THE PIANIST'S RESOURCE GUIDE:

PIANO MUSIC IN PRINT
and
LITERATURE ON THE PIANISTIC ART

JOSEPH REZITS and GERALD DEATSMAN

Kjos PALLMA MUSIC CORP./NEIL A. KJOS JR., PUBLISHER • PARK RIDGE, ILLINOIS 60068

Published by Pallma Music Corp./ Neil A. Kjos Jr., Publisher
Distributed by Neil A. Kjos Music Company
525 Busse Highway, Park Ridge, Illinois 60068

Publisher's Edition Number: PM6
International Standard Book Number: 0-910842-04-3
Library of Congress Catalog Card Number: 74-81297
Printed and Bound in the United States of America

THE PIANIST'S RESOURCE GUIDE:

PIANO MUSIC IN PRINT
and
LITERATURE ON THE PIANISTIC ART

TABLE OF CONTENTS

GUIDE FOR USE ix

PART I—PIANO MUSIC IN PRINT
Composer Index 1
  Single Work Solos 1
  Single Work Solos: Composer/Editor/Arranger
    Unlisted — Works Alphabetized by Title 251
  Collections, Anthologies and
    Instructional Systems or Methods 255
  Collections, Anthologies and Instructional Systems
    or Methods: Composer/Editor/Arranger
    Unlisted — Works Alphabetized by Title 367
  One Piano, Four Hands (Original and Arranged) .. 375
  One Piano, Four Hands (Original and Arranged):
    Composer/Editor/Arranger Unlisted —
    Works Alphabetized by Title 399
  Two Piano, Four Hands (Original and Arranged —
    includes Concertos) 401
  Two Piano, Four Hands (Original and Arranged):
    Composer/Editor/Arranger Unlisted —
    Works Alphabetized by Title 424
  Concertos 426
  Concertos: Composer/Editor/Arranger Unlisted —
    Works Alphabetized by Title 438
  Other Piano Ensembles 439
  Other Piano Ensembles: Composer/Editor/
    Arranger Unlisted — Works Alphabetized by Title 442
  Technical Material 443
  Technical Material: Composer/Editor/Arranger
    Unlisted — Works Alphabetized by Title 458
  Simplified Versions 459
  Simplified Versions: Composer/Editor/Arranger
    Unlisted — Works Alphabetized by Title 471
  Arrangements and Transcriptions 472
  Arrangements and Transcriptions: Composer/
    Editor/Arranger Unlisted — Works Alphabetized
    by Title 516
  Popular Music 519
  Popular Music: Composer/Editor/Arranger
    Unlisted — Works Alphabetized by Title 538
  Folk Music 542
  Folk Music: Composer/Editor/Arranger Unlisted —
    Works Alphabetized by Title 544
  Church Music 545
  Church Music: Composer/Editor/Arranger Unlisted —
    Works Alphabetized by Title 547
  Christmas Music 548
  Christmas Music: Composer/Editor/Arranger Unlisted —
    Works Alphabetized by Title 551
Title Index 552

PART II—LITERATURE ON THE PIANISTIC ART
Author Index 693
Title Index 803
Classification Index 821
  Notable Pianists and Piano Teachers 821
  Keyboard Instruments 824
  Processes of Learning 828
  The Art of Teaching 834
  Piano Technique 838
  Keyboard Skills 842
  Piano Music 846
  The Art of Performing 850
  Ensemble Playing 854
  General Interest 855
Sub-Classification Index 858
  Notable Pianists and Piano Teachers 858
    General 858
    Miscellaneous 858
    Professional Scope 858
    Biography—Narrative 859
    Biography—Historical Survey 860
    Autobiography, Essays, Letters,
      Lectures and Diaries 861
    Critical Review 862
    Interviews 862
  Keyboard Instruments 862
    General 862
    Miscellaneous 863
    History 863
    Selection 864
    Construction 865
    Mechanism 866
    Acoustics 868
    Maintenance, Tuning and Repair 868
    Aesthetic Qualities 869
    Mechanical Pianos 870
    Electronic Instruments 871
    Makers 871
    Pictorial 872
    Early Instruments 873
    Catalogs, Collections, Dictionaries
      and Bibliographies 874
  Processes of Learning 875
    General 875
    Miscellaneous 875
    Psychological Applications 875
    Rudiments, Notation 875
    Analytical Procedures 878
    Listening 878
    Practice Procedures 879
    Memorizing 880
    Repertoire Building 881
    Ear Training 881
    Self-Instruction 882
    Rhythm, Metrics, Tempo 882

(Sub-Classification Index, cont.)
(Processes of Learning, cont.)

Creativity 884
Musicianship, Expression 885
Dynamics 885
The Art of Teaching 886
General 886
Miscellaneous 886
Philosophy and Psychology of Teaching 886
Methods or Systems of Instruction 887
Child Approach 889
Adult Approach 890
Group Teaching 890
Studio Organization and Equipment 891
Student Recitals 892
Testing and Evaluation 892
Teacher Qualifications 892
Master Classes 892
Teacher-Student-Parent Interrelationships 893
Selecting Instructional Materials 893
Piano Technique 893
General 893
Miscellaneous 894
Physiology and Anatomy 894
Physical Attitude 895
Gymnastics 896
Fingering 897
Relaxation 898
Touch-tone 898
Scales, Arpeggios and Chord Formations 900
Exercises for Keyboard Facility 902
Studies 903
History of Technique 903
Compilations of Technical Material 903
Mechanical Devices 903
Keyboard Skills 904
General 904
Miscellaneous 904
Sight Reading 904
Keyboard Harmony and Theory 905
Improvisation—Traditional 907
Improvisation—Jazz 907
Transposition 908
Modulation 908
Score Reading 909
Figured Bass Playing 909
Accompaniment Writing 910
Playing by Ear 910
Piano Music 910
General 910
Miscellaneous 910
Composers and Compositional Techniques 910
Editions 913
Bibliographies 913

(Sub-Classification Index, cont.)
(Piano Music, cont.)

Lists, Graded and Ungraded 913
History 915
Analysis—Theoretical 915
Analysis—Interpretative 917
Criticism 918
Master Lessons 918
Recordings 918
Descriptive Analysis, Program Notes 919
Compositional Forms 919
Guides to Keyboard Literature 920
The Art of Performing 921
General 921
Miscellaneous 921
Performance Practices 921
Interpretation and Style 922
Aesthetics 923
Phrasing, Articulation 924
Ornamentation 924
Pedalling 925
Demeanor and Poise 927
Ensemble Playing 927
General 927
Miscellaneous 927
Chamber Music Playing 927
Duet Playing 927
Two Piano Playing 927
Accompanying and Coaching 928
Concerto Performing 928
General Interest 928
Miscellaneous 928
Appreciation 929
Audiences 929
Recording Procedures 929
Business Aspects 929
Clubs and Organizations 929
Music Therapy 930
Institutional Applications 930
Competitions, Auditions, Examinations
  and Festivals 930
Books for Younger Readers 930
The Amateur Pianist 930
Esoterica 930
Pianistic Careers 931
Research 931
Related Arts 931

PART III—PIANO READER'S GUIDE
Critical Evaluations 933
Topical Index 957

PART IV—PUBLISHERS INDEX 981

APPENDIX—MASTER CODE LIST 991

GUIDE FOR USE

PREFACE

The purpose of *The Pianist's Resource Guide* is to enable the reader to locate books, music and information for and about the piano, piano playing, piano teaching and piano music in print. Directed mainly to the pianist, piano teacher, pedagogical specialist, piano student, musicologist, librarian, music publisher and music dealer, this volume will enable the reader to locate information in a matter of moments. Some specific uses may be as follows: building repertoire lists, bibliographies and chronologies; preparing lectures and reports; finding obscure information; locating music sources and rare books; and as a reading or purchaser's guide.

PART I—PIANO MUSIC IN PRINT

Piano Music in Print is a cross-referenced guide to published piano music currently available and is divided into two main sections:

Composer Index
Title Index

Composer Index

For convenient access, the Composer Index is divided into the following sections:

Single Work Solos
Collections, Anthologies and Instructional Systems or Methods
One Piano, Four Hands (Original and Arranged)
Two Piano, Four Hands (Original and Arranged—Includes Concertos)
Concertos
Other Piano Ensembles
Technical Material
Simplified Versions
Arrangements and Transcriptions
Popular Music
Folk Music
Church Music
Christmas Music

For each entry the following information, if available, is given:

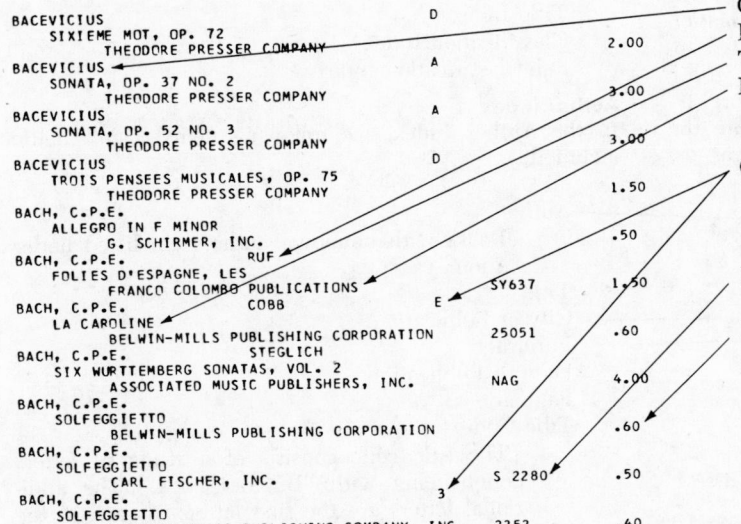

Composer
Editor
Title
Publisher
(The publisher's distributor, if different, may be found in the Publisher's Index on page 981.)
Grade Level
(Grades are listed only as and if given in the publishers' catalogs; no attempt has been made to equalize publishers' gradings.)
Edition Number
(Publisher's Catalog Identification Number)
Price
(Prices are listed as they appeared in the publishers' catalogs at the time of entry into this listing in 1974. Obviously, due to tremendous current price flux, these prices are apt to be higher than listed; they are included as a guideline to the prices at which the publishers sold the music at the time of compilation.)

When the publisher's catalog did not specify or list a composer/editor/arranger for a work, the works are listed alphabetically by title following the alphabetical composer list for that section. Because of computer idiosyncrasies, the grade levels for these works are printed either on the same line as the title entry or one line above the title.

An asterisk (°) following a composer's name indicates a second composer. In some cases the second name is spelled out; in other cases (as the computer seemed to choose arbitrarily), the second name is not given.

Every effort was made to ensure that each composer's name was always listed in the same way. Often, in the publishers' catalogs, only the last name was specified; sometimes one or two initials were used; or, in some instances, the full first name

was listed. In the creating of the master-file for *Piano Music in Print,* the first catalog entry noted for a given composer was retained throughout the work.

Title Index

After locating a work in the Title Index, the reader is referred to the Composer Index for complete details. To keep the Title Index compact, the titles have been restricted to one line entries and then truncated. When there is more than one edition of a particular title (ex. = J. S. Bach "Two-Part Inventions"), the title appears as many times as there are editions in print. When the publishers' catalogs did not specify a composer/editor/arranger, the composer column is blank. The reader should then refer to the alphabetical title listing at the end of the appropriate section of the Composer Index for further information.

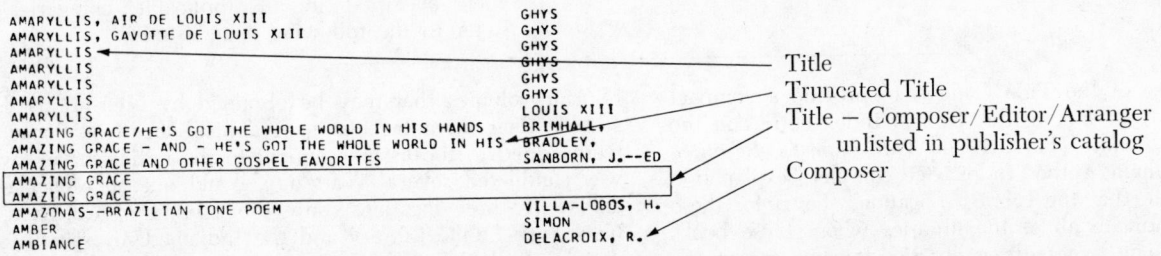

Title
Truncated Title
Title — Composer/Editor/Arranger unlisted in publisher's catalog
Composer

In seeking a particular work, the reader is urged to consider all possible forms of the title, and even the various spellings of the composer's name, if necessary. Different publishers catalog titles in different ways, and, although every attempt has been made to incorporate parallel forms of entry, there are occasions where listings of a given work may not be together. For example, a work with a French title such as Debussy's "La Fille Aux Cheveux de Lin" may also be listed under the English title, "Girl With the Flaxen Hair." Also, a work such as Clementi's "Twelve Sonatinas—Op. 36, 37, 38" may also be listed under "Sonatinas, Op. 36, 37, 38," depending on the title listing in the publishers' catalogs. However, as much as possible, the title listings have been rearranged or revised when necessary to maintain a common order of information. For example, one publisher may specify "Etude, Op. 10, No. 3 in E Major"; another may specify "Etude in E, Opus 10, No. 3"; still another may say only "Etude in E Major." If the titles had been left in this manner, the computer would have indicated a completely different title for each edition and they would not necessarily have appeared together. In order to list all such editions in consecutive places, titles have been made parallel whenever possible.

Ordinarily, titles are listed by key, with the opus number following; e.g., "Etude in E Major, Op. 10 No. 3." However, certain exceptions have been made for the reader's convenience. Beethoven sonatas have the number (1-32) listed first, so that regardless of the language used or of the information in the title, all sonatas with the same number are sorted together. Note that sonatas with numbers below 10 are listed as 01, 02, 03, etc. This is because the computer will "sort" by the first number it sees. If a "0" was not placed before the single digit in a series where more than one digit was ex-

pected, "Sonata No. 10" would be listed before "Sonata No. 2." Mozart sonatas are sorted by Köchel number. Haydn sonatas could not be sorted by "sonata number" because the numbers vary in different editions; therefore, they are sorted by key.

In the interest of keeping instructional systems, collections and anthologies together, editors of such books are listed both in the space reserved for editors and also in the composer's space with "—ED." following the name.

```
AGAY, D.--ED              AGAY, D.
ANTHOLOGY OF PIANO MUSIC, BK. 4 THE TWENTIETH CENTURY
     MUSIC SALES CORPORATION              080044      4.95
```

One more word about the computer. Although impeccable in its accuracy, the computer cannot always alphabetize in the traditional manner. The computer recognizes and alphabetizes letters before spaces. For example, "keyboard" appears before "key," "pianoforte" appears before "piano," "Newton" appears before "New England."

PART II—LITERATURE ON THE PIANISTIC ART

Literature on the Pianistic Art includes over twenty-one hundred books written in English encompassing a span of over two hundred years, and is divided into the following sections:
Author Index
Title Index
Classification Index
Sub-Classification Index

Author Index
In the Author Index, the following items of information are included:

```
ANTRIM, DORAN K.
     TEACHING MUSIC AND MAKING IT PAY
          PHILADELPHIA                1927    113P     BTMAMI
          PRESSER, THEODORE, COMPANY
     IU * LC * NP
     ILL * PHO
     AT1 * AT3 * AT8 * AT9 * AT11 * AT13 * AT14 * GI5

APEL, WILLI
     HISTORY OF KEYBOARD MUSIC TO 1700, THE --TRANSLATED AND REVISED BY
     HANS TISCHLER---1967, IN GERMAN
          BLOOMINGTON, IND.           1972    878P     BHOKMT
          INDIANA UNIVERSITY PRESS
     BR * IU * LC * NP * SA
     APP * BIB * IND * INT * MEX
     NP1 * KI1 * KI3 * KI5 * KI6 * KI9 * KI14 * PM1 * PM3 * PM4 * PM5 *
     PM7 * PM8 * PM9 * PM14

APEL, WILLI
     MASTERS OF THE KEYBOARD
          CAMBRIDGE, MASS.            1947    323P     BMOTK
          HARVARD UNIVERSITY PRESS
     RP * BR * CP * CU * ES * IU * LC * MI * NP * OC * TO * UA * UC * UI
     UK * UM * UO * US * UT * UU * UW * YU
     BIB * ILL * IND * INT * LDR * MEX * MSF * PHO
     KI1 * KI2 * KI5 * KI6 * KI7 * KI9 * KI13 * KI14 * PM3 * PM7 * PM8 *
     PM13 * PM14 * PM15 * AP3 * AP4 * AP5

APPEL, PEARL *
ALEXANDER, RUTH
     HARMONY AT THE PIANO LESSON, A COMPANION TO PIANO STUDY
          CHICAGO                     1940    48P      BHATPL
          APPEL-ALEXANDER
     LC
     INT * MEX
     AT4 * KS4
```

Author
(Books with unknown authors are listed under "Anon.")
Title
City of Publication
Publisher
Date of Publication
Pagination
Title Code
(The title code consists of a string of letters commencing with "B" for "book." The additional letters are the first letters of each of the first five words of the title, excluding the initial definite or indefinite article.)
Library Locations
(A space of two lines is allowed for a two-letter code system used to indicate libraries where the books may be found. A listing of the library codes and their corresponding library names follows.)
Physical Facts
(A space of one line is allowed for a three-letter code system used to identify various facts relating to the physical layout and presentation of each book. A listing of codes follows.)
Classifications and Sub-Classifications
(The last two lines are allowed for a code system of two letters followed by numbers from 1-15 used to identify the specific contents of a particular book. There are ten main classifications, each broken down into more detailed sub-classification categories. Each book has been classified in all applicable categories. Refer to the following code lists.)

The sole purpose of the Title Code is to provide a compact and accurate way of linking the Topical Index entries in the *Piano Reader's Guide* (Part III of *The Pianist's Resource Guide*) to this main Author Index. See complete explanation on page xii. Note that the Library Locations shown for these books do not indicate all of the libraries where these books may be found. The twenty-three libraries selected for survey were chosen for their strength in holdings (especially in out-

of-print volumes that may be obtained by inter-library loan) and/or their advantageous geographical location. Books that were added to the list subsequent to the initial survey, which was conducted several years ago, could not be rechecked at all twenty-three locations; only the Library of Congress, the New York Public Library and the Indiana University Library were rechecked for new listings.

LIBRARY LOCATIONS
Code Library Name
AS   Arizona State University Library
BP   Boston Public Library
BR   British Museum
CP   Chicago Public Library
ES   Eastman School of Music Library
IU   Indiana University Library
LC   Library of Congress
NP   New York Public Library
OC   Oberlin College Library
UA   University of Arizona Library
UC   University of California at Berkeley
       Library
CU   University of Colorado Library
UI   University of Illinois Library
UK   University of Kansas Library
UM   University of Michigan Library
MI   University of Minnesota Library
UO   University of Oregon Library
US   University of Southern California
       Library
UT   University of Texas Library
TO   University of Toronto Library
UU   University of Utah Library
UW   University of Washington Library
YU   Yale University Library

PHYSICAL FACTS
Code Identification
APP   Appendices
BIB   Bibliographies
CHR   Charts, Graphs or Diagrams
CNG   Chronologies
DIS   Discographies
GLO   Glossaries
ILL   Illustrations
IND   Indices
INT   Introduction, Foreword or Preface
LDR   Line Drawings
MEX   Musical Examples
MSF   Manuscript Facsimilies
PHO   Photographs
TAB   Tables

CLASSIFICATIONS AND SUB-CLASSIFICATIONS
Code Identification
NP   Notable Pianists and Piano Teachers
NP1   —General
NP2   —Miscellaneous
NP3   —Professional Scope
NP4   —Biography—Narrative
NP5   —Biography—Historical Survey
NP6   —Autobiography, Essays, Letters,
         Lectures and Diaries
NP7   —Critical Review
NP8   —Interviews

KI   Keyboard Instruments
KI1   —General
KI2   —Miscellaneous
KI3   —History
KI4   —Selection
KI5   —Construction
KI6   —Mechanism
KI7   —Acoustics
KI8   —Maintenance, Tuning and Repair
KI9   —Aesthetic Qualities

Code Identification
(KI Keyboard Instruments, cont.)
KI10   —Mechanical Pianos
KI11   —Electronic Instruments
KI12   —Makers
KI13   —Pictorial
KI14   —Early Instruments
KI15   —Catalogs, Collections, Dictionaries
           and Bibliographies

PL   Processes of Learning
PL1   —General
PL2   —Miscellaneous
PL3   —Psychological Applications
PL4   —Rudiments, Notation
PL5   —Analytical Procedures
PL6   —Listening
PL7   —Practice Procedures
PL8   —Memorizing
PL9   —Repertoire Building
PL10   —Ear Training
PL11   —Self-Instruction
PL12   —Rhythm, Metrics, Tempo
PL13   —Creativity
PL14   —Musicianship, Expression
PL15   —Dynamics

AT   The Art of Teaching
AT1   —General
AT2   —Miscellaneous
AT3   —Philosophy and Psychology of
           Teaching
AT4   —Methods or Systems of
           Instruction
AT5   —Child Approach
AT6   —Adult Approach

AT7   —Group Teaching
AT8   —Studio Organization and
           Equipment
AT9   —Student Recitals
AT10   —Testing and Evaluation
AT11   —Teacher Qualifications
AT12   —Master Classes
AT13   —Teacher-Student-Parent
             Interrelationships
AT14   —Selecting Instructional Materials

PT   Piano Technique
PT1   —General
PT2   —Miscellaneous
PT3   —Physiology and Anatomy
PT4   —Physical Attitude
PT5   —Gymnastics
PT6   —Fingering
PT7   —Relaxation
PT8   —Touch-tone
PT9   —Scales, Arpeggios and Chord
           Formations
PT10   —Exercises for Keyboard Facility
PT11   —Studies
PT12   —History of Technique
PT13   —Compilations of Technical
             Material
PT14   —Mechanical Devices

KS   Keyboard Skills
KS1   —General
KS2   —Miscellaneous

Code Identification
(KS Keyboard Skills, cont.)
KS3   —Sight Reading
KS4   —Keyboard Harmony and Theory
KS5   —Improvisation—Traditional
KS6   —Improvisation—Jazz
KS7   —Transposition
KS8   —Modulation
KS9   —Score Reading
KS10   —Figured Bass Playing
KS11   —Accompaniment Writing
KS12   —Playing by Ear

PM   Piano Music
PM1   —General
PM2   —Miscellaneous
PM3   —Composers and Compositional
           Techniques
PM4   —Editions
PM5   —Bibliographies
PM6   —Lists, Graded and Ungraded
PM7   —History
PM8   —Analysis—Theoretical
PM9   —Analysis—Interpretative
PM10   —Criticism
PM11   —Master Lessons
PM12   —Recordings
PM13   —Descriptive Analysis, Program
             Notes
PM14   —Compositional Forms
PM15   —Guides to Keyboard Literature

AP   The Art of Performing
AP1   —General
AP2   —Miscellaneous
AP3   —Performances Practices
AP4   —Interpretation and Style
AP5   —Aesthetics
AP6   —Phrasing, Articulation
AP7   —Ornamentation
AP8   —Pedalling
AP9   —Demeanor and Poise

EP   Ensemble Playing
EP1   —General
EP2   —Miscellaneous
EP3   —Chamber Music Playing
EP4   —Duet Playing
EP5   —Two Piano Playing
EP6   —Accompanying and Coaching
EP7   —Concerto Performing

GI   General Interest
GI1   —Miscellaneous
GI2   —Appreciation
GI3   —Audiences
GI4   —Recording Procedures
GI5   —Business Aspects
GI6   —Clubs and Organizations
GI7   —Music Therapy
GI8   —Institutional Applications
GI9   —Competitions, Auditions,
           Examinations and Festivals
GI10   —Books for Younger Readers
GI11   —The Amateur Pianist
GI12   —Esoterica
GI13   —Pianistic Careers
GI14   —Research
GI15   —Related Arts

Title Index

Each book in the Author Index of *Literature on the Pianistic Art* is listed a second time in the Title Index. As in the Title Index for the *Piano Music in Print* section, this index acts as a compact referral to the Author Index for complete details. Also, as in the previous Title Index, all titles are truncated in order to keep them one line entries. In this index, all titles with unknown authors are listed as "Anon." and may be found in the Author Index under "Anon.".

Classification Index

The Classification Index lists by author all books having information pertaining to each of the ten specific main classifications:

Notable Pianists and Piano Teachers (NP)
Keyboard Instruments (KI)
Processes of Learning (PL)
The Art of Teaching (AT)
Piano Technique (PT)
Keyboard Skills (KS)
Piano Music (PM)
The Art of Performing (AP)
Ensemble Playing (EP)
General Interest (GI)

Sub-Classification Index

This fourth index breaks down the above information even further and lists by author all of the books having information pertaining to each of the one hundred and twenty-four sub-classifications.

Criteria for Books Included in Literature on the Pianistic Art

The books chosen for inclusion in this section had to meet certain criteria. The explanations, qualifications, limitations, restrictions, etc. are best listed in outline form:

1. Only books relating to the piano, clavichord, harpsichord, spinet, virginals, etc. are included. No books about the organ are listed.
2. In general, only published books are listed; however, there are a number of exceptions (reprints from newspapers and periodicals, yearbooks, unpublished dissertations).
3. No music history, music appreciation or other works of a general nature are included.
4. Composers are represented when they can be identified as pianists and/or composers of piano music. Biographical entries are extensive only for Chopin and Liszt, because of their unique positions.
5. Books for younger readers are emphasized.
6. For some entries the data is incomplete; e.g., date of publication not available.
7. "Methods" are not generally included except for special categories; e.g., group piano instruction.
8. Pagination is sometimes only approximate, noted often by the symbol "+" after the entry.
9. If two editions are sufficiently different in content, they are given separate entries.
10. With a few exceptions, authors are cited and spelled as they exist in the Library of Congress cataloging.
11. Reprint or later edition dates are specified in the space reserved for Date of Publication. The date of the original publication is then found following the title entry.
12. Although the great majority of books were individually examined for purposes of clarification, several could not be located at the time and, consequently, were classified in a general manner.
13. Punctuation marks may be identified or explained as follows:
    a. no question marks are used; they are not possible to enter into the computer.
    b. the colon (:) and semicolon (;) are printed by the computer as . .
    c. parentheses are printed as - -
    d. edited or truncated titles have the symbol . . .
    e. title clarification words follow a triple dash (- - -)
    f. an asterisk (*) following an author's name indicates more than one author

PART III—PIANO READER'S GUIDE

The *Piano Reader's Guide* consists of the following two sections:
Critical Evaluations
Topical Index

Critical Evaluations

One hundred and eighteen books of special professional or historical interest are selected and evaluated by Joseph Rezits. In the selection of books to be reviewed, no attempt was made to select the "118 best books available"; rather, books were chosen from a wide variety of categories and from different periods. The length of a commentary does not necessarily have a direct relationship to the reviewer's opinion of the book, but represents the amount of space needed to give a clear idea of its content. The books evaluated are listed alphabetically by author, and specific information — title, publisher, city of publication, date of publication — is also included.

Topical Index

The Topical Index, constructed with both main headings and sub-headings, is used as a means of locating specific information beyond the more general outlines of the Classification and Sub-Classification Indices of the *Literature on the Pianistic Art* section. Under a given sub-heading, the applicable books are identified by author and a title code. The title code compactly identifies the title of the book and accurately links the entry to the main Author Index of the *Literature on the Pianistic Art* section. For example, if an entry in the Topical Index specifys Matthay, T. as the author, the title code "BOMAPF" would refer the reader to Matthay's book "On Memorizing and Playing From Memory"; the title code "BPFOT" would refer to Matthay's book "Piano Fallacies of Today." The Topical Index contains the following information:

```
ACOUSTICS
    ENSEMBLE PERFORMANCE, IN
        MOORE, G.                    BAITL    P209-10
ACTION AND REACTION
    APPLIED TO MUSCULAR CONTRACTIONS
        CAMPBELL, L.                 BTFORI   P16-17
ADAPTING MOVEMENTS ◄─────────────────────────────── Main Heading
    GEN INFO ◄───────────────────────────────────── Sub-Heading
        GAT, J. ◄──────────────────  BTOPP    P33-36  Author
ADJUDICATION                                          Title Code
    GEN INFO
        HARRISON, S.                 BTNTM    P135-50
ADLER, CLARENCE
    BIOGRAPHICAL MATERIAL
        SALESKI, G.                  BFMOJO   P442-43 ◄ Pages
ADULT BEGINNER
    ANALYZING MUSIC                                    (Exact pages of the book which include
        DILLER, A.                   BSOM     P165-66   information on the topic.)
    APPROACH TO STUDY
        DABREU, G.                   BPTPWC   P23-24
    GEN INFO
        BROUGHTON, J.                BSIPT    P61-62
    LISTENING TO MUSIC
        DILLER, A.                   BSOM     P165-66
```

PART IV—PUBLISHERS INDEX

The final portion of *The Pianist's Resource Guide* lists all names and addresses, when available, of publishers of piano music and books referred to in this volume. The reader should be aware that many publishing houses are no longer in existence; in such cases, the addresses given are the last known place of publication. All publishers addresses are as complete as were available at the publication deadline for this volume. Agents, distributors or representatives of publishers are shown in parentheses.

APPENDIX—MASTER CODE LIST

At the end of this volume, two copies of a complete alphabetical Master Code List are provided as quick reference keys. These pages may be removed from the book and used for constant referral.

PUBLISHER'S NOTE

The authors and publisher have endeavored to take advantage of every means of verifying the accuracy of each entry and item of information; however, many variable factors—constantly changing publishers' catalogs, prices, human error in computer keypunching, the enormous volume of entries involved—have made absolute accuracy impossible. The authors and publisher will not be responsible in any way for errors and omissions; however, corrections are most welcomed and will be used to change, correct and update the next edition of *The Pianist's Resource Guide*. Opinions expressed in the *Piano Reader's Guide* are solely literary evaluations made in a spirit of fair comment and criticism by Joseph Rezits.

1976 EDITION OF THE PIANIST'S RESOURCE GUIDE

Orders are now being accepted for the updated 1976 edition. To reserve a copy of this limited edition, place your order with your music seller or the publisher.

ACKNOWLEDGMENTS

I am most grateful to all persons who, in so many ways, have made significant contributions to this book. My deep appreciation is hereby extended to those who have assisted me:

—To Gerald Deatsman, my co-author and colleague, who, by dint of his incredible bibliographical "sleuthing," found over eight hundred book titles to add to a list I once thought was complete. Mr. Deatsman personally classified the majority of books in *Literature on the Pianistic Art* and is responsible for the editing and critical revision of the entire list.

—to Professor Storm Bull of the University of Colorado who, during the early stages of this work, gave me encouragement and a clarification of direction and purpose.

—to Mary Ann Shaw, Jean Nakhnikian and Dave De-Lauter of the Wrubel Computing Center of Indiana University, who, with infinite patience, guided and instructed me in the methods and problems of information retrieval.

—to the institutions Indiana University and the University of Colorado, which generously provided funds for research and travel.

—to Beverly Barton, Alice Meredith, Marjorie Enix, Chiu-Ling Lin, Susan Bishop, Benjamin Callies, Judy Lin, Diana Wang, Edna Chun, Dennis McGreer, Tanya Gille and Julia Lam for their devoted and efficient catalog editing and keypunching for *Piano Music in Print*.

—to Donald and Helen Pierson for their careful editing of commentaries contained in the *Piano Reader's Guide*.

—to librarians Kent Hurst of the University of Colorado, Dominique René de Lerma of Indiana University, Neal Ratliffe of the New York Public Library, Vincent Duckles of the University of California at Berkeley, Joan Meggett of the University of Southern California, Eulan Brooks of the University of Texas at Austin, Edmund Soule of the University of Oregon, Martin Silver of the University of California at Santa Barbara, and to faculty members and administrators John T. Moore of the University of Washington, Pierre Souvarin of the University of Toronto and Miles Mauney of Oberlin College for their significant help in providing library information.

—to Charles Foreman, Martha Stonequist, Aija Rollis, Drora Pershing Maynard, Joan Benson and Joan Woods, who provided valuable ideas and assistance.

—to Neil A. Kjos Jr., Elsie Karzen and Marcia Broucek of Neil A. Kjos Music Company, whose insight, imagination and enthusiasm were essential ingredients in bringing this project to its completion.

—Joseph Rezits

Single Work Solos

AARON   WILLIAMS, J.   2
    DANCING WAVELETS
        BOSTON MUSIC COMPANY   .50
AARON, M.
    ALL ABOARD
        BELWIN-MILLS PUBLISHING CORPORATION   25006   .60
AARON, M.
    ALPINE HOLIDAY
        BELWIN-MILLS PUBLISHING CORPORATION   25279   .60
AARON, M.
    AT THE SKATING CARNIVAL
        G. SCHIRMER, INC.   .35
AARON, M.
    BALLET STACCATO
        BELWIN-MILLS PUBLISHING CORPORATION   25188   .60
AARON, M.   WILLIAMS
    BANJO SERENADE
        BOSTON MUSIC COMPANY   .50
AARON, M.
    BLITHE SPIRIT
        BELWIN-MILLS PUBLISHING CORPORATION   25265   .60
AARON, M.
    CHICK-A-DEE, THE
        G. SCHIRMER, INC.   .35
AARON, M.
    CIRCUS CLOWNS
        G. SCHIRMER, INC.   .35
AARON, M.
    CLOWNING
        BELWIN-MILLS PUBLISHING CORPORATION   25028   .60
AARON, M.
    COWBOY POKE
        BELWIN-MILLS PUBLISHING CORPORATION   25247   .60
AARON, M.   EASY
    DANCE OF THE DWARFS
        SHAWNEE PRESS, INC.   HB-5008   .40
AARON, M.
    ETUDE IN A
        BELWIN-MILLS PUBLISHING CORPORATION   25189   .60
AARON, M.   EASY
    FAIRY BARQUE, THE
        SHAWNEE PRESS, INC.   HB-5021   .60
AARON, M.   E
    FLOTSAM
        BELWIN-MILLS PUBLISHING CORPORATION   25248   .60
AARON, M.
    HALLOWEEN NIGHT
        G. SCHIRMER, INC.   .40
AARON, M.
    HAUNTED HOUSE
        G. SCHIRMER, INC.   .35
AARON, M.   E
    HOLIDAY PLAY
        BELWIN-MILLS PUBLISHING CORPORATION   25162   .60
AARON, M.
    HOLLAND FESTIVAL
        G. SCHIRMER, INC.   .35
AARON, M.   E
    ICE BALLET
        BELWIN-MILLS PUBLISHING CORPORATION   25263   .60
AARON, M.   E
    ICE CARNIVAL
        BELWIN-MILLS PUBLISHING CORPORATION   25060   .60
AARON, M.   E
    IN OUTER SPACE
        BELWIN-MILLS PUBLISHING CORPORATION   25264   .60
AARON, M.   E
    IN SICILY -- TARANTELLA
        BELWIN-MILLS PUBLISHING CORPORATION   25274   .60
AARON, M.   E
    INDIA
        BELWIN-MILLS PUBLISHING CORPORATION   25062   .60
AARON, M.
    JUMPING-JACKS
        G. SCHIRMER, INC.   .35
AARON, M.   E
    MOON CLOUD
        BELWIN-MILLS PUBLISHING CORPORATION   25245   .60
AARON, M.   E
    PRAIRIE RIDER
        BELWIN-MILLS PUBLISHING CORPORATION   25086   .60
AARON, M.   E
    PRAIRIE SONG
        BELWIN-MILLS PUBLISHING CORPORATION   25281   .60
AARON, M.   E
    REGATTA, THE
        BELWIN-MILLS PUBLISHING CORPORATION   25166   .60
AARON, M.   E
    ROUND THE GIPSY CAMPFIRE
        BELWIN-MILLS PUBLISHING CORPORATION   25192   .60
AARON, M.   E
    SCOTTISH STORY
        BELWIN-MILLS PUBLISHING CORPORATION   25165   .60
AARON, M.   E
    SEA AQUARIUM
        BELWIN-MILLS PUBLISHING CORPORATION   25246   .60
AARON, M.   E
    STORY-BOOK WALTZ
        BELWIN-MILLS PUBLISHING CORPORATION   25103   .60
AARON, M.   E
    SURF RIDERS, THE
        BELWIN-MILLS PUBLISHING CORPORATION   25262   .60
AARON, M.   E
    TATTLETALE -- WITH WORDS
        BELWIN-MILLS PUBLISHING CORPORATION   25107   .60
AARON, M.   E
    TOY BOAT, THE
        BELWIN-MILLS PUBLISHING CORPORATION   25244   .60
AARON, M.   E
    TROPICAL NIGHT
        BELWIN-MILLS PUBLISHING CORPORATION   25280   .60
AARON, M.   E
    VARIATIONS IN C
        BELWIN-MILLS PUBLISHING CORPORATION   25193   .60
AARON, M.   EASY
    WOOD-NYMPH'S FROLIC
        SHAWNEE PRESS, INC.   HB-5015   .40
AARON, M.   EASY
    WOODEN SHOES
        SHAWNEE PRESS, INC.   HB-5018   .60
AARON, M.
    WOODLAND CASCADE
        BELWIN-MILLS PUBLISHING CORPORATION   25122   .60

ABBOTT, A.
    PROSLAMBANOMENOS
        EDITIONS MUSICALES TRANSATLANTIQUES   3.50
ABNHEIM, JOSEPH
    ALBUMBLATT D FLAT 'LEGE WOHL'
        MUSICA OBSCURA   1.00
ABRAMS
    STACCATO, A TECHNICAL DISCUSSION
        CENTURY MUSIC PUBLISHING COMPANY, INC.   3728   .40
ABRAMSKY, A.
    EINFACHE REDE
        UNIVERSAL EDITION   UE 8278   .80
ABRIL
    SONATINA
        ASSOCIATED MUSIC PUBLISHERS, INC.   UME   1.00
ABSIL, J.
    HUMORESQUES
        ELKAN-VOGEL, INC.   LEM   2.50
                                   3
ABTLER
    GAVOTTE DEBUTANTES, SWEET 17
        CENTURY MUSIC PUBLISHING COMPANY, INC.   712   .40
                                   3
ABTLER
    SWEET SEVENTEEN, GAVOTTE
        CENTURY MUSIC PUBLISHING COMPANY, INC.   712   .40
                                   A
ACHRON, J.
    STATUETTES
        THEODORE PRESSER COMPANY   1.25
                                   2
ACKERMANN, D.
    BIG COWBOY AND THE LITTLE COWBOY, THE
        WILLIS MUSIC COMPANY   .40
                                   2
ACKERMANN, D.
    CUBANERA
        WILLIS MUSIC COMPANY   .40
ADAIR, M.   1 1/2
    DANCE OF THE DAFFODILS
        THEODORE PRESSER COMPANY   .50
ADAIR, M.   1
    SONG OF THE PINES
        THEODORE PRESSER COMPANY   .50
ADAIR, Y.
    LITTLE DOG TALES
        BOOSEY AND HAWKES, INC.   .90
ADAIR, Y.
    SKETCHES FROM HANS ANDERSEN
        OXFORD UNIVERSITY PRESS   33.801   1.40
ADAM, A.   STEINER
    CANTIQUE DE NOEL
        G. SCHIRMER, INC.   .50
ADAM, A.   BURNAM   3
    CANTIQUE DE NOEL
        WILLIS MUSIC COMPANY   .35
ADAM, A.   HALL
    GISELLE -- BALLET TOLD IN WORDS AND MUSIC
        BOOSEY AND HAWKES, INC.   1.50
ADAM, A.
    GISELLE -- BALLET-PANTOMINE IN 2 ACTS
        ASSOCIATED MUSIC PUBLISHERS, INC.   ESC   12.75
ADAM, A.   SCHAUM, J.   1
    O HOLY NIGHT
        BELWIN-MILLS PUBLISHING CORPORATION   .50
ADAM, A.   2
    O HOLY NIGHT
        CENTURY MUSIC PUBLISHING COMPANY, INC.   3785   .40
ADAM, A.   PEERY   4
    O HOLY NIGHT
        THEODORE PRESSER COMPANY   .60
ADAM, A.   HESS   5
    O HOLY NIGHT
        THEODORE PRESSER COMPANY   .60
ADAM, A.   BATTMANN   3
    SI J'ETAIS ROI - J'IGNORE SON NOM
        ALPHONSE LEDUC
ADAM, A.   LECARPENTIER, A.   4
    SI J'ETAIS ROI - BAGATELLE
        ALPHONSE LEDUC
ADAM, A.   CROISEZ   5
    SI J'ETAIS ROI - FANTAISIE
        ALPHONSE LEDUC
ADAM, A.   TAVAN   6
    SI J'ETAIS ROI - FANTAISIE
        ALPHONSE LEDUC
ADAM, A.   7
    SI J'ETAIS ROI - OUVERTURE
        ALPHONSE LEDUC
ADAMIS, M.
    SUITE FOR PIANO -- 'IN RITMO ANTICO'
        IMPERO-VERLAG   1.25
ADAMS
    WITCHES IN THE WIND
        SUMMY-BIRCHARD COMPANY   .50
ADAMS, B.   2 1/2
    GYPSY EARRINGS
        BELWIN-MILLS PUBLISHING CORPORATION   .60
ADAMS, B.   2
    INDIAN FUN
        BELWIN-MILLS PUBLISHING CORPORATION   .60
ADAMS, B.   2 1/2
    SNOW BELLS
        BELWIN-MILLS PUBLISHING CORPORATION   .60
ADAMS, G.   M-D
    SONATA IN B MINOR
        C. F. PETERS CORPORATION   6232   1.50
ADAMS, G.   1 1/2
    STAR OF BETHLEHEM
        BELWIN-MILLS PUBLISHING CORPORATION   .50
ADAMS, R. G.   4
    DANCE OF THE SWALLOWS
        VOLKWEIN BROS.   .35
ADAMS, R. G.   2
    MOUNTAIN MAIDEN'S DREAM
        VOLKWEIN BROS.   .30
ADAMS, P. G.   SPENCER, J.   2
    O HOLY NIGHT
        VOLKWEIN BROS.   .30
ADAMS, S.
    HOLY CITY
        ASHLEY DEALERS SERVICE, INC.   ES   .95
ADAMS, S.   GODFREY
    HOLY CITY
        BOOSEY AND HAWKES, INC.   .75
ADAMS, S.   PERRY
    HOLY CITY
        BOOSEY AND HAWKES, INC.   .50
ADAMS, S.   3
    HOLY CITY
        BOSTON MUSIC COMPANY   .50

```
ADAMS, S.                 WALLIS          2
    HOLY CITY, THE
            BOSTON MUSIC COMPANY                                    .50
ADAMS, S.                 ECKSTEIN
    HOLY CITY, THE
            CARL FISCHER, INC.                      P 2378          .75
ADAMS, S.                                 3
    HOLY CITY, THE
            CENTURY MUSIC PUBLISHING COMPANY, INC.  3576            .40
ADAMSON *
    AS THE GIRLS GO
            SAM FOX PUBLISHING COMPANY, INC.                       1.50
ADAMSON *
    AS THE GIRLS GO -- SELECTION
            SOUTHERN MUSIC COMPANY                                 1.50
ADDINSELL
    WALTZ THEME
            SAM FOX PUBLISHING COMPANY, INC.                        .75
ADDINSELL
    WALTZ THEME
            SOUTHERN MUSIC COMPANY                                  .75
ADDINSELL
    WARSAW CONCERTO
            CHAPPELL AND COMPANY, INC.       0017780-1501          1.25
ADDINSELL                 LIBERACE
    WARSAW CONCERTO
            CHAPPELL AND COMPANY, INC.       0021592-1504          1.00
ADDINSELL
    WARSAW CONCERTO -- THEME
            CHAPPELL AND COMPANY, INC.       0017780-1502           .95
ADDINSELL
    WARSAW CONCERTO -- THEME EASY
            CHAPPELL AND COMPANY, INC.       0017798-1503           .95
ADDISON, J.
    REACH FOR THE SKY -- FROM 'REACH FOR THE SKY'
            BELWIN-MILLS PUBLISHING CORPORATION     20220           .85
ADDRISI                   NEALE, J.       EASY
    NEVER MY LOVE
            WARNER BROTHERS PUBLISHERS                              .75
ADLER, M.
    FAWN IN THE FOREST
            SUMMY-BIRCHARD COMPANY                                  .50
ADLER, M.                                 2
    OUR FLAG
            THEODORE PRESSER COMPANY                                .50
ADLER, M.                                 2
    SWAN, THE
            BOSTON MUSIC COMPANY                                    .50
ADLER, M.
    SWIMMING-POOL, THE
            G. SCHIRMER, INC.                                       .40
ADLER, M.
    TWO BUTTERFLIES
            G. SCHIRMER, INC.                                       .40
ADLER, S.
    SONATA BREVE
            OXFORD UNIVERSITY PRESS                 93.215         3.00
AGAY, D.
    BARCAROLETTE
            BOOSEY AND HAWKES, INC.                                 .50
AGAY, D.
    CHROMATIC WALTZ
            MCA MUSIC                                              1.00
AGAY, D.
    DANCING LEAVES
            G. SCHIRMER, INC.                                       .35
AGAY, D.
    EVENING AND MORNING--TWO LITTLE PASTORALES
            G. SCHIRMER, INC.                                       .40
AGAY, D.
    FROLIC
            G. SCHIRMER, INC.                                       .40
AGAY, D.
    GRADUATION WALTZ
            SAM FOX PUBLISHING COMPANY, INC.                        .50
AGAY, D.
    GRADUATION WALTZ
            SOUTHERN MUSIC COMPANY                                  .50
AGAY, D.
    GUARACHA
            G. SCHIRMER, INC.                                       .40
AGAY, D.
    HERE COMES THE CIRCUS
            G. SCHIRMER, INC.                                       .40
AGAY, D.
    LONELY WALTZ
            SAM FOX PUBLISHING COMPANY, INC.                        .50
AGAY, D.
    LONELY WALTZ
            SOUTHERN MUSIC COMPANY                                  .50
AGAY, D.
    MEET MISTER MAMBO
            G. SCHIRMER, INC.                                       .40
AGAY, D.
    PARADE OF THE CLOWNS
            SAM FOX PUBLISHING COMPANY, INC.                        .50
AGAY, D.
    PARADE OF THE CLOWNS
            SOUTHERN MUSIC COMPANY                                  .50
AGAY, D.
    PUPPET POLKA
            SAM FOX PUBLISHING COMPANY, INC.                        .50
AGAY, D.
    PUPPET POLKA
            SOUTHERN MUSIC COMPANY                                  .50
AGAY, D.
    ROCKIN' THE BLUES AWAY
            G. SCHIRMER, INC.                                       .40
AGAY, D.
    SAMBA
            G. SCHIRMER, INC.                                       .40
AGAY, D.
    SERENATA BURLESCA
            BOOSEY AND HAWKES, INC.                                 .75
AGAY, D.
    SHEPHERD'S NIGHT SONG
            G. SCHIRMER, INC.                                       .40
AGAY, D.
    SOLDIERS HOE DOWN
            BOOSEY AND HAWKES, INC.                                 .50
AGAY, D.
    SONATINA HUNGARICA
            MCA MUSIC                                              2.00
AGAY, D.
    SONATINA NO. 03
            SAM FOX PUBLISHING COMPANY, INC.                       1.25

AGAY, D.
    SONATINA NO. 03
            SOUTHERN MUSIC COMPANY                                 1.25
AGAY, D.
    SONATINA TOCCATA
            BOOSEY AND HAWKES, INC.                                 .50
AGAY, D.
    TANGO ROMANCE
            G. SCHIRMER, INC.                                       .35
AGAY, D.
    TWO COUNTRY SKETCHES--FROLIC
            G. SCHIRMER, INC.                                       .40
AGAY, D.
    TWO COUNTRY SKETCHES--SHEPHERD'S NIGHT SONG
            G. SCHIRMER, INC.                                       .40
AGAY, D.                                  3
    TWO IMPROVISATIONS ON HUNGARIAN FOLK SONGS
            THEODORE PRESSER COMPANY                               1.25
AGAY, D.--ED              AGAY, D.        1 1/2
    HE'S GOT THE WHOLE WORLD IN HIS HANDS
            THEODORE PRESSER COMPANY                                .50
AGUERO                                    3
    DREAMING, WALTZ
            CENTURY MUSIC PUBLISHING COMPANY, INC.  2677            .40
AGUIRRE
    HUELLA, OP. 49
            FRANCO COLOMBO PUBLICATIONS             BA6334          .75
AGUIRRE
    INTIMA, OP. 2 NO. 2
            FRANCO COLOMBO PUBLICATIONS             BA6332          .75
AGUIRRE
    ZAMBA, OP. 40
            FRANCO COLOMBO PUBLICATIONS             BA6320          .75
AHMAD, R.                                 1
    ROW ABOUT
            LEE ROBERTS MUSIC PUBLICATIONS, INC.                    .50
AHNELL, E.
    SONATINA FOR PIANO
            COMPOSERS AUTOGRAPH PUBLICATIONS                       3.08
AITKEN, H.
    PIANO FANTASY
            OXFORD UNIVERSITY PRESS                 93.219         5.75
AKIMENKO
    MENUET RUSSE
            FRANCO COLOMBO PUBLICATIONS             SAL            1.75
AKIMENKO
    PETITS TABLEAUX PITTORESQUES POUR LA JEUNESSE - MUGUET, LE
            FRANCO COLOMBO PUBLICATIONS             SAL            1.50
AKIMENKO
    PETITS TABLEAUX PITTORESQUES POUR LA JEUNESSE - PETITE
    BERGERETTE
            FRANCO COLOMBO PUBLICATIONS             SAL            1.50
AKIMENKO
    PETITS TABLEAUX PITTORESQUES POUR LA JEUNESSE - VIENS
            FRANCO COLOMBO PUBLICATIONS             SAL            1.50
AKIMENKO
    REVE DOULOUREUX
            FRANCO COLOMBO PUBLICATIONS             SAL            1.75
AKIMENKO
    SCHERZINO
            FRANCO COLOMBO PUBLICATIONS             SAL            1.75
AKST *
    WHO SAID DREAMS DON'T COME TRUE
            MCA MUSIC                                              1.00
ALABIEFF                  LISZT *
    NIGHTINGALE, THE
            G. SCHIRMER, INC.                                       .50
ALABIEFF                  MAGLIO, DEL
    NIGHTINGALE, THE -- EASY TRANSCRIPTION
            FRANCO COLOMBO PUBLICATIONS             129089          .60
ALABIEFF                  LISZT           6
    NIGHTINGALE, THE, FROM LE ROSSIGNOL
            CENTURY MUSIC PUBLISHING COMPANY, INC.  3342            .40
ALABIEFF *                                6
    NIGHTINGALE, THE
            CENTURY MUSIC PUBLISHING COMPANY, INC.  3342            .40
ALABIEFF *                TAGLIAPIETRA
    NIGHTINGALE, THE
            FRANCO COLOMBO PUBLICATIONS             ER24            .60
ALABIEFF *                TAGLIAPIETRA
    NIGHTINGALE, THE
            FRANCO COLOMBO PUBLICATIONS             ER24            .60
ALABIEFF *                DEIS
    NIGHTINGALE, THE
            G. SCHIRMER, INC.                                       .50
ALABIEFF *                PHILIPP
    ROSSIGNOL,LE--AIR RUSSE AFTER ALABIEFF--
            GERARD BILLAUDOT EDITIONS MUSICALES                    1.30
ALALEONE
    IN TEMPO DI MINUETTO
            FRANCO COLOMBO PUBLICATIONS             DS37           1.25
ALBAM
    JAZZ MAG RAG, THE.
            MCA MUSIC                                              1.00
ALBENIZ, A.
    BULERIAS
            ASSOCIATED MUSIC PUBLISHERS, INC.       UME             .75
ALBENIZ, I.               MONTES
    ALBAICIN, EL -- FROM IBERIA
            FRANCO COLOMBO PUBLICATIONS             BA6249         1.25
ALBENIZ, I.               MONTES
    ALBORADA -- FROM RECUERDOS DE VIAJE
            FRANCO COLOMBO PUBLICATIONS             BA6263          .75
ALBENIZ, I.
    ALBORADA -- NO. 3, FROM RECUERDOS DE VIAJE
            ASSOCIATED MUSIC PUBLISHERS, INC.       UME             .75
ALBENIZ, I.               MONTES
    ALMERIA -- FROM IBERIA
            FRANCO COLOMBO PUBLICATIONS             BA6248         1.25
ALBENIZ, I.               GUARDIA, DE LA
    ARAGON -- FROM SUITE ESPANOLA NO. 1
            FRANCO COLOMBO PUBLICATIONS             BA6017          .75
ALBENIZ, I.               LECHNER
    ARAGON. FANTASIA -- NO. 6, FROM SUITE ESPANOLA NO. 1
            ASSOCIATED MUSIC PUBLISHERS, INC.       UME             .90
ALBENIZ, I.               GUARDIA, DE LA
    ASTURIAS -- FROM SUITE ESPANOLA NO. 1
            FRANCO COLOMBO PUBLICATIONS             BA6016          .75
ALBENIZ, I.
    ASTURIAS -- NO. 2, ESPAGNE -- SOUVENIRS
            ASSOCIATED MUSIC PUBLISHERS, INC.       UME             .90
ALBENIZ, I.               MARCHI, G.
    ASTURIAS FROM 'SUITE ESPANOLA'
            EDIZIONI BERBEN                         1263           1.50
ALBENIZ, I.               LECHNER
    ASTURIAS. LEYENDA -- NO. 5, FROM SUITE ESPANOLA NO. 1
            ASSOCIATED MUSIC PUBLISHERS, INC.       UME            1.25
```

ALBENIZ, I.
  BARCAROLA, OP. 202 -- FROM MALLORCA
    ASSOCIATED MUSIC PUBLISHERS, INC.   UME   .90
ALBENIZ, I.
  BARCAROLA, OP. 23
    ASSOCIATED MUSIC PUBLISHERS, INC.   UME   .75
ALBENIZ, I.   MONTES
  BARCAROLA, OP. 92 NO. 3
    FRANCO COLOMBO PUBLICATIONS   BA6262   .75
ALBENIZ, I.
  BARCAROLLE, CIEL SANS NUAGES, OP. 92, NO. 3 -- FROM 12 PIECES
CARACTERISTIQUES
    ASSOCIATED MUSIC PUBLISHERS, INC.   UME   .60
ALBENIZ, I.
  CADIZ
    BOSTON MUSIC COMPANY   .50
ALBENIZ, I.   GUARDIA, DE LA
  CADIZ -- FROM SUITE ESPANOLA NO. 1
    FRANCO COLOMBO PUBLICATIONS   BA6015   .75
ALBENIZ, I.   LECHNER
  CADIZ. CANCION -- NO. 4, FROM SUITE ESPANOLA NO. 1
    ASSOCIATED MUSIC PUBLISHERS, INC.   UME   .60
ALBENIZ, I.
  CANTOS DE ESPANA - AIRS OF SPAIN - OP. 232
    INTERNATIONAL MUSIC COMPANY   2.00
ALBENIZ, I.   GUARDIA, DE LA
  CASTILLA -- FROM SUITE ESPANOLA NO. 1
    FRANCO COLOMBO PUBLICATIONS   BA6018   .75
ALBENIZ, I.   LECHNER
  CASTILLA. SEGUIDILLAS -- NO. 7, FROM SUITE ESPANOLA NO. 1
    ASSOCIATED MUSIC PUBLISHERS, INC.   UME   1.00
ALBENIZ, I.   GUARDIA, DE LA
  CATALUNA -- FROM SUITE ESPANOLA NO. 1
    FRANCO COLOMBO PUBLICATIONS   BA6013   .75
ALBENIZ, I.   LECHNER
  CATALUNA -- NO. 2, FROM SUITE ESPANOLA NO. 1
    ASSOCIATED MUSIC PUBLISHERS, INC.   UME   .60
ALBENIZ, I.
  CHACONNE NO. 2 -- FROM SUITE ANCIENNE NO. 2 --
    ASSOCIATED MUSIC PUBLISHERS, INC.   UME   .75
ALBENIZ, I.
  CONCHITA, POLKA, OP. 92, NO. 5 -- FROM 12 PIECES
CARACTERISTIQUES
    ASSOCIATED MUSIC PUBLISHERS, INC.   UME   .50
ALBENIZ, I.
  CORDOBA
    EDWARD B. MARKS MUSIC CORPORATION   01.00
ALBENIZ, I.
  CORDOBA--FROM ''SONGS OF SPAIN''
    G. SCHIRMER, INC.   .70
ALBENIZ, I.
  CORDOBA, OP. 232, NO. 4 -- FROM CANTOS DE ESPANA
    ASSOCIATED MUSIC PUBLISHERS, INC.   UME   .75
ALBENIZ, I.   GUARDIA, DE LA
  CORDOBA, OP. 232, NO. 4 -- FROM CANTOS DE ESPANA
    FRANCO COLOMBO PUBLICATIONS   BA6009   .75
ALBENIZ, I.   MONTES
  CORPUS CHRISTI EN SEVILLA -- FROM IBERIA
    FRANCO COLOMBO PUBLICATIONS   BA6246   1.50
ALBENIZ, I.   GUARDIA, DE LA
  CUBA -- FROM SUITE ESPANOLA NO. 1
    FRANCO COLOMBO PUBLICATIONS   BA6019   .75
ALBENIZ, I.   LECHNER
  CUBA. CAPRICE -- NO. 8, FROM SUITE ESPANOLA NO. 1
    ASSOCIATED MUSIC PUBLISHERS, INC.   UME   .75
ALBENIZ, I.
  DESEO, OP. 40 -- CONCERT ETUDE
    ASSOCIATED MUSIC PUBLISHERS, INC.   UME   1.50
ALBENIZ, I.
  EN EL ALHAMBRA -- NO. 4, FROM RECUERDOS DE VIAJE
    ASSOCIATED MUSIC PUBLISHERS, INC.   UME   .75
ALBENIZ, I.
  EN EL MAR -- NO. 1 FROM RECUERDOS DE VIAJE
    ASSOCIATED MUSIC PUBLISHERS, INC.   UME   1.00
ALBENIZ, I.
  EN EL PLAYA -- NO. 7, FROM RECUERDOS DE VIAJE
    ASSOCIATED MUSIC PUBLISHERS, INC.   UME   1.75
ALBENIZ, I.   MONTES
  EN LA ALHAMBRA -- FROM RECUERDOS DE VIAJE
    FRANCO COLOMBO PUBLICATIONS   BA6255   .75
ALBENIZ, I.   MONTES
  ERITANA -- FROM IBERIA
    FRANCO COLOMBO PUBLICATIONS   BA6254   1.00
ALBENIZ, I.
  ESPANA - SIX ALBUM LEAVES - OP. 165
    INTERNATIONAL MUSIC COMPANY   3   2.00
ALBENIZ, I.
  ESPANA, OP. 165
    SCHOTT   1287   2.25
ALBENIZ, I.   3
  ESPANA, OP. 165 NO. 1
    SCHOTT   1287   2.25
ALBENIZ, I.   MONTES
  EVOCACION -- FROM IBERIA
    FRANCO COLOMBO PUBLICATIONS   BA6166   .75
ALBENIZ, I.
  FANTASY NO. 1, FROM ''PEPITA-JIMINEZ''
    ASSOCIATED MUSIC PUBLISHERS, INC.   ESC   1.75
ALBENIZ, I.
  FANTASY NO. 2, FROM ''PEPITA-JIMINEZ''
    ASSOCIATED MUSIC PUBLISHERS, INC.   ESC   2.00
ALBENIZ, I.
  GAVOTTE, OP. 92, NO. 1 -- FROM 12 PIECES CARACTERISTIQUES
    ASSOCIATED MUSIC PUBLISHERS, INC.   UME   .75
ALBENIZ, I.
  GRANADA
    EDWARD B. MARKS MUSIC CORPORATION   01.00
ALBENIZ, I.   GUARDIA, DE LA
  GRANADA -- FROM SUITE ESPANOLA NO. 1
    FRANCO COLOMBO PUBLICATIONS   BA5967   .75
ALBENIZ, I.   MARCHI, G.
  GRANADA FROM 'SUITE ESPANOLA'
    EDIZIONI BERBEN   1262   1.50
ALBENIZ, I.   LECHNER
  GRENADA. SERENATA -- NO. 1, FROM SUITE ESPANOLA NO. 1
    ASSOCIATED MUSIC PUBLISHERS, INC.   UME   .60
ALBENIZ, I.
  IBERIA SUITE, BK. 1
    INTERNATIONAL MUSIC COMPANY   2.50
ALBENIZ, I.
  IBERIA SUITE, BK. 2
    INTERNATIONAL MUSIC COMPANY   2.50
ALBENIZ, I.
  IBERIA SUITE, BK. 3
    INTERNATIONAL MUSIC COMPANY   2.50

ALBENIZ, I.
  IBERIA SUITE, BK. 4
    INTERNATIONAL MUSIC COMPANY   2.50
ALBENIZ, I.
  INTERLUDE, FROM ''PEPITA-JIMINEZ''
    ASSOCIATED MUSIC PUBLISHERS, INC.   ESC   1.75
ALBENIZ, I.   MONTES
  JEREZ -- FROM IBERIA
    FRANCO COLOMBO PUBLICATIONS   BA6253   1.50
ALBENIZ, I.   3
  JOTA ARAGONESA UND TANGO, OP. 164
    SCHOTT   1309   2.00
ALBENIZ, I.
  L'AUTOMNE-VALSE, OP. 170
    ASSOCIATED MUSIC PUBLISHERS, INC.   UME   1.10
ALBENIZ, I.   MONTES
  LAVAPIES -- FROM IBERIA
    FRANCO COLOMBO PUBLICATIONS   BA6251   1.25
ALBENIZ, I.   4
  LEYENDA
    BOSTON MUSIC COMPANY   .60
ALBENIZ, I.
  LEYENDA - ASTURIAS -
    INTERNATIONAL MUSIC COMPANY   1.00
ALBENIZ, I.
  LEYENDA, BARCAROLLE -- NO. 2, FROM RECUERDOS DE VIAJE
    ASSOCIATED MUSIC PUBLISHERS, INC.   UME   .75
ALBENIZ, I.   MONTES
  MALAGA -- FROM IBERIA
    FRANCO COLOMBO PUBLICATIONS   BA6252   1.00
ALBENIZ, I.   SCHAUM, J.   4
  MALAGUENA
    BELWIN-MILLS PUBLISHING CORPORATION   .50
ALBENIZ, I.   4
  MALAGUENA
    CENTURY MUSIC PUBLISHING COMPANY, INC.   3481   .40
ALBENIZ, I.
  MALAGUENA
    EDWARD B. MARKS MUSIC CORPORATION   01.00
ALBENIZ, I.   3
  MALAGUENA NO. 3
    SCHOTT   1702   1.50
ALBENIZ, I.   3
  MALAGUENA, OP. 165 NO. 3
    SCHOTT   1702   1.50
ALBENIZ, I.   MARCHI, G.
  MALAGUENA, OP. 165, NO. 3 FROM 'ESPANA'
    EDIZIONI BERBEN   1260   1.20
ALBENIZ, I.   MONTES
  MALAGUENA, OP. 60, NO. 03--FROM ESPANA
    FRANCO COLOMBO PUBLICATIONS   BA6526   .75
ALBENIZ, I.   MONTES
  MALLORCA, OP. 202
    FRANCO COLOMBO PUBLICATIONS   BA6257   .75
ALBENIZ, I.
  MAZURKA DE SALON, OP. 81
    ASSOCIATED MUSIC PUBLISHERS, INC.   UME   .75
ALBENIZ, I.
  MAZURKA, OP. 80 -- FROM RECUERDOS
    ASSOCIATED MUSIC PUBLISHERS, INC.   UME   1.25
ALBENIZ, I.
  MAZURKA, OP. 92 NO. 10--FROM 12 PIECES CARACTERISTIQUES
    ASSOCIATED MUSIC PUBLISHERS, INC.   UME   .75
ALBENIZ, I.
  MINUET -- FROM SUITE ANCIENNE NO. 3
    ASSOCIATED MUSIC PUBLISHERS, INC.   UME   .60
ALBENIZ, I.
  MINUET NO. 3
    ASSOCIATED MUSIC PUBLISHERS, INC.   UME   .60
ALBENIZ, I.
  MINUET, OP. 111 -- FROM SONATA NO. 7
    ASSOCIATED MUSIC PUBLISHERS, INC.   UME   .75
ALBENIZ, I.
  MINUETTO A SYLVIA, OP. 92, NO. 2 -- FROM 12 PIECES
CARACTERISTIQUES
    ASSOCIATED MUSIC PUBLISHERS, INC.   UME   .60
ALBENIZ, I.
  NAVARRA
    ASSOCIATED MUSIC PUBLISHERS, INC.   UME   1.75
ALBENIZ, I.   PAHISSA
  NAVARRA
    FRANCO COLOMBO PUBLICATIONS   BA8835   1.25
ALBENIZ, I.
  NAVARRA
    INTERNATIONAL MUSIC COMPANY   1.50
ALBENIZ, I.
  ORIENTALE, OP. 232, NO. 2 -- FROM CANTOS DE ESPANA
    ASSOCIATED MUSIC PUBLISHERS, INC.   UME   .75
ALBENIZ, I.   GUARDIA, DE LA
  ORIENTALE, OP. 232, NO. 2 --FROM CANTOS DE ESPANA
    FRANCO COLOMBO PUBLICATIONS   BA6007   .75
ALBENIZ, I.
  PAVANA-CAPRICHO, OP. 12
    ASSOCIATED MUSIC PUBLISHERS, INC.   UME   .90
ALBENIZ, I.   MONTES
  PAVANA-CAPRICHO, OP. 12
    FRANCO COLOMBO PUBLICATIONS   BA6258   .75
ALBENIZ, I.
  PAVANA, OP. 83
    ASSOCIATED MUSIC PUBLISHERS, INC.   UME   .75
ALBENIZ, I.
  PAVANA, OP. 92, NO. 8 -- FROM 12 PIECES CARACTERISTIQUES
    ASSOCIATED MUSIC PUBLISHERS, INC.   UME   .75
ALBENIZ, I.
  PILAR, WALTZ, OP. 92, NO. 6 -- FROM 12 PIECES CARACTERISTIQUES
    ASSOCIATED MUSIC PUBLISHERS, INC.   UME   1.00
ALBENIZ, I.   MONTES
  POLO, EL -- FROM IBERIA
    FRANCO COLOMBO PUBLICATIONS   BA 6250   1.25
ALBENIZ, I.
  POLONESA, OP. 92, NO. 9 -- FROM 12 PIECES CARACTERISTIQUES
    ASSOCIATED MUSIC PUBLISHERS, INC.   UME   1.00
ALBENIZ, I.
  PRELUDE -- NO. 1, AZULEJOS
    ASSOCIATED MUSIC PUBLISHERS, INC.   UME   1.10
ALBENIZ, I.
  PRELUDE, OP. 232 NO. 1--FROM CANTOS DE ESPANA
    ASSOCIATED MUSIC PUBLISHERS, INC.   UME   1.00
ALBENIZ, I.
  PRIERE, OP. 92, NO. 4 -- FROM 12 PIECES CARACTERISTIQUES
    ASSOCIATED MUSIC PUBLISHERS, INC.   UME   .90
ALBENIZ, I.
  PUERTA DE TIERRA -- NO. 5, FROM RECUERDOS DE VIAJE
    ASSOCIATED MUSIC PUBLISHERS, INC.   UME   .75
ALBENIZ, I.
  PUERTO, EL
    ASSOCIATED MUSIC PUBLISHERS, INC.   UME   1.50

ALBENIZ, I.   MONTES
PUERTO, EL -- FROM IBERIA
    FRANCO COLOMBO PUBLICATIONS   BA6167   .75
ALBENIZ, I.
RAPSODIA CUBANA, OP. 66
    ASSOCIATED MUSIC PUBLISHERS, INC.   UME   .65
ALBENIZ, I.
RAPSODIA ESPANOLA
    ASSOCIATED MUSIC PUBLISHERS, INC.   UME   1.50
ALBENIZ, I.
RECUERDOS DE VIAJE - TRAVEL IMPRESSIONS -
    INTERNATIONAL MUSIC COMPANY   2.50
ALBENIZ, I.
RICORDATTI, OP. 96 -- SALON MAZURKA
    ASSOCIATED MUSIC PUBLISHERS, INC.   UME   .60
ALBENIZ, I.   MONTES
RODENA -- FROM IBERIA
    FRANCO COLOMBO PUBLICATIONS   BA6247   1.25
ALBENIZ, I.   MARCHI, G.
RUMORES DE LA CALETA
    EDIZIONI BERBEN   1261   1.50
ALBENIZ, I.
RUMORES DE LA CALETA - MALAGUENAS -
    INTERNATIONAL MUSIC COMPANY   1.00
ALBENIZ, I.   MONTES
RUMORES DE LA CALETA -- FROM RECUERDOS DE VIAJE
    FRANCO COLOMBO PUBLICATIONS   BA6245   .75
ALBENIZ, I.
RUMORES DE LA CALETA, MALAGUENA -- NO. 6, FROM RECUERDOS DE
VIAJE
    ASSOCIATED MUSIC PUBLISHERS, INC.   UME   .75
ALBENIZ, I.
SARABANDE -- NO.1, FROM SUITE ANCIENNE NO. 2
    ASSOCIATED MUSIC PUBLISHERS, INC.   UME   .60
ALBENIZ, I.   5
SEGUIDILLAS
    CENTURY MUSIC PUBLISHING COMPANY, INC.   3732   .40
ALBENIZ, I.
SEGUIDILLAS, OP. 232 NO. 5
    EDWARD B. MARKS MUSIC CORPORATION   01.00
ALBENIZ, I.
SEGUIDILLAS, OP. 232, NO. 5 -- FROM CANTOS DE ESPANA
    ASSOCIATED MUSIC PUBLISHERS, INC.   UME   1.00
ALBENIZ, I.
SERENATA ARABE
    ASSOCIATED MUSIC PUBLISHERS, INC.   UME   .90
ALBENIZ, I.
SERENATA ESPANOLA
    ASSOCIATED MUSIC PUBLISHERS, INC.   UME   .90
ALBENIZ, I.
SEVILLA
    EDWARD B. MARKS MUSIC CORPORATION   01.00
ALBENIZ, I.   GUARDIA, DE LA
SEVILLA -- FROM SUITE ESPANOLA NO. 1
    FRANCO COLOMBO PUBLICATIONS   BA6014   .75
ALBENIZ, I.
SEVILLA -- NO. 2, FROM SUITE ESPANOLA NO. 2
    ASSOCIATED MUSIC PUBLISHERS, INC.   UME   1.00
ALBENIZ, I.   LECHNER
SEVILLA -- NO. 3, FROM SUITE ESPANOLA NO. 1
    ASSOCIATED MUSIC PUBLISHERS, INC.   UME   .60
ALBENIZ, I.
SONATA NO. 03, OP. 68
    ASSOCIATED MUSIC PUBLISHERS, INC.   UME   2.00
ALBENIZ, I.
SONATA NO. 04, OP. 72
    ASSOCIATED MUSIC PUBLISHERS, INC.   UME   1.50
ALBENIZ, I.
SONATA NO. 05, OP. 82
    ASSOCIATED MUSIC PUBLISHERS, INC.   UME   2.25
ALBENIZ, I.
SOUS LE PALMIER, OP. 232, NO. 3 -- FROM CANTOS DE ESPANA
    ASSOCIATED MUSIC PUBLISHERS, INC.   UME   .60
ALBENIZ, I.   GUARDIA, DE LA
SOUS LE PALMIER, OP. 232, NO. 3 --FROM CANTOS DE ESPANA
    FRANCO COLOMBO PUBLICATIONS   BA6008   .75
ALBENIZ, I.
STACCATO, CAPRICE, OP. 92, NO. 11 -- FROM 12 PIECES
CARACTERISTIQUES
    ASSOCIATED MUSIC PUBLISHERS, INC.   UME   1.00
ALBENIZ, I.
SUITE ESPAGNOLE
    EDWIN F. KALMUS   3002   2.00
ALBENIZ, I.   LECHNER   4
SUITE ESPAGNOLE
    SCHOTT   5068   3.50
ALBENIZ, I.   LECHNER   4
SUITE ESPAGNOLE
    SCHOTT   5068   3.50
ALBENIZ, I.   PHILLIPP, I.
SUITE ESPANOLA
    INTERNATIONAL MUSIC COMPANY   2.50
ALBENIZ, I.   GUARDIA, DE LA
SUITE ESPANOLA NO. 1
    FRANCO COLOMBO PUBLICATIONS   BA6273   3.25
ALBENIZ, I.   4
TANGO IN D
    CENTURY MUSIC PUBLISHING COMPANY, INC.   3254   .40
ALBENIZ, I.   3
TANGO NO. 2
    SCHOTT   1701   1.50
ALBENIZ, I.   GODOWSKY   5
TANGO NO. 2. KONZERTTRANSKRIPTION
    SCHOTT   1705   1.75
ALBENIZ, I.   OBERSTADT   3
TANGO NO. 2. TRANSCRIPTION
    SCHOTT   2077   1.25
ALBENIZ, I.   M
TANGO, OP. 165
    C. F. PETERS CORPORATION   5341   1.50
ALBENIZ, I.   ECKSTEIN
TANGO, OP. 165 NO. 2
    CARL FISCHER, INC.   S 2305   1.25
ALBENIZ, I.   3
TANGO, OP. 165 NO. 2
    SCHOTT   1701   1.50
ALBENIZ, I.
TANGO, OP. 165, NO. I -- FROM ESPANA
    ASSOCIATED MUSIC PUBLISHERS, INC.   UME   .60
ALBENIZ, I.   MONTES
TANGO, OP. 60, NO. 2 -- FROM ESPANA
    FRANCO COLOMBO PUBLICATIONS   BA6529   .75
ALBENIZ, I.   MONTES
TORRE BERMEJA, OP. 92 NO. 12
    FRANCO COLOMBO PUBLICATIONS   BA6261   .75

ALBENIZ, I.
TORRE BERMEJA, SERENADE, OP. 92, NO. 12 -- FROM 12 PIECES
CARACTERISTIQUES
    ASSOCIATED MUSIC PUBLISHERS, INC.   UME   1.00
ALBENIZ, I.
TRIANA
    ASSOCIATED MUSIC PUBLISHERS, INC.   UME   .75
ALBENIZ, I.   7
TRIANA
    BOSTON MUSIC COMPANY   .75
ALBENIZ, I.   MONTES
TRIANA -- FROM IBERIA
    FRANCO COLOMBO PUBLICATIONS   BA6168   1.00
ALBENIZ, I.
VEGA, LA -- NO. 1, ALHAMBRA SUITE
    ASSOCIATED MUSIC PUBLISHERS, INC.   ESC   2.00
ALBENIZ, I.
YVONNE EN VISITE
    FRANCO COLOMBO PUBLICATIONS   SAL   2.75
ALBENIZ, I.
ZAMBRA GRANADINA. ORIENTAL DANCE
    ASSOCIATED MUSIC PUBLISHERS, INC.   UME   .60
ALBENIZ, I.
ZAMBRA, OP. 92, NO. 7 -- FROM 12 PIECES CARACTERISTIQUES
    ASSOCIATED MUSIC PUBLISHERS, INC.   UME   .50
ALBENIZ, I.
ZARAGOZA -- NO. 1, FROM SUITE ESPANOLA NO. 2
    ASSOCIATED MUSIC PUBLISHERS, INC.   UME   .75
ALBENIZ, I.
ZORTZICO, OP. 165, NO. 6 -- FROM ESPANA
    ASSOCIATED MUSIC PUBLISHERS, INC.   UME   1.00
ALBENIZ, M.   NIN
SONATA IN D
    ASSOCIATED MUSIC PUBLISHERS, INC.   ESC   .90
ALBENIZ, M.   NIN
SONATA IN D
    ASSOCIATED MUSIC PUBLISHERS, INC.   UME   .75
ALBERS
BASKET OF ROSES
    SAM FOX PUBLISHING COMPANY, INC.   .75
ALBERS
BASKET OF ROSES
    SOUTHERN MUSIC COMPANY   .75
ALBERT, C. D'   4
LA SORELLA
    CENTURY MUSIC PUBLISHING COMPANY, INC.   1154   .40
ALBERT, C. D'   2
PERI WALTZES
    CENTURY MUSIC PUBLISHING COMPANY, INC.   651   .40
ALBERT, E. D'   D
INTERMEZZO AND BALLADE, OP. 16 NO. 3
    C. F. PETERS CORPORATION   2939C   3.00
ALBERT, E. D'
SUITE IN D MINOR, OP. 1
    ASSOCIATED MUSIC PUBLISHERS, INC.   B/H   2.50
ALBERT, E. D'
SUITE, OP. 1--ALLEMANDE, GAVOTTE, MUSETTE
    G. SCHIRMER, INC.   .60
ALBINONI
ADAGIO IN G MINOR
    FRANCO COLOMBO PUBLICATIONS   ER2609   .75
ALBRIGHT, W.
PIANOAGOGO
    ELKAN-VOGEL, INC.   J   2.50
ALDERIGHI
INTRODUCTION, ARIA, AND FINALE
    FRANCO COLOMBO PUBLICATIONS   FOR.11539   2.00
ALDERIGHI
SUITE NO. 1
    FRANCO COLOMBO PUBLICATIONS   FOR.11281   1.75
ALDRED, H.   1
SUNNY MORNING
    BELWIN-MILLS PUBLISHING CORPORATION   .60
ALDRICH   3
LOVE AND FLOWERS
    CENTURY MUSIC PUBLISHING COMPANY, INC.   1319   .40
ALDRICH   4
NEW FLOWER SONG
    CENTURY MUSIC PUBLISHING COMPANY, INC.   1319   .40
ALDROVANDINI   PICCIOLI
ADAGIO AND PASTORALE
    FRANCO COLOMBO PUBLICATIONS   BON.1905   1.00
ALDWINCKLE
PREAMBLE
    ASSOCIATED MUSIC PUBLISHERS, INC.   BER   .40
ALETTER, W.
RENDEVOUS -- INTERMEZZO ROCOCO
    BELWIN-MILLS PUBLISHING CORPORATION   .60
ALEXANDER, H.
SOUNDFIGURES
    ISRAEL MUSIC INSTITUTE   4.00
ALEXANDROV
RUSSIAN FOLK SONG --WITH WEDDING DANCE BY LUBARSKY
    MCA MUSIC   .60
ALEXANDROW, A.
SONATA NO. 05, OP. 22
    UNIVERSAL EDITION   UE 7346   2.55
ALFANO
FOUR RUMANIAN DANCES - NO. 1
    FRANCO COLOMBO PUBLICATIONS   SAL   1.75
ALFANO
FOUR RUMANIAN DANCES - NO. 2
    FRANCO COLOMBO PUBLICATIONS   SAL   1.75
ALFANO
FOUR RUMANIAN DANCES - NO. 3
    FRANCO COLOMBO PUBLICATIONS   SAL   1.75
ALFANO
FOUR RUMANIAN DANCES - NO. 4
    FRANCO COLOMBO PUBLICATIONS   SAL   1.75
ALFANO
TWO PIECES - ARLEQUIN
    FRANCO COLOMBO PUBLICATIONS   SAL   1.75
ALFANO
TWO PIECES - VALSE COQUETTE
    FRANCO COLOMBO PUBLICATIONS   SAL   1.75
ALFOLDY, I.   6
HUNGARIAN CONCERT POLKA
    THEODORE PRESSER COMPANY   .60
ALFONSO
CAPRICCIO IN THE FORM OF A BOLERO
    FRANCO COLOMBO PUBLICATIONS   SAL   2.50
ALFONSO
GUAJIRA
    ASSOCIATED MUSIC PUBLISHERS, INC.   UME   .50
ALFONSO
IMPROMPTU
    ASSOCIATED MUSIC PUBLISHERS, INC.   UME   .75

ALFONSO
  PRELUDE AND TOCCATA
      ASSOCIATED MUSIC PUBLISHERS, INC.   UME   .75
ALFONSO
  SUITE. HOMENAJE A ALBENIZ
      ASSOCIATED MUSIC PUBLISHERS, INC.   UME   2.25
ALFORD, K.
  COLONEL BOGEY
      BOOSEY AND HAWKES, INC.   .75
ALFORD, K.
  COLONEL BOGEY
      BOOSEY AND HAWKES, INC.   .60
ALFORD, K.
  GREAT LITTLE ARMY
      BOOSEY AND HAWKES, INC.   1.50
ALFORD, K.
  MUSICAL SWITCH
      BOOSEY AND HAWKES, INC.   .75
ALFORD, K.   WATTERS
  VOICE OF THE GUNS
      BOOSEY AND HAWKES, INC.   .75
ALFVEN, H.
  SWEDISH POLKA
      BELWIN-MILLS PUBLISHING CORPORATION   -20284   .85
ALKAN
  ALLEGRO BARBARO
      ALEXANDER BROUDE, INC.   2.10
ALKAN
  ALLELUIA, OP. 25
      GERARD BILLAUDOT EDITIONS MUSICALES   2.00
ALKAN
  ALLELUIA, OP. 25
      MUSICA OBSCURA   1.50
ALKAN
  BARCAROLLE, OP. 38 NO. 1
      GERARD BILLAUDOT EDITIONS MUSICALES   1.60
ALKAN
  BARCAROLLE, OP. 38 NO. 2
      GERARD BILLAUDOT EDITIONS MUSICALES   1.60
ALKAN
  BARCAROLLE, OP. 65 NO. 3
      GERARD BILLAUDOT EDITIONS MUSICALES   1.60
ALKAN
  BARCAROLLE, OP. 67 NO. 4
      GERARD BILLAUDOT EDITIONS MUSICALES   1.60
ALKAN
  BARCAROLLE, OP. 70 NO. 5
      GERARD BILLAUDOT EDITIONS MUSICALES   1.60
ALKAN
  CAPRICCIO ALLA SOLIDATESCA, OP. 50 NO. 1
      GERARD BILLAUDOT EDITIONS MUSICALES   3.30
ALKAN
  CHAPEAU BAS
      GERARD BILLAUDOT EDITIONS MUSICALES   3.00
ALKAN
  ETUDE DE CONCERT, OP. 38 NO. 1
      GERARD BILLAUDOT EDITIONS MUSICALES   4.40
ALKAN
  FIRST CONCERTO DA CAMERA IN A MINOR, OP. 10
      GERARD BILLAUDOT EDITIONS MUSICALES   4.10
ALKAN
  GIGUE ET AIR DE BALLET DANS LE STYLE ANCIEN, OP. 24
      GERARD BILLAUDOT EDITIONS MUSICALES   2.50
ALKAN   STIRN, D.
  GRAND PAS CLASSIQUE--PAS DE DEUX--
      GERARD BILLAUDOT EDITIONS MUSICALES   2.20
ALKAN
  GRANDE SONATE, OP. 33
      GERARD BILLAUDOT EDITIONS MUSICALES   6.30
ALKAN
  LE CHEMIN DE FER, OP. 27
      GERARD BILLAUDOT EDITIONS MUSICALES   3.00
ALKAN
  LE FESTIN D'ESOPE, OP. 39
      GERARD BILLAUDOT EDITIONS MUSICALES   3.80
ALKAN
  LE TAMBOUR BAT AUX CHAMPS, OP. 50 NO. 2
      GERARD BILLAUDOT EDITIONS MUSICALES   2.50
ALKAN
  LES MOIS, OP. 74, BK. 1
      GERARD BILLAUDOT EDITIONS MUSICALES   2.00
ALKAN
  LES MOIS, OP. 74, BK. 2
      GERARD BILLAUDOT EDITIONS MUSICALES   2.50
ALKAN
  LES MOIS, OP. 74, BK. 3
      GERARD BILLAUDOT EDITIONS MUSICALES   3.00
ALKAN
  LES MOIS, OP. 74, BK. 4
      GERARD BILLAUDOT EDITIONS MUSICALES   2.50
ALKAN
  MA CHERE LIBERTE, OP. 60 NO. 1
      GERARD BILLAUDOT EDITIONS MUSICALES   2.50
ALKAN
  PERPETUUM MOBILE
      GERARD BILLAUDOT EDITIONS MUSICALES   1.60
ALKAN
  QUASI-CACCIA, OP. 53
      GERARD BILLAUDOT EDITIONS MUSICALES   3.90
ALKAN
  RECONCILIATION, OP. 42
      GERARD BILLAUDOT EDITIONS MUSICALES   2.50
ALKAN
  RIGAUDONS
      GERARD BILLAUDOT EDITIONS MUSICALES   1.60
ALKAN
  SALUT CENDRE DU PAUVRE, OP. 45
      GERARD BILLAUDOT EDITIONS MUSICALES   2.70
ALKAN
  SECOND CONCERTO DA CAMERA IN C SHARP MINOR, OP. 10
      GERARD BILLAUDOT EDITIONS MUSICALES   3.30
ALKAN
  SONATINE IN A MINOR, OP. 61
      GERARD BILLAUDOT EDITIONS MUSICALES   4.40
ALKAN
  SUPER FLUMINA BABYLONIS, OP. 52
      GERARD BILLAUDOT EDITIONS MUSICALES   2.50
ALKAN
  THREE GRANDES ETUDES, OP. 76, NO. 1, FANTAISIE IN A FLAT--LEFT
  HAND ONLY--
      GERARD BILLAUDOT EDITIONS MUSICALES   2.50
ALKAN
  THREE GRANDES ETUDES, OP. 76, NO. 2, INTRODUCTION, VARIATION,
  FINALE--RIGHT HAND ONLY--
      GERARD BILLAUDOT EDITIONS MUSICALES   3.30

ALKAN
  THREE GRANDES ETUDES, OP. 76, NO. 3, MOUVEMENT SEMBLABLE ET
  PERPETUEL--BOTH HANDS--
      GERARD BILLAUDOT EDITIONS MUSICALES   3.30
ALKAN
  TOCCATINA, OP. 75
      GERARD BILLAUDOT EDITIONS MUSICALES   1.60
ALKAN
  TWELVE ETUDES IN MINOR KEYS, NO. 01, COMME LE VENT--A MINOR--
      GERARD BILLAUDOT EDITIONS MUSICALES   3.30
ALKAN
  TWELVE ETUDES IN MINOR KEYS, NO. 02, RYTHME MOLOSSIQUE--D
  MINOR--
      GERARD BILLAUDOT EDITIONS MUSICALES   3.00
ALKAN
  TWELVE ETUDES IN MINOR KEYS, NO. 03, SCHERZO DIABOLICO--G
  MINOR--
      GERARD BILLAUDOT EDITIONS MUSICALES   2.50
ALKAN
  TWELVE ETUDES IN MINOR KEYS, NO. 04, ALLEGRO MODERATO--C MINOR--
      GERARD BILLAUDOT EDITIONS MUSICALES   3.00
ALKAN
  TWELVE ETUDES IN MINOR KEYS, NO. 05, MARCHE FUNEBRE--F MINOR--
      GERARD BILLAUDOT EDITIONS MUSICALES   1.60
ALKAN
  TWELVE ETUDES IN MINOR KEYS, NO. 06, MENUET--B FLAT MINOR--
      GERARD BILLAUDOT EDITIONS MUSICALES   2.50
ALKAN
  TWELVE ETUDES IN MINOR KEYS, NO. 07, FINALE--E FLAT MINOR--
      GERARD BILLAUDOT EDITIONS MUSICALES   3.00
ALKAN
  TWELVE ETUDES IN MINOR KEYS, NO. 08, CONCERTO-ALLEGRO ASSAI--G
  SHARP MINOR--
      GERARD BILLAUDOT EDITIONS MUSICALES   5.70
ALKAN
  TWELVE ETUDES IN MINOR KEYS, NO. 09, CONCERTO-ADAGIO--C SHARP
  MINOR--
      GERARD BILLAUDOT EDITIONS MUSICALES   3.00
ALKAN
  TWELVE ETUDES IN MINOR KEYS, NO. 10, ALLEGRO ALA BARBARESCA--F
  SHARP MINOR--
      GERARD BILLAUDOT EDITIONS MUSICALES   4.40
ALKAN
  TWELVE ETUDES IN MINOR KEYS, NO. 11, OUVERTURE--B MINOR--
      GERARD BILLAUDOT EDITIONS MUSICALES   4.10
ALKAN
  UNE FUSEE, OP. 55--INTRODUCTION ET IMPROMPTU--
      GERARD BILLAUDOT EDITIONS MUSICALES   3.00
ALKAN
  WIND, THE--ETUDE, OP. 15, NO. 2
      G. SCHIRMER, INC.   1.10
ALLEN
  LAMENT
      SUMMY-BIRCHARD COMPANY   .50
ALLEN
  SIESTA AT THE FIESTA
      MCA MUSIC   1.00
ALLEN, C.   ADVANCED
  AMERICAN CAKE WALK
      SHAWNEE PRESS, INC.   HB-132   .60
ALLENDE
  TEMPO DI MINUETTO
      FRANCO COLOMBO PUBLICATIONS   SAL   1.75
ALLIER
  AUX TUILERIES
      FRANCO COLOMBO PUBLICATIONS   SAL   1.50
ALLIER   6
  JOYEUSE ESPAGNE, VALSE BRILLANTE
      ALPHONSE LEDUC
ALLIER
  POLKA DES SOURIS BLANCHES
      FRANCO COLOMBO PUBLICATIONS   SAL   1.50
ALLISON, I.   3 1/2
  FOX CHASE, THE
      WILLIS MUSIC COMPANY   .50
ALLISON, I.   4
  PASTORALE
      WILLIS MUSIC COMPANY   .50
ALLISON, I.   4
  TO A ROSEBUD
      WILLIS MUSIC COMPANY   .50
ALLOWAYS   3-4
  SAD THOUGHTS OF THEE
      CENTURY MUSIC PUBLISHING COMPANY, INC.   2701   .40
ALNAR, F.
  TURKISH DANCE SUITE
      UNIVERSAL EDITION   UE 10867   3.00
ALOYSIUS, SR. MARY   4
  IMPROMPRU
      BELWIN-MILLS PUBLISHING CORPORATION   .60
ALPERT, P.
  DREAM OF A DOLL
      BELWIN-MILLS PUBLISHING CORPORATION   20034   .85
ALPERT, P.
  I WAS KAISER BILL'S BATMAN
      BELWIN-MILLS PUBLISHING CORPORATION   20566   .85
ALPERT, P.
  IVORY TIPS
      BELWIN-MILLS PUBLISHING CORPORATION   20135   .85
ALT
  BUILDING
      EDWARD B. MARKS MUSIC CORPORATION   00.60
ALT
  HIDE AND SEEK
      EDWARD B. MARKS MUSIC CORPORATION   00.60
ALT
  WHAT A LONG FREIGHT TRAIN
      EDWARD B. MARKS MUSIC CORPORATION   00.60
ALT, H.   3
  BEE HIVE, THE
      WILLIS MUSIC COMPANY   .40
ALT, H.   3
  BEE HIVE, THE
      WILLIS MUSIC COMPANY   .40
ALT, H.   1-2
  BICYCLE RIDE
      CENTURY MUSIC PUBLISHING COMPANY, INC.   4252   .40
ALT, H.
  CAT AND THE SQUIRREL, THE
      EDWARD B. MARKS MUSIC CORPORATION   00.60
ALT, H.   3 1/2
  FLICKERING SHADOWS
      WILLIS MUSIC COMPANY   .40
ALT, H.   2-3
  HARE AND THE TORTOISE, THE
      CENTURY MUSIC PUBLISHING COMPANY, INC.   4244   .40

ALT, H.		2	
MARBLES			
THEODORE PRESSER COMPANY			.50
ALT, H.		1	
MY NEW CAR			
CENTURY MUSIC PUBLISHING COMPANY, INC.	4257		.40
ALT, H.		E	
OCEAN, THE			
OXFORD UNIVERSITY PRESS	93.807		1.50
ALT, H.		VE	
PARADE, THE			
OXFORD UNIVERSITY PRESS	93.814		.40
ALT, H.		E	
PING PONG			
COMPOSERS PRESS, INC.			1.00
ALT, H.		VE	
SECRET, THE			
OXFORD UNIVERSITY PRESS	93.313		.40
ALT, H.		2 1/2	
SNOW			
WILLIS MUSIC COMPANY			.40
ALT, H.		2	
SPOOKS			
CENTURY MUSIC PUBLISHING COMPANY, INC.	4272		.40
ALT, H.		1	
WALKING THE DOG			
CENTURY MUSIC PUBLISHING COMPANY, INC.	4336		.40
ALT, H.		1	
WHEELS			
CENTURY MUSIC PUBLISHING COMPANY, INC.	4405		.40
ALTER, L.			
CANDLE IN THE WIND			
THE BIG THREE MUSIC CORPORATION			00.95
ALTER, L.			
MANHATTAN NOONLIGHT			
THE BIG THREE MUSIC CORPORATION			00.95
ALTER, L.			
MANHATTAN SERENADE			
THE BIG THREE MUSIC CORPORATION			00.95
ALTER, L.			
METROPOLITAN NOCTURNE			
THE BIG THREE MUSIC CORPORATION			00.95
ALTER, L.			
SIDE STREET IN GOTHAM			
THE BIG THREE MUSIC CORPORATION			01.25
ALTMAN *			
PLAY FIDDLE PLAY			
EDWARD B. MARKS MUSIC CORPORATION			00.60
AMADEI			
NOSTALGIA			
FRANCO COLOMBO PUBLICATIONS	DS333		1.00
AMADEI			
TOPOLINO			
FRANCO COLOMBO PUBLICATIONS	DS334		1.00
AMENGUAL, R.			
SONATINA			
EDITORIAL COOPERATIVA INTER-AMERICANA			01.25
AMES, J.		3	
BED TIME STORIES			
WILLIS MUSIC COMPANY			.35
AMES, J.		1	
LITTLE ROCKING HORSE, THE			
WILLIS MUSIC COMPANY			.50
AMES, J.		2	
LONGING			
WILLIS MUSIC COMPANY			.35
AMFITEATROF			
PRELUDIO SULL'ANNUNCIAZIONE DI LEONARDO DA VINCI			
FRANCO COLOMBO PUBLICATIONS	DS125		1.75
AMMONS			
BLUEBIRD BOOGIE WOOGIE			
MCA MUSIC			1.00
AMMONS *			
MOVIN' THE BOOGIE			
MCA MUSIC			1.00
AMMONS *			
PINE CREEK			
MCA MUSIC			1.00
AMMONS *			
SIXTH AVENUE EXPRESS			
MCA MUSIC			1.00
AMMONS *			
SIXTH AVENUE EXPRESS			
MCA MUSIC			1.00
AMMONS *			
WALKIN' THE BOOGIE			
MCA MUSIC			1.00
AMOS, L.			
METRONOME, THE			
BRODT MUSIC COMPANY			.50
AMRAM		M	
SONATA			
C. F. PETERS CORPORATION	6685		2.00
AMRAM			
THEMES FROM 'J.B.'			
FRANK MUSIC CORPORATION			.95
AMY, G.			
CAHIERS D'EPIGRAMMES			
HEUGEL ET CIE.			7.25
AMY, G.			
EPIGRAMME POUR PIANO			
HEUGEL ET CIE.			3.90
ANCLIFFE			
NIGHT OF GLADNESS			
EDWARD B. MARKS MUSIC CORPORATION			01.00
ANDERSEN, K.		M	
COLUMBINE AND THE ANNOYED HARLEQUIN			
C. F. PETERS CORPORATION	LY408		.50
ANDERSON		3	
BATTLE OF WATERLOO, THE			
CENTURY MUSIC PUBLISHING COMPANY, INC.	992		.40
ANDERSON *			
HOOTIE'S IGNORANT OIL			
MCA MUSIC			1.00
ANDERSON, G. L.			
PRELUDE ET TOCCATO			
EDITIONS MUSICALES TRANSATLANTIQUES			3.10
ANDERSON, L.		3	
ARIETTA			
WOODBURY MUSIC CORPORATION			.75
ANDERSON, L.		3	
BALLADETTE			
WOODBURY MUSIC CORPORATION			.75
ANDERSON, L.			
BELLE OF THE BALL			
BELWIN-MILLS PUBLISHING CORPORATION	20445		.60

ANDERSON, L.			
BLUE TANGO			
BELWIN-MILLS PUBLISHING CORPORATION	20035		.85
ANDERSON, L.			
BLUEBELLS OF SCOTLAND, THE			
BELWIN-MILLS PUBLISHING CORPORATION	20428		.85
ANDERSON, L.			
BUGLER'S HOLIDAY			
BELWIN-MILLS PUBLISHING CORPORATION	20444		.85
ANDERSON, L.		3	
CAPTAINS AND THE KINGS, THE			
WOODBURY MUSIC CORPORATION			.75
ANDERSON, L.			
CHINA DOLL			
BELWIN-MILLS PUBLISHING CORPORATION	20160		.85
ANDERSON, L.		3-4	
CLARINET CANDY			
WOODBURY MUSIC CORPORATION			.75
ANDERSON, L.			
FIDDLE-FADDLE			
BELWIN-MILLS PUBLISHING CORPORATION	20090		.85
ANDERSON, L.			
FIRST DAY OF SPRING, THE			
BELWIN-MILLS PUBLISHING CORPORATION	20431		.85
ANDERSON, L.			
FOGOTTEN DREAMS			
BELWIN-MILLS PUBLISHING CORPORATION	20412		.85
ANDERSON, L.			
GIRL IN SATIN, THE			
BELWIN-MILLS PUBLISHING CORPORATION	20344		.85
ANDERSON, L.		3-4	
GOLDEN YEARS, THE			
WOODBURY MUSIC CORPORATION			.75
ANDERSON, L.		3	
HOME STRETCH			
WOODBURY MUSIC CORPORATION			.75
ANDERSON, L.			
HORSE AND BUGGY			
BELWIN-MILLS PUBLISHING CORPORATION	20126		.85
ANDERSON, L.			
JAZZ LEGATO			
BELWIN-MILLS PUBLISHING CORPORATION	20448		.85
ANDERSON, L.			
JAZZ PIZZICATO			
BELWIN-MILLS PUBLISHING CORPORATION	20138		.85
ANDERSON, L.			
LADY IN WAITING, THE			
BELWIN-MILLS PUBLISHING CORPORATION	20342		.85
ANDERSON, L.			
PENNY-WHISTLE SONG, THE			
BELWIN-MILLS PUBLISHING CORPORATION	20196		.85
ANDERSON, L.			
PHANTOM REGIMENT, THE			
BELWIN-MILLS PUBLISHING CORPORATION	20438		.85
ANDERSON, L.			
PLINK, PLANK, PLUNK			
BELWIN-MILLS PUBLISHING CORPORATION	20405		.85
ANDERSON, L.			
PROMENADE			
BELWIN-MILLS PUBLISHING CORPORATION	20368		.85
ANDERSON, L.			
PYRAMID DANCE			
BELWIN-MILLS PUBLISHING CORPORATION	20343		.85
ANDERSON, L.			
SANDPAPER BALLET			
BELWIN-MILLS PUBLISHING CORPORATION	20269		.85
ANDERSON, L.			
SARABAND			
BELWIN-MILLS PUBLISHING CORPORATION	20427		.85
ANDERSON, L.			
SERENATA			
BELWIN-MILLS PUBLISHING CORPORATION	20424		.85
ANDERSON, L.			
SLEIGH RIDE			
BELWIN-MILLS PUBLISHING CORPORATION	20250		1.00
ANDERSON, L.	GLOVER, D.		
SLEIGH RIDE			
BELWIN-MILLS PUBLISHING CORPORATION			.60
ANDERSON, L.			
SONG OF THE BELLS			
BELWIN-MILLS PUBLISHING CORPORATION	20398		.85
ANDERSON, L.			
SUMMER SKIES			
BELWIN-MILLS PUBLISHING CORPORATION	20432		.85
ANDERSON, L.			
SYNCOPATED CLOCK, THE			
BELWIN-MILLS PUBLISHING CORPORATION	20286		.85
ANDERSON, L.	KING, S.		
SYNCOPATED CLOCK, THE -- SIMP.			
BELWIN-MILLS PUBLISHING CORPORATION	26037		.75
ANDERSON, L.	KING		
SYNCOPATED CLOCK, THE, SIMP.			
BELWIN-MILLS PUBLISHING CORPORATION			.60
ANDERSON, L.			
TOWN HOUSE MAXIXE -- FROM 'GOLDILOCKS'			
BELWIN-MILLS PUBLISHING CORPORATION	20423		.85
ANDERSON, L.			
TRUMPETER'S LULLABY, A			
BELWIN-MILLS PUBLISHING CORPORATION	20005		.85
ANDERSON, L.			
TURN YE TO ME			
BELWIN-MILLS PUBLISHING CORPORATION	20429		.85
ANDERSON, L.			
TYPEWRITER, THE			
BELWIN-MILLS PUBLISHING CORPORATION	20426		.85
ANDERSON, L.			
WALTZING CAT, THE			
BELWIN-MILLS PUBLISHING CORPORATION	20430		.60
ANDERSON, M.		1	
HOPPING AND RUNNING			
BELWIN-MILLS PUBLISHING CORPORATION			.60
ANDERSON, M.		2	
LULLABY			
BELWIN-MILLS PUBLISHING CORPORATION			.60
ANDERSON, M.			
SKIPS			
BELWIN-MILLS PUBLISHING CORPORATION			.60
ANDRE			
ABC WALTZ, THE			
BOSTON MUSIC COMPANY			.50
ANDRE		1	
ACROBAT			
BELWIN-MILLS PUBLISHING CORPORATION			.60
ANDRE		3 1/2	
MOONLIGHT REVELS			
THEODORE PRESSER COMPANY			.60

ANDRE
  PLAYING JACKS   1
      BELWIN-MILLS PUBLISHING CORPORATION   .60
ANDRE   3
  SLEEPY LAKE
      BELWIN-MILLS PUBLISHING CORPORATION   .60
ANDRE   1
  SPRINGTIME IN THE HILLS
      BELWIN-MILLS PUBLISHING CORPORATION   .60
ANDREWS   2
  TIGHT-ROPE DANCER, THE
      BELWIN-MILLS PUBLISHING CORPORATION   .60
ANDRIESSEN, H.   E
  CANZONETTA. HARPSICHORD
      C. F. PETERS CORPORATION   D458   1.50
ANDRIESSEN, H.   M-D
  PAVANE
      C. F. PETERS CORPORATION   B16   .90
ANDRIESSEN, J.   D
  ASTRAZIONE
      C. F. PETERS CORPORATION   D458   2.00
ANGELL   2
  LITTLE ANTELOPE
      PRO-ART PUBLICATIONS, INC.   156   .50
ANGERER
  STIMMUNGEN -- 1955 --
      ASSOCIATED MUSIC PUBLISHERS, INC.   DOB   1.50
ANSON, G.   2
  BELL TOWER, THE
      WILLIS MUSIC COMPANY   .40
ANSON, G.   2
  BIG BAD WOLF
      PRO-ART PUBLICATIONS, INC.   127   .50
ANSON, G.   3
  BULL IN A CHINA SHOP
      WILLIS MUSIC COMPANY   .40
ANSON, G.
  CHINESE CHATTER
      EDWARD B. MARKS MUSIC CORPORATION   00.60
ANSON, G.   2
  CHINESE SERENADE
      VOLKWEIN BROS.   .30
ANSON, G.
  CLOCK ON THE STAIRS
      BELWIN-MILLS PUBLISHING CORPORATION   25026   .60
ANSON, G.   1
  FOLLOW ME
      WILLIS MUSIC COMPANY   .40
ANSON, G.
  HEAP BIG CHIEF
      EDWARD B. MARKS MUSIC CORPORATION   00.60
ANSON, G.
  HOP-SKIP-AND-JUMP
      SAM FOX PUBLISHING COMPANY, INC.   .50
ANSON, G.
  HOP-SKIP-AND-JUMP
      SOUTHERN MUSIC COMPANY   .50
ANSON, G.   1 1/2
  IN A CONTRARY MOOD
      THEODORE PRESSER COMPANY   .50
ANSON, G.   2
  LITTLE BOY BLUES
      WILLIS MUSIC COMPANY   .50
ANSON, G.   2
  LITTLE TIN TRUMPET
      WILLIS MUSIC COMPANY   .40
ANSON, G.   2
  MAN IN THE MOON
      VOLKWEIN BROS.   .30
ANSON, G.   3
  MYSTERY STORY, A
      WILLIS MUSIC COMPANY   .40
ANSON, G.   2
  OLD WITCH
      THEODORE PRESSER COMPANY   .50
ANSON, G.   1 1/2
  OUT FOR A STROLL
      THEODORE PRESSER COMPANY   .50
ANSON, G.   2 1/2
  PLATINUM PUP, THE
      WILLIS MUSIC COMPANY   .40
ANSON, G.
  SAUNTERING ALONG
      BELWIN-MILLS PUBLISHING CORPORATION   .60
ANSON, G.   1
  SLUMBER STORY
      WILLIS MUSIC COMPANY   .30
ANSON, G.
  SPACE FLIGHT
      SAM FOX PUBLISHING COMPANY, INC.   .50
ANSON, G.
  SPACE FLIGHT
      SOUTHERN MUSIC COMPANY   .50
ANSON, G.
  SPINNING TOP, THE
      BELWIN-MILLS PUBLISHING CORPORATION   25101   .60
ANSON, G.   2
  SPOOK ON THE STAIRS
      WILLIS MUSIC COMPANY   .50
ANSON, G.
  STEPPING HIGH
      BELWIN-MILLS PUBLISHING CORPORATION   .60
ANSON, G.   2
  SUNNY SONATINA, A
      WILLIS MUSIC COMPANY   .40
ANSON, G.   2 1/2
  TEEN-TUNE
      WILLIS MUSIC COMPANY   .50
ANSON, G.   1
  TIRED CUCKOO, THE
      WILLIS MUSIC COMPANY   .40
ANSON, G.   2
  VERY FIRST SONATA, A
      WILLIS MUSIC COMPANY   .40
ANSON, G.   2
  WINTER WIND
      WILLIS MUSIC COMPANY   .50
ANTHEIL, G.
  FOURTH PIANO SONATA
      WEINTRAUB MUSIC COMPANY   070060   2.50
ANTHEIL, G.   A
  SECOND SONATA 'THE AIRPLANE'
      THEODORE PRESSER COMPANY   1.25
ANTHEIL, G.
  TOCCATA NO. 2
      G. SCHIRMER, INC.   .50

ANTHONY, B. R.
  ARRIVAL OF THE BROWNIES   1
      THEODORE PRESSER COMPANY
ANTHONY, B. R.   2
  HOMEWARD BOUND-MARCH
      THEODORE PRESSER COMPANY   .50
ANTHONY, B. R.   3
  MORNING SUNBEAMS
      THEODORE PRESSER COMPANY   .50
ANTHONY, B. R.   3
  OFF TO CAMP
      THEODORE PRESSER COMPANY   .60
ANTHONY, B. R.   2 1/2
  RIPPLING WAVES
      THEODORE PRESSER COMPANY   .50
ANTHONY, B. R.   2 1/2
  SALUTE TO THE COLORS
      THEODORE PRESSER COMPANY   .50
ANTHONY, B. R.   2 1/2
  SPARKLING EYES
      THEODORE PRESSER COMPANY   .60
ANTHONY, B. R.   2 1/2
  UNCLE ZEB WITH HIS FIDDLE
      THEODORE PRESSER COMPANY   .50
ANTONINI
  TWILIGHT SERENADE
      SAM FOX PUBLISHING COMPANY, INC.   .75
ANTONINI
  TWILIGHT SERENADE
      SOUTHERN MUSIC COMPANY   .75
APONTE-LEDEE, R.
  TEMA Y SEIS DIFFERENCIAS
      PEER SOUTHERN ORGANIZATION   02.00
APOSTEL
  PIECE, OP. 8
      ASSOCIATED MUSIC PUBLISHERS, INC.   DOB   1.75
APOSTEL   2 1/2
  SONATA RITMICA, OP. 5
      ASSOCIATED MUSIC PUBLISHERS, INC.   DOB   2.50
APPLEBAUM
  BAGHDAD SUITE
      CENTURY MUSIC PUBLISHING COMPANY, INC.   032   .40
APREA   1
  TOCCATA
      FRANCO COLOMBO PUBLICATIONS   124331   1.25
ARANT, B.
  DUCKS ON THE POND
      THEODORE PRESSER COMPANY   .50
ARBEAU, P.
  BERCEMENT   D
      ELKAN-VOGEL, INC.   .75
ARBOGAST   4
  PARADE OF THE TEMPLARS
      VOLKWEIN BROS.   .35
ARCHER   1A
  JUMPING JACK
      MUSICORD PUBLICATIONS, INC.   .45
ARCHER   1B
  KNIGHTS AND LADIES
      MUSICORD PUBLICATIONS, INC.   .45
ARCHER   1A
  STRAWBERRY HILL
      MUSICORD PUBLICATIONS, INC.   .45
ARCHER, I.   2
  BLUE BALLET
      CENTURY MUSIC PUBLISHING COMPANY, INC.   4188   .40
ARCHER, I.   3
  DOWN ON THE BAYOU
      CENTURY MUSIC PUBLISHING COMPANY, INC.   4198   .40
ARCHER, I.   2-3
  FIESTA IN MEXICO
      CENTURY MUSIC PUBLISHING COMPANY, INC.   4189   .40
ARCHER, I.   2
  GUM DROP TREE
      CENTURY MUSIC PUBLISHING COMPANY, INC.   4059   .40
ARCHER, I.   2
  IN A RED SPANISH SHAWL
      CENTURY MUSIC PUBLISHING COMPANY, INC.   4111   .40
ARCHER, I.   2
  MISCHIEVOUS LEPRECHAUN
      CENTURY MUSIC PUBLISHING COMPANY, INC.   4110   .40
ARCHER, I.   1
  ON CHRISTMAS EVE
      CENTURY MUSIC PUBLISHING COMPANY, INC.   4147   .40
ARCHER, I.   1-2
  RED DANCING SHOES
      CENTURY MUSIC PUBLISHING COMPANY, INC.   4061   .40
ARCHER, I.   1-2
  SHOE SHINE BOY
      CENTURY MUSIC PUBLISHING COMPANY, INC.   4245   .40
ARCHER, I.   1
  TALL TREES
      CENTURY MUSIC PUBLISHING COMPANY, INC.   4238   .40
ARCHER, I.   1-2
  WALTZING FLAMINGOES
      CENTURY MUSIC PUBLISHING COMPANY, INC.   4060   .40
ARCHER, I.   1-2
  WHITE SAILS IN THE MOONLIGHT
      CENTURY MUSIC PUBLISHING COMPANY, INC.   4062   .40
ARCHER, V.   M
  HABITANT SKETCHES
      THEODORE PRESSER COMPANY   .60
ARCHER, V.
  SONATINA NO. 02
      BOOSEY AND HAWKES, INC.   1.00
ARDEVOL, J.
  SONATA NO. 03
      EDITORIAL COOPERATIVA INTER-AMERICANA   01.55
                                   WEYBRIGHT   2
ARDITI
  IL BACIO
      BELWIN-MILLS PUBLISHING CORPORATION   .50
                                   WEYBRIGHT   2
ARDITI
  IL BACIO
      BELWIN-MILLS PUBLISHING CORPORATION   .60
ARDITI
  IL BACIO
      FRANCO COLOMBO PUBLICATIONS   32497   .75
ARDITI   MAGLIO, DEL
  IL BACIO -- EASY TRANSCRIPTION
      FRANCO COLOMBO PUBLICATIONS   124701   .50
ARDITI   2
  IL BACIO -- THE KISS, WALTZ
      CENTURY MUSIC PUBLISHING COMPANY, INC.   877   .40
ARDITI   2
  KISS WALTZ, THE -- IL BACIO
      CENTURY MUSIC PUBLISHING COMPANY, INC.   877   .40

ARENSKY, A.   SCHAUM, J.   2
  ARENSKY WALTZ, THE
        BELWIN-MILLS PUBLISHING CORPORATION   .50
ARENSKY, A.
  ETUDE IN F SHARP MAJOR, OP. 36 NO. 13
        G. SCHIRMER, INC.   .60
ARENSKY, A.   DEIS
  VALSE--FROM SUITE FOR 2 PIANOS, OP. 15
        G. SCHIRMER, INC.   1.25
ARENSKY, A.   5
  VALSE, OP. 36 NO. 7
        CENTURY MUSIC PUBLISHING COMPANY, INC.   2005   .40
ARETZ, I.
  SONATA 1965
        PAN AMERICAN UNION   01.50
ARIAS
  PILARICA, LA -- JOTA
        ASSOCIATED MUSIC PUBLISHERS, INC.   UME   .40
ARIZAGA, R.
  TOCCATA
        PEER SOUTHERN ORGANIZATION   01.00
ARLEN *
  OVER THE RAINBOW
        THE BIG THREE MUSIC CORPORATION   00.95
ARLEN, C.   3
  BALLOONS
        WILLIS MUSIC COMPANY   .40
ARLEN, H.   WALTER
  BLUES IN THE NIGHT
        WARNER BROTHERS PUBLISHERS   1.00
ARLEN, H.   RICHTER   FIRST YEAR
  I LOVE A PARADE
        WARNER BROTHERS PUBLISHERS   .75
ARMA, P.
  LE PIANO INSPIRE DU FOLKLORE
        ELKAN-VOGEL, INC.   LEM   2.50
ARMA, P.
  SONATA DA BALLO
        EDITIONS MUSICALES TRANSATLANTIQUES   3.25
ARMA, P.
  TRANSPARENCE
        EDITIONS MUSICALES TRANSATLANTIQUES   2.50
ARMA, P.
  TROIS EPITAPHES
        EDITIONS MUSICALES TRANSATLANTIQUES   3.60
ARMBRUSTER
  LONESOME PRAIRIE
        CARL FISCHER, INC.   P 3008   .50
ARMBRUSTER
  NATIONAL VELVET - THEME
        THE BIG THREE MUSIC CORPORATION   00.95
ARMOUR   2
  AFTER THE GAME, F MAJOR
        CENTURY MUSIC PUBLISHING COMPANY, INC.   3409   .40
ARMOUR   2
  AT VESPERS
        CENTURY MUSIC PUBLISHING COMPANY, INC.   3403   .40
ARMOUR   1
  BABETTE
        CENTURY MUSIC PUBLISHING COMPANY, INC.   3148   .40
ARMOUR   1
  BELIEVE ME IF ALL THOSE ENDEARING CHARMS
        CENTURY MUSIC PUBLISHING COMPANY, INC.   3461   .40
ARMOUR   1
  CANDLELIGHT
        CENTURY MUSIC PUBLISHING COMPANY, INC.   3410   .40
ARMOUR   1
  CONSOLATION
        CENTURY MUSIC PUBLISHING COMPANY, INC.   3404   .40
ARMOUR   1
  DARTING IN AND OUT, POLKA
        CENTURY MUSIC PUBLISHING COMPANY, INC.   3155   .40
ARMOUR   1
  FORTY FATHOMS
        CENTURY MUSIC PUBLISHING COMPANY, INC.   3405   .40
ARMOUR   2
  FROM COUNTY DERRY
        CENTURY MUSIC PUBLISHING COMPANY, INC.   3411   .40
ARMOUR   1
  GOODNIGHT LADIES
        CENTURY MUSIC PUBLISHING COMPANY, INC.   3463   .40
ARMOUR   1
  IN ROSE TIME
        CENTURY MUSIC PUBLISHING COMPANY, INC.   3154   .40
ARMOUR   1
  INDIAN SUMMER
        CENTURY MUSIC PUBLISHING COMPANY, INC.   3406   .40
ARMOUR   2
  JINGLE BELLS
        CENTURY MUSIC PUBLISHING COMPANY, INC.   3470   .40
ARMOUR   1
  LITTLE DUTCH DANCE, A
        CENTURY MUSIC PUBLISHING COMPANY, INC.   3154   .40
ARMOUR   2
  MARCH TRIUMPHAL
        CENTURY MUSIC PUBLISHING COMPANY, INC.   3412   .40
ARMOUR   1
  MARIE
        CENTURY MUSIC PUBLISHING COMPANY, INC.   3149   .40
ARMOUR   1
  MARIETTA
        CENTURY MUSIC PUBLISHING COMPANY, INC.   3147   .40
ARMOUR   2
  MEDICINE MAN
        CENTURY MUSIC PUBLISHING COMPANY, INC.   3413   .40
ARMOUR   1
  MOONLIGHT WALTZ
        CENTURY MUSIC PUBLISHING COMPANY, INC.   3156   .40
ARMOUR   2
  MY BONNIE LIES OVER THE OCEAN
        CENTURY MUSIC PUBLISHING COMPANY, INC.   3471   .40
ARMOUR   1
  NANNETTE
        CENTURY MUSIC PUBLISHING COMPANY, INC.   3150   .40
ARMOUR   1
  OLD CHURCH ORGAN, THE
        CENTURY MUSIC PUBLISHING COMPANY, INC.   3407   .40
ARMOUR   2
  QUEEN OF THE NIGHT
        CENTURY MUSIC PUBLISHING COMPANY, INC.   3414   .40
ARMOUR   1
  SHEPHERD CALL, THE
        CENTURY MUSIC PUBLISHING COMPANY, INC.   3408   .40
ARMOUR   1
  SHEPHERD'S LULLABY, THE
        CENTURY MUSIC PUBLISHING COMPANY, INC.   3153   .40

ARMOUR   1
  SINGING IN THE GLEN, WALTZ
        CENTURY MUSIC PUBLISHING COMPANY, INC.   3144   .40
ARMOUR   1
  SOLDIERS ALL, MARCH
        CENTURY MUSIC PUBLISHING COMPANY, INC.   3157   .40
ARMOUR   1
  WANDERING MINSTREL, THE
        CENTURY MUSIC PUBLISHING COMPANY, INC.   3152   .40
ARMOUR--ED   ARMOUR   1
  POLLY WOLLY DOODLE
        CENTURY MUSIC PUBLISHING COMPANY, INC.   3466   .40
ARMOUR--ED   ARMOUR   2
  STAR SPANGLED BANNER
        CENTURY MUSIC PUBLISHING COMPANY, INC.   3472   .40
ARNAUD, A.
  GAVOTTE DES BALLERINES
        ELKAN-VOGEL, INC.   D   .50
ARNDT
  MARIONETTE
        SAM FOX PUBLISHING COMPANY, INC.   .75
ARNDT
  MARIONETTE
        SOUTHERN MUSIC COMPANY   .75
ARNDT
  NOLA
        SAM FOX PUBLISHING COMPANY, INC.   1.00
ARNDT   KLICKMANN
  NOLA — EASY ARR.
        SOUTHERN MUSIC COMPANY   .50
ARNDT
  NOLA — ORIGINAL
        SOUTHERN MUSIC COMPANY   ·1.00
ARNDT
  NOLA -- SIMPLIFIED
        SOUTHERN MUSIC COMPANY   1.00
ARNE
  GIG
        FREDERICK HARRIS MUSIC COMPANY   .90
ARNE   GUBITOSI
  SUITE
        FRANCO COLOMBO PUBLICATIONS   ER194   .60
ARNELL
  FOX VARIATIONS, OP. 75
        BELWIN-MILLS PUBLISHING CORPORATION   07045   1.50
ARNELL
  IMPROMPTU
        PEER SOUTHERN ORGANIZATION   01.00
ARNELL   M
  SICILIANA AND FURIANTE
        THEODORE PRESSER COMPANY   .75
ARNELL
  TWENTY-TWO VARIATIONS ON A WELL-KNOWN THEME
        BELWIN-MILLS PUBLISHING CORPORATION   20322   1.00
ARNOLD *   EASY
  CATHEDRAL CHIMES
        SHAWNEE PRESS, INC.   HB-67   .60
ARNOLD, H.   1
  ADVICE TO DOLLY, G MAJOR
        CENTURY MUSIC PUBLISHING COMPANY, INC.   3587   .40
ARNOLD, H.   2
  BALL GAME, A
        CENTURY MUSIC PUBLISHING COMPANY, INC.   3593   .40
ARNOLD, H.   2
  BOY SCOUT PARADE
        CENTURY MUSIC PUBLISHING COMPANY, INC.   3594   .40
ARNOLD, H.   1
  BUSY LITTLE CLOCK
        CENTURY MUSIC PUBLISHING COMPANY, INC.   3589   .40
ARNOLD, H.   1
  GRANDMA'S ROCKING CHAIR
        CENTURY MUSIC PUBLISHING COMPANY, INC.   3590   .40
ARNOLD, H.   1 1/2
  MY TEDDY BEAR
        THEODORE PRESSER COMPANY   .50
ARNOLD, H.   1
  PLAYFUL WIND
        CENTURY MUSIC PUBLISHING COMPANY, INC.   3591   .40
ARNOLD, H.   1
  PROUD MRS. HEN
        CENTURY MUSIC PUBLISHING COMPANY, INC.   3595   .40
ARNOLD, H.   2
  RUN ALONG LITTLE BROOK
        CENTURY MUSIC PUBLISHING COMPANY, INC.   3596   .40
ARNOLD, H.   2
  SPINNING AROUND
        CENTURY MUSIC PUBLISHING COMPANY, INC.   3597   .40
ARNOLD, H.   2
  TOBOGGAN RIDE
        CENTURY MUSIC PUBLISHING COMPANY, INC.   3598   .40
ARNOLD, H.   1
  WHIP-POOR-WILL
        CENTURY MUSIC PUBLISHING COMPANY, INC.   3592   .40
ARNOLD, M.
  MEXICAN HOLIDAY
        BELWIN-MILLS PUBLISHING CORPORATION   20167   .85
ARNOUX, G.
  TARIK LAN LA
        ELKAN-VOGEL, INC.   1.25
ARRIEU
  LITTLE CANARY, THE -- LE PETITE CANARD
        BELWIN-MILLS PUBLISHING CORPORATION   25252   .60
ARRIEU
  MOUVEMENT PERPETUEL
        FRANCO COLOMBO PUBLICATIONS   A121   1.00
ARRIEU
  MUSIQUE POUR PIANO
        FRANCO COLOMBO PUBLICATIONS   SAL   3.25
ARRIEU
  SARABANDE
        ELKAN-VOGEL, INC.   .80
ARRIEU   6
  TOCCATA
        ALPHONSE LEDUC
ARRIEU
  TOCCATA
        ELKAN-VOGEL, INC.   3.75
ARROYO, R.
  LA MARCHANDE D'EAU
        ELKAN-VOGEL, INC.   D   2.10
ASCHER   2
  ALICE, C MAJOR
        CENTURY MUSIC PUBLISHING COMPANY, INC.   1816   .40
ASCHER   4
  LA CASCADE DES ROSES, OP. 80
        CENTURY MUSIC PUBLISHING COMPANY, INC.   1340   .40

ASCHER   5
    SHOWER OF ROSES, OP. 80
        CENTURY MUSIC PUBLISHING COMPANY, INC.   1340   .40
ASCHER   5
    SPANISH DANCE, OP. 24
        CENTURY MUSIC PUBLISHING COMPANY, INC.   1997   .40
ASHLEY, H.   E-M
    CHUGGING DOWN THE RIVER
        COMPOSERS PRESS, INC.   1.00
ATKINS   MAXTED
    HEELIE JEEBIE
        MCA MUSIC   1.00
ATKINS   MAXTED
    I WANT A BIG BUTTER AND EGG MAN
        MCA MUSIC   1.00
ATTWOOD
    SONATINA IN G
        FREDERICK HARRIS MUSIC COMPANY   .60
AUBE   M
    PETITE SUITE '1830'
        C. F. PETERS CORPORATION   C49   1.25
AUBER   CHIESA
    FRA DIAVOLO FANTASY -- EASY TRANSCRIPTION
        FRANCO COLOMBO PUBLICATIONS   107510   .50
AUBERGE, A. D'
    CHRISTMAS CAROL, A
        ALFRED MUSIC COMPANY   657   .85
AUBERGE, A. D'
    IT'S CHRISTMAS TIME
        ALFRED MUSIC COMPANY   659   .85
AUBERT
    COSSACK DANCE
        CARL FISCHER, INC.   P 1992   .50
AUBERT
    DANS LA NUIT -- FROM SILLAGES
        ELKAN-VOGEL, INC.   D   3.00
AUBERT
    ROMANCE
        ELKAN-VOGEL, INC.   D   2.50
AUBERT
    SILLAGES
        ELKAN-VOGEL, INC.   D   3.75
AUBRY
    LUNE QUI DANSE, LA
        FRANCO COLOMBO PUBLICATIONS   SAL   1.50
AUCLERT
    PASTORALE ET GAVOTTE--ALSO FOR HARPSICHORD--
        GERARD BILLAUDOT EDITIONS MUSICALES   2.00
AUCLERT
    PRELUDE AND FUGUE
        FRANCO COLOMBO PUBLICATIONS   A101   1.00
AUCLERT
    QUATRE AIRS A DANSER
        EDITIONS MUSICALES TRANSATLANTIQUES   1.40
AULBACH, F.   3
    HEADIN' FOR THE CORRAL
        WILLIS MUSIC COMPANY   .40
AULBACH, F.   3
    TWILIGHT REVERIE
        WILLIS MUSIC COMPANY   .40
AURIC
    FACHEUX, LES -- BALLET --
        FRANCO COLOMBO PUBLICATIONS   SAL   10.75
AURIC
    FACHEUX, LES -- BALLET -- .. LE MAITRE A DANSER
        FRANCO COLOMBO PUBLICATIONS   SAL   1.75
AURIC
    FACHEUX, LES -- BALLET -- .. LES JOUEURS DE BOULES
        FRANCO COLOMBO PUBLICATIONS   SAL   1.75
AURIC
    FACHEUX, LES -- BALLET -- .. NOCTURNE
        FRANCO COLOMBO PUBLICATIONS   SAL   1.75
AURIC
    LA MARIAGE DE LA TROUHADEC
        HEUGEL ET CIE.   5.65
AURIC
    LA PASTORALE
        HEUGEL ET CIE.   9.25
AURIC
    MARLBOROUGH S'EN VA-T-EN GUERRE
        HEUGEL ET CIE.   2.75
AURIC
    PEINTRE ET SON MODELE, LE -- BALLET --
        FRANCO COLOMBO PUBLICATIONS   SAL   6.25
AURIC
    SONATA IN F
        FRANCO COLOMBO PUBLICATIONS   SAL   8.25
AURIC
    SONATINA
        FRANCO COLOMBO PUBLICATIONS   SAL   3.25
AURIZIO, D'
    SUITE NO. 2
        FRANCO COLOMBO PUBLICATIONS   BON.2534   2.50
AUS DER OHE, A.
    MELODIE--NO. 2--IN G MAJOR. OP. 10, NO. 1
        G. SCHIRMER, INC.   .50
AUS DER OHE, A.
    WALZER, OP. 14
        G. SCHIRMER, INC.   .40
AUSTIN   2-3
    HOT DOGS AND CHILI
        PRO-ART PUBLICATIONS, INC.   599   .50
AUSTIN   2
    INDIAN WARRIOR
        BELWIN-MILLS PUBLISHING CORPORATION   .60
AVERY, R.   1
    HOP SCOTCH
        BELWIN-MILLS PUBLISHING CORPORATION   .60
AVSHALOMOV, J.   MD
    SLOW DANCE
        THEODORE PRESSER COMPANY   .50
AXMANN   3-4
    SONATA NO. 02 'A LA MEMOIRE D'UN GRAND HOMME'
        BARENREITER VERLAG   AP 505
AZZOLA *
    RIVIERA FESTIVAL -- LE FETE DES AS, VALSE BRILLIANTE
        BELWIN-MILLS PUBLISHING CORPORATION   20414   .85
BABBITT   MD
    SEMI-SIMPLE VARIATIONS
        THEODORE PRESSER COMPANY   .50
BABIN
    SONATA NO. 01
        MCA MUSIC   1.50
BABIN
    SONATINA NO. 02
        MCA MUSIC   1.75

BACARISSE
    THEME AND VARIATIONS IN A MINOR, OP. 66
        ASSOCIATED MUSIC PUBLISHERS, INC.   UME   1.50
BACARISSE
    TOREROS
        ASSOCIATED MUSIC PUBLISHERS, INC.   UME   .60
BACEVICIUS   MD
    CAPRICCIO, OP. 28
        THEODORE PRESSER COMPANY   1.00
BACEVICIUS
    DAS ERSTE WORT, OP. 11
        UNIVERSAL EDITION   UE 10970   1.30
BACEVICIUS
    DEUX GROTESQUES, OP. 20
        UNIVERSAL EDITION   UE 10971   1.30
BACEVICIUS   D
    POEME 'CONTEMPLATION', OP. 5
        THEODORE PRESSER COMPANY   1.00
BACEVICIUS   D
    POEME ASTRAL, OP. 7
        THEODORE PRESSER COMPANY   2.00
BACEVICIUS   D
    POEME COSMIQUE, OP. 65
        THEODORE PRESSER COMPANY   1.00
BACEVICIUS   D
    POEME MYSTIQUE, OP. 6
        THEODORE PRESSER COMPANY   1.50
BACEVICIUS   MD
    POEME NO. 40, OP. 10
        THEODORE PRESSER COMPANY   1.00
BACEVICIUS   D
    SIXIEME MOT, OP. 72
        THEODORE PRESSER COMPANY   2.00
BACEVICIUS   A
    SONATA, OP. 37 NO. 2
        THEODORE PRESSER COMPANY   3.00
BACEVICIUS   A
    SONATA, OP. 52 NO. 3
        THEODORE PRESSER COMPANY   3.00
BACEVICIUS   D
    TROIS PENSEES MUSICALES, OP. 75
        THEODORE PRESSER COMPANY   1.50
BACH, C.P.E.
    ALLEGRO IN F MINOR
        G. SCHIRMER, INC.   .50
BACH, C.P.E.   RUF
    FOLIES D'ESPAGNE, LES
        FRANCO COLOMBO PUBLICATIONS   SY637   1.50
BACH, C.P.E.   COBB   E
    LA CAROLINE
        BELWIN-MILLS PUBLISHING CORPORATION   25051   .60
BACH, C.P.E.   STEGLICH
    SIX WURTTEMBERG SONATAS, VOL. 2
        ASSOCIATED MUSIC PUBLISHERS, INC.   NAG   4.00
BACH, C.P.E.
    SOLFEGGIETTO
        BELWIN-MILLS PUBLISHING CORPORATION   .60
BACH, C.P.E.
    SOLFEGGIETTO
        CARL FISCHER, INC.   S 2280   .50
BACH, C.P.E.   3
    SOLFEGGIETTO
        CENTURY MUSIC PUBLISHING COMPANY, INC.   2252   .40
BACH, C.P.E.   POTAMKIN
    SOLFEGGIETTO
        ELKAN-VOGEL, INC.   .50
BACH, C.P.E.   6
    SOLFEGGIETTO
        NOVELLO AND COMPANY, LTD.   55.0032.10 .25
BACH, C.P.E.   3
    SOLFEGGIETTO
        SCHOTT   07996   .75
BACH, C.P.E.   3
    SOLFEGGIETTO
        SCHOTT   07996   .75
BACH, C.P.E.   3
    SOLFEGGIETTO
        VOLKWEIN BROS.   .30
BACH, C.P.E.
    SOLFEGGIETTO --FOR LEFT HAND--
        CARL FISCHER, INC.   S 2181   .50
BACH, C.P.E.   OESTERLE
    SOLFEGGIETTO IN C MINOR
        G. SCHIRMER, INC.   3 1/2   .40
BACH, C.P.E.
    SOLFEGGIETTO IN C MINOR
        THEODORE PRESSER COMPANY   .50
BACH, C.P.E.   PARSONS
    SOLFEGGIETTO IN C MINOR---INCLUDES ARR. FOR LEFT HAND ALONE
        G. SCHIRMER, INC.   .50
BACH, C.P.E.   CESI
    SOLFEGGIO
        FRANCO COLOMBO PUBLICATIONS   ER1059   .50
BACH, C.P.E.   4
    SOLFEGIETTO
        BELWIN-MILLS PUBLISHING CORPORATION   4   .60
BACH, C.P.E.   ZINGEL
    SONATA IN G
        ASSOCIATED MUSIC PUBLISHERS, INC.   B/H   2.75
BACH, C.P.E.   4
    SONATINA IN G
        CENTURY MUSIC PUBLISHING COMPANY, INC.   3789   .40
BACH, C.P.E.   GOEBELS   3
    SONATINE NUOVE, NO. 6
        SCHOTT   5458   1.75
BACH, C.P.E.
    SPRING'S AWAKENING
        FRANCO COLOMBO PUBLICATIONS   127463   .50
BACH, C.P.E.   NEMETH *
    XENOPHONE ET LA SYBILLE
        ASSOCIATED MUSIC PUBLISHERS, INC.   OBV   .60
BACH, J. C. F.   BARBE   E-M
    VARIATIONS ON 'AH, VOUS DIRAI-JE, MAMAN'
        C. F. PETERS CORPORATION   A91   1.25
BACH, J. CHRISTIAN   KUSTER
    SONATA IN A
        ASSOCIATED MUSIC PUBLISHERS, INC.   NAG   3.00
BACH, J. CHRISTIAN   KUSTER
    SONATA IN A, OP. 18 NO. 5
        BARENREITER VERLAG   NMA 115   3.00
BACH, J. CHRISTIAN   4
    SONATA IN D, ALLEGRETTO
        CENTURY MUSIC PUBLISHING COMPANY, INC.   3790   .40
BACH, J. CHRISTIAN   GOEBELS   3
    SONATE G-DUR
        SCHOTT   09663 1/2   1.00

BACH, J. CHRISTIAN   GOEBELS   3
SONATE G-DUR
    SCHOTT   09663   1.00
BACH, J.S.   HESS
ADAGIO, FROM ORGAN TOCCATA NO. 1
    OXFORD UNIVERSITY PRESS   32.039   1.10
BACH, J.S.   4
AIR FOR THE G STRING, C MAJOR
    CENTURY MUSIC PUBLISHING COMPANY, INC.   3378   .40
BACH, J.S.   SCHAUM, J.   3
AIR ON THE G STRING
    BELWIN-MILLS PUBLISHING CORPORATION   .50
BACH, J.S.   JOHNSON
AIR ON THE G STRING, FROM ORCHESTRA SUITE NO. 3
    C. F. PETERS CORPORATION   7110   .60
BACH, J.S.   PARSONS
AIR--FROM ORCHESTRA SUITE, D MAJOR
    G. SCHIRMER, INC.   .40
BACH, J.S.
ALLEGRO
    FREDERICK HARRIS MUSIC COMPANY   .60
BACH, J.S.   BARTH, H.
ALLEMANDE IN A MINOR
    BELWIN-MILLS PUBLISHING CORPORATION   20370   .50
BACH, J.S.   DE ANGELIS
ARIA CON VARIAZIONE IN A MINOR
    FRANCO COLOMBO PUBLICATIONS   DS347   1.25
BACH, J.S.   4
ARIA FROM 'SONATA IN A MINOR'
    THEODORE PRESSER COMPANY   .50
BACH, J.S.   BISCHOFF
ARIA VARIATA A LA MANIERA ITALIANA
    EDWIN F. KALMUS   3052   1.00
BACH, J.S.   D
ARIA VARIATA IN A MINOR, ALLE MANIERA ITALIANA
    C. F. PETERS CORPORATION   215A   1.25
BACH, J.S.   1
ARIETTA
    BELWIN-MILLS PUBLISHING CORPORATION   517   .60
BACH, J.S.   BARTH, H.
ARIETTA IN C
    BELWIN-MILLS PUBLISHING CORPORATION   20020   .60
BACH, J.S.   WALLIS
ARIOSO
    BOSTON MUSIC COMPANY   .50
BACH, J.S.   PIRANI
ARIOSO
    G. SCHIRMER, INC.   .50
BACH, J.S.   ZEPP   4
ARIOSO
    PRO-ART PUBLICATIONS, INC.   265   .50
BACH, J.S.   BILOTTI   4-5
ARIOSO
    PRO-ART PUBLICATIONS, INC.   6   .50
BACH, J.S.
ARIOSO --FROM THE CANTATA NO. 156--
    CARL FISCHER, INC.   S 2316   .50
BACH, J.S.   4
ARIOSO IN G
    CENTURY MUSIC PUBLISHING COMPANY, INC.   3417   .40
BACH, J.S.   CZERNY   D
ART OF THE FUGUE
    C. F. PETERS CORPORATION   218   3.00
BACH, J.S.   CZERNY
ART OF THE FUGUE, THE
    EDWIN F. KALMUS   3051   3.00
BACH, J.S.   BRADLEY
AUTHENTIC 'FIRST BACH'
    FRANCO COLOMBO PUBLICATIONS   LD196   1.00
BACH, J.S.   GOUNOD, C.
AVE MARIA
    CARL FISCHER, INC.   S 1959   .60
BACH, J.S.   SCHER
BADINERIE
    BOSTON MUSIC COMPANY   .50
BACH, J.S.   WEYBRIGHT   4
BIST DU BEI MIR
    BELWIN-MILLS PUBLISHING CORPORATION   .50
BACH, J.S.   WEYBRIGHT   4
BIST DU BEI MIR
    BELWIN-MILLS PUBLISHING CORPORATION   .60
BACH, J.S.   HARRIS
BIST DU BEI MIR
    OXFORD UNIVERSITY PRESS   32.105   .95
BACH, J.S.   ZIMMERMAN
BOUREE IN C MAJOR AND BOURREE IN C MINOR--FROM CELLO SUITE NO. 3
    G. SCHIRMER, INC.   .40
BACH, J.S.   TOURS
BOURREE IN B MINOR--FROM VIOLIN SONATA NO. 2
    G. SCHIRMER, INC.   .40
BACH, J.S.   HEINZE
BOURREE IN G MAJOR--TRS. FROM CELLO SUITE NO. 3
    G. SCHIRMER, INC.   .30
BACH, J.S.   BRADLEY, R.
BRADLEY CLASSICAL SERIES - PRELUDE NO. 1 IN C FROM THE
WELL-TEMPERED CLAVIER
    SCREEN GEMS - COLUMBIA PUBLICATIONS   5713PP2   .85
BACH, J.S.   BRADLEY, R.
BRADLEY CLASSICAL SERIES - TWO-PART INVENTION NO. 1 IN C
    SCREEN GEMS - COLUMBIA PUBLICATIONS   7407TP2   .85
BACH, J.S.   BRADLEY, R.
BRADLEY CLASSICAL SERIES - TWO-PART INVENTION NO. 8 IN F
    SCREEN GEMS - COLUMBIA PUBLICATIONS   7408TP2   .85
BACH, J.S.   M
BRANDENBURG CONCERTO NO. 1
    C. F. PETERS CORPORATION   H304   1.25
BACH, J.S.   D
BRANDENBURG CONCERTO NO. 3
    C. F. PETERS CORPORATION   H305   2.00
BACH, J.S.   KREUTZ   4
CAPRICCIO B-DUR -- DIE ABREISE, BWV 992
    SCHOTT   3862   1.00
BACH, J.S.   KREUTZ   4
CAPRICCIO B-DUR, BWV 992 --DIE ABREISE--
    SCHOTT   0862 1/2   1.00
BACH, J.S.   BUSONI
CAPRICCIO IN B FLAT, S. 992
    ASSOCIATED MUSIC PUBLISHERS, INC.   B/H   1.25
BACH, J.S.   FRISKIN   3
CAPRICCIO ON THE DEPARTURE OF A BELOVED BROTHER
    BELWIN-MILLS PUBLISHING CORPORATION   1.00
BACH, J.S.   BISCHOFF
CAPRICCIO ON THE DEPARTURE OF A BROTHER
    EDWIN F. KALMUS   3050   1.00
BACH, J.S.   TAGLIAPIETRA
CAPRICCIO SOPRA LA LONTANANZA DEL SUO FRATELLO DILLETISSIMO
    FRANCO COLOMBO PUBLICATIONS   128406   1.00

BACH, J.S.   D
CAPRICCIO-- B FLAT -- ON THE DEPARTURE OF HIS BELOVED BROTHER
    C. F. PETERS CORPORATION   208C   1.25
BACH, J.S.   BRAHMS
CHACONNE IN D MINOR-- LEFT HAND
    ASSOCIATED MUSIC PUBLISHERS, INC.   B/H   2.00
BACH, J.S.   BUSONI
CHACONNE IN D MINOR--FROM THE SONATA FOR VIOLIN SOLO, NO. 4
    G. SCHIRMER, INC.   L1597   .75
BACH, J.S.   BUSONI
CHACONNE IN D MINOR, S. 1004E
    ASSOCIATED MUSIC PUBLISHERS, INC.   B/H   1.50
BACH, J.S.   PILLNEY
CHACONNE, S. 1004
    ASSOCIATED MUSIC PUBLISHERS, INC.   B/H   2.25
BACH, J.S.   KAHL
CHORALE
    BOSTON MUSIC COMPANY   .50
BACH, J.S.   KEMPFF
CHORALE -- ''JESU, JOY OF MAN'S DESIRING'' -- FROM CANTATA NO.
147
    ASSOCIATED MUSIC PUBLISHERS, INC.   B/H   1.25
BACH, J.S.   FOGWELL
CHORALE FROM CANTATA 147
    BANKS AND SON LTD.   .55
BACH, J.S.   KREUTZ   6
CHROMAT. FANTASIE UND FUGE, BWV 903
    SCHOTT   01083/4   1.50
BACH, J.S.   KREUTZ   6
CHROMATIC FANTASIE UND FUGE, BWV 903
    SCHOTT   01083-4   1.50
BACH, J.S.   SAUER   D
CHROMATIC FANTASY AND FUGUE
    C. F. PETERS CORPORATION   3514   1.25
BACH, J.S.   BISCHOFF
CHROMATIC FANTASY AND FUGUE
    EDWIN F. KALMUS   3038   1.00
BACH, J.S.   BUELOW *
CHROMATIC FANTASY AND FUGUE
    FRANCO COLOMBO PUBLICATIONS   ER2632   .90
BACH, J.S.   BUELOW
CHROMATIC FANTASY AND FUGUE
    G. SCHIRMER, INC.   1.10
BACH, J.S.   BOGHEN
CHROMATIC FANTASY AND FUGUE
    INTERNATIONAL MUSIC COMPANY   1.50
BACH, J.S.   RONTGEN
CHROMATIC FANTASY AND FUGUE
    UNIVERSAL EDITION   520   1.75
BACH, J.S.   HUBER
CHROMATIC FANTASY AND FUGUE
    UNIVERSAL EDITION   12008   1.70
BACH, J.S.   BUSONI
CHROMATIC FANTASY AND FUGUE IN D MINOR, S. 903
    ASSOCIATED MUSIC PUBLISHERS, INC.   SIM   1.50
BACH, J.S.
CHROMATIC FANTASY AND FUGUE--VIENNA URTEXT EDITION
    UNIVERSAL EDITION   2540   2.35
BACH, J.S.   KELLER   D
CHROMATIC FANTASY AND FUGUE, URTEXT, WITH 2 VARIANTS AND
REVISIONSBERICHT
    C. F. PETERS CORPORATION   9006   2.50
BACH, J.S.   KELBERINE
COME, SWEET DEATH
    ELKAN-VOGEL, INC.   .50
BACH, J.S.   BAUER
COME, SWEET DEATH--KOMM' SUSSER TOD
    G. SCHIRMER, INC.   .50
BACH, J.S.   BUELOW *
CONCERTO IN THE ITALIAN STYLE
    FRANCO COLOMBO PUBLICATIONS   ER2631   .90
BACH, J.S.   BUELOW
CONCERTO IN THE ITALIAN STYLE
    G. SCHIRMER, INC.   .90
BACH, J.S.   HULDBACH
CONTRAPUNCTUS INVERSUS DER FUGA XV FROM 'THE ART OF THE FUGUE'
    FRANCO COLOMBO PUBLICATIONS   DS124   1.25
BACH, J.S.   BARTH, H.
COURANTE
    BELWIN-MILLS PUBLISHING CORPORATION   20380   .60
BACH, J.S.   E-M
ECHO--FRENCH OVERTURE--
    C. F. PETERS CORPORATION   4464C   .90
BACH, J.S.   MORONI   4
ENGLISCHE SUITEN
    BARENREITER VERLAG   CM 20183
BACH, J.S.   10
FANTAISIE IN C MINOR
    THEODORE PRESSER COMPANY   .50
BACH, J.S.   D
FANTASIA AND FUGUE IN A MINOR
    C. F. PETERS CORPORATION   208B   1.25
BACH, J.S.   MONTANI
FANTASIA AND FUGUE IN A MINOR
    FRANCO COLOMBO PUBLICATIONS   128970   1.00
BACH, J.S.   TAGLIAPIETRA
FANTASIA AND FUGUE IN G MINOR FOR ORGAN
    FRANCO COLOMBO PUBLICATIONS   ER628   1.25
BACH, J.S.   D
FANTASIA AND FUGUE--TOCCATA--, IN D
    C. F. PETERS CORPORATION   211A   1.25
BACH, J.S.   PALMER, W. A.
FANTASIA IN C MINOR
    ALFRED MUSIC COMPANY   602   1.25
BACH, J.S.   MONTANI
FANTASIA IN C MINOR
    FRANCO COLOMBO PUBLICATIONS   128395   .75
BACH, J.S.   BUELOW
FANTASIA IN C MINOR
    G. SCHIRMER, INC.   .50
BACH, J.S.
FANTASIA IN C MINOR
    WILLIS MUSIC COMPANY   .35
BACH, J.S.   4
FANTASIA IN C MINOR
    WILLIS MUSIC COMPANY   .35
BACH, J.S.   LISZT *
FANTASIE AND FUGUE IN G MINOR--FOR ORGAN
    G. SCHIRMER, INC.   L1494   .75
BACH, J.S.   KREUTZ   4
FANTASIE IN C-MOLL -- BWV 906
    SCHOTT   0879 1/2   1.00
BACH, J.S.   KREUTZ   4
FANTASIE IN C-MOLL, BWV 906
    SCHOTT   0879 1/2   1.00
BACH, J.S.   BISCHOFF
FANTASY IN C MINOR
    EDWIN F. KALMUS   3040   1.00

BACH, J.S.   SCHAUM, J.   4
   FESTIVAL FUGUE
      BELWIN-MILLS PUBLISHING CORPORATION   .50
BACH, J.S.
   FESTIVAL GROUPS FOR PIANO SELECTED BY ARTHUR BENJAMIN, SERIES 2
   -- PASSEPIED, FROM 'SECOND ENGLISH SUITE'
      BOOSEY AND HAWKES, INC.   .60
BACH, J.S.   DAVID   3
   FRANZ, OUVERTURE C-MOLL
      SCHOTT   2380   1.75
BACH, J.S.   DAVID   3
   FRANZ, OUVERTURE C-MOLL, BWV 831
      SCHOTT   2380   1.75
BACH, J.S.   MORONI   3
   FRANZOSISCHE SUITEN
      BARENREITER VERLAG   CM 20181
BACH, J.S.   4
   FRUEHLINGSERWACHEN
      CENTURY MUSIC PUBLISHING COMPANY, INC.   876   .40
BACH, J.S.   2-3
   FRUEHLINGSERWACHEN, EASY
      CENTURY MUSIC PUBLISHING COMPANY, INC.   2161   .40
BACH, J.S.   6
   FUGUE NO. 5, WELL TEMPERED CLAVICHORD
      CENTURY MUSIC PUBLISHING COMPANY, INC.   3488   .40
BACH, J.S.   SAINT-SAENS
   GAVOTTE IN B MINOR
      WILLIS MUSIC COMPANY   .35
BACH, J.S.   3
   GAVOTTE IN B MINOR, SECOND VIOLIN SONATA
      CENTURY MUSIC PUBLISHING COMPANY, INC.   2400   .40
BACH, J.S.   SAINT-SAENS
   GAVOTTE IN E MAJOR--FROM VIOLIN SONATA NO. 6
      G. SCHIRMER, INC.   .40
BACH, J.S.   2
   GAVOTTE IN G
      BOSTON MUSIC COMPANY   .50
BACH, J.S.   ECKSTEIN
   GAVOTTE IN G FROM 5TH FRENCH SUITE
      CARL FISCHER, INC.   S 1930   .50
BACH, J.S.
   GAVOTTE IN G MINOR
      FREDERICK HARRIS MUSIC COMPANY   .60
BACH, J.S.   BUELOW
   GAVOTTE IN G MINOR--FROM ENGLISH SUITE NO. 3
      G. SCHIRMER, INC.   .35
BACH, J.S.   SAINT-SAENS *
   GAVOTTE--BOURREE--IN B MINOR--FROM VIOLIN SONATA NO. 2
      G. SCHIRMER, INC.   .50
BACH, J.S.
   GAVOTTE, ENGLISH SUITE NO. 3
      FREDERICK HARRIS MUSIC COMPANY   .30
BACH, J.S.
   GAVOTTE, FRENCH SUITE NO. 4
      FREDERICK HARRIS MUSIC COMPANY   .40
BACH, J.S.   3
   GIGUE
      NOVELLO AND COMPANY, LTD.   55.0022.02   .40
BACH, J.S.
   GIGUE IN B FLAT, FROM FIRST PARTITA
      BELWIN-MILLS PUBLISHING CORPORATION   .60
BACH, J.S.
   GIGUE IN B FLAT, FROM THE FIRST PARTITA
      WILLIS MUSIC COMPANY   .35
BACH, J.S.   4
   GIGUE IN B MINOR
      WILLIS MUSIC COMPANY   .30
BACH, J.S.
   GIGUE IN B MINOR, FROM THE THIRD FRENCH SUITE
      WILLIS MUSIC COMPANY   .35
BACH, J.S.   BISCHOFF
   GOLDBERG VARIATIONS
      EDWIN F. KALMUS   3043   2.00
BACH, J.S.   TAGLIAPIETRA
   GOLDBERG VARIATIONS
      FRANCO COLOMBO PUBLICATIONS   ER1470   2.25
BACH, J.S.
   GOLDBERG VARIATIONS
      G. HENLE MUSIKVERLAG   159   2.75
BACH, J.S.   SOLDAN
   GOLDBERG VARIATIONS -- URTEXT --
      C. F. PETERS CORPORATION   4462   2.00
BACH, J.S.   BUSONI *
   GOLDBERG VARIATIONS, S. 998
      ASSOCIATED MUSIC PUBLISHERS, INC.   B/H   2.75
BACH, J.S.   KIRKPATRICK
   GOLDBERG VARIATIONS, THE
      G. SCHIRMER, INC.   3.00
BACH, J.S.   D
   GOLDBERG VARIATIONS, URTEXT
      C. F. PETERS CORPORATION   4462   2.00
BACH, J.S.
   INTRATA
      FREDERICK HARRIS MUSIC COMPANY   .60
BACH, J.S.   4
   INVENTION, 2 PART, NO. 8
      CENTURY MUSIC PUBLISHING COMPANY, INC.   3418   .40
BACH, J.S.   PALMER, W. A.
   ITALIAN CONCERTO
      ALFRED MUSIC COMPANY   573   2.00
BACH, J.S.   BISCHOFF
   ITALIAN CONCERTO
      EDWIN F. KALMUS   3100   1.00
BACH, J.S.
   ITALIAN CONCERTO
      G. HENLE MUSIKVERLAG   160   1.15
BACH, J.S.   ZEPP   3-4
   JESU JOY OF MAN'S DESIRING
      PRO-ART PUBLICATIONS, INC.   559   .75
BACH, J.S.   NIELAND   E-M
   JESU, JOY OF MAN'S DESIRE --FROM CANTATA NO. 147--
      C. F. PETERS CORPORATION   B14   .90
BACH, J.S.   MANSFIELD   E-M
   JESU, JOY OF MAN'S DESIRE --FROM CANTATA NO. 147--
      C. F. PETERS CORPORATION   2648   .80
BACH, J.S.
   JESU, JOY OF MAN'S DESIRING
      ASHLEY DEALERS SERVICE, INC.   1.00
BACH, J.S.   SCHAUM, J.   3
   JESU, JOY OF MAN'S DESIRING
      BELWIN-MILLS PUBLISHING CORPORATION   .50
BACH, J.S.   4
   JESU, JOY OF MAN'S DESIRING
      CENTURY MUSIC PUBLISHING COMPANY, INC.   3729   .40
BACH, J.S.   LIPSCOMB
   JESU, JOY OF MAN'S DESIRING
      G. SCHIRMER, INC.   .60

BACH, J.S.   KARTUN
   JESU, JOY OF MAN'S DESIRING
      LES EDITIONS OUVRIERES   2.00
BACH, J.S.   HESS
   JESU, JOY OF MAN'S DESIRING
      OXFORD UNIVERSITY PRESS   32.049   1.25
BACH, J.S.   BILOTTI   3
   JESU, JOY OF MAN'S DESIRING
      PRO-ART PUBLICATIONS, INC.   7   .50
BACH, J.S.   ELAINE   1
   JESU, JOY OF MAN'S DESIRING -- CHORALE FROM CANTATA NO. 147
      WILLIS MUSIC COMPANY   .40
BACH, J.S.   FREED
   JESU, JOY OF MAN'S DESIRING --CHORALE FROM CANTATA NO. 147--
      CARL FISCHER, INC.   P 2075   .60
BACH, J.S.   BERLIN
   JESU, JOY OF MY LIFE
      FREDERICK HARRIS MUSIC COMPANY   .60
BACH, J.S.   BAUER
   JESUS, JOY OF MAN'S DESIRE--JESUS BLEIBET MEINE FREUDE--FROM
   CHURCH CANTATA 147
      G. SCHIRMER, INC.   .60
BACH, J.S.   PARKER, T.
   JOY
      THE BIG THREE MUSIC CORPORATION   00.95
BACH, J.S.   D
   KLAVIERUEBUNG --URTEXT--. PART 4: GOLDBERG VARIATIONS
      C. F. PETERS CORPORATION   4462   2.00
BACH, J.S.   KEMPFF
   LARGO FROM THE CLAVIER CONCERTO IN F MINOR
      ASSOCIATED MUSIC PUBLISHERS, INC.   B/B   .90
BACH, J.S.   PALMER, W. A.
   LITTLE CLAVIER BOOK
      ALFRED MUSIC COMPANY   603   2.50
BACH, J.S.   2
   MARCH
      NOVELLO AND COMPANY, LTD.   55.0005.02   .40
BACH, J.S.
   MARCH IN D
      FREDERICK HARRIS MUSIC COMPANY   .60
BACH, J.S.   2
   MARCH IN D, ANNA MAGDALENA
      CENTURY MUSIC PUBLISHING COMPANY, INC.   3607   .40
BACH, J.S.   WEYBRIGHT   3
   MARCH, FROM A COLLECTION OF 'PIECES FOR KLAVIER' EDITED FOR SOLO
   PIANO
      BELWIN-MILLS PUBLISHING CORPORATION   .60
BACH, J.S.   3
   MENUET
      LEE ROBERTS MUSIC PUBLICATIONS, INC.   .50
BACH, J.S.
   MENUETT IN G
      FREDERICK HARRIS MUSIC COMPANY   .60
BACH, J.S.   DE ANGELIS
   MINUET
      FRANCO COLOMBO PUBLICATIONS   DS356   1.00
BACH, J.S.   2
   MINUET
      NOVELLO AND COMPANY, LTD.   55.0009.05   .25
BACH, J.S.   ZEPP   3-4
   MINUET
      PRO-ART PUBLICATIONS, INC.   231   .50
BACH, J.S.   4
   MINUET IN B MINOR
      NOVELLO AND COMPANY, LTD.   55.0028.01   .40
BACH, J.S.
   MINUET IN D MINOR
      BELWIN-MILLS PUBLISHING CORPORATION   .60
BACH, J.S.   3
   MINUET IN D MINOR
      NOVELLO AND COMPANY, LTD.   55.0022.02   .40
BACH, J.S.
   MINUET IN F
      FREDERICK HARRIS MUSIC COMPANY   .60
BACH, J.S.   2
   MINUET IN G
      BOSTON MUSIC COMPANY   .50
BACH, J.S.   SCHAUM, J.   2 1/2
   MINUET MEDLEY
      SCHAUM PUBLICATIONS, INC.   .50
BACH, J.S.   2
   MINUET NO. 1, ANNA MAGDALENA
      CENTURY MUSIC PUBLISHING COMPANY, INC.   3709   .40
BACH, J.S.   2
   MINUET NO. 2, ANNA MAGDALENA
      CENTURY MUSIC PUBLISHING COMPANY, INC.   3710   .40
BACH, J.S.
   MINUET, FRENCH SUITE NO. 6
      FREDERICK HARRIS MUSIC COMPANY   .60
BACH, J.S.
   MINUETS IN G MAJOR AND G MINOR NO. 01
      BELWIN-MILLS PUBLISHING CORPORATION   .60
BACH, J.S.   2
   MINUETS IN G MAJOR AND G MINOR NO. 02
      BELWIN-MILLS PUBLISHING CORPORATION   .60
BACH, J.S.   2
   MUSETTE
      CENTURY MUSIC PUBLISHING COMPANY, INC.   3608   .40
BACH, J.S.   2
   MUSETTE IN D
      BOSTON MUSIC COMPANY   .50
BACH, J.S.
   MUSETTE IN D MAJOR
      BELWIN-MILLS PUBLISHING CORPORATION   .60
BACH, J.S.   2
   MUSETTE IN D, ANNA MAGDALENA
      CENTURY MUSIC PUBLISHING COMPANY, INC.   3608   .40
BACH, J.S.   LANDSHOFF
   MUSICAL OFFERING
      C. F. PETERS CORPORATION   4202A   3.50
BACH, J.S.   CZERNY   D
   MUSICAL OFFERING. COMPLETE SCORE IN ORIGINAL CLEFS, INCLUDING
   THE RICERCARE A 6 REDUCED TO TWO OR THREE STAVES FOR PIANO OR
   ORGAN.
      C. F. PETERS CORPORATION   219   3.50
BACH, J.S.   LANDSHOFF   D
   MUSICAL OFFERING--URTEXT--. COMPLETE SCORE IN ORIGINAL CLEFS,
   PLUS SUPPLEMENT OF COMPLETE SCORE IN MODERN CLEFS
      C. F. PETERS CORPORATION   4202   10.00
BACH, J.S.   SAMAROFF
   ORGAN FUGUE IN G MINOR--THE LITTLE
      ELKAN-VOGEL, INC.   .60
BACH, J.S.   SILOTI
   ORGAN PRELUDE IN E MINOR
      CARL FISCHER, INC.   P 1323   .60
BACH, J.S.   SILOTI
   ORGAN PRELUDE IN G MINOR --AFTER SZANTO--
      CARL FISCHER, INC.   P 1397   .75

BACH, J.S.   REGER   6
ORGEL-TOCCATA UND FUGE D-MOLL
    SCHOTT   1075   2.25
BACH, J.S.   REGER   6
ORGEL-TOCCATA UND FUGUE D-MOLL, BWV 565
    SCHOTT   1075   2.25
BACH, J.S.   KARTUN
OVERTURE, CANTATA NO. 29
    LES EDITIONS OUVRIERES   2.25
BACH, J.S.   BAUER
PARTITA IN B FLAT MAJOR
    G. SCHIRMER, INC.   1.50
BACH, J.S.
PARTITA IN D, S. 828
    ASSOCIATED MUSIC PUBLISHERS, INC.   B/H   1.10
BACH, J.S.   PALMER, W. A.
PARTITA NO. 1
    ALFRED MUSIC COMPANY   634   1.50
BACH, J.S.   BISCHOFF
PARTITA NO. 1 IN B FLAT MAJOR
    EDWIN F. KALMUS   3064   1.25
BACH, J.S.   BISCHOFF
PARTITA NO. 1 IN B FLAT MAJOR
    INTERNATIONAL MUSIC COMPANY   1.50
BACH, J.S.   BISCHOFF
PARTITA NO. 2 IN C MINOR
    EDWIN F. KALMUS   3065   1.25
BACH, J.S.   BISCHOFF
PARTITA NO. 5 IN G MAJOR
    EDWIN F. KALMUS   3066   1.25
BACH, J.S.   M-D
PARTITAS --URTEXT--, VOL. 1
    C. F. PETERS CORPORATION   4463A   2.00
BACH, J.S.   SZANTO
PASSACAGLIA IN C MINOR
    FRANCO COLOMBO PUBLICATIONS   SAL   3.50
BACH, J.S.   ALBERT, E. D'
PASSACAGLIA IN C MINOR, S. 582
    ASSOCIATED MUSIC PUBLISHERS, INC.   B/B   2.50
BACH, J.S.   BENJAMIN
PASSEPIED
    BOOSEY AND HAWKES, INC.   .60
BACH, J.S.   BAMPTON, R.   3
PASTORALE FROM 'CHRISTMAS ORATORIO'
    BOSTON MUSIC COMPANY   .50
BACH, J.S.
POLONAISE IN G MINOR
    FREDERICK HARRIS MUSIC COMPANY   .60
BACH, J.S.   GEORGII, W.   5-6
PRALUDIUM 1 UND FUGE 1 -- BWV 846
    SCHOTT   09588   .75
BACH, J.S.   GEORGII, W.   5-6
PRALUDIUM 2 UND FUGE 2 -- BWV 847
    SCHOTT   09589   .75
BACH, J.S.   GEORGII, W.   5-6
PRALUDIUM 21 UND FUGE 21 -- BWV 866
    SCHOTT   09590   .75
BACH, J.S.   HARRIS, R.
PRELUDE AND FUGUE
    BELWIN-MILLS PUBLISHING CORPORATION 20210   1.75
BACH, J.S.   VOGRICH
PRELUDE AND FUGUE IN A MINOR
    G. SCHIRMER, INC.   .70
BACH, J.S.   LISZT *
PRELUDE AND FUGUE IN A MINOR
    G. SCHIRMER, INC.   L1475   1.00
BACH, J.S.   5
PRELUDE AND FUGUE IN C MINOR
    CENTURY MUSIC PUBLISHING COMPANY, INC. 3899   .40
BACH, J.S.   BUSONI
PRELUDE AND FUGUE IN D, S. 532
    ASSOCIATED MUSIC PUBLISHERS, INC.   B/H   1.00
BACH, J.S.   BUSONI
PRELUDE AND FUGUE IN E FLAT, S. 552
    ASSOCIATED MUSIC PUBLISHERS, INC.   SIM   2.00
BACH, J.S.
PRELUDE AND FUGUE IN E MINOR
    BELWIN-MILLS PUBLISHING CORPORATION   .60
BACH, J.S.   FRISKIN
PRELUDE FROM CANTATA 'GOTTES ZEIT IST DIE ALLERBESTE ZEIT'
    BELWIN-MILLS PUBLISHING CORPORATION   .60
BACH, J.S.   SILOTI
PRELUDE IN B MINOR
    MUSICAL SCOPE PUBLISHERS   01.25
BACH, J.S.   3
PRELUDE IN C
    CENTURY MUSIC PUBLISHING COMPANY, INC. 3257   .40
BACH, J.S.   ZEPP   4
PRELUDE IN C
    PRO-ART PUBLICATIONS, INC.   516   .60
BACH, J.S.   OESTERLE
PRELUDE IN C MAJOR--FROM WELL-TEMPERED CLAVICHORD
    G. SCHIRMER, INC.   .40
BACH, J.S.   BUONAMICI
PRELUDE IN C MINOR
    G. SCHIRMER, INC.   .40
BACH, J.S.
PRELUDE IN C, FROM WELL-TEMPERED CLAVICHORD NO. 1
    WILLIS MUSIC COMPANY   .35
BACH, J.S.   M
PRELUDE IN E -- VIOLIN PARTITA NO.3--
    C. F. PETERS CORPORATION   H253   1.25
BACH, J.S.
PRELUDE IN G MAJOR
    BOOSEY AND HAWKES, INC.   .60
BACH, J.S.   BUSONI
PRELUDE, FUGUE AND ALLEGRO IN E FLAT, S. 998
    ASSOCIATED MUSIC PUBLISHERS, INC.   B/H   1.50
BACH, J.S.   PILLNEY
RICERCAR, THREE PART, FROM ''THE MUSICAL OFFERING''
    ASSOCIATED MUSIC PUBLISHERS, INC.   B/H   1.75
BACH, J.S.
RONDEAU, PARTITA NO. 2
    FREDERICK HARRIS MUSIC COMPANY   .30
BACH, J.S.   TURECK, R.
SARABANDE IN C MINOR
    OXFORD UNIVERSITY PRESS   32.924   .90
BACH, J.S.
SARABANDE, FRENCH SUITE NO. 1
    FREDERICK HARRIS MUSIC COMPANY   .40
BACH, J.S.
SHEEP MAY SAFELY GRAZE
    ASHLEY DEALERS SERVICE, INC.   1.00
BACH, J.S.   SCHAUM, J.   4
SHEEP MAY SAFELY GRAZE
    BELWIN-MILLS PUBLISHING CORPORATION   .50

BACH, J.S.   PETRI
SHEEP MAY SAFELY GRAZE
    BOOSEY AND HAWKES, INC.   .60
BACH, J.S.   WHITFORD   3
SHEEP MAY SAFELY GRAZE
    BOSTON MUSIC COMPANY   .50
BACH, J.S.   HOWE
SHEEP MAY SAFELY GRAZE
    OXFORD UNIVERSITY PRESS   32.110   1.20
BACH, J.S.   BARTH, H.
SICILIANA
    BELWIN-MILLS PUBLISHING CORPORATION 20238   .60
BACH, J.S.   M
SICILIANO --FROM FLUTE SONATA NO.2--
    C. F. PETERS CORPORATION   815   .90
BACH, J.S.   KEMPFF
SICILIANO FROM SONATA NO. 2 FOR FLUTE -- S. 1031B
    ASSOCIATED MUSIC PUBLISHERS, INC.   B/H   1.25
BACH, J.S.   HUGHES, E.
SICILIANO--FROM SONATA NO. 2 FOR FLUTE AND HARPSICHORD
    G. SCHIRMER, INC.   .50
BACH, J.S.   HUGHES
SICILIANO--FROM SONATA NO. 2 FOR FLUTE AND HARPSICHORD
    G. SCHIRMER, INC.   .50
BACH, J.S.   WEYBRIGHT   4 1/2
SICILIENNA FROM 'FLUTE AND PIANO SONATA'
    BELWIN-MILLS PUBLISHING CORPORATION   .60
BACH, J.S.   HESS
SLEEPERS, WAKE
    OXFORD UNIVERSITY PRESS   32.201   1.25
BACH, J.S.   ZEPP   4
SOLFEGGIETTO
    PRO-ART PUBLICATIONS, INC.   405   .50
BACH, J.S.   CLOUGH *   3
SOLFEGIETTO IN C MINOR
    BOSTON MUSIC COMPANY   .50
BACH, J.S.   BARTOK
SONATA NO. 06
    KULTURA   1.75
BACH, J.S.   ALKAN
SONATE, SECOND MOVEMENT--HARPSCHORD AND FLUTE--
    GERARD BILLAUDOT EDITIONS MUSICALES   1.60
BACH, J.S.
SONG, A
    FREDERICK HARRIS MUSIC COMPANY   .60
BACH, J.S.   RACHMANINOFF, S.
SUITE FROM THE PARTITA IN E MAJOR FOR VIOLIN --
PRELUDIO-GAVOTTE-GIGUE
    BELWIN-MILLS PUBLISHING CORPORATION   2.00
BACH, J.S.   RIEMENSCHNEIDER
THREE HUNDRED AND SEVENTY ONE HARMONIZED CHORALES AND 69 CHORALE
MELODIES WITH FIGURED BASS
    G. SCHIRMER, INC.   3.50
BACH, J.S.   D
TOCCATA --FANTASIA AND FUGUE--
    C. F. PETERS CORPORATION   211A   1.25
BACH, J.S.   TAUSIG *
TOCCATA AND FUGUE FOR ORGAN IN D MINOR
    G. SCHIRMER, INC.   .80
BACH, J.S.   5
TOCCATA AND FUGUE IN D MINOR
    CENTURY MUSIC PUBLISHING COMPANY, INC. 3558   .40
BACH, J.S.   BUSONI
TOCCATA AND FUGUE IN D MINOR
    G. SCHIRMER, INC.   L1629   1.00
BACH, J.S.   TAUSIG
TOCCATA AND FUGUE IN D MINOR FOR ORGAN
    FRANCO COLOMBO PUBLICATIONS   128322   1.00
BACH, J.S.   PROSTAKOFF
TOCCATA AND FUGUE IN D MINOR--THE DORIAN
    G. SCHIRMER, INC.   L1787   1.25
BACH, J.S.   BUSONI
TOCCATA IN C MAJOR
    G. SCHIRMER, INC.   L1628   1.00
BACH, J.S.   BUSONI
TOCCATA IN C, S. 564
    ASSOCIATED MUSIC PUBLISHERS, INC.   B/H   .60
BACH, J.S.   BAUER
TOCCATA IN D MAJOR
    G. SCHIRMER, INC.   1.25
BACH, J.S.   BUSONI
TOCCATA IN D MINOR, S. 565
    ASSOCIATED MUSIC PUBLISHERS, INC.   B/H   1.50
BACH, J.S.   MONTANI
TOCCATA IN E MINOR
    FRANCO COLOMBO PUBLICATIONS   128969   1.00
BACH, J.S.   KREUTZ   4
TOCCATA UND FUGE IN D-DUR -- BWV 912
    SCHOTT   05504 1/2   1.00
BACH, J.S.   DUMM
TWO MINUETS
    BELWIN-MILLS PUBLISHING CORPORATION 26120   .60
BACH, J.S.
TWO MINUETS
    BELWIN-MILLS PUBLISHING CORPORATION   .60
BACH, J.S.
TWO PART INVENTION NO. 11
    FREDERICK HARRIS MUSIC COMPANY   .45
BACH, J.S.
TWO PART INVENTION NO. 12
    FREDERICK HARRIS MUSIC COMPANY   .30
BACH, J.S.   4
TWO PART INVENTION NO. 8
    CENTURY MUSIC PUBLISHING COMPANY, INC. 3418   .40
BACH, J.S.   3
TWO-PART INVENTION IN F
    BOSTON MUSIC COMPANY   1.00
BACH, J.S.   KREUTZER
TWO-PART INVENTION NO. 04 IN D MINOR
    BRODT MUSIC COMPANY   .50
BACH, J.S.   KREUTZER
TWO-PART INVENTION NO. 08 IN F MAJOR
    BRODT MUSIC COMPANY   .50
BACH, J.S.   KREUTZER
TWO-PART INVENTION NO. 13 IN A MINOR
    BRODT MUSIC COMPANY   .50
BACH, J.S.   KREUTZER
TWO-PART INVENTION NO. 14 IN B FLAT MAJOR
    BRODT MUSIC COMPANY   .50
BACH, J.S. *   1
AVE MARIA
    BELWIN-MILLS PUBLISHING CORPORATION   .50
BACH, J.S. *   3
AVE MARIA
    BELWIN-MILLS PUBLISHING CORPORATION 580   .60

BACH, J.S. *   3
    AVE MARIA
        CENTURY MUSIC PUBLISHING COMPANY, INC. 3487   .40
BACH, J.S. *   3
    AVE MARIA
        CENTURY MUSIC PUBLISHING COMPANY, INC. 3487   .40
BACH, J.S. *   3
    AVE MARIA
        CENTURY MUSIC PUBLISHING COMPANY, INC. 3707   .40
BACH, J.S. *   ZEPP   4
    AVE MARIA
        PRO-ART PUBLICATIONS, INC.   577   .50
BACH, J.S. *   SPENCER, J.   1
    AVE MARIA
        VOLKWEIN BROS.   .25
BACH, J.S. *   MONTANI
    CHACONNE IN D MINOR BY BACH ARRANGED FOR THE LEFT HAND
        FRANCO COLOMBO PUBLICATIONS   128396   .75
BACH, J.S. *   BOGHEN
    FANTASIA AND FUGUE IN G MINOR FOR ORGAN
        FRANCO COLOMBO PUBLICATIONS   ER2371   1.25
BACH, J.S. *   BOGHEN
    FANTASIA AND FUGUE IN G MINOR FOR ORGAN
        FRANCO COLOMBO PUBLICATIONS   ER2371   1.25
BACH, J.S. *   HUGHES
    ORGAN FANTASIE AND FUGUE IN G MINOR
        G. SCHIRMER, INC.   L1494   .75
BACH, J.S. *   HUGHES
    PRELUDE AND FUGUE IN A MINOR
        G. SCHIRMER, INC.   L1475   1.00
BACH, J.S. *   MONTANI
    PRELUDE AND FUGUE IN A MINOR FOR ORGAN
        FRANCO COLOMBO PUBLICATIONS   128426   1.00
BACH, J.S. *   MONTANI
    PRELUDE AND FUGUE IN A MINOR FOR ORGAN
        FRANCO COLOMBO PUBLICATIONS   128426   1.00
BACH, W. F.   DUMM
    RECITAL REFRESHER SERIES -- LAMENTO IN E MINOR
        BELWIN-MILLS PUBLISHING CORPORATION   26109   .60
BACH, W.F.
    ARIA
        FREDERICK HARRIS MUSIC COMPANY   .60
BACH, W.F.   STEINER   2
    BEDTIME STORY
        BELWIN-MILLS PUBLISHING CORPORATION   .50
BACH, W.F.   STEINER   2
    BEDTIME STORY -- LULLABY
        BELWIN-MILLS PUBLISHING CORPORATION   .60
BACH, W.F.
    LAMENTO IN E MINOR
        BELWIN-MILLS PUBLISHING CORPORATION   .85
BACH, W.F.   EASY
    SCHERZO
        SHAWNEE PRESS, INC.   .40
BACHMANN, G.   1
    BABILLAGE
        CENTURY MUSIC PUBLISHING COMPANY, INC. 1002   .40
BACHMANN, G.   7
    CHANSON DU BON VIEUX TEMPS, OP. 28
        ALPHONSE LEDUC
BACHMANN, G.   DEIS
    LES SYLPHES--IMPROMPTU-VALSE
        G. SCHIRMER, INC.   .60
BACHMANN, G.   4
    LES SYLPHES, VALSE
        CENTURY MUSIC PUBLISHING COMPANY, INC. 277   .40
BACHMANN, G.   ROLFE, W.   3
    SYLPHES, LES, EASY
        CENTURY MUSIC PUBLISHING COMPANY, INC. 3365   .40
BACKHELM, P.   VE
    HOBGOBLINS
        OXFORD UNIVERSITY PRESS   93.335   .40
BACON
    FLIGHT
        BOOSEY AND HAWKES, INC.   .60
BACON, E.   3
    CAMP MEETING
        THEODORE PRESSER COMPANY   .50
BACON, E.
    FRIENDS
        FRANCO COLOMBO PUBLICATIONS   NY2262   1.00
BACON, E.
    MAPLE SUGARING
        LAWSON-GOULD MUSIC PUBLISHERS, INC.   2 1/2
BACON, E.   2 1/2
    MELODIOUS SONNET
        THEODORE PRESSER COMPANY   .50
BACON, E.   2 1/2
    SELDOM SEEN HOLLOW
        THEODORE PRESSER COMPANY   .50
BADARZEWSKA, T.   4
    MAIDEN'S PRAYER
        BELWIN-MILLS PUBLISHING CORPORATION   10   .60
BADARZEWSKA, T.   4
    MAIDEN'S PRAYER
        CENTURY MUSIC PUBLISHING COMPANY, INC. 300   .40
BADARZEWSKA, T.   STEINER   3
    MAIDEN'S PRAYER, THE
        BELWIN-MILLS PUBLISHING CORPORATION   .60
BADARZEWSKA, T.
    MAIDEN'S PRAYER, THE
        G. SCHIRMER, INC.   .40
BADINGS   M
    SONATA FOR A CARILLON OF FOUR OCTAVES
        C. F. PETERS CORPORATION   D126   1.50
BADINGS   5
    SONATA I
        SCHOTT   2339   2.75
BADINGS   4
    SONATA II
        SCHOTT   2833   2.75
BADINGS   M
    SONATA NO. 02 --FOR CARILLON--
        C. F. PETERS CORPORATION   D125   1.50
BADINGS   3
    SONATINE
        SCHOTT   2576   2.50
BADINGS   M
    SUITE NO. 4, ON NETHERLANDS FOLK DANCES --FOR CARILLON--
        C. F. PETERS CORPORATION   D127   1.50
BADINGS   M
    SUITE--1943--. FOR CARILLON
        C. F. PETERS CORPORATION   D124   1.50
BADURA-SKODA
    CADENZA TO MOZART CONCERTO IN C, K. 503
        ASSOCIATED MUSIC PUBLISHERS, INC.   DOB   1.25

BAETZ, C.   3 1/2
    HAWAII
        BELWIN-MILLS PUBLISHING CORPORATION   .60
BAETZ, C.   2
    SCATTERING LEAVES
        BELWIN-MILLS PUBLISHING CORPORATION   .60
BAGLEY, E.   STEINER   2
    NATIONAL EMBLEM MARCH
        BELWIN-MILLS PUBLISHING CORPORATION   .60
BAGLEY, E.   SCHAUM, J.   2
    NATIONAL EMBLEM MARCH
        SCHAUM PUBLICATIONS, INC.   .50
BAGLEY, E.
    NATIONAL EMBLEM MARCH
        THE BIG THREE MUSIC CORPORATION   00.95
BAIN, J.   HARRISON
    BROTHER JAMES'S AIR
        OXFORD UNIVERSITY PRESS   32.131   1.20
BAINES, W.   2 1/2
    CAMEL TRAIN
        THEODORE PRESSER COMPANY   .95
BAINES, W.   2 1/2
    COUNTRY GARDENS
        THEODORE PRESSER COMPANY   .50
BAINES, W.   2 1/2
    KING'S REVIEW
        THEODORE PRESSER COMPANY   .50
BAISDEN   2
    GROWING MELODY
        BOSTON MUSIC COMPANY   .50
BAL, R.
    PRELUDIO
        EDICIONES MEXICANAS DE MUSICA, A. C.   01.50
BALADA, L.
    MUSICA EN CUATRO TIEMPOS - MUSIC IN FOUR TEMPOS
        GENERAL MUSIC PUBLISHING COMPANY, INC. 447   3.00
BALAKIREV
    AU JARDIN--IDYLLE ETUDE
        G. SCHIRMER, INC.   .40
BALAKIREV   MONTES
    ISLAMEY
        FRANCO COLOMBO PUBLICATIONS   BA8921   1.50
BALAKIREV
    ISLAMEY. FANTAISIE ORIENTALE
        ASSOCIATED MUSIC PUBLISHERS, INC.   SIM   1.50
BALAKIREV
    L'ALOUETTE--GLINKA
        G. SCHIRMER, INC.   .50
BALAKIREV   D
    SCHERZO IN B MINOR
        C. F. PETERS CORPORATION   ZM1316   2.00
BALAKIREV   D
    SONATA IN B FLAT MINOR
        C. F. PETERS CORPORATION   ZM1027   2.00
BALBO
    IMPROMPTU
        FRANCO COLOMBO PUBLICATIONS   FOR.12286   1.00
BALDWIN, E.   1
    BILLIE BEAVER
        WILLIS MUSIC COMPANY   .50
BALEANI, V.
    ALTRI TEMPI
        EDIZIONI BERBEN   EB 1434   1.20
BALEANI, V.
    ROMANZA
        EDIZIONI BERBEN   EB 1535   1.20
BALES
    TOCCATA
        ASSOCIATED MUSIC PUBLISHERS, INC.   BER   .75
BALFE   2
    BOHEMIAN GIRL, I DREAMT I DWELT
        CENTURY MUSIC PUBLISHING COMPANY, INC. 1778   .40
BALFE   3
    BOHEMIAN GIRL, I DREAMT I DWELT, E FLAT MAJOR
        CENTURY MUSIC PUBLISHING COMPANY, INC. 1570   .40
BALFE   3
    BOHEMIAN GIRL, THEN YOU'LL REMEMBER
        CENTURY MUSIC PUBLISHING COMPANY, INC. 1576   .40
BALLANTINE   7
    VARIATIONS FOR PIANO ON 'MARY HAD A LITTLE LAMB' - SERIES 1
        BOSTON MUSIC COMPANY   1.50
BALLANTINE   7
    VARIATIONS FOR PIANO ON 'MARY HAD A LITTLE LAMB' - SERIES 2
        BOSTON MUSIC COMPANY   1.50
BALLARO, E.
    FIFTY MINI-ESERCIZI
        EDIZIONI BERBEN   EB 1356   1.50
BALLATORE, P.
    DIZZY BUTTERFLY, OP. 99
        G. SCHIRMER, INC.   .35
BALLATORE, P.   2
    GRACIOUS LADY
        PRO-ART PUBLICATIONS, INC.   364   .50
BALLATORE, P.
    LITTLE GOLDFISH
        G. SCHIRMER, INC.   .35
BALLATORE, P.   2-3
    MAGIC CLOCK, THE
        PRO-ART PUBLICATIONS, INC.   401   .50
BALLIF
    BLOC-NOTES, OP. 37
        ASSOCIATED MUSIC PUBLISHERS, INC.   B/B   6.00
BALLIF
    SONATA NO. 01, OP. 18
        ASSOCIATED MUSIC PUBLISHERS, INC.   B/B   5.00
BALOGH
    BLACK KEY WALTZ
        BOOSEY AND HAWKES, INC.   .50
BALOGH
    CIGALE JOYEUSE, LA
        FRANCO COLOMBO PUBLICATIONS   SAL   1.75
BALOGH   2
    CLUMPING ALONG
        CENTURY MUSIC PUBLISHING COMPANY, INC. 4228   .40
BALOGH
    CONVERSATION
        BOOSEY AND HAWKES, INC.   .50
BALOGH
    DEBATE
        BOOSEY AND HAWKES, INC.   .60
BALOGH
    REEL
        BOOSEY AND HAWKES, INC.   .50
BAMPTON, R.   2
    SHEPHERD'S DANCE, THE
        BELWIN-MILLS PUBLISHING CORPORATION   .60

BAMPTON, R.   3
  SPINNER, THE
    PRO-ART PUBLICATIONS, INC.   214   .50
BAMPTON, R.   EASY
  STROLLING RIP
    SHAWNEE PRESS, INC.   .40
BANKS, M.
  BAGPIPES
    G. SCHIRMER, INC.   .35
BANKS, M.
  SWISS SONG
    G. SCHIRMER, INC.   .35
BARATI   M
  INVENTION
    THEODORE PRESSER COMPANY   .50
BARATI   MD
  ROLLING WHEELS
    THEODORE PRESSER COMPANY   .50
BARBELLE, P.
  BELLS OF TIBET
    G. SCHIRMER, INC.   .35
BARBER, S.
  EXCURSIONS, OP. 20
    G. SCHIRMER, INC.   1.25
BARBER, S.
  NOCTURNE
    G. SCHIRMER, INC.   .75
BARBER, S.
  SONATA, OP. 26
    G. SCHIRMER, INC.   2.50
BARBER, S.
  SOUVENIRS--BALLET SUITE, OP. 28
    G. SCHIRMER, INC.   2.00
BARBER, S.   NOEL   EARLY GRADES
  UNDER THE WILLOW TREE--FROM 'VANESSA'
    G. SCHIRMER, INC.   .40
BARBERA
  LITTLE SOLDIERS MARCHING
    FRANCO COLOMBO PUBLICATIONS   124797   1.00
BARBIROLLI
  OBLIO -- SLOW WALTZ --
    FRANCO COLOMBO PUBLICATIONS   SAL   1.75
BARBOT
  FINSON ET FAUVETTE
    FRANCO COLOMBO PUBLICATIONS   SAL   2.00
BARDIN-ROYER   5
  LA GROTTE DE CRISTAL, POLKA-MAZURKA
    ALPHONSE LEDUC
BARILI, E. C.   3 1/2
  APPLE BLOSSOMS
    THEODORE PRESSER COMPANY   .50
BARLOW
  BICHE DANS LA NEIGE
    ASSOCIATED MUSIC PUBLISHERS, INC.   ESC   1.25
BARLOW
  MIDNIGHT
    EDWARD B. MARKS MUSIC CORPORATION   00.60
BARLOW
  PETITE PRINCESSE A REVE, UNE
    ASSOCIATED MUSIC PUBLISHERS, INC.   ESC   1.75
BARLOW, D.
  GENESIS
    NOVELLO AND COMPANY, LTD.   10.0002.00   1.15
BARNES, B.
  DAINTY DOLL
    THE BIG THREE MUSIC CORPORATION   00.95
BARNES, B.
  DAINTY MISS
    THE BIG THREE MUSIC CORPORATION   00.95
BARNES, G. M.
  IN THE CANOE
    BANKS AND SON LTD.   .25
BARNES, M.   2
  SAND CASTLES
    WILLIS MUSIC COMPANY   .40
BARRAINE, E.
  BOITE DE PANDORE, LA
    GERARD BILLAUDOT EDITIONS MUSICALES   6.90
BARRAINE, E.
  FANTASIE FOR CLAVECIN OR PIANO
    EDITIONS MUSICALES TRANSATLANTIQUES   3.00
BARRAUD
  MUSIQUE PUOR PETITES MAINS
    FRANCO COLOMBO PUBLICATIONS   A148   1.00
BARRETT   1
  MY MERRY DRUM
    PRO-ART PUBLICATIONS, INC.   576   .50
BARRETT   3-4
  ROCOCO RONDO
    PRO-ART PUBLICATIONS, INC.   575   .50
BARRY
  LOVE THEME FROM 'MARY, QUEEN OF SCOTS'
    MCA MUSIC   1.00
BARRY
  MAN ALONE, A
    MCA MUSIC   1.00
BARRY
  THEME FROM THE PERSUADERS
    WARNER BROTHERS PUBLISHERS   1.00
BARTA   4
  SONATA NO. 02 -- 1961 --
    BARENREITER VERLAG   AP 887
BARTH, H.   5
  BRONZE STATUE
    BELWIN-MILLS PUBLISHING CORPORATION   .60
BARTH, H.
  BULL DOG
    G. SCHIRMER, INC.   .35
BARTH, H.
  COCKER SPANIEL
    G. SCHIRMER, INC.   .35
BARTH, H.
  FIFTH SONATA, OP. 31
    BELWIN-MILLS PUBLSHING CORPORATION   20092   1.25
BARTH, H.   3
  GAVOTTE
    BELWIN-MILLS PUBLISHING CORPORATION   .60
BARTH, H.   4
  GIGUE
    BELWIN-MILLS PUBLISHING CORPORATION   .60
BARTH, H.
  GREAT DANE
    G. SCHIRMER, INC.   .35
BARTH, H.   2
  INVISIBLE PRINCE, THE
    BELWIN-MILLS PUBLISHING CORPORATION   .60

BARTH, H.   3
  MOONLIGHT MEDITATIONS
    VOLKWEIN BROS.   .25
BARTH, H.
  SCOTTIE
    G. SCHIRMER, INC.   .35
BARTH, H.
  SIXTH SONATA, OP. 32
    BELWIN-MILLS PUBLISHING CORPORATION   20245   1.25
BARTH, H.
  SONATA NO. 04, OP. 30
    BELWIN-MILLS PUBLISHING CORPORATION   20101   1.25
BARTH, H.
  WIRE-HAIRED FOX-TERRIER
    G. SCHIRMER, INC.   .35
BARTH, O.
  WOOD BIRD'S CAROL, OP. 16 NO. 7
    BELWIN-MILLS PUBLISHING CORPORATION   28057   .60
BARTHELSON, J.
  HURRY, HURRY
    BELWIN-MILLS PUBLISHING CORPORATION   .60
BARTHELSON, J.
  WIND IN THE TREES
    BELWIN-MILLS PUBLISHING CORPORATION   .60
BARTLETT, H.   5-6
  GRAND POLKA DE CONCERT
    CENTURY MUSIC PUBLISHING COMPANY, INC.   1481   .40
BARTLETT, H.
  GRANDE POLKA DE CONCERT, OP. 1
    G. SCHIRMER, INC.   .70
BARTLEY, E.
  BALLAD AND TRAINS
    FREDERICK HARRIS MUSIC COMPANY   .60
BARTOK
  ALLEGRO BARBARO
    BOOSEY AND HAWKES, INC.   1.50
BARTOK
  ALLEGRO BARBARO
    UNIVERSAL EDITION   5934   1.50
BARTOK
  BALLAD, FROM 'FIFTEEN HUNGARIAN PEASANT SONGS'
    BOOSEY AND HAWKES, INC.   .60
BARTOK
  BEAR DANCE
    EDWIN F. KALMUS   3124   1.00
BARTOK
  BEAR DANCE, FROM 'TEN EASY PIECES'
    BOOSEY AND HAWKES, INC.   .60
BARTOK
  DANCE SUITE
    BOOSEY AND HAWKES, INC.   3.50
BARTOK
  ETUDE FOR THE LEFT HAND
    EDWIN F. KALMUS   3128   1.25
BARTOK
  EVENING IN THE COUNTRY
    BOOSEY AND HAWKES, INC.   .60
BARTOK   2-3
  EVENING IN THE COUNTRY
    CENTURY MUSIC PUBLISHING COMPANY, INC.   3909   .40
BARTOK   AGAY, D.
  EVENING IN THE COUNTRY
    MCA MUSIC   .60
BARTOK
  FANTASIA NO. 2
    BOOSEY AND HAWKES, INC.   .50
BARTOK
  FIRST TERM AT THE PIANO
    BOOSEY AND HAWKES, INC.   .90
BARTOK
  FROM THE DIARY OF A FLY
    BOOSEY AND HAWKES, INC.   .60
BARTOK
  IMPROVISATIONS, OP. 20
    BOOSEY AND HAWKES, INC.   1.50
BARTOK
  OSTINATO
    BOOSEY AND HAWKES, INC.   .75
BARTOK
  OUT OF DOORS SUITE
    BOOSEY AND HAWKES, INC.   2.50
BARTOK
  PETITE SUITE
    UNIVERSAL EDITION   10987   1.95
BARTOK
  PETITE SUITE, FROM 'FORTY-FOUR DUOS FOR TWO VIOLINS'
    BOOSEY AND HAWKES, INC.   1.00
BARTOK
  RHAPSODY, OP. 1 --FIRST VERSION--
    KULTURA   2.75
BARTOK
  ROUMANIAN DANCE NO. 6
    BOOSEY AND HAWKES, INC.   .60
BARTOK
  RUMANISCHE VOLKSTANZE
    UNIVERSAL EDITION   5802   2.50
BARTOK
  RUMANISCHE WEIHACHTSLIEDER
    UNIVERSAL EDITION   5890   2.85
BARTOK
  SCHERZO -- GMUNDEN, 1903 --
    EDWIN F. KALMUS   3137   1.25
BARTOK
  SONATA
    BOOSEY AND HAWKES, INC.   2.25
BARTOK
  SONATA
    UNIVERSAL EDITION   8772   3.40
BARTOK
  SONATINA
    BOOSEY AND HAWKES, INC.   1.50
BARTOK
  SONATINA
    EDWIN F. KALMUS   3139   1.00
BARTOK   PHILIPP, I.
  SONATINA
    INTERNATIONAL MUSIC COMPANY   1.25
BARTOK
  STUDY FOR THE LEFT HAND
    BOOSEY AND HAWKES, INC.   1.00
BARTOK
  SUITE, OP. 14
    BOOSEY AND HAWKES, INC.   1.00
BARTOK
  SUITE, OP. 14
    UNIVERSAL EDITION   5891   2.70

BARTOK
  TANZSUITE
    UNIVERSAL EDITION   8397   3.40
BARTOK *
  PIANO METHOD
    BOOSEY AND HAWKES, INC.   2.50
BARTOS, J.   3-4
  KLEINE SUITE, OP. 9
    BARENREITER VERLAG   AP 511
BARTOW, N.
  TOCCATA FOR PIANO
    SHAWNEE PRESS, INC.   HB-237   1.50
BARTOW, N.
  VARIATIONS AND FUGUE
    OXFORD UNIVERSITY PRESS   93.209   2.50
BARWINSKY, W.
  MARCH FROM 'UKRANIAN MINIATURES'
    UNIVERSAL EDITION   UE 10964   .50
BASIE
  ONE O'CLOCK JUMP
    THE BIG THREE MUSIC CORPORATION   00.95
BASLER, H. R.   3
  SCHOOL GIRLS' MARCH
    VOLKWEIN BROS.   .40
BASSET, R.   2
  FROG POOL, THE
    WILLIS MUSIC COMPANY   .25
BASSETT   WILLIAMS
  BELLS, THE
    BOSTON MUSIC COMPANY   .50
BASSLER   3
  GOOD EVENING SCHOTTISCHE
    CENTURY MUSIC PUBLISHING COMPANY, INC.   1188   .40
BASTIEN
  BIG RED FIRE ENGINE, THE
    NEIL A. KJOS MUSIC COMPANY   140   .50
BASTIEN
  BLACK CAT TANGO
    NEIL A. KJOS MUSIC COMPANY   100   .50
BASTIEN
  BROKEN CLOCK, THE
    NEIL A. KJOS MUSIC COMPANY   146   .50
BASTIEN
  CARNIVAL CHA CHA
    NEIL A. KJOS MUSIC COMPANY   138   .50
BASTIEN
  CAT AT NIGHT
    NEIL A. KJOS MUSIC COMPANY   139   .50
BASTIEN
  CHINATOWN
    NEIL A. KJOS MUSIC COMPANY   126   .50
BASTIEN
  CHINESE SNOWMAN, THE
    NEIL A. KJOS MUSIC COMPANY   149   .50
BASTIEN
  CHINESE TEA PARTY
    NEIL A. KJOS MUSIC COMPANY   114   .50
BASTIEN
  CLIMBING IN THE CHERRY TREE
    NEIL A. KJOS MUSIC COMPANY   115   .50
BASTIEN
  DUBLIN IRISH JIG
    NEIL A. KJOS MUSIC COMPANY   103   .50
BASTIEN
  DUMP TRUCKS ON PARADE
    NEIL A. KJOS MUSIC COMPANY   112   .50
BASTIEN
  FIFTH AVENUE POODLE
    NEIL A. KJOS MUSIC COMPANY   141   .50
BASTIEN
  FINAL EXAM BLUES
    NEIL A. KJOS MUSIC COMPANY   101   .50
BASTIEN
  FIRST DANCING CLASS, THE
    NEIL A. KJOS MUSIC COMPANY   129   .50
BASTIEN
  FIRST SONATINA, A
    NEIL A. KJOS MUSIC COMPANY   147   1.00
BASTIEN
  GEORGE WASHINGTON
    NEIL A. KJOS MUSIC COMPANY   102   .50
BASTIEN
  GIGUE
    NEIL A. KJOS MUSIC COMPANY   145   .50
BASTIEN
  HAPPY WITCH, THE
    NEIL A. KJOS MUSIC COMPANY   150   .50
BASTIEN
  HAVE YOU SEEN
    NEIL A. KJOS MUSIC COMPANY   125   .50
BASTIEN
  HOLIDAY SERENADE
    NEIL A. KJOS MUSIC COMPANY   142   .50
BASTIEN
  HUSH-A-BYE DOLLY
    NEIL A. KJOS MUSIC COMPANY   111   .50
BASTIEN
  IT'S RAINING OUT
    NEIL A. KJOS MUSIC COMPANY   113   .50
BASTIEN
  JULY 4TH SQUARE DANCE
    NEIL A. KJOS MUSIC COMPANY   104   .50
BASTIEN
  KITTY CAT
    NEIL A. KJOS MUSIC COMPANY   118   .50
BASTIEN
  LATIN HOLIDAY
    NEIL A. KJOS MUSIC COMPANY   105   .50
BASTIEN
  LITTLE DOG, RUNNING
    NEIL A. KJOS MUSIC COMPANY   124   .50
BASTIEN
  MARCH OF THE TROLL DOLLS
    NEIL A. KJOS MUSIC COMPANY   116   .50
BASTIEN
  MARCHING TO SCHOOL
    NEIL A. KJOS MUSIC COMPANY   135   .50
BASTIEN
  MEXICAN FIESTA
    NEIL A. KJOS MUSIC COMPANY   143   .50
BASTIEN
  MY GREEN UMBRELLA
    NEIL A. KJOS MUSIC COMPANY   106   .50
BASTIEN
  MY NEW BIKE
    NEIL A. KJOS MUSIC COMPANY   148   .50

BASTIEN
  ON THE MERRY-GO-ROUND
    NEIL A. KJOS MUSIC COMPANY   132   .50
BASTIEN
  PARAKEETS IN BIRDLAND
    NEIL A. KJOS MUSIC COMPANY   108   .50
BASTIEN
  POODLES PRANCING
    NEIL A. KJOS MUSIC COMPANY   107   .50
BASTIEN
  RED LIGHT, GREEN LIGHT
    NEIL A. KJOS MUSIC COMPANY   137   .50
BASTIEN
  ROCK CONCERT
    NEIL A. KJOS MUSIC COMPANY   144   .50
BASTIEN
  RUN-AWAY BALLOON
    NEIL A. KJOS MUSIC COMPANY   127   .50
BASTIEN
  RUSTLING ASPEN LEAVES
    NEIL A. KJOS MUSIC COMPANY   137   .50
BASTIEN
  SLEEPY ALLIGATOR, THE
    NEIL A. KJOS MUSIC COMPANY   136   .50
BASTIEN
  SONATINA IN G
    NEIL A. KJOS MUSIC COMPANY   155   1.00
BASTIEN
  SPACE EXPLORERS
    NEIL A. KJOS MUSIC COMPANY   130   .50
BASTIEN
  SPOOKS ON HALLOWEEN
    NEIL A. KJOS MUSIC COMPANY   109   .50
BASTIEN
  TO A LONELY SWAYING PINE
    NEIL A. KJOS MUSIC COMPANY   110   .50
BASTIEN
  TUMBLING
    NEIL A. KJOS MUSIC COMPANY   131   .50
BASTIEN
  TURTLE AT THE ZOO
    NEIL A. KJOS MUSIC COMPANY   123   .50
BASTIEN
  WILD DAISIES
    NEIL A. KJOS MUSIC COMPANY   128   .50
BASTIEN
  WISE OLD OWL
    NEIL A. KJOS MUSIC COMPANY   117   .50
BATE, ST.   5
  SEVEN PIECES
    SCHOTT   10012   2.25
BATH
  CORNISH RHAPSODY
    SAM FOX PUBLISHING COMPANY, INC.   1.50
BATH
  CORNISH RHAPSODY
    SAM FOX PUBLISHING COMPANY, INC.   1.00
BATH
  CORNISH RHAPSODY -- COMPLETE
    SOUTHERN MUSIC COMPANY   1.50
BATH
  CORNISH RHAPSODY -- THEME
    SOUTHERN MUSIC COMPANY   1.50
BATISTE, E.   4
  STAR OF HOPE
    THEODORE PRESSER COMPANY   .50
BAUDRIER
  DAME A LA LICORNE, LA
    FRANCO COLOMBO PUBLICATIONS   A111   .90
BAUDUC *
  SOUTH RAMPART STREET PARADE
    THE BIG THREE MUSIC CORPORATION   00.95
BAUER
  CHA-CHA-LITA
    BOSTON MUSIC COMPANY   .50
BAUER   3
  DANDY-LION, THE
    WILLIS MUSIC COMPANY   .40
BAUER   3
  LYRIC DANCE
    BOSTON MUSIC COMPANY   .50
BAUER   2
  MAMBO JAMBO
    BOSTON MUSIC COMPANY   .50
BAUER   3
  MEXICALI PROMENADE
    BOSTON MUSIC COMPANY   .50
BAUER
  SONATINA IN G
    CARL FISCHER, INC.   P 3172   1.50
BAUER   4
  WESTERN SONG
    BOSTON MUSIC COMPANY   .50
BAUER, H.
  TUNES FROM THE 18TH CENTURY, NO. 4--FLOURISH
    G. SCHIRMER, INC.   .50
BAUER, M.
  FIREFLIES
    MCA MUSIC   .75
BAUER, M.   E
  FOR NIMBLE FINGERS
    THEODORE PRESSER COMPANY   .75
BAUER, M.
  RAINY DAY, A
    MCA MUSIC   .60
BAUER, M.   E
  SPRING DAY
    THEODORE PRESSER COMPANY   .50
BAUER, M.
  WATER WHEEL, THE.
    MCA MUSIC   .75
BAUERNFEIND
  LITTLE SUITE -- 1959 --
    ASSOCIATED MUSIC PUBLISHERS, INC.   DOB   2.25
BAUERNFEIND
  SONATINA
    ASSOCIATED MUSIC PUBLISHERS, INC.   DOB   2.25
BAUMER, C.
  GOLLYWOG
    BANKS AND SON LTD.   .25
BAUMFELDER, F.   2
  PEASANT'S DANCE OP. 208
    THEODORE PRESSER COMPANY   .50
BAUMFELDER, F.
  YOUNG OFFICER, THE--OP. 270, NO. 5
    G. SCHIRMER, INC.   .25

BAUR
CAPRICCIO -- 1953 --
ASSOCIATED MUSIC PUBLISHERS, INC.   B/H   1.75
BAUR
SUITE -- 1956 --
ASSOCIATED MUSIC PUBLISHERS, INC.   B/H   3.25
BAVICCHI, J.
TOCCATA, 1965
SEESAW MUSIC CORPORATION   4.00
BAYLEY
TUNE FOR A MUSICAL TOY, A
ASSOCIATED MUSIC PUBLISHERS, INC.   BER   .40
BAYNON, A.
UP HILL AND DOWN DALE
NOVELLO AND COMPANY, LTD.   10.0004.07   1.25
BAZELAIRE
CHANSON D'AUTOMNE
FRANCO COLOMBO PUBLICATIONS   SAL   1.75
BAZELAIRE
CORTEGE
FRANCO COLOMBO PUBLICATIONS   SAL   2.75
BAZELAIRE
GAITE
FRANCO COLOMBO PUBLICATIONS   SAL   1.50
BAZELAIRE
GENTILLESSE
FRANCO COLOMBO PUBLICATIONS   SAL   1.50
BAZELAIRE
PRELUDE IN C MINOR, OP. 75
FRANCO COLOMBO PUBLICATIONS   SAL   2.75
BAZELON, I.
PIANO SONATINA
WEINTRAUB MUSIC COMPANY   070076   2.00
BEALL, J.
PARTITA
COMPOSERS AUTOGRAPH PUBLICATIONS   3.52
BEAMAN, M. L.   2
MORNING SONG
BELWIN-MILLS PUBLISHING CORPORATION   .60
BEATON, C.
DANCE OF THE BRAVES
G. SCHIRMER, INC.   .35
BEATON, C.
WALTZ ON THE GREEN
G. SCHIRMER, INC.   .40
BEAUCAMP   5
BOITE A MUSIQUE
ALPHONSE LEDUC
BEAUCAMP
BON PETIT DIABLE, LE
GERARD BILLAUDOT EDITIONS MUSICALES   1.30
BEAUCAMP
DANSE DE DIABLES
GERARD BILLAUDOT EDITIONS MUSICALES   1.30
BEAUCAMP   7
ESCAPADE, ETUDE
ALPHONSE LEDUC
BEAUCAMP
GRANDS POUR LES PETITS,LES--NO.2 UN SOIR CHEZ ANNA MAGDALENA
BACH--
GERARD BILLAUDOT EDITIONS MUSICALES   1.10
BEAUCAMP
GRANDS POUR LES PETITS,LES--NO.3 LE PETIT SECRET DE ROBERT
SCHUMANN--
GERARD BILLAUDOT EDITIONS MUSICALES   1.10
BEAUCAMP
GRANDS POUR LES PETITS,LES--NO.4 DANS LES JARDINS DE GABRIEL
FAURE--
GERARD BILLAUDOT EDITIONS MUSICALES   1.10
BEAUCAMP
GRANDS POUR LES PETITS,LES--NO.5 LE MIROIR DE CLAUDE DEBUSSY--
GERARD BILLAUDOT EDITIONS MUSICALES   1.10
BEAUCAMP
GRANDS POUR LES PETITS,LES--NO.6 UN PETIT TOUR AVEC MAURICE
RAVEL--
GERARD BILLAUDOT EDITIONS MUSICALES   1.10
BEAUCAMP
PETIT THEME VARIE
GERARD BILLAUDOT EDITIONS MUSICALES   1.30
BEAUCAMP
SUITE ENFANTINE, NO.1 GRAND-PERE BACH
GERARD BILLAUDOT EDITIONS MUSICALES   1.10
BEAUCAMP
SUITE ENFANTINE, NO.2 LE PASSEUR D'EAU
GERARD BILLAUDOT EDITIONS MUSICALES   1.10
BEAUCAMP
SUITE ENFANTINE, NO.3 MARCHANDE DE FLEURS
GERARD BILLAUDOT EDITIONS MUSICALES   1.10
BEAUCAMP
SUITE ENFANTINE, NO.5 HISTOIRE SANS HISTOIRES
GERARD BILLAUDOT EDITIONS MUSICALES   1.10
BEAUCAMP
SUITE ENFANTINE, NO.6 RONDE DES PUCES
GERARD BILLAUDOT EDITIONS MUSICALES   1.10
BEAUCAMP   6, 7
THEME ET VARIATIONS
ALPHONSE LEDUC
BEAULIEU
JUNGLE RHUMBA
MCA MUSIC   1.00
BEAUMONT   1-2
CHIPPY CHIPMUNK
PRO-ART PUBLICATIONS, INC.   537   .50
BEAUMONT   2
FRISKY LAMB, THE
PRO-ART PUBLICATIONS, INC.   212   .50
BEAUMONT   1
JUNE JOY
PRO-ART PUBLICATIONS, INC.   505   .50
BEAUMONT   2-3
KEEP THE STAR-SPANGLED BANNER WAVING
PRO-ART PUBLICATIONS, INC.   284   .50
BEAUMONT   1
MISTER HOP-TOAD
PRO-ART PUBLICATIONS, INC.   504   .50
BEAUMONT   3
SMOOTH SAILING
PRO-ART PUBLICATIONS, INC.   273   .50
BEAUMONT   3
SPRING FEVER
PRO-ART PUBLICATIONS, INC.   213   .50
BEAUMONT, P.   3
CON AMORE
CENTURY MUSIC PUBLISHING COMPANY, INC.   170   .40
BEAUMONT, P.
CON AMORE
G. SCHIRMER, INC.   .50

BEAUMONT, P.   3
CON AMORE
VOLKWEIN BROS.   .35
BEAUMONT, P.
TARENTELLE
G. SCHIRMER, INC.   .50
BEAUMONT, P.   2
WITH MY LOVE, EASY
CENTURY MUSIC PUBLISHING COMPANY, INC.   2589   .40
BEAUMONT, V.   1
JOHNNY JUMP UP
WILLIS MUSIC COMPANY   .40
BEAUMONT, V.   1
JOHNNY JUMP UP
WILLIS MUSIC COMPANY   .40
BEAUMONT, V.   1
LITTLE GOLDEN DAFFODIL
WILLIS MUSIC COMPANY   .40
BEAUMONT, V.   1
LITTLE GOLDEN DAFFODIL
WILLIS MUSIC COMPANY   .40
BECAUD   DAVIS, J. R.   FIRST YEAR
WHAT NOW MY LOVE
WARNER BROTHERS PUBLISHERS   .75
BECAUD *   NEALE, J.   EASY
WHAT NOW MY LOVE
WARNER BROTHERS PUBLISHERS   .75
BECHET
PAY OFF, THE
MCA MUSIC   1.00
BECHTER, K.   2
JOLLY MINSTRELS
THEODORE PRESSER COMPANY   .60
BECK   2 1/2
BIRTHDAY BELLS
THEODORE PRESSER COMPANY   .50
BECK
CAPRICCETTO
FRANCO COLOMBO PUBLICATIONS   NY1123   .30
BECK   3
CHANG-CHUNG
CENTURY MUSIC PUBLISHING COMPANY, INC.   030   .40
BECK   2
CLOWNING
THEODORE PRESSER COMPANY   .50
BECK   2
DANCING ON THE TIGHTROPE
THEODORE PRESSER COMPANY   .50
BECK
DRIFTING SANDS
FRANCO COLOMBO PUBLICATIONS   NY1124   .30
BECK
ETUDE BRILLANTE
FRANCO COLOMBO PUBLICATIONS   NY1125   .40
BECK   3
FOX FIRE
BELWIN-MILLS PUBLISHING CORPORATION   .60
BECK   2 1/2
FULL OF FUN
CENTURY MUSIC PUBLISHING COMPANY, INC.   029   .40
BECK   1
GHOST STALKS AT MIDNIGHT, THE
THEODORE PRESSER COMPANY   .50
BECK   3
IRISH FANCY
BELWIN-MILLS PUBLISHING CORPORATION   .60
BECK
JAPANESE WALTZ
MCA MUSIC   1.00
BECK
LAUGHING WATERS
FRANCO COLOMBO PUBLICATIONS   NY1126   .30
BECK
LEGENDE
BELWIN-MILLS PUBLISHING CORPORATION   .60
BECK
LEGENDS
FRANCO COLOMBO PUBLICATIONS   NY1120   .40
BECK   2
LITTLE BELLS OF KYOTE
BELWIN-MILLS PUBLISHING CORPORATION   .60
BECK   2B
NICKELODEON
MUSICORD PUBLICATIONS, INC.   .45
BECK   2
NIGHT IN BAGDAD
THEODORE PRESSER COMPANY   .50
BECK   2
NIGHT WIND
THEODORE PRESSER COMPANY   .50
BECK   1 1/2
OLD CHIEF POWHATAN
THEODORE PRESSER COMPANY   .50
BECK
ONCE UPON A TIME
BELWIN-MILLS PUBLISHING CORPORATION   .60
BECK
ONCE UPON A TIME
FRANCO COLOMBO PUBLICATIONS   NY1121   .40
BECK
SASSY PIECE
MCA MUSIC   1.00
BECK   2
SHUTTLE COCK
BELWIN-MILLS PUBLISHING CORPORATION   .60
BECK   2
SKIP TO MY LOU
THEODORE PRESSER COMPANY   .50
BECK, C.   4
SONATINE
SCHOTT   2072   2.25
BECK, C.   3
SONATINE 2
SCHOTT   4042   2.00
BECK, F.   E
TRIADS ON PARADE
COMPOSERS PRESS, INC.   1.00
BECK, M.   1
WALTZING IN THE GARDEN
WILLIS MUSIC COMPANY   .40
BECKEL   TCHEREPNIN   E
AMERICAN CIVIL WAR BATTLE PIECE -- THE BATTLE OF GETTYSBURG.
MARCH OF THE GRAND ARMY OF THE POTOMAC-- 1863 --
C. F. PETERS CORPORATION   H218   1.25
BECKEL   TCHEREPNIN   E
MARCH OF THE GRAND ARMY OF THE POTOMAC --1863--
C. F. PETERS CORPORATION   H218   1.25

A

BECKER
SOUND PIECE NO. 5 'SONATA FOR PIANO'
THEODORE PRESSER COMPANY   1.00
BECKWITH
NOVELETTE
ASSOCIATED MUSIC PUBLISHERS, INC.   BER   1.00
BECKWITH
SUITE ON OLD TUNES
ASSOCIATED MUSIC PUBLISHERS, INC.   BER   .75
BECUCCI
ALI DORATE
FRANCO COLOMBO PUBLICATIONS   127751   .50
BECUCCI
FANCIULLI ALLEGRI NO. 1
FRANCO COLOMBO PUBLICATIONS   109321   .50
BECUCCI
FANCIULLI ALLEGRI NO. 2
FRANCO COLOMBO PUBLICATIONS   109322   .50
BECUCCI
FANCIULLI ALLEGRI NO. 3
FRANCO COLOMBO PUBLICATIONS   109323   .50
BECUCCI
LABBRA CORALLINE
FRANCO COLOMBO PUBLICATIONS   54989   .50
BECUCCI
MAZURKA
FRANCO COLOMBO PUBLICATIONS   110107   .60
BECUCCI   3
MY TREASURE WALTZ
CENTURY MUSIC PUBLISHING COMPANY, INC.   1512   .40
BECUCCI
POLKA
FRANCO COLOMBO PUBLICATIONS   110106   .60
BECUCCI
TESORO MIO
FRANCO COLOMBO PUBLICATIONS   96788   .60
BECUCCI
TESORO MIO
FRANCO COLOMBO PUBLICATIONS   111077   .60
BECUCCI   DEL MAGLIO
TESORO MIO
FRANCO COLOMBO PUBLICATIONS   127110   .60
BECUCCI   3
TESORO MIO, WALTZ
CENTURY MUSIC PUBLISHING COMPANY, INC.   1512   .40
BECUCCI
WALTZ
FRANCO COLOMBO PUBLICATIONS   110105   .60
BEDFORD, D.
PIANO PIECE 2
UNIVERSAL EDITION   UE 15314   3.00
BEDFORD, D.
PIANO PIECES 1
UNIVERSAL EDITION   UE 14196   2.00
BEETHOVEN
AANDANTE, WOO 57, F MAJOR
G. HENLE MUSIKVERLAG   21   1.10
BEETHOVEN   DEL MAGLIO
ADAGIO CANTABILE--FROM SONATA, OP. 13
FRANCO COLOMBO PUBLICATIONS   124704   .75
BEETHOVEN   FICHANDLER, W.   3
ADAGIO FROM STRING TRIO, OP. 8
BELWIN-MILLS PUBLISHING CORPORATION   .60
BEETHOVEN   CASELLA
ADAGIO SOSTENUTO--FROM SONATA, OP. 27 NO. 2
FRANCO COLOMBO PUBLICATIONS   127612   .75
BEETHOVEN   DEL MAGLIO
ADAGIO SOSTENUTO--FROM SONATA, OP. 27 NO. 2
FRANCO COLOMBO PUBLICATIONS   124705   .60
BEETHOVEN
ADIEU TO THE PIANO
G. SCHIRMER, INC.   .50
BEETHOVEN
ADIEU TO THE PIANO
WILLIS MUSIC COMPANY   .40
BEETHOVEN
ALBUMBLATT -- FUR ELISE
WILLIS MUSIC COMPANY   .40
BEETHOVEN   DEIS
ALBUMBLATT--FUR ELISE
G. SCHIRMER, INC.   .50
BEETHOVEN
ALBUMBLATT, WO O 59, A MINOR 'FOR ELISE'
G. HENLE MUSIKVERLAG   128   1.10
BEETHOVEN   BRENDEL
ALLA INGHARESE --RAGE OVER THE LOST PENNY--, OP. 129
WIENER URTEXT EDITION   UT 50020   2.00
BEETHOVEN
ALLA INGHARESE QUASI UN CAPRICCIO --THE RAGE OVER THE LOST
PENNY--OP. 129, G MAJOR
G. HENLE MUSIKVERLAG   171   1.15
BEETHOVEN   WERNER
ALLEGRETTO IN B MINOR--CURWEN EDITION
G. SCHIRMER, INC.   .60
BEETHOVEN   4
ALLEGRETTO SCHERZANDO, B FLAT MAJOR, FROM THE EIGHTH SYMPHONY
CENTURY MUSIC PUBLISHING COMPANY, INC.   3643   .40
BEETHOVEN   4
ALLEGRETTO, A MINOR, FROM THE SEVENTH SYMPHONY
CENTURY MUSIC PUBLISHING COMPANY, INC.   3663   .40
BEETHOVEN   2
ALLEGRETTO, A MINOR, FROM THE SEVENTH SYMPHONY -- EASY --
CENTURY MUSIC PUBLISHING COMPANY, INC.   3643   .40
BEETHOVEN   1
ALLEGRETTO, FROM '7TH SYMPHONY IN A MAJOR'
THEODORE PRESSER COMPANY   .50
BEETHOVEN
ALLEMANDE
FREDERICK HARRIS MUSIC COMPANY   .45
BEETHOVEN   4
ANDANTE F-DUR
SCHOTT   0266 1/2   1.00
BEETHOVEN   ROHM
ANDANTE FAVORI IN F
ASSOCIATED MUSIC PUBLISHERS, INC.   OBV   .75
BEETHOVEN   LEBERT
ANDANTE IN F MAJOR
G. SCHIRMER, INC.   .70
BEETHOVEN   BRADLEY
AUTHENTIC 'FIRST BEETHOVEN'
FRANCO COLOMBO PUBLICATIONS   LD197   1.00
BEETHOVEN
BAGATELLE IN A MINOR
BELWIN-MILLS PUBLISHING CORPORATION   .60
BEETHOVEN   3
BAGATELLE IN D, OP.33 NO.6
CENTURY MUSIC PUBLISHING COMPANY, INC.   3910   .40

BEETHOVEN
BAGATELLE IN E FLAT, OP. 33 NO. 1
G. SCHIRMER, INC.   .50
BEETHOVEN
BAGATELLE IN E FLAT, OP. 33 NO. 1
WILLIS MUSIC COMPANY   .35
BEETHOVEN   3
BAGATELLE IN E FLAT, OP.33 NO. 1
CENTURY MUSIC PUBLISHING COMPANY, INC.   3328   .40
BEETHOVEN
BAGATELLE NOUVELLE IN G MINOR, OP. 119 NO. 1
G. SCHIRMER, INC.   .30
BEETHOVEN   RUSSEL
BAGATELLE, OP. 33 NO. 1
BOSTON MUSIC COMPANY   .50
BEETHOVEN   FRUGATTA
BAGATELLES, OP. 33
FRANCO COLOMBO PUBLICATIONS   ER2595   1.00
BEETHOVEN
BONN SONATA NO. 1
BELWIN-MILLS PUBLISHING CORPORATION   20499   .85
BEETHOVEN
BONN SONATA NO. 2
BELWIN-MILLS PUBLISHING CORPORATION   20452   .85
BEETHOVEN   BRADLEY, R.
BRADLEY CLASSICAL SERIES - FUR ELISE
SCREEN GEMS - COLUMBIA PUBLICATIONS   6707FP2   .85
BEETHOVEN   BRADLEY, R.
BRADLEY CLASSICAL SERIES - MOONLIGHT SONATA
SCREEN GEMS - COLUMBIA PUBLICATIONS   4715MP2   .85
BEETHOVEN   BRADLEY, R.
BRADLEY CLASSICAL SERIES - SONATINA NO. 01 IN G
SCREEN GEMS - COLUMBIA PUBLICATIONS   4742SP2   .85
BEETHOVEN
CADENZA TO CONCERTO NO. 02 IN B FLAT, OP. 19
ASSOCIATED MUSIC PUBLISHERS, INC.   DOB   1.00
BEETHOVEN
CADENZA TO CONCERTO NO. 03 IN C MINOR, OP. 37
ASSOCIATED MUSIC PUBLISHERS, INC.   DOB   1.25
BEETHOVEN
CADENZA TO CONCERTO NO. 04 IN G, OP. 58
ASSOCIATED MUSIC PUBLISHERS, INC.   DOB   1.25
BEETHOVEN
CADENZA TO MOZART CONCERTO IN D MINOR, K. 466
ASSOCIATED MUSIC PUBLISHERS, INC.   DOB   1.00
BEETHOVEN   REINECKE
CADENZA TO THE CONCERTO NO. 3 IN C MINOR, OP. 37--FIRST MOVEMENT
G. SCHIRMER, INC.   .70
BEETHOVEN
CLAVIERSTUCK
BELWIN-MILLS PUBLISHING CORPORATION   .85
BEETHOVEN   HESS   D
CONCERTO IN E FLAT. JUGENDKONZERT
C. F. PETERS CORPORATION   Z454   4.70
BEETHOVEN   KULLAK
CONCERTO NO. 05 IN E FLAT MAJOR--OP. 73-- 'EMPEROR'
G. SCHIRMER, INC.   L625   1.00
BEETHOVEN   3
CONGRATULATION MINUET
CENTURY MUSIC PUBLISHING COMPANY, INC.   4015   .40
BEETHOVEN   SEISS   3
CONTRA DANCE
BOSTON MUSIC COMPANY   .50
BEETHOVEN   SEISS   3
CONTRA DANCE
BOSTON MUSIC COMPANY   .50
BEETHOVEN   5
CONTRA DANCE
THEODORE PRESSER COMPANY   .50
BEETHOVEN   SCHAUM, J.   2
COUNTRY DANCE
BELWIN-MILLS PUBLISHING CORPORATION   .50
BEETHOVEN
DIABELLI VARIATIONS
EDWIN F. KALMUS   3196   2.25
BEETHOVEN   D
DIABELLI VARIATIONS, OP. 120
C. F. PETERS CORPORATION   4476   2.50
BEETHOVEN   STEINER   1 1/2
DUKE AND DUCHESS
BELWIN-MILLS PUBLISHING CORPORATION   .60
BEETHOVEN   BUSONI *
ECOSSAISE IN B FLAT
ASSOCIATED MUSIC PUBLISHERS, INC.   AMP   .50
BEETHOVEN   2
ECOSSAISE IN E FLAT
CENTURY MUSIC PUBLISHING COMPANY, INC.   3711   .40
BEETHOVEN
ECOSSAISES
FREDERICK HARRIS MUSIC COMPANY   .90
BEETHOVEN   BUSONI
ECOSSAISES
G. SCHIRMER, INC.   L1509   .50
BEETHOVEN   4
ECOSSAISES
THEODORE PRESSER COMPANY   .50
BEETHOVEN   3
ECOSSAISES IN E FLAT
CENTURY MUSIC PUBLISHING COMPANY, INC.   3744   .40
BEETHOVEN   4
EGMONT OUVERTURE OP. 84
SCHOTT   01749 1/2   1.00
BEETHOVEN   POZZOLI
EGMONT OVERTURE
FRANCO COLOMBO PUBLICATIONS   127807   .50
BEETHOVEN   M
EGMONT, OP. 84. COMPLETE
C. F. PETERS CORPORATION   99   5.00
BEETHOVEN
FANTASY IN G MINOR, OP. 77
INTERNATIONAL MUSIC COMPANY   1.00
BEETHOVEN
FAREWELL TO THE PIANO
CARL FISCHER, INC.   S 10   .50
BEETHOVEN   3
FAREWELL TO THE PIANO
CENTURY MUSIC PUBLISHING COMPANY, INC.   699   .40
BEETHOVEN
FAREWELL TO THE PIANO
FRANCO COLOMBO PUBLICATIONS   128020   .60
BEETHOVEN   DEL MAGLIO
FAREWELL TO THE PIANO
FRANCO COLOMBO PUBLICATIONS   129091   .60
BEETHOVEN
FESTIVAL GROUPS FOR PIANO SELECTED BY ARTHUR BENJAMIN, SERIES 2
-- RONDO, FROM 'SONATINA IN F'
BOOSEY AND HAWKES, INC.   .60

BEETHOVEN	MITTLER	2B		
FIFTH SYMPHONY				
MUSICORD PUBLICATIONS, INC.				.45
BEETHOVEN		3		
FOR ELISE				
BELWIN-MILLS PUBLISHING CORPORATION			19	.60
BEETHOVEN		E-M		
FOR ELISE --FUER ELISE--				
C. F. PETERS CORPORATION			7097	.90
BEETHOVEN	CHIESA			
FUNERAL MARCH, OP. 26				
FRANCO COLOMBO PUBLICATIONS			128121	.50
BEETHOVEN				
FUR ELISE				
ASHLEY DEALERS SERVICE, INC.			ES	.95
BEETHOVEN				
FUR ELISE				
ASSOCIATED MUSIC PUBLISHERS, INC.			OBV	.60
BEETHOVEN				
FUR ELISE				
BANKS AND SON LTD.				.40
BEETHOVEN		3		
FUR ELISE				
BOSTON MUSIC COMPANY				.50
BEETHOVEN	ECKSTEIN			
FUR ELISE				
CARL FISCHER, INC.			S 564	.50
BEETHOVEN		3		
FUR ELISE				
CENTURY MUSIC PUBLISHING COMPANY, INC.			225	.40
BEETHOVEN				
FUR ELISE				
FRANCO COLOMBO PUBLICATIONS			128130	.60
BEETHOVEN	DEL MAGLIO			
FUR ELISE				
FRANCO COLOMBO PUBLICATIONS			128112	.60
BEETHOVEN				
FUR ELISE				
G. SCHIRMER, INC.				.50
BEETHOVEN	WHITFORD	GR. 2 1/2		
FUR ELISE				
ROBERT WHITFORD PUBLICATIONS				.40
BEETHOVEN	SCHAUM, J.	2 1/2		
FUR ELISE				
SCHAUM PUBLICATIONS, INC.				.60
BEETHOVEN		3		
FUR ELISE				
VOLKWEIN BROS.				.25
BEETHOVEN		2		
FUR ELISE --ALBUMBLATT--				
SCHOTT			06641 1/2	1.00
BEETHOVEN				
FUR ELISE ALBUMBLATT				
BELWIN-MILLS PUBLISHING CORPORATION				.60
BEETHOVEN		3		
FUR ELISE OP. 173				
THEODORE PRESSER COMPANY				.50
BEETHOVEN	DEIS			
GAVOTTE IN F MAJOR				
G. SCHIRMER, INC.				.50
BEETHOVEN	ZEPP	4		
GERMAN DANCE				
PRO-ART PUBLICATIONS, INC.			379	.50
BEETHOVEN	BERUMEN			
GERMAN DANCE				
SHAWNEE PRESS, INC.			HB-5025	.60
BEETHOVEN	ECKSTEIN			
GERTRUDE'S DREAM WALTZ				
CARL FISCHER, INC.			S 2053	.50
BEETHOVEN		2		
GERTRUDE'S DREAM WALTZ				
CENTURY MUSIC PUBLISHING COMPANY, INC.			626	.40
BEETHOVEN				
GERTRUDE'S DREAM WALTZ				
G. SCHIRMER, INC.				.40
BEETHOVEN		2		
GERTRUDE'S DREAM WALTZ				
WILLIS MUSIC COMPANY				.35
BEETHOVEN	HARTZELL			
GRANDE SONATA -- AFTER THE STRING TRIO, OP. 3 --				
ASSOCIATED MUSIC PUBLISHERS, INC.			DOB	3.00
BEETHOVEN	MARCHI, G.			
INCONTRO CON BEETHOVEN				
EDIZIONI BERBEN			1314	6.00
BEETHOVEN		4		
LEONOREN-OUV. OP. 72 NO. 3				
SCHOTT			05674 1/2	1.00
BEETHOVEN	BALLATORE			
LITTLE RONDO IN G				
G. SCHIRMER, INC.				.40
BEETHOVEN		3		
LONGING				
CENTURY MUSIC PUBLISHING COMPANY, INC.			818	.40
BEETHOVEN	RUBINSTEIN			
MARCHE A LA TURQUE--FROM THE ''RUINS OF ATHENS''				
G. SCHIRMER, INC.				.60
BEETHOVEN	CHIESA			
MARCHE A LA TURQUE--FROM 'THE RUINS OF ATHENS'				
FRANCO COLOMBO PUBLICATIONS			107506	.50
BEETHOVEN				
MARCHE FUNEBRE--FROM SONATA, OP. 26				
G. SCHIRMER, INC.				.35
BEETHOVEN		2-3		
MARCIA UND GAVOTTA				
SCHOTT			09583 1/2	1.00
BEETHOVEN		1		
MENUET IN G, EASY				
CENTURY MUSIC PUBLISHING COMPANY, INC.			3822	.40
BEETHOVEN		2		
MENUET NO. 2 IN G				
BELWIN-MILLS PUBLISHING CORPORATION			20	.60
BEETHOVEN	ECKSTEIN			
MENUET NO. 2 IN G				
CARL FISCHER, INC.			S 830	.50
BEETHOVEN		3		
MENUET NO. 2 IN G				
THEODORE PRESSER COMPANY				.50
BEETHOVEN		3		
MENUET, FROM SONATA OP. 49 NO. 2				
BELWIN-MILLS PUBLISHING CORPORATION			22	.60
BEETHOVEN		2		
MENUETT G-DUR				
SCHOTT			07536	.75
BEETHOVEN	DEL MAGLIO			
MINUET FROM SONATA, OP. 49 NO. 2				
FRANCO COLOMBO PUBLICATIONS			124706	.60

BEETHOVEN				
MINUET FROM SONATA, OP. 49 NO. 2				
G. SCHIRMER, INC.				.50
BEETHOVEN	BARTH, H.			
MINUET IN C				
BELWIN-MILLS PUBLISHING CORPORATION			20168	.60
BEETHOVEN	BARTH, H.			
MINUET IN E FLAT				
BELWIN-MILLS PUBLISHING CORPORATION			20399	.60
BEETHOVEN				
MINUET IN E FLAT MAJOR				
G. SCHIRMER, INC.				.30
BEETHOVEN				
MINUET IN G				
ASHLEY DEALERS SERVICE, INC.			ES	.95
BEETHOVEN	WEYBRIGHT	2 1/2		
MINUET IN G				
BELWIN-MILLS PUBLISHING CORPORATION				.60
BEETHOVEN		3		
MINUET IN G				
BOSTON MUSIC COMPANY				.50
BEETHOVEN		2		
MINUET IN G				
CENTURY MUSIC PUBLISHING COMPANY, INC.			1891	.40
BEETHOVEN		3		
MINUET IN G				
CENTURY MUSIC PUBLISHING COMPANY, INC.			1891	.40
BEETHOVEN		2		
MINUET IN G				
CENTURY MUSIC PUBLISHING COMPANY, INC.			3498	.60
BEETHOVEN	DEL MAGLIO			
MINUET IN G				
FRANCO COLOMBO PUBLICATIONS			124707	.60
BEETHOVEN		3		
MINUET IN G				
VOLKWEIN BROS.				.25
BEETHOVEN				
MINUET IN G				
WILLIS MUSIC COMPANY				.35
BEETHOVEN		2		
MINUET IN G				
WILLIS MUSIC COMPANY				.35
BEETHOVEN	DEIS			
MINUET IN G MAJOR				
G. SCHIRMER, INC.				.30
BEETHOVEN				
MINUET IN G--OLD EDITION--				
FREDERICK HARRIS MUSIC COMPANY				.30
BEETHOVEN	SCHAUM, J.	4		
MOONLIGHT SONATA				
BELWIN-MILLS PUBLISHING CORPORATION				.50
BEETHOVEN		6		
MOONLIGHT SONATA				
CENTURY MUSIC PUBLISHING COMPANY, INC.			1186	.40
BEETHOVEN	MITTLER	2B		
MOONLIGHT SONATA				
MUSICORD PUBLICATIONS, INC.				.45
BEETHOVEN	ZEPP	5		
MOONLIGHT SONATA				
PRO-ART PUBLICATIONS, INC.			457	.60
BEETHOVEN	WALLIS	2		
MOONLIGHT SONATA THEME				
WILLIS MUSIC COMPANY				.35
BEETHOVEN	ECKSTEIN			
MOONLIGHT SONATA, FIRST MVT.				
CARL FISCHER, INC.			S 2292	.50
BEETHOVEN	ECKSTEIN			
MOONLIGHT SONATA, FIRST MVT.				
CARL FISCHER, INC.			S 2311	.50
BEETHOVEN				
MOONLIGHT SONATA, OP. 27 NO. 2				
ASHLEY DEALERS SERVICE, INC.			ES	1.00
BEETHOVEN		4 - 5		
MOONLIGHT SONATA, OP. 27 NO. 2 - FIRST MOVEMENT				
BOSTON MUSIC COMPANY				.50
BEETHOVEN				
MOONLIGHT SONATA, OP. 27 NO. 2 -- FIRST MOVEMENT				
ASHLEY DEALERS SERVICE, INC.			ES	.95
BEETHOVEN	POZZOLI			
MY FIRST BEETHOVEN				
FRANCO COLOMBO PUBLICATIONS			ER1952	1.00
BEETHOVEN		3		
NEL COR PIU NON MI SIENTO, SIX VARIATIONS				
CENTURY MUSIC PUBLISHING COMPANY, INC.			3494	.40
BEETHOVEN	MULLER			
NEUE VARIATIONEN A-DUR				
SCHOTT			09689 1/2	1.00
BEETHOVEN	THOMPSON, J.	1		
NINTH SYMPHONY				
WILLIS MUSIC COMPANY				.35
BEETHOVEN				
ODE TO JOY				
ASHLEY DEALERS SERVICE, INC.				1.00
BEETHOVEN		1 1/2		
ODE TO JOY				
BELWIN-MILLS PUBLISHING CORPORATION				.60
BEETHOVEN		5		
POLONAISE IN C, OP. 89				
CENTURY MUSIC PUBLISHING COMPANY, INC.			3898	.40
BEETHOVEN				
POLONAISE IN C, OP. 89				
INTERNATIONAL MUSIC COMPANY				1.00
BEETHOVEN	ROHM			
PRELUDE IN F MINOR				
ASSOCIATED MUSIC PUBLISHERS, INC.			OBV	.40
BEETHOVEN		4		
RAGE OVER A LOST PENNY, OP. 129				
CENTURY MUSIC PUBLISHING COMPANY, INC.			3783	.40
BEETHOVEN				
RAGE OVER THE LOST PENNY, OP. 129				
UNIVERSAL EDITION			1314	2.10
BEETHOVEN	DUMM			
RECITAL REFRESHER SERIES -- CLAVIERSTUECK				
BELWIN-MILLS PUBLISHING CORPORATION			26115	.60
BEETHOVEN	SCHOLZ			
ROMANCE IN F, OP. 50				
ASSOCIATED MUSIC PUBLISHERS, INC.			DOB	.60
BEETHOVEN	BUELOW			
RONDO A CAPRICCIO IN G MAJOR, OP. 129				
G. SCHIRMER, INC.				.80
BEETHOVEN		4		
RONDO A CAPRICCIO OP. 129 -- WUT UBER DEN VERLORENEN GROSCHEN				
SCHOTT			0888 1/2	1.00
BEETHOVEN				
RONDO A CAPRICCIO, OP. 129				
EDWIN F. KALMUS			3198	1.00

BEETHOVEN   ROHM
RONDO A CAPRICCIO, OP. 129 -- ''RAGE OVER THE LOST PENNY'' --
ASSOCIATED MUSIC PUBLISHERS, INC.   OBV   .90
BEETHOVEN   FRUGATTA
RONDO A CAPRICCIO, OP. 129 'RAGE OVER THE LOST PENNY'
FRANCO COLOMBO PUBLICATIONS   ER1867   .75
                                            3
BEETHOVEN
RONDO C-DUR, OP. 51 NO. 1
SCHOTT   0278 1/2   1.00
BEETHOVEN   HARDING, R.   3
RONDO FROM FIFTH CONCERTO
WILLIS MUSIC COMPANY   .35
                                            4
BEETHOVEN
RONDO G-DUR, OP. 51 NO. 2
SCHOTT   0279   1.00
BEETHOVEN   ROHM
RONDO IN A
ASSOCIATED MUSIC PUBLISHERS, INC.   OBV   .50
BEETHOVEN
RONDO IN C MAJOR, OP. 51 NO. 1
WILLIS MUSIC COMPANY   .40
                                            3
BEETHOVEN
RONDO IN C, OP. 51 NO. 1
CENTURY MUSIC PUBLISHING COMPANY, INC.   375   .40
BEETHOVEN
RONDO IN C, OP. 51 NO. 1
G. HENLE MUSIKVERLAG   140   1.10
BEETHOVEN   LEBERT
RONDO IN C, OP. 51 NO. 1
G. SCHIRMER, INC.   .50
BEETHOVEN   LEBERT
RONDO IN G, OP. 51 NO. 2
G. SCHIRMER, INC.   .75
BEETHOVEN   KLEINMICHEL
RONDO, OP. 51 NO. 1
FRANCO COLOMBO PUBLICATIONS   129028   1.00
                                            3
BEETHOVEN
RONDO, OP. 51 NO. 2
CENTURY MUSIC PUBLISHING COMPANY, INC.   375   .40
                                            3
BEETHOVEN
RONDO, OP. 51 NO. 2
CENTURY MUSIC PUBLISHING COMPANY, INC.   3345 .40
BEETHOVEN   RUBINSTEIN   5
RUINS OF ATHENS, TURKISH MARCH
CENTURY MUSIC PUBLISHING COMPANY, INC.   2406 .40
BEETHOVEN   MIROVITCH
SCHERZO AND MENUET
ELKAN-VOGEL, INC.   .70
                                            5
BEETHOVEN
SCHERZO, FROM SONATA OP. 2, NO. 3
THEODORE PRESSER COMPANY   .50
                                            2
BEETHOVEN
SECHS LEICHTE VARIATIONEN -- SCHWEIZERLIED F-DUR
SCHOTT   0288 1/2   1.00
                                            3
BEETHOVEN
SECHS LEICHTE VARIATIONEN G-DUR
SCHOTT   0292 1/2   1.00
                                            5
BEETHOVEN
SECHS VARIATIONEN F-DUR, OP. 34
SCHOTT   0291 1/2   1.00
                                            3
BEETHOVEN
SECHS VARIATIONEN UBER 'NEL COR PIU NON MI SENTO'
SCHOTT   0287 1/2   1.00
BEETHOVEN   BENDIK   3
SECHS VARIATIONEN UBER EIN RUS SSISCHES VOLKSLIED OP. 107/7
SCHOTT   09664 1/2   1.00
BEETHOVEN   SINGER   M-D
SEPTET, OP. 20
C. F. PETERS CORPORATION   490   2.50
BEETHOVEN   HARDING, R.   3
SEVENTH SYMPHONY
WILLIS MUSIC COMPANY   .35
                                            3
BEETHOVEN
SIEBEN BAGATELLEN, OP. 33
SCHOTT   0267-8   1.50
BEETHOVEN   DEL MAGLIO
SIX ECOSSAISES
FRANCO COLOMBO PUBLICATIONS   127111   .60
BEETHOVEN
SIX VARIATIONS ON 'NEL COR PIU NON MI SENTO'
CARL FISCHER, INC.   S 1077   .60
BEETHOVEN   KLEINMICHEL
SIX VARIATIONS ON 'NEL COR PIU NON MI SENTO'
FRANCO COLOMBO PUBLICATIONS   ER2568   .75
BEETHOVEN   LEBERT
SIX VARIATIONS ON A SWISS SONG
G. SCHIRMER, INC.   .40
BEETHOVEN   LEBERT
SIX VARIATIONS ON AN ORIGINAL THEME
G. SCHIRMER, INC.   .50
                                            3
BEETHOVEN
SIX VARIATIONS ON NEL COR PIU NON MI SENTO
CENTURY MUSIC PUBLISHING COMPANY, INC.   3494 .40
BEETHOVEN   LEBERT
SIX VARIATIONS ON THE DUET ''NEL COR PIU NON MI SENTO''
G. SCHIRMER, INC.   .75
                                            6
BEETHOVEN
SLOW MOVEMENT, FROM 'MOONLIGHT SONATA OP. 27 NO. 2'
THEODORE PRESSER COMPANY   .50
BEETHOVEN
SONATA NO. 01 IN F MINOR, OP. 2 NO. 1
FRANCO COLOMBO PUBLICATIONS   ER2318   1.00
BEETHOVEN   SCIONTI
SONATA NO. 01 IN F MINOR, OP. 2 NO. 1
FRANCO COLOMBO PUBLICATIONS   NY1462   1.00
BEETHOVEN
SONATA NO. 01 IN F MINOR, OP. 2 NO. 1
G. HENLE MUSIKVERLAG   183   1.15
BEETHOVEN
SONATA NO. 01 IN F MINOR, OP. 2 NO. 1
G. SCHIRMER, INC.   1.10
BEETHOVEN   CHING
SONATA NO. 01 IN F MINOR, OP. 2 NO. 1
GENERAL WORDS AND MUSIC COMPANY   .75
BEETHOVEN   HOEHN, A.   4
SONATA NO. 01 IN F MINOR, OP. 2 NO. 1
SCHOTT   0206 1/2   1.00
BEETHOVEN
SONATA NO. 01 URTEXT
EDWIN F. KALMUS   3166   1.25
BEETHOVEN
SONATA NO. 02 IN A, OP. 2 NO. 2
G. SCHIRMER, INC.   1.10
BEETHOVEN   HOEHN, A.   5
SONATA NO. 02 IN A, OP. 2 NO. 2
SCHOTT   0208 1/2   1.00

BEETHOVEN
SONATA NO. 03 IN C, OP. 2 NO. 3
FRANCO COLOMBO PUBLICATIONS   ER2320   1.25
BEETHOVEN
SONATA NO. 03 IN C, OP. 2 NO. 3
G. SCHIRMER, INC.   1.10
BEETHOVEN   HOEHN, A.   5
SONATA NO. 03 IN C, OP. 2 NO. 3
SCHOTT   0210-1   1.50
BEETHOVEN
SONATA NO. 04 IN E FLAT, OP. 7
FRANCO COLOMBO PUBLICATIONS   ER2321   1.50
BEETHOVEN
SONATA NO. 04 IN E FLAT, OP. 7
G. SCHIRMER, INC.   1.10
BEETHOVEN   SCIONTI
SONATA NO. 05 IN C MINOR, OP. 10 NO. 1
BELWIN-MILLS PUBLISHING CORPORATION   20267   1.00
BEETHOVEN
SONATA NO. 05 IN C MINOR, OP. 10 NO. 1
FRANCO COLOMBO PUBLICATIONS   ER2322   1.00
BEETHOVEN
SONATA NO. 05 IN C MINOR, OP. 10 NO. 1
G. HENLE MUSIKVERLAG   47   1.15
BEETHOVEN
SONATA NO. 05 IN C MINOR, OP. 10 NO. 1
G. SCHIRMER, INC.   .80
BEETHOVEN   HOEHN, A.   5
SONATA NO. 05 IN C MINOR, OP. 10 NO. 1
SCHOTT   0214 1/2   1.00
BEETHOVEN
SONATA NO. 05 URTEXT
EDWIN F. KALMUS   3166   1.25
BEETHOVEN
SONATA NO. 06 IN F, OP. 10 NO. 2
FRANCO COLOMBO PUBLICATIONS   ER2323   1.00
BEETHOVEN
SONATA NO. 06 IN F, OP. 10 NO. 2
G. SCHIRMER, INC.   .90
BEETHOVEN   HOEHN, A.   5
SONATA NO. 06 IN F, OP. 10 NO. 2
SCHOTT   0215 1/2   1.00
BEETHOVEN
SONATA NO. 07 IN D, OP. 10 NO. 3
FRANCO COLOMBO PUBLICATIONS   ER2324   1.00
BEETHOVEN
SONATA NO. 07 IN D, OP. 10 NO. 3
G. SCHIRMER, INC.   1.00
BEETHOVEN   HOEHN, A.   5
SONATA NO. 07 IN D, OP. 10 NO. 3
SCHOTT   0216-7   1.50
BEETHOVEN   ALBERT, D'
SONATA NO. 08 IN C MINOR, OP. 13
CARL FISCHER, INC.   P 53   1.00
BEETHOVEN   CHING
SONATA NO. 08 IN C MINOR, OP. 13
GENERAL WORDS AND MUSIC COMPANY   .75
BEETHOVEN   PODOLSKY, L.
SONATA NO. 08 IN C MINOR, OP. 13
VOLKWEIN BROS.   1.00
BEETHOVEN
SONATA NO. 08 IN C MINOR, OP. 13 - GRANDE SONATA PATHETIQUE
G. HENLE MUSIKVERLAG   48   1.15
                                            5
BEETHOVEN
SONATA NO. 08 IN C MINOR, OP. 13 - PATHETIQUE
CENTURY MUSIC PUBLISHING COMPANY, INC.   1341 .40
BEETHOVEN   SCIONTI
SONATA NO. 08 IN C MINOR, OP. 13 'PATHETIQUE'
BELWIN-MILLS PUBLISHING CORPORATION   20268   1.00
BEETHOVEN
SONATA NO. 08 IN C MINOR, OP. 13 'PATHETIQUE'
FRANCO COLOMBO PUBLICATIONS   ER2325   1.00
BEETHOVEN   HOEHN, A.   5
SONATA NO. 08 IN C MINOR, OP. 13 'PATHETIQUE'
SCHOTT   0218 1/2   1.00
BEETHOVEN   RATZ-SCHENKER
SONATA NO. 08 IN C MINOR, OP. 13 'PATHETIQUE'
UNIVERSAL EDITION   110-40532   1.00
BEETHOVEN
SONATA NO. 08 IN C MINOR, OP. 13, 'PATHETIQUE'
G. SCHIRMER, INC.   1.10
BEETHOVEN
SONATA NO. 08 URTEXT
EDWIN F. KALMUS   3166   1.25
BEETHOVEN   SCIONTI
SONATA NO. 09 IN E, OP. 14 NO. 1
BELWIN-MILLS PUBLISHING CORPORATION   20265   1.00
BEETHOVEN
SONATA NO. 09 IN E, OP. 14 NO. 1
FRANCO COLOMBO PUBLICATIONS   ER2326   1.00
BEETHOVEN
SONATA NO. 09 IN E, OP. 14 NO. 1
G. SCHIRMER, INC.   .90
BEETHOVEN   HOEHN, A.   4
SONATA NO. 09 IN E, OP. 14 NO. 1
SCHOTT   0220 1/2   1.00
                                            4
BEETHOVEN
SONATA NO. 09 IN E, OP. 14 NO. 1, ALLEGRETTO
CENTURY MUSIC PUBLISHING COMPANY, INC.   3794 .40
BEETHOVEN
SONATA NO. 09 URTEXT
EDWIN F. KALMUS   3166   1.25
BEETHOVEN   SCIONTI
SONATA NO. 10 IN G, OP. 14 NO. 2
BELWIN-MILLS PUBLISHING CORPORATION   20262   1.00
BEETHOVEN
SONATA NO. 10 IN G, OP. 14 NO. 2
FRANCO COLOMBO PUBLICATIONS   ER2327   1.00
BEETHOVEN
SONATA NO. 10 IN G, OP. 14 NO. 2
G. SCHIRMER, INC.   .90
BEETHOVEN   HOEHN, A.   4
SONATA NO. 10 IN G, OP. 14 NO. 2
SCHOTT   0221 1/2   1.00
BEETHOVEN
SONATA NO. 10 URTEXT
EDWIN F. KALMUS   3166   1.25
BEETHOVEN
SONATA NO. 11 IN B FLAT, OP. 22
FRANCO COLOMBO PUBLICATIONS   ER2328   1.50
BEETHOVEN
SONATA NO. 11 IN B FLAT, OP. 22
G. SCHIRMER, INC.   1.10
BEETHOVEN
SONATA NO. 12 IN A FLAT, OP. 26
G. SCHIRMER, INC.   1.10

BEETHOVEN
SONATA NO. 12 IN A FLAT, OP. 26 'FUNERAL MARCH'
FRANCO COLOMBO PUBLICATIONS   ER2329   1.00
BEETHOVEN   HOEHN, A.   6
SONATA NO. 12 IN A FLAT, OP. 26 'TRAUERMARSCH'
SCHOTT   0225 1/2   1.00
BEETHOVEN   RATZ-SCHENKER
SONATA NO. 12 IN A FLAT, OP. 26 WITH FUNERAL MARCH
UNIVERSAL EDITION   110-40533   1.00
BEETHOVEN
SONATA NO. 13 IN E FLAT, OP. 27 NO. 1
FRANCO COLOMBO PUBLICATIONS   ER2330   1.00
BEETHOVEN
SONATA NO. 13 IN E FLAT, OP. 27 NO. 1
G. SCHIRMER, INC.   .90
BEETHOVEN   HOEHN, A.   5
SONATA NO. 13 IN E FLAT, OP. 27 NO. 1 'FANTASIE'
SCHOTT   0227 1/2   1.00
BEETHOVEN   RATZ-SCHENKER
SONATA NO. 14 IN C SHARP MINOR 'MOONLIGHT'
UNIVERSAL EDITION   110-40534   .90
BEETHOVEN
SONATA NO. 14 IN C SHARP MINOR, OP. 27 NO. 2
CARL FISCHER, INC.   S 2134   .90
BEETHOVEN   ALBERT, D'
SONATA NO. 14 IN C SHARP MINOR, OP. 27 NO. 2
CARL FISCHER, INC.   P 59   .90
BEETHOVEN   6
SONATA NO. 14 IN C SHARP MINOR, OP. 27 NO. 2
CENTURY MUSIC PUBLISHING COMPANY, INC.   1186   .40
BEETHOVEN   CHING
SONATA NO. 14 IN C SHARP MINOR, OP. 27 NO. 2
GENERAL WORDS AND MUSIC COMPANY   .75
BEETHOVEN
SONATA NO. 14 IN C SHARP MINOR, OP. 27 NO. 2 --FIRST MOVEMENT
ONLY--
G. SCHIRMER, INC.   .50
BEETHOVEN   HOEHN, A.   5
SONATA NO. 14 IN C SHARP MINOR, OP. 27 NO. 2 'MONDSCHEIN'
SCHOTT   0229 1/2   1.00
BEETHOVEN
SONATA NO. 14 IN C SHARP MINOR, OP. 27 NO. 2 'MOONLIGHT'
FRANCO COLOMBO PUBLICATIONS   ER2331   1.00
BEETHOVEN
SONATA NO. 14 IN C SHARP MINOR, OP. 27 NO. 2 'MOONLIGHT'
G. HENLE MUSIKVERLAG   49   1.15
BEETHOVEN
SONATA NO. 14 IN C SHARP MINOR, OP. 27 NO. 2, 'MOONLIGHT'
G. SCHIRMER, INC.   .90
BEETHOVEN
SONATA NO. 14 URTEXT
EDWIN F. KALMUS   3166   1.25
BEETHOVEN   LAMOND
SONATA NO. 15 IN D, OP. 28
ASSOCIATED MUSIC PUBLISHERS, INC.   B/H   1.00
BEETHOVEN
SONATA NO. 15 IN D, OP. 28 'PASTORAL'
FRANCO COLOMBO PUBLICATIONS   ER2332   1.25
BEETHOVEN
SONATA NO. 15 IN D, OP. 28 'PASTORAL'
G. SCHIRMER, INC.   1.10
BEETHOVEN   RATZ-SCHENKER
SONATA NO. 15 IN D, OP. 28 'PASTORAL'
UNIVERSAL EDITION   110-40535   1.00
BEETHOVEN   HOEHN, A.   6
SONATA NO. 15 IN D, OP. 28 'PASTORALE'
SCHOTT   0231-2   1.50
BEETHOVEN
SONATA NO. 16 IN G, OP. 31 NO. 1
FRANCO COLOMBO PUBLICATIONS   ER2333   1.25
BEETHOVEN
SONATA NO. 16 IN G, OP. 31 NO. 1
G. SCHIRMER, INC.   1.10
BEETHOVEN   SCIONTI
SONATA NO. 17 IN D MINOR, OP. 31 NO. 2
BELWIN-MILLS PUBLISHING CORPORATION 20261   1.00
BEETHOVEN
SONATA NO. 17 IN D MINOR, OP. 31 NO. 2
G. SCHIRMER, INC.   1.10
BEETHOVEN   HOEHN, A.   5
SONATA NO. 17 IN D MINOR, OP. 31 NO. 2
SCHOTT   0235-6   1.50
BEETHOVEN
SONATA NO. 17 IN D MINOR, OP. 31 NO. 2 'TEMPEST'
FRANCO COLOMBO PUBLICATIONS   ER2334   1.25
BEETHOVEN
SONATA NO. 18 IN E FLAT, OP. 31 NO. 3
FRANCO COLOMBO PUBLICATIONS   ER2335   1.25
BEETHOVEN
SONATA NO. 18 IN E FLAT, OP. 31 NO. 3
G. SCHIRMER, INC.   1.10
BEETHOVEN
SONATA NO. 19 IN G MINOR, OP. 49 NO 1
FREDERICK HARRIS MUSIC COMPANY   .60
BEETHOVEN   3
SONATA NO. 19 IN G MINOR, OP. 49 NO. 1
CENTURY MUSIC PUBLISHING COMPANY, INC.   398   .40
BEETHOVEN
SONATA NO. 19 IN G MINOR, OP. 49 NO. 1
FRANCO COLOMBO PUBLICATIONS   ER2336   1.00
BEETHOVEN
SONATA NO. 19 IN G MINOR, OP. 49 NO. 1
G. SCHIRMER, INC.   .70
BEETHOVEN   CHING
SONATA NO. 19 IN G MINOR, OP. 49 NO. 1
GENERAL WORDS AND MUSIC COMPANY   .75
BEETHOVEN   HOEHN, A.   2
SONATA NO. 19 IN G MINOR, OP. 49 NO. 1 'SONATINE'
SCHOTT   0239 1/2   1.00
BEETHOVEN
SONATA NO. 20 IN G, OP. 49 NO. 2
CARL FISCHER, INC.   S 1459   .70
BEETHOVEN   3
SONATA NO. 20 IN G, OP. 49 NO. 2
CENTURY MUSIC PUBLISHING COMPANY, INC.   400   .40
BEETHOVEN   LEBERT   3
SONATA NO. 20 IN G, OP. 49 NO. 2
CENTURY MUSIC PUBLISHING COMPANY, INC.   401   .40
BEETHOVEN
SONATA NO. 20 IN G, OP. 49 NO. 2
FRANCO COLOMBO PUBLICATIONS   ER2337   1.00
BEETHOVEN
SONATA NO. 20 IN G, OP. 49 NO. 2
G. SCHIRMER, INC.   .70

BEETHOVEN   CHING
SONATA NO. 20 IN G, OP. 49 NO. 2
GENERAL WORDS AND MUSIC COMPANY   .75
BEETHOVEN   HOEHN, A.   2
SONATA NO. 20 IN G, OP. 49 NO. 2 'SONATINE'
SCHOTT   0240 1/2   1.00
BEETHOVEN   RATZ-SCHENKER
SONATA NO. 21 IN C, OP. 53
UNIVERSAL EDITION   110-40536   1.10
BEETHOVEN
SONATA NO. 21 IN C, OP. 53 'WALDSTEIN'
FRANCO COLOMBO PUBLICATIONS   ER2338   1.50
BEETHOVEN   HOEHN, A.   6
SONATA NO. 21 IN C, OP. 53 'WALDSTEIN'
SCHOTT   0241-2 1/2   1.75
BEETHOVEN
SONATA NO. 21 IN C, OP. 53, 'WALDSTEIN'
G. HENLE MUSIKVERLAG   57   1.40
BEETHOVEN
SONATA NO. 21 IN C, OP. 53, 'WALDSTEIN'
G. SCHIRMER, INC.   1.10
BEETHOVEN
SONATA NO. 22 IN F, OP. 54
FRANCO COLOMBO PUBLICATIONS   ER2339   1.00
BEETHOVEN   RATZ-SCHENKER
SONATA NO. 23 IN F MINOR, OP. 57
UNIVERSAL EDITION   110-40537   1.10
BEETHOVEN
SONATA NO. 23 IN F MINOR, OP. 57 'APPASSIONATA'
FRANCO COLOMBO PUBLICATIONS   ER2340   1.50
BEETHOVEN   HOEHN, A.   6
SONATA NO. 23 IN F MINOR, OP. 57 'APPASSIONATA'
SCHOTT   0245-6   1.50
BEETHOVEN
SONATA NO. 23 IN F MINOR, OP. 57, 'APPASSIONATA'
G. HENLE MUSIKVERLAG   1.40
BEETHOVEN
SONATA NO. 23 IN F MINOR, OP. 57, 'APPASSIONATA'
G. SCHIRMER, INC.   1.10
BEETHOVEN
SONATA NO. 24 IN F SHARP MINOR, OP. 78
G. SCHIRMER, INC.   .80
BEETHOVEN
SONATA NO. 24 IN F SHARP, OP. 78
FRANCO COLOMBO PUBLICATIONS   ER2341   1.00
BEETHOVEN
SONATA NO. 24 IN G, OP. 79
G. HENLE MUSIKVERLAG   59   1.15
BEETHOVEN   4
SONATA NO. 24 IN G, OP. 79 - ANDANTE
CENTURY MUSIC PUBLISHING COMPANY, INC.   3795   .40
BEETHOVEN   4
SONATA NO. 24 UN G, OP. 79
CENTURY MUSIC PUBLISHING COMPANY, INC.   4088   .40
BEETHOVEN
SONATA NO. 25 IN G, OP. 79
FRANCO COLOMBO PUBLICATIONS   ER2342   1.00
BEETHOVEN
SONATA NO. 25 IN G, OP. 79
G. SCHIRMER, INC.   .80
BEETHOVEN   HOEHN, A.   3
SONATA NO. 25 IN G, OP. 79 'SONATINE'
SCHOTT   0249 1/2   1.00
BEETHOVEN
SONATA NO. 26 IN D FLAT, OP. 81A 'LES ADIEUX'
G. SCHIRMER, INC.   1.10
BEETHOVEN
SONATA NO. 26 IN E FLAT, OP. 81A 'LES ADIEUX'
FRANCO COLOMBO PUBLICATIONS   ER2343   1.00
BEETHOVEN   HOEHN, A.   5
SONATA NO. 26 IN E FLAT, OP. 81A 'LES ADIEUX'
SCHOTT   0250 1/2   1.00
BEETHOVEN
SONATA NO. 26 URTEXT
EDWIN F. KALMUS   3166   1.25
BEETHOVEN
SONATA NO. 27 IN E MINOR, OP. 90
FRANCO COLOMBO PUBLICATIONS   ER2344   1.00
BEETHOVEN
SONATA NO. 27 IN E MINOR, OP. 90
G. SCHIRMER, INC.   1.10
BEETHOVEN
SONATA NO. 27 URTEXT
EDWIN F. KALMUS   3166   1.25
BEETHOVEN
SONATA NO. 28 IN A, OP. 101
G. SCHIRMER, INC.   1.10
BEETHOVEN
SONATA NO. 28 IN A, OP.101
FRANCO COLOMBO PUBLICATIONS   ER2345   1.00
BEETHOVEN
SONATA NO. 28 URTEXT
EDWIN F. KALMUS   3166   1.25
BEETHOVEN
SONATA NO. 29 IN B FLAT, OP. 106 'HAMMERKLAVIER'
FRANCO COLOMBO PUBLICATIONS   ER2346   2.00
BEETHOVEN
SONATA NO. 29 IN B FLAT, OP. 106 'HAMMERKLAVIER'
G. SCHIRMER, INC.   1.50
BEETHOVEN   HOEHN, A.   6
SONATA NO. 29 IN B FLAT, OP. 106 'HAMMERKLAVIER'
SCHOTT   0256-8 1/2   2.50
BEETHOVEN
SONATA NO. 29 URTEXT
EDWIN F. KALMUS   3175   1.25
BEETHOVEN
SONATA NO. 30 IN E, OP. 109
FRANCO COLOMBO PUBLICATIONS   ER2347   1.00
BEETHOVEN
SONATA NO. 30 IN E, OP. 109
G. SCHIRMER, INC.   1.10
BEETHOVEN
SONATA NO. 31 IN A FLAT, OP. 110
FRANCO COLOMBO PUBLICATIONS   ER2348   1.00
BEETHOVEN
SONATA NO. 31 IN A FLAT, OP. 110
G. SCHIRMER, INC.   1.10
BEETHOVEN
SONATA NO. 32 IN C MINOR, OP. 111
FRANCO COLOMBO PUBLICATIONS   ER2349   1.25
BEETHOVEN
SONATA NO. 32 IN C MINOR, OP. 111
G. SCHIRMER, INC.   1.00
BEETHOVEN   HOEHN, A.   6
SONATA NO. 32 IN C MINOR, OP. 111
SCHOTT   0264-5   1.50

BEETHOVEN
    SONATA NO. 32 IN C MINOR, OP. 111 -- FACSIMILE
        DOVER PUBLICATIONS, INC.   21983-6   3.00
BEETHOVEN
    SONATA PATHETIQUE, OP. 13
        ASHLEY DEALERS SERVICE, INC.   ES   1.00
                    2
BEETHOVEN
    SONATINA -- G
        WILLIS MUSIC COMPANY   .30
BEETHOVEN   VAN DYCK
    SONATINA IN C--FOR MANDOLIN AND CEMBALO, TRANSCRIBED FOR PIANO
        G. SCHIRMER, INC.   .75
                    2
BEETHOVEN
    SONATINA IN F
        CENTURY MUSIC PUBLISHING COMPANY, INC.   414   .40
BEETHOVEN
    SONATINA IN F MAJOR
        WILLIS MUSIC COMPANY   .40
                    4
BEETHOVEN
    SONATINA IN G
        BOSTON MUSIC COMPANY   .50
                    2
BEETHOVEN
    SONATINA IN G
        CENTURY MUSIC PUBLISHING COMPANY, INC.   413   .40
                    2
BEETHOVEN
    SONATINA IN G
        WILLIS MUSIC COMPANY   .30
                    2
BEETHOVEN
    SONATINA IN G MAJOR
        WILLIS MUSIC COMPANY   .35
BEETHOVEN
    SONATINA NO. 01
        EDWIN F. KALMUS   3184   1.25
BEETHOVEN
    SONATINA NO. 01 IN G
        CARL FISCHER, INC.   S 1467   .50
BEETHOVEN
    SONATINA NO. 01 IN G
        G. SCHIRMER, INC.   .40
BEETHOVEN
    SONATINA NO. 02
        EDWIN F. KALMUS   3185   1.25
                    5
BEETHOVEN
    SONATINA NO. 02 IN F
        BOSTON MUSIC COMPANY   .50
BEETHOVEN
    SONATINA NO. 02 IN F
        CARL FISCHER, INC.   S 1468   .50
BEETHOVEN
    SONATINA NO. 02 IN F
        G. SCHIRMER, INC.   .40
BEETHOVEN
    SONATINA NO. 03
        EDWIN F. KALMUS   3186   1.25
BEETHOVEN
    SONATINA NO. 04
        EDWIN F. KALMUS   3187   1.00
BEETHOVEN
    SONATINA NO. 05
        EDWIN F. KALMUS   3188   1.00
BEETHOVEN
    SONATINA NO. 06
        EDWIN F. KALMUS   3189   1.00
BEETHOVEN   SCHAUM, J.   1
    SONG OF JOY
        SCHAUM PUBLICATIONS, INC.   .60
                    3
BEETHOVEN
    SPIRIT WALTZ
        CENTURY MUSIC PUBLISHING COMPANY, INC.   818   .40
BEETHOVEN
    SYMPHONY NO. 01 IN C, OP. 21
        FRANCO COLOMBO PUBLICATIONS   ER403   1.25
BEETHOVEN
    SYMPHONY NO. 03 IN E FLAT, OP. 55 'EROICA'
        FRANCO COLOMBO PUBLICATIONS   ER405   1.75
BEETHOVEN
    SYMPHONY NO. 05 IN C MINOR
        ASHLEY DEALERS SERVICE, INC.   1.95
BEETHOVEN   GOETSCHIUS, P.
    SYMPHONY NO. 05 IN C MINOR
        THEODORE PRESSER COMPANY   1.75
BEETHOVEN
    SYMPHONY NO. 05 IN C MINOR, OP. 67
        FRANCO COLOMBO PUBLICATIONS   130181   2.75
                    3
BEETHOVEN
    SYMPHONY NO. 05, ALLEGRO CON BRIO
        CENTURY MUSIC PUBLISHING COMPANY, INC. 3532   .40
                    2
BEETHOVEN
    SYMPHONY NO. 05, ANDANTE CON MOTO
        CENTURY MUSIC PUBLISHING COMPANY, INC. 3428   .40
                    3
BEETHOVEN
    SYMPHONY NO. 05, VICTORY THEME
        CENTURY MUSIC PUBLISHING COMPANY, INC. 3532   .40
BEETHOVEN
    SYMPHONY NO. 06 IN F, OP. 68 'PASTORAL'
        FRANCO COLOMBO PUBLICATIONS   130306   2.25
BEETHOVEN
    SYMPHONY NO. 07 IN A, OP. 92
        FRANCO COLOMBO PUBLICATIONS   ER409   1.50
                    4
BEETHOVEN
    SYMPHONY NO. 07, ALLEGRETTO
        CENTURY MUSIC PUBLISHING COMPANY, INC. 129   .40
                    4
BEETHOVEN
    SYMPHONY NO. 08, ALLEGRETTO SCHERZANDO
        CENTURY MUSIC PUBLISHING COMPANY, INC. 3643   .40
BEETHOVEN
    SYMPHONY NO. 09 IN D MINOR, OP. 125 'CHORAL'
        FRANCO COLOMBO PUBLICATIONS   129761   3.25
                    2
BEETHOVEN
    SYMPHONY NO. 09, CHORAL THEME
        CENTURY MUSIC PUBLISHING COMPANY, INC. 3759   .40
BEETHOVEN   WALLIS
    THEME -- FIRST MOVEMENT -- FROM 'MOONLIGHT SONATA'
        BOSTON MUSIC COMPANY   .50
BEETHOVEN   THOMPSON, J.   2
    THEME FROM FIFTH SYMPHONY
        WILLIS MUSIC COMPANY   .40
BEETHOVEN   ECKSTEIN
    THEME FROM FIFTH SYMPHONY --FIRST MVT.--
        CARL FISCHER, INC.   S 2283   .50
BEETHOVEN   RUSSELL   2
    THEME FROM SONATA IN E FLAT, OP. 27 NO. 1
        BOSTON MUSIC COMPANY   .50
BEETHOVEN   HARDING, R.   3
    THEME WITH VARIATIONS FROM OP. 26
        WILLIS MUSIC COMPANY   .35

BEETHOVEN
    THIRTY-TWO VARIATIONS
        EDWIN F. KALMUS   3197   1.50
BEETHOVEN   BUELOW *
    THIRTY-TWO VARIATIONS IN C MINOR
        FRANCO COLOMBO PUBLICATIONS   ER2641   1.25
BEETHOVEN
    THIRTY-TWO VARIATIONS IN C MINOR, WO O 80
        G. HENLE MUSIKVERLAG   61   1.15
BEETHOVEN   BUELOW
    THIRTY-TWO VARIATIONS ON AN ORIGINAL THEME IN C MINOR
        G. SCHIRMER, INC.   L1511   1.25
                    3
BEETHOVEN
    TRAUERMARSCH AUS DER SONATE OP. 26 AS-DUR
        SCHOTT   0284   .75
                    3
BEETHOVEN
    TURKISCHER MARSCH AUS, DIE RUINEN VON ATHEN
        SCHOTT   0285 1/2   1900
                    5
BEETHOVEN
    TURKISH MARCH, RUINS OF ATHENS
        CENTURY MUSIC PUBLISHING COMPANY, INC. 2406   .40
                    3
BEETHOVEN
    VARIATIONS, NEL COR
        CENTURY MUSIC PUBLISHING COMPANY, INC. 3494   .40
                    M
BEETHOVEN
    VIOLIN CONCERTO, OP. 61. ABRIDGED PIANO SOLO ARRANGEMENT
        C. F. PETERS CORPORATION   1898   1.50
BEETHOVEN   BARTH, H.
    WALTZ IN G
        BELWIN-MILLS PUBLISHING CORPORATION   20376   .60
                    6
BEETHOVEN
    ZWEI UND DREIZIG VARIATIONEN C-MOLL
        SCHOTT   0290 1/2   1.00
BEETHOVEN *
    CHANT D'ALLIANCE
        GERARD BILLAUDOT EDITIONS MUSICALES   1.60
BEETHOVEN *
    ECOSSAISES
        CARL FISCHER, INC.   P 1481   .75
                    5
BEETHOVEN *
    TURKISH MARCH--RUINS OF ATHENS
        CENTURY MUSIC PUBLISHING COMPANY, INC. 2406   .40
BEETHOVEN *
    WHIRLING DERVISHES CHORUS
        MUSICAL SCOPE PUBLISHERS   01.25
                    2-3
BEETZ
    HIKING
        PRO-ART PUBLICATIONS, INC.   287   .50
                    3
BEETZ
    MARCH OF THE CLOWNS
        PRO-ART PUBLICATIONS, INC.   288   .50
                    3-4
BEGNAC
    GOOD NIGHT AND LULLABY
        PRO-ART PUBLICATIONS, INC.   26   .50
BEHR, F.   SCHAUM, J.   1
    AFRICAN SAFARI
        BELWIN-MILLS PUBLISHING CORPORATION   .50
                    3
BEHR, F.
    ALPINE MELODY
        CENTURY MUSIC PUBLISHING COMPANY, INC. 1548   .40
                    1
BEHR, F.
    BARCAROLLE
        CENTURY MUSIC PUBLISHING COMPANY, INC. 2255   .40
BEHR, F.   HIRSCHBERG, D.   2A
    CAMP OF THE GYPSIES
        MUSICORD PUBLICATIONS, INC.   .45
                    1
BEHR, F.
    CHILD'S PLAY
        CENTURY MUSIC PUBLISHING COMPANY, INC. 2359   .40
                    3
BEHR, F.
    FIRST VIOLET
        VOLKWEIN BROS.   .25
                    3
BEHR, F.
    FIRST VIOLET, THE
        CENTURY MUSIC PUBLISHING COMPANY, INC. 213   .40
                    1
BEHR, F.
    FRENCH CHILD'S SONG
        CENTURY MUSIC PUBLISHING COMPANY, INC. 1007   .40
                    1
BEHR, F.
    FRENCH CHILD'S SONG
        VOLKWEIN BROS.   .25
                    2
BEHR, F.
    GYPSY ENCAMPMENT, THE
        CENTURY MUSIC PUBLISHING COMPANY, INC. 238   .40
                    1
BEHR, F.
    IN MAY, OP. 575 NO. 2
        BELWIN-MILLS PUBLISHING CORPORATION   31   .60
BEHR, F.
    IN MAY, OP. 575 NO. 2
        G. SCHIRMER, INC.   .35
BEHR, F.
    IN THE GYPSY CAMP, OP. 424, NO. 3
        G. SCHIRMER, INC.   .50
                    1
BEHR, F.
    IN THE MONTH OF MAY
        CENTURY MUSIC PUBLISHING COMPANY, INC. 1014   .40
                    1
BEHR, F.
    IN THE MONTH OF MAY
        VOLKWEIN BROS.   .25
                    1
BEHR, F.
    LITTLE HUNGARIAN MELODY OP. 503 NO. 13
        THEODORE PRESSER COMPANY   .50
BEHR, F.   KAHL   1
    SPRING
        BOSTON MUSIC COMPANY   .50
                    1
BEHR, F.
    TANDELEI, OP. 575 NO. 3
        CENTURY MUSIC PUBLISHING COMPANY, INC. 2559   .40
BEIDERBECKE, B.
    DAVENPORT BLUES
        THE BIG THREE MUSIC CORPORATION   00.95
BEIDERBECKE, B.
    IN A MIST
        THE BIG THREE MUSIC CORPORATION   00.95
BEISSERT
    BLACK BOOTS
        SUMMY-BIRCHARD COMPANY   .50
BEISSERT
    PUPPET PARADE
        G. SCHIRMER, INC.   .35
                    3
BEISSERT
    SPOOKY NIGHTS
        WILLIS MUSIC COMPANY   .35
                    2
BEISSERT
    TOY TOWN BRIGADE
        WILLIS MUSIC COMPANY   .40

BEISSERT   2
  TOYTOWN BRIGADE
    WILLIS MUSIC COMPANY   .40
BELL   1 1/2
  CHILDREN'S MINUET
    BELWIN-MILLS PUBLISHING CORPORATION   .60
BELLINI   PALMERI
  CANTO NAPOLETANO
    G. SCHIRMER, INC.   .50
BELLINI   DEL MAGLIO
  DOLENTE IMAGINE
    FRANCO COLOMBO PUBLICATIONS   128122   .50
BELLINI   BURGMUELLER   2
  MARCH, NORMA
    CENTURY MUSIC PUBLISHING COMPANY, INC.   647   .40
BELLINI
  NORMA - CASTA DIVA
    FRANCO COLOMBO PUBLICATIONS   123380   .60
BELLINI   DEL MAGLIO
  NORMA - CASTA DIVA
    FRANCO COLOMBO PUBLICATIONS   128139   .50
BELLINI   DEL MAGLIO
  NORMA - DELL'AURA TUA PROFETICA
    FRANCO COLOMBO PUBLICATIONS   124708   .60
BELLINI   CHIESA
  NORMA - EASY FANTASIA
    FRANCO COLOMBO PUBLICATIONS   107494   .50
BELLINI
  NORMA - OVERTURE
    FRANCO COLOMBO PUBLICATIONS   128370   1.00
BELLINI
  NORMA -- COMPLETE OPERA --
    FRANCO COLOMBO PUBLICATIONS   41007   5.00
BELLINI   KRUG   2
  NORMA, EASY TRANSCRIPTION
    CENTURY MUSIC PUBLISHING COMPANY, INC.   525   .40
BELLINI   CHIESA
  PURITANI, I - EASY FANTASIA
    FRANCO COLOMBO PUBLICATIONS   107492   .60
BELLINI   CHIESA
  SONNAMBULA, LA - EASY FANTASIA
    FRANCO COLOMBO PUBLICATIONS   107493   .60
BELLISARIO, A.
  TRE PICCOLI PEZZO
    EDIZIONI BERBEN   EB 1740   1.25
BELTON, J.
  TIME MARCHES ON
    BELWIN-MILLS PUBLISHING CORPORATION   20311   .85
BELWOOD, E.   1
  GOBLINS, THE
    WILLIS MUSIC COMPANY   .35
BEN-HAIM
  MELODY AND VARIATIONS
    ALEXANDER BROUDE, INC.   3.50
BEN-HAIM
  MUSIC FOR PIANO - 1957
    ALEXANDER BROUDE, INC.   2.80
BEN-HAIM
  MUSIC FOR PIANO - 1967
    ALEXANDER BROUDE, INC.   3.50
BEN-HAIM
  PIANO SONATA
    ALEXANDER BROUDE, INC.   3.50
BEN-HAIM
  SONATINA, OP. 38
    MCA MUSIC   1.75
BEN-YOHANAN
  PRELUDE AND TOCCATA
    ISRAEL MUSIC INSTITUTE   5.00
BENBOW
  DANCE OF THE ATOMS
    FRANCO COLOMBO PUBLICATIONS   LD451   .60
BENBOW
  PETITE MARCHE
    FRANCO COLOMBO PUBLICATIONS   LD545   .60
BENBOW
  RHAPSODY
    FRANCO COLOMBO PUBLICATIONS   LD550   1.25
BENDA, R.
  DARK EYES
    G. SCHIRMER, INC.   .50
BENDER
  EINE VERGNEUGTE KLAVIERMUSIK
    BARENREITER VERLAG   BA2071   3.00
BENEDICT   MENDEL, S.   1 1/2
  CARNIVAL OF VENICE
    WILLIS MUSIC COMPANY   .40
BENFORD   1-2
  CIRCUS CLOWN
    PRO-ART PUBLICATIONS, INC.   434   .50
BENFORD   2-3
  DOODLING
    PRO-ART PUBLICATIONS, INC.   370   .50
BENFORD   1-2
  EXPLORER '88'
    PRO-ART PUBLICATIONS, INC.   185   .50
BENFORD   1-2
  FLYING SAUCER
    PRO-ART PUBLICATIONS, INC.   184   .50
BENFORD   1-2
  LONESOME GOLDFISH
    PRO-ART PUBLICATIONS, INC.   485   .50
BENFORD   2-3
  MARCHING PIXIE
    PRO-ART PUBLICATIONS, INC.   158   .50
BENFORD   2-3
  MISCHIEVOUS PIXIE
    PRO-ART PUBLICATIONS, INC.   159   .50
BENFORD   2
  MOON JUMP
    PRO-ART PUBLICATIONS, INC.   535   .50
BENFORD   3
  PINWHEELS
    PRO-ART PUBLICATIONS, INC.   93   .50
BENFORD   1-2
  RAINDROPS
    PRO-ART PUBLICATIONS, INC.   369   .50
BENFORD   3
  SWARM OF BEES
    PRO-ART PUBLICATIONS, INC.   95   .50
BENFORD   2
  TEDDY BEAR WALTZ
    PRO-ART PUBLICATIONS, INC.   94   .50
BENGUERREL, X.
  ESTRUCTURA IV, 1966
    SEESAW MUSIC CORPORATION   3.00

BENJAMIN
  CHINOISERIE
    BOOSEY AND HAWKES, INC.   1.25
BENJAMIN
  FANTASIES, BK. 1
    BOOSEY AND HAWKES, INC.   1.50
BENJAMIN
  FESTIVAL GROUPS FOR PIANO SELECTED BY ARTHUR BENJAMIN, SERIES 1
  -- A GAY STUDY
    BOOSEY AND HAWKES, INC.   .60
BENJAMIN
  FESTIVAL GROUPS FOR PIANO SELECTED BY ARTHUR BENJAMIN, SERIES 2
  -- A REST BY THE BROOKLET
    BOOSEY AND HAWKES, INC.   .60
BENJAMIN
  FOREST PEACE
    BOOSEY AND HAWKES, INC.   .40
BENJAMIN
  HAUNTED HOUSE
    BOOSEY AND HAWKES, INC.   .40
BENJAMIN
  JAMAICAN RUMBA
    BOOSEY AND HAWKES, INC.   .60
BENJAMIN
  LET'S GO HIKING
    BOOSEY AND HAWKES, INC.   .90
BENJAMIN
  PASTORALE, ARIOSO AND FINALE
    BOOSEY AND HAWKES, INC.   2.75
BENJAMIN
  RAINY DAY
    BOOSEY AND HAWKES, INC.   .40
BENJAMIN
  SCHERZINO
    BOOSEY AND HAWKES, INC.   1.00
BENJAMIN
  SICILIANA
    BOOSEY AND HAWKES, INC.   .75
BENJAMIN
  SQUIRREL'S PARADE
    BOOSEY AND HAWKES, INC.   .40
BENJAMIN
  TAMBOURIN
    BOOSEY AND HAWKES, INC.   .90
BENJAMIN
  THREE LITTLE PIECES
    BOOSEY AND HAWKES, INC.   .75
BENNER, L.
  DANCING -- 3 PIECES
    BENNER PUBLISHERS   .85
BENNETT   GLOVER, D.
  RED CROSS FOR A BLUE LADY
    BELWIN-MILLS PUBLISHING CORPORATION   .60
BENNETT, R.
  DIVERSIONS FOR PIANO
    UNIVERSAL EDITION   UE 1415E   1.30
BENNETT, R.
  FANTASY
    BELWIN-MILLS PUBLISHING CORPORATION   07036   3.00
BENNETT, R.
  FIREFLIES ON PARADE
    SAM FOX PUBLISHING COMPANY, INC.   .75
BENNETT, R.
  FIREFLIES ON PARADE
    SOUTHERN MUSIC COMPANY   .75
BENNETT, R.
  FIVE STUDIES FOR PIANO
    UNIVERSAL EDITION   UE 12995   2.75
BENNETT, R.
  FOUR FREEDOMS SYMPHONY
    THE BIG THREE MUSIC CORPORATION   03.00
BENNETT, R.
  PARTY PIECE FOR YOUNG PLAYERS, PARTS
    UNIVERSAL EDITION   15425A   6.30
BENNETT, R.
  PIANO CONCERTO
    UNIVERSAL EDITION   UE 14656   5.50
BENNETT, R.
  SEVEN DAYS A WEEK
    BELWIN-MILLS PUBLISHING CORPORATION   07090   1.50
BENNETT, R.
  SONATA
    UNIVERSAL EDITION   UE 12349   2.10
BENNETT, R.
  WEEK OF BIRTHDAYS
    BELWIN-MILLS PUBLISHING CORPORATION   07007   1.50
BENOIST, A.   4
  PRELUDE IN E FLAT
    VOLKWEIN BROS.   .60
BENSON
  IF I COULD BE
    MCA MUSIC   .60
BENSON   WILLIAMS, J.   1
  MARKETING
    BOSTON MUSIC COMPANY   .50
BENSON
  RECIPE FOR A LITTLE GIRL
    MCA MUSIC   .60
BENSON   1
  ROBIN SINGS A MERRY TUNE
    BOSTON MUSIC COMPANY   .50
BENTLEY
  BY THE SEA
    SUMMY-BIRCHARD COMPANY   .50
BENTLEY   3
  CHINESE LANDSCAPE
    BELWIN-MILLS PUBLISHING CORPORATION   .60
BENTLEY   4
  CHRISTMAS CAROL
    THEODORE PRESSER COMPANY   .60
BENTLEY
  DANCE OF THE HOBGOBLINS
    CARL FISCHER, INC.   RS 362   .50
BENTLEY
  DANCE, GYPSY
    SUMMY-BIRCHARD COMPANY   .50
BENTLEY   2
  DANCING BY CANDLELIGHT
    BELWIN-MILLS PUBLISHING CORPORATION   .60
BENTLEY   3
  DAY AT THE BEACH, A
    THEODORE PRESSER COMPANY   .50
BENTLEY
  DRIFTING MOON
    SUMMY-BIRCHARD COMPANY   .50

BENTLEY
  ELF AND THE FAIRY, THE
    SUMMY-BIRCHARD COMPANY   .50
BENTLEY
  HERE, THERE AND EVERYWHERE
    THEODORE PRESSER COMPANY   1.25
BENTLEY   E
  LATVIAN LULLABY
    BELWIN-MILLS PUBLISHING CORPORATION   25127   .60
BENTLEY
  LITTLE HARPIST, THE
    SUMMY-BIRCHARD COMPANY   .50
BENTLEY   2
  MISCHIEVOUS ELF
    BELWIN-MILLS PUBLISHING CORPORATION   .60
BENTLEY
  PRAELUDIUM
    SUMMY-BIRCHARD COMPANY   .40
BENTLEY
  RESTLESS SEA, THE
    SUMMY-BIRCHARD COMPANY   .75
BENTLEY
  SAGEBRUSH SERENADE
    SUMMY-BIRCHARD COMPANY   .50
BENTLEY
  SHIP AHOY
    SUMMY-BIRCHARD COMPANY   .50
BENTLEY   1
  SOFTLY SNOWING
    BELWIN-MILLS PUBLISHING CORPORATION   .60
BENTLEY
  SONATINA IN D MAJOR
    WARNER BROTHERS PUBLISHERS   1.00
BENTLEY   2 1/2
  SONG OF THE BAMBOO TREE
    THEODORE PRESSER COMPANY   .50
BENTLEY
  SONG OF THE WILD BEE
    SUMMY-BIRCHARD COMPANY   .50
BENTLEY   2 1/2
  TALE OF LONG AGO, A
    THEODORE PRESSER COMPANY   .50
BENUSSAN, M.
  NOVELETTE
    BROUDE BROTHERS LTD.   02.00
BERBERIAN, C.
  MORSICATHY
    UNIVERSAL EDITION   UE 15162   6.75
BERENS, H.
  SONATINA, THIRD MOVEMENT
    FREDERICK HARRIS MUSIC COMPANY   .60
BERENY
  KARPATHIA CZARDAS
    FRANCO COLOMBO PUBLICATIONS   SAL   1.50
BERG, A.
  SONATA, OP. 1
    UNIVERSAL EDITION   UE 8812   3.75
BERGENFELD, N.   1
  BUTTERFLY, BUTTERFLY
    PRO-ART PUBLICATIONS, INC.   549   .50
BERGENFELD, N.   1
  SALMON, THE
    PRO-ART PUBLICATIONS, INC.   550   .50
BERGER
  AMOUREUSE
    BELWIN-MILLS PUBLISHING CORPORATION   .60
BERGER
  AMOUREUSE - WALTZ
    FRANCO COLOMBO PUBLICATIONS   NY2113   .60
BERGER   SCHAUM, J.   3
  ANOUREUSE
    BELWIN-MILLS PUBLISHING CORPORATION   .50
BERGER   MD
  RONDO
    THEODORE PRESSER COMPANY   .60
BERGER   6
  SONATINA
    THEODORE PRESSER COMPANY   .85
BERKMAN, V.
  ELVES IN THE FOREST
    BELWIN-MILLS PUBLISHING CORPORATION   25045   .60
BERKMAN, V.
  PRELUDE
    SUMMY-BIRCHARD COMPANY   .45
BERKOWITZ
  GAME OF DANCE
    FRANK MUSIC CORPORATION   .95
BERLA, F.   1
  SNOW SCRAMBLE
    BELWIN-MILLS PUBLISHING CORPORATION   .60
BERLIN, B.
  MERRY-GO-ROUND, THE
    FREDERICK HARRIS MUSIC COMPANY   .45
BERLIN, B.
  SQUIRRELS AT PLAY
    FREDERICK HARRIS MUSIC COMPANY   .60
BERLIN, B.
  VOYAGER'S FAREWELL
    FREDERICK HARRIS MUSIC COMPANY   .60
BERLIN, B.
  YANINA
    FREDERICK HARRIS MUSIC COMPANY   .60
BERLIN, J. D.   E
  SONATINA
    C. F. PETERS CORPORATION   LY8   .60
BERLIOZ   M
  BALLET DES TROYENS A CARTHAGE
    C. F. PETERS CORPORATION   C26   3.00
BERLIOZ *   6
  RAKOCZY MARCH
    CENTURY MUSIC PUBLISHING COMPANY, INC. 370   .40
BERMONT, G.
  ALADDINS LAMP
    EDWARD B. MARKS MUSIC CORPORATION   00.60
BERMONT, G.
  CAROUSEL
    EDWARD B. MARKS MUSIC CORPORATION   00.60
BERMONT, G.
  GOLDFISH IN THE BOWL
    EDWARD B. MARKS MUSIC CORPORATION   00.60
BERMONT, G.
  MARCH OF THE MOON MEN
    EDWARD B. MARKS MUSIC CORPORATION   00.60
BERMONT, G.
  MY FIRST DANCE
    EDWARD B. MARKS MUSIC CORPORATION   00.60

BERMONT, G.   EASY
  WALTZ OF THE TOYS
    SHAWNEE PRESS, INC.   HB-5005   .60
BERMONT, H.   1A
  ALONG THE MOHAWK TRAIL
    MUSICORD PUBLICATIONS, INC.   .45
BERMONT, H.   2A
  AUTUMN NYMPH
    MUSICORD PUBLICATIONS, INC.   .45
BERMONT, H.   1B
  CIRCUS DAYS
    MUSICORD PUBLICATIONS, INC.   .45
BERMONT, H.   2A
  CONCERT IN THE PARK
    MUSICORD PUBLICATIONS, INC.   .45
BERMONT, H.   1A
  HOLIDAY IN MEXICO
    MUSICORD PUBLICATIONS, INC.   .45
BERMONT, H.   2A
  JOLLY MILLER
    MUSICORD PUBLICATIONS, INC.   .45
BERMONT, H.   2A
  JOLLY SAILOR LADS
    MUSICORD PUBLICATIONS, INC.   .45
BERMONT, H.
  JOY TO THE WORLD
    ALFRED MUSIC COMPANY   643   1.25
BERMONT, H.   2A
  PARADE OF THE LOLLIPOPS
    MUSICORD PUBLICATIONS, INC.   .45
BERMONT, H.   2A
  PUPPET POLKA
    MUSICORD PUBLICATIONS, INC.   .45
BERMONT, H.   1B
  WALTZ OF THE PEACOCKS
    MUSICORD PUBLICATIONS, INC.   .45
BERNA
  CHIQUITO -- TANGO
    BOSTON MUSIC COMPANY   .50
BERNA   2
  SPRING FLOWERS
    BOSTON MUSIC COMPANY   .50
BERNA   3
  TO A REDWOOD TREE
    BOSTON MUSIC COMPANY   .50
BERNAL, J.
  ANTIGUA VALLADOLID
    PEER SOUTHERN ORGANIZATION   01.00
BERNAL, J.
  CARTELES
    PEER SOUTHERN ORGANIZATION   02.00
BERNARD, O.
  PROMENADES
    ELKAN-VOGEL, INC.   CON   3.50
BERNHEIM
  AIR ANCIEN
    FRANCO COLOMBO PUBLICATIONS   SAL   2.50
BERNHEIM
  ARLEQUIN
    FRANCO COLOMBO PUBLICATIONS   SAL   2.75
BERNSTEIN, E.
  FROM THE TERRACE
    THE BIG THREE MUSIC CORPORATION   00.95
BERNSTEIN, L.
  FIVE ANNIVERSARIES
    G. SCHIRMER, INC.   1.25
BERNSTEIN, L.
  FOUR ANNIVERSARIES
    G. SCHIRMER, INC.   .75
BERNSTEIN, L.   SINGER
  MARIA, FROM 'WEST SIDE STORY'
    G. SCHIRMER, INC.   .60
BERNSTEIN, L.
  SEVEN ANNIVERSARIES -- CYCLE
    WARNER BROTHERS PUBLISHERS   1.25
BERNSTEIN, L.   SINGER
  TONIGHT, FROM 'WEST SIDE STORY'
    G. SCHIRMER, INC.   .60
BERNSTEIN, M.   4
  PIROUETTE
    BELWIN-MILLS PUBLISHING CORPORATION   .60
BERNSTEIN, S.   M
  KOREAN BLUEBIRD
    COMPOSERS PRESS, INC.   1.00
BERNSTEIN, S.   E
  SAD PUPPET, THE
    COMPOSERS PRESS, INC.   1.00
BERRILL, R.
  LOVE MAKES THE WORLD GO 'ROUND
    THE BIG THREE MUSIC CORPORATION   00.95
BERTHELEMY
  ESQUISSE
    GERARD BILLAUDOT EDITIONS MUSICALES   1.60
BERTRAND, C.   BROWN   2
  ITZY BITZY SPIDER
    WILLIS MUSIC COMPANY   .30
BERTRAND, C.   2
  SKIP TO MY LOU
    WILLIS MUSIC COMPANY   .35
BERVILLY
  TWO PIECES CARACTERISTIQUES - DANSE ORGIAQUE
    FRANCO COLOMBO PUBLICATIONS   SAL   1.75
BERVILLY
  TWO PIECES CARACTERISTIQUES - HUERE TRISTE
    FRANCO COLOMBO PUBLICATIONS   SAL   1.75
BESTHOFF, M.
  BUSY WOODPECKER, THE
    BELWIN-MILLS PUBLISHING CORPORATION   25202   .60
BESTHOFF, M.
  CHINESE SANDMAN
    BELWIN-MILLS PUBLISHING CORPORATION   25021   .60
BESTHOFF, M.
  MARCH IN F
    BELWIN-MILLS PUBLISHING CORPORATION   25070   .60
BETTINELLI
  FANTASIA -- 1955 --
    FRANCO COLOMBO PUBLICATIONS   129216   1.50
BEVERLY
  BUTTERFLY, A
    BOSTON MUSIC COMPANY   .50
BEYER, F.   3
  IDYLLE D'ENFANTS
    ALPHONSE LEDUC
BEYER, F.   QUADRILLE
  LANCIERS, LES
    FRANCO COLOMBO PUBLICATIONS   SAL   1.75

BEYER, F.   1
    PETITE MELODIE
       ALPHONSE LEDUC
BEYER, F.   SCHAUM, J.   2
    POLKA DOT POLKA
       BELWIN-MILLS PUBLISHING CORPORATION   .50
BEYER, F.   DEL CORONA
    SCUOLA PREPARATORIA, OP. 101
       EDIZIONI BERBEN   1154   3.00
BEYER, F.   2
    UNE TOUTE PETITE MATINEE
       ALPHONSE LEDUC
BEYER, F.   2
    UNE TOUTE PETITE SOIREE
       ALPHONSE LEDUC
BEYER, F.--ED   BEYER, F.   4
    MARSEILLAISE, THE
       CENTURY MUSIC PUBLISHING COMPANY, INC.   635   .40
BIALOSKY, M.   3 1/2
    SPRING SONG, A
       THEODORE PRESSER COMPANY   .50
BICHEL, M.   3
    WALTZ FANTASIE
       WILLIS MUSIC COMPANY   .50
BIGELOW, F.
    OUR DIRECTOR
       FREDERICK HARRIS MUSIC COMPANY   .45
BIGELOW, F.   4
    OUR DIRECTOR MARCH
       CENTURY MUSIC PUBLISHING COMPANY, INC.   4372   .40
BIGELOW, F.
    OUR DIRECTOR MARCH
       THE BIG THREE MUSIC CORPORATION   00.95
BILBRO, M.   1
    BIRDS IN OUR GARDEN
       VOLKWEIN BROS.   .25
BILBRO, M.
    BUSY SAW-MILL, THE
       G. SCHIRMER, INC.   .40
BILBRO, M.   EASY
    CLOWN DANCE
       SHAWNEE PRESS, INC.   HB-5012   .60
BILBRO, M.   1
    JUMPING BEAN
       VOLKWEIN BROS.   .25
BILBRO, M.
    JUST STARTING
       G. SCHIRMER, INC.   1.25
BILBRO, M.   2
    NIGHT JASMINE
       VOLKWEIN BROS.   .25
BILBRO, M.   1
    ONE LOVELY MORNING
       VOLKWEIN BROS.   .25
BILBRO, M.   2
    PRETTY MORNING GLORIES
       VOLKWEIN BROS.   .25
BILBRO, M.   2
    SLEEPING TULIP
       VOLKWEIN BROS.   .25
BILLEMA
    GAZOUILLEMENT DES OISEAUX, LE
       FRANCO COLOMBO PUBLICATIONS   SAL   2.50
BILLEMA
    GAZOUILLEMENT DES OISEAUX, LE
       FRANCO COLOMBO PUBLICATIONS   SAL   2.75
BILLEMA   5
    TWITTERING OF THE BIRDS
       CENTURY MUSIC PUBLISHING COMPANY, INC.   993   .40
BILLI
    EVENING BELLS
       BELWIN-MILLS PUBLISHING CORPORATION   .60
BILOHRUD
    NIGHT SHADOWS
       SUMMY-BIRCHARD COMPANY   .50
BILOTTI
    BERCEUSE
       BOOSEY AND HAWKES, INC.   .50
BILOTTI
    FIREFLY
       CARL FISCHER, INC.   P 2232   .50
BILOTTI
    PRELUDE
       BOOSEY AND HAWKES, INC.   .50
BILOTTI
    VALSE
       BOOSEY AND HAWKES, INC.   .50
BINDER   M
    HORA
       THEODORE PRESSER COMPANY   .50
BINDER
    VARIATIONS ON A YEMENITE THEME
       MCA MUSIC   1.00
BINDER, A. W.   E
    BOAT SONG AT DUSK
       THEODORE PRESSER COMPANY   .50
BINDER, A. W.   M
    FLOWER IN THE WIND
       THEODORE PRESSER COMPANY   .50
BINET
    FANTASIE-TARENTELLE
       ELKAN-VOGEL, INC.   D   2.25
BINET   5
    LA PETITE FILEUSE, OP. 114
       ALPHONSE LEDUC
BINKERD
    CONCERT SET FOR PIANO
       BOOSEY AND HAWKES, INC.   1.50
BINKERD
    ENTERTAINMENTS FOR PIANO
       BOOSEY AND HAWKES, INC.   1.50
BINKERD
    PIANO MISCELLANY
       BOOSEY AND HAWKES, INC.   1.25
BINKERD
    SONATA
       BOOSEY AND HAWKES, INC.   2.00
BINKERD
    YOUNG PIANIST
       BOOSEY AND HAWKES, INC.   1.50
BINKLEY
    BOOGIE ETUDE
       SOUTHERN MUSIC COMPANY   .50
BINKLEY
    CORPORAL TIM
       SAM FOX PUBLISHING COMPANY, INC.   .50

BINKLEY
    CORPORAL TIM
       SOUTHERN MUSIC COMPANY   .50
BINKLEY
    DANCE CREOLE
       SAM FOX PUBLISHING COMPANY, INC.   .50
BINKLEY
    DANCE CREOLE
       SOUTHERN MUSIC COMPANY   .50
BIRBECK   3
    PEARLY DEW DROPS, MAZURKA
       CENTURY MUSIC PUBLISHING COMPANY, INC.   650   .40
BIRBECK   3
    PEARLY DEWDROP
       VOLKWEIN BROS.   .25
BIRCSAK, T.   2 1/2
    CHINESE LULLABY
       THEODORE PRESSER COMPANY   .50
BIRCSAK, T.   2
    HIGHLAND COUNTRY DANCE
       THEODORE PRESSER COMPANY   .50
BIRCSAK, T.   2
    HUMMING BIRD, THE
       THEODORE PRESSER COMPANY   .50
BIRCSAK, T.   1 1/2
    MEXICAN JUMPING BEANS
       THEODORE PRESSER COMPANY   .50
BIRTWISTLE, H.
    PRECIS
       UNIVERSAL EDITION   UE 14158   1.70
BISHOP
    HOE DOWN
       CARL FISCHER, INC.   P 3016   .50
BISHOP   2
    HOME, SWEET HOME, VAR.
       CENTURY MUSIC PUBLISHING COMPANY, INC.   2043   .40
BISHOP
    THUMBNAIL SKETCHES
       CARL FISCHER, INC.   P 3207   .75
BISHOP
    WOODEN SHOE DANCE
       CARL FISCHER, INC.   P 2893   .50
BISHOP
    YANKEE DOODLE
       CARL FISCHER, INC.   P 3017   .50
BISHOP *
    WOODCHOPPER'S BALL
       MCA MUSIC   1.00
BISHOP, R.   PRESSER, T.   6
    HOME SWEET HOME
       THEODORE PRESSER COMPANY   .60
BITSCH   8
    SONATINE
       ALPHONSE LEDUC
BITTNER, J.
    AUSTRIAN DANCES
       UNIVERSAL EDITION   UE 5909   1.50
BITTNER, J.
    SOARING DRAGONFLY
       CARL FISCHER, INC.   P 3175   .50
BIVENS *
    JOSEPHINE
       THE BIG THREE MUSIC CORPORATION   00.95
BIZET, G.   3
    ARLESIENNE SUITE, INTERMEZZO
       CENTURY MUSIC PUBLISHING COMPANY, INC.   3562   .40
BIZET, G.   M
    BALLET 'LES BOHEMIENNES' --JOLIE FILLE DE PERTH--
       C. F. PETERS CORPORATION   C44   3.00
BIZET, G.   M
    CARMEN BALLET
       C. F. PETERS CORPORATION   C238   3.50
BIZET, G.   M
    CARMEN. COMPLETE OPERA IN PIANO SOLO ARRANGEMENT
       C. F. PETERS CORPORATION   C339   7.50
BIZET, G.   E
    CARMEN. COMPLETE.
       C. F. PETERS CORPORATION   H639   2.00
BIZET, G.   KRUG   2
    CARMEN, EASY TRANS.
       CENTURY MUSIC PUBLISHING COMPANY, INC.   2146   .40
BIZET, G.   2
    CARMEN, HABANERA
       CENTURY MUSIC PUBLISHING COMPANY, INC.   2336   .40
BIZET, G.   LOEW, J.   3
    CARMEN, MARCH
       CENTURY MUSIC PUBLISHING COMPANY, INC.   1632   .40
BIZET, G.   3
    CARMEN, TOREADOR SONG
       CENTURY MUSIC PUBLISHING COMPANY, INC.   1577   .40
BIZET, G.   BAMPTON, R.   2
    FESTIVAL BELLS
       BOSTON MUSIC COMPANY   .50
BIZET, G.   SCHAUM, J.   5
    GYPSY DANCE FROM 'CARMEN'
       BELWIN-MILLS PUBLISHING CORPORATION   .50
BIZET, G.   LANGE, G.   4
    HABANERA, FROM 'CARMEN'
       CENTURY MUSIC PUBLISHING COMPANY, INC.   2336   .40
BIZET, G.   LANGE
    HABANERA, FROM 'CARMEN'
       G. SCHIRMER, INC.   .60
BIZET, G.   DEXTER, H.
    L'ARLESIENNE
       SAM FOX PUBLISHING COMPANY, INC.   1.00
BIZET, G.   M
    L'ARLESIENNE SUITE NO.1
       C. F. PETERS CORPORATION   C27   3.00
BIZET, G.   M
    L'ARLESIENNE SUITE NO.2
       C. F. PETERS CORPORATION   C28   3.00
BIZET, G.   3
    L'ARLESIENNE, INTERMEZZO
       CENTURY MUSIC PUBLISHING COMPANY, INC.   3562   .40
BIZET, G.   3
    L'ARLESIENNE, INTERMEZZO
       CENTURY MUSIC PUBLISHING COMPANY, INC.   3562   .40
BIZET, G.   4
    L'ARLESIENNE, MINUETTO
       CENTURY MUSIC PUBLISHING COMPANY, INC.   3977   .40
BIZET, G.   BERLIN
    MARCH FROM L'ARLESIENNE
       FREDERICK HARRIS MUSIC COMPANY   .30
BIZET, G.   WEYBRIGHT   3
    MARCH OF THE TOREADORS
       BELWIN-MILLS PUBLISHING CORPORATION   .60

BIZET, G.   LOEW, J.   3
    MARCH, CARMEN
        CENTURY MUSIC PUBLISHING COMPANY, INC.   1632   .40
BIZET, G.   4
    MINUETTO, L'ARLESIENNE
        CENTURY MUSIC PUBLISHING COMPANY, INC.   3977   .40
BIZET, G.   D
    PATRIE. OUVERTURE DRAMATIQUE
        C. F. PETERS CORPORATION   C24   3.50
BIZET, G.   3
    TOREADOR SONG, CARMEN
        CENTURY MUSIC PUBLISHING COMPANY, INC.   1577   .40
BIZET, G.   WEINGARTNER   D
    VARIATIONS CHROMATIQUES, OP. 3 --CONCERT EDITION--
        C. F. PETERS CORPORATION   C436   3.50
BIZZELLI
    MADONNA PURITA -- BALLET --
        FRANCO COLOMBO PUBLICATIONS   DS374   6.50
BIZZELLI
    TWO EASY LITTLE PIECES
        FRANCO COLOMBO PUBLICATIONS   DS331   1.25
BJERCKE   M
    ROMERIKS SUITE
        C. F. PETERS CORPORATION   LY9   .60
BLACHER
    CHIARINA, OP. 33 -- BALLET IN ONE ACT
        ASSOCIATED MUSIC PUBLISHERS, INC.   BOT   5.00
BLACHER
    DEMETER -- 1963 -- BALLET IN 4 SCENES
        ASSOCIATED MUSIC PUBLISHERS, INC.   BOT   10.00
BLACHER
    FEST IM SUEDEN, OP. 6 -- DANCE-DRAMA IN ONE ACT
        ASSOCIATED MUSIC PUBLISHERS, INC.   BOT   6.00
BLACHER
    HAMLET, OP. 35 -- CHORAL BALLET IN ONE PROLOGUE AND 3 TABLEAUX
        ASSOCIATED MUSIC PUBLISHERS, INC.   BOT   6.00
BLACHER
    LYSISTRATA, OP. 34 -- BALLET IN 3 TABLEAUX
        ASSOCIATED MUSIC PUBLISHERS, INC.   BOT   7.50
BLACHER
    ORNAMENTE, OP. 37 -- 1950 --
        ASSOCIATED MUSIC PUBLISHERS, INC.   B/B   2.00
BLACHER
    SONATA, OP. 39
        ASSOCIATED MUSIC PUBLISHERS, INC.   B/B   3.25
BLACHER
    TRISTAN -- 1965 -- BALLET IN 7 SCENES
        ASSOCIATED MUSIC PUBLISHERS, INC.   BOT   12.00
BLACK, M.   1
    FOOTSTEPS OF SPRING
        WILLIS MUSIC COMPANY   .40
BLACK, M.
    LOLLIPOP BRIGADE, THE
        G. SCHIRMER, INC.   .35
BLACK, M.
    PAPER DOLL
        EDWARD B. MARKS MUSIC CORPORATION   01.00
BLACK, M.
    SPOON BREAD
        G. SCHIRMER, INC.   .35
BLACKFORD, V.   1
    BARNYARD FROLICS
        WILLIS MUSIC COMPANY   .35
BLACKWOOD, E.
    THREE SHORT FANTASIES FOR PIANO, OP. 16
        G. SCHIRMER, INC.   2.00
BLAIN
    PRELUDE 1967
        ASSOCIATED MUSIC PUBLISHERS, INC.   BER   .75
BLAKE   SCHAUM, J.   2
    MEMORIES OF YOU
        SCHAUM PUBLICATIONS, INC.   .75
BLAKE, C.   4
    CLAYTON'S GRAND MARCH
        BELWIN-MILLS PUBLISHING CORPORATION   646   .60
BLAKE, C.   3
    CLAYTON'S GRAND MARCH
        CENTURY MUSIC PUBLISHING COMPANY, INC.   3064   .40
BLAKE, C.   WALLIS   3
    CLAYTON'S GRAND MARCH
        WILLIS MUSIC COMPANY   .50
BLAKE, C.   3
    SHEPHERD'S EVENING SONG
        CENTURY MUSIC PUBLISHING COMPANY, INC.   2732   .40
BLAKE, C.   4
    WAVES OF THE OCEAN, GALOP
        CENTURY MUSIC PUBLISHING COMPANY, INC.   531   .40
BLAKE, D.   1
    BANJO PLAYER
        WILLIS MUSIC COMPANY   .40
BLAKE, D.   3
    HUNTERS AWAY
        WILLIS MUSIC COMPANY   .40
BLAKE, D.   3
    HUNTERS AWAY
        WILLIS MUSIC COMPANY   .40
BLAKE, D.   3
    TANGO
        WILLIS MUSIC COMPANY   .40
BLAKE, D.
    VARIATIONS
        OXFORD UNIVERSITY PRESS   32.927   2.00
BLAKE, D. G.   2
    CAPTAIN KIDD
        THEODORE PRESSER COMPANY   .50
BLAKE, D. G.   3
    TAMBOURINE
        WILLIS MUSIC COMPANY   .50
BLAKE, M. D.   1 1/2
    FOLLOW THE LEADER
        THEODORE PRESSER COMPANY   .50
BLANC
    HOMMAGE A MUSSET
        FRANCO COLOMBO PUBLICATIONS   SAL   1.50
BLANC
    NOCTURNE
        FRANCO COLOMBO PUBLICATIONS   SAL   1.50
BLANC
    POUR BERCER
        FRANCO COLOMBO PUBLICATIONS   SAL   1.50
BLANC
    STALACTITE
        MCA MUSIC   1.00
BLANC DE FONTBELLE
    A LA MEMOIRE DE LILY BOULANGER
        FRANCO COLOMBO PUBLICATIONS   SAL   1.75

BLANC DE FONTBELLE
    BROUILLARD MONTAIT DOUCEMENT DANS LA NUIT
        FRANCO COLOMBO PUBLICATIONS   SAL   2.50
BLANC DE FONTBELLE
    TWO POLYTONAL STUDIES - NO. 1
        FRANCO COLOMBO PUBLICATIONS   SAL   4.00
BLANC DE FONTBELLE
    TWO POLYTONAL STUDIES - NO. 2
        FRANCO COLOMBO PUBLICATIONS   SAL   4.00
BLANC DE FONTBELLE
    VENT LEGER COURBE LES BRANCHES, UN
        FRANCO COLOMBO PUBLICATIONS   SAL   2.75
BLANCAFORT
    POLKA DE L'EQUILIBRISTE
        FRANCO COLOMBO PUBLICATIONS   SAL   1.75
BLANCAFORT
    SONATA -- 1955 --
        ASSOCIATED MUSIC PUBLISHERS, INC.   UME   2.00
BLANCHET
    DIVERTIMENTO IN C, OP. 47
        ASSOCIATED MUSIC PUBLISHERS, INC.   ESC   1.60
BLANCO
    AUGUSTINA DE ARAGON. GRAN JOTA ARAGONESA
        ASSOCIATED MUSIC PUBLISHERS, INC.   UME   .65
BLAND   2
    CARRY ME BACK TO OLD VIRGINNY
        CENTURY MUSIC PUBLISHING COMPANY, INC.   3468   .40
BLISS, A.
    BALLET 'ADAM ZERO', PIANO SCORE
        NOVELLO AND COMPANY, LTD.   10.0005.05 4.90
BLISS, A.
    BALLET 'CHECKMATE', PIANO SCORE
        NOVELLO AND COMPANY, LTD.   10.0007.01 6.25
BLISS, A.
    BALLET 'MIRACLE IN THE GORBALS', PIANO SCORE
        NOVELLO AND COMPANY, LTD.   10.0006.03 3.65
BLISS, A.
    LADY OF SHALOTT, THE -- EXCERP FROM THE BALLET
        NOVELLO AND COMPANY, LTD.   10.0008.10 .90
BLISS, A.
    PIANO SONATA
        NOVELLO AND COMPANY, LTD.   10.0010.01 2.75
BLISS, P.   3
    ARBUTUS
        WILLIS MUSIC COMPANY   .50
BLISS, P.   3
    TUMBLE-WEED
        THEODORE PRESSER COMPANY   .75
BLOCH, E.
    CLOWN, THE
        BROUDE BROTHERS LTD.   02.00
BLOCH, E.
    DANSE SACREE
        BROUDE BROTHERS LTD.   02.50
BLOCH, E.
    DIALOGUE AND DANCE OF THE HEAVYWEIGHT AND DWARF
        BROUDE BROTHERS LTD.   02.00
BLOCH, E.
    EX-VOTO
        BROUDE BROTHERS LTD.   01.50
BLOCH, E.
    FIVE SKETCHES IN SEPIA
        G. SCHIRMER, INC.   1.25
BLOCH, E.
    HOMLIEST WOMAN, THE
        BROUDE BROTHERS LTD.   01.75
BLOCH, E.
    IN THE NIGHT
        G. SCHIRMER, INC.   .60
BLOCH, E.
    POEMS OF THE SEA--CYCLE
        G. SCHIRMER, INC.   2.50
BLOCH, E.
    SONATA PER PIANOFORTE
        BELWIN-MILLS PUBLISHING CORPORATION   20411   2.00
BLOCH, E.
    TWO 'BURLINGHAM' BROTHERS, THE
        BROUDE BROTHERS LTD.   02.00
BLOCH, E.
    VISIONS ET PROPHETIES
        G. SCHIRMER, INC.   1.25
BLOCK--ED   BLOCK   2-3
    JARABE TAPATIO, HAT DANCE
        CENTURY MUSIC PUBLISHING COMPANY, INC.   3647   .40
BLOOM
    SOLILOQUY
        BELWIN-MILLS PUBLISHING CORPORATION   20256   .95
BLOOM, R.
    SONG OF THE BAYOU
        THE BIG THREE MUSIC CORPORATION   00.95
BLOSE, J.   5 1/2
    NOCTURNE IN D FLAT
        THEODORE PRESSER COMPANY   .60
BLOWER, M.   7
    SOLITUDE
        NOVELLO AND COMPANY, LTD.   55.0034.06 .25
BLUMENFELD
    TRANSFORMATIONS FOR PIANO, 1963
        SEESAW MUSIC CORPORATION   5.00
BLUMENTHAL   5
    TWO ANGELS, THE
        CENTURY MUSIC PUBLISHING COMPANY, INC.   1101   .40
BLYTH   3
    DANCE AND QUIET TIME
        LEE ROBERTS MUSIC PUBLICATIONS, INC.   .85
BLYTH   6
    TOCCATA
        LEE ROBERTS MUSIC PUBLICATIONS, INC.   .85
BOCAGE *   MAXTED
    MAM'S GONE, GOODBYE
        MCA MUSIC   1.00
BOCCHERINI
    FAMOUS MINUET - FROM QUINTET, OP. 13 NO. 5
        FRANCO COLOMBO PUBLICATIONS   45917   .60
BOCCHERINI   CHIESA
    FAMOUS MINUET - FROM QUINTET, OP. 13 NO. 5
        FRANCO COLOMBO PUBLICATIONS   107478   .60
BOCCHERINI   DEL MAGLIO
    SECOND FAMOUS MINUET
        FRANCO COLOMBO PUBLICATIONS   128151   .50
BOCCHERINI   MAFFIOLETTI   3-4
    SONATE IN E FLAT
        BARENREITER VERLAG   CM 15763
BOCCHERINI, L.   4
    MENUET
        CENTURY MUSIC PUBLISHING COMPANY, INC.   826   .40

```
BOCCHERINI, L.                                        3
    MENUETT
        SCHOTT                              0893        .75
BOCCHERINI, L.
    MINUET IN A MAJOR
        G. SCHIRMER, INC.                               .50
BOCCI
    GIRASOLE BALDANZOSO, IL
        FRANCO COLOMBO PUBLICATIONS         DS962      1.25
BOCCOSI, B.
    SUITE IN FORMA DI VARIAZIONI
        EDIZIONI BERBEN                     EB 1544    5.40
BOCCOSI, BIO
    BIALLO E ROSSO
        EDIZIONI BERBEN                     EB 1270    1.20
BOCCOSI, BIO
    PICCOLO BARCAROLA
        EDIZIONI BERBEN                     EB 1266     .90
BOCK, J.                  SCHAUM, J.         2 1/2
    FIDDLER ON THE ROOF
        SCHAUM PUBLICATIONS, INC.                       .75
BOCK, J.                  SCHAUM, J.         1 1/2
    IF I WERE A RICH MAN
        SCHAUM PUBLICATIONS, INC.                       .75
BOCK, J.                  SCHAUM, J.         2
    MATCHMAKER
        SCHAUM PUBLICATIONS, INC.                       .75
BOCK, J.                  SCHAUM, J.         1
    SUNRISE, SUNSET
        SCHAUM PUBLICATIONS, INC.                       .75
BODYCOMBE, A.                                         4
    VALSE GRACILE
        VOLKWEIN BROS.                                00.50
BOEHME                    WEYBRIGHT          2
    AMERICAN EAGLE MARCH
        BELWIN-MILLS PUBLISHING CORPORATION             .50
BOEHME                    WEYBRIGHT          2
    AMERICAN EAGLE MARCH
        BELWIN-MILLS PUBLISHING CORPORATION             .60
BOEHMER, A.
    VARIATIONS ON A PLAY TUNE
        COMPOSERS AUTOGRAPH PUBLICATIONS               1.54
BOELLMANN, L.
    RONDE FRANCAISE
        ELKAN-VOGEL, INC.                  D           2.25
BOELLMANN, L.
    SUITE GOTHIQUE
        ELKAN-VOGEL, INC.                  D           4.25
BOERO
    SUITE INFANTIL
        FRANCO COLOMBO PUBLICATIONS        BA10218     1.25
BOHM                                                 3
    A LA VALSE, IMPROMPTU, G MAJOR
        CENTURY MUSIC PUBLISHING COMPANY, INC.  1203    .40
BOHM                                                 3
    ALPINE FLOWER
        CENTURY MUSIC PUBLISHING COMPANY, INC.  743     .40
BOHM                                                 3
    ALPINE FLOWER, F MAJOR, OP. 279 NO. 1
        CENTURY MUSIC PUBLISHING COMPANY, INC.  743     .40
BOHM
    ATTAQUE DES UHLANS--GRAND MILITARY GALOP, OP. 213
        G. SCHIRMER, INC.
                          THOMPSON, J.       5          .50
BOHM
    CALM AS THE NIGHT
        WILLIS MUSIC COMPANY                            .40
BOHM                                                 4
    CHARGE OF THE UHLANS
        CENTURY MUSIC PUBLISHING COMPANY, INC.  764     .40
BOHM                                                 4
    DANCE ON THE GREEN
        CENTURY MUSIC PUBLISHING COMPANY, INC.  1331    .40
BOHM                                                 3
    DANCING SPIRITS
        CENTURY MUSIC PUBLISHING COMPANY, INC.  1003    .40
BOHM                                                 3
    ENFANT CHERI - LITTLE DEAREST
        CENTURY MUSIC PUBLISHING COMPANY, INC.  282     .40
BOHM                                                 4
    FADETTE, IMPROMPTU
        CENTURY MUSIC PUBLISHING COMPANY, INC.  1639    .40
BOHM                                                 3
    FAREWELL TO THE ALPS
        CENTURY MUSIC PUBLISHING COMPANY, INC.  1330    .40
BOHM                                                 4
    FLUTTERING BUTTERFLIES
        CENTURY MUSIC PUBLISHING COMPANY, INC.  2326    .40
BOHM                                                 3
    FOUNTAIN, THE
        CENTURY MUSIC PUBLISHING COMPANY, INC.  791     .40
BOHM                      ROLFE, W.          2
    FOUNTAIN, THE, EASY
        CENTURY MUSIC PUBLISHING COMPANY, INC.  3545    .40
BOHM
    FOUNTAIN, THE, OP. 221
        G. SCHIRMER, INC.                               .50
BOHM
    GIPSY MAZURKA, OP. 102
        G. SCHIRMER, INC.                               .50
BOHM                                                 3
    GLISSANDO MAZURKA
        CENTURY MUSIC PUBLISHING COMPANY, INC.  2200    .40
BOHM                                                 4
    GLISSANDO MAZURKA, OP. 259 NO. 2
        BELWIN-MILLS PUBLISHING CORPORATION     43      .60
BOHM
    GLISSANDO MAZURKA, OP. 259 NO. 2
        G. SCHIRMER, INC.                               .50
BOHM                                                 3
    GRACE, LA
        CENTURY MUSIC PUBLISHING COMPANY, INC.  634     .40
BOHM
    GRACE, OP. 302 NO. 5
        G. SCHIRMER, INC.                               .40
BOHM                                                 3
    LA FONTAINE, OP. 221
        CENTURY MUSIC PUBLISHING COMPANY, INC.  791     .40
BOHM                                                 3
    LA GRACE
        CENTURY MUSIC PUBLISHING COMPANY, INC.  634     .40
BOHM                                                 4
    LA ZINGANA, MAZURKA
        CENTURY MUSIC PUBLISHING COMPANY, INC.  275     .40
BOHM                                                 4
    LA ZINGNA MAZURKA
        VOLKWEIN BROS.                                  .25


BOHM                                                 2
    LITTLE DEAREST --GAVOTTE--
        THEODORE PRESSER COMPANY                        .50
BOHM                                                 3
    LITTLE DEAREST, GAVOTTE
        CENTURY MUSIC PUBLISHING COMPANY, INC.  282     .40
BOHM                                                 4
    LOVE IN ARMS, WALTZ
        CENTURY MUSIC PUBLISHING COMPANY, INC.  1355    .40
BOHM                                                 3
    LOVE'S ORACLE, MAZURKA
        CENTURY MUSIC PUBLISHING COMPANY, INC.  1356    .40
BOHM                                                 4
    MOUNTAIN SPRING
        CENTURY MUSIC PUBLISHING COMPANY, INC.  1357    .40
BOHM                                                 4
    MURMURING BROOK
        CENTURY MUSIC PUBLISHING COMPANY, INC.  1649    .40
BOHM                                                 3
    MURMURING SPRING
        THEODORE PRESSER COMPANY                        .50
BOHM                                                 3
    NOVELETTE PETITE
        CENTURY MUSIC PUBLISHING COMPANY, INC.  1946    .40
BOHM                                                 4
    QUEEN OF THE NIGHT, VALSE
        CENTURY MUSIC PUBLISHING COMPANY, INC.  2023    .40
BOHM                                                 4
    SEGUIDILLA, SPANISH DANCE
        CENTURY MUSIC PUBLISHING COMPANY, INC.  1399    .40
BOHM                                                 4
    SILVER STARS
        BELWIN-MILLS PUBLISHING CORPORATION     5       .60
BOHM                                                 4
    SILVER STARS, MAZURKA
        CENTURY MUSIC PUBLISHING COMPANY, INC.  388     .40
BOHM                                                 4
    SONG OF THE SWALLOW
        CENTURY MUSIC PUBLISHING COMPANY, INC.  660     .40
BOHM                                                 4
    SUNDAY MORNING
        CENTURY MUSIC PUBLISHING COMPANY, INC.  2047    .40
BOHM                                                 4
    THROWING KISSES, MAZURKA
        CENTURY MUSIC PUBLISHING COMPANY, INC.  2119    .40
BOHM                                                 3
    TO THE WALTZ, IMPROMPTU
        CENTURY MUSIC PUBLISHING COMPANY, INC.  1203    .40
BOHM                                                 4
    VOICES OF SPRING
        CENTURY MUSIC PUBLISHING COMPANY, INC.  2007    .40
BOHM                                                 4
    ZINGANA, LA -- MAZURKA
        VOLKWEIN BROS.                                  .25
BOHM                      ROLFE, W.          3
    ZINGANA, LA, EASY
        CENTURY MUSIC PUBLISHING COMPANY, INC.  3363    .40
BOHN, J.C.                                           3
    LOVE SPRING
        CENTURY MUSIC PUBLISHING COMPANY, INC.  2112    .40
BOHN, J.C.                                           3
    SWEET RECOLLECTIONS
        CENTURY MUSIC PUBLISHING COMPANY, INC.  2111    .40
BOITO                     CHIESA
    MEFISTOFELE - EASY FANTASIA
        FRANCO COLOMBO PUBLICATIONS         109092      .50
BOIZARD, G.
    MUSETTE
        EDITIONS MUSICALES TRANSATLANTIQUES            1.25
BOIZARD, G.
    PARTITA
        EDITIONS MUSICALES TRANSATLANTIQUES            5.40
BOLCK, O.
    ALLEGRO VITO
        FREDERICK HARRIS MUSIC COMPANY                  .60
BOLCOM, W.
    GRACEFUL GHOST RAG, THE
        EDWARD B. MARKS MUSIC CORPORATION             01.25
BOLCOM, W.
    SEABISCUITS
        EDWARD B. MARKS MUSIC CORPORATION             01.25
BOLDI
    ROMANCE BOHEMIENNE
        FRANCO COLOMBO PUBLICATIONS         SAL        1.75
BOLDON
    MUSICALLY SPEAKING
        MCA MUSIC                                      1.25
BOLDON
    TEN FINGER ORCHESTRA
        MCA MUSIC                                      1.50
BOLLINGTON, A.
    STATE FAIR POLKA
        BELWIN-MILLS PUBLISHING CORPORATION  20421      .85
BOLZONI
    MINUETTO
        FRANCO COLOMBO PUBLICATIONS         49206       .50
BOLZONI                   DEL MAGLIO
    MINUETTO
        FRANCO COLOMBO PUBLICATIONS         127752      .50
BOND                                                 3
    I LOVE YOU TRULY
        BOSTON MUSIC COMPANY                            .60
BOND                                                 3
    PERFECT DAY, A
        BOSTON MUSIC COMPANY                            .60
BOND                      WALLIS             3
    PERFECT DAY, A
        BOSTON MUSIC COMPANY                            .60
BOND                      MOORE              1
    PERFECT DAY, A
        BOSTON MUSIC COMPANY                            .50
BONDON, J.
    LES INSOLITES
        EDITIONS MUSICALES TRANSATLANTIQUES            3.20
BONDS
    TROUBLED WATERS
        SAM FOX PUBLISHING COMPANY, INC.               1.00
BONDS
    TROUBLED WATERS
        SOUTHERN MUSIC COMPANY                         1.25
BONESATTI
    CABALGATA
        FRANCO COLOMBO PUBLICATIONS         BA10359     .75
BONHEUR
    SUR TROIS MARCHES DE MARBRE ROSE
        FRANCO COLOMBO PUBLICATIONS         SAL        4.25
```

BONINCONTRO
  TES YEUX -- I TUOI OCCHI --
    FRANCO COLOMBO PUBLICATIONS   SAL   1.50
BONNAL, E.
  COMPLAINTE POUR L'ENFANT REVEUR
    ELKAN-VOGEL, INC.   D   1.25
BONNEL *
  TURKEY IN THE STRAW
    THE BIG THREE MUSIC CORPORATION   00.95
BONNER
  BETTY BLUE EYES
    CARL FISCHER, INC.   EV 1   .50
BONNIE   1-2
  BATTER UP
    PRO-ART PUBLICATIONS, INC.   467   .50
BONO   NEALE, J.   EASY
  BEAT GOES ON, THE
    WARNER BROTHERS PUBLISHERS   .75
BORASTON, M.   2
  MR. LOLLIPOP AND HIS FRIEND
    BELWIN-MILLS PUBLISHING CORPORATION   .60
BORASTON, M.   2
  PLAYGROUND MARCH
    BELWIN-MILLS PUBLISHING CORPORATION   .60
BORDES
  CAPRICCIO IN 5 MOVEMENTS
    FRANCO COLOMBO PUBLICATIONS   SAL   3.25
BOREL-CLERC, C.
  LA MATTCHICHE--CELEBRATED SPANISH MARCH
    G. SCHIRMER, INC.   .35
BORGI
  IMPLORANDO
    FRANCO COLOMBO PUBLICATIONS   FOR. 10655 .75
BORLENGHI
  PRELUDE, ADAGIO AND FINALE
    FRANCO COLOMBO PUBLICATIONS   FOR. 12290 2.00
BORLENGHI
  SUITE
    FRANCO COLOMBO PUBLICATIONS   Z4738   .60
BORODIN, A.
  AU COUVENT--FROM PETITE SUITE
    G. SCHIRMER, INC.   .35
BORODIN, A.   JADOUL
  IN THE STEPPES OF CENTRAL ASIA
    BOOSEY AND HAWKES, INC.   2.50
BORODIN, A.   3
  INTERMEZZO, PETITE SUITE
    CENTURY MUSIC PUBLISHING COMPANY, INC. 3972   .40
BORODIN, A.   RAGGI
  LITTLE SUITE
    FRANCO COLOMBO PUBLICATIONS   ER2564   1.00
BORODIN, A.   ZEPP   4
  MELODIC THEME FROM POLOVETZIAN DANCE
    PRO-ART PUBLICATIONS, INC.   163   .50
BORODIN, A.   COOMBS
  NOCTURNE, FROM 'SECOND QUARTET'
    BOOSEY AND HAWKES, INC.   .60
BORODIN, A.   SCHAUM, J.   2
  ORIENTAL ROMANCE 'PRINCE IGOR'
    BELWIN-MILLS PUBLISHING CORPORATION   .50
BORODIN, A.   M
  PETITE SUITE
    C. F. PETERS CORPORATION   4320   2.50
BORODIN, A.   POST   1-2
  POLOVETSIAN DANCE, PRINCE IGOR
    CENTURY MUSIC PUBLISHING COMPANY, INC. 4159   .40
BORODIN, A.   BLUMENFELD
  PRINCE IGOR OVERTURE
    BOOSEY AND HAWKES, INC.   2.00
BORODIN, A.   1-2
  PRINCE IGOR, POLOVETSIAN DANCE
    CENTURY MUSIC PUBLISHING COMPANY, INC. 4159   .40
BORODIN, A.   TCHEREPNIN   D
  SCHERZO
    C. F. PETERS CORPORATION   H4320A   1.25
BORODIN, A.
  SCHERZO IN A FLAT
    INTERNATIONAL MUSIC COMPANY   1.50
BORONAT
  PASTORES CHIQUITOS. VILLANICO POPULAR
    ASSOCIATED MUSIC PUBLISHERS, INC.   UME   .40
BOROWSKI, E.   4
  COQUETTE, THE
    CENTURY MUSIC PUBLISHING COMPANY, INC. 2550   .40
BOROWSKI, F.
  VALSETTE
    G. SCHIRMER, INC.   .40
BOSCOVICH
  GOLDEN CHAIN
    ISRAEL MUSIC INSTITUTE   4.00
BOSKOFF
  LEGENDE HEROIQUE
    FRANCO COLOMBO PUBLICATIONS   A150   1.00
BOSKOFF
  NOCTURNE
    FRANCO COLOMBO PUBLICATIONS   A147   1.00
BOSKOFF
  VALSE ROMANTIQUE
    FRANCO COLOMBO PUBLICATIONS   A160   .90
BOSMANS, A.
  SONATA EN COLORES
    EDITORIAL COOPERATIVA INTER-AMERICANA   01.25
BOSMANS, A.
  SONATINA LUSITANA
    EDITORIAL COOPERATIVA INTER-AMERICANA   01.35
BOSSI, F.   4
  CHIAPANECAS
    THEODORE PRESSER COMPANY   .50
BOSSI, F.   4
  EL JALEO DE XERES
    THEODORE PRESSER COMPANY   .50
BOSSI, M. E.
  FIVE EASY PIECES, OP. 139, NO. 1 - PAGLIACCETTO
    FRANCO COLOMBO PUBLICATIONS   BON. 1266 .90
BOSSI, M. E.
  FIVE EASY PIECES, OP. 139, NO. 2 - CAPITAN FRACASSA
    FRANCO COLOMBO PUBLICATIONS   BON. 1267 .90
BOSSI, M. E.
  FIVE EASY PIECES, OP. 139, NO. 3 - PIERROT IN AMBASCIA
    FRANCO COLOMBO PUBLICATIONS   BON. 1268 .90
BOSSI, M. E.
  FIVE EASY PIECES, OP. 139, NO. 4 - LIBELLULE
    FRANCO COLOMBO PUBLICATIONS   BON. 1269 .90
BOSSI, M. E.
  FIVE EASY PIECES, OP. 139, NO. 5 - LA DANZATRICE
    FRANCO COLOMBO PUBLICATIONS   BON. 1270 .90

BOSSI, R.
  FATA MORGANA E L'ORCO, LA, OP. 27
    FRANCO COLOMBO PUBLICATIONS   BON. 1396 1.75
BOSTELMANN
  AT THE CONCERT
    EDWARD B. MARKS MUSIC CORPORATION   00.60
BOSTELMANN
  FEATHER IN MY CAP
    SUMMY-BIRCHARD COMPANY   .45
BOSTELMANN   2
  FIRST FLIGHT OF A LITTLE BIRD, THE
    BOSTON MUSIC COMPANY   .50
BOSTELMANN   2
  LITTLE MINUET
    BOSTON MUSIC COMPANY   .50
BOSTELMANN   2
  LITTLE ORCHESTRA
    BOSTON MUSIC COMPANY   .50
BOSTELMANN   2
  LONELY BIRD, THE
    BOSTON MUSIC COMPANY   .50
BOSTELMANN   2
  SPRING MORNING IN THE WOODS
    BOSTON MUSIC COMPANY   .50
BOSTELMANN
  TRAVELS OF MR. THUMB
    EDWARD B. MARKS MUSIC CORPORATION   00.60
BOTELLI
  GAUCHO
    FRANCO COLOMBO PUBLICATIONS   BA11991 .75
BOTSFORD, G.
  BLACK AND WHITE RAG
    BELWIN-MILLS PUBLISHING CORPORATION 20033   .85
BOTSFORD, G.
  BLACK AND WHITE RAG
    WARNER BROTHERS PUBLISHERS   1.00
BOTTINO, G.
  DUE DANZA BARBARE
    EDIZIONI BERBEN   EB 1616 3.60
BOUCOURECHLIEV
  ARCHIPEL IV
    ALPHONSE LEDUC
BOULANGER, L.
  CORTEGE
    FRANCO COLOMBO PUBLICATIONS   R537   1.50
BOULANGER, L.
  D'UN JARDIN CLAIR
    FRANCO COLOMBO PUBLICATIONS   R534   1.50
BOULANGER, L.
  D'UN VIEUX JARDIN
    FRANCO COLOMBO PUBLICATIONS   R533   1.50
BOULEZ
  SONATA NO. 01
    FRANCO COLOMBO PUBLICATIONS   A153   3.75
BOULEZ
  SONATA NO. 02
    HEUGEL ET CIE.   8.75
BOULEZ
  SONATA NO. 03, 2ND MVT.
    UNIVERSAL EDITION   13292   7.20
BOULEZ
  SONATA NO. 03, 3RD MVT.
    UNIVERSAL EDITION   13293B 12.60
BOULNOIS
  MENUET PASTORAL
    FRANCO COLOMBO PUBLICATIONS   SAL   2.50
BOULNOIS
  PAVANE
    FRANCO COLOMBO PUBLICATIONS   SAL   2.50
BOURGAULT-DUCOUDRAY
  TWO GAVOTTES BRETONNES - NO. 1
    FRANCO COLOMBO PUBLICATIONS   SAL   1.75
BOURGAULT-DUCOUDRAY
  TWO GAVOTTES BRETONNES - NO. 2
    FRANCO COLOMBO PUBLICATIONS   SAL   1.75
BOUSTEAD, A.   M
  LITTLE SUITE
    OXFORD UNIVERSITY PRESS   33.070   1.30
BOUTNIKOFF
  POEME
    FRANCO COLOMBO PUBLICATIONS   SAL   1.25
BOUTRY
  SCHERZO FANTASIE
    FRANCO COLOMBO PUBLICATIONS   SAL   5.50
BOUTRY   8, 9
  SONATA SCHERZO
    ALPHONSE LEDUC
BOUTRY
  SONATINE CLAVECIN
    FRANCO COLOMBO PUBLICATIONS   SAL   4.25
BOUTRY
  VOLEUR D'ETINCELLES, LE
    FRANCO COLOMBO PUBLICATIONS   SAL   3.00
BOWLES, P.   MD
  EL BEJUCO
    THEODORE PRESSER COMPANY   .50
BOWLES, P.   MD
  EL INDIO
    THEODORE PRESSER COMPANY   .50
BOWLES, P.   M
  SIX PRELUDES
    THEODORE PRESSER COMPANY   1.00
BOWN
  G'WON TRAIN
    MCA MUSIC   1.00
BOWN
  HEAD SHAKIN'
    MCA MUSIC   1.00
BOWN, P.
  COWBOY BAND, THE
    BELWIN-MILLS PUBLISHING CORPORATION 25140   .60
BOWN, P.
  DUSTING THE PIANO
    BELWIN-MILLS PUBLISHING CORPORATION 25042   .60
BOYDELL
  DANCE OF AN ANCIENT RITUAL
    FRANCO COLOMBO PUBLICATIONS   LD415   .60
BOYDELL
  SARABANDE
    FRANCO COLOMBO PUBLICATIONS   LD538   .60
BOYDELL
  SLEEPING LEPRECHAUN
    FRANCO COLOMBO PUBLICATIONS   LD416   .60
BOYKIN, H.   2
  SOLILOQUY
    BELWIN-MILLS PUBLISHING CORPORATION   .60

BOZAY, A.
  BAGATELLE, OP. 4
    KULTURA   2.25
BOZI, H. DE
  PAOLINO. TANGO FOR LEFT HAND ALONE
    ASSOCIATED MUSIC PUBLISHERS, INC.   7   ESC   1.00
BOZZA
  PULCINELLA, OP. 53
    ALPHONSE LEDUC   7
BOZZA
  TOCCATA
    ALPHONSE LEDUC   7
BRACCO
  SERENATA
    FRANCO COLOMBO PUBLICATIONS   FOR. 10969   .90
BRACY   5
  UN NID D'AIGLE, POLKA
    ALPHONSE LEDUC
BRADLEY
  BOOK OF RHYTHM
    FRANCO COLOMBO PUBLICATIONS   LD223   1.00
BRADLEY, R.--ARR.   BRADLEY, R.   EASY
  ABRAHAM, MARTIN AND JOHN
    SCREEN GEMS - COLUMBIA PUBLICATIONS   0403AP2   .85
BRADLEY, R.--ARR.   BRADLEY, R.   EASY
  ALLEY CAT
    SCREEN GEMS - COLUMBIA PUBLICATIONS   3733AP2   .85
BRADLEY, R.--ARR.   BRADLEY, R.   EASY
  AM I LOSING YOU
    SCREEN GEMS - COLUMBIA PUBLICATIONS   4002AP2   .85
BRADLEY, R.--ARR.   BRADLEY, R.   EASY
  ARE YOU LONESOME TONIGHT
    SCREEN GEMS - COLUMBIA PUBLICATIONS   5703AP2   .85
BRADLEY, R.--ARR.   BRADLEY, R.   EASY
  AUBREY
    SCREEN GEMS - COLUMBIA PUBLICATIONS   6704AP2   .85
BRADLEY, R.--ARR.   BRADLEY, R.   EASY
  BABY DON'T GET HOOKED ON ME
    SCREEN GEMS - COLUMBIA PUBLICATIONS   0010BP2   .85
BRADLEY, R.--ARR.   BRADLEY, R.   EASY
  BABY I'M-A WANT YOU
    SCREEN GEMS - COLUMBIA PUBLICATIONS   0003BP2   .85
BRADLEY, R.--ARR.   BRADLEY, R.   EASY
  BACK TO CALIFORNIA
    SCREEN GEMS - COLUMBIA PUBLICATIONS   0004BP2   .85
BRADLEY, R.--ARR.   BRADLEY, R.   EASY
  BEAUTIFUL CITY
    SCREEN GEMS - COLUMBIA PUBLICATIONS   1430BP2   .85
BRADLEY, R.--ARR.   BRADLEY, R.   EASY
  BEEN TO CANAAN
    SCREEN GEMS - COLUMBIA PUBLICATIONS   1423BP2   .85
BRADLEY, R.--ARR.   BRADLEY, R.   EASY
  BEN
    SCREEN GEMS - COLUMBIA PUBLICATIONS   1443BP2   .85
BRADLEY, R.--ARR.   BRADLEY, R.   EASY
  BLACK AND WHITE
    SCREEN GEMS - COLUMBIA PUBLICATIONS   3712BP2   .85
BRADLEY, R.--ARR.   BRADLEY, R.   EASY
  BLESS THE BEASTS AND CHILDREN
    SCREEN GEMS - COLUMBIA PUBLICATIONS   3702BP2   .85
BRADLEY, R.--ARR.   BRADLEY, R.   EASY
  BORN FREE
    SCREEN GEMS - COLUMBIA PUBLICATIONS   4701BP2   .85
BRADLEY, R.--ARR.   BRADLEY, R.   BIG NOTE EASY
  BORN FREE
    SCREEN GEMS - COLUMBIA PUBLICATIONS   4701BP3   .85
BRADLEY, R.--ARR.   BRADLEY, R.   INTERMEDIATE
  BORN FREE
    SCREEN GEMS - COLUMBIA PUBLICATIONS   4701BP   1.00
BRADLEY, R.--ARR.   BRADLEY, R.   EASY
  BREAKING UP IS HARD TO DO
    SCREEN GEMS - COLUMBIA PUBLICATIONS   5701BP2   .85
BRADLEY, R.--ARR.   BRADLEY, R.   EASY
  BRIAN'S SONG
    SCREEN GEMS - COLUMBIA PUBLICATIONS   5707BP2   .85
BRADLEY, R.--ARR.   BRADLEY, R.   BIG NOTE EASY
  BRIAN'S SONG
    SCREEN GEMS - COLUMBIA PUBLICATIONS   5707BP3   .85
BRADLEY, R.--ARR.   BRADLEY, R.   EASY
  BY THE TIME I GET TO PHOENIX
    SCREEN GEMS - COLUMBIA PUBLICATIONS   8002BP2   .85
BRADLEY, R.--ARR.   BRADLEY, R.   EASY
  CANDY MAN, THE
    SCREEN GEMS - COLUMBIA PUBLICATIONS   0007CP2   .85
BRADLEY, R.--ARR.   BRADLEY, R.   BIG NOTE EASY
  CANDY MAN, THE
    SCREEN GEMS - COLUMBIA PUBLICATIONS   0007CP3   .85
BRADLEY, R.--ARR.   BRADLEY, R.   BIG NOTE EASY
  CANDY MAN, THE - AND - BORN FREE
    SCREEN GEMS - COLUMBIA PUBLICATIONS   C0016P3   1.00
BRADLEY, R.--ARR.   BRADLEY, R.   EASY
  CHERISH
    SCREEN GEMS - COLUMBIA PUBLICATIONS   2406CP2   .85
BRADLEY, R.--ARR.   BRADLEY, R.   EASY
  CLOUDS
    SCREEN GEMS - COLUMBIA PUBLICATIONS   3709CP2   .85
BRADLEY, R.--ARR.   BRADLEY, R.   EASY
  DAY BY DAY
    SCREEN GEMS - COLUMBIA PUBLICATIONS   0014DP2   .85
BRADLEY, R.--ARR.   BRADLEY, R.   EASY
  DIARY
    SCREEN GEMS - COLUMBIA PUBLICATIONS   2705DP2   .85
BRADLEY, R.--ARR.   BRADLEY, R.   EASY
  DON'T IT MAKE YOU WANTA GO HOME
    SCREEN GEMS - COLUMBIA PUBLICATIONS   4706DP2   .85
BRADLEY, R.--ARR.   BRADLEY, R.   EASY
  EVERYTHING I OWN
    SCREEN GEMS - COLUMBIA PUBLICATIONS   7007EP2   .85
BRADLEY, R.--ARR.   BRADLEY, R.   EASY
  FIRST TIME EVER I SAW YOUR FACE, THE
    SCREEN GEMS - COLUMBIA PUBLICATIONS   2703FP2   .85
BRADLEY, R.--ARR.   BRADLEY, R.   EASY
  FOR ONCE IN MY LIFE
    SCREEN GEMS - COLUMBIA PUBLICATIONS   4717FP2   .85
BRADLEY, R.--ARR.   BRADLEY, R.   EASY
  FUNNY FACE
    SCREEN GEMS - COLUMBIA PUBLICATIONS   6706FP2   .85
BRADLEY, R.--ARR.   BRADLEY, R.   EASY
  GO AWAY LITTLE GIRL
    SCREEN GEMS - COLUMBIA PUBLICATIONS   4702GP2   .85
BRADLEY, R.--ARR.   BRADLEY, R.   EASY
  GOING OUT OF MY HEAD
    SCREEN GEMS - COLUMBIA PUBLICATIONS   4717GP2   .85
BRADLEY, R.--ARR.   BRADLEY, R.   EASY
  GREEN GREEN GRASS OF HOME
    SCREEN GEMS - COLUMBIA PUBLICATIONS   5702GP2   .85

BRADLEY, R.--ARR.   BRADLEY, R.   EASY
  GUITAR MAN, THE
    SCREEN GEMS - COLUMBIA PUBLICATIONS   6704GP2   .85
BRADLEY, R.--ARR.   BRADLEY, R.   EASY
  HANDS OF TIME, THE
    SCREEN GEMS - COLUMBIA PUBLICATIONS   0011HP2   .85
BRADLEY, R.--ARR.   BRADLEY, R.   EASY
  HAPPIEST GIRL IN THE WHOLE U.S.A., THE
    SCREEN GEMS - COLUMBIA PUBLICATIONS   0014HP2   .85
BRADLEY, R.--ARR.   BRADLEY, R.   EASY
  HAVA NAGILA
    SCREEN GEMS - COLUMBIA PUBLICATIONS   0026HP2   .85
BRADLEY, R.--ARR.   BRADLEY, R.   EASY
  HEY, GIRL
    SCREEN GEMS - COLUMBIA PUBLICATIONS   1402HP2   .85
BRADLEY, R.--ARR.   BRADLEY, R.   EASY
  HI-DE-HO --THAT OLD SWEET ROLL--
    SCREEN GEMS - COLUMBIA PUBLICATIONS   2701HP2   .85
BRADLEY, R.--ARR.   BRADLEY, R.   EASY
  HOLLY JOLLY CHRISTMAS, A
    SCREEN GEMS - COLUMBIA PUBLICATIONS   4714HP2   .85
BRADLEY, R.--ARR.   BRADLEY, R.   EASY
  HOME AGAIN
    SCREEN GEMS - COLUMBIA PUBLICATIONS   4703HP2   .85
BRADLEY, R.--ARR.   BRADLEY, R.   EASY
  HOUSE OF THE RISING SUN, THE
    SCREEN GEMS - COLUMBIA PUBLICATIONS   4701HP2   .85
BRADLEY, R.--ARR.   BRADLEY, R.   EASY
  HURTING EACH OTHER
    SCREEN GEMS - COLUMBIA PUBLICATIONS   6704HP2   .85
BRADLEY, R.--ARR.   BRADLEY, R.   EASY
  I BELIEVE IN MUSIC
    SCREEN GEMS - COLUMBIA PUBLICATIONS   0402IP2   .85
BRADLEY, R.--ARR.   BRADLEY, R.   EASY
  I GOT A NAME
    SCREEN GEMS - COLUMBIA PUBLICATIONS   2004IP2   .85
BRADLEY, R.--ARR.   BRADLEY, R.   EASY
  I KNEW YOU WHEN
    SCREEN GEMS - COLUMBIA PUBLICATIONS   3401IP2   .85
BRADLEY, R.--ARR.   BRADLEY, R.   EASY
  I NEVER PROMISED YOU A ROSE GARDEN
    SCREEN GEMS - COLUMBIA PUBLICATIONS   4702RP2   .85
BRADLEY, R.--ARR.   BRADLEY, R.   EASY
  I WILL WAIT FOR YOU
    SCREEN GEMS - COLUMBIA PUBLICATIONS   7408IP2   .85
BRADLEY, R.--ARR.   BRADLEY, R.   EASY
  I WOKE UP IN LOVE THIS MORNING
    SCREEN GEMS - COLUMBIA PUBLICATIONS   7402IP2   .85
BRADLEY, R.--ARR.   BRADLEY, R.   EASY
  IF
    SCREEN GEMS - COLUMBIA PUBLICATIONS   1702IP2   .85
BRADLEY, R.--ARR.   BRADLEY, R.   EASY
  IT'S GOING TO TAKE SOME TIME
    SCREEN GEMS - COLUMBIA PUBLICATIONS   6415IP2   .85
BRADLEY, R.--ARR.   BRADLEY, R.   EASY
  IT'S ONE OF THOSE NIGHTS --YES LOVE--
    SCREEN GEMS - COLUMBIA PUBLICATIONS   6414IP2   .85
BRADLEY, R.--ARR.   BRADLEY, R.   INTERMEDIATE
  IT'S TOO LATE
    SCREEN GEMS - COLUMBIA PUBLICATIONS   6403IP   1.00
BRADLEY, R.--ARR.   BRADLEY, R.   EASY
  JEAN
    SCREEN GEMS - COLUMBIA PUBLICATIONS   1417JP2   .85
BRADLEY, R.--ARR.   BRADLEY, R.   BIG NOTE EASY
  JINGLE BELLS
    SCREEN GEMS - COLUMBIA PUBLICATIONS   2703JP2   .85
BRADLEY, R.--ARR.   BRADLEY, R.   EASY
  JOY
    SCREEN GEMS - COLUMBIA PUBLICATIONS   4706JP2   .85
BRADLEY, R.--ARR.   BRADLEY, R.   EASY
  JOY TO THE WORLD
    SCREEN GEMS - COLUMBIA PUBLICATIONS   4703JP2   .85
BRADLEY, R.--ARR.   BRADLEY, R.   BIG NOTE EASY
  JOY TO THE WORLD
    SCREEN GEMS - COLUMBIA PUBLICATIONS   4703JP3   .85
BRADLEY, R.--ARR.   BRADLEY, R.   EASY
  KNOCKIN' ON HEAVEN'S DOOR
    SCREEN GEMS - COLUMBIA PUBLICATIONS   4703KP2   .85
BRADLEY, R.--ARR.   BRADLEY, R.   EASY
  L-O-V-E
    SCREEN GEMS - COLUMBIA PUBLICATIONS   4704LP2   .85
BRADLEY, R.--ARR.   BRADLEY, R.   EASY
  LAST TIME I SAW HIM
    SCREEN GEMS - COLUMBIA PUBLICATIONS   0042LP2   .85
BRADLEY, R.--ARR.   BRADLEY, R.   EASY
  LITTLE PEOPLE AMERICA
    SCREEN GEMS - COLUMBIA PUBLICATIONS   2703LP2   .85
BRADLEY, R.--ARR.   BRADLEY, R.   EASY
  LIVING TOGETHER, GROWING TOGETHER
    SCREEN GEMS - COLUMBIA PUBLICATIONS   2715LP2   .85
BRADLEY, R.--ARR.   BRADLEY, R.   EASY
  LONG-HAIRED LOVER FROM LIVERPOOL
    SCREEN GEMS - COLUMBIA PUBLICATIONS   4728LP2   .85
BRADLEY, R.--ARR.   BRADLEY, R.   EASY
  LOOK OF LOVE, THE
    SCREEN GEMS - COLUMBIA PUBLICATIONS   4703LP2   .85
BRADLEY, R.--ARR.   BRADLEY, R.   INTERMEDIATE
  LOVE MEANS --YOU NEVER HAVE TO SAY YOU'RE SORRY--
    SCREEN GEMS - COLUMBIA PUBLICATIONS   4717LP   1.00
BRADLEY, R.--ARR.   BRADLEY, R.   EASY
  MISTY
    SCREEN GEMS - COLUMBIA PUBLICATIONS   2728MP2   .85
BRADLEY, R.--ARR.   BRADLEY, R.   EASY
  MORNING AFTER, THE
    SCREEN GEMS - COLUMBIA PUBLICATIONS   4723MP2   .85
BRADLEY, R.--ARR.   BRADLEY, R.   EASY
  MOST BEAUTIFUL GIRL, THE
    SCREEN GEMS - COLUMBIA PUBLICATIONS   4722MP2   .85
BRADLEY, R.--ARR.   BRADLEY, R.   EASY
  MUSIC
    SCREEN GEMS - COLUMBIA PUBLICATIONS   6701MP2   .85
BRADLEY, R.--ARR.   BRADLEY, R.   EASY
  NEVER BEEN TO SPAIN
    SCREEN GEMS - COLUMBIA PUBLICATIONS   1403NP2   .85
BRADLEY, R.--ARR.   BRADLEY, R.   EASY
  NEVER CAN SAY GOODBYE
    SCREEN GEMS - COLUMBIA PUBLICATIONS   1413NP2   .85
BRADLEY, R.--ARR.   BRADLEY, R.   EASY
  ONE TIN SOLDIER
    SCREEN GEMS - COLUMBIA PUBLICATIONS   4438OP2   .85
BRADLEY, R.--ARR.   BRADLEY, R.   EASY
  PAPER ROSES
    SCREEN GEMS - COLUMBIA PUBLICATIONS   0015PP2   .85
BRADLEY, R.--ARR.   BRADLEY, R.   EASY
  POPCORN
    SCREEN GEMS - COLUMBIA PUBLICATIONS   4709PP2   .85

BRADLEY, R.--ARR.   BRADLEY, R.   EASY
   ROCK AND ROLL LULLABY
      SCREEN GEMS - COLUMBIA PUBLICATIONS   4705RP2   .85
BRADLEY, R.--ARR.   BRADLEY, R.   EASY
   ROCKIN' AROUND THE CHRISTMAS TREE
      SCREEN GEMS - COLUMBIA PUBLICATIONS   4711RP2   .85
BRADLEY, R.--ARR.   BRADLEY, R.   BIG NOTE EASY
   RUDOLPH THE RED-NOSED REINDEER
      SCREEN GEMS - COLUMBIA PUBLICATIONS   6706RP3   .85
BRADLEY, R.--ARR.   BRADLEY, R.   EASY
   RUN RUN RUN
      SCREEN GEMS - COLUMBIA PUBLICATIONS   6706RP2   .85
BRADLEY, R.--ARR.   BRADLEY, R.   EASY
   SEATTLE
      SCREEN GEMS - COLUMBIA PUBLICATIONS   1401SP2   .85
BRADLEY, R.--ARR.   BRADLEY, R.   EASY
   SEE YOU IN SEPTEMBER
      SCREEN GEMS - COLUMBIA PUBLICATIONS   1407SP2   .85
BRADLEY, R.--ARR.   BRADLEY, R.   BIG NOTE EASY
   SILENT NIGHT
      SCREEN GEMS - COLUMBIA PUBLICATIONS   2706SP3   .85
BRADLEY, R.--ARR.   BRADLEY, R.   EASY
   SMILE - HAVE A HAPPY DAY
      SCREEN GEMS - COLUMBIA PUBLICATIONS   4002SP2   .85
BRADLEY, R.--ARR.   BRADLEY, R.   EASY
   SNOOPY'S CHRISTMAS
      SCREEN GEMS - COLUMBIA PUBLICATIONS   4405SP2   .85
BRADLEY, R.--ARR.   BRADLEY, R.   EASY
   SO FAR AWAY
      SCREEN GEMS - COLUMBIA PUBLICATIONS   4703SP2   .85
BRADLEY, R.--ARR.   BRADLEY, R.   EASY
   SOME KIND OF WONDERFUL
      SCREEN GEMS - COLUMBIA PUBLICATIONS   4702SP2   .85
BRADLEY, R.--ARR.   BRADLEY, R.   EASY
   SONG OF LONG AGO
      SCREEN GEMS - COLUMBIA PUBLICATIONS   4712SP2   .85
BRADLEY, R.--ARR.   BRADLEY, R.   EASY
   SPANISH EYES
      SCREEN GEMS - COLUMBIA PUBLICATIONS   5002SP2   .85
BRADLEY, R.--ARR.   BRADLEY, R.   EASY
   SWEET SEASONS
      SCREEN GEMS - COLUMBIA PUBLICATIONS   7406SP2   .85
BRADLEY, R.--ARR.   BRADLEY, R.   EASY
   SWEET SURRENDER
      SCREEN GEMS - COLUMBIA PUBLICATIONS   7420SP2   .85
BRADLEY, R.--ARR.   BRADLEY, R.   EASY
   TAPESTRY
      SCREEN GEMS - COLUMBIA PUBLICATIONS   003TP2   .85
BRADLEY, R.--ARR.   BRADLEY, R.   EASY
   THEME FROM NICHOLAS AND ALEXANDRA
      SCREEN GEMS - COLUMBIA PUBLICATIONS   2701NP2   .85
BRADLEY, R.--ARR.   BRADLEY, R.   EASY
   THEME FROM SHAFT
      SCREEN GEMS - COLUMBIA PUBLICATIONS   2422SP2   .85
BRADLEY, R.--ARR.   BRADLEY, R.   EASY
   TOO YOUNG
      SCREEN GEMS - COLUMBIA PUBLICATIONS   4716TP2   .85
BRADLEY, R.--ARR.   BRADLEY, R.   EASY
   TOUCH ME IN THE MORNING
      SCREEN GEMS - COLUMBIA PUBLICATIONS   4738TP2   .85
BRADLEY, R.--ARR.   BRADLEY, R.   EASY
   TRACES
      SCREEN GEMS - COLUMBIA PUBLICATIONS   5701TP2   .85
BRADLEY, R.--ARR.   BRADLEY, R.   EASY
   UP, UP AND AWAY
      SCREEN GEMS - COLUMBIA PUBLICATIONS   5002UP2   .85
BRADLEY, R.--ARR.   BRADLEY, R.   EASY
   WALK A MILE IN MY SHOES
      SCREEN GEMS - COLUMBIA PUBLICATIONS   0005WP2   .85
BRADLEY, R.--ARR.   BRADLEY, R.   EASY
   WAY WE WERE, THE
      SCREEN GEMS - COLUMBIA PUBLICATIONS   0055WP2   .85
BRADLEY, R.--ARR.   BRADLEY, R.   BIG NOTE EASY
   WAY WE WERE, THE
      SCREEN GEMS - COLUMBIA PUBLICATIONS   0055WP3   .85
BRADLEY, R.--ARR.   BRADLEY, R.   INTERMEDIATE
   WAY WE WERE, THE
      SCREEN GEMS - COLUMBIA PUBLICATIONS   0055WP   1.00
BRADLEY, R.--ARR.   BRADLEY, R.   EASY
   WHEN YOU SAY LOVE
      SCREEN GEMS - COLUMBIA PUBLICATIONS   2437WP2   .85
BRADLEY, R.--ARR.   BRADLEY, R.   EASY
   WHERE IS THE LOVE
      SCREEN GEMS - COLUMBIA PUBLICATIONS   2435WP2   .85
BRADLEY, R.--ARR.   BRADLEY, R.   EASY
   WINTER WONDERLAND
      SCREEN GEMS - COLUMBIA PUBLICATIONS   2722WP2   .85
BRADLEY, R.--ARR.   BRADLEY, R.   BIG NOTE EASY
   WINTER WONDERLAND
      SCREEN GEMS - COLUMBIA PUBLICATIONS   2722WP3   .85
BRADLEY, R.--ARR.   BRADLEY, R.   EASY
   WORLD IS A CIRCLE, THE
      SCREEN GEMS - COLUMBIA PUBLICATIONS   4717WP2   .85
BRADLEY, R.--ARR.   BRADLEY, R.   EASY
   YO YO
      SCREEN GEMS - COLUMBIA PUBLICATIONS   4704YP2   .85
BRADLEY, R.--ARR.   BRADLEY, R.   EASY
   YOU'VE GOT A FRIEND
      SCREEN GEMS - COLUMBIA PUBLICATIONS   4702YP2   .85
BRADLEY, R.--ARR.   BRADLEY, R.   INTERMEDIATE
   YOU'VE GOT A FRIEND
      SCREEN GEMS - COLUMBIA PUBLICATIONS   4702YP   1.00
BRADLEY, R.--ARR.   BRADLEY, R.   EASY
   YOUNG LOVE
      SCREEN GEMS - COLUMBIA PUBLICATIONS   4756YP2   .85
BRADY, D.   2
   HIGH ON A HILLTOP
      WILLIS MUSIC COMPANY   .35
BRAGA   WEYBRIGHT   1 1/2
   ANGEL'S SERENADE
      BELWIN-MILLS PUBLISHING CORPORATION   .50
BRAGA   WEYBRIGHT   1 1/2
   ANGEL'S SERENADE
      BELWIN-MILLS PUBLISHING CORPORATION   .60
BRAGA   4
   ANGEL'S SERENADE
      CENTURY MUSIC PUBLISHING COMPANY, INC.   682   .40
BRAGA   3
   ANGEL'S SERENADE, THE
      THEODORE PRESSER COMPANY   .50
BRAGA   SMITH
   LA SERENATA
      G. SCHIRMER, INC.   .60
BRAGA   HITZ
   LA SERENATA
      G. SCHIRMER, INC.   .40

BRAGA   3
   LA SERENATTA -- ANGEL'S SERENADE
      CENTURY MUSIC PUBLISHING COMPANY, INC.   3381   .40
BRAGDON   3
   CANDLE LIGHT WALTZ
      BELWIN-MILLS PUBLISHING CORPORATION   .60
BRAGDON   E
   CASTANETS
      COMPOSERS PRESS, INC.   1.00
BRAGDON   WILLIAMS, J.   1
   CUCKOO'S CALL, THE
      BOSTON MUSIC COMPANY   .50
BRAGDON   2
   FAIRY BELL
      BOSTON MUSIC COMPANY   .50
BRAGDON   E
   IN THE WOODS
      COMPOSERS PRESS, INC.   1.00
BRAGDON   WILLIAMS, J.
   PICKING HOLLY
      BOSTON MUSIC COMPANY   .50
BRAGDON   E
   POLKA DOT POLKA
      COMPOSERS PRESS, INC.   1.00
BRAGDON   E
   RAIN'S MONOTONE, THE
      COMPOSERS PRESS, INC.   1.00
BRAGGIOTTI, M.
   VARIATIONS ON 'YANKEE DOODLE' --IN THE MANNER OF SCARLATTI,
   BEETHOVEN, CHOPIN, DEBUSSY, AND GERSHWIN--
      G. SCHIRMER, INC.   1.50
BRAHE, M.   PERRY
   BLESS THIS HOUSE
      BOOSEY AND HAWKES, INC.   .60
BRAHE, M.   SEDLON
   BLESS THIS HOUSE
      BOOSEY AND HAWKES, INC.   .50
BRAHMS   4
   BALLADE G MOLL, OP. 118 NO. 3
      SCHOTT   07565 1/2   1.00
BRAHMS
   BALLADE IN D MINOR, OP. 10 NO. 1
      G. SCHIRMER, INC.   .50
BRAHMS   5
   BALLADE IN G MINOR, OP. 118 NO. 3
      CENTURY MUSIC PUBLISHING COMPANY, INC.   3733   .40
BRAHMS   MONTANI
   BALLADE IN G MINOR, OP. 118 NO. 3
      FRANCO COLOMBO PUBLICATIONS   128419   .60
BRAHMS
   BALLADE IN G MINOR, OP. 118 NO. 3
      G. SCHIRMER, INC.   .60
BRAHMS   4-5
   BALLADEN OP. 10
      SCHOTT   1636   1.50
BRAHMS   MAIER, G.   3
   BLACKSMITH, THE
      BELWIN-MILLS PUBLISHING CORPORATION   .60
BRAHMS   SCHAUM, J.   1
   BRAHMS LULLABY
      BELWIN-MILLS PUBLISHING CORPORATION   .50
BRAHMS   5
   CAPRICCIO IN B MINOR, OP. 76 NO. 2
      CENTURY MUSIC PUBLISHING COMPANY, INC.   3836   .40
BRAHMS   PHILIPP
   CAPRICCIO IN B MINOR, OP. 76 NO. 2
      G. SCHIRMER, INC.   .50
BRAHMS   3
   CRADLE SONG
      CENTURY MUSIC PUBLISHING COMPANY, INC.   3063   .40
BRAHMS   ROLFE, W.   2
   CRADLE SONG
      CENTURY MUSIC PUBLISHING COMPANY, INC.   3243   .40
BRAHMS   STRIMER, J.   1
   CRADLE SONG
      PRO-ART PUBLICATIONS, INC.   35   .50
BRAHMS   SPENCER, J.   2
   CRADLE SONG
      VOLKWEIN BROS.   .30
BRAHMS   BRENDEL   5
   CRADLE SONG, OP. 49 NO. 4
      THEODORE PRESSER COMPANY   .60
BRAHMS   GRAINGER, P.
   CRADLE-SONG, OP. 49 NO. 4
      G. SCHIRMER, INC.   .50
BRAHMS   DEIS
   CRADLE-SONG, OP. 49 NO. 4
      G. SCHIRMER, INC.   .40
BRAHMS   MAIER, G.   3
   DISAPPOINTED SERENADER, THE
      BELWIN-MILLS PUBLISHING CORPORATION   .60
BRAHMS   4
   DREI INTERMEZZI OP. 117
      SCHOTT   1646   1.00
BRAHMS   STEUERMANN, E.
   FANTASIES, OP. 116
      UNIVERSAL EDITION   2267   1.60
BRAHMS
   FOUR PIECES, OP. 119
      NOVELLO AND COMPANY, LTD.   10.0014.04   1.00
BRAHMS   5
   HUNGARIAN DANCE NO. 01
      CENTURY MUSIC PUBLISHING COMPANY, INC.   2447   .40
BRAHMS   4
   HUNGARIAN DANCE NO. 03
      CENTURY MUSIC PUBLISHING COMPANY, INC.   2395   .40
BRAHMS
   HUNGARIAN DANCE NO. 03 IN F
      BANKS AND SON LTD.   .40
BRAHMS   FLETCHER   2
   HUNGARIAN DANCE NO. 05
      BOSTON MUSIC COMPANY   .50
BRAHMS   KAHL   2
   HUNGARIAN DANCE NO. 05
      BOSTON MUSIC COMPANY   .50
BRAHMS
   HUNGARIAN DANCE NO. 05
      CARL FISCHER, INC.   S 1846   .50
BRAHMS   5
   HUNGARIAN DANCE NO. 05
      CENTURY MUSIC PUBLISHING COMPANY, INC.   2203   .40
BRAHMS   JESTON, I. H.   3
   HUNGARIAN DANCE NO. 05
      VOLKWEIN BROS.   .35
BRAHMS
   HUNGARIAN DANCE NO. 05
      WILLIS MUSIC COMPANY   .35

```
BRAHMS                                                      2
   HUNGARIAN DANCE NO. 05
      WILLIS MUSIC COMPANY                                             .35
BRAHMS                  SCHARFENBERG
   HUNGARIAN DANCE NO. 05 IN F SHARP MINOR
      G. SCHIRMER, INC.                            6                   .40
BRAHMS                                                      6
   HUNGARIAN DANCE NO. 06
      CENTURY MUSIC PUBLISHING COMPANY, INC.   2205                    .40
BRAHMS                                                      6
   HUNGARIAN DANCE NO. 06
      CENTURY MUSIC PUBLISHING COMPANY, INC.   3249                    .40
BRAHMS
   HUNGARIAN DANCE NO. 06 IN D FLAT
      G. SCHIRMER, INC.                                                .50
BRAHMS                  JORDA
   HUNGARIAN DANCE NO. 06 IN D FLAT
      G. SCHIRMER, INC.                                                .35
BRAHMS                                                      4
   HUNGARIAN DANCE NO. 07
      CENTURY MUSIC PUBLISHING COMPANY, INC.   3336                    .40
BRAHMS
   HUNGARIAN DANCE NO. 07 IN F
      G. SCHIRMER, INC.                                                .30
BRAHMS                  KREUTZER                            3
   INTERMEZZO
      BOSTON MUSIC COMPANY                                             .50
BRAHMS                                                      4
   INTERMEZZO IN A FLAT, OP. 76 NO. 3
      CENTURY MUSIC PUBLISHING COMPANY, INC.   3837                    .40
BRAHMS
   INTERMEZZO IN A MINOR, OP. 118 NO. 1
      G. SCHIRMER, INC.                                                .35
BRAHMS
   INTERMEZZO IN A, OP. 118 NO. 2
      G. SCHIRMER, INC.                                                .50
BRAHMS                                                      5
   INTERMEZZO IN C, OP. 119 NO. 3
      CENTURY MUSIC PUBLISHING COMPANY, INC.   3491                    .40
BRAHMS
   INTERMEZZO IN C, OP. 119 NO. 3
      G. SCHIRMER, INC.                                                .50
BRAHMS                                                      7
   INTERMEZZO IN E FLAT
      NOVELLO AND COMPANY, LTD.               55.0033.08               .40
BRAHMS                                                      4
   INTERMEZZO IN E FLAT, OP. 117 NO. 1
      CENTURY MUSIC PUBLISHING COMPANY, INC.   3999                    .40
BRAHMS                                                      5
   INTERMEZZO IN E MINOR, OP. 119 NO. 2
      CENTURY MUSIC PUBLISHING COMPANY, INC.   3734                    .40
BRAHMS
   INTERMEZZO IN E, OP. 116 NO. 4
      G. SCHIRMER, INC.                                                .40
BRAHMS
   INTERMEZZO IN E, OP. 116 NO. 6
      G. SCHIRMER, INC.                                                .35
BRAHMS                                                      4-5
   KLAVIERSTUCKE OP. 118
      SCHOTT                                    1647                   1.00
BRAHMS                                                      4-5
   KLAVIERSTUCKE OP. 119
      SCHOTT                                    1648                   1.50
BRAHMS                                                      4
   LIEBESLIEDER-WALZER OP. 52
      SCHOTT                                    1642                   1.50
BRAHMS                  GEST, E.                            3
   LULLABY
      BOSTON MUSIC COMPANY                                             .50
BRAHMS                  WALLIS                              1
   LULLABY
      BOSTON MUSIC COMPANY                                             .50
BRAHMS                                                      4
   LULLABY
      THEODORE PRESSER COMPANY                                         .50
BRAHMS                  THOMPSON, J.                        1
   LULLABY
      WILLIS MUSIC COMPANY                                             .30
BRAHMS                  ZANON
   LULLABY -- WIEGENLIED -- OP. 49 NO. 4
      FRANCO COLOMBO PUBLICATIONS               127656                 .60
BRAHMS                  DEL MAGLIO
   LULLABY -- WIEGENLIED -- OP. 49 NO. 4
      FRANCO COLOMBO PUBLICATIONS               124711                 .50
BRAHMS                  PERSICHETTI
   ORGAN PRELUDE AND FUGUE IN A MINOR
      ELKAN-VOGEL, INC.                                                .60
BRAHMS                  SCHAUM, J.                          4 1/2
   PAGANINI VARIATIONS
      BELWIN-MILLS PUBLISHING CORPORATION                              .50
BRAHMS
   PAGANINI VARIATIONS
      EDWIN F. KALMUS                           3260                   2.00
BRAHMS                  SAUER          D
   PAGANINI VARIATIONS, OP. 35 BK. 1
      C. F. PETERS CORPORATION                  3663A                  1.50
BRAHMS                  SAUER          D
   PAGANINI VARIATIONS, OP. 35 BK. 2
      C. F. PETERS CORPORATION                  3663B                  1.50
BRAHMS                  SAUER          D
   PAGANINI VARIATIONS, OP. 35 COMPLETE
      C. F. PETERS CORPORATION                  3663                   2.50
BRAHMS                  WINDRUSH
   POPULAR WALTZ
      BANKS AND SON LTD.                                               .40
BRAHMS
   PRESTO NACH J.S. BACH
      ASSOCIATED MUSIC PUBLISHERS, INC.         B/H                    1.50
BRAHMS                                                      4
   RHAPSODIE G-MOLL OP. 79 NO. 2
      SCHOTT                                    07570 1/2              1.00
BRAHMS                                                      4
   RHAPSODIE H-MOLL OP. 79 NO. 1
      SCHOTT                                    07569 1/2              1.50
BRAHMS
   RHAPSODIE IN B MINOR, OP. 79 NO. 1
      G. SCHIRMER, INC.                                                .80
BRAHMS
   RHAPSODIE IN E FLAT, OP. 119 NO. 4
      G. SCHIRMER, INC.                                                .70
BRAHMS
   RHAPSODIE IN G MINOR, OP. 79 NO. 2
      G. SCHIRMER, INC.                                                .60
BRAHMS                                                      4
   RHAPSODY IN E MINOR, OP. 119 NO. 4
      CENTURY MUSIC PUBLISHING COMPANY, INC.   3902                    .40

BRAHMS
   RHAPSODY, OP. 119 NO. 4
      FRANCO COLOMBO PUBLICATIONS               ER1062                 .90
BRAHMS
   RHAPSODY, OP. 79 NO. 2
      WILLIS MUSIC COMPANY                                             .50
BRAHMS
   RONDO NACH C.M. VON WEBER
      ASSOCIATED MUSIC PUBLISHERS, INC.         B/H                    1.50
BRAHMS                                          M
   SAINT ANTHONY CHORALE AND FOUR VARIATIONS
      C. F. PETERS CORPORATION                  7088                   1.25
BRAHMS
   SCHERZO IN E FLAT MINOR, OP. 4
      ASSOCIATED MUSIC PUBLISHERS, INC.         B/H                    1.10
BRAHMS                  OEIS
   SCHERZO IN E FLAT MINOR, OP. 4
      G. SCHIRMER, INC.                                                .90
BRAHMS                  KLASEN, W.
   SCHERZO IN E FLAT MINOR, OP. 4
      UNIVERSAL EDITION                         2257                   1.50
BRAHMS                                                      7
   SCHERZO, FROM SONATA IN F MINOR, OP. 5
      THEODORE PRESSER COMPANY                                         .50
BRAHMS
   SIX PIECES, OP. 118
      NOVELLO AND COMPANY, LTD.                10.0013.06              1.00
BRAHMS
   SIXTEEN WALTZES, OP. 39
      ASSOCIATED MUSIC PUBLISHERS, INC.         B/H                    .90
BRAHMS                  KLASEN, W.
   SONATA IN F MINOR, OP. 5
      UNIVERSAL EDITION                         2103                   1.75
BRAHMS
   SONATA NO. 01 IN C, OP. 1
      ASSOCIATED MUSIC PUBLISHERS, INC.         B/H                    1.25
BRAHMS                                                      5
   SONATA NO. 01 IN C, OP. 1, ANDANTE
      CENTURY MUSIC PUBLISHING COMPANY, INC.   2798                    .40
BRAHMS                  WHITING
   SONATA NO. 01 ON C, OP. 1
      G. SCHIRMER, INC.                         L1360                  1.25
BRAHMS
   SONATA NO. 02 IN F SHARP MINOR, OP. 2
      ASSOCIATED MUSIC PUBLISHERS, INC.         B/H                    1.00
BRAHMS
   SONATA NO. 03 IN F MINOR, OP. 5
      ASSOCIATED MUSIC PUBLISHERS, INC.         B/H                    .75
BRAHMS
   SONATA NO. 03 IN F MINOR, OP. 5
      FRANCO COLOMBO PUBLICATIONS               ER1177                 1.00
BRAHMS                  BAUER
   SONATA NO. 03 IN F MINOR, OP. 5
      G. SCHIRMER, INC.                                                1.25
BRAHMS                  FREY, H.
   THIRD SYMPHONY- THEME
      THE BIG THREE MUSIC CORPORATION                                  00.95
BRAHMS
   THREE INTERMEZZOS, OP. 117
      NOVELLO AND COMPANY, LTD.                10.0012.08              1.00
BRAHMS
   TWO RHAPSODIES, OP. 79
      NOVELLO AND COMPANY, LTD.                10.0011.10              1.00
BRAHMS                  KELLER         4
   UNGARISCHER TANZ
      SCHOTT                                    07593 1/2              1.00
BRAHMS                                                      5
   UNGARISCHER TANZ NO. 05
      SCHOTT                                    07585                  .75
BRAHMS                  KELLER         3
   UNGARISCHER TANZ NO. 05
      SCHOTT                                    07589                  .75
BRAHMS                                                      6
   UNGARISCHER TANZ NO. 06
      SCHOTT                                    07586 1/2              1.00
BRAHMS
   VARIATIONS AND FUGUE ON A THEME BY HANDEL, OP. 24
      ASSOCIATED MUSIC PUBLISHERS, INC.         B/H                    1.10
BRAHMS                  SAUER          D
   VARIATIONS AND FUGUE ON A THEME BY HANDEL, OP. 24
      C. F. PETERS CORPORATION                  3926                   2.00
BRAHMS
   VARIATIONS AND FUGUE ON A THEME BY HANDEL, OP. 24
      G. SCHIRMER, INC.                         L1598                  1.00
BRAHMS
   VARIATIONS AND FUGUE ON A THEME OF HANDEL, OP. 24
      FRANCO COLOMBO PUBLICATIONS               ER1008                 1.25
BRAHMS
   VARIATIONS IN A MINOR ON A THEME BY PAGANNINI, OP. 35
      INTERNATIONAL MUSIC COMPANY                                      2.00
BRAHMS
   VARIATIONS ON A THEME BY HAYDN
      G. SCHIRMER, INC.                         L1662                  1.00
BRAHMS                  STARK
   VARIATIONS ON A THEME BY HAYDN, OP. 56A
      ASSOCIATED MUSIC PUBLISHERS, INC.         SIM                    2.00
BRAHMS
   VARIATIONS ON A THEME BY PAGANINI
      ASSOCIATED MUSIC PUBLISHERS, INC.         B/H                    1.50
BRAHMS                  HUGHES
   VARIATIONS ON A THEME BY PAGANINI, OP. 35, BK. 1
      G. SCHIRMER, INC.                         L1450                  1.00
BRAHMS                  HUGHES
   VARIATIONS ON A THEME BY PAGANINI, OP. 35, BK. 2
      G. SCHIRMER, INC.                         L1451                  1.00
BRAHMS
   VARIATIONS ON A THEME BY SCHUMANN, OP. 9
      ASSOCIATED MUSIC PUBLISHERS, INC.         B/H                    .90
BRAHMS                  MONTANI
   VARIATIONS ON A THEME OF PAGANINI, OP. 35
      FRANCO COLOMBO PUBLICATIONS               ER2464                 1.50
BRAHMS                  MONTANI
   VARIATIONS ON A THEME OF SCHUMANN, OP. 9
      FRANCO COLOMBO PUBLICATIONS               ER1006                 1.00
BRAHMS
   VARIATIONS, OP. 21
      ASSOCIATED MUSIC PUBLISHERS, INC.         B/H                    .90
BRAHMS                  LONG, L.       2
   WALTZ
      WILLIS MUSIC COMPANY                                             .40
BRAHMS                  MOSSMAN
   WALTZ IN A FLAT MAJOR
      BELWIN-MILLS PUBLISHING CORPORATION       26103                  .60
BRAHMS                  BARTH, H.
   WALTZ IN A FLAT, OP. 39 NO. 15
      BELWIN-MILLS PUBLISHING CORPORATION       20395                  .60
```

BRAHMS   CHALOFF
  WALTZ IN A FLAT, OP. 39 NO. 15
    CARL FISCHER, INC.   S 2133   .50
BRAHMS   DEIS
  WALTZ IN A FLAT, OP. 39 NO. 15
    G. SCHIRMER, INC.   .30
BRAHMS   BALLATORE
  WALTZ IN A FLAT, OP. 39 NO. 15
    G. SCHIRMER, INC.   .30
BRAHMS
  WALTZ IN G
    FREDERICK HARRIS MUSIC COMPANY   .60
BRAHMS   RUSSELL   2
  WALTZ, OP. 39 NO. 1
    BOSTON MUSIC COMPANY   .50
BRAHMS
  WALTZ, OP. 39 NO. 15
    FRANCO COLOMBO PUBLICATIONS   ER2563   .75
BRAHMS   DEL MAGLIO
  WALTZ, OP. 39 NO. 15
    FRANCO COLOMBO PUBLICATIONS   124712   .50
BRAHMS   THOMPSON, J.   1
  WALTZ, OP. 39 NO. 15
    WILLIS MUSIC COMPANY   .35
BRAHMS
  WALTZES, OP. 39. SIMPLIFIED
    G. HENLE MUSIKVERLAG   43   1.15
BRAHMS   4
  WALZER OP. 39
    SCHOTT   1641   1.00
BRAHMS   2
  WIEGENLIED OP. 49 NO. 4
    SCHOTT   07635   .75
BRAHMS *   STEINER   1-2
  TWO CAPRICES
    CENTURY MUSIC PUBLISHING COMPANY, INC.   3979   .40
BRAHMS--ED.   PARSONS
  GAVOTTE IN A MAJOR --FROM 'IPHIGENIA IN AULIS' BY GLUCK--
    G. SCHIRMER, INC.   .40
BRAINARD, C. S.   2
  STARLIGHT WALTZ
    CENTURY MUSIC PUBLISHING COMPANY, INC.   1110   .40
BRAINARD, C. S.   2
  STARLIGHT WALTZ
    THEODORE PRESSER COMPANY   .50
BRAND *
  MIDNIGHT IN MOSCOW --YOU CAN'T KEEP ME FROM LOVING YOU--
    TRO SONGWAYS SERVICE, INC.   2042
BRANDSTETTER
  PARTITA, 1958 -- HARPSICHORD OR PIANO --
    ASSOCIATED MUSIC PUBLISHERS, INC.   DOB   2.25
BRANDT, D.   2
  LITTLE DONKEY IN THE SNOW
    BELWIN-MILLS PUBLISHING CORPORATION   .60
BRANNAN   2
  BELLE OF THE BALL, WALTZ
    CENTURY MUSIC PUBLISHING COMPANY, INC.   1259   .40
BRANNAN   RICHTER
  SKIPPING ROPE
    FRANCO COLOMBO PUBLICATIONS   NY1510   .35
BRANT
  BANDA, BANDURRIA
    BELWIN-MILLS PUBLISHING CORPORATION   25221   .60
BRANT
  BOMBARDON CHIFONE
    BELWIN-MILLS PUBLISHING CORPORATION   25130   .60
BRANT
  DANZETTA
    SHAWNEE PRESS, INC.   HB-236   .60
BRANT, A.
  FOUP SQUARE MARCH FOR PIANOS -- EASY SOLO PART
    AMERICAN MUSIC EDITION   .75
BRANT, A.
  TRIPTYCH INTERLOCHEN -- A SUITE FOR PIANO
    FEMA MUSIC PUBLICATIONS   1.35
BRASSARD
  NOISETTES, LES -- NO. 1, FROM ''ORLEANAISES'' SUITE
    ASSOCIATED MUSIC PUBLISHERS, INC.   BER   .75
BRASSARD
  ORATOIRE A LA CROISEE DES CHEMINS -- NO. 2, FROM ''ORLEANAISES''
    SUITE
    ASSOCIATED MUSIC PUBLISHERS, INC.   BER   .75
BRATTON
  TEDDY BEARS' PICNIC, THE
    WARNER BROTHERS PUBLISHERS   1.00
BRATTON   MACLACHLAN   FIRST YEAR
  TEDDY BEARS' PICNIC, THE
    WARNER BROTHERS PUBLISHERS   .75
BRAUN, Y.
  SONATA
    ISRAEL MUSIC INSTITUTE   4.00
BRAUNON   3
  VALSE D'AMOUR
    CENTURY MUSIC PUBLISHING COMPANY, INC.   1309   .40
BRAUTIGAM
  SONATA, OP. 6
    ASSOCIATED MUSIC PUBLISHERS, INC.   B/H   2.40
BRAVIS, B.   2
  LITTLE TAMBOURINES
    THEODORE PRESSER COMPANY   .50
BRAZELTON
  LANTERNS
    WARNER BROTHERS PUBLISHERS   .85
BREAU, L.   1 1/2
  ON THE ISLAND OF KOO-KOO
    BELWIN-MILLS PUBLISHING CORPORATION   .60
BRERO
  TOCCATA
    FRANCO COLOMBO PUBLICATIONS   BA9763   .75
BRES, D. J.   3 1/2
  ALONG THE WAY
    THEODORE PRESSER COMPANY   .50
BRES, D. J.   2
  GAY MOOD
    BELWIN-MILLS PUBLISHING CORPORATION   .60
BRES, D. J.   3
  TRAIL RIDGE
    BOSTON MUSIC COMPANY   .50
BRETON   3
  BUTTERFLY WALTZ, THE
    CENTURY MUSIC PUBLISHING COMPANY, INC.   2504   .40
BRETON   3
  VALSE PAPILLON
    CENTURY MUSIC PUBLISHING COMPANY, INC.   2504   .40
BREWER
  ROMANTICS, THE
    PRO-ART PUBLICATIONS, INC.   521   .50

BRICUSSE *   SCHAUM, J.   2
  CANDY MAN
    SCHAUM PUBLICATIONS, INC.   .75
BRIDGE, F.
  BITTERSWEET
    BOOSEY AND HAWKES, INC.   .60
BRIDGE, F.
  ROSEMARY
    BOOSEY AND HAWKES, INC.   .60
BRIDGE, F.
  VALSE CAPRICIEUSE
    BOOSEY AND HAWKES, INC.   .75
BRIDGE, F.
  WATER NYMPHS
    BOOSEY AND HAWKES, INC.   .75
BRIED, F.   2 1/2
  DRIFTING
    BELWIN-MILLS PUBLISHING CORPORATION   .60
BRIED, F.   2 1/2
  SWISS VILLAGE
    BELWIN-MILLS PUBLISHING CORPORATION   .60
BRIGGS, R.   M
  FACETIOUS
    COMPOSERS PRESS, INC.   1.00
BRIGHT
  FOUR FOR PIANO. A SHORT SUITE
    ASSOCIATED MUSIC PUBLISHERS, INC.   AMP   1.25
BRILLHART   2
  CHANGING SCENES
    PRO-ART PUBLICATIONS, INC.   415   .50
BRIMHALL, J.   2-3
  BIKE RIDE
    PRO-ART PUBLICATIONS, INC.   163   .50
BRIMHALL, J.   1-2
  HANNIBAL'S MARCH
    PRO-ART PUBLICATIONS, INC.   267   .50
BRIMHALL, J.   2
  INTERLUDE
    PRO-ART PUBLICATIONS, INC.   268   .50
BRIMHALL, J.   2-3
  MERRY-GO-ROUND, THE
    PRO-ART PUBLICATIONS, INC.   164   .50
BRIMHALL, J.   2-3
  WANDERING COWBOY, THE
    PRO-ART PUBLICATIONS, INC.   165   .50
BRIMHALL, J.--ED.   BRIMHALL, J.
  ABRAHAM, MARTIN AND JOHN
    CHARLES HANSEN   35960   .85
BRIMHALL, J.--ED.   BRIMHALL, J.
  ALFIE
    CHARLES HANSEN   F30001   .85
BRIMHALL, J.--ED.   BRIMHALL, J.
  ALL KINDS OF PEOPLE
    CHARLES HANSEN   X30114   .85
BRIMHALL, J.--ED.   BRIMHALL, J.
  ALSO SPRACH ZARATHUSTRA
    CHARLES HANSEN   35979   .85
BRIMHALL, J.--ED.   BRIMHALL, J.
  AMAZING GRACE/HE'S GOT THE WHOLE WORLD IN HIS HANDS
    CHARLES HANSEN   35866   .85
BRIMHALL, J.--ED.   BRIMHALL, J.
  APPLAUSE
    CHARLES HANSEN   .85
BRIMHALL, J.--ED.   BRIMHALL, J.
  AROUND THE WORLD
    CHARLES HANSEN   35912   .85
BRIMHALL, J.--ED.   BRIMHALL, J.
  AUTUMN LEAVES
    CHARLES HANSEN   E32018   .85
BRIMHALL, J.--ED.   BRIMHALL, J.
  BABY ELEPHANT WALK
    CHARLES HANSEN   F30066   .85
BRIMHALL, J.--ED.   BRIMHALL, J.
  BATTLE HYMN OF THE REPUBLIC
    CHARLES HANSEN   35968   .85
BRIMHALL, J.--ED.   BRIMHALL, J.
  BEGINNINGS
    CHARLES HANSEN   35883   .85
BRIMHALL, J.--ED.   BRIMHALL, J.
  BIBLE TELLS ME SO, THE
    CHARLES HANSEN   F30069   .85
BRIMHALL, J.--ED.   BRIMHALL, J.
  BLACK AND WHITE
    CHARLES HANSEN   35943   .85
BRIMHALL, J.--ED.   BRIMHALL, J.
  BY THE TIME I GET TO PHOENIX
    CHARLES HANSEN   35163   .85
BRIMHALL, J.--ED.   BRIMHALL, J.
  CANDY MAN, THE
    CHARLES HANSEN   35929   .85
BRIMHALL, J.--ED.   BRIMHALL, J.
  CAROL OF THE BELLS
    CHARLES HANSEN   .85
BRIMHALL, J.--ED.   BRIMHALL, J.
  CHERISH
    CHARLES HANSEN   35906   .85
BRIMHALL, J.--ED.   BRIMHALL, J.
  CHIM CHIM CHER-EE
    CHARLES HANSEN   30007   .85
BRIMHALL, J.--ED.   BRIMHALL, J.
  CHRISTMAS SONG, THE
    CHARLES HANSEN   .85
BRIMHALL, J.--ED.   BRIMHALL, J.
  CLASSICAL GAS
    CHARLES HANSEN   35402   .85
BRIMHALL, J.--ED.   BRIMHALL, J.
  CLOSE TO YOU
    CHARLES HANSEN   X30110   .85
BRIMHALL, J.--ED.   BRIMHALL, J.
  COLOUR MY WORLD
    CHARLES HANSEN   35882   .85
BRIMHALL, J.--ED.   BRIMHALL, J.
  COME SATURDAY MORNING
    CHARLES HANSEN   F30064   .85
BRIMHALL, J.--ED.   BRIMHALL, J.
  CRACKLIN ROSIE
    CHARLES HANSEN   35845   .85
BRIMHALL, J.--ED.   BRIMHALL, J.
  CRAZY HORSES
    CHARLES HANSEN   35961   .85
BRIMHALL, J.--ED.   BRIMHALL, J.
  DEAR WORLD
    CHARLES HANSEN   E32002   .85
BRIMHALL, J.--ED.   BRIMHALL, J.
  DIDN'T WE
    CHARLES HANSEN   35408   .85

BRIMHALL, J.--ED.	BRIMHALL, J.		
DIZZY			
CHARLES HANSEN		35573	.85
BRIMHALL, J.--ED.	BRIMHALL, J.		
DO YOU KNOW THE WAY TO SAN JOSE			
CHARLES HANSEN		X30102	.85
BRIMHALL, J.--ED.	BRIMHALL, J.		
DOWN BY THE LAZY RIVER			
CHARLES HANSEN		35914	.85
BRIMHALL, J.--ED.	BRIMHALL, J.		
DOWNTOWN			
CHARLES HANSEN		35888	.85
BRIMHALL, J.--ED.	BRIMHALL, J.		
DUELING BANJO			
CHARLES HANSEN		35966	.85
BRIMHALL, J.--ED.	BRIMHALL, J.		
EVERYTHING IS BEAUTIFUL			
CHARLES HANSEN		35817	.85
BRIMHALL, J.--ED.	BRIMHALL, J.		
FASCINATION			
CHARLES HANSEN		32262	.85
BRIMHALL, J.--ED.	BRIMHALL, J.		
FOR THE GOOD TIMES			
CHARLES HANSEN		35865	.85
BRIMHALL, J.--ED.	BRIMHALL, J.		
FREE			
CHARLES HANSEN		35864	.85
BRIMHALL, J.--ED.	BRIMHALL, J.		
FUNNY FACE			
CHARLES HANSEN		35956	.85
BRIMHALL, J.--ED.	BRIMHALL, J.		
GENTLE ON MY MIND			
CHARLES HANSEN		35054	.85
BRIMHALL, J.--ED.	BRIMHALL, J.		
GET ME TO THE CHURCH ON TIME			
CHARLES HANSEN		35922	.85
BRIMHALL, J.--ED.	BRIMHALL, J.		
GIRL FROM IPANEMA, THE			
CHARLES HANSEN		35874	.85
BRIMHALL, J.--ED.	BRIMHALL, J.		
GODFATHER WALTZ			
CHARLES HANSEN		F30080	.85
BRIMHALL, J.--ED.	BRIMHALL, J.		
GREEN,GREEN GRASS OF HOME			
CHARLES HANSEN		35837	.85
BRIMHALL, J.--ED.	BRIMHALL, J.		
GREENSLEEVES			
CHARLES HANSEN		35856	.85
BRIMHALL, J.--ED.	BRIMHALL, J.		
GUANTANAMERA			
ASHLEY DEALERS SERVICE, INC.			1.00
BRIMHALL, J.--ED.	BRIMHALL, J.		
GUANTANAMERA			
CHARLES HANSEN		34769	.85
BRIMHALL, J.--ED.	BRIMHALL, J.		
HAVE YOU EVER SEEN THE RAIN			
CHARLES HANSEN		35859	.85
BRIMHALL, J.--ED.	BRIMHALL, J.		
HAWAIIAN WEDDING SONG, THE			
CHARLES HANSEN		35873	.85
BRIMHALL, J.--ED.	BRIMHALL, J.		
HE AIN'T HEAVY...HE'S MY BROTHER			
CHARLES HANSEN		35847	.85
BRIMHALL, J.--ED.	BRIMHALL, J.		
HELLO, DOLLY			
CHARLES HANSEN		E32003	.85
BRIMHALL, J.--ED.	BRIMHALL, J.		
HEY, LOOK ME OVER			
CHARLES HANSEN		E32013	.85
BRIMHALL, J.--ED.	BRIMHALL, J.		
HONEY			
CHARLES HANSEN		3533	.85
BRIMHALL, J.--ED.	BRIMHALL, J.		
HOUSE OF THE RISING SUN, THE			
CHARLES HANSEN		35813	.85
BRIMHALL, J.--ED.	BRIMHALL, J.		
HOW INSENSITIVE			
CHARLES HANSEN		35905	.85
BRIMHALL, J.--ED.	BRIMHALL, J.		
I AM ... I SAID			
CHARLES HANSEN		35870	.85
BRIMHALL, J.--ED.	BRIMHALL, J.		
I AM WOMAN			
CHARLES HANSEN		35964	.85
BRIMHALL, J.--ED.	BRIMHALL, J.		
I LEFT MY HEART IN SAN FRANCISCO			
CHARLES HANSEN		30014	.85
BRIMHALL, J.--ED.	BRIMHALL, J.		
I NEVER PROMISED YOU A ROSE GARDEN			
CHARLES HANSEN		35854	.85
BRIMHALL, J.--ED.	BRIMHALL, J.		
I'LL BE HOME FOR CHRISTMAS			
CHARLES HANSEN			.85
BRIMHALL, J.--ED.	BRIMHALL, J.		
I'LL NEVER FALL IN LOVE AGAIN			
CHARLES HANSEN		E32015	.85
BRIMHALL, J.--ED.	BRIMHALL, J.		
I'VE GROWN ACCUSTOMED TO HER FACE			
CHARLES HANSEN		35923	.85
BRIMHALL, J.--ED.	BRIMHALL, J.		
IMPOSSIBLE DREAM, THE			
CHARLES HANSEN		35841	.85
BRIMHALL, J.--ED.	BRIMHALL, J.		
ISN'T IT A PITY			
CHARLES HANSEN		35849	.85
BRIMHALL, J.--ED.	BRIMHALL, J.		
IT WAS A VERY GOOD YEAR			
CHARLES HANSEN		30015	.85
BRIMHALL, J.--ED.	BRIMHALL, J.		
IT'S A SMALL WORLD			
CHARLES HANSEN		35913	.85
BRIMHALL, J.--ED.	BRIMHALL, J.		
IT'S IMPOSSIBLE			
CHARLES HANSEN		35903	.85
BRIMHALL, J.--ED.	BRIMHALL, J.		
IT'S NOT UNUSUAL			
CHARLES HANSEN		35906	.85
BRIMHALL, J.--ED.	BRIMHALL, J.		
JEAN			
CHARLES HANSEN		T31002	.85
BRIMHALL, J.--ED.	BRIMHALL, J.		
JOIN TOGETHER			
CHARLES HANSEN		35935	.85
BRIMHALL, J.--ED.	BRIMHALL, J.		
JOY TO THE WORLD			
CHARLES HANSEN		35942	.85

BRIMHALL, J.--ED.	BRIMHALL, J.		
KING OF THE ROAD			
CHARLES HANSEN		30018	.85
BRIMHALL, J.--ED.	BRIMHALL, J.		
LET IT BE ME			
CHARLES HANSEN		35887	.85
BRIMHALL, J.--ED.	BRIMHALL, J.		
LET IT SNOW, LET IT SNOW			
CHARLES HANSEN			.85
BRIMHALL, J.--ED.	BRIMHALL, J.		
LET THERE BE PEACE ON EARTH			
CHARLES HANSEN		30046	.85
BRIMHALL, J.--ED.	BRIMHALL, J.		
LITTLE GREEN APPLES			
CHARLES HANSEN		35297	.85
BRIMHALL, J.--ED.	BRIMHALL, J.		
LOVE IS BLUE			
CHARLES HANSEN		35896	.85
BRIMHALL, J.--ED.	BRIMHALL, J.		
LOVE IS ONLY LOVE			
CHARLES HANSEN		E32014	.85
BRIMHALL, J.--ED.	BRIMHALL, J.		
LOVE THEME FROM ROMEO AMD JULIET			
CHARLES HANSEN		35748	.85
BRIMHALL, J.--ED.	BRIMHALL, J.		
LOVE THEME FROM THE GODFATHER			
CHARLES HANSEN		F30079	.85
BRIMHALL, J.--ED.	BRIMHALL, J.		
MAME			
CHARLES HANSEN		E32004	.85
BRIMHALL, J.--ED.	BRIMHALL, J.		
MAMMY BLUE			
CHARLES HANSEN		35895	.85
BRIMHALL, J.--ED.	BRIMHALL, J.		
MAN AND A WOMAN, A			
CHARLES HANSEN		35886	.85
BRIMHALL, J.--ED.	BRIMHALL, J.		
MASTERPIECE, THE			
CHARLES HANSEN			.85
BRIMHALL, J.--ED.	BRIMHALL, J.		
MAY THE GOOD LORD BLESS AND KEEP YOU			
CHARLES HANSEN		35901	.85
BRIMHALL, J.--ED.	BRIMHALL, J.		
ME AND BOBBY MCGEE			
CHARLES HANSEN		35867	.85
BRIMHALL, J.--ED.	BRIMHALL, J.		
MEDITATION			
CHARLES HANSEN		35885	.85
BRIMHALL, J.--ED.	BRIMHALL, J.		
MIDNIGHT COWBOY			
CHARLES HANSEN		E32020	.85
BRIMHALL, J.--ED.	BRIMHALL, J.		
MIMI			
CHARLES HANSEN		F30067	.85
BRIMHALL, J.--ED.	BRIMHALL, J.		
MISSION# IMPOSSIBLE			
CHARLES HANSEN		35335	.85
BRIMHALL, J.--ED.	BRIMHALL, J.		
MISTY			
CHARLES HANSEN		T31020	.85
BRIMHALL, J.--ED.	BRIMHALL, J.		
MOON OVER MIAMI			
CHARLES HANSEN		A51028	.85
BRIMHALL, J.--ED.	BRIMHALL, J.		
MOON RIVER			
CHARLES HANSEN		F30032	.85
BRIMHALL, J.--ED.	BRIMHALL, J.		
MOZART SYMPHONY NO. 40			
CHARLES HANSEN		35872	.85
BRIMHALL, J.--ED.	BRIMHALL, J.		
MY FUNNY VALENTINE			
CHARLES HANSEN		35919	.85
BRIMHALL, J.--ED.	BRIMHALL, J.		
MY SWEET LORD			
CHARLES HANSEN		35840	.85
BRIMHALL, J.--ED.	BRIMHALL, J.		
MY WAY			
CHARLES HANSEN		35697	.85
BRIMHALL, J.--ED.	BRIMHALL, J.		
MY YIDDISCHE MOMMA			
CHARLES HANSEN		35920	.85
BRIMHALL, J.--ED.	BRIMHALL, J.		
NEVER ON SUNDAY			
CHARLES HANSEN		30026	.85
BRIMHALL, J.--ED.	BRIMHALL, J.		
NIGHT THEY DROVE OLD DIXIE DOWN, THE			
CHARLES HANSEN		35898	.85
BRIMHALL, J.--ED.	BRIMHALL, J.		
NOLA			
CHARLES HANSEN		30394	.85
BRIMHALL, J.--ED.	BRIMHALL, J.		
O HOLY NIGHT			
CHARLES HANSEN			.85
BRIMHALL, J.--ED.	BRIMHALL, J.		
ON THE STREET WHERE YOU LIVE			
CHARLES HANSEN		35921	.85
BRIMHALL, J.--ED.	BRIMHALL, J.		
ONE BAD APPLE			
CHARLES HANSEN		35860	.85
BRIMHALL, J.--ED.	BRIMHALL, J.		
ONE LESS BELL TO ANSWER			
CHARLES HANSEN		X30113	.85
BRIMHALL, J.--ED.	BRIMHALL, J.		
ONE NOTE SAMBA			
CHARLES HANSEN		35892	.85
BRIMHALL, J.--ED.	BRIMHALL, J.		
ONE OF THOSE SONGS			
CHARLES HANSEN		35907	.85
BRIMHALL, J.--ED.	BRIMHALL, J.		
OTHER MAN'S GRASS IS ALWAYS GREENER, THE			
CHARLES HANSEN		35908	.85
BRIMHALL, J.--ED.	BRIMHALL, J.		
OVERTURE FROM 'TOMY'			
CHARLES HANSEN		35829	.85
BRIMHALL, J.--ED.	BRIMHALL, J.		
PEACEFUL			
CHARLES HANSEN		35977	.85
BRIMHALL, J.--ED.	BRIMHALL, J.		
PINBALL WIZARD			
CHARLES HANSEN		35965	.85
BRIMHALL, J.--ED.	BRIMHALL, J.		
PROMISES, PROMISES			
CHARLES HANSEN		E32017	.85
BRIMHALL, J.--ED.	BRIMHALL, J.		
PROUD MARY			
CHARLES HANSEN		35855	.85

BRIMHALL, J.--ED.   BRIMHALL, J.
PUT YOUR HAND IN THE HAND
     CHARLES HANSEN   35869   .85
BRIMHALL, J.--ED.   BRIMHALL, J.
QUIET NIGHTS OF QUIET STARS
     CHARLES HANSEN   35893   .85
BRIMHALL, J.--ED.   BRIMHALL, J.
RAIN IN SPAIN, THE
     CHARLES HANSEN   35924   .85
BRIMHALL, J.--ED.   BRIMHALL, J.
RAINDROPS KEEP FALLIN' ON MY HEAD
     CHARLES HANSEN   X30105   .85
BRIMHALL, J.--ED.   BRIMHALL, J.
RUBBER DUCKIE
     CHARLES HANSEN   35836   .85
BRIMHALL, J.--ED.   BRIMHALL, J.
SATURDAY IN THE PARK
     CHARLES HANSEN   35936   .85
BRIMHALL, J.--ED.
SCARBOROUGH FAIR
     ASHLEY DEALERS SERVICE, INC.   1.00
BRIMHALL, J.--ED.   BRIMHALL, J.
SCARBOROUGH FAIR
     CHARLES HANSEN   35490   .85
BRIMHALL, J.--ED.   BRIMHALL, J.
SEPARATE WAYS
     CHARLES HANSEN   35962   .85
BRIMHALL, J.--ED.   BRIMHALL, J.
SILENT NIGHT
     CHARLES HANSEN   .85
BRIMHALL, J.--ED.   BRIMHALL, J.
SILVER BELLS
     CHARLES HANSEN   F30070   .85
BRIMHALL, J.--ED.   BRIMHALL, J.
SNOWBIRD
     CHARLES HANSEN   35848   .85
BRIMHALL, J.--ED.   BRIMHALL, J.
SO NICE
     CHARLES HANSEN   35891   .85
BRIMHALL, J.--ED.   BRIMHALL, J.
SOMEDAY NEVER COMES
     CHARLES HANSEN   35928   .85
BRIMHALL, J.--ED.   BRIMHALL, J.
SOMETHING
     CHARLES HANSEN   35821   .85
BRIMHALL, J.--ED.   BRIMHALL, J.
SOMETHING STUPID
     CHARLES HANSEN   30070   .85
BRIMHALL, J.--ED.   BRIMHALL, J.
SONG FROM MASH
     CHARLES HANSEN   T31024   .85
BRIMHALL, J.--ED.   BRIMHALL, J.
SONG SUNG BLUE
     CHARLES HANSEN   35927   .85
BRIMHALL, J.--ED.   BRIMHALL, J.
SOUND OF MUSIC, THE
     CHARLES HANSEN   35974   .85
BRIMHALL, J.--ED.   BRIMHALL, J.
SPANISH FLEA
     CHARLES HANSEN   30033   .85
BRIMHALL, J.--ED.   BRIMHALL, J.
SPEAK SOFTLY LOVE--THE GODFATHER--
     CHARLES HANSEN   F30081   .85
BRIMHALL, J.--ED.   BRIMHALL, J.
STRANGERS IN THE NIGHT
     CHARLES HANSEN   35889   .85
BRIMHALL, J.--ED.   BRIMHALL, J.
SWEET CAROLINE
     CHARLES HANSEN   35792   .85
BRIMHALL, J.--ED.   BRIMHALL, J.
SWEET HITCH-HIKER
     CHARLES HANSEN   .85
BRIMHALL, J.--ED.   BRIMHALL, J.
TAMMY
     CHARLES HANSEN   35900   .85
BRIMHALL, J.--ED.   BRIMHALL, J.
TASTE OF HONEY, A
     CHARLES HANSEN   30060   .85
BRIMHALL, J.--ED.   BRIMHALL, J.
TENDERLY
     CHARLES HANSEN   E32008   .85
BRIMHALL, J.--ED.   BRIMHALL, J.
THEME FROM LOVE STORY
     CHARLES HANSEN   F30072   .85
BRIMHALL, J.--ED.   BRIMHALL, J.
THIS GUY'S IN LOVE WITH YOU
     CHARLES HANSEN   X30103   .85
BRIMHALL, J.--ED.   BRIMHALL, J.
THIS IS MY COUNTRY
     CHARLES HANSEN   35815   .85
BRIMHALL, J.--ED.   BRIMHALL, J.
THIS IS MY SONG
     CHARLES HANSEN   35909   .85
BRIMHALL, J.--ED.   BRIMHALL, J.
THOROUGHLY MODERN MILLIE
     CHARLES HANSEN   35910   .85
BRIMHALL, J.--ED.   BRIMHALL, J.
TIAJUANA TAXI
     CHARLES HANSEN   30037   .85
BRIMHALL, J.--ED.   BRIMHALL, J.
TIE ME KANGAROO DOWN
     CHARLES HANSEN   35932   .85
BRIMHALL, J.--ED.   BRIMHALL, J.
TIME FOR US, A --ROMEO AND JULIET --
     CHARLES HANSEN   F30071   .85
BRIMHALL, J.--ED.   BRIMHALL, J.
TWELVE DAYS OF CHRISTMAS
     CHARLES HANSEN   .85
BRIMHALL, J.--ED.   BRIMHALL, J.
UNDER PARIS SKIES
     CHARLES HANSEN   35902   .85
BRIMHALL, J.--ED.   BRIMHALL, J.
UP AROUND THE BEND
     CHARLES HANSEN   .85
BRIMHALL, J.--ED.   BRIMHALL, J.
UP, UP AND AWAY
     CHARLES HANSEN   34042   .85
BRIMHALL, J.--ED.   BRIMHALL, J.
WE NEED A LITTLE CHRISTMAS
     CHARLES HANSEN   .85
BRIMHALL, J.--ED.   BRIMHALL, J.
WEDDING SONG
     CHARLES HANSEN   35897   .85
BRIMHALL, J.--ED.   BRIMHALL, J.
WHAT IS A YOUTH --ROMEO AND JULIET --
     CHARLES HANSEN   35747   .85

BRIMHALL, J.--ED.   BRIMHALL, J.
WHAT THE WORLD NEEDS NOW IS LOVE
     CHARLES HANSEN   X30104   .85
BRIMHALL, J.--ED.   BRIMHALL, J.
WHERE DO I BEGIN --LOVE STORY --
     CHARLES HANSEN   F30073   .85
BRIMHALL, J.--ED.   BRIMHALL, J.
WHY
     CHARLES HANSEN   35939   .85
BRIMHALL, J.--ED.   BRIMHALL, J.
WINDY
     CHARLES HANSEN   34041   .85
BRIMHALL, J.--ED.   BRIMHALL, J.
WINTER WONDERLAND
     CHARLES HANSEN   T31021   .85
BRIMHALL, J.--ED.   BRIMHALL, J.
WITCHCRAFT
     CHARLES HANSEN   E32027   .85
BRIMHALL, J.--ED.   BRIMHALL, J.
WITHOUT YOU
     CHARLES HANSEN   35915   .85
BRIMHALL, J.--ED.   BRIMHALL, J.
YOU'RE SO VAIN
     CHARLES HANSEN   35959   .85
BRINKMANN   3
FAR AWAY, REMEMBER ME
     CENTURY MUSIC PUBLISHING COMPANY, INC. 371   .40
BRINKMANN   3
FLEETING HOURS, PASTORALE
     CENTURY MUSIC PUBLISHING COMPANY, INC. 1074   .40
BRINKMANN   3
REMEMBER ME -- FAR AWAY --
     CENTURY MUSIC PUBLISHING COMPANY, INC. 371   .40
BRITAIN   EASY INTER.
ANGEL CHIMES -- EASY INTER.
     AMERICAN MUSIC EDITION   .50
BRITAIN
ENSENADA
     FRANCO COLOMBO PUBLICATIONS   BR2269   .60
BRITTEN, B.
HOLIDAY DIARY, OP. 5
     BOOSEY AND HAWKES, INC.   3.00
BRITTEN, B.
MOZART CADENZAS, K. 482
     FABER MUSIC, LTD.   F0091
BRITTEN, B.
NIGHT PIECE -- NOTTURNO
     BOOSEY AND HAWKES, INC.   1.50
BRODSKY, M.   2
CALL OF THE RANGE
     CENTURY MUSIC PUBLISHING COMPANY, INC. 4201   .40
BRODSKY, M.   2
CALYPSO PARTY
     ELKAN-VOGEL, INC.   .50
BRODSKY, M.   1
CATCH ME
     PRO-ART PUBLICATIONS, INC.   422   .50
BRODSKY, M.   1
CHING-CHEE
     CENTURY MUSIC PUBLISHING COMPANY, INC. 4143   .40
BRODSKY, M.   1
COME OUT, COME OUT
     ELKAN-VOGEL, INC.   .50
BRODSKY, M.   2-3
DANCING IN ISRAEL
     CENTURY MUSIC PUBLISHING COMPANY, INC. 4191   .40
BRODSKY, M.   1
DAY DREAMING
     CENTURY MUSIC PUBLISHING COMPANY, INC. 4303   .40
BRODSKY, M.
ESCAPADE
     BELWIN-MILLS PUBLISHING CORPORATION   .60
BRODSKY, M.   2
FALSE ALARM
     CENTURY MUSIC PUBLISHING COMPANY, INC. 4233   .40
BRODSKY, M.   2
FINGER FROLICS -- 1. CHASING RABBITS
     ELKAN-VOGEL, INC.   .50
BRODSKY, M.   2
FINGER FROLICS -- 2. CUCKOO ON A SPREE
     ELKAN-VOGEL, INC.   .50
BRODSKY, M.   2
FINGER FROLICS -- 4. CAMP SPIRIT
     ELKAN-VOGEL, INC.   .50
BRODSKY, M.   1 1/2
FLAG DAY PARADE
     ELKAN-VOGEL, INC.   .50
BRODSKY, M.
GAY GOUCHO
     ELKAN-VOGEL, INC.   .50
BRODSKY, M.   2
HAND IN HAND
     CENTURY MUSIC PUBLISHING COMPANY, INC. 4200   .40
BRODSKY, M.   1
HAPPY LITTLE MEN
     CENTURY MUSIC PUBLISHING COMPANY, INC. 4234   .40
BRODSKY, M.   2
HOLIDAY HORA
     PRO-ART PUBLICATIONS, INC.   421   .50
BRODSKY, M.   2-3
HOW D'YOU DO, MY PARTNER
     ELKAN-VOGEL, INC.   .50
BRODSKY, M.   2
I SAW A HORSE
     CENTURY MUSIC PUBLISHING COMPANY, INC. 4193   .40
BRODSKY, M.   1
IN GRANDMA'S CLOSET
     BELWIN-MILLS PUBLISHING CORPORATION   .60
BRODSKY, M.   3 1/2
IN THE LAND OF ISRAEL
     THEODORE PRESSER COMPANY   .50
BRODSKY, M.   1
INDIAN BRAVE
     CENTURY MUSIC PUBLISHING COMPANY, INC. 4274   .40
BRODSKY, M.   1
IT'S A DATE
     CENTURY MUSIC PUBLISHING COMPANY, INC. 4411   .40
BRODSKY, M.   2
JOGGIN' ALONG
     BELWIN-MILLS PUBLISHING CORPORATION   .60
BRODSKY, M.   2 1/2
JOLLY BARBER, THE
     ELKAN-VOGEL, INC.   .50
BRODSKY, M.   2
KING LION
     CENTURY MUSIC PUBLISHING COMPANY, INC. 4246   .40

BRODSKY, M.   3
    LADY FAN TAN
        BELWIN-MILLS PUBLISHING CORPORATION   .60
BRODSKY, M.   1B
    LEMONADE FOR SALE
        MUSICORD PUBLICATIONS, INC.   .45
BRODSKY, M.   1
    LISTEN TO THE WOODPECKER
        ELKAN-VOGEL, INC.   .50
BRODSKY, M.   1 1/2
    LOOK AT ME
        CENTURY MUSIC PUBLISHING COMPANY, INC.   013   .40
BRODSKY, M.   3
    MARCH OF THE PHANTOM BRIGADE
        BELWIN-MILLS PUBLISHING CORPORATION   .60
BRODSKY, M.   2
    MI AMIGO PEPITO
        CENTURY MUSIC PUBLISHING COMPANY, INC.   4192   .40
BRODSKY, M.   2
    MY WALKING, TALKING DOLL
        CENTURY MUSIC PUBLISHING COMPANY, INC.   4202   .40
BRODSKY, M.   2
    NEW BOY, THE
        CENTURY MUSIC PUBLISHING COMPANY, INC.   4227   .40
BRODSKY, M.   2
    NO MORE DARK CLOUDS
        CENTURY MUSIC PUBLISHING COMPANY, INC.   4172   .40
BRODSKY, M.   1
    NO ONE TO PLAY WITH
        CENTURY MUSIC PUBLISHING COMPANY, INC.   014   .40
BRODSKY, M.   1
    NOBODY HOME
        CENTURY MUSIC PUBLISHING COMPANY, INC.   4304   .40
BRODSKY, M.   1
    OFF TO SEA
        CENTURY MUSIC PUBLISHING COMPANY, INC.   4144   .40
BRODSKY, M.   2
    OH ME, OH MY
        CENTURY MUSIC PUBLISHING COMPANY, INC.   022   .40
BRODSKY, M.   2 1/2
    POSTLUDE
        THEODORE PRESSER COMPANY   .50
BRODSKY, M.   2
    QUIET ECHOES
        CENTURY MUSIC PUBLISHING COMPANY, INC.   4235   .40
BRODSKY, M.   2
    RAIN, RAIN GO AWAY
        CENTURY MUSIC PUBLISHING COMPANY, INC.   4142   .40
BRODSKY, M.   2
    RING OUT BELLS
        CENTURY MUSIC PUBLISHING COMPANY, INC.   4273   .40
BRODSKY, M.   1-2
    SAID THE WIND TO ME
        CENTURY MUSIC PUBLISHING COMPANY, INC.   4145   .40
BRODSKY, M.   1
    SERGEANT MAJOR
        CENTURY MUSIC PUBLISHING COMPANY, INC.   016   .40
BRODSKY, M.   1
    SING LOW, SING HIGH
        CENTURY MUSIC PUBLISHING COMPANY, INC.   4261   .40
BRODSKY, M.   1-2
    SNOW MOUNTAINS
        CENTURY MUSIC PUBLISHING COMPANY, INC.   4199   .40
BRODSKY, M.   1
    SOUND OF THE DRUMS
        CENTURY MUSIC PUBLISHING COMPANY, INC.   4141   .40
BRODSKY, M.   1-2
    SUCH A FUNNY BUNNY
        CENTURY MUSIC PUBLISHING COMPANY, INC.   4203   .40
BRODSKY, M.   1 1/2 - 2
    THAT'S FOR ME
        ELKAN-VOGEL, INC.   .50
BRODSKY, M.   2 1/2
    TOM FOOLERY
        BELWIN-MILLS PUBLISHING CORPORATION   .60
BRODSKY, M.   2 1/2
    TRAVELS OF A FOLK TUNE
        BELWIN-MILLS PUBLISHING CORPORATION   .60
BRODSKY, M.   1
    WHEN NIGHT BEGINS
        CENTURY MUSIC PUBLISHING COMPANY, INC.   0115   .40
BROGI
    ISABELLA ORSINI - INTERMEZZO
        FRANCO COLOMBO PUBLICATIONS   FOR. 10917 .90
BRONS   D
    IMAGINATIONS
        C. F. PETERS CORPORATION   D417   1.50
BRONSON, M.   1
    JOLLY SAILOR MARCH
        VOLKWEIN BROS.   .25
BRONSON, M.   1
    PLAY THE SCALE OF C
        VOLKWEIN BROS.   .25
BROOM, P.
    ALL THE YEAR ROUND
        BOOSEY AND HAWKES, INC.   1.25
BROOM, P.
    FESTIVAL GROUPS FOR PIANO SELECTED BY ARTHUR BENJAMIN, SERIES 2
    -- THE LITTLE GREEN PIPER
        BOOSEY AND HAWKES, INC.   .60
BROOM, P.
    OVER THE BRIDGE
        BOOSEY AND HAWKES, INC.   1.25
BROUTMAN--ED   BROUTMAN   3
    KUM BAH YAH - AFRICAN FOLK SONG
        PRO-ART PUBLICATIONS, INC.   448   .50
BROUTMAN, E.   3
    FANDANGO
        PRO-ART PUBLICATIONS, INC.   367   .50
BROUTMAN, E.   2
    STAGECOACH TRAIL
        WILLIS MUSIC COMPANY   .40
BROUWERS, S. B.   4
    COMING OF SPRING, THE
        THEODORE PRESSER COMPANY   .60
BROWN   2-3
    FAREWELL
        PRO-ART PUBLICATIONS, INC.   486   .50
BROWN   2
    SULTAN'S BAND, MARCH
        CENTURY MUSIC PUBLISHING COMPANY, INC.   1495   .40
BROWN *
    TEMPTATION
        THE BIG THREE MUSIC CORPORATION   00.95

BROWN *
    WEDDING OF THE PAINTED DOLL
        THE BIG THREE MUSIC CORPORATION   00.95
BROWN *   ZEPP   2
    YOU TELL ME YOUR DREAMS
        PRO-ART PUBLICATIONS, INC.   193   .50
BROWN, A.
    BALLET ON SKATES, OP. 126
        BELWIN-MILLS PUBLISHING CORPORATION   28182   .60
BROWN, A.
    DOLORES -- THE DESERT FLOWER, OP. 86
        BELWIN-MILLS PUBLISHING CORPORATION   28067   .60
BROWN, A.
    IMPROVISATION AND MELODY
        G. SCHIRMER, INC.   .50
BROWN, A.   5
    LOVE DREAMS OP. 4
        THEODORE PRESSER COMPANY   .60
BROWN, A.   E
    PIXIES' GAVOTTE, OP. 32 NO. 9
        BELWIN-MILLS PUBLISHING CORPORATION   28031   .60
BROWN, A.   E
    PIXIES' GOOD-NIGHT SONG, OP. 32 NO. 10
        BELWIN-MILLS PUBLISHING CORPORATION   28032   .60
BROWN, A.   2A
    SPACE EXPLORERS
        MUSICORD PUBLICATIONS, INC.   .45
BROWN, A.   SCHAUM, J.   1
    SPOOKY HOLLOW
        BELWIN-MILLS PUBLISHING CORPORATION   .50
BROWN, A.   2B
    VILLAGE ON THE GREEN
        MUSICORD PUBLICATIONS, INC.   .45
BROWN, C.
    CAPRICCIO
        GERARD BILLAUDOT EDITIONS MUSICALES   1.10
BROWN, C.
    MINUETTO
        GERARD BILLAUDOT EDITIONS MUSICALES   1.10
BROWN, C.
    TAMBOURIN
        GERARD BILLAUDOT EDITIONS MUSICALES   1.10
BROWN, E.   6
    PERSPECTIVES
        SCHOTT   AV4   2.00
BROWN, L.   1
    LITTLE COUNTRY DANCE
        THEODORE PRESSER COMPANY   .50
BROWN, L.   2
    OLD FOLK SONG, AN
        THEODORE PRESSER COMPANY   .50
BROWN, L.   2
    PIRATE'S TALE, A
        THEODORE PRESSER COMPANY   .50
BROWN, L.   2
    REVERIE AT TWILIGHT
        BELWIN-MILLS PUBLISHING CORPORATION   .60
BROWN, N. H.
    DOLL DANCE
        THE BIG THREE MUSIC CORPORATION   00.95
BROWN, N. H.
    RAG DOLL
        THE BIG THREE MUSIC CORPORATION   00.95
BRUCE, M. C.
    ODDS AND ENDS
        BANKS AND SON LTD.   .80
BRUCKNER   D
    ADAGIO --7TH SYMPHONY--
        C. F. PETERS CORPORATION   BR19   1.50
BRUCKNER   OESER, F.   4
    ADAGIO AUS DER SYMPHONIE NO. 07
        BARENREITER VERLAG   AE 292
BRUCKNER   SCHOLZ
    ERINNERUNG
        ASSOCIATED MUSIC PUBLISHERS, INC.   DOB   .60
BRUCKNER   KNAB, A.   3
    IDYLLE -- NACHGELASSENES TRIO ZUR SYMPHONIE NO. 09 --
        BARENREITER VERLAG   AE 224
BRUGMANN, A.   1 1/2
    SADNESS AND MADNESS -- PHRYGIAN AND LOCRIAN MODES
        ELKAN-VOGEL, INC.   .50
BRUGNOLI
    SCENE NAPOLITANE
        FRANCO COLOMBO PUBLICATIONS   FOR. 11691 2.75
BRUNNER
    SONATA
        BARENREITER VERLAG   BA 1984   3.50
BRUNNER   4
    SONATA
        BARENREITER VERLAG   BA 1984
BRUNS, V.
    NEUE ODYSSEE -- BALLET IN 5 TABLEAUX
        ASSOCIATED MUSIC PUBLISHERS, INC.   BRH   12.50
BRUNS, V.
    RECHT DES HERRN, DAS -- BALLET IN 2 TABLEAUX
        ASSOCIATED MUSIC PUBLISHERS, INC.   BRH   4.80
BRUSSELMANS
    PRELUDE AND FUGUE ON A NAME
        FRANCO COLOMBO PUBLICATIONS   SAL   2.50
BRUSSELS, I.
    AT THE CARNIVAL
        G. SCHIRMER, INC.   .50
BRUSSELS, I.
    AT THE FOUNTAIN
        PEER SOUTHERN ORGANIZATION   00.80
BRUSSELS, I.   2 1/2
    AUTUMN LEAVES
        WILLIS MUSIC COMPANY   .40
BRUSSELS, I.
    BY THE BROOK
        PEER SOUTHERN ORGANIZATION   00.80
BRUSSELS, I.
    CAPRICE
        PEER SOUTHERN ORGANIZATION   00.80
BRUSSELS, I.
    CHEERFUL STORY, A
        PEER SOUTHERN ORGANIZATION   00.80
BRUSSELS, I.   1
    CHINESE STORY
        BELWIN-MILLS PUBLISHING CORPORATION   .60
BRUSSELS, I.
    CLOWNS DANCE, THE
        PEER SOUTHERN ORGANIZATION   00.75
BRUSSELS, I.
    DANCING BUTTERFLY, A
        PEER SOUTHERN ORGANIZATION   01.00

BRUSSELS, I.
  DESERT CARAVAN, THE
    PEER SOUTHERN ORGANIZATION   00.80
BRUSSELS, I.
  DREAMY MOOD, A
    BELWIN-MILLS PUBLISHING CORPORATION   25305   .60
BRUSSELS, I.   2
  DRUMMER BOY, THE
    BOSTON MUSIC COMPANY   .50
BRUSSELS, I.   3
  ESCAPADES
    BOSTON MUSIC COMPANY   .50
BRUSSELS, I.
  FROM NEW ORLEANS
    PEER SOUTHERN ORGANIZATION   00.80
BRUSSELS, I.   2
  FUN OF FUN
    BELWIN-MILLS PUBLISHING CORPORATION   .60
BRUSSELS, I.   2
  GRACEFUL BALLET DANCER, THE
    WILLIS MUSIC COMPANY   .40
BRUSSELS, I.   2
  GRACEFUL BALLET DANCER, THE
    WILLIS MUSIC COMPANY   .40
BRUSSELS, I.   2
  HALLOWEEN NIGHT
    BELWIN-MILLS PUBLISHING CORPORATION   .60
BRUSSELS, I.
  HAPPY-GO-LUCKY
    PEER SOUTHERN ORGANIZATION   00.75
BRUSSELS, I.
  IN BLUE TONE
    G. SCHIRMER, INC.   .40
BRUSSELS, I.   2
  IN SPANISH STYLE
    BELWIN-MILLS PUBLISHING CORPORATION   .60
BRUSSELS, I.
  INDIAN POW-WOW
    PEER SOUTHERN ORGANIZATION   00.75
BRUSSELS, I.
  JOIN THE PARADE
    G. SCHIRMER, INC.   .40
BRUSSELS, I.   1
  JUGGLER, THE
    BELWIN-MILLS PUBLISHING CORPORATION   .60
BRUSSELS, I.
  LYRICAL PRELUDE, A
    G. SCHIRMER, INC.   .40
BRUSSELS, I.
  MY LITTLE BROTHER
    PEER SOUTHERN ORGANIZATION   00.80
BRUSSELS, I.   2
  MY PAL AND I
    PRO-ART PUBLICATIONS, INC.   242   .50
BRUSSELS, I.
  MY SCOTTISH FRIEND
    PEER SOUTHERN ORGANIZATION   00.75
BRUSSELS, I.
  NEAR THE BAYOU
    PEER SOUTHERN ORGANIZATION   00.80
BRUSSELS, I.
  NOCTURNAL MOOD
    PEER SOUTHERN ORGANIZATION   00.80
BRUSSELS, I.
  NOCTURNE
    BELWIN-MILLS PUBLISHING CORPORATION   .60
BRUSSELS, I.
  ON THE LAKE
    PEER SOUTHERN ORGANIZATION   00.80
BRUSSELS, I.
  OUR LAST DANCE
    G. SCHIRMER, INC.   .35
BRUSSELS, I.   2
  PLAYFUL LITTLE KITTEN
    WILLIS MUSIC COMPANY   .40
BRUSSELS, I.   2
  PLAYFUL LITTLE KITTEN
    WILLIS MUSIC COMPANY   .40
BRUSSELS, I.
  PLAYING A GAME
    G. SCHIRMER, INC.   .40
BRUSSELS, I.   2 1/2
  QUIET RAIN, THE
    WILLIS MUSIC COMPANY   .40
BRUSSELS, I.
  RHYTHMIC PRELUDE
    PEER SOUTHERN ORGANIZATION   00.80
BRUSSELS, I.   2
  SPRING BREEZES
    WILLIS MUSIC COMPANY   .40
BRUSSELS, I.   E
  SUNDAY IN VERMONT
    BELWIN-MILLS PUBLISHING CORPORATION   25306   .60
BRUSSELS, I.   2
  TARANTELLA
    BOSTON MUSIC COMPANY   .50
BRUSSELS, I.   2
  TICK-TOC, LITTLE CLOCK
    WILLIS MUSIC COMPANY   .40
BRUSSELS, I.
  TOCCATA
    PEER SOUTHERN ORGANIZATION   00.80
BRUSSELS, I.   1 1/2
  TWILIGHT
    WILLIS MUSIC COMPANY   .40
BRUSSELS, I.   E
  WALTZING SUNBEAMS
    BELWIN-MILLS PUBLISHING CORPORATION   25307   .60
BRUSSELS, I.
  WATCHING MY SAIL BOAT
    PEER SOUTHERN ORGANIZATION   00.75
BRYANT   NEALE, J.   EASY
  ALL I HAVE TO DO IS DREAM
    WARNER BROTHERS PUBLISHERS   .75
BRYDSON, J.
  SUITE OF COUNTRY DANCES
    NOVELLO AND COMPANY, LTD.   10.0015.02   1.40
BUCALOSSI   3-4
  GITANA, LA, WALTZES
    CENTURY MUSIC PUBLISHING COMPANY, INC.   2449   .40
BUCALOSSI   3-4
  LA GITANA, WALTZ
    CENTURY MUSIC PUBLISHING COMPANY, INC.   2449   .40
BUCCI, M.   2
  PUPPY IS LOST
    CENTURY MUSIC PUBLISHING COMPANY, INC.   4063   .40

BUCHANAN, R.   4
  GINGERETTE
    THEODORE PRESSER COMPANY   .50
BUESSER   M
  LE SOMMEIL DE L'ENFANT JESUS. BERCEUSE FOR PIANO --CHRISTMAS--
    C. F. PETERS CORPORATION   C91   2.00
BULL   1
  GUITAR PLAYER, THE
    BELWIN-MILLS PUBLISHING CORPORATION   .60
BULL   2 1/2
  OLD BROWN CAYUSE
    BELWIN-MILLS PUBLISHING CORPORATION   .60
BULL
  REFLETS DU PASSE - AH, VOUS DIRAI-JE MAMAN
    FRANCO COLOMBO PUBLICATIONS   SAL   1.75
BULL
  REFLETS DU PASSE - AU CLAIR DE LA LUNE
    FRANCO COLOMBO PUBLICATIONS   SAL   1.75
BULL
  REFLETS DU PASSE - IL PLEUT BERGERE
    FRANCO COLOMBO PUBLICATIONS   SAL   1.75
BULL
  REFLETS DU PASSE - LA MARSEILLAISE
    FRANCO COLOMBO PUBLICATIONS   SAL   1.75
BULL
  REFLETS DU PASSE - LE ROI DAGOBERT
    FRANCO COLOMBO PUBLICATIONS   SAL   1.75
BULL
  REFLETS DU PASSE - MALBOROUGH
    FRANCO COLOMBO PUBLICATIONS   SAL   1.75
BURCH, S.   2
  ASTRONAUTS SALUTE
    BELWIN-MILLS PUBLISHING CORPORATION   .60
BURCH, S.   2
  MARCH OF THE PLASTIC SOLDIERS
    WILLIS MUSIC COMPANY   .40
BURCH, S.   1 1/2
  SWING ALONG
    BELWIN-MILLS PUBLISHING CORPORATION   .60
BURDICK--ED
  HANON VIRTUOSO PIANIST, PART 1
    CENTURY MUSIC PUBLISHING COMPANY, INC.   2379   .40
BURDICK--ED
  HANON VIRTUOSO PIANIST, PART 2
    CENTURY MUSIC PUBLISHING COMPANY, INC.   2380   .40
BUREN, N.
  LULLABY
    G. SCHIRMER, INC.   .35
BURGMUELLER
  BALLADE
    FREDERICK HARRIS MUSIC COMPANY   .60
BURGMUELLER   3
  BALLADE, OP. 100 NO. 15
    WILLIS MUSIC COMPANY   .35
BURGMUELLER
  BOLERO, OP. 76 NO. 2
    G. SCHIRMER, INC.   .50
BURGMUELLER
  LA CHASSE
    FREDERICK HARRIS MUSIC COMPANY   .60
BURGMUELLER
  OISEAUX DE NOTRE-DAME, LES
    FRANCO COLOMBO PUBLICATIONS   SAL   1.75
BURGMUELLER
  RONDO ALLA TURCA, OP. 68
    CARL FISCHER, INC.   S 1323   .50
BURGMUELLER
  RONDO ALLA TURCA, OP. 68 NO. 3
    G. SCHIRMER, INC.   .50
BURGMUELLER   2
  RONDOLETTO IN C, OP. 76 NO. 1
    THEODORE PRESSER COMPANY   .50
BURGMUELLER
  SWALLOW, THE
    FREDERICK HARRIS MUSIC COMPANY   .60
BURGMUELLER *
  PAS DE VENDANGES--PAS DE DEUX--FROM GISELLE
    GERARD BILLAUDOT EDITIONS MUSICALES   2.20
BURKE *   NEALE, J.   EASY
  TIP-TOE THRU' THE TULIPS WITH ME
    WARNER BROTHERS PUBLISHERS   .75
BURKE, F.   2
  DANCING CHORDS
    WILLIS MUSIC COMPANY   .40
BURKE, T.   2
  FIREFLIES
    WILLIS MUSIC COMPANY   .40
BURKHARD, W.
  SONATA, OP. 66
    UNIVERSAL EDITION   UE 11494   2.15
BURKHARD, W.
  WEIHNACHTSSONATINE, OP. 71
    BARENREITER VERLAG   BA 2074   2.25
BURLEIGH, C.   6
  COASTING OP. 9
    THEODORE PRESSER COMPANY   .60
BURLEIGH, C.
  COTTONTAILS, OP. 10
    G. SCHIRMER, INC.   .50
BURLEIGH, C.   3
  WING FOO OP. 1 NO. 1
    THEODORE PRESSER COMPANY   .50
BURNAM   2 1/2
  ALASKAN CRUISE
    WILLIS MUSIC COMPANY   1.00
BURNAM
  AT THE CARNIVAL
    G. SCHIRMER, INC.   .35
BURNAM
  AT THE TYPEWRITER
    SUMMY-BIRCHARD COMPANY   .50
BURNAM   1
  BAGPIPE AND KILT
    WILLIS MUSIC COMPANY   .40
BURNAM   1
  BONNIE, BONNIE LASSIE
    WILLIS MUSIC COMPANY   .40
BURNAM   1
  BUILDING A SNOW MAN
    WILLIS MUSIC COMPANY   .40
BURNAM   2
  BUTTERFLY TIME
    WILLIS MUSIC COMPANY   .40
BURNAM   ADAM
  CANTIQUE DE NOEL -- O HOLY NIGHT
    WILLIS MUSIC COMPANY   .35

BURNAM 1
  CARPENTER'S SONG, THE
    WILLIS MUSIC COMPANY .40
BURNAM 2
  CAVERN BY THE SEA, A
    WILLIS MUSIC COMPANY .50
BURNAM 2 1/2
  CHANGING OF THE GUARD
    WILLIS MUSIC COMPANY .40
BURNAM 1 1/2
  CHIMNEY SMOKE FROM SNOW
    WILLIS MUSIC COMPANY .40
BURNAM
  COCONUT TREES IN HAWAII
    WILLIS MUSIC COMPANY .30
BURNAM 1
  COME, FAIRIES, COME
    WILLIS MUSIC COMPANY .40
BURNAM 1
  COUNT DOWN
    WILLIS MUSIC COMPANY .40
BURNAM 2
  DANCE OF THE RADISHES
    THEODORE PRESSER COMPANY .50
BURNAM 2
  DEEP GORGE, A
    WILLIS MUSIC COMPANY .40
BURNAM 1
  DOLL THAT CRIED, THE
    CENTURY MUSIC PUBLISHING COMPANY, INC. 4101 .40
BURNAM 1
  DOWN IN THE VALLEY
    WILLIS MUSIC COMPANY .35
BURNAM 2 1/2
  ECHOES OF GYPSIES
    WILLIS MUSIC COMPANY .50
BURNAM 2 1/2
  ECHOES OF SCOTLAND
    WILLIS MUSIC COMPANY .40
BURNAM 1
  EDINBURGH CASTLE
    WILLIS MUSIC COMPANY .40
BURNAM 2
  ELEPHANT'S JOKE, THE
    THEODORE PRESSER COMPANY .50
BURNAM
  FIFTEEN MEN IN A PIRATE BOAT
    SUMMY-BIRCHARD COMPANY .50
BURNAM 1
  FLORAL CLOCK, THE
    WILLIS MUSIC COMPANY .40
BURNAM 2
  FLOWERS IN A TEMPLE GARDEN
    WILLIS MUSIC COMPANY .50
BURNAM 3
  FOREST OF JOSHUA TREES
    WILLIS MUSIC COMPANY .40
BURNAM
  FROM A LIGHTHOUSE WINDOW
    SUMMY-BIRCHARD COMPANY .50
BURNAM 2
  HANGING MOSS ON THE BAYOU TREES
    WILLIS MUSIC COMPANY .50
BURNAM 1 1/2
  HAUNTED HOUSE, A
    WILLIS MUSIC COMPANY .75
BURNAM 1
  HIGH IN A TREE
    WILLIS MUSIC COMPANY .35
BURNAM 2
  HORSE DRAWN CARRIAGE
    WILLIS MUSIC COMPANY .50
BURNAM 1
  HULA GIRLS IN HAWAII
    WILLIS MUSIC COMPANY .30
BURNAM 1
  I CAN PLAY WITH A METRONOME
    WILLIS MUSIC COMPANY .35
BURNAM 1
  ICE GLIDING WALTZ
    WILLIS MUSIC COMPANY .40
BURNAM 1
  IN A LITTLE OUTRIGGER CANOE -- WITH WORDS
    WILLIS MUSIC COMPANY .30
BURNAM 1
  IN HONOLULU
    WILLIS MUSIC COMPANY .30
BURNAM
  IN THE FOREST TALL
    SUMMY-BIRCHARD COMPANY .50
BURNAM 2
  IRON LACE BALCONIES
    WILLIS MUSIC COMPANY .50
BURNAM 2 1/2
  LACE MAKER LADY
    WILLIS MUSIC COMPANY .50
BURNAM 2 1/2
  LADIES DRILL MARCH
    WILLIS MUSIC COMPANY .75
BURNAM 2
  LAUNCHING A ROCKET
    WILLIS MUSIC COMPANY .60
BURNAM 2
  LITTLE CHAPEL IN THE MOONLIGHT
    WILLIS MUSIC COMPANY .40
BURNAM 3
  LITTLE SAGEBRUSH ALL AROUND
    WILLIS MUSIC COMPANY .40
BURNAM 2
  LORENA
    WILLIS MUSIC COMPANY .35
BURNAM 1
  LULLABY LAND
    CENTURY MUSIC PUBLISHING COMPANY, INC. 4102 .40
BURNAM 1
  MAILMAN
    WILLIS MUSIC COMPANY .35
BURNAM 2 1/2
  MARDI GRAS
    WILLIS MUSIC COMPANY .50
BURNAM 2
  ON THE SURFACE OF THE MOON, FAR AWAY
    WILLIS MUSIC COMPANY .75
BURNAM 1
  PAINTER'S SONG
    WILLIS MUSIC COMPANY .35

BURNAM 1
  PARADE GOES MARCHING BY
    WILLIS MUSIC COMPANY .35
BURNAM 1
  PARAKEET
    WILLIS MUSIC COMPANY .35
BURNAM 3
  PASTEL DESERT COLORS
    WILLIS MUSIC COMPANY .40
BURNAM 2 1/2
  PICCADILLY CIRCUS
    WILLIS MUSIC COMPANY .40
BURNAM 3
  PLAYGROUND PANORAMA
    WILLIS MUSIC COMPANY .60
BURNAM 2
  RED RIVER VALLEY
    WILLIS MUSIC COMPANY .35
BURNAM 2 1/2
  RIDE OF PAUL REVERE, THE
    WILLIS MUSIC COMPANY .75
BURNAM 1 1/2
  ROCKING CHAIR TRIP
    THEODORE PRESSER COMPANY .50
BURNAM 2 1/2
  RODEO ROUND UP
    THEODORE PRESSER COMPANY .50
BURNAM 1
  SHOVEL THAT SNOW
    WILLIS MUSIC COMPANY .40
BURNAM 1
  SHOVEL THAT SNOW
    WILLIS MUSIC COMPANY .40
BURNAM 3
  SINGING FOUNTAIN, THE
    WILLIS MUSIC COMPANY .50
BURNAM 2
  SINGING IN THE SADDLE
    WILLIS MUSIC COMPANY .40
BURNAM 1 1/2
  SNOW COVERED TREES ON A MOUNTAIN WHITE
    WILLIS MUSIC COMPANY .40
BURNAM 1 1/2
  SNOW COVERED TREES ON A MOUNTAIN WHITE
    WILLIS MUSIC COMPANY .40
BURNAM 2
  SNOW PLOW AND ROTARY
    WILLIS MUSIC COMPANY .35
BURNAM 2
  SPACE TRAVELOGUE
    WILLIS MUSIC COMPANY .60
BURNAM 1
  SPRAY PERFUME
    WILLIS MUSIC COMPANY .50
BURNAM 2
  STILL WATERS
    WILLIS MUSIC COMPANY .50
BURNAM 3
  SUN ON THE SAND
    WILLIS MUSIC COMPANY .50
BURNAM 1
  SURF BOARD RIDER
    WILLIS MUSIC COMPANY .30
BURNAM 2 1/2
  SURGING SEA, THE
    WILLIS MUSIC COMPANY .40
BURNAM 2 1/2
  SURGING SEA, THE
    WILLIS MUSIC COMPANY .50
BURNAM 1 1/2
  SWEET COLLEEN, A
    WILLIS MUSIC COMPANY .50
BURNAM 1 1/2
  TALL, TALL BUILDINGS
    WILLIS MUSIC COMPANY .50
BURNAM 2
  TANGO TIME
    WILLIS MUSIC COMPANY .35
BURNAM 1
  TEDDY BEAR'S GOODNIGHT
    CENTURY MUSIC PUBLISHING COMPANY, INC. 4100 .40
BURNAM 2
  UMBRELLA TIME
    WILLIS MUSIC COMPANY .50
BURNAM
  WEDDING OF THE DOLLS
    G. SCHIRMER, INC. .40
BURNAM 2
  WHEN I RIDE A BUCKING BRONCO -- WITH WORDS
    WILLIS MUSIC COMPANY .35
BURNAM
  WHIRLING LEAVES
    SUMMY-BIRCHARD COMPANY .50
BURNAM 2 1/2
  WHITE CLIFFS OF DOVER, THE
    WILLIS MUSIC COMPANY .40
BURNAM 2 1/2
  WITHIN A JEWEL BOX
    WILLIS MUSIC COMPANY .40
BURNAM--ED   BURNAM 2
  AURA LEE
    WILLIS MUSIC COMPANY .40
BURNAM--ED   BURNAM 2
  CLAP HANDS -- CHIAPANECAS
    WILLIS MUSIC COMPANY .40
BURNAM--ED   BURNAM 1
  CLAP HANDS DANCE -- CHIAPENECAS
    WILLIS MUSIC COMPANY .40
BURNAM--ED   BURNAM 2
  DANNY BOY
    WILLIS MUSIC COMPANY .40
BURNAM--ED   BURNAM 2
  GREENSLEEVES
    WILLIS MUSIC COMPANY .40
BURNAM--ED   BURNAM 1
  HE'S GOT THE WHOLE WORLD IN HIS HANDS
    WILLIS MUSIC COMPANY .40
BURNETT
  STEAMBOAT RAG
    MCA MUSIC 1.00
BURNS 3
  FLOWERS OF THE FOREST
    WILLIS MUSIC COMPANY .40
BURTON 2
  HALLOWE'EN
    BOSTON MUSIC COMPANY .50

BURTON		2		
ICE SKATERS				
BOSTON MUSIC COMPANY				.50
BURTON		1		
LEAP FROG				
BOSTON MUSIC COMPANY				.50
BURTON, L.		3		
SWISS MUSIC BOX, THE				
WILLIS MUSIC COMPANY				.40
BUSH		2 1/2		
OUTER SPACE				
THEODORE PRESSER COMPANY				.50
BUSH		2		
ROUNDELAY, A				
THEODORE PRESSER COMPANY				.50
BUSONI				
ALL'ITALIA				
ASSOCIATED MUSIC PUBLISHERS, INC.	B/H			1.25
BUSONI				
BERCEUSE				
ASSOCIATED MUSIC PUBLISHERS, INC.	B/H			1.25
BUSONI				
CAMPANELLA, LA. ETUDE NO. 3-- PAGANINI-LISZT -- WITH LISZT				
TRANSCRIPTION INCLUDED.				
ASSOCIATED MUSIC PUBLISHERS, INC.	B/H			2.00
BUSONI				
CHAMBER FANTASY ON THEMES FROM BIZET'S ''CARMEN''				
ASSOCIATED MUSIC PUBLISHERS, INC.	B/H			3.25
BUSONI				
CONCERT INTERPRETATION OF OP. 11, NO. 2 BY SCHOENBERG				
UNIVERSAL EDITION			2992	1.10
BUSONI				
FANTASIA IN A MINOR, AFTER J.S. BACH				
ASSOCIATED MUSIC PUBLISHERS, INC.	B/H			3.00
BUSONI				
SONATINA -- ''IN DIEM NATIVITATIS CHRISTI, 1917'' --				
ASSOCIATED MUSIC PUBLISHERS, INC.	B/H			2.00
BUSONI				
SONATINA -- 1910 --				
ASSOCIATED MUSIC PUBLISHERS, INC.	B/H			4.00
BUSONI				
SONATINA AD USUM INFANTIS				
ASSOCIATED MUSIC PUBLISHERS, INC.	B/H			1.75
BUSONI				
SONATINA BREVIS, AFTER BACH				
ASSOCIATED MUSIC PUBLISHERS, INC.	B/H			1.75
BUSONI				
SONATINA NO. 02				
ASSOCIATED MUSIC PUBLISHERS, INC.	B/H			1.50
BUSONI				
TOCCATA				
ASSOCIATED MUSIC PUBLISHERS, INC.	B/H			2.25
BUSSEY, M.		3		
SPANISH DANCE, A				
WILLIS MUSIC COMPANY				.25
BUTLER		2-3		
LONELY AS A STAR				
PRO-ART PUBLICATIONS, INC.			321	.50
BUTLER		1-2		
WEARY PLOWMAN, THE				
PRO-ART PUBLICATIONS, INC.			320	.50
BUTLER, J.		2		
ARABESQUE				
WILLIS MUSIC COMPANY				.40
BUTLER, J.		2		
BARCAROLLE				
WILLIS MUSIC COMPANY				.40
BUTLER, J.		2 1/2		
BAROQUE SUITE IN D MINOR				
WILLIS MUSIC COMPANY				.40
BUTLER, J.		1 1/2		
CANTER				
WILLIS MUSIC COMPANY				.40
BUTLER, J.		2 1/2		
FLIGHT				
WILLIS MUSIC COMPANY				.40
BUTLER, J.		1 1/2		
FROLIC				
WILLIS MUSIC COMPANY				.40
BUTLER, J.		2 1/2		
MIRAGE				
WILLIS MUSIC COMPANY				.40
BUTLER, J.		2 1/2		
NOVELETTE				
WILLIS MUSIC COMPANY				.40
BUTLER, J.		2		
PETITE MELODY				
WILLIS MUSIC COMPANY				.35
BUTLER, J.		2 1/2		
PROMENADE				
WILLIS MUSIC COMPANY				.40
BUTLER, J.		2		
SHENANDOAH				
WILLIS MUSIC COMPANY				.40
BUTLER, J.		2		
STAR FLOWER				
WILLIS MUSIC COMPANY				.40
BUTLER, J.		2		
TAG				
WILLIS MUSIC COMPANY				.40
BUTLER, J.		2 1/2		
TONE POEM				
WILLIS MUSIC COMPANY				.40
BUTTERFIELD		2		
WHEN YOU AND I WERE YOUNG MAGGIE				
CENTURY MUSIC PUBLISHING COMPANY, INC.			2439	.40
BUTTING, M.				
FANTASIA, OP. 28				
UNIVERSAL EDITION			UE 8507	1.70
BUXTEHUDE	PROKOFIEFF			
ORGAN PRELUDE AND FUGUE IN D MINOR				
MCA MUSIC				.60
BUXTEHUDE	PROKOFIEFF			
PRELUDE AND FUGUE IN D MINOR				
INTERNATIONAL MUSIC COMPANY				1.00
BYINGTON		2		
MINUET IN F				
BOSTON MUSIC COMPANY				.50
BYRD, W.	BARTH, H.			
CARMAN'S WHISTLE, THE				
BELWIN-MILLS PUBLISHING CORPORATION			20359	.50
CAAMANO				
VARIACIONES GREGORIANAS, OP. 15				
FRANCO COLOMBO PUBLICATIONS			BA11127	.75
CABLE *				
LITTLEST CLOWN , THE.				
MCA MUSIC				2.50
CABLE *				
THIEF OF BAGDAD				
MCA MUSIC				2.50
CABLE *	PORTNOFF			
THIEF OF BAGDAD				
MCA MUSIC				1.75
CACAVAS		1		
BUZZY BUZZY BEE				
WILLIS MUSIC COMPANY				.40
CACAVAS		1		
CONCERTO PETITE				
WILLIS MUSIC COMPANY				.50
CACAVAS		1		
EVERY DAY IS SATURDAY				
WILLIS MUSIC COMPANY				.35
CACAVAS				
LA NUIT				
WARNER BROTHERS PUBLISHERS				.60
CACAVAS		1		
LULLABY				
WILLIS MUSIC COMPANY				.35
CACAVAS				
LUNA RHAPSODY				
WARNER BROTHERS PUBLISHERS				.60
CACAVAS				
NOCTURNE				
WARNER BROTHERS PUBLISHERS				.60
CACAVAS *				
MANDARIN'S SONG, THE				
SPRATT MUSIC PUBLISHERS				.40
CADERARA				
NINNA-NANNA DELLA BAMBOLA				
FRANCO COLOMBO PUBLICATIONS			BON.1828	.90
CADMAN, C.		3 1/2		
AT DAWNING				
THEODORE PRESSER COMPANY				.60
CADMAN, C.				
LOVE SONG, OP. 40				
BELWIN-MILLS PUBLISHING CORPORATION			28039	.60
CADZOW		2		
JUST SUPPOSE				
CENTURY MUSIC PUBLISHING COMPANY, INC.		E	4030	.40
CADZOW				
LITTLE BEN				
THEODORE PRESSER COMPANY				.50
CADZOW		2		
LULLABY IN THE DARK WIND				
CENTURY MUSIC PUBLISHING COMPANY, INC.			4031	.40
CADZOW		2		
MARCH FOR NEW SHOES				
CENTURY MUSIC PUBLISHING COMPANY, INC.		E	4029	.40
CADZOW				
PRAIRIE LULLABY				
THEODORE PRESSER COMPANY				.50
CAGE				
HPSCHD				
C. F. PETERS CORPORATION			6804	RENTA
CAGGIANO				
CAPRICCIO				
FRANCO COLOMBO PUBLICATIONS			DS284	1.25
CAGNACCI				
CANZONE MONTANARA				
FRANCO COLOMBO PUBLICATIONS			FOR. 10604	.75
CAGNACCI				
CANZONE MONTANARA				
FRANCO COLOMBO PUBLICATIONS			FOR.10605	.75
CAHAN				
MULE DRIVER, THE. --EL MULETERO				
MCA MUSIC				1.00
CAHN *				
THREE COINS IN A FOUNTAIN				
THE BIG THREE MUSIC CORPORATION				00.95
CALABRO, L.				
DIVERSITIES				
ELKAN-VOGEL, INC.				1.50
CALABRO, L.				
SONATINA FOR PIANO				
ELKAN-VOGEL, INC.				1.25
CALABRO, L.				
SUITE OF SEVEN				
ELKAN-VOGEL, INC.				1.00
CALABRO, L.				
YOUNG PEOPLE'S SONATINE				
ELKAN-VOGEL, INC.				.75
CALLAN, L.		2		
COASTER, THE				
BELWIN-MILLS PUBLISHING CORPORATION				.60
CALLINICOS				
NERANTZULA				
MCA MUSIC				.75
CALTABIANO				
LARGO				
FRANCO COLOMBO PUBLICATIONS			BON. 2039	1.50
CALTABIANO				
SONATINA IN D				
FRANCO COLOMBO PUBLICATIONS			BON. 2320	2.25
CALTABIANO				
THEME, VARIATIONS AND FUGUE				
FRANCO COLOMBO PUBLICATIONS			BON. 2130	1.75
CALWELL		2		
PURPLE PEAKS				
BOSTON MUSIC COMPANY				.50
CALWELL		1		
WOODPECKER				
BOSTON MUSIC COMPANY				.50
CAMEO--ED	CAMEO	4		
GREENSLEEVES				
SCHAUM PUBLICATIONS, INC.				.60
CAMEO--ED	CAMEO	4		
JINGLE BELLS JUBILEE				
SCHAUM PUBLICATIONS, INC.				.60
CAMILLERI, C.				
FIVE MALTESE DANCES				
BELWIN-MILLS PUBLISHING CORPORATION			20433	1.50
CAMILLERI, C.				
THREE MALTESE MINIATURES				
BELWIN-MILLS PUBLISHING CORPORATION			20477	1.50
CAMPBELL				
PRINCESS AND THE PIRATE				
CARL FISCHER, INC.			P 2706	.50
CAMPBELL		2		
WALTZ -- THEN MARCH				
BELWIN-MILLS PUBLISHING CORPORATION				.60

CAMPOLIETI
    TOCCATA
        FRANCO COLOMBO PUBLICATIONS   R2189   1.50
CAMPOS-PARSI, H.
    SONATA IN G
        PAN AMERICAN UNION   01.50
CANAL, M.
    PAGES ENFANTINES
        ELKAN-VOGEL, INC.   H   1.25
CANFIELD, J.   1-2
    ACROBATICS
        PRO-ART PUBLICATIONS, INC.   237   .50
CANFIELD, J.   2
    FANCY FREE
        BELWIN-MILLS PUBLISHING CORPORATION   .60
CANFIELD, J.   2
    FIESTA
        WILLIS MUSIC COMPANY   .35
CANFIELD, J.   3
    FISHIN'
        PRO-ART PUBLICATIONS, INC.   177   .50
CANFIELD, J.   1
    GALLOPING PONY
        BOSTON MUSIC COMPANY   .50
CANFIELD, J.   2
    GHOST WALKS, THE
        PRO-ART PUBLICATIONS, INC.   160   .50
CANFIELD, J.   1
    GOBLINS
        WILLIS MUSIC COMPANY   .30
CANFIELD, J.   2
    GYPSY CAMP
        PRO-ART PUBLICATIONS, INC.   79   .50
CANFIELD, J.   2
    HAPPY STORY, A
        CENTURY MUSIC PUBLISHING COMPANY, INC.   4358   .40
CANFIELD, J.   1-2
    IN SPRING
        PRO-ART PUBLICATIONS, INC.   80   .50
CANFIELD, J.   1
    JEEPERS CREEPERS
        BOSTON MUSIC COMPANY   .50
CANFIELD, J.   3
    MELODIC MOOD
        BELWIN-MILLS PUBLISHING CORPORATION   .60
CANFIELD, J.   1
    MERRY-GO-ROUND
        BOSTON MUSIC COMPANY   .50
CANFIELD, J.   2
    OZARK DANCE
        BELWIN-MILLS PUBLISHING CORPORATION   .60
CANFIELD, J.   2
    QUIET HOUR, THE
        WILLIS MUSIC COMPANY   .40
CANFIELD, J.   2
    RODEO
        PRO-ART PUBLICATIONS, INC.   175   .50
CANFIELD, J.   2
    SATURDAY NIGHT
        PRO-ART PUBLICATIONS, INC.   293   .50
CANFIELD, J.   2
    SHADOWS IN THE POOL
        BOSTON MUSIC COMPANY   .50
CANFIELD, J.   2
    SINGING COWBOY
        BOSTON MUSIC COMPANY   .50
CANFIELD, J.   1
    SKIPPING
        BOSTON MUSIC COMPANY   .50
CANFIELD, J.   2
    SPRING DAY
        PRO-ART PUBLICATIONS, INC.   481   .50
CANFIELD, J.   2
    SQUARE DANCING DOLLS
        CENTURY MUSIC PUBLISHING COMPANY, INC.   4357   .40
CANFIELD, J.   2
    TALL TREES
        BOSTON MUSIC COMPANY   .50
CANFIELD, J.   1
    TROTTING PONY
        BOSTON MUSIC COMPANY   .50
CANFIELD, J.   2
    WAVELETS
        BOSTON MUSIC COMPANY   .50
CANICE   1-2
    MAGIC RIVER
        PRO-ART PUBLICATIONS, INC.   437   .50
CANICE   1
    WHITE BUTTERFLY
        PRO-ART PUBLICATIONS, INC.   438   .50
CANNONE
    ENFANTILLAGE
        FRANCO COLOMBO PUBLICATIONS   DS97   1.00
CANTALLOS   NIN
    SONATA IN C MINOR
        ASSOCIATED MUSIC PUBLISHERS, INC.   ESC   .95
CANTELOUBE
    BOURREES D'AUVERGNE
        FRANCO COLOMBO PUBLICATIONS   SAL   3.50
CANTORE   4
    MOONLIGNT MELODY
        CENTURY MUSIC PUBLISHING COMPANY, INC.   2417   .40
CANTORE   4
    PENSEE DE COEUR
        CENTURY MUSIC PUBLISHING COMPANY, INC.   2417   .40
CANTU
    FANTASIA IN E FLAT
        FRANCO COLOMBO PUBLICATIONS   BON. 1316   1.50
CANTU
    NELLA BASILICA DI SAN MARCO
        FRANCO COLOMBO PUBLICATIONS   BON. 1068   1.50
CANTU
    PAVANE BIJOU
        FRANCO COLOMBO PUBLICATIONS   BON. 1315   .90
CANTU
    PICORDANZE D'UNA FESTA CAMPESTRE
        FRANCO COLOMBO PUBLICATIONS   BON. 1069   1.50
CANTU
    RONDO
        FRANCO COLOMBO PUBLICATIONS   BON. 1325   1.50
CANTU
    SUITE ROMANTIQUE
        FRANCO COLOMBO PUBLICATIONS   BON. 1070   1.75
CAPES, D.   4
    DOUBLE-THREADS
        NOVELLO AND COMPANY, LTD.   10.0017.09   1.15

CAPES, D.   4
    TWO-PART FANCIES
        NOVELLO AND COMPANY, LTD.   10.0018.07   1.15
CARABELLA
    GAVOTTA ALL'ANTICA
        FRANCO COLOMBO PUBLICATIONS   DS201   1.25
CARABELLA
    SEDIA EPISCOPALE DELLA CHIESA DEI SS. NEREO E ACHILLEO, LA
        FRANCO COLOMBO PUBLICATIONS   DS221   1.25
CARABELLA
    STUDIO MONORITIMICO
        FRANCO COLOMBO PUBLICATIONS   DS203   1.75
CARABELLA
    TOCCATA
        FRANCO COLOMBO PUBLICATIONS   DS200   1.25
CARDEW
    MEMORIES OF YOU
        UNIVERSAL EDITION   UE 15446   3.50
CARDEW   D
    OCTET FOR JASPER JOHNS
        C. F. PETERS CORPORATION   H771A   1.50
CARDEW
    THREE WINTER POTATOES
        UNIVERSAL EDITION   UE 14200   2.10
CAREY, H.   3
    AMERICA
        THEODORE PRESSER COMPANY   .50
CAREY, H.   WALLIS *   1
    MY COUNTRY 'TIS OF THEE
        WILLIS MUSIC COMPANY   .30
CARLE, F.
    ESTELLE
        BELWIN-MILLS PUBLISHING CORPORATION   20081   .85
CARLE, F. *
    SUNRISE BOOGIE
        BELWIN-MILLS PUBLISHING CORPORATION   20480   .85
CARLE, F. *
    SUNRISE IN NAPOLI
        BELWIN-MILLS PUBLISHING CORPORATION   20280   .85
CARLE, F. *
    SYNCOPATED DOLL, THE
        BELWIN-MILLS PUBLISHING CORPORATION   20287   .85
CARLETON, B.
    GRAB BAG
        THEODORE PRESSER COMPANY   1.25
CARLETON, B.   1 1/2
    MARINES' HYMN
        THEODORE PRESSER COMPANY   .50
CARLETON, B.   1
    MELLOW MOON
        THEODORE PRESSER COMPANY   .50
CARLETON, B.   1
    MERRY MAJORETTE
        THEODORE PRESSER COMPANY   .50
CARLETON, B.   1
    TOMAHAWK DANCE
        THEODORE PRESSER COMPANY   .50
CARLEY, I. M.   2
    HOLIDAY
        BELWIN-MILLS PUBLISHING CORPORATION   .60
CARLEY, I. M.   2
    MAGIC CIRCLE, THE
        BELWIN-MILLS PUBLISHING CORPORATION   .60
CARMAN   5
    A SARAGOSSE
        ALPHONSE LEDUC
CARMAN
    AU TEMPS DES CERISES
        FRANCO COLOMBO PUBLICATIONS   SAL   1.50
CARMAN
    BALLET THEME -- WALTZ -- FROM ''CRUNCH, CRUNCH''
        ASSOCIATED MUSIC PUBLISHERS, INC.   BER   .60
CARMAN   4
    BONJOUR COLOMBINE, OP. 86
        ALPHONSE LEDUC
CARMAN   5
    CHANSON DE MAITRE WOLFF, OP. 97
        ALPHONSE LEDUC
CARMAN
    CONTE DE NOEL
        FRANCO COLOMBO PUBLICATIONS   SAL   1.50
CARMAN   4
    EN CHEMINANT, CHANSON, OP. 90
        ALPHONSE LEDUC
CARMAN   4
    MURMURE, PETITE VALSE, OP. 87
        ALPHONSE LEDUC
CARMAN
    PETITES AQUARELLES MUSICALES - CHANSON D'AUTREFOIS
        FRANCO COLOMBO PUBLICATIONS   SAL   1.50
CARMAN
    PETITES AQUARELLES MUSICALES - DANSE DU 18E SIECLE
        FRANCO COLOMBO PUBLICATIONS   SAL   1.50
CARMAN
    PETITES AQUARELLES MUSICALES - FETE BRETONNE
        FRANCO COLOMBO PUBLICATIONS   SAL   1.50
CARMAN
    PETITES AQUARELLES MUSICALES - MARCHE DU REGIMENT
        FRANCO COLOMBO PUBLICATIONS   SAL   1.50
CARMAN
    PETITES AQUARELLES MUSICALES - MINUETTO CAPRICCIOSO
        FRANCO COLOMBO PUBLICATIONS   SAL   1.50
CARMAN   5
    PETITES AQUARELLES MUSICALES - SCHERZETTINO
        FRANCO COLOMBO PUBLICATIONS   SAL   1.50
CARMAN   5
    PRES DU MOULIN
        ALPHONSE LEDUC
CARMAN
    RENDEZ-VOUS DE CHASSE
        FRANCO COLOMBO PUBLICATIONS   SAL   1.75
CARMAN
    SABOTIERE
        FRANCO COLOMBO PUBLICATIONS   SAL   1.75
CARMAN
    SECRET DE POLICHINELLE
        FRANCO COLOMBO PUBLICATIONS   SAL   1.75
CARMICHAEL   FIELDS, I.
    STAR DUST
        BELWIN-MILLS PUBLISHING CORPORATION   20353   .85
CARMICHAEL   KRENZ, B.
    STAR DUST
        BELWIN-MILLS PUBLISHING CORPORATION   20352   .85
CARMICHAEL   MATTE, J.
    STAR DUST
        BELWIN-MILLS PUBLISHING CORPORATION   20354   .85

CARMICHAEL   DESOLIS
  STAR DUST
    BELWIN-MILLS PUBLISHING CORPORATION   20468   1.00
CARMICHAEL   GLOVER, D.
  STAR DUST
    BELWIN-MILLS PUBLISHING CORPORATION   .60
CARMICHAEL   MOSSMAN, T.
  STAR DUST -- SIMP.
    BELWIN-MILLS PUBLISHING CORPORATION   26077   .50
CARMICHAEL   MALTBY
  STAR DUST MAMBO
    BELWIN-MILLS PUBLISHING CORPORATION   20278   .85
CARNEVALI
  MUSIC BOX
    FRANCO COLOMBO PUBLICATIONS   DS434   1.00
CARNEVALI
  NOTTI VENEZIANE
    FRANCO COLOMBO PUBLICATIONS   DS372   1.25
CARON-LEGRIS
  POEME PASTORAL
    ASSOCIATED MUSIC PUBLISHERS, INC.   BER   .75
CAROSONE
  ICICLE WING-DING
    MCA MUSIC   1.00
CARPENTER, J.
  CONCERTINO IN B MINOR
    G. SCHIRMER, INC.   2.50
CARPENTER, J.
  DANZA
    G. SCHIRMER, INC.   1.00
CARPENTER, J.
  IMPROMPTU
    G. SCHIRMER, INC.   .50
CARPENTER, J.
  LITTLE DANCER
    G. SCHIRMER, INC.   .50
CARPENTER, J.
  POLONAISE AMERICAINE
    G. SCHIRMER, INC.   .60
CARPENTER, J.
  SKYSCRAPERS--BALLET
    G. SCHIRMER, INC.   4.00
CARPENTER, J.
  TANGO AMERICAINE
    G. SCHIRMER, INC.   .80
CARPIO VALDES, R.
  SUITE
    EDITORIAL COOPERATIVA INTER-AMERICANA   01.15
CARRE
  ARAB DANCE
    SAM FOX PUBLISHING COMPANY, INC.   .50
CARRE   3
  ARAB DANCE
    SOUTHERN MUSIC COMPANY   .50
CARRE   E
  CRIMSON DAWN
    BELWIN-MILLS PUBLISHING CORPORATION   .60
CARRE
  DOODLING
    COMPOSERS PRESS, INC.   1.00
CARRE
  HORNPIPE
    SAM FOX PUBLISHING COMPANY, INC.   .50
CARRE   3
  HORNPIPE
    SOUTHERN MUSIC COMPANY   .50
CARRE
  JIMMY BUGS
    BELWIN-MILLS PUBLISHING CORPORATION   .60
CARRE
  PIRATE'S SONG
    SAM FOX PUBLISHING COMPANY, INC.   .50
CARRE   3
  PIRATES' SONG
    SOUTHERN MUSIC COMPANY   .50
CARRE
  WHITECAPS
    BELWIN-MILLS PUBLISHING CORPORATION   .60
CARREL, B.
  NORTHERN LIGHTS
    COMPOSERS AUTOGRAPH PUBLICATIONS   .66
CARREL, B.
  SIMPLICITY
    COMPOSERS AUTOGRAPH PUBLICATIONS   .44
CARREL, B.
  VERDUGO VIEW WALTZ
    COMPOSERS AUTOGRAPH PUBLICATIONS   .44
CARREL, B.
  VISITING GREEK, A
    COMPOSERS AUTOGRAPH PUBLICATIONS   .44
CARRER
  BUTTERFLY, THE
    FRANCO COLOMBO PUBLICATIONS   DS56   1.25
CARRER
  IMPROMPTUS
    FRANCO COLOMBO PUBLICATIONS   DS57   1.75
CARRER
  TEMPO DI MINUETTO
    FRANCO COLOMBO PUBLICATIONS   DS58   1.25
CARROLL   SCHAUM, J.   1 1/2
  BY THE BEAUTIFUL SEA
    SCHAUM PUBLICATIONS, INC.   .75
CARROLL   1 1/2
  MERRY MOMENTS
    WILLIS MUSIC COMPANY   .40
CARROLL   1 1/2
  MERRY MOMENTS
    WILLIS MUSIC COMPANY   .40
CARROLL *
  I'M ALWAYS CHASING RAINBOWS
    THE BIG THREE MUSIC CORPORATION   00.95
CARSON
  ALLEGRO BRILLANTE
    BOSTON MUSIC COMPANY   .50
CARTER
  BOUNCING THE BALL
    SUMMY-BIRCHARD COMPANY   .50
CARTER, B.
  EASTER
    BELWIN-MILLS PUBLISHING CORPORATION   25131   .60
                                         A
CARTER, E.
  PIANO SONATA
    THEODORE PRESSER COMPANY   3.50
CASADESUS, H.
  JARDIN DES AMOURS, LE
    FRANCO COLOMBO PUBLICATIONS   SAL   4.25

CASADESUS, H.
  RECREATIONS A LA CAMPAGNE
    FRANCO COLOMBO PUBLICATIONS   SAL   4.25
CASADESUS, R.
  CADENZAS TO MOZART'S CONCERTO NO. 22 IN E FLAT
    INTERNATIONAL MUSIC COMPANY   1.00
CASADESUS, R.
  SONATA NO. 01
    FRANCO COLOMBO PUBLICATIONS   SAL   4.50
CASADESUS, R.
  TOCCATA, OP. 40
    ELKAN-VOGEL, INC.   D   2.75
CASADESUS, R.
  VARIATIONS ON 'HOMAGE TO DEBUSSY' BY DE FALLA
    FRANCO COLOMBO PUBLICATIONS   R2022   2.50
CASATI
  RHAPSODY
    FRANCO COLOMBO PUBLICATIONS   BON. 2285   1.00
CASELLA, A.
  A NOTTE ALTA - MUSICAL POEM
    FRANCO COLOMBO PUBLICATIONS   117295 1.50
CASELLA, A.
  BARCAROLLE
    FRANCO COLOMBO PUBLICATIONS   R505   1.00
CASELLA, A.
  COCKTAIL'S DANCE
    FRANCO COLOMBO PUBLICATIONS   R505   .90
CASELLA, A.
  LA GIARA
    UNIVERSAL EDITION   UE 7715   14.00
CASELLA, A.
  LA GIARA -- DER GROSSE KRUG
    UNIVERSAL EDITION   UE 7715   14.00
CASELLA, A.
  PAGINE DI GUERRA
    FRANCO COLOMBO PUBLICATIONS   115929 1.50
CASELLA, A.
  PUPAZZETTI
    FRANCO COLOMBO PUBLICATIONS   116742 1.50
CASELLA, A.
  RICERCARE ON THE NAME 'GUIDO M. GATTI'
    FRANCO COLOMBO PUBLICATIONS   DS688   1.00
CASELLA, A.
  SARABANDE
    FRANCO COLOMBO PUBLICATIONS   SAL   3.25
CASELLA, A.   4-5
  SINFONIA, ARIOSO UND TOCCATA, OP. 59
    BARENREITER VERLAG   CM 18778
CASELLA, A.
  SONATINA
    FRANCO COLOMBO PUBLICATIONS   116838 1.50
CASELLA, A.
  TOCCATA
    FRANCO COLOMBO PUBLICATIONS   117017 1.75
CASELLA, A.
  VARIATIONS SUR UNE CHACONNE
    FRANCO COLOMBO PUBLICATIONS   SAL   3.25
CASELLA, E. M.
  NORTENAS
    FRANCO COLOMBO PUBLICATIONS   BA6132 .75
CASELLA, E. M.
  SUITE INCAICA
    FRANCO COLOMBO PUBLICATIONS   BA6097 2.00
CASTALDI, P.
  MOLL
    UNIVERSAL EDITION   UE 14950   6.05
CASTELLINI
  ALBA BRUMOSA
    FRANCO COLOMBO PUBLICATIONS   DS289   1.25
CASTELLINI
  NOCTURNE
    FRANCO COLOMBO PUBLICATIONS   DS240   1.00
CASTELNUOVO-TEDESCO
  ALGHE
    FRANCO COLOMBO PUBLICATIONS   FOR. 10821   1.50
CASTELNUOVO-TEDESCO
  ALT WIEN NO. 1 WALTZ
    FRANCO COLOMBO PUBLICATIONS   FOR. 11014   1.75
CASTELNUOVO-TEDESCO
  ALT WIEN NO. 2 NOCTURNE
    FRANCO COLOMBO PUBLICATIONS   FOR. 11015   1.75
CASTELNUOVO-TEDESCO
  ALT WIEN NO. 3 FOX TROT
    FRANCO COLOMBO PUBLICATIONS   FOR. 11016   1.75
CASTELNUOVO-TEDESCO
  CANDIDE
    MCA MUSIC   2.50
CASTELNUOVO-TEDESCO
  CIPRESSI
    FRANCO COLOMBO PUBLICATIONS   FOR. 10892   2.00
CASTELNUOVO-TEDESCO
  DANZE DEL RE DAVID, LE
    FRANCO COLOMBO PUBLICATIONS   FOR. 11260   4.00
CASTELNUOVO-TEDESCO
  ENGLISH SUITE -- PIANO OR HARPSICHORD
    BELWIN-MILLS PUBLISHING CORPORATION   20363   1.25
CASTELNUOVO-TEDESCO
  EPIGRAFE
    FRANCO COLOMBO PUBLICATIONS   FOR. 11013   1.75
CASTELNUOVO-TEDESCO
  FANDANGO ON THE NAME OF AMPARO ITURBI
    GENERAL MUSIC PUBLISHING COMPANY, INC.   661   2.50
CASTELNUOVO-TEDESCO
  GREETING CARDS - AMPARO ITURBI, OP. 170 NO. 6
    GENERAL MUSIC PUBLISHING COMPANY, INC.   2.50
CASTELNUOVO-TEDESCO
  GREETING CARDS - ANDRE PREVIN, OP. 170 NO. 1
    GENERAL MUSIC PUBLISHING COMPANY, INC.   2.50
CASTELNUOVO-TEDESCO
  GREETING CARDS - GIESEKING, OP. 170 NO. 5
    GENERAL MUSIC PUBLISHING COMPANY, INC.   2.50
CASTELNUOVO-TEDESCO
  MIRAGES ON THE NAME OF GIESEKING
    GENERAL MUSIC PUBLISHING COMPANY, INC.   660   2.50
CASTELNUOVO-TEDESCO
  NAVIGANTI, I
    FRANCO COLOMBO PUBLICATIONS   FOR. 10822   1.75
CASTELNUOVO-TEDESCO
  NINNA-NANNA DEL DOPOGUERRA
    FRANCO COLOMBO PUBLICATIONS   FOR. 12230   1.25
CASTELNUOVO-TEDESCO
  PASSATEMPI
    FRANCO COLOMBO PUBLICATIONS   FOR. 11512   2.00
CASTELNUOVO-TEDESCO
  PIEDIGROTTA 1924
    FRANCO COLOMBO PUBLICATIONS   119916 1.75

CASTELNUOVO-TEDESCO
  QUESTO FU IL CARRO DELLA MORTE
    FRANCO COLOMBO PUBLICATIONS   FOR. 10598 1.25
CASTELNUOVO-TEDESCO
  RAGGIO VERDE, IL
    FRANCO COLOMBO PUBLICATIONS   FOR. 10750 2.00
CASTELNUOVO-TEDESCO
  RICERCARE ON THE NAME 'LUIGI DALLAPICCOLA'
    FRANCO COLOMBO PUBLICATIONS   FOR. 12348 1.75
CASTELNUOVO-TEDESCO
  SEASONS, THE
    FRANCO COLOMBO PUBLICATIONS   FOR. 12222 2.50
CASTELNUOVO-TEDESCO
  SIRENETTA E IL PESCE TURCHINO, LA
    FRANCO COLOMBO PUBLICATIONS   FOR. 10940 2.00
CASTELNUOVO-TEDESCO
  SONATINA ZOOLOGICA
    FRANCO COLOMBO PUBLICATIONS   130266 2.25
CASTELNUOVO-TEDESCO
  TANGO ON THE NAME OF ANDRE PREVIN
    GENERAL MUSIC PUBLISHING COMPANY, INC. 656 2.50
CASTELNUOVO-TEDESCO
  VITALBA E BIANCOSPINO
    FRANCO COLOMBO PUBLICATIONS   FOR. 10958 1.75
CASTEREDE, J.
  SONATA
    ELKAN-VOGEL, INC.   7.00
CASTILLO
  PRELUDIO, DIFFERENCIAS, AND TOCCATA ON A THEME BY ALBENIZ
    ASSOCIATED MUSIC PUBLISHERS, INC. UME 2.25
CASTILLO
  SUITE IN D
    PAN AMERICAN UNION   01.00
CASTILLO, D. 2
  GAVOTTE
    WILLIS MUSIC COMPANY   .40
CASTRO, J. J.
  SONATINA ESPANOLA
    UNIVERSAL EDITION   UE 12444 3.95
CASTRO, J. J.
  TOCCATA
    FRANCO COLOMBO PUBLICATIONS   EAM6 1.25
CASTRO, J. M.
  CORALES CRIOLLOS NO. 1
    PAN AMERICAN UNION   01.85
CASTRO, J. M.
  PEQUENA MARCHA
    PAN AMERICAN UNION   00.75
CASTRO, J. M.
  QUASI POLKA
    PAN AMERICAN UNION   00.85
CASTRO, J. M.
  SONATA DE PRIMAVERA
    PAN AMERICAN UNION   03.00
CASTRO, J. M.
  TANGOS
    PAN AMERICAN UNION   01.75
CASTRO, J. M.
  TOCCATA
    PAN AMERICAN UNION   02.00
CASTRO, J. M.
  VALS MINIATURA
    PAN AMERICAN UNION   00.75
CASTRO, W.
  ARRORO
    PAN AMERICAN UNION   00.75
CASTRO, W.
  CAMPANITAS DE FIESTA
    PAN AMERICAN UNION   00.75
CASTRO, W.
  ERA UN PAJARITO
    PAN AMERICAN UNION   00.85
CASTRO, W.
  HACIENDO NONITO
    PAN AMERICAN UNION   00.75
CASTRO, W.
  INTERMEZZI
    PAN AMERICAN UNION   01.60
CASTRO, W.
  JUEGOS
    PAN AMERICAN UNION   01.00
CASTRO, W.
  RONDA
    PAN AMERICAN UNION   01.00
CATALANI
  EBBEN, N'ANDRO LONTANA
    FRANCO COLOMBO PUBLICATIONS   122420 .50
CATALANI
  IN SOGNO
    FRANCO COLOMBO PUBLICATIONS   64853 1.00
CATALANI
  LORELEY - DANZA DELLE ONDINE
    FRANCO COLOMBO PUBLICATIONS   54308 1.00
CATALANI
  PICCOLO VALZER -- OP. POSTH. --
    FRANCO COLOMBO PUBLICATIONS   Z524 1.00
CATALANI
  WALLY, LA A SERA - PRELUDE TO ACT III
    FRANCO COLOMBO PUBLICATIONS   53496 .60
CATALANI   DEL MAGLIO
  WALLY, LA A SERA - PRELUDE TO ACT III
    FRANCO COLOMBO PUBLICATIONS   127754 .50
CATALANI   CHIESA
  WALLY, LA - 1ST EASY FANTASIA
    FRANCO COLOMBO PUBLICATIONS   113181 .60
CATALANI   CHIESA
  WALLY, LA - 2ND EASY FANTASIA
    FRANCO COLOMBO PUBLICATIONS   113182 .50
CATALANI   CHIESA
  WALLY, LA - 3RD EASY FANTASIA
    FRANCO COLOMBO PUBLICATIONS   113183 .50
CATIZONE, J. M. 1 1/2
  BOUNCING ALONG
    THEODORE PRESSER COMPANY   .50
CATIZONE, J. M. 2
  CRYSTAL
    PRO-ART PUBLICATIONS, INC.   356 .50
CATIZONE, J. M. 1
  EASTER TIME
    PRO-ART PUBLICATIONS, INC.   372 .50
CATIZONE, J. M. 1
  JUST A HUMMIN'
    PRO-ART PUBLICATIONS, INC.   353 .50
CATIZONE, J. M. 1
  LET'S FLY TO THE MOON
    PRO-ART PUBLICATIONS, INC.   355 .50

CATIZONE, J. M. 1
  MILJO
    PRO-ART PUBLICATIONS, INC.   357 .50
CATIZONE, J. M. 3
  MOON CRATER ROCK
    PRO-ART PUBLICATIONS, INC.   432 .50
CATIZONE, J. M. 2-3
  POLAR BEAR POLKA
    PRO-ART PUBLICATIONS, INC.   411 .50
CATIZONE, J. M. 1
  RIDIN' ALONG MANDEVILLE TRAIL
    PRO-ART PUBLICATIONS, INC.   354 .50
CATIZONE, J. M. 1
  TALKING GRACE NOTES
    PRO-ART PUBLICATIONS, INC.   433 .50
CATIZONE, J. M. 1 1/2
  TUNE FOR TWO HANDS
    THEODORE PRESSER COMPANY   .50
CATIZONE, J. M. 2
  ZIPPY
    PRO-ART PUBLICATIONS, INC.   409 .50
CATON, F.
  ITALIAN MARCH
    FREDERICK HARRIS MUSIC COMPANY   .60
CATON, F.
  JIG
    FREDERICK HARRIS MUSIC COMPANY   .60
CATON, F.
  SAILOR TUNE, A
    FREDERICK HARRIS MUSIC COMPANY   .60
CATON, F.
  TWILIGHT
    FREDERICK HARRIS MUSIC COMPANY   .60
CATPE, J. F. 2 1/2
  PETITE BALLET
    BELWIN-MILLS PUBLISHING CORPORATION .60
CAVEZ, F.
  TAMBOO
    BELWIN-MILLS PUBLISHING CORPORATION 20290 .85
CAZDEN, N.
  MR. CZERNY
    AMERICAN MUSIC EDITION   .50
CAZDEN, N. E
  TRAMP AWAY
    THEODORE PRESSER COMPANY   .50
CAZDEN, N. MD
  VARIATIONS
    THEODORE PRESSER COMPANY   .60
CECCARELLI
  SCHERZO NO. 2
    FRANCO COLOMBO PUBLICATIONS   FOR. 11703 .90
CECERE, C. 2
  SWAY GENTLY
    WILLIS MUSIC COMPANY   .40
CECERE, C. 1
  SWAY GENTLY
    WILLIS MUSIC COMPANY   .40
CELE
  PENNY WHISTLE BLUE -- MAGIC GARDENS, THE.
    MCA MUSIC   1.00
CELLA
  QUADRO ANTICO
    FRANCO COLOMBO PUBLICATIONS   BON. 1877 .50
CERVENKA 1
  DANCING FINGERS
    WILLIS MUSIC COMPANY   .35
CHABRIER
  BOUREE FANTASQUE
    FRANCO COLOMBO PUBLICATIONS   ER2658 1.25
CHABRIER
  BOURREE FANTASTIQUE
    EDWARD B. MARKS MUSIC CORPORATION 01.00
CHABRIER 4
  ESPANA
    CENTURY MUSIC PUBLISHING COMPANY, INC. 3605 .40
CHABRIER SCHAUM, J. 2
  ESPANA WALTZ
    BELWIN-MILLS PUBLISHING CORPORATION .50
CHABRIER WEYBRIGHT 3
  HABANERA
    BELWIN-MILLS PUBLISHING CORPORATION .50
CHABRIER PHILIPP, I.
  HABANERA
    INTERNATIONAL MUSIC COMPANY   1.00
CHABRIER SCHAUM, J. 4
  HAVANA NIGHTS
    BELWIN-MILLS PUBLISHING CORPORATION .50
CHABRIER PHILIPP, I.
  IDYLL
    INTERNATIONAL MUSIC COMPANY   1.00
CHABRIER
  SCHERZO VALSE -- PIECES PITTORESQUES, NO. 10
    ELKAN-VOGEL, INC.   ENOCH 1.75
CHABRIER
  SCHERZO-WALTZ
    EDWARD B. MARKS MUSIC CORPORATION 01.00
CHADWICK, G. 1
  CRICKET AND BUMBLE BEE
    CENTURY MUSIC PUBLISHING COMPANY, INC. 4414 .40
CHADWICK, G.
  CRICKET AND THE BUMBLE BEE
    CARL FISCHER, INC.   P 3005 .50
CHADWICK, G. 2
  CRICKET AND THE BUMBLE BEE
    WILLIS MUSIC COMPANY   .40
CHADWICK, G.
  CRICKET AND THE BUMBLE BEE, THE
    G. SCHIRMER, INC.   .40
CHAGRIN
  SERENADE
    FRANCO COLOMBO PUBLICATIONS   LD522 .60
CHAGRIN
  TUSSLE
    FRANCO COLOMBO PUBLICATIONS   LD521 .60
CHAGY 2 1/2
  BALLAD OF THE BELLS
    BELWIN-MILLS PUBLISHING CORPORATION .60
CHAGY
  BICYCLE RIDE
    BOSTON MUSIC COMPANY   .50
CHAGY
  BLUE BALLAD
    BOSTON MUSIC COMPANY   .50
CHAGY 3
  BUTTERFLY BALLET
    BELWIN-MILLS PUBLISHING CORPORATION .60

CHAGY   3
    CHEERY CHIPMUNK
        WILLIS MUSIC COMPANY   .40
CHAGY   2
    DANCE OF THE MEDICINE MAN
        WILLIS MUSIC COMPANY   .35
CHAGY   3
    DESERT SCENE
        THEODORE PRESSER COMPANY   .50
CHAGY   1
    GRAY BIRCH
        BOSTON MUSIC COMPANY   .50
CHAGY   3
    HOLIDAY WALTZ
        PRO-ART PUBLICATIONS, INC.   441   .50
CHAGY   3
    JAPANESE RICKSHA
        BELWIN-MILLS PUBLISHING CORPORATION   .60
CHAGY   3
    JAZZ TANGO
        BOSTON MUSIC COMPANY   .50
CHAGY
    JAZZ TARANTELLA
        EDWARD B. MARKS MUSIC CORPORATION   00.60
CHAGY   2
    MUTED HARP, THE
        BOSTON MUSIC COMPANY   .60
CHAGY   2 1/2
    RIDING BOOTS
        BELWIN-MILLS PUBLISHING CORPORATION   .60
CHAGY   1
    SHEPHERD BOY
        CENTURY MUSIC PUBLISHING COMPANY, INC. 4392   .40
CHAGY   3
    SNOW IS FALLING
        BOSTON MUSIC COMPANY   .50
CHAGY   2 - 3
    TOCCATINA
        BOSTON MUSIC COMPANY   .60
CHAGY   .3
    TRAMPOLINE TRICKS
        BOSTON MUSIC COMPANY   .50
CHAGY   2
    TWILIGHT BELL
        THEODORE PRESSER COMPANY   .50
CHAGY   1
    TWILIGHT WALTZ
        BOSTON MUSIC COMPANY   .50
CHAGY   2
    VILLAGE SQUARE DANCE
        BOSTON MUSIC COMPANY   .50
CHAGY   1
    WALTZ OF THE GHOSTS
        BELWIN-MILLS PUBLISHING CORPORATION   .60
CHAGY   2
    WHIRLY-BIRD
        BOSTON MUSIC COMPANY   .50
CHAGY   3
    YELLOW JACKET
        BOSTON MUSIC COMPANY   .50
CHAILLEY   D
    SONATA BREVE
        C. F. PETERS CORPORATION   C379   2.00
CHAILLY, L.
    IMPROVISATION NO. 02
        FRANCO COLOMBO PUBLICATIONS   FOR. 12380   2.00
CHAILLY, L.
    ISTANTANEE DI ANNA MARIA
        FRANCO COLOMBO PUBLICATIONS   128968   .60
CHAILLY, L.
    TWO ISTANTANEE
        FRANCO COLOMBO PUBLICATIONS   129248   .60
CHAMINADE   4
    AIR DE BALLET -- CALLIRHOE -- G MAJOR
        CENTURY MUSIC PUBLISHING COMPANY, INC. 122   .40
CHAMINADE   5
    AIR DE BALLET -- PAS DES AMORPHES -- B FLAT MAJOR
        CENTURY MUSIC PUBLISHING COMPANY, INC. 1025   .40
CHAMINADE
    AIR DE BALLET NO. 1, OP. 30
        G. SCHIRMER, INC.   .70
CHAMINADE   6-7
    AUTUMN, OP. 35 NO. 2
        CENTURY MUSIC PUBLISHING COMPANY, INC. 2391   .40
CHAMINADE
    AUTUMN, OP. 35 NO. 2
        G. SCHIRMER, INC.   .70
CHAMINADE   5
    FAUNS, THE - SYLVAINS
        CENTURY MUSIC PUBLISHING COMPANY, INC. 2293   .40
CHAMINADE
    FAUNS, THE, OP. 60
        G. SCHIRMER, INC.   .50
CHAMINADE   5
    FLATTERER
        VOLKWEIN BROS.   .25
CHAMINADE
    FLATTERER, THE
        G. SCHIRMER, INC.   .70
CHAMINADE   4
    FLATTERER, THE -- LA LISONJERA
        CENTURY MUSIC PUBLISHING COMPANY, INC. 214   .40
CHAMINADE
    FOUR PIECES POUR PIANO - COLOMBINE
        FRANCO COLOMBO PUBLICATIONS   SAL   2.50
CHAMINADE
    FOUR PIECES POUR PIANO - LES NOCES D'OR
        FRANCO COLOMBO PUBLICATIONS   SAL   1.75
CHAMINADE
    FOUR PIECES POUR PIANO - MARCHE IMPROMPTU
        FRANCO COLOMBO PUBLICATIONS   SAL   1.75
CHAMINADE
    FOUR PIECES POUR PIANO - PAS DES SYLPHES
        FRANCO COLOMBO PUBLICATIONS   SAL   1.75
CHAMINADE
    FOUR PIECES POUR PIANO - PAS DES SYLPHES
        FRANCO COLOMBO PUBLICATIONS   SAL   1.50
CHAMINADE   5
    LA LISONJERA
        CENTURY MUSIC PUBLISHING COMPANY, INC. 214   .40
CHAMINADE   3
    LA LISONJERA, EASY
        CENTURY MUSIC PUBLISHING COMPANY, INC. 2508   .40
CHAMINADE   5
    LES SYLVAINS -- THE FAUNS --
        CENTURY MUSIC PUBLISHING COMPANY, INC. 2293   .40

CHAMINADE
    LISONJERA, LA. OP. 50
        FRANCO COLOMBO PUBLICATIONS   94163   .90
CHAMINADE   5
    PAS DES AMPHORES
        CENTURY MUSIC PUBLISHING COMPANY, INC. 1025   .40
CHAMINADE
    PAS DES AMPHORES--AIR DE BALLET, NO. 2
        G. SCHIRMER, INC.   .50
CHAMINADE
    PIERRETTE, OP. 41
        G. SCHIRMER, INC.   .40
CHAMINADE   4
    SCARF DANCE
        BOSTON MUSIC COMPANY   .50
CHAMINADE   5
    SCARF DANCE
        CENTURY MUSIC PUBLISHING COMPANY, INC. 383   .40
CHAMINADE
    SCARF-DANCE--AIR DE BALLET, NO. 3
        G. SCHIRMER, INC.   .40
CHAMINADE
    SCOTCH DANCE, OP. 151
        BELWIN-MILLS PUBLISHING CORPORATION   20235   1.25
CHAMINADE
    SPINNING-WHEEL, OP. 35 NO. 3
        G. SCHIRMER, INC.   .70
CHAMINADE   5
    SYLVAINS, LES -- THE FAUNS --
        CENTURY MUSIC PUBLISHING COMPANY, INC. 2293   .40
CHAMINADE
    TENDERNESS, OP. 149 -- VALSE TENDRE
        BELWIN-MILLS PUBLISHING CORPORATION   20299   1.00
CHAMPAGNE
    PRELUDE AND FILIGRANE, OP. 4
        ASSOCIATED MUSIC PUBLISHERS, INC.   BER   .75
CHAMPAGNE
    QUADRILHA BRASILEIRA -- 1942 -- ON A MARAJO ISLAND THEME
        ASSOCIATED MUSIC PUBLISHERS, INC.   BER   1.00
CHANAUD
    PAVANE LOUIS XV
        FRANCO COLOMBO PUBLICATIONS   SAL   1.75
CHANDLER *
    CANADIAN CAPERS
        WARNER BROTHERS PUBLISHERS   1.00
CHANLER, T.   MD
    CHILD IN THE HOUSE, A
        THEODORE PRESSER COMPANY   2.00
CHANLER, T.   MD
    TOCCATA
        THEODORE PRESSER COMPANY   .75
CHAPLIN
    MY STAR
        MCA MUSIC   1.00
CHAPLIN   KERR, R.N.
    THIS IS MY SONG
        MCA MUSIC   1.00
CHAPPELL, H.
    MAK, THE SHEEP STEALER
        UNIVERSAL EDITION   UE 14646   6.00
CHARLES
    WALTZ INTERLUDE, 'LET MY SONG FILL YOUR HEART'
        G. SCHIRMER, INC.   .50
CHARPENTIER, G.
    DEPUIS LE JOUR
        HEUGEL ET CIE.   1.95
CHARPENTIER, G.
    LOUISE
        HEUGEL ET CIE.   21.70
CHARPENTIER, J.   8
    ALLEGRO DE CONCERT
        ALPHONSE LEDUC
CHARPENTIER, J.   8
    TOCCATA
        ALPHONSE LEDUC
CHASINS, A.   4
    NOCTURNE IN G MINOR
        BELWIN-MILLS PUBLISHING CORPORATION   .60
CHASINS, A.   4 1/2
    PRELUDE IN B MINOR, OP. 13 NO. 5
        THEODORE PRESSER COMPANY   .50
CHASINS, A.   4
    PRELUDE IN D, OP. 10 NO. 5
        THEODORE PRESSER COMPANY   .50
CHASINS, A.   4
    RUSH-HOUR IN HONG KONG
        BELWIN-MILLS PUBLISHING CORPORATION   .75
CHAUNCEY, R. G.   3 1/2
    CARNIVAL DANCERS
        THEODORE PRESSER COMPANY   .50
CHAUNCEY, R. G.   1 1/2
    IN OUR CHERRY TREE
        THEODORE PRESSER COMPANY   .50
CHAUSSON
    INTERLUDE FROM 'POEME DE L'AMOUR ET DE LA MER'
        FRANCO COLOMBO PUBLICATIONS   SAL   1.75
CHAUSSON
    PAYSAGE
        FRANCO COLOMBO PUBLICATIONS   SAL   1.75
CHAVAGNAT
    ALIES, LES -- VALSE DE SALON --
        FRANCO COLOMBO PUBLICATIONS   SAL   1.75
CHAVARRI
    CUENTO DE LA PRINCESA DEL GUISANTE -- CUENTOS Y FANTASIAS, NO. 6
        ASSOCIATED MUSIC PUBLISHERS, INC.   UME   .65
CHAVARRI
    EL VIEJO CASTILLO MORO
        EDWARD B. MARKS MUSIC CORPORATION   01.00
CHAVARRI
    MARCHA DE LOS SOLDADOS DE PLOMO -- CUENTOS Y FANTASIAS, NO. 1
        ASSOCIATED MUSIC PUBLISHERS, INC.   UME   .50
CHAVARRI
    MENUETTINO-- CUENTOS Y FANTASIAS, NO. 2
        ASSOCIATED MUSIC PUBLISHERS, INC.   UME   .50
CHAVARRI
    MUNECA BAILA, LA -- CUENTOS Y FANTASIAS, NO. 4
        ASSOCIATED MUSIC PUBLISHERS, INC.   UME   .50
CHAVARRI
    SONATA LEVANTINA
        ASSOCIATED MUSIC PUBLISHERS, INC.   UME   1.35
CHAVARRI
    TOREROS DE CARTON -- CUENTOS Y FANTASIAS, NO. 3
        ASSOCIATED MUSIC PUBLISHERS, INC.   UME   .50
CHAVARRI
    VIEJO CASTILLO MORO, IL -- CUENTOS Y FANTASIAS NO. 5
        ASSOCIATED MUSIC PUBLISHERS, INC.   UME   .75

CHAVEZ, C.
CONCERTO FOR PIANO AND ORCHESTRA
G. SCHIRMER, INC.   3.00
CHAVEZ, C.
ESTUDIO HOMENAJE A CHOPIN
EDICIONES MEXICANAS DE MUSICA, A. C.   01.50
CHAVEZ, C.
INVENCION
BOOSEY AND HAWKES, INC.   2.50
CHAVEZ, C.
SIXTH SONATA FOR PIANO
BELWIN-MILLS PUBLISHING CORPORATION   20476   4.25
CHAVEZ, C.
SONATINA
BOOSEY AND HAWKES, INC.   .75
CHAVEZ, C.
TERCERA SONATA
PEER SOUTHERN ORGANIZATION   05.00
CHAVEZ, C.
THREE ETUDES
BELWIN-MILLS PUBLISHING CORPORATION   2.75
CHAYNES   8
CAPRICCIO
ALPHONSE LEDUC
CHAYNES   6, 8
SUBSTANCES CONVERGENTES
ALPHONSE LEDUC
CHEDEVILLE, E. P.   MOFFAT   5
TAMBOURIN CHINOIS
NOVELLO AND COMPANY, LTD.   55.0046.10   .40
CHELU
NAIN JAUNE, LE -- GALOP BRILLANT --
FRANCO COLOMBO PUBLICATIONS   SAL   2.00
CHELU
NAIN JAUNE, LE -- GALOP BRILLANT --
FRANCO COLOMBO PUBLICATIONS   SAL   1.50
CHENEY, T.   M
DIFFICULT DECISION
THEODORE PRESSER COMPANY   .50
CHENEY, T.   M
OUTDOOR MUSIC
THEODORE PRESSER COMPANY   .50
CHENOWETH, W.
CONCERT WALTZ--MEMORIES OF OLD VIENNA
G. SCHIRMER, INC.   .75
CHENOWETH, W.
CORTEGE--PRELUDE
G. SCHIRMER, INC.   .40
CHENOWETH, W.
HIDDEN WATERFALL, THE
G. SCHIRMER, INC.   .60
CHENOWETH, W.
IN A PATIO--SPANISH SERENADE
G. SCHIRMER, INC.   .50
CHENOWETH, W.
PUPPETS ON PARADE
G. SCHIRMER, INC.   .50
CHENOWETH, W.
RUSTIC DANCE
G. SCHIRMER, INC.   .40
CHEVALIER   3
LOVE EN MASQUE, WALTZ
CENTURY MUSIC PUBLISHING COMPANY, INC.   2679   .40
CHIATRI   JESTON, I. H.   2
LA SPAGNOLA
VOLKWEIN BROS.   .35
CHILDERS, L.   *   2
BANJO, THE
BELWIN-MILLS PUBLISHING CORPORATION   .60
CHILDERS, L.   1
MOON SHOT
BELWIN-MILLS PUBLISHING CORPORATION   .60
CHILDERS, L.   M
SONATINA IN G MINOR, NO. 2
COMPOSERS PRESS, INC.   2.00
CHISOLM
SORROW FOR A QUEEN
FRANCO COLOMBO PUBLICATIONS   SAL   1.75
CHISOLM
VIEWED FROM A STARPOINT
FRANCO COLOMBO PUBLICATIONS   SAL   2.50
CHOPIN   ROGERS
AUTUMN REVERIE
BOSTON MUSIC COMPANY   .50
CHOPIN   JOSEFFY
BALLADE IN A FLAT MAJOR, OP. 47
G. SCHIRMER, INC.   .80
CHOPIN   SAUER   5
BALLADE IN A FLAT, OP. 47
SCHOTT   06211 1/2   1.00
CHOPIN
BALLADE IN A-FLAT, OP. 47
FRANCO COLOMBO PUBLICATIONS   ER2518   .75
CHOPIN   JOSEFFY
BALLADE IN F MAJOR, OP. 38
G. SCHIRMER, INC.   .75
CHOPIN
BALLADE IN F MINOR, OP. 52
FRANCO COLOMBO PUBLICATIONS   ER2519   1.00
CHOPIN
BALLADE IN F, OP. 38
FRANCO COLOMBO PUBLICATIONS   ER2517   .75
CHOPIN   SAUER   6
BALLADE IN F, OP. 38
SCHOTT   0362 1/2   1.00
CHOPIN
BALLADE IN G MINOR, OP. 23
FRANCO COLOMBO PUBLICATIONS   ER1868   1.00
CHOPIN   JOSEFFY
BALLADE IN G MINOR, OP. 23
G. SCHIRMER, INC.   .90
CHOPIN   SAUER   6
BALLADE IN G MINOR, OP. 23
SCHOTT   06209 1/2   1.00
CHOPIN   SAUER   6
BARCAROLLE IN F SHARP
SCHOTT   0422 1/2   1.00
CHOPIN   JOSEFFY
BARCAROLLE IN F SHARP MAJOR, OP. 60
G. SCHIRMER, INC.   .75
CHOPIN   MERTKE, E.
BARCAROLLE, OP. 60
EDWIN F. KALMUS   3335   1.00
CHOPIN   BRUGNOLI *
BARCAROLLE, OP. 60
FRANCO COLOMBO PUBLICATIONS   ER2576   .90

CHOPIN   JOSEFFY
BERCEUSE IN D FLAT MAJOR, OP. 57
G. SCHIRMER, INC.   .50
CHOPIN   SAUER   5
BERCEUSE IN D FLAT, OP. 57
SCHOTT   0421 1/2   1.00
CHOPIN   6
BERCEUSE, OP. 57
CENTURY MUSIC PUBLISHING COMPANY, INC.   1403   .40
CHOPIN   BRUGNOLI *
BERCEUSE, OP. 57
FRANCO COLOMBO PUBLICATIONS   ER2577   .75
CHOPIN   5
BLACK KEY ETUDE
CENTURY MUSIC PUBLISHING COMPANY, INC.   2445   .40
CHOPIN   MERTKE, E.
BOLERO, OP. 19
EDWIN F. KALMUS   3336   1.00
CHOPIN   BRUGNOLI
BOLERO, OP. 19
FRANCO COLOMBO PUBLICATIONS   ER1433   1.00
CHOPIN   BRADLEY, R.
BRADLEY CLASSICAL SERIES - MINUTE WALTZ, OP. 64 NO. 1
SCREEN GEMS - COLUMBIA PUBLICATIONS   2718MP2   .85
CHOPIN   BRADLEY, R.
BRADLEY CLASSICAL SERIES - NOCTURNE IN E FLAT, OP. 9 NO. 2
SCREEN GEMS - COLUMBIA PUBLICATIONS   4721NP2   .85
CHOPIN   BRADLEY, R.
BRADLEY CLASSICAL SERIES - PRELUDE IN E MINOR, OP. 28 NO. 4
SCREEN GEMS - COLUMBIA PUBLICATIONS   5714PP2   .85
CHOPIN   SCHAUM, J.   2
BUTTERFLY ETUDE
BELWIN-MILLS PUBLISHING CORPORATION   .50
CHOPIN   5-6
BUTTERFLY ETUDE
CENTURY MUSIC PUBLISHING COMPANY, INC.   2544   .40
CHOPIN   SCHAUM, J.   2 1/2
CANDLELIGHT SERENADE
BELWIN-MILLS PUBLISHING CORPORATION   .50
CHOPIN   TREHARNE
CHOPIN SIMPLIFIED
BOSTON MUSIC COMPANY   1.00
CHOPIN   SCHOEGEL
CHOPIN'S POLONAISE IN BOOGIE
MCA MUSIC   1.00
CHOPIN   M
CONCERTO NO. 01 IN E MINOR, OP. 11
C. F. PETERS CORPORATION   2895AA   1.25
CHOPIN   JOSEFFY
CONCERTO NO. 01 IN E MINOR, OP. 11
G. SCHIRMER, INC.   L1350   1.75
CHOPIN   MIKULI
CONCERTO NO. 01 IN E MINOR, OP. 11
G. SCHIRMER, INC.   L1558   1.50
CHOPIN   JOSEFFY
CONCERTO NO. 02 IN F MINOR, OP. 21
G. SCHIRMER, INC.   L1351   1.75
CHOPIN   MIKULI
CONCERTO NO. 02 IN F MINOR, OP. 21
G. SCHIRMER, INC.   L1557   1.50
CHOPIN   6
CRADLE SONG -- BERCEUSE, OP. 57
CENTURY MUSIC PUBLISHING COMPANY, INC.   1403   .40
CHOPIN   BRUGNOLI *
ECOSSAISE, OP. 72, NO. 3
FRANCO COLOMBO PUBLICATIONS   ER2578   .60
CHOPIN   DEL MAGLIO
ECOSSAISE, OP. 72, NO. 3
FRANCO COLOMBO PUBLICATIONS   127141   .50
CHOPIN   FRIEDHEIM
ETUDE IN A FLAT MAJOR, OP. 25 NO. 1
G. SCHIRMER, INC.   .50
CHOPIN
ETUDE IN A FLAT, OP. 25 NO. 1
FRANCO COLOMBO PUBLICATIONS   ER2615   .60
CHOPIN   FRIEDHEIM
ETUDE IN A MINOR, OP. 10 NO. 2
G. SCHIRMER, INC.   .40
CHOPIN
ETUDE IN A MINOR, OP. 25 NO. 11
FRANCO COLOMBO PUBLICATIONS   128328   .50
CHOPIN   FRIEDHEIM
ETUDE IN A MINOR, OP. 25 NO. 4
G. SCHIRMER, INC.   .35
CHOPIN
ETUDE IN C MINOR, OP. 10 NO. 12
ASHLEY DEALERS SERVICE, INC.   ES   .95
CHOPIN
ETUDE IN C MINOR, OP. 10 NO. 12
FRANCO COLOMBO PUBLICATIONS   128132   .75
CHOPIN   DEL MAGLIO
ETUDE IN C MINOR, OP. 10 NO. 12
FRANCO COLOMBO PUBLICATIONS   127142   .50
CHOPIN   FRIEDHEIM
ETUDE IN C MINOR, OP. 10 NO. 12
G. SCHIRMER, INC.   .50
CHOPIN
ETUDE IN C MINOR, OP. 10 NO. 12
WILLIS MUSIC COMPANY   .35
CHOPIN   6
ETUDE IN C MINOR, OP. 10 NO. 12 - REVOLUTIONARY
CENTURY MUSIC PUBLISHING COMPANY, INC.   2543   .40
CHOPIN   SAUER
ETUDE IN C MINOR, OP. 10 NO. 12 'REVOLUTION'
SCHOTT   09574 1/2   1.00
CHOPIN   FRIEDHEIM
ETUDE IN C SHARP MINOR, OP. 10 NO. 4
G. SCHIRMER, INC.   .60
CHOPIN   FRIEDHEIM
ETUDE IN C SHARP MINOR, OP. 25 NO. 7
G. SCHIRMER, INC.   .50
CHOPIN
ETUDE IN E
WILLIS MUSIC COMPANY   .40
CHOPIN   FRIEDHEIM
ETUDE IN E FLAT MINOR, OP. 10 NO. 6
G. SCHIRMER, INC.   .40
CHOPIN   MOSSMAN
ETUDE IN E MAJOR
BELWIN-MILLS PUBLISHING CORPORATION   26065   .60
CHOPIN   SCHAUM, J.   3
ETUDE IN E MAJOR
SCHAUM PUBLICATIONS, INC.   .60
CHOPIN
ETUDE IN E MAJOR -- TRISTESSE, OP. 10 NO. 3
ASHLEY DEALERS SERVICE, INC.   ES   .95

CHOPIN   FRIEDHEIM
  ETUDE IN E MAJOR, OP. 10 NO. 3
    G. SCHIRMER, INC.   .40
CHOPIN
  ETUDE IN E, OP. 10 NO. 3
    FRANCO COLOMBO PUBLICATIONS   128301   .90
CHOPIN   DEL MAGLIO
  ETUDE IN E, OP. 10 NO. 3
    FRANCO COLOMBO PUBLICATIONS   127484   .60
CHOPIN   SAUER   5
  ETUDE IN E, OP. 10 NO. 3
    SCHOTT   0379 1/2   1.00
CHOPIN   FRIEDHEIM
  ETUDE IN F MINOR, OP. 10 NO. 9
    G. SCHIRMER, INC.   .40
CHOPIN
  ETUDE IN F MINOR, OP. 25 NO. 2
    FRANCO COLOMBO PUBLICATIONS   ER2616   .60
CHOPIN   FRIEDHEIM
  ETUDE IN G FLAT MAJOR, OP. 10 NO. 5
    G. SCHIRMER, INC.   .40
CHOPIN   FRIEDHEIM
  ETUDE IN G FLAT MAJOR, OP. 25 NO. 9
    G. SCHIRMER, INC.   .40
CHOPIN
  ETUDE IN G FLAT, OP. 10 NO. 5
    FRANCO COLOMBO PUBLICATIONS   ER2614   .60
CHOPIN   9
  ETUDE IN G FLAT, OP. 10 NO. 5
    THEODORE PRESSER COMPANY   .50
CHOPIN   5
  ETUDE IN G FLAT, OP. 10 NO. 5 - BLACK KEY
    CENTURY MUSIC PUBLISHING COMPANY, INC.   2445   .40
CHOPIN
  ETUDE IN G FLAT, OP. 25 NO. 9
    FRANCO COLOMBO PUBLICATIONS   ER2617   .60
CHOPIN
  ETUDE IN G FLAT, OP. 25 NO. 9
    WILLIS MUSIC COMPANY   .35
CHOPIN   6
  ETUDE IN G, OP. 25 NO. 9 - BUTTERFLY
    CENTURY MUSIC PUBLISHING COMPANY, INC.   2544   .40
CHOPIN   ECKSTEIN
  FANTASIE IMPROMPTU IN C SHARP MINOR, OP. 66
    CARL FISCHER, INC.   S 2259   .60
CHOPIN   6
  FANTASIE IMPROMPTU, OP. 66
    CENTURY MUSIC PUBLISHING COMPANY, INC.   1180   .40
CHOPIN
  FANTASIE IMPROMPTU, OP. 66 NO. 4
    ASHLEY DEALERS SERVICE, INC.   ES   .95
CHOPIN   BRUGNOLI *
  FANTASIE IN F MINOR, OP. 49
    FRANCO COLOMBO PUBLICATIONS   ER2507   1.25
CHOPIN   JOSEFFY
  FANTASIE IN F MINOR, OP. 49
    G. SCHIRMER, INC.   1.10
CHOPIN   SAUER   6
  FANTASIE IN F MINOR, OP. 49
    SCHOTT   06240 1/2   1.00
CHOPIN
  FANTASIE-IMPROMPTU IN C SHARP MINOR, OP. 66
    G. SCHIRMER, INC.   .60
CHOPIN   SAUER   5
  FANTASIE-IMPROMPTU IN C SHARP MINOR, OP. 66
    SCHOTT   0368 1/2   1.00
CHOPIN
  FANTASIE-IMPROMPTU IN C SHARP MINOR, OP. 66--FROM THE COLLECTION
  OF ARTUR RUBINSTEIN
    G. SCHIRMER, INC.   .75
CHOPIN   BRUGNOLI *
  FANTASIE-IMPROMPTU, OP. 66
    FRANCO COLOMBO PUBLICATIONS   ER2540   .75
CHOPIN
  FANTASIE-IMPROMPTU, OP. 66
    WILLIS MUSIC COMPANY   .50
CHOPIN   6
  FANTASY-IMPROMPTU, OP. 66
    BELWIN-MILLS PUBLISHING CORPORATION   650   .60
CHOPIN   WEYBRIGHT   1
  FAVORITE THEME, A -- FROM FANTASIE IMPROMPTU
    BELWIN-MILLS PUBLISHING CORPORATION   .60
CHOPIN   STEINER   2 1/2
  FRENCH RIVER BOAT, ADAPTED FROM THE NOCTURNE OP. 37 NO. 2
    BELWIN-MILLS PUBLISHING CORPORATION   .60
CHOPIN   GOLINELLI
  FUNERAL MARCH - FROM SONATA, OP. 35
    FRANCO COLOMBO PUBLICATIONS   30530   .90
CHOPIN   DEL MAGLIO
  FUNERAL MARCH - FROM SONATA, OP. 35
    FRANCO COLOMBO PUBLICATIONS   129099   .60
CHOPIN   5
  FUNERAL MARCH -- SONATA NO. 2
    CENTURY MUSIC PUBLISHING COMPANY, INC.   587   .40
CHOPIN   4-5
  GRAND VALSE BRILLANTE, OP. 18
    CENTURY MUSIC PUBLISHING COMPANY, INC.   2444   .40
CHOPIN   SCHAUM, J.   5
  HARP ETUDE
    BELWIN-MILLS PUBLISHING CORPORATION   .50
CHOPIN   JOSEFFY
  IMPROMPTU IN A FLAT MAJOR, OP. 29
    G. SCHIRMER, INC.   .60
CHOPIN   5
  IMPROMPTU IN A FLAT, OP. 29
    CENTURY MUSIC PUBLISHING COMPANY, INC.   254   .40
CHOPIN   SAUER   5
  IMPROMPTU IN A FLAT, OP. 29
    SCHOTT   0365 1/2   1.00
CHOPIN   JOSEFFY
  IMPROMPTU IN C SHARP MINOR, OP. 66
    G. SCHIRMER, INC.   .60
CHOPIN   JOSEFFY
  IMPROMPTU IN F SHARP MAJOR, OP. 36
    G. SCHIRMER, INC.   .60
CHOPIN   PUGNO
  IMPROMPTU IN F, OP. 36
    ASSOCIATED MUSIC PUBLISHERS, INC. AMP   .50
CHOPIN
  IMPROMPTU NO. 1 IN A-FLAT, OP. 29
    FRANCO COLOMBO PUBLICATIONS   ER2570   .60
CHOPIN
  LAST MAZURKA, THE --F MINOR
    EDWARD B. MARKS MUSIC CORPORATION   02.00

CHOPIN   SCHAUM, J.   2
  MAIDEN'S WISH
    BELWIN-MILLS PUBLISHING CORPORATION   .50
CHOPIN   LISZT
  MAIDEN'S WISH
    G. SCHIRMER, INC.   .60
CHOPIN   LONG, L.   2
  MAIDEN'S WISH, THE
    WILLIS MUSIC COMPANY   .35
CHOPIN   5
  MARCHE FUNEBRE
    CENTURY MUSIC PUBLISHING COMPANY, INC.   587   .40
CHOPIN
  MARCHE FUNEBRE--FROM SONATA IN B FLAT MINOR, OP. 35
    G. SCHIRMER, INC.   .40
CHOPIN   JOSEFFY
  MAZURKA IN A FLAT MAJOR, OP. 24 NO. 3
    G. SCHIRMER, INC.   .30
CHOPIN   JOSEFFY
  MAZURKA IN A MINOR, OP. 17 NO. 4
    G. SCHIRMER, INC.   .50
CHOPIN   JOSEFFY
  MAZURKA IN A MINOR, OP. 59 NO. 1
    G. SCHIRMER, INC.   .35
CHOPIN   JOSEFFY
  MAZURKA IN A MINOR, OP. 67 NO. 4
    G. SCHIRMER, INC.   .35
CHOPIN   JOSEFFY
  MAZURKA IN A MINOR, OP. 68 NO. 2
    G. SCHIRMER, INC.   .40
CHOPIN   3
  MAZURKA IN A MINOR, OP. 68 NO. 2
    THEODORE PRESSER COMPANY   .50
CHOPIN   JOSEFFY
  MAZURKA IN A MINOR, OP. 7 NO. 2
    G. SCHIRMER, INC.   .35
CHOPIN   5
  MAZURKA IN B FLAT
    NOVELLO AND COMPANY, LTD.   55.0031.01   .40
CHOPIN   JOSEFFY
  MAZURKA IN B FLAT MAJOR, OP. 17 NO. 1
    G. SCHIRMER, INC.   .30
CHOPIN   JOSEFFY
  MAZURKA IN B FLAT MAJOR, OP. 7 NO. 1
    G. SCHIRMER, INC.   .40
CHOPIN   3
  MAZURKA IN B FLAT, OP. 7 NO. 1
    CENTURY MUSIC PUBLISHING COMPANY, INC.   3251   .40
CHOPIN   3
  MAZURKA IN B FLAT, OP. 7 NO. 1
    THEODORE PRESSER COMPANY   .50
CHOPIN
  MAZURKA IN B FLAT, OP. 7 NO. 1
    WILLIS MUSIC COMPANY   .30
CHOPIN   JOSEFFY
  MAZURKA IN B MAJOR, OP. 63 NO. 1
    G. SCHIRMER, INC.   .30
CHOPIN   JOSEFFY
  MAZURKA IN B MINOR, OP. 33 NO. 4
    G. SCHIRMER, INC.   .50
CHOPIN   JOSEFFY
  MAZURKA IN C MAJOR, OP. 67 NO. 3
    G. SCHIRMER, INC.   .40
CHOPIN   WERNER
  MAZURKA IN D AND CONTREDANSE--CURWEN EDITION
    G. SCHIRMER, INC.   .85
CHOPIN   4
  MAZURKA IN E MINOR, OP. 41 NO. 2
    CENTURY MUSIC PUBLISHING COMPANY, INC.   3838   .40
CHOPIN   JOSEFFY
  MAZURKA IN F MAJOR, OP. 68 NO. 3
    G. SCHIRMER, INC.   .40
CHOPIN   JOSEFFY
  MAZURKA IN F SHARP MINOR, OP. 6 NO. 1
    G. SCHIRMER, INC.   .40
CHOPIN   3
  MAZURKA IN F, OP. 68 NO. 3
    CENTURY MUSIC PUBLISHING COMPANY, INC.   4038   .40
CHOPIN   3
  MAZURKA IN G MINOR, OP. 67 NO. 2
    CENTURY MUSIC PUBLISHING COMPANY, INC.   164   .40
CHOPIN   JOSEFFY
  MAZURKA IN G MINOR, OP. 67 NO. 2
    G. SCHIRMER, INC.   .40
CHOPIN   4
  MAZURKA IN G SHARP MINOR, OP. 33 NO. 1
    CENTURY MUSIC PUBLISHING COMPANY, INC.   3256   .40
CHOPIN
  MAZURKA, OP. 17 NO. 2
    FRANCO COLOMBO PUBLICATIONS   128700   .60
CHOPIN
  MAZURKA, OP. 33 NO. 1
    FRANCO COLOMBO PUBLICATIONS   128701   .60
CHOPIN
  MAZURKA, OP. 67 NO. 4
    FRANCO COLOMBO PUBLICATIONS   128702   .60
CHOPIN
  MAZURKA, OP. 68 NO. 2
    FRANCO COLOMBO PUBLICATIONS   128697   .60
CHOPIN
  MAZURKA, OP. 68 NO. 2
    FREDERICK HARRIS MUSIC COMPANY   .30
CHOPIN
  MAZURKA, OP. 7 NO. 1
    FRANCO COLOMBO PUBLICATIONS   128698   .60
CHOPIN   DEL MAGLIO
  MAZURKA, OP. 7 NO. 1
    FRANCO COLOMBO PUBLICATIONS   129100   .60
CHOPIN
  MAZURKA, OP. 7 NO. 2
    FRANCO COLOMBO PUBLICATIONS   128699   .60
CHOPIN   ZEPP   3
  MELODY AND PRELUDE
    PRO-ART PUBLICATIONS, INC.   150   .50
CHOPIN   4
  MILITARY POLONAISE
    CENTURY MUSIC PUBLISHING COMPANY, INC.   1181   .40
CHOPIN   2
  MILITARY POLONAISE, EASY
    CENTURY MUSIC PUBLISHING COMPANY, INC.   1825   .40
CHOPIN
  MILITARY POLONAISE, OP. 40 NO. 1
    CARL FISCHER, INC.   S 1228   .60
CHOPIN   2
  MINUTE WALTZ, EASY
    CENTURY MUSIC PUBLISHING COMPANY, INC.   2160   .40

CHOPIN   4 - 5
    MINUTE WALTZ, OP. 64 NO. 1
       BOSTON MUSIC COMPANY   .50
CHOPIN   3
    MINUTE WALTZ, OP. 64 NO. 1
       CENTURY MUSIC PUBLISHING COMPANY, INC.   1175   .40
CHOPIN
    MINUTE WALTZ, OP. 64 NO. 1
       WILLIS MUSIC COMPANY   .35
CHOPIN
    MINUTE WALTZ, OP. 64 NO. 1 -- VALSE IN D FLAT
       ASHLEY DEALERS SERVICE, INC.   ES   .95
CHOPIN   POZZOLI
    MY FIRST CHOPIN
       FRANCO COLOMBO PUBLICATIONS   ER2466   1.00
CHOPIN   KREUTZER   3
    NOCTURNE
       BOSTON MUSIC COMPANY   .50
CHOPIN   1
    NOCTURNE
       WILLIS MUSIC COMPANY   .35
CHOPIN   JOSEFFY
    NOCTURNE IN A FLAT MAJOR, OP. 32 NO. 2
       G. SCHIRMER, INC.   .50
CHOPIN   JOSEFFY
    NOCTURNE IN B FLAT MINOR, OP. 9 NO. 1
       G. SCHIRMER, INC.   .40
CHOPIN   JOSEFFY
    NOCTURNE IN B MAJOR, OP. 32 NO. 1
       G. SCHIRMER, INC.   .40
CHOPIN
    NOCTURNE IN B MINOR, OP. 9 NO. 1
       FRANCO COLOMBO PUBLICATIONS   ER2650   .75
CHOPIN   5
    NOCTURNE IN B, OP. 32 NO. 1
       CENTURY MUSIC PUBLISHING COMPANY, INC.   337   .40
CHOPIN   JOSEFFY
    NOCTURNE IN C MINOR, OP. 48 NO. 1
       G. SCHIRMER, INC.   .60
CHOPIN   YORK
    NOCTURNE IN C SHARP MINOR, OP. POSTH.
       G. SCHIRMER, INC.   .50
CHOPIN
    NOCTURNE IN C SHARP MINOR, OP. POSTH.
       INTERNATIONAL MUSIC COMPANY   .75
CHOPIN   JOSEFFY
    NOCTURNE IN D FLAT MAJOR, OP. 27 NO. 2
       G. SCHIRMER, INC.   .40
CHOPIN   6
    NOCTURNE IN D FLAT, OP. 27 NO. 2
       CENTURY MUSIC PUBLISHING COMPANY, INC.   3424   .40
CHOPIN   EDWARDS, C.
    NOCTURNE IN E FLAT
       BELWIN-MILLS PUBLISHING CORPORATION   26034   .60
CHOPIN
    NOCTURNE IN E FLAT MAJOR, OP. 9 NO. 2
       BELWIN-MILLS PUBLISHING CORPORATION   28171   .60
CHOPIN   JOSEFFY
    NOCTURNE IN E FLAT MAJOR, OP. 9 NO. 2
       G. SCHIRMER, INC.   .50
CHOPIN
    NOCTURNE IN E FLAT, OP. 9 NO. 2
       ASHLEY DEALERS SERVICE, INC.   ES   .95
CHOPIN   ECKSTEIN
    NOCTURNE IN E FLAT, OP. 9 NO. 2
       CARL FISCHER, INC.   S 1086   .50
CHOPIN   4
    NOCTURNE IN E FLAT, OP. 9 NO. 2
       CENTURY MUSIC PUBLISHING COMPANY, INC.   1176   .40
CHOPIN
    NOCTURNE IN E FLAT, OP. 9 NO. 2
       FRANCO COLOMBO PUBLICATIONS   ER2596   .60
CHOPIN   DEL MAGLIO
    NOCTURNE IN E FLAT, OP. 9 NO. 2
       FRANCO COLOMBO PUBLICATIONS   124714   .75
CHOPIN   SAUER   4
    NOCTURNE IN E FLAT, OP. 9 NO. 2
       SCHOTT   0343   .75
CHOPIN
    NOCTURNE IN E FLAT, OP. 9 NO. 2
       WILLIS MUSIC COMPANY   .40
CHOPIN   JOSEFFY
    NOCTURNE IN E MAJOR, OP. 62 NO. 2
       G. SCHIRMER, INC.   .40
CHOPIN   JOSEFFY
    NOCTURNE IN E MINOR, OP. 72 NO. 1 --POSTHUMOUS--
       G. SCHIRMER, INC.   .50
CHOPIN   JOSEFFY
    NOCTURNE IN F MAJOR, OP. 15 NO. 1
       G. SCHIRMER, INC.   .40
CHOPIN   5
    NOCTURNE IN F MINOR, OP. 55 NO. 1
       CENTURY MUSIC PUBLISHING COMPANY, INC.   340   .40
CHOPIN   JOSEFFY
    NOCTURNE IN F MINOR, OP. 55 NO. 1
       G. SCHIRMER, INC.   .50
CHOPIN   WHITFORD   GR. 2 1/2
    NOCTURNE IN F SHARP
       ROBERT WHITFORD PUBLICATIONS   .40
CHOPIN   JOSEFFY
    NOCTURNE IN F SHARP MAJOR, OP. 15 NO. 2
       G. SCHIRMER, INC.   .40
CHOPIN   7
    NOCTURNE IN F SHARP, OP. 13 NO. 2
       CENTURY MUSIC PUBLISHING COMPANY, INC.   3343   .40
CHOPIN   JOSEFFY
    NOCTURNE IN G MAJOR, OP. 37 NO. 2
       G. SCHIRMER, INC.   .50
CHOPIN   JOSEFFY
    NOCTURNE IN G MINOR, OP. 15 NO. 3
       G. SCHIRMER, INC.   .40
CHOPIN   JOSEFFY
    NOCTURNE IN G MINOR, OP. 37 NO. 1
       G. SCHIRMER, INC.   .40
CHOPIN   SAUER   4
    NOCTURNE IN G MINOR, OP. 37 NO. 1
       SCHOTT   1.00
CHOPIN   5
    NOCTURNE IN G, OP. 37 NO. 2
       CENTURY MUSIC PUBLISHING COMPANY, INC.   339   .40
CHOPIN   SCHAUM, J.   2 1/2
    NOCTURNE--OP. 09 NO. 2
       BELWIN-MILLS PUBLISHING CORPORATION   .50
CHOPIN
    NOCTURNE, OP. POSTH. IN C-SHARP MINOR
       FRANCO COLOMBO PUBLICATIONS   ER2601   .60

CHOPIN   THOMPSON, J.   4
    NOCTURNE, OP. 15 NO. 2
       WILLIS MUSIC COMPANY   .60
CHOPIN
    NOCTURNE, OP. 15 NO. 2 IN F-SHARP
       FRANCO COLOMBO PUBLICATIONS   128110   .75
CHOPIN
    NOCTURNE, OP. 15 NO. 3
       FREDERICK HARRIS MUSIC COMPANY   .40
CHOPIN
    NOCTURNE, OP. 27 NO. 1 IN C-SHARP MINOR
       FRANCO COLOMBO PUBLICATIONS   129185   .75
CHOPIN
    NOCTURNE, OP. 27 NO. 2 IN D FLAT
       FRANCO COLOMBO PUBLICATIONS   ER2594   .60
CHOPIN   THOMPSON, J.   3
    NOCTURNE, OP. 37 NO. 2
       WILLIS MUSIC COMPANY   .60
CHOPIN   THOMPSON, J.   3
    NOCTURNE, OP. 48 NO. 1
       WILLIS MUSIC COMPANY   .60
CHOPIN   DEL MAGLIO
    NOCTURNE, OP. 55 NO. 1
       FRANCO COLOMBO PUBLICATIONS   124715   .60
CHOPIN
    NOCTURNE, OP. 72 NO. 1 IN E MINOR
       FRANCO COLOMBO PUBLICATIONS   ER2593   .60
CHOPIN   5
    NOCTURNE, OP. 9 NO. 2
       BELWIN-MILLS PUBLISHING CORPORATION   71   .60
CHOPIN   THOMPSON, J.   4
    NOCTURNE, OP. 9 NO. 2
       WILLIS MUSIC COMPANY   .60
CHOPIN
    NOUVELLES ETUDE IN A FLAT MAJOR, NO. 2
       G. SCHIRMER, INC.   .30
CHOPIN
    NOUVELLES ETUDE IN F MINOR, NO. 1
       G. SCHIRMER, INC.   .30
CHOPIN   5
    POLONAISE IN A FLAT
       BOSTON MUSIC COMPANY   1.00
CHOPIN
    POLONAISE IN A FLAT MAJOR, OP. 53
       ASHLEY DEALERS SERVICE, INC.   ES   .95
CHOPIN
    POLONAISE IN A FLAT MAJOR, OP. 53
       G. SCHIRMER, INC.   .75
CHOPIN   SCHAUM, J.   2
    POLONAISE IN A FLAT, OP. 53
       BELWIN-MILLS PUBLISHING CORPORATION   .50
CHOPIN
    POLONAISE IN A FLAT, OP. 53
       CARL FISCHER, INC.   S 1999   .75
CHOPIN   5-6
    POLONAISE IN A FLAT, OP. 53
       CENTURY MUSIC PUBLISHING COMPANY, INC.   3843   .40
CHOPIN   10
    POLONAISE IN A FLAT, OP. 53
       THEODORE PRESSER COMPANY   .75
CHOPIN   SAUER   5
    POLONAISE IN A FLAT, OP. 53 'OCTAVEN'
       SCHOTT   06205 1/2   1.00
CHOPIN
    POLONAISE IN A, OP. 40 NO. 1 --MILITARY--
       G. SCHIRMER, INC.   .60
CHOPIN   BALLATORE
    POLONAISE IN A, OP. 40 NO. 1
       G. SCHIRMER, INC.   .40
CHOPIN
    POLONAISE IN A, OP. 40 NO. 1
       WILLIS MUSIC COMPANY   .40
CHOPIN   4 1/2
    POLONAISE IN A, OP. 40 NO. 1 --MILITAIRE--
       THEODORE PRESSER COMPANY   .50
CHOPIN   SAUER   6
    POLONAISE IN A, OP. 40 NO. 1 'MILITAR'
       SCHOTT   0334 1/2   1.00
CHOPIN
    POLONAISE IN B FLAT, OP. 71 NO. 2
       G. SCHIRMER, INC.   .60
CHOPIN
    POLONAISE IN C MINOR, OP. 40 NO. 2
       G. SCHIRMER, INC.   .60
CHOPIN   8
    POLONAISE IN C MINOR, OP. 40 NO. 2
       THEODORE PRESSER COMPANY   .60
CHOPIN   6
    POLONAISE IN C SHARP MINOR, OP. 26 NO. 1
       CENTURY MUSIC PUBLISHING COMPANY, INC.   1725   .40
CHOPIN
    POLONAISE IN C SHARP MINOR, OP. 26 NO. 1
       G. SCHIRMER, INC.   .60
CHOPIN
    POLONAISE IN C SHARP MINOR, OP. 26 NO. 1
       WILLIS MUSIC COMPANY   .40
CHOPIN   SAUER   5
    POLONAISE IN C SHARP MINOR, OP. 26 NO. 1 'DRAMATISCH'
       SCHOTT   0332 1/2   1.00
CHOPIN   5
    POLONAISE IN E FLAT MINOR, OP. 26 NO. 2
       CENTURY MUSIC PUBLISHING COMPANY, INC.   3483   .40
CHOPIN
    POLONAISE IN E FLAT MINOR, OP. 26 NO. 2
       G. SCHIRMER, INC.   .75
CHOPIN   ECKSTEIN
    POLONAISE MILITAIRE IN A, OP. 40 NO. 1
       CARL FISCHER, INC.   S 1228   .60
CHOPIN   ROLFE, W.   2
    POLONAISE MILITAIRE, EASY
       CENTURY MUSIC PUBLISHING COMPANY, INC.   3221   .40
CHOPIN
    POLONAISE MILITAIRE, OP. 40 NO. 1
       ASHLEY DEALERS SERVICE, INC.   ES   .95
CHOPIN   4
    POLONAISE MILITAIRE, OP. 40 NO. 1
       CENTURY MUSIC PUBLISHING COMPANY, INC.   1181   .40
CHOPIN
    POLONAISE, OP. 22--GRANDE POLONAISE BRILLANTE
       G. SCHIRMER, INC.   1.00
CHOPIN
    POLONAISE, OP. 22, ANDANTE SPINATO AND GRAND POLONAISE BRILLIANTE
       FRANCO COLOMBO PUBLICATIONS   92999   1.25
CHOPIN
    POLONAISE, OP. 26 NO. 1
       FRANCO COLOMBO PUBLICATIONS   127903   .50

CHOPIN
POLONAISE, OP. 40 NO. 1 'MILITARY'
FRANCO COLOMBO PUBLICATIONS   ER2627   .60
CHOPIN
POLONAISE, OP. 44
FRANCO COLOMBO PUBLICATIONS   128758   1.25
CHOPIN   WALLIS   3
POLONAISE, OP. 53
BOSTON MUSIC COMPANY   .50
CHOPIN   FREY, H.
POLONAISE, OP. 53
THE BIG THREE MUSIC CORPORATION   00.75
CHOPIN   CAVALLARO, C.
POLONAISE, OP. 53
THE BIG THREE MUSIC CORPORATION   00.95
CHOPIN   THOMPSON, J.   3
POLONAISE, OP. 53
WILLIS MUSIC COMPANY   .60
CHOPIN
POLONAISE, OP. 53 'HEROIC'
FRANCO COLOMBO PUBLICATIONS   129004   .50
CHOPIN   DEL MAGLIO
POLONAISE, OP. 53 'HEROIC'
FRANCO COLOMBO PUBLICATIONS   129101   .60
CHOPIN
POLONAISES
NOVELLO AND COMPANY, LTD.   10.0022.05 2.00
CHOPIN   SAUER   4
PRALUDIUM IN D FLAT, OP. 28 NO. 15 'REGENTROPFEN'
SCHOTT   09200 1/2   1.00
CHOPIN   5
PRELUDE -- RAINDROP, OP. 28 NO. 15
CENTURY MUSIC PUBLISHING COMPANY, INC.   855   .40
CHOPIN   JOSEFFY
PRELUDE IN A FLAT, OP. 28 NO. 17
G. SCHIRMER, INC.   .40
CHOPIN   THOMPSON, J.   3
PRELUDE IN C MINOR
WILLIS MUSIC COMPANY   .60
CHOPIN
PRELUDE IN C SHARP MINOR, OP. 45
G. SCHIRMER, INC.   .50
CHOPIN
PRELUDE IN D FLAT, OP. 28 NO. 15
G. HENLE MUSIKVERLAG   141   1.10
CHOPIN
PRELUDE IN D FLAT, OP. 28 NO. 15 'RAINDROP'
FRANCO COLOMBO PUBLICATIONS   127658   .60
CHOPIN   JOSEFFY
PRELUDE IN D FLAT, OP. 28 NO. 15 'RAINDROP'
G. SCHIRMER, INC.   .40
CHOPIN
PRELUDE IN D MINOR, OP. 28 NO. 24
FRANCO COLOMBO PUBLICATIONS   127665   .50
CHOPIN   JOSEFFY
PRELUDE IN D MINOR, OP. 28 NO. 24
G. SCHIRMER, INC.   .40
CHOPIN   7
PRELUDE IN E MINOR
NOVELLO AND COMPANY, LTD.   55.0017.06 .25
CHOPIN   JOSEFFY
PRELUDE IN F MINOR, OP. 28 NO. 18
G. SCHIRMER, INC.   .30
CHOPIN   JOSEFFY
PRELUDE IN G SHARP MINOR, OP. 28 NO. 12
G. SCHIRMER, INC.   .40
CHOPIN   JOSEFFY
PRELUDE IN G, OP. 28 NO. 3
G. SCHIRMER, INC.   .35
CHOPIN   5
PRELUDES, OP. 28 NOS. 3 AND 4
CENTURY MUSIC PUBLISHING COMPANY, INC.   853   .40
CHOPIN   SCHAUM, J.   4 1/2
RAINBOW FANTASY
BELWIN-MILLS PUBLISHING CORPORATION   .50
CHOPIN   ROLFE, W.   2
RAINDROP, THE, EASY
CENTURY MUSIC PUBLISHING COMPANY, INC.   3659   .40
CHOPIN   5
RAINDROP, THE, PRELUDE
CENTURY MUSIC PUBLISHING COMPANY, INC.   855   .40
CHOPIN   STEINER   3
ROMANTIC ETUDE, OP. 10 NO. 3
BELWIN-MILLS PUBLISHING CORPORATION   .60
CHOPIN   JOSEFFY
SCHERZO IN B FLAT MINOR, OP. 31
G. SCHIRMER, INC.   1.10
CHOPIN   SAUER   6
SCHERZO IN B FLAT MINOR, OP. 31
SCHOTT   0372 1/2   1.00
CHOPIN   7
SCHERZO IN B FLAT MINOR, OP. 32
CENTURY MUSIC PUBLISHING COMPANY, INC.   3346   .40
CHOPIN   JOSEFFY
SCHERZO IN B MINOR, OP. 20
G. SCHIRMER, INC.   1.10
CHOPIN   SAUER   6
SCHERZO IN B MINOR, OP. 20
SCHOTT   0370 1/2   1.00
CHOPIN   JOSEFFY
SCHERZO IN C SHARP MINOR, OP. 39
G. SCHIRMER, INC.   .90
CHOPIN
SCHERZO NO. 1 IN B MINOR, OP. 20
FRANCO COLOMBO PUBLICATIONS   ER2542   .75
CHOPIN
SCHERZO NO. 2 IN B-FLAT MINOR, OP. 31
FRANCO COLOMBO PUBLICATIONS   ER1467   1.00
CHOPIN
SONATA IN B FLAT MINOR, OP. 35
G. SCHIRMER, INC.   1.10
CHOPIN
SONATA IN B MINOR, OP. 58
G. SCHIRMER, INC.   1.25
CHOPIN
SONATA IN C MINOR, OP. 4
G. SCHIRMER, INC.   1.25
CHOPIN   SAUER   5
SONATA NO. 02 IN B FLAT MINOR, OP. 35
SCHOTT   0398-9   1.50
CHOPIN
SONATA NO. 02, OP. 35
FRANCO COLOMBO PUBLICATIONS   ER1874   1.25
CHOPIN   CORTOT
SONATA NO. 02, OP. 35
FRANCO COLOMBO PUBLICATIONS   SAL   2.75

CHOPIN   CORTOT
SONATA NO. 03, OP. 58
FRANCO COLOMBO PUBLICATIONS   SAL   2.75
CHOPIN   ROGERS   2
SONG OF THE NIGHT
BOSTON MUSIC COMPANY   .50
CHOPIN   KAHL   2
STARS IN THE LAKE -- ETUDE, OP. 10 NO. 3
BOSTON MUSIC COMPANY   .50
CHOPIN   D'ESPOSITO
SYLPHIDES, LES -- BALLET --
FRANCO COLOMBO PUBLICATIONS   BA8897   2.00
CHOPIN   SAUER   5
TARANTELLA IN A FLAT, OP. 43
SCHOTT   0418 1/2   1.00
CHOPIN   BRUGNOLI *
TARANTELLA, OP. 43
FRANCO COLOMBO PUBLICATIONS   ER2579   .90
CHOPIN   JOSEFFY
TARENTELLE IN A FLAT MAJOR, OP. 43
G. SCHIRMER, INC.   .70
CHOPIN   ZEPP   4
THEME FROM ETUDE IN E
PRO-ART PUBLICATIONS, INC.   68   .50
CHOPIN   SAUER   4
TRAUERMARSCH A. D. SONATA, OP. 35
SCHOTT   0400 1/2   1.00
CHOPIN   SAUER   4
TRAUERMARSCH, OP. 72 NO. 2
SCHOTT   0423   .75
CHOPIN
TROIS ECOSSAISES
FREDERICK HARRIS MUSIC COMPANY   .90
CHOPIN   5
VALSE -- POSTHUMOUS, OP. 70 NO. 2
THEODORE PRESSER COMPANY   .50
CHOPIN
VALSE BRILLANTE IN A FLAT, OP. 34 NO. 1
WILLIS MUSIC COMPANY   .50
CHOPIN   4
VALSE BRILLANTE OP. 34 NO. 2
THEODORE PRESSER COMPANY   .50
CHOPIN   WERNER
VALSE IN A MINOR--CURWEN EDITION
G. SCHIRMER, INC.   .60
CHOPIN   5
VALSE IN C SHARP MINOR, OP. 64 NO. 2
BOSTON MUSIC COMPANY   .50
CHOPIN
VALSE IN C SHARP MINOR, OP. 64 NO. 2
WILLIS MUSIC COMPANY   .35
CHOPIN   4
VALSE IN D FLAT
BELWIN-MILLS PUBLISHING CORPORATION   511   .60
CHOPIN
VALSE IN D FLAT -- MINUTE WALTZ, OP. 64 NO. 1
ASHLEY DEALERS SERVICE, INC.   ES   .95
CHOPIN
VALSE IN D FLAT, OP. 64 NO. 1
WILLIS MUSIC COMPANY   .35
CHOPIN   THOMPSON, J.   2
VALSE, OP. 18
WILLIS MUSIC COMPANY   .60
CHOPIN   2
VALSE, OP. 64 NO. 1, EASY
CENTURY MUSIC PUBLISHING COMPANY, INC.   2160   .40
CHOPIN   THOMPSON, J.   3 1/2
VALSE, OP. 64 NO. 2
WILLIS MUSIC COMPANY   .60
CHOPIN   7
VALSE, OP. 64 NO. 3
THEODORE PRESSER COMPANY   .50
CHOPIN   MARCHI, G.
VALZER IN LA MIN.
EDIZIONI BERBEN   1321   .90
CHOPIN   JOSEFFY
WALTZ IN A FLAT MAJOR, OP. 42
G. SCHIRMER, INC.   .70
CHOPIN   JOSEFFY
WALTZ IN A FLAT MAJOR, OP. 64, NO. 3
G. SCHIRMER, INC.   .40
CHOPIN   JOSEFFY
WALTZ IN A FLAT MAJOR, OP. 69, NO. 1
G. SCHIRMER, INC.   .50
CHOPIN   5
WALTZ IN A FLAT, OP. 34 NO. 1
CENTURY MUSIC PUBLISHING COMPANY, INC.   1768   .40
CHOPIN   SAUER   4
WALTZ IN A FLAT, OP. 34 NO. 1
SCHOTT   0294 1/2   1.00
CHOPIN   JOSEFFY
WALTZ IN A FLAT, OP. 34 NO. 1 'VALSE BRILLANTE'
G. SCHIRMER, INC.   .70
CHOPIN   6
WALTZ IN A FLAT, OP. 42
CENTURY MUSIC PUBLISHING COMPANY, INC.   3425   .40
CHOPIN   5
WALTZ IN A FLAT, OP. 64 NO. 3
CENTURY MUSIC PUBLISHING COMPANY, INC.   3255   .40
CHOPIN   3
WALTZ IN A FLAT, OP. 69 NO. 1
CENTURY MUSIC PUBLISHING COMPANY, INC.   3351   .40
CHOPIN   3
WALTZ IN A MINOR, OP. 34 NO. 2
CENTURY MUSIC PUBLISHING COMPANY, INC.   3352   .40
CHOPIN   SAUER   3
WALTZ IN A MINOR, OP. 34 NO. 2
SCHOTT   0295 1/2   1.00
CHOPIN   JOSEFFY
WALTZ IN A MINOR, OP. 34, NO. 2
G. SCHIRMER, INC.   .50
CHOPIN   4-5
WALTZ IN B MINOR, OP. 69 NO. 2
CENTURY MUSIC PUBLISHING COMPANY, INC.   2446   .40
CHOPIN   JOSEFFY
WALTZ IN B MINOR, OP. 69, NO. 2
G. SCHIRMER, INC.   .40
CHOPIN
WALTZ IN C SHARP MINOR, OP. 64 NO. 2
BELWIN-MILLS PUBLISHING CORPORATION   28173   .60
CHOPIN   4
WALTZ IN C SHARP MINOR, OP. 64 NO. 2
CENTURY MUSIC PUBLISHING COMPANY, INC.   1174   .40
CHOPIN   SAUER   4
WALTZ IN C SHARP MINOR, OP. 64 NO. 2
SCHOTT   0299 1/2   1.00

CHOPIN   JOSEFFY
WALTZ IN C SHARP MINOR, OP. 64, NO. 2
    G. SCHIRMER, INC.   .50
CHOPIN   JOSEFFY
WALTZ IN D FLAT MAJOR, OP. 64, NO. 1--MINUTE
    G. SCHIRMER, INC.   .50
CHOPIN   JOSEFFY
WALTZ IN D FLAT MAJOR, OP. 70, NO. 3
    G. SCHIRMER, INC.   .35
CHOPIN   3
WALTZ IN D FLAT, OP. 64 NO. 1 - MINUTE
    CENTURY MUSIC PUBLISHING COMPANY, INC.   1175   .40
CHOPIN   SAUER   5
WALTZ IN D FLAT, OP. 64 NO. 1 'MINUTEN'
    SCHOTT   0298 1/2   1.00
CHOPIN
WALTZ IN D FLAT, OP. 64 NO. 2 --MINUTE--
    CARL FISCHER, INC.   S 1974   .50
CHOPIN   4
WALTZ IN D FLAT, OP. 70 NO. 3
    CENTURY MUSIC PUBLISHING COMPANY, INC.   3486   .40
CHOPIN   JOSEFFY
WALTZ IN E FLAT MAJOR, OP. 18--GRANDE VALSE BRILLIANTE
    G. SCHIRMER, INC.   .70
CHOPIN   JORDA
WALTZ IN E FLAT MAJOR, OP. 18--GRANDE VALSE BRILLIANTE
    G. SCHIRMER, INC.   .50
CHOPIN   4-5
WALTZ IN E FLAT, OP. 18
    CENTURY MUSIC PUBLISHING COMPANY, INC.   2444   .40
CHOPIN   SAUER   5
WALTZ IN E FLAT, OP. 18
    SCHOTT   0293 1/2   1.00
CHOPIN   4
WALTZ IN E FLAT, OP. 70 NO. 2
    CENTURY MUSIC PUBLISHING COMPANY, INC.   3485   .40
CHOPIN
WALTZ IN E MAJOR
    G. SCHIRMER, INC.   .40
CHOPIN
WALTZ IN E MINOR
    G. SCHIRMER, INC.   .50
CHOPIN   4
WALTZ IN E MINOR , NO. 14
    CENTURY MUSIC PUBLISHING COMPANY, INC.   1717   .40
CHOPIN
WALTZ IN E MINOR--POSTH.--
    FREDERICK HARRIS MUSIC COMPANY   .75
CHOPIN   SAUER   5
WALTZ IN E MINOR, OP. POSTHUMOUS
    SCHOTT   0303 1/2   1.00
CHOPIN   JOSEFFY
WALTZ IN F MINOR, OP. 70, NO. 2
    G. SCHIRMER, INC.   .50
CHOPIN   4
WALTZ IN F, OP. 34 NO. 3
    CENTURY MUSIC PUBLISHING COMPANY, INC.   3484   .40
CHOPIN   JOSEFFY
WALTZ IN G FLAT MAJOR, OP. 70, NO. 1
    G. SCHIRMER, INC.   .40
CHOPIN   3
WALTZ IN G FLAT, OP. 70 NO. 1
    CENTURY MUSIC PUBLISHING COMPANY, INC.   3353   .40
CHOPIN
WALTZ, OP. 18 IN E FLAT
    FRANCO COLOMBO PUBLICATIONS   ER2555   .75
CHOPIN   CHIESA
WALTZ, OP. 18 IN E FLAT
    FRANCO COLOMBO PUBLICATIONS   107479   .60
CHOPIN
WALTZ, OP. 34 NO. 1 IN A FLAT
    FRANCO COLOMBO PUBLICATIONS   ER2655   .60
CHOPIN   DEL MAGLIO
WALTZ, OP. 34 NO. 1 IN A FLAT
    FRANCO COLOMBO PUBLICATIONS   127143   .60
CHOPIN
WALTZ, OP. 34 NO. 2 IN A MINOR
    FRANCO COLOMBO PUBLICATIONS   ER2565   .60
CHOPIN   DEL MAGLIO
WALTZ, OP. 34 NO. 2 IN A MINOR
    FRANCO COLOMBO PUBLICATIONS   129104   .60
CHOPIN
WALTZ, OP. 34 NO. 3
    FREDERICK HARRIS MUSIC COMPANY   .40
CHOPIN
WALTZ, OP. 34 NO. 3 IN F
    FRANCO COLOMBO PUBLICATIONS   ER2536   .60
CHOPIN
WALTZ, OP. 42 IN A FLAT
    FRANCO COLOMBO PUBLICATIONS   ER2537   .75
CHOPIN   DEL MAGLIO
WALTZ, OP. 64 NO. 1 IN D FLAT
    FRANCO COLOMBO PUBLICATIONS   127144   .60
CHOPIN
WALTZ, OP. 64 NO. 1 IN D FLAT 'MINUTE'
    FRANCO COLOMBO PUBLICATIONS   129246   .60
CHOPIN   WHITFORD   GR. 2
WALTZ, OP. 64 NO. 2
    ROBERT WHITFORD PUBLICATIONS   .40
CHOPIN
WALTZ, OP. 64 NO. 2 IN C SHARP
    FRANCO COLOMBO PUBLICATIONS   ER2581   .75
CHOPIN   DEL MAGLIO
WALTZ, OP. 64 NO. 2 IN C SHARP
    FRANCO COLOMBO PUBLICATIONS   129105   .60
CHOPIN
WALTZ, OP. 64 NO. 3 IN A FLAT
    FRANCO COLOMBO PUBLICATIONS   ER2551   .60
CHOPIN   PODOLSKY
WALTZ, OP. 69 NO. 1
    FREDERICK HARRIS MUSIC COMPANY   .90
CHOPIN
WALTZ, OP. 69 NO. 1 IN A FLAT
    FRANCO COLOMBO PUBLICATIONS   ER2662   .60
CHOPIN   DEL MAGLIO
WALTZ, OP. 69 NO. 1 IN A FLAT
    FRANCO COLOMBO PUBLICATIONS   127147   .60
CHOPIN
WALTZ, OP. 69 NO. 2 IN B MINOR
    FRANCO COLOMBO PUBLICATIONS   127971   .60
CHOPIN
WALTZ, OP. 70 NO. 2 IN F MINOR
    FRANCO COLOMBO PUBLICATIONS   ER2528   .60
CHOPIN
WALTZ, OP. 70 NO. 3 IN D FLAT
    FRANCO COLOMBO PUBLICATIONS   ER2539   .60

CHOPIN   ROLFE, W.   2 1/2
WALTZING IN THE NIGHT -- FROM NOCTURNE IN E FLAT OP. 9 NO. 2
    THEODORE PRESSER COMPANY   .50
CHOPIN *   JOSEFFY
CHANT POLONAIS, OP. 74 NO. 5
    G. SCHIRMER, INC.   .50
CHOPIN *   JOSEFFY
CHANT POLONAIS, OP. 74 NO. 5
    G. SCHIRMER, INC.   .50
CHOPIN *   4
MAIDEN'S WISH
    CENTURY MUSIC PUBLISHING COMPANY, INC.   3339   .40
CHOPIN *
MAIDEN'S WISH
    G. SCHIRMER, INC.   .60
CHOPIN *   4
MAIDEN'S WISH, THE
    CENTURY MUSIC PUBLISHING COMPANY, INC.   3339   .40
CHORIN
PETOFI CZARDAS
    FRANCO COLOMBO PUBLICATIONS   SAL   1.50
CHOU WEN-CHUNG   M
WILLOWS ARE NEW, THE --AFTER WANG WEI'S YANG KUANG--
    C. F. PETERS CORPORATION   6169   1.25
CHRETIEN
IMAGES SONORES - ARIETTE AILEE
    FRANCO COLOMBO PUBLICATIONS   SAL   1.75
CHRETIEN
IMAGES SONORES - L'OISEAU-FEE
    FRANCO COLOMBO PUBLICATIONS   SAL   1.75
CHRETIEN
IMAGES SONORES - RONDE DES SCOUTS
    FRANCO COLOMBO PUBLICATIONS   SAL   1.75
CHRETIEN
IMAGES SONORES - YASMINA DANSE
    FRANCO COLOMBO PUBLICATIONS   SAL   1.75
CHRETIEN
IMAGES SONORES - YOLE FLEURIE
    FRANCO COLOMBO PUBLICATIONS   SAL   1.75
CHRISTENSEN, A.
SNOW FAIRY
    BELWIN-MILLS PUBLISHING CORPORATION   25093   .60
CHRISTENSEN, A.   2
SWEDISH DANCE
    WILLIS MUSIC COMPANY   .35
CHRISTOPHER, G.   3
AT SUNSET
    WILLIS MUSIC COMPANY   .40
CHRUSZCH, R.
FUGHETTA
    COMPOSERS AUTOGRAPH PUBLICATIONS   1.32
CIAJA, A.
SONATE PER CEMBALO
    BROUDE BROTHERS LTD.   22.50
CIKKER   3
SONATINA, OP. 12 NO. 1
    BARENREITER VERLAG   AP 526
CILEA
ADRIANA LECOUVREUR - INTERMEZZO FROM ACT II
    FRANCO COLOMBO PUBLICATIONS   SON.1110   .90
CILEA
ARLESIANA, L' - LAMENTO DI FEDERICO
    FRANCO COLOMBO PUBLICATIONS   SON.2875   .90
CILEA
BERCEUSE, NO. 20
    FRANCO COLOMBO PUBLICATIONS   125798   .60
CILEA
INVOCAZIONE
    FRANCO COLOMBO PUBLICATIONS   118557   .60
CILEA
SERENATA A DISPETTO
    FRANCO COLOMBO PUBLICATIONS   118558   .75
CILEA
SUITE, OP. 42 'VECCHIO STILE'
    FRANCO COLOMBO PUBLICATIONS   115799   .90
CILEA
TWO PIECES - 1. RISONANZE NOSTALGICHE
    FRANCO COLOMBO PUBLICATIONS   121491   .90
CILEA
TWO PIECES - 2. FESTA SILANA
    FRANCO COLOMBO PUBLICATIONS   121492   .75
CIMAROSA
MATRIMONIO SEGRETO, IL - OVERTURE
    FRANCO COLOMBO PUBLICATIONS   128579   1.00
CIMAROSA   MONTANI
SONATA NO. 28 'PERFIDIA'
    FRANCO COLOMBO PUBLICATIONS   128597   .75
CIMATTI
CANTO DI PRIMAVERA
    FRANCO COLOMBO PUBLICATIONS   DS898   1.25
CIMATTI
DANZA VOTIVA
    FRANCO COLOMBO PUBLICATIONS   DS888   1.25
CIMATTI
SULLA LAGUNA
    FRANCO COLOMBO PUBLICATIONS   DS891   1.00
CINQUE
CIPRESSI
    FRANCO COLOMBO PUBLICATIONS   BA11349   1.00
CINQUE
FRENTE AL PESEBRE
    FRANCO COLOMBO PUBLICATIONS   BA10846   .75
CINTOLESI
MINUZZOLO E LA SUA GIORNATA
    FRANCO COLOMBO PUBLICATIONS   FOR.12030   1.25
CIOFFI
STAIRWAY TO THE SEA --SCALINATELLA
    MCA MUSIC   1.00
CLARABELL   2
YOU AND I WALTZ
    VOLKWEIN BROS.   00.25
CLARE, A.
DESCANSADO
    BELWIN-MILLS PUBLISHING CORPORATION   20436   .85
CLARIBEL   3
COME BACK TO ERIN
    CENTURY MUSIC PUBLISHING COMPANY, INC.   3633   .40
CLARIBEL   2
YOU AND I WALTZ
    CENTURY MUSIC PUBLISHING COMPANY, INC.   459   .40
CLARK, J.   ASCHERBERG *
PONY RIDE, A
    G. SCHIRMER, INC.   .40
CLARK, J.   ASCHERBERG *
TOCCATA BRILLANTE
    G. SCHIRMER, INC.   .75

CLARK, M. E.		2	
ALL NIGHT LONG			
BELWIN-MILLS PUBLISHING CORPORATION			.60
CLARK, M. E.		2 1/2	
LILT			
BELWIN-MILLS PUBLISHING CORPORATION			.60
CLARK, M. E.		1 1/2	
MARCHING ALONG			
BELWIN-MILLS PUBLISHING CORPORATION			.60
CLARK, M. E.		1 1/2	
MING LING			
BELWIN-MILLS PUBLISHING CORPORATION			.60
CLARK, M. E.		1 1/2	
WHO'S THAT KNOCKING			
BELWIN-MILLS PUBLISHING CORPORATION			.60
CLARK, S.		4	
MARCHE AUX FLAMBEAUX			
CENTURY MUSIC PUBLISHING COMPANY, INC.	1700		.40
CLARK, S.		4	
TORCHLIGHT PROCESSION			
CENTURY MUSIC PUBLISHING COMPANY, INC.	1700		.40
CLARK, T.		3	
WALTZ OF THE BLUE FAIRY			
BELWIN-MILLS PUBLISHING CORPORATION			.60
CLASSENS			
NEPOUMUCENE A MEGEVE			
ELKAN-VOGEL, INC.	CON		4.50
CLAUDE, M.			
COURANTS D'AIRS			
GERARD BILLAUDOT EDITIONS MUSICALES			2.00
CLAWSON			
ADVENTURES IN THE PARK --SUITE			
EDWARD B. MARKS MUSIC CORPORATION			01.00
CLAY, S.		1	
BOLD ADVENTURER			
WILLIS MUSIC COMPANY			.60
CLAYTON, R.		3	
COLLEEN			
CENTURY MUSIC PUBLISHING COMPANY, INC.	4140		.40
CLEMENTI	POZZOLI		
MY FIRST CLEMENTI			
FRANCO COLOMBO PUBLICATIONS	ER1953		.25
CLEMENTI			
SONATA IN G MINOR, OP. 50 NO. 3--DIDONE ABBANDONATA--SCENA			
TRAGICA			
G. HENLE MUSIKVERLAG	86		1.95
CLEMENTI			
SONATA OP. 26 NO. 2 IN F SHARP MINOR			
FRANCO COLOMBO PUBLICATIONS	128407		.60
CLEMENTI	MONTANI		
SONATA OP. 26 NO. 3			
FRANCO COLOMBO PUBLICATIONS	128854		1.00
CLEMENTI	MONTANI		
SONATA OP. 50 NO. 2 'DIDONE ABBANDONATA'			
FRANCO COLOMBO PUBLICATIONS	ER2425		1.25
CLEMENTI			
SONATA, OP. 14 NO. 3			
E. C. SCHIRMER MUSIC COMPANY	234		01.00
CLEMENTI			
SONATA, OP. 26 NO. 2			
EDWIN F. KALMUS	3299		1.00
CLEMENTI			
SONATA, OP. 7 NO. 3			
EDWIN F. KALMUS	3298		1.00
CLEMENTI			
SONATINA IN C MAJOR, OP. 36			
G. SCHIRMER, INC.			.40
CLEMENTI			
SONATINA IN C MAJOR, OP. 36			
G. SCHIRMER, INC.			.50
CLEMENTI			
SONATINA IN D MAJOR, OP. 36			
G. SCHIRMER, INC.			.50
CLEMENTI			
SONATINA IN F MAJOR, OP. 36			
G. SCHIRMER, INC.			.50
CLEMENTI			
SONATINA IN G MAJOR, OP. 36			
G. SCHIRMER, INC.			.50
CLEMENTI			
SONATINA IN G MAJOR, OP. 36			
G. SCHIRMER, INC.			.60
CLEMENTI		2	
SONATINA, OP. 36 NO. 1			
CENTURY MUSIC PUBLISHING COMPANY, INC.	1910		.40
CLEMENTI		2	
SONATINA, OP. 36 NO. 2			
CENTURY MUSIC PUBLISHING COMPANY, INC.	1911		.40
CLEMENTI		2	
SONATINA, OP. 36 NO. 3			
CENTURY MUSIC PUBLISHING COMPANY, INC.	1912		.40
CLERGUE		5	
ROMANCE			
ALPHONSE LEDUC			
COATES, D.		6-7	
SCHERZO 'PIP' -- A YORKSHIRE TERRIER			
NOVELLO AND COMPANY, LTD.	10.0024.01		.90
COATES, E.	SCHAUM, J.	2	
SLEEPY LAGOON			
SCHAUM PUBLICATIONS, INC.			.50
COBB			
ARAB HORSEMEN, THE			
SUMMY-BIRCHARD COMPANY			.50
COBB			
BUGGY RIDE, THE			
BELWIN-MILLS PUBLISHING CORPORATION	25153		.60
COBB			
BULL-FROG AND THE TOAD, THE.			
MCA MUSIC			.60
COBB			
CAREFREE			
BELWIN-MILLS PUBLISHING CORPORATION	25251		.60
COBB			
CAROUSEL			
BELWIN-MILLS PUBLISHING CORPORATION	25123		.60
COBB			
CATERPILLAR			
MCA MUSIC			.60
COBB			
CHOCOLATE SOLDIER			
SUMMY-BIRCHARD COMPANY			.50
COBB			
COWBOY			
BELWIN-MILLS PUBLISHING CORPORATION	25030		.60

COBB			
FIRST SONATINA IN F MAJOR -- IN FOUR MOVEMENTS			
BELWIN-MILLS PUBLISHING CORPORATION	25203		.60
COBB			
GOAT AND THE TOM-CAT, THE			
MCA MUSIC			.60
COBB		2	
HALLOWE'EN			
BELWIN-MILLS PUBLISHING CORPORATION			.60
COBB		E	
HAVANA HOLIDAY			
BELWIN-MILLS PUBLISHING CORPORATION	25128		.60
COBB			
HAVANA HOLIDAY			
BELWIN-MILLS PUBLISHING CORPORATION			.60
COBB			
HIPPOPOTAMUS, THE			
MCA MUSIC			.60
COBB		E	
IN THE PINEY WOODS			
BELWIN-MILLS PUBLISHING CORPORATION	25141		.60
COBB		E	
IN THE TREETOPS			
BELWIN-MILLS PUBLISHING CORPORATION	25220		.60
COBB			
IRISH LAD			
EDWARD B. MARKS MUSIC CORPORATION			00.60
COBB			
JOLLY ELEPHANT, THE.			
MCA MUSIC			.60
COBB			
KANGAROO'S POCKET, THE			
MCA MUSIC			.60
COBB		E	
KING'S GUARD, THE			
BELWIN-MILLS PUBLISHING CORPORATION	25219		.60
COBB			
LITTLE BIRDS			
CARL FISCHER, INC.	P 2640		.50
COBB		E	
MANY-A-MILE AWAY			
BELWIN-MILLS PUBLISHING CORPORATION	25068		.60
COBB		E	
MARCH OF THE MIGHTY			
BELWIN-MILLS PUBLISHING CORPORATION	25200		.60
COBB		E	
MARIONETTES			
BELWIN-MILLS PUBLISHING CORPORATION	25100		.60
COBB		E	
MASKED RIDER			
EDWARD B. MARKS MUSIC CORPORATION			00.60
COBB		E	
MOONLIGHT -- PEDAL STUDY			
BELWIN-MILLS PUBLISHING CORPORATION	25376		.60
COBB		E	
MORRIS DANCE			
BELWIN-MILLS PUBLISHING CORPORATION	25057		.60
COBB			
MRS. MOUSIE			
MCA MUSIC			.60
COBB		E	
MY FAVORITE TUNE			
BELWIN-MILLS PUBLISHING CORPORATION	25077		.60
COBB		E	
NOSTALGIQUE			
BELWIN-MILLS PUBLISHING CORPORATION	25012		.60
COBB			
POLL PARROT			
MCA MUSIC			.60
COBB		2	
POMP AND PAGEATRY			
WILLIS MUSIC COMPANY			.50
COBB		E	
SAUCY SAUNTER			
BELWIN-MILLS PUBLISHING CORPORATION	25091		.60
COBB			
SCHOOL BAND			
EDWARD B. MARKS MUSIC CORPORATION			00.60
COBB		E	
SECOND SONATINA IN F MAJOR -- IN THREE MOVEMENTS			
BELWIN-MILLS PUBLISHING CORPORATION	25228		.75
COBB		E	
SHOEMAKER, THE			
BELWIN-MILLS PUBLISHING CORPORATION	25223		.60
COBB			
SONATINA IN A MINOR -- IN THREE MOVEMENTS			
BELWIN-MILLS PUBLISHING CORPORATION	25096		.60
COBB			
SONATINA IN C MAJOR -- IN THREE MOVEMENTS			
BELWIN-MILLS PUBLISHING CORPORATION	25097		.60
COBB		E	
SONATINA IN G MAJOR -- IN THREE MOVEMENTS			
BELWIN-MILLS PUBLISHING CORPORATION	25098		.60
COBB			
SONATINE ALLA SUITE -- FOUR MOVEMENTS			
BELWIN-MILLS PUBLISHING CORPORATION	25138		.85
COBB			
SONATINE CLASSIQUE -- IN THREE MOVEMENTS			
BELWIN-MILLS PUBLISHING CORPORATION	25099		.70
COBB			
SPOTTED GIRAFFE, THE.			
MCA MUSIC			.60
COBB		E	
STADIUM MARCH			
BELWIN-MILLS PUBLISHING CORPORATION	25073		.60
COBB		E	
STEPPING OUT			
BELWIN-MILLS PUBLISHING CORPORATION	25102		.60
COBB			
STYLISH FLAMINGO, THE.			
MCA MUSIC			.60
COBB		2	
SWINGING HIGH AND LOW			
WILLIS MUSIC COMPANY			.35
COBB		2	
SWINGING HIGH AND LOW			
WILLIS MUSIC COMPANY			.35
COBB			
TARANTELLA			
EDWARD B. MARKS MUSIC CORPORATION			00.60
COBB		E	
TERESITA			
BELWIN-MILLS PUBLISHING CORPORATION	25108		.60
COBB		E	
THAT PROMISED LAND -- SPIRITUAL			
BELWIN-MILLS PUBLISHING CORPORATION	25109		.60

COBB		E		
TWIRLING BATONS				
BELWIN-MILLS PUBLISHING CORPORATION			25075	.60
COBB		E		
VALSE RUBATO				
BELWIN-MILLS PUBLISHING CORPORATION			25139	.60
COBB		E		
VALSETTE				
BELWIN-MILLS PUBLISHING CORPORATION			25225	.60
COBB				
WATER WHEEL				
CARL FISCHER, INC.			P 2723	.50
COBB		E		
WHIRLYBIRD				
BELWIN-MILLS PUBLISHING CORPORATION			25064	.60
COBB		E		
WINDING ROAD, THE				
BELWIN-MILLS PUBLISHING CORPORATION			25250	.60
COBB				
YELLOW CHICK				
MCA MUSIC				.60
COBEN	MAXTED			
OLD PIANO ROLL BLUES, THE				
MCA MUSIC				1.00
COBURN				
FROLICKY, ROLLICKY, WIND				
SUMMY-BIRCHARD COMPANY				.50
COBURN *				
WHISPERING				
THE BIG THREE MUSIC CORPORATION				00.95
COELHO, P.M.P.				
SONATINE				
FRANCO COLOMBO PUBLICATIONS			SAL	4.00
COFFEY, J. R.		3 1/2		
CLOWNS				
THEODORE PRESSER COMPANY				.50
COFFEY, J. R.				
SCORPIO				
WARNER BROTHERS PUBLISHERS				1.00
COHAN	WEYBRIGHT	2		
GIVE MY REGARDS TO BROADWAY				
BELWIN-MILLS PUBLISHING CORPORATION				.50
COHAN	WEYBRIGHT	2		
GIVE MY REGARDS TO BROADWAY				
BELWIN-MILLS PUBLISHING CORPORATION				.60
COHAN	SCHAUM, J.	2		
GIVE MY REGARDS TO BROADWAY				
SCHAUM PUBLICATIONS, INC.				.60
COHAN	STEINER	2 1/2		
SO LONG MARY				
BELWIN-MILLS PUBLISHING CORPORATION				.60
COHAN				
YANKEE DOODLE BOY				
EDWARD B. MARKS MUSIC CORPORATION				00.60
COHAN	SCHAUM, J.	2		
YANKEE DOODLE DANDY				
SCHAUM PUBLICATIONS, INC.				.50
COHAN	STEINER	2		
YOU'RE A GRAND OLD FLAG				
BELWIN-MILLS PUBLISHING CORPORATION				.60
COHAN				
YOU'RE A GRAND OLD FLAG				
EDWARD B. MARKS MUSIC CORPORATION				00.60
COHAN	SCHAUM, J.	2		
YOU'RE A GRAND OLD FLAG				
SCHAUM PUBLICATIONS, INC.				.60
COHAN, G. M.				
GIVE MY REGARDS TO BROADWAY				
EDWARD B. MARKS MUSIC CORPORATION				00.60
COHAN, G. M.				
HARRIGAN				
EDWARD B. MARKS MUSIC CORPORATION				00.60
COHAN, G. M.				
MARY'S A GRAND OLD NAME				
EDWARD B. MARKS MUSIC CORPORATION				00.60
COHEN, A.				
FOUR PIECES FOR PIANO				
BELWIN-MILLS PUBLISHING CORPORATION			07043	1.25
COKELY, C.		1		
BOBOLINK				
BELWIN-MILLS PUBLISHING CORPORATION				.60
COKELY, C.		1		
MISTER LITTLE TOAD				
BELWIN-MILLS PUBLISHING CORPORATION				.60
COKELY, C.		3		
SCHERZO				
BELWIN-MILLS PUBLISHING CORPORATION				.60
COLEMAN, C.				
GYPSY SPRING DANCE				
FREDERICK HARRIS MUSIC COMPANY				.60
COLERIDGE-TAYLOR, S.				
PETITE SUITE DE CONCERT				
BOOSEY AND HAWKES, INC.				1.25
COLERIDGE-TAYLOR, S.				
SCENES FROM AN IMAGINARY BALLET				
G. SCHIRMER, INC.				1.50
COLLET				
DANZAS CASTELLANAS				
FRANCO COLOMBO PUBLICATIONS			SAL	2.75
COLLET				
TOREROS, LOS -- BALLET PANTOMIME --				
FRANCO COLOMBO PUBLICATIONS			SAL	6.50
COLLUM				
SUITE -- 1945 --				
ASSOCIATED MUSIC PUBLISHERS, INC.			B/H	2.25
COLOMBATTI, H.				
WOODLANDS				
BANKS AND SON LTD.				.25
COLTRO				
NOCTURNE				
FRANCO COLOMBO PUBLICATIONS			BON.1642	1.00
COLTRO				
TARLO, IL				
FRANCO COLOMBO PUBLICATIONS			BON.1643	1.00
COMMOSS		1		
GOBLIN GO-AROUND				
PRO-ART PUBLICATIONS, INC.			436	.50
COMSTOCK		GR. 3		
BROWN LEAVES OF FALL				
WESTERN INTERNATIONAL MUSIC, INC.			HP201	.75
COMSTOCK		GR. 3		
GARDEN IN SPRING, A				
WESTERN INTERNATIONAL MUSIC, INC.			HP202	.75
COMSTOCK		GR. 3		
SNOWFLAKES OF WINTER, THE				
WESTERN INTERNATIONAL MUSIC, INC.			HP204	.75

COMSTOCK		GR. 3		
SUMMER STROLL, A				
WESTERN INTERNATIONAL MUSIC, INC.			HP203	.75
CONCONE, G.		4		
OCTAVE STUDY, OP. 33				
CENTURY MUSIC PUBLISHING COMPANY, INC.			1669	.40
CONCONE, G.		4		
STUDY IN OCTAVES				
CENTURY MUSIC PUBLISHING COMPANY, INC.			1669	.40
CONCONE, G.		4		
VALSE BRILLANTE				
CENTURY MUSIC PUBLISHING COMPANY, INC.			1669	.40
CONCONE, G.	DEIS			
VALSE BRILLANTE IN OCTAVES, OP. 33				
G. SCHIRMER, INC.				.40
CONFREY, E.				
CHOCOLATE BUNNY'S LOVE SONG				
BELWIN-MILLS PUBLISHING CORPORATION			25022	.60
CONFREY, E.				
FOUR CIRCUS PIECES				
BELWIN-MILLS PUBLISHING CORPORATION			25249	.60
CONFREY, E.				
MARSHMALLOW MINSTRELS				
BELWIN-MILLS PUBLISHING CORPORATION			25072	.60
CONFREY, Z.	SCHAUM, J.	4 1/2		
AFTER THEATER TANGO				
SCHAUM PUBLICATIONS, INC.				.60
CONFREY, Z.				
COAXING THE PIANO				
BELWIN-MILLS PUBLISHING CORPORATION			20053	.85
CONFREY, Z.				
DIZZY FINGERS				
BELWIN-MILLS PUBLISHING CORPORATION			20073	.85
CONFREY, Z.				
FOURTH DIMENSION				
BELWIN-MILLS PUBLISHING CORPORATION			20100	.85
CONFREY, Z.				
GREENWICH WITCH				
BELWIN-MILLS PUBLISHING CORPORATION			20117	.85
CONFREY, Z.				
JACK IN THE BOX				
BELWIN-MILLS PUBLISHING CORPORATION			20136	.85
CONFREY, Z.				
KITTEN ON THE KEYS				
BELWIN-MILLS PUBLISHING CORPORATION			20141	.85
CONFREY, Z.				
MY PET				
BELWIN-MILLS PUBLISHING CORPORATION			20180	.85
CONFREY, Z.				
POOR BUTTERMILK				
BELWIN-MILLS PUBLISHING CORPORATION			20204	.85
CONFREY, Z.				
STUMBLING				
THE BIG THREE MUSIC CORPORATION				00.95
CONN, D.		E		
BY THE FIRESIDE				
COMPOSERS PRESS, INC.				1.00
CONTILLI				
TOCCATA				
FRANCO COLOMBO PUBLICATIONS			DS351	1.25
COOK		3		
MICE IN THREE BLIND KEYS				
BOSTON MUSIC COMPANY				.50
COOK		2 1/2		
MING TOY				
BELWIN-MILLS PUBLISHING CORPORATION				.60
COOK		3		
PLAINT AT SUNDOWN				
BOSTON MUSIC COMPANY				.50
COOK		2		
SOMBRERO				
BELWIN-MILLS PUBLISHING CORPORATION				.60
COOK		2		
THERE'S A CRICKET IN THE HOUSE				
BOSTON MUSIC COMPANY				.50
COOK, P.		M		
FORLANA				
COMPOSERS PRESS, INC.				2.00
COOK, P.		E		
INDIAN SUMMER				
COMPOSERS PRESS, INC.				1.00
COOK, P.		E		
KANAWAHA RIVER				
COMPOSERS PRESS, INC.				1.00
COOK, P.		E		
PADDLE WHEEL, THE				
COMPOSERS PRESS, INC.				1.00
COOK, P.		E-M		
SOUTHWARD FLOWS THE RIVER				
COMPOSERS PRESS, INC.				1.00
COOK, P.		E-M		
TO A SOUTHERN PINE				
COMPOSERS PRESS, INC.				1.00
COOK, P.		E-M		
VESPERS IN SILVARA				
COMPOSERS PRESS, INC.				1.00
COOKE				
DANCE OF THE PUPPETS				
FRANCO COLOMBO PUBLICATIONS			LD424	.60
COOKE				
PASTORALE				
FRANCO COLOMBO PUBLICATIONS			LD423	.60
COOKE		4		
SEA GARDENS				
THEODORE PRESSER COMPANY				.60
COOKE		3		
WHITE ORCHIDS				
THEODORE PRESSER COMPANY				.50
COOKE, A.				
SCHERZO				
NOVELLO AND COMPANY, LTD.			10.0027.06	1.25
COOKE, A.				
SUITE IN C				
OXFORD UNIVERSITY PRESS			32.925	2.45
COOPER, J.				
ELEGY FOR PIANO				
AMERICAN MUSIC EDITION				.50
COOTE		3		
CORNFLOWER WALTZES				
CENTURY MUSIC PUBLISHING COMPANY, INC.			178	.40
COPE, D.				
ICEBERG MEADOW				
COMPOSERS AUTOGRAPH PUBLICATIONS				1.32
COPE, D.				
PIANO SONATA NO. 01				
COMPOSERS AUTOGRAPH PUBLICATIONS				3.96

COPE, D.
  PIANO SONATA NO. 02
    COMPOSERS AUTOGRAPH PUBLICATIONS   2.86
COPE, D.
  PIANO SONATA NO. 03
    COMPOSERS AUTOGRAPH PUBLICATIONS   2.86
COPE, D.
  PIANO SONATA NO. 04
    COMPOSERS AUTOGRAPH PUBLICATIONS   2.64
COPE, D.
  PIANO SONATA NO. 04
    SEESAW MUSIC CORPORATION   5.00
COPELAND, B.   2
  GAY GRETCHEN
    THEODORE PRESSER COMPANY   .50
COPELAND, B.   1 1/2
  SONG OF THE WILLOW
    THEODORE PRESSER COMPANY   .50
COPELAND, C.
  SPANISH DANCER, OP. 14 NO. 6
    BELWIN-MILLS PUBLISHING CORPORATION   28082   .60
COPLAND   FOSS
  BILLY THE KID
    BOOSEY AND HAWKES, INC.   1.50
COPLAND
  CAT AND THE MOUSE
    BOOSEY AND HAWKES, INC.   1.00
COPLAND
  DANCE PANELS
    BOOSEY AND HAWKES, INC.   4.00
COPLAND   SMIT
  DANZON CUBANO
    BOOSEY AND HAWKES, INC.   1.25
COPLAND
  DOWN A COUNTRY LANE
    BOOSEY AND HAWKES, INC.   .60
COPLAND
  EL SALON MEXICO
    BOOSEY AND HAWKES, INC.   1.00
COPLAND   GREEN
  FANTASIA MEXICANA
    BOOSEY AND HAWKES, INC.   .75
COPLAND
  FANTASY
    BOOSEY AND HAWKES, INC.   5.00
COPLAND
  OUR TOWN
    BOOSEY AND HAWKES, INC.   1.00
COPLAND
  PASSACAGLIA
    FRANCO COLOMBO PUBLICATIONS   SAL   1.50
COPLAND
  RODEO
    BOOSEY AND HAWKES, INC.   3.00
COPLAND
  SONATA
    BOOSEY AND HAWKES, INC.   2.00
COPLAND
  VARIATIONS
    BOOSEY AND HAWKES, INC.   1.50
CORBMAN   1
  GRASSHOPPER'S PICNIC
    WILLIS MUSIC COMPANY   .35
CORBRIDGE   2
  PRISCILLA MINUET
    VOLKWEIN BROS.   .25
CORDERO, R.
  SONATA BREVE
    PEER SOUTHERN ORGANIZATION   02.50
CORDERO, R.
  SONATINA RITMICA
    PAN AMERICAN UNION   01.25
CORELLI   MONTANDON
  ADAGIO--FROM SONATA FOR VIOLIN AND CONTINUO, OP. 5 NO. 5
    G. SCHIRMER, INC.   .50
CORELLI   WEYBRIGHT   4
  PASTORAL FROM 'CONCERTO GROSSO NO. 8'
    BELWIN-MILLS PUBLISHING CORPORATION   .60
CORELLI
  SARABANDE
    FREDERICK HARRIS MUSIC COMPANY   .60
CORGHI
  CONTINUALLY
    FRANCO COLOMBO PUBLICATIONS   SON.2877   3.50
CORNISH, W.   3
  TRIP TO NIAGARA, A
    CENTURY MUSIC PUBLISHING COMPANY, INC.   2932   .40
CORONARO
  CUCULO E L'ALBA, IL
    FRANCO COLOMBO PUBLICATIONS   FOR.11795   1.00
CORRADINI
  DIECI BAGATELLE
    EDIZIONI BERBEN   EB 1627   4.20
CORRADINI   MOZZATI
  PRELUDE AND TOCCATA
    FRANCO COLOMBO PUBLICATIONS   130662   2.25
CORRADINI
  SUITE
    FRANCO COLOMBO PUBLICATIONS   101199   3.25
CORTES, R.   MD
  GENIE OF THE WATER, THE
    THEODORE PRESSER COMPANY   .50
CORTES, R.
  SUITE FOR PIANO
    ELKAN-VOGEL, INC.   1.00
CORY, G.
  CITY BY THE BAY, THE
    GENERAL MUSIC PUBLISHING COMPANY, INC.   602   2.00
CORY, G.
  TEA WITH A STRANGER - TABLEAU FOR PIANO
    GENERAL MUSIC PUBLISHING COMPANY, INC.   2.50
CORY, G.
  TEA WITH A TOTAL STRANGER
    GENERAL MUSIC PUBLISHING COMPANY, INC.   1.50
COSME, L.
  CANCAO DO TIO BARNABE
    EDITORIAL COOPERATIVA INTER-AMERICANA   00.75
COSTANTINI
  MORETTI CHE DANZANO
    FRANCO COLOMBO PUBLICATIONS   DS424   1.00
COTTRAU   DEL MAGLIO
  ADDIO A NAPOLI
    FRANCO COLOMBO PUBLICATIONS   127756   .50
COUGILL, B.
  WOOD MAGIC
    G. SCHIRMER, INC.   .40

COULTER, G.
  AIRS AND GRACES
    BANKS AND SON LTD.   .80
COULTHARD
  DAREDEVIL
    ASSOCIATED MUSIC PUBLISHERS, INC.   BER   .75
COULTHARD
  ETUDE NO. 1, ALLEGRO LEGGIERO
    ASSOCIATED MUSIC PUBLISHERS, INC.   BER   1.00
COULTHARD
  ETUDE NO. 2, LENTO
    ASSOCIATED MUSIC PUBLISHERS, INC.   BER   .75
COULTHARD
  ETUDE NO. 3, TOCCATA
    ASSOCIATED MUSIC PUBLISHERS, INC.   BER   .75
COULTHARD
  ETUDE NO. 4, CON FUOCO
    ASSOCIATED MUSIC PUBLISHERS, INC.   BER   .75
COULTHARD
  NOON SIESTA
    ASSOCIATED MUSIC PUBLISHERS, INC.   BER   .40
COULTHARD
  PRELUDE NO. 01 -- LEGGIERO
    ASSOCIATED MUSIC PUBLISHERS, INC.   BER   .60
COULTHARD
  PRELUDE NO. 02 -- TORMENT
    ASSOCIATED MUSIC PUBLISHERS, INC.   BER   .60
COULTHARD
  PRELUDE NO. 03 -- QUEST
    ASSOCIATED MUSIC PUBLISHERS, INC.   BER   2.00
COULTHARD
  SONATA
    ASSOCIATED MUSIC PUBLISHERS, INC.   BER   2.00
COULTHARD
  WHITE CAPS. RONDO FROM SONATINA
    ASSOCIATED MUSIC PUBLISHERS, INC.   BER   .60
COUPERIN, F.
  ART OF PLAYING THE HARPSICHORD, THE -- L'ART DE TOUCHER LE
  CLAVECIN --
    ASSOCIATED MUSIC PUBLISHERS, INC.   B/H   3.50
COUPERIN, F.   CESI
  CARILLON DE CYNTHERE
    FRANCO COLOMBO PUBLICATIONS   ER720   .60
COUPERIN, F.   3-4
  GAVOTTE, LA BOURBONAISE U. RAMEAU, LE TAMBOURINU. GAVOTTE A.,
  ZAIS
    SCHOTT   08863   1.00
COUPERIN, F.
  LA BANDOLINE
    ELKAN-VOGEL, INC.   D   .75
COUPERIN, F.
  LA FLEURIE
    G. SCHIRMER, INC.   .25
COUPERIN, F.
  LE PETIT REIN -- THE TRIFLE
    FREDERICK HARRIS MUSIC COMPANY   .60
COUPERIN, F.
  LE TIC-TOC-CHOC -- OR LES MAILLOTINS
    ELKAN-VOGEL, INC.   D   .75
COUPERIN, F.
  LES BARRICADES MYSTERIEUSES
    ELKAN-VOGEL, INC.   D   1.00
COUPERIN, F.
  LES PETITS MOULINS A VENT
    G. SCHIRMER, INC.   .30
COUPERIN, F.
  LES TRICOTEUSES
    ELKAN-VOGEL, INC.   D   .75
COUPERIN, F.
  PASSEPIED
    FREDERICK HARRIS MUSIC COMPANY   .60
COUPERIN, F.
  REAPERS, THE
    FREDERICK HARRIS MUSIC COMPANY   .60
COUPERIN, F.
  SOEUR MONIQUE--RONDO
    G. SCHIRMER, INC.   .40
COUPERIN, F.   FRIEDMAN
  TENDRE FANCHON
    UNIVERSAL EDITION   5416   .80
COUPERIN, F.
  TIC-TOC-CHOC, LE
    FRANCO COLOMBO PUBLICATIONS   FOR.10672   .50
COUPERIN, L.   BOUVET
  PIECES DE CLAVECIN, VOL. 1
    ASSOCIATED MUSIC PUBLISHERS, INC.   ESC   2.75
COUPERIN, P.   3-4
  BUTTERFLIES, THE
    CENTURY MUSIC PUBLISHING COMPANY, INC.   3903   .40
COUPERIN, P.   4-5
  FICKLE COUNTRY MAID, THE
    CENTURY MUSIC PUBLISHING COMPANY, INC.   3904   .40
COUPERIN, P.   3
  LA BONDOLINE, RONDEAU
    CENTURY MUSIC PUBLISHING COMPANY, INC.   3889   .40
COUPERIN, P.   4
  LITTLE WINDMILLS
    CENTURY MUSIC PUBLISHING COMPANY, INC.   3890   .40
COURSEY, R. DE
  BANNERS HIGH
    ASSOCIATED MUSIC PUBLISHERS, INC.   BER   .40
COURSEY, R. DE
  BUS RIDE
    ASSOCIATED MUSIC PUBLISHERS, INC.   BER   .40
COURSEY, R. DE   3
  GALAWAY FESTIVAL
    CENTURY MUSIC PUBLISHING COMPANY, INC.   4359   .40
COURSEY, R. DE
  MUSETTE
    ASSOCIATED MUSIC PUBLISHERS, INC.   BER   .40
COURSEY, R. DE   1
  OFF TO SCHOOL
    CENTURY MUSIC PUBLISHING COMPANY, INC.   4308   .40
COURSEY, R. DE
  SCOTTISH POEM
    ASSOCIATED MUSIC PUBLISHERS, INC.   BER   .40
COURSEY, R. DE
  STEAMBOAT'S A COMIN'
    ASSOCIATED MUSIC PUBLISHERS, INC.   BER   .40
COURSEY, R. DE   3
  VILLAGE WEDDING
    CENTURY MUSIC PUBLISHING COMPANY, INC.   4360   .40
COUTURE
  A EDVARD GRIEG
    FRANCO COLOMBO PUBLICATIONS   FOR.12092   1.00

COUTURE
A UNA FARFALLA
　　FRANCO COLOMBO PUBLICATIONS　　　　　FOR.12259　　.90
COUTURE
ALLEGRO
　　FRANCO COLOMBO PUBLICATIONS　　　　　FOR.12224　　1.00
COUTURE
ANDANTE
　　FRANCO COLOMBO PUBLICATIONS　　　　　FOR.12298　　1.00
COUTURE
CANZONE, VALZER, BUONA NOTTE
　　FRANCO COLOMBO PUBLICATIONS　　　　　FOR.12321　　1.25
COUTURE
DIVAGAZIONI
　　FRANCO COLOMBO PUBLICATIONS　　　　　FOR.12278　　1.00
COUTURE
IMPRESSIONI
　　FRANCO COLOMBO PUBLICATIONS　　　　　FOR.12156　　1.00
COUTURE
INTERMEZZO NO. 01
　　FRANCO COLOMBO PUBLICATIONS　　　　　FOR.12173　　1.00
COUTURE
INTERMEZZO NO. 02
　　FRANCO COLOMBO PUBLICATIONS　　　　　FOR.12269　　1.00
COUTURE
INTERMEZZO NO. 03
　　FRANCO COLOMBO PUBLICATIONS　　　　　FOR.12364　　1.00
COUTURE
MELODIA
　　FRANCO COLOMBO PUBLICATIONS　　　　　FOR.12210　　1.00
COUTURE
MERIGGIO
　　FRANCO COLOMBO PUBLICATIONS　　　　　FOR.12287　　1.00
COUTURE
MONTETURLI
　　FRANCO COLOMBO PUBLICATIONS　　　　　FOR.12347　　1.00
COUTURE
NELLA NOTTE
　　FRANCO COLOMBO PUBLICATIONS　　　　　FOR.12242　　1.00
COUTURE
NINNA-NANNA DELLA GATTA MEA
　　FRANCO COLOMBO PUBLICATIONS　　　　　FOR.12135　　.75
COUTURE
PRELUDE
　　FRANCO COLOMBO PUBLICATIONS　　　　　FOR.12236　　1.00
COUTURE
QUANDRO ERA PRIMAVERA
　　FRANCO COLOMBO PUBLICATIONS　　　　　FOR.12121　　1.00
COUTURE
QUASI UNA FANTASIA
　　FRANCO COLOMBO PUBLICATIONS　　　　　FOR.12126　　2.00
COUTURE
ROMANZA
　　FRANCO COLOMBO PUBLICATIONS　　　　　FOR.12175　　1.00
COUTURE
SERA D'ESTATE
　　FRANCO COLOMBO PUBLICATIONS　　　　　FOR.12169　　1.00
COUTURE
SERENAMENTE
　　FRANCO COLOMBO PUBLICATIONS　　　　　FOR.12291　　1.25
COUTURE
SUL PRATO GIUCCANO I FIGLI DELLA GATTA MEA
　　FRANCO COLOMBO PUBLICATIONS　　　　　FOR.12206　　.75
COUTURE
TEMPO DI VALZER
　　FRANCO COLOMBO PUBLICATIONS　　　　　FOR.12205　　.75
COUTURE
VILLA DI QUERCETO, LA
　　FRANCO COLOMBO PUBLICATIONS　　　　　FOR.12329　　1.00
COVEY, E.　　　　　　　　　　　　　　　2
GLIDING
　　WILLIS MUSIC COMPANY　　　　　　　　　　　.25
COVINGTON, W.
TAKIN' IT SLOW
　　BELWIN-MILLS PUBLISHING CORPORATION　20437　　.85
COWARD　　　　　MACLACHLAN　　　FIRST YEAR
ZIGEUNER
　　WARNER BROTHERS PUBLISHERS　　　　　　　.75
COWELL　　　　　　　　　　　　　　　　3
ALL DRESSED UP, D MAJOR
　　CENTURY MUSIC PUBLISHING COMPANY, INC.　3946　　.40
COWELL　　　　　　　　　　　　　　　　E
BOUNCE DANCE
　　THEODORE PRESSER COMPANY　　　　　　　　.50
COWELL
DYNAMIC MOTION
　　ASSOCIATED MUSIC PUBLISHERS, INC.　AMP　　1.00
COWELL
EPISODE
　　ASSOCIATED MUSIC PUBLISHERS, INC.　AMP　　1.00
COWELL
FABRIC
　　ASSOCIATED MUSIC PUBLISHERS, INC.　AMP　　.60
COWELL　　　　　　　　　　　　　　　　3
GOOD OLD DAYS, THE
　　CENTURY MUSIC PUBLISHING COMPANY, INC.　3947　　.40
COWELL
HARP OF LIFE, THE
　　ASSOCIATED MUSIC PUBLISHERS, INC.　AMP　　1.00
COWELL　　　　　　　　　　　　　　　　MD
HILARIOUS CURTAIN OPENER AND RITOURNELLE
　　THEODORE PRESSER COMPANY　　　　　　　　1.50
COWELL　　　　　　　　　　　　　　　　3
HOMESICK LILT
　　CENTURY MUSIC PUBLISHING COMPANY, INC.　3948　　.40
COWELL
IRISHMAN DANCES
　　CARL FISCHER, INC.　　　　　　　　P 2115　　.50
COWELL　　　　　　　　　　　　　　　　3
PA JIGS THEM ALL DOWN
　　CENTURY MUSIC PUBLISHING COMPANY, INC.　3949　　.40
COWELL　　　　　　　　　　　　　　　　4
PEGLEG DANCE
　　CENTURY MUSIC PUBLISHING COMPANY, INC.　3950　　.40
COWELL　　　　　　　　　　　　　　　　MD
RITOURNELLE
　　THEODORE PRESSER COMPANY　　　　　　　　1.50
COWELL
SNOWS OF FUJI-YAMA
　　ASSOCIATED MUSIC PUBLISHERS, INC.　AMP　　.60
COWELL　　　　　　　　　　　　　　　　M
SWAY DANCE
　　THEODORE PRESSER COMPANY　　　　　　　　.50
COWELL
WHAT'S THIS
　　ASSOCIATED MUSIC PUBLISHERS, INC.　AMP　　.40

COX
BRAZILIAN SONG
　　FRANCO COLOMBO PUBLICATIONS　　　　LD525　　.60
COX
INDIAN RITUAL DANCE
　　FRANCO COLOMBO PUBLICATIONS　　　　LD523　　.60
CRAIG, P.　　　　　　　　　　　　　　2
SCARECROW WALTZ
　　SCHAUM PUBLICATIONS, INC.　　　　　　　.50
CRAIG, P.—ED　　　　　CRIAG, P.　　　2
THANKSGIVING SCENE
　　SCHAUM PUBLICATIONS, INC.　　　　　　　.60
CRAMER, H.
LE DESIR
　　BANKS AND SON LTD.　　　　　　　　　　.55
CRAMER, H.
LE DESIR, OP. 14
　　G. SCHIRMER, INC.　　　　　　　　　　　.40
CRAMER, J.　　　　　　　　　　　　　4
DESIDERIO, IL
　　CENTURY MUSIC PUBLISHING COMPANY, INC.　1503　　.40
CRAMER, J.
LE PETIT RIEN
　　BANKS AND SON LTD.　　　　　　　　　　.55
CRAMM, H.　　　　　　　　　　　　1 1/2
LITTLE DUTCH DANCE
　　THEODORE PRESSER COMPANY　　　　　　　　.50
CRAMM, H.
TWO LITTLE FROGGIES, OP. 7 NO. 10
　　BELWIN-MILLS PUBLISHING CORPORATION　28027　　.60
CRAS
POLYPHEME -- LE SOMMEIL DE GALATHEE --
　　FRANCO COLOMBO PUBLICATIONS　　　　SAL　　2.50
CRAWFORD　　　　　ECKSTEIN
U. S. AIR FORCE
　　CARL FISCHER, INC.　　　　　　　P 2287　　.60
CRAWFORD　　　　　ECKSTEIN
U. S. AIR FORCE
　　CARL FISCHER, INC.　　　　　　　P 2290　　.75
CRAWFORD, C.
IN FLORIDA MOONLIGHT, OP. 11
　　BELWIN-MILLS PUBLISHING CORPORATION　28083　　.60
CRAWFORD, C.
ON THE ICE AT SWEET BRIAR -- ARPEGGIO WALTZ
　　BELWIN-MILLS PUBLISHING CORPORATION　28045　　.60
CRAWFORD, C.　　　　　　　　　　　　3
ON THE MAGIC LAKE
　　WILLIS MUSIC COMPANY　　　　　　　　　　.40
CRAWFORD, R.　　　　　　　　　　　　A
PIANO STUDY
　　THEODORE PRESSER COMPANY　　　　　　　　2.00
CRAXTON, H.
SICILIANO AND RIGADON
　　OXFORD UNIVERSITY PRESS　　　　　32.116　　1.25
CRAXTON, H.
TWO STUDIES
　　EDWARD B. MARKS MUSIC CORPORATION　　　00.60
CREMIEUX
CHARME D'AMOUR
　　FRANCO COLOMBO PUBLICATIONS　　　　SAL　　1.75
CRERIE, E.　　　　　　　　　　　　　2
BASEBALL GAME
　　VOLKWEIN BROS.　　　　　　　　　　　　.25
CRERIE, E.　　　　　　　　　　　　　2
BOB WHITE
　　VOLKWEIN BROS.　　　　　　　　　　　　.25
CRERIE, E.　　　　　　　　　　　　　2
BREAKERS
　　VOLKWEIN BROS.　　　　　　　　　　　　.30
CRERIE, E.　　　　　　　　　　　　　2
CARNATIONS
　　VOLKWEIN BROS.　　　　　　　　　　　　.25
CREPIE, E.　　　　　　　　　　　　　2
CUCKOO CLOCK
　　VOLKWEIN BROS.　　　　　　　　　　　　.30
CRERIE, E.　　　　　　　　　　　　　3
DANCE OF THE GYPSIES
　　VOLKWEIN BROS.　　　　　　　　　　　　.25
CRERIE, E.　　　　　　　　　　　　　2
DANDELION MARCH
　　VOLKWEIN BROS.　　　　　　　　　　　　.25
CREPIE, E.　　　　　　　　　　　　　2
DROWSY LAND
　　VOLKWEIN BROS.　　　　　　　　　　　　.30
CRERIE, E.　　　　　　　　　　　　　2
EVENING REVERIE
　　VOLKWEIN BROS.　　　　　　　　　　　　.30
CRERIE, E.　　　　　　　　　　　　　2
GERANIUMS
　　VOLKWEIN BROS.　　　　　　　　　　　　.25
CRERIE, E.　　　　　　　　　　　　　2
HAPPY THOUGHTS
　　VOLKWEIN BROS.　　　　　　　　　　　　.25
CRERIE, E.　　　　　　　　　　　　　2
HOW ARE YOU THIS MORNING
　　VOLKWEIN BROS.　　　　　　　　　　　　.25
CRERIE, E.　　　　　　　　　　　　　2
HOW DO YOU DO
　　VOLKWEIN BROS.　　　　　　　　　　　　.30
CRERIE, E.　　　　　　　　　　　　　2
IN MERRY MOOD
　　VOLKWEIN BROS.　　　　　　　　　　　　.25
CRERIE, E.　　　　　　　　　　　　　2
JOLLY BOY
　　VOLKWEIN BROS.　　　　　　　　　　　　.25
CRERIE, E.　　　　　　　　　　　　　2
LILACS
　　VOLKWEIN BROS.　　　　　　　　　　　　.25
CRERIE, E.　　　　　　　　　　　　　2
ON THE TRAPEZE
　　VOLKWEIN BROS.　　　　　　　　　　　　.25
CRERIE, E.　　　　　　　　　　　　　2
ORIENTAL DANCE
　　VOLKWEIN BROS.　　　　　　　　　　　　.40
CRERIE, E.　　　　　　　　　　　　　2
ORIENTAL DANCE, AN
　　VOLKWEIN BROS.　　　　　　　　　　　　.40
CRERIE, E.　　　　　　　　　　　　　2
PLAYFUL PUPPY
　　VOLKWEIN BROS.　　　　　　　　　　　　.30
CRERIE, E.　　　　　　SCHIEFELBEIN, F.　4
SILENT NIGHT VARIATIONS
　　VOLKWEIN BROS.　　　　　　　　　　　00.50
CRERIE, E.　　　　　　　　　　　　　2
SUNSET ON THE WATER
　　VOLKWEIN BROS.　　　　　　　　　　　00.30

CRERIE, E.   2
  TRAMP, TRAMP, TRAMP
    VOLKWEIN BROS.   00.25
CRERIE, E.   2
  TUMBLING
    VOLKWEIN BROS.   00.30
CRERIE, E.   2
  VALSE PETITE
    VOLKWEIN BROS.   00.25
CRERIE, E.   2
  WOODLAND WALTZ
    VOLKWEIN BROS.   00.25
CRERIE, E. *   4
  SILENT NIGHT -- VARIATIONS
    VOLKWEIN BROS.   .40
CRESTON
  FIVE TWO-PART INVENTIONS
    SEESAW MUSIC CORPORATION   3.00
CRESTON
  METAMORPHOSES
    BELWIN-MILLS PUBLISHING CORPORATION   20562   5.00
CRESTON
  PONY RONDO
    BELWIN-MILLS PUBLISHING CORPORATION   20456   .95
                       MD
CRESTON
  PRELUDE AND DANCE NO. 1
    THEODORE PRESSER COMPANY   .60
                       ADVANCED
CRESTON
  PRELUDE AND DANCE, OP. 29 NO. 2
    SHAWNEE PRESS, INC.   HB-123   .75
CRESTON
  RUMBA TARANTELLA
    BELWIN-MILLS PUBLISHING CORPORATION   20434   1.25
                       ADVANCED
CRESTON
  SONATA, OP. 9
    SHAWNEE PRESS, INC.   2.50
CRESTON
  SONG OF SICILY
    BELWIN-MILLS PUBLISHING CORPORATION   20457   .95
CRIST, B.
  FANTASIE IN D
    OXFORD UNIVERSITY PRESS   93.208   1.50
CRIST, D. W.   3
  SCHOOL BOY MARCH
    VOLKWEIN BROS.   .25
CROCKER, D.
  AT THE SEASHORE
    BELWIN-MILLS PUBLISHING CORPORATION   25215   .60
CROCKER, D.   2
  COURT MINUET
    BELWIN-MILLS PUBLISHING CORPORATION   .60
CROCKER, D.   2
  DANCE OF THE WIND
    WILLIS MUSIC COMPANY   .40
CROCKER, D.   1 1/2
  DANCING SUNBEAMS
    WILLIS MUSIC COMPANY   .40
CROCKER, D.   2
  FUN AT THE CIRCUS
    WILLIS MUSIC COMPANY   .40
CROCKER, D.   2 1/2
  HAPPY PIRATE
    BELWIN-MILLS PUBLISHING CORPORATION   .60
CROCKER, D.   1 1/2
  IN THE CANOE
    BELWIN-MILLS PUBLISHING CORPORATION   .60
CROCKER, D.   2 1/2
  JUDY'S BALL
    BELWIN-MILLS PUBLISHING CORPORATION   .60
CROCKER, D.   2 1/2
  PIXIES
    BELWIN-MILLS PUBLISHING CORPORATION   .60
CROCKER, D.   2
  SQUIRRELS AT PLAY
    BELWIN-MILLS PUBLISHING CORPORATION   .60
CROCKER, D.   2
  TOE DANCER
    BELWIN-MILLS PUBLISHING CORPORATION   .60
CROCKER, D.   1 1/2
  WALTZ OF THE DOLLS
    BELWIN-MILLS PUBLISHING CORPORATION   .60
CROCKER, D.   3
  WHIRLWIND
    BELWIN-MILLS PUBLISHING CORPORATION   .60
CROCKER, V.   3
  DREAMS OF SPRING
    CENTURY MUSIC PUBLISHING COMPANY, INC.   1837   .40
CROCKER, V.   3
  MORNING NOON AND NIGHT
    CENTURY MUSIC PUBLISHING COMPANY, INC.   2057   .40
CROCKER, V.   3
  SCALE WALTZ
    CENTURY MUSIC PUBLISHING COMPANY, INC.   2055   .40
CROCKER, V.   3
  VIOLETS AND ROSES
    CENTURY MUSIC PUBLISHING COMPANY, INC.   2051   .40
CROISEZ, A.
  GRAND VENEUR
    FRANCO COLOMBO PUBLICATIONS   SAL   1.75
CROISEZ, A.
  HIRONDELLE ET LE PRISONNIER, L'
    FRANCO COLOMBO PUBLICATIONS   SAL   1.75
CROISEZ, A.
  MARIEE DU MOULIN, LA
    FRANCO COLOMBO PUBLICATIONS   SAL   1.75
CROISEZ, A.
  PASSAGE DU REGIMENT, LE
    FRANCO COLOMBO PUBLICATIONS   SAL   1.75
CROISEZ, A.
  VOYAGE D'UNE HIRONDELLE
    FRANCO COLOMBO PUBLICATIONS   SAL   1.50
CROISEZ, A.
  VOYAGE D'UNE HIRONDELLE
    FRANCO COLOMBO PUBLICATIONS   SAL   1.50
CROOT
  BURLESQUE
    FRANCO COLOMBO PUBLICATIONS   LD445   .60
CROOT
  SCHERZINO
    FRANCO COLOMBO PUBLICATIONS   LD446   .60
CROSBY, M.   2
  BASKET DANCE
    CENTURY MUSIC PUBLISHING COMPANY, INC.   3649   .40
CROSBY, M.   1
  BUGLERS MARCH
    VOLKWEIN BROS.   .25

CROSBY, M.   2
  CIRCUS COMES TO TOWN, THE
    CENTURY MUSIC PUBLISHING COMPANY, INC.   3650   .40
CROSBY, M.   2
  DANCE OF THE MOON FAIRIES
    VOLKWEIN BROS.   .30
CROSBY, M.   2
  FAIRIES' LULLABY
    VOLKWEIN BROS.   .25
CROSBY, M.   2
  FUNNY OLD CLOWN
    CENTURY MUSIC PUBLISHING COMPANY, INC.   3815   .40
CROSBY, M.   2
  JACK BE NIMBLE
    VOLKWEIN BROS.   .25
CROSBY, M.   2
  JACK O'LANTERN PARTY
    VOLKWEIN BROS.   .25
CROSBY, M.   2
  JOLLY LITTLE SAMBO
    CENTURY MUSIC PUBLISHING COMPANY, INC.   3137   .40
CROSBY, M.   2
  OLD FRENCH DANCE, AN
    CENTURY MUSIC PUBLISHING COMPANY, INC.   3140   .40
CROSBY, M.   2
  QUIET SAILING
    CENTURY MUSIC PUBLISHING COMPANY, INC.   3995   .40
CROSBY, M.   2
  SANDMAN'S LULLABY, THE
    CENTURY MUSIC PUBLISHING COMPANY, INC.   3141   .40
CROSBY, M.   2
  SCOUTS ON PARADE
    CENTURY MUSIC PUBLISHING COMPANY, INC.   3139   .40
CROSBY, M.   2
  SHADOW WALTZ
    CENTURY MUSIC PUBLISHING COMPANY, INC.   3135   .40
CROSBY, M.   2
  SKATING WALTZ
    VOLKWEIN BROS.   .25
CROSBY, M.   2
  SKIPPING TO SCHOOL
    CENTURY MUSIC PUBLISHING COMPANY, INC.   3136   .40
CROSBY, M.   2
  SPINNING TO THE TOP
    CENTURY MUSIC PUBLISHING COMPANY, INC.   3142   .40
CROSBY, M.   2
  TUMBLING JACK
    VOLKWEIN BROS.   00.25
CROSBY, M.   2
  WALTZ OF THE FLOWER FAIRIES
    THEODORE PRESSER COMPANY   .50
CRUICKSHANK   2
  EARLY ROBIN
    PRO-ART PUBLICATIONS, INC.   23   .50
CRUICKSHANK   2-3
  PLAYFUL PORPOISE
    PRO-ART PUBLICATIONS, INC.   25   .50
CRUICKSHANK   2
  SILVER MOONBEAMS
    PRO-ART PUBLICATIONS, INC.   48   .50
CRUICKSHANK   2
  SKOOTING ALONG
    BELWIN-MILLS PUBLISHING CORPORATION   .60
        THOMPSON, J.   2
CUI, C.
  ORIENTALE
    WILLIS MUSIC COMPANY   .40
CUI, C.   DEIS
  ORIENTALE, OP. 50, NO. 9
    G. SCHIRMER, INC.   .40
CUI, C.   4
  SPANISH MARIONETTES
    NOVELLO AND COMPANY, LTD.   55.0040.00 .40
CUNNINGHAM, M.
  PIANO SUITE
    COMPOSERS AUTOGRAPH PUBLICATIONS   1.10
CURCIO
  DAY DREAMS
    BELWIN-MILLS PUBLISHING CORPORATION   28086   .60
CURCIO
  HERE COMES THE BAND
    BELWIN-MILLS PUBLISHING CORPORATION   28003   .60
CURCIO
  HERE COMES THE GENERAL
    BELWIN-MILLS PUBLISHING CORPORATION   28088   .60
CURCIO
  RED VELVET WALTZ
    BELWIN-MILLS PUBLISHING CORPORATION   .60
CURCIO
  UP IN THE CLOUDS
    BELWIN-MILLS PUBLISHING CORPORATION   28001   .60
CURRIE, E.   2 1/2
  GHOST ROAMS AT MIDNIGHT, THE
    WILLIS MUSIC COMPANY   .25
CURRIE, E.   3
  GOBLINS
    WILLIS MUSIC COMPANY   .25
CURRIE, E.   2 1/2
  LITTLE LULLABY, A
    WILLIS MUSIC COMPANY   .25
CURRIE, E.   2
  VALSETTE
    WILLIS MUSIC COMPANY   .25
CURRIER
  SLEIGH RIDE -- SIMP.
    BELWIN-MILLS PUBLISHING CORPORATION   90114   1.00
CURTIS   GRACEY
  CARMELA -- FANTASIE --
    FRANCO COLOMBO PUBLICATIONS   SAL   1.75
CURTIS   WALTER
  CARMELA -- WALTZ --
    FRANCO COLOMBO PUBLICATIONS   SAL   1.75
CURTIS *   KERR, R.N.
  LET IT BE ME
    MCA MUSIC   1.00
CURZON, F.
  BOULEVARDIER
    BOOSEY AND HAWKES, INC.   .60
CURZON, F.
  DANCE OF AN OSTRACIZED IMP
    BOOSEY AND HAWKES, INC.   .60
CURZON, F.
  SQUARE DANCING
    BOOSEY AND HAWKES, INC.   .90
CUSTER, A.
  FOUR IDEAS FOR PIANO
    GENERAL MUSIC PUBLISHING COMPANY, INC.   3.00

CUSTER, A.				
RHAPSODALITY BROWN				
GENERAL MUSIC PUBLISHING COMPANY, INC.	531	3.00		
CUSTER, A.				
RHAPSODALITY BROWN				
GENERAL MUSIC PUBLISHING COMPANY, INC.		3.00		
CZAJANEK				
BALLET				
ASSOCIATED MUSIC PUBLISHERS, INC.	OBV	.40		
CZAJANEK				
INTERMEZZO				
ASSOCIATED MUSIC PUBLISHERS, INC.	OBV	.40		
CZERNY	STEINER	2		
HARVEST IN BOHEMIA				
BELWIN-MILLS PUBLISHING CORPORATION		.60		
CZERNY				
NOCTURNE B FLAT, OP. 368 NO. 8				
MUSICA OBSCURA		1.00		
CZERNY				
POLKA				
FREDERICK HARRIS MUSIC COMPANY		.60		
CZERNY	JOSEFFY			
TOCCATA IN C MAJOR, OP. 92				
G. SCHIRMER, INC.		.70		
CZERNY	MOSZKOWSKI			
TOCCATA IN C MAJOR, OP. 92				
G. SCHIRMER, INC.		.50		
CZERNY	ARIAS			
TOCCATA IN C, OP. 92				
MUSICA OBSCURA		2.50		
CZERNY	CESI			
TOCCATA, OP. 090				
FRANCO COLOMBO PUBLICATIONS	ER2603	.90		
CZERNY	D			
TOCCATA, OP. 92				
C. F. PETERS CORPORATION	3174	1.50		
CZERNY				
VARIATIONEN UBER DEN BELIEBTEN WIENER TRAUER-WALZER -- SCHUBERT				
OP. 12				
MUSICA OBSCURA		2.00		
CZERNY				
VARIATIONS --EASY ON 'LA CI DAREM' FROM DON GIOVANNI --MOZART				
OP. 825, NO. 17				
MUSICA OBSCURA		1.50		
CZERNY				
VARIATIONS, 'LA RICORDANZA' , OP. 33				
INTERNATIONAL MUSIC COMPANY		1.50		
CZIBULKA	3			
LOVE'S DREAM AFTER THE BALL				
CENTURY MUSIC PUBLISHING COMPANY, INC.	295	.40		
CZIBULKA	3			
SCENE DE BALLET				
CENTURY MUSIC PUBLISHING COMPANY, INC.	1999	.40		
CZIBULKA	4			
STEPHANIE GAVOTTE				
CENTURY MUSIC PUBLISHING COMPANY, INC.	436	.40		
D'ESPOSITO	LOCATELLI			
PRELUDE AND FUGUE				
FRANCO COLOMBO PUBLICATIONS	BA8857	1.00		
D'HARDELOT	SCHAUM, J.	2 1/2		
BECAUSE				
BELWIN-MILLS PUBLISHING CORPORATION		.50		
D'HARDELOT				
BECAUSE				
CHAPPELL AND COMPANY, INC.	0420000	.95		
D'HARDELOT				
BECAUSE				
CHAPPELL AND COMPANY, .INC.	0420000-170	.60		
D'HARDELOT	4			
BECAUSE, A FLAT MAJOR				
CENTURY MUSIC PUBLISHING COMPANY, INC.	4276	.40		
D'HARDELOT	4			
BECAUSE, B FLAT MAJOR				
CENTURY MUSIC PUBLISHING COMPANY, INC.	4277	.40		
D'HARDELOT	4			
BECAUSE, C MAJOR				
CENTURY MUSIC PUBLISHING COMPANY, INC.	4288	.40		
D'INDY, V.				
FANTASIE				
HEUGEL ET CIE.		4.50		
D'INDY, V.				
SYMPHONY ON A FRENCH MOUNTAIN AIR, OP.25				
INTERNATIONAL MUSIC COMPANY		3.00		
D'INDY, V.				
THEME VARIE, FUGUE ET CHANSON, OP. 85				
FRANCO COLOMBO PUBLICATIONS	SAL	6.50		
D'ORSO	3			
AMUSETTE, POLKA MAZURKA				
CENTURY MUSIC PUBLISHING COMPANY, INC.	1849	.60		
D'ORSO	3			
ANGEL'S DREAM				
CENTURY MUSIC PUBLISHING COMPANY, INC.	1810	.60		
DA-OZ, RAM				
CAPRICCIO				
ISRAEL MUSIC INSTITUTE		2.50		
DA-OZ, RAM				
PROLOGUE, VARIATIONS AND EPILOGUE				
ISRAEL MUSIC INSTITUTE		3.50		
DACRE	MENDEL, S.	1		
BICYCLE BUILT FOR TWO, A				
WILLIS MUSIC COMPANY		.40		
DAGINCOURT, P.	4			
WINDMILL, THE				
CENTURY MUSIC PUBLISHING COMPANY, INC.	3905	.40		
DAHL	MD			
FIRST MARCH -- ALLA MARCIA MODERATO				
THEODORE PRESSER COMPANY		.50		
DAHL	MD			
SECOND MARCH -- ALLA MARCIA FUNEBRE				
THEODORE PRESSER COMPANY		.50		
DAHL				
SONATA PASTORALE				
PEER SOUTHERN ORGANIZATION		02.50		
DAHL	D			
SONATA SERIA				
THEODORE PRESSER COMPANY		3.50		
DAHL	MD			
THIRD MARCH -- ALLA MARCIA ALLEGRO				
THEODORE PRESSER COMPANY		.50		
DAHL				
THREE MARCHES FROM 'SONATINA ALLA MARCIA'				
THEODORE PRESSER COMPANY		.50		
DALAM, H.	3			
SOFT MIST				
BELWIN-MILLS PUBLISHING CORPORATION		.60		

DALCROZE				
CANZONETTA				
FRANCO COLOMBO PUBLICATIONS	SAL	1.75		
DALCROZE				
IMPROMPTU - SCHERZETTO				
FRANCO COLOMBO PUBLICATIONS	SAL	1.75		
DALCROZE				
TWO FEUILLETS D'ALBUM				
FRANCO COLOMBO PUBLICATIONS	SAL	1.75		
DALLA VECCHIA				
MIA OVARIAITONEN				
FRANCO COLOMBO PUBLICATIONS	Z4628	1.75		
DALLINGER				
SONATINA -- 1954 --				
ASSOCIATED MUSIC PUBLISHERS, INC.	DOB	2.25		
DAMASE, J. M.				
DEUXIEME CONCERTO				
EDITIONS MUSICALES TRANSATLANTIQUES		12.25		
DAMASE, J. M.				
GUIRLANDE -- HARPSICHORD				
EDITIONS MUSICALES TRANSATLANTIQUES		3.15		
DAMASE, J. M.				
INTERMEZZO				
EDITIONS MUSICALES TRANSATLANTIQUES		2.00		
DAMASE, J. M.				
LES CHAMEAUX				
ELKAN-VOGEL, INC.	RR	2.30		
DAMASE, J. M.				
MOUVEMENT PERPETUEL				
FRANCO COLOMBO PUBLICATIONS	SAL	2.50		
DAMASE, J. M.				
PASSACAILLE FOR CLAVECIN OR PIANO				
EDITIONS MUSICALES TRANSATLANTIQUES		1.40		
DAMASE, J. M.				
PIECES BREVES				
ELKAN-VOGEL, INC.	LEM	1.80		
DAMASE, J. M.				
PROMENADE				
ELKAN-VOGEL, INC.	RR	2.30		
DAMASE, J. M.				
RITOURNELLES -- OR FOR HARP				
ELKAN-VOGEL, INC.	LEM	2.75		
DAMASE, J. M.				
SONATA				
FRANCO COLOMBO PUBLICATIONS	SAL	6.25		
DAMASE, J. M.				
THEME ET VARIATIONS				
ELKAN-VOGEL, INC.	LEM	3.00		
DAMASE, J. M.				
VARIATIONS SUR UN THEME DE RAMEAU				
EDITIONS MUSICALES TRANSATLANTIQUES		7.70		
DANDELOT				
CREATION DU MONDE,LA, NO.2 LA CREATION				
GERARD BILLAUDOT EDITIONS MUSICALES		1.30		
DANDELOT				
CREATION DU MONDE,LA, NO.4 LA NUIT				
GERARD BILLAUDOT EDITIONS MUSICALES		1.30		
DANDELOT				
JARDIN DE CATHERINE, LE				
ASSOCIATED MUSIC PUBLISHERS, INC.	ESC	2.00		
DANDELOT				
JARDIN DE CLAUDE, LE				
ASSOCIATED MUSIC PUBLISHERS, INC.	ESC	2.25		
DANDELOT				
JARDIN DE SYLVIE, LE				
ASSOCIATED MUSIC PUBLISHERS, INC.	ESC	2.50		
DANDELOT				
SUITE -- 1933 --				
ASSOCIATED MUSIC PUBLISHERS, INC.	ESC	5.50		
DANDRIEU, J.				
LES TOURBILLONS				
NOVELLO AND COMPANY, LTD.	10.0028.04	1.15		
DANDRIEU, P.	4-5			
FIFERS, THE				
CENTURY MUSIC PUBLISHING COMPANY, INC.	3891	.40		
DANDRIEU, P.	GILLOCK	2		
FIFERS, THE				
WILLIS MUSIC COMPANY		.40		
DANFOLD	3-4			
ETUDE				
PRO-ART PUBLICATIONS, INC.	497	.50		
DANFORD, A.	SCHAUM, J.	1		
BLUE GNU				
SCHAUM PUBLICATIONS, INC.		.50		
DANIEL-LESUR				
MINUET, FROM SUITE FRANCAISE				
FRANCO COLOMBO PUBLICATIONS	A103A	.90		
DANIEL-LESUR				
NOCTURNE				
RONGWEN MUSIC, INC.		02.00		
DANIEL-LESUR				
SUITE FRANCAISE				
FRANCO COLOMBO PUBLICATIONS	A103	1.50		
DANIEL, K.	2			
DROWSY JUNE				
WILLIS MUSIC COMPANY		.35		
DANIEL, K.	3			
SINGING FINGERS				
WILLIS MUSIC COMPANY		.35		
DANIEL, K.	3			
SWAYING TREETOPS				
WILLIS MUSIC COMPANY		.40		
DANIEL, K.	3			
WIND CRADLE				
WILLIS MUSIC COMPANY		.35		
DANKS	3			
SILVER THREADS AMONG THE GOLD				
CENTURY MUSIC PUBLISHING COMPANY, INC.	2618	.40		
DAQUIN, C.	4			
COUCOU, LE				
CENTURY MUSIC PUBLISHING COMPANY, INC.	2303	.40		
DAQUIN, C.	CESI *			
COUCOU, LE -- RONDO				
FRANCO COLOMBO PUBLICATIONS	ER2618	.60		
DAQUIN, C.	ECKSTEIN			
COUCOU, LE --PONDEAU--				
CARL FISCHER, INC.	S 316	.50		
DAQUIN, C.	4			
CUCKOO, THE				
CENTURY MUSIC PUBLISHING COMPANY, INC.	2303	.40		
DAQUIN, C.				
CUCKOO, THE--RONDO				
G. SCHIRMER, INC.		.50		
DAQUIN, C.	4			
L'HIRONDELLE -- THE SWALLOW --				
CENTURY MUSIC PUBLISHING COMPANY, INC.	3906	.40		

DAQUIN, C.   3
    LA MELODIEUSE
        CENTURY MUSIC PUBLISHING COMPANY, INC.   3892   .40
DAQUIN, C.
    LE COUCOU
        BANKS AND SON LTD.   .40
DAQUIN, C.
    LE COUCOU
        ELKAN-VOGEL, INC.   D   .75
DAQUIN, C.
    RIGAUDON
        FREDERICK HARRIS MUSIC COMPANY   4   .60
DAQUIN, C.
    SWALLOW, THE
        CENTURY MUSIC PUBLISHING COMPANY, INC.   3906   .40
DARDENELLE, L.
    CHRISTMAS CHIMES
        WILLIS MUSIC COMPANY   .50
DARION *
    IMPOSSIBLE DREAM, THE -- FROM 'MAN OF LA MANCHA'
        SOUTHERN MUSIC COMPANY   1.25
DARION *   AGAY, D.
    IMPOSSIBLE DREAM, THE -- FROM 'MAN OF LA MANCHA'
        SOUTHERN MUSIC COMPANY   1.00
DARION *   AGAY, D.
    MAN OF LA MANCHA
        SAM FOX PUBLISHING COMPANY, INC.   1.75
DART, T.--ED.   DART, T.   M
    PARTHENIA IN-VIOLATA --MAYDEN MUSICKE--
        C. F. PETERS CORPORATION   6133   3.00
DARWEN, J.
    LITTLE CLOCK, THE
        FREDERICK HARRIS MUSIC COMPANY   .60
DASHER, J.
    CHRISTMAS LULLABY
        WILLIS MUSIC COMPANY   .50
DASHER, J.
    CHRISTMAS MEDLEY
        WILLIS MUSIC COMPANY   .50
DASHER, J.
    YULETIDE MEDLEY
        WILLIS MUSIC COMPANY   .50
DAUTREMER, M.
    TOCCATA
        ELKAN-VOGEL, INC.   LEM   2.50
DAVENPORT, G.
    GAVOTTE AND BOURREE
        FREDERICK HARRIS MUSIC COMPANY   .75
DAVENPORT, G.
    PRELUDE AND SARABANDE
        FREDERICK HARRIS MUSIC COMPANY   1.15
DAVID
    ETUDE ET DANSE
        GERARD BILLAUDOT EDITIONS MUSICALES   1.70
DAVID
    EVOCATION VESPERALE -- PRELUDE
        ELKAN-VOGEL, INC.   D   .90
DAVID
    LE MARAIS ET SES MOULINS
        ELKAN-VOGEL, INC.   D   1.25
DAVID, A.   E
    CHORALE IN STYLE OF HANDEL
        COMPOSERS PRESS, INC.   1.00
DAVID, M.   M
    REFLECTIONS
        COMPOSERS PRESS, INC.   1.00
DAVIES, E. J.   3
    IN HANGING GARDENS
        WILLIS MUSIC COMPANY   .45
DAVIES, E. J.   2
    IN HANGING GARDENS
        WILLIS MUSIC COMPANY   .45
DAVIES, E. J.   4
    TEMPUS FUGIT
        VOLKWEIN BROS.   00.40
DAVIS   ECKER   4
    PACIFIC GRAND MARCH
        VOLKWEIN BROS.   00.35
DAVIS   1
    POLLY'S LULLABY
        PRO-ART PUBLICATIONS, INC.   67   .50
DAVIS   1
    RAINY DAY, A
        CENTURY MUSIC PUBLISHING COMPANY, INC.   4401   .40
DAVIS   2
    SIESTA SERENADE
        PRO-ART PUBLICATIONS, INC.   66   .50
DAVIS, A.
    RAZORBACK REEL
        OXFORD UNIVERSITY PRESS   93.211   1.25
DAVIS, J.   2
    CAROUSEL
        THEODORE PRESSER COMPANY   .50
DAVIS, J.   3
    CHING CHONG ALLEY
        BELWIN-MILLS PUBLISHING CORPORATION   .60
DAVIS, J.   1 1/2
    FUN AT THE FAIR
        THEODORE PRESSER COMPANY   .50
DAVIS, J.   GLOVER, D.
    I'LL BE THERE
        BELWIN-MILLS PUBLISHING CORPORATION   .60
DAVIS, J.   2
    JOLLY JUGGLER
        THEODORE PRESSER COMPANY   .50
DAVIS, J.   1-2
    MARCH OF THE LOLLIPOPS
        CENTURY MUSIC PUBLISHING COMPANY, INC.   4197   .40
DAVIS, J.   2 1/2
    OTTO, THE CLOWN
        THEODORE PRESSER COMPANY   .50
DAVIS, J.   2
    POPCORN
        THEODORE PRESSER COMPANY   .50
DAVIS, J.   2 1/2
    RIDIN' THE RANGE
        THEODORE PRESSER COMPANY   .50
DAVIS, J.   2 1/2
    SAMMY THE SAILOR
        THEODORE PRESSER COMPANY   .50
DAVIS, J.   2 1/2
    SPACE PATROL
        THEODORE PRESSER COMPANY   .50
DAVIS, J.   2-3
    WALKING AND WHISTLING
        CENTURY MUSIC PUBLISHING COMPANY, INC.   4196   .40

DAVIS, K.   4
    HORNPIPE
        BELWIN-MILLS PUBLISHING CORPORATION   .60
DAVIS, K.
    INDIAN DRUM
        G. SCHIRMER, INC.   .40
DAVIS, K.
    SICILIENNE
        G. SCHIRMER, INC.   .40
DAVIS, K. *
    LITTLE DRUMMER BOY, THE -- SIMP.
        BELWIN-MILLS PUBLISHING CORPORATION   26071   .50
DAVIS, M.
    ARBUTUS -- INTERMEZZO
        BELWIN-MILLS PUBLISHING CORPORATION   28043   .60
DAVIS, M.   KAHN, M.
    CAROL OF THE DRUM
        BELWIN-MILLS PUBLISHING CORPORATION   28103   .60
DAVIS, M.
    JONQUILS
        BELWIN-MILLS PUBLISHING CORPORATION   28077   .60
DAVIS, M.
    MAGNOLIA -- INTERMEZZO
        BELWIN-MILLS PUBLISHING CORPORATION   28044   .60
DAWES
    MELODY
        WARNER BROTHERS PUBLISHERS   1.00
DAY, R.   3
    BUTTERFLY LAGOON
        WILLIS MUSIC COMPANY   .40
DE ANGELIS VALENTINI
    ARIA CON VARIAZIONI
        FRANCO COLOMBO PUBLICATIONS   BON.1954   .75
DE ANGELIS VALENTINI
    BALLADE IN THE FORM OF VARIATIONS
        FRANCO COLOMBO PUBLICATIONS   BON.1224   1.00
DE ANGELIS VALENTINI
    BALLETTO AD USUM INFANTIS
        FRANCO COLOMBO PUBLICATIONS   BON.1882   1.00
DE ANGELIS VALENTINI
    POEMA AUTUNNALE
        FRANCO COLOMBO PUBLICATIONS   BON.1951   .75
DE ANGELIS VALENTINI
    PRELUDE AND FUGUE ON THE NAME 'BACH'
        FRANCO COLOMBO PUBLICATIONS   DS357   1.75
DE ANGELIS VALENTINI
    SARABANDE ON THE THEME BY NICOLAS SIRET
        FRANCO COLOMBO PUBLICATIONS   DS346   1.00
DE BELLIS
    BAGLIORI
        FRANCO COLOMBO PUBLICATIONS   BON.2229 1.50
DE BOURGUIGNON
    DANS L'ILLE DE PINANG
        FRANCO COLOMBO PUBLICATIONS   SAL   4.25 .
DE CAMPO---ED   DE CAMPO
    CHIAPANECAS
        EDWARD B. MARKS MUSIC CORPORATION   01.00
DE CASTERA
    BERCEUSE
        FRANCO COLOMBO PUBLICATIONS   SAL   1.50
DE CASTERA
    TWO DANSES - DANSE ALLEGRE
        FRANCO COLOMBO PUBLICATIONS   SAL   1.50
DE CASTERA
    TWO DANSES - PETITE VALSE
        FRANCO COLOMBO PUBLICATIONS   SAL   1.50
DE CRESCENZO
    AMAMI, MAMMA
        FRANCO COLOMBO PUBLICATIONS   99843   .60
DE CRESCENZO
    DOLCE APRILE
        FRANCO COLOMBO PUBLICATIONS   98367   .90
DE CRESCENZO
    MAMMA, CARISSIMA
        FRANCO COLOMBO PUBLICATIONS   112047   .60
DE CRESCENZO
    MAMMA, QUANTO T'AMO
        FRANCO COLOMBO PUBLICATIONS   104631   .60
DE CRESCENZO
    ONOMASTICO DEL BABBO, OP. 209
        FRANCO COLOMBO PUBLICATIONS   109183   .60
DE CRESCENZO
    PRIMA CAREZZA
        FRANCO COLOMBO PUBLICATIONS   98717   .60
DE CRESCENZO
    RETOUR DES HIRONDELLES, LE
        FRANCO COLOMBO PUBLICATIONS   99779   .60
DE CRESCENZO
    SERA A SORRETO, UNA
        FRANCO COLOMBO PUBLICATIONS   108149   .60
DE CRESCENZO
    VISIONS D'UN ANGELO
        FRANCO COLOMBO PUBLICATIONS   113149   .60
DE CURTIS   SANFORD
    COME BACK TO SORRENTO
        BOSTON MUSIC COMPANY   .50
DE FRAGUIER
    PAYSAGES
        FRANCO COLOMBO PUBLICATIONS   SAL   4.00
DE FRAGUIER
    RIGAUDON CHAMPETRE
        FRANCO COLOMBO PUBLICATIONS   SAL   2.50
DE FRANCMESNIL
    BERCEUSE
        FRANCO COLOMBO PUBLICATIONS   SAL   1.75
DE FRANCMESNIL
    IMPROMPTU
        FRANCO COLOMBO PUBLICATIONS   SAL   1.75
DE FRANCMESNIL
    LEGENDE
        FRANCO COLOMBO PUBLICATIONS   SAL   1.75
DE FRANCMESNIL
    NOCTURNE
        FRANCO COLOMBO PUBLICATIONS   SAL   1.75
DE GARAUDE
    MARCHE DU SACRE DU PROPHETE
        FRANCO COLOMBO PUBLICATIONS   SAL   1.75
DE GRAU   4
    CORRICOLO, IL, GALOP, OP. 24
        CENTURY MUSIC PUBLISHING COMPANY, INC.   1855   .40
DE GRAU   4
    IL CORRICOLO, GALOP, OP. 24
        CENTURY MUSIC PUBLISHING COMPANY, INC.   1855   .40
DE JONG, C.
    ETENRAKU FOR PIANO OR CARILLON
        SEESAW MUSIC CORPORATION   1.50

DE LA CASINIERE
   SONATA IN B MINOR
      FRANCO COLOMBO PUBLICATIONS   SAL   5.25
DE LA SALLE, SR. M.   3
   SCHERZO
      BELWIN-MILLS PUBLISHING CORPORATION   .60
DE LA TOMBELLE
   JAUNESSE
      FRANCO COLOMBO PUBLICATIONS   SAL   2.50
DE LA TOMBELLE
   PLEIN SOLEIL
      FRANCO COLOMBO PUBLICATIONS   SAL   2.75
DE LEON *
   LEMONS AND LIMES -- A LA LIMA Y AL LIMON
      BELWIN-MILLS PUBLISHING CORPORATION   20150   .85
DE LEONE, F. D.   6
   POLONAISE
      THEODORE PRESSER COMPANY   .75
DE LUCIA, N.
   MEDIEVAL BALLAD
      FRANCO COLOMBO PUBLICATIONS   DS314   1.00
DE LULLI, A.   1
   CHOP STICKS
      WILLIS MUSIC COMPANY   .35
DE LULLI, A.   2
   CHOPSTICKS, WALTZ
      CENTURY MUSIC PUBLISHING COMPANY, INC.   768   .40
DE MARIA
   PRELUDE NO. 02
      FRANCO COLOMBO PUBLICATIONS   RCT111   .75
DE MARIA
   PRELUDE NO. 1
      FRANCO COLOMBO PUBLICATIONS   NY1157   .50
DE MENASCE, J.
   PETITE SUITE
      ELKAN-VOGEL, INC.   D   2.00
DE NARDIS
   CANZONETTA ABRUZZESE
      FRANCO COLOMBO PUBLICATIONS   10567   .60
DE NARDIS
   SALTARELLO ABRUZZESE
      FRANCO COLOMBO PUBLICATIONS   98524   .60
DE NARDIS   DEL MAGLIO
   SALTARELLO ABRUZZESE
      FRANCO COLOMBO PUBLICATIONS   127758   .60
DE NITO
   LYRIC SKETCHES
      FRANCO COLOMBO PUBLICATIONS   BA8039   2.00
DE PRINCE
   JOYFUL CANARY -- JOYEUX CANARI
      BELWIN-MILLS PUBLISHING CORPORATION   20415   .85
DE RIENZO   2
   HOLIDAY IN NAPLES
      CENTURY MUSIC PUBLISHING COMPANY, INC.   4413   .40
DE ROGATIS
   COYAS BAJANDO LA MONTANA
      FRANCO COLOMBO PUBLICATIONS   BA9712   .75
DE ROSE, P.
   AMERICAN WALTZ
      THE BIG THREE MUSIC CORPORATION   00.95
DE ROSE, P.
   AUTUMN SERENADE
      THE BIG THREE MUSIC CORPORATION   00.95
DE ROSE, P.
   DEEP PURPLE
      THE BIG THREE MUSIC CORPORATION   00.95
DE ROSE, P.
   FOUNTAIN IN CENTRAL PARK
      THE BIG THREE MUSIC CORPORATION   00.95
DE ROSE, P.   SCHAUM, J.   2 1/2
   HAVE YOU EVER BEEN LONELY
      SCHAUM PUBLICATIONS, INC.   .75
DE ROSE, P.
   MOONLIGHT MOOD
      THE BIG THREE MUSIC CORPORATION   00.95
DE ROSE, P.
   MUSIC BOX IN BLUE
      THE BIG THREE MUSIC CORPORATION   00.95
DE ROSE, P.
   STARLIT HOUR
      THE BIG THREE MUSIC CORPORATION   00.95
DE ROSE, P.
   WHITE ORCHIDS
      THE BIG THREE MUSIC CORPORATION   00.95
DE RUBERTIS
   GAVOTTE AND MUSETTE
      FRANCO COLOMBO PUBLICATIONS   BA8132   .75
DE RUBERTIS
   GAVOTTE IN A FLAT
      FRANCO COLOMBO PUBLICATIONS   BA8130   .75
DE SAXE
   PARODIETTE
      MCA MUSIC   .60
DE SOLIS
   FIESTA MEXICANA
      BELWIN-MILLS PUBLISHING CORPORATION   20091   1.00
DE SOLIS
   PAGANINI PAYS A VISIT TO BACH
      BELWIN-MILLS PUBLISHING CORPORATION   20189   1.00
DE VILLEBICHOT
   RETRAIT AUX FLAMBEAUX
      FRANCO COLOMBO PUBLICATIONS   SAL   1.75
DE VITO, A.   2 1/2
   BARN DANCE
      THEODORE PRESSER COMPANY   .50
DE VITO, A.   GR. 2
   BIG BASS FIDDLE
      KENYON PUBLICATIONS   .75
DE VITO, A.   2
   BUG BASS TUBA, THE
      THEODORE PRESSER COMPANY   .50
DE VITO, A.   GR. 3
   CONVERSATIONAL PIECES, THREE
      KENYON PUBLICATIONS   .80
DE VITO, A.   2
   COUNTRY DANCE
      PRO-ART PUBLICATIONS, INC.   77   .50
DE VITO, A.   2
   COWBOY LAMENT
      PRO-ART PUBLICATIONS, INC.   92   .50
DE VITO, A.   3-4
   FASCINATION
      PRO-ART PUBLICATIONS, INC.   85   .50
DE VITO, A.   GR. 2
   FROLICKING FAUNS
      KENYON PUBLICATIONS   .75

DE VITO, A.   1-2
   HAPPY TIMES
      PRO-ART PUBLICATIONS, INC.   78   .50
DE VITO, A.
   HOLIDAY MOOD
      BOOSEY AND HAWKES, INC.   .40
DE VITO, A.   3 1/2
   HOLIDAY SONG, A
      THEODORE PRESSER COMPANY   .50
DE VITO, A.
   IRISH MOOD
      BOOSEY AND HAWKES, INC.   .40
DE VITO, A.   1-2
   JOLLY CAPTAIN, THE
      PRO-ART PUBLICATIONS, INC.   82   .50
DE VITO, A.   1
   MELODIC WALTZ
      PRO-ART PUBLICATIONS, INC.   76   .50
DE VITO, A.   GR. 3
   MERRY GO-ROUND
      KENYON PUBLICATIONS   .75
DE VITO, A.   1
   MY FIRST MARCH
      PRO-ART PUBLICATIONS, INC.   74   .50
DE VITO, A.   2
   PETITE WALTZ
      PRO-ART PUBLICATIONS, INC.   75   .50
DE VITO, A.   2
   SINGING CELLO
      PRO-ART PUBLICATIONS, INC.   83   .50
DE WAILLY
   SOUS UN BALCON
      FRANCO COLOMBO PUBLICATIONS   SAL   1.75
DEAN, L. *   DEAN, L.
   ORPHEUS --GLUCK-- ADAPTED AS A CHILDREN'S OPERA-STORY TO BE
   PLAYED, SUNG, OR INFORMALLY DRAMATIZED
      G. SCHIRMER, INC.   .60
DEBPAS, L.
   KLAVIERSTUK NO. 1
      SEESAW MUSIC CORPORATION   2.00
DEBREVILLE
   FANTASIE
      FRANCO COLOMBO PUBLICATIONS   SAL   4.25
DEBREVILLE
   PRELUDE AND FUGUE
      FRANCO COLOMBO PUBLICATIONS   SAL   3.25
DEBREVILLE
   SONATA
      FRANCO COLOMBO PUBLICATIONS   SAL   6.50
DEBUSMAN, E.
   SONATA NO. 01, OP. 17 FOR PIANO SOLO
      AMERICAN MUSIC EDITION   2.00
DEBUSSY
   AFTERNOON OF A FAUN
      ASHLEY DEALERS SERVICE, INC.   ES   1.00
DEBUSSY   SCHAUM, J.   3
   AFTERNOON OF A FAUN
      BELWIN-MILLS PUBLISHING CORPORATION   .50
DEBUSSY   MITTLER   2B
   AFTERNOON OF A FAUN
      MUSICORD PUBLICATIONS, INC.   .45
DEBUSSY   4
   AFTERNOON OF A FAUN, E MAJOR
      CENTURY MUSIC PUBLISHING COMPANY, INC.   3721   .40
DEBUSSY   4
   ALBUM LEAF --PAGE D'ALBUM--
      THEODORE PRESSER COMPANY   .50
DEBUSSY   LEVINE
   ARABESQUE NO. 1
      BOSTON MUSIC COMPANY   .60
DEBUSSY
   ARABESQUE NO. 1
      EDWARD B. MARKS MUSIC CORPORATION   01.00
DEBUSSY
   ARABESQUE NO. 1
      ELKAN-VOGEL, INC.   .75
DEBUSSY   PHILIPP, I.
   ARABESQUE NO. 1
      INTERNATIONAL MUSIC COMPANY   .75
DEBUSSY   LEVINE
   ARABESQUE NO. 2
      BOSTON MUSIC COMPANY   .50
DEBUSSY
   ARABESQUE NO. 2
      EDWARD B. MARKS MUSIC CORPORATION   01.00
DEBUSSY
   ARABESQUE NO. 2
      ELKAN-VOGEL, INC.   .75
DEBUSSY   PHILIPP, I.
   ARABESQUE NO. 2
      INTERNATIONAL MUSIC COMPANY   .75
DEBUSSY
   ARABESQUE NOS. 1 AND 2
      EDWARD B. MARKS MUSIC CORPORATION   01.25
DEBUSSY
   BALLADE
      EDWIN F. KALMUS   3371   1.00
DEBUSSY
   BALLET FROM PETITE SUITE
      ELKAN-VOGEL, INC.   2.25
DEBUSSY
   BERCEUSE HEROIQUE
      ELKAN-VOGEL, INC.   2.25
DEBUSSY
   BROUILLARDS FROM PRELUDES, BK. 2
      ELKAN-VOGEL, INC.   2.25
DEBUSSY
   BRUYERES FROM PRELUDES, BK. 2
      ELKAN-VOGEL, INC.   2.25
DEBUSSY
   CANOPE FROM PRELUDES, BK. 2
      ELKAN-VOGEL, INC.   1.70
DEBUSSY
   CE QU'A VU LE VENT D'OUEST FROM PRELUDES, BK. 1
      ELKAN-VOGEL, INC.   2.50
DEBUSSY
   CLAIR DE LUNE
      ASHLEY DEALERS SERVICE, INC.   ES   1.00
DEBUSSY
   CLAIR DE LUNE
      ASHLEY DEALERS SERVICE, INC.   ES   .95
DEBUSSY   EDWARDS
   CLAIR DE LUNE
      BOSTON MUSIC COMPANY   .75
DEBUSSY   KAHL
   CLAIR DE LUNE
      BOSTON MUSIC COMPANY   .50

DEBUSSY   M
   CLAIR DE LUNE
      C. F. PETERS CORPORATION   7251   .75
DEBUSSY
   CLAIR DE LUNE
      CARL FISCHER, INC.   P 3024   1.00
DEBUSSY   ECKSTEIN
   CLAIR DE LUNE
      CARL FISCHER, INC.   P 3025   .50
DEBUSSY   WATSON
   CLAIR DE LUNE
      CARL FISCHER, INC.   RS 384   .50
DEBUSSY   4
   CLAIR DE LUNE
      CENTURY MUSIC PUBLISHING COMPANY, INC. 4329   .40
DEBUSSY
   CLAIR DE LUNE
      EDWARD B. MARKS MUSIC CORPORATION   01.00
DEBUSSY
   CLAIR DE LUNE
      ELKAN-VOGEL, INC.   .80
DEBUSSY   INTERMEDIATE
   CLAIR DE LUNE
      ELKAN-VOGEL, INC.   .75
DEBUSSY   RICHTER
   CLAIR DE LUNE
      ELKAN-VOGEL, INC.   .60
DEBUSSY   RICHTER   1
   CLAIR DE LUNE
      ELKAN-VOGEL, INC.   .50
DEBUSSY
   CLAIR DE LUNE
      G. SCHIRMER, INC.   .75
DEBUSSY   PHILIPP, I.
   CLAIR DE LUNE
      INTERNATIONAL MUSIC COMPANY   1.00
DEBUSSY
   CLAIR DE LUNE
      NOVELLO AND COMPANY, LTD.   10.0030.06 .90
DEBUSSY   ZEPP   5
   CLAIR DE LUNE
      PRO-ART PUBLICATIONS, INC.   361   .75
DEBUSSY   SCHAUM, J.   4
   CLAIR DE LUNE
      SCHAUM PUBLICATIONS, INC.   .60
DEBUSSY   PODOLSKY, L.
   CLAIR DE LUNE
      SHAWNEE PRESS, INC.   HB-230   .75
DEBUSSY   DAVIS, J. R.   FIRST YEAR
   CLAIR DE LUNE
      WARNER BROTHERS PUBLISHERS   .75
DEBUSSY   THOMPSON   3
   CLAIR DE LUNE
      WILLIS MUSIC COMPANY   .60
DEBUSSY   ANSON, G.   5
   CLAIR DE LUNE
      WILLIS MUSIC COMPANY   .75
DEBUSSY
   CLAIR DE LUNE FROM SUITE BERGAMASQUE
      EDWIN F. KALMUS   3372   1.00
DEBUSSY
   CLOCHES A TRAVERS LES FEUILLES FROM IMAGES, BK. 2
      ELKAN-VOGEL, INC.   2.25
DEBUSSY
   CORTEGE
      ELKAN-VOGEL, INC.   D   2.25
DEBUSSY   D
   D'UN CAHIER D'ESQUISSES
      C. F. PETERS CORPORATION   SCH17   2.00
DEBUSSY
   DANCE OF PUCK FROM PRELUDES, BK. 1
      ELKAN-VOGEL, INC.   2.25
DEBUSSY
   DANCERS OF DELPHES FROM PRELUDES, BK. 1
      ELKAN-VOGEL, INC.   1.30
DEBUSSY   5
   DANSE
      BOSTON MUSIC COMPANY   .75
DEBUSSY
   DANSE
      EDWIN F. KALMUS   3373   1.00
DEBUSSY
   DANSE
      ELKAN-VOGEL, INC.   2.00
DEBUSSY
   DANSE - SACRE ET PROFANE
      ELKAN-VOGEL, INC.   3.00
DEBUSSY   3-4
   DANSE BOHEMIENNE
      SCHOTT   2169   1.75
DEBUSSY
   DANSE DE LA POUPEE FROM LA BOITE A JOUJOUX
      ELKAN-VOGEL, INC.   2.25
DEBUSSY
   DES PAS SUR LA NEIGE FROM PRELUDES, BK. 1
      ELKAN-VOGEL, INC.   1.30
DEBUSSY   M
   DEUX ARABESQUES, NO.1
      C. F. PETERS CORPORATION   7259A   .75
DEBUSSY   M
   DEUX ARABESQUES, NO.2
      C. F. PETERS CORPORATION   7259B   .75
DEBUSSY
   DR. GRADUS AD PARNASSUM FROM THE CHILDREN'S CORNER
      ELKAN-VOGEL, INC.   2.25
DEBUSSY
   EN BATEAU
      ASHLEY DEALERS SERVICE, INC.   ES   1.00
DEBUSSY   PICCIOLI
   EN BATEAU
      INTERNATIONAL MUSIC COMPANY   .75
DEBUSSY   LEVINE   4
   EN BATEAU -- FROM THE 'PETITE SUITE'
      BOSTON MUSIC COMPANY   .60
DEBUSSY
   EN BATEAU, FROM PETITE SUITE
      EDWIN F. KALMUS   3374   1.00
DEBUSSY
   EN BATEAU, FROM PETITE SUITE
      ELKAN-VOGEL, INC.   .75
DEBUSSY   PHILIPP, I.
   ESTAMPES - SUITE OF 3 PIECES-
      INTERNATIONAL MUSIC COMPANY   2.00
DEBUSSY
   ET LA LUNE DESCEND SUR LE TEMPLE FROM IMAGES, BK. 2
      ELKAN-VOGEL, INC.   2.25

DEBUSSY
   EVENING IN GRENADE FROM THE ESTAMPES
      ELKAN-VOGEL, INC.   1.00
DEBUSSY   NERINI, E.
   FANTOCHES
      ELKAN-VOGEL, INC.   D   1.25
DEBUSSY
   FETES, NOCTURNE
      ELKAN-VOGEL, INC.   4.50
DEBUSSY
   FEUILLES MORTES FROM PRELUDES, BK. 2
      ELKAN-VOGEL, INC.   1.70
DEBUSSY
   FIREWORKS--FEUX D'ARTIFICE--   FROM PRELUDES, BK. 2
      ELKAN-VOGEL, INC.   3.00
DEBUSSY
   FIRST ARABESQUE
      ASHLEY DEALERS SERVICE, INC.   ES   .95
DEBUSSY
   FIRST ARABESQUE
      G. SCHIRMER, INC.   .60
DEBUSSY
   GARDENS IN THE RAIN
      ASHLEY DEALERS SERVICE, INC.   ES   1.00
DEBUSSY
   GARDENS IN THE RAIN FROM THE ESTAMPES
      ELKAN-VOGEL, INC.   1.00
DEBUSSY
   GENERAL LAVINE - ECCENTRIC FROM PRELUDES, BK. 2
      ELKAN-VOGEL, INC.   2.50
DEBUSSY
   GIGUES
      ELKAN-VOGEL, INC.   D   2.75
DEBUSSY
   GIRL WITH THE FLAXEN HAIR FROM PRELUDES, BK.1
      ELKAN-VOGEL, INC.   1.30
DEBUSSY
   GOLDFISH--POISSONS D'OR--   FROM IMAGES, BK. 2
      ELKAN-VOGEL, INC.   3.00
DEBUSSY
   GOLLIWOGG'S CAKE-WALK FROM THE CHILDREN'S CORNER
      ELKAN-VOGEL, INC.   2.25
DEBUSSY
   HILLS OF ANACAPRI, THE, FROM PRELUDES, BK. 1
      ELKAN-VOGEL, INC.   2.25
DEBUSSY
   HOMAGE TO HAYDN
      ELKAN-VOGEL, INC.   1.70
DEBUSSY
   HOMMAGE A RAMEAU FROM IMAGES BK. 1
      ELKAN-VOGEL, INC.   2.25
DEBUSSY
   HOMMAGE A S. PICKWICK FROM PRELUDES, BK. 2
      ELKAN-VOGEL, INC.   2.25
DEBUSSY
   IBERIA
      ELKAN-VOGEL, INC.   D   5.00
DEBUSSY   M-D
   JARDINS SOUS LA PLUIE
      C. F. PETERS CORPORATION   7263   1.00
DEBUSSY
   JARDINS SOUS LA PLUIE
      EDWARD B. MARKS MUSIC CORPORATION   01.00
DEBUSSY
   JARDINS SOUS LA PLUIE
      EDWIN F. KALMUS   3380   1.00
DEBUSSY
   JARDINS SOUS LA PLUIE
      G. SCHIRMER, INC.   .75
DEBUSSY   PHILIPP, I.
   JARDINS SOUS LA PLUIE
      INTERNATIONAL MUSIC COMPANY   1.00
DEBUSSY
   JIMBO'S LULLABY FROM THE CHILDREN'S CORNER
      ELKAN-VOGEL, INC.   2.25
DEBUSSY
   KHAMMA
      ELKAN-VOGEL, INC.   D   7.50
DEBUSSY
   L ISLE JOYEUSE
      EDWARD B. MARKS MUSIC CORPORATION   01.25
DEBUSSY   4
   L'APRES-MIDI D'UN FAUNE
      CENTURY MUSIC PUBLISHING COMPANY, INC. 3721   .40
DEBUSSY
   L'ISLE JOYEUSE
      EDWIN F. KALMUS   3379   1.25
DEBUSSY
   L'ISLE JOYEUSE
      ELKAN-VOGEL, INC.   1.00
DEBUSSY
   L'ISLE JOYEUSE
      INTERNATIONAL MUSIC COMPANY   1.25
DEBUSSY
   LA CATHEDRALE ENGLOUTIE FROM PRELUDES, BK. 1
      ELKAN-VOGEL, INC.   2.25
DEBUSSY
   LA MER
      ELKAN-VOGEL, INC.   6.75
DEBUSSY
   LA PLUS QUE LENTE, VALSE
      ELKAN-VOGEL, INC.   2.25
DEBUSSY
   LA PLUS QUE LENTE, VALSE
      ELKAN-VOGEL, INC.   D   2.10
DEBUSSY
   LA PUERTA DEL VINO FROM PRELUDES, BK. 2
      ELKAN-VOGEL, INC.   2.25
DEBUSSY
   LA SERENADE INTERROMPUE FROM PRELUDES, BK. 1
      ELKAN-VOGEL, INC.   2.25
DEBUSSY
   LA TERRASSE DES AUDIENCES FROM PRELUDES, BK. 2
      ELKAN-VOGEL, INC.   2.25
DEBUSSY
   LE BON PASTEUR -- FROM LE MARTYR DE ST. SEBASTIEN
      ELKAN-VOGEL, INC.   D   1.50
DEBUSSY
   LE PETIT NEGRE
      ELKAN-VOGEL, INC.   2.20
DEBUSSY   D
   LE TRIOMPHE DE BACCHUS
      C. F. PETERS CORPORATION   C43   2.50

DEBUSSY
  LES JARDINS DANS LA PLUIE -- GARDENS IN THE RAIN
    ELKAN-VOGEL, INC.   D   1.75
DEBUSSY
  LES SONS ET LES PARFUMS FROM PRELUDES , BK. 1
    ELKAN-VOGEL, INC.   1.70
DEBUSSY
  LINDARAJA
    ELKAN-VOGEL, INC.   J   1.50
DEBUSSY
  LITTLE NEGRO
    ASHLEY DEALERS SERVICE, INC.   ES   1.00
                        3
DEBUSSY
  LITTLE NEGRO, THE
    ALPHONSE LEDUC
DEBUSSY
  LITTLE SHEPHERD, THE, FROM THE CHILDREN'S CORNER
    ELKAN-VOGEL, INC.   1.30
DEBUSSY
  MARCHE ECOSSAISE
    ELKAN-VOGEL, INC.   J   2.00
DEBUSSY
  MASQUES
    ELKAN-VOGEL, INC.   3.00
DEBUSSY
  MAZURKA
    ELKAN-VOGEL, INC.   J   1.80
                        4
DEBUSSY
  MAZURKA IN F MINOR
    CENTURY MUSIC PUBLISHING COMPANY, INC. 3839   .40
                        4
DEBUSSY
  MAZURKA IN F SHARP MINOR
    THEODORE PRESSER COMPANY   .50
DEBUSSY
  MENUET
    ELKAN-VOGEL, INC.   D   2.25
DEBUSSY
  MINSTRELS FROM PRELUDES, BK. 1
    ELKAN-VOGEL, INC.   2.25
DEBUSSY
  NOCTURNE IN D FLAT
    EDWARD B. MARKS MUSIC CORPORATION   01.00
DEBUSSY   PHILIPP
  NOCTURNE IN D FLAT MINOR
    ASSOCIATED MUSIC PUBLISHERS, INC.   ESC   5.50
DEBUSSY
  NUAGES, NOCTURNE
    ELKAN-VOGEL, INC.   2.30
DEBUSSY
  ONDINE FROM PRELUDES, BK. 2
    ELKAN-VOGEL, INC.   2.25
DEBUSSY
  PAGODES FROM THE ESTAMPES
    ELKAN-VOGEL, INC.   2.50
DEBUSSY
  PAGODES, FROM ESTAMPES
    EDWIN F. KALMUS   3382   1.25
DEBUSSY   PICCIOLI
  PETITE SUITE
    INTERNATIONAL MUSIC COMPANY   2.00
DEBUSSY
  POUR LE PIANO
    ASHLEY DEALERS SERVICE, INC.   1.50
DEBUSSY
  POUR LE PIANO
    ELKAN-VOGEL, INC.   1.50
DEBUSSY   PHILIPP, I.
  POUR LE PIANO
    INTERNATIONAL MUSIC COMPANY   1.75
DEBUSSY
  PRELUDE A L'APRES-MIDI D'UNE FAUNE
    EDWARD B. MARKS MUSIC CORPORATION   01.00
DEBUSSY   PHILIPP, I.
  PRELUDE FROM 'POUR LE PIANO'
    INTERNATIONAL MUSIC COMPANY   1.00
DEBUSSY
  PRELUDE IN A MINOR
    ELKAN-VOGEL, INC.   1.00
DEBUSSY
  PRELUDE TO THE
           AFTERNOON OF A FAUN
    ELKAN-VOGEL, INC.   3.00
DEBUSSY
  QUATUOR
    ELKAN-VOGEL, INC.   D   5.00
DEBUSSY
  REFLECTIONS IN THE WATER
    ASHLEY DEALERS SERVICE, INC.   ES   1.00
DEBUSSY
  REFLECTIONS IN THE WATER FROM IMAGES, BK. 1
    ELKAN-VOGEL, INC.   .75
DEBUSSY
  REFLETS DANS L'EAU
    EDWIN F. KALMUS   3385   1.50
DEBUSSY
  REFLETS DANS L'EAU
    G. SCHIRMER, INC.   .75
DEBUSSY   PHILIPP, I.
  REFLETS DANS L'EAU
    INTERNATIONAL MUSIC COMPANY   .75
DEBUSSY
  REFLETS DANS L'EAU --IMAGES--
    CARL FISCHER, INC.   P 3061   .75
DEBUSSY   SCHAUM, J.   3
  REVERIE
    BELWIN-MILLS PUBLISHING CORPORATION   .50
DEBUSSY   ECKSTEIN
  REVERIE
    CARL FISCHER, INC.   S 2277   .50
                        4
DEBUSSY
  REVERIE
    CENTURY MUSIC PUBLISHING COMPANY, INC. 3252   .40
DEBUSSY
  REVERIE
    ELKAN-VOGEL, INC.   1.45
DEBUSSY   BAUER
  REVERIE
    G. SCHIRMER, INC.   .60
DEBUSSY   MOSSMAN, T.
  REVERIE -- SIMP.
    BELWIN-MILLS PUBLISHING CORPORATION 26094   .50
DEBUSSY   3 - 4
  ROMANCE
    BOSTON MUSIC COMPANY   .50

DEBUSSY
  ROMANCES
    ASSOCIATED MUSIC PUBLISHERS, INC.   ESC   3.75
DEBUSSY
  SECOND ARABESQUE
    ASHLEY DEALERS SERVICE, INC.   ES   .95
DEBUSSY
  SECOND ARABESQUE
    G. SCHIRMER, INC.   .60
DEBUSSY
  SERENADE FOR THE DOLL FROM THE CHILDREN'S CORNER
    ELKAN-VOGEL, INC.   2.25
DEBUSSY
  SIRENES, NOCTURNE
    ELKAN-VOGEL, INC.   4.00
DEBUSSY
  SNOW IS DANCING, THE, FROM THE CHILDREN'S CORNER
    ELKAN-VOGEL, INC.   2.25
DEBUSSY   PHILIPP, I.
  SOIREE DANS GRENADE
    INTERNATIONAL MUSIC COMPANY   1.00
DEBUSSY
  SOIREE EN GRENADE, FROM ESTAMPES
    EDWIN F. KALMUS   3386   1.00
DEBUSSY   PALMER, W. A.
  SUITE BERGAMASQUE
    ALFRED MUSIC COMPANY   615   1.50
                      M
DEBUSSY
  SUITE BERGAMASQUE
    C. F. PETERS CORPORATION   7261   1.50
DEBUSSY
  SUITE BERGAMASQUE
    ELKAN-VOGEL, INC.   1.50
DEBUSSY   PHILIPP, I.
  SUITE BERGAMASQUE
    INTERNATIONAL MUSIC COMPANY   1.75
DEBUSSY
  TOCCATA, FROM POUR LE PIANO
    EDWIN F. KALMUS   3388   1.50
DEBUSSY   DUMM   5 - 6
  TWO ARABESQUES
    BOSTON MUSIC COMPANY   .50
DEBUSSY   4
  VALSE ROMANTIQUE
    BOSTON MUSIC COMPANY   .50
DEBUSSY
  VALSE ROMANTIQUE
    ELKAN-VOGEL, INC.   1.75
DEBUSSY
  VOILES FROM PRELUDES, BK. 1
    ELKAN-VOGEL, INC.   2.25
DEBUSSY
  WIND IN THE PLAIN, THE, FROM PRELUDES, BK. 1
    ELKAN-VOGEL, INC.   2.25
DECOLA, F.
  ROCKING HORSE SWING
    G. SCHIRMER, INC.   .35
DECOLA, F.
  RUMBA RASCAL
    G. SCHIRMER, INC.   .35
DECOLA, F.
  RUMBA ROMANCE
    G. SCHIRMER, INC.   .35
DECOLA, F.
  SNAPPY SAMBA
    G. SCHIRMER, INC.   .35
DEE, M.   2
  COMICAL FINGERS
    VOLKWEIN BROS.   .40
DEE, M.   2
  LOPE ALONG COWBOY
    VOLKWEIN BROS.   .35
DEE, M.   3
  RIDING THE RANGE
    VOLKWEIN BROS.   .40
DEE, M.   2
  TWO OF A KIND
    VOLKWEIN BROS.   00.35
DEFAY   7
  SUITE
    ALPHONSE LEDUC
DEFILIPPI, A.
  DANCE RHYTHMS FOR PIANO
    GENERAL MUSIC PUBLISHING COMPANY, INC.   2.00
DEFOSSE
  NOCTURNE
    FRANCO COLOMBO PUBLICATIONS   SAL   1.75
DEGEN
  SONATA NO. 01 -- 1942-47 --
    ASSOCIATED MUSIC PUBLISHERS, INC.   B/H   2.00
DEGEN
  SONATA NO. 02 -- 1945 --
    ASSOCIATED MUSIC PUBLISHERS, INC.   B/H   2.00
DEGEN
  SONATA NO. 04
    ASSOCIATED MUSIC PUBLISHERS, INC.   B/H   2.00
DEGEN   3-4
  SUITE FUR KLAVIER
    BARENREITER VERLAG   SM 1100
DEIS
  FLYING SAUCERS
    G. SCHIRMER, INC.   .40
DEKONTSKI   5
  AWAKENING OF THE LION
    CENTURY MUSIC PUBLISHING COMPANY, INC. 747   .40
DEKOVEN, R.   ROGERS
  OH, PROMISE ME
    G. SCHIRMER, INC.   .50
DEKOVEN, R.   STEINER
  OH, PROMISE ME
    G. SCHIRMER, INC.   .50
DEL CASTILLO   2 1/2
  BABILLAGE
    BELWIN-MILLS PUBLISHING CORPORATION   .60
DEL CORONA
  DANZA E CANZONE A BALLO
    FRANCO COLOMBO PUBLICATIONS   BON.2026   1.00
DEL CORONA
  NOCTURNE
    FRANCO COLOMBO PUBLICATIONS   BON.2211   1.50
DEL CORONA
  PRELUDE
    FRANCO COLOMBO PUBLICATIONS   BON.2175   1.00
DELA
  HOMMAGE
    ASSOCIATED MUSIC PUBLISHERS, INC.   BER   .75

DELA
  VIELLE CAPITALE, LA
    ASSOCIATED MUSIC PUBLISHERS, INC.   BER   1.00
DELABRE
  COLOMBINELLA -- SERENADE --
    FRANCO COLOMBO PUBLICATIONS   SAL   1.50
DELACROIX, R.
  AMBIANCE
    ELKAN-VOGEL, INC.   CON   3.50
DELACROIX, R.
  ESQUISSES
    ELKAN-VOGEL, INC.   CON   3.50
DELACROIX, R.
  UN PEASANT FARDEAU, MON PHARMACIEN
    ELKAN-VOGEL, INC.   CON   3.50
DELANNOY
  BELLE INSOUCIANTE, LA -- LE CAHIER DE SYLVINE, NO. 3
    ASSOCIATED MUSIC PUBLISHERS, INC.   ESC   1.10
DELANNOY
  BERCEUSE CONTRE AVIONS -- LE CAHIER DE SYLVINE, NO. 4
    ASSOCIATED MUSIC PUBLISHERS, INC.   ESC   .85
DELANNOY
  CENDRILLON - VALSE
    ASSOCIATED MUSIC PUBLISHERS, INC.   ESC   1.25
DELANNOY
  CENDRILLON -- CINDERELLA -- BALLET
    ASSOCIATED MUSIC PUBLISHERS, INC.   ESC   6.00
DELANNOY
  DANSE DE NEGRILLONS -- ''LA PANTOUFLE DE VAIR''
    ASSOCIATED MUSIC PUBLISHERS, INC.   ESC   2.00
DELANNOY
  LE FOU DE LA DAME -- SARABANDE
    HEUGEL ET CIE.   8.05
DELANNOY
  LE MARCHAND DE LUNETTES
    HEUGEL ET CIE.   3.25
DELANNOY
  MOMENT MUSICAL -- LE CAHIER DE SYLVINE, NO. 2
    ASSOCIATED MUSIC PUBLISHERS, INC.   ESC   .75
DELANNOY
  NOCES FANTASTIQUES, LES -- BALLET IN 2 ACTS
    ASSOCIATED MUSIC PUBLISHERS, INC.   ESC   12.00
DELANNOY
  ROMANCE -- LE CAHIER DE SYLVINE, NO. 1
    ASSOCIATED MUSIC PUBLISHERS, INC.   ESC   1.10
DELANNOY
  VALSE -- ''LA PANTOUFLE DE VAIR''
    ASSOCIATED MUSIC PUBLISHERS, INC.   ESC   .60
DELBRUCK   3-4
  BERCEUSE -- CRADLE SONG
    CENTURY MUSIC PUBLISHING COMPANY, INC. 2549   .40
DELBRUCK   2-3
  CRADLE SONG -- BERCEUSE
    CENTURY MUSIC PUBLISHING COMPANY, INC. 2549   .40
DELDEN, VAN   M-D
  SONATA
    C. F. PETERS CORPORATION   D205   2.00
DELIBES, L.
  COPPELIA
    HEUGEL ET CIE.   1.50
DELIBES, L.
  COPPELIA
    HEUGEL ET CIE.   15.25
DELIBES, L.   3
  COPPELIA -- TANZ-SUITE
    SCHOTT   08951 1/2   1.50
DELIBES, L.   3
  COPPELIA -- VALSE LENTE
    SCHOTT   08884 1/2   1.00
DELIBES, L.   DEXTER, H.
  COPPELIA BALLET
    SAM FOX PUBLISHING COMPANY, INC.   1.00
DELIBES, L.
  COPPELIA WALTZ
    EDWARD B. MARKS MUSIC CORPORATION   01.50
DELIBES, L.   4
  COPPELIA, VALSE LENTE
    CENTURY MUSIC PUBLISHING COMPANY, INC.   591   .40
DELIBES, L.
  LA SOURCE
    HEUGEL ET CIE.   16.75
DELIBES, L.   SCHAUM, J.   4
  MAIDS OF CADIZ
    BELWIN-MILLS PUBLISHING CORPORATION   .50
DELIBES, L.
  MAILA WALTZ
    EDWARD B. MARKS MUSIC CORPORATION   01.00
DELIBES, L.   3
  NAILA -- LE PAS DE FLEURS
    SCHOTT   08885 1/2   1.00
DELIBES, L.   ROLFE, W.   2
  NAILA WALTZ, EASY
    CENTURY MUSIC PUBLISHING COMPANY, INC. 3547   .40
DELIBES, L.   4
  NAILA, PAS DES FLEURS
    CENTURY MUSIC PUBLISHING COMPANY, INC. 1514   .40
DELIBES, L.
  PAS DES FLEURS--WALTZ FROM ''NAILA''
    G. SCHIRMER, INC.   .70
DELIBES, L.   4
  PAS DES FLEURS, NAILA
    CENTURY MUSIC PUBLISHING COMPANY, INC. 1514   .40
DELIBES, L.
  PASSEPIED FROM ''LE ROI S'AMUSE''
    G. SCHIRMER, INC.   .40
DELIBES, L.   MENDEL, S.   2
  PIZZICATI
    WILLIS MUSIC COMPANY   .40
DELIBES, L.   DEIS
  PIZZICATI FROM ''SYLVIA''
    G. SCHIRMER, INC.   .50
DELIBES, L.   3
  PIZZICATI--BALLET SYLVIA
    VOLKWEIN BROS.   .25
DELIBES, L.   4
  PIZZICATO POLKA
    BELWIN-MILLS PUBLISHING CORPORATION   81   .60
DELIBES, L.   3
  SYLVIA -- PIZZICATI
    SCHOTT   0887 1/2   1.00
DELIBES, L.   DEXGER, H.
  SYLVIA BALLET
    SAM FOX PUBLISHING COMPANY, INC.   1.00
DELIBES, L.   3
  SYLVIA, PIZZICATI
    CENTURY MUSIC PUBLISHING COMPANY, INC. 358   .40

DELIBES, L.   2
  SYLVIA, PIZZICATO, EASY
    CENTURY MUSIC PUBLISHING COMPANY, INC. 2142   .40
DELIBES, L.
  VALSE LENTE FROM ''COPPELIA''
    G. SCHIRMER, INC.   .40
DELIBES, L.
  VALSE LENTE FROM ''SYLVIA''
    G. SCHIRMER, INC.   .50
DELIBES, L.   SCHAUM, J.   3
  VALSE LENTE FROM 'COPPELIA'
    BELWIN-MILLS PUBLISHING CORPORATION   .50
DELIBES, L.   4
  VALSE LENTE, COPPELIA
    CENTURY MUSIC PUBLISHING COMPANY, INC.   591   .40
DELIBES, L.   ROLFE, W.   2
  VALSE LENTE, NAILA, EASY
    CENTURY MUSIC PUBLISHING COMPANY, INC. 3547   .40
DELIOUX
  BOHEMIENS, LES
    FRANCO COLOMBO PUBLICATIONS   SAL   2.50
DELIOUX   6
  MARCH HONGROISE OP. 14
    THEODORE PRESSER COMPANY   .50
DELIUS, F.   FENBY
  AIR AND DANCE
    BOOSEY AND HAWKES, INC.   .60
DELIUS, F.   PERRY
  CALINDA, FROM 'KOANGA'
    BOOSEY AND HAWKES, INC.   1.00
DELIUS, F.
  DANCE FOR HARPSICHORD
    BOOSEY AND HAWKES, INC.   .50
DELIUS, F.   FENBY
  IRMELIN PRELUDE
    BOOSEY AND HAWKES, INC.   1.00
DELIUS, F.
  SERENADE, FROM 'HASSAN'
    BOOSEY AND HAWKES, INC.   .50
DELIUS, F.
  WALK TO THE PARADISE GARDEN, FROM 'A VILLAGE ROMEO AND JULIET'
    BOOSEY AND HAWKES, INC.   .60
DELL'ANNO
  THREE SHORT PIECES
    SOUTHERN MUSIC COMPANY   1.25
DELLO JOIO, N.
  CAPRICCIO ON THE INTERVAL OF A SECOND
    EDWARD B. MARKS MUSIC CORPORATION   02.00
DELLO JOIO, N.
  PRELUDE - TO A YOUNG DANCER
    G. SCHIRMER, INC.   .50
DELLO JOIO, N.
  PRELUDE - TO A YOUNG MUSICIAN
    G. SCHIRMER, INC.   .60
DELLO JOIO, N.
  SONATA NO. 02
    G. SCHIRMER, INC.   1.50
DELLO JOIO, N.
  SUITE FOR PIANO
    G. SCHIRMER, INC.   .80
DELLO JOIO, N.
  SUITE FROM THE BALLET 'ON STAGE'
    G. SCHIRMER, INC.   1.25
DELUGG *
  FRANTIC FOR FIVE
    MCA MUSIC   1.00
DELUNE
  A DOS D'ANE -- NO. 3, FROM FIVE EASY PIECES
    ASSOCIATED MUSIC PUBLISHERS, INC.   ESC   .90
DELUNE
  AUTOMOBILE -- NO. 1, FROM FIVE EASY PIECES
    ASSOCIATED MUSIC PUBLISHERS, INC.   ESC   .75
DELUNE
  CHEVRIER QUI PASSE, LE -- NO. 4, FROM FIVE EASY PIECES
    ASSOCIATED MUSIC PUBLISHERS, INC.   ESC   .40
DELUNE
  GRACIEUSEMENT. WALTZ -- NO. 2, FROM FIVE EASY PIECES
    ASSOCIATED MUSIC PUBLISHERS, INC.   ESC   .50
DELUNE
  SENORITA CONCHITA, LA -- NO. 5, FROM FIVE PIECES
    ASSOCIATED MUSIC PUBLISHERS, INC.   ESC   .60
DEMARQUEZ
  SONATINA
    FRANCO COLOMBO PUBLICATIONS   SAL   4.00
DEMENASCE, J.   A
  SONATINA NO. 02
    THEODORE PRESSER COMPANY   1.00
DEMENASCE, J.   A
  SONATINA NO. 03
    THEODORE PRESSER COMPANY   1.50
DEMIERRE
  PAGES ENFANTINES - CANTILENE AND PETIT FRERE S'ENDORT
    FRANCO COLOMBO PUBLICATIONS   SAL   1.50
DEMIERRE
  PAGES ENFANTINES - PETIT CANON AND POUR NOEL
    FRANCO COLOMBO PUBLICATIONS   SAL   1.50
DEMIERRE
  RYTHMES ET JEUX
    FRANCO COLOMBO PUBLICATIONS   SAL   3.50
DEMIERRE
  TWENTY-FOUR PRELUDES IN ALL THE MAJOR AND MINOR KEYS -
  CLAIRIERES
    FRANCO COLOMBO PUBLICATIONS   SAL   1.50
DEMIERRE
  TWENTY-FOUR PRELUDES IN ALL THE MAJOR AND MINOR KEYS - ESCAPADE
    FRANCO COLOMBO PUBLICATIONS   SAL   1.50
DEMIERRE
  TWENTY-FOUR PRELUDES IN ALL THE MAJOR AND MINOR KEYS - PETITS
  BERGERS
    FRANCO COLOMBO PUBLICATIONS   SAL   1.50
DENARD   4
  SPIRIT OF OUR BOYS
    VOLKWEIN BROS.   .40
DENEE
  VALSE IN C MAJOR
    ASHLEY DEALERS SERVICE, INC.   ES   .95
DENNEE   3
  DANSE MODERNE, OP. 9 NO. 1
    BOSTON MUSIC COMPANY   .50
DENNEE   3
  TARANTELLA IN A MINOR
    BOSTON MUSIC COMPANY   .75
DENNEE   3
  TARANTELLE
    CENTURY MUSIC PUBLISHING COMPANY, INC. 4324   .40

DENZA   CLAUSETTI
  FUNICULI-FUNICULA
    FRANCO COLOMBO PUBLICATIONS   47171   .60
DENZA   DEL MAGLIO
  FUNICULI-FUNICULA
    FRANCO COLOMBO PUBLICATIONS   124716   .60
DENZA   WEYBRIGHT
  FUNICULI-FUNICULA -- SIMP.
    BELWIN-MILLS PUBLISHING CORPORATION   26015   .50
DENZA   DEL MAGLIO
  SE
    FRANCO COLOMBO PUBLICATIONS   128138   .50
DENZA
  SI VOUS L'AVIEZ COMPRIS
    FRANCO COLOMBO PUBLICATIONS   120713   .60
DEPPEN
  DANCE OF THE ROBINS
    SAM FOX PUBLISHING COMPANY, INC.   .75
DEPPEN
  DANCE OF THE ROBINS
    SOUTHERN MUSIC COMPANY   .75
DEPPEN
  JAPANESE SUNSET, A
    SAM FOX PUBLISHING COMPANY, INC.   .75
DEPPEN
  JAPANESE SUNSET, A
    SOUTHERN MUSIC COMPANY   .75
DEPRET, M.   3
  AIR DE BALLET
    WILLIS MUSIC COMPANY   .35
DERE
  KRISHNA
    FRANCO COLOMBO PUBLICATIONS   SAL   4.00
DERE
  NIEGE TOMBE, LA
    FRANCO COLOMBO PUBLICATIONS   SAL   1.50
DERKSEN
  BAVARIAN SUITE, OP. 21
    ASSOCIATED MUSIC PUBLISHERS, INC.   B/B   1.50
DERKSEN
  LUSTIGEN FISCHERJUNG'S, DIE -- OP. 23, NO. 2
    ASSOCIATED MUSIC PUBLISHERS, INC.   B/B   .90
DERKSEN
  MATROSENLIEBCHEN, OP. 23, NO. 1 -- POLKA
    ASSOCIATED MUSIC PUBLISHERS, INC.   B/B   .90
DESCARRIES
  TOCCATA
    ASSOCIATED MUSIC PUBLISHERS, INC.   BER   1.00
DESCAVES, L. *
  NOUVELLE METHODE, LE COUPPEY
    GERARD BILLAUDOT EDITIONS MUSICALES   3.50
DESCHAMPS, J.
  DOUDOU CHIEN SAVANT
    GERARD BILLAUDOT EDITIONS MUSICALES   1.60
DESDEPI   7
  SONATA
    ALPHONSE LEDUC
DESDEPI
  VARIATIONS ON A CHILDREN'S THEME
    FRANCO COLOMBO PUBLICATIONS   128711   .75
DESENCLOS, A.
  CHANSON DE TROUBADOUR
    ELKAN-VOGEL, INC.   D   .80
DESENCLOS, A.
  SUITE BREVE FOR YOUNG PIANISTS
    ELKAN-VOGEL, INC.   D   3.75
DESOLIS
  ETUDE
    FRANCO COLOMBO PUBLICATIONS   NY1306   .60
DESOLIS
  PIERROT'S SERENADE
    BELWIN-MILLS PUBLISHING CORPORATION   20498   .85
DESOLIS
  PORTRAITS D'ESPAGNE - 1. CADIZ
    FRANCO COLOMBO PUBLICATIONS   NY1303   .75
DESOLIS
  PORTRAITS D'ESPAGNE - 2. MADRID
    FRANCO COLOMBO PUBLICATIONS   NY1304   .75
DESOLIS
  PORTRAITS D'ESPAGNE - 3. SEVILLA
    FRANCO COLOMBO PUBLICATIONS   NY1305   1.00
DESOLIS
  SWANEE RIVER -- THEME, VARIATIONS AND FINALE
    BELWIN-MILLS PUBLISHING CORPORATION   20283   1.00
DESORMES   3
  BOULANGER MARCH
    CENTURY MUSIC PUBLISHING COMPANY, INC.   152   .40
DESORMES   5
  CELEBRE SERENADE DE MANDOLINES
    ALPHONSE LEDUC
DESORMES
  EN REVANT DE LA REVEU
    FRANCO COLOMBO PUBLICATIONS   SAL   1.75
DESORMES
  EN REVANT DE LA REVEU
    FRANCO COLOMBO PUBLICATIONS   SAL   1.50
DESORMES   3
  GENERAL BOULANGER'S MARCH
    CENTURY MUSIC PUBLISHING COMPANY, INC.   152   .40
DESPORTES
  FOIRE AUX CROUTES, LA -- 12 LITTLE TABLEAUX
    ASSOCIATED MUSIC PUBLISHERS, INC.   ESC   6.00
DESREZ   8
  A LA BIEN-AIMEE
    ALPHONSE LEDUC
DESREZ   7
  ETOILE, POEME SYMPHONIQUE
    ALPHONSE LEDUC
DESREZ   8
  L'APPEL DU PRINTEMPS, SYMPHONIE
    ALPHONSE LEDUC
DESREZ   7
  QUATRE VARIATIONS SUR UN THEME DE 'PRINTEMPS'
    ALPHONSE LEDUC
DESSAGNES   M
  SONATINE HELLENIQUE
    C. F. PETERS CORPORATION   C437   3.00
DESSAGNES
  TOCCATA
    DELRIEU ET CIE.   2.75
DESSAU
  SONATINA -- 1955 --
    ASSOCIATED MUSIC PUBLISHERS, INC.   B/H   1.75
DESSAUX   5
  BIJOUX CHERIS, PETITE VALSE
    ALPHONSE LEDUC

DESSAUX   2
  BIJOUX CHERIS, PETITE VALSE -- SIMPLIFIED VERSION
    ALPHONSE LEDUC
DESSAUX   5
  BUCEPHALE, PREMIER GALOP
    ALPHONSE LEDUC
DESSAUX   3
  BUCEPHALE, PREMIER GALOP -- SIMPLIFIED VERSION
    ALPHONSE LEDUC
DESSAUX
  DERBY, LE -- GALOP --
    FRANCO COLOMBO PUBLICATIONS   SAL   2.00
DESSAUX
  FLEUR D'ETE -- POLKA --
    FRANCO COLOMBO PUBLICATIONS   SAL   1.75
DESSAUX   5
  GENTILLE A CROQUER, PETITE POLKA
    ALPHONSE LEDUC
DESSAUX   2
  LE PETIT BAISER, VALSE MIGNINNE
    ALPHONSE LEDUC
DESSAUX   1
  LE PETIT BAISER, VALSE MIGNONNE -- SIMPLIFIED VERSION
    ALPHONSE LEDUC
DESSAUX   3
  LE PETIT BOUQUET, POLKA-MAZURKA MIGNONNE
    ALPHONSE LEDUC
DESSAUX   2
  LES PETITS POLKEURS, POLKA MIGNONNE
    ALPHONSE LEDUC
DESSAUX   4
  REVE DE PRINTEMPS, MAZURKA
    ALPHONSE LEDUC
DETT, N.
  JUBA
    SUMMY-BIRCHARD COMPANY   .75
DETT, R.
  MADRIGAL DIVINE
    BELWIN-MILLS PUBLISHING CORPORATION   20155   .85
DEUTSCH
  PLAY FIDDLE PLAY
    EDWARD B. MARKS MUSIC CORPORATION   01.00
DEUTSCH *
  HI-LILI, HI-LO
    THE BIG THREE MUSIC CORPORATION   00.95
DEWDNEY, J. H.
  ORIENTAL SONG
    FREDERICK HARRIS MUSIC COMPANY   .60
DI CURTIS   2
  COME BACK TO SORRENTO
    CENTURY MUSIC PUBLISHING COMPANY, INC.   3617   .40
DI MAJO, G.   5
  CAPRICHOS - 1959
    SCHOTT   5099   2.00
DI MARTINO
  TOCCATA
    FRANCO COLOMBO PUBLICATIONS   DS892   1.75
DIABELLI
  ALLEGRETTO IN C
    FREDERICK HARRIS MUSIC COMPANY   .60
DIABELLI
  RONDO IN C
    FREDERICK HARRIS MUSIC COMPANY   .60
DIAMOND, D.
  GAMBIT
    PEER SOUTHERN ORGANIZATION   01.00
DIAMOND, D.
  MYRIOLOGUE
    PEER SOUTHERN ORGANIZATION   01.50
DIAMOND, D.
  SONATA
    PEER SOUTHERN ORGANIZATION   04.50
DIAMOND, D.   MD
  SONATINA
    THEODORE PRESSER COMPANY   1.00
DIBDIN
  FESTIVAL GROUPS FOR PIANO SELECTED BY ARTHUR BENJAMIN, SERIES 1
  -- COUNTRY DANCE
    BOOSEY AND HAWKES, INC.   .60
DICAPUA   ZEPP   4
  MY LOVE FOR YOU
    PRO-ART PUBLICATIONS, INC.   109   .50
DICAPUA   KALBERT   2
  O SOLE MIO
    BOSTON MUSIC COMPANY   .50
DICAPUA   ROGERS   2
  O SOLE MIO, SIMPLIFIED
    BELWIN-MILLS PUBLISHING CORPORATION   709   .60
DICAPUA   3
  O, SOLE MIO
    CENTURY MUSIC PUBLISHING COMPANY, INC.   1807   .40
DICAPUA   3
  O, SOLE MIO
    CENTURY MUSIC PUBLISHING COMPANY, INC.   3701   .40
DICHIARI   JETSON, I. H.   2
  LA SPAGNOLA
    VOLKWEIN BROS.   .35
DICHLER
  TOCCATA -- ETUDE
    ASSOCIATED MUSIC PUBLISHERS, INC.   DOB   1.00
DICK, M.
  SUITE FOR PIANO
    COMPOSERS AUTOGRAPH PUBLICATIONS   6.60
DICKS, E. A.
  CONCERT STUDY ON THE 'SAILORS HORNPIPE'
    FREDERICK HARRIS MUSIC COMPANY   .90
DIEMENTE, E.   2
  HAPPY WALTZ, A
    THEODORE PRESSER COMPANY   .50
DIEMENTE, E.   MD
  REGINA COELI -- QUEEN OF HEAVEN
    THEODORE PRESSER COMPANY   .50
DIEMENTE, E.   2
  RESTLESS MOTION
    THEODORE PRESSER COMPANY   .50
DIEMENTE, E.   M
  SALVE REGINA -- HAIL, HOLY QUEEN
    THEODORE PRESSER COMPANY   .50
DIEMER
  GAVOTTE
    BOOSEY AND HAWKES, INC.   .50
DIEMER
  GIGUE
    BOOSEY AND HAWKES, INC.   .50
DIEMER
  INVENTION
    BOOSEY AND HAWKES, INC.   .50

DIEMER
    SERENADE
        BOOSEY AND HAWKES, INC.   .50
DIERCKS
    SUITE NO. 1
        MCA MUSIC   2.00
DIERCKS
    THEME AND VARIATIONS
        COMPOSERS AUTOGRAPH PUBLICATIONS   3.96
                                                    D
DIETHELM
    SONATA NO. 07
        C. F. PETERS CORPORATION   N6213   2.00
                                                    M
DIETHELM
    SONATA NO. 09
        C. F. PETERS CORPORATION   N1183   2.00
                                                    2
DIETRICH
    BY THE CRADLE
        PRO-ART PUBLICATIONS, INC.   55   .50
DIETRICH
    LAVENDEL-FUGE
        ASSOCIATED MUSIC PUBLISHERS, INC.   DOB   1.50
                                                    2
DIETRICH
    STUBBORN DONKEY
        PRO-ART PUBLICATIONS, INC.   54   .50
                                                    2
DIETS, J.
    GOOSE CHASE -- THE GALOP
        VOLKWEIN BROS.   .30
                                                    2
DIETS, J.
    IN SHADY NOOK, REVERIE
        VOLKWEIN BROS.   .25
                                                    2
DIETS, J.
    LITTLE DANCING MASTER
        VOLKWEIN BROS.   .30
                                                    2
DIETS, J.
    MOONLIGHT DANCE WALTZ
        VOLKWEIN BROS.   .25
                                                    2
DIETS, J.
    RING AROUND WALTZ
        VOLKWEIN BROS.   .30
DIETZ *   LEVINE
    LOUISIANA HAYRIDE
        WARNER BROTHERS PUBLISHERS   1.00
                                                    E
DIJK, VAN
    PARTITA. HARPSICHORD
        C. F. PETERS CORPORATION   D457   2.00
                                                    GRADE 1
DILLER, A.
    IN DAYS OF OLD--AUGUSTIN
        G. SCHIRMER, INC.   .40
                                                    GRADE 1
DILLER, A.
    IN DAYS OF OLD--GOSSIP JOAN
        G. SCHIRMER, INC.   .40
                                                    GRADE 1
DILLER, A.
    IN DAYS OF OLD--REAP THE FLAX
        G. SCHIRMER, INC.   .35
                                                    GRADE 1
DILLER, A.
    IN DAYS OF OLD--THE JUDGE'S DANCE
        G. SCHIRMER, INC.   .35
DILLER, A.
    MARCH OF THE THREE KINGS--AIRS AND DANCES OF THE 18TH CENTURY
        G. SCHIRMER, INC.   .35
DILLER, A.   SMITH
    STAR-SPANGLED BANNER, THE--ARR. IN A FLAT AND B FLAT
        G. SCHIRMER, INC.   .60
DILLER, A.   SMITH   GRADE 2
    STAR-SPANGLED BANNER, THE--ARR. IN G
        G. SCHIRMER, INC.   .40
                                          GRADE 2
DILLER, A.
    STORY OF SIEGFRIED, THE
        G. SCHIRMER, INC.   1.00
                                          D
DILLON, F.
    BUTTERFLY WINGS
        COMPOSERS PRESS, INC.   1.00
                                          D
DILLON, F.
    CHINESE TEMPLE SCENE
        COMPOSERS PRESS, INC.   1.00
                                          M
DILLON, F.
    WINTER MOONLIGHT
        COMPOSERS PRESS, INC.   1.00
                                          4
DILSNER
    BOLANGO
        BELWIN-MILLS PUBLISHING CORPORATION   .60
                                          2-3
DILSNER
    BOUREE A LA BAGATELLE
        PRO-ART PUBLICATIONS, INC.   383   .50
                                          3
DILSNER
    MINOR MOODS FOR MODERNS
        BOSTON MUSIC COMPANY   .50
                                          2-3
DILSNER
    PETITE GAVOTTE - MUSETTE
        PRO-ART PUBLICATIONS, INC.   365   .50
                                          1-2
DILSNER
    PORPOISES ON PARADE
        PRO-ART PUBLICATIONS, INC.   524   .50
                                          2-3
DILSNER
    TUMBLEWEED
        PRO-ART PUBLICATIONS, INC.   569   .50
DINICU *
    HORA STACCATO
        CARL FISCHER, INC.   P 2380   .80
DIONISI
    MOVIMENTI
        FRANCO COLOMBO PUBLICATIONS   Z4746   2.25
DITTENHAVER
    ABOARD THE SANTE FE
        BRODT MUSIC COMPANY   .50
DITTENHAVER
    AND AWAY WE GO
        BRODT MUSIC COMPANY   .35
DITTENHAVER
    APPALACHIAN REVERIE
        NEIL A. KJOS MUSIC COMPANY   119   1.00
DITTENHAVER
    AT THE COUNTY FAIR
        WARNER BROTHERS PUBLISHERS   .60
DITTENHAVER
    AT THE CRAFTMAN'S FAIR
        BRODT MUSIC COMPANY   .45
DITTENHAVER
    BEAR AND THE OPOSSUM, THE
        BRODT MUSIC COMPANY   .35
DITTENHAVER   1
    BICYCLE TUNE
        BELWIN-MILLS PUBLISHING CORPORATION   .60
DITTENHAVER
    CANOE SONG
        BRODT MUSIC COMPANY   .35

DITTENHAVER   2
    CAROLINA CAKEWALK
        CENTURY MUSIC PUBLISHING COMPANY, INC.   4406   .40
DITTENHAVER
    CASTLE IN THE SAND
        BRODT MUSIC COMPANY   .35
DITTENHAVER
    CHEROKEE BRAVES
        BRODT MUSIC COMPANY   .45
DITTENHAVER
    CHIEF SOARING EAGLE
        BRODT MUSIC COMPANY   .40
DITTENHAVER
    CIRCUS DAY
        NEIL A. KJOS MUSIC COMPANY   120   .50
DITTENHAVER   4 1/2
    CRAGGY GARDENS IN THE SPRING
        BELWIN-MILLS PUBLISHING CORPORATION   .60
DITTENHAVER
    DANCING IN THE WIND
        BRODT MUSIC COMPANY   .35
DITTENHAVER   2
    DREAM WALTZ
        BELWIN-MILLS PUBLISHING CORPORATION   .60
DITTENHAVER
    GALLOPING
        BRODT MUSIC COMPANY   .40
DITTENHAVER
    GENTLE FLIGHT
        EDWARD B. MARKS MUSIC CORPORATION   00.60
DITTENHAVER   2
    HIDE THE THIMBLE
        CENTURY MUSIC PUBLISHING COMPANY, INC.   034   .40
DITTENHAVER
    IN A LOG CABIN
        BRODT MUSIC COMPANY   .35
DITTENHAVER   1
    IN MOMMY'S HIGH HEELS
        CENTURY MUSIC PUBLISHING COMPANY, INC.   4343   .40
DITTENHAVER
    IN THE CASTLE GARDEN
        BRODT MUSIC COMPANY   .45
DITTENHAVER
    IN THE SWISS ALPS
        BRODT MUSIC COMPANY   .35
DITTENHAVER   2
    KITE STORY, A
        CENTURY MUSIC PUBLISHING COMPANY, INC.   035   .40
DITTENHAVER
    LAMBS IN THE VALLEY
        BRODT MUSIC COMPANY   .35
DITTENHAVER
    LITTLE DANCER, THE
        BRODT MUSIC COMPANY   .35
DITTENHAVER
    LITTLE ELF, THE
        BRODT MUSIC COMPANY   .40
DITTENHAVER
    LITTLE JOURNEY
        BRODT MUSIC COMPANY   .45
DITTENHAVER   2
    LYRIC TO THE MOON
        BELWIN-MILLS PUBLISHING CORPORATION   .60
DITTENHAVER
    MAN IN THE MOON, THE
        BRODT MUSIC COMPANY   .40
DITTENHAVER
    MARCH OF THE ASTRONAUTS
        EDWARD B. MARKS MUSIC CORPORATION   00.60
DITTENHAVER   2
    MARDI GRAS
        BELWIN-MILLS PUBLISHING CORPORATION   .60
DITTENHAVER
    MARINES ON PARADE
        BRODT MUSIC COMPANY   .40
DITTENHAVER
    MIMOSA WALTZ
        BRODT MUSIC COMPANY   .35
DITTENHAVER   4 1/2
    MOONLIGHT IN SANTA MARIA
        BELWIN-MILLS PUBLISHING CORPORATION   .60
DITTENHAVER   1
    MORNING IN THE HILLS
        BELWIN-MILLS PUBLISHING CORPORATION   .60
DITTENHAVER
    MOTHER, SHAKE THE CHERRY TREE
        BRODT MUSIC COMPANY   .35
DITTENHAVER
    MY DOG RUSTY
        BRODT MUSIC COMPANY   .35
DITTENHAVER
    MY GIFT
        BRODT MUSIC COMPANY   .35
DITTENHAVER
    NEIGHBORHOOD CIRCUS
        BRODT MUSIC COMPANY   .40
DITTENHAVER
    NOSEGAY
        BRODT MUSIC COMPANY   .35
DITTENHAVER   3
    ON A QUIET SHORE
        CENTURY MUSIC PUBLISHING COMPANY, INC.   036   .40
DITTENHAVER
    ON THE RIVER BOAT
        BRODT MUSIC COMPANY   .40
DITTENHAVER
    PIPER PLAYS A TUNE, THE
        BRODT MUSIC COMPANY   .35
DITTENHAVER
    RAIN DROPS ARE WALTZING
        BRODT MUSIC COMPANY   .40
DITTENHAVER
    RIDE-A-COCK HORSE
        BRODT MUSIC COMPANY   .35
DITTENHAVER
    RING-A-RING
        BRODT MUSIC COMPANY   .40
DITTENHAVER   2
    RIVERSONG
        CENTURY MUSIC PUBLISHING COMPANY, INC.   023   .40
DITTENHAVER   1
    SCOOTER
        CENTURY MUSIC PUBLISHING COMPANY, INC.   010   .40
DITTENHAVER   3
    SILVER SHIP
        CENTURY MUSIC PUBLISHING COMPANY, INC.   037   .40

DITTENHAVER
  SINGING
    BRODT MUSIC COMPANY   .35
DITTENHAVER
  SLEEPY WIND
    BRODT MUSIC COMPANY   .45
DITTENHAVER
  SNOW-WHITE PONY
    BRODT MUSIC COMPANY   .45
DITTENHAVER   1 1/2
  SOCO GAP SQUARE DANCE
    THEODORE PRESSER COMPANY   .50
DITTENHAVER
  SPRING BREEZES
    NEIL A. KJOS MUSIC COMPANY   122   .50
DITTENHAVER
  STARLIGHT LULLABY
    EDWARD B. MARKS MUSIC CORPORATION   00.60
DITTENHAVER
  STRANGE PARTY, A
    BRODT MUSIC COMPANY   .40
DITTENHAVER
  SUNRISE CANTER
    EDWARD B. MARKS MUSIC CORPORATION   00.60
DITTENHAVER
  SUSAN BLUE
    BRODT MUSIC COMPANY   .35
DITTENHAVER   2 1/2
  TOCCATA IN D MINOR
    WILLIS MUSIC COMPANY   .40
DITTENHAVER
  UNDER THE TENT OF THE SKY
    BRODT MUSIC COMPANY   .40
DITTENHAVER
  WALTZ OF THE DREAM FAIRY
    BRODT MUSIC COMPANY   .35
DITTENHAVER
  WALTZING AT SUNDOWN
    EDWARD B. MARKS MUSIC CORPORATION   00.60
DITTENHAVER   1
  WANDERING MINSTREL
    THEODORE PRESSER COMPANY   .50
DITTENHAVER
  WHEN I GO WALKING
    BRODT MUSIC COMPANY   .40
DITTENHAVER   2
  WHERE GO THE CLOUDS
    BELWIN-MILLS PUBLISHING CORPORATION   .60
DITTENHAVER
  WHIRLING DANCERS
    NEIL A. KJOS MUSIC COMPANY   121   .50
DITTENHAVER   1
  WOODPECKER, THE
    CENTURY MUSIC PUBLISHING COMPANY, INC. 4342   .40
DITTERSDORF, K.D. VON   5
  ENGLISH DANCES
    LEE ROBERTS MUSIC PUBLICATIONS, INC.   .50
DIVERNOIS, J. P.   4
  GENTLE BREEZES
    VOLKWEIN BROS.   .30
DIVERNOIS, J. P.   4
  MARGARET POLKA
    VOLKWEIN BROS.   .50
DJEMIL, E.
  PETITE SUITE BRIOCHINE
    ELKAN-VOGEL, INC.   CON   4.00
DOBROWEN, I.
  BALLADE, OP. 9
    UNIVERSAL EDITION   UE 7323   1.10
DOBROWEN, I.
  IMPROMPTU, OP. 14
    UNIVERSAL EDITION   UE 7368   1.10
DOBROWEN, I.
  JUGENDSONATA, OP. 5
    UNIVERSAL EDITION   UE 8184   1.80
DOBROWEN, I.
  MAZURKAS, OP. 4 AND OP. 11
    UNIVERSAL EDITION   UE 7320   1.30
DOBROWEN, I.
  SCHERZO, OP. 7
    UNIVERSAL EDITION   UE 8185   1.10
DOHNANYI
  CAPRICCIO IN B MINOR, OP. 2 NO. 4
    EDWARD B. MARKS MUSIC CORPORATION   01.00
DOHNANYI
  CAPRICCIO IN B MINOR, OP. 2, NO. 4 -- FROM FOUR PIECES
    ASSOCIATED MUSIC PUBLISHERS, INC.   DOB   1.50
DOHNANYI
  CAPRICCIO, OP. 28, NO. 6
    KULTURA   1.50
DOHNANYI
  FOUR RHAPSODIES, NO. 1
    EDWIN F. KALMUS   3406   1.50
DOHNANYI
  FOUR RHAPSODIES, NO. 2
    EDWIN F. KALMUS   3407   1.50
DOHNANYI
  FOUR RHAPSODIES, NO. 3
    EDWIN F. KALMUS   3408   1.50
DOHNANYI
  FUGUE -- 1913 -- LEFT HAND/TWO HANDS
    ASSOCIATED MUSIC PUBLISHERS, INC.   AMP   .60
DOHNANYI
  INTERMEZZO IN A MINOR, OP. 2, NO. 2 -- FROM FOUR PIECES
    ASSOCIATED MUSIC PUBLISHERS, INC.   DOB   2.00
DOHNANYI
  INTERMEZZO IN F MINOR, OP. 2, NO. 3 -- FROM FOUR PIECES
    ASSOCIATED MUSIC PUBLISHERS, INC.   DOB   2.00
DOHNANYI
  MARCH HUMORESQUE -- ON A GROUND BASS -- OP. 17, NO. 1
    ASSOCIATED MUSIC PUBLISHERS, INC.   SIM   .75
DOHNANYI
  PASSACAGLIA, OP. 6
    ASSOCIATED MUSIC PUBLISHERS, INC.   DOB   3.50
DOHNANYI
  POSTLUDIUM
    EDWARD B. MARKS MUSIC CORPORATION   01.00
DOHNANYI
  RHAPSODY IN C, OP. 11 NO. 3
    ASSOCIATED MUSIC PUBLISHERS, INC.   DOB   2.50
DOHNANYI
  RHAPSODY IN E FLAT MINOR, OP. 11 NO. 4
    ASSOCIATED MUSIC PUBLISHERS, INC.   DOB   2.50
DOHNANYI
  RHAPSODY IN F SHARP MINOR, OP. 11 NO. 2
    ASSOCIATED MUSIC PUBLISHERS, INC.   DOB   2.50

DOHNANYI
  RHAPSODY IN F SHARP MINOR, OP. 11 NO. 2
    EDWARD B. MARKS MUSIC CORPORATION   01.00
DOHNANYI
  RHAPSODY IN G MINOR, OP. 11 NO. 1
    ASSOCIATED MUSIC PUBLISHERS, INC.   DOB   2.25
DOHNANYI
  RHAPSODY IN G MINOR, OP. 11 NO. 1
    EDWARD B. MARKS MUSIC CORPORATION   01.00
DOHNANYI
  RURALIA HUNGARICA, OP. 32A
    KULTURA   2.75
DOHNANYI
  SCHERZO IN C SHARP MINOR, OP. 2 NO. 1 -- FROM FOUR PIECES
    ASSOCIATED MUSIC PUBLISHERS, INC.   DOB   1.75
DOHNANYI   BLASSER
  WEDDING-WALTZ FROM ''DER SCHLEIER DER PIERETTE'' -- SIMPLIFIED
  VERSION
    ASSOCIATED MUSIC PUBLISHERS, INC.   DOB   1.25
DOIGE   4-5
  FILIGREE
    PRO-ART PUBLICATIONS, INC.   414   .50
DOIGE   1
  HOUSE IN THE TREE, A
    PRO-ART PUBLICATIONS, INC.   443   .50
DOIGE   1
  I'M AN EDUCATED DOG
    PRO-ART PUBLICATIONS, INC.   456   .50
DOIGE   2-3
  REFLECTION
    PRO-ART PUBLICATIONS, INC.   452   .50
DOIGE   1-2
  RUMPUS ROOM RUMBA
    PRO-ART PUBLICATIONS, INC.   453   .50
DOIGE   2
  SHOESTRING WALTZ
    PRO-ART PUBLICATIONS, INC.   451   .50
DOLGOW, R.   3 - 4
  BASSO OSTINATO
    BOSTON MUSIC COMPANY   .75
DOLIN
  LITTLE TOCCATA
    ASSOCIATED MUSIC PUBLISHERS, INC.   BER   .75
DOLIN
  SLIGHTLY SQUARE ROUND DANCE
    ASSOCIATED MUSIC PUBLISHERS, INC.   BER   .40
DOLIN
  SONATINA
    ASSOCIATED MUSIC PUBLISHERS, INC.   BER   .40
DOLMETCH   5
  VALSE LENTE NO. 02
    CENTURY MUSIC PUBLISHING COMPANY, INC. 1106   .40
DONATO, A.   2 1/2
  NORTHERN LIGHTS
    THEODORE PRESSER COMPANY   .50
DONATO, A.   3
  PAINT BOX, THE
    THEODORE PRESSER COMPANY   .50
DONATO, A.   3
  ROCK CRUSHER
    BELWIN-MILLS PUBLISHING CORPORATION   .60
DONATO, A.   2 1/2
  WISTFUL LITTLE PRINCESS, THE
    THEODORE PRESSER COMPANY   .50
DONENFELD, J.   2
  ANGELICA
    PRO-ART PUBLICATIONS, INC.   475   .50
DONENFELD, J.   3-4
  CONCERTINO
    PRO-ART PUBLICATIONS, INC.   478   .50
DONENFELD, J.   2
  DANCING BELLS
    BELWIN-MILLS PUBLISHING CORPORATION   .60
DONENFELD, J.   3
  GHOST TOWN
    PRO-ART PUBLICATIONS, INC.   477   .50
DONENFELD, J.   1
  LULLABY AND WALTZ
    PRO-ART PUBLICATIONS, INC.   126   .50
DONENFELD, J.   2
  MAZURKA
    BOSTON MUSIC COMPANY   .50
DONENFELD, J.   2
  MELANCHOLY MAZURKA
    PRO-ART PUBLICATIONS, INC.   501   .50
DONENFELD, J.
  MONKEYSHINES
    G. SCHIRMER, INC.   .40
DONENFELD, J.   1
  OOM PAH-PAH WALTZ
    BELWIN-MILLS PUBLISHING CORPORATION   .60
DONENFELD, J.   3
  PEPITA
    PRO-ART PUBLICATIONS, INC.   454   .50
DONENFELD, J.   2
  RODEO RIDER
    PRO-ART PUBLICATIONS, INC.   528   .50
DONENFELD, J.   2
  TAMBOURINE DANCE
    BOSTON MUSIC COMPANY   .50
DONENFELD, J.
  WALTZING FLAMINGO, THE
    G. SCHIRMER, INC.   .35
DONENFELD, J.   2
  WALTZING GIRAFFE, THE
    PRO-ART PUBLICATIONS, INC.   215   .50
DONENFELD, J.   2
  WESTERN WALTZ
    BELWIN-MILLS PUBLISHING CORPORATION   .60
DONENFELD, J.   3
  WHISTLIN' TUNE
    PRO-ART PUBLICATIONS, INC.   476   .50
DONENFELD, J.
  YOUNG AMERICANS
    G. SCHIRMER, INC.   .50
DONIDA   HASTINGS
  AL DI LA
    WARNER BROTHERS PUBLISHERS   1.00
DONIDA   SAMPIETRO   FIRST YEAR
  AL DI LA
    WARNER BROTHERS PUBLISHERS   .75
DONIDA *   NEALE, J.   EASY
  AL DI LA
    WARNER BROTHERS PUBLISHERS   .75

DONIZETTI　　　　　　　LESCHETIZKY
  ANDANTE FINALE FROM ''LUCIA DI LAMMERMOOR''--FOR LEFT HAND ALONE
    G. SCHIRMER, INC.　　　　　　　　　　　　　　　　　　.60
DONIZETTI
  DON PASQUALE, OVERTURE
    FRANCO COLOMBO PUBLICATIONS　　　　　　128623　　1.00
DONIZETTI
  ELISIR D'AMORE, L' - FURTIVA LAGRIMA, UNA
    FRANCO COLOMBO PUBLICATIONS　　　　　　125429　　.60
DONIZETTI　　　　　　　DEL MAGLIO
  ELISIR D'AMORE, L' - FURTIVA LAGRIMA, UNA
    FRANCO COLOMBO PUBLICATIONS　　　　　　128146　　.60
DONIZETTI　　　　　　　CHIESA
  ELISIR D'AMORE, L', EASY FANTASIA
    FRANCO COLOMBO PUBLICATIONS　　　　　　107496　　.50
DONIZETTI　　　　　　　CHIESA
  FAVORITA, LA - EASY FANTASIA
    FRANCO COLOMBO PUBLICATIONS　　　　　　107508　　.50
DONIZETTI　　　　　　　CHIESA
  LINDA DI CHAMONIX - EASY FANTASIA
    FRANCO COLOMBO PUBLICATIONS　　　　　　107504　　.50
DONIZETTI　　　　　　　LEYBACH, I.　　　5
  LUCIA DI LAMMERMOOR
    CENTURY MUSIC PUBLISHING COMPANY, INC.　1178　　.40
DONIZETTI　　　　　　　KRUG　　　　　2
  LUCIA DI LAMMERMOOR
    CENTURY MUSIC PUBLISHING COMPANY, INC.　523　　.40
DONIZETTI　　　　　　　CHIESA
  LUCIA DI LAMMERMOOR - EASY FANTASIA
    FRANCO COLOMBO PUBLICATIONS　　　　　　107495　　.50
DONIZETTI　　　　　　　DEL MAGLIO
  LUCIA DI LAMMERMOOR - VERRANNO A TE AND TU CHE A DIO
    FRANCO COLOMBO PUBLICATIONS　　　　　　128120　　.50
DONIZETTI　　　　　　　BOHM　　　　　3
  LUCIA, SEXTETTE
    CENTURY MUSIC PUBLISHING COMPANY, INC.　1183　　.40
DONIZETTI　　　　　　　JESTON, I. H.　　4
  SEXTET -- LUCIA DI LAMMERMOOR
    VOLKWEIN BROS.　　　　　　　　　　　　　　　.35
DONIZETTI　　　　　　　BOHM　　　　　3
  SEXTETTE, LUCIA
    CENTURY MUSIC PUBLISHING COMPANY, INC.　1183　　.40
DONIZETTI　　　　　　　　　　　　　　2
  SEXTETTE, LUCIA, EASY
    CENTURY MUSIC PUBLISHING COMPANY, INC.　2512　　.40
DONIZETTI *　　　　　　REISER, V.　　　6
  LUCIA DI LAMMERMOOR, SEXTETTE
    CENTURY MUSIC PUBLISHING COMPANY, INC.　1860　　.40
DONOSTIA
  MENUET BASQUE
    ASSOCIATED MUSIC PUBLISHERS, INC.　　ESC　　1.10
DONOVAN, R.　　　　　　　　　　　　3
  ADVENTURE
    THEODORE PRESSER COMPANY　　　　　　　　　.50
DOPPELBAUER
  LITTLE SUITE NO. 1
    ASSOCIATED MUSIC PUBLISHERS, INC.　　DOB　　3.00
DORE, L.　　　　　　　　　　　　　4
  BLUE BUTTERFLIES
    CENTURY MUSIC PUBLISHING COMPANY, INC.　2416　　.40
DORN　　　　　　　　　　　　　　3
  TRIPPING THROUGH THE WOODS
    CENTURY MUSIC PUBLISHING COMPANY, INC.　2188　　.40
DOROLLE, A.
  AIRS AND DANCES FROM HARPSICHORD PERIOD
    BOOSEY AND HAWKES, INC.　　　　　　　　　1.25
DOUCET, C.
  MONTPARNASSE
    UNIVERSAL EDITION　　　　　　　　UE 3464　　2.25
DOUCET, C.
  WIENER LUFT
    UNIVERSAL EDITION　　　　　　　　UE 3463　　2.25
DOUGLAS　　　　　　　　　　　　　2
  FOLLOW ME
    BELWIN-MILLS PUBLISHING CORPORATION　　　.60
DOUGLAS　　　　　　　　　　　　　2
  FROM THE ORIENT
    BELWIN-MILLS PUBLISHING CORPORATION　　　.60
DOUGLAS　　　　　　　　　　　　　1
  GENTLE BREEZE
    BELWIN-MILLS PUBLISHING CORPORATION　　　.60
DOUGLAS　　　　　　　　　　　　　2
  ON THE GRAND CANAL
    BOSTON MUSIC COMPANY　　　　　　　　　　.50
DOUGLAS　　　　　　　　　　　　2 1/2
  PIPES OF PAN
    BELWIN-MILLS PUBLISHING CORPORATION　　　.60
DOURY, P.
  PROMENADE ET TOCCATINA
    GERARD BILLAUDOT EDITIONS MUSICALES　　　1.60
DOYEN, J.　　　　　　　　　　　6, 7
  SUITE EN SI
    ALPHONSE LEDUC
DRAGOI
  LITTLE SUITE OF ROUMANIAN FOLK DANCES
    ASSOCIATED MUSIC PUBLISHERS, INC.　　SIM　　1.50
DRAKE *　　　　　　　　SCHAUM, J.　　2 1/2
  I BELIEVE
    SCHAUM PUBLICATIONS, INC.　　　　　　　.75
DRAKE *
  TORNADO
    MCA MUSIC　　　　　　　　　　　　　　1.00
DRAKEFORD, R.　　　　　　　　　　4-5
  HANDFUL OF PLEASANT DELIGHTS, A
    NOVELLO AND COMPANY, LTD.　　10.0032.02　1.15
DRAO　　　　　　　　　　　　　　2
  BOSSA NOVA ROMA
    PRO-ART PUBLICATIONS, INC.　　　　387　　.50
DRAO　　　　　　　　　　　　　　2
  BOSSA NOVA TIME
    PRO-ART PUBLICATIONS, INC.　　　　318　　.50
DRAO　　　　　　　　　　　　　1-2
  SI, SI, BOSSA NOVA
    PRO-ART PUBLICATIONS, INC.　　　　319　　.50
DRAYTON　　　　　　　　　　　　　2
  LITTLE MISCHIEVOUS
    CENTURY MUSIC PUBLISHING COMPANY, INC.　816　　.40
DRDLA, F.　　　　　　　　　　　　4
  SOUVENIR
    BELWIN-MILLS PUBLISHING CORPORATION　87　　.60
DRDLA, F.　　　　　　　　　　　　4
  SOUVENIR
    CENTURY MUSIC PUBLISHING COMPANY, INC.　1856　　.40

DRDLA, F.
  SOUVENIR
    EDWARD B. MARKS MUSIC CORPORATION　　　01.00
DRDLA, F.　　　　　　　PINTER
  SOUVENIR
    G. SCHIRMER, INC.　　　　　　　　　　　.40
DRDLA, F.　　　　　　　　　　　　5
  SOUVENIR
    VOLKWEIN BROS.　　　　　　　　　　　　.25
DREISBACH
  CAROL, A
    ASSOCIATED MUSIC PUBLISHERS, INC.　　AMP　　.35
DRESSER　　　　　　　　ZEPP　　　2-3
  ON THE BANKS OF THE WABASH
    PRO-ART PUBLICATIONS, INC.　　　　230　　.50
DREYSCHOCK
  PHANTASIESTUCK OP. 113
    MUSICA OBSCURA　　　　　　　　　　　2.00
DREYSCHOCK
  RHAPSODIE G MINOR OP. 46
    MUSICA OBSCURA　　　　　　　　　　　2.00
DRIESSLER
  THREE SONATINAS, OP. 29 NO. 2
    BARENREITER VERLAG　　　　　　　BA 2694　　3.25
DRIGO, R.　　　　　　　WEYBRIGHT　　2
  DRIGO SERENADE
    BELWIN-MILLS PUBLISHING CORPORATION　　　.60
DRIGO, R.　　　　　　　　　　　2-3
  HARLEQUIN SERENADE, EASY
    CENTURY MUSIC PUBLISHING COMPANY, INC.　2468　　.40
DRIGO, R.　　　　　　　　　　　　4
  MILLIONS OF HARLEQUIN
    CENTURY MUSIC PUBLISHING COMPANY, INC.　2016　　.40
DRIGO, R.　　　　　　　GROOMS　　　2
  MILLIONS OF HARLEQUIN, EASY
    CENTURY MUSIC PUBLISHING COMPANY, INC.　2468　　.40
DRIGO, R.　　　　　　　　　　　　4
  PIZZICATO, POLKA, MILLIONS OF HARLEQUIN
    CENTURY MUSIC PUBLISHING COMPANY, INC.　2015　　.40
DRIGO, R.
  SERENADE FROM 'L MILIONI D'ARLECCHINO'
    FRANCO COLOMBO PUBLICATIONS　　　BON.148　　.50
DRIGO, R.　　　　　　　　　　　　4
  SERENADE, MILLIONS OF HARLEQUIN
    CENTURY MUSIC PUBLISHING COMPANY, INC.　2016　　.40
DRIGO, P.　　　　　　　THOMPSON, J.　　5
  VALSE BLUETTE
    WILLIS MUSIC COMPANY　　　　　　　　　.50
DRIGO, R.　　　　　　　　　　　　3
  VALSE BLUETTE, AIR DE BALLET
    CENTURY MUSIC PUBLISHING COMPANY, INC.　2002　　.40
DRIGO, R.　　　　　　　RAPEE
  VALSE-BLUETTE
    G. SCHIRMER, INC.　　　　　　　　　　　.50
DRIGO, R. *
  CORSAIRE,LE--PAS DE DEUX--
    GERARD BILLAUDOT EDITIONS MUSICALES　　　2.70
DRING
  LITTLE WAGON, THE
    FRANCO COLOMBO PUBLICATIONS　　　LD491　　.60
DRING
  SOLDIERS PASS, THE
    EDWARD B. MARKS MUSIC CORPORATION　　00.60
DRING
  SONG OF THE BELLS AND HORNPIPE
    EDWARD B. MARKS MUSIC CORPORATION　　00.60
DRING
  SPRING MORNING AND LITTLE MINUET
    EDWARD B. MARKS MUSIC CORPORATION　　00.60
DRING, M.　　　　　　　　　　　　E
  UP AND AWAY
    OXFORD UNIVERSITY PRESS　　　　33.066　　1.30
DRISCHNER　　　　　　　　　　　E-M
  CHORAL FANTASY ON 'LOBET DEN HERRN'
    C. F. PETERS CORPORATION　　　　VP153　　1.50
DRIVER, P.　　　　　　　　　　　　6
  ARABESQUE
    NOVELLO AND COMPANY, LTD.　　55.0018.04　.25
DRIVER, P.　　　　　　　　　　　　4
  FOUNTAIN, THE
    NOVELLO AND COMPANY, LTD.　　55.0043.05　.25
DRIVER, P.　　　　　　　　　　　　1
  SONG OF THE FLOWER
    NOVELLO AND COMPANY, LTD.　　55.0020.06　.25
DRUMHELLER　　　　　　　　　　　4
  BEAUTIFUL STAR OF HEAVEN
    VOLKWEIN BROS.　　　　　　　　　　　　.60
DRUMHELLER　　　　　　　　　　　4
  GRAND IMPERIAL MARCH
    CENTURY MUSIC PUBLISHING COMPANY, INC.　1386　　.40
DRUMHELLER　　　　　　　　　　　4-5
  LISTEN TO THE MOCKING BIRD -- VARIATION
    VOLKWEIN BROS.　　　　　　　　　　　　.50
DRUMHELLER　　　　　　　　　　　4
  LOVE AND DEVOTION
    VOLKWEIN BROS.　　　　　　　　　　　　.50
DRUMHELLER　　　　　　　　　　　4
  LOVE'S GOLDEN STAR
    VOLKWEIN BROS.　　　　　　　　　　　　.50
DRUMHELLER　　　　　　　　　　　4-5
  NEARER MY GOD TO THEE
    VOLKWEIN BROS.　　　　　　　　　　　　.50
DRUMHELLER　　　　　　　　　　　4-5
  OLD OAKEN BUCKET -- VARIATIONS
    VOLKWEIN BROS.　　　　　　　　　　　　.50
DRUMHELLER　　　　　　　　　　　4
  SILVER TRAY, CAPRICE
    CENTURY MUSIC PUBLISHING COMPANY, INC.　1387　　.40
DRUMHELLER　　　　　　　　　　　4-5
  SWEET BYE AND BYE VARIATIONS
    VOLKWEIN BROS.　　　　　　　　　　　　.50
DRUMHELLER　　　　　　　　　　　4
  SWEET SUSPENSE
    VOLKWEIN BROS.　　　　　　　　　　　　.50
DRUMHELLER　　　　　　　　　　　3
  TEXAS GALOP
    CENTURY MUSIC PUBLISHING COMPANY, INC.　1388　　.40
DRUMHELLER　　　　　　　　　　　4-5
  WHEN YOU AND I WERE YOUNG MAGGIE -- VARIATIONS
    VOLKWEIN BROS.　　　　　　　　　　　　.50
DRUMHELLER　　　　　　　　　　　4
  WHERE MEMORY DWELLS
    VOLKWEIN BROS.　　　　　　　　　　　　.50
DRYE, S. L.
  INTERMEZZO
    BRODT MUSIC COMPANY　　　　　　　　　.50

DRYE, S. L.
SKETCHES IN A MINOR
BRODT MUSIC COMPANY .50
DRYE, S. L.
TOCCATA
BRODT MUSIC COMPANY .50
DUBENSKY
REFLECTIONS ON THE WATER, OP. 5
FRANCO COLOMBO PUBLICATIONS NY1302 .75
DUBOIS
AU PAYS TOURANGEAU
FRANCO COLOMBO PUBLICATIONS SAL 4.00
DUBOIS
POUR ANNE
ELKAN-VOGEL, INC. RR 1.20
DUBOIS, P. M. 6
ARLEQUIN ET PANTALON
ALPHONSE LEDUC
DUBOIS, P. M. 8
FANTAISIE DE CONCERT
ALPHONSE LEDUC
DUBOIS, P. M. 5
HOMMAGE A POULENC
ALPHONSE LEDUC
DUBOIS, P. M. 5
LES FOUS DE BASSAN
ALPHONSE LEDUC
DUBOIS, P. M.
PARTITA -- HARPSICHORD/PIANO
ASSOCIATED MUSIC PUBLISHERS, INC. ESC 3.50
DUBOIS, P. M. 8
POUR LES BELLES ECOUTEUSES, SERENADE
ALPHONSE LEDUC
DUBOIS, P. M. 8
TOCCATA
ALPHONSE LEDUC
DUBOIS, T.
POEMES VIRGILIENS
HEUGEL ET CIE. 3.00
DUBSKY 1-2
OLD WORLD MELODY
CENTURY MUSIC PUBLISHING COMPANY, INC. 4377 .40
DUBSKY 1-2
SQUIRREL, THE
CENTURY MUSIC PUBLISHING COMPANY, INC. 4409 .40
DUBSKY
STREET GAME AND WALTZ IN 5/4
BRODT MUSIC COMPANY .45
DUCELLE, P.
FEATHER DANCE--VALSE-CAPRICE
G. SCHIRMER, INC. .50
DUCHOW
CHANT INTIME
ASSOCIATED MUSIC PUBLISHERS, INC. BER .60
DUCHOW
PASSACAGLIA
ASSOCIATED MUSIC PUBLISHERS, INC. BER .75
DUCLOS, P.
CORTEGE DU BERRY
EDITIONS MUSICALES TRANSATLANTIQUES 1.55
DUCLOS, P. DESCOMBEY, M.
LE RENDEZ-VOUS BALLET
EDITIONS MUSICALES TRANSATLANTIQUES 2.80
DUCLOS, P.
LE RENDEZVOUS
EDITIONS MUSICALES TRANSATLANTIQUES 2.80
DUDLEY, R.
CORONATION MARCH, A
FREDERICK HARRIS MUSIC COMPANY 1.15
DUKAS, P.
L'APPRENTI SORCIER
ELKAN-VOGEL, INC. D 5.35
DUKAS, P.
LA PERI
ELKAN-VOGEL, INC. D 7.00
DUKAS, P.
LA PLAINTE, AU LOIN, DU FAUNE
ELKAN-VOGEL, INC. D 2.10
DUKAS, P.
PRELUDE ELEGIAQUE
ELKAN-VOGEL, INC. D 1.50
DUKAS, P.
SONATE
ELKAN-VOGEL, INC. D 7.00
DUKAS, P. SCHAUM, J. 2
SORCERER'S APPRENTICE
BELWIN-MILLS PUBLISHING CORPORATION .50
DUKAS, P. 4
SORCERER'S APPRENTICE
CENTURY MUSIC PUBLISHING COMPANY, INC. 3799 .40
DUKAS, P. SANDOR
SORCERER'S APPRENTICE, THE
G. SCHIRMER, INC. L1738 1.25
DUKAS, P.
VARIATIONS INTERLUDE ET FINALE
ELKAN-VOGEL, INC. D 6.25
DUKE WHITNEY
APRIL IN PARIS
WARNER BROTHERS PUBLISHERS 1.00
DUKE RICHTER FIRST YEAR
APRIL IN PARIS
WARNER BROTHERS PUBLISHERS .75
DUKE WHITNEY
AUTUMN IN NEW YORK
WARNER BROTHERS PUBLISHERS 1.00
DUKE, H. 4
PROMENADE -- SUITE
NOVELLO AND COMPANY, LTD. 10.0036.05 1.40
DUKE, V.
NEW YORK NOCTURNE
THE BIG THREE MUSIC CORPORATION 00.95
DUKE, V.
PARISIAN SUITE
BROUDE BROTHERS LTD. 03.75
DUKE, V.
SONATA - SOUVENIR DE VENISE
BROUDE BROTHERS LTD. 02.50
DUKELSKY
PRINTEMPS, 1931
BOOSEY AND HAWKES, INC. 1.50
DUKELSKY
SONATA
BOOSEY AND HAWKES, INC. 1.75
DUKELSKY
ZEPHIRE ET FLORE
BOOSEY AND HAWKES, INC. 4.00

DUMAS, L.
IMPROMPTU
FRANCO COLOMBO PUBLICATIONS SAL 2.50
DUMAS, L.
NEIGE
FRANCO COLOMBO PUBLICATIONS SAL 1.75
DUMAS, L.
NOCTURNE
FRANCO COLOMBO PUBLICATIONS SAL 2.50
DUMAS, L.
ROMANCE
FRANCO COLOMBO PUBLICATIONS SAL 2.50
DUMAS, L.
THEME ET VARIATIONS
EDITIONS MUSICALES TRANSATLANTIQUES 4.30
DUMM
BIRTHDAY PARTY
BELWIN-MILLS PUBLISHING CORPORATION 25142 .60
DUMM
BIT OF BLUE, A
BOSTON MUSIC COMPANY .50
DUMM
CHANGING THE GUARD
BELWIN-MILLS PUBLISHING CORPORATION 25143 .60
DUMM
DAY IN-DAY OUT
BELWIN-MILLS PUBLISHING CORPORATION 25177 .60
DUMM E
FORTUNATE FELINE
BELWIN-MILLS PUBLISHING CORPORATION 25144 .60
DUMM 2
TIME MARCHES ON
BOSTON MUSIC COMPANY .50
DUNCAN 2
CYPRESS SWAMP
VOLKWEIN BROS. .30
DUNCOMBE ROWLEY
FESTIVAL GROUPS FOR PIANO SELECTED BY ARTHUR BENJAMIN, SERIES 1
-- SONATINA
BOOSEY AND HAWKES, INC. .60
DUNGAN
AT A FOOTBALL GAME
FRANCO COLOMBO PUBLICATIONS NY1551 .35
DUNGAN 2
BALANESE DANCER
BELWIN-MILLS PUBLISHING CORPORATION .60
DUNGAN
BALKY MULE
BOOSEY AND HAWKES, INC. .40
DUNGAN
BARN DANCE
BELWIN-MILLS PUBLISHING CORPORATION .60
DUNGAN
BARN DANCE
FRANCO COLOMBO PUBLICATIONS NY1480 .40
DUNGAN GORE, G.
BLUE GRAPES
BELWIN-MILLS PUBLISHING CORPORATION .60
DUNGAN
BLUES
BELWIN-MILLS PUBLISHING CORPORATION .60
DUNGAN
BLUES
FRANCO COLOMBO PUBLICATIONS NY1481 .35
DUNGAN
BRONCO PETE
FRANCO COLOMBO PUBLICATIONS NY1552 .40
DUNGAN GORE, G.
CARROT TALKS, THE
BELWIN-MILLS PUBLISHING CORPORATION .60
DUNGAN 3
CHIMES AT PARANA
THEODORE PRESSER COMPANY . .50
DUNGAN
EIGHT CHARACTER STORIES FOR YOUNG FOLKS -- WITH WORDS BY
GERTRUDE GORE -- 1. BLUE GRAPES
FRANCO COLOMBO PUBLICATIONS NY1492 .35
DUNGAN
EIGHT CHARACTER STORIES FOR YOUNG FOLKS -- WITH WORDS BY
GERTRUDE GORE -- 2. THE CARROT TALKS
FRANCO COLOMBO PUBLICATIONS NY1485 .35
DUNGAN
EIGHT CHARACTER STORIES FOR YOUNG FOLKS -- WITH WORDS BY
GERTRUDE GORE -- 3. GREY RABBIT
FRANCO COLOMBO PUBLICATIONS NY1489 .35
DUNGAN
EIGHT CHARACTER STORIES FOR YOUNG FOLKS -- WITH WORDS BY
GERTRUDE GORE -- 4. GROWING PEANUTS
FRANCO COLOMBO PUBLICATIONS NY1488 .35
DUNGAN
EIGHT CHARACTER STORIES FOR YOUNG FOLKS -- WITH WORDS BY
GERTRUDE GORE -- 5. THE SILENT PIG
FRANCO COLOMBO PUBLICATIONS NY1490 .35
DUNGAN
EIGHT CHARACTER STORIES FOR YOUNG FOLKS -- WITH WORDS BY
GERTRUDE GORE -- 6. THE STRAWBERRY TALKS
FRANCO COLOMBO PUBLICATIONS NY1486 .35
DUNGAN
EIGHT CHARACTER STORIES FOR YOUNG FOLKS -- WITH WORDS BY
GERTRUDE GORE -- 7. THREE FAMOUS BEARS
FRANCO COLOMBO PUBLICATIONS NY1487 .35
DUNGAN
EIGHT CHARACTER STORIES FOR YOUNG FOLKS -- WITH WORDS BY
GERTRUDE GORE -- 8. VITAMINS PLUS
FRANCO COLOMBO PUBLICATIONS NY1491 .35
DUNGAN 2 1/2
GLIMPSE OF CUBA
THEODORE PRESSER COMPANY .50
DUNGAN
GRASSHOPPERS
SAM FOX PUBLISHING COMPANY, INC. .50
DUNGAN
GRASSHOPPERS
SOUTHERN MUSIC COMPANY .50
DUNGAN GORE, G.
GRAY RABBIT
BELWIN-MILLS PUBLISHING CORPORATION .60
DUNGAN GORE, G.
GROWING PEANUTS
BELWIN-MILLS PUBLISHING CORPORATION .60
DUNGAN
ICE SKATING
BELWIN-MILLS PUBLISHING CORPORATION .60
DUNGAN
ICE SKATING
FRANCO COLOMBO PUBLICATIONS NY1554 .35

DUNGAN   4
  IMPRESSION OF THE ARGENTINE
    THEODORE PRESSER COMPANY   .50
DUNGAN   2
  JACK-IN THE BOX
    THEODORE PRESSER COMPANY   .50
DUNGAN
  OLD PLANTATION
    BELWIN-MILLS PUBLISHING CORPORATION   .60
DUNGAN
  OLD PLANTATION
    FRANCO COLOMBO PUBLICATIONS   NY1553   .40
DUNGAN
  PEACOCK, THE
    BELWIN-MILLS PUBLISHING CORPORATION   .60
DUNGAN
  PEACOCK, THE
    FRANCO COLOMBO PUBLICATIONS   NY1550   .60
DUNGAN   3
  PINK BALLET
    THEODORE PRESSER COMPANY   .50
DUNGAN
  REFLECTIONS
    BELWIN-MILLS PUBLISHING CORPORATION   .60
DUNGAN
  REFLECTIONS
    FRANCO COLOMBO PUBLICATIONS   NY1482   .50
DUNGAN   3
  REFLECTIONS OF THE MOON
    BELWIN-MILLS PUBLISHING CORPORATION   .60
DUNGAN
  RIDING A WESTERN TRAIL
    BELWIN-MILLS PUBLISHING CORPORATION   .60
DUNGAN
  RIDING A WESTERN TRAIL
    FRANCO COLOMBO PUBLICATIONS   NY1483   .40
DUNGAN   2
  RUMBA
    BOSTON MUSIC COMPANY   .50
DUNGAN   GORE, G.
  SILENT PIG, THE
    BELWIN-MILLS PUBLISHING CORPORATION   .60
DUNGAN
  SINGING CELLO, THE
    BELWIN-MILLS PUBLISHING CORPORATION   25148   .60
DUNGAN   2 1/2
  SOARING GULLS
    THEODORE PRESSER COMPANY   .50
DUNGAN   3
  SPOOKS
    BELWIN-MILLS PUBLISHING CORPORATION   .60
DUNGAN   GORE, G.
  STRAWBERRY TALKS, THE
    BELWIN-MILLS PUBLISHING CORPORATION   .60
DUNGAN
  SUMMER EVENING
    BELWIN-MILLS PUBLISHING CORPORATION   .60
DUNGAN
  SUMMER EVENING
    FRANCO COLOMBO PUBLICATIONS   NY1484   .50
DUNGAN   GORE, G.
  THREE FAMOUS BEARS
    BELWIN-MILLS PUBLISHING CORPORATION   .60
DUNGAN   GORE, G.
  VITAMINS PLUS
    BELWIN-MILLS PUBLISHING CORPORATION   .60
DUNGAN   3 1/2
  WATERFALL
    THEODORE PRESSER COMPANY   .50
DUNGAN   3
  WHITE HERON
    THEODORE PRESSER COMPANY   .50
DUNHILL
  COUNTRY LIFE
    BANKS AND SON LTD.   .80
DUNHILL
  FESTIVAL GROUPS FOR PIANO SELECTED BY ARTHUR BENJAMIN, SERIES 1
  -- BY THE SHADED POOL
    BOOSEY AND HAWKES, INC.   .60
DUNHILL
  FESTIVAL GROUPS FOR PIANO SELECTED BY ARTHUR BENJAMIN, SERIES 2
  -- DULCIMER TUNE
    BOOSEY AND HAWKES, INC.   .60
DUNHILL
  MELODIES IN MINIATURE, BK. 1
    BANKS AND SON LTD.   .80
DUNHILL
  MELODIES IN MINIATURE, BK. 2
    BANKS AND SON LTD.   .70
DUNHILL, T.   1
  BOY'S MARCH
    NOVELLO AND COMPANY, LTD.   55.0039.07   .25
DUNHILL, T.   2
  FAIRY BELLS
    NOVELLO AND COMPANY, LTD.   55.0008.07   .40
DUNHILL, T.   1
  FISHERMAIDEN'S SONG, THE
    NOVELLO AND COMPANY, LTD.   55.0001.10   .25
DUNHILL, T.   3
  LAVENDER LADY, THE
    NOVELLO AND COMPANY, LTD.   55.0024.09   .25
DUNHILL, T.   2
  MANIKINS
    NOVELLO AND COMPANY, LTD.   55.0009.05   .25
DUNLAP, F.   STICKLES
  WEDDING PRAYER
    G. SCHIRMER, INC.   .60
DUNN, H.
  KEYBOARD GAMBOLS--A MERRY CHASE
    G. SCHIRMER, INC.   .35
DUNNAGAN, F.   2
  SURF AND THE SANDPIPERS
    BELWIN-MILLS PUBLISHING CORPORATION   .60
DUNYAN, C.   4
  GYPSY FANTASY
    WILLIS MUSIC COMPANY   .50
DUNYON
  BAND CONCERT, THE
    BOSTON MUSIC COMPANY   .50
DUNYON   2
  JOLLY WALTZ
    BOSTON MUSIC COMPANY   .50
DUNYON   SCHAUM, J.   1
  LEGER LINE CIRCUS
    SCHAUM PUBLICATIONS, INC.   .50

DUPERIER
  FALENCES -- SYMPHONIC SUITE --
    FRANCO COLOMBO PUBLICATIONS   SAL   5.00
DUPERIER
  IMAGES D'EPINAL -- SYMPHONIC SUITE --
    FRANCO COLOMBO PUBLICATIONS   SAL   4.50
DUPIN, M.   3
  GAY CAPRICE, A
    WILLIS MUSIC COMPANY   .40
DUPIN, M.   4
  GYPSY LIFE
    WILLIS MUSIC COMPANY   .50
DUPIN, M.   4
  GYPSY LIFE
    WILLIS MUSIC COMPANY   .50
DUPONT, J.
  CONCERT, POUR PIANO ET ORCHESTRE, OP. 2
    ALPHONSE LEDUC
DUPONT, J.   7, 8
  SCHERZO, OP. 42
    ALPHONSE LEDUC
DUPRE, M.   7
  VARIATIONS EN UT DIESE MINEUR, OP. 22
    ALPHONSE LEDUC
DURAND
  BINIOU, LE
    FRANCO COLOMBO PUBLICATIONS   SAL   1.75
DURAND DE CRAU
  CLOCHETTES -- GALOP --
    FRANCO COLOMBO PUBLICATIONS   SAL   1.75
DURAND DE CRAU
  CORRICOLO, IL -- GALOP --
    FRANCO COLOMBO PUBLICATIONS   SAL   1.75
DURAND DE CRAU
  PLUIE DE CORAIL
    FRANCO COLOMBO PUBLICATIONS   SAL   2.50
DURAND DE CRAU
  PLUIE DE CORAIL, CAPRICE BRILLANT
    FRANCO COLOMBO PUBLICATIONS   SAL   1.75
DURAND, A.   3
  CHACONNE
    CENTURY MUSIC PUBLISHING COMPANY, INC.   160   .40
DURAND, A.   3
  CHACONNE
    VOLKWEIN BROS.   .25
DURAND, A.
  CHACONNE IN A MINOR, OP. 62
    G. SCHIRMER, INC.   .50
DURAND, A.   3
  ERSTER WALZER ES-DUR OP. 83 NO. 1
    SCHOTT   09642   1.00
DURAND, A.   4
  FIRST VALSE OP. 83
    THEODORE PRESSER COMPANY   .50
DURAND, A.
  POMPONNETTE
    ELKAN-VOGEL, INC.   D   2.10
DURAND, A.
  POMPONNETTE--AIR A DANSER, OP. 80
    G. SCHIRMER, INC.   .40
DURAND, A.   4
  POMPONNETTE, AIR DE LOUIS XIV
    CENTURY MUSIC PUBLISHING COMPANY, INC.   1844   .40
DURAND, A.
  PREMIER VALSE
    ELKAN-VOGEL, INC.   D   2.10
DURAND, A.   5
  SECOND VALSE, OP. 86
    CENTURY MUSIC PUBLISHING COMPANY, INC.   1382   .40
DURAND, A.
  VALSE IN A FLAT MAJOR, OP. 86
    G. SCHIRMER, INC.   .60
DURAND, A.   4
  VALSE IN E FLAT
    VOLKWEIN BROS.   .50
DURAND, A.   DEIS
  VALSE IN E FLAT MAJOR, OP. 83
    G. SCHIRMER, INC.   .60
DURAND, A.   3
  VALSE IN E FLAT, OP. 83
    BOSTON MUSIC COMPANY   .50
DURAND, A.   3
  VALSE, NO. 02, EASY
    CENTURY MUSIC PUBLISHING COMPANY, INC.   2520   .40
DURAND, A.
  VALSE, OP. 83
    CARL FISCHER, INC.   S 1686   .60
DURAND, P.
  FANTASIA
    BELWIN-MILLS PUBLISHING CORPORATION   20086   .85
DURAND, P.
  TANGO DE LA ROSA
    BELWIN-MILLS PUBLISHING CORPORATION   20293   .95
DURKO
  PSICOGRAMMA
    KULTURA   2.00
DURNAM   2
  LITTLE SAILBOATS
    PRO-ART PUBLICATIONS, INC.   279   .50
DURNAM   2
  LITTLE WALTZ
    PRO-ART PUBLICATIONS, INC.   252   .50
DUROCHER, L.   SCHAUM, J.   1 1/2
  ABOMINABLE SNOWMAN
    SCHAUM PUBLICATIONS, INC.   .50
DUSCHEK   RHAU
  SONATA IN B FLAT
    ASSOCIATED MUSIC PUBLISHERS, INC.   B/H   .60
DUSSEK, F. X.   RACEK   3
  SONATA PER IL CLAVICEMBALO
    BARENREITER VERLAG   MAB 8
DUSSEK, J.   3
  LES ADIEUX
    SCHOTT   0466 1/2   1.00
DUSSEK, J.   CESI
  MATINEE, LA
    FRANCO COLOMBO PUBLICATIONS   128442   .50
DUSSEK, J.   4-5
  RONDO -- LES ADIEUX --
    CENTURY MUSIC PUBLISHING COMPANY, INC.   2337   .40
DUSSEK, J.   KURZ   4
  SONATA IN E FLAT, OP. 44
    BARENREITER VERLAG   AP 559
DUSSEK, J.   D
  SONATA IN F SHARP MINOR, OP. 61
    C. F. PETERS CORPORATION   6010   1.25

DUSSEK, J.
  SONATINA IN G, OP. 20 NO. 1
    FREDERICK HARRIS MUSIC COMPANY   .60
DUTILLEUX
  SONATE
    ELKAN-VOGEL, INC.   D   10.00
DUTTON, T.
  NIGHT SONG
    G. SCHIRMER, INC.   .30
DUTTON, T.
  TALLY-HO RIDE, THE
    G. SCHIRMER, INC.   .30
DUTTON, T.
  UNDER THE ROSE-ARBOR
    G. SCHIRMER, INC.   .35
DUVAL, P.   4
  DANSE HONGROISE
    THEODORE PRESSER COMPANY   .60
DUVERNOY, J.   2
  BLUETTE VALSE
    CENTURY MUSIC PUBLISHING COMPANY, INC.   2306   .40
DUVERNOY, J.
  BLUETTE-WALTZ, OP. 272 NO. 1
    G. SCHIRMER, INC.   .40
DUVERNOY, J.
  RAPID FIRE. ETUDE, OP. 256--FOR RIGHT HAND ALONE
    G. SCHIRMER, INC.   .40
DUVERNOY, J.
  RAPID FIRE, OP. 256--ETUDE
    G. SCHIRMER, INC.   .40
DVORAK
  BERCEUSE AND CAPRICCIO
    ARTIA   1.50
DVORAK
  DUMKA AND FURIANT, OP. 12
    ARTIA   .50
DVORAK
  DUMKA, OP. 35
    ARTIA   .90
DVORAK   SOLC   3
  DUMKA, OP. 35
    BARENREITER VERLAG   AP 563
DVORAK   3
  FURIANT IN D, OP. 42 NO. 1
    BARENREITER VERLAG   AP 565
DVORAK   3
  FURIANT IN F, OP. 42 NO. 2
    BARENREITER VERLAG   AP 566
DVORAK   3
  GOIN' HOME
    THEODORE PRESSER COMPANY   .50
DVORAK   4
  HUMORESKE
    CENTURY MUSIC PUBLISHING COMPANY, INC.   1601   .40
DVORAK   5
  HUMORESKE
    VOLKWEIN BROS.   .25
DVORAK
  HUMORESKE IN G FLAT MAJOR, OP. 101 NO. 7
    G. SCHIRMER, INC.   .40
DVORAK
  HUMORESKE IN G MAJOR, OP. 101 NO. 7--ORIGINAL IN G FLAT MAJOR--
    G. SCHIRMER, INC.   .40
DVORAK   4
  HUMORESKE OP. 101 NO. 7
    SCHOTT   03692   .75
DVORAK   LECHNER   2-3
  HUMORESKE OP. 101 NO. 7
    SCHOTT   03694   .75
DVORAK   POKORNY   2
  HUMORESKE, OP. 101 NO. 7 -- ERLEICHTERT --
    BARENREITER VERLAG   AP 568
DVORAK   LASKA   3
  HUMORESKE, OP. 101 NO. 7 -- ORIGINAL --
    BARENREITER VERLAG   AP 567
DVORAK   3
  HUMORESKE, TRANSPOSED
    CENTURY MUSIC PUBLISHING COMPANY, INC.   2204   .40
DVORAK   SCHAUM, J.   4 1/2
  HUMORESQUE
    SCHAUM PUBLICATIONS, INC.   .60
DVORAK   THOMPSON, J. 1
  HUMORESQUE
    WILLIS MUSIC COMPANY   .35
DVORAK   4
  HUMORESQUE IN G FLAT, OP. 101 NO. 7 - TRANSPOSED IN G
    THEODORE PRESSER COMPANY   .50
DVORAK
  HUMORESQUE, OP. 101, NO. 7
    ARTIA   .50
DVORAK   POKORNY
  HUMORESQUE, OP. 101, NO. 7
    ARTIA   .50
DVORAK   MONTANI
  HUMORESQUE, OP. 101, NO. 7
    FRANCO COLOMBO PUBLICATIONS   128916   .60
DVORAK   DEL MAGLIO
  HUMORESQUE, OP. 101, NO. 7
    FRANCO COLOMBO PUBLICATIONS   129079   .60
DVORAK
  IN THE OLD CASTLE, OP. 85 NO. 3
    G. SCHIRMER, INC.   .35
DVORAK   LAISTNER
  LARGO
    FREDERICK HARRIS MUSIC COMPANY   .75
DVORAK   3
  LARGO -- NEVER MORE TO ROAM --
    CENTURY MUSIC PUBLISHING COMPANY, INC.   3624   .40
DVORAK   POSA
  LARGO FROM THE ''NEW WORLD'' SYMPHONY
    G. SCHIRMER, INC.   .60
DVORAK   STEINER   1
  LARGO FROM THE 'NEW WORLD SYMPHONY'
    BELWIN-MILLS PUBLISHING CORPORATION   .60
DVORAK   WEYBRIGHT   1 1/2
  LARGO FROM THE 'NEW WORLD SYMPHONY'
    BELWIN-MILLS PUBLISHING CORPORATION   .60
DVORAK   COWDREY   3
  LARGO FROM THE 'NEW WORLD SYMPHONY'
    BOSTON MUSIC COMPANY   .50
DVORAK   6
  LARGO FROM THE NEW WORLD SYMPHONY
    CENTURY MUSIC PUBLISHING COMPANY, INC.   2198   .40
DVORAK   2-3
  MENUETT IN A FLAT, OP. 28 NO. 1
    BARENREITER VERLAG   AP 571

DVORAK   2-3
  MENUETT IN F, OP. 28 NO. 2
    BARENREITER VERLAG   AP 572
DVORAK   6
  NEW WORLD SYMPHONY, LARGO
    CENTURY MUSIC PUBLISHING COMPANY, INC.   2198   .40
DVORAK   ROLFE, W.   2
  NEW WORLD SYMPHONY, LARGO, EASY
    CENTURY MUSIC PUBLISHING COMPANY, INC.   3392   .40
DVORAK
  ON THE HOLY MOUNT, OP. 85 NO. 13
    G. SCHIRMER, INC.   .35
DVORAK
  POETIC IMPRESSIONS, OP. 85 - NO. 8 DANCE OF THE SPRITES
    FRANCO COLOMBO PUBLICATIONS   128915   .60
DVORAK   M
  POLONAISE IN E FLAT
    C. F. PETERS CORPORATION   4525   1.50
DVORAK
  SERENADE, OP. 85 NO. 9
    G. SCHIRMER, INC.   .50
DVORAK   SOLC   3-4
  SINFONIE NO. 08 IN G, OP. 88
    BARENREITER VERLAG   AP 286
DVORAK   SOLC   3
  SINFONIE NO. 09 IN E MINOR, OP. 95, 'AUS DER NEUEN WELT'
    BARENREITER VERLAG   AP 577
DVORAK   LASKA   2-3
  SINFONIE NO. 09 IN E MINOR, OP. 95, 'AUS DER NEUEN WELT' --
  LARGO --
    BARENREITER VERLAG   AP 570
DVORAK
  SLAVIC DANCE IN E MINOR, OP. 72
    G. SCHIRMER, INC.   .50
DVORAK   4
  SLAVONIC DANCE NO. 2
    CENTURY MUSIC PUBLISHING COMPANY, INC.   3641   .40
DVORAK   2
  SLAVONIC DANCE NO. 6, EASY
    CENTURY MUSIC PUBLISHING COMPANY, INC.   3978   .40
DVORAK   3
  SONGS MY MOTHER TAUGHT ME
    CENTURY MUSIC PUBLISHING COMPANY, INC.   2499   .40
DVORAK   3
  SONGS MY MOTHER TAUGHT ME
    CENTURY MUSIC PUBLISHING COMPANY, INC.   3477   .40
DVORAK   BERLIN
  SONGS MY MOTHER TAUGHT ME
    FREDERICK HARRIS MUSIC COMPANY   .30
DVORAK
  SPRING SONG, OP. 85 NO. 4
    G. SCHIRMER, INC.   .50
DVORAK   SOLC   3
  SUITE IN A, OP. 98
    BARENREITER VERLAG   AP 285
DVORAK
  SUITE, OP. 98
    ARTIA   1.75
DVORAK
  SUITE, OP. 98
    ASSOCIATED MUSIC PUBLISHERS, INC.   SIM   2.00
DVORAK   JUON
  SYMPHONY NO. 05 IN E MINOR 'FROM THE NEW WORLD'
    ASSOCIATED MUSIC PUBLISHERS, INC.   SIM   2.50
DVORAK
  SYMPHONY NO. 09 IN E MINOR, OP. 95 FROM 'THE NEW WORLD'
    ARTIA   1.75
DVORAK   MASLO   3
  TEUFELSTANZ AUS 'KANTINKA UND DER TEUFEL'
    BARENREITER VERLAG   AP 578
DVORAK   SOLC   3-4
  THEMA MIT VARIATIONEN, OP. 36
    BARENREITER VERLAG   AP 579
DVORAK
  THEME AND VARIATIONS, OP. 36
    ARTIA   1.25
DVORAK
  WALTZ IN A MAJOR, OP. 54 NO. 1
    G. SCHIRMER, INC.   .40
DVORAK   MONTANI
  WALTZ IN A, OP. 54, NO. 1
    FRANCO COLOMBO PUBLICATIONS   128917   .60
DVORAK *
  INDIAN LAMENT
    CARL FISCHER, INC.   F 2012   1.00
DVORINE   1
  AT CHURCH
    CENTURY MUSIC PUBLISHING COMPANY, INC.   3936   .40
DVORINE   1-2
  BAGPIPE CAPERS
    CENTURY MUSIC PUBLISHING COMPANY, INC.   4025   .40
DVORINE   1
  BAREBACK RIDER, THE
    CENTURY MUSIC PUBLISHING COMPANY, INC.   4019   .40
DVORINE   1-2
  CANDY CANE MARCH
    CENTURY MUSIC PUBLISHING COMPANY, INC.   4162   .40
DVORINE   1-2
  CHICKEN HOP
    CENTURY MUSIC PUBLISHING COMPANY, INC.   413   .40
DVORINE   1
  CHRISTOPHER COLUMBUS
    CENTURY MUSIC PUBLISHING COMPANY, INC.   4149   .40
DVORINE   1
  CONGA, LA
    CENTURY MUSIC PUBLISHING COMPANY, INC.   4020   .40
DVORINE   1
  DOPO THE DONKEY
    CENTURY MUSIC PUBLISHING COMPANY, INC.   3937   .40
DVORINE   1
  DREAMLAND
    CENTURY MUSIC PUBLISHING COMPANY, INC.   4017   .40
DVORINE   1
  HALLOWE'EN NIGHT
    CENTURY MUSIC PUBLISHING COMPANY, INC.   4150   .40
DVORINE   1
  LA CONGA
    CENTURY MUSIC PUBLISHING COMPANY, INC.   4020   .40
DVORINE   1
  LONELY SHORE
    CENTURY MUSIC PUBLISHING COMPANY, INC.   3938   .40
DVORINE   1
  MARCH OF THE SPACE CADETS
    CENTURY MUSIC PUBLISHING COMPANY, INC.   4151   .40
DVORINE   1-2
  MR. PORCUPINE TAKES A WALK
    CENTURY MUSIC PUBLISHING COMPANY, INC.   4152   .40

DVORINE
  PENSIVE NOCTURNE
      BELWIN-MILLS PUBLISHING CORPORATION   20198   .85
                                                 1
DVORINE
  RED SANDS OF MARS
      CENTURY MUSIC PUBLISHING COMPANY, INC. 4204   .40
                                                 1
DVORINE
  SCISSORS MAN, THE
      CENTURY MUSIC PUBLISHING COMPANY, INC. 4018   .40
                                                 1
DVORINE
  SONG OF THE PRAIRIE
      CENTURY MUSIC PUBLISHING COMPANY, INC. 3939   .40
                                                1-2
DVORINE
  TV CIRCUS
      CENTURY MUSIC PUBLISHING COMPANY, INC. 4243   .40
                                                1-2
DVORINE
  WAGON TRAIN, THE
      CENTURY MUSIC PUBLISHING COMPANY, INC. 4205   .40
                                                1-2
DVORINE
  WAGON TRAIN, THE
      CENTURY MUSIC PUBLISHING COMPANY, INC. 4205   .40
                                                 1
DVORINE
  YELLOW BUTTERFLY
      CENTURY MUSIC PUBLISHING COMPANY, INC. 3940   .40
DYKES   WEYBRIGHT   2
  HOLY, HOLY, HOLY
      BELWIN-MILLS PUBLISHING CORPORATION   .50
DYKES   WEYBRIGHT   2
  HOLY, HOLY, HOLY
      BELWIN-MILLS PUBLISHING CORPORATION   .60
                                                 3
DYKES
  LEAD, KINDLY LIGHT
      CENTURY MUSIC PUBLISHING COMPANY, INC. 3619   .40
DYLAN   NEALE, J.   EASY
  BLOWIN' IN THE WIND
      WARNER BROTHERS PUBLISHERS   .75
EARL   SCHAUM, J.   1 1/2
  BEAUTIFUL OHIO
      SCHAUM PUBLICATIONS, INC.   .75
EARLE   3
  CONVERSATION PIECES
      LEE ROBERTS MUSIC PUBLICATIONS, INC.   .85
ECHEVARRIA
  NOCTURNO ANDALUZ
      ASSOCIATED MUSIC PUBLISHERS, INC.   UME   1.50
                                                 2
ECKHARDT, F.
  BEE AND THE BUTTERCUP, THE
      CENTURY MUSIC PUBLISHING COMPANY, INC. 3810   .40
                                                 2
ECKHARDT, F.
  FROM THE RUSSIAN STEPPES
      CENTURY MUSIC PUBLISHING COMPANY, INC. 3811   .40
                                                 2
ECKHARDT, F.
  GRASSHOPPERS HOLIDAY
      CENTURY MUSIC PUBLISHING COMPANY, INC. 3812   .40
                                                 2
ECKHARDT, F.
  PILLOW FIGHT
      CENTURY MUSIC PUBLISHING COMPANY, INC. 3813   .40
                                                 2
ECKHARDT, F.
  SONGS OF AMERICA
      CENTURY MUSIC PUBLISHING COMPANY, INC. 3774   .40
                                                 2
ECKHARDT, F.
  SONGS OF FRANCE
      CENTURY MUSIC PUBLISHING COMPANY, INC. 3776   .40
                                                 2
ECKHARDT, F.
  SONGS OF ITALY
      CENTURY MUSIC PUBLISHING COMPANY, INC. 3777   .40
                                                 2
ECKHARDT, F.
  SONGS OF SCOTLAND
      CENTURY MUSIC PUBLISHING COMPANY, INC. 3 775   .40
                                                 2
ECKHARDT, F.
  SQUIRRELS' PICNIC, THE
      CENTURY MUSIC PUBLISHING COMPANY, INC. 3997   .40
ECKHARDT, F.--ED   ECKHARDT, F.   3
  HEAV'N, HEAV'N
      CENTURY MUSIC PUBLISHING COMPANY, INC. 3786   .40
ECKSTEIN
  AERO FLIGHT
      BOSTON MUSIC COMPANY   .50
ECKSTEIN
  ARPEGGIETTO
      CARL FISCHER, INC.   P 2949   .50
ECKSTEIN
  BALLET PROFILE
      CARL FISCHER, INC.   P 3190   .50
ECKSTEIN
  BELLS OF ANDORRA
      CARL FISCHER, INC.   P 3171   .50
ECKSTEIN
  BLUE FOUNTAIN
      CARL FISCHER, INC.   P 2919   .50
ECKSTEIN
  BY A BLUE LAGOON
      CARL FISCHER, INC.   P 2396   .50
ECKSTEIN
  CAROUSEL WALTZ
      CARL FISCHER, INC.   P 3187   .50
ECKSTEIN
  CHINA DOLL
      CARL FISCHER, INC.   P 2163   .50
ECKSTEIN
  CONCEPTS
      CARL FISCHER, INC.   P 3133   .60
ECKSTEIN
  CRYPTIC
      CARL FISCHER, INC.   P 3134   .60
ECKSTEIN
  DANCE OF THE CLOWNS
      CARL FISCHER, INC.   P 2955   .50
ECKSTEIN
  DANCE OF THE MOON DWELLERS
      CARL FISCHER, INC.   P 2985   .50
ECKSTEIN
  DEBUTANTE
      CARL FISCHER, INC.   P 2269   .50
ECKSTEIN
  DREAM BALLAD
      CARL FISCHER, INC.   P 3049   .50
ECKSTEIN
  DREAM DANCERS
      CARL FISCHER, INC.   P 3206   .60
ECKSTEIN   EASY
  DREAMS OF YESTERDAY
      SHAWNEE PRESS, INC.   HB-5010   .60
ECKSTEIN
  ELEPHANT WALK
      CARL FISCHER, INC.   P 2858   .50

ECKSTEIN
  ENCHANTED NIGHT
      CARL FISCHER, INC.   P 3125   .50
ECKSTEIN
  FIESTA TIME
      CARL FISCHER, INC.   P 2521   .50
                                                 3
ECKSTEIN
  FIRE DANCE
      BOSTON MUSIC COMPANY   .50
                                                 3
ECKSTEIN
  GARDEN AT EVENING, A
      BOSTON MUSIC COMPANY   .50
ECKSTEIN
  GHOST IN THE CHIMNEY
      CARL FISCHER, INC.   P 2052   .50
ECKSTEIN   EASY
  GINGER SNAP BRIGADE, THE
      SHAWNEE PRESS, INC.   HB-5017   .35
ECKSTEIN
  GOLLIWOGS AT PLAY
      SHAWNEE PRESS, INC.   HB-5032   .40
                                                 2
ECKSTEIN
  GYPSY CAMP FIRES
      BOSTON MUSIC COMPANY   .50
                                                 3
ECKSTEIN
  IN THE BAZAAR
      BOSTON MUSIC COMPANY   .50
ECKSTEIN
  INTERMEZZO
      CARL FISCHER, INC.   P 2951   .50
ECKSTEIN
  JEAN AND BABETTE
      CARL FISCHER, INC.   P 1834   .50
ECKSTEIN
  LIGHT AND LIVELY
      CARL FISCHER, INC.   P 3188   .50
                                                 2
ECKSTEIN
  LITTLE LADY
      BOSTON MUSIC COMPANY   .50
                                                 3
ECKSTEIN
  LULLABY FOR A LAMBKIN
      BOSTON MUSIC COMPANY   .50
ECKSTEIN
  MANTILLA
      CARL FISCHER, INC.   P 2057   .50
ECKSTEIN
  OFF TO CAMP
      CARL FISCHER, INC.   P 2162   .50
                                                 3
ECKSTEIN
  ON SUNSET HILL
      BOSTON MUSIC COMPANY   .50
                                                 1
ECKSTEIN
  PICKANINNY SERENADE
      BOSTON MUSIC COMPANY   .50
ECKSTEIN
  PIGGY BANK TUNE
      CARL FISCHER, INC.   P 2923   .50
ECKSTEIN
  PRELUDE IN PASTEL
      CARL FISCHER, INC.   P 2280   .50
ECKSTEIN
  PRINCESS CHARMING
      CARL FISCHER, INC.   P 1974   .50
                                                 3
ECKSTEIN
  RHAPSODIE
      BOSTON MUSIC COMPANY   .75
ECKSTEIN
  SILVER SLIPPERS
      CARL FISCHER, INC.   P 2268   .50
ECKSTEIN
  SNAKE CHARMER
      CARL FISCHER, INC.   P 3166   .50
ECKSTEIN
  SOLDIERS ON PARADE
      CARL FISCHER, INC.   P 1876   .50
ECKSTEIN
  SOMBRERO
      CARL FISCHER, INC.   P 2940   .50
ECKSTEIN
  SONG OF THE BELL
      CARL FISCHER, INC.   P 1873   .50
ECKSTEIN   EASY
  SPANISH ROSES
      SHAWNEE PRESS, INC.   .40
ECKSTEIN
  SPOOKS
      G. SCHIRMER, INC.   .35
ECKSTEIN
  STEEPLECHASE
      CARL FISCHER, INC.   P 3189   .50
ECKSTEIN
  SWINGING LANTERNS --CHINESE DANCE--
      CARL FISCHER, INC.   P 1926   .50
ECKSTEIN
  THREE TROLLS, THE--WITH WORDS
      G. SCHIRMER, INC.   .40
ECKSTEIN
  TRAINS
      CARL FISCHER, INC.   P 2073   .50
                                                 3
ECKSTEIN
  TWINKLETOES
      BOSTON MUSIC COMPANY   .50
ECKSTEIN
  WALTZ REVERIE, A
      CARL FISCHER, INC.   P 2275   .50
ECKSTEIN
  WISHBONE WALTZ
      CARL FISCHER, INC.   P 3165   .50
ECKSTEIN--ARR.   ECKSTEIN
  DOWN IN THE VALLEY
      CARL FISCHER, INC.   P 2857   .50
EDDY   3-4
  ONLY A DREAM, REVERIE
      CENTURY MUSIC PUBLISHING COMPANY, INC. 2729   .40
EDEL, Y.
  CAPRICCIO
      ISRAEL MUSIC INSTITUTE   5.00
EDEL, Y.
  TRIPTYQUE
      ISRAEL MUSIC INSTITUTE   3.75
EDELSON   1-2
  BLUE UMBRELLA
      PRO-ART PUBLICATIONS, INC.   536   .50
EDELSON   1
  GHOST HOUSE
      PRO-ART PUBLICATIONS, INC.   560   .50

EDELSON, E.   2
    TIME FOR BED
        THEODORE PRESSER COMPANY   .50
EDER
    SONATA NO. 01 -- 1950 --
        ASSOCIATED MUSIC PUBLISHERS, INC.   B/H   2.40
EDGINTON   E
    CAT'S DELIGHT
        C. F. PETERS CORPORATION   H880   1.25
EDMONDS
    SEVEN MUSIGRAMS
        SOUTHERN MUSIC COMPANY   1.00
EDMUNDS   M
    SUITE IN G, FOR HARPSICHORD OR PIANO
        C. F. PETERS CORPORATION   H744A 1.50
EDOUARD   3
    MELODIOUS MOMENTS
        CENTURY MUSIC PUBLISHING COMPANY, INC.   1898   .40
EDWARDS
    CLOG DANCE
        EDWARD B. MARKS MUSIC CORPORATION   00.60
EDWARDS
    LAMENT
        EDWARD B. MARKS MUSIC CORPORATION   00.60
EDWARDS, C.   DEIS
    BY THE BEND OF THE RIVER--BARCAROLLE
        G. SCHIRMER, INC.   .60
EDWARDS, C.   ZEPP   2
    IN MY MERRY OLDSMOBILE
        PRO-ART PUBLICATIONS, INC.   380   .50
EDWARDS, G.   SCHAUM, J.   1
    IN MY MERRY OLDSMOBILE
        SCHAUM PUBLICATIONS, INC.   .50
EDWARDS, G.   SCHAUM, J.   1
    SCHOOL DAYS
        SCHAUM PUBLICATIONS, INC.   .75
EELE, M.
    THREE G MAJORS, THE--CURWEN EDITION
        G. SCHIRMER, INC.   .50
EGGE   D
    FANTASY IN SPRING RHYTHM, OP. 12C
        C. F. PETERS CORPORATION   LY182   .60
EGGE   M
    GOATHORN DANCE --GUKKOSLATTEN--
        C. F. PETERS CORPORATION   LY252   .50
EGGE   D
    SONATA NO. 02, OP. 27 --PATETICA--
        C. F. PETERS CORPORATION   LY380   2.00
EGGHARD   2
    TENDER FLOWER, OP. 299 NO. 1
        CENTURY MUSIC PUBLISHING COMPANY, INC.   2358   .40
EGK, W.   4
    SONATA FUR KLAVIER
        SCHOTT   1332   3.75
EHLERT, LOUIS
    TRAUMGEBILE E
        MUSICA OBSCURA   1.00
EHMKE, R.   2
    HAPPY DAYS
        BELWIN-MILLS PUBLISHING CORPORATION   .60
EHRENBERG   EASY
    CLOCK SHOP, THE
        SHAWNEE PRESS, INC.   .35
EHRLICH, G.
    BARCAROLLE IN G MAJOR
        G. SCHIRMER, INC.   .50
EIDT, M.   2
    FAIRY DANCE
        THEODORE PRESSER COMPANY   .50
EIGES
    ROMANCE
        FREDERICK HARRIS MUSIC COMPANY   .60
EILENBERG
    DANCE OF THE CLOWNS, OP. 26 NO. 1
        BELWIN-MILLS PUBLISHING CORPORATION   28055   .60
EILENBERG   4
    LA MANOLA -- SERENADE ESPAGNOLE
        CENTURY MUSIC PUBLISHING COMPANY, INC.   1642   .40
EILENBERG   3
    MANDOLIN SERENADE
        CENTURY MUSIC PUBLISHING COMPANY, INC.   1710   .40
EILENBERG   4
    MANOLA, LA, SERENADE
        CENTURY MUSIC PUBLISHING COMPANY, INC.   1642   .40
EILENBERG
    REGIMENT QUE PASSE, LE
        FRANCO COLOMBO PUBLICATIONS   SAL   1.50
EILENBERG   3
    SERENADE OF THE MANDOLINS
        CENTURY MUSIC PUBLISHING COMPANY, INC.   1710   .40
EINEM, G.
    MEDUSA, OP. 24 -- BALLET IN 3 SCENES
        ASSOCIATED MUSIC PUBLISHERS, INC.   BOT   7.50
EINEM, G.
    PRINZESSIN TURANDOT, OP. 1 -- BALLET IN 2 TABLEAUX
        ASSOCIATED MUSIC PUBLISHERS, INC.   BOT   7.50
EINEM, G.
    RONDO VOM GOLDENEN KALB, OP. 13 -- BALLET IN 3 SCENES
        ASSOCIATED MUSIC PUBLISHERS, INC.   BOT   6.00
EINEM, G.
    TWO SONATINAS
        UNIVERSAL EDITION   UE 11911 3.00
EISBERG, B.   1 1/2
    HAVING FUN
        BELWIN-MILLS PUBLISHING CORPORATION   .60
EISBERG, B.   2
    MARCH OF THE TOY PICCOLOS
        BELWIN-MILLS PUBLISHING CORPORATION   .60
EISBERG, B.   2
    MARCHING MARIONETTES
        BELWIN-MILLS PUBLISHING CORPORATION   .60
EISLER
    SONATA NO. 02 OP. 6 -- IN FORM OF VARIATIONS --
        ASSOCIATED MUSIC PUBLISHERS, INC.   B/H   1.25
EISLER
    SONATA, OP. 1
        UNIVERSAL EDITION   7475   1.95
EISLER
    VARIATIONS -- 1940 --
        ASSOCIATED MUSIC PUBLISHERS, INC.   B/H   2.75
EISLER   2 1/2
    WINTER WIND
        THEODORE PRESSER COMPANY   .50
ELAINE, M.
    BOOGIE BEET
        BELWIN-MILLS PUBLISHING CORPORATION   25302   .60

ELAINE, M.
    FUN TIME
        BELWIN-MILLS PUBLISHING CORPORATION   25301   .60
ELAINE, M.
    HINDU DANCER
        BELWIN-MILLS PUBLISHING CORPORATION   25303   .60
ELAINE, M.
    LULLABY FOR A PAPOOSE
        BELWIN-MILLS PUBLISHING CORPORATION   25198   .60
ELAINE, M.
    MODAL MARCH
        BELWIN-MILLS PUBLISHING CORPORATION   25284   .60
ELAINE, M.
    PIECE IN THE DORIAN MODE
        BELWIN-MILLS PUBLISHING CORPORATION   25290   .60
ELAINE, M.
    SNAKE CHARMER PASSES BY, A
        BELWIN-MILLS PUBLISHING CORPORATION   25304   .60
ELAINE, SR.   3
    GAY SENORITA
        BELWIN-MILLS PUBLISHING CORPORATION   .60
ELAINE, SR.   1
    MARCH OF THE INDIANS
        BELWIN-MILLS PUBLISHING CORPORATION   .60
ELAINE, SR.   3
    SPANISH DANCE
        WILLIS MUSIC COMPANY   .40
ELAINE, SR.   3
    TRIADS ON PARADE
        BELWIN-MILLS PUBLISHING CORPORATION   .60
ELDON, M.   3
    FLICKERING SHADOWS
        VOLKWEIN BROS.   .40
ELGAR, E.
    ADIEU
        SAM FOX PUBLISHING COMPANY, INC.   .75
ELGAR, E.
    ADIEU
        SOUTHERN MUSIC COMPANY   .75
ELGAR, E.
    CHANSON DE MATIN
        NOVELLO AND COMPANY, LTD.   10.0039.10 1.15
ELGAR, E.
    CHANSON DE NUIT
        NOVELLO AND COMPANY, LTD.   10.0040.03 .90
ELGAR, E.   VALBER
    LAND OF HOPE AND GLORY
        BOOSEY AND HAWKES, INC.   .60
ELGAR, E.   WATTERS
    LAND OF HOPE AND GLORY
        BOOSEY AND HAWKES, INC.   .60
ELGAR, E.   PROSTAKOFF
    LAND OF HOPE AND GLORY--THEME FROM POMP AND CIRCUMSTANCE
        G. SCHIRMER, INC.   .40
ELGAR, E.   KAHL   2
    LOVE'S GREETING
        BOSTON MUSIC COMPANY   .50
ELGAR, E.   4
    LOVE'S GREETING
        CENTURY MUSIC PUBLISHING COMPANY, INC.   1229   .40
ELGAR, E.
    LOVE'S GREETING, OP. 12
        G. SCHIRMER, INC.   .40
ELGAR, E.   KAHL   1
    MY VALENTINE -- SALUTE D'AMOUR
        BOSTON MUSIC COMPANY   .50
ELGAR, E.
    NIMROD
        NOVELLO AND COMPANY, LTD.   10.0040.01 .90
ELGAR, E.
    NURSERY SUITE
        SAM FOX PUBLISHING COMPANY, INC.   2.50
ELGAR, E.   ZEPP   2
    POMP AND CIRCUMSTANCE
        PRO-ART PUBLICATIONS, INC.   147   .50
ELGAR, E.   RICHTER
    POMP AND CIRCUMSTANCE
        WARNER BROTHERS PUBLISHERS   .75
ELGAR, E.   THOMPSON, J. 3
    POMP AND CIRCUMSTANCE
        WILLIS MUSIC COMPANY   .50
ELGAR, E.   ZEPP   4
    POMP AND CIRCUMSTANCE - FULL CHORD VERSION
        PRO-ART PUBLICATIONS, INC.   149   .50
ELGAR, E.   ZEPP   3
    POMP AND CIRCUMSTANCE - SMALL CHORD VERSION
        PRO-ART PUBLICATIONS, INC.   148   .50
ELGAR, E.   ECKSTEIN
    POMP AND CIRCUMSTANCE --ORIG--
        CARL FISCHER, INC.   P 2941 .75
ELGAR, E.   ECKSTEIN
    POMP AND CIRCUMSTANCE --THEME--
        CARL FISCHER, INC.   P 2924 .50
ELGAR, E.   SCHAUM, J.   4
    POMP AND CIRCUMSTANCE MARCH
        BELWIN-MILLS PUBLISHING CORPORATION   .50
ELGAR, E.   4
    POMP AND CIRCUMSTANCE MARCH
        CENTURY MUSIC PUBLISHING COMPANY, INC.   4371   .40
ELGAR, E.   PROSTAKOFF
    POMP AND CIRCUMSTANCE MARCH
        G. SCHIRMER, INC.   .75
ELGAR, E.   BELLAIRS
    POMP AND CIRCUMSTANCE MARCH NO. 1 IN D
        BOOSEY AND HAWKES, INC.   .75
ELGAR, E.   SCHMID
    POMP AND CIRCUMSTANCE MARCH NO. 1 IN D
        BOOSEY AND HAWKES, INC.   .75
ELGAR, E.   SCHMID
    POMP AND CIRCUMSTANCE MARCH NO. 4 IN G
        BOOSEY AND HAWKES, INC.   1.25
ELGAR, E.
    POMP AND CIRCUMSTANCE NO. 1 IN D, OP. 39
        ASHLEY DEALERS SERVICE, INC.   ES   .95
ELGAR, E.   SCHAUM, J.   1
    PROCESSIONAL--FROM POMP AND CIRCUMSTANCE, OP. 39 NO. 1
        BELWIN-MILLS PUBLISHING CORPORATION   .50
ELGAR, E.   4
    SALUT D'AMOUR
        CENTURY MUSIC PUBLISHING COMPANY, INC.   1229   .40
ELGAR, E.   WEYBRIGHT   1
    SALUT D'AMOUR -- LOVE'S GREETING
        BELWIN-MILLS PUBLISHING CORPORATION   .60
ELGAR, E.   PALMERI
    SALUT D'AMOUR, OP. 12
        G. SCHIRMER, INC.   .50

ELGAR, E.
  SERENADE
    SAM FOX PUBLISHING COMPANY, INC.   .75
ELGAR, E.
  SERENADE
    SOUTHERN MUSIC COMPANY   .75
ELGAR, E.
  VARIATIONS, OP. 36, 'ENIGMA'
    NOVELLO AND COMPANY, LTD.   10.0042.10   3.25
ELGAR, E.
  WAND OF YOUTH, SUITE 1
    NOVELLO AND COMPANY, LTD.   10.0043.08   2.00
ELGAR, E.
  WAND OF YOUTH, SUITE 2
    NOVELLO AND COMPANY, LTD.   10.0048.09   2.00
                                    2
ELIOT
  CAPRICE
    PRO-ART PUBLICATIONS, INC.   112   .50
                                    2
ELIOT
  MELODY AND VARIATION
    PRO-ART PUBLICATIONS, INC.   114   .50
                                    2
ELIOT
  PRELUDIO
    PRO-ART PUBLICATIONS, INC.   111   .50
                                    2
ELIOT
  REVERIE
    PRO-ART PUBLICATIONS, INC.   113   .50
ELISCU *
  WITHOUT A SONG
    THE BIG THREE MUSIC CORPORATION   00.95
                                    4
ELISIA, SR.
  CHINESE CHASE
    LEE ROBERTS MUSIC PUBLICATIONS, INC.   .50
                                    4
ELISIA, SR.
  ORGAN MAN AND THE MONKEYS, THE
    LEE ROBERTS MUSIC PUBLICATIONS, INC.   .50
ELLINGTON   SINGER
  AZURE
    BELWIN-MILLS PUBLISHING CORPORATION   20022   .85
ELLINGTON
  BIRD OF PARADISE
    THE BIG THREE MUSIC CORPORATION   00.95
ELLINGTON   ELLIS, N.
  IN A SENTIMENTAL MOOD
    BELWIN-MILLS PUBLISHING CORPORATION   20132   .85
ELLINGTON
  MOOD INDIGO
    BELWIN-MILLS PUBLISHING CORPORATION   20266   .85
ELLINGTON   MOSSMAN, R.
  MOOD INDIGO, SIMP.
    BELWIN-MILLS PUBLISHING CORPORATION   .60
ELLINGTON   ELLIS, N.
  PYRAMID
    BELWIN-MILLS PUBLISHING CORPORATION   20216   .85
ELLINGTON
  ROCKIN' IN RHYTHM
    BELWIN-MILLS PUBLISHING CORPORATION   20227   .85
ELLINGTON   ELLIS, N.
  SOLITUDE
    BELWIN-MILLS PUBLISHING CORPORATION   20258   .85
ELLINGTON
  SOPHISTICATED LADY
    BELWIN-MILLS PUBLISHING CORPORATION   20273   .85
                                    3
ELLIOTT
  CONCERT WALTZ
    PRO-ART PUBLICATIONS, INC.   483   .50
                                    3
ELLIOTT
  LOUISIANA LOU
    PRO-ART PUBLICATIONS, INC.   482   .50
                                    1
ELLIOTT
  MY DOG, PAL
    PRO-ART PUBLICATIONS, INC.   507   .50
                                    3
ELLIOTT
  NOCTURNE
    PRO-ART PUBLICATIONS, INC.   506   .50
                                    2-3
ELLIOTT
  POLKA DOT PONY, THE
    PRO-ART PUBLICATIONS, INC.   519   .50
                                    1-2
ELLIOTT
  WHY DON'T DUCKS GET WET
    PRO-ART PUBLICATIONS, INC.   517   .50
ELLIS, E.   PAULL   ADVANCED
  NAPOLEON'S LAST CHARGE
    SHAWNEE PRESS, INC.   HB-61   .60
ELLIS, N.
  BOY MEETS HORN
    BELWIN-MILLS PUBLISHING CORPORATION   20039   .85
ELLMENREICH, A.   SCHAUM, J.   1
  SPINNING SONG
    BELWIN-MILLS PUBLISHING CORPORATION   .50
                                    2
ELLMENREICH, A.
  SPINNING SONG
    CENTURY MUSIC PUBLISHING COMPANY, INC. 990   .40
                                    2
ELLMENREICH, A.
  SPINNING SONG
    VOLKWEIN BROS.   .30
                                    2
ELLMENREICH, A.
  SPINNING SONG, A
    THEODORE PRESSER COMPANY   .50
ELLMENREICH, A.
  SPINNING SONG, OP. 14 NO. 4
    BELWIN-MILLS PUBLISHING CORPORATION   28053   .60
ELLMENREICH, A.   ECKSTEIN
  SPINNING SONG, OP. 14 NO. 4
    CARL FISCHER, INC.   S 1534   .50
ELLMENREICH, A.
  SPINNING SONG, OP. 14 NO. 4
    G. SCHIRMER, INC.   .40
ELLSTEIN, A.
  LOVERS NO MORE
    BELWIN-MILLS PUBLISHING CORPORATION   20455   .85
ELLSTEIN, A.
  NEGEV CONCERTO
    BELWIN-MILLS PUBLISHING CORPORATION   20336   2.00
ELLSWORTH
  SLEEPYHEAD
    CARL FISCHER, INC.   P 2956   .50
ELMER, C.   E
  BIT MISCHIEVOUS, A
    COMPOSERS PRESS, INC.   1.00
ELMER, C.   E-M
  PETITE PAVANE
    COMPOSERS PRESS, INC.   1.00
ELWELL, H.   M
  BUSY DAY
    THEODORE PRESSER COMPANY   .50

ELWELL, H.   E
  PLAINT
    THEODORE PRESSER COMPANY   .50
ELWELL, H.   M
  PROCESSION
    THEODORE PRESSER COMPANY   .50
ELWELL, H.
  SONATA
    OXFORD UNIVERSITY PRESS   93.201   2.00
EMERY
  BREATH OF A BREEZE
    BOSTON MUSIC COMPANY   .50
                                    3
EMERY
  FOREST BROOK
    BOSTON MUSIC COMPANY   .50
EMERY
  HARVEST DANCE
    G. SCHIRMER, INC.   .35
                                    3
EMERY
  SNOW ON THE EVERGREENS
    BOSTON MUSIC COMPANY   .50
EMMANUEL, M.
  SONATINE NO. 04 SUR LES MODES HINDOUS
    ELKAN-VOGEL, INC.   D   3.25
EMMET *   2
  WEARING OF THE GREEN
    CENTURY MUSIC PUBLISHING COMPANY, INC. 2098   .40
EMMETT   WEYBRIGHT   2
  DIXIE
    BELWIN-MILLS PUBLISHING CORPORATION   .50
EMMETT   ARMOUR   2
  DIXIE
    CENTURY MUSIC PUBLISHING COMPANY, INC. 3469   .40
EMMETT   ZEPP   2-3
  DIXIE
    PRO-ART PUBLICATIONS, INC.   197   .50
ENDRES, O.
  IN A SAIL-BOAT
    G. SCHIRMER, INC.   .40
                                    1
ENDRES, O.
  LET'S WATCH THE CLOCK
    BELWIN-MILLS PUBLISHING CORPORATION   .60
                                    3
ENDRES, O.
  PETITE BALLET
    BELWIN-MILLS PUBLISHING CORPORATION   .60
ENDRES, O.
  SINGING BIRDS
    G. SCHIRMER, INC.   .40
ENESCO
  FIRST RUMANIAN RHAPSODY
    PEER SOUTHERN ORGANIZATION   02.75
ENESCO
  PRELUDE AND FUGUE
    FRANCO COLOMBO PUBLICATIONS   SAL   3.50
ENESCO   SCHAUM, J.   2
  ROUMANIAN RHAPSODY
    BELWIN-MILLS PUBLISHING CORPORATION   .50
                                    4
ENESCO
  ROUMANIAN RHAPSODY, NO. 1
    CENTURY MUSIC PUBLISHING COMPANY, INC. 3566   .40
ENESCO
  SONATA NO. 03 IN D MAJOR
    FRANCO COLOMBO PUBLICATIONS   SAL   8.00
ENGEL, L.
  SONATA
    BOOSEY AND HAWKES, INC.   1.50
ENGEL, S.
  CHILDREN'S FESTIVAL, THE--HUNGARIAN DANCE, OP. 31
    G. SCHIRMER, INC.   .30
ENGELMANN, H. U.   1
  HUNGARIAN DANCE
    BOSTON MUSIC COMPANY   .50
ENGELMANN, H. U.   2
  LITTLE BOY BLUE
    BOSTON MUSIC COMPANY   .50
ENGELMANN, H. U.
  MELODY OF LOVE
    ASHLEY DEALERS SERVICE, INC.   ES   .95
ENGELMANN, H. U.   4 - 5
  MELODY OF LOVE
    BOSTON MUSIC COMPANY   .50
ENGELMANN, H. U.
  MELODY OF LOVE
    CARL FISCHER, INC.   S 7677   .50
ENGELMANN, H. U.   3
  MELODY OF LOVE
    THEODORE PRESSER COMPANY   .60
ENGELMANN, H. U.   CARLETON, B. 1 1/2
  MELODY OF LOVE
    THEODORE PRESSER COMPANY   .50
ENGELMANN, H. U.   SINGER   5
  MELODY OF LOVE
    THEODORE PRESSER COMPANY   .60
ENGELMANN, H. U.   RICHTER   FIRST YEAR
  MELODY OF LOVE
    WARNER BROTHERS PUBLISHERS   .75
ENGELMANN, H. U.   BURNAM   2
  MELODY OF LOVE
    WILLIS MUSIC COMPANY   .40
ENGELMANN, H. U.   4
  MESSAGE OF PEACE
    VOLKWEIN BROS.   .50
ENGELMANN, H. U.   1
  MY FIRST DANCE
    THEODORE PRESSER COMPANY   .50
ENGELMANN, H. U.
  NIGHT BEFORE CHRISTMAS, THE
    BOSTON MUSIC COMPANY   .50
ENGELMANN, H. U.   4
  RUSSIAN DANCE OP. 753
    THEODORE PRESSER COMPANY   .60
ENGELMANN, H. U.   6
  TOCCATA
    SCHOTT   4048   1.50
ENGLAND, G.   2
  DREAMTIME
    CENTURY MUSIC PUBLISHING COMPANY, INC. 3331   .40
ENGLEMANN, H. U.   2
  MELODY OF LOVE - CARY
    CENTURY MUSIC PUBLISHING COMPANY, INC. 4289   .40
ENGLEMANN, H. U.   4
  MELODY OF LOVE - ORIGINAL
    CENTURY MUSIC PUBLISHING COMPANY, INC. 4288   .40
ENGLISH, G.   3
  DANCING ANTIQUE
    THEODORE PRESSER COMPANY   .50

EPPEL *   SCHAUM, J.
  MISSOURI WALTZ
    BELWIN-MILLS PUBLISHING CORPORATION   .60
                                  1
ERB
  A-RUB-A-DUB
    THEODORE PRESSER COMPANY   .50
ERB
  AMBITIOUS GOOSE, THE
    BOSTON MUSIC COMPANY   .50
EPB
  BIRD IN THE TREETOP
    BOSTON MUSIC COMPANY   .50
ERB
  BRIGHT BLUE SEA, THE
    G. SCHIRMER, INC.   .35
                                  1
ERB
  CHATTERING BROOK
    VOLKWEIN BROS.   .30
                                  1
ERB
  CHEER LEADER
    VOLKWEIN BROS.   .25
ERB   WILLIAMS
  CHERRY BLOSSOM TIME
    BOSTON MUSIC COMPANY   .50
ERB   WILLIAMS
  CHIMING BELLS
    BOSTON MUSIC COMPANY   .50
ERB
  CIRCUS PARADE, THE -- WITH WORDS
    BOSTON MUSIC COMPANY   .50
                                  1
ERB
  CONTRARY ME
    THEODORE PRESSER COMPANY   .50
                                  2
ERB
  CRICKETS
    THEODORE PRESSER COMPANY   .50
                                  1
ERB
  CUCKOO CLOCK, THE
    THEODORE PRESSER COMPANY   .50
ERB
  DAFFODILS ARE HERE
    BELWIN-MILLS PUBLISHING CORPORATION   25173   .60
                                  1
ERB
  DANCING BEAR, THE
    BOSTON MUSIC COMPANY   .50
ERB
  DANCING ON THE DYKE
    SUMMY-BIRCHARD COMPANY   .50
                                  1 1/2
ERB
  DRUM MAJOR
    THEODORE PRESSER COMPANY   .50
                                  1 1/2
ERB
  DRUMMER BOY
    THEODORE PRESSER COMPANY   .50
                                  1
ERB
  FOLLOW THE LEADER
    BOSTON MUSIC COMPANY   .50
                                  1
ERB
  FOUR MERRY CLOWNS
    BOSTON MUSIC COMPANY   .50
                                  2
ERB
  GAY TARANTELLA
    THEODORE PRESSER COMPANY   .50
                                  1
ERB
  GYPSY CAMP, THE
    BOSTON MUSIC COMPANY   .50
                                  1 1/2
ERB
  HI, SPRING
    THEODORE PRESSER COMPANY   .50
                                  1
ERB
  HIPPITY, HIPPITY, HOP
    CENTURY MUSIC PUBLISHING COMPANY, INC.   026   .40
                                  1
ERB
  HUNGRY PUSSY, THE
    BOSTON MUSIC COMPANY   .50
ERB   WILLIAMS, J.   2
  HURDY GURDY
    BOSTON MUSIC COMPANY   .50
                                  1
ERB
  I WISH I WERE A DUCK
    THEODORE PRESSER COMPANY   .50
                                  1 1/2
ERB
  IN A TREETOP SO TALL
    THEODORE PRESSER COMPANY   .50
                                  1
ERB
  LITTLE BARN DANCE, A
    THEODORE PRESSER COMPANY   .50
                                  2
ERB
  LITTLE DANDY
    VOLKWEIN BROS.   .25
                                  2
ERB
  LITTLE IRISH DANCE, A
    THEODORE PRESSER COMPANY   .50
                                  1
ERB
  LITTLE MISS BLUEBIRD
    BOSTON MUSIC COMPANY   .50
                                  2
ERB
  LITTLE MISS QUACK-QUACK
    VOLKWEIN BROS.   .25
                                  1 1/2
ERB
  LITTLE SHADOW
    THEODORE PRESSER COMPANY   .50
                                  1
ERB
  LITTLE YELLOW DUCKLING
    BOSTON MUSIC COMPANY   .50
                                  1
ERB
  MERRY, MERRY WASH DAY
    CENTURY MUSIC PUBLISHING COMPANY, INC.   027   .40
                                  1
ERB
  MOUSE AND THE CLOCK
    VOLKWEIN BROS.   .30
                                  E
ERB
  MR. AND MRS. WREN
    BELWIN-MILLS PUBLISHING CORPORATION   25172   .60
ERB   WILLIAMS, J.   1
  MRS. CACKLE-CACKLE
    BOSTON MUSIC COMPANY   .50
                                  1
ERB
  MY GALLOPING STEED
    THEODORE PRESSER COMPANY   .50
                                  1
ERB
  MY WISHING STAR
    VOLKWEIN BROS.   .30
                                  1
ERB
  NIGHT ROVER
    VOLKWEIN BROS.   .25

ERB   1 1/2
  PICCADILLY CIRCUS
    THEODORE PRESSER COMPANY   .50
ERB   1 1/2
  PONY RIDE, A
    THEODORE PRESSER COMPANY   .50
ERB   2
  ROGUISHNESS
    VOLKWEIN BROS.   .35
ERB   WILLIAMS, J.   1
  SCISSORS GRINDER
    BOSTON MUSIC COMPANY   .50
ERB   1 1/2
  SLEEPY BIRDS
    THEODORE PRESSER COMPANY   .50
ERB   WILLIAMS, J.   1
  SWING SONG
    BOSTON MUSIC COMPANY   .50
ERB   1
  TRAVELERS OF THE AIR
    VOLKWEIN BROS.   .25
ERB   1 1/2
  TUG OF WAR
    THEODORE PRESSER COMPANY   .50
ERB
  TULIP TIME
    G. SCHIRMER, INC.   .35
ERB   WILLIAMS, J.   1
  WAKE UP
    BOSTON MUSIC COMPANY   .50
ERB   E
  WEE BOBBY ROBIN
    BELWIN-MILLS PUBLISHING CORPORATION   25174   .60
ERB   2
  WHIRLIGIGS
    THEODORE PRESSER COMPANY   .50
ERB   E
  WILD RIDERS
    BELWIN-MILLS PUBLISHING CORPORATION   25175   .60
ERB   1
  WONDERFUL WORLD
    CENTURY MUSIC PUBLISHING COMPANY, INC.   028   .40
ERB, M.
  FROLICKY GRASSHOPPER, THE
    BELWIN-MILLS PUBLISHING CORPORATION   .60
ERB, M.
  HIGH JINKS
    SHAWNEE PRESS, INC.   HB-5024   .60
ERB, M.
  RODEO RIDERS
    SHAWNEE PRESS, INC.   HB-5084   .60
ERB, M.   EASY
  WHIZ, GOES THE TRAIN
    SHAWNEE PRESS, INC.   HB-5013   .40
ERBSE
  EKSTATO, OP. 7 -- 1953 --
    ASSOCIATED MUSIC PUBLISHERS, INC.   B/B   2.25
ERBSE
  RUTH, OP. 16 -- BALLET IN 2 ACTS
    ASSOCIATED MUSIC PUBLISHERS, INC.   BOT   9.00
ERBSE
  SONATA, OP. 6 -- 1953 --
    ASSOCIATED MUSIC PUBLISHERS, INC.   B/B   3.00
ERICOURT   7, 8
  FANTAISIE
    ALPHONSE LEDUC
ERMANN
  DOUZE VARIATIONS ROMANTIQUES
    ASSOCIATED MUSIC PUBLISHERS, INC.   ESC   5.50
ESCOBAR, L.
  SONATINA NO. 02
    PAN AMERICAN UNION   01.00
ESPEN, T.
  DREAMS ON THE BOSPHORUS, OP. 32
    G. SCHIRMER, INC.   .50
ESPEN, T.   3
  FRUEHLINGSERWACHEN
    CENTURY MUSIC PUBLISHING COMPANY, INC.   2206   .40
ESPEN, T.   3
  SPRING'S AWAKENING, OP. 3 NO. 1
    CENTURY MUSIC PUBLISHING COMPANY, INC.   2206   .40
ESPLA
  CHANTS D'ANTAN -- CHILDREN'S SUITE
    ASSOCIATED MUSIC PUBLISHERS, INC.   ESC   2.00
ESPLA
  IMPRESIONES MUSICALES
    ASSOCIATED MUSIC PUBLISHERS, INC.   UME   1.25
ESPLA
  LIRICA ESPANOLA, OP. 54 -- VOL. 1
    ASSOCIATED MUSIC PUBLISHERS, INC.   UME   1.50
ESPLA
  PAJARA PINTA, LA
    ASSOCIATED MUSIC PUBLISHERS, INC.   UME   1.00
ESPLA
  SCHERZO, OP. 5
    ASSOCIATED MUSIC PUBLISHERS, INC.   UME   .80
ESPLA
  SIERRA, LA. FOLKLORE SUITE
    ASSOCIATED MUSIC PUBLISHERS, INC.   ESC   3.00
ESPLA
  SONATA ESPANOLA, OP. 53 -- 1949 --
    ASSOCIATED MUSIC PUBLISHERS, INC.   UME   2.25
ESPLA
  SUITE OF LITTLE PIECES
    ASSOCIATED MUSIC PUBLISHERS, INC.   UME   .80
ESTELLA   2
  TWISTING THE TWIST
    CENTURY MUSIC PUBLISHING COMPANY, INC.   4388   .40
ETHRIDGE
  SUNDAY MORNING
    ASSOCIATED MUSIC PUBLISHERS, INC.   BER   .40
ETLER
  SONATINA
    ALEXANDER BROUDE, INC.   3.00
ETTI
  SONATINA
    ASSOCIATED MUSIC PUBLISHERS, INC.   DOB   2.00
ETTORE, E.
  DANCING MAGPIE
    COMPOSERS AUTOGRAPH PUBLICATIONS   .66
ETTORE, E.
  ELEGIE
    COMPOSERS AUTOGRAPH PUBLICATIONS   .66
ETTORE, E.
  LIFE OF LOVE, THE
    COMPOSERS AUTOGRAPH PUBLICATIONS   .66

ETTORE, E.
  NAME THAT SWINGS, A
    COMPOSERS AUTOGRAPH PUBLICATIONS   1.32
ETTORE, E.
  RONDO FOR PIANO
    COMPOSERS AUTOGRAPH PUBLICATIONS   1.98
ETTORE, E.
  THEME AND VARIATIONS
    COMPOSERS AUTOGRAPH PUBLICATIONS   1.54
ETTORE, E.
  VALSE FOR PIANO
    COMPOSERS AUTOGRAPH PUBLICATIONS   1.10
EVANS   LAMONT
  LADY OF SPAIN
    SOUTHERN MUSIC COMPANY   1.00
EVANS   KLICKMANN
  LADY OF SPAIN -- SIMPLIFIED
    SOUTHERN MUSIC COMPANY   .50
EVANS   2
  LOLA WALTZ
    VOLKWEIN BROS.   .30
EVANS   2
  NINA MARCH
    VOLKWEIN BROS.   .25
EVANS   4
  VARIATIONS ON A NURSERY TUNE, 'THREE BLIND MICE' IN THE STYLES
  OF CORELLI, BACH, MOZART, AND FRANCK
    BOSTON MUSIC COMPANY   .50
EVANS *
  LADY OF SPAIN
    SAM FOX PUBLISHING COMPANY, INC.   1.00
EVANS, M. L.   3
  YELLOW BUTTERFLIES
    THEODORE PRESSER COMPANY   .50
EVETT
  SONATA NO. 02
    PAN AMERICAN UNION   01.60
EWING, M.
  DEW ON THE ROSE, THE
    FREDERICK HARRIS MUSIC COMPANY   .60
EWING, M.
  PRINCESS WALTZ
    FREDERICK HARRIS MUSIC COMPANY   .55
EWING, M.
  SHADOWS OF TWILIGHT, THE
    FREDERICK HARRIS MUSIC COMPANY   .60
EZELL, H.   E
  APRIL
    OXFORD UNIVERSITY PRESS   93.810   .40
EZELL, H.   3
  ARAB RIDERS
    BELWIN-MILLS PUBLISHING CORPORATION   .60
EZELL, H.
  BOUND FOR BIRMINGHAM
    BRODT MUSIC COMPANY   .45
EZELL, H.   2
  CREOLE LULLABY
    WILLIS MUSIC COMPANY   .40
EZELL, H.   E
  DAY IN SPRING
    OXFORD UNIVERSITY PRESS   93.315   .40
EZELL, H.
  LITTLE BUCKAROO
    BRODT MUSIC COMPANY   .45
EZELL, H.
  MOONLIT GARDEN
    SAM FOX PUBLISHING COMPANY, INC.   .50
EZELL, H.
  MOONLIT GARDEN
    SOUTHERN MUSIC COMPANY   .50
EZELL, H.   3
  PROUD MR. GOBBLER
    BELWIN-MILLS PUBLISHING CORPORATION   .60
EZELL, H.
  QUITE CONTRARY
    G. SCHIRMER, INC.   .35
EZELL, H.
  RESTLESS BROOK
    G. SCHIRMER, INC.   .40
EZELL, H.
  RIVER BOAT
    G. SCHIRMER, INC.   .35
EZELL, H.
  SEE SAW
    BRODT MUSIC COMPANY   .45
EZELL, H.
  SMALL FRY
    SAM FOX PUBLISHING COMPANY, INC.   1.25
EZELL, H.
  SOFT LITTLE BREEZE
    BRODT MUSIC COMPANY   .45
EZELL, H.   1
  TIRESOME RAINDROPS
    BELWIN-MILLS PUBLISHING CORPORATION   .60
EZELL, H.
  TRAVELIN' WEST
    G. SCHIRMER, INC.   .40
EZELL, H.   3
  WITCHES PARTY, ON THE BROOMSTICK
    BELWIN-MILLS PUBLISHING CORPORATION   .60
FABER   WEYBRIGHT   2
  FAITH OF OUR FATHERS
    BELWIN-MILLS PUBLISHING CORPORATION   .50
FABER   WEYBRIGHT   2
  FAITH OF OUR FATHERS, A HYMN
    BELWIN-MILLS PUBLISHING CORPORATION   .60
FAGO   M
  TOCCATA FOR HARPSICHORD
    C. F. PETERS CORPORATION   ZA4311   1.50
FAGO
  TOCCATA FOR HARPSICHORD
    FRANCO COLOMBO PUBLICATIONS   Z4311   2.00
FAHNESTOCK   GR. 2 1/2
  CANDY'S DANCE
    KENYON PUBLICATIONS   .75
FAHNESTOCK   E-M
  DELTA, THE
    COMPOSERS PRESS, INC.   1.00
FAHNESTOCK   E
  HAPPY GO LUCKY
    COMPOSERS PRESS, INC.   1.00
FAHNESTOCK   SCHAUM, J.   2
  NIGHT FLIGHT
    SCHAUM PUBLICATIONS, INC.   .50
FAHNESTOCK   3
  QUITE CATCHY
    BOSTON MUSIC COMPANY   .50

FAIN   HASTINGS
  SECRET LOVE
    WARNER BROTHERS PUBLISHERS   1.00
FAIN *
  APRIL LOVE
    THE BIG THREE MUSIC CORPORATION   00.95
FAIN *
  LOVE IS A MANY-SPLENDORED THING
    THE BIG THREE MUSIC CORPORATION   00.95
FAIRCHILD
  CINQ CHANTS NEGRES
    ELKAN-VOGEL, INC.   D   2.25
FAIRCHILD
  EN VOYAGE
    ELKAN-VOGEL, INC.   D   4.50
FAIRCHILD   3
  IRISH MEDLEY
    VOLKWEIN BROS.   .25
FAIRCHILD   3
  IRISH MEDLEY
    VOLKWEIN BROS.   00.50
FAIRCHILD
  POUR LES PETITS -- LE PETIT NEGRE EST TRISTE
    ELKAN-VOGEL, INC.   D   .50
FAITH   ADVANCED
  DARK RIDERS, THE
    SHAWNEE PRESS, INC.   HB-228   1.25
FAITH
  HIGHWAYMAN, THE
    SUMMY-BIRCHARD COMPANY   .50
FAITH
  LEGEND
    SUMMY-BIRCHARD COMPANY   .50
FAITH   ADVANCED
  SONATA NO. 01
    SHAWNEE PRESS, INC.   HB-229   2.00
FAITH *
  SWEDISH RHAPSODY
    TRO SONGWAYS SERVICE, INC.   2054
FALLA, M. DE
  ANDALUZA FROM PIECES ESPAGNOLES
    ELKAN-VOGEL, INC.   2.25
FALLA, M. DE
  ARAGONESA FROM PIECES ESPAGNOLES
    ELKAN-VOGEL, INC.   2.25
FALLA, M. DE
  CUBANA FROM PIECES ESPAGNOLES
    ELKAN-VOGEL, INC.   2.25
FALLA, M. DE
  MONTANESA FROM PIECES ESPAGNOLES
    ELKAN-VOGEL, INC.   2.25
FALLA, M. DE
  NOCTURNE
    ASSOCIATED MUSIC PUBLISHERS, INC.   UME   .75
FALLA, M. DE
  SERENATA ANDALUZA
    ASSOCIATED MUSIC PUBLISHERS, INC.   UME   1.10
FALLA, M. DE
  SERENATA ANDALUZA
    G. SCHIRMER, INC.   .60
FALLA, M. DE   SCHMITZ
  SPANISH DANCE NO. 1 -- FROM ''LA VIE BREVE''
    ASSOCIATED MUSIC PUBLISHERS, INC.   ESC   1.00
FALLA, M. DE   SAMAZEUILH
  SPANISH DANCE NO. 1 -- FROM ''LA VIE BREVE''
    ASSOCIATED MUSIC PUBLISHERS, INC.   ESC   3.00
FALLA, M. DE   SAMAZEUILH
  SPANISH DANCE NO. 2 -- FROM ''LA VIE BREVE''
    ASSOCIATED MUSIC PUBLISHERS, INC.   ESC   .75
FALLA, M. DE
  VALS-CAPRICHO
    ASSOCIATED MUSIC PUBLISHERS, INC.   UME   .90
FANCELLI, L.
  IL PRESEPE
    EDIZIONI BERBEN   EB 165   .90
FANO, G. A.
  ENFANT S'AMUSE, L'
    FRANCO COLOMBO PUBLICATIONS   Z1463   .90
FANO, G. A.
  IMAGO DAL MONTE PELLEGRINO
    FRANCO COLOMBO PUBLICATIONS   122749   1.25
FANO, G. A.
  SOLITUDE
    FRANCO COLOMBO PUBLICATIONS   122750   1.25
FANO, G. A.
  SONATINA, OP. 5
    FRANCO COLOMBO PUBLICATIONS   BON.175   1.00
FARINA   BOCCALLI
  PASTORALI DEL NATALE
    FRANCO COLOMBO PUBLICATIONS   128958   1.75
FARINA
  TWELVE CHARACTERISTIC PIECES, BK. 1 - EASY
    FRANCO COLOMBO PUBLICATIONS   ER2055   1.25
FARINA
  TWELVE CHARACTERISTIC PIECES, BK. 2 - MEDIUM-DIFFICULT
    FRANCO COLOMBO PUBLICATIONS   ER2056   1.50
FARISS, M.
  BARNYARD SAILORS
    G. SCHIRMER, INC.   .30
FARISS, M.
  OUR FEARLESS ASTRONAUTS
    G. SCHIRMER, INC.   .40
FARJEON
  FESTIVAL GROUPS FOR PIANO SELECTED BY ARTHUR BENJAMIN, SERIES 1
  -- PRELUDE
    BOOSEY AND HAWKES, INC.   .60
FARJEON
  FESTIVAL GROUPS FOR PIANO SELECTED BY ARTHUR BENJAMIN, SERIES 1
  -- KATE GREENAWAY
    BOOSEY AND HAWKES, INC.   .60
FARJEON
  SPRITE IN THE GRASS
    FRANCO COLOMBO PUBLICATIONS   LD22   1.00
FARKAS, F.
  BALLADE
    BELWIN-MILLS PUBLISHING CORPORATION   07012   2.50
FARKAS, F.
  CORRESPONDENCES
    BELWIN-MILLS PUBLISHING CORPORATION   07026   2.50
FARQUHAR
  PARTITA
    BOOSEY AND HAWKES, INC.   .75
FARRAR, F. E.   2
  FAIRY FOOTSTEPS
    THEODORE PRESSER COMPANY   .50

FARWELL, A.   A
  NAVAJO WAR DANCE NO. 2
      THEODORE PRESSER COMPANY   .75
FASULLO
  NOCTURNE
      FRANCO COLOMBO PUBLICATIONS   FOR.12123   .90
FAUCHEY
  HESITATION -- WALTZ --
      FRANCO COLOMBO PUBLICATIONS   SAL   1.75
FAURE, G.
  BALLADE, OP. 19
      ELKAN-VOGEL, INC.   3.70
FAURE, G.
  BARCAROLLE NO. 07, OP. 90
      HEUGEL ET CIE.   1.95
FAURE, G.
  BARCAROLLE NO. 08, OP. 96
      HEUGEL ET CIE.   2.45
FAURE, G.
  BARCAROLLE NO. 09, OP. 101
      HEUGEL ET CIE.   2.00
FAURE, G.
  BARCAROLLE NO. 10
      ELKAN-VOGEL, INC.   2.50
FAURE, G.
  BARCAROLLE NO. 11
      ELKAN-VOGEL, INC.   2.00
FAURE, G.
  BARCAROLLE NO. 12
      ELKAN-VOGEL, INC.   2.25
FAURE, G.
  BARCAROLLE NO. 13
      ELKAN-VOGEL, INC.   2.25
FAURE, G.   4
  IMPROMPTU IN F SHARP MINOR, OP. 31 NO. 2
      BOSTON MUSIC COMPANY   .60
FAURE, G.
  IMPROMPTU NO. 1
      ELKAN-VOGEL, INC.   2.30
FAURE, G.
  IMPROMPTU NO. 2
      ELKAN-VOGEL, INC.   2.50
FAURE, G.
  IMPROMPTU NO. 3
      ELKAN-VOGEL, INC.   2.50
FAURE, G.
  IMPROMPTU NO. 4, OP. 91
      HEUGEL ET CIE.   2.00
FAURE, G.
  IMPROMPTU NO. 5, OP. 102
      HEUGEL ET CIE.   2.00
FAURE, G.
  NOCTURNE NO. 04 IN E FLAT, OP. 36
      INTERNATIONAL MUSIC COMPANY   1.00
FAURE, G.
  NOCTURNE NO. 05 IN B FLAT, OP. 37
      INTERNATIONAL MUSIC COMPANY   1.00
FAURE, G.
  NOCTURNE NO. 09, OP. 97
      HEUGEL ET CIE.   1.65
FAURE, G.
  NOCTURNE NO. 10, OP. 99
      HEUGEL ET CIE.   1.65
FAURE, G.
  NOCTURNE NO. 11
      ELKAN-VOGEL, INC.   2.50
FAURE, G.
  NOCTURNE NO. 12
      ELKAN-VOGEL, INC.   3.00
FAURE, G.
  NOCTURNE NO. 13
      ELKAN-VOGEL, INC.   3.00
FAURE, G.
  NOCTURNE, OP. 33 NO. 1
      ELKAN-VOGEL, INC.   2.30
FAURE, G.   FREEMAN   4
  PALMS, THE
      CENTURY MUSIC PUBLISHING COMPANY, INC.   594   .40
FAURE, G.
  PENELOPE-PRELUDE
      HEUGEL ET CIE.   2.40
FAURE, G.
  ROMANCE SANS PAROLES
      EDWIN F. KALMUS   3435   1.25
FAURE, G.
  SICILIENNE, OP. 78
      ELKAN-VOGEL, INC.   HAM   10.00
FAURE, G.
  THEME AND VARIATIONS, OP. 73
      EDWIN F. KALMUS   3436   1.75
FAURE, G.
  THEME AND VARIATIONS, OP. 73
      ELKAN-VOGEL, INC.   4.25
FAURE, G.
  THEME AND VARIATIONS, OP. 73
      INTERNATIONAL MUSIC COMPANY   1.75
FAURE, J.   SCHAUM, J.   1
  PALMS, THE
      BELWIN-MILLS PUBLISHING CORPORATION   .50
FAURE, J.   LEYBACH   5
  PALMS, THE, TRANS.
      CENTURY MUSIC PUBLISHING COMPANY, INC.   526   .40
FAURE, J.   FREEMAN   4
  PALMS, THE, VAR.
      CENTURY MUSIC PUBLISHING COMPANY, INC.   594   .40
FAVRE   4
  DEUX PIECES - AIR BRETON
      ALPHONSE LEDUC
FAVRE   4
  DEUX PIECES - VALSE MELANCOLIQUE
      ALPHONSE LEDUC
FAWCETT   WEYBRIGHT   1 1/2
  BLEST BE THE TIE THAT BINDS
      BELWIN-MILLS PUBLISHING CORPORATION   .50
FAWCETT   WEYBRIGHT   1 1/2
  BLEST BE THE TIE THAT BINDS -- HYMN
      BELWIN-MILLS PUBLISHING CORPORATION   .60
FAYE
  ONLY YESTERDAY
      MCA MUSIC   1.00
FEARIS, J. S.   STEINER   1
  BEAUTIFUL ISLE OF SOMEWHERE
      BELWIN-MILLS PUBLISHING CORPORATION   .60
FEDERE   4
  BUDS AND BLOSSOMS
      CENTURY MUSIC PUBLISHING COMPANY, INC.   1081   .40

FEDERER, R.   3 1/2
  DREAM TIME
      THEODORE PRESSER COMPANY   .50
FEDERER, R.   3
  FADED LOVE LETTER
      THEODORE PRESSER COMPANY   .50
FEDERER, R.   5
  GARDENIAS
      THEODORE PRESSER COMPANY   .50
FEDERER, R.   4
  OLD ROMANCE, AN
      THEODORE PRESSER COMPANY   .50
FEDERER, R.   3
  ON SILVER SKATES
      THEODORE PRESSER COMPANY   .50
FEINBERG, S.
  SONATA NO. 06, OP. 13
      UNIVERSAL EDITION   UE 7342   1.95
FELD, J.   4
  PRAELUDIUM UND TOCCATA
      BARENREITER VERLAG   AP 1652
FELD, J.
  PRELUDIUM AND TOCCATA
      ARTIA   1.00
FELINE
  BERCEUSE
      ASSOCIATED MUSIC PUBLISHERS, INC.   ESC   .40
FELINE
  CARAVANES
      FRANCO COLOMBO PUBLICATIONS   SAL   2.50
FENNER
  SUITE
      FRANCO COLOMBO PUBLICATIONS   NY1081   .60
FENSTOCK, B.
  HEBREW RHAPSODY
      BELWIN-MILLS PUBLISHING CORPORATION   20122   1.00
FENSTOCK, B.
  MEXICAN FIESTA
      WARNER BROTHERS PUBLISHERS   .60
FENTON, R.
  BREAK AWAY
      BANKS AND SON LTD.   .25
FERGUSON, J.
  AIR DE BALLET
      G. SCHIRMER, INC.   .50
FERNANDEZ   DEL MAGLIO
  CIELITO LINDO
      FRANCO COLOMBO PUBLICATIONS   129115   .60
FERNANDEZ GIL
  DIVERTIMENTO, OP. 32
      FRANCO COLOMBO PUBLICATIONS   129462   1.25
FERNANDEZ GIL
  MORT DE ROLAND, OP. 18
      ASSOCIATED MUSIC PUBLISHERS, INC.   ESC   3.25
FERNANDEZ, E. *
  DE ROMERIA. DANZA LEONESA
      ASSOCIATED MUSIC PUBLISHERS, INC.   UME   .75
FERNANDEZ, O.   3
  BEAUTIFUL HEAVEN
      BELWIN-MILLS PUBLISHING CORPORATION   613   .60
FERNANDEZ, O.
  BRASILIAN SUITE 1 - OLD SONG
      PEER SOUTHERN ORGANIZATION   00.60
FERNANDEZ, O.
  BRASILIAN SUITE 1 - SERENADE
      PEER SOUTHERN ORGANIZATION   00.60
FERNANDEZ, O.
  BRASILIAN SUITE 1 - SWEET CRADLE
      PEER SOUTHERN ORGANIZATION   00.60
FERNANDEZ, O.
  BRASILIAN SUITE 2 - DANCE
      PEER SOUTHERN ORGANIZATION   00.90
FERNANDEZ, O.
  BRASILIAN SUITE 2 - PRELUDE
      PEER SOUTHERN ORGANIZATION   00.60
FERNANDEZ, O.
  BRASILIAN SUITE 2 - SONG
      PEER SOUTHERN ORGANIZATION   00.85
FERNANDEZ, O.
  BRASILIAN SUITE 3 - NEGRO DANCE
      PEER SOUTHERN ORGANIZATION   00.75
FERNANDEZ, O.
  BRASILIAN SUITE 3 - SERENADE
      PEER SOUTHERN ORGANIZATION   00.60
FERNANDEZ, O.
  BRASILIAN SUITE 3 - SONG
      PEER SOUTHERN ORGANIZATION   00.75
FERNANDEZ, O.
  CHILDREN'S VISIONS - LITTLE CORTEGE
      PEER SOUTHERN ORGANIZATION   00.75
FERNANDEZ, O.
  CHILDREN'S VISIONS - MYSTERIOUS DANCE
      PEER SOUTHERN ORGANIZATION   00.80
FERNANDEZ, O.
  CHILDREN'S VISIONS - NOCTURNAL ROUND
      PEER SOUTHERN ORGANIZATION   00.80
FERNANDEZ, O.   3
  CIELITO LINDO
      CENTURY MUSIC PUBLISHING COMPANY, INC.   3570   .40
FERNANDEZ, O.   3
  CIELITO LINDO
      CENTURY MUSIC PUBLISHING COMPANY, INC.   2265   .40
FERNANDEZ, O.
  DOLLS - CHOCOLATE CAKE GIRL VENDOR
      PEER SOUTHERN ORGANIZATION   00.75
FERNANDEZ, O.
  DOLLS - ITALIAN PEASANT GIRL
      PEER SOUTHERN ORGANIZATION   00.75
FERNANDEZ, O.
  DOLLS - PORTUGUESE SHEPHERDESS
      PEER SOUTHERN ORGANIZATION   00.75
FERNANDEZ, O.
  DOLLS - RUSSIAN GIRL WOODCUTTER
      PEER SOUTHERN ORGANIZATION   00.75
FERNANDEZ, O.
  DOLLS - SPANISH BALLERINA
      PEER SOUTHERN ORGANIZATION   00.75
FERNANDEZ, O.
  FIREFLIES
      PEER SOUTHERN ORGANIZATION   00.80
FERNANDEZ, O.
  LULLABY OF MEMORIES
      PEER SOUTHERN ORGANIZATION   00.75
FERNANDEZ, O.
  MIRAGE
      PEER SOUTHERN ORGANIZATION   00.80

FERNANDEZ, O.
  NAIVE LITTLE TALE
      PEER SOUTHERN ORGANIZATION   00.75
FERNANDEZ, O.
  NOCTURNE
      PEER SOUTHERN ORGANIZATION   01.25
FERNANDEZ, O.
  REVERIE
      PEER SOUTHERN ORGANIZATION   00.85
FERNANDEZ, O.
  SERENADE OF PRINCE CHARMING
      PEER SOUTHERN ORGANIZATION   00.75
FERNANDEZ, O.
  SNOW WHITE
      PEER SOUTHERN ORGANIZATION   00.80
FERNANDEZ, O.
  SONATA BREVE
      PEER SOUTHERN ORGANIZATION   02.00
FERNANDEZ, O.
  SUITE ON FIVE NOTES
      PEER SOUTHERN ORGANIZATION   01.25
FERNANDEZ, O.
  WOODLAND FAIRY
      PEER SOUTHERN ORGANIZATION   00.85
FERNANDEZ, O.
  YAYA, THE DOLL
      PEER SOUTHERN ORGANIZATION   01.00
FERRARI-TRECATE
  CAMPANE FAN DIN DON
      FRANCO COLOMBO PUBLICATIONS   BON.1729   1.75
FERRARI-TRECATE
  NINNOLI MUSICALI
      FRANCO COLOMBO PUBLICATIONS   127798   1.50
FERRARI-TRECATE
  OMBRE SULLO SCHERMO
      FRANCO COLOMBO PUBLICATIONS   127449   1.50
FERRARI-TRECATE
  PRODE ANSELMO, IL
      FRANCO COLOMBO PUBLICATIONS   123921   1.00
FERRARI-TRECATE
  RIFLESSI LAGUNARI
      FRANCO COLOMBO PUBLICATIONS   127446   1.50
FERRARI-TRECATE
  SBALZI
      FRANCO COLOMBO PUBLICATIONS   125414   1.50
FERRARIS
  PRIMI TOCHI
      FRANCO COLOMBO PUBLICATIONS   FOR.12225   1.25
FERRARIS
  TES YEUX NOIRS
      FRANCO COLOMBO PUBLICATIONS   SAL   1.50
FERRELL, B.   2
  DESERT SANDS
      BOSTON MUSIC COMPANY   .50
FERRELL, B.   2
  FOREST ECHOES
      BOSTON MUSIC COMPANY   .50
FERRELL, B.   2
  HONEY BEE
      BOSTON MUSIC COMPANY   .50
FERRELL, B.   3
  OUTER SPACE
      BOSTON MUSIC COMPANY   .50
FERRELL, B.   3 - 4
  RAMA-JAZZ AND JAZZARAMA
      BOSTON MUSIC COMPANY   .50
FERRELL, B.   1
  SOARING IN THE SKY
      BOSTON MUSIC COMPANY   .50
FERRELL, B.   2
  TOY SOLDIERS
      BOSTON MUSIC COMPANY   .50
FERRER   NIN
  SONATA IN D
      ASSOCIATED MUSIC PUBLISHERS, INC. ESC   .90
FERRERO
  ESTILO
      FRANCO COLOMBO PUBLICATIONS   BA12152   .75
FERROUD, P. O.
  AU PARC MONCEAU - NONCHALANTE
      FRANCO COLOMBO PUBLICATIONS   SAL   1.25
FERTE
  BARCAROLLE
      EDITIONS MUSICALES TRANSATLANTIQUES   3.10
FERTE
  ETUDE FOR PIANO
      EDITIONS MUSICALES TRANSATLANTIQUES   3.10
FERTE
  GAMMES DIATONIQUES ET CHROMATIQUES
      EDITIONS MUSICALES TRANSATLANTIQUES   5.60
FERTE
  IMPROVISATION
      EDITIONS MUSICALES TRANSATLANTIQUES   3.10
FERTE
  NOCTURNE FOR PIANO
      EDITIONS MUSICALES TRANSATLANTIQUES   2.70
FERTE
  PIROUETTES
      EDITIONS MUSICALES TRANSATLANTIQUES   3.50
FERTE
  POUR LE PIANO
      EDITIONS MUSICALES TRANSATLANTIQUES   3.50
FERTE
  TARENTELLE
      EDITIONS MUSICALES TRANSATLANTIQUES   3.10
FERTE
  TOCCATA
      EDITIONS MUSICALES TRANSATLANTIQUES   2.80
FEVRIER   5, 6
  LA BONNE JOURNEE - BAVARDAGE
      ALPHONSE LEDUC
FEVRIER   5, 6
  LA BONNE JOURNEE - JOYEUX REVEIL
      ALPHONSE LEDUC
FEVRIER   5, 6
  LA BONNE JOURNEE - SAUTE-MOUTON
      ALPHONSE LEDUC
FEVRIER   7
  TROIS ESQUISSES - CLIGNE-MUSETTE
      ALPHONSE LEDUC
FEVRIER   6
  TROIS ESQUISSES - SOIR
      ALPHONSE LEDUC
FEVRIER   6
  TROIS ESQUISSES - VALSE
      ALPHONSE LEDUC

FIALA
  AUSTRALIAN SUITE
      ASSOCIATED MUSIC PUBLISHERS, INC.   BER   1.25
FIALA
  LULLABY
      ASSOCIATED MUSIC PUBLISHERS, INC.   BER   .75
FIALA
  MINIATURE SUITE
      ASSOCIATED MUSIC PUBLISHERS, INC.   BER   .75
FIALA
  PRELUDE
      ASSOCIATED MUSIC PUBLISHERS, INC.   BER   .40
FIALA
  SONATINA, OP. 1
      ASSOCIATED MUSIC PUBLISHERS, INC.   BER   1.00
FIBICH, Z.   OSTRAL   3
  AM ABEND, OP. 39
      BARENREITER VERLAG   AP 585A
FIBICH, Z.   SCHAUM, J.   4
  MOONLIGHT POEM
      BELWIN-MILLS PUBLISHING CORPORATION   .50
FIBICH, Z.   3
  POEM
      CENTURY MUSIC PUBLISHING COMPANY, INC. 3240   .40
FIBICH, Z.   RAPEE
  POEM
      G. SCHIRMER, INC.   2   .35
FIBICH, Z.
  POEM -- DRIFTING DOWN THE LAGOON --
      CENTURY MUSIC PUBLISHING COMPANY, INC. 3629   .40
                                            2-3
FIBICH, Z.
  POEM -- ERLEICHTERT -- UND FRUHLING UND JUGEND
      BARENREITER VERLAG   AP 591
                                            3
FIBICH, Z.
  POEM -- ORIGINAL -- UND IMAGE
      BARENREITER VERLAG   AP 590
FIBICH, Z.   DEL MAGLIO
  POEM, OP. 41, NO. 14
      FRANCO COLOMBO PUBLICATIONS   128847   .60
FIBICH, Z.   3
  POEM, ROMANCE
      CENTURY MUSIC PUBLISHING COMPANY, INC. 3240   .40
FIBICH, Z.   2-3
  SONATINE IN D MINOR
      BARENREITER VERLAG   AP 592
FIBICH, Z. *
  POEM --MY MOONLIGHT MADONNA--
      CARL FISCHER, INC.   S 2261   .50
FICHANDLER, W.   2 1/2
  COME AFTER ME
      THEODORE PRESSER COMPANY   .50
FICHANDLER, W.
  COUNTRY DANCE
      BROOT MUSIC COMPANY   .50
FICHANDLER, W.   2 1/2
  DANCING SUNBEAMS
      THEODORE PRESSER COMPANY   .50
FICHANDLER, W.   2
  DEW DROPS
      THEODORE PRESSER COMPANY   .50
FICHANDLER, W.   2
  DONKEY RIDE
      THEODORE PRESSER COMPANY   .50
FICHANDLER, W.
  FIVE THUMBNAIL SKETCHES
      BROOT MUSIC COMPANY   .60
FICHANDLER, W.   3
  GRADUATION DANCE
      PRO-ART PUBLICATIONS, INC.   402   .50
FICHANDLER, W.   2
  HAPPY DANCE
      THEODORE PRESSER COMPANY   .50
FICHANDLER, W.
  LITTLE TANGO
      BROOT MUSIC COMPANY   .60
FICHANDLER, W.   2 1/2
  LULLABY
      BELWIN-MILLS PUBLISHING CORPORATION   .60
FICHANDLER, W.   2
  MY SHADOW
      THEODORE PRESSER COMPANY   .50
FICHANDLER, W.   3
  NOCTURNE FROM "SECOND STRING QUARTET"
      BELWIN-MILLS PUBLISHING CORPORATION   .60
FICHANDLER, W.   1
  PLAYTIME
      BELWIN-MILLS PUBLISHING CORPORATION   .60
FICHANDLER, W.   2 1/2
  PROMENADE
      BELWIN-MILLS PUBLISHING CORPORATION   .60
FICHANDLEP, W.
  PUPPET DANCE
      BROOT MUSIC COMPANY   .50
FICHER
  CANCION TRISTE
      PEER SOUTHERN ORGANIZATION   00.75
FICHER
  EL BURRO FLAUTISTA
      PEER SOUTHERN ORGANIZATION   00.75
FICHER
  EL LEON Y EL RATON
      PEER SOUTHERN ORGANIZATION   00.75
FICHER
  ES DESFILE
      PEER SOUTHERN ORGANIZATION   00.75
FICHER
  LA LIEBRE Y LA TORTUGA
      PEER SOUTHERN ORGANIZATION   00.75
FICHER
  LA MONA Y LOS MONOS
      PEER SOUTHERN ORGANIZATION   01.00
FICHER
  LAS PALOMAS
      PEER SOUTHERN ORGANIZATION   00.75
FICHER
  POLKA
      PEER SOUTHERN ORGANIZATION   00.75
FICHER
  RONDA DE LOS ANIMALES
      PEER SOUTHERN ORGANIZATION   01.25
FICHER
  TRES DANZAS EN ESTILO POPULAR ARGENTINO
      PEER SOUTHERN ORGANIZATION   01.50
FICHTER   MCWHERTOR   2
  CAUSE IT'S CHRISTMAS
      VOLKWEIN BROS.   .50

```
FIEDEL
  TEN WEST
    MCA MUSIC                                              1.00
FIELD, E. *               SCHAUM, J.
  WYNKEN, BLYNKEN AND NOD
    BELWIN-MILLS PUBLISHING CORPORATION    4                .50
FIELD, J.
  FIFTH NOCTURNE
    CENTURY MUSIC PUBLISHING COMPANY, INC.  1338    3       .40
FIELD, J.
  NOCTURNE B-DUR
    SCHOTT                                 0925 1/2   1.00
FIELD, J.               LESCHETIZKY
  NOCTURNE IN B FLAT MAJOR
    G. SCHIRMER, INC.                               3       .50
FIELD, J.               KREUTZER       3
  NOCTURNE IN G
    BOSTON MUSIC COMPANY                                   .50
FIELD, J.               MONTANI
  NOCTURNE NO. 01 IN E FLAT
    FRANCO COLOMBO PUBLICATIONS            128516          .50
FIELD, J.               DEL MAGLIO
  NOCTURNE NO. 01 IN E FLAT
    FRANCO COLOMBO PUBLICATIONS            129080          .50
FIELD, J.               MONTANI
  NOCTURNE NO. 05 IN B FLAT
    FRANCO COLOMBO PUBLICATIONS            128517          .50
FIELD, J.                              4
  NOCTURNE, NO. 05
    CENTURY MUSIC PUBLISHING COMPANY, INC.  1338          .40
FIELDS, I.
  FOGBOUND
    BELWIN-MILLS PUBLISHING CORPORATION    20384          .85
FIELDS, I.
  FRANTIC FINGERS
    BELWIN-MILLS PUBLISHING CORPORATION    20102          .85
FIELDS, I.
  MIAMI BEACH RUMBA
    EDWARD B. MARKS MUSIC CORPORATION             01.00
FIELDS, I.
  MIAMI BEACH RUMBA
    EDWARD B. MARKS MUSIC CORPORATION             00.60
FIELDS, I.
  PUPPET'S HOLIDAY
    BELWIN-MILLS PUBLISHING CORPORATION    20215          .85
FIELDS, I.
  SAO PAULO
    BELWIN-MILLS PUBLISHING CORPORATION    20386          .85
FIELDS, I.
  ST. MORITZ
    BELWIN-MILLS PUBLISHING CORPORATION    20232          .85
FIELDS, I.
  TEN DANCING FINGERS
    BELWIN-MILLS PUBLISHING CORPORATION    20298          .85
FILAS                                  1 1/2
  PECAN NUT
    WILLIS MUSIC COMPANY                                  .40
FILAS                                  2
  PEPPERMINT STICK
    WILLIS MUSIC COMPANY                                  .40
FILAS *
  SHOWBOAT RAG
    BELWIN-MILLS PUBLISHING CORPORATION    20237          .85
FINE, I.
  HOMAGE A MOZART
    BOOSEY AND HAWKES, INC.                       E        .50
FINE, I.                               E
  LULLABY FOR A BABY PANDA
    THEODORE PRESSER COMPANY                              .50
FINE, I.
  MUSIC FOR PIANO
    MCA MUSIC                                             2.00
FINE, I.                               E
  VICTORY MARCH OF THE ELEPHANTS
    THEODORE PRESSER COMPANY                              .50
FINK, W.                               4
  SPRING SHOWERS
    CENTURY MUSIC PUBLISHING COMPANY, INC.  1181          .40
FINK, W.
  SPRING SHOWERS, OP. 174
    G. SCHIRMER, INC.                                     .50
FINKBEINER
  CHACONNE
    ASSOCIATED MUSIC PUBLISHERS, INC.      B/H            1.50
FINKE
  MARIONETTEN-MUSIKEN
    ASSOCIATED MUSIC PUBLISHERS, INC.      B/H            1.75
FINKE
  REITER-BURLESQUE, EINE
    ASSOCIATED MUSIC PUBLISHERS, INC.      B/H            3.00
FINLAYSON, W.
  BOATING SONG
    BOOSEY AND HAWKES, INC.                               .40
FINLAYSON, W.
  JUMPING JACK
    BOOSEY AND HAWKES, INC.                               .40
FINLAYSON, W.
  LITTLE MARCH
    BOOSEY AND HAWKES, INC.                               .40
FINLAYSON, W.
  LITTLE WHITE BURRO
    BOOSEY AND HAWKES, INC.                               .40
FINLAYSON, W.                          2
  ON A SUMMER SEA
    BOSTON MUSIC COMPANY                                  .50
FINLAYSON, W.
  PIANO PICTURES
    BOOSEY AND HAWKES, INC.                               .85
FINLAYSON, W.                          3
  SONG OF THE BELLS
    BOSTON MUSIC COMPANY                                  .50
FINLAYSON, W.                          3
  STARS
    BOSTON MUSIC COMPANY                                  .50
FINNEY
  FANTASY
    BOOSEY AND HAWKES, INC.                               1.50
FINNEY                                 MD
  NOSTALGIC WALTZES
    THEODORE PRESSER COMPANY                              1.50
FINNEY                                 A
  PIANO SONATA IN D MINOR
    THEODORE PRESSER COMPANY                              1.75
FINNEY                                 M-D
  SONATA
    C. F. PETERS CORPORATION               6831           2.00

FINNEY                                 A
  SONATA NO. 04 IN E - CHRISTMAS 1945
    THEODORE PRESSER COMPANY                              1.50
FIRESTONE, I.          LEVINE
  IF I COULD TELL YOU
    G. SCHIRMER, INC.                                     .50
FIRESTONE, I.          DEWS
  IN MY GARDEN
    G. SCHIRMER, INC.                                     .60
FISCHER                                5
  A TRAVEPS BOIS
    ALPHONSE LEDUC
FISCHER                                4
  FAISEZ RISETTE, VALSE MIGNONNE
    ALPHONSE LEDUC
FISCHER
  FAUVETTE, LA -- CAPRICE --
    FRANCO COLOMBO PUBLICATIONS            SAL            1.75
FISCHER                                5
  HOP HOP
    ALPHONSE LEDUC
FISCHER                                5
  LA JOLIE HONGROISE, VALSE
    ALPHONSE LEDUC
FISCHER                                3
  WAYSIDE ROSE, THE, OP. 177
    CENTURY MUSIC PUBLISHING COMPANY, INC.  1105          .40
FISCHER, E.                            4
  BUNTE GEDANKEN IM WALZERTAKT
    SCHOTT                                 1301           1.75
FISCHER, E.                            4
  VERLIEBTE TASTEN
    SCHOTT                                 3875           2.00
FISCHER, H.
  FESTIVAL GROUPS FOR PIANO SELECTED BY ARTHUR BENJAMIN, SERIES 2
  -- ENGLISH BALLET
    BOOSEY AND HAWKES, INC.                               .60
FISHER, E.                             1
  BEDTIME
    WILLIS MUSIC COMPANY                                  .40
FISHER, E.                             1
  LITTLE GIRL'S WALTZ, A
    WILLIS MUSIC COMPANY                                  .25
FISHER, E.                             4
  NIGHTINGALE'S TRILL
    CENTURY MUSIC PUBLISHING COMPANY, INC.  1087          .40
FISHER, E.
  PIPES OF PAN
    G. SCHIRMER, INC.                                     .50
FISHER, G.                             2
  CLOWN DANCE
    WILLIS MUSIC COMPANY                                  .40
FISHER, G.                             2
  GOSSIP
    WILLIS MUSIC COMPANY                                  .40
FISHER, L.                             4
  ROBIN'S DEPARTURE, THE
    CENTURY MUSIC PUBLISHING COMPANY, INC.  1688          .40
FISHER, L.                             4
  ROBIN'S RETURN, THE
    CENTURY MUSIC PUBLISHING COMPANY, INC.  2428          .40
FISHER, L.                             4
  ROBIN'S RETURN, THE
    THEODORE PRESSER COMPANY                              .60
FISHER, T.
  PIANO SONATA NO. 01
    COMPOSERS AUTOGRAPH PUBLICATIONS                      5.28
FITCH, J.                              2
  FIVE PLUS FIVE
    THEODORE PRESSER COMPANY                              .50
FITCH, J.                              2 1/2
  MARCH
    THEODORE PRESSER COMPANY                              .50
FITELBERG
  SONATA NO. 01
    ASSOCIATED MUSIC PUBLISHERS, INC.      ESC            3.50
FITZGERALD
  IRISH JIG
    FRANCO COLOMBO PUBLICATIONS            NY1558         .35
FITZPATRICK, J.J.                      3
  DANCE OF THE GOLDENRODS
    CENTURY MUSIC PUBLISHING COMPANY, INC.  2973          .40
FITZPATRICK, J.J.                      3
  FALLING WATERS, REVERIE
    CENTURY MUSIC PUBLISHING COMPANY, INC.  2992          .40
FITZPATRICK, J.J.                      3
  MOONBEAMS ON THE LAKE
    CENTURY MUSIC PUBLISHING COMPANY, INC.  2972          .40
FLAGELLO, N.
  EPISODES
    GENERAL MUSIC PUBLISHING COMPANY, INC.                2.00
FLAGELLO, N.
  EPISODES
    NOVELLO AND COMPANY, LTD.                             1.40
FLAGELLO, N.
  PRELUDE, OSTINATO AND FUGUE
    GENERAL MUSIC PUBLISHING COMPANY, INC.  65            2.50
FLAGELLO, N.
  PRELUDE, OSTINATO AND FUGUE
    GENERAL MUSIC PUBLISHING COMPANY, INC.                3.00
FLAGELLO, N.
  PRELUDE, OSTINATO AND FUGUE
    NOVELLO AND COMPANY, LTD.                             2.50
FLAGELLO, N.
  SONATA
    GENERAL MUSIC PUBLISHING COMPANY, INC.  164           4.00
FLAGELLO, N.
  SONATA
    GENERAL MUSIC PUBLISHING COMPANY, INC.                5.00
FLAGELLO, N.
  SONATA 1962
    NOVELLO AND COMPANY, LTD.                             3.00
FLANAGAN, W.
  SONATA
    PEER SOUTHERN ORGANIZATION                           01.25
FLAXLAND
  ALBUM DE COPINNE - FLANERIE
    FRANCO COLOMBO PUBLICATIONS            SAL            1.50
FLAXLAND
  ALBUM DE CORINNE - WALZETTA
    FRANCO COLOMBO PUBLICATIONS            SAL            1.50
FLAXLAND
  ALBUM DE CORRINE - ANDANTE
    FRANCO COLOMBO PUBLICATIONS            SAL            1.50
FLAXLAND
  ALBUM DE CORRINE - AU COUVENT
    FRANCO COLOMBO PUBLICATIONS            SAL            1.50
```

FLAXLAND
   ALBUM DE CORRINE - CAPRICE SICILIEN AU BAL
      FRANCO COLOMBO PUBLICATIONS   SAL   1.50
FLAXLAND
   ALBUM DE CORRINE - CHANSON ESPAGNOL
      FRANCO COLOMBO PUBLICATIONS   SAL   1.50
FLAXLAND
   ALBUM DE CORRINE - LA PROCESSION
      FRANCO COLOMBO PUBLICATIONS   SAL   1.50
FLAXLAND
   ALBUM DE CORRINE - PRINTEMPS
      FRANCO COLOMBO PUBLICATIONS   SAL   1.50
FLAXLAND
   ALBUM DE CORRINE - RETRAITE MILITAIRE
      FRANCO COLOMBO PUBLICATIONS   SAL   1.50
FLEITES, V.
   PEQUENA SUITE
      PEER SOUTHERN ORGANIZATION   00.75
FLETCHER   2
   FOLLOW THE BAND
      BOSTON MUSIC COMPANY   .50
FLETCHER   2
   ICE BALLET, THE
      BOSTON MUSIC COMPANY   .50
FLETCHER   3
   NOBODY KNOWS THE TROUBLE I'VE SEEN
      BOSTON MUSIC COMPANY   .50
FLETCHER   1
   PLAY AWAY SUITE NO. 1
      BOSTON MUSIC COMPANY   .75
FLETCHER   1
   PLAY AWAY SUITE NO. 2
      BOSTON MUSIC COMPANY   .75
FLETCHER   2
   PLAY AWAY SUITE NO. 3
      BOSTON MUSIC COMPANY   .75
FLETCHER   2
   PLAY AWAY SUITE NO. 4
      BOSTON MUSIC COMPANY   .75
FLETCHER   1
   SHOEMAKER'S SHOP
      BOSTON MUSIC COMPANY   .50
FLETCHER   3
   TANGO
      BOSTON MUSIC COMPANY   .50
FLETCHER *
   SUGAR BLUES
      MCA MUSIC   1.00
FLETCHER, G.   2
   HABABERA, A
      THEODORE PRESSER COMPANY   .50
FLETCHER, G.   E
   MARCHING MUSIC FOR JOHNNY APPLESEED
      THEODORE PRESSER COMPANY   .50
FLETCHER, L.   EASY
   WATER SPRITES
      SHAWNEE PRESS, INC.   HB-5002   .50
FLOOD
   RECESS BELL, THE
      BELWIN-MILLS PUBLISHING CORPORATION   .60
FLOOD
   RECESS BELL, THE
      FRANCO COLOMBO PUBLICATIONS   NY1434   .35
FLORSHEIM   4
   ELEVATION
      CENTURY MUSIC PUBLISHING COMPANY, INC.   2210   .40
FLOTOW   KRUG   2
   MARTHA, EASY TRANSCRIPTION
      CENTURY MUSIC PUBLISHING COMPANY, INC.   524   .40
FLOTOW   DORN   4
   MARTHA, FANTASIE, OP. 39
      CENTURY MUSIC PUBLISHING COMPANY, INC.   306   .40
FLOYD, C.
   SONATA
      BOOSEY AND HAWKES, INC.   2.50
FLYNN *   3-4
   WITH YOU, MY OWN
      CENTURY MUSIC PUBLISHING COMPANY, INC.   2556   .40
FOLDEN
   TOYMAKERS DREAM
      EDWARD B. MARKS MUSIC CORPORATION   00.60
FOLDES   2 1/2
   FROM A STORY BOOK
      CENTURY MUSIC PUBLISHING COMPANY, INC.   024   .40
FOLDES   2
   INVENTION
      CENTURY MUSIC PUBLISHING COMPANY, INC.   4032   .40
FOLDES   1
   IT'S RAINING
      CENTURY MUSIC PUBLISHING COMPANY, INC.   3867   .40
FOLDES   4
   KADENZA ZU KLAVIERKONZERT IN C, K467 BY W. A. MOZART
      BARENREITER VERLAG   BA 3823
FOLDES   4
   KADENZA ZU KLAVIERKONZERT IN C, K503 BY W. A. MOZART
      BARENREITER VERLAG   BA 3822
FOLDES   4
   KADENZA ZU KLAVIERKONZERT IN E FLAT, K482 BY W. A. MOZART
      BARENREITER VERLAG   BA 3908
FOLDES   4
   KADENZA ZU KLAVIERKONZERT IN G, K453 BY W. A. MOZART
      BARENREITER VERLAG   BA 3821
FOLDES   1
   LET'S PLAY TAG
      CENTURY MUSIC PUBLISHING COMPANY, INC.   3870   .40
FOLDES   1
   LITTLE BOATS ON THE POND
      CENTURY MUSIC PUBLISHING COMPANY, INC.   3868   .40
FOLDES   2
   LITTLE VALSE
      CENTURY MUSIC PUBLISHING COMPANY, INC.   3991   .40
FOLDES   2
   MARCHING HOME
      CENTURY MUSIC PUBLISHING COMPANY, INC.   3992   .40
FOLDES   1
   ORGAN GRINDER, THE
      CENTURY MUSIC PUBLISHING COMPANY, INC.   3869   .40
FOLDES   1
   TAKING A WALK
      CENTURY MUSIC PUBLISHING COMPANY, INC.   3866   .40
FOLSOM   2
   ANCHORED, MARCH
      CENTURY MUSIC PUBLISHING COMPANY, INC.   584   .60
FONTAINE   3
   SWING SONG
      CENTURY MUSIC PUBLISHING COMPANY, INC.   2096   .40

FONTAINE, L. J.   4
   DANSE BIZARRE, OP. 107 NO. 2
      THEODORE PRESSER COMPANY   .50
FONTANA
   CAPRICCIO
      FRANCO COLOMBO PUBLICATIONS   NY1070   .50
FONTANA
   ROMANCE
      FRANCO COLOMBO PUBLICATIONS   NY946   .50
FONTENAILLES
   NID DANS LES ROSES
      FRANCO COLOMBO PUBLICATIONS   SAL   1.75
FONTPIERE, G.
   LITTLE SUITE
      NOVELLO AND COMPANY, LTD.   1.90
FONTRIERE, G.
   LITTLE SUITE FOR PIANO
      GENERAL MUSIC PUBLISHING COMPANY, INC.   1.50
FORBES
   BRUNE ET BLONDE
      FRANCO COLOMBO PUBLICATIONS   SAL   1.75
FORBES, M.   2
   ELFIN COBBLER, THE
      WILLIS MUSIC COMPANY   .40
FORESYTHE, R.
   SERENADE FOR A WEALTHY WIDOW
      THE BIG THREE MUSIC CORPORATION   1 1/2   00.95
FORREST, S.   1
   FROG AND THE POLLIWOG, THE
      THEODORE PRESSER COMPANY   .50
FORREST, S.   1
   PARADE OF THE TIN SOLDIERS
      THEODORE PRESSER COMPANY   .50
FORSMAN
   SONATA NO. 04
      BARENREITER VERLAG   BA 3501   3.25
FORSMAN   4
   SONATA NO. 04
      BARENREITER VERLAG   BA 3501
FORSMAN
   SONATA VARIATO - NO. 3
      BARENREITER VERLAG   BA 3503   3.50
FORSMAN   4
   SONATA VARIATO -- NO. 03 --
      BARENREITER VERLAG   BA 3503
FORTNER, W.   4-5
   EPIGRAMME FUR KLAVIER - 1964
      SCHOTT   4810   3.00
FORTNER, W.   4
   KAMMERMUSIK
      SCHOTT   2219   2.50
FORTNER, W.   3-4
   SONATINA
      SCHOTT   2345   2.75
FOSS, L.
   FANTASY RONDO
      G. SCHIRMER, INC.   1.50
FOSSATI
   BAJO UN ALERO
      FRANCO COLOMBO PUBLICATIONS   BA10609   1.50
FOSSEY, E.   2
   CINDERELLA'S MINUET
      WILLIS MUSIC COMPANY   .40
FOSSEY, E.   1
   RIDE LITTLE COWBOY
      WILLIS MUSIC COMPANY   .40
FOSTER   3
   BEAUTIFUL DREAMER
      CENTURY MUSIC PUBLISHING COMPANY, INC.   3244   .40
FOSTER   4
   BEAUTIFUL DREAMER
      THEODORE PRESSER COMPANY   .50
FOSTER   SCHIEFELBEIN, F.   2
   BEAUTIFUL DREAMER
      VOLKWEIN BROS.   .25
FOSTER   1
   CAMPTOWN RACES
      CENTURY MUSIC PUBLISHING COMPANY, INC.   3462   .40
FOSTER   1
   CLASSIC GEMS OF STEPHEN FOSTER
      CENTURY MUSIC PUBLISHING COMPANY, INC.   3531   .40
FOSTER   SCHIEFELBEIN, F.   2
   COME WHERE MY LOVE LIES DREAMING
      VOLKWEIN BROS.   .25
FOSTER
   DAINTY LADY
      EDWARD B. MARKS MUSIC CORPORATION   00.60
FOSTER   WEYBRIGHT   1
   DE CAMPTOWN RACES
      BELWIN-MILLS PUBLISHING CORPORATION   .60
FOSTER   SCHIEFELBEIN, F.   2
   GENTLE ANNIE
      VOLKWEIN BROS.   .25
FOSTER   WEYBRIGHT   2
   GLENDY BURKE, THE
      BELWIN-MILLS PUBLISHING CORPORATION   .50
FOSTER   WEYBRIGHT   2
   GLENDY BURKE, THE
      BELWIN-MILLS PUBLISHING CORPORATION   .60
FOSTER   SCHIEFELBEIN, F.   2
   HARD TIMES COME AGAIN NO MORE
      VOLKWEIN BROS.   .25
FOSTER   3
   I DREAMED OF JEANIE
      CENTURY MUSIC PUBLISHING COMPANY, INC.   3247   .40
FOSTER   3
   JEANIE WITH LIGHT BROWN HAIR
      CENTURY MUSIC PUBLISHING COMPANY, INC.   3247   .40
FOSTER   WEYBRIGHT   2
   JEANNIE WITH THE LIGHT BROWN HAIR
      BELWIN-MILLS PUBLISHING CORPORATION   .50
FOSTER   WEYBRIGHT   2
   JEANNIE WITH THE LIGHT BROWN HAIR
      BELWIN-MILLS PUBLISHING CORPORATION   .60
FOSTER   BERLIN, B.
   JEANNIE WITH THE LIGHT BROWN HAIR
      FREDERICK HARRIS MUSIC COMPANY   .30
FOSTER   ZEPP   4
   JEANNIE WITH THE LIGHT BROWN HAIR
      PRO-ART PUBLICATIONS, INC.   152   .50
FOSTER   1 1/2
   JEANNIE WITH THE LIGHT BROWN HAIR
      THEODORE PRESSER COMPANY   .50
FOSTER
   LULLABY
      EDWARD B. MARKS MUSIC CORPORATION   00.60

FOSTER	BERLIN, B.			
MASSA'S IN DE COLD, COLD GROUND				
FREDERICK HARRIS MUSIC COMPANY				.30
FOSTER	SCHIEFELBEIN, F.	2		
MASSA'S IN THE COLD, COLD GROUND				
VOLKWEIN BROS.				.25
FOSTER	SCHIEFELBEIN, F.	2		
MY OLD KENTUCKY HOME				
VOLKWEIN BROS.				.25
FOSTER	SPENCER, J.	2		
MY OLD KENTUCKY HOME				
VOLKWEIN BROS.				.25
FOSTER	DRUMHELLER	5		
MY OLD KENTUCKY HOME -- VARIATIONS				
VOLKWEIN BROS.				.50
FOSTER	DRUMHELLER	2		
NELLY WAS A LADY				
VOLKWEIN BROS.				.25
FOSTER	ARMOUR	1		
OH SUSANNA				
CENTURY MUSIC PUBLISHING COMPANY, INC.		3464		.40
FOSTER	SCHIEFELBEIN, F.	2		
OH SUSANNA				
VOLKWEIN BROS.				.25
FOSTER	FLETCHER	2		
OLD BLACK JOE				
BOSTON MUSIC COMPANY				.50
FOSTER	SCHIEFELBEIN, F.	2		
OLD BLACK JOE				
VOLKWEIN BROS.				.25
FOSTER	SPENCER, J.	1		
OLD BLACK JOE				
VOLKWEIN BROS.				.25
FOSTER	DRUMHELLER	4-5		
OLD BLACK JOE -- VARIATIONS				
VOLKWEIN BROS.				.50
FOSTER	SCHIEFELBEIN, F.	2		
OLD DOG TRAY				
VOLKWEIN BROS.				.25
FOSTER	ARMOUR	1		
OLD FOLKS AT HOME				
CENTURY MUSIC PUBLISHING COMPANY, INC.		3465		.40
FOSTER	MEACHAM, F.	4		
OLD FOLKS AT HOME				
CENTURY MUSIC PUBLISHING COMPANY, INC.		1046		.40
FOSTER	DRUMHELLER	4-5		
OLD FOLKS AT HOME				
VOLKWEIN BROS.				.50
FOSTER	SCHIEFELBEIN, F.	2		
OLD FOLKS AT HOME				
VOLKWEIN BROS.				.25
FOSTER	SPENCER, J.	2		
OLD FOLKS AT HOME				
VOLKWEIN BROS.				.25
FOSTER	ZEPP	3-4		
SWANEE MOOD				
PRO-ART PUBLICATIONS, INC.		151		.50
FOSTER	SCHIEFELBEIN, F.	2		
UNCLE NED				
VOLKWEIN BROS.				00.25
FOSTER	MEACHAM, F.	4		
WAY DOWN UPON THE SWANEE RIVER				
CENTURY MUSIC PUBLISHING COMPANY, INC.		1046		.40
FOSTER	SCHIEFELBEIN, F.	2		
WILLIE WE HAVE MISSED YOU				
VOLKWEIN BROS.				00.25
FOSTER, I. R.				
BEDTIME TUNE, A				
FRANCO COLOMBO PUBLICATIONS		LD489		.60
FOSTER, I. R.				
BUSY BIRDS				
BANKS AND SON LTD.				.25
FOSTER, I. R.				
LITTLE GAVOTTE, A				
FRANCO COLOMBO PUBLICATIONS		LD490		.60
FOSTER, I. R.				
ON THE LAWN				
BANKS AND SON LTD.				.25
FOSTER, I. R.				
STATELY PINE TREE, THE				
FRANCO COLOMBO PUBLICATIONS		LD488		.60
FOUNTAIN *				
OH DIDN'T HE RAMBLE				
MCA MUSIC				1.00
FOURDRAIN				
ANNIVERSAIRE				
FRANCO COLOMBO PUBLICATIONS		SAL		1.75
FOURDRAIN				
CREPUSCULE				
FRANCO COLOMBO PUBLICATIONS		SAL		1.75
FOURDRAIN				
EFFET DU SOLEIL				
FRANCO COLOMBO PUBLICATIONS		SAL		1.75
FOURDRAIN				
MARINE				
FRANCO COLOMBO PUBLICATIONS		SAL		1.75
FOURDRAIN				
NENUPHARS, LES				
FRANCO COLOMBO PUBLICATIONS		SAL		1.75
FOURDRAIN				
PROMENADE -- 1915 --				
ASSOCIATED MUSIC PUBLISHERS, INC.		ESC		.90
FOURDRAIN				
SIUTE PITTORESQUE - DANSE GUERRIERE				
FRANCO COLOMBO PUBLICATIONS		SAL		1.75
FOURDRAIN				
SUITE PITTORESQUE - DIMANCHE SOIR				
FRANCO COLOMBO PUBLICATIONS		SAL		1.75
FOURDRAIN				
SUITE PITTORESQUE - DIVERTISSEMENT ORIENTAL				
FRANCO COLOMBO PUBLICATIONS		SAL		1.75
FOURDRAIN				
SUITE PITTORESQUE - FANTASIE BALLET				
FRANCO COLOMBO PUBLICATIONS		SAL		1.75
FOURDRAIN				
SUITE PITTORESQUE - FETE JAPONAISE				
FRANCO COLOMBO PUBLICATIONS		SAL		1.75
FOURDRAIN				
SUITE PITTORESQUE - VIEUX SOUVENIR				
FRANCO COLOMBO PUBLICATIONS		SAL		1.75
FOURDRAIN				
VALSE ALSACIENNE				
FRANCO COLOMBO PUBLICATIONS		SAL		1.75
FOX		EASY		
HOP O'MY THUMB				
SHAWNEE PRESS, INC.				.35

FOX	2			
PAGODA BELLS				
BOSTON MUSIC COMPANY				.50
FRACKENPOHL, A.	1 1/2			
AIR WITH CANON				
ELKAN-VOGEL, INC.				.50
FRACKENPOHL, A.	3			
BERCEUSE AND DIALOGUE				
LEE ROBERTS MUSIC PUBLICATIONS, INC.				.50
FRACKENPOHL, A.	1			
DORIAN TUNE				
LEE ROBERTS MUSIC PUBLICATIONS, INC.				.50
FRACKENPOHL, A.	3			
GLIDING				
LEE ROBERTS MUSIC PUBLICATIONS, INC.				.50
FRACKENPOHL, A.				
LULLABY AND A HAPPY TUNE				
SAM FOX PUBLISHING COMPANY, INC.				.50
FRACKENPOHL, A.				
LULLABY AND A HAPPY TUNE				
SOUTHERN MUSIC COMPANY				.50
FRACKENPOHL, A.	3			
MARCH ON, AND PARADE				
LEE ROBERTS MUSIC PUBLICATIONS, INC.				.50
FRACKENPOHL, A.	1 1/2			
SAD WALTZ				
ELKAN-VOGEL, INC.				.50
FRACKENPOHL, A.	2			
SHARP FOUR				
LEE ROBERTS MUSIC PUBLICATIONS, INC.				.50
FRACKENPOHL, A.	3			
WALKING TUNE, A				
LEE ROBERTS MUSIC PUBLICATIONS, INC.				.50
FRAENKEL				
VARIATIONS AND FANTASIA ON A THEME OF SCHOENBERG, OP. 19 NO. 3				
UNIVERSAL EDITION		UE 12549		4.20
FRAGGI				
ETUDE ROMANTIQUE				
FRANCO COLOMBO PUBLICATIONS		SAL		3.50
FRAGGI				
JEUX DE BEAUTE				
FRANCO COLOMBO PUBLICATIONS		SAL		3.50
FRANCAIX *				
LADY L - THEME				
THE BIG THREE MUSIC CORPORATION				00.95
FRANCAIX, J.				
CARILLON DE FLANDRE				
FRANCO COLOMBO PUBLICATIONS		SAL		1.75
FRANCAIX, J.	4-5			
DANSE DE TROIS ARLEQUINS				
EDITIONS MUSICALES TRANSATLANTIQUES				2.25
FRANCAIX, J.	4			
ELOGE DE LA DANSE				
SCHOTT		4016		2.50
FRANCAIX, J.				
L'INSECTARIUM FUR CEMBALO -- KLAVIER				
SCHOTT		4977		2.50
FRANCAIX, J.				
LA DAME DANS LA LUNE				
EDITIONS MUSICALES TRANSATLANTIQUES				8.00
FRANCAIX, J.				
LA DAME DANS LA LUNE				
EDITIONS MUSICALES TRANSATLANTIQUES				8.00
FRANCAIX, J.				
MARCHE DES ECOSSAIS				
FRANCO COLOMBO PUBLICATIONS		SAL		1.75
FRANCAIX, J.				
MON RECITAL - LE COUCOU AND EN BERCANT CLAUDE				
FRANCO COLOMBO PUBLICATIONS		SAL		1.50
FRANCAIX, J.	4			
SCHERZO				
SCHOTT		2477		1.75
FRANCAIX, J.				
SI VERSAILLES M'ETAIT CONTE				
EDITIONS MUSICALES TRANSATLANTIQUES				5.25
FRANCAIX, J.				
SIX GRAND MARCHES IN THE STYLE OF THE FIRST EMPIRE				
EDITIONS MUSICALES TRANSATLANTIQUES				5.25
FRANCAIX, J.				
SOIR DE TOUSSAINT EN CAMBRESIS				
FRANCO COLOMBO PUBLICATIONS		SAL		2.50
FRANCAIX, J.	5			
SONATA				
SCHOTT		5082		2.50
FRANCE				
BEAUTY AND THE BEAST				
FREDERICK HARRIS MUSIC COMPANY				.60
FRANCE				
JIG				
ASSOCIATED MUSIC PUBLISHERS, INC.		BER		.60
FRANCHETTI				
CANZONETTA				
FRANCO COLOMBO PUBLICATIONS		BON.2400		1.25
FRANCHETTI	M			
CHANT				
THEODORE PRESSER COMPANY				.50
FRANCHETTI				
SONATA				
FRANCO COLOMBO PUBLICATIONS		BON.2410		2.25
FRANCK, C.				
CHORALE, PRELUDE, FUGUE				
EDWIN F. KALMUS		3447		1.25
FRANCK, C.	MONTANI			
DANZA LENTA				
FRANCO COLOMBO PUBLICATIONS		128421		.50
FRANCK, C.	2			
DOLL'S LAMENT, THE				
CENTURY MUSIC PUBLISHING COMPANY, INC.		3235		.40
FRANCK, C.	WILLAN			
DOLL'S LAMENT, THE				
FREDERICK HARRIS MUSIC COMPANY				.55
FRANCK, C.	2			
LAMENTATION OF A DOLL				
CENTURY MUSIC PUBLISHING COMPANY, INC.		3235		.40
FRANCK, C.	SCHAUM, J.	3		
PANIS ANGELICUS				
BELWIN-MILLS PUBLISHING CORPORATION				.50
FRANCK, C.				
PLAINTES D'UNE POUPEE				
FRANCO COLOMBO PUBLICATIONS		127456		.60
FRANCK, C.	4			
PRALUDIUM, CHORAL UND FUGE				
SCHOTT		08860 1/2		1.00
FRANCK, C.	ROSSI			
PRELUDE, AIR AND FINALE				
FRANCO COLOMBO PUBLICATIONS		ER2105		1.25

FRANCK, C.   BAUER   4 - 6
  PRELUDE, ARIA AND FINALE
    BOSTON MUSIC COMPANY   1.25
FRANCK, C.   SAUER   M-D
  PRELUDE, ARIA, AND FINALE
    C. F. PETERS CORPORATION   3740B   2.50
FRANCK, C.   SAUER   M-D
  PRELUDE, CHORALE AND FUGUE
    C. F. PETERS CORPORATION   3740A   1.25
FRANCK, C.   ROSSI
  PRELUDE, CHORALE AND FUGUE
    FRANCO COLOMBO PUBLICATIONS   ER2094   1.25
FRANCK, C.   PINTER
  PRELUDE, CHORALE AND FUGUE
    G. SCHIRMER, INC.   L1232   1.00
FRANCK, C.   BAUER
  PRELUDE, FUGUE AND VARIATIONS
    ELKAN-VOGEL, INC.   3.00
FRANCK, C.
  PREMIER GRAND CAPRICE
    ELKAN-VOGEL, INC.   LEM   4.50
FRANCK, C.   DUMM
  RECITAL REFRESHER SERIES -- THE DOLL'S COMPLAINT
    BELWIN-MILLS PUBLISHING CORPORATION   26116   .60
FRANCK, C.   JEMAIN
  REDEMPTION - MORCEAU SYMPHONIQUE
    HEUGEL ET CIE.   2.40
FRANCK, C.   SCHAUM, J.   4 1/2
  SYMPHONIC RHAPSODY
    SCHAUM PUBLICATIONS, INC.   .50
FRANCK, C.   M
  SYMPHONIC VARIATIONS
    C. F. PETERS CORPORATION   3741A   1.25
FRANCK, C.   MASON
  SYMPHONY IN D MINOR--MUSIC LOVER'S SYMPHONY SERIES, NO. 6
    G. SCHIRMER, INC.   1.25
FRANCK, C.   3
  THEME FROM SYMPHONY IN D MINOR
    CENTURY MUSIC PUBLISHING COMPANY, INC. 3612   .40
FRANCK, C.   PHILIPP
  VARIATIONS SYMPHONIQUES
    G. SCHIRMER, INC.   L1407   1.50
FRANCK, C,   4
  PANIS ANGELICUS
    CENTURY MUSIC PUBLISHING COMPANY, INC. 3730   .40
FRANCO, C.   2
  PIANO FANTASIE
    COMPOSERS AUTOGRAPH PUBLICATIONS   2.64
FRANCO, J.
  AT THE CIRCUS
    THEODORE PRESSER COMPANY   .50
FRANCO, J.
  EVOCACION MALAGUENA
    FRANCO COLOMBO PUBLICATIONS   SAL   4.00
FRANCO, J.   3 1/2
  SUNRISE AT SEA
    THEODORE PRESSER COMPANY   .50
FRANCO, J.   2 1/2
  THREE PIANO SKETCHES
    THEODORE PRESSER COMPANY   .50
FRANCO, J.   2 1/2
  TOCCATA
    THEODORE PRESSER COMPANY   .50
FRANGIPANE--ED   2
  SWEET ROSIE O'GRADY NUGENT
    CENTURY MUSIC PUBLISHING COMPANY, INC. 4298   .40
FRANGIPANE--ED   2
  WHEN THE SAINTS GO MARCHING
    CENTURY MUSIC PUBLISHING COMPANY, INC. 4299   .40
FRANK
  BAGATELLE
    MCA MUSIC   .60
FRANK
  CATHEDRAL CHIMES
    MCA MUSIC   .60
FRANK
  COSMIC CLOUDS
    SAM FOX PUBLISHING COMPANY, INC.   .50
FRANK
  COSMIC CLOUDS
    SOUTHERN MUSIC COMPANY   .50
FRANK
  COSMIC LIGHTS
    MCA MUSIC   .60
FRANK
  FLIGHT OF FANCY
    MCA MUSIC   .60
FRANK
  MUSING
    MCA MUSIC   .60
FRANK
  PIROUETTE
    MCA MUSIC   .60
FRANK, M.   FRANK, M.
  RED SKELTON -- HIS PIANO BOOK
    SAM FOX PUBLISHING COMPANY, INC.   1.75
FRANKE, M.   3
  INTERMEZZO RUSSE, OP. 136
    CENTURY MUSIC PUBLISHING COMPANY, INC. 1699   .40
FRANKE, T.   3
  RUSSIAN INTERMEZZO, OP. 136
    CENTURY MUSIC PUBLISHING COMPANY, INC. 1699   .40
FRANKELL   D
  SEA PICTURE, A
    C. F. PETERS CORPORATION   H277   .90
FRANKELL   E-M
  THREE DAYS SONATINA
    C. F. PETERS CORPORATION   H1435   1.25
FRANTZ, C.   SCHAUM, J.   1
  TUMBLEWEED TRAIL
    SCHAUM PUBLICATIONS, INC.   .60
FRANTZEN   WEYBRIGHT   2
  COLLEGE LIFE MARCH
    BELWIN-MILLS PUBLISHING CORPORATION   .50
FRANTZEN   WEYBRIGHT   2
  COLLEGE LIFE, MARCH
    BELWIN-MILLS PUBLISHING CORPORATION   .60
FRAZEE, G. F.   2
  MARCH OF THE CHORDS
    WILLIS MUSIC COMPANY   .40
FRAZEE, G. F.   5
  WOODLAND WATERFALL
    THEODORE PRESSER COMPANY   .50
FRAZZI
  MADRIGAL
    FRANCO COLOMBO PUBLICATIONS   FOR.11285   1.25

FRAZZI
  TOCCATA
    FRANCO COLOMBO PUBLICATIONS   FOR.10847   1.25
FREDERICKS   1
  ADESTE FIDELIS
    VOLKWEIN BROS.   .25
FREDERICKS   2-3
  AT PLAY
    VOLKWEIN BROS.   .25
FREDERICKS   2
  AT THE TULIP FESTIVAL
    VOLKWEIN BROS.   .40
FREDERICKS   2
  COUNTRY GARDENS -- EASY
    VOLKWEIN BROS.   .30
FREDERICKS   2
  MERRY GO ROUND
    VOLKWEIN BROS.   .25
FREDERICKS   2
  OFF TO CAMP
    VOLKWEIN BROS.   .30
FREDERICKS   2
  ON GREEN MEADOWS
    VOLKWEIN BROS.   .30
FREDERICKS   3
  SAD STORY
    VOLKWEIN BROS.   .25
FREDERICKS   1
  SILENT NIGHT, HOLY NIGHT
    VOLKWEIN BROS.   .25
FREDERICKS   2
  SUNSET HOUR
    VOLKWEIN BROS.   00.30
FREDERICKS   2
  THROUGH WOOD AND DALE
    VOLKWEIN BROS.   00.25
FREED, I.
  FETE FANTASQUE, UNE
    FRANCO COLOMBO PUBLICATIONS   SAL   2.75
FREED, I.   E
  INCA WAR SONG
    THEODORE PRESSER COMPANY   .50
FREED, I.
  SONATA -- 1933 --
    ASSOCIATED MUSIC PUBLISHERS, INC.   ESC   5.00
FREED, I.
  SONATINA NO. 01
    PEER SOUTHERN ORGANIZATION   00.85
FREED, I.
  SONORITES RYTHMIQUES
    FRANCO COLOMBO PUBLICATIONS   SAL   5.00
FREED, I.   M
  TOCCATINA - THE WIND
    THEODORE PRESSER COMPANY   .50
FREED, I.   E
  WALTZ ON WHITE KEYS
    THEODORE PRESSER COMPANY   .50
FREED, S.   3
  WILD HORSES
    THEODORE PRESSER COMPANY   .50
FREEMAN   4
  BELIEVE ME ENDEARING CHARMS
    CENTURY MUSIC PUBLISHING COMPANY, INC. 749   .40
FREEMAN   4
  CALVARY, TRANSCRIPTION
    CENTURY MUSIC PUBLISHING COMPANY, INC. 683   .40
FREEMAN   4
  COME ALL YE FAITHFUL
    CENTURY MUSIC PUBLISHING COMPANY, INC. 615   .40
FREEMAN   4
  EASTER HYMN, TRANS.
    CENTURY MUSIC PUBLISHING COMPANY, INC. 623   .40
FREEMAN   4
  JERUSALEM, THE GOLDEN
    CENTURY MUSIC PUBLISHING COMPANY, INC. 632   .70
FREEMAN   3
  KATHLEEN MAVOURNEEN, TRANS.
    CENTURY MUSIC PUBLISHING COMPANY, INC. 809   .40
FREEMAN   3
  MY OLD KENTUCKY HOME
    CENTURY MUSIC PUBLISHING COMPANY, INC. 835   .40
FREEMAN   4
  NEARER, MY GOD, TO THEE
    CENTURY MUSIC PUBLISHING COMPANY, INC. 646   .40
FREEMAN--ED.   FREEMAN   4
  ABIDE WITH ME, G MAJOR
    CENTURY MUSIC PUBLISHING COMPANY, INC. 614   .40
FREEMAN--ED.   FREEMAN   4
  ADESTE FIDELIS, A FLAT MAJOR
    CENTURY MUSIC PUBLISHING COMPANY, INC. 615   .40
FREEMAN--ED.   FREEMAN   4
  LEAD, KINDLY LIGHT
    CENTURY MUSIC PUBLISHING COMPANY, INC. 637   .40
FREEMAN--ED.   FREEMAN   3
  OLD KENTUCKY HOME
    CENTURY MUSIC PUBLISHING COMPANY, INC. 835   .40
FREEMAN--ED.
  SONGS OF FAITH
    BOOSEY AND HAWKES, INC.   1.00
FREIRE
  AY-AY-AY -- FAMOUS SERENADE --
    FRANCO COLOMBO PUBLICATIONS   SAL   1.50
FRESCOBALDI   MONTANI
  FRESCOBALDA, LA
    FRANCO COLOMBO PUBLICATIONS   128431   .50
FRESCOBALDI   RESPIGHI
  PASSACAGLIA -- ORGAN --
    FRANCO COLOMBO PUBLICATIONS   117143   .90
FRESCOBALDI   RESPIGHI
  PRELUDE AND FUGUE IN G MINOR -- ORGAN --
    FRANCO COLOMBO PUBLICATIONS   117144   .75
FRESCOBALDI   CERHA
  TOCCATA AND CANZONE -- VCL AD LIB
    ASSOCIATED MUSIC PUBLISHERS, INC.   00B   2.00
FRESCOBALDI   BRUGNOLI
  TOCCATA AND FUGUE IN A MINOR -- ORGAN --
    FRANCO COLOMBO PUBLICATIONS   ER413   1.00
FRESCOBALDI   RESPIGHI
  TOCCATA AND FUGUE IN A MINOR -- ORGAN --
    FRANCO COLOMBO PUBLICATIONS   117145   1.00
FREUNDORFER
  SINGING ZITHER, THE
    MCA MUSIC   1.00
FREY
  VALSE-ARABESQUE
    G. SCHIRMER, INC.   .65

FRICK   2
    PARADE OF THE PANDAS
        BOSTON MUSIC COMPANY   .50
FRICKER, P.   5
    VARIATIONEN, OP. 31
        SCHOTT   10704   2.75
FRIEDMAN   1 1/2
    LET ME CALL YOU SWEETHEART
        SCHAUM PUBLICATIONS, INC.   .75
FRIEDMAN   SCHAUM, J.   1
    SUN DANCE
        BELWIN-MILLS PUBLISHING CORPORATION   .50
FRIEDMAN   GARTNER
    VIENNESE DANCE, NO. 4
        UNIVERSAL EDITION   8312   1.30
FRIEDMAN   GARTNER
    VIENNESE DANCE, NO. 5
        UNIVERSAL EDITION   8313   1.30
FRIEDMAN   GARTNER
    VIENNESE DANCE, NO. 6
        UNIVERSAL EDITION   9904   1.30
FRIML, R.   STEINER
    ALLAH'S HOLIDAY--''KATINKA''
        G. SCHIRMER, INC.   .40
FRIML, R.   LEVINE
    ALLAH'S HOLIDAY--''KATINKA''
        G. SCHIRMER, INC.   .50
FRIML, R.   LEVINE
    ALLAH'S HOLIDAY--''KATINKA''
        G. SCHIRMER, INC.   .50
FRIML, R.   KAPLAN
    ALLAH'S HOLIDAY--''KATINKA''--FOX-TROT
        G. SCHIRMER, INC.   .50
FRIML, R.
    AMOUR COQUET
        G. SCHIRMER, INC.   .50
FRIML, R.   LEVINE
    BUBBLE, THE--''HIGH JINKS''
        G. SCHIRMER, INC.   .50
FRIML, R.
    BUTTERFLIES
        G. SCHIRMER, INC.   .50
FRIML, R.
    CHANSON
        G. SCHIRMER, INC.   .50
FRIML, R.   2-3
    CREPUSCULE OP. 36 NO. 2
        SCHOTT   1.25
FRIML, R.   KOVACS
    DONKEY SERENADE, THE
        G. SCHIRMER, INC.   .50
FRIML, R.   WHITE
    DONKEY SERENADE, THE
        G. SCHIRMER, INC.   .50
FRIML, R.   LEVINE
    DONKEY SERENADE, THE
        G. SCHIRMER, INC.   .50
FRIML, R.   MELVIN, B.
    DONKEY SERENADE, THE--ARRANGED FOR EITHER HAND ALONE, OR BOTH
    HANDS TOGETHER
        G. SCHIRMER, INC.   .35
FRIML, R.
    ECHOES OF SPRING
        G. SCHIRMER, INC.   .60
FRIML, R.
    ETUDE--A GLEE, OP. 85 BIS, NO. 5
        G. SCHIRMER, INC.   .50
FRIML, R.   1
    FOXY KITTEN
        WILLIS MUSIC COMPANY   .40
FRIML, R.
    FROM MY GARDEN
        G. SCHIRMER, INC.   1.25
FRIML, R.   LEVINE
    GIANNINA MIA--''THE FIREFLY''
        G. SCHIRMER, INC.   .50
FRIML, R.   PALMERI
    GIANNINA MIA--''THE FIREFLY''
        G. SCHIRMER, INC.   .50
FRIML, R.   LEVINE
    HE WHO LOVES AND RUNS AWAY--''THE FIREFLY''
        G. SCHIRMER, INC.   .50
FRIML, R.   RICHTER
    INDIAN LOVE CALL
        WARNER BROTHERS PUBLISHERS   .75
FRIML, R.   MOKREJS
    INDIAN LOVE CALL
        WARNER BROTHERS PUBLISHERS   1.00
FRIML, R.   WHITNEY
    INDIAN LOVE CALL
        WARNER BROTHERS PUBLISHERS   1.00
FRIML, R.   LEVINE
    KATINKA--''KATINKA''
        G. SCHIRMER, INC.   .50
FRIML, R.   LEVINE
    LOVE IS LIKE A FIREFLY--''THE FIREFLY''
        G. SCHIRMER, INC.   .50
FRIML, R.   LEVINE
    LOVE'S OWN KISS--''HIGH JINKS''
        G. SCHIRMER, INC.   .50
FRIML, R.   4
    MOON DAWN
        THEODORE PRESSER COMPANY   .50
FRIML, R.
    MOONLIGHT ON THE LAGOON
        G. SCHIRMER, INC.   .50
FRIML, R.
    PONY RACE, OP. 70
        G. SCHIRMER, INC.   .75
FRIML, R.   LEVINE
    RACKETY COO--''KATINKA''
        G. SCHIRMER, INC.   .50
FRIML, R.   RIEGGER
    ROSE MARIE
        WARNER BROTHERS PUBLISHERS   1.00
FRIML, R.
    RUSSIAN DANCE--''KATINKA''
        G. SCHIRMER, INC.   .50
FRIML, R.
    RUSSIAN ROMANCE, OP. 30
        G. SCHIRMER, INC.   .50
FRIML, R.   LEVINE
    SOMETHING SEEMS TINGLE-ING-ING--''HIGH JINKS''
        G. SCHIRMER, INC.   .50
FRIML, R.   PINTER
    SYMPATHY WALTZ--''THE FIREFLY''
        G. SCHIRMER, INC.   .60

FRIML, R.   PALMERI
    SYMPATHY WALTZ--''THE FIREFLY''
        G. SCHIRMER, INC.   .35
FRIML, R.   LEVINE
    SYMPATHY WALTZ--''THE FIREFLY''
        G. SCHIRMER, INC.   .50
FRIML, R.   4
    VALSE CHRISTINE
        THEODORE PRESSER COMPANY   .50
FRIML, R.
    VALSE LUCILLE, OP. 85 BIS, NO. 1
        G. SCHIRMER, INC.   .50
FRIML, R.   LEVINE
    VALSE LUCILLE, OP. 85 BIS, NO. 1
        G. SCHIRMER, INC.   .50
FRIML, R.
    VALSE PARISIENNE
        G. SCHIRMER, INC.   .50
FRIML, R.   LEVINE
    WHEN A MAID COMES KNOCKING AT YOUR HEART--''THE FIREFLY''
        G. SCHIRMER, INC.   .50
FRIML, R.   LEVINE
    WOMAN'S KISS, A--''THE FIREFLY''
        G. SCHIRMER, INC.   .50
FRONTIERE, D.
    HANG 'EM HIGH
        THE BIG THREE MUSIC CORPORATION   00.95
FRONTIERE, D.
    LA CHAMADE
        THE BIG THREE MUSIC CORPORATION   00.95
FRONTIERE, D.
    TWELVE O'CLOCK HIGH - THEME
        THE BIG THREE MUSIC CORPORATION   00.95
FRONTINI
    BARCAROLLE NO. 02
        FRANCO COLOMBO PUBLICATIONS   FOR.9943   .90
FRONTINI
    IVRESSE
        FRANCO COLOMBO PUBLICATIONS   FOR.10246 .90
FRONTINI   MARTIN
    LITTLE MUSICIANS
        BOOSEY AND HAWKES, INC.   .60
FRONTINI
    VALSE D'AMOUR
        FRANCO COLOMBO PUBLICATIONS   FOR.9840   .90
FRONTINI
    VALSE VOLUPTUEUX
        FRANCO COLOMBO PUBLICATIONS   FOR.10013 .90
FRONTINI
    VALZER IDEAL
        FRANCO COLOMBO PUBLICATIONS   FOR.9842   .90
FROSCHAUER
    TOCCATA -- 1956 --
        ASSOCIATED MUSIC PUBLISHERS, INC.   DOB   1.75
FROST   1
    BEADED MOCCASINS
        BELWIN-MILLS PUBLISHING CORPORATION   .60
FROST
    BELL AT THE FOUNTAIN
        BOSTON MUSIC COMPANY   .50
FROST
    BUSY BUGLER, THE
        BOSTON MUSIC COMPANY   .50
FROST   1
    CART WHEELS
        BELWIN-MILLS PUBLISHING CORPORATION   .60
FROST
    CHIMES THROUGH THE MIST
        SUMMY-BIRCHARD COMPANY   .50
FROST
    COME AND PLAY
        G. SCHIRMER, INC.   .35
FROST   1
    CONTENTMENT
        BOSTON MUSIC COMPANY   .50
FROST   1
    CONTENTMENT
        BOSTON MUSIC COMPANY   .50
FROST   2
    GAY PROMENADE, A
        BOSTON MUSIC COMPANY   .50
FROST
    HOP-TOAD, THE
        G. SCHIRMER, INC.   .35
FROST   2
    IMPRESSIONS
        BOSTON MUSIC COMPANY   .50
FROST   1
    IN A SPACE SHIP
        BELWIN-MILLS PUBLISHING CORPORATION   .60
FROST   1
    KANGAROO HOPS
        BELWIN-MILLS PUBLISHING CORPORATION   .60
FROST   1
    LOOKING GLASS LAKE
        BOSTON MUSIC COMPANY   .50
FROST   1
    MARCH OF THE WILD GEESE
        BOSTON MUSIC COMPANY   .50
FROST   2
    MINSTREL MAN, THE
        BOSTON MUSIC COMPANY   .50
FROST   2
    MOUNTAIN SUNRISE
        BOSTON MUSIC COMPANY   .50
FROST   1
    PLEASANT DAY, A
        BOSTON MUSIC COMPANY   .50
FROST
    PONY RACE
        G. SCHIRMER, INC.   .40
FROST   1
    RED UMBRELLA
        BOSTON MUSIC COMPANY   .50
FROST
    SKATING LADY
        G. SCHIRMER, INC.   .35
FROST   2
    SONATINA IN G MAJOR
        BELWIN-MILLS PUBLISHING CORPORATION   .75
FROST   1
    TO A CYPRESS TREE
        BOSTON MUSIC COMPANY   .50
FROST   2
    TO A PARADE
        BOSTON MUSIC COMPANY   .50

FROST   2
    TUMBLING CLOWNS
        BOSTON MUSIC COMPANY   .50
FROST   2
    WALTZ REFLECTIONS
        BOSTON MUSIC COMPANY   .50
FROST   1
    WALTZING BIRD, THE
        BELWIN-MILLS PUBLISHING CORPORATION   .60
FROST   3 .
    WHITE SWAN
        BOSTON MUSIC COMPANY   .50
FUCIK   3
    BALLETTOUVERTURE, OP. 319
        BARENREITER VERLAG   AP 598
FUCIK
    ENTREE DES GLADIATEURS -- MARCH --
        FRANCO COLOMBO PUBLICATIONS   SAL   1.50
FUCIK
    ENTRY OF THE GLADIATORS
        BOOSEY AND HAWKES, INC.   .60
FUCIK
    MARCHE DES HEROS HONGROIS
        FRANCO COLOMBO PUBLICATIONS   SAL   1.50
FUERST, P. W.
    DORIAN GRAY -- BALLET IN 6 SCENES
        ASSOCIATED MUSIC PUBLISHERS, INC.   DOB   10.00
FUGA
    DIVERTIMENTO
        FRANCO COLOMBO PUBLICATIONS   128272   3.50
FUGA
    SONATA -- 1957 --
        FRANCO COLOMBO PUBLICATIONS   129669   1.75
FUGA
    SONATINA
        FRANCO COLOMBO PUBLICATIONS   123945   1.50
FUGA
    TOCCATA
        FRANCO COLOMBO PUBLICATIONS   123607   1.50
FUGA
    VARIAZIONI GIOCONDE -- 1957 --
        FRANCO COLOMBO PUBLICATIONS   129618   2.25
FUGAZZA
    PIERINO SI DIVERTE
        EDIZIONI BERBEN   EB 1245   2.10
FULEIHAN, A.
    AIR AND FUGUE ON WHITE KEYS
        PEER SOUTHERN ORGANIZATION   01.00
FULEIHAN, A.
    CAGE DANCER
        PEER SOUTHERN ORGANIZATION   00.85
FULEIHAN, A.
    CONCERTO NO. 02
        G. SCHIRMER, INC.   3.00
FULEIHAN, A.
    DANCING
        PEER SOUTHERN ORGANIZATION   00.85
FULEIHAN, A.
    EPITHALAMIUM -- VARIATIONS FOR PIANO AND STRING ORCHESTRA
        G. SCHIRMER, INC.   2.00
FULEIHAN, A.
    GIRL FROM PAPHOS, THE
        PEER SOUTHERN ORGANIZATION   00.85
FULEIHAN, A.
    HARVEST CHANT
        PEER SOUTHERN ORGANIZATION   00.75
FULEIHAN, A.
    KYRENIA
        PEER SOUTHERN ORGANIZATION   00.85
FULEIHAN, A.
    PIANO SONATA NO. 11
        BOOSEY AND HAWKES, INC.   2.00
FULEIHAN, A.
    PIANO SONATA NO. 12
        BOOSEY AND HAWKES, INC.   2.00
FULEIHAN, A.
    PIANO SONATA NO. 14
        BOOSEY AND HAWKES, INC.   2.00
FULEIHAN, A.
    SERENADE
        PEER SOUTHERN ORGANIZATION   00.85
FULEIHAN, A.
    SONATA NO. 01
        PEER SOUTHERN ORGANIZATION   03.50
FULEIHAN, A.
    SONATA NO. 02
        PEER SOUTHERN ORGANIZATION   02.50
FULEIHAN, A.
    SONATA NO. 03
        PEER SOUTHERN ORGANIZATION   02.50
FULEIHAN, A.
    SONATA NO. 04
        PEER SOUTHERN ORGANIZATION   03.00
FULEIHAN, A.
    SONATA NO. 09
        PEER SOUTHERN ORGANIZATION   01.75
FULEIHAN, A.
    SYRTOS
        PEER SOUTHERN ORGANIZATION   00.85
FULEIHAN, A.
    TWILIGHT MOOD
        PEER SOUTHERN ORGANIZATION   00.75
FULLER
    SCATTER SHIELD
        MCA MUSIC   1.00
FULLER
    WAIKIKI RUN
        MCA MUSIC   1.00
FURGERI
    SONATA IN C
        FRANCO COLOMBO PUBLICATIONS   BON.2514   5.25
FURGERI
    SUITE PER GIOCONDA
        FRANCO COLOMBO PUBLICATIONS   Z4828   4.25
FURZE
    THINGS I REMEMBER
        EDWARD B. MARKS MUSIC CORPORATION   00.60
FURZE
    TOWN AND COUNTRY
        EDWARD B. MARKS MUSIC CORPORATION   00.60
FURZE
    WINDMILL LAND
        EDWARD B. MARKS MUSIC CORPORATION   00.60
FUSSAN
    SONATINA NO. 02, OP. 11
        ASSOCIATED MUSIC PUBLISHERS, INC.   B/B   1.25

FUX   AHLGRIMM
    CAPRICCIO AND FUGUE
        ASSOCIATED MUSIC PUBLISHERS, INC.   DOB   2.00
GABRIEL, M.   3
    CINQUANTAINE, LA
        CENTURY MUSIC PUBLISHING COMPANY, INC.   1345   .40
GABRIEL, M.   2
    CINQUANTAINE, LA, EASY
        CENTURY MUSIC PUBLISHING COMPANY, INC.   2596   .40
GABRIEL, M.   2
    GOLDEN WEDDING, EASY
        CENTURY MUSIC PUBLISHING COMPANY, INC.   2596   .40
GABRIEL, M.   3
    GOLDEN WEDDING, THE
        CENTURY MUSIC PUBLISHING COMPANY, INC.   1345   .40
GABRIEL, M.   3
    LA CINQUANTAINE
        CENTURY MUSIC PUBLISHING COMPANY, INC.   1345   .40
GABRIEL, M. *
    CINQUANTAINE, LA
        CARL FISCHER, INC.   S 287   .50
GABRILOWITSCH, OSSIP
    CAPRICE-BURLESQUE OP. 3
        MUSICA OBSCURA   2.50
GADE, N.   M
    AQUARELLES, OP. 19
        C. F. PETERS CORPORATION   3532   1.50
GADE, N.
    BOY' ROUND DANCE
        BANKS AND SON LTD.   .25
GADE, N.
    BOY'S MERRY-GO-ROUND
        G. SCHIRMER, INC.   .35
GADE, N.   3
    CHRISTMAS BELLS
        CENTURY MUSIC PUBLISHING COMPANY, INC.   4089   .40
GADE, N.   M
    IDYLS, OP. 34
        C. F. PETERS CORPORATION   3534   2.00
GADE, N.   LEVINE
    JALOUSIE
        WARNER BROTHERS PUBLISHERS   1.00
GADE, N.
    JALOUSIE
        WARNER BROTHERS PUBLISHERS   1.00
GADE, N.   RICHTER
    JALOUSIE
        WARNER BROTHERS PUBLISHERS   .75
GAEL
    SUR LA PLAGE - BLONDINETTE
        FRANCO COLOMBO PUBLICATIONS   SAL   1.50
GAEL
    SUR LA PLAGE - L'HORLOGE A MUSIQUE
        FRANCO COLOMBO PUBLICATIONS   SAL   1.50
GAEL
    SUR LA PLAGE - MUSETTA
        FRANCO COLOMBO PUBLICATIONS   SAL   1.50
GAEL
    SUR LA PLAGE - VALSE DES VAGUES
        FRANCO COLOMBO PUBLICATIONS   SAL   1.50
GAGNEUR
    PETIT ALBUM FACILE - MA POUPEE PLEURE AND MA POUPEE DANSE
        FRANCO COLOMBO PUBLICATIONS   SAL   1.50
GAIL   RICHTER
    FOR MY DOLLY
        BELWIN-MILLS PUBLISHING CORPORATION   .60
GAIL   RICHTER
    FOR MY DOLLY
        FRANCO COLOMBO PUBLICATIONS   NY1514   .35
GAIL   RICHTER
    SCHOOL BAND, THE
        BELWIN-MILLS PUBLISHING CORPORATION   .60
GAIL   RICHTER
    SCHOOL BAND, THE
        FRANCO COLOMBO PUBLICATIONS   NY1513   .35
GAIL   RICHTER
    SWING ME
        BELWIN-MILLS PUBLISHING CORPORATION   .60
GAIL   RICHTER
    SWING ME
        FRANCO COLOMBO PUBLICATIONS   NY1512   .35
GAILLARD
    CANCIONERO, EL
        FRANCO COLOMBO PUBLICATIONS   SAL   4.00
GAILLARD
    DOULCES NOSTALGIES -- 1935 --
        ASSOCIATED MUSIC PUBLISHERS, INC.   ESC   2.00
GAILLARD
    MAYA MALDITA, LA
        FRANCO COLOMBO PUBLICATIONS   SAL   4.00
GAILLARD
    SUITE ANGLAISE -- 1930 --
        ASSOCIATED MUSIC PUBLISHERS, INC.   ESC   1.60
GAILLARD
    VERS LES ETOILES
        FRANCO COLOMBO PUBLICATIONS   SAL   4.00
GAITO
    CARAVAN, OP. 30, NO. 1
        FRANCO COLOMBO PUBLICATIONS   BA7640   .75
GAITO
    FANTASTIC DANCES, OP. 18, NO. 1
        FRANCO COLOMBO PUBLICATIONS   BA6704   1.00
GAITO
    FANTASTIC DANCES, OP. 18, NO. 2
        FRANCO COLOMBO PUBLICATIONS   BA6705   1.00
GAITO
    FANTASTIC DANCES, OP. 18, NO. 3
        FRANCO COLOMBO PUBLICATIONS   BA6706   1.00
GAL, H.
    THREE SKETCHES, OP. 7
        UNIVERSAL EDITION   UE 6509   1.30
GALDIERI *
    LOVE THEME FROM 'LA STRADA'
        MCA MUSIC   1.00
GALLEZ   2
    CALLIOPE
        WILLIS MUSIC COMPANY   .40
GALLEZ
    TEASING
        SUMMY-BIRCHARD COMPANY   .50
GALLINI   KAHL   1
    OUR ZOO
        BOSTON MUSIC COMPANY   .50
GALLON, J.
    BERCEUSE
        FRANCO COLOMBO PUBLICATIONS   SAL   3.00

GALLON, J.
CHANSON DU VENT
FRANCO COLOMBO PUBLICATIONS   SAL   1.75
GALLON, J.
GAVOTTE AND MINUETTINO
FRANCO COLOMBO PUBLICATIONS   SAL   1.75
GALLON, J.
POUR UNE ARBRE DE NOEL - CHEVEUX D'ANGES
FRANCO COLOMBO PUBLICATIONS   SAL   1.75
GALLON, J.
POUR UNE ARBRE DE NOEL - CLOCHES D'ALLEGRESSE
FRANCO COLOMBO PUBLICATIONS   SAL   1.75
GALLON, J.
POUR UNE ARBRE DE NOEL - DIVINE CRECHE
FRANCO COLOMBO PUBLICATIONS   SAL   1.75
GALLON, J.
POUR UNE ARBRE DE NOEL - MAISON DE NEIGE
FRANCO COLOMBO PUBLICATIONS   SAL   1.75
GALLON, J.
POUR UNE ARBRE DE NOEL - MOULIN ENCHANTE
FRANCO COLOMBO PUBLICATIONS   SAL   1.75
GALLON, J.
POUR UNE ARBRE DE NOEL - PETIT OISEAU
FRANCO COLOMBO PUBLICATIONS   SAL   1.75
GALLON, J.
POUR UNE ARBRE DE NOEL - ROIS MAGES
FRANCO COLOMBO PUBLICATIONS   SAL   1.75
GALLON, J.
POUR UNE ARBRE DE NOEL - TAMBOURS ET TROMPETTES
FRANCO COLOMBO PUBLICATIONS   SAL   1.75
GALLON, J.
SCHERZETTO
FRANCO COLOMBO PUBLICATIONS   SAL   1.75
GALLON, J.
SOURCE DE MON PAYS, LA
FRANCO COLOMBO PUBLICATIONS   SAL   1.75
GALLON, J.
THEME VARIE
GERARD BILLAUDOT EDITIONS MUSICALES   1.30
GALLUB, B.   2
MASK OF THE AFICAN KING
BELWIN-MILLS PUBLISHING CORPORATION   .60
GALOS   5
A L'APPROCHE DU SOIR
ALPHONSE LEDUC
GALOS   5
AU MATIN SUR LES CIMES
ALPHONSE LEDUC
GALOS   4
CLOCHES DANS LE SOIR
ALPHONSE LEDUC
GALOS   5
DOLOROSA
ALPHONSE LEDUC
GALOS   4
EN REGARDANT LE CIEL
ALPHONSE LEDUC
GALOS   4
L'ENFANT EN PRIERE
ALPHONSE LEDUC
GALOS   6
L'ORAGE DANS LES ALPES
ALPHONSE LEDUC
GALOS   4
LAC DE GARDE, LE
ALPHONSE LEDUC
GALOS   4
LANGAGE DES FLEURS, LE
ALPHONSE LEDUC
GALOS   6
LE CHANT DU BATELIER
ALPHONSE LEDUC
GALOS   4
LE CHANT DU BERGER
ALPHONSE LEDUC
GALOS   5
LE LAC DE COME
ALPHONSE LEDUC
GALOS   5
PRINCE CHARMANT, LE
ALPHONSE LEDUC
GALOS   5
SOUVENIR DES CHAMPS
ALPHONSE LEDUC
GALOS   6
SUR LE LAC MAJEUR
ALPHONSE LEDUC
GALOS   3
UN SOIR A NAPLES
ALPHONSE LEDUC
GALUPPI   TAGLIAPIETRA
SONATA NO. 02
FRANCO COLOMBO PUBLICATIONS   129124   .90
GALUPPI   GALLON, N.
SONATE EN RE
ELKAN-VOGEL, INC.   CON   1.75
GALUPPI   MCCLANAHAN
TOCCATA -- HARMONIC STUDY EDITION WITH OPTIONAL SECOND PIANO
BELWIN-MILLS PUBLISHING CORPORATION 20315 3   .85
GAMBETTI
ITALIAN ROYAL MARCH
CENTURY MUSIC PUBLISHING COMPANY, INC. 1677   .40
GAMBETTI   3
ROYAL MARCH OF ITALY
CENTURY MUSIC PUBLISHING COMPANY, INC. 1677   .40
GAMSE   2
DOWN SOUTH, MYDDLETON
CENTURY MUSIC PUBLISHING COMPANY, INC. 4294   .40
GANDINI
AVE MARIS STELLA
FRANCO COLOMBO PUBLICATIONS   BON.2382   1.50
GANDINI
VARIATIONS ON 'VERA LANGUORES'
FRANCO COLOMBO PUBLICATIONS   BON.2532   5.25
GANNE
AUBADE FLEURIE
FRANCO COLOMBO PUBLICATIONS   SAL   1.75
GANNE   3 1/2
CZARINA, LA
BELWIN-MILLS PUBLISHING CORPORATION   .50
GANNE   3
CZARINE, MAZURKA RUSSE
CENTURY MUSIC PUBLISHING COMPANY, INC. 269   .40
GANNE   3
FATHER VICTORY, FRENCH MARCH
CENTURY MUSIC PUBLISHING COMPANY, INC. 1937   .40

GANNE   WEYBRIGHT   3 1/2
LA CZARINA -- MAZURKA
BELWIN-MILLS PUBLISHING CORPORATION   .60
GANNE   3
LA CZARINE
CENTURY MUSIC PUBLISHING COMPANY, INC. 269   .40
GANNE   2
LA CZARINE, MAZURKA, EASY
CENTURY MUSIC PUBLISHING COMPANY, INC. 2138   .40
GANNE   4
LA TZIGANE
CENTURY MUSIC PUBLISHING COMPANY, INC. 2060   .40
GANNE   3
LE PERE LA VICTOIRE, MARCH
CENTURY MUSIC PUBLISHING COMPANY, INC. 1937   .40
GANNE   4
MARCH RUSSE
CENTURY MUSIC PUBLISHING COMPANY, INC. 1938   .40
GANNE   4
RUSSIAN MARCH
CENTURY MUSIC PUBLISHING COMPANY, INC. 1938   .40
GANNE   4
TZIGANE, LA, MAZURKA
CENTURY MUSIC PUBLISHING COMPANY, INC. 2060   .40
GANSCHALS   3
IN THE TWILIGHT
BOSTON MUSIC COMPANY   .50
GANSCHALS   3
IN TWILIGHT
CENTURY MUSIC PUBLISHING COMPANY, INC. 1012   .40
GANZ   E
BIG FEET JOHNNIE
COMPOSERS PRESS, INC.   1.00
GANZ   E
BOY SOLDIER
COMPOSERS PRESS, INC.   1.00
GANZ   E
CLOCK FROM OVER THERE
COMPOSERS PRESS, INC.   1.00
GANZ   4
QUI VIVE
CENTURY MUSIC PUBLISHING COMPANY, INC. 1246   .40
GANZ   E
WISTFUL LITTLE GIRL
COMPOSERS PRESS, INC.   1.00
GARCIA ACEVEDO   KALUYO
DANZA
FRANCO COLOMBO PUBLICATIONS   BA12030   .75
GARCIA MORILLO
DANCE OF HARRILD
FRANCO COLOMBO PUBLICATIONS   BA10014   .75
GARCIA MORILLO
SONATA NO. 02
FRANCO COLOMBO PUBLICATIONS   BA12458   1.50
GARCIA MORILLO
SONATA NO. 03, OP. 14
FRANCO COLOMBO PUBLICATIONS   BA9878   1.50
GARCIA MORILLO
SONATA NO. 04, OP. 26
FRANCO COLOMBO PUBLICATIONS   BA11814   2.00
GARCIA MORILLO
VARIACIONES APOLINEAS, OP. 25
FRANCO COLOMBO PUBLICATIONS   BA11932   2.00
GARCIA MORILLO
VARIACIONES 1942, OP. 10
FRANCO COLOMBO PUBLICATIONS   BA8864   .75
GARCIN, M.
BEAU JEUDI,UN
GERARD BILLAUDOT EDITIONS MUSICALES   2.00
GARCIN, M.
COFFRE A JOUETS,LE
GERARD BILLAUDOT EDITIONS MUSICALES   1.60
GARDNER   2
MARIONETTES
VOLKWEIN BROS.   .30
GARLAND   SCHAUM, J.   2
IN THE MOOD
SCHAUM PUBLICATIONS, INC.   .75
GARROW   2
BANJO BILL
VOLKWEIN BROS.   .35
GARROW
CATCH ME
BOSTON MUSIC COMPANY   .50
GARROW   1
DOWN THE WAGON TRAIL
BOSTON MUSIC COMPANY   .50
GARROW
LION, THE
BRODT MUSIC COMPANY   .40
GARROW   1
LITTLE BROWN HEN
BOSTON MUSIC COMPANY   .50
GARROW
LONDON BRIDGE
BRODT MUSIC COMPANY   .45
GARROW   2
ROUND WE GO
BOSTON MUSIC COMPANY   .50
GARROW
RUN MOUSE, RUN
BRODT MUSIC COMPANY   .40
GARROW
THREE LITTLE DUCKS
BRODT MUSIC COMPANY   .40
GARROW   1
TV COWBOY
BOSTON MUSIC COMPANY   .50
GARROW   2
TWO MOODS
VOLKWEIN BROS.   .35
GARROW   2
UPSY-DAISY
BOSTON MUSIC COMPANY   .50
GARROW
WEE 3 MARTIANS
CARL FISCHER, INC.   P 3101   .50
GARROW   2
WHISTLING COWBOY
BOSTON MUSIC COMPANY   .50
GARROW, L.   4
ADVENTURES OF A GHOST
BELWIN-MILLS PUBLISHING CORPORATION   .60
GARROW, L.   2 1/2
AGENT 402
BELWIN-MILLS PUBLISHING CORPORATION   .60

GARROW, L.   3
     AT THE BALLET
          BELWIN-MILLS PUBLISHING CORPORATION   .60
GARROW, L.   1
     AT THE TRADING POST
          BELWIN-MILLS PUBLISHING CORPORATION   .60
                                              PRIM.
GARROW, L.
     BATTER UP
          BELWIN-MILLS PUBLISHING CORPORATION   .60
GARROW, L.   2
     BOOGIE ON THE BRIDGE
          BELWIN-MILLS PUBLISHING CORPORATION   .60
GARROW, L.   2
     BOY WITH GUITAR
          BELWIN-MILLS PUBLISHING CORPORATION   .60
                                              PRIM.
GARROW, L.
     CALICO WALTZ
          BELWIN-MILLS PUBLISHING CORPORATION   .60
                                              PRIM.
GARROW, L.
     CALLIOPE
          BELWIN-MILLS PUBLISHING CORPORATION   .60
                                              PRIM.
GARROW, L.
     CHASE ME
          BELWIN-MILLS PUBLISHING CORPORATION   .60
                                              2 1/2
GARROW, L.
     CHOPSTICKS DE LUXE
          BELWIN-MILLS PUBLISHING CORPORATION   .60
GARROW, L.   3
     COOL BLUE
          BELWIN-MILLS PUBLISHING CORPORATION   .60
GARROW, L.   3
     DANCING BURRO
          BELWIN-MILLS PUBLISHING CORPORATION   .60
GARROW, L.   2
     DREAM BOAT
          BELWIN-MILLS PUBLISHING CORPORATION   .60
GARROW, L.   2
     FOX AND HOUNDS
          BELWIN-MILLS PUBLISHING CORPORATION   .60
                                              PRIM.
GARROW, L.
     HERE COMES THE BAND
          BELWIN-MILLS PUBLISHING CORPORATION   .60
GARROW, L.   1
     ICE SKATING
          BELWIN-MILLS PUBLISHING CORPORATION   .60
GARROW, L.   2
     LE BEAU PAPILLON
          BELWIN-MILLS PUBLISHING CORPORATION   .60
GARROW, L.   2
     LEFT, RIGHT MARCH
          BELWIN-MILLS PUBLISHING CORPORATION   .60
                                              1 1/2
GARROW, L.
     LITTLE FROG, THE
          BELWIN-MILLS PUBLISHING CORPORATION   .60
GARROW, L.   2
     MARCH OF THE ANIMALS
          BELWIN-MILLS PUBLISHING CORPORATION   .60
GARROW, L.   3
     MEXICAN SERENADE
          BELWIN-MILLS PUBLISHING CORPORATION   .60
GARROW, L.   1
     NOISY WOODPECKER
          BELWIN-MILLS PUBLISHING CORPORATION   .60
GARROW, L.   2
     PAPER BOY
          BELWIN-MILLS PUBLISHING CORPORATION   .60
                                              PRIM.
GARROW, L.
     PICNIC IN THE PARK
          BELWIN-MILLS PUBLISHING CORPORATION   .60
                                              2 1/2
GARROW, L.
     POLLY WOLLY BOOGIE
          BELWIN-MILLS PUBLISHING CORPORATION   .60
GARROW, L.   4
     POLYNESIAN SUNSET
          BELWIN-MILLS PUBLISHING CORPORATION   .60
GARROW, L.   1
     RACING SEA HORSES
          BELWIN-MILLS PUBLISHING CORPORATION   .60
GARROW, L.   4
     SECRET
          BELWIN-MILLS PUBLISHING CORPORATION   .60
GARROW, L.   4
     SHADOWS ON THE MOON
          BELWIN-MILLS PUBLISHING CORPORATION   .60
GARROW, L.   2
     SUMMER EVENING
          BELWIN-MILLS PUBLISHING CORPORATION   .60
GARROW, L.   1
     SWANS
          BELWIN-MILLS PUBLISHING CORPORATION   .60
GARROW, L.   4
     SWING THE BLUES
          BELWIN-MILLS PUBLISHING CORPORATION   .60
GARROW, L.   4
     TAKE OFF
          BELWIN-MILLS PUBLISHING CORPORATION   .60
                                              2 1/2
GARROW, L.
     TORTILLAS FOR SALE
          BELWIN-MILLS PUBLISHING CORPORATION   .60
GARROW, L.   2
     TRICKY TRAFFIC
          BELWIN-MILLS PUBLISHING CORPORATION   .60
GARROW, L.   2
     WALKING THE DOG
          BELWIN-MILLS PUBLISHING CORPORATION   .60
GARROW, L.   1
     WALTZING POODLE
          BELWIN-MILLS PUBLISHING CORPORATION   .60
GARROW, L.   2
     WANDA, THE WALTZING WALRUS
          BELWIN-MILLS PUBLISHING CORPORATION   .60
GARROW, L.   2
     WHIRLY BIRD
          BELWIN-MILLS PUBLISHING CORPORATION   .60
GARROW, L.   3
     WINDING RIVER
          BELWIN-MILLS PUBLISHING CORPORATION   .60
GARTENLAUB, O.
     GRAVE TOCCATA
          ELKAN-VOGEL, INC.   RR   2.00
GARTENLAUB, O.
     LE COIN DES ENFANTS
          ELKAN-VOGEL, INC.   RR   4.75
GARTENLAUB, O.
     PETITE ETUDE POUR LES MAINS ALTERNEES
          ELKAN-VOGEL, INC.   RR   1.20

GARTENLAUB, O.
     PETITE ETUDE POUR LES TIERCES
          ELKAN-VOGEL, INC.   RR   1.20
GARTENLAUB, O.
     PREPARATION AU DECHIFFRAGE PIANISTIQUE
          ELKAN-VOGEL, INC.   RR   4.00
GAUBERT, P.
     LE CHEVALIER ET LA DAMOISELLE
          HEUGEL ET CIE.   8.00
GAUTIER, L.
     BLUETTE
          FRANCO COLOMBO PUBLICATIONS   SAL   1.50
GAUTIER, L.
     CELESTE PRIERE -- REVERIE --
          FRANCO COLOMBO PUBLICATIONS   SAL   1.50
GAUTIER, L.
     CHARMES DE L'ETUDE, LES - COLIBRI
          FRANCO COLOMBO PUBLICATIONS   SAL   1.50
GAUTIER, L.
     CHARMES DE L'ETUDE, LES - EN FORET
          FRANCO COLOMBO PUBLICATIONS   SAL   1.50
GAUTIER, L.
     CHARMES DE L'ETUDE, LES - GIRALDA
          FRANCO COLOMBO PUBLICATIONS   SAL   1.50
GAUTIER, L.
     CHARMES DE L'ETUDE, LES - JOUR DE FETE
          FRANCO COLOMBO PUBLICATIONS   SAL   1.50
GAUTIER, L.
     CHARMES DE L'ETUDE, LES - LA BONNE FEE
          FRANCO COLOMBO PUBLICATIONS   SAL   1.50
GAUTIER, L.
     CHARMES DE L'ETUDE, LES - LE MASCARET
          FRANCO COLOMBO PUBLICATIONS   SAL   1.50
GAUTIER, L.
     CHARMES DE L'ETUDE, LES - LEGER PAPILLON
          FRANCO COLOMBO PUBLICATIONS   SAL   1.50
GAUTIER, L.
     CHARMES DE L'ETUDE, LES - MISS ALICE
          FRANCO COLOMBO PUBLICATIONS   SAL   1.50
GAUTIER, L.
     CHARMES DE L'ETUDE, LES - PENSEE FUGITIVE
          FRANCO COLOMBO PUBLICATIONS   SAL   1.50
GAUTIER, L.
     CHARMES DE L'ETUDE, LES - PERLES DU MATIN
          FRANCO COLOMBO PUBLICATIONS   SAL   1.50
GAUTIER, L.
     CHARMES DE L'ETUDE, LES - SOUS LES ORANGERS
          FRANCO COLOMBO PUBLICATIONS   SAL   1.50
GAUTIER, L.
     CHARMES DE L'ETUDE, LES - VOL D'OISEAUX
          FRANCO COLOMBO PUBLICATIONS   SAL   1.50
GAUTIER, L.
     COMMENCEMENT DU PIANO, LE - BAL D'ENFANTS
          FRANCO COLOMBO PUBLICATIONS   SAL   1.50
GAUTIER, L.
     COMMENCEMENT DU PIANO, LE - LA SAINTE CATHERINE
          FRANCO COLOMBO PUBLICATIONS   SAL   1.50
GAUTIER, L.
     COMMENCEMENT DU PIANO, LE - LE SAINTE NICOLAS
          FRANCO COLOMBO PUBLICATIONS   SAL   1.50
GAUTIER, L.
     COMMENCEMENT DU PIANO, LE - LES PETITS BATEAUX
          FRANCO COLOMBO PUBLICATIONS   SAL   1.50
GAUTIER, L.
     COMMENCEMENT DU PIANO, LE - LES PETITS TOURISTS
          FRANCO COLOMBO PUBLICATIONS   SAL   1.50
GAUTIER, L.
     COMMENCEMENT DU PIANO, LE - UNE SURPRISE A PETIT PERE
          FRANCO COLOMBO PUBLICATIONS   SAL   1.50
GAUTIER, L.
     LE SECRET
          BELWIN-MILLS PUBLISHING CORPORATION 28200   .70
GAUTIER, L.   3
     LE SECRET
          CENTURY MUSIC PUBLISHING COMPANY, INC. 276   .40
GAUTIER, L.   3
     LE SECRET
          VOLKWEIN BROS.   .25
GAUTIER, L.   3
     LE SECRET
          VOLKWEIN BROS.   .25
GAUTIER, L.
     LE SECRET, INTERMEZZO-PIZZICATO
          G. SCHIRMER, INC.   .60
GAUTIER, L.
     REGRET, UN -- REVERIE --
          FRANCO COLOMBO PUBLICATIONS   SAL   1.75
GAUTIER, L.
     RENDEZ-VOUS DE CHASSE, LE
          FRANCO COLOMBO PUBLICATIONS   SAL   1.75
GAUTIER, L.
     REPENTIR -- REVERIE --
          FRANCO COLOMBO PUBLICATIONS   SAL   1.75
GAUTIER, L.
     REVE, UN -- REVERIE NOCTURNE --
          FRANCO COLOMBO PUBLICATIONS   SAL   1.75
GAUTIER, L.   ROLFE, W.   2
     SECRET, THE, EASY
          CENTURY MUSIC PUBLISHING COMPANY, INC. 3364   .40
GAUTIER, L.   3
     SECRET, THE, INTERMEZZO
          CENTURY MUSIC PUBLISHING COMPANY, INC. 276   .40
GAUTIER, L.
     SOUS L'OMBRAGE -- WALTZ --
          FRANCO COLOMBO PUBLICATIONS   SAL   1.75
GAUTIER, L.
     VERTIGE, LE -- GALOP --
          FRANCO COLOMBO PUBLICATIONS   SAL   1.50
GAY   2 1/2
     LONELY LULLABY
          WILLIS MUSIC COMPANY   .40
GAY   2-3
     TREASURE CHEST
          PRO-ART PUBLICATIONS, INC.   566   .50
GAY
     WINDSOR MELODY, THE
          BELWIN-MILLS PUBLISHING CORPORATION 20333   .85
GAY *   E-M
     BEGGAR'S OPERA. ABRIDGED.
          C. F. PETERS CORPORATION   H1728   1.50
GAY, A.   E-M
     BALLOONS
          COMPOSERS PRESS, INC.   1.00
GAY, G.   2 1/2
     CONTENTED CLOCK
          WILLIS MUSIC COMPANY   .40

GAYFER, J. M.
  NONCHALANCE
    FREDERICK HARRIS MUSIC COMPANY   .75
GAYNOR   SCHAUM, J.
  CANDY DOLLY
    BELWIN-MILLS PUBLISHING CORPORATION   .50
GAYNOR   3
  ELF MAN'S SERENADE, THE
    THEODORE PRESSER COMPANY   .50
GAYNOR   2
  GUITAR SERENADE, THE
    THEODORE PRESSER COMPANY   .50
GAYNOR
  GUITAR, THE
    SUMMY-BIRCHARD COMPANY   .50
GAYNOR   2
  MARCH OF THE WEE FOLK
    THEODORE PRESSER COMPANY   .50
GAYNOR   2 1/2
  STORY OF THE OLD HOUSE IN THE WOODS
    THEODORE PRESSER COMPANY   .50
GAYNOR   SCHAUM, J.   1 1/2
  THANKSGIVING SONG
    BELWIN-MILLS PUBLISHING CORPORATION   .50
GAYRHOS, E.
  ETUDE IN A MINOR
    BELWIN-MILLS PUBLISHING CORPORATION   .60
GEERSH, E.
  PASO DOBLE NO. 1
    BELWIN-MILLS PUBLISHING CORPORATION 20194 .85
GEGENHEIMER, C.   3
  GALLOPING
    BELWIN-MILLS PUBLISHING CORPORATION   .60
GEIBEL   2
  KENTUCKY BABE
    CENTURY MUSIC PUBLISHING COMPANY, INC. 4079 .40
GEIBEL *   ZEPP   2-3
  KENTUCKY BABE
    PRO-ART PUBLICATIONS, INC.   195 .50
GEIGER   2
  COSSACK DANCE
    CENTURY MUSIC PUBLISHING COMPANY, INC. 4286 .40
GEIGER   1
  LITTLE GAVOTTE, A
    CENTURY MUSIC PUBLISHING COMPANY, INC. 4285 .40
GEIGER   1
  LITTLE HILDER
    CENTURY MUSIC PUBLISHING COMPANY, INC. 4386 .40
GEIGER   1
  PENNY WHISTLE
    CENTURY MUSIC PUBLISHING COMPANY, INC. 4387 .40
GEISER
  SUITE, OP. 41
    BARENREITER VERLAG   BA 1981 4.50
GEISER   4
  SUITE, OP. 41
    BARENREITER VERLAG   BA 1981
GEISSLER
  PIGMENT -- BALLET IN 5 TABLEAUX
    ASSOCIATED MUSIC PUBLISHERS, INC.   BRH 10.00
GELBER
  CATCH ME
    CARL FISCHER, INC.   P 3051 .50
GELBER
  REFLECTIONS
    CARL FISCHER, INC.   P 3050 .50
GELLAR *   NEVIN
  ABERGAVENNY
    BELWIN-MILLS PUBLISHING CORPORATION   .60
GENZMER   3-4
  CAPRICCIO -- SONATINA NO. 02
    SCHOTT   4288 2.00
GENZMER   2-3
  KLEINES KLAVIERBUCH
    SCHOTT   1054 2.50
GENZMER   3
  SONATA NO. 01
    SCHOTT   2886 2.25
GENZMER   5
  SONATA NO. 02
    SCHOTT   3951 2.50
GENZMER   2
  SONATINA NO. 03, 1959
    SCHOTT   5067 2.00
GENZMER   5
  SUITE IN C
    SCHOTT   4023 2.25
GEORGE   VE
  CRISS CROSS
    OXFORD UNIVERSITY PRESS   93.312 .40
GEORGE
  DISTANT CHIMES
    SUMMY-BIRCHARD COMPANY   .50
GEORGE   VE
  ECHO SONG
    OXFORD UNIVERSITY PRESS   93.310 .40
GEORGE
  FRONTIER TOWN
    SUMMY-BIRCHARD COMPANY   .50
GEORGE
  INTERMEZZO
    ELKAN-VOGEL, INC.   .50
GEORGE   VE
  KANGAROOS
    OXFORD UNIVERSITY PRESS   93.311 .40
GEORGE
  LENTO
    OXFORD UNIVERSITY PRESS   93.213 .60
GEORGE   2
  MONARCH BUTTERFLY
    BOSTON MUSIC COMPANY   .50
GEORGE   VE
  PLAYING JACKS
    OXFORD UNIVERSITY PRESS   93.309 .40
GEORGE   2
  PUPPY DOG GALOP
    BOSTON MUSIC COMPANY   .50
GEORGE
  QUIET LAGOON
    SUMMY-BIRCHARD COMPANY   .50
GEORGE
  SONATINA IN F MAJOR
    SUMMY-BIRCHARD COMPANY   .75
GEORGE
  SONATINA IN G MAJOR
    SUMMY-BIRCHARD COMPANY   .75

GEORGE
  TURTLE TALK
    SUMMY-BIRCHARD COMPANY   .50
GEORGE,
  BANJO SERENADE
    OXFORD UNIVERSITY PRESS   93.210 1.25
GERARD, J.
  MUSIC BOX CONCERTO, THE
    FREDERICK HARRIS MUSIC COMPANY   .60
GERMAN, E.
  THREE DANCES FROM 'HENRY VIII'
    NOVELLO AND COMPANY, LTD.   10.0056.10 1.25
GERSCHEFSKI, E.   M
  SONG OF THE MOUNTAINS
    THEODORE PRESSER COMPANY   .50
GERSHWIN   DALY
  AMERICAN IN PARIS, AN
    WARNER BROTHERS PUBLISHERS   4.00
GERSHWIN   WHITNEY
  AMERICAN IN PARIS, AN - IN MINIATURE
    WARNER BROTHERS PUBLISHERS   1.50
GERSHWIN   LEVINE
  EMBRACEABLE YOU
    WARNER BROTHERS PUBLISHERS   1.00
GERSHWIN   WALTER
  EMBRACEABLE YOU
    WARNER BROTHERS PUBLISHERS   1.00
GERSHWIN   RICHTER   FIRST YEAR
  EMBRACEABLE YOU
    WARNER BROTHERS PUBLISHERS   .75
GERSHWIN   STONE
  FASCINATING RHYTHM
    WARNER BROTHERS PUBLISHERS   1.00
GERSHWIN
  GERSHWIN, THE BEST OF HOLLYWOOD
    CHAPPELL AND COMPANY, INC.   0021675 1.50
GERSHWIN   LEVINE
  I GOT RHYTHM
    WARNER BROTHERS PUBLISHERS   1.00
GERSHWIN
  IT AIN'T NECESSARILY SO
    CHAPPELL AND COMPANY, INC.   2762524 .95
GERSHWIN   LEVINE
  LIZA
    WARNER BROTHERS PUBLISHERS   1.00
GERSHWIN   LEVINE
  MAN I LOVE, THE
    WARNER BROTHERS PUBLISHERS   1.00
GERSHWIN   GRAINGER, P.
  MAN I LOVE, THE
    WARNER BROTHERS PUBLISHERS   1.00
GERSHWIN   RICHTER   FIRST YEAR
  MAN I LOVE, THE
    WARNER BROTHERS PUBLISHERS   .75
GERSHWIN   LEVINE
  OH, LADY BE GOOD
    WARNER BROTHERS PUBLISHERS   1.00
GERSHWIN   LEVINE
  SOMEONE TO WATCH OVER ME
    WARNER BROTHERS PUBLISHERS   1.00
GERSHWIN   WHITNEY
  SOMEONE TO WATCH OVER ME
    WARNER BROTHERS PUBLISHERS   1.00
GERSHWIN   RICHTER   FIRST YEAR
  SOMEONE TO WATCH OVER ME
    WARNER BROTHERS PUBLISHERS   .75
GERSHWIN   LEVINE
  STRIKE UP THE BAND
    WARNER BROTHERS PUBLISHERS   1.00
GERSHWIN
  SUMMERTIME
    CHAPPELL AND COMPANY, INC.   5565023 .60
GERSTER, O.   3-4
  INTRODUCTION UND PERPETUUM
    SCHOTT   4114 2.00
GERSTER, O.   3
  SONATINE
    BARENREITER VERLAG   SM 1265
GEST, E.   WILLIAMS, J.   1
  FIREFLIES
    BOSTON MUSIC COMPANY   .50
GEST, E.   1
  PUDDLES
    BOSTON MUSIC COMPANY   .50
GEST, E.   1
  SNOW BIRD
    BELWIN-MILLS PUBLISHING CORPORATION   .60
GEST, E.   1
  SUN DOWN
    BELWIN-MILLS PUBLISHING CORPORATION   .60
GEST, E.   WILLIAMS, J.   1
  SUNSHOWER
    BOSTON MUSIC COMPANY   .50
GETTY, G.   3
  BERCEUSE
    BELWIN-MILLS PUBLISHING CORPORATION   .60
GETTY, G.   2
  GHOST WALTZ
    BELWIN-MILLS PUBLISHING CORPORATION   .60
GETTY, G.   2 1/2
  GIGA
    BELWIN-MILLS PUBLISHING CORPORATION   .60
GETTY, G.   3 1/2
  NIGHT HORSES
    BELWIN-MILLS PUBLISHING CORPORATION   .60
GETTY, G.   3 1/2
  SEASCAPE
    BELWIN-MILLS PUBLISHING CORPORATION   .60
GHEDINI
  DIVERTIMENTO CONTRAPPUNTISTICO
    FRANCO COLOMBO PUBLICATIONS   125298 1.50
GHIKA   4
  PARFUM D'EVENTAIL
    ALPHONSE LEDUC
GHYS   ROLFE   2
  AIR OF LOUIS XIII, C MAJOR
    CENTURY MUSIC PUBLISHING COMPANY, INC. 3213 .40
GHYS   4
  AIR OF LOUIS XIII, E MAJOR
    CENTURY MUSIC PUBLISHING COMPANY, INC. 132 .40
GHYS   WEYBRIGHT   2
  AMARYLLIS
    BELWIN-MILLS PUBLISHING CORPORATION   .50
GHYS   4
  AMARYLLIS
    BELWIN-MILLS PUBLISHING CORPORATION 121 .60

GHYS   BRISSON
  AMARYLLIS
    G. SCHIRMER, INC.   .60
GHYS
  AMARYLLIS, AIR DE LOUIS XIII
    CARL FISCHER, INC.   S 58   .50
GIACCHINO CUSENZA
  BASSO OSTINATO
    FRANCO COLOMBO PUBLICATIONS   124320   1.00
GIACCHINO CUSENZA
  CHORALE AND VARIATIONS
    FRANCO COLOMBO PUBLICATIONS   129015   1.50
GIACCHINO CUSENZA
  PRELUDE AND FUGUE IN G MINOR
    FRANCO COLOMBO PUBLICATIONS   123654   1.25
GIACCHINO CUSENZA
  STUDIO CANONICO IN OTTAVE
    FRANCO COLOMBO PUBLICATIONS   128783   .60
GIACCHINO CUSENZA
  STUDIO ESATONICO
    FRANCO COLOMBO PUBLICATIONS   128784   1.00
GIACOBETTI *
  RICORDATE MARCELLINO
    MCA MUSIC   1.00
GIANNEO
  CAMINITO DE BELEN
    PEER SOUTHERN ORGANIZATION   00.75
GIANNEO
  SONATINA
    PEER SOUTHERN ORGANIZATION   02.00
GIANNEO
  VILLANCICO
    PEER SOUTHERN ORGANIZATION   00.75
GIANNINI
  MODAL VARIATIONS FOR PIANO
    AMERICAN MUSIC EDITION   1.50
GIANNINI
  SONATA
    FRANCO COLOMBO PUBLICATIONS   NY2462   2.50
GIANNINI
  SONATA FOR PIANOFORTE
    BELWIN-MILLS PUBLISHING CORPORATION   2.50
GIANNINI
  SONATINA FOR PIANO
    AMERICAN MUSIC EDITION   1.25
GIARD, C.   4
  HUMMING BIRD, THE
    BELWIN-MILLS PUBLISHING CORPORATION   .60
GIARD, C.   3
  SKETCH
    BELWIN-MILLS PUBLISHING CORPORATION   .60
GIASSON, P.
  AFTER DARK
    GENERAL MUSIC PUBLISHING COMPANY, INC.   702   .75
GIASSON, P.
  ANDALUSIAN SERENADE
    GENERAL MUSIC PUBLISHING COMPANY, INC.   544   975
GIASSON, P.
  ANDALUSIAN SERENADE - FROM SEVEN FLOWERS FROM A PIANIST'S GARDEN
    GENERAL MUSIC PUBLISHING COMPANY, INC.   .60
GIASSON, P.
  AUTUMN THOUGHTS
    GENERAL MUSIC PUBLISHING COMPANY, INC.   547   .75
GIASSON, P.
  AUTUMN THOUGHTS - FROM SEVEN FLOWERS FROM A PIANIST'S GARDEN
    GENERAL MUSIC PUBLISHING COMPANY, INC.   .60
GIASSON, P.
  CANADIAN CHILDHOOD - SUITE
    GENERAL MUSIC PUBLISHING COMPANY, INC.   460   2.50
GIASSON, P.
  CANADIAN CHILDHOOD - SUITE
    GENERAL MUSIC PUBLISHING COMPANY, INC.   2.50
GIASSON, P.
  CHATTERBOX
    GENERAL MUSIC PUBLISHING COMPANY, INC.   543   .75
GIASSON, P.
  CHATTERBOX - FROM SEVEN FLOWERS FROM A PIANIST'S GARDEN
    GENERAL MUSIC PUBLISHING COMPANY, INC.   .75
GIASSON, P.
  GOLDEN COACH, THE
    GENERAL MUSIC PUBLISHING COMPANY, INC.   542   .75
GIASSON, P.
  INDIAN SUMMER - SUITE
    GENERAL MUSIC PUBLISHING COMPANY, INC.   410   1.50
GIASSON, P.
  INDIAN SUMMER - SUITE
    GENERAL MUSIC PUBLISHING COMPANY, INC.   1.50
GIASSON, P.   3
  MERRIE MUSIC BOX
    BOSTON MUSIC COMPANY   .50
GIASSON, P.
  NEW ENGLAND SEASCAPE
    GENERAL MUSIC PUBLISHING COMPANY, INC.   548   .75
GIASSON, P.
  NEW ENGLAND SEASCAPE - FROM SEVEN FLOWERS FROM A PIANIST'S
  GARDEN
    GENERAL MUSIC PUBLISHING COMPANY, INC.   .60
GIASSON, P.
  NEW HORIZONS
    GENERAL MUSIC PUBLISHING COMPANY, INC.   31   1.25
GIASSON, P.
  NEW HORIZONS
    GENERAL MUSIC PUBLISHING COMPANY, INC.   1.25
GIASSON, P.
  PARISIAN PROMENADE
    GENERAL MUSIC PUBLISHING COMPANY, INC.   462   1.00
GIASSON, P.
  PORTRAIT IN BLUE
    GENERAL MUSIC PUBLISHING COMPANY, INC.   35   .75
GIASSON, P.
  PORTRAIT IN BLUE
    GENERAL MUSIC PUBLISHING COMPANY, INC.   1.00
GIASSON, P.
  PORTRAIT OF A CITY
    GENERAL MUSIC PUBLISHING COMPANY, INC.   703   .75
GIASSON, P.
  PRAISIAN PROMENADE
    GENERAL MUSIC PUBLISHING COMPANY, INC.   1.00
GIASSON, P.
  REFLECTIONS
    GENERAL MUSIC PUBLISHING COMPANY, INC.   546   .75
GIASSON, P.
  REFLECTIONS - FROM SEVEN FLOWERS FROM A PIANIST'S GARDEN
    GENERAL MUSIC PUBLISHING COMPANY, INC.   .75
GIASSON, P.
  SUMMER SOLILOQUY
    GENERAL MUSIC PUBLISHING COMPANY, INC.   683   .75

GIASSON, P.
  VELVET NOCTURNE
    GENERAL MUSIC PUBLISHING COMPANY, INC.   545   .75
GIASSON, P.
  VELVET NOCTURNE - FROM SEVEN FLOWERS FROM A PIANIST'S GARDEN
    GENERAL MUSIC PUBLISHING COMPANY, INC.   .60
GIASSON, P.
  VIENNA-ON-THE-HUDSON
    GENERAL MUSIC PUBLISHING COMPANY, INC.   684   .75
GIASSON, P.
  WALTZ FOR CINDERELLA, A
    GENERAL MUSIC PUBLISHING COMPANY, INC.   44   1.00
GIASSON, P.
  WALTZ FOR CINDERELLA, A
    GENERAL MUSIC PUBLISHING COMPANY, INC.   1.25
GIASSON, P.
  WALTZ IN JAZZ TIME
    GENERAL MUSIC PUBLISHING COMPANY, INC.   461   1.00
GIASSON, P.
  WALTZ IN JAZZ TIME
    GENERAL MUSIC PUBLISHING COMPANY, INC.   1.00
GIAZOTTO
  AU TOMBEAU DE RAVEL
    FRANCO COLOMBO PUBLICATIONS   129762   1.50
GIBBS
  DUSK
    BOOSEY AND HAWKES, INC.   .75
GIDEON, M.   MD
  CANZONA
    THEODORE PRESSER COMPANY   1.00
GIFFORD
  SMOKE RINGS
    BELWIN-MILLS PUBLISHING CORPORATION   20251   .85
GIGGY, F.
  PIANO SONATA NO. 01
    COMPOSERS AUTOGRAPH PUBLICATIONS   3.96
GIL-MARCHEX
  LUNE D'AUTOMNE A IDZUOMO -- NO. 1, FROM DEUX IMAGES DU VIEUX
  JAPAN
    ASSOCIATED MUSIC PUBLISHERS, INC.   UME   1.00
GIL-MARCHEX
  RETOUR DE YOSHIWARA -- NO. 2, FROM DEUX IMAGES DU VIEUX JAPAN
    ASSOCIATED MUSIC PUBLISHERS, INC.   UME   2.00
GILARDI
  CANTARES DE MI CANTAR
    FRANCO COLOMBO PUBLICATIONS   BA9418   1.50
GILARDI
  CHACARERA
    FRANCO COLOMBO PUBLICATIONS   BA8602   .75
GILARDI
  FIRMEZA, LA
    FRANCO COLOMBO PUBLICATIONS   BA8603   .75
GILARDI
  NOVIANDO
    FRANCO COLOMBO PUBLICATIONS   BA7262   .75
GILARDI
  TANGO
    FRANCO COLOMBO PUBLICATIONS   BA12333   .75
GILBERT *   STEINER   2
  I'VE GOT A LITTLE LIST
    BELWIN-MILLS PUBLISHING CORPORATION   .60
GILBERT AND SULLIVAN   STEINER   1
  PIRATE KING, THE
    BELWIN-MILLS PUBLISHING CORPORATION   .60
GILBERT, G. V.   2 1/2
  ARABESQUE, OP. 17 NO. 1
    THEODORE PRESSER COMPANY   .50
GILBOA
  LITTLE INSECTS
    ALEXANDER BROUDE, INC.   4.20
GILIO, L.
  L'ALLEGRO SCIATORE
    EDIZIONI BERBEN   EB 1210   .90
GILIO, L.
  MARCIA NUZIALE
    EDIZIONI BERBEN   EB 1629   1.20
GILLET, E.   3
  ECHOES OF THE BALL
    CENTURY MUSIC PUBLISHING COMPANY, INC.   294   .40
GILLET, E.
  ECHOES OF THE BALL
    G. SCHIRMER, INC.   .50
GILLET, E.   2
  ECHOES OF THE BALL
    VOLKWEIN BROS.   .25
GILLET, E.   3
  LOIN DE BAL
    CENTURY MUSIC PUBLISHING COMPANY, INC.   294   .40
GILLET, E.
  PENDANT LE BAL -- INTERMEZZO --
    FRANCO COLOMBO PUBLICATIONS   SAL   1.75
GILLET, E.
  REPONSE A MANON -- INTERMEZZO --
    FRANCO COLOMBO PUBLICATIONS   SAL   1.75
GILLEY, E.   3
  CHATTERING CHIPMUNKS
    WILLIS MUSIC COMPANY   .40
GILLNESS
  LAKE BY MOONLIGHT
    CARL FISCHER, INC.   P 3198   .50
GILLNESS
  PONY TROT
    CARL FISCHER, INC.   P 3202   .50
GILLOCK   4
  ADAGIO ESOTICO
    WILLIS MUSIC COMPANY   .40
GILLOCK   2 1/2
  ADAGIO ESOTICO
    WILLIS MUSIC COMPANY   .40
GILLOCK
  AEOLIAN HARP
    SUMMY-BIRCHARD COMPANY   .50
GILLOCK   2 1/2
  ARIEL
    WILLIS MUSIC COMPANY   .40
GILLOCK   2 1/2
  ARIEL
    WILLIS MUSIC COMPANY   .40
GILLOCK   2
  AT THE BALLET
    WILLIS MUSIC COMPANY   .40
GILLOCK   2
  AT THE BALLET
    WILLIS MUSIC COMPANY   .40
GILLOCK   2
  AUTUMN IS HERE
    WILLIS MUSIC COMPANY   .35

GILLOCK		
AUTUMN IS HERE	1	
WILLIS MUSIC COMPANY		.40
GILLOCK	4	
BAGDAD		
WILLIS MUSIC COMPANY		.40
GILLOCK	2 1/2	
BAGDAD		
WILLIS MUSIC COMPANY		.40
GILLOCK	2	
BARCAROLLE		
WILLIS MUSIC COMPANY		.40
GILLOCK	2	
BARCAROLLE		
WILLIS MUSIC COMPANY		.40
GILLOCK	2	
BLUE BUTTERFLY		
VOLKWEIN BROS.		.35
GILLOCK	2	
BLUE MOOD		
WILLIS MUSIC COMPANY		.75
GILLOCK	2 1/2	
BY A SYLVAN LAKE		
WILLIS MUSIC COMPANY		.40
GILLOCK	2 1/2	
BY A SYLVAN LAKE		
WILLIS MUSIC COMPANY		.40
GILLOCK	2 1/2	
CAPRICCIETTO		
WILLIS MUSIC COMPANY		.40
GILLOCK	2 1/2	
CAPRICCIETTO		
WILLIS MUSIC COMPANY		.40
GILLOCK	4	
CARNIVAL IN RIO		
WILLIS MUSIC COMPANY		.40
GILLOCK	2 1/2	
CARNIVAL IN RIO		
WILLIS MUSIC COMPANY		.40
GILLOCK	4	
CASTANETS		
WILLIS MUSIC COMPANY		.40
GILLOCK	2	
CASTANETS		
WILLIS MUSIC COMPANY		.40
GILLOCK		
CLASSIC CARNIVAL		
WILLIS MUSIC COMPANY		.50
GILLOCK	3	
CLASSIC CARNIVAL -- 3 MOVEMENT		
WILLIS MUSIC COMPANY		.50
GILLOCK	1 1/2	
CLOWNS		
WILLIS MUSIC COMPANY		.50
GILLOCK	1	
DAY DREAMS		
BELWIN-MILLS PUBLISHING CORPORATION		.60
GILLOCK	4	
ELECTRONIC COMPUTER, THE		
WILLIS MUSIC COMPANY		.40
GILLOCK	2	
ELECTRONIC COMPUTER, THE		
WILLIS MUSIC COMPANY		.40
GILLOCK	2	
ETUDE IN E MINOR		
WILLIS MUSIC COMPANY		.75
GILLOCK	2	
FANTASY WHIRLWIND		
VOLKWEIN BROS.		.40
GILLOCK		
FESTIVE PIECE		
WILLIS MUSIC COMPANY		.40
GILLOCK	2	
FIESTA		
WILLIS MUSIC COMPANY		.40
GILLOCK	2	
FIESTA		
WILLIS MUSIC COMPANY		.40
GILLOCK	4	
FLAMENCO		
WILLIS MUSIC COMPANY		.40
GILLOCK	2	
FLAMENCO		
WILLIS MUSIC COMPANY		.40
GILLOCK	4	
FOUNTAIN IN THE RAIN		
WILLIS MUSIC COMPANY		.40
GILLOCK	4	
FOUNTAIN IN THE RAIN		
WILLIS MUSIC COMPANY		.40
GILLOCK	3	
FRENCH DOLL		
WILLIS MUSIC COMPANY		.40
GILLOCK	1 1/2	
FRENCH DOLL		
WILLIS MUSIC COMPANY		.40
GILLOCK	1 1/2	
GLASS SLIPPER, THE		
WILLIS MUSIC COMPANY		.50
GILLOCK	3	
GOLDFISH		
WILLIS MUSIC COMPANY		.40
GILLOCK	3	
GOLDFISH		
WILLIS MUSIC COMPANY		.40
GILLOCK	2	
HAPPY HOLIDAY		
WILLIS MUSIC COMPANY		.35
GILLOCK	1	
HAPPY HOLIDAY		
WILLIS MUSIC COMPANY		.40
GILLOCK	1	
HAPPY HOLIDAY		
WILLIS MUSIC COMPANY		.40
GILLOCK	4	
HARLEQUIN		
WILLIS MUSIC COMPANY		.40
GILLOCK	2 1/2	
HARLEQUIN		
WILLIS MUSIC COMPANY		.40
GILLOCK	2 1/2	
HAUNTED TREE, THE		
WILLIS MUSIC COMPANY		.40
GILLOCK	2	
HORSEBACK RIDE		
WILLIS MUSIC COMPANY		.40

GILLOCK	2	
HORSEBACK RIDE		
WILLIS MUSIC COMPANY		.40
GILLOCK	2 1/2	
IN OLD VIENNA		
WILLIS MUSIC COMPANY		.40
GILLOCK	2 1/2	
IN OLD VIENNA		
WILLIS MUSIC COMPANY		.40
GILLOCK	2	
JUGGLER		
WILLIS MUSIC COMPANY		.40
GILLOCK	2	
JUGGLER, THE		
WILLIS MUSIC COMPANY		.40
GILLOCK		
LAST SPRING		
WILLIS MUSIC COMPANY		.40
GILLOCK	2 1/2	
LAST SPRING		
WILLIS MUSIC COMPANY		.10
GILLOCK	2 1/2	
LAST SPRING		
WILLIS MUSIC COMPANY		.40
GILLOCK	3	
MISSION BELLS		
WILLIS MUSIC COMPANY		.40
GILLOCK	2	
MISSION BELLS		
WILLIS MUSIC COMPANY		.40
GILLOCK		
MY LADY'S HARPSICHORD		
CARL FISCHER, INC.	RS 363	.50
GILLOCK	1 1/2	
MY TOY DUCK		
BELWIN-MILLS PUBLISHING CORPORATION		.60
GILLOCK		
NOCTURNE		
G. SCHIRMER, INC.		.35
GILLOCK	2	
OLD PLANTATION		
WILLIS MUSIC COMPANY		.40
GILLOCK	2	
OLD PLANTATION		
WILLIS MUSIC COMPANY		.40
GILLOCK		
PINWHEELS		
SUMMY-BIRCHARD COMPANY		.75
GILLOCK	3	
POLYNESIAN NOCTURNE		
WILLIS MUSIC COMPANY		.40
GILLOCK	2 1/2	
PORTRAIT OF PARIS		
WILLIS MUSIC COMPANY		.50
GILLOCK		
PORTRAIT OF PARIS -- SECOND PIANO PART AVAILABLE		
WILLIS MUSIC COMPANY		.50
GILLOCK	3	
PROMENADE		
WILLIS MUSIC COMPANY		.40
GILLOCK	2	
PROMENADE		
WILLIS MUSIC COMPANY		.40
GILLOCK	2	
PROWLING PUSSYCAT, THE		
WILLIS MUSIC COMPANY		.35
GILLOCK	1	
PROWLING PUSSYCAT, THE		
WILLIS MUSIC COMPANY		.35
GILLOCK		
SARABANDE		
WILLIS MUSIC COMPANY		.40
GILLOCK	2	
SARABANDE		
WILLIS MUSIC COMPANY		.40
GILLOCK	2	
SARABANDE		
WILLIS MUSIC COMPANY		.40
GILLOCK	3	
SING, LITTLE PUSSY CAT		
WILLIS MUSIC COMPANY		.35
GILLOCK	3	
SLEIGH BELLS IN THE SNOW		
WILLIS MUSIC COMPANY		.40
GILLOCK	2	
SLEIGH RIDE		
BELWIN-MILLS PUBLISHING CORPORATION		.60
GILLOCK		
SONATINA IN CLASSIC STYLE		
WILLIS MUSIC COMPANY		.60
GILLOCK	3	
SONATINA IN CLASSIC STYLE		
WILLIS MUSIC COMPANY		.60
GILLOCK	3	
SONATINA IN CLASSIC STYLE		
WILLIS MUSIC COMPANY		.60
GILLOCK	3	
SONATINE		
WILLIS MUSIC COMPANY		.60
GILLOCK	3	
SONATINE		
WILLIS MUSIC COMPANY		.60
GILLOCK	2 1/2	
SUNSET		
WILLIS MUSIC COMPANY		.40
GILLOCK	2 1/2	
SUNSET		
WILLIS MUSIC COMPANY		.40
GILLOCK	2	
TARANTELLA		
WILLIS MUSIC COMPANY		.40
GILLOCK	2	
TARANTELLA		
WILLIS MUSIC COMPANY		.40
GILLOCK		
TROPIC ISLAND, A		
G. SCHIRMER, INC.		.40
GILLOCK	2 1/2	
VALSE ETUDE		
WILLIS MUSIC COMPANY		.60
GILLOCK	2	
VALSE TRISTE		
WILLIS MUSIC COMPANY		.40
GILLOCK	2	
VALSE TRISTE		
WILLIS MUSIC COMPANY		.40

GILLOCK	3		
WHIRLWIND			
VOLKWEIN BROS.			.40
GILLOCK	2		
WOOD LAND LEGEND, A			
WILLIS MUSIC COMPANY			.40
GILLOCK	2		
WOODLAND LEGEND, A			
WILLIS MUSIC COMPANY			.40
GIMBEL			
BURSTING BUBBLES			
EDWARD B. MARKS MUSIC CORPORATION			00.60
GIMBEL *	KERR, R.N.		
GIRL FROM IPANEMA			
MCA MUSIC			1.00
GIMBEL *	KERR, R.N.		
HOW INSENSITIVE			
MCA MUSIC			1.00
GIMINEZ			
INTERMEDIO -- NO. 4, FROM ''EL BAILE DE LUIS ALONSO''			
ASSOCIATED MUSIC PUBLISHERS, INC.		UME	1.00
GIMINEZ			
INTERMEDIO -- NO. 4, FROM ''LA BODA DE LUIS ALONSO''			
ASSOCIATED MUSIC PUBLISHERS, INC.		UME	1.50
GINASTERA			
DANZAS ARGENTINAS			
ELKAN-VOGEL, INC.		D	3.75
GINASTERA			
ESTANCIA			
BOOSEY AND HAWKES, INC.			6.50
GINASTERA			
MALAMBO			
FRANCO COLOMBO PUBLICATIONS		BA8449	1.00
GINASTERA			
MILONGA			
FRANCO COLOMBO PUBLICATIONS		BA9928	.75
GINASTERA			
PEQUENA DANZA, FROM 'ESTANCIA'			
BOOSEY AND HAWKES, INC.			.75
GINASTERA			
RONDO ON ARGENTINE CHILDREN'S FOLK TUNES			
BOOSEY AND HAWKES, INC.			.75
GINASTERA			
SONATA			
BOOSEY AND HAWKES, INC.			4.00
GINASTERA			
SUITE DE DANZAS CRIOLLAS			
BOOSEY AND HAWKES, INC.			3.00
GIORDANI	DEL MAGLIO		
CARO MIO BEN			
FRANCO COLOMBO PUBLICATIONS		128119	.50
GIORDANO	MARCIANO		
ANDREA CHENIER - MADDALENA'S ARIA			
FRANCO COLOMBO PUBLICATIONS		SON.936	.90
GIORDANO			
FEDORA - INTERLUDIO			
FRANCO COLOMBO PUBLICATIONS		SON.994	.90
GIORDANO	DE CHRISTOFARO		
SIBERIA - DANCE OF THE BALALAIKAS			
FRANCO COLOMBO PUBLICATIONS		SON.1921	.90
GIORDANO *			
ANNA			
TRO SONGWAYS SERVICE, INC.		2003	
GIORZA	DEL MAGLIO		
DAGHELA AVANTI UN PASSO			
FRANCO COLOMBO PUBLICATIONS		127837	.50
GIOVANNI	2A		
AVIATORS ON PARADE			
MUSICORD PUBLICATIONS, INC.			.45
GIOVANNI	1		
BAMBOO GROVE			
CENTURY MUSIC PUBLISHING COMPANY, INC.		3750	.40
GIOVANNI	2B		
CATHEDRAL REVERIE			
MUSICORD PUBLICATIONS, INC.			.45
GIOVANNI	2		
HAPPY SAM THE BANJO MAN			
BOSTON MUSIC COMPANY			.50
GIOVANNI	1		
MARIE ANTOINETTE'S MUSIC BOX			
CENTURY MUSIC PUBLISHING COMPANY, INC.		3681	.40
GIOVANNI	1A		
MING LING LAUNDRYMAN			
MUSICORD PUBLICATIONS, INC.			.45
GIOVANNI	2		
MR. TURKEY GOES TO TOWN			
BOSTON MUSIC COMPANY			.50
GIOVANNI	1		
PIRATE BOLD, A			
CENTURY MUSIC PUBLISHING COMPANY, INC.		3751	.40
GIOVANNI	3		
TARANTELLA VICO			
BOSTON MUSIC COMPANY			.50
GIOVANNI	1B		
TOY SOLDIERS ON PARADE			
MUSICORD PUBLICATIONS, INC.			.45
GIRALDI			
NOCTURNE			
FRANCO COLOMBO PUBLICATIONS		DS519	1.25
GIRARD	4		
VALLEY OF FRANCE, MEDITATION			
CENTURY MUSIC PUBLISHING COMPANY, INC.		2414	.40
GIRAUD			
UNDER PARIS SKIES			
MCA MUSIC			1.00
GIURANNA			
SONATINA			
FRANCO COLOMBO PUBLICATIONS		123421	1.00
GIURANNA			
TOCCATA			
FRANCO COLOMBO PUBLICATIONS		123917	.90
GLADKOVSKY			
LITTLE BALLERINA			
MCA MUSIC			.60
GLASER	PODOLSKY, L.		
MINUETTO			
FREDERICK HARRIS MUSIC COMPANY			.60
GLAZOUNOW, A.			
AUTUMN, FROM 'THE SEASONS'			
BOOSEY AND HAWKES, INC.			3.25
GLAZOUNOW, A.			
CHANT DES BATELIERS DE LA VOLGA, OP. 97			
BOOSEY AND HAWKES, INC.			.75
GLAZOUNOW, A.	FREDERICKS		
CONCERTO THEME FROM PIANO CONCERTO, OP. 92			
MCA MUSIC			.75

GLAZOUNOW, A.			
GRAND VALSE DE CONCERT, OP. 41			
BOOSEY AND HAWKES, INC.			2.50
GLAZOUNOW, A.			
PIZZICATO, FROM 'RAYMONDA'			
BOOSEY AND HAWKES, INC.			1.25
GLAZOUNOW, A.			
PRELUDE AND FUGUE, OP. 62			
BOOSEY AND HAWKES, INC.			2.50
GLAZOUNOW, A.	DEIS		
PRELUDIO E FUGA IN E MINOR			
G. SCHIRMER, INC.			1.00
GLAZOUNOW, A.			
SONATA NO. 01, OP. 74			
BOOSEY AND HAWKES, INC.			4.00
GLAZOUNOW, A.			
SONATA NO. 02, OP. 75			
BOOSEY AND HAWKES, INC.			4.00
GLAZOUNOW, A.			
THEME AND VARIATIONS, OP. 72			
BOOSEY AND HAWKES, INC.			2.75
GLAZOUNOW, A.			
THEME AND VARIATIONS, OP. 72			
INTERNATIONAL MUSIC COMPANY			1.75
GLAZOUNOW, A.			
THREE ETUDES, OP. 31 NO. 1 IN C			
BOOSEY AND HAWKES, INC.			1.50
GLAZOUNOW, A.			
THREE ETUDES, OP. 31 NO. 2 IN E			
BOOSEY AND HAWKES, INC.			1.75
GLAZOUNOW, A.			
THREE ETUDES, OP. 31 NO. 3 'LA NUIT'			
BOOSEY AND HAWKES, INC.			1.50
GLAZOUNOW, A.			
WALTZ, OP. 23			
BOOSEY AND HAWKES, INC.			1.50
GLAZOUNOW, A.			
WALTZ, OP. 44 NO. 3			
BOOSEY AND HAWKES, INC.			3.00
GLEDHILL, C.			
FIDDLE TUNE			
FREDERICK HARRIS MUSIC COMPANY			.90
GLIERE			
DANCE OF THE RUSSIAN SAILORS			
EDWARD B. MARKS MUSIC CORPORATION			01.00
GLIERE	SWARENSKI		
DANCE OF THE RUSSIAN SAILORS			
MCA MUSIC			.75
GLIERE			
FESTIVAL GROUPS FOR PIANO SELECTED BY ARTHUR BENJAMIN, SERIES 1			
-- MELODIE IN A FLAT			
BOOSEY AND HAWKES, INC.			.60
GLIERE			
HAPPY LIFE, A			
MCA MUSIC			.60
GLIERE	85		
ORIENTAL SONG			
BELWIN-MILLS PUBLISHING CORPORATION			.60
GLIERE			
PRELUDE IN D FLAT, OP. 43 NO. 1			
FREDERICK HARRIS MUSIC COMPANY			.60
GLIERE	DUMM		
RECITAL REFRESHER SERIES -- ORIENTAL SONG			
BELWIN-MILLS PUBLISHING CORPORATION		26119	.85
GLIERE	5		
RED POPPY BALLET, DANCE			
CENTURY MUSIC PUBLISHING COMPANY, INC.		3482	.40
GLIERE			
WALTZ FROM -- THE BRONZE HORSEMAN			
MCA MUSIC			.75
GLINKA	BALAKIREV	5	
L'ALOUETTE TRANSKRIPTION			
SCHOTT		10392	.75
GLINKA	BALAKIREV	5	
LARK, THE			
CENTURY MUSIC PUBLISHING COMPANY, INC.		2581	.40
GLINKA	BALAKIREV	9	
LARK, THE			
THEODORE PRESSER COMPANY			.50
GLINKA			
NOCTURNE IN F MINOR 'LA SEPARATION'			
MUSICA OBSCURA			1.50
GLINKA			
RUSSLAN AND LUDMILLA			
CENTURY MUSIC PUBLISHING COMPANY, INC.			1.25
GLINKA			
VARIATIONS ON 'THE LAST ROSE OF SUMMER'			
MUSICA OBSCURA			2.00
GLINKA			
VARIATIONS ON A RUSSIAN SONG			
MUSICA OBSCURA			1.75
GLOVER			
FORWARD MARCH			
EDWARD B. MARKS MUSIC CORPORATION			00.60
GLOVER			
KNIVES AND FORKS			
EDWARD B. MARKS MUSIC CORPORATION			00.60
GLOVER			
LITTLE BIRD'S SONG, THE			
EDWARD B. MARKS MUSIC CORPORATION			00.60
GLOVER			
LITTLE LEAD GENERAL, THE			
SUMMY-BIRCHARD COMPANY			.50
GLOVER			
REAL COOL BOOGIE			
EDWARD B. MARKS MUSIC CORPORATION			00.60
GLOVER	2		
ROSE OF TRALEE, THE			
CENTURY MUSIC PUBLISHING COMPANY, INC.		3702	.40
GLOVER			
SUNDAY MORNING			
EDWARD B. MARKS MUSIC CORPORATION			00.60
GLOVER, D.	2		
BANJO ON MY KNEE			
BELWIN-MILLS PUBLISHING CORPORATION			.60
GLOVER, D.	1		
BLUE WINDMILLS			
BELWIN-MILLS PUBLISHING CORPORATION			.60
GLOVER, D.	2		
CANDLELIGHT SUPPER CLUB			
VOLKWEIN BROS.			.35
GLOVER, D.	PRIM.		
CAPTAIN CANDY			
BELWIN-MILLS PUBLISHING CORPORATION			.60
GLOVER, D.	1 1/2		
CAT TALE			
VOLKWEIN BROS.			.35

GLUCK   SGAMBATI *
  MELODY FROM ''ORFEO''
    G. SCHIRMER, INC.   .50
GLUCK   DEL MAGLIO
  ORFEO - CHE FARO SENZA EURIDICE
    FRANCO COLOMBO PUBLICATIONS   128123   .60
                          2-3
GLUCK
  ORPHEUS UND EURYDIKE -- REIGEN SELIGER GEISTER UND GAVOTTE
    SCHOTT   01100   .75
GLUCK   DEAN, L.
  ORPHEUS--ADAPTED AS A CHILDREN'S OPERA-STORY TO BE PLAYED, READ,
    SUNG OR INFORMALLY DRAMATIZED
    G. SCHIRMER, INC.   .60
GNESSINA
  MARCH
    MCA MUSIC   .60
GNESSINA
  SAD LITTLE TUNE, A
    MCA MUSIC   .60
GOBBAERTS   3
  DANCING LEAVES
    CENTURY MUSIC PUBLISHING COMPANY, INC.   185   .40
GODARD, B.   4
  AU MATIN
    CENTURY MUSIC PUBLISHING COMPANY, INC.   512   .40
GODARD, B.   4
  AU MATIN -- AT MORN
    VOLKWEIN BROS.   .25
GODARD, B.
  AU MATIN, OP. 83
    G. SCHIRMER, INC.   .40
GODARD, B.   5
  BARCAROLLE VENETIENNE
    CENTURY MUSIC PUBLISHING COMPANY, INC.   1767   .40
GODARD, B.   MENDEL, S.   2
  BERCEUSE
    WILLIS MUSIC COMPANY   .40
GODARD, B.
  BERCEUSE FROM 'JOCELYN'
    BELWIN-MILLS PUBLISHING CORPORATION   28049   .60
GODARD, B.   KLEINPAUL
  BERCEUSE FROM 'JOCELYN'
    G. SCHIRMER, INC.   .50
GODARD, B.   5
  BERCEUSE, JOCELYN
    CENTURY MUSIC PUBLISHING COMPANY, INC.   1322   .40
GODARD, B.   ROLFE, W.   2
  CHROMATIC WALTZ, EASY
    CENTURY MUSIC PUBLISHING COMPANY, INC.   3555   .40
GODARD, B.
  DEUXIEME MAZURKA IN B FLAT, OP. 54
    G. SCHIRMER, INC.   .60
GODARD, B.
  DEUXIEME VALSE BRILLANTE IN B FLAT, OP. 56
    G. SCHIRMER, INC.   .60
GODARD, B.   ROLFE, W.   2
  FIFTH WALTZ, EASY
    CENTURY MUSIC PUBLISHING COMPANY, INC.   3555   .40
GODARD, B.   4
  FIRST MAZURKA, OP. 25
    CENTURY MUSIC PUBLISHING COMPANY, INC.   1635   .40
GODARD, B.   4
  FIRST WALTZ
    CENTURY MUSIC PUBLISHING COMPANY, INC.   3237   .40
GODARD, B.   5
  FOURTH BARCAROLLE
    CENTURY MUSIC PUBLISHING COMPANY, INC.   1767   .40
GODARD, B.   3
  JOCELYN, BERCEUSE, EASY
    CENTURY MUSIC PUBLISHING COMPANY, INC.   2518   .40
GODARD, B.
  JUGGLERY--ETUDE, OP. 107 NO. 3
    G. SCHIRMER, INC.   .50
GODARD, B.
  LE CAVALIER FANTASTIQUE--ETUDE ARTISTIQUE, OP. 42, NO. 1
    G. SCHIRMER, INC.   .50
GODARD, B.   5
  LULLABY, JOCELYN
    CENTURY MUSIC PUBLISHING COMPANY, INC.   1322   .40
GODARD, B.   3
  LULLABY, JOCELYN, EASY
    CENTURY MUSIC PUBLISHING COMPANY, INC.   2518   .40
GODARD, B.   4
  MAZURKA NO. 1
    CENTURY MUSIC PUBLISHING COMPANY, INC.   1635   .40
GODARD, B.   4
  MAZURKA NO. 2
    CENTURY MUSIC PUBLISHING COMPANY, INC.   189   .40
GODARD, B.   4
  MEDITATION, THE ANGELUS
    CENTURY MUSIC PUBLISHING COMPANY, INC.   2197   .40
GODARD, B.
  QUATRIEME MAZURKA IN B FLAT, OP. 103 NO. 4
    G. SCHIRMER, INC.   .60
GODARD, B.   4
  SECOND MAZURKA
    CENTURY MUSIC PUBLISHING COMPANY, INC.   189   .40
GODARD, B.   4
  SECOND MAZURKA
    VOLKWEIN BROS.   .25
GODARD, B.
  SECOND MAZURKA, OP. 54
    BELWIN-MILLS PUBLISHING CORPORATION   28176   .70
GODARD, B.   4
  SECOND VALSE
    VOLKWEIN BROS.   .25
GODARD, B.   4
  SECOND VALSE, OP. 56
    CENTURY MUSIC PUBLISHING COMPANY, INC.   695   .40
GODARD, B.   6
  SECOND WALTZ
    BELWIN-MILLS PUBLISHING CORPORATION   128   .60
GODARD, B.   5
  VALSE CHROMATIQUE
    BELWIN-MILLS PUBLISHING CORPORATION   17   .60
GODARD, B.   5
  VALSE CHROMATIQUE
    CENTURY MUSIC PUBLISHING COMPANY, INC.   1497   .40
GODARD, B.
  VALSE CHROMATIQUE --5TH WALTZ-- IN G, OP. 88
    CARL FISCHER, INC.   S 1763   .75
GODARD, B.
  VALSE CHROMATIQUE, OP. 88
    G. SCHIRMER, INC.   .75
GODARD, B.   3
  VALSE NO. 02, EASY
    CENTURY MUSIC PUBLISHING COMPANY, INC.   2592   .40

GODARD, B.   ROLFE, W.   2
  VALSE, OP. 88 NO. 5, EASY
    CENTURY MUSIC PUBLISHING COMPANY, INC.   3555   .40
GODARD, B.
  VENITIENNE--FOURTH BARCAROLLE, OP. 110 NO. 2
    G. SCHIRMER, INC.   .60
GODARD, B.   5
  VENITIENNE, 4TH, BARCAROLLE
    CENTURY MUSIC PUBLISHING COMPANY, INC.   1767   .40
GODARD, B.   4
  WALTZ NO. 01
    CENTURY MUSIC PUBLISHING COMPANY, INC.   3237   .40
GODARD, B.   4
  WALTZ NO. 02
    CENTURY MUSIC PUBLISHING COMPANY, INC.   695   .40
GODARD, B.   4
  WOODCHOPPER AND THE LINNET
    CENTURY MUSIC PUBLISHING COMPANY, INC.   .40
GODARD, C.   4
  ANGELUS, THE
    CENTURY MUSIC PUBLISHING COMPANY, INC.   2197   .40
GODARD, C.   4
  BUTTERFLY DANCE, OP. 69
    CENTURY MUSIC PUBLISHING COMPANY, INC.   1583   .40
GODARD, C.   4
  DANCE OF THE STARS
    CENTURY MUSIC PUBLISHING COMPANY, INC.   1584   .40
GODARD, C.
  ECHOES FROM SCOTIA
    FREDERICK HARRIS MUSIC COMPANY   .75
GODDARD, B.
  MAZURKA NO. 01, OP. 25
    FRANCO COLOMBO PUBLICATIONS   SAL   2.00
GODDARD, B.
  WALTZ NO. 01, OP. 26
    FRANCO COLOMBO PUBLICATIONS   SAL   2.00
GODDARD, W.
  BIG BASS DRUM
    G. SCHIRMER, INC.   .35
GODDARD, W.
  FUNNY FROG
    G. SCHIRMER, INC.   .35
GODDARD, W.
  JUMPIEST GRASSHOPPER, THE
    G. SCHIRMER, INC.   .40
GODDEN, R.
  BLACKBERRY JACK
    FREDERICK HARRIS MUSIC COMPANY   .90
GODDEN, R.
  DANCE
    FREDERICK HARRIS MUSIC COMPANY   .60
GODDEN, R.
  HIKERS SONG, THE
    FREDERICK HARRIS MUSIC COMPANY   .60
GODDEN, R.
  HOPPING SPARROW, THE
    FREDERICK HARRIS MUSIC COMPANY   .60
GODDEN, R.
  LINDA ROSE
    FREDERICK HARRIS MUSIC COMPANY   .60
GODDEN, R.
  LITTLE HANS
    FREDERICK HARRIS MUSIC COMPANY   .60
GODDEN, R.
  MOZART ON TIPTOE
    FREDERICK HARRIS MUSIC COMPANY   .60
GODDEN, R.
  VALSE LENTE
    FREDERICK HARRIS MUSIC COMPANY   .60
GODDEN, R.
  VESPERS
    FREDERICK HARRIS MUSIC COMPANY   .75
GODOWSKY, L.
  ALT-WIEN--FROM TRIAKONTAMERON
    G. SCHIRMER, INC.   .60
GODOWSKY, L.   STEINER
  ALT-WIEN--FROM TRIAKONTAMERON
    G. SCHIRMER, INC.   .50
GODOWSKY, L.
  MELODIE MEDITATIVE IN E FLAT OP. 15, NO. 1
    MUSICA OBSCURA   1.00
GODOWSKY, L.
  NOCTURNAL TANGIER
    G. SCHIRMER, INC.   .50
GODOWSKY, L.
  TOCCATA IN G FLAT 'MOTO PERPETUO' OP. 13
    MUSICA OBSCURA   2.50
GOEB, R.   M
  JESTING
    THEODORE PRESSER COMPANY   .50
GOEDICKE
  DANCE, OP. 36 NO. 21
    FREDERICK HARRIS MUSIC COMPANY   .60
GOEDICKE
  DANCE, REVERIE, MAZURKA, OP. 36
    MCA MUSIC   .60
GOEDICKE
  RIGAUDON, OP. 46 NO. 1
    FREDERICK HARRIS MUSIC COMPANY   .60
GOEDICKE
  SHORT PIECE, OP. 6 NO. 2
    FREDERICK HARRIS MUSIC COMPANY   .60
GOEHR, A.   6
  CAPRICCIO, OP. 6
    SCHOTT   10674   1.50
GOEHR, A.   5
  SONATA, OP. 2
    SCHOTT   10417   2.00
GOEPDELER, R.   4
  CHRISTMAS CHIMES
    THEODORE PRESSER COMPANY   .50
GOERDELER, R.
  YULETIDE BELLS
    BOSTON MUSIC COMPANY   .50
GOERNER
  SONATA BALLATA, OP. 21
    ASSOCIATED MUSIC PUBLISHERS, INC.   SIM   2.25
GOETSCHY
  ESPOIR DU RETOUR, L' -- CAPRICE --
    FRANCO COLOMBO PUBLICATIONS   SAL   1.75
GOETSCHY
  ESPOIR DU RETOUR, L' -- CAPRICE --
    FRANCO COLOMBO PUBLICATIONS   SAL   1.50
GOLD
  EXODUS, MAIN THEME
    CHAPPELL AND COMPANY, INC.   1405026   .95

GOLDFARB   2
    SNOWFLAKE WALTZ
        PRO-ART PUBLICATIONS, INC.   523   .50
GOLDMAN, R.   MD
    AUBADES
        THEODORE PRESSER COMPANY   1.00
GOLDMAN, R.   MD
    LEE RIGG, THE
        THEODORE PRESSER COMPANY   .50
GOLDMAN, R.   M
    SONATINA
        THEODORE PRESSER COMPANY   1.00
GOLDSCHMIDT
    CAPRICCIO, OP. 11
        UNIVERSAL EDITION   UE 9551   1.10
GOLDSCHMIDT
    FROM THE BALLET
        FRANCO COLOMBO PUBLICATIONS   LD418   .60
GOLDSCHMIDT
    SCHERZO
        FRANCO COLOMBO PUBLICATIONS   LD417   .60
GOLDSCHMIDT
    SONATA, OP. 10
        UNIVERSAL EDITION   UE 8925   3.20
GOLDSMITH, J.
    BLUE MAX, THE
        THE BIG THREE MUSIC CORPORATION   00.95
GOLDSMITH, J.
    LILA'S THEME - THE STRIPPER
        THE BIG THREE MUSIC CORPORATION   00.95
GOLDSMITH, J.
    MAN FROM U.N.C.L.E. - THEME
        THE BIG THREE MUSIC CORPORATION   00.95
GOLDSMITH, J.
    OUR MAN FLINT
        THE BIG THREE MUSIC CORPORATION   00.95
GOLDSMITH, J.
    PRIZE, THE
        THE BIG THREE MUSIC CORPORATION   00.95
GOLDSMITH, J.
    VON RYAN MARCH
        THE BIG THREE MUSIC CORPORATION   00.95
GOLZ   M
    ETUDE
        COMPOSERS PRESS, INC.   1.00
GOLZ
    ETUDE JOYEUSE
        FRANCO COLOMBO PUBLICATIONS   NY1565   .60
GOMBAU
    DANZA DEL DESTINO
        ASSOCIATED MUSIC PUBLISHERS, INC.   UME   .55
GOMBAU
    ESCENA Y DANZA CHARRA
        ASSOCIATED MUSIC PUBLISHERS, INC.   UME   .55
GOMES
    GUARANY, IL - OVERTURE
        FRANCO COLOMBO PUBLICATIONS   127730   1.00
GOMEZ CARRILLO
    DANZA DEL CUERVO
        FRANCO COLOMBO PUBLICATIONS   BA11525   .7P
GOMEZ CARRILLO
    DANZA SANTIAGUENA
        FRANCO COLOMBO PUBLICATIONS   BA6098   1.00
GOMEZ CARRILLO
    HUAHUA, LA
        FRANCO COLOMBO PUBLICATIONS   BA9411   .75
GOMEZ CARRILLO
    MISTOLERO, EL
        FRANCO COLOMBO PUBLICATIONS   BA6099   .75
GOMEZ CARRILLO
    RAPSODIA SANTIAGUENA
        FRANCO COLOMBO PUBLICATIONS   BA6279   1.50
GOMEZ CARRILLO
    SIETE DE ABRIL
        FRANCO COLOMBO PUBLICATIONS   BA10276   .75
GOMEZ CARRILLO
    SUMAJ
        FRANCO COLOMBO PUBLICATIONS   BA9716   .75
GOMEZ CARRILLO
    TUNANTE CATAMARQUENO, EL
        FRANCO COLOMBO PUBLICATIONS   BA11493   .75
GOODMAN *
    STOMPING AT THE SAVOY
        THE BIG THREE MUSIC CORPORATION   00.95
GOODMAN, J.   2
    COLONIAL MANSION
        CENTURY MUSIC PUBLISHING COMPANY, INC.   4114   .40
GOODMAN, J.   2
    MASQUERADE
        CENTURY MUSIC PUBLISHING COMPANY, INC.   4206   .40
GOODMAN, J.   2
    OLD-WORLD DANCE, AN
        CENTURY MUSIC PUBLISHING COMPANY, INC.   4183   .40
GOODMAN, J.   2
    SCURRY UP
        CENTURY MUSIC PUBLISHING COMPANY, INC.   4182   .40
GOODMAN, J.   2
    SLOW MINUET
        CENTURY MUSIC PUBLISHING COMPANY, INC.   4184   .40
GOODMAN, J.   2
    SNOW AT DUSK
        CENTURY MUSIC PUBLISHING COMPANY, INC.   4115   .40
GOODRICH
    CAPRICE IN C
        SUMMY-BIRCHARD COMPANY   .75
GOODRICH
    WATER SPRITE
        SUMMY-BIRCHARD COMPANY   .50
GOODWIN, R.
    OF HUMAN BONDAGE - THEME
        THE BIG THREE MUSIC CORPORATION   00.95
GOSSEC   2
    GAVOTTE
        BELWIN-MILLS PUBLISHING CORPORATION   .50
GOSSEC   WEYBRIGHT   2
    GAVOTTE
        BELWIN-MILLS PUBLISHING CORPORATION   .60
GOSSEC   2
    GAVOTTE
        CENTURY MUSIC PUBLISHING COMPANY, INC.   1971   .40
GOSSEC   3
    GAVOTTE D-DUR UND MARTINI, GAVOTTE
        SCHOTT   0917 1/2 1.00
GOTTSCHALK   5
    DYING POET
        VOLKWEIN BROS.   .25

GOTTSCHALK   4
    DYING POET, THE
        CENTURY MUSIC PUBLISHING COMPANY, INC.   1047   .40
GOTTSCHALK   REEG, G. A.   3
    LAST HOPE
        VOLKWEIN BROS.   .35
GOTTSCHALK   6
    LAST HOPE, THE, OP. 16
        CENTURY MUSIC PUBLISHING COMPANY, INC.   636   .40
GOTTSCHALK   D
    SOUVENIR DE PORTO RICO
        THEODORE PRESSER COMPANY   1.50
GOULD, E.
    BLOWING BELL AND SNOW WHIRL
        ELKAN-VOGEL, INC.   .50
GOULD, E.
    FIRST FLIGHT
        ELKAN-VOGEL, INC.   .50
GOULD, M.
    AMERICAN SYMPHONETTE NO. 1 -- FIRST MOV'T
        BELWIN-MILLS PUBLISHING CORPORATION   20010   .50
GOULD, M.
    AMERICAN SYMPHONETTE NO. 1 -- THIRD MOV'T
        BELWIN-MILLS PUBLISHING CORPORATION   20011   .85
GOULD, M.
    AMERICAN SYMPHONETTE NO. 2 -- FIRST MOV'T
        BELWIN-MILLS PUBLISHING CORPORATION   20012   .85
GOULD, M.
    AMERICAN SYMPHONETTE NO. 2 -- THIRD MOV'T
        BELWIN-MILLS PUBLISHING CORPORATION   20013   .85
GOULD, M.
    AMERICAN SYMPHONETTE NO. 3 -- FIRST MOV'T
        BELWIN-MILLS PUBLISHING CORPORATION   20014   .85
GOULD, M.
    BALLERINA, THE
        BELWIN-MILLS PUBLISHING CORPORATION   20025   .85
GOULD, M.
    BLUES, FROM 'INTERPLAY'
        BELWIN-MILLS PUBLISHING CORPORATION   .85
GOULD, M.
    BOOGIE THE WOOGIE
        BELWIN-MILLS PUBLISHING CORPORATION   20036   .85
GOULD, M.
    BOOGIE WOOGIE ETUDE
        BELWIN-MILLS PUBLISHING CORPORATION   20037   .85
GOULD, M.
    COLONIAL PORTRAIT
        BELWIN-MILLS PUBLISHING CORPORATION   20054   .85
GOULD, M.
    CONTINENTAL SERENADE
        BELWIN-MILLS PUBLISHING CORPORATION   20060   .85
GOULD, M.
    CRINOLINE AND LACE
        BELWIN-MILLS PUBLISHING CORPORATION   20063   .85
GOULD, M.
    DESERTED BALLROOM
        BELWIN-MILLS PUBLISHING CORPORATION   20070   .85
GOULD, M.
    GUARACHA, THIRD MOV'T FROM LATIN-AMERICAN SYMPHONETTE
        BELWIN-MILLS PUBLISHING CORPORATION   20118   .85
GOULD, M.
    PAVANNE
        BELWIN-MILLS PUBLISHING CORPORATION   20195   .85
GOULD, M.
    POP'S SERENADE
        BELWIN-MILLS PUBLISHING CORPORATION   20206   .85
GOULD, M.
    PRELUDE AND TOCCATA
        BELWIN-MILLS PUBLISHING CORPORATION   20209   .85
GOULD, M.
    PRIMA DONNA, THE
        BELWIN-MILLS PUBLISHING CORPORATION   20213   .85
GOULD, M.
    SONATINA FOR PIANO
        BELWIN-MILLS PUBLISHING CORPORATION   20270   1.50
GOULD, M.
    TROPICAL
        BELWIN-MILLS PUBLISHING CORPORATION   20320   .85
GOUNOD, C.
    AVE MARIA
        FRANCO COLOMBO PUBLICATIONS   33759   .50
GOUNOD, C.   6
    BAL D'ENFANTS, LE, VALSE
        ALPHONSE LEDUC
GOUNOD, C.   3
    BALLET NO. 1, FAUST
        CENTURY MUSIC PUBLISHING COMPANY, INC.   2052   .40
GOUNOD, C.   M
    FAUST
        C. F. PETERS CORPORATION   C281   7.50
GOUNOD, C.   M
    FAUST
        C. F. PETERS CORPORATION   H640   2.00
GOUNOD, C.   CHIESA
    FAUST - EASY FANTASIA
        FRANCO COLOMBO PUBLICATIONS   109094   .50
GOUNOD, C.   MILICI
    FAUST - WALTZ
        FRANCO COLOMBO PUBLICATIONS   BA8329   .75
GOUNOD, C.   BURGMUELLER
    FAUST - WALTZES
        FRANCO COLOMBO PUBLICATIONS   64451   .75
GOUNOD, C.   M
    FAUST BALLET
        C. F. PETERS CORPORATION   C25   3.50
GOUNOD, C.   3
    FAUST BALLET, NO. 1
        CENTURY MUSIC PUBLISHING COMPANY, INC.   2052   .40
GOUNOD, C.   3
    FAUST BALLET, NO. 6
        CENTURY MUSIC PUBLISHING COMPANY, INC.   2054   .40
GOUNOD, C.   BURGMUELLER
    FAUST WALTZ
        FRANCO COLOMBO PUBLICATIONS   64452   1.25
GOUNOD, C.   2
    FAUST, FLOWER SONG
        CENTURY MUSIC PUBLISHING COMPANY, INC.   1565   .40
GOUNOD, C.   3
    FAUST, SOLDIERS' CHORUS
        CENTURY MUSIC PUBLISHING COMPANY, INC.   1575   .40
GOUNOD, C.
    FUNERAL MARCH OF A MARIONETTE
        ASHLEY DEALERS SERVICE, INC.   ES   .95
GOUNOD, C.   SCHAUM, J.   2 1/2
    FUNERAL MARCH OF A MARIONETTE
        SCHAUM PUBLICATIONS, INC.   .60

GOUNOD, C.   2
    JULIET'S VALSE
        CENTURY MUSIC PUBLISHING COMPANY, INC.   2044   .40
GOUNOD, C.   SCHAUM, J.   2
    MAGNIFICENT PROCESSION, THE
        BELWIN-MILLS PUBLISHING CORPORATION   .50
GOUNOD, C.   RICHARDS, B.   4
    MARCH, FAUST
        CENTURY MUSIC PUBLISHING COMPANY, INC.   1544   .40
GOUNOD, C.
    MARCHE FUNEBRE D'UNE MARIONNETTE
        G. SCHIRMER, INC.   .60
GOUNOD, C.
    MARCHE PONTIFICALE
        ASHLEY DEALERS SERVICE, INC.   ES   .95
GOUNOD, C.
    MARCHE PONTIFICALE
        G. SCHIRMER, INC.   .40
GOUNOD, C.
    MEDITATION ON THE FIRST PRELUDE BY J. S. BACH
        G. SCHIRMER, INC.   .60
GOUNOD, C.
    MEDITATION ON THE FIRST PRELUDE BY J. S. BACH
        G. SCHIRMER, INC.   .40
GOUNOD, C.   2
    MIREILLE, WALTZ SONG
        CENTURY MUSIC PUBLISHING COMPANY, INC.   2040   .40
GOUNOD, C.   SCHAUM, J.   1
    NAZARETH
        BELWIN-MILLS PUBLISHING CORPORATION   .50
GOUNOD, C.   M
    QUEEN OF SHEBA BALLET
        C. F. PETERS CORPORATION   C51   3.50
GOUNOD, C.   M
    ROMEO AND JULIET BALLET
        C. F. PETERS CORPORATION   C209   3.50
GOUNOD, C.   2
    ROMEO AND JULIET, WALTZ
        CENTURY MUSIC PUBLISHING COMPANY, INC.   2044   .40
GOUNOD, C.   WEYBRIGHT   2
    SEND OUT THY LIGHT -- ANTHEM
        BELWIN-MILLS PUBLISHING CORPORATION   .60
GOUNOD, C.   DEL MAGLIO
    SERENADE
        FRANCO COLOMBO PUBLICATIONS   124717   .50
GOUNOD, C.   4, 6
    SIX MORCEAUX FACILES
        ALPHONSE LEDUC
GOUNOD, C.   SCHAUM, J.   2
    SOLDIERS' CHORUS FROM 'FAUST'
        BELWIN-MILLS PUBLISHING CORPORATION   .50
GOUNOD, C.   LANGE
    WALTZ FROM 'FAUST', OP. 196 NO. 1
        BELWIN-MILLS PUBLISHING CORPORATION   28159   .70
GOUNOD, C.   LANGE, G.   2
    WALTZ SONG, MIREILLE
        CENTURY MUSIC PUBLISHING COMPANY, INC.   2040   .40
GOUNOD, C.   LANGE
    WALTZ--FROM ''FAUST''
        G. SCHIRMER, INC.   .70
GOUNOD, C. *   2
    AVE MARIA
        BELWIN-MILLS PUBLISHING CORPORATION   .50
GOUNOD, C. *
    FAUST, VALSE
        G. SCHIRMER, INC.   1.10
GOUNOD, C. *
    VALSE--'FAUST'
        G. SCHIRMER, INC.   1.10
GRADI, R. G.   2 1/2
    DREAMER, THE
        THEODORE PRESSER COMPANY   .60
GRADY, J.
    TWELVE DAYS OF CHRISTMAS, THE
        FEMA MUSIC PUBLICATIONS   2.50
GRAHAM
    BARN DANCE
        CARL FISCHER, INC.   P 3180   .50
GRAHAM   1
    OWL IN THE BELFRY
        CENTURY MUSIC PUBLISHING COMPANY, INC.   4346   .40
GRAHAM
    SEASCAPE
        WARNER BROTHERS PUBLISHERS   .60
GRAHAM
    SKIP TAG
        CARL FISCHER, INC.   P 3181   .50
GRAHAM, R.
    BEAR AND THE BEEHIVES, THE
        ELKAN-VOGEL, INC.   .50
GRAHAM, R.   1 1/2
    BLACK CAT, THE
        WILLIS MUSIC COMPANY   .40
GRAHAM, R.   1
    BLOSSOMS IN A POOL
        BELWIN-MILLS PUBLISHING CORPORATION   .60
GRAHAM, R.   1 1/2
    GORILLA, THE
        ELKAN-VOGEL, INC.   .50
GRAHAM, R.   1 1/2
    GRASSHOPPER REEL
        WILLIS MUSIC COMPANY   .40
GRAHAM, R.   1
    INDIAN SUMMER
        BELWIN-MILLS PUBLISHING CORPORATION   .60
GRAHAM, R.
    KITE AND THE PIGEONS, THE
        ELKAN-VOGEL, INC.   .50
GRAHAM, R.
    MANDARIN AND THE MULE, THE
        BELWIN-MILLS PUBLISHING CORPORATION   .60
GRAHAM, R.   1
    OWL IN THE BELFRY
        CENTURY MUSIC PUBLISHING COMPANY, INC.   4336   .40
GRAHAM, R.   2
    RAIN
        BELWIN-MILLS PUBLISHING CORPORATION   .60
GRAHAM, R.   1 1/2 - 2
    SEA GULL
        ELKAN-VOGEL, INC.   .50
GRAHAM, R.   1
    SLEIGH RIDE
        BELWIN-MILLS PUBLISHING CORPORATION   .60
GRAHAM, R.   1
    SUMMERTIME
        BELWIN-MILLS PUBLISHING CORPORATION   .60

GRAHAM, R.
    TWO DESERT SKETCHES -- PAPAGO FLUTE AND DESERT RAINFALL
        BROOT MUSIC COMPANY   .50
GRAINGER, P.
    CHILDREN'S MARCH- OVER THE HILLS AND FAR AWAY
        G. SCHIRMER, INC.   .50
GRAINGER, P.
    COUNTRY GARDENS--EASY VERSION--
        G. SCHIRMER, INC.   .60
GRAINGER, P.
    COUNTRY GARDENS--ENGLISH MORRIS-DANCE TUNE--
        G. SCHIRMER, INC.   .60
GRAINGER, P.
    COUNTRY GARDENS--ESPECIALLY EASY VERSION--
        G. SCHIRMER, INC.   .50
GRAINGER, P.
    FREE SETTING OF BRAHMS' CRADLE SONG, OP. 49, NO. 4
        G. SCHIRMER, INC.   .50
GRAINGER, P.
    GRIEG'S PIANO CONCERTO, FIRST MOVEMENT--CONCERT TRANSCRIPTION OF
    MAIN THEMES AND EPISODES--
        G. SCHIRMER, INC.   .80
GRAINGER, P.
    IRISH TUNE FROM COUNTY DERRY
        G. SCHIRMER, INC.   .50
GRAINGER, P.   5
    LANDLICHE GARTEN
        SCHOTT   1726   1.00
GRAINGER, P.
    LET'S DANCE GAY
        FABER MUSIC, LTD.   F0093
GRAINGER, P.   5
    PARAPHPASE UBER TSCHAIKOWSKYS BLUMEN-WALZER
        SCHOTT   1727   1.50
GRAINGER, P.
    RACHMANINOFF'S PIANO CONCERTO NO. 2 IN C MINOR, OP. 18, THIRD
    MOVEMENT--CONCERT TRANSCRIPTION OF MAIN THEMES AND EPISODES--
        G. SCHIRMER, INC.   1.00
GRAINGER, P.
    SCHUMANN'S PIANO CONCERTO, FIRST MOVEMENT--CONCERT TRANSCRIPTION
    OF MAIN THEMES AND EPISODES--
        G. SCHIRMER, INC.   1.25
GRAINGER, P.
    SCOTCH STRATHSPEY AND REEL
        G. SCHIRMER, INC.   1.00
GRAINGER, P.
    SHEPHERD'S HEY--ENGLISH MORRIS-DANCE TUNE--ORIGINAL VERSION
        G. SCHIRMER, INC.   .75
GRAINGER, P.
    TSCHAIKOWSKY'S PIANO CONCERT IN B FLAT MINOR--TRANSCRIPTION OF
    THE OPENING--
        G. SCHIRMER, INC.   .50
GRAITZER, G.
    RONDO
        PEER SOUTHERN ORGANIZATION   00.75
GRAMATGES
    SUITE CUBANA PARA NINOS
        FRANCO COLOMBO PUBLICATIONS   BA11570   1.00
GRANADOS
    A LA PRADERA
        ASSOCIATED MUSIC PUBLISHERS, INC.   UME   1.00
GRANADOS
    ALLEGRO DE CONCIERTO
        ASSOCIATED MUSIC PUBLISHERS, INC.   UME   1.10
GRANADOS
    ALLEGRO DE CONCIERTO
        G. SCHIRMER, INC.   1.50
GRANADOS   MARCHI, G.
    ANDALUZA FROM 'DANZAS ESPANOLAS'
        EDIZIONI BERBEN   1264   1.20
GRANADOS
    ANORANZA -- NO. 1, FROM SIX PIECES ON SPANISH FOLK SONGS
        ASSOCIATED MUSIC PUBLISHERS, INC.   UME   .90
GRANADOS
    APARICION
        ASSOCIATED MUSIC PUBLISHERS, INC.   UME   .90
GRANADOS
    BARCAROLLE, OP. 45
        ASSOCIATED MUSIC PUBLISHERS, INC.   UME   .75
GRANADOS
    CAPRICHO ESPANOL, OP. 39
        ASSOCIATED MUSIC PUBLISHERS, INC.   UME   .75
GRANADOS
    CAREZZA. WALTZ, OP. 39
        ASSOCIATED MUSIC PUBLISHERS, INC.   UME   .50
GRANADOS
    CARTAS DE AMOR -- VALSES INTIMOS -- OP. 44
        ASSOCIATED MUSIC PUBLISHERS, INC.   UME   .75
GRANADOS
    CUENTOS DE LA JUVENTUD, OP. 1
        ASSOCIATED MUSIC PUBLISHERS, INC.   UME   2.00
GRANADOS   4
    DANZA IRISTE
        CENTURY MUSIC PUBLISHING COMPANY, INC.   3840   .40
GRANADOS
    DANZA LENTA
        ASSOCIATED MUSIC PUBLISHERS, INC.   UME   1.00
GRANADOS
    DANZAS ESPANOLAS, OP. 37
        G. SCHIRMER, INC.   .75
GRANADOS
    ECOS DE LA PARRANDA -- NO. 2, FROM SIX PIECES ON SPANISH FOLK
    SONGS
        ASSOCIATED MUSIC PUBLISHERS, INC.   UME   .75
GRANADOS
    EL PELELE
        G. SCHIRMER, INC.   .90
GRANADOS
    ELISENDA SUITE -- EL JARDI
        ASSOCIATED MUSIC PUBLISHERS, INC.   UME   .60
GRANADOS
    GOYESCAS - SUITE OF 6 PIECES-
        INTERNATIONAL MUSIC COMPANY   3.75
GRANADOS
    INTERMEZZO FROM 'GOYESCAS'
        G. SCHIRMER, INC.   .50
GRANADOS   2
    LAST PAVANE, THE
        CENTURY MUSIC PUBLISHING COMPANY, INC.   3973   .40
GRANADOS
    MAIDEN AND THE NIGHTINGALE
        EDWARD B. MARKS MUSIC CORPORATION   01.00
GRANADOS   PHILIPP, I.
    MAIDEN AND THE NIGHTINGALE, THE
        INTERNATIONAL MUSIC COMPANY   1.00
GRANADOS
    MARCHA ORIENTAL -- NO. 4, FROM SIX PIECES ON SPANISH FOLK SONGS
        ASSOCIATED MUSIC PUBLISHERS, INC.   UME   .90

GRANADOS   MARCHI, G.
    ORIENTAL FROM 'DANZAS ESPANOLAS'
        EDIZIONI BERBEN   1265   1.20
GRANADOS
    PAISAJE, OP. 35
        ASSOCIATED MUSIC PUBLISHERS, INC.   UME   .90
GRANADOS   4 1/2
    PLAYERA --E MINOR--
        THEODORE PRESSER COMPANY   4   .50
GRANADOS
    PLAYERA, OP. 5 NO. 5
        CENTURY MUSIC PUBLISHING COMPANY, INC.   3480   .40
GRANADOS
    QUEJAS O LA MAJA Y EL RUISENOR -- NO. 4, FROM GOYESCAS
        ASSOCIATED MUSIC PUBLISHERS, INC.   UME   .75
GRANADOS   DEIS
    QUEJAS, O LA MAJA Y EL RUISENOR, FROM 'GOYESCAS'
        G. SCHIRMER, INC.   .75
GRANADOS
    RAPSODIA ARAGONESA
        ASSOCIATED MUSIC PUBLISHERS, INC.   UME   1.50
GRANADOS
    REQUIEBROS, LOS -- NO. 1, FROM GOYESCAS
        ASSOCIATED MUSIC PUBLISHERS, INC.   UME   1.00
GRANADOS
    SEVEN VALSES POETICOS WITH PRELUDE AND POSTLUDE
        ASSOCIATED MUSIC PUBLISHERS, INC.   UME   .90
GRANADOS   5
    SPANISH DANCE
        BOSTON MUSIC COMPANY   .50
GRANADOS
    VASCONGADA -- NO. 3, FROM SIX PIECES ON SPANISH FOLK SONGS
        ASSOCIATED MUSIC PUBLISHERS, INC.   UME   .90
GRANADOS
    ZAMBRA -- NO. 5, FROM SIX PIECES ON SPANISH FOLK SONGS
        ASSOCIATED MUSIC PUBLISHERS, INC.   UME   .90
GRANADOS
    ZAPATEADO -- NO. 6, FROM SIX PIECES ON SPANISH FOLK SONGS
        ASSOCIATED MUSIC PUBLISHERS, INC.   UME   .90
GRANFIELD, A.   2 1/2
    ORANGE BLOSSOMS
        THEODORE PRESSER COMPANY   .50
GRANT, G. A.   SCHAEFER   2
    MARCH OF THE BOY SCOUTS
        THEODORE PRESSER COMPANY   .50
GRANT, J.
    FOOT IT FEATLY
        EDWARD B. MARKS MUSIC CORPORATION   00.60
GRANT, J.
    MARCHING TOWARDS MORNING
        EDWARD B. MARKS MUSIC CORPORATION   00.60
GRANT, J.   1
    ON MY BIKE
        BELWIN-MILLS PUBLISHING CORPORATION   .60
GRANT, J.   1
    ON MY POGO STICK
        BELWIN-MILLS PUBLISHING CORPORATION   .60
GRANT, J.   2
    ON THE MERRY-GO-ROUND
        ELKAN-VOGEL, INC.   .50
GRATTON
    CREPESCULE
        ASSOCIATED MUSIC PUBLISHERS, INC.   BER   1.00
GRATTON
    FAIRY TALE
        ASSOCIATED MUSIC PUBLISHERS, INC.   BER   .60
GRAUN
    GIGUE IN B FLAT MINOR
        BANKS AND SON LTD.   .55
GRAUPNER
    SLUMBER
        FREDERICK HARRIS MUSIC COMPANY   .60
GRAY, D.
    CAROLLERS
        BOOSEY AND HAWKES, INC.   1.00
GRAY, D.
    COME AND PLAY
        BOOSEY AND HAWKES, INC.   1.00
GRAY, D.
    FROM MY WINDOW
        BOOSEY AND HAWKES, INC.   .90
GRAY, D.
    FUN OF THE FAIR
        BOOSEY AND HAWKES, INC.   1.00
GRAY, D.
    LORD MAYOR'S SHOW
        BOOSEY AND HAWKES, INC.   .90
GRAY, D.
    MAYTIME
        BOOSEY AND HAWKES, INC.   1.00
GRAY, D.
    MUSICA VARIATA
        BOOSEY AND HAWKES, INC.   1.25
GRAY, D.
    MUSICAL GATEWAY
        BOOSEY AND HAWKES, INC.   1.00
GRAY, D.
    PETER PIPER
        BOOSEY AND HAWKES, INC.   .85
GRAY, D.
    TUNES OF ALL TIME
        BOOSEY AND HAWKES, INC.   1.00
GRAZIANI
    PICCOLI PIANISTI
        FRANCO COLOMBO PUBLICATIONS   FOR.11385B   2.00
GREAVES, T.   E
    MOON MINIATURES
        OXFORD UNIVERSITY PRESS   33.071   .75
GREEN   LEVINE
    BODY AND SOUL
        WARNER BROTHERS PUBLISHERS   1.00
GREEN   WALTER
    BODY AND SOUL
        WARNER BROTHERS PUBLISHERS   1.00
GREEN
    JOHN AND JULIE
        MCA MUSIC   1.00
GREEN   3
    ROBOTS
        BELWIN-MILLS PUBLISHING CORPORATION   .60
GREEN
    SAILS AT SUNDOWN
        BELWIN-MILLS PUBLISHING CORPORATION   .60
GREEN
    SEE THE EMPEROR
        BELWIN-MILLS PUBLISHING CORPORATION   .60

GREEN
    SHADOW BALLET
        CARL FISCHER, INC.   P 3197   .50
GREEN
    SNOW FLURRIES
        EDWARD B. MARKS MUSIC CORPORATION   00.60
GREEN   3
    SONG OF THE RANGE
        BELWIN-MILLS PUBLISHING CORPORATION   .60
GREEN *
    COQUETTE
        THE BIG THREE MUSIC CORPORATION   00.95
GREEN, H.   1 1/2
    THAR SHE BLOWS
        WILLIS MUSIC COMPANY   .40
GREEN, P.   EASY INTER.
    BALLERINA WALTZ
        AMERICAN MUSIC EDITION   .40
GREEN, R.   INTER.
    COWBOY SONATINA
        AMERICAN MUSIC EDITION   .40
GREEN, R.
    DANCE SET NO. 1 AN AMERICAN BOURREE
        AMERICAN MUSIC EDITION   .75
GREEN, R.
    DANCE SET NO. 2 AN AMERICAN PASTROAL
        AMERICAN MUSIC EDITION   .75
GREEN, R.
    DANCE SET NO. 3 AN AMERICAN RIGAUDON
        AMERICAN MUSIC EDITION   1.00
GREEN, R.
    DANCE THEME AND VARIATIONS
        AMERICAN MUSIC EDITION   3.00
GREEN, R.
    FESTIVAL FUGUES
        AMERICAN MUSIC EDITION   3.00
GREEN, R.   EASY INTER.
    HAPPY HOLIDAY
        AMERICAN MUSIC EDITION   .40
GREEN, R.   INTER.
    MARCH SONATINA NO. 1
        AMERICAN MUSIC EDITION   .50
GREEN, R.   EASY INTER.
    OFFBEAT POLKA
        AMERICAN MUSIC EDITION   .40
GREEN, R.   1
    OLYMPIC STAR
        AMERICAN MUSIC EDITION   .40
GREEN, R.   INTER.
    PIECES FOR CHILDREN AND FOR GROWNUPS TO MAKE A NOTE OF ...
        AMERICAN MUSIC EDITION   .75
GREEN, R.   EASY INTER.
    POLKA SONATINA NO. 1
        AMERICAN MUSIC EDITION   .50
GREEN, R.   EASY INTER.
    POLKA SONATINA NO. 2
        AMERICAN MUSIC EDITION   .50
GREEN, R.   INTER.
    POLKA SONATINA NO. 3
        AMERICAN MUSIC EDITION   .50
GREEN, R.
    PRELUDE BLUES FOR PIANO SOLO -- TO GEORGE GERSHWIN FROM
    'DEDICATIONS'
        AMERICAN MUSIC EDITION   .75
GREEN, R.
    QUARTET -- FOUR PRELUDES FOR PIANO OOLO
        AMERICAN MUSIC EDITION   1.50
GREEN, P.   1
    RAG DOLL WALTZ
        AMERICAN MUSIC EDITION   .35
GREEN, R.
    RAINDROPS
        AMERICAN MUSIC EDITION   .35
GREEN, R.   2
    RAINY DAY
        AMERICAN MUSIC EDITION   .40
GREEN, R.
    RHAPSODIC INTERLUDE -- TO BELA BARTOK FROM 'DEDICATIONS'
        AMERICAN MUSIC EDITION   .60
GREEN, R.
    SHORT SONATA IN A -- NO. 10 IN A SERIES 12
        AMERICAN MUSIC EDITION   1.50
GREEN, R.
    SHORT SONATA IN C -- NO. 01 IN A SERIES OF 12
        AMERICAN MUSIC EDITION   1.25
GREEN, R.
    SHORT SONATA IN C -- SECOND EDITION
        AMERICAN MUSIC EDITION   .75
GREEN, R.
    SHORT SONATA IN D -- NO. 11 IN A SERIES OF 12
        AMERICAN MUSIC EDITION   1.75
GREEN, R.
    SHORT SONATA IN F -- NO. 02 IN A SERIES OF 12
        AMERICAN MUSIC EDITION   1.25
GREEN, R.   EMERICH, P.
    SONATA BREVIS -- FORMERLY ENTITLED 'SONATINA FOR PIANO SOLO'
        AMERICAN MUSIC EDITION   1.50
GREEN, R.   INTER.
    SONG SONATINA
        AMERICAN MUSIC EDITION   .60
GREEN, R.   INTER.
    SQUARE DANCE SONATINA
        AMERICAN MUSIC EDITION   .50
GREEN, R.   EASY INTER.
    SUMMER SMOKE
        AMERICAN MUSIC EDITION   .50
GREEN, R.
    SUMMER SUNSET -- TO EDWARD MACDOWELL FROM 'DEDICATIONS'
        AMERICAN MUSIC EDITION   .60
GREEN, R.   2
    TOYMAKER'S SHOP
        AMERICAN MUSIC EDITION   .50
GREEN, R.
    TWELVE INVENTIONS FOR PIANO SOLO
        AMERICAN MUSIC EDITION   2.00
GREEN, R.   EASY INTER.
    WESTERN SKY
        AMERICAN MUSIC EDITION   .50
GREENAWAY *   E
    I WAS KAISER BILL'S BATMAN
        BELWIN-MILLS PUBLISHING CORPORATION   20566   .60
GREENE   2
    PLAYFUL RONDO
        CENTURY MUSIC PUBLISHING COMPANY, INC.   1111   .40
GREENE, H.   E
    WHITE NOTES, THE
        THEODORE PRESSER COMPANY   .75

GREENHILL, H.
    COUNTRY SNAPSHOTS
        BANKS AND SON LTD.   .80
GREENHILL, H.   3
    DIVERSION
        NOVELLO AND COMPANY, LTD.   55.0010.09   .40
GREENHILL, H.   4
    PIPER OF SPRING, THE
        NOVELLO AND COMPANY, LTD.   55.0041.09   .40
GREENWALD, M.   1
    ANGELINA, NOCTURNE
        CENTURY MUSIC PUBLISHING COMPANY, INC.   1589   .40
GREENWALD, M.   1
    BARBARA, WALTZ
        CENTURY MUSIC PUBLISHING COMPANY, INC.   1590   .40
GREENWALD, M.   4
    CENTURY OVERTURE, OPERA GEMS
        CENTURY MUSIC PUBLISHING COMPANY, INC.   1384   .40
GREENWALD, M.
    CHAPEL CHIMES
        THE BIG THREE MUSIC CORPORATION   00.95
GREENWALD, M.   1
    CHILDREN AT PLAY, CAPRICE
        CENTURY MUSIC PUBLISHING COMPANY, INC.   1419   .40
GREENWALD, M.   3
    CLAUDIA, WALTZ
        CENTURY MUSIC PUBLISHING COMPANY, INC.   1414   .40
GREENWALD, M.   3
    DANCE OF THE BUTTERFLIES
        CENTURY MUSIC PUBLISHING COMPANY, INC.   1372   .40
GREENWALD, M.   3-4
    DANCE OF THE MIDGETS
        CENTURY MUSIC PUBLISHING COMPANY, INC.   2692   .40
GREENWALD, M.   1
    DANCERS, THE
        CENTURY MUSIC PUBLISHING COMPANY, INC.   1417   .40
GREENWALD, M.   1
    DEMETRIUS, MARCH
        CENTURY MUSIC PUBLISHING COMPANY, INC.   1592   .40
GREENWALD, M.   1
    ETHELINDA, MAZURKA
        CENTURY MUSIC PUBLISHING COMPANY, INC.   1593   .40
GREENWALD, M.   1
    FERNANDO, SCHOTT
        CENTURY MUSIC PUBLISHING COMPANY, INC.   1594   .40
GREENWALD, M.   3
    HOME GUARD, THE
        CENTURY MUSIC PUBLISHING COMPANY, INC.   2693   .40
GREENWALD, M.   4
    IRON MASTER
        VOLKWEIN BROS.   .40
GREENWALD, M.   1
    LITTLE BLUE EYES
        CENTURY MUSIC PUBLISHING COMPANY, INC.   3076   .40
GREENWALD, M.   3
    LOVE DREAMS, WALTZ
        CENTURY MUSIC PUBLISHING COMPANY, INC.   3133   .40
GREENWALD, M.   2
    LOVE THOUGHTS, WALTZES
        CENTURY MUSIC PUBLISHING COMPANY, INC.   2680   .40
GREENWALD, M.   1
    MARCH MILITAIRE
        CENTURY MUSIC PUBLISHING COMPANY, INC.   1416   .40
GREENWALD, M.   1
    MEDITATION
        CENTURY MUSIC PUBLISHING COMPANY, INC.   1721   .40
GREENWALD, M.   1
    MY DARLING, WALTZ
        CENTURY MUSIC PUBLISHING COMPANY, INC.   1719   .40
GREENWALD, M.   1
    PRETTY BUTTERFLIES, RONDO
        CENTURY MUSIC PUBLISHING COMPANY, INC.   1600   .40
GREENWALD, M.   1
    PRETTY DEWDROPS, MAZURKA
        CENTURY MUSIC PUBLISHING COMPANY, INC.   1596   .40
GREENWALD, M.   1
    PRETTY MOONBEAMS, MARCH
        CENTURY MUSIC PUBLISHING COMPANY, INC.   1598   .40
GREENWALD, M.   1
    PRETTY RAINBOW, REVERIE
        CENTURY MUSIC PUBLISHING COMPANY, INC.   1599   .40
GREENWALD, M.   1
    PRETTY STARLIGHT, GAVOTTE
        CENTURY MUSIC PUBLISHING COMPANY, INC.   1595   .40
GREENWALD, M.   1
    PRETTY SUNSHINE, WALTZ
        CENTURY MUSIC PUBLISHING COMPANY, INC.   1597   .40
GREENWALD, M.   3
    REVERIE
        CENTURY MUSIC PUBLISHING COMPANY, INC.   1316   .40
GREENWALD, M.   3
    SPANISH DANCE
        CENTURY MUSIC PUBLISHING COMPANY, INC.   1317   .40
GREENWALD, M.   3
    VICTORIA, MARCH
        CENTURY MUSIC PUBLISHING COMPANY, INC.   1415   .40
GREENWALD, M.--ED   GREENWALD, M.   4
    OPERATIC GEMS OVERTURE
        CENTURY MUSIC PUBLISHING COMPANY, INC.   1384   .40
GREENWALD, M.--ED   GREENWALD, M.   3
    RUSSIAN FOLK SONG
        CENTURY MUSIC PUBLISHING COMPANY, INC.   1903   .40
GREENWALD, M.--ED   GREENWALD, M.   3
    SONG OF THE VOLGA BOATMAN
        CENTURY MUSIC PUBLISHING COMPANY, INC.   1903   .40
GREENWALD, M.--ED   GREENWALD, M.   3
    VOLGA BOAT SONG
        CENTURY MUSIC PUBLISHING COMPANY, INC.   1903   .40
GREENWOOD   2
    LITTLE SALLY WATERS
        CENTURY MUSIC PUBLISHING COMPANY, INC.   1922   .40
GREENWOOD   2
    WATER, WATER, WILDFLOWER
        CENTURY MUSIC PUBLISHING COMPANY, INC.   1925   .40
GREER, J.
    FLAPPERETTE
        BELWIN-MILLS PUBLISHING CORPORATION   20392   .85
GREGG   3
    JIGS AND REELS
        CENTURY MUSIC PUBLISHING COMPANY, INC.   1328   .40
GREGG   3
    REELS AND JIGS
        CENTURY MUSIC PUBLISHING COMPANY, INC.   1328   .40
GREGH
    AVANT PRINTEMPS, OP. 99
        FRANCO COLOMBO PUBLICATIONS   SAL   1.75

GREGH
    GAVOTTE MIGNONNE
        FRANCO COLOMBO PUBLICATIONS   SAL   1.50
GREGH
    JOYEUX PAPILLONS, LES -- CAPRICE -- OP. 8
        FRANCO COLOMBO PUBLICATIONS   SAL   2.50
GREGH
    PARAIS A TA FENETRE, OP. 28
        FRANCO COLOMBO PUBLICATIONS   SAL   2.00
GREGH
    RETOUR DES MOISSONNEURS, LE OP. 13
        FRANCO COLOMBO PUBLICATIONS   SAL   2.00
GREGH
    SALTARELLE, OP. 49
        FRANCO COLOMBO PUBLICATIONS   SAL   2.00
GREGH   3
    SHEPHERD'S DANCE, OP. 5
        CENTURY MUSIC PUBLISHING COMPANY, INC.   1942   .40
GRETCHANINOFF   2
    AT THE CIRCUS
        BELWIN-MILLS PUBLISHING CORPORATION   .60
GRETCHANINOFF
    AU FOYER, OP. 183
        BOOSEY AND HAWKES, INC.   .60
GRETCHANINOFF   2
    CHANSON MILITAIRE
        BELWIN-MILLS PUBLISHING CORPORATION   .60
GRETCHANINOFF   PALMER, W. A.
    CHILDREN'S BOOK
        ALFRED MUSIC COMPANY   629   1.50
GRETCHANINOFF   2
    DER TAG DES KINDES OP. 109
        SCHOTT   1414   2.50
GRETCHANINOFF   2
    ETUDE
        CENTURY MUSIC PUBLISHING COMPANY, INC.   3773   .40
GRETCHANINOFF   3
    FLUCHTIGE GEDANKEN OP. 115
        SCHOTT   2071   2.25
GRETCHANINOFF   AGAY, D.
    GLASS BEADS, OP. 123
        MCA MUSIC   1.25
GRETCHANINOFF   2
    IM GRUNEN OP. 99
        SCHOTT   1125   2.25
GRETCHANINOFF   GILLOCK   1 1/2
    MARCH OF THE TIN SOLDIERS
        WILLIS MUSIC COMPANY   .40
GRETCHANINOFF   2
    POLKA
        CENTURY MUSIC PUBLISHING COMPANY, INC.   3780   .40
GRETCHANINOFF   PAJOT
    RAPSODIE RUSSE
        ASSOCIATED MUSIC PUBLISHERS, INC.   ENO   1.00
GRETCHANINOFF   2
    ROMANCE
        CENTURY MUSIC PUBLISHING COMPANY, INC.   3779   .40
GRETCHANINOFF   2
    RUSSIAN DANCE
        CENTURY MUSIC PUBLISHING COMPANY, INC.   3782   .40
GRETCHANINOFF   GILLOCK   2
    SEVEN DWARVES, THE
        WILLIS MUSIC COMPANY   .40
GRETCHANINOFF   BERLIN
    SLUMBER SONG--BERCEUSE--
        FREDERICK HARRIS MUSIC COMPANY   .30
GRETCHANINOFF   ADVANCED
    SONATA NO. 02, OP. 174
        SHAWNEE PRESS, INC.   1.50
GRETCHANINOFF
    SONATE G-MOLL OP. 129
        SCHOTT   2164   2.25
GRETCHANINOFF   3
    SONATINE, OP. 110 NO. 1 G-DUR
        SCHOTT   1297   2.25
GRETCHANINOFF   3
    SONATINE, OP. 110 NO. 2 F-DUR
        SCHOTT   1298   2.25
GRETCHANINOFF   2
    TAUTROPFEN OP. 127A
        SCHOTT   2176   2.25
GRETCHANINOFF   1
    WALTZ
        BELWIN-MILLS PUBLISHING CORPORATION   .60
GRETCHANINOFF   2
    WISTFUL MAZURKA
        CENTURY MUSIC PUBLISHING COMPANY, INC.   3781   .40
GREVER *
    WHAT A DIFFERENCE A DAY MADE
        EDWARD B. MARKS MUSIC CORPORATION   01.00
GREVI
    VALZER ALL'ANTICA
        FRANCO COLOMBO PUBLICATIONS   FOR.11861   .90
GREY, F.
    COQUETTERIE
        BOOSEY AND HAWKES, INC.   .50
GREY, F.   2 1/2
    HAWAIIAN NIGHTS
        THEODORE PRESSER COMPANY   .50
GREY, F.   4
    LEGEND OF THE WATERS
        THEODORE PRESSER COMPANY   .50
GREY, F.   2
    LITTLE ATTIC OF DREAMS
        THEODORE PRESSER COMPANY   .50
GREY, F.   3
    MEMORY OF MAYTIME
        THEODORE PRESSER COMPANY   .50
GREY, F.   3 1/2
    UNDER THE HAWAIIAN MOON
        THEODORE PRESSER COMPANY   .50
GRIEG   4
    ALBUM LEAF
        VOLKWEIN BROS.   .25
GRIEG   3
    ALBUM LEAF -- ALBUMBLATT -- E MINOR
        CENTURY MUSIC PUBLISHING COMPANY, INC.   125   .40
GRIEG
    ALBUM-LEAF IN E MINOR, OP. 12, NO. 7
        G. SCHIRMER, INC.   .30
GRIEG   OESTERLE
    ALBUM-LEAVES, OP. 28
        G. SCHIRMER, INC.   L771   .75
GRIEG   5
    AN DEN FRUEHLING -- TO SPRING
        CENTURY MUSIC PUBLISHING COMPANY, INC.   1035   .60

GRIEG   ROLFE, W.   3
    AN DEN FRUEHLING, EASY
        CENTURY MUSIC PUBLISHING COMPANY, INC.   3225   .60
GRIEG   SCHAUM, J.   2 1/2
    ANITRA'S DANCE
        BELWIN-MILLS PUBLISHING CORPORATION   .50
GRIEG   THOMPSON, J.   3
    ANITRA'S DANCE
        WILLIS MUSIC COMPANY   .40
GRIEG   MOSSMAN
    ANITRA'S DANCE -- FROM PEER GYNT SUITE
        BELWIN-MILLS PUBLISHING CORPORATION   26106   .60
GRIEG   M-D
    ANITRA'S DANCE --PEER GYNT SUITE NO.1--
        C. F. PETERS CORPORATION   2423   .90
GRIEG   4
    ANITRA'S DANCE FROM 'FIRST PEER GYNT SUITE'
        THEODORE PRESSER COMPANY   .50
GRIEG   4
    ANITRA'S DANCE FROM THE PEER GYNT SUITE, OP. 46
        CENTURY MUSIC PUBLISHING COMPANY, INC.   136   .40
GRIEG   M-D
    ARABIAN DANCE --PEER GYNT SUITE NO.2--
        C. F. PETERS CORPORATION   2653   1.50
GRIEG   M-D
    ASE'S DEATH --PEER GYNT SUITE NO.1--
        C. F. PETERS CORPORATION   2420B   .90
GRIEG   .   4
    ASE'S DEATH FROM THE PEER GYNT SUITE, OP. 46
        CENTURY MUSIC PUBLISHING COMPANY, INC.   2360   .40
GRIEG
    ASE'S DEATH, OP. 46 NO. 2
        G. SCHIRMER, INC.   .30
GRIEG   D
    BALLADE, OP. 24
        C. F. PETERS CORPORATION   1470   1.25
GRIEG   HUGHES
    BALLADE, OP. 24
        G. SCHIRMER, INC.   L1373   1.00
GRIEG   M
    BERCEUSE --CRADLE SONG--, OP. 41 NO. 1
        C. F. PETERS CORPORATION   3129A   .90
GRIEG   M
    BERCEUSE --LULLABY--, OP. 38 NO. 1
        C. F. PETERS CORPORATION   2426   .90
GRIEG
    BERCEUSE IN G MAJOR, OP. 38 NO. 4
        G. SCHIRMER, INC.   .35
GRIEG   M-D
    BERGLIOT, OP. 42
        C. F. PETERS CORPORATION   2263A   3.00
GRIEG   4
    BIRDLING, OP. 43 NO. 4
        CENTURY MUSIC PUBLISHING COMPANY, INC.   3841   .40
GRIEG
    BIRDLING, OP. 43 NO. 4
        G. SCHIRMER, INC.   .40
GRIEG
    BIRDLING, OP. 43 NO. 4
        WILLIS MUSIC COMPANY   .35
GRIEG   7
    BUTTERFLY OP. 43 NO. 1 --PAPILLON--
        THEODORE PRESSER COMPANY   .50
GRIEG   6
    BUTTERFLY PAPILLON
        VOLKWEIN BROS.   .25
GRIEG
    BUTTERFLY, OP. 43 NO. 1
        BELWIN-MILLS PUBLISHING CORPORATION   28198   .50
GRIEG   M-D
    BUTTERFLY, OP. 43 NO. 1
        C. F. PETERS CORPORATION   2540   .90
GRIEG
    BUTTERFLY, OP. 43 NO. 1
        CARL FISCHER, INC.   S 219   .50
GRIEG   5
    BUTTERFLY, OP. 43 NO. 1
        CENTURY MUSIC PUBLISHING COMPANY, INC.   1000   .40
GRIEG
    BUTTERFLY, OP. 43 NO. 1
        G. SCHIRMER, INC.   .40
GRIEG   5
    BUTTERFLY, OP. 43 NO. 1
        WILLIS MUSIC COMPANY   .40
GRIEG
    CONCERTO IN A MINOR
        ASHLEY DEALERS SERVICE, INC.   1.95
GRIEG   NIELSON
    CONCERTO IN A MINOR
        BOOSEY AND HAWKES, INC.   1.50
GRIEG   THOMPSON, J.   2
    CONCERTO IN A MINOR
        WILLIS MUSIC COMPANY   .35
GRIEG
    CONCERTO IN A MINOR -- OPENING THEME
        ASHLEY DEALERS SERVICE, INC.   ES   .95
GRIEG   M
    CONCERTO IN A MINOR, OP. 16
        C. F. PETERS CORPORATION   2164B   1.25
GRIEG   GRAINGER, P.
    CONCERTO IN A MINOR, OP. 16
        G. SCHIRMER, INC.   L1399   2.50
GRIEG   M
    CONCERTO IN A MINOR, OP. 16. ABRIDGED PIANO SOLO ARRANGEMENT
        C. F. PETERS CORPORATION   2164B   1.25
GRIEG   GRAINGER, P.
    CONCERTO, FIRST MOVEMENT--CONCERT TRANSCRIPTION OF MAIN THEMES
    AND EPISODES
        G. SCHIRMER, INC.   .80
GRIEG   4
    CONCERTO, THEME
        CENTURY MUSIC PUBLISHING COMPANY, INC.   3533   .40
GRIEG   M-D
    COWKEEPER'S TUNE AND COUNTRY DANCE, OP. 63 NO. 2
        C. F. PETERS CORPORATION   2855B   .90
GRIEG   4
    DANCE CAPRICE, OP. 28 NO. 3
        CENTURY MUSIC PUBLISHING COMPANY, INC.   1940   .40
GRIEG
    DANCE CAPRICE, OP. 28 NO. 3
        WILLIS MUSIC COMPANY   .35
GRIEG
    DANCE OF ANITRA, OP. 46 NO. 3
        G. SCHIRMER, INC.   .40
GRIEG
    DANCE OF ELVES, OP. 12 NO. 4
        BELWIN-MILLS PUBLISHING CORPORATION   28193   .60

GRIEG
    DANCE-CAPRICE, OP. 28 NO. 3
        G. SCHIRMER, INC.   .50
GRIEG   M-D
    DEATH OF ASE --PEER GYNT SUITE NO.1--
        C. F. PETERS CORPORATION   2420B   .90
GRIEG   M
    ELFENTANZ, OP. 12 NO. 4
        C. F. PETERS CORPORATION   1269D   .90
GRIEG   3
    ELFENTANZ, OP. 12 NO. 4
        CENTURY MUSIC PUBLISHING COMPANY, INC.   1314   .40
GRIEG
    ELFIN DANCE, OP. 12 NO. 4
        G. SCHIRMER, INC.   .40
GRIEG
    ELFIN DANCE, OP. 12 NO. 4
        WILLIS MUSIC COMPANY   .35
GRIEG
    EROTIK, OP. 43 NO. 5
        G. SCHIRMER, INC.   .50
GRIEG   M-D
    EROTIKON, OP. 43 NO. 5
        C. F. PETERS CORPORATION   2425   .90
GRIEG   M
    FAIRY DANCE, OP. 12 NO. 4
        C. F. PETERS CORPORATION   1269D   .90
GRIEG   3
    FOLKSONG, OP. 12 NO. 5
        CENTURY MUSIC PUBLISHING COMPANY, INC.   3974   .40
GRIEG   M-D
    FRENCH SERENADE, OP. 62 NO. 3
        C. F. PETERS CORPORATION   3126   1.25
GRIEG   STERNBERG
    FROM HOLBERG'S TIME, OP. 40
        G. SCHIRMER, INC.   1.00
GRIEG
    GRANDMOTHER'S MINUET, OP. 68 NO. 2
        G. SCHIRMER, INC.   .40
GRIEG   MITTLER   3B
    GRIEG CONCERTO
        MUSICORD PUBLICATIONS, INC.   .45
GRIEG   5
    HOCHZEISTAG AUF TROLDHAUGEN OP. 65 NO. 6
        SCHOTT   09595 1/2 1.00
GRIEG   5
    HOCHZEITSTAG AUF TROLDHAGEN
        CENTURY MUSIC PUBLISHING COMPANY, INC.   2325   .40
GRIEG   M
    HOLBERG SUITE, OP. 40
        C. F. PETERS CORPORATION   2151   1.25
GRIEG   5
    HULDIGUNGSMARSCH AUS, SIGURD JORSALFAR
        SCHOTT   09597 1/2 1.00
GRIEG   D
    HULDIGUNGSMARSCH, OP. 56 NO. 3
        C. F. PETERS CORPORATION   2656   1.25
GRIEG   OESTERLE
    HUMORESKEN, OP. 6
        G. SCHIRMER, INC.   L199   1.00
GRIEG   3
    I LOVE THEE
        CENTURY MUSIC PUBLISHING COMPANY, INC.   3613   .40
GRIEG
    I LOVE THEE
        WILLIS MUSIC COMPANY   .40
GRIEG   5
    I LOVE THEE, OP. 41 NO. 3
        BELWIN-MILLS PUBLISHING CORPORATION   28191   .60
GRIEG   5
    I LOVE THEE, OP. 41 NO. 3
        CENTURY MUSIC PUBLISHING COMPANY, INC.   1011   .40
GRIEG
    I LOVE THEE, OP. 41 NO. 3
        G. SCHIRMER, INC.   .40
GRIEG   3
    ICH LIEBE DICH
        CENTURY MUSIC PUBLISHING COMPANY, INC.   3613   .40
GRIEG   ZEPP   5
    ICH LIEBE DICH
        PRO-ART PUBLICATIONS, INC.   434   .50
GRIEG   5
    ICH LIEBE DICH, OP. 41 NO. 3
        CENTURY MUSIC PUBLISHING COMPANY, INC.   1011   .40
GRIEG   D
    IMPROVISATA --ON 2 NORWEGIAN FOLK SONGS--, OP. 29
        C. F. PETERS CORPORATION   1871   1.75
GRIEG   M
    IN AUTUMN, CONCERT OVERTURE, OP. 11
        C. F. PETERS CORPORATION   3225   2.50
GRIEG   KING, S.
    IN THE HALL OF THE MOUNTAIN KING --A STUDY IN STACCATO--
        SHAWNEE PRESS, INC.   HB-5040   .40
GRIEG   M-D
    IN THE HALL OF THE MOUNTAIN KING --PEER GYNT SUITE NO.1--
        C. F. PETERS CORPORATION   2420   1.50
GRIEG   4
    IN THE HALL OF THE MOUNTAIN KING FROM THE PEER GYNT SUITE, OP.
    46
        CENTURY MUSIC PUBLISHING COMPANY, INC.   3338   .40
GRIEG
    IN THE HALL OF THE MOUNTAIN KING, OP. 46 NO. 4
        CARL FISCHER, INC.   S 741   .50
GRIEG
    IN THE HALL OF THE MOUNTAIN-KING, OP. 46 NO. 4
        G. SCHIRMER, INC.   .50
GRIEG   M-D .
    INGRID'S LAMENT --PEER GYNT SUITE 2--
        C. F. PETERS CORPORATION   2653   1.50
GRIEG   M-D
    KOBOLD, OP. 71 NO. 3
        C. F. PETERS CORPORATION   2985A   .90
GRIEG   M-D
    LAST SPRING, OP. 34 NO. 2
        C. F. PETERS CORPORATION   2265B   .90
GRIEG   M-D
    LITTLE BIRD, OP. 43 NO. 4
        C. F. PETERS CORPORATION   3093   .90
GRIEG   3
    LYRISCHE STUCKE 1 OP. 12
        SCHOTT   4696   1.00
GRIEG   4-5
    LYRISCHE STUCKE 3 -- AN D. FRUHLING OP. 43 NO. 6
        SCHOTT   09592   .75
GRIEG   4-5
    LYRISCHE STUCKE 3 OP. 43
        SCHOTT   4698   1.00

GRIEG   4
    MARCH OF DWARFS, OP. 54 NO. 3
        CENTURY MUSIC PUBLISHING COMPANY, INC.   2290   .40
GRIEG   SCHAUM, J.   3
    MARCH OF THE DWARFS
        BELWIN-MILLS PUBLISHING CORPORATION   .50
GRIEG
    MARCH OF THE DWARFS
        CARL FISCHER, INC.   S 929   .50
GRIEG   M-D
    MARCH OF THE DWARFS, OP. 54 NO. 3
        C. F. PETERS CORPORATION   2834   .90
GRIEG
    MARCH OF THE DWARFS, OP. 54 NO. 3
        G. SCHIRMER, INC.   .60
GRIEG
    MARCH OF THE DWARFS, OP. 54 NO. 3
        WILLIS MUSIC COMPANY   .50
GRIEG   4
    MORNING
        CENTURY MUSIC PUBLISHING COMPANY, INC.   2328   .40
GRIEG   KING, S.
    MORNING MOOD
        SHAWNEE PRESS, INC.   HB-5033   .40
GRIEG   M-D
    MORNING MOOD --PEER GYNT SUITE NO. 1--
        C. F. PETERS CORPORATION   2420A   .90
GRIEG
    MORNING OP. 46 NO. 1
        BELWIN-MILLS PUBLISHING CORPORATION   28190   .60
GRIEG
    MORNING-MOOD, OP. 46 NO. 1
        G. SCHIRMER, INC.   .50
GRIEG   POZZOLI
    MY FIRST GRIEG
        FRANCO COLOMBO PUBLICATIONS   ER2600   1.25
GRIEG   WEYBRIGHT   2 1/2
    NATIONAL SONG
        BELWIN-MILLS PUBLISHING CORPORATION   .60
GRIEG   M-D
    NOCTURNE, OP. 54 NO. 4
        C. F. PETERS CORPORATION   2652   .90
GRIEG
    NOCTURNE, OP. 54 NO. 4
        G. SCHIRMER, INC.   .50
GRIEG
    NOCTURNE, OP. 54 NO. 4
        WILLIS MUSIC COMPANY   .30
GRIEG
    NOCTURNE, OP. 54 NO. 4 --SUMMER NIGHT--
        CARL FISCHER, INC.   S 1103   .50
GRIEG   3
    NORWEGIAN BRAUTZUG OP. 19 NO. 2
        SCHOTT   09596 1/2 1.00
GRIEG   5
    NORWEGIAN BRIDAL PARTY, OP. 19 NO. 2
        CENTURY MUSIC PUBLISHING COMPANY, INC.   1023   .40
GRIEG   6
    NORWEGIAN BRIDAL PROCESSION OP. 19 NO. 2
        THEODORE PRESSER COMPANY   .50
GRIEG   E-M
    NORWEGIAN BRIDAL PROCESSION, OP. 19 NO. 2
        C. F. PETERS CORPORATION   2153   1.25
GRIEG
    NORWEGIAN BRIDAL PROCESSION, OP. 19 NO. 2
        G. SCHIRMER, INC.   .50
GRIEG   SCHAUM, J.   4 1/2
    NORWEGIAN CONCERTO
        BELWIN-MILLS PUBLISHING CORPORATION   .50
GRIEG
    NORWEGIAN DANCE IN A MAJOR, OP. 35 NO. 2
        G. SCHIRMER, INC.   .40
GRIEG
    NORWEGIAN DANCE, OP. 35 NO. 2
        CARL FISCHER, INC.   S 1101   .50
GRIEG   4
    NORWEGIAN DANCE, OP. 35 NO. 2
        CENTURY MUSIC PUBLISHING COMPANY, INC.   3479   .40
GRIEG   M-D
    NOTTURNO, OP. 54 NO. 4
        C. F. PETERS CORPORATION   2652   .90
GRIEG   4
    NOTTURNO, OP. 54 NO. 4
        CENTURY MUSIC PUBLISHING COMPANY, INC.   3250   .40
GRIEG   5
    PAPILLON -- BUTTERFLY --
        CENTURY MUSIC PUBLISHING COMPANY, INC.   1000   .40
GRIEG   2
    PATRIOTIC SONG
        CENTURY MUSIC PUBLISHING COMPANY, INC.   2264   .40
GRIEG
    PATRIOTIC SONG, OP. 12 NO. 8
        G. SCHIRMER, INC.   .35
GRIEG   RICHTER, A.
    PEER GYNT SUITE - A STORY WITH
        THEODORE PRESSER COMPANY   1.25
GRIEG   M-D
    PEER GYNT SUITE NO. 1, OP. 46
        C. F. PETERS CORPORATION   2420   1.50
GRIEG
    PEER GYNT SUITE NO. 1, OP. 46
        G. SCHIRMER, INC.   L205   1.00
GRIEG   M-D
    PEER GYNT SUITE NO. 2, OP. 55
        C. F. PETERS CORPORATION   2653   1.50
GRIEG
    PEER GYNT SUITE NO. 2, OP. 55
        G. SCHIRMER, INC.   L1420   1.00
GRIEG
    PEER GYNT SUITE 1
        EDWIN F. KALMUS   3483   1.25
GRIEG   M-D
    PEER GYNT.
        C. F. PETERS CORPORATION   3709   7.50
GRIEG   4
    PEER-GYNT-SUITE 1 -- ANITRAS TANZ OP. 46 NO. 3
        SCHOTT   09593   .75
GRIEG   FREY, H.
    PIANO CONCERTO
        THE BIG THREE MUSIC CORPORATION   00.75
GRIEG   MOSSMAN
    PIANO CONCERTO IN A MINOR -- FIRST MOVEMENT
        BELWIN-MILLS PUBLISHING CORPORATION   26089   .60
GRIEG   4
    PIANO CONCERTO IN A MINOR, THEME
        CENTURY MUSIC PUBLISHING COMPANY, INC.   3533   .40

GRIEG   KREUTZER   3
    POETIC TONE PICTURE
        BOSTON MUSIC COMPANY   .50
GRIEG   5
    PUCK, OP. 71 NO. 3
        BELWIN-MILLS PUBLISHING CORPORATION   642   .60
GRIEG   M-D
    PUCK, OP. 71 NO. 3
        C. F. PETERS CORPORATION   2985A   .90
GRIEG
    PUCK, OP. 71 NO. 3
        CARL FISCHER, INC.   S 7643   .50
GRIEG
    PUCK, OP. 71 NO. 3
        G. SCHIRMER, INC.   .40
GRIEG   DUMM
    RECITAL REFRESHER SERIES -- FOLK SONG
        BELWIN-MILLS PUBLISHING CORPORATION   26117   .60
GRIEG   M-D
    RIGAUDON --HOLBERG SUITE--, OP. 40 NO. 5
        C. F. PETERS CORPORATION   2151E   .90
GRIEG
    SAILOR'S SONG, OP. 68 NO. 1
        CARL FISCHER, INC.   S 1352   .50
GRIEG
    SAILOR'S SONG, OP. 68 NO. 1
        G. SCHIRMER, INC.   .40
GRIEG   M-D
    SCHERZO-IMPROMPTU, OP. 73 NO. 2
        C. F. PETERS CORPORATION   3125A   .90
GRIEG
    SOLITARY WANDERER, OP. 43 NO. 2
        G. SCHIRMER, INC.   .35
GRIEG   3-4
    SOLVEJG'S SONG, OP. 52 NO. 4
        CENTURY MUSIC PUBLISHING COMPANY, INC.   2353   .40
GRIEG
    SOLVEJG'S SONG, OP. 52 NO. 4
        G. SCHIRMER, INC.   .35
GRIEG
    SONATA IN E MINOR, OP. 7
        ASSOCIATED MUSIC PUBLISHERS, INC.   B/H   1.50
GRIEG   D
    SONATA IN E MINOR, OP. 7
        C. F. PETERS CORPORATION   2278   2.00
GRIEG   GALLICO
    SONATA IN E MINOR, OP. 7
        G. SCHIRMER, INC.   L892   1.00
GRIEG   5
    SONATE E-MOLL OP. 7
        SCHOTT   4694   1.75
GRIEG   2
    SONG OF THE FATHERLAND, OP. 12 NO. 8
        CENTURY MUSIC PUBLISHING COMPANY, INC.   2264   .40
GRIEG   ECKSTEIN
    THEME FROM PIANO CONCERTO, OP. 16
        CARL FISCHER, INC.   S 2295   .50
GRIEG   4
    THEME FROM THE FIRST MOVEMENT OF PIANO CONCERTO IN A MINOR
        BOSTON MUSIC COMPANY   .50
GRIEG   WALLIS   2
    THEME FROM THE FIRST MOVEMENT OF PIANO CONCERTO IN A MINOR
        BOSTON MUSIC COMPANY   .50
GRIEG   LEVINE   5
    THEME, FROM PIANO CONCERTO IN A MINOR
        THEODORE PRESSER COMPANY   .50
GRIEG   TRUXELL, E.   3 1/2
    THEMES FROM PIANO CONCERTO
        VOLKWEIN BROS.   00.40
GRIEG   M
    THOUGHTS OF LOVE --LIEBESLIED--
        C. F. PETERS CORPORATION   7001   .80
GRIEG   MOSSMAN
    TO SPRING
        BELWIN-MILLS PUBLISHING CORPORATION   26101   .60
GRIEG   KAHL   2
    TO SPRING
        BOSTON MUSIC COMPANY   .50
GRIEG   M-D
    TO SPRING, OP. 43 NO. 6
        C. F. PETERS CORPORATION   2422   .90
GRIEG   E
    TO SPRING, OP. 43 NO. 6
        C. F. PETERS CORPORATION   2422A   .90
GRIEG
    TO SPRING, OP. 43 NO. 6
        CARL FISCHER, INC.   S 1636   .50
GRIEG   5
    TO SPRING, OP. 43 NO. 6
        CENTURY MUSIC PUBLISHING COMPANY, INC.   1035   .40
GRIEG
    TO SPRING, OP. 43 NO. 6
        G. SCHIRMER, INC.   .40
GRIEG
    TO THE SPRING, OP. 43 NO. 6
        WILLIS MUSIC COMPANY   .35
GRIEG   D
    TRIUMPHAL MARCH --SIGURD JORSALFAR--, OP. 56 NO. 3
        C. F. PETERS CORPORATION   2656   1.25
GRIEG   ROLFE, W.   2
    TROLDTOG, EASY
        CENTURY MUSIC PUBLISHING COMPANY, INC.   3657   .40
GRIEG   4
    TROLDTOG, OP. 54 NO. 3
        CENTURY MUSIC PUBLISHING COMPANY, INC.   2290   .40
GRIEG   3
    VALSE IN A MINOR
        VOLKWEIN BROS.   .25
GRIEG   3
    WACHTERLIED, OP. 12 NO. 3
        CENTURY MUSIC PUBLISHING COMPANY, INC.   2257   .40
GRIEG   BARTH, H.   3
    WALTZ IN A MINOR
        BELWIN-MILLS PUBLISHING CORPORATION   .60
GRIEG   3
    WALTZ IN A MINOR, OP. 12 NO. 2
        CENTURY MUSIC PUBLISHING COMPANY, INC.   3745   .40
GRIEG
    WALTZ IN A MINOR, OP. 12 NO. 2
        G. SCHIRMER, INC.   .40
GRIEG
    WALTZ IN E MINOR, OP. 38 NO. 7
        G. SCHIRMER, INC.   .30
GRIEG   M-D
    WALTZ IN E MINOR, OP. 38, NO. 7
        C. F. PETERS CORPORATION   2150A   .90

GRIEG   3
    WATCHMAN'S SONG, OP. 12 NO. 3
        CENTURY MUSIC PUBLISHING COMPANY, INC.   2257   .40
GRIEG
    WATCHMAN'S SONG, OP. 12 NO. 3
        G. SCHIRMER, INC.   .30
GRIEG
    WEDDING DAY AT TROLDHAUGEN, OP. 65 NO. 6
        C. F. PETERS CORPORATION   2922   .90
GRIEG   E-M
    WEDDING DAY AT TROLDHAUGEN, OP. 65 NO. 6
        C. F. PETERS CORPORATION   2922A   .80
GRIEG   5
    WEDDING DAY AT TROLDHAUGEN, OP. 65 NO. 6
        CENTURY MUSIC PUBLISHING COMPANY, INC.   2325   .40
GRIEG
    WEDDING-DAY AT TROLDHAUGEN
        G. SCHIRMER, INC.   .70
GRIFFES, C.
    DANCE SONG
        G. SCHIRMER, INC.   .40
GRIFFES, C.
    FANTASY PIECES, OP. 6--BARCAROLLE--
        G. SCHIRMER, INC.   1.00
GRIFFES, C.
    FANTASY PIECES, OP. 6--NOTTURNO--
        G. SCHIRMER, INC.   1.00
GRIFFES, C.
    FANTASY PIECES, OP. 6--SCHERZO--
        G. SCHIRMER, INC.   1.00
GRIFFES, C.
    MARCH
        G. SCHIRMER, INC.   .35
GRIFFES, C.
    MARCHING SONG
        G. SCHIRMER, INC.   .35
GRIFFES, C.
    ROMAN SKETCHES, OP. 7--CLOUDS
        G. SCHIRMER, INC.   .75
GRIFFES, C.
    ROMAN SKETCHES, OP. 7--FOUNTAIN OF ACQUA PAOLA, THE
        G. SCHIRMER, INC.   .80
GRIFFES, C.
    ROMAN SKETCHES, OP. 7--NIGHTFALL
        G. SCHIRMER, INC.   .80
GRIFFES, C.
    ROMAN SKETCHES, OP. 7--WHITE PEACOCK, THE
        G. SCHIRMER, INC.   .80
GRIFFES, C.
    SONATA IN F MAJOR
        G. SCHIRMER, INC.   2.50
GRIFFES, C.
    THREE TONE PICTURES, OP. 5--LAKE AT EVENING, THE
        G. SCHIRMER, INC.   .60
GRIFFES, C.
    THREE TONE PICTURES, OP. 5--NIGHT WINDS, THE
        G. SCHIRMER, INC.   .75
GRIFFES, C.
    THREE TONE PICTURES, OP. 5--VALE OF DREAMS, THE
        G. SCHIRMER, INC.   .50
GRIFFIN, A.   2 1/2
    EASY-GOING WALTZ
        BELWIN-MILLS PUBLISHING CORPORATION   .60
GRIFFIS, E.   M
    BRIEF STANZA
        COMPOSERS PRESS, INC.   1.00
GRIFFIS, E.   M
    CHILD ASLEEP, A
        COMPOSERS PRESS, INC.   1.00
GRIFFIS, E.   E
    FOR A BROKEN DOLL
        COMPOSERS PRESS, INC.   1.00
GRIFFIS, E.   M-D
    IMPROVISATION
        COMPOSERS PRESS, INC.   1.00
GRIFFIS, E.   M
    INTRATA
        COMPOSERS PRESS, INC.   1.00
GRIFFIS, E.   M
    JULIANNE
        COMPOSERS PRESS, INC.   2.00
GRIFFIS, E.   M-D
    ROUSSEAU VARIATIONS
        COMPOSERS PRESS, INC.   4.00
GRIFFIS, E.   M-D
    SET OF EIGHT
        COMPOSERS PRESS, INC.   6.00
GRIFFIS, E.   M
    TANGO ESPANOL
        COMPOSERS PRESS, INC.   1.50
GRISELLF, T.
    TWO AMERICAN SKETCHES
        THE BIG THREE MUSIC CORPORATION   01.25
GRISOLIA
    SONATINA
        FRANCO COLOMBO PUBLICATIONS   BA9361   1.50
GROBE   3
    AMERICAN MEDLEY
        CENTURY MUSIC PUBLISHING COMPANY, INC.   1251   .60
GROBE   4
    DIXIE LAND, VARIATIONS
        CENTURY MUSIC PUBLISHING COMPANY, INC.   1004   .40
GROBE   3
    MUSIC OF THE UNION
        CENTURY MUSIC PUBLISHING COMPANY, INC.   1251   .40
GROFE, F.
    ALICE BLUE
        THE BIG THREE MUSIC CORPORATION   00.95
GROFE, F.
    AVIATION SUITE
        THE BIG THREE MUSIC CORPORATION   03.00
GROFE, F.
    BLACK SAPPHIRE
        THE BIG THREE MUSIC CORPORATION   00.95
GROFE, F.
    BROADWAY AT NIGHT
        THE BIG THREE MUSIC CORPORATION   01.25
GROFE, F.
    CHRISTMAS EVE
        THE BIG THREE MUSIC CORPORATION   00.95
GROFE, F.
    FATHER OF WATERS
        THE BIG THREE MUSIC CORPORATION   00.95
GROFE, F.
    FESTIVIANA
        THE BIG THREE MUSIC CORPORATION   01.25

GROFE, F.
    FREE AIR
        THE BIG THREE MUSIC CORPORATION   00.95
GROFE, F.
    GRAND CANYON SUITE
        THE BIG THREE MUSIC CORPORATION   03.00
GROFE, F.
    KILLARNEY
        THE BIG THREE MUSIC CORPORATION   01.25
GROFE, F.
    KNUTE ROCKNE
        THE BIG THREE MUSIC CORPORATION   01.25
GROFE, F.
    MARCH FOR AMERICANS
        THE BIG THREE MUSIC CORPORATION   00.95
GROFE, F.
    MARDI GRAS
        THE BIG THREE MUSIC CORPORATION   00.95
GROFE, F.
    MISSISSIPPI SUITE
        THE BIG THREE MUSIC CORPORATION   02.50
GROFE, F.
    ON THE TRAIL
        THE BIG THREE MUSIC CORPORATION   00.95
GROFE, F.
    PAVILIONS OF INDUSTRY - THEME
        THE BIG THREE MUSIC CORPORATION   00.95
GROFE, F.
    SERENADE
        THE BIG THREE MUSIC CORPORATION   00.95
GROFE, F.
    SKY LINE
        THE BIG THREE MUSIC CORPORATION   00.95
GROFE, F.
    SYMPHONY IN STEEL
        THE BIG THREE MUSIC CORPORATION   01.25
GROFE, F.
    TABLOID
        THE BIG THREE MUSIC CORPORATION   03.00
GROFE, F.
    WHEELS
        THE BIG THREE MUSIC CORPORATION   03.00
GROFE, F.
    WORLD'S FAIR SUITE
        THE BIG THREE MUSIC CORPORATION   03.00
GROOMS   3
    ANNIE LAURIE, TRANS.
        CENTURY MUSIC PUBLISHING COMPANY, INC.   2537   .60
GROOMS   2-3
    CLARINET, THE
        CENTURY MUSIC PUBLISHING COMPANY, INC.   2278   .40
GROOMS   3
    COUNTRY GARDENS, ENGLISH DANCE
        CENTURY MUSIC PUBLISHING COMPANY, INC.   3123   .40
GROOMS   3-4
    DVORAKANA, FOX TROT, FANTASIE
        CENTURY MUSIC PUBLISHING COMPANY, INC.   2557   .40
GROOMS   2-3
    FLUTE, THE
        CENTURY MUSIC PUBLISHING COMPANY, INC.   2276   .40
GROOMS   3-4
    GRIEGIOLA, FOX TROT FANTASIE
        CENTURY MUSIC PUBLISHING COMPANY, INC.   2554   .40
GROOMS   2-3
    MANDOLIN AND GUITAR, THE
        CENTURY MUSIC PUBLISHING COMPANY, INC.   2275   .40
GROOMS   3
    NOBODY KNOWS DE TROUBLE I SEE
        CENTURY MUSIC PUBLISHING COMPANY, INC.   2579   .40
GROOMS   3-4
    WAGNERIANA
        CENTURY MUSIC PUBLISHING COMPANY, INC.   2558   .40
GROOMS--ED   GROOMS   3
    AY, AY, AY, TRANS.
        CENTURY MUSIC PUBLISHING COMPANY, INC.   2542   .40
GROOMS--ED   GROOMS   3
    DARK EYES
        CENTURY MUSIC PUBLISHING COMPANY, INC.   2671   .40
GROOMS--ED   GROOMS   3
    DEEP RIVER, TRANS.
        CENTURY MUSIC PUBLISHING COMPANY, INC.   2541   .40
GROOMS--ED   GROOMS   3
    IN THE GLOAMING, TRANS.
        CENTURY MUSIC PUBLISHING COMPANY, INC.   2536   .40
GROOMS--ED   GROOMS   3
    LAST ROSE OF SUMMER
        CENTURY MUSIC PUBLISHING COMPANY, INC.   2539   .40
GROOMS--ED   GROOMS   3
    LONDONDERRY AIR
        CENTURY MUSIC PUBLISHING COMPANY, INC.   2535   .40
GROOMS--ED   GROOMS   3
    MINSTREL BOY, THE
        CENTURY MUSIC PUBLISHING COMPANY, INC.   2538   .40
GROOMS--ED   GROOMS   3
    TURKEY IN THE STRAW
        CENTURY MUSIC PUBLISHING COMPANY, INC.   2496   .40
GROOMS--ED   GROOMS   3
    TWO GUITARS
        CENTURY MUSIC PUBLISHING COMPANY, INC.   2670   .40
GROSZ, W.
    SYMPHONIC VARIATIONS ON AN ORIGINAL THEME, OP. 9
        UNIVERSAL EDITION   UE 6484   2.75
GROTON, F.   3 1/2
    CHARMANTE
        THEODORE PRESSER COMPANY   .60
GROTON, F.   1
    SUMMER AND WINTER, OP. C NO. 1
        THEODORE PRESSER COMPANY   .50
GROVE
    BLUES MOTIF
        SUMMY-BIRCHARD COMPANY   .50
GROVE
    BUCCANEER
        SUMMY-BIRCHARD COMPANY   .50
GROVE   3
    CELEBRATION
        PRO-ART PUBLICATIONS, INC.   555   .50
GROVE   1-2
    CLOCK SERENADE
        PRO-ART PUBLICATIONS, INC.   555   .50
GROVE   2
    FANCY FREE
        WILLIS MUSIC COMPANY   .40
GROVE   2-3
    HIGH SPIRITS
        PRO-ART PUBLICATIONS, INC.   553   .50

GROVE   2
  JOLLY JALOPY
    BOSTON MUSIC COMPANY   .50
GROVE   1 - 2
  MAGIC MIRRORS
    BOSTON MUSIC COMPANY   .50
GROVE   1 1/2
  TIRELESS TRAVELER, THE
    WILLIS MUSIC COMPANY   .50
GROVE, R.   1 1/2
  BOOGIE BRIGADE
    BELWIN-MILLS PUBLISHING CORPORATION   .60
GROVE, R.   2
  HAPPY TIME
    BELWIN-MILLS PUBLISHING CORPORATION   .60
GROVE, R.   3 1/2
  MARCH
    BELWIN-MILLS PUBLISHING CORPORATION   .60
GROVE, R.   2
  MELODY
    BELWIN-MILLS PUBLISHING CORPORATION   .60
GROVE, R.   2
  MERRY JUGGLER, THE
    WILLIS MUSIC COMPANY   .40
GROVE, R.   2 1/2
  RIDING THE WAVES
    BELWIN-MILLS PUBLISHING CORPORATION   .60
GROVE, R.   3 1/2
  VILLAGE FAIR
    BELWIN-MILLS PUBLISHING CORPORATION   .60
GROVLEZ
  IMPRESSIONS
    HEUGEL ET CIE.   1.00
GROVLEZ
  VALSE-CAPRICE
    ASSOCIATED MUSIC PUBLISHERS, INC.   ESC   2.50
GRUBER, E.   1
  CAISSONS GO ROLLING ALONG, THE
    WILLIS MUSIC COMPANY   .35
GRUBER, F.   HENLEIN
  HOLY NIGHT
    WILLIS MUSIC COMPANY   .30
GRUBER, F.   KRUG   3
  HOLY NIGHT, SILENT NIGHT
    CENTURY MUSIC PUBLISHING COMPANY, INC.   1633   .40
GRUBER, F.   2
  HOLY NIGHT, SILENT NIGHT, EASY
    CENTURY MUSIC PUBLISHING COMPANY, INC.   2159   .40
GRUBER, F.   SCHAUM, J.   1 1/2
  SILENT NIGHT
    BELWIN-MILLS PUBLISHING CORPORATION   .50
GRUBER, F.
  SILENT NIGHT
    FRANCO COLOMBO PUBLICATIONS   BA9679   .75
GRUBER, F.   KOHLMANN, C.   5
  SILENT NIGHT
    THEODORE PRESSER COMPANY   .60
GRUBER, F.   SPENCER, J.   2
  SILENT NIGHT
    VOLKWEIN BROS.   .35
GRUBER, F.   RICHTER   FIRST YEAR
  SILENT NIGHT
    WARNER BROTHERS PUBLISHERS   .75
GRUBER, F.   WOODE
  SILENT NIGHT
    WILLIS MUSIC COMPANY   .30
GRUBER, F.   HARVEY   2
  SILENT NIGHT -- CHRISTMAS MEDLEY
    VOLKWEIN BROS.   .25
GRUBER, F.   2
  SILENT NIGHT, HOLY NIGHT
    CENTURY MUSIC PUBLISHING COMPANY, INC.   2159   .40
GRUBER, F.   KRUG   3
  SILENT NIGHT, HOLY NIGHT
    CENTURY MUSIC PUBLISHING COMPANY, INC.   1633   .40
GRUBER, F.   ADLER, M.   1 1/2
  SILENT NIGHT, HOLY NIGHT
    THEODORE PRESSER COMPANY   .50
GRUBER, F.   WEBER, H.
  SILENT NIGHT, HOLY NIGHT
    WILLIS MUSIC COMPANY   .35
GRUENBERG, L.
  JAZZ MASKS NO. 2, OP. 30A
    UNIVERSAL EDITION   UE 9644   2.10
GRUENBERG, L.
  POLYCHROMATICS, OP. 16
    UNIVERSAL EDITION   UE 7127   4.65
GRUENFELD   4
  LITTLE SERENADE
    CENTURY MUSIC PUBLISHING COMPANY, INC.   2148   .40
GRUENFELD   SCHNEIDER
  SOIREE DE VIENNE, OP. 56 -- CONCERT PARAPHRASE ON WALTZES OF
  STRAUSS
    ASSOCIATED MUSIC PUBLISHERS, INC.   B/B   1.75
GRUENFELD
  VOICES OF SPRING, OP. 57 -- CONCERT PARAPHRASE ON STRAUSS
    ASSOCIATED MUSIC PUBLISHERS, INC.   B/B   1.00
GRUNENWALD
  FANTASMAGORIE -- SCHERZO --
    FRANCO COLOMBO PUBLICATIONS   SAL   4.00
GRUNENWALD
  PARTITA
    ELKAN-VOGEL, INC.   RR   3.00
GRUNENWALD
  SUITE DE DANSES
    FRANCO COLOMBO PUBLICATIONS   SAL   5.00
GRUNEWALD   8
  CAPRICCIO
    ALPHONSE LEDUC
GRUNEWALD   6
  MELODIE INTERIEURE, LA
    ALPHONSE LEDUC
GRUNEWALD   5
  PRELUDE
    ALPHONSE LEDUC
GRUNEWALD   6, 7
  THEME ET VARIATIONS
    ALPHONSE LEDUC
GRUNN, H.
  HUMORESQUE NEGRE
    G. SCHIRMER, INC.   .50
GRUNN, H.   4
  TIS RAINING
    THEODORE PRESSER COMPANY   .60
GRUSIN
  IT TAKES A THIEF
    MCA MUSIC   1.00
GRUSIN
  IT'S NOT UNUSUAL
    MCA MUSIC   1.00
GRUSIN
  NAME OF THE GAME, THE
    MCA MUSIC   1.00
GUARINO, C.
  BARUFFE DI PIERROT E PIERETTE, LE
    FRANCO COLOMBO PUBLICATIONS   BON.1844   .90
GUARINO, C.
  CANZONE BARBERA
    FRANCO COLOMBO PUBLICATIONS   BON.1977   .90
GUARINO, C.
  CAPRICCI DI MASCHERE
    FRANCO COLOMBO PUBLICATIONS   BON.1750   2.25
GUARINO, C.
  DANZA DE LA CAPA ROJA
    FRANCO COLOMBO PUBLICATIONS   BON.1868   1.50
GUARINO, C.
  PRELUDE
    FRANCO COLOMBO PUBLICATIONS   BON.2352   1.00
GUARINO, C.
  SONATA FANTASIA
    FRANCO COLOMBO PUBLICATIONS   BON.1846   1.75
GUARINO, C.
  SUITE
    FRANCO COLOMBO PUBLICATIONS   BON.2354   3.00
GUARINO, C.
  TOCCATA AND FUGUE
    FRANCO COLOMBO PUBLICATIONS   BON.2355   3.00
GUARNIERI
  ACALANT - FROM 'SUITE IV CENTENARIO'
    FRANCO COLOMBO PUBLICATIONS   BR2158   .60
GUARNIERI
  CANCAO SERTANEJA
    FRANCO COLOMBO PUBLICATIONS   BR1662   .75
GUARNIERI
  CHORO TORTURADO
    ASSOCIATED MUSIC PUBLISHERS, INC.   AMP   1.00
GUARNIERI
  DANSA BRASILEIRA
    ASSOCIATED MUSIC PUBLISHERS, INC.   AMP   .65
GUARNIERI
  DANSA BRASILIERA
    FRANCO COLOMBO PUBLICATIONS   BR627   .75
GUARNIERI
  DANSA NEGRA
    ASSOCIATED MUSIC PUBLISHERS, INC.   AMP   .90
GUARNIERI
  DANSA NEGRA
    FRANCO COLOMBO PUBLICATIONS   BR667   .90
GUARNIERI
  FICARAS SOSINHA
    FRANCO COLOMBO PUBLICATIONS   BR629   .60
GUARNIERI   M
  FICARAS SOSINHA
    THEODORE PRESSER COMPANY   .60
GUARNIERI
  IMPROVISO
    FRANCO COLOMBO PUBLICATIONS   BR2159   .75
GUARNIERI
  LITTLE HORSE WITH THE BROKEN LEG, THE -- O CAVALINHO DE PERNA
  QUEBRADA -- 1932
    ASSOCIATED MUSIC PUBLISHERS, INC.   AMP   .40
GUARNIERI
  LUNDU
    FRANCO COLOMBO PUBLICATIONS   BR770   1.00
GUARNIERI   M
  MARIA LUCIA
    THEODORE PRESSER COMPANY   .60
GUARNIERI
  O CAVALINHO DE PERNA QUEBRADA
    FRANCO COLOMBO PUBLICATIONS   BR628   .75
GUARNIERI
  SONATINA NO. 03 IN THE TREBLE CLEF
    ASSOCIATED MUSIC PUBLISHERS, INC.   AMP   1.75
GUARNIERI
  SUITE MIRIM
    FRANCO COLOMBO PUBLICATIONS   BA11096   1.00
GUARNIERI
  TOCCATA
    FRANCO COLOMBO PUBLICATIONS   BR772   1.00
GUARNIERI
  TOCCATA -- 1935 --
    ASSOCIATED MUSIC PUBLISHERS, INC.   AMP   1.00
GUARNIERI
  VALSA NO. 6
    FRANCO COLOMBO PUBLICATIONS   BR2163   .75
GUARNIERI
  VALSA NO. 7
    FRANCO COLOMBO PUBLICATIONS   BR2146   .75
GUARNIERI
  VALSA NO. 8
    FRANCO COLOMBO PUBLICATIONS   BR2157   .75
GUARNIERI
  VALSA NO. 9
    FRANCO COLOMBO PUBLICATIONS   BR2244   .75
GUASTAVINO
  BAILECITO
    FRANCO COLOMBO PUBLICATIONS   BA8701   .75
GUASTAVINO
  ESTILO
    FRANCO COLOMBO PUBLICATIONS   BA10549   .75
GUASTAVINO
  GATO
    FRANCO COLOMBO PUBLICATIONS   BA8277   .75
GUASTAVINO
  MIS AMIGOS
    FRANCO COLOMBO PUBLICATIONS   BA12586   2.00
GUASTAVINO
  PAMPEANO
    FRANCO COLOMBO PUBLICATIONS   BA10574   .75
GUASTAVINO
  PRESENCIAS, LAS, NO. 1 LODUVINA
    FRANCO COLOMBO PUBLICATIONS   BA11832   .75
GUASTAVINO
  PRESENCIAS, LAS, NO. 2 ORTEGA
    FRANCO COLOMBO PUBLICATIONS   BA11901   .75
GUASTAVINO
  PRESENCIAS, LAS, NO. 3 FEDERICO IGNACIO CESPEDES VILLEGA
    FRANCO COLOMBO PUBLICATIONS   BA12126   .75
GUASTAVINO
  PRESENCIAS, LAS, NO. 4 MARIANA
    FRANCO COLOMBO PUBLICATIONS   BA12172   .75
GUASTAVINO
  PRESENCIAS, LAS, NO. 5 HORACIO LAVALLE
    FRANCO COLOMBO PUBLICATIONS   BA12173   .75

GUASTAVINO
  PUEBLITO, MI PUEBLO
    FRANCO COLOMBO PUBLICATIONS   BA11521   .75
GUASTAVINO
  ROMANCE DE CUYO
    FRANCO COLOMBO PUBLICATIONS   BA10881   1.00
GUASTAVINO
  ROMANCES NUEVOS, NO. 1 +LA NINA DEL RIO DULCE
    FRANCO COLOMBO PUBLICATIONS   BA11077   1.25
GUASTAVINO
  ROMANCES NUEVOS, NO. 2 EL CHICO QUE VINO DEL SUR
    FRANCO COLOMBO PUBLICATIONS   BA11101   .75
GUASTAVINO
  SIESTA, LA
    FRANCO COLOMBO PUBLICATIONS   BA9868   1.00
GUASTAVINO
  SONATA
    FRANCO COLOMBO PUBLICATIONS   BA10914   2.00
GUASTAVINO
  SONATINA
    FRANCO COLOMBO PUBLICATIONS   BA10268   1.25
GUASTAVINO
  SUITE ARGENTINA
    FRANCO COLOMBO PUBLICATIONS   BA10866   1.50
GUASTAVINO
  TARDE EN RINCON, LA
    FRANCO COLOMBO PUBLICATIONS   BA10796   .75
GUASTAVINO
  TIERRA LINDA
    FRANCO COLOMBO PUBLICATIONS   BA8450   .75
GUENIFFEY
  ALLEE JONCHEE DE ROSES, L'
    FRANCO COLOMBO PUBLICATIONS   SAL   1.50
GUENIFFEY
  CE QUE CHANTE L'EAU VIVE
    FRANCO COLOMBO PUBLICATIONS   SAL   1.50
GUENIFFEY
  FLORYSE EN SA TOURELLE
    FRANCO COLOMBO PUBLICATIONS   SAL   1.50
GUENIFFEY
  SEMEUR D'ILLUSIONS, LE
    FRANCO COLOMBO PUBLICATIONS   SAL   1.50
GUENIFFEY
  SUR LES MONTS BAIGNES D'AZUR
    FRANCO COLOMBO PUBLICATIONS   SAL   1.50
GUENTHER   2
  CAPTAIN JINKS
    CENTURY MUSIC PUBLISHING COMPANY, INC.   4035   .40
GUENTHER   GRIEG   3-4
  DREAM, A
    CENTURY MUSIC PUBLISHING COMPANY, INC.   3916   .40
GUENTHER   E
  FOUR BREVITIES
    THEODORE PRESSER COMPANY   .50
GUENTHER   1-2
  JELLY JIG - WILSON CLOG
    CENTURY MUSIC PUBLISHING COMPANY, INC.   4034   .40
GUENTHER   2
  KATE KEARNEY WALTZ
    CENTURY MUSIC PUBLISHING COMPANY, INC.   4036   .40
GUENTHER   3
  SAMBA, YERBA BUENA
    CENTURY MUSIC PUBLISHING COMPANY, INC.   3981   .40
GUENTHER   1-2
  WILSON CLOG AND JELLY JIG
    CENTURY MUSIC PUBLISHING COMPANY, INC.   4034   .40
GUENTHER   3
  YERBA BUENA, SAMBA
    CENTURY MUSIC PUBLISHING COMPANY, INC.   3981   .40
GUERRERO, A.
  TANGO
    FREDERICK HARRIS MUSIC COMPANY   .90
GUERRINI, G.
  ARABESQUE
    FRANCO COLOMBO PUBLICATIONS   BON.2256   .90
GUERRINI, G.
  NOSTALGIE DI NOVIZZE
    FRANCO COLOMBO PUBLICATIONS   BON.1300   1.50
GUERRINI, G.
  PASSEGGIATA NE CHIOSTRO, LA
    FRANCO COLOMBO PUBLICATIONS   BON.1962   1.50
GUERRINI, G.
  PETTEGOLEZZO IN REFETTORIO
    FRANCO COLOMBO PUBLICATIONS   BON.1961   1.50
GUIDA
  PASTORALE
    FRANCO COLOMBO PUBLICATIONS   DS435   1.00
GUILLAUME
  AT THE SEA - SHINING MORNING, THE ROCKEY BEACH, ROUGH SEA
    FRANCO COLOMBO PUBLICATIONS   SAL   4.25
GUILLAUME
  SUITE WALLONNE - PROMENADE A LA CAMPAGNE, AU CABARET, LE PECHEUR
  A LA LIGNE, A LA VEILLEE, LES PAYSANS
    FRANCO COLOMBO PUBLICATIONS   SAL   6.50
GUILLOU, J.   8
  TOCCATA
    ALPHONSE LEDUC
GUION, D.
  ARKANSAS TRAVELER--OLD FIDDLER'S BREAKDOWN
    G. SCHIRMER, INC.   .75
GUION, D.
  COUNTRY JIG IN C MAJOR
    G. SCHIRMER, INC.   .50
GUION, D.
  COUNTRY JIG IN D MAJOR
    G. SCHIRMER, INC.   .50
GUION, D.
  HARMONICA-PLAYER, THE--FROM ''ALLEY TUNES''
    G. SCHIRMER, INC.   .60
GUION, D.
  PRAIRIE DUSK--NOCTURNE
    G. SCHIRMER, INC.   .50
GUION, D.
  SHEEP AND GOAT WALKIN' TO THE PASTURE--COWBOYS' AND OLD FIDDLERS
  BREAKDOWN
    G. SCHIRMER, INC.   .50
GUION, D.
  TURKEY IN THE STRAW--COWBOYS' AND OLD FIDDLERS' BREAKDOWN
    G. SCHIRMER, INC.   .50
GUIRAUD
  QUERELLE DE FAUVETTES -- CAPRICE --
    FRANCO COLOMBO PUBLICATIONS   SAL   1.75
GULDA
  CADENZA TO MOZART CONCERTO IN C, K. 503
    ASSOCIATED MUSIC PUBLISHERS, INC.   DOB   .75

GULDA
  CADENZA TO MOZART CONCERTO IN D, K. 537 -- CORONATION --
    ASSOCIATED MUSIC PUBLISHERS, INC.   DOB   .75
GUNST
  PRELUDE
    FRANCO COLOMBO PUBLICATIONS   SAL   1.75
GURLITT   2
  BUTTERFLIES, OP. 158 NO. 1
    G. SCHIRMER, INC.   .50
GURLITT   2
  BY THE SPRING
    CENTURY MUSIC PUBLISHING COMPANY, INC.   1001   .40
GURLITT   1
  FAIR KIRMESS
    VOLKWEIN BROS.   .25
GURLITT   2
  FAIR, THE -- KERMESSE
    CENTURY MUSIC PUBLISHING COMPANY, INC.   2213   .40
GURLITT   2
  FAIR, THE--OP. 101 NO. 8
    G. SCHIRMER, INC.   .35
GURLITT   GILLOCK   2
  FESTIVE DANCE
    WILLIS MUSIC COMPANY   .40
GURLITT   GILLOCK   2
  FESTIVE DANCE
    WILLIS MUSIC COMPANY   .40
GURLITT   2
  HUNTING SON
    CENTURY MUSIC PUBLISHING COMPANY, INC.   1010   .40
GURLITT   1
  HUNTING SONG, OP. 101 NO. 19
    G. SCHIRMER, INC.   .40
GURLITT   2
  KERMESSE -- THE FAIR
    CENTURY MUSIC PUBLISHING COMPANY, INC.   2213   .40
GURLITT
  SLUMBER-SONG, OP. 101 NO. 6
    G. SCHIRMER, INC.   .35
GURLITT   2
  VALSE IN A FLAT MAJOR, OP. 62 NO. 11
    G. SCHIRMER, INC.   .35
GURLITT   2
  WALTZ, OP. 101 NO. 11
    CENTURY MUSIC PUBLISHING COMPANY, INC.   1042   .40
GURLITT   2
  WALTZ, OP. 101 NO. 11
    THEODORE PRESSER COMPANY   .50
GUTHRIE
  THIS LAND IS YOUR LAND
    TRO SONGWAYS SERVICE, INC.   2082   .85
GUTIERREZ-PONCE   4
  BALLADE MAURESQUE
    ASSOCIATED MUSIC PUBLISHERS, INC.   ESC   .90
GUY
  TWILIGHT REVERIE
    CENTURY MUSIC PUBLISHING COMPANY, INC.   1327   .40
GWYNN, F.
  PERSIMMONS--A NEGRO REVEL
    G. SCHIRMER, INC.   .40
GWYNN, F.
  UP AND DOWN THE MOUNTAINSIDE
    SHAWNEE PRESS, INC.   HB-5042   .40
GWYNN, F.
  WOODLAND WALTZ
    G. SCHIRMER, INC.   .40
GWYNN, F. *   EASY
  PENNY WHISTLE
    SHAWNEE PRESS, INC.   HB-5027   .60
GYLDMARK, S.   5
  CRAZY COMPOSER
    BELWIN-MILLS PUBLISHING CORPORATION   20062   .85
HAAS   4
  ALTE UNNENNB. TAGE OP. 42
    SCHOTT   2632   2.25
HAAS
  DEUTSCHE REIGEN UND ROMANZEN OP. 51
    SCHOTT   2633   2.25
HAAS   3
  FLYING LEAVES, OP. 16
    ASSOCIATED MUSIC PUBLISHERS, INC.   SIM   1.25
HAAS   5
  GESPENSTER OP. 34
    SCHOTT   2627   2.25
HAAS   5
  SONATE A-MOLL OP. 61 NO. 2
    SCHOTT   1730   2.50
HAAS   5
  SONATE D-DUR OP. 61 NO. 1
    SCHOTT   1729   2.50
HAAS   3
  WICHTELMANNCHEN OP. 27
    SCHOTT   2626   2.25
HACKH, O.
  CLOWN, THE
    G. SCHIRMER, INC.   .50
HACKH, O.   2
  ON THE SEA
    WILLIS MUSIC COMPANY   .40
HACKH, O.   1 1/2
  TIN SOLDIER, THE
    WILLIS MUSIC COMPANY   .40
HACKNEY, B. L.
  GAY PARADE, THE
    BELWIN-MILLS PUBLISHING CORPORATION   .60
HAEHNEL
  CAREFREE
    FREDERICK HARRIS MUSIC COMPANY   .60
HAHN, C.   3 1/2
  GREEN CATHEDRAL, THE
    THEODORE PRESSER COMPANY   .60
HAHN, R.   4
  HAD MY VERSES WINGS
    CENTURY MUSIC PUBLISHING COMPANY, INC.   3920   .40
HAHN, R.
  L'HEURE EXQUISE
    HEUGEL ET CIE.   1.30
HAHN, R.   4
  SI MES VERS AVAIENT DES AILES
    CENTURY MUSIC PUBLISHING COMPANY, INC.   3920   .40
HAIEFF, A.
  GIFTS AND SEMBLANCES
    BOOSEY AND HAWKES, INC.   1.50
HAINES, E.   1
  TWILIGHT LULLABY
    WILLIS MUSIC COMPANY   .35

HAINES, H.			
PLAYMATES			
G. SCHIRMER, INC.			.35
HAJDU, M.			
SONATINA			
KULTURA			1.25
HALFFTER, C.			
INTRODUCTION, FUGUE, AND FINALE, OP. 15 -- 1957 --			
ASSOCIATED MUSIC PUBLISHERS, INC.		UME	1.75
HALFFTER, C.			
SONATA IN A			
ASSOCIATED MUSIC PUBLISHERS, INC.		UME	1.00
HALFFTER, E.			
HABANERA			
ASSOCIATED MUSIC PUBLISHERS, INC.		ESC	2.00
HALFFTER, E.			
MARCHE JOYEUSE			
ASSOCIATED MUSIC PUBLISHERS, INC.		UME	.75
HALFFTER, E.			
PREGON. CUBA			
ASSOCIATED MUSIC PUBLISHERS, INC.		ESC	1.50
HALFFTER, E.			
SONATA			
ASSOCIATED MUSIC PUBLISHERS, INC.		ESC	3.75
HALFFTER, E.			
SONATINA -- BALLET IN ONE ACT			
ASSOCIATED MUSIC PUBLISHERS, INC.		ESC	9.00
HALFFTER, E.			
SONATINA BALLET, DANCE OF THE GYPSY			
ASSOCIATED MUSIC PUBLISHERS, INC.		ESC	1.50
HALFFTER, E.			
SONATINA BALLET, DANCE OF THE SHEPHERDESS			
ASSOCIATED MUSIC PUBLISHERS, INC.		ESC	3.00
HALFFTER, R.			
PRELUDE AND FUGUE -- 1932			
ASSOCIATED MUSIC PUBLISHERS, INC.		UME	.75
HALFFTER, R.			
SONATA NO. 02			
PAN AMERICAN UNION			02.00
HALFFTER, R.			
SONATA, OP. 16			
ASSOCIATED MUSIC PUBLISHERS, INC.		UME	1.50
HALFFTER, R.			
TERCERA SONATA			
EDICIONES MEXICANAS DE MUSICA, A. C.			03.00
HALL	D		
ETUDE FOR PIANO			
C. F. PETERS CORPORATION		H273	1.25
HALL *			
JOHNSON RAG			
THE BIG THREE MUSIC CORPORATION			00.95
HALL, E.	E		
TOLD AT TWIGHLIGHT			
COMPOSERS PRESS, INC.			1.00
HALL, F.	3-4		
LADS AND LASSIES GAY			
CENTURY MUSIC PUBLISHING COMPANY, INC.		2760	.40
HALL, F.			
OFFICER OF THE DAY			
ASHLEY DEALERS SERVICE, INC.		ES	.95
HALL, F.	3		
VENETIAN REVERIE, A			
CENTURY MUSIC PUBLISHING COMPANY, INC.		2759	.40
HALL, F.			
WEDDING OF THE WINDS			
ASHLEY DEALERS SERVICE, INC.		ES	.95
HALL, F.	SCHAUM, J.	2	
WEDDING OF THE WINDS			
BELWIN-MILLS PUBLISHING CORPORATION			.50
HALL, F.	3		
WEDDING OF THE WINDS			
CENTURY MUSIC PUBLISHING COMPANY, INC.		4292	.40
HALLBAUER, H.	E		
END OF DAY			
COMPOSERS PRESS, INC.			1.00
HALLMAYR			
INNO PONTIFICIO			
FRANCO COLOMBO PUBLICATIONS		102726	.60
HALLSTROM *			
TINIEST ANGEL, THE			
WILLIS MUSIC COMPANY			.40
HAMER, G. F.	4		
MAJESTY OF THE DEEP			
THEODORE PRESSER COMPANY			.60
HAMILTON *			
MAIDS OF MADRID, THE.			
MCA MUSIC			1.00
HAMILTON, I.	D		
PIANO SONATA NO. 01			
THEODORE PRESSER COMPANY			2.95
HAMMERSTEIN *			
CINDERELLA			
MCA MUSIC			2.50
HAMMERSTEIN *	PORTNOFF		
CINDERELLA			
MCA MUSIC			1.50
HAMMERSTEIN *	GLOVER		
CLIMB EV'RY MOUNTAIN			
MCA MUSIC			.85
HAMMERSTEIN *	GLOVER		
EDELWEISS			
MCA MUSIC			.85
HAMMERSTEIN *			
FLOWER DRUM SONG			
MCA MUSIC			2.50
HAMMERSTEIN *	PORTNOFF		
FLOWER DRUM SONG			
MCA MUSIC			1.50
HAMMERSTEIN *	RITTMAN		
GETTING TO KNOW YOU			
MCA MUSIC			1.00
HAMMERSTEIN *	RITTMAN		
HELLO, YOUNG LOVERS			
MCA MUSIC			1.00
HAMMERSTEIN *	RITTMAN		
I WHISTLE A HAPPY TUNE			
MCA MUSIC			1.00
HAMMERSTEIN *	PORTNOFF		
I WHISTLE A HAPPY TUNE			
MCA MUSIC			.85
HAMMERSTEIN *	RITTMAN		
IT MIGHT AS WELL BE SPRING			
MCA MUSIC			1.00
HAMMERSTEIN *			
IT MIGHT AS WELL BE SPRING			
MCA MUSIC			1.00
HAMMERSTEIN *	SINGER		
IT'S A GRAND NIGHT FOR SINGING			
MCA MUSIC			1.00
HAMMERSTEIN *	SIRMAY		
IT'S A GRAND NIGHT FOR SINGING			
MCA MUSIC			.85
HAMMERSTEIN *			
KING AND I, THE			
MCA MUSIC			2.50
HAMMERSTEIN *	STICKLES		
KING AND I, THE			
MCA MUSIC			1.50
HAMMERSTEIN *	SIRMAY		
MARCH OF THE SIAMESE CHILDREN			
MCA MUSIC			.85
HAMMERSTEIN *			
MARCH OF THE SIAMESE CHILDREN, THE			
MCA MUSIC			1.00
HAMMERSTEIN *			
ME AND JULIET			
MCA MUSIC			1.00
HAMMERSTEIN *	SINGER		
MY FAVORITE THINGS			
MCA MUSIC			1.00
HAMMERSTEIN *	RITTMAN		
MY FAVORITE THINGS			
MCA MUSIC			1.00
HAMMERSTEIN *	SIRMAY		
NO OTHER LOVE			
MCA MUSIC			1.00
HAMMERSTEIN *	RITTMAN		
OH WHAT A BEAUTIFUL MORNIN'			
MCA MUSIC			1.00
HAMMERSTEIN *	SIRMAY		
OH, WHAT A BEAUTIFUL MORNIN'			
MCA MUSIC			.85
HAMMERSTEIN *			
OKLAHOMA			
MCA MUSIC			2.50
HAMMERSTEIN *	STICKLES		
OKLAHOMA			
MCA MUSIC			1.50
HAMMERSTEIN *	RITTMAN		
OUT OF MY DREAMS			
MCA MUSIC			1.00
HAMMERSTEIN *	RITTMAN		
PEOPLE WILL SAY WE'RE IN LOVE			
MCA MUSIC			1.00
HAMMERSTEIN *			
PIPE DREAM			
MCA MUSIC			2.50
HAMMERSTEIN *	RITTMAN		
SOME ENCHANTED EVENING			
MCA MUSIC			1.00
HAMMERSTEIN *	PORTNOFF		
SOME ENCHANTED EVENING			
MCA MUSIC			.85
HAMMERSTEIN *	PORTNOFF		
SOUND OF MUSIC, THE.			
MCA MUSIC			1.50
HAMMERSTEIN *	SINGER		
SOUND OF MUSIC, THE.			
MCA MUSIC			1.00
HAMMERSTEIN *	GLOVER		
SOUND OF MUSIC, THE.			
MCA MUSIC			.85
HAMMERSTEIN *			
SOUND OF MUSIC, THE.			
MCA MUSIC			2.50
HAMMERSTEIN *			
SOUTH PACIFIC			
MCA MUSIC			2.50
HAMMERSTEIN *	STICKLES		
SOUTH PACIFIC			
MCA MUSIC			1.50
HAMMERSTEIN *	STICKLES		
STATE FAIR			
MCA MUSIC			1.50
HAMMERSTEIN *			
STATE FAIR			
MCA MUSIC			2.50
HAMMERSTEIN *	SINGER		
STRANGE MUSIC			
MCA MUSIC			1.00
HAMMERSTEIN *			
SURREY WITH THE FRINGE ON TOP			
MCA MUSIC			1.00
HAMMERSTEIN *	SIRMAY		
SURREY WITH THE FRINGE ON TOP			
MCA MUSIC			.85
HAMMERSTEIN *			
WALTZ FOR A BALL			
MCA MUSIC			1.00
HAMMERSTEIN *	RITTMAN		
WE KISS IN A SHADOW			
MCA MUSIC			1.00
HAMMERSTEIN *			
WHERE IS CINDERELLA			
MCA MUSIC			1.00
HAMMERSTEIN *	RITTMAN		
WONDERFUL GUY, THE			
MCA MUSIC			1.00
HAMMERSTEIN *			
YOU ARE BEAUTIFUL			
MCA MUSIC			1.00
HAMMERSTEIN *	SINGER		
YOU ARE BEAUTIFUL			
MCA MUSIC			1.00
HAMMERSTEIN *	RITTMAN		
YOUNGER THAN SPRINGTIME			
MCA MUSIC			1.00
HAMPTON, L.			
HAMPS BOOGIE-WOOGIE			
THE BIG THREE MUSIC CORPORATION			00.95
HANDEL	3		
ADAGIO, BOUREE			
CENTURY MUSIC PUBLISHING COMPANY, INC.		3913	.40
HANDEL	3		
AIR			
CENTURY MUSIC PUBLISHING COMPANY, INC.		3914	.40
HANDEL	PALMER, W. A.		
AIR AND VARIATIONS FROM SUITE NO. 5			
ALFRED MUSIC COMPANY		570	1.50
HANDEL	BUELOW		
AIR AND VARIATIONS--HARMONIOUS BLACKSMITH			
G. SCHIRMER, INC.			.50

HANDEL   3
    AIR IN G MAJOR, SUITE 14
        CENTURY MUSIC PUBLISHING COMPANY, INC.   3975   .40
HANDEL   BEARD
    AIR VARIE FROM CONCERTO GROSSO NO. 2
        ELKAN-VOGEL, INC.   .50
HANDEL   BARTH, H.
    ALLEGRO IN C
        BELWIN-MILLS PUBLISHING CORPORATION   20369   .60
HANDEL   4
    ALLEGRO IN D MINOR
        NOVELLO AND COMPANY, LTD.   55.0026.05 .25
HANDEL
    ALLEGRO IN G MAJOR, FROM SUITE NO. 14
        BELWIN-MILLS PUBLISHING CORPORATION   .60
HANDEL
    ALLEGRO IN G MINOR
        BANKS AND SON LTD.   .25
HANDEL   4
    ALLEGRO IN G MINOR
        NOVELLO AND COMPANY, LTD.   55.0011.07 .40
HANDEL   SHELDON
    AND WITH HIS STRIPES WE ARE HEALED -- MESSIAH CHORUS
        BELWIN-MILLS PUBLISHING CORPORATION   20016   .60
HANDEL   3
    ANDANTE, HORNPIPE
        CENTURY MUSIC PUBLISHING COMPANY, INC.   3915   .40
HANDEL   BAUER
    ARIA CON VARIAZIONI--HARMONIOUS BLACKSMITH
        G. SCHIRMER, INC.   .80
HANDEL   2
    ARIA MIT VARIATIONEN --BRAHMS-VARIATIONEN--
                            SCHOTT   0470 1/2 1.00
HANDEL   M
    ARRIVAL OF THE QUEEN OF SHEBA, FROM 'SOLOMON'
        C. F. PETERS CORPORATION   H375A   1.25
HANDEL   M
    ARRIVAL OF THE QUEEN OF SHEBA, FROM 'SOLOMON'. CONCERT VERSION.
        C. F. PETERS CORPORATION   H375   1.25
HANDEL   BRADLEY
    AUTHENTIC 'FIRST HANDEL'
        FRANCO COLOMBO PUBLICATIONS   LD204   1.00
HANDEL   3
    BERUHMTES LARGO
                            SCHOTT   0475   .75
HANDEL   2
    BERUHMTES LARGO -- ERLEICHTERT
                            SCHOTT   06667   .75
HANDEL   BARTH, H.
    BOURREE
        BELWIN-MILLS PUBLISHING CORPORATION   .60
HANDEL   3
    BOURREE
        NOVELLO AND COMPANY, LTD.   55.0024.09 .25
HANDEL   3
    CHACONNE F-DUR
                            SCHOTT   09579 1/2 1.00
HANDEL   3
    CHACONNE G-DUR
                            SCHOTT   09578 1/2 1.00
HANDEL   MONTANI
    CHACONNE IN G
        FRANCO COLOMBO PUBLICATIONS   129170   .90
HANDEL   PHILIPP, I.
    CHACONNE IN G
        INTERNATIONAL MUSIC COMPANY   1.25
HANDEL   M-D
    CHACONNE WITH 62 VARIATIONS IN G
        C. F. PETERS CORPORATION   4E   1.50
HANDEL
    CORRENTE IN G
        FREDERICK HARRIS MUSIC COMPANY   .45
HANDEL   CHISOLM
    CUCKOO AND NIGHTINGALE
        FRANCO COLOMBO PUBLICATIONS   SAL   4.25
HANDEL
    FANFARE
        BELWIN-MILLS PUBLISHING CORPORATION   .85
HANDEL
    FESTIVAL GROUPS FOR PIANO SELECTED BY ARTHUR BENJAMIN, SERIES 1
    -- ALLEGRO IN G, FROM 'FOURTEENTH SUITE'
        BOOSEY AND HAWKES, INC.   .60
HANDEL   3
    GAVOTTE
        NOVELLO AND COMPANY, LTD.   55.0023.00 .25
HANDEL   SIVRAI, DE
    GAVOTTE IN B FLAT
        G. SCHIRMER, INC.   .50
HANDEL   4
    GROBSCHMIED-VARIATIONEN
                            SCHOTT   0473 1/2 1.00
HANDEL   ZEPP
    HALLELUJAH CHORUS
        PRO-ART PUBLICATIONS, INC.   359   .50
HANDEL   SCHAUM, J.   3
    HALLELUJAH CHORUS
        SCHAUM PUBLICATIONS, INC.   .60
HANDEL   SHELDON
    HALLELUJAH CHORUS -- FROM 'MESSIAH'
        BELWIN-MILLS PUBLISHING CORPORATION   20121   .60
HANDEL   4
    HALLELUJAH CHORUS, FROM MESSIAH
        CENTURY MUSIC PUBLISHING COMPANY, INC.   3723   .40
HANDEL
    HALLELUJAH, FROM 'MESSIAH'
        G. SCHIRMER, INC.   .50
HANDEL   SCHAUM, J.   3
    HANDEL'S MESSIAH
        SCHAUM PUBLICATIONS, INC.   1.50
HANDEL   5
    HARMONIOUS BLACKSMITH
        CENTURY MUSIC PUBLISHING COMPANY, INC.   1172   .40
HANDEL
    HARMONIOUS BLACKSMITH
        FREDERICK HARRIS MUSIC COMPANY   .90
HANDEL   MARCIANO
    HARMONIOUS BLACKSMITH, THE
        FRANCO COLOMBO PUBLICATIONS   100772   .50
HANDEL   6
    HARMONIOUS BLACKSMITH, THE
        THEODORE PRESSER COMPANY   .50
HANDEL   BUELOW
    HARMONIOUS BLACKSMITH, THE -- VARIATIONS
        ASSOCIATED MUSIC PUBLISHERS, INC.   B/B   .50
HANDEL   4
    LARGO
        BELWIN-MILLS PUBLISHING CORPORATION   153   .60

HANDEL
    LARGO
        CARL FISCHER, INC.   S 794   .50
HANDEL   3
    LARGO
        CENTURY MUSIC PUBLISHING COMPANY, INC.   272   .40
HANDEL   VITALI
    LARGO FROM 'SERSE'
        FRANCO COLOMBO PUBLICATIONS   48092   .60
HANDEL   DEL MAGLIO
    LARGO FROM 'SERSE'
        FRANCO COLOMBO PUBLICATIONS   124718   .60
HANDEL   PARSONS
    LARGO FROM 'XERXES'
        G. SCHIRMER, INC.   .40
HANDEL   DEIS
    LARGO FROM 'XERXES'
        G. SCHIRMER, INC.   .35
HANDEL   HERRMANN
    LITTLE PIANO BOOK
        ASSOCIATED MUSIC PUBLISHERS, INC.   B/B   1.00
HANDEL   DEXTER, H.
    MESSIAH
        SAM FOX PUBLISHING COMPANY, INC.   1.00
HANDEL   4
    MESSIAH, THE, HALLELUJAH CHORUS
        CENTURY MUSIC PUBLISHING COMPANY, INC.   3723   .40
HANDEL
    MINUET FROM 'ALCINA'
        FREDERICK HARRIS MUSIC COMPANY   .60
HANDEL   PHILLIPS, D.
    MINUET IN G MINOR
        BELWIN-MILLS PUBLISHING CORPORATION   .60
HANDEL   PHILLIPS, D.   3
    MINUET IN G MINOR
        BELWIN-MILLS PUBLISHING CORPORATION   .60
HANDEL   POZZOLI
    MY FIRST HANDEL
        FRANCO COLOMBO PUBLICATIONS   ER1954   1.25
HANDEL   SHAW, W.
    OVERTURE 'MESSIAH'
        NOVELLO AND COMPANY, LTD.   01.0078.01 .50
HANDEL   MONTANI
    PASSACAGLIA - FROM SUITE NO. 7
        FRANCO COLOMBO PUBLICATIONS   128953   .90
HANDEL   DUMM
    RECITAL REFRESHER SERIES -- FANFARE
        BELWIN-MILLS PUBLISHING CORPORATION   26113   .60
HANDEL   BARTH, H.
    SARABANDE IN F
        BELWIN-MILLS PUBLISHING CORPORATION   20390   .60
HANDEL   3
    SARABANDE WITH VARIATIONS, SUITE 11,WATER MUSIC
        CENTURY MUSIC PUBLISHING COMPANY, INC.   3746   .40
HANDEL
    SEVEN PIECES, NO. 5
        FREDERICK HARRIS MUSIC COMPANY   .50
HANDEL   BAUER, M.   MEDIUM
    SIX LITTLE FUGUES
        SHAWNEE PRESS, INC.   HB-203   1.25
HANDEL   3
    SONATINA
        NOVELLO AND COMPANY, LTD.   55.0023.00 .40
HANDEL
    WATER MUSIC
        NOVELLO AND COMPANY, LTD.   10.0062.04 1.25
HANDEL   3
    WATER MUSIC, ADAGIO-BOURREE
        CENTURY MUSIC PUBLISHING COMPANY, INC.   3913   .40
HANDEL   3
    WATER MUSIC, ANDANTE-HORNPIPE
        CENTURY MUSIC PUBLISHING COMPANY, INC.   3915   .40
HANDEL   2
    XERXES, LARGO, EASY
        CENTURY MUSIC PUBLISHING COMPANY, INC.   2465   .40
HANDEL *
    CHOEUR DES PRETRES DE DAGON
        GERARD BILLAUDOT EDITIONS MUSICALES   1.60
HANLEY, J.   SCHAUM, J.   2
    BACK HOME AGAIN IN INDIANA
        SCHAUM PUBLICATIONS, INC.   .75
HANLEY, J.   SCHAUM, J.   2 1/2
    SECOND HAND ROSE
        SCHAUM PUBLICATIONS, INC.   .75
HANN, R.
    LA FETE CHEZ THERESE
        HEUGEL ET CIE.   9.00
HANNA   3
    ADVENTURES OF A TRITONE
        PRO-ART PUBLICATIONS, INC.   590   .50
HANNA   3
    CABLE CAR CAPER
        PRO-ART PUBLICATIONS, INC.   613   .50
HANNA   3
    INVENTION IN SYNCOPATION
        PRO-ART PUBLICATIONS, INC.   591   .50
HANNA   3
    MEDIEVAL FANTASY
        PRO-ART PUBLICATIONS, INC.   592   .50
HANNA   2
    MERRY MOTHER GOOSE SUITE
        PRO-ART PUBLICATIONS, INC.   593   .60
HANSEN   1
    SONG WITHOUT WORDS
        BOSTON MUSIC COMPANY   .50
HANSON
    BELL, THE
        CARL FISCHER, INC.   P 2263   .50
HANSON
    CLOG DANCE
        CARL FISCHER, INC.   P 2387   .60
HANSON
    FOR THE FIRST TIME
        CARL FISCHER, INC.   O 4642   1.50
HANSON   4
    MARCH CARILLON
        THEODORE PRESSER COMPANY   .60
HANSON
    THREE MINIATURES
        CARL FISCHER, INC.   P 2393   .75
HANSON *
    ENCHANTMENT
        CARL FISCHER, INC.   P 2128   .50
HANUS, J.
    MUSIC OF NATURE, THE
        GENERAL MUSIC PUBLISHING COMPANY, INC.   3.00

HARDING, M.   2 1/2
    STROLLING HARP PLAYER, THE
        THEODORE PRESSER COMPANY   .50
HARDING, R.
    HARK THE HERALD ANGELS SING
        WILLIS MUSIC COMPANY   .30
HARDING, R.
    I SAW THREE SHIPS
        WILLIS MUSIC COMPANY   .25
HARDING, R.
    O LITTLE TOWN OF BETHLEHEM
        WILLIS MUSIC COMPANY   .35
HARKER, F.   3 1/2
    PEASANT'S SONG, THE
        THEODORE PRESSER COMPANY   .50
HARKER, F.
    SWINGING IN FAIRYLAND
        G. SCHIRMER, INC.   .50
HARMON, M. S.
    JUGGLERS, THE
        BRODT MUSIC COMPANY   .40
HARPER
    LA PLAYA DE MALAGA
        BOSTON MUSIC COMPANY   3
HARPER, M.   4
    FIESTA GITANA, LA
        BELWIN-MILLS PUBLISHING CORPORATION   .60
HARPER, M.   2
    FLOWER MARKET IN SPAIN, A
        BELWIN-MILLS PUBLISHING CORPORATION   .60
HARPER, M.   1 1/2
    IN A HINDUSTANI MARKET
        BELWIN-MILLS PUBLISHING CORPORATION   .60
HARPER, M.   2 1/2
    IN A SYRIAN BAZAAR
        BELWIN-MILLS PUBLISHING CORPORATION   .60
HARPER, M.   2 1/2
    IN THE HILLS OF PALESTINE
        BELWIN-MILLS PUBLISHING CORPORATION   .60
HARPER, M.   1 1/2
    MEMORIES OF MALAGA
        BELWIN-MILLS PUBLISHING CORPORATION   .60
HARPER, M.
    OLE, GYPSY
        BOOSEY AND HAWKES, INC.   .40
HARPER, M.   1 1/2
    ON THE PANCHO
        BELWIN-MILLS PUBLISHING CORPORATION   .60
HARPER, M.
    PANCHO'S SERENADE
        BOOSEY AND HAWKES, INC.   .40
HARPER, M.   2
    UNDER THE CRESCENT MOON
        BELWIN-MILLS PUBLISHING CORPORATION   .60
HARPER, M.   2
    VISIT TO ARGENTINA, A
        BELWIN-MILLS PUBLISHING CORPORATION   .60
HARPER, M.   2
    VISIT TO MEXICO
        BELWIN-MILLS PUBLISHING CORPORATION   .60
HARPER, M.   1 1/2
    VISIT TO PUERTO RICO, A
        BELWIN-MILLS PUBLISHING CORPORATION   .60
HARPER, M.   2 1/2
    VISIT TO SPAIN
        BELWIN-MILLS PUBLISHING CORPORATION   .60
HARRIS   KAHL
    AFTER THE BALL
        BOSTON MUSIC COMPANY   .50
HARRIS   HASTINGS
    FOOTPRINTS ON THE MOON
        WARNER BROTHERS PUBLISHERS   1.00
HARRIS
    VERY IMPORTANT PERSON
        SUMMY-BIRCHARD COMPANY   .50
HARRIS, C.
    MINUET
        BANKS AND SON LTD.   .55
HARRIS, C.
    VALSE HONGROISE
        BANKS AND SON LTD.   .55
HARRIS, C. K.   SCHAUM, J.   2
    AFTER THE BALL
        BELWIN-MILLS PUBLISHING CORPORATION   .50
HARRIS, C. K.   1-2
    AFTER THE BALL, F MAJOR
        CENTURY MUSIC PUBLISHING COMPANY, INC. 4078   .40
HARRIS, C. K.   3
    INTRODUCTION AND FUGATO
        WILLIS MUSIC COMPANY   .60
HARRIS, R.
    LITTLE SUITE
        G. SCHIRMER, INC.   .50
HARRIS, R.   CUMPSON
    SONATA, OP. 1
        ASSOCIATED MUSIC PUBLISHERS, INC.   AMP   2.00
HARRISON, L.
    FESTIVAL GROUPS FOR PIANO SELECTED BY ARTHUR BENJAMIN, SERIES 1
    -- DANCE IN THE CHERRY ORCHARD
        BOOSEY AND HAWKES, INC.   .60
HARRISON, L.   D
    SUITE FOR PIANO
        C. F. PETERS CORPORATION   6427 2.00
HARSANYI
    BABY DANCING
        FRANCO COLOMBO PUBLICATIONS   SAL   4.25
HARSANYI
    NOVELETTE
        FRANCO COLOMBO PUBLICATIONS   SAL   2.50
HARSANYI
    PETITE SUITE POUR ENFANTS
        FRANCO COLOMBO PUBLICATIONS   SAL   4.25
HARSANYI
    RHAPSODIE
        FRANCO COLOMBO PUBLICATIONS   SAL   2.75
HARSANYI
    SONATA
        UNIVERSAL EDITION   9487 1.95
HART   2-3
    MAJORETTES, THE
        PRO-ART PUBLICATIONS, INC.   315   .50
HART   2-3
    PLAYING TAG
        PRO-ART PUBLICATIONS, INC.   314   .50
HART *
    BLUE MOON
        THE BIG THREE MUSIC CORPORATION   00.95

HART *
    SPRING IS HERE
        THE BIG THREE MUSIC CORPORATION   00.95
HART, F.
    DOLPHINS
        G. SCHIRMER, INC.   .35
HART, F. *
    MANHATTAN
        EDWARD B. MARKS MUSIC CORPORATION   01.00
HART, F. *
    MANHATTAN
        EDWARD B. MARKS MUSIC CORPORATION   00.60
HART, G. R.
    CLOUDS FLOATING BY
        BRODT MUSIC COMPANY   .40
HART, G. R.
    DANCE OF THE SNOWMAN
        BRODT MUSIC COMPANY   .40
HART, G. R.
    JOHNNY-JUMP-UP
        BRODT MUSIC COMPANY   .40
HART, G. R.
    KITTEN AND THE MOUSE, THE
        BRODT MUSIC COMPANY   .40
HART, G. R.
    MORNING BLORIES
        BRODT MUSIC COMPANY   .40
HART, G. R.
    SONG OF THE MOCKING BIRD
        BRODT MUSIC COMPANY   .45
HART, G. R.
    VOICES IN THE WOODS
        BRODT MUSIC COMPANY   .45
HART, N.   1
    COWBOY AND HIS BANJO, THE
        WILLIS MUSIC COMPANY   .40
HARTEVELD
    ELEGY
        FRANCO COLOMBO PUBLICATIONS   SAL   2.50
HARTEVELD
    NOCTURNE
        FRANCO COLOMBO PUBLICATIONS   SAL   2.50
HARTEVELD
    PRELUDE
        FRANCO COLOMBO PUBLICATIONS   SAL   2.50
HARTIG
    LITTLE SONATA, OP. 27 -- 1957
        ASSOCIATED MUSIC PUBLISHERS, INC.   B/B   2.25
HARTIG
    SCHWARZE SONNE, OP. 31 -- BALLET IN 9 TABLEAUX
        ASSOCIATED MUSIC PUBLISHERS, INC.   BOT   7.50
HARTIG
    VARIATIONS EN METRES VARIABLES, OP. 12
        ASSOCIATED MUSIC PUBLISHERS, INC.   B/B   4.50
HARTLEY   D
    SONATA NO. 02
        THEODORE PRESSER COMPANY   3.00
HARTLEY, W.
    CARILLON
        FEMA MUSIC PUBLICATIONS   1.00
HARTLEY, W.
    IMPROVISATIONS
        FEMA MUSIC PUBLICATIONS   1.50
HARTLEY, W.
    JOTA
        FEMA MUSIC PUBLICATIONS   1.50
HARTLEY, W.
    LITTLE DUET FOR PIANO
        FEMA MUSIC PUBLICATIONS   1.00
HARTLEY, W.
    MINIATURE SUITE
        FEMA MUSIC PUBLICATIONS   1.50
HARTLEY, W.
    SONATA IN A
        FEMA MUSIC PUBLICATIONS   4.00
HARTLEY, W.
    THREE PIANO PIECES
        FEMA MUSIC PUBLICATIONS   2.50
HARTLEY, W.
    TWO PIECES FOR PIANO
        FEMA MUSIC PUBLICATIONS   3.00
HARTMANN
    BLACK LIGHTS, OP. 74
        BOOSEY AND HAWKES, INC.   2.50
HARTMANN
    RUSSIAN FAIRY TALES, OP. 58
        BOOSEY AND HAWKES, INC.   2.50
HARTMANN
    SONATA NO. 01, OP. 67
        BOOSEY AND HAWKES, INC.   2.00
HARTMANN
    SONATA NO. 02, OP. 82
        BOOSEY AND HAWKES, INC.   4.50
HARTMANN
    TWO NOCTURNES, OP. 84
        BOOSEY AND HAWKES, INC.   1.25
HARVEY   2
    GLENDALE WALTZ
        VOLKWEIN BROS.   .IK
HARVEY   1
    GOLDENROD
        VOLKWEIN BROS.   .25
HARVEY   3
    JINGLE BELLS MARCH
        VOLKWEIN BROS.   .25
HARVEY   2
    JINGLE BELLS MARCH
        VOLKWEIN BROS.   00.25
HARVEY, PATRICK
    MUSIC FOR TWO DANCERS
        FRANCO COLOMBO PUBLICATIONS   LD540 .60
HARVEY, PATRICK
    SALUTE TO SAMUEL PEPYS
        FRANCO COLOMBO PUBLICATIONS   LD518 .60
HARVEY, PAUL R.
    RHUMBA TOCCATA
        FRANCO COLOMBO PUBLICATIONS   LD503 .75
HARVEY, VIVIEN
    CAPRICCIO
        FRANCO COLOMBO PUBLICATIONS   NY1347 .35
HARVEY, VIVIEN
    CHINESE TEMPLE GONGS
        BELWIN-MILLS PUBLISHING CORPORATION   .60
HARVEY, VIVIEN
    CHINESE TEMPLE GONGS
        FRANCO COLOMBO PUBLICATIONS   NY1346 .50

HARVEY, VIVIEN
    GREENSLEEVES
        BELWIN-MILLS PUBLISHING CORPORATION   .75
HARVEY, VIVIEN
    LET'S PLAY TAG
        FRANCO COLOMBO PUBLICATIONS   NY1345   .30
HARVEY, VIVIEN
    OLD FASHIONED DANCE, AN
        FRANCO COLOMBO PUBLICATIONS   NY1344   .30
HARVEY, VIVIEN
    OLD MILL, THE
        FRANCO COLOMBO PUBLICATIONS   NY1348   .30
HARVEY, VIVIEN
    PASTORALE
        BELWIN-MILLS PUBLISHING CORPORATION   .60
HARVEY, VIVIEN
    PASTORALE
        FRANCO COLOMBO PUBLICATIONS   NY1349   .35
HARVEY, VIVIEN
    STRATHSPEY AND AIR
        BELWIN-MILLS PUBLISHING CORPORATION   .60
HARVEY, VIVIEN
    STRATHSPEY AND AIR
        FRANCO COLOMBO PUBLICATIONS   NY1388   .35
HARVEY, VIVIEN
    TANGLEWOOD AND TALES
        FRANCO COLOMBO PUBLICATIONS   NY2072   1.50
HARVEY, VIVIEN
    VARIATIONS IN GREENSLEEVES
        FRANCO COLOMBO PUBLICATIONS   NY1493   .75
HASKELL
    RENDEZVOUS
        CARL FISCHER, INC.   P 3146   .50
HASLINGER, T.
    SONATINA, SECOND MOVEMENT
        FREDERICK HARRIS MUSIC COMPANY   .60
HASSE, J.   2
    BARBERINI'S MINUET
        CENTURY MUSIC PUBLISHING COMPANY, INC. 3189   .40
HASSLER, H.   KISS
    VARIATIONEN 'ICH GIENG EINMAL SPATIEREN' FUR CEMBALO
        SCHOTT   6226
HASSLER, J.   2-3
    DER TONKREIS
        SCHOTT   2577   2.25
HATCH   KERR, R. N.
    DOWNTOWN
        MCA MUSIC   1.00
HATCH   KERR, R.N.
    SIGN OF THE TIMES, THE.
        MCA MUSIC   1.00
HATCH
    SPANISH CARNIVAL
        SUMMY-BIRCHARD COMPANY   .50
HATRAK   2
    CHIP'S BOOGIE-WOOGIE
        BELWIN-MILLS PUBLISHING CORPORATION   .60
HATRAK   2
    HOP SCOTCH POLKA
        BELWIN-MILLS PUBLISHING CORPORATION   .60
HAUBENSTOCK-RAMATI, R.
    CATCH 1 -- CEMBALO SOLO
        UNIVERSAL EDITION   UE 14784   7.25
HAUBENSTOCK-RAMATI, R.
    CATCH 2
        UNIVERSAL EDITION   UE 14881   11.00
HAUBENSTOCK-RAMATI, R.
    KLAVIERSTUCKE
        UNIVERSAL EDITION   UE 14255   2.85
HAUBIEL, C.   D
    AMERICAN RHAPSODIE
        COMPOSERS PRESS, INC.   6.00
HAUBIEL, C.   D
    CAPRICCIO
        COMPOSERS PRESS, INC.   1.50
HAUBIEL, C.   E
    DANCE OF THE DORIAN YOUTH
        COMPOSERS PRESS, INC.   1.00
HAUBIEL, C.   D
    DAWN MISTS
        COMPOSERS PRESS, INC.   3.00
HAUBIEL, C.   M
    EIGHTEEN SIXTY-FIVE A.D.
        COMPOSERS PRESS, INC.   1.50
HAUBIEL, C.   M
    ELEGIAC NOCTURNE
        COMPOSERS PRESS, INC.   1.00
HAUBIEL, C.   M-D
    ELVES SPINNING
        COMPOSERS PRESS, INC.   1.50
HAUBIEL, C.   M-D
    EVOCACION
        COMPOSERS PRESS, INC.   2.00
HAUBIEL, C.   E-M
    FAIRY SPINNING WHEEL
        COMPOSERS PRESS, INC.   1.00
HAUBIEL, C.   M
    FESTIVAL
        COMPOSERS PRESS, INC.   1.00
HAUBIEL, C.   M
    FESTIVAL OF THE DRAGON
        COMPOSERS PRESS, INC.   1.50
HAUBIEL, C.   M
    FOX AHEAD
        COMPOSERS PRESS, INC.   1.50
HAUBIEL, C.   M
    GAIETY
        COMPOSERS PRESS, INC.   1.00
HAUBIEL, C.   3
    GAILY
        BELWIN-MILLS PUBLISHING CORPORATION   .60
HAUBIEL, C.   3
    GENTLY
        BELWIN-MILLS PUBLISHING CORPORATION   .60
HAUBIEL, C.   M
    GOTHIC DANCE
        COMPOSERS PRESS, INC.   1.00
HAUBIEL, C.   D
    IDILLIO
        COMPOSERS PRESS, INC.   2.00
HAUBIEL, C.   E-M
    IN A PAGODA
        COMPOSERS PRESS, INC.   1.00
HAUBIEL, C.   E
    KEYBOARD PICTURES
        COMPOSERS PRESS, INC.   2.00

HAUBIEL, C.   E
    LONELY ELF
        COMPOSERS PRESS, INC.   1.00
HAUBIEL, C.   M
    LULLABY
        COMPOSERS PRESS, INC.   1.00
HAUBIEL, C.   M
    MADONNA
        COMPOSERS PRESS, INC.   1.00
HAUBIEL, C.   D
    METAMORPHOSES
        COMPOSERS PRESS, INC.   3.00
HAUBIEL, C.   3
    MYSTERIOUSLY
        BELWIN-MILLS PUBLISHING CORPORATION   .60
HAUBIEL, C.   E
    MYSTERY, A
        COMPOSERS PRESS, INC.   1.00
HAUBIEL, C.   M-D
    NOCHE EN ESPANA
        COMPOSERS PRESS, INC.   1.50
HAUBIEL, C.   M
    NOSTALGIA
        COMPOSERS PRESS, INC.   1.50
HAUBIEL, C.   E
    NOW I LAY ME TO SLEEP
        COMPOSERS PRESS, INC.   1.00
HAUBIEL, C.   M
    OF BYGONE DAYS
        COMPOSERS PRESS, INC.   1.00
HAUBIEL, C.   D
    PERPETUAL MOTION
        COMPOSERS PRESS, INC.   2.00
HAUBIEL, C.   D
    PIANO BEYOND, THE
        COMPOSERS PRESS, INC.   4.00
HAUBIEL, C.   M
    RIDE THROUGH THE NIGHT
        COMPOSERS PRESS, INC.   1.50
HAUBIEL, C.   D
    SCHERZO
        COMPOSERS PRESS, INC.   3.00
HAUBIEL, C.   E
    SHADOWS
        COMPOSERS PRESS, INC.   1.00
HAUBIEL, C.   M
    SHADOWS -- CONCERT VERSION
        COMPOSERS PRESS, INC.   1.00
HAUBIEL, C.   E
    SNOWFLAKES
        COMPOSERS PRESS, INC.   1.00
HAUBIEL, C.   M
    SUMMER CHURCHYARD
        COMPOSERS PRESS, INC.   1.50
HAUBIEL, C.   E
    TEN FOR PLEASURE
        COMPOSERS PRESS, INC.   4.00
HAUBIEL, C.   D
    TOCCATA
        COMPOSERS PRESS, INC.   3.00
HAUBIEL, C.   M
    VOODOO
        COMPOSERS PRESS, INC.   1.00
HAUBIEL, C.   E-M
    WEDDING RING WALTZ
        COMPOSERS PRESS, INC.   1.00
HAUBIEL, C.   E
    WHERE THE SHADOW LIES
        COMPOSERS PRESS, INC.   1.00
HAUBIEL, C.   M
    WHIRLING DERVISH
        COMPOSERS PRESS, INC.   1.50
HAUDEBERT
    CAHIER D'ELISABETH, LE
        FRANCO COLOMBO PUBLICATIONS   SAL   4.00
HAUDEBERT
    CAHIER D'EVE, LE
        FRANCO COLOMBO PUBLICATIONS   SAL   2.50
HAUDEBERT
    DIEU VAINQUEUR -- FINAL FUGUE --
        FRANCO COLOMBO PUBLICATIONS   SAL   2.75
HAUFRECHT   E
    SONG OF THE VALLEY
        THEODORE PRESSER COMPANY   .50
HAUFRECHT
    TICK-TOCK TOCCATA -- A 'TIMEPIECE'
        MCA MUSIC   .60
HAUPT, L. VON
    HANSEL AND GRETEL--ADAPTED FROM HUMPERDINCK AS A CHILDREN'S
    OPERA-STORY
        G. SCHIRMER, INC.   .75
HAUSER   2
    BERCEUSE -- CRADLE SONG
        CENTURY MUSIC PUBLISHING COMPANY, INC. 2056   .40
HAUSER   2
    CRADLE SONG -- BERCEUSE
        CENTURY MUSIC PUBLISHING COMPANY, INC. 2056   .40
HAUSER   THOMPSON, J.   4
    HUNGARIAN
        WILLIS MUSIC COMPANY   .40
HAUSER   2
    WIEGENLIED -- CRADLE SONG --
        CENTURY MUSIC PUBLISHING COMPANY, INC. 2056   .40
HAUSERMAN, J.   E
    LEGENDE
        THEODORE PRESSER COMPANY   .75
HAVEN   3
    OCEAN BY MOONLIGHT, THE
        CENTURY MUSIC PUBLISHING COMPANY, INC. 2730   .40
HAWES, J.
    BURLESQUE AND PASTORALE
        NOVELLO AND COMPANY, LTD.   10.0063.02   .90
HAWLEY   2
    COLLEGE MARCH MEDLEY
        CENTURY MUSIC PUBLISHING COMPANY, INC. 2994   .40
HAWLEY   3
    EXCELSIOR, SACRED SONG MED.
        CENTURY MUSIC PUBLISHING COMPANY, INC. 2993   .40
HAWTHORNE, A.   SCHAUM, J.   2
    WHISPERING HOPE
        BELWIN-MILLS PUBLISHING CORPORATION   .50
HAWTHORNE, A.   DEWS
    WHISPERING HOPE
        G. SCHIRMER, INC.   .50
HAWTHORNE, A.   BURNAM   1 1/2
    WHISPERING HOPE
        WILLIS MUSIC COMPANY   .35

HAWTHORNE, A.   2
  WHISPERING HOPE
    WILLIS MUSIC COMPANY   .35
HAYASHI, H.
  SONATA
    ONGAKU NO TOMO SHA   3.50
HAYDN
  AIR   4
    DELRIEU ET CIE.   1.00
HAYDN
  ALLEGRETTO
    THEODORE PRESSER COMPANY   .50
HAYDN
  ALLEGRETTO IN B FLAT MAJOR
    G. SCHIRMER, INC.   .40
HAYDN
  ALLEGRO IN F
    FREDERICK HARRIS MUSIC COMPANY   .30
HAYDN   LEBERT
  ANDANTE CON VARIAZIONI IN F MINOR
    G. SCHIRMER, INC.   .70
HAYDN   DELIOUX
  ANDANTE FROM ''SURPRISE'' SYMPHONY IN G MAJOR
    G. SCHIRMER, INC.   .60
HAYDN   2
  ARIETTA CON VARIAZIONI -- HOBOKEN 17-2
    SCHOTT   09662 1/2   1.00
HAYDN   STEINER   2 1/2
  BIRD CALLS
    BELWIN-MILLS PUBLISHING CORPORATION   .50
HAYDN   LANDOWSKA, W.
  CADENZA - CONCERTO IN D, OP. 21
    BROUDE BROTHERS LTD.   02.00
HAYDN
  CAPRICCIO
    FREDERICK HARRIS MUSIC COMPANY   .60
HAYDN   GANZ
  CONCERTO IN D MAJOR
    G. SCHIRMER, INC.   L1700   1.75
HAYDN
  COUNTRY DANCE
    FREDERICK HARRIS MUSIC COMPANY   .60
HAYDN   3
  DEUTSCHLAND-LIED
    SCHOTT   07150 1/2   1.00
HAYDN
  DIVERTIMENTO IN D MAJOR
    BELWIN-MILLS PUBLISHING CORPORATION 25229 .60
HAYDN
  FANTASIA IN C
    EDWIN F. KALMUS   3535   1.00
HAYDN   BUELOW
  FANTASIA IN C MAJOR
    G. SCHIRMER, INC.   .75
HAYDN   3
  FANTASIE C-DUR -- HOBOKEN 17-4
    SCHOTT   09661 1/2   1.00
HAYDN
  FANTASIE IN C MAJOR, H. XVII-4
    G. HENLE MUSIKVERLAG   69   1.10
HAYDN
  FANTASY IN C MAJOR
    KULTURA   .80
HAYDN   SCHOBERLECHNER
  FESTIVAL GROUPS FOR PIANO SELECTED BY ARTHUR BENJAMIN, SERIES 2
  -- MENUETT
    BOOSEY AND HAWKES, INC.   .60
HAYDN
  FINALE IN A FLAT, FROM SONATA NO. 8
    BELWIN-MILLS PUBLISHING CORPORATION   .60
HAYDN   ECKSTEIN
  GIPSY RONDO
    CARL FISCHER, INC.   S 598   .50
HAYDN   KOEHLER
  GIPSY RONDO
    G. SCHIRMER, INC.   .50
HAYDN   4
  GYPSY RONDO
    BELWIN-MILLS PUBLISHING CORPORATION 159   .60
HAYDN   3
  GYPSY RONDO
    CENTURY MUSIC PUBLISHING COMPANY, INC. 628 .40
HAYDN   4
  GYPSY RONDO
    WILLIS MUSIC COMPANY   .50
HAYDN   SCHAUM, J.   2
  HAYDN GO-SEEK
    BELWIN-MILLS PUBLISHING CORPORATION   .50
HAYDN   MARCHI, G.
  INCONTRO CON HAYDN
    EDIZIONI BERBEN   1304   4.50
HAYDN
  MINUET AND TRIO
    FREDERICK HARRIS MUSIC COMPANY   .60
HAYDN
  MINUETTO AND TRIO
    FREDERICK HARRIS MUSIC COMPANY   .60
HAYDN   BARTH, H.
  MINUETTO GIOCOSO
    BELWIN-MILLS PUBLISHING CORPORATION 20169 .60
HAYDN
  MINUETTO GIOCOSO IN C MAJOR
    G. SCHIRMER, INC.   .40
HAYDN   3-4
  MY MOTHER BIDS ME BIND MY HAIR
    CENTURY MUSIC PUBLISHING COMPANY, INC. 3919 .40
HAYDN   CURRIE, E.   3 1/2
  NEW SONATAS BY HAYDN - SONATA NO. 01
    WILLIS MUSIC COMPANY   1.10
HAYDN   CURRIE, E.   3
  NEW SONATAS BY HAYDN - SONATA NO. 02
    WILLIS MUSIC COMPANY   .80
HAYDN   CURRIE, E.   2 1/2
  NEW SONATAS BY HAYDN - SONATA NO. 03
    WILLIS MUSIC COMPANY   .80
HAYDN   CURRIE, E.   2 1/2
  NEW SONATAS BY HAYDN - SONATA NO. 04
    WILLIS MUSIC COMPANY   .60
HAYDN   CURRIE, E.   2
  NEW SONATAS BY HAYDN - SONATA NO. 05
    WILLIS MUSIC COMPANY   .85
HAYDN   CURRIE, E.   2 1/2
  NEW SONATAS BY HAYDN - SONATA NO. 06
    WILLIS MUSIC COMPANY   .70
HAYDN   CURRIE, E.   2 1/2
  NEW SONATAS BY HAYDN - SONATA NO. 07
    WILLIS MUSIC COMPANY   .85

HAYDN   CURRIE, E.   2 1/2
  NEW SONATAS BY HAYDN - SONATA NO. 08
    WILLIS MUSIC COMPANY   .85
HAYDN   CURRIE, E.   3
  NEW SONATAS BY HAYDN - SONATA NO. 09
    WILLIS MUSIC COMPANY   .80
HAYDN   CURRIE, E.   2 1/2
  NEW SONATAS BY HAYDN - SONATA NO. 10
    WILLIS MUSIC COMPANY   .60
HAYDN   WEYBRIGHT   2
  O WORSHIP THE KING -- A HYMN
    BELWIN-MILLS PUBLISHING CORPORATION   .60
HAYDN   VOSS   3
  OCHSEN-MENUETT -- HOBOKEN 9-27
    SCHOTT   0509 1/2   1.00
HAYDN
  OLD ENGLISH SONG -- I HAD A LITTLE NUT TREE
    FREDERICK HARRIS MUSIC COMPANY   .60
HAYDN   2
  OXEN MINUET
    CENTURY MUSIC PUBLISHING COMPANY, INC. 3712 .40
HAYDN   MONTANI
  OXEN MINUET
    FRANCO COLOMBO PUBLICATIONS 128443   .50
HAYDN   STEINER   2 1/2
  PERPETUUM MOBILE, OP. 64 NO. 5 -- PERPETUAL MOTION
    BELWIN-MILLS PUBLISHING CORPORATION   .60
HAYDN   LECHNER   2-3
  RONDO ALL' ONGARESE -- HOBOKEN 15-25
    SCHOTT   09641 102   1.00
HAYDN
  RONDO IN A MAJOR
    G. SCHIRMER, INC.   .50
HAYDN   GOEBELS   3
  SONATA IN A FLAT, SHO 0502 1/2, H 46
    SCHOTT   0502 1/2   1.00
HAYDN
  SONATA IN B FLAT--SCH NO. 18
    G. SCHIRMER, INC.   .50
HAYDN
  SONATA IN C MAJOR, H. XVI-35
    G. HENLE MUSIKVERLAG   176   1.10
HAYDN   GOEBELS   3
  SONATA IN C MINOR, SHO 09660 1/2, H20
    SCHOTT   09660 1/2   1.00
HAYDN
  SONATA IN C SHARP MINOR--SCH NO. 06
    G. SCHIRMER, INC.   .70
HAYDN   GOEBELS   3
  SONATA IN C SHARP MINOR, SHO 0492 1/2, H 36
    SCHOTT   0492 1/2   1.00
HAYDN
  SONATA IN C--SCH NO. 05
    G. SCHIRMER, INC.   .75
HAYDN   GOEBELS   3
  SONATA IN C, SHO 0485 1/2, H 35
    SCHOTT   0485 1/2   1.00
HAYDN   GOEBELS   2
  SONATA IN C, SHO 09659 1/2, H 15
    SCHOTT   09659 1/2   1.00
HAYDN
  SONATA IN D MAJOR, H. XVI-37
    G. HENLE MUSIKVERLAG   177   1.10
HAYDN
  SONATA IN D--SCH NO. 07
    G. SCHIRMER, INC.   .60
HAYDN
  SONATA IN D--SCH NO. 09
    G. SCHIRMER, INC.   .80
HAYDN
  SONATA IN D--SCH NO. 19
    G. SCHIRMER, INC.   .75
HAYDN
  SONATA IN D, NO. 07
    FREDERICK HARRIS MUSIC COMPANY   .60
HAYDN   GOEBELS   3
  SONATA IN D, SHO 0488 1/2, H 37
    SCHOTT   0488 1/2   1.00
HAYDN   GOEBELS   3
  SONATA IN D, SHO 3497 1/2, H 19
    SCHOTT   0497 1/2   1.00
HAYDN
  SONATA IN E FLAT--SCH NO. 01
    G. SCHIRMER, INC.   1.00
HAYDN
  SONATA IN E FLAT--SCH NO. 03
    G. SCHIRMER, INC.   .80
HAYDN
  SONATA IN E FLAT, NO. 03
    FREDERICK HARRIS MUSIC COMPANY   .75
HAYDN   GOEBELS   3
  SONATA IN E FLAT, SHO 0499 1/2, H 49
    SCHOTT   0499 1/2   1.00
HAYDN   GOEBELS   3
  SONATA IN E FLAT, SHO 0503 1/2, H 52
    SCHOTT   0503 1/2   1.00
HAYDN
  SONATA IN E MINOR--SCH NO. 02
    G. SCHIRMER, INC.   .70
HAYDN   6
  SONATA IN E MINOR, COTTA NO. 7
    THEODORE PRESSER COMPANY   .70
HAYDN   GOEBELS   3
  SONATA IN E MINOR, SHO 0491 1/2, H34
    SCHOTT   0491 1/2   1.00
HAYDN
  SONATA IN E--SCH NO. 17
    G. SCHIRMER, INC.   .60
HAYDN
  SONATA IN F--SCH NO. 13
    G. SCHIRMER, INC.   .70
HAYDN
  SONATA IN F--SCH NO. 20
    G. SCHIRMER, INC.   .70
HAYDN   GOEBELS   3
  SONATA IN F, SHO 0486 1/2, H 23
    SCHOTT   0486 1/2   1.00
HAYDN
  SONATA IN G MINOR--SCH NO. 04
    G. SCHIRMER, INC.   .60
HAYDN
  SONATA IN G--SCH NO. 11
    G. SCHIRMER, INC.   .75
HAYDN   GOEBELS   3
  SONATA IN G, SHO 0484 1/2, H 27
    SCHOTT   0484 1/2   1.00

HAYDN   3
    SONATA NO. 01
        CENTURY MUSIC PUBLISHING COMPANY, INC.   402   .40
HAYDN   ECKSTEIN
    SONATA NO. 01 IN C
        CARL FISCHER, INC.   S 1460   .75
HAYDN
    SONATA NO. 05 IN C
        FRANCO COLOMBO PUBLICATIONS   ER717   1.00
HAYDN   ECKSTEIN
    SONATA NO. 07 IN D
        CARL FISCHER, INC.   S 2262   .75
HAYDN   4
    SONATA NO. 07, FINALE
        CENTURY MUSIC PUBLISHING COMPANY, INC.   3793   .40
HAYDN   CHING
    SONATA NO. 27 IN G
        GENERAL WORDS AND MUSIC COMPANY   .75
HAYDN   CHING
    SONATA NO. 34 IN E MINOR
        GENERAL WORDS AND MUSIC COMPANY   .75
HAYDN   CHING
    SONATA NO. 35 IN C
        GENERAL WORDS AND MUSIC COMPANY   .75
HAYDN   THOMPSON, J.   1
    SURPRISE SYMPHONY, THE
        WILLIS MUSIC COMPANY   .35
HAYDN   GOETSCHIUS, P.
    SYMPHONY NO. 16 IN G MAJOR
        THEODORE PRESSER COMPANY   .75
HAYDN
    TEMA CON VARIAZIONI IN C MAJOR
        FREDERICK HARRIS MUSIC COMPANY   .40
HAYDN   1
    THEME FROM SURPRISE SYMPHONY
        CENTURY MUSIC PUBLISHING COMPANY, INC.   3606   .40
HAYDN
    THEME WITH SIX VARIATIONS
        BROOT MUSIC COMPANY   .50
HAYDN   4
    VARIATIONEN F-MOLL -- HOBOKEN 17-6
        SCHOTT   0511 1/2   1.00
HAYDN   HERNADI
    VARIATIONS IN F MINOR
        KULTURA   1.00
HAYDN
    VARIATIONS IN F, H. XVII-6
        G. HENLE MUSIKVERLAG   70   1.10
HAYDN *
    MENUET--FROM QUARTET,OP.76--
        GERARD BILLAUDOT EDITIONS MUSICALES   1.60
HAYES   1-2
    ACROBAT, THE, G MAJOR
        CENTURY MUSIC PUBLISHING COMPANY, INC.   4385   .40
HAYES   2
    AT THE BALLET
        BELWIN-MILLS PUBLISHING CORPORATION   .60
HAYES   3
    AUTUMN SHADES
        CENTURY MUSIC PUBLISHING COMPANY, INC.   4207   .40
HAYES   2
    BLACK STEPPING STONES
        CENTURY MUSIC PUBLISHING COMPANY, INC.   4222   .40
HAYES
    CELLO PLAYER
        BROOT MUSIC COMPANY   .35
HAYES
    COUNTY FAIR
        BROOT MUSIC COMPANY   .40
HAYES   2
    ETUDE
        BELWIN-MILLS PUBLISHING CORPORATION   .60
HAYES   2
    ETUDE MELODIC
        BELWIN-MILLS PUBLISHING CORPORATION   .60
HAYES   2
    GRAY MULE, THE
        CENTURY MUSIC PUBLISHING COMPANY, INC.   4345   .40
HAYES   2
    HAPPY HOBO
        CENTURY MUSIC PUBLISHING COMPANY, INC.   4271   .40
HAYES   2-3
    LAME DUCK, THE
        CENTURY MUSIC PUBLISHING COMPANY, INC.   4156   .40
HAYES   3
    LITTLE GAVOTTE
        WILLIS MUSIC COMPANY   .40
HAYES   2
    LITTLE PUPPETS ON PARADE
        BELWIN-MILLS PUBLISHING CORPORATION   .60
HAYES   2
    LITTLE SHEPHERD
        BELWIN-MILLS PUBLISHING CORPORATION   .60
HAYES   1
    LITTLE SLEEPY SONG -- RUN AND SKIP
        CENTURY MUSIC PUBLISHING COMPANY, INC.   4155   .40
HAYES   1-2
    MUSICAL POWDER BOX
        CENTURY MUSIC PUBLISHING COMPANY, INC.   4067   .40
HAYES   2
    NONAME -- CHROMATIC WALTZ
        BOSTON MUSIC COMPANY   .50
HAYES   2-3
    ONE HAND WALTZ
        CENTURY MUSIC PUBLISHING COMPANY, INC.   4230   .40
HAYES   3
    PERPETUAL MOTION
        CENTURY MUSIC PUBLISHING COMPANY, INC.   4259   .40
HAYES   2
    PIPER'S TUNE, A
        CENTURY MUSIC PUBLISHING COMPANY, INC.   4220   .40
HAYES
    PIXY PRANKS
        BROOT MUSIC COMPANY   .45
HAYES   1 1/2
    POPPING CORN
        WILLIS MUSIC COMPANY   .40
HAYES   2
    ROLLER SKATING
        CENTURY MUSIC PUBLISHING COMPANY, INC.   4109   .40
HAYES
    ROUND AND ROUND
        BROOT MUSIC COMPANY   .40
HAYES   1
    RUN AND SKIP -- LITTLE SLEEPY SONG
        CENTURY MUSIC PUBLISHING COMPANY, INC.   4155   .40

HAYES   2
    SKIPPING ALONG
        THEODORE PRESSER COMPANY   .50
HAYES   1
    SLEEPY HEAD
        CENTURY MUSIC PUBLISHING COMPANY, INC.   4157   .40
HAYES   2
    SWING SONG
        BELWIN-MILLS PUBLISHING CORPORATION   .60
HAYES   2 1/2
    VALSE LENTE
        BELWIN-MILLS PUBLISHING CORPORATION   .60
HAYES   2-3
    WALL CLOCK, THE
        CENTURY MUSIC PUBLISHING COMPANY, INC.   4256   .40
HAYMAN, R.
    HER NAME IS SUZANNE
        BELWIN-MILLS PUBLISHING CORPORATION   20348   .85
HAYMAN, R.
    HOLIDAY IN HAITI
        BELWIN-MILLS PUBLISHING CORPORATION   20417   .85
HAYMAN, R.
    MARYELLEN
        BELWIN-MILLS PUBLISHING CORPORATION   20410   .85
HAYMAN, R.
    REGENCY WALTZ
        BELWIN-MILLS PUBLISHING CORPORATION   20470   .85
HAYS   2
    HALF STEP WALTZ
        BOSTON MUSIC COMPANY   .50
HAYS, D.
    HELP COMPOSE FOR PIANO AND AUDIENCE
        SEESAW MUSIC CORPORATION   1.00
HAZELL   1 1/2
    WOOD CUTTER
        BELWIN-MILLS PUBLISHING CORPORATION   .60
HAZELLE   2 1/2
    BAMBA BOOGIE
        BELWIN-MILLS PUBLISHING CORPORATION   .60
HAZELLE   2-3
    HAPPY HOBO
        PRO-ART PUBLICATIONS, INC.   244   .50
HAZELLE   3
    MARCH OF THE PUPPETS
        PRO-ART PUBLICATIONS, INC.   317   .50
HAZELLE   2
    PONY TAIL
        PRO-ART PUBLICATIONS, INC.   297   .50
HAZELLE   2
    WAR CHIEF BOOGIE
        BELWIN-MILLS PUBLISHING CORPORATION   .60
HEADINGTON
    CHEERFUL TUNE, THE
        EDWARD B. MARKS MUSIC CORPORATION   00.60
HEAPS, S.   2
    BROWNIE'S COURTSHIP
        CENTURY MUSIC PUBLISHING COMPANY, INC.   3687   .40
HEAPS, S.   3
    FRIENDSHIP
        CENTURY MUSIC PUBLISHING COMPANY, INC.   3374   .40
HEAPS, S.   1
    FROM MY GARDEN
        CENTURY MUSIC PUBLISHING COMPANY, INC.   3990   .40
HEAPS, S.   2
    PRANCING CLOWN
        CENTURY MUSIC PUBLISHING COMPANY, INC.   3377   .40
HEARN, E. F.   2
    RAINY DAY
        BELWIN-MILLS PUBLISHING CORPORATION   .60
HEDGE, E.   E-M
    REMEMBRANCES
        COMPOSERS PRESS, INC.   1.00
HEDGES
    MASQUERADE
        UNIVERSAL EDITION   UE 12933   1.20
HEDGES
    PLAYGROUND
        UNIVERSAL EDITION   UE 12319   1.25
HEDGES
    SCHERZETTO
        FRANCO COLOMBO PUBLICATIONS   LD537   .60
HEFTI, N.
    BATMAN THEME
        THE BIG THREE MUSIC CORPORATION   00.95
HEGEDUS, A.   M
    FLOWERS I HAVE SEEN
        OXFORD UNIVERSITY PRESS   93.805   1.50
HEIDEN
    SONATA NO. 02 -- 1952
        ASSOCIATED MUSIC PUBLISHERS, INC.   AMP   2.00
HEIDER   D
    INVENTIO THREE FOR HARPSICHORD
        C. F. PETERS CORPORATION   4848   2.50
HEIM, J.   SCHAUM, J.   PREP
    PENGUINS AT PLAY
        SCHAUM PUBLICATIONS, INC.   .50
HEIMLER
    TRUMPET MARCH
        FRANCO COLOMBO PUBLICATIONS   LD450   .60
HEINDOT   4
    IN THE GARDEN OF LOVE
        VOLKWEIN BROS.   .50
HEINS
    BLACK-FOREST CLOCK, THE--SALON POLKA, OP. 224
        G. SCHIRMER, INC.   .40
HEINS, C.   4
    AM WEIHNACHTSABEND, OP. 43
        CENTURY MUSIC PUBLISHING COMPANY, INC.   1348   .60
HEINS, C.   4
    BELL TONES, OP. 81
        CENTURY MUSIC PUBLISHING COMPANY, INC.   1812   .40
HEINS, C.   4
    CARILLON
        THEODORE PRESSER COMPANY   .50
HEINS, C.   3
    CASCADE, THE, OP. 233
        CENTURY MUSIC PUBLISHING COMPANY, INC.   2018   .40
HEINS, C.   4
    CHRISTMAS EVE
        THEODORE PRESSER COMPANY   .60
HEINS, C.   3
    CHRISTMAS EVE, OP. 43
        BELWIN-MILLS PUBLISHING CORPORATION   169   .60
HEINS, C.   4
    CHRISTMAS EVE, OP. 43
        CENTURY MUSIC PUBLISHING COMPANY, INC.   1348   .40

HEINS, C.   3
    COUNTRY DANCE
        CENTURY MUSIC PUBLISHING COMPANY, INC.   3424   .40
HEINS, C.   2
    DANCE OF BEARS --BAERTANZ--
        CENTURY MUSIC PUBLISHING COMPANY, INC.   1715   .40
HEINS, C.   4
    DANCING GIRL, THE
        THEODORE PRESSER COMPANY   .50
HEINS, C.   SWEET VIOLET   4
    EDELVEILCHEN
        CENTURY MUSIC PUBLISHING COMPANY, INC.   2212   .40
HEINS, C.   3
    ELFIN DANCE
        CENTURY MUSIC PUBLISHING COMPANY, INC.   1108   .40
HEINS, C.   3
    EVENING CHIMES, OP. 201
        CENTURY MUSIC PUBLISHING COMPANY, INC.   1862   .40
HEINS, C.   3
    GITANA, OP. 156
        CENTURY MUSIC PUBLISHING COMPANY, INC.   2331   .40
HEINS, C.   2
    GOLDFISH, OP. 158
        CENTURY MUSIC PUBLISHING COMPANY, INC.   1687   .40
HEINS, C.   3
    HERDSMAN'S COTTAGE, THE
        CENTURY MUSIC PUBLISHING COMPANY, INC.   1499   .40
HEINS, C.   2
    IN A GONDOLA
        CENTURY MUSIC PUBLISHING COMPANY, INC.   1861   .40
HEINS, C.   4
    KISS YOUR HAND, MAZURKA, OP. 127
        CENTURY MUSIC PUBLISHING COMPANY, INC.   1498   .40
HEINS, C.   3
    LA CASCADE, OP. 223
        CENTURY MUSIC PUBLISHING COMPANY, INC.   2018   .40
HEINS, C.   4
    LES SYLPHIDES
        CENTURY MUSIC PUBLISHING COMPANY, INC.   1194   .40
HEINS, C.   3
    MUSIC
        WILLIS MUSIC COMPANY   .35
HEINS, C.   3
    MUSIC BOX, THE
        CENTURY MUSIC PUBLISHING COMPANY, INC.   2398   .40
HEINS, C.
    MUSIC-BOX, THE
        G. SCHIRMER, INC.   .30
HEINS, C.   3-4
    PHILOPENA MAZURKA
        VOLKWEIN BROS.   .50
HEINS, C.   3
    REAPER'S PARTING KISS
        CENTURY MUSIC PUBLISHING COMPANY, INC.   1349   .40
HEINS, C.   3
    ROSE FAY, OP. 185
        CENTURY MUSIC PUBLISHING COMPANY, INC.   1030   .40
HEINS, C.
    ROSE-FAY, THE--MAZURKA-CAPRICE, OP. 185
        G. SCHIRMER, INC.   .40
HEINS, C.   ROLFE, W.   2
    SENNERS TRAUM, EASY
        CENTURY MUSIC PUBLISHING COMPANY, INC.   3370   .40
HEINS, C.   3
    SENNERS TRAUM, OP. 171
        CENTURY MUSIC PUBLISHING COMPANY, INC.   1112   .40
HEINS, C.
    SHEPHERD'S DREAM, OP. 171
        G. SCHIRMER, INC.   .35
HEINS, C.   3
    SHEPHERD'S DREAM, OP.171
        CENTURY MUSIC PUBLISHING COMPANY, INC.   1112   .40
HEINS, C.   4
    SILVER NYMPH
        BELWIN-MILLS PUBLISHING CORPORATION   173   .60
HEINS, C.   4
    SILVER NYMPH, THE
        CENTURY MUSIC PUBLISHING COMPANY, INC.   1333   .40
HEINS, C.
    SILVER NYMPH, THE--MAZURKA BRILLANTE, OP. 164
        G. SCHIRMER, INC.   .40
HEINS, C.   4
    SWEET VIOLET
        CENTURY MUSIC PUBLISHING COMPANY, INC.   2212   .40
HEINS, C.   4
    SYLPHIDES, LES, CAPRICE
        CENTURY MUSIC PUBLISHING COMPANY, INC.   1194   .40
HEINS, C.   4
    THROWING KISSES
        CENTURY MUSIC PUBLISHING COMPANY, INC.   1498   .40
HEINS, C.   3
    WATERFALL, THE --LA CASCADE--
        CENTURY MUSIC PUBLISHING COMPANY, INC.   2018   .40
HEINS, P.   3
    POET'S REVERIE
        CENTURY MUSIC PUBLISHING COMPANY, INC.   2110   .40
HEINS, P.
    VILLAGE BLACKSMITH, THE
        CENTURY MUSIC PUBLISHING COMPANY, INC.   2109   .40
HEISER-DAILY   STEINER   1
    DREAMING
        BELWIN-MILLS PUBLISHING CORPORATION   .60
HEISS
    CHACONNE
        ASSOCIATED MUSIC PUBLISHERS, INC.   B/H   1.00
HELFER, W.
    ELEGIAC SONATA
        UNIVERSAL EDITION   UE 10291 1.70
HELLARD, R. A.   2 1/2
    LITTLE ADMIRAL
        THEODORE PRESSER COMPANY   .50
HELLARD, R. A.   3 1/2
    TIDBITS
        THEODORE PRESSER COMPANY   .60
HELLER   2
    POLACCA
        WILLIS MUSIC COMPANY   .40
HELLER, A.
    PRELUDE -- ''HAPPY BIRTHDAY''
        ASSOCIATED MUSIC PUBLISHERS, INC.   AMP   .60
HELLER, E.   1
    CROCODILE, THE
        CENTURY MUSIC PUBLISHING COMPANY, INC.   4132   .40
HELLER, E.   1
    LIGHTHOUSE, THE
        CENTURY MUSIC PUBLISHING COMPANY, INC.   4239   .40

HELLER, E.   1
    LITTLE BROWN THRUSH, THE
        CENTURY MUSIC PUBLISHING COMPANY, INC.   4260   .40
HELLER, E.   1
    RAIN ON A RICE PADDY
        CENTURY MUSIC PUBLISHING COMPANY, INC.   4134   .40
HELLER, E.   2
    ROLLER COASTER RIDE
        CENTURY MUSIC PUBLISHING COMPANY, INC.   4122   .40
HELLER, E.   1
    SLEEPY CUCKOO
        CENTURY MUSIC PUBLISHING COMPANY, INC.   4133   .40
HELLER, E.   1
    WINDOW WASHER, THE
        CENTURY MUSIC PUBLISHING COMPANY, INC.   4208   .40
HELLER, P.   1 1/2
    BUTTERFLY CHASE
        WILLIS MUSIC COMPANY   .40
HELLER, S.
    AVALANCHE
        BOSTON MUSIC COMPANY   .50
HELLER, S.
    AVALANCHE IN A MINOR, OP. 45 NO. 2
        G. SCHIRMER, INC.   .40
HELLER, S.
    AVALANCHE, L', OP. 45 NO. 2
        CARL FISCHER, INC.   S 130   .50
HELLER, S.   3
    AVALANCHE, OP. 45 NO. 2
        CENTURY MUSIC PUBLISHING COMPANY, INC.   746   .40
HELLER, S.   M
    AVALANCHE, OP. 45, NO. 2
        C. F. PETERS CORPORATION   H236   .50
HELLER, S.   MONTANI
    BROOKLET, THE, OP. 81, NO. 3
        FRANCO COLOMBO PUBLICATIONS   128954   .60
HELLER, S.   E-M
    CONTEMPLATION, OP. 47, NO. 23
        C. F. PETERS CORPORATION   H233   .60
HELLER, S.   3
    CURIOUS STORY
        CENTURY MUSIC PUBLISHING COMPANY, INC.   1336   .40
HELLER, S.   2
    CURIOUS STORY
        WILLIS MUSIC COMPANY   .35
HELLER, S.   2
    CURIOUS STORY
        WILLIS MUSIC COMPANY   .35
HELLER, S.
    CURIOUS STORY IN F MAJOR, OP. 138 NO. 9
        G. SCHIRMER, INC.   .30
HELLER, S.
    CURIOUS STORY, OP. 138 NO. 9
        CARL FISCHER, INC.   S 332   .50
HELLER, S.
    ETUDES, OP. 125 NO. 1 AND 21
        BELWIN-MILLS PUBLISHING CORPORATION   .60
HELLER, S.
    IMPATIENCE, OP. 45 NO. 18
        G. SCHIRMER, INC.   .30
HELLER, S.
    MESSAGE--FROM ''FLOWER-FRUIT-AND-THORN-PIECES''
        G. SCHIRMER, INC.   .35
HELLER, S.   3
    PETITE TARANTELLE
        CENTURY MUSIC PUBLISHING COMPANY, INC.   2259   .40
HELLER, S.
    PETITE TARANTELLE IN E MINOR, OP. 46 NO. 7
        G. SCHIRMER, INC.   .40
HELLER, S.   4
    POSTLUDE - WARRIOR'S SONG
        CENTURY MUSIC PUBLISHING COMPANY, INC.   2260   .40
HELLER, S.
    SAILOR'S SONG, OP. 45 NO. 14
        G. SCHIRMER, INC.   .30
HELLER, S.
    SONATINA NO. 01
        FRANCO COLOMBO PUBLICATIONS   ER740   1.25
HELLER, S.   MAYER *
    TARANTELLA IN A FLAT, OP. 85 NO. 2
        ASSOCIATED MUSIC PUBLISHERS, INC.   B/H   .65
HELLER, S.
    TARANTELLA, OP. 85 NO. 2
        FREDERICK HARRIS MUSIC COMPANY   .60
HELLER, S.   4
    TARANTELLE, OP. 85
        CENTURY MUSIC PUBLISHING COMPANY, INC.   440   .40
HELLER, S.   4
    TARANTELLE, OP. 85 NO. 2
        BELWIN-MILLS PUBLISHING CORPORATION   179   .60
HELLER, S.
    TARENTELLE IN A FLAT MAJOR, OP. 85 NO. 2
        G. SCHIRMER, INC.   .50
HELLER, S.   SCHAUM, J.   3
    WARRIOR'S SONG
        BELWIN-MILLS PUBLISHING CORPORATION   .50
HELLER, S.
    WARRIOR'S SONG, OP. 45 NO. 15
        BELWIN-MILLS PUBLISHING CORPORATION   28038   .60
HELLER, S.   4
    WARRIOR'S SONG, OP. 45 NO. 15
        CARL FISCHER, INC.   S 1774   .50
HELLER, S.   4
    WARRIOR'S SONG, OP. 45 NO. 15
        CENTURY MUSIC PUBLISHING COMPANY, INC.   2260   .40
HELLER, S.   DEIS
    WARRIOR'S SONG, OP. 45 NO. 15
        G. SCHIRMER, INC.   .40
HELPS   M-D
    PORTRAIT
        C. F. PETERS CORPORATION   6997   1.25
HELPS   D
    RECOLLECTIONS
        C. F. PETERS CORPORATION   66167   1.25
HELTMAN   2
    BETTY JANE WALTZ
        VOLKWEIN BROS.   .25
HELTMAN   5
    HER KISS VALSE
        VOLKWEIN BROS.   .25
HELTMAN   2
    MARY JANE WALTZ
        VOLKWEIN BROS.   .25
HELTMAN   2
    MERRY CHRISTMAS MARCH
        VOLKWEIN BROS.   00.25

HELYER, M.   3
  CONTRASTS
    NOVELLO AND COMPANY, LTD.   10.0136.01 1.25
HELYER, M.   PRELIM.
  DOWN A COUNTRY LANE
    NOVELLO AND COMPANY, LTD.   10.0066.07 1.25
HELYER, M.   1
  GAY PICTURES
    NOVELLO AND COMPANY, LTD.   10.0067.05 1.25
HELYER, M.   PRELIM-1
  OVER THE HILLS
    NOVELLO AND COMPANY, LTD.   10.0068.03 1.25
HELYER, M.   2
  SHIP AHOY
    NOVELLO AND COMPANY, LTD.   10.0069.01 1.25
HEMMER, E.   INTER.
  AMERICAN WALTZ FOR PIANO SOLO
    AMERICAN MUSIC EDITION   .50
HENDERSON   WALTER
  BIRTH OF THE BLUES, THE
    WARNER BROTHERS PUBLISHERS   1.00
HENDERSON   MACLACHLAN   FIRST YEAR
  BIRTH OF THE BLUES, THE
    WARNER BROTHERS PUBLISHERS   .75
HENDERSON   1-2
  CAROUSEL
    PRO-ART PUBLICATIONS, INC.   373   .50
HENDERSON   2
  CIRCUS WALTZ
    PRO-ART PUBLICATIONS, INC.   208   .50
HENDERSON
  JANIE IS HER NAME
    BELWIN-MILLS PUBLISHING CORPORATION 20349   .95
HENDERSON   1
  SCHOOLDAY SUITE
    PRO-ART PUBLICATIONS, INC.   278   .50
HENDRICKS *
  DESAFINADO
    TRO SONGWAYS SERVICE, INC.   2019
HENKEMANS   D
  SONATA --1958--
    C. F. PETERS CORPORATION   D176   2.50
HENKLE, M.
  MY MUSIC DIARY
    BOOSEY AND HAWKES, INC.   1.25
HENRY, C.   6, 7
  JOUEUSES D'OSSELETS
    ALPHONSE LEDUC
HENRY, C.   6, 7
  SUITE PERSANE
    ALPHONSE LEDUC
HENSEL, R.   1
  LITTLE DANCE, A
    WILLIS MUSIC COMPANY   .40
HENSEL, R.   1
  LITTLE DANCE, A
    WILLIS MUSIC COMPANY   .40
HENSEL, R.
  SONATA FOR PIANO NO. 01
    COMPOSERS AUTOGRAPH PUBLICATIONS   3.96
HENSELT, A.   4-5
  CHANSON DE PRINTEMPS
    CENTURY MUSIC PUBLISHING COMPANY, INC. 2441 .40
HENSELT, A.   5-6
  ETUDE -- IF I WERE A BIRD
    CENTURY MUSIC PUBLISHING COMPANY, INC. 252   .40
HENSELT, A.   6
  IF I WERE A BIRD
    CENTURY MUSIC PUBLISHING COMPANY, INC. 252   .40
HENSELT, A.
  PETITE WALTZ
    MUSICAL SCOPE PUBLISHERS   01.25
HENSELT, A.
  PREAMBULES DANS TOUS LES TONS
    MUSICA OBSCURA   2.00
HENSELT, A.   4-5
  SPRING SONG, OP. 15
    CENTURY MUSIC PUBLISHING COMPANY, INC. 2441 .40
HENSELT, A.   JONAS
  WERE I A BIRD, OP. 2 NO. 6
    G. SCHIRMER, INC.   .40
HENZE, H.   5
  LUCY ESCOTT VARIATIONS FOR HARPSICHORD, 1963 - KLAVIERFASSUNG
    SCHOTT   5453   3.50
HENZE, H.   6
  SONATA
    SCHOTT   5084   4.50
HENZE, H.   5
  VARIATIONEN, OP. 13
    SCHOTT   4046   2.50
HERBERT   LEVINE
  AH, SWEET MYSTERY OF LIFE
    WARNER BROTHERS PUBLISHERS   1.00
HERBERT   WEYBRIGHT   3
  AL FRESCO
    BELWIN-MILLS PUBLISHING CORPORATION   .50
HERBERT   WEYBRIGHT   3
  AL FRESCO
    BELWIN-MILLS PUBLISHING CORPORATION   .60
HERBERT   SCHAUM, J.   3
  BADINAGE
    BELWIN-MILLS PUBLISHING CORPORATION   .50
HERBERT
  DAGGER DANCE--FROM ''NATOMA''
    G. SCHIRMER, INC.   .50
HERBERT   BURNAM   3
  GYPSY LOVE SONG
    WILLIS MUSIC COMPANY   .40
HERBERT   MENDEL, S.   1 1-2
  GYPSY LOVE SONG
    WILLIS MUSIC COMPANY   .40
HERBERT   SCHAUM, J.   4
  GYPSY SWEETHEART
    BELWIN-MILLS PUBLISHING CORPORATION   .50
HERBERT   STEINER   1 1/2
  IN OLD NEW YORK, FROM 'THE RED MILL'
    BELWIN-MILLS PUBLISHING CORPORATION   .60
HERBERT   STEINER   1
  IN THE LAND OF THE EMIR
    BELWIN-MILLS PUBLISHING CORPORATION   .60
HERBERT
  INDIAN SUMMER
    WARNER BROTHERS PUBLISHERS   1.00
HERBERT   SCHAUM, J.   4
  KISS ME AGAIN
    SCHAUM PUBLICATIONS, INC.   .60

HERBERT
  MARCH OF THE TOYS
    ASHLEY DEALERS SERVICE, INC.   ES   .95
HERBERT   3
  MARCH OF THE TOYS
    CENTURY MUSIC PUBLISHING COMPANY, INC. 4415 .40
HERBERT   SCHAUM, J.   4
  MARCH OF THE TOYS
    SCHAUM PUBLICATIONS, INC.   .60
HERBERT
  MARCH OF THE TOYS
    WARNER BROTHERS PUBLISHERS   1.00
HERBERT   RICHTER
  MARCH OF THE TOYS
    WARNER BROTHERS PUBLISHERS   .75
HERBERT   BURNAM   2 1/2
  MARCH OF THE TOYS
    WILLIS MUSIC COMPANY   .35
HERBERT   BURNAM   2 1/2
  MARCH OF THE TOYS
    WILLIS MUSIC COMPANY   .35
HERBERT
  MARCH OF THE TOYS -- SIMP.
    ASHLEY DEALERS SERVICE, INC.   ES   .95
HERBERT   ECKSTEIN
  MARCH OF THE TOYS --FROM BABES IN TOYLAND--
    CARL FISCHER, INC.   P 2992   .50
HERBERT   GAMSE   1
  MARCH OF THE TOYS, SIMPLIFIED
    CENTURY MUSIC PUBLISHING COMPANY, INC. 4416 .40
HERBERT   SCHAUM, J.   2 1/2
  PAN AMERICANA
    BELWIN-MILLS PUBLISHING CORPORATION   .50
HERBERT   SCHAUM, J.   5
  ROMANY LIFE
    BELWIN-MILLS PUBLISHING CORPORATION   .50
HERBERT   STEINER   3
  SWEETHEARTS--WALTZ
    G. SCHIRMER, INC.   .60
HERBERT   STEINER   3
  TOYLAND
    BELWIN-MILLS PUBLISHING CORPORATION   .60
HERBERT   ZEPP   2
  TOYLAND
    PRO-ART PUBLICATIONS, INC.   228   .50
HERBERT   SCHAUM, J.   4
  TOYLAND
    SCHAUM PUBLICATIONS, INC.   .60
HERBERT   RICHTER
  TOYLAND
    WARNER BROTHERS PUBLISHERS   .75
HERBERT   STEINER   2 1/2
  WIZARD OF THE NILE, THE
    BELWIN-MILLS PUBLISHING CORPORATION   .60
HERNANDEZ NONCADA, E.
  COSTENA
    EDICIONES MEXICANAS DE MUSICA, A. C.   01.30
HEROLD   LANCHBERY
  CLOG DANCE FROM LA FILLE MAL GARDEE
    OXFORD UNIVERSITY PRESS   32.141   1.50
HEROLD   3
  OVERTURE, ZAMPA, EASY
    CENTURY MUSIC PUBLISHING COMPANY, INC. 2121 .40
HEROLD
  ZAMPA OVERTURE
    FRANCO COLOMBO PUBLICATIONS   28625   1.00
HERRARTE, M.
  THREE DANCES
    PAN AMERICAN UNION   00.90
HERRMANN, H.
  CHERUBINISCHE SONATA
    FRANCO COLOMBO PUBLICATIONS   SIK.396   2.00
HERTEL
  SONATA IN D MINOR FOR HARPSICHORD OR PIANO
    BARENREITER VERLAG   HM 49   3.00
HERTEL   ERDMANN   3
  SONATE IN D MINOR FOR CEMBALO ODER KLAVIER
    BARENREITER VERLAG   HM 49   3.00
HERTRICH   4
  GREETINGS OF SPRING, OP. 16
    CENTURY MUSIC PUBLISHING COMPANY, INC. 2001 .40
HERTRICH   4
  SALUT DU PRINTEMPS, OP. 16
    CENTURY MUSIC PUBLISHING COMPANY, INC. 2001 .40
HERZ, H.
  GRANDE VALSE BRILLANTE, OP. 37
    FRANCO COLOMBO PUBLICATIONS   SAL   2.00
HERZ, H.
  PETIT DEMON, LE
    FRANCO COLOMBO PUBLICATIONS   67977   .60
HERZ, H.
  VARIATIONS BRILLIANTES SUR ' THE LAST ROSE OF SUMMER ' OP. 159
    MUSICA OBSCURA   2.00
HERZ, H.
  VARIATIONS ON LA CENERENTOLA
    MUSICAL SCOPE PUBLISHERS   01.25
HERZ, H.
  VARIATIONS ON NON PIU MESTA FROM ROSSINI'S LA CENERENTOLA FOR
  PIANO
    MUSIC TREASURE PUBLICATIONS   5.00
HERZER, R.   3
  HOCH HEIDECKSBURG, MARSCH - OP. 10
    SCHOTT   1.25
HERZER, R.   2
  HOCH HEIDECKSBURG, MARSCH - OP. 10, ERLEICHTERT
    SCHOTT   1.25
HESSENBERG, K.   3-4
  SONATINE, OP. 17
    BARENREITER VERLAG   SM 1038
HEUBERGER *
  MIDNIGHT BELLS
    CARL FISCHER, INC.   F 2019   1.00
HEYKENS
  CELEBRE SERENADE, OP. 21
    FRANCO COLOMBO PUBLICATIONS   SAL   1.50
HEYNE
  PETITE GAVOTTE, LA
    MCA MUSIC   1.00
HEYNE
  PETITE WALTZ, THE
    MCA MUSIC   1.00
HIBBS, C.   2 1/2
  BOOGIE-BOO-YOU
    BELWIN-MILLS PUBLISHING CORPORATION   .60
HIBBS, C.   1 1/2
  CATCH ME IF YOU CAN
    BELWIN-MILLS PUBLISHING CORPORATION   .60

HIBBS, C.   2
  CATCHING THE SCHOOL BUS
    BELWIN-MILLS PUBLISHING CORPORATION   .60
HIBBS, C.   2
  CUBAN NIGHTS
    VOLKWEIN BROS.   .35
HIBBS, C.   1
  DRIFTING ALONG
    THEODORE PRESSER COMPANY   .50
HIBBS, C.   1 1/2
  FOLLOW THE LEADER
    THEODORE PRESSER COMPANY   .50
HIBBS, C.   3
  FROG AND THE BUTTERFLY, THE
    BELWIN-MILLS PUBLISHING CORPORATION   25050   .60
HIBBS, C.   2
  GRANDEUR OF THE SEA
    VOLKWEIN BROS.   .30
HIBBS, C.   2
  HAPPY GO LUCKY
    VOLKWEIN BROS.   .35
HIBBS, C.   1 1/2
  HAPPY HOLIDAY
    BELWIN-MILLS PUBLISHING CORPORATION   .60
HIBBS, C.   2
  HELTER SKELTER
    VOLKWEIN BROS.   .30
HIBBS, C.   2
  IN THE FOREST
    VOLKWEIN BROS.   .30
HIBBS, C.   2
  LET'S WALTZ
    BELWIN-MILLS PUBLISHING CORPORATION   .60
HIBBS, C.   2
  MARCH OF THE LILLIPUTIANS
    THEODORE PRESSER COMPANY   .50
HIBBS, C.   2
  MARIONETTE BALLET
    VOLKWEIN BROS.   .30
HIBBS, C.   1 1/2
  MAY I HAVE THIS DANCE
    BELWIN-MILLS PUBLISHING CORPORATION   .60
HIBBS, C.   3
  MIST
    BELWIN-MILLS PUBLISHING CORPORATION   .60
HIBBS, C.   2
  OLD FRENCH DANCE - GAVOTTE
    VOLKWEIN BROS.   .30
HIBBS, C.   2
  OLD FRENCH DANCE AND GOVOTTE
    VOLKWEIN BROS.   .30
HIBBS, C.   2
  ONCE UPON A TIME
    VOLKWEIN BROS.   .30
HIBBS, C.   2
  POTTER'S WHEEL
    VOLKWEIN BROS.   .35
HIBBS, C.   1
  SAILING ALONG THE SHORE
    BELWIN-MILLS PUBLISHING CORPORATION   .60
HIBBS, C.   1 1/2
  TOPSY-TURVY
    BELWIN-MILLS PUBLISHING CORPORATION   .60
HIBBS, C.   2
  WALTZ MODERNE
    VOLKWEIN BROS.   00.40
HIBBS, C.   2
  WESTERN NOCTURNE
    VOLKWEIN BROS.   00.35
HIBBS, C.   2
  WHITE MICE
    VOLKWEIN BROS.   00.40
HIER, E.   M-D
  ASOLO BELLS
    COMPOSERS PRESS, INC.   1.50
HIER, E.   M
  BADINAGE
    COMPOSERS PRESS, INC.   1.50
HIER, E.
  DAY IN THE PETERBOROUGH WOODS, A--BOBOLINK
    G. SCHIRMER, INC.   .50
HIER, E.
  DAY IN THE PETERBOROUGH WOODS, A--SUNSET AT HILLCREST
    G. SCHIRMER, INC.   .60
HIER, E.
  DAY IN THE PETERBOROUGH WOODS, A--WHIPPOORWILL, THE
    G. SCHIRMER, INC.   .60
HIER, E.
  DAY IN THE PETERBOROUGH WOODS, A--WOOD-THRUSH, THE
    G. SCHIRMER, INC.   .50
HIER, E.   M
  PRELUDE
    COMPOSERS PRESS, INC.   1.00
HIER, E.   2
  SKI PARTY
    CENTURY MUSIC PUBLISHING COMPANY, INC.   4280   .40
HIER, E.   2
  TALLY HO
    CENTURY MUSIC PUBLISHING COMPANY, INC.   4281   .40
HIER, E.   1
  WALTZ TIME
    CENTURY MUSIC PUBLISHING COMPANY, INC.   4282   .40
HIGGINS   2
  ONCE AND THEN AGAIN
    BOSTON MUSIC COMPANY   .50
HIGGINS   WILLIAMS, J.   2
  STREET ACROBATS, THE
    BOSTON MUSIC COMPANY   .50
HILGER
  ONE FINGER PIANO
    EDWARD B. MARKS MUSIC CORPORATION   00.60
HILL
  CHRISTMAS BELLS WALTZ
    VOLKWEIN BROS.   .35
HILL   3
  EVENTIDE
    BOSTON MUSIC COMPANY   .50
HILL   3
  EVERGLADES
    BOSTON MUSIC COMPANY   .50
HILL   HAMBRO
  HAPPY BIRTHDAY, DEAR LUDWIG -- VARIATIONS IN THE STYLE OF
  BEETHOVEN ON ''HAPPY BIRTHDAY TO YOU'' --
    SUMMY-BIRCHARD COMPANY   1.00
HILL--ARR.   HILL
  HAPPY BIRTHDAY TO YOU --WITH WORDS--
    SUMMY-BIRCHARD COMPANY   .50

HILL, B.   SCHAUM, J.   2 1/2
  GLORY OF LOVE
    SCHAUM PUBLICATIONS, INC.   .75
HILL, M.   1
  PETITE WALTZ
    CENTURY MUSIC PUBLISHING COMPANY, INC.   4300   .40
HILL, M.   1
  POW WOW
    CENTURY MUSIC PUBLISHING COMPANY, INC.   4301   .40
HILLER   D
  SCHERZO FOR PIANO
    THEODORE PRESSER COMPANY   2.50
HILLER
  TWELVE-TONE VARIATIONS FOR PIANO
    THEODORE PRESSER COMPANY   5.00
HILLER   GLOVER, D.
  UNITED WE STAND
    BELWIN-MILLS PUBLISHING CORPORATION   .60
HILSHER, F.   4
  CUNNING CUPID
    VOLKWEIN BROS.   .50
HILSHER, F.   3
  KISS
    VOLKWEIN BROS.   .50
HILSHER, F.   3
  OUR SQUADRON MARCH
    VOLKWEIN BROS.   .35
HINDEMITH   5
  DREI KLAVIER-SONATEN, 1936, NO. 01 IN A
    SCHOTT   2518   3.00
HINDEMITH   4
  DREI KLAVIER-SONATEN, 1936, NO. 02 IN G
    SCHOTT   2519   3.00
HINDEMITH   4
  DREI KLAVIER-SONATEN, 1936, NO. 03 IN B FLAT
    SCHOTT   2521   3.00
HINDEMITH
  KONZERT FUR KLAVIER UND ORCHESTER, 1945 -- KLAVIERAUSZUG
    SCHOTT   3838   6.00
HINDEMITH   4-5
  SUITE '1922', OP. 26
    SCHOTT   1732   2.75
HINDEMITH   3
  TUTTIFANTCHEN - TANZ DER HOLZPUPPEN
    SCHOTT   1734   1.50
HINES, C.   3
  THROWING KISSES
    VOLKWEIN BROS.   00.25
HINSON, M.   3
  FIDDLER ON THE GREEN
    BELWIN-MILLS PUBLISHING CORPORATION   .60
HIRSCHBERG, D.   1B
  LITTLE CHINESE FISHERMAN
    MUSICORD PUBLICATIONS, INC.   .45
HIRSCHBERG, D.   1B
  MOONLIGHT MELODY
    MUSICORD PUBLICATIONS, INC.   .45
HIRSCHBERG, D.   1B
  SCALES FOR JUNIORS - PART 1 MAJOR
    MUSICORD PUBLICATIONS, INC.   .45
HIRSCHBERG, D.   1B
  SCALES FOR JUNIORS - PART 2 MINOR
    MUSICORD PUBLICATIONS, INC.   .45
HIRSCHBERG, D.   1B
  SUNBEAMS AND ROBINS
    MUSICORD PUBLICATIONS, INC.   .45
HITZ, F.
  A TRAVERS BOIS -- REVERIE -- OP. 151
    FRANCO COLOMBO PUBLICATIONS   SAL   1.75
HITZ, F.
  DANS LE BOIS
    FRANCO COLOMBO PUBLICATIONS   SAL   1.75
HITZ, F.   5
  GAIS BATELIERS, CHANSON
    ALPHONSE LEDUC
HITZ, F.
  LA SERENATA--TRANSCRIPTION AFTER MELODY BY BRAGA
    G. SCHIRMER, INC.   .40
HITZEL--ED   HITZEL   2
  LAST ROSE OF SUMMER
    CENTURY MUSIC PUBLISHING COMPANY, INC.   2045   .40
HLAVAC, M.
  STENOGRAMS
    GENERAL MUSIC PUBLISHING COMPANY, INC.   5.00
HOBSON, M.
  WATERFALL, THE--ARPEGGIO WALTZ
    G. SCHIRMER, INC.   .50
HODDINOTT, A.
  SECOND NOCTURNE, OP. 16 NO. 1
    NOVELLO AND COMPANY, LTD.   10.0070.05   .90
HODDINOTT, A.
  SONATA NO. 01
    OXFORD UNIVERSITY PRESS   32.138   3.25
HODDINOTT, A.
  SONATA NO. 02, OP. 27
    NOVELLO AND COMPANY, LTD.   10.0071.03   1.75
HODDINOTT, A.
  SONATA NO. 03, OP. 40
    NOVELLO AND COMPANY, LTD.   10.0072.01   2.25
HODDINOTT, A.
  SONATA NO. 04
    OXFORD UNIVERSITY PRESS   32.150   3.00
HODDINOTT, A.
  SONATA NO. 05
    OXFORD UNIVERSITY PRESS   32.157   4.60
HODGSON, H.
  POLKA DOTS
    BRODT MUSIC COMPANY   .75
HOELLER   3-4
  SUITE, OP. 2
    BARENREITER VERLAG   SM 1264
HOELZEL   4
  SONG WITHOUT WORDS
    CENTURY MUSIC PUBLISHING COMPANY, INC.   874   .40
HOFER   3
  REDEMPTION POLKA
    CENTURY MUSIC PUBLISHING COMPANY, INC.   2093   .40
HOFER, M.
  TOCCATA -- THE MACHINE
    UNIVERSAL EDITION   UE 11293   1.70
HOFFER, P.   4
  TANZVARIATIONEN
    SCHOTT   2648   3.00
HOFFMAN   5
  LISTEN TO THE MOCKING BIRD
    CENTURY MUSIC PUBLISHING COMPANY, INC.   1237   .40

HOFFMANN, E. T. A. SCHNAPP				
SONATA IN A				
BARENREITER VERLAG			BA 19105	4.00
HOFFMANN, E. T. A. SCHNAPP	4			
SONATA IN A -- 1805 --				
BARENREITER VERLAG			NMA 222	
HOFFMANN, PH. K.	M			
CADENZA TO MOZART CONCERTO K.467				
C. F. PETERS CORPORATION			H1756A	2.00
HOFFMANN, PH. K.	M			
CADENZA TO MOZART CONCERTO K.482				
C. F. PETERS CORPORATION			H1756B	2.00
HOFFMANN, PH. K.	M			
CADENZA TO MOZART CONCERTO K.488				
C. F. PETERS CORPORATION			H1756C	2.00
HOFFMANN, PH. K.	M			
CADENZA TO MOZART CONCERTO K.491				
C. F. PETERS CORPORATION			H1756D	2.00
HOFFMANN, PH. K.	M			
CADENZA TO MOZART CONCERTO K.503				
C. F. PETERS CORPORATION			H1756E	2.00
HOFFMANN, PH. K.	M			
CADENZA TO MOZART CONCERTO K.595				
C. F. PETERS CORPORATION			H1756F	2.00
HOFSTAD, M.	1			
CIRCUS COMES TO TOWN, THE				
WILLIS MUSIC COMPANY				.40
HOFSTAD, M.				
COPY-CAT				
G. SCHIRMER, INC.				.35
HOFSTAD, M.	1			
FLY AWAY KITE				
WILLIS MUSIC COMPANY				.40
HOFSTAD, M.	1			
FLYING SQUIRRELS' PLAYTIME				
THEODORE PRESSER COMPANY				.50
HOFSTAD, M.				
HOOTY THE OWL				
CARL FISCHER, INC.			P 2686	.50
HOFSTAD, M.				
JOLLY LITTLE SAILOR				
CARL FISCHER, INC.			P 2687	.50
HOFSTAD, M.		1		
LITTLE BEAR CUB SEES THE WORLD ON HIS OWN				
THEODORE PRESSER COMPANY				.50
HOFSTAD, M.	1			
LITTLE COWBOY RIDES AGAIN				
THEODORE PRESSER COMPANY				.50
HOFSTAD, M.				
MEET THE MASTERS				
WILLIS MUSIC COMPANY				1.00
HOFSTAD, M.	1			
MOON MUSIC				
WILLIS MUSIC COMPANY				.40
HOFSTAD, M.				
MR. AND MRS. PETER RABBIT				
WILLIS MUSIC COMPANY				.60
HOFSTAD, M.				
MY ENGINE				
G. SCHIRMER, INC.				.40
HOFSTAD, M.	1			
RUN LITTLE INDIAN				
WILLIS MUSIC COMPANY				.40
HOFSTAD, M.	1			
SEA PRINCESS, THE				
THEODORE PRESSER COMPANY				.50
HOFSTAD, M.				
SUNSHINY SHOWER, A				
G. SCHIRMER, INC.				.35
HOFSTAD, M.	1			
WHAT COLOR IS THE TREE TOAD				
THEODORE PRESSER COMPANY				.50
HOIBY, L.				
CAPRICCIO ON FIVE NOTES, OP. 23				
BOOSEY AND HAWKES, INC.				1.00
HOLCMAN, J.	3			
THREE ECHOES				
THEODORE PRESSER COMPANY				.95
HOLLAENDER	3			
CANZONETTA				
VOLKWEIN BROS.				.25
HOLLAENDER	4			
FRUEHLINGSLIED, STUDY				
CENTURY MUSIC PUBLISHING COMPANY, INC.			1400	.40
HOLLANDER				
BIG BASS VIOL				
EDWARD B. MARKS MUSIC CORPORATION				00.60
HOLLANDER	1			
GRANDPAPA PLAYS IN THE MONDAY NIGHT BAND				
PRO-ART PUBLICATIONS, INC.			217	.50
HOLLANDER	1			
HAPPY SKATERS, THE				
PRO-ART PUBLICATIONS, INC.			186	.50
HOLLANDER				
PARADE				
SUMMY-BIRCHARD COMPANY				.50
HOLLANDER	2			
RUFFLES AND LACE				
PRO-ART PUBLICATIONS, INC.			187	.50
HOLLANDER				
SWING				
BOOSEY AND HAWKES, INC.				.40
HOLLANDER	1			
VILLAGE CHOIR, THE				
PRO-ART PUBLICATIONS, INC.			218	.50
HOLLER, K.	2			
SONATA, OP. 58 NO. 01				
SCHOTT			4817	2.00
HOLLER, K.	3			
SONATA, OP. 58 NO. 02				
SCHOTT			4818	2.00
HOLLER, K.	4			
TESSINER KLAVIERBUCH, OP. 57				
SCHOTT			4750	2.50
HOLLIDAY, J.				
CARAVAN, THE				
G. SCHIRMER, INC.				.50
HOLLINS, A. CHAMBERS, H. A.				
SPRING SONG				
NOVELLO AND COMPANY, LTD.			10.0073.10	1.15
HOLLOWAY, J.	3			
HOLIDAY IN SWITZERLAND				
BELWIN-MILLS PUBLISHING CORPORATION				.60
HOLLOWAY, J.	3 1/2			
SHADOW DANCE OF A BALLERINA				
BELWIN-MILLS PUBLISHING CORPORATION				.60

HOLST				
DANCE OF THE DEMON				
ASHLEY DEALERS SERVICE, INC.			ES	.95
HOLST	4			
DIANA				
WILLIS MUSIC COMPANY				.60
HOLST	1			
RIPE APPLES				
BELWIN-MILLS PUBLISHING CORPORATION				.60
HOLST	3 1/2			
SONATINA OP. 48 NO. 3 -- SPRINGTIME				
VOLKWEIN BROS.				.75
HOLST				
TWO PIECES FOR PIANO				
FABER MUSIC, LTD.			F0003	
HOLST SCHAUM, J.	2 1/2			
WHIRLWIND POLKA				
BELWIN-MILLS PUBLISHING CORPORATION				.50
HOLT * KERR, R.N.				
ONE OF THOSE SONGS				
MCA MUSIC				1.00
HOLT, EILSEL	3			
AT THE LAWN FETE				
CENTURY MUSIC PUBLISHING COMPANY, INC.			2560	.40
HOLT, EILSFL	4			
CASTILIAN AFTERNOON				
CENTURY MUSIC PUBLISHING COMPANY, INC.			2639	.40
HOLT, EILSEL	3-4			
DISTANT BELLS AT EVENING				
CENTURY MUSIC PUBLISHING COMPANY, INC.			2562	.40
HOLT, EILSEL	3			
DREAMS OF HAPPY HOURS				
CENTURY MUSIC PUBLISHING COMPANY, INC.			2561	.40
HOLT, EILSEL	3			
FLOWER IN THE CRANNIED WALL				
CENTURY MUSIC PUBLISHING COMPANY, INC.			2637	.40
HOLT, EILSEL	3-4			
IN A SPANISH GARDEN				
CENTURY MUSIC PUBLISHING COMPANY, INC.			2559	.40
HOLT, EILSEL	3			
IN CREOLE COMPANY				
CENTURY MUSIC PUBLISHING COMPANY, INC.			2683	.40
HOLT, EILSEL	3			
IN THE QUEEN'S COMPANY				
CENTURY MUSIC PUBLISHING COMPANY, INC.			2644	.40
HOLT, EILSEL	3			
LADY CAPRICE				
CENTURY MUSIC PUBLISHING COMPANY, INC.			2563	.40
HOLT, EILSEL	3-4			
LADY GRACEFUL				
CENTURY MUSIC PUBLISHING COMPANY, INC.			2566	.40
HOLT, EILSEL	3-4			
MAID OF THE DAWN				
CENTURY MUSIC PUBLISHING COMPANY, INC.			2635	.40
HOLT, EILSEL	3			
MELODIE CHARMANTE				
CENTURY MUSIC PUBLISHING COMPANY, INC.			3232	.40
HOLT, EILSEL	3			
MEMORIES OF SUMMER DAYS				
CENTURY MUSIC PUBLISHING COMPANY, INC.			2565	.40
HOLT, EILSEL	4			
MEMORY CHEST, A				
CENTURY MUSIC PUBLISHING COMPANY, INC.			3232	.40
HOLT, EILSEL	4			
ON THE LEVEE				
CENTURY MUSIC PUBLISHING COMPANY, INC.			3231	.40
HOLT, EILSEL	3			
PENSIVE FLOWERET				
CENTURY MUSIC PUBLISHING COMPANY, INC.			2640	.40
HOLT, EILSEL	3			
POLISH FESTIVAL DAY				
CENTURY MUSIC PUBLISHING COMPANY, INC.			2641	.40
HOLT, EILSEL	3			
TWAS NIGHT IN VENICE				
CENTURY MUSIC PUBLISHING COMPANY, INC.			2567	.40
HOLT, EILSEL	3			
UNDER THE CATHEDRAL TOWER				
CENTURY MUSIC PUBLISHING COMPANY, INC.			2568	.40
HOLT, ERNEST				
DANCING SUNBEAMS				
CENTURY MUSIC PUBLISHING COMPANY, INC.			2185	.40
HOLZMANN, A.				
BLAZE AWAY				
THE BIG THREE MUSIC CORPORATION				00.95
HOLZMANN, R.				
PEQUENA SUITE				
EDITORIAL COOPERATIVA INTER-AMERICANA				01.05
HONEGGER, A.				
AVENTURES DU ROI PAUSOLE, LES -- SUITE --				
FRANCO COLOMBO PUBLICATIONS			SAL	4.25
HONEGGER, A.				
CAHIER ROMAND, LE				
FRANCO COLOMBO PUBLICATIONS			SAL	1.50
HONEGGER, A.				
DEUX ESQUISSES				
ELKAN-VOGEL, INC.			D	1.15
HONEGGER, A.				
HOMMAGE A ALBERT ROUSSEL				
FRANCO COLOMBO PUBLICATIONS			SAL	2.00
HONEGGER, A.				
LE CANTIQUE DES CANTIQUES -- BALLET CHANTE				
HEUGEL ET CIE.				8.90
HONEGGER, A.				
MIRACLE DE NOTRE-DAME -- INCIDENTAL MUSIS TO THE PLAY BY ST.				
GEORGE DE BOUHELIER --				
FRANCO COLOMBO PUBLICATIONS			SAL	20.00
HONEGGER, A.				
NEIGE SUR ROME, LA				
FRANCO COLOMBO PUBLICATIONS			SAL	1.75
HONEGGER, A.	E			
PRELUDE, ARIOSO ET FUGHETTE SUR LE NOM DE BACH				
FRANCO COLOMBO PUBLICATIONS			SAL	2.75
HONEGGER, A.				
SOUVENIR DE CHOPIN				
C. F. PETERS CORPORATION			C50	1.50
HONEGGER, A.				
TOCCATA AND VARIATIONS				
FRANCO COLOMBO PUBLICATIONS			SAL	1.50
HOOK ROWLEY				
FESTIVAL GROUPS FOR PIANO SELECTED BY ARTHUR BENJAMIN, SERIES 1				
-- MENUET				
BOOSEY AND HAWKES, INC.				.60
HOPKINS, H.	1			
SWING SONG, NOVELLETE				
CENTURY MUSIC PUBLISHING COMPANY, INC.			3006	.40

HOPKINS, H.   1
  PAPER SOLDIERS, MARCH
    CENTURY MUSIC PUBLISHING COMPANY, INC.   2977   .40
HOPKINS, H.   1
  PASSING THE CHURCH
    CENTURY MUSIC PUBLISHING COMPANY, INC.   3099   .40
HOPKINS, H.   2
  PETIT TANGO
    CENTURY MUSIC PUBLISHING COMPANY, INC.   3059   .40
HOPKINS, H.   2
  PLAYING SOLDIERS, MARCH
    CENTURY MUSIC PUBLISHING COMPANY, INC.   3113   .40
HOPKINS, H.   2
  ROBIN REDBREAST, WALTZ
    CENTURY MUSIC PUBLISHING COMPANY, INC.   3054   .40
HOPKINS, H.   1
  SANTA CLAUS, XMAS TALE
    CENTURY MUSIC PUBLISHING COMPANY, INC.   3050   .40
HOPKINS, H.   1
  SCHOOL PICTURES, WALTZ
    CENTURY MUSIC PUBLISHING COMPANY, INC.   2740   .40
HOPKINS, H.   2
  SEVEN FROGGIES, GAVOTTE
    CENTURY MUSIC PUBLISHING COMPANY, INC.   3052   .40
HOPKINS, H.   1
  SHOOGY-SHOO, LITTLE TALE
    CENTURY MUSIC PUBLISHING COMPANY, INC.   2975   .40
HOPKINS, H.   1
  SILVER STARS, REVERIE
    CENTURY MUSIC PUBLISHING COMPANY, INC.   3106   .40
HOPKINS, H.   1
  SKIP AND DANCE, WALTZ
    CENTURY MUSIC PUBLISHING COMPANY, INC.   3039   .40
HOPKINS, H.   1
  SKIPPING ROPE, DANCE
    CENTURY MUSIC PUBLISHING COMPANY, INC.   3105   .40
HOPKINS, H.   1
  SONG FOR ANNIE LOU
    CENTURY MUSIC PUBLISHING COMPANY, INC.   3802   .40
HOPKINS, H.   1
  STARRY WAY
    CENTURY MUSIC PUBLISHING COMPANY, INC.   3989   .40
HOPKINS, H.   2
  SUMMER
    CENTURY MUSIC PUBLISHING COMPANY, INC.   3578   .40
HOPKINS, H.   1
  SUMMER DAYS
    CENTURY MUSIC PUBLISHING COMPANY, INC.   3679   .40
HOPKINS, H.   2
  TELL ME, PUSSY
    CENTURY MUSIC PUBLISHING COMPANY, INC.   3060   .40
HOPKINS, H.   1
  TOMMY'S MARCH
    CENTURY MUSIC PUBLISHING COMPANY, INC.   3680   .40
HOPKINS, H.   1
  TWINKLE TOES, DANCE
    CENTURY MUSIC PUBLISHING COMPANY, INC.   2983   .40
HOPKINS, H.   3
  VALSE D'AMOUR
    CENTURY MUSIC PUBLISHING COMPANY, INC.   3415   .40
HOPKINS, H.   1
  WATCHING THE SOLDIERS
    CENTURY MUSIC PUBLISHING COMPANY, INC.   2747   .40
HOPKINS, H.   1
  WIGWAM DANCE
    THEODORE PRESSER COMPANY   .50
HOPKINS, H.   1
  WINDY DAY, A, CAPRICE
    CENTURY MUSIC PUBLISHING COMPANY, INC.   3042   .40
HOPKINS, H.   1
  WYNKUM AND BLYNKUM
    CENTURY MUSIC PUBLISHING COMPANY, INC.   2979   .40
HOPKINS, K.
  HUSTLER, THE -THEME
    THE BIG THREE MUSIC CORPORATION   00.95
HOPSON, E.   2
  COME, LET'S DANCE
    PRO-ART PUBLICATIONS, INC.   135   .50
HOPSON, E.
  DANCING BUTTERCUPS
    G. SCHIRMER, INC.   .50
HOPSON, E.   1
  GLISTENING GLIDER
    THEODORE PRESSER COMPANY   .50
HOPSON, E.
  HUNTING SONG
    G. SCHIRMER, INC.   .40
HOPSON, E.
  LITTLE CHIEF RED FEATHER
    G. SCHIRMER, INC.   .35
HOPSON, E.   EASY
  MARCH OF THE CANDY SOLDIERS
    SHAWNEE PRESS, INC.   HB-5011   .35
HOPSON, E.   2
  MERRY CHASE
    PRO-ART PUBLICATIONS, INC.   259   .50
HOPSON, E.
  PARADE OF THE MIDGETS
    G. SCHIRMER, INC.   .50
HOPSON, E.
  RIDING ON A CAMEL
    G. SCHIRMER, INC.   .35
HOPSON, E.   1-2
  SPEEDING SATELLITE
    PRO-ART PUBLICATIONS, INC.   137   .50
HORNE   2
  ADVENTURE, AN
    PRO-ART PUBLICATIONS, INC.   429   .50
HORNSTEIN
  MINNELIED IN B FLAT
    MUSICA OBSCURA   .75
HOSER *   3
  ES SINGT DER RHEIN
    SCHOTT   2.00
HOSKINS, W.
  NOCTURNELLE
    BELWIN-MILLS PUBLISHING CORPORATION   25241   .60
HOSKINS, W.   3 1/2
  RUSHIN' DANCE
    THEODORE PRESSER COMPANY   .50
HOSSEIN, A.
  PRELUDE ET LEGENDE PERSANE
    EDITIONS MUSICALES TRANSATLANTIQUES   2.00
HOTCHKISS, J.
  WALTZ OF THE TOREADORS, THE
    BELWIN-MILLS PUBLISHING CORPORATION   20459   .85

HOUDRET
  PAVANE
    FRANCO COLOMBO PUBLICATIONS   SAL   2.75
HOUSE, A.   1
  DANCING CRICKET
    ELKAN-VOGEL, INC.   .50
HOUSE, A.
  I AM A HAPPY CLOWN
    BROOT MUSIC COMPANY   .45
HOUSE, A.
  LITTLE BIRD AT MY WINDOW
    BROOT MUSIC COMPANY   .45
HOUSE, A.
  LITTLE POLISH DANCE, A
    BROOT MUSIC COMPANY   .45
HOUSE, A.
  LIVELY RABBIT, THE
    BROOT MUSIC COMPANY   .45
HOUSE, A.
  MARCHING IN THE PARADE
    BROOT MUSIC COMPANY   .45
HOUSE, A.
  PUMPKIN MAN, THE
    BROOT MUSIC COMPANY   .40
HOUSE, A.
  TARANTELLE
    BROOT MUSIC COMPANY   .40
HOUSE, A.
  TWIRLING BATON
    BROOT MUSIC COMPANY   .45
HOVHANESS, A.
  ACHTAMAR
    PEER SOUTHERN ORGANIZATION   01.35
HOVHANESS, A.   M
  ARTINIS
    C. F. PETERS CORPORATION   66408   1.25
HOVHANESS, A.   D
  BARDO SONATA
    C. F. PETERS CORPORATION   6425   1.50
HOVHANESS, A.   M
  BARE NOVEMBER DAY. HARPSICHORD
    C. F. PETERS CORPORATION   66022   1.25
HOVHANESS, A.   M
  DARK RIVER AND DISTANT BELL. HARPSICHORD
    C. F. PETERS CORPORATION   66024   .60
HOVHANESS, A.   D
  DO YOU REMEMBER THE LAST SILENCE
    C. F. PETERS CORPORATION   6293   1.25
HOVHANESS, A.   D
  FANTASY
    C. F. PETERS CORPORATION   6482   1.25
HOVHANESS, A.
  FANTASY ON AN OSSETIN TUNE
    PEER SOUTHERN ORGANIZATION   01.25
HOVHANESS, A.   D
  FAREWELL TO THE MOUNTAINS
    C. F. PETERS CORPORATION   6573B   .60
HOVHANESS, A.
  HYMN TO A CELESTIAL MUSICIAN
    PEER SOUTHERN ORGANIZATION   01.00
HOVHANESS, A.
  JHALA
    PEER SOUTHERN ORGANIZATION   01.50
HOVHANESS, A.   D
  LAKE OF VAN SONATA
    C. F. PETERS CORPORATION   6209   1.50
HOVHANESS, A.   MD
  LOUSNAG KISHER -- MOONLIGHT NIGHT
    THEODORE PRESSER COMPANY   .50
HOVHANESS, A.   M
  MACEDONIAN MOUNTAIN DANCE
    C. F. PETERS CORPORATION   6199   .90
HOVHANESS, A.   D
  MADRAS SONATA
    C. F. PETERS CORPORATION   6210   1.50
HOVHANESS, A.   D
  MAZERT NMAN REHANI -- THY HAIR IS LIKE BASIL LEAF--
    C. F. PETERS CORPORATION   6640A   .90
HOVHANESS, A.   M
  MOUNTAIN DANCE NO. 2
    C. F. PETERS CORPORATION   6278   .60
HOVHANESS, A.   E
  MYSTIC FLUTE
    C. F. PETERS CORPORATION   6470   .60
HOVHANESS, A.
  ORBIT NO. 2
    PEER SOUTHERN ORGANIZATION   01.50
HOVHANESS, A.
  PASTORAL NO. 1
    PEER SOUTHERN ORGANIZATION   01.10
HOVHANESS, A.   D
  POSEIDON SONATA
    C. F. PETERS CORPORATION   6292   1.50
HOVHANESS, A.   D
  SHALIMAR. SUITE
    C. F. PETERS CORPORATION   6214   1.50
HOVHANESS, A.   D
  SONATA RICERCARE
    C. F. PETERS CORPORATION   6585   2.00
HOVHANESS, A.   D
  SONATA, OP. 145
    C. F. PETERS CORPORATION   6290   1.50
HOVHANESS, A.   M
  SONATINA
    C. F. PETERS CORPORATION   6529   .90
HOVHANESS, A.   D
  SUITE
    C. F. PETERS CORPORATION   6554   1.50
HOVHANESS, A.   M
  TOCCATA AND FUGUE NO. 5
    C. F. PETERS CORPORATION   6478   1.50
HOVHANESS, A.   M
  VANADOUR
    C. F. PETERS CORPORATION   6573A   .60
HOVLAND   M
  RONDINO, OP. 29, NO. 2
    C. F. PETERS CORPORATION   LY370   .60
HOVLAND   M
  SCHERZO, OP. 29, NO. 1
    C. F. PETERS CORPORATION   LY369   .60
HOWARD
  FLY ME TO THE MOON --BOSSA NOVA--
    TRO SONGWAYS SERVICE, INC.   2024
HOWARD, J.   SCHAUM, J.   2
  GOODBY MY LADY LOVE
    SCHAUM PUBLICATIONS, INC.   .50

HOWARD, M. B.   4
    FRIENDSHIP MARCH
        VOLKWEIN BROS.   .35
HOWE   STEFFE *
    BATTLE HYMN OF THE REPUBLIC
        CARL FISCHER, INC.   P 2973   .50
HOWE   STEFFE *   4
    BATTLE HYMN OF THE REPUBLIC
        PRO-ART PUBLICATIONS, INC.   579   .50
HOWE   STEFFE *   1
    BATTLE HYMN OF THE REPUBLIC
        WILLIS MUSIC COMPANY   .30
HOWE   STEFFE *   2
    BATTLE HYMN OF THE REPUBLIC, THE
        WILLIS MUSIC COMPANY   .35
HOWE, J. W.   2
    GLORY, GLORY HALLELUJAH
        BELWIN-MILLS PUBLISHING CORPORATION   .60
HOWELL   1 1/2
    AT THE CARNIVAL
        BELWIN-MILLS PUBLISHING CORPORATION   .60
HOWELL   2 1/2
    AT THE FOUNTAIN
        BELWIN-MILLS PUBLISHING CORPORATION   .60
HOWELL   2
    CANDLELIGHT MOODS
        VOLKWEIN BROS.   .40
HOWELL   2
    DRIFTING CLOUDS
        VOLKWEIN BROS.   .40
HOWELL   3
    GOLLIWOG'S DANCE
        WILLIS MUSIC COMPANY   .30
HOWELL   4
    IMPETUOSO
        VOLKWEIN BROS.   .40
HOWELL   3
    INTERMEZZO
        VOLKWEIN BROS.   .40
HOWELL   2
    LILAC TIME
        BELWIN-MILLS PUBLISHING CORPORATION   .60
HOWELL   2
    MUSIC BOX
        BELWIN-MILLS PUBLISHING CORPORATION   .60
HOWELL   2
    PLAYING HOPSCOTCH
        BELWIN-MILLS PUBLISHING CORPORATION   .60
HOWELL   1 1/2
    RAIN DROPS
        BELWIN-MILLS PUBLISHING CORPORATION   .60
HOWELL   2
    RIPPLING BOOKLET
        BELWIN-MILLS PUBLISHING CORPORATION   .60
HOWELL   2 1/2
    SEA GULLS IN FLIGHT
        BELWIN-MILLS PUBLISHING CORPORATION   .60
HOWELL   3
    SINGING SURF
        VOLKWEIN BROS.   .40
HOWELL   2
    SPRINGTIME SERENADE
        VOLKWEIN BROS.   .40
HOWELL   2
    VALSE MIGNON
        VOLKWEIN BROS.   .30
HOWELL   2
    WATER SPRITES AT PLAY
        BELWIN-MILLS PUBLISHING CORPORATION   .60
HOWELL   4
    WHIRLWIND
        WILLIS MUSIC COMPANY   .40
HOWELL   4
    WIND IN THE PINES
        WILLIS MUSIC COMPANY   .50
HOWELL, C. R.   SCHAUM, J.   2
    BARN DANCE
        BELWIN-MILLS PUBLISHING CORPORATION   .50
HOWELL, C. R.   1
    PICKING PLUMS
        PRO-ART PUBLICATIONS, INC.   20   .50
HOWELL, C. R.   1-2
    PLAYMATES
        PRO-ART PUBLICATIONS, INC.   157   .50
HOWELL, C. R.
    RUSTIC DANCE
        BELWIN-MILLS PUBLISHING CORPORATION   28189   .60
HOWELL, C. R.   ECKSTEIN
    RUSTIC DANCE
        CARL FISCHER, INC.   S 2189   .50
HOWELL, C. R.   3
    RUSTIC DANCE
        CENTURY MUSIC PUBLISHING COMPANY, INC. 681   .40
HOWELL, C. R.   3
    RUSTIC DANCE
        G. SCHIRMER, INC.   .40
HOWELL, C. R.   3
    RUSTIC DANCE
        VOLKWEIN BROS.   .30
HOWELL, C. R.   3
    RUSTIC DANCE
        WILLIS MUSIC COMPANY   .35
HOWELL, C. R.   BURNAM   2
    RUSTIC DANCE
        WILLIS MUSIC COMPANY   .35
HOWELL, C. R.   1 1/2
    TOYSHOP PARADE
        PRO-ART PUBLICATIONS, INC.   21   .50
HOWELL, D.
    KNIGHT FORLORN AND OFF TO THE TOURNEY, THE
        BANKS AND SON LTD.   .25
HOWELL, I.   1 1/2
    BOLD PIRATE
        BELWIN-MILLS PUBLISHING CORPORATION   .60
HOWELL, I.   1
    CAPERS OF A CLOWN
        BELWIN-MILLS PUBLISHING CORPORATION   .60
HOWELL, I.   2
    EASTER LILY
        BELWIN-MILLS PUBLISHING CORPORATION   .60
HOWELL, I.   2
    FLIGHT OF THE FIREFLY, THE
        BELWIN-MILLS PUBLISHING CORPORATION   .60
HOWELL, I.   1 1/2
    FLOWER QUIZ, A
        BELWIN-MILLS PUBLISHING CORPORATION   .60

HOWELL, I.   2
    MR. AND MRS. WOODPECKER
        BELWIN-MILLS PUBLISHING CORPORATION   .60
HOWELL, I.   2
    SLEIGH BELLS IN THE SNOW
        BELWIN-MILLS PUBLISHING CORPORATION   .60
HRUBY, V.   2
    GREEK DANCE
        PRO-ART PUBLICATIONS, INC.   531   .50
HRUBY, V.   3
    SAILING
        PRO-ART PUBLICATIONS, INC.   532   .50
HRUBY, V.   3
    SEA GULLS
        PRO-ART PUBLICATIONS, INC.   530   .50
HUBBELL   WHITNEY
    POOR BUTTERFLY
        WARNER BROTHERS PUBLISHERS   1.00
HUBER   5
    LA CHACE FUR CEMBALO SOLO
        SCHOTT   5429   3.00
HUBICKI, M.   ASCHERBERG *
    I KNOW A BANK
        G. SCHIRMER, INC.   .40
HUBICKI, M.   ASCHERBERG *
    ST. CRISPIN'S DAY
        G. SCHIRMER, INC.   .40
HUDSON *
    MOONGLOW
        BELWIN-MILLS PUBLISHING CORPORATION   20406   .85
HUDSON *
    MR. GHOST GOES TO TOWN
        BELWIN-MILLS PUBLISHING CORPORATION   20175   .85
HUDSON *
    ORGAN GRINDER'S SWING
        BELWIN-MILLS PUBLISHING CORPORATION   20186   .85
HUE, G.
    RETOUR D'ULYSSE, LE
        FRANCO COLOMBO PUBLICATIONS   SAL   4.25
HUE, G.
    SIANG-SIN
        HEUGEL ET CIE.   9.25
HUENTEN
    RONDOLETTO IN C MAJOR, OP. 15
        G. SCHIRMER, INC.   .50
HUERTER, C.
    FIRE DANCE
        G. SCHIRMER, INC.   .50
HUGHES, H.
    BRIAN BORU'S MARCH--AN IRISH PATROL
        G. SCHIRMER, INC.   .40
HUGON, G.
    EAUX-FORTEX -- SUITE
        EDITIONS MUSICALES TRANSATLANTIQUES   6.50
HUGON, G.
    PROMENADE, AU BORD DE L'ETANG
        EDITIONS MUSICALES TRANSATLANTIQUES   1.35
HUGUET Y TAGELL
    DESDE LA REJA
        FRANCO COLOMBO PUBLICATIONS   SAL   1.50
HUGUET Y TAGELL
    GUITARRERIAS
        FRANCO COLOMBO PUBLICATIONS   SAL   4.25
HUMBERT, G.   1
    ALLERLEI SPIELZEUG
        SCHOTT   2605   2.00
HUMBERT, G.   1
    KUNTERBUNT
        SCHOTT   2485   2.00
HUMBERT, G.   2
    SONATINA NO. 02 IN G
        SCHOTT   2788   2.00
HUMBERT, G.   1
    ZAUBERSTUNDEN
        SCHOTT   2379   2.00
HUMES, D.   2 1/2
    RAINDROPS IN THE WIND
        THEODORE PRESSER COMPANY   .50
HUMMEL, J. N.
    GOD SAVE THE KING, AIR VARIE
        MUSICA OBSCURA   2.00
HUMMEL, J. N.
    LARGHETTO A CAPRICCIO
        MUSICAL SCOPE PUBLISHERS   01.25
HUMMEL, J. N.
    PREAMBULES DANS TOUS LES TONS, OP. 67
        MUSICA OBSCURA   2.00
HUMMEL, J. N.   2 1/2
    RONDINO GALOP
        WILLIS MUSIC COMPANY   .40
HUMMEL, J. N.
    RONDO
        DELRIEU ET CIE.   1.00
HUMMEL, J. N.
    RONDO IN E FLAT, OP. 11
        G. SCHIRMER, INC.   .50
HUMMEL, J. N.   M-D
    RONDO, OP. 11
        C. F. PETERS CORPORATION   7045   .90
HUMMEL, J. N.   2 1/2
    SCHERZO
        WILLIS MUSIC COMPANY   .40
HUMPERDINCK, E.   STEINER   APPR.
    CHILDREN'S DANCE FROM 'HANSEL AND GRETEL'
        BELWIN-MILLS PUBLISHING CORPORATION   .60
HUMPERDINCK, E.   WEYBRIGHT   1 1/2
    CHILDREN'S PRAYER, THE -- FROM HANSEL AND GRETEL
        BELWIN-MILLS PUBLISHING CORPORATION   .60
HUMPERDINCK, E.
    EVENING PRAYER, FROM 'HANSEL AND GRETEL'
        CENTURY MUSIC PUBLISHING COMPANY, INC. 3402   .40
HUMPERDINCK, E.   BOHN, J. C.
    HANSEL AND GRETEL SUITE
        BOSTON MUSIC COMPANY   .90
HUMPERDINCK, E.   HAUPT, L. VON
    HANSEL AND GRETEL--ADAPTED AS A CHILDREN'S OPERA-STORY
        G. SCHIRMER, INC.   .75
HUMPERDINCK, E.   2
    HANSEL AND GRETEL, PRAYER
        CENTURY MUSIC PUBLISHING COMPANY, INC. 3402   .40
HUMPERDINCK, E.   3
    HANSEL AND GRETEL, SUSY LITTLE SUSY
        CENTURY MUSIC PUBLISHING COMPANY, INC. 3433   .40
HUMPERDINCK, E.   3
    HANSEL AND GRETEL, THE LITTLE MAN
        CENTURY MUSIC PUBLISHING COMPANY, INC. 3435   .40

HUMPERDINCK, E.   4
    HANSEL UND GRETEL -- ABENDSEGEN UND ENGELREIGEN
        SCHOTT   1.50
HUMPERDINCK, E.   4
    HANSEL UND GRETEL -- KNUSPERWALZER
        SCHOTT   1.50
HUMPERDINCK, E.   5
    HANSEL UND GRETEL -- VORSPIEL
        SCHOTT   1.75
HUMPERDINCK, E.   3
    LITTLE MAN, THE, HANSEL AND GRETEL
        CENTURY MUSIC PUBLISHING COMPANY, INC.   3435   .40
HUMPERDINCK, E.   2
    PRAYER, HANSEL AND GRETEL
        CENTURY MUSIC PUBLISHING COMPANY, INC.   3402   .40
HUMPERDINCK, E.   3
    SUSY LITTLE SUSY, HANSEL AND GRETEL
        CENTURY MUSIC PUBLISHING COMPANY, INC.   3433   .40
HUMPERDINCK, E.   WEYBRIGHT   1 1/2
    SUSY, LITTLE SUSY -- GERMAN FOLK SONG, USED IN THE OPERA 'HANSEL
    AND GRETEL'
        BELWIN-MILLS PUBLISHING CORPORATION   .60
HUMPERDINCK, E.   3
    THERE STANDS A LITTLE MAN
        CENTURY MUSIC PUBLISHING COMPANY, INC.   3435   .40
HUMPHREYS   2 1/2
    GOOD MORNIN' MRS. SIPPI
        WILLIS MUSIC COMPANY   .40
HUNEKE   2
    GAY SENORITA
        BOSTON MUSIC COMPANY   .50
HUNEKE   1-2
    POP-CORN
        PRO-ART PUBLICATIONS, INC.   299   .50
HUNEKE   1-2
    SAD LITTLE CLOWN
        PRO-ART PUBLICATIONS, INC.   298   .50
HUNEKE   2-3
    SLEIGH RIDE
        PRO-ART PUBLICATIONS, INC.   295   .50
HUNKE   1
    MY SHADOW
        BOSTON MUSIC COMPANY   .50
HUNTEN, F.
    SONG IN THE WOODS, A
        FREDERICK HARRIS MUSIC COMPANY   .60
HUNTLEY, H.   2 1/2
    HOE DOWN
        WILLIS MUSIC COMPANY   .40
HURD, E.
    FIRST BUD, OP. 15 NO. 1
        BELWIN-MILLS PUBLISHING CORPORATION   25065   .60
HURE
    AIR DE BALLET
        FRANCO COLOMBO PUBLICATIONS   SAL   1.75
HURE
    CHANT DE GUERRE
        FRANCO COLOMBO PUBLICATIONS   SAL   1.75
HURE
    ELEGIE
        FRANCO COLOMBO PUBLICATIONS   SAL   1.75
HURE
    SONATA NO. 01
        FRANCO COLOMBO PUBLICATIONS   SAL   4.00
HURE
    SONATA NO. 02
        FRANCO COLOMBO PUBLICATIONS   SAL   5.00
HURST, G.
    DANCE PRELUDES--NO. 1
        ASSOCIATED MUSIC PUBLISHERS, INC.   BER   .50
HURST, G.
    DANCE PRELUDES--NO. 2
        ASSOCIATED MUSIC PUBLISHERS, INC.   BER   .60
HURST, G.
    DANCE PRELUDES--NO. 3
        ASSOCIATED MUSIC PUBLISHERS, INC.   BER   .60
HURST, G.
    DANCE PRELUDES--NO. 4
        ASSOCIATED MUSIC PUBLISHERS, INC.   BER   .75
HURST, G.
    MASQUE
        ASSOCIATED MUSIC PUBLISHERS, INC.   BER   .65
HURST, G.
    TOCCATA
        ASSOCIATED MUSIC PUBLISHERS, INC.   BER   .75
HUSA, K.   5
    ELEGIE
        ALPHONSE LEDUC
HUSA, K.   6
    SONATA, OP. 11
        SCHOTT   4348   3.00
HUZELLA
    CAMBIATE PER PIANOFORTE
        KULTURA   1.25
HYDE *   SINGER
    LITTLE GIRL
        MCA MUSIC   .60
HYDE, F.
    BATTLE OF THE SEWING MACHINES, THE --1874--
        MUSICA OBSCURA   2.50
HYMAN, D.
    BARDOLINO
        BELWIN-MILLS PUBLISHING CORPORATION   20347   .85
HYMAN, D.
    DOWN HOME MELODY
        BELWIN-MILLS PUBLISHING CORPORATION   20345   .85
IBBOTSON, E. M.   2
    IN OLD MADRID
        WILLIS MUSIC COMPANY   .40
IBBOTSON, E. M.   1
    SONG OF THE CLOCK
        WILLIS MUSIC COMPANY   .40
IBBOTSON, E. M.   3 1/2
    WINTER FROLIC
        THEODORE PRESSER COMPANY   .50
IBERT
    AMOURS DE JUPITER, LES -- BALLET --
        FRANCO COLOMBO PUBLICATIONS   SAL   7.25
IBERT
    DIVERTISSEMENT
        ELKAN-VOGEL, INC.   D   4.50
IBERT   E
    FELICIE NANTEUIL, VALSE
        C. F. PETERS CORPORATION   C344   1.25
IBERT   7
    FERRIQUE
        ALPHONSE LEDUC

IBERT   6
    FRANCAISE
        ALPHONSE LEDUC
IBERT
    GIDDY GIRL, A
        ELKAN-VOGEL, INC.   LED   2.75
IBERT
    LE JARDINIER DE SAMOS
        HEUGEL ET CIE.   4.75
IBERT   7, 8
    LES RENCONTRES
        ALPHONSE LEDUC
IBERT
    LITTLE WHITE DONKEY
        ELKAN-VOGEL, INC.   LED   3.50
IBERT   6
    MATIN SUR L'EAU
        ALPHONSE LEDUC
IBERT   4
    SCHERZETTO
        ALPHONSE LEDUC
IBERT   6
    TOCCATA SUR LE NOM D'ALBERT ROUSSEL
        ALPHONSE LEDUC
IBERT
    VALSE FROM L'EVENTAIL DE JEANNE
        HEUGEL ET CIE.   1.25
IBERT   6
    VENT DANS LES RUINES, LE --EN CHAMPAGNE, 1915--
        ALPHONSE LEDUC
ICINI
    SUMMERTIME IN VENICE
        MCA MUSIC   1.00
IGLESIAS VILLOUD
    BAILECITO
        FRANCO COLOMBO PUBLICATIONS   BA9931   .75
IGLESIAS VILLOUD   LOCATELLI
    BRUJO AYMARA
        FRANCO COLOMBO PUBLICATIONS   BA8870   .75
IGLESIAS VILLOUD
    CANCION
        FRANCO COLOMBO PUBLICATIONS   BA10128   .75
IGLESIAS VILLOUD
    CATA ARQUENA
        EDITORIAL COOPERATIVA INTER-AMERICANA   00.85
IGLESIAS VILLOUD
    CHOLA APASIONADA, LA
        FRANCO COLOMBO PUBLICATIONS   BA8410   1.00
IGLESIAS VILLOUD   LOCATELLI
    DANZA DE LOS 'LAIKAS'
        FRANCO COLOMBO PUBLICATIONS   BA8871   .75
IGLESIAS VILLOUD
    HUAINO
        FRANCO COLOMBO PUBLICATIONS   BA9347   .75
ILJINSKY, A.
    BERCEUSE IN G FLAT MAJOR, OP. 13
        G. SCHIRMER, INC.   .40
ILJINSKY, A.   MOSSMAN, T.
    BERCEUSE, OP. 13 NO. 7
        BELWIN-MILLS PUBLISHING CORPORATION   26105   .50
ILJINSKY, A.   3
    BERCEUSE, OP. 13 NO. 7
        CENTURY MUSIC PUBLISHING COMPANY, INC.   2017   .40
ILJINSKY, A.   3
    LULLABY, OP. 13 NO. 7
        CENTURY MUSIC PUBLISHING COMPANY, INC.   2017   .40
INDY, V. D'
    SONATE EN MI
        ELKAN-VOGEL, INC.   D   6.25
INFANTE
    DANSES ANDALOUSES - 1. RITMO
        FRANCO COLOMBO PUBLICATIONS   SAL   4.00
INFANTE
    GITANERIAS
        FRANCO COLOMBO PUBLICATIONS   SAL   4.00
INFANTE   7
    GUADALQUIVIR
        ALPHONSE LEDUC
INFANTE
    SEVILLANA
        FRANCO COLOMBO PUBLICATIONS   SAL   4.00
INFANTE
    VITO, EL -- EDITION A - ORIGINAL --
        FRANCO COLOMBO PUBLICATIONS   SAL   4.25
INFANTE
    VITO, EL -- EDITION B - SIMPLIFIED --
        FRANCO COLOMBO PUBLICATIONS   SAL   2.75
INGHELBRECHT, D. E.
    GRECO, EL
        FRANCO COLOMBO PUBLICATIONS   SAL   7.00
INGHELBRECHT, D. E.
    LE DIABLE DANS LE BEFROI
        HEUGEL ET CIE.   7.30
INGHELBRECHT, D. E.
    MARINE
        FRANCO COLOMBO PUBLICATIONS   SAL   1.75
INGHELBRECHT, D. E.
    METAMORPHOSE D'EVE -- BALLET --
        FRANCO COLOMBO PUBLICATIONS   SAL   7.00
INGHELBRECHT, D. E.
    METAMORPHOSE D'EVE SUITE
        FRANCO COLOMBO PUBLICATIONS   SAL   4.25
INGHELBRECHT, D. E.
    SERRE AUX NENUPHARS
        FRANCO COLOMBO PUBLICATIONS   SAL   4.25
INGHELBRECHT, D. E.
    THREE DANCE POEMS NO. 1 REVE
        UNIVERSAL EDITION   UE 9922   1.95
INGHELBRECHT, D. E.
    THREE DANCE POEMS NO. 2 LA DANSE POUR LES OISEAUX
        UNIVERSAL EDITION   UE 9923   1.30
INGHELBRECHT, D. E.
    THREE DANCE POEMS NO. 3 L'ALBUM AUX PORTRAITS
        UNIVERSAL EDITION   UE 9924   1.50
INGLE   NEALE, J.   EASY
    IN-A-GADDA-DA-VIDA
        WARNER BROTHERS PUBLISHERS   .75
IPPOLITOV-IVANOV, M.
    CAUCASIAN SKETCHES, OP. 10--SUITE IN 4 PARTS
        G. SCHIRMER, INC.   L1531   1.25
IPPOLITOV-IVANOV, M.   5-6
    CORTEGE DU SARDAR
        CENTURY MUSIC PUBLISHING COMPANY, INC.   3182   .40
IPPOLITOV-IVANOV, M.   5
    MARCH OF THE SARDAR
        CENTURY MUSIC PUBLISHING COMPANY, INC.   3182   .40

IPPOLITOV-IVANOV, M.   4
    PROCESSION OF THE SARDAR
        THEODORE PRESSER COMPANY   .50
IPPOLITOV-IVANOV, M.   MOSSMAN
    PROCESSION OF THE SARDAR -- FROM 'CAUCASIAN SKETCHES'
        BELWIN-MILLS PUBLISHING CORPORATION   26093   .60
IRELAND, J.
    BALLADE OF LONDON NIGHTS
        BOOSEY AND HAWKES, INC.   1.75
IRELAND, J.
    FIRE OF SPRING
        BOOSEY AND HAWKES, INC.   1.00
IRELAND, J.
    HOLY BOY
        BOOSEY AND HAWKES, INC.   .60
IRELAND, J.
    RHAPSODY
        BOOSEY AND HAWKES, INC.   1.75
IRELAND, J.
    SONATINA
        OXFORD UNIVERSITY PRESS   32.036   2.00
IRVING
    CAROUSEL AND FERRIS WHEEL --PIANO SOLO OR 2 PIANOS, 4 HANDS--
        SUMMY-BIRCHARD COMPANY   1.00
IRVING, M.   2 1/2
    DANCE OF SPAIN
        WILLIS MUSIC COMPANY   .40
ISSERLIS, J.
    FAIRY TALES, OP. 6
        UNIVERSAL EDITION   UE 8844   .95
ISSERLIS, J.
    MEMORIES OF YOUTH, OP. 11
        UNIVERSAL EDITION   UE 10099   1.30
ISSERLIS, J.
    RUSSIAN DANCE, OP. 7
        UNIVERSAL EDITION   UE 9467   .95
ISSERLIS, J.
    SOUVENIR RUSSE, OP. 9
        UNIVERSAL EDITION   UE 1110   .95
ITURBI, J.
    PEQUENA DANZA ESPANOLA
        G. SCHIRMER, INC.   .50
ITURBI, J.
    THREE BLIND MICE - 3 INTERPRETATIONS
        THE BIG THREE MUSIC CORPORATION   00.95
IVANOVICI, J.
    CARMEN SYLVA
        FRANCO COLOMBO PUBLICATIONS   BA8451   .75
IVANOVICI, J.
    CLAIR DE LUNE
        FRANCO COLOMBO PUBLICATIONS   BA8679   .75
IVANOVICI, J.   3
    DANUBE WAVES, WALTZES
        CENTURY MUSIC PUBLISHING COMPANY, INC.   453   .40
IVANOVICI, J.
    WAVES OF THE DANUBE
        ASHLEY DEALERS SERVICE, INC.   ES   .95
IVANOVICI, J.   SCHAUM, J.   1
    WAVES OF THE DANUBE
        BELWIN-MILLS PUBLISHING CORPORATION   .50
IVANOVICI, J.   3
    WAVES OF THE DANUBE
        CENTURY MUSIC PUBLISHING COMPANY, INC.   453   .40
IVANOVICI, J.
    WAVES OF THE DANUBE
        FRANCO COLOMBO PUBLICATIONS   105061   .60
IVANOVICI, J.   CHIESA
    WAVES OF THE DANUBE
        FRANCO COLOMBO PUBLICATIONS   107481   .50
IVANOVICI, J.   CARLETON   1 1/2
    WAVES OF THE DANUBE
        THEODORE PRESSER COMPANY   .50
IVANOVICI, J.   MOSSMAN
    WAVES OF THE DANUBE -- BOOGIE WOOGIE
        BELWIN-MILLS PUBLISHING CORPORATION   26061   .90
IVANOVICI, J.   JESTON, I. H.   2
    WAVES OF THE DANUBE WALTZ
        VOLKWEIN BROS.   00.35
IVANOVICI, J.
    WAVES OF THE DANUBE--WALTZ
        G. SCHIRMER, INC.   .60
IVANOVICI, J. *   MEDIUM
    WAVES OF THE DANUBE
        SHAWNEE PRESS, INC.   .50
IVANOW   2
    MARCH OF THE SARDAR, EASY
        CENTURY MUSIC PUBLISHING COMPANY, INC.   3384   .40
IVANOW   5-6
    PROCESSION OF THE SARDAR
        CENTURY MUSIC PUBLISHING COMPANY, INC.   3182   .40
IVANOW   ROLFE, W.   2
    PROCESSION OF THE SARDAR, EASY
        CENTURY MUSIC PUBLISHING COMPANY, INC.   3384   .40
IVES, C.   A
    ANTI-ABOLITIONIST RIOTS
        THEODORE PRESSER COMPANY   1.00
IVES, C.   A
    SOME SOUTHPAW PITCHING
        THEODORE PRESSER COMPANY   .75
IVES, C.
    SONATA NO. 01
        PEER SOUTHERN ORGANIZATION   04.00
IVES, C.
    SONATA NO. 02 -- 'CONCORD, MASS., 1843-60'
        ASSOCIATED MUSIC PUBLISHERS, INC.   AMP   7.00
IVES, C.   KIRKPATRICK
    STUDY NO. 22
        THEODORE PRESSER COMPANY   1.25
IVES, C.   A
    THREE PAGE SONATA
        THEODORE PRESSER COMPANY   1.50
IVES, C.   KIRKPATRICK   D
    VARIED AIR AND VARIATIONS
        THEODORE PRESSER COMPANY   2.50
IVEY   2
    SLEEPY TIME AND WATER WHEEL
        LEE ROBERTS MUSIC PUBLICATIONS, INC.   .50
JACKSON, H.
    PICNIC FOR PELICANS
        BELWIN-MILLS PUBLISHING CORPORATION   20491   .85
JACOB, G.
    FROGS, THE
        OXFORD UNIVERSITY PRESS   32.921   1.15
JACOB, G.
    SUITE FOR THE VIRGINAL
        OXFORD UNIVERSITY PRESS   32.923   2.70

JACOBI   MEDIUM
    PRELUDE IN E MINOR
        SHAWNEE PRESS, INC.   .75
JACOBI, W.
    SONATA NO. 02
        ASSOCIATED MUSIC PUBLISHERS, INC.   LEU   2.75
JACOBI, W.
    SONATA NO. 03
        ASSOCIATED MUSIC PUBLISHERS, INC.   LEU   3.25
JACOBI, W.   M-D
    SONATINA FOR HARPSICHORD
        C. F. PETERS CORPORATION   FK34   1.50
JACOBS *   ZEPP   2
    I LOVE YOU TRULY
        PRO-ART PUBLICATIONS, INC.   229   .50
JACOBUS, D.   2
    CHORD FROLIC
        WILLIS MUSIC COMPANY   .35
JADASSOHN, S.
    REMEMBRANCE, OP. 71 NO. 6
        FREDERICK HARRIS MUSIC COMPANY   .40
JADASSOHN, S.
    TALE, A
        FREDERICK HARRIS MUSIC COMPANY   .30
JAELL   5-6
    DANSE DES FEES, POLKA
        CENTURY MUSIC PUBLISHING COMPANY, INC.   2440   .40
JAELL   5-6
    LA DANSE DES FEES, POLKA
        CENTURY MUSIC PUBLISHING COMPANY, INC.   2440   .40
JAHN, C.   2
    AT THE MASQUERADE
        CENTURY MUSIC PUBLISHING COMPANY, INC.   1869   .40
JAHN, C.   2
    DREAM OF A WALTZ
        CENTURY MUSIC PUBLISHING COMPANY, INC.   1864   .40
JAHN, C.   2
    INVITATION TO THE DANCE
        CENTURY MUSIC PUBLISHING COMPANY, INC.   1865   .40
JAHN, C.   2
    MENUET
        CENTURY MUSIC PUBLISHING COMPANY, INC.   1868   .40
JAHN, C.   2
    OLD ENGLISH DANCE, MENUET
        CENTURY MUSIC PUBLISHING COMPANY, INC.   1868   .40
JAHN, C.   2
    SEMPER FIDELIS
        CENTURY MUSIC PUBLISHING COMPANY, INC.   1866   .40
JAMES, E. L.   2
    MY SHADOW
        BELWIN-MILLS PUBLISHING CORPORATION   .60
JAMES, M.   1
    OFF FOR A TRIP
        CENTURY MUSIC PUBLISHING COMPANY, INC.   3850   .40
JAMES, M.   1
    ON THE OPEN ROAD
        CENTURY MUSIC PUBLISHING COMPANY, INC.   3809   .40
JAMES, M.   1
    YO YO
        CENTURY MUSIC PUBLISHING COMPANY, INC.   3807   .40
JAMES, W. G.
    FAIRY FLUTE, THE
        FRANCO COLOMBO PUBLICATIONS   LD493   .60
JAMES, W. G.
    HIDE AND SEEK
        FRANCO COLOMBO PUBLICATIONS   LD494   .60
JANACEK
    IN THE MISTS
        ARTIA   1.75
JANACEK   4
    INDRODUKTION UND FUGE, OP. 22
        BARENREITER VERLAG
JANACEK
    LACHIAN DANCES
        ARTIA   2.25
JANACEK
    MORAVIAN FOLK SONGS
        ARTIA   1.00
JANACEK
    ON AN OVERGROWN PATH
        ARTIA   3.50
JANACEK   3
    PILKY
        BARENREITER VERLAG   AP 1548
JANACEK
    SONATA -- 1. 10. 1905
        ARTIA   1.50
JANACEK   4
    SONATE DER STRASSE -- 1. 10. 1905 --
        BARENREITER VERLAG   AP 608
JANACEK   3-4
    THEMA MIT VARIATIONEN
        BARENREITER VERLAG   AP 617
JANACEK
    THEME AND VARIATIONS -- ZDENKA'S VARIATIONS
        ARTIA   .75
JANECEK   3
    STIMME DER RUHE, OP. 14
        BARENREITER VERLAG   AP 615
JANECEK   3-4
    SUITE, OP. 18
        BARENREITER VERLAG   AP 616
JANKE, G.
    ALLA TURCA
        G. SCHIRMER, INC.   .25
JAQUE, R.
    DANCE
        ASSOCIATED MUSIC PUBLISHERS, INC.   BER   .40
JAQUE, R.
    JESTING--BADINERIE
        ASSOCIATED MUSIC PUBLISHERS, INC.   BER   .40
JAQUE, R.
    RUSTIC DANCE
        ASSOCIATED MUSIC PUBLISHERS, INC.   BER   .40
JARNACH, P.   4
    DAS AMRUMER TAGEBUCH, OP. 30
        SCHOTT   3958   2.00
JARNACH, P.   4-5
    SONATA NO. 02
        SCHOTT   4387   2.25
JARRE, M.
    GRAND PRIX - THEME
        THE BIG THREE MUSIC CORPORATION   00.95
JARRE, M.
    LARA'S THEME - 'DOCTOR ZHIVAGO'
        THE BIG THREE MUSIC CORPORATION   00.95

JARVIS
  HOPES ADRIFT   3
    VOLKWEIN BROS.   .25
JAY   2
  THIS OLD MAN
    WILLIS MUSIC COMPANY   .40
JAY *
  VIENNESE LANTERN WALTZ
    MCA MUSIC   1.00
JEAN, E.   2
  BROOKLET IS SINGING, THE
    CENTURY MUSIC PUBLISHING COMPANY, INC. 3439   .40
JEAN, E.   2
  HAPPINESS
    CENTURY MUSIC PUBLISHING COMPANY, INC. 3440   .40
JEAN, E.   2
  IN SHADOW TOWN
    CENTURY MUSIC PUBLISHING COMPANY, INC. 3441   .40
JEAN, E.   2
  LULLABY
    CENTURY MUSIC PUBLISHING COMPANY, INC. 3442   .40
JEAN, E.   2
  OLD PICTURE, AN
    CENTURY MUSIC PUBLISHING COMPANY, INC. 3437   .40
JEAN, E.   2
  POSTMAN, THE
    CENTURY MUSIC PUBLISHING COMPANY, INC. 3443   .40
JEAN, E.   2
  SEASONS, THE
    CENTURY MUSIC PUBLISHING COMPANY, INC. 3444   .40
JEAN, E.   2
  SQUIRREL
    CENTURY MUSIC PUBLISHING COMPANY, INC. 3445   .40
JEAN, E.   2
  SUMMER AND WINTER
    CENTURY MUSIC PUBLISHING COMPANY, INC. 3446   .40
JEAN, E.   2
  SWING SONG
    CENTURY MUSIC PUBLISHING COMPANY, INC. 3447   .40
JEAN, E.   2
  WOODLAND ORCHESTRA
    CENTURY MUSIC PUBLISHING COMPANY, INC. 3448   .40
JEANNERET
  SONATA
    FRANCO COLOMBO PUBLICATIONS   SAL   4.25
JEFFRIES *   SINGER
  CANDY STORE BLUES
    MCA MUSIC   .60
JELESNIK, E.
  J. F. K. MARCH
    BELWIN-MILLS PUBLISHING CORPORATION 20454 .85
JELINEK, H.
  SONATINA, OP. 9 NO. 4
    UNIVERSAL EDITION   UE 11916 2.35
JELINEK, H.
  TWELVE-TONE MUSIC, OP. 15 BK. 5, SUITE IN E
    UNIVERSAL EDITION   UE 12024 2.35
JEMNITZ, A.
  DANCE -- SONATA, OP. 23
    UNIVERSAL EDITION   UE 6691   3.00
JEMNITZ, A.
  SONATA NO. 03, OP. 26
    UNIVERSAL EDITION   UE 9929   1.95
JENKINS, M.   1
  DAILY DOZEN, THE
    CENTURY MUSIC PUBLISHING COMPANY, INC. 4393   .40
JENKINS, M.
  KALEIDOSCOPE
    MCA MUSIC   1.00
JENKINS, M.
  LOVE THEME FROM 'MANHATTAN TOWER'
    MCA MUSIC   1.00
JENSEN, A.   3
  DIE MUHLE OP. 17 NO. 3
    SCHOTT   01577 1/2 1.00
JENSEN, A.   3
  ELFIN DANCE
    WILLIS MUSIC COMPANY   .35
JENSEN, A.
  ELFIN DANCE, OP. 33 NO. 5
    G. SCHIRMER, INC.   .30
JENSEN, A.   4
  ELFIN DANCE, OP. 33 NO. 5
    THEODORE PRESSER COMPANY   .50
JENSEN, A.
  MILL, THE
    G. SCHIRMER, INC.   .50
JENSEN, A.
  MILL, THE, OP. 17 NO. 3
    BANKS AND SON LTD.   .55
JENSEN, A.
  MILL, THE, OP. 17 NO. 3
    FRANCO COLOMBO PUBLICATIONS BA6467   .75
JENSEN, A.   VOSS   3
  MURMELNDES LUFTCHEN, FANTASIE OP. 21 NO. 4
    SCHOTT   01961 1/2 1.00
JENSEN, A.   NIEMANN
  MURMURING ZEPHYRS
    G. SCHIRMER, INC.   .40
JENSEN, A.
  SCENES OF TRAVEL, OP. 17
    FRANCO COLOMBO PUBLICATIONS BA10839 2.00
JENSEN, A.   4
  SERENADE
    CENTURY MUSIC PUBLISHING COMPANY, INC. 2403   .40
JEREMIAS   4
  SONATE NO. 02 IN D MINOR, OP. 10
    BARENREITER VERLAG   AP 620
JESSE, M.
  BALLERINA
    G. SCHIRMER, INC.   .40
JESSE, M.   3
  BANJO PETE
    WILLIS MUSIC COMPANY   .40
JESSE, M.
  BAVARIAN YODELER
    SAM FOX PUBLISHING COMPANY, INC.   .50
JESSE, M.
  BAVARIAN YODELER
    SOUTHERN MUSIC COMPANY   .50
JESSE, M.
  BUSY MILL WHEEL, THE
    G. SCHIRMER, INC.   .40
JESSE, M.
  CAPTAIN WEATHERBRAVE OF THE SEA
    G. SCHIRMER, INC.   .35

JESSE, M.
  CAROUSEL
    G. SCHIRMER, INC.   .35
JESSE, M.
  COUNTRY DANCE
    G. SCHIRMER, INC.   .40
JESSE, M.
  DRUM CORPS
    G. SCHIRMER, INC.   .40
JESSE, M.
  I LOVE A PARADE
    G. SCHIRMER, INC.   .35
JESSE, M.
  LISTEN TO THE RAIN
    G. SCHIRMER, INC.   .35
JESSE, M.
  LITTLE BIRD IN SPRING, A
    G. SCHIRMER, INC.   .35
JESSE, M.
  OLD UNCLE JOE PLAYS A CAKE-WALK TUNE
    G. SCHIRMER, INC.   .35
JESSE, M.
  OVER THE HILLS IN A SLEIGH
    SAM FOX PUBLISHING COMPANY, INC.   .50
JESSE, M.
  OVER THE HILLS IN A SLEIGH
    SOUTHERN MUSIC COMPANY   .50
JESSE, M.
  RIDING ON A CAMEL
    G. SCHIRMER, INC.   .35
JESSE, M.
  SERENADE
    G. SCHIRMER, INC.   .40
JESSE, M.
  TICK TOCK, SONG OF THE CLOCK
    G. SCHIRMER, INC.   .35
JESSE, M.
  WHEN MARIA SINGS AND PLAYS HER GUITAR
    G. SCHIRMER, INC.   .40
JESSE, M.
  WIGWAM LULLABY
    G. SCHIRMER, INC.   .35
JESSE, M.
  YO HO, FOR THE SAILOR BOY
    G. SCHIRMER, INC.   .35
JESSEL   SCHAUM, J.   1 1/2
  PARADE OF THE TOY SOLDIERS
    SCHAUM PUBLICATIONS, INC.   .50
JESSEL
  PARADE OF THE WOODEN SOLDIERS
    ASHLEY DEALERS SERVICE, INC.   ES   .95
JESSEL
  PARADE OF THE WOODEN SOLDIERS
    EDWARD B. MARKS MUSIC CORPORATION   01.00
JESSEL
  PARADE OF THE WOODEN SOLDIERS
    EDWARD B. MARKS MUSIC CORPORATION   01.00
JESSEL
  PARADE OF THE WOODEN SOLDIERS
    EDWARD B. MARKS MUSIC CORPORATION   00.60
JESSEL
  PARADE OF THE WOODEN SOLDIERS -- SIMP.
    ASHLEY DEALERS SERVICE, INC.   ES   .95
JESSEL   ZEPP   2
  WOODEN SOLDIERS ON PARADE
    PRO-ART PUBLICATIONS, INC.   322   .50
JESTON, I. H.   3-4
  DANCING SUNBEAMS
    VOLKWEIN BROS.   .50
JEVONS
  ALICIA'S DANCE
    FRANCO COLOMBO PUBLICATIONS LD42   1.00
JIRAK   2-3
  KLEINE KLAVIERSUITE, OP. 12
    BARENREITER VERLAG   AP 628
JIRAK   3-4
  SUITE IM ALTEN STIL, OP. 21
    BARENREITER VERLAG   AP 631
JIRKO   4
  SONATE
    BARENREITER VERLAG   AP 2108
JOACHIM, O.
  L'ECLOSION
    ASSOCIATED MUSIC PUBLISHERS, INC. BER 1.50
JOHANNESEN, G.
  IMPROVISATION ON A MORMON HYMN, 'COME, COME, YE SAINTS'
    OXFORD UNIVERSITY PRESS   93.218 .75
JOHANNING   3
  MADAME POMPADOUR
    CENTURY MUSIC PUBLISHING COMPANY, INC. 1691   .40
JOHANNING   3
  YELLOW JONQUILS
    CENTURY MUSIC PUBLISHING COMPANY, INC. 4370   .40
JOHANNING   3
  YELLOW JONQUILS
    WILLIS MUSIC COMPANY   .50
JOHNSON   3-4
  ENCANTADA
    PRO-ART PUBLICATIONS, INC.   352   .50
JOHNSON, C.
  DILL-PICKLES
    BELWIN-MILLS PUBLISHING CORPORATION 20072 .85
JOHNSON, H.   A
  PIANO SONATA
    THEODORE PRESSER COMPANY   2.50
JOHNSON, J. R.   SCHAUM, J.   2
  LIFT EV'RY VOICE AND SING
    SCHAUM PUBLICATIONS, INC.   .60
JOHNSON, L.   MD
  CHACONNE
    THEODORE PRESSER COMPANY   .75
JOHNSON, R.   STEINER   4
  LAZY MOON -- PIANO SOLO WITH WORDS
    BELWIN-MILLS PUBLISHING CORPORATION   .60
JOHNSON, R.
  PIANO SONATA NO. 01
    OXFORD UNIVERSITY PRESS   32.151 4.60
JOHNSON, R.
  PIANO SONATA NO. 02
    OXFORD UNIVERSITY PRESS   32.155 5.25
JOHNSON, S.
  BOOGIN' ON THE DOWNBEAT
    MCA MUSIC   1.00
JOHNSON, S.   3
  DRIFTING ON
    CENTURY MUSIC PUBLISHING COMPANY, INC. 2555   .40

JOHNSON, S.
    GOING AWAY BLUES
        MCA MUSIC   1.00
JOHNSON, S.
    HOLLYWOOD BOOGIE
        MCA MUSIC   1.00
JOHNSON, S.
    KANSAS CITY FAREWELL
        MCA MUSIC   1.00
JOHNSON, S.
    OVER THE BARS
        MCA MUSIC   1.00
JOHNSON, S.
    PETE'S MIXTURE
        MCA MUSIC   1.00
JOHNSON, S.
    ROLL 'EM PETE
        MCA MUSIC   1.00
JOHNSON, S. *
    DEATH RAY BOOGIE
        MCA MUSIC   1.00
JOHNSON, S. *
    IT'S A LOW DOWN DIRTY SHAME
        MCA MUSIC   1.00
JOHNSON, S. *
    LAST GOODBYE BLUES
        MCA MUSIC   1.00
JOHNSON, S. *
    OH WEE BABY BLUES
        MCA MUSIC   1.00
JOHNSTON, R.
    ROCKING
        ASSOCIATED MUSIC PUBLISHERS, INC.   BER   .40
JOLAS, B.
    AUTOUR
        HEUGEL ET CIE.   5.00
JOLAS, B.
    CHANSON D'APPROCHE
        HEUGEL ET CIE.   5.00
JOLIVET, A.
    BERCEUSE DANS UN HAMAC
        GERARD BILLAUDOT EDITIONS MUSICALES   1.10
JOLIVET, A.
    CHANSONS NAIVES
        GERARD BILLAUDOT EDITIONS MUSICALES   2.00
JOLIVET, A.
    DEUXIEME SONATE POUR PIANO
        HEUGEL ET CIE.   5.50
JOLIVET, A.
    ETUDE SUR DES MODES ANTIQUES
        ELKAN-VOGEL, INC.   D   1.70
JOLIVET, A.
    GUIGNOL ET PANDORE -- BALLET IN ONE ACT
        ASSOCIATED MUSIC PUBLISHERS, INC.   ESC   5.40
JOLIVET, A.
    SONATA FOR PIANO
        UNIVERSAL EDITION   UE 11827   3.65
JOLIVET, A.
    SONATA POUR PIANO NO. 2
        HEUGEL ET CIE.   7.30
JOLIVET, A.
    THREE TEMPS NO. 1
        FRANCO COLOMBO PUBLICATIONS   SAL   4.00
JOLLES
    PIANO BAZAAR
        EDWARD B. MARKS MUSIC CORPORATION   01.25
JOLLES
    PIANO SET
        EDWARD B. MARKS MUSIC CORPORATION   01.00
JOLSON *   SCHAUM, J.   1
    ANNIVERSARY SONG
        SCHAUM PUBLICATIONS, INC.   .75
JONASSOHN   2-3
    CUCKOO SONG
        CENTURY MUSIC PUBLISHING COMPANY, INC.   4090   .40
JONES
    IRONSIDE
        MCA MUSIC   1.00
JONES *
    CHRISTMAS CAROLS ROCK
        ALFRED MUSIC COMPANY   644   1.50
JONES, C.   D
    THREE PIECES
        THEODORE PRESSER COMPANY   1.50
JONES, J.   2
    LITTLE TRAPEZE GIRL
        WILLIS MUSIC COMPANY   .40
JONES, S.   STEINER   2
    GEISHA, THE
        BELWIN-MILLS PUBLISHING CORPORATION   .60
JONES, S. T.   ROWLEY
    FESTIVAL GROUPS FOR PIANO SELECTED BY ARTHUR BENJAMIN, SERIES 2
    -- IN MINUET TIME
        BOOSEY AND HAWKES, INC.   .60
JONES, S. T.
    THEME AND VARIATIONS ON A GERMAN FOLK TUNE
        FRANCO COLOMBO PUBLICATIONS   NY2128   1.00
JONGEN, J.
    DEUX PIECES
        ELKAN-VOGEL, INC.   D   3.10
JONGEN, J.
    SERENADE, OP. 19
        FRANCO COLOMBO PUBLICATIONS   SAL   2.75
JONGEN, L.
    ESQUISSES - 1. RHAPSODIE
        FRANCO COLOMBO PUBLICATIONS   SAL   2.00
JONGEN, L.
    ESQUISSES - 2. POLICHINELLE
        FRANCO COLOMBO PUBLICATIONS   SAL   2.00
JONGEN, L.
    ESQUISSES - 3. BERCEUSE POUR UN COEUR LASSE
        FRANCO COLOMBO PUBLICATIONS   SAL   2.00
JONGEN, L.
    ESQUISSES - 4. POCHADE
        FRANCO COLOMBO PUBLICATIONS   SAL   2.00
JONGEN, L.
    ESQUISSES - 5. RYTHMES DE DANSES
        FRANCO COLOMBO PUBLICATIONS   SAL   2.50
JONGEN, L.
    ESQUISSES - 6. FANTASQUE
        FRANCO COLOMBO PUBLICATIONS   SAL   2.00
JONGEN, L.
    ESQUISSES - 7. MASCARADE
        FRANCO COLOMBO PUBLICATIONS   SAL   3.25
JONNASSON   SCHAUM, J.   2 1/2
    CUCKOO WALTZ
        BELWIN-MILLS PUBLISHING CORPORATION   .50

JONSON   ZEPP   4
    DRINK TO ME ONLY WITH THINE EYES
        PRO-ART PUBLICATIONS, INC.   234   .50
JOPLIN, S.   SCHAUM, J.   2 1/2
    ENTERTAINER, THE
        SCHAUM PUBLICATIONS, INC.   .75
JOPLIN, S.
    MAPLE LEAF RAG
        ASHLEY DEALERS SERVICE, INC.   ES   .95
JOPLIN, S.   3
    MAPLE LEAF RAG
        CENTURY MUSIC PUBLISHING COMPANY, INC.   4328   .40
JOPLIN, S.
    MAPLE LEAF RAG
        EDWARD B. MARKS MUSIC CORPORATION   01.00
JOPLIN, S.   ZEPP   4-5
    MAPLE LEAF RAG
        PRO-ART PUBLICATIONS, INC.   328   .50
JOPLIN, S.
    MAPLE LEAF RAG
        THE BIG THREE MUSIC CORPORATION   00.95
JOPLIN, S.   3
    MAPLE LEAF RAG
        WILLIS MUSIC COMPANY   .50
JOPLIN, S.
    NEW RAG
        EDWARD B. MARKS MUSIC CORPORATION   01.00
JOPLIN, S.
    PINEAPPLE RAG
        BELWIN-MILLS PUBLISHING CORPORATION   20202   .85
JOPLIN, S.
    WEEPING WILLOW
        BELWIN-MILLS PUBLISHING CORPORATION   20465   .85
JORDA, L.
    CARNIVAL OF VENICE
        G. SCHIRMER, INC.   .35
JORDA, L.
    DANCE FROM BALLET-MUSIC FOR 'ROSAMUNDE'
        G. SCHIRMER, INC.   .35
JORDAN, J.
    LITTLE RED MONKEY
        THE BIG THREE MUSIC CORPORATION   00.95
JOSEFFY, R.
    ARIETTA DI BALLETTO--GLUCK
        G. SCHIRMER, INC.   .50
JOSEFFY, R.
    SECOND MELODY IN E FLAT
        G. SCHIRMER, INC.   .50
JOSEPHUS, SR. MARY   3
    HOBGOBLINS
        BELWIN-MILLS PUBLISHING CORPORATION   .60
JOSTEN, W.
    SONATA FOR PIANO
        AMERICAN MUSIC EDITION   2.00
JOUBERT, J.
    DANCE SUITE
        NOVELLO AND COMPANY, LTD.   10.0077.02   1.25
JOUBERT, J.
    SONATA IN ONE MOVEMENT
        NOVELLO AND COMPANY, LTD.   10.0079.09   1.40
JOUBERTI
    BAL CHEZ LE MINISTRE, UN -- MAZURKA --
        FRANCO COLOMBO PUBLICATIONS   SAL   1.75
JOUBERTI
    BAL CHEZ LE MINISTRE, UN -- MAZURKA --
        FRANCO COLOMBO PUBLICATIONS   SAL   1.50
JOYNER, B.   1
    BROWN-EYED DOLLY
        THEODORE PRESSER COMPANY   .50
JOYNER, B.
    DEAR SANTA
        WILLIS MUSIC COMPANY   .35
JOYNER, B.   1
    DRIFTING
        WILLIS MUSIC COMPANY   .30
JOYNER, B.   1 1/2
    ECHO
        THEODORE PRESSER COMPANY   .50
JOYNER, B.   1
    GLIDING
        WILLIS MUSIC COMPANY   .35
JOYNER, B.   1
    GRASSHOPPER, THE
        WILLIS MUSIC COMPANY   .35
JOYNER, B.   1
    HOLIDAY MARCH
        WILLIS MUSIC COMPANY   .30
JOYNER, B.   3
    JAZZETTE
        WILLIS MUSIC COMPANY   .40
JOYNER, B.   1
    JUMP JOHNNY JUMP
        THEODORE PRESSER COMPANY   .50
JOYNER, B.   1
    LITTLEST REINDEER, THE
        WILLIS MUSIC COMPANY   .40
JOYNER, B.   1
    MARCHING FINGERS
        WILLIS MUSIC COMPANY   .35
JOYNER, B.   2 1/2
    MELODY WALTZ
        WILLIS MUSIC COMPANY   .40
JOYNER, B.   1 1/2
    MERRY LITTLE MILLWHEEL
        THEODORE PRESSER COMPANY   .50
JOYNER, B.   1
    OUR MAPLE TREE
        THEODORE PRESSER COMPANY   .50
JOYNER, B.   1 1/2
    RUN, LITTLE SQUIRREL
        WILLIS MUSIC COMPANY   .35
JOYNER, B.   3
    SHADOW DANCERS
        WILLIS MUSIC COMPANY   .40
JOYNER, B.   1 1/2
    SNOW ON THE HILLSIDE
        WILLIS MUSIC COMPANY   .40
JOYNER, B.   2 1/2
    TALE OF HALLOWEEN
        THEODORE PRESSER COMPANY   .50
JOYNER, B.   1 1/2
    THIS IS THE NIGHT OF HALLOWEEN
        THEODORE PRESSER COMPANY   .50
JOYNER, B.   3
    THOUGHTS OF SPRING
        WILLIS MUSIC COMPANY   .40

JOYNER, B.	1		
TROT, PONY TROT			
WILLIS MUSIC COMPANY			.30
JOYNER, B.	1		
WALTZ FOR JUDY			
WILLIS MUSIC COMPANY			.35
JOYNER, B.	1		
WALTZING BALLERINA			
WILLIS MUSIC COMPANY			.50
JOYNER, B.	1		
WHISTLING BOY			
WILLIS MUSIC COMPANY			.30
JUDD, A.	3		
BABBLING BROOK, A			
CENTURY MUSIC PUBLISHING COMPANY, INC.		1684	.40
JUDD, A.	3		
BARN DANCE			
CENTURY MUSIC PUBLISHING COMPANY, INC.		1413	.40
JUDD, A.	3		
COQUETA, LA, FANDANGO			
CENTURY MUSIC PUBLISHING COMPANY, INC.		1683	.40
JUDD, A.			
COUNTRY DANCE			
FRANCO COLOMBO PUBLICATIONS		LD520	.60
JUDD, A.	3		
FROST ON THE PUMPKINS			
CENTURY MUSIC PUBLISHING COMPANY, INC.		1413	.40
JUDD, A.	4		
IN THE MONTH OF ROSES			
CENTURY MUSIC PUBLISHING COMPANY, INC.		1678	.40
JUDD, A.	3		
VALSE NOVELETTE			
CENTURY MUSIC PUBLISHING COMPANY, INC.		1679	.40
JUDD, A.			
WISTFUL TUNE			
FRANCO COLOMBO PUBLICATIONS		LD519	.60
JUNAYEVSKY *			
SNOWFLAKES			
MCA MUSIC			1.00
JUNGMAN, A.	4		
CHAPEL IN THE FOREST			
CENTURY MUSIC PUBLISHING COMPANY, INC.		985	.40
JUNGMAN, A.	3		
IN THE FORGE			
CENTURY MUSIC PUBLISHING COMPANY, INC.		2588	.40
JUNGMAN, A.	5		
LA HARPE -- HARP SOUNDS			
CENTURY MUSIC PUBLISHING COMPANY, INC.		2291	.40
JUNGMAN, A.	3		
LONGING FOR HOME			
CENTURY MUSIC PUBLISHING COMPANY, INC.		640	.40
JUNGMAN, A.	4		
WILL O' THE WISP			
CENTURY MUSIC PUBLISHING COMPANY, INC.		1381	.40
JUNGMANN, A.			
WILL-O'-THE-WISP--CAPRICCIETTO			
G. SCHIRMER, INC.			.40
JURAFSKY			
TOCCATA			
FRANCO COLOMBO PUBLICATIONS		BA12511	1.25
JUREK, W. A.			
DEUTSCHMEISTER REGIMENTS-MARSCH			
UNIVERSAL EDITION		UE 4042	.95
JUROWSKY	4		
KLAVIER-SUITE, OP. 2			
BARENREITER VERLAG		AP 632	
KABALEVSKY	MIROVITCH, A.		
CLOWN, A COZY WALTZ, THE			
MCA MUSIC			.60
KABALEVSKY			
CLOWNS			
FREDERICK HARRIS MUSIC COMPANY			.60
KABALEVSKY			
COMEDIAN'S GALLOP, OP. 26			
MCA MUSIC			1.00
KABALEVSKY	MIROVITCH, A.		
CRADLE SONG, OP. 27			
MCA MUSIC			.60
KABALEVSKY			
DANCE			
MCA MUSIC			.60
KABALEVSKY	MIROVITCH, A.		
ETUDE, OP. 27			
MCA MUSIC			.60
KABALEVSKY			
GALLOPING COMEDIANS			
MCA MUSIC			.75
KABALEVSKY			
GAY MARCH, A			
FREDERICK HARRIS MUSIC COMPANY			.60
KABALEVSKY			
HOPPING			
FREDERICK HARRIS MUSIC COMPANY			.60
KABALEVSKY	MIROVITCH, A.		
HORSEMAN, OP. 27, THE.			
MCA MUSIC			.60
KABALEVSKY	FOLDES		
INTERMEZZO FROM 'THE COMEDIANS'			
MCA MUSIC			.60
KABALEVSKY	FOLDES		
LITTLE LYRICAL SCENE, A			
MCA MUSIC			.60
KABALEVSKY			
LITTLE SONG, A			
FREDERICK HARRIS MUSIC COMPANY			.60
KABALEVSKY			
NIGHT ON THE RIVER			
FREDERICK HARRIS MUSIC COMPANY			.60
KABALEVSKY	MIROVITCH, A.		
PLAYING BALL, OP. 27			
MCA MUSIC			.60
KABALEVSKY	D		
RONDO, OP. 59			
C. F. PETERS CORPORATION		4766	2.00
KABALEVSKY			
RONDO, OP. 59			
INTERNATIONAL MUSIC COMPANY			1.25
KABALEVSKY			
RONDO, OP. 59			
MCA MUSIC			1.25
KABALEVSKY			
RUSSIAN FOLK SONG			
FREDERICK HARRIS MUSIC COMPANY			.60
KABALEVSKY			
SONATA NO. 01			
MCA MUSIC			2.00

KABALEVSKY			
SONATA NO. 02			
EDWIN F. KALMUS		3571	2.00
KABALEVSKY			
SONATA NO. 02 OP. 45			
MCA MUSIC			3.00
KABALEVSKY			
SONATA NO. 02, OP. 45			
G. SCHIRMER, INC.			2.00
KABALEVSKY	PHILIPP, I.		
SONATA NO. 02, OP. 45			
INTERNATIONAL MUSIC COMPANY			2.00
KABALEVSKY	D		
SONATA NO. 02, OP. 45 --NEW VERSION--			
C. F. PETERS CORPORATION		4763	4.00
KABALEVSKY			
SONATA NO. 03			
EDWIN F. KALMUS		3572	2.00
KABALEVSKY	M-D		
SONATA NO. 03, OP. 46			
C. F. PETERS CORPORATION		4731	3.00
KABALEVSKY			
SONATA NO. 03, OP. 46			
G. SCHIRMER, INC.			1.50
KABALEVSKY	PHILIPP, I.		
SONATA NO. 03, OP. 46			
INTERNATIONAL MUSIC COMPANY			2.00
KABALEVSKY			
SONATA, OP. 6			
EDWIN F. KALMUS		357 0	1.50
KABALEVSKY	MIROVITCH, A.		
SONATINA IN A MINOR, OP. 27			
MCA MUSIC			1.25
KABALEVSKY	PHILIPP, I.		
SONATINA NO. 01 IN C, OP. 13			
INTERNATIONAL MUSIC COMPANY			1.25
KABALEVSKY			
SONATINA NO. 01 IN C, OP. 13 NO. 1			
G. SCHIRMER, INC.			.75
KABALEVSKY			
SONATINA, OP. 13 NO. 1			
ASHLEY DEALERS SERVICE, INC.		ES	1.00
KABALEVSKY			
SONATINA, OP. 13 NO. 1 IN C MAJOR			
MCA MUSIC			1.25
KABALEVSKY			
SONATINA, OP. 13 NO. 2 IN G MAJOR			
MCA MUSIC			1.25
KABALEVSKY	M		
SONATINA, OP. 13, NO. 1			
C. F. PETERS CORPORATION		4708	2.00
KABALEVSKY	2-3		
SONATINE IN A MINOR			
CENTURY MUSIC PUBLISHING COMPANY, INC.		3911	.40
KABALEVSKY			
SPRING GAMES AND DANCE			
MCA MUSIC			2.00
KABALEVSKY	M		
THEME AND VARIATIONS, OP. 40, NO. 2			
C. F. PETERS CORPORATION		4707B	1.25
KABALEVSKY			
TOCCATINA			
FREDERICK HARRIS MUSIC COMPANY			.60
KABALEVSKY	MIROVITCH, A.		
TOCCATINA, OP. 27			
MCA MUSIC			.60
KABALEVSKY	E		
VARIATIONS IN D, OP. 40, NO. 1			
C. F. PETERS CORPORATION		4707A	1.25
KABALEVSKY			
VARIATIONS ON AN AMERICAN FOLK SONG			
MCA MUSIC			1.00
KABALEVSKY	PHILIPP, I.		
VARIATIONS, OP. 40			
INTERNATIONAL MUSIC COMPANY			1.25
KABALEVSKY			
VARIATIONS, OP. 43			
MCA MUSIC			1.25
KABALEVSKY *			
LITTLE JOKE, A, OP. 27			
MCA MUSIC			.60
KADOSA			
AL FRESCO, OP. 11A			
KULTURA			1.75
KADOSA			
CAPRICCIO, OP. 23H			
KULTURA			1.25
KADOSA			
EPIGRAMME, OP. 8			
KULTURA			1.00
KADOSA			
ESQUISSES, OP. 28B			
KULTURA			1.50
KADOSA			
FOLK SONG SUITE, OP. 21			
KULTURA			1.25
KADOSA			
KALEIDOSCOPE, OP. 61			
KULTURA			1.50
KADOSA			
RHAPSODIE, OP. 28A			
UNIVERSAL EDITION		UE 11698	1.30
KADOSA			
SIX PETITE PRELUDES, OP. 35A			
UNIVERSAL EDITION		UE 11727	1.30
KADOSA			
SONATA NO. 01, OP. 7			
KULTURA			2.75
KADOSA			
SONATA NO. 02, OP. 9			
KULTURA			2.00
KADOSA			
SONATA NO. 03, OP. 13			
KULTURA			1.50
KADOSA			
SONATA NO. 04, OP. 54			
KULTURA			3.00
KADOSA			
SONATINA			
KULTURA			.75
KADOSA			
SONATINA ON HUNGARIAN FOLKSONGS, OP. 23D			
KULTURA			1.50
KADOSA			
SONATINA, OP. 11B			
KULTURA			.90

KADOSA
    SUITE FOR PIANO NO. 2, OP. 1 NO. 2
        KULTURA   1.00
KADOSA
    THREE SMALL PIECES
        KULTURA   .80
KADOSA
    THREE TRISTIA, OP. 38B
        KULTURA   .90
KAGEL, M.
    METAPIECE -- MIMETICS
        UNIVERSAL EDITION   UE 14919   20.75
KAHAL *   RITTMAN
    I'LL BE SEEING YOU
        MCA MUSIC   1.00
KAHAL *   LIBERACE
    I'LL BE SEEING YOU
        MCA MUSIC   1.00
KAHAL *   SINGER
    I'LL BE SEEING YOU
        MCA MUSIC   1.00
KAHALI, V.
    GARGOYLES
        BELWIN-MILLS PUBLISHING CORPORATION   20568   .60
KAHL
    AIRPLANE RIDE, AN
        BOSTON MUSIC COMPANY   .50
KAHL
    BLACK MAGIC
        BOSTON MUSIC COMPANY   .50
KAHL
    BUTTERFLY WALTZ
        BOSTON MUSIC COMPANY   .50
KAHL   SCHAUM, J.   2 1/2
    CARAVAN
        SCHAUM PUBLICATIONS, INC.   .60
KAHL   2
    ECHO WALTZ
        BELWIN-MILLS PUBLISHING CORPORATION   .60
KAHL   2
    FIREFLIES
        BOSTON MUSIC COMPANY   .50
KAHL   1
    LEARNING TO DANCE
        BOSTON MUSIC COMPANY   .50
KAHL   1
    TALKING CLOCK, THE
        BOSTON MUSIC COMPANY   .50
KAHL   2
    TWINKLING STAR
        BOSTON MUSIC COMPANY   .50
KAHN, E.I.
    CIACCONA DEI TEMPI DI GUERRA--1943
        ASSOCIATED MUSIC PUBLISHERS, INC.   BMP   4.00
KAHN, E.I.
    SHORT PIANO PIECE
        ASSOCIATED MUSIC PUBLISHERS, INC.   BMP   .75
KAHN, M.
    CASCADING STARS
        BELWIN-MILLS PUBLISHING CORPORATION   25294   .60
KAHN, M.
    COOL MULE
        BELWIN-MILLS PUBLISHING CORPORATION   25273   .60
KAHN, M.
    CORN FLAKES
        BELWIN-MILLS PUBLISHING CORPORATION   25312   .60
KAHN, M.
    GASLIGHT BLUES
        BELWIN-MILLS PUBLISHING CORPORATION   25288   .60
KAHN, M.
    GOIN' TO TOWN
        BELWIN-MILLS PUBLISHING CORPORATION   25005   .60
KAHN, M.
    JAZZ SUITE
        BELWIN-MILLS PUBLISHING CORPORATION   25293   .75
KAHN, M.
    JUMPIN' JUPITER
        BELWIN-MILLS PUBLISHING CORPORATION   25155   .60
KAHN, M.
    LAZY DAZE
        BELWIN-MILLS PUBLISHING CORPORATION   25156   .60
KAHN, M.
    ON THE PONY EXPRESS
        BELWIN-MILLS PUBLISHING CORPORATION   25154   .60
KAHN, M.
    OUTWARD BOUND
        BELWIN-MILLS PUBLISHING CORPORATION   25283   .60
KAHN, M.
    PERCEPTION
        BELWIN-MILLS PUBLISHING CORPORATION   25291   .60
KAHN, M.
    SCARECROW ON A HOLIDAY
        BELWIN-MILLS PUBLISHING CORPORATION   25179   .60
KAHN, M.
    SCARECROW ON A HOLIDAY
        BELWIN-MILLS PUBLISHING CORPORATION   .60
KAHN, M.
    SPANISH BLUES
        BELWIN-MILLS PUBLISHING CORPORATION   25055   .60
KAHN, M.
    SPECTRUM
        BELWIN-MILLS PUBLISHING CORPORATION   25002   .60
KAHN, M.
    STRICTLY SOLID
        BELWIN-MILLS PUBLISHING CORPORATION   25205   .60
KAHN, M.
    SUNDAY TRAFFIC
        BELWIN-MILLS PUBLISHING CORPORATION   25169   .60
KAHN, M.--ED   KAHN, M.
    DOES YOUR CHEWING GUM LOSE ITS FLAVOR ON THE BEDPOST OVERNIGHT
    -- SIMP.
        BELWIN-MILLS PUBLISHING CORPORATION   26074   .50
KAHN, M.--ED   KAHN, M.
    HAVAH NAGILAH
        BELWIN-MILLS PUBLISHING CORPORATION   20404   .85
KAHN, M.--ED   KAHN, M.
    I WAS KAISER BILL'S BATMAN -- SIMP.
        BELWIN-MILLS PUBLISHING CORPORATION   26121   .50
KAHN, M.--ED   KAHN, M.
    JUST BEGUINE-ING
        BELWIN-MILLS PUBLISHING CORPORATION   25257   .60
KAHNAU
    SONATA NO. 02
        EDWARD B. MARKS MUSIC CORPORATION   02.00

KAIHAN *
    NOW IS THE HOUR
        MCA MUSIC   1.00
KAIHAN *
    NOW IS THE HOUR
        MCA MUSIC   .60
KAINE   4
    DUTCH WALTZ
        VOLKWEIN BROS.   .30
KAISER   1
    LITTLE DRUMMER BOY
        PRO-ART PUBLICATIONS, INC.   400   .50
KAISER   3
    NATIONAL AIRS, MEDLEY MARCH
        CENTURY MUSIC PUBLISHING COMPANY, INC. 978   .40
KALBERT   3
    MURMURING WAVES
        BOSTON MUSIC COMPANY   .50
KALINNIKOFF   M-D
    ELEGIE
        C. F. PETERS CORPORATION   F49   1.50
KALKBRENNER
    SONATA FOR LEFT HAND OP. 40
        MUSICA OBSCURA   3.50
KALKBRENNER
    VARIATIONS ON 'RULE BRITANICA' FROM ALFRED --DR. ARNE OP. 53
        MUSICA OBSCURA   2.50
KALMAN   SIRMAY
    PLAY GYPSIES - DANCE GYPSIES
        WARNER BROTHERS PUBLISHERS   1.00
KALMAN   RICHTER   FIRST YEAR
    PLAY GYPSIES - DANCE GYPSIES
        WARNER BROTHERS PUBLISHERS   .75
KALMAN
    SARI
        EDWARD B. MARKS MUSIC CORPORATION   01.00
KALMAN, C.
    NEW YORK IMPRESSIONS
        GENERAL MUSIC PUBLISHING COMPANY, INC. 33   1.50
KALMAN, C.
    NEW YORK IMPRESSIONS - LIGHT SUITE
        GENERAL MUSIC PUBLISHING COMPANY, INC.   1.50
KALMANOFF
    BOUNCING THE BALL
        SAM FOX PUBLISHING COMPANY, INC.   .50
KALMANOFF
    BOUNCING THE BALL
        SOUTHERN MUSIC COMPANY   .50
KALMANOFF
    LITTLE SAILBOAT, THE
        SAM FOX PUBLISHING COMPANY, INC.   .50
KALMANOFF
    LITTLE SAILBOAT, THE
        SOUTHERN MUSIC COMPANY   .50
KALMANOFF
    UP ON A PLAYGROUND SWING
        SAM FOX PUBLISHING COMPANY, INC.   .50
KALMANOFF
    UP ON A PLAYGROUND SWING
        SOUTHERN MUSIC COMPANY   .50
KANN, H.
    ABSCHNITT 37
        ASSOCIATED MUSIC PUBLISHERS, INC.   DOB   1.50
KANN, H.
    SONATINA--1954
        ASSOCIATED MUSIC PUBLISHERS, INC.   DOB   1.75
KAPER, B.
    CONFETTI
        THE BIG THREE MUSIC CORPORATION   00.95
KAPER, B.
    INVITATION
        THE BIG THREE MUSIC CORPORATION   00.95
KAPER, B.
    MUTINY ON THE BOUNTY
        THE BIG THREE MUSIC CORPORATION   00.95
KAPER, B.
    TWO LOVES - THEME
        THE BIG THREE MUSIC CORPORATION   00.95
KAPLAN   2
    CHINESE DANCE
        BELWIN-MILLS PUBLISHING CORPORATION   .60
KAPLAN   1
    GAY KANGAROO, THE
        BELWIN-MILLS PUBLISHING CORPORATION   .60
KAPR   4
    SONATA NO. 01
        BARENREITER VERLAG   AP 637
KAPRAL   3-4
    FANTASIE
        BARENREITER VERLAG   AP 638
KAPRAL   3
    ROMANTISCHE SUITE
        BARENREITER VERLAG   AP 305
KAPRAL   3
    SONATINA BUCOLICA
        BARENREITER VERLAG   AP 639
KAPRAL   3-4
    SONATINE -- 1930 --
        BARENREITER VERLAG   AP 641
KAPRAL   3
    SONATINE -- 1944 --
        BARENREITER VERLAG   AP 640
KAPRAL   3
    SUITE BUCOLICA
        BARENREITER VERLAG   AP 642
KARAM, F.
    SCHERZO IN B MINOR
        ASSOCIATED MUSIC PUBLISHERS, INC.   BER   .60
KARGANOFF   2
    GRANDFATHER'S CLOCK
        WILLIS MUSIC COMPANY   .40
KARGANOFF   4
    SERENADE
        CENTURY MUSIC PUBLISHING COMPANY, INC. 2355   .40
KARGANOFF   4
    SOUVENIR
        CENTURY MUSIC PUBLISHING COMPANY, INC. 2163   .40
KARGANOFF
    VALSE MINIATURE
        FREDERICK HARRIS MUSIC COMPANY   .60
KAROLYI
    TOCCATA FURIOSA
        KULTURA   1.50
KARP   2
    BUGLES ON PARADE
        PRO-ART PUBLICATIONS, INC.   572   .50

```
KARP                               2
    CANON HILL
        PRO-ART PUBLICATIONS, INC.          606      .50
KARP                               2-3
    CHASIDIC TUNE
        PRO-ART PUBLICATIONS, INC.          617      .50
KARP                               2-3
    CIRCLE DANCE
        PRO-ART PUBLICATIONS, INC.          597      .50
KARP                               1 1/2
    CROSS OVER THE BRIDGE
        WILLIS MUSIC COMPANY                         .40
KARP                               2-3
    DANCE ALLEGRO
        PRO-ART PUBLICATIONS, INC.          601      .50
KARP                               2-3
    DANCE, DANCE THE HORA
        PRO-ART PUBLICATIONS, INC.          545      .50
KARP                               2
    DANCING ALONG
        PRO-ART PUBLICATIONS, INC.          494      .50
KARP                               2
    DASHING ALONG
        PRO-ART PUBLICATIONS, INC.          565      .50
KARP                               1-2
    DOWNTOWN STREET MARCH
        PRO-ART PUBLICATIONS, INC.          584      .50
KARP                               2
    EMERALD DANCE
        PRO-ART PUBLICATIONS, INC.          547      .50
KARP                               2-3
    EMERALD TANGO
        PRO-ART PUBLICATIONS, INC.          514      .50
KARP                               2-3
    FANTASY
        PRO-ART PUBLICATIONS, INC.          571      .50
KARP                               2-3
    GEMINI
        PRO-ART PUBLICATIONS, INC.          618      .50
KARP                               2
    GLIDING ALONG
        PRO-ART PUBLICATIONS, INC.          515      .50
KARP                               2-3
    HEBREW DANCE
        PRO-ART PUBLICATIONS, INC.          586      .50
KARP                               1-2
    HORA TIME
        PRO-ART PUBLICATIONS, INC.          581      .50
KARP                               2
    JEWISH DANCE
        WILLIS MUSIC COMPANY                         .40
KARP                               2-3
    JOYOUS DANCE
        PRO-ART PUBLICATIONS, INC.          594      .50
KARP                               2
    LONESOME PUPPET
        PRO-ART PUBLICATIONS, INC.          605      .50
KARP                               1-2
    LONG JOURNEY, A
        PRO-ART PUBLICATIONS, INC.          567      .50
KARP                               2-3
    LONG WAIT, A
        PRO-ART PUBLICATIONS, INC.          493      .50
KARP                               2-3
    MERRY GO ROUND RIDE
        PRO-ART PUBLICATIONS, INC.          533      .50
KARP                               1-2
    MERRY GO ROUND WALTZ
        PRO-ART PUBLICATIONS, INC.          583      .50
KARP                               2
    MOON BUGGY
        PRO-ART PUBLICATIONS, INC.          588      .50
KARP                               2-3
    MR. SCARLATTI
        PRO-ART PUBLICATIONS, INC.          492      .50
KARP                               1-2
    MY KITE
        PRO-ART PUBLICATIONS, INC.          580      .50
KARP                               2-3
    ORIENTAL DANCE
        PRO-ART PUBLICATIONS, INC.          582      .50
KARP                               2
    PAINTED SOLDIER
        PRO-ART PUBLICATIONS, INC.          557      .50
KARP                               2
    PLEASANT DREAMS
        PRO-ART PUBLICATIONS, INC.          587      .50
KARP                               1-2
    PUPPET ON A STRING
        PRO-ART PUBLICATIONS, INC.          616      .50
KARP                               1-2
    PUPPET'S TALE
        PRO-ART PUBLICATIONS, INC.          520      .50
KARP                               1 1/2
    RUNNING ALONG
        WILLIS MUSIC COMPANY                         .40
KARP                               2-3
    SNAKE CHARMER
        PRO-ART PUBLICATIONS, INC.          604      .50
KARP                               2
    STROLLING ALONG
        PRO-ART PUBLICATIONS, INC.          487      .50
KARP                               1
    SWINGING IN THE PARK
        PRO-ART PUBLICATIONS, INC.          529      .50
KARP                               2
    TANZ
        WILLIS MUSIC COMPANY                         .50
KARP                               1
    TOY BALLOON
        PRO-ART PUBLICATIONS, INC.          558      .50
KARP                               1-2
    TRAVELING ALONG
        PRO-ART PUBLICATIONS, INC.          570      .50
KARP                               1-2
    WALKING ALONG
        PRO-ART PUBLICATIONS, INC.          495      .50
KARP, D.                           2
    BUSY LITTLE TRAIN, THE
        LEE ROBERTS MUSIC PUBLICATIONS, INC.         .50
KARST                              1-2
    DE TULPENFEEST
        PRO-ART PUBLICATIONS, INC.          470      .50
KARST                              1
    IT'S SNOWING
        PRO-ART PUBLICATIONS, INC.          375      .50

KARST                              1-2
    MY LITTLE DOG
        PRO-ART PUBLICATIONS, INC.          469      .50
KARST                              1
    SLEEP, PRETTY SUSAN
        PRO-ART PUBLICATIONS, INC.          376      .50
KARTUN
    CAPRICE RHYTHMIQUE -- ON A THEME BY PAGANINI --
        FRANCO COLOMBO PUBLICATIONS          SAL     3.00
KASILAG, L.
    THEME AND VARIATIONS
        PEER SOUTHERN ORGANIZATION                   01.50
KASNER                             2
    BAION
        PRO-ART PUBLICATIONS, INC.          348      .50
KASSCHAU, H.
    MAMBO MARITA
        SAM FOX PUBLISHING COMPANY, INC.             .50
KASSCHAU, H.
    MAMBO MARITA
        SOUTHERN MUSIC COMPANY                       .50
KASSCHAU, H.
    MERRY VARIATIONS
        SAM FOX PUBLISHING COMPANY, INC.             .50
KASSCHAU, H.
    MERRY VARIATIONS
        SOUTHERN MUSIC COMPANY                       .50
KASSCHAU, H.
    MY FIRST WALTZ
        SAM FOX PUBLISHING COMPANY, INC.             .50
KASSCHAU, H.
    MY FIRST WALTZ
        SOUTHERN MUSIC COMPANY                       .50
KASSCHAU, H.
    RHUMBA RIO
        SAM FOX PUBLISHING COMPANY, INC.             .50
KASSCHAU, H.
    RHUMBA RIO
        SOUTHERN MUSIC COMPANY                       .50
KASSCHAU, H.
    SAMBA SENORITA
        SAM FOX PUBLISHING COMPANY, INC.             .50
KASSCHAU, H.
    SAMBA SENORITA
        SOUTHERN MUSIC COMPANY                       .50
KASSCHAU, H.
    SHEEP MAY SAFELY GRAZE
        SOUTHERN MUSIC COMPANY                       .50
KASSCHAU, H.
    VICAR OF BRAY, THE
        SAM FOX PUBLISHING COMPANY, INC.             .50
KASSCHAU, H.
    VICAR OF BRAY, THE
        SOUTHERN MUSIC COMPANY                       .50
KASSCHAU, H.--ED.        KASSCHAU, H.
    HE'S GOT THE WHOLE WORLD IN HIS HAND
        SOUTHERN MUSIC COMPANY                       .75
KASSCHAU, H.--ED.        KASSCHAU, H.
    HE'S GOT THE WHOLE WORLD IN HIS HANDS
        SAM FOX PUBLISHING COMPANY, INC.             .75
KASSCHAU, H.--ED.        KASSCHAU, H.
    SHEEP MAY SAFELY GRAZE
        SAM FOX PUBLISHING COMPANY, INC.             .50
KASTLE
    PRELUDE, NOCTURNE AND DANCE
        BELWIN-MILLS PUBLISHING CORPORATION          1.75
KASTLE
    PRELUDE, NOCTURNE AND DANCE
        FRANCO COLOMBO PUBLICATIONS         NY2226   1.75
KASTLER, A.             SCHAUM, J.          3
    CANDY CANE LANE
        SCHAUM PUBLICATIONS, INC.                    .60
KASZNER                            3
    BRAZILIAN SAMBA
        PRO-ART PUBLICATIONS, INC.          349      .50
KASZNER                            3
    LITTLE RONDEAU
        PRO-ART PUBLICATIONS, INC.          346      .50
KASZNER                            3
    MONKEY'S PACHANGA
        PRO-ART PUBLICATIONS, INC.          347      .50
KASZYCKI
    SONATINA
        EDWARD B. MARKS MUSIC CORPORATION            01.60
KATCHER                RICHTER          FIRST YEAR
    WHEN DAY IS DONE
        WARNER BROTHERS PUBLISHERS                   .75
KATTNIGG, R.
    FOUR PRELUDES AND FUGUES IN OLDEN STYLE , OP. 7
        UNIVERSAL EDITION                   UE 8506  2.80
KATTNIGG, R.
    THREE PIANO PIECES, OP. 1
        UNIVERSAL EDITION                   UE 10204 1.30
KAY                                3
    SWEET MEDITATIONS
        CENTURY MUSIC PUBLISHING COMPANY, INC. 2686  .40
KAYE, E.
    MUSICAL CROSSWORD, A
        OXFORD UNIVERSITY PRESS             33.058   .75
KAYE, L.                           1 1/2
    OUR WALTZ
        BELWIN-MILLS PUBLISHING CORPORATION          .60
KAYSER, P.                         M
    SUITE POUR PIANO
        C. F. PETERS CORPORATION            H186     1.50
KEAN, H.
    DAWN OF A SPRING
        G. SCHIRMER, INC.                            .35
KEENAN
    THRUMMING AND HUMMING
        CARL FISCHER, INC.                  P 2008   .50
KEISER                             4
    FLOWERS AND FERNS
        CENTURY MUSIC PUBLISHING COMPANY, INC. 2179  .60
KEISER                             4
    FLOWERS AND FERNS, TONE POEM
        CENTURY MUSIC PUBLISHING COMPANY, INC. 1070  .40
KEISER                             3
    IRISH AIRS, MEDLEY MARCH
        CENTURY MUSIC PUBLISHING COMPANY, INC. 1093  .40
KELEMEN                            D
    SONATA
        C. F. PETERS CORPORATION            5866     4.00
KELER BELA                         4
    OVERTURE, LUSTSPIEL
        CENTURY MUSIC PUBLISHING COMPANY, INC. 642   .40
```

KELKEL
    MINIATURES POUR PETIT ALEXANDRE
        FRANCO COLOMBO PUBLICATIONS   R2213   2.50
KELKEL
    TOCCATA
        FRANCO COLOMBO PUBLICATIONS   R1391   1.50
KELLER, B.   4
    LUSTSPIEL OVERTURE
        CENTURY MUSIC PUBLISHING COMPANY, INC.   642   .40
KELLEY   1
    FOREIGN AGENT
        PRO-ART PUBLICATIONS, INC.   447   .50
KELLEY
    JACK TAR
        CARL FISCHER, INC.   P 2984   .50
KELLEY, R.   1-2
    DESERT DRUMS
        CENTURY MUSIC PUBLISHING COMPANY, INC.   4412   .40
KELLEY, R.   1-2
    FIFE AND DRUM CORPS
        CENTURY MUSIC PUBLISHING COMPANY, INC.   4240   .40
KELLEY, R.   2-3
    MONKEY SHINES
        CENTURY MUSIC PUBLISHING COMPANY, INC.   4137   .40
KELLEY, R.   2-3
    WHODUNIT
        CENTURY MUSIC PUBLISHING COMPANY, INC.   4209   .40
KELLEY, S.   M
    SKY LINE
        COMPOSERS PRESS, INC.   1.50
KELTERBORN
    MONOSONATA
        BARENREITER VERLAG   BA 4142   6.00
KELTERBORN   5
    MONOSONATA
        BARENREITER VERLAG   BA 4142
KENINS
    DREAMING
        FREDERICK HARRIS MUSIC COMPANY   .60
KENNAWAY   M
    VARIATIONS ON A TRADITIONAL MELODY --DRINK TO ME ONLY WITH THINE
    EYES--
        C. F. PETERS CORPORATION   H755   1.50
KENNEDY *   SCHAUM, J.   2
    SOUTH OF THE BORDER
        SCHAUM PUBLICATIONS, INC.   .75
KENNEDY, A.   3
    STAR OF HOPE, REVERIE
        CENTURY MUSIC PUBLISHING COMPANY, INC.   981   .40
KENNEDY, A.
    STAR OF THE SEA
        ASHLEY DEALERS SERVICE, INC.   ES   .95
KENNEDY, A.   4
    STAR OF THE SEA
        CENTURY MUSIC PUBLISHING COMPANY, INC.   .40
KENNEDY, A.
    STAR OF THE SEA
        THE BIG THREE MUSIC CORPORATION   00.50
KENNEDY, A.   3
    STAR OF THE SEA
        WILLIS MUSIC COMPANY   .40
KENNEDY, A.   3
    STARS OF GLORY
        CENTURY MUSIC PUBLISHING COMPANY, INC.   1076   .40
KENNEDY, A.   4
    STARS OF THE SEA
        CENTURY MUSIC PUBLISHING COMPANY, INC.   3493   .40
KENNINS
    DIVERSITIES
        MCA MUSIC   2.00
KENSLER   1
    NANCY'S LULLABY
        PRO-ART PUBLICATIONS, INC.   286   .50
KENT, A.   2 1/2
    ALPINE BOOGIE
        BELWIN-MILLS PUBLISHING CORPORATION   .60
KENT, A.   2
    BROWN BEAR BOOGIE
        BELWIN-MILLS PUBLISHING CORPORATION   .60
KENT, A.   2 1/2
    CARILLON BELLS
        BELWIN-MILLS PUBLISHING CORPORATION   .60
KENT, A.   1 1/2
    HAPPY BEE, THE
        BELWIN-MILLS PUBLISHING CORPORATION   .60
KENT, A.   2
    HONG KONG BOOGIE
        BELWIN-MILLS PUBLISHING CORPORATION   .60
KENT, A.   3
    JAZZ FESTIVAL BOOGIE
        BELWIN-MILLS PUBLISHING CORPORATION   .60
KENT, A.   2
    JUKEBOX BOOGIE
        BELWIN-MILLS PUBLISHING CORPORATION   .60
KENT, A.   3
    LA FIESTA BOOGIE
        BELWIN-MILLS PUBLISHING CORPORATION   .60
KENT, A.   3 1/2
    LOI KRATHONG
        BELWIN-MILLS PUBLISHING CORPORATION   .60
KENT, A.   2
    LOTUS DANCE, THE
        BELWIN-MILLS PUBLISHING CORPORATION   .60
KENT, A.   2 1/2
    MONKEY CAPERS
        BELWIN-MILLS PUBLISHING CORPORATION   .60
KENT, H.   1 1/2
    CHICO' BOOGIE WOOGIE
        BELWIN-MILLS PUBLISHING CORPORATION   .60
KERN, C. W.   3 1/2
    ARIEL, OP. 151 -- SCHERZO VALSE
        THEODORE PRESSER COMPANY   .60
KERN, C. W.   2
    CLOWN, THE
        THEODORE PRESSER COMPANY   .50
KERN, C. W.   2 1/2
    JUGGLER, THE OP. 192 NO. 6
        THEODORE PRESSER COMPANY   .50
KERR   2
    LITTLE HARPIST
        BOSTON MUSIC COMPANY   .50
KERR   WILLIAMS, J.   2
    WATCH YOUR STEP
        BOSTON MUSIC COMPANY   .50
KERR, H.   MD
    FRONTIER DAY
        THEODORE PRESSER COMPANY   .50

KERR, H.
    SONATA NO. 02
        BOOSEY AND HAWKES, INC.   1.50
KERR, R. N.   3
    BALLERINA
        VOLKWEIN BROS.   .40
KERR, R. N.   1-2
    BE WISE
        CENTURY MUSIC PUBLISHING COMPANY, INC.   4178   .40
KERR, R. N.   2
    CAN YOU
        CENTURY MUSIC PUBLISHING COMPANY, INC.   4179   .40
KERR, R. N.   1
    MY FIRST PIECE
        THEODORE PRESSER COMPANY   .50
KERR, R. N.   2
    ON THE ICE
        VOLKWEIN BROS.   .35
KERR, R. N.   1
    SUNDAY IN THE PARK
        CENTURY MUSIC PUBLISHING COMPANY, INC.   4120   .40
KERR, R. N.   2
    SWING IN OUR YARD, THE
        CENTURY MUSIC PUBLISHING COMPANY, INC.   4119   .40
KERR, R. N.   2
    WOODS AT DAWN
        WILLIS MUSIC COMPANY   .40
KERSEY
    BOOGIE WOOGIE COCKTAIL
        MCA MUSIC   1.00
KETELBEY, A.
    DEVOTION
        BELWIN-MILLS PUBLISHING CORPORATION   20071   .85
KETELBEY, A.
    DREAM OF CHRISTMAS, A
        BELWIN-MILLS PUBLISHING CORPORATION   .75
KETELBEY, A.
    IN A MONASTERY GARDEN
        WARNER BROTHERS PUBLISHERS   1.00
KETELBEY, A.   RICHTER   FIRST YEAR
    IN A MONASTERY GARDEN
        WARNER BROTHERS PUBLISHERS   .75
KETELBEY, A.   SCHAUM, J.
    SANCTUARY OF THE HEART
        BELWIN-MILLS PUBLISHING CORPORATION   .60
KETTERER, E.   3
    BANJO SONG
        THEODORE PRESSER COMPANY   .50
KETTERER, E.   1
    BELL AND THE LITTLE BELL, THE
        THEODORE PRESSER COMPANY   .50
KETTERER, E.   1
    BOBOLINK
        THEODORE PRESSER COMPANY   .50
KETTERER, E.   3
    BRAVE KNIGHT, THE
        THEODORE PRESSER COMPANY   .50
KETTERER, E.   3
    BUCCANEER, THE
        THEODORE PRESSER COMPANY   .50
KETTERER, E.   3
    CADETS ON PARADE
        THEODORE PRESSER COMPANY   .50
KETTERER, E.   1
    CAT TAILS
        VOLKWEIN BROS.   .25
KETTERER, E.   3
    DAINTY BALLET DANCER
        THEODORE PRESSER COMPANY   .50
KETTERER, E.   1
    FLEDGLINGS, THE
        THEODORE PRESSER COMPANY   .50
KETTERER, E.   2
    GAY CAVALIER, THE
        BOSTON MUSIC COMPANY   .50
KETTERER, E.
    HUNGARIAN CAPRICE, OP. 7
        FRANCO COLOMBO PUBLICATIONS   BA6407   .75
KETTERER, E.   2
    HUSHABY
        VOLKWEIN BROS.   .25
KETTERER, E.   2
    ICE CARNIVAL
        VOLKWEIN BROS.   .30
KETTERER, E.   2
    JACK AND JILL
        THEODORE PRESSER COMPANY   .50
KETTERER, E.   4
    L'ARGENTINE -- SILVERY WHISTLE
        CENTURY MUSIC PUBLISHING COMPANY, INC.   271   .40
KETTERER, E.   1
    LEFT, RIGHT, MARCH ALONG
        THEODORE PRESSER COMPANY   .50
KETTERER, E.   1
    LITTLE BOAT SONG, A
        THEODORE PRESSER COMPANY   .50
KETTERER, E.   2
    MARCH OF THE GNOMES
        THEODORE PRESSER COMPANY   .50
KETTERER, E.   2 1/2
    MARCH OF THE JACK O'LANTERNS
        THEODORE PRESSER COMPANY   .50
KETTERER, E.   2
    MARCH OF THE SCOUTS
        THEODORE PRESSER COMPANY   .50
KETTERER, E.   1
    MOON BOAT, THE
        THEODORE PRESSER COMPANY   .50
KETTERER, E.   2
    ON A SUMMER SEA
        WILLIS MUSIC COMPANY   .40
KETTERER, E.   2
    ON A SUMMER SEA
        WILLIS MUSIC COMPANY   .40
KETTERER, E.   2
    ON A SUMMER SEA
        WILLIS MUSIC COMPANY   .40
KETTERER, E.   3
    ON SKATES
        THEODORE PRESSER COMPANY   .50
KETTERER, E.   3
    PETITE MAZURKA
        THEODORE PRESSER COMPANY   .50
KETTERER, E.   3
    POLISH DANCE
        THEODORE PRESSER COMPANY   .50

KETTERER, E. 2 1/2
SILVER BLADES
THEODORE PRESSER COMPANY .50

KETTERER, E. 4
SILVERY THISTLE -- L'ARGENTINE --
CENTURY MUSIC PUBLISHING COMPANY, INC. 271 .40

KETTERER, E. 3
SPANISH DANCE
THEODORE PRESSER COMPANY .50

KETTERER, E. 3
SPARKLES
THEODORE PRESSER COMPANY .50

KETTERER, E. 2
SPINNING TOP, THE
THEODORE PRESSER COMPANY .50

KETTERER, E. 2 1/2
SWEETLY SINGS THE BROOKLET
THEODORE PRESSER COMPANY .50

KETTERER, E. 1
TICK TOCK
VOLKWEIN BROS. .25

KETTERER, E. 3
VALSE MELODIQUE
THEODORE PRESSER COMPANY .50

KETTERER, E. 3
VALSE PETITE
THEODORE PRESSER COMPANY .50

KETTERING, K. E
SUGAR AND SPICE
THEODORE PRESSER COMPANY .50

KEVAN 1
APACHE DANCE
PRO-ART PUBLICATIONS, INC. 180 .50

KEVAN 1 1/2
AT THE ICE PALACE
PRO-ART PUBLICATIONS, INC. 51 .50

KEVAN 1-2
BOUNCING BALL
PRO-ART PUBLICATIONS, INC. 181 .50

KEVAN 1-2
CAMEL RIDE, THE
PRO-ART PUBLICATIONS, INC. 183 .50

KEVAN 2
GRANDPA'S ROCKING CHAIR
PRO-ART PUBLICATIONS, INC. 49 .50

KEVAN 1-2
INDIAN WAR DANCE
PRO-ART PUBLICATIONS, INC. 271 .50

KEVAN 1-2
POGO STICK, THE
PRO-ART PUBLICATIONS, INC. 182 .50

KEVAN 2
SPOOKS ON PARADE
PRO-ART PUBLICATIONS, INC. 53 .50

KEVAN 1-2
TOY BAND, THE
PRO-ART PUBLICATIONS, INC. 179 .50

KEVAN
TRAINS A COMIN'
EDWARD B. MARKS MUSIC CORPORATION 00.60

KEVAN, G. A. 1 1/2
LITTLE TRUMPETER, THE
THEODORE PRESSER COMPANY .50

KEVAN, G. A. 1 1/2
PIRATES CAVE
THEODORE PRESSER COMPANY .50

KEVAN, G. A. 2
PRANCING PONY, THE
THEODORE PRESSER COMPANY .50

KEYSER, I. 2 1/2
MARCH OF THE TROLLS
THEODORE PRESSER COMPANY .50

KEYSOR, C. 1
RAIN ON THE LEAVES
THEODORE PRESSER COMPANY .50

KEYSOR, C. 1
SUMMER EVENING
THEODORE PRESSER COMPANY .50

KEYSOR, C. 1
WATER-WHEEL, THE
BELWIN-MILLS PUBLISHING CORPORATION .60

KHATCHATURIAN FLATO
ARMEN'S VARIATION
MCA MUSIC .60

KHATCHATURIAN FLATO
DANCE OF AYSHE
MCA MUSIC .60

KHATCHATURIAN SWARENSKI
DANCE OF THE ROSE MAIDENS
MCA MUSIC .60

KHATCHATURIAN FLATO
DANCE OF THE YOUNG KURDS
MCA MUSIC .60

KHATCHATURIAN
EVENING SONG
FREDERICK HARRIS MUSIC COMPANY .60

KHATCHATURIAN MIROVITCH, A.
EVENING SONG
MCA MUSIC .60

KHATCHATURIAN
GALOP FROM 'MASQUERADE' SUITE
MCA MUSIC .60

KHATCHATURIAN
IVAN SINGS
FREDERICK HARRIS MUSIC COMPANY .60

KHATCHATURIAN MIROVITCH, A.
IVAN SINGS
MCA MUSIC .60

KHATCHATURIAN SINGER
LEGINKA
MCA MUSIC .60

KHATCHATURIAN
ORIENTAL DANCE
MCA MUSIC .60

KHATCHATURIAN
POEM
MCA MUSIC 1.25

KHATCHATURIAN
SABRE DANCE
ASHLEY DEALERS SERVICE, INC. ES .95

KHATCHATURIAN
SABRE DANCE
EDWIN F. KALMUS 3579 .90

KHATCHATURIAN BERLIN
SABRE DANCE
FREDERICK HARRIS MUSIC COMPANY .60

KHATCHATURIAN SANDOR
SABRE DANCE
MCA MUSIC 1.25

KHATCHATURIAN LEVANT
SABRE DANCE
MCA MUSIC 1.00

KHATCHATURIAN SINGER
SABRE DANCE
MCA MUSIC 1.00

KHATCHATURIAN
SABRE DANCE -- SIMP.
ASHLEY DEALERS SERVICE, INC. ES .95

KHATCHATURIAN D
SABRE DANCE --FROM GAYNE--
C. F. PETERS CORPORATION 4768 1.50

KHATCHATURIAN
SABRE DANCE BOOGIE
MCA MUSIC 1.00

KHATCHATURIAN LEVINE
SABRE DANCE FROM 'GAYNE BALLET'
G. SCHIRMER, INC. .50

KHATCHATURIAN 3-4
SABRE DANCE, GAYNE BALLET
CENTURY MUSIC PUBLISHING COMPANY, INC. 4016 .40

KHATCHATURIAN D
SONATA
C. F. PETERS CORPORATION 4787 5.00

KHATCHATURIAN
SONATA
EDWIN F. KALMUS 3581 2.50

KHATCHATURIAN
SONATA
MCA MUSIC 3.50

KHATCHATURIAN M-D
SONATINA
C. F. PETERS CORPORATION 4758 2.50

KHATCHATURIAN
SONATINA
EDWIN F. KALMUS 3583 2.25

KHATCHATURIAN
SONATINA --1959
MCA MUSIC 2.00

KHATCHATURIAN SCHAUM, J. 3
SWORD DANCE
BELWIN-MILLS PUBLISHING CORPORATION .50

KHATCHATURIAN KING, S.
SWORD DANCE -- FROM BALLET 'GAYNE'
BELWIN-MILLS PUBLISHING CORPORATION 26054 .60

KHATCHATURIAN
TOCCATA
ASHLEY DEALERS SERVICE, INC. ES 1.00

KHATCHATURIAN D
TOCCATA
C. F. PETERS CORPORATION 4734 2.50

KHATCHATURIAN
TOCCATA
EDWIN F. KALMUS 3580 1.00

KHATCHATURIAN
TOCCATA
G. SCHIRMER, INC. .75

KHATCHATURIAN PHILIPP, I.
TOCCATA
INTERNATIONAL MUSIC COMPANY 1.25

KHATCHATURIAN
TOCCATA
MCA MUSIC 1.25

KHATCHATURIAN
WALTZ FROM -- MASQUERADE SUITE
MCA MUSIC .75

KHATCHTURIAN FRANK
LITTLE PIECE
MCA MUSIC .60

KILPATRICK 2 1/2
IKE MILLER'S REEL
BELWIN-MILLS PUBLISHING CORPORATION .60

KILPATRICK 2 1/2
RUSTLERS, BEWARE
BELWIN-MILLS PUBLISHING CORPORATION .60

KILPINEN, Y.
SONATA, OP. 85
ASSOCIATED MUSIC PUBLISHERS, INC. BRH 1.50

KIMES, K. 1
CHEROKEE CLAM-BAKE
BELWIN-MILLS PUBLISHING CORPORATION .60

KING
BUTTERFLY WINGS
BOSTON MUSIC COMPANY .50

KING
BY A BLUE LAGOON
SUMMY-BIRCHARD COMPANY .50

KING
CAROLINA WALTZ
BOSTON MUSIC COMPANY .50

KING
CAROUSEL IN PARIS
CARL FISCHER, INC. P 3208 .50

KING
CHARTREUSE KITTEN
CARL FISCHER, INC. P 3176 .50

KING
CHERRY BLOSSOM TIME
BOSTON MUSIC COMPANY .50

KING 2
CROOKED MARCH, A
LEE ROBERTS MUSIC PUBLICATIONS, INC. .50

KING 2
FROLICSOME FINGERS
BOSTON MUSIC COMPANY .50

KING 2
HERE COMES THE TRAIN
LEE ROBERTS MUSIC PUBLICATIONS, INC. .50

KING 2
IN AN OLD CHALET
BOSTON MUSIC COMPANY .50

KING 2
JUMPIN' AND COMIN' DOWN THE RIVER
LEE ROBERTS MUSIC PUBLICATIONS, INC. .60

KING 4
LA PRIMA DONNA, SCHOT.
CENTURY MUSIC PUBLISHING COMPANY, INC. 977 .40

KING 1
OLD WATER-WHEEL
BOSTON MUSIC COMPANY .50

KING 2
ON A NIGHT IN JUNE
BOSTON MUSIC COMPANY .50

KING		2	
ON SKATES			
BOSTON MUSIC COMPANY			.50
KING		4	
PRIMA DONNA, LA, SCHOTTISCHE			
CENTURY MUSIC PUBLISHING COMPANY, INC.	977		.40
KING			
RUNNYMEDE RHAPSODY --WHERE THE WATERLILIES DREAM			
MCA MUSIC			1.00
KING		1	
SAD THING, A			
LEE ROBERTS MUSIC PUBLICATIONS, INC.			.50
KING			
SONG OF THE ISLANDS			
EDWARD B. MARKS MUSIC CORPORATION			01.00
KING			
SONG OF THE ISLANDS			
EDWARD B. MARKS MUSIC CORPORATION			00.60
KING		2	
SPIRIT OF LIBERTY			
BOSTON MUSIC COMPANY			.50
KING, C.	BRADLEY, R.	EASY	
GOLD, UPDATED			
SCREEN GEMS - COLUMBIA PUBLICATIONS	P0086P2		2.95
KING, C.	BRADLEY, R.	EASY	
TAPESTRY			
SCREEN GEMS - COLUMBIA PUBLICATIONS	P0039P2		2.50
KING, M.			
FIVE GAY FINGERS			
G. SCHIRMER, INC.			.40
KING, M.			
STEPPING STONES			
G. SCHIRMER, INC.			.40
KING, S.		3	
APRIL MOOD			
THEODORE PRESSER COMPANY			.50
KING, S.		2	
BELLS OF NORMANDY			
THEODORE PRESSER COMPANY			.50
KING, S.		EASY	
CORN PONE SHUFFLE			
SHAWNEE PRESS, INC.			.35
KING, S.			
DANCE OF THE CHINA DOLL			
BELWIN-MILLS PUBLISHING CORPORATION	25035		.60
KING, S.			
DANCE OF THE CLOCKS			
THEODORE PRESSER COMPANY			2
KING, S.			
DANCE OF THE DUTCH DOLL			
BELWIN-MILLS PUBLISHING CORPORATION	25036		.60
KING, S.		2	
DAWN ON LOTUS LAKE			
THEODORE PRESSER COMPANY			.50
KING, S.		2	
FIDDLE-FADDLE -- SIMP.			
BELWIN-MILLS PUBLISHING CORPORATION	26013		.50
KING, S.		2 1/2	
GAY MASQUERADE			
THEODORE PRESSER COMPANY			.50
KING, S.		2 1/2	
GRAY MOONLIGHT			
THEODORE PRESSER COMPANY			.50
KING, S.		3	
JEALOUS EYES			
THEODORE PRESSER COMPANY			.50
KING, S.		1	
LOTUS FESTIVAL			
THEODORE PRESSER COMPANY			.50
KING, S.		2 1/2	
NIGHT WINDS			
THEODORE PRESSER COMPANY			.50
KING, S.		1 1/2	
PATIO PARTY			
THEODORE PRESSER COMPANY			.50
KING, S.			
PONY TROT			
G. SCHIRMER, INC.			.35
KING, S.			
PROGRESSIVE JAZZ FOR JUNIORS			
THEODORE PRESSER COMPANY			1.25
KING, S.		2	
RAIN DANCE			
THEODORE PRESSER COMPANY			.50
KING, S.		4	
SCHERZO HUMORESQUE			
THEODORE PRESSER COMPANY			.50
KING, S.		3	
SPRINGTIME IN SORRENTO			
THEODORE PRESSER COMPANY			.50
KING, S.		3 1/2	
STAR DREAMS			
THEODORE PRESSER COMPANY			.50
KING, S.		EASY	
SWISS WALTZ			
SHAWNEE PRESS, INC.	HB-5009		.60
KING, S.			
TRAVEL SCENES			
THEODORE PRESSER COMPANY			1.50
KING, S.		2	
TUMBLING			
THEODORE PRESSER COMPANY			.50
KING, S.		E	
WHISPERING WINDS			
BELWIN-MILLS PUBLISHING CORPORATION	25120		.60
KING, S.--ED.	KING, S.		
BLUE TANGO -- SIMP.			
BELWIN-MILLS PUBLISHING CORPORATION	26067		.50
KING, S.--ED.	KING, S.	EASY	
COUNTRY GARDENS			
SHAWNEE PRESS, INC.	HB-5029		.60
KING, S.--ED.	KING, S.		
DOWN BY THE STATION -- SIMP.			
BELWIN-MILLS PUBLISHING CORPORATION	26063		.50
KING, S.--ED.	KING, S.		
RED ROSES FOR A BLUE LADY --SIMP.			
BELWIN-MILLS PUBLISHING CORPORATION	26064		.50
KING, S.--ED.	KING, S.		
SLEIGH RIDE -- SIMP.			
BELWIN-MILLS PUBLISHING CORPORATION	26047		.50
KING, S.--ED.	KING, S.		
THAT OLD TIME BEAT			
THEODORE PRESSER COMPANY			1.25
KING, S.--ED.	KING, S.		
THAT'S MY DESIRE -- SIMP.			
BELWIN-MILLS PUBLISHING CORPORATION	26056		.50

KINKEL, C.			
BAISER D'UN ANGE -- NOCTURNE --			
FRANCO COLOMBO PUBLICATIONS		SAL	1.75
KINKEL, C.		4	
FLITTINGS FROM THE PAST			
CENTURY MUSIC PUBLISHING COMPANY, INC.	1231		.40
KINKEL, C.		3	
MOUNTAIN BELLE			
WILLIS MUSIC COMPANY			.30
KINKEL, C.		3	
MOUNTAIN BELLE SCHOTTISCHE			
BELWIN-MILLS PUBLISHING CORPORATION	195		.60
KINKEL, C.		3	
MOUNTAIN BELLE SCHOTTISCHE			
CENTURY MUSIC PUBLISHING COMPANY, INC.	1226		.40
KINKEL, C.		3	
MOUNTAIN BELLE SCHOTTISCHE			
THEODORE PRESSER COMPANY			.50
KINKEL, C.		3	
MOUNTAIN BELLE SCHOTTISCHE			
VOLKWEIN BROS.			.25
KINKEL, C.			
SERENADE DES ANGES			
FRANCO COLOMBO PUBLICATIONS		SAL	1.75
KINKEL, C.		2	
SWEET KISS, POLKA			
CENTURY MUSIC PUBLISHING COMPANY, INC.	1393		.40
KINKEL, C.		3	
WHISPERINGS OF LOVE, VALSE			
CENTURY MUSIC PUBLISHING COMPANY, INC.	1228		.40
KIRBY-MASON, B.			
PAPER BOATS			
BANKS AND SON LTD.			.25
KIRBY-MASON, B.			
SIX SKETCHES			
BANKS AND SON LTD.			.80
KIRCHNER, L.		M	
LITTLE SUITE			
THEODORE PRESSER COMPANY			1.00
KIRCHNER, L.			
SONATA, 1948			
ASSOCIATED MUSIC PUBLISHERS, INC.		BMP	4.00
KIRK			
BELLS			
BOSTON MUSIC COMPANY			.50
KIRK			
PETITE BOLERO			
MCA MUSIC			1.00
KIRKPATRICK		2	
BAR-Z BARN DANCE			
BELWIN-MILLS PUBLISHING CORPORATION			.60
KIRNBERGER, J. P.			
LUTE, THE			
FREDERICK HARRIS MUSIC COMPANY			.60
KIRNBERGER, J. P.			
TWO PARROTS, THE			
FREDERICK HARRIS MUSIC COMPANY			.60
KISH, A.		2	
GIVE AND TAKE			
THEODORE PRESSER COMPANY			.50
KITTREDGE, M.			
VILLAGE PARADE			
G. SCHIRMER, INC.			.35
KJERULF		3	
CRADLE SONG			
CENTURY MUSIC PUBLISHING COMPANY, INC.	3234		.40
KLARKE		3	
SILVER BAND MARCH			
CENTURY MUSIC PUBLISHING COMPANY, INC.	2728		.40
KLAUS, N.		3	
ORGAN-GRINDER IN THE RAIN			
THEODORE PRESSER COMPANY			.50
KLAUSS, N.		3	
PIN WHEELS			
THEODORE PRESSER COMPANY			.50
KLEBE, G.			
MENAGERIE, OP. 31 -- BALLET IN 5 TABLEAUX			
ASSOCIATED MUSIC PUBLISHERS, INC.		BOT	6.00
KLEBER		3	
RAINBOW SCHOTTISCHE			
CENTURY MUSIC PUBLISHING COMPANY, INC.	1254		.40
KLEIMAN, S.			
PATTERNS, 1970			
SEESAW MUSIC CORPORATION			3.00
KLEIN, B.			
MAZURKA, OP. 55 NO. 4			
G. SCHIRMER, INC.			.50
KLEIN, B.			
OLD ADVENT HYMN, OP. 55 NO. 3			
G. SCHIRMER, INC.			.25
KLEIN, B.			
VIVACE NON TANTO, OP. 19 NO. 3			
G. SCHIRMER, INC.			.60
KLEINMAN, A.		1 1/2	
BOOGIE AT THE FAIR			
BELWIN-MILLS PUBLISHING CORPORATION			.60
KLEINMAN, A.		2	
BRASS BAND OF PARADE			
CENTURY MUSIC PUBLISHING COMPANY, INC.	4340		.40
KLEINMAN, A.		2 1/2	
DANCING AT THE FAIR			
BELWIN-MILLS PUBLISHING CORPORATION			.60
KLEINMAN, A.		2	
FIRST PROM WALTZ			
BELWIN-MILLS PUBLISHING CORPORATION			.60
KLEINMAN, A.		2	
FUN AT THE FAIR			
THEODORE PRESSER COMPANY			.50
KLEINMAN, A.		2-3	
GONE HUNTING			
CENTURY MUSIC PUBLISHING COMPANY, INC.	4210		.40
KLEINMAN, A.		1 1/2	
IN MERRY MOOD			
BELWIN-MILLS PUBLISHING CORPORATION			.60
KLEINMAN, A.		1	
JAMIE'S MUSIC BOX			
CENTURY MUSIC PUBLISHING COMPANY, INC.	4384		.40
KLEINMAN, A.			
JANIE'S FIRST WALTZ			
G. SCHIRMER, INC.			.40
KLEINMAN, A.		2 1/2	
LET'S DO THE POLKA			
BELWIN-MILLS PUBLISHING CORPORATION			.60
KLEINMAN, A.		2	
LITTLE MEXICAN BURRO			
CENTURY MUSIC PUBLISHING COMPANY, INC.	4283		.40

KLEINMAN, A.   2
    LITTLE TARANTELLE
        BELWIN-MILLS PUBLISHING CORPORATION   .60
KLEINMAN, A.   2
    MEXICAN BURRO, THE
        CENTURY MUSIC PUBLISHING COMPANY, INC.   4283   .40
KLEINMAN, A.   1 1/2
    MUSIC BOX CHANSONETTE
        BELWIN-MILLS PUBLISHING CORPORATION   .60
KLEINMAN, A.   2
    MUSIC BOX DANCE
        BELWIN-MILLS PUBLISHING CORPORATION   .60
KLEINMAN, A.   2 1/2
    ORIENTAL DANCE
        BELWIN-MILLS PUBLISHING CORPORATION   .60
KLEINMAN, A.   2
    ORIENTAL JUGGLERS
        BELWIN-MILLS PUBLISHING CORPORATION   .60
KLEINMAN, A.   1
    PLEASE DO COME TO THE FAIR
        CENTURY MUSIC PUBLISHING COMPANY, INC.   4341   .40
KLEINMAN, A.   2
    POLKA MAZURKA
        BELWIN-MILLS PUBLISHING CORPORATION   .60
KLEINMAN, A.   1 1/2
    STREET PARADE
        BELWIN-MILLS PUBLISHING CORPORATION   .60
KLEINMAN, A.   3
    SUNDAY MORNING STROLL
        BELWIN-MILLS PUBLISHING CORPORATION   .60
KLEINMAN, A.   1
    UP IN A SWING
        BELWIN-MILLS PUBLISHING CORPORATION   .60
KLEINMAN, A.   2
    WALTZES ON A MUSIC BOX
        CENTURY MUSIC PUBLISHING COMPANY, INC.   4284   .40
KLEINSINGER, G.
    PEE-WEE THE PICCOLO--WITH NARRATOR
        G. SCHIRMER, INC.   .75
KLEMM, E.   E
    DESERT DANCE
        COMPOSERS PRESS, INC.   1.00
KLEMM, G.   4
    INDIAN SUNSET
        THEODORE PRESSER COMPANY   .50
KLEMM, G.   1
    QUIZ GAME
        BELWIN-MILLS PUBLISHING CORPORATION   .60
KLENAU, P. V.
    LITTLE IDA'S FLOWERS OVERTURE
        UNIVERSAL EDITION   UE 5714   1.50
KLENAU, P. V.
    LITTLE IDA'S WALTZ
        UNIVERSAL EDITION   UE 5720   1.30
KLICKMANN   EASY
    SABBATH CHIMES
        SHAWNEE PRESS, INC.   HB-62   .60
KLOHR, J. N.   4
    BILLBOARD MARCH, THE
        THEODORE PRESSER COMPANY   .50
KLOTZMAN, D. H.   M
    SONATINE
        THEODORE PRESSER COMPANY   1.00
KNAB, A.   4
    SONATA IN E
        SCHOTT   2368   2.25
KNAUER
    CANADIAN DANCE SUITE
        FRANCO COLOMBO PUBLICATIONS SIK.509   2.25
KNAUER
    MONTREAL
        MCA MUSIC   1.00
KNIGHT   2
    DANCE OF THE BROWNIES
        VOLKWEIN BROS.   .25
KNIGHT   2
    GINNY'S DANCE
        VOLKWEIN BROS.   .25
KNIGHT   2
    JOYS OF YOUTH
        VOLKWEIN BROS.   .25
KNIGHT   KERR, R.N.
    WONDER OF YOU, THE
        MCA MUSIC   1.00
KNIGHTON   EASY
    TALL TALE
        SHAWNEE PRESS, INC.   .40
KNIPPER   2
    MEADOWLAND
        CENTURY MUSIC PUBLISHING COMPANY, INC.   3766   .40
KNORR, E.L. VON   3
    KLEINE SONATE IN D
        BARENREITER VERLAG   SM 1861
KNORR, E.L. VON
    SONATINA IN A, 1947
        ASSOCIATED MUSIC PUBLISHERS, INC.   SIM   1.00
KNOWLTON, D.   1 1/2
    RAINDROP TAG
        THEODORE PRESSER COMPANY   .50
KOCH, E.   2
    COTTONTAIL PARADE
        BELWIN-MILLS PUBLISHING CORPORATION   .60
KOCH, E.   3
    DANCING BONES
        BELWIN-MILLS PUBLISHING CORPORATION   .60
KOCH, E.   2
    IMPISH PRANKS
        THEODORE PRESSER COMPANY   .50
KOCH, E.   2 1/2
    PARADE OF THE MANNEQUINS
        BELWIN-MILLS PUBLISHING CORPORATION   .60
KOCH, E.   2 1/2
    PEASANT DANCE
        BELWIN-MILLS PUBLISHING CORPORATION   .60
KOCH, E.   1 1/2
    SNOWMEN ON PARADE
        BELWIN-MILLS PUBLISHING CORPORATION   .60
KOCH, E.
    VARIANTI VIRTUOSO 1965
        NOVELLO AND COMPANY, LTD.   10.0175.02   2.25
KOCH, F.   3 1/2
    ANNIVERSARY TOCCATA
        THEODORE PRESSER COMPANY   1.00
KOCH, F.   2
    DANCE OF THE MOON MEN
        BELWIN-MILLS PUBLISHING CORPORATION   .60

KOCH, F.   2
    DOG AND HIS TAIL
        BOSTON MUSIC COMPANY   .50
KOCH, F.   D
    DREAMY MELODY
        COMPOSERS PRESS, INC.   1.00
KOCH, F.   E
    FROM THE HIGHLANDS
        COMPOSERS PRESS, INC.   1.00
KOCH, F.
    SONATINA NO. 2
        SEESAW MUSIC CORPORATION   3.00
KOCH, F.   M
    SONATINA, 1950
        COMPOSERS PRESS, INC.   2.00
KOCH, J.
    ANDANTE AND SCHERZO
        GENERAL MUSIC PUBLISHING COMPANY, INC.   439   1.20
KOCH, J.
    FINALE GAUDIOSO - NO. 3 FROM SUITE FOR PIANO
        GENERAL MUSIC PUBLISHING COMPANY, INC.   2.00
KOCH, J.
    FINALE GRANDIOSO
        GENERAL MUSIC PUBLISHING COMPANY, INC.   440   1.80
KOCH, J.
    FROM THE COUNTRY
        GENERAL MUSIC PUBLISHING COMPANY, INC.   597   2.00
KOCH, J.
    FROM THE COUNTRY - PICTURES FOR THE YOUNG PIANIST
        GENERAL MUSIC PUBLISHING COMPANY, INC.   2.00
KOCH, J.
    IMPROMPTU
        GENERAL MUSIC PUBLISHING COMPANY, INC.   438   1.80
KOCH, J.
    IMPROMPTU - NO. 1 FROM SUITE FOR PIANO
        GENERAL MUSIC PUBLISHING COMPANY, INC.   2.00
KOCVARA
    CELEBRATED 'BATTLE OF PRAGUE, THE.' --CA. 1788
        MUSICA OBSCURA   2.00
KODALY, E.
    PIANO VARIATIONS
        KULTURA   2.75
KODALY, E.
    VALSES VIENNOISES
        BOOSEY AND HAWKES, INC.   1.50
KODALY, Z.
    DANCES FROM GALANTA
        UNIVERSAL EDITION   UE 10671   3.00
KODALY, Z.
    DANCES OF MAROSSZEK
        UNIVERSAL EDITION   UE 8213   5.75
KODALY, Z.
    MEDITATION ON A MOTIF OF C. DEBUSSY
        UNIVERSAL EDITION   UE 7799   3.00
KODALY, Z.
    SEVEN PIANO PIECES, OP. 11
        UNIVERSAL EDITION   UE 6653   5.00
KODALY, Z.   FOLDES, A.
    SONG FROM 'HARY JANOS'
        UNIVERSAL EDITION   UE 12192   1.00
KODALY, Z.
    VALSETTE
        KULTURA   1.00
KODALY, Z.   FOLDES, A.
    VIENNESE CLOCK FROM 'HARY JANOS'
        UNIVERSAL EDITION   UE 10671   3.00
KOECHLIN, C.
    ECOLE DU JEU LIE, L'
        FRANCO COLOMBO PUBLICATIONS SAL   4.25
KOECHLIN, C.
    PASTORALES
        FRANCO COLOMBO PUBLICATIONS SAL   3.25
KOECHLIN, C.
    SARABANDE
        FRANCO COLOMBO PUBLICATIONS SAL   2.00
KOECHLIN, C.
    SONATINAS SERIES I, NO. 1
        FRANCO COLOMBO PUBLICATIONS SAL   2.75
KOECHLIN, C.
    SONATINAS SERIES I, NO. 2
        FRANCO COLOMBO PUBLICATIONS SAL   3.25
KOECHLIN, C.
    SONATINAS SERIES I, NO. 3
        FRANCO COLOMBO PUBLICATIONS SAL   3.25
KOECHLIN, C.
    SONATINAS SERIES I, NO. 4
        FRANCO COLOMBO PUBLICATIONS SAL   5.00
KOECHLIN, C.
    SONATINAS SERIES I, NO. 5
        FRANCO COLOMBO PUBLICATIONS SAL   5.00
KOECHLIN, C.
    SONATINAS SERIES II -- NEW -- NO. 1
        FRANCO COLOMBO PUBLICATIONS SAL   2.50
KOECHLIN, C.
    SONATINAS SERIES II -- NEW -- NO. 2
        FRANCO COLOMBO PUBLICATIONS SAL   2.50
KOECHLIN, C.
    SONATINAS SERIES II -- NEW -- NO. 3
        FRANCO COLOMBO PUBLICATIONS SAL   2.50
KOECHLIN, C.
    SONATINAS SERIES II -- NEW -- NO. 4
        FRANCO COLOMBO PUBLICATIONS SAL   2.50
KOECHLIN, C.
    TEN EASY PIECES - LA JOLIE FLEUR DU JARDIN
        FRANCO COLOMBO PUBLICATIONS SAL   1.50
KOECHLIN, C.
    TWELVE LITTLE PIECES - LA BALLE
        FRANCO COLOMBO PUBLICATIONS SAL   1.50
KOEHLER   3
    ALADDIN
        WILLIS MUSIC COMPANY   .40
KOEHLER
    RONDINO
        FREDERICK HARRIS MUSIC COMPANY   .60
KOEHLER, C.   3
    BARN DANCE TONIGHT
        WILLIS MUSIC COMPANY   .40
KOEHLER, C.   3
    BARN DANCE TONIGHT
        WILLIS MUSIC COMPANY   .40
KOEHLER, C.   2 1/2
    CLOWN DANCE, THE
        WILLIS MUSIC COMPANY   .40
KOEHLER, C.   2 1/2
    CLOWN DANCE, THE
        WILLIS MUSIC COMPANY   .40

KOEHLER, C.	3	
LITTLE PACKBURRO, THE		
WILLIS MUSIC COMPANY		.40
KOEHLER, C.	3	
LITTLE PACKBURRO, THE		
WILLIS MUSIC COMPANY		.40
KOELLING		
ALBUM LEAF IN A MINOR		
SUMMY-BIRCHARD COMPANY		.50
KOELLING		
FLUTTERING LEAVES IN A MINOR, OP. 147 NO. 2		
CARL FISCHER, INC.	S 2263	.50
KOELLING		
FLUTTERING LEAVES IN D, OP. 147, NO. 3		
CARL FISCHER, INC.	S 1956	.60
KOELLING		
FLYING LEAVES, OP. 147--ALLEGRO IN C		
G. SCHIRMER, INC.		.35
KOELLING		
FLYING LEAVES, OP. 147--ALLEGRO MOLTO IN A MINOR		
G. SCHIRMER, INC.		.40
KOELLING		
FLYING LEAVES, OP. 147--PRESTISSIMO IN D		
G. SCHIRMER, INC.		.60
KOELLING PODOLSKY, L.		
HUNGARY --RHAPSODIE MIGNONNE--		
SHAWNEE PRESS, INC.	HB-223	.75
KOELLING	4 1/2	
HUNGARY, RAPSODIE MIGNONNE, OP. 410		
THEODORE PRESSER COMPANY		1.75
KOELLING	4	
LA CHASSE INFERNALE, GALOP		
CENTURY MUSIC PUBLISHING COMPANY, INC.	1326	.40
KOELLING	3	
TWO FLOWERS --ZWEI BLUMEN OP. 364--		
THEODORE PRESSER COMPANY		.50
KOELLREUTTER, J.		
MUSICA 1941		
EDITORIAL COOPERATIVA INTER-AMERICANA		01.15
KOERPPEN, A.		
JAHRMARKT, DER		
ASSOCIATED MUSIC PUBLISHERS, INC.	BRH	2.25
KOFFLER, J.		
FIFTEEN VARIATIONS ON A 12 TONE SERIES		
FRANCO COLOMBO PUBLICATIONS	SAL	2.75
KOFFLER, J.		
MUSIQUE DE BALLET		
FRANCO COLOMBO PUBLICATIONS	SAL	2.75
KOFFLER, J.		
MUSIQUE QUASI UNA SONATA		
FRANCO COLOMBO PUBLICATIONS	SAL	2.75
KOFFLER, J.		
SONATINA, OP. 12		
UNIVERSAL EDITION	UE 7267	1.30
KOFFLER, J.		
VARIATIONS ON A WALTZ BY JOHANN STRAUSS		
UNIVERSAL EDITION	UE 10796	1.30
KOHLER, F.	1	
BLACK EYED SUSAN		
CENTURY MUSIC PUBLISHING COMPANY, INC.	2348	.40
KOHLER, F.	1	
CLOVER BLOSSOMS		
CENTURY MUSIC PUBLISHING COMPANY, INC.	2344	.40
KOHLER, F.	1	
DAINTY DAFFODILS		
CENTURY MUSIC PUBLISHING COMPANY, INC.	2347	.40
KOHLER, F.	1	
JUNE ROSES		
CENTURY MUSIC PUBLISHING COMPANY, INC.	2345	.40
KOHLER, F.	2	
KOHLER'S SCALES AND CHORDS		
CENTURY MUSIC PUBLISHING COMPANY, INC.	1312	.40
KOHLER, F.	1	
MORNING GLORY		
CENTURY MUSIC PUBLISHING COMPANY, INC.	2342	.40
KOHLER, F.	1	
PANSY FACES		
CENTURY MUSIC PUBLISHING COMPANY, INC.	2346	.40
KOHLER, F.	1	
SPRING TULIPS		
CENTURY MUSIC PUBLISHING COMPANY, INC.	2349	.40
KOHLER, F.	1	
SWEET VIOLETS		
CENTURY MUSIC PUBLISHING COMPANY, INC.	2343	.40
KOHLER, F.	1	
WATER LILIES		
CENTURY MUSIC PUBLISHING COMPANY, INC.	2350	.40
KOHS, E. B.	M	
FORLANE		
THEODORE PRESSER COMPANY		.50
KOHS, E. B.	A	
PIANO VARIATIONS		
THEODORE PRESSER COMPANY		1.25
KOHS, E. B.	M	
SCHERZO		
THEODORE PRESSER COMPANY		.50
KOHS, E. B.	A	
TOCCATA		
THEODORE PRESSER COMPANY		1.25
KOHS, E. B.	A	
VARIATIONS ON L'HOMME ARME		
THEODORE PRESSER COMPANY		1.50
KOLINSKI		
TIN SOLDIER'S WEDDING MARCH		
MCA MUSIC		.60
KOLLING, C.	4	
CHASSE INTERNALE		
CENTURY MUSIC PUBLISHING COMPANY, INC.	1326	.40
KOLLING, C.	4	
FLUTTERING LEAVES		
CENTURY MUSIC PUBLISHING COMPANY, INC.	2150	.40
KOLLING, C.	3	
FLYING LEAVES		
CENTURY MUSIC PUBLISHING COMPANY, INC.	2214	.40
KOLLING, C.	5	
LARK'S MORNING SONG		
CENTURY MUSIC PUBLISHING COMPANY, INC.	2283	.40
KOLZ, E.		
EMOTION		
UNIVERSAL EDITION	UE 12404	1.10
KOLZ, E.		
PARTITA, FOR PIANO OR HARPSICHORD		
ASSOCIATED MUSIC PUBLISHERS, INC.	DOB	1.50
KOLZ, E.		
SONATA		
UNIVERSAL EDITION	UE 12065	1.30

KOMZAK	2		
FAIRY TALE			
BELWIN-MILLS PUBLISHING CORPORATION			.50
KONOWITZ, B.			
JAZZ SPOOKS			
LEE ROBERTS MUSIC PUBLICATIONS, INC.			.50
KONOWITZ, B.			
JAZZ WALTZ			
LEE ROBERTS MUSIC PUBLICATIONS, INC.			.50
KONOWITZ, B.			
RAGA ROCK			
LEE ROBERTS MUSIC PUBLICATIONS, INC.			.50
KONOWITZ, B.			
SURF SWING			
LEE ROBERTS MUSIC PUBLICATIONS, INC.			.50
KONOWITZ, B.			
TIME CHANGES			
LEE ROBERTS MUSIC PUBLICATIONS, INC.			.50
KONT, P.			
DIVERTISSEMENT			
ASSOCIATED MUSIC PUBLISHERS, INC.	DOB	2.50	
KONT, P.			
EGEGH			
ASSOCIATED MUSIC PUBLISHERS, INC.	DOB	1.75	
KONT, P.			
KLEINE SALONMUSIK			
ASSOCIATED MUSIC PUBLISHERS, INC.	DOB	2.00	
KONT, P.			
TANTSTUCK			
ASSOCIATED MUSIC PUBLISHERS, INC.	DOB	1.60	
KOPTAGEL, Y.			
EPITAFIO			
ASSOCIATED MUSIC PUBLISHERS, INC.	BOT	.75	
KOPTAGEL, Y.			
TAMZARA--TURKISH DANCE			
ASSOCIATED MUSIC PUBLISHERS, INC.	ESC	1.75	
KOPTAGEL, Y.			
TOCCATA			
ASSOCIATED MUSIC PUBLISHERS, INC.	ESC	2.75	
KORN, P.			
BAGATELLE, OP. 11 NO. 1 BALLADE			
BOOSEY AND HAWKES, INC.		1.00	
KORN, P.			
BAGATELLE, OP. 11 NO. 2 SCHERZO			
BOOSEY AND HAWKES, INC.		1.00	
KORN, P.			
BAGATELLE, OP. 11 NO. 3 PRELUDE			
BOOSEY AND HAWKES, INC.		1.00	
KORN, P.			
BAGATELLE, OP. 11 NO. 4 BURLESKE			
BOOSEY AND HAWKES, INC.		1.00	
KORN, P.			
BAGATELLE, OP. 11 NO. 5 INTERMEZZO			
BOOSEY AND HAWKES, INC.		1.00	
KORN, P.			
BAGATELLE, OP. 11 NO. 6 DANCE			
BOOSEY AND HAWKES, INC.		1.00	
KORN, P.			
BAGATELLE, OP. 11 NO. 7 TORCH SONG			
BOOSEY AND HAWKES, INC.		1.00	
KORN, P.			
BAGATELLE, OP. 11 NO. 8 PASSACAGLIA POLKA			
BOOSEY AND HAWKES, INC.		1.00	
KORN, P.			
SONATA NO. 01			
BOOSEY AND HAWKES, INC.		1.50	
KORNGOLD, E. W.	5		
KLAVIERSUITE AUS 'VIEL LARMEN UM NICHTS', OP. 11			
SCHOTT	1740	2.25	
KORNGOLD, E. W.	5		
MARCHENBILDER, OP. 3 NO. 2 'DIE PRINZESSIN AUF DER ERBSE'			
SCHOTT	1742	1.25	
KORNGOLD, E. W.	5		
MARCHENBILDER, OP. 3 NO. 7 'DAS MARCHEN SPRICHT DEN EPILOG'			
SCHOTT	1747	1.25	
KORNGOLD, E. W.			
SONATA IN D MINOR			
UNIVERSAL EDITION	UE 2765	2.15	
KORTE	4		
SONATE			
BARENREITER VERLAG	AP 646		
KORTE, K.	2		
MARCHING ON TIPTOES			
BELWIN-MILLS PUBLISHING CORPORATION			.60
KOSA, G.			
BAGATELLES			
UNIVERSAL EDITION	UE 8559	1.30	
KOSA, G.			
KLEIN JUTKA -- 12 PIECES			
UNIVERSAL EDITION	UE 9711	1.50	
KOSMA, J.			
DANSE DES AUTOMATES			
FRANCO COLOMBO PUBLICATIONS	SAL	2.50	
KOSSENDO			
SCHERZINO, OP. 15			
MCA MUSIC			.60
KOUGELL, A.			
DANSE KURDE, OP. 52			
ASSOCIATED MUSIC PUBLISHERS, INC.	ESC	1.10	
KOUGUELL			
PASTORALE			
SAM FOX PUBLISHING COMPANY, INC.			.50
KOUGUELL			
PASTORALE			
SOUTHERN MUSIC COMPANY			.50
KOUNTZ, R.	2		
COME, LITTLE BLUEBIRD			
THEODORE PRESSER COMPANY			.50
KOUNTZ, R.			
LITTLE ORPHAN WALTZ			
G. SCHIRMER, INC.			.35
KOUNTZ, R.			
LITTLE SHEPHERD, THE			
G. SCHIRMER, INC.			.35
KOUNTZ, R.	2 1/2		
VIENNA ROSES			
THEODORE PRESSER COMPANY			.50
KOUNTZ, R.			
WOODEN SHOE DANCE			
G. SCHIRMER, INC.			.35
KOUTZEN, B.	M		
CLOWN'S REVERIE AND DANCE			
THEODORE PRESSER COMPANY			.50
KOUTZEN, B.			
EIDOLONS			
GENERAL MUSIC PUBLISHING COMPANY, INC.	58	2.50	

KOUTZEN, B.
  EIDOLONS
     GENERAL MUSIC PUBLISHING COMPANY, INC.   3.00
KOUTZEN, B.
  EIDOLONS
     NOVELLO AND COMPANY, LTD.   2.50
KOUTZEN, B.
  SONATINA
     GENERAL MUSIC PUBLISHING COMPANY, INC.   3.00
KOUTZEN, B.
  SONATINA 1931
     NOVELLO AND COMPANY, LTD.   1.90
KOVACS, S.
  FLEDERMAUS PARAPHRASE--ON AIRS FROM 'THE BAT' BY J. STRAUSS
     G. SCHIRMER, INC.   .90
KOWALSKI, H.
  CORTEGE ORIENTAL
     FRANCO COLOMBO PUBLICATIONS   SAL   4.00
KOWALSKI, H.   6
  HUNGARIAN MARCH
     CENTURY MUSIC PUBLISHING COMPANY, INC. 1369   .40
KOWALSKI, H.   2
  HUNGARIAN MARCH, EASY
     CENTURY MUSIC PUBLISHING COMPANY, INC. 2133   .40
KOWALSKI, H.
  HUNGARIAN MARCH, OP. 13
     FRANCO COLOMBO PUBLICATIONS   BA9092 .75
KOWALSKI, H.   6
  SALUT A PESTH
     CENTURY MUSIC PUBLISHING COMPANY, INC. 1369   .40
KOWALSKI, H.
  SALUT A PESTH--MARCHE HONGROISE DE CONCERT
     G. SCHIRMER, INC.   .70
KOX   M-D
  SONATA NO. 02
     C. F. PETERS CORPORATION   D208   2.00
KOX   M
  SONATINA. HARPSICHORD
     C. F. PETERS CORPORATION   D463   2.00
KRAEHENBUEHL
  ELEGY
     SUMMY-BIRCHARD COMPANY   .50
KRAEHENBUEHL
  NOTTURNO
     SUMMY-BIRCHARD COMPANY   .50
KRAEHENBUEHL
  SPANISH WALTZ
     SUMMY-BIRCHARD COMPANY   .50
KRAFT   2
  LITTLE PRELUDE
     CENTURY MUSIC PUBLISHING COMPANY, INC. 018   .40
KRAFT, L.   1
  COME OUT KIDS
     CENTURY MUSIC PUBLISHING COMPANY, INC. 3805   .40
KRAFT, L.   1
  OUTDOOR SONG
     CENTURY MUSIC PUBLISHING COMPANY, INC. 3985   .40
KRAFT, L.
  PARTITA FOR PIANO
     GENERAL MUSIC PUBLISHING COMPANY, INC.   3.00
KRAFT, L.
  PARTITA NO. 1
     GENERAL MUSIC PUBLISHING COMPANY, INC. 426   3.00
KRAFT, L.   M
  PERKY PETE
     THEODORE PRESSER COMPANY   .50
KRAFT, L.   1
  SHORT SONATA NO. 1
     GENERAL MUSIC PUBLISHING COMPANY, INC.   2.00
KRAFT, L.   1 1/2
  TIC-TAC-TOE
     CENTURY MUSIC PUBLISHING COMPANY, INC. 4062   .40
KRAFT, L.
  TIMOTHY MIXOLYDIAN
     THEODORE PRESSER COMPANY   .50
KRAMER, A. W.
  CYPRESSES
     OXFORD UNIVERSITY PRESS   93.207 1.50
KRAMER, A. W.
  INTERMEZZO, OP. 40 NO. 1
     BELWIN-MILLS PUBLISHING CORPORATION   .60
KRAMER, A. W.   3
  MARCH OF THE IMPS
     BELWIN-MILLS PUBLISHING CORPORATION   .60
KRAMER, A. W.   2
  ON MY WAY TO CHURCH
     BELWIN-MILLS PUBLISHING CORPORATION   .60
KRAMER, A. W.   2
  PLAINTIVE AIR
     BELWIN-MILLS PUBLISHING CORPORATION   .60
KRAMER, A. W.   3
  PROCESSIONAL
     BELWIN-MILLS PUBLISHING CORPORATION   .60
KRAUKAUER *
  PARADISE
     CARL FISCHER, INC.   F 2021   .80
KREBS
  JESTER, THE
     FREDERICK HARRIS MUSIC COMPANY   .60
KREBS   SOLDAN   M
  KLAVIERUEBUNG
     C. F. PETERS CORPORATION   4178   2.50
KREBS
  TOCCATA IN E
     FREDERICK HARRIS MUSIC COMPANY   .60
KREBS, S.   E
  ROLLER SKATING
     COMPOSERS PRESS, INC.   1.00
KREIDER, N.
  STUDY, OP. 6 NO. 1
     G. SCHIRMER, INC.   .75
KREIN, J.
  EIGHT PIECES, OP. 9
     UNIVERSAL EDITION   2.15
KREIN, J.
  FOUR PIANO PIECES, OP. 14
     UNIVERSAL EDITION   UE 9449 1.70
KREIN, J.
  RHAPSODY, OP. 17
     UNIVERSAL EDITION   UE 9468 1.30
KREISLER   4
  ALT-WIENER TANZWEISEN, LIEBESFREUD
     SCHOTT   1.75
KREISLER   4
  ALT-WIENER TANZWEISEN, LIEBESLIED
     SCHOTT   1.75

KREISLER   4
  ALT-WIENER TANZWEISEN, SCHON ROSMARIN
     SCHOTT   1.75
KREISLER   5
  ALT-WIENER TANZWEISEN, TRANSKRIPTION -- RACHMANINOFF
     SCHOTT   1757   2.00
KREISLER   5
  ALT-WIENER TANZWEISEN, TRANSKRIPTION -- RACHMANINOFF
     SCHOTT   1758   2.00
KREISLER   BRANDL   4
  ALTER REFRAIN -- DU ALTER STEPHANSTURM
     SCHOTT
KREISLER   5
  ANDANTINO IM STILE VON P. MARTINI
     SCHOTT   1.75
KREISLER
  CAPRICE VIENNOIS
     CARL FISCHER, INC.   F 2005   1.25
KREISLER   3
  CAPRICE VIENNOIS
     SCHOTT   1.75
KREISLER   MAIER
  CAPRICE VIENNOIS --STUDENT EDITION--
     CARL FISCHER, INC.   F 2057   .65
KREISLER   4
  IM PARADIES-WIENER VOLKSLIED
     SCHOTT   1.75
KREISLER   3
  LA PRECIEUSE IM STILE VON COUPERIN
     SCHOTT   1.75
KREISLER   RACHMANINOFF, S.
  LIEBESFREUD
     BELWIN-MILLS PUBLISHING CORPORATION   1.50
KREISLER
  LIEBESFREUD
     CARL FISCHER, INC.   F 2015   1.00
KREISLER   MAIER
  LIEBESFREUD --STUDENT EDITION--
     CARL FISCHER, INC.   F 2055   .65
KREISLER   RACHMANINOFF, S.
  LIEBESLIED
     BELWIN-MILLS PUBLISHING CORPORATION   1.50
KREISLER
  LIEBESLIED
     CARL FISCHER, INC.   F 2017   1.00
KREISLER   FLETCHER
  LIEBESLIED --STUDENT EDITION--
     CARL FISCHER, INC.   F 2315   .65
KREISLER   MAIER
  MIDNIGHT BELLS --STUDENT EDITION--
     CARL FISCHER, INC.   F 2056   .65
KREISLER
  OLD REFRAIN, THE
     CARL FISCHER, INC.   F 2038   1.00
KREISLER
  PRECIEUSE, LA
     CARL FISCHER, INC.   F 2014   .80
KREISLER   GODOWSKY, L.   3
  RONDINO VON BEETHOVEN
     SCHOTT   1755   1.75
KREISLER
  SCHON ROSMARIN
     CARL FISCHER, INC.   F 2029   .65
KREISLER   FLETCHER
  SCHON ROSMARIN
     CARL FISCHER, INC.   F 2061   .65
KREISLER
  SHEPHERD'S MADRIGAL
     CARL FISCHER, INC.   F 2030   .80
KREISLER   MAIER
  SHEPHERD'S MADRIGAL
     CARL FISCHER, INC.   F 2054   .65
KREISLER
  TAMBOURIN CHINOIS
     CARL FISCHER, INC.   F 2034   1.25
KREISLER   CHALOFF   5
  TAMBOURIN CHINOIS
     SCHOTT   1756   1.75
KREISLER *
  LIEBESFREUD
     CARL FISCHER, INC.   F 2016   1.50
KREISLER *
  RONDINO ON A THEME OF BEETHOVEN
     CARL FISCHER, INC.   F 2026   1.25
KREJCI, M.   3-4
  AUS DEM LEBEN, OP. 11
     BARENREITER VERLAG   AP 648
KRENEK, E.
  ECHOES FROM AUSTRIA
     RONGWEN MUSIC, INC.   02.50
KRENEK, E.
  GEORGE WASHINGTON VARIATIONS
     EDITORIAL COOPERATIVA INTER-AMERICANA   01.75
KRENEK, E.
  SONATA NO. 01 IN E FLAT, OP. 2
     UNIVERSAL EDITION   6496   3.40
KRENEK, E.
  SONATA NO. 02, OP. 59
     UNIVERSAL EDITION   8836   3.00
KRENEK, E.
  SONATA NO. 03, OP. 92 NO. 4 --1943--
     ASSOCIATED MUSIC PUBLISHERS, INC. AMP   2.00
KRENEK, E.
  SONATA NO. 04 -- 1948
     ASSOCIATED MUSIC PUBLISHERS, INC. BMP   4.00
KRENEK, E.
  TOCCATA AND CHACONNE, OP. 13
     UNIVERSAL EDITION   7210   3.60
KRENTZLIN, R.   2 1/2
  AT THE CAMPFIRE, OP. 124
     THEODORE PRESSER COMPANY   .60
KRENTZLIN, R.   2
  AUS DEM JUGENDLANDE
     SCHOTT   3960   2.00
KRENTZLIN, R.   3
  IN SCHUBERT'S DAY, OP. 109
     THEODORE PRESSER COMPANY   .50
KRENTZLIN, R.
  TURKISH RONDO
     SUMMY-BIRCHARD COMPANY   .50
KRENZ, B.
  BARBER SHOP RAG
     BELWIN-MILLS PUBLISHING CORPORATION 20028 .85
KRENZ, B.
  DARK EYES
     BELWIN-MILLS PUBLISHING CORPORATION 20068 .85

KRENZ, B.
    MUD CAT RAG
        BELWIN-MILLS PUBLISHING CORPORATION   20177   .85
KRENZ, B.
    PIANOLA RAG
        BELWIN-MILLS PUBLISHING CORPORATION   20199   .85
KRENZ, B.
    RAMBLIN' RAG
        BELWIN-MILLS PUBLISHING CORPORATION   20219   .85
KRENZ, B.
    ROUNDHOUSE CAPRICCIOSO
        BELWIN-MILLS PUBLISHING CORPORATION   20228   .85
KRENZ, B.
    WHISPERING RAIN
        BELWIN-MILLS PUBLISHING CORPORATION   20466   .85
                            MD
KREUTZ
    STUDY IN JAZZ
        THEODORE PRESSER COMPANY   .60
KREUTZER
    HAPPY HAMSTERS
        BRODT MUSIC COMPANY   .45
                            E
KREUTZER
    MARBLES
        COMPOSERS PRESS, INC.   1.00
                            1
KREUTZER
    MY PIGGY BANK
        THEODORE PRESSER COMPANY   .50
KREUTZER
    SCHERZETTO
        BRODT MUSIC COMPANY   .40
KREVIT, W.
    BARE BACK RIDER, THE
        G. SCHIRMER, INC.   .35
KREVIT, W.   2
    BUCKING BRONCO
        CENTURY MUSIC PUBLISHING COMPANY, INC.   4027   .40
KREVIT, W.   1
    CLOWNS, THE
        CENTURY MUSIC PUBLISHING COMPANY, INC.   3942   .40
KREVIT, W.   1
    CLOWNS, THE
        CENTURY MUSIC PUBLISHING COMPANY, INC.   3942   .40
KREVIT, W.   1
    CRACKER JACK
        CENTURY MUSIC PUBLISHING COMPANY, INC.   4057   .40
KREVIT, W.   1
    LITTLE LOST BEAR
        CENTURY MUSIC PUBLISHING COMPANY, INC.   3941   .40
                            E
KREVIT, W.
    MINUET A LA BACH
        BELWIN-MILLS PUBLISHING CORPORATION   25074   .60
KREVIT, W.   1-2
    MORNING CHIMES
        CENTURY MUSIC PUBLISHING COMPANY, INC.   4175   .40
KREVIT, W.   1-2
    ON THE FLOAT
        CENTURY MUSIC PUBLISHING COMPANY, INC.   4139   .40
KREVIT, W.   1
    PICNIC PARTY
        CENTURY MUSIC PUBLISHING COMPANY, INC.   3943   .40
KREVIT, W.   1
    PIED PIPERS MARCH
        CENTURY MUSIC PUBLISHING COMPANY, INC.   4058   .40
KREVIT, W.   2
    SAMBALINA
        CENTURY MUSIC PUBLISHING COMPANY, INC.   4028   .40
KREVIT, W.   1
    TRAPEZE WALTZ
        CENTURY MUSIC PUBLISHING COMPANY, INC.   3944   .40
KREVIT, W.   1
    YES, I WILL
        CENTURY MUSIC PUBLISHING COMPANY, INC.   4138   .40
KRICKA   3
    LAUNE, OP. 11
        BARENREITER VERLAG   AP 650
KROEGER, E. R.   STEINER   2
    CIRCUS ELEPHANTS
        BELWIN-MILLS PUBLISHING CORPORATION   .60
KROGMANN, C. W.
    CHRISTMAS SONG
        WILLIS MUSIC COMPANY   .40
KROGMANN, C. W.   1
    FIRST LESSON, THE
        THEODORE PRESSER COMPANY   .50
KROGMANN, C. W.
    L'INGENUE--VALSE, OP. 81 NO. 1--FOR LEFT HAND ALONE--
        G. SCHIRMER, INC.   .50
KROGMANN, C. W.
    ZEPHYRS FROM MELODYLAND, OP. 15--MERRY BOBOLINK
        G. SCHIRMER, INC.   .40
KROGMANN, C. W.
    ZEPHYRS FROM MELODYLAND, OP. 15--LITTLE PRINCE
        G. SCHIRMER, INC.   .40
KROGMANN, C. W.
    ZEPHYRS FROM MELODYLAND, OP. 15--ROBIN'S LULLABY
        G. SCHIRMER, INC.   .50
KROGMANN, C. W.
    ZEPHYRS FROM MELODYLAND, OP. 15--SANTA CLAUS GUARDS
        G. SCHIRMER, INC.   .40
KROL, B.
    EVOLUZIONI, OP. 19
        ASSOCIATED MUSIC PUBLISHERS, INC.   SIM   3.00
KRUGER   5
    AEOLIAN HARP, THE, A FLAT MAJOR, OP. 25
        CENTURY MUSIC PUBLISHING COMPANY, INC.   2580   .40
KRUL   1
    BUTTERFLIES
        PRO-ART PUBLICATIONS, INC.   311   .50
KRUL   2
    DREAMING
        PRO-ART PUBLICATIONS, INC.   310   .50
KRUL   1
    IN THE PLAYROOM
        PRO-ART PUBLICATIONS, INC.   309   .50
KUBIK, G.
    CELEBRATIONS AND EPILOGUE
        EDITORIAL COOPERATIVA INTER-AMERICANA   02.50
KUBIK, G.   MD
    DANCE SOLILOQUY
        THEODORE PRESSER COMPANY   .90
KUBIK, G.   M
    QUIET TIME
        THEODORE PRESSER COMPANY   .50
KUBIK, G.
    SONATA
        EDITORIAL COOPERATIVA INTER-AMERICANA   03.50

KUBIK, G.   MD
    SONATINA
        THEODORE PRESSER COMPANY   1.50
KUBIK, G.   MD
    WHISTLING TUNE -- OSTINATO
        THEODORE PRESSER COMPANY   .50
KUESTER, H.   4
    SCHWARZ UND WEISS
        SCHOTT   4018   2.00
KUHE, W.
    ON THE SEA--BARCAROLLE
        G. SCHIRMER, INC.   .50
KUHLAU, F.
    ALLEGRO IN A MINOR, OP. 88 NO. 3
        BANKS AND SON LTD.   .40
KUHLAU, F.
    ALLEGRO VIVACE
        FREDERICK HARRIS MUSIC COMPANY   .60
KUHLAU, F.
    LITTLE GYPSY, THE, OP. 55 NO. 1
        BANKS AND SON LTD.   .40
KUHLAU, F.
    SONATINA IN A MINOR, OP. 88 NO. 3
        G. SCHIRMER, INC.   .45
KUHLAU, F.
    SONATINA IN A, OP. 59 NO. 1
        G. SCHIRMER, INC.   .75
KUHLAU, F.
    SONATINA IN A, OP. 60 NO. 2
        G. SCHIRMER, INC.   .60
KUHLAU, F.
    SONATINA IN C, OP. 20 NO. 1
        G. SCHIRMER, INC.   .50
KUHLAU, F.
    SONATINA IN C, OP. 55 NO. 1
        G. SCHIRMER, INC.   .40
KUHLAU, F.
    SONATINA IN C, OP. 55 NO. 3
        G. SCHIRMER, INC.   .50
KUHLAU, F.
    SONATINA IN F, OP. 20 NO. 3
        G. SCHIRMER, INC.   .60
KUHLAU, F.
    SONATINA IN G, OP. 20 NO. 2
        G. SCHIRMER, INC.   .60
KUHLAU, F.
    SONATINA IN G, OP. 55 NO. 2
        G. SCHIRMER, INC.   .50
KUHLAU, F.
    SONATINA NO. 01
        EDWIN F. KALMUS   3599   1.50
KUHLAU, F.
    SONATINA NO. 02
        EDWIN F. KALMUS   3600   1.50
KUHLAU, F.   3
    SONATINA OP. 55 NO. 1
        THEODORE PRESSER COMPANY   .50
KUHLAU, F.   2
    SONATINA, OP. 55 NO. 1
        CENTURY MUSIC PUBLISHING COMPANY, INC.   1913   .40
KUHLAU, F.   2
    SONATINA, OP. 55 NO. 2
        CENTURY MUSIC PUBLISHING COMPANY, INC.   1914   .40
KUHLAU, F.   2
    SONATINA, OP. 55 NO. 3
        CENTURY MUSIC PUBLISHING COMPANY, INC.   1915   .40
KUHLAU, F.
    SONATINA, OP. 55 NO. 6
        FREDERICK HARRIS MUSIC COMPANY   .90
KUHLAU, F.
    SONATINA, OP. 88 NO. 2--OLD EDITION--
        FREDERICK HARRIS MUSIC COMPANY   .40
KUHNAU, J.   HALFORD
    BIBLICAL SONATA NO. 5
        ALFRED MUSIC COMPANY   683   1.75
KUHNAU, J.   NIEMANN   E
    BIBLICAL SONATAS‡ NO. 1 -- THE BATTLE BETWEEN DAVID AND
    GOLIATH--
        C. F. PETERS CORPORATION   4434   1.50
KUHNAU, J.   E
    BIBLICAL SONATAS‡ NO. 1--THE BATTLE BETWEEN DAVID AND GOLIATH--
        C. F. PETERS CORPORATION   4840A   1.50
KUHNAU, J.   E
    BIBLICAL SONATAS‡ NO. 2 -- SAUL CURED BY DAVID WITH THE HELP OF
    MUSIC--
        C. F. PETERS CORPORATION   4840B   1.50
KUHNAU, J.   E
    BIBLICAL SONATAS‡ NO. 3 -- THE WEDDING OF JACOB--
        C. F. PETERS CORPORATION   4840C   1.50
KUHNAU, J.   E
    BIBLICAL SONATAS‡ NO. 4 -- HEZEKIAH WHO, BEING SICK UNTO DEATH,
    IS RESTORED AGAIN TO HEALTH--
        C. F. PETERS CORPORATION   4840D   1.25
KUHNAU, J.   E
    BIBLICAL SONATAS‡ NO. 5 -- GIDEON, THE DELIVERER OF ISRAEL
        C. F. PETERS CORPORATION   4840E   1.25
KUHNAU, J.   E
    BIBLICAL SONATAS‡ NO. 6 -- THE DEATH AND BURIAL OF JACOB
        C. F. PETERS CORPORATION   4840F   1.25
KUHNAU, J.
    BOURREE
        FREDERICK HARRIS MUSIC COMPANY   .60
KUHNAU, J.
    SONATA, DAVID AND GOLIATH
        EDWIN F. KALMUS   3601   1.50
KULLAK, T.   2
    CLOCK, THE
        CENTURY MUSIC PUBLISHING COMPANY, INC.   2546   .40
KULLAK, T.   3
    DANCE ON THE LAWN
        CENTURY MUSIC PUBLISHING COMPANY, INC.   2258   .40
KULLAK, T.
    GHOST IN THE CHIMNEY
        BELWIN-MILLS PUBLISHING CORPORATION   28019   .60
KULLAK, T.
    GHOST IN THE CHIMNEY, THE--OP. 81 NO. 10
        G. SCHIRMER, INC.   .35
KULLAK, T.
    MORNING PRAYER
        FREDERICK HARRIS MUSIC COMPANY   .60
KULLAK, T.   4
    PRAYER
        NOVELLO AND COMPANY, LTD.   55.0042.07   .40
KULLMANN
    BARCAROLLE
        FRANCO COLOMBO PUBLICATIONS   SAL   2.75

KULLMANN
  EFFLUVES
    FRANCO COLOMBO PUBLICATIONS   SAL   2.75
KULLMANN
  NOSTALGIES
    FRANCO COLOMBO PUBLICATIONS   SAL   2.50
KUNC, B.
  HURDY-GURDY
    RONGWEN MUSIC, INC.   01.50
KUNKILL   3
  SONG OF THE MOUNTAIN BROOK
    CENTURY MUSIC PUBLISHING COMPANY, INC. 2190   .40
KUPFERMAN, M.
  LITTLE SONATA
    GENERAL MUSIC PUBLISHING COMPANY, INC. 72   2.00
KUPFERMAN, M.
  LITTLE SONATA
    GENERAL MUSIC PUBLISHING COMPANY, INC.   3.00
KUPFERMAN, M.
  LITTLE SONATA
    GENERAL MUSIC PUBLISHING COMPANY, INC.   4.00
KUPFERMAN, M.
  LITTLE SONATA
    NOVELLO AND COMPANY, LTD.   2.15
KUPFERMAN, M.
  PARTITA
    GENERAL MUSIC PUBLISHING COMPANY, INC. 34   2.50
KUPFERMAN, M.
  RECITATIVE
    GENERAL MUSIC PUBLISHING COMPANY, INC. 37   2.00
KUPFERMAN, M.
  RECITATIVE - 1951
    GENERAL MUSIC PUBLISHING COMPANY, INC.   2.00
KUPFERMAN, M.
  SHORT SUITE
    GENERAL MUSIC PUBLISHING COMPANY, INC. 427   2.00
KUPFERMAN, M.
  SHORT SUITE
    GENERAL MUSIC PUBLISHING COMPANY, INC.   2.00
KUPFERMAN, M.
  SONATA ON JAZZ ELEMENTS
    GENERAL MUSIC PUBLISHING COMPANY, INC. 40   4.00
KUPFERMAN, M.
  SONATA ON JAZZ ELEMENTS
    GENERAL MUSIC PUBLISHING COMPANY, INC.   5.00
KUPFERMAN, M.
  SONATA ON JAZZ ELEMENTS
    NOVELLO AND COMPANY, LTD.   1.90
KUPFERMAN, M.
  VARIATIONS
    NOVELLO AND COMPANY, LTD.   1.50
KUPFERMAN, M.
  VARIATIONS - SUITE
    GENERAL MUSIC PUBLISHING COMPANY, INC. 78   2.00
KUPFERMAN, M.
  VARIATIONS - SUITE
    GENERAL MUSIC PUBLISHING COMPANY, INC.   2.50
KURKA, R.   A
  FOR THE PIANO
    THEODORE PRESSER COMPANY   1.50
KURKA, R.
  PIANO SONATA, OP. 6
    WEINTRAUB MUSIC COMPANY   070110   1.25
KURKA, R.
  PIANO SONATINA FOR YOUNG PERSONS
    WEINTRAUB MUSIC COMPANY   070111   1.50
KURTAG, G.
  ACHT KLAVIERSTUCKE, OP. 3
    UNIVERSAL EDITION   UE 14140 3.10
KURTZ, E.
  ANIMATIONS
    ELKAN-VOGEL, INC.   J   6.25
KVAPIL   3
  SONATINE
    BARENREITER VERLAG   AP 654
KVELVE   1
  BIRDS IN SPRINGTIME
    VOLKWEIN BROS.   .25
KVELVE   2
  BOY SCOUTS MARCH
    VOLKWEIN BROS.   .25
KVELVE   1
  NORWEGIAN LULLABY
    VOLKWEIN BROS.   .25
KVELVE   1
  TICK TOCK
    VOLKWEIN BROS.   00.25
L'HERVILLIERS
  PAS DE DEUX
    FRANCO COLOMBO PUBLICATIONS   SAL   1.75
LA ROCCA *
  AT THE JAZZ BAND BALL
    THE BIG THREE MUSIC CORPORATION   00.95
LABEY
  PETITE RONDE SUR UNE CHANSON
    FRANCO COLOMBO PUBLICATIONS   SAL   1.75
LABEY
  SIX PIECES - DANS LE PRE FLEURI
    FRANCO COLOMBO PUBLICATIONS   SAL   1.50
LABEY
  SIX PIECES - RONDE
    FRANCO COLOMBO PUBLICATIONS   SAL   1.50
LABITZKY, A.
  ALP-MAID'S DREAM, THE--OP. 45
    G. SCHIRMER, INC.   .40
LABITZKY, A.   4
  HERD GIRL'S DREAM, THE
    CENTURY MUSIC PUBLISHING COMPANY, INC. 1673   .40
LABITZKY, A.   2-3
  SHEPHERDESS' DREAM, EASY
    CENTURY MUSIC PUBLISHING COMPANY, INC. 2515   .40
LABITZKY, A.   4
  SHEPHERDESS' DREAM, THE
    CENTURY MUSIC PUBLISHING COMPANY, INC. 1673   .40
LABUNSKI, W.
  FOUR VARIATIONS ON A THEME BY PAGANINI
    CARL FISCHER, INC.   P 2300   .75
LABUNSKI, W.   3
  SECOND IMPROMPTU
    CENTURY MUSIC PUBLISHING COMPANY, INC. 3853   .40
LACALLE
  AMAPOLA
    EDWARD B. MARKS MUSIC CORPORATION   01.00
LACK   3, 4
  SONATE PASTORALE, OP. 253
    ALPHONSE LEDUC

LACK, J.   4
  DANSE FLORENTINE
    THEODORE PRESSER COMPANY   .50
LACK, T.
  BOLERO IN A MINOR, OP. 27
    G. SCHIRMER, INC.   .50
LACK, T.   4
  CABALETTA
    VOLKWEIN BROS.   .25
LACK, T.   4
  CABALETTA, OP. 83
    CENTURY MUSIC PUBLISHING COMPANY, INC. 694   .40
LACK, T.
  CABALETTA, OP. 83
    G. SCHIRMER, INC.   .40
LACK, T.   5
  IDILIO
    VOLKWEIN BROS.   .25
LACK, T.
  IDILIO IN A FLAT, OP. 134
    G. SCHIRMER, INC.   .35
LACK, T.   4
  IDILIO, OP. 134
    CENTURY MUSIC PUBLISHING COMPANY, INC. 803   .40
LACK, T.
  LES CLASSIQUES FAVORIS DU PIANO
    ELKAN-VOGEL, INC.   LEM   5.25
LACK, T.
  PENDANT LA VALSE--CAPRICE, OP. 73
    G. SCHIRMER, INC.   .50
LACK, T.
  SALTARELLO
    FRANCO COLOMBO PUBLICATIONS   SAL   1.75
LACK, T.   5
  SONG OF THE BROOK
    CENTURY MUSIC PUBLISHING COMPANY, INC. 1352   .40
LACK, T.   4
  SONG OF THE BROOK
    THEODORE PRESSER COMPANY   .50
LACK, T.
  SONG OF THE BROOK, OP. 92
    G. SCHIRMER, INC.   .50
LACK, T.
  THREE AIRS A DANSER - GAVOTTE ET MUSETTE
    FRANCO COLOMBO PUBLICATIONS   SAL   1.50
LACK, T.
  THREE AIRS A DANSER - GIGUE ECOSSAISE
    FRANCO COLOMBO PUBLICATIONS   SAL   1.50
LACK, T.
  THREE AIRS A DANSER - MENUET ALSACIEN
    FRANCO COLOMBO PUBLICATIONS   SAL   1.50
LACK, T.   5
  VALSE ARABESQUE, OP. 82
    CENTURY MUSIC PUBLISHING COMPANY, INC. 1041   .40
LACK, T.   5
  VALSE ARABESQUE, OP. 82
    VOLKWEIN BROS.   .25
LACK, T.
  VALSE-ARABESQUE IN E FLAT, OP. 82
    G. SCHIRMER, INC.   .75
LACK, T.
  WHILE WALTZING, OP. 73
    G. SCHIRMER, INC.   .40
LACROIX, N.
  THEME ET VARIATIONS
    EDITIONS MUSICALES TRANSATLANTIQUES   4.60
LADERMAN, E.
  PIANO SONATA NO. 01
    OXFORD UNIVERSITY PRESS   93.214   4.00
LADERMAN, E.
  PIANO SONATA NO. 02
    OXFORD UNIVERSITY PRESS   93.212   5.00
LAFORGE, F.
  ROMANCE
    G. SCHIRMER, INC.   .50
LAFORTUNE, L.
  PRELUDE
    ASSOCIATED MUSIC PUBLISHERS, INC.   BER   .60
LAI, F.
  LIVE FOR LIFE
    THE BIG THREE MUSIC CORPORATION   00.95
LAIRD
  MINUET AND TRIO
    FRANCO COLOMBO PUBLICATIONS   LD501   .60
LAIRD
  PASTORALE AND DANCE
    FRANCO COLOMBO PUBLICATIONS   LD499   .60
LAIRD
  PRAIRIE SONG AND COVERED WAGON
    FRANCO COLOMBO PUBLICATIONS   LD500   .60
LAIS   1
  HOUR OF SONG, THE
    PRO-ART PUBLICATIONS, INC.   42   .50
LAIS   1
  TICK TOCK
    PRO-ART PUBLICATIONS, INC.   46   .50
LAJTHA   5
  CONTES POUR LE PIANO
    ALPHONSE LEDUC
LAKE
  APRIL RAIN -- LARGE NOTES
    BOSTON MUSIC COMPANY   .50
LAKE   1
  I LIKE FROGS
    BOSTON MUSIC COMPANY   .50
LAKE   2
  IT'S A GUMDROP TREE
    BOSTON MUSIC COMPANY   .50
LAKE   2
  MUSIC IN MY FINGERS
    BOSTON MUSIC COMPANY   .50
LAKE, G.   1
  BALLERINA
    WILLIS MUSIC COMPANY   .35
LAKE, G.   1
  CANCY CANE CAPERS
    WILLIS MUSIC COMPANY   .40
LAKE, G.   1
  CANDY PARADE
    WILLIS MUSIC COMPANY   .40
LAKE, G.   1
  CANDY TOWN
    WILLIS MUSIC COMPANY   .40
LAKE, G.   1
  CAT AND MOUSE
    WILLIS MUSIC COMPANY   .35

LAKE, G.		1		
CHICKADEE				
WILLIS MUSIC COMPANY				.35
LAKE, G.		2		
CLOWNS				
WILLIS MUSIC COMPANY				.40
LAKE, G.				
FAMILY PETS				
WILLIS MUSIC COMPANY				.65
LAKE, G.		1		
FUNNY FOX				
WILLIS MUSIC COMPANY				.35
LAKE, G.		1		
LITTLE BUNNY				
WILLIS MUSIC COMPANY				.35
LAKE, G.		3		
PEACOCK WALK				
WILLIS MUSIC COMPANY				.40
LAKE, G.		1		
RIDING ON A BUFFALO				
WILLIS MUSIC COMPANY				.30
LAKE, G.		2		
TREE SQUIRREL, THE				
WILLIS MUSIC COMPANY				.30
LAKE, G.		1		
TURKEY, TURKEY				
WILLIS MUSIC COMPANY				.35
LAKE, G.		1		
WIND AND SAIL				
WILLIS MUSIC COMPANY				.40
LAKS				
SONATINA				
FRANCO COLOMBO PUBLICATIONS		SAL		4.25
LAMARCHE, P.				
FOLK TUNE--HOMAGE TO GRIEG				
ASSOCIATED MUSIC PUBLISHERS, INC.		BER		.40
LAMARCHE, P.				
WALTZ				
ASSOCIATED MUSIC PUBLISHERS, INC.		BER		.40
LAMBERT		2		
SIDE SHOW				
CENTURY MUSIC PUBLISHING COMPANY, INC.	4403			.40
LAMBERT--ED. LAMBERT		2		
ON TOP OF OLD SMOKY				
CENTURY MUSIC PUBLISHING COMPANY, INC.	4026			.40
LAMBERT, C.		2		
DANCING LESSON				
CENTURY MUSIC PUBLISHING COMPANY, INC.	4351			.40
LAMBERT, C.				
ELEGY				
OXFORD UNIVERSITY PRESS	32.032			1.00
LAMBERT, C.		3		
MAD MARCH WINDS				
BELWIN-MILLS PUBLISHING CORPORATION				.60
LAMBERT, C.		D		
PROCESSIONAL				
COMPOSERS PRESS, INC.				1.00
LAMBERT, C.		2		
RED BALLOON, THE				
CENTURY MUSIC PUBLISHING COMPANY, INC.	4361			.40
LAMONT		4		
CHRISTMAS TREE FAIRY				
THEODORE PRESSER COMPANY				.50
LAMONTAINE, J.		E		
QUESTIONING				
OXFORD UNIVERSITY PRESS	93.336			1.00
LAMONTAINE, J.				
TOCCATA				
BROUDE BROTHERS LTD.				02.00
LAMOTHE				
CHANSON ARABE				
FRANCO COLOMBO PUBLICATIONS		SAL		1.75
LAMOTHE				
MADRIGAL DE FRANCOIS I				
FRANCO COLOMBO PUBLICATIONS		SAL		1.75
LANARO, L.				
MINIATURA				
EDIZIONI BERBEN	EB 394			.90
LANCEN		M-D		
CONCERTINO FOR PIANO				
C. F. PETERS CORPORATION	H371			2.00
LANCEN		D		
DOMINO --SUITE FANTASTIQUE--				
C. F. PETERS CORPORATION	H57			1.25
LANCEN		D		
FANTAISIE SUR UN THEME ANCIEN				
C. F. PETERS CORPORATION	H1904			1.25
LANCEN		M		
MOINS QUE RIEN				
C. F. PETERS CORPORATION	H1901			.90
LANCEN		M		
VALSE 1900				
C. F. PETERS CORPORATION	H1900			.90
LANCEN		M		
ZWIEFACHE --A LA MEMOIRE DE FRANZ SCHUBERT--				
C. F. PETERS CORPORATION	H1902			1.25
LANCIANNI		2-3		
EARLY MORN				
CENTURY MUSIC PUBLISHING COMPANY, INC.	2399			.40
LANDOWSKI				
SONATINA				
FRANCO COLOMBO PUBLICATIONS		SAL		4.00
LANDRY				
APRES LA MOISSON -- TWO RUSTIC SKETCHES --				
FRANCO COLOMBO PUBLICATIONS		SAL		1.75
LANDRY		5		
BERGERES DE TRIANON, GAVOTTE, OP. 209				
ALPHONSE LEDUC				
LANDRY				
BERGERETTE				
FRANCO COLOMBO PUBLICATIONS		SAL		1.75
LANDRY				
FRAIS VALLON				
FRANCO COLOMBO PUBLICATIONS		SAL		1.75
LANDRY		5		
HIDALGO, DANSE ANDALOUSE, OP. 214				
ALPHONSE LEDUC				
LANDRY				
MARCHE PERSANE				
FRANCO COLOMBO PUBLICATIONS		SAL		1.75
LANDRY				
PETITES VIOLONS DU ROI LOUIS XV, LES				
FRANCO COLOMBO PUBLICATIONS		SAL		1.75
LANDRY				
SOUVENIR DU TYROL - WALTZ NO. 1				
FRANCO COLOMBO PUBLICATIONS		SAL		1.75

LANDRY			
WALTZ NO. 02			
FRANCO COLOMBO PUBLICATIONS	SAL		1.75
LANE, E.		4	
CRAPSHOOTERS, THE			
BELWIN-MILLS PUBLISHING CORPORATION			.60
LANE, J.		2	
APRIL ENCHANTMENT			
THEODORE PRESSER COMPANY			.50
LANE, J.			
JOHN LANE PLAYS BIG MOVIE HITS			
THE BIG THREE MUSIC CORPORATION			03.95
LANE, J.		3 1/2	
MOON SHADOWS			
THEODORE PRESSER COMPANY			.50
LANE, J.		2 1/2	
MOSS ROSES			
THEODORE PRESSER COMPANY			.50
LANE, J.			
PENGUIN, THE			
CARL FISCHER, INC.		P 3142	.60
LANE, J.		3	
TWILIGHT IN SLEEPY HOLLOW			
THEODORE PRESSER COMPANY			.50
LANE, J.		2 1/2	
WHITE SAILS			
THEODORE PRESSER COMPANY			.50
LANE, J.		3	
WHITE TULIPS			
THEODORE PRESSER COMPANY			.50
LANE, J.--ED. LANE, J.			
ALICE BLUE GOWN			
THE BIG THREE MUSIC CORPORATION			00.70
LANE, J.--ED. LANE, J.			
ALL I EVER NEED IS YOU			
THE BIG THREE MUSIC CORPORATION			00.85
LANE, J.--ED. LANE, J.			
AMERICAN PIE			
THE BIG THREE MUSIC CORPORATION			00.70
LANE, J.--ED. LANE, J.			
ANCHORS AWEIGH			
THE BIG THREE MUSIC CORPORATION			00.70
LANE, J.--ED.			
ANY TIME			
THE BIG THREE MUSIC CORPORATION			00.70
LANE, J.--ED. LANE, J.			
APRIL LOVE			
THE BIG THREE MUSIC CORPORATION			00.70
LANE, J.--ED. LANE, J.			
AQUARIUS			
THE BIG THREE MUSIC CORPORATION			00.70
LANE, J.--ED. LANE, J.			
ARRIVEDERCI, ROMA			
THE BIG THREE MUSIC CORPORATION			00.70
LANE, J.--ED. LANE, J.			
AT SUNDOWN			
THE BIG THREE MUSIC CORPORATION			00.70
LANE, J.--ED. LANE, J.			
BATMAN THEME			
THE BIG THREE MUSIC CORPORATION			00.70
LANE, J.--ED. LANE, J.			
BEAUTIFUL SUNDAY			
THE BIG THREE MUSIC CORPORATION			00.85
LANE, J.--ED. LANE, J.			
BECAUSE YOU'RE MINE			
THE BIG THREE MUSIC CORPORATION			00.70
LANE, J.--ED. LANE, J.			
BEYOND THE SUNSET			
THE BIG THREE MUSIC CORPORATION			00.70
LANE, J.--ED. LANE, J.			
BIG SPENDER			
THE BIG THREE MUSIC CORPORATION			00.70
LANE, J.--ED. LANE, J.			
BLUE MOON			
THE BIG THREE MUSIC CORPORATION			00.70
LANE, J.--ED. LANE, J.			
CANDIDA			
THE BIG THREE MUSIC CORPORATION			00.70
LANE, J.--ED. LANE, J.			
CERTAIN SMILE, A			
THE BIG THREE MUSIC CORPORATION			00.70
LANE, J.--ED. LANE, J.			
CHARMAINE			
THE BIG THREE MUSIC CORPORATION			00.70
LANE, J.--ED. LANE, J.			
CHATTANOOGA CHOO CHOO			
THE BIG THREE MUSIC CORPORATION			00.70
LANE, J.--ED. LANE, J.			
CHILDREN'S MARCHING SONG			
THE BIG THREE MUSIC CORPORATION			00.70
LANE, J.--ED. LANE, J.			
CHITTY CHITTY BANG BANG			
THE BIG THREE MUSIC CORPORATION			00.70
LANE, J.--ED. LANE, J.			
CIRCUS WORLD			
THE BIG THREE MUSIC CORPORATION			00.70
LANE, J.--ED. LANE, J.			
CRYING IN THE CHAPEL			
THE BIG THREE MUSIC CORPORATION			00.70
LANE, J.--ED. LANE, J.			
DARKTOWN STRUTTERS' BALL			
THE BIG THREE MUSIC CORPORATION			00.70
LANE, J.--ED. LANE, J.			
DAY IN THE LIFE OF A FOOL, A			
THE BIG THREE MUSIC CORPORATION			.70
LANE, J.--ED. LANE, J.			
DEEP PURPLE			
THE BIG THREE MUSIC CORPORATION			00.70
LANE, J.--ED. LANE, J.			
DELILAH			
THE BIG THREE MUSIC CORPORATION			00.85
LANE, J.--ED. LANE, J.			
DELILAH			
THE BIG THREE MUSIC CORPORATION			00.85
LANE, J.--ED. LANE, J.			
DIAMONDS ARE FOREVER			
THE BIG THREE MUSIC CORPORATION			00.70
LANE, J.--ED. LANE, J.			
DIANE			
THE BIG THREE MUSIC CORPORATION			00.70
LANE, J.--ED. LANE, J.			
DOLL DANCE			
THE BIG THREE MUSIC CORPORATION			00.70
LANE, J.--ED. LANE, J.			
DON'T BLAME ME			
THE BIG THREE MUSIC CORPORATION			00.70

LANGE, G.   3
  IN THE ALPINE HUT, OP. 240
    CENTURY MUSIC PUBLISHING COMPANY, INC.   1305   .40
LANGE, G.   2
  IN THE MEADOW, OP. 243
    CENTURY MUSIC PUBLISHING COMPANY, INC.   258   .40
LANGE, G.   2
  LITTLE WANDERER
    CENTURY MUSIC PUBLISHING COMPANY, INC.   292   .40
LANGE, G.   3
  LOVING HEARTS MUST PART
    CENTURY MUSIC PUBLISHING COMPANY, INC.   625   .40
LANGE, G.   4
  NEW SPRING
    CENTURY MUSIC PUBLISHING COMPANY, INC.   1396   .40
LANGE, G.   4
  PEARLS OF FOAM
    CENTURY MUSIC PUBLISHING COMPANY, INC.   649   .40
LANGE, G.   BURNAM   2 1/2
  PURE AS SNOW
    WILLIS MUSIC COMPANY   .35
LANGE, G.   SCHAUM, J.   1 1/2
  ROCKET RANGER
    BELWIN-MILLS PUBLISHING CORPORATION   .50
LANGE, G.   3
  RUSTLING LEAVES
    CENTURY MUSIC PUBLISHING COMPANY, INC.   2199   .40
LANGE, G.   4
  SECRET WISHES
    CENTURY MUSIC PUBLISHING COMPANY, INC.   1360   .40
LANGE, G.   5
  SILENT LOVE
    CENTURY MUSIC PUBLISHING COMPANY, INC.   1485   .40
LANGE, G.   4
  SWEET DREAMS
    CENTURY MUSIC PUBLISHING COMPANY, INC.   1402   .40
LANGE, G.   4
  THINE OWN - DEIN ELGEN
    CENTURY MUSIC PUBLISHING COMPANY, INC.   886   .40
LANGE, G.   4
  UNDER MY LOVED ONE'S WINDOW
    CENTURY MUSIC PUBLISHING COMPANY, INC.   1361   .40
LANGE, P.   3
  IN THE ROSE GARDEN
    CENTURY MUSIC PUBLISHING COMPANY, INC.   2108   .40
LANGE, P.   3
  MEMORIES OF DAYS GONE BY
    CENTURY MUSIC PUBLISHING COMPANY, INC.   2107   .40
LANGENFELD
  BLUE CLARINET
    BELWIN-MILLS PUBLISHING CORPORATION   20561   .85
LANGEY   3
  MANDOLINA, MEXICAN SERENADE
    CENTURY MUSIC PUBLISHING COMPANY, INC.   2253   .40
LANGLOIS, T.
  A UNE MAIN--FOR THE LEFT HAND ALONE
    ASSOCIATED MUSIC PUBLISHERS, INC.   ESC   2.25
LANGSTROTH, I.
  SONATINA
    NOVELLO AND COMPANY, LTD.   10.0087.10   1.40
LANJEAN, M.
  DANSES ANCIENNES
    EDITIONS MUSICALES TRANSATLANTIQUES   1.60
LANNACCONE, A.
  KEYBOARD ESSAYS
    SEESAW MUSIC CORPORATION   3.00
LANNER, J. F. C.   LANDOWSKA
  VALSES VIENNOISES
    G. SCHIRMER, INC.   .75
LANSDELL, C.
  FLEUR DE LYS
    BANKS AND SON LTD.   .40
LANSING   3
  DARKIE'S DREAM, THE
    CENTURY MUSIC PUBLISHING COMPANY, INC.   2397   .40
LANTIER, P.
  PRELUDE A DANSER
    GERARD BILLAUDOT EDITIONS MUSICALES   1.30
LANZA, A.
  PLECTROS I -- 1962-II, FOR ONE OR TWO PIANOS
    BOOSEY AND HAWKES, INC.   1.00
LANZA, A.
  PLECTROS II -- 1966-I, FOR PIANO AND ELECTRONIC SOUNDS
    BOOSEY AND HAWKES, INC.   1.50
LAPARRA, R.
  GITANERIAS
    FRANCO COLOMBO PUBLICATIONS   SAL   4.75
LAPARRA, R.
  JUERGAS
    FRANCO COLOMBO PUBLICATIONS   SAL   4.25
LAPARRA, R.
  PASEOS
    FRANCO COLOMBO PUBLICATIONS   SAL   4.50
LAPARRA, R.
  SUENOS
    FRANCO COLOMBO PUBLICATIONS   SAL   4.50
LAPARRA, R.
  THREE WALTZES
    FRANCO COLOMBO PUBLICATIONS   SAL   3.25
LAPEYRE, T.
  BALLADE DANS LE COSMOS
    EDITIONS MUSICALES TRANSATLANTIQUES   2.30
LAPEYRE, T.
  DEUX PIECES
    EDITIONS MUSICALES TRANSATLANTIQUES   2.00
LAPEYRE, T.
  SCHERZO PARISIEN
    EDITIONS MUSICALES TRANSATLANTIQUES   2.50
LARA, A.
  GRANADA
    EDITORIAL COOPERATIVA INTER-AMERICANA   01.00
LARA, A.
  GRANADA - SIMPLIFIED
    EDITORIAL COOPERATIVA INTER-AMERICANA   00.85
LARA, A.
  GRANADA - TEACHING EDITION
    EDITORIAL COOPERATIVA INTER-AMERICANA   00.85
LARENNE, L.
  HUMORESQUE
    BANKS AND SON LTD.   .25
LARREGLA, J.
  JOTA
    EDWARD B. MARKS MUSIC CORPORATION   01.00
LARREGLA, J.
  VIVA NAVARRA--JOTA DE CONCIERTO
    ASSOCIATED MUSIC PUBLISHERS, INC.   UME   1.00

LARSON   2 1/2
  AUTUMN COLOR
    BELWIN-MILLS PUBLISHING CORPORATION   .60
LARSON   2
  HAPPY-GO-LUCKY
    PRO-ART PUBLICATIONS, INC.   50   .50
LARSON   1
  LITTLE DANCER
    BELWIN-MILLS PUBLISHING CORPORATION   .60
LARSON   2
  STUDENTS ON PARADE
    BELWIN-MILLS PUBLISHING CORPORATION   .60
LARSSON, L. E.
  SONATINA, OP. 16
    UNIVERSAL EDITION   UE 10994   3.35
LASALA
  CANTAR
    FRANCO COLOMBO PUBLICATIONS   BA10227   .75
LASALA
  IMPRESIONES DE MI TIERRA
    FRANCO COLOMBO PUBLICATIONS   BA11532   2.00
LASALA
  LEYENDA DEL VIEJO APARCERO
    FRANCO COLOMBO PUBLICATIONS   BA9717   .75
LASALA
  PAMPEANA
    FRANCO COLOMBO PUBLICATIONS   BA11024   .75
LASALA
  SERRANA
    FRANCO COLOMBO PUBLICATIONS   BA9348   .75
LASSON, P.   4
  CRESCENDO
    CENTURY MUSIC PUBLISHING COMPANY, INC.   2165   .40
LASSON, P.
  CRESCENDO
    G. SCHIRMER, INC.   .40
LASSON, P.   ZEPP   4
  CRESCENDO
    PRO-ART PUBLICATIONS, INC.   458   .50
LASSON, P.   3
  CRESCENDO
    SCHOTT   07313   .75
LAST, J.   E
  BARCAROLLE AND POLKA
    OXFORD UNIVERSITY PRESS   33.927   .90
LAST, J.   E
  CARNIVAL PROCESSION
    OXFORD UNIVERSITY PRESS   33.931   1.20
LAST, J.   E
  CATS
    OXFORD UNIVERSITY PRESS   33.929   1.25
LAST, J.   VE
  COUNTRY OUTING
    OXFORD UNIVERSITY PRESS   33.934   1.00
LAST, J.   E
  COURANTE FROM 'IN CLASSIC STYLE'
    OXFORD UNIVERSITY PRESS   93.308   .40
LAST, J.   VE
  DAY WITH PETER AND PENNY
    OXFORD UNIVERSITY PRESS   33.910   .40
LAST, J.   E
  DOWN TO THE SEA
    OXFORD UNIVERSITY PRESS   33.918   1.40
LAST, J.   E
  DOWNLAND
    OXFORD UNIVERSITY PRESS   33.001   1.25
LAST, J.   VE
  DRUID'S CIRCLE FROM 'DOWNLAND'
    OXFORD UNIVERSITY PRESS   93.301   .40
LAST, J.   E
  FAR TO GO FROM 'MONDAY'S CHILD'
    OXFORD UNIVERSITY PRESS   93.306   .40
LAST, J.   E
  FARMYARD CAT , FROM 'FARMYARD PARADE'
    OXFORD UNIVERSITY PRESS   93.302   .40
LAST, J.   E
  FARMYARD PARADE
    OXFORD UNIVERSITY PRESS   33.916   1.25
LAST, J.   VE
  FIRST CONCERT
    OXFORD UNIVERSITY PRESS   33.903   1.30
LAST, J.   VE
  FUN FAIR
    OXFORD UNIVERSITY PRESS   33.919   1.25
LAST, J.   E
  IN A GARDEN GAY
    OXFORD UNIVERSITY PRESS   33.917   1.50
LAST, J.   E
  IN CLASSIC STYLE
    OXFORD UNIVERSITY PRESS   33.912   1.00
LAST, J.   E
  LETS GO TO THE THEATRE
    OXFORD UNIVERSITY PRESS   33.915   1.50
LAST, J.   E
  LONDON TODAY
    OXFORD UNIVERSITY PRESS   33.933   1.20
LAST, J.   E
  MAGIC CIRCLE
    OXFORD UNIVERSITY PRESS   33.932   1.20
LAST, J.   VE
  MARCH OF THE SHADOW-MEN, FROM THE 'FIRST CONCERT'
    OXFORD UNIVERSITY PRESS   93.303   .40
LAST, J.   E
  MINIATURE DANCE SUITE
    OXFORD UNIVERSITY PRESS   33.925   .90
LAST, J.   E
  MONDAY'S CHILD
    OXFORD UNIVERSITY PRESS   33.036   1.50
LAST, J.   ME
  MOTO PERPETUO
    OXFORD UNIVERSITY PRESS   33.922   1.00
LAST, J.   VE
  ONE-A-PENNY
    OXFORD UNIVERSITY PRESS   33.911   1.55
LAST, J.   VE
  PANTOMIME PICTURES
    OXFORD UNIVERSITY PRESS   34.713   1.00
LAST, J.
  PUCK'S PIECES
    BOOSEY AND HAWKES, INC.   1.50
LAST, J.   E
  SPRING SERENADE
    OXFORD UNIVERSITY PRESS   33.928   1.00
LAST, J.
  TOAD GOES FOR A RIDE, FROM 'LET'S GO TO THE THEATRE'
    OXFORD UNIVERSITY PRESS   93.304   .40

LAST, J.
  TREE PICTURES
    OXFORD UNIVERSITY PRESS   33.920   1.25
                                         1 1/2
LAST, J.
  VALSE CHANSON
    WILLIS MUSIC COMPANY   .40
                                         1 1/2
LAST, J.
  VALSE DE BALLET
    WILLIS MUSIC COMPANY   .40
LAST, J.
  VALSE GAIE
    OXFORD UNIVERSITY PRESS   33.921   1.00
LAUDER, H.   SCHAUM, J.   2
  I LOVE A LASSIE
    SCHAUM PUBLICATIONS, INC.   .50
LAUDISA
  MINUET
    FRANCO COLOMBO PUBLICATIONS   DS134   1.00
LAUFMAN
  SINGING PINES
    FRANCO COLOMBO PUBLICATIONS   NY1545   .35
LAUNAY, E.
  SHE IS LOVELY--VALSE-BOSTON, OP. 208
    G. SCHIRMER, INC.   .40
LAUSNAY, G.
  TROIS PETITS PIANOS
    GERARD BILLAUDOT EDITIONS MUSICALES   1.30
LAVAGNE
  BOITE DE COULEURS--NO. 01, CADMIUM ORANGE
    GERARD BILLAUDOT EDITIONS MUSICALES   1.10
LAVAGNE
  BOITE DE COULEURS--NO. 09, MAUVE
    GERARD BILLAUDOT EDITIONS MUSICALES   1.10
LAVAGNE
  BOITE DE COULEURS--NO. 11, INDIGO
    GERARD BILLAUDOT EDITIONS MUSICALES   1.10
LAVAGNE
  BOITE DE COULEURS--NO. 12, ARC EN CIEL
    GERARD BILLAUDOT EDITIONS MUSICALES   1.10
LAVAGNINO
  PASTORALE
    FRANCO COLOMBO PUBLICATIONS   BON.2139   .90
LAVAGNINO
  TOCCATA
    FRANCO COLOMBO PUBLICATIONS   Z3306   1.25
LAVALLEE, C.
  BUTTERFLY
    CARL FISCHER, INC.   S 220   .60
LAVALLEE, C.
  BUTTERFLY -- LE PAPILLON
    BELWIN-MILLS PUBLISHING CORPORATION   28172   .60
                                         5
LAVALLEE, C.
  BUTTERFLY, THE
    CENTURY MUSIC PUBLISHING COMPANY, INC.   999   .40
LAVALLEE, C.
  LE PAPILLON--ETUDE DE CONCERT
    G. SCHIRMER, INC.   .60
LAVALLEE, C.   ROLFE, W.   3
  PAPILLON, EASY
    CENTURY MUSIC PUBLISHING COMPANY, INC.   3215   .40
                                         5
LAVALLEE, C.
  PAPILLON, ETUDE DE CONCERT
    CENTURY MUSIC PUBLISHING COMPANY, INC.   999   .40
LAWLOR, G.
  BUSY DRUMMER
    BOOSEY AND HAWKES; INC.   .40
LAWLOR, G.
  CHINESE DREAM
    BOOSEY AND HAWKES, INC.   .40
                                         1-2
LAWLOR, G.
  EAST SIDE, WEST SIDE
    CENTURY MUSIC PUBLISHING COMPANY, INC.   4077   .40
LAWLOR, G.
  JUST POLIN' ALONG
    BELWIN-MILLS PUBLISHING CORPORATION   .60
LAWLOR, G.
  TWO SHEPHERDS
    BOOSEY AND HAWKES, INC.   .40
LAWLOR, G. *   1-2
  SIDEWALKS OF NEW YORK
    CENTURY MUSIC PUBLISHING COMPANY, INC.   4077   .40
LAWLOR, G. *   KLICKMANN   EASY
  SIDEWALKS OF NEW YORK
    SHAWNEE PRESS, INC.   .35
LAWLOR, G. *   SCHAUM, J.   2
  SIDEWALKS OF NEW YORK, THE
    BELWIN-MILLS PUBLISHING CORPORATION   .50
LAWLOR, G. *   CURCIO   1
  SIDEWALKS OF NEW YORK, THE
    BOSTON MUSIC COMPANY   .50
LAWNER, M.
  IT WON'T STOP RAINING
    WEINTRAUB MUSIC COMPANY   070083   .50
LAWNER, M.
  SCHOOLS OUT
    WEINTRAUB MUSIC COMPANY   070084   .50
LAWNER, M.
  SQUARE DANCE
    WEINTRAUB MUSIC COMPANY   070080   .40
LAWNER, M.
  TARANTELLA
    WEINTRAUB MUSIC COMPANY   070082   .60
LAWNER, M.
  WALTZ
    WEINTRAUB MUSIC COMPANY   070081   .50
LAWSON, P.   2
  RIPPLES
    THEODORE PRESSER COMPANY   .50
LAWSON, P.   2
  ROSE PETALS
    THEODORE PRESSER COMPANY   .50
LAWTON   1 1/2
  SPRING IS HERE
    WILLIS MUSIC COMPANY   .75
LAZAR, F.
  SONATE
    ELKAN-VOGEL, INC.   D   5.25
LAZAR, F.
  SUITE NO. 1
    UNIVERSAL EDITION   UE 8299   1.30
LAZAR, F.
  SUITE NO. 2
    UNIVERSAL EDITION   UE 8316   1.30
LAZARE-LEVY
  SANS OCTAVES -- 12 LITTLE PIECES -- VALSE LENTE
    FRANCO COLOMBO PUBLICATIONS   SAL   1.50

LAZARE-LEVY
  SONATINA NO. 03
    FRANCO COLOMBO PUBLICATIONS   SAL   4.00
LAZARUS
  FANTASY
    FRANCO COLOMBO PUBLICATIONS   SAL   2.75
LAZARUS, D.
  CARNAVAL HEROIQUE -- RYTHMES DE GUERRE
    ELKAN-VOGEL, INC.   D   3.00
LAZZARI   6
  PETITE ESQUISSE
    ALPHONSE LEDUC
LE DUC   3
  CHATELAINE, LA
    CENTURY MUSIC PUBLISHING COMPANY, INC.   162   .40
LE DUC   3
  LA CHATELAINE
    CENTURY MUSIC PUBLISHING COMPANY, INC.   162   .40
LEACOCK, L.
  TIC TOCCATINA
    FREDERICK HARRIS MUSIC COMPANY   .75
LEANDER *   KERR, R.N.
  EARLY IN THE MORNING
    MCA MUSIC   1.00
LEBEGUE   2
  NOELS VARIES -- VARIATIONEN UBER WEIHNACHTSSTUCKE --
    BARENREITER VERLAG
LECHNER--ED   LECHNER
  TONLEITERN UND AKKORDE DURCH ALLE DUR-UND MOLL-TONARTEN
    SCHOTT   04312 1/2   1.00
LECONTE, G. W.
  CHANSON POUR UN AUTRE TEMPS
    EDITIONS MUSICALES TRANSATLANTIQUES   1.55
LECOUPPEY, F.
  AGILITE, L', OP. 20
    FRANCO COLOMBO PUBLICATIONS   BA6100   2.00
LECOUPPEY, F.   GILLOCK   1 1/2
  CHORAL PRELUDE
    WILLIS MUSIC COMPANY   .40
LECOUPPEY, F. *   1 1/2
  BELLS OF NOTRE DAME
    WILLIS MUSIC COMPANY   .40
LECUONA
  AHI VIENE EL CHINO
    EDWARD B. MARKS MUSIC CORPORATION   01.00
LECUONA
  ALHAMBRA
    EDWARD B. MARKS MUSIC CORPORATION   01.00
LECUONA
  AMOROSA
    EDWARD B. MARKS MUSIC CORPORATION   01.00
LECUONA
  ANDALUCIA
    EDWARD B. MARKS MUSIC CORPORATION   01.00
LECUONA
  ANDALUCIA
    EDWARD B. MARKS MUSIC CORPORATION   01.00
LECUONA   SUGARMAN
  ANDALUCIA
    EDWARD B. MARKS MUSIC CORPORATION   00.60
LECUONA
  ANTE EL ESCORIAL
    EDWARD B. MARKS MUSIC CORPORATION   01.00
LECUONA
  ANTE EL ESCORIAL
    EDWARD B. MARKS MUSIC CORPORATION   01.00
LECUONA
  ARAGON
    EDWARD B. MARKS MUSIC CORPORATION   01.00
LECUONA
  ARAGONESA
    EDWARD B. MARKS MUSIC CORPORATION   01.00
LECUONA
  CANTO DEL GUAJIRO
    EDWARD B. MARKS MUSIC CORPORATION   01.00
LECUONA
  COMPARSA, LA
    EDWARD B. MARKS MUSIC CORPORATION   01.00
LECUONA
  COMPARSA, LA
    EDWARD B. MARKS MUSIC CORPORATION   01.00
LECUONA
  CORDOBA
    EDWARD B. MARKS MUSIC CORPORATION   01.00
LECUONA
  CORDOBA
    EDWARD B. MARKS MUSIC CORPORATION   01.00
LECUONA
  DANZA LUCUMI
    EDWARD B. MARKS MUSIC CORPORATION   01.00
LECUONA
  DANZA NEGRA
    EDWARD B. MARKS MUSIC CORPORATION   01.00
LECUONA
  EL MIRINAQUE
    EDWARD B. MARKS MUSIC CORPORATION   01.00
LECUONA
  EN TRES POR CUATRO
    EDWARD B. MARKS MUSIC CORPORATION   01.00
LECUONA
  GITANERIAS
    EDWARD B. MARKS MUSIC CORPORATION   01.00
LECUONA
  GITANERIAS
    EDWARD B. MARKS MUSIC CORPORATION   01.00
LECUONA
  GRANADA
    EDWARD B. MARKS MUSIC CORPORATION   01.25
LECUONA
  GUADALQUIVIR
    EDWARD B. MARKS MUSIC CORPORATION   01.00
LECUONA
  JUNGLE DRUMS
    EDWARD B. MARKS MUSIC CORPORATION   01.00
LECUONA
  LA HABANERA
    EDWARD B. MARKS MUSIC CORPORATION   01.00
LECUONA
  MALAGUENA
    EDWARD B. MARKS MUSIC CORPORATION   01.25
LECUONA
  MALAGUENA
    EDWARD B. MARKS MUSIC CORPORATION   01.00
LECUONA
  MALAGUENA
    EDWARD B. MARKS MUSIC CORPORATION   00.60

LECUONA
   MAZURKA GLISSANDO
      EDWARD B. MARKS MUSIC CORPORATION   01.00
LECUONA
   RAPSODIA NEGRA
      EDWARD B. MARKS MUSIC CORPORATION   01.25
LECUONA
   SAN FRANCISCO EL GRANDE
      EDWARD B. MARKS MUSIC CORPORATION   01.00
LECUONA   SCHAFER
   SAY 'SI SI'
      EDWARD B. MARKS MUSIC CORPORATION   01.00
LECUONA
   SIBONEY
      THE BIG THREE MUSIC CORPORATION   00.95
LECUONA
   VALS ROMANTICO
      EDWARD B. MARKS MUSIC CORPORATION   01.00
LECUONA
   Y LA MEGRA BAILABA
      EDWARD B. MARKS MUSIC CORPORATION   01.00
LECUONA
   YO TE QUIERO SIEMPRE
      EDWARD B. MARKS MUSIC CORPORATION   01.00
LECUONA
   ZAMBRA GITANA
      EDWARD B. MARKS MUSIC CORPORATION   01.00
LEDUC, A.   5
   LANCERS, THE
      ALPHONSE LEDUC
LEDUC, A.   3
   MALVINA, VALSE MIGNONNE
      ALPHONSE LEDUC
LEDUC, A.   3
   PETITS BRETONS, LES, QUADRILLE MIGNON
      ALPHONSE LEDUC
LEE
   WEST COUNTRY SUITE
      FRANCO COLOMBO PUBLICATIONS   LD39   1.00
LEE *   SCHAUM, J.   1
   PENNSYLVANIA POLKA
      SCHAUM PUBLICATIONS, INC.   .75
LEE, DAI-KEONG
   SONATINA -- IN THREE MOVEMENTS
      BELWIN-MILLS PUBLISHING CORPORATION 20271   .85
LEE, DAI-KEONG
   THREE PRELUDES
      BOOSEY AND HAWKES, INC.   .75
LEE, E.   1 1/2
   MARCH OF THE ELEPHANTS
      WILLIS MUSIC COMPANY   .35
LEE, E.   1
   PARADE OF THE GOBLINS
      CENTURY MUSIC PUBLISHING COMPANY, INC. 4354   .40
LEE, E.   1
   PLAYFUL NYMPHS
      CENTURY MUSIC PUBLISHING COMPANY, INC. 4376   .40
LEE, E.
   PROCESSION
      BOOSEY AND HAWKES, INC.   .90
LEE, E.   2
   SPACE FLIGHT
      WILLIS MUSIC COMPANY   .35
LEE, E.   2
   TURKISH REVELS
      WILLIS MUSIC COMPANY   .35
LEE, E. M.
   BOSUN, THE
      BANKS AND SON LTD.   .25
LEE, E. M.
   FROM THE BEGINNING
      BANKS AND SON LTD.   .80
LEE, E. M.
   MOVING ALONG
      BANKS AND SON LTD.   .95
LEE, E. M.
   UPWARD WAY, THE
      BANKS AND SON LTD.   .95
LEE, N.
   EUNICE CAPRICE, THE
      COMPOSERS AUTOGRAPH PUBLICATIONS   1.32
LEE, N.
   FANTASIA IN D MINOR
      COMPOSERS AUTOGRAPH PUBLICATIONS   2.86
LEE, N.
   SONATA NO. 01
      COMPOSERS AUTOGRAPH PUBLICATIONS   1.32
LEE, N.
   SONATA NO. 02
      COMPOSERS AUTOGRAPH PUBLICATIONS   2.64
LEE, N.
   VARIATIONS
      COMPOSERS AUTOGRAPH PUBLICATIONS   2.20
LEEDS, R.
   FIVE FINGERPRINTS
      G. SCHIRMER, INC.   .75
LEEDS, R.   1
   ONCE UPON A TIME, SUITE
      BELWIN-MILLS PUBLISHING CORPORATION   .60
LEEDS, R.   1
   RAMPLESTILTSKIN
      ELKAN-VOGEL, INC.   .50
LEEDS, R.   1 1/2
   RAPUNZEL
      ELKAN-VOGEL, INC.   .50
LEEMANS
   MARCH OF THE BELGIAN PARATROOPS
      MCA MUSIC   1.00
LEES *   KERR, R.N.
   QUIET NIGHTS OF QUIET STARS
      MCA MUSIC   1.00
LEES, B.
   FANTASIA
      BOOSEY AND HAWKES, INC.   1.50
LEES, B.
   KALEIDOSCOPES
      BOOSEY AND HAWKES, INC.   1.50
LEES, B.
   PIANO SONATA NO. 04
      BOOSEY AND HAWKES, INC.   3.75
LEES, B.
   SONATA BREVE
      BOOSEY AND HAWKES, INC.   2.00
LEES, B.
   THREE PRELUDES
      BOOSEY AND HAWKES, INC.   1.75

LEEUW, T.   M-D
   VARIATIONS ON A FRENCH FOLKSONG. PIANO --HARPSICHORD--
      C. F. PETERS CORPORATION   D462   2.00
LEFEVRE, A.
   VILLANELLE
      GERARD BILLAUDOT EDITIONS MUSICALES   1.10
LEGE, W.
   BUTTERFLIES, OP. 59 NO. 2
      G. SCHIRMER, INC.   .40
LEGE, W.   2
   BUTTERFLY, THE
      CENTURY MUSIC PUBLISHING COMPANY, INC. 1103   .40
LEGRAND   TERRY
   THEME FROM SUMMER OF '42
      WARNER BROTHERS PUBLISHERS   1.00
LEGRAND *   BALL   EASY
   SUMMER KNOWS, THE
      WARNER BROTHERS PUBLISHERS   .75
LEHAR
   FRASQUITA SERENADE
      EDWARD B. MARKS MUSIC CORPORATION   01.00
LEHAR   WEYBRIGHT   1 1/2
   GOLD AND SILVER WALTZ
      BELWIN-MILLS PUBLISHING CORPORATION   .50
LEHAR   WEYBRIGHT   1 1/2
   GOLD AND SILVER WALTZ
      BELWIN-MILLS PUBLISHING CORPORATION   .60
LEHAR
   GOLD AND SILVER WALTZ
      BOOSEY AND HAWKES, INC.   .60
LEHAR   3
   GOLD AND SILVER WALTZ
      CENTURY MUSIC PUBLISHING COMPANY, INC. 3333   .40
LEHAR   SCHAUM, J.   5
   MERRY WIDOW
      BELWIN-MILLS PUBLISHING CORPORATION   .50
LEHAR   WALLIS   2
   MERRY WIDOW WALTZ
      BOSTON MUSIC COMPANY   .50
LEHAR   3
   MERRY WIDOW WALTZ
      CENTURY MUSIC PUBLISHING COMPANY, INC. 3621   .40
LEHAR
   MERRY WIDOW WALTZ
      CHAPPELL AND COMPANY, INC.   3735008   .95
LEHAR
   MERRY WIDOW WALTZ
      FRANCO COLOMBO PUBLICATIONS   128116   .60
LEHAR   MITTLER   2A
   MERRY WIDOW WALTZ
      MUSICORD PUBLICATIONS, INC.   .45
LEHAR   ROGERS   2
   MERRY WIDOW WALTZ, SIMPLIFIED
      BELWIN-MILLS PUBLISHING CORPORATION 717   .60
LEHAR   4
   MERRY WIDOW, SELECTION
      CENTURY MUSIC PUBLISHING COMPANY, INC. 1311   .40
LEHAR   3
   MERRY WIDOW, VILIA
      CENTURY MUSIC PUBLISHING COMPANY, INC. 3350   .40
LEHAR   STEINER   1
   ROYAL BALLET
      BELWIN-MILLS PUBLISHING CORPORATION   .60
LEHAR   2
   VILIA
      CENTURY MUSIC PUBLISHING COMPANY, INC. 3350   .40
LEIGHTON
   FANTASIA CONTRAPPUNTISTICA
      FRANCO COLOMBO PUBLICATIONS   129470   1.50
LEIGHTON
   JACK-IN-THE-BOX
      FRANCO COLOMBO PUBLICATIONS   LD444   .60
LEIGHTON
   VARIATIONS
      NOVELLO AND COMPANY, LTD.   10.0090.10   1.40
LEKEU
   SONATA
      FRANCO COLOMBO PUBLICATIONS   SAL   4.25
LELEU   7
   PAR LES RUES ECLATANTES
      ALPHONSE LEDUC
LELEU   7
   SUITE SYMPHONIQUE
      ALPHONSE LEDUC
LELEU   7
   TRANSPARENCES, NO. 2, MIROUR D'EAU
      ALPHONSE LEDUC
LELEU   4, 5
   UN PEU DE TOUT
      ALPHONSE LEDUC
LEMAIRE
   GAVOTTE DES MATHURINS
      FRANCO COLOMBO PUBLICATIONS   SAL   1.50
LEMAIRE
   GAVOTTE DES MATHURINS
      FRANCO COLOMBO PUBLICATIONS   SAL   1.50
LEMAIRE
   GAVOTTE NO. 2
      FRANCO COLOMBO PUBLICATIONS   SAL   1.75
LEMAIRE
   MAZURKA NO. 02
      FRANCO COLOMBO PUBLICATIONS   SAL   1.75
LEMAIRE
   RETRAITE SLAVE
      FRANCO COLOMBO PUBLICATIONS   SAL   1.75
LEMAIRE
   SCINTILLEMENT D'ETOILES
      FRANCO COLOMBO PUBLICATIONS   SAL   1.75
LEMARE, E.   SCHAUM, J.   2 1/2
   ANDANTINO
      BELWIN-MILLS PUBLISHING CORPORATION   .50
LEMARE, E.   ARMOUR   3
   ANDANTINO
      CENTURY MUSIC PUBLISHING COMPANY, INC. 3627   .60
LEMARE, E.
   ANDANTINO
      NOVELLO AND COMPANY, LTD.   10.0091.08   1.15
LEMARE, E.   MOSSMAN, T.
   ANDANTINO IN D FLAT -- SIMP.
      BELWIN-MILLS PUBLISHING CORPORATION 26107   .50
LEMARE, E.   3-4
   CATHEDRAL MEDITATION -- ANDANTINO
      CENTURY MUSIC PUBLISHING COMPANY, INC. 2422   .40
LEMARE, E.   2
   CATHEDRAL MEDITATION, EASY
      CENTURY MUSIC PUBLISHING COMPANY, INC. 3383   .40

LEMARE, E.   WALDO, J.   1
    THEME FROM ANDANTINO
        WILLIS MUSIC COMPANY   .30
LEMOINE, H.   STEINER   2
    DANCE OF THE DEBUTANTES, OP. 37 NO. 25
        BELWIN-MILLS PUBLISHING CORPORATION   .60
LEMOINE, H.
    ETUDES ENFANTINES, OP. 37
        FRANCO COLOMBO PUBLICATIONS   ER 894   1.75
                                          2 1/2
LEMONT, C. W.
    ELFIN FROLIC, OP. 59 NO. 6
        THEODORE PRESSER COMPANY   .50
LEMONT, C. W.   2
    GRACEFUL LADY, THE
        BOSTON MUSIC COMPANY   .50
LEMONT, C. W.
    ORGANIST, THE
        CARL FISCHER, INC.   P 2138   .50
LEMONT, C. W.   WILLIAMS, J.   3
    RONDINO
        BOSTON MUSIC COMPANY   .50
LEMONT, C. W.   3
    WITCHES' DANCE
        THEODORE PRESSER COMPANY   .50
LENG, A.
    SONATA
        PAN AMERICAN UNION   01.25
LENNON *   NEALE, J.   EASY
    ALL TOGETHER NOW
        WARNER BROTHERS PUBLISHERS   .75
LENNON *   NEALE, J.   EASY
    ALL YOU NEED IS LOVE
        WARNER BROTHERS PUBLISHERS   .75
LENNON *   NEALE, J.   EASY
    HEY JUDE
        WARNER BROTHERS PUBLISHERS   .75
LENNON *   NEALE, J.   EASY
    LET IT BE
        WARNER BROTHERS PUBLISHERS   .75
LENNON *   NEALE, J.   EASY
    LONG AND WINDING ROAD, THE
        WARNER BROTHERS PUBLISHERS   .75
LENNON *   NEALE, J.   EASY
    MICHELLE
        WARNER BROTHERS PUBLISHERS   .75
LENNON *   NEALE, J.   EASY
    YESTERDAY
        WARNER BROTHERS PUBLISHERS   .75
LEO, L.   MCCLANAHAN, R.
    GIGA -- HARMONIC STUDY EDITION
        BELWIN-MILLS PUBLISHING CORPORATION   20341   .85
LEO, L.   MCCLANAHAN, R.
    SONATA PER CEMBALO, HARMONIC STUDY EDITION -- WITH OPTIONAL
    SECOND PIANO
        BELWIN-MILLS PUBLISHING CORPORATION   20263   .85
LEONCAVALLO   CORONARO
    BOHEME, LA - IO NON CHE UNA POVERA STANZETTA
        FRANCO COLOMBO PUBLICATIONS   SON.970   .90
LEONCAVALLO
    GAVOTTE
        FRANCO COLOMBO PUBLICATIONS   SAL   1.75
LEONCAVALLO
    INTERMEZZO FROM PAGLIACCI
        FREDERICK HARRIS MUSIC COMPANY   .50
LEONCAVALLO   ZEPP   4
    IT REALLY CAN HAPPEN
        PRO-ART PUBLICATIONS, INC.   407   .50
LEONCAVALLO   BALLATORE, P.   2
    LA MATTINATA
        PRO-ART PUBLICATIONS, INC.   395   .50
LEONCAVALLO
    MENUETTO E GAVOTTA FROM PAGLIACI
        FREDERICK HARRIS MUSIC COMPANY   .75
LEONCAVALLO
    PAGLIACCI - ARIOSO
        FRANCO COLOMBO PUBLICATIONS   SON.1908   .90
LEONCAVALLO
    PAGLIACCI - INTERMEZZO
        FRANCO COLOMBO PUBLICATIONS   SON.732   .90
LEONCAVALLO   DE CRISTOFARO
    PAGLIACCI - INTERMEZZO AND UN TAL GIOCO
        FRANCO COLOMBO PUBLICATIONS   SON.1845   1.00
LEONCAVALLO   DE CRISTOFARO
    PAGLIACCI - MINUET AND SERENATA
        FRANCO COLOMBO PUBLICATIONS   SON.1844   1.00
LEONCAVALLO
    PAGLIACCI - PROLOGUE
        FRANCO COLOMBO PUBLICATIONS   SON.1902   1.25
LEONCAVALLO
    PAGLIACCI -- COMPLETE OPERA --
        FRANCO COLOMBO PUBLICATIONS   SON.656   8.75
LEONCAVALLO
    SERENADE
        FRANCO COLOMBO PUBLICATIONS   SAL   1.75
LEONCAVALLO
    ZINGARI
        FRANCO COLOMBO PUBLICATIONS   SON.1899   1.25
LEONI, F.
    SAVAGE DANCE, A
        G. SCHIRMER, INC.   .30
LEOZ, J.G.
    SONATINA
        ASSOCIATED MUSIC PUBLISHERS, INC.   UME   1.75
LEPITRE
    GAVOTTE DANS LE STYLE DE JADIS
        FRANCO COLOMBO PUBLICATIONS   SAL   1.50
LERMYTE
    SIX PIECES FOR CHILDREN - CHEZ GUIGNOL
        FRANCO COLOMBO PUBLICATIONS   SAL   1.50
LERMYTE
    SIX PIECES FOR CHILDREN - LA PETITE FUTEE
        FRANCO COLOMBO PUBLICATIONS   SAL   1.50
LERMYTE
    SIX PIECES FOR CHILDREN - LE PETIT BALLON ROUGE
        FRANCO COLOMBO PUBLICATIONS   SAL   1.50
LERMYTE
    SIX PIECES FOR CHILDREN - LES CLOCHETTES
        FRANCO COLOMBO PUBLICATIONS   SAL   1.50
LERMYTE
    SIX PIECES FOR CHILDREN - PETIT MENUET
        FRANCO COLOMBO PUBLICATIONS   SAL   1.50
LERMYTE
    SIX PIECES FOR CHILDREN - REVERIE
        FRANCO COLOMBO PUBLICATIONS   SAL   1.50

LESCHETIZKY
    ANDANTE FINALE DE 'LUCIA DI LAMMERMOOR'--FOR THE LEFT HAND
    ALONE--OP. 13
        G. SCHIRMER, INC.   .60
LESCHETIZKY
    ARABESQUE EN FORME D'ETUDE, OP. 45 NO. 1
        G. SCHIRMER, INC.   .50
LESCHETIZKY   5
    CAPRICE - ARABESQUE EN FORME D'UN ETUDE
        CENTURY MUSIC PUBLISHING COMPANY, INC. 3329   .40
LESCHETIZKY   5
    DEUX ALOUETTES - TWO LARKS
        CENTURY MUSIC PUBLISHING COMPANY, INC. 188   .40
LESCHETIZKY
    INTERMEZZO IN OCTAVES, OP. 44 NO. 4
        G. SCHIRMER, INC.   .50
LESCHETIZKY   5
    MAZURKA, OP. 24 NO. 2
        CENTURY MUSIC PUBLISHING COMPANY, INC. 1017   .40
LESCHETIZKY   6
    SEXTET, LUCIA - FOR LEFT HAND
        CENTURY MUSIC PUBLISHING COMPANY, INC. 1860   .40
LESCHETIZKY   6
    STUDY FOR LEFT HAND, LUCIA
        CENTURY MUSIC PUBLISHING COMPANY, INC. 1860   .40
LESCHETIZKY   5
    TWO LARKS
        CENTURY MUSIC PUBLISHING COMPANY, INC. 188   .40
LESCHETIZKY
    TWO LARKS, THE--IMPROMPTU, OP. 2 NO. 1
        G. SCHIRMER, INC.   .60
LESLIE   COWLRICK
    MEXICANA
        FRANCO COLOMBO PUBLICATIONS   LD134   1.00
LESLIE
    NIGHT FLIGHT TO MADRID
        BELWIN-MILLS PUBLISHING CORPORATION   28100   .85
LESSARD, J.
    LITTLE CONCERT -- SUITE
        NOVELLO AND COMPANY, LTD.   2.25
LESSARD, J.
    LITTLE CONCERT SUITE
        GENERAL MUSIC PUBLISHING COMPANY, INC. 53   2.50
LESSARD, J.
    MASK
        GENERAL MUSIC PUBLISHING COMPANY, INC. MD   2.50
LESSARD, J.
    MASK
        THEODORE PRESSER COMPANY   1.00
LESSARD, J.
    PERPETUAL MOTION
        GENERAL MUSIC PUBLISHING COMPANY, INC. 266 2.00
LESSARD, J.
    PERPETUAL MOTION
        GENERAL MUSIC PUBLISHING COMPANY, INC.   2.00
LESSARD, J.
    TOCCATA
        GENERAL MUSIC PUBLISHING COMPANY, INC. 43   3.00
LESSARD, J.
    TOCCATA IN FOUR MOVEMENTS
        GENERAL MUSIC PUBLISHING COMPANY, INC.   3.00
LESSARD, J.
    TOCCATA IN FOUR MOVEMENTS FOR HARPSICHORD OR PIANO
        NOVELLO AND COMPANY, LTD.   3.15
LESTER, I.   4
    CRIMSON BLUSHES
        CENTURY MUSIC PUBLISHING COMPANY, INC. 968   .40
LESTRANGE--ED   LESTRANGE
    BELLS OF ST. MARY'S, WALTZ
        CHAPPELL AND COMPANY, INC.   0437509-1501 .95
LESUR, D.
    CARILLONS, LES
        FRANCO COLOMBO PUBLICATIONS   SAL   3.50
LESUR, D.
    LE BAL. SUITE
        EDITIONS MUSICALES TRANSATLANTIQUES   3.00
LESUR, D.
    MOMENT MUSICAL
        EDITIONS MUSICALES TRANSATLANTIQUES   1.75
LETELIER, A.
    VARIATIONS EN FA
        BOOSEY AND HAWKES, INC.   3.00
LEUKAUF, R.
    FUGENSONATE NO. 1, OP. 11
        ASSOCIATED MUSIC PUBLISHERS, INC.   DOB   2.00
                                          2-3
LEVENSON, B.
    GRACEFUL MAIDS
        CENTURY MUSIC PUBLISHING COMPANY, INC. 2674   .40
                                          3
LEVENSON, B.
    LA MEMOIRE
        CENTURY MUSIC PUBLISHING COMPANY, INC. 2673   .40
                                          3
LEVENSON, B.
    O'ER THE MOONLIT WATER
        CENTURY MUSIC PUBLISHING COMPANY, INC. 2672   .40
                                          2-3
LEVENSON, B.
    REMBRANCE OF POLAND
        CENTURY MUSIC PUBLISHING COMPANY, INC. 2675   .40
                                          4
LEVINE
    HUMORESKE
        BOSTON MUSIC COMPANY   .60
LEVINE, H.   PALMER, W. A.
    THEMES WITHOUT VARIATIONS
        ALFRED MUSIC COMPANY   622   2.50
LEVITON
    PROMENADE
        SUMMY-BIRCHARD COMPANY   .40
LEVITZKI, M.
    VALSE, OP. 2
        G. SCHIRMER, INC.   .50
LEVITZKI, M.   LEVINE
    VALSE, OP. 2
        G. SCHIRMER, INC.   .50
LEVY, E.
    DANSE HUMORISTIQUE
        FRANCO COLOMBO PUBLICATIONS   SAL   2.50
LEVY, E.
    JEUX DE NUAGES
        FRANCO COLOMBO PUBLICATIONS   SAL   2.50
LEVY, E.
    VIVA MARIA
        FRANCO COLOMBO PUBLICATIONS   SAL   2.50
LEVY, S.   SCHAUM, J.
    NAUGHTY WALTZ, THAT
        BELWIN-MILLS PUBLISHING CORPORATION   .60
                                          MD
LEWINE, R.
    TERRIBLE TEMPERED CLAVICHORD, THE
        THEODORE PRESSER COMPANY   .50

LEWIS
ROCK LIZA
LEE ROBERTS MUSIC PUBLICATIONS, INC. .85
LEWIS
ROCKIN' LITTLE TALE, A
LEE ROBERTS MUSIC PUBLICATIONS, INC. .75
1
LEWIS
SAILOR'S DELIGHT
LEE ROBERTS MUSIC PUBLICATIONS, INC. .85
LEWIS
SIX WHEEL CHASER
MCA MUSIC 1.00
LEWIS
TANGANA
LEE ROBERTS MUSIC PUBLICATIONS, INC. 1.00
LEWIS *
BOOGIE WOOGIE PRAYER
MCA MUSIC 1.00
LEWIS, E. M
ARIOSA
THEODORE PRESSER COMPANY .60
LEWIS, M. 1
DOLLY'S DREAM
THEODORE PRESSER COMPANY .50
LEWIS, M. 1
PRETTY LITTLE DAISY
THEODORE PRESSER COMPANY .50
LEWIS, R. H.
FIVE MOVEMENTS FOR PIANO, 1960
SEESAW MUSIC CORPORATION 6.00
LEY, S.
DANZA EXOTICA
PAN AMERICAN UNION 01.50
LEYBACH, I. 6
CAPRICE BRILLANTE
CENTURY MUSIC PUBLISHING COMPANY, INC. 1253 .40
LEYBACH, I. 4
DIABOLIQUE, LA, ETUDE
CENTURY MUSIC PUBLISHING COMPANY, INC. 776 .40
LEYBACH, I. 5
FIFTH NOCTURNE
BELWIN-MILLS PUBLISHING CORPORATION 226 .60
LEYBACH, I. 4
FIFTH NOCTURNE
CENTURY MUSIC PUBLISHING COMPANY, INC. 209 .40
LEYBACH, I. DEIS
FIFTH NOCTURNE IN A FLAT, OP. 52
G. SCHIRMER, INC. .70
LEYBACH, I. 4
FIFTH NOCTURNE, OP. 52
THEODORE PRESSER COMPANY .70
LEYBACH, I. 4
LA DIABOLIQUE, ETUDE
CENTURY MUSIC PUBLISHING COMPANY, INC. 776 .40
LEYBACH, I. 2
MERRY MOOD - FROHER SINN
CENTURY MUSIC PUBLISHING COMPANY, INC. 1315 .40
LEYBACH, I. 2-3
NOCTURNE, NO. 05, EASY
CENTURY MUSIC PUBLISHING COMPANY, INC. 2507 .40
LEYBACH, I. 5
NOCTURNE, OP. 4 NO. 2
CENTURY MUSIC PUBLISHING COMPANY, INC. 1378 .40
LEYBACH, I. 4
NOCTURNE, OP. 52 NO. 5
CENTURY MUSIC PUBLISHING COMPANY, INC. 209 .40
LEYBACH, I. 5
NOCTURNE, OP. 9 NO. 6
CENTURY MUSIC PUBLISHING COMPANY, INC. 1200 .40
LEYBACH, I. 5
SECOND NOCTURNE, OP. 4
CENTURY MUSIC PUBLISHING COMPANY, INC. 1378 .40
LEYBACH, I. 5
SIXTH NOCTURNE, OP. 91
CENTURY MUSIC PUBLISHING COMPANY, INC. 1200 .40
LIADOW, A.
BALLADE, OP. 21
BOOSEY AND HAWKES, INC. 1.75
LIADOW, A.
BARCAROLLE, OP. 44
BOOSEY AND HAWKES, INC. 1.75
LIADOW, A.
EIGHT POPULAR RUSSIAN SONGS, OP. 58
BOOSEY AND HAWKES, INC. 2.00
LIADOW, A.
ETUDE IN A FLAT, OP. 5
G. SCHIRMER, INC. .50
LIADOW, A.
ETUDE, OP. 37
BOOSEY AND HAWKES, INC. 1.25
LIADOW, A.
MARIONNETTES, OP. 29
BOOSEY AND HAWKES, INC. 1.50
LIADOW, A. OLDENBURG, E. 2
MUSICAL SNUFF BOX
BOSTON MUSIC COMPANY .50
LIADOW, A. 3-4
MUSICAL SNUFF BOX
CENTURY MUSIC PUBLISHING COMPANY, INC. 3609 .40
LIADOW, A.
MUSICAL SNUFF BOX, OP. 32
BOOSEY AND HAWKES, INC. .60
LIADOW, A. OESTERLE
MUSICAL SNUFF-BOX, THE--VALSE-BADINAGE, OP. 32
G. SCHIRMER, INC. .50
LIADOW, A.
NOVELLETTE, OP. 20
BOOSEY AND HAWKES, INC. 1.50
LIADOW, A.
ON THE PRAIRIE, OP. 23
BOOSEY AND HAWKES, INC. 1.00
LIADOW, A. 3
PRELUDE IN B FLAT MINOR
CENTURY MUSIC PUBLISHING COMPANY, INC. 3912 .40
LIADOW, A.
VARIATIONS ON A POPULAR POLISH THEME, OP. 51
BOOSEY AND HAWKES, INC. 2.75
LIADOW, A.
VARIATIONS ON A THEME OF GLINKA, OP. 35
BOOSEY AND HAWKES, INC. 3.75
LIAPUNOFF D
VARIATIONS SUR UN THEME RUSSE, OP. 49
C. F. PETERS CORPORATION ZM1384 2.50
LIBBY, R. 1
SWEET STORY
THEODORE PRESSER COMPANY .50

LIBERACE--ED LIBERACE
SEPTEMBER SONG
CHAPPELL AND COMPANY, INC. 5060009-1502 .95
LICHNER, H. 2
AT HOME
CENTURY MUSIC PUBLISHING COMPANY, INC. 618 .40
LICHNER, H. 3
AUF WIEDERSEHN
CENTURY MUSIC PUBLISHING COMPANY, INC. 2298 .40
LICHNER, H. 2
BUNTE BLUMEN OP. 111
SCHOTT 1680 1.00
LICHNER, H. 2
FROHER SINN -- MERRY MOOD
CENTURY MUSIC PUBLISHING COMPANY, INC. 1315 .40
LICHNER, H.
GIPSY DANCE--FROM SONATINA, OP. 149 NO. 6
G. SCHIRMER, INC. .40
LICHNER, H. 3
GYPSY DANCE
CENTURY MUSIC PUBLISHING COMPANY, INC. 627 .40
LICHNER, H. 2
HELIOTROPE
CENTURY MUSIC PUBLISHING COMPANY, INC. 1492 .40
LICHNER, H.
IN THE MEADOW, OP. 95 NO. 2
G. SCHIRMER, INC. .40
LICHNER, H. 2
KLEINE BLUMEN, KLEINE BLATTER OP. 64
SCHOTT 1.00
LICHNER, H. 2
LILY
CENTURY MUSIC PUBLISHING COMPANY, INC. 638 .40
LICHNER, H. STEINER 2 1/2
MAZURKA IN A MINOR
BELWIN-MILLS PUBLISHING CORPORATION .60
LICHNER, H. 1
MORNING PRAYER
CENTURY MUSIC PUBLISHING COMPANY, INC. 1909 .40
LICHNER, H. 2
ON PARADE
CENTURY MUSIC PUBLISHING COMPANY, INC. 1711 .40
LICHNER, H. 2
ON THE MEADOW
CENTURY MUSIC PUBLISHING COMPANY, INC. 1024 .40
LICHNER, H. 2
PINK
CENTURY MUSIC PUBLISHING COMPANY, INC. 653 .40
LICHNER, H. 3
SANTA LUCIA
CENTURY MUSIC PUBLISHING COMPANY, INC. 380 .40
LICHNER, H.
SONATINA IN C, OP. 4 NO. 1
G. SCHIRMER, INC. .60
LICHNER, H.
SONATINA IN C, OP. 66 NO. 1
G. SCHIRMER, INC. .40
LICHNER, H. 2
SONATINE, OP. 49 NO. 1
CENTURY MUSIC PUBLISHING COMPANY, INC. 427 .40
LICHNER, H. 2
SONATINE, OP. 49 NO. 2
CENTURY MUSIC PUBLISHING COMPANY, INC. 428 .40
LICHNER, H. 3
SUMMER
CENTURY MUSIC PUBLISHING COMPANY, INC. 1350 .40
LICHNER, H. 2
TULIP
CENTURY MUSIC PUBLISHING COMPANY, INC. 1037 .40
LICHNER, H.
TULIP, OP. 111 NO. 4
G. SCHIRMER, INC. .35
LICHNER, H. 2
TYROLESE AND HIS CHILD
CENTURY MUSIC PUBLISHING COMPANY, INC. 447 .40
LICHNER, P. 2
ARRIVAL OF THE FRIENDS
CENTURY MUSIC PUBLISHING COMPANY, INC. 1430 .40
LICHNER, P. 2
AS THE DANCE GOES ON
CENTURY MUSIC PUBLISHING COMPANY, INC. 1431 .40
LICHNER, P. 2
DREAMING
CENTURY MUSIC PUBLISHING COMPANY, INC. 1433 .40
LICHNER, P. 3
LETTER FROM AUNTIE
CENTURY MUSIC PUBLISHING COMPANY, INC. 1429 .40
LICHNER, P. 2
TILL WE MEET AGAIN
CENTURY MUSIC PUBLISHING COMPANY, INC. 2298 .40
LICHNER, P. 2
WAITING FOR THE MAIL
CENTURY MUSIC PUBLISHING COMPANY, INC. 1428 .40
LICHNER, R. 1
VACATION TIME
CENTURY MUSIC PUBLISHING COMPANY, INC. 3077 .40
LIDDIARD, I.
FUN AT THE CIRCUS
BOOSEY AND HAWKES, INC. .85
LIDDLE, S. PERRY
ABIDE WITH ME
BOOSEY AND HAWKES, INC. .50
LIEBERMAN, F.
SONATINA
E. C. SCHIRMER MUSIC COMPANY 232 01.00
LIEBERMAN, F.
SUITE
E. C. SCHIRMER MUSIC COMPANY 233 01.00
LIEBERMANN, R.
SONATA
UNIVERSAL EDITION UE 12055 2.55
LIEBICH 4
MUSIC BOX, CAPRICE
CENTURY MUSIC PUBLISHING COMPANY, INC. 988 .40
LIER M-D
SONATINA NO. 02
C. F. PETERS CORPORATION D209 1.25
LIGETI, G.
CONTINUUM FUR CEMBALO
SCHOTT 6111
LIGHT, F. M. 1
BETTY'S FIRST WALTZ
THEODORE PRESSER COMPANY .50
LIGHT, F. M. 1
BETTY'S HIGH CHAIR
THEODORE PRESSER COMPANY .50

LIGHT, F. M.   2
    BETTY'S WOODEN SHOE DANCE
        THEODORE PRESSER COMPANY   .50
LIGHTFOOT   NEALE, J.   EASY
    IF YOU COULD READ MY MIND
        WARNER BROTHERS PUBLISHERS   .75
LILIUOKALANI   2
    ALOHA OE
        BELWIN-MILLS PUBLISHING CORPORATION   239   .60
LIMA *
    DANZA DE NEGROS
        FRANCO COLOMBO PUBLICATIONS   2.50
LINCKE, P.
    GAVOTTE DES VERS LUISANTS
        FRANCO COLOMBO PUBLICATIONS   SAL   1.50
LINCKE, P.
    GLOW WORM
        ASHLEY DEALERS SERVICE, INC.   ES   .95
LINCKE, P.   4
    GLOW WORM
        BOSTON MUSIC COMPANY   .50
LINCKE, P.
    GLOW WORM
        EDWARD B. MARKS MUSIC CORPORATION   01.00
LINCKE, P.
    GLOW WORM
        EDWARD B. MARKS MUSIC CORPORATION   01.00
LINCKE, P.   SUGARMAN
    GLOW WORM
        EDWARD B. MARKS MUSIC CORPORATION   00.60
LINCKE, P.   RICHTER   FIRST YEAR
    GLOW WORM
        WARNER BROTHERS PUBLISHERS   .75
LINCKE, P.   BURNAM   2
    GLOW WORM
        WILLIS MUSIC COMPANY   .40
LINCKE, P.
    GLOW WORM -- EASY
        CENTURY MUSIC PUBLISHING COMPANY, INC.   4291   .40
LINCKE, P.
    GLOW WORM -- SIMP.
        ASHLEY DEALERS SERVICE, INC.   ES   .95
LINCKE, P.
    GLOW WORM-- ORIGINAL
        CENTURY MUSIC PUBLISHING COMPANY, INC.   4290   .40
LINCKE, P.   ECKSTEIN
    GLOW WORM, THE
        CARL FISCHER, INC.   P 2943   .50
LINCKE, P.   ZEPP   3-4
    GLOW WORM, THE
        PRO-ART PUBLICATIONS, INC.   199   .50
LINCKE, P.
    SPRING BEAUTIFUL SPRING
        EDWARD B. MARKS MUSIC CORPORATION   01.00
LINCKE, P.   SCHAUM, J.   1
    SPRING, SWEET SPRING
        SCHAUM PUBLICATIONS, INC.   .50
LINCOLN   PAULL   MEDIUM
    MENUET DU SOIR
        SHAWNEE PRESS, INC.   .60
LINCOLN, H.
    FIRE DRILL
        BELWIN-MILLS PUBLISHING CORPORATION   20093   .85
LINCOLN, H.
    GARDEN OF DREAMS
        BELWIN-MILLS PUBLISHING CORPORATION   20106   .85
LINCOLN, H.
    MIDNIGHT FIRE ALARM
        ASHLEY DEALERS SERVICE, INC.   ES   .95
LINCOLN, H.   3
    MIDNIGHT FIRE ALARM
        CENTURY MUSIC PUBLISHING COMPANY, INC.   4378   .40
LINCOLN, H.   PAULL   ADVANCED
    MIDNIGHT FIRE ALARM
        SHAWNEE PRESS, INC.   HB-58   .60
LINCOLN, H.   3 1/2
    MIDNIGHT FIRE ALARM, THE
        WILLIS MUSIC COMPANY   .50
LINCOLN, H.
    REPASZ BAND
        ASHLEY DEALERS SERVICE, INC.   ES   .95
LINCOLN, H.
    REPASZ BAND
        BELWIN-MILLS PUBLISHING CORPORATION   20224   .85
LINCOLN, H.   2 1/2
    REPASZ BAND MARCH
        WILLIS MUSIC COMPANY   .35
LINCOLN, H.   2
    REPAZ BAND
        CENTURY MUSIC PUBLISHING COMPANY, INC.   4417   .40
LINCOLN, H.
    SILENT THOUGHTS
        BELWIN-MILLS PUBLISHING CORPORATION   20243   .85
LIND, L. S.   2 1/2
    DARK NIGHT
        THEODORE PRESSER COMPANY   .50
LIND, L. S.
    OLD INDIAN TRAIL
        BELWIN-MILLS PUBLISHING CORPORATION   .60
LIND, L. S.   2 1/2
    RIDING ON A STAR
        THEODORE PRESSER COMPANY   .50
LINDFORS
    CRADLED CLOUD
        BELWIN-MILLS PUBLISHING CORPORATION   25031   .60
LINDFORS
    LULLABY LAND
        BELWIN-MILLS PUBLISHING CORPORATION   25151   .60
LINDFORS
    SNOWFLAKE CHASE
        BELWIN-MILLS PUBLISHING CORPORATION   25149   .60
LINDFORS
    TO A BUTTERFLY
        BELWIN-MILLS PUBLISHING CORPORATION   25111   .60
LINDFORS, E.   1
    DUTCH DANCERS AND IN THE CLOCK STORE
        BELWIN-MILLS PUBLISHING CORPORATION   .60
LINDFORS, E.   1-2
    FUN AT THE CIRCUS
        PRO-ART PUBLICATIONS, INC.   419   .50
LINDFORS, E.   2
    GOLLIWOG'S PARADE
        WILLIS MUSIC COMPANY   .35
LINDFORS, E.   1
    IN THE CLOCK STORE AND DUTCH DANCERS
        BELWIN-MILLS PUBLISHING CORPORATION   .60

LINDFORS, E.
    INDIAN DANCE
        BRODT MUSIC COMPANY   .40
LINDFORS, E.   2
    MUSINGS
        WILLIS MUSIC COMPANY   .40
LINDFORS, E.   2 1/2
    PASTORAL
        WILLIS MUSIC COMPANY   .40
LINDFORS, E.
    SKY BOATS
        BRODT MUSIC COMPANY   .45
LINDFORS, E.
    TAP DANCE
        BELWIN-MILLS PUBLISHING CORPORATION   .60
LINDFORS, E.   1
    TO A LOST PET
        WILLIS MUSIC COMPANY   .40
LINDO, S.
    METHODE DE PIANO
        EDITIONS MUSICALES TRANSATLANTIQUES   5.40
LINK, J.D.
    SONATA NO. 02 IN E MINOR, 1946
        ASSOCIATED MUSIC PUBLISHERS, INC.   BRH   2.50
LIPATTI, D.
    NOCTURNE IN F SHARP MINOR
        FRANCO COLOMBO PUBLICATIONS   SAL   2.00
LIPATTI, D.
    SONATINA FOR THE LEFT HAND
        FRANCO COLOMBO PUBLICATIONS   SAL   3.50
LIPSCOMB
    HURDY-GURDY MAN, THE
        AMERICAN MUSIC EDITION   .50
LIPSCOMB
    SKIPPING SONG
        AMERICAN MUSIC EDITION   .50
LISZT   4
    ANNEES DE PELERINAGE -- AU BORD D'UNE SOURCE
        SCHOTT   06270 1/2   1.00
LISZT   5
    ANNEES DE PELERINAGE -- LES JEUX D'EAUX A LA VILLA D'ESTE
        SCHOTT   06297 1/2   1.00
LISZT   MONTANI
    ANNEES DE PELERINAGE, 1ST YEAR, SWITZERLAND - AU BORD D'UNE
    SOURCE
        FRANCO COLOMBO PUBLICATIONS   128389   .75
LISZT   TAGLIAPIETRA
    ANNEES DE PELERINAGE, 1ST YEAR, SWITZERLAND - CHAPELLE DE
    GUILLAUME TELL
        FRANCO COLOMBO PUBLICATIONS   ER722   .60
LISZT   TAGLIAPIETRA
    ANNEES DE PELERINAGE, 1ST YEAR, SWITZERLAND - CLOCHES DE GENEVE,
    LES
        FRANCO COLOMBO PUBLICATIONS   ER723   .75
LISZT   TAGLIAPIETRA
    ANNEES DE PELERINAGE, 1ST YEAR, SWITZERLAND - EGLOGUE
        FRANCO COLOMBO PUBLICATIONS   EP757   .60
LISZT   TAGLIAPIETRA
    ANNEES DE PELERINAGE, 2ND YEAR, ITALY - GONDOLIERA
        FRANCO COLOMBO PUBLICATIONS   128006   .90
LISZT   TAGLIAPIETRA
    ANNEES DE PELERINAGE, 2ND YEAR, ITALY - SPOSALIZIO
        FRANCO COLOMBO PUBLICATIONS   127766   .60
LISZT   TAGLIAPIETRA
    ANNEES DE PELERINAGE, 2ND YEAR, ITALY - SUPPLEMENT, VENEZIA E
    NAPOLI
        FRANCO COLOMBO PUBLICATIONS   ER76   1.75
LISZT   SEAK
    ANNEES DE PELERINAGE, 3RD YEAR - BALLADE NO. 1
        FRANCO COLOMBO PUBLICATIONS   ER2544   .90
LISZT   TAGLIAPIETRA
    ANNEES DE PELERINAGE, 3RD YEAR - JEUX D'EAUX A LA VILLA D'ESTE,
    LE
        FRANCO COLOMBO PUBLICATIONS   ER760   1.25
LISZT   CORTOT
    APRES UNE LECTURE DU DANTE
        FRANCO COLOMBO PUBLICATIONS   SAL   3.25
LISZT
    AU BORD D'UNE SOURCE
        EDWIN F. KALMUS   3623   1.00
LISZT   CORTOT
    AU BORD D'UNE SOURCE
        FRANCO COLOMBO PUBLICATIONS   SAL   2.50
LISZT
    AU BORD D'UNE SOURCE
        KULTURA   1.00
LISZT
    AU BORD D'UNE SOURCE--FROM PREMIERE ANNEE DE PELERINAGE
        G. SCHIRMER, INC.   .60
LISZT   4
    AVE MARIA
        CENTURY MUSIC PUBLISHING COMPANY, INC.   585   .40
LISZT
    BAGATELLE SANS TONALITE
        KULTURA   .75
LISZT   CORTOT
    BALLADE NO. 2
        FRANCO COLOMBO PUBLICATIONS   SAL   3.00
LISZT   CORTOT
    BENEDICTION DE DIEU DANS LA SOLITUDE
        FRANCO COLOMBO PUBLICATIONS   SAL   2.75
LISZT   4
    BY THE LAKE OF WALLENSTADT
        CENTURY MUSIC PUBLISHING COMPANY, INC.   4003   .40
LISZT
    CAMPANELLA, LA
        FRANCO COLOMBO PUBLICATIONS   128471   1.00
LISZT   JOSEFFY
    CANTIQUE D'AMOUR--HARMONIES POETIQUES ET RELIGIEUSES, BK. 7 NO.
    10
        G. SCHIRMER, INC.   .70
LISZT
    CANZONE--FROM VENEZIA E NAPOLI
        G. SCHIRMER, INC.   .75
LISZT   STREABBOG
    CARNIVAL OF VENICE
        FRANCO COLOMBO PUBLICATIONS   BA1751   .75
LISZT   PLANTE, FR.   8
    CELEBRE MELODIE HONGROISE EN SI FLAT
        ALPHONSE LEDUC
LISZT
    CHASSE, LA -- 1ST AND 2ND VERSIONS --
        FRANCO COLOMBO PUBLICATIONS   128472   1.25
LISZT   PHILIPP
    CHASSE, LA--NO. 5 OF THE ETUDES AFTER PAGANINI--
        GERARD BILLAUDOT EDITIONS MUSICALES   1.30

LISZT   M
  CHRISTMAS TREE
    THEODORE PRESSER COMPANY   1.25
LISZT   BUSONI-DA MOTTA
  CONCERT ETUDE NO. 3 IN D FLAT
    ASSOCIATED MUSIC PUBLISHERS, INC.   BRH   .75
LISZT   JOSEFFY
  CONCERTO NO. 01 IN E FLAT
    G. SCHIRMER, INC.   L1057   1.75
LISZT   JOSEFFY
  CONCERTO NO. 02 IN A
    G. SCHIRMER, INC.   L1058   2.50
LISZT   HUGHES
  CONCERTO PATHETIQUE IN E MINOR
    G. SCHIRMER, INC.   L1534   1.50
LISZT
  CONSOLATIONS
    KULTURA   1.00
LISZT   FRIEDMAN
  CONSOLATIONS
    UNIVERSAL EDITION   5879   .80
LISZT   JOSEFFY
  CONSOLATIONS NO. 3 IN D FLAT
    G. SCHIRMER, INC.   .50
LISZT   JOSEFFY
  CONSOLATIONS NO. 5 IN E
    G. SCHIRMER, INC.   .40
LISZT   7
  CONSOLATIONS, NO. 1
    NOVELLO AND COMPANY, LTD.   55.0015.10   .40
LISZT   5
  CONSOLATIONS, NO. 3
    CENTURY MUSIC PUBLISHING COMPANY, INC.   173   .40
LISZT
  CZARDAS MACABRE
    KULTURA   1.00
LISZT   3
  DREAM OF LOVE
    CENTURY MUSIC PUBLISHING COMPANY, INC.   3625   .40
LISZT   THOMPSON, J.   5
  DREAM OF LOVE
    WILLIS MUSIC COMPANY   .50
LISZT
  DREAM OF LOVE -- LIEBESTRAUM NO. 3 IN A FLAT
    ASHLEY DEALERS SERVICE, INC.   ES   .95
LISZT   GROOMS   3
  DREAM OF LOVE, EASY
    CENTURY MUSIC PUBLISHING COMPANY, INC.   2467   .40
LISZT   ECKSTEIN
  DREAMS OF LOVE NO. 3 IN A FLAT --LIEBESTRAUME--
    CARL FISCHER, INC.   S 802   .50
LISZT   7
  ETUDE DE CONCERT IN D FLAT --UN SOSPIRO--
    THEODORE PRESSER COMPANY   .70
LISZT   FRAEMCKE
  ETUDE DE CONCERT IN F MINOR
    G. SCHIRMER, INC.   .80
LISZT   PAUER
  ETUDE IN D FLAT--UN SOSPIRO
    G. SCHIRMER, INC.   .70
LISZT
  ETUDE NO. 02 IN A MINOR
    ASSOCIATED MUSIC PUBLISHERS, INC.   BRH   .50
LISZT
  ETUDE NO. 12 IN B FLAT MINOR--'CHASSE NEIGE'
    ASSOCIATED MUSIC PUBLISHERS, INC.   BRH   .60
LISZT   BRUGNOLI
  ETUDES D'EXECUTION TRANSCENDANTE
    FRANCO COLOMBO PUBLICATIONS   ER9   5.50
LISZT
  ETUDES D'EXECUTION TRANSCENDANTE - EROICA
    FRANCO COLOMBO PUBLICATIONS   ER619   .75
LISZT
  ETUDES D'EXECUTION TRANSCENDANTE - MAZEPPA
    FRANCO COLOMBO PUBLICATIONS   ER882   1.00
LISZT   CORTOT
  FANTASY AND FUGUE ON THE NAME B-A-C-H
    FRANCO COLOMBO PUBLICATIONS   SAL   3.00
LISZT   CORTOT
  FANTASY ON MOZART'S 'DON GIOVANNI'
    FRANCO COLOMBO PUBLICATIONS   SAL   5.50
LISZT   PHILIPP
  FEUX FOLLETS--NO.5 OF THE TRANSCENDENTAL ETUDES--
    GERARD BILLAUDOT EDITIONS MUSICALES   1.60
LISZT   SCHAUM, J.   4
  FORGOTTEN WALTZ
    SCHAUM PUBLICATIONS, INC.   .60
LISZT   6
  FORGOTTEN WALTZ NO. 4 -- QUATRIEME VALSE OUBLIEE
    THEODORE PRESSER COMPANY   1.00
LISZT
  FUNERAILLES
    EDWIN F. KALMUS   3620   1.50
LISZT
  FUNERAILLES
    FRANCO COLOMBO PUBLICATIONS   128449   1.00
LISZT   CORTOT
  FUNERAILLES
    FRANCO COLOMBO PUBLICATIONS   SAL   2.50
LISZT   BUSONI-DA MOTTA
  GNOMENREIGEN--CONCERT ETUDE
    ASSOCIATED MUSIC PUBLISHERS, INC.   BRH   .75
LISZT   JOSEFFY
  GNOMENREIGEN--CONCERT ETUDE
    G. SCHIRMER, INC.   .75
LISZT   D
  GOD SAVE THE QUEEN --PARAPHRASE--
    C. F. PETERS CORPORATION   H1953   1.50
LISZT   FRAEMCKE
  GRAND GALOP CHROMATIQUE, OP. 12
    G. SCHIRMER, INC.   .70
LISZT   SAUER   M
  HUNGARIAN FANTASY
    C. F. PETERS CORPORATION   3612A   1.25
LISZT   JOSEFFY
  HUNGARIAN FANTASY
    G. SCHIRMER, INC.   L1056   1.25
LISZT
  HUNGARIAN RHAPSODY NO. 01
    EDWIN F. KALMUS   3630   1.00
LISZT   BENDEL
  HUNGARIAN RHAPSODY NO. 02
    ASSOCIATED MUSIC PUBLISHERS, INC.   BRH   .50
LISZT   SCHAUM, .J   4
  HUNGARIAN RHAPSODY NO. 02
    BELWIN-MILLS PUBLISHING CORPORATION   .50

LISZT   KRENZ
  HUNGARIAN RHAPSODY NO. 02
    BELWIN-MILLS PUBLISHING CORPORATION   20127   .95
LISZT
  HUNGARIAN RHAPSODY NO. 02
    CARL FISCHER, INC.   S 681   1.00
LISZT   BENDEL *
  HUNGARIAN RHAPSODY NO. 02
    CARL FISCHER, INC.   S 682   .80
LISZT   7
  HUNGARIAN RHAPSODY NO. 02
    CENTURY MUSIC PUBLISHING COMPANY, INC.   1179   .40
LISZT
  HUNGARIAN RHAPSODY NO. 02
    EDWIN F. KALMUS   3631   1.00
LISZT   CORTOT
  HUNGARIAN RHAPSODY NO. 02
    FRANCO COLOMBO PUBLICATIONS   SAL   3.00
LISZT   7
  HUNGARIAN RHAPSODY NO. 02
    FRANCO COLOMBO PUBLICATIONS   ER2569   1.25
LISZT   THOMPSON, J.   3
  HUNGARIAN RHAPSODY NO. 02
    THEODORE PRESSER COMPANY   1.25
LISZT
  HUNGARIAN RHAPSODY NO. 02
    WILLIS MUSIC COMPANY   .50
LISZT   7
  HUNGARIAN RHAPSODY NO. 06
    CARL FISCHER, INC.   S 2200   .90
LISZT   7
  HUNGARIAN RHAPSODY NO. 06
    CENTURY MUSIC PUBLISHING COMPANY, INC.   2582   .40
LISZT   CORTOT
  HUNGARIAN RHAPSODY NO. 06
    CENTURY MUSIC PUBLISHING COMPANY, INC.   2582   .40
LISZT   CORTOT
  HUNGARIAN RHAPSODY NO. 06
    FRANCO COLOMBO PUBLICATIONS   SAL   2.50
LISZT   CORTOT
  HUNGARIAN RHAPSODY NO. 09
    FRANCO COLOMBO PUBLICATIONS   SAL   3.25
LISZT   CORTOT
  HUNGARIAN RHAPSODY NO. 10
    FRANCO COLOMBO PUBLICATIONS   SAL   2.75
LISZT   CORTOT
  HUNGARIAN RHAPSODY NO. 11
    FRANCO COLOMBO PUBLICATIONS   SAL   2.50
LISZT   CORTOT
  HUNGARIAN RHAPSODY NO. 12
    FRANCO COLOMBO PUBLICATIONS   SAL   2.75
LISZT   CORTOT
  HUNGARIAN RHAPSODY NO. 13
    FRANCO COLOMBO PUBLICATIONS   SAL   2.50
LISZT
  JEUX D'EAU DE LA VILLA D'ESTE
    EDWIN F. KALMUS   3632   1.25
LISZT
  JEUX D'EAUX A LA VILLA D'ESTE
    KULTURA   3.00
LISZT   CORTOT
  JEUX D'EAUX A LA VILLA D'ESTE, LES
    FRANCO COLOMBO PUBLICATIONS   SAL   2.75
LISZT   5
  KONZERT-ETUDE - GNOMENREIGEN
    SCHOTT   06455 1/2   1.00
LISZT   5
  KONZERT-ETUDE - UN SOSPIRO
    SCHOTT   06779 1/2   1.00
LISZT   5
  KONZERT-ETUDE - WALDESRAUSCHEN
    SCHOTT   06454 1/2   1.00
LISZT   SCHAUM, J.   3
  LA CAMPANELLA
    BELWIN-MILLS PUBLISHING CORPORATION   .50
LISZT   PAGANINI *   3
  LA CAMPANELLA
    BELWIN-MILLS PUBLISHING CORPORATION   .50
LISZT
  LA CAMPANELLA
    EDWIN F. KALMUS   3624   1.00
LISZT   6
  LA REGATTA VENETIANA
    CENTURY MUSIC PUBLISHING COMPANY, INC.   1480   .40
LISZT   OESTERLE
  LEGENDES NO. 2--ST. FRANCOIS DE PAULE, MARCHANT SUR LES FLOTS
    G. SCHIRMER, INC.   .90
LISZT   STRADAL
  LES PRELUDES--SYMPHONIC POEM NO. 3
    ASSOCIATED MUSIC PUBLISHERS, INC.   BRH   2.00
LISZT   SCHAUM, J.   4
  LIEBESTRAUM
    BELWIN-MILLS PUBLISHING CORPORATION   .50
LISZT   MITTLER   2B
  LIEBESTRAUM
    MUSICORD PUBLICATIONS, INC.   .45
LISZT   ZEPP   4-5
  LIEBESTRAUM
    PRO-ART PUBLICATIONS, INC.   358   .50
LISZT   WHITFORD   GR. 2
  LIEBESTRAUM
    ROBERT WHITFORD PUBLICATIONS   .40
LISZT   HODSON   3 1/2
  LIEBESTRAUM
    THEODORE PRESSER COMPANY   .50
LISZT   3
  LIEBESTRAUM -- LOVE DREAMS --
    CENTURY MUSIC PUBLISHING COMPANY, INC.   3625   .40
LISZT   6
  LIEBESTRAUM, NO. 1
    CENTURY MUSIC PUBLISHING COMPANY, INC.   2117   .40
LISZT   WEYBRIGHT   2
  LIEBESTRAUME
    BELWIN-MILLS PUBLISHING CORPORATION   .60
LISZT
  LIEBESTRAUME
    EDWIN F. KALMUS   3635   1.25
LISZT   5
  LIEBESTRAUME -- NO. 1 AS-DUR
    SCHOTT   06480 1/2   1.00
LISZT   5
  LIEBESTRAUME -- NO. 2 E-DUR
    SCHOTT   06481 1/2   1.00
LISZT   5
  LIEBESTRAUME -- NO. 3 AS-DUR
    SCHOTT   06482 1/2   1.00

LISZT
    LIEBESTRAUME NO. 2 IN E
        G. SCHIRMER, INC.   .50
                                6
LISZT
    LIEBESTRAUME NO. 3
        BELWIN-MILLS PUBLISHING CORPORATION   238   .60
LISZT
    LIEBESTRAUME NO. 3 IN A FLAT
        G. SCHIRMER, INC.   .50
LISZT   JAUME
    LIEBESTRAUME NO. 3 IN A FLAT
        G. SCHIRMER, INC.   .50
LISZT
    MEFISTO VALSE
        EDWIN F. KALMUS   3636   2.00
LISZT   CORTOT
    MEPHISTO WALTZ
        FRANCO COLOMBO PUBLICATIONS   SAL   3.50
LISZT   TAGLIAPIETRA
    MEPHISTO WALTZ NO. 1
        FRANCO COLOMBO PUBLICATIONS   ER1468   1.50
LISZT   BUSONI
    MEPHISTO WALTZ--EPISODE FROM LENAU'S 'FAUST', DANCE IN THE
    VILLAGE INN
        G. SCHIRMER, INC.   L1649   1.50
LISZT
    PAGANINI-ETUDES--NO. 2 IN E FLAT
        ASSOCIATED MUSIC PUBLISHERS, INC.   BRH   .50
LISZT
    PAGANINI-ETUDES--NO. 3 IN G-SHARP MINOR-- LA CAMPANELLA
        ASSOCIATED MUSIC PUBLISHERS, INC.   BRH   .75
LISZT   BUSONI
    PAGANINI-ETUDES--NO. 3 IN G-SHARP MINOR--CONCERT TRANSCRIPTION
        ASSOCIATED MUSIC PUBLISHERS, INC.   BRH   .75
LISZT
    PAGANINI-ETUDES--NO. 4 IN E
        ASSOCIATED MUSIC PUBLISHERS, INC.   BRH   .50
LISZT
    PASTORELLA DELLE ALPI
        KULTURA   1.00
LISZT
    PAYSAGE--ETUDE NO. 3
        ASSOCIATED MUSIC PUBLISHERS, INC.   BRH   .60
LISZT   JOSEFFY
    POLONAISE NO. 02 IN E
        G. SCHIRMER, INC.   1.00
LISZT   CORTOT
    POLONAISE NO. 2
        FRANCO COLOMBO PUBLICATIONS   SAL   2.75
LISZT
    PORTRAITS HONGROIS HISTORIQUES
        KULTURA   1.50
LISZT   KLUSSMANN
    PRELUDES, LES
        FRANCO COLOMBO PUBLICATIONS   SIK.194   2.25
LISZT
    PREMIERE VALSE OUBLIEE
        KULTURA   .90
                                6
LISZT
    QUATRIEME VALSE OUBLIEE -- FORGOTTEN WALTZ
        THEODORE PRESSER COMPANY   1.00
LISZT   THOMPSON, J.   3
    RAKOCZY MARCH
        WILLIS MUSIC COMPANY   .60
LISZT   PHILIPP
    RAPSODIE HONGROISE NO.12
        GERARD BILLAUDOT EDITIONS MUSICALES   2.00
LISZT   BUSONI
    REMINISCENCES DE DON JUAN-- CONCERT-FANTASY ON MOTIFS FROM
    MOZART'S 'DON GIOVANNI' --CRITICAL EDITION WITH ORIGINAL LISZT AND
    BUSONI VERSIONS
        ASSOCIATED MUSIC PUBLISHERS, INC.   BRH   2.00
LISZT   CORTOT
    RHAPSODIE ESPAGNOLE
        FRANCO COLOMBO PUBLICATIONS   3.25
LISZT
    RHAPSODIE HONGROISE NO. 02
        ASHLEY DEALERS SERVICE, INC.   ES   1.00
LISZT
    RHAPSODIE HONGROISE NO. 02 -- SIMP.
        ASHLEY DEALERS SERVICE, INC.   ES   1.00
LISZT
    RHAPSODIE HONGROISE, NO. 2
        BELWIN-MILLS PUBLISHING CORPORATION   28170   1.25
LISZT
    RHAPSODIE NO. 01
        FRANCO COLOMBO PUBLICATIONS   ER241   1.25
LISZT
    RHAPSODIE NO. 02
        FRANCO COLOMBO PUBLICATIONS   ER242   1.25
LISZT   BENDEL
    RHAPSODIE NO. 02
        FRANCO COLOMBO PUBLICATIONS   108077   1.25
LISZT   DEL MAGLIO
    RHAPSODIE NO. 02
        FRANCO COLOMBO PUBLICATIONS   129106   .90
LISZT
    RHAPSODIE NO. 03
        FRANCO COLOMBO PUBLICATIONS   ER243   .75
LISZT
    RHAPSODIE NO. 05
        FRANCO COLOMBO PUBLICATIONS   ER245   .75
LISZT
    RHAPSODIE NO. 06
        FRANCO COLOMBO PUBLICATIONS   ER246   .75
LISZT
    RHAPSODIE NO. 08
        FRANCO COLOMBO PUBLICATIONS   ER248   1.00
LISZT
    RHAPSODIE NO. 11
        FRANCO COLOMBO PUBLICATIONS   ER251   .75
LISZT
    RHAPSODIE NO. 12
        FRANCO COLOMBO PUBLICATIONS   ER252   1.00
LISZT
    RHAPSODIE NO. 14
        FRANCO COLOMBO PUBLICATIONS   ER254   .75
LISZT
    RHAPSODIE NO. 20 -- RHAPSODIE ESPAGNOLE --
        FRANCO COLOMBO PUBLICATIONS   ER260   1.50
LISZT   KREUTZER   3
    RHAPSODIE ZINGARESE
        BOSTON MUSIC COMPANY   .50
LISZT
    RHAPSODIES HONGROISES NO. 02
        G. SCHIRMER, INC.   .90

LISZT   BENDEL
    RHAPSODIES HONGROISES NO. 02
        G. SCHIRMER, INC.   .90
LISZT
    RHAPSODIES HONGROISES NO. 03
        G. SCHIRMER, INC.   .50
LISZT
    RHAPSODIES HONGROISES NO. 05
        G. SCHIRMER, INC.   .60
LISZT
    RHAPSODIES HONGROISES NO. 06
        G. SCHIRMER, INC.   .75
LISZT
    RHAPSODIES HONGROISES NO. 09
        G. SCHIRMER, INC.   1.25
LISZT
    RHAPSODIES HONGROISES NO. 10
        G. SCHIRMER, INC.   .80
LISZT
    RHAPSODIES HONGROISES NO. 11
        G. SCHIRMER, INC.   .70
LISZT
    RHAPSODIES HONGROISES NO. 12
        G. SCHIRMER, INC.   .90
LISZT
    RHAPSODIES HONGROISES NO. 13
        G. SCHIRMER, INC.   .80
LISZT
    RHAPSODIES HONGROISES NO. 14
        G. SCHIRMER, INC.   1.10
LISZT
    RHAPSODIES HONGROISES NO. 15
        G. SCHIRMER, INC.   1.25
LISZT   BENDEL   4
    SECOND HUNGARIAN RHAPSODY
        CENTURY MUSIC PUBLISHING COMPANY, INC.   1645   .40
LISZT   MITTLER   3B
    SECOND HUNGARIAN RHAPSODY
        MUSICORD PUBLICATIONS, INC.   .45
LISZT
    SECOND VALSE OUBLIEE
        ELKAN-VOGEL, INC.   D   .90
LISZT   DEL MAGLIO
    SIX CONSOLATIONS, NO. 3
        FRANCO COLOMBO PUBLICATIONS   127149   .60
LISZT
    SIX ETUDES CONCERT - LEGGIEREZZA, LA
        FRANCO COLOMBO PUBLICATIONS   128363   1.00
LISZT
    SIX ETUDES DE CONCERT - GNOMENREIGNEN
        FRANCO COLOMBO PUBLICATIONS   128394   .60
LISZT
    SIX ETUDES DE CONCERT - SOSPIRO, UN
        FRANCO COLOMBO PUBLICATIONS   128438   1.00
LISZT
    SIX ETUDES DE CONCERT - WALDESRAUSCHEN
        FRANCO COLOMBO PUBLICATIONS   128018   1.00
LISZT
    SOIREES DE VIENNE NO. 6
        G. SCHIRMER, INC.   .75
LISZT   3
    SOIREES DE VIENNE, WIENER ABENDE NACH KOMP. VON F. SCHUBERT NO.
    6 A-DUR
        SCHOTT   06562 1/2   1.00
LISZT   SAUER   D
    SONATA IN B MINOR
        C. F. PETERS CORPORATION   3611   1.50
LISZT
    SONATA IN B MINOR
        EDWIN F. KALMUS   3639   1.50
LISZT   MONTANI
    SONATA IN B MINOR
        FRANCO COLOMBO PUBLICATIONS   ER2424   1.50
LISZT   CORTOT
    SONATA IN B MINOR
        FRANCO COLOMBO PUBLICATIONS   SAL   5.50
LISZT   JOSEFFY
    SONATA IN B MINOR
        G. SCHIRMER, INC.   L861   1.25
LISZT
    SONETTO 104 DEL PETRARCA--FROM DEUXIEME ANNEE DE PELERINAGE
        G. SCHIRMER, INC.   .60
LISZT
    SONETTO 123 DEL PETRARCA--FROM DEUXIEME ANNEE DE PELERINAGE
        G. SCHIRMER, INC.   .50
LISZT   BUSONI
    SPANISH RHAPSODY--ARRANGED FOR PIANO AND ORCHESTRA
        G. SCHIRMER, INC.   L1252   2.50
LISZT
    SPOSALIZIO--FROM DEUXIEME ANNEE DE PELERINAGE
        G. SCHIRMER, INC.   .50
LISZT
    ST. FRANCIS BIRD SERMON
        EDWIN F. KALMUS   3633   1.00
LISZT
    ST. FRANCIS WALKING OVER THE WAVES
        EDWIN F. KALMUS   3634   1.25
LISZT
    SUNT LACRIMAE RERUM
        KULTURA   .75
LISZT
    TARANTELLA--FROM VENEZIA E NAPOLI
        G. SCHIRMER, INC.   1.00
LISZT
    TARENTELLE DE CESAR CUI
        ELKAN-VOGEL, INC.   D   2.20
LISZT   ECKSTEIN
    THEME FROM HUNGARIAN RHAPSODY NO. 2
        CARL FISCHER, INC.   S 2303   .50
LISZT   ECKSTEIN
    THEME FROM LIEBESTRAUME
        CARL FISCHER, INC.   S 2286   .50
LISZT   THOMPSON, J.   2
    THEME FROM LIEBESTRAUME
        WILLIS MUSIC COMPANY   .35
LISZT
    THREE LIEBESTRAEUME - NO. 3
        FRANCO COLOMBO PUBLICATIONS   128156   .90
LISZT   DEL MAGLIO
    THREE LIEBESTRAEUME - NO. 3
        FRANCO COLOMBO PUBLICATIONS   127203   .60
LISZT   TAGLIAPIETRA
    TWO LEGENDES - 1. ST. FRANCOIS D'ASSISE - LA PREDICATION AUX
    OISEAUX
        FRANCO COLOMBO PUBLICATIONS   ER186   1.00

LISZT	BOGHEN			
TWO LEGENDES - 2. ST. FRANCOIS DE PAULE MARCHANT SUR LES FLOTS				
FRANCO COLOMBO PUBLICATIONS		ER133		1.25
LISZT			6	
UNGARISCHE RHAPSODIE NO. 02, M. D. BER. KADENZ				
SCHOTT		06414 1/2		1.00
LISZT			6	
UNGARISCHE RHAPSODIEN NO. 01				
SCHOTT		06412 1/2		1.00
LISZT	BENDEL		3	
UNGARISCHE RHAPSODIEN NO. 02, M. D. BER. KADENZ				
SCHOTT		06435 1/2		1.00
LISZT			5	
UNGARISCHE RHAPSODIEN NO. 05, HEROIDE-ELEGIAQUE				
SCHOTT		06418 1/2		1.00
LISZT			6	
UNGARISCHE RHAPSODIEN NO. 06				
SCHOTT		06419 1/2		1.00
LISZT			6	
UNGARISCHE RHAPSODIEN NO. 14				
SCHOTT		06431 1/2		1.00
LISZT			6	
UNGARISCHE RHAPSODIEN NO. 15, RACOCZY-MARSCH				
SCHOTT		06433 1/2		1.00
LISZT			6	
VALSE IMPROMPTU				
SCHOTT		06548 1/2		1.00
LISZT	DEIS			
VALSE OUBLIEE				
G. SCHIRMER, INC.				.70
LISZT			4	
VALSE OUBLIEE				
SCHOTT		07042 102		1.00
LISZT				
VALSE-IMPROMPTU IN A FLAT				
G. SCHIRMER, INC.				.80
LISZT				
VARIATION ON A WALTZ BY DIABELLI --1822 SEARLE 147				
MUSICA OBSCURA				1.00
LISZT	CORTOT			
VARIATIONS ON BACH'S "WEININ, KLAGEN"				
FRANCO COLOMBO PUBLICATIONS		SAL		3.00
LISZT			4	
VENEZIA E NAPOLI -- GONDOLIERA				
SCHOTT		06287 1/2		1.00
LISZT			5	
VENEZIA E NAPOLI -- TARANTELLA				
SCHOTT		06290 1/2		1.00
LISZT			5	
VERSCHIEDENE WERKE -- CAMPANELLA, N. PAGANINI				
SCHOTT		06550 1/2		1.00
LISZT			3-4	
VERSCHIEDENE WERKE -- CONSOLATIONS				
SCHOTT		06474 1/2		1.00
LISZT			5	
VERSCHIEDENE WERKE -- FUNERAILLES				
SCHOTT		06468 1/2		1.00
LISZT			4	
VERSCHIEDENE WERKE -- LA REGATA VENEZIANA				
SCHOTT		06303 1/2		1.00
LISZT			6	
VERSCHIEDENE WERKE -- LEGENDE NO. 1				
SCHOTT		06476 1/2		1.00
LISZT			6	
VERSCHIEDENE WERKE -- LEGENDE NO. 2				
SCHOTT		06478 1/2		1.00
LISZT			6	
VERSCHIEDENE WERKE -- MEPHISTO-WALZER				
SCHOTT		06488-9		1.50
LISZT			5	
VERSCHIEDENE WERKE -- POLONAISE NO. 2 E-DUR				
SCHOTT		06543 1/2		1.00
LISZT			6	
VERSCHIEDENE WERKE -- RIGOLETTO-PARAPHRASE				
SCHOTT		06810 1/2		1.00
LISZT				
WALDESRAUSCHEN -- FOREST MURMURS--				
EDWIN F. KALMUS		3640		1.25
LISZT	JOSEFFY			
WALDESRAUSCHEN--CONCERT ETUDE				
G. SCHIRMER, INC.				.75
LISZT *	GALLICO			
LA CAMPANELLA				
G. SCHIRMER, INC.				.80
LISZT *	GALLICO			
LA CAMPANELLA				
G. SCHIRMER, INC.				.80
LISZT *				
LEISE FLEHEN				
G. SCHIRMER, INC.				.75
LISZT *	TAGLIAPIETRA			
NIGHTINGALE, THE				
FRANCO COLOMBO PUBLICATIONS		ER24		.60
LISZT *				
REGATA VENEZIANA, LA				
FRANCO COLOMBO PUBLICATIONS		128857		.90
LISZT *			6	
REGATTA VENETIANA				
CENTURY MUSIC PUBLISHING COMPANY, INC.		1480		.40
LISZT *				
SPRING NIGHT				
FRANCO COLOMBO PUBLICATIONS		128430		.50
LITER, M.				
TWO BOP IMPRESSIONS				
BOOSEY AND HAWKES, INC.				.90
LITER, M.				
VALSE MELANCOLIQUE				
BOOSEY AND HAWKES, INC.				.75
LITOLFF	CUPZON			
SCHERSO CONCERTO				
BOOSEY AND HAWKES, INC.				1.25
LITOLFF	JOHNSON		M	
SCHERZO --FROM CONCERTO SYMPHONIQUE NO. 4--				
C. F. PETERS CORPORATION		H1462		1.25
LITTLEWOOD, R.	SCHAUM, J.		1 1/2	
POPPO THE PORPOISE				
SCHAUM PUBLICATIONS, INC.				.60
LITTOFF				
DANCER, THE				
CARL FISCHER, INC.		P 1959		.50
LITTOFF				
LITTLE NAVAJO				
CARL FISCHER, INC.		P 1848		.50
LITTOFF				
UP IN A SWING				
CARL FISCHER, INC.		P 1861		.50

LIUZZI				
GAIOLA E MARECHIARO				
FRANCO COLOMBO PUBLICATIONS		FOR.10996		1.75
LIVELY, K.		1A		
CHIEF RED FEATHER				
MUSICORD PUBLICATIONS, INC.				.45
LIVELY, K.				
CIRCUS PONY				
G. SCHIRMER, INC.				.50
LIVELY, K. *		EASY		
SING-LEE, CHINA-BOY				
SHAWNEE PRESS, INC.		HB-5014		.60
LLONGUERAS, J.				
MIA, 6 IMPRESSIONS, NO. 2--MIA JUGA				
ASSOCIATED MUSIC PUBLISHERS, INC.		UME		.25
LLONGUERAS, J.				
MIA, 6 IMPRESSIONS, NO. 3--MIA DANCA				
ASSOCIATED MUSIC PUBLISHERS, INC.		UME		.25
LLONGUERAS, J.				
MIA, 6 IMPRESSIONS, NO. 4--MIA CANTA				
ASSOCIATED MUSIC PUBLISHERS, INC.		UME		.25
LLONGUERAS, J.				
MIA, 6 IMPRESSIONS, NO. 6--MIA DORM				
ASSOCIATED MUSIC PUBLISHERS, INC.		UME		.25
LLONGUERAS, J.				
YAN, 6 IMPRESSIONS, NO. 1--YAN PREGA				
ASSOCIATED MUSIC PUBLISHERS, INC.		UME		.25
LLONGUERAS, J.				
YAN, 6 IMPRESSIONS, NO. 2--YAN JUGA				
ASSOCIATED MUSIC PUBLISHERS, INC.		UME		.25
LLONGUERAS, J.				
YAN, 6 IMPRESSIONS, NO. 3--YAN DANCA				
ASSOCIATED MUSIC PUBLISHERS, INC.		UME		.25
LLONGUERAS, J.				
YAN, 6 IMPRESSIONS, NO. 4--YAN CANTA				
ASSOCIATED MUSIC PUBLISHERS, INC.		UME		.25
LLONGUERAS, J.				
YAN, 6 IMPRESSIONS, NO. 5--YAN PLORA				
ASSOCIATED MUSIC PUBLISHERS, INC.		UME		.25
LLONGUERAS, J.				
YAN, 6 IMPRESSIONS, NO. 6--YAN DORM				
ASSOCIATED MUSIC PUBLISHERS, INC.		UME		.25
LLOYD, L.		2 1/2		
HEADS UP				
THEODORE PRESSER COMPANY				.50
LLOYD, N.		A		
SONATA FOR PIANO				
THEODORE PRESSER COMPANY				2.50
LOBO *				
REZA				
MCA MUSIC				1.00
LOBODA, S.				
FREEDOMS FOUNDATION MARCH				
BELWIN-MILLS PUBLISHING CORPORATION		20064		.85
LOCKE		2 1/2		
LILY PADS				
THEODORE PRESSER COMPANY				.50
LOCKWOOD, N.		MD		
LYRIC ARABESQUE				
THEODORE PRESSER COMPANY				.50
LOCKYER				
FIDDLERS BOOGIE, THE				
MCA MUSIC				1.00
LODGE, H.				
TEMPTATION RAG				
BELWIN-MILLS PUBLISHING CORPORATION		20297		.85
LOESSER, F.	RICHTER		2 1/2 - 3	
ADELAIDE'S LAMENT				
FRANK MUSIC CORPORATION				.75
LOESSER, F.				
ON A SLOW BOAT TO CHINA				
FRANK MUSIC CORPORATION				.75
LOEWE, F.				
RAIN IN SPAIN, THE				
CHAPPELL AND COMPANY, INC.		4790002		.95
LOGIS *				
HAPPY WALTZ, THE				
MCA MUSIC				1.00
LOMAS, W.				
TARANTELLA IN E MINOR				
G. SCHIRMER, INC.				.60
LONG, L.		2		
BOGEY MAN, THE				
WILLIS MUSIC COMPANY				.40
LONG, L.		2		
IN THE BIRD SHOP				
WILLIS MUSIC COMPANY				.35
LONG, L.		3		
MEMORY, A				
WILLIS MUSIC COMPANY				.40
LONG, L.		1		
MOCCASIN DANCE				
WILLIS MUSIC COMPANY				.50
LONG, L.		2		
NEPTUNE'S CAVE				
WILLIS MUSIC COMPANY				.40
LONG, L.		1		
PROCESSION OF THE SEVEN DWARFS				
WILLIS MUSIC COMPANY				.40
LONGAS				
ARAGON				
EDWARD B. MARKS MUSIC CORPORATION				01.00
LONGAS				
ARAGON				
FRANCO COLOMBO PUBLICATIONS		SAL		3.00
LONGAS				
BOLERO RITMICO				
EDWARD B. MARKS MUSIC CORPORATION				01.00
LONGAS				
BULERIAS				
EDWARD B. MARKS MUSIC CORPORATION				01.00
LONGAS				
HABANERA				
FRANCO COLOMBO PUBLICATIONS		SAL		2.50
LONGAS				
RECUERDO				
FRANCO COLOMBO PUBLICATIONS		SAL		1.50
LONGAS				
THREE PETITES PIECES ESPAGNOLES - SIESTE ANDALOUSE				
FRANCO COLOMBO PUBLICATIONS		SAL		1.50
LONGHI				
MARCH -- WITH SILVERI - RELIGIOUS HARMONY --				
FRANCO COLOMBO PUBLICATIONS		102699		.75
LONGMIRE				
ANIMAL CHARACTERS				
BOOSEY AND HAWKES, INC.				.85

LONGMIRE
  IN THE CASTLE
    BOOSEY AND HAWKES, INC.   .90
LONGMIRE
  LONDON CALLING
    FRANCO COLOMBO PUBLICATIONS   LD428   .75
LONGMIRE
  TOCCATINA
    BANKS AND SON LTD.   .25
LONGO, A.
  EASY SONATA IN D
    FRANCO COLOMBO PUBLICATIONS   BON.1829   2.25
                                         MD
LOPATNIKOFF
  DANCE PIECE FOR PIANO
    THEODORE PRESSER COMPANY   .50
                                         3
LOPATNIKOFF
  DIALOGE
    SCHOTT   2240   1.75
                                         4
LOPATNIKOFF
  FUNF KONTRASTE, OP. 16
    SCHOTT   2136   7.50
LOPATNIKOFF
  SONATINA, OP. 7
    BOOSEY AND HAWKES, INC.   1.50
LOPEZ BUCHARDO
  BAILECITO
    FRANCO COLOMBO PUBLICATIONS   BA7245   .75
LOPEZ BUCHARDO
  CAMPERS
    FRANCO COLOMBO PUBLICATIONS   BA7081   .75
LOPEZ BUCHARDO
  CANCION DEL CARRETERO
    FRANCO COLOMBO PUBLICATIONS   BA11125   .75
LOPEZ BUCHARDO
  NOCTURNE
    FRANCO COLOMBO PUBLICATIONS   BA9052   .75
LOPEZ BUCHARDO
  SONATINA
    FRANCO COLOMBO PUBLICATIONS   BA10103   1.00
LOPEZ BUCHARDO
  VIDALA
    FRANCO COLOMBO PUBLICATIONS   BA9349   .75
                                         ADVANCED
LORA
  WALTZ IN G FLAT MAJOR
    SHAWNEE PRESS, INC.   .60
                                         3
LORAINE, P.
  BLUE GARDEN, THE
    CENTURY MUSIC PUBLISHING COMPANY, INC. 2763   .40
                                         3
LORAINE, P.
  SILVER CHIMES, INTERMEZZO
    CENTURY MUSIC PUBLISHING COMPANY, INC. 2764   .40
                                         3
LORAINE, P.
  SKATES, THE -- LES PATINEURS
    CENTURY MUSIC PUBLISHING COMPANY, INC. 2762   .40
                                         3
LORAINE, W.
  PADISHA, THE
    CENTURY MUSIC PUBLISHING COMPANY, INC. 3375   .40
LORDANSKY
  DANCE
    MCA MUSIC   .60
                                         3
LORMER
  FERNANDE, VALSE LENTE
    CENTURY MUSIC PUBLISHING COMPANY, INC. 2672   .40
LOSAVIO, G.
  IL CLAINETTO
    EDIZIONI BERBEN   EB 1622   2.10
                                         5
LOSEY
  BLACK AND WHITE
    VOLKWEIN BROS.   .50
LOSEY   WEYBRIGHT   2 1/2
  GLORIA MARCH
    BELWIN-MILLS PUBLISHING CORPORATION   .50
LOSEY   WEYBRIGHT   2 1/2
  GLORIA, MARCH
    BELWIN-MILLS PUBLISHING CORPORATION   .60
LOTTINI
  CHITARRATA
    FRANCO COLOMBO PUBLICATIONS   FOR.11473   .90
LOUIS XIII
  AIR--GAVOTTE--
    FRANCO COLOMBO PUBLICATIONS   BA8822   .75
                                         3
LOUKA, M.
  CAPTAIN GENERAL
    VOLKWEIN BROS.   .25
                                         4
LOUKA, M.
  DANCE OF THE DEW DROPS
    VOLKWEIN BROS.   .40
                                         4
LOUKA, M.
  DANCE OF THE DEWDROPS
    VOLKWEIN BROS.   00.60
                                         4
LOUKA, M.
  DANCE OF THE SNOWFLAKES
    VOLKWEIN BROS.   .40
                                         3
LOUKA, M.
  FIRE AND FLAME
    VOLKWEIN BROS.   .35
                                         3
LOUKA, M.
  FLEETING HOURS
    VOLKWEIN BROS.   .35
                                         3
LOUKA, M.
  HOUR OF PRAYER
    VOLKWEIN BROS.   .40
                                         4
LOUKA, M.
  JAPANESE FIRE DANCE
    VOLKWEIN BROS.   .35
                                         4
LOUKA, M.
  OCEAN SPRAY
    VOLKWEIN BROS.   .40
                                         4
LOUKA, M.
  RAJAH MARCH
    VOLKWEIN BROS.   .35
                                         4
LOUKA, M.
  SILENT PRAYER
    VOLKWEIN BROS.   .40
                                         3-4
LOUMEY, A.
  SHADOWS ON THE LAKE
    CENTURY MUSIC PUBLISHING COMPANY, INC. 3128   .40
LOURIE
  GIGUE
    FRANCO COLOMBO PUBLICATIONS   SAL   2.25
LOURIE
  MARCH
    FRANCO COLOMBO PUBLICATIONS   SAL   1.75
LOURIE
  SHORT SUITE IN F
    RONGWEN MUSIC, INC.   02.00

LOURIE
  TOCCATA
    FRANCO COLOMBO PUBLICATIONS   SAL   3.50
LOURIE
  WALTZ
    FRANCO COLOMBO PUBLICATIONS   SAL   2.50
LOUVIER
  QUATRE PRELUDES POUR CORDES
    ALPHONSE LEDUC
                                         2 1/2
LOVEJOY
  LITTLE GIRL, BIG GIRL
    WILLIS MUSIC COMPANY   .40
                                         2
LOW, J.
  CAVATINA
    WILLIS MUSIC COMPANY   .40
LOWE   SHEARING
  I'LL NEVER SMILE AGAIN
    MCA MUSIC   1.00
LOWENSTEIN
  BEYOND THE RIO GRANDE
    BOSTON MUSIC COMPANY   .50
                                         3
LOWENSTEIN
  JUBILO
    BOSTON MUSIC COMPANY   .50
                                         2
LOWENSTEIN
  SHIP AHOY
    BOSTON MUSIC COMPANY   .50
LOYND, G. M.
  MIDNIGHT REVELS
    BANKS AND SON LTD.   .25
LUBARSKY
  WEDDING DANCE --WITH RUSSIAN FOLK SONG BY ALEXANDROV
    MCA MUSIC   .60
                                         2
LUBIN, E.
  LITTLE PASTORALE
    CENTURY MUSIC PUBLISHING COMPANY, INC. 4402   .40
                                         2
LUBIN, E.
  MOODS
    CENTURY MUSIC PUBLISHING COMPANY, INC. 4339   .40
                                         2
LUBIN, E.
  PASTORALE
    WILLIS MUSIC COMPANY   .40
                                         3
LUBIN, E.
  PORTRAIT IN A GARDEN
    CENTURY MUSIC PUBLISHING COMPANY, INC. 4187   .40
                                         2 1/2
LUBIN, E.
  TWO OLD DANCES
    CENTURY MUSIC PUBLISHING COMPANY, INC. 033   .40
                                         2
LUBIN, E.
  WILLOWS ARE WALTZING
    CENTURY MUSIC PUBLISHING COMPANY, INC. 4068   .40
LUBOFF, N.   RICHTER   2 1/2 - 3
  YELLOW BIRD
    FRANK MUSIC CORPORATION   .75
LUBOFF, N.   TERRY, F.
  YELLOW BIRD
    FRANK MUSIC CORPORATION   .95
LUCAS, G.   ANDERSON
  PRELUDE AND TOCCATA
    EDITIONS MUSICALES TRANSATLANTIQUES   3.10
LUCAS, M.
  INSECTES DANSENT,LES
    GERARD BILLAUDOT EDITIONS MUSICALES   1.70
LUCAS, T.
  ABERRATIONS N. VII FOR PIANO
    COMPOSERS AUTOGRAPH PUBLICATIONS   4.40
LUCAS, T.
  SONETTE
    COMPOSERS AUTOGRAPH PUBLICATIONS   2.42
LUDOVIC
  GALOP DU DIABLE, OP. 42
    FRANCO COLOMBO PUBLICATIONS   69130   .75
LUDOVIC
  REVE D'UN ANGE, OP. 44
    FRANCO COLOMBO PUBLICATIONS   69132   .60
LUDOVIC, G.
  ANGEL'S DREAM, OP. 44
    G. SCHIRMER, INC.   .40
                                         3
LUDOVIC, G.
  BUTTERFLY WALTZ
    CENTURY MUSIC PUBLISHING COMPANY, INC. 1195   .40
                                         3
LUDOVIC, G.
  CARNIVAL OF VENICE
    CENTURY MUSIC PUBLISHING COMPANY, INC. 760   .40
                                         3
LUDOVIC, G.
  CONVENT BELLS
    CENTURY MUSIC PUBLISHING COMPANY, INC. 175   .40
                                         3
LUDOVIC, G.
  CONVENT BELLS
    VOLKWEIN BROS.   .25
                                         3
LUDOVIC, G.
  FLORES DE NARANJO
    FRANCO COLOMBO PUBLICATIONS   BA6551   .75
                                         3
LUDOVIC, G.
  ORANGE BLOSSOMS
    CENTURY MUSIC PUBLISHING COMPANY, INC. 350   .40
                                         4
LUDOVIC, G.
  PEARLS AND LACES
    CENTURY MUSIC PUBLISHING COMPANY, INC. 1054   .40
                                         3
LUDOVIC, G.
  TARANTELLE
    CENTURY MUSIC PUBLISHING COMPANY, INC. 662   .40
                                         3
LUDOVIC, G.
  VALSE DES PAPILLONS, OP. 108
    CENTURY MUSIC PUBLISHING COMPANY, INC. 1195   .40
                                         3
LUDWIG
  DANCING CHECKERS
    BELWIN-MILLS PUBLISHING CORPORATION   .60
                                         MD
LUENING, O.
  EIGHT PRELUDES -- WITH FIVE SKETCHES, PISK
    THEODORE PRESSER COMPANY   2.00
                                         E
LUENING, O.
  GAY PICTURE
    THEODORE PRESSER COMPANY   .50
                                         M
LUENING, O.
  TWO INVENTIONS
    THEODORE PRESSER COMPANY   .60
LUIGINI   RIES
  BALLET EGYPTIEN -- SUITE 1 --
    BOSTON MUSIC COMPANY   1.00
                                         4
LULLI, A. DE
  AU CLAIR DE LA LUNE
    ALPHONSE LEDUC
LULLY
  COURANTE
    FREDERICK HARRIS MUSIC COMPANY   .60

LULLY
  FAMOUS GAVOTTE
    FRANCO COLOMBO PUBLICATIONS   69134   .60
LULLY
  MENUET DU BOURGEOIS GENTILHOMME
    ELKAN-VOGEL, INC.   D   .70
LULLY, P.   3
  COURANTE IN E MINOR
    CENTURY MUSIC PUBLISHING COMPANY, INC. 3893   .40
LUMSDAINE, D.
  KELLY GROUND
    UNIVERSAL EDITION   UE 14226 4.00
LUNDIE, K.   2 1/2
  PEPPERMIT POPCORN
    BELWIN-MILLS PUBLISHING CORPORATION
               3   .60
LUTZ
  FAUST UP TO DATE
    CENTURY MUSIC PUBLISHING COMPANY, INC. 391   .40
LUZZATTI
  AIRE DE MILONGA
    FRANCO COLOMBO PUBLICATIONS   BA9718   .75
LUZZATTI
  DANZA CAPRICHO
    FRANCO COLOMBO PUBLICATIONS   BA9223   .75
LUZZI
  SOGNO, UN
    FRANCO COLOMBO PUBLICATIONS   FOR.10544   .75
LYBBERT   D
  SONATA BREVIS
    C. F. PETERS CORPORATION   6542   1.50
LYNES
  STORY BY THE MOUSE, THE
    SUMMY-BIRCHARD COMPANY
             2 1/2   .50
LYON
  AT THE FRENCH COURT
    BELWIN-MILLS PUBLISHING CORPORATION
               1   .60
LYON
  FIDDLE BOOGIE DEE
    BELWIN-MILLS PUBLISHING CORPORATION
               2   .60
LYON
  LAGOON BOOGIE
    BELWIN-MILLS PUBLISHING CORPORATION
               1   .60
LYON
  LITTLE BOOGIE TUCKER
    BELWIN-MILLS PUBLISHING CORPORATION
               1   .60
LYON
  LITTLE BOOGIE WALL CLOCK
    BELWIN-MILLS PUBLISHING CORPORATION
               1   .60
LYON
  RIDE A BOOGIE HORSE
    BELWIN-MILLS PUBLISHING CORPORATION
             1 1/2   .60
LYON
  SADDLE BOY BOOGIE
    BELWIN-MILLS PUBLISHING CORPORATION
               5   .60
LYSBERG, C. B.
  BALADINE, LA, CAPRICE
    CENTURY MUSIC PUBLISHING COMPANY, INC. 2427   .40
LYSBERG, C. B.
  ILYLLE, OP. 62
    G. SCHIRMER, INC.
             5-6   .50
LYSBERG, C. B.
  LA BALADINE
    CENTURY MUSIC PUBLISHING COMPANY, INC. 2427   .40
LYSBERG, C. B.   6
  LA FONTAINE, ODYLLE, OP. 31
    CENTURY MUSIC PUBLISHING COMPANY, INC. 4401   .40
MACBETH   4
  LOVE IN IDLENESS
    CENTURY MUSIC PUBLISHING COMPANY, INC. 2287   .40
MACBETH   4
  SERENATA, LOVE IN IDLENESS
    CENTURY MUSIC PUBLISHING COMPANY, INC. 2287   .40
MACCHI
  MINUET
    FRANCO COLOMBO PUBLICATIONS   DS290   1.00
MACCHI
  PRELUDE
    FRANCO COLOMBO PUBLICATIONS   DS205   1.00
MACCHI
  PRELUDE AND FUGUE IN B
    FRANCO COLOMBO PUBLICATIONS   DS298   1.25
MACDONALD
  ENTRY OF THE ZANIES
    FRANCO COLOMBO PUBLICATIONS   LD449   .60
MACDONALD
  MAZOVIAN WEDDING
    FRANCO COLOMBO PUBLICATIONS   LD448   .60
MACDONALD
  ON THE AVENIDA
    FRANCO COLOMBO PUBLICATIONS   LD447   .60
MACDOWELL
  ALLA TARANTELLA
    ASHLEY DEALERS SERVICE, INC.   ES   .95
MACDOWELL
  ALLA TARANTELLA
    BOSTON MUSIC COMPANY
                          .50
MACDOWELL
  ARABESKE
    BOSTON MUSIC COMPANY
                          .50
MACDOWELL
  BARCAROLLE, OP. 18 NO. 1
    G. SCHIRMER, INC.
                          .40
MACDOWELL
  BLUETTE IN E FLAT, OP. 46 NO. 8
    ASSOCIATED MUSIC PUBLISHERS, INC. BRH   .60
MACDOWELL   HUGHES
  CONCERTO NO. 02, OP. 23
    G. SCHIRMER, INC.   L1462   2.50
MACDOWELL
  CZARDAS, OP. 24 NO. 4
    G. SCHIRMER, INC.   M   .50
MACDOWELL
  EAGLE, THE
    COMPOSERS PRESS, INC.
                        1.00
MACDOWELL
  ELFIN DANCE, OP. 46 NO. 5
    ASSOCIATED MUSIC PUBLISHERS, INC. BRH   .60
MACDOWELL
  ETUDE DE CONCERT, OP. 36
    CARL FISCHER, INC.   S 7651   .75
MACDOWELL
  FOUR LITTLE POEMS, OP. 32--REV. 1906
    ASSOCIATED MUSIC PUBLISHERS, INC. AMP   1.00
MACDOWELL
  FOUR LITTLE POEMS, OP. 32, REV. 1906, NO. 1--THE EAGLE
    ASSOCIATED MUSIC PUBLISHERS, INC. AMP   .60

MACDOWELL
  FOUR LITTLE POEMS, OP. 32, REV. 1906, NO. 2--THE BROOK
    ASSOCIATED MUSIC PUBLISHERS, INC. AMP   .60
MACDOWELL
  FOUR LITTLE POEMS, OP. 32, REV. 1906, NO. 3--MOONSHINE
    ASSOCIATED MUSIC PUBLISHERS, INC. AMP   .60
MACDOWELL
  FOUR LITTLE POEMS, OP. 32, REV. 1906, NO. 4--WINTER
    ASSOCIATED MUSIC PUBLISHERS, INC. AMP   .60
MACDOWELL
  GEDICHTE NACH HEINRICH HEINE--OP. 31 NO. 2 IN F MINOR--'SCOTCH POEM'
    G. SCHIRMER, INC.
             6   .50
MACDOWELL
  HEXENTANZ -- WITCHES DANCE
    CENTURY MUSIC PUBLISHING COMPANY, INC. 1043   .40
MACDOWELL   ROLFE, W.   3
  HEXENTANZ, EASY
    CENTURY MUSIC PUBLISHING COMPANY, INC. 3372   .40
MACDOWELL   5
  HUNGARIAN
    BOSTON MUSIC COMPANY
                          .50
MACDOWELL   ECKSTEIN
  HUNGARIAN
    CARL FISCHER, INC.   P 2771   .60
MACDOWELL   4
  HUNGARIAN
    CENTURY MUSIC PUBLISHING COMPANY, INC. 4322   .40
MACDOWELL   PHILIPP, I.
  HUNGARIAN, OP. 39 NO. 12
    INTERNATIONAL MUSIC COMPANY
                         1.00
MACDOWELL
  MODERN SUITE NO. 1, OP. 10--INTERMEZZO
    ASSOCIATED MUSIC PUBLISHERS, INC. AMP   .60
MACDOWELL
  MODERN SUITE NO. 1, OP. 10--PRELUDE
    ASSOCIATED MUSIC PUBLISHERS, INC. AMP   .75
MACDOWELL
  NEW ENGLAND IDYLLS
    EDWIN F. KALMUS   3654   2.50
MACDOWELL   BAMPTON, R.   4
  OF A TAILOR AND A BEAR
    BOSTON MUSIC COMPANY
                           .50
MACDOWELL   PODOLSKY, L.
  PRAELUDIUM, FROM 1ST MODERN SUITE, OP. 10, NO. 1
    SHAWNEE PRESS, INC.   HB-234   1.00
MACDOWELL   DUMM
  RECITAL REFRESHER SERIES -- TO A HUMMING BIRD
    BELWIN-MILLS PUBLISHING CORPORATION 26110   .60
MACDOWELL   KREUTZER   3
  ROMANZ
    BOSTON MUSIC COMPANY
                          .50
MACDOWELL   5
  SCOTCH POEM, OP. 31 NO. 2
    BELWIN-MILLS PUBLISHING CORPORATION 241   .60
MACDOWELL
  SCOTCH POEM, OP. 31 NO. 2
    CARL FISCHER, INC.   S 1859   .50
MACDOWELL   5
  SCOTCH POEM, OP. 31 NO. 2
    CENTURY MUSIC PUBLISHING COMPANY, INC. 2094   .40
MACDOWELL
  SEA PIECES
    EDWIN F. KALMUS   3650   1.50
MACDOWELL
  SHADOW DANCE
    ASHLEY DEALERS SERVICE, INC.   ES   .95
MACDOWELL   4 - 5
  SHADOW DANCE
    BOSTON MUSIC COMPANY
                          .50
MACDOWELL   4
  SHADOW DANCE
    CENTURY MUSIC PUBLISHING COMPANY, INC. 4321   .40
MACDOWELL   ECKSTEIN
  SHADOW DANCE, OP. 39 NO. 8
    CARL FISCHER, INC.   P 2770   .60
MACDOWELL   PHILIPP, I.
  SHADOW DANCE, OP. 39 NO. 8
    INTERNATIONAL MUSIC COMPANY
                         1.00
MACDOWELL   HUGHES
  SONATA EROICA IN G MINOR, OP. 50
    G. SCHIRMER, INC.
                        2.50
MACDOWELL
  SONATA EROICA NO. 02 IN G MINOR, OP. 50
    ASSOCIATED MUSIC PUBLISHERS, INC. BRH   1.50
MACDOWELL
  SONATA EROICA, OP. 50
    EDWIN F. KALMUS   3651   2.50
MACDOWELL
  SONATA NO. 03, OP. 57
    EDWIN F. KALMUS   3652   3.00
MACDOWELL
  SONATA NO. 04
    EDWIN F. KALMUS   3653   2.50
MACDOWELL   HUGHES
  SONATA TRAGICA IN G MINOR, OP. 45
    G. SCHIRMER, INC.
                        2.00
MACDOWELL
  TO A HUMMING BIRD
    BELWIN-MILLS PUBLISHING CORPORATION
               4   .85
MACDOWELL
  TO A WATER LILY
    CENTURY MUSIC PUBLISHING COMPANY, INC. 4094   .40
MACDOWELL   MENDEL, S.   2 1/2
  TO A WATER LILY
    WILLIS MUSIC COMPANY
                          .40
MACDOWELL   SCHAUM, J.   1
  TO A WILD ROSE
    BELWIN-MILLS PUBLISHING CORPORATION
                          .50
MACDOWELL   LEVINE   3
  TO A WILD ROSE
    BOSTON MUSIC COMPANY
                          .50
MACDOWELL
  TO A WILD ROSE
    CARL FISCHER, INC.   P 2776   .50
MACDOWELL   ECKSTEIN
  TO A WILD ROSE
    CARL FISCHER, INC.   P 2777   .50
MACDOWELL   3
  TO A WILD ROSE
    CENTURY MUSIC PUBLISHING COMPANY, INC. 4093   .40
MACDOWELL
  TO A WILD ROSE
    EDWARD B. MARKS MUSIC CORPORATION
                        00.60
MACDOWELL   BERMONT, H.   2A
  TO A WILD ROSE
    MUSICORD PUBLICATIONS, INC.
                        .45

MACDOWELL   WHITFORD   GR. 2
  TO A WILD ROSE
    ROBERT WHITFORD PUBLICATIONS   .40
MACDOWELL   3
  TO A WILD ROSE
    VOLKWEIN BROS.   .50
MACDOWELL   MENDEL, S.   2
  TO A WILD ROSE
    WILLIS MUSIC COMPANY   .40
MACDOWELL
  TO A WILD ROSE, OP. 51
    ASHLEY DEALERS SERVICE, INC.   ES   .95
MACDOWELL
  TWELVE VIRTUOSO STUDIES, OP. 46--NO. 1, NOVELETTE
    ASSOCIATED MUSIC PUBLISHERS, INC.   AMP   .60
MACDOWELL
  TWELVE VIRTUOSO STUDIES, OP. 46--NO. 10, MARCH WIND
    ASSOCIATED MUSIC PUBLISHERS, INC.   AMP   .60
MACDOWELL
  TWELVE VIRTUOSO STUDIES, OP. 46--NO. 11, IMPROMPTU
    ASSOCIATED MUSIC PUBLISHERS, INC.   AMP   .60
MACDOWELL
  TWELVE VIRTUOSO STUDIES, OP. 46--NO. 12, POLONAISE
    ASSOCIATED MUSIC PUBLISHERS, INC.   AMP   .60
MACDOWELL
  TWELVE VIRTUOSO STUDIES, OP. 46--NO. 2, MOTO PERPETUO
    ASSOCIATED MUSIC PUBLISHERS, INC.   AMP   .60
MACDOWELL
  TWELVE VIRTUOSO STUDIES, OP. 46--NO. 4, IMPROVISATION
    ASSOCIATED MUSIC PUBLISHERS, INC.   AMP   .60
MACDOWELL
  TWELVE VIRTUOSO STUDIES, OP. 46--NO. 7, BURLESQUE
    ASSOCIATED MUSIC PUBLISHERS, INC.   AMP   .60
MACDOWELL   SCHAUM, J.   2
  UNCLE REMUS--OP. 51, OP. 7--
    BELWIN-MILLS PUBLISHING CORPORATION   .50
MACDOWELL
  WITCHES' DANCE
    EDWIN F. KALMUS   3655   1.00
MACDOWELL
  WITCHES' DANCE --HEXENTANZ--, OP. 17, NO. 2
    CARL FISCHER, INC.   S 1801   .50
MACDOWELL   6
  WITCHES' DANCE, OP. 17
    THEODORE PRESSER COMPANY   .70
MACDOWELL   6
  WITCHES' DANCE, OP. 17 NO. 2
    CENTURY MUSIC PUBLISHING COMPANY, INC. 1043   .40
MACDOWELL
  WOODLAND SKETCHES
    EDWIN F. KALMUS   3649   1.50
MACDOWELL
  WOODLAND SKETCHES, OP. 51
    G. SCHIRMER, INC.   L1805   1.00
MACDOWELL   PHILIPP, I.
  WOODLAND SKETCHES, OP. 51
    INTERNATIONAL MUSIC COMPANY   1.50
MACFADYEN, A.   5
  COUNTRY DANCE
    THEODORE PRESSER COMPANY   .60
MACFADYEN, A.
  ROLLING STONES
    G. SCHIRMER, INC.   .50
MACGREGOR   WILLIAMS, J.   1
  DANCE OF THE WOODEN SHOES
    BOSTON MUSIC COMPANY   .50
MACGREGOR   WILLIAMS, J.   1
  FIVE PICKANINNIES
    BOSTON MUSIC COMPANY   .50
MACGREGOR   WILLIAMS, J.   2
  MERRY DANCE
    BOSTON MUSIC COMPANY   .50
MACGREGOR   WILLIAMS, J.   1
  ON PARADE
    BOSTON MUSIC COMPANY   .50
MACK, E.   3
  GENERAL GRANT'S GRAND MARCH
    BELWIN-MILLS PUBLISHING CORPORATION   244   .60
MACK, E.   3
  GENERAL GRANT'S GRAND MARCH
    CENTURY MUSIC PUBLISHING COMPANY, INC. 1109   .40
MACK, E.   SCHIEFELBEIN, F. 3
  GENERAL GRANT'S GRAND MARCH
    VOLKWEIN BROS.   .25
MACK, E.   WOODE   2
  GENERAL GRANT'S GRAND MARCH
    WILLIS MUSIC COMPANY   .35
MACK, E.   1
  MARY'S PET WALTZ
    CENTURY MUSIC PUBLISHING COMPANY, INC. 1394   .40
MACK, E.   3-4
  PURITY
    CENTURY MUSIC PUBLISHING COMPANY, INC. 2456   .40
MACK, F.   1
  LITTLE FLATTERER
    CENTURY MUSIC PUBLISHING COMPANY, INC. 1421   .40
MACK, F.   1
  MILL WHEEL, THE
    CENTURY MUSIC PUBLISHING COMPANY, INC. 1422   .40
MACKAY
  SHOEMAKER'S HOLIDAY, THE
    MCA MUSIC   1.00
MACKOWN
  PITTER PATTER
    SAM FOX PUBLISHING COMPANY, INC.   .50
MACKOWN
  PITTER PATTER
    SOUTHERN MUSIC COMPANY   .50
MACKOWN
  SAIL BOAT
    CARL FISCHER, INC.   P 2789   .50
MACKOWN, M.
  BROKEN ROCKING HORSE, THE
    OXFORD UNIVERSITY PRESS   93.322   .40
MACLACHIAN, T.
  BANJO-BOUNCE
    SHAWNEE PRESS, INC.   HB-5023   .60
MACLACHIAN, T.   EASY
  CLIMBING
    SHAWNEE PRESS, INC.   HB-5001   .65
MACLACHIAN, T.
  FAIR, THE
    SHAWNEE PRESS, INC.   HB-5037   .40
MACLACHIAN, T.   EASY
  VIENNESE WALTZ
    SHAWNEE PRESS, INC.   HB-5019   .60

MACLACHLAN   2
  LITTLE TARANTELLE
    BOSTON MUSIC COMPANY   .50
MACLACHLAN   WILLIAMS, J.   2
  TOY SOLDIERS ON PARADE
    BOSTON MUSIC COMPANY   .50
MACLACHLAN   WILLIAMS, J.   2
  YELLOW BUTTERFLY
    BOSTON MUSIC COMPANY   .50
MACLACHLIN, T.
  BIRTHDAY PARTY
    G. SCHIRMER, INC.   .35
MACLACHLIN, T.
  CASCADES, THE--WITH PRELIMINARY STUDIES--
    G. SCHIRMER, INC.   .50
MACLACHLIN, T.
  HONG KONG NIGHTS
    G. SCHIRMER, INC.   .40
MACLACHLIN, T.
  IN THE COTTON-FIELDS
    G. SCHIRMER, INC.   .40
MACLACHLIN, T.
  JOYOUS WALTZ
    G. SCHIRMER, INC.   .40
MACLACHLIN, T.
  LITTLE BUGLER, THE
    G. SCHIRMER, INC.   .35
MACLACHLIN, T.
  MILL BY THE BROOK, THE
    G. SCHIRMER, INC.   .40
MACLACHLIN, T.
  RIDING THE CLOUDS
    G. SCHIRMER, INC.   .40
MACLACHLIN, T.
  SAILOR-BOY
    G. SCHIRMER, INC.   .40
MACONCHY   E
  COUNTRY TOWN, A. SUITE
    C. F. PETERS CORPORATION   H613   1.25
MACONCHY   D
  IMPROMPTU
    C. F. PETERS CORPORATION   H23   1.25
MACONCHY
  MILL RACE
    FRANCO COLOMBO PUBLICATIONS   LD517   .60
MACONCHY
  YAFFLE, THE
    FRANCO COLOMBO PUBLICATIONS   LD502   .60
MADURO, C.
  ESPANA
    ASSOCIATED MUSIC PUBLISHERS, INC.   ESC   1.25
MADURO, C.
  SCHERZO ESPAGNOL
    ASSOCIATED MUSIC PUBLISHERS, INC.   ESC   1.00
MAGIN, M.
  IMAGES D'ENFANTS
    ELKAN-VOGEL, INC.   D   4.75
MAGLIONI
  MAY 24, 1915
    FRANCO COLOMBO PUBLICATIONS   FOR.10557 1.25
MAGLIONI
  SARABANDE
    FRANCO COLOMBO PUBLICATIONS   FOR.11999 1.25
MAGNARD
  SYMPHONY NO. 03
    FRANCO COLOMBO PUBLICATIONS   SAL   6.50
MAGNEY, R.   1 1/2
  LIGHT AS A FEATHER
    WILLIS MUSIC COMPANY   .40
MAGONE
  DORMI CARLA
    FRANCO COLOMBO PUBLICATIONS   BON.2370   .90
MAGONE
  TOCCATA
    FRANCO COLOMBO PUBLICATIONS   BON.2416   2.25
MAHLER   SINGER   D
  SYMPHONY NO. 05
    C. F. PETERS CORPORATION   3760   6.00
MAILLARD   6, 7
  ETUDE EN MI FLAT
    ALPHONSE LEDUC
MAILLARD VERGER
  HOMMAGE A PROKOFIEFF
    FRANCO COLOMBO PUBLICATIONS   SAL   2.00
MAILLARD, P.
  CAPRICE
    ELKAN-VOGEL, INC.   D   1.10
MAILLARD, P.
  PETITE SUITE POUR PIANO
    ELKAN-VOGEL, INC.   D   2.70
MAILMAN, M.
  PETITE PARTITA
    BELWIN-MILLS PUBLISHING CORPORATION   20381   1.25
MAINI
  ISOLE
    FRANCO COLOMBO PUBLICATIONS   DS626   1.75
MAINVILLE
  BLUE BUTTERFLIES
    SUMMY-BIRCHARD COMPANY   .50
MAINVILLE   1
  GRANDPERE'S CLOCK
    PRO-ART PUBLICATIONS, INC.   189   .50
MAINVILLE   1
  I HAVE A LITTLE SHADOW
    PRO-ART PUBLICATIONS, INC.   188   .50
MAINVILLE   4
  VALSE CHARMANTE
    WILLIS MUSIC COMPANY   .50
MAIXANDEAU, M. V.
  SONATA NO. 02
    ASSOCIATED MUSIC PUBLISHERS, INC.   ESC   7.00
MAIZTEGUI, I.
  ESCARCEO CRIOLLO
    EDITORIAL COOPERATIVA INTER-AMERICANA   01.15
MALATS
  SERENATA ESPANOLA
    FRANCO COLOMBO PUBLICATIONS   SAL   1.50
MALAWSKI
  TRIPTYQUE MONTAGNARD
    EDWARD B. MARKS MUSIC CORPORATION   02.25
MALDEN, G.
  CRADLE SONG
    G. SCHIRMER, INC.   .35
MALEINGRAU
  SUITE ENFANTINE
    FRANCO COLOMBO PUBLICATIONS   SAL   2.25

MALEZIEUX
  POLCHINELLE
    FRANCO COLOMBO PUBLICATIONS — SAL — 1.75
MALHERBE, C.
  PETITE ETUDE
    ELKAN-VOGEL, INC. — D — 1.00
MALIPIERO, G. F.
  ARMENIA
    FRANCO COLOMBO PUBLICATIONS — SAL — 3.00
MALIPIERO, G. F.
  CAVALCATE
    FRANCO COLOMBO PUBLICATIONS — SAL — 2.75
MALIPIERO, G. F.
  CINQUE STUDI PER DOMANI
    UNIVERSAL EDITION — UE 13063 — 2.85
MALIPIERO, G. F.
  PASQUA DI RESURREZIONE
    FRANCO COLOMBO PUBLICATIONS — SAL — 3.25
MALIPIERO, G. F.
  PAUSE DEL SILENCIO
    FRANCO COLOMBO PUBLICATIONS — BON.1119 — 3.50
MALIPIERO, G. F.
  POEMETTI LUNARI
    FRANCO COLOMBO PUBLICATIONS — SAL — 5.00
MALIPIERO, G. F.
  PRELUDI AUTUNNALI
    FRANCO COLOMBO PUBLICATIONS — SAL — 3.25
MALIPIERO, G. F.
  RISONANZE
    FRANCO COLOMBO PUBLICATIONS — BON.1130 — 1.00
MALIPIERO, G. F.
  SIESTA, LA, 1920
    ASSOCIATED MUSIC PUBLISHERS, INC. — ESC — 2.75
MALIPIERO, G. F.
  TARLO, IL
    FRANCO COLOMBO PUBLICATIONS — SAL — 3.25
MALLARD, C. S.   1 1/2
  LITTLE PLAYMATES
    THEODORE PRESSER COMPANY — .50
MALNECK *
  DREAM STREET
    THE BIG THREE MUSIC CORPORATION — 00.95
MALNECK *
  PARK AVENUE FANTASY
    THE BIG THREE MUSIC CORPORATION — 00.95
MALOOF
  NOCTURNE IN G FLAT
    FRANCO COLOMBO PUBLICATIONS — NY1402 — .60
MALOTTE, A.   DEIS
  LORD'S PRAYER, THE
    G. SCHIRMER, INC. — .60
MALOTTE, A.   DEWS
  LORD'S PRAYER, THE
    G. SCHIRMER, INC. — .60
MALOTTE, A.   LEVINE
  LORD'S PRAYER, THE
    G. SCHIRMER, INC. — .50
MALSIO, J.
  PRELUDE AND TOCCATA
    PAN AMERICAN UNION — 00.80
MALTZMAN   2-3
  ECHO WALTZ
    PRO-ART PUBLICATIONS, INC. — 209 — .50
MALTZMAN   3
  FLIGHT
    PRO-ART PUBLICATIONS, INC. — 257 — .50
MALTZMAN   3
  JUST WANDERING
    PRO-ART PUBLICATIONS, INC. — 256 — .50
MALTZMAN   3
  WHISPERING WIND, THE
    PRO-ART PUBLICATIONS, INC. — 258 — .50
MAMEN, C.
  ARABESQUES
    GERARD BILLAUDOT EDITIONS MUSICALES — 2.20
MAMORSKY, M.
  BALLET IN BLUE
    RONGWEN MUSIC, INC. — 01.50
MANA-ZUCCA   3
  BLUE DAISIES OP. 140
    THEODORE PRESSER COMPANY — .50
MANA-ZUCCA
  CLOUDY DAY, A
    G. SCHIRMER, INC. — .40
MANA-ZUCCA
  DANCING IN THE MOONLIGHT
    G. SCHIRMER, INC. — .35
MANA-ZUCCA
  DIP IN THE POOL, A
    G. SCHIRMER, INC. — .40
MANA-ZUCCA
  JOLLY WALTZ, A
    G. SCHIRMER, INC. — .35
MANA-ZUCCA
  JUST FOOLING
    G. SCHIRMER, INC. — .40
MANA-ZUCCA
  LITTLE PUSSY-CAT
    G. SCHIRMER, INC. — .30
MANA-ZUCCA
  LITTLE SPARROW, THE
    G. SCHIRMER, INC. — .35
MANA-ZUCCA
  MR. FUNNY MAN
    G. SCHIRMER, INC. — .35
MANA-ZUCCA
  RIPPLING WATER, THE, FROM 'NATURE PIECES'
    G. SCHIRMER, INC. — .35
MANA-ZUCCA
  STARLIGHT, FROM 'LIGHT PIECES'
    G. SCHIRMER, INC. — .25
MANA-ZUCCA
  SUNLIGHT, FROM 'LIGHT PIECES'
    G. SCHIRMER, INC. — .40
MANA-ZUCCA
  TAKING IT EASY
    G. SCHIRMER, INC. — .35
MANA-ZUCCA
  VALSE BRILLANTE
    G. SCHIRMER, INC. — .80
MANAS
  ILES DES PRINCES, LES
    FRANCO COLOMBO PUBLICATIONS — SAL — 4.25
MANCINI   HASTINGS
  DAYS OF WINE AND ROSES
    WARNER BROTHERS PUBLISHERS — 1.00

MANCINI   DAVIS, J. R.   FIRST YEAR
  DAYS OF WINE AND ROSES
    WARNER BROTHERS PUBLISHERS — .75
MANCINI
  HIGH TIME
    THE BIG THREE MUSIC CORPORATION — 00.95
MANCINI
  LOVE THEME FROM 'THE GLENN MILLER STORY'
    MCA MUSIC — 1.00
MANCINI
  MR. HOBBS THEME
    THE BIG THREE MUSIC CORPORATION — 00.95
MANCINI
  MYSTERY MOVIE THEME
    MCA MUSIC — 1.00
MANCINI
  PINK PANTHER
    CIMINO PUBLICATIONS, INC. — NOR — 1.25
MANCINI
  PINK PANTHER
    CIMINO PUBLICATIONS, INC. — NOR — 1.00
MANCINI
  TANGO AMERICANO
    MCA MUSIC — 1.00
MANCINI *   NEALE, J.   EASY
  DAYS OF WINE AND ROSES
    WARNER BROTHERS PUBLISHERS — .75
MANCINI *
  TOY TIGER
    MCA MUSIC — 1.00
MANCUSO, S.   2 1/2
  ROCKING LULLABY
    BELWIN-MILLS PUBLISHING CORPORATION — .60
MANEN, C.   D
  DANSE
    C. F. PETERS CORPORATION — C393 — .90
MANENTI
  LAI
    FRANCO COLOMBO PUBLICATIONS — 129128 — .60
MANENTI
  SUITE
    FRANCO COLOMBO PUBLICATIONS — BON.2467 — 1.50
MANENTI
  TOCCATA
    FRANCO COLOMBO PUBLICATIONS — 129662 — 1.00
MANICKE, D.
  SONATA
    ASSOCIATED MUSIC PUBLISHERS, INC. — SIM — 3.50
MANN   3-4
  BY THE SEA
    PRO-ART PUBLICATIONS, INC. — 378 — .50
MANN, M.
  COVERED WAGON, THE
    BELWIN-MILLS PUBLISHING CORPORATION — 25207 — .60
MANN, M.
  LITTLE FROG, A
    BELWIN-MILLS PUBLISHING CORPORATION — 25176 — .60
MANN, M.
  TOCO, MY SHETLAND PONY
    BELWIN-MILLS PUBLISHING CORPORATION — 25191 — .60
MANNEY, C.
  VIENNESE POPULAR SONG -- THE OLD REFRAIN
    BELWIN-MILLS PUBLISHING CORPORATION — 28069 — .60
MANNING   SINGER
  PUSSY CAT SONG
    MCA MUSIC — .60
MANNING, K.   DEIS
  IN THE LUXEMBOURG GARDENS--REVERIE
    G. SCHIRMER, INC. — .50
MANNINO, V.
  CHROMATIC STUDY
    FRANCO COLOMBO PUBLICATIONS — DS466 — 1.75
MANNINO, V.
  MINUET AND BURLESQUE
    FRANCO COLOMBO PUBLICATIONS — DS467 — 2.00
MANTOVANI
  GYPSY LEGEND
    BELWIN-MILLS PUBLISHING CORPORATION — 20120 — .85
MANTOVANI
  SERENATA D'AMORE
    THE BIG THREE MUSIC CORPORATION — 00.95
MANZIARLY, M. DE
  IMPRESSIONS DE MER
    FRANCO COLOMBO PUBLICATIONS — SAL — 4.00
MARAVILLA, L.
  SONATA IN E, 1945
    ASSOCIATED MUSIC PUBLISHERS, INC. — UME — .50
MARC, E.
  CHANSON DE LA FILEUSE
    ELKAN-VOGEL, INC. — LEM — .90
MARC, E.
  SUITE MINIATURE
    ELKAN-VOGEL, INC. — LEM — 1.80
MARC, E.
  TROIS PIECES BREVES
    ELKAN-VOGEL, INC. — LEM — 3.00
MARCEL, G.
  ROSE LEAVES
    BANKS AND SON LTD. — .55
MARCEL, G.
  SUMMER HOLIDAY, A
    BANKS AND SON LTD. — .80
MARCEL, G.
  SWALLOW'S RETURN, THE
    BANKS AND SON LTD. — .55
MARCEL, L. A.
  TOCCATA -- IMPROVISANO-PERCOSSO
    EDITIONS MUSICALES TRANSATLANTIQUES — 4.80
MARCELLO   MONTANI
  ADAGIO
    FRANCO COLOMBO PUBLICATIONS — FOR.11919 — .75
MARCELLO   TAGLIAPIETRA
  SONATA DA CEMBALO IN G MINOR
    FRANCO COLOMBO PUBLICATIONS — Z3375 — 1.25
MARCELLO   MAFFIOLETTI *   3
  SONATA IN B FLAT
    BARENREITER VERLAG — CM 15574
MARCELLO *   M
  CONCERTO IN D MINOR
    C. F. PETERS CORPORATION — 217D — 1.50
MARCHESE
  BOZZETTI SICILIANI
    FRANCO COLOMBO PUBLICATIONS — 128986 — 1.75
MARCHETTI, F.
  FASCINATION
    ASHLEY DEALERS SERVICE, INC. — ES — .95

MARCHETTI, F.   2
  FASCINATION
        CENTURY MUSIC PUBLISHING COMPANY, INC.   4396   .40
MARCHETTI, F.   ZEPP   4
  FASCINATION
        PRO-ART PUBLICATIONS, INC.   264   .50
MARCHETTI, F.   RICHTER   FIRST YEAR
  FASCINATION
        WARNER BROTHERS PUBLISHERS   .75
MARCHETTI, F.
  FASCINATION -- SIMP.
        ASHLEY DEALERS SERVICE, INC.   ES   .95
MARCHETTI, F.   SCHAUM, J.   2
  FASCINATION WALTZ
        SCHAUM PUBLICATIONS, INC.   .60
MARCHETTI, F.   1
  FASCINATION-GAMSE
        CENTURY MUSIC PUBLISHING COMPANY, INC.   4397   .40
MARCHI
  LITTLE MUSICAL ZOO, THE
        FRANCO COLOMBO PUBLICATIONS   129635   3.50
MARCHI, G.
  IL CIGNO
        EDIZIONI BERBEN   EB 1275   .90
MARCHI, G.
  TEMPO DI GAVOTTA
        EDIZIONI BERBEN   EB 1241   .90
MARCKHL, E.
  SONATA IN E, 1945
        ASSOCIATED MUSIC PUBLISHERS, INC.   OBV   1.25
MARCUS   3
  BAISEZ, MIGNON, PETITE VALSE
        ALPHONSE LEDUC
MARENCO   CHIESA
  EXCELSIOR - EASY FANTASY
        FRANCO COLOMBO PUBLICATIONS   109098   .60
MARESCOTTI, A. F.
  CROQUIS
        ELKAN-VOGEL, INC.   J   1.60
MARESCOTTI, A. F.
  FANTASQUE
        ELKAN-VOGEL, INC.   J   2.50
MARESCOTTI, A. F.
  SECOND SUITE EN UT
        ELKAN-VOGEL, INC.   J   3.00
MARESCOTTI, A. F.
  SUITE EN SOL
        ELKAN-VOGEL, INC.   J   2.10
MARET, L.
  BARCAROLLE
        ASSOCIATED MUSIC PUBLISHERS, INC.   ESC   2.50
MARGAT, Y.
  EN CARRIOLE
        ELKAN-VOGEL, INC.   D   .75
MARGAT, Y.
  IMPROMPTU VALSE
        ELKAN-VOGEL, INC.   D   1.25
MARGAT, Y.
  LE PETIT TRAIN DE PAIMPOL
        ELKAN-VOGEL, INC.   D   1.00
MARGAT, Y.
  UNE VALSE POUR PIANO
        ELKAN-VOGEL, INC.   D   1.25
MARGIS, A.
  VALSE BLANCHE
        FRANCO COLOMBO PUBLICATIONS   SAL   1.75
MARGIS, A.
  VALSE BLANCHE
        FRANCO COLOMBO PUBLICATIONS   SAL   1.50
MARGIS, A.   3
  VALSE BLEUE
        BELWIN-MILLS PUBLISHING CORPORATION   492   .60
MARGIS, A.   3
  VALSE BLEUE
        CENTURY MUSIC PUBLISHING COMPANY, INC.   595   .40
MARGIS, A.   3
  VALSE BLEUE
        VOLKWEIN BROS.   .25
MARGIS, A.
  VALSE BLEUE IN E FLAT
        G. SCHIRMER, INC.   .50
MARGOLA
  MOSAIC
        FRANCO COLOMBO PUBLICATIONS   BON.2318   3.00
MARGOLA
  SONATA NO. 01 -- 1956 --
        FRANCO COLOMBO PUBLICATIONS   129332   1.00
MARGOLA
  SONATA NO. 02
        FRANCO COLOMBO PUBLICATIONS   BON.2456   3.50
MARGOLA
  SONATA NO. 03 -- 1957 --
        FRANCO COLOMBO PUBLICATIONS   129726   1.50
MARGOLA
  SONATA NO. 04
        FRANCO COLOMBO PUBLICATIONS   BON.2470   3.50
MARI, P.
  NICOLAS AND PIMPRENELLE
        EDITIONS MUSICALES TRANSATLANTIQUES   1.55
MARIANI, L. L.
  AL PIE DE LA REJA, OP. 33
        ASSOCIATED MUSIC PUBLISHERS, INC.   UME   .50
MARIANI, L. L.
  ALMA ANDALUZA, NO. 1--EN LA FERIA
        ASSOCIATED MUSIC PUBLISHERS, INC.   UME   .50
MARIANI, L. L.
  ALMA ANDALUZA, NO. 2--LA MACARENA
        ASSOCIATED MUSIC PUBLISHERS, INC.   UME   .60
MARIANI, L. L.
  ALMA ANDALUZA, NO. 3--EL FLORERO
        ASSOCIATED MUSIC PUBLISHERS, INC.   UME   .50
MARIANI, L. L.
  ALMA ANDALUZA, NO. 4--ZAPATEADO
        ASSOCIATED MUSIC PUBLISHERS, INC.   UME   .60
MARIANI, L. L.
  ALMA ANDALUZA, NO. 5--SERENATA
        ASSOCIATED MUSIC PUBLISHERS, INC.   UME   .50
MARIE   WEYBRIGHT   1
  CINQUANTAINE, LA
        BELWIN-MILLS PUBLISHING CORPORATION   .50
MARIE   WEYBRIGHT   2
  CINQUANTAINE, LA
        BELWIN-MILLS PUBLISHING CORPORATION   .60
MARIE
  CINQUANTAINE, LA
        GERARD BILLAUDOT EDITIONS MUSICALES   1.30

MARIE
  LA CINQUANTAINE
        G. SCHIRMER, INC.   .40
MARIE
  MARCHE FUNEBRE D'UNE MOUSME
        FRANCO COLOMBO PUBLICATIONS   SAL   1.75
MARIE   WEYBRIGHT   2 1/2
  PETITE GAVOTTE
        BELWIN-MILLS PUBLISHING CORPORATION   .60
MARIE
  SERENADE BADINE
        GERARD BILLAUDOT EDITIONS MUSICALES   1.30
MARINIER
  BONSOIR, MADAME LA LUNE
        FRANCO COLOMBO PUBLICATIONS   SAL   1.75
MARINUZZI   RAMELLA
  VALZER CAMPESTRE
        FRANCO COLOMBO PUBLICATIONS   115743   .75
MARKEWITCH
  NOCES
        FRANCO COLOMBO PUBLICATIONS   SAL   1.75
MARKOWITZ, R.
  HONDO
        THE BIG THREE MUSIC CORPORATION   00.95
MARLAND, A.
  MEXICAN FIRE DANCE
        BELWIN-MILLS PUBLISHING CORPORATION   20339   .85
MAROS, R.
  EAST EUROPEAN FOLKSONG SUITE
        PAN AMERICAN UNION   02.00
MARPURG, F. W.
  MENUET
        FREDERICK HARRIS MUSIC COMPANY   .60
MARQUINA
  ESPANA CANI
        EDWARD B. MARKS MUSIC CORPORATION   01.00
MARROQUIN, J.
  CHAPINIANA
        PEER SOUTHERN ORGANIZATION   01.60
MARRYOTT, R. E.   4
  SWIRLING WATERS
        THEODORE PRESSER COMPANY   .50
MARSCHALL   LOEPKE   3
  STARLIGHT
        VOLKWEIN BROS.   .35
MARSDEN, E.
  OLD KITCHEN CLOCK, THE
        FREDERICK HARRIS MUSIC COMPANY   .60
MARSDEN, E.
  SKATING CARNIVAL, THE
        FREDERICK HARRIS MUSIC COMPANY   .60
MARSDEN, E.
  STAMPEDE
        FREDERICK HARRIS MUSIC COMPANY   .60
MARSDEN, E.
  TARANTELLE
        FREDERICK HARRIS MUSIC COMPANY   .60
MARSHALL   KERR, R.N.
  HAWAIIAN WEDDING SONG
        MCA MUSIC   1.00
MARSHALL
  THUNDER ROAD CHASE
        MCA MUSIC   1.00
MARSHALL, L.   E
  COUNTRY LANE
        COMPOSERS PRESS, INC.   1.00
MARSHALL, L.   E-M
  IN A CANOE
        COMPOSERS PRESS, INC.   1.00
MARSICK
  FOUR PIECES - AU CREPUSCULE
        FRANCO COLOMBO PUBLICATIONS   SAL   2.00
MARSICK
  FOUR PIECES - LES ELFES
        FRANCO COLOMBO PUBLICATIONS   SAL   2.00
MARSICK
  FOUR PIECES - LES PLAINTES D'ATYS
        FRANCO COLOMBO PUBLICATIONS   SAL   2.00
MARSICK
  FOUR PIECES - SCHERZO
        FRANCO COLOMBO PUBLICATIONS   SAL   2.00
MARTELLI, H.
  GUITARE
        FRANCO COLOMBO PUBLICATIONS   SAL   2.75
MARTELLI, H.
  SECOND PETITE SUITE
        GERARD BILLAUDOT EDITIONS MUSICALES   1.60
MARTELLI, M.   D
  CONCERTO, OP. 56
        C. F. PETERS CORPORATION   C404   3.00
MARTIN   WILLIAMS   3
  COTTON PICKER
        BOSTON MUSIC COMPANY   .50
MARTIN   WILLIAMS, J.   3
  COTTON PICKERS
        BOSTON MUSIC COMPANY   .50
MARTIN
  DANCE OF THE PUPPETS
        CARL FISCHER, INC.   P 2041   .50
MARTIN
  WHISTLING GONDOLIER, THE
        SAM FOX PUBLISHING COMPANY, INC.   .50
MARTIN, E.   SEDLON
  COME TO THE FAIR
        BOOSEY AND HAWKES, INC.   .40
MARTIN, E.
  EVENSONG
        BOOSEY AND HAWKES, INC.   .60
MARTIN, E.
  EVENSONG IN F
        BOOSEY AND HAWKES, INC.   .60
MARTIN, E.   2
  HAPPY CHILDREN
        CENTURY MUSIC PUBLISHING COMPANY, INC.   4177   .40
MARTIN, E.   1
  LITTLE RANGE RIDER, THE
        WILLIS MUSIC COMPANY   .40
MARTIN, E.   1
  LITTLE RANGE RIDER, THE
        WILLIS MUSIC COMPANY   .30
MARTIN, E.
  WHISTLING GONDOLIER, THE
        SOUTHERN MUSIC COMPANY   .50
MARTIN, G.   1
  AT THE COUNTY FAIR, MARCH
        CENTURY MUSIC PUBLISHING COMPANY, INC.   2076   .40

MARTIN, G.		1	
AT THE DANCE			
CENTURY MUSIC PUBLISHING COMPANY, INC.		1758	.40
MARTIN, G.		1	
BETTY'S WALTZ			
CENTURY MUSIC PUBLISHING COMPANY, INC.		1606	.40
MARTIN, G.		1	
BUNCH OF DAISIES, A			
CENTURY MUSIC PUBLISHING COMPANY, INC.		1963	.40
MARTIN, G.		1	
CARNIVAL OF ROSES			
CENTURY MUSIC PUBLISHING COMPANY, INC.		3074	.40
MARTIN, G.		2	
CHA CHA DOLL			
CENTURY MUSIC PUBLISHING COMPANY, INC.		38	.40
MARTIN, G.		2	
CHA CHA DOLL			
CENTURY MUSIC PUBLISHING COMPANY, INC.		038	.40
MARTIN, G.		1	
CONTENTMENT WALTZ			
CENTURY MUSIC PUBLISHING COMPANY, INC.		1956	.40
MARTIN, G.		1	
CUCKOO SONG			
CENTURY MUSIC PUBLISHING COMPANY, INC.		1608	.40
MARTIN, G.		1	
DANCE POLONAISE			
CENTURY MUSIC PUBLISHING COMPANY, INC.		1612	.40
MARTIN, G.		1	
DANCE OF THE PANSIES			
CENTURY MUSIC PUBLISHING COMPANY, INC.		1957	.40
MARTIN, G.		1	
DOLL'S BALL, THE			
CENTURY MUSIC PUBLISHING COMPANY, INC.		3073	.40
MARTIN, G.		1	
DREAMING OF SANTA CLAUS			
CENTURY MUSIC PUBLISHING COMPANY, INC.		2079	.40
MARTIN, G.		1	
EASTER LILLIES, REVERIE			
CENTURY MUSIC PUBLISHING COMPANY, INC.		2071	.40
MARTIN, G.		1	
ELIZABETH WALTZ			
CENTURY MUSIC PUBLISHING COMPANY, INC.		1614	.40
MARTIN, G.		1	
FAIRIES' LULLABY			
CENTURY MUSIC PUBLISHING COMPANY, INC.		1958	.40
MARTIN, G.		1	
FIRECRACKER, GALOP			
CENTURY MUSIC PUBLISHING COMPANY, INC.		2074	.40
MARTIN, G.		1	
FLORAL PARADE, THE, VALSE			
CENTURY MUSIC PUBLISHING COMPANY, INC.		1959	.40
MARTIN, G.		1	
FOX AND GOOSE			
CENTURY MUSIC PUBLISHING COMPANY, INC.		1603	.40
MARTIN, G.		2	
GHOST STORY, A			
CENTURY MUSIC PUBLISHING COMPANY, INC.		1757	.40
MARTIN, G.		1-2	
GYPSY TANGO			
CENTURY MUSIC PUBLISHING COMPANY, INC.		4400	.40
MARTIN, G.		1	
HALLOWE'EN PRANKS, CAPRICE			
CENTURY MUSIC PUBLISHING COMPANY, INC.		2077	.40
MARTIN, G.		1	
HAPPY CHILDHOOD			
CENTURY MUSIC PUBLISHING COMPANY, INC.		1610	.40
MARTIN, G.		1	
HAPPY YOUTH, POLKA			
CENTURY MUSIC PUBLISHING COMPANY, INC.		1961	.40
MARTIN, G.		1	
IN MAY, LITTLE FOLKSONG			
CENTURY MUSIC PUBLISHING COMPANY, INC.		1604	.40
MARTIN, G.		2	
IN SPRINGTIME			
CENTURY MUSIC PUBLISHING COMPANY, INC.		1757	.40
MARTIN, G.		1	
IN THE GARDEN			
CENTURY MUSIC PUBLISHING COMPANY, INC.		1962	.40
MARTIN, G.		2	
JIMMIE CRACK CORN, BOOGIE			
CENTURY MUSIC PUBLISHING COMPANY, INC.		4302	.40
MARTIN, G.		1	
LITTLE RONDO			
CENTURY MUSIC PUBLISHING COMPANY, INC.		1913	.40
MARTIN, G.		1	
MARCH OF THE BOY SCOUTS			
CENTURY MUSIC PUBLISHING COMPANY, INC.		1911	.40
MARTIN, G.		1	
MAY POLE DANCE			
CENTURY MUSIC PUBLISHING COMPANY, INC.		2072	.40
MARTIN, G.		1	
MEADOW BROOK, THE, ETUDE			
CENTURY MUSIC PUBLISHING COMPANY, INC.		1967	.40
MARTIN, G.		1	
ON A VISIT, MARCH			
CENTURY MUSIC PUBLISHING COMPANY, INC.		1964	.40
MARTIN, G.		1	
PLAYING IN THE SUNLIGHT			
CENTURY MUSIC PUBLISHING COMPANY, INC.		1965	.40
MARTIN, G.		2	
ROCK AND ROLL BLUES			
CENTURY MUSIC PUBLISHING COMPANY, INC.		39	.40
MARTIN, G.		3	
ROCK AND ROLL BLUES			
CENTURY MUSIC PUBLISHING COMPANY, INC.		039	.40
MARTIN, G.		1	
ROCK AND ROLL LULLABY			
THEODORE PRESSER COMPANY			.50
MARTIN, G.		1	
SCHOOL IS OUT, MARCH			
CENTURY MUSIC PUBLISHING COMPANY, INC.		2073	.40
MARTIN, G.		1	
ST. PATRICK'S DAY PARADE			
CENTURY MUSIC PUBLISHING COMPANY, INC.		2070	.40
MARTIN, G.		2	
TARANTELLE			
CENTURY MUSIC PUBLISHING COMPANY, INC.		1758	.40
MARTIN, G.		1	
VALENTINE PARTY, WALTZ			
CENTURY MUSIC PUBLISHING COMPANY, INC.		2069	.40
MARTIN, G.		1	
VIOLETS AND ROSES			
CENTURY MUSIC PUBLISHING COMPANY, INC.		1966	.40
MARTIN, G.		2	
WOODLAND VOICE			
CENTURY MUSIC PUBLISHING COMPANY, INC.		3075	.40

MARTIN, G. B.	DEL MAGLIO		
GAVOTTE			
FRANCO COLOMBO PUBLICATIONS		129093	.60
MARTIN, H.			
AUTUMN FANTASY			
BELWIN-MILLS PUBLISHING CORPORATION		25038	.60
MARTIN, H.		3	
BALLERINA, THE			
BELWIN-MILLS PUBLISHING CORPORATION			.60
MARTIN, H.			
BLUEBELLS IN SPRING			
BELWIN-MILLS PUBLISHING CORPORATION		25157	.60
MARTIN, H.			
BOOGIE FUN FOR THE PIANO			
BELWIN-MILLS PUBLISHING CORPORATION		11060	1.25
MARTIN, H.		E	
BUTTERFLY WALTZ, THE			
BELWIN-MILLS PUBLISHING CORPORATION			.60
MARTIN, H.		1	
CALICO CLOWN, THE			
BELWIN-MILLS PUBLISHING CORPORATION		25212	.60
MARTIN, H.			
CAMP OF THE GYPSIES			
VOLKWEIN BROS.			.25
MARTIN, H.			
CANDLELIGHT AND CRINOLINE			
BELWIN-MILLS PUBLISHING CORPORATION		25259	.60
MARTIN, H.			
DANCING ON A CLOUD			
BELWIN-MILLS PUBLISHING CORPORATION		25230	.60
MARTIN, H.			
DANISH DANCER, THE			
BELWIN-MILLS PUBLISHING CORPORATION		25184	.60
MARTIN, H.			
ENCHANTED DANCER, THE			
BELWIN-MILLS PUBLISHING CORPORATION		25209	.60
MARTIN, H.			
ENCHANTED FOREST, THE			
BELWIN-MILLS PUBLISHING CORPORATION		25158	.60
MARTIN, H.			
ENCHANTED PRINCESS, THE			
BELWIN-MILLS PUBLISHING CORPORATION		25210	.60
MARTIN, H.			
FOREST FAIRYLAND			
BELWIN-MILLS PUBLISHING CORPORATION		25277	.60
MARTIN, H.			
GHOST WALKS, THE			
BELWIN-MILLS PUBLISHING CORPORATION		25053	.60
MARTIN, H.			
GOBLIN'S NIGHT OUT			
BELWIN-MILLS PUBLISHING CORPORATION		25275	.60
MARTIN, H.			
GRANDMA'S MUSIC BOX			
BELWIN-MILLS PUBLISHING CORPORATION		25258	.60
MARTIN, H.			
HAPPY HOP-A-LONG			
BELWIN-MILLS PUBLISHING CORPORATION		25278	.60
MARTIN, H.			
HOLIDAY IN MEXICO			
BELWIN-MILLS PUBLISHING CORPORATION		25125	.60
MARTIN, H.			
HONKY TONK BOOGIE			
BELWIN-MILLS PUBLISHING CORPORATION		25190	.60
MARTIN, H.			
JAMAICAN TANGO			
BELWIN-MILLS PUBLISHING CORPORATION		25231	.60
MARTIN, H.			
JET MARCH, THE			
BELWIN-MILLS PUBLISHING CORPORATION		25204	.60
MARTIN, H.			
JUST TRAVELIN' ALONG			
BELWIN-MILLS PUBLISHING CORPORATION		25211	.60
MARTIN, H.		2A	
MAGIC HOUR, THE			
MUSICORD PUBLICATIONS, INC.			.45
MARTIN, H.		2	
MAGNOLIA TIME			
VOLKWEIN BROS.			.40
MARTIN, H.			
MARCH OF THE CANDY CANES			
BELWIN-MILLS PUBLISHING CORPORATION		25084	.60
MARTIN, H.			
PINAFORE BALLET			
BELWIN-MILLS PUBLISHING CORPORATION		25276	.60
MARTIN, H.		2	
PINAFORE POLKA, THE			
BELWIN-MILLS PUBLISHING CORPORATION		25260	.60
MARTIN, H.			
POPCORN POLKA			
VOLKWEIN BROS.			.35
MARTIN, H.			
SNOW PARTY, THE			
BELWIN-MILLS PUBLISHING CORPORATION		25178	.60
MARTIN, H.			
SUMMER NIGHT			
BELWIN-MILLS PUBLISHING CORPORATION		25261	.60
MARTIN, H.			
SUMMER STARLIGHT			
BELWIN-MILLS PUBLISHING CORPORATION		25160	.60
MARTIN, H.			
TANGO MODERNE			
BELWIN-MILLS PUBLISHING CORPORATION		25106	.60
MARTIN, H.		3 1/2	
TANGO TIME IN RIO			
BELWIN-MILLS PUBLISHING CORPORATION			.60
MARTIN, R. C.			
APRES LA CLASSE			
ELKAN-VOGEL, INC.		D	.70
MARTIN, R. C.			
APRES LES DEVOIRS			
ELKAN-VOGEL, INC.		J	2.25
MARTIN, R. C.			
QUEL DIABLE			
ELKAN-VOGEL, INC.		D	2.25
MARTINA			
WILLY-NILLY WALTZ			
MCA MUSIC			.60
MARTINI, G.			
GAVOTTE UND GOSSEC, GAVOTTE D-DUR			
SCHOTT		0917 1/2	1.00
MARTINI, G.		3	
PLAISIR D'AMOUR			
CENTURY MUSIC PUBLISHING COMPANY, INC.		3432	.40
MARTINI, G.			
PLAISIR D'AMOUR			
FRANCO COLOMBO PUBLICATIONS		69436	.60

MARTINI, G. LEVINE			
PLAISIR D'AMOUR			
G. SCHIRMER, INC.			.50
MARTINI, G.			
SONATE D'INTAVOLATURA - L'ORGANO E 'L CEMBALO			
BROUDE BROTHERS LTD.			27.50
MARTINO CALYPSO			
CHILI-BEAN			
MCA MUSIC			.60
MARTINO			
EASTER SERENADE			
MCA MUSIC			.60
MARTINO			
GOSPEL MEETING			
MCA MUSIC			.60
MARTINO			
HANKY-PANKY			
MCA MUSIC			.60
MARTINO 2			
HEADIN' HOME			
PRO-ART PUBLICATIONS, INC.	518		.50
MARTINO			
MOONBEAMS			
MCA MUSIC			.60
MARTINO			
PIANO FANTASY			
E. C. SCHIRMER MUSIC COMPANY	1434		02.50
MARTINO			
WINDMILLS			
MCA MUSIC			.60
MARTINON, J.			
EPILOGUE D'UN CONTE D'AMOUR--BERCEUSE--,OP.35 NO.1			
GERARD BILLAUDOT EDITIONS MUSICALES			1.30
MARTINON, J.			
INTRODUCTION ET TOCCATA			
GERARD BILLAUDOT EDITIONS MUSICALES			2.50
MARTINON, J.			
SONATINE NO. 03			
GERARD BILLAUDOT EDITIONS MUSICALES			2.00
MARTINU, B.			
BAGATELLE			
ASSOCIATED MUSIC PUBLISHERS, INC.	ESC		2.00
MARTINU, B.			
DUMKA, OP. POSTH.			
ASSOCIATED MUSIC PUBLISHERS, INC.	ESC		2.50
MARTINU, B. 5			
ESQUISSES DE DANSES			
SCHOTT	2327		2.50
MARTINU, B.			
FABLES			
ARTIA			1.25
MARTINU, B. 5			
FENETRE SUR LE JARDIN			
ALPHONSE LEDUC			
MARTINU, B.			
FILM IN MINIATURE			
ARTIA			1.25
MARTINU, B.			
LES BOUQUINISTES DU QUAI MALAQUAIS			
HEUGEL ET CIE.			1.25
MARTINU, B. 5			
LES RITOURNELLES			
SCHOTT	2326		2.50
MARTINU, B.			
MAZURKA			
BOOSEY AND HAWKES, INC.			1.00
MARTINU, B. 5			
REVUE DE CUISINE, LE, SUITE			
ALPHONSE LEDUC			
MARTINU, B.			
SONATA, 1958			
ASSOCIATED MUSIC PUBLISHERS, INC.	ESC		9.50
MARTINU, B.			
SPRING IN THE GARDEN			
ARTIA			1.75
MARTINU, B.			
TWO DANCES			
ARTIA			1.50
MARTINU, B.			
TWO PIECES FOR CLAVECIN			
UNIVERSAL EDITION	UE 13431		2.90
MARTUCCI			
BARCAROLLE NO. 01, OP. 20			
FRANCO COLOMBO PUBLICATIONS	44509		.60
MARTUCCI			
CAPRICE NO. 1, OP. 2			
FRANCO COLOMBO PUBLICATIONS	53018		.90
MARTUCCI			
CAPRICE NO. 2, OP. 3			
FRANCO COLOMBO PUBLICATIONS	44527		.75
MARTUCCI			
FANTASY, OP. 51			
FRANCO COLOMBO PUBLICATIONS	ER2178		1.25
MARTUCCI			
FIORELLINO, OP. 43 NO. 5			
FRANCO COLOMBO PUBLICATIONS	46241		.60
MARTUCCI CESI			
IMPROMPTU, OP. 17			
FRANCO COLOMBO PUBLICATIONS	127611		.60
MARTUCCI LONGO			
NOCTURNE IN F SHARP MINOR, OP. 70 NO. 2			
FRANCO COLOMBO PUBLICATIONS	127767		.75
MARTUCCI			
NOCTURNE IN G FLAT, OP. 70 NO. 1			
FRANCO COLOMBO PUBLICATIONS	128152		.60
MARTUCCI LONGO			
SCHERZO, OP. 53 NO. 2			
FRANCO COLOMBO PUBLICATIONS	128001		.90
MARTUCCI			
STUDIO DI CONCERTO, OP. 9			
FRANCO COLOMBO PUBLICATIONS	44526		1.25
MARTUCCI			
STUDIO, OP. 47			
FRANCO COLOMBO PUBLICATIONS	122755		1.00
MARTUCCI			
TARANTELLA, OP. 44 NO. 6			
FRANCO COLOMBO PUBLICATIONS	128330		1.25
MARTUCCI			
TEMPO DI MAZURKA, OP. 11			
FRANCO COLOMBO PUBLICATIONS	44489		.75
MARTUCCI LONGO			
THEME AND VARIATIONS, OP. 58			
FRANCO COLOMBO PUBLICATIONS	ER2144		1.25
MARTY 4			
REVEIL DU PRINTEMPS			
ALPHONSE LEDUC			

MARWICK, M. *			
ON THE OTHER HAND			
LEE ROBERTS MUSIC PUBLICATIONS, INC.			.85
MARWICK, M. *			
SUMP'N SWEET			
LEE ROBERTS MUSIC PUBLICATIONS, INC.			.85
MARX 3			
SONATINE IN A, OP. 48 NO. 1			
BARENREITER VERLAG	BA 2076		
MASCAGNI, A.			
SONATINA			
FRANCO COLOMBO PUBLICATIONS	Z4804		2.50
MASCAGNI, P. DE CRISTOFARO			
AMICO FRITZ, L' - CHERRY DUET			
FRANCO COLOMBO PUBLICATIONS	SON.1727		1.00
MASCAGNI, P. AZZONI			
AMICO FRITZ, L' - INTERMEZZO			
FRANCO COLOMBO PUBLICATIONS	SON.620		.90
MASCAGNI, P. DE CRISTOFARO			
AMICO FRITZ, L' - INTERMEZZO -- FINGERED --			
FRANCO COLOMBO PUBLICATIONS	SON.1816		.90
MASCAGNI, P.			
AMICO FRITZ, L' - INTERMEZZO -- ORIGINAL --			
FRANCO COLOMBO PUBLICATIONS	SON.703		.90
MASCAGNI, P.			
CAVALLERIA RUSTICANA - GRAND FANTASY			
FRANCO COLOMBO PUBLICATIONS	SON.1764		1.50
MASCAGNI, P. FUMAGALLI			
CAVALLERIA RUSTICANA - INTERMEZZO			
FRANCO COLOMBO PUBLICATIONS	SON.522		.90
MASCAGNI, P. DE SIMONE			
CAVALLERIA RUSTICANA - INTERMEZZO			
FRANCO COLOMBO PUBLICATIONS	SON.1348		.90
MASCAGNI, P.			
CAVALLERIA RUSTICANA - INTERMEZZO -- ORIGINAL --			
FRANCO COLOMBO PUBLICATIONS	SON.509		.90
MASCAGNI, P.			
CAVALLERIA RUSTICANA - PRELUDE			
FRANCO COLOMBO PUBLICATIONS	SON.613		1.00
MASCAGNI, P.			
CAVALLERIA RUSTICANA -- COMPLETE OPERA --			
FRANCO COLOMBO PUBLICATIONS	SON.493		8.75
MASCAGNI, P. 3			
CAVALLERIA RUSTICANA 'INTERMEZZO'			
BELWIN-MILLS PUBLISHING CORPORATION	245		.60
MASCAGNI, P.			
CAVALLERIA RUSTICANA--FANTASIA--			
FREDERICK HARRIS MUSIC COMPANY			.50
MASCAGNI, P. 3			
CAVALLERIA RUSTICANA, INTERMEZZO			
CENTURY MUSIC PUBLISHING COMPANY, INC.	158		.40
MASCAGNI, P. 2			
CAVALLERIA RUSTICANA, INTERMEZZO, EASY			
CENTURY MUSIC PUBLISHING COMPANY, INC.	1784		.40
MASCAGNI, P.			
DANZA ESOTICA			
FRANCO COLOMBO PUBLICATIONS	SON.590		1.25
MASCAGNI, P. GALLI			
GUGLIELMO RATCLIFF - DREAM OF RATCLIFF			
FRANCO COLOMBO PUBLICATIONS	SON.902		.90
MASCAGNI, P.			
INTERMEZZO SINFONICO--'CAVALLERIA RUSTICANA'			
G. SCHIRMER, INC.			.35
MASCAGNI, P. 3			
INTERMEZZO, CAV. RUSTICANA			
CENTURY MUSIC PUBLISHING COMPANY, INC.	158		.40
MASCAGNI, P. 2			
INTERMEZZO, CAV. RUSTICANA			
CENTURY MUSIC PUBLISHING COMPANY, INC.	1784		.40
MASCAGNI, P. CHIESA			
IRIS - EASY FANTASIA			
FRANCO COLOMBO PUBLICATIONS	111262		.50
MASCAGNI, P.			
IRIS - HYMN TO THE SUN			
FRANCO COLOMBO PUBLICATIONS	102335		1.00
MASCAGNI, P.			
ISABEAU -- COMPLETE OPERA --			
FRANCO COLOMBO PUBLICATIONS	SON.1644		11.50
MASCAGNI, P. MIRRI			
LODOLETTA - SERENATA			
FRANCO COLOMBO PUBLICATIONS	SON.2105		.90
MASCAGNI, P.			
LODOLETTA -- COMPLETE OPERA --			
FRANCO COLOMBO PUBLICATIONS	SON.2032		11.50
MASCAGNI, P.			
MASCHERE, LE - OVERTURE			
FRANCO COLOMBO PUBLICATIONS	SON.1933		1.25
MASCAGNI, P.			
MASCHERE, LE - PRELUDIETTO TO ACT II			
FRANCO COLOMBO PUBLICATIONS	SON.1938		.90
MASCAGNI, P.			
PICCOLI MARAT, IL -- COMPLETE OPERA --			
FRANCO COLOMBO PUBLICATIONS	SON.2206		11.50
MASCAGNI, P.			
PRELUDE AND SICILIANA FROM CAVALLERIA RUSTICANA			
FREDERICK HARRIS MUSIC COMPANY			.60
MASCAGNI, P. BUMMERI			
SILVANO - EASY FANTASY NO. 1			
FRANCO COLOMBO PUBLICATIONS	SON.1707		.90
MASCAGNI, P. BUCCERI			
SILVANO - EASY FANTASY NO. 2			
FRANCO COLOMBO PUBLICATIONS	SON.1708		.90
MASCAGNI, P.			
SILVANO - NOCTURNE			
FRANCO COLOMBO PUBLICATIONS	SON.2796		.90
MASDEA, V. 2			
DIVINE STAR			
VOLKWEIN BROS.			.30
MASDEA, V. 2			
HAPPY HOUR WALTZ			
VOLKWEIN BROS.			.30
MASDEA, V. 2			
REMEMBER ME			
VOLKWEIN BROS.			.30
MASETTI			
CAPANNA, UNA BIMBA, UNA STELLA, UNA			
FRANCO COLOMBO PUBLICATIONS	BON.1728		.90
MASETTI			
GIOCO DEL CUCU, IL			
FRANCO COLOMBO PUBLICATIONS	BON.1836		1.00
MASETTI			
NOCTURNE			
FRANCO COLOMBO PUBLICATIONS	BON.2316		1.50
MASKELL, C. H. 4			
I WANT THE TWILIGHT AND YOU			
VOLKWEIN BROS.			.50

MASKELL, C. H.   4
  LOVE'S GOLDEN MEMORIES
    VOLKWEIN BROS.   .50
MASKELL, C. H.   4
  TWILIGHT SERENADE
    VOLKWEIN BROS.   00.50
MASON, I.
  LEGENDE DE NUIT
    BELWIN-MILLS PUBLISHING CORPORATION   25282   .60
MASON, I.
  MEJESKA DANCE, OP. 30 NO. 2
    BELWIN-MILLS PUBLISHING CORPORATION   25272   .60
MASON, I.
  SAILS FROM 'SEA SKETCHES'
    BELWIN-MILLS PUBLISHING CORPORATION   25196   .60
MASON, I.
  SEA MISTS FROM 'SEA SKETCHES'
    BELWIN-MILLS PUBLISHING CORPORATION   25197   .60
MASON, I.
  SEA SHANTY 'A SENTIMENTAL SAILOR' FROM 'SEA SKETCHES'
    BELWIN-MILLS PUBLISHING CORPORATION   25195   .60
MASON, I.   INTERMEDIATE
  SKIDMORE MODERN KEYBOARD SERIES - PASTELS
    SHAPIRO, BERNSTEIN ORGANIZATION   .75
MASON, I.   INTERMEDIATE
  SKIDMORE MODERN KEYBOARD SERIES -MALEKULA MOON DANCE
    SHAPIRO, BERNSTEIN ORGANIZATION   .75
MASON, L.   STEINER   APP.
  FATHER, IN THY MYSTERIOUS PRESENCE KNEELING
    BELWIN-MILLS PUBLISHING CORPORATION   .60
MASON, L.   4
  NEARER, MY GOD, TO THEE
    THEODORE PRESSER COMPANY   .50
MASON, W.
  GAVOTTE IN D FROM THE 6TH 'CELLO-SONATA OF BACH
    G. SCHIRMER, INC.   .50
MASON, W.   6
  SILVER SPRING
    CENTURY MUSIC PUBLISHING COMPANY, INC.   1253   .40
MASON, W.   5
  SPRING DAWN
    CENTURY MUSIC PUBLISHING COMPANY, INC.   1253   .40
MASSENET, J.   BARTH, H.   3
  ARAGONAISE
    BELWIN-MILLS PUBLISHING CORPORATION   .60
MASSENET, J.   3
  ARAGONAISE
    VOLKWEIN BROS.   .25
MASSENET, J.   SCHAUM, J.   2
  ARAGONAISE 'LE CID'
    BELWIN-MILLS PUBLISHING CORPORATION   .50
MASSENET, J.
  ARAGONAISE--FROM THE BALLET 'LE CID'
    G. SCHIRMER, INC.   .50
MASSENET, J.
  ARAGONAISE, FROM LE CID
    CARL FISCHER, INC.   S 94   .50
MASSENET, J.   5
  ARAGONAISE, LE CID
    CENTURY MUSIC PUBLISHING COMPANY, INC.   138   .40
MASSENET, J.   HOFFMAN   4
  ARGONAISE
    WILLIS MUSIC COMPANY   .35
MASSENET, J.
  CID, LE - ARAGONAISE
    FRANCO COLOMBO PUBLICATIONS   BA6481   .75
MASSENET, J.   DEL MAGLIO
  CID, LE - ARAGONAISE
    FRANCO COLOMBO PUBLICATIONS   BA10206   .75
MASSENET, J.   4
  DERNIER SOMMEIL DE LA VIERGE, LE
    CENTURY MUSIC PUBLISHING COMPANY, INC.   2352   .40
MASSENET, J.
  ELEGIE IN E MINOR, OP. 10
    G. SCHIRMER, INC.   .40
MASSENET, J.   4
  ELEGIE, MELODIE
    CENTURY MUSIC PUBLISHING COMPANY, INC.   1018   .40
MASSENET, J.   3
  ELEGY
    BOSTON MUSIC COMPANY   .50
MASSENET, J.   JETSON, I. H.   4
  ELEGY
    VOLKWEIN BROS.   .35
MASSENET, J.
  ELEGY, OP. 10
    FRANCO COLOMBO PUBLICATIONS   BA6475   .75
MASSENET, J.
  GAVOTTE FROM 'MANON'
    HEUGEL ET CIE.   1.95
MASSENET, J.
  HERODIADE -- BALLET EXTRACT
    HEUGEL ET CIE.   2.40
MASSENET, J.
  LA VIERGE-DERNIER SOMMEIL
    HEUGEL ET CIE.   1.30
MASSENET, J.   4
  LAST DREAM OF THE VIRGIN
    CENTURY MUSIC PUBLISHING COMPANY, INC.   2352   .40
MASSENET, J.
  LE CID -- BALLET EXTRACT
    HEUGEL ET CIE.   3.75
MASSENET, J.
  LE GRILLON DU FOYER
    HEUGEL ET CIE.   3.25
MASSENET, J.
  MANON
    HEUGEL ET CIE.   11.00
MASSENET, J.   KING, S.
  MEDITATION -- FROM 'THAIS'
    BELWIN-MILLS PUBLISHING CORPORATION   26029   .60
MASSENET, J.
  MEDITATION --FROM THAIS
    EDWARD B. MARKS MUSIC CORPORATION   01.00
MASSENET, J.
  MEDITATION 'THAIS'
    ASHLEY DEALERS SERVICE, INC.   ES   .95
MASSENET, J.   3
  MEDITATION FROM 'THAIS'
    BOSTON MUSIC COMPANY   .60
MASSENET, J.
  MEDITATION FROM 'THAIS'
    HEUGEL ET CIE.   1.45
MASSENET, J.
  MEDITATION FROM THAIS
    CARL FISCHER, INC.   P 2294   .75

MASSENET, J.   3
  MEDITATION, THAIS
    CENTURY MUSIC PUBLISHING COMPANY, INC.   4 004   .40
MASSENET, J.
  MELODIE -- ELEGY, OP. 10
    BELWIN-MILLS PUBLISHING CORPORATION   28167   .60
MASSENET, J.   4
  MELODIE 'ELEGIE' OP. 10
    BELWIN-MILLS PUBLISHING CORPORATION   248   .60
MASSENET, J.   4
  MELODIE, ELEGIE
    CENTURY MUSIC PUBLISHING COMPANY, INC.   1018   .40
MASSENET, J.   2
  MELODIE, ELEGIE, EASY
    CENTURY MUSIC PUBLISHING COMPANY, INC.   3216   .40
MASSENET, J.   3
  PHADRA -- OUVERTURE
    SCHOTT   1.75
MASSENET, J.
  THAIS
    HEUGEL ET CIE.   9.75
MASSENET, J.
  THAIS - MEDITATION
    FRANCO COLOMBO PUBLICATIONS   BA6476   .75
MASSENET, J.   DEL MAGLIO
  THAIS - MEDITATION
    FRANCO COLOMBO PUBLICATIONS   BA10205   .75
MASSENET, J.   SCHAUM, J.   4
  THAIS 'MEDITATION'
    BELWIN-MILLS PUBLISHING CORPORATION   .50
MASSENET, J.   3
  THAIS, MEDITATION
    CENTURY MUSIC PUBLISHING COMPANY, INC.   4004   .40
MASSENET, J.
  WERTHER
    HEUGEL ET CIE.   8.75
MASSEY, G.
  SNAPSHOTS IN SOUND
    BANKS AND SON LTD.   .80
MASSIAS, G.
  ALICE AU PAYS DES MERVEILLES
    GERARD BILLAUDOT EDITIONS MUSICALES   2.50
MASTERS
  CHAPEL BELLS
    CARL FISCHER, INC.   P 1998   .50
MATA, E.
  SONATA
    EDICIONES MEXICANAS DE MUSICA, A. C.   02.00
MATHESON   RICHTER
  CHICKADEE
    FRANCO COLOMBO PUBLICATIONS   NY1511   .35
MATHESON   RICHTER
  CHICKADEE, THE
    BELWIN-MILLS PUBLISHING CORPORATION   2 1/2   .60
MATHEWS, B. D.
  MARCH OF THE YOUNG CADETS
    THEODORE PRESSER COMPANY   .50
MATHIAS
  TOCCATA ALLA DANZA
    OXFORD UNIVERSITY PRESS   32.928   1.40
MATHIAS, W.
  PIANO SONATA
    OXFORD UNIVERSITY PRESS   32.142   3.30
MATHIEU
  THREE PIECES FOR CHILDREN - BERCEUSE
    FRANCO COLOMBO PUBLICATIONS   SAL   1.50
MATHIEU
  THREE PIECES FOR CHILDREN - HOMMAGE A MOZART
    FRANCO COLOMBO PUBLICATIONS   SAL   1.50
MATHIEU
  THREE PIECES FOR CHILDREN - TRISTESSE
    FRANCO COLOMBO PUBLICATIONS   SAL   1.50
MATHIEU
  THREE PIECES PITTORESQUES - DANSE SAUVAGE
    FRANCO COLOMBO PUBLICATIONS   SAL   2.50
MATHIEU
  THREE PIECES PITTORESQUES - LES MOUETTES
    FRANCO COLOMBO PUBLICATIONS   SAL   2.50
MATHIEU
  THREE PIECES PITTORESQUES - PROCESSION D'ELEPHANTS
    FRANCO COLOMBO PUBLICATIONS   SAL   2.50
MATICIC
  DANSES GROTESQUES
    FRANCO COLOMBO PUBLICATIONS   A181   1.75
MATOS RODRIGUEZ
  CUMPARSITA, LA
    FRANCO COLOMBO PUBLICATIONS   120357   .75
MATOS RODRIGUEZ   DEL MAGLIO
  CUMPARSITA, LA
    FRANCO COLOMBO PUBLICATIONS   127204   .60
MATSUSHITA, S.
  SPECTRA
    UNIVERSAL EDITION   UE 14700   2.75
MATTEI   9
  TOURBILLON, LE, FIRST GRANDE VALSE, OP. 15
    ALPHONSE LEDUC
MATTEI   5
  TOURBILLON, VALSE DE CONCERT
    CENTURY MUSIC PUBLISHING COMPANY, INC.   235   .40
MATTEI   3
  TOURBILLON, VALSE DE CONCERT, EASY
    CENTURY MUSIC PUBLISHING COMPANY, INC.   2516   .40
MATTEL, T.   5
  GRAND VALSE DE CONCERT
    CENTURY MUSIC PUBLISHING COMPANY, INC.   235   .40
MATTHESON, J.
  AIR
    FREDERICK HARRIS MUSIC COMPANY   .60
MATTHEWS, H. A.   4
  PINES, THE
    THEODORE PRESSER COMPANY   .75
MATTHEWS, H. A.   3
  SUNSET
    THEODORE PRESSER COMPANY   .50
MATTINGLY, J.   3
  ON THE BLUE LAGOON
    WILLIS MUSIC COMPANY   .40
MATTINGLY, J.   2
  SPARKLING FIREFLIES
    WILLIS MUSIC COMPANY   .40
MATTINGLY, J.   1
  TICK-TOCK
    WILLIS MUSIC COMPANY   .35
MAURAT, E.
  BALLADE, OP. 12
    ASSOCIATED MUSIC PUBLISHERS, INC.   ESC   3.25

MAURAT, E.
    IMPROMPTU NO. 1, OP. 32
        ASSOCIATED MUSIC PUBLISHERS, INC.   ESC   1.75
MAURAT, E.
    IMPROMPTU NO. 2, OP. 34
        ASSOCIATED MUSIC PUBLISHERS, INC.   ESC   2.25
MAURAT, E.
    IMPROMPTU NO. 3, OP. 36
        ASSOCIATED MUSIC PUBLISHERS, INC.   ESC   2.75
MAURAT, E.
    NOCTURNE NO. 01, OP. 17
        ASSOCIATED MUSIC PUBLISHERS, INC.   ESC   1.10
MAURAT, E.
    NOCTURNE NO. 04, OP. 38
        ASSOCIATED MUSIC PUBLISHERS, INC.   ESC   3.00
MAURAT, E.
    PRELUDES--OP. 04 NO. 01--INTRODUCIMENTO
        ASSOCIATED MUSIC PUBLISHERS, INC.   ESC   .80
MAURAT, E.
    PRELUDES--OP. 04 NO. 02--CON SCLANCIO
        ASSOCIATED MUSIC PUBLISHERS, INC.   ESC   .75
MAURAT, E.
    PRELUDES--OP. 04 NO. 03--FRETTOLOSAMENTE
        ASSOCIATED MUSIC PUBLISHERS, INC.   ESC   .80
MAURAT, E.
    PRELUDES--OP. 04 NO. 04--DOLCEMENTE FERVOROSO
        ASSOCIATED MUSIC PUBLISHERS, INC.   ESC   .80
MAURAT, E.
    PRELUDES--OP. 04 NO. 05--ARDITAMENTE
        ASSOCIATED MUSIC PUBLISHERS, INC.   ESC   .80
MAURAT, E.
    PRELUDES--OP. 04 NO. 08--SDRUCCIOLONE
        ASSOCIATED MUSIC PUBLISHERS, INC.   ESC   .55
MAURAT, E.
    PRELUDES--OP. 04 NO. 09--PER LA SINISTRA--FOR THE LEFT HAND
        ASSOCIATED MUSIC PUBLISHERS, INC.   ESC   .55
MAUPAT, E.
    PRELUDES--OP. 04 NO. 10--LANGUIDAMENTE
        ASSOCIATED MUSIC PUBLISHERS, INC.   ESC   .75
MAURAT, E.
    PRELUDES--OP. 04 NO. 11--SERPEGGIANDO
        ASSOCIATED MUSIC PUBLISHERS, INC.   ESC   .55
MAURAT, E.
    PRELUDES--OP. 04 NO. 12--QUASI IMPROVISATO
        ASSOCIATED MUSIC PUBLISHERS, INC.   ESC   1.20
MAURAT, E.
    PRELUDES--OP. 27 NO. 32
        ASSOCIATED MUSIC PUBLISHERS, INC.   ESC   .95
MAURAT, E.
    PRELUDES--OP. 27 NO. 33
        ASSOCIATED MUSIC PUBLISHERS, INC.   ESC   1.25
MAUPAT, E.
    PRELUDES--OP. 27 NO. 34
        ASSOCIATED MUSIC PUBLISHERS, INC.   ESC   .95
MAUPAT, E.
    PRELUDES--OP. 27 NO. 35
        ASSOCIATED MUSIC PUBLISHERS, INC.   ESC   1.90
MAUPAT, E.
    PRELUDES--OP. 27 NO. 36
        ASSOCIATED MUSIC PUBLISHERS, INC.   ESC   .95
MAURICE, P.
    IL ETAIT UNE FOIS
        GERARD BILLAUDOT EDITIONS MUSICALES   1.60
MAURICE, P.
    MEMOIRES D'UN CHAT
        ELKAN-VOGEL, INC.   D   3.00
MAXIM, F.   SCHAUM, J.   1 1/2
    GRANDFATHER'S CLOCK
        SCHAUM PUBLICATIONS, INC.   .50
MAXIM, F.   1
    GRANDFATHER'S CLOCK, THE
        BOSTON MUSIC COMPANY   .50
MAXIM, F.
    ROOSTER, THE--FROM 'THE DANCING SCHOOL IN NOAH'S ARK
        G. SCHIRMER, INC.   .35
MAXWELL
    EBB TIDE
        THE BIG THREE MUSIC CORPORATION   00.95
MAXWELL *
    SHANGRI-LA
        THE BIG THREE MUSIC CORPORATION   00.95
MAXWELL, D.
    MY NOAH'S ARK
        BANKS AND SON LTD.   .80
MAY   1B
    GOING TO A PARTY
        MUSICORD PUBLICATIONS, INC.   .45
MAY   3
    SHOWER OF ROSES, REVERIE
        CENTURY MUSIC PUBLISHING COMPANY, INC.   2689   .40
MAY *
    BAL MASQUE CHEZ LES OIES
        FRANCO COLOMBO PUBLICATIONS   SAL   1.50
MAY, M.
    PLAYTIME
        BANKS AND SON LTD.   .40
MAYER   3
    BARN DANCE, 'SIS HOPKINS'
        CENTURY MUSIC PUBLISHING COMPANY, INC.   1412   .40
MAYER   MD
    DISTANT TIMES, DISTANT PLACES
        THEODORE PRESSER COMPANY   .75
MAYER   2
    MIDWAY MARCH
        CENTURY MUSIC PUBLISHING COMPANY, INC.   025   .40
MAYER   MD
    MOST IMPORTANT TRAIN, A
        THEODORE PRESSER COMPANY   .85
MAYER   3
    SIS HOPKINS, BARN DANCE
        CENTURY MUSIC PUBLISHING COMPANY, INC.   1412   .40
MAYER   MD
    SUBWAY IN THE SUNLIGHT
        THEODORE PRESSER COMPANY   .75
MAYER   HASTINGS
    SUMMER WIND
        WARNER BROTHERS PUBLISHERS   1.00
MAYER, C.
    GRACE, OP. 149 NO. 5
        BANKS AND SON LTD.   .55
MAYKAPAR
    IN THE GARDEN, WALTZ
        MCA MUSIC   .60
MAYKAPAR
    LITTLE SHEPHERD
        FREDERICK HARRIS MUSIC COMPANY   .60

MAYKAPAR
    PASSING FANCE, THE MOTH
        MCA MUSIC   .60
MAYKAPAR
    POLKA
        FREDERICK HARRIS MUSIC COMPANY   .60
MAYKAPAR
    POLKA
        MCA MUSIC   .60
MAYKAPAR
    STUDENT PIECE, DEWDROPS
        MCA MUSIC   .60
MAYOR   3
    MOTHER'S LOVE, MELODY
        CENTURY MUSIC PUBLISHING COMPANY, INC.   1894   .40
MAYR   DEL MAGLIO
    BIONDA IN GONDOLETTA, LA
        FRANCO COLOMBO PUBLICATIONS   129081   .60
MAYUZUMI
    BIBLE, THE
        THE BIG THREE MUSIC CORPORATION   00.95
MAZELLIER, J.
    BERCELONNETTE
        GERARD BILLAUDOT EDITIONS MUSICALES   1.10
MCADAMS, G.   2
    BEAUTIFUL MOONLIGHT
        VOLKWEIN BROS.   .25
MCADAMS, G.   2
    BUDDING BLOSSOMS
        VOLKWEIN BROS.   .30
MCADAMS, G.   2
    DREAM BIRD
        VOLKWEIN BROS.   .30
MCADAMS, G.   3
    GOLDEN DAWN
        VOLKWEIN BROS.   .25
MCADAMS, G.   2
    HOUR OF PARTING
        VOLKWEIN BROS.   .25
MCADAMS, G.   2
    LOUISE
        VOLKWEIN BROS.   .30
MCADAMS, G.   4
    LOVE'S LAST GREETING
        VOLKWEIN BROS.   .25
MCADAMS, G.   2
    MAYFLOWER
        VOLKWEIN BROS.   .25
MCADAMS, G.   2
    MINOTA
        VOLKWEIN BROS.   .30
MCADAMS, G.   3
    SWEET MEMORIES
        VOLKWEIN BROS.   00.35
MCADAMS, G.   4
    SWEET RECOLLECTIONS
        VOLKWEIN BROS.   00.40
MCADAMS, G.   4
    SWEET THOUGHTS OF YESTERDAY
        VOLKWEIN BROS.   00.35
MCADAMS, G.   2
    VIRDORA
        VOLKWEIN BROS.   00.25
MCADAMS, G.   2
    VISION OF GOLDEN SUNSET
        VOLKWEIN BROS.   00.25
MCBRIDE, R.   M
    SCHOOL BUS -- STOP
        THEODORE PRESSER COMPANY   .50
MCBRIDE, R.   M
    TALL IN THE SADDLE
        THEODORE PRESSER COMPANY   .50
MCCABE, J.
    FANTASY ON A THEME OF LISZT 1967
        NOVELLO AND COMPANY, LTD.   10.0176.00   2.25
MCCABE, J.
    VARIATIONS, OP. 22
        NOVELLO AND COMPANY, LTD.   10.0094.02   2.25
MCCARTHY *
    IRENE
        THE BIG THREE MUSIC CORPORATION   01.50
MCCLEARY
    JUMPING BEANS
        SHAWNEE PRESS, INC.   HB-5057   .60
MCCLUSKY
    BALL THREE
        BOSTON MUSIC COMPANY   .50
MCCLUSKY   2
    INDIAN SUN DANCE
        BOSTON MUSIC COMPANY   .50
MCCLUSKY   2
    NOVELETTE
        BOSTON MUSIC COMPANY   .50
MCCLUSKY   2
    PLAYFUL PONIES
        BOSTON MUSIC COMPANY   .50
MCCLUSKY   2
    SHADOW PLAY
        BOSTON MUSIC COMPANY   .50
MCCLUSKY   2
    SONG OF THE WANDERER
        BOSTON MUSIC COMPANY   .50
MCCLUSKY   2
    WIND IS WILD, THE
        PRO-ART PUBLICATIONS, INC.   542   .50
MCCREARY, D.   SCHAUM, J.   1
    PONY RIDE
        SCHAUM PUBLICATIONS, INC.   .50
MCCULLEN, A.   SCHAUM, J.   PREP
    BUBBLE GUM
        SCHAUM PUBLICATIONS, INC.   .50
MCDONALD, H.
    MONKEY SHINES NO. 1
        ELKAN-VOGEL, INC.   .50
MCDONALD, H.
    TONE PORTRAIT, A
        ASSOCIATED MUSIC PUBLISHERS, INC.   AMP   1.00
MCDOUGLE, A.
    LITTLE BALLAD
        G. SCHIRMER, INC.   .40
MCGINLEY
    PIANO SESSIONS - KINDERGARTEN SERIES‡ DANCING IN THE SQUARE
    --SUPP. MUSIC FOR MR. AND MRS. MIDDLE--
        SHAWNEE PRESS, INC.   .35
MCGINLEY
    PIANO SESSIONS - KINDERGARTEN SERIES‡ FIRST WALTZ --SUPP. MUSIC
    FOR MR. AND MRS. MIDDLE--
        SHAWNEE PRESS, INC.   .35

MCGINLEY
PIANO SESSIONS - KINDERGARTEN SERIES‡ FUN AT THE FAIR --SUPP.
MUSIC FOR TRUDY TREBLE AND TOM--
SHAWNEE PRESS, INC. .25
MCGINLEY
PIANO SESSIONS - KINDERGARTEN SERIES‡ LITTLE NOCTURNE --SUPP.
MUSIC FOR TRUDY TREBLE AND TOM--
SHAWNEE PRESS, INC. .25
MCGINLEY
PIANO SESSIONS - KINDERGARTEN SERIES‡ LONG, LONG AGO --SUPP.
MUSIC FOR MR. AND MRS. MIDDLE--
SHAWNEE PRESS, INC. .35
MCGINLEY
PIANO SESSIONS - KINDERGARTEN SERIES‡ ON TOP OF OLD SMOKY
--SUPP. MUSIC FOR MR. AND MRS. MIDDLE--
SHAWNEE PRESS, INC. .35
MCGINLEY
PIANO SESSIONS - KINDERGARTEN SERIES‡ RED RIVER VALLEY --SUPP.
MUSIC FOR MR. AND MRS. MIDDLE--
SHAWNEE PRESS, INC. .35
MCGINLEY
PIANO SESSIONS - KINDERGARTEN SERIES‡ TWINKLE, TWINKLE LITTLE
STAR --SUPP. MUSIC FOR TRUDY TREBLE AND TOM--
SHAWNEE PRESS, INC. .25
MCGINLEY
PIANO SESSIONS - KINDERGARTEN SERIES‡ WALK IN THE WOODS, A
--SUPP. MUSIC FOR MR. AND MRS. MIDDLE--
SHAWNEE PRESS, INC. .35
MCGRATH
WITCHES AT MIDNIGHT
CARL FISCHER, INC. P 1985 .50
MCGRAW 1
ANTIQUE SNUFFBOX, THE
ELKAN-VOGEL, INC. .50
MCGRAW 1 1/2
ANTIQUE SNUFFBOX, THE
ELKAN-VOGEL, INC. .50
MCGRAW
APPALACHIAN SONG
BOSTON MUSIC COMPANY .50
MCGRAW
BAGATELLE
BOSTON MUSIC COMPANY .50
MCGRAW
BLACK NOTE POLKA
BOSTON MUSIC COMPANY .50
MCGRAW 2
IN A CANOE
BELWIN-MILLS PUBLISHING CORPORATION .60
MCGRAW 2
JACK RABBIT
BOSTON MUSIC COMPANY .50
MCGRAW 1
JUGGLER CLOWN, THE
CENTURY MUSIC PUBLISHING COMPANY, INC. 4408 .40
MCGRAW 1
KANGAROO, THE
CENTURY MUSIC PUBLISHING COMPANY, INC. 4363 .40
MCGRAW 2
LITTLE ARGUMENT, A
THEODORE PRESSER COMPANY .50
MCGRAW 2
LOWLAND LULLABY
BOSTON MUSIC COMPANY .50
MCGRAW 1 1/2
MARCH OF THE PENGUINS
THEODORE PRESSER COMPANY .50
MCGRAW 2
MINUET
THEODORE PRESSER COMPANY .50
MCGRAW 1 1/2 - 2
PING PONG
ELKAN-VOGEL, INC. .50
MCGRAW 1-2
PING-PONG
ELKAN-VOGEL, INC. .50
MCGRAW 1
PIRATES HORNPIPE
CENTURY MUSIC PUBLISHING COMPANY, INC. 4362 .40
MCGRAW 1
SONG OF THE SAGEBRUSH
BOSTON MUSIC COMPANY .50
MCGRAW 2
STROLLING ALONG
BOSTON MUSIC COMPANY .50
MCGRAW 3
WHIRLING ALONG
WILLIS MUSIC COMPANY .40
MCGRAW 1
WISTFUL WALTZ
BOSTON MUSIC COMPANY .50
MCHALE, M. 2-3
ARABIAN CAMPFIRE
CENTURY MUSIC PUBLISHING COMPANY, INC. 4171 .40
MCHALE, M. 3
CORN HUSKIN'
THEODORE PRESSER COMPANY .50
MCHALE, M. 2
DUTCH DANCE
BELWIN-MILLS PUBLISHING CORPORATION .60
MCHALE, M. 2-3
GRASSHOPPERS
CENTURY MUSIC PUBLISHING COMPANY, INC. 4229 .40
MCHALE, M. 2
HARVEST DANCE
CENTURY MUSIC PUBLISHING COMPANY, INC. 4223 .40
MCHALE, M. 2
HOP TOADS
CENTURY MUSIC PUBLISHING COMPANY, INC. 4170 .40
MCHALE, M.
ICICLES
G. SCHIRMER, INC. .35
MCHALE, M. 3
IN THE DAYS OF CHOPIN
THEODORE PRESSER COMPANY .50
MCHALE, M. 1
JOLLY POSTMAN, THE
THEODORE PRESSER COMPANY .50
MCHALE, M. 2
JUMPING BEANS
BELWIN-MILLS PUBLISHING CORPORATION .60
MCHALE, M.
MARCH OF THE CORNSTALKS
G. SCHIRMER, INC. .35
MCHALE, M. 1 1/2
PRIVATE PETE
BELWIN-MILLS PUBLISHING CORPORATION .60

MCHALE, M.
PUSSY WILLOWS
G. SCHIRMER, INC. .40
MCHALE, M. 3
QUILTIN' BEE
CENTURY MUSIC PUBLISHING COMPANY, INC. 4211 .40
MCHALE, M. 3
RIPPLING STREAM
THEODORE PRESSER COMPANY .50
MCHALE, M. 2
SCARED SPOOK, THE
THEODORE PRESSER COMPANY .50
MCHALE, M. 1
WALTZING PUSSYCATS
BELWIN-MILLS PUBLISHING CORPORATION .60
MCHALE, M. 2 1/2
WESTWARD HO
THEODORE PRESSER COMPANY .50
MCHALE, M. 2 1/2
ZOO PARADE, THE
THEODORE PRESSER COMPANY .50
MCHUGH SCHAUM, J. 2
EXACTLY LIKE YOU
SCHAUM PUBLICATIONS, INC. .75
MCHUGH SCHAUM, J. 2 1/2
ON THE SUNNY SIDE OF THE STREET
SCHAUM PUBLICATIONS, INC. .75
MCINTYRE, E.
CELLO PLAYER, OP. 12 NO. 5
BELWIN-MILLS PUBLISHING CORPORATION 28158 .60
MCINTYRE, E. 2
INDIAN DANCE IN THE FIRELIGHT
BOSTON MUSIC COMPANY .50
MCKAY, G. 1
CALL OF THE CANYON
THEODORE PRESSER COMPANY .50
MCKAY, G. E
DANCE PASTORALLE -- RONDINO
THEODORE PRESSER COMPANY .50
MCKAY, G. MD
DANCE SUITE NO. 2
THEODORE PRESSER COMPANY .50
MCKAY, G. 2 1/2
ECHOING LAUGHTER
CENTURY MUSIC PUBLISHING COMPANY, INC. 031 .40
MCKAY, G. M
EXCURSION
THEODORE PRESSER COMPANY .50
MCKAY, G.
FOLK SONG STORIES
BOOSEY AND HAWKES, INC. .85
MCKAY, G. VE
FROM THE NORTH WOODS
OXFORD UNIVERSITY PRESS 93.325 .40
MCKAY, G. 1 1/2
MEN AT WORK
THEODORE PRESSER COMPANY .50
MCKAY, G. 2
MY WISH FOR YOUR HAPPINESS
BELWIN-MILLS PUBLISHING CORPORATION .60
MCKAY, G. 2 1/2
NAVAJO LULLABY
THEODORE PRESSER COMPANY .50
MCKAY, G. 3
ON A MAY MORNING
BELWIN-MILLS PUBLISHING CORPORATION .60
MCKAY, G. 2
PRAIRIE VISTA
THEODORE PRESSER COMPANY .50
MCKAY, G.
PROCESSION TRISTE
FRANCO COLOMBO PUBLICATIONS SAL 1.75
MCKAY, G. 3
PROMENADE
BOSTON MUSIC COMPANY .50
MCKAY, G. 3
REMEMBERED HAPPINESS, A
BELWIN-MILLS PUBLISHING CORPORATION .60
MCKAY, G.
SAGEBRUSH COUNTRY
SAM FOX PUBLISHING COMPANY, INC. 1.50
MCKAY, G. 2
TRAIN TRACKS
THEODORE PRESSER COMPANY .50
MCKAY, G.
VISTAS
SAM FOX PUBLISHING COMPANY, INC. 1.00
MCKEE
CECILE WALTZ
BELWIN-MILLS PUBLISHING CORPORATION .60
MCKEE
CECILE WALTZ
FRANCO COLOMBO PUBLICATIONS 116067 .50
MCKEE
MILLICENT WALTZ
FRANCO COLOMBO PUBLICATIONS 116112 .50
MCKEE
MINOR AND MAJOR - ORIENTAL WALTZ
FRANCO COLOMBO PUBLICATIONS 116061 .50
MCKINNEY 2
CHRISTMAS LULLABY, A
BELWIN-MILLS PUBLISHING CORPORATION .60
MCKUEN
MIDNIGHT PETE
MCA MUSIC 1.00
MCLEAN, D.
AMERICAN PIE
THE BIG THREE MUSIC CORPORATION 00.95
MCQUATTIE, S. ASCHERBERG *
SICILIANA
G. SCHIRMER, INC. .40
MCSHANN
VINE STREET BOOGIE
MCA MUSIC 1.00
MCSHANN *
HOOTIE BLUES
MCA MUSIC 1.00
MCSHANN *
SWINGMATISH
MCA MUSIC 1.00
MCSWEEN, F. W. 2
DANCE OF THE PAPER DOLLS
BELWIN-MILLS PUBLISHING CORPORATION .60
MCSWEEN, F. W. 3 1/2
HAWAIIAN GUITARS
BELWIN-MILLS PUBLISHING CORPORATION .60

MCSWEEN, F. W.   4
  HINDU DANCING GIRL
    BELWIN-MILLS PUBLISHING CORPORATION   .60
MCSWEEN, F. W.   2 1/2
  JOHNNY-JUMP-UPS
    BELWIN-MILLS PUBLISHING CORPORATION   .60
MCSWEEN, F. W.   3
  MARCH OF THE BAGPIPES
    BELWIN-MILLS PUBLISHING CORPORATION   .60
MCSWEEN, F. W.   3
  MOSQUITO
    BELWIN-MILLS PUBLISHING CORPORATION   .60
MCSWEEN, F. W.   3 1/2
  ON THE LAGOON
    BELWIN-MILLS PUBLISHING CORPORATION   .60
MCSWEEN, F. W.   2 1/2
  POGO STICK PARADE
    BELWIN-MILLS PUBLISHING CORPORATION   .60
MCSWEEN, F. W.   2 1/2
  SWAYING DAFFODILS
    BELWIN-MILLS PUBLISHING CORPORATION   .60
MCSWEEN, F. W.   2 1/2
  WHISTLING BOY
    BELWIN-MILLS PUBLISHING CORPORATION   .60
MEACHAM, F.
  AMERICAN PATROL
    ASHLEY DEALERS SERVICE, INC.   ES   .95
MEACHAM, F.   4
  AMERICAN PATROL
    CENTURY MUSIC PUBLISHING COMPANY, INC. 3478   .40
MEACHAM, F.   4
  AMERICAN PATROL
    VOLKWEIN BROS.   .50
MEACHAM, F.   MESSINA, J.   1
  AMERICAN PATROL
    VOLKWEIN BROS.   .35
MEACHAM, F.   4
  AMERICAN PATROL
    VOLKWEIN BROS.   .75
MEACHAM, F.   WALLIS   2
  AMERICAN PATROL
    WILLIS MUSIC COMPANY   .40
MEACHAM, F.   SCHAUM, J.   1 1/2
  AMERICAN PATROL MARCH
    BELWIN-MILLS PUBLISHING CORPORATION   .50
MEACHAM, F.   ECKSTEIN
  AMERICAN PATROL MARCH
    CARL FISCHER, INC.   S 2279   .60
MEACHAM, F.   MITTLER   2A
  AMERICAN PATROL MARCH
    MUSICORD PUBLICATIONS, INC.   .45
MEACHAM, F.   KING, S.
  AMERICAN PATROL MARCH
    SHAWNEE PRESS, INC.   HB-5047   .40
MEACHAM, F.   ECISTEIN
  AMERICAN PATROL MARCH --SIMPLIFIED--
    CARL FISCHER, INC.   P 2960   .50
MEACHAM, F.   4
  COME BACK TO ERIN, TRANSPOSED
    CENTURY MUSIC PUBLISHING COMPANY, INC. 1061   .40
MEACHAM, F.   4
  LISTEN TO THE MOCKING BIRD
    CENTURY MUSIC PUBLISHING COMPANY, INC. 1060   .40
MEACHAM, F.--ED   MEACHAM, F.   3
  MARCHING THRU GEORGIA
    CENTURY MUSIC PUBLISHING COMPANY, INC. 1263   .40
MEACHAM, F.--ED   MEACHAM, F.   4
  OLD BLACK JOE, VARIATIONS
    CENTURY MUSIC PUBLISHING COMPANY, INC. 1045   .40
MEACHAM, F.--ED   MEACHAM, F.   4
  OLD OAKEN BUCKET, THE
    CENTURY MUSIC PUBLISHING COMPANY, INC. 1062   .40
MEARES, J. C.   3
  LOVE'S PARADISE
    VOLKWEIN BROS.   .35
MECHEM, K.
  SONATA
    E. C. SCHIRMER MUSIC COMPANY   240   01.00
MECHEM, K.
  SUITE
    E. C. SCHIRMER MUSIC COMPANY   239   01.00
MEDINA--ED.   MEDINA
  DARK EYES
    ASSOCIATED MUSIC PUBLISHERS, INC.   UME   .50
MEDINA--ED.   MEDINA
  TWO GUITARS
    ASSOCIATED MUSIC PUBLISHERS, INC.   UME   .50
MEDTNER, N.   D
  DANZA FESTIVA, OP. 38, NO. 3
    C. F. PETERS CORPORATION   ZM1701 2.00
MEDTNER, N.
  FAIRY TALE, OP. 20 NO. 1
    BOOSEY AND HAWKES, INC.   .90
MEDTNER, N.
  FAIRY TALE, OP. 26 NO. 1
    EDWARD B. MARKS MUSIC CORPORATION   01.00
MEDTNER, N.
  FAIRY TALE, OP. 26 NO. 1
    EDWARD B. MARKS MUSIC CORPORATION   01.00
MEDTNER, N.
  FAIRY TALE, OP. 26 NO. 2
    EDWARD B. MARKS MUSIC CORPORATION   01.00
MEDTNER, N.
  FAIRY TALE, OP. 26 NO. 4
    EDWARD B. MARKS MUSIC CORPORATION   01.00
MEDTNER, N.   D
  FAIRY TALE, OP. 51, NO. 1
    C. F. PETERS CORPORATION   ZM1020 1.25
MEDTNER, N.   D
  FAIRY TALE, OP. 51, NO. 2
    C. F. PETERS CORPORATION   ZM1021 1.25
MEDTNER, N.   D
  FAIRY TALE, OP. 51, NO. 3
    C. F. PETERS CORPORATION   ZM1022 1.25
MEDTNER, N.   M-D
  FAIRY TALE, OP. 51, NO. 4
    C. F. PETERS CORPORATION   ZM1023 1.25
MEDTNER, N.   D
  FAIRY TALE, OP. 51, NO. 5
    C. F. PETERS CORPORATION   ZM1024 1.25
MEDTNER, N.   D
  FAIRY TALE, OP. 51, NO. 6
    C. F. PETERS CORPORATION   ZM1025 1.25
MEDTNER, N.
  FAIRY TALES, OP. 26 --COMPLETE
    EDWARD B. MARKS MUSIC CORPORATION   01.25

MEDTNER, N.
  FOUR FAIRY TALES, OP. 26
    BOOSEY AND HAWKES, INC.   1.75
MEDTNEP, N.
  IMPROVISATION, OP. 31 NO. 1
    BOOSEY AND HAWKES, INC.   1.50
MEDTNER, N.
  NOVELETTE, OP. 17 NO. 1
    BOOSEY AND HAWKES, INC.   .90
MEDTNER, N.
  SONATA-CONTE, OP. 25 NO. 1
    BOOSEY AND HAWKES, INC.   2.00
MEDTNER, N.
  SONATA, OP. 5
    BOOSEY AND HAWKES, INC.   3.00
MEDTNER, N.   FREY
  SONATEN-TRIADE, OP. 11 NO. 3
    ASSOCIATED MUSIC PUBLISHERS, INC.   SIM   2.00
MEEK
  TELSTAR
    EDWARD B. MARKS MUSIC CORPORATION   01.00
MEHEGAN, J.
  JAZZ BOURREE
    SOUTHERN MUSIC COMPANY   .75
MEHEGAN, J.
  STYLES FOR THE JAZZ PIANIST, BK. 2
    SAM FOX PUBLISHING COMPANY, INC.   3.00
MEHUL, E. H.
  MINUET
    BANKS AND SON LTD.   .40
MEISTER, W.   2
  FORGET ME NOT
    WILLIS MUSIC COMPANY   .40
MELACHRINO, G.
  PORTRAIT OF A LADY
    BELWIN-MILLS PUBLISHING CORPORATION 20207   .85
MELACHRINO, G.
  SONG OF THE ORCHID
    BELWIN-MILLS PUBLISHING CORPORATION 20272   .85
MELECCI, A.
  BALLERINA
    FREDERICK HARRIS MUSIC COMPANY   .60
MELECCI, A.
  DANCE CAPRICE
    FREDERICK HARRIS MUSIC COMPANY   .60
MELECCI, A.
  DUTCH DANCE
    FREDERICK HARRIS MUSIC COMPANY   .60
MELECCI, A.
  HUMORESQUE
    FREDERICK HARRIS MUSIC COMPANY   .55
MELECCI, A.
  INTRODUCTION TO HANON
    FREDERICK HARRIS MUSIC COMPANY   .90
MELECCI, A.
  JENNY LIND WALTZ
    FREDERICK HARRIS MUSIC COMPANY   .60
MELECCI, A.
  KITES IN THE WIND
    FREDERICK HARRIS MUSIC COMPANY   .60
MELECCI, A.
  L'HABITANT EN ROUTE
    FREDERICK HARRIS MUSIC COMPANY   .60
MELECCI, A.
  LA PETITE POLKA CANADIENNE
    FREDERICK HARRIS MUSIC COMPANY   .60
MELECCI, A.   BERLIN, B.
  MAGIC PIANO IN ORCHESTRA LAND, THE
    FREDERICK HARRIS MUSIC COMPANY   1.50
MELECCI, A.
  MUSIC BOX SONATINA, THE
    FREDERICK HARRIS MUSIC COMPANY   .60
MELECCI, A.
  POODLE DANCE
    FREDERICK HARRIS MUSIC COMPANY   .60
MELECCI, A.
  PRELUDE
    FREDERICK HARRIS MUSIC COMPANY   .60
MELECCI, A.
  ROCKY MOUNTAIN SKETCHES
    FREDERICK HARRIS MUSIC COMPANY   1.15
MELECCI, A.
  SONATINA
    FREDERICK HARRIS MUSIC COMPANY   .60
MELECCI, A.
  SONATINA IN THE STYLE OF MOZART
    FREDERICK HARRIS MUSIC COMPANY   .60
MELECCI, A.
  SOUTH OF THE BORDER
    FREDERICK HARRIS MUSIC COMPANY   .75
MELECCI, A.
  SUNNY SKIES
    FREDERICK HARRIS MUSIC COMPANY   .60
MELECCI, A.
  TEDDY BEARS ON PARADE
    FREDERICK HARRIS MUSIC COMPANY   .60
MELECCI, A.
  TO THE SETTING SUN
    FREDERICK HARRIS MUSIC COMPANY   .60
MELECCI, A.
  TOBOGGAN RIDE
    FREDERICK HARRIS MUSIC COMPANY   .60
MELECCI, A.
  TOY SOLDIER
    FREDERICK HARRIS MUSIC COMPANY   .60
MELECCI, A.
  TOYS ON PARADE
    FREDERICK HARRIS MUSIC COMPANY   .60
MELECCI, A.
  WALTZ OF THE SHADOWS
    FREDERICK HARRIS MUSIC COMPANY   .60
MELECCI, A.
  WILLOWS, THE
    FREDERICK HARRIS MUSIC COMPANY   .60
MELECCI, A.
  ZOO, THE
    FREDERICK HARRIS MUSIC COMPANY   .60
MELIS, J.
  VOLARE
    THE BIG THREE MUSIC CORPORATION   00.95
MELLERS, W.   3-5
  CAT CHARMS
    NOVELLO AND COMPANY, LTD.   21.0024.10 1.15
MELLICHAMP, N.   1
  GNOME PASSES BY, A
    CENTURY MUSIC PUBLISHING COMPANY, INC. 4176   .40

MELLICHAMP, N.   1
  SOLDIERS MARCH
    CENTURY MUSIC PUBLISHING COMPANY, INC.   4356   .40
MELLICHAMP, N.   2
  SQUIRRELS
    CENTURY MUSIC PUBLISHING COMPANY, INC.   4242   .40
MELO GORIGOYTIA, H.
  MANCHAS DE COLOR
    EDITORIAL COOPERATIVA INTER-AMERICANA   00.85
MELOCCHI, V.
  QUADRETTI ARMONIOSI
    EDIZIONI BERBEN   EB 228   1.50
MELVIN, B.   3
  BUGLER'S NIGHTMARE
    BELWIN-MILLS PUBLISHING CORPORATION   .60
MELVIN, B.   4
  CAPRICE MODERNE
    BELWIN-MILLS PUBLISHING CORPORATION   .60
MELVIN, B.   2-3
  FLYING BIRDS
    PRO-ART PUBLICATIONS, INC.   131   .50
MELVIN, B.   3
  FRISKY FAWN
    PRO-ART PUBLICATIONS, INC.   313   .50
MELVIN, B.   1
  HAPPY FROGMEN
    PRO-ART PUBLICATIONS, INC.   154   .50
MELVIN, B.   2
  HYDROFOIL RIDE
    PRO-ART PUBLICATIONS, INC.   282   .50
MELVIN, B.   2
  ICEBERG BOOGIE
    BELWIN-MILLS PUBLISHING CORPORATION   .60
MELVIN, B.   2-3
  IL CAVALLINO DA CORSA - THE LITTLE RACEHORSE
    PRO-ART PUBLICATIONS, INC.   155   .50
MELVIN, B.   2
  IL GUITARRISTA
    BELWIN-MILLS PUBLISHING CORPORATION   .60
MELVIN, B.   4
  LA CUCARACHA BAILARINA
    BELWIN-MILLS PUBLISHING CORPORATION   .60
MELVIN, B.   3
  LI'L RED CABBOSE
    BELWIN-MILLS PUBLISHING CORPORATION   .60
MELVIN, B.   3 1/2
  MOOD MODERNE
    BELWIN-MILLS PUBLISHING CORPORATION   .60
MELVIN, B.   1
  MY BUDGIE
    PRO-ART PUBLICATIONS, INC.   130   .50
MELVIN, B.   2-3
  POLTERGEIST, THE
    PRO-ART PUBLICATIONS, INC.   249   .50
MELVIN, B.   1 1/2
  RIDING THE RANGE
    BELWIN-MILLS PUBLISHING CORPORATION   .60
MELVIN, B.   2
  ROLLING WAVES
    BELWIN-MILLS PUBLISHING CORPORATION   .60
MELVIN, B.   2
  SAIL BOATS ON PARADE
    BELWIN-MILLS PUBLISHING CORPORATION   .60
MELVIN, B.   1
  SEA WALTZ, THE
    BELWIN-MILLS PUBLISHING CORPORATION   .60
MELVIN, B.   2 1/2
  SHIMMERING IVORIES
    BELWIN-MILLS PUBLISHING CORPORATION   .60
MELVIN, B.   2
  STAGECOACH ADVENTURE
    BELWIN-MILLS PUBLISHING CORPORATION   .60
MELVIN, B.   2
  SWING THE SCALE
    BELWIN-MILLS PUBLISHING CORPORATION   .60
MELVIN, B.   2
  TRIP TO MARS
    PRO-ART PUBLICATIONS, INC.   132   .50
MENDEL, S.   2
  COUNTRY GARDENS
    WILLIS MUSIC COMPANY   .40
MENDEL, S.   1 1-2
  GREENSLEEVES
    WILLIS MUSIC COMPANY   .40
MENDEL, S.   2 1/2
  HYMN TO THE SUN
    WILLIS MUSIC COMPANY   .40
MENDEL, S.--ED   MENDEL, S.   2
  AFTER THE BALL IS OVER
    WILLIS MUSIC COMPANY   .40
MENDELSSOHN
  ALLEGRETTO, OP. 72 NO. 3
    FREDERICK HARRIS MUSIC COMPANY   .30
MENDELSSOHN
  ALLEGRO ASSAI
    NOVELLO AND COMPANY, LTD.   10.0096.09   1.15
MENDELSSOHN
  ANDANTE AND RONDO CAPRICCIOSO
    NOVELLO AND COMPANY, LTD.   10.0097.07   1.15
MENDELSSOHN   5
  ANDANTE AND RONDO CAPRICCIOSO, OP. 14
    CENTURY MUSIC PUBLISHING COMPANY, INC.   376   .40
MENDELSSOHN   3
  ANDANTE CANTABILE, VIOLIN CONCERTO
    CENTURY MUSIC PUBLISHING COMPANY, INC.   1916   .40
MENDELSSOHN   ROLFE, W.   3
  ATHALIA, PRIESTS' MARCH, EASY
    CENTURY MUSIC PUBLISHING COMPANY, INC.   3395   .40
MENDELSSOHN   KREUTZER
  BOAT SONG
    BOSTON MUSIC COMPANY   .50
MENDELSSOHN   STERNBERG
  CAPPICCIO BRILLANTE
    G. SCHIRMER, INC.   L1187   1.25
MENDELSSOHN   CORTOT
  CAPRICCIO IN F-SHARP MINOR, OP. 5
    FRANCO COLOMBO PUBLICATIONS   SAL   3.00
MENDELSSOHN   4
  CAPRICCIO, SCHERZO
    CENTURY MUSIC PUBLISHING COMPANY, INC.   2443   .40
MENDELSSOHN   RUTHARDT
  CONCERTO NO. 01 IN G MINOR, OP. 25
    G. SCHIRMER, INC.   L61   1.25
MENDELSSOHN   RUTHARDT
  CONCERTO NO. 02 IN D MINOR, OP. 40
    G. SCHIRMER, INC.   L62   1.50

MENDELSSOHN   4
  CONFIDENCE, OP. 19 NO. 4
    CENTURY MUSIC PUBLISHING COMPANY, INC.   171   .40
MENDELSSOHN   4
  CONSOLATION
    WILLIS MUSIC COMPANY   .30
MENDELSSOHN   4
  CONSOLATION, OP. 30 NO. 3
    CENTURY MUSIC PUBLISHING COMPANY, INC.   174   .40
MENDELSSOHN   SAUER   4
  EIN SOMMERNACHTS TRAUM -- HOCHZEITSMARSCH OP. 61 NO. 9
    SCHOTT   06707 1/2   1.00
MENDELSSOHN   CORTOT
  ETUDE IN F, OP. 104 NO. 2
    FRANCO COLOMBO PUBLICATIONS   SAL   2.50
MENDELSSOHN   MONTANI
  FANTASY, OP. 28
    FRANCO COLOMBO PUBLICATIONS   ER2423   .75
MENDELSSOHN
  FINGAL'S CAVE -- THE HEBRIDES -- OVERTURE
    CENTURY MUSIC PUBLISHING COMPANY, INC.   1.25
MENDELSSOHN   2-3
  FRUEHLINGSLIED, EASY
    CENTURY MUSIC PUBLISHING COMPANY, INC.   2158   .40
MENDELSSOHN   GOERDELER   4
  HARK THE HERALD ANGELS SING
    THEODORE PRESSER COMPANY   .50
MENDELSSOHN   5
  HUNTING SONG, OP. 19 NO. 3
    CENTURY MUSIC PUBLISHING COMPANY, INC.   1674   .40
MENDELSSOHN   4
  MARCH OF THE PRIESTS, ATHALIA
    CENTURY MUSIC PUBLISHING COMPANY, INC.   1531   .40
MENDELSSOHN   ROLFE, W.   3
  MARCH OF THE PRIESTS, EASY
    CENTURY MUSIC PUBLISHING COMPANY, INC.   3395   .40
MENDELSSOHN   5
  MARCH, FROM CAPRICCIO, OP. 22
    THEODORE PRESSER COMPANY   .50
MENDELSSOHN   SMITH   5
  MIDSUMMER NIGHT'S DREAM
    CENTURY MUSIC PUBLISHING COMPANY, INC.   1332   .40
MENDELSSOHN   M
  MIDSUMMER NIGHT'S DREAM. COMPLETE. ENGLISH-FRENCH TEXT
    C. F. PETERS CORPORATION   C95   10.00
MENDELSSOHN   M
  MIDSUMMER NIGHT'S DREAM. COMPLETE. GERMAN TEXT
    C. F. PETERS CORPORATION   1751   6.00
MENDELSSOHN   TAGLIAPIETRA
  MIDSUMMER NIGHT'S DREAM, A - OVERTURE
    FRANCO COLOMBO PUBLICATIONS   ER1002   1.00
MENDELSSOHN
  MIDSUMMER NIGHT'S DREAM, A - WEDDING MARCH
    FRANCO COLOMBO PUBLICATIONS   128358   1.00
MENDELSSOHN   CHIESA
  MIDSUMMER NIGHT'S DREAM, A - WEDDING MARCH
    FRANCO COLOMBO PUBLICATIONS   107507   .60
MENDELSSOHN   KLAUSER
  MIDSUMMER NIGHT'S DREAM, A - WEDDING MARCH
    G. SCHIRMER, INC.   .50
MENDELSSOHN   ROLFE   3
  MIDSUMMER NIGHT'S DREAM, NOCTURNE
    CENTURY MUSIC PUBLISHING COMPANY, INC.   4160   .40
MENDELSSOHN   SMITH   5
  MIDSUMMER NIGHT'S DREAM, OP. 76 - PARAPHRASE DE CONCERT
    THEODORE PRESSER COMPANY   .60
MENDELSSOHN   STEINER   3
  MOMENTS WITH MENDELSSOHN
    BELWIN-MILLS PUBLISHING CORPORATION   .60
MENDELSSOHN   ROLFE, W.   3
  NOCTURNE, MIDSUMMER NIGHT'S DREAM
    CENTURY MUSIC PUBLISHING COMPANY, INC.   4160   .40
MENDELSSOHN
  ON WINGS OF SONG
    CARL FISCHER, INC.   S 1133   .50
MENDELSSOHN   DEL MAGLIO
  ON WINGS OF SONG
    FRANCO COLOMBO PUBLICATIONS   129092   .60
MENDELSSOHN   LOEW *
  ON WINGS OF SONG
    G. SCHIRMER, INC.   .50
MENDELSSOHN   THOMPSON, J.   5
  ON WINGS OF SONG
    WILLIS MUSIC COMPANY   .40
MENDELSSOHN
  PHANTASIE IN F SHARP MINOR, OP. 28
    G. SCHIRMER, INC.   .90
MENDELSSOHN
  PRAELUDIUM IN E MINOR
    G. SCHIRMER, INC.   .50
MENDELSSOHN   CORTOT
  PRELUDE AND FUGUE IN E MINOR, OP. 35 NO. 1
    FRANCO COLOMBO PUBLICATIONS   SAL   2.50
MENDELSSOHN
  PRELUDE AND FUGUE IN E MINOR, OP. 35 NO. 1
    G. SCHIRMER, INC.   .80
MENDELSSOHN   CORTOT
  PRESTO FROM THE FANTASY IN F-SHARP MINOR, OP. 28
    FRANCO COLOMBO PUBLICATIONS   SAL   2.75
MENDELSSOHN   4
  PRIESTS' MARCH, ATHALIA
    CENTURY MUSIC PUBLISHING COMPANY, INC.   1531   .40
MENDELSSOHN   STERNBERG
  RONDO BRILLANTE, OP. 29
    G. SCHIRMER, INC.   L1188   1.25
MENDELSSOHN   ECKSTEIN
  RONDO CAPRICCIOSO IN E, OP. 14
    CARL FISCHER, INC.   S 1327   .75
MENDELSSOHN   SAUER   5
  RONDO CAPRICCIOSO OP. 14
    SCHOTT   0537 1/2   1.00
MENDELSSOHN   KULLAK   M-D
  RONDO CAPRICCIOSO, OP. 14
    C. F. PETERS CORPORATION   1704F   1.25
MENDELSSOHN   MONTANI
  RONDO CAPRICCIOSO, OP. 14
    FRANCO COLOMBO PUBLICATIONS   128448   1.00
MENDELSSOHN   CORTOT
  RONDO CAPRICCIOSO, OP. 14
    FRANCO COLOMBO PUBLICATIONS   SAL   2.50
MENDELSSOHN
  RONDO CAPRICCIOSO, OP. 14
    G. SCHIRMER, INC.   .75
MENDELSSOHN   ROMANIELLO
  SCHERZO A CAPPICCIO IN F-SHARP MINOR
    FRANCO COLOMBO PUBLICATIONS   128413   .75

MENDELSSOHN　　　　　CESI
　SCHERZO IN E MINOR, OP. 16 NO. 2
　　FRANCO COLOMBO PUBLICATIONS　　　　BA8896　　.75
MENDELSSOHN　　　　　CORTOT
　SCHERZO IN E MINOR, OP. 16 NO. 2
　　FRANCO COLOMBO PUBLICATIONS　　　　SAL　　　2.25
MENDELSSOHN　　　　　OESTERLE
　SCHERZO IN E MINOR, OP. 16 NO. 2
　　G. SCHIRMER, INC.　　　　　　　　　　　　　.50
MENDELSSOHN　　　　　SAUER　　　　　5
　SCHERZO IN E-MOLL OP. 16 NO. 2
　　SCHOTT　　　　　　　　　　　　　0540 1/2　1.00
MENDELSSOHN　　　　　　　　　　　4
　SCHERZO, CAPRICCIO, OP. 16 NO. 2
　　CENTURY MUSIC PUBLISHING COMPANY, INC.　2443　　.40
MENDELSSOHN　　　　　RACHMANINOFF, S.
　SCHERZO, FROM A MIDSUMMER NIGHT'S DREAM
　　BELWIN-MILLS PUBLISHING CORPORATION　　　1.50
MENDELSSOHN　　　　　　　　　　　6
　SCHERZO, OP. 16 NO. 2
　　THEODORE PRESSER COMPANY　　　　　　　.50
MENDELSSOHN
　SONGS WITHOUT WORDS, NO. 01--SWEET REMEMBRANCE, OP. 19 NO. 1
　　G. SCHIRMER, INC.　　　　　　　　　　　　.40
MENDELSSOHN
　SONGS WITHOUT WORDS, NO. 03--HUNTING-SONG, OP. 19 NO. 3
　　G. SCHIRMER, INC.　　　　　　　　　　　　.50
MENDELSSOHN
　SONGS WITHOUT WORDS, NO. 04--CONFIDENCE, OP. 19 NO. 4
　　G. SCHIRMER, INC.　　　　　　　　　　　　.35
MENDELSSOHN
　SONGS WITHOUT WORDS, NO. 06--VENETIAN BOAT-SONG NO. 1, OP. 19
　NO. 6
　　G. SCHIRMER, INC.　　　　　　　　　　　　.40
MENDELSSOHN
　SONGS WITHOUT WORDS, NO. 09--CONSOLATION, OP. 30 NO. 3
　　G. SCHIRMER, INC.　　　　　　　　　　　　.30
MENDELSSOHN
　SONGS WITHOUT WORDS, NO. 11--THE BROOK, OP. 30 NO. 5
　　G. SCHIRMER, INC.　　　　　　　　　　　　.30
MENDELSSOHN
　SONGS WITHOUT WORDS, NO. 12--VENETIAN BOAT-SONG NO. 2, OP. 30
　NO. 6
　　G. SCHIRMER, INC.　　　　　　　　　　　　.35
MENDELSSOHN
　SONGS WITHOUT WORDS, NO. 18--DUET, OP. 38 NO. 6
　　,G. SCHIRMER, INC.　　　　　　　　　　　　.50
MENDELSSOHN
　SONGS WITHOUT WORDS, NO. 29--VENETIAN BOAT-SONG NO. 3, OP. 62
　NO. 5
　　G. SCHIRMER, INC.　　　　　　　　　　　　.30
MENDELSSOHN
　SONGS WITHOUT WORDS, NO. 30--SPRING-SONG, OP. 62 NO. 6
　　G. SCHIRMER, INC.　　　　　　　　　　　　.50
MENDELSSOHN
　SONGS WITHOUT WORDS, NO. 34--SPINNING-SONG, OP. 67 NO. 4
　　G. SCHIRMER, INC.　　　　　　　　　　　　.50
MENDELSSOHN
　SONGS WITHOUT WORDS, NO. 45--TARANTELLA, OP. 102 NO. 3
　　G. SCHIRMER, INC.　　　　　　　　　　　　.30
MENDELSSOHN　　　　　　　　　　　5
　SONGS WITHOUT WORDS, OP. 19 NO. 3
　　CENTURY MUSIC PUBLISHING COMPANY, INC.　1674　　.40
MENDELSSOHN　　　　　　　　　　　4
　SONGS WITHOUT WORDS, OP. 19 NO. 4
　　CENTURY MUSIC PUBLISHING COMPANY, INC.　171　　.40
MENDELSSOHN　　　　　　　　　　　3
　SONGS WITHOUT WORDS, OP. 19 NO. 6
　　CENTURY MUSIC PUBLISHING COMPANY, INC.　1177　　.40
MENDELSSOHN　　　　　　　　　　　4
　SONGS WITHOUT WORDS, OP. 30 NO. 3
　　CENTURY MUSIC PUBLISHING COMPANY, INC.　174　　.40
MENDELSSOHN　　　　　　　　　　　4
　SONGS WITHOUT WORDS, OP. 30 NO. 34
　　CENTURY MUSIC PUBLISHING COMPANY, INC.　433　　.40
MENDELSSOHN　　　　　　　　　　　4
　SPINNING SONG, S.W.W., 34
　　CENTURY MUSIC PUBLISHING COMPANY, INC.　433　　.40
MENDELSSOHN　　　　　JETSON, I. H.　　2
　SPRING SONG
　　VOLKWEIN BROS.　　　　　　　　　　　.35
MENDELSSOHN　　　　　　　　　　　4
　SPRING SONG
　　WILLIS MUSIC COMPANY　　　　　　　　.35
MENDELSSOHN　　　　　　　　　　　4
　SPRING SONG
　　WILLIS MUSIC COMPANY　　　　　　　　.35
MENDELSSOHN
　SPRING SONG, OP. 62 NO. 6
　　FRANCO COLOMBO PUBLICATIONS　　　　122188　　.60
MENDELSSOHN　　　　　DEL MAGLIO
　SPRING SONG, OP. 62 NO. 6
　　FRANCO COLOMBO PUBLICATIONS　　　　128844　　.60
MENDELSSOHN　　　　　　　　　　　4
　SPRING SONG, S.W.W., 39
　　CENTURY MUSIC PUBLISHING COMPANY, INC.　435　　.40
MENDELSSOHN　　　　　STEINER　　　　1
　SPRING'S GREETING
　　BELWIN-MILLS PUBLISHING CORPORATION　　　.60
MENDELSSOHN　　　　　GOETSCHIUS, P.
　SYMPHONY NO. 04 IN A MAJOR
　　THEODORE PRESSER COMPANY　　　　　　　1.25
MENDELSSOHN　　　　　　　　　　　3
　TARANTELLA, S.W.W., 45
　　CENTURY MUSIC PUBLISHING COMPANY, INC.　4087　　.40
MENDELSSOHN
　VARIATIONS SERIEUSES
　　EDWIN F. KALMUS　　　　　　　　　3677　　1.00
MENDELSSOHN　　　　　　　　　　　D
　VARIATIONS SERIEUSES, OP. 54
　　C. F. PETERS CORPORATION　　　　　1704G　　1.25
MENDELSSOHN　　　　　ROMANIELLO
　VARIATIONS SERIEUSES, OP. 54
　　FRANCO COLOMBO PUBLICATIONS　　　　ER2422　　1.00
MENDELSSOHN　　　　　CORTOT
　VARIATIONS SERIEUSES, OP. 54
　　FRANCO COLOMBO PUBLICATIONS　　　　SAL　　　3.00
MENDELSSOHN　　　　　HUGHES
　VARIATIONS SERIEUSES, OP. 54
　　G. SCHIRMER, INC.　　　　　　　　L1526　　1.00
MENDELSSOHN　　　　　SAUER　　　　　5
　VARIATIONS SERIEUSES, OP. 54
　　SCHOTT　　　　　　　　　　　　　0566 1/2　1.00
MENDELSSOHN　　　　　CORTOT
　VARIATIONS, OP. 32
　　FRANCO COLOMBO PUBLICATIONS　　　　SAL　　　3.00

MENDELSSOHN
　VENETIAN BOAT SONG, OP. 19 NO. 6
　　FRANCO COLOMBO PUBLICATIONS　　　　128414　　.60
MENDELSSOHN　　　　　DEL MAGLIO
　VENETIAN BOAT SONG, OP. 19 NO. 6
　　FRANCO COLOMBO PUBLICATIONS　　　　124719　　.60
MENDELSSOHN　　　　　　　　　　　4
　VENETIAN BOAT SONG, OP. 19 NO. 6 -- SONG WITHOUT WORDS
　　THEODORE PRESSER COMPANY　　　　　　　.50
MENDELSSOHN
　VENETIAN BOAT SONG, OP. 30 NO. 6
　　FRANCO COLOMBO PUBLICATIONS　　　　122187　　.60
MENDELSSOHN　　　　　DEL MAGLIO
　VENETIAN BOAT SONG, OP. 30 NO. 6
　　FRANCO COLOMBO PUBLICATIONS　　　　124720　　.60
MENDELSSOHN　　　　　　　　　　　3
　VENETIAN BOAT SONG, S.W.W., 6
　　CENTURY MUSIC PUBLISHING COMPANY, INC.　1177　　.40
MENDELSSOHN　　　　　　　　　　　M
　VIOLIN CONCERTO, OP. 64. ABRIDGED PIANO SOLO ARR.
　　C. F. PETERS CORPORATION　　　　　17318　　1.50
MENDELSSOHN　　　　　　　　　　　2 1/2
　WANDERING
　　WILLIS MUSIC COMPANY　　　　　　　　.40
MENDELSSOHN　　　　　　　　　　　4
　WAR MARCH OF THE PRIESTS
　　CENTURY MUSIC PUBLISHING COMPANY, INC.　1531　　.40
MENDELSSOHN
　WAR MARCH OF THE PRIESTS -- ATHALIE
　　BELWIN-MILLS PUBLISHING CORPORATION　28177　　.60
MENDELSSOHN
　WAR MARCH OF THE PRIESTS FROM 'ATHALIA', OP. 74
　　CARL FISCHER, INC.　　　　　　　　S 1773　　.50
MENDELSSOHN　　　　　ROLFE, W.　　　3
　WAR MARCH OF THE PRIESTS, EASY
　　CENTURY MUSIC PUBLISHING COMPANY, INC.　3395　　.40
MENDELSSOHN　　　　　PAUER
　WAR MARCH OF THE PRIESTS, FROM 'ATHALIA'
　　G. SCHIRMER, INC.　　　　　　　　　　　.60
MENDELSSOHN
　WAR MARCH OF THE PRIESTS, OP. 74
　　ASHLEY DEALERS SERVICE, INC.　　　ES　　　.95
MENDELSSOHN　　　　　　　　　　　4
　WAR MARCH OF THE PRIETS 'ATHALIA'
　　BELWIN-MILLS PUBLISHING CORPORATION　251　　.60
MENDELSSOHN
　WEDDING MARCH
　　ASHLEY DEALERS SERVICE, INC.　　　ES　　　.95
MENDELSSOHN　　　　　　　　　　　4
　WEDDING MARCH
　　BELWIN-MILLS PUBLISHING CORPORATION　254　　.60
MENDELSSOHN　　　　　　　　　　　5
　WEDDING MARCH
　　CENTURY MUSIC PUBLISHING COMPANY, INC.　455　　.40
MENDELSSOHN
　WEDDING MARCH
　　FRANCO COLOMBO PUBLICATIONS　　　　34558　　.60
MENDELSSOHN　　　　　　　　　　　3
　WEDDING MARCH
　　WILLIS MUSIC COMPANY　　　　　　　　.40
MENDELSSOHN
　WEDDING MARCH FROM 'MIDSUMMER NIGHT'S DREAM'
　　CARL FISCHER, INC.　　　　　　　　S 1784　　.50
MENDELSSOHN　　　　　WEYBRIGHT　　　3
　WEDDING MARCH, FROM 'MID-SUMMER NIGHT'S DREAM'
　　BELWIN-MILLS PUBLISHING CORPORATION　　　.60
MENDELSSOHN *
　MAID OF GANGES, THE
　　G. SCHIRMER, INC.　　　　　　　　　　　.60
MENDELSSOHN *
　MAID OF THE GANGES, THE
　　G. SCHIRMER, INC.　　　　　　　　　　　.60
MENDELSSOHN *　　　　　　　　　　5
　ON WINGS OF SONG
　　CENTURY MUSIC PUBLISHING COMPANY, INC.　2434　　.40
MENDELSSOHN *　　　　TAGLIAPIETRA
　ON WINGS OF SONG
　　FRANCO COLOMBO PUBLICATIONS　　　　127926　　.90
MENDELSSOHN *　　　　TAGLIAPIETRA
　ON WINGS OF SONG
　　FRANCO COLOMBO PUBLICATIONS　　　　127926　　.90
MENDELSSOHN *　　　　TAGLIAPIETRA
　ON WINGS OF SONGS
　　FRANCO COLOMBO PUBLICATIONS　　　　127926　　.90
MENDOZA-NAVA, J.
　GITANA
　　RONGWEN MUSIC, INC.　　　　　　　　　02.50
MENOTTI　　　　　　　　LEVINE
　BARCAROLLE FROM THE BALLET 'SEBASTIAN'
　　FRANCO COLOMBO PUBLICATIONS　　　　NY2055　　.50
MENOTTI　　　　　　　　LEVINE
　BARCAROLLE FROM THE BALLET 'SEBASTIAN'
　　FRANCO COLOMBO PUBLICATIONS　　　　NY2056　　.75
MENOTTI　　　　　　　　LEVINE, H.
　BARCAROLLE, FROM THE BALLET 'SEBASTIAN'
　　BELWIN-MILLS PUBLISHING CORPORATION　　　.60
MENOTTI
　POEMETTI
　　BELWIN-MILLS PUBLISHING CORPORATION　　　1.50
MENOTTI
　RICERCARE AND TOCCATA
　　BELWIN-MILLS PUBLISHING CORPORATION　　　1.50
MENOTTI
　RICERCARE AND TOCCATA ON A THEME FROM 'THE OLD MAID AND THE
　THIEF'
　　FRANCO COLOMBO PUBLICATIONS　　　　NY1538　　1.25
MERANG
　MARQUISE, LA
　　GERARD BILLAUDOT EDITIONS MUSICALES　　　1.30
MERANG
　MISS HAUMON
　　GERARD BILLAUDOT EDITIONS MUSICALES　　　1.30
MERIGOT, F.
　DANSE POUR PIERROT
　　ELKAN-VOGEL, INC.　　　　　　　　D　　　.90
MERIGOT, F.
　JOYEUX MATIN
　　ELKAN-VOGEL, INC.　　　　　　　　D　　　1.00
MERIGOT, F.
　MADRIGAL
　　ELKAN-VOGEL, INC.　　　　　　　　D　　　1.00
MERIGOT, F.
　PETIT CARNAVAL
　　ELKAN-VOGEL, INC.　　　　　　　　D　　　.75
MERIGOT, F.
　PIECE ROMANTIQUE
　　ELKAN-VOGEL, INC.　　　　　　　　D　　　.75

MERIGOT, F.
POUR DIX PETITS DOIGTS D'ENFANTS
ELKAN-VOGEL, INC.   D   .70
MERIGOT, F.
POUR LES TOUTS PETITS
ELKAN-VOGEL, INC.   D   .40
MERIGOT, F.
POUR MA POUPEE
ELKAN-VOGEL, INC.   D   .50
MERKEL, G.   3
BUTTERFLY
CENTURY MUSIC PUBLISHING COMPANY, INC.   1704   .40
MERKEL, G.
BUTTERFLY, OP. 81 NO. 4
BELWIN-MILLS PUBLISHING CORPORATION   28021   .50
MERKEL, G.
BUTTERFLY, OP. 81 NO. 4
CARL FISCHER, INC.   S 221   .50
MERKEL, G.
BUTTERFLY, OP. 81 NO. 4--BAGATELLE
G. SCHIRMER, INC.   .40
MERKEL, G.   3
PAPILLON -- BUTTERFLY --
CENTURY MUSIC PUBLISHING COMPANY, INC.   1704   .40
MERKEL, G.   ROLFE, W.   2
PAPILLON, EASY
CENTURY MUSIC PUBLISHING COMPANY, INC.   3357   .40
MERKEL, G.
SPRING SONG, OP. 18 NO. 1
BELWIN-MILLS PUBLISHING CORPORATION   28153   .50
MERKEL, N.   3
MARCH SLAV BOOGIE
THEODORE PRESSER COMPANY   .50
MERKEL, N.   3
SHUFFLE BOOGIE
THEODORE PRESSER COMPANY   .50
MERKUR
AND AWAY WE GO
BELWIN-MILLS PUBLISHING CORPORATION   20487   .50
MERKUR
FRENCH MUSICAL CLOCK, A
BELWIN-MILLS PUBLISHING CORPORATION   25271   .60
MERKUR
INDIAN WAR DANCE -- FROM THREE PIECES FOR THE PIANO
BELWIN-MILLS PUBLISHING CORPORATION   25234   .60
MERKUR
IRIS -- FROM THREE PIECES FOR THE PIANO
BELWIN-MILLS PUBLISHING CORPORATION   25236   .60
MERKUR
JAPANESE JUGGLER
BELWIN-MILLS PUBLISHING CORPORATION   25034   .60
MERKUR
MR. AND MRS. STACCATO
BELWIN-MILLS PUBLISHING CORPORATION   25299   .60
MERKUR
SAILOR'S SONG AND HORNPIPE -- FROM THREE PIECES FOR THE PIANO
BELWIN-MILLS PUBLISHING CORPORATION   25233   .60
MERLET   9
SONATINE
ALPHONSE LEDUC
MERRICK, F.
BONNIE BLUE BELL, THE
NOVELLO AND COMPANY, LTD.   10.0100.00   1.15
MERRICK, F.
HARES ON THE MOUNTAINS
NOVELLO AND COMPANY, LTD.   10.0173.06   .90
MERRILL, B.
CARNIVAL
THE BIG THREE MUSIC CORPORATION   01.50
MERZ, O.   2
PRINCESA, LA -- SPANISH DANCE, OP. 5 NO. 2
THEODORE PRESSER COMPANY   .50
MESEROLE, H. T.   2
CHARLES THE CHESTY CHIPMUNK
BELWIN-MILLS PUBLISHING CORPORATION   .60
MESEROLE, H. T.   2
PAUL THE POKEY PORCUPINE
BELWIN-MILLS PUBLISHING CORPORATION   .60
MESEROLE, H. T.   2
ROBERT THE RAMBLIN' RABBIT
BELWIN-MILLS PUBLISHING CORPORATION   .60
MESEROLE, H. T.
WALLACE THE WADDING WOODCHUCK
BELWIN-MILLS PUBLISHING CORPORATION   .60
MESSIAEN, O.
CANTEYODJAYA
UNIVERSAL EDITION   UE 12127   6.50
MESSIAEN, O.
FANTASIE BURLESQUE
ELKAN-VOGEL, INC.   D   5.35
MESSIAEN, O.
ILE DE FEU NO. 1
ELKAN-VOGEL, INC.   D   1.70
MESSIAEN, O.
ILE DE FEU NO. 2
ELKAN-VOGEL, INC.   D   3.00
MESSIAEN, O.
LE BAISER DE L'ENFANT-JESUS
ELKAN-VOGEL, INC.   D   1.80
MESSIAEN, O.
LES OFFRANDES OUBLIEES
ELKAN-VOGEL, INC.   D   3.10
MESSIAEN, O.
MODE DE VALEURS ET D'INTENSITES
ELKAN-VOGEL, INC.   D   2.30
MESSIAEN, O.
NEUMES RYTHMIQUES
ELKAN-VOGEL, INC.   D   3.10
MESSIAEN, O.
OISEAUX EXOTIQUES -- PIANO SOLO PART
UNIVERSAL EDITION   UE 13008P   6.50
MESSIAEN, O.   8
RONDEAU
ALPHONSE LEDUC
MESSIAEN, O.
RONDEAU
ELKAN-VOGEL, INC.   LED   3.50
MESSIAEN, O.   9
SEPT HAIKAI
ALPHONSE LEDUC
MESSINA, J.   4
LOVE AND PASSION
VOLKWEIN BROS.   .50
MESSINA, J.   4
VALLEY OF ROSES WALTZ
VOLKWEIN BROS.   00.50

METCALF, J.   2
SACK WALTZ
BELWIN-MILLS PUBLISHING CORPORATION   258   .60
METCALF, J.   2
SACK WALTZ
VOLKWEIN BROS.   .25
METCALF, J.   2
SACK WALTZ
WILLIS MUSIC COMPANY   .35
METCALF, J.   2
SACK WALTZ, THE
CENTURY MUSIC PUBLISHING COMPANY, INC.   1068   .40
METIS, F.
ENCHANTED SEA
VOLKWEIN BROS.   .85
METRA
SERENATA
FRANCO COLOMBO PUBLICATIONS   BA9083   .75
METRA   DEL MAGLIO
SERENATA
FRANCO COLOMBO PUBLICATIONS   129107   .60
METRA   4
VALSE SERENADE
CENTURY MUSIC PUBLISHING COMPANY, INC.   1714   .40
METRA   2
VALSE SERENADE, EASY
CENTURY MUSIC PUBLISHING COMPANY, INC.   2141   .40
METRA, O.
LA SERENADE
HEUGEL ET CIE.   2.00
METRA, O.   4
SERENADE, VALSE ESPAGNOLE
CENTURY MUSIC PUBLISHING COMPANY, INC.   1714   .40
MEUTTMAN, M.   1B
BUGLE CALL
MUSICORD PUBLICATIONS, INC.   .45
MEUTTMAN, M.   1 1/2
RIDING THE MOUNTAIN PONY
WILLIS MUSIC COMPANY   .35
MEUTTMAN, M.   1
WALKING IN THE WOODS
WILLIS MUSIC COMPANY   .35
MEUX
MARCH OF THE ASTRONAUTS
CARL FISCHER, INC.   RS 385   .50
MEUX
SPANISH SURF
CARL FISCHER, INC.   RS 422   .50
MEUX
WEB OF LOVELINESS
CARL FISCHER, INC.   RS 415   .50
MEYER
FIRST SONATA
EDWARD B. MARKS MUSIC CORPORATION   03.00
MEYER
SONATA NO. 02
EDWARD B. MARKS MUSIC CORPORATION   02.50
MEYER *   WALTER
CRAZY RHYTHM
WARNER BROTHERS PUBLISHERS   1.00
MEYER *
PAS DE QUATRE
FRANCO COLOMBO PUBLICATIONS   SAL   1.75
MEYER-HELMUND   4
MAZURKA
CENTURY MUSIC PUBLISHING COMPANY, INC.   309   .40
MEYER-LUTZ
PAS DE QUATRE
FRANCO COLOMBO PUBLICATIONS   SAL   1.50
MEYERBEER, G.   WERNER
ALBUMLEAF IN A FLAT--CURWEN EDITION
G. SCHIRMER, INC.   .60
MEYERBEER, G.   SCHAUM, J.   2
CORONATION MARCH
BELWIN-MILLS PUBLISHING CORPORATION   .50
MEYERBEER, G.
CORONATION MARCH--'LE PROPHETE'
G. SCHIRMER, INC.   .50
MEYERBEER, G.   4
CORONATION MARCH, PROPHET
CENTURY MUSIC PUBLISHING COMPANY, INC.   1650   .40
MEYERBEER, G.   SMITH   5
HUGENOTS, FANTASIE
CENTURY MUSIC PUBLISHING COMPANY, INC.   1171   .40
MEYERBEER, G.   4
HUGENOTS, THE, PAGE'S SONG
CENTURY MUSIC PUBLISHING COMPANY, INC.   2215   .40
MEYERBEER, G.   4
PROPHETE, CORONATION MARCH
CENTURY MUSIC PUBLISHING COMPANY, INC.   1650   .40
MEYERBEER, G.   2
PROPHETE, CORONATION MARCH, EASY
CENTURY MUSIC PUBLISHING COMPANY, INC.   3760   .40
MEYEROWITZ
BALLADE
EDWARD B. MARKS MUSIC CORPORATION   01.50
MIASKOVSKY
RECOLLECTIONS, OP. 29
UNIVERSAL EDITION   UE 9431   2.35
MIASKOVSKY   M
SONATA, OP. 84
C. F. PETERS CORPORATION   4709   3.00
MICHAELIDES
SUITE GRECQUE POUR PIANO
SEESAW MUSIC CORPORATION   6.00
MICHAELIS, J.   3
BLACKSMITH IN THE WOODS
CENTURY MUSIC PUBLISHING COMPANY, INC.   150   .40
MICHAELIS, J.   3
FORGE IN THE FOREST, THE
CENTURY MUSIC PUBLISHING COMPANY, INC.   150   .40
MICHEELSEN
KLEINE SPIELMUSIK
BARENREITER VERLAG   BA 1337   2.25
MICHEUZ, G.
ALLELUIA DES OISEAUX
FRANCO COLOMBO PUBLICATIONS   SAL   1.75
MICHEUZ, G.
BAISERS D'OISEAUX
FRANCO COLOMBO PUBLICATIONS   SAL   1.75
MICHEUZ, G.
BOURDONNEMENT D'ABEILLES
FRANCO COLOMBO PUBLICATIONS   SAL   1.75
MICHEUZ, G.   5
CAROLLING OF THE BIRDS, OP. 156
CENTURY MUSIC PUBLISHING COMPANY, INC.   .40

MICHEUZ, G.	3		
CAROLLING OF THE BIRDS, OP. 156			
THEODORE PRESSER COMPANY			.50
MICHIELS			
BOHEMA CZARDAS			
FRANCO COLOMBO PUBLICATIONS		SAL	1.75
MICHIELS			
DIVERTISSEMENT HONGROIS			
FRANCO COLOMBO PUBLICATIONS		SAL	1.75
MICUCCI			
MINUETTO ANTICO			
FRANCO COLOMBO PUBLICATIONS		DS112	.90
MIDDLEBROOK	2		
GAIETY			
BOSTON MUSIC COMPANY			.50
MIDDLEBROOK	3		
INDIAN SUMMER			
BOSTON MUSIC COMPANY			.50
MIDDLEBROOK	3		
SLEIGHING			
BOSTON MUSIC COMPANY			.50
MIDDLEBROOK	1		
UMBRELLAS			
BOSTON MUSIC COMPANY			.50
MIDDLEBROOK	2		
WATER LILIES			
BOSTON MUSIC COMPANY			.50
MIGHAM, M.	4		
IMPROVISATION			
THEODORE PRESSER COMPANY			.50
MIGNONE			
MICROBINHO			
EDWIN F. KALMUS		3683	1.25
MIGOT	5, 6		
FETE DE LA BERGERE, LA			
ALPHONSE LEDUC			
MIGOT	5		
LA 'NIMURA', DANSE			
ALPHONSE LEDUC			
MIGOT	6		
PRELUDE A UN			
ALPHONSE LEDUC			
MIGOT	5		
PRELUDE POUR UN POETE			
ALPHONSE LEDUC			
MIGOT	6		
SEGUE, LA, DANSE LENTE			
ALPHONSE LEDUC			
MIGOT	7		
SONATE			
ALPHONSE LEDUC			
MIGOT	4		
SONATINE			
ALPHONSE LEDUC			
MIGOT	7		
SUITE EN 3 PARTIES			
ALPHONSE LEDUC			
MIGOT	6		
TOMBEAU DE DU FAULT, LE			
ALPHONSE LEDUC			
MIHALOVICI			
ALTERNAMENTI -- BALLET --			
FRANCO COLOMBO PUBLICATIONS		R1591	9.00
MIHALOVICI			
DEUXIEME SONATE POUR PIANO			
HEUGEL ET CIE.			5.50
MIHALOVICI			
RICERCARI			
HEUGEL ET CIE.			6.65
MIHALOVICI	8		
SONATE			
ALPHONSE LEDUC			
MILANO, R.	MD		
TOCCATA			
THEODORE PRESSER COMPANY			1.00
MILDENBERG, A.			
ARABIAN NIGHT--ROMANCE			
G. SCHIRMER, INC.			.50
MILES			
BUTTERFLY DANCE			
SAM FOX PUBLISHING COMPANY, INC.			.75
MILES			
BUTTERFLY DANCE			
SOUTHERN MUSIC COMPANY			.75
MILES			
CAPTAIN HOOK OF THE PIRATE BAND			
CARL FISCHER, INC.		P 1999	.50
MILES			
DAINTY DAFFODILS			
SAM FOX PUBLISHING COMPANY, INC.			.75
MILES			
DAINTY DAFFODILS			
SOUTHERN MUSIC COMPANY			.75
MILES			
SPARKLETS			
SAM FOX PUBLISHING COMPANY, INC.			1.00
MILES			
SPARKLETS			
SOUTHERN MUSIC COMPANY			1.00
MILES			
WATER BUG, THE			
SAM FOX PUBLISHING COMPANY, INC.			.75
MILES			
WATER BUG, THE			
SOUTHERN MUSIC COMPANY			.75
MILES *			
ANCHORS AWEIGH			
THE BIG THREE MUSIC CORPORATION			00.95
MILEY *			
BLACK AND TAN FANTASY			
BELWIN-MILLS PUBLISHING CORPORATION		20555	.85
MILHAUD, D.			
ACCUEIL AMICAL			
HEUGEL ET CIE.			1.60
MILHAUD, D.			
ADAME MIROIR			
HEUGEL ET CIE.			2.75
MILHAUD, D.	MD		
ALAMEDA FROM 'FOUR SKETCHES'			
THEODORE PRESSER COMPANY			.60
MILHAUD, D.			
AUTOMNE, L'			
FRANCO COLOMBO PUBLICATIONS		SAL	4.00
MILHAUD, D.			
FLOWERS - FROM 'A CHILD LOVES'			
MCA MUSIC			.60

MILHAUD, D.	MD		
FOUR SKETCHES -- ECLOGUE, MADRIGAL, ALAMEDA, SOBFE LA LOMA			
THEODORE PRESSER COMPANY			2.00
MILHAUD, D.			
HILD LOVES, A			
MCA MUSIC			1.25
MILHAUD, D.			
HOUSEHOLD MUSE, THE			
ELKAN-VOGEL, INC.		D	1.60
MILHAUD, D.			
LE TRAIN BLEU			
HEUGEL ET CIE.			14.70
MILHAUD, D.	MD		
MADRIGAL FROM 'FOUR SKETCHES'			
THEODORE PRESSER COMPANY			.60
MILHAUD, D.	MD		
ONE DAY -- UNE JOURNEE			
THEODORE PRESSER COMPANY			1.00
MILHAUD, D.			
POLKA -- L'EVENTAIL DE JEANNE			
HEUGEL ET CIE.			1.45
MILHAUD, D.			
SALADE -- BALLET CHANTE			
HEUGEL ET CIE.			14.60
MILHAUD, D. SCHMITZ			
SAUDADES DO BRAZIL--SUITE--NO. 3, LEME			
ASSOCIATED MUSIC PUBLISHERS, INC.		ESC	.75
MILHAUD, D.			
SAUDADES DO BRAZIL--SUITE--NO. 5, IPANEMA			
ASSOCIATED MUSIC PUBLISHERS, INC.		ESC	.75
MILHAUD, D.			
SEVEN-BRANCHED CANDELABRA, THE			
PEER SOUTHERN ORGANIZATION			01.75
MILHAUD, D.			
SONATA			
FRANCO COLOMBO PUBLICATIONS		SAL	5.25
MILHAUD, D.			
SONATA NO. 02			
HEUGEL ET CIE.			6.75
MILHAUD, D.			
SONATINE			
EDITIONS MUSICALES TRANSATLANTIQUES			3.85
MILHAUD, D.			
SONGES, LES -- BALLET --			
FRANCO COLOMBO PUBLICATIONS		SAL	6.00
MILHAUD, D.			
SUITE FOR THE PIANO			
ELKAN-VOGEL, INC.		D	6.60
MILHAUD, D.			
TANGO DES FRATELLINI FROM 'BOEUF SUR LE TOIT'			
ASSOCIATED MUSIC PUBLISHERS, INC.		ESC	2.00
MILHAUD, D.			
THREE RAG-CAPRICES			
UNIVERSAL EDITION		UE 6562	2.65
MILHAUD, D.	MD		
UNE JOURNEE			
THEODORE PRESSER COMPANY			.50
MILICI			
DANZAS DE LAS NUSTAS			
FRANCO COLOMBO PUBLICATIONS		BA10827	.75
MILICI			
MALAMBO			
FRANCO COLOMBO PUBLICATIONS		BA10828	.75
MILICI			
TILCARENO, EL			
FRANCO COLOMBO PUBLICATIONS		BA10410	.75
MILKEY, E.			
BAGPIPES AND DRUMS			
BELWIN-MILLS PUBLISHING CORPORATION		25079	.60
MILLER	4-5		
IMPROMPTU			
PRO-ART PUBLICATIONS, INC.		371	.60
MILLER	6		
IMPROMPTU IN E FLAT MINOR			
THEODORE PRESSER COMPANY			.75
MILLER	2		
MIST			
PRO-ART PUBLICATIONS, INC.		396	.50
MILLER	1		
PELICANS ON PARADE			
WILLIS MUSIC COMPANY			.35
MILLER	2-3		
PETITE RONDO			
PRO-ART PUBLICATIONS, INC.		427	.50
MILLER GLOVER, D.			
PLACE IN THE SUN, A			
BELWIN-MILLS PUBLISHING CORPORATION			.60
MILLER	4		
SPARKLING FINGERS			
WILLIS MUSIC COMPANY			.40
MILLER	2		
TWINKLE TOES			
WILLIS MUSIC COMPANY			.40
MILLER *	1		
LITTLE DEER, THE			
PRO-ART PUBLICATIONS, INC.		435	.50
MILLER *			
MOONLIGHT SERENADE			
THE BIG THREE MUSIC CORPORATION			00.95
MILLER, H.	2 1/2		
LITTLE BALLADE			
BELWIN-MILLS PUBLISHING CORPORATION			.60
MILLER, J.	4		
FANTASIE			
BELWIN-MILLS PUBLISHING CORPORATION			1.25
MILLER, J.			
FIVE MOVEMENTS FOR PIANO			
SEESAW MUSIC CORPORATION			15.00
MILLER, L.			
DRIFTWOOD			
BELWIN-MILLS PUBLISHING CORPORATION		25145	.60
MILLER, L.			
FUNNY BUNNY			
BELWIN-MILLS PUBLISHING CORPORATION		25235	.60
MILLER, L.			
MONKEY'S MARCH, THE			
BELWIN-MILLS PUBLISHING CORPORATION		25168	.60
MILLER, L.			
PINEAPPLES AND PALM TREES			
BELWIN-MILLS PUBLISHING CORPORATION		25024	.60
MILLER, L.			
SWAN, THE			
BELWIN-MILLS PUBLISHING CORPORATION		25167	.60
MILLER, L.			
VENEZUELA VALSE			
BELWIN-MILLS PUBLISHING CORPORATION		25011	.60

MILLER, S.
  DAY DREAMS
    BELWIN-MILLS PUBLISHING CORPORATION 28084 .60
MILLIGAN   RICHTER
  ALIDA'S DANCE
    BELWIN-MILLS PUBLISHING CORPORATION   .60
MILLIGAN   RICHTER
  ALIDA'S DANCE
    FRANCO COLOMBO PUBLICATIONS   NY1505 .40
MILLIGAN   2 1/2
  CAROUSEL RIDE
    THEODORE PRESSER COMPANY   .50
MILLIGAN   RICHTER
  CLOUD PATTERNS
    FRANCO COLOMBO PUBLICATIONS   NY1506 .35
MILLIGAN   2 1/2
  JUNIE THE JITTERBUG
    THEODORE PRESSER COMPANY   .50
MILLIGAN   2 1/2
  KEEP IN STEP
    THEODORE PRESSER COMPANY   .50
MILLIGAN   2
  WAGON TRAILS
    THEODORE PRESSER COMPANY   .50
MILLIGAN   1
  WALTZ OF THE BLUE FAIRY
    THEODORE PRESSER COMPANY   .60
MILLIGAN   RICHTER
  WHISTLING FARM BOY
    FRANCO COLOMBO PUBLICATIONS   NY1507 .35
MILLS   1
  IT'S RAINING
    LEE ROBERTS MUSIC PUBLICATIONS, INC.   .50
MILLS   2
  PHRYGIAN FABLE
    LEE ROBERTS MUSIC PUBLICATIONS, INC.   .50
MILLS   6
  TARANTELLE, OP. 13 NO. 1
    CENTURY MUSIC PUBLISHING COMPANY, INC. 1232 .40
MILLS *   KERR, R.N.
  IT'S NOT UNUSUAL
    MCA MUSIC   1.00
MILLS, D.
  PACE HORSE
    FREDERICK HARRIS MUSIC COMPANY   .60
MILLS, K.   SCHAUM, J.   1
  AT A DARKY CAMP MEETING
    BELWIN-MILLS PUBLISHING CORPORATION   .50
MILLS, K.
  AT A GEORGIA CAMP MEETING
    BELWIN-MILLS PUBLISHING CORPORATION 20021 .85
MILLS, K.   MEDIUM
  RED WING
    SHAWNEE PRESS, INC.   HB-74 .50
MILLWARD   4
  ROCK OF AGES, TRANSCRIPTION
    CENTURY MUSIC PUBLISHING COMPANY, INC. 654 .40
MILNER, A.
  HOBGOBLIN
    NOVELLO AND COMPANY, LTD.   10.0101.09 .90
MILNES   3
  AFTER A SUMMER RAIN, F MAJOR
    CENTURY MUSIC PUBLISHING COMPANY, INC. 4212 .40
MILNES   3
  CARILLON, THE
    CENTURY MUSIC PUBLISHING COMPANY, INC. 4383 .40
MILNES   3
  GREEN REFLECTIONS
    CENTURY MUSIC PUBLISHING COMPANY, INC. 4254 .40
MILOIEVITCH
  DANS MON PAYS, OP. 16
    FRANCO COLOMBO PUBLICATIONS   SAL 3.25
MILOSZ *
  IMAGES D'ENFANTS
    ELKAN-VOGEL, INC.   D 5.00
MIMAROGLU, I.
  MONOLOGUE IV FOR THE RIGHT HAND
    SEESAW MUSIC CORPORATION   4.00
MIMAROGLU, I.
  PIANO SONATA, 1966
    SEESAW MUSIC CORPORATION   12.00
MINGOTE, A.
  MANOJICO
    ASSOCIATED MUSIC PUBLISHERS, INC.   UME .75
MINKUS, L. *
  DON QUICHOTTE--PAS DE DEUX--
    GERARD BILLAUDOT EDITIONS MUSICALES   1.70
MINKUS, L. *
  PAS DE TROIS--DE PAQUITA--
    GERARD BILLAUDOT EDITIONS MUSICALES   2.20
MIRANDOLLE   6
  SONATINE
    ALPHONSE LEDUC
MIRANTE   2-3
  MUSICAL JOURNEY, A
    PRO-ART PUBLICATIONS, INC.   502 .50
MIRO, F.
  MERCEDES--VALSE ESPAGNOLE
    G. SCHIRMER, INC.   .90
MIROUZE   4, 6
  SUITE DANS LE STYLE ANCIEN
    ALPHONSE LEDUC
MIRSALIS, W.
  IN THE VILLAGE
    FREDERICK HARRIS MUSIC COMPANY   .60
MISSLER   5
  RAMAGE D'OISEAUX, OP. 80
    ALPHONSE LEDUC
MITCHELL, M. A.   1 1/2
  LITTLE INDIAN BRAVE
    WILLIS MUSIC COMPANY   .40
MITTLER   1A
  BOAT RIDE AT SILVER SPRINGS
    MUSICORD PUBLICATIONS, INC.   .45
MITTLER   3A
  BOLERO IN BLUE
    MUSICORD PUBLICATIONS, INC.   .45
MITTLER   3A
  BOOGIE WOOGIE IN BLUE
    MUSICORD PUBLICATIONS, INC.   .45
MITTLER   3A
  ONE FINGER POLKA
    MUSICORD PUBLICATIONS, INC.   .45
MITTLER   3A
  SERENADE IN BLUE
    MUSICORD PUBLICATIONS, INC.   .45

MITTLER   3A
  WALTZ IN BLUE
    MUSICORD PUBLICATIONS, INC.   .45
MITTLER--ED   MITTLER   2A
  COUNTRY GARDENS
    MUSICORD PUBLICATIONS, INC.   .45
MITTLER--ED   MITTLER   1B
  MARINES' HYMN
    MUSICORD PUBLICATIONS, INC.   .45
MITTLER--ED   MITTLER   2B
  TWO GUITARS
    MUSICORD PUBLICATIONS, INC.   .45
MODONA
  EASY NOTEBOOK NO. 3
    FRANCO COLOMBO PUBLICATIONS   FOR.11405 1.75
MODONA
  PRELUDE ON THE WHITE KEYS
    FRANCO COLOMBO PUBLICATIONS   FOR.11643 1.25
MODONA
  RONDINI
    FRANCO COLOMBO PUBLICATIONS   FOR.11642 1.25
MODONA
  WALTZ ON 2 NOTES
    FRANCO COLOMBO PUBLICATIONS   FOR.11955 .75
MOESCHINGER   4
  D'UN CAHIER VALAISAN -- AUS EINEM WALLISER SKIZZENBUCH --
  KLAVIERSUITE, OP. 63
    BARENREITER VERLAG   BA 2083
MOESCHINGER
  PIANO SUITE OP. 63
    BARENREITER VERLAG   BA 2083 2.75
MOESCHINGER
  TOCCATA NO. 1, OP. 30A
    BARENREITER VERLAG   BA 2247 2.25
MOESCHINGER   4
  TOCCATA NO. 1, OP. 30A
    BARENREITER VERLAG   BA-2247
MOESCHINGER
  TOCCATA NO. 2, OP. 30B
    BARENREITER VERLAG   BA 2248 2.25
MOESCHINGER   4
  TOCCATA NO. 2, OP. 30B
    BARENREITER VERLAG   BA 2248
MOESCHINGER
  TOCCATA NO. 3, OP. 72
    BARENREITER VERLAG   BA 2249 4.50
MOESCHINGER   4
  TOCCATA NO. 3, OP. 72
    BARENREITER VERLAG   BA 2249
MOEVS, R.
  FANTASIA SOPRA UN MOTIVO, 1951
    ASSOCIATED MUSIC PUBLISHERS, INC.   ESC 3.00
MOEVS, R.
  PHOENIX
    EDWARD B. MARKS MUSIC CORPORATION   02.50
MOEVS, R.
  SONATA, 1950
    ASSOCIATED MUSIC PUBLISHERS, INC.   ESC 4.75
MOFFAT--ED   7
  VAUDEVILLE A DANSER
    NOVELLO AND COMPANY, LTD.   55.0015.10 .40
MOHAUPT, R.
  MAX AND MORITZ -- A MUSICAL STORY
    ASSOCIATED MUSIC PUBLISHERS, INC.   AMP 3.25
MOHLER   4-5
  KONZERTSTUCKE, OP. 21
    BARENREITER VERLAG   SM 1705
MOHO-NALI   3
  WAHOO, INDIAN DANCE
    CENTURY MUSIC PUBLISHING COMPANY, INC. 1086 .40
MOISSE, S.
  NOCTURNE
    ASSOCIATED MUSIC PUBLISHERS, INC.   BER .75
MOISSE, S.
  VARIATIONS SUR UN THEME HURON
    ASSOCIATED MUSIC PUBLISHERS, INC.   BER 2.00
MOJSISOVICS, R.
  PEASANT DANCE
    UNIVERSAL EDITION   UE 3057 .85
MOKREJS   2
  BAREFOOT BOY
    BELWIN-MILLS PUBLISHING CORPORATION   .60
MOKREJS   2
  BLINKING OWLS
    BELWIN-MILLS PUBLISHING CORPORATION   .60
MOKREJS   3
  SHIMMERING SEA
    BELWIN-MILLS PUBLISHING CORPORATION   .60
MOKREJS
  VALCIK IN D FLAT
    ASHLEY DEALERS SERVICE, INC.   ES .95
MOKREJS
  VALCIK IN D FLAT
    CARL FISCHER, INC.   P 2998 .60
MOKRJES   5
  VALCIK IN D FLAT
    WILLIS MUSIC COMPANY   .50
MOLFETTA
  NINNA-NANNA
    FRANCO COLOMBO PUBLICATIONS   DS353 2.00
MOLLER *
  HAPPY WANDERER, THE
    SAM FOX PUBLISHING COMPANY, INC.   .50
MOLLER *
  HAPPY WANDERER, THE
    SAM FOX PUBLISHING COMPANY, INC.   .75
MOLLER *
  HAPPY WANDERER, THE -- SIMP. VERSION
    SOUTHERN MUSIC COMPANY   .50
MOLLER *
  HAPPY WANDERER, THE -- TRANSCRIPTION
    SOUTHERN MUSIC COMPANY   .75
MOLLOY, J. L.   PERRY
  KERRY DANCE
    BOOSEY AND HAWKES, INC.   .50
MOLLOY, J. L.   STEINER 1 1/2
  OH, THE DAYS OF THE KERRY DANCING
    BELWIN-MILLS PUBLISHING CORPORATION   .60
MOLLOY, J. L.--ED   MOLLOY, J. L. 3
  LOVE'S OLD SWEET SONG
    CENTURY MUSIC PUBLISHING COMPANY, INC. 2438 .40
MOLLOY, J. L.--ED   MOLLOY, J. L. 2
  LOVE'S OLD SWEET SONG
    CENTURY MUSIC PUBLISHING COMPANY, INC. 2061 .40
MOMPOU, F.
  CANCION Y DANZA, NO. 1--QUASI MODERATO
    ASSOCIATED MUSIC PUBLISHERS, INC.   UME .75

MOMPOU, F.
  CANCION Y DANZA, NO. 2--LENTO
    ASSOCIATED MUSIC PUBLISHERS, INC.   UME   .90
MOMPOU, F.
  CANCION Y DANZA, NO. 3--MODERE
    ASSOCIATED MUSIC PUBLISHERS, INC.   UME   .75
MOMPOU, F.
  CANCION Y DANZA, NO. 4--MODERATO
    ASSOCIATED MUSIC PUBLISHERS, INC.   UME   .90
MOMPOU, F.
  CANCION Y DANZA, NO. 5
    EDWARD B. MARKS MUSIC CORPORATION   01.00
MOMPOU, F.
  CANCION Y DANZA, NO. 7
    EDWARD B. MARKS MUSIC CORPORATION   01.00
MOMPOU, F.
  CANCION Y DANZA, NO. 8
    EDWARD B. MARKS MUSIC CORPORATION   01.00
MOMPOU, F.
  CANCO I DANSA
    EDWARD B. MARKS MUSIC CORPORATION   01.00
MOMPOU, F.
  CHANSON ET DANSE NO. 09
    FRANCO COLOMBO PUBLICATIONS   SAL   2.50
MOMPOU, F.
  CHANSON ET DANSE NO. 10
    FRANCO COLOMBO PUBLICATIONS   SAL   2.50
MOMPOU, F.
  FETES LOINTAINES
    FRANCO COLOMBO PUBLICATIONS   SAL   1.50
MOMPOU, F.
  SCENES D'ENFANTS
    FRANCO COLOMBO PUBLICATIONS   SAL   1.25
MOMPOU, F.
  SUBURBIS
    FRANCO COLOMBO PUBLICATIONS   SAL   1.25
MOMPOU, F.
  VARIATIONS ON A THEME BY CHOPIN
    FRANCO COLOMBO PUBLICATIONS   SAL   5.50
MONATH
  PRELUDE
    SAM FOX PUBLISHING COMPANY, INC.   1.00
MONATH
  PRELUDE
    SOUTHERN MUSIC COMPANY   1.00
MONFRED
  ENAMOURED WATCHMAKER, THE
    FRANCO COLOMBO PUBLICATIONS   SAL   1.50
MONFRED
  JEUNE FILLE FRANCAISE, UNE -- LITTLE SUITE --
    FRANCO COLOMBO PUBLICATIONS   SAL   5.00
MONFRED
  PRELUDE INTERMEZZO AND FUGUE
    FRANCO COLOMBO PUBLICATIONS   SAL   4.00
MONFRED
  SERAIT-CE L'AMOUR
    FRANCO COLOMBO PUBLICATIONS   SAL   1.75
MONK--ED.   MONK   3
  ABIDE WITH ME, C MAJOR
    CENTURY MUSIC PUBLISHING COMPANY, INC.   3619   .40
MONNIKENDAM
  CAPILLON DE CYNTHERE, LE
    FRANCO COLOMBO PUBLICATIONS   SAL   2.00
MONRI, V.   DEL MAGLIO
  CZARDAS NO. 1
    FRANCO COLOMBO PUBLICATIONS   127211   .60
MONTAINE   4
  UP IN A SWING
    CENTURY MUSIC PUBLISHING COMPANY, INC.   984   .40
MONTALBAN, R.
  EL CORRO DE LAS NINAS
    ASSOCIATED MUSIC PUBLISHERS, INC.   UME   2.25
MONTANARI
  BEBE DORME
    FRANCO COLOMBO PUBLICATIONS   127554   .60
MONTANARI
  BIMBI SOLDATI
    FRANCO COLOMBO PUBLICATIONS   127552   .60
MONTANARI
  CINESINA
    FRANCO COLOMBO PUBLICATIONS   127563   .60
MONTANARI
  MARTITA
    FRANCO COLOMBO PUBLICATIONS   127564   .60
MONTANARI
  PICCOLA GIAPPONESE
    FRANCO COLOMBO PUBLICATIONS   127551   .60
MONTANARI
  SULL'ALTALENA
    FRANCO COLOMBO PUBLICATIONS   127553   .60
MONTANARO
  SCENES FROM CHILDHOOD - 1. BAGATELLA
    FRANCO COLOMBO PUBLICATIONS   DS378   1.25
MONTANARO
  SCENES FROM CHILDHOOD - 2. LA CANZONE DEL RUSCELLO
    FRANCO COLOMBO PUBLICATIONS   DS379   1.25
MONTANARO
  SCENES FROM CHILDHOOD - 3. LA TROTTOLA
    FRANCO COLOMBO PUBLICATIONS   DS380   1.25
MONTANARO
  SCENES FROM CHILDHOOD - 4. DAMINE
    FRANCO COLOMBO PUBLICATIONS   DS381   1.25
MONTANARO
  SCENES FROM CHILDHOOD - 5. PICCOLO ARABO
    FRANCO COLOMBO PUBLICATIONS   DS382   1.25
MONTANARO
  SCENES FROM CHILDHOOD - 6. PICCOLE PATTUGLIE
    FRANCO COLOMBO PUBLICATIONS   DS383   1.25
MONTANARO
  SIX EASY PIECES ON 5 NOTES - 1. MEDITANDO
    FRANCO COLOMBO PUBLICATIONS   DS411   1.00
MONTANARO
  SIX EASY PIECES ON 5 NOTES - 2. NOSTALGIA SLAVA
    FRANCO COLOMBO PUBLICATIONS   DS412   1.00
MONTANARO
  SIX EASY PIECES ON 5 NOTES - 3. IL SUONATORE DI CORNAMUSA
    FRANCO COLOMBO PUBLICATIONS   DS413   1.00
MONTANARO
  SIX EASY PIECES ON 5 NOTES - 4. IL CARILLON DI LOLETTE
    FRANCO COLOMBO PUBLICATIONS   DS414   1.00
MONTANARO
  SIX EASY PIECES ON 5 NOTES - 5. IL COMPLEANNO
    FRANCO COLOMBO PUBLICATIONS   DS415   1.00
MONTANARO
  SIX EASY PIECES ON 5 NOTES - 6. IN MORTE DEL PASSEROTTO
    FRANCO COLOMBO PUBLICATIONS   DS416   1.00

MONTANARO
  SIX RECREATIONAL PIECES - 1. MARIONETTE INNAMORATE
    FRANCO COLOMBO PUBLICATIONS   DS650   1.00
MONTANARO
  SIX RECREATIONAL PIECES - 2. CANZONE DELLA LAGUNA
    FRANCO COLOMBO PUBLICATIONS   DS651   1.00
MONTANARO
  SIX RECREATIONAL PIECES - 3. AMABILITA
    FRANCO COLOMBO PUBLICATIONS   DS652   1.00
MONTANARO
  SIX RECREATIONAL PIECES - 4. PICCOLA ARABA
    FRANCO COLOMBO PUBLICATIONS   DS653   1.00
MONTANARO
  SIX RECREATIONAL PIECES - 5. TARANTELLA
    FRANCO COLOMBO PUBLICATIONS   DS654   1.00
MONTANARO
  SIX RECREATIONAL PIECES - 6. FIORE ANDALUSO
    FRANCO COLOMBO PUBLICATIONS   DS655   1.00
MONTANI
  ARCA DI NOE, L' - 1. CAPRICCIO DEL CUCU
    FRANCO COLOMBO PUBLICATIONS   125496   .75
MONTANI
  ARCA DI NOE, L' - 2. IN MORTE DI UNA CUCCIOLA
    FRANCO COLOMBO PUBLICATIONS   125497   .75
MONTANI
  ARCA DI NOE, L' - 3. QUEL ROSIGNUOL CHE SI SOAVE PIANGE
    FRANCO COLOMBO PUBLICATIONS   125810   .75
MONTANI
  CHARACTERISTIC STUDIES - FANTASY
    FRANCO COLOMBO PUBLICATIONS   122642   1.00
MONTANI
  GAUDIA RURIS
    FRANCO COLOMBO PUBLICATIONS   BON.1225   1.50
MONTBRUN, G.   8
  ALLEGRO
    ALPHONSE LEDUC   1
MONTE, M.
  FAIRY QUEEN GAVOTTE
    CENTURY MUSIC PUBLISHING COMPANY, INC.   2385   .40
MONTE, M.   1
  FAIRY QUEEN MARCH
    CENTURY MUSIC PUBLISHING COMPANY, INC.   2384   .40
MONTE, M.   1
  FAIRY QUEEN MAZURKA
    CENTURY MUSIC PUBLISHING COMPANY, INC.   2383   .40
MONTE, M.   1
  FAIRY QUEEN REVERIES
    CENTURY MUSIC PUBLISHING COMPANY, INC.   2389   .40
MONTE, M.   1
  FAIRY QUEEN WALTZ
    CENTURY MUSIC PUBLISHING COMPANY, INC.   2381   .40
MONTERDE, B.
  MACARENA
    PEER SOUTHERN ORGANIZATION   01.00
MONTGOMERY, L.   2
  CELLO SONG
    CENTURY MUSIC PUBLISHING COMPANY, INC.   3816   .40
MONTGOMERY, L.   2
  ON THE MERRY GO ROUND
    CENTURY MUSIC PUBLISHING COMPANY, INC.   3817   .40
MONTI, V.
  AUBADE D'MOUR
    FRANCO COLOMBO PUBLICATIONS   104127   .60
MONTI, V.
  CZARDAS
    ASHLEY DEALERS SERVICE, INC.   ES   .95
MONTI, V.   4
  CZARDAS
    CENTURY MUSIC PUBLISHING COMPANY, INC.   3423   .40
MONTI, V.   RAMELLA
  CZARDAS NO. 1
    FRANCO COLOMBO PUBLICATIONS   118669   .75
MONTI, V. *
  CSARDAS
    CARL FISCHER, INC.   P 2225   .75
MONTPELLIER, P.
  SUITE LOUIS XVI
    EDITIONS MUSICALES TRANSATLANTIQUES   2.90
MOONEY
  SWAMP-FIRE
    MCA MUSIC   1.00
MOORE   SCHAUM, J.   4
  CHRISTMAS FANTASY
    SCHAUM PUBLICATIONS, INC.   .60
MOORE   M
  DANCE FOR A HOLIDAY
    THEODORE PRESSER COMPANY   .50
MOORE   2B
  GREMLINS
    MUSICORD PUBLICATIONS, INC.   .45
MOORE   3 1/2
  IN A LAZY SPRING
    THEODORE PRESSER COMPANY   .50
MOORE   3
  JUNGLE CARAVEN
    CENTURY MUSIC PUBLISHING COMPANY, INC.   041   .40
MOORE   3
  MY PRAYER
    BELWIN-MILLS PUBLISHING CORPORATION   .60
MOORE   M
  PRELUDE
    THEODORE PRESSER COMPANY   .50
MOORE
  RED SQUARE
    MCA MUSIC   1.00
MOORE   3
  RHAPSODIC MELODY
    BELWIN-MILLS PUBLISHING CORPORATION   .60
MOORE   2 1/2
  ROMANTIC REVERIE
    BELWIN-MILLS PUBLISHING CORPORATION   .60
MOORE
  SHOO-SHOO BABY
    MCA MUSIC   1.00
MOORE *
  FIDDLIN' JOE
    CARL FISCHER, INC.   P 2119   .50
MOPPER, I.   E
  DIVERSIONS
    THEODORE PRESSER COMPANY   .50
MOPPER, I.   MD
  SONATINA NO. 02
    THEODORE PRESSER COMPANY   .75
MORALES   SINGER
  JUNGLE FANTASY
    MCA MUSIC   1.00

MORAWETZ
  FANTASY ELEGY AND TOCCATA
    MCA MUSIC   2.50
MOREAU
  SUR LA MER LOINTAINE
    FRANCO COLOMBO PUBLICATIONS   SAL   1.75
                                             8
MOREAU
  VARIATIONS A DANSER
    ALPHONSE LEDUC
MOREL, F.
  RONDE ENFANTINE
    ASSOCIATED MUSIC PUBLISHERS, INC.   BER   .60
                                             3
MOREL, G.
  INTERMEZZO VENETIEN
    CENTURY MUSIC PUBLISHING COMPANY, INC.   2765   .40
                                             3
MOREL, G.
  LADY POMPADOUR
    CENTURY MUSIC PUBLISHING COMPANY, INC.   2368   .40
                                             3
MOREL, G.
  NORWEGIAN CRADLE SONG
    CENTURY MUSIC PUBLISHING COMPANY, INC.   2308   .40
MORENO GANS, J.
  GAVOTTE IN B MINOR
    ASSOCIATED MUSIC PUBLISHERS, INC.   UME   .50
MORENO GANS, J.
  HOMENAJE A ALBENIZ
    ASSOCIATED MUSIC PUBLISHERS, INC.   UME   1.25
MORENO GANS, J.
  PASTORAL
    ASSOCIATED MUSIC PUBLISHERS, INC.   UME   .60
                                             E
MOREY, F.
  BOATMAN'S SONG, THE
    COMPOSERS PRESS, INC.   1.00
                                             E
MOREY, F.
  DOLL'S DANCE
    COMPOSERS PRESS, INC.   1.00
                                             E
MOREY, F.
  JACK AND JILL IN HAPPYLAND
    COMPOSERS PRESS, INC.   1.00
                                             E
MOREY, F.
  MAMMY'S LULLABY
    COMPOSERS PRESS, INC.   •   1.00
                                             E
MOREY, F.
  MARCH OF THE BOY SCOUTS
    COMPOSERS PRESS, INC.   1.00
                                             E-M
MOREY, F.
  TANGLEFOOT'S MAD CHASE
    COMPOSERS PRESS, INC.   1.00
MORGEN, M.
  CHILDREN AT PLAY
    FREDERICK HARRIS MUSIC COMPANY   .60
MORGEN, M.
  LITTLE DUTCH DANCE
    FREDERICK HARRIS MUSIC COMPANY   .60
MORGEN, M.
  MERRY TUNE, A
    FREDERICK HARRIS MUSIC COMPANY   .60
MORGEN, M.
  MUSIC BOX
    FREDERICK HARRIS MUSIC COMPANY   .60
MORILLO, R.
  MARLBOROUGH'S RETURN
    PEER SOUTHERN ORGANIZATION   00.85
                                             MD
MORITZ, E.
  FRONTIER
    THEODORE PRESSER COMPANY   .60
                                             E
MORITZ, E.
  KEYBOARD CARICATURES
    THEODORE PRESSER COMPANY   .50
                                             M
MORITZ, E.
  LAKE MIRROR
    THEODORE PRESSER COMPANY   .60
MORLEY, G.
  NOCTURNE
    ASSOCIATED MUSIC PUBLISHERS, INC.   BER   .75
MORRICONE, E.
  GOOD, THE BAD, AND THE UGLY, THE
    THE BIG THREE MUSIC CORPORATION   00.95
MORRIS, C.   3
  MEDITATION, OP. 84
    CENTURY MUSIC PUBLISHING COMPANY, INC.   2189   .40
MORRIS, C.
  PLAY THE THING
    MCA MUSIC   1.00
                                             M
MORRIS, H.
  BALLET
    COMPOSERS PRESS, INC.   1.00
                                             D
MORRIS, H.
  SONATA NO. 04
    COMPOSERS PRESS, INC.   5.00
                                             3
MORRISON, C.
  MEDITATION
    CENTURY MUSIC PUBLISHING COMPANY, INC.   4099   .40
                                             4
MORRISON, C.
  MEDITATION
    THEODORE PRESSER COMPANY   .50
                                             4
MORRISON, C.
  MEDITATION
    VOLKWEIN BROS.   .50
MORRISON, C.
  MEDITATION, OP. 90
    ASHLEY DEALERS SERVICE, INC.   ES   .95
                                             2
MORRISON, C.
  MEDITATIONS
    WILLIS MUSIC COMPANY   .35
MORTARI
  STUDI GALANTI
    FRANCO COLOMBO PUBLICATIONS   FOR.11958   1.75
MOSCHELES, I.
  CANON A LA SEPTIEME, PUBLISHED WITH AMY FAY DEPPE EXERCISES
    MUSICA OBSCURA   2.50
MOSCHELES, I.
  LA CARINA
    BANKS AND SON LTD.   .55
MOSCHELES, I.
  RECOLLECTIONS OF SCOTLAND, OP. 80
    MUSICA OBSCURA   4.00
MOSER, C.
  MINUETTO E INTERMEZZO
    EDIZIONI BERBEN   EB 1366   1.20
                                             2
MOSHER
  ALOUETTE, G MAJOR
    CENTURY MUSIC PUBLISHING COMPANY, INC.   4382   .40
                                             2
MOSHER
  LARK, THE
    CENTURY MUSIC PUBLISHING COMPANY, INC.   4382   .40

MOSKOWITZ   3
  CZARA
    CENTURY MUSIC PUBLISHING COMPANY, INC.   969   .40
MOSS, E.
  CALYPSO BOY
    FREDERICK HARRIS MUSIC COMPANY   .60
                                             3
MOSS, E.
  LINGERING MEMORIES
    CENTURY MUSIC PUBLISHING COMPANY, INC.   2415   .40
MOSS, E.
  LITTLE LAMB
    FREDERICK HARRIS MUSIC COMPANY   .60
MOSS, L.
  FANTASY FOR PIANO
    ELKAN-VOGEL, INC.   3.50
MOSS, L.
  FOUR SCENES FOR PIANO, 1961
    SEESAW MUSIC CORPORATION   4.00
MOSSMAN, T.
  AIN'T MISBEHAVIN' -- SIMP.
    BELWIN-MILLS PUBLISHING CORPORATION   26003   .50
                                             2
MOSSMAN, T.
  ARKANSAS FIDDLER
    BELWIN-MILLS PUBLISHING CORPORATION   .60
MOSSMAN, T.
  AT A GEORGIA CAMP MEETING -- SIMP.
    BELWIN-MILLS PUBLISHING CORPORATION   26004   .50
MOSSMAN, T.
  BELLS OF AVALON, THE -- SIMP.
    BELWIN-MILLS PUBLISHING CORPORATION   26066   .50
                                             2
MOSSMAN, T.
  BIG ROCK CANDY MOUNTAIN
    BELWIN-MILLS PUBLISHING CORPORATION   .60
                                             2 1/2
MOSSMAN, T.
  BLOW THE MAN DOWN
    BELWIN-MILLS PUBLISHING CORPORATION   .60
MOSSMAN, T.
  BUGLE CALL RAG -- SIMP.
    BELWIN-MILLS PUBLISHING CORPORATION   26072   .50
MOSSMAN, T.
  CENTRAL PARK ROMANCE
    THE BIG THREE MUSIC CORPORATION   00.95
MOSSMAN, T.
  COMPOSING A RONDO WITH BEETHOVEN -- SIMP.
    BELWIN-MILLS PUBLISHING CORPORATION   26079   .50
                                             1
MOSSMAN, T.
  DAY OF JUBILO
    BELWIN-MILLS PUBLISHING CORPORATION   .60
                                             2
MOSSMAN, T.
  DEEP RIVER
    BELWIN-MILLS PUBLISHING CORPORATION   .60
MOSSMAN, T.
  FLAPPERETTE -- SIMP.
    BELWIN-MILLS PUBLISHING CORPORATION   26014   .50
MOSSMAN, T.
  FOR ME AND MY GAL -- SIMP.
    BELWIN-MILLS PUBLISHING CORPORATION   26075   .50
MOSSMAN, T.
  HANDEL PLAYS FOR THE KING -- SIMP.
    BELWIN-MILLS PUBLISHING CORPORATION   26017   .50
MOSSMAN, T.
  HANDS ACROSS THE TABLE -- SIMP.
    BELWIN-MILLS PUBLISHING CORPORATION   26069   .50
MOSSMAN, T.
  HAYDN GOES HUNTING -- SIMP.
    BELWIN-MILLS PUBLISHING CORPORATION   26018   .50
MOSSMAN, T.
  HOME -- SIMP.
    BELWIN-MILLS PUBLISHING CORPORATION   26020   .50
MOSSMAN, T.
  I CAN'T GIVE YOU ANYTHING BUT LOVE -- SIMP.
    BELWIN-MILLS PUBLISHING CORPORATION   26021   .50
MOSSMAN, T.
  IN SUNNY SOUTH AMERICAN -- SIMP.
    BELWIN-MILLS PUBLISHING CORPORATION   26078   .50
MOSSMAN, T.
  MARGIE -- SIMP.
    BELWIN-MILLS PUBLISHING CORPORATION   26027   .50
MOSSMAN, T.
  MARY LOU -- SIMP.
    BELWIN-MILLS PUBLISHING CORPORATION   26028   .50
                                             2
MOSSMAN, T.
  MOHEE
    BELWIN-MILLS PUBLISHING CORPORATION   .60
MOSSMAN, T.
  ODE TO GERSHWIN
    THE BIG THREE MUSIC CORPORATION   00.95
MOSSMAN, T.
  ONE MORNING IN MAY -- SIMP.
    BELWIN-MILLS PUBLISHING CORPORATION   26035   .50
MOSSMAN, T.
  REPASZ BAND -- SIMP.
    BELWIN-MILLS PUBLISHING CORPORATION   26041   .50
MOSSMAN, T.
  SCHOOL DAYS -- SIMP.
    BELWIN-MILLS PUBLISHING CORPORATION   26042   .50
MOSSMAN, T.
  SOARING WITH SCHUMANN -- SIMP.
    BELWIN-MILLS PUBLISHING CORPORATION   26048   .50
MOSSMAN, T.
  SOLITUDE -- SIMP.
    BELWIN-MILLS PUBLISHING CORPORATION   26049   .50
MOSSMAN, T.
  SOPHISTICATED LADY -- SIMP.
    BELWIN-MILLS PUBLISHING CORPORATION   26050   .50
                                             2
MOSSMAN, T.
  SUZETTE
    BELWIN-MILLS PUBLISHING CORPORATION   .60
MOSSMAN, T.
  WALTZING WITH STRAUSS
    BELWIN-MILLS PUBLISHING CORPORATION   26059   .50
MOSSMAN, T.--ED   MOSSMAN, T.
  HANDS ACROSS THE TABLE, SIMPLIFIED
    BELWIN-MILLS PUBLISHING CORPORATION   .60
MOSSMAN, T.--ED   MOSSMAN, T.
  KITTEN ON THE KEYS -- SIMP.
    BELWIN-MILLS PUBLISHING CORPORATION   26023   .50
MOSSMAN, T.--ED   MOSSMAN, T.
  ORGAN GRINDER'S SWING -- SIMP.
    BELWIN-MILLS PUBLISHING CORPORATION   26068   .50
MOSSMAN, T.--ED   MOSSMAN, T.
  PAVANNE -- SIMP.
    BELWIN-MILLS PUBLISHING CORPORATION   26036   .50
MOSSMAN, T.--ED   MOSSMAN, T.
  SERENADE IN THE NIGHT -- SIMP.
    BELWIN-MILLS PUBLISHING CORPORATION   26092   .50

MOSSMAN, T.--ED   MOSSMAN, T.
  SHEIK OF ARABY, THE -- SIMP.
    BELWIN-MILLS PUBLISHING CORPORATION   .50
MOSSMAN, T.--ED   MOSSMAN, T.
  SWEET LORRAINE -- SIMP.
    BELWIN-MILLS PUBLISHING CORPORATION   26052 .50
MOSSMAN, T.--ED   MOSSMAN, T.
  SWEET ROSIE O'GRADY SIMP.
    BELWIN-MILLS PUBLISHING CORPORATION   26053 .50
MOSSMAN, T.--ED   MOSSMAN, T.
  TAKE ME IN YOUR ARMS -- SIMP.
    BELWIN-MILLS PUBLISHING CORPORATION   26055 .50
MOSSMAN, T.--ED   MOSSMAN, T.
  WHEN IT'S SLEEPY TIME DOWN SOUTH -- SIMP.
    BELWIN-MILLS PUBLISHING CORPORATION   26062 .50
MOSSOLOW, A.
  TWO NOCTURNES, OP. 15
    UNIVERSAL EDITION   UE 9571 1.10
MOSZKOWSKI
  AIR DE BALLET IN G MINOR, OP. 36 NO. 5
    G. SCHIRMER, INC.   .70
MOSZKOWSKI   SCHAUM, J.   3
  BOLERO
    BELWIN-MILLS PUBLISHING CORPORATION   .50
MOSZKOWSKI   4
  BOLERO, OP. 12 NO. 5
    CENTURY MUSIC PUBLISHING COMPANY, INC. 1766 .40
MOSZKOWSKI   LOCATELLI
  BOLERO, OP. 12 NO. 5
    FRANCO COLOMBO PUBLICATIONS   BA11285 .75
MOSZKOWSKI   M
  CAPRICE ESPAGNOL
    C. F. PETERS CORPORATION   2218A .90
MOSZKOWSKI   M-D
  CAPRICE ESPAGNOL, OP. 37
    C. F. PETERS CORPORATION   2218   1.25
MOSZKOWSKI   5
  CAPRICE ESPAGNOL, OP. 37
    CENTURY MUSIC PUBLISHING COMPANY, INC. 1775 .40
MOSZKOWSKI
  CAPRICE ESPAGNOL, OP. 37
    FRANCO COLOMBO PUBLICATIONS   BA7998 1.00
MOSZKOWSKI
  CAPRICE ESPAGNOL, OP. 37
    G. SCHIRMER, INC.   .80
MOSZKOWSKI
  CHANSON BOHEME DE CARMEN --BIZET
    MUSICA OBSCURA   2.50
MOSZKOWSKI   5
  EN AUTONNE, OP. 36 NO. 4
    CENTURY MUSIC PUBLISHING COMPANY, INC. 3337 .40
MOSZKOWSKI
  ETINCELLES--MORCEAU CARACTERISTIQUE, OP. 36 NO. 6
    G. SCHIRMER, INC.   .80
MOSZKOWSKI   3
  ETUDE DE LEGATO OP. 81 NO. 3
    SCHOTT   1.25
MOSZKOWSKI
  ETUDE IN D, OP. 32 NO. 2
    G. SCHIRMER, INC.   .50
MOSZKOWSKI
  ETUDE IN G, OP. 18 NO. 3
    G. SCHIRMER, INC.   .50
MOSZKOWSKI   PAUER
  FROM FOREIGN PARTS, OP. 23--GERMANY
    G. SCHIRMER, INC.   .35
MOSZKOWSKI   4
  GONDOLIERA
    CENTURY MUSIC PUBLISHING COMPANY, INC. 3238 .40
MOSZKOWSKI   LOCATELLI
  GONDOLIERA, OP. 41
    FRANCO COLOMBO PUBLICATIONS   BA11198 .75
MOSZKOWSKI   M-D
  GUITAR, OP. 45 NO. 2
    C. F. PETERS CORPORATION   2223   1.50
MOSZKOWSKI   E
  GUITAR, OP. 45 NO. 2
    C. F. PETERS CORPORATION   2223A .90
MOSZKOWSKI   LOCATELLI
  GUITAR, OP. 45 NO. 2
    FRANCO COLOMBO PUBLICATIONS   BA11199 .75
MOSZKOWSKI   4
  GUITARRE, OP. 45 NO. 2
    CENTURY MUSIC PUBLISHING COMPANY, INC. 3334 .40
MOSZKOWSKI   D
  HABANERA, OP. 65, NO. 3
    C. F. PETERS CORPORATION   3021   .90
MOSZKOWSKI
  IN AUTUMN, OP. 36 NO. 4
    G. SCHIRMER, INC.   .60
MOSZKOWSKI   D
  JUGGLERESS, OP. 52, NO. 4
    C. F. PETERS CORPORATION   2840   .90
MOSZKOWSKI   D
  LOVE WALTZ, OP. 57, NO. 5
    C. F. PETERS CORPORATION   2907   .90
MOSZKOWSKI
  MALAGUENA - FROM 'BOABDIL'
    FRANCO COLOMBO PUBLICATIONS   BA11200 .75
MOSZKOWSKI   D
  MALAGUENA --FROM BOABDIL--
    C. F. PETERS CORPORATION   2616   .90
MOSZKOWSKI   3
  MENUETT OP. 77 NO. 10
    SCHOTT   1.25
MOSZKOWSKI   LOCATELLI
  MINUET, OP. 77 NO. 10
    FRANCO COLOMBO PUBLICATIONS   BA11201 .75
MOSZKOWSKI
  PANTOMIME--FROM 'PIECES MIGNONNES', OP. 77
    G. SCHIRMER, INC.   .50
MOSZKOWSKI
  POLONAISE IN D, OP. 17 NO. 1
    MUSICA OBSCURA   2.50
MOSZKOWSKI
  SCHERZINO IN F, OP. 18 NO. 2
    G. SCHIRMER, INC.   .50
MOSZKOWSKI   M
  SCHERZO-VALSE, OP. 40
    C. F. PETERS CORPORATION   2219   1.50
MOSZKOWSKI   KAHL   2
  SERENATA
    BOSTON MUSIC COMPANY   .50
MOSZKOWSKI
  SERENATA IN D, OP. 15 NO. 1
    G. SCHIRMER, INC.   .35

MOSZKOWSKI   LOCATELLI
  SERENATA, OP. 15 NO. 1
    FRANCO COLOMBO PUBLICATIONS   BA11202 .75
MOSZKOWSKI   4
  SERENATA, OP. 15 NO. 2
    CENTURY MUSIC PUBLISHING COMPANY, INC. 386   .40
MOSZKOWSKI   5
  SPANISH CAPRICE
    CENTURY MUSIC PUBLISHING COMPANY, INC. 1775 .40
MOSZKOWSKI   4
  SPANISH DANCE NO. 1
    CENTURY MUSIC PUBLISHING COMPANY, INC. 1764 .40
MOSZKOWSKI   4
  SPANISH DANCE NO. 2
    CENTURY MUSIC PUBLISHING COMPANY, INC. 1765 .40
MOSZKOWSKI   4
  SPANISH DANCE NO. 4
    CENTURY MUSIC PUBLISHING COMPANY, INC. 2011 .40
MOSZKOWSKI   4
  SPANISH DANCE NO. 5
    CENTURY MUSIC PUBLISHING COMPANY, INC. 1766 .40
MOSZKOWSKI
  SPANISH DANCE OP. 12 NO. 1
    VOLKWEIN BROS.   .25
MOSZKOWSKI
  SPANISH DANCE, OP. 12 NO. 1
    CARL FISCHER, INC.   S 2093 .50
MOSZKOWSKI
  SPANISH DANCES, OP. 12 NO. 1
    G. SCHIRMER, INC.   .40
MOSZKOWSKI
  SPANISH DANCES, OP. 12 NO. 5--BOLERO
    G. SCHIRMER, INC.   .40
MOSZKOWSKI   5
  SPARKS
    CENTURY MUSIC PUBLISHING COMPANY, INC. 3348 .40
MOSZKOWSKI   5
  VALSE BRILLANTE AS-DUR
    SCHOTT   1778   1.50
MOSZKOWSKI
  VALSE BRILLANTE IN A FLAT
    G. SCHIRMER, INC.   .75
MOSZKOWSKI   5
  VALSE BRILLIANTE
    CENTURY MUSIC PUBLISHING COMPANY, INC. 1647 .40
MOSZKOWSKI
  VALSE D'MOUR, OP. 57 NO. 5
    FRANCO COLOMBO PUBLICATIONS   BA11203 .75
MOSZKOWSKI
  VALSE IN E, OP. 34 NO. 1
    G. SCHIRMER, INC.   1.00
MOSZKOWSKI   6
  VALSE IN E, OP. 34 NO. 1
    THEODORE PRESSER COMPANY   .50
MOTTU
  CHARMEUSE DE PEINES
    FRANCO COLOMBO PUBLICATIONS   SAL   5.50
MOTTU
  LIVRE D'HEURES
    FRANCO COLOMBO PUBLICATIONS   SAL   4.25
MOURAVIEFF, L.
  THREE POEMS
    BOOSEY AND HAWKES, INC.   2.75
MOUSSORGSKY   KREUTZ   5
  BILDER EINER AUSSTELLUNG
    SCHOTT   525   3.00
MOUSSORGSKY
  CHILDREN'S JEST, A
    ASSOCIATED MUSIC PUBLISHERS, INC.   SIM   1.50
MOUSSORGSKY   4
  GOPAK
    CENTURY MUSIC PUBLISHING COMPANY, INC. 3610 .40
MOUSSORGSKY   MOSSMAN, T.
  GOPAK FROM 'THE FAIR AT SOROCHINSK' -- SIMP.
    BELWIN-MILLS PUBLISHING CORPORATION   26080 .50
MOUSSORGSKY   RACHMANINOFF, S.
  HOPAK
    BELWIN-MILLS PUBLISHING CORPORATION   1.00
MOUSSORGSKY   CLOUGH *   3
  HOPAK
    BOSTON MUSIC COMPANY   .60
MOUSSORGSKY   ECKSTEIN
  HOPAK
    CARL FISCHER, INC.   S 2306 .60
MOUSSORGSKY
  PICTURES AT AN ART EXHIBITION
    ASHLEY DEALERS SERVICE, INC.   1.50
MOUSSORGSKY   D
  PICTURES AT AN EXHIBITION
    C. F. PETERS CORPORATION   3727A 2.50
MOUSSORGSKY
  PICTURES AT AN EXHIBITION
    EDWIN F. KALMUS   3688   1.75
MOUSSORGSKY   CASELLA
  PICTURES AT AN EXHIBITION
    FRANCO COLOMBO PUBLICATIONS   ER2251 2.25
MOUSSORGSKY
  PICTURES AT AN EXHIBITION
    INTERNATIONAL MUSIC COMPANY   2.50
MOUSSORGSKY   BAUER
  PICTURES AT AN EXPOSITION
    G. SCHIRMER, INC.   1.50
MOUSSORGSKY
  PICTURES FROM AN EXHIBITION
    EDWARD B. MARKS MUSIC CORPORATION   01.25
MOUSSORGSKY   DEXTER, H.
  PICTURES FROM AN EXHIBITION
    SAM FOX PUBLISHING COMPANY, INC.   1.00
MOUSSORGSKY
  SCHERZINO
    EDWARD B. MARKS MUSIC CORPORATION   01.10
MOUSSORGSKY   DANIEL, R. M.
  TABLEAUX D'UNE EXPOSITION
    ELKAN-VOGEL, INC.   CON   3.50
MOUSSORGSKY   GRATIA, L. E.
  TABLEAUX D'UNE EXPOSITION
    ELKAN-VOGEL, INC.   CON   2.75
MOWPEY, D.
  FESTIVAL
    G. SCHIRMER, INC.   .50
MOWPEY, D.
  LAZY PICCANINNY
    G. SCHIRMER, INC.   .50
MOWPEY, D.
  SCHERZO IN DOUBLE-NOTES
    G. SCHIRMER, INC.   .80

```
MOWREY, D.
    SERENADE
        G. SCHIRMER, INC.                                    .75
MOWREY, D.
    SPANISH GYPSY DANCE
        G. SCHIRMER, INC.                                    .60
MOWREY, D.
    TANGO
        G. SCHIRMER, INC.                                    .60
MOWREY, D.
    TRAPEZE PERFORMERS, THE
        G. SCHIRMER, INC.                                    .50
MOY
    FESTIVAL GROUPS FOR PIANO SELECTED BY ARTHUR BENJAMIN, SERIES 2
    -- THE MERRY SHEPHERD
        BOOSEY AND HAWKES, INC.                              .60
MOY, E.
    SONATINA
        NOVELLO AND COMPANY, LTD.         10.0102.07   1.25
MOYZES, A.                        3-4
    DIVERTIMENTO, OP. 11
        BARENREITER VERLAG               AP 660
MOYZES, M.                        4
    SONATINE
        BARENREITER VERLAG               AP 662
MOZART, L.                        4
    PASSEPIED -- FROM NOTEBOOK FOR WOLFGANG
        LEE ROBERTS MUSIC PUBLICATIONS, INC.                 .50
MOZART, L.          STEINER       2 1/2
    POLONAISE IN C
        BELWIN-MILLS PUBLISHING CORPORATION                  .60
MOZART, W. A.
    ADAGIO DE LA SONATA NO. 6
        EDITIONS MUSICALES TRANSATLANTIQUES           3.25
MOZART, W. A.
    ADAGIO FOR PIANOFORTE, B MINOR, K540
        G. HENLE MUSIKVERLAG            137       1.10
MOZART, W. A.          STEINER    1
    AIR OF THE SHEPHERDESS
        BELWIN-MILLS PUBLISHING CORPORATION                  .50
MOZART, W. A.          STEINER    1
    AIR OF THE SHEPHERDESS
        BELWIN-MILLS PUBLISHING CORPORATION                  .60
MOZART, W. A.
    ALLA TURCA RONDO
        BELWIN-MILLS PUBLISHING CORPORATION                  .60
MOZART, W. A.                     4
    ALLA TURCA, A MINOR, FROM THE SONATA IN A MINOR
        CENTURY MUSIC PUBLISHING COMPANY, INC.   17 2        .40
MOZART, W. A.                     2
    ALLA TURCA, A MINOR, FROM THE SONATA IN A MINOR--EASY--
        CENTURY MUSIC PUBLISHING COMPANY, INC.   3653        .40
MOZART, W. A.                     3
    ALLEGRO IN B FLAT MAJOR
        LEE ROBERTS MUSIC PUBLICATIONS, INC.                 .50
MOZART, W. A.                     4
    ALLEGRO IN F MAJOR
        LEE ROBERTS MUSIC PUBLICATIONS, INC.                 .50
MOZART, W. A.          MONTANI
    ANDANTE CON VARIAZIONI, K501
        FRANCO COLOMBO PUBLICATIONS     128955    1.00
MOZART, W. A.
    ANDANTE FOR A SMALL MECHANICAL ORGAN, K616
        G. HENLE MUSIKVERLAG            232       1.15
MOZART, W. A.          DEL MAGLIO
    ANDANTE FROM SONATA NO. 15
        FRANCO COLOMBO PUBLICATIONS     124724    .50
MOZART, W. A.          BUSONI
    ANDANTINO FROM PIANO CONCERTO K271
        ASSOCIATED MUSIC PUBLISHERS, INC.   BRH   1.20
MOZART, W. A.
    ANDANTINO, K236
        BRODT MUSIC COMPANY                       .35
MOZART, W. A.                     1
    AVE VERUM -- MIT TEXT K.V. 618
        SCHOTT                          05757     .75
MOZART, W. A.                     2
    BERUHMTES MENUETT AUS DEM D-DUR DIVERTIMENTO -- K.V. 334
        SCHOTT                          07792     .75
MOZART, W. A.
    BOUREF
        FREDERICK HARRIS MUSIC COMPANY            .60
MOZART, W. A.                     3
    BOUREE
        LEE ROBERTS MUSIC PUBLICATIONS, INC.      .50
MOZART, W. A.          POTAMKIN
    BREAD AND BUTTER WALTZ
        ELKAN-VOGEL, INC.                         .50
MOZART, W. A.          LANDOWSKA, W.
    CADENZA - SONATA K333 IN B FLAT
        BROUDE BROTHERS LTD.                      01.75
MOZART, W. A.
    CONCERTO IN C MAJOR, NO. 21 -- THEME FROM 'ELVIRA MADIGAN'
        ASHLEY DEALERS SERVICE, INC.              1.00
MOZART, W. A.                     M
    CONCERTO K488 IN A
        C. F. PETERS CORPORATION        3309EE    1.25
MOZART, W. A.          PIETSCH
    CRADLE SONG
        G. SCHIRMER, INC.                         .35
MOZART, W. A.          STEINER    2
    DAINTY DANCE
        BELWIN-MILLS PUBLISHING CORPORATION       .60
MOZART, W. A.                     M
    DON GIOVANNI
        C. F. PETERS CORPORATION        H631      2.00
MOZART, W. A.          DEL MAGLIO
    DON GIOVANNI - DEH VIENI ALLA FINESTRA
        FRANCO COLOMBO PUBLICATIONS     124722    .50
MOZART, W. A.          CHIESA
    DON GIOVANNI - EASY FANTASIA
        FRANCO COLOMBO PUBLICATIONS     107486    .50
MOZART, W. A.                     2
    DON JUAN MINUET
        THEODORE PRESSER COMPANY                  .50
MOZART, W. A.          ROSATI, G.
    DUE VALZER
        EDIZIONI BERBEN                 EB 1637   1.25
MOZART, W. A.          STARK
    EINE KLEINE NACHTMUSIK--SERENADE--K525
        ASSOCIATED MUSIC PUBLISHERS, INC.   BRH   .90
MOZART, W. A.          CLASSENS
    EINE KLEINE NACHTMUSIK, A LITTLE NIGHT MUSIC
        ELKAN-VOGEL, INC.                         1.60
MOZART, W. A.                     E-M
    EINE KLEINE NACHTMUSIK, K525
        C. F. PETERS CORPORATION        3957      1.50

MOZART, W. A.          ZANON
    EINE KLEINE NACHTMUSIK, K525
        FRANCO COLOMBO PUBLICATIONS     ER2270    1.25
MOZART, W. A.                     3
    EINE KLEINE NACHTMUSIK, K525
        SCHOTT                          1630      1.00
MOZART, W. A.                     4
    EINE KLEINE NACHTMUSIK, ROMANZE
        CENTURY MUSIC PUBLISHING COMPANY, INC.   3490   .40
MOZART, W. A.
    EINE KLEINE NACHTMUSIK, K525
        FRANCO COLOMBO PUBLICATIONS     ER2059    1.00
MOZART, W. A.                     5
    FANTASIA IN C MINOR
        CENTURY MUSIC PUBLISHING COMPANY, INC.   3492   .40
MOZART, W. A.          CASELLA
    FANTASIA IN C MINOR, K475
        FRANCO COLOMBO PUBLICATIONS     128405    1.00
MOZART, W. A.
    FANTASIA IN D MINOR
        ASHLEY DEALERS SERVICE, INC.    ES        .95
MOZART, W. A.                     3
    FANTASIA IN D MINOR
        CENTURY MUSIC PUBLISHING COMPANY, INC.   3332   .40
MOZART, W. A.          CASELLA
    FANTASIA IN D MINOR, K397
        FRANCO COLOMBO PUBLICATIONS     ER2575    .60
MOZART, W. A.          BUELOW
    FANTASIA K396 IN C MINOR
        G. SCHIRMER, INC.                         .70
MOZART, W. A.          BUONAMICI
    FANTASIA K397 IN D MINOR
        G. SCHIRMER, INC.                         .50
MOZART, W. A.          EPSTEIN
    FANTASIA K475 IN C MINOR
        G. SCHIRMER, INC.                         .70
MOZART, W. A.                     4
    FANTASIA K475, AND SONATA K457 IN C MINOR, SCH NO. 18
        G. SCHIRMER, INC.                         1.10
MOZART, W. A.                     4
    FANTASIE C-MOLL -- K.V. 396
        SCHOTT                          0968 1/2  1.00
MOZART, W. A.                     4
    FANTASIE C-MOLL -- K.V. 475
        SCHOTT                          0636 1/2  1.00
MOZART, W. A.                     3
    FANTASIE D-MOLL -- K.V. 397
        SCHOTT                          0969 1/2  1.00
MOZART, W. A.                     5
    FANTASIE UND FUGE C-DUR -- K.V. 394
        SCHOTT                          0970 1/2  1.00
MOZART, W. A.
    FANTASY IN D MINOR, K397
        ASSOCIATED MUSIC PUBLISHERS, INC.   BRH   .60
MOZART, W. A.          PODOLSKY, L.
    FANTASY IN D MINOR, K397
        SHAWNEE PRESS, INC.             HB-232    .75
MOZART, W. A.          MONTANI
    FUGUE IN G MINOR, K401
        FRANCO COLOMBO PUBLICATIONS     128956    .90
MOZART, W. A.          PODOLSKY, L.
    GERMAN DANCE NO. 2
        FREDERICK HARRIS MUSIC COMPANY            .60
MOZART, W. A.          STEINER    2
    HAPPY HARVEST
        BELWIN-MILLS PUBLISHING CORPORATION       .60
MOZART, W. A.          ROLFE, W.    EASY
    HARPSICHORD PLAYER, THE --SONATA IN C--
        SHAWNEE PRESS, INC.             HB-5006    .60
MOZART, W. A.
    LANDLER
        FREDERICK HARRIS MUSIC COMPANY            .60
MOZART, W. A.
    LE PETITS RIEN
        HEUGEL ET CIE.                            5.65
MOZART, W. A.                     2
    LULLABY
        CENTURY MUSIC PUBLISHING COMPANY, INC.   3918   .40
MOZART, W. A.                     M
    MAGIC FLUTE, ABRIDGED
        C. F. PETERS CORPORATION        H633      2.00
MOZART, W. A.                     3
    MAGIC FLUTE, PRIESTS' MARCH
        CENTURY MUSIC PUBLISHING COMPANY, INC.   454    .40
MOZART, W. A.          BARTOK
    MARCH ALLA TURCA
        KULTURA                                   .75
MOZART, W. A.                     3
    MARCH OF THE PRIESTS, MAGIC FLUTE
        CENTURY MUSIC PUBLISHING COMPANY, INC.   454    .40
MOZART, W. A.                     M
    MARRIAGE OF FIGARO, ABRIDGED
        C. F. PETERS CORPORATION        H632      2.00
MOZART, W. A.                     4
    MENUET
        WILLIS MUSIC COMPANY                      .35
MOZART, W. A.                     4
    MENUET AND TRIO, SYMPHONY NO. 39 IN E FLAT
        CENTURY MUSIC PUBLISHING COMPANY, INC.   2334   .40
MOZART, W. A.
    MENUET FROM SYMPHONY IN E FLAT
        CARL FISCHER, INC.              S 88      .50
MOZART, W. A.                     3
    MENUETT AUS D. ES-DUR-SYMPHONIE -- K.V. 543
        SCHOTT                          07782     .75
MOZART, W. A.                     2
    MENUETTO AND AIR
        CENTURY MUSIC PUBLISHING COMPANY, INC.   3713   .40
MOZART, W. A.                     1
    MINUET
        NOVELLO AND COMPANY, LTD.       55.0038.09  .40
MOZART, W. A.          SCHULHOFF
    MINUET AND TRIO FROM SYMPHONY IN E FLAT
        BELWIN-MILLS PUBLISHING CORPORATION   28160   .60
MOZART, W. A.
    MINUET FROM 'DON GIOVANNI'
        G. SCHIRMER, INC.                         .30
MOZART, W. A.                     2
    MINUET FROM DON GIOVANNI
        CENTURY MUSIC PUBLISHING COMPANY, INC.   1813   .40
MOZART, W. A.          POTAMKIN
    MINUET FROM DON JUAN
        ELKAN-VOGEL, INC.                         .50
```

MOZART, W. A. SCHULHOFF
  MINUET FROM SYMPHONY NO. 39
    ASSOCIATED MUSIC PUBLISHERS, INC. LEU .75
MOZART, W. A. CHIESA
  MINUET FROM SYMPHONY NO. 39
    FRANCO COLOMBO PUBLICATIONS 107487 .60
MOZART, W. A. MONTANI
  MINUET IN D FROM DIVERTIMENTO NO. 17
    FRANCO COLOMBO PUBLICATIONS 128417 .60
MOZART, W. A.
  MINUET K001 IN G--WITH TRIO
    G. SCHIRMER, INC. .30
MOZART, W. A.
  MINUET K355 IN D
    G. SCHIRMER, INC. .30
MOZART, W. A. DEIS
  MINUET--FROM DIVERTIMENTO K334 IN D
    G. SCHIRMER, INC. .40
MOZART, W. A. SCHULHOFF
  MINUET--FROM SYMPHONY K543 IN E FLAT
    G. SCHIRMER, INC. .40
MOZART, W. A. 1
  MINUETTO 'DON GIOVANNI', SIMPLIFIED
    BELWIN-MILLS PUBLISHING CORPORATION 527 .60
MOZART, W. A.
  NINE VARIATIONS ON A MINUET BY DUPORT, K573
    G. HENLE MUSIKVERLAG 190 1.10
MOZART, W. A.
  NOZZE DI FIGARO, LE - OVERTURE
    FRANCO COLOMBO PUBLICATIONS 128009 1.00
MOZART, W. A. SCHAUM, J. 2
  OVERTURE TO MARRIAGE OF FIGARO
    BELWIN-MILLS PUBLISHING CORPORATION .50
MOZART, W. A.
  PASTORALE VARIEE K209B--ATTRIBUTED TO MOZART
    G. SCHIRMER, INC. .70
MOZART, W. A.
  ROMANZA K205 IN A FLAT--ATTRIBUTED TO MOZART
    G. SCHIRMER, INC. .40
MOZART, W. A. 4
  ROMANZE AS-DUR -- K.V. 205
    SCHOTT 08232 1/2 1.00
MOZART, W. A. 4
  RONDO A-MOLL -- K.V. 511
    SCHOTT 0971 1/2 1.00
MOZART, W. A.
  RONDO ALLA TURCA FROM SONATA NO. 11
    FRANCO COLOMBO PUBLICATIONS 43744 .60
MOZART, W. A. CHIESA
  RONDO ALLA TURCA FROM SONATA NO. 11
    FRANCO COLOMBO PUBLICATIONS 107488 .60
MOZART, W. A.
  RONDO ALLA TURCA--FROM SONATA K331 IN A
    G. SCHIRMER, INC. .40
MOZART, W. A. ECKSTEIN
  RONDO ALLA TURCA, FROM A MAJOR SONATA
    CARL FISCHER, INC. S 932 .50
MOZART, W. A. 2
  RONDO D-DUR -- K.V. 485
    SCHOTT 0972 1/2 1.00
MOZART, W. A. KLEE
  RONDO K485 IN D
    G. SCHIRMER, INC. .50
MOZART, W. A. KLEE
  RONDO K511 IN A MINOR
    G. SCHIRMER, INC. .60
MOZART, W. A.
  RONDO, K. 485, D MAJOR
    G. HENLE MUSIKVERLAG 53 1.10
MOZART, W. A.
  RONDO, K. 511, A MINOR
    G. HENLE MUSIKVERLAG 54 1.10
MOZART, W. A. BACKHAUS
  SERENADE--'DON GIOVANNI'
    G. SCHIRMER, INC. .50
MOZART, W. A.
  SONATA FACILE K545 IN C
    G. HENLE MUSIKVERLAG 164 1.15
MOZART, W. A. WHITFORD GR. 3
  SONATA IN C
    ROBERT WHITFORD PUBLICATIONS .40
MOZART, W. A.
  SONATA K135 IN F, SCH NO. 13
    G. SCHIRMER, INC. .70
MOZART, W. A. GEORGII, W. 3
  SONATA K135ANH. IN F, SHO NO. 0611 1/2
    SCHOTT 0611 1/2 1.00
MOZART, W. A.
  SONATA K279 IN C, SCH NO. 8
    G. SCHIRMER, INC. .70
MOZART, W. A. GEORGII, W. 3
  SONATA K279 IN C, SHO NO. 0612 1/2
    SCHOTT 0612 1/2 1.00
MOZART, W. A.
  SONATA K280 IN F, SCH NO. 2
    G. SCHIRMER, INC. .75
MOZART, W. A. GEORGII, W. 4
  SONATA K280 IN F, SHO NO. 0613 1/2
    SCHOTT 0613 1/2 1.00
MOZART, W. A.
  SONATA K282 IN E FLAT
    G. HENLE MUSIKVERLAG 60 1.15
MOZART, W. A.
  SONATA K282 IN E FLAT, SCH NO. 17
    G. SCHIRMER, INC. .75
MOZART, W. A. GEORGII, W. 3
  SONATA K282 IN E FLAT, SHO NO. 0639 1/2
    SCHOTT 0639 1/2 1.00
MOZART, W. A.
  SONATA K283 IN G, SCH NO. 5
    G. SCHIRMER, INC. .80
MOZART, W. A. GEORGII, W. 3
  SONATA K283 IN G, SHO NO. 0608 1/2
    SCHOTT 0608 1/2 1.00
MOZART, W. A.
  SONATA K284 IN D, SCH NO. 9
    G. SCHIRMER, INC. 1.10
MOZART, W. A.
  SONATA K309 IN C, SCH NO. 10
    G. SCHIRMER, INC. .90
MOZART, W. A. GEORGII, W. 4
  SONATA K309 IN C, SHO NO. 0622 1/2
    SCHOTT 0622 1/2 1.00
MOZART, W. A.
  SONATA K310 IN A MINOR, SCH NO. 14
    G. SCHIRMER, INC. 1.00

MOZART, W. A. GEORGII, W. 4
  SONATA K310 IN A MINOR, SHO NO. 0632 1/2
    SCHOTT 0632 1/2 1.00
MOZART, W. A.
  SONATA K311 IN D, SCH NO. 12
    G. SCHIRMER, INC. 1.00
MOZART, W. A. GEORGII, W. 4
  SONATA K311 IN D, SHO NO. 0626 1/2
    SCHOTT 0626 1/2 1.00
MOZART, W. A.
  SONATA K330 IN C, SCH NO. 11
    G. SCHIRMER, INC. .80
MOZART, W. A. GEORGII, W. 3
  SONATA K330 IN C, SHO NO. 0609 1/2
    SCHOTT 0609 1/2 1.00
MOZART, W. A.
  SONATA K331 IN A
    EDWARD B. MARKS MUSIC CORPORATION 01.50
MOZART, W. A.
  SONATA K331 IN A
    G. HENLE MUSIKVERLAG 50 1.15
MOZART, W. A. CHING
  SONATA K331 IN A
    GENERAL WORDS AND MUSIC COMPANY .75
MOZART, W. A.
  SONATA K331 IN A, FRA NO. 11
    FRANCO COLOMBO PUBLICATIONS 128404 1.25
MOZART, W. A.
  SONATA K331 IN A, SCH NO. 16
    G. SCHIRMER, INC. 1.00
MOZART, W. A. GEORGII, W. 4
  SONATA K331 IN A, SHO NO. 0618 1/2
    SCHOTT 0618 1/2 1.00
MOZART, W. A.
  SONATA K332 IN F
    G. HENLE MUSIKVERLAG 178 1.15
MOZART, W. A.
  SONATA K332 IN F, FRA NO. 12
    FRANCO COLOMBO PUBLICATIONS ER730 .75
MOZART, W. A.
  SONATA K332 IN F, SCH NO. 1
    G. SCHIRMER, INC. .90
MOZART, W. A. GEORGII, W. 4
  SONATA K332 IN F, SHO NO. 0614 1/2
    SCHOTT 0614 1/2 1.00
MOZART, W. A. 4
  SONATA K333 IN B FLAT, ALLEGRO
    CENTURY MUSIC PUBLISHING COMPANY, INC. 3791 .40
MOZART, W. A.
  SONATA K333 IN B FLAT, SCH NO. 7
    G. SCHIRMER, INC. 1.10
MOZART, W. A.
  SONATA K457 IN C MINOR
    EDWARD B. MARKS MUSIC CORPORATION 01.50
MOZART, W. A.
  SONATA K457 IN C MINOR, SCH NO. 18, AND FANTASIA K475
    G. SCHIRMER, INC. 1.10
MOZART, W. A. GEORGII, W. 4
  SONATA K457 IN C MINOR, SHO NO. 0637 1/2
    SCHOTT 0637 1/2 1.00
MOZART, W. A.
  SONATA K533 IN F, SCH NO. 4
    G. SCHIRMER, INC. 1.00
MOZART, W. A. CHING
  SONATA K545 IN C
    GENERAL WORDS AND MUSIC COMPANY .75
MOZART, W. A.
  SONATA K545 IN C, FRA NO. 15
    FRANCO COLOMBO PUBLICATIONS 128354 1.00
MOZART, W. A.
  SONATA K545 IN C, SCH NO. 3
    G. SCHIRMER, INC. .70
MOZART, W. A. GEORGII, W. 2
  SONATA K545 IN C, SHO NO. 0607 1/2
    SCHOTT 0607 1/2 1.00
MOZART, W. A.
  SONATA K570 IN B FLAT
    BELWIN-MILLS PUBLISHING CORPORATION 20259 .95
MOZART, W. A. GEORGII, W. 3
  SONATA K570 IN B FLAT, SHO NO. 0709 1/2
    SCHOTT 0706 1/2 1.00
MOZART, W. A.
  SONATA K576 IN D, SCH NO. 15
    G. SCHIRMER, INC. .90
MOZART, W. A.
  SONATA NO. 01 IN C
    ASHLEY DEALERS SERVICE, INC. ES .95
MOZART, W. A. ECKSTEIN
  SONATA NO. 01 IN C
    CARL FISCHER, INC. S 1466 .75
MOZART, W. A. 3
  SONATA NO. 01 IN C
    CENTURY MUSIC PUBLISHING COMPANY, INC. 403 .40
MOZART, W. A. 6
  SONATA NO. 03 IN C
    THEODORE PRESSER COMPANY .75
MOZART, W. A. 5 1/2
  SONATA NO. 04 IN F
    THEODORE PRESSER COMPANY .60
MOZART, W. A. 5
  SONATA NO. 06 IN F
    THEODORE PRESSER COMPANY .50
MOZART, W. A.
  SONATA NO. 19 IN F, K.ANH. 135 AND 138A
    FRANCO COLOMBO PUBLICATIONS 128332 1.00
MOZART, W. A. 3
  SONATINA -- VIENNESE -- NO. 01, RONDO
    CENTURY MUSIC PUBLISHING COMPANY, INC. 3792 .40
MOZART, W. A. 4
  SYMPHONY IN E FLAT, MINUET
    CENTURY MUSIC PUBLISHING COMPANY, INC. 317 .40
MOZART, W. A. 3
  SYMPHONY IN E FLAT, MINUET
    CENTURY MUSIC PUBLISHING COMPANY, INC. 2334 .40
MOZART, W. A. GOETSCHIUS, P.
  SYMPHONY NO. 38 IN D -- WITHOUT MINUET
    THEODORE PRESSER COMPANY .75
MOZART, W. A. DE LOS RIOS
  SYMPHONY NO. 40 - THEMES
    THE BIG THREE MUSIC CORPORATION 00.95
MOZART, W. A. SCHAUM, J. 2
  SYMPHONY NO. 40 -- FIRST THEME
    SCHAUM PUBLICATIONS, INC. .50
MOZART, W. A. MONTANI
  TARTINA DI BURRO, LA
    FRANCO COLOMBO PUBLICATIONS 128519 .60

MOZART, W. A.   2
  TEMPO DI MINUETTO
    LEE ROBERTS MUSIC PUBLICATIONS, INC.   .50
MOZART, W. A.   FISCHER
  TEN VARIATIONS IN G, K. 45--'UNSER DUMMER POBEL MEINT'
    ASSOCIATED MUSIC PUBLISHERS, INC.   NAG   1.50
MOZART, W. A.   FISCHER, K. VON
  TEN VARIATIONS IN G, K455
    BARENREITER VERLAG   NMA 228   1.75
MOZART, W. A.
  TEN VARIATIONS ON ''UNSER DUMMER   POBEL MEINT'', K. 455
    G. HENLE MUSIKVERLAG   189   1.15
MOZART, W. A.   RUSSELL   2
  THEME FROM 'DON JUAN'
    BOSTON MUSIC COMPANY   .50
MOZART, W. A.   ECKSTEIN
  THEME FROM SONATA IN C, FIRST MVT.
    CARL FISCHER, INC.   S 2291   .50
MOZART, W. A.   3
  TURKISCHER MARSCH -- K.V. 331
    SCHOTT   0640 1/2 1.00
MOZART, W. A.   SCHAUM, J.   2 1/2
  TURKISH MARCH
    SCHAUM PUBLICATIONS, INC.   .60
MOZART, W. A.
  TURKISH MARCH FROM SONATA IN A
    FRANCO COLOMBO PUBLICATIONS   43745   .60
MOZART, W. A.   ROLFE, W.   2
  TURKISH MARCH, EASY
    CENTURY MUSIC PUBLISHING COMPANY, INC.   3653   .40
MOZART, W. A.   FISCHER
  TWELVE VARIATIONS IN C ON 'AH VOUS DIRAI-JE MAMAN,' K265
    ASSOCIATED MUSIC PUBLISHERS, INC.   NAG   1.25
MOZART, W. A.   MONTANI
  TWELVE VARIATIONS IN C ON 'AH VOUS DIRAIJE, MAMAN,' K. 265
    FRANCO COLOMBO PUBLICATIONS   128399   1.00
MOZART, W. A.   FISCHER, K. VON
  TWELVE VARIATIONS IN C, K265
    BARENREITER VERLAG   NMA 227   1.00
MOZART, W. A.   POTAMKIN
  VALSE FAVORITE
    ELKAN-VOGEL, INC.   .50
MOZART, W. A.   MONTANI
  VALZER FAVORITO
    FRANCO COLOMBO PUBLICATIONS   128520   .60
MOZART, W. A.   2
  VARIATIONEN UBER, AH, VOUS DIRAI-JE-MAMAN -- K.V. 265
    SCHOTT   09197 1/2 1.00
MOZART, W. A.   BRUELL
  VARIATIONS - COMPLETE-
    INTERNATIONAL MUSIC COMPANY   3.75
MOZART, W. A.
  VARIATIONS COMPLETE
    EDWIN F. KALMUS   3694   3.50
MOZART, W. A.
  VARIATIONS ON 'AH, VOUS DIRAI-JE MAMAN' K265
    G. HENLE MUSIKVERLAG   165   1.10
MOZART, W. A.   M
  VARIATIONS ON 'AH, VOUS DIRAI-JE, MAMAN, K.265
    C. F. PETERS CORPORATION   273B   .90
MOZART, W. A.
  VARIATIONS ON 'AH, VOUS DIRAI-JE, MAMAN'
    EDWIN F. KALMUS   3701   1.25
MOZART, W. A.
  VARIATIONS ON 'AH, VOUS DIRAI-JE, MAMAN'
    INTERNATIONAL MUSIC COMPANY   1.00
MOZART, W. A.   M-D
  VARIATIONS ON A MINUET BY FISCHER, K.179
    C. F. PETERS CORPORATION   .90
MOZART, W. A.   STEINER   2
  VIENNESE MINUET
    BELWIN-MILLS PUBLISHING CORPORATION   .60
MOZART, W. A.   HENDERSON
  WALTZ IN D
    BOOSEY AND HAWKES, INC.   .60
MOZART, W. A.   BARTH, H.
  WALTZ K600 NO. 1
    BELWIN-MILLS PUBLISHING CORPORATION   20460   .60
MOZART, W. A.   1
  WIEGENLIED -- MIT TEXT
    SCHOTT   05758   .75
MOZART, W. A. *
  ANDANTE--FROM THE EIGHTH QUARTET--
    GERARD BILLAUDOT EDITIONS MUSICALES   2.50
MOZART, W. A. *
  NE CINIS ET PULVIS SUPERBE--MOTET--
    GERARD BILLAUDOT EDITIONS MUSICALES   2.50
MOZART, W. A. *
  SERENADE--EINE KLEINE NACHTMUSIK--
    GERARD BILLAUDOT EDITIONS MUSICALES   2.00
MUCZYNSKI, R.
  SONATA IN F
    ASSOCIATED MUSIC PUBLISHERS, INC.   AMP   1.00
MUCZYNSKI, R.
  SUITE, OP. 13
    G. SCHIRMER, INC.   1.50
MUCZYNSKI, R.
  SUMMER JOURNAL, A, OP. 19
    G. SCHIRMER, INC.   1.50
MUELLER, C.   4
  AUTUMN REVERIE
    CENTURY MUSIC PUBLISHING COMPANY, INC.   1230   .40
MUELLER, C.   STEINER   PREPARATORY
  AWAY IN A MANGER
    BELWIN-MILLS PUBLISHING CORPORATION   .50
MUELLER, C.   STEINER   JR. APPR.
  AWAY IN A MANGER
    BELWIN-MILLS PUBLISHING CORPORATION   .60
MUELLER, C.   4
  CHRISTMAS FASTASIA
    THEODORE PRESSER COMPANY   .60
MUELLER, C.   4
  FALLING LEAVES, REVERIE
    CENTURY MUSIC PUBLISHING COMPANY, INC.   1230   .40
MULE   PICCIOLI
  LARGO
    FRANCO COLOMBO PUBLICATIONS   BON.1949   .90
MULE   MORINI
  LARGO
    FRANCO COLOMBO PUBLICATIONS   BON.2030   .90
MULE   MORINI
  LARGO
    FRANCO COLOMBO PUBLICATIONS   BON.2029   .90
MUNGER, S.
  I FEEL SAD
    CENTURY MUSIC PUBLISHING COMPANY, INC.   4305   .40

MUNGER, S.   2
  LULLABY TO A FRENCH DOLL
    CENTURY MUSIC PUBLISHING COMPANY, INC.   4225   .40
MUNGER, S.   3
  PROCESSION OF THE MAGYARS
    WILLIS MUSIC COMPANY   .40
MUNN, W.
  AFTER DARK IN OLD JAPAN
    G. SCHIRMER, INC.   .50
MUNN, W.
  AT THE STROKE OF MIDNIGHT
    BELWIN-MILLS PUBLISHING CORPORATION   28079   .60
MUNN, W.
  CY AND CINDY
    CARL FISCHER, INC.   P 3140   .50
MUNN, W.   2
  DREAMY-TIME SONG
    WILLIS MUSIC COMPANY   .40
MUNN, W.   1 1/2
  EAST INDIAN DANCER
    WILLIS MUSIC COMPANY   .40
MUNN, W.
  FESTIVAL GROUPS FOR PIANO SELECTED BY ARTHUR BENJAMIN, SERIES 2
    -- THE ANGRY MAN
    BOOSEY AND HAWKES, INC.   .60
MUNN, W.
  IN MEXICO
    CARL FISCHER, INC.   P 3143   .50
MUNN, W.
  IN MY WHITE BOAT
    SAM FOX PUBLISHING COMPANY, INC.   .50
MUNN, W.
  IN MY WHITE BOAT
    SOUTHERN MUSIC COMPANY   .50
MUNN, W.   1
  MARCH OF THE TINY SOLDIERS
    WILLIS MUSIC COMPANY   .30
MUNN, W.
  MY WOODEN SHOES
    G. SCHIRMER, INC.   .40
MUNN, W.   3
  PRELUDE ROMANTIQUE
    BELWIN-MILLS PUBLISHING CORPORATION   .60
MUNN, W.   2
  SANDMAN'S SONG
    WILLIS MUSIC COMPANY   .40
MUNN, W.   2
  SANTA CLAUS IS IN TOWN
    BELWIN-MILLS PUBLISHING CORPORATION   .60
MUNN, W.   3
  SCHOOL AND FRATERNITY MARCH
    BOSTON MUSIC COMPANY   .50
MUNN, W.   E
  SENORITA
    BELWIN-MILLS PUBLISHING CORPORATION   28072   .60
MUNN, W.
  SINGING TOWER, THE
    G. SCHIRMER, INC.   .50
MUNN, W.
  SLEEPY TOWN
    G. SCHIRMER, INC.   .35
MUNN, W.
  SNAKE CHARMER, THE
    G. SCHIRMER, INC.   .35
MUNN, W.
  STRAW HAT AND CANE
    CARL FISCHER, INC.   P 3137   .50
MUNN, W.
  WHISTLING DOWN THE ROAD I GO
    G. SCHIRMER, INC.   .35
MUNN, W.   1 1/2
  WINDMILLS AND TULIPS
    WILLIS MUSIC COMPANY   .40
MUNRO, R.
  MUSICAL TYPIST
    BELWIN-MILLS PUBLISHING CORPORATION   20179   .85
MUNSON, C.   E-M
  DANCING ELVES
    COMPOSERS PRESS, INC.   1.00
MURILLO, E.
  CANCION DEL AIRE
    G. SCHIRMER, INC.   .60
MURRAY   3
  MIX-A-MODE
    LEE ROBERTS MUSIC PUBLICATIONS, INC.   .50
MURRAY   1
  OLD BEGGARS, THE
    LEE ROBERTS MUSIC PUBLICATIONS, INC.   .50
MURRAY   4
  TRES Y CINCO
    LEE ROBERTS MUSIC PUBLICATIONS, INC.   .50
MURRAY, B.
  FIVE AMUSEMENTS
    ELKAN-VOGEL, INC.   .80
MURRAY, B.   1 1/2
  WITCH, THE
    THEODORE PRESSER COMPANY   .50
MUSEMECI, D.
  STUDIO IN RITMO
    EDIZIONI BERBEN   EB 1242   .90
MUSSO
  ELEGY
    FRANCO COLOMBO PUBLICATIONS   FOR.732   .90
MYDDLETON   SCHAUM, J.   3
  COTTON PICKIN' BOOGIE
    SCHAUM PUBLICATIONS, INC.   .50
MYDDLETON
  DOWN SOUTH
    EDWARD B. MARKS MUSIC CORPORATION   00.60
MYERS, F.   4
  BUNTE RHYTHMEN
    SCHOTT   2609   2.00
MYERS, T.
  WIND DOTH BLOW, THE
    COMPOSERS AUTOGRAPH PUBLICATIONS   1.10
MYROW
  AUTUMN NOCTURNE
    WARNER BROTHERS PUBLISHERS   1.00
MYROW, F.
  PALM CANYON
    BELWIN-MILLS PUBLISHING CORPORATION   20191   .85
MYROW, F.
  THEME AND VARIATIONS
    BELWIN-MILLS PUBLISHING CORPORATION   20300   1.75
MYROW, J.
  L'AFFAIRE
    BELWIN-MILLS PUBLISHING CORPORATION   20144   .85

NABERT, C.
    GLOCK OU L'HISTOIRE D'UN CLOWN
        ELKAN-VOGEL, INC.   CON   2.50
NABOKOFF, N.
    DON QUIXOTE -- COMPLETE BALLET
        BOOSEY AND HAWKES, INC.   15.00
NABOKOFF, N.
    SONATA
        FRANCO COLOMBO PUBLICATIONS   SAL   5.00
NABOKOFF, N.
    SONATA NO. 02
        BOOSEY AND HAWKES, INC.   2.50
                                    4
NAGY, M.
    ONE HANDED SOLITAIRE, NO. 1, 2 AND 3
        LEE ROBERTS MUSIC PUBLICATIONS, INC.   1.00
NAPOLI
    OMAGGIO A SCARLATTI
        EDIZIONI BERBEN   EB 1311   1.20
NAPOLI
    SCENES OF CHILDHOOD
        FRANCO COLOMBO PUBLICATIONS   120251   2.25
NAPOLITANO
    CHACARERA, OP. 8 NO. 1
        FRANCO COLOMBO PUBLICATIONS   BA10543   .75
NAPOLITANO
    DANZA DE LAS BAILARINAS CORTESANAS - FROM 'APURIMAC', OP. 5
        FRANCO COLOMBO PUBLICATIONS   BA9109   .75
NAPOLITANO
    GATO
        FRANCO COLOMBO PUBLICATIONS   BA11388   .75
NAPOLITANO
    GATO, OP. 8 NO. 3
        FRANCO COLOMBO PUBLICATIONS   BA9350   .75
NAPOLITANO   RICHTER
    GATO, OP. 8 NO. 3
        FRANCO COLOMBO PUBLICATIONS   NY1571   .40
NAPOLITANO
    TRISTE, OP. 8 NO. 2
        FRANCO COLOMBO PUBLICATIONS   BA 9841   .75
NAPOLITANO
    VIDALITAY, OP. 8 NO. 4
        FRANCO COLOMBO PUBLICATIONS   BA10229   .75
NAPOLITANO
    YARAVI - FROM 'APURIMAC', OP. 5
        FRANCO COLOMBO PUBLICATIONS   BA8979   .75
NARDINI   ZUELLI *
    ADAGIO
        FRANCO COLOMBO PUBLICATIONS   BON.562   .90
NASCIMBENE
    FRANCIS OF ASSISI - THEME
        THE BIG THREE MUSIC CORPORATION   00.95
NASCIMBENE
    ROMANOFF AND JULIET
        MCA MUSIC   1.00
NASH, J.
    I CAN SEE CLEARLY NOW
        THE BIG THREE MUSIC CORPORATION   02.95
NASSANN   MEDIUM
    CONNECTICUT MARCH
        SHAWNEE PRESS, INC.   HB-60   .60
NAT, Y.
    CLOWN
        FRANCO COLOMBO PUBLICATIONS   SAL   2.75
NAT, Y.
    POUR UNE PETIT MOUJICK
        FRANCO COLOMBO PUBLICATIONS   SAL   2.00
NAT, Y.
    SIX PRELUDES - B MINOR
        FRANCO COLOMBO PUBLICATIONS   SAL   3.25
NAT, Y.
    SIX PRELUDES - B-FLAT
        FRANCO COLOMBO PUBLICATIONS   SAL   3.25
NAT, Y.
    SIX PRELUDES - F-SHARP MAJOR
        FRANCO COLOMBO PUBLICATIONS   SAL   3.25
NAT, Y.
    SIX PRELUDES - LE BUCHARON
        FRANCO COLOMBO PUBLICATIONS   SAL   3.25
NAT, Y.
    SIX PRELUDES - LE TEMPETE
        FRANCO COLOMBO PUBLICATIONS   SAL   3.25
NAT, Y.
    SIX PRELUDES - PRELUDES A L'AUTOMNE
        FRANCO COLOMBO PUBLICATIONS   SAL   3.25
NAVARRO, L.
    FAIRY SNOWFLAKES
        BANKS AND SON LTD.   .25
NAZARETH, E.
    DENGOZA--BRAZILIAN MAXIXE-TANGO
        G. SCHIRMER, INC.   .35
NEARING, H.
    KUTZTOWN REEL -- A PA. DUTCH FOLK TUNE
        BELWIN-MILLS PUBLISHING CORPORATION   20143   .85
NEGLIA, F.
    L'ARPISTA FANTASTIC, OP. 93 'P'
        EDIZIONI BERBEN   EB 1412   1.50
NEGLIA, F.
    SONATINA IN UN TEMPO, OP. 15 'P'
        EDIZIONI BERBEN   EB 1449   1.50
NEGRETE WOOLCOCK, S.
    RITMICA
        EDITORIAL COOPERATIVA INTER-AMERICANA   00.85
NEIDLINGER, W. H.   STEINER
    BIRTHDAY OF A KING, THE
        G. SCHIRMER, INC.   .35
NEIDLINGER, W. H.   ZEPP   4-5
    BIRTHDAY TO A KING
        PRO-ART PUBLICATIONS, INC.   508   .50
NEIDLINGER, W. H.
    FAIRY STORIES--DANCING UNDER THE MAY-APPLES
        G. SCHIRMER, INC.   .30
NEIDLINGER, W. H.
    FAIRY STORIES--WATER-SPRITES' BARCAROLE, THE
        G. SCHIRMER, INC.   .30
NELSON
    AFTER SCHOOL --SUITE--
        SCHMITT, HALL AND MCCREARY COMPANY   9549   1.00
NERINI, E.
    ESQUISSES ENFANTINES, BK. 1
        GERARD BILLAUDOT EDITIONS MUSICALES   1.30
NERINI, E.
    ESQUISSES ENFANTINES, BK. 2
        GERARD BILLAUDOT EDITIONS MUSICALES   1.30
NERINI, E.
    L'ART D'ETRE GRAND-PERE, BK. 1
        GERARD BILLAUDOT EDITIONS MUSICALES   2.50

NERINI, E.
    L'ART D'ETRE GRAND-PERE, BK. 2
        GERARD BILLAUDOT EDITIONS MUSICALES   2.50
NERINI, E.
    PAGES D'ALBUM - FEUX FOLLETS
        FRANCO COLOMBO PUBLICATIONS   SAL   1.50
NERINI, E.
    PAGES D'ALBUM - LA FILEUSE
        FRANCO COLOMBO PUBLICATIONS   SAL   1.50
NERINI, E.
    PAGES D'ALBUM - LA SOURCE
        FRANCO COLOMBO PUBLICATIONS   SAL   1.50
NERINI, E.
    PAGES D'ALBUM - PRELUDE
        FRANCO COLOMBO PUBLICATIONS   SAL   1.50
NERINI, E.
    PAGES D'ALBUM - REVERIE
        FRANCO COLOMBO PUBLICATIONS   SAL   1.50
NERINI, E.
    PAGES D'ALBUM - ROMANCE SANS PAROLES
        FRANCO COLOMBO PUBLICATIONS   SAL   1.50
NERINI, E.
    RONDE DES LUTINS
        FRANCO COLOMBO PUBLICATIONS   SAL   2.50
NERINI, E.
    SCHERZO ROMANTIQUE
        FRANCO COLOMBO PUBLICATIONS   SAL   2.50
NERINI, E.
    WALTZ NO. 01
        FRANCO COLOMBO PUBLICATIONS   SAL   2.00
NERO
    HOT CANARY, THE
        MCA MUSIC   1.00
NESCI
    AMANCAY
        FRANCO COLOMBO PUBLICATIONS   BA10798   .75
NEUSTEDT
    GAVOTTE FAVORITE DE MARIE-ANTOINETTE
        FRANCO COLOMBO PUBLICATIONS   SAL   1.75
NEVIN
    ALPHABET WALTZ
        EDWARD B. MARKS MUSIC CORPORATION   00.60
NEVIN   SCHAUM, J.   3
    AMERICAN IN VENICE
        BELWIN-MILLS PUBLISHING CORPORATION   .50
NEVIN
    BARCHETTA
        BOSTON MUSIC COMPANY   .60
NEVIN
    BOLSHOI BAGATELLE
        BELWIN-MILLS PUBLISHING CORPORATION   .60
NEVIN
    CANZONETTA
        EDWARD B. MARKS MUSIC CORPORATION   00.60
NEVIN
    CHIRIBIRI-BINGO
        BELWIN-MILLS PUBLISHING CORPORATION   25297   .60
NEVIN
    CHORD PRELUDE
        BELWIN-MILLS PUBLISHING CORPORATION   25311   .60
NEVIN
    CHORD PRELUDE
        BELWIN-MILLS PUBLISHING CORPORATION
                         2   .60
NEVIN
    CHROMATIC HEY-DAY
        BELWIN-MILLS PUBLISHING CORPORATION   .60
NEVIN
    DAY IN VENICE --SUITE--
        CARL FISCHER, INC.   O 3946   1.50
NEVIN
    DAY IN VENICE, A --VENEZIA--
        THEODORE PRESSER COMPANY   1.50
NEVIN   RICHTER, A.
    DAY IN VENICE, A --VENEZIA--
        THEODORE PRESSER COMPANY   1.50
NEVIN
    DREAM INTERLUDE
        BELWIN-MILLS PUBLISHING CORPORATION   25308   .60
                         2 1/2
NEVIN
    ESPANITA
        BELWIN-MILLS PUBLISHING CORPORATION   .60
                         1 1/2
NEVIN
    FIFE AND DRUM DORPS
        BELWIN-MILLS PUBLISHING CORPORATION   1.00
                         2 1/2
NEVIN
    FLAMENCO
        BELWIN-MILLS PUBLISHING CORPORATION   .85
                         2
NEVIN
    FOLK TUNE BOOGIE
        BELWIN-MILLS PUBLISHING CORPORATION   .60
                         1
NEVIN
    FOLLOW ME
        BELWIN-MILLS PUBLISHING CORPORATION   .60
                         E
NEVIN
    GERRY GIRAFFE
        BELWIN-MILLS PUBLISHING CORPORATION   28205   .60
                         E
NEVIN
    GO TELL AUNT RHODY
        BELWIN-MILLS PUBLISHING CORPORATION   .60
                         4
NEVIN
    GONDOLIERS
        BOSTON MUSIC COMPANY   .50
NEVIN   LEVINE   3
    GONDOLIERS
        BOSTON MUSIC COMPANY   .50
                         E
NEVIN
    GOOFY MONKEY
        BELWIN-MILLS PUBLISHING CORPORATION   28091   .60
                         E
NEVIN
    HANDSPRINGS
        BELWIN-MILLS PUBLISHING CORPORATION   28114   .60
                         1
NEVIN
    HAPPY GO LUCKY
        BELWIN-MILLS PUBLISHING CORPORATION   .60
                         2
NEVIN
    HELICOPTER, THE
        BELWIN-MILLS PUBLISHING CORPORATION   .60
                         E
NEVIN
    HONG KONG HOLIDAY
        BELWIN-MILLS PUBLISHING CORPORATION   28104   .60
                         E
NEVIN
    HOPAK
        BELWIN-MILLS PUBLISHING CORPORATION   28121   .60
                         E
NEVIN
    I LIKE MUSIC
        BELWIN-MILLS PUBLISHING CORPORATION   28129   .60

NEVIN　　　　　　　　　　　　　　　　　　　　　　　5
　　IN MY NEIGHBOR'S GARDEN
　　　　BOSTON MUSIC COMPANY
NEVIN　　　　　　　　　　　　　　　　2 1/2　　　　　　　.60
　　ISRAELI WALTZ
　　　　BELWIN-MILLS PUBLISHING CORPORATION
NEVIN　　　　　　　　　　　　　　　　E　　　　　　　　　.60
　　JAZZ ALLEGRETTO
　　　　BELWIN-MILLS PUBLISHING CORPORATION　28138　　.60
NEVIN　　　　　　　　　　　　　　　　E
　　JAZZ ANDANTINO
　　　　BELWIN-MILLS PUBLISHING CORPORATION　28137　　.60
NEVIN　　　　　　　　　　　　　　　　2
　　JAZZ FINGERS
　　　　BELWIN-MILLS PUBLISHING CORPORATION　　　　　.60
NEVIN　　　　　　　　　　　　　　　　E
　　JAZZ MINIATURE
　　　　BELWIN-MILLS PUBLISHING CORPORATION　28113　　.60
NEVIN　　　　　　　　　　　　　　　　E
　　JAZZ PRELUDE
　　　　BELWIN-MILLS PUBLISHING CORPORATION　28096　　.60
NEVIN　　　　　　　　　　　　　　　　E
　　JETAWAY
　　　　BELWIN-MILLS PUBLISHING CORPORATION　28143　　.60
NEVIN
　　JOGGING
　　　　EDWARD B. MARKS MUSIC CORPORATION　　　　　00.60
NEVIN　　　　　　　　　　　　　　　　2
　　JOLLY ASTRONAUT, THE
　　　　BELWIN-MILLS PUBLISHING CORPORATION　　　　　.60
NEVIN　　　　　　　　　　　　　　　　E
　　JOLLY FINGERS
　　　　BELWIN-MILLS PUBLISHING CORPORATION　28122　　.60
NEVIN　　　　　　　　　　　　　　　　E
　　JUMPIN' JALOPY
　　　　BELWIN-MILLS PUBLISHING CORPORATION　28093　　.60
NEVIN　　　　　　　　　　　　　　　　E
　　KANGAROO HOP
　　　　BELWIN-MILLS PUBLISHING CORPORATION　25298　　.60
NEVIN　　　　　　　　　　　　　　　　E
　　KRISS KROSS KAPERS
　　　　BELWIN-MILLS PUBLISHING CORPORATION　28141　　.60
NEVIN　　　　　　　　　　　　　　　　E
　　KWAZY WABBIT
　　　　BELWIN-MILLS PUBLISHING CORPORATION　28090　　.60
NEVIN　　　　　　　　　　　　　　　　E
　　MANHATTAN BLUES
　　　　BELWIN-MILLS PUBLISHING CORPORATION　28120　　.60
NEVIN　　　　　　　　　　　　　　　　E
　　MARCH OF THE TRIADS
　　　　BELWIN-MILLS PUBLISHING CORPORATION　　　　　.60
NEVIN　　　　　　SCHAUM, J.　　　　　2
　　MIGHTY LAK' A ROSE
　　　　BELWIN-MILLS PUBLISHING CORPORATION　　　　　.50
NEVIN　　　　　　LEVINE　　　　　　　4
　　MIGHTY LAK' A ROSE
　　　　BOSTON MUSIC COMPANY
NEVIN　　　　　　LEVINE　　　　　　　2　　　　　　　　.50
　　MIGHTY LAK' A ROSE
　　　　BOSTON MUSIC COMPANY
NEVIN　　　　　　FELTON　　　　　　　3　　　　　　　　.50
　　MIGHTY LAK' A ROSE
　　　　THEODORE PRESSER COMPANY
NEVIN　　　　　　　　　　　　　　　　2　　　　　　　　.50
　　MINI-SCHERZO
　　　　BELWIN-MILLS PUBLISHING CORPORATION　　　　　.60
NEVIN　　　　　　　　　　　　　　　　E
　　MISTER HIPPO
　　　　BELWIN-MILLS PUBLISHING CORPORATION　28204　　.60
NEVIN　　　　　　　　　　　　　　　　3
　　MODERN SWANEE RIVER, THE
　　　　BELWIN-MILLS PUBLISHING CORPORATION　　　　　.60
NEVIN
　　MOONOCTURNE
　　　　BELWIN-MILLS PUBLISHING CORPORATION　　　　　.60
NEVIN　　　　　　　　　　　　　　　　E
　　MUSETTA'S WALTZ
　　　　BELWIN-MILLS PUBLISHING CORPORATION　28095　　.60
NEVIN　　　　　　　　　　　　　　　　4
　　NARCISSUS
　　　　BOSTON MUSIC COMPANY　　　　　　　　　　　.50
NEVIN　　　　　　LOTH　　　　　　　　2
　　NARCISSUS
　　　　BOSTON MUSIC COMPANY　　　　　　　　　　　.50
NEVIN　　　　　　ANDERTON　　　　　　2
　　NARCISSUS
　　　　BOSTON MUSIC COMPANY　　　　　　　　　　　.50
NEVIN　　　　　　　　　　　　　　　　3
　　NARCISSUS
　　　　CENTURY MUSIC PUBLISHING COMPANY, INC.　3849　.40
NEVIN　　　　　　　　　　　　　　　　4
　　NARCISSUS
　　　　THEODORE PRESSER COMPANY　　　　　　　　.50
NEVIN　　　　　　　　　　　　　　　　4
　　NARCISSUS
　　　　VOLKWEIN BROS.　　　　　　　　　　　　　.50
NEVIN
　　NARCISSUS, OP. 13 NO. 4
　　　　ASHLEY DEALERS SERVICE, INC.　　　ES　　　.95
NEVIN
　　NARCISSUS, OP. 13 NO. 4
　　　　BANKS AND SON LTD.　　　　　　　　　　　.55
NEVIN　　　　　　ECKSTEIN
　　NARCISSUS, OP. 13 NO. 4
　　　　CARL FISCHER, INC.　　　　　　S 7652　　.50
NEVIN
　　NARCISSUS, OP. 13 NO. 4
　　　　FRANCO COLOMBO PUBLICATIONS　　128420　　.60
NEVIN　　　　　　DEL MAGLIO
　　NARCISSUS, OP. 13 NO. 4
　　　　FRANCO COLOMBO PUBLICATIONS　　128846　　.60
NEVIN　　　　　　WEYBRIGHT　　　　　2
　　NARCISSUS, THEME
　　　　BELWIN-MILLS PUBLISHING CORPORATION　　　　　.60
NEVIN　　　　　　　　　　　　　　　　E
　　NOCTURNE FOR MODERNS
　　　　BELWIN-MILLS PUBLISHING CORPORATION　28094　　.60
NEVIN
　　NOCTURNETTE
　　　　BELWIN-MILLS PUBLISHING CORPORATION　　　　　.60
NEVIN　　　　　　　　　　　　　　　　E
　　PAGLIACCI -- PROLOGUE, VESTI LA GUIBBA
　　　　BELWIN-MILLS PUBLISHING CORPORATION　28132　　.60
NEVIN
　　PANTOMIME
　　　　BELWIN-MILLS PUBLISHING CORPORATION　　　　　.60

NEVIN　　　　　　　　　　　　　　　　E
　　PARADE OF THE TIN SOLDIERS
　　　　BELWIN-MILLS PUBLISHING CORPORATION　28092　　.60
NEVIN
　　PARISIENNE
　　　　BELWIN-MILLS PUBLISHING CORPORATION　　　　　.60
NEVIN　　　　　　　　　　　　　　　　E
　　PEEK A BOO, I SEE YOU
　　　　BELWIN-MILLS PUBLISHING CORPORATION　28118　　.60
NEVIN　　　　　　　　　　　　　　　　1
　　PUPPET SHOW
　　　　BELWIN-MILLS PUBLISHING CORPORATION　　　　　.60
NEVIN　　　　　　　　　　　　　　　　E
　　RICKSHAW MAN
　　　　BELWIN-MILLS PUBLISHING CORPORATION　28105　　.60
NEVIN　　　　　　　　　　　　　　　　E
　　RIGOLLETTO -- LA DONNA E MOBILE, QUARTET
　　　　BELWIN-MILLS PUBLISHING CORPORATION　28131　　.60
NEVIN　　　　　　SCHAUM, J.　　　　　1 1/2
　　ROSARY, THE
　　　　BELWIN-MILLS PUBLISHING CORPORATION　　　　　.50
NEVIN　　　　　　LOEPKE　　　　　　　2
　　ROSARY, THE
　　　　BOSTON MUSIC COMPANY　　　　　　　　　　　.60
NEVIN　　　　　　WHELPLEY　　　　　　3
　　ROSARY, THE
　　　　BOSTON MUSIC COMPANY　　　　　　　　　　　.60
NEVIN　　　　　　MOORE　　　　　　　　1
　　ROSARY, THE
　　　　BOSTON MUSIC COMPANY　　　　　　　　　　　.50
NEVIN　　　　　　　　　　　　　　　　2
　　SAILOR'S JIG
　　　　CENTURY MUSIC PUBLISHING COMPANY, INC.　4213　.40
NEVIN
　　SHADES OF BLUE
　　　　BELWIN-MILLS PUBLISHING CORPORATION　　　　　.60
NEVIN　　　　　　　　　　　　　　　　E
　　SIXTH SENSE
　　　　BELWIN-MILLS PUBLISHING CORPORATION　25309　　.60
NEVIN　　　　　　　　　　　　　　　　E
　　SPACE FLIGHT
　　　　BELWIN-MILLS PUBLISHING CORPORATION　28126　　.60
NEVIN
　　SWEET SIXTEEN
　　　　BELWIN-MILLS PUBLISHING CORPORATION　　　　　.60
NEVIN　　　　　　　　　　　　　　　　E
　　TANGO BONGO
　　　　BELWIN-MILLS PUBLISHING CORPORATION　28112　　.60
NEVIN　　　　　　　　　　　　　　　　E
　　TEN CONCERT VARIATIONS
　　　　BELWIN-MILLS PUBLISHING CORPORATION　25310　　.70
NEVIN
　　TEN CONCERT VARIATIONS
　　　　BELWIN-MILLS PUBLISHING CORPORATION　25310　　.70
NEVIN　　　　　　　　　　　　　　　　E
　　THREE SWINGY BOATMEN
　　　　BELWIN-MILLS PUBLISHING CORPORATION　28130　　.60
NEVIN　　　　　　　　　　　　　　　　E
　　TIA JUANA TANGO
　　　　BELWIN-MILLS PUBLISHING CORPORATION　28128　　.60
NEVIN　　　　　　　　　　　　　　　　E
　　TOKYO TOCCATINA
　　　　BELWIN-MILLS PUBLISHING CORPORATION　25313　　.60
NEVIN　　　　　　　　　　　　　　　　E
　　TOY POODLE
　　　　BELWIN-MILLS PUBLISHING CORPORATION　25300　　.60
NEVIN　　　　　　　　　　　　　　　　E
　　TOYLAND
　　　　BELWIN-MILLS PUBLISHING CORPORATION　28107　　.60
NEVIN　　　　　　　　　　　　　　　　E
　　TWO PART 'INTENTION'
　　　　BELWIN-MILLS PUBLISHING CORPORATION　28119　　.60
NEVIN　　　　　　　　　　　　　　　　E
　　VARIATIONS ON 'OH SUSANNA'
　　　　BELWIN-MILLS PUBLISHING CORPORATION　28111　　.60
NEVIN　　　　　　　　　　　　　　　　4
　　VENETIAN LOVE SONG
　　　　BOSTON MUSIC COMPANY　　　　　　　　　　　.10
NEVIN　　　　　　　　　　　　　　　　E
　　WALTZING BALLERINA
　　　　BELWIN-MILLS PUBLISHING CORPORATION　28127　　.60
NEVIN　　　　　　　　　　　　　　　　1
　　WE WISH YOU A MERRY CHRISTMAS
　　　　BELWIN-MILLS PUBLISHING CORPORATION　　　　　.60
NEVIN--ED　　　　　　　　NEVIN
　　CARMEN -- TOREADOR SONG, HABANEA
　　　　BELWIN-MILLS PUBLISHING CORPORATION　28135　　.60
NEWLAND, R.　　　　　　　　　　　　4
　　VALSE CAPRICE
　　　　CENTURY MUSIC PUBLISHING COMPANY, INC.　4326　.40
NEWLAND, R.　　　　　　　　　　　　4
　　VALSE CAPRICE
　　　　WILLIS MUSIC COMPANY　　　　　　　　　　　.60
NEWMAN, A.
　　STREET SCENE
　　　　THE BIG THREE MUSIC CORPORATION　　　　　00.95
NEWMAN, L.
　　HONG KONG
　　　　THE BIG THREE MUSIC CORPORATION　　　　　00.95
NEWMAN, M.
　　CONCERTO SENTIMENTO
　　　　BELWIN-MILLS PUBLISHING CORPORATION　20458　　.85
NEWMAN, W.　　　　　SCHAUM, J.　　　1 1/2
　　SEAGULL
　　　　SCHAUM PUBLICATIONS, INC.　　　　　　　　.50
NEWTON, E.
　　SMUGGLERS OF ROMNEY MARSH, THE
　　　　BANKS AND SON LTD.　　　　　　　　　　　.80
NICHOL *　　　　　　　　　　　　　　1
　　CLOCKS -- WHAT TIME IS IT
　　　　VOLKWEIN BROS.　　　　　　　　　　　　　.50
NICHOL *　　　　　　　　　　　　　　1
　　SKY FAIRIES
　　　　VOLKWEIN BROS.　　　　　　　　　　　　　.50
NICHOL *　　　　　　　　　　　　　　1
　　TIP MY DOG
　　　　VOLKWEIN BROS.　　　　　　　　　　　　00.50
NICHOLAS　　　　　　　　　　　　　　3
　　JINGLE BELLS
　　　　CENTURY MUSIC PUBLISHING COMPANY, INC.　2617　.40
NICHOLLS, H.
　　CHERRY BLOSSOM
　　　　BANKS AND SON LTD.　　　　　　　　　　　.25
NICHOLLS, H.
　　NORTH, SOUTH, EAST AND WEST
　　　　BANKS AND SON LTD.　　　　　　　　　　　1.10

NICHOLLS, H.
  VIENNESE SKETCHES
    BANKS AND SON LTD.   .95
NIEDT *
  UNDER THE LINDEN TREE
    MCA MUSIC   1.00
NIEL   3
  LONDONDERRY AIR
    BOSTON MUSIC COMPANY   .50
NIELSEN, C.   D
  SUITE FOR THE PIANO, OP. 45
    C. F. PETERS CORPORATION   3808   2.50
NIELSEN, R.
  SONATINA IN SIGNO MAGNI ARNOLD
    FRANCO COLOMBO PUBLICATIONS   BON.2401   2.25
NIELSEN, R.
  SONATINA PERBREVIS AD USUM PETRI ET KAROLI MARIAE
    FRANCO COLOMBO PUBLICATIONS   BON.2402   1.50
NIEMANN   M
  BARREL ORGAN, OP. 107, NO. 9
    C. F. PETERS CORPORATION   3864B   .60
NIEMANN   E-M
  CHRISTMAS BELLS, OP. 129
    C. F. PETERS CORPORATION   4272A   1.50
NIEMANN   M-D
  GARDEN MUSIC, OP. 117
    C. F. PETERS CORPORATION   3867   .90
NIEMANN   M
  GARDENS IN SPRING, OP. 112, NO. 6
    C. F. PETERS CORPORATION   3864D   .60
NIEMANN
  IMPRESSIONS OF THE FAR EAST--IN THE CHINESE CITY
    G. SCHIRMER, INC.   .50
NIEMANN
  MAGIC BOOK, THE, OP. 76--6 PHANTASMAGORIAS--NO. 1, THE HUMMING
  BIRD
    ASSOCIATED MUSIC PUBLISHERS, INC.   SIM   .90
NIEMANN
  MAGIC BOOK, THE, OP. 92--6 PHANTASMAGORIAS--NO. 6, SILVER
  CASCADE
    ASSOCIATED MUSIC PUBLISHERS, INC.   SIM   .75
NIEMANN
  MIRROR LAKE, THE
    G. SCHIRMER, INC.   .50
NIEMANN
  ORCHID GARDEN, THE, OP. 76--10 IMPRESSIONS OF THE FAR EAST--NO.
  5, BIRD OF PARADISE AT THE WATERFALL
    ASSOCIATED MUSIC PUBLISHERS, INC.   SIM   .65
NIEMANN
  SONATA GIOCOSA, OP. 96
    ASSOCIATED MUSIC PUBLISHERS, INC.   SIM   3.00
NIEMANN
  WEIHNACHTSABEND, DER, OP. 137
    ASSOCIATED MUSIC PUBLISHERS, INC.   BRH   2.50
NIGG, S.
  SONATA NO. 02
    ELKAN-VOGEL, INC.   J   5.00
NIGG, S.
  STREPITOSO
    ELKAN-VOGEL, INC.   J   3.75
NILES, J.
  I WONDER AS I WANDER--APPALACHIAN FOLK CAROL
    G. SCHIRMER, INC.   .35
NILES, J.
  LITTLE LYKING, THE
    G. SCHIRMER, INC.   .50
NILSSON, BO
  QUANTITATEN -- FACSIMILE EDITION
    UNIVERSAL EDITION   UE 12873   2.00
NIN
  BERCEUSE POUR LES ORPHELINS D'ESPAGNE--1938
    ASSOCIATED MUSIC PUBLISHERS, INC.   ESC   1.75
NIN
  MESSAGE A CLAUDE DEBUSSY, 1929
    ASSOCIATED MUSIC PUBLISHERS, INC.   ESC   2.25
NIN
  THREE SPANISH DANCES--1938--NO. 1, DANSE MURCIENNE
    ASSOCIATED MUSIC PUBLISHERS, INC.   ESC   2.25
NIN
  THREE SPANISH DANCES--1938--NO. 2, DANSE ANDALOUSE
    ASSOCIATED MUSIC PUBLISHERS, INC.   ESC   4.00
NIN
  THREE SPANISH DANCES--1938--NO. 3, DANSE IBERIENNE NO. 2
    ASSOCIATED MUSIC PUBLISHERS, INC.   ESC   3.00
NIN
  VARIATIONS SUR UN THEME FRIVOLE--'1830'--1934
    ASSOCIATED MUSIC PUBLISHERS, INC.   ESC   3.00
NIN-CULMELL, J.
  SONATA BREVE
    RONGWEN MUSIC, INC.   02.50
NIN-CULMELL, J.
  TROMPEUR DE SEVILLE, LE -- BALLET IN ONE ACT
    ASSOCIATED MUSIC PUBLISHERS, INC.   ESC   10.75
NIRELLA, D.   4
  ALLEGIANCE TO THE U. S. A.
    VOLKWEIN BROS.   .50
NIRELLA, D.   4
  CHAMBER OF COMMERCE MARCH
    VOLKWEIN BROS.   .50
NIRELLA, D.   4
  LIBERTY FAIR MARCH
    VOLKWEIN BROS.   .35
NIRELLA, D.   4
  ONE HUNDRED SEVENTH FIELD ARTILLERY
    VOLKWEIN BROS.   .50
NIRELLA, D.   4
  RAINBOW DIVISION MARCH
    VOLKWEIN BROS.   .40
NIRELLA, D.   4
  ROTARY MARCH
    VOLKWEIN BROS.   .35
NIRELLA, D.   4
  YANKEES IN FRANCE
    VOLKWEIN BROS.   00.35
NIVELET   4
  MA BERGERE --OU LE PATRE DES MONTAGNES--
    ALPHONSE LEDUC
NIVERD, L.
  DANS LA CLAIRE NUIT
    FRANCO COLOMBO PUBLICATIONS   SAL   1.50
NIVERD, L.
  DANS LE SOMBRE NUIT
    FRANCO COLOMBO PUBLICATIONS   SAL   1.50
NIVERD, L.
  IMPRESSIONS ET REFLETS
    FRANCO COLOMBO PUBLICATIONS   SAL   4.25

NIVERD, L.
  SIX PIECES CLAIRES ET BIEN AEREES - CLAIRIERE ENSOLEILLEE
    FRANCO COLOMBO PUBLICATIONS   SAL   2.50
NIVERD, L.
  SIX PIECES CLAIRES ET BIEN AEREES - CRINCRINS ET CARILLONS
    FRANCO COLOMBO PUBLICATIONS   SAL   2.50
NIVERD, L.
  SIX PIECES CLAIRES ET BIEN AEREES - HALTE SOUS L'OMBRAGE
    FRANCO COLOMBO PUBLICATIONS   SAL   2.50
NIVERD, L.
  SIX PIECES CLAIRES ET BIEN AEREES - LE BOURRIQUET RECALCITRANT
    FRANCO COLOMBO PUBLICATIONS   SAL   2.50
NIVERD, L.
  SIX PIECES CLAIRES ET BIEN AEREES - LE MOULIN DU VAL
    FRANCO COLOMBO PUBLICATIONS   SAL   2.50
NIVERD, L.
  SIX PIECES CLAIRES ET BIEN AEREES - SOIR DE FETE AUX MOISSONS
    FRANCO COLOMBO PUBLICATIONS   SAL   2.50
NOACK, K.   3
  HEINZELMANNCHENS WACHTPARADE, OP. 5
    SCHOTT   1.25
NOACK, K.   2
  HEINZELMANNCHENS WACHTPARADE, OP. 5, ERLEICHTERT
    SCHOTT   1.25
NOBLE   SCHAUM, J.   2
  CHEROKEE
    SCHAUM PUBLICATIONS, INC.   .75
NOBLES, O.
  LULLABY FOR A SLEEPY DOLL
    BELWIN-MILLS PUBLISHING CORPORATION   28078   .60
NOBLES, O.
  MERMAIDS
    BELWIN-MILLS PUBLISHING CORPORATION   20567   .60
NOBLITT, K.   2
  WALTZ MOOD
    WILLIS MUSIC COMPANY   .35
NOBLITT, K. M.   2 1/2
  MARCH OF THE AMERICANS
    BELWIN-MILLS PUBLISHING CORPORATION   .60
NOBLITT, K. M.   SCHAUM, J.   1
  WINDSHIELD WIPER ROCK
    SCHAUM PUBLICATIONS, INC.   .60
NOEL, H.
  GAMBOLING
    G. SCHIRMER, INC.   .40
NOEL, H.
  MAZURKA
    G. SCHIRMER, INC.   .35
NOEL, H.   3
  MY WORK IS OVER
    LEE ROBERTS MUSIC PUBLICATIONS, INC.   .50
NOEL, H.
  NEARBY A CAROUSEL--AMUSEMENT
    G. SCHIRMER, INC.   .35
NOEL, H.
  NEARBY A CAROUSEL--CONVERSATION
    G. SCHIRMER, INC.   .35
NOEL, H.
  NEARBY A CAROUSEL--MARCH
    G. SCHIRMER, INC.   .40
NOEL, H.
  NEARBY A CAROUSEL--WALTZ
    G. SCHIRMER, INC.   .40
NOEL, H.   2
  ONE BY ONE, TWO BY TWO
    THEODORE PRESSER COMPANY   .50
NOEL, H.   3
  PANTOMINE
    BELWIN-MILLS PUBLISHING CORPORATION   .60
NOEL, P. *
  FABLIAU
    GERARD BILLAUDOT EDITIONS MUSICALES   1.10
NOEL, P. *
  FIRST VALSE-IMPROMPTU
    GERARD BILLAUDOT EDITIONS MUSICALES   2.00
NOEL, P. *
  GUIRLANDES
    GERARD BILLAUDOT EDITIONS MUSICALES   1.30
NOEL, P. *
  PAGES ENFANTINES
    GERARD BILLAUDOT EDITIONS MUSICALES   1.30
NOEL, P. *
  REVERIE
    GERARD BILLAUDOT EDITIONS MUSICALES   1.10
NOEL, P. *
  RONDO CLASSIQUE
    GERARD BILLAUDOT EDITIONS MUSICALES   1.30
NOEL, P. *
  SECOND VALSE-IMPROMPTU
    GERARD BILLAUDOT EDITIONS MUSICALES   1.60
NOEL, P. *
  TOCCATA
    GERARD BILLAUDOT EDITIONS MUSICALES   2.00
NOETEL
  SONATA
    BARENREITER VERLAG   BA 1983   2.25
NOETEL   4
  SONATE
    BARENREITER VERLAG   BA 1983
NOETEL   4
  VARIATIONEN
    BARENREITER VERLAG   BA 1838
NOETEL
  VARIATIONS
    BARENREITER VERLAG   BA 1838   2.50
NOLLET, E.
  ELEGIE IN C SHARP MINOR, OP. 88
    BELWIN-MILLS PUBLISHING CORPORATION   28154   .50
NOLLET, E.
  ELEGIE IN C SHARP MINOR, OP. 88
    G. SCHIRMER, INC.   .40
NOLLET, E.   5
  ELEGY, OP. 88
    CENTURY MUSIC PUBLISHING COMPANY, INC.   2305   .40
NOLLET, E.
  HEURE DU COUVRE-FEU, L' OP. 56
    FRANCO COLOMBO PUBLICATIONS   SAL   1.75
NOLLET, E.
  TARENTELLE IN D, OP. 77
    G. SCHIRMER, INC.   .70
NOONA, W.   2 1/2
  ALL BY MYSELF
    BELWIN-MILLS PUBLISHING CORPORATION   .60
NOONA, W.   2
  BIG CHIEF HIC-CUP
    BELWIN-MILLS PUBLISHING CORPORATION   .60

NOONA, W.   3 1/2
    CARTAGENA
        BELWIN-MILLS PUBLISHING CORPORATION   .60
NOONA, W.   1 1/2
    DARING COSSACK
        BELWIN-MILLS PUBLISHING CORPORATION   .60
NOONA, W.   3
    FLAMING TAMBOURINE
        BELWIN-MILLS PUBLISHING CORPORATION   .60
NOONA, W.   2 1/2
    I FOUND A STAR
        BELWIN-MILLS PUBLISHING CORPORATION   .60
NOONA, W.   2 1/2
    KNIGHT, THE
        BELWIN-MILLS PUBLISHING CORPORATION   .60
NOONA, W.   1 1/2
    MY ROCKING CHAIR
        BELWIN-MILLS PUBLISHING CORPORATION   .60
NOONA, W.   2
    RED DRUM
        BELWIN-MILLS PUBLISHING CORPORATION   .60
NOONA, W.   6
    REFLECTIONS IN THE RAIN
        BELWIN-MILLS PUBLISHING CORPORATION   .60
NOONA, W.   4 1/2
    SAMARAI SWORD DANCE
        BELWIN-MILLS PUBLISHING CORPORATION   .60
NOONA, W.   3
    SPIDER DANCE
        BELWIN-MILLS PUBLISHING CORPORATION   .60
NORDIO   KESSYANA
    HUMORESKE
        FRANCO COLOMBO PUBLICATIONS   123382   1.25
NORDOFF, P.   M
    APPALACHIAN DANCE
        THEODORE PRESSER COMPANY   .50
NORDOFF, P.   M
    HILL SONG
        THEODORE PRESSER COMPANY   .50
NORDORFF, P.   INTER.
    FOURTH SINGS, THE
        AMERICAN MUSIC EDITION   .50
NORMAN
    FOREIGN INTRIGUE CONCERTO
        MCA MUSIC   1.00
NORMAN
    THEME FROM FOREIGN INTRIGUE CONCERTO -- SIMPLIFIED EDITION
        MCA MUSIC   1.00
NORMAN *
    FANFARE TANGO
        MCA MUSIC   1.00
NORMAN *
    LONELY WHISTLER, THE
        MCA MUSIC   1.00
NORTH, A.
    ANTONY AND CLEOPATRA THEME
        THE BIG THREE MUSIC CORPORATION   00.95
NORTH, A.
    CAESAR AND CLEOPATRA THEME
        THE BIG THREE MUSIC CORPORATION   00.95
NORTH, A.
    GRANDFATHER'S THEME
        BELWIN-MILLS PUBLISHING CORPORATION   20115   .85
NORTH, A.
    OUTRAGE, THE - THEME
        THE BIG THREE MUSIC CORPORATION   00.95
NORTH, A.
    RECONCILIATION
        THE BIG THREE MUSIC CORPORATION   00.95
NORTH, A.
    SHOES OF THE FISHERMAN, THE
        THE BIG THREE MUSIC CORPORATION   00.95
NORTH, M.   PERRY
    SUCH LOVELY THINGS
        BOOSEY AND HAWKES, INC.   .75
NOSSE   1
    PRINCE CHARMING WALTZ
        PRO-ART PUBLICATIONS, INC.   460   .50
NOVAK   3
    SLOWAKISCHE SUITE, OP. 32
        BARENREITER VERLAG   AP 666
NOVAK   3-4
    SONATA EROICA, OP. 24
        BARENREITER VERLAG   AP 665
NOVAK   4
    VARIATIONEN UBER EIN THEMA VON ROBERT SCHUMANN, OP. 68
        BARENREITER VERLAG   AP 669
NOVARO
    INNO DI MAMELI -- WITH WORDS --
        FRANCO COLOMBO PUBLICATIONS   126839   .60
NOVARO   DEL MAGLIO
    INNO DI MAMELI -- WITH WORDS --
        FRANCO COLOMBO PUBLICATIONS   127212   .60
NOVICH, C.   E
    IN THE ORIENT
        COMPOSERS PRESS, INC.   1.00
NOVIKOFF
    FANTASY
        FRANCO COLOMBO PUBLICATIONS   DS260   1.75
NOVIKOFF
    GONDOLIERA
        FRANCO COLOMBO PUBLICATIONS   DS350   1.25
NOVIKOFF
    NOSTALGIA
        FRANCO COLOMBO PUBLICATIONS   DS279   .75
NOVIKOFF
    SCHERZO
        FRANCO COLOMBO PUBLICATIONS   DS299   1.25
NOVIKOFF
    SPRING
        FRANCO COLOMBO PUBLICATIONS   DS276   1.00
NOVIKOFF
    SUITE
        FRANCO COLOMBO PUBLICATIONS   DS269   2.00
NOVIKOFF
    VALSE BERCEUSE
        FRANCO COLOMBO PUBLICATIONS   DS215   1.00
NUNES, E.
    LITANIES DU FEU ET DE LA MER NO. 1
        ELKAN-VOGEL, INC.   J   3.75
O'NEILL, C.   COVERT
    REGIMENTAL MARCH OF THE ROYAL CANADIAN MOUNTED POLICE
        FREDERICK HARRIS MUSIC COMPANY   .75
OAKLAND, B.
    NEWS BEAT
        BELWIN-MILLS PUBLISHING CORPORATION   20158   .85

OAKLAND, B.
    VALSE MODERNE
        THE BIG THREE MUSIC CORPORATION   00.95
OBENCHAIN, V.
    CHURCH MOUSE, THE
        G. SCHIRMER, INC.   .35
OBENCHAIN, V.
    EASTER BUNNY, THE
        G. SCHIRMER, INC.   .30
OBENCHAIN, V.   2-3
    KATHY'S WALTZ
        PRO-ART PUBLICATIONS, INC.   99   .50
OBENCHAIN, V.
    LET'S HAVE FUN
        G. SCHIRMER, INC.   .30
OBENCHAIN, V.   1
    MISTER BUNNY
        THEODORE PRESSER COMPANY   .50
OBENCHAIN, V.   1
    MOUSE GOES TO CHURCH, A
        BOSTON MUSIC COMPANY   .50
OBENCHAIN, V.
    PEPPERMINT CANDY
        G. SCHIRMER, INC.   .35
OBENCHAIN, V.
    POLISH WEDDING DANCE
        G. SCHIRMER, INC.   .35
OBENCHAIN, V.
    PUMPKIN FACES
        BELWIN-MILLS PUBLISHING CORPORATION   25088   .60
OBENCHAIN, V.   2-3
    TURKEY GOBBLER, THE
        PRO-ART PUBLICATIONS, INC.   100   .50
OBENCHAIN, V.   1-2
    WITCHES IN THE SKY
        PRO-ART PUBLICATIONS, INC.   178   .50
OBERG, O. S.   3
    FADED MEMORIES
        THEODORE PRESSER COMPANY   .50
OCHS   3
    S KOMMT EIN VOGEL GEFLOGEN. IM STILE ALTERER UND NEUERER MEISTER
    HUMORISTISCH BEARBEITET
        BARENREITER VERLAG   SM 959
OESTEN   4
    ALPINE GLOW
        CENTURY MUSIC PUBLISHING COMPANY, INC. 1051   .40
OESTEN   4
    CARNIVAL OF VENICE
        CENTURY MUSIC PUBLISHING COMPANY, INC. 157   .40
OESTEN   2
    DOLL'S DREAM
        CENTURY MUSIC PUBLISHING COMPANY, INC. 190   .40
OESTEN   2
    DOLL'S DREAM
        VOLKWEIN BROS.   .25
OESTEN
    DOLLIE'S DREAM
        G. SCHIRMER, INC.   .50
OESTEN
    DOLLY'S DREAM AND AWAKENING
        CARL FISCHER, INC.   S 373   .50
OETTING, H.   4
    BARCAROLLE
        VOLKWEIN BROS.   .40
OETTING, H.   4
    MEDITATION -- A PEDAL STUDY
        VOLKWEIN BROS.   .40
OFFENBACH   3
    APACHE DANCE
        CENTURY MUSIC PUBLISHING COMPANY, INC. 3648   .40
OFFENBACH   SEIDT   4
    BACAROLLE -- TALES OF HOFFMAN
        VOLKWEIN BROS.   .35
OFFENBACH
    BARBE-BLEUE
        HEUGEL ET CIE.   12.00
OFFENBACH   NICHOLLS
    BARCAROLLE
        BANKS AND SON LTD.   .40
OFFENBACH   WEYBRIGHT   2 1/2
    BARCAROLLE
        BELWIN-MILLS PUBLISHING CORPORATION   .50
OFFENBACH   WEYBRIGHT   2 1/2
    BARCAROLLE
        BELWIN-MILLS PUBLISHING CORPORATION   .60
OFFENBACH   4
    BARCAROLLE
        WILLIS MUSIC COMPANY   .30
OFFENBACH   3
    BARCAROLLE, BEAUTIFUL NIGHT
        CENTURY MUSIC PUBLISHING COMPANY, INC. 3623   .40
OFFENBACH   3
    BARCAROLLE, TALES OF HOFFMANN
        CENTURY MUSIC PUBLISHING COMPANY, INC. 1321   .40
OFFENBACH   LEVINE
    CAN CAN
        BOSTON MUSIC COMPANY   .50
OFFENBACH   3
    CAN CAN
        CENTURY MUSIC PUBLISHING COMPANY, INC. 3564   .40
OFFENBACH
    CAN CAN DANCE
        ASHLEY DEALERS SERVICE, INC.   ES   .95
OFFENBACH
    DRAGONETTE
        HEUGEL ET CIE.   6.50
OFFENBACH
    LA BELLE HELENE
        HEUGEL ET CIE.   9.75
OFFENBACH
    LA CHANSON DE FORTUNIO
        HEUGEL ET CIE.   7.30
OFFENBACH
    LA CHANSON DE FORTUNIO
        HEUGEL ET CIE.   7.30
OFFENBACH
    LES CONTES D'HOFFMANN--BARCAROLLE. INTERMEZZO
        G. SCHIRMER, INC.   .35
OFFENBACH   SPINDLER
    LES CONTES D'HOFFMANN--BARCAROLLE. O BELLE NUIT
        G. SCHIRMER, INC.   .60
OFFENBACH
    ORPHEE AUX ENFERS
        HEUGEL ET CIE.   24.00
OFFENBACH
    OVERTURE ON THEMES FROM 'ORPHEUS'
        G. SCHIRMER, INC.   .70

OFFENBACH	SCHAUM, J.	1	
RIDE RANGER RIDE			
BELWIN-MILLS PUBLISHING CORPORATION			.50
OFFENBACH		2	
TALES OF HOFFMAN, BARCAROLLE			
CENTURY MUSIC PUBLISHING COMPANY, INC.		2505	.40
OFFENBACH	SEAK		
TALES OF HOFFMANN - BARCAROLLE			
FRANCO COLOMBO PUBLICATIONS		129189	.50
OFFENBACH	SAMMARTINO		
TALES OF HOFFMANN - BARCAROLLE			
FRANCO COLOMBO PUBLICATIONS		BA9218	.75
OFFENBACH		1	
TALES OF HOFFMANN - BARCAROLLE, SIMP.			
BELWIN-MILLS PUBLISHING CORPORATION		514	.60
OFFENBACH		E-M	
VALSE CHALOUPEE --APACHE DANCE--			
C. F. PETERS CORPORATION		C85	1.50
OFFENBACH *			
ORPHEUS IN THE UNDERWORLD -- QUADRILLE			
HEUGEL ET CIE.			2.05
OFFUTT		3	
MARCH EROICA			
BELWIN-MILLS PUBLISHING CORPORATION			.60
OFFUTT			
PEPPERMINT GUARD, THE			
BRODT MUSIC COMPANY			.45
OGILVY, F.		5	
CAPRICE			
NOVELLO AND COMPANY, LTD.		55.0045.01	.25
OGILVY, F.		3	
FROLIC			
NOVELLO AND COMPANY, LTD.		55.0027.03	.25
OGILVY, F.		3	
HUMORESQUE			
NOVELLO AND COMPANY, LTD.		55.0029.10	.40
OGILVY, F.		3	
MELODY AND STATELY DANCE			
NOVELLO AND COMPANY, LTD.		10.0174.04	.90
OGILVY, F.		4	
REVELRY			
NOVELLO AND COMPANY, LTD.		55.0028.01	.40
OGILVY, F.		3	
WALTZ IN D			
NOVELLO AND COMPANY, LTD.		55.0027.03	.25
OGILVY, F.		3	
WEIRD STORY, A			
NOVELLO AND COMPANY, LTD.		55.0029.10	.40
OGLE, J.		M	
ECCENTRIC DANCE			
COMPOSERS PRESS, INC.			1.00
OGLE, L.		3	
DANCING CASTANETS			
PRO-ART PUBLICATIONS, INC.		425	.50
OGLE, L.		2	
DANCING WITH THE BREEZE			
WILLIS MUSIC COMPANY			.40
OGLE, L.		3	
LATIN WITH BAGPIPE			
PRO-ART PUBLICATIONS, INC.		426	.50
OGLE, L.		2	
MOTHER'S LULLABY			
CENTURY MUSIC PUBLISHING COMPANY, INC.		4121	.40
OHANA, M.			
SONATINE MONODIQUE			
GERARD BILLAUDOT EDITIONS MUSICALES			3.15
OHLSON, M.		2	
HONEYSUCKLE			
BELWIN-MILLS PUBLISHING CORPORATION			.60
OHLSON, M.			
MARCHE			
BELWIN-MILLS PUBLISHING CORPORATION			.60
OLCOTT	CURCIO	1	
MY WILD IRISH ROSE			
BOSTON MUSIC COMPANY			.50
OLDENBURG, E.		1	
BUDDY SQUIRREL			
PRO-ART PUBLICATIONS, INC.		122	.50
OLDENBURG, E.		2-3	
FARMER DANCE			
PRO-ART PUBLICATIONS, INC.		91	.50
OLDENBURG, E.		2-3	
FIESTA TIME			
PRO-ART PUBLICATIONS, INC.		63	.50
OLDENBURG, E.		2	
FINGER FLIGHT			
PRO-ART PUBLICATIONS, INC.		124	.50
OLDENBURG, E.		3	
FINGER TRICKS			
THEODORE PRESSER COMPANY			.50
OLDENBURG, E.		1	
LITTLE BIRD IN THE TREE			
PRO-ART PUBLICATIONS, INC.		88	.50
OLDENBURG, E.		2	
MING TOY			
PRO-ART PUBLICATIONS, INC.		123	.50
OLDENBURG, E.		2	
MONOLOGUE			
PRO-ART PUBLICATIONS, INC.		81	.50
OLDENBURG, E.		3 1/2	
PAGODA LAND			
THEODORE PRESSER COMPANY			.50
OLDENBURG, E.		1	
QUACK, QUACK			
PRO-ART PUBLICATIONS, INC.		121	.50
OLDENBURG, E.		1-2	
ROBIN, ROBIN			
PRO-ART PUBLICATIONS, INC.		90	.50
OLDENBURG, E.		1-2	
STRANGE STORY, A			
PRO-ART PUBLICATIONS, INC.		89	.50
OLEMAN, A.		3-4	
BLUE BIRD WALTZ -- HESITATION			
VOLKWEIN BROS.			.50
OLIVER			
PRELUDE TO THE STARS			
SAM FOX PUBLISHING COMPANY, INC.			.75
OLIVER			
PRELUDE TO THE STARS			
SOUTHERN MUSIC COMPANY			.75
OLIVER	LOWRY		
STUDIO ONE CONCERTO			
SAM FOX PUBLISHING COMPANY, INC.			1.00
OLIVER *			
EASY DOES IT			
MCA MUSIC			1.00

OLIVER *			
STUDIO ONE CONCERTO			
SOUTHERN MUSIC COMPANY			1.00
OLIVIERI			
GARIBALDI HYMN -- WITH WORDS --			
FRANCO COLOMBO PUBLICATIONS		126840	.60
OLIVIERI	DEL MAGLIO		
GARIBALDI HYMN -- WITH WORDS --			
FRANCO COLOMBO PUBLICATIONS		127213	.50
OLIVIERO			
ALL			
EDWARD B. MARKS MUSIC CORPORATION			00.60
OLIVIERO *			
MORE			
EDWARD B. MARKS MUSIC CORPORATION			01.00
OLIVIERO *			
MORE			
EDWARD B. MARKS MUSIC CORPORATION			01.00
OLIVIERO *			
MORE			
EDWARD B. MARKS MUSIC CORPORATION			00.60
OLLONE, M. D'			
LE TEMPLE ABANDONNE			
HEUGEL ET CIE.			5.00
OLSEN, A. L.		1 1/2	
TWO JAPANESE FOLK SONGS			
THEODORE PRESSER COMPANY			.50
OLSEN, O.			
BERCEUSE			
G. SCHIRMER, INC.			.25
OLSEN, O.			
SERENADE, OP. 19 NO. 2			
G. SCHIRMER, INC.			.30
OLSEN, P.		D	
MEDARDUS --SUITE--			
C. F. PETERS CORPORATION		EN13	3.00
OLSEN, S.		E-M	
ANDANTE FUNEBRE			
C. F. PETERS CORPORATION		LY164	.60
OLSON			
BRIEF ENCOUNTER			
CARL FISCHER, INC.		P 3204	.60
OLSON			
CARIBBEAN BLUE			
CARL FISCHER, INC.		P 3203	.60
OLSON			
CEREMONIAL			
SUMMY-BIRCHARD COMPANY			.50
OLSON			
FIRST SONATA			
CARL FISCHER, INC.		P 3201	.75
OLSON		3-4	
IN FOURTEEN HUNDRED NINETY-TWO			
PRO-ART PUBLICATIONS, INC.		247	.50
OLSON			
MAKE IT SNAPPY			
CARL FISCHER, INC.		P 3169	.50
OLSON		E	
MENAGERIE			
OXFORD UNIVERSITY PRESS		93.806	1.00
OLSON			
NIGHT CLOUDS			
SUMMY-BIRCHARD COMPANY			.50
OLSON			
OASIS, THE			
CARL FISCHER, INC.		P 3167	.50
OLSON			
OLE			
SUMMY-BIRCHARD COMPANY			.50
OLSON			
ON THE HIGH SEA			
CARL FISCHER, INC.		P 3205	.60
OLSON			
PAGODA			
SUMMY-BIRCHARD COMPANY			.50
OLSON			
RATHER BLUE			
G. SCHIRMER, INC.			.40
OLSON			
SECRET MISSION			
CARL FISCHER, INC.		P 3170	.50
OLSON			
SOUSAPHONE SERENADE			
CARL FISCHER, INC.		P 3200	.50
OLSON			
SPANISH SERENADE			
SUMMY-BIRCHARD COMPANY			.50
OLSON			
SUAVE SCHERZO			
CARL FISCHER, INC.		P 3191	.50
OLSON		3	
SUGARLOAF			
PRO-ART PUBLICATIONS, INC.		248	.50
OLSON			
SWEET DREAMS			
CARL FISCHER, INC.		P 3199	.50
OLSON			
TEMPLE CHIMES			
CARL FISCHER, INC.		P 3168	.50
OLSON			
WHEELS			
CARL FISCHER, INC.		P 3192	.50
OLSON, R.		3	
WALTZING CHIMPANZEE, THE			
BELWIN-MILLS PUBLISHING CORPORATION			.60
OMALLEY		E	
SIX SHORT DANCE VARIATIONS			
C. F. PETERS CORPORATION		H1540	1.25
OMER, BRO.		3	
SOUNDS OF AUTUMN, REVERIE			
CENTURY MUSIC PUBLISHING COMPANY, INC.		1888	.40
OPRESKA		2-3	
MEMORY, A			
PRO-ART PUBLICATIONS, INC.		471	.50
ORBON, J.			
TOCCATA			
EDITORIAL COOPERATIVA INTER-AMERICANA			01.15
OREFICE, G.			
CREPUSCOLI			
FRANCO COLOMBO PUBLICATIONS		130142	1.50
OREFICE, G.			
MIRAGGI			
FRANCO COLOMBO PUBLICATIONS		130150	2.75
OREFICE, G.			
PRELUDE AND FUGUE			
FRANCO COLOMBO PUBLICATIONS		117618	1.00

OREFICE, G.
   PRELUDI DEL MAR
      FRANCO COLOMBO PUBLICATIONS   130146   3.75
OREFICE, G.
   QUADRI DI BOEKLIN
      FRANCO COLOMBO PUBLICATIONS   130147   2.50
OREM, P. W.   8
   AMERICAN INDIAN RHAPSODY
      THEODORE PRESSER COMPANY   1.00
ORLAND, H.
   BREVISSIME PRETEXTE, BAGATELLE ET ETUDE
      SEESAW MUSIC CORPORATION   1.50
ORLAND, H.
   FANTASY, OP. 2
      SEESAW MUSIC CORPORATION   4.00
ORLAND, H.
   NOCTURNAL DANCE, OP. 3
      SEESAW MUSIC CORPORATION   2.00
ORLAND, H.
   SONATA FOR PIANO, OP. 20
      SEESAW MUSIC CORPORATION   7.00
ORLANDO, S.
   RONDA DI STRUMENTI
      EDIZIONI BERBEN   EB 1684   1.80
ORNSTEIN, L.
   CHINOISE, A LA, OP. 39
      ASSOCIATED MUSIC PUBLISHERS, INC.   AMP   1.25
ORNSTEIN, L.
   MEXICANA, A LA, OP. 35
      ASSOCIATED MUSIC PUBLISHERS, INC.   AMP   1.00
ORNSTEIN, L.
   SCHERZINO, OP. 5 NO. 2
      ASSOCIATED MUSIC PUBLISHERS, INC.   AMP   .50
ORNSTEIN, L.
   SERENADE, OP. 5 NO. 1
      ASSOCIATED MUSIC PUBLISHERS, INC.   AMP   .50
ORREGO SALAS, J.
   RUSTICA
      PAN AMERICAN UNION   00.65
ORREGO SALAS, J.
   SONATA, OP. 60
      PEER SOUTHERN ORGANIZATION   02.50
ORREGO SALAS, J.
   SUITE NO. 1, OP. 14
      BOOSEY AND HAWKES, INC.   1.75
ORREGO SALAS, J.
   SUITE NO. 2, OP. 32
      BOOSEY AND HAWKES, INC.   2.50
ORREGO SALAS, J.
   VARIATIONS AND FUGUE
      BOOSEY AND HAWKES, INC.   1.75
ORTALI
   SONATA NO. 03
      FRANCO COLOMBO PUBLICATIONS   BON.2508   3.50
ORTHEL   M-D
   SONATINA NO. 03, OP. 28
      C. F. PETERS CORPORATION   AL7   1.25
ORTOLANI
   ECCO WALTZ, THE
      EDWARD B. MARKS MUSIC CORPORATION   01.00
ORTOLANI
   ELOISE
      THE BIG THREE MUSIC CORPORATION   00.95
ORTOLANI
   MAE
      THE BIG THREE MUSIC CORPORATION   00.95
ORTOLANI
   MAYA
      THE BIG THREE MUSIC CORPORATION   00.95
ORTOLANI
   YELLOW ROLLS-ROYCE - THEME
      THE BIG THREE MUSIC CORPORATION   00.95
OSBORNE
   PLUIE DE PERLES, LA -- WALTZ --
      FRANCO COLOMBO PUBLICATIONS   SAL   1.75
OSBORNE   5
   SHOWER OF PEARLS, VALSE
      CENTURY MUSIC PUBLISHING COMPANY, INC.   1329   .40
OSBORNE *
   BETWEEN 18TH AND 19TH ON CHESTNUT STREET
      MCA MUSIC   1.00
OSBORNE, W.   3 1/2
   CONTRASTS
      THEODORE PRESSER COMPANY   .50
OSBORNE, W.   2
   FOLK DANCE
      THEODORE PRESSER COMPANY   .50
OSBORNE, W.   3 1/2
   PUPPET DANCE
      THEODORE PRESSER COMPANY   .50
OSBORNE, W.
   SONATINA
      BOOSEY AND HAWKES, INC.   1.25
OSBORNE, W.   2 1/2
   TWO QUIET SONGS
      THEODORE PRESSER COMPANY   .50
OSSER *
   KATHY'S THEME
      MCA MUSIC   1.00
OSTRCIL   3
   TSCHECHISCHE BALLADE, OP. 9
      BARENREITER VERLAG   AP 673
OSWALT, C.   E-M
   DREAM OF THE SANDMAN
      COMPOSERS PRESS, INC.   1.00
OTTE, H.
   TROPISMEN
      UNIVERSAL EDITION   UE 13645   3.65
OVERPLADE, A. R.   3 1/2
   SWAYING DAFFODILS
      THEODORE PRESSER COMPANY   .60
OVERSTREET
   THERE'LL BE SOME CHANGES MADE
      EDWARD B. MARKS MUSIC CORPORATION   00.60
OWEN
   DORIAN DUDE, THE
      ROCHESTER MUSIC PUBLISHERS, INC.   .50
OWENS
   CALIFORNIA SONATA
      FRANCO COLOMBO PUBLICATIONS   SIK.565   2.00
OWENS
   CARNIVAL
      FRANCO COLOMBO PUBLICATIONS   SIK.661   4.00
PABLO, L. DE
   SONATA, OP. 3
      ASSOCIATED MUSIC PUBLISHERS, INC.   UME   1.25

PABST   2
   GAVOTTE
      VOLKWEIN BROS.   .25
PACCAGNINI, A.
   RECREATION, SUITE ENFANTINE
      UNIVERSAL EDITION   UE 13714   1.65
PACE, R.   1
   FOLK SONG SETTINGS
      LEE ROBERTS MUSIC PUBLICATIONS, INC.   .85
PACE, R.   1
   THROUGH THE KEYS
      LEE ROBERTS MUSIC PUBLICATIONS, INC.   1.00
PACHER, J. A.   3
   AUSTRIAN SONG, OP. 69
      CENTURY MUSIC PUBLISHING COMPANY, INC. 140   .40
PACHER, J. A.
   MEI HERZIGES DIRNDL--AUSTRIAN FOLK-SONG, OP. 69 NO. 1
      G. SCHIRMER, INC.   .60
PACHETTI
   EGYPTIAN BALLET
      FRANCO COLOMBO PUBLICATIONS   DS166   1.00
PADEREWSKI, I. J.
   CAPRICE A LA SCARLATTI, OP. 14, NO. 3
      MUSICA OBSCURA   1.75
PADEREWSKI, I. J.
   CELEBRATED MINUET, OP. 14 NO. 1
      BELWIN-MILLS PUBLISHING CORPORATION 28015   .50
PADEREWSKI, I. J.
   CHANT D'AMOUR, OP. 10 NO. 2
      G. SCHIRMER, INC.   .30
PADEREWSKI, I. J.   5
   CRACOVIENNE FANTASTIQUE
      BOSTON MUSIC COMPANY   .60
PADEREWSKI, I. J.   5
   CRACOVIENNE FANTASTIQUE
      BOSTON MUSIC COMPANY   .60
PADEREWSKI, I. J.
   MELODIE FROM 'CHANTS DU VOYAGEUR', OP. 8 NO. 3
      G. SCHIRMER, INC.   .50
PADEREWSKI, I. J.   3
   MELODIE, OP. 8 NO. 3
      CENTURY MUSIC PUBLISHING COMPANY, INC. 314   .40
PADEREWSKI, I. J.
   MENUET A L'ANTIQUE, OP. 14 NO. 1
      ASHLEY DEALERS SERVICE, INC.   ES   .95
PADEREWSKI, I. J.   MASON, W.   6
   MENUET A L'ANTIQUE, OP. 14 NO. 1
      THEODORE PRESSER COMPANY   .75
PADEREWSKI, I. J.
   MENUET IN G, OP. 14 NO. 1
      G. SCHIRMER, INC.   .50
PADEREWSKI, I. J.   ECKSTEIN
   MENUET, OP. 14 NO. 1
      CARL FISCHER, INC.   S 991   .50
PADEREWSKI, I. J.   5
   MENUET, OP. 14 NO. 1
      VOLKWEIN BROS.   .25
PADEREWSKI, I. J.   2
   MENUET, SIMPLIFIED
      BELWIN-MILLS PUBLISHING CORPORATION 710   .60
PADEREWSKI, I. J.   KING, S.   EASY
   MINUET
      SHAWNEE PRESS, INC.   HB-5034   .40
PADEREWSKI, I. J.   4
   MINUET
      WILLIS MUSIC COMPANY   .40
PADEREWSKI, I. J.   3 - 4
   MINUET A L'ANTIQUE
      BOSTON MUSIC COMPANY   .50
PADEREWSKI, I. J.
   MINUET, OP. 14, NO. 1
      CARL FISCHER, INC.   S 991   .50
PADEREWSKI, I. J.
   NOCTURNE IN B FLAT, OP. 16 NO. 4
      G. SCHIRMER, INC.   .40
PADEREWSKI, I. J.
   THEME VARIE, OP. 16 NO. 3
      ASSOCIATED MUSIC PUBLISHERS, INC.   BOT   1.50
PADEREWSKI, I. J.
   THEME WITH VARIATIONS
      G. SCHIRMER, INC.   .80
PADEREWSKI, I.J.   4
   MENUET A L'ANTIQUE
      CENTURY MUSIC PUBLISHING COMPANY, INC. 315   .40
PADILLA, J.
   BIEN AMADA, LA--VALENCIA
      ASSOCIATED MUSIC PUBLISHERS, INC.   UME   .50
PADILLA, J.   3
   EL RELICARIO
      CENTURY MUSIC PUBLISHING COMPANY, INC. 3614   .40
PADWA, V.
   ELECTRIC
      G. SCHIRMER, INC.   .60
PADWA, V.   3 1/2
   MARCH OF THE MINUTE MEN
      THEODORE PRESSER COMPANY   .50
PADWA, V.   3
   PARADE OF THE POOKAS
      THEODORE PRESSER COMPANY   .50
PADWA, V.   5
   ROMAN SUITE
      THEODORE PRESSER COMPANY   .75
PADWA, V.
   SIX LITTLE PRELUDES--NO. 1, DIALOGUE
      ASSOCIATED MUSIC PUBLISHERS, INC.   AMP   .40
PADWA, V.
   SIX LITTLE PRELUDES--NO. 2, INTERLUDE
      ASSOCIATED MUSIC PUBLISHERS, INC.   AMP   .40
PADWA, V.
   SIX LITTLE PRELUDES--NO. 3, LITTLE MARCH
      ASSOCIATED MUSIC PUBLISHERS, INC.   AMP   .40
PADWA, V.
   SIX LITTLE PRELUDES--NO. 5, SHADOWS
      ASSOCIATED MUSIC PUBLISHERS, INC.   AMP   .40
PAGANINI, N.   CHIESA
   CARNIVAL OF VENICE
      FRANCO COLOMBO PUBLICATIONS   107490   .60
PAGANINI, N. *
   MOTO PERPETUO, OP. 11 -- TRANSCRIPTION --
      G. SCHIRMER, INC.   1.00
PAHISSA
   BODAS EN LA MONTANA
      FRANCO COLOMBO PUBLICATIONS   BA10882   1.50
PAHISSA   DIA FELIZ
   EIGHT POETIC PIECES - JOYOUS DAY
      FRANCO COLOMBO PUBLICATIONS   NY1575   .50

PAHISSA
NOCHE DE NAVIDAD
FRANCO COLOMBO PUBLICATIONS   BA11294   .75
PAHISSA
RONDINO - FROM 7 CHILDREN'S PIECES
FRANCO COLOMBO PUBLICATIONS   NY1574   .50
PAITA, F.
BALLADE DU LAC BLANC
ASSOCIATED MUSIC PUBLISHERS, INC.   ESC   2.50
PAITA, F.
NOCTURNE NO. 02 IN B MINOR
ASSOCIATED MUSIC PUBLISHERS, INC.   ESC   2.25
PALAU, M.
EVOCACION DE ANDALUCIA
ASSOCIATED MUSIC PUBLISHERS, INC.   UME   .60
PALAU, M.
TOCCATA IN E MINOR
ASSOCIATED MUSIC PUBLISHERS, INC.   UME   .65
PALMA   LOCATELLI
PRELUDE
FRANCO COLOMBO PUBLICATIONS   BA10890   .75
PALMA
VIDALA
FRANCO COLOMBO PUBLICATIONS   BA9932   .75
PALMER
BOOK OF CHIMES
FRANCO COLOMBO PUBLICATIONS   LD378   1.25
PALMER   M
EVENING MUSIC
THEODORE PRESSER COMPANY   .50
PALMER
TOCCATA OSTINATO
ELKAN-VOGEL, INC.   .75
PALMER *
SERENADE TO AN EMPTY ROOM
MCA MUSIC   1.00
PALMER, W. A.
CHRISTMAS HOLIDAY
ALFRED MUSIC COMPANY   658   1.25
PALMGREN, S.   3
CRADLE SONG
BOSTON MUSIC COMPANY   .50
PALMGREN, S.
MAY NIGHT
ASHLEY DEALERS SERVICE, INC.   ES   .95
PALMGREN, S.   5
MAY NIGHT
BOSTON MUSIC COMPANY   .50
PALMGREN, S.   4
MAY NIGHT
CENTURY MUSIC PUBLISHING COMPANY, INC.   3122   .40
PALMGREN, S.
MAY NIGHT
G. SCHIRMER, INC.   .40
PALMGREN, S.
MAY NIGHT, OP. 27 NO. 4
CARL FISCHER, INC.   S 2264   .50
PALMGREN, S.   5
SEA, THE
BOSTON MUSIC COMPANY   .50
PALMGREN, S.   5
SLUMBER SONG
BOSTON MUSIC COMPANY   .50
PALMGREN, S.   4
SWAN, THE
BOSTON MUSIC COMPANY   .60
PALOMBI
DANZA SPAGNOLA
FRANCO COLOMBO PUBLICATIONS   DS47   1.00
PALOMBI
NOCTURNE NO. 01
FRANCO COLOMBO PUBLICATIONS   DS48   1.25
PALOMBI
NOCTURNE NO. 02
FRANCO COLOMBO PUBLICATIONS   DS301   1.25
PANELLA, L.   2
ASTERS
VOLKWEIN BROS.   .25
PANELLA, L.   2
AT THE DANCE
VOLKWEIN BROS.   .30
PANELLA, L.   2
BUTTERCUPS
VOLKWEIN BROS.   .25
PANELLA, L.   2
DAFFODILS
VOLKWEIN BROS.   .25
PANELLA, L.   2
DAHLIAS
VOLKWEIN BROS.   .25
PANELLA, L.   4
DAINTY DAMOZEL
VOLKWEIN BROS.   .40
PANELLA, L.   2
DANCE OF THE KEWPIES
VOLKWEIN BROS.   .30
PANELLA, L.   2
DREAM MELODY
VOLKWEIN BROS.   .25
PANELLA, L.   4
ECHOES OF THE CHIMES
VOLKWEIN BROS.   .35
PANELLA, L.   4
FRESHMAN MARCH
VOLKWEIN BROS.   .40
PANELLA, L.   2
GLADIOLAS
VOLKWEIN BROS.   .25
PANELLA, L.   3
GOLDEN SHOWERS
VOLKWEIN BROS.   .35
PANELLA, L.   2
IN COMMAND -- SIMPLIFIED
VOLKWEIN BROS.   .30
PANELLA, L.   2
IN THE PIRATE'S CAVE
VOLKWEIN BROS.   .30
PANELLA, L.   4
JUNIOR MARCH
VOLKWEIN BROS.   .40
PANELLA, L.   2
LARKSPURS
VOLKWEIN BROS.   .25
PANELLA, L.   2
LOVE TOKENS -- SIMPLIFIED
VOLKWEIN BROS.   .40

PANELLA, L.   2
LULLABY
VOLKWEIN BROS.   .25
PANELLA, L.   2
MARIGOLDS
VOLKWEIN BROS.   .25
PANELLA, L.   2
MOONBEAMS
VOLKWEIN BROS.   .35
PANELLA, L.   2
OMAR
VOLKWEIN BROS.   .30
PANELLA, L.   2
ORCHIDS
VOLKWEIN BROS.   .25
PANELLA, L.   2
OWL
VOLKWEIN BROS.   .25
PANELLA, L.   2
PANSY BLOSSOMS
VOLKWEIN BROS.   .30
PANELLA, L.   2-3
PLAYTIME
VOLKWEIN BROS.   .25
PANELLA, L.   2
POPPIES
VOLKWEIN BROS.   .25
PANELLA, L.   2
ROLLING WAVES
VOLKWEIN BROS.   .30
PANELLA, L.   4
SENIOR MARCH
VOLKWEIN BROS.   .40
PANELLA, L.   4
SOPHOMORE MARCH
VOLKWEIN BROS.   .40
PANELLA, L.   4
SPIRIT OF AMERICA
VOLKWEIN BROS.   .50
PANELLA, L.   4
TECH TARTAN
VOLKWEIN BROS.   00.50
PANELLA, L.   2
WOODPECKER
VOLKWEIN BROS.   00.25
PANELLA, L.   2
ZEPHRS
VOLKWEIN BROS.   00.30
PANZANI
SCHIZZI
FRANCO COLOMBO PUBLICATIONS   BON.2233   1.50
PAPARELLI
NEWTON'S BOOGIE WOOGIE
MCA MUSIC   1.00
PAPE, W.   6
IRISH AIRS
CENTURY MUSIC PUBLISHING COMPANY, INC.   1198   .40
PAPINEAU-COUTURE, J.
ARIA
ASSOCIATED MUSIC PUBLISHERS, INC.   BER   .40
PAPINEAU-COUTURE, J.
ETUDE IN SI FLAT
PEER SOUTHERN ORGANIZATION   01.25
PAPINEAU-COUTURE, J.
MOUVEMENT PERPETUEL
ASSOCIATED MUSIC PUBLISHERS, INC.   BER   .60
PAPINEAU-COUTURE, J.
SUITE--RONDO
ASSOCIATED MUSIC PUBLISHERS, INC.   BER   1.00
PAPP, L.
VARIATIONS
KULTURA   2.00
PARADIES, P. D.
GIGA IN B FLAT
BANKS AND SON LTD.   .40
PARADIES, P. D.   TARENGLEI   3
TOCCATA
BARENREITER VERLAG   CM 13736
PARADIES, P. D.
TOCCATA
CARL FISCHER, INC.   S 1841   .50
PARADIES, P. D.   4
TOCCATA
CENTURY MUSIC PUBLISHING COMPANY, INC.   3735   .40
PARADIES, P. D.   CESI
TOCCATA
FRANCO COLOMBO PUBLICATIONS   102754   .50
PARADIES, P. D.   HUGHES
TOCCATA IN A
G. SCHIRMER, INC.   .50
PARADIES, P. D.   4
TOCCATA IN A
SCHOTT   0908 1/2   1.00
PARAY, P.
D'UNE AME
ELKAN-VOGEL, INC.   J   6.00
PARAY, P.
THEME ET VARIATIONS
ELKAN-VOGEL, INC.   J   2.75
PARDAVE
MEGRA CONSENTIDA
EDWARD B. MARKS MUSIC CORPORATION   01.00
PARENTE, SR. E.
FAIRYLAND WALTZ
G. SCHIRMER, INC.   .35
PARENTE, SR. E.
FROLIC
G. SCHIRMER, INC.   .35
PARENTE, SR. E.   2
MITZY'S RENDEZVOUS
WILLIS MUSIC COMPANY   .40
PARENTE, SR. E.   2
SWINGING ALONG
WILLIS MUSIC COMPANY   .40
PARENTE, SR. E.
WALTZ WITH ME
G. SCHIRMER, INC.   .35
PARISH, M. *   GLOVER, D.
SYNCOPATED CLOCK
BELWIN-MILLS PUBLISHING CORPORATION   .60
PARK   2
AT THE BALLET
CENTURY MUSIC PUBLISHING COMPANY, INC.   019   .40
PARK   2
SHADOWS
CENTURY MUSIC PUBLISHING COMPANY, INC.   020   .40

PARK, S.   1
    CLOUDS
        ELKAN-VOGEL, INC.   .50
PARK, S.   3
    HOLIDAY
        WILLIS MUSIC COMPANY   .50
PARK, S.
    TOBOGGAN RIDE
        BELWIN-MILLS PUBLISHING CORPORATION   25181 .60
PARK, S.   1
    TREES
        ELKAN-VOGEL, INC.   .50
PARKER, J.   2
    HOLIDAY IN TOWN
        BELWIN-MILLS PUBLISHING CORPORATION   .60
PARKER, J.   1
    WHISTLING PARAKEET, THE
        BELWIN-MILLS PUBLISHING CORPORATION   .60
PARMICIANO
    DEA MORTA DELL'ACROPOLI, UNA
        FRANCO COLOMBO PUBLICATIONS   FOR.11749 1.00
PARNES *   GLOVER, D.
    HAPPINESS IS
        BELWIN-MILLS PUBLISHING CORPORATION   .60
PARRA, B. G. DE LA
    CASTELLANAS
        ASSOCIATED MUSIC PUBLISHERS, INC.   UME   .75
PARSONS
    BOHEMIAN FOLK SONG
        FREDERICK HARRIS MUSIC COMPANY   .60
PARTICHALA
    MEXICAN HAT DANCE
        ASHLEY DEALERS SERVICE, INC.   ES   .95
PARTOS, O.
    PIECE FOR PIANO
        ISRAEL MUSIC INSTITUTE   2.50
PARTOS, O.
    PRELUDE
        ISRAEL MUSIC INSTITUTE   2.25
PASCAL, A.
    POUR LES PETITES MAINS
        EDITIONS MUSICALES TRANSATLANTIQUES   1.25
PASCAL, C.
    L'ALBUM DE LISETTE ET POULOT
        ELKAN-VOGEL, INC.   D   4.25
PASCAL, C.
    LE DOUX SOMMEIL DES FEES -- FROM 'L'ALBUM DE LISETTE ET POULOT'
        ELKAN-VOGEL, INC.   D   .80
PASCAL, C.
    SUITE FOR PIANO
        ELKAN-VOGEL, INC.   D   12.00
PASCAL, C.
    TOCCATA
        ELKAN-VOGEL, INC.   D   2.25
PASQUET, J.   3
    ARABESQUE
        WILLIS MUSIC COMPANY   .40
PASQUET, J.   4
    ON A MOONLIT LAKE
        WILLIS MUSIC COMPANY   .40
PASQUET, J.   2 1/2
    STORMY WEATHER
        WILLIS MUSIC COMPANY   .40
PASQUINI   CANINO, B.
    SONATA NO. 10 IN MI MINORE
        EDIZIONI BERBEN   EB 1312   1.25
PASQUINI
    TOCCATA ON THE CUCKOO'S SONG
        FRANCO COLOMBO PUBLICATIONS   128241   .75
PATTISON, L.   M
    PRELUDE
        COMPOSERS PRESS, INC.   1.00
PAUER
    CASCADE, LA OP. 37
        FRANCO COLOMBO PUBLICATIONS   SAL   1.75
PAUER   6
    CASCADE, OP. 37
        CENTURY MUSIC PUBLISHING COMPANY, INC. 1182 .40
PAUER   6
    LA CASCADE, OP. 37
        CENTURY MUSIC PUBLISHING COMPANY, INC. 1182 .40
PAUL   5
    BABY-POLKA
        ALPHONSE LEDUC
PAULL   ADVANCED
    BATTLE OF GETTYSBURG
        SHAWNEE PRESS, INC.   .50
PAULL
    BEN HUR CHARIOT RACE
        ASHLEY DEALERS SERVICE, INC.   ES   .95
PAULL   3
    BEN HUR CHARIOT RACE
        CENTURY MUSIC PUBLISHING COMPANY, INC. 4320 .40
PAULL   MENDEL, S.   2 1/2
    BEN HUR CHARIOT RACE
        WILLIS MUSIC COMPANY   .40
PAULL   2
    BEN HUR CHARIOT RACE
        WILLIS MUSIC COMPANY   .50
PAULL   ADVANCED
    BEN HUR CHARIOT RACE MARCH
        SHAWNEE PRESS, INC.   HB-83   .60
PAULL   3
    BURNING OF ROME
        CENTURY MUSIC PUBLISHING COMPANY, INC. 4323 .40
PAULL   ADVANCED
    BURNING OF ROME
        SHAWNEE PRESS, INC.   HB-66   .60
PAULL   3
    BURNING OF ROME MARCH
        ASHLEY DEALERS SERVICE, INC.   ES   .95
PAULL   3
    NAPOLEON'S LAST CHARGE
        CENTURY MUSIC PUBLISHING COMPANY, INC. 4375 .40
PAULL   ADVANCED
    PAUL REVERE'S RIDE
        SHAWNEE PRESS, INC.   HB-65   .50
PAULL   ADVANCED
    SILVER SLEIGH BELLS
        SHAWNEE PRESS, INC.   HB-6   .50
PAYMER, A.   3
    HAPPY BUGLER, THE
        THEODORE PRESSER COMPANY   .50
PAYNE, W.
    CAROLS YOU KNOW
        BANKS AND SON LTD.   .95

PAYTON, P.
    DANCING LEAVES
        G. SCHIRMER, INC.   .35
PAZ, J.
    TERCERA SONATINA
        EDITORIAL COOPERATIVA INTER-AMERICANA   01.05
PECHMAN   2
    AFTER DARK
        WILLIS MUSIC COMPANY   .40
PECHMAN   2
    AFTER DARK
        WILLIS MUSIC COMPANY   .40
PECHMAN   1
    FIVE FINGER FUN
        PRO-ART PUBLICATIONS, INC.   538   .50
PECHMAN   2
    FRIENDLY DEER
        PRO-ART PUBLICATIONS, INC.   491   .50
PECHMAN   1
    FRIENDS
        PRO-ART PUBLICATIONS, INC.   540   .50
PECHMAN   1-2
    GHOST MARCH
        PRO-ART PUBLICATIONS, INC.   339   .50
PECHMAN   3
    HAPPY GUY
        BOSTON MUSIC COMPANY   .50
PECHMAN   2
    HOTEL CARIBBEAN
        WILLIS MUSIC COMPANY   .40
PECHMAN   2
    LADY IN VELVET
        WILLIS MUSIC COMPANY   .40
PECHMAN   1
    SUNNY DAY, A
        PRO-ART PUBLICATIONS, INC.   541   .50
PECHMAN   2
    THROUGH THE WOODS
        PRO-ART PUBLICATIONS, INC.   539   .50
PECHMAN   2
    TRANQUIL MOOD
        WILLIS MUSIC COMPANY   .40
PECK, L.
    NORSEMAN'S SONG
        BANKS AND SON LTD.   .25
PECK, R.
    SUSPENDED SENTENCE
        ELKAN-VOGEL, INC.   J   4.00
PEDERSON-KRAG   1
    FOUR BY EIGHT
        CENTURY MUSIC PUBLISHING COMPANY, INC. 3935 .40
PEDRELL, C.
    SURLES BORES DU DOURO, 1922
        ASSOCIATED MUSIC PUBLISHERS, INC.   ESC   2.75
PEERSON, C.
    ARIA
        FREDERICK HARRIS MUSIC COMPANY   .60
PEERY, R. R.   5
    DARK EYES
        THEODORE PRESSER COMPANY   .50
PEETERS   D
    TOCCATA, OP. 51A
        C. F. PETERS CORPORATION   6396   .90
PELS, W.   2-3
    BROWN-EYED SUZY
        PRO-ART PUBLICATIONS, INC.   341   .50
PELS, W.   2
    CAREFREE BUTTERFLY
        PRO-ART PUBLICATIONS, INC.   340   .50
PELS, W.   2-3
    DAFFODILS
        CENTURY MUSIC PUBLISHING COMPANY, INC. 4258 .40
PELS, W.   2-3
    FAIRY TALE
        PRO-ART PUBLICATIONS, INC.   342   .50
PELS, W.   2
    HERE COMES THE TUBA
        WILLIS MUSIC COMPANY   .50
PELS, W.   2-3
    JAMBOREE
        PRO-ART PUBLICATIONS, INC.   331   .50
PELS, W.   1-2
    ONE, TWO THREE DANCE WITH ME
        PRO-ART PUBLICATIONS, INC.   332   .50
PELS, W.   2-3
    PARTY POLKA
        PRO-ART PUBLICATIONS, INC.   343   .50
PELS, W.   2
    PIANO TUNER
        PRO-ART PUBLICATIONS, INC.   330   .50
PELS, W.   2
    ROUND AND ROUND AND ROUND IT GOES
        CENTURY MUSIC PUBLISHING COMPANY, INC. 4263 .40
PELS, W.   3
    TWICE TOLD TALE
        BOSTON MUSIC COMPANY   .50
PELZ   1-2
    BELLS, BELLS, BELLS
        CENTURY MUSIC PUBLISHING COMPANY, INC. 4395 .40
PELZ, W.   2
    DOUBLE FEATURE
        BELWIN-MILLS PUBLISHING CORPORATION   .60
PELZ, W.   2
    TWIN TUNES
        BELWIN-MILLS PUBLISHING CORPORATION   .60
PENAU
    NOCTURNE
        FRANCO COLOMBO PUBLICATIONS   SAL   1.75
PENNINGTON, S.
    DANCE OF THE FIREFLIES, OP. 21
        BELWIN-MILLS PUBLISHING CORPORATION   28202 .60
PENNINGTON, S.
    VILLAGE DANCE -- DANCE VILLAGEOISE, OP. 10 NO. 1
        BELWIN-MILLS PUBLISHING CORPORATION   28041 .60
PENTLAND, B.
    DIRGE
        ASSOCIATED MUSIC PUBLISHERS, INC.   BER   .60
PENTLAND, B.
    FANTASY
        ASSOCIATED MUSIC PUBLISHERS, INC.   BER   1.25
PENTLAND, B.
    TOCCATA
        ASSOCIATED MUSIC PUBLISHERS, INC.   BER   1.00
PEPPING, E.
    PHANTASIEN FUR KLAVIER
        BARENREITER VERLAG   BA 2256   7.50

PEPPING, E.   4
  SONATA NO. 03
    SCHOTT   2623   3.00
PEPPING, E.
  SONATA NO. 04
    BARENREITER VERLAG   BA 2257   5.50
PEPPING, E.   4
  SONATA NO. 04
    BARENREITER VERLAG   BA 2257
PEPPING, E.   3
  SONATINA
    SCHOTT   2180   2.75
PEPPING, E.   3
  VARIATIONEN 1
    BARENREITER VERLAG   BA 2254
PEPPING, E.   3
  VARIATIONEN 2
    BARENREITER VERLAG   BA 2255
PEPPING, E.
  VARIATIONS NO. 1
    BARENREITER VERLAG   BA 2254   2.50
PEPPING, E.
  VARIATIONS NO. 2
    BARENREITER VERLAG   BA 2255   2.50
PEPPING, E.
  ZUHAUSE -- VARIATIONS IN 4 MOVEMENTS
    BARENREITER VERLAG   BA 2270   6.00
PEPPING, E.   3-4
  ZWEI SONATEN, NO. 01
    SCHOTT   2584   2.75
PEPPING, E.   3-4
  ZWEI SONATEN, NO. 02
    SCHOTT   2585   2.75
PEPUSCH   E-M
  BEGGAR'S OPERA, ABRIDGED
    C. F. PETERS CORPORATION   H1728   1.50
PERAGALLO, M.
  FANTASIA
    UNIVERSAL EDITION   UE 12137   1.90
PERCUOCO
  BAILECITO
    FRANCO COLOMBO PUBLICATIONS   BA10230   .75
PERCUOCO
  DUERMETE NINO
    FRANCO COLOMBO PUBLICATIONS   BA9351   .75
PERCUOCO
  SOLDADITOS DE PLOMO
    FRANCO COLOMBO PUBLICATIONS   BA10556   .75
PERGOLESI   DEL MAGLIO
  SE TU M'AMI
    FRANCO COLOMBO PUBLICATIONS   128124   .50
PERGOLESI   ZECCHI *   3
  SONATA IN F
    BARENREITER VERLAG   CM 21818
PERGOLESI   MONTANI
  SONATAS AND SUITES - NO. 3 FIRST SONATA IN G
    FRANCO COLOMBO PUBLICATIONS   128400   .75
PERILHOU
  CHANSON DE JANE-LA-GAILLARDE
    FRANCO COLOMBO PUBLICATIONS   SAL   1.75
PERIN, H.   3
  TARANTELLE IN E MINOR
    WILLIS MUSIC COMPANY   .40
PERKINS, F.
  BARBARA
    BELWIN-MILLS PUBLISHING CORPORATION   20027   .85
PERKINS, F.
  FANDANGO
    BELWIN-MILLS PUBLISHING CORPORATION   20085   .85
PERKINS, F.
  FELICIANA
    BELWIN-MILLS PUBLISHING CORPORATION   20089   .85
PERKINS, F.
  FRUSTRATED FLOORWALKER
    BELWIN-MILLS PUBLISHING CORPORATION   20104   .85
PERKINS, F.
  KENTUCKY TROTTER
    BELWIN-MILLS PUBLISHING CORPORATION   S 140   .85
PERKINS, F.
  MUSIC FOR MY LADY
    BELWIN-MILLS PUBLISHING CORPORATION   20178   .85
PERKINS, F.
  PALACE OF THE GRAND PANJANDRUM, THE -- AN ORIENTAL PARADE
    BELWIN-MILLS PUBLISHING CORPORATION   20190   .85
PERKINS, F.
  PICCADILLY WILLY
    BELWIN-MILLS PUBLISHING CORPORATION   20473   .85
PERKINS, F.
  POP GUN PATROL
    BELWIN-MILLS PUBLISHING CORPORATION   20205   .85
PERKINS, F.
  WALTZ FOR MILADY
    BELWIN-MILLS PUBLISHING CORPORATION   20331   .60
PERLE, G.   M
  INTERRUPTED STORY
    THEODORE PRESSER COMPANY   .50
PERLE, G.   D
  SHORT SONATA
    THEODORE PRESSER COMPANY   1.75
PERLE, G.
  SONATA
    EDITORIAL COOPERATIVA INTER-AMERICANA   00.95
PERRIN   2
  BALLET DANCER
    BELWIN-MILLS PUBLISHING CORPORATION   .60
PERRIN   1
  BELLS AT EVENING
    BELWIN-MILLS PUBLISHING CORPORATION   .60
PERRIN   1
  CLOCK IN MY ROOM
    BELWIN-MILLS PUBLISHING CORPORATION   .60
PERRIN   EASY
  IN CARACAS
    SHAWNEE PRESS, INC.   HB-5020   .40
PERRIN   2 1/2
  MANOLETTO'S DANCE
    BELWIN-MILLS PUBLISHING CORPORATION   .60
PERRIN   1
  MY NEW HAT
    BELWIN-MILLS PUBLISHING CORPORATION   .60
PERRIN   2
  OLD DESERTED HOUSE
    BELWIN-MILLS PUBLISHING CORPORATION   .60
PERRIN   2
  RUNNING ON TIPTOES
    BELWIN-MILLS PUBLISHING CORPORATION   .60

PERRIN   1 1/2
  SCISSORS GRINDER
    BELWIN-MILLS PUBLISHING CORPORATION   .60
PERRIN   2
  TRAIN, THE
    BELWIN-MILLS PUBLISHING CORPORATION   .60
PERROT
  CAPRICES DE PIERRETTE, LES
    FRANCO COLOMBO PUBLICATIONS   SAL   1.75
PERROT
  REVE D'ARLEQUIN
    FRANCO COLOMBO PUBLICATIONS   SAL   1.75
PERRY, N.   E
  COUNTRY COTTAGE
    OXFORD UNIVERSITY PRESS   33.923   1.15
PERRY, N.   E
  THROUGH THE KALEIDOSCOPE
    OXFORD UNIVERSITY PRESS   33.057   1.25
PERRY, P.   1B
  AT THE OLD SWIMMIN HOLE
    MUSICORD PUBLICATIONS, INC.   .45
PERRY, P.   2
  CEDAR BROOK WALTZ
    CENTURY MUSIC PUBLISHING COMPANY, INC.   1684   .40
PERSICHETTI
  CONCERTINO
    ELKAN-VOGEL, INC.   2.50
PERSICHETTI
  LITTLE PIANO BOOK
    ELKAN-VOGEL, INC.   1.25
PERSICHETTI
  PARADES, OP. 57
    ELKAN-VOGEL, INC.   .90
PERSICHETTI
  PIANO SONATA NO. 03
    ELKAN-VOGEL, INC.   2.50
PERSICHETTI
  PIANO SONATA NO. 04
    ELKAN-VOGEL, INC.   3.00
PERSICHETTI
  PIANO SONATA NO. 05
    ELKAN-VOGEL, INC.   2.00
PERSICHETTI
  PIANO SONATA NO. 06
    ELKAN-VOGEL, INC.   2.50
PERSICHETTI
  PIANO SONATA NO. 07
    ELKAN-VOGEL, INC.   2.00
PERSICHETTI
  PIANO SONATA NO. 08
    ELKAN-VOGEL, INC.   2.50
PERSICHETTI
  PIANO SONATA NO. 09
    ELKAN-VOGEL, INC.   2.50
PERSICHETTI
  PIANO SONATA NO. 10
    ELKAN-VOGEL, INC.   3.50
PERSICHETTI
  PIANO SONATA NO. 11
    ELKAN-VOGEL, INC.   3.50
PERSICHETTI
  SERENADE NO. 02
    ELKAN-VOGEL, INC.   .90
PERSICHETTI   2 1/2 - 3
  SERENADE NO. 07
    ELKAN-VOGEL, INC.   1.25
PERSICHETTI
  SERENADE NO. 08, OP. 62
    ELKAN-VOGEL, INC.   1.25
PERSICHETTI
  SONATA FOR HARPSICHORD
    ELKAN-VOGEL, INC.   3.50
PERSICHETTI   M
  VARIATIONS FOR AN ALBUM
    THEODORE PRESSER COMPANY   .75
PESSARD   6
  ANDALOUSE
    ALPHONSE LEDUC
PESSE
  AMUSANTE HISTOIRE, L'
    FRANCO COLOMBO PUBLICATIONS   SAL   1.50
PESSE   6
  CHANSON DU MULETIER, LA
    ALPHONSE LEDUC
PESSE
  GAVOTTE DES PETITS
    FRANCO COLOMBO PUBLICATIONS   SAL   1.75
PESSE
  GENTIL PRINTEMPS
    FRANCO COLOMBO PUBLICATIONS   SAL   1.50
PESTALOZZA   3
  CIRBIRIBIN, WALTZ
    CENTURY MUSIC PUBLISHING COMPANY, INC.   1511   .40
PETER, C.   3
  JOLLY COPPERSMITH, THE
    CENTURY MUSIC PUBLISHING COMPANY, INC.   1705   .40
PETERS, F.   1 1/2
  MERRY CHASE, A
    WILLIS MUSIC COMPANY   .40
PETERS, F.   1
  UP IN THE CLOUDS
    WILLIS MUSIC COMPANY   .40
PETIT, P.   8
  CAPRICCIO
    ALPHONSE LEDUC
PETIT, P.
  DEUX ETUDES, NO.1, BROUILLAGE
    GERARD BILLAUDOT EDITIONS MUSICALES   1.30
PETIT, P.
  DEUX ETUDES, NO.2 MOULIN A CAFE
    GERARD BILLAUDOT EDITIONS MUSICALES   1.30
PETRALIA
  MEMORIE
    FRANCO COLOMBO PUBLICATIONS   FOR.11416   .75
PETRALIA
  VENDEMMIA
    FRANCO COLOMBO PUBLICATIONS   FOR.11431   .75
PETRASSI
  RITRATTO DI DON CHISCIOTTE
    UNIVERSAL EDITION   UE 11841   4.05
PETRASSI
  RITRATTO DI DON CHISCIOTTE
    UNIVERSAL EDITION   UE 11841   4.05
PETRASSI
  TOCCATA
    FRANCO COLOMBO PUBLICATIONS   122924   1.25

PETRICH, F. C.   3
  GENERAL WITH THE PAPER HAT, THE
    THEODORE PRESSER COMPANY   .50
PETRICH, F. C.   2 1/2
  GOOD SHIP ROVER, THE
    THEODORE PRESSER COMPANY   .50
PETRIE   SCHAUM, J.   2 1/2
  ASLEEP IN THE DEEP
    BELWIN-MILLS PUBLISHING CORPORATION   .50
PETRIE-WINGATE   STEINER   2 1/2
  BACKYARD BOOGIE
    BELWIN-MILLS PUBLISHING CORPORATION   .60
PETRZELKA   4
  SUITE FUR KLAVIER, OP. 22
    BARENREITER VERLAG   AP 677
PETYREK, F.
  CHORALE, VARIATIONS AND SONATINA
    UNIVERSAL EDITION   UE 7621   1.70
PETYREK, F.
  HUNGARIAN FOLK SONGS
    UNIVERSAL EDITION   UE 6165   3.50
PETYREK, F.
  VARIATIONS AND FUGUE IN C MAJOR
    UNIVERSAL EDITION   UE 6825   1.70
PETYREK, R.
  SONATA, 1944
    ASSOCIATED MUSIC PUBLISHERS, INC.   DOB   2.25
PETYREK, R.
  SONATINA IN C, 1947
    ASSOCIATED MUSIC PUBLISHERS, INC.   OBV   1.50
PFEIFFER, A.
  MAZURKA DE SALON NO. 4
    FRANCO COLOMBO PUBLICATIONS   SAL   2.50
PFEIFFER, A.
  THREE FEUILLETS D'ALBUM, OP. 47 - CONTE
    FRANCO COLOMBO PUBLICATIONS   SAL   1.75
PFEIFFER, A.
  THREE FEUILLETS D'ALBUM, OP. 47 - MENUET
    FRANCO COLOMBO PUBLICATIONS   SAL   1.75
PFEIFFER, A.
  THREE FEUILLETS D'ALBUM, OP. 47 - MUSETTE
    FRANCO COLOMBO PUBLICATIONS   SAL   1.75
PHILIPP, I.   DEIS
  FEUX-FOLLETS, OP. 24 NO. 3
    G. SCHIRMER, INC.   .70
PHILIPP, I.
  POUR LES PETITS
    ELKAN-VOGEL, INC.   D   4.25
PHILIPP, I.
  PROMENADE AU ZOO
    ELKAN-VOGEL, INC.   LEM   3.75
PHILIPP, I.
  TWO OLD ITALIAN AIRS
    G. SCHIRMER, INC.   .50
PHILIPP, I.--ED.   PHILIPP, I.
  QUATRE PIECES DE CONCERT, NO. 1, TARTINI--DANCE
    ASSOCIATED MUSIC PUBLISHERS, INC.   ESC   .85
PHILIPP, I.--ED.   PHILIPP, I.
  QUATRE PIECES DE CONCERT, NO. 2, TARTINI--BALLET
    ASSOCIATED MUSIC PUBLISHERS, INC.   ESC   .85
PHILIPP, I.--ED.   PHILIPP, I.
  QUATRE PIECES DE CONCERT, NO. 3, VERACINI--DIVERTISSEMENT
    ASSOCIATED MUSIC PUBLISHERS, INC.   ESC   1.00
PHILIPP, I.--ED.   PHILIPP, I.
  QUATRE PIECES DE CONCERT, NO. 4, VERACINI--DANSE VILLAGEOISE
    ASSOCIATED MUSIC PUBLISHERS, INC.   ESC   .65
PHILLIPS   2
  IN A SEA CRADLE
    THEODORE PRESSER COMPANY   .50
PHILLIPS, B.
  FIVE VARIOUS AND SUNDRY
    ELKAN-VOGEL, INC.   .75
PHILLIPS, B.
  LITTLE SONG
    ELKAN-VOGEL, INC.   .50
PHILLIPS, B.   1 1/2 - 2
  SEASHORE GAME, A
    ELKAN-VOGEL, INC.   .50
PHILLIPS, B.   2
  SILLY SEA HORSE
    ELKAN-VOGEL, INC.   .50
PHILLIPS, B.   E
  TOY RONDO
    OXFORD UNIVERSITY PRESS   93.316   1.25
PHILLIPS, D.
  CONCERTO IN JAZZ
    BELWIN-MILLS PUBLISHING CORPORATION   20402   2.00
PHILLIPS, D.
  CONCERTO IN JAZZ
    BELWIN-MILLS PUBLISHING CORPORATION   2.00
PHILLIPS, D.
  CONCERTO IN JAZZ -- THEMES
    BELWIN-MILLS PUBLISHING CORPORATION   20401   .85
PHILLIPS, D.
  ISRAELI CARNIVAL
    BELWIN-MILLS PUBLISHING CORPORATION   20134   .85
PHILLIPS, D.
  MERMAID -- MELODY FROM THE SEA
    BELWIN-MILLS PUBLISHING CORPORATION   20355   .85
PHILLIPS, D.
  STREET OF A THOUSAND MEMORIES
    BELWIN-MILLS PUBLISHING CORPORATION   20246   .85
PHILLIPS, D.
  SWINGING SLEIGH BELLS
    BELWIN-MILLS PUBLISHING CORPORATION   20422   .85
PHILLIPS, D.
  TONI'S TUNE
    BELWIN-MILLS PUBLISHING CORPORATION   20442   .85
PHILLIPS, D.
  WALTZING ON ICE
    BELWIN-MILLS PUBLISHING CORPORATION   20330   .60
PHILLIPS, R.
  JE JOUE DU PIANO
    ELKAN-VOGEL, INC.   CON   3.50
PHILLIPS, S.
  NIGHT RIDE, THE
    BELWIN-MILLS PUBLISHING CORPORATION   20181   .85
PHIPPENY
  CANDY BAND
    SUMMY-BIRCHARD COMPANY   .50
PIAF *
  MORE, MORE, AND MORE -- UN GRAND AMOUR
    MCA MUSIC   1.00
PIAGET, A.   2
  FAIRY LAND MUSIC
    WILLIS MUSIC COMPANY   .35

PICCIOLI
  BOZZETTI
    FRANCO COLOMBO PUBLICATIONS   BON.2168   1.75
PICCIOLI
  NOCTURNE
    FRANCO COLOMBO PUBLICATIONS   BON.567   1.00
PICCIOLI
  PAVANA E MINUETTO   *
    FRANCO COLOMBO PUBLICATIONS   BON.1906   .90
PICCIOLI
  PETITE VALSE E STORIELLA
    FRANCO COLOMBO PUBLICATIONS   BON.1907   .90
PICCIOLI
  QUADRETTI
    FRANCO COLOMBO PUBLICATIONS   BON.1767   3.00
PICCIOLI
  SCENES OF CHILDHOOD
    FRANCO COLOMBO PUBLICATIONS   BON.1767   1.50
PICHA   3
  SCHERZO
    BARENREITER VERLAG   AP 678
PICK-MANGIAGALLI
  CARILLON MAGICO, IL -- BALLET --
    FRANCO COLOMBO PUBLICATIONS   4.50
PICK-MANGIAGALLI
  MIGNARDISES
    FRANCO COLOMBO PUBLICATIONS   112519   .75
PICK-MANGIAGALLI
  PRELUDE AND TOCCATA, OP. 27
    FRANCO COLOMBO PUBLICATIONS   116795   1.00
PICK-MANGIAGALLI
  SILHOUETTES DE CARNEVAL - 1. MASQUERADES
    FRANCO COLOMBO PUBLICATIONS   109932   2.00
PICK-MANGIAGALLI
  SILHOUETTES DE CARNEVAL - 2. CHANSON-SERENADE A COLOMBINE
    FRANCO COLOMBO PUBLICATIONS   109933   1.75
PICK-MANGIAGALLI
  SILHOUETTES DE CARNEVAL - 3. ET PIERRETTE DANSAIT
    FRANCO COLOMBO PUBLICATIONS   109934   1.75
PICK-MANGIAGALLI
  SILHOUETTES DE CARNEVAL - 4. LA RONDE DES ARLEQUINS
    FRANCO COLOMBO PUBLICATIONS   109935   1.75
PICK-MANGIAGALLI
  TWO LUNAIRES, OP. 33 - 1. COLLOQUE AU CLAIR DE LUNE
    FRANCO COLOMBO PUBLICATIONS   120571   1.00
PICK-MANGIAGALLI
  TWO LUNAIRES, OP. 33 - 2. LA DANSE D'OLAF
    FRANCO COLOMBO PUBLICATIONS   120572   1.00
PICKENS, M.   2
  PRANCING PONY
    WILLIS MUSIC COMPANY   .35
PIECZONKA, A.   4
  TARANTELLA
    CENTURY MUSIC PUBLISHING COMPANY, INC. 663   .40
PIECZONKA, A.   3
  TARANTELLA
    WILLIS MUSIC COMPANY   .50
PIECZONKA, A.   4
  TARANTELLA
    WILLIS MUSIC COMPANY   .50
PIECZONKA, A.
  TARANTELLA IN A MINOR
    CARL FISCHER, INC.   S 1599   .60
PIECZONKA, A.
  TARANTELLA IN A MINOR
    G. SCHIRMER, INC.   .60
PIERNE   5
  CACHE-CACHE, OP. 3 NO. 12
    ALPHONSE LEDUC
PIERNE
  CHANSON DE LA GRAND'MAMAN, OP. 3 NO. 2
    ALPHONSE LEDUC
PIERNE
  CHORAL A L'EGLISE, OP. 3 NO. 8
    ALPHONSE LEDUC
PIERNE   5
  FANTASMAGORIE, OP. 3 NO. 3
    ALPHONSE LEDUC
PIERNE   7
  IMPROMPTU-CAPRICE, OP. 9
    ALPHONSE LEDUC
PIERNE   4
  MARCH OF THE LEAD SOLDIERS
    CENTURY MUSIC PUBLISHING COMPANY, INC. 3239   .40
PIERNE
  PASSACAGLIA
    FRANCO COLOMBO PUBLICATIONS   SAL   4.25
PIERNE
  PRELUDE DE 'CATHEDRALES'
    FRANCO COLOMBO PUBLICATIONS   SAL   2.50
PIERNE   3
  SERENADE
    CENTURY MUSIC PUBLISHING COMPANY, INC. 1945   .40
PIERNE   5
  SERENADE, OP. 7
    ALPHONSE LEDUC
PIERNE   6
  TARENTELLE, OP. 3 NO. 15
    ALPHONSE LEDUC
PIERNE   7
  VALSE NO. 2 EN SOL, OP. 15
    ALPHONSE LEDUC
PIERNE   6
  VALSE, OP. 3 NO. 13
    ALPHONSE LEDUC
PIERNE
  VIENNOISE -- SUITE --
    FRANCO COLOMBO PUBLICATIONS   SAL   4.25
PIERNE, P.
  BADINAGE
    FRANCO COLOMBO PUBLICATIONS   SAL   1.75
PIERNE, P.
  CAPRICE
    FRANCO COLOMBO PUBLICATIONS   SAL   1.75
PIERNE, P.
  CHANT D'AUTOMNE
    FRANCO COLOMBO PUBLICATIONS   SAL   1.75
PIERNE, P.
  CHANT DU PRINTEMPS
    FRANCO COLOMBO PUBLICATIONS   SAL   1.75
PIERNE, P.
  CROQUIS DE ROUTE
    FRANCO COLOMBO PUBLICATIONS   SAL   1.75
PIERNE, P.
  JEU DE LA CACHETTE
    FRANCO COLOMBO PUBLICATIONS   SAL   1.75

PIERNE, P.			
JEUX DE BARRES			
FRANCO COLOMBO PUBLICATIONS	SAL		1.75
PIERNE, P.			
PASSEPIED			
FRANCO COLOMBO PUBLICATIONS	SAL		1.75
PIERNE, P.			
PASSEPIED AND GIGUE			
FRANCO COLOMBO PUBLICATIONS	SAL		1.75
PIERNE, P.			
PETITES PIECES POMPADOUR - GAVOTTE			
FRANCO COLOMBO PUBLICATIONS	SAL		1.50
PIERNE, P.			
REVERIE			
FRANCO COLOMBO PUBLICATIONS	SAL		1.75
PIERNE, P.			
SAUT A LA CORDE, LE			
FRANCO COLOMBO PUBLICATIONS	SAL		1.75
PIERNE, P.			
SCENE D'ALSACE			
FRANCO COLOMBO PUBLICATIONS	SAL		1.75
PIERNE, P.			
TRISTESSE			
FRANCO COLOMBO PUBLICATIONS	SAL		1.75
PIERSON		3	
RIPPLING WATERS			
BELWIN-MILLS PUBLISHING CORPORATION			.60
PIERSON, A.	E-M		
JOY			
COMPOSERS PRESS, INC.			1.00
PIERSON, A.	E-M		
ROMANCE			
COMPOSERS PRESS, INC.			1.00
PIERSON, A.	M		
THINK OF ME			
COMPOSERS PRESS, INC.			1.00
PIERSON, A.	E		
VALSE GENTILE			
COMPOSERS PRESS, INC.			1.00
PIETSCH, E.	1		
DOLLY'S LULLABY			
THEODORE PRESSER COMPANY			.50
PIETSCH, E.			
WALTZ FOR ONE HAND--FOR EITHER HAND ALONE			
G. SCHIRMER, INC.			.35
PIJPER	E		
PASSEPIED			
C. F. PETERS CORPORATION	D123		1.50
PIJPER	D		
SONATA			
C. F. PETERS CORPORATION	D143		1.50
PIJPER	M-D		
SONATINA NO. 01			
C. F. PETERS CORPORATION	D144		2.00
PILLING			
PIPER AT THE GATES OF DAWN, THE			
FRANCO COLOMBO PUBLICATIONS	LD498		.60
PILLOIS			
IMPROMPTU			
FRANCO COLOMBO PUBLICATIONS	SAL		2.50
PINCKARD	2		
JUMPIN' JACK RABBIT			
BOSTON MUSIC COMPANY			.50
PINCKARD	2		
SERENADE TO A BREEZE			
BOSTON MUSIC COMPANY			.50
PINCKARD	2		
SIT DOWN, SISTER			
BOSTON MUSIC COMPANY			.50
PINKHAM	M		
PARTITA. HARPSICHORD			
C. F. PETERS CORPORATION	6519		3.00
PINTO, O.			
CHILDREN'S FESTIVAL--LITTLE SUITE			
G. SCHIRMER, INC.			.75
PINTO, O.			
MARCHA DO PEQUENO POLEGAR			
G. SCHIRMER, INC.			.50
PINTO, O.			
SCENAS INFANTIS--MARCH, LITTLE SOLDIER			
G. SCHIRMER, INC.			.50
PINTO, O.			
SCENAS INFANTIS--RUN, RUN			
G. SCHIRMER, INC.			.50
PIRANI			
BEBE			
FRANCO COLOMBO PUBLICATIONS	FOR.51		.75
PIRIOU			
JEUX D'ENFANTS			
FRANCO COLOMBO PUBLICATIONS	SAL		3.00
PIRIOU			
PAVANE FOR MELISANDE			
FRANCO COLOMBO PUBLICATIONS	SAL		2.75
PIRIOU			
PETITES HISTOIRES			
FRANCO COLOMBO PUBLICATIONS	SAL		2.75
PIRIOU			
SCHERZO-DANSE			
FRANCO COLOMBO PUBLICATIONS	SAL		4.00
PISK	M		
DANCE FROM THE RIO GRANDE VALLEY			
THEODORE PRESSER COMPANY			.50
PISK			
ENGINE ROOM			
MCA MUSIC			.75
PISK			
FIVE PIECE SET			
BELWIN-MILLS PUBLISHING CORPORATION	20096		1.00
PISK			
SONATINA - DEATH VALLEY			
EDITORIAL COOPERATIVA INTER-AMERICANA			01.05
PISK *	MD		
FIVE SKETCHES -- WITH EIGHT PRELUDES			
THEODORE PRESSER COMPANY			2.00
PISTON, W.	MD		
PASSACAGLIA			
THEODORE PRESSER COMPANY			.75
PITFIELD	M		
HOMAGE TO TCHAIKOVSKY			
OXFORD UNIVERSITY PRESS	33.068		1.10
PITTALUGA			
CUCKOLD'S FAIR, THE -- LA ROMERIA DE LOS CORNUDOS -- BALLET IN			
ONE ACT			
ASSOCIATED MUSIC PUBLISHERS, INC.	UME		2.00
PIXIS			
FANTAISIE MILITAIRE OP. 121			
MUSICA OBSCURA			4.00

PIZZETTI			
PISANELLA, LA - 1. LA QUAI DU PORT DU FAMAGOUSTE			
FRANCO COLOMBO PUBLICATIONS	FOR.11045		1.75
PIZZETTI			
PISANELLA, LA - 2. LA DANZA DELLO SPARVIERO			
FRANCO COLOMBO PUBLICATIONS	FOR.11046		1.75
PIZZETTI			
PISANELLA, LA - 3. L'ESTAMPIE ROYALE			
FRANCO COLOMBO PUBLICATIONS	FOR.11047		1.25
PIZZETTI			
PISANELLA, LA - 4. LA DANSE DE L'AMOUR ET DE LA MORT PARFUMEE			
FRANCO COLOMBO PUBLICATIONS	FOR.11048		2.50
PIZZINI			
BUON PIERINO, IL			
FRANCO COLOMBO PUBLICATIONS	DS321		1.25
PIZZINI			
C'ERA UN RE			
FRANCO COLOMBO PUBLICATIONS	DS420		1.25
PIZZINI			
NEL GIARDINO SETTECENTESCO			
FRANCO COLOMBO PUBLICATIONS	DS159		1.25
PIZZINI			
NINNA-NANNA DI NATALE			
FRANCO COLOMBO PUBLICATIONS	DS421		1.00
PIZZINI			
NOSTALGIA ALPINA			
FRANCO COLOMBO PUBLICATIONS	DS320		1.00
PIZZINI			
SERAFINO			
FRANCO COLOMBO PUBLICATIONS	DS403		1.75
PIZZINI			
TOPOLINO VA SOLDATO			
FRANCO COLOMBO PUBLICATIONS	DS363		1.25
PLACE		3	
SONG OF THE RAILS			
BELWIN-MILLS PUBLISHING CORPORATION			.60
PLANK, E.	SCHAUM, J.	1	
CHEERLEADER, THE			
SCHAUM PUBLICATIONS, INC.			.60
PLANQUETTE		3	
CHIMES OF NORMANDY, SEL. 1			
CENTURY MUSIC PUBLISHING COMPANY, INC.	2101		.40
PLANQUETTE		3	
CHIMES OF NORMANDY, SEL. 2			
CENTURY MUSIC PUBLISHING COMPANY, INC.	2102		.40
PLANQUETTE		3	
CHIMES OF NORMANDY, SEL. 3			
CENTURY MUSIC PUBLISHING COMPANY, INC.	2103		.40
PLANTE	MEDIUM		
WALTZ IN A MAJOR, OP. 16			
SHAWNEE PRESS, INC.			.60
PLATANIA, P.	CULTRERA, G.		
DIVAGANDO			
EDIZIONI BERBEN	EB 1679		1.40
PLATZMAN		4	
DANCE OF THE SEA NYMPHS			
CENTURY MUSIC PUBLISHING COMPANY, INC.	1079		.40
PLEYEL			
MINUET AND TRIO			
FREDERICK HARRIS MUSIC COMPANY			.60
PLEYEL			
RONDO IN C			
FREDERICK HARRIS MUSIC COMPANY			.60
PLEYEL			
RONDO IN G			
FREDERICK HARRIS MUSIC COMPANY		3 1/2	.60
PODESKA, I.			
SHADOWS OF THE NIGHT			
THEODORE PRESSER COMPANY			.65
POGLIETTI	GOEBELS	3-4	
IL ROSSIGNOLO. ARIA CON VARIAZIONI ED ARIA BIZARRA			
BARENREITER VERLAG	SM 2482		
POHL, V.			
POEME FOR LEFT HAND, OP. 17			
BOOSEY AND HAWKES, INC.			1.25
POHL, V.			
VALSE IMPROMPTU, OP. 19 NO. 1 FOR LEFT HAND			
BOOSEY AND HAWKES, INC.			1.00
POHL, V.			
VALSE ROMANTIQUE, OP. 19 NO. 2 FOR LEFT HAND			
BOOSEY AND HAWKES, INC.			1.00
POISE		5	
JOLI GILLES, ENTR'ACTE			
ALPHONSE LEDUC			
POLDINI, E.			
BIRDS OF PASSAGE			
G. SCHIRMER, INC.			.35
POLDINI, E.			
DAINTY MARCH, OP. 15 NO. 2			
G. SCHIRMER, INC.			.50
POLDINI, E.			
DANCE OF THE GNOMES			
G. SCHIRMER, INC.			.30
POLDINI, E.		4	
DANCING DOLL			
BELWIN-MILLS PUBLISHING CORPORATION	281		.60
POLDINI, E.		4	
DANCING DOLL			
CENTURY MUSIC PUBLISHING COMPANY, INC.	1697		.40
POLDINI, E.	MENDEL, S.	2	
DANCING DOLL			
WILLIS MUSIC COMPANY			.40
POLDINI, E.		2 1/2	
GENERAL BOOM BOOM			
WILLIS MUSIC COMPANY			.40
POLDINI, E.		2	
GENERAL BUM-BUM			
CENTURY MUSIC PUBLISHING COMPANY, INC.	1843		.40
POLDINI, E.			
JAPANESE STUDY, OP. 27 NO. 2			
G. SCHIRMER, INC.			.40
POLDINI, F.			
MERRY ALBUM FOR THE YOUNG, A, OP. 122			
UNIVERSAL EDITION	UE 9385		2.15
POLDINI, E.			
MOMENTS MUSICAUX, OP. 80			
UNIVERSAL EDITION	UE 7724		3.40
POLDINI, E.		2	
MUSIC BOX			
BELWIN-MILLS PUBLISHING CORPORATION	630		.60
POLDINI, E.	STERNBERG		
MUSIC-BOX, THE			
G. SCHIRMER, INC.			.35
POLDINI, E.			
POESIES, OP. 74--AU CHEMIN SEME DE ROSES			
G. SCHIRMER, INC.			.60

POLDINI, E.
POESIES, OP. 74--CONTE PLAISANT
G. SCHIRMER, INC. .60
POLDINI, E.
POUPEE VALSANTE
BELWIN-MILLS PUBLISHING CORPORATION 4 .60
POUPEE VALSANTE
CENTURY MUSIC PUBLISHING COMPANY, INC. 1697 .40
POLDINI, E. ROLFE, W. 2
POUPEE VALSANTE
CENTURY MUSIC PUBLISHING COMPANY, INC. 3543 .40
POLDINI, E.
POUPEE VALSANTE
FRANCO COLOMBO PUBLICATIONS 103871 .50
POLDINI, E. 4
POUPEE VALSANTE
VOLKWEIN BROS. .25
POLDINI, E. ECKSTEIN
POUPEE VALSANTE --WALTZING DOLL--
CARL FISCHER, INC. S 1236 .50
POLDINI, E.
POUPEE VALSANTE--WALTZ
G. SCHIRMER, INC. .50
POLDINI, E.
SONATINA NO. 01
UNIVERSAL EDITION UE 8874 1.20
POLDINI, E.
SONATINA NO. 02
UNIVERSAL EDITION UE 8875 1.20
POLDINI, E.
SONATINA NO. 03
UNIVERSAL EDITION UE 8876 1.20
POLDINI, E.
TWENTY-FIVE POETIC ETUDES, OP. 96
UNIVERSAL EDITION UE 8135 3.85
POLDINI, E. 2
VALSE SERENADE
CENTURY MUSIC PUBLISHING COMPANY, INC. 2004 .40
POLDINI, E. 4
WALTZING DOLL
CENTURY MUSIC PUBLISHING COMPANY, INC. 1697 .40
POLDINI, E. 4
WALTZING DOLL -- POUPEE VALSANTE
VOLKWEIN BROS. 00.25
POLDINI, E. ROLFE, W. 2
WALTZING DOLL, EASY
CENTURY MUSIC PUBLISHING COMPANY, INC. 3543 .40
POLIN, C.
OUT OF CHILDHOOD
SEESAW MUSIC CORPORATION 3.00
POLIVKA 3
AKKORDE -- ETUDENWERK --
BARENREITER VERLAG AP 679
POLIVKA 2-3
LUSTIGE MUSIK
BARENREITER VERLAG AP 680
POLIVKA 3
SONATE
BARENREITER VERLAG AP 681
POLLA, W.--ED POLLA, W. 5
TWO GUITARS
BELWIN-MILLS PUBLISHING CORPORATION 473 .60
POLLACK *
DIANE
THE BIG THREE MUSIC CORPORATION 00.95
POLONIO
SOUVENIR DU BRESIL, OP. 10
FRANCO COLOMBO PUBLICATIONS SAL 1.75
POLOWINKIN, L. A.
EREIGNIS 3, OP. 10
UNIVERSAL EDITION UE 7345 1.30
POLOWINKIN, L. A.
EREIGNISSE 4 AND 5, OP. 12
UNIVERSAL EDITION UE 8277 1.10
POLOWINKIN, L. A.
SONATA NO. 02, OP. 13
UNIVERSAL EDITION UE 8283 3.20
PONC 2-3
KLEINE SUITE
BARENREITER VERLAG AP 682
PONCE, E.
HOLIDAY
THE BIG THREE MUSIC CORPORATION 00.95
PONCE, M.
ELEGIA DE LA AUSENCIA
EDITORIAL COOPERATIVA INTER-AMERICANA 00.90
PONCE, M. 4
ESTRELLITA
BELWIN-MILLS PUBLISHING CORPORATION 543 .60
PONCE, M. TREHARNE 3
ESTRELLITA
BOSTON MUSIC COMPANY .50
PONCE, M. 3
ESTRELLITA
CENTURY MUSIC PUBLISHING COMPANY, INC. 3630 .40
PONCE, M. ROLFE, W. 3
ESTRELLITA
CENTURY MUSIC PUBLISHING COMPANY, INC. 3630 .40
PONCE, M.
ESTRELLITA
EDITORIAL COOPERATIVA INTER-AMERICANA 00.75
PONCE, M. 4
GAVOTA
EDITORIAL COOPERATIVA INTER-AMERICANA 00.75
PONCE, M.
INTERMEZZO NO. 2
EDITORIAL COOPERATIVA INTER-AMERICANA 00.80
PONCE, M.
MOMENTO DOLOROSO
EDITORIAL COOPERATIVA INTER-AMERICANA 00.75
PONCE, M.
PRELUDE ET FUGUE POUR LA MAIN GAUCHE SEULE
EDITORIAL COOPERATIVA INTER-AMERICANA 01.25
PONCE, M.
PRELUDIO TRAGICO
PEER SOUTHERN ORGANIZATION 01.25
PONCE, M.
PRELUDIO Y FUGA SOBRE UN TEMA DE HANDEL
PEER SOUTHERN ORGANIZATION 01.25
PONCE, M.
PRELUDIO Y FUGA SOBRE UN TEMA DE J. S. BACH
PEER SOUTHERN ORGANIZATION 02.00
PONCE, M.
SONATA NO. 02
PEER SOUTHERN ORGANIZATION 03.00

PONCHIELLI MENDEL, S. 1 1/2
DANCE OF THE HOURS
WILLIS MUSIC COMPANY .40
PONCHIELLI ZEPP 3-4
DANCE OF THE HOURS - FROM THE OPERA 'LA GIOCANDA'
PRO-ART PUBLICATIONS, INC. 404 .50
PONCHIELLI
DANCE OF THE HOURS--BALLET FROM 'LA GIOCCONDA'
G. SCHIRMER, INC. L1396 1.00
PONCHIELLI 4
DANCE OF THE HOURS, GIOCONDA
CENTURY MUSIC PUBLISHING COMPANY, INC. 1902 .40
PONCHIELLI 4
GIOCONDA BALLET
CENTURY MUSIC PUBLISHING COMPANY, INC. 1902 .40
PONCHIELLI
GIOCONDA, LA - DANCE OF THE HOURS
FRANCO COLOMBO PUBLICATIONS 44836 .75
PONCHIELLI CHIESA
GIOCONDA, LA - DANCE OF THE HOURS
FRANCO COLOMBO PUBLICATIONS 109093 .60
PONCHIELLI DEL MAGLIO
GIOCONDA, LA - DANCE OF THE HOURS
FRANCO COLOMBO PUBLICATIONS 45389 .60
PONCHIELLI CHIESA
GIOCONDA, LA - EASY FANTASIA
FRANCO COLOMBO PUBLICATIONS 109097 .50
PONCHIELLI TAVAN
GIOCONDA, LA - FANTASIA
FRANCO COLOMBO PUBLICATIONS 128785 1.00
PONCHIELLI 4
LA GIOCONDA, DANCE OF HOURS
CENTURY MUSIC PUBLISHING COMPANY, INC. 1902 .40
POND, S.
ROCKING DOLLY TO SLEEP
BELWIN-MILLS PUBLISHING CORPORATION 28186 .60
POOLE, C.
BLACK FOREST OWL, THE
FREDERICK HARRIS MUSIC COMPANY .60
POOLE, C.
BUFFALO HUNT, THE
FREDERICK HARRIS MUSIC COMPANY .60
POOLE, C.
INDIANS ON THE WARPATH
FREDERICK HARRIS MUSIC COMPANY .60
POOLE, C. 1 1/2
MARCH OF THE FINGER SNAPS
WILLIS MUSIC COMPANY .40
POOLE, C.
MUSIC BOX
FREDERICK HARRIS MUSIC COMPANY .60
POOLE, C.
POP CORN AND COVERED WAGON
FREDERICK HARRIS MUSIC COMPANY .60
POOLE, C.
POP GOES THE WEASEL
FREDERICK HARRIS MUSIC COMPANY .60
POOLE, C. 1 1/2
SPAIN
WILLIS MUSIC COMPANY .50
POOLE, C.
SPOOKS
FREDERICK HARRIS MUSIC COMPANY .60
POOLE, C.
VARIATIONS ON 'O DEAR WHAT CAN THE MATTER BE'
FREDERICK HARRIS MUSIC COMPANY .60
POOLE, C.
WAR DANCE AND THE SAD INDIAN BOY
FREDERICK HARRIS MUSIC COMPANY .60
POOT, M.
BALLADE
ASSOCIATED MUSIC PUBLISHERS, INC. ESC 3.75
POOT, M.
ETUDE--1951
ASSOCIATED MUSIC PUBLISHERS, INC. ESC 3.00
POOT, M.
SONATA--1927
ASSOCIATED MUSIC PUBLISHERS, INC. ESC 2.75
POOT, M.
SUITE
UNIVERSAL EDITION UE 11375 2.90
POOT, M.
VARIATIONS
UNIVERSAL EDITION UE 11643 1.70
POPP *
PORTUGUESE WASHERWOMEN, THE
WARNER BROTHERS PUBLISHERS 1.00
POPY
VALSE POUDREE
FRANCO COLOMBO PUBLICATIONS SAL 1.75
POPY
VIVA EL TORERO -- SPANISH MARCH --
FRANCO COLOMBO PUBLICATIONS SAL 1.75
PORRINO
MONDO-TONDO -- BALLET --
FRANCO COLOMBO PUBLICATIONS 126085 4.50
PORTER M
DAY DREAMS
THEODORE PRESSER COMPANY .50
PORTER 4
PRELUDE IN D MINOR
BOSTON MUSIC COMPANY .60
PORTER M-D
SONATA
C. F. PETERS CORPORATION 6669 2.00
PORTER, C. LEVINE
BEGIN THE BEGUINE
WARNER BROTHERS PUBLISHERS 1.00
PORTER, C. WALTER
BEGIN THE BEGUINE
WARNER BROTHERS PUBLISHERS 1.00
PORTER, C. HEYWOOD
BEGIN THE BEGUINE
WARNER BROTHERS PUBLISHERS 1.00
PORTER, C. RICHTER FIRST YEAR
BEGIN THE BEGUINE
WARNER BROTHERS PUBLISHERS .75
PORTER, C. 2
MARCH OF THE SPOOKS
BELWIN-MILLS PUBLISHING CORPORATION .60
PORTER, C. HASTINGS
NIGHT AND DAY
WARNER BROTHERS PUBLISHERS 1.00
PORTER, C. MACLACHLAN FIRST YEAR
NIGHT AND DAY
WARNER BROTHERS PUBLISHERS .75

PORTER, C.   2 1/2
    PESKY FLY
        BELWIN-MILLS PUBLISHING CORPORATION   .60
PORTER, C.   2 1/2
    PINK CLOVER
        BELWIN-MILLS PUBLISHING CORPORATION   .60
PORTER, C.
    SO IN LOVE
        CIMINO PUBLICATIONS, INC.   H   1.25
PORTER, W.   1
    DOWN BY THE MERRY MATANZIE
        CENTURY MUSIC PUBLISHING COMPANY, INC. 3682   .40
PORTER, W.   1
    HERE WE GO
        CENTURY MUSIC PUBLISHING COMPANY, INC. 3684   .40
PORTER, W.   1
    I SAW A LITTLE BIRD
        CENTURY MUSIC PUBLISHING COMPANY, INC. 1737   .40
PORTER, W.   1
    MY DOGGIE
        CENTURY MUSIC PUBLISHING COMPANY, INC. 1736   .40
PORTER, W.   1
    POOR FIDO
        CENTURY MUSIC PUBLISHING COMPANY, INC. 3683   .40
PORTER, W.   1
    PUSSY'S LESSON
        CENTURY MUSIC PUBLISHING COMPANY, INC. 1739   .40
PORTER, W.   1
    SCHOOL DRILL
        CENTURY MUSIC PUBLISHING COMPANY, INC. 3685   .40
PORTER, W.   4
    SWEET DREAMS
        CENTURY MUSIC PUBLISHING COMPANY, INC. 1838   .40
PORTER, W.   3
    VESPER BELLS ARE RINGING
        CENTURY MUSIC PUBLISHING COMPANY, INC. 1840   .40
PORTER, W.   4
    YOUTH AND BEAUTY DANCE
        CENTURY MUSIC PUBLISHING COMPANY, INC. 1839   .40
POSCA
    BY THE SEA
        BOSTON MUSIC COMPANY   .50
POSCA   4
    BY THE SEA
        CENTURY MUSIC PUBLISHING COMPANY, INC. 4325   .40
POSCA   5
    BY THE SEA
        THEODORE PRESSER COMPANY   .60
POSER
    BAGATELLES, OP. 1
        FRANCO COLOMBO PUBLICATIONS   SIK.118   2.00
POSER
    DANCE VARIATIONS ON CHILDREN'S SONGS
        FRANCO COLOMBO PUBLICATIONS   SIK.493   2.00
POSER
    SONATA NO. 01
        FRANCO COLOMBO PUBLICATIONS   SIK.178   3.50
POSER
    SONATINA NO. 01, OP. 12 NO. 1
        FRANCO COLOMBO PUBLICATIONS   SIK.120   1.50
POSER
    SONATINA NO. 02, OP. 12 NO. 2
        FRANCO COLOMBO PUBLICATIONS   SIK.121   1.50
POSER
    SONATINA NO. 03, OP. 44 NO. 1
        FRANCO COLOMBO PUBLICATIONS   SIK.505   1.75
POSER
    SONATINA NO. 04, OP. 44 NO. 2
        FRANCO COLOMBO PUBLICATIONS   SIK.506   1.75
POST--ED   POST   1-2
    THANKSGIVING HYMN
        CENTURY MUSIC PUBLISHING COMPANY, INC. 4158   .40
POST--ED   POST   1-2
    WE GATHER TOGETHER
        CENTURY MUSIC PUBLISHING COMPANY, INC. 4158   .40
POSTON, E.   3-4
    LULLABY AND FESTA
        NOVELLO AND COMPANY, LTD.   10.0105.01   1.15
POTTER, E.   E
    LITTLE SWISS MUSIC BOX
        COMPOSERS PRESS, INC.   1.00
POTTERBAUM, W.   1 1/2
    MERRY-GO-RONDO
        THEODORE PRESSER COMPANY   .50
POUISHNOFF, L.
    MUSICAL BOX
        BOOSEY AND HAWKES, INC.   .75
POULENC, F.
    ANIMAUX MODELES, LES -- BALLET IN ONE ACT
        ASSOCIATED MUSIC PUBLISHERS, INC.   ESC   12.50
POULENC, F.
    AUBADE -- PIANO SOLO PART
        FRANCO COLOMBO PUBLICATIONS   SAL   6.25
POULENC, F.
    AUBADE -- PIANO REDUCTION --
        FRANCO COLOMBO PUBLICATIONS   SAL   8.75
POULENC, F.
    BADINAGE
        FRANCO COLOMBO PUBLICATIONS   SAL   1.75
POULENC, F.
    CAPRICE -- BASED ON FINALE OF 'BAL MASQUE' --
        FRANCO COLOMBO PUBLICATIONS   SAL   3.25
POULENC, F.
    EIGHT NOCTURNES
        HEUGEL ET CIE.   5.25
POULENC, F.
    HUMORESQUE
        FRANCO COLOMBO PUBLICATIONS   SAL   1.75
POULENC, F.
    IMPROVISATION NO. 01
        FRANCO COLOMBO PUBLICATIONS   SAL   1.25
POULENC, F.
    IMPROVISATION NO. 02
        FRANCO COLOMBO PUBLICATIONS   SAL   1.25
POULENC, F.
    IMPROVISATION NO. 03
        FRANCO COLOMBO PUBLICATIONS   SAL   1.25
POULENC, F.
    IMPROVISATION NO. 04
        FRANCO COLOMBO PUBLICATIONS   SAL   1.25
POULENC, F.
    IMPROVISATION NO. 05
        FRANCO COLOMBO PUBLICATIONS   SAL   1.25
POULENC, F.
    IMPROVISATION NO. 06
        FRANCO COLOMBO PUBLICATIONS   SAL   1.25

POULENC, F.
    IMPROVISATION NO. 07
        FRANCO COLOMBO PUBLICATIONS   SAL   1.25
POULENC, F.
    IMPROVISATION NO. 08
        FRANCO COLOMBO PUBLICATIONS   SAL   1.25
POULENC, F.
    IMPROVISATION NO. 09
        FRANCO COLOMBO PUBLICATIONS   SAL   1.25
POULENC, F.
    IMPROVISATION NO. 10
        FRANCO COLOMBO PUBLICATIONS   SAL   1.25
POULENC, F.
    IMPROVISATION NO. 13
        FRANCO COLOMBO PUBLICATIONS   SAL   2.00
POULENC, F.
    IMPROVISATION NO. 14
        FRANCO COLOMBO PUBLICATIONS   SAL   2.00
POULENC, F.
    IMPROVISATION NO. 15
        FRANCO COLOMBO PUBLICATIONS   SAL   2.00
POULENC, F.
    INTERMEDE IN D MINOR
        FRANCO COLOMBO PUBLICATIONS   SAL   2.00
POULENC, F.
    INTERMEZZO IN A FLAT--1943
        ASSOCIATED MUSIC PUBLISHERS, INC.   ESC   3.00
POULENC, F.
    INTERMEZZO NO. 1 IN C
        FRANCO COLOMBO PUBLICATIONS   SAL   2.00
POULENC, F.
    INTERMEZZO NO. 2 IN D-FLAT
        FRANCO COLOMBO PUBLICATIONS   SAL   2.00
POULENC, F.
    LES BICHES -- ADAGIETTO NO. 2
        HEUGEL ET CIE.   2.50
POULENC, F.
    LES BICHES -- ANDANTINO NO. 3
        HEUGEL ET CIE.   2.75
POULENC, F.
    LES BICHES -- BALLET
        HEUGEL ET CIE.   13.00
POULENC, F.
    LES BICHES -- COMPLETE
        HEUGEL ET CIE.   22.00
POULENC, F.
    LES BICHES -- OVERTURE NO. 1
        HEUGEL ET CIE.   2.25
POULENC, F.
    LES SOIREES DE NAZELLES
        ELKAN-VOGEL, INC.   D   7.00
POULENC, F.
    MELANCOLIE--1940
        ASSOCIATED MUSIC PUBLISHERS, INC.   ESC   3.75
POULENC, F.
    NOCTURNE NO. 05
        HEUGEL ET CIE.   1.60
POULENC, F.
    NOCTURNE NO. 08 IN G
        HEUGEL ET CIE.   .90
POULENC, F.
    PASTORALE
        ASHLEY DEALERS SERVICE, INC.   ES   .95
POULENC, F.
    PASTORALE FROM THREE PIECES
        HEUGEL ET CIE.   1.25
POULENC, F.   5
    PASTORALE, NO. 1 OF TROIS PIECES
        THEODORE PRESSER COMPANY   .95
POULENC, F.
    PASTOURELLE FROM L'EVENTAIL DE JEANNE
        HEUGEL ET CIE.   1.30
POULENC, F.   4 1/2
    PASTOURELLE, FROM THE BALLET 'L'EVENTAIL DE JEANNE'
        THEODORE PRESSER COMPANY   .50
POULENC, F.   6
    PIECE BREVE SUR LE NOM D'ALBERT ROUSSEL
        ALPHONSE LEDUC
POULENC, F.
    PRESTO IN B-FLAT
        FRANCO COLOMBO PUBLICATIONS   SAL   .75
POULENC, F.
    QUATRIEMME NOCTURNE IN C MINOR
        HEUGEL ET CIE.   1.25
POULENC, F.
    SIXIEME NOCTURNE
        HEUGEL ET CIE.   1.30
POULENC, F.
    SUITE FRANCAISE
        ELKAN-VOGEL, INC.   D   2.75
POULENC, F.   6
    TOCCATA NO. 2 OF TROIS PIECES
        THEODORE PRESSER COMPANY   .95
POULENC, F.
    VILLAGEOISES - POLKA AND LITTLE RONDO
        FRANCO COLOMBO PUBLICATIONS   SAL   1.50
POULENC, F.
    VILLAGEOISES - VALSE TYROLIENNE
        FRANCO COLOMBO PUBLICATIONS   SAL   .80
POULENC, F.
    WALTZ--1919
        ASSOCIATED MUSIC PUBLISHERS, INC.   ESC   2.00
POUSSEUR, H.
    APOSTROPHE ET SIX REFLECTIONS
        UNIVERSAL EDITION   UE 14773   3.75
POUSSEUR, H.
    CARACTERES
        UNIVERSAL EDITION   UE 13452   9.00
POUSSEUR, H.
    MIROIR DE VOTRE FAUST
        UNIVERSAL EDITION   UE 14254   15.50
POWELL
    SUITE SUDISTE - COLIBRIS
        FRANCO COLOMBO PUBLICATIONS   SAL   1.75
POWELL
    SUITE SUDISTE - ELEGIE NEGRE
        FRANCO COLOMBO PUBLICATIONS   SAL   1.75
POWELL
    SUITE SUDISTE - POEME EROTIQUE
        FRANCO COLOMBO PUBLICATIONS   SAL   1.75
POWELL, A.
    OVER HILL AND DALE
        G. SCHIRMER, INC.   .50
POWELL, J.   3
    ROSE WALTZ
        BELWIN-MILLS PUBLISHING CORPORATION   .60

POWELL, MEL
  SONATINA
    FRANCO COLOMBO PUBLICATIONS   NY1688   1.50
POWELL, W.   3
  RIGHT ABOUT MARCH
    VOLKWEIN BROS.   .40
POWELL, W.   3
  SCENTED POSIES
    CENTURY MUSIC PUBLISHING COMPANY, INC.   1410   .40
POWER, H. B.
  MAY DAY ON THE GREEN
    BANKS AND SON LTD.   .80
POWERS, M.   E
  DANCE TUNE
    THEODORE PRESSER COMPANY   .50
POWERS, M.   2
  HUMORESKE
    BELWIN-MILLS PUBLISHING CORPORATION   .60
POWERS, M.   E
  MARIONETTE WALTZ
    THEODORE PRESSER COMPANY   .50
POWERS, M.   E
  MISCHIEF MAKERS
    THEODORE PRESSER COMPANY   .50
POWERS, M.   M
  PATTERNS
    THEODORE PRESSER COMPANY   .60
POWERS, M.   E
  STROLLING WITH MY DOG
    THEODORE PRESSER COMPANY   .50
POZORO, J.
  PIANO SONATA NO. 02
    COMPOSERS AUTOGRAPH PUBLICATIONS   4.84
POZZOLI
  BERCEUSE
    FRANCO COLOMBO PUBLICATIONS   128153   .60
POZZOLI
  EASY SONATINA IN THE CLASSIC STYLE
    FRANCO COLOMBO PUBLICATIONS   129753   .75
POZZOLI
  PINOCCHIO SUITE
    FRANCO COLOMBO PUBLICATIONS   129061   1.50
PRATELLA
  GUERRA, LA
    FRANCO COLOMBO PUBLICATIONS   BON.1114   1.00
PRATELLA
  ROMAGNA - 1. CANZONI DI PRIMAVERA
    FRANCO COLOMBO PUBLICATIONS   BON.1167   2.25
PRATELLA
  ROMAGNA - 2. NOTTI, EBBREZZE E SANGUE
    FRANCO COLOMBO PUBLICATIONS   BON.1168   2.50
PRATELLA
  ROMAGNA - 3. VORTICI DI DANZE
    FRANCO COLOMBO PUBLICATIONS   BON.1169   2.25
PRATELLA
  ROMAGNA - 4. BACCANALE D'AUTUNNO
    FRANCO COLOMBO PUBLICATIONS   BON.1170   2.50
PRATELLA
  ROMAGNA - 5. LA NOTTE DI NATALE
    FRANCO COLOMBO PUBLICATIONS   BON.1171   2.50
PRATELLA
  TRITTICO LIRICO - 1. LA RONDA NOTTURNA
    FRANCO COLOMBO PUBLICATIONS   BON.2112   1.00
PRATELLA
  TRITTICO LIRICO - 2. LA CONZONE DI LUISA
    FRANCO COLOMBO PUBLICATIONS   BON.2113   1.00
PRATELLA
  TRITTICO LIRICO - 3. PIFFERATA INVERNALE
    FRANCO COLOMBO PUBLICATIONS   BON.2114   1.00
PRESLE   6
  PARADE FANTASQUE
    ALPHONSE LEDUC
PRESLE   5
  PETITE BERCEUSE
    ALPHONSE LEDUC
PRESLE   8
  THEME ET VARIATIONS
    ALPHONSE LEDUC
PRESS
  DIS-CONCERTO
    MCA MUSIC   1.25
PRESS
  SPICECAKE WALK
    WEINTRAUB MUSIC COMPANY   070103   .60
PRESS
  WEDDING DANCE
    WEINTRAUB MUSIC COMPANY   070101   .60
PRESS
  WEDDING DANCE
    WEINTRAUB MUSIC COMPANY   070100   .75
PRESTON, M. L.   1 1/2
  TOMMY'S NEW DRUM
    THEODORE PRESSER COMPANY   .50
PREVIN, A.
  BIRTHDAY PARTY
    THE BIG THREE MUSIC CORPORATION   01.50
PREVIN, A.
  LIKE BLUE
    THE BIG THREE MUSIC CORPORATION   00.95
PREVIN, A.
  LIKE YOUNG
    THE BIG THREE MUSIC CORPORATION   00.95
PREVIN, A.
  LONG DAY'S JOURNEY INTO NIGHT, THEME FROM
    MCA MUSIC   1.00
PRIANO
  CAROVANA
    FRANCO COLOMBO PUBLICATIONS   BON.1588   .90
PRIANO
  DANZA DELLE BAMBOLE
    FRANCO COLOMBO PUBLICATIONS   BON.1587   .90
PRICE, F.   3 1/2
  TICKLIN' TOES
    THEODORE PRESSER COMPANY   .60
PRICHARD
  TI JACQUES SUITE
    BELWIN-MILLS PUBLISHING CORPORATION   1.75
PRIGGE, O.   1
  BICYCLE STUNTS
    WILLIS MUSIC COMPANY   .35
PRIGGE, O.   1
  CUB SCOUT MARCH
    WILLIS MUSIC COMPANY   .35
PRIGGE, O.   1 1/2
  DOWN IN THE VALLEY
    WILLIS MUSIC COMPANY   .40

PRIGGE, O.   1
  SINGING BIRD, THE
    WILLIS MUSIC COMPANY   .35
PRIGGE, O.   1
  SKIP TO MY LOU
    WILLIS MUSIC COMPANY   .35
PRITCHARD
  TI JACQUES SUITE
    FRANCO COLOMBO PUBLICATIONS   NY2457   1.75
PROCTER, A.   2
  JAUNT TO TOWN
    ELKAN-VOGEL, INC.   .50
PROCTOR   3
  PENTATONE
    BOSTON MUSIC COMPANY   .50
PROEHL, H.   2
  BETTY LOU, MINUET
    CENTURY MUSIC PUBLISHING COMPANY, INC.   3536   .40
PROEHL, H.   2
  OLD TIME BARN DANCE
    CENTURY MUSIC PUBLISHING COMPANY, INC.   3537   .40
PROEHL, H.   2
  POLLY AND PEGGY
    CENTURY MUSIC PUBLISHING COMPANY, INC.   3534   .40
PROEHL, H.   2
  TWILIGHT DREAMS
    CENTURY MUSIC PUBLISHING COMPANY, INC.   3535   .40
PROKOFIEFF   FREY
  BITTERER SPOTT, OP. 17
    ASSOCIATED MUSIC PUBLISHERS, INC.   SIM   1.50
PROKOFIEFF   FREY
  CAPRICE, OP. 12 NO. 5
    ASSOCIATED MUSIC PUBLISHERS, INC.   SIM   .60
PROKOFIEFF
  CHOSE EN SOI 'A', OP. 45A
    BOOSEY AND HAWKES, INC.   1.50
PROKOFIEFF
  CHOSE EN SOI 'B', OP. 45B
    BOOSEY AND HAWKES, INC.   2.00
PROKOFIEFF
  CINDERELLA'S WALTZ, FROM 'CINDERELLA' BALLET
    MCA MUSIC   .75
PROKOFIEFF
  CLASSICAL SYMPHONY
    EDWIN F. KALMUS   3787   2.50
PROKOFIEFF
  CLASSICAL SYMPHONY, OP. 25
    BOOSEY AND HAWKES, INC.   1.50
PROKOFIEFF   FREY
  DEVILISH INSPIRATION, OP. 4 NO. 4
    ASSOCIATED MUSIC PUBLISHERS, INC.   SIM   .60
PROKOFIEFF
  DIVERTIMENTO, OP. 43
    BOOSEY AND HAWKES, INC.   1.50
PROKOFIEFF
  DIVERTISSEMENT, OP. 43B
    BOOSEY AND HAWKES, INC.   2.00
PROKOFIEFF
  DIVERTISSMENT, OP. 43B
    MCA MUSIC   1.25
PROKOFIEFF
  EPISODES, OP. 12
    MCA MUSIC   2.00
PROKOFIEFF   D
  ETUDE OP. 2 NO. 1
    C. F. PETERS CORPORATION   F62   1.25
PROKOFIEFF   D
  ETUDE OP. 2 NO. 2
    C. F. PETERS CORPORATION   F63   1.25
PROKOFIEFF   D
  ETUDE OP. 2 NO. 3
    C. F. PETERS CORPORATION   F64   1.25
PROKOFIEFF   D
  ETUDE OP. 2 NO. 4
    C. F. PETERS CORPORATION   F65   1.25
PROKOFIEFF   WOLMAN
  EVENING, OP. 65
    MCA MUSIC   .60
PROKOFIEFF   SCHAUM, J.   2
  F.B.I. MARCH
    BELWIN-MILLS PUBLISHING CORPORATION   .50
PROKOFIEFF   WOLMAN
  FAIRY TALE, OP. 65, NO. 3
    MCA MUSIC   .60
PROKOFIEFF   FREY
  FLUCHTIGE ERSCHEINUNGEN, OP. 22
    ASSOCIATED MUSIC PUBLISHERS, INC.   SIM   1.50
PROKOFIEFF
  FOURTH GAVOTTE, OP. 77
    EDWIN F. KALMUS   3801   1.75
PROKOFIEFF   PHILIPP, I.
  GAVOTTE IN F SHARP
    INTERNATIONAL MUSIC COMPANY   1.00
PROKOFIEFF
  GAVOTTE, FROM 'CLASSICAL SYMPHONY'
    BOOSEY AND HAWKES, INC.   .50
PROKOFIEFF   3
  GAVOTTE, FROM CLASSICAL SYMPHONY
    CENTURY MUSIC PUBLISHING COMPANY, INC.   4086   .40
PROKOFIEFF
  GAVOTTE, OP. 12
    EDWARD B. MARKS MUSIC CORPORATION   01.00
PROKOFIEFF
  GAVOTTE, OP. 12 NO. 2
    ASSOCIATED MUSIC PUBLISHERS, INC.   SIM   .75
PROKOFIEFF
  GAVOTTE, OP. 32 NO. 3
    BOOSEY AND HAWKES, INC.   1.25
PROKOFIEFF
  GAVOTTE, OP. 77 NO. 4
    BOOSEY AND HAWKES, INC.   .75
PROKOFIEFF   FREY
  IN DESPAIR, OP. 4
    ASSOCIATED MUSIC PUBLISHERS, INC.   SIM   .80
PROKOFIEFF   FREY
  LEGEND, OP. 12 NO. 6
    ASSOCIATED MUSIC PUBLISHERS, INC.   SIM   .60
PROKOFIEFF   4
  LOVE OF THREE ORANGES, MARCH
    CENTURY MUSIC PUBLISHING COMPANY, INC.   4014   .40
PROKOFIEFF
  LT. KIJE SUITE
    CENTURY MUSIC PUBLISHING COMPANY, INC.   1.00
PROKOFIEFF   SINGER
  MARCH FROM 'PETER AND THE WOLF'
    MCA MUSIC   .60

PROKOFIEFF　　　　　　　　　　　　　　　　　4
　　MARCH FROM 'THE LOVE OF THREE ORANGES', OP. 33
　　　　BOSTON MUSIC COMPANY　　　　　　　　　　　　　.50
PROKOFIEFF　　　　　　　　　　　　　　　　　4
　　MARCH FROM THE LOVE OF THREE ORANGES
　　　　CENTURY MUSIC PUBLISHING COMPANY, INC.　4014　　.40
PROKOFIEFF　　　　　　SCHNEIDER
　　MARCH, FROM 'LOVE OF THE THREE ORANGES'
　　　　BOOSEY AND HAWKES, INC.　　　　　　　　　.75
PROKOFIEFF　　　　　　FREY
　　MARCH, OP. 12 NO. 1
　　　　ASSOCIATED MUSIC PUBLISHERS, INC.　　SIM　　.90
PROKOFIEFF
　　MARCH, OP. 12 NO. 1
　　　　G. SCHIRMER, INC.　　　　　　　　　　　　.50
PROKOFIEFF　　　　　　WOLMAN
　　MARCH, OP. 65, NO. 10
　　　　MCA MUSIC　　　　　　　　　　　　　　　.60
PROKOFIEFF
　　MARCHE--LOVE OF THREE ORANGES
　　　　EDWARD B. MARKS MUSIC CORPORATION　　　00.75
PROKOFIEFF　　　　　　FREY
　　MAZURKA, OP. 12 NO. 4
　　　　ASSOCIATED MUSIC PUBLISHERS, INC.　　SIM　　.90
PROKOFIEFF　　　　　　WOLMAN
　　MOONLIT MEADOWS, OP. 65
　　　　MCA MUSIC　　　　　　　　　　　　　　　.60
PROKOFIEFF　　　　　　　　　　　　　　　　　2
　　MORNING
　　　　CENTURY MUSIC PUBLISHING COMPANY, INC.　3976　　.40
PROKOFIEFF
　　OLD GRANDMOTHER'S TALES, OP. 31
　　　　BOOSEY AND HAWKES, INC.　　　　　　　　1.25
PROKOFIEFF
　　PARADE OF THE GRASSHOPPERS, OP. 65
　　　　MCA MUSIC　　　　　　　　　　　　　　　.60
PROKOFIEFF
　　PAYSAGE, OP. 59 NO. 2
　　　　BOOSEY AND HAWKES, INC.　　　　　　　　1.00
PROKOFIEFF
　　PENSEES, OP. 62
　　　　BOOSEY AND HAWKES, INC.　　　　　　　　1.00
PROKOFIEFF　　　　　　WALLIS　　　　　　3
　　PETER AND THE WOLF
　　　　BOSTON MUSIC COMPANY　　　　　　　　　1.00
PROKOFIEFF　　　　　　HIRSCHBERG, D.　　3A
　　PETER AND THE WOLF
　　　　MUSICORD PUBLICATIONS, INC.　　　　　.45
PROKOFIEFF　　　　　　ECKSTEIN
　　PETER AND THE WOLF --TRIUMPHAL MARCH--
　　　　CARL FISCHER, INC.　　　　　　　　P 3071　　.60
PROKOFIEFF　　　　　　DUNHILL
　　PETER AND THE WOLF, OP. 67
　　　　BOOSEY AND HAWKES, INC.　　　　　　　1.25
PROKOFIEFF　　　　　　　　　　　　　　　　　4
　　PETER AND THE WOLF, TRIUMPHANT MARCH
　　　　CENTURY MUSIC PUBLISHING COMPANY, INC.　3560　　.40
PROKOFIEFF
　　PRELUDE IN C, OP. 12 NO. 7
　　　　G. SCHIRMER, INC.　　　　　　　　　　.50
PROKOFIEFF
　　PRELUDE IN C, OP. 12 NO. 7
　　　　MCA MUSIC　　　　　　　　　　　　　　.75
PROKOFIEFF　　　　　　FREY
　　PRELUDE, OP. 17 NO. 7
　　　　ASSOCIATED MUSIC PUBLISHERS, INC.　　SIM　　.90
PROKOFIEFF
　　PROMENADE, OP. 59 NO. 1
　　　　BOOSEY AND HAWKES, INC.　　　　　　　1.00
PROKOFIEFF
　　PROMENADE, OP. 65
　　　　MCA MUSIC　　　　　　　　　　　　　　.60
PROKOFIEFF　　　　　　FREY
　　REMEMBRANCES, OP. 4 NO. 1
　　　　ASSOCIATED MUSIC PUBLISHERS, INC.　　SIM　　1.00
PROKOFIEFF
　　RIGAUDON, OP. 12 NO. 3
　　　　ASSOCIATED MUSIC PUBLISHERS, INC.　　SIM　　.90
PROKOFIEFF　　　　　　FREY
　　SCHERZO HUMORISTIQUE, OP. 12 NO. 9
　　　　ASSOCIATED MUSIC PUBLISHERS, INC.　　SIM　　.60
PROKOFIEFF
　　SCHERZO, OP. 12 NO. 10
　　　　ASSOCIATED MUSIC PUBLISHERS, INC.　　SIM　　.75
PROKOFIEFF
　　SINFONIETTA, OP. 5
　　　　BOOSEY AND HAWKES, INC.　　　　　　　5.00
PROKOFIEFF
　　SIX MORCEAUX, OP. 52 NO. 1 INTERMEZZO
　　　　BOOSEY AND HAWKES, INC.　　　　　　　1.00
PROKOFIEFF
　　SIX MORCEAUX, OP. 52 NO. 2 RONDO
　　　　BOOSEY AND HAWKES, INC.　　　　　　　1.00
PROKOFIEFF
　　SIX MORCEAUX, OP. 52 NO. 3 ETUDE
　　　　BOOSEY AND HAWKES, INC.　　　　　　　1.00
PROKOFIEFF
　　SIX MORCEAUX, OP. 52 NO. 4 SCHERZINO
　　　　BOOSEY AND HAWKES, INC.　　　　　　　1.00
PROKOFIEFF
　　SIX MORCEAUX, OP. 52 NO. 5 ANDANTE
　　　　BOOSEY AND HAWKES, INC.　　　　　　　1.00
PROKOFIEFF
　　SIX MORCEAUX, OP. 52 NO. 6 SCHERZO
　　　　BOOSEY AND HAWKES, INC.　　　　　　　1.00
PROKOFIEFF　　　　　　PADWA
　　SIX PIECES, OP. 52--NO. 2, RONDO
　　　　ASSOCIATED MUSIC PUBLISHERS, INC.　　AMP　　.75
PROKOFIEFF　　　　　　PADWA
　　SIX PIECES, OP. 52--NO. 6, SCHERZO
　　　　ASSOCIATED MUSIC PUBLISHERS, INC.　　AMP　　.75
PROKOFIEFF　　　　　　FREY
　　SOARING, OP. 4 NO. 2
　　　　ASSOCIATED MUSIC PUBLISHERS, INC.　　SIM　　.80
PROKOFIEFF　　　　　　FREY
　　SONATA NO. 01
　　　　ASSOCIATED MUSIC PUBLISHERS, INC.　　SIM　　1.25
PROKOFIEFF
　　SONATA NO. 01
　　　　EDWIN F. KALMUS　　　　　　　　3778　　2.00
　　　　　　　　　　　　　　　　　　　D
PROKOFIEFF
　　SONATA NO. 01 IN F MINOR, OP. 1
　　　　C. F. PETERS CORPORATION　　　　F48　　3.00
PROKOFIEFF
　　SONATA NO. 01 IN F MINOR, OP. 1
　　　　INTERNATIONAL MUSIC COMPANY　　　　1.75

PROKOFIEFF　　　　　　SANDOR
　　SONATA NO. 01 IN F MINOR, OP. 1
　　　　MCA MUSIC　　　　　　　　　　　　2.00
PROKOFIEFF
　　SONATA NO. 02
　　　　EDWIN F. KALMUS　　　　　　　　3779　　2.50
PROKOFIEFF　　　　　　FREY
　　SONATA NO. 02 IN D MINOR, OP. 14
　　　　ASSOCIATED MUSIC PUBLISHERS, INC.　　SIM　　2.00
PROKOFIEFF　　　　　　　　　　　　　　　　D
　　SONATA NO. 02 IN D MINOR, OP. 14
　　　　C. F. PETERS CORPORATION　　　　F27　　3.00
PROKOFIEFF
　　SONATA NO. 02 IN D MINOR, OP. 14
　　　　INTERNATIONAL MUSIC COMPANY　　　　2.00
PROKOFIEFF　　　　　　SANDOR
　　SONATA NO. 02 IN D MINOR, OP. 14
　　　　MCA MUSIC　　　　　　　　　　　　3.50
PROKOFIEFF
　　SONATA NO. 03
　　　　EDWIN F. KALMUS　　　　　　　　3780　　2.00
PROKOFIEFF　　　　　　PHILIPP, I.
　　SONATA NO. 03 IN A MINOR , OP. 28
　　　　INTERNATIONAL MUSIC COMPANY　　　　2.00
PROKOFIEFF
　　SONATA NO. 03 IN A MINOR, OP. 28
　　　　BOOSEY AND HAWKES, INC.　　　　　1.00
PROKOFIEFF　　　　　　FREY
　　SONATA NO. 03, OP. 28
　　　　ASSOCIATED MUSIC PUBLISHERS, INC.　　SIM　　2.00
PROKOFIEFF　　　　　　FREY
　　SONATA NO. 03, OP. 28
　　　　ASSOCIATED MUSIC PUBLISHERS, INC.　　AMP　　1.50
PROKOFIEFF
　　SONATA NO. 04
　　　　EDWIN F. KALMUS　　　　　　　　3781　　2.50
PROKOFIEFF
　　SONATA NO. 04 IN C MINOR, OP. 29
　　　　BOOSEY AND HAWKES, INC.　　　　　1.25
PROKOFIEFF　　　　　　SANDOR
　　SONATA NO. 04 IN C MINOR, OP. 29
　　　　MCA MUSIC　　　　　　　　　　　　3.00
PROKOFIEFF
　　SONATA NO. 05
　　　　EDWIN F. KALMUS　　　　　　　　3782　　3.00
PROKOFIEFF
　　SONATA NO. 05 IN C MINOR, OP. 38
　　　　BOOSEY AND HAWKES, INC.　　　　　2.50
PROKOFIEFF
　　SONATA NO. 05 IN C, OP. 36
　　　　INTERNATIONAL MUSIC COMPANY　　　　2.00
PROKOFIEFF　　　　　　SANDOR
　　SONATA NO. 05 IN C, OP. 39
　　　　MCA MUSIC　　　　　　　　　　　　3.50
PROKOFIEFF
　　SONATA NO. 06
　　　　EDWIN F. KALMUS　　　　　　　　3783　　3.00
PROKOFIEFF　　　　　　SANDOR
　　SONATA NO. 06 IN A MAJOR, OP. 82
　　　　MCA MUSIC　　　　　　　　　　　　4.00
PROKOFIEFF　　　　　　　　　　　　　　　　D
　　SONATA NO. 06, OP. 82
　　　　C. F. PETERS CORPORATION　　　　4788　　4.50
PROKOFIEFF
　　SONATA NO. 07
　　　　EDWIN F. KALMUS　　　　　　　　3784　　3.00
PROKOFIEFF　　　　　　SANDOR
　　SONATA NO. 07 IN B FLAT MAJOR, OP. 83
　　　　MCA MUSIC　　　　　　　　　　　　3.00
PROKOFIEFF　　　　　　PHILIPP, I.
　　SONATA NO. 07 IN B FLAT, OP. 83
　　　　INTERNATIONAL MUSIC COMPANY　　　　2.00
PROKOFIEFF　　　　　　　　　　　　　　　　D
　　SONATA NO. 07, OP. 83
　　　　C. F. PETERS CORPORATION　　　　4745　　3.50
PROKOFIEFF
　　SONATA NO. 08
　　　　EDWIN F. KALMUS　　　　　　　　3785　　3.00
PROKOFIEFF　　　　　　SANDOR
　　SONATA NO. 08 IN B FLAT MAJOR, OP. 84
　　　　MCA MUSIC　　　　　　　　　　　　4.00
PROKOFIEFF　　　　　　　　　　　　　　　　D
　　SONATA NO. 08, OP. 84
　　　　C. F. PETERS CORPORATION　　　　4732　　4.50
PROKOFIEFF　　　　　　SANDOR
　　SONATA NO. 09 IN C MAJOR, OP. 103
　　　　MCA MUSIC　　　　　　　　　　　　3.00
PROKOFIEFF　　　　　　　　　　　　　　　　D
　　SONATA NO. 09, OP. 103
　　　　C. F. PETERS CORPORATION　　　　4769　　4.00
PROKOFIEFF
　　SONATA NO. 09, OP. 103
　　　　EDWIN F. KALMUS　　　　　　　　3786　　3.50
PROKOFIEFF
　　SONATINA IN E MINOR, OP. 54 NO. 1
　　　　BOOSEY AND HAWKES, INC.　　　　　.75
PROKOFIEFF
　　SONATINA IN G, OP. 54 NO. 2
　　　　BOOSEY AND HAWKES, INC.　　　　　.75
PROKOFIEFF
　　SONATINE PASTORALLE, OP. 59 NO. 3
　　　　BOOSEY AND HAWKES, INC.　　　　　1.00
PROKOFIEFF　　　　　　　　　　　　　　　　2
　　TARANTELLA
　　　　CENTURY MUSIC PUBLISHING COMPANY, INC.　3714　　.40
PROKOFIEFF　　　　　　WOLMAN
　　TARANTELLA, OP. 65
　　　　MCA MUSIC　　　　　　　　　　　　.60
PROKOFIEFF　　　　　　　　　　　　　　　　D
　　TOCCATA, OP. 11
　　　　C. F. PETERS CORPORATION　　　　F35　　1.50
PROKOFIEFF
　　TOCCATA, OP. 11
　　　　EDWIN F. KALMUS　　　　　　　　379　　1.50
PROKOFIEFF
　　TOCCATA, OP. 11
　　　　INTERNATIONAL MUSIC COMPANY　　　　1.25
PROKOFIEFF
　　TOCCATA, OP. 11
　　　　MCA MUSIC　　　　　　　　　　　　1.25
PROKOFIEFF　　　　　　　　　　　　　　　　4
　　TRIUMPHANT MARCH, PETER AND THE WOLF
　　　　CENTURY MUSIC PUBLISHING COMPANY, INC.　3560　　.40
PROKOFIEFF　　　　　　GEEHL
　　TRUMPET VOLUNTARY
　　　　BOOSEY AND HAWKES, INC.　　　　　.60

PROKOFIEFF
  VALSE, OP. 32 NO. 4
    BOOSEY AND HAWKES, INC.   1.00
PROKOFIEFF
  WALTZ FROM CINDERELLA
    EDWIN F. KALMUS   3793   1.50
PROKOFIEFF   E-M
  WALTZ FROM CINDERELLA BALLET
    C. F. PETERS CORPORATION   4774   2.00
PROKOFIEFF   WOLMAN
  WALTZ, OP. 65
    MCA MUSIC   .60
PROKOFIEFF *   2
  PETER AND THE WOLF
    BELWIN-MILLS PUBLISHING CORPORATION   .50
PROTOPOPOFF, S.
  SONATA NO. 02, OP. 5
    UNIVERSAL EDITION   UE 8747   3.30
PRUTTING   3
  TRAILING ARBUTUS
    BOSTON MUSIC COMPANY   .50
PRYOR
  SIFFLEUR ET SON CHIEN, LE
    FRANCO COLOMBO PUBLICATIONS   SAL   1.50
PRYOR   ECKSTEIN
  WHISTLER AND HIS DOG
    CARL FISCHER, INC.   P 2282   .50
PRYOR   SCHAUM, J.   4
  WHISTLER AND HIS DOG
    SCHAUM PUBLICATIONS, INC.   .60
PUCCINI   MARCIANO
  BOHEME, LA - CHE GELIDA MANINA
    FRANCO COLOMBO PUBLICATIONS   99747   .90
PUCCINI   RICHTER
  BOHEME, LA - CHE GELIDA MANINA
    FRANCO COLOMBO PUBLICATIONS   NY1530   .60
PUCCINI   CHIESA
  BOHEME, LA - EASY FANTASIA
    FRANCO COLOMBO PUBLICATIONS   109096   .60
PUCCINI   TAVAN
  BOHEME, LA - FANTASIA
    FRANCO COLOMBO PUBLICATIONS   128786   1.00
PUCCINI   WOLFF
  BOHEME, LA - FANTASIA
    FRANCO COLOMBO PUBLICATIONS   100951   1.50
PUCCINI
  BOHEME, LA - MUSETTA'S WALTZ SONG
    FRANCO COLOMBO PUBLICATIONS   99441   .60
PUCCINI
  BOHEME, LA - MUSETTA'S WALTZ SONG
    FRANCO COLOMBO PUBLICATIONS   114029   .75
PUCCINI   ALASSIO
  BOHEME, LA - MUSETTA'S WALTZ SONG
    FRANCO COLOMBO PUBLICATIONS   99483   .60
PUCCINI   RICHTER
  BOHEME, LA - MUSETTA'S WALTZ SONG
    FRANCO COLOMBO PUBLICATIONS   NY1529   .60
PUCCINI   MARCIANO
  BOHEME, LA - SI, MI CHIAMANO MIMI
    FRANCO COLOMBO PUBLICATIONS   99748   .60
PUCCINI   ALASSIO
  BOHEME, LA - SI, MI CHIAMANO MIMI
    FRANCO COLOMBO PUBLICATIONS   99482   .50
PUCCINI
  BOHEME, LA -- COMPLETE OPERA --
    FRANCO COLOMBO PUBLICATIONS   99001   6.00
PUCCINI   3
  BOHEME, LA -- MUSETTA'S WALTZ
    CENTURY MUSIC PUBLISHING COMPANY, INC.   4085   .40
PUCCINI   DEL MAGLIO
  E L'UCCELLINO - BERCEUSE
    FRANCO COLOMBO PUBLICATIONS   124726   .50
PUCCINI   DEL MAGLIO
  FANCIULLA DEL WEST, LA - 1ST EASY FANTASIA
    FRANCO COLOMBO PUBLICATIONS   125419   .50
PUCCINI   DEL MAGLIO
  FANCIULLA DEL WEST, LA - 2ND EASY FANTASIA
    FRANCO COLOMBO PUBLICATIONS   125420   .50
PUCCINI   DEL MAGLIO
  GIANNI SCHICCHI - O MIO BABBINO CARO
    FRANCO COLOMBO PUBLICATIONS   127760   .60
PUCCINI   RICHTER
  I'LL HOLD YOUR HAND IN MY HAND -- FROM 'LA BOHEME'
    BELWIN-MILLS PUBLISHING CORPORATION   .60
PUCCINI   3
  LA BOHEME, MUSETTA'S WALTZ
    CENTURY MUSIC PUBLISHING COMPANY, INC.   4085   .40
PUCCINI
  LA BOHEME, SELECTION
    BELWIN-MILLS PUBLISHING CORPORATION   .60
PUCCINI   TAVAN
  MADAMA BUTTERFLY - FANTASIA
    FRANCO COLOMBO PUBLICATIONS   128787   1.00
PUCCINI   GRAZIANI-WALTER
  MADAMA BUTTERFLY - FANTASIA APPASSIONATA
    FRANCO COLOMBO PUBLICATIONS   110996   1.00
PUCCINI
  MADAMA BUTTERFLY - FINALE OF ACT II -- HUMMING CHORUS --
    FRANCO COLOMBO PUBLICATIONS   11013   .75
PUCCINI
  MADAMA BUTTERFLY - ONE FINE DAY
    FRANCO COLOMBO PUBLICATIONS   117171   .75
PUCCINI   GODFREY, JR.
  MADAMA BUTTERFLY - SELECTION
    FRANCO COLOMBO PUBLICATIONS   110877   1.25
PUCCINI   CHIESA
  MADAMA BUTTERFLY - 1ST EASY FANTASIA
    FRANCO COLOMBO PUBLICATIONS   113184   .60
PUCCINI   CHIESA
  MADAMA BUTTERFLY - 2ND EASY FANTASIA
    FRANCO COLOMBO PUBLICATIONS   113185   .60
PUCCINI   CHIESA
  MADAMA BUTTERFLY - 3RD EASY FANTASIA
    FRANCO COLOMBO PUBLICATIONS   113186   .60
PUCCINI
  MADAMA BUTTERFLY -- COMPLETE OPERA --
    FRANCO COLOMBO PUBLICATIONS   110001   6.00
PUCCINI   TAVAN
  MANON LESCAUT - FANTASIA
    FRANCO COLOMBO PUBLICATIONS   128788   1.00
PUCCINI   DEL MAGLIO
  MANON LESCAUT - IN QUELLE TRINE MORBIDE
    FRANCO COLOMBO PUBLICATIONS   127761   .60
PUCCINI
  MANON LESCAUT - INTERMEZZO ACT III
    FRANCO COLOMBO PUBLICATIONS   97402   .75

PUCCINI   RICHARDSON   2
  MUSETTA'S WALTZ
    WILLIS MUSIC COMPANY   .35
PUCCINI   ECKSTEIN
  MUSETTA'S WALTZ --LA BOHEME--
    CARL FISCHER, INC.   P 2779   .50
PUCCINI   RICHTER
  MUSETTA'S WALTZ SONG -- LA BOHEME
    BELWIN-MILLS PUBLISHING CORPORATION   3   .60
PUCCINI   3
  MUSETTA'S WALTZ, LA BOHEME
    CENTURY MUSIC PUBLISHING COMPANY, INC.   4085   .40
PUCCINI   BECUCCI
  TOSCA - CAPRICCIO-FANTASIA
    FRANCO COLOMBO PUBLICATIONS   103328   1.25
PUCCINI
  TOSCA - E LUCEVAN LE STELLE
    FRANCO COLOMBO PUBLICATIONS   114595   .75
PUCCINI   GODFREY, JR.
  TOSCA - FANTASIA
    FRANCO COLOMBO PUBLICATIONS   103332   1.25
PUCCINI   TAVAN
  TOSCA - FANTASIA
    FRANCO COLOMBO PUBLICATIONS   127613   1.00
PUCCINI   ALASSIO
  TOSCA - O DOLCI BACI
    FRANCO COLOMBO PUBLICATIONS   103325   .60
PUCCINI   WOLFF
  TOSCA - POT-POURRI
    FRANCO COLOMBO PUBLICATIONS   103335   1.25
PUCCINI   SERRA
  TOSCA - VISSI D'ARTE, VISSI D'AMORE
    FRANCO COLOMBO PUBLICATIONS   103316   .90
PUCCINI   CHIESA
  TOSCA - 1ST EASY FANTASIA
    FRANCO COLOMBO PUBLICATIONS   111263   .60
PUCCINI   CHIESA
  TOSCA - 2ND EASY FANTASIA
    FRANCO COLOMBO PUBLICATIONS   111264   .60
PUCCINI
  TOSCA -- COMPLETE OPERA --
    FRANCO COLOMBO PUBLICATIONS   103051   6.00
PUCCINI   STEINER   3 1/2
  TOSCA, CONCERT MEDLEY
    BELWIN-MILLS PUBLISHING CORPORATION   .60
PUCCINI   DEL MAGLIO
  TURANDOT - 1ST EASY FANTASIA
    FRANCO COLOMBO PUBLICATIONS   125421   .60
PUCCINI   DEL MAGLIO
  TURANDOT - 2ND EASY FANTASIA
    FRANCO COLOMBO PUBLICATIONS   125422   .60
PUI KAI   3
  LULLABY
    BELWIN-MILLS PUBLISHING CORPORATION   .60
PULFORD, W.   3
  MINUET IN F
    NOVELLO AND COMPANY, LTD.   55.0025.07   .25
PURCELL, H.
  MINUET IN G
    FREDERICK HARRIS MUSIC COMPANY   .60
PURCELL, H.   BARTOK
  PRELUDE IN G
    MCA MUSIC   .60
PURCELL, H.   DUMM
  RECITAL REFRESHER SERIES -- TRUMPET TUNE IN C MAJOR
    BELWIN-MILLS PUBLISHING CORPORATION   26111   .60
PURCELL, H.   DUMM
  RECITAL REFRESHER SERIES -- TRUMPET TUNE IN D MAJOR
    BELWIN-MILLS PUBLISHING CORPORATION   26112   .60
PURCELL, H.
  RONDEAU FROM 'ABDELAZER'
    OXFORD UNIVERSITY PRESS   32.139   1.10
PURCELL, H.   GUBITOSI
  SUITE
    FRANCO COLOMBO PUBLICATIONS   129645   1.00
PURCELL, H.   GUBITOSI
  TOCCATA
    FRANCO COLOMBO PUBLICATIONS   129646   1.00
PURCELL, H.   3
  TRUMPET PIECE AND AIR IN D
    CENTURY MUSIC PUBLISHING COMPANY, INC.   3380   .40
PURCELL, H.   NORDEN   3
  TRUMPET TUNE
    BOSTON MUSIC COMPANY   .50
PURCELL, H.
  TRUMPET TUNE IN D MAJOR
    BELWIN-MILLS PUBLISHING CORPORATION   .85
PURCELL, H.   NICHOLLS
  TRUMPET VOLUNTARY AND TRUMPET TUNE
    BANKS AND SON LTD.   .40
PUTSCHE, T.
  THREE BUGS FOR PIANO
    SEESAW MUSIC CORPORATION   2.00
QUAILE, E.   PRELIMINARY GRADE
  VERY FIRST PIANO BOOK, A--THE STORY OF TONY IN WORDS AND
  MUSIC--FOR CLASS AND INDIVIDUAL INSTRUCTION
    G. SCHIRMER, INC.   1.25
QUAPATINO
  RAPSODIA ARGENTINA
    FRANCO COLOMBO PUBLICATIONS   123882   1.00
QUILTER
  FESTIVAL GROUPS FOR PIANO SELECTED BY ARTHUR BENJAMIN, SERIES 2
  -- SHEPHERD'S SONG
    BOOSEY AND HAWKES, INC.   .60
QUINCKE, W.   2
  APRIL HEYDAY
    CENTURY MUSIC PUBLISHING COMPANY, INC.   3514   .40
QUINCKE, W.   2
  BUSY FINGERS
    CENTURY MUSIC PUBLISHING COMPANY, INC.   3515   .40
QUINCKE, W.   2
  IN MY GARDEN
    CENTURY MUSIC PUBLISHING COMPANY, INC.   3516   .40
QUINCKE, W.   2
  MAY TIME
    CENTURY MUSIC PUBLISHING COMPANY, INC.   3517   .40
QUINCKE, W.   2
  SINGING AND SWINGING
    CENTURY MUSIC PUBLISHING COMPANY, INC.   3518   .40
QUINCKE, W.   2
  SUNSET HOUR
    CENTURY MUSIC PUBLISHING COMPANY, INC.   3519   .40
QUINCKE, W.   2
  THEY'RE OFF
    CENTURY MUSIC PUBLISHING COMPANY, INC.   3520   .40

QUINCKE, W.   2
  WILD BLOSSOMS
        CENTURY MUSIC PUBLISHING COMPANY, INC.   3521   .40
QUINN   3
  CLOWN PRANKS, CAPRICE
        CENTURY MUSIC PUBLISHING COMPANY, INC.   1083   .40
QUIST   2 1/2
  OLD RIVER BOAT, THE
        BELWIN-MILLS PUBLISHING CORPORATION   .60
QUIST   1
  POPSICLE FROLIC
        BELWIN-MILLS PUBLISHING CORPORATION   .60
QUIXLEY, F.
  AUTUMN LEAVES
        G. SCHIRMER, INC.   .35
QUIXLEY, F.
  BOUNCING THE BALL
        G. SCHIRMER, INC.   .35
RABEY, P.
  SCENES PASTORALES -- CHOEUR DES MOISSONNEURS
        ELKAN-VOGEL, INC.   D   .90
RABINOFF, S.   M
  RIKA
        COMPOSERS PRESS, INC.   1.00
RACHMANINOFF, S.   5
  BELLS OF MOSCOW
        CENTURY MUSIC PUBLISHING COMPANY, INC.   1028   .40
RACHMANINOFF, S.   2
  BELLS OF MOSCOW, EASY
        CENTURY MUSIC PUBLISHING COMPANY, INC.   3222   .40
RACHMANINOFF, S.   HOLCMAN, J.
  CADENZA TO THE LISZT 2ND HUNGARIAN RHAPSODY
        THEODORE PRESSER COMPANY   1.00
RACHMANINOFF, S.
  CANTABILE
        EDWARD B. MARKS MUSIC CORPORATION   01.00
RACHMANINOFF, S.
  CONCERTO NO. 01 IN F SHARP MINOR, OP. 1
        G. SCHIRMER, INC.   L1655   2.00
RACHMANINOFF, S.   SCHAUM, J.   2
  CONCERTO NO. 02
        BELWIN-MILLS PUBLISHING CORPORATION   .50
RACHMANINOFF, S.   DEIS
  CONCERTO NO. 02 IN C MINOR, OP. 18--THEMES FROM 1ST MOVEMENT
        G. SCHIRMER, INC.   .60
RACHMANINOFF, S.   DEIS
  CONCERTO NO. 02 IN C MINOR, OP. 18--THEMES FROM 3RD MOVEMENT
        G. SCHIRMER, INC.   .60
RACHMANINOFF, S.   GRAINGER, P.   D
  CONCERTO NO. 02 IN C MINOR, OP. 18--THEMES FROM 3RD MOVEMENT
        G. SCHIRMER, INC.   1.00
RACHMANINOFF, S.   ECKSTEIN
  CONCERTO NO. 02, THEME FROM 1ST MOVEMENT
        CARL FISCHER, INC.   S 2313   .50
RACHMANINOFF, S.   ECKSTEIN
  CONCERTO NO. 02, THEMES FROM ALL 3 MVTS.
        CARL FISCHER, INC.   P 2889   1.00
RACHMANINOFF, S.
  DAISIES
        BELWIN-MILLS PUBLISHING CORPORATION   1.00
RACHMANINOFF, S.   EICHHORN, H. W.
  EIGHTEENTH VARIATION, FROM RAPSODIE ON A THEME OF PAGANINI
        BELWIN-MILLS PUBLISHING CORPORATION   1.00
RACHMANINOFF, S.   LAMBERT
  EIGHTEENTH VARIATION, FROM RAPSODIE ON A THEME OF PAGANINI
        BELWIN-MILLS PUBLISHING CORPORATION   1.00
RACHMANINOFF, S.   4
  ELEGIE OP. 3 NO. 1
        SCHOTT   01648 1/2 1.75
RACHMANINOFF, S.
  ELEGIE, OP. 3 NO. 1
        BOOSEY AND HAWKES, INC.   .75
RACHMANINOFF, S.
  ELEGIE, OP. 3 NO. 1
        G. SCHIRMER, INC.   .50
RACHMANINOFF, S.
  ETUDE TABLEAU IN A MINOR, OP. 39 NO. 2
        BOOSEY AND HAWKES, INC.   1.00
RACHMANINOFF, S.
  ETUDE TABLEAU IN A MINOR, OP. 39 NO. 6
        BOOSEY AND HAWKES, INC.   1.00
RACHMANINOFF, S.
  ETUDE TABLEAU IN B MINOR, OP. 39 NO. 4
        BOOSEY AND HAWKES, INC.   1.00
RACHMANINOFF, S.
  ETUDE TABLEAU IN C MAJOR, OP. 33
        BELWIN-MILLS PUBLISHING CORPORATION   1.00
RACHMANINOFF, S.
  ETUDE TABLEAU IN C MINOR, OP. 39 NO. 1
        BOOSEY AND HAWKES, INC.   1.00
RACHMANINOFF, S.
  ETUDE TABLEAU IN C MINOR, OP. 39 NO. 7
        BOOSEY AND HAWKES, INC.   1.00
RACHMANINOFF, S.
  ETUDE TABLEAU IN D MAJOR, OP. 39 NO. 9
        BOOSEY AND HAWKES, INC.   1.00
RACHMANINOFF, S.
  ETUDE TABLEAU IN D MINOR, OP. 39 NO. 8
        BOOSEY AND HAWKES, INC.   1.00
RACHMANINOFF, S.
  ETUDE TABLEAU IN E FLAT MINOR, OP. 39 NO. 5
        BOOSEY AND HAWKES, INC.   1.00
RACHMANINOFF, S.
  ETUDE TABLEAU IN F SHARP MINOR, OP. 39 NO. 3
        BOOSEY AND HAWKES, INC.   4   1.00
RACHMANINOFF, S.
  HUMORESKE, OP. 10 NO. 5
        CENTURY MUSIC PUBLISHING COMPANY, INC.   3335   .40
RACHMANINOFF, S.
  HUMORESKE, OP. 10 NO. 5
        G. SCHIRMER, INC.   .75
RACHMANINOFF, S.
  HUMORESQUE
        BELWIN-MILLS PUBLISHING CORPORATION   1.00
RACHMANINOFF, S.   SILOTI
  ITALIAN POLKA
        BOOSEY AND HAWKES, INC.   .90
RACHMANINOFF, S.
  ITALIAN POLKA
        EDWARD B. MARKS MUSIC CORPORATION   01.00
RACHMANINOFF, S.
  LILACS
        BELWIN-MILLS PUBLISHING CORPORATION   1.00
RACHMANINOFF, S.
  LILACS, OP. 21 NO. 5
        BOOSEY AND HAWKES, INC.   1.00

RACHMANINOFF, S.
  MELODIE
        BELWIN-MILLS PUBLISHING CORPORATION   1.00
RACHMANINOFF, S.
  MELODIE IN E MINOR, OP. 10 NO. 4
        G. SCHIRMER, INC.   .40
RACHMANINOFF, S.
  MELODIE, OP. 3 NO. 3
        CARL FISCHER, INC.   S 2182   .50
RACHMANINOFF, S.   4
  MELODIE, OP. 3 NO. 3
        SCHOTT   01649 1/2 1.00
RACHMANINOFF, S.
  MOMENT MUSICAL
        BELWIN-MILLS PUBLISHING CORPORATION   .60
RACHMANINOFF, S.   1.00
  ORIENTAL SKETCH
        BELWIN-MILLS PUBLISHING CORPORATION   .60
RACHMANINOFF, S.
  PIANO CONCERTO NO. 02
        ASHLEY DEALERS SERVICE, INC.   2.50
RACHMANINOFF, S.   MOSSMAN
  PIANO CONCERTO NO. 02 IN C MINOR -- THIRD MOVEMENT
        BELWIN-MILLS PUBLISHING CORPORATION   26090   .60
RACHMANINOFF, S.   3
  PIANO CONCERTO, THEME
        CENTURY MUSIC PUBLISHING COMPANY, INC.   3764   .40
RACHMANINOFF, S.   SCHAUM, J.   3
  POLICHINELLE
        BELWIN-MILLS PUBLISHING CORPORATION   .50
RACHMANINOFF, S.   6
  POLICHINELLE
        CENTURY MUSIC PUBLISHING COMPANY, INC.   2324   .40
RACHMANINOFF, S.   4
  POLICHINELLE
        SCHOTT   07039 1/2 1.00
RACHMANINOFF, S.
  POLICHINELLE, OP. 3 NO. 4
        BELWIN-MILLS PUBLISHING CORPORATION   28175   .70
RACHMANINOFF, S.
  POLICHINELLE, OP. 3 NO. 4
        CARL FISCHER, INC.   S 1210   .75
RACHMANINOFF, S.
  POLICHINELLE, OP. 3 NO. 4
        G. SCHIRMER, INC.   5   .60
RACHMANINOFF, S.
  PRELUDE CIS-MOLL, OP. 3 NO. 2
        SCHOTT   01650 1/2 1.00
RACHMANINOFF, S.
  PRELUDE IN A FLAT, OP. 23 NO. 8
        BOOSEY AND HAWKES, INC.   .75
RACHMANINOFF, S.
  PRELUDE IN A MINOR, OP. 32 NO. 8
        BOOSEY AND HAWKES, INC.   .75
RACHMANINOFF, S.
  PPELUDE IN A, OP. 32 NO. 9
        BOOSEY AND HAWKES, INC.   .75
RACHMANINOFF, S.
  PRELUDE IN B FLAT MINOR, OP. 23 NO. 2
        BOOSEY AND HAWKES, INC.   .75
RACHMANINOFF, S.
  PRELUDE IN B FLAT MINOR, OP. 32 NO. 2
        BOOSEY AND HAWKES, INC.   .75
RACHMANINOFF, S.
  PRELUDE IN B MINOR, OP. 32 NO. 10
        BOOSEY AND HAWKES, INC.   .75
RACHMANINOFF, S.
  PRELUDE IN B, OP. 32 NO. 11
        BOOSEY AND HAWKES, INC.   .75
RACHMANINOFF, S.
  PRELUDE IN C MINOR, OP. 23 NO. 7
        BOOSEY AND HAWKES, INC.   .75
RACHMANINOFF, S.   5
  PRELUDE IN C SHARP MINOR
        CENTURY MUSIC PUBLISHING COMPANY, INC.   1028   .40
RACHMANINOFF, S.   MITTLER   3B
  PRELUDE IN C SHARP MINOR
        MUSICORD PUBLICATIONS, INC.   .45
RACHMANINOFF, S.   7
  PRELUDE IN C SHARP MINOR
        VOLKWEIN BROS.   .25
RACHMANINOFF, S.
  PRELUDE IN C SHARP MINOR, OP. 3 NO. 2
        ASHLEY DEALERS SERVICE, INC.   ES   .95
RACHMANINOFF, S.
  PRELUDE IN C SHARP MINOR, OP. 3 NO. 2
        BOOSEY AND HAWKES, INC.   .75
RACHMANINOFF, S.
  PRELUDE IN C SHARP MINOR, OP. 3 NO. 2
        CARL FISCHER, INC.   S 1246   .60
RACHMANINOFF, S.   ECKSTEIN
  PRELUDE IN C SHARP MINOR, OP. 3 NO. 2
        CARL FISCHER, INC.   S 2319   .50
RACHMANINOFF, S.   ESPOSITO
  PRELUDE IN C SHARP MINOR, OP. 3 NO. 2
        FRANCO COLOMBO PUBLICATIONS   129066   .60
RACHMANINOFF, S.   DEL MAGLIO
  PRELUDE IN C SHARP MINOR, OP. 3 NO. 2
        FRANCO COLOMBO PUBLICATIONS   129082   .60
RACHMANINOFF, S.
  PRELUDE IN C SHARP MINOR, OP. 3 NO. 2
        G. SCHIRMER, INC.   .60
RACHMANINOFF, S.
  PRELUDE IN C, OP. 32 NO. 1
        BOOSEY AND HAWKES, INC.   .75
RACHMANINOFF, S.
  PRELUDE IN D FLAT, OP. 32 NO. 13
        BOOSEY AND HAWKES, INC.   .75
RACHMANINOFF, S.
  PRELUDE IN D MINOR, OP. 23 NO. 4
        BOOSEY AND HAWKES, INC.   .75
RACHMANINOFF, S.
  PRELUDE IN D, OP. 23 NO. 3
        BOOSEY AND HAWKES, INC.   .75
RACHMANINOFF, S.
  PRELUDE IN E FLAT MINOR, OP. 23 NO. 9
        BOOSEY AND HAWKES, INC.   .75
RACHMANINOFF, S.
  PRELUDE IN E FLAT, OP. 23 NO. 6
        BOOSEY AND HAWKES, INC.   .75
RACHMANINOFF, S.
  PRELUDE IN E FLAT, OP. 23, NO. 6
        G. SCHIRMER, INC.   .50
RACHMANINOFF, S.
  PRELUDE IN E MAJOR, OP. 32
        BELWIN-MILLS PUBLISHING CORPORATION   1.00

RACHMANINOFF, S.
  PRELUDE IN E MINOR, OP. 32 NO. 4
    BOOSEY AND HAWKES, INC.   .75
RACHMANINOFF, S.
  PRELUDE IN E, OP. 32 NO. 3
    BOOSEY AND HAWKES, INC.   .75
RACHMANINOFF, S.
  PRELUDE IN F MINOR, OP. 32 NO. 6
    BOOSEY AND HAWKES, INC.   .75
RACHMANINOFF, S.
  PRELUDE IN F SHARP MINOR, OP. 23 NO. 1
    BOOSEY AND HAWKES, INC.   .75
RACHMANINOFF, S.
  PRELUDE IN F, OP. 32 NO. 7
    BOOSEY AND HAWKES, INC.   .75
RACHMANINOFF, S.
  PRELUDE IN G FLAT, OP. 23 NO. 10
    BOOSEY AND HAWKES, INC.   .75
RACHMANINOFF, S.   PALMERI
  PRELUDE IN G MINOR
    G. SCHIRMER, INC.   .40
RACHMANINOFF, S.
  PRELUDE IN G MINOR, OP. 23 NO. 5
    BOOSEY AND HAWKES, INC.   .75
RACHMANINOFF, S.   5
  PRELUDE IN G MINOR, OP. 23 NO. 5
    BOSTON MUSIC COMPANY   .50
RACHMANINOFF, S.   ECKSTEIN
  PRELUDE IN G MINOR, OP. 23 NO. 5
    CARL FISCHER, INC.   S 1247   .50
RACHMANINOFF, S.
  PRELUDE IN G MINOR, OP. 23 NO. 5
    G. SCHIRMER, INC.   .60
RACHMANINOFF, S.
  PRELUDE IN G SHARP MINOR, OP. 32 NO. 12
    BOOSEY AND HAWKES, INC.   .75
RACHMANINOFF, S.   4
  PRELUDE IN G SHARP MINOR, OP. 32 NO. 12
    BOSTON MUSIC COMPANY   .50
RACHMANINOFF, S.
  PRELUDE IN G, OP. 32 NO. 5
    BOOSEY AND HAWKES, INC.   .75
RACHMANINOFF, S.
  PRELUDE, F MAJOR, OP. 32
    BELWIN-MILLS PUBLISHING CORPORATION   1.00
RACHMANINOFF, S.
  PRELUDE, F MINOR, OP. 32
    BELWIN-MILLS PUBLISHING CORPORATION   1.00
RACHMANINOFF, S.   5
  PRELUDE, OP. 23 NO. 5
    CENTURY MUSIC PUBLISHING COMPANY, INC.   2126   .40
RACHMANINOFF, S.   SCHAUM, J.   4
  PRELUDE, OP. 3 NO. 2
    BELWIN-MILLS PUBLISHING CORPORATION   .50
RACHMANINOFF, S.   6
  PUNCHINELLO, OP. 3 NO. 4
    CENTURY MUSIC PUBLISHING COMPANY, INC.   2324   .40
RACHMANINOFF, S.   ROLFE, W.   3
  PUNCHINELLO, OP. 3 NO. 4, EASY
    CENTURY MUSIC PUBLISHING COMPANY, INC.   3394   .40
RACHMANINOFF, S.   MITTLER   3A
  RACHMANINOFF CONCERTO
    MUSICORD PUBLICATIONS, INC.   .45
RACHMANINOFF, S.
  SECOND PIANO CONCERTO - THEMES
    THE BIG THREE MUSIC CORPORATION   00.75
RACHMANINOFF, S.   SILOTI
  SERENADE IN B FLAT MINOR, OP. 3 NO. 5
    G. SCHIRMER, INC.   .40
RACHMANINOFF, S.
  SONATA NO. 01 IN D MINOR, OP. 28
    BOOSEY AND HAWKES, INC.   2.50
RACHMANINOFF, S.
  SONATA NO. 01 IN D MINOR, OP. 28
    INTERNATIONAL MUSIC COMPANY   2.50
RACHMANINOFF, S.
  SONATA NO. 02 IN B FLAT MINOR, OP 36
    INTERNATIONAL MUSIC COMPANY   2.50
RACHMANINOFF, S.   ECKSTEIN
  THEME FROM SECOND PIANO CONCERTO, OP. 18
    CARL FISCHER, INC.   S 2313   .50
RACHMANINOFF, S.   THORNE
  THEME, FROM 'CONCERTO NO. 02'
    BOOSEY AND HAWKES, INC.   .60
RACHMANINOFF, S.   3 1/2
  THEME, FROM PIANO CONCERTO IN C MINOR
    THEODORE PRESSER COMPANY   .50
RACHMANINOFF, S.   TRUXELL, E.   3 1/2
  THEMES FROM PIANO CONCERTO
    VOLKWEIN BROS.   00.40
RACHMANINOFF, S.   4
  VALSE A-DUR OP. 10 NO. 2
    SCHOTT   01651 1/2   1.00
RACHMANINOFF, S.   4
  VALSE IN A, OP. 10 NO. 2
    CENTURY MUSIC PUBLISHING COMPANY, INC.   3354   .40
RACHMANINOFF, S.
  VARIATIONS ON A THEME BY CHOPIN, OP. 22
    INTERNATIONAL MUSIC COMPANY   2.50
RACHMANINOFF, S.
  VARIATIONS ON A THEME OF CORELLI
    BELWIN-MILLS PUBLISHING CORPORATION   2.00
RACHMANINOFF, S.   RICHARDSON
  VOCALISE, OP. 34 NO. 14
    BOOSEY AND HAWKES, INC.   .75
RAEZER, C.
  ALL ON A CIRCUS DAY
    G. SCHIRMER, INC.   .35
RAEZER, C.
  BECKYS WALTZ
    EDWARD B. MARKS MUSIC CORPORATION   00.60
RAEZER, C.
  BIG BROWN BEAR
    G. SCHIRMER, INC.   .35
RAEZER, C.
  CARNIVAL, THE
    BELWIN-MILLS PUBLISHING CORPORATION   25019   .60
RAEZER, C.
  CUT THE PIGEON WING
    BELWIN-MILLS PUBLISHING CORPORATION   25033   .60
RAEZER, C.
  DANCE LIGHTLY
    G. SCHIRMER, INC.   .35
RAEZER, C.
  DREAM CLOUDS
    G. SCHIRMER, INC.   .35

RAEZER, C.   1
  FAIRY QUEEN WALTZ
    WILLIS MUSIC COMPANY   .25
RAEZER, C.
  FORGET-ME-NOT
    G. SCHIRMER, INC.   .40
RAEZER, C.
  GAY LARKS GO MODERN, THE
    G. SCHIRMER, INC.   .35
RAEZER, C.   1
  HIDE AND SEEK
    WILLIS MUSIC COMPANY   .40
RAEZER, C.
  HOBBY HORSES
    EDWARD B. MARKS MUSIC CORPORATION   00.60
RAEZER, C.
  IN A FAIRY GARDEN
    G. SCHIRMER, INC.   .35
RAEZER, C.
  IN A GYPSY TENT
    G. SCHIRMER, INC.   .35
RAEZER, C.
  JOY DANCERS
    G. SCHIRMER, INC.   .35
RAEZER, C.
  LITTLE SKATING STAR
    G. SCHIRMER, INC.   .40
RAEZER, C.   1
  MAGIC GARDEN
    G. SCHIRMER, INC.   .35
RAEZER, C.   1
  PLAYFUL PRANKS
    WILLIS MUSIC COMPANY   .30
RAEZER, C.
  PONIES PARADE
    EDWARD B. MARKS MUSIC CORPORATION   00.60
RAEZER, C.
  POP-CORN
    G. SCHIRMER, INC.   .35
RAEZER, C.
  SHOW TIME
    G. SCHIRMER, INC.   .35
RAEZER, C.
  SKIP AROUND AND SING
    G. SCHIRMER, INC.   .40
RAEZER, C.
  SOARING HIGH
    EDWARD B. MARKS MUSIC CORPORATION   00.60
RAEZER, C.
  SPRING VIOLETS
    G. SCHIRMER, INC.   .35
RAEZER, C.
  STRUTTERS FROLIC
    EDWARD B. MARKS MUSIC CORPORATION   00.60
RAEZER, C.
  STRUTTERS FROLIC
    EDWARD B. MARKS MUSIC CORPORATION   00.60
RAEZER, C.
  WEE FOLKS' MARCH
    G. SCHIRMER, INC.   .35
RAFF   6
  LA FILLEUSE
    CENTURY MUSIC PUBLISHING COMPANY, INC.   1190   .40
RAFF, J.   3
  FABLIAU OP. 75 NO. 2
    SCHOTT   01652 1/2   1.00
RAFF, J.
  FANTAISIE MILITAIRE SUR LES HUGUENOTS --MEYERBEER--
    MUSICA OBSCURA   2.50
RAFF, J.
  FILEUSE, LA, OP. 157 NO. 2
    FRANCO COLOMBO PUBLICATIONS   ER2246   .75
RAFF, J.
  GIGA CON VARIAZIONI FROM SUITE IN D MINOR, OP. 91
    MUSICA OBSCURA   4.00
RAFF, J.   HENSELT, A. V.
  LA FILEUSE F SHARP, OP. 157 NO. 2
    MUSICA OBSCURA   2.00
RAFF, J.   4
  LA FILEUSE OP. 157 NO. 2
    SCHOTT   01657 1/2   1.00
RAFF, J.   HENSELT
  LA FILEUSE, OP. 157 NO. 2
    G. SCHIRMER, INC.   .60
RAFF, J.
  NOCTURNE IN A FLAT, OP. 17
    MUSICA OBSCURA   1.50
RAFF, J.   6
  SPINNING WHEEL, ETUDE
    CENTURY MUSIC PUBLISHING COMPANY, INC.   1190   .40
RAGANINI, A.
  DEER IN THE CLEARING
    BELWIN-MILLS PUBLISHING CORPORATION   .60
RAGANINI, A.   1
  RACOON, THE ROBBER
    BELWIN-MILLS PUBLISHING CORPORATION   .60
RAGANINI, A.   1
  SQUIRRELS IN THE NUT TREE
    BELWIN-MILLS PUBLISHING CORPORATION   .60
RAGAS *
  CLARINET MARMALADE
    THE BIG THREE MUSIC CORPORATION   00.95
RAHIM, G. A.
  VARIATIONS ON AN EGYPTIAN FOLKSONG
    ASSOCIATED MUSIC PUBLISHERS, INC.   DOB   2.50
RAKSIN, D.
  BAD AND THE BEAUTIFUL, THE
    THE BIG THREE MUSIC CORPORATION   00.95
RALSTON, F.   M
  AVOWAL
    COMPOSERS PRESS, INC.   1.00
RALSTON, F.   M
  ESTRANGEMENT
    COMPOSERS PRESS, INC.   1.00
RALSTON, F.   M
  RECONCILIATION
    COMPOSERS PRESS, INC.   1.00
RAMEAU   4-5
  EGYPTIAN GIRL, THE
    CENTURY MUSIC PUBLISHING COMPANY, INC.   3894   .40
RAMEAU   GODOWSKY, L.
  ELEGY
    SHAWNEE PRESS, INC.   HB-235   .75
RAMEAU
  GAVOTTE
    ELKAN-VOGEL, INC.   D   .85

RAMEAU   PHILIPP, I.
  GAVOTTE WITH VARIATIONS IN A MINOR
    INTERNATIONAL MUSIC COMPANY   1.25
                            4

RAMEAU
  HEN, THE -- LA POULE
    CENTURY MUSIC PUBLISHING COMPANY, INC.   3907   .40
                            6

RAMEAU   MOFFAT
  LA BOURREE DE VINCENT
    NOVELLO AND COMPANY, LTD.   55.0016.08   .40
                            4

RAMEAU
  LA POULE
    CENTURY MUSIC PUBLISHING COMPANY, INC.   3907   .40

RAMEAU
  LA POULE
    ELKAN-VOGEL, INC.   D   .90

RAMEAU
  LA POULE
    G. SCHIRMER, INC.   .40

RAMEAU   THOMPSON, J.   1
  LE TAMBORIN
    WILLIS MUSIC COMPANY   .35

RAMEAU
  LE TAMBOURIN
    G. SCHIRMER, INC.   .30

RAMEAU
  LES CYCLOPS
    ELKAN-VOGEL, INC.   D   1.00

RAMEAU
  LES INDES GALANTES -- FIRST SUITE
    ELKAN-VOGEL, INC.   D   2.10

RAMEAU
  LES SAUVAGES
    ELKAN-VOGEL, INC.   D   .75

RAMEAU
  MINUET
    BELWIN-MILLS PUBLISHING CORPORATION   .85

RAMEAU
  MINUET
    FREDERICK HARRIS MUSIC COMPANY   .60

RAMEAU
  PIECES CHOISIES
    HEUGEL ET CIE.   2.65
                            4

RAMEAU
  POULE, LA -- THE HEN --
    CENTURY MUSIC PUBLISHING COMPANY, INC.   3907   .40

RAMEAU
  RAPPEL DES OISEAUX
    UNIVERSAL EDITION   UE 5417   .80

RAMEAU   FRIEDMAN
  RAPPEL DES OIXEAUX
    UNIVERSAL EDITION   5417   .80

RAMEAU   DUMM
  RECITAL REFRESHER SERIES -- MINUET
    BELWIN-MILLS PUBLISHING CORPORATION   26118   .60
                            3

RAMEAU
  RIGAUDON
    CENTURY MUSIC PUBLISHING COMPANY, INC.   3747   .40
                            3

RAMEAU
  RIGAUDON
    SCHOTT   0910 1/2   1.00

RAMEAU
  RIGAUDON DES DARDANUS
    ELKAN-VOGEL, INC.   D   .90

RAMEAU
  TAMBOURIN
    CARL FISCHER, INC.   S 2035   .50
                            3

RAMEAU
  TAMBOURIN
    CENTURY MUSIC PUBLISHING COMPANY, INC.   3639   .40

RAMEAU   LONGO
  TAMBOURIN
    FRANCO COLOMBO PUBLICATIONS   127928   .60

RAMEY *
  SO YOU WON'T JUMP
    MCA MUSIC   1.00

RAMEY, P.
  EPIGRAMS
    BOOSEY AND HAWKES, INC.   1.50

RAMOS, E.   HARRIS   3-4
  PAQUITA MIA
    VOLKWEIN BROS.   .30

RAMOS, E.   HARRIS   4
  YOLANDA
    VOLKWEIN BROS.   00.30

RAMSIER, P.
  MY HAMSTER CRAWLS -- CASE BOUND
    BOOSEY AND HAWKES, INC.   2.95

RAMSIER, P.
  MY HAMSTER CRAWLS -- PAPER
    BOOSEY AND HAWKES, INC.   1.50

RAMSIER, P.
  PIED PIPER
    BOOSEY AND HAWKES, INC.   1.25

RAN, S.
  SHORT PIANO PIECES
    ISRAEL MUSIC INSTITUTE   2.75

RAN, S.
  SONATA NO. 02
    ISRAEL MUSIC INSTITUTE   3.50

RANDS, R.
  TRE EXPRESSIONI
    UNIVERSAL EDITION   UE 14229   2.25

RANSOME, F.
  NATIONAL AIRS
    BANKS AND SON LTD.   .80

RANSOME, F.
  NEGRO AIRS
    BANKS AND SON LTD.   .80

RAPHAEL, G.
  SONATA NO. 01, OP. 38 NO. 1--1939
    ASSOCIATED MUSIC PUBLISHERS, INC.   BRH   2.00

RAPHAEL, G.
  SONATA NO. 02, OP. 38 NO. 2--1939
    ASSOCIATED MUSIC PUBLISHERS, INC.   BRH   2.00
                          3-4

RAPHAEL, G.
  SONATINA SERIA, OP. 51 NO. 1
    BARENREITER VERLAG   SM 1629

RAPHLING
  AMUSEMENT PARK - SUITE
    GENERAL MUSIC PUBLISHING COMPANY, INC.   229   2.00

RAPHLING
  BAGATELLE CUBANA
    SAM FOX PUBLISHING COMPANY, INC.   .50

RAPHLING
  BAGATELLE CUBANA
    SOUTHERN MUSIC COMPANY   .50

RAPHLING
  BAGATELLE ISRAELI
    SAM FOX PUBLISHING COMPANY, INC.   .50

RAPHLING
  BAGATELLE ISRAELI
    SOUTHERN MUSIC COMPANY   .50

RAPHLING
  BIRTHDAY PARTY
    GENERAL MUSIC PUBLISHING COMPANY, INC.   601   1.50

RAPHLING
  BIRTHDAY PARTY
    GENERAL MUSIC PUBLISHING COMPANY, INC.   1.50

RAPHLING
  BLUE STREAK
    BELWIN-MILLS PUBLISHING CORPORATION   28009   .60

RAPHLING
  CAKE WALK
    BELWIN-MILLS PUBLISHING CORPORATION   25185   .60

RAPHLING
  CANDID CAMERA - FOR THE YOUNGEST PIANISTS
    GENERAL MUSIC PUBLISHING COMPANY, INC.   2.25

RAPHLING
  DANCE OF THE DHASSIDIM
    BELWIN-MILLS PUBLISHING CORPORATION   25285   .60

RAPHLING
  DANZON
    BELWIN-MILLS PUBLISHING CORPORATION   25289   .60

RAPHLING
  FERRIS WHEEL
    BELWIN-MILLS PUBLISHING CORPORATION   28010   .60

RAPHLING
  HAPPENING
    GENERAL MUSIC PUBLISHING COMPANY, INC.   2.00
                            M

RAPHLING
  INTRODUCTION AND RAG
    THEODORE PRESSER COMPANY   .60

RAPHLING
  JAZZ TOCCATA
    BELWIN-MILLS PUBLISHING CORPORATION   25286   .60

RAPHLING
  MAGIC EYE, THE
    GENERAL MUSIC PUBLISHING COMPANY, INC.   281   1.50

RAPHLING
  MARCH OF THE ATHLETES
    BELWIN-MILLS PUBLISHING CORPORATION   25296   .60

RAPHLING
  MARCH OF THE TWIRLERS
    MCA MUSIC   .60

RAPHLING
  MILL ON THE FLOSS
    BELWIN-MILLS PUBLISHING CORPORATION   28012   .60

RAPHLING
  MOMENTS TO REMEMBER
    GENERAL MUSIC PUBLISHING COMPANY, INC.   633   2.00

RAPHLING
  MOMENTS TO REMEMBER
    GENERAL MUSIC PUBLISHING COMPANY, INC.   2.50
                            M

RAPHLING
  NOCTURNAL PRELUDE
    THEODORE PRESSER COMPANY   .50

RAPHLING
  NOVELTY SUITE
    BELWIN-MILLS PUBLISHING CORPORATION   20183   .85

RAPHLING
  PASSACAGLIA EBRAICA
    GENERAL MUSIC PUBLISHING COMPANY, INC.   3.00

RAPHLING
  PENNY ARCADE
    BELWIN-MILLS PUBLISHING CORPORATION   28011   .60
                           MD

RAPHLING
  PIANO SONATA NO. 03
    THEODORE PRESSER COMPANY   2.00

RAPHLING
  PONY RIDE
    BELWIN-MILLS PUBLISHING CORPORATION   25292   .60

RAPHLING
  RIDE OF THE ASTRONAUT
    BELWIN-MILLS PUBLISHING CORPORATION   25287   .60

RAPHLING
  SEVEN MOBILES
    GENERAL MUSIC PUBLISHING COMPANY, INC.   2.00

RAPHLING
  SIDE SHOW
    BELWIN-MILLS PUBLISHING CORPORATION   28013   .60

RAPHLING
  SONATA NO. 01
    BELWIN-MILLS PUBLISHING CORPORATION   20400   3.00

RAPHLING
  SONATA NO. 05
    GENERAL MUSIC PUBLISHING COMPANY, INC.   391   3.50

RAPHLING
  SONATA NO. 05
    GENERAL MUSIC PUBLISHING COMPANY, INC.   4.50
                            MD

RAPHLING
  SONATINA NO. 01
    THEODORE PRESSER COMPANY   1.00

RAPHLING
  SONATINA NO. 02
    GENERAL MUSIC PUBLISHING COMPANY, INC.   378   3.50

RAPHLING
  SONATINA NO. 02
    GENERAL MUSIC PUBLISHING COMPANY, INC.   3.50

RAPHLING
  SQUARE DANCE CALLER
    BELWIN-MILLS PUBLISHING CORPORATION   25295   .60

RAPHLING
  TRIP TO THE MOON, A
    BELWIN-MILLS PUBLISHING CORPORATION   25240   .60

RAPHLING
  TWO BLUES
    FRANCO COLOMBO PUBLICATIONS   NY2260   1.00
                            3

RASBACH, O.
  DAY DREAMS
    WILLIS MUSIC COMPANY   .60
                           3

RASBACH, O.
  DAY DREAMS
    WILLIS MUSIC COMPANY   .40

RASBACH, O.
  DRIFTING CLOUDS
    WARNER BROTHERS PUBLISHERS   .60

RASBACH, O.
  EARLY CALIFORNIA   ELEMENTARY GRADE
    G. SCHIRMER, INC.   .80

RASBACH, O.
  EL BURRITO
    G. SCHIRMER, INC.   .50

RASBACH, O.
FROM 'WAY DOWN SOUTH--TURKEY IN DE STRAW
G. SCHIRMER, INC. .40
RASBACH, O. INTERMEDIATE GRADE
FROM DIXIELAND
G. SCHIRMER, INC. .80
RASBACH, O. LOWER ADVANCED GRADE
IN COLONIAL DAYS
G. SCHIRMER, INC. .90
RASBACH, O.
MARCH OF THE CADETS
G. SCHIRMER, INC. .40
RASBACH, O. RASBACH, O.
TREES
G. SCHIRMER, INC. .50
TREES
G. SCHIRMER, INC. DEIS .50
TREES
G. SCHIRMER, INC. .50
RASBACH, O. DEIS
TREES
G. SCHIRMER, INC. .50
RASBACH, O.
VALSE ELAINE
G. SCHIRMER, INC. .50
RASBACH, O.
WALTZ IMPROVISATION
G. SCHIRMER, INC. .50
RASBACH, O.
WOODS AT NIGHT
G. SCHIRMER, INC. .50
RASCHIG 1-2
JOLLY JIM
PRO-ART PUBLICATIONS, INC. 308 .50
RASKIN, D.
LAURA
THE BIG THREE MUSIC CORPORATION 00.95
RATHAUS, K.
BALLADE, OP. 40--VARIATIONS ON A HURDY-GURDY THEME
ASSOCIATED MUSIC PUBLISHERS, INC. BMP 4.00
RATHAUS, K. D
FOUR STUDIES AFTER DOMENICO SCARLATTI, OP. 56
THEODORE PRESSER COMPANY 2.00
RATHAUS, K.
SIX LITTLE PIECES, OP. 11
UNIVERSAL EDITION UE 8415 2.90
RATHAUS, K.
THREE MAZURKAS, OP. 24
UNIVERSAL EDITION UE 9654 2.15
RATHBONE, G. 2
JOLLY BOY, THE
NOVELLO AND COMPANY, LTD. 55.0004.04 .25
RATHBONE, G. 2
LAKE, THE
NOVELLO AND COMPANY, LTD. 55.0007.09 .25
RATHBONE, G. 2
LITTLE WALTZ, A
NOVELLO AND COMPANY, LTD. 55.0006.00 .40
RATHBONE, G. 7
ROMANCE
NOVELLO AND COMPANY, LTD. 55.0036.02 .25
RATHBONE, G. 5
SAILORS' DANCE
NOVELLO AND COMPANY, LTD. 55.0030.03 .25
RATHGEBER, V. STEGLICH
MUSIKALISCHER ZEITVERTREIB AUF DEM KLAVIER
BARENREITER VERLAG NMA 105 3.00
RAVEL
A LA MANIERE DE BORODINE
FRANCO COLOMBO PUBLICATIONS SAL 2.00
RAVEL
A LA MANIERE DE CHABRIER
FRANCO COLOMBO PUBLICATIONS SAL 1.75
RAVEL
ADAGIO
ELKAN-VOGEL, INC. D 2.10
RAVEL
ALBORADA DEL GRACIOSO
EDWIN F. KALMUS 3827 1.00
RAVEL
ALBORADA DEL GRACIOSO, FROM MIROIRS
ASSOCIATED MUSIC PUBLISHERS, INC. ESC 4.00
RAVEL SCHMITZ
ALBORADA DEL GRACIOSO, FROM MIROIRS
ASSOCIATED MUSIC PUBLISHERS, INC. ESC 1.25
RAVEL
ALBORADA DEL GRACIOSO, FROM MIROIRS
G. SCHIRMER, INC. .80
RAVEL
BERCEUSE SUR LE NOM DE FAURE
ELKAN-VOGEL, INC. D 1.25
RAVEL
BOLERO
ELKAN-VOGEL, INC. 2.25
RAVEL
CONCERTO FOR THE LEFT HAND--SOLO PART
ELKAN-VOGEL, INC. 6.75
RAVEL
DAPHNIS ET CHLOE
ELKAN-VOGEL, INC. D 4.15
RAVEL
FIVE O'CLOCK FOX-TROT
ELKAN-VOGEL, INC. 2.25
RAVEL
HABANERA - RAPSODIE ESPAGNOLE
ELKAN-VOGEL, INC. 1.70
RAVEL
INTRODUCTION ET ALLEGRO
ELKAN-VOGEL, INC. D 3.40
RAVEL
JEUX D'EAU
ASSOCIATED MUSIC PUBLISHERS, INC. ESC 4.75
RAVEL SCHMITZ
JEUX D'EAU
ASSOCIATED MUSIC PUBLISHERS, INC. ESC 1.00
RAVEL
JEUX D'EAU
EDWARD B. MARKS MUSIC CORPORATION 01.00
RAVEL
JEUX D'EAU
EDWIN F. KALMUS 3839 1.00
RAVEL
JEUX D'EAU
G. SCHIRMER, INC. .80
RAVEL 5
JEUX D'EAU
SCHOTT 1787 2.50

RAVEL
KADDISCH -- MELODIE HEBRAIQUE
ELKAN-VOGEL, INC. D 2.25
RAVEL
L'ENFANT ET LES SORTILEGES
ELKAN-VOGEL, INC. D 2.50
RAVEL
L'HEURE ESPAGNOLE
ELKAN-VOGEL, INC. D 3.00
RAVEL
LA VALSE
ELKAN-VOGEL, INC. 5.00
RAVEL
LE GIBET FROM GASPARD DE LA NUIT
ELKAN-VOGEL, INC. 1.70
RAVEL
MENUET
ELKAN-VOGEL, INC. 1.70
RAVEL
MENUET
ELKAN-VOGEL, INC. PHILIPP, I. D 1.75
RAVEL
MENUET ANTIQUE
INTERNATIONAL MUSIC COMPANY 1.25
RAVEL
MENUET ON NAME OF HAYDN
ELKAN-VOGEL, INC. 1.20
RAVEL
MINUET ANTIQUE
EDWIN F. KALMUS 3829 1.50
RAVEL 5
MIROIRS, NO. 5 LA VALLEE DES CLOCHES
SCHOTT 1785 1.75
RAVEL
MOTHER GOOSE SUITE
ELKAN-VOGEL, INC. 3.40
RAVEL
NOCTUELLES
EDWIN F. KALMUS 3828 1.00
RAVEL
NOCTUELLES, FROM MIROIRS
ASSOCIATED MUSIC PUBLISHERS, INC. ESC 3.50
RAVEL
OISEAUX TRISTES
EDWIN F. KALMUS 3835 1.00
RAVEL
OISEAUX TRISTES, FROM MIROIRS
ASSOCIATED MUSIC PUBLISHERS, INC. ESC 2.75
RAVEL
ONDINE FROM GASPARD DE LA NUIT
ELKAN-VOGEL, INC. 3.00
RAVEL 4
PAVANE
BOSTON MUSIC COMPANY .60
RAVEL 5
PAVANE
CENTURY MUSIC PUBLISHING COMPANY, INC. 3422 .40
RAVEL 4
PAVANE
SCHOTT 1788 2.25
RAVEL
PAVANE POUR UNE INFANTE DEFUNTE
ASSOCIATED MUSIC PUBLISHERS, INC. ESC 2.50
RAVEL SCHMITZ
PAVANE POUR UNE INFANTE DEFUNTE
ASSOCIATED MUSIC PUBLISHERS, INC. ESC .75
RAVEL
PAVANE POUR UNE INFANTE DEFUNTE
EDWARD B. MARKS MUSIC CORPORATION 01.00
RAVEL
PAVANE POUR UNE INFANTE DEFUNTE
THE BIG THREE MUSIC CORPORATION 00.95
RAVEL DUMESNIL, M. 6
PIECE EN FORME DE HABANERA
ALPHONSE LEDUC
RAVEL
PRELUDE
ELKAN-VOGEL, INC. 1.50
RAVEL
QUATUOR
ELKAN-VOGEL, INC. D 7.00
RAVEL
RAPSODIE ESPAGNOLE
ELKAN-VOGEL, INC. 4.25
RAVEL
RIGAUDON
ELKAN-VOGEL, INC. 2.25
RAVEL
SCARBO FROM GASPARD DE LA NUIT
ELKAN-VOGEL, INC. 4.10
RAVEL
SONATINE
CARL FISCHER, INC. P 3062 2.00
RAVEL
SONATINE
EDWIN F. KALMUS 3838 1.50
RAVEL
SONATINE
ELKAN-VOGEL, INC. 1.25
RAVEL
SONATINE
G. SCHIRMER, INC. L1815 1.50
RAVEL PHILIPP, I.
SONATINE IN F SHARP
INTERNATIONAL MUSIC COMPANY 1.50
RAVEL
TOCCATA
ELKAN-VOGEL, INC. 3.00
RAVEL
UNE BARQUE SUR L'OCEAN
EDWIN F. KALMUS 3837 1.00
RAVEL
UNE BARQUE SUR L'OCEAN, FROM MIROIRS
ASSOCIATED MUSIC PUBLISHERS, INC. ESC 4.00
RAVEL
VALLEE DES CLOCHES
EDWIN F. KALMUS 3836 1.00
RAVEL
VALLEE DES CLOCHES, FROM MIROIRS
ASSOCIATED MUSIC PUBLISHERS, INC. ESC 2.25
RAVEL
VALSES -- DANSE DES RAINETTE
ELKAN-VOGEL, INC. D 1.75
RAVEL
VALSES NOBLES ET SENTIMENTALES
ELKAN-VOGEL, INC. 6.00

RAVINA, H.   4
    CALINERIE, MELODIE ENFANTINE, OP. 86
        ALPHONSE LEDUC
RAVINA, H.   SCHAUM, J.   3
    CARRIER PIGEON
        BELWIN-MILLS PUBLISHING CORPORATION   .50
RAVINA, H.   4
    ETUDE DE STYLE
        CENTURY MUSIC PUBLISHING COMPANY, INC.   1116   .40
RAVINA, H.   2 1/2
    FLATTERY
        WILLIS MUSIC COMPANY   .40
RAVINA, H.
    LITTLE BOLERO, OP. 62
        G. SCHIRMER, INC.   .60
RAVINA, H.   4
    PETITE BOLERO
        CENTURY MUSIC PUBLISHING COMPANY, INC.   625   .40
RAVINA, H.
    RONDO VILLAGEOIS
        FRANCO COLOMBO PUBLICATIONS   SAL   2.50
RAWICZ
    SNOW FLAKES
        BELWIN-MILLS PUBLISHING CORPORATION   20252   .85
RAWICZ
    SPINNING WHEEL
        BELWIN-MILLS PUBLISHING CORPORATION   20276   .85
RAWSTHORNE, A.
    BALLADE
        OXFORD UNIVERSITY PRESS   32.149   3.30
RAWSTHORNE, A.
    SONATINA FOR PIANO
        OXFORD UNIVERSITY PRESS   32.001   3.00
RAYE
    DOWN THE ROAD A PIECE
        MCA MUSIC   1.00
RAYE
    DOWN THE ROAD A PIECE
        MCA MUSIC   1.00
RAYE
    SCRUB ME MAMA --WITH A BOOGIE BEAT--
        MCA MUSIC   1.00
RAYE *
    COW-COW BOOGIE
        MCA MUSIC   1.00
RAYE *
    MISTER FIVE BY FIVE
        MCA MUSIC   1.00
RAYE *
    RHUMBOOGIE
        MCA MUSIC   1.00
RAYE *
    STRUTTIN' WITH SOME BARBECUE
        MCA MUSIC   1.00
RAYMOND   2
    WINTER
        BOSTON MUSIC COMPANY   .50
RAYMOND, J.   2
    AUTUMN
        BELWIN-MILLS PUBLISHING CORPORATION   .60
RAYMOND, J.   3
    MARCH OF THE WHITE KEYS
        BELWIN-MILLS PUBLISHING CORPORATION   .60
RAYMOND, J.   2
    MEXICAN SUNDAY
        BOSTON MUSIC COMPANY   .50
RAYMOND, J.
    SOLITUDE FOR PIANO SOLO
        AMERICAN MUSIC EDITION   .50
RAYMOND, J.   3
    SUMMER
        BOSTON MUSIC COMPANY   .50
RAYMOND, J.   3
    WALTZ INTERLUDE
        BOSTON MUSIC COMPANY   .50
RAZIGADE
    ECOUTEZ CETTE HISTOIRE
        FRANCO COLOMBO PUBLICATIONS   SAL   1.50
REA
    LINNET, THE
        SUMMY-BIRCHARD COMPANY   .50
REA
    WOOD NYMPH'S HARP, THE
        SUMMY-BIRCHARD COMPANY   .50
READ, G.   3
    ANCIENT DANCE, AN
        BELWIN-MILLS PUBLISHING CORPORATION   .60
READ, G.
    DANCE OF THE LOCOMOTIVES, OP. 57
        SEESAW MUSIC CORPORATION   2.00
READ, G.   E
    DAY'S END
        THEODORE PRESSER COMPANY   .50
READ, G.   3
    LITTLE SOLDIERS, THE
        BELWIN-MILLS PUBLISHING CORPORATION   .60
READ, G.   2
    MARCH OF THE TIN SOLDIERS
        VOLKWEIN BROS.   .30
READ, G.   2
    OLD COURT DANCE, AN
        BELWIN-MILLS PUBLISHING CORPORATION   .60
READ, G.   2
    ON PARADE
        VOLKWEIN BROS.   .30
READ, G.   3
    POEME
        BELWIN-MILLS PUBLISHING CORPORATION   .60
READ, G.
    SONATA DA CHIESA FOR PIANO
        SEESAW MUSIC CORPORATION   5.00
READ, G.   4
    TALLY-HO
        BELWIN-MILLS PUBLISHING CORPORATION   .60
READ, G.
    THREE SATIRICAL SARCASMS
        SEESAW MUSIC CORPORATION   2.00
READ, G.
    TOUCH PIECE FOR PIANO
        SEESAW MUSIC CORPORATION   6.00
READ, G.   3
    TOY PARADE
        BELWIN-MILLS PUBLISHING CORPORATION   .60
READING, H.--ED   READING, H.
    ADESTE FIDELIS
        WILLIS MUSIC COMPANY   .30

REBE
    ALPINE SPINNING WHEEL
        BELWIN-MILLS PUBLISHING CORPORATION   .60
REBE   2
    CADET'S REVIEW, THE
        WILLIS MUSIC COMPANY   .35
REBE   WILLIAMS
    CASTANETS
        BOSTON MUSIC COMPANY   .50
REBE   2
    CINDERELLA DANCES
        THEODORE PRESSER COMPANY   .50
REBE
    CIRCUS RIDER, THE
        SUMMY-BIRCHARD COMPANY   .50
REBE   1
    COBBLER, COBBLER
        WILLIS MUSIC COMPANY   .35
REBE   3
    COSSACKS
        WILLIS MUSIC COMPANY   .40
REBE
    DANCING DAFFODILS
        WARNER BROTHERS PUBLISHERS   .60
REBE   3
    DANCING RAINDROPS
        WILLIS MUSIC COMPANY   .40
REBE   2
    DAPPLE GRAY
        THEODORE PRESSER COMPANY   .50
REBE   WILLIAMS, J.   4
    GAY VIENNA
        BOSTON MUSIC COMPANY   .60
REBE
    GREENSLEEVES
        SUMMY-BIRCHARD COMPANY   .50
REBE
    HEATHERED HILLS
        WARNER BROTHERS PUBLISHERS   .60
REBE   1
    HERE'S THE CHURCH
        THEODORE PRESSER COMPANY   .50
REBE   2
    HUSH BABY, MY DARLING
        VOLKWEIN BROS.   .30
REBE   2 1/2
    IN THE MOONLIGHT
        CENTURY MUSIC PUBLISHING COMPANY, INC.   040   .40
REBE   WILLIAMS, J.   1
    LET'S DANCE AND SING
        BOSTON MUSIC COMPANY   .50
REBE   2
    LITTLE BIRD
        VOLKWEIN BROS.   .30
REBE   WILLIAMS, J.   3
    MANTILLA
        BOSTON MUSIC COMPANY   .50
REBE   2
    MARCH OF THE CUB SCOUTS
        THEODORE PRESSER COMPANY   .50
REBE   WILLIAMS, J.   3
    POLISH PEASANTS
        BOSTON MUSIC COMPANY   .50
REBE   WILLIAMS, J.   2
    PONIES
        BOSTON MUSIC COMPANY   .50
REBE
    PRELUDE IN B MINOR
        BELWIN-MILLS PUBLISHING CORPORATION   .60
REBE   2
    SEE-SAW MARGERY DAW
        VOLKWEIN BROS.   .30
REBE   2
    SILVER BELLS
        CENTURY MUSIC PUBLISHING COMPANY, INC.   4117   .40
REBE   2
    SWAN ON THE MOONLIT LAKE
        WILLIS MUSIC COMPANY   .35
REBE   1
    SWING LOW, SWING HIGH
        BELWIN-MILLS PUBLISHING CORPORATION   .60
REBE   2
    TO HORSE AND AWAY
        VOLKWEIN BROS.   .30
REBE   1
    TO MARKET, TO MARKET
        VOLKWEIN BROS.   .30
REBE   2
    TOY CAROUSEL
        BOSTON MUSIC COMPANY   .50
REBE   2B
    TULIP TIME
        MUSICORD PUBLICATIONS, INC.   .45
REBER   3-4
    REMEMBRANCE
        CENTURY MUSIC PUBLISHING COMPANY, INC.   2340   .40
REBER   3-4
    ROMANCE SANS PAROLES
        CENTURY MUSIC PUBLISHING COMPANY, INC.   2340   .40
REBIKOV
    BEAR, PLAYING SOLDIERS, THE
        MCA MUSIC   .60
REBIKOV   PHILIPP, I.
    SILHOUETTES, OP. 31
        INTERNATIONAL MUSIC COMPANY   1.25
REBIKOV
    SOLDIERS PASS, THE
        FREDERICK HARRIS MUSIC COMPANY   .60
RECLI
    DANZA DEL BURATINO E DELLA BAMBOLA, LA
        FRANCO COLOMBO PUBLICATIONS   BON.2404 1.75
RECLI
    SOGNO DI NICOLETTA
        FRANCO COLOMBO PUBLICATIONS   BON.1995 1.00
REDDING, E.   3
    DISTANT PANORAMA
        BELWIN-MILLS PUBLISHING CORPORATION   .60
REED, D.
    MARCH OF THE GINGERBREAD MEN, OP. 12 NO. 1
        BELWIN-MILLS PUBLISHING CORPORATION   28064   .60
REED, H.   2
    AT THE BALL GAME, MARCH
        CENTURY MUSIC PUBLISHING COMPANY, INC.   1434   .40
REED, H.   2
    AT THE CIRCUS, GALOP
        CENTURY MUSIC PUBLISHING COMPANY, INC.   1435   .40

REED, H.   2
    CHASING SQUIRRELS, SCHOTTISCHE
        CENTURY MUSIC PUBLISHING COMPANY, INC. 1438   .40
REED, H.   2
    DANCE ON THE LAWN
        CENTURY MUSIC PUBLISHING COMPANY, INC. 1437   .40
REED, H.
    EL MUCHACHO
        BELWIN-MILLS PUBLISHING CORPORATION   20446   .60
REED, H.   SINGER
    GYPSY, THE
        MCA MUSIC
                                                            .60
REED, H.   2
    PONY RIDE, THE - WALTZ
        CENTURY MUSIC PUBLISHING COMPANY, INC. 1436   .40
REEG, G. A.   2
    DANCE OF THE DOLLS
        VOLKWEIN BROS.   .25
REEG, G. A.   4
    EMBLEM OF PEACE -- MARCH
        VOLKWEIN BROS.   .35
REEG, G. A.   4
    GOLDEN AUTUMN
        VOLKWEIN BROS.   .40
REEG, G. A.   4
    MELODY OF THE FLOWERS
        VOLKWEIN BROS.   .35
REEG, G. A.   4
    REFLECTIONS
        VOLKWEIN BROS.   .40
REEL   WEYBRIGHT   2 1/2
    IRISH WASHERWOMAN
        BELWIN-MILLS PUBLISHING CORPORATION   .60
REES   2
    MAJOLICA, POLKA
        CENTURY MUSIC PUBLISHING COMPANY, INC. 1987   .40
REES   2
    WATER LILIES, GAVOTTE
        CENTURY MUSIC PUBLISHING COMPANY, INC. 1939   .40
REEVES, R.   3 1/2
    BLUE MIST
        BELWIN-MILLS PUBLISHING CORPORATION   .60
REEVES, R.   2
    CALYPSO DANCE
        BELWIN-MILLS PUBLISHING CORPORATION   .60
REEVES, R.   2
    DANCING CLOCK
        BELWIN-MILLS PUBLISHING CORPORATION   .60
REEVES, R.   3
    IN ARPEGGIO LAND
        BELWIN-MILLS PUBLISHING CORPORATION   .60
REEVES, R.   2
    LITTLE SONATINA
        BELWIN-MILLS PUBLISHING CORPORATION   .60
REEVES, R.   2
    MIDWAY AT THE FAIR
        BELWIN-MILLS PUBLISHING CORPORATION   .60
REEVES, R.   3
    MOMENT ORIENTALE
        BELWIN-MILLS PUBLISHING CORPORATION   .60
REEVES, R.   3
    ON A TEXAS TRAIL
        BELWIN-MILLS PUBLISHING CORPORATION   .60
REEVES, R.   2
    PEASANT DANCE
        BELWIN-MILLS PUBLISHING CORPORATION   .60
REEVES, R.   2
    ROCK AND ROLL MELODY
        BELWIN-MILLS PUBLISHING CORPORATION   .60
REEVES, R.   1 1/2
    TOY PARADE
        BELWIN-MILLS PUBLISHING CORPORATION   .60
REEVES, R.   2 1/2
    WOODEN SHOE POLKA
        BELWIN-MILLS PUBLISHING CORPORATION   .60
REGER
    BUNTE BLATTER, OP. 36 - BK. 1
        UNIVERSAL EDITION   1199   2.25
REGER
    BUNTE BLATTER, OP. 36 - BK. 2
        UNIVERSAL EDITION   1200   2.25
REGER
    HUMORESQUE, OP. 79 NO. 2
        G. SCHIRMER, INC.   .40
REGER   D
    IMPROVISATION ON BLUE DANUBE
        C. F. PETERS CORPORATION   3950   3.50
REGER
    MOMENT MUSICAL, OP. 44 NO. 3
        UNIVERSAL EDITION   10963   .55
REGER   D
    MOZART VARIATIONS AND FUGUE, OP. 132
        C. F. PETERS CORPORATION   3975   3.50
REGER
    SIHOUETTES, OP. 53
        UNIVERSAL EDITION   1250   1.90
REGER
    SONATINA IN A MINOR, OP. 89 NO. 4
        ASSOCIATED MUSIC PUBLISHERS, INC.   BOT   3.00
REGER
    SONATINA IN D, OP. 89 NO. 2
        ASSOCIATED MUSIC PUBLISHERS, INC.   BOT   2.25
REGER
    SONATINA IN E MINOR, OP. 89 NO. 1
        ASSOCIATED MUSIC PUBLISHERS, INC.   BOT   2.00
REGER
    SONATINA IN F, OP. 89 NO. 3
        ASSOCIATED MUSIC PUBLISHERS, INC.   BOT   3.00
REGER   D
    TELEMANN VARIATIONS AND FUGUE, OP. 134
        C. F. PETERS CORPORATION   3979   2.50
REGER   M
    VALSE D'AMOUR, OP. 130 NO. 5
        C. F. PETERS CORPORATION   3388   .90
REGER
    VIRGIN'S SLUMBER SONG, THE, MARIA WIEGENLIED, OP. 76 NO. 52
        ASSOCIATED MUSIC PUBLISHERS, INC.   BOT   1.00
REGER   3
    WEIHNACHTSTRAUM, FANTASIE UBER, STILLE NACHT OP. 17 NO. 9,
    ST.-V.S. 29
        SCHOTT   1.25
REICH, J.
    MOSAIC--1967
        ASSOCIATED MUSIC PUBLISHERS, INC.   BER   2.50
REICH, M.   SCHAUM, J.   PREP
    PLAYFUL POODLE
        SCHAUM PUBLICATIONS, INC.   .50

REID   1
    BE HAPPY - BE LUCKY
        PRO-ART PUBLICATIONS, INC.   412   .50
REID   1-2
    CON AMORE
        PRO-ART PUBLICATIONS, INC.   449   .50
REID   1 1/2
    GET MOVING BOOGIE
        BELWIN-MILLS PUBLISHING CORPORATION   .60
REID   3 1/2
    LET'S GO BOOGIE
        BELWIN-MILLS PUBLISHING CORPORATION   .60
REID   2 1/2
    LOTS OF LUCK BOOGIE
        BELWIN-MILLS PUBLISHING CORPORATION   .60
REID   1
    OOM-PAH MARCH
        PRO-ART PUBLICATIONS, INC.   403   .50
REID   2 1/2
    PINCH A PENNY BOOGIE
        BELWIN-MILLS PUBLISHING CORPORATION   .60
REID   2
    PINK POODLE POLKA
        PRO-ART PUBLICATIONS, INC.   211   .50
REID   1
    RAIN IN THE NIGHT
        PRO-ART PUBLICATIONS, INC.   450   .50
REID   3
    SAO PAULO BOOGIE
        BELWIN-MILLS PUBLISHING CORPORATION   .60
REID   1
    SUMMER SNOW FLOWERS
        PRO-ART PUBLICATIONS, INC.   413   .50
REID--ED   REID   1
    JESUS LOVES ME, THIS I KNOW
        BELWIN-MILLS PUBLISHING CORPORATION   .60
REIF, P.
    SEVEN MUSICAL MOMENTS
        GENERAL MUSIC PUBLISHING COMPANY, INC.   3.00
REIN
    SONATINA IN B-FLAT
        FRANCO COLOMBO PUBLICATIONS   SIK.195   1.75
REINECKE   HUGHES
    CADENZA TO THE BEETHOVEN CONCERTO IN CM, OP. 37, FIRST
    MOVEMENT--OP. 87 NO. 3
        G. SCHIRMER, INC.   .70
REINECKE
    NOCTURNO IN A FLAT
        MUSICA OBSCURA   1.50
REINECKE   D
    SONATA FOR LEFT HAND ALONE, OP. 179
        C. F. PETERS CORPORATION   3314   2.50
REINER   3-4
    SONATA NO. 03
        BARENREITER VERLAG   AP 360
REINHOLD, H.
    HUNGARIAN DANCE
        G. SCHIRMER, INC.   .30
REINHOLD, H.   2
    HUNGARIAN DANCE
        WILLIS MUSIC COMPANY   .40
REINHOLD, H.
    IMPROMPTU IN C SHARP MINOR, OP. 28 NO. 3
        G. SCHIRMER, INC.   .70
REINHOLD, H.   7
    IMPROMPTU, OP. 28 NO. 3
        THEODORE PRESSER COMPANY   .70
REISER, V.   2
    BLUE BALLET
        PRO-ART PUBLICATIONS, INC.   260   .50
REISER, V.   2
    CARNIVAL
        PRO-ART PUBLICATIONS, INC.   611   .50
REISER, V.   1-2
    CATHEDRAL CHIMES
        PEER SOUTHERN ORGANIZATION   00.85
REISER, V.   2-3
    CHIT-CHAT
        CENTURY MUSIC PUBLISHING COMPANY, INC. 4185   .40
REISER, V.   3
    DANCING SHADOWS
        CENTURY MUSIC PUBLISHING COMPANY, INC. 4249   .40
REISER, V.   3
    DANCING SNOWFLAKES
        CENTURY MUSIC PUBLISHING COMPANY, INC. 4250   .40
REISER, V.   2
    ECHOES OF VIENNA
        BELWIN-MILLS PUBLISHING CORPORATION   .60
REISER, V.   2
    ENCHANTMENT
        WILLIS MUSIC COMPANY   .40
REISER, V.   2
    EVENING IN SEVILLE
        WILLIS MUSIC COMPANY   .40
REISER, V.   2-3
    FANCY FROLIC
        BOSTON MUSIC COMPANY   .50
REISER, V.   2
    GARDEN PARTY
        PRO-ART PUBLICATIONS, INC.   374   .50
REISER, V.   2
    GAY GYPSY
        CENTURY MUSIC PUBLISHING COMPANY, INC. 4381   .40
REISER, V.   1-2
    GIPSY REVELS
        VOLKWEIN BROS.   .35
REISER, V.   3
    GLOW WORM
        CENTURY MUSIC PUBLISHING COMPANY, INC. 4291   .40
REISER, V.   M
    GOSSIPS, THE
        BELWIN-MILLS PUBLISHING CORPORATION   .60
REISER, V.
    IMPROMPTU
        THEODORE PRESSER COMPANY   .75
REISER, V.
    IN A GYPSY TEA ROOM
        SAM FOX PUBLISHING COMPANY, INC.   .50
REISER, V.   2 1/2
    IN A GYPSY TEA ROOM
        SOUTHERN MUSIC COMPANY   .50
REISER, V.
    IN A SPANISH VILLAGE
        THEODORE PRESSER COMPANY   .50
REISER, V.   3
    IN GAY MADRID
        CENTURY MUSIC PUBLISHING COMPANY, INC. 4214   .40

REISER, V.　　　　　　　　　　　　　　　　2
　IN SUNNY SPAIN
　　WILLIS MUSIC COMPANY　　　　　　　　　　　　　　.60
REISER, V.　　　　　　　　　　　　　　　　2
　JOLLY JUGGLER, THE
　　WILLIS MUSIC COMPANY　　　　　　　　　　　　　　.40
REISER, V.　　　　　　　　　　　　　　　　1
　JUGGLER, THE
　　CENTURY MUSIC PUBLISHING COMPANY, INC.　4136　.40
REISER, V.
　KITTEN GAMES
　　CENTURY MUSIC PUBLISHING COMPANY, INC.　4215　.40
REISER, V.　　　　　　　　　　　　　　　　2
　LA DANZARINA
　　WILLIS MUSIC COMPANY　　　　　　　　　　　　　　.75
REISER, V.　　　　　　　　　　　　　　　　1-2
　MELODY OF LOVE
　　CENTURY MUSIC PUBLISHING COMPANY, INC.　4289　.40
REISER, V.　　　　　　　　　　　　　　　　2
　MERRYMAKERS
　　PRO-ART PUBLICATIONS, INC.　　　　　　612　.50
REISER, V.　　　　　　　　　　　　　　　　2
　MOONLIT MORNING
　　WILLIS MUSIC COMPANY　　　　　　　　　　　　　　.75
REISER, V.　　　　　　　　　　　　　　　　M
　MOTIVATION
　　THEODORE PRESSER COMPANY　　　　　　　　　　　　.60
REISER, V.　　　　　　　　　　　　EARLY ADVANCED
　NEW DAWN FANTASY
　　MUSICORD PUBLICATIONS, INC.　　　　　　　　　　　.60
REISER, V.　　　　　　　　　　　　　　　　1
　OLD ROCKING CHAIR, THE
　　CENTURY MUSIC PUBLISHING COMPANY, INC.　4135　.40
REISER, V.　　　　　　　　　　　　　　　　2
　PENGUIN PARADE, THE
　　CENTURY MUSIC PUBLISHING COMPANY, INC.　4338　.40
REISER, V.　　　　　　　　　　　　　　　　2-3
　PLANTATION PICNIC
　　PRO-ART PUBLICATIONS, INC.　　　　　　207　.50
REISER, V.　　　　　　　　　　　　　　　　1-2
　SILVER STREAMLETS
　　CENTURY MUSIC PUBLISHING COMPANY, INC.　4287　.40
REISER, V.　　　　　　　　　　　　　　　　2
　SPANISH SERENADE
　　WILLIS MUSIC COMPANY　　　　　　　　　　　　　　.40
REISER, V.　　　　　　　　　　　　　　　　3
　SPRING MOOD
　　CENTURY MUSIC PUBLISHING COMPANY, INC.　4266　.40
REISER, V.　　　　　　　　　　　　　　　　2
　SUMMER IN SICILY
　　WILLIS MUSIC COMPANY　　　　　　　　　　　　　　.40
REISER, V.　　　　　　　　　　　　　　　　2
　SWAYING PALMS
　　CENTURY MUSIC PUBLISHING COMPANY, INC.　4221　.40
REISER, V.　　　　　　　　　　　　　　　　2
　TINSEL TOES
　　WILLIS MUSIC COMPANY　　　　　　　　　　　　　　.60
REISER, V.　　　　　　　　　　　　　　　　1-2
　TO AND FRO - AND TO AGAIN
　　CENTURY MUSIC PUBLISHING COMPANY, INC.　4186　.40
REISER, V.　　　　　　　　　　　　　　　　2
　TOY SOLDIERS ON PARADE
　　BELWIN-MILLS PUBLISHING CORPORATION　　　　　　.60
REISER, V.　　　　　　　　　　　　　　　　3
　VALSE BLUETTE
　　PRO-ART PUBLICATIONS, INC.　　　　　　610　.50
REISER, V.
　VALSE ELEGANTE
　　SAM FOX PUBLISHING COMPANY, INC.　　　　　　　　.50
REISER, V.
　VALSE ELEGANTE
　　SOUTHERN MUSIC COMPANY　　　　　　　　　　　　　.50
REISER, V.　　　　　　　　　　　　　　　　1 1/2
　WALTZING WILLOWS
　　VOLKWEIN BROS.　　　　　　　　　　　　　　　　　.35
REISER, V.　　　　　　　　　　　　　　　　2-3
　WHIRLPOOL
　　PRO-ART PUBLICATIONS, INC.　　　　　　366　.50
REISFELD　　　　　　　　　　　　　　　　　M
　COBBLESTONES
　　THEODORE PRESSER COMPANY　　　　　　　　　　　1.00
REISFELD　　　　　　　　　　　　　　　　　3
　LA CHUPADERO, RHUMBA
　　CENTURY MUSIC PUBLISHING COMPANY, INC.　3980　.40
REISFELD　　　　　　　　　　　　　　　　　3
　LA MANO ABAJO, CONGA
　　CENTURY MUSIC PUBLISHING COMPANY, INC.　3980　.40
REISFELD　　　　　　　　　　　　　　　　　2
　NOBODY KNOWS DE TROUBLE I'VE SEEN
　　CENTURY MUSIC PUBLISHING COMPANY, INC.　3831　.40
REISFELD　　　　　　　　　　　　　　　　　M
　NOCTURNE ON THE PRAIRIE
　　THEODORE PRESSER COMPANY　　　　　　　　　　　　.50
REISFELD　　　　　　　　　　　　　　　　　3
　RHUMBA, LA CHUPADERO
　　CENTURY MUSIC PUBLISHING COMPANY, INC.　3980　.40
REISFELD　　　　　　　　　　　　　　　　　M
　VARIATIONS IN SEARCH OF A THEME
　　THEODORE PRESSER COMPANY　　　　　　　　　　　　.60
REISFELD--ED　　　　　　REISFELD　　　　　　2
　DEEP RIVER
　　CENTURY MUSIC PUBLISHING COMPANY, INC.　3830　.40
REISFELD--ED　　　　　　REISFELD　　　　　　2
　ROLL, JORDAN, ROLL
　　CENTURY MUSIC PUBLISHING COMPANY, INC.　3832　.40
REISFELD--ED　　　　　　REISFELD　　　　　　2
　STANDIN' IN THE NEED OF PRAYER
　　CENTURY MUSIC PUBLISHING COMPANY, INC.　3835　.40
REISINGER, O.
　TINGLE-TANGLE
　　BELWIN-MILLS PUBLISHING CORPORATION　20312　.85
REISSIGER
　DANSE DES ELFES, OP. 18
　　BANKS AND SON LTD.　　　　　　　　　　　　　　　.40
REISTRUP, J.　　　　　　　　　　　　　　　M
　EPISODE OF THE TOAD
　　COMPOSERS PRESS, INC.　　　　　　　　　　　　　1.00
REISTRUP, J.　　　　　　　　　　　　　　　M
　ETUDE
　　COMPOSERS PRESS, INC.　　　　　　　　　　　　　1.00
REISTRUP, J.　　　　　　　　　　　　　　　M
　FIELD MOUSE
　　COMPOSERS PRESS, INC.　　　　　　　　　　　　　1.50
REISTRUP, J.　　　　　　　　　　　　　　　M
　FLOATING
　　COMPOSERS PRESS, INC.　　　　　　　　　　　　　1.00

REISTRUP, J.　　　　　　　　　　　　　　　M
　MOLE, THE
　　COMPOSERS PRESS, INC.　　　　　　　　　　　　　1.50
REISTRUP, J.　　　　　　　　　　　　　　　M-D
　SOARING
　　COMPOSERS PRESS, INC.　　　　　　　　　　　　　2.00
REISTRUP, J.　　　　　　　　　　　　　　　E
　SUNDAY MORNING
　　COMPOSERS PRESS, INC.　　　　　　　　　　　　　1.00
REISTRUP, J.　　　　　　　　　　　　　　　M
　TO THE SWALLOW
　　COMPOSERS PRESS, INC.　　　　　　　　　　　　　1.00
REISTRUP, J.　　　　　　　　　　　　　　　M
　TOMMELISE'S SONG
　　COMPOSERS PRESS, INC.　　　　　　　　　　　　　1.00
REISTRUP, J.　　　　　　　　　　　　　　　M-D
　WITH THE BEETLES
　　COMPOSERS PRESS, INC.　　　　　　　　　　　　　1.50
REITER, A.
　SONATINA
　　ASSOCIATED MUSIC PUBLISHERS, INC.　　DOB　1.50
REIZENSTEIN, F.　　　　　　　　　　　　　M
　STUDY IN IRREGULAR RHYTHM
　　OXFORD UNIVERSITY PRESS　　　　　　33.060　1.20
REIZENSTEIN, F.
　SUITE
　　BOOSEY AND HAWKES, INC.　　　　　　　　　　　3.25
REIZENSTEIN, F.
　ZODIAN
　　MCA MUSIC　　　　　　　　　　　　　　　　　　2.50
RENARD, P.　　　　　　　　　　　　　　　　3 1/2
　IRIS -- INTERMEZZO
　　THEODORE PRESSER COMPANY　　　　　　　　　　　　.60
RENDANO　　　　　　　　　　　　　　　　　3-4
　CHANT DU PAYSEN
　　CENTURY MUSIC PUBLISHING COMPANY, INC.　2552　.40
RENDANO　　　　　　　　　　　　　　　　　3-4
　PEASANT'S SONG
　　CENTURY MUSIC PUBLISHING COMPANY, INC.　2552　.40
RENNARD　　　　　　　　　　　　　　　　　1
　BABY'S LULLABY
　　CENTURY MUSIC PUBLISHING COMPANY, INC.　4237　.40
RENNARD　　　　　　　　　　　　　　　　　1
　DAINTY LITTLE MISS
　　CENTURY MUSIC PUBLISHING COMPANY, INC.　4307　.40
RENNARD　　　　　　　　　　　　　　　　　2
　EVENING MIST
　　CENTURY MUSIC PUBLISHING COMPANY, INC.　4364　.40
RENNARD　　　　　　　　　　　　　　　　　1
　FOLLOW THE LEADER
　　CENTURY MUSIC PUBLISHING COMPANY, INC.　4365　.40
RENNARD　　　　　　　　　　　　　　　　　1
　FUN IN THE SNOW - OPTIONAL 2ND PIANO PART
　　BOSTON MUSIC COMPANY　　　　　　　　　　　　　.50
RENNARD　　　　　　　　　　　　　　　　　2
　GAY DANCE
　　BOSTON MUSIC COMPANY　　　　　　　　　　　　　.50
RENNARD　　　　　　　　　　　　　　　　　1
　HAPPY COWBOY
　　BOSTON MUSIC COMPANY　　　　　　　　　　　　　.50
RENNARD　　　　　　　　　　　　　　　　　2 1/2
　HUMMINGBIRD, THE
　　WILLIS MUSIC COMPANY　　　　　　　　　　　　　.40
RENNARD　　　　　　　　　　　　　　　　　2
　MODERN MUSIC BOX
　　BOSTON MUSIC COMPANY　　　　　　　　　　　　　.50
RENNARD　　　　　　　　　　　　　　　　　1
　ON A BRIGHT SPRING MORN
　　CENTURY MUSIC PUBLISHING COMPANY, INC.　4404　.40
RENNARD　　　　　　　　　　　　　　　　　1
　RAIN CLOUDS AND SUNSHINE
　　BOSTON MUSIC COMPANY　　　　　　　　　　　　　.50
RENNARD　　　　　　　　　　　　　　　　　1
　SHADOWS ON THE WALL
　　CENTURY MUSIC PUBLISHING COMPANY, INC.　4269　.40
RENNARD　　　　　　　　　　　　　　　　　2
　SUMMER ROMANCE
　　BOSTON MUSIC COMPANY　　　　　　　　　　　　　.50
RENNICK, E.
　MERRILY WE PLAY AND SING
　　BELWIN-MILLS PUBLISHING CORPORATION　11294　1.00
RENNICK, E.
　MERRILY WE PLAY AND SWAY
　　BELWIN-MILLS PUBLISHING CORPORATION　11295　1.00
RENTON, V.　　　　　　　　　　　　　　　　3
　MARCH OF THE CANDY DOLLS
　　THEODORE PRESSER COMPANY　　　　　　　　　　　.50
RENTON, V.　　　　　　　　　　　　　　　　3 1/2
　STAR SAPPHIRES
　　THEODORE PRESSER COMPANY　　　　　　　　　　　.60
RENZI
　SONATINA IN TRE DIVERTIMENTI
　　FRANCO COLOMBO PUBLICATIONS　　　　　DS700　2.75
RESPIGHI
　CANON
　　FRANCO COLOMBO PUBLICATIONS　　　　BON.184　1.00
RESPIGHI
　ETUDE
　　FRANCO COLOMBO PUBLICATIONS　　　　BON.187　1.00
RESPIGHI
　MINUETTO
　　FRANCO COLOMBO PUBLICATIONS　　　　BON.186　1.00
RESPIGHI
　NOCTURNE
　　FRANCO COLOMBO PUBLICATIONS　　　　BON.185　1.00
RESPIGHI
　NOTTURNO
　　G. SCHIRMER, INC.　　　　　　　　　　　　　　.50
RESPIGHI
　RE ENZO - INTERMEZZO
　　FRANCO COLOMBO PUBLICATIONS　　　　BON.235　1.00
RESPIGHI　　　　　　　　　　ZUCCOLI
　UCCELLI, GLI -- THE BIRDS --
　　FRANCO COLOMBO PUBLICATIONS　　　　129891　3.50
RESPIGHI
　VALSE CARESSANTE
　　FRANCO COLOMBO PUBLICATIONS　　　　BON.183　1.00
RETI, R.
　TRAUME, LIEBE, TANZE, OP. 4
　　UNIVERSAL EDITION　　　　　　　　　UE 7237　2.15
REYNA
　SIEMPRE FLOR
　　FRANCO COLOMBO PUBLICATIONS　　　　SAL　1.50
REYNALD, G.　　　　　　　　　　　　　　　4
　FOUNTAIN, OP. 6 NO. 1
　　CENTURY MUSIC PUBLISHING COMPANY, INC.　221　.40

REYNALD, G.
PEARLY DEW, OP. 6 NO. 3
     G. SCHIRMER, INC.   .35
REYNARD
BOWL OF PANSIES
     SAM FOX PUBLISHING COMPANY, INC.   .75
REYNARD
BOWL OF PANSIES
     SOUTHERN MUSIC COMPANY   .75
REYNOLDS   D
EPIGRAMS AND EVOLUTION
     C. F. PETERS CORPORATION   6618   2.00
REZNICEK
DONNA DIANA, OVERTURE
     UNIVERSAL EDITION   UE 9407   1.50
RHEINHOLD, H.
IMPROMPTU IN C SHARP MINOR, OP. 28 NO. 3
     CARL FISCHER, INC.   S 703   .75
RHENE-BATON
ALBUM ROSE, EASY LITTLE PIECES, NO. 1--PETITE MELODIE
     ASSOCIATED MUSIC PUBLISHERS, INC.   ESC   .75
RHENE-BATON
ALBUM ROSE, EASY LITTLE PIECES, NO. 2--BLUETTE
     ASSOCIATED MUSIC PUBLISHERS, INC.   ESC   .75
RHENE-BATON
ALBUM ROSE, EASY LITTLE PIECES, NO. 3--INTERMEZZO
     ASSOCIATED MUSIC PUBLISHERS, INC.   ESC   .75
RHENE-BATON
ALBUM ROSE, EASY LITTLE PIECES, NO. 4--PETIT CHORAL
     ASSOCIATED MUSIC PUBLISHERS, INC.   ESC   .75
RHENE-BATON
ALBUM ROSE, EASY LITTLE PIECES, NO. 5--VIEILLE ROMANCE
     ASSOCIATED MUSIC PUBLISHERS, INC.   ESC   .75
RHENE-BATON
ALBUM ROSE, EASY LITTLE PIECES, NO. 6--MUSETTE
     ASSOCIATED MUSIC PUBLISHERS, INC.   ESC   .75
RHENE-BATON
FILEUSES PRES DE CARANTEC, OP. 13 NO. 5
     ELKAN-VOGEL, INC.   D   2.10
RHENE-BATON
PRELUDE IN D MINOR
     ASSOCIATED MUSIC PUBLISHERS, INC.   ESC   1.50
RIBARI, A.
ALL ANTICA - SUITE
     GENERAL MUSIC PUBLISHING COMPANY, INC.   516   3.00
RIBARI, A.
ALL' ANTICA - SUITE
     GENERAL MUSIC PUBLISHING COMPANY, INC.   3.00
RIBARI, A.
SONATA
     GENERAL MUSIC PUBLISHING COMPANY, INC.   4.00
RIBAULT, A.
BADINERIE
     ELKAN-VOGEL, INC.   CON   1.25
RIBERT, J.   3 1/2
DAWN IN NORMANDY
     THEODORE PRESSER COMPANY   .50
RICCARDI, J.   2
LITTLE PRELUDE
     THEODORE PRESSER COMPANY   .50
RICCARDI, J.
LONELY SWAN
     ELKAN-VOGEL, INC.   .50
RICCARDI, J.
PLAYFUL KITTEN
     ELKAN-VOGEL, INC.   .50
RICCARDI, J.   2
RECESS TIME
     THEODORE PRESSER COMPANY   .50
RICCI, F. R.
CANZONETTA
     FREDERICK HARRIS MUSIC COMPANY   .60
RICE *   KERR, R.N.
I DON'T KNOW HOW TO LOVE HIM
     MCA MUSIC   1.00
RICE *   AGAY, D.
JESUS CHRIST SUPERSTAR
     MCA MUSIC   1.50
RICHARDS
ALLA SERA
     FRANCO COLOMBO PUBLICATIONS   FOR.10719   .50
RICHARDS, B.   1
GOLDEN SUNSET WALTZ -- SOLO - DUET
     VOLKWEIN BROS.   .25
RICHARDS, B.   2
O COME ALL FAITHFUL -- SANTA CLAUS
     VOLKWEIN BROS.   .30
RICHARDS, B.   2
SANTA CLAUS MARCH AND O COME ALL
     VOLKWEIN BROS.   .25
RICHARDS, B.   1
SILVER MOONBEAMS -- SOLO OR DUET
     VOLKWEIN BROS.   .25
RICHARDS, B.   4
WARBLINGS AT EVE
     CENTURY MUSIC PUBLISHING COMPANY, INC.   665   .40
RICHARDS, S.
SEA SHANTIES
     BANKS AND SON LTD.   .80
RICHARDSON
ACROSS THE BORDER
     FRANCO COLOMBO PUBLICATIONS   LD420   .60
RICHARDSON
PENDULUM, THE
     FRANCO COLOMBO PUBLICATIONS   LD419   .60
RICHARDSON, A.
RUNNING OFF THE RAILS --A LOCO-MOTIF
     MCA MUSIC   1.00
RICHARDSON, A.   2-3
TOY MARCH
     CENTURY MUSIC PUBLISHING COMPANY, INC.   4216   .40
RICHARDSON, C.
BEACHCOMBER
     BOOSEY AND HAWKES, INC.   .60
RICHARDSON, G. D.   4
DANCE OF THE PINK PETALS
     THEODORE PRESSER COMPANY   .50
RICHARDSON, W. H.
HARLEQUIN
     BANKS AND SON LTD.   .55
RICHARDSON, W. H.
MISS MODERN
     BANKS AND SON LTD.   .55
RICHARTZ   3
ALTD. WIEGENLIED, OP. 66
     SCHOTT   2889   1.50

RICHARTZ   3
FRUHLING AN DER BERGSTRASSE, OP. 72
     SCHOTT   2839   1.50
RICHARTZ   3
GALANTE GAVOTTE, OP. 43
     SCHOTT   2880   1.50
RICHARTZ   3
KLEINES MENUETT
     SCHOTT   2677   1.25
RICHARTZ
TWO LITTLE PIECES
     FRANCO COLOMBO PUBLICATIONS   SIK.370   1.50
RICHMAN, A.   2
CLOWNING
     THEODORE PRESSER COMPANY   .50
RICHMAN, A.   2
CRICKET, THE
     CENTURY MUSIC PUBLISHING COMPANY, INC.   4398   .40
RICHMAN, A.   2
FROM A WINDOW
     THEODORE PRESSER COMPANY   .50
RICHMAN, A.   2
MAGIC LAMP, THE
     THEODORE PRESSER COMPANY   .50
RICHMAN, A.   1
MEADOW LARK, THE
     BELWIN-MILLS PUBLISHING CORPORATION   .60
RICHMAN, A.   2
MISTER POSSUM
     THEODORE PRESSER COMPANY   .50
RICHMAN, A.
MULE, THE
     BRODT MUSIC COMPANY   .45
RICHMAN, A.   1
PEPPERMINT STICK
     PRO-ART PUBLICATIONS, INC.   333   .50
RICHMAN, A.   2
PICCOLO, THE
     PRO-ART PUBLICATIONS, INC.   312   .50
RICHMAN, A.   2
PRIMROSE, THE
     THEODORE PRESSER COMPANY   .50
RICHMAN, A.   2
PRIMROSE, THE
     THEODORE PRESSER COMPANY   .50
RICHMAN, A.
PRISM
     G. SCHIRMER, INC.   .35
RICHMAN, A.   3
RELUCTANT BALLERINA
     BOSTON MUSIC COMPANY   .50
RICHMAN, A.
STATELY DANCE
     G. SCHIRMER, INC.   .40
RICHMOND
DANCE OF THE HONEYBEES
     EDWARD B. MARKS MUSIC CORPORATION   01.00
RICHTER   2
AIRPLANE RIDE, AN, D MAJOR
     CENTURY MUSIC PUBLISHING COMPANY, INC.   3165   .40
RICHTER   1
ALL ABOARD, G MAJOR
     CENTURY MUSIC PUBLISHING COMPANY, INC.   3158   .40
RICHTER   2
AT THE BARBER SHOP
     ELKAN-VOGEL, INC.   .50
RICHTER   2
BOUNCE THE BALL
     CENTURY MUSIC PUBLISHING COMPANY, INC.   3166   .40
RICHTER   2
BUSY LITTLE BEE
     CENTURY MUSIC PUBLISHING COMPANY, INC.   3168   .40
RICHTER
CHEER-UP
     CARL FISCHER, INC.   P 2388   .50
RICHTER
CLOCK, THE--WITH WORDS
     G. SCHIRMER, INC.   .35
RICHTER   2
DREAM OF LITTLE BOY BLUE
     CENTURY MUSIC PUBLISHING COMPANY, INC.   3449   .40
RICHTER   1-2
EASIER THAN EASY
     ELKAN-VOGEL, INC.   1.00
RICHTER   2
ELEPHANT'S TRUNK, THE
     CENTURY MUSIC PUBLISHING COMPANY, INC.   345 0   .40
RICHTER   1-2
FERRIS WHEEL, THE
     ELKAN-VOGEL, INC.   .50
RICHTER
FOOTSTEPS
     BOOSEY AND HAWKES, INC.   .35
RICHTER   2
GUESS WHO
     CENTURY MUSIC PUBLISHING COMPANY, INC.   3160   .40
RICHTER   2
HIKING
     CENTURY MUSIC PUBLISHING COMPANY, INC.   3451   .40
RICHTER
HURDY GURDY
     BOOSEY AND HAWKES, INC.   .35
RICHTER   2
IMP IN THE CLOCK
     CENTURY MUSIC PUBLISHING COMPANY, INC.   3163   .40
RICHTER
IN A FIELD OF DAISIES
     WARNER BROTHERS PUBLISHERS   .60
RICHTER   1
IN MY ROCKING CHAIR
     BOSTON MUSIC COMPANY   .50
RICHTER   2
INDIAN BOY
     CENTURY MUSIC PUBLISHING COMPANY, INC.   3452   .40
RICHTER   1
IT'S RAINING
     BOSTON MUSIC COMPANY   .50
RICHTER   2
JOLLY SANTA CLAUS
     CENTURY MUSIC PUBLISHING COMPANY, INC.   3159   .40
RICHTER   2
JUMPING ROPE
     CENTURY MUSIC PUBLISHING COMPANY, INC.   3162   .40
RICHTER
LITTLE PENGUIN
     BOOSEY AND HAWKES, INC.   .25

RICHTER
    LITTLE SONG
        BOOSEY AND HAWKES, INC.   .35
RICHTER
    MARCH OF THE CRUSADERS
        BOOSEY AND HAWKES, INC.   .35
RICHTER
    MISTER BUFFALO
        BOOSEY AND HAWKES, INC.   .25
RICHTER
    MISTER HIPPO'S BIG MOUTH
        BOOSEY AND HAWKES, INC.   .25
RICHTER
    MONKEY CHATTER
        BOOSEY AND HAWKES, INC.   .25
RICHTER   2
    MOTORCYCLE RIDE
        BOSTON MUSIC COMPANY   .50
RICHTER   2
    MR. THIRD TAKES A WALK
        CENTURY MUSIC PUBLISHING COMPANY, INC. 3 164 .40
RICHTER
    ON A TRAPEZE
        BELWIN-MILLS PUBLISHING CORPORATION   .60
RICHTER   2
    ON THE MERRY-GO-ROUND
        CENTURY MUSIC PUBLISHING COMPANY, INC. 34 53 .40
RICHTER   1
    OUR SCHOOL BAND
        BOSTON MUSIC COMPANY   .50
RICHTER   2
    PLAYFUL ECHO, THE
        CENTURY MUSIC PUBLISHING COMPANY, INC. 3454 .40
RICHTER   1
    PRANCING PONY
        BOSTON MUSIC COMPANY   .50
RICHTER   2
    PUSSY WILLOW
        CENTURY MUSIC PUBLISHING COMPANY, INC. 3169 .40
RICHTER   2
    RIDDLE, A
        CENTURY MUSIC PUBLISHING COMPANY, INC. 3455 .40
RICHTER   2
    ROBIN'S SONG, THE
        CENTURY MUSIC PUBLISHING COMPANY, INC. 3456 .40
RICHTER   2
    SAIL ON LITTLE BOAT
        CENTURY MUSIC PUBLISHING COMPANY, INC. 3161 .40
RICHTER   2
    SCHOOL BELL
        CENTURY MUSIC PUBLISHING COMPANY, INC. 3167 .40
RICHTER   2
    SEE SAW
        CENTURY MUSIC PUBLISHING COMPANY, INC. 3457 .40
RICHTER   2
    SNOWFLAKE'S STORY. THE
        CENTURY MUSIC PUBLISHING COMPANY, INC. 3 458 .40
RICHTER
    THREE BLIND MICE
        WARNER BROTHERS PUBLISHERS   .60
RICHTER   1-2
    TRAFFIC COP, THE
        ELKAN-VOGEL, INC.   .50
RICHTER
    TROTTING
        BOOSEY AND HAWKES, INC.   .35
RICHTER   1
    WHEN MY BIRTHDAY COMES
        CENTURY MUSIC PUBLISHING COMPANY, INC. 3 459 .40
RICHTER   2
    WOODPECKER, THE
        CENTURY MUSIC PUBLISHING COMPANY, INC. 3460 .40
RICHTER, A.   2
    AND THE BAND PLAYED ON
        THEODORE PRESSER COMPANY   .50
RICHTER, A.
    AWAY IN A MANGER
        THEODORE PRESSER COMPANY   .50
RICHTER, A.   2
    BABY MOUSE
        FRANCO COLOMBO PUBLICATIONS   NY1471 .30
RICHTER, A.
    CATERPILLAR RIDE
        THEODORE PRESSER COMPANY   .50
RICHTER, A.
    CHRISTMAS TREE
        THEODORE PRESSER COMPANY   .50
RICHTER, A.
    CINDERELLA
        THEODORE PRESSER COMPANY   1.25
RICHTER, A.   2
    COWBOY ON THE TRAIL
        THEODORE PRESSER COMPANY   .50
RICHTER, A.
    FIRST CHRISTMAS - A STORY WITH MUSIC
        THEODORE PRESSER COMPANY   1.25
RICHTER, A.
    FIRST EASTER - A STORY WITH MUSIC
        THEODORE PRESSER COMPANY   1.00
RICHTER, A.
    HARE AND THE TORTOISE - A STORY WITH MUSIC
        THEODORE PRESSER COMPANY   1.25
RICHTER, A.   1 1/2
    IN A SAILBOAT
        THEODORE PRESSER COMPANY   .50
RICHTER, A.   1 1/2
    IN MY AIRPLANE
        THEODORE PRESSER COMPANY   .50
RICHTER, A.   1 1/2
    INDIAN MEDICINE MAN
        THEODORE PRESSER COMPANY   .50
RICHTER, A.
    JACK AND THE BEANSTALK - A STORY WITH MUSIC
        THEODORE PRESSER COMPANY   1.25
RICHTER, A.   1 1/2
    JINGLE BELLS FROM THE THREE CHRISTMAS SONGS
        THEODORE PRESSER COMPANY   .50
RICHTER, A.   1 1/2
    JOLLY OLD SAINT NICHOLAS FROM THE THREE CHRISTMAS SONGS
        THEODORE PRESSER COMPANY   .50
RICHTER, A.   1 1/2
    JOY TO THE WORLD FROM THE THREE YULETIDE MELODIES
        THEODORE PRESSER COMPANY   .50
RICHTER, A.
    LION AND THE MOUSE, THE - A STORY WITH MUSIC
        THEODORE PRESSER COMPANY   1.25

RICHTER, A.   1
    LITTLE PET DUCK
        THEODORE PRESSER COMPANY   .50
RICHTER, A.
    MARCH OF THE TELEVISION PUPPETS
        FRANCO COLOMBO PUBLICATIONS   NY1472 .35
RICHTER, A.
    MORE STUNTS
        THEODORE PRESSER COMPANY   1.25
RICHTER, A.
    MY FIRST SONG BOOK
        THEODORE PRESSER COMPANY   1.25
RICHTER, A.   1
    MY FIRST TOYS -- ROY POLY, AIRPLANE, DRUM
        THEODORE PRESSER COMPANY   .50
RICHTER, A.   1 1/2
    MY POPGUN
        THEODORE PRESSER COMPANY   .50
RICHTER, A.   2
    NIBBLE MOUSE
        THEODORE PRESSER COMPANY   .50
RICHTER, A.   1 1/2
    OLD CHRISTMAS TREE
        THEODORE PRESSER COMPANY   .50
RICHTER, A.   1 1/2
    ON A DOUBLE-DECKER BUS
        THEODORE PRESSER COMPANY   .50
RICHTER, A.
    ON A TRAPEZE
        FRANCO COLOMBO PUBLICATIONS   NY1469 .30
RICHTER, A.   2
    ORGAN GRINDER MAN
        THEODORE PRESSER COMPANY   .50
RICHTER, A.
    PETER RABBIT - A STORY WITH MUSIC
        THEODORE PRESSER COMPANY   1.25
RICHTER, A.   2 1/2
    REVELRY
        THEODORE PRESSER COMPANY   .50
RICHTER, A.   1
    RIDDLE, A
        THEODORE PRESSER COMPANY   .50
RICHTER, A.   2 1/2
    SILENT NIGHT
        THEODORE PRESSER COMPANY   .50
RICHTER, A.   2
    SLEEP-A-LOT LAND
        THEODORE PRESSER COMPANY   .50
RICHTER, A.   1
    STEP CAREFULLY
        THEODORE PRESSER COMPANY   .50
RICHTER, A.
    STUNTS FOR PIANO
        THEODORE PRESSER COMPANY   1.25
RICHTER, A.
    THREE LITTLE PIGS - A STORY WITH MUSIC
        THEODORE PRESSER COMPANY   1.25
RICHTER, A.   1
    WAKE UP
        THEODORE PRESSER COMPANY   .50
RICHTER, A.   3 1/2
    WALTZ FOR A BALLERINA
        THEODORE PRESSER COMPANY   .50
RICHTER, A.
    WALTZING BEAR, THE
        FRANCO COLOMBO PUBLICATIONS   NY1470 .30
RICHTER, A.   1 1/2
    WHY DAISIES DANCE
        THEODORE PRESSER COMPANY   .50
RICKER   1-2
    AARDY THE AARDVARK
        PRO-ART PUBLICATIONS, INC.   345 .50
RICKER   2-3
    AT THE CONCERT HALL
        PRO-ART PUBLICATIONS, INC.   389 .50
RICKER   2
    DANCE OF THE DOLLS
        PRO-ART PUBLICATIONS, INC.   281 .50
RICKER   3-4
    DREAM DANCE
        PRO-ART PUBLICATIONS, INC.   300 .50
RICKER   1-2
    DRESS PARADE
        PRO-ART PUBLICATIONS, INC.   390 .50
RICKEP   1
    HAPPY SONG
        PRO-ART PUBLICATIONS, INC.   388 .50
RICKER   1
    HOPSCOTCH
        PRO-ART PUBLICATIONS, INC.   294 .50
RICKER   2-3
    MARCH OF THE MARTIANS
        PRO-ART PUBLICATIONS, INC.   391 .50
RICKER   2-3
    PETITE GYPSY DANCE
        PRO-ART PUBLICATIONS, INC.   305 .50
RICKER, E.   1
    ANIMAL LAND -- SQUIRRELS, LITTLE MOUNTAIN BURRO, ELEPHANTS
        LEE ROBERTS MUSIC PUBLICATIONS, INC.   .85
RICKER, E.   1
    DISTANT BELL AND DESERTED COTTAGE, A
        LEE ROBERTS MUSIC PUBLICATIONS, INC.   .85
RICKER, E.   2
    DUTCH DANCE
        THEODORE PRESSER COMPANY   .50
RICKER, E.   3
    ESCAPE TO SHERWOOD
        LEE ROBERTS MUSIC PUBLICATIONS, INC.   .50
RICKER, E.   2
    GHOSTS ON THE STAIRS
        LEE ROBERTS MUSIC PUBLICATIONS, INC.   .50
RICKER, E.   3
    HERO'S MARCH
        LEE ROBERTS MUSIC PUBLICATIONS, INC.   .50
RICKER, E.   1
    IN A PARADE
        BELWIN-MILLS PUBLISHING CORPORATION   .60
RICKER, E.   2
    LEGEND OF AN ANCIENT LAND
        LEE ROBERTS MUSIC PUBLICATIONS, INC.   .85
RICKER, E.   1
    LITTLE ROGUISH CLOWN
        LEE ROBERTS MUSIC PUBLICATIONS, INC.   .50
RICKER, E.   2
    LONESOME PRAIRIE, THE
        LEE ROBERTS MUSIC PUBLICATIONS, INC.   .50

RICKER, E.   2
  LULLABY
    BOSTON MUSIC COMPANY   .50
RICKER, E.   3
  OLD VALENTINE, AN
    BELWIN-MILLS PUBLISHING CORPORATION   .60
RICKER, E.   1
  OVER THE FENCE IS OUT
    BELWIN-MILLS PUBLISHING CORPORATION   .60
RICKER, E.   1
  PHANTOM RIDER, THE
    BOSTON MUSIC COMPANY   .50
RICKER, E.   1
  SADDLE SONG
    LEE ROBERTS MUSIC PUBLICATIONS, INC.   .50
RICKER, E.   2
  SHEPHERD'S FLUTE, A
    LEE ROBERTS MUSIC PUBLICATIONS, INC.   .50
RICKMAN   2-3
  GNOME IN THE METRONOME, THE
    PRO-ART PUBLICATIONS, INC.   280   .50
RIDDLE
  PROFILES IN COURAGE --THEME
    EDWARD B. MARKS MUSIC CORPORATION   01.00
RIDDLE, N.
  THEME FROM 'THE UNTOUCHABLES'
    FRANK MUSIC CORPORATION   .95
RIDLEY, S. C.
  MODEST VIOLET
    BANKS AND SON LTD.   .25
RIDLEY, S. C.
  SWEET WILLIAM
    BANKS AND SON LTD.   .25
RIEGGER, W.
  FOUR TONE PICTURES FOR PIANO SOLO
    AMERICAN MUSIC EDITION   1.00
RIEGGER, W.
  NEW AND OLD
    BOOSEY AND HAWKES, INC.   3.00
RIEGGER, W.
  NEW DANCE
    ASSOCIATED MUSIC PUBLISHERS, INC.   AMP   .75
RIEGGER, W.   M
  PETITE ETUDE
    THEODORE PRESSER COMPANY   .50
RIEGGER, W.
  TOCCATA, FROM 'NEW AND OLD'
    BOOSEY AND HAWKES, INC.   .75
RIEMANN, A.
  SONATA NO. 01--1958
    ASSOCIATED MUSIC PUBLISHERS, INC.   BOT   3.75
RIEMANN, A.
  SPEKTREN FUR KLAVIER
    SCHOTT   AV 31
RIEMANN, A.
  STOFFRESTE -- BALLET IN ONE ACT
    ASSOCIATED MUSIC PUBLISHERS, INC.   BOT   7.50
RIESCO, C.
  SEMBLANZAS CHILENAS
    EDITORIAL COOPERATIVA INTER-AMERICANA   00.95
RIETI
  ARABESQUE
    FRANCO COLOMBO PUBLICATIONS   BON.1392   1.00
RIETI
  BRICCIOLE
    FRANCO COLOMBO PUBLICATIONS   BON.1394   1.00
RIETI
  CANON - VALSETTE
    GENERAL MUSIC PUBLISHING COMPANY, INC.   29   .60
RIETI
  CANON-VALSETTE - FROM FIVE PIECES FOR YOUNG PIANISTS
    GENERAL MUSIC PUBLISHING COMPANY, INC.   .75
RIETI
  CONTRASTS
    GENERAL MUSIC PUBLISHING COMPANY, INC.   279   2.50
RIETI
  CONTRASTS FOR PIANO
    GENERAL MUSIC PUBLISHING COMPANY, INC.   3.00
RIETI
  FIVE PIECES FOR YOUNG PIANISTS -- 1. PRELUDE
    NOVELLO AND COMPANY, LTD.   .75
RIETI
  FIVE PIECES FOR YOUNG PIANISTS -- 2. CANON
    NOVELLO AND COMPANY, LTD.   1.00
RIETI
  FIVE PIECES FOR YOUNG PIANISTS -- 3. VALSETTE
    NOVELLO AND COMPANY, LTD.   1.00
RIETI
  FIVE PIECES FOR YOUNG PIANISTS -- 4. TARANTELLA
    NOVELLO AND COMPANY, LTD.   1.00
RIETI
  FIVE PIECES FOR YOUNG PIANISTS -- 5. SILLY POLKA
    NOVELLO AND COMPANY, LTD.   .75
RIETI
  MADRIGAL
    FRANCO COLOMBO PUBLICATIONS   SAL   4.25
RIETI
  MEDIEVAL VARIATIONS
    NOVELLO AND COMPANY, LTD.   1.65
RIETI
  MEDIEVAL VARIATIONS - SUITE
    GENERAL MUSIC PUBLISHING COMPANY, INC.   32   1.50
RIETI
  MEDIEVAL VARIATIONS - SUITE
    GENERAL MUSIC PUBLISHING COMPANY, INC.   2.50
RIETI
  PASTORALE
    FRANCO COLOMBO PUBLICATIONS   BON.1393   1.00
RIETI
  PEOMA FIESOLANO
    UNIVERSAL EDITION   UE 6808   2.00
RIETI
  PRELUDE
    GENERAL MUSIC PUBLISHING COMPANY, INC.   36   .60
RIETI
  PRELUDE - FROM FIVE PIECES FOR YOUNG PIANISTS
    GENERAL MUSIC PUBLISHING COMPANY, INC.   .60
RIETI
  PRELUDE-NOCTURNE
    FRANCO COLOMBO PUBLICATIONS   BON.1390   1.00
RIETI
  SILLY POLKA
    GENERAL MUSIC PUBLISHING COMPANY, INC.   38   .40
RIETI
  SILLY POLKA - FROM FIVE PIECES FOR YOUNG PIANISTS
    GENERAL MUSIC PUBLISHING COMPANY, INC.   .60

RIETI
  SIX SHORT PIECES FOR PIANO
    GENERAL MUSIC PUBLISHING COMPANY, INC.   3.00
RIETI
  SONATA ALL' ANTICA
    BROUDE BROTHERS LTD.   03.00
RIETI
  SONATA IN A FLAT
    GENERAL MUSIC PUBLISHING COMPANY, INC.   383   3.50
RIETI
  SONATA IN A FLAT
    GENERAL MUSIC PUBLISHING COMPANY, INC.   4.00
RIETI
  SONATA IN A FLAT
    NOVELLO AND COMPANY, LTD.   4.40
RIETI
  SONATINA
    UNIVERSAL EDITION   UE 8287   1.65
RIETI
  TARANTELLA
    GENERAL MUSIC PUBLISHING COMPANY, INC.   43   .60
RIETI
  TARANTELLA - FROM FIVE PIECES FOR YOUNG PIANISTS
    GENERAL MUSIC PUBLISHING COMPANY, INC.   .75
RIETI
  THREE MARCHES FOR ANIMALS
    FRANCO COLOMBO PUBLICATIONS   BON.1391   1.75
RIETI
  VARIATIONS ACADEMIQUES
    FRANCO COLOMBO PUBLICATIONS   NY2026   2.00
RIETI
  VARIATIONS ACADEMIQUES
    GENERAL MUSIC PUBLISHING COMPANY, INC.   323   2.50
RIETI
  VARIATIONS ACADEMIQUES - SUITE
    GENERAL MUSIC PUBLISHING COMPANY, INC.   3.50
RIGUETTE   1
  JAUNTY STROLL
    CENTURY MUSIC PUBLISHING COMPANY, INC.   4309   .40
RIGUETTE   1
  JUMPING BUNS
    CENTURY MUSIC PUBLISHING COMPANY, INC.   4309   .40
RILEY, D.   2 1/2
  FOLK DANCE -- IN HUNGARIAN STYLE
    THEODORE PRESSER COMPANY   .50
RILEY, D.   2
  MELODY
    THEODORE PRESSER COMPANY   .50
RIMSKY-KORSAKOFF
  BUMBLE-BEE, THE
    BELWIN-MILLS PUBLISHING CORPORATION   1.00
RIMSKY-KORSAKOFF
  CAPRICCIO ESPAGNOL
    EDWARD B. MARKS MUSIC CORPORATION   01.25
RIMSKY-KORSAKOFF   SCHAUM, J.   4
  CAPRICCIO ESPAGNOL, OP. 34
    BELWIN-MILLS PUBLISHING CORPORATION   .50
RIMSKY-KORSAKOFF   WINKLER
  CAPRICCIO ESPAGNOL, OP. 34
    BOOSEY AND HAWKES, INC.   3.25
RIMSKY-KORSAKOFF   MONTES
  CAPRICCIO ESPAGNOL, OP. 34
    FRANCO COLOMBO PUBLICATIONS   BA9106   1.50
RIMSKY-KORSAKOFF   BUSH   2-3
  CELEBRATIONS IN THE SACRED FOREST
    PRO-ART PUBLICATIONS, INC.   22   .50
RIMSKY-KORSAKOFF   4
  CHANSON INDOUE, E FLAT MAJOR
    CENTURY MUSIC PUBLISHING COMPANY, INC.   2115   .40
RIMSKY-KORSAKOFF   2
  CHANSON INDOUE, G MAJOR
    CENTURY MUSIC PUBLISHING COMPANY, INC.   2466   .40
RIMSKY-KORSAKOFF   6
  COQ D'OR, HYMN TO SUN
    CENTURY MUSIC PUBLISHING COMPANY, INC.   2299   .40
RIMSKY-KORSAKOFF   4
  FESTIVAL AT BAGDAD, SCHEHEREZADE
    CENTURY MUSIC PUBLISHING COMPANY, INC.   3722   .40
RIMSKY-KORSAKOFF   SCHAUM, J.   1
  FESTIVAL IN BRAZIL
    BELWIN-MILLS PUBLISHING CORPORATION   .50
RIMSKY-KORSAKOFF
  FLIGHT OF THE BUMBLE BEE
    ASHLEY DEALERS SERVICE, INC.   ES   .95
RIMSKY-KORSAKOFF   SCHAUM, J.   4
  FLIGHT OF THE BUMBLE BEE
    BELWIN-MILLS PUBLISHING CORPORATION   .50
RIMSKY-KORSAKOFF   ECKSTEIN
  FLIGHT OF THE BUMBLE BEE
    CARL FISCHER, INC.   S 2278   .50
RIMSKY-KORSAKOFF   5
  FLIGHT OF THE BUMBLE BEE
    CENTURY MUSIC PUBLISHING COMPANY, INC.   3184   .40
RIMSKY-KORSAKOFF
  FLIGHT OF THE BUMBLE BEE
    EDWARD B. MARKS MUSIC CORPORATION   01.00
RIMSKY-KORSAKOFF
  FLIGHT OF THE BUMBLE BEE
    EDWARD B. MARKS MUSIC CORPORATION   01.00
RIMSKY-KORSAKOFF   FELTON, W.   5
  FLIGHT OF THE BUMBLE BEE
    THEODORE PRESSER COMPANY   .50
RIMSKY-KORSAKOFF   3
  FLIGHT OF THE BUMBLE BEE, THE
    BOSTON MUSIC COMPANY   .50
RIMSKY-KORSAKOFF   MONTES
  GOLDEN COCKEREL, THE - HYMN TO THE SUN
    FRANCO COLOMBO PUBLICATIONS   BA8924   .75
RIMSKY-KORSAKOFF   LECHNER   2
  HINDU-LIED AUS SADKO
    SCHOTT   09623   .75
RIMSKY-KORSAKOFF   6
  HYMN TO THE SUN
    CENTURY MUSIC PUBLISHING COMPANY, INC.   2299   .40
RIMSKY-KORSAKOFF   M
  HYMN TO THE SUN GOD --LE COQ D'OR--
    C. F. PETERS CORPORATION   H1954   .90
RIMSKY-KORSAKOFF   LECHNER   3
  HYMNE AN DIE SONNE AUS DER GOLDENE HAHN
    SCHOTT   09624 1/2   1.00
RIMSKY-KORSAKOFF   SCHAUM, J.   1
  IN THE SULTAN'S PALACE
    BELWIN-MILLS PUBLISHING CORPORATION   .50
RIMSKY-KORSAKOFF   3
  ROMANCE IN A FLAT
    CENTURY MUSIC PUBLISHING COMPANY, INC.   2394   .40

RIMSKY-KORSAKOFF
RUSSIAN EASTER FESTIVAL, OP. 36
BOOSEY AND HAWKES, INC.   3.25
RIMSKY-KORSAKOFF   MONTES
SADKO - SONG OF INDIA
FRANCO COLOMBO PUBLICATIONS   BA7498   .75
RIMSKY-KORSAKOFF   MOSSMAN
SCHEHERAZADE
BELWIN-MILLS PUBLISHING CORPORATION   26097   .60
RIMSKY-KORSAKOFF   GILSON
SCHEHERAZADE, OP. 35
BOOSEY AND HAWKES, INC.   3.50
RIMSKY-KORSAKOFF   FUCHS
SCHEHERAZADE, OP. 35
FRANCO COLOMBO PUBLICATIONS   BA10441   3.25
                                        4
RIMSKY-KORSAKOFF
SCHEHERAZADE, FESTIVAL AT BAGDAD
CENTURY MUSIC PUBLISHING COMPANY, INC.   3722   .40
RIMSKY-KORSAKOFF   GILSON *
SHEHERAZADE--SYMPHONIC SUITE, OP. 35
G. SCHIRMER, INC.   L1348   1.50
RIMSKY-KORSAKOFF
SIX VARIATIONS ON B-A-C-H, OP. 10
BOOSEY AND HAWKES, INC.   2.00
RIMSKY-KORSAKOFF   MOSSMAN
SONG OF INDIA
BELWIN-MILLS PUBLISHING CORPORATION   26098   .60
RIMSKY-KORSAKOFF   TCHEREPNIN
SONG OF INDIA
BOOSEY AND HAWKES, INC.   .75
                                        4
RIMSKY-KORSAKOFF
SONG OF INDIA
CENTURY MUSIC PUBLISHING COMPANY, INC.   2115   .40
RIMSKY-KORSAKOFF
SONG OF INDIA -- SIMP.
BOOSEY AND HAWKES, INC.   .60
RIMSKY-KORSAKOFF   DEIS
SONG OF INDIA--FROM 'SADKO'
G. SCHIRMER, INC.   .50
                                        3
RIMSKY-KORSAKOFF
SONG OF INDIA, A
CENTURY MUSIC PUBLISHING COMPANY, INC.   3626   .40
                                        5
RIMSKY-KORSAKOFF
SONG OF INDIA, A FROM 'SADKO'
THEODORE PRESSER COMPANY   .50
RIMSKY-KORSAKOFF   THOMPSON, J.   3
YOUNG PRINCE AND PRINCESS, THE
WILLIS MUSIC COMPANY   .35
RIMSKY-KORSAKOFF   MONTES
ZAR SULTAN - FLIGHT OF THE BUMBLE BEE
FRANCO COLOMBO PUBLICATIONS   BA7499   .75
RIPPEL, M.   E
INDIAN WAR DANCE
COMPOSERS PRESS, INC.   1.00
RISHER, A. P.   1 1/2
SONG OF THE DRUM
THEODORE PRESSER COMPANY   .50
RISHER, A. P.   1
SONG OF THE SEESAW
THEODORE PRESSER COMPANY   .50
RITCHIE--ED   RITCHIE   3
CLAIR DE LUNE
CENTURY MUSIC PUBLISHING COMPANY, INC.   4330   .40
RITTMAN--ED   RITTMAN
YESTERDAYS
CIMINO PUBLICATIONS, INC.   H   1.25
RIVIER, J.
NOCTURNE
FRANCO COLOMBO PUBLICATIONS   SAL   2.25
RIVIER, J.
POUR DES MAINS AMIES -- SONATA IN FIVE MOVEMENTS
EDITIONS MUSICALES TRANSATLANTIQUES   5.70
RIVIER, J.
POUR DES MAINS AMIES -- SUITE OF 5 NUMBERS
EDITIONS MUSICALES TRANSATLANTIQUES   3.00
RIVIER, J.
SONATE POUR PIANO EN CINQ MOUVEMENTS
EDITIONS MUSICALES TRANSATLANTIQUES   5.70
RIVIER, J.
STRIDENCES
GERARD BILLAUDOT EDITIONS MUSICALES   2.50
RIVIER, J.
TORRENTS
EDITIONS MUSICALES TRANSATLANTIQUES   3.00
RIXNER
RAGAMUFFIN
MCA MUSIC   1.00
RIXNER, J.   3
SPANISCHER MARSCH
SCHOTT   1.25
RIZO, M.
TOCCATA-ZAPATEO
BELWIN-MILLS PUBLISHING CORPORATION   20350   1.00
ROBBINS   1-2
GYPSY WAGONS
PRO-ART PUBLICATIONS, INC.   479   .50
ROBBINS   2 1/2
LITTLE HARPIST
BELWIN-MILLS PUBLISHING CORPORATION   .60
ROBBINS   2
LULLABY FOR A DOLL
WILLIS MUSIC COMPANY   .40
ROBBINS   1 1/2
PIECE IN THE OLDEN STYLE
BELWIN-MILLS PUBLISHING CORPORATION   .60
ROBBINS
TRY AND CATCH ME
SUMMY-BIRCHARD COMPANY   .50
ROBBINS   2
TWO FROGS
BELWIN-MILLS PUBLISHING CORPORATION   .60
ROBBINS, L.   1 1/2
WALTZ REVERIE
WILLIS MUSIC COMPANY   .40
ROBERTS   2-3
AROUND THE CAMPFIRE
PRO-ART PUBLICATIONS, INC.   96   .50
ROBERTS   2-3
AUTUMN TIME
PRO-ART PUBLICATIONS, INC.   97   .50
ROBERTS   2
ENCHANTED PLANET, THE
PRO-ART PUBLICATIONS, INC.   138   .50
ROBERTS   2
GREMLIN HOP
PRO-ART PUBLICATIONS, INC.   143   .50

ROBERTS   3
MARCH OF THE ROBOTS
PRO-ART PUBLICATIONS, INC.   141   .50
ROBERTS
MUSIC BOX RAG
EDWARD B. MARKS MUSIC CORPORATION   01.00
ROBERTS   2
PUPPET WALTZ, THE
PRO-ART PUBLICATIONS, INC.   139   .50
ROBERTS   2-3
ROUND UP
PRO-ART PUBLICATIONS, INC.   98   .50
ROBERTS
SONATA
NOVELLO AND COMPANY, LTD.   10.0117.05 2.40
ROBERTS
SONATINA
NOVELLO AND COMPANY, LTD.   10.0118.03 1.25
ROBERTS   2
TUMBLING STREAM
PRO-ART PUBLICATIONS, INC.   140   .50
ROBERTSON   4
VARIATIONS ON 'LONDON BRIDGE IS FALLING DOWN'
BOSTON MUSIC COMPANY   .50
ROBIN *   SHEARING
UNDECIDED
MCA MUSIC   1.00
ROBIN *
UNDECIDED
MCA MUSIC   1.00
ROBINSON   2 1/2
HECTIC HIGHWAY
BELWIN-MILLS PUBLISHING CORPORATION   .60
ROBINSON
OWL IN THE MOONLIGHT
CARL FISCHER, INC.   P 2844   .50
ROBINSON, A.   2
CASTANETS, THE
THEODORE PRESSER COMPANY   .50
ROBINSON, A.   2
CHINESE LULLABY
THEODORE PRESSER COMPANY   .50
ROBINSON, A.   2
CLOWN ANTICS
THEODORE PRESSER COMPANY   .50
ROBINSON, A.   2
DAY DREAMS
CENTURY MUSIC PUBLISHING COMPANY, INC.   4212   .40
ROBINSON, A.
DROWSY COWBOY
SAM FOX PUBLISHING COMPANY, INC.   .50
ROBINSON, A.
DROWSY COWBOY
SOUTHERN MUSIC COMPANY   .50
ROBINSON, A.   3
DROWSY TIME
CENTURY MUSIC PUBLISHING COMPANY, INC.   4265   .40
ROBINSON, A.   1
EVENING SHADOWS
THEODORE PRESSER COMPANY   .50
ROBINSON, A.   1
FIRST MARCH
CENTURY MUSIC PUBLISHING COMPANY, INC.   4268   .40
ROBINSON, A.   1A
FLUFFY AND DUFFY
MUSICORD PUBLICATIONS, INC.   .45
ROBINSON, A.
FOREST NOCTURNE
SAM FOX PUBLISHING COMPANY, INC.   .50
ROBINSON, A.
FOREST NOCTURNE
SOUTHERN MUSIC COMPANY   .50
ROBINSON, A.   2-3
FUN ON THE 4TH
CENTURY MUSIC PUBLISHING COMPANY, INC.   4226   .40
ROBINSON, A.
FUNNY PELICAN
SAM FOX PUBLISHING COMPANY, INC.   .50
ROBINSON, A.
FUNNY PELICAN
SOUTHERN MUSIC COMPANY   .50
ROBINSON, A.   2
GOLDENROD
THEODORE PRESSER COMPANY   .50
ROBINSON, A.   2
HERE COMES THE RODEO PARADE
CENTURY MUSIC PUBLISHING COMPANY, INC.   4103   .40
ROBINSON, A.   1
IN THE HAMMOCK
CENTURY MUSIC PUBLISHING COMPANY, INC.   4104   .40
ROBINSON, A.
JUMPIN' JALOPY
SAM FOX PUBLISHING COMPANY, INC.   .50
ROBINSON, A.
JUMPIN' JALOPY
SOUTHERN MUSIC COMPANY   .50
ROBINSON, A.   2-3
JUST LOAFIN'
CENTURY MUSIC PUBLISHING COMPANY, INC.   4155   .40
ROBINSON, A.   2
LONELY COWBOY, THE
WILLIS MUSIC COMPANY   .35
ROBINSON, A.
LONELY DESERT
SAM FOX PUBLISHING COMPANY, INC.   .50
ROBINSON, A.
LONELY DESERT
SOUTHERN MUSIC COMPANY   .50
ROBINSON, A.   1
MARCHING ALONG
WILLIS MUSIC COMPANY   .30
ROBINSON, A.   1
MINUET
WILLIS MUSIC COMPANY   .40
ROBINSON, A.   2
MONKEY ANTICS
CENTURY MUSIC PUBLISHING COMPANY, INC.   4105   .40
ROBINSON, A.
MR. LION
SAM FOX PUBLISHING COMPANY, INC.   .50
ROBINSON, A.
MR. LION
SOUTHERN MUSIC COMPANY   .50
ROBINSON, A.
MR. SNOWMAN
SAM FOX PUBLISHING COMPANY, INC.   .50

ROBINSON, A.				
MR. SNOWMAN				
SOUTHERN MUSIC COMPANY				.50
ROBINSON, A.		1 1/2		
MY PICCOLO				
THEODORE PRESSER COMPANY				.50
ROBINSON, A.				
NERVOUS GHOST				
SAM FOX PUBLISHING COMPANY, INC.				.50
ROBINSON, A.				
NERVOUS GHOST				
SOUTHERN MUSIC COMPANY				.50
ROBINSON, A.		2A		
PLAYING COWBOY				
MUSICORD PUBLICATIONS, INC.				.45
ROBINSON, A.		1		
POOR PIGGY BANK				
CENTURY MUSIC PUBLISHING COMPANY, INC.	426 4			.40
ROBINSON, A.		1 1/2		
SAILOR BOY				
THEODORE PRESSER COMPANY				.50
ROBINSON, A.		1		
SCHOOL BELL, THE				
THEODORE PRESSER COMPANY				.50
ROBINSON, A.		3		
SPANISH LULLABY				
THEODORE PRESSER COMPANY				.50
ROBINSON, A.		2		
SPOOKY HALLOWE'EN				
CENTURY MUSIC PUBLISHING COMPANY, INC.	4 174			.40
ROBINSON, A.		2		
SWINGIN' 'N SWAYIN'				
WILLIS MUSIC COMPANY				.40
ROBINSON, A.		2		
TANGOLETTA				
WILLIS MUSIC COMPANY				.40
ROBINSON, A.		1		
TOY DRUM				
WILLIS MUSIC COMPANY				.40
ROBINSON, A.		2		
VIENNESE MELODY				
THEODORE PRESSER COMPANY				.50
ROBINSON, A.		1		
WESTERN LULLABY				
WILLIS MUSIC COMPANY				.35
ROBINSON, A.				
WINTER WINDS				
G. SCHIRMER, INC.				.40
ROBINSON, A. *				
BRAZILIAN POLKA				
SAM FOX PUBLISHING COMPANY, INC.				.75
ROBINSON, A. *				
BRAZILIAN POLKA				
SOUTHERN MUSIC COMPANY				.75
ROBINSON, E.				
DO IT NOW				
BELWIN-MILLS PUBLISHING CORPORATION	10009			1.00
ROBINSON, W. E.		3		
DREAM TIME				
THEODORE PRESSER COMPANY				.50
ROBINSON, W. E.		2		
LAZY LIZ				
BELWIN-MILLS PUBLISHING CORPORATION				.60
ROBINSON, W. E.		1		
LITTLE DUTCH DANCE				
THEODORE PRESSER COMPANY				.50
ROBINSON, W. E.		1A		
LITTLE SAILBOAT				
MUSICORD PUBLICATIONS, INC.				.45
ROBINSON, W. E.		1		
MY ROCKING HORSE				
WILLIS MUSIC COMPANY				.35
ROBINSON, W. E.		2		
SCHERZO PETITE				
WILLIS MUSIC COMPANY				.35
ROBINSON, W. E.		3		
SONG OF THE CELLO				
BELWIN-MILLS PUBLISHING CORPORATION				.60
ROBISION				
TREE TOP SERENADE				
MCA MUSIC				1.00
ROBLES				
EL CONDOR PASA				
EDWARD B. MARKS MUSIC CORPORATION				01.00
ROBLES				
EL CONDOR PASA				
EDWARD B. MARKS MUSIC CORPORATION				01.00
ROBOTTI	MAGNAINI, D.			
TWELVE ESERCIZI				
EDIZIONI BERBEN		EB 1581		2.40
ROBYN		3		
ANSWER				
CENTURY MUSIC PUBLISHING COMPANY, INC.	3628			.40
ROBYN		3		
BALLET MINIATURE				
CENTURY MUSIC PUBLISHING COMPANY, INC.	3230			.40
ROBYN		3		
JAPANESE DOLL DANCE				
CENTURY MUSIC PUBLISHING COMPANY, INC.	3229			.40
ROBYN, A.				
MANZANILLO				
THE BIG THREE MUSIC CORPORATION				00.95
ROCERETO, M.		2		
BLUE RIDGE DIVISION				
VOLKWEIN BROS.				.40
ROCERETO, M.		4		
CATHEDRAL OF LEARNING				
VOLKWEIN BROS.				.40
ROCERETO, M.		4		
OUR FIGHTING MEN				
VOLKWEIN BROS.				.40
ROCHBERG, G.		MD		
ARIOSO				
THEODORE PRESSER COMPANY				.50
ROCHBERG, G.		MD		
BARTOKIANA				
THEODORE PRESSER COMPANY				.50
ROCHBERG, G.		D		
NACH BACH -- FANTASY FOR HARPSICHORD OR PIANO				
THEODORE PRESSER COMPANY				2.00
ROCHBERG, G.		D		
PRELUDE ON 'HAPPY BIRTHDAY'				
THEODORE PRESSER COMPANY				1.00
ROCHBERG, G.		D		
SONATA FANTASIA				
THEODORE PRESSER COMPANY				3.50

ROCKWOOD, G.		2			
GAY GAVOTTE, A					
WILLIS MUSIC COMPANY					.40
ROCKWOOD, G.		2			
GAY GAVOTTE, A					
WILLIS MUSIC COMPANY					.40
RODGERS	MACLACHLAN	FIRST YEAR			
BLUE ROOM, THE					
WARNER BROTHERS PUBLISHERS					.75
RODGERS					
GREAT ADVENTURE, THE					
MCA MUSIC					1.00
RODGERS					
GUADALCANAL MARCH					
MCA MUSIC					1.00
RODGERS					
MOON MIST					
SUMMY-BIRCHARD COMPANY					.50
RODGERS					
NO STRINGS					
MCA MUSIC					2.50
RODGERS	PORTNOFF				
NO STRINGS					
MCA MUSIC					1.50
RODGERS					
REGENTS MARCH, THE. --SALIANT YEARS, MAIN THEME, THE.					
MCA MUSIC					1.00
RODGERS					
SLAUGHTER ON TENTH AVENUE					
CHAPPELL AND COMPANY, INC.			0017756-1501		1.25
RODGERS	LIBERACE				
SLAUGHTER ON TENTH AVENUE					
CHAPPELL AND COMPANY, INC.			0017764-1502		1.00
RODGERS					
SLAUGHTER ON TENTH AVENUE -- THEMES					
CHAPPELL AND COMPANY, INC.			0017756-1502		.95
RODGERS					
SUNRISE IN THE VALLEY					
CARL FISCHER, INC.			P 2061		.50
RODGERS		3			
SUNSET					
BOSTON MUSIC COMPANY					.50
RODGERS	SINGER				
SWEETEST SOUNDS, THE					
MCA MUSIC					1.00
RODGERS					
VALIENT YEARS, THE. --REGENT MARCH					
MCA MUSIC					1.00
RODGERS					
VICTORY AT SEA					
MCA MUSIC					1.25
RODGERS					
VICTORY AT SEA --THEME					
MCA MUSIC					1.00
RODGERS		1			
WATERFALL					
BOSTON MUSIC COMPANY					.50
RODGERS	RICHTER	FIRST YEAR			
WITH A SONG IN MY HEART					
WARNER BROTHERS PUBLISHERS					.75
RODGERS *	RITTMAN				
MARCH OF THE SIAMESE CHILDREN					
MCA MUSIC					.75
RODGERS *	RITTMAN				
SURREY WITH THE FRINGE ON TOP					
MCA MUSIC					.75
RODGERS *	MILLER, M.				
TWO BY TWO					
MCA MUSIC					1.50
RODGERS, I.		1			
AT THE ICE BALLET					
WILLIS MUSIC COMPANY					.40
RODGERS, I.		3			
BY A ROADSIDE FIRE					
WILLIS MUSIC COMPANY					.35
RODGERS, I.					
DANCING RAINDROPS					
BELWIN-MILLS PUBLISHING CORPORATION			25039		.60
RODGERS, I.		3			
IN A VANITY BOX					
WILLIS MUSIC COMPANY					.40
RODGERS, I.					
VALSE MELODIE					
BELWIN-MILLS PUBLISHING CORPORATION			25115		.60
RODGERS, I.					
WALTZ OF THE ROSES					
BELWIN-MILLS PUBLISHING CORPORATION			25116		.60
RODRIGO, J.					
A L'OMBRE DE ''TORRE BERMEJA''					
ASSOCIATED MUSIC PUBLISHERS, INC.			UME		1.10
RODRIGO, J.					
BAGATELLE					
FRANCO COLOMBO PUBLICATIONS			SAL		2.00
RODRIGO, J.					
BERCEUSE D'AUTOMNE					
FRANCO COLOMBO PUBLICATIONS			SAL		1.75
RODRIGO, J.					
BERCEUSE DE PRINTEMPS					
FRANCO COLOMBO PUBLICATIONS			SAL		2.00
RODRIGO, J.					
PASTORAL					
ASSOCIATED MUSIC PUBLISHERS, INC.			UME		.50
RODRIGO, J.					
PRELUDE AU COQ MATINAL					
FRANCO COLOMBO PUBLICATIONS			SAL		3.25
RODRIGO, J.					
SARABANDE LOINTAINE					
ASSOCIATED MUSIC PUBLISHERS, INC.			ESC		1.00
RODRIGO, J.					
SERENATA					
FRANCO COLOMBO PUBLICATIONS			SAL		3.25
RODRIGO, J.					
SONADA DE ADIOS					
ASSOCIATED MUSIC PUBLISHERS, INC.			ESC		3.00
RODRIGO, M.					
COPLA INTRUSA, LA					
ASSOCIATED MUSIC PUBLISHERS, INC.			UME		.80
RODRIGUEZ, C.		5 1/2			
PRELUDE IN F MINOR					
BELWIN-MILLS PUBLISHING CORPORATION					.60
RODRIGUEZ, C.		3			
SONATINA					
BELWIN-MILLS PUBLISHING CORPORATION					.60
RODRIGUEZ, P.		3			
CUMPARSITA, LA					
CENTURY MUSIC PUBLISHING COMPANY, INC.			3615		.40

RODRIGUEZ, R.   3
  LA CHUMPARSITA
    CENTURY MUSIC PUBLISHING COMPANY, INC.   3615   .40
RODRIGUEZ, R.
  LA CUMPARSITA
    EDWARD B. MARKS MUSIC CORPORATION   01.00
RODRIGUEZ, R.
  SONATINA
    ASSOCIATED MUSIC PUBLISHERS, INC.   ESC   5.50
ROEDER   3
  GONDOLIER WALTZES
    CENTURY MUSIC PUBLISHING COMPANY, INC.   233   .40
ROEMHELD, H.
  RUBY
    THE BIG THREE MUSIC CORPORATION   00.95
ROESGEN-CHAMPION
  SONATINA FOR HARPSICHORD
    FRANCO COLOMBO PUBLICATIONS   SAL   5.50
ROESSING, H.   2
  BIRDS ON A BOUGH
    VOLKWEIN BROS.   .30
ROESSING, H.   2
  POP-CORN BALLS
    BELWIN-MILLS PUBLISHING CORPORATION   .60
ROESSING, H.   3
  SKIING
    BELWIN-MILLS PUBLISHING CORPORATION   .60
ROFF   3
  IN THE PARK
    WILLIS MUSIC COMPANY   .40
ROFF   3
  MERRY FROLIC
    WILLIS MUSIC COMPANY   .40
ROGER-DUCASSE
  ESQUISSES
    ELKAN-VOGEL, INC.   D   1.50
ROGER-DUCASSE
  IMPROMPTU
    ELKAN-VOGEL, INC.   D   3.00
ROGER-DUCASSE
  PETITE SUITE
    ELKAN-VOGEL, INC.   D   2.00
ROGER-DUCASSE
  QUATRE ETUDES
    ELKAN-VOGEL, INC.   D   6.25
ROGERS   3-4
  CHARMANTE
    PRO-ART PUBLICATIONS, INC.   337   .50
ROGERS   3
  CHINATOWN
    THEODORE PRESSER COMPANY   .50
ROGERS   3
  FIESTA
    BOSTON MUSIC COMPANY   .50
ROGERS   3
  FOURTH OF JULY PARADE
    PRO-ART PUBLICATIONS, INC.   335   .50
ROGERS   2-3
  MOUNTAIN LAUREL
    PRO-ART PUBLICATIONS, INC.   384   .50
ROGERS   1
  PARADE
    BOSTON MUSIC COMPANY   .50
ROGERS   2-3
  RHUMBATINA
    PRO-ART PUBLICATIONS, INC.   334   .50
ROGERS   4
  ROCK-A-BOGGIE
    PRO-ART PUBLICATIONS, INC.   336   .50
ROGERS   2
  SPRING BOUQUET
    BOSTON MUSIC COMPANY   .50
ROGERS
  STARTIME
    BELWIN-MILLS PUBLISHING CORPORATION 20364 .95
ROGERS   1-2
  SWING HIGH, SWING LOW
    PRO-ART PUBLICATIONS, INC.   307   .50
ROGERS   3
  TA'IAMIM
    PRO-ART PUBLICATIONS, INC.   442   .50
ROGERS   3
  TARANTELLA
    BOSTON MUSIC COMPANY   .50
ROGERS   1-2
  TIDDLY WINKS
    PRO-ART PUBLICATIONS, INC.   338   .50
ROGERS   2
  VARIATIONS ON 'SKIP TO MY LOU'
    BOSTON MUSIC COMPANY   .50
ROGERS   3
  WITCHCRAFT
    PRO-ART PUBLICATIONS, INC.   385   .50
ROGERS   2
  YANKEE DOODLE DANDIED
    BOSTON MUSIC COMPANY   .50
ROGERS, B.   MD
  BELLS
    THEODORE PRESSER COMPANY   .50
ROGERS, E.   1
  CHOO, CHOO, CHOO
    CENTURY MUSIC PUBLISHING COMPANY, INC. 4124 .40
ROGERS, E.   1
  CIRCUS SCENES
    CENTURY MUSIC PUBLISHING COMPANY, INC. 4051 .40
ROGERS, E.   1-2
  COWBOY NOCTURNE
    CENTURY MUSIC PUBLISHING COMPANY, INC. 4164 .40
ROGERS, E.   2
  CROW'S FEET
    LEE ROBERTS MUSIC PUBLICATIONS, INC.   .50
ROGERS, E.   2
  DINOSAURS
    CENTURY MUSIC PUBLISHING COMPANY, INC. 021 .40
ROGERS, E.   1
  DRESSING FOR SCHOOL
    CENTURY MUSIC PUBLISHING COMPANY, INC. 012 .40
ROGERS, E.   1
  EARLY MORNING ROOSTER
    CENTURY MUSIC PUBLISHING COMPANY, INC. 4045 .40
ROGERS, E.   1
  EXPLORING THE ATTIC
    CENTURY MUSIC PUBLISHING COMPANY, INC. 011 .40
ROGERS, E.   2
  FUN
    CENTURY MUSIC PUBLISHING COMPANY, INC. 4168 .40

ROGERS, E.   2
  JAYBIRDS JIG
    CENTURY MUSIC PUBLISHING COMPANY, INC. 4247 .40
ROGERS, E.   5
  KING'S JESTER, THE
    LEE ROBERTS MUSIC PUBLICATIONS, INC.   .50
ROGERS, E.   4
  KNIGHT IN ARMOR
    LEE ROBERTS MUSIC PUBLICATIONS, INC.   .50
ROGERS, E.   1
  MARCH OF RUBBER BOOTS
    CENTURY MUSIC PUBLISHING COMPANY, INC. 4046 .40
ROGERS, E.   1
  MISTER ECHO
    CENTURY MUSIC PUBLISHING COMPANY, INC. 4165 .40
ROGERS, E.   1-2
  MOONLIGHT CRUISE
    CENTURY MUSIC PUBLISHING COMPANY, INC. 4253 .40
ROGERS, E.   2
  MY TOY TRUMPET
    CENTURY MUSIC PUBLISHING COMPANY, INC. 4053 .40
ROGERS, E.   2
  ON A HOBBY HORSE
    THEODORE PRESSER COMPANY   .50
ROGERS, E.   1
  PARAKEET POLKA
    CENTURY MUSIC PUBLISHING COMPANY, INC. 4248 .40
ROGERS, E.   2
  POW WOW
    LEE ROBERTS MUSIC PUBLICATIONS, INC.   .50
ROGERS, E.   1
  PUNCH AND JUDY
    CENTURY MUSIC PUBLISHING COMPANY, INC. 4047 .40
ROGERS, E.   1
  RAIN ON THE ROOF
    CENTURY MUSIC PUBLISHING COMPANY, INC. 4048 .40
ROGERS, E.   1
  RIDING MY BIKE
    CENTURY MUSIC PUBLISHING COMPANY, INC. 4126 .40
ROGERS, E.   1
  ROMANCE IN RIO
    BELWIN-MILLS PUBLISHING CORPORATION   .60
ROGERS, E.   1
  SAILING IN THE TUB
    CENTURY MUSIC PUBLISHING COMPANY, INC. 41 23 .40
ROGERS, E.   2
  SCALE SONG
    CENTURY MUSIC PUBLISHING COMPANY, INC. 4056 .40
ROGERS, E.   1
  SEE SAW
    CENTURY MUSIC PUBLISHING COMPANY, INC. 4125 .40
ROGERS, E.   1
  SHOWING OFF
    CENTURY MUSIC PUBLISHING COMPANY, INC. 4167 .40
ROGERS, E.   1
  SIDEWALK CRACKS
    CENTURY MUSIC PUBLISHING COMPANY, INC. 4127 .40
ROGERS, E.   1
  SPELLING FUN
    CENTURY MUSIC PUBLISHING COMPANY, INC. 4052 .40
ROGERS, E.   1
  SQUARE DANCE TUNE
    CENTURY MUSIC PUBLISHING COMPANY, INC. 412 9 .40
ROGERS, E.   1
  SUNDAY RIDE
    CENTURY MUSIC PUBLISHING COMPANY, INC. 4166 .40
ROGERS, E.   2
  TAG
    CENTURY MUSIC PUBLISHING COMPANY, INC. 4054 .40
ROGERS, E.   1
  TIDDLYWINKS
    CENTURY MUSIC PUBLISHING COMPANY, INC. 4049 .40
ROGERS, E.   2
  TILT TOP
    BELWIN-MILLS PUBLISHING CORPORATION   .60
ROGERS, E.   2 1/2
  TOPSY-TURVY-TOY
    THEODORE PRESSER COMPANY   .50
ROGERS, E.   3
  TROUBADOUR, THE
    LEE ROBERTS MUSIC PUBLICATIONS, INC.   .50
ROGERS, E.   1
  TWO WINTER PIECES
    CENTURY MUSIC PUBLISHING COMPANY, INC. 412 8 .40
ROGERS, E.   1
  WESTERN STORY, A
    CENTURY MUSIC PUBLISHING COMPANY, INC. 4050 .40
ROGERS, E.   2
  WHISTLING TUNE
    CENTURY MUSIC PUBLISHING COMPANY, INC. 4055 .40
ROGERS, F.
  SPANISH DANCE
    G. SCHIRMER, INC.   .35
ROGERS, J.
  ETUDE MELODIQUE
    G. SCHIRMER, INC.   .60
ROGERS, J.   3 1/2
  INTERMEZZO ORIENTALE
    THEODORE PRESSER COMPANY   .60
ROGERS, J.
  VALSE-CAPRICE
    G. SCHIRMER, INC.   .50
ROGERS, J.
  VALZER GLISSANDO
    G. SCHIRMER, INC.   .40
ROHDE, E.   2 1/2
  MARIONETTES
    WILLIS MUSIC COMPANY   .40
ROIG
  YOURS --QUIEREME MUCHO
    EDWARD B. MARKS MUSIC CORPORATION   01.00
ROIG
  YOURS--QUIEREME MUCHO
    EDWARD B. MARKS MUSIC CORPORATION   00.60
ROLAND   MANUEL
  CANARIE FROM L'EVENTAIL DE JEANNE
    HEUGEL ET CIE.   1.95
ROLAND *
  L'ECRAN DES JEUNES FILLES
    HEUGEL ET CIE.   8.10
ROLAND *
  LE TOURNOI SINGULIER
    HEUGEL ET CIE.   2.75
ROLCAN, A.
  MULATO
    PEER SOUTHERN ORGANIZATION   00.90

ROLCAN, A.
  PRELUDIO CUBANO
    PEER SOUTHERN ORGANIZATION   00.90
ROLFE   2
  BIG BASS SINGER, THE
    THEODORE PRESSER COMPANY   .50
ROLFE   2
  DADDY'S WALTZ
    THEODORE PRESSER COMPANY   .50
ROLFE
  DANCE OF THE CRICKETS
    THEODORE PRESSER COMPANY   3
ROLFE
  VALE OF SONG
    SUMMY-BIRCHARD COMPANY   .50
ROLFE, W.   2
  ANIMAL CRACKERS WALTZ
    VOLKWEIN BROS.   .30
ROLFE, W.
  AUTUMN SPLENDOR
    SAM FOX PUBLISHING COMPANY, INC.   .50
ROLFE, W.
  AUTUMN SPLENDOR
    SOUTHERN MUSIC COMPANY   .50
ROLFE, W.   1
  BAA, BAA, BLACK SHEEP
    CENTURY MUSIC PUBLISHING COMPANY, INC.   3208   .40
ROLFE, W.
  BELLS AT TWILIGHT
    SHAWNEE PRESS, INC.   HB-5035   .35
ROLFE, W.   2
  BUTTERFLY, BUTTERFLY AND SHIP A-SAILING
    CENTURY MUSIC PUBLISHING COMPANY, INC.   3204   .40
ROLFE, W.   BEETHOVEN   2
  CHICADEE FROM BEETHOVEN'S SYMPHONY NO. 8
    CENTURY MUSIC PUBLISHING COMPANY, INC.   3179   .40
ROLFE, W.
  CHILD'S PRIMER, A.
    SAM FOX PUBLISHING COMPANY, INC.   1.50
ROLFE, W.   2
  CRUSADER MARCH
    VOLKWEIN BROS.   .30
ROLFE, W.   CHOPIN   2
  DANCING THE MENUET FROM CHOPIN'S PRELUDE, OP. 28
    CENTURY MUSIC PUBLISHING COMPANY, INC.   3170   .40
ROLFE, W.   2
  DRIFTING AND DREAMING
    VOLKWEIN BROS.   .25
ROLFE, W.   CHOPIN   2
  EVENING SHADOWS FROM CHOPIN'S NOCTURNE
    CENTURY MUSIC PUBLISHING COMPANY, INC.   3174   .40
ROLFE, W.   1
  FREE AND EASY MARCH
    VOLKWEIN BROS.   .25
ROLFE, W.   2
  GOING TO MARKET
    CENTURY MUSIC PUBLISHING COMPANY, INC.   3691   .40
ROLFE, W.   1
  GOOSEY GOOSEY GANDER AND PRETTY MAID
    CENTURY MUSIC PUBLISHING COMPANY, INC.   3212   .40
ROLFE, W.
  HARBINGER OF SPRING
    SAM FOX PUBLISHING COMPANY, INC.   .50
ROLFE, W.
  HARBINGER OF SPRING
    SOUTHERN MUSIC COMPANY   .50
ROLFE, W.   1
  HEY, DIDDLE, DIDDLE AND POOR DOG
    CENTURY MUSIC PUBLISHING COMPANY, INC.   3201   .40
ROLFE, W.   1
  HUMPTY DUMPTY AND PETER, PETER
    CENTURY MUSIC PUBLISHING COMPANY, INC.   3202   .40
ROLFE, W.   1
  HUSH, BE STILL AND MARY'S LAMB
    CENTURY MUSIC PUBLISHING COMPANY, INC.   3203   .40
ROLFE, W.   1
  I SAW SHIP A'SAILING AND BUTTERFLY
    CENTURY MUSIC PUBLISHING COMPANY, INC.   3204   .40
ROLFE, W.   1
  JACK AND JILL AND POLLY FLINDERS
    CENTURY MUSIC PUBLISHING COMPANY, INC.   3206   .40
ROLFE, W.   3
  KISS OF SPRING
    BOSTON MUSIC COMPANY   .50
ROLFE, W.   CHOPIN   2
  LACES AND FRILLS FROM CHOPIN'S MAZURKA
    CENTURY MUSIC PUBLISHING COMPANY, INC.   3173   .40
ROLFE, W.
  LARKSPUR
    CARL FISCHER, INC.   EV 16   .50
ROLFE, W.   CHOPIN   2
  LITTLE BALLAD FROM CHOPIN'S OP. 47
    CENTURY MUSIC PUBLISHING COMPANY, INC.   3171   .40
ROLFE, W.   1
  LITTLE BO-PEEP
    CENTURY MUSIC PUBLISHING COMPANY, INC.   3205   .40
ROLFE, W.   1
  LITTLE POLLY FLINDERS
    CENTURY MUSIC PUBLISHING COMPANY, INC.   3206   .40
ROLFE, W.   1 1/2
  LITTLE SWEETHEART WALTZ
    THEODORE PRESSER COMPANY   .50
ROLFE, W.   2
  LOTS OF FUN
    CENTURY MUSIC PUBLISHING COMPANY, INC.   3692   .40
ROLFE, W.   1
  MARY'S LITTLE LAMB
    CENTURY MUSIC PUBLISHING COMPANY, INC.   3203   .40
ROLFE, W.   3 1/2
  MOON ROCKET, THE
    THEODORE PRESSER COMPANY   .75
ROLFE, W.
  MOON SHADOWS
    SAM FOX PUBLISHING COMPANY, INC.   .50
ROLFE, W.
  MOON SHADOWS
    SOUTHERN MUSIC COMPANY   .50
ROLFE, W.   1
  OLD MOTHER HUBBARD
    CENTURY MUSIC PUBLISHING COMPANY, INC.   3209   .40
ROLFE, W.   1
  OLD WOMAN LIVED IN A SHOE
    CENTURY MUSIC PUBLISHING COMPANY, INC.   3211   .40
ROLFE, W.   1
  ONE HE LOVES AND PUSSY CAT
    CENTURY MUSIC PUBLISHING COMPANY, INC.   3207   .40

ROLFE, W.   1
  PETER, PETER AND HUMPTY DUMPTY
    CENTURY MUSIC PUBLISHING COMPANY, INC.   3202   .40
ROLFE, W.   1
  POLKA DOT
    CENTURY MUSIC PUBLISHING COMPANY, INC.   3986   .40
ROLFE, W.   1
  POOR DOG BRIGHT AND HEY DIDDLE
    CENTURY MUSIC PUBLISHING COMPANY, INC.   3201   .40
ROLFE, W.   BEETHOVEN   2
  PRAYER FROM BEETHOVEN'S SYMPHONY NO. 2, A
    CENTURY MUSIC PUBLISHING COMPANY, INC.   3180   .40
ROLFE, W.   1
  PUG NOSE
    CENTURY MUSIC PUBLISHING COMPANY, INC.   3987   .40
ROLFE, W.   1
  RATS AND MICE
    CENTURY MUSIC PUBLISHING COMPANY, INC.   3210   .40
ROLFE, W.
  ROSES
    CARL FISCHER, INC.   EV 23   .50
ROLFE, W.   EASY
  RUSTIC CHAPEL
    SHAWNEE PRESS, INC.   HB-5004   .60
ROLFE, W.   1
  SCHOOL CARNIVAL MARCH
    BOSTON MUSIC COMPANY   .50
ROLFE, W.   2
  SEA SPRAY
    CENTURY MUSIC PUBLISHING COMPANY, INC.   3693   .40
ROLFE, W.   1
  SING A SONG OF SIXPENCE
    CENTURY MUSIC PUBLISHING COMPANY, INC.   3209   .40
ROLFE, W.   2
  SOARING
    THEODORE PRESSER COMPANY   .50
ROLFE, W.   1
  SPRING FEVER
    CENTURY MUSIC PUBLISHING COMPANY, INC.   3988   .40
ROLFE, W.   EASY
  SPRING FLOWERS
    SHAWNEE PRESS, INC.   HB-5007   .60
ROLFE, W.   EASY
  STAR GAZERS, THE
    SHAWNEE PRESS, INC.   HB-5016   .40
ROLFE, W.   1
  STARRY WAY
    CENTURY MUSIC PUBLISHING COMPANY, INC.   3989   .40
ROLFE, W.   BEETHOVEN   2
  STOP, STOP, PRETTY WATER FROM BEETHOVEN'S SONATA, OP. 49 NO. 1
    CENTURY MUSIC PUBLISHING COMPANY, INC.   3181   .40
ROLFE, W.   1
  THERE WAS A LITTLE GIRL
    CENTURY MUSIC PUBLISHING COMPANY, INC.   3211   .40
ROLFE, W.   2
  VALSE JESSICA
    BOSTON MUSIC COMPANY   .50
ROLFE, W.   CHOPIN   2
  VALSE TRISTE FROM CHOPIN'S OP. 34 NO. 2
    CENTURY MUSIC PUBLISHING COMPANY, INC.   3172   .40
ROLFE, W.   MOZART, W.A.   2
  VIOLET FROM MOZART'S SONATA NO. 12, THE
    CENTURY MUSIC PUBLISHING COMPANY, INC.   3177   .40
ROLFE, W.   1
  WHERE ARE YOU GOING PRETTY MAID
    CENTURY MUSIC PUBLISHING COMPANY, INC.   3212   .40
ROLFE, W.   BEETHOVEN   2
  WISH FROM BEETHOVEN'S SYMPHONY NO. 3, A
    CENTURY MUSIC PUBLISHING COMPANY, INC.   3178   .40
ROLFE, W.   3
  WITH CHARMING GRACE
    BOSTON MUSIC COMPANY   .50
ROLFE, W.--ED   ROLFE, W.   2
  AY, AY, AY
    CENTURY MUSIC PUBLISHING COMPANY, INC.   3575   .40
ROLFE, W.--ED   ROLFE, W.   3
  BRITISH GRENADIERS
    CENTURY MUSIC PUBLISHING COMPANY, INC.   3616   .40
ROLFE, W.--ED   ROLFE, W.   2
  CHRISTMAS CAROLS
    CENTURY MUSIC PUBLISHING COMPANY, INC.   3724   .40
ROLFE, W.--ED   ROLFE, W.   2
  CHRISTMAS HYMNS
    CENTURY MUSIC PUBLISHING COMPANY, INC.   3725   .40
ROLFE, W.--ED   ROLFE, W.   1
  DEEP RIVER
    CENTURY MUSIC PUBLISHING COMPANY, INC.   3476   .40
ROLFE, W.--ED   ROLFE, W.   2
  GEMS OF STEPHEN FOSTER
    CENTURY MUSIC PUBLISHING COMPANY, INC.   3531   .40
ROLFE, W.--ED   ROLFE, W.   3
  GOD BE WITH YOU TILL WE MEET AGAIN
    CENTURY MUSIC PUBLISHING COMPANY, INC.   3699   .40
ROLFE, W.--ED   ROLFE, W.   2
  HOME ON THE RANGE
    CENTURY MUSIC PUBLISHING COMPANY, INC.   3475   .40
ROLFE, W.--ED   ROLFE, W.   2
  KERRY DANCE, THE
    CENTURY MUSIC PUBLISHING COMPANY, INC.   3572   .40
ROLFE, W.--ED   ROLFE, W.   2
  LOCH LOMMOND
    CENTURY MUSIC PUBLISHING COMPANY, INC.   3765   .40
ROLFE, W.--ED   ROLFE, W.   1
  LONDONDERRY AIR
    CENTURY MUSIC PUBLISHING COMPANY, INC.   3474   .40
ROLFE, W.--ED   ROLFE, W.   2
  MOTHER HUBBARD AND SONG OF SIXPENCE
    CENTURY MUSIC PUBLISHING COMPANY, INC.   3209   .40
ROLFE, W.--ED   ROLFE, W.   1
  OLD VIENNESE MELODY
    CENTURY MUSIC PUBLISHING COMPANY, INC.   3574   .40
ROLFE, W.--ED   ROLFE, W.   3
  POLLY PUT THE KETTLE ON
    CENTURY MUSIC PUBLISHING COMPANY, INC.   3210   .40
ROLFE, W.--ED   ROLFE, W.   1
  RED RIVER VALLEY
    CENTURY MUSIC PUBLISHING COMPANY, INC.   3571   .40
ROLFE, W.--ED   ROLFE, W.   3
  ROCK-A-BYE BABY
    CENTURY MUSIC PUBLISHING COMPANY, INC.   3208   .40
ROLFE, W.--ED   ROLFE, W.   3
  SHORTNIN' BREAD
    CENTURY MUSIC PUBLISHING COMPANY, INC.   3573   .40
ROLFE, W.--ED   ROLFE, W.   3
  SONG OF THE VOLGA BOATMAN
    CENTURY MUSIC PUBLISHING COMPANY, INC.   3634   .40

ROLLINS			3	
MISCHIEF MAKER				
BOSTON MUSIC COMPANY				.50
ROLLINS, G.			2	
GENTLE IS THE BREEZE				
WILLIS MUSIC COMPANY				.40
ROLLINS, G.			2	
GENTLE IS THE BREEZE				
WILLIS MUSIC COMPANY				.40
ROLLINS, G.			2	
RUNNING, RUNNING				
WILLIS MUSIC COMPANY				.40
ROLLINS, G.			2	
WALKING HOME				
THEODORE PRESSER COMPANY				.50
ROLSETH, B.				
ARPEGGIO WALTZ				
G. SCHIRMER, INC.				.35
ROLSETH, B.				
BALLET-DANCER, THE				
G. SCHIRMER, INC.				.50
ROLSETH, B.				
DANCING LESSON, THE				
G. SCHIRMER, INC.				.35
ROLSETH, B.				
FAIRY DOLL, THE				
G. SCHIRMER, INC.				.30
ROLSETH, B.				
INDIAN WAR-DANCE				
G. SCHIRMER, INC.				.35
ROLSETH, B.				
MY FIRST WALTZ				
G. SCHIRMER, INC.				.35
ROLSETH, B.				
NORWEGIAN COUNTRY DANCE				
G. SCHIRMER, INC.				.40
ROLSETH, B.				
OLD CLOCK, THE				
G. SCHIRMER, INC.				.35
ROLSETH, B.				
ON PARADE				
G. SCHIRMER, INC.				.35
ROLSETH, B.				
SPOOKY NIGHTMARE				
G. SCHIRMER, INC.				.30
ROLSETH, B.				
STROLLING				
G. SCHIRMER, INC.				.30
ROMANETTE, J.				
TOCCATA, OP. 7				
ASSOCIATED MUSIC PUBLISHERS, INC.	ESC			1.60
ROMBERG, S.				
BLOSSOM TIME				
THE BIG THREE MUSIC CORPORATION				01.50
ROMBERG, S.	RICHTER	FIRST YEAR		
DESERT SONG, THE				
WARNER BROTHERS PUBLISHERS				.75
ROMBERG, S.	RIEGGER			
SERENADE				
WARNER BROTHERS PUBLISHERS				1.00
ROMBERG, S.	RICHTER	FIRST YEAR		
SERENADE				
WARNER BROTHERS PUBLISHERS				.75
ROMBERG, S.	RICHTER	FIRST YEAR		
STOUTHEARTED MEN				
WARNER BROTHERS PUBLISHERS				.75
ROMBERG, S.	KAPLAN			
WILL YOU REMEMBER--FROM 'MAYTIME'				
G. SCHIRMER, INC.				.50
ROMBERG, S.	DEIS			
WILL YOU REMEMBER--FROM 'MAYTIME'				
G. SCHIRMER, INC.				.40
ROMBERG, S.	LEVINE			
WILL YOU REMEMBER--FROM 'MAYTIME'				
G. SCHIRMER, INC.				.50
ROMBERG, S.	LEVINE			
WILL YOU REMEMBER--FROM 'MAYTIME'				
G. SCHIRMER, INC.				.50
ROMBERG, S. *				
UP IN CENTRAL PARK				
MCA MUSIC				2.50
ROME *				
ON GUARD MARCH				
MCA MUSIC				1.00
ROMERO, M. *				
CANTANDO VAN LOS PASTORES--VILLANCICO				
ASSOCIATED MUSIC PUBLISHERS, INC.	UME			.40
RONNEFELD, P.				
PETER SCHLEMIHL				
UNIVERSAL EDITION	UE 12475			8.10
ROOSEVELT			4	
UNDER THE STARS AND STRIPES				
CENTURY MUSIC PUBLISHING COMPANY, INC.	983			.40
ROOT	SCHAUM, J.	1		
BATTLE CRY OF FREEDOM				
BELWIN-MILLS PUBLISHING CORPORATION				.50
ROOT, F. W.			2 1/2	
FLY-AWAY				
THEODORE PRESSER COMPANY				.50
ROOT, G.			2	
JESUS LOVES THE LITTLE CHILDREN				
BELWIN-MILLS PUBLISHING CORPORATION				.60
ROPARTZ				
CHORAL VARIE				
FRANCO COLOMBO PUBLICATIONS	SAL			2.00
ROPARTZ				
CROQUIS D'AUTOMNE - DANSE AU VILLAGE				
FRANCO COLOMBO PUBLICATIONS	SAL			2.00
ROPARTZ				
CROQUIS D'AUTOMNE - JOYEUSE AUBADE				
FRANCO COLOMBO PUBLICATIONS	SAL			2.50
ROPARTZ				
CROQUIS D'AUTOMNE - SOIR DE TOUSSAINT				
FRANCO COLOMBO PUBLICATIONS	SAL			2.00
ROPARTZ				
CROQUIS D'AUTOMNE - UN PATRE CHANTE				
FRANCO COLOMBO PUBLICATIONS	SAL			2.00
ROPARTZ				
CROQUIS D'AUTOMNE - UNE ENFANT REVE				
FRANCO COLOMBO PUBLICATIONS	SAL			2.00
ROPARTZ				
CROQUIS D'ETE - PETITE RONDE FRANCAISE				
FRANCO COLOMBO PUBLICATIONS	SAL			2.50
ROPARTZ				
DANS L'OMBRE DE LA MONTAGNE -- PAYSAGE				
ELKAN-VOGEL, INC.	D			.80

ROPARTZ				
DANS L'OMBRE DE LA MONTAGNE -- QUAND LA LUMIERE S'EN EST ALLEE				
ELKAN-VOGEL, INC.	D			2.25
ROPARTZ				
DANS L'OMBRE DE LA MONTAGNE -- RONDE				
ELKAN-VOGEL, INC.	D			2.25
ROPARTZ				
DANS L'OMBRE DE LA MONTAGNE -- SUR LA ROUTE				
ELKAN-VOGEL, INC.	D			.70
ROPARTZ				
DANS L'OMBRE DE LA MONTAGNE -- VIEILLE EGLISE				
ELKAN-VOGEL, INC.	D			1.70
ROPARTZ				
JEUNES FILLES				
ELKAN-VOGEL, INC.	D			3.50
ROPARTZ				
L'INDISCRET				
ELKAN-VOGEL, INC.	D			3.00
ROPARTZ				
MUSIQUES AU JARDIN				
ELKAN-VOGEL, INC.	D			3.60
ROPARTZ				
NOCTURNE				
FRANCO COLOMBO PUBLICATIONS	SAL			3.25
ROPARTZ				
SERENADE				
FRANCO COLOMBO PUBLICATIONS	SAL			2.00
ROPARTZ				
UN PRELUDE DOMINICAL ET SIX PIECES A DANSER				
ELKAN-VOGEL, INC.	D			4.00
ROREM, N.				
QUIET AFTERNOON, A				
PEER SOUTHERN ORGANIZATION				01.50
ROREM, N.				
SECOND SONATE				
GERARD BILLAUDOT EDITIONS MUSICALES				3.00
ROREM, N.				
SONATA NO. 02				
BOOSEY AND HAWKES, INC.				5.00
ROREM, N.				
SPIDERS, FOR HARPSICHORD				
BOOSEY AND HAWKES, INC.				1.50
ROREM, N.	M-D			
TOCCATA				
C. F. PETERS CORPORATION	6263			.90
ROSAS			2	
OVER THE WAVES				
BOSTON MUSIC COMPANY				.50
ROSAS				
OVER THE WAVES				
FRANCO COLOMBO PUBLICATIONS	106146			.90
ROSAS	CHIESA			
OVER THE WAVES				
FRANCO COLOMBO PUBLICATIONS	109199			.60
ROSAS	JESTON, I. H.	2		
OVER THE WAVES WALTZ				
VOLKWEIN BROS.				.35
ROSAS				
SOBRE LAS OLAS--WALTZ				
G. SCHIRMER, INC.				.70
ROSAS			3	
SOBRE LAS OLAS, VALSE				
CENTURY MUSIC PUBLISHING COMPANY, INC.	352			.40
ROSAS			2	
SOBRE LAS OLAS, VALSE, EASY				
CENTURY MUSIC PUBLISHING COMPANY, INC.	2137			.40
ROSE, D.				
HOMBRE				
THE BIG THREE MUSIC CORPORATION				00.95
ROSE, E.	STEINER	2		
GEORGIA MINSTREL BAND				
BELWIN-MILLS PUBLISHING CORPORATION				.60
ROSELLEN			4	
TREMOLO, REVERIE				
CENTURY MUSIC PUBLISHING COMPANY, INC.	1036			.40
ROSENFELD, G.				
SONATA--1968				
ASSOCIATED MUSIC PUBLISHERS, INC.	DVM			2.50
ROSENSTOCK, J.				
SONATA IN E MINOR, OP. 3				
UNIVERSAL EDITION	UE 5542			2.75
ROSENTHAL, L.				
COMEDIANS, THE				
THE BIG THREE MUSIC CORPORATION				00.95
ROSENTHAL, M.				
PAPILLONS				
BOOSEY AND HAWKES, INC.				1.50
ROSENTHAL, M.	BROWNING			
PAPILLONS				
MUSICA OBSCURA				2.50
ROSETTA, G.				
BOUQUET				
EDIZIONI BERBEN	EB 1546			3.60
ROSMAN, M.				
DANCE TO THE CLASSICS				
BOOSEY AND HAWKES, INC.				1.00
ROSNER			2B	
CAT AND THE MUSIC BOX				
MUSICORD PUBLICATIONS, INC.				.45
ROSNER			1B	
CHINESE CHATTER				
MUSICORD PUBLICATIONS, INC.				.45
ROSNER			3A	
CLEMENTINE CAPERS				
MUSICORD PUBLICATIONS, INC.				.45
ROSNER			3B	
GYPSY RHAPSODY				
MUSICORD PUBLICATIONS, INC.				.45
ROSNER			2B	
IN A DONKEY CART				
MUSICORD PUBLICATIONS, INC.				.45
ROSNER			2A	
LITTLE BOOGIE WOOGIE				
MUSICORD PUBLICATIONS, INC.				.45
ROSNER			1B	
LITTLE COWBOY				
MUSICORD PUBLICATIONS, INC.				.45
ROSNER			3A	
PUCK				
MUSICORD PUBLICATIONS, INC.				.45
ROSNER			2B	
RED PEPPER POLKA				
MUSICORD PUBLICATIONS, INC.				.45
ROSS				
MAGIC HORN, THE				
MCA MUSIC				1.00

ROSSE, F.
    ALBUM
        BOOSEY AND HAWKES, INC.   1.25
ROSSELLINI
    PAGAN POEMS
        FRANCO COLOMBO PUBLICATIONS   123454   1.50
ROSSELLINI
    RACCONTO D'INVERNO -- WINTER TALE -- -- BALLET --
        FRANCO COLOMBO PUBLICATIONS   128607   2.25
ROSSELLINI   M. SALTA
    SICILIAN SCHERZO
        FRANCO COLOMBO PUBLICATIONS   NY1396   .60
ROSSELLINI
    SONGS OF THE GULF OF NAPLES
        FRANCO COLOMBO PUBLICATIONS   NY1701   1.50
ROSSI   4
    SPIN, SPIN, ESTHONIAN FOLK SONG
        CENTURY MUSIC PUBLISHING COMPANY, INC.   2288   .40
ROSSI, G.   4
    ESTHONIAN FOLK SONG
        CENTURY MUSIC PUBLISHING COMPANY, INC.   2288   .40
ROSSI, G.   4
    FANTASIE, SPIN, SPIN
        CENTURY MUSIC PUBLISHING COMPANY, INC.   2288   .40
ROSSI, M. A.   MARCIANO
    ANDANTINO AND ALLEGRO
        FRANCO COLOMBO PUBLICATIONS   104257   .60
ROSSI, R.
    NINNA-NANNA A GIANNI
        FRANCO COLOMBO PUBLICATIONS   DS311   1.00
ROSSI, R.
    PRELUDE AND FUGUE
        FRANCO COLOMBO PUBLICATIONS   DS312   1.25
ROSSINI *
    DANZA, LA
        FRANCO COLOMBO PUBLICATIONS   128321   1.00
ROSSINI *
    REGATA VENEZIANA, LA
        FRANCO COLOMBO PUBLICATIONS   128857   .90
ROSSINI, G.
    ASSEDIO DI CORINTO, L' - OVERTURE
        FRANCO COLOMBO PUBLICATIONS   127768   1.00
ROSSINI, G.   E-M
    BARBER OF SEVILLE, ABRIDGED
        C. F. PETERS CORPORATION   H638   2.00
ROSSINI, G.   KRUG   2
    BARBER OF SEVILLE, TRANS.
        CENTURY MUSIC PUBLISHING COMPANY, INC.   513   .40
ROSSINI, G.   CHIESA
    BARBIERE DI SIVIGLIA, IL - CAVATINA - UNA VOCE POCO FA
        FRANCO COLOMBO PUBLICATIONS   107483   .60
ROSSINI, G.
    BARBIERE DI SIVIGLIA, IL - OVERTURE
        FRANCO COLOMBO PUBLICATIONS   127659   1.00
ROSSINI, G.
    BARBIERE DI SIVIGLIA, IL -- COMPLETE OPERA --
        FRANCO COLOMBO PUBLICATIONS   124061   6.00
ROSSINI, G.   5
    CUJUS ANIMAM FROM STABAT MATER
        CENTURY MUSIC PUBLISHING COMPANY, INC.   182   .40
ROSSINI, G.   LISZT
    DANZA, LA
        FRANCO COLOMBO PUBLICATIONS   128321   1.00
ROSSINI, G.   DEL MAGLIO
    DANZA, LA
        FRANCO COLOMBO PUBLICATIONS   124727   .60
ROSSINI, G.   ECKSTEIN
    FANFARE FROM 'WILLIAM TELL'
        CARL FISCHER, INC.   S 2288   .50
ROSSINI, G.   WERNER
    FANFARE POUR CHASSE--CURWEN EDITION
        G. SCHIRMER, INC.   .75
ROSSINI, G.
    GAZZA LADRA, LA - OVERTURE
        FRANCO COLOMBO PUBLICATIONS   127997   1.25
ROSSINI, G.   CHIESA
    GUILLAUME TELL - EASY FANTASIA
        FRANCO COLOMBO PUBLICATIONS   107499   .50
ROSSINI, G.
    GUILLAUME TELL - OVERTURE
        FRANCO COLOMBO PUBLICATIONS   128081   1.00
ROSSINI, G.   DEL MAGLIO
    GUILLAUME TELL - PASTORALE FROM THE OVERTURE
        FRANCO COLOMBO PUBLICATIONS   128145   .50
ROSSINI, G.
    ITALIANA IN ALGERI, L' - OVERTURE
        FRANCO COLOMBO PUBLICATIONS   127585   1.00
ROSSINI, G.   SCHAUM, J.   4
    LA DANZA
        SCHAUM PUBLICATIONS, INC.   .60
ROSSINI, G.   PERONI
    MATILDE DI SHABRAN - OVERTURE
        FRANCO COLOMBO PUBLICATIONS   129243   1.00
ROSSINI, G.
    MOSE - DAL TUO STELLATO SOGLIO
        FRANCO COLOMBO PUBLICATIONS   42195   .60
ROSSINI, G.   DEL MAGLIO
    MOSE - DAL TUO STELLATO SOGLIO
        FRANCO COLOMBO PUBLICATIONS   124728   .60
ROSSINI, G.
    OVERTURE FROM 'WILLIAM TELL'
        G. SCHIRMER, INC.   .80
ROSSINI, G.   5
    OVERTURE, WILLIAM TELL
        CENTURY MUSIC PUBLISHING COMPANY, INC.   1529   .40
ROSSINI, G.   ROLFE, W.   2
    OVERTURE, WILLIAM TELL
        CENTURY MUSIC PUBLISHING COMPANY, INC.   3401   .40
ROSSINI, G.   3
    OVERTURE, WILLIAM TELL, EASY
        CENTURY MUSIC PUBLISHING COMPANY, INC.   2513   .40
ROSSINI, G.   MONTANI
    PETIT CAPRICE IN THE STYLE OF OFFENBACH
        FRANCO COLOMBO PUBLICATIONS   129058   .75
ROSSINI, G.   TOMEKKERI
    PETIT MESSE SOLENNELLE - PRELUDIO RELIGIOSO
        FRANCO COLOMBO PUBLICATIONS   129033   .75
ROSSINI, G.   MONTANI
    PETIT TRAIN DE PLAISIR, UN
        FRANCO COLOMBO PUBLICATIONS   129059   1.00
ROSSINI, G.   LISZT
    REGATA VENEZIANA, LA
        FRANCO COLOMBO PUBLICATIONS   128857   .90
ROSSINI, G.
    SCALA DI SETA, LA - OVERTURE
        FRANCO COLOMBO PUBLICATIONS   127769   1.00

ROSSINI, G.
    SEMIRAMIDE - OVERTURE
        FRANCO COLOMBO PUBLICATIONS   128645   .75
ROSSINI, G.   5
    STABAT MATER, CUJUS ANIMAM
        CENTURY MUSIC PUBLISHING COMPANY, INC.   182   .40
ROSSINI, G.
    TANCREDI - OVERTURE
        FRANCO COLOMBO PUBLICATIONS   127904   .60
ROSSINI, G.
    UNE REJOUISSANCE
        FABER MUSIC, LTD.   F0045
ROSSINI, G.   ZEPP   2-3
    WILLIAM TELL
        PRO-ART PUBLICATIONS, INC.   325   .50
ROSSINI, G.   BERMONT, H.   1B
    WILLIAM TELL -- FANFARE
        MUSICORD PUBLICATIONS, INC.   .45
ROSSINI, G.   KRUG   2
    WILLIAM TELL OVERTURE, EASY
        CENTURY MUSIC PUBLISHING COMPANY, INC.   532   .40
ROSSINI, G. *
    DANZA, LA
        FRANCO COLOMBO PUBLICATIONS   128321   1.00
ROSSINI, G. *   6
    LA REGATTA VENITIANA
        CENTURY MUSIC PUBLISHING COMPANY, INC.   1480   .40
ROSSMAN, F. A.
    HOP TOAD
        BELWIN-MILLS PUBLISHING CORPORATION   .60
ROSSMAN, F. A.   2
    LITTLE SWISS CLOCK, THE
        BELWIN-MILLS PUBLISHING CORPORATION   .60
ROSZA
    BEAUTY AND GRACE
        THE BIG THREE MUSIC CORPORATION   00.95
ROSZA
    BEN-HUR
        THE BIG THREE MUSIC CORPORATION   00.95
ROSZA
    KING OF KINGS, THE
        THE BIG THREE MUSIC CORPORATION   00.95
ROSZA
    LYDIA
        SAM FOX PUBLISHING COMPANY, INC.   .75
ROSZA
    LYDIA
        SOUTHERN MUSIC COMPANY   .75
ROSZA
    SPELLBOUND CONCERTO -- THEME
        CHAPPELL AND COMPANY, INC.   0023341-1502 .95
ROSZA
    VARIATIONS
        FRANCO COLOMBO PUBLICATIONS   SAL   4.25
ROSZA
    VINTNERS DAUGHTER, THE
        BROUDE BROTHERS LTD.   04.25
ROTA   COLE
    CLOWNS MARCH
        EDWARD B. MARKS MUSIC CORPORATION   01.00
ROTA
    LEGEND OF THE GLASS MOUNTAIN, THE
        SAM FOX PUBLISHING COMPANY, INC.   1.25
ROTA
    LEGEND OF THE GLASS MOUNTAIN, THE
        SOUTHERN MUSIC COMPANY   1.25
ROTA *
    ZAMPANO
        MCA MUSIC   1.00
ROTHGEB, M.   2
    GYPSY ECHOES
        WILLIS MUSIC COMPANY   .35
ROTHGEB, M.   1
    HOP SCOTCH
        WILLIS MUSIC COMPANY   .35
ROTSCHER, K.
    VENEZIANISCHER KARNEVAL, OP. 21 -- BALLET IN 7 PARTS ON THEMES
    OF D'ALBERT
        ASSOCIATED MUSIC PUBLISHERS, INC.   BOT   7.50
ROUBIER, H.
    CHACONNE, OP. 59
        G. SCHIRMER, INC.   .50
ROUBIER, H.
    MARCHE DES TROUBADOURS, OP. 32
        GERARD BILLAUDOT EDITIONS MUSICALES   1.30
ROUBIER, H.
    UNE FETE A TRIANON, OP. 52
        G. SCHIRMER, INC.   .50
ROUBIER, H.
    UNE FETE A TRIANON, OP. 52
        GERARD BILLAUDOT EDITIONS MUSICALES   1.30
ROUGET DE LISLE
    MARSEILLAISE, LA
        FRANCO COLOMBO PUBLICATIONS   SAL   1.50
ROUGNON
    JOYEUX PRINTEMPS
        FRANCO COLOMBO PUBLICATIONS   SAL   1.75
ROUSE, E.
    SNOW QUEEN
        BOOSEY AND HAWKES, INC.   1.00
ROUSSEL, A.
    DOUTE
        ELKAN-VOGEL, INC.   D   .90
ROUSSEL, A.
    LE FESTIN DE L'ARAIGNEE, OP. 17
        ELKAN-VOGEL, INC.   D   5.75
ROUSSEL, A.
    PETIT CANON PERPETUAL
        ELKAN-VOGEL, INC.   D   1.50
ROUSSEL, A.
    PRELUDE AND FUGUE, OP. 46
        ELKAN-VOGEL, INC.   D   2.75
ROUSSEL, A.
    PRINTEMPS
        ELKAN-VOGEL, INC.   D   4.00
ROUSSEL, A.
    RESURECTION
        FRANCO COLOMBO PUBLICATIONS   SAL   4.50
ROUSSEL, A.
    RETOUR DE FETE -- FROM RUSTIQUES, OP. 5
        ELKAN-VOGEL, INC.   D   1.80
ROUSSEL, A.
    RUSTIQUES, OP. 5
        ELKAN-VOGEL, INC.   D   5.00
ROUSSEL, A.
    SONATINE, OP. 16
        ELKAN-VOGEL, INC.   D   5.35

ROUSSEL, A.
    SUITE POUR PIANO
        FRANCO COLOMBO PUBLICATIONS   SAL   3.00
ROUSSEL, A.
    THREE PIECES, OP. 49
        ELKAN-VOGEL, INC.   D   3.00
ROVENGER   2
    BIG INDIAN CHIEF
        THEODORE PRESSER COMPANY   .50
ROVICS, H.
    THREE STUDIES FOR PIANO
        SEESAW MUSIC CORPORATION   4.00
ROWE, D.   2 1/2
    CHEERFULNESS
        THEODORE PRESSER COMPANY   .50
ROWLAND   ADVANCED
    DANSA BRASILEIRA
        SHAWNEE PRESS, INC.   .60
ROWLEY   3
    ANDALUSIAN DANCE
        BELWIN-MILLS PUBLISHING CORPORATION   .60
ROWLEY
    AQUARELLES
        BOOSEY AND HAWKES, INC.   1.00
ROWLEY   E
    CANZONETTA
        C. F. PETERS CORPORATION   H61   .90
ROWLEY
    CONCERT ETUDE NO. 2
        BOOSEY AND HAWKES, INC.   1.25
ROWLEY
    DOCK-SIDE SUITE
        BOOSEY AND HAWKES, INC.   1.25
ROWLEY
    EARLY ENGLISH SONATINAS
        BOOSEY AND HAWKES, INC.   1.50
ROWLEY
    FESTIVAL GROUPS FOR PIANO SELECTED BY ARTHUR BENJAMIN, SERIES 2
    -- AIR, OP. 25
        BOOSEY AND HAWKES, INC.   .60
ROWLEY
    FROM ANCIENT TO MODERN
        BOOSEY AND HAWKES, INC.   .90
ROWLEY
    HAPPENINGS
        BANKS AND SON LTD.   .95
ROWLEY
    HEDGE OF BRACKEN, A
        BANKS AND SON LTD.   .25
ROWLEY
    HORNPIPE
        BOOSEY AND HAWKES, INC.   .40
ROWLEY   2
    JUMPING JACK
        BELWIN-MILLS PUBLISHING CORPORATION   .60
ROWLEY
    MARIONETTES
        BANKS AND SON LTD.   .95
ROWLEY
    NOCTURNE NO. 01 IN B MINOR
        BOOSEY AND HAWKES, INC.   .90
ROWLEY
    NOCTURNE NO. 04 IN E
        BOOSEY AND HAWKES, INC.   .90
ROWLEY
    NOCTURNE NO. 05 IN F
        BOOSEY AND HAWKES, INC.   1.00
ROWLEY
    OLD ENGLISH WORTHIES
        BOOSEY AND HAWKES, INC.   1.25
ROWLEY   4
    ON THE HILLSIDE
        NOVELLO AND COMPANY, LTD.   55.0042.07 .40
ROWLEY
    POLKA-BURLESQUE
        BOOSEY AND HAWKES, INC.   1.25
ROWLEY   2
    SPRING IS DANCING
        BELWIN-MILLS PUBLISHING CORPORATION   .60
ROWLEY
    SUITE
        ELKAN-VOGEL, INC.   D   3.40
ROWLEY   4
    SUNLIT VALLEY
        NOVELLO AND COMPANY, LTD.   55.0013.03 .40
ROYAL--ED   ROYAL   3
    CAISSON SONG
        CENTURY MUSIC PUBLISHING COMPANY, INC.   3727   .40
ROYAL--ED   ROYAL   3
    FIELD ARTILLERY SONG
        CENTURY MUSIC PUBLISHING COMPANY, INC.   3727   .40
ROZIN
    BIT OF FOLKSY, A
        BOSTON MUSIC COMPANY   .50
ROZIN   2
    BURRO TRAIL
        CENTURY MUSIC PUBLISHING COMPANY, INC.   4380   .40
ROZIN   2
    CARNIVAL DAYS
        CENTURY MUSIC PUBLISHING COMPANY, INC.   4351   .40
ROZIN   2
    CELLO REVERIE
        CENTURY MUSIC PUBLISHING COMPANY, INC.   4190   .40
ROZIN   2
    CHOP SUEY BOOGIE
        BELWIN-MILLS PUBLISHING CORPORATION   .60
ROZIN   2
    CLOUDY SKIES
        BELWIN-MILLS PUBLISHING CORPORATION   .60
ROZIN   3 1/2
    CLOWN CAPERS
        BELWIN-MILLS PUBLISHING CORPORATION   .60
ROZIN   2-3
    COLOR GUARDS
        CENTURY MUSIC PUBLISHING COMPANY, INC.   4148   .40
ROZIN
    CONTINENTAL POLKA
        BOOSEY AND HAWKES, INC.   .40
ROZIN   1 1/2
    COPY ME
        BELWIN-MILLS PUBLISHING CORPORATION   .60
ROZIN   3
    EXAMINATION BLUES
        BOSTON MUSIC COMPANY   .50
ROZIN   3
    FAIR AND WARM
        BELWIN-MILLS PUBLISHING CORPORATION   .60

ROZIN   3
    GINGERBREAD HOUSE, THE
        BOSTON MUSIC COMPANY   .50
ROZIN   2
    GRASSHOPPERS
        PRO-ART PUBLICATIONS, INC.   496   .50
ROZIN
    GYPSY TALES
        BRODT MUSIC COMPANY   .45
ROZIN   1
    HALLOWEEN PRANKS
        CENTURY MUSIC PUBLISHING COMPANY, INC.   4337   .40
ROZIN   3 1/2
    HAPPY NEW YEAR
        BELWIN-MILLS PUBLISHING CORPORATION   .60
ROZIN   2
    HOP-ALONG POLKA
        THEODORE PRESSER COMPANY   .50
ROZIN   3
    HURRICANE HILDA
        BELWIN-MILLS PUBLISHING CORPORATION   .60
ROZIN   2
    JAMBOREE
        BELWIN-MILLS PUBLISHING CORPORATION   .60
ROZIN   2
    JOCKO
        BELWIN-MILLS PUBLISHING CORPORATION   .60
ROZIN   1 1/2
    LOOK AT THAT
        THEODORE PRESSER COMPANY   .50
ROZIN   2 1/2
    MELODY CORNER
        BELWIN-MILLS PUBLISHING CORPORATION   .60
ROZIN   2
    MIRRORS AND ME
        CENTURY MUSIC PUBLISHING COMPANY, INC.   4169   .40
ROZIN   2 1/2
    OVERCAST
        BELWIN-MILLS PUBLISHING CORPORATION   .60
ROZIN   1
    PEEK-A-BOO
        BOSTON MUSIC COMPANY   .50
ROZIN   2
    PING-PONG
        PRO-ART PUBLICATIONS, INC.   424   .50
ROZIN
    PLANTATION ECHOES
        BRODT MUSIC COMPANY   .45
ROZIN   3
    SLEEPY TOWN
        BELWIN-MILLS PUBLISHING CORPORATION   .60
ROZIN   2-3
    SOMBRERO DANCE
        PRO-ART PUBLICATIONS, INC.   468   .50
ROZIN   2
    SPIN, SPIN, SPIN
        PRO-ART PUBLICATIONS, INC.   423   .50
ROZIN
    SUBWAY RUSH
        BOOSEY AND HAWKES, INC.   .40
ROZIN   3
    SUMMER SHOWERS
        BELWIN-MILLS PUBLISHING CORPORATION   .60
ROZIN   2 1/2
    TAMBOURINE
        THEODORE PRESSER COMPANY   .50
ROZIN   2
    TOCCATINA
        BOSTON MUSIC COMPANY   .50
ROZIN
    TWO COUNTRYSIDE SKETCHES
        SOUTHERN MUSIC COMPANY   .50
ROZIN   3
    WALTZ OF THE WINDS
        BELWIN-MILLS PUBLISHING CORPORATION   .60
ROZIN
    WALTZING KEYS
        BRODT MUSIC COMPANY   .45
ROZSA, M.
    SONATA--1948
        ASSOCIATED MUSIC PUBLISHERS, INC.   BRH   3.00
RUBINSTEIN   5
    APOLLO ETUDE
        CENTURY MUSIC PUBLISHING COMPANY, INC.   1770   .40
RUBINSTEIN
    DIE NACHT, ROMANZE OP. 44 NO. 1
        SCHOTT   07117   .75
RUBINSTEIN
    EL DACHTERAN, MARCHE ORIENTALE--FROM 'MINIATURES'
        G. SCHIRMER, INC.   .30
RUBINSTEIN   SCHAUM, J.   4 1/2
    KAMENNOI-OSTROW
        BELWIN-MILLS PUBLISHING CORPORATION   .50
RUBINSTEIN   WEYBRIGHT   1 1/2
    KAMENNOI-OSTROW
        BELWIN-MILLS PUBLISHING CORPORATION   .60
RUBINSTEIN   5
    KAMENNOI-OSTROW
        CENTURY MUSIC PUBLISHING COMPANY, INC.   1051   .40
RUBINSTEIN   DEIS
    KAMENNOI-OSTROW
        G. SCHIRMER, INC.   .70
RUBINSTEIN
    KAMENNOI-OSTROW
        MCA MUSIC   1.00
RUBINSTEIN
    KAMENNOI-OSTROW --REVE ANGELIQUE--, OP. 10 NO. 22
        CARL FISCHER, INC.   S 782   .60
RUBINSTEIN   3
    LICHTERTANZ DER BRAUTE
        SCHOTT   07124 102 1.00
RUBINSTEIN   4
    MELODIE F-DUR OP. 3 NO. 1
        SCHOTT   01665 1/2 1.00
RUBINSTEIN   5
    MELODIE IN F, OP. 3 NO. 1
        BELWIN-MILLS PUBLISHING CORPORATION   296   .60
RUBINSTEIN
    MELODIE IN F, OP. 3 NO. 1
        G. SCHIRMER, INC.   .50
RUBINSTEIN   SCHAUM, J.   2 1/2
    MELODY IN F
        SCHAUM PUBLICATIONS, INC.   .60
RUBINSTEIN   JESTON, I. H.   3
    MELODY IN F
        VOLKWEIN BROS.   .35

RUBINSTEIN	2		
MELODY IN F -- SIMPLIFIED			
VOLKWEIN BROS.			.25
RUBINSTEIN	4		
MELODY IN F, OP. 23 NO. 2			
CENTURY MUSIC PUBLISHING COMPANY, INC.		313	.40
RUBINSTEIN			
MELODY IN F, OP. 3 NO. 1			
CARL FISCHER, INC.		S 979	.50
RUBINSTEIN CESI			
MELODY IN F, OP. 3 NO. 1			
FRANCO COLOMBO PUBLICATIONS		ER2245	.50
RUBINSTEIN DEL MAGLIO			
MELODY IN F, OP. 3 NO. 1			
FRANCO COLOMBO PUBLICATIONS		127354	.50
RUBINSTEIN	5		
OCTAVE STUDY IN C			
CENTURY MUSIC PUBLISHING COMPANY, INC.		177 0	.40
RUBINSTEIN	5		
POLKA BOHEME, OP. 82 NO. 7			
CENTURY MUSIC PUBLISHING COMPANY, INC.		1644	.40
RUBINSTEIN WALLIS	3		
ROMANCE IN E FLAT			
BOSTON MUSIC COMPANY			.50
RUBINSTEIN DEL MAGLIO			
ROMANCE IN E FLAT, OP. 44			
FRANCO COLOMBO PUBLICATIONS		127355	.50
RUBINSTEIN DEIS			
ROMANCE IN E FLAT, OP. 44 NO. 1			
G. SCHIRMER, INC.			.40
RUBINSTEIN	4		
ROMANCE, OP.44 NO. 1			
CENTURY MUSIC PUBLISHING COMPANY, INC.		373	.40
RUBINSTEIN	3		
SONG OF LOVE -- ROMANCE OP. 44, NO. 1			
THEODORE PRESSER COMPANY			.50
RUBINSTEIN	5		
STACCATO ETUDE IN C			
CENTURY MUSIC PUBLISHING COMPANY, INC.		1770	.40
RUBINSTEIN			
TURKISH MARCH FROM 'THE RUINS OF ATHENS'--BEETHOVEN			
G. SCHIRMER, INC.			.60
RUBINSTEIN	5-6		
VALSE CAPRICE IN E FLAT			
CENTURY MUSIC PUBLISHING COMPANY, INC.		2425	.40
RUBINSTEIN			
VALSE-CAPRICE IN E FLAT			
G. SCHIRMER, INC.			.70
RUBINSTEIN--ED RUBINSTEIN			
BESS YOU IS MY WOMAN			
CHAPPELL AND COMPANY, INC.		0447524	1.00
RUBINSTEIN--ED RUBINSTEIN			
I GOT PLENTY O' NUTTIN'			
CHAPPELL AND COMPANY, INC.		2230027-1502	.95
RUBINSTEIN--ED RUBINSTEIN			
SUMMERTIME, RUBENSTEIN CONCERT ARR.			
CHAPPELL AND COMPANY, INC.		5565023-1503	1.00
RUBINSTEIN, B. SCHAUM, J.	2		
CAVALRY TROT			
BELWIN-MILLS PUBLISHING CORPORATION			.50
RUBINSTEIN, B.			
WHIRLIGIG			
OXFORD UNIVERSITY PRESS		93.205	1.25
RUDAN			
BOZZETTI			
FRANCO COLOMBO PUBLICATIONS		BON.2023	1.50
RUDAN			
DIVERTIMENTO			
FRANCO COLOMBO PUBLICATIONS		BON.2425	1.75
RUDAN			
HERBARIUM			
FRANCO COLOMBO PUBLICATIONS		BON.2517	3.00
RUDAN			
RICHIAMI DEL MARE			
FRANCO COLOMBO PUBLICATIONS		BON.2427	2.25
RUDAN			
SCHERZO			
FRANCO COLOMBO PUBLICATIONS		BON.2380	.90
RUDAN			
SUITE LIBURNICA			
FRANCO COLOMBO PUBLICATIONS		BON.2480	2.25
RUDHYAR, D.	A		
GRANITES			
THEODORE PRESSER COMPANY			1.25
RUDHYAR, D.	A		
GRANITES -- THREE PAEANS			
THEODORE PRESSER COMPANY			2.50
RUEFF	7		
PRELUDE ET TOCCATA			
ALPHONSE LEDUC			
RUGER, J.			
SKETCHES AT THE BALLET			
BELWIN-MILLS PUBLISHING CORPORATION		20247	.85
RUGGLES, C.			
EVOCATIONS -- FOUR CHANTS FOR PIANO			
AMERICAN MUSIC EDITION			2.00
RUGGLES, C.			
EVOCATIONS -- FOUR CHANTS FOR PIANO, SPECIAL EDITION			
AMERICAN MUSIC EDITION			5.00
RUIZ ARMENGOL, M.			
LAS FRIAS MONTANAS			
EDICIONES MEXICANAS DE MUSICA, A. C.			01.25
RUIZ ARMENGOL, M.			
SONATINA			
EDITORIAL COOPERATIVA INTER-AMERICANA			01.25
RUIZ DEL PORTAL			
RETRAITE ESPAGNOL			
FRANCO COLOMBO PUBLICATIONS		SAL	1.75
RUIZ-PIPO			
KALEIDOSCOPE			
MCA MUSIC			1.75
RUNGEE	1		
ACROSS AN AZURE SKY, F MAJOR			
CENTURY MUSIC PUBLISHING COMPANY, INC.		2372	.40
RUNGEE	1		
BY THE BROOKLET			
CENTURY MUSIC PUBLISHING COMPANY, INC.		2374	.40
RUNGEE	1		
GOLDEN GLOW			
CENTURY MUSIC PUBLISHING COMPANY, INC.		2373	.40
RUNGEE	1		
GRASSY DELLS			
CENTURY MUSIC PUBLISHING COMPANY, INC.		2369	.40
RUNGEE	1		
HILL TOPS FAIRY			
CENTURY MUSIC PUBLISHING COMPANY, INC.		2377	.40

RUNGEE	1		
SKY AND FOREST			
CENTURY MUSIC PUBLISHING COMPANY, INC.		2378	.40
RUNGEE	1		
TO THE SUNRISE			
CENTURY MUSIC PUBLISHING COMPANY, INC.		2371	.40
RUNGEE	1		
WOODLAND PINES			
CENTURY MUSIC PUBLISHING COMPANY, INC.		2370	.40
RUSH, L.			
OH, SUSANNA			
ELKAN-VOGEL, INC.		J	2.50
RUSSELL	4		
BLUE LAGOON			
THEODORE PRESSER COMPANY			.50
RUSSELL STEINER	4		
BOOGIE ON THE SHANNON RIVER			
BELWIN-MILLS PUBLISHING CORPORATION			.60
RUSSELL	1		
BUBBLE GUM			
PRO-ART PUBLICATIONS, INC.		472	.50
RUSSELL	2-3		
CALYPSO INTERLUDE			
PRO-ART PUBLICATIONS, INC.		607	.50
RUSSELL	2-3		
CARIBBEAN LOVE SONG			
PRO-ART PUBLICATIONS, INC.		608	.50
RUSSELL	3		
CHA CHA ON THE BEACH			
PRO-ART PUBLICATIONS, INC.		609	.50
RUSSELL	1 1/2		
FIFE AND DRUM			
WILLIS MUSIC COMPANY			.40
RUSSELL	1 1/2		
FIFE AND DRUM, THE			
WILLIS MUSIC COMPANY			.40
RUSSELL	1-2		
FIRST NOCTURNE			
PRO-ART PUBLICATIONS, INC.		368	.50
RUSSELL	1		
FOR A LITTLE GIRL			
BOSTON MUSIC COMPANY			.50
RUSSELL	1		
FOUR RIDDLES			
BOSTON MUSIC COMPANY			.50
RUSSELL			
ISLAND SONG			
BELWIN-MILLS PUBLISHING CORPORATION			.60
RUSSELL	3		
MILLER BOY -- VARIATIONS ON AN AMERICAN FOLK SONG			
BOSTON MUSIC COMPANY			.50
RUSSELL	1		
RECREATIONS			
BOSTON MUSIC COMPANY			.50
RUSSELL	2		
ROCKIN' THE SCALES			
BOSTON MUSIC COMPANY			.50
RUSSELL	1		
ROPE TRICKS			
PRO-ART PUBLICATIONS, INC.		446	.50
RUSSELL	3		
RUNAWAY COLT			
BOSTON MUSIC COMPANY			.50
RUSSELL	2		
SEA SHELLS			
BELWIN-MILLS PUBLISHING CORPORATION			.60
RUSSELL	2		
SINGING TEA KETTLE			
BELWIN-MILLS PUBLISHING CORPORATION			.60
RUSSELL	2-3		
SINGING WATER			
PRO-ART PUBLICATIONS, INC.		329	.50
RUSSELL	3		
STAMPEDE			
BOSTON MUSIC COMPANY			.50
RUSSELL	2		
TIME MACHINE, THE			
PRO-ART PUBLICATIONS, INC.		600	.50
RUSSELL SCHAUM, J.	2 1/2		
WHERE THE RIVER SHANNON FLOWS			
SCHAUM PUBLICATIONS, INC.			.60
RUSSELL	3		
WITCHES FLIGHT, B FLAT			
CENTUPY MUSIC PUBLISHING COMPANY, INC.		4398	.40
RUST			
SONATA NO. 01			
FRANCO COLOMBO PUBLICATIONS		SAL	1.75
RUST			
SONATA NO. 02			
FRANCO COLOMBO PUBLICATIONS		SAL	1.75
RUST			
SONATA NO. 03			
FRANCO COLOMBO PUBLICATIONS		SAL	1.75
RUST			
SONATA NO. 04			
FRANCO COLOMBO PUBLICATIONS		SAL	1.75
RUST			
SONATA NO. 05			
FRANCO COLOMBO PUBLICATIONS		SAL	1.75
RUST			
SONATA NO. 06			
FRANCO COLOMBO PUBLICATIONS		SAL	1.75
RUST			
SONATA NO. 07			
FRANCO COLOMBO PUBLICATIONS		SAL	1.75
RUST			
SONATA NO. 08			
FRANCO COLOMBO PUBLICATIONS		SAL	1.75
RUST			
SONATA NO. 09			
FRANCO COLOMBO PUBLICATIONS		SAL	1.75
RUST			
SONATA NO. 10			
FRANCO COLOMBO PUBLICATIONS		SAL	1.75
RUST			
SONATA NO. 11			
FRANCO COLOMBO PUBLICATIONS		SAL	1.75
RUST			
SONATA NO. 12			
FRANCO COLOMBO PUBLICATIONS		SAL	1.75
RUTINI PERINELLO	3		
SONATA, OP. 5 NO. 5			
BARENREITER VERLAG		CM 14423	
RUYNEMAN			
KLEINE SONATE			
UNIVERSAL EDITION		UE 8224	1.30

RUYNEMAN　　　　　　　　　　　　　　　　　　　　　　　M
　SONATINA
　　C. F. PETERS CORPORATION　　　　　　　　B420　　1.25
　　　　　　　　　　　　　　　　　　　　　　4
RYDER
　SONG OF THE ALPS, OP. 51
　　CENTURY MUSIC PUBLISHING COMPANY, INC.　2586　　.40
　　　　　　　　　　　　　　　　　　　　　　2
SADLON
　AUTUMN BREEZES
　　BELWIN-MILLS PUBLISHING CORPORATION　　　　　　.60
　　　　　　　　　　　　　　　　　　　　　　2 1/2
SADLON
　DANCE OF THE WOODSPRITES
　　BELWIN-MILLS PUBLISHING CORPORATION　　　　　　.60
　　　　　　　　　　　　　　　　　　　　　　2
SADLON
　PUPPETS ON THE MARCH
　　BELWIN-MILLS PUBLISHING CORPORATION　　　　　　.60
　　　　　　　　　　　　　　　　　　　　　　2 1/2
SADLON
　WALTZ 'JOY'
　　BELWIN-MILLS PUBLISHING CORPORATION　　　　　　.60
　　　　　　　　　　　　　　　　　　　　　　1
SAEGEL
　COUCOU, LE
　　ALPHONSE LEDUC
　　　　　　　　　　　　　　　　　　　　　　3
SAEGER
　THROUGH THE ASTEROIDS
　　BOSTON MUSIC COMPANY　　　　　　　　　　　　.50
SAENZ
　JUGUETES
　　FRANCO COLOMBO PUBLICATIONS　　　　　BA9194　　1.00
SAENZ
　NORTENA
　　FRANCO COLOMBO PUBLICATIONS　　　　　BA9720　　.75
SAENZ
　VARIATIONS
　　FRANCO COLOMBO PUBLICATIONS　　　　　BA10349　.75
SAINT-SAENS
　AFRICA, OP. 89 -- FANTASIE FOR PIANO AND ORCH., PIANO RED.
　　ELKAN-VOGEL, INC.　　　　　　　　　　D　　4.15
SAINT-SAENS
　ALBUM, OP. 72 NO. 1 -- PRELUDE
　　ELKAN-VOGEL, INC.　　　　　　　　　　D　　1.60
SAINT-SAENS
　ALBUM, OP. 72 NO. 2 -- CARILLON
　　ELKAN-VOGEL, INC.　　　　　　　　　　D　　1.70
SAINT-SAENS
　ALBUM, OP. 72 NO. 3 -- TOCCATA
　　ELKAN-VOGEL, INC.　　　　　　　　　　D　　2.25
SAINT-SAENS
　ALBUM, OP. 72 NO. 4 -- VALSE
　　ELKAN-VOGEL, INC.　　　　　　　　　　D　　3.65
SAINT-SAENS
　ALBUM, OP. 72 NO. 5 -- CHANSON NAPOLITAINE
　　ELKAN-VOGEL, INC.　　　　　　　　　　D　　1.40
SAINT-SAENS
　ALBUM, OP. 72 NO. 6 -- FINAL
　　ELKAN-VOGEL, INC.　　　　　　　　　　D　　1.80
SAINT-SAENS
　ALLEGRO APPASSIONATO, OP. 70
　　ELKAN-VOGEL, INC.　　　　　　　　　　　　　3.00
SAINT-SAENS
　ALLEGRO APPASSIONATO, OP. 70
　　INTERNATIONAL MUSIC COMPANY　　　　　　　　1.75
SAINT-SAENS　　　　　　　　　　BIZET
　ALLEGRO SCHERZANDO, OP. 22
　　ELKAN-VOGEL, INC.　　　　　　　　　　D　　2.75
SAINT-SAENS
　BENEDICTION NUPTIALE, OP. 9
　　ELKAN-VOGEL, INC.　　　　　　　　　　D　　1.00
SAINT-SAENS
　BOURREE FOR THE LEFT HAND, OP. 135, NO. 4
　　ELKAN-VOGEL, INC.　　　　　　　　　　　　　2.75
SAINT-SAENS
　CAPRICE ON THE AIRS DE BALLET FROM GLUCK'S 'ALCESTE'
　　G. SCHIRMER, INC.　　　　　　　　　　　　　1.10
SAINT-SAENS　　　　　　　　　　BENFELD, A.
　CAPRICE-VALSE -- FROM 'WEDDING CAKE', OP. 76
　　ELKAN-VOGEL, INC.　　　　　　　　　　D　　4.00
SAINT-SAENS
　CAPRICE, OP. 4
　　ELKAN-VOGEL, INC.　　　　　　　　　　J　　2.50
　　　　　　　　　　　　　　　　　　　　　　4
SAINT-SAENS
　CYGNE, LE
　　CENTURY MUSIC PUBLISHING COMPANY, INC.　1693　　.40
　　　　　　　　　　　　　　　　　　　　　　2
SAINT-SAENS
　CYGNE, LE
　　CENTURY MUSIC PUBLISHING COMPANY, INC.　2140　　.40
　　　　　　　　　　　　　　　　　　　　　　3
SAINT-SAENS
　DANCE MACABRE
　　CENTURY MUSIC PUBLISHING COMPANY, INC.　3330　　.40
　　　　　　　　　　　　　　　　　　　　　　3
SAINT-SAENS
　DANCE MACABRE
　　WILLIS MUSIC COMPANY　　　　　　　　　　　　.60
SAINT-SAENS　　　　　　　　　　LISZT
　DANSE MACABRE
　　ELKAN-VOGEL, INC.　　　　　　　　　　　　　4.00
SAINT-SAENS　　　　　　　　　　LISZT
　DANSE MACABRE
　　ELKAN-VOGEL, INC.　　　　　　　　　　D　　5.35
SAINT-SAENS　　　　　　　　　　CRAMER
　DANSE MACABRE
　　G. SCHIRMER, INC.　　　　　　　　　　　　　.90
SAINT-SAENS　　　　　　　　　　SCHAUM, J.　　3
　DANSE MACABRE
　　SCHAUM PUBLICATIONS, INC.　　　　　　　　　.50
SAINT-SAENS　　　　　　　　　　CRAMER
　DANSE MACABRE, OP. 40
　　ELKAN-VOGEL, INC.　　　　　　　　　　　　　2.75
SAINT-SAENS　　　　　　　　　　CRAMER, J.
　DANSE MACABRE, OP. 40
　　ELKAN-VOGEL, INC.　　　　　　　　　　D　　3.00
SAINT-SAENS　　　　　　　　　　ECKSTEIN
　EXCERPT FROM 'DANSE MACABRE'
　　CARL FISCHER, INC.　　　　　　　　　　S 2290　.50
SAINT-SAENS
　GAVOTTE -- FROM SUITE, OP. 90
　　ELKAN-VOGEL, INC.　　　　　　　　　　D　　1.75
SAINT-SAENS　　　　　　　　　　LEVY
　GAVOTTE IN B MINOR FROM VIOLIN SONATA NO. 2--BACH
　　G. SCHIRMER, INC.　　　　　　　　　　　　　.50
SAINT-SAENS
　GAVOTTE IN E FROM VIOLIN SONATA NO. 6--BACH
　　G. SCHIRMER, INC.　　　　　　　　　　　　　.40
SAINT-SAENS
　JAVOTTE
　　ELKAN-VOGEL, INC.　　　　　　　　　　　　　9.50
SAINT-SAENS
　LA JEUNESS D'HERCULE, OP. 50
　　ELKAN-VOGEL, INC.　　　　　　　　　　D　　2.30

SAINT-SAENS
　LE CARNAVAL DES ANIMAUX -- COMPLETE
　　ELKAN-VOGEL, INC.　　　　　　　　　　D　　4.60
SAINT-SAENS
　LE CARNAVAL DES ANIMAUX, NO. 01 -- INTRODUCTION ET MARCHE ROYALE DU LION
　　ELKAN-VOGEL, INC.　　　　　　　　　　D　　1.50
SAINT-SAENS
　LE CARNAVAL DES ANIMAUX, NO. 02 -- POULES ET COQS
　　ELKAN-VOGEL, INC.　　　　　　　　　　D　　.60
SAINT-SAENS
　LE CARNAVAL DES ANIMAUX, NO. 03 -- HEMIONES
　　ELKAN-VOGEL, INC.　　　　　　　　　　D　　.75
SAINT-SAENS
　LE CARNAVAL DES ANIMAUX, NO. 04 -- TORTUES
　　ELKAN-VOGEL, INC.　　　　　　　　　　D　　1.20
SAINT-SAENS
　LE CARNAVAL DES ANIMAUX, NO. 05 -- L'ELEPHANT
　　ELKAN-VOGEL, INC.　　　　　　　　　　D　　1.25
SAINT-SAENS
　LE CARNAVAL DES ANIMAUX, NO. 06 -- KANGOUROUS
　　ELKAN-VOGEL, INC.　　　　　　　　　　D　　1.25
SAINT-SAENS
　LE CARNAVAL DES ANIMAUX, NO. 07 -- AQUARIUM
　　ELKAN-VOGEL, INC.　　　　　　　　　　D　　1.25
SAINT-SAENS
　LE CARNAVAL DES ANIMAUX, NO. 08 -- PERSONNAGES A LONGUES OREILLES
　　ELKAN-VOGEL, INC.　　　　　　　　　　D　　.75
SAINT-SAENS
　LE CARNAVAL DES ANIMAUX, NO. 09 -- LE COUCOU AU FOND DES BOIS
　　ELKAN-VOGEL, INC.　　　　　　　　　　D　　.90
SAINT-SAENS
　LE CARNAVAL DES ANIMAUX, NO. 10 -- VOLIERE
　　ELKAN-VOGEL, INC.　　　　　　　　　　D　　1.50
SAINT-SAENS
　LE CARNAVAL DES ANIMAUX, NO. 11 -- PIANISTES
　　ELKAN-VOGEL, INC.　　　　　　　　　　D　　.60
SAINT-SAENS
　LE CARNAVAL DES ANIMAUX, NO. 12 -- FOSSILES
　　ELKAN-VOGEL, INC.　　　　　　　　　　D　　1.00
SAINT-SAENS
　LE CARNAVAL DES ANIMAUX, NO. 13 -- LE CYGNE
　　ELKAN-VOGEL, INC.　　　　　　　　　　D　　1.70
SAINT-SAENS
　LE CARNAVAL DES ANIMAUX, NO. 14 -- FINAL
　　ELKAN-VOGEL, INC.　　　　　　　　　　D　　1.25
SAINT-SAENS
　MARCHE MILITAIRE FRANCAISE DE LA SUITE ALGERIENNE, OP. 60
　　ELKAN-VOGEL, INC.　　　　　　　　　　D　　3.50
SAINT-SAENS
　MARCHE-SCHERZO, OP. 2
　　ELKAN-VOGEL, INC.　　　　　　　　　　D　　1.50
SAINT-SAENS
　MENUET ET VALSE, OP. 56
　　ELKAN-VOGEL, INC.　　　　　　　　　　D　　1.50
　　　　　　　　　　　　　　　　　　　　　　4
SAINT-SAENS
　MY HEART AT THY SWEET VOICE
　　BELWIN-MILLS PUBLISHING CORPORATION　299　　.60
　　　　　　　　　　　　　　　　　　　　　　3
SAINT-SAENS
　MY HEART AT THY SWEET VOICE
　　CENTURY MUSIC PUBLISHING COMPANY, INC.　2013　　.40
　　　　　　　　　　　　　　　　　　　　　　3
SAINT-SAENS
　MY HEART AT THY SWEET VOICE
　　CENTURY MUSIC PUBLISHING COMPANY, INC.　2013　　.40
SAINT-SAENS
　ORATORIO DE NOEL
　　ELKAN-VOGEL, INC.　　　　　　　　　　D　　1.10
SAINT-SAENS
　PRELUDE LE DELUGE
　　ELKAN-VOGEL, INC.　　　　　　　　　　D　　1.25
SAINT-SAENS
　PREMIER MAZURKA, OP. 21
　　ELKAN-VOGEL, INC.　　　　　　　　　　D　　1.75
SAINT-SAENS　　　　　　　　　　DURAND, A.
　REVERIE DU SOIR DE LA SUITE ALGERIENNE, OP. 60
　　ELKAN-VOGEL, INC.　　　　　　　　　　D　　1.70
SAINT-SAENS
　RHAPSODIE D'AUVERGNE, OP. 73
　　ELKAN-VOGEL, INC.　　　　　　　　　　D　　4.50
　　　　　　　　　　　　　　　　　　　　　　3
SAINT-SAENS
　ROMANCE SANS PAROLES
　　CENTURY MUSIC PUBLISHING COMPANY, INC.　3344　　.40
　　　　　　　　　　　　　　　　　　　　　　3
SAINT-SAENS
　SAMSON AND DELILA, MY HEART
　　CENTURY MUSIC PUBLISHING COMPANY, INC.　2013　　.40
SAINT-SAENS
　SAMSON ET DALILA
　　ELKAN-VOGEL, INC.　　　　　　　　　　D　　3.00
SAINT-SAENS
　SIX ETUDES POUR LA MAIN GAUCHE SEULE, OP. 135 -- BOUREE
　　ELKAN-VOGEL, INC.　　　　　　　　　　D　　3.25
SAINT-SAENS
　SIX ETUDES POUR LA MAIN GAUCHE SEULE, OP. 135 -- ELEGIE
　　ELKAN-VOGEL, INC.　　　　　　　　　　D　　2.00
SAINT-SAENS
　SIX ETUDES POUR LA MAIN GAUCHE SEULE, OP. 135 -- MOTO PERPETUO
　　ELKAN-VOGEL, INC.　　　　　　　　　　D　　1.05
SAINT-SAENS
　SIX ETUDES POUR LE PIANO, BK. 1, NO. 01 -- PRELUDE
　　ELKAN-VOGEL, INC.　　　　　　　　　　D　　1.75
SAINT-SAENS
　SIX ETUDES POUR LE PIANO, BK. 1, NO. 02 -- POUR L'INDEPENDANCE DES DOIGTS
　　ELKAN-VOGEL, INC.　　　　　　　　　　D　　.75
SAINT-SAENS
　SIX ETUDES POUR LE PIANO, BK. 1, NO. 03 -- PRELUDE ET FUGUE EN FA MINEUR
　　ELKAN-VOGEL, INC.　　　　　　　　　　D　　2.00
SAINT-SAENS
　SIX ETUDES POUR LE PIANO, BK. 1, NO. 04 -- ETUDE DE RYTHME
　　ELKAN-VOGEL, INC.　　　　　　　　　　D　　1.50
SAINT-SAENS
　SIX ETUDES POUR LE PIANO, BK. 1, NO. 05 -- PRELUDE ET FUGUE EN LA MAJEUR
　　ELKAN-VOGEL, INC.　　　　　　　　　　D　　1.60
SAINT-SAENS
　SIX ETUDES POUR LE PIANO, BK. 1, NO. 06 -- EN FORME DE VALSE
　　ELKAN-VOGEL, INC.　　　　　　　　　　D　　4.50
SAINT-SAENS
　SIX ETUDES POUR LE PIANO, BK. 2, NO. 01 -- TIERCES MAJEURES ET MINEURES
　　ELKAN-VOGEL, INC.　　　　　　　　　　D　　1.60
SAINT-SAENS
　SIX ETUDES POUR LE PIANO, BK. 2, NO. 02 -- TRAITS CHROMATIQUES
　　ELKAN-VOGEL, INC.　　　　　　　　　　D　　1.25

SAINT-SAENS
    SIX ETUDES POUR LE PIANO, BK. 2, NO. 03 -- PRELUDE ET FUGUE
        ELKAN-VOGEL, INC.   D   1.50
SAINT-SAENS
    SIX ETUDES POUR LE PIANO, BK. 2, NO. 04 -- LES CLOCHES DE LAS
    PALMAS
        ELKAN-VOGEL, INC.   D   1.25
SAINT-SAENS
    SIX ETUDES POUR LE PIANO, BK. 2, NO. 05 -- TIERCES MAJEURES
    CHROMATIQUES
        ELKAN-VOGEL, INC.   D   1.25
SAINT-SAENS
    SIX ETUDES POUR LE PIANO, BK. 2, NO. 06 -- TOCCATA D'APRES LE
    CINQUIEME CONCERTO
        ELKAN-VOGEL, INC.   D   3.00
SAINT-SAENS   SCHAUM, J.   2
    SPINNING WHEEL OF OMPHALE
        BELWIN-MILLS PUBLISHING CORPORATION   .50
SAINT-SAENS
    SUITE, OP. 90
        ELKAN-VOGEL, INC.   D   3.40
SAINT-SAENS   4
    SWAN
        BELWIN-MILLS PUBLISHING CORPORATION   300   .60
SAINT-SAENS   4
    SWAN, THE
        CENTURY MUSIC PUBLISHING COMPANY, INC.   1693   .40
SAINT-SAENS   ZEPP   4
    SWAN, THE
        PRO-ART PUBLICATIONS, INC.   382   .50
SAINT-SAENS   THOMPSON, J.   1
    SWAN, THE
        WILLIS MUSIC COMPANY   .40
SAINT-SAENS   PALMERI
    SWAN, THE--FROM 'CARNAVAL DES ANIMAUX'
        G. SCHIRMER, INC.   .35
SAINT-SAENS   LEVINE
    SWAN, THE--FROM 'CARNAVAL DES ANIMAUX'
        G. SCHIRMER, INC.   .50
SAINT-SAENS   HOSKIER
    SWAN, THE--MELODY FROM THE 'CARNAVAL DES ANIMAUX'
        G. SCHIRMER, INC.   .50
SAINT-SAENS   PHILIPP, I.
    TOCCATA - ETUDE NO. 6 -,OP. 222
        INTERNATIONAL MUSIC COMPANY   1.75
SAINT-SAENS
    TOCCATA, OP. 111, NO. 6
        ELKAN-VOGEL, INC.   3.00
SAINT-SAENS
    TROISIEME MAZURKA, OP. 66
        ELKAN-VOGEL, INC.   D   2.50
SAINT-SAENS
    VALSE NONCHALANTE, OP. 110
        ELKAN-VOGEL, INC.   D   2.25
SALMHOFER, FR.
    KLAVIERSTUCK IN QUARTEN, OP. 3
        UNIVERSAL EDITION   UE 7140   1.10
SALMHOFER, FR.
    SCHERZO, OP. 4
        UNIVERSAL EDITION   UE 7141   1.10
SALMHOFER, FR.
    SONATA IN C MAJOR
        UNIVERSAL EDITION   UE 12129   2.55
SALTA
    NOCTURNE
        FRANCO COLOMBO PUBLICATIONS   NY1318   .60
SALTA
    SORROW OF A LONELY HEART
        BELWIN-MILLS PUBLISHING CORPORATION   20275   .85
SALTER, L.
    SPOOKS
        FRANCO COLOMBO PUBLICATIONS   LD524   .60
SALUTRINSKAYA
    LULLABY -- WITH DANCE BY GERCHIK
        MCA MUSIC   .60
SALVATORI
    DANZA MATTUTINA
        FRANCO COLOMBO PUBLICATIONS   FOR.11966   1.00
SALVATORI
    TOCCATA
        FRANCO COLOMBO PUBLICATIONS   FOR.11967   1.00
SALZAR, A.
    SONATA
        PAN AMERICAN UNION   01.25
SAMAZEUILH
    CHANSON A MA POUPEE
        ELKAN-VOGEL, INC.   D   1.60
SAMAZEUILH
    ESQUISSES
        ELKAN-VOGEL, INC.   D   3.50
SAMAZEUILH
    EVOCATION
        ELKAN-VOGEL, INC.   D   .90
SAMAZEUILH
    LE CHANT DE LA MER
        ELKAN-VOGEL, INC.   D   6.00
SAMAZEUILH
    SERENADE
        ELKAN-VOGEL, INC.   D   2.30
SAMGIORGI
    INTRODUCTION
        FRANCO COLOMBO PUBLICATIONS   FOR.12032   .90
SAMINSKY
    CONTE NO. 2
        FRANCO COLOMBO PUBLICATIONS   SAL   2.50
SAMINSKY
    DANSE RITUELLE DU SABBATH
        FRANCO COLOMBO PUBLICATIONS   SAL   4.00
SAMINSKY
    GAILLARDE D'UNE PESTE JOYEUSE -- OPERA-BALLET --
        FRANCO COLOMBO PUBLICATIONS   SAL   7.00
SAMINSKY
    LAMENTATIONS DE RACHEL
        FRANCO COLOMBO PUBLICATIONS   SAL   7.00
SAMINSKY
    VISION
        FRANCO COLOMBO PUBLICATIONS   SAL   2.50
SAMPSON, G.   3
    BAGATELLE
        NOVELLO AND COMPANY, LTD.   55.0004.04   .25
SAMPSON, G.   3
    COUNTRY DANCE, A
        NOVELLO AND COMPANY, LTD.   55.0005.02   .40
SAMUEL ROUSSEAU
    CHANSON POUR BERCER
        FRANCO COLOMBO PUBLICATIONS   SAL   1.75

SANCAN, P.
    CAPRICE ROMANTIQUE
        ELKAN-VOGEL, INC.   D   1.50
SANCAN, P.
    TOCCATA
        ELKAN-VOGEL, INC.   D   3.50
SANCHEZ GAVITO, J.
    SUITE DE VALSES NO. 1
        ASSOCIATED MUSIC PUBLISHERS, INC.   UME   .75
SANCHEZ GAVITO, J.
    SUITE DE VALSES NO. 2
        ASSOCIATED MUSIC PUBLISHERS, INC.   UME   .50
SANCHEZ GAVITO, J.
    SUITE DE VALSES NO. 3
        ASSOCIATED MUSIC PUBLISHERS, INC.   UME   .50
SANDBOURNE   2
    CAMPING AT NIGHT
        CENTURY MUSIC PUBLISHING COMPANY, INC.   4316   .40
SANDBOURNE   1
    FOUR LITTLE TUNES
        PRO-ART PUBLICATIONS, INC.   58   .50
SANDBOURNE   2
    PLAYING WITH PHRASES
        PRO-ART PUBLICATIONS, INC.   61   .50
SANDBOURNE   3
    SNAPPY AND SMOOTH
        PRO-ART PUBLICATIONS, INC.   72   .50
SANDBOURNE   1-2
    WAITING ON THE CORNER
        PRO-ART PUBLICATIONS, INC.   71   .50
SANDERS, J.
    IMPROVISATIONS
        THE BIG THREE MUSIC CORPORATION   01.50
SANDOVAL
    LA MARIPOSA
        EDWARD B. MARKS MUSIC CORPORATION   01.00
SANDOVAL
    PICTURE OF A MAN AND WIFE CONVERSING
        MCA MUSIC   1.25
SANGIORGI
    IN MODO DI TARANTELLA
        FRANCO COLOMBO PUBLICATIONS   FOR.12255   1.25
SANGIORGI
    LITTLE SUITE
        FRANCO COLOMBO PUBLICATIONS   FOR.12273   1.75
SANGIORGI
    MAZURKA
        FRANCO COLOMBO PUBLICATIONS   FOR.12272   1.25
SANGIORGI   CULTRERA, G.
    PICCOLA SUITE
        EDIZIONI BERBEN   EBA 1680   1.50
SANGIORGI
    PRELUDE
        FRANCO COLOMBO PUBLICATIONS   FOR.12027   1.25
SANGIORGI
    PRELUDE AND DIVERTIMENTO
        FRANCO COLOMBO PUBLICATIONS   FOR.12034   1.25
SANGIORGI
    RONDO BURLESCO
        FRANCO COLOMBO PUBLICATIONS   FOR.12029   1.25
SANGIORGI
    TOCCATA
        FRANCO COLOMBO PUBLICATIONS   FOR.12033   1.25
SANGIORGI
    VALZER AND IN MODO DI RUMBA
        FRANCO COLOMBO PUBLICATIONS   FOR.12256   1.25
SANJUAN, P.   MD
    TOCCATA
        THEODORE PRESSER COMPANY   1.00
SANTLY   3-4
    DRIFTING ON, FOX TROT
        CENTURY MUSIC PUBLISHING COMPANY, INC.   2555   .40
SANTOLIQUIDO
    GIARDINI NOTTURNI
        FRANCO COLOMBO PUBLICATIONS   FOR.11743   1.75
SANTOLIQUIDO
    IMPROMPTU IN C
        FRANCO COLOMBO PUBLICATIONS   FOR.11397   1.75
SANTOLIQUIDO
    THREE MINIATURES FOR CHILDREN
        FRANCO COLOMBO PUBLICATIONS   FOR.11743   1.75
SANTOLIQUIDO
    TWO ACQUEFORTI TUNISINE - LA DANZARTRICE ARABA
        FRANCO COLOMBO PUBLICATIONS   FOR.10802   1.25
SANTOLIQUIDO
    TWO ACQUEFORTI TUNISINE - 1. LA NOTTE SAHARIANA
        FRANCO COLOMBO PUBLICATIONS   FOR.10801   1.25
SANTONJA, O.
    DORMIDITO LE VI YO
        ASSOCIATED MUSIC PUBLISHERS, INC.   UME   .50
SANTORO, C.
    INTERMITENCIAS
        ELKAN-VOGEL, INC.   J   2.00
SANTORSOLA, G.
    CANCAO TRISTE E DANCA BRASILEIRA
        EDIZIONI BERBEN   EB 1626   3.60
SANTORSOLA, G.
    CHORO
        PEER SOUTHERN ORGANIZATION   00.60
SAPELLNIKOFF
    DANCE OF THE ELVES, OP. 3
        MUSICA OBSCURA   3.25
SAPP, G.
    ERSTE SONATA FUR KLAVIER
        SEESAW MUSIC CORPORATION   5.00
SARACENI
    RICERCARE
        FRANCO COLOMBO PUBLICATIONS   DS566   1.00
SARAI, T.
    SONATINA
        KULTURA   .75
SARASATE
    GIPSY AIRS, OP. 20
        G. SCHIRMER, INC.   .70
SARASATE   SCHAUM, J.   4
    GYPSY RHAPSODY, OP. 20
        BELWIN-MILLS PUBLISHING CORPORATION   .50
SARASATE
    ZAPATEADO, OP. 23 NO. 2
        FRANCO COLOMBO PUBLICATIONS   BA7643   1.00
SARDA, A.
    FIVE PIECES FOR PIANO, 1970
        SEESAW MUSIC CORPORATION   2.00
SARDI, S.
    PICCOLO VALZER PER ROSARIA
        EDIZIONI BERBEN   EB 1539   1.20

SARDI, S.
    QUATRO VEZZEGGIATIVI IN MI-DO-RE
        EDIZIONI BERBEN   EB 1392   1.50
SARIA, T.
    RONDOLETTO
        KULTURA   .60
SARNO
    REFLEXOES HARMONICAS NO. 4
        FRANCO COLOMBO PUBLICATIONS   DS833   3.25
SAROLA   3-4
    ALASKAN TWILIGHT, F MAJOR
        CENTURY MUSIC PUBLISHING COMPANY, INC.   2501   .40
SAROLA   5
    IN GOLDEN AUTUMN
        CENTURY MUSIC PUBLISHING COMPANY, INC.   2502   .40
SARTORIO   3
    TORCHLIGHT DANCE
        CENTURY MUSIC PUBLISHING COMPANY, INC.   2207   .40
SARTORIO   2
    UNDER THE LINDENS, MAZURKA
        CENTURY MUSIC PUBLISHING COMPANY, INC.   1039   .40
SAS, A.
    MELODIA Y AIRE VARIADO
        PEER SOUTHERN ORGANIZATION   01.50
SAS, A.
    PRELUDIO Y TOCCATA
        PEER SOUTHERN ORGANIZATION   01.10
SAS, A.
    SONATA, OP. 47
        PEER SOUTHERN ORGANIZATION   01.85
SATIE, E.
    AVANT DERNIERES PENSES
        FRANCO COLOMBO PUBLICATIONS   SAL   2.50
SATIE, E.
    BUREAUCRATIC SONATINA
        ELKAN-VOGEL, INC.   CON   3.00
SATIE, E.
    DANSES GOTHIQUES
        FRANCO COLOMBO PUBLICATIONS   SAL   1.00
SATIE, E.
    DIVA DE L'EMPIRE, LA
        FRANCO COLOMBO PUBLICATIONS   SAL   2.00
SATIE, E.
    FILS DES ETIOLES, LE
        FRANCO COLOMBO PUBLICATIONS   SAL   4.25
SATIE, E.   MILHAUD, D.
    FIVE GRIMACES, OP. POSTH.
        UNIVERSAL EDITION   UE 9915   3.75
SATIE, E.
    GNOSSIENNE NO. 1
        CARL FISCHER, INC.   HO 521   .50
SATIE, E.
    GNOSSIENNE NO. 1
        FRANCO COLOMBO PUBLICATIONS   SAL   1.00
SATIE, E.
    GNOSSIENNE NO. 2
        FRANCO COLOMBO PUBLICATIONS   SAL   1.00
SATIE, E.
    GNOSSIENNE NO. 3
        FRANCO COLOMBO PUBLICATIONS   SAL   1.00
SATIE, E.
    GYMNOPEDIE NO. 1
        EDWARD B. MARKS MUSIC CORPORATION   01.00
SATIE, E.
    GYMNOPEDIE NO. 1
        FRANCO COLOMBO PUBLICATIONS   SAL   1.75
SATIE, E.
    GYMNOPEDIE NO. 2
        EDWARD B. MARKS MUSIC CORPORATION   01.00
SATIE, E.
    GYMNOPEDIE NO. 2
        FRANCO COLOMBO PUBLICATIONS   SAL   1.75
SATIE, E.
    GYMNOPEDIE NO. 3
        CARL FISCHER, INC.   HO 526   .60
SATIE, E.
    GYMNOPEDIE NO. 3
        EDWARD B. MARKS MUSIC CORPORATION   01.00
SATIE, E.
    GYMNOPEDIE NO. 3
        FRANCO COLOMBO PUBLICATIONS   SAL   1.75
SATIE, E.
    JACK IN THE BOX, OP. POSTH.
        UNIVERSAL EDITION   UE 9914   3.00
SATIE, E.
    JE TE VEUX
        FRANCO COLOMBO PUBLICATIONS   SAL   1.00
SATIE, E.
    MESSE DES PAUVRES
        FRANCO COLOMBO PUBLICATIONS   SAL   3.25
SATIE, E.
    MINUET NO. 1
        ASSOCIATED MUSIC PUBLISHERS, INC.   ESC   1.50
SATIE, E.
    NOCTURNE NO. 04
        ASSOCIATED MUSIC PUBLISHERS, INC.   ESC   1.75
SATIE, E.
    NOCTURNE NO. 05
        ASSOCIATED MUSIC PUBLISHERS, INC.   ESC   1.75
SATIE, E.
    OGIVES
        MCA MUSIC   .75
SATIE, E.
    PANTINS DANSENT, LES
        FRANCO COLOMBO PUBLICATIONS   SAL   1.75
SATIE, E.
    PASSACAILLE
        FRANCO COLOMBO PUBLICATIONS   SAL   2.50
SATIE, E.
    PIECES FROIDES - AIR A FAIRE FUIR
        FRANCO COLOMBO PUBLICATIONS   SAL   2.75
SATIE, E.
    PIECES FROIDES - DANSE DE TRAVERS
        FRANCO COLOMBO PUBLICATIONS   SAL   2.75
SATIE, E.
    PRELUDE DE LA PORTE HEROIQUE DU CIEL
        FRANCO COLOMBO PUBLICATIONS   SAL   1.50
SATIE, E.
    PRELUDE EN TAPISSERIE
        FRANCO COLOMBO PUBLICATIONS   SAL   1.75
SATIE, E.
    RAG-TIME PARADE
        FRANCO COLOMBO PUBLICATIONS   SAL   1.75
SATIE, E.
    RELACHE -- BALLET --
        FRANCO COLOMBO PUBLICATIONS   SAL   11.50

SATIE, E.
    REVERIE DE L'ENFANCE DE PANTAGRUEL
        ASSOCIATED MUSIC PUBLISHERS, INC.   ESC   1.75
SATIE, E.
    SONNERIES DE LA ROSE-CROIX
        FRANCO COLOMBO PUBLICATIONS   SAL   4.25
SATIE, E.
    THREE NOCTURNES - NO. 1
        FRANCO COLOMBO PUBLICATIONS   SAL   1.00
SATIE, E.
    THREE NOCTURNES - NO. 2
        FRANCO COLOMBO PUBLICATIONS   SAL   1.00
SATIE, E.
    THREE NOCTURNES - NO. 3
        FRANCO COLOMBO PUBLICATIONS   SAL   1.00
SATIE, E.
    THREE SARABANDES - NO. 1
        FRANCO COLOMBO PUBLICATIONS   SAL   1.75
SATIE, E.
    THREE SARABANDES - NO. 2
        FRANCO COLOMBO PUBLICATIONS   SAL   1.75
SATIE, E.
    THREE SARABANDES - NO. 3
        FRANCO COLOMBO PUBLICATIONS   SAL   1.75
SATIE, E.
    VEXATIONS
        MUSICA OBSCURA   1.00
SAUER   5
    KONZERT-ETUDE -- COUPLET SANS PAROLES
        SCHOTT   1.50
SAUER   5
    KONZERT-ETUDE -- NO. 26 PREGHIERA
        SCHOTT   1.50
SAUER   5
    KONZERT-ETUDE -- NO. 6 FRISSON DE FEUILLES
        SCHOTT   1.50
SAUER   5
    LES DELICES DE VIENNE, VALSE
        SCHOTT   2.00
SAUER   5
    SPIELDOSE -- ORIGINAL
        SCHOTT   1.50
SAUGUET
    CHATTE, LA -- BALLET --
        FRANCO COLOMBO PUBLICATIONS   SAL   7.50
SAUGUET
    CHATTE, LA -- BALLET -- .. HYMNE FINAL
        FRANCO COLOMBO PUBLICATIONS   SAL   1.75
SAUGUET
    CHATTE, LA -- BALLET -- .. INVOCATION A APHRODITE
        FRANCO COLOMBO PUBLICATIONS   SAL   1.75
SAUGUET
    DAVID -- BALLET --
        FRANCO COLOMBO PUBLICATIONS   SAL   9.00
SAUGUET
    FEUILLETS D'ALBUM -- UN NOCTURNE
        ELKAN-VOGEL, INC.   J   1.25
SAUGUET
    FEUILLETS D'ALBUM -- UN SCHERZO
        ELKAN-VOGEL, INC.   J   1.75
SAUGUET
    FEUILLETS D'ALBUM -- UNE VALSE
        ELKAN-VOGEL, INC.   J   2.00
SAUGUET
    FORAINS, LES -- BALLET --
        FRANCO COLOMBO PUBLICATIONS   SAL   10.75
SAUGUET
    LE RECONTRE
        HEUGEL ET CIE.   6.00
SAUGUET
    LES CINQ ETAGES
        HEUGEL ET CIE.   3.00
SAUGUET
    MIRAGES, LES -- BALLET --
        FRANCO COLOMBO PUBLICATIONS   SAL   7.25
SAUGUET
    NUIT, LA -- BALLET --
        FRANCO COLOMBO PUBLICATIONS   SAL   4.25
SAUGUET
    PRES DU BAL -- SUITE --
        FRANCO COLOMBO PUBLICATIONS   SAL   4.25
SAUGUET
    ROMANCE IN C
        FRANCO COLOMBO PUBLICATIONS   SAL   1.75
SAUGUET
    SONATA IN D
        FRANCO COLOMBO PUBLICATIONS   SAL   5.75
SAUGUET
    VALSE LENT D'AMOUR INQUIET
        FRANCO COLOMBO PUBLICATIONS   R1690   1.25
SAUNDERS, N.
    PASSACAGLIA
        NOVELLO AND COMPANY, LTD.   10.0212.03   1.40
SAUVREZIS
    CHANT SANS PAROLES
        FRANCO COLOMBO PUBLICATIONS   SAL   2.50
SAUVREZIS
    CLOCHES DE PAQUES
        FRANCO COLOMBO PUBLICATIONS   SAL   1.75
SAUVREZIS
    GESTES D'ENFANTS - A LA VOLEE
        FRANCO COLOMBO PUBLICATIONS   SAL   1.50
SAVAGE   3
    JET BOMBER
        BOSTON MUSIC COMPANY   .50
SAVAGE   4
    SUNSET ON THE SOUND
        BOSTON MUSIC COMPANY   .50
SAVAGE, H. S.   2
    RIDING THE RAPIDS
        VOLKWEIN BROS.   .30
SAVAGE, H. S.   2
    SCISSORS GRINDER
        VOLKWEIN BROS.   .25
SAVAGE, H. S.   4
    VALSE CAPRICE
        VOLKWEIN BROS.   00.50
SAVAGNONE
    DRAGO ROSSO, IL -- BALLET --
        FRANCO COLOMBO PUBLICATIONS   DS423   5.00
SAVAGNONE
    PRELUDE NO. 01
        FRANCO COLOMBO PUBLICATIONS   129982   1.25
SAVASTA
    NOCTURNE
        FRANCO COLOMBO PUBLICATIONS   116812   .90

SAVASTA
  SCHERZO
          FRANCO COLOMBO PUBLICATIONS   116813   1.00
SAVILLE, A.
  PETER PENGUIN'S PIANOFORTE BOOK
          BANKS AND SON LTD.   .95
SAVINIO
  VITA DELL'UOMO -- BALLET --
          FRANCO COLOMBO PUBLICATIONS   128135   5.00
SAVINO
  STUDY IN BLUE
          THE BIG THREE MUSIC CORPORATION   00.95
SAVINO
  TWILIGHT HOUR
          G. SCHIRMER, INC.   .50
SAVINO
  VALSE SIMPLE
          G. SCHIRMER, INC.   .50
SAVINO--ED.   SAVINO
  CHIAPANECAS
          THE BIG THREE MUSIC CORPORATION   00.75
SAVINO--ED.   SAVINO
  WALTZ YOU SAVED FOR ME
          THE BIG THREE MUSIC CORPORATION   00.95
SAVINO--ED.   SAVINO
  WONDERFUL ONE
          THE BIG THREE MUSIC CORPORATION   00.95
SAWTELL, P.
  VOYAGE TO THE BOTTOM OF THE SEA
          THE BIG THREE MUSIC CORPORATION   00.95
SAXMAN   2
  TUMBLEWEED
          BOSTON MUSIC COMPANY   .50
SAXTON
  MUSIC BOX, THE
          G. SCHIRMER, INC.   .35
SAXTON
  POPEYE'S HORNPIPE
          G. SCHIRMER, INC.   .35
SAYGUN, A.
  ANADOLU DAN
          PEER SOUTHERN ORGANIZATION   02.00
SAYGUN, A.
  INCI NIN KITABI
          PEER SOUTHERN ORGANIZATION   01.25
SAYGUN, A.
  SONATINA
          PEER SOUTHERN ORGANIZATION   02.25
SCALFATI
  SUITE
          FRANCO COLOMBO PUBLICATIONS   DS285   1.25
SCALINO
  CHOPSTICKS
          FRANCO COLOMBO PUBLICATIONS   NY1572   .35
SCARLATTI, A.   BARTH, H.
  PASTORAL SONATA
          BELWIN-MILLS PUBLISHING CORPORATION   20373   .60
SCARLATTI, A.   BARTH, H.
  SONATA IN D MAJOR
          BELWIN-MILLS PUBLISHING CORPORATION   20377   .60
SCARLATTI, A.   TAGLIAPIETRA
  TOCCATA IN A MINOR
          FRANCO COLOMBO PUBLICATIONS   128191   .50
SCARLATTI, A.   TAGLIAPIETRA
  VARIATIONS ON 'FOLLIA DI SPAGNA'
          FRANCO COLOMBO PUBLICATIONS   128111   1.00
SCARLATTI, D.   TAUSIG
  CAPRICCIO IN E, LONGO 10--TRANSCRIBED FOR CONCERT-USE
          G. SCHIRMER, INC.   .40
SCARLATTI, D.   BUELOW
  CAT-FUGUE, LONGO 499
          G. SCHIRMER, INC.   .50
SCARLATTI, D.   M
  CAT'S FUGUE
          C. F. PETERS CORPORATION   7098   .75
SCARLATTI, D.
  COMPLETE WORKS FOR CLAVICEMBALO - NO. 10 IN C MINOR
          FRANCO COLOMBO PUBLICATIONS   LD   .60
SCARLATTI, D.
  COMPLETE WORKS FOR CLAVICEMBALO - NO. 108 IN D MINOR
          FRANCO COLOMBO PUBLICATIONS   LD   .60
SCARLATTI, D.
  COMPLETE WORKS FOR CLAVICEMBALO - NO. 114 IN E-FLAT
          FRANCO COLOMBO PUBLICATIONS   LD   .60
SCARLATTI, D.
  COMPLETE WORKS FOR CLAVICEMBALO - NO. 14 IN D
          FRANCO COLOMBO PUBLICATIONS   LD   .60
SCARLATTI, D.
  COMPLETE WORKS FOR CLAVICEMBALO - NO. 142 IN E-FLAT
          FRANCO COLOMBO PUBLICATIONS   LD   .60
SCARLATTI, D.
  COMPLETE WORKS FOR CLAVICEMBALO - NO. 23 IN E 'CORTEGE'
          FRANCO COLOMBO PUBLICATIONS   128378   .75
SCARLATTI, D.
  COMPLETE WORKS FOR CLAVICEMBALO - NO. 256 IN C-SHARP MINOR
          FRANCO COLOMBO PUBLICATIONS   LD   .60
SCARLATTI, D.
  COMPLETE WORKS FOR CLAVICEMBALO - NO. 263 IN B MINOR 'BOURREE'
          FRANCO COLOMBO PUBLICATIONS   LD   .60
SCARLATTI, D.
  COMPLETE WORKS FOR CLAVICEMBALO - NO. 265 IN D
          FRANCO COLOMBO PUBLICATIONS   LD   .60
SCARLATTI, D.
  COMPLETE WORKS FOR CLAVICEMBALO - NO. 33 IN B MINOR
          FRANCO COLOMBO PUBLICATIONS   LD   .60
SCARLATTI, D.
  COMPLETE WORKS FOR CLAVICEMBALO - NO. 345 IN A
          FRANCO COLOMBO PUBLICATIONS   NY1412   .60
SCARLATTI, D.
  COMPLETE WORKS FOR CLAVICEMBALO - NO. 387 IN G
          FRANCO COLOMBO PUBLICATIONS   LD   .60
SCARLATTI, D.
  COMPLETE WORKS FOR CLAVICEMBALO - NO. 413 IN D MINOR 'PASTORALE'
          FRANCO COLOMBO PUBLICATIONS   LD150   .60
SCARLATTI, D.
  COMPLETE WORKS FOR CLAVICEMBALO - NO. 422 IN D MINOR 'TOCCATA'
          FRANCO COLOMBO PUBLICATIONS   128439   .75
SCARLATTI, D.
  COMPLETE WORKS FOR CLAVICEMBALO - NO. 433 IN F 'SICILIANA'
          FRANCO COLOMBO PUBLICATIONS   LD151   .60
SCARLATTI, D.
  COMPLETE WORKS FOR CLAVICEMBALO - NO. 449 IN B MINOR
          FRANCO COLOMBO PUBLICATIONS   NY1228   .60
SCARLATTI, D.
  COMPLETE WORKS FOR CLAVICEMBALO - NO. 46 IN B-FLAT
          FRANCO COLOMBO PUBLICATIONS   LD   .60

SCARLATTI, D.
  COMPLETE WORKS FOR CLAVICEMBALO - NO. 463 IN D
          FRANCO COLOMBO PUBLICATIONS   LD   .60
SCARLATTI, D.   MONTANI
  COMPLETE WORKS FOR CLAVICEMBALO - NO. 463 IN D
          FRANCO COLOMBO PUBLICATIONS   128415   .50
SCARLATTI, D.
  COMPLETE WORKS FOR CLAVICEMBALO - NO. 49 IN G MINOR
          FRANCO COLOMBO PUBLICATIONS   NY1219   .60
SCARLATTI, D.
  COMPLETE WORKS FOR CLAVICEMBALO - NO. 494 IN A
          FRANCO COLOMBO PUBLICATIONS   LD   .60
SCARLATTI, D.
  COMPLETE WORKS FOR CLAVICEMBALO - NO. 499 IN G MINOR 'CAT'S
  FUGUE'
          FRANCO COLOMBO PUBLICATIONS   128369   .90
SCARLATTI, D.   5
  KATZENFUGE
          SCHOTT   0982 1/2   1.00
SCARLATTI, D.
  MINUET IN E MINOR
          FREDERICK HARRIS MUSIC COMPANY   .60
SCARLATTI, D.   4
  PASTORALE
          CENTURY MUSIC PUBLISHING COMPANY, INC.   3640   .40
SCARLATTI, D.   TAUSIG *
  PASTORALE -- L.413 -- AND CAPRICCIO -- L. 375 --
          FRANCO COLOMBO PUBLICATIONS   128312   1.00
SCARLATTI, D.   ECKSTEIN
  PASTORALE --SONATA NO. 1--
          CARL FISCHER, INC.   S 1842   .50
SCARLATTI, D.   4
  PASTORALE D-MOLL
          SCHOTT   0984   .75
SCARLATTI, D.   TAUSIG
  PASTORALE, LONGO 413--ARRANGED FOR CONCERT-USE
          G. SCHIRMER, INC.   .40
SCARLATTI, D.   LONGO
  SONATA IN A MAJOR, NO. 345
          BELWIN-MILLS PUBLISHING CORPORATION   .60
SCARLATTI, D.   LONGO
  SONATA IN A MAJOR, NO. 494
          BELWIN-MILLS PUBLISHING CORPORATION   .75
SCARLATTI, D.   LESCHETIZKY
  SONATA IN A, LONGO 345
          G. SCHIRMER, INC.   .60
SCARLATTI, D.
  SONATA IN C MAJOR
          BELWIN-MILLS PUBLISHING CORPORATION   .60
SCARLATTI, D.   3
  SONATA IN C MAJOR
          CENTURY MUSIC PUBLISHING COMPANY, INC.   4001   .40
SCARLATTI, D.   PALMER, W. A.
  SONATA IN D MINOR
          ALFRED MUSIC COMPANY   569   1.50
SCARLATTI, D.   3
  SONATA IN E MAJOR
          CENTURY MUSIC PUBLISHING COMPANY, INC.   4037   .40
SCARLATTI, D.   PALMER, W. A.
  SONATA NO. 30 -- THE CAT'S FUGUE
          ALFRED MUSIC COMPANY   566   1.50
SCARLATTI, D.   WURMSER, L.
  TOCCATA DI BRAVURA
          ELKAN-VOGEL, INC.   CON   3.75
SCARLINO
  JUMPING FROG
          FRANCO COLOMBO PUBLICATIONS   NY1573   .35
SCARMOLIN   1
  A B C
          PRO-ART PUBLICATIONS, INC.   47   .50
SCARMOLIN   1
  BEHIND THE DOOR
          PRO-ART PUBLICATIONS, INC.   45   .50
SCARMOLIN   2
  BLACK EBONY
          THEODORE PRESSER COMPANY   .50
SCARMOLIN   1
  BOOM BOOM
          CENTURY MUSIC PUBLISHING COMPANY, INC.   3522   .40
SCARMOLIN   M
  CAPRICCIO
          COMPOSERS PRESS, INC.   1.50
SCARMOLIN
  CHOPSTICKS -- HUMORESQUE
          BELWIN-MILLS PUBLISHING CORPORATION   .60
SCARMOLIN   2
  FABLE, A
          BELWIN-MILLS PUBLISHING CORPORATION   .60
SCARMOLIN   1 1/2
  FROGGIE AND THE FISHES, THE
          THEODORE PRESSER COMPANY   .50
SCARMOLIN   2
  HARMONICA JOE
          CENTURY MUSIC PUBLISHING COMPANY, INC.   4106   .40
SCARMOLIN   1 1/2
  JIM DOLAN, PRIVATE EYE
          THEODORE PRESSER COMPANY   .50
SCARMOLIN   1
  LICORICE STICKS
          CENTURY MUSIC PUBLISHING COMPANY, INC.   4107   .40
SCARMOLIN   1
  LOOK BEFORE YOU LEAP
          PRO-ART PUBLICATIONS, INC.   43   .50
SCARMOLIN   1 1/2
  MEXICAN DANCE
          THEODORE PRESSER COMPANY   .50
SCARMOLIN   E
  MID-DAY SIESTA
          COMPOSERS PRESS, INC.   1.00
SCARMOLIN   2
  MISTY EVENING
          CENTURY MUSIC PUBLISHING COMPANY, INC.   3993   .40
SCARMOLIN   1 1/2
  MR. B FLAT, OP. 86 NO. 3
          THEODORE PRESSER COMPANY   .50
SCARMOLIN   1
  ON THE SWING
          CENTURY MUSIC PUBLISHING COMPANY, INC.   3523   .40
SCARMOLIN   1
  ORGAN GRINDER
          PRO-ART PUBLICATIONS, INC.   28   .50
SCARMOLIN   1
  OVER AND UNDER
          PRO-ART PUBLICATIONS, INC.   205   .50
SCARMOLIN   1
  PAPER BOATS
          CENTURY MUSIC PUBLISHING COMPANY, INC.   3524   .40

SCARMOLIN   1 1/2
  PENNY SHOW
    THEODORE PRESSER COMPANY   .50
SCARMOLIN   1
  PONY RIDE
    CENTURY MUSIC PUBLISHING COMPANY, INC.   3525   .40
SCARMOLIN   1
  RAINBOW IN THE SKY
    PRO-ART PUBLICATIONS, INC.   125   .50
SCARMOLIN   1
  ROLLING STONE GATHERS NO MOSS
    PRO-ART PUBLICATIONS, INC.   33   .50
SCARMOLIN   2
  SCOTCH PLAID
    CENTURY MUSIC PUBLISHING COMPANY, INC.   3814   .40
SCARMOLIN   1
  SEA SHELLS
    CENTURY MUSIC PUBLISHING COMPANY, INC.   4108   .40
SCARMOLIN   1
  SOME DAY
    PRO-ART PUBLICATIONS, INC.   44   .50
SCARMOLIN   1
  STITCH IN TIME SAVES NINE
    PRO-ART PUBLICATIONS, INC.   32   .50
SCARMOLIN   M
  TARANTELLE BRILLANTE
    COMPOSERS PRESS, INC.   1.50
SCARMOLIN   E
  TWO CUCKOO CLOCKS, THE
    COMPOSERS PRESS, INC.   1.00
SCARMOLIN   M
  VALSE GRACIEUSE
    COMPOSERS PRESS, INC.   1.50
SCARMOLIN   1
  WHOO'S WHOO
    THEODORE PRESSER COMPANY   .50
SCELSI
  CAPRICCIO
    FRANCO COLOMBO PUBLICATIONS   DS712   2.00
SCELSI
  POEMI
    FRANCO COLOMBO PUBLICATIONS   DS726   2.25
SCELSI
  SONATA
    FRANCO COLOMBO PUBLICATIONS   DS694   4.00
SCELSI
  VARIATIONS AND FUGUE
    FRANCO COLOMBO PUBLICATIONS   DS706   2.75
SCHAEUBLE, H.
  SONATA, OP. 39--1953-4--
    ASSOCIATED MUSIC PUBLISHERS, INC.   BOT   3.00
SCHALE, C. F.
  MINUETTO
    FREDERICK HARRIS MUSIC COMPANY   .60
SCHARWENKA, P.
  TEMPO DI MINUETTO IN D
    G. SCHIRMER, INC.   .25
SCHARWENKA, X.
  BALLADE IN F SHARP MINOR, OP. 85 NO. 1
    ASSOCIATED MUSIC PUBLISHERS, INC.   LEU   3.25
SCHARWENKA, X.
  BARCAROLLE, OP. 62 NO. 4
    G. SCHIRMER, INC.   .30
SCHARWENKA, X.   HILL   5
  POLISH DANCE
    CENTURY MUSIC PUBLISHING COMPANY, INC.   363   .40
SCHARWENKA, X.   4
  POLISH DANCE
    VOLKWEIN BROS.   .25
SCHARWENKA, X.   5
  POLISH DANCE NO. 1
    CENTURY MUSIC PUBLISHING COMPANY, INC.   849   .40
SCHARWENKA, X.
  POLISH DANCE, OP. 3 NO. 1
    BELWIN-MILLS PUBLISHING CORPORATION   28196   .60
SCHARWENKA, X.
  POLISH DANCE, OP. 3 NO. 1
    CARL FISCHER, INC.   S 192   .50
SCHARWENKA, X.
  POLISH DANCE, OP. 3 NO. 1
    G. SCHIRMER, INC.   .50
SCHARWENKA, X.
  POLISH NATIONAL DANCE, OP. 3 NO. 1
    ASSOCIATED MUSIC PUBLISHERS, INC.   BRH   .75
SCHAT   M-D
  INSCRIPTIONS
    C. F. PETERS CORPORATION   D214   1.25
SCHATZ   4
  LOVE'S REPROACHES
    CENTURY MUSIC PUBLISHING COMPANY, INC.   2286   .40
SCHAUM, J.   2
  BEACH BALL BOOGIE
    SCHAUM PUBLICATIONS, INC.   .50
SCHAUM, J.   1 1/2
  BEAUTIFUL OHIO
    SCHAUM PUBLICATIONS, INC.   .60
SCHAUM, J.   PREP
  BIKE HIKE
    SCHAUM PUBLICATIONS, INC.   .50
SCHAUM, J.   SCHAUM, J.   1 1/2
  CABBAGE WALTZ, THE
    BELWIN-MILLS PUBLISHING CORPORATION   .50
SCHAUM, J.   3
  CORSAGE WALTZ
    SCHAUM PUBLICATIONS, INC.   .60
SCHAUM, J.   1
  DINOSAUR DITTIES
    SCHAUM PUBLICATIONS, INC.   1.25
SCHAUM, J.   2 1/2
  DRY BONES
    BELWIN-MILLS PUBLISHING CORPORATION   .50
SCHAUM, J.   PREP TO 1
  FESTIVAL OF SOLOS
    SCHAUM PUBLICATIONS, INC.   1.25
SCHAUM, J.   2 1/2
  HAVE YOU EVER BEEN LONELY
    SCHAUM PUBLICATIONS, INC.   .60
SCHAUM, J.   3
  HAWAIIAN NOCTURNE
    SCHAUM PUBLICATIONS, INC.   .60
SCHAUM, J.   SCHAUM, J.   2
  HORN BOOGIE
    BELWIN-MILLS PUBLISHING CORPORATION   .50
SCHAUM, J.   1 1/2
  HOUR GLASS WALTZ
    SCHAUM PUBLICATIONS, INC.   .60

SCHAUM, J.   PREP
  HYMN PRIMER
    SCHAUM PUBLICATIONS, INC.   1.25
SCHAUM, J.   2 1/2
  I BELIEVE
    SCHAUM PUBLICATIONS, INC.   .60
SCHAUM, J.   SCHAUM, J.   1
  JOHNNY APPLESEED
    BELWIN-MILLS PUBLISHING CORPORATION   .50
SCHAUM, J.   1 1/2
  JUMPING ROPE
    SCHAUM PUBLICATIONS, INC.   .50
SCHAUM, J.   1 1/2
  LET ME CALL YOU SWEETHEART
    SCHAUM PUBLICATIONS, INC.   .60
SCHAUM, J.   PREP
  LOLLIPOP WALTZ
    SCHAUM PUBLICATIONS, INC.   .50
SCHAUM, J.   1
  LUMBERJACK SONG
    SCHAUM PUBLICATIONS, INC.   .50
SCHAUM, J.   1
  MARINES' HYMN, THE
    BOSTON MUSIC COMPANY   .50
SCHAUM, J.   2
  MEMORIES OF YOU
    SCHAUM PUBLICATIONS, INC.   .60
SCHAUM, J.   2
  POLLUTION SOLUTION
    SCHAUM PUBLICATIONS, INC.   .50
SCHAUM, J.   PREP
  PREPOSTEROUS RHINOCEROS
    SCHAUM PUBLICATIONS, INC.   .50
SCHAUM, J.   2
  ROAD RUNNER
    SCHAUM PUBLICATIONS, INC.   .60
SCHAUM, J.   2 1/2
  SANTA'S ON HIS WAY
    SCHAUM PUBLICATIONS, INC.   .60
SCHAUM, J.   1 1/2
  SEAGULL
    SCHAUM PUBLICATIONS, INC.   .60
SCHAUM, J.   2
  TAP DANCER, THE
    BOSTON MUSIC COMPANY   .50
SCHAUM, J.--ED.   SCHAUM, J.   3
  AMERI-CONGA, THE
    BELWIN-MILLS PUBLISHING CORPORATION   .50
SCHAUM, J.--ED.   SCHAUM, J.   2
  APACHE INDIAN DANCE
    BELWIN-MILLS PUBLISHING CORPORATION   .50
SCHAUM, J.--ED.   SCHAUM, J.   2
  AT MY TEACHER'S STUDIO
    BELWIN-MILLS PUBLISHING CORPORATION   .50
SCHAUM, J.--ED.   SCHAUM, J.   2 1/2
  BAGDAD BOOGIE
    BELWIN-MILLS PUBLISHING CORPORATION   .50
SCHAUM, J.--ED.   SCHAUM, J.   1
  BASEBALL LEAGUE, THE
    BELWIN-MILLS PUBLISHING CORPORATION   .50
SCHAUM, J.--ED.   SCHAUM, J.   1 1/2
  BASKETBALL PEP SONG
    BELWIN-MILLS PUBLISHING CORPORATION   .50
SCHAUM, J.--ED.   SCHAUM, J.
  BATTLE HYMN OF THE REPUBLIC
    BELWIN-MILLS PUBLISHING CORPORATION   .50
SCHAUM, J.--ED.   SCHAUM, J.   3
  BE-BOP BOOGIE
    BELWIN-MILLS PUBLISHING CORPORATION   .50
SCHAUM, J.--ED.   SCHAUM, J.
  BLACK BEAUTY
    BELWIN-MILLS PUBLISHING CORPORATION   .50
SCHAUM, J.--ED.   SCHAUM, J.   2
  BLACKIE AND WHITEY
    BELWIN-MILLS PUBLISHING CORPORATION   .50
SCHAUM, J.--ED.   SCHAUM, J.   2
  BLUE BOOGIE
    BELWIN-MILLS PUBLISHING CORPORATION   .50
SCHAUM, J.--ED.   SCHAUM, J.   3
  BLUE TAIL FLY
    BELWIN-MILLS PUBLISHING CORPORATION   .50
SCHAUM, J.--ED.   SCHAUM, J.   3
  BOOGIE EXPRESS
    BELWIN-MILLS PUBLISHING CORPORATION   .50
SCHAUM, J.--ED.   SCHAUM, J.   2
  BOOGIE MAN, THE
    BELWIN-MILLS PUBLISHING CORPORATION   .50
SCHAUM, J.--ED.   SCHAUM, J.   1
  BRISK WINDS
    BELWIN-MILLS PUBLISHING CORPORATION   .50
SCHAUM, J.--ED.   SCHAUM, J.   5
  CAISSONS GO ROLLING ALONG
    BELWIN-MILLS PUBLISHING CORPORATION   .50
SCHAUM, J.--ED.   SCHAUM, J.   2
  CARNIVAL OF VENICE
    BELWIN-MILLS PUBLISHING CORPORATION   .50
SCHAUM, J.--ED.   SCHAUM, J.
  CHICKEN REEL
    BELWIN-MILLS PUBLISHING CORPORATION   .50
SCHAUM, J.--ED.   SCHAUM, J.   2
  CHINA CLIPPER
    BELWIN-MILLS PUBLISHING CORPORATION   .50
SCHAUM, J.--ED.   SCHAUM, J.   3
  CHOO CHOO BOOGIE
    BELWIN-MILLS PUBLISHING CORPORATION   .50
SCHAUM, J.--ED.   SCHAUM, J.   1
  CHOP BOOGIE
    BELWIN-MILLS PUBLISHING CORPORATION   .50
SCHAUM, J.--ED.   SCHAUM, J.   5
  CHOP STICKS
    BELWIN-MILLS PUBLISHING CORPORATION   .50
SCHAUM, J.--ED.   SCHAUM, J.   2
  CHRISTMAS RHAPSODY
    BELWIN-MILLS PUBLISHING CORPORATION   .50
SCHAUM, J.--ED.   SCHAUM, J.   2
  COWBOY AND HIS BANJO, THE
    BELWIN-MILLS PUBLISHING CORPORATION   .50
SCHAUM, J.--ED.   SCHAUM, J.   2
  COWBOY BOOGIE
    BELWIN-MILLS PUBLISHING CORPORATION   .50
SCHAUM, J.--ED.   SCHAUM, J.   2 1/2
  CRICKET AND BUMBLE BEE
    BELWIN-MILLS PUBLISHING CORPORATION   .50
SCHAUM, J.--ED.   SCHAUM, J.
  CUBAN MAMBO
    BELWIN-MILLS PUBLISHING CORPORATION   .50

SCHAUM, W.--ED   SCHAUU, W.   1
  TWELVE DAYS OF CHRISTMAS
    SCHAUM PUBLICATIONS, INC.   .50
SCHAUM, W.--ED   SCHAUM, W.   1
  WHAT CHILD IS THIS
    SCHAUM PUBLICATIONS, INC.   .50
SCHECHTMAN
  RECREATION FOR PIANO
    MCA MUSIC   2.00
SCHEIDT   AULER   3-4
  LIEDVARIATIONEN
    SCHOTT   2828   2.25
SCHELLING, E.
  UN PETIT RIEN
    G. SCHIRMER, INC.   .75
SCHER, W.
  ACROBATS
    CARL FISCHER, INC.   RS 397   .50
SCHER, W.   2
  AT THE BARBER SHOP
    PRO-ART PUBLICATIONS, INC.   377   .50
SCHER, W.
  AT THE BAZAAR
    BELWIN-MILLS PUBLISHING CORPORATION 25008   .60
SCHER, W.   2
  AT THE CIRCUS
    CENTURY MUSIC PUBLISHING COMPANY, INC. 4355   .40
SCHER, W.   1-2
  AT THE ICE SKATING RINK
    PRO-ART PUBLICATIONS, INC.   500   .50
SCHER, W.   2-3
  BALALAIKA
    PRO-ART PUBLICATIONS, INC.   585   .50
SCHER, W.
  BALLET OF THE DOLLS
    CARL FISCHER, INC.   P 3033   .50
SCHER, W.
  BALLOON MAN
    SAM FOX PUBLISHING COMPANY, INC.   .50
SCHER, W.
  BALLOON MAN
    SOUTHERN MUSIC COMPANY   .50
SCHER, W.
  BEAR DANCE
    BELWIN-MILLS PUBLISHING CORPORATION 25253   .60
SCHER, W.   2
  BEE AND THE BUTTERFLY, THE
    THEODORE PRESSER COMPANY   .50
SCHER, W.   1
  BEE HAPPY
    CENTURY MUSIC PUBLISHING COMPANY, INC. 4312   .40
SCHER, W.
  BEE IN THE CLOCK, THE
    BOSTON MUSIC COMPANY   .50
SCHER, W.
  BEES A-BUZZIN'
    EDWARD B. MARKS MUSIC CORPORATION   00.60
SCHER, W.
  BLUE BALLET SHOES
    CARL FISCHER, INC.   RS 412   .50
SCHER, W.   3
  BUFFOON
    THEODORE PRESSER COMPANY   .50
SCHER, W.   1
  BULLFIGHTER, THE
    PRO-ART PUBLICATIONS, INC.   115   .50
SCHER, W.   1
  BUMPY JEEP, THE
    PRO-ART PUBLICATIONS, INC.   117   .50
SCHER, W.
  BUST BUTTERFLIES
    EDWARD B. MARKS MUSIC CORPORATION   00.60
SCHER, W.
  BUSY BUNNY AND DADDY'S NEW CAR
    EDWARD B. MARKS MUSIC CORPORATION   00.60
SCHER, W.   3
  BUSY LITTLE RICKSHAW BOY
    THEODORE PRESSER COMPANY   .50
SCHER, W.
  CANDY SUITE
    EDWARD B. MARKS MUSIC CORPORATION   00.60
SCHER, W.
  CARNIVAL CAPERS
    SAM FOX PUBLISHING COMPANY, INC.   .50
SCHER, W.
  CARNIVAL CAPERS
    SOUTHERN MUSIC COMPANY   .50
SCHER, W.   2
  CARNIVAL IN SPAIN
    BOSTON MUSIC COMPANY   .50
SCHER, W.   2
  CAUCASIAN MARCH
    PRO-ART PUBLICATIONS, INC.   296   .50
SCHER, W.   2
  CHIEF RED FEATHER
    THEODORE PRESSER COMPANY   .50
SCHER, W.   2 1/2
  CHINESE CHATTER
    BELWIN-MILLS PUBLISHING CORPORATION   .60
SCHER, W.   2
  CHINESE MARKET PLACE, A
    PRO-ART PUBLICATIONS, INC.   162   .50
SCHER, W.
  CHITARRATA ITALIENNE
    BOSTON MUSIC COMPANY   .50
SCHER, W.   2-3
  CHROMATIC POLKA
    PRO-ART PUBLICATIONS, INC.   512   .50
SCHER, W.   1
  CIRCUS DAYS
    PRO-ART PUBLICATIONS, INC.   118   .50
SCHER, W.   2-3
  COME DANCE THE POLKA
    PRO-ART PUBLICATIONS, INC.   202   .50
SCHER, W.
  COSSACKS
    WARNER BROTHERS PUBLISHERS   .60
SCHER, W.
  COTTON PICKIN' PETE
    CARL FISCHER, INC.   RS 356   .50
SCHER, W.
  CUCKOO IN THE CLOCK
    CARL FISCHER, INC.   P 2916   .50
SCHER, W.   3-4
  CZARDAS FANTASY
    PRO-ART PUBLICATIONS, INC.   474   .50

SCHER, W.
  CZARDAS RHAPSODY
    CARL FISCHER, INC.   RS 395   .50
SCHER, W.   1
  DANCING GRASSHOPPERS
    ELKAN-VOGEL, INC.   .50
SCHER, W.
  DANCING NORTH WIND, THE
    BELWIN-MILLS PUBLISHING CORPORATION   .60
SCHER, W.   3
  DANCING PUPPETS
    THEODORE PRESSER COMPANY   .50
SCHER, W.   3
  DANCING SCARECROW
    CENTURY MUSIC PUBLISHING COMPANY, INC. 4113   .40
SCHER, W.   2
  DANCING SENORITAS
    PRO-ART PUBLICATIONS, INC.   204   .50
SCHER, W.   2
  DANCING SPIDERS
    ELKAN-VOGEL, INC.   .50
SCHER, W.   3
  DANSE RUSSE
    THEODORE PRESSER COMPANY   .50
SCHER, W.   1
  DAY WITH GRANDMA, A
    CENTURY MUSIC PUBLISHING COMPANY, INC. 4313   .40
SCHER, W.   2
  DESERT DANCE
    BELWIN-MILLS PUBLISHING CORPORATION   .60
SCHER, W.   3
  DESERTED ISLE, A
    BOSTON MUSIC COMPANY   .50
SCHER, W.
  DONKEY RIDE
    BELWIN-MILLS PUBLISHING CORPORATION 25040   .60
SCHER, W.   2 1/2
  DREAM OF THE TIN SOLDIER
    BELWIN-MILLS PUBLISHING CORPORATION   .60
SCHER, W.
  DREAMING OF OLD VIENNA
    BELWIN-MILLS PUBLISHING CORPORATION 25041   .60
SCHER, W.   2
  EVENING IN HAWAII
    PRO-ART PUBLICATIONS, INC.   235   .50
SCHER, W.   3
  FESTIVAL
    PRO-ART PUBLICATIONS, INC.   562   .50
SCHER, W.
  FLAMENCO
    SUMMY-BIRCHARD COMPANY   .50
SCHER, W.
  FRISKY SQUIRRELS AND TO A LITTLE INDIAN
    EDWARD B. MARKS MUSIC CORPORATION   00.60
SCHER, W.   1 1/2
  FROM NOAH'S ARK
    THEODORE PRESSER COMPANY   .50
SCHER, W.   2
  FUNFARE
    THEODORE PRESSER COMPANY   .50
SCHER, W.   2
  GARDEN IN THE SEA
    ELKAN-VOGEL, INC.   .50
SCHER, W.   E
  GIPSIES ARE COMING, THE
    BELWIN-MILLS PUBLISHING CORPORATION 25266   .60
SCHER, W.   3
  GOLDEN HARP, THE
    BOSTON MUSIC COMPANY   .50
SCHER, W.   E
  GRACEFUL BALLERINA
    BELWIN-MILLS PUBLISHING CORPORATION 25268   .60
SCHER, W.   2-3
  GRACEFUL GAZELLE, THE
    PRO-ART PUBLICATIONS, INC.   203   .50
SCHER, W.
  GREEN LANTERNS
    CARL FISCHER, INC.   P 2859   .50
SCHER, W.
  GRETEL AMD HANS
    CARL FISCHER, INC.   P 2938   .50
SCHER, W.
  GYPSY STRINGS
    CARL FISCHER, INC.   RS 396   .50
SCHER, W.   2
  HAPPY PUPPY, THE
    PRO-ART PUBLICATIONS, INC.   116   .50
SCHER, W.   2
  HOLIDAY IN NAPLES
    PRO-ART PUBLICATIONS, INC.   236   .50
SCHER, W.   4
  HUNGARIAN FANTASY
    THEODORE PRESSER COMPANY   .60
SCHER, W.
  ICE CARNIVAL IN VIENNA
    CARL FISCHER, INC.   P 3119   .50
SCHER, W.   2
  IN HINDULAND
    BELWIN-MILLS PUBLISHING CORPORATION   .60
SCHER, W.   2-3
  IN THE LAND OF THE DWARFS
    CENTURY MUSIC PUBLISHING COMPANY, INC. 4146   .40
SCHEP, W.   2-3
  JAPANESE LANTERNS
    PRO-ART PUBLICATIONS, INC.   561   .50
SCHER, W.   2 1/2
  JOLLY LITTLE MANNEQUIN
    BELWIN-MILLS PUBLISHING CORPORATION   .60
SCHER, W.   3
  JOLLY RICKSHA BOY
    BELWIN-MILLS PUBLISHING CORPORATION   .60
SCHER, W.   2-3
  LAUGHING CLOWN
    PRO-ART PUBLICATIONS, INC.   473   .50
SCHER, W.   3 1/2
  LAUGHING GIANT
    BELWIN-MILLS PUBLISHING CORPORATION   .60
SCHER, W.
  LITTLE ALMOND EYES
    SAM FOX PUBLISHING COMPANY, INC.   .50
SCHER, W.
  LITTLE ALMOND EYES
    SOUTHERN MUSIC COMPANY   .50
SCHER, W.   2
  LITTLE BANDMASTER, THE
    PRO-ART PUBLICATIONS, INC.   161   .50

SCHER, W.
    LITTLE CONCERT POLKA
        G. SCHIRMER, INC.   .40
SCHER, W.   2
    LITTLE MISS DANCER
        CENTURY MUSIC PUBLISHING COMPANY, INC.   4112   .40
SCHER, W.   1-2
    LITTLE NOCTURNE
        PRO-ART PUBLICATIONS, INC.   498   .50
SCHER, W.   2
    LOLA DANCES
        PRO-ART PUBLICATIONS, INC.   548   .50
SCHER, W.   1-2
    LONELY DOLPHIN, THE
        PRO-ART PUBLICATIONS, INC.   596   .50
SCHER, W.   3 1/2
    LOTUS FLOWERS IN THE WIND
        BELWIN-MILLS PUBLISHING CORPORATION   .60
SCHER, W.   2
    LUIGI'S TARANTELLA
        PRO-ART PUBLICATIONS, INC.   394   .50
SCHER, W.   2
    MARCH OF THE GREEN BERETS
        PRO-ART PUBLICATIONS, INC.   466   .50
SCHER, W.   E
    MARCHING ELEPHANTS
        BELWIN-MILLS PUBLISHING CORPORATION   25256   .60
SCHER, W.   2
    MARCHING MARIONETTES
        THEODORE PRESSER COMPANY   .50
SCHER, W.   E
    MEMORIES OF HUNGARY
        BELWIN-MILLS PUBLISHING CORPORATION   25270   .60
SCHER, W.
    MERRY LITTLE CLOCK
        SAM FOX PUBLISHING COMPANY, INC.   .50
SCHER, W.
    MERRY LITTLE CLOCK
        SOUTHERN MUSIC COMPANY   .50
SCHER, W.   1
    MERRY LITTLE RAINDROPS
        ELKAN-VOGEL, INC.   .50
SCHER, W.   2
    MERRY OLD SALT
        PRO-ART PUBLICATIONS, INC.   574   .50
SCHER, W.   2
    MERRY SCISSOR GRINDER
        THEODORE PRESSER COMPANY   .50
SCHER, W.   2-3
    MEXICAN JUMPING BEAN
        PRO-ART PUBLICATIONS, INC.   465   .50
SCHER, W.   2 1/2
    MIDNIGHT RIDERS
        THEODORE PRESSER COMPANY   .50
SCHER, W.   2-3
    MINSTRELS
        PRO-ART PUBLICATIONS, INC.   614   .50
SCHER, W.   2-3
    MYSTERIOUS TALE, A
        PRO-ART PUBLICATIONS, INC.   251   .50
SCHER, W.   E
    NAUGHTY LITTLE RAINDROPS
        BELWIN-MILLS PUBLISHING CORPORATION   25269   .60
SCHER, W.   E
    NYMPHS
        BELWIN-MILLS PUBLISHING CORPORATION   25267   .60
SCHER, W.   1
    ON MY POLO STICK
        CENTURY MUSIC PUBLISHING COMPANY, INC.   4352   .40
SCHER, W.   2
    ON MY WOODEN HORSE
        ELKAN-VOGEL, INC.   .50
SCHER, W.
    ORGAN GRINDER'S TARANTELLA
        CARL FISCHER, INC.   P 3037   .50
SCHER, W.   2-3
    ORIENTAL MYSTERY
        PRO-ART PUBLICATIONS, INC.   201   .50
SCHER, W.   2
    OUR SCHOOL BAND
        PRO-ART PUBLICATIONS, INC.   499   .50
SCHER, W.
    PEDRO DANCES
        G. SCHIRMER, INC.   .35
SCHER, W.   2
    PENGUINS
        BOSTON MUSIC COMPANY   .50
SCHER, W.   1
    PINK PETAL
        CENTURY MUSIC PUBLISHING COMPANY, INC.   4270   .40
SCHER, W.   1-2
    POLLY WANTS A CRACKER
        CENTURY MUSIC PUBLISHING COMPANY, INC.   4173   .40
SCHER, W.   3
    POLONAISE ROMANTIQUE
        PRO-ART PUBLICATIONS, INC.   573   .50
SCHER, W.   3
    PRELUDE PATHETIQUE
        PRO-ART PUBLICATIONS, INC.   551   .50
SCHER, W.
    PROCESSION OF THE NIGHT
        CARL FISCHER, INC.   P 3069   .50
SCHER, W.   2 1/2
    PUPPETS ON PARADE
        BELWIN-MILLS PUBLISHING CORPORATION   .60
SCHER, W.
    PUPPETS ON PARADE
        BELWIN-MILLS PUBLISHING CORPORATION   .60
SCHER, W.   E
    ROMANCE TZIGANE
        BELWIN-MILLS PUBLISHING CORPORATION   25255   .60
SCHER, W.
    SAD CLOWN
        EDWARD B. MARKS MUSIC CORPORATION   00.60
SCHER, W.
    SAD LITTLE PUPPY
        CARL FISCHER, INC.   P 2856   .50
SCHER, W.
    SEA FANTASY
        CARL FISCHER, INC.   RS 407   .50
SCHER, W.
    SERENADE ROMANTIQUE
        CARL FISCHER, INC.   R 4091   .50
SCHER, W.
    SERENADE TO A MANDARIN
        CARL FISCHER, INC.   P 3150   .50

SCHER, W.   2-3
    SERENATA
        PRO-ART PUBLICATIONS, INC.   464   .50
SCHER, W.
    SHEPHERD'S SONG AND DANCE
        G. SCHIRMER, INC.   .40
SCHER, W.   2
    SICILIAN TARANTELLA
        THEODORE PRESSER COMPANY   .50
SCHER, W.
    SLAVONIC DANCE
        G. SCHIRMER, INC.   .40
SCHER, W.   1
    SNAKE CHARMER
        CENTURY MUSIC PUBLISHING COMPANY, INC.   4224   .40
SCHER, W.   2 1/2
    SNOW TIME
        THEODORE PRESSER COMPANY   .50
SCHER, W.   2
    SPANISH GUITARS
        PRO-ART PUBLICATIONS, INC.   239   .50
SCHER, W.   2
    SPANISH GYPSY
        BOSTON MUSIC COMPANY   .50
SCHER, W.   1-2
    SPOOKY FAIRY TALE, A
        PRO-ART PUBLICATIONS, INC.   240   .50
SCHER, W.   2-3
    SWEET SIXTEEN WALTZ
        PRO-ART PUBLICATIONS, INC.   269   .50
SCHER, W.   2
    TELL ME PRETTY DAISY
        BOSTON MUSIC COMPANY   .50
SCHER, W.   2
    TIMID LITTLE BEE, THE
        ELKAN-VOGEL, INC.   .50
SCHER, W.   1 1/2
    TO A DAISY
        THEODORE PRESSER COMPANY   .50
SCHER, W.
    TO MY FRENCH DOLL
        EDWARD B. MARKS MUSIC CORPORATION   00.60
SCHER, W.
    TO MY LITTLE WHITE KITTEN
        EDWARD B. MARKS MUSIC CORPORATION   00.60
SCHER, W.   1
    TONY'S TARANTELLE
        CENTURY MUSIC PUBLISHING COMPANY, INC.   4236   .40
SCHER, W.   2
    TOY SHOP FROLICS
        BOSTON MUSIC COMPANY   .50
SCHER, W.
    TRICK OR TREAT
        SAM FOX PUBLISHING COMPANY, INC.   .50
SCHER, W.
    TRICK OR TREAT
        SOUTHERN MUSIC COMPANY   .50
SCHER, W.   2
    TULIP TIME IN HOLLAND
        WILLIS MUSIC COMPANY   .40
SCHER, W.   2
    TURKISH DANCE
        PRO-ART PUBLICATIONS, INC.   392   .50
SCHER, W.   2
    TWIDDLE DEE DEE
        PRO-ART PUBLICATIONS, INC.   595   .50
SCHER, W.   2
    TWO LITTLE WOODPECKERS
        CARL FISCHER, INC.   P 2917   .50
SCHER, W.   2
    TWO WOODEN PUPPETS ON A STRING
        CENTURY MUSIC PUBLISHING COMPANY, INC.   4353   .40
SCHER, W.   1-2
    VALSE NOCTURNE
        CENTURY MUSIC PUBLISHING COMPANY, INC.   4407   .40
SCHER, W.   3
    VEIL DANCE
        CENTURY MUSIC PUBLISHING COMPANY, INC.   4231   .40
SCHER, W.   2
    VENETIAN HOLIDAY -- TARANTELLA
        BOSTON MUSIC COMPANY   .50
SCHER, W.   2
    VOICES OF SPRING
        PRO-ART PUBLICATIONS, INC.   513   .50
SCHER, W.   1-2
    WALTZ OF THE BELLS
        PRO-ART PUBLICATIONS, INC.   167   .50
SCHER, W.   1 1/2
    WALTZING BEAR
        THEODORE PRESSER COMPANY   .50
SCHER, W.
    WALTZING BY CANDLELIGHT
        CARL FISCHER, INC.   P 3149   .50
SCHER, W.
    WALTZING DAFFODILS/LET'S DANCE GRANDMA
        EDWARD B. MARKS MUSIC CORPORATION   00.60
SCHER, W.
    WALTZING GYPSIES
        CARL FISCHER, INC.   RS 414   .50
SCHER, W.   2
    WALTZING JUGGLER
        WILLIS MUSIC COMPANY   .40
SCHER, W.   1-2
    WALTZING PUPPET
        PRO-ART PUBLICATIONS, INC.   563   .50
SCHER, W.   3
    WANDERING CARAVAN
        PRO-ART PUBLICATIONS, INC.   344   .50
SCHER, W.   1 1/2
    WEEPING WILLOW, THE
        THEODORE PRESSER COMPANY   .50
SCHER, W.--ED   SCHER, W.   2-3
    MINKA
        PRO-ART PUBLICATIONS, INC.   168   .50
SCHICKELE, P.
    IN MY NINE LIVES
        ELKAN-VOGEL, INC.   2.00
SCHICKELE, P.
    THREE FOLK SETTINGS
        ELKAN-VOGEL, INC.   .75
SCHIEFELBEIN, F.   2
    ADESTE FIDELIS
        VOLKWEIN BROS.   .25
SCHIEFELBEIN, F.   2
    BOY SCOUTS MARCH
        VOLKWEIN BROS.   .25

SCHIEFELBEIN, F.   2
    BROKEN RING
        VOLKWEIN BROS.   .30
SCHIEFELBEIN, F.   2
    CAPTAIN'S COMMAND
        VOLKWEIN BROS.   .30
SCHIEFELBEIN, F.   3
    COUNTRY GARDENS
        VOLKWEIN BROS.   .30
SCHIEFELBEIN, F.   4
    DANCE OF THE MAYBELLS
        VOLKWEIN BROS.   .40
SCHIEFELBEIN, F.   4
    DREAM THOUGHTS
        VOLKWEIN BROS.   .40
SCHIEFELBEIN, F.   2
    FIR TREE
        VOLKWEIN BROS.   .IK
SCHIEFELBEIN, F.   3
    FLEETING FANCIES
        VOLKWEIN BROS.   .40
SCHIEFELBEIN, F.   2
    FROST KING
        VOLKWEIN BROS.   .50
SCHIEFELBEIN, F.   3
    GATHERING DAISIES
        VOLKWEIN BROS.   .40
SCHIEFELBEIN, F.   2
    HUNTERS JOY
        VOLKWEIN BROS.   .30
SCHIEFELBEIN, F.   2
    IN THE COUNTRY
        VOLKWEIN BROS.   .25
SCHIEFELBEIN, F.   2
    IN THE GARDEN
        VOLKWEIN BROS.   .25
SCHIEFELBEIN, F.   2
    JINGLE BELLS
        VOLKWEIN BROS.   .35
SCHIEFELBEIN, F.   2
    JINGLE BELLS
        VOLKWEIN BROS.   00.40
SCHIEFELBEIN, F.   2
    JOYFUL MESSAGE
        VOLKWEIN BROS.   .30
SCHIEFELBEIN, F.   2
    LAUTERBACH
        VOLKWEIN BROS.   .30
SCHIEFELBEIN, F.   4
    LAZY RIVER
        VOLKWEIN BROS.   .40
SCHIEFELBEIN, F.   4
    LEFT FOOT, RIGHT FOOT -- ORIGINAL
        VOLKWEIN BROS.   .30
SCHIEFELBEIN, F.   2
    LEFT FOOT, RIGHT FOOT -- SIMPLIFIED
        VOLKWEIN BROS.   .30
SCHIEFELBEIN, F.   4
    LEFT FOOT, RIGHT FOOT MARCH
        VOLKWEIN BROS.   00.50
SCHIEFELBEIN, F.   2
    LITTLE RECRUIT
        VOLKWEIN BROS.   .25
SCHIEFELBEIN, F.   2
    LORELEI
        VOLKWEIN BROS.   .30
SCHIEFELBEIN, F.   4
    LOVE'S LULLABY
        VOLKWEIN BROS.   .35
SCHIEFELBEIN, F.   3
    MARDI GRAS PARADE
        VOLKWEIN BROS.   .40
SCHIEFELBEIN, F.   2
    OH MY DEAR AUGUSTIN
        VOLKWEIN BROS.   .30
SCHIEFELBEIN, F.   2
    PARTING SONG
        VOLKWEIN BROS.   .30
SCHIEFELBEIN, F.   2
    RUSSIAN PEASANT DANCE
        VOLKWEIN BROS.   .40
SCHIEFELBEIN, F.   2
    SANCTISSIMA
        VOLKWEIN BROS.   .25
SCHIEFELBEIN, F.   2
    SHEPHERD'S REST
        VOLKWEIN BROS.   .25
SCHIEFELBEIN, F.   2
    SILENT NIGHT, HOLY NIGHT
        VOLKWEIN BROS.   .25
SCHIEFELBEIN, F.   2
    SILENT NIGHT, HOLY NIGHT
        VOLKWEIN BROS.   00.40
SCHIEFELBEIN, F.   3
    SONG OF THE BROOK
        VOLKWEIN BROS.   .25
SCHIEFELBEIN, F.   2
    THOU FILLEST MY
        VOLKWEIN BROS.   00.30
SCHIEFELBEIN, F.   2
    TO A VIOLET
        VOLKWEIN BROS.   00.35
SCHIEFELBEIN, F.   2
    TO A VIOLET
        VOLKWEIN BROS.   00.50
SCHIEFELBEIN, F.   2
    TRUE LOVE
        VOLKWEIN BROS.   00.30
SCHIEFELBEIN, F.   2
    VILLAGE BELLS
        VOLKWEIN BROS.   00.30
SCHIEFELBEIN, F.   2
    WEIRD TALE
        VOLKWEIN BROS.   00.40
SCHIFF, H.
    SONATA IN E MINOR
        ASSOCIATED MUSIC PUBLISHERS, INC.   BRH   2.40
SCHIFF, H.
    SONATINA NO. 02--FUR DIE JUGEND
        ASSOCIATED MUSIC PUBLISHERS, INC.   DOB   2.00
SCHIFRIN   1 1/2
    BLUE-PINK
        WILLIS MUSIC COMPANY   .40
SCHIFRIN   HASTINGS
    BULLITT, THEME FROM
        WARNER BROTHERS PUBLISHERS   1.00

SCHIFRIN
    FOX, THE, THEME FROM
        WARNER BROTHERS PUBLISHERS   1.00
SCHIFRIN, L.
    HAUNTING
        THE BIG THREE MUSIC CORPORATION   00.95
SCHIFRIN, L.
    MIMA
        EDWARD B. MARKS MUSIC CORPORATION   01.25
SCHIFRIN, L.
    RHINO - THEME
        THE BIG THREE MUSIC CORPORATION   00.95
SCHILINGER
    LITTLE WALTZ
        MCA MUSIC   .60
SCHILLER, F.   1
    BLACK BIRD, A TALE
        CENTURY MUSIC PUBLISHING COMPANY, INC.   1213   .40
SCHILLER, F.   1
    BLUE BIRD, MELODIE
        CENTURY MUSIC PUBLISHING COMPANY, INC.   1216   .40
SCHILLER, F.   2
    BOBOLINK, POLKA
        CENTURY MUSIC PUBLISHING COMPANY, INC.   1221   .40
SCHILLER, F.   2
    HUMMING BIRD, WALTZ
        CENTURY MUSIC PUBLISHING COMPANY, INC.   1222   .40
SCHILLER, F.   1
    ROBIN REDBREAST
        CENTURY MUSIC PUBLISHING COMPANY, INC.   1215   .40
SCHILLER, F.   1
    SWALLOW, VALSETTE
        CENTURY MUSIC PUBLISHING COMPANY, INC.   1212   .40
SCHILLER, W.   5
    FAWN, THE
        BELWIN-MILLS PUBLISHING CORPORATION   .60
SCHILLINGS   M-D
    WITCH SONG, THE. MELODRAMA
        C. F. PETERS CORPORATION   F4   3.50
SCHININA, L.
    ESERCIZI DI OTTAVE IN TUTTE LE TONALITA, OP. 28
        EDIZIONI BERBEN   EB 1735   9.00
SCHIRMER, R.
    UNITED STATES VICTORY MARCH
        G. SCHIRMER, INC.   .75
SCHISKE, K.
    RHAPSODY, OP. 20--1945
        ASSOCIATED MUSIC PUBLISHERS, INC.   DOB   1.65
SCHISKE, K.
    SONATA, OP. 3--1936
        ASSOCIATED MUSIC PUBLISHERS, INC.   DOB   3.50
SCHISKE, K.
    SONATINA, OP. 42--1954
        ASSOCIATED MUSIC PUBLISHERS, INC.   DOB   1.75
SCHLOSS, J.
    TWELVE-TONE SUITE
        PEER SOUTHERN ORGANIZATION   02.00
SCHLOSS, J.
    TWENTY-THREE PIECES FOR CHILDREN
        PEER SOUTHERN ORGANIZATION   02.00
SCHLOSS, J.
    TWENTY-THREE STUDIES FOR CHILDREN
        PEER SOUTHERN ORGANIZATION   02.00
SCHMIDT, F.   WUEHRER
    INTERMEZZO
        ASSOCIATED MUSIC PUBLISHERS, INC.   DOB   2.25
SCHMIDT, F.   WUEHRER
    TOCCATA
        ASSOCIATED MUSIC PUBLISHERS, INC.   DOB   2.50
SCHMITT
    BALLADE DE LA NEIGE
        FRANCO COLOMBO PUBLICATIONS   SAL   2.00
SCHMITT
    CORTEGE DES ADORATEURS DU FEU
        FRANCO COLOMBO PUBLICATIONS   SAL   2.00
SCHMITT
    DANSE DES MILLIARDS
        FRANCO COLOMBO PUBLICATIONS   SAL   2.00
SCHMITT
    MENUET VIF
        FRANCO COLOMBO PUBLICATIONS   SAL   2.00
SCHMITT
    RITOURNELLES
        FRANCO COLOMBO PUBLICATIONS   SAL   2.00
SCHMITT
    SONATINE
        FREDERICK HARRIS MUSIC COMPANY   .60
SCHMITT, A.   1
    FIVE FINGER EXERCISES, PART 1
        CENTURY MUSIC PUBLISHING COMPANY, INC.   1207   .40
SCHMITT, A.   1
    FIVE FINGER EXERCISES, PART 2
        CENTURY MUSIC PUBLISHING COMPANY, INC.   1208   .40
SCHMITT, A.   KNECHT
    PREPARATORY EXERCISES. 5-FINGER EXERCISES. OP. 16
        G. SCHIRMER, INC.   L434   .85
SCHMITT, F.
    CLAVECIN OBTEMPERANT SUITE, OP. 107
        ELKAN-VOGEL, INC.   D   4.25
SCHMITT, F.
    LA TRAGEDIE DE SOLOME
        ELKAN-VOGEL, INC.   D   6.00
SCHMITT, F.
    LE PETIT ELFE 'FERME-L'OEIL'
        ELKAN-VOGEL, INC.   D   7.00
SCHMITT, F.
    PUPAZZI
        FRANCO COLOMBO PUBLICATIONS   SAL   4.25
SCHMITT, F.
    SOIRS
        ELKAN-VOGEL, INC.   D   5.35
SCHMITT, J.
    SONATINA IN G, OP. 249 NO. 2
        FREDERICK HARRIS MUSIC COMPANY   .60
SCHMOLL, A.   2
    CYMBALS AND CASTANETS
        CENTURY MUSIC PUBLISHING COMPANY, INC.   1708   .40
SCHMOLL, A.   2 1/2
    CYMBALS AND CASTANETS
        WILLIS MUSIC COMPANY   .40
SCHMOLL, A.   3
    MARCH OF THE RECRUITS
        CENTURY MUSIC PUBLISHING COMPANY, INC.   2307   .40
SCHNEIDER-TRNAVSKY   3
    SLOWAKISCHE SONATINE, OP. 75
        BARENREITER VERLAG   AP 693

SCHOECK
  RITORNELLE UND FUGHETTEN, OP. 68
    FRANCO COLOMBO PUBLICATIONS   SY496 2.00
SCHOEN
  MY POEM
    MCA MUSIC 1.00
SCHOENBERG
  PIANO PIECE, OP. 33A
    UNIVERSAL EDITION   UE 9773 2.75
SCHOENBERG
  PIANO PIECE, OP. 33B
    UNIVERSAL EDITION   UE 15165 7.00
SCHOENBERG
  SIX LITTLE PIANO PIECES, OP. 19
    UNIVERSAL EDITION   UE 5069 3.75
SCHOENBERG
  SUITE, OP. 25
    UNIVERSAL EDITION   UE 7627 3.50
SCHOENBERG
  THREE PIANO PIECES, OP. 11
    UNIVERSAL EDITION   UE 2991 3.25
SCHOLZ
  ROMANTISCHE STUDIE--''ERWARTUNG''
    ASSOCIATED MUSIC PUBLISHERS, INC.   DOB 1.50
SCHOLZ
  SONATA NO. 03, OP. 52
    ASSOCIATED MUSIC PUBLISHERS, INC.   DOB 4.00
SCHOLZ
  TOCCATA--1959
    ASSOCIATED MUSIC PUBLISHERS, INC.   DOB 1.75
SCHRAMM
  BHARATE SANGITA--INDIAN MUSIC--
    MCA MUSIC 2.00
SCHRAMM   2
  JAVALI
    THEODORE PRESSER COMPANY .50
SCHRAMM
  KIRAVANI-RAMAPRIYA LOTUS DANCE
    AMERICAN MUSIC EDITION .50
SCHRAMM
  NATYAMALIKA - DANCE SUITE
    GENERAL MUSIC PUBLISHING COMPANY, INC. 270 1.25
SCHRAMM
  NATYAMALIKA - DANCE SUITE
    GENERAL MUSIC PUBLISHING COMPANY, INC. 1.75
SCHRAMM
  VERTICAL CONSTRUCTION
    GENERAL MUSIC PUBLISHING COMPANY, INC. 271 1.25
SCHRAMM
  VERTICAL CONSTRUCTION
    GENERAL MUSIC PUBLISHING COMPANY, INC. 1.25
SCHREIBER, FR.
  SEVENTEEN SMALL PIECES, OP. 23
    UNIVERSAL EDITION   UE 6039 1.70
SCHROEDER, H.   4-5
  KLAVIERSONATA NO. 02 - 1953
    SCHOTT   4540 1.75
SCHROEDER, H.   4
  SONATA IN A MINOR
    SCHOTT   4123 1.75
SCHROETER, H.
  SONATINA, OP. 8
    ASSOCIATED MUSIC PUBLISHERS, INC.   BOT 3.00
SCHUBERT   KREUTZER
  ALLEGRETTO IN C MINOR
    BOSTON MUSIC COMPANY .50
SCHUBERT   DEL MAGLIO
  AN DEN MOND
    FRANCO COLOMBO PUBLICATIONS 128143 .50
SCHUBERT   SCHAUM, J.   1
  AVE MARIA
    BELWIN-MILLS PUBLISHING CORPORATION .50
SCHUBERT   WALLIS
  AVE MARIA
    BOSTON MUSIC COMPANY .50
SCHUBERT
  AVE MARIA
    CARL FISCHER, INC.   S 2038 .50
SCHUBERT   HELLER
  AVE MARIA
    G. SCHIRMER, INC. .40
SCHUBERT   SCHAUM, J.   4
  AVE MARIA
    SCHAUM PUBLICATIONS, INC. .60
SCHUBERT   HODSON   3
  AVE MARIA
    THEODORE PRESSER COMPANY .50
SCHUBERT   BURNAM   1
  AVE MARIA
    WILLIS MUSIC COMPANY .40
SCHUBERT   HELLER   3
  AVE MARIA
    WILLIS MUSIC COMPANY .40
SCHUBERT
  AVE MARIA, OP. 52 NO. 6
    FRANCO COLOMBO PUBLICATIONS 121560 .60
SCHUBERT   DEL MAGLIO
  AVE MARIA, OP. 52 NO. 6
    FRANCO COLOMBO PUBLICATIONS 128149 .60
SCHUBERT   4
  AVE MARIA, WORDS
    CENTURY MUSIC PUBLISHING COMPANY, INC. 3185 .40
SCHUBERT   FISCHHOF *
  BALLET MUSIC FROM 'ROSAMUNDE', OP. 26
    G. SCHIRMER, INC.   L1146 .75
SCHUBERT   4
  BALLET MUSIC, ROSAMUND
    CENTURY MUSIC PUBLISHING COMPANY, INC. 2003 .40
SCHUBERT   5
  BALLETT MUSIK 2 G-DUR AUS ROSAMUNDE
    SCHOTT   0707 1/2 1.00
SCHUBERT   4
  BEE, THE
    CENTURY MUSIC PUBLISHING COMPANY, INC. 3645 .40
SCHUBERT   2
  BOY AND THE ROSE, THE
    CENTURY MUSIC PUBLISHING COMPANY, INC. 3824 .40
SCHUBERT   MILLER   4
  BY THE SEA
    CENTURY MUSIC PUBLISHING COMPANY, INC. 133 .40
SCHUBERT   STEINER   2
  CHARM OF CHAMBER MUSIC
    BELWIN-MILLS PUBLISHING CORPORATION .60
SCHUBERT   1
  CRADLE SONG
    BELWIN-MILLS PUBLISHING CORPORATION 541 .60

SCHUBERT   3-4
  DER LINDENBAUM
    CENTURY MUSIC PUBLISHING COMPANY, INC. 3917 .40
SCHUBERT   HELLER   5
  DIE FORELLE
    SCHOTT   08004 1/2 1.00
SCHUBERT   HELLER *
  DIE FORELLE--THE TROUT
    G. SCHIRMER, INC. .70
SCHUBERT
  ECCOSSAISES
    EDWIN F. KALMUS   3879 1.50
SCHUBERT   SCHAUM, J.   5
  ERL KING, THE
    BELWIN-MILLS PUBLISHING CORPORATION .50
SCHUBERT   BUONAMICI
  FANTASIA IN C, OP. 15--'WANDERER'
    G. SCHIRMER, INC. 1.10
SCHUBERT   BUONAMICI
  FANTASIA OR SONATA IN G, OP. 78
    G. SCHIRMER, INC. 1.10
SCHUBERT   LANGE   4
  FANTASIE
    SCHOTT   08724 1/2 1.00
SCHUBERT   DURR, W.   4-5
  FANTASIE IN C -- 'GRAZER FANTASIE' --
    BARENREITER VERLAG 19 101
SCHUBERT   BADURA-SKODA
  FANTASY C MAJOR --'WANDERER FANTASIE'--, D 760
    WIENER URTEXT EDITION UT 50010 2.50
SCHUBERT   DURR, W.
  FANTASY FOR PIANO --'GRAZER FANTASIE'
    BARENREITER VERLAG BA19101 6.00
SCHUBERT
  FANTASY IN C MAJOR - WANDERER FANTASIA
    UNIVERSAL EDITION 13368E 1.80
SCHUBERT   CORTOT
  FANTASY IN C, OP. 15
    FRANCO COLOMBO PUBLICATIONS SAL 5.00
SCHUBERT   DEL MAGLIO
  FORELLE
    FRANCO COLOMBO PUBLICATIONS 128142 .50
SCHUBERT   2
  HEIDENROESLEIN
    CENTURY MUSIC PUBLISHING COMPANY, INC. 3824 .40
SCHUBERT   DEL MAGLIO
  HEIDENROESLEIN, OP. 3 NO. 3
    FRANCO COLOMBO PUBLICATIONS 128125 .50
SCHUBERT   5
  IMPROMPTU AS-DUR, OP. 142 NO. 2
    SCHOTT   0692 1/2 1.00
SCHUBERT   5
  IMPROMPTU AS-DUR, OP. 90 NO. 4
    SCHOTT   0689 1/2 1.00
SCHUBERT   5
  IMPROMPTU B-DUR, OP. 142 NO. 3
    SCHOTT   0693 1.00
SCHUBERT   5
  IMPROMPTU C-MOLL, OP. 90 NO. 1
    SCHOTT   0686 1/2 1.00
SCHUBERT   BUELOW
  IMPROMPTU ELEGIAQUE, OP. 90 NO. 3
    G. SCHIRMER, INC. .70
SCHUBERT   5
  IMPROMPTU ES-DUR, OP. 90 NO. 2
    SCHOTT   0687 102 1.00
SCHUBERT   3
  IMPROMPTU G-DUR, OP. 90
    SCHOTT   0688 102 1.00
SCHUBERT   4-5
  IMPROMPTU GES-DUR, OP. 90 NO. 3
    SCHOTT   0654 1/2 1.00
SCHUBERT   5
  IMPROMPTU IN A FLAT, OP. 142 NO. 2
    BELWIN-MILLS PUBLISHING CORPORATION 309 .60
SCHUBERT   4
  IMPROMPTU IN A FLAT, OP. 142 NO. 2
    CENTURY MUSIC PUBLISHING COMPANY, INC. 2251 .40
SCHUBERT   BUONAMICI
  IMPROMPTU IN A FLAT, OP. 142 NO. 2
    G. SCHIRMER, INC. .40
SCHUBERT   CHING
  IMPROMPTU IN A FLAT, OP. 142 NO. 2
    GENERAL WORDS AND MUSIC COMPANY .75
SCHUBERT   BUONAMICI
  IMPROMPTU IN A FLAT, OP. 142 NO. 4
    G. SCHIRMER, INC. .90
SCHUBERT   SCHAUM, J.   3
  IMPROMPTU IN A FLAT, OP. 90 NO. 4
    BELWIN-MILLS PUBLISHING CORPORATION .50
SCHUBERT
  IMPROMPTU IN A FLAT, OP. 90 NO. 4
    FRANCO COLOMBO PUBLICATIONS 128669 1.25
SCHUBERT   BUONAMICI
  IMPROMPTU IN A FLAT, OP. 90 NO. 4
    G. SCHIRMER, INC.
SCHUBERT   CHING
  IMPROMPTU IN A FLAT, OP. 90 NO. 4
    GENERAL WORDS AND MUSIC COMPANY .75
SCHUBERT
  IMPROMPTU IN A FLAT, OP. 90 NO. 4
    WILLIS MUSIC COMPANY .50
SCHUBERT   5
  IMPROMPTU IN B FLAT, OP. 142 NO. 3
    CENTURY MUSIC PUBLISHING COMPANY, INC. 2335 .40
SCHUBERT
  IMPROMPTU IN B FLAT, OP. 142 NO. 3
    FRANCO COLOMBO PUBLICATIONS 128385 .75
SCHUBERT   BUONAMICI
  IMPROMPTU IN B FLAT, OP. 142 NO. 3
    G. SCHIRMER, INC. .60
SCHUBERT   BUONAMICI
  IMPROMPTU IN C MINOR, OP. 90 NO. 1
    G. SCHIRMER, INC. .70
SCHUBERT   4
  IMPROMPTU IN E FLAT, OP. 90
    CENTURY MUSIC PUBLISHING COMPANY, INC. 3489 .40
SCHUBERT
  IMPROMPTU IN E FLAT, OP. 90 NO. 2
    FRANCO COLOMBO PUBLICATIONS 128131 .60
SCHUBERT   BUONAMICI
  IMPROMPTU IN E FLAT, OP. 90 NO. 2
    G. SCHIRMER, INC. .75
SCHUBERT   BUONAMICI
  IMPROMPTU IN F MINOR, OP. 142 NO. 1
    G. SCHIRMER, INC. .80

SCHUBERT   DEL MAGLIO
   IMPROMPTU IN G FLAT, OP. 90 NO. 3
      FRANCO COLOMBO PUBLICATIONS   124730   .50
SCHUBERT   BUONAMICI
   IMPROMPTU IN G FLAT, OP. 90 NO. 3
      G. SCHIRMER, INC.   .70
SCHUBERT
   IMPROMPTU IN G FLAT, OP. 90 NO. 3 -- TRANSPOSED IN G --
      FRANCO COLOMBO PUBLICATIONS   128087   .90
SCHUBERT   3-4
   LINDEN TREE, THE -- LINDENBAUM --
      CENTURY MUSIC PUBLISHING COMPANY, INC. 3917   .40
SCHUBERT   2
   LITTLE WALTZES FROM OP. 9A
      CENTURY MUSIC PUBLISHING COMPANY, INC. 3715   .40
SCHUBERT   3
   MARCH MILITAIRE, OP. 51
      CENTURY MUSIC PUBLISHING COMPANY, INC. 1648   .40
SCHUBERT
   MARCH MILITAIRE, OP. 51 NO. 1
      CARL FISCHER, INC.   S 1022   .50
SCHUBERT   TAGLIAPIETRA
   MARCHE MILITAIRE, OP. 51 NO. 1
      FRANCO COLOMBO PUBLICATIONS   127897   .60
SCHUBERT   DEL MAGLIO
   MARCHE MILITAIRE, OP. 51 NO. 1
      FRANCO COLOMBO PUBLICATIONS   124731   .60
SCHUBERT
   MENUETTO IN B MINOR
      G. SCHIRMER, INC.   .40
SCHUBERT   6
   MENUETTO IN B MINOR, OP. 78
      THEODORE PRESSER COMPANY   .50
SCHUBERT
   MENUETTO, OP. 78
      WILLIS MUSIC COMPANY   .30
SCHUBERT   4
   MILITARMARSCH D-DUR OP. 51 NO. 1
      SCHOTT   0704 1/4   1.00
SCHUBERT   KRENTZLIN   2
   MILITARMARSCH D-DUR OP. 51 NO. 1
      SCHOTT   08260 1/2   1.00
SCHUBERT   DIETRICH
   MILITARY MARCH IN D
      G. SCHIRMER, INC.   .40
SCHUBERT   ROLFE, W.   2
   MILITARY MARCH, EASY
      CENTURY MUSIC PUBLISHING COMPANY, INC. 3176   .40
SCHUBERT   3
   MILITARY MARCH, NO. 1
      CENTURY MUSIC PUBLISHING COMPANY, INC. 1648   .40
SCHUBERT
   MILITARY MARCH, OP. 51 NO. 1
      BELWIN-MILLS PUBLISHING CORPORATION 28166   .60
SCHUBERT   3 1/2
   MILITARY MARCH, OP. 51 NO. 1
      THEODORE PRESSER COMPANY   .50
SCHUBERT
   MILITARY MARCH, OP. 51 NO. 1
      WILLIS MUSIC COMPANY   .75
SCHUBERT
   MINUET IN B MINOR, OP. 78
      FREDERICK HARRIS MUSIC COMPANY   .35
SCHUBERT   STRIMER, J.   1
   MOMENT MUSICAL
      PRO-ART PUBLICATIONS, INC.   34   .50
SCHUBERT   SCHAUM, J.   2 1/2
   MOMENT MUSICAL
      SCHAUM PUBLICATIONS, INC.   .50
SCHUBERT   7
   MOMENT MUSICAL IN F MINOR
      NOVELLO AND COMPANY, LTD.   55.0047.08   .25
SCHUBERT   3
   MOMENT MUSICAL NO. 3
      BELWIN-MILLS PUBLISHING CORPORATION 308   .60
SCHUBERT   4
   MOMENT MUSICAL, OP. 94 NO. 1
      CENTURY MUSIC PUBLISHING COMPANY, INC. 3900   .40
SCHUBERT   4
   MOMENT MUSICAL, OP. 94 NO. 2
      CENTURY MUSIC PUBLISHING COMPANY, INC. 4039   .40
SCHUBERT   BUONAMICI
   MOMENT MUSICAL, OP. 94 NO. 2
      G. SCHIRMER, INC.   .40
SCHUBERT   2
   MOMENT MUSICAL, OP. 94 NO. 3
      CENTURY MUSIC PUBLISHING COMPANY, INC. 2164   .40
SCHUBERT   MONTANI
   MOMENT MUSICAL, OP. 94 NO. 3
      FRANCO COLOMBO PUBLICATIONS   46179   .60
SCHUBERT   DEL MAGLIO
   MOMENT MUSICAL, OP. 94 NO. 3
      FRANCO COLOMBO PUBLICATIONS   124732   .50
SCHUBERT   CORTOT
   MOMENT MUSICAL, OP. 94 NO. 3
      FRANCO COLOMBO PUBLICATIONS   SAL   1.75
SCHUBERT   BAUER
   MOMENT MUSICAL, OP. 94 NO. 3
      G. SCHIRMER, INC.   .30
SCHUBERT   BUONAMICI
   MOMENT MUSICAL, OP. 94 NO. 3
      G. SCHIRMER, INC.   .35
SCHUBERT   4
   MOMENT MUSICAL, OP. 94 NO. 3
      VOLKWEIN BROS.   .25
SCHUBERT   BUONAMICI
   MOMENT MUSICAL, OP. 94 NO. 4
      G. SCHIRMER, INC.   .50
SCHUBERT   4
   MOMENT MUSICAL, OP. 94 NO. 5
      CENTURY MUSIC PUBLISHING COMPANY, INC. 3736   .40
SCHUBERT   4
   MOMENT MUSICAL, OP. 94 NO. 6
      CENTURY MUSIC PUBLISHING COMPANY, INC. 4040   .40
SCHUBERT   BUONAMICI
   MOMENT MUSICAL, OP. 94 NO. 6
      G. SCHIRMER, INC.   .40
SCHUBERT   5
   MOMENT MUSICAL, OP. 94 NO. 6
      THEODORE PRESSER COMPANY   .50
SCHUBERT   5
   MOMENTS MUSICAUX OP. 94 NO. 2 AS-DUR
      SCHOTT   0696 1/2   1.00
SCHUBERT   5
   MOMENTS MUSICAUX OP. 94 NO. 3 F-MOLL
      SCHOTT   0697   .75

SCHUBERT   M-D
   QUINTET, OP. 114 'TROUT'
      C. F. PETERS CORPORATION   1307A   2.50
SCHUBERT   3
   ROSAMUND, BALLET MUSIC
      CENTURY MUSIC PUBLISHING COMPANY, INC. 2003   .40
SCHUBERT   SCHAUM, J.   2
   ROSAMUNDE 'BALLET MUSIC'
      BELWIN-MILLS PUBLISHING CORPORATION   .50
SCHUBERT
   SCHERZO
      WILLIS MUSIC COMPANY   .35
SCHUBERT   4
   SCHERZO IN B FLAT - POSTH.
      CENTURY MUSIC PUBLISHING COMPANY, INC. 3737   .40
SCHUBERT
   SCHERZO IN B FLAT--POSTHUMOUS
      G. SCHIRMER, INC.   .40
SCHUBERT   LANGE
   SCHERZO IN B FLAT--POSTHUMOUS
      G. SCHIRMER, INC.   .50
SCHUBERT   LISZT
   SCHERZO IN B FLAT--POSTHUMOUS
      G. SCHIRMER, INC.   .75
SCHUBERT   MAY *
   SCHERZO NO. 01 IN B FLAT
      ASSOCIATED MUSIC PUBLISHERS, INC.   DOB   .60
SCHUBERT   LISZT   6
   SERENADE
      CENTURY MUSIC PUBLISHING COMPANY, INC. 696   .40
SCHUBERT
   SERENADE
      FRANCO COLOMBO PUBLICATIONS   121561   .60
SCHUBERT   DEL MAGLIO
   SERENADE
      FRANCO COLOMBO PUBLICATIONS   128150   .60
SCHUBERT   DEL MAGLIO
   SERENADE
      FRANCO COLOMBO PUBLICATIONS   43123   .90
SCHUBERT   WHITFORD   GR. 2
   SERENADE
      ROBERT WHITFORD PUBLICATIONS   .40
SCHUBERT   JESTON, I. H.   3
   SERENADE
      VOLKWEIN BROS.   .35
SCHUBERT   3
   SERENADE
      WILLIS MUSIC COMPANY   .35
SCHUBERT   3
   SERENADE - STAENDCHEN
      CENTURY MUSIC PUBLISHING COMPANY, INC. 2196   .40
SCHUBERT   LANGE
   SERENADE, OP. 90 NO. 11
      CARL FISCHER, INC.   P 3185   .75
SCHUBERT
   SLUMBER SONG
      FREDERICK HARRIS MUSIC COMPANY   .60
SCHUBERT   BUONAMICI
   SONATA IN A MINOR, OP. 42
      G. SCHIRMER, INC.   1.00
SCHUBERT   BUONAMICI
   SONATA IN A, OP. 120
      G. SCHIRMER, INC.   1.00
SCHUBERT   BUONAMICI
   SONATA IN D, OP. 53
      G. SCHIRMER, INC.   1.50
SCHUBERT   BUONAMICI
   SONATA IN E FLAT, OP. 122
      G. SCHIRMER, INC.   .75
SCHUBERT
   SONATA IN F SHARP MINOR
      CHAPPELL AND COMPANY, INC.   0016816   2.00
SCHUBERT   BUONAMICI
   SONATA NO. 03 IN B FLAT, OP. POSTH.
      G. SCHIRMER, INC.   1.50
SCHUBERT   BAUER
   SONATA NO. 03 IN B FLAT, OP. POSTH.
      G. SCHIRMER, INC.   L1367   1.00
SCHUBERT   BUONAMICI
   SONATA OR FANTASIA IN G, OP. 78
      G. SCHIRMER, INC.   1.10
SCHUBERT
   SONATA, OP. POST. 120, D. 664, A MAJOR
      G. HENLE MUSIKVERLAG   157   1.10
SCHUBERT   4
   SONATA, OP. 120, ANDANTE
      CENTURY MUSIC PUBLISHING COMPANY, INC. 3796   .40
SCHUBERT
   SONATA, OP. 42, D. 845, A MINOR
      G. HENLE MUSIKVERLAG   156   1.40
SCHUBERT   GEORGII, W.   5
   SONATE IN A-DUR OP. 120
      SCHOTT   0664 1/2   1.00
SCHUBERT   GEORGII, W.   5
   SONATE IN A-MOLL OP. 42
      SCHOTT   0655-6 1/2   1.75
SCHUBERT   GEORGII, W.   3
   SONATE IN G-DUR OP. 78 DARAUS -- MENUETT
      SCHOTT   0663   .75
SCHUBERT   GEORGII, W.   6
   SONATE IN G-DUR OP. 78 FANTASIE
      SCHOTT   0661-2   1.50
SCHUBERT   LANGE   3
   STANDCHEN, LEISE FLEHEN, FANTASIE
      SCHOTT   07539 1/2   1.00
SCHUBERT   MAIER   4
   STARS, THE
      THEODORE PRESSER COMPANY   .50
SCHUBERT   5
   SYMPHONIE H-MOLL -- UNVOLL.
      SCHOTT   128   1.50
SCHUBERT   TAGLIAPIETRA
   SYMPHONY IN B MINOR 'UNFINISHED'
      FRANCO COLOMBO PUBLICATIONS   ER617   .75
SCHUBERT   DEL MAGLIO
   SYMPHONY IN B MINOR 'UNFINISHED' -- THEMES IN EASY TRANSCR. --
      FRANCO COLOMBO PUBLICATIONS   128144   .50
SCHUBERT   DEIS
   SYMPHONY IN B MINOR, NO. 8--'UNFINISHED'
      G. SCHIRMER, INC.   L1408   1.00
SCHUBERT   M
   SYMPHONY NO. 08
      C. F. PETERS CORPORATION   1311   1.25
SCHUBERT   M
   SYMPHONY NO. 09 IN C
      C. F. PETERS CORPORATION   126   4.00

SCHUBERT   GOETSCHIUS, P.
    SYMPHONY NO. 10 IN C MAJOR
      THEODORE PRESSER COMPANY   1.25
SCHUBERT   3
    SYMPHONY, UNFINISHED, THEME
      CENTURY MUSIC PUBLISHING COMPANY, INC.   3434   .40
SCHUBERT   ECKSTEIN
    THEME FROM 'UNFINISHED SYMPHONY'
      CARL FISCHER, INC.   S 2287   .50
SCHUBERT   RUSSELL   2
    THEME FROM RONDO IN D, OP. 53 NO. 2
      BOSTON MUSIC COMPANY   .50
SCHUBERT   HELLER
    TROUT, THE
      WILLIS MUSIC COMPANY   .60
SCHUBERT   3
    UNFINISHED SYMPHONY, 2 THEMES
      CENTURY MUSIC PUBLISHING COMPANY, INC.   3434   .40
SCHUBERT   D
    WANDERER FANTASIE, OP. 15
      C. F. PETERS CORPORATION   716A   2.00
SCHUBERT   6
    WANDERER-FANTASIE OP. 15
      SCHOTT   0684-5   1.50
SCHUBERT   SCHAUM, J.   2 1/2
    WHO IS SYLVIA
      BELWIN-MILLS PUBLISHING CORPORATION   .50
SCHUBERT   2
    WIEGENLIED
      SCHOTT   07021   .75
SCHUBERT   DEL MAGLIO
    WOHIN OP. 25 NO. 2
      FRANCO COLOMBO PUBLICATIONS   128126   .50
SCHUBERT *
    AVE MARIA
      ELKAN-VOGEL, INC.   D   .50
SCHUBERT *
    AVE MARIA
      G. SCHIRMER, INC.   .60
SCHUBERT *   DEIS
    AVE MARIA
      G. SCHIRMER, INC.   .60
SCHUBERT *   DEIS
    DIE LORELEI
      G. SCHIRMER, INC.   .60
SCHUBERT *
    DU BIST DIE RUH'
      G. SCHIRMER, INC.   .50
SCHUBERT *
    DU BIST DIE RUH'
      G. SCHIRMER, INC.   .50
SCHUBERT *   6
    ERL KING, THE
      CENTURY MUSIC PUBLISHING COMPANY, INC.   1193   .40
SCHUBERT *   6
    ERL KING, THE
      CENTURY MUSIC PUBLISHING COMPANY, INC.   1193   .40
SCHUBERT *
    ERLKING
      G. SCHIRMER, INC.   .60
SCHUBERT *
    ERLKING
      G. SCHIRMER, INC.   .60
SCHUBERT *   6
    HARK, HARK THE LARK
      CENTURY MUSIC PUBLISHING COMPANY, INC.   1335   .40
SCHUBERT *   6
    HARK, HARK THE LARK
      CENTURY MUSIC PUBLISHING COMPANY, INC.   1335   .40
SCHUBERT *   PARSONS
    HARK, HARK, THE LARK
      G. SCHIRMER, INC.   .60
SCHUBERT *   PARSONS
    HARK, HARK, THE LARK
      G. SCHIRMER, INC.   .60
SCHUBERT *
    HARK, HARK, THE LARK
      WILLIS MUSIC COMPANY   .50
SCHUBERT *
    LEISE FLEHEN--SERENADE
      G. SCHIRMER, INC.   .75
SCHUBERT *
    MARGUERITE AU ROUET
      ELKAN-VOGEL, INC.   D   .50
SCHUBERT *
    MILITARY MARCH IN D FLAT, OP. 51 NO. 1
      G. SCHIRMER, INC.   .80
SCHUBERT   D
    SONATA IN C. 1825. COMPLETED BY A. KNAB
      C. F. PETERS CORPORATION   9014   3.50
SCHUBERT, T.   PETIT, L.
    TEN VARIATIONS
      EDITIONS MUSICALES TRANSATLANTIQUES   3.85
SCHUETT   3
    A LA BIEN AIMEE
      BELWIN-MILLS PUBLISHING CORPORATION   .50
SCHUETT   6
    A LA BIEN AIMEE -- LOVE WALTZ -- D MAJOR
      CENTURY MUSIC PUBLISHING COMPANY, INC.   1324   .40
SCHUETT   2
    A LA BIEN AIMEE, C MAJOR
      CENTURY MUSIC PUBLISHING COMPANY, INC.   2521   .40
SCHUETT
    A LA BIEN-AIMEE. VALSE, OP. 59 NO. 2
      G. SCHIRMER, INC.   .70
SCHUETT
    CANZONETTA IN D, OP. 28 NO. 2
      G. SCHIRMER, INC.   .50
SCHUETT
    ETUDE MIGNONNE IN D, OP. 16 NO. 1
      G. SCHIRMER, INC.   .40
SCHUETT   6
    LOVE WALTZ, OP. 59 NO. 2
      CENTURY MUSIC PUBLISHING COMPANY, INC.   1324   .40
SCHUETT   3
    LOVE WALTZ, OP. 59 NO. 2 - EASY
      CENTURY MUSIC PUBLISHING COMPANY, INC.   2521   .40
SCHUETT   6
    PAPILLONS D'AMOUR, VALSE
      CENTURY MUSIC PUBLISHING COMPANY, INC.   1324   .40
SCHUETT
    PRELUDE IN A FLAT, OP. 35 NO. 4
      G. SCHIRMER, INC.   .25
SCHUETT   4
    VALSE LENTE, OP. 17 NO. 2
      CENTURY MUSIC PUBLISHING COMPANY, INC.   1974   .40

SCHULDT, M.   2
    DANCE OF THE WOODEN SHOES
      BELWIN-MILLS PUBLISHING CORPORATION   .60
SCHULDT, M.   2
    HAPPY BANJO
      BELWIN-MILLS PUBLISHING CORPORATION   .60
SCHULDT, M.   2
    LITTLE CHIPPEWA INDIAN
      BELWIN-MILLS PUBLISHING CORPORATION   .60
SCHULDT, M.   1
    MARCH OF THE CATTAILS
      BELWIN-MILLS PUBLISHING CORPORATION   .60
SCHULDT, M.   2
    MR. AND MRS. CUCKOO
      BELWIN-MILLS PUBLISHING CORPORATION   .60
SCHULDT, M.   1
    MY FIRST SONATA
      BELWIN-MILLS PUBLISHING CORPORATION   .60
SCHULHOF, O.
    THREE TRANSCRIPTIONS ON MOTIFS BY JOHANN STRAUSS, OP. 9--NO. 1
      ASSOCIATED MUSIC PUBLISHERS, INC.   DOB   1.25
SCHULHOF, O.
    THREE TRANSCRIPTIONS ON MOTIFS BY JOHANN STRAUSS, OP. 9--NO. 2
      ASSOCIATED MUSIC PUBLISHERS, INC.   DOB   1.25
SCHULHOF, O.
    THREE TRANSCRIPTIONS ON MOTIFS BY JOHANN STRAUSS, OP. 9--NO. 3
      ASSOCIATED MUSIC PUBLISHERS, INC.   DOB   1.25
SCHULHOFF
    BOSTON 'PARTITA'
      UNIVERSAL EDITION   10967   .85
SCHULHOFF   4
    SONATA NO. 03 -- 1927 --
      BAERENREITER VERLAG   AP 134
SCHULTZE   COLE
    LILLI MARLENE
      EDWARD B. MARKS MUSIC CORPORATION   01.00
SCHULTZE
    LILLI MARLENE
      EDWARD B. MARKS MUSIC CORPORATION   01.00
SCHULZ-EVLER   GALLICO
    BY THE BEAUTIFUL BLUE DANUBE--J. STRAUSS--CONCERT ARABESQUE
      G. SCHIRMER, INC.   .90
SCHULZ-WELDA   2
    LONGING -- SEHNSUCHT --
      CENTURY MUSIC PUBLISHING COMPANY, INC.   2402   .40
SCHULZ-WELDA   3
    LOVE SONG -- MINNELIED --
      CENTURY MUSIC PUBLISHING COMPANY, INC.   2401   .40
SCHULZ-WELDA   2
    SEHNSUCHT -- LONGING --
      CENTURY MUSIC PUBLISHING COMPANY, INC.   2402   .40
SCHULZ, F. A.
    SCALES AND CHORDS IN ALL THE MAJOR AND MINOR KEYS
      G. SCHIRMER, INC.   L392   .75
SCHUMAN, W.   MD
    THREE PIANO MOODS
      THEODORE PRESSER COMPANY   .50
SCHUMAN, W.   MD
    THREE PIANO MOODS. NO. 1, LYRICAL
      THEODORE PRESSER COMPANY   .50
SCHUMAN, W.   MD
    THREE PIANO MOODS. NO. 2, PENSIVE
      THEODORE PRESSER COMPANY   .50
SCHUMAN, W.   MD
    THREE PIANO MOODS. NO. 3, DYNAMIC
      THEODORE PRESSER COMPANY   .50
SCHUMAN, W.
    THREE-SCORE SET
      G. SCHIRMER, INC.   .50
SCHUMANN, J.   3
    WOOD SPRITE, THE
      WILLIS MUSIC COMPANY   .40
SCHUMANN, R.
    ABEGG VARIATIONS
      EDWIN F. KALMUS   3898   1.50
SCHUMANN, R.   CORTOT
    ABEGG VARIATIONS, OP. 1
      FRANCO COLOMBO PUBLICATIONS   SAL   2.75
SCHUMANN, R.   DEL MAGLIO
    ABENDLIED, OP. 85 NO. 12
      FRANCO COLOMBO PUBLICATIONS   128845   .60
SCHUMANN, R.   LORENZONI
    ALBUM FUER DIE JUGEND -- ALBUM FOR THE YOUNG --, OP. 68
      FRANCO COLOMBO PUBLICATIONS   ER688   1.75
SCHUMANN, R.
    ALBUM FUER DIE JUGEND -- ALBUM FOR THE YOUNG --, OP. 68 NO. 10 -
    THE HAPPY FARMER
      FRANCO COLOMBO PUBLICATIONS   127458   .60
SCHUMANN, R.   DEL MAGLIO
    ALBUM FUER DIE JUGEND -- ALBUM FOR THE YOUNG --, OP. 68 NO. 10 -
    THE HAPPY FARMER
      FRANCO COLOMBO PUBLICATIONS   .60
SCHUMANN, R.
    ALBUM LEAVES, OP. 124
      EDWIN F. KALMUS   3899   1.25
SCHUMANN, R.
    ALBUM LEAVES, OP. 124
      UNIVERSAL EDITION   562   1.55
SCHUMANN, R.   CESI
    ALBUMBLAETTER, OP. 124
      FRANCO COLOMBO PUBLICATIONS   ER1303   1.75
SCHUMANN, R.   DEL MAGLIO
    ALBUMBLAETTER, OP. 124 NO. 16
      FRANCO COLOMBO PUBLICATIONS   129084   .60
SCHUMANN, R.
    ALLEGRO, FROM SONATA, OP. 118 NO. 1
      BELWIN-MILLS PUBLISHING CORPORATION   .60
SCHUMANN, R.   BAUER
    ALLEGRO, OP. 8
      G. SCHIRMER, INC.   L1167   1.00
SCHUMANN, R.   PAUER, M.   5
    ARABESKE OP. 18
      SCHOTT   0725 1/2   1.00
SCHUMANN, R.   BAUER
    ARABESQUE IN C, OP. 18
      G. SCHIRMER, INC.   .70
SCHUMANN, R.   SCHUMANN, C. *
    ARABESQUE, OP. 18
      ASSOCIATED MUSIC PUBLISHERS, INC.   BRH   .75
SCHUMANN, R.   SAUER   M
    ARABESQUE, OP. 18
      C. F. PETERS CORPORATION   2304A   .80
SCHUMANN, R.
    ARABESQUE, OP. 18
      EDWIN F. KALMUS   3900   1.00
SCHUMANN, R.   MONTANI
    ARABESQUE, OP. 18
      FRANCO COLOMBO PUBLICATIONS   128388   .90

```
SCHUMANN, R.          CORTOT
   ARABESQUE, OP. 18
      FRANCO COLOMBO PUBLICATIONS              SAL        1.75
SCHUMANN, R.
   ARABESQUE, OP. 18
      G. HENLE MUSIKVERLAG                     84         1.10
                                        8
SCHUMANN, R.
   ARABESQUE, OP. 18
      THEODORE PRESSER COMPANY                             .70
                                        5
SCHUMANN, R.
   AUFSCHWUNG - SOARING
      CENTURY MUSIC PUBLISHING COMPANY, INC.   1724        .40
                                        5
SCHUMANN, R.
   AUFSCHWUNG -- SOARING
      CENTURY MUSIC PUBLISHING COMPANY, INC.   1724        .40
SCHUMANN, R.
   AUFSCHWUNG, OP. 12 NO. 2--FANTASIESTUCKE
      G. SCHIRMER, INC.                                    .50
                                        3
SCHUMANN, R.
   BILDER AUS DEM OSTEN OP. 66
      SCHOTT                                   01042-3 1/2 1.75
                                        8
SCHUMANN, R.
   BIRD AS PROPHET, OP. 82 NO. 7
      THEODORE PRESSER COMPANY                             .50
SCHUMANN, R.          SAUER           M-D
   BLUMENSTUECK, OP. 19
      C. F. PETERS CORPORATION                 2304B       .80
SCHUMANN, R.          CORTOT
   BLUMENSTUECK, OP. 19
      FRANCO COLOMBO PUBLICATIONS              SAL        1.75
SCHUMANN, R.
   BLUMENSTUECK, OP. 19
      G. HENLE MUSIKVERLAG                     90         1.10
SCHUMANN, R.          BRADLEY, R.
   BRADLEY CLASSICAL SERIES - HAPPY FARMER, THE
      SCREEN GEMS - COLUMBIA PUBLICATIONS      0027HP2     .85
SCHUMANN, R.          BRADLEY, R.
   BRADLEY CLASSICAL SERIES - HUNTING SONG
      SCREEN GEMS - COLUMBIA PUBLICATIONS      6707HP2     .85
SCHUMANN, R.          BRADLEY, R.
   BRADLEY CLASSICAL SERIES - SOLDIER'S MARCH
      SCREEN GEMS - COLUMBIA PUBLICATIONS      4749SP2     .85
SCHUMANN, R.          BRADLEY, R.
   BRADLEY CLASSICAL SERIES - WILD HORSEMAN, THE
      SCREEN GEMS - COLUMBIA PUBLICATIONS      2716WP2     .85
SCHUMANN, R.          SCHAUM, J.      2 1/2
   BUCKING BRONCO BOOGIE
      BELWIN-MILLS PUBLISHING CORPORATION                  .50
SCHUMANN, R.          PAUER, M.       5-6
   CARNAVAL OP. 9
      SCHOTT                                   09188-9 1/2 1.75
SCHUMANN, R.          SAUER           D
   CARNAVAL, OP. 9
      C. F. PETERS CORPORATION                 2307       1.50
SCHUMANN, R.
   CARNAVAL, OP. 9
      EDWIN F. KALMUS                          3903       2.00
SCHUMANN, R.          MORONI
   CARNAVAL, OP. 9
      FRANCO COLOMBO PUBLICATIONS              ER2122     2.00
SCHUMANN, R.          CORTOT
   CARNAVAL, OP. 9
      FRANCO COLOMBO PUBLICATIONS              SAL        4.00
SCHUMANN, R.
   CARNAVAL, OP. 9
      G. HENLE MUSIKVERLAG                     187        1.80
SCHUMANN, R.          BAUER
   CARNAVAL, OP. 9
      G. SCHIRMER, INC.                        L89        1.50
SCHUMANN, R.
   CARNAVAL, OP. 9
      UNIVERSAL EDITION                        360        1.40
SCHUMANN, R.
   COLORED LEAVES, OP. 99
      EDWIN F. KALMUS                          3904       1.50
SCHUMANN, R.
   COLORED LEAVES, OP. 99
      G. HENLE MUSIKVERLAG                     81         1.80
                                        M
SCHUMANN, R.
   CONCERTO IN A MINOR, OP. 54. ABRIDGED
      C. F. PETERS CORPORATION                 2898A      1.25
SCHUMANN, R.          GRAINGER
   CONCERTO, FIRST MOVEMENT--CONCERT TRANSCRIPTION
      G. SCHIRMER, INC.                                   1.25
                                        2
SCHUMANN, R.
   CRADLE SONG, OP. 124 NO. 6
      CENTURY MUSIC PUBLISHING COMPANY, INC.   181         .40
                                        2
SCHUMANN, R.
   CRADLE SONG, OP. 124 NO. 6
      CENTURY MUSIC PUBLISHING COMPANY, INC.   181         .40
SCHUMANN, R.          CORTOT
   DAVIDSBUENDLER DANCES, OP. 6
      FRANCO COLOMBO PUBLICATIONS              SAL        5.00
SCHUMANN, R.          SAUER           D
   DAVIDSBUENDLERTAENZE, OP. 6
      C. F. PETERS CORPORATION                 2306       1.25
SCHUMANN, R.
   DAVIDSBUNDLER, OP. 6
      UNIVERSAL EDITION                        532        2.10
SCHUMANN, R.
   DES ABENDS, OP. 12 NO. 1--FANTASIESTUCKE
      G. SCHIRMER, INC.                                    .35
SCHUMANN, R.
   DREAMING - TRAUMEREI, OP. 15 NO. 7
      BANKS AND SON LTD.                                   .40
SCHUMANN, R.
   FABEL, OP. 12 NO. 6--FANTASIESTUCKE
      G. SCHIRMER, INC.                                    .35
SCHUMANN, R.          BAUER
   FANTASIA, OP. 17
      G. SCHIRMER, INC.                        L1163      1.00
SCHUMANN, R.          BUONAMICI
   FANTASIESTUCKE -- FANTASY PIECES --, OP. 12
      FRANCO COLOMBO PUBLICATIONS              ER639      1.75
SCHUMANN, R.          MONTANI
   FANTASIESTUCKE -- FANTASY PIECES --, OP. 12 NO. 2 - AUFSCHWUNG
      FRANCO COLOMBO PUBLICATIONS              ER2584      .60
SCHUMANN, R.          PAUER M.        5
   FANTASIESTUCKE OP. 12 NO. 2 AUFSCHWUNG
      SCHOTT                                   0737 102   1.00
SCHUMANN, R.
   FANTASIESTUCKE, OP. 12
      G. HENLE MUSIKVERLAG                     91         1.80
SCHUMANN, R.          WERNER
   FANTASIESTUCKE, OP. 12 NO. 9--CURWEN EDITION
      G. SCHIRMER, INC.                                    .75

SCHUMANN, R.          CORTOT
   FANTASIESTUECK, OP. 12
      FRANCO COLOMBO PUBLICATIONS              SAL        5.00
SCHUMANN, R.          MONTANI
   FANTASY IN C, OP. 17
      FRANCO COLOMBO PUBLICATIONS              ER2597     1.75
SCHUMANN, R.          SAUER           D
   FANTASY, OP. 17
      C. F. PETERS CORPORATION                 2314       2.00
SCHUMANN, R.
   FANTASY, OP. 17
      EDWIN F. KALMUS                          3905       1.50
SCHUMANN, R.          CORTOT
   FANTASY, OP. 17
      FRANCO COLOMBO PUBLICATIONS              SAL        3.25
SCHUMANN, R.          CORTOT
   FASCHINGSSCHWANK AUS WIEN -- CARNAVAL OF VIENNA -- OP. 26
      FRANCO COLOMBO PUBLICATIONS              SAL        4.00
SCHUMANN, R.          BUONAMICI
   FASCHINGSSCHWANK AUS WIEN -- CARNIVAL JEST FROM VIENNA --, OP. 26
      FRANCO COLOMBO PUBLICATIONS              ER1465     1.00
SCHUMANN, R.          SAUER           M-D
   FASCHINGSSCHWANK AUS WIEN, OP. 26
      C. F. PETERS CORPORATION                 2312       1.25
SCHUMANN, R.
   FASCHINGSSCHWANK AUS WIEN, OP. 26
      G. HENLE MUSIKVERLAG                     186        1.80
SCHUMANN, R.          BAUER
   FASCHINGSSCHWANK AUS WIEN, OP. 26
      G. SCHIRMER, INC.                        L99        1.25
SCHUMANN, R.
   FASCHINGSSCHWANK WIEN, OP. 26
      EDWIN F. KALMUS                          3907       1.50
SCHUMANN, R.          PAUER, M.       4
   FASCHINGSSCHWANK, OP. 26
      SCHOTT                                   08210-1    1.50
SCHUMANN, R.
   FASCHINGSSCHWANK, OP. 26
      UNIVERSAL EDITION                        438        2.30
                                        2
SCHUMANN, R.
   FIRST LOSS, OP. 68 NO. 16
      CENTURY MUSIC PUBLISHING COMPANY, INC.   3716        .40
                                        2
SCHUMANN, R.
   FIRST LOSS, OP. 68 NO. 16
      CENTURY MUSIC PUBLISHING COMPANY, INC.   3716        .40
SCHUMANN, R.          BAUER
   FIRST LOSS, OP. 68 NO. 16--ALBUM FOR THE YOUNG
      G. SCHIRMER, INC.                                    .30
SCHUMANN, R.
   FOREST SCENES, OP. 82
      EDWIN F. KALMUS                          3908       1.25
SCHUMANN, R.          CORTOT
   FOREST SCENES, OP. 82
      FRANCO COLOMBO PUBLICATIONS              SAL        3.25
SCHUMANN, R.
   FOREST SCENES, OP. 82
      G. HENLE MUSIKVERLAG                     83         1.65
SCHUMANN, R.          SCHUMANN, C. *
   GRAND SONATA NO. 1 IN F-SHARP MINOR, OP. 11
      ASSOCIATED MUSIC PUBLISHERS, INC.        BRH        1.25
SCHUMANN, R.
   GRAND SONATA NO. 1, OP. 11
      EDWIN F. KALMUS                          3912       1.50
                                        4
SCHUMANN, R.
   GRILLEN, OP. 12 NO. 4
      CENTURY MUSIC PUBLISHING COMPANY, INC.   2304        .40
SCHUMANN, R.
   GRILLEN, OP. 12 NO. 4--FANTASIESTUCKE
      G. SCHIRMER, INC.                                    .50
SCHUMANN, R.
   HAPPY FARMER, OP. 68 NO. 10
      CARL FISCHER, INC.                       S 1009      .50
                                        2
SCHUMANN, R.
   HAPPY FARMER, OP. 68 NO. 10
      CENTURY MUSIC PUBLISHING COMPANY, INC.   268         .40
                                        2
SCHUMANN, R.
   HAPPY FARMER, OP. 68 NO. 10
      CENTURY MUSIC PUBLISHING COMPANY, INC.   268         .40
SCHUMANN, R.          HARDING
   HAPPY FARMER, THE
      BOSTON MUSIC COMPANY                                 .50
SCHUMANN, R.          HARTL           4
   HAPPY FARMER, TRANS.
      CENTURY MUSIC PUBLISHING COMPANY, INC.   2116        .40
SCHUMANN, R.          STEINER         2 1/2
   HE, THE NOBLIEST OF ALL
      BELWIN-MILLS PUBLISHING CORPORATION                  .60
SCHUMANN, R.                          1
   HUMMING SONG
      NOVELLO AND COMPANY, LTD.                55.0039.07  .25
SCHUMANN, R.          BAUER
   HUMORESKE, OP. 20
      G. SCHIRMER, INC.                        L102       1.00
SCHUMANN, R.          SAUER           D
   HUMORESQUE, OP. 20
      C. F. PETERS CORPORATION                 2311       2.50
SCHUMANN, R.          CORTOT
   HUMORESQUE, OP. 20
      FRANCO COLOMBO PUBLICATIONS              SAL        3.25
SCHUMANN, R.
   HUMORESQUE, OP. 20
      UNIVERSAL EDITION                        529        1.40
                                        3
SCHUMANN, R.
   HUNTING SONG
      NOVELLO AND COMPANY, LTD.                55.0025.07  .25
                                        2
SCHUMANN, R.
   HUNTING SONG, OP. 68 NO. 7
      CENTURY MUSIC PUBLISHING COMPANY, INC.   2356        .40
                                        2
SCHUMANN, R.
   HUNTING SONG, OP. 68 NO. 7
      CENTURY MUSIC PUBLISHING COMPANY, INC.   2356        .40
SCHUMANN, R.          BAUER
   IMPORTANT EVENT, OP. 15 NO. 6--SCENES FROM CHILDHOOD
      G. SCHIRMER, INC.                                    .30
                                        7
SCHUMANN, R.
   INN, THE, FROM 'FOREST SCENES'
      NOVELLO AND COMPANY, LTD.                55.0035.04  .25
                                        2
SCHUMANN, R.
   JAGERLIEDCHEN, OP. 68 NO. 7
      CENTURY MUSIC PUBLISHING COMPANY, INC.   2356        .40
SCHUMANN, R.          HARTL           4
   JOYFUL PEASANT
      CENTURY MUSIC PUBLISHING COMPANY, INC.   2116        .40
                                        2
SCHUMANN, R.
   JOYOUS FARMER
      CENTURY MUSIC PUBLISHING COMPANY, INC.   268         .40
```

SCHUMANN, R.   LORENZONI
KINDERSCENEN -- SCENES FROM CHILDHOOD --, OP. 15
   FRANCO COLOMBO PUBLICATIONS   ER689   1.00
SCHUMANN, R.
KINDERSCENEN -- SCENES FROM CHILDHOOD --, OP. 15 NO. 7 -
TRAEUMEPEI
   FRANCO COLOMBO PUBLICATIONS   127459   .60
SCHUMANN, R.   DEL MAGLIO
KINDERSCENEN -- SCENES FROM CHILDHOOD --, OP. 15 NO. 7 -
TRAEUMEREI
   FRANCO COLOMBO PUBLICATIONS   128129   .60
SCHUMANN, R.   STEGLICH
KINDERSZENEN
   BARENREITER VERLAG   BA 345   1.00
SCHUMANN, R.   SCHAUM, J.   2
KNIGHT RUPERT
   BELWIN-MILLS PUBLISHING CORPORATION   .50
SCHUMANN, R.   BAUER
KNIGHT RUPERT, OP. 68 NO. 12--ALBUM FOR THE YOUNG
   G. SCHIRMER, INC.   .40
SCHUMANN, R.   SAUER   D
KREISLERIANA, OP. 16
   C. F. PETERS CORPORATION   2310   1.25
SCHUMANN, R.
KREISLERIANA, OP. 16
   EDWIN F. KALMUS   3909   1.25
SCHUMANN, R.   TAGLIAPIETRA
KREISLERIANA, OP. 16
   FRANCO COLOMBO PUBLICATIONS   ER1324   1.75
SCHUMANN, R.   CORTOT
KREISLERIANA, OP. 16
   FRANCO COLOMBO PUBLICATIONS   SAL   5.00
SCHUMANN, R.
KREISLERIANA, OP. 16
   G. HENLE MUSIKVERLAG   253
SCHUMANN, R.   BAUER
KREISLERIANA, OP. 16
   G. SCHIRMER, INC.   L95   1.00
SCHUMANN, R.
KREISLERIANA, OP. 16
   UNIVERSAL EDITION   481   1.80
SCHUMANN, R.   2
LADY BUG
   CENTURY MUSIC PUBLISHING COMPANY, INC.   3829   .40
SCHUMANN, R.   2
LADY BUG
   CENTURY MUSIC PUBLISHING COMPANY, INC.   3829   .40
SCHUMANN, R.   2
LITTLE HUNTING SONG
   CENTURY MUSIC PUBLISHING COMPANY, INC.   2356   .40
SCHUMANN, R.   1
LITTLE PIECE, A
   NOVELLO AND COMPANY, LTD.   55.0038.09   .40
SCHUMANN, R.   BAUER
LITTLE PRELUDE AND FUGUE, OP. 68 NO. 40--ALBUM FOR THE YOUNG
   G. SCHIRMER, INC.   .35
SCHUMANN, R.   6
LONELY FLOWERS, FROM 'FOREST SCENES'
   NOVELLO AND COMPANY, LTD.   55.0019.02   .40
SCHUMANN, R.   2
MARIENWUERMCHEN
   CENTURY MUSIC PUBLISHING COMPANY, INC.   3829   .40
SCHUMANN, R.   BAUER
MELODIE, OP. 68 NO. 01--ALBUM FOR THE YOUNG
   G. SCHIRMER, INC.   .30
SCHUMANN, R.   1
MELODY
   NOVELLO AND COMPANY, LTD.   55.0001.10   .40
SCHUMANN, R.   1
MELODY NO. 1 OP. 68
   THEODORE PRESSER COMPANY   .50
SCHUMANN, R.   BAUER
MERRY FARMER, THE, OP. 68 NO. 10--ALBUM FOR THE YOUNG
   G. SCHIRMER, INC.   .30
SCHUMANN, R.
MERRY PEASANT AND HUNTING SONG
   BELWIN-MILLS PUBLISHING CORPORATION   28155   .60
SCHUMANN, R.   2
MERRY PEASANT, THE
   NOVELLO AND COMPANY, LTD.   55.0006.00   .40
SCHUMANN, R.
MERRY PEASANT, THE, AND HUNTING SONG
   BANKS AND SON LTD.   .40
SCHUMANN, R.   5
NACHTSTUCK, OP. 23 NO. 4
   CENTURY MUSIC PUBLISHING COMPANY, INC.   1196   .40
SCHUMANN, R.   5
NACHTSTUCK, OP. 23 NO. 4
   CENTURY MUSIC PUBLISHING COMPANY, INC.   1196   .40
SCHUMANN, R.   5
NACHTSTUCK, OP. 23 NO. 4
   CENTURY MUSIC PUBLISHING COMPANY, INC.   1196   .40
SCHUMANN, R.
NACHTSTUCKE, OP. 23
   G. HENLE MUSIKVERLAG   104   1.65
SCHUMANN, R.   BAUER
NACHTSTUCKE, OP. 23 NO. 4
   G. SCHIRMER, INC.   .40
SCHUMANN, R.   BAUER
NEW YEAR'S EVE, OP. 68 NO. 43--ALBUM FOR THE YOUNG
   G. SCHIRMER, INC.   .30
SCHUMANN, R.   KREUTZER   3
NIGHT PIECE
   BOSTON MUSIC COMPANY   .50
SCHUMANN, R.
NIGHT SONG, A
   FREDERICK HARRIS MUSIC COMPANY   .60
SCHUMANN, R.   5
NOCTURNE -- NACHTSTUCK --
   CENTURY MUSIC PUBLISHING COMPANY, INC.   1354   .40
SCHUMANN, R.   5
NOCTURNE, OP. 23 NO. 4
   CENTURY MUSIC PUBLISHING COMPANY, INC.   1196   .40
SCHUMANN, R.   BAUER
NORSE SONG, OP. 68 NO. 41--ALBUM FOR THE YOUNG
   G. SCHIRMER, INC.   .35
SCHUMANN, R.
NORTHERN SONG
   FREDERICK HARRIS MUSIC COMPANY   .60
SCHUMANN, R.   5
NOVELETTE, OP. 21 NO. 7
   CENTURY MUSIC PUBLISHING COMPANY, INC.   4002   .40
SCHUMANN, R.   5
NOVELETTE, OP. 21 NO. 7
   CENTURY MUSIC PUBLISHING COMPANY, INC.   4002   .40

SCHUMANN, R.   5
NOVELETTE, OP. 99 NO. 9
   CENTURY MUSIC PUBLISHING COMPANY, INC.   838   .40
SCHUMANN, R.   5
NOVELETTE, OP. 99 NO. 9
   CENTURY MUSIC PUBLISHING COMPANY, INC.   838   .40
SCHUMANN, R.
NOVELLETTE IN B MINOR, OP. 99 NO. 3
   G. SCHIRMER, INC.   .40
SCHUMANN, R.   BAUER
NOVELLETTE IN E, OP. 21 NO. 7
   G. SCHIRMER, INC.   .60
SCHUMANN, R.   BAUER
NOVELLETTE IN F, OP. 21 NO. 1
   G. SCHIRMER, INC.   .60
SCHUMANN, R.   SAUER   D
PAPILLONS, OP. 2
   C. F. PETERS CORPORATION   2315B   .90
SCHUMANN, R.
PAPILLONS, OP. 2
   EDWIN F. KALMUS   3910   1.25
SCHUMANN, R.   BUONAMICI
PAPILLONS, OP. 2
   FRANCO COLOMBO PUBLICATIONS   ER2309   1.00
SCHUMANN, R.   LORENZONI
PAPILLONS, OP. 2
   FRANCO COLOMBO PUBLICATIONS   ER2653   1.00
SCHUMANN, R.   CORTOT
PAPILLONS, OP. 2
   FRANCO COLOMBO PUBLICATIONS   SAL   2.75
SCHUMANN, R.
PAPILLONS, OP. 2
   G. HENLE MUSIKVERLAG   105   1.15
SCHUMANN, R.   BAUER
PAPILLONS, OP. 2
   G. SCHIRMER, INC.   L1544   1.00
SCHUMANN, R.   PAUER, M.   5
PAPILLONS, OP. 2
   SCHOTT   0770 1/2   1.00
SCHUMANN, R.   MUELLER *
PAPILLONS, OP. 2
   WIENER URTEXT EDITION   UT 50014   2.00
SCHUMANN, R.   LORENZONI
PAPILLONS, OP. 2 -- WITH VARIATIONS ON THE NAME 'ABEGG' --
   FRANCO COLOMBO PUBLICATIONS   ER224   1.25
SCHUMANN, R.   SCHAUM, J.   1
PLEASANT PEASANT
   BELWIN-MILLS PUBLISHING CORPORATION   .50
SCHUMANN, R.   4
PROPHET BIRD, OP. 82 NO. 7
   CENTURY MUSIC PUBLISHING COMPANY, INC.   2357   .40
SCHUMANN, R.   4
PROPHET BIRD, OP. 82 NO. 7
   CENTURY MUSIC PUBLISHING COMPANY, INC.   2357   .40
SCHUMANN, R.   DEIS
PROPHET BIRD, THE, OP. 82 NO. 7--FOREST SCENES
   G. SCHIRMER, INC.   .50
SCHUMANN, R.   MONTANI
ROMANCE IN D MINOR, OP. 32 NO. 3
   FRANCO COLOMBO PUBLICATIONS   129422   .50
SCHUMANN, R.   4
ROMANCE, OP. 15 NO. 7
   CENTURY MUSIC PUBLISHING COMPANY, INC.   443   .40
SCHUMANN, R.   5
ROMANCE, OP. 28 NO. 2
   CENTURY MUSIC PUBLISHING COMPANY, INC.   3844   .40
SCHUMANN, R.   BAUER
ROMANCE, OP. 28 NO. 2
   G. SCHIRMER, INC.   .35
SCHUMANN, R.   7
ROMANCE, OP. 28 NO. 2
   THEODORE PRESSER COMPANY   .50
SCHUMANN, R.   PAUER, M.   5
ROMANZE FIS-DUR OP. 28 NO. 2
   SCHOTT   0773   .75
SCHUMANN, R.   4
ROMANZE, OP. 15 NO. 7
   CENTURY MUSIC PUBLISHING COMPANY, INC.   443   .40
SCHUMANN, R.   5
ROMANZE, OP. 28 NO. 2
   CENTURY MUSIC PUBLISHING COMPANY, INC.   3844   .40
SCHUMANN, R.   BAUER
RUSTIC SONG, OP. 68 NO. 20--ALBUM FOR THE YOUNG
   G. SCHIRMER, INC.   .30
SCHUMANN, R.   PALMER, W. A.
SCENES FROM CHILDHOOD
   ALFRED MUSIC COMPANY   632   1.25
SCHUMANN, R.
SCENES FROM CHILDHOOD
   EDWIN F. KALMUS   3896   1.00
SCHUMANN, R.   CORTOT
SCENES FROM CHILDHOOD, OP. 15
   FRANCO COLOMBO PUBLICATIONS   SAL   3.00
SCHUMANN, R.
SCENES FROM CHILDHOOD, OP. 15
   G. HENLE MUSIKVERLAG   44   1.15
SCHUMANN, R.
SCENES FROM CHILDHOOD, OP. 15
   UNIVERSAL EDITION   362   .80
SCHUMANN, R.   BAUER
SCHERZO, GIGUE, ROMANCE, AND FUGHETTA, OP. 32
   G. SCHIRMER, INC.   L1715   .75
SCHUMANN, R.   2
SHORT STUDY, A
   NOVELLO AND COMPANY, LTD.   55.0002.08   .25
SCHUMANN, R.   2
SICILIENNE, OP. 68 NO. 11
   CENTURY MUSIC PUBLISHING COMPANY, INC.   3717   .40
SCHUMANN, R.   2
SICILIENNE, OP. 68 NO. 11
   CENTURY MUSIC PUBLISHING COMPANY, INC.   3717   .40
SCHUMANN, R.   BAUER
SICILIENNE, OP. 68 NO. 11--ALBUM FOR THE YOUNG
   G. SCHIRMER, INC.   .35
SCHUMANN, R.   BAUER
SLUMBER-SONG, OP. 124 NO. 16--ALBUM-LEAVES
   G. SCHIRMER, INC.   .40
SCHUMANN, R.   5
SOARING -- AUFSCHWUNG --
   CENTURY MUSIC PUBLISHING COMPANY, INC.   1724   .40
SCHUMANN, R.   2
SOLDIERS MARCH
   VOLKWEIN BROS.   .25
SCHUMANN, R.   1
SOLDIERS MARCH, OP. 68 NO. 2 ALSO MELODY NO. 1
   THEODORE PRESSER COMPANY   .50

SCHUMANN, R.   1
    SOLDIERS' MARCH
        NOVELLO AND COMPANY, LTD.   55.0037.00   .40
SCHUMANN, R.
    SOLDIERS' MARCH AND THE WILD RIDER
        BELWIN-MILLS PUBLISHING CORPORATION   28165   .60
SCHUMANN, R.   BAUER
    SOLDIERS' MARCH, OP. 68 NO. 02--ALBUM FOR THE YOUNG
        G. SCHIRMER, INC.   .30
SCHUMANN, R.   2
    SOLDIERS' MARCH, OP. 68 NO. 2
        CENTURY MUSIC PUBLISHING COMPANY, INC.   2450   .40
SCHUMANN, R.   2
    SOLDIERS' MARCH, OP. 68 NO. 2
        CENTURY MUSIC PUBLISHING COMPANY, INC.   2450   .40
SCHUMANN, R.   CESI
    SONATA NO. 01 IN F SHARP MINOR, OP. 11
        FRANCO COLOMBO PUBLICATIONS   ER818   2.25
SCHUMANN, R.   CORTOT
    SONATA NO. 01 IN F SHARP MINOR, OP. 11
        FRANCO COLOMBO PUBLICATIONS   SAL   5.00
SCHUMANN, R.   BAUER
    SONATA NO. 01 IN F SHARP MINOR, OP. 11
        G. SCHIRMER, INC.   L103   1.25
SCHUMANN, R.   SCHUMANN, C. *
    SONATA NO. 02 IN G MINOR, OP. 22
        ASSOCIATED MUSIC PUBLISHERS, INC.   BRH   1.00
SCHUMANN, R.   CESI
    SONATA NO. 02 IN G MINOR, OP. 22
        FRANCO COLOMBO PUBLICATIONS   ER819   1.50
SCHUMANN, R.   CORTOT
    SONATA NO. 02 IN G MINOR, OP. 22
        FRANCO COLOMBO PUBLICATIONS   SAL   5.50
SCHUMANN, R.
    SONATA NO. 02, OP. 22
        EDWIN F. KALMUS   3914   1.25
SCHUMANN, R.   CORTOT
    SONATA NO. 03 IN F MINOR, OP. 14
        FRANCO COLOMBO PUBLICATIONS   SAL   5.50
SCHUMANN, R.   BAUER
    SONATA NO. 03 IN G MINOR, AND PRESTO PASSIONATA, OP. 22
        G. SCHIRMER, INC.   L105   1.25
SCHUMANN, R.
    SONATA NO. 03, OP. 14
        EDWIN F. KALMUS   3913   1.50
SCHUMANN, R.   3
    SONATA, OP. 118 NO. 1, ALLEGRO
        CENTURY MUSIC PUBLISHING COMPANY, INC.   3797   .40
SCHUMANN, R.   3
    SONATA, OP. 118 NO. 1, ALLEGRO
        CENTURY MUSIC PUBLISHING COMPANY, INC.   3797   .40
SCHUMANN, R.   D
    SONATA, OP. 14
        C. F. PETERS CORPORATION   2327   3.50
SCHUMANN, R.   SAUER   D
    STUDIES AFTER CAPRICES BY PAGANINI, OP. 3
        C. F. PETERS CORPORATION   2323   1.25
SCHUMANN, R.   MORONI
    SYMPHONIC ETUDES, OP. 13
        FRANCO COLOMBO PUBLICATIONS   ER2107   1.50
SCHUMANN, R.   CORTOT
    SYMPHONIC ETUDES, OP. 13
        FRANCO COLOMBO PUBLICATIONS   SAL   5.50
SCHUMANN, R.   SCHUMANN, R. *
    TOCCATA IN C, OP. 7
        ASSOCIATED MUSIC PUBLISHERS, INC.   BRH   .75
SCHUMANN, R.   SAUER   D
    TOCCATA, OP. 7
        C. F. PETERS CORPORATION   2316A   1.50
SCHUMANN, R.
    TOCCATA, OP. 7
        EDWIN F. KALMUS   3917   1.25
SCHUMANN, R.   MONTANI
    TOCCATA, OP. 7
        FRANCO COLOMBO PUBLICATIONS   ER2585   1.00
SCHUMANN, R.   CORTOT
    TOCCATA, OP. 7
        FRANCO COLOMBO PUBLICATIONS   SAL   2.50
SCHUMANN, R.
    TOCCATA, OP. 7
        G. HENLE MUSIKVERLAG   201   1.15
SCHUMANN, R.   BAUER
    TOCCATA, OP. 7
        G. SCHIRMER, INC.   L1266   .75
SCHUMANN, R.
    TRAUMEREI AND ROMANCE
        BELWIN-MILLS PUBLISHING CORPORATION   28161   .60
SCHUMANN, R.   4
    TRAUMEREI AND ROMANCE, OP. 15 NO. 7
        CENTURY MUSIC PUBLISHING COMPANY, INC.   443   .40
SCHUMANN, R.   4
    TRAUMEREI AND ROMANCE, OP. 15, NO. 7
        CENTURY MUSIC PUBLISHING COMPANY, INC.   443   .40
SCHUMANN, R.
    TRAUMEREI, OP. 15 NO. 7--SCENES FROM CHILDHOOD
        G. SCHIRMER, INC.   .35
SCHUMANN, R.   SAUER   D
    TWELVE SYMPHONIC ETUDES, OP. 13
        C. F. PETERS CORPORATION   2313   2.00
SCHUMANN, R.   BAUER
    TWELVE SYMPHONIC STUDIES, OP. 13
        G. SCHIRMER, INC.   L96   1.00
SCHUMANN, R.   PHILLIPS, M.
    VALSE MODERATO, OP. 124 NO. 10
        BELWIN-MILLS PUBLISHING CORPORATION   .60
SCHUMANN, R.
    VARIATIONS AND PAPILLONS, OP. 1/2
        UNIVERSAL EDITION   436   1.60
SCHUMANN, R.   M
    VARIATIONS IN E FLAT ON AN ORIGINAL THEME
        C. F. PETERS CORPORATION   H70   1.25
SCHUMANN, R.   BAUER
    VARIATIONS ON THE MANE 'ABEGG', OP. 1
        G. SCHIRMER, INC.   L1695   1.00
SCHUMANN, R.
    VARIATIONS ON THE NAME ''ABEGG'', OP. 1
        G. HENLE MUSIKVERLAG   87   1.15
SCHUMANN, R.   SAUER   D
    VARIATIONS ON THE NAME 'ABEGG', OP. 1
        C. F. PETERS CORPORATION   2315A   1.25
SCHUMANN, R.   LORENZONI
    VARIATIONS ON THE NAME 'ABEGG', OP. 1
        FRANCO COLOMBO PUBLICATIONS   ER2652   1.00
SCHUMANN, R.   LORENZONI
    VARIATIONS ON THE NAME 'ABEGG', OP. 1 -- WITH PAPILLONS --
        FRANCO COLOMBO PUBLICATIONS   ER224   1.25

SCHUMANN, R.   4
    VOGELS ALS PROPHET, OP. 82 NO. 7
        CENTURY MUSIC PUBLISHING COMPANY, INC.   2357   .40
SCHUMANN, R.   BUONAMICI
    WALDSCENEN -- FOREST SCENES --, OP. 82
        FRANCO COLOMBO PUBLICATIONS   ER1211   1.25
SCHUMANN, R.
    WARUM, OP. 12 NO. 3--FANTASIESTUCKE
        G. SCHIRMER, INC.   .40
SCHUMANN, R.   4
    WHIMS - GRILLEN, OP. 12 NO. 4
        CENTURY MUSIC PUBLISHING COMPANY, INC.   2304   .40
SCHUMANN, R.   4
    WHIMS -- GRILLEN, OP. 12 NO. 4
        CENTURY MUSIC PUBLISHING COMPANY, INC.   2304   .40
SCHUMANN, R.   7
    WHY
        NOVELLO AND COMPANY, LTD.   55.0017.06   .25
SCHUMANN, R.   LISZT
    WIDMUNG -- DEDICATION --, OP. 25 NO. 1
        FRANCO COLOMBO PUBLICATIONS   127908   .50
SCHUMANN, R.   BAUER
    WILD HORSEMAN, THE, OP. 68 NO. 08--ALBUM FOR THE YOUNG
        G. SCHIRMER, INC.   .30
SCHUMANN, R.   2
    WILD HORSEMAN, THE, OP. 68 NO. 8
        CENTURY MUSIC PUBLISHING COMPANY, INC.   2356   .40
SCHUMANN, R.   2
    WILD HORSEMAN, THE, OP. 68 NO. 8
        CENTURY MUSIC PUBLISHING COMPANY, INC.   2356   .40
SCHUMANN, R.   3
    WILD RIDER, THE
        NOVELLO AND COMPANY, LTD.   55.0008.07   .40
SCHUMANN, R.   DE VITO, A.   2
    WILD RIDER, THE
        PRO-ART PUBLICATIONS, INC.   84   .50
SCHUMANN, R. *
    DEDICATION
        G. SCHIRMER, INC.   .70
SCHUMANN, R. *
    DEDICATION
        G. SCHIRMER, INC.   .70
SCHUMANN, R. *
    SMUGGLER, THE
        MUSICAL SCOPE PUBLISHERS   01.25
SCHUMANN, R. *
    SPRING NIGHT
        FRANCO COLOMBO PUBLICATIONS   128430   .50
SCHUMANN, R. *   MONTANI
    SPRING NIGHT
        FRANCO COLOMBO PUBLICATIONS   128430   .50
SCHUMANN, R. *
    WIDMUNG
        FRANCO COLOMBO PUBLICATIONS   127908   .50
SCHUMANN, R. *
    WIDMUNG
        FRANCO COLOMBO PUBLICATIONS   127908   .50
SCHUNKE   2
    WALTZING THIRDS
        BOSTON MUSIC COMPANY   .50
SCHUSTER   WILLIAMS, W.   MEDIUM
    FLOREINE WALTZ
        SHAWNEE PRESS, INC.   HB-79   .50
SCHUYLER
    RUMPELSTILTSKIN
        FRANCO COLOMBO PUBLICATIONS   BA   1.00
SCHWAB   2
    AT THE PLAYGROUND
        CENTURY MUSIC PUBLISHING COMPANY, INC.   3694   .40
SCHWAB   3
    EVENING SONG
        CENTURY MUSIC PUBLISHING COMPANY, INC.   1951   .40
SCHWAB   3
    MILITARY PARADE
        CENTURY MUSIC PUBLISHING COMPANY, INC.   1950   .40
SCHWAB   3
    MILL WHEEL, THE
        CENTURY MUSIC PUBLISHING COMPANY, INC.   1952   .40
SCHWAB   2
    PARTY CLOTHES
        CENTURY MUSIC PUBLISHING COMPANY, INC.   3695   .40
SCHWAB   3
    POLONAISE D'AMOUR
        CENTURY MUSIC PUBLISHING COMPANY, INC.   1947   .40
SCHWAB   3
    POPPY FIELD, THE, IDYLLE
        CENTURY MUSIC PUBLISHING COMPANY, INC.   1948   .40
SCHWAB   3
    UNDER THE LEAVES
        CENTURY MUSIC PUBLISHING COMPANY, INC.   1949   .40
SCHWALM, R.
    DAILY EXERCISES
        G. SCHIRMER, INC.   L796   1.25
SCHWARTZ, H.   E-M
    BARCAROLLE
        COMPOSERS PRESS, INC.   1.00
SCHWARTZ, S.   SCHAUM, J.   1 1/2
    DAY BY DAY
        SCHAUM PUBLICATIONS, INC.   .75
SCHWARZ   2
    VARIATIONEN UBER EIN ALTES BAUERNLIED
        BARENREITER VERLAG   BA 1429
SCHWARZ
    VARIATIONS ON AN OLD PEASANT SONG
        BARENREITER VERLAG   BA 1429   1.75
SCHWARZ-SCHILLING, R.
    SONATA--1968
        ASSOCIATED MUSIC PUBLISHERS, INC.   BOT   5.50
SCHWARZ-SCHILLING, R.
    SONATINA
        BARENREITER VERLAG   BA 2084   3.50
SCHWARZ-SCHILLING, R.   3
    SONATINE
        BARENREITER VERLAG   BA 2084
SCHYTTE
    BERCEUSE IN G
        G. SCHIRMER, INC.   .35
SCHYTTE
    ETUDE IN B MINOR, OP. 15 NO. 12--'GHOST'
        G. SCHIRMER, INC.   .40
SCHYTTE
    ON THE SEA, OP. 22 NO. 6
        G. SCHIRMER, INC.   .40
SCHYTTE   3
    WITCHES REVEL
        CENTURY MUSIC PUBLISHING COMPANY, INC.   3908   .40

SCHYTTE
  WITCHES' DANCE, OP. 74
      G. SCHIRMER, INC.
                                                    3   .30
SCHYTTE
  WITCHES' REVELS
      BOSTON MUSIC COMPANY
                                                                        .50
SCHYTTE
  WITCHES' REVELS, OP. 66 NO. 24
      CARL FISCHER, INC.   S 7663   .50
SCIAMMARELLA
  HOMENAJE A FALLA
      FRANCO COLOMBO PUBLICATIONS   BA12377   1.25
SCIORTINO, E.
  EVOCATION, OP. 6
      GERARD BILLAUDOT EDITIONS MUSICALES   2.50
SCRIABINE, A.   7
  PRELUDE, OP. 9 NO. 1
      THEODORE PRESSER COMPANY
                                                                        .50
SCOTT-BAKER
  PANTOMIME
      NOVELLO AND COMPANY, LTD.   10.0125.06   1.15
SCOTT, C.   5
  AGYPTEN
      SCHOTT   1436   2.50
SCOTT, C.
  ALLEGRO, FROM 'TWO PIERROT PIECES'
      BOOSEY AND HAWKES, INC.
                                                                        .60
SCOTT, C.
  DANSE NEGRE, OP. 58 NO. 5
      ASHLEY DEALERS SERVICE, INC.   ES   .95
SCOTT, C.   3-4
  DANSE ORIENTALE, OP. 74 NO. 1
      SCHOTT   1802   1.75
SCOTT, C.   5
  INDISCHE SUITE
      SCHOTT   1438   2.25
SCOTT, C.
  LENTO
      ASHLEY DEALERS SERVICE, INC.   ES   .95
SCOTT, C.   ARNOLD
  LENTO
      BOOSEY AND HAWKES, INC.
                                                                        .35
SCOTT, C.   4 - 5
  LENTO
      BOSTON MUSIC COMPANY
                                                                        .50
SCOTT, C.   5
  LENTO
      CENTURY MUSIC PUBLISHING COMPANY, INC.   4373   .40
SCOTT, C.   SCHAUM, J.   4
  LENTO
      SCHAUM PUBLICATIONS, INC.
                                                                        .60
SCOTT, C.   5
  LENTO
      WILLIS MUSIC COMPANY
                                                                        .60
SCOTT, C.
  LENTO, FROM 'TWO PIERROT PIECES'
      BOOSEY AND HAWKES, INC.
                                                                        .75
SCOTT, C.   ZEPP   5
  LOTUS LAND
      PRO-ART PUBLICATIONS, INC.   459   .60
SCOTT, C.   SCHAUM, J.   4 1/2
  LOTUS LAND
      SCHAUM PUBLICATIONS, INC.
                                                                        .60
SCOTT, C.
  LOTUS LAND, OP. 47 NO. 1
      ASHLEY DEALERS SERVICE, INC.   ES   .95
SCOTT, C.
  LOTUS LAND, OP. 47 NO. 1
      CARL FISCHER, INC.   P 3059   .75
SCOTT, C.   5
  LOTUS LAND, OP. 47 NO. 1
      WILLIS MUSIC COMPANY
                                                                        .60
SCOTT, C.   5
  LOTUS-LAND
      CENTURY MUSIC PUBLISHING COMPANY, INC.   4374   .40
SCOTT, C.   4
  LOTUSLAND, OP. 47 NO. 1
      SCHOTT   1804   2.75
SCOTT, C.   5
  POEMS
      SCHOTT   1440   2.50
SCOTT, C.
  SONG FROM THE EAST, A, OP. 54 NO. 2
      ASHLEY DEALERS SERVICE, INC.   ES   .95
SCOTT, C.   RICHTER
  TOY TRUMPET
      WARNER BROTHERS PUBLISHERS
                                                                        .75
SCOTT, C.
  TWO PIANO PIECES
      BOOSEY AND HAWKES, INC.
                                                                        .85
SCOTT, C.   2
  ZOO, TIERE FUR KLAVIER
      SCHOTT   2115   2.50
SCOTT, H.
  HAZEL'S BOOGIE WOOGIE
      MCA MUSIC
                                                                       1.00
SCOVILL
  CELLIST, THE
      CARL FISCHER, INC.   P 1837   .50
SCRIABINE, A.
  ALLEGRO APPASSIONATO, OP. 4
      BOOSEY AND HAWKES, INC.
                                                                       2.50
SCRIABINE, A.   D
  ETUDE IN B FLAT, OP. 65 NO. 1
      C. F. PETERS CORPORATION   F50   1.25
SCRIABINE, A.
  ETUDE IN C SHARP MINOR, OP. 2 NO. 1
      G. SCHIRMER, INC.
                                                                        .40
SCRIABINE, A.   D
  ETUDE IN C SHARP, OP. 65 NO. 2
      C. F. PETERS CORPORATION   F51   1.25
SCRIABINE, A.   FRIEDHEIM
  ETUDE IN D SHARP MINOR, OP. 8 NO. 12
      G. SCHIRMER, INC.
                                                                        .50
SCRIABINE, A.   D
  ETUDE IN G, OP. 65 NO. 3
      C. F. PETERS CORPORATION   F52   1.25
SCRIABINE, A.   D
  ETUDE, OP. 2 NO. 1
      C. F. PETERS CORPORATION   F61   .90
SCRIABINE, A.
  FANTASY IN B MINOR, OP. 28
      INTERNATIONAL MUSIC COMPANY
                                                                       1.75
SCRIABINE, A.
  FLAMMES SOMBRES, OP. 73
      INTERNATIONAL MUSIC COMPANY
                                                                       1.25

SCRIABINE, A.   FREY
  IMPROMPTU A LA MAZUR, OP. 2 NO. 3
      ASSOCIATED MUSIC PUBLISHERS, INC.   SIM   1.00
SCRIABINE, A.
  NOCTURNE FOR THE LEFT HAND ALONE, OP. 9 NO. 2
      G. SCHIRMER, INC.
                                                                        .50
SCRIABINE, A.   5
  NOCTURNE IN D FLAT
      THEODORE PRESSER COMPANY
                                                                        .50
SCRIABINE, A.
  POEME IN F SHARP, OP. 32 NO. 1
      BOOSEY AND HAWKES, INC.
                                                                       1.25
SCRIABINE, A.
  POEME IN FORME D'UNE SONATE, OP. POSTH.
      MUSICA OBSCURA
                                                                       4.00
SCRIABINE, A.
  POEME SATANIQUE, OP. 36
      BOOSEY AND HAWKES, INC.
                                                                       2.00
SCRIABINE, A.
  POEME TRAGIQUE, OP. 34
      BOOSEY AND HAWKES, INC.
                                                                       2.75
SCRIABINE, A.   D
  POEME, OP. 71 NO. 1
      C. F. PETERS CORPORATION   F82   1.25
SCRIABINE, A.
  POLONAISE IN B FLAT MINOR, OP. 21
      MUSICA OBSCURA
                                                                       2.50
SCRIABINE, A.
  POLONAISE, OP. 21
      INTERNATIONAL MUSIC COMPANY
                                                                       1.50
SCRIABINE, A.
  PRELUDE AND NOCTURNE FOR LEFT HAND, OP. 9
      BOOSEY AND HAWKES, INC.
                                                                       1.50
SCRIABINE, A.
  PRELUDE FOR THE LEFT HAND ALONE, OP. 9 NO. 1
      G. SCHIRMER, INC.
                                                                        .40
SCRIABINE, A.   FREY
  PRELUDE, OP. 2 NO. 2
      ASSOCIATED MUSIC PUBLISHERS, INC.   SIM   .50
SCRIABINE, A.
  SATANIC POEM
      EDWIN F. KALMUS   3944   1.25
SCRIABINE, A.
  SATANIC POEM, OP. 36
      INTERNATIONAL MUSIC COMPANY
                                                                       1.25
SCRIABINE, A.
  SONATA NO. 01, OP. 6
      BOOSEY AND HAWKES, INC.
                                                                       3.25
SCRIABINE, A.
  SONATA NO. 02 IN G SHARP MINOR, OP.19
      INTERNATIONAL MUSIC COMPANY
                                                                       1.75
SCRIABINE, A.   PHILIPP, I.
  SONATA NO. 03 IN F SHARP MINOR, OP. 23
      INTERNATIONAL MUSIC COMPANY
                                                                       1.75
SCRIABINE, A.
  SONATA NO. 03, OP. 23
      BOOSEY AND HAWKES, INC.
                                                                       3.25
SCRIABINE, A.
  SONATA NO. 04 IN F SHARP MINOR, OP. 23
      INTERNATIONAL MUSIC COMPANY
                                                                       1.75
SCRIABINE, A.
  SONATA NO. 04, OP. 30
      BOOSEY AND HAWKES, INC.
                                                                       1.75
SCRIABINE, A.
  SONATA NO. 05 IN F SHARP MINOR, OP. 53
      INTERNATIONAL MUSIC COMPANY
                                                                       1.75
SCRIABINE, A.
  SONATA NO. 05, OP. 53
      BOOSEY AND HAWKES, INC.
                                                                       3.50
SCRIABINE, A.
  SONATA NO. 07, OP. 64
      BOOSEY AND HAWKES, INC.
                                                                       2.00
SCRIABINE, A.   D
  SONATA NO. 08, OP. 66
      C. F. PETERS CORPORATION   F95   2.00
SCRIABINE, A.
  SONATA NO. 09 IN F, OP. 68
      INTERNATIONAL MUSIC COMPANY
                                                                       1.75
SCRIABINE, A.   D
  SONATA NO. 09, OP. 68
      C. F. PETERS CORPORATION   F53   2.00
SCRIABINE, A.
  SONATA NO. 10 IN C, OP. 70
      INTERNATIONAL MUSIC COMPANY
                                                                       1.75
SCRIABINE, A.   D
  SONATA NO. 10, OP. 70
      C. F. PETERS CORPORATION   F54   2.00
SCRIABINE, A.
  SONATA-FANTASY NO. 2, OP. 19
      BOOSEY AND HAWKES, INC.
                                                                       4.00
SCRIABINE, A.
  TRAGIC POEM, OP. 34
      EDWIN F. KALMUS   3943   1.25
SCRIABINE, A.
  TRAGIC POEM, OP. 34
      INTERNATIONAL MUSIC COMPANY
                                                                       1.25
SCRIABINE, A.
  VERS LA FLAMME
      EDWIN F. KALMUS   3940   1.25
SCRIABINE, A.
  VERS LA FLAMME, OP. 72
      ASSOCIATED MUSIC PUBLISHERS, INC.   SIM   1.50
SCRIABINE, A.
  VERS LA FLAMME, OP. 72
      INTERNATIONAL MUSIC COMPANY
                                                                       1.25
SCRIABINE, A.
  WALTZ, OP. 38
      BOOSEY AND HAWKES, INC.
                                                                       2.00
SCUDERI
  CASTELNUOVO SUL CARSO 1915
      FRANCO COLOMBO PUBLICATIONS   BON.1506   1.75
SCUDERI
  PRELUDE-PRESTO IN A-FLAT MINOR
      FRANCO COLOMBO PUBLICATIONS   BON.1505   1.75
SEARLE, H.
  PIANO SONATA
      OXFORD UNIVERSITY PRESS   32.901   3.50
SEARLE, H.
  PRELUDE FOR PIANO
      FABER MUSIC, LTD.   F0209
SEBASTIANI, P.
  CANCION DE CUNA PARA BIBI
      PEER SOUTHERN ORGANIZATION   00.60
SEGAL, J.   GLOVER, D.
  SCARLET RIBBONS
      BELWIN-MILLS PUBLISHING CORPORATION   .60

SEIBER, M.	5			
SCHERZANDO CAPRICCIOSO				
SCHOTT		10247		1.00
SEIDER, S.	1 1/2			
DONKEY AND THE ZEBRA				
BELWIN-MILLS PUBLISHING CORPORATION				.60
SEIDER, S.	1 1/2			
TINKER BELL AND THE PIRATE				
BELWIN-MILLS PUBLISHING CORPORATION				.60
SEIDT, J.	4			
AZALEA				
VOLKWEIN BROS.				.40
SEIDT, J.	2			
DOLLIE'S MARCH				
VOLKWEIN BROS.				.25
SEIDT, J.	2			
DOLLIE'S POLKA				
VOLKWEIN BROS.				.25
SEIDT, J.	1			
DOLLIE'S SONG				
VOLKWEIN BROS.				.25
SEIDT, J.	1			
DOLLIE'S WALTZ				
VOLKWEIN BROS.				.25
SEIDT, J.	4			
DYING WAIF -- THE FANTASIA				
VOLKWEIN BROS.				.50
SEIDT, J.	4			
GUARDIAN ANGEL				
VOLKWEIN BROS.				.50
SEIDT, J.	4			
LOVE'S DEPARTURE				
VOLKWEIN BROS.				.50
SEIDT, J.	4			
LOVE'S GREETING				
VOLKWEIN BROS.				.50
SEIDT, J.	4			
LOVE'S MEDITATION				
VOLKWEIN BROS.				.50
SEIDT, J.	4			
LOVE'S QUARREL				
VOLKWEIN BROS.				.50
SEIDT, J.	4-5			
LOVE'S TRIUMPH				
VOLKWEIN BROS.				.50
SEIDT, J.	3			
MOONLIGHT ON THE RIVER WALTZ				
VOLKWEIN BROS.				.50
SEIDT, J.	4-5			
MOONLIGHT ON THE WATER				
VOLKWEIN BROS.				00.50
SEIDT, J.	4			
STARLIGHT REVERIE				
VOLKWEIN BROS.				.50
SEIDT, J.	4			
THOUGHTS AT TWILIGHT REVERIE				
VOLKWEIN BROS.				00.50
SEIDT, J.	4			
VALSE CAPRICE				
VOLKWEIN BROS.				00.40
SEIDT, J.	4			
WOODLAND ECHOES REVERIES				
VOLKWEIN BROS.				00.40
SEINBERG	1-2			
BOASTFUL LITTLE MONKEY				
PRO-ART PUBLICATIONS, INC.		397		.50
SEINBERG	1-2			
JACK IN THE BOX				
PRO-ART PUBLICATIONS, INC.		398		.50
SEINBERG				
MASQUERADE WALTZ				
CARL FISCHER, INC.		P 3145		.50
SEISS				
SONATINA IN D, OP. 8 NO. 1				
G. SCHIRMER, INC.				.70
SELBY, V.	3			
DRUM MAJOR, THE				
WILLIS MUSIC COMPANY				.40
SELIVANOV				
LITTLE SCHERZO, OP. 3, NO. 3				
MCA MUSIC				.60
SELLENICK	5			
MARCHE INDIENNE				
ALPHONSE LEDUC				
SENTER, G.	2 1/2			
INTERLUDE				
BELWIN-MILLS PUBLISHING CORPORATION				.60
SENTER, G.	2			
MINOR PRELUDE, A				
BELWIN-MILLS PUBLISHING CORPORATION				.60
SENTER, G.	1 1/2			
PEANUT BRITTLE				
BELWIN-MILLS PUBLISHING CORPORATION				.60
SERAFINI, C.				
HANON, OGGI				
EDIZIONI BERBEN		EB 1529		3.00
SEREBRIER, J.				
SONATA				
PEER SOUTHERN ORGANIZATION				02.00
SERENDERO, D.				
REINHILD - RHAPSODY				
PAN AMERICAN UNION				02.00
SERLY				
FOX TROT				
MCA MUSIC				1.00
SERLY				
SONATA IN MODUS LACSIVUS				
PEER SOUTHERN ORGANIZATION				04.00
SEROUX				
DIVERTISSEMENT				
FRANCO COLOMBO PUBLICATIONS		SAL		2.50
SEROUX				
HOMMAGE A CLAUDE DEBUSSY				
FRANCO COLOMBO PUBLICATIONS		SAL		2.75
SEROUX				
NOCTURNE				
FRANCO COLOMBO PUBLICATIONS		SAL		2.50
SERRADELL	3			
GOLONDRINA, LA				
CENTURY MUSIC PUBLISHING COMPANY, INC.		2097		.40
SERRADELL	3			
GOLONDRINA, LA				
CENTURY MUSIC PUBLISHING COMPANY, INC.		3569		.40
SERRADELL	3			
LA GOLONDRINA				
BELWIN-MILLS PUBLISHING CORPORATION		135		.60
SERRADELL	WALLIS	3		
LA GOLONDRINA				
BOSTON MUSIC COMPANY				.50
SERRADELL	3			
LA GOLONDRINA -- THE SWALLOW				
CENTURY MUSIC PUBLISHING COMPANY, INC.		2097		.40
SERRADELL	3			
LA GOLONDRINA -- THE SWALLOW, EASY				
CENTURY MUSIC PUBLISHING COMPANY, INC.		3569		.40
SERRADELL	3			
SWALLOW, THE -- LA GOLONDRINA --				
CENTURY MUSIC PUBLISHING COMPANY, INC.		2097		.40
SERRADELL	3			
SWALLOW, THE -- LA GOLONDRINA --				
CENTURY MUSIC PUBLISHING COMPANY, INC.		3569		.40
SERRANO, G.				
EVOCACION GOYESCA				
ASSOCIATED MUSIC PUBLISHERS, INC.		UME		.65
SERRANO, G.				
EVOCACION GOYESCA -- BALLET				
ASSOCIATED MUSIC PUBLISHERS, INC.		UME		.65
SESSIONS, P.				
FROM MY DIARY				
EDWARD B. MARKS MUSIC CORPORATION				03.00
SESSIONS, P.	5			
SONATA				
SCHOTT		2163		3.25
SESSIONS, R.				
SONATA NO. 03				
EDWARD B. MARKS MUSIC CORPORATION				05.00
SETACCIOLI				
RETOUR DU BERGER, LE				
FRANCO COLOMBO PUBLICATIONS		DS95		.65
SETER, M.				
CHACONNE AND SCHERZO				
ISRAEL MUSIC INSTITUTE				4.00
SEUEL *				
BLACK PIRATES				
SUMMY-BIRCHARD COMPANY				.50
SEUEL-HOLST, M.				
FANCIES FREE. TONE-POEMS FOR YOUNG PIANISTS--SINGING BELLS				
G. SCHIRMER, INC.				.35
SEUEL-HOLST, M.				
FANCIES FREE. TONE-POEMS FOR YOUNG PIANISTS--THREE AND TWENTY PIRATES				
G. SCHIRMER, INC.				.40
SEUEL-HOLST, M.	2			
IN THE FOOTHILLS				
WILLIS MUSIC COMPANY				.75
SEUEL-HOLST, M.	2			
IN THE NORTHLAND				
WILLIS MUSIC COMPANY				1.00
SEUEL-HOLST, M.				
MARCH OF THE DOMINOS				
SUMMY-BIRCHARD COMPANY				.50
SEVERAC				
BAIGNEUSES AU SOLEIL				
FRANCO COLOMBO PUBLICATIONS		SAL		2.50
SEVERAC				
CERDANA - EN TARTANE				
FRANCO COLOMBO PUBLICATIONS		SAL		4.25
SEVERAC				
CERDANA - LE RETOUR DES MULETIERS				
FRANCO COLOMBO PUBLICATIONS		SAL		1.25
SEVERAC				
CERDANA - LES FETES				
FRANCO COLOMBO PUBLICATIONS		SAL		3.25
SEVERAC				
CERDANA - LES MULETIERS DEVANT LE CHRIST DE LLIVIA				
FRANCO COLOMBO PUBLICATIONS		SAL		2.50
SEVERAC				
CERDANA - MENETRIERS ET GLANEUSES				
FRANCO COLOMBO PUBLICATIONS		SAL		3.25
SEVERAC				
EN LANGUEDOC - A CHEVAL DANS LA PRAIRIE				
FRANCO COLOMBO PUBLICATIONS		SAL		2.50
SEVERAC				
EN LANGUEDOC - LE JOUR DE LA FOIRE AU MAS				
FRANCO COLOMBO PUBLICATIONS		SAL		3.25
SEVERAC				
EN LANGUEDOC - SUR L'ETANG, LE SOIR				
FRANCO COLOMBO PUBLICATIONS		SAL		2.50
SEVERAC				
EN LANGUEDOC - VERS LA MAS EN FETE				
FRANCO COLOMBO PUBLICATIONS		SAL		3.25
SEVERAC				
EN VACANCES, BK. 1 - INVOCATION A SCHUMANN				
FRANCO COLOMBO PUBLICATIONS		SAL		1.75
SEVERAC				
EN VACANCES, BK. 1 - LES CARESSES DE GRAND-MAMAN				
FRANCO COLOMBO PUBLICATIONS		SAL		1.75
SEVERAC				
EN VACANCES, BK. 1 - LES PETITES VOISINES ENVISITE				
FRANCO COLOMBO PUBLICATIONS		SAL		1.75
SEVERAC				
EN VACANCES, BK. 1 - OU L'ON ENTEND UNE VIEILLE BOITE A MUSIQUE				
FRANCO COLOMBO PUBLICATIONS		SAL		1.75
SEVERAC				
EN VACANCES, BK. 1 - RONDE DANS LE PARC				
FRANCO COLOMBO PUBLICATIONS		SAL		1.75
SEVERAC				
EN VACANCES, BK. 1 - TOTO DEGUISE EN SUISSE D'EGLISE AND MIMI SE DEGUISE EN MARQUISE				
FRANCO COLOMBO PUBLICATIONS		SAL		1.75
SEVERAC				
EN VACANCES, BK. 1 - VALSE ROMANTIQUE				
FRANCO COLOMBO PUBLICATIONS		SAL		1.75
SEVERAC				
EN VACANCES, BK. 2 - LA VASQUE AUX COLOMBES				
FRANCO COLOMBO PUBLICATIONS		SAL		1.75
SEVERAC				
EN VACANCES, BK. 2 - LES 2 MOUSQUETAIRES				
FRANCO COLOMBO PUBLICATIONS		SAL		1.75
SEVERAC				
NAIADES ET LE FAUNE INDISCRET, LES				
FRANCO COLOMBO PUBLICATIONS		SAL		2.75
SEVERAC				
PIPPERMINT GET -- WALTZ --				
FRANCO COLOMBO PUBLICATIONS		SAL		2.50
SEVERAC				
SOUS LES LAURIERS ROSES				
FRANCO COLOMBO PUBLICATIONS		SAL		5.50
SEVERAC				
STANCES DE MADAME DE POMPADOUR				
FRANCO COLOMBO PUBLICATIONS		SAL		2.50
SEWELL	1			
GOOD NIGHT				
CENTURY MUSIC PUBLISHING COMPANY, INC.		1663		.40

SEWELL   1
    IN SUNNY SPAIN
        CENTURY MUSIC PUBLISHING COMPANY, INC.   1665   .40
SEWELL   1
    VALSE PETITE
        CENTURY MUSIC PUBLISHING COMPANY, INC.   1664   .40
SGAMBATI
    BOITE A MUSIQUE
        FRANCO COLOMBO PUBLICATIONS   116787   .90
SGAMBATI
    CAMPANE A FESTA. EPITHALAMIUM, OP. 12 NO. 8
        G. SCHIRMER, INC.   .35
SGAMBATI
    ETUDE MELODIQUE OP. 21 NO. 5
        SCHOTT   4
SGAMBATI
    FUNFTE NOCTURNE OP. 31
        SCHOTT   5
                                                1809   1.25
SGAMBATI
    GAVOTTE AS-MOLL OP. 14
        SCHOTT   4
                                                1808   1.25
SGAMBATI
    GLUCK, MELODIE
        SCHOTT   6
                                                1816   1.25
SGAMBATI
    KONZERT-ETUDE FIS-MOLL OP. 10 NO. 2
        SCHOTT   1.25
SGAMBATI   BAUER
    MELODY--FROM 'ORFEO' BY GLUCK
        G. SCHIRMER, INC.   4
                                                             .50
SGAMBATI
    NENIA OP. 18 NO. 3
        SCHOTT   1813   1.25
SGAMBATI
    PIANISTS' GUIDE
        FRANCO COLOMBO PUBLICATIONS   ER49   2.75
SGAMBATI   4
    PRUDENT OP. 41 INTRODUCTION ET ETUDE BRILLANTE
        SCHOTT   1810   1.25
SGAMBATI   5
    SECHSTE NOCTURNE OP. 33
        SCHOTT   1.25
SGAMBATI   4
    VECCHIO MINUETTO OP. 18 NO. 2
        SCHOTT   1812   1.25
SHAPERO, H.
    SONATA IN F MINOR
        PEER SOUTHERN ORGANIZATION   04.50
SHAPERO, H.   M
    SONG WITHOUT WORDS
        THEODORE PRESSER COMPANY   .50
SHAPERO, H.   M
    STACCATO DANCE
        THEODORE PRESSER COMPANY   .50
SHAPERO, H.
    VARIATIONS IN C MINOR
        PEER SOUTHERN ORGANIZATION   02.50
SHARP   RICHTER
    HIDING IN THE GARDEN
        BELWIN-MILLS PUBLISHING CORPORATION   .60
SHARP   RICHTER
    HIDING IN THE GARDEN
        FRANCO COLOMBO PUBLICATIONS   NY1508   .35
SHARP   RICHTER
    JUMPING JACKS
        BELWIN-MILLS PUBLISHING CORPORATION   .60
SHARP   RICHTER
    JUMPING JACKS
        FRANCO COLOMBO PUBLICATIONS   NY1509   .35
SHAW
    PASTEL BLUES
        MCA MUSIC   1.00
SHAW, C.   4
    ASH GROVE, THE
        THEODORE PRESSER COMPANY   .50
SHAW, C.   5
    THIRD STREET RHUMBA
        THEODORE PRESSER COMPANY   .50
SHAW, E. B.   2 1/2
    KITE CAPERS
        THEODORE PRESSER COMPANY   .50
SHAW, M.   3
    CANON IN A MINOR
        NOVELLO AND COMPANY, LTD.   55.0023.00   .25
SHCHDRIN
    SONATA FOR PIANO
        MCA MUSIC   1.50
SHCHDRIN
    TOCCATINA
        MCA MUSIC   1.50
SHEARING, G.
    CONSTERNATION
        BELWIN-MILLS PUBLISHING CORPORATION   20058   1.00
SHEARING, G.
    FOURTH DEUCE, THE
        BELWIN-MILLS PUBLISHING CORPORATION   20099   1.00
SHEARING, G.
    MAN FROM MINTON'S, THE
        BELWIN-MILLS PUBLISHING CORPORATION   20383   1.00
SHEFFER
    SHIPBUILDERS, THE
        SUMMY-BIRCHARD COMPANY   .50
SHEPHERD
    CAPRICCIO NO. 2
        FRANCO COLOMBO PUBLICATIONS   NY1641   1.25
SHEPHERD
    EXOTIC DANCE
        OXFORD UNIVERSITY PRESS   93.203   .75
SHEPHERD
    SECOND SONATA
        OXFORD UNIVERSITY PRESS   93.206   2.50
SHEPHERD   1 1/2
    WAY UP NORTH
        THEODORE PRESSER COMPANY   .50
SHERIFF, N.
    SONATA--1961
        ASSOCIATED MUSIC PUBLISHERS, INC.   BOT   4.50
SHERMAN, N.
    TOCCATA--1956
        ASSOCIATED MUSIC PUBLISHERS, INC.   BER   2.50
SHIFFERLY, R.   3
    SCOTTISH ECHOES
        BELWIN-MILLS PUBLISHING CORPORATION   .60
SHIFFERLY, R.   3
    SUNDAY MORNING
        BELWIN-MILLS PUBLISHING CORPORATION   .60

SHIFRIN   D
    TRAEUERMUSIK
        C. F. PETERS CORPORATION   5872   2.50
SHLONSKY, V.
    YOUTH SUITE FOR PIANO
        BELWIN-MILLS PUBLISHING CORPORATION   20475   1.50
SHOEMAKER   2
    SWING AND SWAY
        BELWIN-MILLS PUBLISHING CORPORATION   .60
SHORES--ED.   SHORES
    BATTLE HYMN OF THE REPUBLIC
        SUMMY-BIRCHARD COMPANY   .50
SHOSTAKOVITCH   SANDOR
    DANCE FROM 'THE GOLDEN AGE' BALLET, OP. 22
        MCA MUSIC   .75
SHOSTAKOVITCH
    DANCE OF THE DOLLS
        EDWIN F. KALMUS   3968   1.50
SHOSTAKOVITCH
    DANCE, FROM THE BALLET 'THE GOLDEN AGE,' OP. 22
        UNIVERSAL EDITION   13141   1.30
SHOSTAKOVITCH   WOLMAN
    HAPPY FAIRY TALE, A
        MCA MUSIC   .60
SHOSTAKOVITCH   WOLMAN
    MECHANICAL DOLL, THE
        MCA MUSIC   .60
SHOSTAKOVITCH
    PETITE BALLERINA, THE - FROM DANCE OF THE DOLLS
        MCA MUSIC   .60
SHOSTAKOVITCH
    PETITS CONTES
        GERARD BILLAUDOT EDITIONS MUSICALES   2.10
SHOSTAKOVITCH   SCHAUM, J.   3
    POLKA FROM THE 'GOLDEN AGE'
        BELWIN-MILLS PUBLISHING CORPORATION   .50
SHOSTAKOVITCH
    POLKA FROM THE BALLET 'L'AGE D'OR', OP. 22
        G. SCHIRMER, INC.   .50
SHOSTAKOVITCH   4
    POLKA, AGE D'OR
        CENTURY MUSIC PUBLISHING COMPANY, INC.   3644   .40
SHOSTAKOVITCH
    POLKA, FROM THE BALLET 'THE GOLDEN AGE, OP. 22
        UNIVERSAL EDITION   13144   .85
SHOSTAKOVITCH
    SONATA NO. 01, OP. 12
        MCA MUSIC   2.50
SHOSTAKOVITCH
    SONATA NO. 02, OP. 64
        EDWIN F. KALMUS   3960   1.75
SHOSTAKOVITCH
    SONATA, OP. 12
        EDWIN F. KALMUS   3959   2.00
SHOSTAKOVITCH   D
    SONATA, OP. 64
        C. F. PETERS CORPORATION   4726   5.00
SHOSTAKOVITCH
    SPANISH DANCE
        MCA MUSIC   .75
SHOSTAKOVITCH
    THREE FANTASTIC DANCES, OP. 1
        G. SCHIRMER, INC.   .60
SHOSTAKOVITCH *
    POLKA, FROM THE BALLET 'L'AGE D' OR', OP. 22
        CARL FISCHER, INC.   S 2294   .50
SHULMAN
    CRADLE SONG
        WEINTRAUB MUSIC COMPANY   070085   .50
SHULMAN
    HUES OF BLUES
        SAM FOX PUBLISHING COMPANY, INC.   .50
SHULMAN
    HUES OF BLUES
        SOUTHERN MUSIC COMPANY   .50
SHULMAN
    LOPSIDED
        WEINTRAUB MUSIC COMPANY   070087   .50
SHULMAN
    MEXICAN MOUNTAIN CLIMB
        SAM FOX PUBLISHING COMPANY, INC.   .50
SHULMAN
    MEXICAN MOUNTAIN CLIMB
        SOUTHERN MUSIC COMPANY   .50
SHULMAN
    ONE MAN SHOW
        SAM FOX PUBLISHING COMPANY, INC.   1.50
SHULMAN
    PASTORALE
        WEINTRAUB MUSIC COMPANY   070086   .50
SHUMAKER, F. M.   3
    HUMPTY DUMPTY
        THEODORE PRESSER COMPANY   .50
SIBELIUS
    ANDANTE FESTIVO
        PEER SOUTHERN ORGANIZATION   00.85
SIBELIUS   GARTNER
    BARDE, DER, OP. 64--ORCH
        ASSOCIATED MUSIC PUBLISHERS, INC.   BRH   1.00
SIBELIUS
    BELLS OF BERGHALL CHURCH, THE, OP. 65B
        ASSOCIATED MUSIC PUBLISHERS, INC.   BRH   .60
SIBELIUS   PALMGREN
    BLACK ROSES, OP. 36 NO. 1
        ASSOCIATED MUSIC PUBLISHERS, INC.   BRH   1.20
SIBELIUS   TAUBMANN
    CANZONETTA, OP. 62A--STR ORCH
        ASSOCIATED MUSIC PUBLISHERS, INC.   BRH   .90
SIBELIUS
    EKLOGE NO. 1
        ASSOCIATED MUSIC PUBLISHERS, INC.   BRH   .90
SIBELIUS   ECKSTEIN
    FINLANDIA
        CARL FISCHER, INC.   S 2298   .75
SIBELIUS   6
    FINLANDIA
        CENTURY MUSIC PUBLISHING COMPANY, INC.   3236   .40
SIBELIUS
    FINLANDIA, OP. 26 NO. 7
        ASSOCIATED MUSIC PUBLISHERS, INC.   AMP   .75
SIBELIUS
    FINLANDIA, OP. 26 NO. 7
        ASSOCIATED MUSIC PUBLISHERS, INC.   BRH   1.25
SIBELIUS
    FINLANDIA, OP. 26 NO. 7
        G. SCHIRMER, INC.   .75

SIBELIUS   EKMAN
    GESANG VON DER KREUZSPINNE, DER, OP. 27 NO. 4
        ASSOCIATED MUSIC PUBLISHERS, INC.   BRH   1.20
SIBELIUS   EKMAN
    GESANG VON DER KREUZSPINNE, OP. 27 NO. 4--WITH SUPERLINEAR TEXT
        ASSOCIATED MUSIC PUBLISHERS, INC.   BRH   .75
SIBELIUS
    IDYLL, OP. 24 NO. 6
        ASSOCIATED MUSIC PUBLISHERS, INC.   BRH   .80
SIBELIUS
    KARELIA SUITE, OP. 11
        ASSOCIATED MUSIC PUBLISHERS, INC.   BRH   2.00
SIBELIUS   TAUBMANN
    KING CHRISTIAN SUITE--BALLADE
        ASSOCIATED MUSIC PUBLISHERS, INC.   BRH   1.20
SIBELIUS   PALMGREN
    MADCHEN KAM VOM STELLDICHEIN, OP. 37 NO. 5
        ASSOCIATED MUSIC PUBLISHERS, INC.   BRH   1.20
SIBELIUS
    RAKASTAVA
        PEER SOUTHERN ORGANIZATION   02.25
SIBELIUS
    REVERIE, OP. 58 NO. 1
        ASSOCIATED MUSIC PUBLISHERS, INC.   BRH   .75
SIBELIUS   PODOLSKY, L.
    ROMANCE
        SHAWNEE PRESS, INC.   HB-231   .75
SIBELIUS   4
    ROMANCE IN D FLAT
        BOSTON MUSIC COMPANY   .60
SIBELIUS
    ROMANCE IN D FLAT, OP. 24 NO. 9
        ASSOCIATED MUSIC PUBLISHERS, INC.   AMP   .40
SIBELIUS   5
    ROMANCE IN D FLAT, OP. 24 NO. 9
        BELWIN-MILLS PUBLISHING CORPORATION   323   .60
SIBELIUS   ECKSTEIN
    ROMANCE, OP. 24 NO. 9
        CARL FISCHER, INC.   S 1309   .75
SIBELIUS   5
    ROMANCE, OP. 24 NO. 9
        CENTURY MUSIC PUBLISHING COMPANY, INC.   1972   .40
SIBELIUS
    RONDINO, OP. 68, NO. 1
        UNIVERSAL EDITION   3848   .85
SIBELIUS   PALMGREN
    SCHILFROHR, SAUSLE, OP. 36 NO. 4
        ASSOCIATED MUSIC PUBLISHERS, INC.   BRH   1.20
SIBELIUS   TAUBMANN
    SWAN OF TUONELA, OP. 22 NO. 3--ORCH
        ASSOCIATED MUSIC PUBLISHERS, INC.   BRH   1.50
SIBELIUS   WALLIS   2
    THEME FROM FINLANDIA
        BOSTON MUSIC COMPANY   .50
SIBELIUS   ZEPP   4
    THEME FROM FINLANDIA
        PRO-ART PUBLICATIONS, INC.   261   .50
SIBELIUS   TAUBMANN
    VALSE ROMANTIQUE, OP. 62B--SM ORCH
        ASSOCIATED MUSIC PUBLISHERS, INC.   BRH   .90
SIBELIUS   5
    VALSE TRISTE
        BELWIN-MILLS PUBLISHING CORPORATION   131   .60
SIBELIUS   SCHAUM, J.   3
    VALSE TRISTE
        SCHAUM PUBLICATIONS, INC.   .60
SIBELIUS   THOMPSON, J.   1
    VALSE TRISTE
        WILLIS MUSIC COMPANY   .35
SIBELIUS   ECKSTEIN
    VALSE TRISTE, OP. 44
        CARL FISCHER, INC.   S 2228   .50
SIBELIUS   4-5
    VALSE TRISTE, OP. 44
        CENTURY MUSIC PUBLISHING COMPANY, INC.   2452   .40
SIBELIUS   4-5
    VALSE TRISTE, OP. 44
        CENTURY MUSIC PUBLISHING COMPANY, INC.   2452   .40
SIBELIUS
    VALSE TRISTE, OP. 44
        G. SCHIRMER, INC.   .50
SIBELIUS   2
    VALSETTE
        CENTURY MUSIC PUBLISHING COMPANY, INC.   3749   .40
SIBELIUS
    VALSETTE IN E MINOR, OP. 40 NO. 1
        ASSOCIATED MUSIC PUBLISHERS, INC.   BRH   .90
SICCARDI, H.
    EL COSACO ANSIOSO
        PEER SOUTHERN ORGANIZATION   01.25
SICILIANI
    CARNAVALITO
        FRANCO COLOMBO PUBLICATIONS   BA11761   .75
SICILIANI
    DANZA CRIOLLA
        FRANCO COLOMBO PUBLICATIONS   BA10922   .75
SICILIANI
    DANZA DEL GURI
        FRANCO COLOMBO PUBLICATIONS   BA9355   .75
SICILIANI
    NOCHE SERRANA
        FRANCO COLOMBO PUBLICATIONS   BA10463   .75
SICILIANI
    NORMA
        FRANCO COLOMBO PUBLICATIONS   BA11320   .75
SICILIANI
    PRELUDE
        FRANCO COLOMBO PUBLICATIONS   BA11321   .75
SICILIANI
    SERIE ARGENTINA DE DANZAS
        FRANCO COLOMBO PUBLICATIONS   BA10923   1.00
SICILIANI
    SERRANITA
        FRANCO COLOMBO PUBLICATIONS   BA9721   .75
SIEFERT
    SONATA IN C MINOR
        FRANCO COLOMBO PUBLICATIONS   SAL   8.75
SIEGL, O.
    PARTITA--1953
        ASSOCIATED MUSIC PUBLISHERS, INC.   DOB   2.75
SIEGMEISTER
    AMERICAN KALEIDOSCOPE
        SAM FOX PUBLISHING COMPANY, INC.   1.75
SIEGMEISTER
    BOOGIE
        SOUTHERN MUSIC COMPANY   .50

SIEGMEISTER   E
    LONESOME SONG
        THEODORE PRESSER COMPANY   .50
SIEGMEISTER
    SONATA NO. 02
        MCA MUSIC   2.50
SIEWART   3
    MAY BELLS RINGING
        VOLKWEIN BROS.   .25
SIFLER, P.   3
    SONATINA NO. 01
        BOSTON MUSIC COMPANY   .75
SIFLER, P.   VE
    UGLY DUCKLING, THE
        OXFORD UNIVERSITY PRESS   93.334   .40
SIGNORELLI *
    BLUES SERENADE, A
        BELWIN-MILLS PUBLISHING CORPORATION   20001   .85
SIGTENHORST-MEYER
    PRELUDE
        FRANCO COLOMBO PUBLICATIONS   SAL   2.50
SILAS, E.
    GIGUE IN A MINOR
        G. SCHIRMER, INC.   .50
SILCHER   DAHMEN   3
    VARIATIONEN FUR KLAVIER UBER 'GIB MIR DIE BLUMEN'
        BARENREITER VERLAG   EN 1219
SILCHER   DAHMEN
    VARIATIONS FOR PIANO ON 'GIB MIR DIE BLUMEN'
        BARENREITER VERLAG   EN 1219   2.00
SILVA
    NINNA-NANNA
        FRANCO COLOMBO PUBLICATIONS   DS352   1.00
SILVERI
    RELIGIOUS HARMONY -- WITH LONGHI - MARCH --
        FRANCO COLOMBO PUBLICATIONS   102699   .75
SILVERMAN
    DANCE FROM FAR AWAY, A
        EDWARD B. MARKS MUSIC CORPORATION   00.60
SILVERS   RIEGGER
    APRIL SHOWERS
        WARNER BROTHERS PUBLISHERS   1.00
SILVERS   RICHTER   FIRST YEAR
    APRIL SHOWERS
        WARNER BROTHERS PUBLISHERS   .75
SILVERS *
    INTERLUDE
        MCA MUSIC   1.00
SILVESTER, F. C.
    LINCOLNSHIRE POACHER
        FREDERICK HARRIS MUSIC COMPANY   .60
SILVESTER, F. C.
    MY LADY GREENSLEEVES
        FREDERICK HARRIS MUSIC COMPANY   .60
SILVESTRI
    FAVILLE CAPRICCIO
        FRANCO COLOMBO PUBLICATIONS   124984   1.00
SIMMONS, H.
    TWO MODERN BAROQUE DANCES
        VOLKWEIN BROS.   00.75
SIMMONS, T.   3
    JUNGLE FLOWER, THE
        BELWIN-MILLS PUBLISHING CORPORATION   .60
SIMMS
    ROCK 'EM BOOGIE
        SOUTHERN MUSIC COMPANY   .50
SIMMS
    ROLL 'EM BOOGIE
        SOUTHERN MUSIC COMPANY   .50
SIMON
    EMERALDS
        MCA MUSIC   1.00
SIMON
    MOONSTONES
        MCA MUSIC   1.00
SIMON   SILVERMAN
    POINCIANA
        EDWARD B. MARKS MUSIC CORPORATION   00.60
SIMON
    RUBIES
        MCA MUSIC   1.00
SIMON
    SAPPHIRES
        MCA MUSIC   1.00
SIMONETTI
    MADRIGAL
        FRANCO COLOMBO PUBLICATIONS   97848   .60
SIMONETTI   DEL MAGLIO
    MADRIGAL
        FRANCO COLOMBO PUBLICATIONS   124733   .50
SIMONETTI
    MADRIGALE IN D
        G. SCHIRMER, INC.   .30
SIMONS
    PEANUT VENDOR, THE
        EDWARD B. MARKS MUSIC CORPORATION   01.00
SIMONS
    PEANUT VENDOR, THE
        EDWARD B. MARKS MUSIC CORPORATION   01.00
SIMPSON
    LAUGHING TROMBONE POLKA
        MCA MUSIC   1.00
SIMS
    CONTRASTS
        SHAWNEE PRESS, INC.   .50
SINATRA, R.
    BOOGIE-WOOGIE IN THE KITCHEN
        THE BIG THREE MUSIC CORPORATION   00.95
SINATRA, R.
    BOOGIE-WOOGIE IN THE PARLOR
        THE BIG THREE MUSIC CORPORATION   00.95
SINCIRT, H.   STEINER   JR. APPR.
    LITTLE BIRD, THE
        BELWIN-MILLS PUBLISHING CORPORATION   .60
SINDING
    A LA MENUETTO, OP. 125 NO. 2
        ASSOCIATED MUSIC PUBLISHERS, INC.   AMP   .60
SINDING
    CON FUOCO, OP. 125 NO. 1
        ASSOCIATED MUSIC PUBLISHERS, INC.   AMP   .60
SINDING
    CON FUOCO, OP. 25 NO. 1
        G. SCHIRMER, INC.   .60
SINDING   5
    FRUEHLINGSRAUCHEN
        CENTURY MUSIC PUBLISHING COMPANY, INC.   1096   .40

SINGERY
    POUR UNE PETITE BIEN SAGE - ARIETTE AND PASTORALE
        FRANCO COLOMBO PUBLICATIONS   SAL   1.50
SINGERY
    POUR UNE PETITE BIEN SAGE - VALSETTE AND PETITE MARCHE
        FRANCO COLOMBO PUBLICATIONS   SAL   1.50
SINGLETON *   KERR, R.N.
    STRANGERS IN THE NIGHT
        MCA MUSIC   1.00
SINTON, J.   1
    THIS OLD MAN
        WILLIS MUSIC COMPANY   .35
SIROONI   GR. 4
    PRELUDE IN E MINOR
        KENYON PUBLICATIONS   .85
SIROONI   GR. 5
    RONDO IN E FLAT
        KENYON PUBLICATIONS   .85
SKAAGS   2
    LITTLE BLUE LADY
        CENTURY MUSIC PUBLISHING COMPANY, INC.   4391   .40
SKAAGS   2
    MERRY CRICKET, THE
        CENTURY MUSIC PUBLISHING COMPANY, INC.   4344   .40
SKAGGS
    BASKETBALL
        BOSTON MUSIC COMPANY   .50
SKAGGS   2
    DANCE OF THE MARTIANS
        BELWIN-MILLS PUBLISHING CORPORATION   .60
SKAGGS
    LITTLE GIRL FROM MARS
        CARL FISCHER, INC.   P 3120   .50
SKAGGS   2
    LITTLE INVENTION
        BOSTON MUSIC COMPANY   .50
SKAGGS
    PETITE BALLERINA
        SAM FOX PUBLISHING COMPANY, INC.   .50
SKAGGS
    PETITE BALLERINA
        SOUTHERN MUSIC COMPANY   .50
SKALKOTTAS, N.
    FIFTEEN LITTLE VARIATIONS
        UNIVERSAL EDITION   UE 12729   1.80
SKALKOTTAS, N.
    PASSACAGLIA
        UNIVERSAL EDITION   UE 12370   1.80
SKALKOTTAS, N.
    SUITE NO. 3
        UNIVERSAL EDITION   UE 13611   1.50
SKALKOTTAS, N.
    SUITE NO. 4
        UNIVERSAL EDITION   UE 12428   1.95
SKIPPER
    GETTING THERE AND TRIAD STOMP
        NATIONAL KEYBOARD ARTS ASSOCIATES   .50
SKORZENY, F.
    SONATA--1962
        ASSOCIATED MUSIC PUBLISHERS, INC.   DOB   3.75
SLACK   3
    HOME, SWEET HOME, VAR.
        CENTURY MUSIC PUBLISHING COMPANY, INC.   244   .40
SLATER, N.
    FALLING SNOW
        ASSOCIATED MUSIC PUBLISHERS, INC.   BER   .40
SLATES, P.   2 1/2
    LAZY STROLL, A
        THEODORE PRESSER COMPANY   .50
SLATES, P.   2
    TEMPLE PRICESSIONAL AND DANCE
        THEODORE PRESSER COMPANY   .50
SLATES, P.   2 1/2
    UPS AND DOWNS
        THEODORE PRESSER COMPANY   .50
SLONIMSKY   MEDIUM
    COUNTRY DANCE
        SHAWNEE PRESS, INC.   .40
SLONIMSKY   MEDIUM
    DREAMS AND DRUMS
        SHAWNEE PRESS, INC.   .40
SLONIMSKY   MEDIUM
    HAUNTING HORN, THE
        SHAWNEE PRESS, INC.   .40
SLONIMSKY   MEDIUM
    KIDDIES ON THE KEYS
        SHAWNEE PRESS, INC.   .40
SLONIMSKY   MEDIUM
    RUSSIAN PRELUDE
        SHAWNEE PRESS, INC.   .50
SLONIMSKY   MEDIUM
    VARIATIONS ON A KINDERGARTEN TUNE --MY TOY BALLOON--
        SHAWNEE PRESS, INC.   .75
SLONIMSKY, N.   MD
    STUDIES IN BLACK AND WHITE
        THEODORE PRESSER COMPANY   1.50
SMALL, A.   2
    BILL BAILEY
        CENTURY MUSIC PUBLISHING COMPANY, INC.   4331   .40
SMALL, A.   2
    GIVE MY REGARDS TO BROADWAY
        CENTURY MUSIC PUBLISHING COMPANY, INC.   4332   .40
SMALL, A.   2
    GREENSLEEVES
        CENTURY MUSIC PUBLISHING COMPANY, INC.   4334   .40
SMALL, A.   2
    MY GAL SAL
        CENTURY MUSIC PUBLISHING COMPANY, INC.   4335   .40
SMALL, A.--ED   2
    HE'S GOT THE WHOLE WORLD IN HIS HANDS
        CENTURY MUSIC PUBLISHING COMPANY, INC.   4327   .40
SMALLEY, R.
    MONODY
        FABER MUSIC, LTD.   F0503
SMALLWOOD   4
    FAIRY BARQUE
        CENTURY MUSIC PUBLISHING COMPANY, INC.   1006   .40
SMALLWOOD   2
    HARE BELL
        CENTURY MUSIC PUBLISHING COMPANY, INC.   1008   .40
SMALLWOOD   2
    SWEET VIOLET
        CENTURY MUSIC PUBLISHING COMPANY, INC.   1487   .40
SMALLWOOD   2
    WOODBINE
        CENTURY MUSIC PUBLISHING COMPANY, INC.   1044   .40

SMETANA   3-4
    AM MEERESSTRAND. KONZERTETUDE, OP. 17
        BARENREITER VERLAG   AP 701
SMETANA
    BAL VISION
        ARTIA   .90
SMETANA   3-4
    BALL-VISION
        BARENREITER VERLAG   AP 705
SMETANA   4
    BARTERED BRIDE, POLKA
        CENTURY MUSIC PUBLISHING COMPANY, INC.   3719   .40
SMETANA
    BETTINA'S POLKA
        ARTIA   .90
SMETANA   3
    BETTINAS POLKA
        BARENREITER VERLAG   AP 706
SMETANA
    BLANIK
        ARTIA   1.25
SMETANA   M-D
    BOHEMIAN DANCE NO. 2# 'THE LITTLE PULLET'
        C. F. PETERS CORPORATION   4435A   .90
SMETANA   SCHAUM, J.   5
    BOHEMIAN POLKA
        BELWIN-MILLS PUBLISHING CORPORATION   .50
SMETANA   JOSEFFY
    BY THE SEASHORE--CONCERT ETUDE
        G. SCHIRMER, INC.   .75
SMETANA   KREUTZER
    CHANSON
        BOSTON MUSIC COMPANY   .50
SMETANA   2-3
    DALIBOR. POTPOURRI AUS DER OPER
        BARENREITER VERLAG   AP 707
SMETANA   4-5
    DIE MOLDAU
        SCHOTT   4345   1.75
SMETANA   3
    DREI SALONPOLKAS, OP. 7 NO. 1 IN F SHARP
        BARENREITER VERLAG   AP 699
SMETANA   2-3
    ERINNERUNGEN AN PILSEN
        BARENREITER VERLAG   AP 322
SMETANA
    FABLE, OP. 2 NO. 2
        BELWIN-MILLS PUBLISHING CORPORATION   .85
SMETANA
    FROM BOHEMIA'S WOODS AND FIELDS
        ARTIA   1.25
SMETANA   5
    FURIANT
        SCHOTT   07011 1/2   1.00
SMETANA
    GEORGINE'S POLKA
        ARTIA   1.25
SMETANA   2-3
    GEORGINEN-POLKA IN D
        BARENREITER VERLAG   AP 712
SMETANA   2-3
    HOCHZEITSSZENEN
        BARENREITER VERLAG   AP 713
SMETANA
    IN BOHEMIA
        ARTIA   .75
SMETANA
    IN THE HALL
        ARTIA   .75
SMETANA
    LOUISA'S POLKA
        ARTIA   .75
SMETANA   3
    LUISENS POLKA IN E FLAT
        BARENREITER VERLAG   AP 715
SMETANA   KAAN   3
    MEIN VATERLAND, HEFT 1 - VYSEHRAD
        BARENREITER VERLAG   AP 717A
SMETANA   KAAN   3
    MEIN VATERLAND, HEFT 2 - DIE MOLDAU
        BARENREITER VERLAG   AP 717B
SMETANA   PEK   3
    MEIN VATERLAND, HEFT 3 - SARKA
        BARENREITER VERLAG   AP 717C
SMETANA   PEK   3
    MEIN VATERLAND, HEFT 4 - AUS BOHMENS HAIN UND FLUR
        BARENREITER VERLAG   AP 717D
SMETANA   PEK   3
    MEIN VATERLAND, HEFT 5 - TABOR
        BARENREITER VERLAG   AP 717E
SMETANA   PEK   3
    MEIN VATERLAND, HEFT 6 - BLANIK
        BARENREITER VERLAG   AP 717F
SMETANA   KLUSSMANN
    MOLDAU, THE
        FRANCO COLOMBO PUBLICATIONS   SIK.192   2.00
SMETANA   4
    MOLDAU, THE -- THEME
        CENTURY MUSIC PUBLISHING COMPANY, INC.   3846   .40
SMETANA
    ON THE SEA SHORE
        ARTIA   .75
SMETANA
    PENSEE FUGITIVE
        ARTIA   .75
SMETANA   3
    PENSEE FUGITIVE
        BARENREITER VERLAG   AP 719
SMETANA   SIN   2-3
    POLKA AUS DER OPER 'DIE VERKAUFTE BRAUT'
        BARENREITER VERLAG   AP 294
SMETANA   5
    POLKA IN A MINOR
        CENTURY MUSIC PUBLISHING COMPANY, INC.   3842   .40
SMETANA
    POLKA IN F SHARP MAJOR, OP. 7, NO. 1
        ARTIA   .75
SMETANA   4
    POLKA, BARTERED BRIDE
        CENTURY MUSIC PUBLISHING COMPANY, INC.   3719   .40
SMETANA   DUMM
    RECITAL REFRESHER SERIES -- FABLE, OP. 2 NO. 2
        BELWIN-MILLS PUBLISHING CORPORATION   26114   .60
SMETANA
    REVES
        ARTIA   2.75

SMETANA   3-4
  REVES. 6 CHARAKTERSTUCKE
    BARENREITER VERLAG   AP 342
SMETANA   3
  SECHS ALBUMBLATTER, OP. 2 - NO. 1, 'A ROBERT SCHUMANN'
    BARENREITER VERLAG   AP 327
SMETANA
  SIX ALBUM LEAVES, OP. 2
    ARTIA   .75
SMETANA
  SIX CHARACTERISTIC PIECES, OP. 1
    ARTIA   1.25
SMETANA   3
  SKIZZEN, OP. 4 UND 5
    BARENREITER VERLAG   AP 698
SMETANA
  SONATA
    ARTIA   2.50
SMETANA   3
  SONATA
    BARENREITER VERLAG   AP 720
SMETANA   3
  SPRINGTANZ
    BARENREITER VERLAG   AP 972
SMETANA
  TO OUR GIRLS
    ARTIA   .75
SMETANA
  TO ROBERT SCHUMANN
    ARTIA   .75
SMETANA
  TROIS POLKAS DE SALON, OP. 7
    ARTIA   1.25
SMETANA
  TSCHECHISCHE TANZE 1 AND 2
    BARENREITER VERLAG   AP 722
SMETANA
  UNSEREN MADCHEN
    BARENREITER VERLAG   AP 724
SMETANA
  VYSHERAD
    ARTIA   1.25
SMETANA
  WEDDING SCENES
    ARTIA   1.00
SMIT SIBINGA   D
  TOCCATA. HARPSICHORD
    C. F. PETERS CORPORATION   D460   3.00
SMIT, L.
  FANTASY - THE FAREWELL
    BROUDE BROTHERS LTD.   02.50
SMIT, L.
  SONATA
    BELWIN-MILLS PUBLISHING CORPORATION   20564   4.50
SMIT, L.
  VARIATIONS IN G
    BOOSEY AND HAWKES, INC.   1.75
SMITH   4
  ANGEL'S SERENADE
    CENTURY MUSIC PUBLISHING COMPANY, INC. 682   .60
SMITH   2
  AT THE PARTY
    PRO-ART PUBLICATIONS, INC.   462   .50
SMITH
  COTTON FLUFF
    SUMMY-BIRCHARD COMPANY   .50
SMITH   1
  CRISS CROSS
    BOSTON MUSIC COMPANY   .50
SMITH   2
  ELF DANCES, THE
    BOSTON MUSIC COMPANY   .50
SMITH   3-4
  MAY POLE DANCE
    CENTURY MUSIC PUBLISHING COMPANY, INC. 2341   .40
SMITH
  MINUET IN SWING
    MCA MUSIC   1.00
SMITH   3
  MOONLIGHT ON VENUS
    BOSTON MUSIC COMPANY   .50
SMITH
  PINETOP'S BLUES
    MCA MUSIC   1.00
SMITH   1B
  STEPPING HIGH
    MUSICORD PUBLICATIONS, INC.   .45
SMITH   2
  TRIAD TUNE
    BOSTON MUSIC COMPANY   .50
SMITH   3
  WHIMS
    BOSTON MUSIC COMPANY   .50
SMITH--ED   SMITH   2
  STAR SPANGLED BANNER
    BOSTON MUSIC COMPANY   .50
SMITH-MASTERS
  QUIET DANCE
    FRANCO COLOMBO PUBLICATIONS   LD421   .60
SMITH, H.
  DRAGONFLY, THE, OP. 11 NO. 4
    G. SCHIRMER, INC.   .25
SMITH, H.   M-D
  EVOCATION
    C. F. PETERS CORPORATION   6875   .60
SMITH, H.   1
  LET'S BUY A CLOCK
    CENTURY MUSIC PUBLISHING COMPANY, INC. 4368   .40
SMITH, H.   1
  MAKE BELIEVE
    CENTURY MUSIC PUBLISHING COMPANY, INC. 4367   .40
SMITH, H.
  PLANTATION MELODY, OP. 11 NO. 3
    G. SCHIRMER, INC.   .30
SMITH, J.   MD
  CHARACTERISTIC SUITE
    THEODORE PRESSER COMPANY   2.00
SMITH, J.   4
  PRELUDE
    THEODORE PRESSER COMPANY   .60
SMITH, J.   DILLER
  STAR-SPANGLED BANNER, THE
    G. SCHIRMER, INC.   .40
SMITH, J.   DILLER
  STAR-SPANGLED BANNER, THE----ARRANGED IN TWO KEYS, WITH A BRIEF
  SKETCH OF THE ORIGIN OF THE WORDS AND MUSIC
    G. SCHIRMER, INC.   .60

SMITH, L.   3
  CHAPEL IN THE MOUNTAINS
    CENTURY MUSIC PUBLISHING COMPANY, INC. 2105   .40
SMITH, S.   3
  DOROTHY
    CENTURY MUSIC PUBLISHING COMPANY, INC. 192   .40
SMITH, S.   3
  DOROTHY -- OLD ENGLISH DANCE
    VOLKWEIN BROS.   .25
SMITH, S.
  DOROTHY--OLD ENGLISH DANCE
    G. SCHIRMER, INC.   .50
SMITH, S.
  RUSSIAN SONG
    FRANCO COLOMBO PUBLICATIONS   127464   .50
SMITH, SYDNEY   5
  AEOLIAN HARP, E FLAT MAJOR
    CENTURY MUSIC PUBLISHING COMPANY, INC. 1052   .40
SMITH, SYDNEY   ROLFE, W.   2
  CHANSON RUSSE, EASY
    CENTURY MUSIC PUBLISHING COMPANY, INC. 3396   .40
SMITH, SYDNEY   4
  CHANSON RUSSE, OP. 31
    CENTURY MUSIC PUBLISHING COMPANY, INC. 2192   .40
SMITH, SYDNEY
  CHANSON RUSSE, OP. 31
    G. SCHIRMER, INC.   .50
SMITH, SYDNEY   5
  DANCE DES FANTOMES
    CENTURY MUSIC PUBLISHING COMPANY, INC. 1841   .40
SMITH, SYDNEY   4
  GAITE DU COEUR
    CENTURY MUSIC PUBLISHING COMPANY, INC. 1696   .40
SMITH, SYDNEY   5
  HARPE EOLIENNE
    CENTURY MUSIC PUBLISHING COMPANY, INC. 1052   .40
SMITH, SYDNEY   4
  LILY OF THE VALLEY, OP. 14
    CENTURY MUSIC PUBLISHING COMPANY, INC. 278   .40
SMITH, SYDNEY   5
  MOUNTAIN STREAM, THE, OP. 13
    CENTURY MUSIC PUBLISHING COMPANY, INC. 1048   .40
SMITH, SYDNEY   3-4
  PREMIER MAI, OP. 45
    CENTURY MUSIC PUBLISHING COMPANY, INC. 2341   .40
SMITH, SYDNEY   4
  RUSSIAN SONG, OP. 31
    CENTURY MUSIC PUBLISHING COMPANY, INC. 2192   .40
SMITH, W.
  JOYOUS MOMENTS. VALSE, OP. 87 NO. 2
    G. SCHIRMER, INC.   .75
SMOLANOFF
  CHILDRENS SUITE FOR PIANO
    SEESAW MUSIC CORPORATION   1.00
SMOLANOFF
  PRELUDES FOR PIANO
    BELWIN-MILLS PUBLISHING CORPORATION   20565   1.75
SMOLANOFF
  VARIATIONS FOR PIANO
    SEESAW MUSIC CORPORATION   5.00
SMOLIN, H.
  GREEN GOBLINS, THE
    G. SCHIRMER, INC.   .35
SMOLIN, H.
  MERRY MOUNTAINEERS, THE
    G. SCHIRMER, INC.   .35
SNYDER   MEDIUM
  NOCTURNE, OP. 6 NO. 1
    SHAWNEE PRESS, INC.   .60
SNYDER, W.
  FASCINATION -- VARIATIONS ON THE THEME FOR PIANO
    ASHLEY DEALERS SERVICE, INC.   1.00
SNYDER, W.
  GREENSLEEVES -- VARIATIONS ON THE THEME FOR PIANO
    ASHLEY DEALERS SERVICE, INC.   1.00
SNYDER, W.
  GUANTAMERA
    ASHLEY DEALERS SERVICE, INC.   1.00
SNYDER, W.
  MY PONY MACARONI
    BELWIN-MILLS PUBLISHING CORPORATION   28140   .50
SNYDER, W.
  ON THE TOP OF OLD SMOKY -- IMPROVISATIONS FOR PIANO
    ASHLEY DEALERS SERVICE, INC.   1.00
SOCHTING   GILLOCK   1 1/2
  CUCKOO'S CALL
    WILLIS MUSIC COMPANY   .40
SOEGIJO, P. G.
  KLAVIERSTUDIE NO. 1--1968
    ASSOCIATED MUSIC PUBLISHERS, INC.   BOT   5.50
SOENSTEVOLD   D
  BASSO OSTINATO
    C. F. PETERS CORPORATION   LY249   .60
SOHY
  SIX LITTLE PIECES - IL PLEUT
    FRANCO COLOMBO PUBLICATIONS   SAL   1.50
SOLER, A.   MARVIN
  FANDANGO
    ALEXANDER BROUDE, INC.   2.75
SOLER, A.   MARVIN, F.
  FANDANGO
    BELWIN-MILLS PUBLISHING CORPORATION   07031   2.50
SOMERS, H.
  STRANGENESS OF HEART
    ASSOCIATED MUSIC PUBLISHERS, INC.   BER   .75
SOMMI
  FAVOLE DI PERAULT
    FRANCO COLOMBO PUBLICATIONS   FOR.11197   1.75
SORET
  BARCAROLLE
    FRANCO COLOMBO PUBLICATIONS   SAL   2.75
SORIANO, A. P.
  JOTA ARAGONESA IN A
    ASSOCIATED MUSIC PUBLISHERS, INC.   UME   .75
SOSNIK, H.
  GAYETY
    THE BIG THREE MUSIC CORPORATION   00.95
SOUBEYRAN
  CROQUIS D'ENFANTS - A LA CAMPAGNE
    FRANCO COLOMBO PUBLICATIONS   SAL   2.50
SOUBEYRAN
  CROQUIS D'ENFANTS - A LA MAISON
    FRANCO COLOMBO PUBLICATIONS   SAL   2.50
SOUBEYRAN
  CROQUIS D'ENFANTS - LA MAISON ENDORMIE
    FRANCO COLOMBO PUBLICATIONS   SAL   1.50

SOUBEYRAN
    CROQUIS D'ENFANTS - LA RETOUR DE L'ECOLE
        FRANCO COLOMBO PUBLICATIONS   SAL   1.50
SOUBEYRAN
    CROQUIS D'ENFANTS - PRIERE DU SOIR
        FRANCO COLOMBO PUBLICATIONS   SAL   1.50
SOUERS
    AWAY TO THE WOODS
        MCA MUSIC   .60
SOUERS   4
    IMPROMPTU
        WILLIS MUSIC COMPANY   .50
SOUERS   2 1/2
    OFF TO THE PICNIC
        WILLIS MUSIC COMPANY   .40
SOUERS   2
    PASSACAGLIA
        WILLIS MUSIC COMPANY   .40
SOUERS   3
    SNOWFALL
        WILLIS MUSIC COMPANY   .40
SOUERS
    SOFT SHADOWS
        MCA MUSIC   .60
SOUERS
    SQUIRREL'S FROLIC
        MCA MUSIC   .60
SOUERS   3
    TOCCATA BREVE
        WILLIS MUSIC COMPANY   .50
SOUERS   2 1/2
    WANDERING BROOK, THE
        WILLIS MUSIC COMPANY   .40
SOULAGE
    VARIATIONS ON A POPULAR SONG -- L'AVOCAT --
        FRANCO COLOMBO PUBLICATIONS   SAL   4.25
SOULE   2
    BALLAD
        BELWIN-MILLS PUBLISHING CORPORATION   .60
SOULE   2
    DANCE IN THE BARN
        BELWIN-MILLS PUBLISHING CORPORATION   .60
SOULE   1
    NIGHT SONG
        BELWIN-MILLS PUBLISHING CORPORATION   .60
SOULE   2
    SCHERZO
        BELWIN-MILLS PUBLISHING CORPORATION   .60
SOUSA   LEVINE   3 1/2
    EL CAPITAN
        THEODORE PRESSER COMPANY   .50
SOUSA   WEYBRIGHT   2
    LIBERTY BELL, THE, MARCH
        BELWIN-MILLS PUBLISHING CORPORATION   .60
SOUSA   SCHAUM, J.   2 1/2
    SEMPER FIDELIS
        BELWIN-MILLS PUBLISHING CORPORATION   .50
SOUSA   3-4
    SEMPER FIDELIS
        CENTURY MUSIC PUBLISHING COMPANY, INC.   3737   .40
SOUSA   LEVINE   3 1/2
    SEMPER FIDELIS
        THEODORE PRESSER COMPANY   .50
SOUSA
    STARS AND STRIPES FOREVER
        ASHLEY DEALERS SERVICE, INC.   ES   .95
SOUSA   SCHAUM, J.   4
    STARS AND STRIPES FOREVER
        BELWIN-MILLS PUBLISHING CORPORATION   .50
SOUSA   4
    STARS AND STRIPES FOREVER
        CENTURY MUSIC PUBLISHING COMPANY, INC.   4130   .40
SOUSA   ZEPP   2
    STARS AND STRIPES FOREVER
        PRO-ART PUBLICATIONS, INC.   144   .50
SOUSA   ZEPP   4
    STARS AND STRIPES FOREVER
        PRO-ART PUBLICATIONS, INC.   145   .50
SOUSA
    STARS AND STRIPES FOREVER
        THEODORE PRESSER COMPANY   .50
SOUSA   RICHTER   2
    STARS AND STRIPES FOREVER
        THEODORE PRESSER COMPANY   .50
SOUSA   SCHAUM   2 1/2
    STARS AND STRIPES FOREVER
        THEODORE PRESSER COMPANY   .50
SOUSA   4
    STARS AND STRIPES FOREVER
        THEODORE PRESSER COMPANY   .50
SOUSA   1 1/2
    STARS AND STRIPES FOREVER
        WILLIS MUSIC COMPANY   .40
SOUSA   3
    STARS AND STRIPES FOREVER
        WILLIS MUSIC COMPANY   .50
SOUSA   PELS, W.   1B
    STARS AND STRIPES FOREVER -- FINALE THEME
        MUSICORD PUBLICATIONS, INC.   .45
SOUSA   CARLETON   1 1/2
    STARS AND STRIPES FOREVER --TRIO THEME--
        THEODORE PRESSER COMPANY   .50
SOUSA   ECKSTEIN
    STARS AND STRIPES FOREVER, THE
        CARL FISCHER, INC.   P 2802   .60
SOUSA   SCHAUM, J.   2
    THUNDERER
        BELWIN-MILLS PUBLISHING CORPORATION   .50
SOUSA
    WASHINGTON POST MARCH
        ASHLEY DEALERS SERVICE, INC.   ES   .95
SOUSA   3-4
    WASHINGTON POST MARCH
        CENTURY MUSIC PUBLISHING COMPANY, INC.   3787   .40
SOUSA   THOMPSON, J.   1
    WASHINGTON POST MARCH
        WILLIS MUSIC COMPANY   .35
SOUSA   KING, S.
    WASHINGTON POST MARCH, THE
        BELWIN-MILLS PUBLISHING CORPORATION   26060   .60
SOUSA   3
    WASHINGTON POST, THE
        BOSTON MUSIC COMPANY   .50
SOUTHAM, A.
    QUODLIBET
        ASSOCIATED MUSIC PUBLISHERS, INC.   BER   .40

SOUTHAM, A.
    SEA FLEA
        ASSOCIATED MUSIC PUBLISHERS, INC.   BER   .40
SOWERBY, L.   E
    FANCY, A
        THEODORE PRESSER COMPANY   .50
SOWERBY, L.   4
    IRISH WASHERWOMAN
        BOSTON MUSIC COMPANY   .50
SPAULDING, G. L.   1
    AIRY FAIRIES
        THEODORE PRESSER COMPANY   .75
SPAULDING, G. L.   1 1/2
    PRETTY LITTLE SONG BIRD
        THEODORE PRESSER COMPANY   .50
SPAULDING, G. L.   SCHAUM, J.   2
    SING, ROBIN SING
        SCHAUM PUBLICATIONS, INC.   .50
SPAULDING, G. L.   1
    SING, ROBIN SING
        THEODORE PRESSER COMPANY   .50
SPAULDING, G. L.--ED   SPAULDING, G. L.
    BELLS OF ST. MARY'S, WALTZ
        CHAPPELL AND COMPANY, INC.   0437509-1503   .95
SPEAKS, O.   DEIS
    ON THE ROAD TO MANDALAY
        G. SCHIRMER, INC.   .60
SPEAKS, O.   DEIS
    SYLVIA
        G. SCHIRMER, INC.   .60
SPEARE-LUTYENS, S.
    ENCORE
        COMPOSERS AUTOGRAPH PUBLICATIONS   1.54
SPECTOR   2
    LADYBUG WALTZ
        CENTURY MUSIC PUBLISHING COMPANY, INC.   4267   .40
SPENCER, C.   6-7
    ADVENTURES OF CHANTICLEER AND PARTLET, THE
        NOVELLO AND COMPANY, LTD.   10.0127.02   1.25
SPENCER, E. B.   4-5
    SUNNYSIDE -- SCHOTTISCHE DE CONCERT
        VOLKWEIN BROS.   .35
SPENCER, J.   2
    ADESTE FIDELIS AND FIRST NOEL
        VOLKWEIN BROS.   .30
SPENCER, J.   2
    ADESTE FIDELIS AND SANTA CLAUS MARCH
        VOLKWEIN BROS.   .35
SPENCER, J.   1
    AMERICA
        VOLKWEIN BROS.   .30
SPENCER, J.   1
    ANNIE LAURIE
        VOLKWEIN BROS.   .25
SPENCER, J.   2
    COME ALL YE FAITHFUL AND FIRST NOEL
        VOLKWEIN BROS.   .30
SPENCER, J.   2
    COME ALL YE FAITHFUL AND SANTA CLAUS
        VOLKWEIN BROS.   .35
SPENCER, J.   1
    COUNTRY GARDENS
        VOLKWEIN BROS.   .25
SPENCER, J.   1
    DRINK TO ME ONLY WITH THINE EYES
        VOLKWEIN BROS.   .25
SPENCER, J.   2
    FIRST NOEL AND COME ALL YE FAITHFUL
        VOLKWEIN BROS.   .30
SPENCER, J.   1
    HOME ON THE RANGE -- AMERICAN COWBOY
        VOLKWEIN BROS.   .30
SPENCER, J.   2
    MARINES' HYMN
        VOLKWEIN BROS.   .30
SPENCER, J.   2
    O COME ALL FAITHFUL -- FIRST NOEL
        VOLKWEIN BROS.   .30
SPENCER, J.   3
    PETITE RHAPSODY
        BELWIN-MILLS PUBLISHING CORPORATION   .60
SPENCER, J.   1
    STAR SPANGLED BANNER
        VOLKWEIN BROS.   .30
SPENDIAROW
    BERCEUSE
        BOSTON MUSIC COMPANY   .60
SPIEGLEMAN
    MORSELS --'KOUSOCHKI'
        MCA MUSIC   2.50
SPIELER
    FLASHING PEARLS
        MCA MUSIC   1.00
SPIES, C.
    IMPROMPTU
        ELKAN-VOGEL, INC.   .60
SPIES, L.
    SONATINA--1958
        ASSOCIATED MUSIC PUBLISHERS, INC.   BRH   1.00
SPILIOS   D
    BALLADE IN B FLAT
        C. F. PETERS CORPORATION   H595A   1.25
SPINDLER   4
    CHARGE DES AMAZONS
        CENTURY MUSIC PUBLISHING COMPANY, INC.   1851   .40
SPINDLER   4
    CHARGE OF THE HUSSARS
        CENTURY MUSIC PUBLISHING COMPANY, INC.   763   .40
SPINDLER   2
    FAIRY POLKA, OP. 93 NO. 3
        CENTURY MUSIC PUBLISHING COMPANY, INC.   785   .40
SPINDLER   2
    FLORA WALTZ, OP. 294
        CENTURY MUSIC PUBLISHING COMPANY, INC.   789   .40
SPINDLER   4
    FLYING LEAF, OP. 123
        CENTURY MUSIC PUBLISHING COMPANY, INC.   1065   .40
SPINDLER
    FLYING LEAF, OP. 123 NO. 10
        G. SCHIRMER, INC.   .35
SPINDLER   2
    HUNTING SONG
        CENTURY MUSIC PUBLISHING COMPANY, INC.   1202   .40
SPINDLER   2
    PRIMROSE POLKA, OP. 294
        CENTURY MUSIC PUBLISHING COMPANY, INC.   856   .40

SPINDLER   4
    RIDE OF THE AMAZONS, OP. 321
        CENTURY MUSIC PUBLISHING COMPANY, INC.   1851   .40
SPINDLER   2 1/2
    TRUMPETER'S SERENADE
        WILLIS MUSIC COMPANY   .40
SPINDLER   3
    VALSE BRILLIANTE, OP. 148
        CENTURY MUSIC PUBLISHING COMPANY, INC.   2008   .40
SPINNER
    FANTASY FOR PIANO, OP. 9
        BOOSEY AND HAWKES, INC.   2.25
SPINNER
    INVENTIONS, OP. 13
        BOOSEY AND HAWKES, INC.   1.50
SPINNER
    SONATA, OP. 3
        UNIVERSAL EDITION   UE 12155   1.50
SPITZMULLER, A.
    CONSTRUCTION HUMAINE, OP. 49 -- ABSTRACT BALLET
        ASSOCIATED MUSIC PUBLISHERS, INC.   BOT   7.50
SPITZMULLER, A.
    PRELUDE AND DOUBLE FUGUE, OP. 7
        UNIVERSAL EDITION   UE 10428   1.25
SPITZMULLER, A.
    VARIATIONS ON AN ORIGINAL THEME, OP. 3
        UNIVERSAL EDITION   UE 10401   2.15
SPIVAK, S.   3
    BOOGIE BUGLE
        BELWIN-MILLS PUBLISHING CORPORATION   .60
SPIVAK, S.   2
    BOOGIE WOOGIE BARBECUE
        BELWIN-MILLS PUBLISHING CORPORATION   .60
SPIVAK, S.   3
    BOOGIE WOOGIE CARNIVAL
        BELWIN-MILLS PUBLISHING CORPORATION   .60
SPIVAK, S.   2
    BOOGIE WOOGIE COASTER
        BELWIN-MILLS PUBLISHING CORPORATION   .60
SPIVAK, S.   1
    BOOGIE WOOGIE MAYPOLE
        BELWIN-MILLS PUBLISHING CORPORATION   .60
SPIVAK, S.   3
    BOOGIE WOOGIE NOCTURNE
        BELWIN-MILLS PUBLISHING CORPORATION   .60
SPIVAK, S.   2
    BOOGIE WOOGIE PARADE
        BELWIN-MILLS PUBLISHING CORPORATION   .60
SPIVAK, S.   2
    GOING TO TOWN BOOGIE
        BELWIN-MILLS PUBLISHING CORPORATION   .60
SPIVAK, S.   2
    LONDON BRIDGE BOOGIE
        BELWIN-MILLS PUBLISHING CORPORATION   .60
SPIVAK, S.   3 1/2
    SCANDINAVIAN BOOGIE
        BELWIN-MILLS PUBLISHING CORPORATION   .60
SPRINGER, M.
    MIDNIGHT SUN, OP. 33
        UNIVERSAL EDITION   UE 6051   1.30
SPRINGER, M.
    THREE PIANO PIECES, OP. 34
        UNIVERSAL EDITION   UE 6052   1.30
SPRINGER, M.
    TONE PICTURES, OP. 35
        UNIVERSAL EDITION   UE 6053   1.30
SPURLING, C.   2
    NOCTURNE
        NOVELLO AND COMPANY, LTD.   55.0037.00   .40
SROM   4
    SCHWARZWEISSE TOCCATA
        BARENREITER VERLAG   AP 330
SRS. OF ST. JOSEPH   2
    SWEET CARNATIONS, WALTZ
        CENTURY MUSIC PUBLISHING COMPANY, INC.   1509   .40
ST. QUENTIN--ED   ST. QUENTIN
    BELLS OF ST. MARY'S, WALTZ
        CHAPPELL AND COMPANY, INC.   0437509-1502 .95
STAIRS, L.
    AIRPLANES
        EDWARD B. MARKS MUSIC CORPORATION   00.60
STAIRS, L.
    AMERICAN FOLK TUNE, AN
        THEODORE PRESSER COMPANY   1 1/2
STAIRS, L.   1 1/2
    ANIMAL CRACKERS
        THEODORE PRESSER COMPANY   .50
STAIRS, L.   1 1/2
    ANXIOUS TULIP, THE
        THEODORE PRESSER COMPANY   .50
STAIRS, L.   1 1/2
    BUNNY TRACKS
        THEODORE PRESSER COMPANY   .50
STAIRS, L.   1 1/2
    CIRCUS BAND, THE
        THEODORE PRESSER COMPANY   .50
STAIRS, L.
    CLOCK IN THE HALL
        EDWARD B. MARKS MUSIC CORPORATION   00.60
STAIRS, L.   1
    COWSLIP BELLS
        THEODORE PRESSER COMPANY   .50
STAIRS, L.   2
    DANCING LEPPRECHAUNS
        THEODORE PRESSER COMPANY   .50
STAIRS, L.   1 1/2
    DING DONG BELL
        THEODORE PRESSER COMPANY   .50
STAIRS, L.   1
    I HEARD A BLUEBIRD
        THEODORE PRESSER COMPANY   .50
STAIRS, L.   1
    I LOVE LITTLE PUSSY
        THEODORE PRESSER COMPANY   .50
STAIRS, L.   1 1/2
    MISTRESS MARY
        THEODORE PRESSER COMPANY   .50
STAIRS, L.   2
    MORNING PRAYER
        THEODORE PRESSER COMPANY   .50
STAIRS, L.
    MY COWBOY BOOTS
        EDWARD B. MARKS MUSIC CORPORATION   00.60
STAIRS, L.   2
    MY EASTER BONNET
        THEODORE PRESSER COMPANY   .50

STAIRS, L.
    MY POLLYWOG
        EDWARD B. MARKS MUSIC CORPORATION   00.60
STAIRS, L.   1 1/2
    NEST OF BABY BUNNIES, A
        THEODORE PRESSER COMPANY   .50
STAIRS, L.   1 1/2
    PONY RIDE, A
        THEODORE PRESSER COMPANY   .50
STAIRS, L.   1 1/2
    REG-WINGED BLACKBIRDS
        THEODORE PRESSER COMPANY   .50
STAIRS, L.   1 1/2
    RUSTIC DANCE
        THEODORE PRESSER COMPANY   .50
STAIRS, L.   1
    SAILBOATS
        THEODORE PRESSER COMPANY   .50
STAIRS, L.   2
    SCAMPERING CHIPMUNKS
        THEODORE PRESSER COMPANY   .50
STAIRS, L.   1
    SOLDIERS AT PLAY
        THEODORE PRESSER COMPANY   .50
STAIRS, L.
    SPRING BLOSSOMS
        EDWARD B. MARKS MUSIC CORPORATION   00.60
STAIRS, L.   1 1/2
    UNDER MY WINDOW
        THEODORE PRESSER COMPANY   .50
STAIRS, L.   1 1/2
    WISE OLD OWL, THE
        THEODORE PRESSER COMPANY   .50
STAMATY, C.
    RHYTHMIC TRAINING FOR THE FINGERS, OP. 3--IN SPANISH AND ENGLISH
        G. SCHIRMER, INC.   L1136   2.00
STAMATY, C.
    SINGING TOUCH AND TECHNIQUE--25 EASY STUDIES FOR SMALL HANDS,
    OP. 37
        G. SCHIRMER, INC.   L858   1.50
STANLEY   3
    BLUE FLAME, BLUES
        CENTURY MUSIC PUBLISHING COMPANY, INC.   3509   .40
STANLEY   3
    CARACAS, CONGA
        CENTURY MUSIC PUBLISHING COMPANY, INC.   3511   .40
STANLEY   2
    DEEP RHYTHM, BOOGIE-WOOGIE
        CENTURY MUSIC PUBLISHING COMPANY, INC.   3510   .40
STANLEY   3
    OUR ROMANCE, WALTZ
        CENTURY MUSIC PUBLISHING COMPANY, INC.   3513   .40
STANLEY   3
    VECINOS BUENOS, TANGO
        CENTURY MUSIC PUBLISHING COMPANY, INC.   3508   .40
STANLEY--ED   STANLEY   3
    AULD LANG SYNE
        CENTURY MUSIC PUBLISHING COMPANY, INC.   3769   .40
STANLEY--ED   STENLEY   3
    COMIN' THRU THE RYE
        CENTURY MUSIC PUBLISHING COMPANY, INC.   3770   .40
STANLEY--ED   STANLEY   3
    GOODNIGHT LADIES
        CENTURY MUSIC PUBLISHING COMPANY, INC.   3769   .40
STANLEY--ED   STANLEY   3
    HAND ME DOWN MY WALKIN' CANE
        CENTURY MUSIC PUBLISHING COMPANY, INC.   3771   .40
STANLEY--ED   STANLEY   3
    LITTLE BROWN JUG
        CENTURY MUSIC PUBLISHING COMPANY, INC.   3768   .40
STANLEY--ED   STANLEY   3
    OLD GRAY MARE, THE
        CENTURY MUSIC PUBLISHING COMPANY, INC.   3768   .40
STANLEY--ED   STANLEY   3
    OLD MACDONALD HAD A FARM
        CENTURY MUSIC PUBLISHING COMPANY, INC.   3772   .40
STANLEY--ED   STANLEY   3
    SHE'LL BE COMIN' ROUND THE MOUNTAIN
        CENTURY MUSIC PUBLISHING COMPANY, INC.   3771   .40
STANTON, E.   1
    FLOATING
        CENTURY MUSIC PUBLISHING COMPANY, INC.   3983   .40
STANTON, E.   1
    STRUTTING
        CENTURY MUSIC PUBLISHING COMPANY, INC.   3808   .40
STAPER   M
    BUGLE, DRUM AND FIFE
        THEODORE PRESSER COMPANY   .50
STARER
    FANTASIA
        IMPERO-VERLAG   1.75
STAREP
    FANTASIA CONCERTANTE
        MCA MUSIC   2.00
STARER
    HEXAHEDRON
        MCA MUSIC   1.25
STARER
    SONATA
        MCA MUSIC   2.50
STAPER
    SONATA NO. 02
        MCA MUSIC   2.50
STAPER   3
    SYNCOPATED SERENADE
        LEE ROBERTS MUSIC PUBLICATIONS, INC.   .50
STAPEP   M
    TELEGRAPH, THE
        THEODORE PRESSER COMPANY   .50
STARR   STEINER   1 1/2
    STARR SONG -- SOMEBODY LOVES ME
        BELWIN-MILLS PUBLISHING CORPORATION   .60
STAUB, V.
    GAIEMENT
        ELKAN-VOGEL, INC.   D   1.70
STAUB, V.
    SOUS BOIS, OP. 6
        ASHLEY DEALERS SERVICE, INC.   ES   1.00
STAUB, V.
    SOUS BOIS, OP. 6
        ELKAN-VOGEL, INC.   D   2.75
STEADMAN, A.   1
    CURIOUS CAT, THE
        WILLIS MUSIC COMPANY   .40
STEADMAN, A.   1
    SILVER SLIPPERS
        WILLIS MUSIC COMPANY   .40

STEARNS, P. P.
  PARTITA--1961
    ASSOCIATED MUSIC PUBLISHERS, INC.   AMP   1.25
STECHER *
  HOLIDAY IN HAIFA
    SUMMY-BIRCHARD COMPANY   .50
STECHER *
  I AM FROM SIAM
    SCHMITT, HALL AND MCCREARY COMPANY   9971   .50
STECHER *
  JAZZ A GOGO
    SUMMY-BIRCHARD COMPANY   .50
STECHER *
  LITTLE CABALLERO
    SCHMITT, HALL AND MCCREARY COMPANY   9972   .50
STECHER *
  MARCH OF THE MINI-MARTIANS
    SCHMITT, HALL AND MCCREARY COMPANY   9975   .50
STECHER *
  TERRAIN OF SPAIN, THE
    SUMMY-BIRCHARD COMPANY   .50
STECHER *
  UNDER THE BIG TOP
    SUMMY-BIRCHARD COMPANY   .50
STECHER *
  WAGGIN' TRAIN
    SCHMITT, HALL AND MCCREARY COMPANY   9976   .50
STEEL   2
  BELL SONATINA
    VOLKWEIN BROS.   .45
STEEL   5
  JACOBEAN SUITE
    NOVELLO AND COMPANY, LTD.   10.0129.09 1.15
STEEL   2
  LULLABY
    VOLKWEIN BROS.   .35
STEEL
  SLEEPY HEAD AND THE CLOCKS ON THE STAIRS
    FRANCO COLOMBO PUBLICATIONS   LD422   .60
STEEL
  SONATINA NO. 01
    NOVELLO AND COMPANY, LTD.   10.0045.04 1.25
STEEL
  SONATINA NO. 02
    NOVELLO AND COMPANY, LTD.   10.0046.02 1.15
STEELE, G.   E
  SHORT SUITE
    THEODORE PRESSER COMPANY   .60
STEFFAN, J. A.
  CAPRICCI
    G. HENLE MUSIKVERLAG   227
STEFFEN, W.
  SONATA, OP. 21
    ASSOCIATED MUSIC PUBLISHERS, INC.   BOT   3.00
STEFFENS, W.
  PLUIE DE FEU
    PEER SOUTHERN ORGANIZATION   02.50
STEIBELT
  SONATINA IN C
    BANKS AND SON LTD.   .55
STEIN, G. M.
  SOLDIERS ON PARADE
    BELWIN-MILLS PUBLISHING CORPORATION   .60
STEIN, L.   E
  HOLIDAY
    THEODORE PRESSER COMPANY   .50
STEIN, L.   E
  MELODY
    THEODORE PRESSER COMPANY   .50
STEINER   1 1/2
  ALPINE YODEL
    BELWIN-MILLS PUBLISHING CORPORATION   .50
STEINER   2
  ANCIENT CHARIOT RACE
    BELWIN-MILLS PUBLISHING CORPORATION   .50
STEINER   2
  ANCIENT CHARIOT RACE
    BELWIN-MILLS PUBLISHING CORPORATION   .60
STEINER   1
  AURA LEE
    BELWIN-MILLS PUBLISHING CORPORATION   .60
STEINER   PREPARATORY
  BABY GRAND, THE
    BELWIN-MILLS PUBLISHING CORPORATION   .50
STEINER   JR. APPR.
  BABY GRAND, THE
    BELWIN-MILLS PUBLISHING CORPORATION   .60
STEINER   2 1/2
  BACKYARD BOOGIE
    BELWIN-MILLS PUBLISHING CORPORATION   .50
STEINER   JR. APPR.
  BEAUTIFUL SAVIOUR
    BELWIN-MILLS PUBLISHING CORPORATION   .60
STEINER   3
  BIG BOY BOOGIE
    BELWIN-MILLS PUBLISHING CORPORATION   .60
STEINER   3
  BLUE MONDAY
    BELWIN-MILLS PUBLISHING CORPORATION   .60
STEINER   2
  BONNIE BOOGIE
    BELWIN-MILLS PUBLISHING CORPORATION   .60
STEINER   2
  BY CANDLELIGHT
    BELWIN-MILLS PUBLISHING CORPORATION   .60
STEINER   3 1/2
  CAPRICE IN A MINOR
    BELWIN-MILLS PUBLISHING CORPORATION   .60
STEINER   3
  CATTLE ROUNDUP
    BELWIN-MILLS PUBLISHING CORPORATION   .60
STEINER   2
  CAUCASIAN SHEPHERD
    CENTURY MUSIC PUBLISHING COMPANY, INC.   3754   .40
STEINER   1 1/2
  CHANGE OF THE GUARDS -- ENGLISH FOLK MELODIES
    BELWIN-MILLS PUBLISHING CORPORATION   .60
STEINER   JR. APPROACH
  CHERRIES RIPE
    BELWIN-MILLS PUBLISHING CORPORATION   .60
STEINER   2
  CHRISTMAS LULLABY
    BELWIN-MILLS PUBLISHING CORPORATION   .60
STEINER   JR. APPR.
  CHRISTOPHER COLOMBUS
    BELWIN-MILLS PUBLISHING CORPORATION   .60

STEINER   3 1/2
  CHROMATIC NOCTURNE
    BELWIN-MILLS PUBLISHING CORPORATION   .60
STEINER   1 1/2
  COCKLES AND MUSSELS
    BELWIN-MILLS PUBLISHING CORPORATION   .60
STEINER   1
  CRAWDAD, THE
    BELWIN-MILLS PUBLISHING CORPORATION   .60
STEINER   2
  CROCODILE TEARS
    BELWIN-MILLS PUBLISHING CORPORATION   .60
STEINER   3
  DANCE FLOOR WHISPERS
    BELWIN-MILLS PUBLISHING CORPORATION   .60
STEINER   2
  DANISH PASTRY
    BELWIN-MILLS PUBLISHING CORPORATION   .60
STEINER   2 1/2
  DANUBE BOOGIE
    BELWIN-MILLS PUBLISHING CORPORATION   .60
STEINER   3 1/2
  DOCTOR FAUSTUS
    BELWIN-MILLS PUBLISHING CORPORATION   .60
STEINER   1 1/2
  DRUMSTICKS
    BELWIN-MILLS PUBLISHING CORPORATION   .60
STEINER   1
  ELEVATOR OPERATOR
    BELWIN-MILLS PUBLISHING CORPORATION   .60
STEINER   4
  EVENING OF GLAMOUR
    BELWIN-MILLS PUBLISHING CORPORATION   .60
STEINER   1 1/2
  EXPECTATION WALTZ
    BELWIN-MILLS PUBLISHING CORPORATION   .60
STEINER   2 1/2
  FEAST IN THE EAST
    BELWIN-MILLS PUBLISHING CORPORATION   .60
STEINER   1
  FIRST NOEL, THE
    BELWIN-MILLS PUBLISHING CORPORATION   .60
STEINER   JR. APPR.
  FOLLOW WASHINGTON
    BELWIN-MILLS PUBLISHING CORPORATION   .60
STEINER   1 1/2
  FORT TICONDEROGA
    BELWIN-MILLS PUBLISHING CORPORATION   .60
STEINER   2
  FRIENDSHIP SERENADE
    BELWIN-MILLS PUBLISHING CORPORATION   .60
STEINER   2
  GARDEN PARTY
    BELWIN-MILLS PUBLISHING CORPORATION   .60
STEINER   2
  GASLIGHT WALTZ
    CENTURY MUSIC PUBLISHING COMPANY, INC.   4181   .40
STEINER   2
  HANDKERCHIEF DANCE
    BELWIN-MILLS PUBLISHING CORPORATION   .60
STEINER   JR. APPR.
  HARVEST HYMN
    BELWIN-MILLS PUBLISHING CORPORATION   .60
STEINER   2
  HAWAIIAN DELIGHT -- FOLK MELODIES
    BELWIN-MILLS PUBLISHING CORPORATION   .60
STEINER   2
  HOCUS POCUS
    BELWIN-MILLS PUBLISHING CORPORATION   .60
STEINER   2
  HOLIDAY IN LISBON, FOLK DANCE
    BELWIN-MILLS PUBLISHING CORPORATION   .60
STEINER   2 1/2
  IDA, SWEET AS APPLE CIDER
    BELWIN-MILLS PUBLISHING CORPORATION   .60
STEINER   1
  IT AIN'T GONNA RAIN
    BELWIN-MILLS PUBLISHING CORPORATION   .60
STEINER   1
  JOY OF LIFE
    BELWIN-MILLS PUBLISHING CORPORATION   .60
STEINER   2 1/2
  JUBILATION, RECITAL ETUDE
    BELWIN-MILLS PUBLISHING CORPORATION   .60
STEINER   2-3
  KALEIDOSCOPE
    CENTURY MUSIC PUBLISHING COMPANY, INC.   4180   .40
STEINER   3
  KNICK-KNACKS
    BELWIN-MILLS PUBLISHING CORPORATION   .60
STEINER   3
  LA CUCARACHA BOOGIE
    BELWIN-MILLS PUBLISHING CORPORATION   .60
STEINER   2
  LIFE ON THE OCEAN WAVE, A -- SAILORS' MARCH
    BELWIN-MILLS PUBLISHING CORPORATION   .60
STEINER   2
  LITTLE GHOSTS ARE MARCHING
    CENTURY MUSIC PUBLISHING COMPANY, INC.   3529   .40
STEINER   1 1/2
  LOVE THAT BOOGIE
    BELWIN-MILLS PUBLISHING CORPORATION   .60
STEINER   1
  MAID OF SORRENTO
    BELWIN-MILLS PUBLISHING CORPORATION   .60
STEINER   2
  MARCH ON THE BLACK KEYS
    CENTURY MUSIC PUBLISHING COMPANY, INC.   3527   .40
STEINER   2
  MELLOW CELLO, THE
    BELWIN-MILLS PUBLISHING CORPORATION   .60
STEINER   2
  MICHAEL FINNIGAN -- FOLK TUNE
    BELWIN-MILLS PUBLISHING CORPORATION   .60
STEINER   2
  MOCCASIN FLOWER
    BELWIN-MILLS PUBLISHING CORPORATION   .60
STEINER   JR. APPR.
  MUSIC OUTDOORS
    BELWIN-MILLS PUBLISHING CORPORATION   .60
STEINER   2
  OAK AND THE ASH, THE -- PIANO SOLO WITH WORDS
    BELWIN-MILLS PUBLISHING CORPORATION   .60
STEINER   JR. APPR.
  OLD ABE LINCOLN
    BELWIN-MILLS PUBLISHING CORPORATION   .60

STEINER   1
      PARACHUTISTS, THE
         CENTURY MUSIC PUBLISHING COMPANY, INC.   3755   .40
STEINER   1
      PARASOL PARADE
         BELWIN-MILLS PUBLISHING CORPORATION   .60
STEINER   1
      PING PONG
         CENTURY MUSIC PUBLISHING COMPANY, INC.   3756   .40
STEINER   3
      PIROUETTES
         BELWIN-MILLS PUBLISHING CORPORATION   .60
STEINER   2
      PUPPET SHOW, THE
         CENTURY MUSIC PUBLISHING COMPANY, INC.   3696   .40
STEINER   2
      QUEEN OF THE RODEO
         CENTURY MUSIC PUBLISHING COMPANY, INC.   3994   .40
STEINER   2
      RIDE IN A JEEP, A
         CENTURY MUSIC PUBLISHING COMPANY, INC.   3757   .40
STEINER   2 1/2
      ROMANCE OF THE SPACE AGE
         BELWIN-MILLS PUBLISHING CORPORATION   .60
STEINER   JR. APPR.
      ROSE OF TRALEE, THE
         BELWIN-MILLS PUBLISHING CORPORATION   .60
STEINER   2
      RUFF AND TUFF
         CENTURY MUSIC PUBLISHING COMPANY, INC.   3996   .40
STEINER   3
      RUMPUS ROOM
         BELWIN-MILLS PUBLISHING CORPORATION   .60
STEINER   2
      SCOUT CAMPOREE
         BELWIN-MILLS PUBLISHING CORPORATION   .60
STEINER   2
      SONG FROM OLD CHINATOWN
         CENTURY MUSIC PUBLISHING COMPANY, INC.   3526   .40
STEINER   2
      SONG OF THE MARINER
         CENTURY MUSIC PUBLISHING COMPANY, INC.   3698   .40
STEINER   3 1/2
      ST. LOUIS IMPROVISATIONS
         BELWIN-MILLS PUBLISHING CORPORATION   .60
STEINER   3 1/2
      SWEET SIXTEEN
         BELWIN-MILLS PUBLISHING CORPORATION   .60
STEINER   1
      SWINGING IN A HAMMOCK
         BELWIN-MILLS PUBLISHING CORPORATION   .60
STEINER   FREEMAN
      TARA THEME
         WARNER BROTHERS PUBLISHERS   1.00
STEINER   RICHTER
      TARA THEME -- MY OWN TRUE LOVE
         WARNER BROTHERS PUBLISHERS   .75
STEINER
      THEME FROM A SUMMER PLACE
         WARNER BROTHERS PUBLISHERS   1.00
STEINER   RICHTER
      THEME FROM A SUMMER PLACE
         WARNER BROTHERS PUBLISHERS   .75
STEINER   1 1/2
      THERE'S A HOLE IN MY BUCKET
         BELWIN-MILLS PUBLISHING CORPORATION   .60
STEINER   3
      THOROUGHBREDS
         BELWIN-MILLS PUBLISHING CORPORATION   .60
STEINER   2
      THREE CHEERS FOR THE TEAM
         CENTURY MUSIC PUBLISHING COMPANY, INC.   3998   .40
STEINER   E
      TOCCATA
         BELWIN-MILLS PUBLISHING CORPORATION   25136   .60
STEINER   3
      TOCCATA
         BELWIN-MILLS PUBLISHING CORPORATION   .60
STEINER   2 1/2
      TOMBOYS
         BELWIN-MILLS PUBLISHING CORPORATION   .60
STEINER   2
      TOPSY TURVY
         CENTURY MUSIC PUBLISHING COMPANY, INC.   3697   .40
STEINER   3
      TRAILING THE LONESOME ROAD
         BELWIN-MILLS PUBLISHING CORPORATION   .60
STEINER   3 1/2
      TSCHAIKOWSKY GEMS
         BELWIN-MILLS PUBLISHING CORPORATION   .60
STEINER   3
      TWILIGHT INTERLUDE
         BELWIN-MILLS PUBLISHING CORPORATION   .60
STEINER   2 1/2
      VIGNETTE
         BELWIN-MILLS PUBLISHING CORPORATION   .60
STEINER   2
      VIVE LA COMPAGNIE
         BELWIN-MILLS PUBLISHING CORPORATION   .60
STEINER   2
      WALK THROUGH THE PARK, A
         CENTURY MUSIC PUBLISHING COMPANY, INC.   3528   .40
STEINER   1 1/2
      WAYFARING STRANGER
         BELWIN-MILLS PUBLISHING CORPORATION   .60
STEINER   1 1/2
      WHITE AND BLACK IVORIES
         BELWIN-MILLS PUBLISHING CORPORATION   .60
STEINER   2
      WITCHCRAFT
         CENTURY MUSIC PUBLISHING COMPANY, INC.   4033   .40
STEINER   2
      WON'T YOU COME HOME, BILL BAILEY
         BELWIN-MILLS PUBLISHING CORPORATION   .60
STEINER   1 1/2
      YOU TELL ME YOUR DREAMS
         BELWIN-MILLS PUBLISHING CORPORATION   .60
STEINER *   NEALE, J.   EASY
      SUMMER PLACE, A, THEME FROM
         WARNER BROTHERS PUBLISHERS   .75
STEINER--ED.   STEINER   1 1/2
      ALPINE YODEL, FOLK MELODY
         BELWIN-MILLS PUBLISHING CORPORATION   .60
STEINER--ED.   STEINER   1
      AURA LEE
         BELWIN-MILLS PUBLISHING CORPORATION   .50

STEINER--ED.   STEINER   1
      BEAUTIFUL ISLE OF SOMEWHERE
         BELWIN-MILLS PUBLISHING CORPORATION   .50
STEINER--ED.   STEINER   PREPARATORY
      BEAUTIFUL SAVIOUR
         BELWIN-MILLS PUBLISHING CORPORATION   .50
STEINER--ED.   STEINER
      FORGOTTEN DREAMS -- SIMP.
         BELWIN-MILLS PUBLISHING CORPORATION   26070   .50
STEINER--ED.   STEINER   2
      GIVE ME THAT OLD-TIME RELIGION -- SPIRITUAL
         BELWIN-MILLS PUBLISHING CORPORATION   .60
STEINER--ED.   STEINER
      HEY, MR. BANJO
         BELWIN-MILLS PUBLISHING CORPORATION   25092   .50
STEINER--ED.   STEINER   1
      PARISIAN SCENE FROM 'MANON'
         CENTURY MUSIC PUBLISHING COMPANY, INC.   4314   .40
STEINER--ED.   STEINER   1
      POLONAISE FROM 'MIGNON'
         CENTURY MUSIC PUBLISHING COMPANY, INC.   4315   .40
STEINER--ED.   STEINER
      SLEIGH RIDE -- CHILDREN'S EDITION
         BELWIN-MILLS PUBLISHING CORPORATION   25133   .50
STEINER--ED.   STEINER
      SYNCOPATED CLOCK, THE -- CHILDREN'S EDITION
         BELWIN-MILLS PUBLISHING CORPORATION   25134   .50
STEINER--ED.   STEINER
      WALTZING CAT, THE
         BELWIN-MILLS PUBLISHING CORPORATION   25135   .50
STEINER, G.
      FANTASY PIECE FOR PIANO, 1966
         SEESAW MUSIC CORPORATION   4.00
STEINER, G.
      PIANO SONATA, 1964
         SEESAW MUSIC CORPORATION   6.00
STEINER, G.
      THREE PIECES FOR PIANO, 1961
         SEESAW MUSIC CORPORATION   3.00
STEINERT, A.
      BARCAROLLE
         UNIVERSAL EDITION   UE 10407   .95
STEINERT, A.
      SONATA
         UNIVERSAL EDITION   UE 9998   2.55
STEPAN
      MENUETTE
         BARENREITER VERLAG   MVH 9
STEPAN
      REVES NOSTALGIQUES -- FANTASY IN THE FORM OF VARIATIONS --
         FRANCO COLOMBO PUBLICATIONS   SAL   5.50
STEPHENS, A.   2
      LITTLE GOLDEN HARP, THE
         WILLIS MUSIC COMPANY   .40
STEPHENS, A.   2
      LITTLE GOLDEN HARP, THE
         WILLIS MUSIC COMPANY   .40
STERN
      ALHAMBRA
         BOSTON MUSIC COMPANY   .50
STERNBERG   M-D
      CAPRICE HIPPIQUE
         C. F. PETERS CORPORATION   3161C   .90
STERNKLAR, A.   2 1/2
      BAMIDBAR -- IN THE DESERT
         THEODORE PRESSER COMPANY   .50
STERNKLAR, A.   2 1/2
      BRISK MARCH, A
         THEODORE PRESSER COMPANY   .50
STERNKLAR, A.
      NORTHERN LIGHTS
         SUMMY-BIRCHARD COMPANY   .50
STERNKLAR, A.   2
      SAD LITTLE CAT
         THEODORE PRESSER COMPANY   .50
STEVENS
      BALLERINA
         CARL FISCHER, INC.   .   RS 343   .50
STEVENS
      CELLO SERENADE
         CARL FISCHER, INC.   RS 344   .50
STEVENS
      COME BACK TO SORRENTO
         CARL FISCHER, INC.   RS 367   .50
STEVENS
      COMMANCHE
         CARL FISCHER, INC.   RS 356   .50
STEVENS
      DISTANT HILLS, THE
         CARL FISCHER, INC.   RS403   .50
STEVENS
      FUNNY ESKIMO
         CARL FISCHER, INC.   P 2875   .50
STEVENS
      HOMAGE TO RAVEL
         CARL FISCHER, INC.   RS 457   .50
STEVENS
      ONCE UPON A TIME
         CARL FISCHER, INC.   P 2890   .50
STEVENS
      OZARK REEL
         FRANCO COLOMBO PUBLICATIONS   NY1607   .35
STEVENS
      PRAIRIE SUNSET
         CARL FISCHER, INC.   RS 376   .50
STEVENS
      TRAIL OF THE COVERED WAGON
         CARL FISCHER, INC.   RS 421   .50
STEVENS
      TWILIGHT WALTZ
         CARL FISCHER, INC.   P 3011   .50
STEVENS
      WHITE CLOUDS
         CARL FISCHER, INC.   P 2854   .50
STEVENS, E.   2
      ANIMAL PARADE
         BELWIN-MILLS PUBLISHING CORPORATION   .60
STEVENS, E.   2 1/2
      AUTUMN FIELDS
         THEODORE PRESSER COMPANY   .50
STEVENS, E.   1 1/2 - 2
      BIRD CHATTER
         ELKAN-VOGEL, INC.   .50
STEVENS, E.   3
      BUCK 'N' WING
         BELWIN-MILLS PUBLISHING CORPORATION   .60

STEVENS, E.   2
    DRUM MAJOR, THE
        THEODORE PRESSER COMPANY   .50
STEVENS, E.   2
    DRUMS FROM A DISTANCE
        THEODORE PRESSER COMPANY   .50
STEVENS, E.   2
    EVENING SERENADE
        THEODORE PRESSER COMPANY   .50
STEVENS, E.   E
    FIVE O'CLOCK TRAFFIC
        BELWIN-MILLS PUBLISHING CORPORATION   25129   .60
STEVENS, E.   1 - 1/2
    IN AUTUMN
        ELKAN-VOGEL, INC.   .50
STEVENS, E.   2
    JO-JO THE JUGGLER
        BELWIN-MILLS PUBLISHING CORPORATION   .60
STEVENS, E.   1
    LET'S HAVE FUN
        CENTURY MUSIC PUBLISHING COMPANY, INC.   4366   .40
STEVENS, E.   2
    LITTLE SHEPHERDESS, THE
        THEODORE PRESSER COMPANY   .50
STEVENS, E.   2 1/2
    MORNING MIST
        THEODORE PRESSER COMPANY   .50
STEVENS, E.   1
    OF LONG AGO
        VOLKWEIN BROS.   .35
STEVENS, E.   2
    ON A HAYRIDE
        THEODORE PRESSER COMPANY   .50
STEVENS, E.   EASY
    PARADE OF THE PENGUINS
        SHAWNEE PRESS, INC.   HB-5003   .60
STEVENS, E.   2 1/2
    PLAYTIME
        THEODORE PRESSER COMPANY   .50
STEVENS, E.   2 1/2
    SET OF THREE
        THEODORE PRESSER COMPANY   .50
STEVENS, E.   2 1/2
    SOFT RAIN
        THEODORE PRESSER COMPANY   .50
STEVENS, E.   2
    SONG FROM THE HILLS
        THEODORE PRESSER COMPANY   .50
STEVENS, E.   2 1/2
    TOY WALTZ
        THEODORE PRESSER COMPANY   .50
STEVENS, E.   2
    TUNES IN FOLK STYLE
        THEODORE PRESSER COMPANY   .50
STEVENS, E.   1
    UP IN THE SWING
        WILLIS MUSIC COMPANY   .35
STEVENS, E.   1 1/2
    WALTZ FOR A LITTLE DOLL
        THEODORE PRESSER COMPANY   .50
STEVENS, E.   1
    YELLOW BUTTERFLIES
        CENTURY MUSIC PUBLISHING COMPANY, INC.   4306   .40
STEVENS, H.   M
    LYRIC PIECE
        THEODORE PRESSER COMPANY   .50
STEVENS, H.
    PARTITA
        PEER SOUTHERN ORGANIZATION   02.00
STEVENS, H.
    SONATA NO. 03 FOR PIANOFORTE
        AMERICAN MUSIC EDITION   2.00
STEVENS, L.   E
    LET'S LOOK OUTDOORS
        COMPOSERS PRESS, INC.   1.50
STEVENS, M.   1
    APRIL FLOWERS
        THEODORE PRESSER COMPANY   .50
STEVENS, M.   5
    GAY DAFFODILS
        THEODORE PRESSER COMPANY   .50
STEVENS, M.   2 1/2
    LIVELY DANCE, A
        THEODORE PRESSER COMPANY   .50
STEVENS, M.   2 1/2
    NODDING POPPIES
        THEODORE PRESSER COMPANY   .50
STEVENS, M.   2 1/2
    ON A BRIGHT BLUE SEA
        THEODORE PRESSER COMPANY   .60
STEVENS, M.   1 1/2
    ROLLING HOOPS
        THEODORE PRESSER COMPANY   .50
STEVENS, R.   3
    DANCE OF THE CANNIBALS
        BELWIN-MILLS PUBLISHING CORPORATION   .60
STEVENSON, R.
    PASSACAGLIA ON D-S-C-H-
        OXFORD UNIVERSITY PRESS   32.147   12.00
STEVENSON, R.
    PRELUDE, FUGUE AND FANTASY
        NOVELLO AND COMPANY, LTD.   10.0172.08 3.75
STEWART
    ECHO TANGO
        MCA MUSIC   1.00
STEWART, H.
    INTERLUDE
        COMPOSERS AUTOGRAPH PUBLICATIONS   .88
STEWART, H.
    ROMANCE
        COMPOSERS AUTOGRAPH PUBLICATIONS   .66
STIEFEL, E.   E
    DANCING DOLL
        COMPOSERS PRESS, INC.   1.00
STIEFEL, E.   E
    HAPPY BIRTHDAY
        COMPOSERS PRESS, INC.   1.00
STIEFEL, E.   E
    LITTLE TOCCATA
        COMPOSERS PRESS, INC.   1.00
STIEFEL, E.   E
    LONDON BRIDGE IS FALLING, THE
        COMPOSERS PRESS, INC.   1.00
STIEFEL, E.   E
    MY PRANDING PONY
        COMPOSERS PRESS, INC.   1.00

STIEFEL, E.   E
    YANKEE DOODLE
        COMPOSERS PRESS, INC.   1.00
STILL
    MARIONETTE
        MCA MUSIC   .75
STILWELL
    ATTIC PLAYROOM, THE
        EDWARD B. MARKS MUSIC CORPORATION   00.60
STILWELL   WILLIAMS
    BANJO PLAYER, THE
        BOSTON MUSIC COMPANY   .50
STILWELL
    CHIMING BELLS
        EDWARD B. MARKS MUSIC CORPORATION   00.60
STILWELL
    HOP TOAD
        CARL FISCHER, INC.   P 2707   .50
STILWELL
    JOLLY MEN ARE WE
        EDWARD B. MARKS MUSIC CORPORATION   00.60
STILWELL
    MARCHING TO THE MUSIC
        EDWARD B. MARKS MUSIC CORPORATION   00.60
STILWELL
    MOSEYIN' ALONG
        EDWARD B. MARKS MUSIC CORPORATION   00.60
STILWELL
    PINK LADY
        CARL FISCHER, INC.   P 2708   .50
STILWELL
    SWINGING IN THE GARDEN
        EDWARD B. MARKS MUSIC CORPORATION   00.60
STILWELL   WILLIAMS, J.   3
    TARANTELL
        BOSTON MUSIC COMPANY   .50
STOCKBRIDGE, J.   1 1/2
    INDIAN RAIN DANCE
        THEODORE PRESSER COMPANY   .50
STOCKHAUSEN, K.
    FROM THE SEVEN DAYS
        UNIVERSAL EDITION   UE 14790 6.25
STOCKHAUSEN, K.
    NO. 2 PIANO PIECES 1-4
        UNIVERSAL EDITION   UE 12251 4.00
STOCKHAUSEN, K.
    NO. 4 PIANO PIECES 10
        UNIVERSAL EDITION   UE 13675F 9.45
STOCKHAUSEN, K.
    NO. 4 PIANO PIECES 5
        UNIVERSAL EDITION   UE 13675A 3.55
STOCKHAUSEN, K.
    NO. 4 PIANO PIECES 6
        UNIVERSAL EDITION   UE 13675B 9.45
STOCKHAUSEN, K.
    NO. 4 PIANO PIECES 7
        UNIVERSAL EDITION   UE 13675C 4.20
STOCKHAUSEN, K.
    NO. 4 PIANO PIECES 8
        UNIVERSAL EDITION   UE 13675D 4.50
STOCKHAUSEN, K.
    NO. 4 PIANO PIECES 9
        UNIVERSAL EDITION   UE 13675E 4.20
STOCKHAUSEN, K.
    NO. 7 PIANO PIECES 11 -- IN ROLL WITH STAND
        UNIVERSAL EDITION   UE 12654B 21.75
STOCKHAUSEN, K.
    NO. 7 PIANO PIECES 11 -- IN ROLL WITHOUT STAND
        UNIVERSAL EDITION   UE 12654A 4.90
STODDARD   2
    EVERGREEN WALTZ
        CENTURY MUSIC PUBLISHING COMPANY, INC.   1005   .40
STOHR, R.
    FIVE PIANO PIECES, OP. 23
        UNIVERSAL EDITION   UE 3054   2.75
STOHR, R.
    VON DEN MADCHEN, OP. 64 -- 12 PIECES
        UNIVERSAL EDITION   UE 6625   2.75
STOJOWSKI, S.   4
    VALSE, OP. 12 NO. 2 -- DANSE HUMORESQUE
        THEODORE PRESSER COMPANY   .50
STOKER
    POET'S NOTEBOOK, A
        MCA MUSIC   1.25
STOLZ
    HARBOR ROMANCE
        MCA MUSIC   1.00
STOLZE, R.   M
    GREEN EARTH
        COMPOSERS PRESS, INC.   2.00
STOLZE, R.   M-D
    MINIATURES
        COMPOSERS PRESS, INC.   2.00
STOLZE, R.   M-D
    TRAFFIC DANCE
        COMPOSERS PRESS, INC.   2.00
STOLZEL
    MINUET IN G MINOR
        FREDERICK HARRIS MUSIC COMPANY   .60
STONE, C.
    CHINESE BOY, THE
        FREDERICK HARRIS MUSIC COMPANY   .60
STONE, E.   2
    DEW DROP
        CENTURY MUSIC PUBLISHING COMPANY, INC.   3806   .40
STONE, E.   2
    HARVEST TIME
        CENTURY MUSIC PUBLISHING COMPANY, INC.   3851   .40
STONE, E.   2
    LIGHT AND SHADOW
        CENTURY MUSIC PUBLISHING COMPANY, INC.   3852   .40
STONE, E.   2
    ON TIPTOES
        CENTURY MUSIC PUBLISHING COMPANY, INC.   3818   .40
STONE, E.   2
    SOUTHERN SONATINA
        CENTURY MUSIC PUBLISHING COMPANY, INC.   3945   .40
STONE, E.   2
    SWORD DANCE, THE
        CENTURY MUSIC PUBLISHING COMPANY, INC.   3819   .40
STONE, E.--ED   STONE, E.
    I GOT PLENTY O' NUTTIN'
        CHAPPELL AND COMPANY, INC.   2230027-1501 .95
STONE, E.--ED   STONE, E.
    SUMMERTIME
        CHAPPELL AND COMPANY, INC.   5565023   .95

STONE, E.--ED   STONE, E.
  SUMMERTIME, STONE CONCERT ARR.
    CHAPPELL AND COMPANY, INC.   5565023-502 1.00
STONE, E.--ED   STONE, E.
  YESTERDAYS
    CIMINO PUBLICATIONS, INC.   H   1.25
STONE, M.
  VARIATIONS ON THE THEME, LITTLE SUZI
    COMPOSERS AUTOGRAPH PUBLICATIONS   1.76
                                 2
STORR, S.
  BACK COUNTRY BALLAD
    BELWIN-MILLS PUBLISHING CORPORATION   .60
STORR, S.   1 1/2
  CHANT OF THE BIRD WOMAN
    THEODORE PRESSER COMPANY   .50
STORR, S.   2
  DIGGING IN YUCCA FLAT
    THEODORE PRESSER COMPANY   .50
STORR, S.
  ECHO IN THE CANYON
    BELWIN-MILLS PUBLISHING CORPORATION   .60
STORR, S.   3
  ELYSIAN SUITE
    BELWIN-MILLS PUBLISHING CORPORATION   1.00
STORR, S.   2
  GRECIAN SUITE
    BOSTON MUSIC COMPANY   .60
STORR, S.   1
  KABUKI DANCE
    CENTURY MUSIC PUBLISHING COMPANY, INC. 4399   .40
STORR, S.
  KING MIDAS
    BRODT MUSIC COMPANY   .40
STORR, S.
  LULLABY FOR A CHERUB
    BRODT MUSIC COMPANY   .40
STORR, S.   2
  ON A VICTORIAN VERANDA
    BOSTON MUSIC COMPANY   .50
STORR, S.
  SCARECROW SHUFFLE
    BRODT MUSIC COMPANY   .40
STORR, S.
  SONATINE
    BRODT MUSIC COMPANY   1.00
STORR, S.   2 1/2
  TONTO TRAIL
    THEODORE PRESSER COMPANY   .50
STOWE, F.   2
  SWAYING PALMS
    THEODORE PRESSER COMPANY   .50
STRADELLA   DEL MAGLIO
  PRAYER
    FRANCO COLOMBO PUBLICATIONS   128141   .50
STRAIGHT, W.
  STRUCTURE FOR PIANO
    BOOSEY AND HAWKES, INC.   1.00
STRATEGIER   M-D
  SONATINA
    C. F. PETERS CORPORATION   D215   1.25
STRAUS, J.   SCHAUM, J.   2
  DRAGON FLY, THE
    BELWIN-MILLS PUBLISHING CORPORATION   .50
STRAUS, O.   SCHAUM, J.   2
  WALTZ DREAM
    BELWIN-MILLS PUBLISHING CORPORATION   .50
STRAUS, O.   3-4
  WALTZ DREAM, A
    CENTURY MUSIC PUBLISHING COMPANY, INC. 2458   .40
STRAUSS, J.
  ACCELERATION WALTZ
    MCA MUSIC   .60
STRAUSS, J.   3
  ACCELERATION WALTZ
    THEODORE PRESSER COMPANY   .50
STRAUSS, J.
  ACCELERATIONS, OP. 234
    FRANCO COLOMBO PUBLICATIONS   BA6608   .75
STRAUSS, J.   DEL MAGLIO
  ACCELERATIONS, OP. 234
    FRANCO COLOMBO PUBLICATIONS   124734   .50
STRAUSS, J.   3
  ANNEN POLKA
    CENTURY MUSIC PUBLISHING COMPANY, INC. 3379   .60
STRAUSS, J.   SCHAUM, J.   4 1/2
  ARTIST'S LIFE
    BELWIN-MILLS PUBLISHING CORPORATION   .50
STRAUSS, J.
  ARTIST'S LIFE
    FRANCO COLOMBO PUBLICATIONS   SAL   1.50
STRAUSS, J.   5
  ARTIST'S LIFE
    WILLIS MUSIC COMPANY   .40
STRAUSS, J.
  ARTIST'S LIFE, OP. 316
    FRANCO COLOMBO PUBLICATIONS   BA6656   .75
STRAUSS, J.   DEL MAGLIO
  ARTIST'S LIFE, OP. 316
    FRANCO COLOMBO PUBLICATIONS   124737   .60
STRAUSS, J.
  ARTISTS' LIFE--WALTZ, OP. 316
    G. SCHIRMER, INC.   .70
STRAUSS, J.   4
  ARTISTS'S LIFE
    CENTURY MUSIC PUBLISHING COMPANY, INC. 3495   .40
STRAUSS, J.
  BAT, THE
    EDWARD B. MARKS MUSIC CORPORATION   01.00
STRAUSS, J.   4
  BEAUTIFUL BLUE DANUBE
    CENTURY MUSIC PUBLISHING COMPANY, INC. 514   .40
STRAUSS, J.   4
  BEAUTIFUL BLUE DANUBE
    CENTURY MUSIC PUBLISHING COMPANY, INC. 514   .40
STRAUSS, J.   THOMPSON, J.   5
  BEAUTIFUL BLUE DANUBE
    WILLIS MUSIC COMPANY   .60
STRAUSS, J.   3
  BEAUTIFUL BLUE DANUBE IN C
    CENTURY MUSIC PUBLISHING COMPANY, INC. 3622   .40
STRAUSS, J.   DEL MAGLIO
  BEAUTIFUL MAY, OP. 375
    FRANCO COLOMBO PUBLICATIONS   124742   .60
STRAUSS, J.
  BLUE DANUBE
    FRANCO COLOMBO PUBLICATIONS   SAL   1.50

STRAUSS, J.
  BLUE DANUBE
    FRANCO COLOMBO PUBLICATIONS   SAL   1.50
STRAUSS, J.   SCHAUM, J.   3
  BLUE DANUBE
    SCHAUM PUBLICATIONS, INC.   .60
STRAUSS, J.   TRUXELL, E.   1 1/2
  BLUE DANUBE
    VOLKWEIN BROS.   .30
STRAUSS, J.   SCHAUM, J.   2
  BLUE DANUBE IN REVERSE
    BELWIN-MILLS PUBLISHING CORPORATION   .50
STRAUSS, J.   4
  BLUE DANUBE OP. 314
    THEODORE PRESSER COMPANY   .50
STRAUSS, J.   WEYBRIGHT   1 1/2
  BLUE DANUBE WALTZ
    BELWIN-MILLS PUBLISHING CORPORATION   .50
STRAUSS, J.   WALLIS
  BLUE DANUBE WALTZ
    BOSTON MUSIC COMPANY   .50
STRAUSS, J.
  BLUE DANUBE WALTZ
    CARL FISCHER, INC.   S 1118   .50
STRAUSS, J.   ECKSTEIN
  BLUE DANUBE WALTZ
    CARL FISCHER, INC.   S 2285   .50
STRAUSS, J.   STREABBOG   2
  BLUE DANUBE WALTZ
    CENTURY MUSIC PUBLISHING COMPANY, INC. 3242   .40
STRAUSS, J.   3
  BLUE DANUBE WALTZ
    CENTURY MUSIC PUBLISHING COMPANY, INC. 3622   .40
STRAUSS, J.   MITTLER   2B
  BLUE DANUBE WALTZ
    MUSICORD PUBLICATIONS, INC.   .45
STRAUSS, J.   KING, S.
  BLUE DANUBE WALTZ
    SHAWNEE PRESS, INC.   HB-5030   .60
STRAUSS, J.
  BLUE DANUBE WALTZ --SIMPLIFIED--
    CARL FISCHER, INC.   S 1120   .60
STRAUSS, J.   4
  BLUE DANUBE WALTZ, D MAJOR
    CENTURY MUSIC PUBLISHING COMPANY, INC. 514   .40
STRAUSS, J.   2
  BLUE DANUBE WALTZ, EASY
    CENTURY MUSIC PUBLISHING COMPANY, INC. 2122   .40
STRAUSS, J.   ZEPP   2-3
  BLUE DANUBE WALTZ, THE
    PRO-ART PUBLICATIONS, INC.   194   .50
STRAUSS, J.
  CLEAR THE TRACK POLKA
    MCA MUSIC   .60
STRAUSS, J.   3
  DRAGON FLY, POLKA MAZURKA
    CENTURY MUSIC PUBLISHING COMPANY, INC. 2587   .40
STRAUSS, J.   4
  DREAMING, REVERIE
    CENTURY MUSIC PUBLISHING COMPANY, INC. 2351   .40
STRAUSS, J.   STEINER
  DRINKING SONG -- FROM 'DIE FLEDERMAUS'
    BELWIN-MILLS PUBLISHING CORPORATION 26012   .60
STRAUSS, J.   4
  DU UND DU -- FLEDERMAUS WALTZ
    CENTURY MUSIC PUBLISHING COMPANY, INC. 3426   .40
STRAUSS, J.   SCHAUM, J.   2
  EMPEROR WALTZ
    BELWIN-MILLS PUBLISHING CORPORATION   .50
STRAUSS, J.   PENNARIO
  EMPEROR WALTZ
    BELWIN-MILLS PUBLISHING CORPORATION 20078   1.50
STRAUSS, J.   WALLIS   2
  EMPEROR WALTZ
    BOSTON MUSIC COMPANY   .50
STRAUSS, J.   4
  EMPEROR WALTZ
    CENTURY MUSIC PUBLISHING COMPANY, INC. 3430   .40
STRAUSS, J.
  EMPEROR WALTZ
    EDWARD B. MARKS MUSIC CORPORATION   01.75
STRAUSS, J.   ZEPP   3
  EMPEROR WALTZ
    PRO-ART PUBLICATIONS, INC.   196   .50
STRAUSS, J.
  EMPEROR WALTZ, OP. 437
    FRANCO COLOMBO PUBLICATIONS   .75
STRAUSS, J.   DEL MAGLIO
  EMPEROR WALTZ, OP. 437
    FRANCO COLOMBO PUBLICATIONS   124748   .60
STRAUSS, J.
  EMPEROR WALTZ, THE, OP. 437
    G. SCHIRMER, INC.   .75
STRAUSS, J.   KOVACS, S.
  FLEDERMAUS PARAPHRASE--ON AIRS FROM 'THE BAT'
    G. SCHIRMER, INC.   .90
STRAUSS, J.   WEYBRIGHT   2 1/2
  FLEDERMAUS, DIE
    BELWIN-MILLS PUBLISHING CORPORATION   .50
STRAUSS, J.   WEYBRIGHT   2 1/2
  FLEDERMAUS, DIE
    BELWIN-MILLS PUBLISHING CORPOPATION   .60
STRAUSS, J.   DORATI
  GRADUATION BALL
    BELWIN-MILLS PUBLISHING CORPORATION 07047   4.00
STRAUSS, J.
  GYPSY BARON OVERTURE, THE
    MCA MUSIC   .60
STRAUSS, J.   STEINER   2
  GYPSY BARON POLKA
    BELWIN-MILLS PUBLISHING CORPORATION   .60
STRAUSS, J.   3
  GYPSY BARON WALTZES
    CENTURY MUSIC PUBLISHING COMPANY, INC. 237   .40
STRAUSS, J.   DEL MAGLIO
  KISS WALTZ, OP. 411
    FRANCO COLOMBO PUBLICATIONS   124744   .60
STRAUSS, J.   DEL MAGLIO
  LAGOON WALTZ, OP. 411
    FRANCO COLOMBO PUBLICATIONS   124746   .60
STRAUSS, J.   STEINER
  LAUGHING SONG -- FROM 'DIE FLEDERMAUS'
    BELWIN-MILLS PUBLISHING CORPORATION 26025   .60
STRAUSS, J.
  MORNING PAPERS, OP. 279
    FRANCO COLOMBO PUBLICATIONS   BA6646   .75

STRAUSS, J.   DEL MAGLIO
    MORNING PAPERS, OP. 279
        FRANCO COLOMBO PUBLICATIONS   .60
STRAUSS, J.   4
    NIGHT IN VENICE, WALTZES
        CENTURY MUSIC PUBLISHING COMPANY, INC.   3342   .40
STRAUSS, J.   DEIS *
    ON THE BEAUTIFUL BLUE DANUBE
        G. SCHIRMER, INC.   .60
STRAUSS, J.   SCHULZ-EVLER
    ON THE BEAUTIFUL BLUE DANUBE--CONCERT ARABESQUE
        G. SCHIRMER, INC.   .90
STRAUSS, J.
    ON THE BEAUTIFUL BLUE DANUBE, OP. 314
        FRANCO COLOMBO PUBLICATIONS   40735   1.00
STRAUSS, J.
    ON THE BEAUTIFUL BLUE DANUBE, OP. 314
        FRANCO COLOMBO PUBLICATIONS   40967   .60
STRAUSS, J.   DEL MAGLIO
    ON THE BEAUTIFUL BLUE DANUBE, OP. 314
        FRANCO COLOMBO PUBLICATIONS   124736   .60
STRAUSS, J.
    ON THE BEAUTIFUL BLUE DANUBE, OP. 314
        G. SCHIRMER, INC.   .70
STRAUSS, J.   3
    ONE HEART, ONE SOUL
        CENTURY MUSIC PUBLISHING COMPANY, INC.   347   .40
STRAUSS, J.   3
    PIZZICATO POLKA
        CENTURY MUSIC PUBLISHING COMPANY, INC.   359   .40
STRAUSS, J.   PALMERI
    PIZZICATO POLKA
        G. SCHIRMER, INC.   .40
STRAUSS, J.   STEINER
    PRINCE ORLOFSKY'S SONG -- FROM 'DIE FLEDERMAUS'
        BELWIN-MILLS PUBLISHING CORPORATION   26039   .60
STRAUSS, J.
    QUADRILLE ON OFFENBACH'S 'LA VIE PARISIENNE'
        FRANCO COLOMBO PUBLICATIONS   SAL   1.75
STRAUSS, J.   4
    ROSES FROM THE SOUTH
        CENTURY MUSIC PUBLISHING COMPANY, INC.   1493   .40
STRAUSS, J.
    ROSES FROM THE SOUTH, OP. 388
        FRANCO COLOMBO PUBLICATIONS   BA6583   .75
STRAUSS, J.   DEL MAGLIO
    ROSES FROM THE SOUTH, OP. 388
        FRANCO COLOMBO PUBLICATIONS   124743   .60
STRAUSS, J.
    SIEHE, TANZE UND MARSCHE, SEITE 15
        SCHOTT
STRAUSS, J.   3
    SWEETHEART WALTZES, GYPSY BARON
        CENTURY MUSIC PUBLISHING COMPANY, INC.   237   .40
STRAUSS, J.   FLETCHER   2
    TALES FROM THE VIENNA WOODS
        BOSTON MUSIC COMPANY   .50
STRAUSS, J.   WALLIS   3
    TALES FROM THE VIENNA WOODS
        BOSTON MUSIC COMPANY   .50
STRAUSS, J.   4
    TALES FROM THE VIENNA WOODS
        CENTURY MUSIC PUBLISHING COMPANY, INC.   3241   .40
STRAUSS, J.
    TALES FROM THE VIENNA WOODS
        FRANCO COLOMBO PUBLICATIONS   SAL   1.50
STRAUSS, J.   MITTLER   2B
    TALES FROM THE VIENNA WOODS
        MUSICORD PUBLICATIONS, INC.   .45
STRAUSS, J.   TRUXELL, E.   2
    TALES FROM THE VIENNA WOODS
        VOLKWEIN BROS.   00.40
STRAUSS, J.
    TALES FROM THE VIENNA WOODS --WALTZ--, OP. 325
        CARL FISCHER, INC.   S 2047   .60
STRAUSS, J.   SCHAUM, J.   5
    TALES FROM THE VIENNA WOODS WALTZ
        BELWIN-MILLS PUBLISHING CORPORATION   .50
STRAUSS, J.   ECKSTEIN
    TALES FROM THE VIENNA WOODS WALTZ
        CARL FISCHER, INC.   S 2284   .50
STRAUSS, J.   TRUXELL, E.   3
    TALES FROM THE VIENNA WOODS WALTZ
        VOLKWEIN BROS.   00.50
STRAUSS, J.   PALMERI
    TALES FROM THE VIENNA WOODS--WALTZ
        G. SCHIRMER, INC.   .50
STRAUSS, J.
    TALES FROM THE VIENNA WOODS--WALTZ, OP. 325
        G. SCHIRMER, INC.   .75
STRAUSS, J.
    TALES FROM THE VIENNA WOODS, OP. 325
        FRANCO COLOMBO PUBLICATIONS   .75
STRAUSS, J.   DEL MAGLIO
    TALES FROM THE VIENNA WOODS, OP. 325
        FRANCO COLOMBO PUBLICATIONS   .60
STRAUSS, J.   BOHM   2
    TALES FROM VIENNA WOODS
        CENTURY MUSIC PUBLISHING COMPANY, INC.   894   .40
STRAUSS, J.   3
    TALES FROM VIENNA WOODS
        CENTURY MUSIC PUBLISHING COMPANY, INC.   3703   .40
STRAUSS, J.   4
    THOUSAND AND ONE NIGHTS
        CENTURY MUSIC PUBLISHING COMPANY, INC.   2442   .40
STRAUSS, J.
    THOUSAND AND ONE NIGHTS, OP. 346
        FRANCO COLOMBO PUBLICATIONS   BA6601   .75
STRAUSS, J.   SCHAUM, J.   2
    TIMBER AUCTION POLKA
        BELWIN-MILLS PUBLISHING CORPORATION   .50
STRAUSS, J.
    TREASURE WALTZ, OP. 418
        FRANCO COLOMBO PUBLICATIONS   BA6655   .75
STRAUSS, J.   DEL MAGLIO
    TREASURE WALTZ, OP. 418
        FRANCO COLOMBO PUBLICATIONS   124747   .60
STRAUSS, J.
    TRITSCH TRATSCH POLKA
        MCA MUSIC   .60
STRAUSS, J.   SCHAUM, J.   3
    TRITSCH TRATSCH POLKA, OP. 214
        BELWIN-MILLS PUBLISHING CORPORATION   .50
STRAUSS, J.   SCHAUM, J.   3
    VARSOVIANA
        BELWIN-MILLS PUBLISHING CORPORATION   .50

STRAUSS, J.
    VIENNA BLOOD, OP. 354
        FRANCO COLOMBO PUBLICATIONS   BA6581   .75
STRAUSS, J.   DEL MAGLIO
    VIENNA BLOOD, OP. 354
        FRANCO COLOMBO PUBLICATIONS   124740   .60
STRAUSS, J.   4
    VIENNA LIFE
        CENTURY MUSIC PUBLISHING COMPANY, INC.   3496   .40
STRAUSS, J.   THOMPSON, J.   5
    VIENNA LIFE
        WILLIS MUSIC COMPANY   .40
STRAUSS, J.   SCHAUM, J.   2
    VOICES OF SPRING
        BELWIN-MILLS PUBLISHING CORPORATION   .50
STRAUSS, J.   4
    VOICES OF SPRING
        CENTURY MUSIC PUBLISHING COMPANY, INC.   3436   .40
STRAUSS, J.
    VOICES OF SPRING
        FRANCO COLOMBO PUBLICATIONS   SAL   1.50
STRAUSS, J.
    VOICES OF SPRING--WALTZ, OP. 410
        G. SCHIRMER, INC.   .60
STRAUSS, J.
    VOICES OF SPRING, OP. 410
        FRANCO COLOMBO PUBLICATIONS   BA6587   .75
STRAUSS, J.   DEL MAGLIO
    VOICES OF SPRING, OP. 410
        FRANCO COLOMBO PUBLICATIONS   124745   .60
STRAUSS, J.
    WALDMEISTER--OVERTURE
        ASSOCIATED MUSIC PUBLISHERS, INC.   DOB   .90
STRAUSS, J.   TAUSIG
    WALTZ CAPRICE
        UNIVERSAL EDITION   3340   .60
STRAUSS, J.   4
    WALTZ FROM FLEDERMAUS
        CENTURY MUSIC PUBLISHING COMPANY, INC.   3426   .40
STRAUSS, J.   STEINER   2 1/2
    WEDDING CAKE
        BELWIN-MILLS PUBLISHING CORPORATION   .60
STRAUSS, J.
    WHERE THE CITRONS BLOOM
        MCA MUSIC   .60
STRAUSS, J.
    WIENER BLUT
        FRANCO COLOMBO PUBLICATIONS   SAL   1.50
STRAUSS, J.
    WINE, WOMEN AND SONG, OP. 333
        FRANCO COLOMBO PUBLICATIONS   BA6596   .75
STRAUSS, J.   DEL MAGLIO
    WINE, WOMEN AND SONG, OP. 333
        FRANCO COLOMBO PUBLICATIONS   124739   .50
STRAUSS, J.   DEL MAGLIO
    YOU AND YOU FROM 'FLEDERMAUS'
        FRANCO COLOMBO PUBLICATIONS   124741   .60
STRAUSS, J.   RASBACH, O.
    YOU AND YOU--WALTZES FROM 'THE BAT'
        G. SCHIRMER, INC.   .50
STRAUSS, J. *
    FLEDERMAUS - CONCERT PARAPHRASE
        PEER SOUTHERN ORGANIZATION   02.50
STRAUSS, J. *
    KUNSTLERIEBEN
        PEER SOUTHERN ORGANIZATION   02.75
STRAUSS, J. *   6
    ROSEN AUS DEM SUDEN, KONZERTWALZER
        SCHOTT   3712   2.00
STRAUSS, J. *
    WIEN, WEIB UND GESANG
        PEER SOUTHERN ORGANIZATION   02.50
STRAUSS, R.   SINGER
    ALPENSINFONIE, EINE, OP. 64
        ASSOCIATED MUSIC PUBLISHERS, INC.   LEU   6.00
STRAUSS, R.   PHILIPP, I.
    BURLESQUE
        INTERNATIONAL MUSIC COMPANY   2.50
STRAUSS, R.   SINGER
    CONCERT WALTZ, FROM 'DER ROSENKAVALIER'
        BOOSEY AND HAWKES, INC.   1.50
STRAUSS, R.   SINGER
    DANCE OF THE SEVEN VEILS, FROM 'SALOME'
        BOOSEY AND HAWKES, INC.   3.50
STRAUSS, R.   D
    DEATH AND TRANSFIGURATION, OP. 24
        C. F. PETERS CORPORATION   4193B   4.00
STRAUSS, R.   D
    DON JUAN, OP. 20
        C. F. PETERS CORPORATION   4193A   4.00
STRAUSS, R.   D
    DON QUIXOTE, OP. 35
        C. F. PETERS CORPORATION   4193E   4.00
STRAUSS, R.   4
    DREAM AT TWILIGHT
        CENTURY MUSIC PUBLISHING COMPANY, INC.   3921   .40
STRAUSS, R.   D
    ENOCH ARDEN, OP. 38. MELODRAMA
        C. F. PETERS CORPORATION   F59   3.50
STRAUSS, R.   4
    FLEDERMAUS, DIE, WALTZ
        CENTURY MUSIC PUBLISHING COMPANY, INC.   3426   .40
STRAUSS, R.   GIESEKING
    SERENADE, OP. 17, NO. 2
        BOOSEY AND HAWKES, INC.   .60
STRAUSS, R.
    SONATA IN B MINOR, OP. 5
        UNIVERSAL EDITION   1006   4.40
STRAUSS, R.
    STIMMUNGSBILDER, OP. 9
        UNIVERSAL EDITION   1017   3.00
STRAUSS, R.
    SUITE FROM ''DER BURGER ALS EDELMANN''--ORCH
        ASSOCIATED MUSIC PUBLISHERS, INC.   LEU   5.00
STRAUSS, R.   D
    THUS SPAKE ZARATHUSTRA, OP. 30
        C. F. PETERS CORPORATION   4193D   4.00
STRAUSS, R.   SCHAUM, J.   5
    TILL EULENSPIEGEL'S MERRY PRANKS
        BELWIN-MILLS PUBLISHING CORPORATION   .50
STRAUSS, R.   D
    TILL EULENSPIEGEL'S MERRY PRANKS, OP. 28
        C. F. PETERS CORPORATION   4193C   3.50
STRAUSS, R.   JOHNSON   M
    TILL EULENSPIEGEL'S MERRY PRANKS, OP. 28. ABRIDGED
        C. F. PETERS CORPORATION   H410   1.25

STRAUSS, R.
  TRAUMEREI, OP. 9, NO. 4
    UNIVERSAL EDITION   1012   1.50
STRAVINSKY, I.
  APOLLON MUSAGETE
    BOOSEY AND HAWKES, INC.   2.50
STRAVINSKY, I.
  BERCEUSE AND FINALE --FIREBIRD
    EDWARD B. MARKS MUSIC CORPORATION   01.00
STRAVINSKY, I.
  CHANT DU ROSSIGNOL
    BOOSEY AND HAWKES, INC.   3.25
STRAVINSKY, I.   5
  CIRCUS-POLKA
    SCHOTT   4282   1.75
STRAVINSKY, I.   BURNAM   3
  DANCE RUSSE
    WILLIS MUSIC COMPANY   .35
STRAVINSKY, I.   BURNAM   2
  DANCE RUSSE -- PETROUSHKA
    WILLIS MUSIC COMPANY   .35
STRAVINSKY, I.
  DANSE INFERNALE--FIREBIRD
    EDWARD B. MARKS MUSIC CORPORATION   01.00
STRAVINSKY, I.   WILLMS   3
  DER FEUERVOGEL -- BERCEUSE
    SCHOTT   3712   2.00
STRAVINSKY, I.   AGOSTI   6
  DER FEUERVOGEL -- DANSE INFERNALE, BERCEUSE ET FINALE
    SCHOTT   2378   3.00
STRAVINSKY, I.   WILLMS   3
  DER FEUFPVOGEL -- RONDE DES PRINCESSES
    SCHOTT   2548   1.75
STRAVINSKY, I.
  FAIRY'S KISS -- REVISED 1950 VERSION
    BOOSEY AND HAWKES, INC.   6.00
STRAVINSKY, I.   4
  FIREBIRD, RONDE DES PRINCESSES
    CENTURY MUSIC PUBLISHING COMPANY, INC.   3563   .40
STRAVINSKY, I.   FREY
  FOUR ETUDES, OP. 7--NO. 1 IN C MINOR
    ASSOCIATED MUSIC PUBLISHERS, INC.   SIM   .90
STRAVINSKY, I.   FREY
  FOUR ETUDES, OP. 7--NO. 2 IN D
    ASSOCIATED MUSIC PUBLISHERS, INC.   SIM   .90
STRAVINSKY, I.   FREY
  FOUR ETUDES, OP. 7--NO. 3 IN E MINOR
    ASSOCIATED MUSIC PUBLISHERS, INC.   SIM   .90
STRAVINSKY, I.   FREY
  FOUR ETUDES, OP. 7--NO. 4 IN F-SHARP
    ASSOCIATED MUSIC PUBLISHERS, INC.   SIM   .90
STRAVINSKY, I.   LOURIE
  OCTET FOR WIND INSTRUMENTS
    BOOSEY AND HAWKES, INC.   2.50
STRAVINSKY, I.   SPINNER
  ORPHEUS
    BOOSEY AND HAWKES, INC.   2.50
STRAVINSKY, I.   SCHAUM, J.   3
  PETROUCHKA
    BELWIN-MILLS PUBLISHING CORPORATION   .50
STRAVINSKY, I.   STRAVINSKY, I.
  PETROUCHKA - 3 MOVEMENTS -
    INTERNATIONAL MUSIC COMPANY   2.50
STRAVINSKY, I.   4
  PETRUSHKA, DANSE RUSSE
    CENTURY MUSIC PUBLISHING COMPANY, INC.   3720   .40
STRAVINSKY, I.
  SCHERZO AND SONATA
    FABER MUSIC, LTD.   F0507
STRAVINSKY, I.
  SERENADE IN A
    BOOSEY AND HAWKES, INC.   2.50
STRAVINSKY, I.
  SONATA
    BOOSEY AND HAWKES, INC.   2.50
STRAVINSKY, I.   3
  TANGO
    SCHOTT   1917   1.50
STRAVINSKY, I.   MD
  TANGO
    THEODORE PRESSER COMPANY   .60
STREABBOG   2
  ADONIS GALOP, G MAJOR
    CENTURY MUSIC PUBLISHING COMPANY, INC.   121   .40
STREABBOG   2
  ALICE WALTZ
    CENTURY MUSIC PUBLISHING COMPANY, INC.   128   .40
STREABBOG   2
  ASTER SCHOTTISCHE
    CENTURY MUSIC PUBLISHING COMPANY, INC.   139   .40
STREABBOG   1
  AUTUMN FLOWERS, WALTZ
    CENTURY MUSIC PUBLISHING COMPANY, INC.   1427   .40
STREABBOG
  BIRDS OF PARADISE--VALSE MIGNONNE, OP. 78 NO. 1
    G. SCHIRMER, INC.   .30
STREABBOG   2
  BIRDS OF PARADISE, WALTZ
    CENTURY MUSIC PUBLISHING COMPANY, INC.   2457   .40
STREABBOG   3
  BLANC ET NOIR, VALSE, OP. 314 NO. 2
    ALPHONSE LEDUC
STREABBOG
  BOLERO -- BOUQUET DE PENSEES --
    FRANCO COLOMBO PUBLICATIONS   SAL   1.75
STREABBOG
  BOUQUETIERE, LA
    FRANCO COLOMBO PUBLICATIONS   SAL   1.75
STREABBOG   3
  CENDRILLON, VALSE, OP. 279
    ALPHONSE LEDUC
STREABBOG   3
  CERISETTE, POLKA-MAZURKA, OP. 280
    ALPHONSE LEDUC
STREABBOG   3
  CHEZ GRAND-PAPA
    ALPHONSE LEDUC
STREABBOG   2
  CHEZ GRAND'MAMAN
    ALPHONSE LEDUC
STREABBOG   2
  CHILDREN'S CARNIVAL
    CENTURY MUSIC PUBLISHING COMPANY, INC.   815   .40
STREABBOG   4
  CLOCHETTE, LA, RONDINO, OP. 241
    ALPHONSE LEDUC

STREABBOG   2
  CORA, WALTZ
    CENTURY MUSIC PUBLISHING COMPANY, INC.   177   .40
STREABBOG   2
  COUCOU, LE
    ALPHONSE LEDUC
STREABBOG   2
  CYPRUS, WALTZ
    CENTURY MUSIC PUBLISHING COMPANY, INC.   183   .40
STREABBOG   2
  DAHLIA POLKA
    CENTURY MUSIC PUBLISHING COMPANY, INC.   184   .40
STREABBOG   2
  DAHLIA POLKA
    VOLKWEIN BROS.   .25
STREABBOG
  DO, RE, MI, FA WALTZ, OP. 138
    FRANCO COLOMBO PUBLICATIONS   127639   .50
STREABBOG   2
  DORA POLKA
    CENTURY MUSIC PUBLISHING COMPANY, INC.   191   .40
STREABBOG   2
  DREAMS OF THE PAST, WALTZ
    CENTURY MUSIC PUBLISHING COMPANY, INC.   194   .40
STREABBOG   2
  ECHO WALTZ
    VOLKWEIN BROS.   .25
STREABBOG   2
  ECHO, WALTZ
    CENTURY MUSIC PUBLISHING COMPANY, INC.   197   .40
STREABBOG   2
  FIRST FLOWER
    VOLKWEIN BROS.   .25
STREABBOG   2
  FLORENCE POLKA
    CENTURY MUSIC PUBLISHING COMPANY, INC.   216   .40
STREABBOG   3
  FRASQUITA, BOLERO, OP. 276
    ALPHONSE LEDUC
STREABBOG   2
  FRISKY GALOP
    CENTURY MUSIC PUBLISHING COMPANY, INC.   223   .40
STREABBOG   2
  GARLAND OF ROSES
    CENTURY MUSIC PUBLISHING COMPANY, INC.   3188   .40
STREABBOG   3
  GAVOTTE DE LA POUPEE, OP. 203
    ALPHONSE LEDUC
STREABBOG
  GITANE, LA -- SOUVENIR D'ESPAGNE --
    FRANCO COLOMBO PUBLICATIONS   SAL   1.75
STREABBOG   2
  GOLDEN STAR POLKA
    CENTURY MUSIC PUBLISHING COMPANY, INC.   231   .40
STREABBOG   2
  GOLDEN STAR WALTZ
    CENTURY MUSIC PUBLISHING COMPANY, INC.   521   .40
STREABBOG   2
  GUARDS' MARCH
    CENTURY MUSIC PUBLISHING COMPANY, INC.   236   .40
STREABBOG   2
  HONEY BELL, POLKA MAZ
    CENTURY MUSIC PUBLISHING COMPANY, INC.   245   .40
STREABBOG   2
  HONEYSUCKLE, WALTZ
    CENTURY MUSIC PUBLISHING COMPANY, INC.   246   .40
STREABBOG   3
  IDA, POLKA
    CENTURY MUSIC PUBLISHING COMPANY, INC.   251   .40
STREABBOG   3
  INFATIGABLES, LES, GALOP, OP. 243
    ALPHONSE LEDUC
STREABBOG   3
  JOYEUSE BANDE, MARCHE, OP. 277
    ALPHONSE LEDUC
STREABBOG
  LANGAGE DE MARGUERITES, LE
    FRANCO COLOMBO PUBLICATIONS   SAL   1.75
STREABBOG   2
  LE PETIT CARNIVAL, SCHOTTISCHE
    CENTURY MUSIC PUBLISHING COMPANY, INC.   690   .40
STREABBOG   2
  LES PIERROTS, WALTZ
    CENTURY MUSIC PUBLISHING COMPANY, INC.   691   .40
STREABBOG   1
  LILY POLKA
    VOLKWEIN BROS.   .25
STREABBOG   2
  LILY, POLKA
    CENTURY MUSIC PUBLISHING COMPANY, INC.   279   .40
STREABBOG   2
  LITTLE CARNIVAL, GALOP
    CENTURY MUSIC PUBLISHING COMPANY, INC.   689   .40
STREABBOG   2
  LITTLE DANCER
    CENTURY MUSIC PUBLISHING COMPANY, INC.   2302   .40
STREABBOG   2
  LITTLE FAIRY MARCH
    BELWIN-MILLS PUBLISHING CORPORATION   347   .60
STREABBOG   2
  LITTLE FAIRY MARCH
    CENTURY MUSIC PUBLISHING COMPANY, INC.   639   .40
STREABBOG   2
  LITTLE FAIRY MARCH
    VOLKWEIN BROS.   .25
STREABBOG   2
  LITTLE FAIRY POLKA
    CENTURY MUSIC PUBLISHING COMPANY, INC.   815   .40
STREABBOG   2
  LITTLE FAIRY POLKA
    VOLKWEIN BROS.   .25
STREABBOG   2
  LITTLE FAIRY SCHOTTISCHE
    CENTURY MUSIC PUBLISHING COMPANY, INC.   283   .40
STREABBOG   2
  LITTLE FAIRY SCHOTTISCHE
    VOLKWEIN BROS.   .25
STREABBOG   2
  LITTLE FAIRY WALTZ
    BELWIN-MILLS PUBLISHING CORPORATION   436   .60
STREABBOG   2
  LITTLE FAIRY WALTZ
    CENTURY MUSIC PUBLISHING COMPANY, INC.   284   .40
STREABBOG   2
  LITTLE FAIRY WALTZ
    VOLKWEIN BROS.   .25

STREABBOG   2
    LITTLE FAIRY WALTZ
        WILLIS MUSIC COMPANY   .35
STREABBOG
    LITTLE FAIRY WALTZ, OP. 105 NO. 1
        G. SCHIRMER, INC.   .40
STREABBOG   2
    MARCH MILITAIRE
        CENTURY MUSIC PUBLISHING COMPANY, INC.   304   .40
STREABBOG   2
    MARCH OF THE GUARDS
        VOLKWEIN BROS.   .25
STREABBOG   3
    MARCHE MILITAIRE
        BELWIN-MILLS PUBLISHING CORPORATION   407   .60
STREABBOG   2
    MIGNONETTE POLKA
        VOLKWEIN BROS.   .25
STREABBOG   2
    MINNIE WALTZ
        CENTURY MUSIC PUBLISHING COMPANY, INC.   324   .40
STREABBOG   2
    MORNING PRAYER
        CENTURY MUSIC PUBLISHING COMPANY, INC.   328   .40
STREABBOG   2
    MORNING PRAYER
        VOLKWEIN BROS.   .25
STREABBOG
    MORNING PRAYER, OP. 130 NO. 1
        G. SCHIRMER, INC.   .50
STREABBOG   2
    MYRTLE GALOP
        CENTURY MUSIC PUBLISHING COMPANY, INC.   333   .40
STREABBOG   2
    OISEAUX DE PARADIS, WALTZ
        CENTURY MUSIC PUBLISHING COMPANY, INC.   2457   .40
STREABBOG   2
    PETIT CARNIVAL, GALOP
        CENTURY MUSIC PUBLISHING COMPANY, INC.   689   .40
STREABBOG   2
    PETIT CARNIVAL, SCHOTTISCHE
        CENTURY MUSIC PUBLISHING COMPANY, INC.   690   .40
STREABBOG   4
    PETITE TYROLIENNE, OP. 242
        ALPHONSE LEDUC
STREABBOG   4
    PETITS CONSCRITS, LES, MARCHE MILITAIRE, OP. 202
        ALPHONSE LEDUC
STREABBOG   3
    PETITS JONGLEURS, LES, AIR DE BALLET, OP. 314 NO. 1
        ALPHONSE LEDUC
STREABBOG   2
    PIERROTS, LES, WALTZ
        CENTURY MUSIC PUBLISHING COMPANY, INC.   691   .40
STREABBOG   2
    PINK, WALTZ
        CENTURY MUSIC PUBLISHING COMPANY, INC.   357   .40
STREABBOG   2
    ROMANCE SANS PAROLES
        CENTURY MUSIC PUBLISHING COMPANY, INC.   1210   .40
STREABBOG   4
    ROMANCE SANS PAROLES --SONG WITHOUT WORDS, OP. 97 NO. 3--
        THEODORE PRESSER COMPANY   .50
STREABBOG   3
    ROSETTE, VALSE, OP. 275
        ALPHONSE LEDUC
STREABBOG   3
    SABRES DE BOIS, LES, OP. 314 NO. 3
        ALPHONSE LEDUC
STREABBOG   2
    SHOWER OF ROSES
        VOLKWEIN BROS.   .25
STREABBOG   2
    SHOWER OF ROSES, SCHOTTISCHE
        CENTURY MUSIC PUBLISHING COMPANY, INC.   656   .40
STREABBOG   2
    SHOWER OF ROSES, WALTZ
        CENTURY MUSIC PUBLISHING COMPANY, INC.   657   .40
STREABBOG   3
    SONG WITHOUT WORDS, OP. 97
        CENTURY MUSIC PUBLISHING COMPANY, INC.   1210   .40
STREABBOG   3
    SONG WITHOUT WORDS, OP. 97 NO. 3
        G. SCHIRMER, INC.   .40
STREABBOG   4
    SONG WITHOUT WORDS, OP. 97 NO. 3 --ROMANCE SANS PAROLES--
        THEODORE PRESSER COMPANY   .50
STREABBOG   1
    SPRINGTIME
        CENTURY MUSIC PUBLISHING COMPANY, INC.   1426   .40
STREABBOG   2
    VIOLET WALTZ
        CENTURY MUSIC PUBLISHING COMPANY, INC.   450   .40
STREABBOG   2
    VIOLET WALTZ
        VOLKWEIN BROS.   .25
STREET, A. A.
    DROWSY DILEMMA
        ASSOCIATED MUSIC PUBLISHERS, INC.   SIM   .40
STREET, A. A.
    ROMANCE, A
        ASSOCIATED MUSIC PUBLISHERS, INC.   BER   .75
STRELEZKI
    LE VENT --ETUDE DE CONCERT, OP. 10 NO. 1
        MUSICA OBSCURA   2.00
STRELEZKI   4
    SERENADE ESPAGNOLE
        CENTURY MUSIC PUBLISHING COMPANY, INC.   2049   .40
STRELEZKI   4
    SPANISH SERENADE
        CENTURY MUSIC PUBLISHING COMPANY, INC.   2049   .40
STRICKLAND, L.   5
    IMPROMPTU
        THEODORE PRESSER COMPANY   .60
STRICKLAND, L.   2
    LITTLE INDIAN CHIEF
        THEODORE PRESSER COMPANY   .50
STRIMER
    ALBUM DE MAROUSSIA - AU CINEMA
        FRANCO COLOMBO PUBLICATIONS   SAL   1.50
STRIMER
    ALBUM DE MAROUSSIA - CASTAGNETTES
        FRANCO COLOMBO PUBLICATIONS   SAL   1.50
STRIMER
    ALBUM DE MAROUSSIA - JAVA
        FRANCO COLOMBO PUBLICATIONS   SAL   1.50

STRIMER
    ALBUM DE MAROUSSIA - JOURS D'AUTREFOIS
        FRANCO COLOMBO PUBLICATIONS   SAL   1.50
STRIMER
    ALBUM DE MAROUSSIA - LATENDRE EMMA
        FRANCO COLOMBO PUBLICATIONS   SAL   1.50
STRIMER
    ALBUM DE MAROUSSIA - LE PETIT SAVANT
        FRANCO COLOMBO PUBLICATIONS   SAL   1.50
STRIMER
    ALBUM DE MAROUSSIA - MARIONNETTES
        FRANCO COLOMBO PUBLICATIONS   SAL   1.50
STRIMER
    ALBUM DE MAROUSSIA - PETITS POUSSINS
        FRANCO COLOMBO PUBLICATIONS   SAL   1.50
STRIMER
    ALBUM DE MAROUSSIA - PROCESSION
        FRANCO COLOMBO PUBLICATIONS   SAL   1.50
STRIMER
    ALBUM DE MAROUSSIA - ROSEE MATINALE
        FRANCO COLOMBO PUBLICATIONS   SAL   1.50
STRIMER
    ALBUM DE MAROUSSIA - TOURMENT
        FRANCO COLOMBO PUBLICATIONS   SAL   1.50
STRIMER
    ALBUM DE MAROUSSIA - VALSE DE MAROUSSIA
        FRANCO COLOMBO PUBLICATIONS   SAL   1.50
STRIMER
    ALBUM DE NATACHA - AU PRINTEMPS
        FRANCO COLOMBO PUBLICATIONS   SAL   1.50
STRIMER
    ALBUM DE NATACHA - CARILLON
        FRANCO COLOMBO PUBLICATIONS   SAL   1.50
STRIMER
    ALBUM DE NATACHA - DANSE DE LA MOUCHE
        FRANCO COLOMBO PUBLICATIONS   SAL   1.50
STRIMER
    ALBUM DE NATACHA - DOUMKA AND HOPAK
        FRANCO COLOMBO PUBLICATIONS   SAL   1.50
STRIMER
    ALBUM DE NATACHA - EN VALSANT
        FRANCO COLOMBO PUBLICATIONS   SAL   1.50
STRIMER
    ALBUM DE NATACHA - PROMENADE
        FRANCO COLOMBO PUBLICATIONS   SAL   1.50
STRIMER
    ALBUM DE NATACHA - TANGO ARGENTIN
        FRANCO COLOMBO PUBLICATIONS   SAL   1.50
STRIMER
    ALBUM DE NATACHA - TENDRESSE AND SOUVENIR LOINTAIN
        FRANCO COLOMBO PUBLICATIONS   SAL   1.50
STRIMER
    ALBUM DE NATACHA - VALSE DE NATACHA
        FRANCO COLOMBO PUBLICATIONS   SAL   1.50
STRIMER
    ALBUM DE TANIA - AMUSETTE
        FRANCO COLOMBO PUBLICATIONS   SAL   1.50
STRIMER
    ALBUM DE TANIA - IN A MINOR
        FRANCO COLOMBO PUBLICATIONS   SAL   1.50
STRIMER
    ALBUM DE TANIA - LA PETITE VIENNOISE
        FRANCO COLOMBO PUBLICATIONS   SAL   1.50
STRIMER
    ALBUM DE TANIA - PAYS LOINTAIN
        FRANCO COLOMBO PUBLICATIONS   SAL   1.50
STRIMER
    ALBUM DE TANIA - PLAINTE
        FRANCO COLOMBO PUBLICATIONS   SAL   1.50
STRIMER
    ALBUM DE TANIA - RONDE JOYEUSE
        FRANCO COLOMBO PUBLICATIONS   SAL   1.50
STRIMER
    DANS LA FORET - L'ECHO
        FRANCO COLOMBO PUBLICATIONS   SAL   1.50
STRIMER
    DANS LA FORET - LA ROSEE
        FRANCO COLOMBO PUBLICATIONS   SAL   1.50
STRIMER
    DANS LA FORET - PETITE FLEUR SOLITAIRE
        FRANCO COLOMBO PUBLICATIONS   SAL   1.50
STRIMER
    DANS LA FORET - RONDE NOCTURNE
        FRANCO COLOMBO PUBLICATIONS   SAL   1.50
STRIMER
    DANS LA FORET - SOIR PAISIBLE
        FRANCO COLOMBO PUBLICATIONS   SAL   1.50
STRIMER
    DANS LA RUE - AU MANEGE
        FRANCO COLOMBO PUBLICATIONS   SAL   1.50
STRIMER
    DANS LA RUE - AU SON DU MOTEUR
        FRANCO COLOMBO PUBLICATIONS   SAL   1.75
STRIMER
    DANS LA RUE - CATHERINETTE
        FRANCO COLOMBO PUBLICATIONS   SAL   1.75
STRIMER
    DANS LA RUE - ORGUE DE BARBARIE
        FRANCO COLOMBO PUBLICATIONS   SAL   1.50
STRIMER
    DANS LA RUE - SUR LE BANC D'UN PETIT SQUARE
        FRANCO COLOMBO PUBLICATIONS   SAL   1.50
STRIMER
    MARCH PARAPHRASE ON A THEME OF BACH
        FRANCO COLOMBO PUBLICATIONS   SAL   2.00
STRIMER, J.   1
    ENCHANTED BOATMAN
        PRO-ART PUBLICATIONS, INC.   18   .50
STRIMER, J.   2
    GAVOTTE
        BOSTON MUSIC COMPANY   .50
STRIMER, J.   1
    PINK MUSIC BOX
        PRO-ART PUBLICATIONS, INC.   29   .50
STRIMER, J.   1
    SLUMBER SERENADE
        PRO-ART PUBLICATIONS, INC.   17   .50
STRINGFIELD, L.
    SHOUT FREEDOM
        BROOT MUSIC COMPANY   .35
STROHBACH, S.
    SPIELDOSE, DIE--1951
        ASSOCIATED MUSIC PUBLISHERS, INC.   BRH   1.75
STROHBACH, S.
    SPIELZEUGKISTE, DIE--1952
        ASSOCIATED MUSIC PUBLISHERS, INC.   BRH   1.75

STROUSE			
DITTO			
MCA MUSIC			.60
STROUSE	1		
DONKEY RIDE, A			
BOSTON MUSIC COMPANY			.50
STROUSE			
SIXTH FINGER TUNE			
FRANK MUSIC CORPORATION			.95
STRUM, E.	2		
TRAPEZE ACT			
WILLIS MUSIC COMPANY			.40
STRUM, E.	2		
TRAPEZE ACT			
WILLIS MUSIC COMPANY			.40
STRUM, E.	2 1/2		
WINTER SUNSET			
WILLIS MUSIC COMPANY			.40
STUART, P.			
MOON PASSING BEHIND THE CLOUDS, THE			
G. SCHIRMER, INC.			.50
STUBBLEFIELD	1		
CONFIDENCE			
WILLIS MUSIC COMPANY			.35
STUBBLEFIELD	1		
HAPPY DAYS			
WILLIS MUSIC COMPANY			.35
STUBBLEFIELD	1		
MELODY IN C			
WILLIS MUSIC COMPANY			.35
STUBBLEFIELD	1		
SONG OF SPRING, A			
WILLIS MUSIC COMPANY			.35
STULTS SCHAUM, J.	3		
SWEETEST STORY EVER TOLD, THE			
BELWIN-MILLS PUBLISHING CORPORATION			.50
STULTS	2		
SWEETEST STORY EVER TOLD, THE			
CENTURY MUSIC PUBLISHING COMPANY, INC.		4080	.40
STURTEVANT	3		
PEACEMAKER, THE, MARCH			
CENTURY MUSIC PUBLISHING COMPANY, INC.		1155	.40
STUTSCHEWSKY, J.			
HASSIDIC DANCES			
SEESAW MUSIC CORPORATION			4.00
STUTSCHEWSKY, J.			
LANDSCAPES OF ISRAEL			
SEESAW MUSIC CORPORATION			12.00
STUTSCHEWSKY, J.			
QUATRE INATTENDUS POUR PIANO			
SEESAW MUSIC CORPORATION			4.00
SUCHON, E.			
HIGHLANDER SUITE			
ARTIA			1.75
SUCHON, E.			
I AM LITTLE			
ARTIA			.90
SUCHON, E.			
SONATA RUSTICA			
ARTIA			1.50
SUCHON, E.			
WHEN WOLVES MET			
ARTIA			.90
SUDDARDS			
AMOS			
CARL FISCHER, INC.		P 2274	.50
SUDDARDS	1 1/2		
BUTTERSCOTCH HOP, THE			
ELKAN-VOGEL, INC.			.50
SUDDARDS RICHTER			
HAPPY HUFF			
FRANCO COLOMBO PUBLICATIONS		NY1504	.35
SUDDARDS RICHTER			
HAPPY HUFF, THE			
BELWIN-MILLS PUBLISHING CORPORATION			.60
SUDDARDS	1 1/2		
LITTLE RED HEN AND THE PEPPERMINT STICK, THE			
ELKAN-VOGEL, INC.			.50
SUDDARDS			
MISTER WOOF			
WARNER BROTHERS PUBLISHERS			.60
SUDDARDS	1 1/2 - 2		
PAIR OF DANDY LIONS, A			
ELKAN-VOGEL, INC.			.50
SUDDARDS RICHTER			
SQUIRREL CHASE			
BELWIN-MILLS PUBLISHING CORPORATION			.60
SUDDARDS RICHTER			
SQUIRREL CHASE			
FRANCO COLOMBO PUBLICATIONS		NY1503	.35
SUDDARDS			
SUPPOSE			
CARL FISCHER, INC.		P 2939	.50
SUDDARDS			
WILLIE THE WAFFLE			
CARL FISCHER, INC.		P 2900	.50
SUDERBURG, R.	D		
SIX MOMENTS FOR PIANO			
THEODORE PRESSER COMPANY			1.00
SUESSE, D.	MD		
ONE HUNDRED AND TENTH ST. RHUMBA			
THEODORE PRESSER COMPANY			.60
SUESSE, D.	MD		
SERENADE TO A SKYSCRAPER			
THEODORE PRESSER COMPANY			.60
SUGARMAN	1A		
OLD ORGAN GRINDER			
MUSICORD PUBLICATIONS, INC.			.45
SUGARMAN	1B		
RAIN, RAIN GO AWAY			
MUSICORD PUBLICATIONS, INC.			.45
SUK			
DORFSERENADE			
BARENREITER VERLAG		AP 735	
SUK			
FANTASIE-POLONAISE, OP. 5			
BARENREITER VERLAG		AP 737	
SUK			
FRUHLING, OP. 22A			
BARENREITER VERLAG		AP 738	
SUK	3		
IDYLLE, OP. 7 NO. 4			
BARENREITER VERLAG		AP 739	
SUK	3		
IN NEUES LEBEN -- SOKOL-FEST-MARSCH --			
BARENREITER VERLAG		AP 740	
SUK	3		
LIEBESLIED, OP. 7 NO. 1			
BARENREITER VERLAG		AP 743	
SUK SOLC	3		
MENUETT AUS DER SUITE, OP. 21			
BARENREITER VERLAG		AP 1702	
SUK	3		
OH FREUNDSCHAFT, OP. 36			
BARENREITER VERLAG		AP 747	
SUK			
SUITE, OP. 21			
BARENREITER VERLAG		AP 746	
SUKMAN, H.			
ELEVENTH HOUR			
THE BIG THREE MUSIC CORPORATION			00.95
SULLIVAN, A. PERRY			
LOST CHORD			
BOOSEY AND HAWKES, INC.			.50
SULLIVAN, A.	3		
LOST CHORD, THE			
CENTURY MUSIC PUBLISHING COMPANY, INC.		2065	.40
SULLIVAN, A.	3		
MIKADO, THE, TIT WILLOW			
CENTURY MUSIC PUBLISHING COMPANY, INC.		3706	.40
SULLIVAN, A.	2		
ONWARD CHRISTIAN SOLDIERS			
CENTURY MUSIC PUBLISHING COMPANY, INC.		2062	.40
SULLIVAN, A.	3		
TIT WILLOW, THE MIKADO			
CENTURY MUSIC PUBLISHING COMPANY, INC.		3706	.40
SULLIVAN, J.			
LITTLE ROCK GETAWAY			
THE BIG THREE MUSIC CORPORATION			00.95
SULLIVAN, J. STEINER	2		
OLD HAT BOOGIE			
BELWIN-MILLS PUBLISHING CORPORATION			.60
SULLIVAN, J.	3		
ONWARD, CHRISTIAN SOLDIERS			
CENTURY MUSIC PUBLISHING COMPANY, INC.		3618	.40
SULPIZI, F.			
ALBUM PER DANIELA, OP. 15			
EDIZIONI BERBEN		EB 1598	3.60
SULPIZI, F.			
EPIGRAMMATA ALIA, OP. 21			
EDIZIONI BERBEN		EB 1769	3.00
SUMMERS	2		
CAGED LION, THE			
PRO-ART PUBLICATIONS, INC.		420	.50
SUNSHINE *			
ENLLORO -- VOODOO- MOON			
MCA MUSIC			1.00
SUNY, S.			
IMPROMPTU AND TOCCATA, 1965			
SEESAW MUSIC CORPORATION			8.00
SUPPE. F. MENDEL, S.	2		
POET AND PEASANT OVERTURE			
WILLIS MUSIC COMPANY			.40
SUPPE, F.	2		
DICHTER UND BAUER, EASY			
CENTURY MUSIC PUBLISHING COMPANY, INC.		2123	.40
SUPPE, F.	5		
LIGHT CAVALRY OVERTURE			
CENTURY MUSIC PUBLISHING COMPANY, INC.		1528	.40
SUPPE, F.			
OVERTURE FROM 'POET AND PEASANT'			
G. SCHIRMER, INC.			.75
SUPPE, F.	5		
OVERTURE, LIGHT CAVALRY			
CENTURY MUSIC PUBLISHING COMPANY, INC.		1528	.40
SUPPE, F.	2		
OVERTURE, LIGHT CAVALRY			
CENTURY MUSIC PUBLISHING COMPANY, INC.		3668	.40
SUPPE, F.	4		
OVERTURE, POET AND PEASANT			
CENTURY MUSIC PUBLISHING COMPANY, INC.		361	.40
SUPPE, F.	3		
OVERTURE, POET AND PEASANT, EASY			
CENTURY MUSIC PUBLISHING COMPANY, INC.		2123	.40
SUPPE, F.	4		
POET AND PEASANT OVERTURE			
CENTURY MUSIC PUBLISHING COMPANY, INC.		361	.40
SUPPE, F.			
POET AND PEASANT OVERTURE			
FRANCO COLOMBO PUBLICATIONS		128157	1.00
SUPPE, F. DEL MAGLIO			
POET AND PEASANT OVERTURE			
FRANCO COLOMBO PUBLICATIONS		128675	.60
SURFARIS			
POINT PANIC			
MCA MUSIC			1.00
SURINACH, C.			
ACROBATS OF GOD -- 5 DANCES FROM THE BALLET			
ASSOCIATED MUSIC PUBLISHERS, INC.		AMP	2.50
SURINACH, C.			
SONATINA			
PEER SOUTHERN ORGANIZATION			01.75
SURPEY, C.	3		
SONG OF THE TREES			
WILLIS MUSIC COMPANY			.40
SUTERMEISTER, H.	4		
HOMMAGE A ARTHUR HONEGGER - 1955			
SCHOTT		5755	2.50
SUTERMEISTER, H.	5		
SONATINA IN E FLAT			
SCHOTT		4119	2.00
SUTHERLAND, J.	3		
HAWAIIAN FAREWELL			
WILLIS MUSIC COMPANY			.40
SWAN	4		
SONATA			
NOVELLO AND COMPANY, LTD.		10.0081.00	.90
SWAN *			
MUCHACHACHA			
MCA MUSIC			1.00
SWAN *			
ROCK AND ROLL CHA CHA CHA			
MCA MUSIC			1.00
SWANSON			
CUCKOO, THE			
MCA MUSIC			1.00
SWANSON			
PIANO SONATA			
WEINTRAUB MUSIC COMPANY		070008	2.00
SWEELINCK DOFLEIN	3		
LIEDVARIATIONEN			
SCHOTT		2482	2.25

SWEELINCK		M	
VARIATIONS ON 'MY YOUNG LIFE HATH AN END'			
C. F. PETERS CORPORATION		4301C	1.50
SWEET, A.		3	
ANGEL VOICES EVER NEAR			
CENTURY MUSIC PUBLISHING COMPANY, INC.		2733	.40
SWEET, A.		3	
LA MADONNA			
CENTURY MUSIC PUBLISHING COMPANY, INC.		2702	.40
SWEET, A.		3	
MADONNA, LA			
CENTURY MUSIC PUBLISHING COMPANY, INC.		2702	.40
SWEET, A.		3	
SONG OF HEAVEN			
CENTURY MUSIC PUBLISHING COMPANY, INC.		2700	.40
SWIFT, F.		2	
TAG WALTZ			
CENTURY MUSIC PUBLISHING COMPANY, INC.		1257	.40
SWIFT, N.		2	
PERSIAN BAZAAR			
BELWIN-MILLS PUBLISHING CORPORATION			.60
SWINSTEAD, F.		2	
AFTER THE DANCE			
NOVELLO AND COMPANY, LTD.		55.0007.09	.25
SWINSTEAD, F.			
EN COURANT			
BOOSEY AND HAWKES, INC.			.50
SWINSTEAD, F.			
FIVE FINGERS PIECES			
BANKS AND SON LTD.			.70
SWINSTEAD, F.		1	
GAVOTTE			
NOVELLO AND COMPANY, LTD.		55.0020.06	.25
SWINSTEAD, F.			
GAY DANCE, A			
EDWARD B. MARKS MUSIC CORPORATION			00.60
SWINSTEAD, F.			
HUNTING SONG			
EDWARD B. MARKS MUSIC CORPORATION			00.60
SWINSTEAD, F.			
MARCH PAST			
EDWARD B. MARKS MUSIC CORPORATION			00.60
SWINSTEAD, F.			
MASQUE DANCE			
EDWARD B. MARKS MUSIC CORPORATION			00.60
SWINSTEAD, F.		1	
SING A SONG OF SIXPENCE			
NOVELLO AND COMPANY, LTD.		55.0001.10	.40
SWINSTEAD, F.		1	
TINKER, TAILOR			
NOVELLO AND COMPANY, LTD.		55.0038.09	.40
SWINSTEAD, F.		E	
TO THE MOON			
OXFORD UNIVERSITY PRESS		33.901	.75
SWINSTEAD, F.		1	
TRAMP, THE			
NOVELLO AND COMPANY, LTD.		55.0037.00	.40
SYDEMAN			
SONATA			
E. C. SCHIRMER MUSIC COMPANY		235	02.00
SYDEMAN, W.			
CONCERTINO FOR OBOE, PIANO AND STRINGS			
SEESAW MUSIC CORPORATION			13.00
SYDERMAN			
VARIATIONS, OP. 40			
MCA MUSIC			2.00
SYMONS			
BELINDA'S SUITE NO. 1			
FRANCO COLOMBO PUBLICATIONS		SAL	4.00
SYMONS			
BELINDA'S SUITE NO. 2			
FRANCO COLOMBO PUBLICATIONS		SAL	4.25
SYMONS			
BIRD SONG AT MORNING			
FRANCO COLOMBO PUBLICATIONS		SAL	1.75
SYMONS			
LITTLE FANTASY			
FRANCO COLOMBO PUBLICATIONS		SAL	2.50
SYMONS			
MINIATURE SUITE			
FRANCO COLOMBO PUBLICATIONS		SAL	2.50
SYMONS			
MODERN SUITE			
FRANCO COLOMBO PUBLICATIONS		SAL	4.00
SYMONS			
RIGGADOON			
FRANCO COLOMBO PUBLICATIONS		SAL .	1.75
SYMONS			
SPRING SUITE			
FRANCO COLOMBO PUBLICATIONS		SAL	4.00
SZANTO			
ETUDE NO. 04 -- IN FIFTHS --			
FRANCO COLOMBO PUBLICATIONS		SAL	2.75
SZANTO			
ETUDE ORIENTAL NO. 3 -- IN FOURTHS --			
FRANCO COLOMBO PUBLICATIONS		SAL	2.75
SZANTO		M-D	
NUBANUSIT			
COMPOSERS PRESS, INC.			2.00
SZANTO		M-D	
PORTRAIT OF A DANCER			
COMPOSERS PRESS, INC.			1.00
SZANTO			
TWO JAPANESE MELODIES			
UNIVERSAL EDITION		UE 8440	.80
SZANTO			
VARIATIONS AND FINALE IN D			
UNIVERSAL EDITION		UE 7249	2.80
SZCZENIOWSKI, B.			
GENTLE WIND, THE			
ASSOCIATED MUSIC PUBLISHERS, INC.		BER	.50
SZELL, G.			
THREE LITTLE PIANO PIECES, OP. 6			
UNIVERSAL EDITION		UE 6996	2.35
SZONYI, E.			
STUBBORN PRINCESS			
KULTURA			1.50
SZONYI, E.			
TOCCATINA			
KULTURA			1.50
SZYMANOWSKI			
ETUDE IN B FLAT MINOR, OP. 4 NO. 3			
UNIVERSAL EDITION		UE 3856	1.75
SZYMANOWSKI			
NOCTURNE IN B FLAT			
EDWARD B. MARKS MUSIC CORPORATION			01.60

SZYMANOWSKI			
PRELUDE, OP. 1 NO. 1			
UNIVERSAL EDITION		UE 3853	2.50
SZYMANOWSKI			
SONATA NO. 03, OP. 36			
UNIVERSAL EDITION		UE 3859	7.50
SZYMANOWSKI			
VALSE ROMANTIQUE			
EDWARD B. MARKS MUSIC CORPORATION			01.75
SZYMANOWSKI			
VARIATIONS ON A POLISH FOLK SONG, OP. 10			
UNIVERSAL EDITION		UE 3859	2.55
TAILLEFERRE, G.		E	
FLEURS DE FRANCE			
ELKAN-VOGEL, INC.		LEM	2.75
TAILLEFERRE, G.			
MARCHAND DES OISEAUX			
HEUGEL ET CIE.			2.25
TAILLEFERRE, G.			
PARTITA			
RONGWEN MUSIC, INC.			02.50
TAILLEFERRE, G.			
PASTORALE IN C			
HEUGEL ET CIE.			3.10
TAKACS, J.		2	
BUSY BIRDFEEDER, THE			
WILLIS MUSIC COMPANY			.40
TAKACS, J.		2	
DANCE OF THE FAIRIES			
WILLIS MUSIC COMPANY			.40
TAKACS, J.		2	
FAIRY QUEEN, THE			
WILLIS MUSIC COMPANY			.40
TAKACS, J.			
HUMORESQUE			
ASSOCIATED MUSIC PUBLISHERS, INC.		DOB	1.50
TAKACS, J.			
LITTLE SONATA, OP. 51			
ASSOCIATED MUSIC PUBLISHERS, INC.		DOB	2.25
TAKACS, J.			
PARTITA, OP. 58			
ASSOCIATED MUSIC PUBLISHERS, INC.		DOB	2.75
TAKACS, J.		2	
PIXIES' MARCH, THE			
WILLIS MUSIC COMPANY			.40
TAKACS, J.		2 1/2	
POLKA BAND, THE			
WILLIS MUSIC COMPANY			.40
TAKACS, J.		2 1/2	
SHEPHERD'S BAGPIPES, THE			
WILLIS MUSIC COMPANY			.40
TAKACS, J.		2 1/2	
SHEPHERD'S BAGPIPES, THE			
WILLIS MUSIC COMPANY			.40
TAKACS, J.			
TOCCATA, OP. 54--1946			
ASSOCIATED MUSIC PUBLISHERS, INC.		DOB	2.75
TAKAHASHI			
CHROMAMORPHE 2			
C. F. PETERS CORPORATION		66237	2.00
TAKAHASHI			
METATHESES			
C. F. PETERS CORPORATION		66243	2.00
TAKAHASHI			
ROSACE 2			
C. F. PETERS CORPORATION		66241	2.00
TAL, J.			
SONATA FOR PIANO			
ALEXANDER BROUDE, INC.			3.50
TALBOT		1	
BALLOONS			
BELWIN-MILLS PUBLISHING CORPORATION			.60
TALBOT		1	
FAIRY TALES			
BELWIN-MILLS PUBLISHING CORPORATION			.60
TALBOT		1	
MARCH OF THE PENGUINS			
BELWIN-MILLS PUBLISHING CORPORATION			.60
TALBOT		1	
SUNSET			
BOSTON MUSIC COMPANY			.50
TALEXY			
MUSIDORA -- MAZURKA --			
FRANCO COLOMBO PUBLICATIONS		SAL	1.50
TAMBURINI			
TOCCATA			
FRANCO COLOMBO PUBLICATIONS		128566	1.25
TANGEN		E-M	
TUSSEDANS --GNOME DANCE--			
C. F. PETERS CORPORATION		LY2	.90
TANSMAN, A.			
BALLAD NO. 1--1941			
ASSOCIATED MUSIC PUBLISHERS, INC.		ESC	1.00
TANSMAN, A.			
BALLAD NO. 2--1941			
ASSOCIATED MUSIC PUBLISHERS, INC.		ESC	1.00
TANSMAN, A.			
BALLAD NO. 3--1941			
ASSOCIATED MUSIC PUBLISHERS, INC.		ESC	1.25
TANSMAN, A.			
BRIC-A-BRAC -- 1935 -- BALLET			
ASSOCIATED MUSIC PUBLISHERS, INC.		ESC	4.00
TANSMAN, A.			
EIGHT NOVELETTES--NO. 1, CAPRICE			
ASSOCIATED MUSIC PUBLISHERS, INC.		ESC	1.25
TANSMAN, A.			
EIGHT NOVELETTES--NO. 2, ETUDE			
ASSOCIATED MUSIC PUBLISHERS, INC.		ESC	1.25
TANSMAN, A.			
EIGHT NOVELETTES--NO. 3, EXOTIQUE--DANSE JAVANAISE			
ASSOCIATED MUSIC PUBLISHERS, INC.		ESC	1.75
TANSMAN, A.			
EIGHT NOVELETTES--NO. 4, DANSE TZIGANE			
ASSOCIATED MUSIC PUBLISHERS, INC.		ESC	1.75
TANSMAN, A.			
EIGHT NOVELETTES--NO. 5, OBERTAS--DANSE POLONAISE			
ASSOCIATED MUSIC PUBLISHERS, INC.		ESC	1.75
TANSMAN, A.			
EIGHT NOVELETTES--NO. 6, BLUES			
ASSOCIATED MUSIC PUBLISHERS, INC.		ESC	.90
TANSMAN, A.			
EIGHT NOVELETTES--NO. 7, PRELUDE AND FUGUE			
ASSOCIATED MUSIC PUBLISHERS, INC.		ESC	1.75
TANSMAN, A.			
EIGHT NOVELETTES--NO. 8, IMPROVISATION			
ASSOCIATED MUSIC PUBLISHERS, INC.		ESC	1.50

TANSMAN, A.
   ETUDE
      ASSOCIATED MUSIC PUBLISHERS, INC.   ESC   4.00
TANSMAN, A.
   ETUDE SCHERZO
      FRANCO COLOMBO PUBLICATIONS   SAL   1.75
TANSMAN, A.   BARTH
   FIFTEEN MODERATELY EASY PIECES FOR THE YOUNG PIANIST--BERCEUSE
      ASSOCIATED MUSIC PUBLISHERS, INC.   ESC   .40
TANSMAN, A.   BARTH
   FIFTEEN MODERATELY EASY PIECES FOR THE YOUNG PIANIST--DANCING
   LESSON, THE
      ASSOCIATED MUSIC PUBLISHERS, INC.   ESC   .35
TANSMAN, A.   BARTH
   FIFTEEN MODERATELY EASY PIECES FOR THE YOUNG PIANIST--HIDE AND
   SEEK
      ASSOCIATED MUSIC PUBLISHERS, INC.   ESC   .35
TANSMAN, A.   BARTH
   FIFTEEN MODERATELY EASY PIECES FOR THE YOUNG PIANIST--IN A
   VENETIAN GONDOLA
      ASSOCIATED MUSIC PUBLISHERS, INC.   ESC   .35
TANSMAN, A.   BARTH
   FIFTEEN MODERATELY EASY PIECES FOR THE YOUNG PIANIST--MARCHE
   MILITAIRE
      ASSOCIATED MUSIC PUBLISHERS, INC.   ESC   .35
TANSMAN, A.
   JE JOUE POUR MAMAN--NO. 01, PETIT AIR
      ASSOCIATED MUSIC PUBLISHERS, INC.   ESC   .75
TANSMAN, A.
   JE JOUE POUR MAMAN--NO. 02, AIR BOHEMIEN
      ASSOCIATED MUSIC PUBLISHERS, INC.   ESC   .75
TANSMAN, A.
   JE JOUE POUR MAMAN--NO. 03, JEU
      ASSOCIATED MUSIC PUBLISHERS, INC.   ESC   .75
TANSMAN, A.
   JE JOUE POUR MAMAN--NO. 04, ORIENTALE
      ASSOCIATED MUSIC PUBLISHERS, INC.   ESC   .75
TANSMAN, A.
   JE JOUE POUR MAMAN--NO. 05, VALSE
      ASSOCIATED MUSIC PUBLISHERS, INC.   ESC   .75
TANSMAN, A.
   JE JOUE POUR MAMAN--NO. 06, MELODIE
      ASSOCIATED MUSIC PUBLISHERS, INC.   ESC   .75
TANSMAN, A.
   JE JOUE POUR MAMAN--NO. 07, BOURREE
      ASSOCIATED MUSIC PUBLISHERS, INC.   ESC   .75
TANSMAN, A.
   JE JOUE POUR MAMAN--NO. 08, FANFARE
      ASSOCIATED MUSIC PUBLISHERS, INC.   ESC   .75
TANSMAN, A.
   JE JOUE POUR MAMAN--NO. 09, MELOPEE ARABE
      ASSOCIATED MUSIC PUBLISHERS, INC.   ESC   .75
TANSMAN, A.
   JE JOUE POUR MAMAN--NO. 10, MENUET
      ASSOCIATED MUSIC PUBLISHERS, INC.   ESC   .75
TANSMAN, A.
   JE JOUE POUR MAMAN--NO. 11, POLKA
      ASSOCIATED MUSIC PUBLISHERS, INC.   ESC   .75
TANSMAN, A.
   JE JOUE POUR MAMAN--NO. 12, AIR HONGROIS
      ASSOCIATED MUSIC PUBLISHERS, INC.   ESC   .75
TANSMAN, A.
   JE JOUE POUR PAPA--NO. 01, AUX CHAMPS
      ASSOCIATED MUSIC PUBLISHERS, INC.   ESC   .60
TANSMAN, A.
   JE JOUE POUR PAPA--NO. 02, ORGUE DE BARBARIE
      ASSOCIATED MUSIC PUBLISHERS, INC.   ESC   .60
TANSMAN, A.
   JE JOUE POUR PAPA--NO. 03, A LA PECHE
      ASSOCIATED MUSIC PUBLISHERS, INC.   ESC   .60
TANSMAN, A.
   JE JOUE POUR PAPA--NO. 04, AIR FAMILIER DE PAPA
      ASSOCIATED MUSIC PUBLISHERS, INC.   ESC   .75
TANSMAN, A.
   JE JOUE POUR PAPA--NO. 05, LES PETITS SOLDATS
      ASSOCIATED MUSIC PUBLISHERS, INC.   ESC   .60
TANSMAN, A.
   JE JOUE POUR PAPA--NO. 06, BATEAUX A VOILE
      ASSOCIATED MUSIC PUBLISHERS, INC.   ESC   .60
TANSMAN, A.
   JE JOUE POUR PAPA--NO. 07, L'OURSON
      ASSOCIATED MUSIC PUBLISHERS, INC.   ESC   .60
TANSMAN, A.
   JE JOUE POUR PAPA--NO. 08, PETITE POLKA
      ASSOCIATED MUSIC PUBLISHERS, INC.   ESC   .60
TANSMAN, A.
   JE JOUE POUR PAPA--NO. 09, VALSETTE
      ASSOCIATED MUSIC PUBLISHERS, INC.   ESC   .60
TANSMAN, A.
   JE JOUE POUR PAPA--NO. 10, A TROIS TEMPS
      ASSOCIATED MUSIC PUBLISHERS, INC.   ESC   .60
TANSMAN, A.
   JE JOUE POUR PAPA--NO. 11, PETIT PROBLEME
      ASSOCIATED MUSIC PUBLISHERS, INC.   ESC   .60
TANSMAN, A.
   JE JOUE POUR PAPA--NO. 12, AIR SERIEUX
      ASSOCIATED MUSIC PUBLISHERS, INC.   ESC   .60
TANSMAN, A.
   LITTLE SUITE
      ASSOCIATED MUSIC PUBLISHERS, INC.   ESC   3.50
TANSMAN, A.
   OUVERTURE SYMPHONIQUE--ORCH
      ASSOCIATED MUSIC PUBLISHERS, INC.   ESC   2.00
TANSMAN, A.
   RAPSODIE HEBRAIQUE--1938
      ASSOCIATED MUSIC PUBLISHERS, INC.   ESC   1.75
TANSMAN, A.
   RESSURECTION -- BALLET
      ASSOCIATED MUSIC PUBLISHERS, INC.   ESC   9.00
TANSMAN, A.
   SEXTUOR -- 1923 -- BALLET-BOUFFE
      ASSOCIATED MUSIC PUBLISHERS, INC.   ESC   2.50
TANSMAN, A.
   SONATA NO. 04--1941--
      ASSOCIATED MUSIC PUBLISHERS, INC.   5SC   2.00
TANSMAN, A.
   SONATA NO. 05
      UNIVERSAL EDITION   UE 12498   3.00
TANSMAN, A.
   SONATINA
      FRANCO COLOMBO PUBLICATIONS   SAL   2.75
TANSMAN, A.
   SONATINA NO. 03--1933--
      ASSOCIATED MUSIC PUBLISHERS, INC.   ESC   3.50
TANSMAN, A.
   SONATINE TRANSATLANTIQUE
      ALPHONSE LEDUC

7

TANSMAN, A.
   SUITE DANS LE STYLE ANCIEN
      ASSOCIATED MUSIC PUBLISHERS, INC.   ESC   4.50
TANSMAN, A.
   SUITE VARIEE
      UNIVERSAL EDITION   UE 12401   2.65
TANSMAN, A.
   TEMPO AMERICANO FROM ''SYMPHONIE CONCERTANTE''
      ASSOCIATED MUSIC PUBLISHERS, INC.   ESC   2.50
TANSMAN, A.
   TEN DIVERSIONS FOR THE YOUNG PIANIST--TOCCATA
      ASSOCIATED MUSIC PUBLISHERS, INC.   AMP   .40
TANTILLO
   BERCEUSE
      FRANCO COLOMBO PUBLICATIONS   DS433   1.25
TANTILLO
   BURATTINI IN MARCIA
      FRANCO COLOMBO PUBLICATIONS   DS431   1.25
TANTILLO
   PICCOLA DANZA
      FRANCO COLOMBO PUBLICATIONS   DS432   1.25
TARCAN, B.
   SUITE FOR PIANO -- NOSTALGIE, RONDINO, ETE, DANSEUSE, RHAPSODE,
   LA MER NOIRE
      IMPERO-VERLAG   6.75
TARDOS, B.
   MINIATURES
      KULTURA   .90
TARDOS, B.
   RAINBOW
      KULTURA   1.25
TARDOS, B.
   SONATINA
      KULTURA   2.00
TARDOS, B.
   SUITE
      KULTURA   1.50
TARENGHI
   BURLESCA, OP. 81 NO. 3
      FRANCO COLOMBO PUBLICATIONS   115984   .75
TARENGHI
   CARILLON
      FRANCO COLOMBO PUBLICATIONS   112452   .75
TARENGHI
   CHILDHOOD SCENES, OP. 70
      FRANCO COLOMBO PUBLICATIONS   ER88   1.00
TAURIELLO, A.
   TOCCATA
      BOOSEY AND HAWKES, INC.   1.00
TAUSIG
   BALLADE IN A MINOR 'DAS GEISTERSCHIFF' OP. 1
      MUSICA OBSCURA   2.50
TAUSIG
   REMINISCENCES DE HALKA --MONIUSZKO   OP. 2
      MUSICA OBSCURA   3.00
TAUSIG
   UNGARISCHE ZIGEUNERWEISEN
      MUSICA OBSCURA   4.25
TAUTENHAHN, G.
   EXPOSITIONS FOR PIANO
      COMPOSERS AUTOGRAPH PUBLICATIONS   1.54
TAUTENHAHN, G.
   MOODS, 1973
      SEESAW MUSIC CORPORATION   2.00
TAUTENHAHN, G.
   PRELUDE FOR PIANO
      SEESAW MUSIC CORPORATION   1.00
TAYLOR   2-3
   BIRCH-BARK CANOE
      PRO-ART PUBLICATIONS, INC.   480   .50
TAYLOR   2
   CELLO WALTZES
      VOLKWEIN BROS.   .35
TAYLOR   2
   LITTLE BALLERINA
      BOSTON MUSIC COMPANY   .50
TAYLOR
   LITTLE GYPSY RHAPSODY
      CARL FISCHER, INC.   P 3138   .50
TAYLOR   2
   MELLO CELLO
      VOLKWEIN BROS.   .35
TAYLOR   1-2
   MIDNIGHT WALTZ
      PRO-ART PUBLICATIONS, INC.   444   .50
TAYLOR   3
   MOONLIT CASTLE
      BOSTON MUSIC COMPANY   .50
TAYLOR
   SARAH
      CARL FISCHER, INC.   P 3162   .50
TAYLOR   PAULL   MEDIUM
   SIGNAL FROM MARS, A
      SHAWNEE PRESS, INC.   .50
TAYLOR
   SMUGGLERS, THE
      CARL FISCHER, INC.   P 2132   .50
TAYLOR
   SUMMER CLOUDS
      CARL FISCHER, INC.   P 3036   .50
TAYLOR
   YES, THEY LOVE ME
      CARL FISCHER, INC.   P 3161   .50
TAYLOR, C.   2
   DANCE OF JULIE
      NOVELLO AND COMPANY, LTD.   55.0054.00   .40
TAYLOR, C.   2-3
   FOUR PRELETUDES -- 1. WATERMEADOWS
      NOVELLO AND COMPANY, LTD.   55.0049.04   .40
TAYLOR, C.   2
   FOUR PRELETUDES -- 2. DANCE, A
      NOVELLO AND COMPANY, LTD.   55.0050.08   .40
TAYLOR, C.   3
   FOUR PRELETUDES -- 3. FAREWELL, A
      NOVELLO AND COMPANY, LTD.   55.0051.06   .40
TAYLOR, C.   2-3
   FOUR PRELETUDES -- 4. PUNCH AND JUDY
      NOVELLO AND COMPANY, LTD.   55.0052.04   .40
TAYLOR, C.   ME
   PUCK
      OXFORD UNIVERSITY PRESS   33.056   1.10
TAYLOR, C.
   WHIMSIES
      BOOSEY AND HAWKES, INC.   1.00
TAYLOR, C.   2
   WINTER LANDSCAPE
      NOVELLO AND COMPANY, LTD.   55.0053.02   .40

TAYLOR, E.
   TWO PIANO PORTRAITS
      SOUTHERN MUSIC COMPANY   .50
TAYLOR, EDNA   3 1/2
   AFTER THE SHOWER
      THEODORE PRESSER COMPANY   .50
TAYLOR, EDNA
   FRANCINE DANCES
      FRANCO COLOMBO PUBLICATIONS   NY1531   .35
TAYLOR, EDNA
   HILLTOP DANCE
      BELWIN-MILLS PUBLISHING CORPORATION 25152   .60
TAYLOR, EDNA
   NEAPOLITAN DANCE
      BELWIN-MILLS PUBLISHING CORPORATION 25214   .60
TAYLOR, EDNA
   SINGING FOUNTAIN, THE
      BROOT MUSIC COMPANY   .45
TAYLOR, EDNA   2 1/2
   SONG AT TWILIGHT
      BELWIN-MILLS PUBLISHING CORPORATION   .60
TAYLOR, EDNA
   SPRINGTIME WALTZ
      FRANCO COLOMBO PUBLICATIONS   NY1608   .35
TAYLOR, S. C.   4
   THREE DREAM DANCES - NO. 02
      WILLIS MUSIC COMPANY   .60
TAYLOR, S. C.   4
   THREE-FOURS - NO. 06
      WILLIS MUSIC COMPANY   .75
TAYLOR, S. C.   3
   VALSE BOHEMIENE
      WILLIS MUSIC COMPANY   .60
TAYLOR, S. C.   4
   VALSE DE LA REINE
      WILLIS MUSIC COMPANY   .60
TAYLOR, S. C.   4
   VALSE MAURESQUE
      WILLIS MUSIC COMPANY   .60
TAYLOR, S. C.   3
   VALSE RUSTIQUE
      WILLIS MUSIC COMPANY   .60
TCHEREPNIN   D
   ABYSS --DER ABGRUND--. BALLET AFTER A NOVEL BY L. ANDRIEFF
      C. F. PETERS CORPORATION   6511   5.00
TCHEREPNIN   D
   BADINAGE
      C. F. PETERS CORPORATION   LY110   .60
TCHEREPNIN   BECKEL, J. G.   E
   BATTLE OF GETTYSBURG
      C. F. PETERS CORPORATION   H218   1.25
TCHEREPNIN
   CHANT ET REFRAIN
      ELKAN-VOGEL, INC.   D   2.00
TCHEREPNIN
   CZECH SONG, OP. 27, NO. 5
      HEUGEL ET CIE.   2.00
TCHEREPNIN
   DANCE IN F, OP. 2, NO. 2
      BOOSEY AND HAWKES, INC.   1.00
TCHEREPNIN
   DANSE EN MI FLAT MINEUR
      ELKAN-VOGEL, INC.   D   2.30
TCHEREPNIN
   ENTRETIENS, OP. 46
      ELKAN-VOGEL, INC.   D   1.90
TCHEREPNIN   PHILIPP, I.
   FEUILLES LIBRES
      ELKAN-VOGEL, INC.   D   1.90
TCHEREPNIN   5
   FUNF KONZERT-ETUDEN OP. 52 -- DIE LAUTE
      SCHOTT   4278   1.25
TCHEREPNIN   5
   FUNF KONZERT-ETUDEN OP. 52 -- KASPERLSPIEL
      SCHOTT   4280   1.25
TCHEREPNIN   5
   FUNF KONZERT-ETUDEN OP. 52 -- LOBGES
      SCHOTT   4281   1.25
TCHEREPNIN   5
   FUNF KONZERT-ETUDEN OP. 52 -- SCHATTENSPIIEL
      SCHOTT   4277   1.25
TCHEREPNIN   5
   FUNF KONZERT-ETUDEN OP. 52 -- WIDMUNG AN CHINA
      SCHOTT   4279   1.25
TCHEREPNIN
   HISTOIRE DE LA PETITE THERESE DE L'ENFANT-JESUS
      ELKAN-VOGEL, INC.   D   2.50
TCHEREPNIN
   MESSAGE, OP. 39
      UNIVERSAL EDITION   8611   3.00
TCHEREPNIN
   NOCTURNE DE RUBINSTEIN
      ELKAN-VOGEL, INC.   D   1.60
TCHEREPNIN
   NOCTURNE IN G SHARP, OP. 2, NO. 1
      BOOSEY AND HAWKES, INC.   .75
TCHEREPNIN
   NOCTURNE IN MI MINEUR
      ELKAN-VOGEL, INC.   D   2.10
TCHEREPNIN   PHILIPP, I.
   PETITE SUITE
      ELKAN-VOGEL, INC.   D   3.25
TCHEREPNIN
   PIANO SONATA, OP. 94 NO. 2
      BOOSEY AND HAWKES, INC.   2.00
TCHEREPNIN
   PIECES AN TITRES
      ELKAN-VOGEL, INC.   D   2.00
TCHEREPNIN   ADVANCED
   POLKA
      SHAWNEE PRESS, INC.   HB-138   .75
TCHEREPNIN
   RUSSIAN SONG, OP. 27, NO. 2
      HEUGEL ET CIE.   2.40
TCHEREPNIN
   SHOWCASE, OP. 75
      BOOSEY AND HAWKES, INC.   1.75
TCHEREPNIN
   SONATINE ROMANTIQUE
      ELKAN-VOGEL, INC.   D   4.25
TCHEREPNIN
   SUITE IN C MAJOR, OP. 51, NO. 1
      HEUGEL ET CIE.   1.75
TCHEREPNIN
   SUITE IN C MAJOR, OP. 51, NO. 2
      HEUGEL ET CIE.   3.00

TCHEREPNIN   D
   SUITE, OP. 100. HARPSICHORD
      C. F. PETERS CORPORATION   6879   1.50
TCHEREPNIN
   TOCCATA IN D MINOR, OP. 1
      BOOSEY AND HAWKES, INC.   1.00
TCHEREPNIN
   VOEUX
      ELKAN-VOGEL, INC.   D   3.40
TCHEREPNIN, N.
   PAVILLION D'ARMIDE -- COMPLETE BALLET
      BOOSEY AND HAWKES, INC.   6.00
TCHEREPNIN, S.
   INVENTIONEN
      BOOSEY AND HAWKES, INC.   2.00
TEBOLDI
   BALLAD
      FRANCO COLOMBO PUBLICATIONS   123237 .75
TEBOLDI
   DOLL HOUSE, THE
      FRANCO COLOMBO PUBLICATIONS   123349 .75
TEIKE, C.
   OLD COMRADES
      BOOSEY AND HAWKES, INC.   .60
TEITELBAUM   2
   ORIENTAL NIGHTS
      BELWIN-MILLS PUBLISHING CORPORATION   .60
TELEMANN, G.P.   CANIN   5
   FANTASY IN D MAJOR
      LEE ROBERTS MUSIC PUBLICATIONS, INC.   .60
TELEMANN, G.P.   CANIN   5
   FANTASY IN E MAJOR
      LEE ROBERTS MUSIC PUBLICATIONS, INC.   .60
TELEMANN, G.P. *   M
   ALLEGRO
      C. F. PETERS CORPORATION   7007   .60
TELEMANN, G.P. *   M-D
   CONCERTO IN G MINOR
      C. F. PETERS CORPORATION   217B   3.00
TEMPLETON   MEDIUM
   BIG BEN BOUNCE
      SHAWNEE PRESS, INC.   .60
TEMPLETON   MEDIUM
   FLIGHTS OF FANCY
      SHAWNEE PRESS, INC.   .75
TEMPLETON   ADVANCED
   FOUR CHARACTER STUDIES
      SHAWNEE PRESS, INC.   .75
TEMPLETON
   PRELUDE IN C
      SHAWNEE PRESS, INC.   .75
TEMPLETON, A.
   MENDELSSOHN MOWS 'EM DOWN
      THE BIG THREE MUSIC CORPORATION   00.95
TEMPLETON, A.
   REDWOODS AT BOHEMIAN GROVE
      THE BIG THREE MUSIC CORPORATION   00.95
TEMPLETON, S.
   ALL HAIL THE POWER
      BANKS AND SON LTD.   .70
TEMPLETON, V.
   FINGER TALK
      BELWIN-MILLS PUBLISHING CORPORATION 25049   .60
TEMPLETON, V.
   JUMPING BEANS
      BELWIN-MILLS PUBLISHING CORPORATION 25063   .60
TEMPLETON, V.
   TOY BUGLE
      BELWIN-MILLS PUBLISHING CORPORATION   .60
TERNI
   BALLAD NO. 3
      FRANCO COLOMBO PUBLICATIONS   DS823 2.75
TERNI
   SONATA
      FRANCO COLOMBO PUBLICATIONS   DS902 4.00
TERZIAN, A.
   DANZA CRIOLLA, OP. 1
      BOOSEY AND HAWKES, INC.   .75
THALBERG
   FANTAISIE SUR LES HUGUENOTS   --MEYERBEER OP. 20
      MUSICA OBSCURA   4.00
THALBERG
   GRANDE SONATE C MINOR OP. 56 --1844
      MUSICA OBSCURA   7.00
THALBERG
   GRAZIOSA --ROMANCE SANS PAROLES
      MUSICA OBSCURA   1.00
THALBERG
   HOME SWEET HOME OP. 72
      MUSICA OBSCURA   2.50
THARALDSEN   2
   MIDGET MARCH
      PRO-ART PUBLICATIONS, INC.   463   .50
THARICHEN, W.
   SONATA, OP. 28
      ASSOCIATED MUSIC PUBLISHERS, INC. BOT 2.50
THEODORAKIS, M.
   ZORBA THE GREEK - THEME
      THE BIG THREE MUSIC CORPORATION   00.95
THIELMANS
   VALSE JOLIE, LA. --PRETTY WALTZ, THE.
      MCA MUSIC   1.00
THILMAN   4
   SONATINA PATETICA, OP. 39
      BARENREITER VERLAG
THIMAN
   CHESHIRE ROUNDS
      BANKS AND SON LTD.   .25
THIMAN
   COUNTRY GARLAND, A
      BANKS AND SON LTD.   .95
THIRIET
   SONATINA
      FRANCO COLOMBO PUBLICATIONS   SAL 3.25
THOMA   4
   POLISH DANCE, OP. 52
      CENTURY MUSIC PUBLISHING COMPANY, INC. 1857   .40
THOMAS, A.   WEYBRIGHT   2 1/2
   GAVOTTE 'MIGNON'
      BELWIN-MILLS PUBLISHING CORPORATION   .60
THOMAS, A.   WEYBRIGHT   2 1/2
   GAVOTTE, FROM ''MIGNON''
      BELWIN-MILLS PUBLISHING CORPORATION   .50
THOMAS, A.   3
   GAVOTTE, MIGNON
      CENTURY MUSIC PUBLISHING COMPANY, INC. 1941   .40

THOMAS, A.
    HAMLET
        HEUGEL ET CIE.
THOMAS, A.   11.00
    HAMLET -- LA FETE DU PRINTEMPS
        HEUGEL ET CIE.
THOMAS, A.   4.40
    MIGNON
        HEUGEL ET CIE.
THOMAS, A.   3   11.00
    MIGNON, GAVOTTE
        CENTURY MUSIC PUBLISHING COMPANY, INC.   1941   .40
THOMAS, A.   5
    OVERTURE, RAYMOND
        CENTURY MUSIC PUBLISHING COMPANY, INC.   1579   .40
THOMAS, A.   3
    OVERTURE, RAYMOND, EASY
        CENTURY MUSIC PUBLISHING COMPANY, INC.   2095   .40
THOMAS, A.   6
    POLONAISE
        THEODORE PRESSER COMPANY
THOMAS, A.   5   .50
    RAYMOND OVERTURE
        CENTURY MUSIC PUBLISHING COMPANY, INC.   1579   .40
THOMAS, A.   3
    SANCTISSIMA
        THEODORE PRESSER COMPANY
THOMAS, A.   .50
    STACCATO BRETON--1948
        ASSOCIATED MUSIC PUBLISHERS, INC.   ESC   1.35
THOMAS, A.
    STEPPING OUT
        BANKS AND SON LTD.
THOMAS, A.--ED.   THOMAS, A.   3   .80
    O SANCTISSIMA - SICILIAN MARINERS' HYMN
        THEODORE PRESSER COMPANY
THOMAS, C. J.   .50
    CLOCKWORK DOLL, THE
        BRODT MUSIC COMPANY
THOMAS, C. J.   .30
    COCK A DOODLE DO
        BRODT MUSIC COMPANY
THOMAS, C. J.   .30
    COPY CAT
        BRODT MUSIC COMPANY
THOMAS, C. J.   .30
    IN CHURCH
        BRODT MUSIC COMPANY
THOMAS, C. J.   .30
    IN THE WOOD
        BRODT MUSIC COMPANY
THOMAS, C. J.   .30
    LITTLE BROOK, THE
        BRODT MUSIC COMPANY
THOMAS, C. J.   .40
    LITTLE TRUMPETER, THE
        BRODT MUSIC COMPANY
THOMAS, C. J.   .30
    MUSICAL BOX, THE
        BRODT MUSIC COMPANY
THOMAS, C. J.   .30
    NODDING TOY-CHINAMAN, THE
        BRODT MUSIC COMPANY
THOMAS, C. J.   .30
    PLAYTIME
        BRODT MUSIC COMPANY
THOMAS, C. J.   .30
    SKIPPY
        BRODT MUSIC COMPANY
THOMAS, C. J.   .30
    SNAKE CHARMER, THE
        BRODT MUSIC COMPANY
THOMAS, C. J.   .30
    SWING, THE
        BRODT MUSIC COMPANY
THOMAS, C. J.   .30
    WALTZ
        BRODT MUSIC COMPANY
THOMAS, F.   1 1/2   .30
    CHOCOLATE RIPPLE
        WILLIS MUSIC COMPANY
THOMAS, J. J.   1   .40
    BICYCLE RIDE
        THEODORE PRESSER COMPANY
THOMAS, J. J.   1   .50
    LITTLE BOBOLINK
        THEODORE PRESSER COMPANY
THOMAS, J. J.   2   .50
    MERRYMAKERS, THE
        THEODORE PRESSER COMPANY
THOMAS, J. J.   JESTON, I. H.   3   .50
    RAYMOND FANTASIA
        VOLKWEIN BROS.
THOMAS, J. J.   1 1/2   .35
    SLEEPY BIRD
        THEODORE PRESSER COMPANY
THOMAS, J. M.   .50
    NOEL TRISTE--BERCEUSE
        ASSOCIATED MUSIC PUBLISHERS, INC.   ESC   .60
THOMASON, E.   1
    BALLOON WALTZ
        CENTURY MUSIC PUBLISHING COMPANY, INC.   4217   .40
THOMASON, E.   1
    TUMBLERS, THE
        CENTURY MUSIC PUBLISHING COMPANY, INC.   4251   .40
THOME, F.   5
    ARAGONAISE, VALSE
        CENTURY MUSIC PUBLISHING COMPANY, INC.   1383   .40
THOME, F.   5
    MANDOLINE, SERENADE ESPAGNE
        CENTURY MUSIC PUBLISHING COMPANY, INC.   2284   .40
THOME, F.   1 1/2
    MELODIE
        WILLIS MUSIC COMPANY
THOME, F.   2   .40
    MELODY
        CENTURY MUSIC PUBLISHING COMPANY, INC.   3420   .40
THOME, F.
    PAPILLONS ROSES--IMPROMPTU, OP. 59 NO. 2
        G. SCHIRMER, INC.
THOME, F.   2 1/2   .50
    REMEMBRANCE
        WILLIS MUSIC COMPANY
THOME, F.   4   .40
    SIMPLE AVEU
        VOLKWEIN BROS.
                                                              .25

THOME, F.   4
    SIMPLE AVEU -- CONFESSION
        CENTURY MUSIC PUBLISHING COMPANY, INC.   389   .40
THOME, F.
    SIMPLE AVEU--ROMANCE SANS PAROLES, OP. 25
        G. SCHIRMER, INC.   .50
THOME, F.   4
    SIMPLE CONFESSION
        WILLIS MUSIC COMPANY   .60
THOME, F.   4
    SIMPLE CONFESSION -- SIMPLE AVEU, OP. 25
        BELWIN-MILLS PUBLISHING CORPORATION   28195   .60
THOME, F.   4
    SIREN, VALSE
        CENTURY MUSIC PUBLISHING COMPANY, INC.   1998   .40
THOME, F.   4
    UNDER THE LEAVES
        BELWIN-MILLS PUBLISHING CORPORATION   358   .60
THOME, F.   4
    UNDER THE LEAVES
        CENTURY MUSIC PUBLISHING COMPANY, INC.   994   .40
THOME, F.
    UNDER THE LEAVES, OP. 29
        G. SCHIRMER, INC.   .40
THOME, F.   4
    UNE FETE MADRID
        THEODORE PRESSER COMPANY   .50
THOMPSON, A. A.   2
    PRAM FLEET
        BELWIN-MILLS PUBLISHING CORPORATION   .60
THOMPSON, A. A.   1 1/2
    TRIPPING ALONG
        THEODORE PRESSER COMPANY   .50
THOMPSON, A. A.   2
    TURNING HAND SPRINGS
        BELWIN-MILLS PUBLISHING CORPORATION   .60
THOMPSON, J.   3
    AIR DE BALLET
        WILLIS MUSIC COMPANY   .50
THOMPSON, J.   3
    ANDANTINO FROM CONCERTO IN D MINOR
        WILLIS MUSIC COMPANY   .40
THOMPSON, J.   3
    ARIZONA SUITE
        WILLIS MUSIC COMPANY   2.50
THOMPSON, J.   3
    BA-BA- BLACK SHEEP
        WILLIS MUSIC COMPANY   .50
THOMPSON, J.   5
    BLACK EYES
        WILLIS MUSIC COMPANY   .50
THOMPSON, J.   2
    BROWNIES' CARNIVAL
        WILLIS MUSIC COMPANY   .35
THOMPSON, J.   1
    BURRO, THE
        WILLIS MUSIC COMPANY   .40
THOMPSON, J.   1
    CARAVAN, THE
        WILLIS MUSIC COMPANY   .40
THOMPSON, J.   3
    CASTANETS AND TAMBOURINES
        WILLIS MUSIC COMPANY   .40
THOMPSON, J.   3 1/2
    DESERT SUNSET
        WILLIS MUSIC COMPANY   .50
THOMPSON, J.   1
    DUBLIN TOWN
        WILLIS MUSIC COMPANY   .35
THOMPSON, J.   1
    DUTCH DANCE
        WILLIS MUSIC COMPANY   .40
THOMPSON, J.   3
    EVENING HARMONIES
        WILLIS MUSIC COMPANY   .40
THOMPSON, J.   2
    EVENING IN HAVANA
        WILLIS MUSIC COMPANY   .40
THOMPSON, J.   3
    FAIRIES' FROLIC
        WILLIS MUSIC COMPANY   .40
THOMPSON, J.   1
    FAIRIES' HARP, THE
        WILLIS MUSIC COMPANY   .35
THOMPSON, J.   3
    FOLK TUNE SONATA
        WILLIS MUSIC COMPANY   1.00
THOMPSON, J.   1
    FOREST DAWN
        WILLIS MUSIC COMPANY   .35
THOMPSON, J.   1
    FOREST DAWN
        WILLIS MUSIC COMPANY   .35
THOMPSON, J.   TURNER, J.   3
    GRAND CANYON
        WILLIS MUSIC COMPANY   .35
THOMPSON, J.   3 1/2
    GRAND CANYON
        WILLIS MUSIC COMPANY   .50
THOMPSON, J.   3 1/2
    GRAND CANYON
        WILLIS MUSIC COMPANY   .50
THOMPSON, J.   2
    GYPSY CAMP, THE
        WILLIS MUSIC COMPANY   .35
THOMPSON, J.   3
    HOME ON THE RANGE
        WILLIS MUSIC COMPANY   .35
THOMPSON, J.   3
    LAGOON
        WILLIS MUSIC COMPANY   .40
THOMPSON, J.   3
    LES CLOCHETTES
        WILLIS MUSIC COMPANY   .50
THOMPSON, J.   2
    LITTLE SLAVONIC RHAPSODY
        WILLIS MUSIC COMPANY   .35
THOMPSON, J.   3 1/2
    LOFTY PEAKS
        WILLIS MUSIC COMPANY   .50
THOMPSON, J.   3
    LONDONDERRY AIR
        WILLIS MUSIC COMPANY   .35
THOMPSON, J.   3
    MARACAS
        WILLIS MUSIC COMPANY   .40

THOMPSON, J.   3
   MARIONETTE, THE
     WILLIS MUSIC COMPANY   .40
THOMPSON, J.   3
   MARY HAD A LITTLE LAMB -- VARIATIONS
     WILLIS MUSIC COMPANY   .60
THOMPSON, J.   3 1/2
   MISSION BELLS
     WILLIS MUSIC COMPANY   .50
THOMPSON, J.   2
   MOTHS
     WILLIS MUSIC COMPANY   .40
THOMPSON, J.   3 1/2
   OLD PUEBLOS
     WILLIS MUSIC COMPANY   .50
THOMPSON, J.   5
   PETITE RUSSIAN RHAPSODIE
     WILLIS MUSIC COMPANY   .40
THOMPSON, J.   4
   RHAPSODIE HONGROISE
     WILLIS MUSIC COMPANY   .50
THOMPSON, J.   3
   SONATINA
     WILLIS MUSIC COMPANY   .75
THOMPSON, J.   3 1/2
   SONATINA IN G
     WILLIS MUSIC COMPANY   .60
THOMPSON, J.   2
   SONATINE IN A MINOR
     WILLIS MUSIC COMPANY   .75
THOMPSON, J.   4
   SONATINE IN HARPSICHORD STYLE
     WILLIS MUSIC COMPANY   .75
THOMPSON, J.   1
   SPANISH FIESTA, A
     WILLIS MUSIC COMPANY   .35
THOMPSON, J.   2
   SPARKS
     WILLIS MUSIC COMPANY   .35
THOMPSON, J.   3
   TANGO CARIOCA
     WILLIS MUSIC COMPANY   .40
THOMPSON, J.   2
   TARANTELLA
     WILLIS MUSIC COMPANY   .35
THOMPSON, J.   1
   TIRESOME WOODPECKER, THE
     WILLIS MUSIC COMPANY   .35
THOMPSON, J.   1
   TULIP TIME
     WILLIS MUSIC COMPANY   .35
THOMPSON, J.   3
   TURKEY IN THE STRAW
     WILLIS MUSIC COMPANY   .50
THOMPSON, J.   2
   TWO GUITARS
     WILLIS MUSIC COMPANY   .35
THOMPSON, J.   2 1/2
   VALSE BURLESQUE
     WILLIS MUSIC COMPANY   .50
THOMPSON, J.   2 1/2
   VALSE BURLESQUE
     WILLIS MUSIC COMPANY   .50
THOMPSON, J.   3
   VALSE CHROMATIQUE
     WILLIS MUSIC COMPANY   .40
THOMPSON, J.   3
   VIENNESE MELODY
     WILLIS MUSIC COMPANY   .40
THOMPSON, J.--ED   THOMPSON, J.   3
   CIELITO LINDO
     WILLIS MUSIC COMPANY   .35
THOMPSON, J.--ED   THOMPSON, J.   2
   HE'S GOT THE WHOLE WORLD IN HIS HANDS
     WILLIS MUSIC COMPANY   .40
THOMPSON, J.--ED   THOMPSON, J.   3
   RECOLLECTIONS OF JOHANN STRAUSS
     WILLIS MUSIC COMPANY   .60
THOMPSON, J.--ED   THOMPSON, J.   2
   STAR-SPANGLED BANNER, THE
     WILLIS MUSIC COMPANY   .35
THOMSON, V.
   FILLING STATION
     BOOSEY AND HAWKES, INC.   2.25
THORNE
   HE DOES - SHE DOESN'T
     GENERAL MUSIC PUBLISHING COMPANY, INC.   685   2.00
THORNTON
   APRIL DAYS
     BANKS AND SON LTD.   .55
THORNTON
   FIRST BOUQUET OF WALTZES, A
     BANKS AND SON LTD.   .80
THORNTON
   FUN AND FROLIC
     BANKS AND SON LTD.   .80
THORNTON
   IRIS
     BANKS AND SON LTD.   .25
THORNTON
   JOY TUNES
     BANKS AND SON LTD.   .80
THORNTON
   JOYFUL DAYS
     BANKS AND SON LTD.   .40
THORNTON   STEINER   1
   MAN IN THE MOON, THE
     BELWIN-MILLS PUBLISHING CORPORATION   .60
THORNTON   ZEPP   2
   MY SWEETHEART'S THE MAN IN THE MOON
     PRO-ART PUBLICATIONS, INC.   324   .50
THORNTON
   PLEASURE PIECES
     BANKS AND SON LTD.   .80
THORNTON
   REVELRY
     BANKS AND SON LTD.   .55
THORNTON
   SUMMER GLORY
     BANKS AND SON LTD.   .80
THORNTON
   THREE FLORAL SCENES
     BANKS AND SON LTD.   .80
THUILLIER   2
   FRILEUSE, LA, VALSE
     ALPHONSE LEDUC

THUILLIER   4
   PETIT CARILLON, ESQUISSE
     ALPHONSE LEDUC
THUILLIER   5
   SOUS LES CHENES, VALSE
     ALPHONSE LEDUC
THUILLIER   4
   TARENTELLE
     ALPHONSE LEDUC
THUILLIER
   TRILBY -- GALOP BRILLIANT --
     FRANCO COLOMBO PUBLICATIONS   SAL   1.75
TIBBITTS, A.   1
   MY SNOWMAN
     THEODORE PRESSER COMPANY   .50
TIBBITTS, A.   2
   TURNING WHEELS
     THEODORE PRESSER COMPANY   .50
TIDES, A.   4
   PRETTY LILLIES MORCEAU
     VOLKWEIN BROS.   .50
TIDES, A.   4
   REVEL OF THE ELVES -- MORCEAU
     VOLKWEIN BROS.   .50
TIDES, A.   4-5
   REVEL OF THE ELVES -- MORCEAU
     VOLKWEIN BROS.   00.60
TIEMAN, J.   3
   HAWAIIAN TWILIGHT
     THEODORE PRESSER COMPANY   .50
TIESSEN, H.
   SIX PIANO PIECES, OP. 37
     UNIVERSAL EDITION   UE 9687   1.95
TILLERY, H.   2
   RAMBLIN' RABBIT
     THEODORE PRESSER COMPANY   .50
TILLERY, H.   4
   SUMMER NIGHT
     THEODORE PRESSER COMPANY   .50
TILLERY, H.   2
   TOMAHAWK TRAIL
     THEODORE PRESSER COMPANY   .50
TILLERY, H.   2
   TRICK OR TREAT
     THEODORE PRESSER COMPANY   .50
TILLETT, J.   3
   BATON TWIRLER
     WILLIS MUSIC COMPANY   .40
TILLETT, J.   3
   FUN IN THE POOL
     WILLIS MUSIC COMPANY   .40
TILLETT, J.   2 1/2
   SONATINA NO. 01 IN C MAJOR
     BELWIN-MILLS PUBLISHING CORPORATION   .60
TILLETT, J.   1 1/2
   SONG OF THE BELLS
     BELWIN-MILLS PUBLISHING CORPORATION   .60
TILLETT, J.   3
   TARANTELLA
     WILLIS MUSIC COMPANY   .40
TIOMKIN, D.
   GREEN LEAVES OF SUMMER, THE
     THE BIG THREE MUSIC CORPORATION   00.95
TIOMKIN, D.   RICHTER   FIRST YEAR
   HIGH AND THE MIGHTY, THE
     WARNER BROTHERS PUBLISHERS   .75
TIPPETT, M.   5
   SONATA
     SCHOTT   10123   2.00
TIPPETT, M.   5
   SONATA NO. 02 IN EINEM SATZ
     SCHOTT   10815   2.75
TIRINDELLI   DEL MAGLIO
   O PRIMAVERA
     FRANCO COLOMBO PUBLICATIONS   127762   .50
TISNE, A.
   CIMAISE
     GERARD BILLAUDOT EDITIONS MUSICALES   6.30
TISNE, A.
   EPIGRAPHE POUR UNE STELE
     GERARD BILLAUDOT EDITIONS MUSICALES   2.20
TISNE, A.
   SOLIELS NOIRS
     GERARD BILLAUDOT EDITIONS MUSICALES   3.20
TISNE, A.
   SONATE
     GERARD BILLAUDOT EDITIONS MUSICALES   6.30
TITL   4
   SERENADE
     CENTURY MUSIC PUBLISHING COMPANY, INC.   2338   .40
TJEKNAVORIAN, L. Z.
   SONATINA NO. 01, OP. 7--1961
     ASSOCIATED MUSIC PUBLISHERS, INC.   DOB   2.50
TJEKNAVORIAN, L. Z.
   SONATINA NO. 02, OP. 10--1962
     ASSOCIATED MUSIC PUBLISHERS, INC.   DOB   2.50
TJEKNAVORIAN, L. Z.
   SRING-ATHRE, OP. 9--1962
     ASSOCIATED MUSIC PUBLISHERS, INC.   DOB   2.50
TOBANI
   HEARTS AND FLOWERS
     ASHLEY DEALERS SERVICE, INC.   ES   .95
TOBANI   KING, S.
   HEARTS AND FLOWERS
     BELWIN-MILLS PUBLISHING CORPORATION   26019   .50
TOBANI   3
   HEARTS AND FLOWERS
     BOSTON MUSIC COMPANY   .50
TOBANI   WOODE   1
   HEARTS AND FLOWERS
     BOSTON MUSIC COMPANY   .50
TOBANI   MENDEL, S.   2
   HEARTS AND FLOWERS
     WILLIS MUSIC COMPANY   .40
TOBANI   MENDEL, S.   2
   HEARTS AND FLOWERS
     WILLIS MUSIC COMPANY   .40
TOBIN, R.   E
   READ AND REMEMBER
     OXFORD UNIVERSITY PRESS   33.050   1.80
TOBIN, R.   VE
   REMEMBER
     OXFORD UNIVERSITY PRESS   93.305   .40
TOBIN, R.
   ROUND THE VILLAGE GREEN
     BANKS AND SON LTD.   .95

TOCABEN, L.   2
    ON PARADE
        CENTURY MUSIC PUBLISHING COMPANY, INC.   1533   .40
TOCABEN, L.   2
    SPRINGTIME
        CENTURY MUSIC PUBLISHING COMPANY, INC.   1532   .40
TOCH, E.   5
    BURLESKEN, OP. 31 NO. 3, DER JONGLEUR
        SCHOTT   1823   1.50
TOCH, E.
    REFLECTIONS -- FIVE PIECES FOR PIANO, OP. 86
        BELWIN-MILLS PUBLISHING CORPORATION   20418   1.00
TOCH, E.   5
    SONATA, OP. 47
        SCHOTT   2065   3.00
TOCH, E.
    THREE LITTLE DANCES FOR PIANO, OP. 85
        BELWIN-MILLS PUBLISHING CORPORATION   20378   1.00
TODD   2
    SAMBO'S BANJO
        BELWIN-MILLS PUBLISHING CORPORATION   .60
TODD   1
    SWISS VILLAGE
        BELWIN-MILLS PUBLISHING CORPORATION   .60
TOEBOSCH   M-D
    SONATA NO. 01, OP. 29
        C. F. PETERS CORPORATION   D216   2.00
TOKUNAGA, H.   A
    THREE INTERLUDES FOR PIANO
        THEODORE PRESSER COMPANY   .50
TOLDRA, E. E.
    TAMARIU--SARDANA
        ASSOCIATED MUSIC PUBLISHERS, INC.   UME   .75
TOLLEFSEN, A.   M
    DIRGE
        COMPOSERS PRESS, INC.   1.00
TOLLEFSEN, A.   M
    GAIETY
        COMPOSERS PRESS, INC.   1.00
TOLLEFSEN, A.   E
    NORWEGIAN DANCE
        COMPOSERS PRESS, INC.   1.00
TOLLEFSEN, A.   D
    VAGUE MEMORIES
        COMPOSERS PRESS, INC.   2.00
TOLLEFSEN, A.   E-M
    WATER SPRITE
        COMPOSERS PRESS, INC.   1.00
TOMASI, H.   7
    BERCEUSE
        ALPHONSE LEDUC
TOMASI, H.
    FANTOCHES
        FRANCO COLOMBO PUBLICATIONS   SAL   2.50
TOMASI, H.
    LA GRISI
        HEUGEL ET CIE.   2.75
TOMASI, H.   7
    TARENTELLE
        ALPHONSE LEDUC
TON-THAT, T.
    AI VAN 1
        ELKAN-VOGEL, INC.   J   4.00
TON-THAT, T.
    BA DOAN KHUC
        EDITIONS MUSICALES TRANSATLANTIQUES   3.15
TONNER, P.   1
    GRIZZLY BEAR, THE
        CENTURY MUSIC PUBLISHING COMPANY, INC.   4310   .40
TORJUSSEN
    TO THE RISING SUN
        SUMMY-BIRCHARD COMPANY   .50
TORRANDELL
    SEGUIDILLAS
        FRANCO COLOMBO PUBLICATIONS   SAL   2.00
TORRANDELL
    SEVILLANAS
        FRANCO COLOMBO PUBLICATIONS   SAL   2.00
TORROBA, F. M.
    MOSAICO SEVILLANO
        ASSOCIATED MUSIC PUBLISHERS, INC.   UME   .60
TORROBA, F.M.
    NOCHE SEVILLANAS
        EDWARD B. MARKS MUSIC CORPORATION   01.00
TOSAR
    SONATINA NO. 02
        FRANCO COLOMBO PUBLICATIONS   BA11715   2.50
TOSAR ERRECART, H.
    IMPROVISACION
        EDITORIAL COOPERATIVA INTER-AMERICANA   00.95
TOSAR, H.
    DANZA CRIOLLA
        BROUDE BROTHERS LTD.   02.50
TOSATTI
    ALLEGRO DA CONCERTO
        FRANCO COLOMBO PUBLICATIONS   128878   .90
TOSELLI   SCHAUM, J.   3
    NEAPOLITAN SERENADE
        SCHAUM PUBLICATIONS, INC.   .60
TOSELLI   BROWER   3
    SERENADE
        BOSTON MUSIC COMPANY   .60
TOSELLI   WEST   3
    SERENADE
        BOSTON MUSIC COMPANY   .60
TOSTI   SANDRON
    IDEALE
        FRANCO COLOMBO PUBLICATIONS   117157   .50
TOSTI   DEL MAGLIO
    IDEALE
        FRANCO COLOMBO PUBLICATIONS   124749   .50
TOSTI
    MALIA
        FRANCO COLOMBO PUBLICATIONS   117158   .50
TOSTI   DEL MAGLIO
    MALIA
        FRANCO COLOMBO PUBLICATIONS   124750   .50
TOSTI   SANDRON
    MARECHIARE
        FRANCO COLOMBO PUBLICATIONS   117159   .60
TOSTI   DEL MAGLIO
    MARECHIARE
        FRANCO COLOMBO PUBLICATIONS   124751   .60
TOSTI   DEL MAGLIO
    NON T'AMO PIU
        FRANCO COLOMBO PUBLICATIONS   128148   .50

TOSTI
    SERENATA
        FRANCO COLOMBO PUBLICATIONS   117167   .50
TOSTI   DEL MAGLIO
    VORREI
        FRANCO COLOMBO PUBLICATIONS   128137   .50
TOURS   4-5
    BY THE BROOKSIDE
        CENTURY MUSIC PUBLISHING COMPANY, INC.   2426   .40
TOURS   3
    GAVOTTE MODERNE
        CENTURY MUSIC PUBLISHING COMPANY, INC.   1953   .40
TOWNSEND
    BUSY CARPENTER, THE
        G. SCHIRMER, INC.   .35
TOWNSEND   1-2
    BUSY TRACTOR MAN, THE
        PRO-ART PUBLICATIONS, INC.   223   .50
TOWNSEND   2-3
    COCK-A-DOODLE DOO
        PRO-ART PUBLICATIONS, INC.   222   .50
TOWNSEND   2-3
    COOL REVEILLE
        PRO-ART PUBLICATIONS, INC.   225   .50
TOWNSEND   2
    COWGIRL, THE
        BELWIN-MILLS PUBLISHING CORPORATION   .60
TOWNSEND   3
    CROW AND THE SCARECROW, THE
        PRO-ART PUBLICATIONS, INC.   220   .50
TOWNSEND   1 1/2
    DIDDLE DE DUM
        BELWIN-MILLS PUBLISHING CORPORATION   .60
TOWNSEND   2 1/2
    DIXIE WITH A BEAT
        BELWIN-MILLS PUBLISHING CORPORATION   .60
TOWNSEND   2
    FISH SCALES
        BELWIN-MILLS PUBLISHING CORPORATION   .60
TOWNSEND   1 1/2
    GEORGE THE GIANT
        BELWIN-MILLS PUBLISHING CORPORATION   .60
TOWNSEND   1 1/2
    GUS THE GRASSHOPPER
        BELWIN-MILLS PUBLISHING CORPORATION   .60
TOWNSEND   2
    HANON WITH A BEAT
        BELWIN-MILLS PUBLISHING CORPORATION   .60
TOWNSEND   2
    HOT POTATOES
        BELWIN-MILLS PUBLISHING CORPORATION   .60
TOWNSEND   1 1/2
    JUMPING DUCK
        BELWIN-MILLS PUBLISHING CORPORATION   .60
TOWNSEND   3 1/2
    LET'S CALYPSO
        BELWIN-MILLS PUBLISHING CORPORATION   .60
TOWNSEND   2 1/2
    LITTLE CUBAN BOY
        BELWIN-MILLS PUBLISHING CORPORATION   .60
TOWNSEND   2 1/2
    LITTLE FRENCH BOY
        BELWIN-MILLS PUBLISHING CORPORATION   .60
TOWNSEND   2
    LITTLE ISRAELI BOY
        BELWIN-MILLS PUBLISHING CORPORATION   .60
TOWNSEND   2
    LITTLE SCOTCH BOY
        BELWIN-MILLS PUBLISHING CORPORATION   .60
TOWNSEND   3
    LITTLE SPANISH BOY
        BELWIN-MILLS PUBLISHING CORPORATION   .60
TOWNSEND   2
    LITTLE SWISS BOY
        BELWIN-MILLS PUBLISHING CORPORATION   .60
TOWNSEND   2-3
    MERRY MEADOWLARK, THE
        PRO-ART PUBLICATIONS, INC.   221   .50
TOWNSEND   1-2
    RIVERBOAT CAPTAIN, THE
        PRO-ART PUBLICATIONS, INC.   224   .50
TOWNSEND   3
    ROADRUNNER
        BELWIN-MILLS PUBLISHING CORPORATION   .60
TOWNSEND   3
    U. S. MARSHALL
        PRO-ART PUBLICATIONS, INC.   219   .50
TRACY, G.   1
    TOM TOM PARADE
        BELWIN-MILLS PUBLISHING CORPORATION   .60
TRAEGER   1-2
    CAROUSEL, THE
        PRO-ART PUBLICATIONS, INC.   603   .50
TRAEGER   1-2
    SLEEPYTIME
        PRO-ART PUBLICATIONS, INC.   602   .50
TRANSLETEUR
    MARIAGE A LILLIPUT, UN
        FRANCO COLOMBO PUBLICATIONS   SAL   1.50
TRAPP, M.
    SONATINA, OP. 25
        ASSOCIATED MUSIC PUBLISHERS, INC.   LEU   3.00
TRAUX, J.   3
    FALLING WATERS
        BELWIN-MILLS PUBLISHING CORPORATION   362   .60
TRAUX, J.   4
    FALLING WATERS
        CENTURY MUSIC PUBLISHING COMPANY, INC.   1304   .40
TRAVIS, B.   1 1/2
    BICYCLE RACE, A
        THEODORE PRESSER COMPANY   .50
TRAVIS, B.   1 1/2
    COUNTRY FIDDLER, THE
        THEODORE PRESSER COMPANY   .50
TRAVIS, B.   MD
    FIVE PRELUDES FOR PIANO
        THEODORE PRESSER COMPANY   1.25
TRAVIS, B.   1
    FLYING AN AIRPLANE
        THEODORE PRESSER COMPANY   .50
TRAVIS, B.   1 1/2
    IN LICORICE CANDY LAND
        THEODORE PRESSER COMPANY   .50
TRAVIS, B.
    LITTLE RACE HORSE, THE
        G. SCHIRMER, INC.   .35

TRAVIS, B.
  MARCH OF THE CANDY-STICK MEN
    G. SCHIRMER, INC.   .35
TRAVIS, B.
  PUPPET CARNIVAL
    BELWIN-MILLS PUBLISHING CORPORATION   28183   .60
TRAVIS, B.
  SCALING A FENCE
    BELWIN-MILLS PUBLISHING CORPORATION   28185   .60
TRAVIS, B.   1 1/2
  SLEEPY EYES
    THEODORE PRESSER COMPANY   .50
TRAVIS, B.   1 1/2
  WALTZ OF THE PEPPERMINT STICKS
    THEODORE PRESSER COMPANY   .50
TREBINSKY, A.
  SUITE FRANCAISE POUR PIANO
    EDITIONS MUSICALES TRANSATLANTIQUES   4.90
TREHDE--ED   TREHDE   4
  DOVE, THE -- LA PALOMA
    CENTURY MUSIC PUBLISHING COMPANY, INC.   687   .40
TREPANIER   1-2
  BAGATELLES
    PRO-ART PUBLICATIONS, INC.   272   .50
TREVARTHEN, R. R.
  BERNA
    BRODT MUSIC COMPANY   .45
TREVARTHEN, R. R.
  BLUMLISALP -- RASPBERRY ROSE
    BRODT MUSIC COMPANY   .45
TREVARTHEN, R. R.
  BROTHERS
    BRODT MUSIC COMPANY   .45
TREVARTHEN, R. R.
  FIVE MINIATURES FOR PIANO
    BRODT MUSIC COMPANY   1.00
TREVARTHEN, R. R.
  FUZZY BEAR
    BRODT MUSIC COMPANY   .45
TREVARTHEN, R. R.
  JENNY'S GONE
    BRODT MUSIC COMPANY   .50
TREVARTHEN, R. R.
  LAURA LEE
    BRODT MUSIC COMPANY   .50
TREVARTHEN, R. R.
  MAPLE HILL FARM
    BRODT MUSIC COMPANY   .50
TREVARTHEN, R. R.
  OSTENTATIOUS OSTRICH, THE
    BRODT MUSIC COMPANY   .45
TREVARTHEN, R. R.
  SHIRLEY PINECONE
    BRODT MUSIC COMPANY   .45
TREVARTHEN, R. R.
  SWEETEN CREEK
    BRODT MUSIC COMPANY   .50
TREVARTHEN, R. R.
  THIRDS
    BRODT MUSIC COMPANY   .40
TREVARTHEN, R. R.
  THREE RHAPSODIES ON FOUR NOTES
    BRODT MUSIC COMPANY   1.00
TREVARTHEN, R. R.
  TURKEY KNOB
    BRODT MUSIC COMPANY   .60
TRIGGS
  MAMA, PAPA IS WOUNDED, FROM THE SUITE, 'SIX SURREALIST
  AFTERLUDES'
    BELWIN-MILLS PUBLISHING CORPORATION   1.00
TRIMBLE
  PETIT CONCERT. HARPSICHORD, MEDIUM VOICE, VIOLIN, OBOE
    C. F. PETERS CORPORATION   66069   5.00
TROIANI   LOCATELLI
  DANCE
    FRANCO COLOMBO PUBLICATIONS   BA9200   .75
TROIANI
  RITMOS ARGENTINOS
    FRANCO COLOMBO PUBLICATIONS   BA217   1.25
TROJA   4
  CHERRY BLOSSOMS
    CENTURY MUSIC PUBLISHING COMPANY, INC.   1078   .40
TROJE-MILLER   2 1/2
  BLUEBIRDS
    BELWIN-MILLS PUBLISHING CORPORATION   .60
TROJE-MILLER   2
  BUBBLE SONG
    BELWIN-MILLS PUBLISHING CORPORATION   .60
TROJE-MILLER   1
  LUCKY FOUR-LEAF CLOVER
    BELWIN-MILLS PUBLISHING CORPORATION   .60
TROJE-MILLER   3
  MARCH OF THE MARTIANS
    BELWIN-MILLS PUBLISHING CORPORATION   .60
TROJE-MILLER   3
  PRETTY CAT
    BELWIN-MILLS PUBLISHING CORPORATION   .60
TROJE-MILLER--ED   TROJE-MILLER   2 1/2
  LET'S GO TO THE SYMPHONY
    BELWIN-MILLS PUBLISHING CORPORATION   .60
TROJELLI
  PETITES MAINS, LES - GENTIL SOURIRE
    FRANCO COLOMBO PUBLICATIONS   SAL   1.50
TROJELLI
  PETITES MAINS, LES - LES MARIONNETTES
    FRANCO COLOMBO PUBLICATIONS   SAL   1.50
TROJELLI
  PETITES MAINS, LES - PRES D'UNE MERE
    FRANCO COLOMBO PUBLICATIONS   SAL   1.50
TROJELLI
  PETITES MAINS, LES - RETOUR DE CLASSE
    FRANCO COLOMBO PUBLICATIONS   SAL   1.50
TROJELLI
  PETITES MAINS, LES - SIMPLETTE
    FRANCO COLOMBO PUBLICATIONS   SAL   1.50
TROJELLI
  PETITES MAINS, LES - UN PETIT BAL
    FRANCO COLOMBO PUBLICATIONS   SAL   1.50
TROJELLI
  SIX PIECES MIGNONNES POUE LES PETITES MAINS - EN FAMILLE
    FRANCO COLOMBO PUBLICATIONS   SAL   1.50
TROJELLI
  SIX PIECES MIGNONNES POUR LES PETITES MAINS - CACHECACHE
    FRANCO COLOMBO PUBLICATIONS   SAL   1.50
TROJELLI
  SIX PIECES MIGNONNES POUR LES PETITES MAINS - COUCOU
    FRANCO COLOMBO PUBLICATIONS   SAL   1.50

TROJELLI
  SIX PIECES MIGNONNES POUR LES PETITES MAINS - LA SOURIS BLANCHE
    FRANCO COLOMBO PUBLICATIONS   SAL   1.50
TROJELLI
  SIX PIECES MIGNONNES POUR LES PETITES MAINS - PAPILLON VOLE
    FRANCO COLOMBO PUBLICATIONS   SAL   1.50
TROJELLI
  SIX PIECES MIGNONNES POUR LES PETITES MAINS - PAUVRE TOUTOU
    FRANCO COLOMBO PUBLICATIONS   SAL   1.50
TROMPEO
  NOTRE DAME DES ERMITES
    FRANCO COLOMBO PUBLICATIONS   DS389   1.25
TROWBRIDGE, L.   E
  CROCODILE
    COMPOSERS PRESS, INC.   1.00
TROWBRIDGE, L.   E
  DADDY LONGLEGS
    COMPOSERS PRESS, INC.   1.00
TROWBRIDGE, L.   E-M
  FIREFLY
    COMPOSERS PRESS, INC.   1.00
TROWBRIDGE, L.   E
  HOOTIE THE OWL
    COMPOSERS PRESS, INC.   1.00
TROWBRIDGE, L.   E
  PETER RABBIT
    COMPOSERS PRESS, INC.   1.00
TROWBRIDGE, L.   E-M
  ROBIN REDBREAST
    COMPOSERS PRESS, INC.   1.00
TROWBRIDGE, L.   E-M
  WILL O' THE WISP
    COMPOSERS PRESS, INC.   1.00
TRUAX, J.   4 1/2
  FALLING WATERS
    THEODORE PRESSER COMPANY   .60
TRUAX, J.   3 1/2
  FALLING WATERS
    WILLIS MUSIC COMPANY   .35
TRUAX, J.   4
  WATERS OF YOSEMITE
    CENTURY MUSIC PUBLISHING COMPANY, INC.   1304   .40
TRUED   3
  JALOPY JUNCTION
    PRO-ART PUBLICATIONS, INC.   431   .50
TRUNK, R.
  AMMERSEE-SUITE, OP. 85
    ASSOCIATED MUSIC PUBLISHERS, INC.   LEU   2.00
TRUXELL, E.   1 1/2
  BABY KANGAROO
    VOLKWEIN BROS.   .35
TRUXELL, E.   3
  CHARMING PRINCESS
    VOLKWEIN BROS.   .40
TRUXELL, E.   2
  DANCING WATERS
    VOLKWEIN BROS.   .40
TRUXELL, E.   2
  FIDDLE STICKS
    VOLKWEIN BROS.   .50
TRUXELL, E.   1 1/2
  I'M A LITTLE BLACK SHEEP
    VOLKWEIN BROS.   .35
TRUXELL, E.   2
  LEAPING SQUIRREL
    VOLKWEIN BROS.   .35
TRUXELL, E.   2
  LITTLE JUMBO
    VOLKWEIN BROS.   .35
TRUXELL, E.   2
  MONKEY SHINES
    VOLKWEIN BROS.   .35
TRUXELL, E.   3
  NIGHT FIREWORKS
    VOLKWEIN BROS.   .40
TRUXELL, E.   3
  NOCTURNE IN SPRINGTIME
    VOLKWEIN BROS.   .40
TRUXELL, E.   2
  ONCE UPON A TIME
    VOLKWEIN BROS.   .35
TRUXELL, E.   2
  PLEASANT DAY
    VOLKWEIN BROS.   .35
TRUXELL, E.   2
  POP GOES THE WEASEL
    VOLKWEIN BROS.   .40
TRUXELL, E.   3
  POP GOES THE WEASEL
    VOLKWEIN BROS.   00.60
TRUXELL, E.   2
  RANGERS ON PATROL
    VOLKWEIN BROS.   .35
TRUXELL, E.   3
  RHYTHMIC FEET -- SOFT SHOE DANCE
    VOLKWEIN BROS.   .40
TRUXELL, E.   2
  RIDING THE SUNSET
    VOLKWEIN BROS.   .40
TRUXELL, E.   4
  ROMANCE AND MUSIC
    VOLKWEIN BROS.   .75
TRUXELL, E.   3
  SILVER ANNIVERSARY WALTZ
    VOLKWEIN BROS.   .50
TRUXELL, E.   4
  SPRINGTIME IN THE AIR
    VOLKWEIN BROS.   .50
TRUXELL, E.   1
  STAR SPANGLED BANNER
    VOLKWEIN BROS.   .30
TRUXELL, E.   4
  SUMMER NIGHT
    VOLKWEIN BROS.   .50
TRUXELL, E.   4
  TANGO
    VOLKWEIN BROS.   00.50
TRUXELL, E.   4
  VALSE CHANTEE
    VOLKWEIN BROS.   00.50
TSCHAIKOWSKY   MARCIANO
  ALBUM FOR THE YOUNG, OP. 39
    FRANCO COLOMBO PUBLICATIONS   EP 523   1.25
TSCHAIKOWSKY   ANDERTON
  ANDANTE --FROM THE FIFTH SYMPHONY--
    BELWIN-MILLS PUBLISHING CORPORATION   28147   .60

TSCHAIKOWSKY   KLINDWORTH
    ANDANTE CANTABILE IN B FLAT--FROM THE STRING QUARTET, OP. 11
        G. SCHIRMER, INC.   .50
TSCHAIKOWSKY   WEYBRIGHT   2 1/2
    ANDANTE CANTABILE, EXCERPT
        BELWIN-MILLS PUBLISHING CORPORATION
                         5   .50
TSCHAIKOWSKY
    ARAB DANCE FROM 'NUTCRACKER SUITE'
        BELWIN-MILLS PUBLISHING CORPORATION   498   .60
TSCHAIKOWSKY   4-5
    ARAB DANCE, G MINOR FROM NUTCRACKER SUITE
        CENTURY MUSIC PUBLISHING COMPANY, INC.   2664   .40
TSCHAIKOWSKY   STEINER   3
    ARABIAN DANCE, FROM ''THE NUTCRACKER SUITE''
        BELWIN-MILLS PUBLISHING CORPORATION   .50
TSCHAIKOWSKY
    BALLET -- LE LAC DES CYGNES
        NOVELLO AND COMPANY, LTD.   10.0085.03   7.50
TSCHAIKOWSKY   4
    BARCAROLLE, JUNE
        CENTURY MUSIC PUBLISHING COMPANY, INC.   748   .40
TSCHAIKOWSKY   MIKELA   4-5
    CAPRICCIO ITALIEN
        BARENREITER VERLAG   AP 1701
TSCHAIKOWSKY   SCHAUM, J.   5
    CAPRICCIO ITALIEN
        BELWIN-MILLS PUBLISHING CORPORATION
                         5   .50
TSCHAIKOWSKY
    CAPRICCIO ITALIEN OP. 45
        SCHOTT   2381   1.75
TSCHAIKOWSKY   DEXTER, H.
    CASSE NOISETTE
        SAM FOX PUBLISHING COMPANY, INC.   1.00
TSCHAIKOWSKY
    CASSE-NOISETTE, OP. 71
        GERARD BILLAUDOT EDITIONS MUSICALES   2.50
TSCHAIKOWSKY
    CHANSON TRISTE IN G MINOR, OP. 40 NO. 2
        G. SCHIRMER, INC.
                         3   .40
TSCHAIKOWSKY
    CHANSON TRISTE OP. 40 NO. 2
        SCHOTT   01722   .75
TSCHAIKOWSKY   3
    CHANSON TRISTE, OP. 40 NO. 2
        CENTURY MUSIC PUBLISHING COMPANY, INC.   2393   .40
TSCHAIKOWSKY   MARCIANO
    CHANSON TRISTE, OP. 40 NO. 2
        FRANCO COLOMBO PUBLICATIONS   128155   .50
TSCHAIKOWSKY
    CHANSON TRISTE, OP. 40 NO. 2
        GERARD BILLAUDOT EDITIONS MUSICALES   1.10
TSCHAIKOWSKY   4
    CHANT SANS PAROLES OP. 2 NO. 3
        SCHOTT   01690 1/2   1.00
TSCHAIKOWSKY   4
    CHANT SANS PAROLES, OP. 2 NO. 3
        CENTURY MUSIC PUBLISHING COMPANY, INC.   762   .40
TSCHAIKOWSKY   SCHAUM, J.   2
    CHINESE DANCE 'NUTCRACKER SUITE'
        BELWIN-MILLS PUBLISHING CORPORATION   .50
TSCHAIKOWSKY   4
    CHINESE DANCE IN B FLAT FROM NUTCRACKER SUITE
        CENTURY MUSIC PUBLISHING COMPANY, INC.   2365   .40
TSCHAIKOWSKY   SCHIEFELBEIN   2 1/2
    CONCERTO NO. 01 -- OPENING THEME
        VOLKWEIN BROS.   .25
TSCHAIKOWSKY
    CONCERTO NO. 01 IN B FLAT MINOR
        ASHLEY DEALERS SERVICE, INC.   1.95
TSCHAIKOWSKY   4
    CONCERTO NO. 01 IN B FLAT MINOR
        CENTURY MUSIC PUBLISHING COMPANY, INC.   3530   .40
                                          M
TSCHAIKOWSKY
    CONCERTO NO. 01 IN B FLAT MINOR, OP. 23   ABRIDGED
        C. F. PETERS CORPORATION   3775A   1.25
TSCHAIKOWSKY   FREY, H.
    CONCERTO NO. 02
        THE BIG THREE MUSIC CORPORATION   00.75
TSCHAIKOWSKY   DEIS *
    DANCE OF THE CANDY FAIRY--FROM NUTCRACKER SUITE
        G. SCHIRMER, INC.   .50
TSCHAIKOWSKY   4-5
    DANCE OF THE REED FLUTES IN D FROM NUTCRACKER SUITE
        CENTURY MUSIC PUBLISHING COMPANY, INC.   2365   .40
TSCHAIKOWSKY   DEIS *
    DANCE OF THE REED-FLUTES--FROM NUTCRACKER SUITE
        G. SCHIRMER, INC.   .40
TSCHAIKOWSKY   STEINER   3 1/2
    DANCE OF THE SUGAR PLUM FAIRY -- FROM 'THE NUTCRACKER SUITE'
        BELWIN-MILLS PUBLISHING CORPORATION   .60
TSCHAIKOWSKY   4-5
    DANCE OF THE SUGAR PLUM FAIRY, E MINOR FROM NUTCRACKER SUITE
        CENTURY MUSIC PUBLISHING COMPANY, INC.   2362   .40
                                          4-5
TSCHAIKOWSKY
    DANCE, CANDY FAIRY
        CENTURY MUSIC PUBLISHING COMPANY, INC.   2362   .40
TSCHAIKOWSKY
    DANSE RUSSE TREPAK, OP. 71
        GERARD BILLAUDOT EDITIONS MUSICALES   1.10
TSCHAIKOWSKY
    DANSE RUSSE, OP. 40 NO. 10
        GERARD BILLAUDOT EDITIONS MUSICALES   1.30
TSCHAIKOWSKY   4
    DIE JAHRESZEITEN OP. 37 -- APRIL--SCHNEEGLOCKCHEN
        SCHOTT   01704 1/2   1.00
TSCHAIKOWSKY   4
    DIE JAHRESZEITEN OP. 37 -- JUNI--BARCAROLE
        SCHOTT   01706 1/2   1.00
TSCHAIKOWSKY   5
    DIE JAHRESZEITEN OP. 37 -- NOVEMBER--TROIKA
        SCHOTT   0711 1/2   1.00
TSCHAIKOWSKY   4
    DIE JAHRESZEITEN OP. 37 -- OKTOBER--HERBSTLIED
        SCHOTT   01710 1/2   1.00
TSCHAIKOWSKY   4
    DIE JAHRESZEITEN OP. 37 --DEZEMBER--WEIHNACHTEN
        SCHOTT   01712 1/2   1.00
TSCHAIKOWSKY   SCHAUM, J.   2
    DREAM SHIP
        BELWIN-MILLS PUBLISHING CORPORATION   .50
TSCHAIKOWSKY   PHILIPP, I.
    DUMKA, OP. 59
        INTERNATIONAL MUSIC COMPANY   1.50
TSCHAIKOWSKY   3-4
    EIGHTEEN TWELVE OVERTURE
        CENTURY MUSIC PUBLISHING COMPANY, INC.   3561   .40

TSCHAIKOWSKY
    EIGHTEEN TWELVE OVERTURE
        EDWARD B. MARKS MUSIC CORPORATION   01.25
TSCHAIKOWSKY   4
    EIGHTEEN TWELVE OVERTURE, OP. 49
        SCHOTT   1682   1.50
TSCHAIKOWSKY   LISZT
    EUGEN ONEGIN--POLONAISE
        ASSOCIATED MUSIC PUBLISHERS, INC.   SIM   1.10
TSCHAIKOWSKY   ZEPP   3-4
    FAREWELL TO A HERO
        PRO-ART PUBLICATIONS, INC.   525   .50
TSCHAIKOWSKY   WEITZMANN   D
    GRAND SONATA IN G, OP. 37
        C. F. PETERS CORPORATION   4995   4.50
TSCHAIKOWSKY   BARTH, H.
    HAND ORGAN MAN, THE
        BELWIN-MILLS PUBLISHING CORPORATION   20396   .60
                                          2
TSCHAIKOWSKY
    HAPPY DREAM
        NOVELLO AND COMPANY, LTD.   55.0045.01   .25
TSCHAIKOWSKY
    HUMORESQUE IN G, OP. 10 NO. 2
        G. SCHIRMER, INC.   .40
TSCHAIKOWSKY   4
    HUMORESQUE, OP. 10 NO. 2
        CENTURY MUSIC PUBLISHING COMPANY, INC.   3845   .40
TSCHAIKOWSKY
    HUMORESQUE, OP. 10, NO. 2
        GERARD BILLAUDOT EDITIONS MUSICALES   1.30
TSCHAIKOWSKY   KREUTZER   3
    IMPROMPTU
        BOSTON MUSIC COMPANY   .50
TSCHAIKOWSKY   SCHARFENBERG
    JUNE. BARCAROLLE IN G MINOR, OP. 37 NO. 6
        G. SCHIRMER, INC.   .50
TSCHAIKOWSKY   4
    JUNE, BARCAROLLE
        CENTURY MUSIC PUBLISHING COMPANY, INC.   748   .40
TSCHAIKOWSKY   4
    LARK'S SONG, ALBUM FOR THE YOUNG
        CENTURY MUSIC PUBLISHING COMPANY, INC.   2149   .40
TSCHAIKOWSKY   3
    LOVE THEME, ROMEO AND JULIET
        CENTURY MUSIC PUBLISHING COMPANY, INC.   3431   .40
TSCHAIKOWSKY   RACHMANINOFF, S.
    LULLABY
        BELWIN-MILLS PUBLISHING CORPORATION   1.00
TSCHAIKOWSKY   4
    MARCH IN G FROM NUTCRACKER SUITE
        CENTURY MUSIC PUBLISHING COMPANY, INC.   2366   .40
TSCHAIKOWSKY   2
    MARCH OF THE TOY SOLDIERS
        CENTURY MUSIC PUBLISHING COMPANY, INC.   2451   .40
TSCHAIKOWSKY
    MARCH SLAV
        FREDERICK HARRIS MUSIC COMPANY   .60
TSCHAIKOWSKY   PALMERI
    MARCH SLAVE
        G. SCHIRMER, INC.   .50
                                          3
TSCHAIKOWSKY
    MARCH SLAVE, OP. 31
        CENTURY MUSIC PUBLISHING COMPANY, INC.   3340   .40
TSCHAIKOWSKY   THOMPSON   1
    MARCHE SLAV
        WILLIS MUSIC COMPANY   .35
TSCHAIKOWSKY   BARTH, H.
    MAZURKA
        BELWIN-MILLS PUBLISHING CORPORATION   20374   .60
TSCHAIKOWSKY
    NOCTURNE IN F MINOR, OP. 10 NO. 1
        GERARD BILLAUDOT EDITIONS MUSICALES   2.00
TSCHAIKOWSKY   MOSSMAN
    NONE BUT THE LONELY HEART
        BELWIN-MILLS PUBLISHING CORPORATION   26086   .60
TSCHAIKOWSKY   3
    NONE BUT THE LONELY HEART
        CENTURY MUSIC PUBLISHING COMPANY, INC.   3245   .40
TSCHAIKOWSKY   RIEFLING   E
    NONE BUT THE LONELY HEART, OP. 6 NO. 6
        C. F. PETERS CORPORATION   LY366   .50
TSCHAIKOWSKY   DEL MAGLIO
    NONE BUT THE LONELY HEART, OP. 6 NO. 6
        FRANCO COLOMBO PUBLICATIONS   127114   .60
TSCHAIKOWSKY   DEIS
    NONE BUT THE LONELY HEART, OP. 6 NO. 6
        G. SCHIRMER, INC.   .50
                                          5
TSCHAIKOWSKY
    NOVEMBER, TROIKA RIDE
        CENTURY MUSIC PUBLISHING COMPANY, INC.   1703   .40
                                          6
TSCHAIKOWSKY
    NUSSKNACKER-SUITE OP. 71A
        SCHOTT   2394   2.25
TSCHAIKOWSKY   BANTOCK, G.
    NUTCRACKER SUITE
        BELWIN-MILLS PUBLISHING CORPORATION   09471   2.00
TSCHAIKOWSKY
    NUTCRACKER SUITE
        EDWIN F. KALMUS   4316   1.50
TSCHAIKOWSKY   RICHTER, A.
    NUTCRACKER SUITE -- A STORY WITH MUSIC
        THEODORE PRESSER COMPANY   1.25
TSCHAIKOWSKY   2
    NUTCRACKER SUITE, OP. 71A - DANCE OF THE REED FLUTES
        CENTURY MUSIC PUBLISHING COMPANY, INC.   4084   .40
TSCHAIKOWSKY   4
    NUTCRACKER SUITE, OP. 71A - ARAB DANCE
        CENTURY MUSIC PUBLISHING COMPANY, INC.   2364   .40
TSCHAIKOWSKY   4
    NUTCRACKER SUITE, OP. 71A - CHINESE DANCE, EASY
        CENTURY MUSIC PUBLISHING COMPANY, INC.   4083   .40
TSCHAIKOWSKY   4
    NUTCRACKER SUITE, OP. 71A - MARCH
        CENTURY MUSIC PUBLISHING COMPANY, INC.   2366   .40
TSCHAIKOWSKY   2
    NUTCRACKER SUITE, OP. 71A - MARCH, EASY
        CENTURY MUSIC PUBLISHING COMPANY, INC.   3828   .40
TSCHAIKOWSKY   2
    NUTCRACKER SUITE, OP. 71A - TREPAK, EASY
        CENTURY MUSIC PUBLISHING COMPANY, INC.   3673   .40
TSCHAIKOWSKY   2
    NUTCRACKER SUITE, OP. 71A - WALTZ OF THE FLOWERS, EASY
        CENTURY MUSIC PUBLISHING COMPANY, INC.   3227   .40
TSCHAIKOWSKY   NESTLER
    NUTCRACKER SUITE, OP. 71A--WALTZ OF THE FLOWERS
        ASSOCIATED MUSIC PUBLISHERS, INC.   SIM   .60

TSCHAIKOWSKY
 VALSE IN E FLAT, OP. 39 NO. 8
  G. SCHIRMER, INC.
TSCHAIKOWSKY   4   .30
 VALSE LENTE FROM THE SLEEPING BEAUTY BALLET
  CENTURY MUSIC PUBLISHING COMPANY, INC.   3183   .40
TSCHAIKOWSKY
 VALSE SENTIMENTALE IN F MINOR, OP. 51 NO. 6
  ASSOCIATED MUSIC PUBLISHERS, INC.   AMP   .75
TSCHAIKOWSKY
 VALSE SENTIMENTALE IN F MINOR, OP. 51 NO. 6
  ASSOCIATED MUSIC PUBLISHERS, INC.   SIM   .75
TSCHAIKOWSKY   2
 VIOLIN CONCERTO, THEME
  CENTURY MUSIC PUBLISHING COMPANY, INC.   3847   .40
TSCHAIKOWSKY   SCHAUM, J.   2
 WALTZ FROM SERENADE FOR STRINGS
  BELWIN-MILLS PUBLISHING CORPORATION
TSCHAIKOWSKY   5   .50
 WALTZ FROM SERENADE FOR STRINGS
  CENTURY MUSIC PUBLISHING COMPANY, INC.   3559   .40
TSCHAIKOWSKY   CASTELNUOVO-TEDESCO
 WALTZ FROM SERENADE FOR STRINGS, OP. 48
  MCA MUSIC   1.50
TSCHAIKOWSKY   DEIS
 WALTZ FROM SERENADE, OP. 48
  G. SCHIRMER, INC.   .60
TSCHAIKOWSKY   WEYBRIGHT   1 1/2
 WALTZ FROM THE BALLET 'THE SLEEPING BEAUTY'
  BELWIN-MILLS PUBLISHING CORPORATION   .60
TSCHAIKOWSKY   SCHAUM, J.   3
 WALTZ OF THE FLOWERS
  BELWIN-MILLS PUBLISHING CORPORATION   .50
TSCHAIKOWSKY
 WALTZ OF THE FLOWERS
  CARL FISCHER, INC.   S 2249   .75
TSCHAIKOWSKY   TRUXELL, E.   2
 WALTZ OF THE FLOWERS
  VOLKWEIN BROS.   00.40
TSCHAIKOWSKY   TRUXELL, E.   2 1/2
 WALTZ OF THE FLOWERS
  VOLKWEIN BROS.   00.50
TSCHAIKOWSKY
 WALTZ OF THE FLOWERS FROM 'NUTCRACKER'
  FRANCO COLOMBO PUBLICATIONS   127072   .75
TSCHAIKOWSKY   DEL MAGLIO
 WALTZ OF THE FLOWERS FROM 'NUTCRACKER'
  FRANCO COLOMBO PUBLICATIONS   127115   .60
TSCHAIKOWSKY   ECKSTEIN
 WALTZ OF THE FLOWERS FROM THE 'NUTCRACKER SUITE'
  CARL FISCHER, INC.   S 2300   .50
                                                       4
 WALTZ OF THE FLOWERS IN D FROM NUTCRACKER SUITE
  CENTURY MUSIC PUBLISHING COMPANY, INC.   2367   .40
TSCHAIKOWSKY   DEIS *
 WALTZ OF THE FLOWERS--FROM NUTCRACKER SUITE
  G. SCHIRMER, INC.   .75
TSCHAIKOWSKY   4
 WALTZ, FROM SERENADE FOR STRINGS
  THEODORE PRESSER COMPANY   .50
TSCHAIKOWSKY *
 EUGEN ONEGIN--POLONAISE
  ASSOCIATED MUSIC PUBLISHERS, INC.   DOB   .90
TSCHAIKOWSKY *
 LULLABY
  CARL FISCHER, INC.   F 2059   .75
TUCCI
 LOLA FLORES
  EDWARD B. MARKS MUSIC CORPORATION   01.00
TUCKER *   3
 SWEET GENEVIEVE, TRANSCRIPTION
  CENTURY MUSIC PUBLISHING COMPANY, INC.   2470   .40
TUERK   2
 RONDO
  LEE ROBERTS MUSIC PUBLICATIONS, INC.   .50
TURINA, J.   *
 CICLO PIANISTICO--CASTILLO DE ALMODOVAR, EL, OP. 88
  ASSOCIATED MUSIC PUBLISHERS, INC.   UME   2.00
TURINA, J.
 CICLO PIANISTICO--CONCERTO WITHOUT ORCHESTRA, OP. 88
  ASSOCIATED MUSIC PUBLISHERS, INC.   UME   1.00
TURINA, J.
 CICLO PIANISTICO--PARTITA IN C, OP. 57
  ASSOCIATED MUSIC PUBLISHERS, INC.   UME   1.75
TURINA, J.
 CICLO PIANISTICO--PIEZA ROMANTICA, OP. 64
  ASSOCIATED MUSIC PUBLISHERS, INC.   1.00
TURINA, J.
 CICLO PIANISTICO--RINCONES DE SANLUCAR, OP. 78
  ASSOCIATED MUSIC PUBLISHERS, INC.   UME   .80
TURINA, J.
 CICLO PIANISTICO--TOCCATA AND FUGUE, OP. 50
  ASSOCIATED MUSIC PUBLISHERS, INC.   UME   1.50
TURINA, J.
 CICLO PLATERESCO--FANTASIA CINEMATOGRAFICA, OP. 103
  ASSOCIATED MUSIC PUBLISHERS, INC.   UME   1.25
TURINA, J.
 CICLO PLATERESCO--LINTERNA MAGICA, OP. 101
  ASSOCIATED MUSIC PUBLISHERS, INC.   UME   1.00
TURINA, J.
 COINS DE SEVILLE--SUITE NO. 1
  ASSOCIATED MUSIC PUBLISHERS, INC.   ESC   3.25
TURINA, J.
 CONTEMPLACION, OP. 99
  ASSOCIATED MUSIC PUBLISHERS, INC.   UME   1.25
TURINA, J.
 CONTES D'ESPAGNE, BK. 1 - DANS LES JARDINS DE MURCIA
  FRANCO COLOMBO PUBLICATIONS   SAL   2.00
TURINA, J.
 CONTES D'ESPAGNE, BK. 1 - DEVANT LA TOUR DE CLAVERO
  FRANCO COLOMBO PUBLICATIONS   SAL   2.00
TURINA, J.
 CONTES D'ESPAGNE, BK. 1 - LA CALETA
  FRANCO COLOMBO PUBLICATIONS   SAL   2.00
TURINA, J.
 CONTES D'ESPAGNE, BK. 1 - MIRAMAR, LE CHEMIN DE LA ALHAMBRA
  FRANCO COLOMBO PUBLICATIONS   SAL   2.00
TURINA, J.
 CONTES D'ESPAGNE, BK. 1 - ROMPEOLAS
  FRANCO COLOMBO PUBLICATIONS   SAL   2.25
TURINA, J.
 CONTES D'ESPAGNE, BK. 1 - UNE VIEILLE EGLISE A LOGRONO
  FRANCO COLOMBO PUBLICATIONS   SAL   2.00
TURINA, J.
 CONTES D'ESPAGNE, BK. 2 - BUVEURS DE MANZANILLA
  FRANCO COLOMBO PUBLICATIONS   SAL   1.75

TURINA, J.
 CONTES D'ESPAGNE, BK. 2 - CHANSON MAURESQUE
  FRANCO COLOMBO PUBLICATIONS   SAL   1.75
TURINA, J.
 CONTES D'ESPAGNE, BK. 2 - CHANSONS DE LA NUIT
  FRANCO COLOMBO PUBLICATIONS   SAL   1.75
TURINA, J.
 CONTES D'ESPAGNE, BK. 2 - CORDOUE EN FETE
  FRANCO COLOMBO PUBLICATIONS   SAL   1.75
TURINA, J.
 CONTES D'ESPAGNE, BK. 2 - LA MOSQUEE
  FRANCO COLOMBO PUBLICATIONS   SAL   1.75
TURINA, J.
 CONTES D'ESPAGNE, BK. 2 - PROMENADE
  FRANCO COLOMBO PUBLICATIONS   SAL   1.75
TURINA, J.
 CONTES D'ESPAGNE, BK. 2 - TOURNOI CHEVALERESQUE
  FRANCO COLOMBO PUBLICATIONS   SAL   1.75
TURINA, J.
 CRISTO DE LA CALAVERA, EL, OP. 30
  ASSOCIATED MUSIC PUBLISHERS, INC.   UME   1.25
TURINA, J.
 DANSES GITANES, BK. 1 - SACRO-MONTE
  FRANCO COLOMBO PUBLICATIONS   SAL   1.00
TURINA, J.
 DANZAS FANTASTICAS, OP. 22--NO. 1, EXALTACION
  ASSOCIATED MUSIC PUBLISHERS, INC.   UME   1.25
TURINA, J.
 DANZAS FANTASTICAS, OP. 22--NO. 2, ENSUENO
  ASSOCIATED MUSIC PUBLISHERS, INC.   UME   1.00
TURINA, J.
 DANZAS FANTASTICAS, OP. 22--NO. 3, ORGIA
  ASSOCIATED MUSIC PUBLISHERS, INC.   UME   .60
TURINA, J.
 DESDE MI TERRAZA, OP. 104
  ASSOCIATED MUSIC PUBLISHERS, INC.   UME   1.75
TURINA, J.
 FANTASIA ITALIANA, OP. 75
  ASSOCIATED MUSIC PUBLISHERS, INC.   UME   1.25
TURINA, J.
 FANTASIA ON FIVE NOTES--''ARBOS''--OP. 83
  ASSOCIATED MUSIC PUBLISHERS, INC.   UME   1.50
TURINA, J.
 LEYENDA DE LA GIRALDA, LA, OP. 40
  ASSOCIATED MUSIC PUBLISHERS, INC.   UME   1.00
TURINA, J.
 MALLORCA - NUIT SUR LA BAIE DE PALMA
  FRANCO COLOMBO PUBLICATIONS   SAL   1.75
TURINA, J.
 MUSAS DE ANDALUCIA, LAS, OP. 93--NO. 1, CLIO
  ASSOCIATED MUSIC PUBLISHERS, INC.   UME   .50
TURINA, J.
 MUSAS DE ANDALUCIA, LAS, OP. 93--NO. 7, URANIA
  ASSOCIATED MUSIC PUBLISHERS, INC.   UME   .50
TURINA, J.
 MUSAS DE ANDALUCIA, LAS, OP. 93--NO. 8, TERPISCORE
  ASSOCIATED MUSIC PUBLISHERS, INC.   UME   .50
TURINA, J.
 NAVIDAD -- MIRACLE PANTOMINE IN 2 ACTS
  ASSOCIATED MUSIC PUBLISHERS, INC.   UME   1.00
TURINA, J.
 NAVIDAD FROM ''MILAGRO IN 2 CUADROS'', OP. 16
  ASSOCIATED MUSIC PUBLISHERS, INC.   UME   1.50
TURINA, J.
 NINERIAS, BK. 1 - A LA MEMOIRE D'UN BEBE
  FRANCO COLOMBO PUBLICATIONS   SAL   1.50
TURINA, J.
 NINERIAS, BK. 1 - BERCEUSE
  FRANCO COLOMBO PUBLICATIONS   SAL   1.50
TURINA, J.
 NINERIAS, BK. 1 - CE QU'ON VOIT SUR LA GIRALDA
  FRANCO COLOMBO PUBLICATIONS   SAL   1.50
TURINA, J.
 NINERIAS, BK. 1 - DANSE DES POUPEES
  FRANCO COLOMBO PUBLICATIONS   SAL   1.50
TURINA, J.
 NINERIAS, BK. 1 - DEFILE DES SOLDATS DE PLOMB
  FRANCO COLOMBO PUBLICATIONS   SAL   1.50
TURINA, J.
 NINERIAS, BK. 1 - JEUX
  FRANCO COLOMBO PUBLICATIONS   SAL   1.50
TURINA, J.
 NINERIAS, BK. 1 - PRELUDE AND FUGUE
  FRANCO COLOMBO PUBLICATIONS   SAL   1.50
TURINA, J.
 NINERIAS, BK. 2 - A L'ECOLE
  FRANCO COLOMBO PUBLICATIONS   SAL   1.50
TURINA, J.
 NINERIAS, BK. 2 - CARNAVAL DES ENFANTS
  FRANCO COLOMBO PUBLICATIONS   SAL   1.50
TURINA, J.
 NINERIAS, BK. 2 - CONCHITA PLEURE
  FRANCO COLOMBO PUBLICATIONS   SAL   1.50
TURINA, J.
 NINERIAS, BK. 2 - CONCHITA REVE
  FRANCO COLOMBO PUBLICATIONS   SAL   1.50
TURINA, J.
 NINERIAS, BK. 2 - COURSE FEERIQUE
  FRANCO COLOMBO PUBLICATIONS   SAL   1.50
TURINA, J.
 NINERIAS, BK. 2 - DIVERTISSEMENT
  FRANCO COLOMBO PUBLICATIONS   SAL   1.50
TURINA, J.
 NINERIAS, BK. 2 - ENTREE DE COCHITA
  FRANCO COLOMBO PUBLICATIONS   SAL   1.50
TURINA, J.
 NINERIAS, BK. 2 - PARADE
  FRANCO COLOMBO PUBLICATIONS   SAL   1.50
TURINA, J.
 ORACION DEL TORERO, LA, OP. 34
  ASSOCIATED MUSIC PUBLISHERS, INC.   UME   1.00
TURINA, J.
 POEMA FANTASTICO, OP. 98
  ASSOCIATED MUSIC PUBLISHERS, INC.   UME   1.75
TURINA, J.
 POR LAS CALLES DE SEVILLA, OP. 96
  ASSOCIATED MUSIC PUBLISHERS, INC.   UME   .80
TURINA, J.
 PROCESSION DU ROCIO, LA
  FRANCO COLOMBO PUBLICATIONS   SAL   1.50
TURINA, J.
 QUARTIER DE SANTA-CRUZ, LE
  FRANCO COLOMBO PUBLICATIONS   SAL   5.50
TURINA, J.   3
 RADIO MADRID, SUITE
  SCHOTT   2148   2.50

TURINA, J.
  RINCON MAGICO, OP. 97--DESFILE EN FORMA DE SONATA
    ASSOCIATED MUSIC PUBLISHERS, INC.   UME   1.60
TURINA, J.
  RITMOS -- FANTASIA COREOGRAFICA
    ASSOCIATED MUSIC PUBLISHERS, INC.   UME   1.00
                                                  4
TURINA, J.
  SEEREISE, SUITE
    SCHOTT   2107   2.50
TURINA, J.
  SEGUIDILLAS
    OXFORD UNIVERSITY PRESS   32.136   1.00
TURINA, J.
  SEVILLA, SUITE PITTORESQUE--NO. 1, SOUS LES ORANGERS
    ASSOCIATED MUSIC PUBLISHERS, INC.   ESC   1.50
TURINA, J.
  SEVILLA, SUITE PITTORESQUE--NO. 2, LE JEUDI SAINT A MINUIT
    ASSOCIATED MUSIC PUBLISHERS, INC.   ESC   1.10
TURINA, J.
  SEVILLA, SUITE PITTORESQUE--NO. 3, LA FERIA
    ASSOCIATED MUSIC PUBLISHERS, INC.   ESC   2.00
TURINA, J.
  SILHOUETTES - L'AQUEDUC
    FRANCO COLOMBO PUBLICATIONS   SAL   1.75
TURINA, J.
  SILHOUETTES - LA PHARE DE CADIX
    FRANCO COLOMBO PUBLICATIONS   SAL   1.75
TURINA, J.
  SILHOUETTES - LA PUERTA DEL SOL
    FRANCO COLOMBO PUBLICATIONS   SAL   1.75
TURINA, J.
  SILHOUETTES - LA TOUR DE L'OR
    FRANCO COLOMBO PUBLICATIONS   SAL   1.75
TURINA, J.
  SILHOUETTES - LA TOUR DE LA VELA
    FRANCO COLOMBO PUBLICATIONS   SAL   1.75
TURINA, J.
  SONATA FANTASIA, OP. 59
    ASSOCIATED MUSIC PUBLISHERS, INC.   UME   2.00
TURINA, J.
  SONATA ROMANTIQUE ON A SPANISH THEME
    ASSOCIATED MUSIC PUBLISHERS, INC.   ESC   6.25
TURINA, J.
  SONLUCAR DE BARRAMEDA--PROGRAM SONATA, OP. 24
    ASSOCIATED MUSIC PUBLISHERS, INC.   UME   3.25
TURINA, J.
  SOUVENIRS DE L'ANCIENNE ESPAGNE - DON JUAN
    FRANCO COLOMBO PUBLICATIONS   SAL   1.75
TURINA, J.
  SOUVENIRS DE L'ANCIENNE ESPAGNE - ESTUDIANTINA
    FRANCO COLOMBO PUBLICATIONS   SAL   1.75
TURINA, J.
  SOUVENIRS DE L'ANCIENNE ESPAGNE - HABANERA
    FRANCO COLOMBO PUBLICATIONS   SAL   1.75
TURINA, J.
  SOUVENIRS DE L'ANCIENNE ESPAGNE - L'ETERNELLE CARMEN
    FRANCO COLOMBO PUBLICATIONS   SAL   1.75
TURINA, J.
  TRILOGIA--EL POEMA INFINITO, OP. 77
    ASSOCIATED MUSIC PUBLISHERS, INC.   UME   .80
TURINA, J.
  TRILOGIA--HIPOCRATES, OP. 86
    ASSOCIATED MUSIC PUBLISHERS, INC.   UME   1.00
TURINA, J.
  TRILOGIA--OFRENDA, OP. 85
    ASSOCIATED MUSIC PUBLISHERS, INC.   UME   .80
TURINA, J.
  VENTA DE LOS GATOS, LA, OP. 32
    ASSOCIATED MUSIC PUBLISHERS, INC.   UME   1.25
                                                  3
TURINA, J.
  ZIRKUS, SUITE
    SCHOTT   2226   1.50
                                                  2
TURNER, J.
  BARN DANCE
    CENTURY MUSIC PUBLISHING COMPANY, INC.   1370   .40
                                                  2
TURNER, J.
  FAIRY WEDDING
    CENTURY MUSIC PUBLISHING COMPANY, INC.   1225   .40
                                                  3
TURNER, J.
  FAIRY WEDDING WALTZ
    VOLKWEIN BROS.   .25
                                                  3
TURNER, J.
  FAIRY WEDDING WALTZ, OP. 120
    THEODORE PRESSER COMPANY   .50
TURNER, O.
  BEAR, THE
    BANKS AND SON LTD.   .25
TURNER, O.
  ZOOLOGICAL COMICALITIES
    BANKS AND SON LTD.   .80
TUTTLE, T. K.   1
  FOG HORN WARNINGS
    BELWIN-MILLS PUBLISHING CORPORATION   .60
TUTTLE, T. K.   3
  MOODS
    BELWIN-MILLS PUBLISHING CORPORATION   .60
TUTTLE, T. K.   2
  NOCTURNE
    BELWIN-MILLS PUBLISHING CORPORATION   .60
TUTTLE, T. K.   1
  SHADOWS IN THE LAGOON
    BELWIN-MILLS PUBLISHING CORPORATION   .60
TUTTLE, T. K.   2
  SLEEPY BUGLER, THE
    BELWIN-MILLS PUBLISHING CORPORATION   .60
TUTTLE, T. K.   2
  UMBRELLA IN THE WIND
    BELWIN-MILLS PUBLISHING CORPORATION   .60
TWINNING, W. L.
  BRITISH GRENADIERS AND HERE'S A HEALTH UNTO HIS MAJESTY
    BANKS AND SON LTD.   .25
TWITCHELL--ED   TWITCHELL   4
  DOVE, THE -- LA PALOMA
    CENTURY MUSIC PUBLISHING COMPANY, INC.   270   .40
TWITTENHOFF   2
  SECHS TIMES SECHS VARIATIONEN UBER TANZLIEDER
    SCHOTT   3946   1.75
TYERS, W.
  PANAMA
    THE BIG THREE MUSIC CORPORATION   00.95
UGARTE
  ARRULLO
    FRANCO COLOMBO PUBLICATIONS   BA9722   .75
UGARTE
  DE MI TIERRA, SUITE NO. 1
    FRANCO COLOMBO PUBLICATIONS   BA9367   1.25

UGARTE
  DE MI TIERRA, SUITE NO. 2
    FRANCO COLOMBO PUBLICATIONS   BA10501   2.00
UGARTE
  LAMENTO CAMPERO
    FRANCO COLOMBO PUBLICATIONS   BA10153   .75
UGARTE
  PRELUDE IN G MINOR
    FRANCO COLOMBO PUBLICATIONS   BA10154   .75
UGARTE
  PONPONCITOS
    FRANCO COLOMBO PUBLICATIONS   BA10931   1.00
UGARTE
  VIDALA
    FRANCO COLOMBO PUBLICATIONS   BA10155   .75
ULEHLA, L.
  FIVE OVER TWELVE
    GENERAL MUSIC PUBLISHING COMPANY, INC.   297   1.50
UMILIANI
  MAH-NA, MAH-NA
    EDWARD B. MARKS MUSIC CORPORATION   01.00
UPCRAFT, M.
  VALSE-IMPROMPTU
    G. SCHIRMER, INC.   .50
URAY, E. L.
  MELODISCH-HARMONISCHE STUDIE, EINE
    ASSOCIATED MUSIC PUBLISHERS, INC.   DOB   1.00
URAY, E. L.
  SONATA BREVE NO. 1 IN D
    ASSOCIATED MUSIC PUBLISHERS, INC.   DOB   2.50
URAY, E. L.
  SONATA BREVE NO. 2 IN E MINOR
    ASSOCIATED MUSIC PUBLISHERS, INC.   DOB   3.00
URAY, E. L.
  THEME, VARIATIONS AND FUGUE
    UNIVERSAL EDITION   UE 11098   1.70
URBANCIC, V.
  SONATINA IN G
    ASSOCIATED MUSIC PUBLISHERS, INC.   DOB   2.50
URBANNER, E.
  ADAGIO--1966
    ASSOCIATED MUSIC PUBLISHERS, INC.   DOB   2.75
                                                  6
USMANBAS, I.
  SIX PRELUDES
    THEODORE PRESSER COMPANY   .85
                                                  1
UTZLER
  FANFARE, SICK ON SATURDAY, JUGGLING -- TWELVE-TONE SET
    LEE ROBERTS MUSIC PUBLICATIONS, INC.   .60
                                                  2
UTZLER
  HURRY UP, MOON DREAMING, MOTORCYCLES -- TWELVE-TONE SET
    LEE ROBERTS MUSIC PUBLICATIONS, INC.   .60
VACHEY
  THREE VARIATIONS ON 'CADET ROUSSELLE'
    DELRIEU ET CIE.   2.75
VACKAR   3-4
  EXTEMPORE, OP. 24
    BARENREITER VERLAG   AP 753
VADON
  SUITE
    FRANCO COLOMBO PUBLICATIONS   SAL   2.50
VALCARCEL, T.
  DANZA DEL COMBATE
    EDITORIAL COOPERATIVA INTER-AMERICANA   00.95
                                                  D
VALEN
  INTERMEZZO, OP. 36
    C. F. PETERS CORPORATION   LY226   .60
                                                  D
VALEN
  PRELUDE, OP. 29 NO. 1
    C. F. PETERS CORPORATION   LY100   .60
                                                  D
VALEN
  PRELUDE, OP. 29 NO. 2
    C. F. PETERS CORPORATION   LY95   .60
                                                  D
VALEN
  SONATA NO. 02, OP. 38
    C. F. PETERS CORPORATION   LY304   3.00
                                                  D
VALEN
  VARIATIONS FOR PIANO, OP. 23
    C. F. PETERS CORPORATION   LY151   .90
                                                  2
VALENTI, M.
  CANCION POQUITA
    FRANK MUSIC CORPORATION   .60
                                                  2
VALENTI, M.
  DOWN A COUNTRY LANE
    FRANK MUSIC CORPORATION   .60
                                                  2
VALENTI, M.
  JUMPING BEANS
    FRANK MUSIC CORPORATION   .60
                                                  3
VALENTI, M.
  LEAVES IN THE WIND
    FRANK MUSIC CORPORATION   .60
                                                  2
VALENTI, M.
  LITTLE JAZZ WALTZ
    FRANK MUSIC CORPORATION   .60
                                                  3
VALENTI, M.
  PRETTY VISIONS
    FRANK MUSIC CORPORATION   .60
                                                  3
VALENTI, M.
  SHORT AND SWEET
    FRANK MUSIC CORPORATION   .60
                                                  2
VALENTI, M.
  TICKLING THOUGHT, A
    FRANK MUSIC CORPORATION   .60
                                                  2
VALENTI, M.
  TRAVELING TUNE, A
    FRANK MUSIC CORPORATION   .60
                                                  3
VALENTI, M.
  WESTERN SERENADE
    FRANK MUSIC CORPORATION   .60
VALENTINE, J.
  PENNSYLVANIA TURNPIKE
    BELWIN-MILLS PUBLISHING CORPORATION   20197   .85
VALSEN *
  SNOWFLOWER
    MCA MUSIC   1.00
VALVERDE, J.
  ALEGRIAS, PASO DOBLE FLAMENCO
    G. SCHIRMER, INC.   .50
VAN ALSTYNE, E.   STEINER   2 1/2
  IN THE SHADE OF THE OLD APPLE TREE
    BELWIN-MILLS PUBLISHING CORPORATION   .60
VAN ALSTYNE, E.   STEINER   1 1/2
  WON'T YOU COME OVER TO MY HOUSE
    BELWIN-MILLS PUBLISHING CORPORATION   .60
                                                  2
VAN DYKE
  SWISS YODEL SONG
    BELWIN-MILLS PUBLISHING CORPORATION   .60

VAN GAEL, H.   2
  VOICE OF THE HEART, THE
    CENTURY MUSIC PUBLISHING COMPANY, INC.   1377   .40
VAN HEUSEN, J.   SCHAUM, J.   2 1/2
  DARN THAT DREAM
    SCHAUM PUBLICATIONS, INC.   .75
VAN HULSE, C.   4
  DANCING LETTERS TO LEDA
    WILLIS MUSIC COMPANY   .50
VAN HULSE, C.   3
  DEBUTANTE
    WILLIS MUSIC COMPANY   .50
VAN HULSE, C.   D
  VARIATIONS, OP. 26
    COMPOSERS PRESS, INC.   3.00
VANBIENE, A.   3
  BROKEN MELODY, THE
    CENTURY MUSIC PUBLISHING COMPANY, INC.   2046   .40
VANDELLE   8
  MARINES
    ALPHONSE LEDUC
VANDERBECK, F.   3
  EDELWEISS GLIDE
    BELWIN-MILLS PUBLISHING CORPORATION   370   .60
VANDERBECK, F.
  EDELWEISS GLIDE
    CARL FISCHER, INC.   S 2190   .50
VANDERBECK, F.   4
  EDELWEISS GLIDE
    CENTURY MUSIC PUBLISHING COMPANY, INC.   1385   .40
VANDERBECK, F.   3
  EDELWEISS GLIDE
    WILLIS MUSIC COMPANY   .40
VANDERBECK, F.
  EDELWEISS GLIDE WALTZ
    ASHLEY DEALERS SERVICE, INC.   ES   .95
VANDERBECK, F.   4
  EDELWEISS GLIDE WALTZ
    VOLKWEIN BROS.   .25
VANDERSLOOT, F.
  CHRISTMAS CHIMES
    BELWIN-MILLS PUBLISHING CORPORATION   20051   .85
VANDERSLOOT, F.
  GENERAL PERSHING -- MARCH
    BELWIN-MILLS PUBLISHING CORPORATION   20108   .85
VANDEVERE, J. L.   1 1/2
  COWBOY CHARLEY
    THEODORE PRESSER COMPANY   .50
VANDEVERE, J. L.   1A
  HERE SPOT
    MUSICORD PUBLICATIONS, INC.   .45
VANHALL, J. B.   PODOLSKY, L.
  MINUET IN G
    FREDERICK HARRIS MUSIC COMPANY   .60
VANNORT, I.   2
  BANJO SERENADER
    WILLIS MUSIC COMPANY   .35
VANNORT, I.
  BUSY LITTLE CLOCK, THE -- WITH WORDS
    BELWIN-MILLS PUBLISHING CORPORATION   25015   .60
VANNORT, I.
  CINDERELLA AT THE BALL
    BELWIN-MILLS PUBLISHING CORPORATION   25025   .60
VANNORT, I.
  ENCHANTED SLIPPER, THE
    BELWIN-MILLS PUBLISHING CORPORATION   25046   .60
VANNORT, I.
  FLOWER FAIRY, THE
    EDWARD B. MARKS MUSIC CORPORATION   00.60
VANNORT, I.
  GAY BUTTERFLIES IN SPRINGTIME
    BELWIN-MILLS PUBLISHING CORPORATION   25052   .60
VANNORT, I.
  ICE SKATERS' FROLIC, THE
    G. SCHIRMER, INC.   .35
VANNORT, I.
  LITTLE MISS MUFFET
    BELWIN-MILLS PUBLISHING CORPORATION   25066   .60
VANNORT, I.
  LITTLE PRELUDE
    BELWIN-MILLS PUBLISHING CORPORATION   25067   .60
VANNORT, I.
  MY PAL--WITH WORDS
    G. SCHIRMER, INC.   .35
VANNORT, I.
  NODDING TULIPS
    BELWIN-MILLS PUBLISHING CORPORATION   25078   .60
VANNORT, I.
  PAL'S BRIGADE, THE
    BELWIN-MILLS PUBLISHING CORPORATION   25080   .60
VANNORT, I.
  PLAYING TAG
    BELWIN-MILLS PUBLISHING CORPORATION   25083   .60
VANNORT, I.
  SINGING BIRDS--WITH WORDS
    G. SCHIRMER, INC.   .35
VANNORT, I.
  SOLDIERS ON PARADE--WITH WORDS
    G. SCHIRMER, INC.   .35
VANNORT, I.
  STEPPING HIGH
    EDWARD B. MARKS MUSIC CORPORATION   00.60
VANNORT, I.
  SWING
    BELWIN-MILLS PUBLISHING CORPORATION   25104   .60
VANNORT, I.   1
  WALTZ OF THE WEE FINGERS
    WILLIS MUSIC COMPANY   .35
VANNORT, I.
  WHIRLING AND TWIRLING
    BELWIN-MILLS PUBLISHING CORPORATION   25119   .60
VANNORT, I.   1
  WHISTLING FARMER BOY, THE
    G. SCHIRMER, INC.   .40
VANNORT, I.
  WISHING STAR, THE
    WILLIS MUSIC COMPANY   .35
VANNORT, I.
  WITH FRILLS AND BOWS--WITH WORDS
    G. SCHIRMER, INC.   .35
VARGAS
  GARDEN DANCE, A
    SAM FOX PUBLISHING COMPANY, INC.   .75
VARGAS
  GARDEN DANCE, A
    SOUTHERN MUSIC COMPANY   .75

VARGUES
  DERNIERE GAVOTTE, LA
    FRANCO COLOMBO PUBLICATIONS   SAL   1.75
VARGUES
  MOUSTACHE POLKA
    FRANCO COLOMBO PUBLICATIONS   SAL   1.75
VASQUEZ, C.
  CANCION MEXICANA
    PEER SOUTHERN ORGANIZATION   00.85
VASSEUR
  AIR FAVORI DE LA REINE MARIE LECZINSKA
    FRANCO COLOMBO PUBLICATIONS   SAL   1.75
VASSEUR
  HAPPE DES ANGES
    FRANCO COLOMBO PUBLICATIONS   SAL   1.75
VAUGHAN WILLIAMS, R.   MULLINAR
  ENGLISH FOLK SONG SUITE
    BOOSEY AND HAWKES, INC.   1.50
VAUGHAN WILLIAMS, R.
  GREENSLEEVES
    OXFORD UNIVERSITY PRESS   32.115   1.10
VAUGHAN WILLIAMS, R.
  HYMN-TUNE PRELUDE
    OXFORD UNIVERSITY PRESS   33.705   1.25
VAUGHAN WILLIAMS, R.
  LAKE IN THE MOUNTAINS
    OXFORD UNIVERSITY PRESS   32.069   1.25
VAUGHAN WILLIAMS, R.   PERRY, P.
  LINDEN LEA
    BOOSEY AND HAWKES, INC.   .50
VAUGHN, J.
  GO FOR BAROQUE
    BELWIN-MILLS PUBLISHING CORPORATION   20111   .85
VELLONES, P.
  AU JARDIN DES BETES SAUVAGES, VOL. 1 -- LA BETE A BON DIEU
    ELKAN-VOGEL, INC.   D   .75
VELLONES, P.
  AU JARDIN DES BETES SAUVAGES, VOL. 1 -- LA MEDUSE
    ELKAN-VOGEL, INC.   D   .75
VELLONES, P.
  AU JARDIN DES BETES SAUVAGES, VOL. 1 -- LE CRABE DES COCOTIERS
    ELKAN-VOGEL, INC.   D   1.10
VELLONES, P.
  AU JARDIN DES BETES SAUVAGES, VOL. 1 -- LE LEZARD VERT
    ELKAN-VOGEL, INC.   D   .90
VELLONES, P.
  AU JARDIN DES BETES SAUVAGES, VOL. 1 -- LE POU DE MER
    ELKAN-VOGEL, INC.   D   .60
VELLONES, P.
  AU JARDIN DES BETES SAUVAGES, VOL. 1 -- LES CROCODILES
    ELKAN-VOGEL, INC.   D   .75
VELLONES, P.
  AU JARDIN DES BETES SAUVAGES, VOL. 1 -- LES DAUPHINS
    ELKAN-VOGEL, INC.   D   .90
VELLONES, P.
  AU JARDIN DES BETES SAUVAGES, VOL. 1 -- LES TORTUES MARINES
    ELKAN-VOGEL, INC.   D   .60
VELLONES, P.
  AU JARDIN DES BETES SAUVAGES, VOL. 2 -- L'AUTRUCHE
    ELKAN-VOGEL, INC.   D   .75
VELLONES, P.
  AU JARDIN DES BETES SAUVAGES, VOL. 2 -- L'HAMADRYAS
    ELKAN-VOGEL, INC.   D   1.25
VELLONES, P.
  AU JARDIN DES BETES SAUVAGES, VOL. 2 -- L'HIPPOPOTAME
    ELKAN-VOGEL, INC.   D   1.00
VELLONES, P.
  AU JARDIN DES BETES SAUVAGES, VOL. 2 -- L'OISEAU LYRE
    ELKAN-VOGEL, INC.   D   .90
VELLONES, P.
  AU JARDIN DES BETES SAUVAGES, VOL. 2 -- LA BICHE
    ELKAN-VOGEL, INC.   D   .90
VELLONES, P.
  AU JARDIN DES BETES SAUVAGES, VOL. 2 -- LE CACATOES A HUPPE ROSE
    ELKAN-VOGEL, INC.   D   .90
VELLONES, P.
  AU JARDIN DES BETES SAUVAGES, VOL. 2 -- LES PINGOUINS
    ELKAN-VOGEL, INC.   D   1.00
VELLONES, P.
  AU JARDIN DES BETES SAUVAGES, VOL. 2 -- LES VERS LUISANTS
    ELKAN-VOGEL, INC.   D   .75
VELUCCI
  SWISS HOP
    CARL FISCHER, INC.   RS 426   .50
VENTICINQUE
  DANZA DI GALATEA
    FRANCO COLOMBO PUBLICATIONS   FOR.12091 1.25
VERDI   CHIESA
  AIDA - EASY FANTASIA
    FRANCO COLOMBO PUBLICATIONS   109085   .60
VERDI   TAVAN
  AIDA - FANTASIA
    FRANCO COLOMBO PUBLICATIONS   128789   1.00
VERDI
  AIDA - HYMN AND TRIUMPHAL MARCH
    FRANCO COLOMBO PUBLICATIONS   42519   .60
VERDI   AUBEL, D'   6
  AIDA - MARCHE DES TROMPETTES
    ALPHONSE LEDUC
VERDI   BATTMANN   4
  AIDA - MARCHE DES TROMPETTES
    ALPHONSE LEDUC
VERDI
  AIDA -- COMPLETE OPERA --
    FRANCO COLOMBO PUBLICATIONS   44551   5.00
VERDI   HITZEL   2
  AIDA -- GRAND MARCH -- EASY, G MAJOR
    CENTURY MUSIC PUBLISHING COMPANY, INC.   2144   .40
VERDI   3
  AIDA -- GRAND MARCH -- F MAJOR
    CENTURY MUSIC PUBLISHING COMPANY, INC.   1707   .40
VERDI   E-M
  AIDA, ABRIDGED
    C. F. PETERS CORPORATION   H634   2.00
VERDI   TAVAN   6
  AIDA, FANTAISIE
    ALPHONSE LEDUC
VERDI   3
  ANVIL CHORUS FROM 'IL TROVATORE'
    CENTURY MUSIC PUBLISHING COMPANY, INC.   511   .40
VERDI   CHIESA
  BALLO IN MASCHERA, UN - EASY FANTASIA
    FRANCO COLOMBO PUBLICATIONS   109083   .60
VERDI   SMITH
  BRILLIANT FANTASIA FROM 'IL TROVATORE'
    G. SCHIRMER, INC.   .85

VERDI				4
CELEBRATED WALTZ IL TROVATORE				
VOLKWEIN BROS.				.30
VERDI				2
DONNA E MOBILE, RIGOLETTO				
CENTURY MUSIC PUBLISHING COMPANY, INC.			2041	.40
VERDI	CHIESA			
ERNANI - EASY FANTASIA				
FRANCO COLOMBO PUBLICATIONS			109088	.50
VERDI				3 1/2
FANTAISIE FACILE, OP. 39 NO. 3				
THEODORE PRESSER COMPANY				.50
VERDI	DORN			
FANTASIA FROM 'IL TROVATORE'				
G. SCHIRMER, INC.				.60
VERDI	DORN			
FANTASIA FROM 'RIGOLETTO'				
G. SCHIRMER, INC.				.70
VERDI				
FORZA DEL DESTINO, LA - OVERTURE				
FRANCO COLOMBO PUBLICATIONS			128333	.75
VERDI	DEL MAGLIO			
FORZA DEL DESTINO, LA - VERGINE DEGLI ANGELI, LA				
FRANCO COLOMBO PUBLICATIONS			124754	.90
VERDI				2
GYPSY SONG, FROM 'IL TROVATORE'				
CENTURY MUSIC PUBLISHING COMPANY, INC.			1566	.40
VERDI				3
HOME TO OUR MOUNTAINS				
CENTURY MUSIC PUBLISHING COMPANY, INC.			1568	.40
VERDI				4
IL TROVATORE WALTZ				
VOLKWEIN BROS.				.30
VERDI				3
IL TROVATORE, ANVIL CHORUS				
CENTURY MUSIC PUBLISHING COMPANY, INC.			511	.40
VERDI				2
IL TROVATORE, ANVIL CHORUS, EASY				
CENTURY MUSIC PUBLISHING COMPANY, INC.			3654	.40
VERDI	KRUG			2
IL TROVATORE, EASY TRANS.				
CENTURY MUSIC PUBLISHING COMPANY, INC.			530	.40
VERDI				5
IL TROVATORE, FANTASIE				
BELWIN-MILLS PUBLISHING CORPORATION			84	.60
VERDI	DORN			4
IL TROVATORE, FANTASIE				
CENTURY MUSIC PUBLISHING COMPANY, INC.			253	.40
VERDI	SMITH			5
IL TROVATORE, FANTASIE				
CENTURY MUSIC PUBLISHING COMPANY, INC.			1168	.40
VERDI				2
IL TROVATORE, GYPSY SONG				
CENTURY MUSIC PUBLISHING COMPANY, INC.			1566	.40
VERDI				3
IL TROVATORE, HOME TO OUR MOUNTAINS				
CENTURY MUSIC PUBLISHING COMPANY, INC.			1566	.40
VERDI	TZORR			3
IL TROVATORE, MISERERE				
CENTURY MUSIC PUBLISHING COMPANY, INC.			1530	.40
VERDI				2
IL TROVATORE, MISERERE, EASY				
CENTURY MUSIC PUBLISHING COMPANY, INC.			2153	.40
VERDI	KING, S.		EASY	
LA DONNA E MOBILE				
SHAWNEE PRESS, INC.				.30
VERDI	SMITH			5
LA TRAVIATA, FANTASIE				
CENTURY MUSIC PUBLISHING COMPANY, INC.			1169	.40
VERDI				4
LA TRAVIATA, PRELUDE				
CENTURY MUSIC PUBLISHING COMPANY, INC.			1784	.40
VERDI	DEL MAGLIO			
LOMBARDI, I - O SIGNORE DAL TETTO NATIO				
FRANCO COLOMBO PUBLICATIONS			124755	.60
VERDI				3
MARCH, AIDA				
CENTURY MUSIC PUBLISHING COMPANY, INC.			4707	.40
VERDI				2
MISERERE, IL TROVATORE, EASY				
CENTURY MUSIC PUBLISHING COMPANY, INC.			2153	.40
VERDI	CHIESA			
NABUCCO - EASY FANTASIA				
FRANCO COLOMBO PUBLICATIONS			109089	.60
VERDI				
NABUCCO - VA, PENSIERO				
FRANCO COLOMBO PUBLICATIONS			13894	.60
VERDI	CHIESA			
OTELLO - EASY FANTASIA				
FRANCO COLOMBO PUBLICATIONS			111265	.75
VERDI				4
PRELUDE, TRAVIATA				
CENTURY MUSIC PUBLISHING COMPANY, INC.			3784	.40
VERDI	SPINDLER			4
QUARTET, RIGOLETTO				
CENTURY MUSIC PUBLISHING COMPANY, INC.			1634	.40
VERDI	LISZT			
RIGOLETTO - CONCERT PARAPHRASE				
FRANCO COLOMBO PUBLICATIONS			35588	.75
VERDI	CHIESA			
RIGOLETTO - EASY FANTASIA				
FRANCO COLOMBO PUBLICATIONS			109087	.60
VERDI	TAVAN			
RIGOLETTO - FANTASIA				
FRANCO COLOMBO PUBLICATIONS			127845	1.00
VERDI				
RIGOLETTO -- COMPLETE OPERA --				
FRANCO COLOMBO PUBLICATIONS			42221	5.00
VERDI			E-M	
RIGOLETTO, ABRIDGED				
C. F. PETERS CORPORATION			H635	2.00
VERDI				2
RIGOLETTO, DONNA E MOBILE				
CENTURY MUSIC PUBLISHING COMPANY, INC.			2041	.40
VERDI				2
RIGOLETTO, DONNA E MOBILE, EASY				
CENTURY MUSIC PUBLISHING COMPANY, INC.			2156	.40
VERDI	SPINDLER			4
RIGOLETTO, QUARTETTE				
CENTURY MUSIC PUBLISHING COMPANY, INC.			1634	.40
VERDI	DEL MAGLIO			
SPAZZACAMINO, LO				
FRANCO COLOMBO PUBLICATIONS			128127	.50
VERDI	THOMPSON, J.			2
THEME FROM 'IL TROVATORE'				
WILLIS MUSIC COMPANY				.40

VERDI	STEINER			3
THREE WITCHES, FROM 'MACBETH'				
BELWIN-MILLS PUBLISHING CORPORATION				.60
VERDI			E-M	
TRAVIATA, ABRIDGED				
C. F. PETERS CORPORATION			H636	2.00
VERDI	KRUG			2
TRAVIATA, EASY TRANSCRIPTION				
CENTURY MUSIC PUBLISHING COMPANY, INC.			2145	.40
VERDI	SMITH			5
TRAVIATA, FANTASIE				
CENTURY MUSIC PUBLISHING COMPANY, INC.			1169	.40
VERDI	MENOZZI			
TRAVIATA, LA - BRINDISI				
FRANCO COLOMBO PUBLICATIONS			52554	.60
VERDI	CHIESA			
TRAVIATA, LA - EASY FANTASIA				
FRANCO COLOMBO PUBLICATIONS			109086	.60
VERDI	TAVAN			
TRAVIATA, LA - FANTASIA				
FRANCO COLOMBO PUBLICATIONS			127488	1.00
VERDI				
TRAVIATA, LA - PRELUDE TO ACT I				
FRANCO COLOMBO PUBLICATIONS			25121	.60
VERDI				
TRAVIATA, LA - PRELUDE TO ACT III AND ADDIO, DEL PASSATO				
FRANCO COLOMBO PUBLICATIONS			25122	.75
VERDI				
TRAVIATA, LA -- COMPLETE OPERA --				
FRANCO COLOMBO PUBLICATIONS			42222	5.00
VERDI				4
TRAVIATA, LA, PRELUDE				
CENTURY MUSIC PUBLISHING COMPANY, INC.			3784	.40
VERDI				
TRIUMPHAL MARCH FROM 'AIDA'				
G. SCHIRMER, INC.				.60
VERDI				4
TRIUMPHAL MARCH FROM 'AIDA'				
WILLIS MUSIC COMPANY				.60
VERDI	ROBBINS			3
TRIUMPHAL MARCH FROM 'AIDA'				
WILLIS MUSIC COMPANY				.35
VERDI			E-M	
TROVATORE, ABRIDGED				
C. F. PETERS CORPORATION			H637	2.00
VERDI	CHIESA			
TROVATORE, IL - EASY FANTASIA				
FRANCO COLOMBO PUBLICATIONS			109084	.60
VERDI	TAVAN			
TROVATORE, IL - FANTASIA				
FRANCO COLOMBO PUBLICATIONS			128790	1.00
VERDI				
TROVATORE, IL - MISERERE				
FRANCO COLOMBO PUBLICATIONS			128942	.75
VERDI				
TROVATORE, IL -- COMPLETE OPERA --				
FRANCO COLOMBO PUBLICATIONS			128790	5.00
VERDI				3
TROVATORE, IL, ANVIL CHORUS				
CENTURY MUSIC PUBLISHING COMPANY, INC.			511	.40
VERDI	ROLFE, W.			2
TROVATORE, IL, ANVIL CHORUS, EASY				
CENTURY MUSIC PUBLISHING COMPANY, INC.			3654	.40
VERDI	KRUG			2
TROVATORE, IL, EASY TRANSCRIPTION				
CENTURY MUSIC PUBLISHING COMPANY, INC.			530	.40
VERDI	DORN			4
TROVATORE, IL, FANTASIE				
CENTURY MUSIC PUBLISHING COMPANY, INC.			253	.40
VERDI	SMITH			5
TROVATORE, IL, FANTASIE				
CENTURY MUSIC PUBLISHING COMPANY, INC.			1168	.40
VERDI				2
TROVATORE, IL, GYPSY SONG				
CENTURY MUSIC PUBLISHING COMPANY, INC.			1566	.40
VERDI				3
TROVATORE, IL, HOME TO OUR MOUNTAINS				
CENTURY MUSIC PUBLISHING COMPANY, INC.			1568	.40
VERDI	TZORR			3
TROVATORE, IL, MISERERE				
CENTURY MUSIC PUBLISHING COMPANY, INC.			1530	.40
VERDI	CHIESA			
VESPRI SICILIANI, I - OVERTURE				
FRANCO COLOMBO PUBLICATIONS			127999	.75
VERDI *				
CONCERT PARAPHRASE ON 'RIGOLETTO'				
FRANCO COLOMBO PUBLICATIONS			35588	.75
VERDI *				
CONCERT PARAPHRASE ON 'RIGOLETTO'				
FRANCO COLOMBO PUBLICATIONS			35588	.75
VERDI *	DEIS			
RIGOLETTO--PARAPHRASE				
G. SCHIRMER, INC.				.80
VERDI *				7
RIGOLETTO, PARAPHRASE				
CENTURY MUSIC PUBLISHING COMPANY, INC.			1201	.40
VERDI *	DEIS			
RIGOLETTO, PARAPHRASE				
G. SCHIRMER, INC.				.80
VERETTI				
GALANTE TIRATORE, IL -- BALLET --				
FRANCO COLOMBO PUBLICATIONS				4.50
VERETTI				
SONATINA				
FRANCO COLOMBO PUBLICATIONS			129532	1.50
VERETTI				
TOCCATA IN D				
FRANCO COLOMBO PUBLICATIONS			BON.1467	1.50
VERGANTI				
DREAM, A - 10 FANTASIES -- ILLUSTRATED --				
FRANCO COLOMBO PUBLICATIONS			129661	4.50
VERGANTI				
MUSICAL TALES - 7 PIECES				
FRANCO COLOMBO PUBLICATIONS			130272	2.00
VERHAAR			M-D	
MUZIEK FOR HARPSICHORD				
C. F. PETERS CORPORATION			D465	2.50
VERHEY, T.				
MAZURKA IN A MINOR				
G. SCHIRMER, INC.				.35
VERNE				1
CITY SET				
LEE ROBERTS MUSIC PUBLICATIONS, INC.				.85
VERNE				
PHRYGIAN TOCCATA				
SUMMY-BIRCHARD COMPANY				.50

VERNY, F.
  LA CLE DU PIANISTE
    ELKAN-VOGEL, INC.   J   2.50
VERPALL, J.   1
  CONFIDENCE
    THEODORE PRESSER COMPANY   .50
VERRALL, J.   1 1/2
  GAY JIG, A
    THEODORE PRESSER COMPANY   .50
VERRALL, J.   1
  IN THE AUTUMN
    THEODORE PRESSER COMPANY   .50
VERRALL, J.   1
  LONELINESS
    THEODORE PRESSER COMPANY   .50
VI CHIARI   3
  LA SPAGNOLA -- SPAN. MAIDEN
    CENTURY MUSIC PUBLISHING COMPANY, INC. 1808 .40
VI CHIARI   3
  SPANISH MAIDEN -- LA SPAGNOLA --
    CENTURY MUSIC PUBLISHING COMPANY, INC. 1808 .40
VIADANA, DA   PRAETELLA
  SINFONIE MUSICALI, OP. 18 NOS. 1-6
    FRANCO COLOMBO PUBLICATIONS   BON.1749 3.00
VICTORY, G.
  FIVE TALES FROM ANDERSEN
    BANKS AND SON LTD.   .95
VIDUSSO
  FANTASIA CINESE
    FRANCO COLOMBO PUBLICATIONS   Z3001 2.25
VIEU
  CHANT DE BERGER
    FRANCO COLOMBO PUBLICATIONS   SAL 1.75
VILBRE   4
  HEAVENWARD, MARCH RELIGIOSO
    CENTURY MUSIC PUBLISHING COMPANY, INC. 1391 .40
VILLA-LOBOS, H.
  A HISTORIA DA CAIPIRINHA
    PEER SOUTHERN ORGANIZATION   00.75
VILLA-LOBOS, H.
  A MANHA DA PIERRETTE
    EDWARD B. MARKS MUSIC CORPORATION   01.00
VILLA-LOBOS, H.
  A MAO DIREITA TEM UMA ROSEIRA
    PEER SOUTHERN ORGANIZATION   00.75
VILLA-LOBOS, H.
  A MODA DA CARRANQUINHA
    PEER SOUTHERN ORGANIZATION   00.75
VILLA-LOBOS, H.
  A POBRESINHA SERTANEJA
    PEER SOUTHERN ORGANIZATION   00.75
VILLA-LOBOS, H.
  ALMA BRASILEIRA - CHOROS NO. 5
    MUSIC SALES CORPORATION   040932 1.00
VILLA-LOBOS, H.
  ALNILAM
    CARL FISCHER, INC.   P 2259 .50
VILLA-LOBOS, H.
  ALNITAH
    CARL FISCHER, INC.   P 2258 .50
VILLA-LOBOS, H.
  AMAZONAS--BRAZILIAN TONE POEM
    ASSOCIATED MUSIC PUBLISHERS, INC. ESC 5.50
VILLA-LOBOS, H.
  ASSIM NINAVA MAMAN
    PEER SOUTHERN ORGANIZATION   00.75
VILLA-LOBOS, H.
  BABY'S FAMILY--A PROLE DO BEBE, SERIES 2--NO. 1, LITTLE PAPER
  BUG--A BARATINHA DE PAPEL
    ASSOCIATED MUSIC PUBLISHERS, INC. ESC .60
VILLA-LOBOS, H.
  BABY'S FAMILY--A PROLE DO BEBE, SERIES 2--NO. 2, LITTLE
  CARDBOARD CAT--O GATINHO DE PAPELAO
    ASSOCIATED MUSIC PUBLISHERS, INC. ESC .60
VILLA-LOBOS, H.
  BABY'S FAMILY--A PROLE DO BEBE, SERIES 2--NO. 3, THE LITTLE TOY
  MOUSE--O CAMUNDONGO DE MASSA
    ASSOCIATED MUSIC PUBLISHERS, INC. ESC 3.75
VILLA-LOBOS, H.
  BABY'S FAMILY--A PROLE DO BEBE, SERIES 2--NO. 4, THE LITTLE
  RUBBER DOG--O CACHORRINHO DE BORRACHA
    ASSOCIATED MUSIC PUBLISHERS, INC. ESC 2.25
VILLA-LOBOS, H.
  BABY'S FAMILY--A PROLE DO BEBE, SERIES 2--NO. 5, THE LITTLE
  WOODEN HORSE--O CAVALINHO DE PAU
    ASSOCIATED MUSIC PUBLISHERS, INC. ESC 2.75
VILLA-LOBOS, H.
  BABY'S FAMILY--A PROLE DO BEBE, SERIES 2--NO. 6, THE LITTLE TIN
  OX--O BOISINHO DE CHUMBO
    ASSOCIATED MUSIC PUBLISHERS, INC. ESC 2.25
VILLA-LOBOS, H.
  BABY'S FAMILY--A PROLE DO BEBE, SERIES 2--NO. 7, THE LITTLE
  CLOTH BIRD--O PASSARINHO DE PANNO
    ASSOCIATED MUSIC PUBLISHERS, INC. ESC 2.50
VILLA-LOBOS, H.
  BABY'S FAMILY--A PROLE DO BEBE, SERIES 2--NO. 8, THE LITTLE
  COTTON BEAR--O URSOZINHO DE ALGODAO
    ASSOCIATED MUSIC PUBLISHERS, INC. ESC 3.50
VILLA-LOBOS, H.
  BABY'S FAMILY--A PROLE DO BEBE, SERIES 2--NO. 9, THE LITTLE
  GLASS WOLF--O LOBOSINHO DE VIDRO
    ASSOCIATED MUSIC PUBLISHERS, INC. ESC 3.25
VILLA-LOBOS, H.
  BABY'S FAMILY, THE -- A PROLE DO BEBE, BK. 1
    EDWIN F. KALMUS   4027 2.00
VILLA-LOBOS, H.
  BACHIANAS BRASILEIRAS - SUITE NO. 4 , DANCE
    MUSIC SALES CORPORATION   040936 .75
VILLA-LOBOS, H.
  BACHIANAS BRASILEIRAS - SUITE NO. 4 , PRELUDE
    MUSIC SALES CORPORATION   040947 .75
VILLA-LOBOS, H.
  BACHIANAS BRASILEIRAS - SUITE NO. 4 , SONG
    MUSIC SALES CORPORATION   040931 .75
VILLA-LOBOS, H.
  BACHIANAS BRASILEIRAS - SUITE NO. 4 , SONG OF THE JUNGLE
    MUSIC SALES CORPORATION   040935 .75
VILLA-LOBOS, H.
  BROKEN LITTLE MUSIC BOX, THE
    MUSIC SALES CORPORATION   040934 1.00
VILLA-LOBOS, H.
  CARNABAL DAS CRIANCAS BRASILEIRAS -- PEIRRETTE'S HANDS
    MUSIC SALES CORPORATION   040933 .75
VILLA-LOBOS, H.
  CARNABAL DAS CRIANCAS BRASILEIRAS -THE DEVIL'S WHIP
    MUSIC SALES CORPORATION   040944 .75

VILLA-LOBOS, H.
  CHOROS NO. 5--ALMA BRASILEIRA
    ASSOCIATED MUSIC PUBLISHERS, INC. ESC 4.75
VILLA-LOBOS, H.
  CICLO BRASILEIRO - DANCE OF THE WHITE INDIAN
    MUSIC SALES CORPORATION   040929 1.00
VILLA-LOBOS, H.
  CICLO BRASILEIRO - JUNGLE FESTIVAL
    MUSIC SALES CORPORATION   040937 1.00
VILLA-LOBOS, H.
  CICLO BRASILEIRO - MINSTREL IMPRESSIONS
    MUSIC SALES CORPORATION   040941 1.00
VILLA-LOBOS, H.
  CICLO BRASILEIRO - NATIVE PLANTING SONG
    MUSIC SALES CORPORATION   040930 1.00
VILLA-LOBOS, H.   BRANDAO
  FIVE PRELUDES FOR GUITAR
    ASSOCIATED MUSIC PUBLISHERS, INC. ESC 3.25
VILLA-LOBOS, H.   BRANDAO
  FIVE PRELUDES FOR GUITAR--NO. 1
    ASSOCIATED MUSIC PUBLISHERS, INC. ESC 3.25
VILLA-LOBOS, H.   BRANDAO
  FIVE PRELUDES FOR GUITAR--NO. 2
    ASSOCIATED MUSIC PUBLISHERS, INC. ESC 3.25
VILLA-LOBOS, H.   BRANDAO
  FIVE PRELUDES FOR GUITAR--NO. 3
    ASSOCIATED MUSIC PUBLISHERS, INC. ESC 2.50
VILLA-LOBOS, H.   BRANDAO
  FIVE PRELUDES FOR GUITAR--NO. 5
    ASSOCIATED MUSIC PUBLISHERS, INC. ESC 3.25
VILLA-LOBOS, H.
  FRANCETTE ET PIA--NO. 01, PIA EST VENU EN FRANCE
    ASSOCIATED MUSIC PUBLISHERS, INC. ESC 1.50
VILLA-LOBOS, H.
  FRANCETTE ET PIA--NO. 02, PIA A VU FRANCETTE
    ASSOCIATED MUSIC PUBLISHERS, INC. ESC 1.50
VILLA-LOBOS, H.
  FRANCETTE ET PIA--NO. 03, PIA A PARLE A FRANCETTE
    ASSOCIATED MUSIC PUBLISHERS, INC. ESC 1.50
VILLA-LOBOS, H.
  FRANCETTE ET PIA--NO. 04, PIA ET FRANCETTE JOUENT ENSEMBLE
    ASSOCIATED MUSIC PUBLISHERS, INC. ESC 1.50
VILLA-LOBOS, H.
  FRANCETTE ET PIA--NO. 05, FRANCETTE EST FACHEE
    ASSOCIATED MUSIC PUBLISHERS, INC. ESC 1.50
VILLA-LOBOS, H.
  FRANCETTE ET PIA--NO. 06, PIA EST PARTI POUR LA GUERRE
    ASSOCIATED MUSIC PUBLISHERS, INC. ESC 1.00
VILLA-LOBOS, H.
  FRANCETTE ET PIA--NO. 07, FRANCETTE EST TRISTE
    ASSOCIATED MUSIC PUBLISHERS, INC. ESC 1.00
VILLA-LOBOS, H.
  FRANCETTE ET PIA--NO. 08, PIA REVIENT DE LA GUERRE
    ASSOCIATED MUSIC PUBLISHERS, INC. ESC 1.50
VILLA-LOBOS, H.
  FRANCETTE ET PIA--NO. 09, FRANCETTE EST CONTENTE
    ASSOCIATED MUSIC PUBLISHERS, INC. ESC 1.50
VILLA-LOBOS, H.
  FRANCETTE ET PIA--NO. 10, FRANCETTE ET PIA JOUENT POUR TOUJOURS
    ASSOCIATED MUSIC PUBLISHERS, INC. ESC 3.50
VILLA-LOBOS, H.
  GARIBALDI FOI A MISSA
    PEER SOUTHERN ORGANIZATION   00.75
VILLA-LOBOS, H.
  HOMMAGE A CHOPIN--1949
    ASSOCIATED MUSIC PUBLISHERS, INC. ESC 6.00
VILLA-LOBOS, H.
  LE POLICHINELLE
    ASHLEY DEALERS SERVICE, INC. ES .95
VILLA-LOBOS, H.   LEVINE
  LITTLE TRAIN OF CAIPIRA, THE - TOCCATA FROM 'BACHIANAS
  BRASILEIRAS NO. 2'
    FRANCO COLOMBO PUBLICATIONS   NY2066 .75
VILLA-LOBOS, H.   LEVINE, H.
  LITTLE TRAIN OF THE CAIPIRA, THE -- TOCCATA, FROM 'BACHIANAS
  BRASILEIRAS' NO. 2
    BELWIN-MILLS PUBLISHING CORPORATION   .75
VILLA-LOBOS, H.
  MINTIKA
    CARL FISCHER, INC.   P 2260 .50
VILLA-LOBOS, H.
  NEW YORK SKY LINE
    ASSOCIATED MUSIC PUBLISHERS, INC. ESC 3.25
VILLA-LOBOS, H.
  O POLICHINELLO
    FRANCO COLOMBO PUBLICATIONS   BA9320 .75
VILLA-LOBOS, H.
  OS TRES CAVALHEIROSINHOS
    PEER SOUTHERN ORGANIZATION   00.75
VILLA-LOBOS, H.
  POEMA SINGELO
    MUSIC SALES CORPORATION   040946 1.00
VILLA-LOBOS, H.
  POLICHINELLE, LA
    EDWARD B. MARKS MUSIC CORPORATION   01.00
VILLA-LOBOS, H.
  PROLE DO BEBE - LITTLE PAPER DOLL
    MUSIC SALES CORPORATION   040942 .75
VILLA-LOBOS, H.
  PROLE DO BEBE - LITTLE RUBBER DOLL
    MUSIC SALES CORPORATION   040943 .75
VILLA-LOBOS, H.
  PROLE DO BEBE - PUNCHINELLO
    MUSIC SALES CORPORATION   040945 .75
VILLA-LOBOS, H.
  RUDEPOEMA
    ASSOCIATED MUSIC PUBLISHERS, INC. ESC 7.75
VILLA-LOBOS, H.
  SACY
    PEER SOUTHERN ORGANIZATION   00.75
VILLA-LOBOS, H.
  TIRA O SEU PESINHO
    PEER SOUTHERN ORGANIZATION   00.75
VILLA-LOBOS, H.
  UMA, DUAS ANGOLINHAS
    PEER SOUTHERN ORGANIZATION   00.75
VILLA-LOBOS, H.
  VAMOS TODOS CIRANDAR
    PEER SOUTHERN ORGANIZATION   00.75
VILLA-LOBOS, H.
  VESTIDINHO BRANCO
    PEER SOUTHERN ORGANIZATION   00.75
VILLOLDO   3
  EL CHOCLO
    BELWIN-MILLS PUBLISHING CORPORATION 565 .60
VILLOLDO   3
  EL CHOCLO, TANGO ARGENTINE
    CENTURY MUSIC PUBLISHING COMPANY, INC. 2738 .40

VIOLLE, B.
    POLAR BEARS, OP. 22 NO. 1
        G. SCHIRMER, INC.   .40
VIRGILIO, N.
    CINQUE BREVI IMPRESSIONI
        EDIZIONI BERBEN   5   EB 1639   1.50
VITTADINI
    ELEGIE
        ALPHONSE LEDUC
VIVALDI   FARINA
    FOUR SEASONS, THE
        FRANCO COLOMBO PUBLICATIONS   129190   2.25
VIVIANI   2
    SILVER TRUMPETS
        CENTURY MUSIC PUBLISHING COMPANY, INC.   3895   .40
VLAD   TERRY
    ROMEO AND JULIET SUITE
        FRANCO COLOMBO PUBLICATIONS   NY1731   1.25
VOGEL
    EPITAPH TO ALBAN BERG
        FRANCO COLOMBO PUBLICATIONS   128798   1.50
VOGEL
    GAI LABOUREUR, LE
        DELRIEU ET CIE.   1.00
VOGEL   3
    STILLE, NACHT, HEILIGE NACHT
        BARENREITER VERLAG   SM 439
VOLKART-SCHLAGER, K.   2-3
    KLEINE WELT
        SCHOTT   3947   1.75
VOLKART, H.
    BAND, THE -- MARCH
        BELWIN-MILLS PUBLISHING CORPORATION   25010   .60
VOLKART, H.
    CALLIOPE, THE
        BELWIN-MILLS PUBLISHING CORPORATION   25016   .60
VOLKART, H.
    DANCE OF THE MARIONETTES
        BELWIN-MILLS PUBLISHING CORPORATION   25037   .60
VOLKART, H.
    FROG, THE
        BELWIN-MILLS PUBLISHING CORPORATION   25238   .60
VOLKART, H.
    LITTLE LULLABY, A
        BELWIN-MILLS PUBLISHING CORPORATION   25004   .60
VOLKART, H.
    RIDIN' ALONG
        BELWIN-MILLS PUBLISHING CORPORATION   25239   .60
VOLPATTI
    BANDERILLEROS, LES
        FRANCO COLOMBO PUBLICATIONS   SAL   1.75
VOLPATTI
    BLACK AND WHITE
        FRANCO COLOMBO PUBLICATIONS   SAL   1.75
VOLPATTI
    MA BLONDE AIMEE
        FRANCO COLOMBO PUBLICATIONS   SAL   1.75
VOLPATTI
    PLUIE DE BRILLANTS
        FRANCO COLOMBO PUBLICATIONS   SAL   1.75
VOLPATTI
    SERENADE D'ENFANTS
        FRANCO COLOMBO PUBLICATIONS   SAL   1.75
VOLPATTI
    SORRENTINA
        FRANCO COLOMBO PUBLICATIONS   SAL   1.75
VOLPATTI
    ZOETTE
        FRANCO COLOMBO PUBLICATIONS   SAL   1.75
VOLTI   3
    CITIZEN'S GALOP, THE
        CENTURY MUSIC PUBLISHING COMPANY, INC.   769   .40
VOLZ, H.   1
    ALPINE WALTZ
        WILLIS MUSIC COMPANY   .40
VOLZ, H.   2
    ANTELOPE ANTICS
        PRO-ART PUBLICATIONS, INC.   243   .50
VOLZ, H.   1 1/2
    BALLERINA IN WHITE
        WILLIS MUSIC COMPANY   .40
VOLZ, H.   1 1/2
    BALLERINA IN WHITE
        WILLIS MUSIC COMPANY   .40
VOLZ, H.   3
    BI-CENTENNIAL MARCH
        BELWIN-MILLS PUBLISHING CORPORATION   .60
VOLZ, H.   1
    CHANT TO AUTUMN MOON
        CENTURY MUSIC PUBLISHING COMPANY, INC.   4390   .40
VOLZ, H.   1
    CONCERT OF THE BEES
        PRO-ART PUBLICATIONS, INC.   490   .50
VOLZ, H.   2
    EGYPTIAN DANCERS
        PRO-ART PUBLICATIONS, INC.   255   .50
VOLZ, H.   2
    EVENING STAR
        PRO-ART PUBLICATIONS, INC.   129   .50
VOLZ, H.   1 1/2
    FOREST LULLABY, OP. 1056
        BELWIN-MILLS PUBLISHING CORPORATION   .60
VOLZ, H.   1 1/2
    FROG DANCE, OP. 1010 NO. 8
        BELWIN-MILLS PUBLISHING CORPORATION   .60
VOLZ, H.   2-3
    GAY VIENNA
        PRO-ART PUBLICATIONS, INC.   350   .50
VOLZ, H.   2-3
    MANICHORD CAPRICE
        PRO-ART PUBLICATIONS, INC.   351   .50
VOLZ, H.   1
    PARTY TIME
        PRO-ART PUBLICATIONS, INC.   489   .50
VOLZ, H.
    PHANTOM OF THE SEA
        COMPOSERS PRESS, INC.   1.00
VOLZ, H.   2
    SHOOTING STARS
        PRO-ART PUBLICATIONS, INC.   440   .50
VOLZ, H.   E
    SLAVONIC RHAPSODIE
        COMPOSERS PRESS, INC.   1.00
VOLZ, H.   1
    SLEEP BABY SLEEP
        PRO-ART PUBLICATIONS, INC.   488   .50

VOLZ, H.   3
    SWISS VALSE
        BELWIN-MILLS PUBLISHING CORPORATION   .60
VOLZ, H.   E
    TYROLESE WALTZ
        COMPOSERS PRESS, INC.   1.00
VOLZ, H.   3
    VIENNA VALSE
        VOLKWEIN BROS.   .50
VOMACKA   4
    INTERMEZZO, OP. 6
        BARENREITER VERLAG   AP 757
VOMACKA   3-4
    NACHTSTIMMUNG
        BARENREITER VERLAG   AP 758
VOMACKA   4
    SONATA QUASI FANTASIA, OP. 40
        BARENREITER VERLAG
VOMACKA   4
    SONATA, OP. 7
        BARENREITER VERLAG   AP 759
VONBLON, F.   3
    SERENADE SICILIETTA
        CENTURY MUSIC PUBLISHING COMPANY, INC.   2124   .40
VONBLON, F.   3
    SIZILIETTA SERENADE
        CENTURY MUSIC PUBLISHING COMPANY, INC.   2124   .40
VOORMOLEN
    BERCEUSE
        FRANCO COLOMBO PUBLICATIONS   SAL   1.75
VOORMOLEN
    ELEPHANTS, LES
        FRANCO COLOMBO PUBLICATIONS   SAL   1.75
VOORMOLEN
    FALBALAS
        FRANCO COLOMBO PUBLICATIONS   SAL   2.50
VOORMOLEN
    SCENE ET DANSE EROTIQUES
        FRANCO COLOMBO PUBLICATIONS   SAL   2.50
VOORMOLEN
    SONNET
        FRANCO COLOMBO PUBLICATIONS   SAL   1.50
VOORMOLEN
    SUITE NO. 1
        FRANCO COLOMBO PUBLICATIONS   SAL   3.25
VORISEK   KENADERA   3-4
    SONATA, OP. 20
        BARENREITER VERLAG   MAB 4
VOTACEK   4
    TEMA CON VARIAZIONI
        BARENREITER VERLAG   AP 764
VOVK   3
    HOPAK
        WILLIS MUSIC COMPANY   .40
VOVK   2
    LULLABY FOR EVELINE
        THEODORE PRESSER COMPANY   .50
VOVK
    TOY PARADE
        WARNER BROTHERS PUBLISHERS   .60
VOYE   3
    SINGING BIRDS, POLKA
        CENTURY MUSIC PUBLISHING COMPANY, INC.   880   .40
VRANA   3-4
    PRALUDIUM UND PASSACAGLIA
        BARENREITER VERLAG   AP 765
VRANA   3-4
    SONATA, OP. 11
        BARENREITER VERLAG   AP 766
VUATAZ
    PAIN QUOTIDIEN
        FRANCO COLOMBO PUBLICATIONS   SAL   4.25
VUIK, J.
    TOY SHOP RAG
        BELWIN-MILLS PUBLISHING CORPORATION   20382   .85
WACHS, F.
    LOISIRS DU JEUNE AGE, LES - A FONTAINEBLEAU
        FRANCO COLOMBO PUBLICATIONS   SAL   1.50
WACHS, F.
    LOISIRS DU JEUNE AGE, LES - A LA FETE DE ST. CLOUD
        FRANCO COLOMBO PUBLICATIONS   SAL   1.50
WACHS, F.
    LOISIRS DU JEUNE AGE, LES - ARLEQUIN ET COLOMBINE
        FRANCO COLOMBO PUBLICATIONS   SAL   1.50
WACHS, F.
    LOISIRS DU JEUNE AGE, LES - CARMEN
        FRANCO COLOMBO PUBLICATIONS   SAL   1.50
WACHS, F.
    LOISIRS DU JEUNE AGE, LES - COQUETTE
        FRANCO COLOMBO PUBLICATIONS   SAL   1.50
WACHS, F.
    LOISIRS DU JEUNE AGE, LES - DOUX AVEU
        FRANCO COLOMBO PUBLICATIONS   SAL   1.50
WACHS, F.
    LOISIRS DU JEUNE AGE, LES - FETE A SORRENTE
        FRANCO COLOMBO PUBLICATIONS   SAL   1.50
WACHS, F.
    LOISIRS DU JEUNE AGE, LES - LE PREMIER BAL
        FRANCO COLOMBO PUBLICATIONS   SAL   1.50
WACHS, F.
    LOISIRS DU JEUNE AGE, LES - MIREILLE
        FRANCO COLOMBO PUBLICATIONS   SAL   1.50
WACHS, F.
    LOISIRS DU JEUNE AGE, LES - RETOUR DU PRINTEMPS
        FRANCO COLOMBO PUBLICATIONS   SAL   1.50
WACHS, F.
    LOISIRS DU JEUNE AGE, LES - SOUS LES ETOILES
        FRANCO COLOMBO PUBLICATIONS   SAL   1.50
WACHS, F.
    LOISIRS DU JEUNE AGE, LES - UN SOIR A SEVILLE
        FRANCO COLOMBO PUBLICATIONS   SAL   1.50
WACHS, P.   5
    A MON MOULIN, PIECE IMITATIVE
        ALPHONSE LEDUC
WACHS, P.
    ALICANTE
        FRANCO COLOMBO PUBLICATIONS   SAL   1.75
WACHS, P.   4
    BALANCELLE, IN THE SWING
        CENTURY MUSIC PUBLISHING COMPANY, INC.   2296   .40
WACHS, P.   8
    BERRICHONNE, LA, DANSE CARACTERISTIQUE
        ALPHONSE LEDUC
WACHS, P.
    BIEN GENTILLE
        FRANCO COLOMBO PUBLICATIONS   SAL   1.75

WAGNER   DEL MAGLIO
  WALKUERE, DIE - SIEGMUND'S SPRING SONG
    FRANCO COLOMBO PUBLICATIONS   128128   .50
WAGNER
  WEDDING MARCH FROM 'LOHENGRIN'
    CARL FISCHER, INC.   S 207   .50
WAGNER   PAUER
  WEDDING MARCH FROM 'LOHENGRIN'
    G. SCHIRMER, INC.   .60
WAGNER *   6
  EVENING STAR
    CENTURY MUSIC PUBLISHING COMPANY, INC.   692   .40
WAGNER *   6
  EVENING STAR -- TANNHAUSER
    CENTURY MUSIC PUBLISHING COMPANY, INC.   692   .40
WAGNER *   TAGLIAPIETRA
  LOHENGRIN - CHORUS AND WEDDING MARCH
    FRANCO COLOMBO PUBLICATIONS   ER318   1.00
WAGNER *   TAGLIAPIETRA
  TANNHAEUSER - PILGRIMS' CHORUS
    FRANCO COLOMBO PUBLICATIONS   128792   .50
WAGNER *
  TANNHAEUSER OVERTURE -- FREE TRANSCRIPTION --
    FRANCO COLOMBO PUBLICATIONS   SAL   7.00
WAGNER *
  TANNHAUSER--MARCH. ENTRANCE OF THE GUESTS INTO THE WARTBURG
    G. SCHIRMER, INC.   1.00
WAGNER *
  TANNHAUSER--MARCH. ENTRANCE OF THE GUESTS INTO THE WARTBURG
    G. SCHIRMER, INC.   1.00
WAGNER *
  TRISTAN AND ISOLDE--ISOLDE'S LOVE-DEATH
    G. SCHIRMER, INC.   .60
WAGNER *   TAGLIAPIETRA
  TRISTAN UND ISOLDE - LIEBESTOD
    FRANCO COLOMBO PUBLICATIONS   127795   1.00
WAGNER *
  TRISTAN UND ISOLDE--ISOLDE'S LOVE-DEATH
    G. SCHIRMER, INC.   .60
WAGNER, J.
  FROM THE MONADNOCK REGION
    SEESAW MUSIC CORPORATION   4.00
WAGNER, J.
  JOY PEAL
    SEESAW MUSIC CORPORATION   1.00
WAGNER, J.
  PIANO PIANO DIVERTISSMENTS
    SEESAW MUSIC CORPORATION   3.00
WAGNER, J.
  RADIO CITY SNAPSHOTS
    BELWIN-MILLS PUBLISHING CORPORATION   20217   1.25
WAGNER, J.
  ROMANTIC MOMENTS
    SEESAW MUSIC CORPORATION   1.00
WAGNER, J.
  SONATA IN B MINOR
    PEER SOUTHERN ORGANIZATION   02.25
WAGNER, J.
  SONATINA
    FRANCO COLOMBO PUBLICATIONS   SAL   1.75
WAGNER, J.   SCHAUM, J.   4
  UNDER THE DOUBLE EAGLE
    BELWIN-MILLS PUBLISHING CORPORATION   .50
WAGNER, J.
  UNDER THE DOUBLE EAGLE
    BOOSEY AND HAWKES, INC.   .50
WAGNER, J.   3
  UNDER THE DOUBLE EAGLE
    CENTURY MUSIC PUBLISHING COMPANY, INC.   449   .40
WAGNER, J.   3
  UNDER THE DOUBLE EAGLE
    THEODORE PRESSER COMPANY   .50
WAGNER, J.   3
  UNDER THE DOUBLE EAGLE
    WILLIS MUSIC COMPANY   .35
WAGNER, J.
  UNDER THE DOUBLE EAGLE -- MARCH
    BELWIN-MILLS PUBLISHING CORPORATION   28018   .60
WAGNER, J.
  UNDER THE DOUBLE EAGLE --MARCH--
    CARL FISCHER, INC.   S 1676   .50
WAGNER, J.   3
  UNDER THE DOUBLE EAGLE MARCH
    VOLKWEIN BROS.   .25
WAGNER, J.
  UNDER THE DOUBLE EAGLE, OP. 159
    G. SCHIRMER, INC.   .40
WAGNER, W.
  SONATINA
    FRANCO COLOMBO PUBLICATIONS   BA12500   1.25
WAGNES, F.
  DIE BOSNIAKEN KOMMEN -- MARCH
    UNIVERSAL EDITION   UE 4043   .85
WAGNESS   3
  CATHEDRAL AT TWILIGHT, THE
    THEODORE PRESSER COMPANY   .50
WAGNESS   2 1/2
  GLIDER, THE
    THEODORE PRESSER COMPANY   .50
WAGNESS   2
  GYPSY LIFE
    THEODORE PRESSER COMPANY   .50
WAGNESS   2
  MARCH OF VICTORY
    THEODORE PRESSER COMPANY   .50
WAGNESS   1
  SEA CHANTEY, A
    THEODORE PRESSER COMPANY   .50
WALDO, J.   2
  CAPTAIN KIDD
    WILLIS MUSIC COMPANY   .35
WALDO, J.   1
  IN THE SWING
    WILLIS MUSIC COMPANY   .35
WALDO, J.   3
  MARCH OF THE CHAMPIONS
    WILLIS MUSIC COMPANY   .50
WALDO, J.   3
  MARCH OF THE CHAMPIONS
    WILLIS MUSIC COMPANY   .50
WALDTEUFEL, E.   E
  A TOI, OP. 150
    C. F. PETERS CORPORATION   5805   .90
WALDTEUFEL, E.   3
  ANGEL OF LOVE, WALTZES
    CENTURY MUSIC PUBLISHING COMPANY, INC.   135   .60

WALDTEUFEL, E.   4
  CHARMING WALTZES
    CENTURY MUSIC PUBLISHING COMPANY, INC.   1494   .40
WALDTEUFEL, E.   E
  DOLORES, OP. 170
    C. F. PETERS CORPORATION   5807   .90
WALDTEUFEL, E.   4
  DOLORES, SP. WALTZ
    CENTURY MUSIC PUBLISHING COMPANY, INC.   1587   .40
WALDTEUFEL, E.   E
  ESPANA, OP. 236
    C. F. PETERS CORPORATION   5806   .90
WALDTEUFEL, E.   4
  ESPANA, SP. WALTZ
    CENTURY MUSIC PUBLISHING COMPANY, INC.   1631   .40
WALDTEUFEL, E.   E
  ESTUDIANTINA, OP. 191
    C. F. PETERS CORPORATION   5101   .90
WALDTEUFEL, E.   3
  ESTUDIANTINA, WALTZES
    CENTURY MUSIC PUBLISHING COMPANY, INC.   1482   .40
WALDTEUFEL, E.   SCHAUM, J.   2
  JUNIOR PROM WALTZ
    BELWIN-MILLS PUBLISHING CORPORATION   .50
WALDTEUFEL, E.   4
  LES PATINEURS, SKATERS
    CENTURY MUSIC PUBLISHING COMPANY, INC.   390   .40
WALDTEUFEL, E.   E
  MON REVE, OP. 151
    C. F. PETERS CORPORATION   5802   .90
WALDTEUFEL, E.   4
  PATINEURS, LES -- SKATERS --
    CENTURY MUSIC PUBLISHING COMPANY, INC.   390   .40
WALDTEUFEL, E.   E
  PATINEURS, LES --THE SKATES--, OP. 183
    C. F. PETERS CORPORATION   5100   .90
WALDTEUFEL, E.   ROLFE, W.   2
  PATINEURS, LES, EASY
    CENTURY MUSIC PUBLISHING COMPANY, INC.   3191   .40
WALDTEUFEL, E.   E
  PLUIE DE DIAMANTS --SPARKLING SHOWERS--, OP. 160
    C. F. PETERS CORPORATION   5804   .90
WALDTEUFEL, E.   E
  SIRENES, LES, OP. 154
    C. F. PETERS CORPORATION   5800   .90
WALDTEUFEL, E.
  SKATER'S WALTZ
    ASHLEY DEALERS SERVICE, INC.   ES   .95
WALDTEUFEL, E.   WEYBRIGHT
  SKATER'S WALTZ, THE
    BELWIN-MILLS PUBLISHING CORPORATION   26046   .60
WALDTEUFEL, E.   SCHAUM, J.   2
  SKATERS WALTZ
    BELWIN-MILLS PUBLISHING CORPORATION   .50
WALDTEUFEL, E.   MITTLER   2B
  SKATERS WALTZ
    MUSICORD PUBLICATIONS, INC.   .45
WALDTEUFEL, E.   RASBACH
  SKATERS, THE
    G. SCHIRMER, INC.   .50
WALDTEUFEL, E.   4
  SKATERS, THE
    WILLIS MUSIC COMPANY   .40
WALDTEUFEL, E.   4
  SKATERS, THE
    WILLIS MUSIC COMPANY   .40
WALDTEUFEL, E.   4
  SKATERS' WALTZ
    CENTURY MUSIC PUBLISHING COMPANY, INC.   390   .40
WALDTEUFEL, E.   3
  SPANISH STUDENTS, WALTZES
    CENTURY MUSIC PUBLISHING COMPANY, INC.   1482   .40
WALDTEUFEL, E.   2
  SPANISH STUDENTS, WALTZES, EASY
    CENTURY MUSIC PUBLISHING COMPANY, INC.   3666   .40
WALDTEUFEL, E.   4
  TRES JOLIF
    CENTURY MUSIC PUBLISHING COMPANY, INC.   1494   .40
WALDTEUFEL, E.   E
  TRES JOLIE --CHARMING--, OP. 159
    C. F. PETERS CORPORATION   5801   .90
WALDTEUFEL, E.   E
  VIOLETTES, OP. 148
    C. F. PETERS CORPORATION   5803   .90
WALFORD DAVIES, H.
  R. A. F. MARCH PAST
    BOOSEY AND HAWKES, INC.   .50
WALFORD DAVIES, H.
  SOLEMN MELODY
    NOVELLO AND COMPANY, LTD.   10.0029.02   .90
WALKER   NEALE, J.   EASY
  MR. BOJANGLES
    WARNER BROTHERS PUBLISHERS   .75
WALKER   2
  PARADE OF THE CHINESE DOLLS
    PRO-ART PUBLICATIONS, INC.   86   .50
WALKER, G.
  SONATA NO. 01
    GENERAL MUSIC PUBLISHING COMPANY, INC.   727   6.00
WALKER, G.
  SONATA NO. 01
    GENERAL MUSIC PUBLISHING COMPANY, INC.   6.00
WALKER, G.
  SONATA NO. 01 FOR PIANO
    COMPOSERS AUTOGRAPH PUBLICATIONS   5.94
WALKER, G.
  SPATIALS - VARIATIONS FOR PIANO
    GENERAL MUSIC PUBLISHING COMPANY, INC.   652   2.50
WALKER, G.
  SPATIALS - VARIATIONS FOR PIANO
    GENERAL MUSIC PUBLISHING COMPANY, INC.   2.50
WALKER, G.
  SPEKTRA
    GENERAL MUSIC PUBLISHING COMPANY, INC.   662   4.00
WALKER, G.
  SPEKTRA
    GENERAL MUSIC PUBLISHING COMPANY, INC.   4.00
WALLACE   2
  MARITANA, SCENES THAT ARE BRIGHTEST
    CENTURY MUSIC PUBLISHING COMPANY, INC.   1787   .40
WALLACE   2
  SCENES THAT ARE BRIGHTEST
    CENTURY MUSIC PUBLISHING COMPANY, INC.   1787   .40
WALLER, F.
  BUGLE CALL RAG
    BELWIN-MILLS PUBLISHING CORPORATION   20360   .85

WALLER, T.
  JITTERBUG WALTZ
    THE BIG THREE MUSIC CORPORATION — 00.95
WALLINGTON, G.
  FAIRYLAND
    BELWIN-MILLS PUBLISHING CORPORATION — 20483 — .85
WALLINGTON, G.
  GODCHILD
    BELWIN-MILLS PUBLISHING CORPORATION — 20112 — .85
WALLINGTON, G.
  KNOCKOUT
    BELWIN-MILLS PUBLISHING CORPORATION — 20142 — .85
WALLINGTON, G.
  LEMON DROP
    BELWIN-MILLS PUBLISHING CORPORATION — 20151 — .85
WALLINGTON, G.
  VARIATIONS
    BELWIN-MILLS PUBLISHING CORPORATION — 20329 — 1.00
WALLIS   WEBER, H. *   1
  AMERICA THE BEAUTIFUL
    WILLIS MUSIC COMPANY — .30
WALLIS
  GOOD KING WENCESLAS
    WILLIS MUSIC COMPANY — .25
WALLIS
  JOY TO THE WORLD
    WILLIS MUSIC COMPANY — .30
WALLIS   WEBER, H.   1
  STAR-SPANGLED BANNER, THE
    WILLIS MUSIC COMPANY — .30
WALLIS   WEBER   1
  YANKEE DOODLE
    WILLIS MUSIC COMPANY — .30
WALLIS--ED   WALLIS
  ADESTE FIDELES
    BOSTON MUSIC COMPANY — .50
WALLIS--ED   WALLIS
  FIRST NOEL, THE
    BOSTON MUSIC COMPANY — .50
WALLIS--ED   WALLIS   3
  HOME ON THE RANGE
    BOSTON MUSIC COMPANY — .50
WALSH *
  BLACK HAWK WALTZ
    CARL FISCHER, INC. — S 7638 — .50
WALSH, M.   2
  BLACK HAWK WALTZ
    CENTURY MUSIC PUBLISHING COMPANY, INC. — 147 — .40
WALSH, M.   3
  BLACK HAWK WALTZ
    THEODORE PRESSER COMPANY — .50
WALSH, M.   2
  BLACK HAWK WALTZ
    VOLKWEIN BROS. — .25
WALSH, M.   3
  BLACK HAWK WALTZ
    WILLIS MUSIC COMPANY — .35
WALSH, M.
  BLACK HAWK WALTZ, THE
    ASHLEY DEALERS SERVICE, INC. — ES — .95
WALTER
  APRES LE BAL
    FRANCO COLOMBO PUBLICATIONS — SAL — 1.75
WALTER
  CARMELA
    FRANCO COLOMBO PUBLICATIONS — SAL — 1.75
WALTER
  CE QUE DANSAIT GRAND'MERE
    FRANCO COLOMBO PUBLICATIONS — SAL — 1.75
WALTER
  GAZOUILLIS D'OISEAUX
    FRANCO COLOMBO PUBLICATIONS   1-2   SAL — 1.75
WALTER
  MILITARY MARCH
    PRO-ART PUBLICATIONS, INC. — 430 — .50
WALTER
  OHE, MAMAN
    FRANCO COLOMBO PUBLICATIONS — SAL — 1.75
WALTER
  PAUVRES FOUS
    FRANCO COLOMBO PUBLICATIONS — SAL — 1.75
WALTER
  QUAND L'OISEAU CHANTE
    FRANCO COLOMBO PUBLICATIONS — SAL — 1.75
WALTER
  REVEIL AU COUVENT
    FRANCO COLOMBO PUBLICATIONS — SAL — 1.75
WALTER
  TA-RA-RA-BOUM DER-E
    FRANCO COLOMBO PUBLICATIONS — SAL — 1.75
WALTERS   4
  SOUNDS FROM THE RINGING ROCKS
    CENTURY MUSIC PUBLISHING COMPANY, INC. — 1505 — .40
WALTHEW, R.   7
  LYRICAL
    NOVELLO AND COMPANY, LTD. — 55.0048.06 — .25
WALTON, W.
  CROWN IMPERIAL
    OXFORD UNIVERSITY PRESS — 32.071 — 1.25
WALTON, W.
  FACADE EXCERPTS -- FOX TROT
    OXFORD UNIVERSITY PRESS — 34.042 — 1.55
WALTON, W.
  ORB AND SCEPTRE
    OXFORD UNIVERSITY PRESS — 32.903 — 1.25
WALZEL, L. M.
  SONATINA GRAZIOSA, OP. 21 NO 1
    ASSOCIATED MUSIC PUBLISHERS, INC. — DOB — 1.50
WANDERMAN   2
  IN A VIENNESE GARDEN
    BOSTON MUSIC COMPANY — .50
WANDERMAN   2
  LITTLE FRENCH CAFE
    BOSTON MUSIC COMPANY — .50
WANDERMAN   2
  PLAYFUL MOUSE, THE
    BOSTON MUSIC COMPANY — .50
WANSBOROUGH, H.
  IN AN ORIENTAL MARKET PLACE
    BELWIN-MILLS PUBLISHING CORPORATION   3   .60
WARD
  AMERICA THE BEAUTIFUL
    CENTURY MUSIC PUBLISHING COMPANY, INC. — 3568 — .60
WARD   KAHL
  BAND PLAYED ON, THE
    BOSTON MUSIC COMPANY — .50

WARD   1
  DUTCH TWINS
    WILLIS MUSIC COMPANY — .40
WARD   2
  GYPSY DANCERS
    PRO-ART PUBLICATIONS, INC. — 104 — .50
WARD   1-2
  HIPPITY-HOP
    PRO-ART PUBLICATIONS, INC. — 107 — .50
WARD   1
  HUMPTY DUMPTY
    BOSTON MUSIC COMPANY — .50
WARD   A
  LAMENTATION
    THEODORE PRESSER COMPANY — .60
WARD   1
  LITTLE MOUSE, A
    BOSTON MUSIC COMPANY — .50
WARD   2
  MARCH STACCATO
    PRO-ART PUBLICATIONS, INC. — 106 — .50
WARD   4
  MAY NIGHT
    THEODORE PRESSER COMPANY — .60
WARD   1-2
  MERRY ELF, THE
    PRO-ART PUBLICATIONS, INC. — 103 — .50
WARD   1-2
  PORCELAIN DOLL, THE
    PRO-ART PUBLICATIONS, INC. — 101 — .50
WARD   1-2
  RESTLESS WIND
    PRO-ART PUBLICATIONS, INC. — 275 — .50
WARD   2
  SAD SEA, THE
    PRO-ART PUBLICATIONS, INC. — 102 — .50
WARD   SCHAUM, J.
  STRIKE UP THE BAND
    BELWIN-MILLS PUBLISHING CORPORATION — .50
WARD   1-2
  SWINGING
    PRO-ART PUBLICATIONS, INC. — 274 — .50
WARD   2
  WALTZ IN F
    PRO-ART PUBLICATIONS, INC. — 277 — .50
WARD-STEINMAN, D.   6
  IMPROVISATIONS ON CHILDREN'S SONGS
    LEE ROBERTS MUSIC PUBLICATIONS, INC. — 1.00
WARE   SCHAUM, J.   2
  BAND PLAYED ON
    BELWIN-MILLS PUBLISHING CORPORATION — .50
WARE, H.
  VICTORY PRELUDE
    G. SCHIRMER, INC. — .50
WARFEL, P.   SCHAUM, J.   2
  SKI SLOPE
    SCHAUM PUBLICATIONS, INC. — .60
WARMS
  FLEURS DES CHAMPS
    FRANCO COLOMBO PUBLICATIONS — SAL — 2.50
WARREN   WEYBRIGHT   2
  GOD OF OUR FATHERS
    BELWIN-MILLS PUBLISHING CORPORATION — .50
WARREN   3
  SONG OF THE ROBIN
    CENTURY MUSIC PUBLISHING COMPANY, INC. — 2193 — .40
WARREN   5
  TAM O'SHANTER
    CENTURY MUSIC PUBLISHING COMPANY, INC. — 1033 — .40
WARREN
  TAM O'SHANTER
    G. SCHIRMER, INC. — .50
WARREN   5
  TAM O'SHANTER
    THEODORE PRESSER COMPANY — .50
WARREN
  THAT HAPPY FEELING
    MCA MUSIC — 1.00
WASHBURN, G.
  TIABEOC FOR PIANO
    SEESAW MUSIC CORPORATION — 1.00
WATERMAN   2 1/2
  BARCAROLLE
    BELWIN-MILLS PUBLISHING CORPORATION — .60
WATERMAN   2 1/2
  PETITE MENUET
    BELWIN-MILLS PUBLISHING CORPORATION — .60
WATKINS   2-3
  BEEHIVE, THE
    PRO-ART PUBLICATIONS, INC. — 445 — .50
WATSON
  ALBORADA
    CARL FISCHER, INC. — RS 431 — .50
WATSON
  ASH GROVE, THE
    CARL FISCHER, INC. — RS 370 — .50
WATSON
  FROG HE WOULD A-WOOING GO
    CARL FISCHER, INC. — RS 333 — .50
WATSON   2
  FROLIC OF THE FROGS, WALTZ
    CENTURY MUSIC PUBLISHING COMPANY, INC. — 224 — .40
WATSON
  GREENSLEEVES
    CARL FISCHER, INC. — RS 352 — .50
WATSON
  LITTLE SONATA
    CARL FISCHER, INC. — RS 336 — .50
WATSON
  MARCH OF THE MOON FOLK
    CARL FISCHER, INC. — RS 420 — .50
WATSON   2 1/2
  MOUNTAIN AIR
    THEODORE PRESSER COMPANY — .50
WATSON
  MY POODLE FIFI
    CARL FISCHER, INC. — RS 430 — .50
WATSON   1
  PALOMINO
    CARL FISCHER, INC. — RS 413 — .50
WATSON
  PIRATES BOLD
    THEODORE PRESSER COMPANY — .50
WATSON
  RAIN DANCE
    CARL FISCHER, INC. — RS 382 — .50

WATSON
    SATELLITE
        CARL FISCHER, INC.   RS 380   .50
WATSON
    SPANISH DANCERS
        CARL FISCHER, INC.   RS 381   .50
                                    2 1/2
WATSON
    WALTZ FOR A PENNY, A
        THEODORE PRESSER COMPANY   .50
WATSON
    WHEN JOHNNY COMES MARCHING HOME --CONCERT VARIATIONS--
        CARL FISCHER, INC.   RS 339   .60
WATSON
    WHIRLING DANCERS
        CARL FISCHER, INC.   RS 358   .50
WATSON, G.   3
    SEVEN PASTORALS
        NOVELLO AND COMPANY, LTD.   10.0108.06   1.15
WATSON, S.
    HIGHLAND CRADLE
        BELWIN-MILLS PUBLISHING CORPORATION   .60
WATSON, S.   2
    HIGHLAND ECHO
        BELWIN-MILLS PUBLISHING CORPORATION   .60
WATSON, S.
    SEVEN VARIATIONS ON A THEME BY HAYDN
        G. SCHIRMER, INC.   .50
WATSON, S.
    THREE AMERICAN TUNES--COTTON-EYE JO, THE BLUE BIRD, GRANNY DOES
    YOUR DOG BITE
        G. SCHIRMER, INC.   .50
WAXMAN
    CHARM BRACELET, THE
        MCA MUSIC   .75
WAXMAN   1
    HIPPOPOTAMUS
        BOSTON MUSIC COMPANY   .50
WAXMAN
    TOY TRAIN CHOO-CHOO--WITH WORDS
        G. SCHIRMER, INC.   .35
WEAVER, P.
    HILL-BILLY TUNE
        G. SCHIRMER, INC.   .50
WEBB
    BALKY DONKEY, THE
        MCA MUSIC   .60
WEBB
    BALLERINA OF THE ICE
        MCA MUSIC   .60
WEBB
    HOP SCOTCH
        EDWARD B. MARKS MUSIC CORPORATION   00.60
WEBB
    INDIAN FEATHER
        MCA MUSIC   .60
WEBER   MD
    NEW ADVENTURE
        THEODORE PRESSER COMPANY   .50
WEBER, A.
    ETUDES ACROSTICHES EN FORME DE VARIATIONS
        ALPHONSE LEDUC
WEBER, B.   A
    FIVE BAGATELLES
        THEODORE PRESSER COMPANY   1.25
WEBER, H.
    ADESTE FIDELIS
        WILLIS MUSIC COMPANY   .30
WEBER, H.   5
    STORM, THE
        CENTURY MUSIC PUBLISHING COMPANY, INC.   661   .40
WEBER, VON   GEORGII, W.   3
    AUFFORDERUNG ZUM TANZ -- C-DUR OP. 65
        SCHOTT   0794   1.00
WEBER, VON   GEORGII   5
    AUFFORDERUNG ZUM TANZ -- DES-DUR OP. 65
        SCHOTT   0792 102 1.00
WEBER, VON   2
    BARCAROLLE, OBERON
        CENTURY MUSIC PUBLISHING COMPANY, INC. 1788   .40
WEBER, VON   BARNET   4
    BARCAROLLE, OBERON
        CENTURY MUSIC PUBLISHING COMPANY, INC. 2585   .40
WEBER, VON   WEBSTER, B.
    CONCERTPIECE IN F MINOR OP. 79
        INTERNATIONAL MUSIC COMPANY   2.50
WEBER, VON   LEYBACH, I.   5
    DER FREISCHUTZ, FANTASIE
        CENTURY MUSIC PUBLISHING COMPANY, INC. 793   .40
WEBER, VON   5
    DER FREIZCHUTZ, TRANS.
        CENTURY MUSIC PUBLISHING COMPANY, INC. 2295   .40
WEBER, VON   6
    FANTAISIE BRILLANTE
        THEODORE PRESSER COMPANY   .50
WEBER, VON
    FANTASIA
        EDWARD B. MARKS MUSIC CORPORATION   01.50
WEBER, VON   LEYBACH, I.   5
    FREISCHUTZ, FANTASIE
        CENTURY MUSIC PUBLISHING COMPANY, INC. 793   .40
WEBER, VON   5
    FREISCHUTZ, PRAYER
        CENTURY MUSIC PUBLISHING COMPANY, INC. 2295   .40
WEBER, VON   SEAK
    GRAND POLONAISE, OP. 21
        FRANCO COLOMBO PUBLICATIONS   ER2545   .75
WEBER, VON   GEORGII, W.   5
    GRANDE POLONAISE ES-DUR
        SCHOTT   0789 1/2 1.00
WEBER, VON   WEYBRIGHT   3
    INVITATION TO THE DANCE
        BELWIN-MILLS PUBLISHING CORPORATION   .50
WEBER, VON   5
    INVITATION TO THE DANCE
        CENTURY MUSIC PUBLISHING COMPANY, INC. 698   .40
WEBER, VON
    INVITATION TO THE DANCE IN D FLAT, OP. 65
        G. SCHIRMER, INC.   .70
WEBER, VON
    INVITATION TO THE DANCE, OP. 65
        BELWIN-MILLS PUBLISHING CORPORATION   28157   .80
WEBER, VON   M-D
    INVITATION TO THE DANCE, OP. 65
        C. F. PETERS CORPORATION   2879   1.25
WEBER, VON   BUELOW
    INVITATION TO THE DANCE, OP. 65
        CARL FISCHER, INC.   S 753   .75

WEBER, VON   DEL MAGLIO
    INVITATION TO THE DANCE, OP. 65
        FRANCO COLOMBO PUBLICATIONS   124756   .50
WEBER, VON   CORTOT
    INVITATION TO THE DANCE, OP. 65
        FRANCO COLOMBO PUBLICATIONS   SAL   2.75
WEBER, VON   6
    INVITATION TO THE DANCE, OP. 65
        THEODORE PRESSER COMPANY   .70
WEBER, VON   MONTANI
    LAST MUSICAL THOUGHTS
        FRANCO COLOMBO PUBLICATIONS   128423   .50
WEBER, VON   3
    LAST WALTZ
        CENTURY MUSIC PUBLISHING COMPANY, INC. 454   .40
WEBER, VON   CORTOT
    MOMENTO CAPRICCIOSO, OP. 12
        FRANCO COLOMBO PUBLICATIONS   SAL   2.25
WEBER, VON   5
    MOTO PERPETUO
        CENTURY MUSIC PUBLISHING COMPANY, INC. 1771   .40
WEBER, VON   CORTOT
    MOTO PERPETUO -- RONDO FROM SONATA, OP. 24 --
        FRANCO COLOMBO PUBLICATIONS   SAL   2.50
WEBER, VON   TAGLIAPIETRA
    MOTO PERPETUO FROM SONATA, OP. 24
        FRANCO COLOMBO PUBLICATIONS   128331   1.00
WEBER, VON   2
    OBERON, BARCAROLLE
        CENTURY MUSIC PUBLISHING COMPANY, INC. 1788   .40
WEBER, VON   BARNET   4
    OBERON, BARCAROLLE
        CENTURY MUSIC PUBLISHING COMPANY, INC. 2585   .40
WEBER, VON
    PERPETUAL MOTION--RONDO FROM THE SONATA, OP. 24
        G. SCHIRMER, INC.   .80
WEBER, VON   5
    PERPETUAL MOTION, OP. 24
        CENTURY MUSIC PUBLISHING COMPANY, INC. 1771   .40
WEBER, VON   GEORGII, W.   5
    PERPETUUM MOBILE OP. 24
        SCHOTT   0790 1/2 1.00
WEBER, VON   GEORGII, W.   6
    POLACCA BRILLANTE OP. 72
        SCHOTT   0795 1/2 1.00
WEBER, VON   KROLL
    POLONAISE BRILLANTE IN E-FLAT, OP. 72
        FRANCO COLOMBO PUBLICATIONS   128680   .60
WEBER, VON   CORTOT
    POLONAISE, OP. 72
        FRANCO COLOMBO PUBLICATIONS   SAL   2.50
WEBER, VON   5
    PRAYER, DER FREISCHUTZ
        CENTURY MUSIC PUBLISHING COMPANY, INC. 2295   .40
WEBER, VON   GEORGII, W.   6
    RONDO BRILL. ES-DUR OP. 62
        SCHOTT   0791 1/2 1.00
WEBER, VON   KROLL
    RONDO BRILLANTE IN E-FLAT, OP. 62 'LAGAITE'
        FRANCO COLOMBO PUBLICATIONS   93582   .75
WEBER, VON
    RONDO BRILLANTE, OP. 62
        BANKS AND SON LTD.   .80
WEBER, VON   6
    RONDO BRILLIANTE, OP. 62
        CENTURY MUSIC PUBLISHING COMPANY, INC. 1406   .40
WEBER, VON   CORTOT
    SONATA NO. 02 IN A FLAT MAJOR, OP. 39
        FRANCO COLOMBO PUBLICATIONS   SAL   5.00
WEBER, VON
    SONATA NO. 03 IN D MINOR, OP. 49
        G. SCHIRMER, INC.   1.25
WEBER, VON   WERNER
    WALTZER IN E FLAT--CURWEN EDITION
        G. SCHIRMER, INC.   .75
WEBER, VON *
    CHOEUR-BARCAROLLE FROM OBERON
        GERARD BILLAUDOT EDITIONS MUSICALES   1.30
WEBER, VON *
    INVITATION TO THE DANCE, OP. 65
        FRANCO COLOMBO PUBLICATIONS   ER1039   1.00
WEBER, VON *
    SCHERZO FROM TRIO, OP. 63
        GERARD BILLAUDOT EDITIONS MUSICALES   3.80
WEBERN, A.
    KLAVIERSTUCK, OP. POSTH.
        UNIVERSAL EDITION   UE 13490 3.00
WEBERN, A.
    VARIATIONS, OP. 27
        UNIVERSAL EDITION   UE 10881 4.50
WEBSTER   SAMPIETRO   FIRST YEAR
    SECRET LOVE
        WARNER BROTHERS PUBLISHERS   .75
WEBSTER   STIER   3
    SWEET BY AND BY, THE
        THEODORE PRESSER COMPANY   .60
WEBSTER   3
    SWEET BYE AND BYE, THE
        CENTURY MUSIC PUBLISHING COMPANY, INC. 1660   .40
WEBSTER, J.   3
    CHIMING BELLS
        CENTURY MUSIC PUBLISHING COMPANY, INC. 1686   .40
WEBSTER, J.   1
    IN THE SWEET BYE AND BYE
        CENTURY MUSIC PUBLISHING COMPANY, INC. 1660   .40
WEBSTER, J.   1
    INDIAN RAIN DANCE
        WILLIS MUSIC COMPANY   .35
WEDBERG, G.   1-2
    HOP SCOTCH
        CENTURY MUSIC PUBLISHING COMPANY, INC. 4024   .40
WEDBERG, G.   1
    PUZZLE PIECE NO. 1
        CENTURY MUSIC PUBLISHING COMPANY, INC. 4022   .40
WEDBERG, G.   1
    SEESAW UP - SEESAW DOWN
        CENTURY MUSIC PUBLISHING COMPANY, INC. 4023   .40
WEIGL, K.
    PICTURES AND TALES, OP. 2 -- 6 PIECES
        UNIVERSAL EDITION   UE 2796   2.60
WEIGL, K.
    TWENTY-EIGHT VARIATIONS, OP. 15
        UNIVERSAL EDITION   UE 6367   1.70
WEIGL, V.   2 1/2
    LONESOME KITTEN
        THEODORE PRESSER COMPANY   .50

WEILL, K.
    BEGGAR'S OPERA
        UNIVERSAL EDITION   UE 13832   9.00
WEILL, K.
    MACK THE KNIFE
        WARNER BROTHERS PUBLISHERS   1.00
WEILL, K.   RICHTER   FIRST YEAR
    MACK THE KNIFE
        WARNER BROTHERS PUBLISHERS   .75
WEILL, K.
    TANGO BALLAD -- DREIGROSCHENOPER
        UNIVERSAL EDITION   UE 8848   2.75
WEINBERGER, J.   MD
    CZECH RHAPSODY
        THEODORE PRESSER COMPANY   .75
WEINBERGER, J.   3
    SCHERZO
        PRO-ART PUBLICATIONS, INC.   556   .50
WEINER
    SONATA FOR PIANO, OP. 5
        MCA MUSIC   3.95
WEINER   2
    TANGO D'AMOUR
        BOSTON MUSIC COMPANY   .50
WEISGALL, H.   5
    SINE NOMINE -- GRAVEN IMAGES NO. 3
        THEODORE PRESSER COMPANY   .75
WEISGALL, H.   6
    TWO IMPROVISATIONS -- GRAVEN IMAGES NO. 6
        THEODORE PRESSER COMPANY   1.00
WEISLEDER, A.   1 1/2
    AT A CELLO RECITAL
        BELWIN-MILLS PUBLISHING CORPORATION   .60
WEISLEDER, A.   1 1/2
    AT THE DANCE RECITAL
        BELWIN-MILLS PUBLISHING CORPORATION   .60
WEISLEDER, A.   3
    COLORED LEAVES
        BELWIN-MILLS PUBLISHING CORPORATION   .60
WEISLEDER, A.   2 1/2
    DANCING GNOMES
        BELWIN-MILLS PUBLISHING CORPORATION   .60
WEISLEDER, A.   2 1/2
    DOLITA, SPANISH DANCE
        BELWIN-MILLS PUBLISHING CORPORATION   .60
WEISLEDER, A.   1 1/2
    DOLLY'S MINUET
        BELWIN-MILLS PUBLISHING CORPORATION   .60
WEISLEDER, A.   2
    FIREFLY AND THE FROG, THE
        BELWIN-MILLS PUBLISHING CORPORATION   .60
WEISLEDER, A.   2
    MAZURKA TIME
        PRO-ART PUBLICATIONS, INC.   339   .50
WEISLEDER, A.   2
    MOTHER'S LULLABY
        PRO-ART PUBLICATIONS, INC.   439   .50
WEISLEDER, A.   1 1/2
    PLAYING CHECKERS
        BELWIN-MILLS PUBLISHING CORPORATION   .60
WEISLEDER, A.   2
    WALTZING SNOW MAN
        BELWIN-MILLS PUBLISHING CORPORATION   .60
WEISMANN, J.   D
    PARTITA ON 'ES IST EIN ROS ENTSPRUNGEN'
        C. F. PETERS CORPORATION   4596   2.00
WEISMANN, J.   3
    PARTITA PRIMAVERILE, OP. 132
        BARENREITER VERLAG   SM 1293
WEISMANN, J.   4-5
    SONATA IN A MINOR, OP. 87
        SCHOTT   2898   2.25
WEISMANN, J.   4
    SONATA IN B FLAT, OP. 127
        SCHOTT   2883   2.00
WEISMANN, J.   3-4
    SUITE, OP. 95
        BARENREITER VERLAG   SM 390
WELLESZ, E.
    EPIGRAMME -- 5 PIECES, OP. 17
        UNIVERSAL EDITION   UE 6965   1.50
WELLESZ, E.
    FIVE DANCE PIECES, OP. 42
        UNIVERSAL EDITION   UE 9696   2.35
WELLESZ, E.
    IDYLS, 5 PIANO PIECES, OP. 21
        UNIVERSAL EDITION   UE 6091   3.85
WELY, L.   4
    MONASTERY BELLS
        CENTURY MUSIC PUBLISHING COMPANY, INC.   327   .40
WENRICH, P.   3
    HAPPY HOURS
        THEODORE PRESSER COMPANY   .50
WERLE, F.
    SONATA BREVIS NO. 2
        RONGWEN MUSIC, INC.   02.50
WERLE, F.
    TOCCATA
        RONGWEN MUSIC, INC.   02.50
WERMEL   2
    AROUND THE BEEHIVE
        THEODORE PRESSER COMPANY   .50
WERMEL
    AT THE BALLET SCHOOL
        CARL FISCHER, INC.   P 3139   .50
WERMEL   2
    AT THE FLEA CIRCUS
        THEODORE PRESSER COMPANY   .50
WERMEL   1-2
    AT THE MOVIES
        PRO-ART PUBLICATIONS, INC.   246   .50
WERMEL
    BARCELONA BAZAAR
        BOSTON MUSIC COMPANY   .50
WERMEL   1-2
    BLUE RHYTHM
        PRO-ART PUBLICATIONS, INC.   428   .50
WERMEL   1-2
    BUBBLES
        PRO-ART PUBLICATIONS, INC.   245   .50
WERMEL   2
    BUTTERFLIES AND BEES
        PRO-ART PUBLICATIONS, INC.   615   .50
WERMEL   2
    CARNIVAL DANCER
        PRO-ART PUBLICATIONS, INC.   543   .50

WERMEL
    CHINESE CARNIVAL
        BOSTON MUSIC COMPANY   .50
WERMEL   1
    DANCING SNOWMAN
        CENTURY MUSIC PUBLISHING COMPANY, INC.   4379   .40
WERMEL   2
    FUNNY LITTLE MANNIKINS
        PRO-ART PUBLICATIONS, INC.   238   .50
WERMEL   1
    GRASSHOPPER SERENADE
        PRO-ART PUBLICATIONS, INC.   544   .50
WERMEL   3
    HUNGARIAN FESTIVAL
        BOSTON MUSIC COMPANY   .50
WERMEL   2
    PING-PONG PLAYERS
        THEODORE PRESSER COMPANY   .50
WERMEL   2
    QUIET STORY
        THEODORE PRESSER COMPANY   .50
WERMEL   2-3
    RIO RHYTHM
        PRO-ART PUBLICATIONS, INC.   270   .50
WERMEL   3
    ROLLING WAVES
        BOSTON MUSIC COMPANY   .50
WERMEL   2
    SAILOR DANCES
        BOSTON MUSIC COMPANY   .50
WERMEL   2
    SAILORS SHINDIG
        BELWIN-MILLS PUBLISHING CORPORATION   .60
WERNER, F.   SCHIEFELBEIN, F.   2
    HEDGE ROSE
        VOLKWEIN BROS.   .30
WERNER, J.
    PREMIERE SONATE
        EDITIONS MUSICALES TRANSATLANTIQUES   5.40
WERNER, J.
    PRINTANIERES
        GERARD BILLAUDOT EDITIONS MUSICALES   1.60
WESLEY, C.   FINZI   M
    CONCERTO NO. 04 IN C. HARPSICHORD SOLO PART
        C. F. PETERS CORPORATION   H290A   1.50
WESLY
    CONFIDENCES
        FRANCO COLOMBO PUBLICATIONS   SAL   1.75
WESLY
    EBREZZA D'AMORE
        FRANCO COLOMBO PUBLICATIONS   SAL   1.75
WESLY
    FIANCAILLES
        FRANCO COLOMBO PUBLICATIONS   SAL   1.75
WESLY
    HEURE DU REVE, L'
        FRANCO COLOMBO PUBLICATIONS   SAL   1.75
WESLY
    HYMENEE
        FRANCO COLOMBO PUBLICATIONS   SAL   1.75
WESLY
    MARCHE SOLEMNELLE
        FRANCO COLOMBO PUBLICATIONS   SAL   1.75
WESLY
    REVERIE D'AUTOMNE
        FRANCO COLOMBO PUBLICATIONS   SAL   1.75
WESLY
    SERENADE HONGROISE
        FRANCO COLOMBO PUBLICATIONS   SAL   1.75
WESLY
    SONGES ROSES
        FRANCO COLOMBO PUBLICATIONS   SAL   1.75
WESLY
    SUITE PRINTANIERE - AUBADE
        FRANCO COLOMBO PUBLICATIONS   SAL   1.75
WESLY
    SUITE PRINTANIERE - FLEURS ET PAPILLONS
        FRANCO COLOMBO PUBLICATIONS   SAL   1.75
WESLY
    SUITE PRINTANIERE - IMPROMPTU
        FRANCO COLOMBO PUBLICATIONS   SAL   1.77
WESLY
    SUITE PRINTANIERE - NOCTURNE
        FRANCO COLOMBO PUBLICATIONS   SAL   1.75
WESLY
    SUITE PRINTANIERE - RONDE VILLAGEOISE
        FRANCO COLOMBO PUBLICATIONS   SAL   1.75
WESLY
    TWO PIECES CARACTERISTIQUES - FESTA NAPOLITANA
        FRANCO COLOMBO PUBLICATIONS   SAL   1.75
WESLY
    TWO PIECES CARACTERISYIQUES - TORMENTO DE AMORE
        FRANCO COLOMBO PUBLICATIONS   SAL   1.75
WESTENDORFF   2
    I'LL TAKE YOU HOME AGAIN, KATHLEEN
        CENTURY MUSIC PUBLISHING COMPANY, INC.   3708   .40
WESTERHOUT
    MA BELLE QUI DANSE
        FRANCO COLOMBO PUBLICATIONS   53716   .50
WESTERHOUT   DEL MAGLIO
    MA BELLE QUI DANSE
        FRANCO COLOMBO PUBLICATIONS   127763   .50
WESTERHOUT
    RONDE D'AMOUR
        FRANCO COLOMBO PUBLICATIONS   52966   .75
WESTERHOUT   DEL MAGLIO
    RONDE D'AMOUR
        FRANCO COLOMBO PUBLICATIONS   127764   .50
WESTERMAN, G. VON
    SONATA NO. 02, OP. 25
        ASSOCIATED MUSIC PUBLISHERS, INC.   3   BOT   2.00
WESTERVELT, M.   3
    CANAL STREET BOOGIE
        THEODORE PRESSER COMPANY   .50
WESTIN, P.
    SONATA FOR PIANO
        COMPOSERS AUTOGRAPH PUBLICATIONS   7.70
WESTON, L.   SCHAUM, J.   3
    HAWAIIAN NOCTURNE
        SCHAUM PUBLICATIONS, INC.   .60
WESTON, P.   3
    GOPHER HOLE DANCE
        BELWIN-MILLS PUBLISHING CORPORATION   .60
WESTON, P.   3
    GREEN WILLOW DANCE
        BELWIN-MILLS PUBLISHING CORPORATION   .60

WEYBRIGHT   2 1/2
    SPANISH DANCE, OP. 12 NO. 1
        BELWIN-MILLS PUBLISHING CORPORATION   .60
WEYBRIGHT   2
    SQUARE DANCE, THE
        BELWIN-MILLS PUBLISHING CORPORATION   .60
WEYBRIGHT   3 1/2
    STARLIGHT FANTASIE -- IN POPULAR STYLE
        BELWIN-MILLS PUBLISHING CORPORATION   .60
WEYBRIGHT   1 1/2
    STODOLA PUMPA
        BELWIN-MILLS PUBLISHING CORPORATION   .60
WEYBRIGHT   2
    SUNSET IN THE HILLS
        BELWIN-MILLS PUBLISHING CORPORATION   .60
WEYBRIGHT   2
    SUNSET TRAIL, THE
        BELWIN-MILLS PUBLISHING CORPORATION   .60
WEYBRIGHT   2
    SWISS MOUNTAIN SONG -- SWISS FOLK SONG
        BELWIN-MILLS PUBLISHING CORPORATION   .60
WEYBRIGHT   2 1/2
    TEXAS COWBOY'S SONG
        BELWIN-MILLS PUBLISHING CORPORATION   .60
WEYBRIGHT   1
    THINGS WE DO, THE
        BELWIN-MILLS PUBLISHING CORPORATION   .60
WEYBRIGHT   1 1/2
    THIS OLD MAN
        BELWIN-MILLS PUBLISHING CORPORATION   .60
WEYBRIGHT   E
    THOUSANDS OF MILLIONS OF STARS
        BELWIN-MILLS PUBLISHING CORPORATION   25110   .60
WEYBRIGHT   2
    TO AN ICE SKATER -- LEFT HAND ALONE
        BELWIN-MILLS PUBLISHING CORPORATION   .60
WEYBRIGHT   2
    TRAIL TO MEXICO, THE
        BELWIN-MILLS PUBLISHING CORPORATION   .60
WEYBRIGHT   2
    TRIPLETTA
        BELWIN-MILLS PUBLISHING CORPORATION   .60
WEYBRIGHT   2
    TROPIC CARNIVAL
        BELWIN-MILLS PUBLISHING CORPORATION   .60
WEYBRIGHT   2
    TROPICANA
        BELWIN-MILLS PUBLISHING CORPORATION   .60
WEYBRIGHT   2
    TUMBLING
        BELWIN-MILLS PUBLISHING CORPORATION   .60
WEYBRIGHT   1 1/2
    TWO FOLK SONGS -- DANCING AND BAGPIPES PLAYING
        BELWIN-MILLS PUBLISHING CORPORATION   .60
WEYBRIGHT   1 1/2
    TWO PIECES FOR SOLO PIANO -- THE TIME FOR FUN AND WHEN
    SUMMERTIME IS OVER
        BELWIN-MILLS PUBLISHING CORPORATION   .60
WEYBRIGHT   1 1/2
    TWO STRAUSS WALTZES
        BELWIN-MILLS PUBLISHING CORPORATION   .60
WEYBRIGHT   1 1/2
    VIENNESE WALTZ, A
        BELWIN-MILLS PUBLISHING CORPORATION   .60
WEYBRIGHT   1
    WALKING TO SCHOOL
        BELWIN-MILLS PUBLISHING CORPORATION   .60
WEYBRIGHT   1 1/2
    WALTZ TIME
        BELWIN-MILLS PUBLISHING CORPORATION   .60
WEYBRIGHT   2
    WEATHER CONVERSATION
        BELWIN-MILLS PUBLISHING CORPORATION   .60
WEYBRIGHT   1 1/2
    WHAT SHALL WE DO WHEN WE ALL GO OUT
        BELWIN-MILLS PUBLISHING CORPORATION   .60
WEYBRIGHT   1
    WHIRLIGIG
        BELWIN-MILLS PUBLISHING CORPORATION   .60
WEYBRIGHT   1 1/2
    WHO'S THAT TAPPING AT MY WINDOW
        BELWIN-MILLS PUBLISHING CORPORATION   .60
WEYBRIGHT   3 1/2
    WINSOME
        BELWIN-MILLS PUBLISHING CORPORATION   .60
WEYBRIGHT   1
    WINTER FROST
        BELWIN-MILLS PUBLISHING CORPORATION   .60
WEYBRIGHT   3
    WORRIED MAN BLUES, THE -- AN EARLY AMERICAN TUNE
        BELWIN-MILLS PUBLISHING CORPORATION   .60
WEYBRIGHT--ED.   WEYBRIGHT   3
    ALOUETTE
        BELWIN-MILLS PUBLISHING CORPORATION   .50
WEYBRIGHT--ED.   WEYBRIGHT   1 1/2
    ALPHABET SONG
        BELWIN-MILLS PUBLISHING CORPORATION   .50
WEYBRIGHT--ED.   WEYBRIGHT   2
    AROUND THE MULBERRY BUSH
        BELWIN-MILLS PUBLISHING CORPORATION   .50
WEYBRIGHT--ED.   WEYBRIGHT   2
    BANJO SONG
        BELWIN-MILLS PUBLISHING CORPORATION   .50
WEYBRIGHT--ED.   WEYBRIGHT   2
    BILLY THE KID
        BELWIN-MILLS PUBLISHING CORPORATION   .50
WEYBRIGHT--ED.   WEYBRIGHT   2
    BRITISH GRENADIERS, THE
        BELWIN-MILLS PUBLISHING CORPORATION   .50
WEYBRIGHT--ED.   WEYBRIGHT   2
    BRITISH GRENADIERS, THE
        BELWIN-MILLS PUBLISHING CORPORATION   .60
WEYBRIGHT--ED.   WEYBRIGHT   2
    CARA NINA
        BELWIN-MILLS PUBLISHING CORPORATION   .50
WEYBRIGHT--ED.   WEYBRIGHT   2
    CARA NINA
        BELWIN-MILLS PUBLISHING CORPORATION   .60
WEYBRIGHT--ED.   WEYBRIGHT   2
    CHILEAN FOLK SONG
        BELWIN-MILLS PUBLISHING CORPORATION   .50
WEYBRIGHT--ED.   WEYBRIGHT   2
    CHILEAN FOLK SONG, A
        BELWIN-MILLS PUBLISHING CORPORATION   .60
WEYBRIGHT--ED.   WEYBRIGHT   1 1/2
    COSSACK DANCE
        BELWIN-MILLS PUBLISHING CORPORATION   .50

WEYBRIGHT--ED.   WEYBRIGHT   2 1/2
    CRIPPLE CREEK
        BELWIN-MILLS PUBLISHING CORPORATION   .50
WEYBRIGHT--ED.   WEYBRIGHT   2
    CRUSADERS' HYMN
        BELWIN-MILLS PUBLISHING CORPORATION   .50
WEYBRIGHT--ED.   WEYBRIGHT   2
    DUTCH SPINNING SONG
        BELWIN-MILLS PUBLISHING CORPORATION   .50
WEYBRIGHT--ED.   WEYBRIGHT   3 1/2
    EVERY NIGHT WHEN THE SUN GOES DOWN
        BELWIN-MILLS PUBLISHING CORPORATION   .50
WEYBRIGHT--ED.   WEYBRIGHT   2
    FARM MEDLEY, A
        BELWIN-MILLS PUBLISHING CORPORATION   .50
WEYBRIGHT--ED.   WEYBRIGHT   2
    FARMER COMES TO TOWN, A
        BELWIN-MILLS PUBLISHING CORPORATION   .50
WEYBRIGHT--ED.   WEYBRIGHT   1
    FARMER IN THE DELL, THE
        BELWIN-MILLS PUBLISHING CORPORATION   .50
WEYBRIGHT--ED.   WEYBRIGHT   2
    FOGGY DEW
        BELWIN-MILLS PUBLISHING CORPORATION   .50
WEYBRIGHT--ED.   WEYBRIGHT   2
    FOGGY DEW, THE -- AN IRISH FOLK SONG
        BELWIN-MILLS PUBLISHING CORPORATION   .60
WEYBRIGHT--ED.   WEYBRIGHT   1 1/2
    FOLK FROM THE VILLAGE, THE
        BELWIN-MILLS PUBLISHING CORPORATION   .50
WEYBRIGHT--ED.   WEYBRIGHT   1 1/2
    FOLK FROM THE VILLAGE, THE -- A GERMAN FOLK TUNE FOR SOLO PIANO
        BELWIN-MILLS PUBLISHING CORPORATION   .60
WEYBRIGHT--ED.   WEYBRIGHT   1 1/2
    FREDERIKA
        BELWIN-MILLS PUBLISHING CORPORATION   .50
WEYBRIGHT--ED.   WEYBRIGHT   1 1/2
    FUN WITH MY LOU
        BELWIN-MILLS PUBLISHING CORPORATION   .50
WEYBRIGHT--ED.   WEYBRIGHT   1 1/2
    FUN WITH MY LOU
        BELWIN-MILLS PUBLISHING CORPORATION   .60
WEYBRIGHT--ED.   WEYBRIGHT   1 1/2
    GAILY THEY DANCE
        BELWIN-MILLS PUBLISHING CORPORATION   .50
WEYBRIGHT--ED.   WEYBRIGHT   1 1/2
    GERMAN 'CLAP HANDS' DANCE
        BELWIN-MILLS PUBLISHING CORPORATION   .60
WEYBRIGHT--ED.   WEYBRIGHT   1 1/2
    GERMAN CLAP DANCE
        BELWIN-MILLS PUBLISHING CORPORATION   .50
WEYBRIGHT--ED.   WEYBRIGHT   2
    GOD OF OUR FATHERS
        BELWIN-MILLS PUBLISHING CORPORATION   .60
WEYBRIGHT--ED.   WEYBRIGHT   1 1/2
    GOOD MORROW, GOSSIP JOAN
        BELWIN-MILLS PUBLISHING CORPORATION   .50
WEYBRIGHT--ED.   WEYBRIGHT   1 1/2
    GOOD MORROW, GOSSIP JOAN
        BELWIN-MILLS PUBLISHING CORPORATION   .60
WEYBRIGHT--ED.   WEYBRIGHT   1 1/2
    GOODBYE OLD PAINT
        BELWIN-MILLS PUBLISHING CORPORATION   .50
WEYBRIGHT--ED.   WEYBRIGHT   1 1/2
    GOODBYE, OLD PAINT
        BELWIN-MILLS PUBLISHING CORPORATION   .60
WEYBRIGHT--ED.   WEYBRIGHT   1 1/2
    HOP, HOP, HOP
        BELWIN-MILLS PUBLISHING CORPORATION   .50
WEYBRIGHT--ED.   WEYBRIGHT   2 1/2
    IRISH WASHERWOMAN, THE
        BELWIN-MILLS PUBLISHING CORPORATION   .50
WEYBRIGHT--ED.   WEYBRIGHT   3
    ISLAND FLOWER
        BELWIN-MILLS PUBLISHING CORPORATION   .50
WEYBRIGHT--ED.   WEYBRIGHT   1 1/2
    JOHNNY GET YOUR HAIR CUT
        BELWIN-MILLS PUBLISHING CORPORATION   .50
WEYBRIGHT--ED.   WEYBRIGHT   2
    JOSHUA FIT DE BATTLE OB JERICHO
        BELWIN-MILLS PUBLISHING CORPORATION   .50
WEYBRIGHT--ED.   WEYBRIGHT   2
    JOSHUA FIT DE BATTLE OF JERICHO
        BELWIN-MILLS PUBLISHING CORPORATION   .60
WEYBRIGHT--ED.   WEYBRIGHT   2
    JUBILO
        BELWIN-MILLS PUBLISHING CORPORATION   .50
WEYBRIGHT--ED.   WEYBRIGHT
    SKIP TO MY LOU
        SUMMY-BIRCHARD COMPANY   .50
WEYRAUCH, J.
    SONATA IN F--1959
        ASSOCIATED MUSIC PUBLISHERS, INC.   BRH   1.25
WHEELER, V. B.   3
    AT FULL SPEED
        VOLKWEIN BROS.   .30
WHEELER, V. B.   2
    CRADLE SONG
        VOLKWEIN BROS.   .25
WHEELER, V. B.   2
    IN THE TWILIGHT
        VOLKWEIN BROS.   .30
WHEELER, V. B.   2-3
    SPARKLING STARS
        VOLKWEIN BROS.   .25
WHITE   2
    BUS STOP
        CENTURY MUSIC PUBLISHING COMPANY, INC. 4116   .40
WHITE   3
    HARVEST DANCE
        BOSTON MUSIC COMPANY   .50
WHITE   1
    TEETER TOTTER
        BOSTON MUSIC COMPANY   .50
WHITE, G.   E
    BLACK MAGIC
        COMPOSERS PRESS, INC.   1.00
WHITE, J.   7
    SONATA NO. 01
        ALPHONSE LEDUC
WHITE, J.   7
    SONATA NO. 05
        ALPHONSE LEDUC
WHITE, R.   E-M
    BYE-LOW TUNE
        COMPOSERS PRESS, INC.   1.00

WHITFORD   GR. 2 1/2
    ACCENT ON RHYTHM --MODERN RHYTHMIC CLASSICS--
        ROBERT WHITFORD PUBLICATIONS   .40
WHITFORD   GR. 3
    ADORATION
        ROBERT WHITFORD PUBLICATIONS   .40
WHITFORD   GR. 5
    AMERICAN RHAPSODY
        ROBERT WHITFORD PUBLICATIONS   .40
WHITFORD   GR. 4
    ARTISTRY IN JAZZ --MODERN RHYTHMIC CLASSICS--
        ROBERT WHITFORD PUBLICATIONS   .40
WHITFORD   GR. 3
    AUTUMN
        ROBERT WHITFORD PUBLICATIONS   .40
WHITFORD   GR. 3
    BISCAYNE BOOGIE --MODERN RHYTHMIC CLASSICS--
        ROBERT WHITFORD PUBLICATIONS   .40
WHITFORD   GR. 2
    BLUE HORIZON
        ROBERT WHITFORD PUBLICATIONS   .40
WHITFORD   GR. 3
    BOOGIE WOOGIE IN C --MODERN RHYTHMIC CLASSICS--
        ROBERT WHITFORD PUBLICATIONS   .40
WHITFORD   GR. 2
    BOUQUET
        ROBERT WHITFORD PUBLICATIONS   .40
WHITFORD   GR. 4
    BUSINESS IN E FLAT --MODERN RHYTHMIC CLASSICS--
        ROBERT WHITFORD PUBLICATIONS   .40
WHITFORD   GR. 2 1/2
    CARNIVAL --MODERN RHYTHMIC CLASSICS--
        ROBERT WHITFORD PUBLICATIONS   .40
WHITFORD   GR. 2 1/2
    CAROUSEL
        ROBERT WHITFORD PUBLICATIONS   .40
WHITFORD   GR. 3
    CHA CHA --MODERN RHYTHMIC CLASSICS--
        ROBERT WHITFORD PUBLICATIONS   .40
WHITFORD   GR. 1 1/2
    CHINESE MAIDEN
        ROBERT WHITFORD PUBLICATIONS   .40
WHITFORD   GR. 2
    CLOCK AND THE PIANO, THE
        ROBERT WHITFORD PUBLICATIONS   .40
WHITFORD   GR. 3
    CUBAN CAPERS --MODERN RHYTHMIC CLASSICS--
        ROBERT WHITFORD PUBLICATIONS   .40
WHITFORD   GR. 3
    DANCE MARDI GRAS
        ROBERT WHITFORD PUBLICATIONS   .40
WHITFORD   GR. 4
    DANCE, THE
        ROBERT WHITFORD PUBLICATIONS   .40
WHITFORD   GR. 3
    DANCING STRINGS
        ROBERT WHITFORD PUBLICATIONS   .40
WHITFORD   GR. 2 1/2
    DAYBREAK
        ROBERT WHITFORD PUBLICATIONS   .40
WHITFORD   GR. 3
    DEEP BLUE --MODERN RHYTHMIC CLASSICS--
        ROBERT WHITFORD PUBLICATIONS   .40
WHITFORD   GR. 3 1/2
    DESIRE
        ROBERT WHITFORD PUBLICATIONS   .40
WHITFORD   GR. 3
    DIVERSION
        ROBERT WHITFORD PUBLICATIONS   .40
WHITFORD   GR. 3
    DIXIELAND STOMP --MODERN RHYTHMIC CLASSICS--
        ROBERT WHITFORD PUBLICATIONS   .40
WHITFORD   GR. 2
    DREAM WALTZ
        ROBERT WHITFORD PUBLICATIONS   .40
WHITFORD   GR. 1 1/2
    DREAMLAND
        ROBERT WHITFORD PUBLICATIONS   .40
WHITFORD   GR. 3
    DREAMS
        ROBERT WHITFORD PUBLICATIONS   .40
WHITFORD   GR. 3
    ECLIPSE
        ROBERT WHITFORD PUBLICATIONS   .40
WHITFORD   GR. 4
    ECSTASY
        ROBERT WHITFORD PUBLICATIONS   .40
WHITFORD   GR. 3
    ESCAPADE
        ROBERT WHITFORD PUBLICATIONS   .40
WHITFORD   GR. 2 1/2
    FALLING PETALS
        ROBERT WHITFORD PUBLICATIONS   .40
WHITFORD   GR. 3
    FESTIVAL
        ROBERT WHITFORD PUBLICATIONS   .40
WHITFORD   GR. 3
    GOING LATIN --MODERN RHYTHMIC CLASSICS--
        ROBERT WHITFORD PUBLICATIONS   .40
WHITFORD   GR. 2 1/2
    HOLIDAY
        ROBERT WHITFORD PUBLICATIONS   .40
WHITFORD   GR. 3
    ILLUSION
        ROBERT WHITFORD PUBLICATIONS   .40
WHITFORD   GR. 4
    IMPRESSIONS
        ROBERT WHITFORD PUBLICATIONS   .40
WHITFORD   GR. 3
    IMPROMPTU
        ROBERT WHITFORD PUBLICATIONS   .40
WHITFORD   GR. 4
    IMPROVISATION --MODERN RHYTHMIC CLASSICS--
        ROBERT WHITFORD PUBLICATIONS   .40
WHITFORD   GR. 3 1/2
    IN A PENSIVE MOOD --MODERN RHYTHMIC CLASSICS--
        ROBERT WHITFORD PUBLICATIONS   .40
WHITFORD   GR. 2 1/2
    INSPIRATION
        ROBERT WHITFORD PUBLICATIONS   .40
WHITFORD   GR. 3
    INTERMEZZO
        ROBERT WHITFORD PUBLICATIONS   .40
WHITFORD   GR. 2 1/2
    INTRIGUE
        ROBERT WHITFORD PUBLICATIONS   .40

WHITFORD   GR. 3 1/2
    JAMAICA --MODERN RHYTHMIC CLASSICS--
        ROBERT WHITFORD PUBLICATIONS   .40
WHITFORD   GR. 3
    JAZZ PRELUDE --MODERN RHYTHMIC CLASSICS--
        ROBERT WHITFORD PUBLICATIONS   .40
WHITFORD   GR. 5
    JAZZ SERENADE --MODERN RHYTHMIC CLASSICS--
        ROBERT WHITFORD PUBLICATIONS   .40
WHITFORD   GR. 3 1/2
    LOLLIPOPS --MODERN RHYTHMIC CLASSICS--
        ROBERT WHITFORD PUBLICATIONS   .40
WHITFORD   GR. 3
    MANHATTAN INTERLUDE --MODERN RHYTHMIC CLASSICS--
        ROBERT WHITFORD PUBLICATIONS   .40
WHITFORD   GR. 3
    MANHATTAN RHYTHM --MODERN RHYTHMIC CLASSICS--
        ROBERT WHITFORD PUBLICATIONS   .40
WHITFORD   GR. 3
    MASQUERADE
        ROBERT WHITFORD PUBLICATIONS   .40
WHITFORD   GR. 3 1/2
    MIDNIGHT IN NEW YORK --MODERN RHYTHMIC CLASSICS--
        ROBERT WHITFORD PUBLICATIONS   .40
WHITFORD   GR. 3
    MIRAGE
        ROBERT WHITFORD PUBLICATIONS   .40
WHITFORD   GR. 4
    MODERNE
        ROBERT WHITFORD PUBLICATIONS   .40
WHITFORD   GR. 3
    MORNING MOOD
        ROBERT WHITFORD PUBLICATIONS   .40
WHITFORD   GR. 3 1/2
    MOTION
        ROBERT WHITFORD PUBLICATIONS   .40
WHITFORD   GR. 1 1/2
    MY MUSIC BOX
        ROBERT WHITFORD PUBLICATIONS   .40
WHITFORD   GR. 3
    NIGHT
        ROBERT WHITFORD PUBLICATIONS   .40
WHITFORD   GR. 3
    OUR SERENADE --MODERN RHYTHMIC CLASSICS--
        ROBERT WHITFORD PUBLICATIONS   .40
WHITFORD   GR. 3 1/2
    PERRY SQUARE BOOGIE --MODERN RHYTHMIC CLASSICS--
        ROBERT WHITFORD PUBLICATIONS   .40
WHITFORD   GR. 2 1/2
    PURPLE DUST
        ROBERT WHITFORD PUBLICATIONS   .40
WHITFORD   GR. 3
    RAMROD RAG --MODERN RHYTHMIC CLASSICS--
        ROBERT WHITFORD PUBLICATIONS   .40
WHITFORD   GR. 3 1/2
    REFLECTIONS
        ROBERT WHITFORD PUBLICATIONS   .40
WHITFORD   GR. 2
    RENDEZVOUS
        ROBERT WHITFORD PUBLICATIONS   .40
WHITFORD   GR. 4
    RHAPSODY IN E FLAT
        ROBERT WHITFORD PUBLICATIONS   .40
WHITFORD   GR. 3 1/2
    RHAPSODY IN RHYTHM --MODERN RHYTHMIC CLASSICS--
        ROBERT WHITFORD PUBLICATIONS   .40
WHITFORD   GR. 3 1/2
    RHYTHM INTERLUDE --MODERN RHYTHMIC CLASSICS--
        ROBERT WHITFORD PUBLICATIONS   .40
WHITFORD   GR. 4
    RHYTHM LULLABY --MODERN RHYTHMIC CLASSICS--
        ROBERT WHITFORD PUBLICATIONS   .40
WHITFORD   GR. 3
    ROMANCE
        ROBERT WHITFORD PUBLICATIONS   .40
WHITFORD   GR. 3
    ROSES
        ROBERT WHITFORD PUBLICATIONS   .40
WHITFORD   GR. 2
    SAFARI --MODERN RHYTHMIC CLASSICS--
        ROBERT WHITFORD PUBLICATIONS   .40
WHITFORD   GR. 2 1/2
    SEA, THE
        ROBERT WHITFORD PUBLICATIONS   .40
WHITFORD   GR. 3
    SERENADE
        ROBERT WHITFORD PUBLICATIONS   .40
WHITFORD   GR. 2
    SHADOWS
        ROBERT WHITFORD PUBLICATIONS   .40
WHITFORD   GR. 3
    SILHOUETTE
        ROBERT WHITFORD PUBLICATIONS   .40
WHITFORD   GR. 3
    SOLILOQUY
        ROBERT WHITFORD PUBLICATIONS   .40
WHITFORD   GR. 2
    STARLIGHT SERENADE
        ROBERT WHITFORD PUBLICATIONS   .40
WHITFORD   GR. 2
    SUMMER NOCTURNE
        ROBERT WHITFORD PUBLICATIONS   .40
WHITFORD   GR. 3
    SUSPENSION
        ROBERT WHITFORD PUBLICATIONS   .40
WHITFORD   GR. 3 1/2
    SYMPHONETTE
        ROBERT WHITFORD PUBLICATIONS   .40
WHITFORD   GR. 2 1/2
    TAHITI --MODERN RHYTHMIC CLASSICS--
        ROBERT WHITFORD PUBLICATIONS   .40
WHITFORD   GR. 3
    TANTALIZING --MODERN RHYTHMIC CLASSICS--
        ROBERT WHITFORD PUBLICATIONS   .40
WHITFORD   GR. 3 1/2
    TEASIN' THE IVORIES --MODERN RHYTHMIC CLASSICS--
        ROBERT WHITFORD PUBLICATIONS   .40
WHITFORD   GR. 3
    TOMMY CAT --MODERN RHYTHMIC CLASSICS--
        ROBERT WHITFORD PUBLICATIONS   .40
WHITFORD   GR. 2 1/2
    TROPIC NIGHTS --MODERN RHYTHMIC CLASSICS--
        ROBERT WHITFORD PUBLICATIONS   .40
WHITFORD   GR. 2
    TWILIGHT SERENADE
        ROBERT WHITFORD PUBLICATIONS   .40

WHITFORD   GR. 2 1/2
  VISIONS
    ROBERT WHITFORD PUBLICATIONS   .40
WHITFORD   GR. 2 1/2
  WHITE VIOLETS
    ROBERT WHITFORD PUBLICATIONS   .40
WHITFORD--ED.   WHITFORD   GR. 3
  BADINAGE
    ROBERT WHITFORD PUBLICATIONS   .40
WHITFORD--ED.   WHITFORD   GR. 2 1/2
  DANCE OF THE FLOWERS
    ROBERT WHITFORD PUBLICATIONS   .40
WHITFORD--ED.   WHITFORD   GR. 2 1/2
  EVENING STAR
    ROBERT WHITFORD PUBLICATIONS   .40
WHITFORD--ED.   WHITFORD   GR. 3
  FRANKIE AND JOHNNY BOOGIE
    ROBERT WHITFORD PUBLICATIONS   .40
WHITFORD--ED.   WHITFORD   GR. 4
  IDA --JAZZ ARR.--
    ROBERT WHITFORD PUBLICATIONS   .40
WHITFORD--ED.   WHITFORD   GR. 2
  MARINES' HYMN
    ROBERT WHITFORD PUBLICATIONS   .40
WHITFORD--ED.   WHITFORD   GR. 2
  SWANEE RIVER BOOGIE
    ROBERT WHITFORD PUBLICATIONS   .40
WHITSON *   KLICKMANN   EASY
  LET ME CALL YOU SWEETHEART --LARGE NOTE--
    SHAWNEE PRESS, INC.   HB-53   .85
WIDOR, CH.
  CONTE D'AVRIL
    HEUGEL ET CIE.   10.00
WIDOR, CH.
  LA KORRIGANE
    HEUGEL ET CIE.   13.00
WIENIAWSKI   4
  MAZURKA NO. 2
    CENTURY MUSIC PUBLISHING COMPANY, INC. 1709   .40
WIENIAWSKI   4
  POLISH NATIONAL DANCE
    CENTURY MUSIC PUBLISHING COMPANY, INC. 1709   .40
WIENIAWSKI   4
  SECOND MAZURKA
    CENTURY MUSIC PUBLISHING COMPANY, INC. 1709   .40
WIGGINS, M.
  CATHEDRAL BELLS
    G. SCHIRMER, INC.   .30
WIGGINS, M.
  FROLICKING WAVES
    G. SCHIRMER, INC.   .35
WIGGINS, M.
  GHOST, THE--WITH WORDS
    G. SCHIRMER, INC.   .30
WIGGINS, M.   1-2
  JESTER, THE
    PRO-ART PUBLICATIONS, INC.   64   .50
WIGGINS, M.
  MIDNIGHT -- PRELUDE FOR LEFT HAND
    AMERICAN MUSIC EDITION   .50
WIGGINS, M.   1-2
  ON A RIVER BOAT
    PRO-ART PUBLICATIONS, INC.   119   .50
WIGGINS, M.   1-2
  PRANKS
    PRO-ART PUBLICATIONS, INC.   120   .50
WIGGINS, M.   2
  WATER WHEEL, THE
    PRO-ART PUBLICATIONS, INC.   65   .50
WIGHAM, M.   3
  BACHETTE
    THEODORE PRESSER COMPANY   .50
WIGHAM, M.
  BRILLIANTE
    CARL FISCHER, INC.   RS 393   .50
WIGHAM, M.   2 1/2
  CAREFREE
    WILLIS MUSIC COMPANY   .40
WIGHAM, M.   3 1/2
  GAY CAPRICE
    WILLIS MUSIC COMPANY   .40
WIGHAM, M.   2
  HAPPITAT
    THEODORE PRESSER COMPANY   .50
WIGHAM, M.   1 1/2
  HAVING FUN
    THEODORE PRESSER COMPANY   .50
WIGHAM, M.   1 1/2
  HOP ALONG LITTLE FROGGIE
    CENTURY MUSIC PUBLISHING COMPANY, INC. 017   .40
WIGHAM, M.   1 1/2
  I WONDER WHERE THE ROBINS GO
    THEODORE PRESSER COMPANY   .50
WIGHAM, M.   4
  INTRODUCTION AND SONATINA
    THEODORE PRESSER COMPANY   .50
WIGHAM, M.   3 1/2
  JOYOUS ETUDE
    WILLIS MUSIC COMPANY   .50
WIGHAM, M.   3
  LITTLE MILL, THE
    THEODORE PRESSER COMPANY   .50
WIGHAM, M.   2
  LITTLE MISCHIEF
    THEODORE PRESSER COMPANY   .50
WIGHAM, M.   3
  LITTLEST BALLERINA
    CENTURY MUSIC PUBLISHING COMPANY, INC. 4218   .40
WIGHAM, M.   3
  MERRILY O'ER THE HILLS
    WILLIS MUSIC COMPANY   .40
WIGHAM, M.   1 1/2
  MUSICAL PLAYMATES
    THEODORE PRESSER COMPANY   .50
WIGHAM, M.
  NORTHLAND INTERMEZZO
    CARL FISCHER, INC.   RS 394   .50
WIGHAM, M.   2
  O, SO HAPPY
    THEODORE PRESSER COMPANY   .50
WIGHAM, M.
  OLD COWBOY TRAIL
    G. SCHIRMER, INC.   .35
WIGHAM, M.   3
  ON SWAN LAKE
    THEODORE PRESSER COMPANY   .50

WIGHAM, M.   3
  PUPPY'S TALE
    THEODORE PRESSER COMPANY   .50
WIGHAM, M.   4
  RHAPSODY
    WILLIS MUSIC COMPANY   .60
WIGHAM, M.   2
  SCAMPERING WHOLE STEPS
    THEODORE PRESSER COMPANY   .50
WIGHAM, M.
  SCHERZINO
    BELWIN-MILLS PUBLISHING CORPORATION   .60
WIGHAM, M.
  SCHERZINO
    FRANCO COLOMBO PUBLICATIONS   NY1570   .50
WIGHAM, M.   1
  SEE AND GEE
    THEODORE PRESSER COMPANY   .50
WIGHAM, M.
  SO SLEEPY
    G. SCHIRMER, INC.   .35
WIGHAM, M.   3
  STATELY PRELUDE
    WILLIS MUSIC COMPANY   .40
WIGHAM, M.
  SUMMERTIME PRELUDE
    CARL FISCHER, INC.   RS 401   .50
WIJDEVELD   M-D
  ESCAPADES
    C. F. PETERS CORPORATION   D217   1.50
WIJDEVELD   M-D
  NOTITIEBOEK V. HARPSICHORD
    C. F. PETERS CORPORATION   D461   3.00
WILDGANS, F.
  ETUDE--1949
    ASSOCIATED MUSIC PUBLISHERS, INC.   DOB   1.50
WILDMAN
  LOVE THEME FROM 'MADAME X,' -- SWEDISH RHAPSODY
    MCA MUSIC   1.00
WILDMAN
  STOCKHOLM CONCERTO
    MCA MUSIC   1.00
WILDMAN
  SWEDISH RHAPSODY
    MCA MUSIC   1.50
WILDMAN
  SWEDISH RHAPSODY -- THEME
    MCA MUSIC   1.00
WILDMAN
  SWEDISH RHAPSODY --THEME
    MCA MUSIC   1.00
WILDMAN *
  TANGO PICASSO
    MCA MUSIC   1.00
WILKINSON, P.   4
  DANCE AND BE MERRY -- A LITTLE SUITE
    NOVELLO AND COMPANY, LTD.   10.0109.04   1.15
WILKINSON, P.   4
  FOUR DANCE MINIATURES
    NOVELLO AND COMPANY, LTD.   10.0110.08   1.15
WILKINSON, P.   4
  OUT AND ABOUT
    NOVELLO AND COMPANY, LTD.   10.0111.06   1.25
WILLAN
  PETER'S BOOK
    FREDERICK HARRIS MUSIC COMPANY   .90
WILLAUME
  GAVOTTE LOUIS XV
    FRANCO COLOMBO PUBLICATIONS   SAL   1.50
WILLAUME
  NOCE BRETONNE, LA
    FRANCO COLOMBO PUBLICATIONS   SAL   1.50
WILLIAMS
  CINDERELLA
    SAM FOX PUBLISHING COMPANY, INC.   .75
WILLIAMS
  CINDERELLA
    SOUTHERN MUSIC COMPANY   .75
WILLIAMS
  DREAM OF OLWEN, THE
    BELWIN-MILLS PUBLISHING CORPORATION   20075   .60
                                           3 1/2
WILLIAMS
  JUBILEE MARCH
    THEODORE PRESSER COMPANY   .50
WILLIAMS
  SALLY TRIES THE BALLET -- A MUSICAL PICTURE
    BELWIN-MILLS PUBLISHING CORPORATION   20231   .95
WILLIAMS
  SECRET WAYS, THE
    MCA MUSIC   1.00
WILLIAMS
  TISHOMINGO BLUES
    EDWARD B. MARKS MUSIC CORPORATION   01.00
WILLIAMS--ED.   WILLIAMS   3
  COUNTRY GARDENS
    BOSTON MUSIC COMPANY   .50
WILLIAMS, C.   SCHAUM, J.   4
  JOURNEY TO BETHLEHEM
    SCHAUM PUBLICATIONS, INC.   .60
WILLIAMS, C.   GLOVER, D.
  THEME FROM 'THE APARTMENT
    BELWIN-MILLS PUBLISHING CORPORATION   .60
WILLIAMS, C.
  THEME FROM 'THE APARTMENT'
    BELWIN-MILLS PUBLISHING CORPORATION   20413   .85
WILLIAMS, C.   NEVIN
  THEME FROM 'THE APARTMENT' -- SIMP.
    BELWIN-MILLS PUBLISHING CORPORATION   26108   .50
WILLIAMS, F.   3
  DANCE OF THE GNOMES, OP. 95 NO. 3
    THEODORE PRESSER COMPANY   .50
WILLIAMS, F.   3 1/2
  MARCH OF PROGRESS
    THEODORE PRESSER COMPANY   .60
WILLIAMS, F.   3 1/2
  ON THE LAKE, OP. 48
    THEODORE PRESSER COMPANY   .60
WILLIAMS, H.   SCHAUM, J.   2
  RED SAILS IN THE SUNSET
    SCHAUM PUBLICATIONS, INC.   .75
WILLIAMS, J.   3
  COUNTRY GARDENS
    BOSTON MUSIC COMPANY   .50
WILLIAMS, J.   2
  LITTLE DRUM MAJOR, THE
    BELWIN-MILLS PUBLISHING CORPORATION   .60

WILLIAMS, J.   3
  LONDONDERRY AIR
      BOSTON MUSIC COMPANY   .50
WILLIAMS, L. A.   2
  TROPIC NIGHT
      BELWIN-MILLS PUBLISHING CORPORATION   .60
WILLIAMS, M.
  AEROPLANE STUNTS
      G. SCHIRMER, INC.   .35
WILLIAMS, M.
  YO-YO, THE
      G. SCHIRMER, INC.   .35
WILLIAMS, R.--ED   WILLIAMS, R.
  TILL
      CHAPPELL AND COMPANY, INC.   6057509   .95
WILLIAMS, R.--ED.   WILLIAMS, R.
  AFFAIR TO REMEMBER, AN
      THE BIG THREE MUSIC CORPORATION   1.25
WILLIAMS, R.--ED.   WILLIAMS, R.
  ANASTASIA
      THE BIG THREE MUSIC CORPORATION   01.25
WILLIAMS, R.--ED.   WILLIAMS, R.
  ARRIVEDERCI, ROMA
      THE BIG THREE MUSIC CORPORATION   01.25
WILLIAMS, R.--ED.   WILLIAMS, R.
  DAY IN THE LIFE OF A FOOL, A
      THE BIG THREE MUSIC CORPORATION   1.25
WILLIAMS, R.--ED.   WILLIAMS, R.
  DEEP PURPLE
      THE BIG THREE MUSIC CORPORATION   01.25
WILLIAMS, R.--ED.   WILLIAMS, R.
  GENTLE ON MY MIND
      THE BIG THREE MUSIC CORPORATION   01.25
WILLIAMS, R.--ED.   WILLIAMS, R.
  GREEN LEAVES OF SUMMER
      THE BIG THREE MUSIC CORPORATION   1.25
WILLIAMS, R.--ED.   WILLIAMS, R.
  LARA'S THEME - DOCTOR ZHIVAGO
      THE BIG THREE MUSIC CORPORATION   1.25
WILLIAMS, R.--ED.   WILLIAMS, R.
  LOVE MAKES THE WORLD GO 'ROUND
      THE BIG THREE MUSIC CORPORATION   1.25
WILLIAMS, R.--ED.   WILLIAMS, R.
  MOONLIGHT AND ROSES
      THE BIG THREE MUSIC CORPORATION   01.25
WILLIAMS, R.--ED.   WILLIAMS, R.
  MORE THAN A MIRACLE
      THE BIG THREE MUSIC CORPORATION   01.25
WILLIAMS, R.--ED.   WILLIAMS, R.
  ON THE TRAIL
      THE BIG THREE MUSIC CORPORATION   01.25
WILLIAMS, R.--ED.   WILLIAMS, R.
  OVER THE RAINBOW
      THE BIG THREE MUSIC CORPORATION   01.25
WILLIAMS, R.--ED.   WILLIAMS, R.
  SHADOW OF YOUR SMILE
      THE BIG THREE MUSIC CORPORATION   1.25
WILLIAMS, R.--ED.   WILLIAMS, R.
  SUNNY
      THE BIG THREE MUSIC CORPORATION   01.25
WILLIAMS, T.   STEINER   JR. OR SR. APPR.
  LIFT UP YOUR HEADS
      BELWIN-MILLS PUBLISHING CORPORATION   .60
WILLIAMSON, M.
  SONATA
      BOOSEY AND HAWKES, INC.   2.00
WILLNER, A.
  PIANO AS ORCHESTRA, THE -- STUDIES IN SONORITIES
      NOVELLO AND COMPANY, LTD.   10.0112.04   1.40
WILLNER, A.
  PIANO SONATA NO. 02, OP. 26
      UNIVERSAL EDITION   UE 7701   1.70
WILLNER, A.
  TANZWEISEN, OP. 25, BK. 1
      UNIVERSAL EDITION   UE 6543   1.70
WILLNER, A.
  TANZWEISEN, OP. 25, BK. 2
      UNIVERSAL EDITION   UE 6544   1.70
WILLSON, M.
  I AIN'T DOWN YET
      FRANK MUSIC CORPORATION   .95
WILLSON, M.
  O.O.MCINTYRE SUITE
      THE BIG THREE MUSIC CORPORATION   01.50
WILLSON, M.   RICHTER   2 1/2 - 3
  SEVENTY SIX TROMBONES
      FRANK MUSIC CORPORATION   .75
WILLSON, M.   RICHTER   2 1/2 - 3
  TILL THERE WAS YOU
      FRANK MUSIC CORPORATION   .75
WILM, M. VON
  DROLLERIES, OP. 12 NO. 5
      G. SCHIRMER, INC.   .35
WILM, N. VON   2
  MAZURKA
      WILLIS MUSIC COMPANY   .40
WILSON   2
  CACTUS JACK
      CENTURY MUSIC PUBLISHING COMPANY, INC.   4350   .40
WILSON   4
  CARMENA, VALSE
      CENTURY MUSIC PUBLISHING COMPANY, INC.   1805   .40
WILSON   1
  COTTON SHUFFLE
      CENTURY MUSIC PUBLISHING COMPANY, INC.   4348   .40
WILSON
  HOMMAGE A ALBAN BERG
      FRANCO COLOMBO PUBLICATIONS   LD505   .60
WILSON   1
  JET PILOTS
      CENTURY MUSIC PUBLISHING COMPANY, INC.   4349   .40
WILSON
  MARY HAD A LITTLE LAMB
      CARL FISCHER, INC.   RS 387   .50
WILSON
  NIGHT FLOWER
      CARL FISCHER, INC.   RS 406   .50
WILSON
  PINK LEMONADE
      CARL FISCHER, INC.   RS 432   .50
WILSON   2
  POOL OF WATER LILIES
      BOSTON MUSIC COMPANY   .50
WILSON
  REVERIE
      FRANCO COLOMBO PUBLICATIONS   LD504   .60

WILSON
  SLEEPY BAYOU
      CARL FISCHER, INC.   RS 400   .50
WILSON
  STREAMLINER
      CARL FISCHER, INC.   RS 386   .50
WILSON   2
  SUNSET IN THE MOUNTAINS
      BOSTON MUSIC COMPANY   .50
WILSON
  TZIGANE
      FRANCO COLOMBO PUBLICATIONS   LD506   .60
WILSON   1
  WATER WHEELS
      CENTURY MUSIC PUBLISHING COMPANY, INC.   4347   .40
WILSON *
  IN THE LITTLE RED SCHOOL HOUSE
      EDWARD B. MARKS MUSIC CORPORATION   00.60
WILSON *
  PRANKS
      BANKS AND SON LTD.   .25
WILSON, G.   3
  AT SUNDOWN, REVERIE
      CENTURY MUSIC PUBLISHING COMPANY, INC.   2685   .40
WILSON, G.
  FANTASY FOR PIANO
      COMPOSERS AUTOGRAPH PUBLICATIONS   2.42
WILSON, G.   4-5
  MOONLIGHT ON THE HUDSON
      CENTURY MUSIC PUBLISHING COMPANY, INC.   2713   .40
WILSON, G.   3
  SHEPHERD BOY
      BELWIN-MILLS PUBLISHING CORPORATION   396   .60
WILSON, G.   3
  SHEPHERD BOY, THE
      CENTURY MUSIC PUBLISHING COMPANY, INC.   655   .40
WILSON, G.   4
  WAYSIDE CHAPEL
      BELWIN-MILLS PUBLISHING CORPORATION   467   .60
WILSON, G.   3-4
  WAYSIDE CHAPEL, THE
      CENTURY MUSIC PUBLISHING COMPANY, INC.   2696   .40
WILSON, G.   3
  WAYSIDE CHAPEL, THE
      THEODORE PRESSER COMPANY   .50
WILSON, G.   4
  WAYSIDE CHAPEL, THE
      WILLIS MUSIC COMPANY   .40
WILSON, H.
  PRAYING
      BELWIN-MILLS PUBLISHING CORPORATION   25242   .60
WILSON, M.   1-2
  AIRPLANE FLIGHT, AN, C MAJOR
      CENTURY MUSIC PUBLISHING COMPANY, INC.   2569   .40
WILSON, M.   1
  ANTIQUE
      CENTURY MUSIC PUBLISHING COMPANY, INC.   2650   .40
WILSON, M.   1-2
  BALLET SCENE, THE
      CENTURY MUSIC PUBLISHING COMPANY, INC.   2572   .40
WILSON, M.   1-2
  BASKET OF PRIZE KITTENS, A
      CENTURY MUSIC PUBLISHING COMPANY, INC.   2571   .40
WILSON, M.   2
  BY THE FOUNTAIN
      CENTURY MUSIC PUBLISHING COMPANY, INC.   2573   .40
WILSON, M.   1
  CHARMING
      CENTURY MUSIC PUBLISHING COMPANY, INC.   2654   .40
WILSON, M.   1
  FAITHFUL
      CENTURY MUSIC PUBLISHING COMPANY, INC.   2653   .40
WILSON, M.   1
  FANCIFUL
      CENTURY MUSIC PUBLISHING COMPANY, INC.   2648   .40
WILSON, M.   2
  IN THE JUNGLE
      CENTURY MUSIC PUBLISHING COMPANY, INC.   2578   .40
WILSON, M.   1 1/2
  IT'S BEGINNING TO LOOK LIKE CHRISTMAS
      SCHAUM PUBLICATIONS, INC.   .75
WILSON, M.   1
  JOLITY
      CENTURY MUSIC PUBLISHING COMPANY, INC.   2652   .40
WILSON, M.   1
  MAJESTIC
      CENTURY MUSIC PUBLISHING COMPANY, INC.   2646   .40
WILSON, M.   1
  ON THE RACE TRACK
      CENTURY MUSIC PUBLISHING COMPANY, INC.   2577   .40
WILSON, M.   1
  PRELUDE
      CENTURY MUSIC PUBLISHING COMPANY, INC.   2645   .40
WILSON, M.   2
  SWINGING
      CENTURY MUSIC PUBLISHING COMPANY, INC.   2649   .40
WILSON, M.   2
  TEPEES AND TOTEM POLES
      CENTURY MUSIC PUBLISHING COMPANY, INC.   2574   .40
WILSON, M.   2
  WITH A NOTE OF SADNESS
      CENTURY MUSIC PUBLISHING COMPANY, INC.   2575   .40
WILSON, R. J.   5
  PRELUDE IN D FLAT
      THEODORE PRESSER COMPANY   .50
WILSON, R. J.   5
  PRELUDE IN D FLAT
      THEODORE PRESSER COMPANY   .50
WILSON, R. J.   5
  PRELUDE IN D FLAT
      THEODORE PRESSER COMPANY   .50
WILSON, S.   1
  RUN LITTLE LAMB
      THEODORE PRESSER COMPANY   .50
WILSON, S.   2 1/2
  VILLAGE NIGHTFALL
      THEODORE PRESSER COMPANY   .50
WILSON, S.   2 1/2
  WATER LILIES
      WILLIS MUSIC COMPANY   .50
WINDRUSH, P.
  OLD IRELAND
      BANKS AND SON LTD.   .80
WINDRUSH, P.
  OLD WALES
      BANKS AND SON LTD.   1.10

WINDSOR, B.
   OLDE LAVENDER
      BANKS AND SON LTD.   .25
WISE   3
   DANCE OF THE BUTTERFLIES
      CENTURY MUSIC PUBLISHING COMPANY, INC.   2691   .40
WISOFF, G.   MD
   SONATINA
      THEODORE PRESSER COMPANY   1.00
WISSMER, P.
   SONATE
      GERARD BILLAUDOT EDITIONS MUSICALES   3.00
WITTMAN
   SERENADE A MAGALI
      FRANCO COLOMBO PUBLICATIONS   SAL   1.75
WLADIGEROFF, P.
   SCHUMEN MINIATURE, OP. 29
      UNIVERSAL EDITION   UE 10812   2.15
WOLCOTT, C.
   CAT ON A HOT TIN ROOF
      THE BIG THREE MUSIC CORPORATION   00.95
WOLCOTT, C.
   RUBY-DUBY-DU
      THE BIG THREE MUSIC CORPORATION   00.95
WOLCOTT, J. T.   3
   BOBOLINK POLKA
      THEODORE PRESSER COMPANY   .50
WOLF-FERRARI, E.
   INQUISITIVE WOMEN--PIANO SCORE WITH SUPERLINEAR TEXT
      G. SCHIRMER, INC.   3.00
WOLF-FERRARI, E.   FOLK
   SUZANNE'S SECRET--PIANO SCORE WITH SUPERLINEAR GERMAN TEXT
      G. SCHIRMER, INC.   2.00
WOLFE, J.   EASY
   SHORT'NIN' BREAD
      SHAWNEE PRESS, INC.   .35
WOLFF, B.   2
   RONDO
      WILLIS MUSIC COMPANY   .40
WOLFF, C.   D
   FOR PIANO 1
      C. F. PETERS CORPORATION   6497   2.00
WOLFF, C.   MD
   FOR PREPARED PIANO
      THEODORE PRESSER COMPANY   1.00
WOLFF, C.   D
   SUITE FOR PREPARED PIANO
      C. F. PETERS CORPORATION   6500   2.00
WOLFORD, D.   3
   PASTELS
      BELWIN-MILLS PUBLISHING CORPORATION   .60
WOLLENHAUPT   5
   ETUDE, OP. 22 NO. 1
      CENTURY MUSIC PUBLISHING COMPANY, INC.   1204   .40
WOLLENHAUPT   4
   GAZELLE, LA, POLKA
      CENTURY MUSIC PUBLISHING COMPANY, INC.   811   .40
WOLLENHAUPT   5
   GRANDE MARCH DE CONCERT
      CENTURY MUSIC PUBLISHING COMPANY, INC.   1501   .40
WOLLENHAUPT   5
   LAST SMILE, THE
      CENTURY MUSIC PUBLISHING COMPANY, INC.   1245   .40
WOLLENHAUPT   5
   MARCHE DE CONCERT
      CENTURY MUSIC PUBLISHING COMPANY, INC.   1501   .40
WOLLENHAUPT
   MORCEAUX CARACTERISTIQUE EN FORME D'ETUDES, OP. 22 NO. 1, IN A
   FLAT
      G. SCHIRMER, INC.   .40
WOLLENHAUPT
   NOCTURNE, OP. 29 NO. 10
      G. SCHIRMER, INC.   .25
WOLPAW   2
   IMPS AND FAIRIES
      CENTURY MUSIC PUBLISHING COMPANY, INC.   1653   .40
WOLPAW   2
   MUSIC BOX, THE
      CENTURY MUSIC PUBLISHING COMPANY, INC.   1655   .40
WOLPE
   CHACONNE
      BOOSEY AND HAWKES, INC.   .75
WOLPE
   FORM 4# BROKEN SEQUENCES --IN PREPARATION--
      C. F. PETERS CORPORATION   6562
WOOD, L.
   SUMMER'S WONDERLAND
      BANKS AND SON LTD.   .95
WOOD, O.   VE
   LITTLE SUITE
      OXFORD UNIVERSITY PRESS   33.063   1.10
WOOD, W.   3
   ALOHA OE, G MAJOR
      CENTURY MUSIC PUBLISHING COMPANY, INC.   2676   .40
WOOD, W.   3
   AUTUMN LEAVES
      CENTURY MUSIC PUBLISHING COMPANY, INC.   2682   .40
WOOD, W.   3
   LET'ER GO
      CENTURY MUSIC PUBLISHING COMPANY, INC.   2694   .40
WOOD, W.   3-4
   WHOOP 'ER UP
      CENTURY MUSIC PUBLISHING COMPANY, INC.   2695   .40
WOODS, H.   SCHAUM, J.   2
   SIDE BY SIDE
      SCHAUM PUBLICATIONS, INC.   .75
WOOLLETT
   CROQUIS DE ROUTE - EN CUEILLANT DES FLEURS
      FRANCO COLOMBO PUBLICATIONS   SAL   1.50
WOOLLETT
   CROQUIS DE ROUTE - LE BUCHERON AND LE BERGER
      FRANCO COLOMBO PUBLICATIONS   SAL   1.50
WOOLLETT
   CROQUIS DE ROUTE - LE JOUEUR DE VIELLE
      FRANCO COLOMBO PUBLICATIONS   SAL   1.50
WOOLLETT
   IMPRESSIONS DE VOYAGE
      FRANCO COLOMBO PUBLICATIONS   SAL   4.25
WORK   ADVANCED
   APPALACHIA
      SHAWNEE PRESS, INC.   1.00
WORK   ADVANCED
   SCUPPERNONG
      SHAWNEE PRESS, INC.   .75
WORONOFF, W.   A
   SONNET POUR DALLAPICCOLA
      THEODORE PRESSER COMPANY   1.25

WORTLEY
   ENGLISH COUNTRYSIDE, AN
      BELWIN-MILLS PUBLISHING CORPORATION   .60
WORTZMAN, N.   1
   EASTERN DANCE
      BELWIN-MILLS PUBLISHING CORPORATION   .60
WORTZMAN, N.   1 1/2
   PRAIRIE WAGON
      BELWIN-MILLS PUBLISHING CORPORATION   .60
WORTZMAN, N.   2
   PRINTING PRESS
      PRO-ART PUBLICATIONS, INC.   73   .50
WORTZMAN, N.   2
   RAMBLING RHYTHM
      PRO-ART PUBLICATIONS, INC.   166   .50
WORTZMAN, N.
   TWO ALPINE SINGERS
      G. SCHIRMER, INC.   .35
WOZENCRAFT, M.
   TWO EASY TWIN PIECES WHICH CAN BE PLAYED SEPARATELY AS SOLOS OR
   TOGETHER AT TWO PIANOS--WALTZ ME AROUND, AND WALTZ ME AROUND, TOO
      G. SCHIRMER, INC.   .40
WOZENCRAFT, M.
   WALTZ ME AROUND
      G. SCHIRMER, INC.   .40
WOZENCRAFT, M.
   WALTZ ME AROUND, TOO
      G. SCHIRMER, INC.   .40
WRAGG
   PHANTOM FOUNTAIN, THE
      MCA MUSIC   1.00
WRAY, J.   2
   NIP AND TUCK
      WILLIS MUSIC COMPANY   .35
WRAY, J.   2
   TRILL WALTZ
      WILLIS MUSIC COMPANY   .35
WRAY, J.   1
   WOODEN SHOE DANCE
      WILLIS MUSIC COMPANY   .35
WRIGHT
   CHORALE PRELUDE
      BOSTON MUSIC COMPANY   .50
WRIGHT   1
   NIGHTFALL
      WILLIS MUSIC COMPANY   .35
WRIGHT   WILLIAMS, J.   3
   WOODEN SHOE DANCE
      BOSTON MUSIC COMPANY   .50
WRIGHT, G.
   RED BALLOONS
      G. SCHIRMER, INC.   .35
WRIGHT, K.   2
   HOP, SKIP AND PLAY
      CENTURY MUSIC PUBLISHING COMPANY, INC.   4128   .40
WRIGHT, K.   1
   LITTLE GRAY SQUIRREL
      CENTURY MUSIC PUBLISHING COMPANY, INC.   4194   .40
WRIGHT, K.   1-2
   PARADE OF THE PLANETS
      CENTURY MUSIC PUBLISHING COMPANY, INC.   4195   .40
WRIGHT, K.   1-2
   TRUMPET MARCH
      CENTURY MUSIC PUBLISHING COMPANY, INC.   4154   .40
WRIGHT, L.   4
   AT EVENING
      WILLIS MUSIC COMPANY   .30
WRIGHT, L.   2
   BANJO PICKER, THE
      WILLIS MUSIC COMPANY   .40
WRIGHT, L.   2 1/2
   CELLIST
      BELWIN-MILLS PUBLISHING CORPORATION   .60
WRIGHT, L.   M
   CONCERTO WALTZ
      COMPOSERS PRESS, INC.   1.50
WRIGHT, L.   3
   FROM THE ORGAN LOFT
      WILLIS MUSIC COMPANY   .40
WRIGHT, L.   1 1/2
   MARCHING WITH THE BAND
      BELWIN-MILLS PUBLISHING CORPORATION   .60
WRIGHT, L.   2
   ROLLER COASTER
      BELWIN-MILLS PUBLISHING CORPORATION   .60
WRIGHT, L.   2
   SLUMBER SONG
      BELWIN-MILLS PUBLISHING CORPORATION   .60
WRIGHT, L.   E-M
   WINDY WEATHER
      COMPOSERS PRESS, INC.   1.00
WRIGHT, M.
   INDIAN WAR-CALL
      G. SCHIRMER, INC.   .30
WRIGHT, N.
   AIR DE BALLET
      G. SCHIRMER, INC.   .40
WRIGHT, N.
   BALLET WALTZ, A
      G. SCHIRMER, INC.   .40
WRIGHT, N.   3
   BELLS ACROSS THE VALLEY
      THEODORE PRESSER COMPANY   .50
WRIGHT, N.   1
   CIRCLING 'ROUND
      THEODORE PRESSER COMPANY   .50
WRIGHT, N.
   CONCERT STUDIES, IN C
      G. SCHIRMER, INC.   .50
WRIGHT, N.
   EASY IMPROMPTUS--A MELODY AFTER MENDELSSOHN, OP. 34
      G. SCHIRMER, INC.   .40
WRIGHT, N.
   EASY IMPROMPTUS--WALTZ IN B FLAT, OP. 32
      G. SCHIRMER, INC.   .40
WRIGHT, N.   4 1/2
   GLORY TO GOD
      THEODORE PRESSER COMPANY   .50
WRIGHT, N.
   HUMMING BIRD
      G. SCHIRMER, INC.   .50
WRIGHT, N.
   IN SPRINGTIME, OP. 36 NO. 3--THE BUTTERFLY
      G. SCHIRMER, INC.   .40
WRIGHT, N.   2
   LITTLE BALLET
      CENTURY MUSIC PUBLISHING COMPANY, INC.   4065   .40

WRIGHT, N.   1 1/2
    LITTLE MARCH, A
        THEODORE PRESSER COMPANY   .50
WRIGHT, N.
    MAGNOLIA
        G. SCHIRMER, INC.   .50
WRIGHT, N.   2
    PLACID LAKE
        CENTURY MUSIC PUBLISHING COMPANY, INC.   4066   .40
WRIGHT, N.   2
    PLACID LAKE
        CENTURY MUSIC PUBLISHING COMPANY, INC.   4066   .40
WRIGHT, N.   WILLIAMS, J.   2
    PRELUDE IN E FLAT
        BOSTON MUSIC COMPANY   .50
WRIGHT, N.
    PRELUDE IN E FLAT, OP. 25 NO. 3
        G. SCHIRMER, INC.   .30
WRIGHT, N.   3
    SONG WITHOUT WORDS
        CENTURY MUSIC PUBLISHING COMPANY, INC.   4369   .40
WRIGHT, N.   3-4
    SONG WITHOUT WORDS
        CENTURY MUSIC PUBLISHING COMPANY, INC.   .40
WRIGHT, N.
    TRIP TO VENICE, A--THE BELL
        G. SCHIRMER, INC.   .30
WRIGHT, N.
    VALSE VIENNOISE
        G. SCHIRMER, INC.   .40
WRIGHT, N.
    VEIL DANCE
        G. SCHIRMER, INC.   .30
WRIGHT, N.   4
    VIENNESE WHISPERS
        THEODORE PRESSER COMPANY   .50
WRIGHT, N.
    WE GO MARCHING
        G. SCHIRMER, INC.   .35
WRIGHT, N.   4
    WIND OVER THE PINES
        THEODORE PRESSER COMPANY   .60
WUENSCH
    MINI SUITE NO. 1
        MCA MUSIC   1.50
WUENSCH
    SPECTRUM
        MCA MUSIC   3.50
WUORINEN
    HARPSICHORD DIVISIONS --IN PREPARATION--
        C. F. PETERS CORPORATION   66370
WUORINEN
    PIANO SONATA -- IN PREPARATION--
        C. F. PETERS CORPORATION   66371
WURMSER, L.
    BALLADE
        FRANCO COLOMBO PUBLICATIONS   SAL   4.00
WURMSER, L.
    CINQ IMPRESSIONS ENFANTINES
        EDITIONS MUSICALES TRANSATLANTIQUES   2.20
WURMSER, L.
    CREPUSCULE
        EDITIONS MUSICALES TRANSATLANTIQUES   1.35
WURMSER, L.
    DEUX AIRS A DANSER, NO.1
        GERARD BILLAUDOT EDITIONS MUSICALES   1.10
WURMSER, L.
    DEUX AIRS A DANSER, NO.2
        GERARD BILLAUDOT EDITIONS MUSICALES   1.10
WURMSER, L.
    GRADUS MODERNE, LE--NO. 1, MOUVEMENT
        ASSOCIATED MUSIC PUBLISHERS, INC.   ESC   1.00
WURMSER, L.
    GRADUS MODERNE, LE--NO. 2, MAIN GAUCHE SEULE
        ASSOCIATED MUSIC PUBLISHERS, INC.   ESC   1.50
WURMSER, L.
    GRADUS MODERNE, LE--NO. 3, PAPILLONS BLANCS
        ASSOCIATED MUSIC PUBLISHERS, INC.   ESC   1.50
WURMSER, L.
    GRADUS MODERNE, LE--NO. 4, PETITE TOCCATA
        ASSOCIATED MUSIC PUBLISHERS, INC.   ESC   1.50
WURMSER, L.
    GRADUS MODERNE, LE--NO. 5, L'ENJOUEE
        ASSOCIATED MUSIC PUBLISHERS, INC.   ESC   1.50
WURMSER, L.
    GRADUS MODERNE, LE--NO. 6, ARABESQUES
        ASSOCIATED MUSIC PUBLISHERS, INC.   ESC   1.50
WURMSER, L.
    SCENES PITTORESQUES -- 1. RECUEILLEMENT
        EDITIONS MUSICALES TRANSATLANTIQUES   1.25
WURMSER, L.
    SCENES PITTORESQUES -- 2. SCHERZETTO
        EDITIONS MUSICALES TRANSATLANTIQUES   1.25
WURMSER, L.
    SCENES PITTORESQUES -- 3. SPLEEN
        EDITIONS MUSICALES TRANSATLANTIQUES   1.25
WURMSER, L.
    SCENES PITTORESQUES -- 4. SOUVENIR
        EDITIONS MUSICALES TRANSATLANTIQUES   1.25
WURMSER, L.
    SCENES PITTORESQUES -- 5. PRIERE
        EDITIONS MUSICALES TRANSATLANTIQUES   1.00
WURMSER, L.
    SCENES PITTORESQUES -- 6. JEUX
        EDITIONS MUSICALES TRANSATLANTIQUES   1.25
WURMSER, L.
    TROIS PIECES -- NO. 1 ELEGIE
        EDITIONS MUSICALES TRANSATLANTIQUES   1.35
WURMSER, L.
    TROIS PIECES -- NO. 2 INTERLUDE
        EDITIONS MUSICALES TRANSATLANTIQUES   1.95
WURMSER, L.
    TROIS PIECES -- NO. 3 AIR DE BALLET
        EDITIONS MUSICALES TRANSATLANTIQUES   1.95
WYMAN, A.   4
    CHRISTMAS BELLS MARCH, OP. 17
        THEODORE PRESSER COMPANY   .60
WYMAN, A.
    CHRISTMAS BELLS MARCH, OP. 17
        VOLKWEIN BROS.   .25
WYMAN, A.   4
    MUSIC AMONG THE PINES
        CENTURY MUSIC PUBLISHING COMPANY, INC.   1504   .40
WYMAN, A.   4
    MUSIC AMONG THE PINES
        CENTURY MUSIC PUBLISHING COMPANY, INC.   1504   .40

WYMAN, A.   4
    SILVERY WAVES
        CENTURY MUSIC PUBLISHING COMPANY, INC.   529   .40
WYMAN, A.   4
    SILVERY WAVES
        CENTURY MUSIC PUBLISHING COMPANY, INC.   529   .40
WYMAN, A.   3
    WOODLAND DREAMS, OP. 65
        CENTURY MUSIC PUBLISHING COMPANY, INC.   2184   .40
WYMAN, A.   4
    WOODLAND ECHOES
        CENTURY MUSIC PUBLISHING COMPANY, INC.   1392   .40
WYMAN, A.   4
    WOODLAND ECHOES, OP. 34
        BELWIN-MILLS PUBLISHING CORPORATION   400   .60
WYMAN, A.   5
    WOODLAND ECHOES, OP. 34
        THEODORE PRESSER COMPANY   .60
WYMAN, D. C.
    EASEMENTS FOR PIANO
        SEESAW MUSIC CORPORATION   2.00
XENAKIS, I.
    HERMA
        BOOSEY AND HAWKES, INC.   3.75
YAMADA, C.
    JAPANESE BALLADE
        G. SCHIRMER, INC.   1.00
YANNAY, Y.
    MUSIC FOR PIANO
        ISRAEL MUSIC INSTITUTE   4.75
YARDUMIAN, R.
    CHROMATIC SONATA
        ELKAN-VOGEL, INC.   2.00
YARDUMIAN, R.
    PRELUDE AND CHORALE
        ELKAN-VOGEL, INC.   .50
YARDUMIAN, R.
    THREE PRELUDES
        ELKAN-VOGEL, INC.   1.00
YARROW   NEALE, J.   EASY
    DAY IS DONE
        WARNER BROTHERS PUBLISHERS   .75
YARROW *   NEALE, J.   EASY
    PUFF, THE MAGIC DRAGON
        WARNER BROTHERS PUBLISHERS   .75
YARROW *   DAVIS, J. R.   FIRST YEAR
    PUFF, THE MAGIC DRAGON
        WARNER BROTHERS PUBLISHERS   .75
YON, P. A.   2
    GESU BAMBINO, GRADE 02
        BELWIN-MILLS PUBLISHING CORPORATION   .75
YON, P. A.   3
    GESU BAMBINO, GRADE 03
        BELWIN-MILLS PUBLISHING CORPORATION   .75
YON, P. A.   4
    GESU BAMBINO, GRADE 04
        BELWIN-MILLS PUBLISHING CORPORATION   .75
YON, S. C.
    CAMELLIA-MELODIE
        BELWIN-MILLS PUBLISHING CORPORATION   .60
YORKE, P.
    MISTY VALLEY
        THE BIG THREE MUSIC CORPORATION   00.95
YOUMANS   LEVINE
    TEA FOR TWO
        WARNER BROTHERS PUBLISHERS   1.00
YOUMANS   WALTER
    TEA FOR TWO
        WARNER BROTHERS PUBLISHERS   1.00
YOUMANS   RICHTER   FIRST YEAR
    TEA FOR TWO
        WILLIS MUSIC COMPANY   .75
YOUNG   1-2
    CALM IN THE FOREST
        PRO-ART PUBLICATIONS, INC.   416   .50
YOUNG   3
    IN THE HEATHER
        PRO-ART PUBLICATIONS, INC.   418   .50
YOUNG
    THEME AND VARIATIONS
        SUMMY-BIRCHARD COMPANY   .50
YOUNG   2
    TONE POEM
        PRO-ART PUBLICATIONS, INC.   417   .50
YOUNG, V.
    PEARLS ON VELVET
        THE BIG THREE MUSIC CORPORATION   00.95
YOUNG, V.   SCHAUM, J.   1 1/2
    SWEET SUE - JUST YOU
        SCHAUM PUBLICATIONS, INC.   .75
YOUNG, V.
    TWILIGHT NOCTURNE
        BELWIN-MILLS PUBLISHING CORPORATION   20325   .85
YRADIER   3
    DOVE, THE -- LA PALOMA
        CENTURY MUSIC PUBLISHING COMPANY, INC.   3636   .40
YRADIER   2
    DOVE, THE -- LA PALOMA, EASY
        CENTURY MUSIC PUBLISHING COMPANY, INC.   2139   .40
YRADIER   TWITCHELL   4
    LA PALOMA
        CENTURY MUSIC PUBLISHING COMPANY, INC.   270   .40
YRADIER   3
    LA PALOMA
        CENTURY MUSIC PUBLISHING COMPANY, INC.   3636   .40
YRADIER   TREHDE   4
    LA PALOMA -- THE DOVE
        CENTURY MUSIC PUBLISHING COMPANY, INC.   687   .40
YRADIER   CHIESA
    PALOMA, LA
        FRANCO COLOMBO PUBLICATIONS   105260   .60
YRADIER   CHIESA
    PALOMA, LA
        FRANCO COLOMBO PUBLICATIONS   107485   .60
YSOT, D'
    SCHERZO
        FRANCO COLOMBO PUBLICATIONS   DS562   1.25
YSOT, D'
    SCHERZO FANTASTIQUE
        FRANCO COLOMBO PUBLICATIONS   DS552   1.25
YSOT, D'
    VALSE LENTE
        FRANCO COLOMBO PUBLICATIONS   DS561   1.25
YUILL, M.
    NODDING BUTTERCUPS, NO. 3
        BELWIN-MILLS PUBLISHING CORPORATION   28181   .60

YUILL, M.
  WOOD NYMPH'S SERENADE, NO. 2
    BELWIN-MILLS PUBLISHING CORPORATION   28179   .60
YUILL, M.
  WOODLAND ECHOES, NO. 1
    BELWIN-MILLS PUBLISHING CORPORATION   28180   .60
YUNG
  REVERIES DE MARGUERITE, LES
    FRANCO COLOMBO PUBLICATIONS   SAL   1.75
YVOIRE
  SKI-HIGH --FROM THE ST. MORITZ SUITE
    MCA MUSIC   1.00
ZABRACK, H.
  SCHERZO
    BOOSEY AND HAWKES, INC.   .75
ZACHARIAS
  INNOCENTS ABROAD
    MCA MUSIC   1.00
ZACHARIAS
  SLAP HAPPY
    BELWIN-MILLS PUBLISHING CORPORATION   20249   .85
ZAFRED
  SONATA NO. 03
    FRANCO COLOMBO PUBLICATIONS   128357   2.00
ZAGON
  JEUX DE VAGUES
    FRANCO COLOMBO PUBLICATIONS   SAL   2.50
ZAMANA
  SONATA PER AMEDEO MODIGLIANA
    FRANCO COLOMBO PUBLICATIONS   Z4727   3.50
ZAMECNIK
  CHINA DOLL PARADE
    SAM FOX PUBLISHING COMPANY, INC.   .75
ZAMECNIK
  CHINA DOLL PARADE
    SOUTHERN MUSIC COMPANY   .75
ZAMECNIK   KLICKMANN
  NEAPOLITAN NIGHTS -- SIMPLIFIED
    SOUTHERN MUSIC COMPANY   .50
ZAMECNIK
  POLLY
    SAM FOX PUBLISHING COMPANY, INC.   1.00
ZAMECNIK
  POLLY
    SOUTHERN MUSIC COMPANY   1.00
ZANELLA
  SONATA, OP. 70
    FRANCO COLOMBO PUBLICATIONS   BON.1133   3.00
ZANINELLI
  ENCHANTED LAKE -- BALLET --
    FRANCO COLOMBO PUBLICATIONS   NY1702   1.50
ZANINELLI
  FANTASIA
    ELKAN-VOGEL, INC.   1.50
ZANOTTI *
  PRELUDE AND FANTASY
    FRANCO COLOMBO PUBLICATIONS   FOR.11746   1.75
ZANOTTI *
  SONATINA IN 2 MOVEMENTS
    FRANCO COLOMBO PUBLICATIONS   FOR.11745   1.75
ZANUTTA
  SPIGOLATRICI, LE
    FRANCO COLOMBO PUBLICATIONS   BON.1218   .90
ZBINDEN, J. F.
  JAZZ SONATINA, OP. 11
    ASSOCIATED MUSIC PUBLISHERS, INC.   BRH   2.50
ZECCA, G.
  FOUR PENNELATE IN WALTZ TEMPO
    EDIZIONI BERBEN   EB 1491   1.50
ZEISL, E.
  SONATA BAROCCA--JULY, 1949
    ASSOCIATED MUSIC PUBLISHERS, INC.   DOB   4.00
ZELLER
  WALTZ FROM 'THE BIRDCATCHER'
    FRANCO COLOMBO PUBLICATIONS   128380   .50
ZEPP
  FARMER BOOGIE - BASED ON THE HAPPY FARMER OF SCHUMANN
    PRO-ART PUBLICATIONS, INC.   406   .50
ZEPP--ED   ZEPP   2
  AMERICAN PATROL
    PRO-ART PUBLICATIONS, INC.   323   .50
ZEPP--ED   ZEPP   2
  ARKANSAS TRAVELER, THE
    PRO-ART PUBLICATIONS, INC.   192   .50
ZEPP--ED   ZEPP   2-3
  DIXIE BOOGIE
    PRO-ART PUBLICATIONS, INC.   108   .50
ZEPP--ED   ZEPP   4
  GO DOWN MOSES
    PRO-ART PUBLICATIONS, INC.   233   .50
ZEPP--ED   ZEPP   3
  GREENSLEEVES - WHAT CHILD IS THIS
    PRO-ART PUBLICATIONS, INC.   198   .50
ZEPP--ED   ZEPP   2
  HAVA NAGILA
    PRO-ART PUBLICATIONS, INC.   362   .50
ZEPP--ED   ZEPP   4
  HAVA NAGILA
    PRO-ART PUBLICATIONS, INC.   363   .50
ZEPP--ED   ZEPP   3-4
  HE'S GOT THE WHOLE WORLD IN HIS HANDS
    PRO-ART PUBLICATIONS, INC.   326   .50
ZEPP--ED   ZEPP   2
  JOSHUA FIT DE BATTLE OF JERICHO
    PRO-ART PUBLICATIONS, INC.   262   .50
ZEPP--ED   ZEPP   4
  JOSHUA FIT DE BATTLE OF JERICHO
    PRO-ART PUBLICATIONS, INC.   200   .50
ZEPP--ED   ZEPP   3
  JUGGLE BOOGIE - LITTLE BROWN JUG
    PRO-ART PUBLICATIONS, INC.   69   .50
ZEPP--ED   ZEPP   3-4
  LONDONDERRY AIR
    PRO-ART PUBLICATIONS, INC.   232   .50
ZEPP--ED   ZEPP   1-2
  MARINES' HYMN, THE
    PRO-ART PUBLICATIONS, INC.   226   .50
ZEPP--ED   ZEPP   1-2
  OH, DEAR - WHAT CAN THE MATTER BE
    PRO-ART PUBLICATIONS, INC.   227   .50
ZEPP--ED   ZEPP   2
  OVER THE RIVER AND THROUGH THE WOODS - THANKSGIVING SONG
    PRO-ART PUBLICATIONS, INC.   191   .50
ZEPP--ED   ZEPP   3-4
  POOR WAYFARING STRANGER
    PRO-ART PUBLICATIONS, INC.   266   .50

ZEPP--ED   ZEPP   4
  SCARBOROUGH FAIR
    PRO-ART PUBLICATIONS, INC.   526   .50
ZEPP--ED   ZEPP   4
  SHENANDOAH
    PRO-ART PUBLICATIONS, INC.   527   .50
ZEPP--ED   ZEPP   3
  SHINE BOOGIE
    PRO-ART PUBLICATIONS, INC.   57   .50
ZEPP--ED   ZEPP   1
  SHORT'NIN' BREAD
    PRO-ART PUBLICATIONS, INC.   60   .50
ZEPP--ED   ZEPP   4
  SPACE BOOGIE
    PRO-ART PUBLICATIONS, INC.   153   .50
ZEPP--ED   ZEPP   4
  TARANTELLA
    PRO-ART PUBLICATIONS, INC.   327   .50
ZEPP--ED   ZEPP   3
  UPSIDE DOWN CAKE
    PRO-ART PUBLICATIONS, INC.   70   .50
ZEPP--ED   ZEPP   2
  WHERE ARE THOSE PIRATES BOLD
    PRO-ART PUBLICATIONS, INC.   146   .50
ZEPP--ED   ZEPP   3-4
  YOUNG MACDONALD HAD A FARM
    PRO-ART PUBLICATIONS, INC.   59   .50
ZIEGLER   2
  PRETTY PONY
    BOSTON MUSIC COMPANY   .50
ZIEHRER   5
  JOLIES VIENNOISES, LES
    ALPHONSE LEDUC
ZILCHER   3
  GARCON MEUNIER, LE
    ALPHONSE LEDUC
ZILCHER
  LITTLE SPINNER, THE, OP. 114
    BANKS AND SON LTD.   .25
ZILLIG
  SERENADE NO. 3
    BARENREITER VERLAG   BA 3506   1.75
ZILLIG   4
  SERENADE NO. 3
    BARENREITER VERLAG   BA 3506
ZIPOLI   MONTANI
  COURENTE
    FRANCO COLOMBO PUBLICATIONS   128627   .50
ZIPOLI   LONGO
  SUITE IN B MINOR
    FRANCO COLOMBO PUBLICATIONS   ER462   .75
ZIPP   M
  SONATINA FOR PIANO OR HARPSICHORD
    C. F. PETERS CORPORATION   N3164   1.25
ZONDADARI
  PRELUDE IN C MINOR
    FRANCO COLOMBO PUBLICATIONS
ZUCCA
  KALISTOE
    FRANCO COLOMBO PUBLICATIONS   SAL   2.75
ZULAWSKI
  SONATINA
    EDWARD B. MARKS MUSIC CORPORATION   01.60
ZUPKO   4
  BURLESQUE
    LEE ROBERTS MUSIC PUBLICATIONS, INC.   .60
ZUPKO   4
  EVENING SONG
    LEE ROBERTS MUSIC PUBLICATIONS, INC.   .50
ZUPKO   4
  MARCH
    LEE ROBERTS MUSIC PUBLICATIONS, INC.   .50
ZUR, M.
  FANTASY FOR PIANO, 1972
    SEESAW MUSIC CORPORATION   3.00

Single Work Solos:
Composer/Editor/Arranger Unlisted—Works Alphabetized by Title

A CANZONE'E NAPULE
    MUSIC SALES CORPORATION   040987   1.00

A TAZZA,' CAFE
    MUSIC SALES CORPORATION   040990   1.00

ABBY VARIATIONS
    CHAPPELL AND COMPANY, INC.   0021279-150   1.00

ADDIO, SIGNORA
    MUSIC SALES CORPORATION   040988   1.00

ALAMEIN CONCERTO -- THEME
    CHAPPELL AND COMPANY, INC.   0014258-1502   .95

ALL THE THINGS YOU ARE
    CIMINO PUBLICATIONS, INC.   H   1.25

ALL THE THINGS YOU ARE
    CIMINO PUBLICATIONS, INC.   H   1.25

ALL THE THINGS YOU ARE -- SHOWCASE
    CIMINO PUBLICATIONS, INC.   H   1.25

ALLEZ-VOUS EN, GO AWAY
    CHAPPELL AND COMPANY, INC.   0175000   .95

AMAZING GRACE
    BELWIN-MILLS PUBLISHING CORPORATION   .60

AMAZING GRACE
    MUSIC SALES CORPORATION   060999   .95

APPLES AND BANANAS
    CIMINO PUBLICATIONS, INC.   B   1.25

APRIL IN PORTUGAL
    CHAPPELL AND COMPANY, INC.   0028008   .95

ARABESQUE
    CIMINO PUBLICATIONS, INC.   SOU   1.25

AREN'T YOU GLAD YOU'RE YOU
    MUSIC SALES CORPORATION   050999   .95

BABY, BABY ALL THE TIME
    MUSIC SALES CORPORATION   010990   .95

BALLAD OF THE GREEN BERETS		
CIMINO PUBLICATIONS, INC.	MM	1.00
BELLS OF ST. MARY'S		
CHAPPELL AND COMPANY, INC.	0437509	.60
BEWITCHED		
CHAPPELL AND COMPANY, INC.	0460006	.95
BEYOND THE SEA		
CIMINO PUBLICATIONS, INC.	H	1.25
BILL		
CIMINO PUBLICATIONS, INC.	H	1.25
BIRD SONGS AT EVENTIDE		
CHAPPELL AND COMPANY, INC.	0492504	.95
BIRTHDAY BOUQUET -- THEME AND VARIATIONS 2 1/2		
SCHAUM PUBLICATIONS, INC.		.60
BLUE CHRISTMAS		
CIMINO PUBLICATIONS, INC.	B	1.00
BLUE VELVET		
CIMINO PUBLICATIONS, INC.	V	1.25
BLUE VELVET		
CIMINO PUBLICATIONS, INC.	V	1.00
BRAZILIAN SLEIGH BELLS		
CIMINO PUBLICATIONS, INC.	LT	1.25
BREAD AND BUTTER 3		
CENTURY MUSIC PUBLISHING COMPANY, INC.	3429	.40
BUNNY LAKE IS MISSING, MAIN THEME		
CHAPPELL AND COMPANY, INC.	0630004	.95
BUT BEAUTIFUL		
MUSIC SALES CORPORATION	050998	.95
BY HECK		
EDWARD B. MARKS MUSIC CORPORATION		01.00
BY THE SLEEPY LAGOON		
CHAPPELL AND COMPANY, INC.	0016725	.95
BYE, BYE BABY		
MUSIC SALES CORPORATION	040998	.95
CAFE MOZART WALTZ		
CHAPPELL AND COMPANY, INC.	0670000	.95
CAN'T HELP LOVIN' DAT MAN -- SHOWCASE		
CIMINO PUBLICATIONS, INC.	H	1.25
CANADIAN SUNSET		
CIMINO PUBLICATIONS, INC.	V	1.25
CANADIAN SUNSET		
CIMINO PUBLICATIONS, INC.	V	1.00
CARDINAL STAY WITH ME, THE		
CHAPPELL AND COMPANY, INC.	5490008	.60
CARDINAL, THE -- MAIN THEME		
CHAPPELL AND COMPANY, INC.	0720011	.95
CARIOCA		
CIMINO PUBLICATIONS, INC.	H	1.25
CARIOCA -- SHOWCASE		
CIMINO PUBLICATIONS, INC.	H	1.25
CAROLINA ON MY MIND		
MUSIC SALES CORPORATION	060998	.95
CAROUSEL WALTZ		
CIMINO PUBLICATIONS, INC.	H	1.50
CHARADE		
CIMINO PUBLICATIONS, INC.	SOU	1.25
CHARLOTTE IN APRIL		
CHAPPELL AND COMPANY, INC.	0022046	.95
CHERRY PINK AND APPLE BLOSSOM WHITE		
CHAPPELL AND COMPANY, INC.	0817502	.95
COME PIOVEVA		
MUSIC SALES CORPORATION	040979	1.00
COUNTRY GARDENS		
ASHLEY DEALERS SERVICE, INC.	ES	.95
COUNTRY ROAD		
MUSIC SALES CORPORATION	060997	.95
COUNTRY STYLE		
MUSIC SALES CORPORATION	050997	.95
CUTE		
CIMINO PUBLICATIONS, INC.	NH	1.25
DEAR HEART		
CIMINO PUBLICATIONS, INC.	NOR	1.25
DEAR HEART		
CIMINO PUBLICATIONS, INC.	NOR	1.00
DEARLY BELOVED -- SHOWCASE		
CIMINO PUBLICATIONS, INC.	H	1.25
DIAMONDS ARE A GIRL'S BEST FRIEND		
MUSIC SALES CORPORATION	040997	.95
DICITENCELLO VUIE		
MUSIC SALES CORPORATION	040977	1.00
DON'T EVER LEAVE ME -- SHOWCASE		
CIMINO PUBLICATIONS, INC.	H	1.25
DRUM WALTZ		
CHAPPELL AND COMPANY, INC.	0021337	.95
EARLY ONE MORNING		
FREDERICK HARRIS MUSIC COMPANY		.60
EASTER MORNING		
CHAPPELL AND COMPANY, INC.	0021345	.95
EASY TO LOVE		
CHAPPELL AND COMPANY, INC.	1315001	.95
EL MEXICANITO		
CIMINO PUBLICATIONS, INC.	CP	1.25
ELEPHANT'S MEMORY		
THE BIG THREE MUSIC CORPORATION		03.95
EN MI VIEJO SAN JUAN		
MUSIC SALES CORPORATION	050996	.95
ESPANA CANI		
CARL FISCHER, INC.	HO 517	.75
EVERYTHING HAPPENS TO ME		
MUSIC SALES CORPORATION	050995	.95
EXPERIMENT IN TERROR		
CIMINO PUBLICATIONS, INC.	SOU	1.25
FALLING IN LOVE WITH LOVE		
CHAPPELL AND COMPANY, INC.	1427509	.60
FANNY, MAIN THEME		
CHAPPELL AND COMPANY, INC.	1435015	.95
FESTIVAL		
CHAPPELL AND COMPANY, INC.	0015024	.95
FIRE AND RAIN		
MUSIC SALES CORPORATION	060996	.95
FIRST THANKSGIVING, THE		
CHAPPELL AND COMPANY, INC.	0021386	.95
FIVE MINUTES WITH MR. THORNHILL		
CHAPPELL AND COMPANY, INC.	0019737	1.00
FORTY-NINERS' CAN-CAN		
CHAPPELL AND COMPANY, INC.	0015156	1.00
FOURTH OF JULY		
CHAPPELL AND COMPANY, INC.	1585009	.95
GEORGY GIRL		
CHAPPELL AND COMPANY, INC.	1662501	.60
GOIN' OUT OF MY HEAD		
CIMINO PUBLICATIONS, INC.	V	1.25
GOIN' OUT OF MY HEAD		
CIMINO PUBLICATIONS, INC.	V	1.25
GOING MY WAY		
MUSIC SALES CORPORATION	050994	.95
GREAT IMPOSTER, THE		
CIMINO PUBLICATIONS, INC.	SOU	1.25
HALLOWEEN		
CHAPPELL AND COMPANY, INC.	0021410	.95
HAPPY BAREFOOT BOY		
CIMINO PUBLICATIONS, INC.	NOR	1.25
HAPPY BLUEBIRD 2		
BELWIN-MILLS PUBLISHING CORPORATION		.60
HAPPY ORGAN		
MUSIC SALES CORPORATION	010999	.95
HARBOR LIGHTS		
CHAPPELL AND COMPANY, INC.	1900000	.60
HARP OF THE MERMAID, THE 3		
BELWIN-MILLS PUBLISHING CORPORATION		.60
HAVA NAGILA -- ISRAELI FOLK DANCE 2		
SCHAUM PUBLICATIONS, INC.		.60
HERE'S THAT RAINY DAY		
MUSIC SALES CORPORATION	050993	.95
HOCUS POCUS		
CIMINO PUBLICATIONS, INC.	RAD	1.25
HOME FOR CHRISTMAS		
CHAPPELL AND COMPANY, INC.	0021436	.95
HOW ARE THINGS IN GLOCCA MORRA		
CHAPPELL AND COMPANY, INC.	20600002	.60
I COULD WRITE A BOOK		
CHAPPELL AND COMPANY, INC.	2182509	.95
I DREAM OF YOU		
MUSIC SALES CORPORATION	010998	.95
I GOT PLENTY O' NUTTIN'		
CHAPPELL AND COMPANY, INC.	2230027	.60
I THINK OF YOU		
MUSIC SALES CORPORATION	010997	.95
I WANT A GIRL		
CIMINO PUBLICATIONS, INC.	B	1.25
I WILL WAIT FOR YOU		
CIMINO PUBLICATIONS, INC.	V	1.25
I WILL WAIT FOR YOU		
CIMINO PUBLICATIONS, INC.	V	1.25
I'VE TOLD EV'RY LITTLE STAR		
CIMINO PUBLICATIONS, INC.	H	1.25
I'VE TOLD EV'RY LITTLE STAR		
CIMINO PUBLICATIONS, INC.	H	1.25
IF I LOVED YOU		
CIMINO PUBLICATIONS, INC.	H	1.25
IL SILENZIO		
MUSIC SALES CORPORATION	010996	.95

IM VIOLINSCHLUSSEL -- FIFTEEN LEICHTE STUCKE [1]
SCHOTT 2604 2.00

IMAGINATION
MUSIC SALES CORPORATION 050992 .95

INTERMEZZO
ASHLEY DEALERS SERVICE, INC. 1.00

IRISH AIR -- ST. PATRICK WAS A GENTLEMAN
FREDERICK HARRIS MUSIC COMPANY .60

ISLE OF CAPRI
CIMINO PUBLICATIONS, INC. H 1.25

IT STARTED ALL OVER AGAIN
MUSIC SALES CORPORATION 010995 .95

IT'S DELIGHTFUL DOWN IN CHILE
MUSIC SALES CORPORATION 040996 .95

IT'S IMPOSSIBLE
CIMINO PUBLICATIONS, INC. SU 1.00

ITALIAN FOLK SONG
FREDERICK HARRIS MUSIC COMPANY .60

JAZZ ME BLUES
EDWARD B. MARKS MUSIC CORPORATION 01.00

JERSEY BOUNCE
ASHLEY DEALERS SERVICE, INC. 1.00
LANE, J.

JINGLE BELL ROCK
THE BIG THREE MUSIC CORPORATION 00.70

JOEY
MUSIC SALES CORPORATION 010994 .95

JUMPING BEAN
CHAPPELL AND COMPANY, INC. 2975001 .95

JUST A KISS APART
MUSIC SALES CORPORATION 040995 .95

JUST AS THOUGH YOU WERE HERE
MUSIC SALES CORPORATION 050991 .95

KID FROM RED BANK
CIMINO PUBLICATIONS, INC. NH 1.25

KNIGHTSBRIDGE MARCH
CHAPPELL AND COMPANY, INC. 3092509 .95
LANE, J.

KNOCK THREE TIMES
THE BIG THREE MUSIC CORPORATION 00.70

KOBOLDSTANZ, OP. 85 NO. 8 [3-4]
BARENREITER VERLAG AP 351

KOL NIDRE [3]
CENTURY MUSIC PUBLISHING COMPANY, INC. 3646 .40

LAND OF DREAMS
CIMINO PUBLICATIONS, INC. V 1.25

LANGUAGE, THE
MUSIC SALES CORPORATION 050972 .95

LAST RHAPSODY THEME, THE
CHAPPELL AND COMPANY, INC. 0015735 .95

LET'S GET AWAY FROM IT ALL
MUSIC SALES CORPORATION 050990 .95

LI'L DARLIN'
CIMINO PUBLICATIONS, INC. NH 1.25

LIES
CIMINO PUBLICATIONS, INC. V 1.25

LIGHT MY FIRE
MUSIC SALES CORPORATION 060995 .95

LIKE SOMEONE IN LOVE
MUSIC SALES CORPORATION 050989 .95

LITTLE GIRL BLUE -- SHOWCASE
CIMINO PUBLICATIONS, INC. H 1.25

LITTLE GIRL FROM LITTLE ROCK, A
MUSIC SALES CORPORATION 040994 .95

LITTLE GREY HOME IN THE WEST
CHAPPELL AND COMPANY, INC. 3305000 .95

LONDON AGAIN SUITE
CHAPPELL AND COMPANY, INC. 3360005 2.00

LONDON BRIDGE IS FALLING DOWN
FREDERICK HARRIS MUSIC COMPANY .60

LONDON FANTASIA
CHAPPELL AND COMPANY, INC. 3370004-1501 1.25

LONDON FANTASIA -- THEME
CHAPPELL AND COMPANY, INC. 3370004-1502 .95

LONDON SUITE
CHAPPELL AND COMPANY, INC. 3380003 2.00

LONG AGO AND FAR AWAY -- SHOWCASE
CIMINO PUBLICATIONS, INC. 8 1.25

LONG ISLAND RHAPSODY
CHAPPELL AND COMPANY, INC. 0013300 .95

LOOK FOR THE SILVER LINING
CIMINO PUBLICATIONS, INC. H 1.25

LOOK FOR THE SILVER LINING -- SHOWCASE
CIMINO PUBLICATIONS, INC. H 1.25

LORELEI, THE
MUSIC SALES CORPORATION 050988 .95

LOSS OF LOVE
CIMINO PUBLICATIONS, INC. NOR 1.25

LOST LOVE
CIMINO PUBLICATIONS, INC. V 1.25

LOVE HER MADLY
MUSIC SALES CORPORATION 060994 .95

LOVE WALKED IN
CHAPPELL AND COMPANY, INC. 3515004 .95

MAKE BELIEVE
CIMINO PUBLICATIONS, INC. H 1.25

MAKE BELIEVE
CIMINO PUBLICATIONS, INC. H 1.25

MAKE BELIEVE
CIMINO PUBLICATIONS, INC. H 1.00

MANCINI GENERATION
CIMINO PUBLICATIONS, INC. LSM 1.25

MAY I NEVER LOVE AGAIN
MUSIC SALES CORPORATION 050987 .95

MEDIC THEME
CHAPPELL AND COMPANY, INC. 3715000 .95

MEDITERRANEAN CONCERTO
CHAPPELL AND COMPANY, INC. 3717501-1501 1.25

MEDITERRANEAN CONCERTO -- THEMES
CHAPPELL AND COMPANY, INC. 3717501-1502 .95

MELANCHOLY SERENADE
CIMINO PUBLICATIONS, INC. SS 1.25

MEXICAN HAT DANCE
EDWARD B. MARKS MUSIC CORPORATION 01.00

MOONLIGHT SONATA
CIMINO PUBLICATIONS, INC. SOU 1.25

MOST BEAUTIFUL GIRL IN THE WORLD
CIMINO PUBLICATIONS, INC. H 1.25

MR. LUCKY
CIMINO PUBLICATIONS, INC. SOU 1.25

MUNASTERIO'E SANTA CHIARA
MUSIC SALES CORPORATION 040986 1.00

MY BEAUTIFUL LADY
CHAPPELL AND COMPANY, INC. 3905007 .60

MY ROMANCE
CIMINO PUBLICATIONS, INC. H 1.25

NA SERA'E MAGGIO
MUSIC SALES CORPORATION 040981 1.00

NEVADA
MUSIC SALES CORPORATION 050986 .95

NIGHT THEY INVENTED CHAMPAGNE, THE
CHAPPELL AND COMPANY, INC. 4090007 .60

NIGHT WAS MADE FOR LOVE -- SHOWCASE
CIMINO PUBLICATIONS, INC. 8 1.25

NIGHT WATCH
CHAPPELL AND COMPANY, INC. 4095006 .95

NIGHT WE CALLED IT A DAY
MUSIC SALES CORPORATION 050985 .95

NIGHTY NIGHT
MUSIC SALES CORPORATION 050984 .95

O PAESE D'O SOLE
MUSIC SALES CORPORATION 040991 1.00

OH, YOU CRAZY MOON
MUSIC SALES CORPORATION 050983 .95

OL' MAN RIVER
CIMINO PUBLICATIONS, INC. H 1.25

OL' MAN RIVER
CIMINO PUBLICATIONS, INC. H 1.00

OPUS ONE
MUSIC SALES CORPORATION 010993 .95

ORCHIDS IN THE MOONLIGHT
CIMINO PUBLICATIONS, INC. H 1.25

ORCHIDS IN THE MOONLIGHT -- SHOWCASE
CIMINO PUBLICATIONS, INC. 1.25

PARTHENIA IN-VIOLATA --MAYDEN MUSICKE--. FACSIMILE EDITION PUB.
BY THE NEW YORK PUBLIC LIBRARY
C. F. PETERS CORPORATION 6133A 9.00

PERRY MASON THEME
CIMINO PUBLICATIONS, INC. 8 1.25

PERSONALITY
MUSIC SALES CORPORATION 050982 .95

PETER GUNN
CIMINO PUBLICATIONS, INC. NOR 1.25

PIANOVATIONS OF JOSE MELIS
SAM FOX PUBLISHING COMPANY, INC. 1.75

POLKA DOTS AND MOONBEAMS
MUSIC SALES CORPORATION 050981 .95

POWDERED WIG
CIMINO PUBLICATIONS, INC. SOU 1.25

PRESIDENT KENNEDY MARCH
CIMINO PUBLICATIONS, INC. 8 1.25

PROLOGUE
CHAPPELL AND COMPANY, INC. 1473503 .95

PROMENADE
CHAPPELL AND COMPANY, INC. 4737508 .95

ROSES OF PICARDY
CHAPPELL AND COMPANY, INC. 4930004 .95

SAINTS' WHEEL
CHAPPELL AND COMPANY, INC. 0016527 1.50

Title	Publisher	Number	Price
SCALINATELLA	MUSIC SALES CORPORATION	040978	1.00
SCARBOROUGH FAIR	MUSIC SALES CORPORATION	060992	.95
SEA SHANTEY -- BLOW THE MAN DOWN	FREDERICK HARRIS MUSIC COMPANY		.60
SENZA NISCIUNO	MUSIC SALES CORPORATION	040983	1.00
SEPTEMBER SONG	CHAPPELL AND COMPANY, INC.	5060009-1501	.95
SEPTEMBER SONG	CHAPPELL AND COMPANY, INC.	5060009	.60
SHADOW WALTZ	CHAPPELL AND COMPANY, INC.	5080007	.95
SHE DIDN'T SAY YES -- SHOWCASE	CIMINO PUBLICATIONS, INC.	H	1.25
SHOE SHINE BOY	MUSIC SALES CORPORATION	050980	.95
SHOOTING STAR	CHAPPELL AND COMPANY, INC.	5132501	.95
SHOT IN THE DARK	CIMINO PUBLICATIONS, INC.	TWI	1.25
SILENZIO CANTATORE	MUSIC SALES CORPORATION	040985	1.00
SLEEPY LAGOON	CHAPPELL AND COMPANY, INC.	5225008	.95
SLEEPY LAGOON	CHAPPELL AND COMPANY, INC.	5225008	.60
SMOKE GETS IN YOUR EYES	CIMINO PUBLICATIONS, INC.	H	1.25
SMOKE GETS IN YOUR EYES	CIMINO PUBLICATIONS, INC.	H	1.25
SMOKE GETS IN YOUR EYES	CIMINO PUBLICATIONS, INC.	H	1.25
SMOKE GETS IN YOUR EYES -- SHOWCASE	CIMINO PUBLICATIONS, INC.	H	1.25
SMOKE RINGS	MUSIC SALES CORPORATION	050979	.95
SNOWFALL	CHAPPELL AND COMPANY, INC.	5247507	.95
SOLDIER IN THE RAIN	CIMINO PUBLICATIONS, INC.	EAS	1.25
SOLILOQUY AT MIDNIGHT	CHAPPELL AND COMPANY, INC.	0020016	.95
SOMEBODY'S KNOCKIN' AT YOUR DOOR 2	CENTURY MUSIC PUBLISHING COMPANY, INC.	3833	.40
SOMETIMES I FEEL LIKE A MOTHERLESS CHILD 2	CENTURY MUSIC PUBLISHING COMPANY, INC.	3834	.40
SONG IS YOU	CIMINO PUBLICATIONS, INC.	H	1.25
SONG OF SONGS	CHAPPELL AND COMPANY, INC.	5362504	.95
LANE, J.			
SONGMAN	THE BIG THREE MUSIC CORPORATION		00.85
SOUL MAKOSSA	CIMINO PUBLICATIONS, INC.	RA	1.25
SPY WITH A COLD NOSE	CIMINO PUBLICATIONS, INC.	JEL	1.25
STRANGE MUSIC	CHAPPELL AND COMPANY, INC.	5520002	.60
STRIPPER, THE	CIMINO PUBLICATIONS, INC.	DR	1.25
STUDY IN BROWN	CIMINO PUBLICATIONS, INC.	SOU	1.25
SUNDAY, MONDAY OR ALWAYS	MUSIC SALES CORPORATION	050978	.95
SUNRISE SERENADE	MUSIC SALES CORPORATION	050977	.95
SUNRISE SERENADE -- PIANO SOLO	MUSIC SALES CORPORATION	050976	.95
SWEET BABY JAMES	MUSIC SALES CORPORATION	060993	.95
SWEETHEART TREE	CIMINO PUBLICATIONS, INC.	EAS	1.25
SWINGING ON A STAR	MUSIC SALES CORPORATION	050975	.95
TAKE HER TO JAMAICA	MUSIC SALES CORPORATION	040993	.95
TAP DANCE CONCERTO	CHAPPELL AND COMPANY, INC.	5695002	2.50
THANK HEAVEN FOR LITTLE GIRLS	CHAPPELL AND COMPANY, INC.	5740006	.60
THEME FROM 'LION IN WINTER'	CIMINO PUBLICATIONS, INC.	JEL	1.25
THEME FROM 'THE DEADLY TRAP'	CIMINO PUBLICATIONS, INC.	H	1.25
THEME FROM 'Z'	CIMINO PUBLICATIONS, INC.	BL	1.25
THEME VARIE--1951	ASSOCIATED MUSIC PUBLISHERS, INC.	ESC	4.50
THERE ARE SUCH THINGS	MUSIC SALES CORPORATION	050974	.95
THEY CALL THE WIND MARIA	CHAPPELL AND COMPANY, INC.	5930003	.75
THEY DIDN'T BELIEVE ME	CIMINO PUBLICATIONS, INC.	H	1.25
THIRD MAN THEME	CHAPPELL AND COMPANY, INC.	5947502	.95
THIS LOVE OF MINE	MUSIC SALES CORPORATION	010992	.95
TIGER RAG	THE BIG THREE MUSIC CORPORATION		00.95
TORNA AL PAESELLO	MUSIC SALES CORPORATION	040982	1.00
TOUCH OF YOUR HAND	CIMINO PUBLICATIONS, INC.	H	1.25
TRACY'S THEME	TRO SONGWAYS SERVICE, INC.	2057	
TRUE LOVE	CHAPPELL AND COMPANY, INC.	6165005	.60
TU, CA NUN CHIAGNE	MUSIC SALES CORPORATION	040984	1.00
TUXEDO JUNCTION	ASHLEY DEALERS SERVICE, INC.		1.00
VANESSA	CIMINO PUBLICATIONS, INC.	V	1.25
VARCA NAPULITANA	MUSIC SALES CORPORATION	040989	1.00
VERADERO	CIMINO PUBLICATIONS, INC.	V	1.25
VIENNA ECHOES	CIMINO PUBLICATIONS, INC.	B	1.25
VIOLETS FOR YOUR FURS	MUSIC SALES CORPORATION	050973	.95
VURRIA	MUSIC SALES CORPORATION	040980	1.00
WALTZ AT MAXIM'S	CHAPPELL AND COMPANY, INC.	6335004	.95
WALTZING BUGLE BOY	CHAPPELL AND COMPANY, INC.	6450003	.95
WATCH WHAT HAPPENS	CIMINO PUBLICATIONS, INC.	V	1.25
WATCH WHAT HAPPENS	CIMINO PUBLICATIONS, INC.	V	1.00
WATUSI TRUMPETS	CIMINO PUBLICATIONS, INC.	MP	1.25
WAYWARD WIND	CIMINO PUBLICATIONS, INC.	V	1.00
WHAT HAVE THEY DONE TO MY SONG, MA	CIMINO PUBLICATIONS, INC.	KR	1.00
WHERE OR WHEN	CHAPPELL AND COMPANY, INC.	6592505	.95
WHO	CIMINO PUBLICATIONS, INC.	H	1.25
WHY DO I LOVE YOU	CIMINO PUBLICATIONS, INC.	H	1.25
WHY TRY TO CHANGE ME NOW	MUSIC SALES CORPORATION	040992	.95
WHY WAS I BORN	CIMINO PUBLICATIONS, INC.	H	1.25
WILL YOU STILL BE MINE	MUSIC SALES CORPORATION	050972	.95
WINDJAMMER	CHAPPELL AND COMPANY, INC.	6682504	.95
WORLD IS WAITING FOR THE SUNRISE, THE	CHAPPELL AND COMPANY, INC.	6755003	.95
WUNDERBAR -- SHOWCASE	CIMINO PUBLICATIONS, INC.	H	1.25
YES INDEED	MUSIC SALES CORPORATION	010991	.95
YOU DON'T HAVE TO KNOW	MUSIC SALES CORPORATION	050972	.95
YOU'LL NEVER WALK ALONE	CIMINO PUBLICATIONS, INC.	H	1.25
YOU'LL NEVER WALK ALONE	CIMINO PUBLICATIONS, INC.	H	1.25
YOU'LL NEVER WALK ALONE	CIMINO PUBLICATIONS, INC.	H	1.00
YOU'LL NEVER WALK ALONE -- SHOWCASE	CIMINO PUBLICATIONS, INC.	H	1.25
YOUNGER THAN SPRINGTIME	CHAPPELL AND COMPANY, INC.	6925002	.95
ZANZIBAR	CHAPPELL AND COMPANY, INC.	0020081	.95

Collections, Anthologies and Instructional Systems or Methods

AARON, M.
ADULT PIANO COURSE, BK. 1
    BELWIN-MILLS PUBLISHING CORPORATION   11006   1.75

AARON, M.
ADULT PIANO COURSE, BK. 2
    BELWIN-MILLS PUBLISHING CORPORATION   11007   1.75

AARON, M.
COURS DE PIANO POUR ADULTES.   PREMIER LIVRE
    BELWIN-MILLS PUBLISHING CORPORATION   11018   1.75

AARON, M.
NOTE READER
    BELWIN-MILLS PUBLISHING CORPORATION   11013   1.50

AARON, M.
PIANO ALBUM - ORIGINAL PIECES FOR READING, RECITAL AND
RECREATION
    BELWIN-MILLS PUBLISHING CORPORATION   11012   1.50

AARON, M.
PIANO COURSE - GRADE ONE, FRENCH EDITION
    BELWIN-MILLS PUBLISHING CORPORATION   11017   1.75

AARON, M.   1
PIANO COURSE - GRADE 1
    BELWIN-MILLS PUBLISHING CORPORATION   11001   1.75

AARON, M.   2
PIANO COURSE - GRADE 2
    BELWIN-MILLS PUBLISHING CORPORATION   11002   1.75

AARON, M.
PIANO COURSE - GRADE 2, FRENCH EDITION
    BELWIN-MILLS PUBLISHING CORPORATION   11016   1.75

AARON, M.   3
PIANO COURSE - GRADE 3
    BELWIN-MILLS PUBLISHING CORPORATION   11003   1.75

AARON, M.
PIANO COURSE - GRADE 3, FRENCH EDITION
    BELWIN-MILLS PUBLISHING CORPORATION   11015   1.75

AARON, M.   4
PIANO COURSE - GRADE 4
    BELWIN-MILLS PUBLISHING CORPORATION   11004   1.75

AARON, M.   5
PIANO COURSE - GRADE 5
    BELWIN-MILLS PUBLISHING CORPORATION   11005   1.75

AARON, M.
PIANO PRIMER
    BELWIN-MILLS PUBLISHING CORPORATION   11008   1.50

AARON, M.
PRIMAIRE - FRENCH EDITION
    BELWIN-MILLS PUBLISHING CORPORATION   11014   1.50

ABENDROTH
TWELVE LITTLE RECITAL PIECES
    FRANCO COLOMBO PUBLICATIONS   SIK.101   1.25

ABRAMS
SCALES IN DOUBLE NOTES -- THIRDS --
    CENTURY MUSIC PUBLISHING COMPANY, INC.   3637   .40

ABRAMS
STACCATO, A TECHNICAL DISCUSSION
    CENTURY MUSIC PUBLISHING COMPANY, INC.   3728   .40

ABRIL
THREE PIECES, OP. 32, RIGHT HAND ALONE
    ASSOCIATED MUSIC PUBLISHERS, INC.   ESC   5.00

ABSIL, J.
DU RYTHME A L'EXPRESSION, BK. 1
    ELKAN-VOGEL, INC.   LEM   3.75

ABSIL, J.
DU RYTHME A L'EXPRESSION, BK. 2
    ELKAN-VOGEL, INC.   LEM   2.50

ADAMS
FOLK ROCK
    BELWIN-MILLS PUBLISHING CORPORATION   1.25

ADLER, M.
FINGER FUN
    THEODORE PRESSER COMPANY   .85

ADLER, R. *   EASY
HITS FROM 'DAMN YANKEES'
    FRANK MUSIC CORPORATION   1.25

ADLER, R. *
PAJAMA GAME, THE
    FRANK MUSIC CORPORATION   1.25

ADLER, R. *   PACE, R.   EASY
SONGS FROM 'THE PAJAMA GAME'
    FRANK MUSIC CORPORATION   1.25

ADLER, S.
GRADUS, BK. 1
    OXFORD UNIVERSITY PRESS   93.808   3.00

ADLER, S.
GRADUS, BK. 2
    OXFORD UNIVERSITY PRESS   93.809   3.00

AGAY, D.
EASY PIANO PIECES FOR CHILDREN, BK. 2
    ASHLEY DEALERS SERVICE, INC.   1.50

AGAY, D.
FIFTEEN LITTLE PIECES ON FIVE-NOTE PATTERNS
    BOSTON MUSIC COMPANY   2.50

AGAY, D.
FIRST RECITAL, THE
    MUSIC SALES CORPORATION   080050   .85

AGAY, D.
FOR PIANO AND METRONOME
    MUSIC SALES CORPORATION   080065   .85

AGAY, D.
LITTLE RHAPSODIES ON FOLK-THEMES
    MUSIC SALES CORPORATION   080054   .85

AGAY, D.
MOSAICS -- SIX PIANO PIECES ON HEBREW FOLK THEMES--
    MCA MUSIC   2.50

AGAY, D.
NINE EASY MINIATURES
    SAM FOX PUBLISHING COMPANY, INC.   1.25

AGAY, D.
SKIDMORE MODERN KEYBOARD SERIES --SECONDARY --HAUNTED HOUSE
BOOGIE
    SHAPIRO, BERNSTEIN ORGANIZATION   .75

AGAY, D.
SKIDMORE MODERN KEYBOARD SERIES --SECONDARY --PASTORALE A LA
'MODE'
    SHAPIRO, BERNSTEIN ORGANIZATION   .75

AGAY, D.
SKIDMORE MODERN KEYBOARD SERIES --SECONDARY --STREET CORNER
WALTZ
    SHAPIRO, BERNSTEIN ORGANIZATION   .75

AGAY, D.   3 1/2
THREE RECITAL DANCES -- PARADE POLKA, WALTZ SERENADE, MARDI GRAS
BOLERO
    THEODORE PRESSER COMPANY   .75

AGAY, D.
TWO BAGATELLES
    MCA MUSIC   .60

AGAY, D.
VERY EASY PIANO PIECES FOR CHILDREN, BK. 1
    ASHLEY DEALERS SERVICE, INC.   1.50

AGAY, D.   AGAY, D.
YOUNG VIRTUOSO, THE   -- FOR THE EARLY GRADES
    SAM FOX PUBLISHING COMPANY, INC.   1.75

AGAY, D.   AGAY, D.
YOUR FIRST SOLO BOOK -- ELEMENTARY
    SAM FOX PUBLISHING COMPANY, INC.   1.50

AGAY, D.
YOUR SECOND SOLO BOOK
    SAM FOX PUBLISHING COMPANY, INC.   1.50

AGAY, D.--ED   AGAY, D.
ANTHOLOGY OF PIANO MUSIC, BK. 1 THE BAROQUE PERIOD
    MUSIC SALES CORPORATION   080040   4.95

AGAY, D.--ED   AGAY, D.
ANTHOLOGY OF PIANO MUSIC, BK. 2 THE CLASSICAL PERIOD
    MUSIC SALES CORPORATION   080042   4.95

AGAY, D.--ED   AGAY, D.
ANTHOLOGY OF PIANO MUSIC, BK. 3 THE ROMANTIC PERIOD
    MUSIC SALES CORPORATION   080043   4.95

AGAY, D.--ED   AGAY, D.
ANTHOLOGY OF PIANO MUSIC, BK. 4 THE TWENTIETH CENTURY
    MUSIC SALES CORPORATION   080044   4.95

AGAY, D.--ED   AGAY, D.
BOOGIE AND BLUES
    MUSIC SALES CORPORATION   080056   .85

AGAY, D.--ED   AGAY, D.   A
BROADWAY CLASSICS FOR PIANO, BK. 1
    WARNER BROTHERS PUBLISHERS   YPL 3   1.50

AGAY, D.--ED   B
BROADWAY CLASSICS FOR PIANO, BK. 2
    WARNER BROTHERS PUBLISHERS   YPL 3   1.50

AGAY, D.--ED   AGAY, D.   C
BROADWAY CLASSICS FOR PIANO, BK. 3
    WARNER BROTHERS PUBLISHERS   YPL 3   1.50

AGAY, D.--ED   AGAY, D.   A
BROADWAY SHOWCASE OF FAMOUS MELODIES, BK. 1
    WARNER BROTHERS PUBLISHERS   YPL 9   1.50

AGAY, D.--ED   B
BROADWAY SHOWCASE OF FAMOUS MELODIES, BK. 2
    WARNER BROTHERS PUBLISHERS   YPL 9   1.50

AGAY, D.--ED   AGAY, D.   C
BROADWAY SHOWCASE OF FAMOUS MELODIES, BK. 3
    WARNER BROTHERS PUBLISHERS   YPL 9   1.50

AGAY, D.--ED   AGAY, D.
CHRISTMAS RECITAL
    MUSIC SALES CORPORATION   08006   .85

AGAY, D.--ED   AGAY, D.
CURTAIN TIME -- MELODIES FROM THE MODERN THEATRE
    FRANK MUSIC CORPORATION   2.00

AGAY, D.--ED   AGAY, D.   1-2
DANCES -- BAROQUE TO JAZZ NO. 13, BK. 1
    WARNER BROTHERS PUBLISHERS   1.95

AGAY, D.--ED   AGAY, D.   2-3
DANCES -- BAROQUE TO JAZZ NO. 13, BK. 2
    WARNER BROTHERS PUBLISHERS   1.95

AGAY, D.--ED   AGAY, D.   3-4 1/2
DANCES -- BAROQUE TO JAZZ NO. 13, BK. 3
    WARNER BROTHERS PUBLISHERS   1.95

AGAY, D.--ED   AGAY, D.
DANCING KEYBOARD, THE
    WARNER BROTHERS PUBLISHERS   1.25

AGAY, D.--ED   AGAY, D.
FIESTA
    MUSIC SALES CORPORATION   080057   .85

AGAY, D.--ED   AGAY, D.
FIRST CLASSICS, THE
    MUSIC SALES CORPORATION   080051   .85

AGAY, D.--ED   AGAY, D.   A
FOLK SONGS AND FOLK DANCES, BK. 1
    WARNER BROTHERS PUBLISHERS   YPL 5   1.50

AGAY, D.--ED   AGAY, D.   B
FOLK SONGS AND FOLK DANCES, BK. 2
    WARNER BROTHERS PUBLISHERS   YPL 5   1.50

AGAY, D.--ED   C
FOLK SONGS AND FOLK DANCES, BK. 3
    WARNER BROTHERS PUBLISHERS   YPL 5   1.50

AGAY, D.--ED   AGAY, D.   A
FROM BACH TO BARTOK, BK. 1
    WARNER BROTHERS PUBLISHERS   YPL 1   1.25

AGAY, D.--ED   B
FROM BACH TO BARTOK, BK. 2
    WARNER BROTHERS PUBLISHERS   YPL 1   1.50

AGAY, D.--ED   AGAY, D.   C
FROM BACH TO BARTOK, BK. 3
    WARNER BROTHERS PUBLISHERS   YPL 1   1.50

AGAY, D.--ED   AGAY, D.
FROM RAGTIME TO ROCK AND ROLL
    SAM FOX PUBLISHING COMPANY, INC.   1.50

AGAY, D.--ED   AGAY, D.   A
FUN WITH SIGHT READING, BK. 1
    WARNER BROTHERS PUBLISHERS   YPL 10   1.50

AGAY, D.--ED   AGAY, D.   B
FUN WITH SIGHT READING, BK. 2
    WARNER BROTHERS PUBLISHERS   YPL 10   1.50

AGAY, D.--ED   AGAY, D.   C
FUN WITH SIGHT READING, BK. 3
    WARNER BROTHERS PUBLISHERS   YPL 10   1.50

AGAY, D.--ED *
HAVING A BALL
    SAM FOX PUBLISHING COMPANY, INC.   1.50

AGAY, D.--ED   AGAY, D.
HIGHLIGHTS OF FAMILIAR MUSIC, BK. 1
    THEODORE PRESSER COMPANY   1.75

AGAY, D.--ED   AGAY, D.
HIGHLIGHTS OF FAMILIAR MUSIC, BK. 2
    THEODORE PRESSER COMPANY   1.50

AGAY, D.--ED   AGAY, D.
JAZZ SOLOS
    MUSIC SALES CORPORATION   080058   .85

AGAY, D.--ED   AGAY, D.
JOY OF BACH
    MUSIC SALES CORPORATION   080011   1.75

AGAY, D.--ED   AGAY, D.
JOY OF BOOGIE AND BLUES, THE
    MUSIC SALES CORPORATION   080010   1.75

AGAY, D.--ED   AGAY, D.
JOY OF CLASSICS, THE
    MUSIC SALES CORPORATION   080005   1.75

AGAY, D.--ED   AGAY, D.
JOY OF FOLK SONGS, THE
    MUSIC SALES CORPORATION   080006   1.75

```
AGAY, D.--ED            AGAY, D.
  JOY OF JAZZ, THE
    MUSIC SALES CORPORATION              080004    1.75
AGAY, D.--ED            AGAY, D.
  JOY OF PIANO
    MUSIC SALES CORPORATION              080002    1.75
AGAY, D.--ED            AGAY, D.      EASY
  MATINEE MELODIES
    FRANK MUSIC CORPORATION                        1.50
AGAY, D.--ED            AGAY, D.
  MODERN MINIATURES
    MUSIC SALES CORPORATION              080052     .85
AGAY, D.--ED            AGAY, D.
  POP CONCERT
    MUSIC SALES CORPORATION              080053     .85
AGAY, D.--ED            AGAY, D.
  POPULAR CHOICE -- PIANO TEACHING PIECES
    MCA MUSIC                                      3.95
AGAY, D.--ED            AGAY, D.
  POPULAR MASTERPIECES
    MUSIC SALES CORPORATION              080055     .85
AGAY, D.--ED            AGAY, D.      A
  POPULAR RECITAL PIECES FOR PIANO, BK. 1
    WARNER BROTHERS PUBLISHERS           YPL 4     1.50
AGAY, D.--ED            AGAY, D.
  POPULAR RECITAL PIECES FOR PIANO, BK. 2
    WARNER BROTHERS PUBLISHERS           YPL 4     1.50
AGAY, D.--ED            AGAY, D.      C
  POPULAR RECITAL PIECES FOR PIANO, BK. 3
    WARNER BROTHERS PUBLISHERS           YPL 3     1.50
AGAY, D.--ED            AGAY, D.
  PRESSER PIANO 'POPS' -- FAVORITE HIT MELODIES OLD AND NEW NO. 1
    THEODORE PRESSER COMPANY                       1.00
AGAY, D.--ED            AGAY, D.
  PRESSER PIANO 'POPS' -- FAVORITE HIT MELODIES OLD AND NEW NO. 2
    THEODORE PRESSER COMPANY                       1.00
AGAY, D.--ED            AGAY, D.
  PRESSER PIANO 'POPS' -- FAVORITE HIT MELODIES OLD AND NEW NO. 3
    THEODORE PRESSER COMPANY                       1.00
AGAY, D.--ED            AGAY, D.
  PRESSER PIANO 'POPS' -- FAVORITE HIT MELODIES OLD AND NEW NO. 4
    THEODORE PRESSER COMPANY                       1.00
AGAY, D.--ED            AGAY, D.
  PRESSER PIANO 'POPS' -- FAVORITE HIT MELODIES OLD AND NEW NO. 5
    THEODORE PRESSER COMPANY                       1.00
AGAY, D.--ED            AGAY, D.
  PROGRAM OF CLASSICS, A
    MUSIC SALES CORPORATION              080063     .85
AGAY, D.--ED            AGAY, D.
  ROMANCING KEYBOARD, THE
    WARNER BROTHERS PUBLISHERS                     1.25
AGAY, D.--ED            AGAY, D.
  SMILING KEYBOARD, THE
    WARNER BROTHERS PUBLISHERS                     1.25
AGAY, D.--ED            AGAY, D.      A
  SOLO PIECES OF TODAY, BK. 1
    WARNER BROTHERS PUBLISHERS           YPL 7     1950
AGAY, D.--ED            AGAY, D.      B
  SOLO PIECES OF TODAY, BK. 2
    WARNER BROTHERS PUBLISHERS           YPL 7     1950
AGAY, D.--ED            AGAY, D.      A
  SONATINAS FOR PIANO, BK. 1
    WARNER BROTHERS PUBLISHERS           YPL 2     1.50
AGAY, D.--ED            AGAY, D.      B
  SONATINAS FOR PIANO, BK. 2
    WARNER BROTHERS PUBLISHERS           YPL 2     1.50
AGAY, D.--ED            AGAY, D.      C
  SONATINAS FOR PIANO, BK. 3
    WARNER BROTHERS PUBLISHERS           YPL 2     1.50
AGAY, D.--ED            AGAY, D.
  SPRING RECITAL
    MUSIC SALES CORPORATION              080060     .85
AGAY, D.--ED            AGAY, D.      A
  TECHNIC TREASURY, BK. 1
    WARNER BROTHERS PUBLISHERS           YPL 8     1.50
AGAY, D.--ED            AGAY, D.      B
  TECHNIC TREASURY, BK. 2
    WARNER BROTHERS PUBLISHERS           YPL 8     1.50
AGAY, D.--ED            AGAY, D.      C
  TECHNIC TREASURY, BK. 3
    WARNER BROTHERS PUBLISHERS           YPL 8     1.50
AGAY, D.--ED            AGAY, D.
  THEMES WITH VARIATIONS
    MUSIC SALES CORPORATION              080064     .85
AGAY, D.--ED            AGAY, D.      A
  THEORY GUIDE BOOK, BK. 1
    WARNER BROTHERS PUBLISHERS           YPL 12    1.50
AGAY, D.--ED            AGAY, D.      B
  THEORY GUIDE BOOK, BK. 2
    WARNER BROTHERS PUBLISHERS           YPL 12    1.50
AGAY, D.--ED            AGAY, D.      C
  THEORY GUIDE BOOK, BK. 3
    WARNER BROTHERS PUBLISHERS           YPL 12    1.50
AGAY, D.--ED            AGAY, D.
  THIRTY-THREE HITS FROM BROADWAY
    FRANK MUSIC CORPORATION                        2.50
AGAY, D.--ED            AGAY, D.
  THIRTY-TWO MORE HITS FROM BROADWAY
    FRANK MUSIC CORPORATION                        2.50
AGAY, D.--ED            AGAY, D.      1-2 1/2
  VERY EASY PIANO PIECES, VOL. 1
    CENTURY MUSIC PUBLISHING COMPANY, INC.         1.50
AGAY, D.--ED            AGAY, D.
  VERY EASY PIANO PIECES, VOL. 2
    CENTURY MUSIC PUBLISHING COMPANY, INC.         1.50
AGAY, D.--ED            AGAY, D.
  WELL-PAMPERED PIANIST, THE
    WARNER BROTHERS PUBLISHERS                     1.25
AGAY, D.--ED            AGAY, D.
  YOUNG PIANIST'S FIRST BOOK
    WARNER BROTHERS PUBLISHERS                     1.25
AGUILA--ED              AGUILA
  DOCE HABANERAS POPULARES
    ASSOCIATED MUSIC PUBLISHERS, INC.    UME       1.50
AGUILAR
  AIRES REGIONALES -- FOUR EASY PIECES IN TREBLE CLEF
    ASSOCIATED MUSIC PUBLISHERS, INC.    UME        .50
AGUILAR
  JUGUETES DE BAZAR -- BK. 1, SIX EASY PIECES
    ASSOCIATED MUSIC PUBLISHERS, INC.    UME        .50
AGUILAR
  JUGUETES DE BAZAR -- BK. 3, SIX EASY PIECES
    ASSOCIATED MUSIC PUBLISHERS, INC.    UME        .50
AGUILAR
  SOLDADITOS DE CARTON -- SIX VERY EASY PIECES, PART 2
    ASSOCIATED MUSIC PUBLISHERS, INC.    UME        .50

AGUILAR
  SOLDADITOS DE CARTON-- SIX VERY EASY PIECES, PART 1
    ASSOCIATED MUSIC PUBLISHERS, INC.    UME        .50
AGUIRRE
  ARGENTINE NATIONAL AIRS, OP. 17 - BK. 1
    FRANCO COLOMBO PUBLICATIONS          BA6328    1.00
AGUIRRE
  ARGENTINE NATIONAL AIRS, OP. 17 - BK. 2
    FRANCO COLOMBO PUBLICATIONS          BA 6329   1.00
AGUIRRE
  TRES AIRES CRIOLLOS
    FRANCO COLOMBO PUBLICATIONS          BA6321     .75
AGUIRRE
  TRES AIRES POPULARES ARGENTINOS
    FRANCO COLOMBO PUBLICATIONS          BA9110     .75
AHEARN *
  YOUNG AMERICA AT THE PIANO, BK. 1
    SUMMY-BIRCHARD COMPANY                         2.50
AHRENS
  KLEINES SPIELBUCH
    BARENREITER VERLAG                   BA 1725   1.75
AHRENS                            2-3
  KLEINES SPIELBUCH
    BARENREITER VERLAG                   BA 1725
AIKEN
  MODERN TECHNIC
    WILLIS MUSIC COMPANY                           1.25
AISBERG, D. S.
  DEUX ETUDES DE CONCERT EN OCTAVES -- D'APRES LES ETUDES EN LA
  MINEUR ET DO MINEUR DE CHOPIN
    ELKAN-VOGEL, INC.                              1.60
AITKEN, H.
  THREE CONNECTED PIECES
    OXFORD UNIVERSITY PRESS              93.216    1.50
AKIMENKO
  PETITS TABLEAUX PITTORESQUES POUR LA JEUNESSE
    FRANCO COLOMBO PUBLICATIONS          SAL       3.00
ALAIN, J.                         4, 6
  L'OEUVRE DE PIANO IN 3 VOLUMES, VOL. 1
    ALPHONSE LEDUC
ALAIN, J.                         5, 8
  L'OEUVRE DE PIANO IN 3 VOLUMES, VOL. 2
    ALPHONSE LEDUC
ALAIN, J.                         7, 9
  L'OEUVRE DE PIANO IN 3 VOLUMES, VOL. 3
    ALPHONSE LEDUC
ALAIN, M.                         E
  COCKTAIL PARTY FOR THE YOUNG
    C. F. PETERS CORPORATION             SCH102    1.25
ALAIN, M.                         E
  DANCE PARTY FOR THE YOUNG
    C. F. PETERS CORPORATION             SCH103    1.25
ALAIN, M.                         E
  SURPRISE PARTY FOR THE YOUNG
    C. F. PETERS CORPORATION             SCH104    1.25
ALBENIZ, I.
  ALBENIZ MASTERPIECES
    EDWARD B. MARKS MUSIC CORPORATION              02.50
ALBENIZ, I.
  CANTOS DE ESPANA, OP. 232 -- COMPLETE
    ASSOCIATED MUSIC PUBLISHERS, INC.    UME       3.00
ALBENIZ, I.                       5, 7
  DIX PIECES IN ONE BOOK
    ALPHONSE LEDUC
ALBENIZ, I.        WEITZMANN      M
  ESPANA, OP. 165
    C. F. PETERS CORPORATION             4946      3.00
ALBENIZ, I.
  ESPANA, OP. 165 -- COMPLETE
    ASSOCIATED MUSIC PUBLISHERS, INC.    UME       1.75
ALBENIZ, I.
  IBERIA, BK. 1
    EDWARD B. MARKS MUSIC CORPORATION              01.50
ALBENIZ, I.
  IBERIA, BK. 2
    EDWARD B. MARKS MUSIC CORPORATION              01.50
ALBENIZ, I.
  IBERIA, BK. 3
    EDWARD B. MARKS MUSIC CORPORATION              01.50
ALBENIZ, I.
  IBERIA, VOL. 1
    ASSOCIATED MUSIC PUBLISHERS, INC.    UME       3.50
ALBENIZ, I.
  IBERIA, VOL. 1
    EDWIN F. KALMUS                      3004      1.50
ALBENIZ, I.
  IBERIA, VOL. 2
    ASSOCIATED MUSIC PUBLISHERS, INC.    UME       3.50
ALBENIZ, I.
  IBERIA, VOL. 2
    EDWIN F. KALMUS                      3005      1.50
ALBENIZ, I.
  IBERIA, VOL. 3
    ASSOCIATED MUSIC PUBLISHERS, INC.    UME       3.50
ALBENIZ, I.
  IBERIA, VOL. 3
    EDWIN F. KALMUS                      3006      1.50
ALBENIZ, I.
  IBERIA, VOL. 4
    ASSOCIATED MUSIC PUBLISHERS, INC.    UME       3.50
ALBENIZ, I.
  IBERIA, VOL. 4
    EDWIN F. KALMUS                      3007      1.50
ALBENIZ, I.                       3
  JOTA ARAGONESA UND TANGO, OP. 164
    SCHOTT                               1309      2.00
ALBENIZ, I. *
  PIANO MUSIC FROM SPAIN -- 15 PIECES FOR PIANO SOLO
    ASSOCIATED MUSIC PUBLISHERS, INC.    AMP       2.50
ALBENIZ, I.
  SEVEN STUDIES, OP. 65
    ASSOCIATED MUSIC PUBLISHERS, INC.    UME       3.50
ALBENIZ, I.
  SIETE MAZURKAS DE SALON, OP. 81
    ASSOCIATED MUSIC PUBLISHERS, INC.    UME       1.50
ALBENIZ, I.
  SIX SPANISH DANCES
    ASSOCIATED MUSIC PUBLISHERS, INC.    UME       1.75
ALBENIZ, I.
  SIX SPANISH DANCES
    EDWIN F. KALMUS                      3003      1.25
ALBENIZ, I.        LECHNER
  SUITE ESPANOLA NO. 1 -- COMPLETE
    ASSOCIATED MUSIC PUBLISHERS, INC.    UME       4.00
ALBENIZ, I.        MAGLIO, DEL
  TEN SELECTED PIECES -- EASY TRANSCRIPTION
    FRANCO COLOMBO PUBLICATIONS          BA9814    2.00
```

ALBENIZ, I.	LUDOVICI		
TWELVE FAMOUS PIECES			
FRANCO COLOMBO PUBLICATIONS		DS37	2.00
ALBENIZ, I.		E-M	
TWO SPANISH DANCES			
C. F. PETERS CORPORATION		5342	2.00
ALBENIZ, M. *			
SPANISH COMPOSERS ALBUM			
EDWIN F. KALMUS		3985	2.50
ALBERT, D'--ED	ALBERT, D'	M	
MASTERS BETWEEN BAROQUE AND ROMANTIC PERIODS			
C. F. PETERS CORPORATION		F80	2.00
ALBERT, E. D'			
FIVE BAGATELLES, OP. 29			
ASSOCIATED MUSIC PUBLISHERS, INC.		B/H	4.00
ALBRIGHT, W.			
THREE NOVELTY RAGS			
ELKAN-VOGEL, INC.		J	6.75
ALDERIGHI			
ELEVEN PRELUDES			
FRANCO COLOMBO PUBLICATIONS		FOR.11282	4.00
ALEXANDER, J.			
PLAYTHINGS FOR PIANO			
GENERAL MUSIC PUBLISHING COMPANY, INC.			4.00
ALEXANDER, J.			
TWELVE BAGATELLES			
GENERAL MUSIC PUBLISHING COMPANY, INC.		418	3.50
ALEXANDER, J.			
TWELVE BAGATELLES			
GENERAL MUSIC PUBLISHING COMPANY, INC.			4.50
ALEXANDER, J.			
TWELVE BAGATELLES			
NOVELLO AND COMPANY, LTD.			6.25
ALFASSY, L.--ED	ALFASSY, L.		
CHILDREN'S JAZZ PIECES			
MUSIC SALES CORPORATION		040056	2.95
ALFASSY, L.--ED	ALFASSY, L.		
JUST BLUES			
MUSIC SALES CORPORATION		040055	2.95
ALFORD, K.			
COLONEL BOGEY MARCH ALBUM			
BOOSEY AND HAWKES, INC.			1.25
ALKAN			
ESQUISSES 48 MOTIFS, OP. 63, BK. 1			
GERARD BILLAUDOT EDITIONS MUSICALES			4.10
ALKAN			
ESQUISSES 48 MOTIFS, OP. 63, BK. 2			
GERARD BILLAUDOT EDITIONS MUSICALES			3.80
ALKAN			
ESQUISSES 48 MOTIFS, OP. 63, BK. 3			
GERARD BILLAUDOT EDITIONS MUSICALES			4.40
ALKAN			
ESQUISSES 48 MOTIFS, OP. 63, BK. 4			
GERARD BILLAUDOT EDITIONS MUSICALES	LEWENTHAL, R.		4.40
ALKAN			
PIANO MUSIC OF ALKAN, THE			
G. SCHIRMER, INC.			3.00
ALKAN			
THIRTY CHANTS, 2ND SUITE, SIX CHANTS, OP. 38			
GERARD BILLAUDOT EDITIONS MUSICALES			4.90
ALKAN			
THIRTY CHANTS, 3RD SUITE, SIX CHANTS, OP. 65			
GERARD BILLAUDOT EDITIONS MUSICALES			4.10
ALKAN			
THIRTY CHANTS, 4TH SUITE, SIX CHANTS, OP. 67			
GERARD BILLAUDOT EDITIONS MUSICALES			5.20
ALKAN			
THIRTY CHANTS, 5TH SUITE, SIX CHANTS, OP. 70			
GERARD BILLAUDOT EDITIONS MUSICALES			5.20
ALKAN			
THREE ETUDES DE BRAVOURE, OP. 16--SCHERZI--			
GERARD BILLAUDOT EDITIONS MUSICALES			3.80
ALKAN			
THREE ETUDES DE BRAVOURE, OP.12--IMPROVISATIONS--			
GERARD BILLAUDOT EDITIONS MUSICALES			3.00
ALKAN			
THREE MARCHES--QUASI DA CAVALLERIA--, OP. 37			
GERARD BILLAUDOT EDITIONS MUSICALES			6.30
ALKAN			
THREE MENUETS, OP. 51			
GERARD BILLAUDOT EDITIONS MUSICALES			3.00
ALKAN	PHILIPP		
THREE NOCTURNES			
GERARD BILLAUDOT EDITIONS MUSICALES			3.80
ALKAN			
TROIS ANDANTES ROMANTIQUES, OP. 13			
GERARD BILLAUDOT EDITIONS MUSICALES			3.80
ALKAN			
TROIS MORCEAUX DANS LE GENRE PATHETIQUE, OP. 15			
GERARD BILLAUDOT EDITIONS MUSICALES			3.30
ALKAN			
TROIS PETITES FANTAISIES, OP. 41			
GERARD BILLAUDOT EDITIONS MUSICALES			3.80
ALKAN			
TWELVE ETUDES IN MINOR KEYS, BK. 1			
GERARD BILLAUDOT EDITIONS MUSICALES			13.90
ALKAN			
TWELVE ETUDES IN MINOR KEYS, BK. 2			
GERARD BILLAUDOT EDITIONS MUSICALES			12.30
ALKAN			
TWENTY-FIVE PRELUDES, OP. 31			
GERARD BILLAUDOT EDITIONS MUSICALES			6.95
ALLENDE			
SIX ETUDES			
FRANCO COLOMBO PUBLICATIONS		SAL	4.25
ALLENDE			
SIX GREEK MINIATURES			
FRANCO COLOMBO PUBLICATIONS		SAL	2.50
ALLENDE			
TWELVE TONADAS IN POPULAR CHILEAN STYLE			
FRANCO COLOMBO PUBLICATIONS		SAL	7.00
ALLENDE			
TWO PRELUDES			
FRANCO COLOMBO PUBLICATIONS		SAL	2.50
ALLISON *			
GUILD REPERTOIRE - ELEMENTARY A			
SUMMY-BIRCHARD COMPANY			1.75
ALLISON *			
GUILD REPERTOIRE - ELEMENTARY B			
SUMMY-BIRCHARD COMPANY			1.75
ALLISON *			
GUILD REPERTOIRE - ELEMENTARY C			
SUMMY-BIRCHARD COMPANY			1.75
ALLISON *			
GUILD REPERTOIRE - ELEMENTARY D			
SUMMY-BIRCHARD COMPANY			1.75

ALLISON *			
GUILD REPERTOIRE - INTERMEDIATE A			
SUMMY-BIRCHARD COMPANY			2.00
ALLISON *			
GUILD REPERTOIRE - INTERMEDIATE B			
SUMMY-BIRCHARD COMPANY			2.00
ALLISON *			
GUILD REPERTOIRE - INTERMEDIATE C			
SUMMY-BIRCHARD COMPANY			2.00
ALLISON *			
GUILD REPERTOIRE - INTERMEDIATE D			
SUMMY-BIRCHARD COMPANY			2.00
ALLISON *			
GUILD REPERTOIRE - INTERMEDIATE E			
SUMMY-BIRCHARD COMPANY			2.00
ALLISON *			
GUILD REPERTOIRE - INTERMEDIATE F			
SUMMY-BIRCHARD COMPANY			2.00
ALLISON *			
GUILD REPERTOIRE - PREPARATORY A			
SUMMY-BIRCHARD COMPANY			2.50
ALLISON *			
GUILD REPERTOIRE - PREPARATORY B			
SUMMY-BIRCHARD COMPANY			2.75
ALLISON *			
GUILD REPERTOIRE - PREPARATORY C			
SUMMY-BIRCHARD COMPANY			1.75
ALLISON *			
GUILD REPERTOIRE - PREPARATORY D			
SUMMY-BIRCHARD COMPANY			2.25
ALLISON, I.			
LET'S LEARN ALL THE NOTES AND READ BETTER			
WILLIS MUSIC COMPANY			1.25
ALLISON, I.			
TWO SONATAS AND LITTLE ROMANCE			
WILLIS MUSIC COMPANY			1.25
ALLISON, I.--ED	ALLISON, I.		
IRL ALLISON PIANO LIBRARY -- ELEMENTARY A, PRG 01			
WILLIS MUSIC COMPANY		9568	1.25
ALLISON, I.--ED	ALLISON, I.		
IRL ALLISON PIANO LIBRARY -- ELEMENTARY A, PRG 02			
WILLIS MUSIC COMPANY		9569	1.25
ALLISON, I.--ED	ALLISON, I.		
IRL ALLISON PIANO LIBRARY -- ELEMENTARY B			
WILLIS MUSIC COMPANY		9570	1.25
ALLISON, I.--ED	ALLISON, I.		
IRL ALLISON PIANO LIBRARY -- ELEMENTARY C			
WILLIS MUSIC COMPANY		9571	1.25
ALLISON, I.--ED	ALLISON, I.		
IRL ALLISON PIANO LIBRARY -- ELEMENTARY D			
WILLIS MUSIC COMPANY		9572	1.25
ALLISON, I.--ED	ALLISON, I.		
IRL ALLISON PIANO LIBRARY -- INTERMEDIATE A, PRG 01			
WILLIS MUSIC COMPANY		9548	1.50
ALLISON, I.--ED	ALLISON, I.		
IRL ALLISON PIANO LIBRARY -- INTERMEDIATE A, PRG 02			
WILLIS MUSIC COMPANY		9549	1.50
ALLISON, I.--ED	ALLISON, I.		
IRL ALLISON PIANO LIBRARY -- INTERMEDIATE B, PRG 01			
WILLIS MUSIC COMPANY		9550	1.50
ALLISON, I.--ED	ALLISON, I.		
IRL ALLISON PIANO LIBRARY -- INTERMEDIATE B, PRG 02			
WILLIS MUSIC COMPANY		9551	1.50
ALLISON, I.--ED	ALLISON, I.		
IRL ALLISON PIANO LIBRARY -- INTERMEDIATE C, PRG 01			
WILLIS MUSIC COMPANY		9552	1.50
ALLISON, I.--ED	ALLISON, I.		
IRL ALLISON PIANO LIBRARY -- INTERMEDIATE C, PRG 02			
WILLIS MUSIC COMPANY		9553	1.50
ALLISON, I.--ED	ALLISON, I.		
IRL ALLISON PIANO LIBRARY -- INTERMEDIATE D, PRG 01			
WILLIS MUSIC COMPANY		9554	1.50
ALLISON, I.--ED	ALLISON, I.		
IRL ALLISON PIANO LIBRARY -- INTERMEDIATE D, PRG 02			
WILLIS MUSIC COMPANY		9555	1.50
ALLISON, I.--ED	ALLISON, I.		
IRL ALLISON PIANO LIBRARY -- INTERMEDIATE E, PRG 01			
WILLIS MUSIC COMPANY		9556	1.50
ALLISON, I.--ED	ALLISON, I.		
IRL ALLISON PIANO LIBRARY -- INTERMEDIATE E, PRG 02			
WILLIS MUSIC COMPANY		9557	1.50
ALLISON, I.--ED	ALLISON, I.		
IRL ALLISON PIANO LIBRARY -- INTERMEDIATE F, PRG 01			
WILLIS MUSIC COMPANY		9558	1.50
ALLISON, I.--ED	ALLISON, I.		
IRL ALLISON PIANO LIBRARY -- INTERMEDIATE F, PRG 02			
WILLIS MUSIC COMPANY		9559	1.50
ALLISON, I.--ED	ALLISON, I.		
IRL ALLISON PIANO LIBRARY -- PREPARATORY A, PRG 01			
WILLIS MUSIC COMPANY		9560	1.75
ALLISON, I.--ED	ALLISON, I.		
IRL ALLISON PIANO LIBRARY -- PREPARATORY A, PRG 02			
WILLIS MUSIC COMPANY		9561	1.75
ALLISON, I.--ED	ALLISON, I.		
IRL ALLISON PIANO LIBRARY -- PREPARATORY B, PRG 01			
WILLIS MUSIC COMPANY		9562	1.75
ALLISON, I.--ED	ALLISON, I.		
IRL ALLISON PIANO LIBRARY -- PREPARATORY B, PRG 02			
WILLIS MUSIC COMPANY		9563	1.75
ALLISON, I.--ED	ALLISON, I.		
IRL ALLISON PIANO LIBRARY -- PREPARATORY C, PRG 01			
WILLIS MUSIC COMPANY		9564	1.75
ALLISON, I.--ED	ALLISON, I.		
IRL ALLISON PIANO LIBRARY -- PREPARATORY C, PRG 02			
WILLIS MUSIC COMPANY		9565	1.75
ALLISON, I.--ED	ALLISON, I.		
IRL ALLISON PIANO LIBRARY -- PREPARATORY D, PRG 01			
WILLIS MUSIC COMPANY		9566	1.75
ALLISON, I.--ED	ALLISON, I.		
IRL ALLISON PIANO LIBRARY -- PREPARATORY D, PRG 02			
WILLIS MUSIC COMPANY		9567	1.75
ALLISON, I.--ED	ALLISON, I.		
MY VERY FIRST PIANO PROGRAM			
WILLIS MUSIC COMPANY			1.25
ALLWOOD *	STEVENS	3	
ALTENGLISCHE KLAVIERMUSIK - 14 STUCKE			
BARENREITER VERLAG		BA 2663	
ALOTIN, Y.			
SIX PIANO PIECES FOR CHILDREN			
ISRAEL MUSIC INSTITUTE			2.25
ALOTIN, Y.			
THREE PRELUDES			
ISRAEL MUSIC INSTITUTE			3.75
ALT, H.			
AFTERNOONS -- 14 EARLY-GRADE PIANO PIECES BASED ON THE WHITE KEY			
MAJOR AND MINOR CHORDS--			
THEODORE PRESSER COMPANY			1.25

ALT, H.
    MY MUSICAL DIARY
        EDWARD B. MARKS MUSIC CORPORATION   01.00
ALT, H.
    WEIGHTLESS, AND MECHANICAL MAN
        OXFORD UNIVERSITY PRESS   93.337   .40
ALT, H.--ED   ALT, H.
    SONGS OF A SWISS SUMMER
        WILLIS MUSIC COMPANY   1.50
AMMONS
    FIVE BOOGIE WOOGIE PIANO SOLOS
        MCA MUSIC   1.00
ANDERGASSEN
    THREE PIECES, OP. 84
        ASSOCIATED MUSIC PUBLISHERS, INC.   DOB   1.50
ANDERSON, G.
    THREE PRELUDES FOR PIANO
        AMERICAN MUSIC EDITION   1.00
ANDERSON, L.   NEVIN
    LEROY ANDERSON'S BEST
        BELWIN-MILLS PUBLISHING CORPORATION   2.00
ANDERSON, L.
    MUSIC OF LEROY ANDERSON, THE -- BK. 1
        BELWIN-MILLS PUBLISHING CORPORATION   11331   1.25
ANDREWS--ED   ANDREWS   AI
    TIME TO PLAY WALTZES
        WILLIS MUSIC COMPANY   1.00
ANDRIESSEN, J.   E
    FOUR SONATINAS
        C. F. PETERS CORPORATION   B646   1.50
ANDRIESSEN, J.   M
    THREE BAGATELLES
        C. F. PETERS CORPORATION   B816   .90
ANDRIESSEN, J.   E
    THREE DANCES
        C. F. PETERS CORPORATION   B770   1.25
ANDRIESSEN, J.   D
    TWO ETUDES
        C. F. PETERS CORPORATION   D204   1.50
ANGLES   CLIMENT
    SONATA IN E MINOR AND SONATA IN F
        ASSOCIATED MUSIC PUBLISHERS, INC.   UME   1.75
ANSON, G.
    CHRISTMAS BOOK FOR PIANISTS
        ELKAN-VOGEL, INC.   1.50
ANSON, G.
    PEDAL PATTERNS
        WILLIS MUSIC COMPANY   1.25
ANSON, G.
    PEDAL PUSHERS
        WILLIS MUSIC COMPANY   1.25
ANSON, G.
    SHAPE OF THINGS, THE
        WILLIS MUSIC COMPANY   1.25
ANSON, G.
    TECHNIC TWISTERS
        PRO-ART PUBLICATIONS, INC.   306   .85
ANSON, G.
    TEN TUNES FOR TEN FINGERS
        ELKAN-VOGEL, INC.   .85
ANSON, G.--ED   ANSON, G.
    ANSON INTRODUCES THE SONATA SAMPLER, BK. 1
        WILLIS MUSIC COMPANY   1.50
ANSON, G.--ED   ANSON, G.
    ANSON INTRODUCES THE SONATA SAMPLER, BK. 2
        WILLIS MUSIC COMPANY   1.25
ANSON, G.--ED   ANSON, G.
    ANSON INTRODUCES THE SONATA SAMPLER, BK. 3
        WILLIS MUSIC COMPANY   2.00
ANSON, G.--ED   ANSON, G.   ELEMENTARY
    HAPPY HOLIDAY
        WILLIS MUSIC COMPANY   1.00
ANSON, G.--ED   ANSON, G.
    NEW DIRECTIONS
        WILLIS MUSIC COMPANY   1.25
ANSON, G.--ED   ANSON, G.
    NIGHT MUSIC
        WILLIS MUSIC COMPANY   1.50
ANSON, G.--ED   ANSON, G.
    SURVEY OF PIANO LITERATURE -- LEVEL 1, BK.2 -- THE ROMANTIC
    COMPOSERS
        ELKAN-VOGEL, INC.   1.25
ANSON, G.--ED   ANSON, G.
    SURVEY OF PIANO LITERATURE -- LEVEL 1, BK.3 -- THE CONTEMPORARY
    COMPOSERS
        ELKAN-VOGEL, INC.   1.10
ANSON, G.--ED   ANSON, G.
    SURVEY OF PIANO LITERATURE-- LEVEL 1, BK. 1 -- EARLY KEYBOARD
    MUSIC
        ELKAN-VOGEL, INC.   1.75
ANSON, G.--ED   ANSON, G.
    THIRTY PIECES IN THIRTY KEYS, BK. 1
        WILLIS MUSIC COMPANY   1.00
ANSON, G.--ED   ANSON, G.
    THIRTY PIECES IN THIRTY KEYS, BK. 2
        WILLIS MUSIC COMPANY   1.00
ANTHEIL, G.
    PIANO PASTELS
        WEINTRAUB MUSIC COMPANY   070061   2.50
ANTHONY, G. W.
    CIRCUS PARTY
        THEODORE PRESSER COMPANY   1.00
ANTHONY, G. W.
    LITTLE PIANO SCENES
        THEODORE PRESSER COMPANY   1.25
ANTHONY, G. W.--ED   ANTHONY, G. W.
    COMPOSERS FOR THE KEYBOARD -- FROM BEETHOVEN TO SHOSTAKOVICH,
    EASY BK. 2
        THEODORE PRESSER COMPANY   1.75
ANTHONY, G. W.--ED   ANTHONY, G. W.
    COMPOSERS FOR THE KEYBOARD -- FROM BYRD TO BEETHOVEN,
    INTERMEDIATE BK. 1
        THEODORE PRESSER COMPANY   1.95
ANTHONY, G. W.--ED   ANTHONY, G. W.
    COMPOSERS FOR THE KEYBOARD -- FROM PURCELL TO MOZART, EASY BK. 1
        THEODORE PRESSER COMPANY   1.75
ANTHONY, G. W.--ED   ANTHONY, G. W.
    COMPOSERS FOR THE KEYBOARD -- FROM SCHUBERT TO SHOSTAKOVICH,
    INTERMEDIATE BK. 2
        THEODORE PRESSER COMPANY   1.75
ANTHONY, G. W.--ED   ANTHONY, G. W.
    EASY ALBUM FOR BOYS
        THEODORE PRESSER COMPANY   1.25
ANTHONY, G. W.--ED   ANTHONY, G. W.
    EASY ALBUM FOR GIRLS
        THEODORE PRESSER COMPANY   1.25

ANTHONY, G. W.--ED   ANTHONY, G. W.
    HIGHLIGHTS OF FAMILIAR HYMNS IN TRANSCRIPTION
        THEODORE PRESSER COMPANY   2.95
ANTHONY, G. W.--ED   ANTHONY, G. W.
    HIGHLIGHTS OF FAMILIAR MUSIC, BK. 1, INTERNATIONAL EDITION
        THEODORE PRESSER COMPANY   1.50
ANTHONY, G. W.--ED   ANTHONY, G. W.
    HIGHLIGHTS OF FAMILIAR MUSIC, BK. 2, INTERNATIONAL EDITION
        THEODORE PRESSER COMPANY   1.25
ANTHONY, G. W.--ED   ANTHONY, G. W.
    HIGHLIGHTS OF FAMILIAR REPERTOIRE
        THEODORE PRESSER COMPANY   2.00
ANTHONY, G. W.--ED   ANTHONY, G. W.
    HIGHLIGHTS OF FAMILIAR SACRED MUSIC
        THEODORE PRESSER COMPANY   2.95
ANTHONY, G. W.--ED   ANTHONY, G. W.
    MOMENTS AT THE PIANO
        THEODORE PRESSER COMPANY   1.25
ANTHONY, G. W.--ED   ANTHONY, G. W.
    MUSICAL VISIT TO FOREIGN LANDS, A -- 13 RECITAL AND RECREATIONAL
    PIECES
        THEODORE PRESSER COMPANY   1.25
ANTHONY, G. W.--ED   ANTHONY, G. W.
    MUSICAL VISIT TO OUTER SPACE, A -- 9 RECITAL AND RECREATIONAL
    PIECES
        THEODORE PRESSER COMPANY   1.25
ANTHONY, G. W.--ED   ANTHONY, G. W.
    MUSICAL VISIT TO THE CITY, A -- 12 RECITAL AND RECREATIONAL
    PIECES
        THEODORE PRESSER COMPANY   1.25
ANTHONY, G. W.--ED   ANTHONY, G. W.
    MUSICAL VISIT TO THE COUNTRY, A -- 14 RECITAL AND RECREATIONAL
    PIECES
        THEODORE PRESSER COMPANY   1.25
ANTHONY, G. W.--ED   ANTHONY, G. W.
    MUSICAL VISIT TO THE PARK, A -- 15 RECITAL AND RECREATIONAL
    PIECES
        THEODORE PRESSER COMPANY   1.25
ANTHONY, G. W.--ED   ANTHONY, G. W.
    ON THE MOVE -- SEVEN EASY ACTIVITIES
        THEODORE PRESSER COMPANY   1.25
ANTHONY, G. W.--ED   ANTHONY, G. W.
    PIANO DIVERSIONS, BK. 1
        THEODORE PRESSER COMPANY   1.25
ANTHONY, G. W.--ED   ANTHONY, G. W.
    PIANO DIVERSIONS, BK. 2
        THEODORE PRESSER COMPANY   1.25
ANTHONY, G. W.--ED   ANTHONY, G. W.
    REAL COOL PIANO
        THEODORE PRESSER COMPANY   1.25
ANTHONY, G. W.--ED   ANTHONY, G. W.
    YOUR FAVORITE SOLOS
        THEODORE PRESSER COMPANY   2.00
ANTHONY, G. W.--ED   ANTHONY, G. W.
    YOUR FAVORITE SOLOS FOR ADVANCED PIANISTS
        THEODORE PRESSER COMPANY   1.50
ANTHONY, G. W.--ED   ANTHONY, G. W.
    YOUR VERY FIRST FAVORITE SOLOS
        THEODORE PRESSER COMPANY   1.50
APEL, W.--ED   APEL, W.   2-3
    MUSIK AUS FRUHER ZEIT -- 1350-1650, BAND 01 - DEUTSCHLAND UND
    ITALIEN
        SCHOTT   2341   2.50
APEL, W.--ED   APEL, W.   2-3
    MUSIK AUS FRUHER ZEIT -- 1350-1650, BAND 02 - ENGLAND,
    FRANKRICH, SPANIEN
        SCHOTT   2342   2.50
APOSTEL
    FOUR LITTLE PIECES, OP. 31A, AND FANTASY, OP. 31B
        ASSOCIATED MUSIC PUBLISHERS, INC.   DOB   2.00
APOSTEL
    KUBINIANA OP. 13 --10 PIECES--
        UNIVERSAL EDITION   11776   3.60
APOSTEL
    SUITE 'CONCISE'--7 PIECES--
        UNIVERSAL EDITION   12512   1.50
APREA
    JUVENILIA -- THIRTY-FIVE LITTLE PIECES FOR THE BEGINNER
        FRANCO COLOMBO PUBLICATIONS   128504   3.25
ARANY--ED   ARANY
    HAVE FUN PLAYING PIANO
        MUSIC SALES CORPORATION   040033   2.95
ARCHER, V.
    ELEVEN SHORT PIECES
        EDITORIAL COOPERATIVA INTER-AMERICANA   01.60
ARCHER, V.
    MINUTE MUSIC FOR SMALL HANDS
        PEER SOUTHERN ORGANIZATION   01.50
ARDEVOL, J.
    SEIS PIEZAS
        PEER SOUTHERN ORGANIZATION   01.50
ARENSKY, A.   MIROVITCH, A.
    SIX RECITAL PIECES FOR PIANO DUET, OP. 34-- VOL. 3 OF THE
    STUDENT PIANIST
        MCA MUSIC   1.50
ARISTA--ED   ARISTA
    COLLECCION DE BAILES POPULARES ESPANOLES -- 26 POPULAR SPANISH
    DANCES
        ASSOCIATED MUSIC PUBLISHERS, INC.   UME   3.75
ARMA, P.
    TOUR OF THE WORLD IN TWENTY MINUTES --18 EASY PIECES--
        LES EDITIONS OUVRIERES   3.00
ARMOUR
    MODERN PIANO METHOD FOR BEGINNERS, A, PART 1, LEARNING THE
    LETTERS ON THE KEYBOARD
        CENTURY MUSIC PUBLISHING COMPANY, INC. 3196   .40
ARMOUR
    MODERN PIANO METHOD FOR BEGINNERS, A, PART 2, NOTES, BARS,
    MEASURES, TIME SIGNATURES
        CENTURY MUSIC PUBLISHING COMPANY, INC. 3197   .40
ARMOUR
    MODERN PIANO METHOD FOR BEGINNERS, A, PART 3, WRITING AND FIVE
    FINGER EXERCISES
        CENTURY MUSIC PUBLISHING COMPANY, INC. 3198   .40
ARMOUR
    MODERN PIANO METHOD FOR BEGINNERS, A, PART 4, THE 2/4 TIME
    SIGNATURE
        CENTURY MUSIC PUBLISHING COMPANY, INC. 3199   .40
ARMOUR
    MODERN PIANO METHOD FOR BEGINNERS, A, PART 5, INTRODUCING THE
    EIGTH NOTE
        CENTURY MUSIC PUBLISHING COMPANY, INC. 3200   .40
ARNELL   E
    FOUR IN D
        C. F. PETERS CORPORATION   H724   .90
ARNO--ED.   ARNO
    SACRED HOUR AT THE PIANO
        CARL FISCHER, INC.   O 3255   2.00

ARNOLD, F.
  CHILD'S CZERNY
    THEODORE PRESSER COMPANY   1.75
ARRIAGA, J. C. DE
  ESTUDIOS O CAPRICHOS
    ASSOCIATED MUSIC PUBLISHERS, INC.   UME   1.75
ARRIEU
  IMPROVISATIONS
    FRANCO COLOMBO PUBLICATIONS   A146   1.00
ARRIEU
  QUATRE ETUDES-CAPRICES
    FRANCO COLOMBO PUBLICATIONS   R1413   2.25
ASCHER, L.
  TWO PIANO PIECES
    BOOSEY AND HAWKES, INC.   .50
ASHFORD
  PIANO VOLUNTARIES NO. 1
    LORENZ PUBLISHING COMPANY   2.50
ASINS ARBO
  FLAMENCO -- THREE PIECES
    ASSOCIATED MUSIC PUBLISHERS, INC.   UME   1.00
ASINS ARBO
  FOUR POPULAR CASTILIAN MELODIES
    ASSOCIATED MUSIC PUBLISHERS, INC.   UME   .75
ATKINS
  TWO PIECES
    FRANCO COLOMBO PUBLICATIONS   SAL   2.75
AUBERGE, A. D'
  PIANO COURSE, BK. 1
    ALFRED MUSIC COMPANY   502   1.50
AUBERGE, A. D'
  PIANO COURSE, BK. 2
    ALFRED MUSIC COMPANY   504   1.50
AUBERGE, A. D'
  PIANO COURSE, BK. 3
    ALFRED MUSIC COMPANY   506   1.50
AUBERGE, A. D'
  PIANO COURSE, BK. 4
    ALFRED MUSIC COMPANY   507   1.50
AUBERGE, A. D'
  PIANO COURSE, BK. 5
    ALFRED MUSIC COMPANY   508   1.50
AUBERGE, A. D'
  PIANO COURSE, BK. 6
    ALFRED MUSIC COMPANY   509   1.50
AUBERGE, A. D'
  RECITAL BOOKS, BK. 1
    ALFRED MUSIC COMPANY   510   1.25
AUBERGE, A. D'
  RECITAL BOOKS, BK. 2
    ALFRED MUSIC COMPANY   511   1.25
AUBERGE, A. D'
  RECITAL BOOKS, BK. 3
    ALFRED MUSIC COMPANY   512   1.25
AUCLERT
  THREE SHORT PIECES
    FRANCO COLOMBO PUBLICATIONS   R1846   1.50
AULD, W. J.
  CHRISTMAS TRANSCRIPTIONS FOR PIANO
    LILLENAS PUBLISHING COMPANY   MC-203   1.95
AULD, W. J.
  HANDBOOK FOR CHURCH PIANIST
    LILLENAS PUBLISHING COMPANY   MB-061   1.50
AULD, W. J.
  PIANO HYMNSCRIPTIONS NO. 1
    LILLENAS PUBLISHING COMPANY   MB-148   2.50
AULD, W. J.
  PIANO HYMNSCRIPTIONS NO. 2
    LILLENAS PUBLISHING COMPANY   MB-149   2.50
AULD, W. J.
  SACRED TRANSCRIPTIONS -- PIANO NO. 1
    LILLENAS PUBLISHING COMPANY   MB-178   2.95
AULD, W. J.
  SACRED TRANSCRIPTIONS -- PIANO NO. 2
    LILLENAS PUBLISHING COMPANY   MB-179   2.95
AULD, W. J.
  SACRED TRANSCRIPTIONS -- PIANO NO. 3
    LILLENAS PUBLISHING COMPANY   MB-180   2.95
AURIC *
  ALBUM DES 'SIX' --THE FRENCH SIX--
    ASSOCIATED MUSIC PUBLISHERS, INC.   ESC   5.00
AURIC
  NINE SHORT PIECES -- 1941 --
    ASSOCIATED MUSIC PUBLISHERS, INC.   ESC   4.75
AURIC
  PETITE SUITE
    HEUGEL ET CIE.   2.00
AURIC
  THREE IMPROMPTUS -- 1940 --
    ASSOCIATED MUSIC PUBLISHERS, INC.   ESC   3.50
AXMANN *   1
  ALBUM MODERNER TSCHECHISCHER KOMPONISTEN 1947 - BAND 2, 16
  KLAVIERSTUCKE
    BARENREITER VERLAG   AP 500B
AXMANN   3
  SIEBEN KLAVIERKOMPOSITIONEN
    BARENREITER VERLAG   AP 503
BABBITT
  THREE COMPOSITIONS
    ASSOCIATED MUSIC PUBLISHERS, INC.   BMP   3.00
BABIN
  THREE PIANO PIECES
    MCA MUSIC   1.75
BACARISSE
  HERALDOS -- THREE PIECES
    ASSOCIATED MUSIC PUBLISHERS, INC.   UME   1.00
BACARISSE
  TWENTY-FOUR PRELUDES, OP. 34
    ASSOCIATED MUSIC PUBLISHERS, INC.   UME   1.50
BACH, C.P.E.   KREBS *
  DIE SECHS SAMMLUNGEN VON SONATEN, FREIEN FANTASIEN AND RONDOS
  FUR KENNER UND LIEBHABER--VOL 1.
    ASSOCIATED MUSIC PUBLISHERS, INC.   B/H   2.25
BACH, C.P.E.   KREBS *
  DIE SECHS SAMMLUNGEN VON SONATEN, FREIEN FANTASIEN UND RONDOS
  FUR KENNER UND LIEBHABER--VOL. 2
    ASSOCIATED MUSIC PUBLISHERS, INC.   B/H   2.25
BACH, C.P.E.   KREBS *
  DIE SECHS SAMMLUNGEN VON SONATEN, FREIEN FANTASIEN UND RONDOS
  FUR KENNER UND LIEBHABER--VOL. 3
    ASSOCIATED MUSIC PUBLISHERS, INC.   B/H   2.25
BACH, C.P.E.   KREBS *
  DIE SECHS SAMMLUNGEN VON SONATEN, FREIEN FANTASIEN UND RONDOS
  FUR KENNER UND LIEBHABER--VOL. 4
    ASSOCIATED MUSIC PUBLISHERS, INC.   B/H   2.25

BACH, C.P.E.   KREBS *
  DIE SECHS SAMMLUNGEN VON SONATEN, FREIEN FANTASIEN UND RONDOS
  FUR KENNER UND LIEBHABER--VOL. 5
    ASSOCIATED MUSIC PUBLISHERS, INC.   B/H   2.25
BACH, C.P.E.   KREBS *
  DIE SECHS SAMMLUNGEN VON SONATEN, FREIEN FANTASIEN UND RONDOS
  FUR KENNER UND LIEBHABER--VOL. 6
    ASSOCIATED MUSIC PUBLISHERS, INC.   B/H   2.25
BACH, C.P.E.   ZUERCHER   2-3
  DREI LEICHTE KLAVIERSONATEN
    SCHOTT   4707   2.25
BACH, C.P.E.   ZURCHER   2-3
  DREI LEICHTE KLAVIERSONATEN
    SCHOTT   4707   2.25
BACH, C.P.E.   VRIESLANDER
  EASY SONATAS, WQ 22
    BARENREITER VERLAG   NMA 93   4.00
BACH, C.P.E.   VRIESLANDER
  FOUR EASY SONATAS
    ASSOCIATED MUSIC PUBLISHERS, INC.   NAG   4.00
BACH, C.P.E.   FISCHER, HANS *   E-M
  GERMAN KEYBOARD MUSIC OF THE SEVENTEENTH AND EIGHTEENTH
  CENTURIES, VOL. 7* C. P. E. BACH
    C. F. PETERS CORPORATION   V126   2.00
BACH, C.P.E.   VRIESLANDER   2-3
  KLEINE STUCKE FUR KLAVIER -- 10 STUCKE AUS 'MUSIKALISCHES
  VIELERLEY', 7 STUCKE AUS 'CLAVIERSTUCKE VERSCHIEDENER ART', ARIOSO
  CON VARIAZIONI WQ 118-4, SEI SONATINE NUOVE --
    BARENREITER VERLAG   NMA 65
BACH, C.P.E.   JONAS
  KURZE AND LEICHTE STUCKE
    UNIVERSAL EDITION   13311   3.85
BACH, C.P.E.   VRIESLANDER   2-3
  LEICHTE SONATEN -- G, A MINOR, G MINOR, D, WQ 22, 33, 11, 14 --
    BARENREITER VERLAG   NMA 90
BACH, C.P.E.   VRIESLANDER
  LITTLE KEYBOARD PIECES
    BARENREITER VERLAG   NMA 65   3.00
BACH, C.P.E.   E-M
  MUSIKALISCHES MANCHERLEI--6 PIECES PUBLISHED FOR THE FIRST
  TIME--
    C. F. PETERS CORPORATION   N3121   1.50
BACH, C.P.E.   SCHENKER, H.
  PIANO COMPOSITIONS, BK. 1
    UNIVERSAL EDITION   548A   4.30
BACH, C.P.E.   SCHENKER, H.
  PIANO COMPOSITIONS, BK. 2
    UNIVERSAL EDITION   548B   4.30
BACH, C.P.E.   WUHRER
  POLONAISES, NOS. 03 AND 04
    ASSOCIATED MUSIC PUBLISHERS, INC.   OBV   .50
BACH, C.P.E.   STEGLICH   3
  PREUSSISCHEN SONATEN, DIE, WQ 48, HEFT 1 -- B, B FLAT, E --
    BARENREITER VERLAG   NMA 6
BACH, C.P.E.   STEGLICH   3
  PREUSSISCHEN SONATEN, DIE, WQ 48, HEFT 2 -- C MINOR, C, A --
    BARENREITER VERLAG   NMA 15
BACH, C.P.E.   STEGLICH
  PREUSSISCHEN SONATEN, VOL. 1
    ASSOCIATED MUSIC PUBLISHERS, INC.   NAG   3.50
BACH, C.P.E.   STEGLICH
  PREUSSISCHEN SONATEN, VOL. 2
    ASSOCIATED MUSIC PUBLISHERS, INC.   NAG   3.50
BACH, C.P.E.   STEGLICH
  PRUSSIAN SONATAS WQ 48, BK. 1
    BARENREITER VERLAG   NMA 6   3.25
BACH, C.P.E.   STEGLICH
  PRUSSIAN SONATAS WQ 48, BK. 2
    BARENREITER VERLAG   NMA 15   3.50
BACH, C.P.E.   DOFLEIN   3
  SECHS SONATEN ZU DEM VERSUCH UBER DIE WAHRE ART, DAS CLAVIER ZU
  SPIELEN, BK. 1
    SCHOTT   2353   2.25
BACH, C.P.E.   DOFLEIN   3
  SECHS SONATEN ZU DEM VERSUCH UBER DIE WAHRE ART, DAS CLAVIER ZU
  SPIELEN, BK. 2
    SCHOTT   2354   2.25
BACH, C.P.E.   DOFLEIN   3
  SECHS SONATEN ZU DEM, VERSUCH UBER DIE WAHRE ART, DAS CLAVIER ZU
  SPIELEN, BK. 1
    SCHOTT   2353   2.25
BACH, C.P.E.   DOFLEIN   3
  SECHS SONATEN ZU DEM, VERSUCH UBER DIE WAHRE ART, DAS CLAVIER ZU
  SPIELEN, BK. 2
    SCHOTT   2354   2.25
BACH, C.P.E.   LUITHLEN AND KRAUS
  SELECTED PIANO PIECES
    UNIVERSAL EDITION   11015   1.80
BACH, C.P.E.
  SIX PRUSSIAN SONATAS, BK. 1
    EDWIN F. KALMUS   3090   2.00
BACH, C.P.E.
  SIX PRUSSIAN SONATAS, BK. 2
    EDWIN F. KALMUS   3091   2.00
BACH, C.P.E.   HOFFMAN *
  SIX SONATAS
    ASSOCIATED MUSIC PUBLISHERS, INC.   B/H   3.75
BACH, C.P.E.   BUELOW
  SIX SONATAS
    FRANCO COLOMBO PUBLICATIONS   ER139   2.25
BACH, C.P.E.   BUELOW
  SIX SONATAS
    INTERNATIONAL MUSIC COMPANY   3.50
BACH, C.P.E.   FEDTKE   M
  SIX SONATAS--A, B FLAT, F, A MINOR, D, G MINOR--
    C. F. PETERS CORPORATION   8339A   5.00
BACH, C.P.E.   BUELOW   M-D
  SIX SONATAS--F MINOR, A MINOR, A, G, D MINOR, A FLAT--
    C. F. PETERS CORPORATION   276   5.00
BACH, C.P.E.
  SIX WURTTEMBERG SONATAS, BK. 1
    EDWIN F. KALMUS   3088   2.00
BACH, C.P.E.
  SIX WURTTEMBERG SONATAS, BK. 2
    EDWIN F. KALMUS   3089   2.00
BACH, C.P.E.   STEGLICH
  SIX WURTTEMBERG SONATAS, VOL. 1
    ASSOCIATED MUSIC PUBLISHERS, INC.   NAG   4.00
BACH, C.P.E.   HERMANN
  SONATAS AND PIECES, URTEXT--4 SONATAS, 12 VARIATIONS ON LA FOLIE
  D'ESPAGNE, RONDO IN E FLAT, 4 ALLEGROS, LA STAHL--
    C. F. PETERS CORPORATION   4188   2.00
BACH, C.P.E.
  SONATAS, FANTASIES, AND RONDOS, BK. 1
    EDWIN F. KALMUS   3092   3.50
BACH, C.P.E.
  SONATAS, FANTASIES, AND RONDOS, BK. 2
    EDWIN F. KALMUS   3093   3.50

BACH, C.P.E.   VRIESLANDER
TWENTY-FOUR LITTLE PIECES
        ASSOCIATED MUSIC PUBLISHERS, INC.   NAG   4.00
BACH, C.P.E.   VRIESLANDER
TWENTY-FOUR PIECES
        INTERNATIONAL MUSIC COMPANY   1.75
BACH, C.P.E.   STEGLICH
WURTEMBERG SONATAS WQ 49, BK. 1
        BARENREITER VERLAG   NMA 21   4.00
BACH, C.P.E.   STEGLICH
WURTEMBERG SONATAS WQ 49, BK. 2
        BARENREITER VERLAG   NMA 22   4.00
BACH, C.P.E.   STEGLICH   3
WURTTEMBERGISCHEN SONATEN, DIE, WQ 49, HEFT 1 -- A MINOR, A
FLAT, E MINOR --
        BARENREITER VERLAG   NMA 21
BACH, C.P.E.   STEGLICH   3
WURTTEMBERGISCHEN SONATEN, DIE, WQ 49, HEFT 2 -- B FLAT, E FLAT,
B MINOR --
        BARENREITER VERLAG   NMA 22
BACH, C.P.E.   KREUTZ   3
ZWEI KLAVIERSTUCKE -- FANTASIEFIS-MOLL-RONDO E-MOLL UND D. E.
GROTTHUSS, RONDO
        SCHOTT   4013   2.25
BACH, C.P.E. *   KREUTZ   3
ZWEI KLAVIERSTUCKE --FANTASIE FIS-MOLL, RONDO E-MOLL-- UND RONDO
--GROTTHUSS--
        SCHOTT   4013   2.25
BACH, C.P.E.   KREUTZ   3
ZWEI SONATEN
        SCHOTT   2826   2.25
BACH, C.P.E.   KREUTZ   3
ZWEI SONATEN -- F-ES --
        SCHOTT   2826   2.25
BACH, J. CHRISTIAN *
METHODE OU RECUEIL DE CONNOISANCES ELEMENTAIRES POUR LE
FORTEPIANO OU CLAVECIN
        BROUDE BROTHERS LTD.   27.50
BACH, J. CHRISTIAN   LANDSHOFF   M
SONATAS, VOL. 1
        C. F. PETERS CORPORATION   3831A   1.50
BACH, J. CHRISTIAN   LANDSHOFF   M
SONATAS, VOL. 2
        C. F. PETERS CORPORATION   3831B   1.50
BACH, J. CHRISTIAN *   NEWMAN, W.   MD
SONS OF BACH -- THREE SONATAS FOR KEYBOARD
        THEODORE PRESSER COMPANY   1.50
BACH, J. CHRISTOPH   KREUTZ   2-3
LEICHTE KLAVIERSTUCKE A. D., MUSIKALISCHEN NEBENSTUNDEN
        SCHOTT   3768   1.75
BACH, J. CHRISTOPH   RUF *   3-4
SECHS LEICHTE SONATEN -- AUCH CEMBALO
        SCHOTT   5773   3.25
BACH, J.S.   HEINZE
ALBUM--TWENTY-ONE FAVORITE PIECES
        G. SCHIRMER, INC.   L12   1.25
BACH, J.S.   HEINZE   E-M
ALBUM, 21 FAVORITE PIECES FROM SUITES, PARTITAS, ETC.
        C. F. PETERS CORPORATION   1820   2.00
BACH, J.S.   KELLER
ANNA MAGDALENA BACH'S MUSIC BOOK -- URTEXT -- COMPLETE, WITH
BOARD COVER
        C. F. PETERS CORPORATION   4546   5.00
BACH, J.S.   SAUER   E
ANNA MAGDALENA BACH'S MUSIC BOOK--20 PIECES--
        C. F. PETERS CORPORATION   3829   1.25
BACH, J.S.   KELLER   M
ANNA MAGDALENA BACH'S MUSIC BOOK, COMPLETE, URTEXT. HARD COVER
        C. F. PETERS CORPORATION   4546   5.00
BACH, J.S.   ANSON, G.   INTERMEDIATE
ANSON INTRODUCES BACH - DANCE FORMS FROM THE SUITES
        WILLIS MUSIC COMPANY   1.25
BACH, J.S.   ANSON, G.
ANSON INTRODUCES BACH - SELECTIONS FROM THE .ANNA MAGDALENA BACH
NOTEBOOK
        WILLIS MUSIC COMPANY   1.00
BACH, J.S.   ANSON, G.   INTERMEDIATE
ANSON INTRODUCES BACH - TWELVE LITTLE PRELUDES
        WILLIS MUSIC COMPANY   1.25
BACH, J.S.   TOVEY, D.
ART OF THE FUGUE
        OXFORD UNIVERSITY PRESS   32.064   5.00
BACH, J.S.   3-4
AUSWAHL --25 AUSGEWAHLTE STUCKE--
        SCHOTT   5180   1.75
BACH, J.S.
BACH
        ASHLEY DEALERS SERVICE, INC.   HG 06   2.95
BACH, J.S.   HEINZE
BACH ALBUM
        CARL FISCHER, INC.   L 562   1.50
BACH, J.S.   WAGNESS   GR. 2-3
BACH FAMILY, THE. VOL. 1
        SHAWNEE PRESS, INC.   2.00
BACH, J.S.   WAGNESS   GR. 2-3
BACH FAMILY, THE. VOL. 2
        SHAWNEE PRESS, INC.   2.00
BACH, J.S.   VINCENT
BACH FOR BEGINNERS, BK. 1
        BOOSEY AND HAWKES, INC.   .90
BACH, J.S.   VINCENT
BACH FOR BEGINNERS, BK. 2
        BOOSEY AND HAWKES, INC.   .90
BACH, J.S.   TREHARNE
BACH FOR EARLY GRADES, BOOK 1
        BOSTON MUSIC COMPANY   1.25
BACH, J.S.   TREHARNE
BACH FOR EARLY GRADES, BOOK 2
        BOSTON MUSIC COMPANY   1.25
BACH, J.S.   TREHARNE
BACH FOR EARLY GRADES, BOOK 3
        BOSTON MUSIC COMPANY   1.25
BACH, J.S.   HIRSCHBERG, D.
BACH IS FUN
        MUSICORD PUBLICATIONS, INC.   1.25
BACH, J.S.   HARRIS, R.
BACH ORGAN PRELUDES
        BELWIN-MILLS PUBLISHING CORPORATION   20023   1.25
BACH, J.S.   PALMER, W. A.
BACH--AN INTRODUCTION TO HIS PIANO WORKS
        ALFRED MUSIC COMPANY   638   2.50
BACH, J.S.   SCHAUM, J.   2 1/2
BACH-SCHAUM, BK. 1
        BELWIN-MILLS PUBLISHING CORPORATION   1.25
BACH, J.S.   SCHAUM, J.   2 1/2
BACH-SCHAUM, BK. 1
        BELWIN-MILLS PUBLISHING CORPORATION   1.50

BACH, J.S.   SCHAUM, J.   3-4
BACH-SCHAUM, BK. 2
        BELWIN-MILLS PUBLISHING CORPORATION   1.25
BACH, J.S.   SCHAUM, J.   3-4
BACH-SCHAUM, BK. 2
        BELWIN-MILLS PUBLISHING CORPORATION   1.50
BACH, J.S. *
BACH, BEETHOVEN AND BRAHMS
        MUSIC SALES CORPORATION   020009   2.95
BACH, J.S.   TREDE   2-3
BACHBUCHLEIN FUR CLAVIER
        SCHOTT   3945   1.75
BACH, J.S.   TREDE   2-3
BACHBUCHLEIN FUR CLAVIER
        SCHOTT   3945   1.75
BACH, J.S.   SCHAUM, J.   2 1/2
BEST OF BACH
        SCHAUM PUBLICATIONS, INC.   1.25
BACH, J.S.   ZIMMERMAN
BOURREE IN C AND BOURREE IN C MINOR
        WILLIS MUSIC COMPANY   .35
BACH, J.S.   BRADLEY, R.
BRADLEY CLASSICAL SERIES - TWO MINUETS IN G
        SCREEN GEMS - COLUMBIA PUBLICATIONS   C0020TP2   .85
BACH, J.S.   M
BRANDENBURG CONCERTO NO. 1
        C. F. PETERS CORPORATION   H304   1.25
BACH, J.S.   D
CAPRICCIO, FANTASY, SONATA, FUGUES, MINUETS
        C. F. PETERS CORPORATION   216   2.50
BACH, J.S.   ERK   E
CHORALES AND SACRED ARIAS--317--MEHRSTIMIGE CHORAELE. NEWLY
REVISED EDITION BY FRIEDRICH SMEND, IN 2 VOLUMES. VOL. 1, 195
CHORALES AND SACRED ARIAS
        C. F. PETERS CORPORATION   4264A   6.00
BACH, J.S.   ERK   E
CHORALES AND SACRED ARIAS--317--MERHSTIMMIGE CHORAELE. NEWLY
REVISED EDITION BY FRIEDRICH SMEND, IN 2 VOLUMES. VOL. 2, 122
CHORALES AND SACRED ARIAS
        C. F. PETERS CORPORATION   4264B   6.00
BACH, J.S.   BUELOW
CHROMATIC FANTASY AND FUGUE, CONCERTO IN THE ITALIAN STYLE,
FANTASY IN C MINOR, PRELUDE AND FUGUE IN A MINOR
        G. SCHIRMER, INC.   L22   1.25
BACH, J.S.   TREDE   2-3
CLAVIER-BUCHLEIN VOR W. FR. BACH
        SCHOTT   3944   1.50
BACH, J.S.   TREDE   2-3
CLAVIER-BUCHLEIN VOR W.F. BACH
        SCHOTT   3944   1.50
BACH, J.S.
CLAVIER-UEBUNG -- KEYBOARD PRACTICE --   PARTS 2-4
        G. HENLE MUSIKVERLAG   129   4.65
BACH, J.S.
CLAVIER-UEBUNG -- KEYBOARD PRACTICE --   PARTS 2-4 -- CLOTH
        G. HENLE MUSIKVERLAG   130   7.70
BACH, J.S.   KELLER   3
DREI FUGEN FUR KLAVIER NACH J. A. REINKEN -- BWV 965, 2, BWV
966, 2, BWV 954
        BARENREITER VERLAG   BA 474
BACH, J.S.   KREUTZ   3
DREISTG. SINFONIEN -- INVENTIONEN, BWV 787-801
        SCHOTT   01096-7   1.75
BACH, J.S.   KREUTZ   3
DREISTG. SINFONIEN --INVENTIONEN-- BWV 787-801
        SCHOTT   01096/7 1/2 1.75
BACH, J.S.   M
DUETS --4-- URTEXT. FOR PIANO SOLO
        C. F. PETERS CORPORATION   4465   1.25
BACH, J.S.   ARMA, P.
EIGHT LITTLE PRELUDES AND FUGUES FOR ORGAN
        EDITIONS MUSICALES TRANSATLANTIQUES   2.80
BACH, J.S.   HENDERSON
EIGHT ORGAN CHORALE-PRELUDES
        G. SCHIRMER, INC.   L1087   1.00
BACH, J.S.   BUONAMICI
EIGHTEEN LITTLE PRELUDES AND FUGUES
        G. SCHIRMER, INC.   L424   1.50
BACH, J.S.   PALMER, W. A.
EIGHTEEN SHORT PRELUDES
        ALFRED MUSIC COMPANY   601   2.00
BACH, J.S.   MUGELLINI
ENGLISH SUITES
        FRANCO COLOMBO PUBLICATIONS   ER2374   2.50
BACH, J.S.
ENGLISH SUITES
        G. HENLE MUSIKVERLAG   100   4.25
BACH, J.S.   BISCHOFF
ENGLISH SUITES
        EDWIN F. KALMUS   3039   2.50
BACH, J.S.
ENGLISH SUITES -- CLOTH
        G. HENLE MUSIKVERLAG   101   7.35
BACH, J.S.   KREUTZ
ENGLISH SUITES -- URTEXT -- VOL. 1
        C. F. PETERS CORPORATION   4580A   2.00
BACH, J.S.   KREUTZ
ENGLISH SUITES -- URTEXT -- VOL. 2
        C. F. PETERS CORPORATION   4580B   2.00
BACH, J.S.
ENGLISH SUITES --URTEXT--, COMPLETE IN 1 VOL. CLOTH-BOUND
        C. F. PETERS CORPORATION   10.00
BACH, J.S.
ENGLISH SUITES 1-3
        G. HENLE MUSIKVERLAG   102   2.35
BACH, J.S.
ENGLISH SUITES 4-6
        G. HENLE MUSIKVERLAG   103   2.35
BACH, J.S.   CZERNY
ENGLISH SUITES--BK. 1, SUITES 1-3
        G. SCHIRMER, INC.   L17   1.50
BACH, J.S.   CZERNY
ENGLISH SUITES--BK. 2, SUITES 4-6
        G. SCHIRMER, INC.   L18   1.50
BACH, J.S.   M-D
ENGLISH SUITES--URTEXT--, VOL. 1
        C. F. PETERS CORPORATION   4580A   2.00
BACH, J.S.   M-D
ENGLISH SUITES--URTEXT--, VOL. 2
        C. F. PETERS CORPORATION   4583B   2.00
BACH, J.S.   RONTGEN
ENGLISH SUITES, BK. 1
        UNIVERSAL EDITION   328   3.60
BACH, J.S.   RONTGEN
ENGLISH SUITES, BK. 2
        UNIVERSAL EDITION   327   3.10

BACH, J.S.   BUSONI *
  ENGLISH SUITES, S. 806-811, VOL. 1
    ASSOCIATED MUSIC PUBLISHERS, INC.   B/H   4.00
BACH, J.S.   BUSONI *
  ENGLISH SUITES, S. 806-811, VOL. 2
    ASSOCIATED MUSIC PUBLISHERS, INC.   B/H   4.00
BACH, J.S.   KREUTZ
  ENGLISH SUITES, ORNAMENTATION, GERMAN TEXT
    C. F. PETERS CORPORATION   4580C   1.25
                                      D
BACH, J.S.
  FANTASIA IN C MINOR AND PRELUDIO CON FUGA IN A MINOR
    C. F. PETERS CORPORATION   207C   2.25
BACH, J.S.
  FANTASIA IN C MINOR, PRELUDIO CON FUGA IN A MINOR, ITALIAN
  CONCERTO IN F, FANTASIA CROMATICA CON FUGA IN D MINOR
    C. F. PETERS CORPORATION   207   3.00
                                      D
BACH, J.S.
  FANTASIAS AND FUGUES, VOL. 1
    C. F. PETERS CORPORATION   212A   2.50
                                      D
BACH, J.S.
  FANTASIAS AND FUGUES, VOL. 2
    C. F. PETERS CORPORATION   212B   2.50
BACH, J.S.   BUSONI *
  FANTASIES AND FUGUES
    ASSOCIATED MUSIC PUBLISHERS, INC.   B/H   1.75
BACH, J.S.
  FANTASIES, PRELUDES AND FUGUES
    G. HENLE MUSIKVERLAG   219
BACH, J.S.
  FANTASIES, PRELUDES AND FUGUES -- CLOTH
    G. HENLE MUSIKVERLAG   220
BACH, J.S.   CZERNY
  FIFTEEN THREE-PART INVENTIONS
    CARL FISCHER, INC.   L 255   1.00
BACH, J.S.   CZERNY
  FIFTEEN TWO-PART INVENTIONS
    CARL FISCHER, INC.   L 254   1.00
                                    BEGINNER
BACH, J.S.
  FIRST BOOK
    EDWIN F. KALMUS   3069   1.25
BACH, J.S.   BRADLEY
  FIRST COMPOSERS - BACH
    FRANCO COLOMBO PUBLICATIONS   LD196   1.00
BACH, J.S.   CARROLL
  FIRST LESSONS IN BACH, BK. 1
    G. SCHIRMER, INC.   L1436   .75
BACH, J.S.   CARROLL
  FIRST LESSONS IN BACH, BK. 2
    G. SCHIRMER, INC.   L1437   .75
BACH, J.S.   CARROLL
  FIRST LESSONS, BK. 1
    CARL FISCHER, INC.   L 917   1.00
BACH, J.S.   CARROLL
  FIRST LESSONS, BK. 1
    THEODORE PRESSER COMPANY   .75
BACH, J.S.   CARROLL
  FIRST LESSONS, BK. 2
    CARL FISCHER, INC.   L 918   .75
BACH, J.S.   CLOUGH *
  FIRST STEPS IN BACH
    BOSTON MUSIC COMPANY   1.00
BACH, J.S.   RUTHARDT   BEGINNER
  FIRST STUDENT, THE, VOL. 1
    EDWIN F. KALMUS   3082   1.25
BACH, J.S.   RUTHARDT   BEGINNER
  FIRST STUDENT, THE, VOL. 2
    EDWIN F. KALMUS   3083   1.25
BACH, J.S.   RUTHARDT   M
  FIRST STUDIES, VOL. 1
    C. F. PETERS CORPORATION   2668A   2.00
BACH, J.S.   RUTHARDT   M
  FIRST STUDIES, VOL. 2
    C. F. PETERS CORPORATION   2668B   2.00
BACH, J.S.   FOOTE
  FIRST YEAR BACH
    SUMMY-BIRCHARD COMPANY   1.25
BACH, J.S.
  FIVE PIECES FROM THE FIRST STUDY OF BACH
    FREDERICK HARRIS MUSIC COMPANY   .30
BACH, J.S.   BUSONI
  FOUR CLAVIER COMPOSITIONS
    ASSOCIATED MUSIC PUBLISHERS, INC.   B/H   3.50
BACH, J.S.
  FOUR DUETS
    G. HENLE MUSIKVERLAG   161   1.55
BACH, J.S.   MUGELLINI
  FOUR PARTITAS AND OVERTURE
    FRANCO COLOMBO PUBLICATIONS   ER2231   4.50
                                      M-D
BACH, J.S.
  FRENCH OVERTURE AND ITALIAN CONCERTO, URTEXT
    C. F. PETERS CORPORATION   4594   2.00
BACH, J.S.   MUGELLINI
  FRENCH SUITES
    FRANCO COLOMBO PUBLICATIONS   ER445B   2.50
BACH, J.S.
  FRENCH SUITES
    G. HENLE MUSIKVERLAG   71   2.70
BACH, J.S.   BISCHOFF
  FRENCH SUITES
    EDWIN F. KALMUS   3041   2.00
BACH, J.S.   CZERNY
  FRENCH SUITES
    G. SCHIRMER, INC.   L19   1.00
BACH, J.S.   RONTGEN
  FRENCH SUITES
    UNIVERSAL EDITION   325   3.80
BACH, J.S.
  FRENCH SUITES -- CLOTH
    G. HENLE MUSIKVERLAG   72   5.80
BACH, J.S.   KELLER
  FRENCH SUITES -- URTEXT --
    C. F. PETERS CORPORATION   4594   2.00
BACH, J.S.
  FRENCH SUITES --URTEXT--, COMPLETE IN 1 VOL. CLOTH-BOUND
    C. F. PETERS CORPORATION   10.00
                                      M
BACH, J.S.
  FRENCH SUITES, URTEXT
    C. F. PETERS CORPORATION   4594   2.00
BACH, J.S.   BISCHOFF
  FUGUES OF THE WELL-TEMPERED CLAVIER
    EDWIN F. KALMUS   3042   3.00
                                      3-4
BACH, J.S.
  FUNFUNDZWANZIG AUSGEWAHLTE STUCKE
    SCHOTT   5180   1.75
BACH, J.S. *   LONGO
  GOLDEN LIBRARY, BK. 7 - BACH, HANDE
    FRANCO COLOMBO PUBLICATIONS   112505   5.50

BACH, J.S.   SAMUEL
  INTRODUCTION TO BACH
    CARL FISCHER, INC.   PT 478   1.00
BACH, J.S.   MIROVITCH, A.
  INTRODUCTION TO THE STUDY OF BACH, VOL. 1
    G. SCHIRMER, INC.   1.25
BACH, J.S.   MIROVITCH, A.
  INTRODUCTION TO THE STUDY OF BACH, VOL. 2
    G. SCHIRMER, INC.   1.25
BACH, J.S.   CZERNY   M-D
  INVENTIONS
    C. F. PETERS CORPORATION   201   2.00
BACH, J.S.   BUSONI
  INVENTIONS -- SINFONIAS -- IN THREE PARTS, S. 787-801
    ASSOCIATED MUSIC PUBLISHERS, INC.   B/H   1.75
BACH, J.S.
  INVENTIONS --URTEXT--, COMPLETE IN 1 VOL. CLOTH-BOUND
    C. F. PETERS CORPORATION   7.50
BACH, J.S.   DADELSEN, G. VON
  INVENTIONS AND SINFONIAS
    BARENREITER VERLAG   BA 5035   9.50
BACH, J.S.
  INVENTIONS AND SINFONIAS
    G. HENLE MUSIKVERLAG   64   2.35
BACH, J.S.
  INVENTIONS AND SINFONIAS -- CLOTH
    G. HENLE MUSIKVERLAG   65   5.40
BACH, J.S.   LANDSHOFF
  INVENTIONS AND SINFONIAS -- URTEXT --
    C. F. PETERS CORPORATION   4201   1.75
BACH, J.S.   FUESSL *
  INVENTIONS AND SINFONIAS --2 AND 3 PART INVENTIONS, BWV
  722-801--, WITHOUT COMMENTARIES
    WIENER URTEXT EDITION   UT 50042A 3.25
BACH, J.S.   FUESSL *
  INVENTIONS AND SINFONIAS --2 AND 3 PART INVENTIONS, BWV
  772-801--
    WIENER URTEXT EDITION   UT 50042   7.50
BACH, J.S.   BUSONI
  INVENTIONS IN TWO PARTS, S. 772-786
    ASSOCIATED MUSIC PUBLISHERS, INC.   AMP   1.00
BACH, J.S.   BUSONI
  INVENTIONS IN TWO PARTS, S. 772-786
    ASSOCIATED MUSIC PUBLISHERS, INC.   B/H   1.00
                                      M
BACH, J.S.
  INVENTIONS. SUPPLEMENT 1‡ SINFONIAS 4, 5, 7, 9, 11 WITH TABLE OF
  EMBELLISHMENTS AND REMARKS FOR RECITAL, MUSICAL EXAMPLES --GERMAN
  TEXT--
    C. F. PETERS CORPORATION   4201B   1.50
BACH, J.S.
  INVENTIONS, FACSIMILE, WITH FOREWORD BY RALPH KIRKPATRICK
    C. F. PETERS CORPORATION   4201A   10.00
BACH, J.S.   LANDSHOFF   M-D
  INVENTIONS, URTEXT. 15 2-PART INVENTIONS AND 15 3-PART
  INVENTIONS--SINFONIAS--
    C. F. PETERS CORPORATION   4201   1.75
BACH, J.S.   MUGELLINI
  INVENTIONS, 2 PART
    FRANCO COLOMBO PUBLICATIONS   ER2266B   1.50
BACH, J.S.   MUGELLINI
  INVENTIONS, 3 PART
    FRANCO COLOMBO PUBLICATIONS   ER2267B   1.50
BACH, J.S.   SOLDAN
  ITALIAN CONCERTO AND FRENCH OVERTURE -- URTEXT --
    C. F. PETERS CORPORATION   4464   2.00
BACH, J.S.   M-D
  ITALIAN CONCERTO AND FRENCH OVERTURE--URTEXT--
    C. F. PETERS CORPORATION   4464   2.00
BACH, J.S.   PETRI
  ITALIAN CONCERTO, S. 971, AND PARTITA IN B MINOR, S. 831
    ASSOCIATED MUSIC PUBLISHERS, INC.   B/H   2.25
BACH, J.S.   PASQUET
  JOHANN SEBASTIAN BACH, BK. 1 -- EARLY INTERMEDIATE
    WILLIS MUSIC COMPANY   1.00
BACH, J.S.   PASQUET
  JOHANN SEBASTIAN BACH, BK. 2 -- ADVANCING INTERMEDIATE
    WILLIS MUSIC COMPANY   1.25
BACH, J.S.   PASQUET
  JOHANN SEBASTIAN BACH, BK. 3 -- EARLY ADVANCED
    WILLIS MUSIC COMPANY   1.00
BACH, J.S.
  KEYBOARD MUSIC -- BACH GESELLSCHAFT EDITION
    DOVER PUBLICATIONS, INC.   22360-4   5.00
BACH, J.S.   DADELSEN, G. VON   3
  KLAVIERBUCHLEIN FUR ANNA MAGDALENA BACH VON 1722 UND 1725 --
  NEUE BACH-AUSGABE --
    BARENREITER VERLAG   BA 5008
BACH, J.S.   DADELSEN, G. VON
  KLAVIERBUCHLEIN FUR ANNA MAGDALENA BACH, 1725 -- BIBLIOPHILE
  AUSGABE NACH DEM URTEXT DER 'NEUEN BACH-AUSGABE' IN
  ORIGINALGETREUEM EINBAND --
    BARENREITER VERLAG   BA 5115
BACH, J.S.   PLATH, W.
  KLAVIERBUCHLEIN FUR WILHELM FRIEDEMANN BACH -- NEUE BACH-AUSGABE
  --
    BARENREITER VERLAG   BA 5021
BACH, J.S.   4
  KLAVIERUBUNG, TEIL 3
    BARENREITER VERLAG   BA 5033
BACH, J.S.   M-D
  KLAVIERUEBUNG --URTEXT--. PART 1‡ PARTITAS, VOL. 1
    C. F. PETERS CORPORATION   4463A   2.00
BACH, J.S.   M-D
  KLAVIERUEBUNG --URTEXT--. PART 1‡ PARTITAS, VOL. 2
    C. F. PETERS CORPORATION   4463B   2.00
BACH, J.S.   M-D
  KLAVIERUEBUNG --URTEXT--. PART 2‡ ITALIAN CONCERTO AND FRENCH
  OVERTURE
    C. F. PETERS CORPORATION   4464   2.00
BACH, J.S.   M
  KLAVIERUEBUNG --URTEXT--. PART 3‡ 4 DUETS --FOR PIANO SOLO--
    C. F. PETERS CORPORATION   4465   1.25
BACH, J.S.   DOFLEIN   1 - 2-3
  KLEINEN KLAVIERSTUCKE, DIE - 27 STUCKE, MEIST AUS DEN
  KLAVIERBUCHLEIN FUR ANNA MAGDALENA UND FRIEDEMANN BACH UND 6 KLEINE
  PRAELUDIEN, BWV 933-938
    BARENREITER VERLAG   BA 1766
BACH, J.S.
  LARGER PIANO COMPOSITIONS, BK. 2
    THEODORE PRESSER COMPANY   5.00
BACH, J.S.   HERMANN
  LITTLE DANCES
    FRANCO COLOMBO PUBLICATIONS   SIK.102   1.50
BACH, J.S.   DOFLEIN
  LITTLE KEYBOARD PIECES, BWV 933-938
    BARENREITER VERLAG   BA 1766   2.50

BACH, J.S.   BISCHOFF
LITTLE KNOWN PIECES
    EDWIN F. KALMUS   3053   1.25
BACH, J.S.   PHILIPP, I.
LITTLE MUSIC BOOK OF ANNA MAGDALENA - 12 SELECTED PIECES -
INTERNATIONAL MUSIC COMPANY   1.25
BACH, J.S.   SAUER   E
LITTLE MUSIC BOOK OF ANNA MAGDALENA BACH --20 PIECES--
    C. F. PETERS CORPORATION   3829   1.25
BACH, J.S.   STEURER   E
LITTLE PIANO BOOK --18 PIECES--
    C. F. PETERS CORPORATION   L5012   1.25
BACH, J.S.
LITTLE PRELUDES
    CENTURY MUSIC PUBLISHING COMPANY,.INC.   4000   .40
BACH, J.S.
LITTLE PRELUDES AND FUGUES
    G. HENLE MUSIKVERLAG   106   2.35
BACH, J.S.   GRIEPENKERL *   M
LITTLE PRELUDES AND FUGUES
    C. F. PETERS CORPORATION   200   2.00
BACH, J.S.   KELLER   M
LITTLE PRELUDES AND FUGUES
    C. F. PETERS CORPORATION   200A   3.00
BACH, J.S.   DEHNHARD
LITTLE PRELUDES AND FUGUES
    WIENER URTEXT EDITION   UT 50041   3.50
BACH, J.S.
LITTLE PRELUDES AND FUGUES -- CLOTH
    G. HENLE MUSIKVERLAG   107   5.40
BACH, J.S.   RUTHARDT   M
LITTLE PRELUDES AND FUGUES --24--
    C. F. PETERS CORPORATION   2791   1.50
BACH, J.S.   BUSONI
LITTLE PRELUDES AND OTHER WORKS
    ASSOCIATED MUSIC PUBLISHERS, INC.   B/H   1.25
BACH, J.S.   HUGHES
MASTER SERIES FOR THE YOUNG--VOL. 01--BACH
    G. SCHIRMER, INC.   1.25
BACH, J.S.   M
MENUETTO, POLACCA, 2 TRIOS --FROM BRANDENBURG CONCERTO NO.1--
    C. F. PETERS CORPORATION   H304   1.25
BACH, J.S.   POZZOLI
MY FIRST BACH-12 PIECES
    FRANCO COLOMBO PUBLICATIONS   ER1951   1.00
BACH, J.S.   WACKERNAGEL
NEUES BACH BUCH
    BOOSEY AND HAWKES, INC.   1.00
BACH, J.S.   DOFLEIN
NEUES BACH-HEFT
    BARENREITER VERLAG   BA 1143   1.75
BACH, J.S.   DOFLEIN   3
NEUES BACH-HEFT. 5 WENIG BEKANNTE STUCKE FUR CEMBALO ODER
KLAVIER
    BARENREITER VERLAG   BA 1143
BACH, J.S.   DOFLEIN   3
NEUES BACH-HEFT. 5 WENIG BEKANNTE STUCKE FUR CEMBALO ODER
KLAVIER
    BARENREITER VERLAG   BA 1143
BACH, J.S.   CHING   EASY
NEW EASY GRADED CLASSIC ALBUM - BACH
    GENERAL WORDS AND MUSIC COMPANY   1.25
BACH, J.S.   BUSONI
NINE CHORALE PRELUDES, VOL. 1
    ASSOCIATED MUSIC PUBLISHERS, INC.   B/H   1.75
BACH, J.S.   BUSONI
NINE CHORALE PRELUDES, VOL. 2
    ASSOCIATED MUSIC PUBLISHERS, INC.   B/H   1.75
BACH, J.S.   BISCHOFF   BEGINNER
NOTEBOOK FOR ANNA MAGDALENA BACH
    EDWIN F. KALMUS   3055   3.50
BACH, J.S.   FREY
NOTEBOOK FOR ANNA MAGDALENA, 1725
    FRANCO COLOMBO PUBLICATIONS   SIK.103   1.75
BACH, J.S.   CANINO
NOTEBOOK FOR ANNA MAGDALENA, 1725 -- 19 EASY PIECES
    FRANCO COLOMBO PUBLICATIONS   ER2687   1.00
BACH, J.S.   ROSSI
NOTEBOOK FOR ANNA MAGDALENA, 1725 -- 19 EASY PIECES
    FRANCO COLOMBO PUBLICATIONS   ER2027   1.00
BACH, J.S.   BEGINNER
NOTEBOOK FOR W.F. BACH
    EDWIN F. KALMUS   3067   3.50
BACH, J.S.   PLATH, W.
NOTEBOOK FOR WILHELM FRIEDEMANN BACH
    BARENREITER VERLAG   BA 5021   14.00
BACH, J.S.   LANNING
NOTEBOOK OF ANNA MAGDALENA BACH
    MUSICORD PUBLICATIONS, INC.   1.50
BACH, J.S.   DADELSEN, G. VON
NOTEBOOKS FOR ANNA MAGDALENA BACH OF 1722 AND 1725
    BARENREITER VERLAG   BA 5008   20.00
BACH, J.S.   DADELSEN, G. VON
NOTEBOOKS FOR ANNA MAGDALENA BACH, 1725
    BARENREITER VERLAG   BA 5115   6.75
BACH, J.S.   LUDWIG   2
NOTENBUCHLEIN FUR ANNA MAGDALENA BACH -- BWV 933
    SCHOTT   2698   1.50
BACH, J.S.   LUDWIG   2
NOTENBUCHLEIN FUR ANNA MAGDALENA BACH, BWV 933
    SCHOTT   2698   1.50
BACH, J.S.
ONE HUNDRED ONE CHORALES
    ELKAN-VOGEL, INC.   3.00
BACH, J.S.   REGER   M-D
ORCHESTRAL SUITES
    C. F. PETERS CORPORATION   3181   3.50
BACH, J.S.   BUSONI
ORGAN CHORAL PRELUDES, BK. 1
    CARL FISCHER, INC.   O 3496   1.50
BACH, J.S.   BUSONI
ORGAN CHORAL PRELUDES, BK. 2
    CARL FISCHER, INC.   O 3508   1.50
BACH, J.S.   MURDOCH
ORGAN CHORALE PRELUDES -- BK 1-4
    SCHOTT   SL   EA.
BACH, J.S. *   SAUER   D
ORGAN COMPOSITIONS BY BACH TRANSCRIBED FOR PIANO BY LISZT, VOL. 1
    C. F. PETERS CORPORATION   222   2.50
BACH, J.S. *   SAUER   D
ORGAN COMPOSITIONS BY BACH TRANSCRIBED FOR PIANO BY LISZT, VOL. 2
    C. F. PETERS CORPORATION   223   2950
BACH, J.S.   SAUER   D
ORGAN COMPOSITIONS TRANSCRIBED FOR PIANO BY LISZT. VOL. 1,
PRELUDES AND FUGUES NOS. 1-3--A MINOR, C, C MINOR--
    C. F. PETERS CORPORATION   222   2.50

BACH, J.S.   SAUER   D
ORGAN COMPOSITIONS TRANSCRIBED FOR PIANO BY LISZT. VOL. 2,
PRELUDES AND FUGUES NOS. 4-6--C, E MINOR, BMINOR--
    C. F. PETERS CORPORATION   223   2.50
BACH, J.S.   D
OVERTURE --F--, ARIA VARIATA --A MINOR--, FANTASIAS --G MINOR, A
MINOR--, TOCCATA --G--
    C. F. PETERS CORPORATION   215   2.50
BACH, J.S.   PETRI
PARTITA IN B MINOR, S. 831, AND ITALIAN CONCERTO, S. 971
    ASSOCIATED MUSIC PUBLISHERS, INC.   B/H   2.00
BACH, J.S.   TAGLIAPIETRA
PARTITA IN C MINOR--FRENCH OVERTURE-- AND FANTASY AND FUGUE IN A
MINOR
    FRANCO COLOMBO PUBLICATIONS   ER1441   1.00
BACH, J.S.   SOLDAN
PARTITAS -- URTEXT -- VOL. 1
    C. F. PETERS CORPORATION   4463A   2.00
BACH, J.S.   SOLDAN
PARTITAS -- URTEXT -- VOL. 2
    C. F. PETERS CORPORATION   4463B   2.00
BACH, J.S.   M-D
PARTITAS --URTEXT--, VOL. 2
    C. F. PETERS CORPORATION   4463B   2.00
BACH, J.S.
PARTITAS 1-3
    G. HENLE MUSIKVERLAG   30   2.35
BACH, J.S.
PARTITAS 4-6
    G. HENLE MUSIKVERLAG   31   2.35
BACH, J.S.   CZERNY
PARTITAS--BK. 1--NOS. 1-3
    G. SCHIRMER, INC.   L20   1.50
BACH, J.S.   CZERNY
PARTITAS--BK. 2--NOS. 4-6
    G. SCHIRMER, INC.   L21   1.50
BACH, J.S.   RONTGEN
PARTITAS, BK. 1
    UNIVERSAL EDITION   328   3.80
BACH, J.S.   RONTGEN
PARTITAS, BK. 2
    UNIVERSAL EDITION   329   3.50
BACH, J.S.   ASHBY
PIANISTS BOOK OF BACH CHORALES
    OXFORD UNIVERSITY PRESS   33.055   2.75
BACH, J.S.
PIANO COMPOSITIONS, BK. 2
    THEODORE PRESSER COMPANY   5.00
BACH, J.S.   KELLER   M-D
PIANO WORKS - SUPPLEMENT --URTEXT--. CAPRICCIOS--B FLAT, E--.
ARIA VARIATA, FANTASIAS, FUGUES, STUDIES TO THE WELL-TEMPERED
CLAVIER. PIECES FROM KLAVIERBUECHLEIN FOR W.F. BACH
    C. F. PETERS CORPORATION   9043   6.00
BACH, J.S.   MARTIENSSEN   M
PRELIMINARY STUDIES --25 ORIGINAL PIECES--
    C. F. PETERS CORPORATION   4230   1.25
BACH, J.S.   BUSONI
PRELUDES AND FUGUES
    ASSOCIATED MUSIC PUBLISHERS, INC.   B/H   2.25
BACH, J.S.   BUSONI
PRELUDES AND FUGUES--NOS. 1 IN C MAJOR, 2 IN C MINOR, 21 IN B
FLAT MAJOR--FROM WELL-TEMPERED CLAVICHORD
    G. SCHIRMER, INC.   .60
BACH, J.S.   BUSONI *
PRELUDES, FUGHETTAS, AND FUGUES
    ASSOCIATED MUSIC PUBLISHERS, INC.   B/H   1.50
BACH, J.S.   M-D
PRELUDES, FUGUES, SUITES
    C. F. PETERS CORPORATION   214   3.50
BACH, J.S.   D
PRELUDIO CON FUGA -- A MINOR--, FANTASIA --C MINOR--
    C. F. PETERS CORPORATION   207C   1.25
BACH, J.S.   DAVID
RICERCAR A 3--THREE-PART FUGUE--RICERCAR A 6--SIX-PART FUGUE--IN
''MUSICAL OFFERING''
    G. SCHIRMER, INC.   3.00
BACH, J.S.   KREUTZ   3
SECHS KLEINE PRALUDIEN FUR ANFANGER -- BWV 933-938
    SCHOTT   01068 1/2   1.00
BACH, J.S.   PALMER, W. A.
SELECTIONS FROM ANNA MAGDALENA'S NOTEBOOK
    ALFRED MUSIC COMPANY   605   1.50
BACH, J.S.   BISCHOFF
SEVEN TOCCATAS
    EDWIN F. KALMUS   3105   2.00
BACH, J.S.   KELLER
SEVEN TOCCATAS AND FUGUES -- URTEXT --
    C. F. PETERS CORPORATION   4665   3.50
BACH, J.S.
SEVEN TOCCATAS AND FUGUES --URTEXT--, COMPLETE IN 1 VOL.
CLOTH-BOUND
    C. F. PETERS CORPORATION   10.00
BACH, J.S.   MUGELLINI *
SEVENTEEN LITTLE PRELUDES AND FUGUES
    FRANCO COLOMBO PUBLICATIONS   ER2373   1.00
BACH, J.S.   KABALEVSKY
SHORT ORGAN PRELUDES AND FUGUES
    MCA MUSIC   3.50
BACH, J.S.   BISCHOFF
SHORT PRELUDES AND FUGUES
    EDWIN F. KALMUS   3104   2.00
BACH, J.S.   GRIEPENKERL *   M
SHORT PRELUDES AND FUGUES
    C. F. PETERS CORPORATION   200   2.00
BACH, J.S.   KELLER   M
SHORT PRELUDES AND FUGUES
    C. F. PETERS CORPORATION   200A   3.00
BACH, J.S.   MASON
SHORT PRELUDES AND FUGUES
    G. SCHIRMER, INC.   L15   1.00
BACH, J.S.   RONTGEN
SHORT PRELUDES AND FUGUES
    UNIVERSAL EDITION   323   3.00
BACH, J.S.   ANSON
SHORT PRELUDES AND FUGUES
    WILLIS MUSIC COMPANY   1.25
BACH, J.S.   ANSON, G.
SHORT PRELUDES AND FUGUES
    WILLIS MUSIC COMPANY   1.00
BACH, J.S.   RUTHARDT   M
SHORT PRELUDES AND FUGUES --24--
    C. F. PETERS CORPORATION   2791   1.50
BACH, J.S.
SHORTER PIANO COMPOSITIONS, BK. 1
    THEODORE PRESSER COMPANY   5.00

BACH, J.S. *
SILHOUETTES -- A COLLECTION OF 40 DANCES FROM J.S. BACH TO
THIELE
ASSOCIATED MUSIC PUBLISHERS, INC.   BRH   5.00
BACH, J.S.   KELLER   D
SIX FANTASIAS AND FUGUES, URTEXT
C. F. PETERS CORPORATION   9009   4.50
BACH, J.S.   BUSONI *
SIX FRENCH SUITES, S. 812-817
ASSOCIATED MUSIC PUBLISHERS, INC.   B/H   3.50
BACH, J.S.   3-4
SIX LITTLE PRELUDES
CENTURY MUSIC PUBLISHING COMPANY, INC.   4000   .40
BACH, J.S.   BISCHOFF
SIX LITTLE PRELUDES
EDWIN F. KALMUS   3103   1.00
BACH, J.S.   PERRACHIO
SIX ORGAN CHORALES
FRANCO COLOMBO PUBLICATIONS   ER1317   1.25
BACH, J.S.   MONTANI
SIX PARTITAS
FRANCO COLOMBO PUBLICATIONS   ER2628   3.50
BACH, J.S.   BISCHOFF
SIX PARTITAS AND FRENCH OVERTURE
EDWIN F. KALMUS   3101   2.50
BACH, J.S.
SIX PARTITAS, CLAVIER-UEBUNG, PART 1
G. HENLE MUSIKVERLAG   28   4.25
BACH, J.S.
SIX PARTITAS, CLAVIER-UEBUNG, PART 1 -- CLOTH
G. HENLE MUSIKVERLAG   29   7.35
BACH, J.S.   BUSONI *
SIX PARTITAS, S. 825-830, VOL. 1
ASSOCIATED MUSIC PUBLISHERS, INC.   B/H   3.75
BACH, J.S.   BUSONI *
SIX PARTITAS, S. 825-830, VOL. 2
ASSOCIATED MUSIC PUBLISHERS, INC.   B/H   3.50
BACH, J.S.   BUSONI *
SIX SUITES
ASSOCIATED MUSIC PUBLISHERS, INC.   B/H   3.00
BACH, J.S.   BECKER
SIXTY-NINE CHORALES WITH FIGURED BASS
ASSOCIATED MUSIC PUBLISHERS, INC.   B/H   1.50
BACH, J.S.   BISCHOFF
SIXTY-NINE CHORALES WITH FIGURED BASS
EDWIN F. KALMUS   3046   1.00
BACH, J.S.   D
SONATAS -- A MINOR, C, D MINOR--
C. F. PETERS CORPORATION   213   2.50
BACH, J.S.   KELLER   D
SONATAS AND SONATA MOVEMENTS --URTEXT--
C. F. PETERS CORPORATION   9066   5.00
BACH, J.S.   MANSFIELD
STEPS TO THE MASTERS
BANKS AND SON LTD.   1.35
BACH, J.S.   KELLER   M-D
SUITES --6-- AND SUITE MOVEMENTS --2--. URTEXT.
C. F. PETERS CORPORATION   9007   4.00
BACH, J.S.   BUSONI *
SUITES AND SONATAS
ASSOCIATED MUSIC PUBLISHERS, INC.   B/H   2.25
BACH, J.S.   BARTOK
THIRTEEN EASY SHORT PIANO PIECES, FROM 'NOTEBOOK FOR ANNA
MAGDALENA BACH'
KULTURA   .75
BACH, J.S.   KELLER
THREE FUGUES FOR PIANO ON THEMES BY J.A. REINKEN BWV 965, 966,
954
BARENREITER VERLAG   BA 474   3.00
BACH, J.S.
THREE HUNDRED SEVENTY-ONE CHORALES
ASSOCIATED MUSIC PUBLISHERS, INC.   B/H   2.50
BACH, J.S.   BISCHOFF
THREE HUNDRED SEVENTY-ONE CHORALES, VOL. 1
EDWIN F. KALMUS   3047   1.25
BACH, J.S.   BISCHOFF
THREE HUNDRED SEVENTY-ONE CHORALES, VOL. 2
EDWIN F. KALMUS   3048   1.25
BACH, J.S.   BUSONI *
THREE SONATAS, CONCERTO IN C MINOR, AND MISCELLANEOUS PIECES
ASSOCIATED MUSIC PUBLISHERS, INC.   B/H   2.25
BACH, J.S.   FRISKIN
THREE-PART INVENTIONS
BELWIN-MILLS PUBLISHING CORPORATION   3.00
BACH, J.S.   BUSONI
THREE-PART INVENTIONS
CARL FISCHER, INC.   L 898   1.00
BACH, J.S.   BUSONI
THREE-PART INVENTIONS
G. SCHIRMER, INC.   L1498   1.00
BACH, J.S.   MASON
THREE-PART INVENTIONS
G. SCHIRMER, INC.   L380   1.00
BACH, J.S.   D
TOCCATA AND FUGUE --G MINOR--. PRELUDE AND FUGUE --A MINOR--.
FANTASIA AND FUGUE --D--
C. F. PETERS CORPORATION   211   3.00
BACH, J.S.   BRISKIER
TOCCATA, ADAGIO AND FUGA
CARL FISCHER, INC.   O 4777   2.50
BACH, J.S.
TOCCATAS
G. HENLE MUSIKVERLAG   126   3.85
BACH, J.S.   HUGHES
TOCCATAS
G. SCHIRMER, INC.   L1538   2.00
BACH, J.S.
TOCCATAS -- CLOTH
G. HENLE MUSIKVERLAG   127   6.95
BACH, J.S.   D
TOCCATAS AND FUGUES --4--
C. F. PETERS CORPORATION   210   2.00
BACH, J.S.   KELLER   D
TOCCATAS AND FUGUES --7-- COMPLETE
C. F. PETERS CORPORATION   4665   3.50
BACH, J.S.   MUGELLINI
TOCCATAS AND SONATAS
FRANCO COLOMBO PUBLICATIONS   ER416   2.75
BACH, J.S.   BUSONI
TOCCATAS, AND FANTASY AND FUGUE IN A MINOR
ASSOCIATED MUSIC PUBLISHERS, INC.   B/H   2.00
BACH, J.S.   BUSONI *
TOCCATAS, S. 910-13
ASSOCIATED MUSIC PUBLISHERS, INC.   B/H   3.25
BACH, J.S.   BISCHOFF
TWELVE LITTLE PRELUDES
EDWIN F. KALMUS   3102   1.00

BACH, J.S.   REINECKE
TWELVE LITTLE PRELUDES
G. SCHIRMER, INC.   .80
BACH, J.S.   BEGINNER
TWENTY EASY PIECES FROM NOTEBOOK FOR ANNA MAGDALENA BACH
EDWIN F. KALMUS   3054   1.00
BACH, J.S.   MAIER, G.
TWENTY PIECES FROM BACH'S BOOK FOR HIS SON FRIEDMANN
BELWIN-MILLS PUBLISHING CORPORATION   1.50
BACH, J.S.   MONTANARI AND
TWENTY-FOUR PEZZI DAL LIBRO DI ANNA MAGDALENA
UNIVERSAL EDITION   323   3.90
BACH, J.S.
TWENTY-FOUR SHORT PRELUDES AND FUGUES --URTEXT--, COMPLETE IN 1
VOL. CLOTH-BOUND
C. F. PETERS CORPORATION   10.00
BACH, J.S.   MUGELLINI
TWENTY-THREE EASY PIECES
FRANCO COLOMBO PUBLICATIONS   ER2363   1.00
BACH, J.S.   PALMER, W. A.
TWO AND THREE PART INVENTIONS
ALFRED MUSIC COMPANY   606   3.00
BACH, J.S.   CZERNY
TWO AND THREE PART INVENTIONS
CARL FISCHER, INC.   L 304   1.50
BACH, J.S.   BISCHOFF
TWO AND THREE PART INVENTIONS
EDWIN F. KALMUS   3044   1.50
BACH, J.S.   BUSONI
TWO AND THREE PART INVENTIONS
G. SCHIRMER, INC.   L1574   1.50
BACH, J.S.   CZERNY
TWO AND THREE PART INVENTIONS
G. SCHIRMER, INC.   L813   1.50
BACH, J.S.   BISCHOFF
TWO AND THREE PART INVENTIONS
G. SCHIRMER, INC.   L1771   1.00
BACH, J.S.   RONTGEN
TWO AND THREE PART INVENTIONS
UNIVERSAL EDITION   324   3.35
BACH, J.S.
TWO AND THREE PART INVENTIONS -- FACSIMILE
DOVER PUBLICATIONS, INC.   21982-8   4.00
BACH, J.S.   BISCHOFF
TWO PART INVENTIONS
EDWIN F. KALMUS   3045   1.00
BACH, J.S.
TWO PART INVENTIONS--NOS. 01, 03, 04--
FREDERICK HARRIS MUSIC COMPANY   .60
BACH, J.S.   PALMER, W. A.
TWO-PART INVENTIONS
ALFRED MUSIC COMPANY   604   1.50
BACH, J.S.   FRISKIN
TWO-PART INVENTIONS
BELWIN-MILLS PUBLISHING CORPORATION   2.50
BACH, J.S.   BUSONI
TWO-PART INVENTIONS
CARL FISCHER, INC.   L 897   1.00
BACH, J.S.   BUSONI
TWO-PART INVENTIONS
G. SCHIRMER, INC.   L1512   .85
BACH, J.S.   CZERNY
TWO-PART INVENTIONS
G. SCHIRMER, INC.   L850   1.00
BACH, J.S.   MASON
TWO-PART INVENTIONS
G. SCHIRMER, INC.   L379   1.00
BACH, J.S.
TWO-PART INVENTIONS
WILLIS MUSIC COMPANY   1.25
BACH, J.S.   THOMPSON, J.   4
TWO-PART INVENTIONS
WILLIS MUSIC COMPANY   3.00
BACH, J.S.   ANSON, G.
TWO-PART INVENTIONS
WILLIS MUSIC COMPANY   1.25
BACH, J.S.   BUSONI
VARIATIONS
ASSOCIATED MUSIC PUBLISHERS, INC.   B/H   1.25
BACH, J.S.   BISCHOFF
VARIOUS WORKS, VOL. 1
EDWIN F. KALMUS   3106   3.00
BACH, J.S.   BISCHOFF
VARIOUS WORKS, VOL. 2
EDWIN F. KALMUS   3107   3.00
BACH, J.S.   MUGELLINI
WELL-TEMPERED CLAVICHORD, BK. 1
CARL FISCHER, INC.   O 3692   4.50
BACH, J.S.   BARTOK
WELL-TEMPERED CLAVICHORD, BK. 1
KULTURA   2.50
BACH, J.S.   MUGELLINI
WELL-TEMPERED CLAVICHORD, BK. 2
CARL FISCHER, INC.   O 3693   4.50
BACH, J.S.   BARTOK
WELL-TEMPERED CLAVICHORD, BK. 2
KULTURA   2.50
BACH, J.S.   CZERNY
WELL-TEMPERED CLAVICHORD, THE--BK. 1
G. SCHIRMER, INC.   L13   2.25
BACH, J.S.   HUGHES
WELL-TEMPERED CLAVICHORD, THE--BK. 1
G. SCHIRMER, INC.   L1483   3.00
BACH, J.S.   CZERNY
WELL-TEMPERED CLAVICHORD, THE--BK. 2
G. SCHIRMER, INC.   L14   2.25
BACH, J.S.   HUGHES
WELL-TEMPERED CLAVICHORD, THE--BK. 2
G. SCHIRMER, INC.   L1484   3.00
BACH, J.S.   BUSONI
WELL-TEMPERED CLAVICHORD, THE--FIRST 24 PRELUDES AND FUGUES WITH
SUPPLEMENT
G. SCHIRMER, INC.   5.00
BACH, J.S.   BUSONI
WELL-TEMPERED CLAVICHORD, THE--FIRST 24 PRELUDES AND FUGUES--BK.
1
G. SCHIRMER, INC.   2.00
BACH, J.S.   BUSONI
WELL-TEMPERED CLAVICHORD, THE--FIRST 24 PRELUDES AND FUGUES--BK.
2
G. SCHIRMER, INC.   2.00
BACH, J.S.   BUSONI
WELL-TEMPERED CLAVICHORD, THE--FIRST 24 PRELUDES AND FUGUES--BK.
3
G. SCHIRMER, INC.   2.00
BACH, J.S.
WELL-TEMPERED CLAVICHORD, THE, BK. 1
FRANCO COLOMBO PUBLICATIONS   SAL   10.00

BACH, J.S.   KROLL
WELL-TEMPERED CLAVIER --URTEXT--, COMPLETE IN 2 VOLS.
CLOTH-BOUND
      C. F. PETERS CORPORATION   10.00
BACH, J.S.   KREUTZ *
WELL-TEMPERED CLAVIER --URTEXT--, COMPLETE IN 2 VOLS.
CLOTH-BOUND
      C. F. PETERS CORPORATION   12.50
BACH, J.S.
WELL-TEMPERED CLAVIER, THE -- PART 1
      G. HENLE MUSIKVERLAG   14   4.65
BACH, J.S.
WELL-TEMPERED CLAVIER, THE -- PART 1 -- CLOTH
      G. HENLE MUSIKVERLAG   15   7.70
BACH, J.S.
WELL-TEMPERED CLAVIER, THE -- PART 1 -- WITHOUT FINGERING
      G. HENLE MUSIKVERLAG   256   4.85
BACH, J.S.
WELL-TEMPERED CLAVIER, THE -- PART 1 -- WITHOUT FINGERING --
CLOTH
      G. HENLE MUSIKVERLAG   257   8.40
BACH, J.S.
WELL-TEMPERED CLAVIER, THE -- PART 2
      G. HENLE MUSIKVERLAG   16   4.65
BACH, J.S.
WELL-TEMPERED CLAVIER, THE -- PART 2 -- CLOTH
      G. HENLE MUSIKVERLAG   17   7.70
BACH, J.S.
WELL-TEMPERED CLAVIER, THE -- PART 2 -- WITHOUT FINGERING
      G. HENLE MUSIKVERLAG   258   4.85
BACH, J.S.
WELL-TEMPERED CLAVIER, THE -- PART 2 -- WITHOUT FINGERING --
CLOTH
      G. HENLE MUSIKVERLAG   259   8.40
BACH, J.S.   MUGELLINI
WELL-TEMPERED CLAVIER, THE--VOL. 1
      ASSOCIATED MUSIC PUBLISHERS, INC.   B/H   4.00
BACH, J.S.   BUSONI
WELL-TEMPERED CLAVIER, THE--VOL. 1
      ASSOCIATED MUSIC PUBLISHERS, INC.   B/H   1.75
BACH, J.S.   MUGELLINI
WELL-TEMPERED CLAVIER, THE--VOL. 2
      ASSOCIATED MUSIC PUBLISHERS, INC.   B/H   4.00
BACH, J.S.   BUSONI
WELL-TEMPERED CLAVIER, THE--VOL. 2
      ASSOCIATED MUSIC PUBLISHERS, INC.   B/H   1.75
BACH, J.S.   BUSONI
WELL-TEMPERED CLAVIER, THE--VOL. 3
      ASSOCIATED MUSIC PUBLISHERS, INC.   B/H   1.75
BACH, J.S.   BUSONI
WELL-TEMPERED CLAVIER, THE--VOL. 4
      ASSOCIATED MUSIC PUBLISHERS, INC.   B/H   1.75
BACH, J.S.   BUSONI
WELL-TEMPERED CLAVIER, THE--VOL. 5
      ASSOCIATED MUSIC PUBLISHERS, INC.   B/H   1.75
BACH, J.S.   BUSONI
WELL-TEMPERED CLAVIER, THE--VOL. 6
      ASSOCIATED MUSIC PUBLISHERS, INC.   B/H   1.75
BACH, J.S.   BUSONI
WELL-TEMPERED CLAVIER, THE--VOL. 7
      ASSOCIATED MUSIC PUBLISHERS, INC.   B/H   1.75
BACH, J.S.   BUSONI
WELL-TEMPERED CLAVIER, THE--VOL. 8
      ASSOCIATED MUSIC PUBLISHERS, INC.   B/H   1.75
BACH, J.S.
WELL-TEMPERED CLAVIER, THE, BK. 1
      MUSIC SALES CORPORATION   020144   2.95
BACH, J.S.   BISCHOFF
WELL-TEMPERED CLAVIER, THE, BK. 1
      G. SCHIRMER, INC.   L1759   2.50
BACH, J.S.   RONTGEN
WELL-TEMPERED CLAVIER, THE, BK. 1
      UNIVERSAL EDITION   1547   5.20
BACH, J.S.
WELL-TEMPERED CLAVIER, THE, BK. 2
      MUSIC SALES CORPORATION   020145   2.95
BACH, J.S.   BISCHOFF
WELL-TEMPERED CLAVIER, THE, BK. 2
      G. SCHIRMER, INC.   L1760   2.50
BACH, J.S.   RONTGEN
WELL-TEMPERED CLAVIER, THE, BK. 2
      UNIVERSAL EDITION   1548   4.00
BACH, J.S.   BUSTINI
WELL-TEMPERED CLAVIER, THE, VOL. 1
      FRANCO COLOMBO PUBLICATIONS   DS427   5.00
BACH, J.S.   LONGO
WELL-TEMPERED CLAVIER, THE, VOL. 1
      FRANCO COLOMBO PUBLICATIONS   ER190   3.75
BACH, J.S.   MONTANI
WELL-TEMPERED CLAVIER, THE, VOL. 1
      FRANCO COLOMBO PUBLICATIONS   ER2375   3.75
BACH, J.S.   TAGLIAPIETRA
WELL-TEMPERED CLAVIER, THE, VOL. 1
      FRANCO COLOMBO PUBLICATIONS   ER807   3.75
BACH, J.S.   BISCHOFF
WELL-TEMPERED CLAVIER, THE, VOL. 1
      EDWIN F. KALMUS   3036   2.90
BACH, J.S.   KROLL   D
WELL-TEMPERED CLAVIER, THE, VOL. 1
      C. F. PETERS CORPORATION   1A   3.50
BACH, J.S.   KREUTZ *   D
WELL-TEMPERED CLAVIER, THE, VOL. 1
      C. F. PETERS CORPORATION   4691A   6.00
BACH, J.S.   CZERNY   D
WELL-TEMPERED CLAVIER, THE, VOL. 1
      C. F. PETERS CORPORATION   1   3.50
BACH, J.S.   KROLL
WELL-TEMPERED CLAVIER, THE, VOL. 1 --URTEXT--
      C. F. PETERS CORPORATION   1A   3.50
BACH, J.S.   BUSTINI
WELL-TEMPERED CLAVIER, THE, VOL. 2
      FRANCO COLOMBO PUBLICATIONS   DS428   5.00
BACH, J.S.   LONGO
WELL-TEMPERED CLAVIER, THE, VOL. 2
      FRANCO COLOMBO PUBLICATIONS   ER191   4.50
BACH, J.S.   MONTANI
WELL-TEMPERED CLAVIER, THE, VOL. 2
      FRANCO COLOMBO PUBLICATIONS   ER2376   4.50
BACH, J.S.   TAGLIAPIETRA
WELL-TEMPERED CLAVIER, THE, VOL. 2
      FRANCO COLOMBO PUBLICATIONS   ER808   4.50
BACH, J.S.   BISCHOFF
WELL-TEMPERED CLAVIER, THE, VOL. 2
      EDWIN F. KALMUS   3037   2.90
BACH, J.S.   KROLL   D
WELL-TEMPERED CLAVIER, THE, VOL. 2
      C. F. PETERS CORPORATION   1B   3.50

BACH, J.S.   KREUTZ *   D
WELL-TEMPERED CLAVIER, THE, VOL. 2
      C. F. PETERS CORPORATION   4691C   6.00
BACH, J.S.   CZERNY   D
WELL-TEMPERED CLAVIER, THE, VOL. 2
      C. F. PETERS CORPORATION   2   3.50
BACH, J.S.   KROLL
WELL-TEMPERED CLAVIER, THE, VOL. 2 --URTEXT--
      C. F. PETERS CORPORATION   1B   3.50
BACH, J.S.   SPIELBUCH   M
WORKS FOR KEYBOARD INSTRUMENTS
      C. F. PETERS CORPORATION   4510   2.50
BACH, J.S.   DAVIES
YOUNG PIANIST'S BACH, THE
      OXFORD UNIVERSITY PRESS   33.005   1.90
BACH, J.S.   MAIER, G.
YOUR BACH BOOK
      BELWIN-MILLS PUBLISHING CORPORATION   11527   2.50
BACH, J.S.   KREUTZ   2-3
ZWEISTG. INVENTIONEN -- BWV 772-786
      SCHOTT   01092-3 1/2   1.75
BACH, J.S.   KREUTZ   3
ZWOLF KLEINE PRALUDIEN -- BWV 924-930, 939-942, 999
      SCHOTT   0849 1/2   1.00
BACH, JAN
THREE BAGATELLES
      COMPOSERS AUTOGRAPH PUBLICATIONS   4.62
BACH, P.D.Q. *
NOTEBOOK FOR BETTY-SUE BACH
      THEODORE PRESSER COMPANY   2.50
BACH, W.F.   BLUME
COMPLETE PIANO SONATAS, BK. 1
      BARENREITER VERLAG   NMA 63   4.25
BACH, W.F.   BLUME
COMPLETE PIANO SONATAS, BK. 2
      BARENREITER VERLAG   NMA 78   4.00
BACH, W.F.   BLUME
COMPLETE PIANO SONATAS, BK. 3
      BARENREITER VERLAG   NMA 156   3.50
BACH, W.F.   FEDTKE   M
EIGHT FUGUES FOR ORGAN OR CLAVIER, 3 THREE-PART FUGUES FOR
ORGAN--2 STAVES--
      C. F. PETERS CORPORATION   8010A   3.50
BACH, W.F.   NIEMANN   M
FUGUES AND POLONAISES--12--
      C. F. PETERS CORPORATION   750   1.50
BACH, W.F.   WUHRER
POLONAISES, NOS. 01 AND 02
      ASSOCIATED MUSIC PUBLISHERS, INC.   OBV   .75
BACH, W.F.   WUHRER
POLONAISES, NOS. 05 AND 06
      ASSOCIATED MUSIC PUBLISHERS, INC.   OBV   .75
BACH, W.F.   WUHRER
POLONAISES, NOS. 07 AND 08
      ASSOCIATED MUSIC PUBLISHERS, INC.   OBV   1.00
BACH, W.F.   WUHRER
POLONAISES, NOS. 09 AND 10
      ASSOCIATED MUSIC PUBLISHERS, INC.   OBV   1.00
BACH, W.F.   WUHRER
POLONAISES, NOS. 11 AND 12
      ASSOCIATED MUSIC PUBLISHERS, INC.   OBV   .75
BACH, W.F.   SCHLEUNING
SAMTLICHE KLAVIERFANTASIEN
      SCHOTT   6122
BACH, W.F.   BLUME   3-4
SAMTLICHE KLAVIERSONATEN, HEFT 1 - SONATEN G, A, B FLAT
      BARENREITER VERLAG   NMA 63
BACH, W.F.   BLUME   3-4
SAMTLICHE KLAVIERSONATEN, HEFT 2 - SONATEN D, D, E FLAT
      BARENREITER VERLAG   NMA 78
BACH, W.F.   BLUME   3-4
SAMTLICHE KLAVIERSONATEN, HEFT 3 - SONATEN C, C, F
      BARENREITER VERLAG   NMA 156
BACH, W.F.   BLUME
SONATAS, VOL. 1
      ASSOCIATED MUSIC PUBLISHERS, INC.   NAG   4.25
BACH, W.F.
SONATAS, VOL. 1
      EDWIN F. KALMUS   3112   1.25
BACH, W.F.   BLUME
SONATAS, VOL. 2
      ASSOCIATED MUSIC PUBLISHERS, INC.   NAG   4.00
BACH, W.F.
SONATAS, VOL. 2
      EDWIN F. KALMUS   3113   1.25
BACH, W.F.   BLUME
SONATAS, VOL. 3
      ASSOCIATED MUSIC PUBLISHERS, INC.   NAG   3.00
BACH, W.F.
SONATAS, VOL. 3
      EDWIN F. KALMUS   3114   1.25
BACH, W.F.
TWELVE POLONAISIES
      EDWARD B. MARKS MUSIC CORPORATION   03.00
BACHARACH   LANE
JOHN LANE PLAYS BACHARACH HITS
      THE BIG THREE MUSIC CORPORATION   2.95
BACON
MY WORLD
      SUMMY-BIRCHARD COMPANY   1.25
BACON, E.
BYWAYS
      G. SCHIRMER, INC.   1.50
BACON, E.
FOUR NOTES
      FRANCO COLOMBO PUBLICATIONS   NY2261   1.00
BACON, E.--ED   BACON, E.
PATRIOTIC AMERICAN MELODIES
      THEODORE PRESSER COMPANY   1.25
BADEN   E
TEN EASY PIECES
      C. F. PETERS CORPORATION   LY447   .60
BADINGS   2-3
REIHE KL. KLAVIERSTUCKE
      SCHOTT   2897   2.00
BADINGS   1
ZEHN FUNFTONSTUCKE AUF ZEHN TASTEN, HEFT 2
      SCHOTT   4177   2.00
BADINGS
ZEHN FUNFTONSTUCKE AUF ZEHN WEISSEN TASTEN, HEFT 1
      SCHOTT   4176   2.00
BADINGS   2
ZEHN KLEINE STUCKE OHNE DAUMENUNTERSATZ, HEFT 3
      SCHOTT   4178   2.00
BADURA-SKODA
CADENZA AND INTRODUCTIONS TO MOZART CONCERTO IN C MINOR, K. 491
      ASSOCIATED MUSIC PUBLISHERS, INC.   D08   1.25

BADURA-SKODA			
CADENZAS TO HAYDN CONCERTO IN D			
ASSOCIATED MUSIC PUBLISHERS, INC.	DOB		1.25
BADURA-SKODA			
CADENZAS TO MOZART CONCERTO IN D MINOR, K. 466			
ASSOCIATED MUSIC PUBLISHERS, INC.	DOB		1.25
BADURA-SKODA			
CADENZAS TO MOZART CONCERTO IN E FLAT, K. 482			
ASSOCIATED MUSIC PUBLISHERS, INC.	DOB		1.25
BADURA-SKODA			
CADENZAS TO MOZART'S PIANO CONCERTI			
BARENREITER VERLAG	BA 4461		10.00
BADURA-SKODA	4-5		
KADENZEN ZU MOZARTS KLAVIERKONZERTEN K175, 238, 415, 449, 453,			
456, 467, 482, 491, 503, 537, AND 595			
BARENREITER VERLAG	BA 4461		
BAEZ, J.			
AMERICAN BALLADS AND FOLKSONGS			
MUSIC SALES CORPORATION	040974		2.95
BAEZ, J.			
BRITISH BALLADS AND FOLK SONGS			
MUSIC SALES CORPORATION	040975		2.95
BAEZ, J.			
JOAN BAEZ SONGBOOK, THE			
MUSIC SALES CORPORATION	040973		4.95
BAEZ, J.			
NOEL			
MUSIC SALES CORPORATION	040976		2.95
BAEZ, J.			
SONGS FOR OUR TIMES			
MUSIC SALES CORPORATION	040972		2.95
BAKER			
ON A SMALL SCALE -- 28 SHORT PIECES BASED ON THE MAJOR SCALES			
BOSTON MUSIC COMPANY			2.50
BALADA, L.			
MUSICA EN CUARTO TIEMPOS - MUSIC IN FOUR TEMPOS			
GENERAL MUSIC PUBLISHING COMPANY, INC.			3.00
BALBO			
PICCIOLI-5 SHORT PIECES			
FRANCO COLOMBO PUBLICATIONS	FOR.12276		1.75
BALOGH--ED	BALOGH		
TOCCATA ALBUM			
G. SCHIRMER, INC.	L1793		3.00
BARBERA			
THREE PIECES			
FRANCO COLOMBO PUBLICATIONS	129463		.90
BARESEL, A.	E		
ONE HUNDRED PEDAL EXERCISES WITH ELEMENTARY PEDAL MANUAL			
C. F. PETERS CORPORATION	ZM1246		2.00
BARESEL, A.--ED.	BARESEL, A.		
EUROPEAN NATIONAL ANTHEMS			
FRANCO COLOMBO PUBLICATIONS	SIK.206		3.00
BARNETT			
FOUR INTERLUDES			
FRANCO COLOMBO PUBLICATIONS	SAL		7.00
BARNETT			
THREE INTERLUDES			
FRANCO COLOMBO PUBLICATIONS	SAL		4.25
BARRAUD			
SIX IMPROMPTUS			
FRANCO COLOMBO PUBLICATIONS	A104/9		2.25
BARRETT			
CINDERELLA SUITE			
PRO-ART PUBLICATIONS, INC.	1195		1.00
BARRETT--ED	BARRETT		
JUNIOR HYMNAL FOR PIANO			
SCHUBERTH CO.			1.95
BARROZO	BRUGNOLI		
TWENTY STUDIES IN VELOCITY			
FRANCO COLOMBO PUBLICATIONS	ER892		1.75
BART	GREEN		
OLIVER - EASY PIANO			
TRO SONGWAYS SERVICE, INC.			1.95
BART	GREEN		
OLIVER - PIANO SELECTIONS			
TRO SONGWAYS SERVICE, INC.			1.95
BARTA	3		
ACHT KOMPOSITIONEN FUR JUNGE PIANISTEN			
BARENREITER VERLAG	AP 1763		
BARTH, H.			
KEYBOARD MUSIC OF THE SEVENTEENTH CENTURY			
BELWIN-MILLS PUBLISHING CORPORATION	11257		1.25
BARTH, H.			
SIX TWO-PART INVENTIONS			
BELWIN-MILLS PUBLISHING CORPORATION	20371		.95
BARTHOLOMEE			
INVENTION, PREMIER DOUBLE			
C. F. PETERS CORPORATION	SCH160		1.25
BARTLEY			
TWO DANCES			
ASSOCIATED MUSIC PUBLISHERS, INC.	BER		1.00
BARTOK *	BEGINNER		
ALBUM OF EASY PIECES BY MODERN COMPOSERS, AN			
EDWIN F. KALMUS	3008		2.75
BARTOK			
ALBUM, BK. 1			
KULTURA			2.00
BARTOK			
ALBUM, BK. 2			
KULTURA			2.00
BARTOK	ANSON, G.	ELEMENTARY	
ANSON INTRODUCES BARTOK, BK. 1			
WILLIS MUSIC COMPANY			1.00
BARTOK	ANSON, G.	INTERMEDIATE	
ANSON INTRODUCES BARTOK, BK. 2			
WILLIS MUSIC COMPANY			1.00
BARTOK			
BARTOK ALBUM			
EDWIN F. KALMUS	3118		2.50
BARTOK	AGAY, D.		
BARTOK IS EASY - 15 MELODIOUS PIECES FOR THE YOUNG PIANIST			
THEODORE PRESSER COMPANY			1.25
BARTOK			
DEUX IMAGES			
BOOSEY AND HAWKES, INC.			2.00
BARTOK			
DREI RONDOS UBER VOLKSWEISEN			
UNIVERSAL EDITION	9508		3.30
BARTOK			
FIFTEEN HUNGARIAN PEASANT SONGS			
BOOSEY AND HAWKES, INC.			1.75
BARTOK	BEGINNER		
FIRST TERM			
EDWIN F. KALMUS	3122		1.00
BARTOK			
FOR CHILDREN--EIGHTY-FIVE PIECES WITHOUT OCTAVES FOR			
BEGINNERS--VOL. 1			
G. SCHIRMER, INC.	L1780		1.50

BARTOK			
FOR CHILDREN--EIGHTY-FIVE PIECES WITHOUT OCTAVES FOR			
BEGINNERS--VOL. 2			
G. SCHIRMER, INC.	L1781		1.50
BARTOK			
FOR CHILDREN, BK. 1			
BOOSEY AND HAWKES, INC.			2.00
BARTOK			
FOR CHILDREN, BK. 2			
BOOSEY AND HAWKES, INC.			2.00
BARTOK		BEGINNER	
FOR CHILDREN, VOL. 1			
EDWIN F. KALMUS	3119		1.00
BARTOK		BEGINNER	
FOR CHILDREN, VOL. 2			
EDWIN F. KALMUS	3120		1.00
BARTOK *	AGAY		
FORTY-THREE LITTLE PIECES AND STUDIES			
THEODORE PRESSER COMPANY			2.00
BARTOK			
FOUR DIRGES			
BOOSEY AND HAWKES, INC.			1.25
BARTOK			
FOUR DIRGES			
EDWIN F. KALMUS	3126		1.25
BARTOK			
FOUR NENIES, OP. 8B			
EDWIN F. KALMUS	3132		1.25
BARTOK			
FOURTEEN BAGATELLES, OP. 6			
BOOSEY AND HAWKES, INC.			2.50
BARTOK			
FOURTEEN BAGATELLES, OP. 6			
EDWIN F. KALMUS	3123		2.00
BARTOK			
FUNFZEHN UNGARISCHE BAUERNLIEDER			
UNIVERSAL EDITION	6370		1.95
BARTOK			
IM FREIEN -- 5 PIECES, BK. 1			
UNIVERSAL EDITION	8892A		3.60
BARTOK			
IM FREIEN -- 5 PIECES, BK. 2			
UNIVERSAL EDITION	8892B		3.60
BARTOK			
MIKROKOSMOS, BKS. 1 AND 2			
BOOSEY AND HAWKES, INC.			EA.
BARTOK			
MIKROKOSMOS, BKS. 3, 4, 5 AND 6			
BOOSEY AND HAWKES, INC.			EA.
BARTOK			
NEUNE KLEINE KLAVIERSTUCKE, BK. 1			
UNIVERSAL EDITION	8920		1.95
BARTOK			
NEUNE KLEINE KLAVIERSTUCKE, BK. 1			
UNIVERSAL EDITION	8922		1.95
BARTOK			
NEUNE KLEINE KLAVIERSTUCKE, BK. 2			
UNIVERSAL EDITION	8921		1.95
BARTOK			
NINE LITTLE PIECES, BKS. 1, 2 AND 3			
BOOSEY AND HAWKES, INC.			EA.
BARTOK *			
PIANO METHOD			
BOOSEY AND HAWKES, INC.			2.50
BARTOK	PALMER, W.A.		
PIECES FOR CHILDREN			
ALFRED MUSIC COMPANY	575		2.00
BARTOK			
ROUMANIAN CHRISTMAS CAROLS			
BOOSEY AND HAWKES, INC.			1.50
BARTOK			
ROUMANIAN FOLK DANCES			
BOOSEY AND HAWKES, INC.			1.25
BARTOK	PARLMER, W. A.		
SELECTED CHILDREN'S PIECES			
ALFRED MUSIC COMPANY	623		1.00
BARTOK			
SELECTED WORKS FOR THE PIANO			
G. SCHIRMER, INC.	L1741		3.50
BARTOK			
SEVEN SKETCHES, OP. 9			
BOOSEY AND HAWKES, INC.			1.00
BARTOK			
SIX DANCES IN BULGARIAN RHYTHM			
BOOSEY AND HAWKES, INC.			1.25
BARTOK	PHILIPP, I.		
SIXTEEN PIECES FOR CHILDREN			
INTERNATIONAL MUSIC COMPANY			1.50
BARTOK			
SKETCHES, OP. 9			
EDWIN F. KALMUS	3138		1.25
BARTOK	PALMER, W. A.		
TEN EASY PIECES			
ALFRED MUSIC COMPANY	574		1.25
BARTOK			
TEN EASY PIECES			
BOOSEY AND HAWKES, INC.			1.25
BARTOK		BEGINNER	
TEN EASY PIECES			
EDWIN F. KALMUS	3121		1.00
BARTOK	AGAY, D.		
TEN EASY PIECES FOR PIANO			
MCA MUSIC			1.25
BARTOK	DOFLEIN		
THIRTY-TWO PIECES FROM 'FOR CHILDREN'			
BOOSEY AND HAWKES, INC.			1.25
BARTOK			
THREE BURLESQUES, OP. 8C			
BOOSEY AND HAWKES, INC.			1.25
BARTOK			
THREE BURLESQUES, OP. 8C			
EDWIN F. KALMUS	3125		1.25
BARTOK			
THREE HUNGARIAN FOLK TUNES			
BOOSEY AND HAWKES, INC.			.60
BARTOK			
THREE HUNGARIAN FOLKSONGS			
EDWIN F. KALMUS	3130		1.00
BARTOK			
THREE POPULAR HUNGARIAN SONGS			
BOOSEY AND HAWKES, INC.			.60
BARTOK			
THREE RONDOS ON FOLK TUNES			
BOOSEY AND HAWKES, INC.			1.50
BARTOK			
THREE STUDIES, OP. 18			
BOOSEY AND HAWKES, INC.			1.50

BARTOK
    TWO ELEGIES, OP. 8B
        BOOSEY AND HAWKES, INC.   1.25
BARTOK
    TWO ELEGIES, OP. 8B
        EDWIN F. KALMUS   3127   1.25
BARTOK
    TWO FANTASIES -- GMUNDEN, 1903 --
        EDWIN F. KALMUS   3129   1.25
BARTOK
    TWO IMAGES, OP. 10
        EDWIN F. KALMUS   3131   2.50
BARTOK
    TWO ROUMANIAN DANCES, OP. 8A
        BOOSEY AND HAWKES, INC.   1.00
BARTOK
    TWO ROUMANIAN DANCES, OP. 8A
        EDWIN F. KALMUS   3134   1.75
BARTOK
    WOODEN PRINCE --COMPLETE BALLET--
        BOOSEY AND HAWKES, INC.   7.50
BARTOK
    YOUNG PEOPLE AT THE PIANO, BKS. 1 AND 2
        BOOSEY AND HAWKES, INC.   EA.
BARTOS, J.   2-3
    ACHT BAGATELLEN, OP. 3
        BARENREITER VERLAG   AP 510
BARTOS, J. *   4
    ALBUM MODERNER TSCHECHISCHER KOMPONISTEN 1947 - BAND 1, 19
    KLAVIERSTUCKE
        BARENREITER VERLAG   AP 500A
BARTOS, J.   3
    FUNF CAPRICCI
        BARENREITER VERLAG   AP 512
BARTOS, J.   2
    WEIHNACHTEN - 6 LEICHTE KLAVIERSTUCKE, OP. 20
        BARENREITER VERLAG   AP 513
BARTOS, J. Z.   2-3
    BAGATELLEN -- BERCEUSE, SCHERZANDO, MELODIE, BARCAROLLA, MARCIA
    FUNEBRE, SLOVACKA --
        BARENREITER VERLAG   AP 508
BARTOS, J. Z.   2-3
    VIER ZWEISTIMMIGE INVENTIONEN, OP. 5
        BARENREITER VERLAG   AP 509
BASESCU, B.
    MUSIC READING FOR BEGINNERS
        THEODORE PRESSER COMPANY   3.50
BASTIEN
    BEGINNING PIANO FOR ADULTS
        NEIL A. KJOS MUSIC COMPANY   23   6.95
BASTIEN
    FIRST READING EXPERIENCES
        NEIL A. KJOS MUSIC COMPANY   35   1.75
BASTIEN
    MULTI-KEY READING
        NEIL A. KJOS MUSIC COMPANY   29   1.95
BASTIEN
    MUSIC FLASHCARDS
        NEIL A. KJOS MUSIC COMPANY   27   1.45
BASTIEN
    MUSIC NOTEBOOK
        NEIL A. KJOS MUSIC COMPANY   16   1.25
BASTIEN
    PLAYTIME AT THE PIANO, BK.1
        NEIL A. KJOS MUSIC COMPANY   18   1.25
BASTIEN
    PLAYTIME AT THE PIANO, BK.2
        NEIL A. KJOS MUSIC COMPANY   19   1.25
BASTIEN
    PRE-READING EXPERIENCES
        NEIL A. KJOS MUSIC COMPANY   1   1.95
BASTIEN
    PRE-READING SOLOS
        NEIL A. KJOS MUSIC COMPANY   36   1.25
BASTIEN
    READING, BK.1
        NEIL A. KJOS MUSIC COMPANY   2   1.50
BASTIEN
    READING, BK.2
        NEIL A. KJOS MUSIC COMPANY   4   1.50
BASTIEN
    READING, BK.3
        NEIL A. KJOS MUSIC COMPANY   6   1.50
BASTIEN   1
    VERY YOUNG PIANIST
        NEIL A. KJOS MUSIC COMPANY   34   3.45
BASTIEN   2
    VERY YOUNG PIANIST
        NEIL A. KJOS MUSIC COMPANY   51   3.45
BASTIEN   3
    VERY YOUNG PIANIST
        NEIL A. KJOS MUSIC COMPANY   52   3.45
BASTIEN
    VERY YOUNG PIANIST, WORKBOOK A
        NEIL A. KJOS MUSIC COMPANY   53   1.50
BASTIEN
    VERY YOUNG PIANIST, WORKBOOK B
        NEIL A. KJOS MUSIC COMPANY   54   1.50
BASTIEN--ED.   BASTIEN
    FOLK TUNES FOR FUN
        NEIL A. KJOS MUSIC COMPANY   21   1.25
BASTIEN--ED.   BASTIEN
    HYMNS FOR PIANO, BK. 1
        NEIL A. KJOS MUSIC COMPANY   24   1.00
BASTIEN--ED.   BASTIEN
    HYMNS FOR PIANO, BK. 2
        NEIL A. KJOS MUSIC COMPANY   25   1.25
BASTIEN--ED.   BASTIEN
    MAJOR SCALES AND PIECES
        NEIL A. KJOS MUSIC COMPANY   11   1.50
BASTIEN--ED.   BASTIEN
    MERRY CHRISTMAS, BK.1
        NEIL A. KJOS MUSIC COMPANY   8   .95
BASTIEN--ED.   BASTIEN
    MERRY CHRISTMAS, BK.2
        NEIL A. KJOS MUSIC COMPANY   17   1.00
BASTIEN--ED.   BASTIEN
    MERRY CHRISTMAS, BK.3
        NEIL A. KJOS MUSIC COMPANY   41   1.25
BASTIEN--ED.   BASTIEN
    MINOR SCALES AND PIECES
        NEIL A. KJOS MUSIC COMPANY   12   1.50
BASTIEN--ED.   BASTIEN
    MORE FOLK TUNES FOR FUN
        NEIL A. KJOS MUSIC COMPANY   26   1.25
BASTIEN--ED.   BASTIEN
    PIANO LITERATURE
        NEIL A. KJOS MUSIC COMPANY   10   1.25

BASTIEN--ED.   BASTIEN
    PIANO LITERATURE FOR THE INTERMEDIATE GRADES, BK. 3
        NEIL A. KJOS MUSIC COMPANY   20   1.95
BASTIEN--ED.   BASTIEN
    PIANO LITERATURE, BK.1
        NEIL A. KJOS MUSIC COMPANY   9   1.25
BASTIEN--ED.   BASTIEN
    POP, ROCK 'N BLUES, BK. 1
        NEIL A. KJOS MUSIC COMPANY   37   1.25
BASTIEN--ED.   BASTIEN
    POP, ROCK 'N BLUES, BK. 2
        NEIL A. KJOS MUSIC COMPANY   38   1.25
BASTIEN--ED.   BASTIEN
    POP, ROCK 'N BLUES, BK. 3
        NEIL A. KJOS MUSIC COMPANY   39   1.25
BASTIEN--ED.   BASTIEN
    ROCK 'N BLUES FOR FUN
        NEIL A. KJOS MUSIC COMPANY   56   1.25
BASTIEN--ED.   BASTIEN
    WALT DISNEY FAVORITES
        NEIL A. KJOS MUSIC COMPANY   28   1.50
BAUER
    FROM A COMPOSER'S NOTE BOOK
        CHAPPELL AND COMPANY, INC.   0014910   1.00
BAUER, H. *   PRELIMINARY GRADE
    BAUER-DILLER-QUAILE COURSE--PIANO METHOD FOR CLASS AND
    INDIVIDUAL INSTRUCTION, BK. 1
        G. SCHIRMER, INC.   1.25
BAUER, H. *   GRADE 1
    BAUER-DILLER-QUAILE COURSE--PIANO METHOD FOR CLASS AND
    INDIVIDUAL INSTRUCTION, BK. 2
        G. SCHIRMER, INC.   1.25
BAUER, M.
    FOUR PIANO PIECES
        BOOSEY AND HAWKES, INC.   1.00
BAUER, M.
    SUMMERTIME SUITE -- EIGHT PIECES FOR STUDENTS
        MCA MUSIC   1.50
BAUM--ED *   BAUM *   2-3
    KLAVIERCHORALBUCH. 206 KLAVIERSATZE ZUM EVANGELISCHEN
    KIRCHENGESANGBUCH
        BARENREITER VERLAG   BA 3499
BAUM--ED.   BAUM
    ALTE WEIHNACHTSMUSIK
        BARENREITER VERLAG   BA 826   2.75
BAUM--ED. *   BAUM *
    BRUDER SINGER
        BARENREITER VERLAG   BA 2999   7.00
BAUM--ED. *   BAUM *   2
    BRUDER SINGER. 270 LIEDER UNSERES VOLKES IN LEICHTEN
    KLAVIERSATZEN
        BARENREITER VERLAG   BA 2999
BAUM--ED. *   BAUM *
    KLAVIERCHORALBUCH
        BARENREITER VERLAG   BA 3499   6.50
BAUM--ED.   BAUM
    NEW CHRISTMAS MUSIC
        BARENREITER VERLAG   BA 1371   2.75
BAUR
    APHORISMEN. TWELVE PIECES
        ASSOCIATED MUSIC PUBLISHERS, INC.   B/H   2.25
                                                  6
BAXTER
    NATIVITY, THE -- 5 PIECES
        NOVELLO AND COMPANY, LTD.   10.0003.09   1.25
BAZELON, I.
    FIVE PIANO PIECES
        WEINTRAUB MUSIC COMPANY   070077   1.25
BAZELON, I.
    SUITE FOR YOUNG PEOPLE, BK. 1
        PEER SOUTHERN ORGANIZATION   01.00
BAZELON, I.
    SUITE FOR YOUNG PEOPLE, BK. 2
        PEER SOUTHERN ORGANIZATION   02.00
BEACH, H. H. A.   M-D
    FIVE IMPROVISATIONS
        COMPOSERS PRESS, INC.   EA.
BEAUCAMP
    TROIS ENFANTINES
        GERARD BILLAUDOT EDITIONS MUSICALES   1.30
                                                  4
BECK, C.   4
    KLAVIERSTUCKE 1, 6 STUCKE
        SCHOTT   2109   2.50
BECK, C.   4
    KLAVIERSTUCKE 2, 5 STUCKE
        SCHOTT   2145   2.50
BECKLER, S.
    NINE LITTLE PIECES FOR PIANO
        COMPOSERS AUTOGRAPH PUBLICATIONS   2.20
BECKWITH
    INTERVAL STUDIES
        ASSOCIATED MUSIC PUBLISHERS, INC.   BER   .40
BECVAROVSKY *   SYKORA   2-3
    TSCHECHISCHE KLASSIKER, BAND 1 - 16 STUCKE
        BARENREITER VERLAG   MAB 14
BEER, L. J.--ED   BEER, L. J.
    SIXTEEN MASTERWORKS FOR PIANO
        THEODORE PRESSER COMPANY   1.50
BEETHOVEN
    ALBUM, BKS. 1 AND 2
        KULTURA   EA.
BEETHOVEN   DUMM
    ALLEMANDES, WALTZES, SONGS
        BOSTON MUSIC COMPANY   1.00
BEETHOVEN *   FERTE   M-D
    ANTHOLOGY, VOL. 4: 15 PIECES BY MOZART AND BEETHOVEN
        C. F. PETERS CORPORATION   SCH44   2.50
BEETHOVEN   3-4
    AUSWAHL - 14 BEL. STUCKE
        SCHOTT   502   1.00
BEETHOVEN
    BAGATELLES
        G. HENLE MUSIKVERLAG   158   2.70
BEETHOVEN
    BAGATELLES, OP. 119
        INTERNATIONAL MUSIC COMPANY   1.00
BEETHOVEN   M-D
    BAGATELLES, OP. 119
        C. F. PETERS CORPORATION   7080   .90
BEETHOVEN
    BAGATELLES, OP. 119 AND OP. 126
        G. SCHIRMER, INC.   1.50
BEETHOVEN
    BAGATELLES, OP. 126
        INTERNATIONAL MUSIC COMPANY   1.00
BEETHOVEN
    BEETHOVEN
        ASHLEY DEALERS SERVICE, INC.   HG 07   2.95

BEETHOVEN   THORNE
   BEETHOVEN FOR EVERYBODY
     BOOSEY AND HAWKES, INC.   1.75

BEETHOVEN   ROVENGER
   BEETHOVEN FOR THE YOUNG
     RUBANK, INC.   1.50

BEETHOVEN   ECKHARDT, F.   1
   BEETHOVEN FOR THE YOUNG PIANIST
     CENTURY MUSIC PUBLISHING COMPANY, INC.   3957   .40

BEETHOVEN   HIRSCHBERG, D.
   BEETHOVEN IS FUN
     MUSICORD PUBLICATIONS, INC.   1.25

BEETHOVEN
   BEETHOVEN OVERTURES, THE -- EGMONT, CORIOLANUS, LEONORE NO. 3 --
     CENTURY MUSIC PUBLISHING COMPANY, INC.   1.25

BEETHOVEN
   BEETHOVEN'S BEST KNOWN PIANO SONATAS
     ASHLEY DEALERS SERVICE, INC.   WFS NO. 57   2.95

BEETHOVEN   SCHAUM, J.   2 1/2
   BEST OF BEETHOVEN
     SCHAUM PUBLICATIONS, INC.   1.50

BEETHOVEN   4
   BONN SONATAS, THE
     ASHLEY DEALERS SERVICE, INC.   1.00

BEETHOVEN   4
   BONN SONATAS, THE
     CENTURY MUSIC PUBLISHING COMPANY, INC.   1.00

BEETHOVEN   BRADLEY, R.
   BRADLEY CLASSICAL SERIES - ECCOSSAISES
     SCREEN GEMS - COLUMBIA PUBLICATIONS   0702EP2   .85

BEETHOVEN   KEMPFF
   CADENZAS TO CONCERTI NOS. 1-4
     ASSOCIATED MUSIC PUBLISHERS, INC.   DOB   3.50

BEETHOVEN   BUSONI   D
   CADENZAS TO CONCERTOS 1, 3, 4
     C. F. PETERS CORPORATION   N798   2.00

BEETHOVEN
   CADENZAS TO PIANO CONCERTOS BY BEETHOVEN HIMSELF
     EDWIN F. KALMUS   3195   2.00

BEETHOVEN *   GOLDBERGER, D. *
   CLASSIC DANCES OF MOZART AND BEETHOVEN
     CONSOLIDATED MUSIC PUBLISHERS, INC.   040118   1.50

BEETHOVEN *   E-M
   CLASSIC VARIATIONS
     C. F. PETERS CORPORATION   3013   2.50

BEETHOVEN   SEISS
   CONTRA DANCES
     CARL FISCHER, INC.   P 2865   1.00

BEETHOVEN   SEISS
   CONTRA-DANCES
     G. SCHIRMER, INC.   L1528   .75

BEETHOVEN
   CONTRE DANCES
     EDWIN F. KALMUS   3191   1.00

BEETHOVEN   HERRMANN
   DANCES AND PIECES
     FRANCO COLOMBO PUBLICATIONS   SIK.105   1.75

BEETHOVEN *   SARAUER *   3
   DIE KLASSIKER UND IHRE ZEITGENOSSEN
     BARENREITER VERLAG   AP 1722

BEETHOVEN   BENDIK   3-4
   DREI VARIATIONEN UBER EIN IRISCHES VOLKSLIED OP. 105-4 UND SECHS
   VARIATIONEN UBER EIN OSTERREICHISCHES VOLKSLIED OP. 105-3
     SCHOTT   09665 1/2   1.00

BEETHOVEN   ROWLEY   E-M
   EASIEST ORIGINAL PIECES
     C. F. PETERS CORPORATION   H1   1.50

BEETHOVEN   FRUGATTA
   EASY COMPOSITIONS
     FRANCO COLOMBO PUBLICATIONS   ER87   3.25

BEETHOVEN   LONGO
   EASY COMPOSITIONS
     FRANCO COLOMBO PUBLICATIONS   ER2680   1.75

BEETHOVEN   BEGINNER
   EASY COMPOSITIONS
     EDWIN F. KALMUS   3206   1.25

BEETHOVEN   BUELOW *
   EASY COMPOSITIONS
     G. SCHIRMER, INC.   L5   1.50

BEETHOVEN   RUTHARDT   E
   EASY COMPOSITIONS --8--
     C. F. PETERS CORPORATION   758   3.00

BEETHOVEN   STEURER   E
   EASY PIANO PIECES --12--
     C. F. PETERS CORPORATION   L5005   1.25

BEETHOVEN
   ECOSSAISE AND RONDINO
     DELRIEU ET CIE.   1.00

BEETHOVEN   BUSONI
   ECOSSAISES
     EDWIN F. KALMUS   3190   1.00

BEETHOVEN   M
   ECOSSAISES --6-- AND GERMAN DANCES --12--
     C. F. PETERS CORPORATION   4336   1.50

BEETHOVEN   PALMER, W. A.
   ELEVEN BAGATELLES
     ALFRED MUSIC COMPANY   624   1.50

BEETHOVEN   ETTLER
   ELEVEN VIENNESE DANCES
     ASSOCIATED MUSIC PUBLISHERS, INC.   B/H   .75

BEETHOVEN   KRAUSE
   FIFTEEN EASY PIECES
     ASSOCIATED MUSIC PUBLISHERS, INC.   B/H   .75

BEETHOVEN   SPIVAK, S.
   FINEST MUSIC SERIES -- BEETHOVEN
     SCHUBERTH CO.   NO. 01   1.50

BEETHOVEN   BEGINNER
   FIRST BOOK, A
     EDWIN F. KALMUS   3204   1.25

BEETHOVEN   BRADLEY
   FIRST COMPOSERS - BEETHOVEN
     FRANCO COLOMBO PUBLICATIONS   LD197   1.00

BEETHOVEN   D
   FIVE CONCERTI AND CHORAL FANTASY, OP. 80
     C. F. PETERS CORPORATION   144   10.00

BEETHOVEN   KUHLSTROM   3
   FUNFZEHN WALZER
     SCHOTT   438   2.00

BEETHOVEN *
   GERMAN DANCES
     G. SCHIRMER, INC.   L1653   .75

BEETHOVEN   M
   GERMAN DANCES --12-- AND ECOSSAISES --6--
     C. F. PETERS CORPORATION   4336   1.50

BEETHOVEN *   LONGO
   GOLDEN LIBRARY, BK. 2 - BEETHOVEN, HAYDN, MOZART
     FRANCO COLOMBO PUBLICATIONS   112500   5.50

BEETHOVEN   NICHOLS
   INTRODUCTION TO BEETHOVEN
     CARL FISCHER, INC.   PT 448   1.00

BEETHOVEN   PALMER, W. A.
   INTRODUCTION TO HIS PIANO WORKS, AN
     ALFRED MUSIC COMPANY   607   2.00

BEETHOVEN   FISCHER, E.
   KADENZEN ZU DEN KLAVIERKONZERTEN OP. 15 U. 58--1. SATZ, U. OP. 37
     SCHOTT   4946   2.50

BEETHOVEN   ZEITLIN *
   LITTLE KNOWN PIANO PIECES
     BOSTON MUSIC COMPANY   2.00

BEETHOVEN   HUGHES
   MASTER SERIES FOR THE YOUNG, VOL. 05--BEETHOVEN
     G. SCHIRMER, INC.   1.25

BEETHOVEN *   E-M
   MASTERS FOR THE YOUNG, VOL. 2
     C. F. PETERS CORPORATION   2711   2.50

BEETHOVEN   CHING   EASY
   NEW EASY GRADED CLASSIC ALBUM - BEETHOVEN
     GENERAL WORDS AND MUSIC COMPANY   1.25

BEETHOVEN
   ORIGINAL CADENZAS TO THE PIANO CONCERTI
     ASSOCIATED MUSIC PUBLISHERS, INC.   B/H   2.75

BEETHOVEN   HESS
   ORIGINAL PIANO REDUCTIONS
     ASSOCIATED MUSIC PUBLISHERS, INC.   B/H   32.00

BEETHOVEN
   PIANO COMPOSITIONS, BK. 1
     THEODORE PRESSER COMPANY   5.00

BEETHOVEN
   PIANO COMPOSITIONS, BK. 2
     THEODORE PRESSER COMPANY   5.00

BEETHOVEN
   PIANO PIECES
     G. HENLE MUSIKVERLAG   12   5.80

BEETHOVEN   BRENDEL
   PIANO PIECES
     WIENER URTEXT EDITION   UT 50003   8.00

BEETHOVEN
   PIANO PIECES -- CLOTH
     G. HENLE MUSIKVERLAG   13   8.80

BEETHOVEN   WEINER
   PIANO SONATAS, BKS. 1, 2 AND 3
     KULTURA   EA.

BEETHOVEN
   PIECES FOR THE MUSICAL CLOCK
     EDWIN F. KALMUS   3193   1.00

BEETHOVEN
   RADIO CITY ALBUM
     EDWARD B. MARKS MUSIC CORPORATION   01.50

BEETHOVEN   3
   SECHS BAGATELLEN OP. 126
     SCHOTT   0273 1/2   1.00

BEETHOVEN   FRICKERT   2-3
   SECHS CONTRETANZE
     SCHOTT   09622 1/2   1.00

BEETHOVEN   GEORGII, W.   3
   SECHS ECOSSAISEN
     SCHOTT   09580 1/2   1.00

BEETHOVEN   2
   SECHS MENUETTE
     SCHOTT   0277 1/2   1900

BEETHOVEN   HOEHN   2-4
   SECHS SONATINEN
     SCHOTT   4940   2.50

BEETHOVEN
   SECHS VARIIERTE THEMEN, OP. 105 -- VOL. 1
     ASSOCIATED MUSIC PUBLISHERS, INC.   B/H   2.50

BEETHOVEN
   SECHS VARIIERTE THEMEN, OP. 105 -- VOL. 2
     ASSOCIATED MUSIC PUBLISHERS, INC.   B/H   2.50

BEETHOVEN   2
   SEHNSUCHTS, SCHMERZENS- UND HOFFNUNGWALZER
     SCHOTT   0282 1/2   1.00

BEETHOVEN   CESI
   SELECTED COMPOSITIONS
     FRANCO COLOMBO PUBLICATIONS   ER2669   2.25

BEETHOVEN   FRUGATTA
   SELECTED COMPOSITIONS
     FRANCO COLOMBO PUBLICATIONS   ER183   4.00

BEETHOVEN
   SELECTED VARIATIONS FOR PIANOFORTE
     G. HENLE MUSIKVERLAG   132   1.15

BEETHOVEN   SCHOLZ
   SEVEN BAGATELLES, OP. 33
     ASSOCIATED MUSIC PUBLISHERS, INC.   DOB   1.50

BEETHOVEN
   SEVEN BAGATELLES, OP. 33
     G. HENLE MUSIKVERLAG   20   1.40

BEETHOVEN
   SEVEN BAGATELLES, OP. 33, BK. 1
     G. SCHIRMER, INC.   L970   1.25

BEETHOVEN   BEGINNER
   SEVEN EASY PIECES
     EDWIN F. KALMUS   3205   1.25

BEETHOVEN
   SIX ECOSSAISES
     FRANCO COLOMBO PUBLICATIONS   128266   .75

BEETHOVEN   BEGINNER
   SIX GERMAN DANCES
     EDWIN F. KALMUS   3203   1.00

BEETHOVEN   FRUGATTA
   SIX SONATINAS
     FRANCO COLOMBO PUBLICATIONS   ER65   2.50

BEETHOVEN   VITALI
   SIX WALTZES
     FRANCO COLOMBO PUBLICATIONS   129125   1.00

BEETHOVEN *
   SONATA ALBUM--26 SONATAS BY HAYDN, MOZART, AND BEETHOVEN--BK. 1
     G. SCHIRMER, INC.   L329   3.50

BEETHOVEN *
   SONATA ALBUM--26 SONATAS BY HAYDN, MOZART, AND BEETHOVEN--BK. 2
     G. SCHIRMER, INC.   L340   3.50

BEETHOVEN *   M-D
   SONATA ALBUM, VOL. 1
     C. F. PETERS CORPORATION   2114A   3.00

BEETHOVEN *   M-D
   SONATA ALBUM, VOL. 2
     C. F. PETERS CORPORATION   2114B   3.00

BEETHOVEN   CHING
   SONATA NO. 01 IN F MINOR, OP. 2 NO. 1
     GENERAL WORDS AND MUSIC COMPANY   .75

BEETHOVEN   CHING
   SONATA NO. 08 IN C MINOR, OP. 13
     GENERAL WORDS AND MUSIC COMPANY   .75

BEETHOVEN   CHING
SONATA NO. 14 IN C SHARP MINOR, OP. 27 NO. 2
  GENERAL WORDS AND MUSIC COMPANY   .75
BEETHOVEN   CHING
SONATA NO. 19 IN G MINOR, OP. 49 NO. 1
  GENERAL WORDS AND MUSIC COMPANY   .75
BEETHOVEN   CHING
SONATA NO. 20 IN G, OP. 49 NO. 2
  GENERAL WORDS AND MUSIC COMPANY   .75
BEETHOVEN   MARTIENSSEN
SONATAS --URTEXT--, COMPLETE IN 2 VOLS. CLOTH-BOUND
  C. F. PETERS CORPORATION   12.50
BEETHOVEN
SONATAS FOR THE ELECTOR, WO O 47
  G. HENLE MUSIKVERLAG   255
BEETHOVEN
SONATAS URTEXT COMPLETE, BK. 1
  EDWIN F. KALMUS   3154   6.00
BEETHOVEN
SONATAS URTEXT COMPLETE, BK. 1A, 1-7
  EDWIN F. KALMUS   3155   2.50
BEETHOVEN
SONATAS URTEXT COMPLETE, BK. 1B, 8-15
  EDWIN F. KALMUS   3156   2.50
BEETHOVEN
SONATAS URTEXT COMPLETE, BK. 2
  EDWIN F. KALMUS   3157   6.00
BEETHOVEN   BUELOW *
SONATAS, BK. 1
  G. SCHIRMER, INC.   L1   5.00
BEETHOVEN   BUELOW *
SONATAS, BK. 1
  G. SCHIRMER, INC.   L301   3.50
BEETHOVEN   KREBS
SONATAS, BK. 1--"URTEXT" EDITION
  G. SCHIRMER, INC.   L1769   5.00
BEETHOVEN   BUELOW *
SONATAS, BK. 2
  G. SCHIRMER, INC.   L2   5.00
BEETHOVEN   BUELOW *
SONATAS, BK. 2
  G. SCHIRMER, INC.   L302   3.50
BEETHOVEN   KREBS
SONATAS, BK. 2--"URTEXT" EDITION
  G. SCHIRMER, INC.   L1770   5.00
BEETHOVEN   BUELOW *
SONATAS, BK. 3
  G. SCHIRMER, INC.   L303   3.50
BEETHOVEN   KOEHLER *
SONATAS, COMPLETE IN 2 VOLS. CLOTH-BOUND
  C. F. PETERS CORPORATION   10.00
BEETHOVEN
SONATAS, OP. 14, NO. 1, E MAJOR AND NO. 2, G MAJOR
  G. HENLE MUSIKVERLAG   170   1.55
BEETHOVEN
SONATAS, VOL. 1
  G. HENLE MUSIKVERLAG   32   7.70
BEETHOVEN   KOEHLER *   D
SONATAS, VOL. 1
  C. F. PETERS CORPORATION   296A   4.50
BEETHOVEN   MARTIENSSEN   D
SONATAS, VOL. 1
  C. F. PETERS CORPORATION   1802A   6.50
BEETHOVEN
SONATAS, VOL. 1 -- CLOTH
  G. HENLE MUSIKVERLAG   33   10.80
BEETHOVEN   CASELLA
SONATAS, VOL. 1 -- 1-12 --
  FRANCO COLOMBO PUBLICATIONS   ER1B   4.50
BEETHOVEN   LAMOND
SONATAS, VOL. 1--CLOTH--
  ASSOCIATED MUSIC PUBLISHERS, INC.   B/H   7.50
BEETHOVEN   LAMOND
SONATAS, VOL. 1--PAPER--
  ASSOCIATED MUSIC PUBLISHERS, INC.   B/H   4.75
BEETHOVEN
SONATAS, VOL. 2
  G. HENLE MUSIKVERLAG   34   7.70
BEETHOVEN   KOEHLER *   D
SONATAS, VOL. 2
  C. F. PETERS CORPORATION   296B   4.50
BEETHOVEN   MARTIENSSEN   D
SONATAS, VOL. 2
  C. F. PETERS CORPORATION   1802B   6.50
BEETHOVEN
SONATAS, VOL. 2 -- CLOTH
  G. HENLE MUSIKVERLAG   35   10.80
BEETHOVEN   CASELLA
SONATAS, VOL. 2 -- 13-23 --
  FRANCO COLOMBO PUBLICATIONS   ER2B   4.50
BEETHOVEN   LAMOND
SONATAS, VOL. 2--CLOTH--
  ASSOCIATED MUSIC PUBLISHERS, INC.   B/H   7.50
BEETHOVEN   LAMOND
SONATAS, VOL. 2--PAPER--
  ASSOCIATED MUSIC PUBLISHERS, INC.   B/H   4.75
BEETHOVEN   CASELLA
SONATAS, VOL. 3 -- 24-32 --
  FRANCO COLOMBO PUBLICATIONS   ER3B   4.50
BEETHOVEN   BEGINNER
SONATINAS
  EDWIN F. KALMUS   3199   2.00
BEETHOVEN   E-M
SONATINAS --6-- COMPLETE
  C. F. PETERS CORPORATION   1231   2.00
BEETHOVEN
SONATINAS COMPLETE
  EDWIN F. KALMUS   3199   2.00
BEETHOVEN   MANSFIELD
STEPS TO THE MASTERS
  BANKS AND SON LTD.   1.35
BEETHOVEN   SCHUNEMANN   3
STUCKE FUR DIE SPIELUHR
  SCHOTT   2890   2.00
BEETHOVEN   POZZOLI
SYMPHONIES BK. 1 -- 1-5 --
  FRANCO COLOMBO PUBLICATIONS   ER401   5.00
BEETHOVEN   POZZOLI
SYMPHONIES BK. 2 -- 6-9 --
  FRANCO COLOMBO PUBLICATIONS   ER402   5.00
BEETHOVEN   SINGER
SYMPHONIES, BK. 1--NOS. 1-5
  G. SCHIRMER, INC.   L1562   4.50
BEETHOVEN   SINGER
SYMPHONIES, BK. 2--NOS. 6-9
  G. SCHIRMER, INC.   L1563   4.50

BEETHOVEN   SINGER   M-D
SYMPHONIES, VOL. 1
  C. F. PETERS CORPORATION   196A   6.00
BEETHOVEN   SINGER   M-D
SYMPHONIES, VOL. 2
  C. F. PETERS CORPORATION   196B   6.00
BEETHOVEN   HOLLANDER
THEMES I'LL REMEMBER
  BOOSEY AND HAWKES, INC.   .75
BEETHOVEN   SCHNABEL, A.
THIRTY-TWO SONATAS FOR THE PIANOFORTE --IN TWO VOLUMES--
  SIMON AND SCHUSTER, PUBLISHERS
BEETHOVEN   BOGHEN *
THREE CONTRADANCES
  ASSOCIATED MUSIC PUBLISHERS, INC.   ESC   3.25
BEETHOVEN   BARTH, H.
THREE COUNTRY DANCES
  BELWIN-MILLS PUBLISHING CORPORATION   20304   .60
BEETHOVEN
THREE GERMAN DANCES
  EDWIN F. KALMUS   3192   1.00
BEETHOVEN   KREUTZER
TWELVE GERMAN DANCES
  BRODT MUSIC COMPANY   1.50
BEETHOVEN
TWO EASY SONATAS, OP. 49 NO. 1 IN G MINOR AND NO. 2 IN G
  G. HENLE MUSIKVERLAG   56   1.10
BEETHOVEN   BARTH, H.
TWO ECOSSAISES
  BELWIN-MILLS PUBLISHING CORPORATION   20365   .60
BEETHOVEN   ROHM
TWO PRELUDES IN ALL MAJOR KEYS, OP. 39
  ASSOCIATED MUSIC PUBLISHERS, INC.   OBV   .60
BEETHOVEN
TWO SONATINAS IN G AND F
  FRANCO COLOMBO PUBLICATIONS   129184 .90
BEETHOVEN   RATZ, E.
VARIATIONS FOR PIANO, BK. 1
  UNIVERSAL EDITION   13300   4.80
BEETHOVEN   HOLL, M.
VARIATIONS FOR PIANO, BK. 2
  UNIVERSAL EDITION   13320   4.80
BEETHOVEN   HOLL *
VARIATIONS FOR PIANO, VOL. 1
  WIENER URTEXT EDITION   UT 50024 9.00
BEETHOVEN   HOLL *
VARIATIONS FOR PIANO, VOL. 2
  WIENER URTEXT EDITION   UT 50025 7.50
BEETHOVEN
VARIATIONS FOR PIANOFORTE, COMPLETE, VOL. 1
  G. HENLE MUSIKVERLAG   142   5.00
BEETHOVEN
VARIATIONS FOR PIANOFORTE, COMPLETE, VOL. 1 -- CLOTH
  G. HENLE MUSIKVERLAG   143   8.10
BEETHOVEN
VARIATIONS FOR PIANOFORTE, COMPLETE, VOL. 2
  G. HENLE MUSIKVERLAG   144   5.00
BEETHOVEN
VARIATIONS FOR PIANOFORTE, COMPLETE, VOL. 2--CLOTH
  G. HENLE MUSIKVERLAG   145   8.10
BEETHOVEN   FRUGATTA
VARIATIONS VOL. 1
  FRANCO COLOMBO PUBLICATIONS   ER111   3.50
BEETHOVEN   FRUGATTA
VARIATIONS VOL. 2
  FRANCO COLOMBO PUBLICATIONS   ER112   3.50
BEETHOVEN   BUELOW *
VARIATIONS, BK. 1
  G. SCHIRMER, INC.   L6   3.00
BEETHOVEN   BUELOW *
VARIATIONS, BK. 2
  G. SCHIRMER, INC.   L7   3.00
BEETHOVEN
VARIATIONS, VOL. 1
  EDWIN F. KALMUS   3158   3.50
BEETHOVEN
VARIATIONS, VOL. 2
  EDWIN F. KALMUS   3159   3.50
BEETHOVEN   D
VARIATIONS, VOL.1
  C. F. PETERS CORPORATION   298A   3.50
BEETHOVEN   M-D
VARIATIONS, VOL.2
  C. F. PETERS CORPORATION   298B   3.50
BEETHOVEN   KELLER
VARIOUS PIECES --URTEXT-- IN 2 VOLUMES, VOL.1
  C. F. PETERS CORPORATION   297A   4.00
BEETHOVEN   KELLER
VARIOUS PIECES --URTEXT-- IN 2 VOLUMES, VOL.2
  C. F. PETERS CORPORATION   297B   4.00
BEETHOVEN
VARIOUS PIECES INCLUDING COMPLETE BAGATELLES
  EDWIN F. KALMUS   3194   4.00
BEETHOVEN
ZEHN VARIIERTE THEMEN, OP. 107 -- VOL. 1
  ASSOCIATED MUSIC PUBLISHERS, INC.   B/H   2.50
BEETHOVEN
ZEHN VARIIERTE THEMEN, OP. 107 -- VOL. 2
  ASSOCIATED MUSIC PUBLISHERS, INC.   B/H   2.50
BEETHOVEN
ZEHN VARIIERTE THEMEN, OP. 107 -- VOL. 3
  ASSOCIATED MUSIC PUBLISHERS, INC.   B/H   2.50
BEETHOVEN   FREY   2-3
ZWANZIG KLEINE TANZE
  SCHOTT   2583   1.75
BEETHOVEN   2
ZWEI LEICHTE SONATEN
  SCHOTT   0281 1/2 1.00
BEETHOVEN   HOEHN, A.   2
ZWEI LEICHTE SONATEN IN G AND F
  SCHOTT   0281 1/2 1.00
BEETHOVEN   LUTZ   3
ZWOLF DEUTSCHE TANZE
  SCHOTT   3746   1900
BELAUBRE, L.
POETIQUE DU PIANO, VOL.1
  GERARD BILLAUDOT EDITIONS MUSICALES   3.30
BELAUBRE, L.
POETIQUE DU PIANO, VOL.2
  GERARD BILLAUDOT EDITIONS MUSICALES   3.80
BELL, W.--ARR.   BELL, W.   EASY
JUST FOR FUN - HIT TUNES EVERYBODY KNOWS
  SCREEN GEMS - COLUMBIA PUBLICATIONS   F0126P4 1.95
BELL, W.--ARR.   BELL, W.   EASY
JUST FOR FUN - MELODIES EVERYBODY KNOWS
  SCREEN GEMS - COLUMBIA PUBLICATIONS   F0125P4 1.95

BELL, W.--ARR.   BELL, W.   EASY
     JUST FOR FUN - POPS EVERYBODY KNOWS
          SCREEN GEMS - COLUMBIA PUBLICATIONS   F0081P4   1.50
BELL, W.--ARR.   BELL, W.   EASY
     JUST FOR FUN - SHOW TUNES EVERYBODY KNOWS
          SCREEN GEMS - COLUMBIA PUBLICATIONS   F0107P4   1.95
BELLINI *   LONGO
     GOLDEN LIBRARY, BK. 5 - BELLINI, DONIZETTI, ROSSINI, VERDI
          FRANCO COLOMBO PUBLICATIONS   112503   5.50
BELLINI
     SELECTED OVERTURES -- WITH ROSSINI - SELECTED OVERTURES --
          FRANCO COLOMBO PUBLICATIONS   ER1163   4.25
BEMETZRIEDER, A.
     LECONS DE CLAVECIN
          BROUDE BROTHERS LTD.   30.00
BEN-HAIM
     FIVE COUNTRY DANCES
          MCA MUSIC   1.50
BEN-HAIM
     THREE SONGS WITHOUT WORDS
          ALEXANDER BROUDE, INC.   3.50
BENARY
     SIX MINIATURES FOR PIANO
          MCA MUSIC   1.25
BENDA, R.   FISCHER, HANS *   E-M
     GERMAN KEYBOARD MUSIC OF THE SEVENTEENTH AND EIGHTEENTH
     CENTURIES, VOL. 6# BENDA
          C. F. PETERS CORPORATION   V125   2.00
BENDA, R.   SYKORA   3
     SIXTEEN SONATEN
          BARENREITER VERLAG   MAB 24
BENDA, R. *   EMINGEROVA *   3
     SONATINEN ALTER TSCHECHISCHER MEISTER, 22 STUCKE
          BARENREITER VERLAG   MVH 5
BENDA, R.   RACEK *   3
     THIRTY-FOUR SONATINEN
          BARENREITER VERLAG   MAB 37
BENDER   2-3
     EINE VERGNUGTE KLAVIERMUSIK
          BARENREITER VERLAG   BA 2071
BENDER   2
     KLEINE CHORALVORSPIELE ZUM GOTTESDIENSTLICHEN GEBRAUCH, HEFT 1 -
     30 CHORALVORSPIELE
          BARENREITER VERLAG   BA 2431
BENDER   2
     KLEINE CHORALVORSPIELE ZUM GOTTESDIENSTLICHEN GEBRAUCH, HEFT 2 -
     30 CHORALVORSPIELE
          BARENREITER VERLAG   BA 2434
BENDER   2
     KLEINE CHORALVORSPIELE ZUM GOTTESDIENSTLICHEN GEBRAUCH, HEFT 3 -
     30 CHORALVORSPIELE
          BARENREITER VERLAG   BA 2429
BENDER
     KLEINE CHORALVORSPIELE, BK. 1
          BARENREITER VERLAG   BA 2431   3.25
BENDER
     KLEINE CHORALVORSPIELE, BK. 2
          BARENREITER VERLAG   BA 2434   3.25
BENDER
     KLEINE CHORALVORSPIELE, BK. 3
          BARENREITER VERLAG   BA 2429   3.25
BENDER   MOD. EASY
     THIRTEEN SERVICE PIECES FOR THE CHURCH PIANIST
          ABINGDON PRESS   1.50
BENDER   MOD. DIFF.
     THIRTEEN VOLUNTARIES FOR THE CHURCH PIANIST
          ABINGDON PRESS   3.00
BENFORD--ED   BENFORD
     MEET THE MASTERS
          PRO-ART PUBLICATIONS, INC.   989   1.00
BENJAMIN
     FANTASIES, BK. 2
          BOOSEY AND HAWKES, INC.   1.50
BENJAMIN
     THREE NEW FANTASIES
          BOOSEY AND HAWKES, INC.   1.00
BENNER, L.
     FISH STORIES -- 4 PIECES
          BENNER PUBLISHERS   .85
BENNER, L.
     IN THE WOODS -- 4 PIECES
          BENNER PUBLISHERS   .85
BENNER, L.
     MAKE YOUR OWN SCALES AND ARPEGGIOS
          G. SCHIRMER, INC.   1.25
BENNER, L.
     MUSIC FOR PIANO STUDENTS
          BENNER PUBLISHERS   3.00
BENNER, L.
     THEORY FOR PIANO STUDENTS, BK. 1
          G. SCHIRMER, INC.   1.50
BENNER, L.
     THEORY FOR PIANO STUDENTS, BK. 2
          G. SCHIRMER, INC.   1.50
BENNER, L.
     THEORY FOR PIANO STUDENTS, BK. 3
          G. SCHIRMER, INC.   1.50
BENNER, L.
     THEORY FOR PIANO STUDENTS, BK. 4
          G. SCHIRMER, INC.   1.50
BENNETT, E. *
     COMPLETE SERIES OF SIGHT READING AND EAR TESTS, BK. 1
          FREDERICK HARRIS MUSIC COMPANY   1.15
BENNETT, E. *
     COMPLETE SERIES OF SIGHT READING AND EAR TESTS, BK. 2
          FREDERICK HARRIS MUSIC COMPANY   1.15
BENNETT, E. *
     COMPLETE SERIES OF SIGHT READING AND EAR TESTS, BK. 3
          FREDERICK HARRIS MUSIC COMPANY   1.15
BENNETT, E. *
     COMPLETE SERIES OF SIGHT READING AND EAR TESTS, BK. 4
          FREDERICK HARRIS MUSIC COMPANY   1.15
BENNETT, E. *
     COMPLETE SERIES OF SIGHT READING AND EAR TESTS, BK. 5
          FREDERICK HARRIS MUSIC COMPANY   1.15
BENNETT, E. *
     COMPLETE SERIES OF SIGHT READING AND EAR TESTS, BK. 6
          FREDERICK HARRIS MUSIC COMPANY   1.15
BENNETT, E. *
     COMPLETE SERIES OF SIGHT READING AND EAR TESTS, BK. 7
          FREDERICK HARRIS MUSIC COMPANY   1.15
BENSON
     THREE MACEDONIAN MINIATURES
          BOOSEY AND HAWKES, INC.   .75
BENTLEY
     BENTLEY ALBUM, A
          SUMMY-BIRCHARD COMPANY   1.75

BENTLEY
     BENTLEY SECOND ALBUM
          SUMMY-BIRCHARD COMPANY   1.50
BENTLEY
     FOUR AND TWENTY MELODIES
          SUMMY-BIRCHARD COMPANY   2.25
BENTLEY
     GAY TUNES
          SUMMY-BIRCHARD COMPANY   1.50
BENTLEY
     HAPPY TIMES --25 SHORT PIECES FOR DEVELOPING TECHNIC AND STYLE
     FOR PIANO--
          THEODORE PRESSER COMPANY   1.25
BENTLEY
     LITTLE SONGS TO PLAY AND SING
          SUMMY-BIRCHARD COMPANY   1.75
BENTLEY
     RONDOLETTES
          SUMMY-BIRCHARD COMPANY   2.00
BENTLEY
     SEVEN IMPRESSIONS FOR PIANO
          THEODORE PRESSER COMPANY   1.00
BENUSSAN, M.
     BULGARIAN SONGS AND DANCES, BK. 1
          BROUDE BROTHERS LTD.   02.50
BENUSSAN, M.
     BULGARIAN SONGS AND DANCES, BK. 2
          BROUDE BROTHERS LTD.   02.50
BENUSSAN, M.
     CIRCUS SCRAP BOOK
          BROUDE BROTHERS LTD.   02.50
BENUSSAN, M.
     THREE PIECES
          BROUDE BROTHERS LTD.   02.50
BERENS, H.   PHILIPP, I.   6-7
     EXERCISES ET ETUDES POUR LA MAIN GAUCHE SEULE, OP. 89
          ALPHONSE LEDUC
BERENS, H.
     FIFTY PIECES WITHOUT OCTAVES FOR BEGINNERS, OP. 70
          G. SCHIRMER, INC.   L504   1.25
BERENS, H.
     NEW SCHOOL OF VELOCITY, BK. 1 -- 1-14 --
          FRANCO COLOMBO PUBLICATIONS   ER733   1.50
BERENS, H.
     NEW SCHOOL OF VELOCITY, BK. 2 -- 15-26 --
          FRANCO COLOMBO PUBLICATIONS   ER734   1.25
BERENS, H.
     NEW SCHOOL OF VELOCITY, BK. 3 -- 27-33 --
          FRANCO COLOMBO PUBLICATIONS   ER735   1.25
BERENS, H.
     NEW SCHOOL OF VELOCITY, OP. 61 - 40 EXERCISES, COMPLETE
          FRANCO COLOMBO PUBLICATIONS   ER456   2.50
BERENS, H.   M-D
     SCHOOL OF VELOCITY, VOL. 1# NOS. 1-14
          C. F. PETERS CORPORATION   3187A   1.25
BERENS, H.   M-D
     SCHOOL OF VELOCITY, VOL. 2# NOS. 15-26
          C. F. PETERS CORPORATION   3187B   1.25
BERENS, H.   M-D
     SCHOOL OF VELOCITY, VOL. 3# NOS. 27-33
          C. F. PETERS CORPORATION   3187C   1.50
BERENS, H.   M-D
     SCHOOL OF VELOCITY, VOL. 4# NOS. 34-40
          C. F. PETERS CORPORATION   3187D   1.50
BERENS, H.   M-D
     TRAINING OF THE LEFT HAND, OP. 89
          C. F. PETERS CORPORATION   3188   2.50
BERENS, H.
     TWENTY CHILDREN-STUDIES WITHOUT OCTAVES, OP. 79
          G. SCHIRMER, INC.   L508   1.00
BERGENFELD, N.
     INTROS, BREAKS, FILLERS AND FADEOUTS
          PRO-ART PUBLICATIONS, INC.   1259   2.00
BERINGER, O. *   BRIMHALL, J.
     DAILY PIANOFORTE EXERCISES
          CHARLES HANSEN   H413   .99
BERIOT   5-6
     LA LECTURE AU PIANO, VOL. 1 - 86 EXERCISES
          ALPHONSE LEDUC
BERIOT   8
     THIRTY-SIX ETUDES DE DIFFICULTE TRANSCENDANTE
          ALPHONSE LEDUC
BERKOWITZ
     JAZZETTES
          FRANK MUSIC CORPORATION   4.95
BERKOWITZ
     NINE FOLK SONG PRELUDES
          FRANK MUSIC CORPORATION   2.75
BERLIN, B.
     ABC OF PIANO PLAYING, BK. 1
          BOOSEY AND HAWKES, INC.   1.15
BERLIN, B.
     ABC OF PIANO PLAYING, BK. 2
          BOOSEY AND HAWKES, INC.   1.15
BERLIN, B.
     ABC OF PIANO PLAYING, BK. 3
          BOOSEY AND HAWKES, INC.   1.15
BERLIN, B.   1
     FOUR STAR SIGHT READING, GRADE 1, REVISED EDITION
          BOOSEY AND HAWKES, INC.   1.15
BERLIN, B. *   2
     FOUR STAR SIGHT READING, GRADE 2
          BOOSEY AND HAWKES, INC.   .75
BERLIN, B. *   3
     FOUR STAR SIGHT READING, GRADE 3
          BOOSEY AND HAWKES, INC.   .75
BERLIN, B.   4
     FOUR STAR SIGHT READING, GRADE 4, REVISED EDITION
          BOOSEY AND HAWKES, INC.   1.15
BERLIN, B.   5
     FOUR STAR SIGHT READING, GRADE 5
          FREDERICK HARRIS MUSIC COMPANY   .90
BERLIN, B.   6
     FOUR STAR SIGHT READING, GRADE 6
          FREDERICK HARRIS MUSIC COMPANY   .90
BERLIN, B.   7
     FOUR STAR SIGHT READING, GRADE 7
          FREDERICK HARRIS MUSIC COMPANY   1.15
BERLIN, B.   8
     FOUR STAR SIGHT READING, GRADE 8
          FREDERICK HARRIS MUSIC COMPANY   1.15
BERLIN, B.
     LESSONS IN MUSIC WRITING, PART 1
          FREDERICK HARRIS MUSIC COMPANY   .90
BERLIN, B.
     LESSONS IN MUSIC WRITING, PART 2
          FREDERICK HARRIS MUSIC COMPANY   .90

BERLIN, B.
LESSONS IN MUSIC WRITING, PART 3
FREDERICK HARRIS MUSIC COMPANY .90
BERLIN, B.
NEW MODERN PIANO STUDENT, BK. 1
FREDERICK HARRIS MUSIC COMPANY 1.90
BERLIN, B.
PETER, JUDY AND SQUEAKY, FIRST PIANO BOOK
BOOSEY AND HAWKES, INC. 1.15
BERLIN, B.
PETER, JUDY AND SQUEAKY, SECOND PIANO BOOK
FREDERICK HARRIS MUSIC COMPANY 1.15
BERLIN, B.
WORLD FAMOUS CHRISTMAS CAROLS
FREDERICK HARRIS MUSIC COMPANY .90
BERLIN, B. *
YOUNG PIANISTS' JOYFUL HOUR, BK. 1
FREDERICK HARRIS MUSIC COMPANY 1.90
BERLIN, B. *
YOUNG PIANISTS' JOYFUL HOUR, BK. 2
FREDERICK HARRIS MUSIC COMPANY 1.90
BERLIN, I.
POINTER LIBRARY - WORDS AND MUSIC BY IRVING BERLIN, VOL. 1
POINTER PUBLICATIONS 2.95
BERLIN, I.
POINTER LIBRARY - WORDS AND MUSIC BY IRVING BERLIN, VOL. 2
POINTER PUBLICATIONS 2.95
BERMONT, G.
ECHOES OF THE CIVIL WAR
BELWIN-MILLS PUBLISHING CORPORATION 11139 1.25
BERMONT, H.
ANYONE CAN PLAY PIANO
MUSICORD PUBLICATIONS, INC. 2.00
BERMONT, H.
PLAY POPULAR - BE POPULAR
MUSICORD PUBLICATIONS, INC. 2.00
BERMONT, H.--ED BERMONT, H.
ALL-AMERICAN FOLK SONGS, BK. 1
MUSICORD PUBLICATIONS, INC. 1.50
BERMONT, H.--ED BERMONT, H.
ALL-AMERICAN FOLK SONGS, BK. 2
MUSICORD PUBLICATIONS, INC. 1.50
BERMONT, H.--ED BERMONT, H.
HYMNS WE LOVE
MUSICORD PUBLICATIONS, INC. 1.25
BERMONT, H.--ED BERMONT, H.
LETS PLAY CAROLS
MUSICORD PUBLICATIONS, INC. 1.00
BERMONT, H.--ED BERMONT, H.
MINUTE MELODIES - BK. 1
MUSICORD PUBLICATIONS, INC. 1.25
BERMONT, H.--ED BERMONT, H.
MINUTE MELODIES - BK. 2
MUSICORD PUBLICATIONS, INC. 1.25
BERMONT, H.--ED BERMONT, H.
PLAY THAT TUNE, BK. 1
MUSICORD PUBLICATIONS, INC. 1.25
BERMONT, H.--ED BERMONT, H.
PLAY THAT TUNE, BK. 2
MUSICORD PUBLICATIONS, INC. 1.25
BERMONT, H.--ED BERMONT, H.
PLAY THAT TUNE, BK. 3
MUSICORD PUBLICATIONS, INC. 1.25
BERMONT, H.--ED BERMONT, H.
PLAY THAT TUNE, BK. 4
MUSICORD PUBLICATIONS, INC. 1.25
BERMONT, H.--ED BERMONT, H.
TUNEFUL VARIETIES, BK. 1
MUSICORD PUBLICATIONS, INC. 1.25
BERMONT, H.--ED BERMONT, H.
TUNEFUL VARIETIES, BK. 2
MUSICORD PUBLICATIONS, INC. 1.25
BERMONT, H.--ED BERMONT, H.
TWENTY-EIGHT STAR MELODIES, BK. 1
MUSICORD PUBLICATIONS, INC. 1.25
BERMONT, H.--ED BERMONT, H.
YOUR HIT TUNES - GREEN BOOK
MUSICORD PUBLICATIONS, INC. 1.25
BERMONT, H.--ED BERMONT, H.
YOUR HIT TUNES - RED BOOK
MUSICORD PUBLICATIONS, INC. 1.25
BERNSTEIN, L.
WEST SIDE STORY, SELECTIONS FROM
G. SCHIRMER, INC. 1.50
BERNSTEIN, L. STICKLES
WEST SIDE STORY, SELECTIONS FROM
G. SCHIRMER, INC. 1.25
BERTINI GERMER
FIFTY SELECTED STUDIES, FROM OP. 29, 32, 100
G. SCHIRMER, INC. L795 1.50
BERTINI BUONAMICI *
FIFTY SELECTED STUDIES, FROM OP. 29, 32, 100, 134 --PREPARATORY
TO CRAMER-BUELOW STUDIES--
G. SCHIRMER, INC. L1588 1.50
BERTINI
FORTY-EIGHT STUDIES, OP. 29 - BK. 1
UNIVERSAL EDITION 129 1.40
BERTINI
FORTY-EIGHT STUDIES, OP. 32 - BK. 2
UNIVERSAL EDITION 130 1.40
BERTINI SCHARWENKA
TWELVE EASY PIECES, OP. 84
ASSOCIATED MUSIC PUBLISHERS, INC. B/H .75
BERTINI VOGRICH
TWELVE LITTLE PIECES AND PRELUDES
G. SCHIRMER, INC. L135 1.00
BERTINI E
TWELVE SHORT PIECES AND PRELUDES FOR BEGINNERS
C. F. PETERS CORPORATION 181A 2.00
BERTINI VOGRICH *
TWENTY-FIVE EASY STUDIES WITHOUT OCTAVES, OP. 100
G. SCHIRMER, INC. L136 1.00
BERTINI E
TWENTY-FIVE EASY STUDIES WITHOUT OCTAVES, OP.100
C. F. PETERS CORPORATION 181B 2.00
BERTINI
TWENTY-FIVE ELEMENTARY STUDIES, OP. 137
FRANCO COLOMBO PUBLICATIONS ER2426 1.50
BERTINI OESTERLE
TWENTY-FIVE PRIMARY ETUDES, OP. 166
G. SCHIRMER, INC. L691 1.00
BERTINI
TWENTY-FIVE STUDIES FOR SMALL HANDS, OP. 100
UNIVERSAL EDITION 132 1.20
BERTINI MUGELLINI
TWENTY-FIVE STUDIES FOR THE 1ST GRADE, OP. 100
FRANCO COLOMBO PUBLICATIONS ER493 1.25

BERTINI MUGELLINI
TWENTY-FIVE STUDIES FOR THE 2ND GRADE, OP. 29
FRANCO COLOMBO PUBLICATIONS ER494 1.75
BERTINI MUGELLINI
TWENTY-FIVE STUDIES FOR THE 3RD GRADE, OP. 32
FRANCO COLOMBO PUBLICATIONS ER495 2.50
BERTINI MUGELLINI
TWENTY-FIVE STUDIES FOR THE 4TH GRADE, OP. 134
FRANCO COLOMBO PUBLICATIONS ER496 3.50
BERTINI
TWENTY-FOUR MELODIOUS PIECES, OP. 101
G. SCHIRMER, INC. L758 1.25
BERTINI M
TWENTY-FOUR STUDIES, OP. 29 --PREPARATORY SONATINAS TO CRAMER,
PART 1--
C. F. PETERS CORPORATION 182A 2.00
BERTINI M
TWENTY-FOUR STUDIES, OP. 29 --PREPARATORY SONATINAS TO CRAMER,
PART 1--
C. F. PETERS CORPORATION 182B 2.50
BERTINI VOGRICH *
TWENTY-FOUR STUDIES, OP. 29 --PREPARATORY TO THE CRAMER
STUDIES--
G. SCHIRMER, INC. L137 1.00
BERTINI VOGRICH *
TWENTY-FOUR STUDIES, OP. 32 --SEQUEL TO OP. 29--
G. SCHIRMER, INC. L138 1.00
BESTHOFF, M.
MERRY CHRISTMAS CAROLS TO SING AND PLAY
BELWIN-MILLS PUBLISHING CORPORATION 1.00
BETTS
EIGHT RECITAL PIECES FOR YOUNG PIANISTS, BK. 1-A LITTLE MARCH,
NIGHT SONG
MCA MUSIC .60
BETTS
EIGHT RECITAL PIECES FOR YOUNG PIANISTS, BK. 2 - SERENADE, FOLK
SONG
MCA MUSIC .60
BETTS
EIGHT RECITAL PIECES FOR YOUNG PIANISTS, BK. 3 - WALTZ, SLOW
DANCE
MCA MUSIC .60
BETTS
EIGHT RECITAL PIECES FOR YOUNG PIANISTS, BK. 4 - TARENTELLA,
CHORALE PRELUDE ON 'AWAY IN THE MANGER'
MCA MUSIC .60
BEUCHTGER
THREE PIECES FOR PIANO
BARENREITER VERLAG BE 340 2.25
BEYER, F. SCHARFENBERG
ELEMENTARY INSTRUCTION BOOK
G. SCHIRMER, INC. 1.00
BEYER, F. E
ELEMENTARY INSTRUCTION BOOK, OP. 101
C. F. PETERS CORPORATION 2721 2.50
BEYER, F.
ELEMENTARY METHOD
CARL FISCHER, INC. O 70 1.00
BEYER, F. POZZOLI
PREPARATORY SCHOOL FOR YOUNG STUDENTS, OP. 101
FRANCO COLOMBO PUBLICATIONS ER104 1.75
BEYER, F.
PREPARATORY SCHOOL, OP. 101 --GERMAN, ENGLISH, FRENCH--
UNIVERSAL EDITION 167 2.25
BIALIS * GOEBELS 3
NEUE CEMBALOMUSIK, HEFT 1
BARENREITER VERLAG BA 3804
BIEHL, A.
ELEMENTS OF PIANO-PLAYING, OP. 30
G. SCHIRMER, INC. L530 .75
BIEHL, A.
TWENTY-FIVE EASY AND PROGRESSIVE STUDIES WITH SPECIAL REFERENCES
TO THE LEFT HAND, OP. 44, BK. 1
G. SCHIRMER, INC. L497 1.00
BIEHL, A.
TWENTY-FIVE EASY AND PROGRESSIVE STUDIES WITH SPECIAL REFERENCES
TO THE LEFT HAND, OP. 44, BK. 2
G. SCHIRMER, INC. L498 1.00
BIEHL, A.
TWENTY-FIVE EASY AND PROGRESSIVE STUDIES WITH SPECIAL REFERENCES
TO THE LEFT HAND, OP. 44, BK. 3
G. SCHIRMER, INC. L499 1.00
BILBRO, M.
FIRST MELODY LESSONS
BOSTON MUSIC COMPANY 1.00
BILBRO, M.
FUN IN SCALE PLAYING
WILLIS MUSIC COMPANY .80
BILBRO, M.
HAPPY HALF HOURS IN MELODYLAND
WILLIS MUSIC COMPANY 1.00
BILBRO, M. 1
PIANO DUETS FOR TWO YOUNG PUPILS
WILLIS MUSIC COMPANY .90
BILBRO, M.
PRISCILLA'S WEEK -- SEVEN LITTLE CHARACTERISTIC PIECES
THEODORE PRESSER COMPANY .90
BILBRO, M.
SECOND MELODY LESSONS
BOSTON MUSIC COMPANY 1.25
BILBRO, M.
SPELLING LESSONS IN TIME AND NOTATION
THEODORE PRESSER COMPANY 1.00
BINET 2, 3
LES LILLIPUTIENNES, OP. 125
ALPHONSE LEDUC
BINET 2, 3
LES PAGINETTES, OP. 133
ALPHONSE LEDUC
BISHOP
CHORDS IN ACTION
CARL FISCHER, INC. O 4007 1.75
BISQUERTT
THREE ESQUISSES
FRANCO COLOMBO PUBLICATIONS SAL 2.75
BITSCH 7
HOMMAGE A DOMENICO SCARLATTI
ALPHONSE LEDUC
BITSCH 3
LE LIVRE DE NOEMIE, 10 ETUDES FACILES
ALPHONSE LEDUC
BITSCH 4
LES SONGES MERVEILLEUX
ALPHONSE LEDUC
BIZET, G.
JEUX D'ENFANTS
ELKAN-VOGEL, INC. 5.60

BIZET, G.   4
    L'ARLESIENNE-SUITE 1-2
        SCHOTT   1408   2.25
BIZET, G.
    L'ARLESIENNE, 2 CONCERT SUITES
        G. SCHIRMER, INC.   L357   1.50
BLACHER
    THREE PIANO PIECES
        UNIVERSAL EDITION   11628   2.50
BLACHER
    TWO SONATINAS, OP. 14
        ASSOCIATED MUSIC PUBLISHERS, INC.   B/B   4.00
BLAKE
    ADVENTURES IN STYLE
        WILLIS MUSIC COMPANY   1.25
BLAKE
    DOWN SOUTH
        WILLIS MUSIC COMPANY   .75
BLAKE
    EIGHT INTERVALS, THE
        WILLIS MUSIC COMPANY   .80
BLAKE
    KEYBOARD SECRETS
        WILLIS MUSIC COMPANY   1.25
BLAKE
    LET'S PLAY WITH TWO HANDS
        WILLIS MUSIC COMPANY   1.00
BLAKE
    MELODY BOOK, BK. 1
        WILLIS MUSIC COMPANY   1.50
BLAKE
    MELODY BOOK, BK. 2
        WILLIS MUSIC COMPANY   1.50
BLAKE
    THRU' THE CASTLE GATE
        WILLIS MUSIC COMPANY   .80
BLAKE
    WHEN NOTES GO SKIPPING
        WILLIS MUSIC COMPANY   1.25
BLAKE
    WHEN NOTES GO WALKING
        WILLIS MUSIC COMPANY   1.50
BLAKE--ED   BLAKE
    COMPANIONS AT THE KEYBOARD
        WILLIS MUSIC COMPANY   .90
BLAKE--ED   BLAKE
    TALES AND TUNES FROM GRAND OPERA
        WILLIS MUSIC COMPANY   1.50
BLAKE, J. *
    FIRST GRADE PIANO PIECES
        BOOSEY AND HAWKES, INC.   1.00
BLAKE, J. *
    MAKING MUSIC
        BOOSEY AND HAWKES, INC.   1.50
BLAKE, J. *
    PIANO TIME
        BOOSEY AND HAWKES, INC.   1.00
BLAKE, J. *
    SECOND GRADE PIANO PIECES
        BOOSEY AND HAWKES, INC.   1.00
BLANCAFORT
    CHANTIS INTIMES - BK. 1
        FRANCO COLOMBO PUBLICATIONS   SAL   2.75
BLANCAFORT
    CHANTIS INTOMES - BK. 2
        FRANCO COLOMBO PUBLICATIONS   SAL   3.25
BLANCARD
    ELEMENTARY PRINCIPLES OF PIANO TECHNIQUE
        FRANCO COLOMBO PUBLICATIONS   SAL   3.25
BLANCHET
    EIGHT CONCERT ETUDES, OP. 55
        ASSOCIATED MUSIC PUBLISHERS, INC.   ESC   3.25
BLANCHET
    SIXTY-FOUR PRELUDES, OP. 41--VOL. 2--
        ASSOCIATED MUSIC PUBLISHERS, INC.   ESC   4.50
BLANCHET
    SIXTY-FOUR PRELUDES, OP. 41--VOL. 3--
        ASSOCIATED MUSIC PUBLISHERS, INC.   ESC   4.50
BLANCHET
    SIXTY-FOUR PRELUDES, OP. 64--VOL. 1 --
        ASSOCIATED MUSIC PUBLISHERS, INC.   ESC   4.50
BLANCHET
    THIRTEEN STUDIES FOR THE LEFT HAND ALONE, OP. 53
        ASSOCIATED MUSIC PUBLISHERS, INC.   ESC   3.50
BLANCHET
    TREIZE ETUDES CONTRAPUNTIQUES, OP. 43
        ASSOCIATED MUSIC PUBLISHERS, INC.   ESC   3.00
BLANCHET
    TWO PIECES, OP. 44
        ASSOCIATED MUSIC PUBLISHERS, INC.   ESC   1.50
BLASCO DE NEBRA   PARRIS
    SIX SONATAS
        ASSOCIATED MUSIC PUBLISHERS, INC.   UME   4.75
BLOCH, E.
    ENFANTINES
        CARL FISCHER, INC.   O 2916   1.50
BLOCH, W. *   MARCKHL
    STYRIAN COMPOSERS, WORKS FOR PIANO -- BK. 1
        ASSOCIATED MUSIC PUBLISHERS, INC.   OBV   1.25
BLOCH, W.
    ZWOLF MINIATUREN
        ASSOCIATED MUSIC PUBLISHERS, INC.   DOB   1.50
BLOOM   BLOOM
    RUBE BLOOM'S GUIDE TO MODERN PIANO PLAYING
        THE BIG THREE MUSIC CORPORATION   1.50
BLOOM   BLOOM
    RUBE BLOOM'S MODERN JAZZ PIANO COURSE
        THE BIG THREE MUSIC CORPORATION   1.50
BLOW   E
    SONG TUNE, THEATRE TUNE
        C. F. PETERS CORPORATION   H9   1.50
BOCK, F.
    SACRED SONGS FOR THE PIANO
        BROADMAN MUSIC   4571-08   2.50
BOCK, F.
    YOUNG WORLD PIANIST
        LILLENAS PUBLISHING COMPANY   MB-260   2.50
BOCK, F.--ED   BOCK. F.
    HOW GREAT THOU ART
        THEODORE PRESSER COMPANY   2.95
BOCK, F.--ED   BOCK. F.
    SONGS I SING IN SUNDAY SCHOOL
        THEODORE PRESSER COMPANY   1.25
BOEHM, G. *   BUCHMAYER
    EARLY KEYBOARD WORKS -- BK. 5
        ASSOCIATED MUSIC PUBLISHERS, INC.   BRH   2.00

BOERO
    POPULAR ARGENTINE AIRS, BK. 1
        FRANCO COLOMBO PUBLICATIONS   BA7298   1.00
BOERO
    POPULAR ARGENTINE AIRS, BK. 2
        FRANCO COLOMBO PUBLICATIONS   BA 8038   1.00
BOERO
    POPULAR ARGENTINE AIRS, BK. 3
        FRANCO COLOMBO PUBLICATIONS   BA8687   1.00
BOGHEN
    TOCCATAS BY OLD ITALIAN MASTERS
        FRANCO COLOMBO PUBLICATIONS   ER22   6.75
BOGIN
    UNDER THE BIG TOP SERIES -BALLOONS FOR SALE
        MCA MUSIC   .60
BOGIN
    UNDER THE BIG TOP SERIES -BIG TOP PARADE
        MCA MUSIC   .60
BOGIN
    UNDER THE BIG TOP SERIES -MARCH OF THE ELEPHANTS
        MCA MUSIC   .60
BOGIN
    UNDER THE BIG TOP SERIES -PONY WALTZ
        MCA MUSIC   .60
BOGIN
    UNDER THE BIG TOP SERIES -PUPS ON A SEESAW
        MCA MUSIC   .60
BOGIN
    UNDER THE BIG TOP SERIES -SAD CLOWN, THE.
        MCA MUSIC   .60
BOGIN
    UNDER THE TOP SERIES -JUGGLER, THE.
        MCA MUSIC   .60
BOHM *   BAUM   2-3
    ALTE WEIHNACHTSMUSIK - 13 WEIHNACHTSCHORALE UND
    CHORALVARIATIONEN
        BARENREITER VERLAG   BA 826
BOHM
    COLLECTED KEYBOARD WORKS, VOL. 1
        ASSOCIATED MUSIC PUBLISHERS, INC.   B/H   7.50
BOHM
    COLLECTED KEYBOARD WORKS, VOL. 2
        ASSOCIATED MUSIC PUBLISHERS, INC.   B/H   7.50
BOHME--ED   BOHME   2-3
    WEIHNACHTSMUSIK FUR KLAVIER
        SCHOTT   5450   2.25
BOISMORTIER, J. B. DE   JACOBI
    FOUR SUITES, OP. 59
        ASSOCIATED MUSIC PUBLISHERS, INC.   LEU   5.00
BOIZARD, G.
    FIVE PIECES -- SELECTED FOR UFAM CONTESTANTS
        EDITIONS MUSICALES TRANSATLANTIQUES   2.15
BOIZARD, G.
    FOUR PIECES -- SELECTED FOR UFAM CONTESTANTS
        EDITIONS MUSICALES TRANSATLANTIQUES   2.25
BOIZARD, G.
    QUATRE PIECES
        EDITIONS MUSICALES TRANSATLANTIQUES   5.40
BOLCOM, W.
    TWELVE ETUDES FOR PIANO
        THEODORE PRESSER COMPANY   7.50
BONIS
    NINE EASY PIECES
        ASSOCIATED MUSIC PUBLISHERS, INC.   ESC   1.25
BONNEAU
    SIX PETITS CROQUIS
        ASSOCIATED MUSIC PUBLISHERS, INC.   ESC   1.50
BOONE, D.
    BEAUTIFUL SUNDAY
        THE BIG THREE MUSIC CORPORATION   02.95
BORDES
    DANSES, MARCHES ET CORTEGES POPULAIRES DU PAYS BASQUE ESPAGNOL
        FRANCO COLOMBO PUBLICATIONS   SAL   4.25
BORDES
    FOUR RHYTHMIC FANTASIES
        FRANCO COLOMBO PUBLICATIONS   SAL   4.25
BORKOVEC   3-4
    ZWEI KLAVIERKOMPOSITIONEN
        BARENREITER VERLAG   AP 520
BORLENGHI
    THREE IMMAGINI
        FRANCO COLOMBO PUBLICATIONS   FOR. 12268 1.75
BORNEFELD
    BEGLEITSATZE - DAS CHORALWERK, BK. 1
        BARENREITER VERLAG   BA 2212   3.50
BORNEFELD
    BEGLEITSATZE - DAS CHORALWERK, BK. 2
        BARENREITER VERLAG   BA 2213   3.50
BORNEFELD
    BEGLEITSATZE - DAS CHORALWERK, BK. 3
        BARENREITER VERLAG   BA 2214   3.50
BORNEFELD
    BEGLEITSATZE - DAS CHORALWERK, BK. 4
        BARENREITER VERLAG   BA 2215   3.50
BORNEFELD
    BEGLEITSATZE - DAS CHORALWERK, BK. 5
        BARENREITER VERLAG   BA 2216   3.50
BORNEFELD
    BEGLEITSATZE - DAS CHORALWERK, BK. 6
        BARENREITER VERLAG   BA 2217   3.50
BORNEFELD   1-2
    BEGLEITSATZE -- DAS CHORALWERK -- HEFT 1, 25 SATZE ZU ADVENT,
    WEIHNACHTEN, JAHRESSCHLUSS UND ERSCHEINUNGSFEST
        BARENREITER VERLAG   BA 2212
BORNEFELD   1-2
    BEGLEITSATZE -- DAS CHORALWERK -- HEFT 2, 28 SATZE ZU PASSION,
    OSTERN, HIMMELFAHRT, PFINGSTEN UND DREIEINIGKEIT
        BARENREITER VERLAG   BA 2213
BORNEFELD   1-2
    BEGLEITSATZE -- DAS CHORALWERK -- HEFT 3, 31 SATZE, KIRCHE,
    WORT, SAKRAMENT
        BARENREITER VERLAG   BA 2214
BORNEFELD   1-2
    BEGLEITSATZE -- DAS CHORALWERK -- HEFT 4, 29 SATZE, PSALMEN,
    GEBETE
        BARENREITER VERLAG   BA 2215
BORNEFELD   1-2
    BEGLEITSATZE -- DAS CHORALWERK -- HEFT 5, 30 SATZE, LOB UND
    DANK, GLAUBE
        BARENREITER VERLAG   BA 2216
BORNEFELD   1-2
    BEGLEITSATZE -- DAS CHORALWERK -- HEFT 6, 32 SATZE ZU MORGEN,
    ABEND, BERUF, TOD UND EWIGKEIT
        BARENREITER VERLAG   BA 2217
BORNEFELD *   BAUM   2-3
    NEUE WEIHNACHTSMUSIK. 18 WEIHNACHTSLIEDER IN 24 SATZEN
        BARENREITER VERLAG   BA 908

271

BORODIN, A.   7, 9
    PETITE SUITE
        ALPHONSE LEDUC
BORODIN, A.
    POLOVETSIAN DANCES, FROM 'PRINCE IGOR'
        BOOSEY AND HAWKES, INC.   3.00
BORODIN, A. *
    RUSSIAN MASTERS -- 14 ORIGINAL COMPOSITIONS BY BORODIN,
    MUSSORGSKY, PROKOFIEFF, STRAVINSKY AND OTHERS
        ASSOCIATED MUSIC PUBLISHERS, INC.   SIM   2.00
BORTKIEWICZ
    FOUR PIECES, OP. 65
        ASSOCIATED MUSIC PUBLISHERS, INC.   DOB   2.75
BORTKIEWICZ
    FROM ANDERSEN'S FAIRY TALES, OP. 30
        ASSOCIATED MUSIC PUBLISHERS, INC.   SIM   1.50
BORTKIEWICZ
    MARIONETTES, OP. 54 -- NINE EASY PIECES
        ASSOCIATED MUSIC PUBLISHERS, INC.   SIM   1.50
BORTKIEWICZ
    TEN ETUDES, OP. 15
        ASSOCIATED MUSIC PUBLISHERS, INC.   SIM   3.25
BORTKIEWICZ
    TRAVEL PIECES, OP. 21
        ASSOCIATED MUSIC PUBLISHERS, INC.   SIM   1.25
BOSSI   3
    JUGEND-ALBUM OP. 122, BK. 1
        SCHOTT   2099 2.00
BOSSI   3
    JUGEND-ALBUM OP. 122, BK. 2
        SCHOTT   2100 2.00
BOTTINO, G.
    TRE PERSONAGGI IN CERCA DI REQUIEM
        EDIZIONI BERBEN   EB 1506 3.00
BOUD, R.
    RON BOUD PIANO STYLINGS
        HOPE PUBLISHING COMPANY   2.00
BOUTNIKOFF
    TWO PRELUDES
        FRANCO COLOMBO PUBLICATIONS   SAL   4.00
BOUTRY
    EN IMAGES - BK. 1
        FRANCO COLOMBO PUBLICATIONS   SAL   3.00
BOUTRY
    EN IMAGES - BK. 2
        FRANCO COLOMBO PUBLICATIONS   SAL   3.50
BOUTRY
    LES DANSES EXTRAVAGANTES DU GNOME FARCEUR
        ASSOCIATED MUSIC PUBLISHERS, INC.   ESC   3.75
BOWLES, P.
    TUNE FOR A BOY GOING TO SCHOOL AND TUNE FOR A BOY COMING FROM
    SCHOOL
        EDWARD B. MARKS MUSIC CORPORATION   00.60
BOZZA   2
    DEUX PIECES FACILES
        ALPHONSE LEDUC
BRADLEY
    DEFINITE PURPOSE STUDIES, BK. 1 - PRELIMINARY
        FRANCO COLOMBO PUBLICATIONS   LD261 1.00
BRADLEY
    DEFINITE PURPOSE STUDIES, BK. 2 - PRIMARY
        FRANCO COLOMBO PUBLICATIONS   LD262 1.00
BRADLEY
    DEFINITE PURPOSE STUDIES, BK. 3 - ELEMENTARY
        FRANCO COLOMBO PUBLICATIONS   LD263 1.00
BRADLEY
    FIRST CLASSICS, BK. 1 - PRELIMINARY
        FRANCO COLOMBO PUBLICATIONS   LD210 1.00
BRADLEY
    FIRST CLASSICS, BK. 2 - PRIMARY
        FRANCO COLOMBO PUBLICATIONS   LD211 1.00
BRADLEY
    FIRST CLASSICS, BK. 3 - ELEMENTARY-TRANSITIONAL
        FRANCO COLOMBO PUBLICATIONS   LD212 1.00
BRADLEY
    FIRST COURSE, BK. 1 - PREPARATORY
        FRANCO COLOMBO PUBLICATIONS   LD232 1.00
BRADLEY
    FIRST COURSE, BK. 2 - PRELIMINARY
        FRANCO COLOMBO PUBLICATIONS   LD233 1.00
BRADLEY
    FIRST COURSE, BK. 3 - PRIMARY
        FRANCO COLOMBO PUBLICATIONS   LD234 1.00
BRADLEY
    FIRST COURSE, BK. 4 - ELEMENTARY
        FRANCO COLOMBO PUBLICATIONS   LD235 1.00
BRADLEY
    GOOD MORNING - 12 PIECES
        FRANCO COLOMBO PUBLICATIONS   LD38 1.00
BRADLEY
    LIGHT CLASSICS, BK. 1
        FRANCO COLOMBO PUBLICATIONS   LD226 1.00
BRADLEY
    LIGHT CLASSICS, BK. 2
        FRANCO COLOMBO PUBLICATIONS   LD227 1.00
BRADLEY
    LIGHT CLASSICS, BK. 3
        FRANCO COLOMBO PUBLICATIONS   LD228 1.00
BRADLEY
    LITTLE TECHNICS
        FRANCO COLOMBO PUBLICATIONS   LD219 1.00
BRADLEY
    PROGRESSIVE STUDIES AND PIECES - HIGHER
        FRANCO COLOMBO PUBLICATIONS   LD209 1.00
BRADLEY
    PROGRESSIVE STUDIES AND PIECES - PRIMARY
        FRANCO COLOMBO PUBLICATIONS   LD206 1.00
BRADLEY
    TRAINING IN MUSIC, BK. 1
        FRANCO COLOMBO PUBLICATIONS   LD314 1.00
BRADLEY
    TRAINING IN MUSIC, BK. 2
        FRANCO COLOMBO PUBLICATIONS   LD315 1.00
BRADLEY
    TRAINING IN MUSIC, BK. 3
        FRANCO COLOMBO PUBLICATIONS   LD316 1.00
BRADLEY
    TRAINING IN MUSIC, BK. 4
        FRANCO COLOMBO PUBLICATIONS   LD317 1.00
BRADLEY
    TWO-PART AURAL PRACTICE BOOK
        FRANCO COLOMBO PUBLICATIONS   LD191 1.00
BRADLEY, R.--ARR.   BRADLEY, R.   BIG NOTE EASY
    AMAZING GRACE - AND - HE'S GOT THE WHOLE WORLD IN HIS HANDS
        SCREEN GEMS - COLUMBIA PUBLICATIONS   C0019P3 1.00
BRADLEY, R.--ARR.   BRADLEY, R.   BIG NOTE EASY
    BLACK AND WHITE - AND - BRIAN'S SONG
        SCREEN GEMS - COLUMBIA PUBLICATIONS   C0015P3 1.00

BRADLEY, R.--ARR.   BRADLEY, R.   EASY
    BRADLEY - LIKE IT IS TODAY - EASY PIANO HIT PARADE NO. 1
        SCREEN GEMS - COLUMBIA PUBLICATIONS   F0025P2 1.25
BRADLEY, R.--ARR.   BRADLEY, R.   EASY
    BRADLEY - LIKE IT IS TODAY - EASY PIANO HIT PARADE NO. 2
        SCREEN GEMS - COLUMBIA PUBLICATIONS   F0051P2 1.50
BRADLEY, R.--ARR.   BRADLEY, R.   EASY
    BRADLEY - LIKE IT IS TODAY - EASY PIANO HIT PARADE NO. 3
        SCREEN GEMS - COLUMBIA PUBLICATIONS   F0075P2 1.75
BRADLEY, R.--ARR.   BRADLEY, R.   EASY
    BRADLEY - LIKE IT IS TODAY - EASY PIANO HIT PARADE NO. 4
        SCREEN GEMS - COLUMBIA PUBLICATIONS   F0100P2 1.75
BRADLEY, R.--ARR.   BRADLEY, R.   EASY
    BRADLEY'S BEST OF THE BEST - BREAD
        SCREEN GEMS - COLUMBIA PUBLICATIONS   F0108P2 1.75
BRADLEY, R.--ARR.   BRADLEY, R.   EASY
    BRADLEY'S BEST OF THE BEST - BROADWAY
        SCREEN GEMS - COLUMBIA PUBLICATIONS   F0077P2 1.75
BRADLEY, R.--ARR.   BRADLEY, R.   EASY
    BRADLEY'S BEST OF THE BEST - CAROLE KING
        SCREEN GEMS - COLUMBIA PUBLICATIONS   F0027P2A 1.75
BRADLEY, R.--ARR.   BRADLEY, R.   EASY
    BRADLEY'S BEST OF THE BEST - CHRISTMAS CAROLS
        SCREEN GEMS - COLUMBIA PUBLICATIONS   F0211P2 1.75
BRADLEY, R.--ARR.   BRADLEY, R.   EASY
    BRADLEY'S BEST OF THE BEST - COUNTRY HITS
        SCREEN GEMS - COLUMBIA PUBLICATIONS   F0029P2 1.50
BRADLEY, R.--ARR.   BRADLEY, R.   EASY
    BRADLEY'S BEST OF THE BEST - MOTION PICTURE HITS
        SCREEN GEMS - COLUMBIA PUBLICATIONS   F0037P2 1.50
BRADLEY, R.--ARR.   BRADLEY, R.   EASY
    BRADLEY'S BEST OF THE BEST - POP TEACHING PIECES
        SCREEN GEMS - COLUMBIA PUBLICATIONS   F0230P2 1.75
BRADLEY, R.--ARR.   BRADLEY, R.   EASY
    BRADLEY'S BEST OF THE BEST - POPULAR SACRED SONGS
        SCREEN GEMS - COLUMBIA PUBLICATIONS   F0135P2 1.50
BRADLEY, R.--ARR.   BRADLEY, R.   BIG NOTE EASY
    BRADLEY'S BIG NOTE BLOCKBUSTERS
        SCREEN GEMS - COLUMBIA PUBLICATIONS   F0233P3 2.95
BRADLEY, R.--ARR.   BRADLEY, R.   EASY
    BRADLEY'S CHRISTMAS JOY - ISSUE NO. 1
        SCREEN GEMS - COLUMBIA PUBLICATIONS   F0213P2 1.75
BRADLEY, R.--ARR.   BRADLEY, R.   EASY
    BRADLEY'S COUNTRY JOY - ISSUE NO. 1
        SCREEN GEMS - COLUMBIA PUBLICATIONS   F0189P2 1.50
BRADLEY, R.--ARR.   BRADLEY, R.   EASY
    BRADLEY'S HYMN JOY - ISSUE NO. 1
        SCREEN GEMS - COLUMBIA PUBLICATIONS   F0275P2 1.50
BRADLEY, R.--ARR.   BRADLEY, R.   EASY
    BRADLEY'S POPULAR JOY - ISSUE NO. 1
        SCREEN GEMS - COLUMBIA PUBLICATIONS   F0128P2 1.50
BRADLEY, R.--ARR.   BRADLEY, R.   EASY
    BRADLEY'S POPULAR JOY - ISSUE NO. 2
        SCREEN GEMS - COLUMBIA PUBLICATIONS   F0187P2 1.50
BRADLEY, R.--ARR.   BRADLEY, R.   EASY
    BRADLEY'S POPULAR JOY - ISSUE NO. 3
        SCREEN GEMS - COLUMBIA PUBLICATIONS   F0216P2 1.50
BRADLEY, R.--ARR.   BRADLEY, R.   EASY
    BRADLEY'S POPULAR JOY - ISSUE NO. 4
        SCREEN GEMS - COLUMBIA PUBLICATIONS   F0261P2 1.50
BRADLEY, R.--ARR.   BRADLEY, R.   EASY
    BRADLEY'S SUPER POPULAR MUSIC
        SCREEN GEMS - COLUMBIA PUBLICATIONS   F0016P2 2.50
BRADLEY, R.--ARR.   BRADLEY, R.   EASY
    BRADLEY'S SUPERSTARS
        SCREEN GEMS - COLUMBIA PUBLICATIONS   F0223P2 2.50
BRADLEY, R.--ARR.   BRADLEY, R.   INTERMEDIATE
    BRADLEY'S TODAY'S SOUND PIANO SOLOS
        SCREEN GEMS - COLUMBIA PUBLICATIONS   F0035P   2.95
BRADLEY, R.--ARR.   BRADLEY, R.   EASY
    COUNTRY POPS
        SCREEN GEMS - COLUMBIA PUBLICATIONS   F0244P2 2.95
BRADLEY, R.--ARR.   BRADLEY, R.   EASY
    IN TUNE WITH THE TIMES
        SCREEN GEMS - COLUMBIA PUBLICATIONS   F0145P2 2.95
BRADLEY, R.--ARR.   BRADLEY, R.   BIG NOTE EASY
    LIVING TOGETHER, GROWING TOGETHER - AND - QUESTION ME AN ANSWER
        SCREEN GEMS - COLUMBIA PUBLICATIONS   C0030P3 1.00
BRADLEY, R.--ARR.   BRADLEY, R.   EASY
    LOST HORIZON
        SCREEN GEMS - COLUMBIA PUBLICATIONS   F0158P2 2.50
BRADLEY, R.--ARR.   BRADLEY, R.   EASY
    MORE 24 CARAT GOLD
        SCREEN GEMS - COLUMBIA PUBLICATIONS   F0268P2 3.95
BRADLEY, R.--ARR.   BRADLEY, R.   EASY
    MORE 24 CARAT GOLD
        SCREEN GEMS - COLUMBIA PUBLICATIONS   F0268P2 3.95
BRADLEY, R.--ARR.   BRADLEY, R.   EASY
    MOVIE POPS
        SCREEN GEMS - COLUMBIA PUBLICATIONS   F0259P2 2.50
BRADLEY, R.--ARR.   BRADLEY, R.   EASY
    PARTRIDGE FAMILY, THE - AT HOME WITH THEIR GREATEST HITS
        SCREEN GEMS - COLUMBIA PUBLICATIONS   P0036P2 2.50
BRADLEY, R.--ARR.   BRADLEY, R.   EASY
    POPS MADE EASY FOR PIANO
        SCREEN GEMS - COLUMBIA PUBLICATIONS   F0167P2 2.95
BRADLEY, R.--ARR.   BRADLEY, R.   EASY
    POPULAR TEACHER'S CHOICE
        SCREEN GEMS - COLUMBIA PUBLICATIONS   F0112P21 3.95
BRADLEY, R.--ARR.   BRADLEY, R.   EASY
    SENSATIONAL 70 FOR THE 70'S
        SCREEN GEMS - COLUMBIA PUBLICATIONS   F0050P2A 4.95
BRADLEY, R.--ARR.   BRADLEY, R.   EASY
    SIMON AND GARFUNKEL'S GREATEST HITS
        SCREEN GEMS - COLUMBIA PUBLICATIONS   P0037P2 2.50
BRADLEY, R.--ARR.   BRADLEY, R.   BIG NOTE EASY
    SIMPLY BRADLEY - CHRISTMAS CAROLS
        SCREEN GEMS - COLUMBIA PUBLICATIONS   F0105P3 1.50
BRADLEY, R.--ARR.   BRADLEY, R.   BIG NOTE EASY
    SIMPLY BRADLEY - FOLK BOOK
        SCREEN GEMS - COLUMBIA PUBLICATIONS   F0054P3 1.50
BRADLEY, R.--ARR.   BRADLEY, R.   BIG NOTE EASY
    SIMPLY BRADLEY - HYMN BOOK
        SCREEN GEMS - COLUMBIA PUBLICATIONS   F0048P3 1.50
BRADLEY, R.--ARR.   BRADLEY, R.   BIG NOTE EASY
    SIMPLY BRADLEY - MOVIE BOOK
        SCREEN GEMS - COLUMBIA PUBLICATIONS   F0095P3 1.50
BRADLEY, R.--ARR.   BRADLEY, R.   BIG NOTE EASY
    SIMPLY BRADLEY - POP BOOK
        SCREEN GEMS - COLUMBIA PUBLICATIONS   F0188P3 1.50
BRADLEY, R.--ARR.   BRADLEY, R.   BIG NOTE EASY
    SIMPLY BRADLEY - RUDOLPH THE RED-NOSED REINDEER AND OTHER
    CHRISTMAS FAVORITES
        SCREEN GEMS - COLUMBIA PUBLICATIONS   F0111P3 1.50
BRADLEY, R.--ARR.   BRADLEY, R.   BIG NOTE EASY
    SIMPLY BRADLEY - SECOND POP BOOK, THE
        SCREEN GEMS - COLUMBIA PUBLICATIONS   F0269P3 1.50

BRADLEY, R.--ARR.   BRADLEY, R.   BIG NOTE EASY
SIMPLY BRADLEY - THE PARTRIDGE FAMILY
    SCREEN GEMS - COLUMBIA PUBLICATIONS   P0018P3   1.50
BRADLEY, R.--ARR.   BRADLEY, R.   EASY
SIXTY-SEVEN BRADLEY POP TEACHING PIECES FOR PIANO
    SCREEN GEMS - COLUMBIA PUBLICATIONS   F0245P2   4.95
BRADLEY, R.--ARR.   BRADLEY, R.   EASY
SUPER POPULAR MUSIC
    SCREEN GEMS - COLUMBIA PUBLICATIONS   F0042P2   2.50
BRADLEY, R.--ARR.   BRADLEY, R.   EASY
SUPER 77, THE
    SCREEN GEMS - COLUMBIA PUBLICATIONS   F0199P2   4.95
BRADLEY, R.--ARR.   BRADLEY, R.   EASY
TWENTY-FOUR CARAT GOLD
    SCREEN GEMS - COLUMBIA PUBLICATIONS   F0257P2   3.95
BRADLEY, R.--ARR.   BRADLEY, R.   BIG NOTE EASY
WORLD IS A CIRCLE, THE - AND - REFLECTIONS
    SCREEN GEMS - COLUMBIA PUBLICATIONS   C0031P3   1.00
BRADY--ED   BRADY
CAROLS FOR CHRISTMAS
    BOSTON MUSIC COMPANY   1.50
BRAHMS
ALBUM
    KULTURA   2.00
BRAHMS   WHITING
ALBUM OF FAVORITE PIECES
    G. SCHIRMER, INC.   L1347   3.00
                    3-5
BRAHMS
AUSWAHL - 14 AUSGEWAHLTE STUCKE
    SCHOTT   1433   1.75
BRAHMS
BALLADES, OP. 10
    FRANCO COLOMBO PUBLICATIONS   ER1296   1.00
BRAHMS
BRAHMS
    ASHLEY DEALERS SERVICE, INC.   HG 02   2.95
BRAHMS
BRAHMS AT THE PIANO
    ASHLEY DEALERS SERVICE, INC.   1.00
                    2
BRAHMS
BRAHMS AT THE PIANO
    CENTURY MUSIC PUBLISHING COMPANY, INC.   1.00
BRAHMS   ECKHARDT, F.   1
BRAHMS FOR THE YOUNG PIANIST
    CENTURY MUSIC PUBLISHING COMPANY, INC.   3958   .40
BRAHMS   LEVINE, H.
BRAHMS WALTZES SIMPLIFIED
    ALFRED MUSIC COMPANY   546   1.25
BRAHMS   WHITING
CAPRICCIOS AND INTERMEZZOS, OP. 76
    G. SCHIRMER, INC.   L1261   1.25
BRAHMS   COIT, L. E. *
CHILDHOOD DAYS OF FAMOUS COMPOSERS -- CHILD BRAHMS
    THEODORE PRESSER COMPANY   1.00
BRAHMS
CLAVIERSTUECKE, OP. 76
    FRANCO COLOMBO PUBLICATIONS   ER1457   .75
BRAHMS
COMPLETE PIANO SONATAS AND VARIATIONS FOR SOLO PIANO
    DOVER PUBLICATIONS, INC.   22650-6   4.00
BRAHMS
COMPLETE PIANO TRANSCRIPTIONS, CADENZAS, AND EXERCISES
    DOVER PUBLICATIONS, INC.   22652-2   4.00
BRAHMS
COMPLETE PIANO WORKS--VOL. 1
    ASSOCIATED MUSIC PUBLISHERS, INC.   B/H   3.75
BRAHMS
COMPLETE PIANO WORKS--VOL. 2--
    ASSOCIATED MUSIC PUBLISHERS, INC.   B/H   3.75
BRAHMS
COMPLETE PIANO WORKS--VOL. 3--
    ASSOCIATED MUSIC PUBLISHERS, INC.   B/H   3.75
BRAHMS
COMPLETE SHORTER WORKS FOR PIANO
    DOVER PUBLICATIONS, INC.   22651-4   4.00
BRAHMS   MANDYCZEWSKI
COMPLETE WORKS FOR PIANO SOLO IN 3 VOLS. --THE SET, EACH VOL.
CLOTH-BOUND, BOXED--
    G. SCHIRMER, INC.   15.00
BRAHMS   MANDYCZEWSKI
COMPLETE WORKS FOR PIANO SOLO, BK. 1
    G. SCHIRMER, INC.   L1728   3.00
BRAHMS   MANDYCZEWSKI
COMPLETE WORKS FOR PIANO SOLO, BK. 2
    G. SCHIRMER, INC.   L1729   3.00
BRAHMS   MANDYCZEWSKI
COMPLETE WORKS FOR PIANO SOLO, BK. 3
    G. SCHIRMER, INC.   L1730   3.00
BRAHMS
COMPLETE WORKS, BK. 1
    FRANCO COLOMBO PUBLICATIONS   ER2559   6.25
BRAHMS
COMPLETE WORKS, BK. 2
    FRANCO COLOMBO PUBLICATIONS   ER2560   6.25
BRAHMS
EIGHT PIECES --CAPRICCI AND INTERMEZZI-- OP. 76
    INTERNATIONAL MUSIC COMPANY   1.50
BRAHMS   D
EIGHT PIECES --CAPRICCIOS AND INTERMEZZI-- OP. 76
    C. F. PETERS CORPORATION   3928   1.50
BRAHMS
EIGHT PIECES, OP. 76
    ASSOCIATED MUSIC PUBLISHERS, INC.   B/H   1.00
BRAHMS
EIGHTEEN LOVE SONG WALTZES, OP. 52 -- SATB AD LIB
    ASSOCIATED MUSIC PUBLISHERS, INC.   SIM   1.50
BRAHMS   MILLER
ELEVEN CHORALE PRELUDES, OP. 122
    ASSOCIATED MUSIC PUBLISHERS, INC.   B/H   2.00
BRAHMS
FANTASIES, OP. 116
    G. HENLE MUSIKVERLAG   120   1.40
BRAHMS   DEIS
FANTASIES, OP. 116
    G. SCHIRMER, INC.   L1499   1.25
BRAHMS   LEVINE, H.
FAVORITE BRAHMS HUNGARIAN DANCES
    ALFRED MUSIC COMPANY   684   1.50
BRAHMS
FIFTY-ONE ETUDES
    EDWIN F. KALMUS   3261   1.50
BRAHMS
FIFTY-ONE EXERCISES
    INTERNATIONAL MUSIC COMPANY   2.00
BRAHMS
FIFTY-ONE EXERCISES
    G. SCHIRMER, INC.   L1600   1.25

BRAHMS   POZZOLI
FIFTY-ONE EXERCISES, OP. POSTH. BK. 1
    FRANCO COLOMBO PUBLICATIONS   ER2126   2.00
BRAHMS   POZZOLI
FIFTY-ONE EXERCISES, OP. POSTH. BK. 2
    FRANCO COLOMBO PUBLICATIONS   ER2163   1.75
BRAHMS
FIFTY-ONE STUDIES
    ASSOCIATED MUSIC PUBLISHERS, INC.   B/H   2.00
BRAHMS   MAYER *
FIVE STUDIES, VOL. 1
    ASSOCIATED MUSIC PUBLISHERS, INC.   SIM   .90
BRAHMS   MAYER *
FIVE STUDIES, VOL. 2
    ASSOCIATED MUSIC PUBLISHERS, INC.   SIM   .90
BRAHMS   MAYER *
FOUR BALLADES, OP. 10
    ASSOCIATED MUSIC PUBLISHERS, INC.   B/H   1.00
BRAHMS   SAUER   D
FOUR BALLADES, OP. 10
    C. F. PETERS CORPORATION   3924   1.50
BRAHMS
FOUR BALLADES, OP. 10
    G. SCHIRMER, INC.   L1599   1.00
BRAHMS   STEUERMANN, E.
FOUR BALLADS, OP. 10
    UNIVERSAL EDITION   2258   1.20
BRAHMS
FOUR PIANO PIECES, OP. 119
    EDWIN F. KALMUS   3259   1.50
BRAHMS   DEIS
FOUR PIANO PIECES, OP. 119
    G. SCHIRMER, INC.   L1502   .75
BRAHMS   STEUERMANN, E.
FOUR PIANO PIECES, OP. 119
    UNIVERSAL EDITION   2355   1.20
BRAHMS
FOUR PIECES, OP. 119
    ASSOCIATED MUSIC PUBLISHERS, INC.   B/H   .60
BRAHMS
FOUR PIECES, OP. 119
    INTERNATIONAL MUSIC COMPANY   1.50
BRAHMS   SAUER   D
FOUR PIECES, OP. 119
    C. F. PETERS CORPORATION   3933   2.00
BRAHMS
HUNGARIAN DANCES NOS. 5, 6 AND 7
    FRANCO COLOMBO PUBLICATIONS   ER1030   .75
BRAHMS
HUNGARIAN DANCES NOS. 5, 6, 7
    FRANCO COLOMBO PUBLICATIONS   ER1031   .90
BRAHMS
HUNGARIAN DANCES 1-10
    G. HENLE MUSIKVERLAG   55   1.95
BRAHMS   MARCIANO
HUNGARIAN DANCES, BK. 1
    FRANCO COLOMBO PUBLICATIONS   ER98   1.75
BRAHMS   CESI
HUNGARIAN DANCES, BK. 1 - 1-10
    FRANCO COLOMBO PUBLICATIONS   ER99   1.75
BRAHMS   SCHARFENBERG
HUNGARIAN DANCES, BK. 1, NOS. 1-10
    G. SCHIRMER, INC.   L256   1.25
BRAHMS   MARCIANO
HUNGARIAN DANCES, BK. 2
    FRANCO COLOMBO PUBLICATIONS   ER1523   1.75
BRAHMS   CESI
HUNGARIAN DANCES, BK. 2 - 11-21
    FRANCO COLOMBO PUBLICATIONS   ER1524   2.25
BRAHMS   SCHARFENBERG
HUNGARIAN DANCES, BK. 2, NOS. 11-21
    G. SCHIRMER, INC.   L431   1.00
BRAHMS   SINGER   M-D
HUNGARIAN DANCES, VOL. 1
    C. F. PETERS CORPORATION   2101A   2.00
BRAHMS   SINGER   M-D
HUNGARIAN DANCES, VOL. 2
    C. F. PETERS CORPORATION   2101B   2.00
BRAHMS
PIANO PIECES
    G. HENLE MUSIKVERLAG   36   4.70
BRAHMS
PIANO PIECES --CLOTH--
    G. HENLE MUSIKVERLAG   37   7.70
BRAHMS
PIANO PIECES, OP. 118
    G. HENLE MUSIKVERLAG   122   1.15
BRAHMS
PIANO PIECES, OP. 119
    G. HENLE MUSIKVERLAG   123   1.40
BRAHMS
PIANO PIECES, OP. 76
    G. HENLE MUSIKVERLAG   118   1.15
BRAHMS   SAUER
PIANO WORKS --2 VOLS.--. CLOTH-BOUND
    C. F. PETERS CORPORATION   10.00
BRAHMS
PIANO WORKS, BK. 1
    INTERNATIONAL MUSIC COMPANY   5.00
BRAHMS
PIANO WORKS, BK. 1, --OP. 1 TO OP. 24--
    EDWIN F. KALMUS   3254   5.00
BRAHMS
PIANO WORKS, BK. 2
    INTERNATIONAL MUSIC COMPANY   5.00
BRAHMS
PIANO WORKS, BK. 2 --INCLUDES OP. 119 AND 5 ETUDES--
    EDWIN F. KALMUS   3255   4.00
BRAHMS
PIANO WORKS, BK. 3
    INTERNATIONAL MUSIC COMPANY   5.00
BRAHMS
PIANO WORKS, BK. 3 -- 2 PIANO CONCERTI, PAGANINI VARIATIONS, WALTZES
    EDWIN F. KALMUS   3256   6.00
BRAHMS   SAUER   D
PIANO WORKS, VOL. 1
    C. F. PETERS CORPORATION   3300A   3.00
BRAHMS   SAUER
PIANO WORKS, VOL. 1
    G. SCHIRMER, INC.   L1757   3.00
BRAHMS   SAUER   D
PIANO WORKS, VOL. 2
    C. F. PETERS CORPORATION   3300B   3.00
BRAHMS   SAUER
PIANO WORKS, VOL. 2
    G. SCHIRMER, INC.   L1758   3.00

BRAHMS
RADIO CITY ALBUM
EDWARD B. MARKS MUSIC CORPORATION 02.00
BRAHMS
RHAPSODIES, OP. 79, NOS. 1 AND 2
FRANCO COLOMBO PUBLICATIONS ED1061 1.25
BRAHMS JOSSEFFY, R.
SELECTED PIANO COMPOSITIONS
THEODORE PRESSER COMPANY 5.00
BRAHMS LEVINE, H.
SELECTED WORKS
ALFRED MUSIC COMPANY 625 3.00
BRAHMS SAUER D
SEVEN FANTASIES, OP. 116
C. F. PETERS CORPORATION 3930 1.50
BRAHMS BUSONI
SIX CHORALE PRELUDES FROM OP. 12
ASSOCIATED MUSIC PUBLISHERS, INC. SIM 1.50
BRAHMS
SIX PIANO PIECES, OP. 118
EDWIN F. KALMUS 3258 1.50
BRAHMS DEIS
SIX PIANO PIECES, OP. 118
G. SCHIRMER, INC. L1501 1.00
BRAHMS STEUERMANN, E.
SIX PIANO PIECES, OP. 118
UNIVERSAL EDITION 2354 1.50
BRAHMS SAUER D
SIX PIECES , OP. 118
C. F. PETERS CORPORATION 3932 1.50
BRAHMS
SIX PIECES, OP. 118
ASSOCIATED MUSIC PUBLISHERS, INC. B/H .60
BRAHMS
SIX PIECES, OP. 118
INTERNATIONAL MUSIC COMPANY 1.50
BRAHMS
SIXTEEN WALTZES, OP. 39
FRANCO COLOMBO PUBLICATIONS ER1156 1.75
BRAHMS SAUER D
SONATAS, OP. 1, 2, 5
C. F. PETERS CORPORATION 3923 3.50
BRAHMS
SONATAS, SCHERZO AND BALLADES
G. HENLE MUSIKVERLAG 38 5.50
BRAHMS
SONATAS, SCHERZO AND BALLADES --CLOTH--
G. HENLE MUSIKVERLAG 39 8.55
BRAHMS MONTANI
STUDIES AFTER BACH CHOPIN AND WEBER
FRANCO COLOMBO PUBLICATIONS ER2454 1.75
BRAHMS SINGER M-D
SYMPHONIES --4--
C. F. PETERS CORPORATION 3934 6.00
BRAHMS
TEN HUNGARIAN DANCES
ASSOCIATED MUSIC PUBLISHERS, INC. B/H 1.25
BRAHMS
THREE INTERMEZZI, OP. 117
ASSOCIATED MUSIC PUBLISHERS, INC. B/H .60
BRAHMS
THREE INTERMEZZI, OP. 117
FRANCO COLOMBO PUBLICATIONS ER1174 .75
BRAHMS
THREE INTERMEZZI, OP. 117
G. HENLE MUSIKVERLAG 121 1.15
BRAHMS
THREE INTERMEZZI, OP. 117
EDWIN F. KALMUS 3257 1.50
BRAHMS SAUER D
THREE INTERMEZZI, OP. 117
C. F. PETERS CORPORATION 3931 1.50
BRAHMS DEIS
THREE INTERMEZZI, OP. 117
G. SCHIRMER, INC. L1500 1.00
BRAHMS STEUERMANN, E.
THREE INTERMEZZI, OP. 117
UNIVERSAL EDITION 2294 1.00
BRAHMS MUELLER *
THREE INTERMEZZI, OP. 117
WIENER URTEXT EDITION UT 50023 1.75
BRAHMS WHITING
THREE SONATAS
G. SCHIRMER, INC. L1368 3.00
BRAHMS
TWO RHAPSODIES, OP. 79
ASSOCIATED MUSIC PUBLISHERS, INC. B/H .90
BRAHMS
TWO RHAPSODIES, OP. 79
G. HENLE MUSIKVERLAG 1 19 1.40
BRAHMS SAUER D
TWO RHAPSODIES, OP. 79
C. F. PETERS CORPORATION 3929 1.50
BRAHMS GEBHARD
TWO RHAPSODIES, OP. 79
G. SCHIRMER, INC. L1080 1.00
BRAHMS KLASEN, W.
TWO RHAPSODIES, OP. 79
UNIVERSAL EDITION 2277 1.75
BRAHMS STOCKMAN *
TWO RHAPSODIES, OP. 79
WIENER URTEXT EDITION UT 50007 2.25
BRAHMS M
TWO SARABANDES AND GIGUES
C. F. PETERS CORPORATION H11 1.25
BRAHMS
TWO SARABANDES, OP. POSTH.
ASSOCIATED MUSIC PUBLISHERS, INC. SIM .75
BRAHMS * D
TWO STUDIES --PERPETUUM MOBILE-- IN D.
C. F. PETERS CORPORATION 4831 2.00
BRAHMS BARTH, H.
TWO WALTZES
BELWIN-MILLS PUBLISHING CORPORATION 20327 .60
BRAHMS SCHUTT 5
UNGARISCHER TANZE NO. 11-21
SCHOTT 1428 2.25
BRAHMS
VARIATIONS, OP. 21, NOS. 1 AND 2
FRANCO COLOMBO PUBLICATIONS ER1007 1.00
BRAHMS
WALTZES
INTERNATIONAL MUSIC COMPANY 1.25
BRAHMS SAUER M-D
WALTZES
C. F. PETERS CORPORATION 3666 1.50

BRAHMS LEVINE, H.
WALTZES FOR PIANO SOLO 1. ADAPTED BY THE COMPOSER FROM HIS
PIANO DUETS 2. SIMPLIFIED BY COMPOSER
ALFRED MUSIC COMPANY 572 2.00
BRAHMS
WALTZES, OP. 39
CARL FISCHER, INC. L 919 1.00
BRAHMS
WALTZES, OP. 39
FRANCO COLOMBO PUBLICATIONS ER1155 1.25
BRAHMS
WALTZES, OP. 39
G. HENLE MUSIKVERLAG 42 1.15
BRAHMS
WALTZES, OP. 39
EDWIN F. KALMUS 3263 1.50
BRAHMS WHITING
WALTZES, OP. 39
G. SCHIRMER, INC. L1260 1.00
BRAHMS SAUER
WALTZES, OP. 39
UNIVERSAL EDITION 1108 1.50
BRAHMS
WALTZES, OP. 39. SIMPLIFIED
G. HENLE MUSIKVERLAG 43 1.15
BRAHMS 5
WALTZES, 1,2,8,15, OP. 39
CENTURY MUSIC PUBLISHING COMPANY, INC. 2448 .48
BRANT
FOUR SHORT NATURE PIECES
MCA MUSIC .75
BRAUER, F.
TWELVE STUDIES FOR DEVELOPMENT OF VELOCITY, OP. 15 --PREPARATION
TO CZERNY'S SCHOOL OF VELOCITY--
G. SCHIRMER, INC. L494 1.00
BREEN--ED BREEN
SIX IRISH PIECES -- WORKS FROM THE 17TH AND 18TH CENTURIES
ASSOCIATED MUSIC PUBLISHERS, INC. ESC 2.50
BREIG--ED BREIG
LIED- UND TANZVARIATIONEN DER SWEELINCK-SCHULE
SCHOTT 6030
BRENDEL
CADENZAS TO MOZART CONCERTO IN D MINOR, K. 466
ASSOCIATED MUSIC PUBLISHERS, INC. DOB 1.00
BRERO
SEVEN PRELUDES
FRANCO COLOMBO PUBLICATIONS BA11085 1.50
BRESGEN M
BALKAN IMPRESSIONS, IN 2 VOLS., VOL. 1, 10 PIECES FROM BULGARIA,
GREECE, YUGOSLAVIA
C. F. PETERS CORPORATION 5967A 2.50
BRESGEN M
BALKAN IMPRESSIONS, IN 2 VOLS., VOL. 2, 10 PIECES FROM ALBANIA,
HUNGARY, ROMANIA
C. F. PETERS CORPORATION 5967B 2.50
BRESGEN
STUDIES 1. EASY STUDIES FOR CHILDREN
ASSOCIATED MUSIC PUBLISHERS, INC. DOB 2.25
BRICUSSE *
STOP THE WORLD - I WANT TO GET OFF --EASY PIANO--
TRO SONGWAYS SERVICE, INC. 1.50
BRIDGE, F.
MINIATURE PASTORALS, BK. 1
BOOSEY AND HAWKES, INC. 1.50
BRIDGE, F.
MINIATURE PASTORALS, BK. 2
BOOSEY AND HAWKES, INC. 1.50
BRIDGE, F.
THREE SKETCHES
BOOSEY AND HAWKES, INC. 1.75
BRIMHALL, J.--ED. BRIMHALL, J.
BACHARACH AND DAVID'S TOP TEN
CHARLES HANSEN K401 1.95
BRIMHALL, J.--ED. BRIMHALL, J.
BEST OF BRIMHALL, BK. 1
CHARLES HANSEN 0171 2.95
BRIMHALL, J.--ED. BRIMHALL, J.
BEST OF BRIMHALL, BK. 2
CHARLES HANSEN 0170 2.95
BRIMHALL, J.--ED. BRIMHALL, J.
BEST OF BRIMHALL, BK. 3
CHARLES HANSEN 0171 2.95
BRIMHALL, J.--ED. BRIMHALL, J.
BEST OF SACRED MUSIC
CHARLES HANSEN H446 1.50
BRIMHALL, J.--ED. BRIMHALL, J.
BRIGADOON
CHARLES HANSEN T95 1.50
BRIMHALL, J.--ED. BRIMHALL, J.
BRIMHALL ISSUE NO. 01
CHARLES HANSEN H003 1.50
BRIMHALL, J.--ED. BRIMHALL, J.
BRIMHALL ISSUE NO. 02
CHARLES HANSEN H004 1.50
BRIMHALL, J.--ED. BRIMHALL, J.
BRIMHALL ISSUE NO. 03
CHARLES HANSEN H005 1.50
BRIMHALL, J.--ED. BRIMHALL, J.
BRIMHALL ISSUE NO. 04
CHARLES HANSEN H006 1.50
BRIMHALL, J.--ED. BRIMHALL, J.
BRIMHALL ISSUE NO. 05
CHARLES HANSEN H028 1.50
BRIMHALL, J.--ED. BRIMHALL, J.
BRIMHALL ISSUE NO. 06
CHARLES HANSEN H321 1.50
BRIMHALL, J.--ED. BRIMHALL, J.
BRIMHALL ISSUE NO. 07
CHARLES HANSEN H356 1.50
BRIMHALL, J.--ED. BRIMHALL, J.
BRIMHALL ISSUE NO. 08
CHARLES HANSEN H362 1.50
BRIMHALL, J.--ED. BRIMHALL, J.
BRIMHALL ISSUE NO. 09
CHARLES HANSEN H402 1.50
BRIMHALL, J.--ED. BRIMHALL, J.
BRIMHALL ISSUE NO. 10
CHARLES HANSEN H386 1.50
BRIMHALL, J.--ED. BRIMHALL, J.
BRIMHALL ISSUE NO. 11
CHARLES HANSEN H460 1.50
BRIMHALL, J.--ED. BRIMHALL, J.
BRIMHALL ISSUE NO. 12
CHARLES HANSEN H470 1.50
BRIMHALL, J.--ED. BRIMHALL, J.
BRIMHALL ISSUE NO. 14
CHARLES HANSEN H458 1.95

BRIMHALL, J.--ED. BRIMHALL, J.
BRIMHALL ISSUE NO. 15
CHARLES HANSEN H514 1.95

BRIMHALL, J.--ED. BRIMHALL, J.
BRIMHALL ISSUE NO. 16
CHARLES HANSEN H517 1.95

BRIMHALL, J.--ED. BRIMHALL, J.
BRIMHALL ISSUE NO. 17
CHARLES HANSEN H520 1.95

BRIMHALL, J.--ED. BRIMHALL, J.
BRIMHALL ISSUE NO. 18 AN APPLE FOR THE TEACHER
CHARLES HANSEN H540 1.50

BRIMHALL, J.--ED. BRIMHALL, J.
BRIMHALL ISSUE NO. 20
CHARLES HANSEN H587 1.50

BRIMHALL, J.--ED. BRIMHALL, J.
BRIMHALL'S ENCYCLOPEDIA OF SCALES AND ARPEGGIOS
CHARLES HANSEN T81 1.50

BRIMHALL, J.--ED. BRIMHALL, J.
BRIMHALL'S LOVE THEMES FROM THE GODFATHER AND OTHER POPULAR PIANO PIECES
CHARLES HANSEN M429 2.95

BRIMHALL, J.--ED. BRIMHALL, J.
BRIMHALL'S POPULAR LATIN TEACHING PIECES, NO. 1
CHARLES HANSEN T323 1.50

BRIMHALL, J.--ED. BRIMHALL, J.
BRIMHALL'S POPULAR LATIN TEACHING PIECES, NO. 2
CHARLES HANSEN T324 1.50

BRIMHALL, J.--ED. BRIMHALL, J.
BRIMHALL'S POPULAR LATIN TEACHING PIECES, NO. 3
CHARLES HANSEN T324 1.50

BRIMHALL, J.--ED. BRIMHALL, J.
BRIMHALL'S SACRED MUSIC OF TODAY
CHARLES HANSEN T329 1.50

BRIMHALL, J.--ED. BRIMHALL, J.
BRIMHALL'S 62 EASY-TO-PLAY POP PIANO PIECES
CHARLES HANSEN 0191 3.45

BRIMHALL, J.--ED. BRIMHALL, J.
BRIMHALL'S 64 POPULAR PIANO TEACHING PIECES
CHARLES HANSEN 0335 3.95

BRIMHALL, J.--ED. BRIMHALL, J. 2
CHILDREN'S PIANO PIECES -- POPULAR EDITION
CHARLES HANSEN H361 1.50

BRIMHALL, J.--ED. BRIMHALL, J.
CINDERELLA
CHARLES HANSEN T61 1.50

BRIMHALL, J.--ED. BRIMHALL, J.
DELUXE WALT DISNEY SONGBOOK
CHARLES HANSEN E052 5.95

BRIMHALL, J.--ED. BRIMHALL, J.
EASY POPULAR PIANO TEACHING PIECES, ISSUE NO. 1
CHARLES HANSEN H390 1.50

BRIMHALL, J.--ED. BRIMHALL, J.
EASY POPULAR PIANO TEACHING PIECES, ISSUE NO. 2
CHARLES HANSEN H391 1.50

BRIMHALL, J.--ED. BRIMHALL, J.
FIFTY POPULAR BIGNOTE PIANO TEACHING PIECES, BK. 1
CHARLES HANSEN 030 2.95

BRIMHALL, J.--ED. BRIMHALL, J.
FIFTY POPULAR BIGNOTE PIANO TEACHING PIECES, BK. 2
CHARLES HANSEN 0172 2.95

BRIMHALL, J.--ED. BRIMHALL, J.
FIFTY POPULAR TEACHING PIECES FOR EASY PIANO
CHARLES HANSEN 0236 3.45

BRIMHALL, J.--ED. BRIMHALL, J.
FIRST FUN AT THE PIANO
CHARLES HANSEN T2 1.95

BRIMHALL, J.--ED. BRIMHALL, J.
FIRST POPULAR PIANO PIECES, NO. 1
CHARLES HANSEN H164 1.50

BRIMHALL, J.--ED. BRIMHALL, J.
FIRST POPULAR PIANO PIECES, NO. 2
CHARLES HANSEN L117 1.50

BRIMHALL, J.--ED. BRIMHALL, J.
FIRST POPULAR PIANO PIECES, NO. 3
CHARLES HANSEN H538 1.50

BRIMHALL, J.--ED. BRIMHALL, J.
FORTY-EIGHT BRIMHALL WORLD FAMOUS 3-CHORD PIANO SONGS
CHARLES HANSEN 0117 2.95

BRIMHALL, J.--ED. BRIMHALL, J.
FORTY-FOUR NOW SOUNDS - JOHN BRIMHALL, EASY PIANO
CHARLES HANSEN M418 2.95

BRIMHALL, J.--ED. BRIMHALL, J.
FORTY-SEVEN FAMOUS PIANO PIECES
CHARLES HANSEN D94 4.95

BRIMHALL, J.--ED. BRIMHALL, J.
GOLDEN SONGS OF RODGERS AND HAMMERSTEIN
CHARLES HANSEN D168 5.95

BRIMHALL, J.--ED. BRIMHALL, J.
HELLO, DOLLY
CHARLES HANSEN E8444 1.50

BRIMHALL, J.--ED. BRIMHALL, J.
HERB ALPERT AND THE TIAJUANA BRASS
CHARLES HANSEN H30 1.25

BRIMHALL, J.--ED. BRIMHALL, J.
HOW TO PLAY POPULAR MUSIC
CHARLES HANSEN K192 1.95

BRIMHALL, J.--ED. BRIMHALL, J.
JOHN BRIMHALL GOLD
CHARLES HANSEN M505 3.45

BRIMHALL, J.--ED. BRIMHALL, J.
JOHN BRIMHALL HAWIIAN WEDDING SONG AMD OTHER HITS
CHARLES HANSEN M446 2.95

BRIMHALL, J.--ED. BRIMHALL, J.
JOHN BRIMHALL OMNIBUS OF POPULAR PIANO TEACHING PIECES
CHARLES HANSEN D57 3.95

BRIMHALL, J.--ED. BRIMHALL, J.
JOHN BRIMHALL PIANO METHOD - IN FRENCH, PRIMER
CHARLES HANSEN T451 1.50

BRIMHALL, J.--ED. BRIMHALL, J.
JOHN BRIMHALL PIANO METHOD - IN SPANISH, BK. 1
CHARLES HANSEN T100 2.00

BRIMHALL, J.--ED. BRIMHALL, J.
JOHN BRIMHALL PIANO METHOD, BK. 1
CHARLES HANSEN T101 1.75

BRIMHALL, J.--ED. BRIMHALL, J.
JOHN BRIMHALL PIANO METHOD, BK. 2
CHARLES HANSEN T401 2.00

BRIMHALL, J.--ED. BRIMHALL, J.
JOHN BRIMHALL PIANO METHOD, BK. 2
CHARLES HANSEN T102 1.50

BRIMHALL, J.--ED. BRIMHALL, J.
JOHN BRIMHALL PIANO METHOD, BK. 3
CHARLES HANSEN T103 1.50

BRIMHALL, J.--ED. BRIMHALL, J.
JOHN BRIMHALL PIANO METHOD, BK. 4
CHARLES HANSEN T104 1.75

BRIMHALL, J.--ED. BRIMHALL, J.
JOHN BRIMHALL PIANO METHOD, BK. 5
CHARLES HANSEN T105 1.95

BRIMHALL, J.--ED. BRIMHALL, J.
JOHN BRIMHALL PIANO METHOD, THE PRIMER
CHARLES HANSEN T100 1.50

BRIMHALL, J.--ED. BRIMHALL, J.
JOHN BRIMHALL'S APPLE FOR THE TEACHER NO. 2
CHARLES HANSEN H543 1.50

BRIMHALL, J.--ED. BRIMHALL, J.
JOHN BRIMHALL'S BEST OF BLUES, BOOGIE AND JAZZ
CHARLES HANSEN H439 1.50

BRIMHALL, J.--ED. BRIMHALL, J.
JOHN BRIMHALL'S BEST OF BROADWAY SHOW TUNES
CHARLES HANSEN H445 1.50

BRIMHALL, J.--ED. BRIMHALL, J.
JOHN BRIMHALL'S BEST OF COUNTRY SONGS
CHARLES HANSEN H441 1.50

BRIMHALL, J.--ED. BRIMHALL, J.
JOHN BRIMHALL'S BEST OF FOLK - POPS
CHARLES HANSEN H443 1.50

BRIMHALL, J.--ED. BRIMHALL, J.
JOHN BRIMHALL'S BEST OF MOTION PICTURE THEMES
CHARLES HANSEN H444 1.50

BRIMHALL, J.--ED. BRIMHALL, J.
JOHN BRIMHALL'S BEST OF POP WALTZES
CHARLES HANSEN H440 1.50

BRIMHALL, J.--ED. BRIMHALL, J.
JOHN BRIMHALL'S COLOUR MY WORLD
CHARLES HANSEN K353 2.95

BRIMHALL, J.--ED. BRIMHALL, J.
JOHN BRIMHALL'S ENO TEACHING PIECES, ISSUE NO. 3
CHARLES HANSEN H414 1.50

BRIMHALL, J.--ED. BRIMHALL, J.
JOHN BRIMHALL'S ENO TEACHING PIECES, ISSUE NO. 4
CHARLES HANSEN H415 1.50

BRIMHALL, J.--ED. BRIMHALL, J.
JOHN BRIMHALL'S EXERCISES IN RHYTHM
CHARLES HANSEN T82 1.50

BRIMHALL, J.--ED. BRIMHALL, J.
JOHN BRIMHALL'S INTERMEDIATE CLASSICAL SOLOS
CHARLES HANSEN D172 3.95

BRIMHALL, J.--ED. BRIMHALL, J.
JOHN BRIMHALL'S INTERMEDIATE PIANO SOLOS
CHARLES HANSEN M408 2.95

BRIMHALL, J.--ED. BRIMHALL, J.
JOHN BRIMHALL'S LATEST GROOVY PIANO PIECES
CHARLES HANSEN M123 2.95

BRIMHALL, J.--ED. BRIMHALL, J.
JOHN BRIMHALL'S PIANO POWER
CHARLES HANSEN D113 3.95

BRIMHALL, J.--ED. BRIMHALL, J.
JOHN BRIMHALL'S POPULAR PIANO PIECES
CHARLES HANSEN T309 1.95

BRIMHALL, J.--ED. BRIMHALL, J.
JOHN BRIMHALL'S THE ARISTOCATS
CHARLES HANSEN K422 1.95

BRIMHALL, J.--ED. BRIMHALL, J.
JOHN BRIMHALL'S WORLD'S GREATEST HITS OF POPULAR PIANO PIECES
CHARLES HANSEN D197 3.95

BRIMHALL, J.--ED. BRIMHALL, J.
JOHN BRIMHALL'S 101 EASY-TO-PLAY 'POPS'
CHARLES HANSEN M65 3.45

BRIMHALL, J.--ED. BRIMHALL, J.
JOHN BRIMHALL'S 62 CHILDREN'S PIANO PIECES
CHARLES HANSEN 0188 2.95

BRIMHALL, J.--ED. BRIMHALL, J.
JUNGLE BOOK, THE
CHARLES HANSEN T71 1.50

BRIMHALL, J.--ED. BRIMHALL, J.
MARY POPPINS
CHARLES HANSEN T60 1.50

BRIMHALL, J.--ED. BRIMHALL, J.
MI ALBUM DE CUBA
CHARLES HANSEN T361 1.50

BRIMHALL, J.--ED. BRIMHALL, J. 1
MY FAVORITE CLASSICS
CHARLES HANSEN 0114 2.95

BRIMHALL, J.--ED. BRIMHALL, J. 2
MY FAVORITE CLASSICS
CHARLES HANSEN 0124 2.95

BRIMHALL, J.--ED. BRIMHALL, J.
NINETY-NINE POPULAR PIANO TEACHING PIECES
CHARLES HANSEN M480 3.45

BRIMHALL, J.--ED. BRIMHALL, J.
PETER PAN
CHARLES HANSEN T63 1.50

BRIMHALL, J.--ED. BRIMHALL, J.
PETER RABBIT AND THE TALES OF BEATRIX PORTER
CHARLES HANSEN T318 1.50

BRIMHALL, J.--ED. BRIMHALL, J.
PLAY BY TWOS BK. 1
CHARLES HANSEN H530 1.25

BRIMHALL, J.--ED. BRIMHALL, J.
PLAY BY TWOS BK. 2
CHARLES HANSEN H531 1.25

BRIMHALL, J.--ED. BRIMHALL, J.
POPS OF THE 70'S
CHARLES HANSEN M368 4.95

BRIMHALL, J.--ED. BRIMHALL, J.
POPULAR CHORD INSTRUCTOR
CHARLES HANSEN T59 1.75

BRIMHALL, J.--ED. BRIMHALL, J.
POPULAR MUSIC OF TODAY, NO. 1
CHARLES HANSEN T390 1.75

BRIMHALL, J.--ED. BRIMHALL, J.
POPULAR MUSIC OF TODAY, NO. 2
CHARLES HANSEN T391 1.75

BRIMHALL, J.--ED. BRIMHALL, J.
SELECTIONS FROM MAN OF LA MANCHA
CHARLES HANSEN T83 1.50

BRIMHALL, J.--ED. BRIMHALL, J.
SIXTY-THREE BEST OF THE YEAR -- BRIMHALL EASY PIANO --
CHARLES HANSEN D122 3.95

BRIMHALL, J.--ED. BRIMHALL, J.
SIXTY-TWO POPULAR TEACHING PIECES
CHARLES HANSEN 0197 3.95

BRIMHALL, J.--ED. BRIMHALL, J.
SOUNDS OF THE SEVENTIES
CHARLES HANSEN D71 3.95

BRIMHALL, J.--ED. BRIMHALL, J.
STANDARD MUSIC OF TODAY
CHARLES HANSEN T68 1.50

BRIMHALL, J.--ED. BRIMHALL, J.
TEACHING FINGERS HOW TO PLAY POPS, ISSUE 1
CHARLES HANSEN H525 1.25

BRIMHALL, J.--ED.　　　　BRIMHALL, J.
TEACHING FINGERS HOW TO PLAY POPS, ISSUE 2
　　CHARLES HANSEN　　　　　　　　　H526　　1.25
BRIMHALL, J.--ED.　　　　BRIMHALL, J.
TEACHING FINGERS HOW TO PLAY POPS, ISSUE 3
　　CHARLES HANSEN　　　　　　　　　H527　　1.25
BRIMHALL, J.--ED.　　　　BRIMHALL, J.
TEACHING FINGERS HOW TO PLAY POPS, ISSUE 4
　　CHARLES HANSEN　　　　　　　　　H528　　1.25
BRIMHALL, J.--ED.　　　　BRIMHALL, J.
TEACHING FINGERS HOW TO PLAY SONGS FOR LITTLE NEIGHBORS, ISSUE 7
　　CHARLES HANSEN　　　　　　　　　H612　　1.25
BRIMHALL, J.--ED.　　　　BRIMHALL, J.
THIS IS OUR COUNTRY
　　CHARLES HANSEN　　　　　　　　　H532　　1.50
BRIMHALL, J.--ED.　　　　BRIMHALL, J.
TOP TEN BRIMHALL KIDDIE SHEETS ARRANGEMENTS
　　CHARLES HANSEN　　　　　　　　　T374　　1.95
BRIMHALL, J.--ED.　　　　BRIMHALL, J.
TOP TEN CLASSICAL PIANO SOLOS, BK. 1
　　CHARLES HANSEN　　　　　　　　　K556　　1.95
BRIMHALL, J.--ED.　　　　BRIMHALL, J.
WALT DISNEY 50 HAPPY YEARS, 50 HAPPY HITS
　　CHARLES HANSEN　　　　　　　　　D229　　3.95
BRIMHALL, J.--ED.　　　　BRIMHALL, J.
WALT DISNEY'S BAMBI
　　CHARLES HANSEN　　　　　　　　　T62　　1.50
BRIMHALL, J.--ED.　　　　BRIMHALL, J.
WALT DISNEY'S MARY POPPINS
　　CHARLES HANSEN　　　　　　　　　H29　　1.25
BRIMHALL, J.--ED.　　　　BRIMHALL, J.
WALT DISNEY'S PIANO CLASSICS, NO. 1 MICKEY MOUSE
　　CHARLES HANSEN　　　　　　　　　G018　　.75
BRIMHALL, J.--ED.　　　　BRIMHALL, J.
WALT DISNEY'S PIANO CLASSICS, NO. 2 PETER PAN
　　CHARLES HANSEN　　　　　　　　　G019　　.75
BRIMHALL, J.--ED.　　　　BRIMHALL, J.
WALT DISNEY'S PIANO CLASSICS, NO. 3 ALICE IN WONDERLAND
　　CHARLES HANSEN　　　　　　　　　G020　　.75
BRIMHALL, J.--ED.　　　　BRIMHALL, J.
WALT DISNEY'S PIANO CLASSICS, NO. 4 BABES IN TOYLAND
　　CHARLES HANSEN　　　　　　　　　G021　　.75
BRIMHALL, J.--ED.　　　　BRIMHALL, J.
WALT DISNEY'S PIANO CLASSICS, NO. 5 CINDERELLA
　　CHARLES HANSEN　　　　　　　　　G022　　.75
BRIMHALL, J.--ED.　　　　BRIMHALL, J.
WALT DISNEY'S PIANO CLASSICS, NO. 6 LADY AND THE TRAMP
　　CHARLES HANSEN　　　　　　　　　G023　　.75
BRIMHALL, J.--ED.　　　　BRIMHALL, J.
WORLDS GREATEST BOOK OF CLASSIC THEMES
　　CHARLES HANSEN　　　　　　　　　D210　　3.95
BRIMHALL, J.--ED.　　　　BRIMHALL, J.
WORLDS GREATEST BOOK OF WEDDING SONGS
　　CHARLES HANSEN　　　　　　　　　D203　　3.95
BRIMHALL, J.--ED.　　　　BRIMHALL, J.
WORLDS GREATEST DIXIELAND PIANO SOLOS
　　CHARLES HANSEN　　　　　　　　　D208　　3.95
BRIMHALL, J.--ED.　　　　BRIMHALL, J.
WORLDS GREATEST HITS FOR CHORD PLAYING
　　CHARLES HANSEN　　　　　　　　　D152　　5.95
BRIMHALL, J.--ED.　　　　BRIMHALL, J.
WORLDS GREATEST HITS FROM 1900-1919
　　CHARLES HANSEN　　　　　　　　　D201　　3.95
BRIMHALL, J.--ED.　　　　BRIMHALL, J.
WORLDS GREATEST HITS OF COUNTRY MUSIC
　　CHARLES HANSEN　　　　　　　　　D214　　3.95
BRIMHALL, J.--ED.　　　　BRIMHALL, J.
WORLDS GREATEST HITS OF POPULAR CHORALS
　　CHARLES HANSEN　　　　　　　　　D204　　2.95
BRIMHALL, J.--ED.　　　　BRIMHALL, J.
WORLDS GREATEST HITS OF THE WONDERFUL CHILD
　　CHARLES HANSEN　　　　　　　　　D194　　3.95
BRIMHALL, J.--ED.　　　　BRIMHALL, J.
WORLDS GREATEST JAZZ PIANO SOLOS AND SONGS
　　CHARLES HANSEN　　　　　　　　　D206　　3.95
BRIMHALL, J.--ED.　　　　BRIMHALL, J.
WORLDS GREATEST NATIONAL ANTHEMS
　　CHARLES HANSEN　　　　　　　　　D195　　3.95
BRISMAN, H.
SOUVENIRS FOR PIANO
　　ISRAEL MUSIC INSTITUTE　　　　　　　　　　2.50
BRITTEN, B.
FIVE WALTZES
　　FABER MUSIC, LTD.　　　　　　　　　F0074
BROGI
FIVE COMPOSITIONS
　　FRANCO COLOMBO PUBLICATIONS　　FOR. 10691　1.75
BROWN--ED　　　　BROWN
PLAY AND SING YOUR FAVORITE SONGS
　　WILLIS MUSIC COMPANY　　　　　　　　　　1.25
BROWN, E.　　　　　　　　　　　　5
DREI STUCKE --1951--
　　SCHOTT　　　　　　　　　　10702　　1.50
BROWN, E.
FOLIO -- 1952/53 -- AND FOUR SYSTEMS -- 1954 --
　　ASSOCIATED MUSIC PUBLISHERS, INC.　AMP　7.50
BROZ　　　　　　　　　　　　　　4
DREI CAPRICCI
　　BARENREITER VERLAG　　　　　　　AP 2102
BRUBECK　　　　　　　　　　　　ADVANCED
BRUBECK, VOL. 1
　　SHAWNEE PRESS, INC.　　　　　　　　　　2.00
BRUBECK　　　　　　　　　　　　ADVANCED
BRUBECK, VOL. 2
　　SHAWNEE PRESS, INC.　　　　　　　　　　2.00
BRUBECK　　　　　　　　　　　　ADVANCED
JAZZ IMPRESSIONS OF JAPAN
　　SHAWNEE PRESS, INC.　　　　　　　　　　2.50
BRUBECK
JAZZ IMPRESSIONS OF NEW YORK
　　EDWARD B. MARKS MUSIC CORPORATION　　　02.00
BRUBECK　　　　　　　　　　　　EASY
THEMES FROM EURASIA
　　SHAWNEE PRESS, INC.　　　　　　　　　　2.00
BRUBECK　　　　　　　　　　　　ADVANCED
TIME CHANGES
　　SHAWNEE PRESS, INC.　　　　　　　　　　2.50
BRUCKNER　　　　SINGER　　　　D
SELECTED MOVEMENTS FROM THE SYMPHONIES NOS. 1, 2, 3, 4, 7
　　C. F. PETERS CORPORATION　　　　3847　　3.50
BRUGMANN, A.
PIANO MUSIC READER, BK. 1
　　ELKAN-VOGEL, INC.　　　　　　　　　　2.00
BRUGMANN, A.
PIANO MUSIC READER, BK. 2
　　ELKAN-VOGEL, INC.　　　　　　　　　　2.00

BRUNET, J.
ENFANTAISIES
　　ELKAN-VOGEL, INC.　　　　　　　CON　　3.25
BRUSSELS, I.
TWELVE PIANO SKETCHES
　　WILLIS MUSIC COMPANY　　　　　　　　　1.00
BRUSSELS, I.　　　　　　　　　AI
TWELVE PIANO SKETCHES
　　WILLIS MUSIC COMPANY　　　　　　　　　1.00
BRUSSELS, I.
TWO PRELUDES FOR PIANO
　　MCA MUSIC　　　　　　　　　　　　　1.00
BUECHTGER　　　　　　　　　　　4
DREI KLAVIERSTUCKE
　　BARENREITER VERLAG　　　　　　　BE 340
BUECHTGER　　　　　　　　　　　1
SPIELBUCH FUR UTE. 50 KINDERLIEDER FUR DEN ERSTEN UNTERRICHT
　　BARENREITER VERLAG　　　　　　　SM 2326
BUGBEE, L. A.
SECOND GRADE BOOK OF MELODIC STUDIES
　　THEODORE PRESSER COMPANY　　　　　　　.90
BULL
COMPOSITIONS
　　EDWIN F. KALMUS　　　　　　　3273　　1.50
BULL
FROM HERE TO THERE
　　CARL FISCHER, INC.　　　　　　O 4888
BULL
MUSIC FOR HAIKU
　　CARL FISCHER, INC.　　　　　　O 4862　　1.50
BULL, J.　　　　　　　　　　　E-M
FIVE HARPSICHORD PIECES FROM DR. JOHN BULL'S FLEMISH TABULATURA
　　C. F. PETERS CORPORATION　　　N3075　　1.50
BUNDERVOET
TROIS PIECES EN FORME DE
　　EDITIONS MUSICALES TRANSATLANTIQUES　　2.00
BUOGO
STUDIES FOR THE BEGINNER
　　FRANCO COLOMBO PUBLICATIONS　　ER1810　2.75
BURCHENAL, E.
AMERICAN COUNTRY-DANCES
　　G. SCHIRMER, INC.　　　　　　　　　3.00
BURCHENAL, E.
DANCES OF THE PEOPLE
　　G. SCHIRMER, INC.　　　　　　　　　3.50
BURCHENAL, E. *
FOLK-DANCE MUSIC --ADAPTED FOR USE IN PHYSICAL EDUCATION AND
PLAY--
　　G. SCHIRMER, INC.　　　　　　　　　1.75
BURCHENAL, E.
FOLK-DANCES AND SINGING GAMES
　　G. SCHIRMER, INC.　　　　　　　　　3.50
BURCHENAL, E.
FOLK-DANCES FROM OLD HOMELANDS
　　G. SCHIRMER, INC.　　　　　　　　　3.50
BURGMUELLER　　　　GERMER　　　3-4
ACHTZEHN GENRE-ETUDEN OP. 109
　　SCHOTT　　　　　　　　　　175　　2.50
BURGMUELLER
BALLADE, OP. 100
　　WILLIS MUSIC COMPANY　　　　　　　　.80
BURGMUELLER　　　SCHAUM, J.　　2 1/2
BURGMUELLER-SCHAUM, BK. 1
　　BELWIN-MILLS PUBLISHING CORPORATION　1.50
BURGMUELLER　　　SCHAUM, J.　　5
BURGMUELLER-SCHAUM, BK. 2
　　BELWIN-MILLS PUBLISHING CORPORATION　1.50
BURGMUELLER　　　　　　　　　M-D
EIGHTEEN CHARACTERISTIC STUDIES, OP. 109
　　C. F. PETERS CORPORATION　　　3103　　1.50
BURGMUELLER　　　OESTERLE
EIGHTEEN CHARACTERISTIC STUDIES, OP. 109
　　G. SCHIRMER, INC.　　　　　　　L752　　1.00
BURGMUELLER
EIGHTEEN CHARACTERISTIC STUDIES, OP. 109
　　UNIVERSAL EDITION　　　　　　　1544　　1.00
BURGMUELLER
EIGHTEEN STUDIES, OP. 109
　　FRANCO COLOMBO PUBLICATIONS　　ER419　.75
BURGMUELLER　　　GERMER　　　　1-2
FUNF UND ZWANZIG LEICHTE ETUDEN OP. 100
　　SCHOTT　　　　　　　　　　173　　2.50
BURGMUELLER　　　OESTERLE
TWELVE BRILLIANT AND MELODIOUS STUDIES, OP. 105
　　G. SCHIRMER, INC.　　　　　　　L755　　1.00
BURGMUELLER
TWELVE BRILLIANT STUDIES, OP. 105
　　FRANCO COLOMBO PUBLICATIONS　　ER815　.75
BURGMUELLER　　　　　　　　　M-D
TWELVE STUDIES, OP. 105
　　C. F. PETERS CORPORATION　　　3102　　2.00
BURGMUELLER
TWENTY SELECTED STUDIES FROM OP. 100
　　BOSTON MUSIC COMPANY　　　　　　　　1.00
BURGMUELLER　　　　　　　　　E
TWENTY-FIVE EASY AND PROGRESSIVE STUDIES, OP. 100
　　C. F. PETERS CORPORATION　　　3101　　2.00
BURGMUELLER　　　OESTERLE
TWENTY-FIVE EASY AND PROGRESSIVE STUDIES, OP. 100
　　G. SCHIRMER, INC.　　　　　　　L500　　.85
BURGMUELLER
TWENTY-FIVE EASY AND PROGRESSIVE STUDIES, OP. 100--BK. 1
　　G. SCHIRMER, INC.　　　　　　　L977　　.75
BURGMUELLER
TWENTY-FIVE EASY AND PROGRESSIVE STUDIES, OP. 100--BK. 2
　　G. SCHIRMER, INC.　　　　　　　L978　　.75
BURGMUELLER
TWENTY-FIVE EASY ETUDES, OP. 100
　　CARL FISCHER, INC.　　　　　　L 324　　1.00
BURGMUELLER
TWENTY-FIVE EASY STUDIES, OP. 100
　　ASHLEY DEALERS SERVICE, INC.　　　　1.25
BURGMUELLER
TWENTY-FIVE EASY STUDIES, OP. 100
　　CENTURY MUSIC PUBLISHING COMPANY, INC.　1.25
BURGMUELLER
TWENTY-FIVE EASY STUDIES, OP. 100
　　UNIVERSAL EDITION　　　　　　　1542　　1.40
BURGMUELLER　　　PALMER, W. A.
TWENTY-FIVE PROGRESSIVE PIECES
　　ALFRED MUSIC COMPANY　　　　　608　　1.50
BURGMUELLER
TWENTY-FIVE STUDIES, OP. 100
　　BANKS AND SON LTD.　　　　　　　　　1.50
BURGMUELLER
TWENTY-FIVE STUDIES, OP. 100
　　FRANCO COLOMBO PUBLICATIONS　　ER429　1.75

BURGMUELLER GERMER 3-4			
ZWOLF ETUDEN OP. 105			
SCHOTT		174	2.50
BURKARD, J. A.			
NEUE ANLEITUNG FUR DAS KLAVIERSPIEL, BAND 01			
SCHOTT		2690	2.75
BURKARD, J. A.			
NEUE ANLEITUNG FUR DAS KLAVIERSPIEL, BAND 02			
SCHOTT		2691	2.75
BURKARD, J. A. 1-2			
NEUE ANLEITUNG FUR DAS KLAVIERSPIEL, BEIHEFT 01,			
VOLKSLIEDBUCHLEIN			
SCHOTT		2692	1.75
BURKARD, J. A. 1-2			
NEUE ANLEITUNG FUR DAS KLAVIERSPIEL, BEIHEFT 02, TANZBUCHLEIN			
SCHOTT		2693	1.75
BURKHARD, W. 2			
ACHT LEICHTE KLAVIERSTUCKE			
BARENREITER VERLAG		BA 2070	
BURKHARD, W.			
EIGHT EASY PIANO PIECES			
BARENREITER VERLAG		BA 2070	2.00
BURKHARD, W.			
ELEVEN LITTLE PIECES FOR PIANO, OP. 31			
BARENREITER VERLAG		BA 4141	2.50
BURKHARD, W. 2-3			
ELF KLEINE STUCKE FUR KLAVIER, OP. 31			
BARENREITER VERLAG		BA 4141	
BURKHARD, W.			
SIX PRELUDES, OP. 99			
BARENREITER VERLAG		BA 3504	3.25
BURKHARD, W. 3-4			
SIX PRELUDES, OP. 99			
BARENREITER VERLAG		BA 3504	
BURKHARD, W.			
WAS DIE HIRTEN ALLES ERLEBTEN			
BARENREITER VERLAG		BA 1875	1.75
BURKHARD, W. 1			
WAS DIE HIRTEN ALLES ERLEBTEN -- WEIHNACHTSMUSIK FUR URSULA --			
BARENREITER VERLAG		BA 1875	
BURKHARD, W. 2			
WEIHNACHTSSONATINE, OP. 71 NO. 1			
BARENREITER VERLAG		BA 2074	
BURNAM			
BURNAM BOOK, THE			
SUMMY-BIRCHARD COMPANY			1.75
BURNAM			
DOZEN FOLK TUNES FROM VARIOUS LANDS, A			
WILLIS MUSIC COMPANY			1.00
BURNAM			
DOZEN PIANO DUETS, BK. 2			
WILLIS MUSIC COMPANY			1.00
BURNAM			
DOZEN PIANO PIECES IN VARIOUS STYLES, BK. 1			
WILLIS MUSIC COMPANY			1.00
BURNAM			
DOZEN PIANO PIECES IN VARIOUS STYLES, BK. 2			
WILLIS MUSIC COMPANY			1.00
BURNAM			
DOZEN PIANO PIECES IN VARIOUS STYLES, BK. 3			
WILLIS MUSIC COMPANY			1.00
BURNAM			
DOZEN PIANO PIECES IN VARIOUS STYLES, BK. 4			
WILLIS MUSIC COMPANY			1.25
BURNAM			
DOZEN WALTZES			
WILLIS MUSIC COMPANY			.90
BURNAM			
FAMILY HYMN BOOK, THE			
WILLIS MUSIC COMPANY			1.00
BURNAM			
FOR YOU ALONE			
WILLIS MUSIC COMPANY			.90
BURNAM			
HELP YOURSELF TO HARMONY, BK. 1			
WILLIS MUSIC COMPANY			1.00
BURNAM			
HELP YOURSELF TO HARMONY, BK. 2			
WILLIS MUSIC COMPANY			1.00
BURNAM			
I KNOW THAT THEME, BK. 1			
WILLIS MUSIC COMPANY			1.00
BURNAM			
I KNOW THAT THEME, BK. 2			
WILLIS MUSIC COMPANY			1.00
BURNAM			
MEXICO			
WILLIS MUSIC COMPANY			1.00
BURNAM			
MUSIC WE WILL HAVE			
WILLIS MUSIC COMPANY			1.25
BURNAM			
PLAY ALL THE TIME SIGNATURES			
WILLIS MUSIC COMPANY			1.00
BURNAM			
SONGS WITH HAPPY THOUGHTS			
WILLIS MUSIC COMPANY			1.00
BURNAM			
STEP-BY-STEP PIANO COURSE, BK. 1			
WILLIS MUSIC COMPANY			1.00
BURNAM			
STEP-BY-STEP PIANO COURSE, BK. 2			
WILLIS MUSIC COMPANY			1.00
BURNAM			
STEP-BY-STEP PIANO COURSE, BK. 3			
WILLIS MUSIC COMPANY			1.25
BURNAM			
STEP-BY-STEP PIANO COURSE, BK. 4			
WILLIS MUSIC COMPANY			1.00
BURNAM			
STEP-BY-STEP PIANO COURSE, BK. 5			
WILLIS MUSIC COMPANY			1.25
BURNAM			
STEP-BY-STEP PIANO COURSE, BK. 6			
WILLIS MUSIC COMPANY			1.25
BURNS *			
JAZZ, ROCK, POP AND BLUES PIANO IMPROVISATION METHOD, BK.1			
NEIL A. KJOS MUSIC COMPANY			1.50
BURNS *			
JAZZ, ROCK, POP AND BLUES PIANO IMPROVISATION METHOD, BK.2			
NEIL A. KJOS MUSIC COMPANY			1.50
BURNS *			
JAZZ, ROCK, POP AND BLUES PIANO IMPROVISATION METHOD, BK.3			
NEIL A. KJOS MUSIC COMPANY			1.50
BURNS *			
JAZZ, ROCK, POP AND BLUES PIANO IMPROVISATION METHOD, BK.4			
NEIL A. KJOS MUSIC COMPANY			1.50

BURNS *			
JAZZ, ROCK, POP AND BLUES PIANO IMPROVISATION METHOD, BK.5			
NEIL A. KJOS MUSIC COMPANY			1.50
BURNS *			
JAZZ, ROCK, POP AND BLUES PIANO IMPROVISATION METHOD, BK.6			
NEIL A. KJOS MUSIC COMPANY			1.50
BURROWS *			
ADULT EXPLORER AT THE PIANO, THE			
WILLIS MUSIC COMPANY			1.25
BURROWS *			
LET'S WRITE AND PLAY			
WILLIS MUSIC COMPANY			1.25
BURROWS *			
YOUNG EXPLORER AT THE PIANO, THE			
WILLIS MUSIC COMPANY			1.25
BUSCHBAUM *			
KINDER SPIELEN ZUR WEIHNACHT			
BARENREITER VERLAG		EN 803	6.00
BUSH--ED. BUSH			
ELEVEN FRENCH FAVORITES			
PRO-ART PUBLICATIONS, INC.		988	1.00
BUSH--ED. BUSH			
FAMOUS FRENCH COMPOSERS			
PRO-ART PUBLICATIONS, INC.		936	1.00
BUSONI			
ACHT ETUDEN VON CRAMER			
ASSOCIATED MUSIC PUBLISHERS, INC.		B/H	2.75
BUSONI			
ELEGIES			
ASSOCIATED MUSIC PUBLISHERS, INC.		B/H	4.00
BUSONI			
INDIANISCHES TAGEBUCH, VOL. 1			
ASSOCIATED MUSIC PUBLISHERS, INC.		B/H	2.50
BUSONI GOEBELS			
NEW BUSONI. EXERCISES AND STUDIES FROM THE 'KLAVIERUEBUNG', VOL. 1			
ASSOCIATED MUSIC PUBLISHERS, INC.		B/H	4.00
BUSONI GOEBELS			
NEW BUSONI, THE. EXERCISES AND STUDIES FROM THE 'KLAVIERUEBUNG', VOL. 2			
ASSOCIATED MUSIC PUBLISHERS, INC.		B/H	4.00
BUSONI GOEBELS			
NEW BUSONI, THE--EXERCISES AND STUDIES FROM ''KLAVIERUBUNG''--BK. 1			
ASSOCIATED MUSIC PUBLISHERS, INC.		BRH	4.00
BUSONI GOEBELS			
NEW BUSONI, THE--EXERCISES AND STUDIES FROM ''KLAVIERUBUNG''--BK. 2			
ASSOCIATED MUSIC PUBLISHERS, INC.		BRH	4.00
BUSONI			
SECHS KURZE STUECKE ZUR PFLEGE DES POLYPHONEN SPIELS			
ASSOCIATED MUSIC PUBLISHERS, INC.		B/H	2.50
BUSONI			
SIX EXERCISES AND PRELUDES			
ASSOCIATED MUSIC PUBLISHERS, INC.		B/H	3.00
BUSONI TAGLIAPIETRA			
TWENTY-FOUR PRELUDES, OP. 37 BK. 1			
FRANCO COLOMBO PUBLICATIONS		ER694	1.75
BUSONI TAGLIAPIETRA			
TWENTY-FOUR PRELUDES, OP. 37 BK. 2			
FRANCO COLOMBO PUBLICATIONS		ER695	1.75
BUTLER, A.			
CREATIVE KEYBOARD SOUNDS			
GWYN PUBLISHING COMPANY			3.50
BUTLER, J. E			
ALL ABOUT FUN			
WILLIS MUSIC COMPANY			.75
BUTTING, M.			
FIVE SHORT PIECES, OP. 33			
UNIVERSAL EDITION		UE 9489	1.70
BUUS, J. M			
RICERCARI 3, 4 --DELL'INTABULATURA D'ORGANO, VENICE, 1549--			
C. F. PETERS CORPORATION		HU1185	1.50
BUXTEHUDE			
COMPOSITIONS			
EDWIN F. KALMUS		3281	2.00
BUXTEHUDE M			
FOUR SUITES* 'FOR CLAVICHORD OR LUTE'			
C. F. PETERS CORPORATION		EN4	3.00
BUXTEHUDE HAASCKE			
SELECTED WORKS, URTEXT -- FOR ORGAN, PIANO, OR HARPSICHORD			
ASSOCIATED MUSIC PUBLISHERS, INC.		B/H	3.25
BYRD, W. * RUZICKOVA 2-3			
KOMPOSITIONEN FUR CEMBALO. 9 STUCKE			
BARENREITER VERLAG		MVH 8	
BYRD, W.			
MY LADYE NEVELLS BOOKE			
BROUDE BROTHERS LTD.			25.00
BYRD, W. ANDREWS, H.			
MY LADYE NEVELLS BOOKE OF VIRGINAL MUSIC			
DOVER PUBLICATIONS, INC.		22246-2	4.00
BYRD, W. *			
PARTHENIA			
BROUDE BROTHERS LTD.			09.00
BYRDE, W.			
COMPOSITIONS			
EDWIN F. KALMUS		3282	2.00
CAAMANO			
SIX PRELUDES, OP. 6, BK. 1			
BOOSEY AND HAWKES, INC.			1.50
CAAMANO			
SIX PRELUDES, OP. 6, BK. 2			
BOOSEY AND HAWKES, INC.			1.50
CABEZON, A. KASTNER			
CLAVIERMUSIK			
SCHOTT		4286	3.50
CABEZON, A. KASTNER 3			
TIENTOS UND FUGEN A. D. 'OBRAS DE MUSICA'			
SCHOTT		4948	3.25
CAGE D			
AMORES. TWO PIECES FOR PREPARED PIANO --AND TWO PERCUSSION PIECES			
C. F. PETERS CORPORATION		6264	5.00
CAGE D			
MUSIC OF CHANGES, VOL. 1			
C. F. PETERS CORPORATION		6256	1.50
CAGE D			
MUSIC OF CHANGES, VOL. 2			
C. F. PETERS CORPORATION		6257	3.00
CAGE D			
MUSIC OF CHANGES, VOL. 3			
C. F. PETERS CORPORATION		6258	2.50
CAGE D			
MUSIC OF CHANGES, VOL. 4			
C. F. PETERS CORPORATION		6259	2.50
CAGE D			
SONATAS AND INTERLUDES --PREPARED PIANO--			
C. F. PETERS CORPORATION		6755	10.00

```
CAHN
    BASIC TECHNIQUE FOR JAZZ PIANO
        BELWIN-MILLS PUBLISHING CORPORATION                    1.50
CAHN
    BASIC TECHNIQUE FOR POPULAR PIANO
        BELWIN-MILLS PUBLISHING CORPORATION                    1.50
CAMBISSA, G.
    SEVEN LITTLE STUDIES
        EDIZIONI BERBEN                         EB 1443        3.00
CAMILLERI, C.
    INTRODUCTORY PIANO EXERCISES FOR CONTEMPORARY MUSIC -- BK. 2
        BELWIN-MILLS PUBLISHING CORPORATION     11245          1.25
CAMMAROTA
    TWELVE STUDI DA CONCERTO
        FRANCO COLOMBO PUBLICATIONS             BON. 2510      4.25
CANNON, P.                                          8
    L'ENFANT S'AMUSE -- SUITE OF 5 PIECES
        NOVELLO AND COMPANY, LTD.               10.0016.00     1.50
CANTELOUBE
    DANSES BRETONNES, BK. 1
        FRANCO COLOMBO PUBLICATIONS             SAL            3.50
CAPDEVIELLE
    TROIS INSTANTS MUSICAUX -- 1927 --
        ASSOCIATED MUSIC PUBLISHERS, INC.       ESC            2.00
CAPPETTI
    THREE COMPOSITIONS
        FRANCO COLOMBO PUBLICATIONS             FOR.10529      1.75
CAPUS
    FIABA ARMONIOSA - 7 PIECES
        FRANCO COLOMBO PUBLICATIONS             FOR. 12260     2.00
CARABELLA
    DANCES FOR THE LITTLE PIANIST, BK. 1
        FRANCO COLOMBO PUBLICATIONS             DS671          2.75
CARABELLA
    DANCES FOR THE LITTLE PIANIST, BK. 2
        FRANCO COLOMBO PUBLICATIONS             DS672          2.75
CARABELLA
    THREE ROMAN CLOISTERS
        FRANCO COLOMBO PUBLICATIONS             DS204          2.00
CARDEW                                              D
    FEBRUARY PIECES FOR PIANO, AND OCTET '61 FOR JASPER JOHNS
        C. F. PETERS CORPORATION                H771           5.00
CARLE, F.
    FRANKIE CARLE'S METHOD OF PIANO STYLING
        BELWIN-MILLS PUBLISHING CORPORATION                    1.50
CARLE, F.
    FRANKIE CARLE'S PIANO CONCEPTIONS
        BELWIN-MILLS PUBLISHING CORPORATION                    1.00
CARLE, F.
    FRANKIE CARLE'S PIANO STYLINGS
        BELWIN-MILLS PUBLISHING CORPORATION                    1.00
CARLE, F.
    METHOD OF PIANO STYLING FOR BEGINNERS OR ADVANCED STUDENTS
        BELWIN-MILLS PUBLISHING CORPORATION     11195          1.75
CAROL--ED.              CAROL              EASY
    TWO AMERICAN CHRISTMAS CAROLS
        DELRIEU ET CIE.                                         .85
CARPENTER, J.
    DIVERSIONS
        G. SCHIRMER, INC.                                      2.00
CARRA
    FOUR SHORT PIECES
        ASSOCIATED MUSIC PUBLISHERS, INC.       UME            1.00
CARREIRA                                            M
    THREE FANTASIAS
        C. F. PETERS CORPORATION                HU1695         1.50
CARRIER *
    MODERN PIANO METHOD
        FRANCO COLOMBO PUBLICATIONS             SAL            5.75
CARTER
    KEYBOARD HARMONY
        SUMMY-BIRCHARD COMPANY                                 2.25
CARVER--ED              CARVER
    CHAPPELL'S FAMOUS MELODIES
        CHAPPELL AND COMPANY, INC.              0021964        1.00
CASADESUS, R.
    CADENZAS FOR 3 CONCERTI -- BEETHOVEN, MOZART --
        FRANCO COLOMBO PUBLICATIONS             SAL            4.00
CASADESUS, G.
    EIGHT ETUDES FOR THE PIANO
        G. SCHIRMER, INC.                                      1.50
CASADESUS, R.
    HUIT ETUDES
        ELKAN-VOGEL, INC.                       D              12.00
CASADESUS, R.
    TWENTY-FOUR PRELUDES -- 1924 -- VOL. 1
        ASSOCIATED MUSIC PUBLISHERS, INC.       ESC            2.25
CASADESUS, R.
    TWENTY-FOUR PRELUDES -- 1924 -- VOL. 2
        ASSOCIATED MUSIC PUBLISHERS, INC.       ESC            2.25
CASADESUS, R.
    TWENTY-FOUR PRELUDES -- 1924 -- VOL. 3
        ASSOCIATED MUSIC PUBLISHERS, INC.       ESC            2.25
CASADESUS, R.
    TWENTY-FOUR PRELUDES -- 1924 -- VOL. 4
        ASSOCIATED MUSIC PUBLISHERS, INC.       ESC            4.00
CASANOVA, A.
    FOUR INTERMEZZI
        GERARD BILLAUDOT EDITIONS MUSICALES                    3.20
CASELLA, A. *
    A LA MANIERE DE ... BORODIN, D'INDY, CHABRIER, RAVEL
        FRANCO COLOMBO PUBLICATIONS             SAL            4.00
CASELLA, A.
    A LA MANIERE DE ... WAGNER, FAURE, BRAHMS, DEBUSSY, STRAUSS,
    FRANCK
        FRANCO COLOMBO PUBLICATIONS             SAL            4.00
CASELLA, A.
    ANTOLOGIA PIANISTICA
        FRANCO COLOMBO PUBLICATIONS             FOR.12349      3.75
CASELLA, A.
    ELEVEN CHILDREN'S PIECES
        UNIVERSAL EDITION                       UE 6878        2.75
CASELLA, A.
    TWO RICERCARE ON THE NAME 'BACH'
        FRANCO COLOMBO PUBLICATIONS             122713         1.50
CASH              LANE
    JOHN LANE PLAYS JOHNNY CASH HITS
        THE BIG THREE MUSIC CORPORATION                        1.95
CASHMAN *
    FOLIO
        THE BIG THREE MUSIC CORPORATION                        03.95
CASSIDY, D.
    ROCK ME BABY
        THE BIG THREE MUSIC CORPORATION                        03.95
CASTELLI
    THEORY IS FUN - SET 1
        BOSTON MUSIC COMPANY                                   1.00
```

```
CASTELLI
    THEORY IS FUN - SET 2
        BOSTON MUSIC COMPANY                                   1.00
CASTELNUOVO-TEDESCO
    ALT WIEN
        FRANCO COLOMBO PUBLICATIONS             FOR. 11017     4.00
CASTELNUOVO-TEDESCO
    EVANGELION, PART 1
        FRANCO COLOMBO PUBLICATIONS             FOR. 12343     3.25
CASTELNUOVO-TEDESCO
    EVANGELION, PART 2
        FRANCO COLOMBO PUBLICATIONS             FOR. 12344     3.25
CASTELNUOVO-TEDESCO
    EVANGELION, PART 3
        FRANCO COLOMBO PUBLICATIONS             FOR. 12345     3.25
CASTELNUOVO-TEDESCO
    EVANGELION, PART 4
        FRANCO COLOMBO PUBLICATIONS             FOR. 12346     3.25
CASTELNUOVO-TEDESCO                                 4-5
    MEDIA DIFFICOLTA - VIER STUCKE
        BARENREITER VERLAG                      CM 16477
CASTELNUOVO-TEDESCO
    ONDE - 2 STUDIES
        FRANCO COLOMBO PUBLICATIONS             123636         1.25
CASTELNUOVO-TEDESCO
    SIX CANONS, OP. 142
        MCA MUSIC                                              1.50
CASTELNUOVO-TEDESCO
    SIX PIECES IN FORM OF CANONS, OP. 156
        FRANCO COLOMBO PUBLICATIONS             NY1623         2.00
CASTELNUOVO-TEDESCO
    THREE POEMA CAMPESTRI
        FRANCO COLOMBO PUBLICATIONS             FOR. 11354     4.00
CASTELNUOVO-TEDESCO
    TWO FILM STUDIES
        FRANCO COLOMBO PUBLICATIONS             122608         1.25
CASTRO, J. M.
    TEN SHORT PIECES
        BOOSEY AND HAWKES, INC.                                1.25
CAVALHO, R.
    SCALE PATTERNS FOR YOUNG PIANISTS
        ASSOCIATED MUSIC PUBLISHERS, INC.       BER            1.50
CAVALLARO
    CAVALLARO'S KEYBOARD CREATIONS
        WARNER BROTHERS PUBLISHERS                             1.95
CAVALLARO--ED.              CAVALLARO
    CARMEN CAVALLARO -- MODERN INTERPRETATIONS FOR PIANO
        THE BIG THREE MUSIC CORPORATION                        1.95
CAVALLARO--ED.              CAVALLARO
    CARMEN CAVALLARO'S PARADE OF HITS
        THE BIG THREE MUSIC CORPORATION                        1.50
CAZDEN, N.
    AMERICAN FOLK SONGS FOR PIANO --64 SONGS--
        SPRATT MUSIC PUBLISHERS                                1.75
CAZDEN, N.
    EIGHT PRELUDES, OP. 11
        BOOSEY AND HAWKES, INC.                                1.00
CAZDEN, N.
    TWENTY ONE EVOLUTIONS, OP. 4
        BOOSEY AND HAWKES, INC.                                1.00
CERVANTES, E.
    SIX CUBAN DANCES
        G. SCHIRMER, INC.                                       .60
CERVENKA
    FUN IN SONG
        WILLIS MUSIC COMPANY                                    .60
CERVENKA
    MORE FUN IN SONG
        WILLIS MUSIC COMPANY                                    .75
CESI, B.
    PRACTICAL THEORETICAL METHOD, BK. 01. ELEMENTS AND 20 EXERCISES
        FRANCO COLOMBO PUBLICATIONS             ER2351          .75
CESI, B.
    PRACTICAL THEORETICAL METHOD, BK. 02. EXERCISES AND SCALES
        FRANCO COLOMBO PUBLICATIONS             ER2352         2.25
CESI, B.
    PRACTICAL THEORETICAL METHOD, BK. 03. ARPEGGIOS
        FRANCO COLOMBO PUBLICATIONS             ER2353         2.25
CESI, B.
    PRACTICAL THEORETICAL METHOD, BK. 04. EQUALIZATION OF THE HANDS
        FRANCO COLOMBO PUBLICATIONS             ER2354         2.25
CESI, B.
    PRACTICAL THEORETICAL METHOD, BK. 05. REPEATED NOTES
        FRANCO COLOMBO PUBLICATIONS             ER2355         3.25
CESI, B.
    PRACTICAL THEORETICAL METHOD, BK. 06. WRIST MOVEMENT
        FRANCO COLOMBO PUBLICATIONS             ER2356         1.50
CESI, B.
    PRACTICAL THEORETICAL METHOD, BK. 07. OCTAVE TECHNIQUE
        FRANCO COLOMBO PUBLICATIONS             ER2357         3.75
CESI, B.
    PRACTICAL THEORETICAL METHOD, BK. 08. LEGATO
        FRANCO COLOMBO PUBLICATIONS             ER2358         1.50
CESI, B.
    PRACTICAL THEORETICAL METHOD, BK. 09. THIRDS--LEGATO--
        FRANCO COLOMBO PUBLICATIONS             ER2359         2.00
CESI, B.
    PRACTICAL THEORETICAL METHOD, BK. 10. DOUBLE NOTES
        FRANCO COLOMBO PUBLICATIONS             ER2360         1.75
CESI, B.
    PRACTICAL THEORETICAL METHOD, BK. 11. SIXTHS
        FRANCO COLOMBO PUBLICATIONS             ER2361         1.75
CESI, B.
    PRACTICAL THEORETICAL METHOD, BK. 12. ADVANCED MECHANISM
        FRANCO COLOMBO PUBLICATIONS             ER2362         4.00
CESI, B.
    TWELVE LITTLE PIECES FOR BEGINNERS
        FRANCO COLOMBO PUBLICATIONS             100539          .75
CESI, S. *
    PIANO ANTHOLOGY FOR THE YOUNG, BK. 01 - 27 PIECES
        FRANCO COLOMBO PUBLICATIONS             ER820          1.75
CESI, S. *
    PIANO ANTHOLOGY FOR THE YOUNG, BK. 02 - 10 PIECES
        FRANCO COLOMBO PUBLICATIONS             ER821          1.75
CESI, S. *
    PIANO ANTHOLOGY FOR THE YOUNG, BK. 03 - 10 PIECES
        FRANCO COLOMBO PUBLICATIONS             ER822          1.75
CESI, S. *
    PIANO ANTHOLOGY FOR THE YOUNG, BK. 04 - 23 PIECES
        FRANCO COLOMBO PUBLICATIONS             ER823          1.75
CESI, S. *
    PIANO ANTHOLOGY FOR THE YOUNG, BK. 05 - 10 PIECES
        FRANCO COLOMBO PUBLICATIONS             ER824          1.75
CESI, S. *
    PIANO ANTHOLOGY FOR THE YOUNG, BK. 06 - 10 PIECES
        FRANCO COLOMBO PUBLICATIONS             ER825          2.25
```

CESI, S. *
  PIANO ANTHOLOGY FOR THE YOUNG, BK. 07 - 13 PIECES
    FRANCO COLOMBO PUBLICATIONS   ER826   2.50
CESI, S. *
  PIANO ANTHOLOGY FOR THE YOUNG, BK. 08 - 15 PIECES
    FRANCO COLOMBO PUBLICATIONS   ER827   3.25
CESI, S. *
  PIANO ANTHOLOGY FOR THE YOUNG, BK. 10 - 14 PIECES
    FRANCO COLOMBO PUBLICATIONS   ER829   3.50
CESI, S. *
  PIANO ANTHOLOGY FOR THE YOUNG, BK. 11 - 13 PIECES
    FRANCO COLOMBO PUBLICATIONS   ER830   3.50
CESI, S. *
  PIANO ANTHOLOGY FOR THE YOUNG, BK. 12 - 14 PIECES
    FRANCO COLOMBO PUBLICATIONS   ER831   3.50
CHABRIER   WEBSTER, B.
  PIECES PITTORESQUES
    INTERNATIONAL MUSIC COMPANY   2.50
CHAILLEY
  CARNET DE DESSINS - 20 EASY PIECES
    FRANCO COLOMBO PUBLICATIONS   SAL   3.00
CHAMBONNIERES, J. *   SETKOVA   2-3
  ALTE TANZE DES 17. UND 18. JAHRHUNDERTS, 27 STUCKE
    BARENREITER VERLAG   AP 1728
CHAMBONNIERES, J.
  LES PIECES DE CLAVESSIN
    BROUDE BROTHERS LTD.   22.50
CHAMBONNIERES, J.
  OEUVRES COMPLETES
    BROUDE BROTHERS LTD.   25.00
CHAMINADE
  SELECTED COMPOSITIONS, BK. 1
    G. SCHIRMER, INC.   L211   1.50
CHAMINADE
  SELECTED COMPOSITIONS, BK. 2
    G. SCHIRMER, INC.   L212   1.50
CHANLER, T.
  THREE SHORT PIECES
    BOOSEY AND HAWKES, INC.   .75
CHARLES
  RAY CHARLES INSTRUMENTAL FOLIO
    THE BIG THREE MUSIC CORPORATION   2.00
CHARPENTIER, J.
  SEVENTY-TWO ETUDES KARNATIQUES
    ALPHONSE LEDUC
CHATHAM, B. J.--ED   CHATHAM, B. J.
  GOSPEL SONG FAVORITES FOR THE PIANO
    BROADMAN MUSIC   4571-06   2.25
CHAUMONT   3-4
  ALBUM DE LA JEUNESSE
    ALPHONSE LEDUC
CHAUSSON
  QUELQUES DANSES, OP. 26 - DEDICACE ET SARABANDE, PAVANE, FORLANE
    FRANCO COLOMBO PUBLICATIONS   SAL   5.50
CHAVEZ, C.
  LEFT HAND INVERSIONS OF FIVE CHOPIN ETUDES FOR PIANO
    BELWIN-MILLS PUBLISHING CORPORATION   11602   6.25
CHAVEZ, C.
  SEVEN PIECES
    BELWIN-MILLS PUBLISHING CORPORATION   11431   2.50
CHAVEZ, C.
  SEVEN PIECES FOR PIANO
    BELWIN-MILLS PUBLISHING CORPORATION   11431   2.75
CHAVEZ, C.
  TEN PRELUDES
    G. SCHIRMER, INC.   2.50
CHAZARRETA, A. A.
  ARTE NATIVO ARGENTINO, BK. 01
    FRANCO COLOMBO PUBLICATIONS   BA9514   2.00
CHAZARRETA, A. A.
  ARTE NATIVO ARGENTINO, BK. 02
    FRANCO COLOMBO PUBLICATIONS   BA9513   2.00
CHAZARRETA, A. A.
  ARTE NATIVO ARGENTINO, BK. 03
    FRANCO COLOMBO PUBLICATIONS   BA9515   2.00
CHAZARRETA, A. A.
  ARTE NATIVO ARGENTINO, BK. 04
    FRANCO COLOMBO PUBLICATIONS   BA9554   2.00
CHAZARRETA, A. A.
  ARTE NATIVO ARGENTINO, BK. 09
    FRANCO COLOMBO PUBLICATIONS   BA10170   2.00
CHAZARRETA, A. A.
  ARTE NATIVO ARGENTINO, BK. 10
    FRANCO COLOMBO PUBLICATIONS   BA10739   2.00
CHAZARRETA, A. A.
  ARTE NATIVO ARGENTINO, BK. 11
    FRANCO COLOMBO PUBLICATIONS   BA11759   2.00
CHEYETTE, I.
  BASIC PIANO FOR THE MUSIC EDUCATOR AND CLASSROOM TEACHER
    THEODORE PRESSER COMPANY   2.50
CHIESA *
  EASY FANTASIES FROM FAMOUS OPERAS, BK. 1
    FRANCO COLOMBO PUBLICATIONS   127571   1.75
CHIESA *
  EASY FANTASIES FROM FAMOUS OPERAS, BK. 2
    FRANCO COLOMBO PUBLICATIONS   127572   1.75
CHIESA *
  MUSICAL PEARLS - EASY TRANSCRIPTION OF FAMOUS PIECES, BK. 1
    FRANCO COLOMBO PUBLICATIONS   127548   1.75
CHIESA *
  MUSICAL PEARLS - EASY TRANSCRIPTION OF FAMOUS PIECES, BK. 2
    FRANCO COLOMBO PUBLICATIONS   127549   1.75
CHILDE, M.
  TECHNICAL AIDS TO THE PLAYING OF SCALES, BROKEN CHORDS, AND
  ARPEGGIOS, BK. 1
    OXFORD UNIVERSITY PRESS   39.605   .80
CHILDE, M.
  TECHNICAL AIDS TO THE PLAYING OF SCALES, BROKEN CHORDS, AND
  ARPEGGIOS, BK. 2
    OXFORD UNIVERSITY PRESS   39.606   .80
CHILDE, M.
  TECHNICAL AIDS TO THE PLAYING OF SCALES, BROKEN CHORDS, AND
  ARPEGGIOS, BK. 3
    OXFORD UNIVERSITY PRESS   39.607   .80
CHILKOVSKY, N.
  TEN DANCES IN LABANOTATION
    THEODORE PRESSER COMPANY   2.50
CHING
  CANDIDATES COMPANION, ELEMENTARY
    GENERAL WORDS AND MUSIC COMPANY   1.25
CHING
  CANDIDATES COMPANION, PRIMARY
    GENERAL WORDS AND MUSIC COMPANY   1.25
CHING
  NEW GRADED PEDALLING, BK. 1
    GENERAL WORDS AND MUSIC COMPANY   1.25

CHING
  NEW GRADED PEDALLING, BK. 2
    GENERAL WORDS AND MUSIC COMPANY   1.25
CHING
  NEW GRADED PIECES, BK. 1
    GENERAL WORDS AND MUSIC COMPANY   1.25
CHING
  NEW GRADED PIECES, BK. 2
    GENERAL WORDS AND MUSIC COMPANY   1.25
CHING
  NEW GRADED PIECES, BK. 3
    GENERAL WORDS AND MUSIC COMPANY   1.25
CHING
  NEW GRADED PIECES, BK. 4
    GENERAL WORDS AND MUSIC COMPANY   1.25
CHING
  NEW GRADED PIECES, BK. 5
    GENERAL WORDS AND MUSIC COMPANY   1.25
CHING
  NEW GRADED SIGHT-READING, BK. 1
    GENERAL WORDS AND MUSIC COMPANY   1.25
CHING
  NEW GRADED SIGHT-READING, BK. 2
    GENERAL WORDS AND MUSIC COMPANY   1.25
CHING
  NEW GRADED STUDIES, BK. 1
    GENERAL WORDS AND MUSIC COMPANY   1.25
CHING
  NEW GRADED STUDIES, BK. 2
    GENERAL WORDS AND MUSIC COMPANY   1.25
CHING
  NEW GRADED STUDIES, BK. 3
    GENERAL WORDS AND MUSIC COMPANY   1.25
CHING
  NEW GRADED STUDIES, BK. 4
    GENERAL WORDS AND MUSIC COMPANY   1.25
CHING
  NEW GRADED STUDIES, BK. 5
    GENERAL WORDS AND MUSIC COMPANY   1.25
CHING
  NEW GRADED TIME EXERCISES
    GENERAL WORDS AND MUSIC COMPANY   1.25
CHING
  PIANO PRIMER
    GENERAL WORDS AND MUSIC COMPANY   1.25
CHING
  SCALE AND ARPEGGIO BOOK
    GENERAL WORDS AND MUSIC COMPANY   1.25
CHING--ED.   CHING   EASY
  NEW EASY GRADED CLASSIC ALBUM - OLD ENGLISH MASTERS
    GENERAL WORDS AND MUSIC COMPANY   1.25
CHING--ED.   CHING   EASY
  NEW EASY GRADED CLASSIC ALBUM - OLD FRENCH AND FLEMISH MASTERS
    GENERAL WORDS AND MUSIC COMPANY   1.25
CHING--ED.   CHING   EASY
  NEW EASY GRADED CLASSIC ALBUM - SONATINA MOVEMENTS
    GENERAL WORDS AND MUSIC COMPANY   1.25
CHITI, G.
  THREE PIECES
    EDIZIONI BERBEN   EB 1493   3.00
CHLUBNA   4
  FUNF NOCTURNOS, OP. 36
    BARENREITER VERLAG   AP 525
CHOPIN
  ALBUM
    KULTURA   2.00
CHOPIN
  ALBUM OF 12 SELECTED PIECES
    NOVELLO AND COMPANY, LTD.   10.0019.05   1.75
CHOPIN   SCHOLTZ   M-D
  ALBUM. 32 FAVORITE PIECES
    C. F. PETERS CORPORATION   1926   4.00
CHOPIN   JOSEFFY
  ALBUM--33 FAVORITE COMPOSITIONS
    G. SCHIRMER, INC.   L39   2.75
CHOPIN   FRIEDMAN
  ALBUM, VOL. 1
    ASSOCIATED MUSIC PUBLISHERS, INC.   B/H   2.00
CHOPIN   SCHOLTZ
  ALBUM, VOL. 1
    EDWIN F. KALMUS   3337   2.50
CHOPIN   FRIEDMAN
  ALBUM, VOL. 2
    ASSOCIATED MUSIC PUBLISHERS, INC.   B/H   2.00
CHOPIN   SCHOLTZ
  ALBUM, VOL. 2
    EDWIN F. KALMUS   3338   2.50
CHOPIN   ANSON, G.
  ANSON INTRODUCES CHOPIN
    WILLIS MUSIC COMPANY   1.50
CHOPIN   3-5
  AUSWAHL - 38 BEL. STUCKE, BK. 1
    SCHOTT   503   1.75
CHOPIN   3-5
  AUSWAHL - 38 BEL. STUCKE, BK. 2
    SCHOTT   504   1.75
CHOPIN   BRUGNOLI *
  BALLADES
    FRANCO COLOMBO PUBLICATIONS   ER2520   2.50
CHOPIN   LISZT
  BALLADES
    EDWIN F. KALMUS   3326   2.00
CHOPIN
  BALLADES
    EDWARD B. MARKS MUSIC CORPORATION   03.50
CHOPIN   MERRICK, F.
  BALLADES
    NOVELLO AND COMPANY, LTD.   10.0020.09   1.50
CHOPIN   JOSEFFY
  BALLADES
    G. SCHIRMER, INC.   L31   1.50
CHOPIN   MIKULI
  BALLADES
    G. SCHIRMER, INC.   L1552   1.50
CHOPIN   CORTOT
  BALLADES -- ENGLISH TEXT --
    FRANCO COLOMBO PUBLICATIONS   SAL   6.00
CHOPIN   CORTOT
  BALLADES -- FR. TEXT --
    FRANCO COLOMBO PUBLICATIONS   SAL   6.00
CHOPIN   SCHOLTZ   D
  BALLADES --4-- AND IMPROMPTUS --3--
    C. F. PETERS CORPORATION   1905   2.50
CHOPIN   SCHAUM, J.   3
  BEST OF CHOPIN
    SCHAUM PUBLICATIONS, INC.   1.50

CHOPIN   BRADLEY, R.
BRADLEY CLASSICAL SERIES - PRELUDE IN A - AND - PRELUDE IN C
MINOR
    SCREEN GEMS - COLUMBIA PUBLICATIONS   5715PP2   .85
CHOPIN
CHAMBER MUSIC
    EDWARD B. MARKS MUSIC CORPORATION   06.50
CHOPIN   COIT, L. E. *
CHILDHOOD DAYS OF FAMOUS COMPOSERS -- CHILD CHOPIN
    THEODORE PRESSER COMPANY   1.00
CHOPIN
CHOPIN
    ASHLEY DEALERS SERVICE, INC.   HG 04   2.95
CHOPIN
CHOPIN ALBUM
    MUSIC SALES CORPORATION   020056   2.95
CHOPIN   THORNE
CHOPIN FOR EVERYBODY
    BOOSEY AND HAWKES, INC.   1.50
CHOPIN   ROVENGER
CHOPIN FOR THE YOUNG
    RUBANK, INC.   1.50
CHOPIN   ECKHARDT, F.   2
CHOPIN FOR THE YOUNG PIANIST
    CENTURY MUSIC PUBLISHING COMPANY, INC.   3959   .40
CHOPIN   MALOOF
CHOPIN IN MINIATURE
    CARL FISCHER, INC.   P 3296   1.25
CHOPIN   SMALL, A.
CHOPIN SAMPLER
    ALFRED MUSIC COMPANY   520   3.95
CHOPIN   CHING
CHOPIN SELECTED WALTZES
    GENERAL WORDS AND MUSIC COMPANY   1.25
CHOPIN   SCHAUM, J.   2 1/2
CHOPIN-SCHAUM, BK. 1
    BELWIN-MILLS PUBLISHING CORPORATION   1.25
CHOPIN   SCHAUM, J.   2 1/2
CHOPIN-SCHAUM, BK. 1
    BELWIN-MILLS PUBLISHING CORPORATION   1.50
CHOPIN   SCHAUM, J.   4 1/2
CHOPIN-SCHAUM, BK. 2
    BELWIN-MILLS PUBLISHING CORPORATION   1.25
CHOPIN   SCHUAM, J.   4 1/2
CHOPIN-SCHAUM, BK. 2
    BELWIN-MILLS PUBLISHING CORPORATION   1.50
CHOPIN
CHOPIN, MUSIC TO REMEMBER
    ASHLEY DEALERS SERVICE, INC.   1.50
CHOPIN
COMPLETE PIANO WORKS IN 3 VOLS. CLOTH-BOUND
    C. F. PETERS CORPORATION   15.00
CHOPIN   SCHOLTZ   D
COMPLETE PIANO WORKS, VOL. 1
    C. F. PETERS CORPORATION   1900A   12.50
CHOPIN   SCHOLTZ   D
COMPLETE PIANO WORKS, VOL. 2
    C. F. PETERS CORPORATION   1900B   12.50
CHOPIN   SCHOLTZ   D
COMPLETE PIANO WORKS, VOL. 3
    C. F. PETERS CORPORATION   1900C   12.50
CHOPIN   D
CONCERT PIECES, OP. 2, 13, 14, 22 --ARR. FOR PIANO SOLO--
    C. F. PETERS CORPORATION   1912   6.00
CHOPIN   SAUER   4
DREI ECOSSAISES, OP. 72 NO. 3
    SCHOTT   0424 1/2   1.00
CHOPIN
DREI KLAVIERSTUCKE
    SCHOTT   10984   1.00
CHOPIN   ROWLEY   E-M
EASIEST ORIGINAL PIECES FOR PIANO
    C. F. PETERS CORPORATION   H2   1.50
CHOPIN   FRIEDMAN
ETUDES
    ASSOCIATED MUSIC PUBLISHERS, INC.   B/H   2.75
CHOPIN
ETUDES
    G. HENLE MUSIKVERLAG   124   4.25
CHOPIN   LISZT
ETUDES
    EDWIN F. KALMUS   3327   3.00
CHOPIN
ETUDES
    EDWARD B. MARKS MUSIC CORPORATION   05.00
CHOPIN   FRIEDHEIM
ETUDES
    G. SCHIRMER, INC.   L33   2.00
CHOPIN   MIKULI
ETUDES
    G. SCHIRMER, INC.   L1551   1.75
CHOPIN
ETUDES -- CLOTH
    G. HENLE MUSIKVERLAG   229   7.35
CHOPIN   SCHOLTZ   D
ETUDES --27-- COMPLETE
    C. F. PETERS CORPORATION   1907   2.50
CHOPIN   CORTOT
ETUDES BK. 1 - OP. 10 -- ENGLISH TEXT --
    FRANCO COLOMBO PUBLICATIONS   SAL   6.50
CHOPIN   CORTOT
ETUDES BK. 1 - OP. 10 -- FR. TEXT --
    FRANCO COLOMBO PUBLICATIONS   SAL   6.50
CHOPIN   CORTOT
ETUDES BK. 2 - OP. 25 -- ENGLISH TEXT --
    FRANCO COLOMBO PUBLICATIONS   SAL   6.50
CHOPIN   CORTOT
ETUDES BK. 2 - OP. 25 -- FR. TEXT --
    FRANCO COLOMBO PUBLICATIONS   SAL   6.50
CHOPIN   4
ETUDES IN F MINOR, A FLAT, D FLAT -- POST.
    CENTURY MUSIC PUBLISHING COMPANY, INC.   3901   .40
CHOPIN   ESTEBAN
ETUDES, OP. 10
    ALFRED MUSIC COMPANY   576   3.00
CHOPIN   BADURA-SKODA
ETUDES, OP. 10
    WIENER URTEXT EDITION   UT 50030   3.50
CHOPIN   BRUGNOLI *
ETUDES, OP. 10 AND 25
    FRANCO COLOMBO PUBLICATIONS   ER2575   4.00
CHOPIN   BADURA-SKODA
ETUDES, OP. 25
    WIENER URTEXT EDITION   UT 50031   3.50
CHOPIN
FANTASIA, BERCEUSE, BARCAROLLE
    EDWARD B. MARKS MUSIC CORPORATION   03.00

CHOPIN   PUGNO
FIFTY-ONE MARZURKAS
    UNIVERSAL EDITION   342   6.00
CHOPIN   LISZT
FIFTY-SIX MAZURKAS
    EDWIN F. KALMUS   3328   3.25
CHOPIN   KREUTZER
FIRST CHOPIN
    BOSTON MUSIC COMPANY   1.00
CHOPIN
FORTY PIANO COMPOSITIONS
    THEODORE PRESSER COMPANY   5.00
CHOPIN   PUGNO
FOUR BALLADES AND FOUR IMPROMPTUS
    UNIVERSAL EDITION   345   4.15
CHOPIN   JOSEFFY
FOUR CONCERT PIECES
    G. SCHIRMER, INC.   L38   1.75
CHOPIN   MIKULI
FOUR CONCERT PIECES
    G. SCHIRMER, INC.   L1546   2.50
CHOPIN *
FOUR ETUDES TRANSCRIBED FOR THE LEFT HAND
    FRANCO COLOMBO PUBLICATIONS   SAL   4.25
CHOPIN
FOUR FAVORITE PRELUDES- OP.28, NOS.4, 6, 7, 20
    ELKAN-VOGEL, INC.   .50
CHOPIN   PUGNO
FOURTEEN WALTZES
    UNIVERSAL EDITION   341   3.80
CHOPIN   BRUGNOLI *
IMPROMPTUS
    FRANCO COLOMBO PUBLICATIONS   ER2543   1.75
CHOPIN   CORTOT
IMPROMPTUS
    FRANCO COLOMBO PUBLICATIONS   SAL   2.75
CHOPIN
IMPROMPTUS
    EDWARD B. MARKS MUSIC CORPORATION   03.00
CHOPIN   MERRICK, F.
IMPROMPTUS
    NOVELLO AND COMPANY, LTD.   10.0021.07   1.15
CHOPIN   JOSEFFY
IMPROMPTUS
    G. SCHIRMER, INC.   L1039   .85
CHOPIN   MIKULI
IMPROMPTUS
    G. SCHIRMER, INC.   L1553   1.00
CHOPIN   SCHOLTZ   D
IMPROMPTUS --4--
    C. F. PETERS CORPORATION   1905B   1.50
CHOPIN   MIROVITCH, A.
INTRODUCTION TO CHOPIN, VOL. 1--56 COMPOSITIONS ARRANGED IN
ORDER OF DIFFICULTY
    G. SCHIRMER, INC.   2.50
CHOPIN   MIROVITCH, A.
INTRODUCTION TO CHOPIN, VOL. 2--56 COMPOSITIONS ARRANGED IN
ORDER OF DIFFICULTY
    G. SCHIRMER, INC.   2.50
CHOPIN   PALMER, W. A.
INTRODUCTION TO HIS PIANO WORKS
    ALFRED MUSIC COMPANY   635   2.00
CHOPIN   MONTANI
LITTLE KNOWN PIECES
    FRANCO COLOMBO PUBLICATIONS   ER2625   1.50
CHOPIN   HUGHES
MASTER SERIES FOR THE YOUNG, VOL. 10--CHOPIN
    G. SCHIRMER, INC.   1.25
CHOPIN   E-M
MASTERS FOR THE YOUNG. VOL. 4
    C. F. PETERS CORPORATION   2706   2.50
CHOPIN   SAUER   4
MAZURKA IN B FLAT, OP. 7 NO. 1 AND MAZURKA IN A MINOR, OP. 7 NO.
2
    SCHOTT   0305 1/2   1.00
CHOPIN   FRIEDMAN
MAZURKAS
    ASSOCIATED MUSIC PUBLISHERS, INC.   B/H   3.00
CHOPIN   LEVINE
MAZURKAS
    BOSTON MUSIC COMPANY   1.50
CHOPIN   BRUGNOLI *
MAZURKAS
    FRANCO COLOMBO PUBLICATIONS   ER2485   4.50
CHOPIN
MAZURKAS
    EDWARD B. MARKS MUSIC CORPORATION   07.00
CHOPIN   JOSEFFY
MAZURKAS
    G. SCHIRMER, INC.   L28   3.00
CHOPIN   MIKULI
MAZURKAS
    G. SCHIRMER, INC.   L1548   3.00
CHOPIN   SCHOLTZ   D
MAZURKAS --51--
    C. F. PETERS CORPORATION   1902   2.50
CHOPIN   CORTOT
MAZURKAS, BK. 1 .. OP. 6, 7, 17, 24, 30
    FRANCO COLOMBO PUBLICATIONS   SAL   5.00
CHOPIN   CORTOT
MAZURKAS, BK. 2 .. OP. 33, 41, 50, 56
    FRANCO COLOMBO PUBLICATIONS   SAL   4.00
CHOPIN   CORTOT
MAZURKAS, BK. 3 .. OP. 59, 63, 67, 68
    FRANCO COLOMBO PUBLICATIONS   SAL   4.00
CHOPIN
MINOR WORKS
    EDWARD B. MARKS MUSIC CORPORATION   05.00
CHOPIN   JOSEFFY
MISCELLANEOUS COMPOSITIONS
    G. SCHIRMER, INC.   L36   2.00
CHOPIN   MIKULI
MISCELLANEOUS COMPOSITIONS
    G. SCHIRMER, INC.   L1555   1.75
CHOPIN
MY FAVORITE CHOPIN
    ASHLEY DEALERS SERVICE, INC.   2.95
CHOPIN   CHING   EASY
NEW EASY GRADED CLASSIC ALBUM - CHOPIN
    GENERAL WORDS AND MUSIC COMPANY   1.25
CHOPIN   PUGNO
NINETEEN NOCTURNES
    UNIVERSAL EDITION   344   2.80
CHOPIN   MARCHI, G.
NOCTURNE IN C SHARP MINOR, AND IN C MINOR
    EDIZIONI BERBEN   1320   1.20

```
CHOPIN              SAUER       5
  NOCTURNE IN C SHARP MINOR, OP. 27 NO. 1 AND NOCTURNE IN D FLAT,
  OP. 27 NO. 2
            SCHOTT                                      0334 1/2    1.00
CHOPIN              FRIEDMAN
  NOCTURNES
            ASSOCIATED MUSIC PUBLISHERS, INC.           B/H         3.00
CHOPIN              PINTER
  NOCTURNES
            CARL FISCHER, INC.                          L 743       1.50
CHOPIN              BRUGNOLI *
  NOCTURNES
            FRANCO COLOMBO PUBLICATIONS                 ER2524      2.50
CHOPIN
  NOCTURNES
            G. HENLE MUSIKVERLAG                        185         3.50
CHOPIN              LISZT
  NOCTURNES
            EDWIN F. KALMUS                             3329        2.00
CHOPIN              MERTKE, E.
  NOCTURNES
            EDWIN F. KALMUS                             3333        2.00
CHOPIN
  NOCTURNES
            EDWARD B. MARKS MUSIC CORPORATION                       05.00
CHOPIN              SCHOLTZ        D
  NOCTURNES
            C. F. PETERS CORPORATION                    1904        2.50
CHOPIN              JOSEFFY
  NOCTURNES
            G. SCHIRMER, INC.                           L30         1.50
CHOPIN              MIKULI
  NOCTURNES
            G. SCHIRMER, INC.                           L1550       1.75
CHOPIN              CORTOT
  NOCTURNES - BK. 1 .. OP. 9, 15, 27, 32
            FRANCO COLOMBO PUBLICATIONS                 SAL         4.25
CHOPIN              CORTOT
  NOCTURNES - BK. 2 .. OP. 37, 48, 55, 62
            FRANCO COLOMBO PUBLICATIONS                 SAL         4.25
CHOPIN
  NOCTURNES -- CLOTH
            G. HENLE MUSIKVERLAG                        233         6.55
CHOPIN
  NOCTURNES--CRITICAL COMMENTARY
            G. HENLE MUSIKVERLAG                        203         3.10
CHOPIN              SCHOLTZ *      D
  PIANO PIECES --11--
            C. F. PETERS CORPORATION                    1910        3.00
CHOPIN              FRIEDMAN
  POLONAISES
            ASSOCIATED MUSIC PUBLISHERS, INC.           B/H         3.00
CHOPIN              BRUGNOLI *
  POLONAISES
            FRANCO COLOMBO PUBLICATIONS                 ER2490      4.25
CHOPIN              CORTOT
  POLONAISES
            FRANCO COLOMBO PUBLICATIONS                 SAL         6.00
CHOPIN
  POLONAISES
            G. HENLE MUSIKVERLAG                        217         4.65
CHOPIN              LISZT
  POLONAISES
            EDWIN F. KALMUS                             3330        2.00
CHOPIN              MERTKE, E.
  POLONAISES
            EDWIN F. KALMUS                             3334        2.00
CHOPIN
  POLONAISES
            EDWARD B. MARKS MUSIC CORPORATION                       05.00
CHOPIN              MIKULI
  POLONAISES
            G. SCHIRMER, INC.                           L29         1.50
CHOPIN
  POLONAISES -- CLOTH
            G. HENLE MUSIKVERLAG                        218         7.70
CHOPIN              SCHOLTZ        D
  POLONAISES --10--
            C. F. PETERS CORPORATION                    1903        2.50
CHOPIN
  POLONAISES--CRITICAL COMMENTARY
            G. HENLE MUSIKVERLAG                        249
CHOPIN              CORTOT
  POSTHUMOUS WORKS
            FRANCO COLOMBO PUBLICATIONS                 SAL         6.00
CHOPIN              PALMER, W. A.
  PRELUDES
            ALFRED MUSIC COMPANY                        610         2.00
CHOPIN
  PRELUDES
            CARL FISCHER, INC.                          L 924       1.25
CHOPIN
  PRELUDES
            G. HENLE MUSIKVERLAG                        73          2.70
CHOPIN              LISZT
  PRELUDES
            EDWIN F. KALMUS                             3343        1.50
CHOPIN              MERTKE, E.
  PRELUDES
            EDWIN F. KALMUS                             3332        1.50
CHOPIN
  PRELUDES
            EDWARD B. MARKS MUSIC CORPORATION                       03.00
CHOPIN              JOSEFFY
  PRELUDES
            G. SCHIRMER, INC.                           L34         1.00
CHOPIN              MIKULI
  PRELUDES
            G. SCHIRMER, INC.                           L1547       1.50
CHOPIN              JOSEFFY
  PRELUDES - OP. 28 NO. 1 IN C MAJOR AND NO. 2 IN A MINOR
            G. SCHIRMER, INC.                                       .30
CHOPIN              JOSEFFY
  PRELUDES - OP. 28 NO. 20 IN C MINOR AND NO. 21 IN B FLAT MAJOR
            G. SCHIRMER, INC.                                       .40
CHOPIN              JOSEFFY
  PRELUDES - OP. 28 NO. 4 IN E MINOR AND NO. 5 IN D MAJOR
            G. SCHIRMER, INC.                                       .35
CHOPIN              JOSEFFY
  PRELUDES - OP. 28 NO. 6 IN B MINOR AND NO. 7 IN A MAJOR
            G. SCHIRMER, INC.                                       .35
CHOPIN              JOSEFFY
  PRELUDES - OP. 28 NO. 8 IN F SHARP MINOR AND NO. 9 IN E MAJOR
            G. SCHIRMER, INC.                                       .40
CHOPIN
  PRELUDES -- CLOTH
            G. HENLE MUSIKVERLAG                        228         5.80

CHOPIN              CORTOT
  PRELUDES -- ENGLISH TEXT --
            FRANCO COLOMBO PUBLICATIONS                 SAL         6.50
CHOPIN              CORTOT
  PRELUDES -- FR. TEXT --
            FRANCO COLOMBO PUBLICATIONS                 SAL         6.50
CHOPIN              SCHOLTZ        D
  PRELUDES --25--
            C. F. PETERS CORPORATION                    1908A       1.25
CHOPIN              SCHOLTZ        D
  PRELUDES --25-- AND RONDOS --3--
            C. F. PETERS CORPORATION                    1908        2.50
CHOPIN
  PRELUDES--CRITICAL COMMENTARY
            G. HENLE MUSIKVERLAG                        226         1.95
CHOPIN              BRUGNOLI *
  PRELUDES, OP. 28
            FRANCO COLOMBO PUBLICATIONS                 ER2521      1.75
CHOPIN              MORONI     4-5
  PRELUDES, OP. 28 UND OP. 45
            BARENREITER VERLAG                          CM 20090
CHOPIN              5
  PRELUDES, OP. 28, NOS. 6, 7, 9, 20
            CENTURY MUSIC PUBLISHING COMPANY, INC.      854         .40
CHOPIN              3
  PRELUDES, THREE FAVORITE -- IN B MINOR, OP. 28 NO. 6 - IN A, OP.
  28 NO. 7 - IN G MINOR, OP. 28 NO. 20
            BOSTON MUSIC COMPANY                                    .50
CHOPIN
  RADIO CITY ALBUM, BK. 1
            EDWARD B. MARKS MUSIC CORPORATION                       02.50
CHOPIN
  RADIO CITY ALBUM, BK. 2
            EDWARD B. MARKS MUSIC CORPORATION                       01.50
CHOPIN              CORTOT
  RONDOS
            FRANCO COLOMBO PUBLICATIONS                 SAL         4.25
CHOPIN
  RONDOS
            EDWARD B. MARKS MUSIC CORPORATION                       05.00
CHOPIN              JOSEFFY
  RONDOS
            G. SCHIRMER, INC.                           L1184       1.50
CHOPIN              MIKULI
  RONDOS
            G. SCHIRMER, INC.                           L1554       1.25
CHOPIN              SCHOLTZ        D
  RONDOS --3--
            C. F. PETERS CORPORATION                    1908B       1.25
CHOPIN              LISZT
  RONDOS, FANTASY
            EDWIN F. KALMUS                             3339        1.00
CHOPIN              CORTOT
  SCHERZI
            FRANCO COLOMBO PUBLICATIONS                 SAL         6.00
CHOPIN              SCHOLTZ        D
  SCHERZI --4-- AND FANTASY
            C. F. PETERS CORPORATION                    1906        2.50
CHOPIN              JOSEFFY
  SCHERZI AND FANTASY IN F MINOR, OP. 49
            G. SCHIRMER, INC.                           L32         2.00
CHOPIN              MIKULI
  SCHERZI AND FANTASY IN F MINOR, OP. 49
            G. SCHIRMER, INC.                           L1556       2.00
CHOPIN              LISZT
  SCHERZI, FANTASY IN F MINOR
            EDWIN F. KALMUS                             3340        2.00
CHOPIN              BRUGNOLI *
  SCHERZOS
            FRANCO COLOMBO PUBLICATIONS                 ER2549      3.25
CHOPIN
  SCHERZOS
            EDWARD B. MARKS MUSIC CORPORATION                       05.00
CHOPIN              MERRICK, F.
  SCHERZOS
            NOVELLO AND COMPANY, LTD.              10.0023.03       1.50
CHOPIN
  SELECTED EASY PIECES
            EDWARD B. MARKS MUSIC CORPORATION                       03.00
CHOPIN              PALMER, W. A.
  SELECTED FAVORITES
            ALFRED MUSIC COMPANY                        611         3.00
CHOPIN              FLATO
  SIX CELEBRATED COMPOSITIONS
            MCA MUSIC                                               1.25
CHOPIN              THOMPSON, J.    4
  SIX CHOPIN ETUDES
            WILLIS MUSIC COMPANY                                    1.00
CHOPIN              LISZT *
  SIX POLISH SONGS
            FRANCO COLOMBO PUBLICATIONS                 ER941       1.00
CHOPIN *            TAGLIAPIETRA
  SIX POLISH SONGS
            FRANCO COLOMBO PUBLICATIONS                 ER941       1.00
CHOPIN *            TAGLIAPIETRA
  SIX POLISH SONGS
            FRANCO COLOMBO PUBLICATIONS                 ER941       1.00
CHOPIN              BRUGNOLI *
  SONATAS
            FRANCO COLOMBO PUBLICATIONS                 ER2501      4.25
CHOPIN
  SONATAS
            EDWARD B. MARKS MUSIC CORPORATION                       05.00
CHOPIN              SCHOLTZ *       D
  SONATAS
            C. F. PETERS CORPORATION                    1909        3.00
CHOPIN              MIKULI
  SONATAS
            G. SCHIRMER, INC.                           L35         1.75
CHOPIN              3 *
  SONG GEMS FROM CHOPIN
            SHAPIRO, BERNSTEIN ORGANIZATION                         1.00
CHOPIN
  SONGS
            EDWARD B. MARKS MUSIC CORPORATION                       06.00
CHOPIN              MANSFIELD
  STEPS TO THE MASTERS
            BANKS AND SON LTD.                                      1.50
CHOPIN              HALL
  SYLPHIDES
            BOOSEY AND HAWKES, INC.                                 1.50
CHOPIN              PUGNO
  THIRTEEN POLONAISES
            UNIVERSAL EDITION                           343         2.80
CHOPIN
  THREE ECOSSAISES, OP. 72
            G. SCHIRMER, INC.                                       .50
```

CHOPIN   4
  THREE ETUDES
    CENTURY MUSIC PUBLISHING COMPANY, INC.   3901   .40
CHOPIN   LISZT
  THREE SONATAS
    EDWIN F. KALMUS   3341   3.00
CHOPIN   PUGNO
  TWENTY-FIVE ETUDES
    UNIVERSAL EDITION   347   4.50
CHOPIN   PUGNO
  TWENTY-FIVE PRELUDES
    UNIVERSAL EDITION   348A   3.00
CHOPIN   HANSEN *
  TWENTY-FOUR PRELUDES, OP. 28
    WIENER URTEXT EDITION   UT 50005 4.00
CHOPIN   BRUGNOLI *
  TWENTY-ONE PIECES
    FRANCO COLOMBO PUBLICATIONS   ER2630   3.00
CHOPIN
  TWO FORGOTTEN PIECES
    EDWARD B. MARKS MUSIC CORPORATION   01.35
CHOPIN   DEIS
  TWO PRELUDES - OP. 28 NOS. 7 AND 20
    G. SCHIRMER, INC.   .30
CHOPIN   DEIS
  TWO PRELUDES - OP. 28 NOS. 7 AND 20
    G. SCHIRMER, INC.   .50
CHOPIN
  TWO PRELUDES, OP. 28 NOS. 20 AND 21
    BELWIN-MILLS PUBLISHING CORPORATION   28168   .60
CHOPIN   CORTOT
  VARIOUS PIECES - BK. 1
    FRANCO COLOMBO PUBLICATIONS   SAL   5.00
CHOPIN   CORTOT
  VARIOUS PIECES - BK. 2
    FRANCO COLOMBO PUBLICATIONS   SAL   6.00
CHOPIN   SAUER   4
  WALTZ IN A FLAT, OP. 69 NO. 1 AND WALTZ IN B MINOR, OP. 69 NO. 2
    SCHOTT   0301 1/2 1.00
CHOPIN   SAUER   4
  WALTZ IN G FLAT, OP. 70 NO. 1 - WALTZ IN A FLAT, OP. 70 NO. 2 -
  WALTZ IN D FLAT, OP. 70 NO. 3
    SCHOTT   0302 1/2 1.00
CHOPIN   FRIEDMAN
  WALTZES
    ASSOCIATED MUSIC PUBLISHERS, INC.   B/H   2.50
CHOPIN
  WALTZES
    ASHLEY DEALERS SERVICE, INC.   WFS NO. 52 2.95
CHOPIN   BRUGNOLI *
  WALTZES
    FRANCO COLOMBO PUBLICATIONS   ER2488   2.00
CHOPIN   CORTOT
  WALTZES
    FRANCO COLOMBO PUBLICATIONS   SAL   5.00
CHOPIN
  WALTZES
    G. HENLE MUSIKVERLAG   131   3.50
CHOPIN   LISZT
  WALTZES
    EDWIN F. KALMUS   3342   1.50
CHOPIN   MERTKE, E.
  WALTZES
    EDWIN F. KALMUS   3331   1.50
CHOPIN
  WALTZES
    EDWARD B. MARKS MUSIC CORPORATION   05.00
CHOPIN   JOSEFFY
  WALTZES
    G. SCHIRMER, INC.   L27   1.50
CHOPIN   MIKULI
  WALTZES
    G. SCHIRMER, INC.   L1549   1.25
CHOPIN
  WALTZES -- CLOTH
    G. HENLE MUSIKVERLAG   230   6.55
CHOPIN   SCHOLTZ   D
  WALTZES --14--
    C. F. PETERS CORPORATION   1804   2.50
CHOPIN   3-4
  WALZER
    BARENREITER VERLAG   CM 20177
CHOPIN   MAIER, G.
  YOUR CHOPIN BOOK
    BELWIN-MILLS PUBLISHING CORPORATION   11539   2.50
CHRETIEN
  IMAGES SONORES
    FRANCO COLOMBO PUBLICATIONS   SAL   4.00
CHRETIEN
  PETITS PRELUDES RECREATIFS - PRES DU RUISSEAU, BEBE S'ENDORT,
  PETIT NUAGE, PIERROT SAUTILLE, A L'EGLISE, PARLONS BAS
    FRANCO COLOMBO PUBLICATIONS   SAL   2.00
CHRISTIANSEN
  TRIP THROUGH YELLOWSTONE PARK, A
    BELWIN-MILLS PUBLISHING CORPORATION   1.00
CIMAROSA   BOGHEN *
  THIRTY-TWO SONATAS, VOL. 1
    ASSOCIATED MUSIC PUBLISHERS, INC.   ESC   3.75
CIMAROSA   BOGHEN *
  THIRTY-TWO SONATAS, VOL. 2
    ASSOCIATED MUSIC PUBLISHERS, INC.   ESC   4.50
CIMAROSA   BOGHEN *
  THIRTY-TWO SONATAS, VOL. 3
    ASSOCIATED MUSIC PUBLISHERS, INC.   ESC   5.50
CIMAROSA   LIGTELIJN   M
  TWENTY-FOUR SONATAS, VOL. 1
    C. F. PETERS CORPORATION   B861   2.00
CIMAROSA   LIGTELIJN   M
  TWENTY-FOUR SONATAS, VOL. 2
    C. F. PETERS CORPORATION   B871   2.00
CIMAROSA   RUPERINK   M
  TWENTY-FOUR SONATAS, VOL. 3
    C. F. PETERS CORPORATION   B872   2.00
CINTOLESI
  FIVE PIECES
    FRANCO COLOMBO PUBLICATIONS   FOR.12159 1.25
CINTOLESI
  SIX LITTLE PIECES
    FRANCO COLOMBO PUBLICATIONS   128484   .60
CINTOLESI
  TWO STUDIES FOR REPEATED NOTES
    FRANCO COLOMBO PUBLICATIONS   FOR.12127 .90
CLARK, F.
  A B C PAPERS
    SUMMY-BIRCHARD COMPANY   2.00
CLARK, F.
  LOOK AND LISTEN, PART A -- ELEMENTARY SERIES, BASIC --
    SUMMY-BIRCHARD COMPANY   2.50

CLARK, F.
  LOOK AND LISTEN, PART B -- ELEMENTARY SERIES, BASIC --
    SUMMY-BIRCHARD COMPANY   2.50
CLARK, F.
  LOOK AND LISTEN, PART C -- ELEMENTARY SERIES, BASIC --
    SUMMY-BIRCHARD COMPANY   2.50
CLARK, F.
  LOOK AND LISTEN, PART D -- ELEMENTARY SERIES, BASIC --
    SUMMY-BIRCHARD COMPANY   2.50
CLARK, F.
  PENCIL PLAY, PART A
    SUMMY-BIRCHARD COMPANY   1.75
CLARK, F.
  PENCIL PLAY, PART B
    SUMMY-BIRCHARD COMPANY   1.75
CLARK, F.
  PENCIL PLAY, PART C
    SUMMY-BIRCHARD COMPANY   1.75
CLARK, F.
  PENCIL PLAY, PART D
    SUMMY-BIRCHARD COMPANY   1.25
CLARK, F.
  READER, PART A
    SUMMY-BIRCHARD COMPANY   1.50
CLARK, F.
  READER, PART B
    SUMMY-BIRCHARD COMPANY   1.50
CLARK, F.
  READER, PART C
    SUMMY-BIRCHARD COMPANY   1.50
CLARK, F.
  READER, PART D
    SUMMY-BIRCHARD COMPANY   1.50
CLARK, F.
  READING TECHNIQUE
    SUMMY-BIRCHARD COMPANY   2.50
CLARK, F.
  TIME TO BEGIN -- ELEMENTARY SERIES, BASIC --
    SUMMY-BIRCHARD COMPANY   3.00
CLARK, F.--ED.   CLARK, F.
  CONTEMPORARY PIANO LITERATURE, BK. 1
    SUMMY-BIRCHARD COMPANY   1.75
CLARK, F.--ED.   CLARK, F.
  CONTEMPORARY PIANO LITERATURE, BK. 2
    SUMMY-BIRCHARD COMPANY   1.75
CLARK, F.--ED.   CLARK, F.
  CONTEMPORARY PIANO LITERATURE, BK. 3
    SUMMY-BIRCHARD COMPANY   2.25
CLARK, F.--ED.   CLARK, F.
  CONTEMPORARY PIANO LITERATURE, BK. 4
    SUMMY-BIRCHARD COMPANY   2.50
CLARK, F.--ED.   CLARK, F.
  CONTEMPORARY PIANO LITERATURE, BK. 5
    SUMMY-BIRCHARD COMPANY   2.25
CLARK, F.--ED.   CLARK, F.
  CONTEMPORARY PIANO LITERATURE, BK. 6
    SUMMY-BIRCHARD COMPANY   2.50
CLARK, F.--ED.   CLARK, F.
  JAZZ AND BLUES - 12 INCH LP RECORD --BOOKS 1-6--
    SUMMY-BIRCHARD COMPANY   6.00
CLARK, F.--ED.   CLARK, F.
  JAZZ AND BLUES, BK. 1
    SUMMY-BIRCHARD COMPANY   1.50
CLARK, F.--ED.   CLARK, F.
  JAZZ AND BLUES, BK. 2
    SUMMY-BIRCHARD COMPANY   1.50
CLARK, F.--ED.   CLARK, F.
  JAZZ AND BLUES, BK. 3
    SUMMY-BIRCHARD COMPANY   1.50
CLARK, F.--ED.   CLARK, F.
  JAZZ AND BLUES, BK. 4
    SUMMY-BIRCHARD COMPANY   1.50
CLARK, F.--ED.   CLARK, F.
  JAZZ AND BLUES, BK. 5
    SUMMY-BIRCHARD COMPANY   1.50
CLARK, F.--ED.   CLARK, F.
  JAZZ AND BLUES, BK. 6
    SUMMY-BIRCHARD COMPANY   1.50
CLARK, F.--ED.   CLARK, F.
  KEYBOARD THEORY, BK. 1
    SUMMY-BIRCHARD COMPANY   2.50
CLARK, F.--ED.   CLARK, F.
  KEYBOARD THEORY, BK. 2
    SUMMY-BIRCHARD COMPANY   2.50
CLARK, F.--ED.   CLARK, F.
  KEYBOARD THEORY, BK. 3
    SUMMY-BIRCHARD COMPANY   2.50
CLARK, F.--ED.   CLARK, F.
  KEYBOARD THEORY, BK. 4
    SUMMY-BIRCHARD COMPANY   2.50
CLARK, F.--ED.   CLARK, F.
  KEYBOARD THEORY, BK. 5
    SUMMY-BIRCHARD COMPANY   2.75
CLARK, F.--ED.   CLARK, F.
  KEYBOARD THEORY, BK. 6
    SUMMY-BIRCHARD COMPANY   2.75
CLARK, F.--ED.   CLARK, F.
  MUSIC WORKBOOK - BK. 1A
    SUMMY-BIRCHARD COMPANY   3.00
CLARK, F.--ED.   CLARK, F.
  MUSIC WORKBOOK - BK. 1B
    SUMMY-BIRCHARD COMPANY   2.75
CLARK, F.--ED.   CLARK, F.
  MUSIC WORKBOOK - BK. 2
    SUMMY-BIRCHARD COMPANY   2.50
CLARK, F.--ED.   CLARK, F.
  MUSIC WORKBOOK - BK. 3
    SUMMY-BIRCHARD COMPANY   1.85
CLARK, F.--ED.   CLARK, F.
  PIANO LITERATURE, BK. 1
    SUMMY-BIRCHARD COMPANY   2.00
CLARK, F.--ED.   CLARK, F.
  PIANO LITERATURE, BK. 2
    SUMMY-BIRCHARD COMPANY   2.00
CLARK, F.--ED.   CLARK, F.
  PIANO LITERATURE, BK. 3
    SUMMY-BIRCHARD COMPANY   2.25
CLARK, F.--ED.   CLARK, F.
  PIANO LITERATURE, BK. 4 A
    SUMMY-BIRCHARD COMPANY   2.25
CLARK, F.--ED.   CLARK, F.
  PIANO LITERATURE, BK. 4 B
    SUMMY-BIRCHARD COMPANY   2.00
CLARK, F.--ED.   CLARK, F.
  PIANO LITERATURE, BK. 5 A
    SUMMY-BIRCHARD COMPANY   2.50

CLARK, F.--ED.	CLARK, F.			
PIANO LITERATURE, BK. 5 B				
SUMMY-BIRCHARD COMPANY				2.50
CLARK, F.--ED.	CLARK, F.			
PIANO LITERATURE, BK. 6 A				
SUMMY-BIRCHARD COMPANY				1.85
CLARK, F.--ED.	CLARK, F.			
PIANO LITERATURE, BK. 6 B				
SUMMY-BIRCHARD COMPANY				3.50
CLARK, F.--ED.	CLARK, F.			
PIANO TECHNIC, BK. 1				
SUMMY-BIRCHARD COMPANY				2.50
CLARK, F.--ED.	CLARK, F.			
PIANO TECHNIC, BK. 2				
SUMMY-BIRCHARD COMPANY				2.25
CLARK, F.--ED.	CLARK, F.			
PIANO TECHNIC, BK. 3				
SUMMY-BIRCHARD COMPANY				2.25
CLARK, F.--ED.	CLARK, F.			
PIANO TECHNIC, BK. 4				
SUMMY-BIRCHARD COMPANY				2.25
CLARK, F.--ED.	CLARK, F.			
PIANO TECHNIC, BK. 5				
SUMMY-BIRCHARD COMPANY				2.50
CLARK, F.--ED.	CLARK, F.			
PIANO TECHNIC, BK. 6				
SUMMY-BIRCHARD COMPANY				1.50
CLARK, F.--ED.	CLARK, F.			
TECHNIC TIME - PART A				
SUMMY-BIRCHARD COMPANY				2.50
TECHNIC TIME - PART B				
SUMMY-BIRCHARD COMPANY				2.50
CLARK, F.--ED.	CLARK, F.			
THEMES FROM MASTERWORKS, BK. 1				
SUMMY-BIRCHARD COMPANY				1.50
CLARK, F.--ED.	CLARK, F.			
THEMES FROM MASTERWORKS, BK. 2				
SUMMY-BIRCHARD COMPANY				1.50
CLARK, F.--ED.	CLARK, F.			
THEMES FROM MASTERWORKS, BK. 3				
SUMMY-BIRCHARD COMPANY				1.50
CLARK, F.--ED.	CLARK, F.			
TUNE TIME - PART B				
SUMMY-BIRCHARD COMPANY				2.50
CLARK, F.--ED.	CLARK, F.			
TUNE TIME - PART B				
SUMMY-BIRCHARD COMPANY				2.50
CLARK, F.--ED.	CLARK, F.			
WRITE AND PLAY TIME - PART A				
SUMMY-BIRCHARD COMPANY				3.00
CLARK, F.--ED.	CLARK, F.			
WRITE AND PLAY TIME - PART B				
SUMMY-BIRCHARD COMPANY				3.00
CLARK, M.--ED.	CLARK, M.			
CRIMSON SET				
MYKLAS PRESS				2.50
CLARK, M.--ED.	CLARK, M.			
JADE SET				
MYKLAS PRESS				2.50
CLARK, M.--ED.	CLARK, M.			
ORCHID SET				
MYKLAS PRESS				2.50
CLARK, M.--ED.	CLARK, M.			
SAPPHIRE SET				
MYKLAS PRESS				2.50
CLARK, M.--ED.	CLARK, M.			
SUNSHINE SET				
MYKLAS PRESS				2.50
CLARK, R. *	CURWEN			
EXPRESSIVE RHYTHMIC ACTIVITIES FOR CHILDREN				
G. SCHIRMER, INC.				.75
CLARKE *	SARAUER		2	
ALBUM ALTER MEISTER - 24 TANZE UND KLEINE STUCKE				
BARENREITER VERLAG		AP 1648		
CLASSENS				
LE PIANO CLASSIQUE, VOL. A				
ELKAN-VOGEL, INC.		CON		3.00
CLASSENS				
LE PIANO CLASSIQUE, VOL. B				
ELKAN-VOGEL, INC.		CON		3.00
CLASSENS				
LE PIANO CLASSIQUE, VOL. C				
ELKAN-VOGEL, INC.		CON		3.00
CLASSENS				
LE PIANO CLASSIQUE, VOL. D				
ELKAN-VOGEL, INC.		CON		3.00
CLASSENS				
LE PIANO CLASSIQUE, VOL. E				
ELKAN-VOGEL, INC.		CON		3.00
CLASSENS				
LE PIANO CLASSIQUE, VOL. F				
ELKAN-VOGEL, INC.		CON		6.25
CLASSENS				
LE PIANO CLASSIQUE, VOL. G				
ELKAN-VOGEL, INC.		CON		6.25
CLASSENS				
MUSIQUE ET MUSICIENS D'AUJOURD'HUI, BK. 1				
ELKAN-VOGEL, INC.		CON		1.70
CLASSENS				
MUSIQUE ET MUSICIENS D'AUJOURD'HUI, BK. 2				
ELKAN-VOGEL, INC.		CON		2.50
CLASSENS				
MUSIQUE ET MUSICIENS D'AUJOURD'HUI, BK. 3				
ELKAN-VOGEL, INC.		CON		2.50
CLEMENTI			M-D	
CELEBRATED SONATAS --24-- IN 4 VOLS., VOL. 1				
C. F. PETERS CORPORATION		146A		4.00
CLEMENTI			M-D	
CELEBRATED SONATAS --24-- IN 4 VOLS., VOL. 2				
C. F. PETERS CORPORATION		146B		4.50
CLEMENTI			M-D	
CELEBRATED SONATAS --24-- IN 4 VOLS., VOL. 3				
C. F. PETERS CORPORATION		146C		4.50
CLEMENTI			M-D	
CELEBRATED SONATAS --24-- IN 4 VOLS., VOL. 4				
C. F. PETERS CORPORATION		146D		4.50
CLEMENTI	SCHUNGELER		3-5	
DER NEUE GRADUS AD PARNASSUM, BK. 1				
SCHOTT		2770A		2.50
CLEMENTI	SCHUNGELER		3-5	
DER NEUE GRADUS AD PARNASSUM, BK. 2				
SCHOTT		2770B		2.50
CLEMENTI	TAUSIG			
FIVE FUNDAMENTAL STUDIES FOR DAILY EXERCISE, FROM ''GRADUS AD PARNASSUM''				
G. SCHIRMER, INC.				.60

CLEMENTI	TAUSIG	D		
GRADUS AD PARNASSUM. 29 SELECTED STUDIES				
C. F. PETERS CORPORATION		3013		4.50
CLEMENTI	VOGRICH			
GRADUS AD PARNASSUM--100 EXERCISES, BK. 1				
G. SCHIRMER, INC.		L167		2.50
CLEMENTI	VOGRICH			
GRADUS AD PARNASSUM--100 EXERCISES, BK. 2				
G. SCHIRMER, INC.		L168		2.50
CLEMENTI	TAUSIG			
GRADUS AD PARNASSUM--29 SELECTED STUDIES, PLUS SCALES IN ALL MAJOR AND MINOR KEYS				
G. SCHIRMER, INC.		L780		2.25
CLEMENTI	TAUSIG			
GRADUS AD PARNASSUM--29 SELECTED STUDIES, PLUS SCALES IN ALL MAJOR AND MINOR KEYS--IN SPANISH, FRENCH, AND ENGLISH				
G. SCHIRMER, INC.		L1112		2.00
CLEMENTI	CESI *			
GRADUS AD PARNASSUM, BK. 1				
FRANCO COLOMBO PUBLICATIONS		ER136		3.75
CLEMENTI	CESI *			
GRADUS AD PARNASSUM, BK. 2				
FRANCO COLOMBO PUBLICATIONS		ER137		4.00
CLEMENTI	CESI *			
GRADUS AD PARNASSUM, BK. 3				
FRANCO COLOMBO PUBLICATIONS		ER138		5.50
CLEMENTI	MARCHI, G.			
INCONTRO CON CLEMENTI--BK. 1, 6 PICCOLI PEZZI, OP. 42 AND 6 SONATINE, OP. 36				
EDIZIONI BERBEN		1302		4.50
CLEMENTI	MARCHI, G.			
INCONTRO CON CLEMENTI--BK. 2, 24 VALZER, OP. 38, 39				
EDIZIONI BERBEN		2303		4.50
CLEMENTI	MUGELLINI			
PRELUDES AND EXERCISES				
FRANCO COLOMBO PUBLICATIONS		ER590		1.75
CLEMENTI	VOGRICH			
PRELUDES AND EXERCISES IN ALL THE MAJOR AND MINOR KEYS--SCHOOL OF SCALES				
G. SCHIRMER, INC.		L376		1.75
CLEMENTI	MIROVITCH, A.			
REDISCOVERED MASTERWORKS, BK. 1				
EDWARD B. MARKS MUSIC CORPORATION				02.50
CLEMENTI	MIROVITCH, A.			
REDISCOVERED MASTERWORKS, BK. 2				
EDWARD B. MARKS MUSIC CORPORATION				02.50
CLEMENTI	MIROVITCH, A.			
REDISCOVERED MASTERWORKS, BK. 3				
EDWARD B. MARKS MUSIC CORPORATION				02.50
CLEMENTI	MORONI	2		
SECHS SONATINEN, OP. 36				
BARENREITER VERLAG		CM 18326		
CLEMENTI				
SEVEN SONATAS, VOL. 1				
EDWIN F. KALMUS		3302		2.50
CLEMENTI	PALMER, W. A.			
SIX SONATINAS				
ALFRED MUSIC COMPANY		609		2.00
CLEMENTI				
SIX SONATINAS, OP. 36				
CARL FISCHER, INC.		L 589		1.25
CLEMENTI				
SIX SONATINAS, OP. 36				
EDWIN F. KALMUS		3300		1.50
CLEMENTI	KOEHLER, L.			
SIX SONATINAS, OP. 36				
G. SCHIRMER, INC.		L811		.85
CLEMENTI	GOETSCHIUS, P.			
SIX SONATINAS, OP. 36				
THEODORE PRESSER COMPANY				1.75
CLEMENTI	KLEINMICHEL			
SONATINAS BY CLEMENTI AND OTHER COMPOSERS, BK. 1				
FRANCO COLOMBO PUBLICATIONS		ER1454		3.00
CLEMENTI	KLEINMICHEL			
SONATINAS BY CLEMENTI AND OTHER COMPOSERS, BK. 2				
FRANCO COLOMBO PUBLICATIONS		ER1455		3.50
CLEMENTI		E-M		
SONATINAS, OP. 36				
C. F. PETERS CORPORATION		3346		2.00
CLEMENTI		E-M		
SONATINAS, OP. 36, 37, 38				
C. F. PETERS CORPORATION		145		2.50
CLEMENTI		1-2		
SONATINEN OP. 36				
SCHOTT		182		2.50
CLEMENTI *	KURZ	2-3		
SONATINEN UND RONDI, HEFT 1				
BARENREITER VERLAG		AP 1618		
CLEMENTI	CESI			
TWELVE SONATAS, BK. 1				
FRANCO COLOMBO PUBLICATIONS		ER669		2.75
CLEMENTI	BUONAMICI			
TWELVE SONATAS, BK. 1--NOS. 1-7				
G. SCHIRMER, INC.		L385		2.50
CLEMENTI	CESI			
TWELVE SONATAS, BK. 2				
FRANCO COLOMBO PUBLICATIONS		ER670		4.25
CLEMENTI	BUONAMICI			
TWELVE SONATAS, BK. 2--NOS. 8-12				
G. SCHIRMER, INC.		L386		2.50
CLEMENTI	KOEHLER, L.			
TWELVE SONATINAS--OP. 36, 37, 38				
G. SCHIRMER, INC.		L40		1.25
CLEMENTI	MARCIANO			
TWELVE SONATINAS, BK. 1 -- OP. 36 --				
FRANCO COLOMBO PUBLICATIONS		ER18		1.50
CLEMENTI	MUGELLINI			
TWELVE SONATINAS, BK. 1 -- OP. 36 --				
FRANCO COLOMBO PUBLICATIONS		ER797		1.50
CLEMENTI	MARCIANO			
TWELVE SONATINAS, BK. 2 -- OP. 37 AND 38 --				
FRANCO COLOMBO PUBLICATIONS		ER19		2.00
CLEMENTI				
TWELVE SONATINAS, OP. 36-37-38				
CARL FISCHER, INC.		L 302		1.50
CLEMENTI				
TWELVE SONATINAS, OP. 36, 37, 38				
EDWIN F. KALMUS		3301		2.00
CLEMENTI	MUGELLINI			
TWELVE SONATINAS, OP. 36, 37, 38 COMPLETE				
FRANCO COLOMBO PUBLICATIONS		ER623		2.75
CLEMENTI	PICCIOLI			
TWELVE SONATINAS, OP. 36, 37, 38 COMPLETE				
FRANCO COLOMBO PUBLICATIONS		BON.2223		2.25
CLEMENTI	BUSTINI			
TWENTY-THREE STUDIES FROM 'GRADUS AD PARNASSUM'				
FRANCO COLOMBO PUBLICATIONS		DS445		3.25

CLEMENTI　　　　　MONTANI
TWENTY-THREE STUDIES FROM "GRADUS AD PARNASSUM"
　　FRANCO COLOMBO PUBLICATIONS　　　　ER2317　　2.75
CLEMENTI *　　　　　ALATI　　　　　2
ZWEIHUNDDREISSIG SONATINEN UND RONDO, HEFT 1 - SONATINEN
　　BARENREITER VERLAG　　　　　　　CM 18321
CLEMENTS--ED.　　CLEMENTS　　　INTERMEDIATE
HANS BRINKER, OR THE SILVER SKATES
　　POINTER PUBLICATIONS　　　　　　　　　　　2.95
COATES, E.
ALBUM OF PIANO PIECES
　　BOOSEY AND HAWKES, INC.　　　　　　　　　1.25
COBB
ALL OVER THE KEYBOARD
　　BELWIN-MILLS PUBLISHING CORPORATION　11031　1.50
COBB
AROUND THE KEYS
　　SUMMY-BIRCHARD COMPANY　　　　　　　　　2.00
COBB
AROUND THE KEYS AGAIN
　　SUMMY-BIRCHARD COMPANY　　　　　　　　　1.75
COBB
DO IT YOURSELF ON THE NINE GOLDEN KEYS TO EASY READING
　　BELWIN-MILLS PUBLISHING CORPORATION　11126　1.50
COBB
FAMILIAR MELODIES
　　SUMMY-BIRCHARD COMPANY　　　　　　　　　1.25
COBB
FIRST SOLO BOOK
　　BELWIN-MILLS PUBLISHING CORPORATION　11168　1.50
COBB
GETTING ACQUAINTED AT THE PIANO -- BK. 1 -- PRACTICE PATTERNS
　　BELWIN-MILLS PUBLISHING CORPORATION　11208　1.75
COBB
LOOK AND LEARN
　　BELWIN-MILLS PUBLISHING CORPORATION　11280　1.75
COBB
LOOK AND LEARN WORKBOOK, BK. 1
　　BELWIN-MILLS PUBLISHING CORPORATION　11281　1.50
COBB
LOOK AND LEARN WORKBOOK, BK. 2
　　BELWIN-MILLS PUBLISHING CORPORATION　11282　1.25
COBB
MAJOR MINIATURES FOR PIANO
　　BELWIN-MILLS PUBLISHING CORPORATION　11661　1.75
COBB
MID-TERM READER
　　BELWIN-MILLS PUBLISHING CORPORATION　11298　1.25
COBB　　　　　　　　　　　　　　　　　　　E
MOONLIGHT -- PEDAL STUDY
　　BELWIN-MILLS PUBLISHING CORPORATION　25376　.60
COBB
NINE GOLDEN KEYS TO EASY READING
　　BELWIN-MILLS PUBLISHING CORPORATION　11352　1.25
COBB
RHYTHM TO COUNT, SING AND PLAY
　　BELWIN-MILLS PUBLISHING CORPORATION　11416　1.25
COBB
RHYTHM WITH RHYME AND REASON
　　BELWIN-MILLS PUBLISHING CORPORATION　11417　1.75
COBB
SECOND SOLO BOOK
　　BELWIN-MILLS PUBLISHING CORPORATION　11426　1.25
COBB
SONATINA ALBUM - FOUR SONATINAS FOR THE YOUNG PIANIST
　　BELWIN-MILLS PUBLISHING CORPORATION　11463　1.25
COBB
TECHNIQUE BUILDERS
　　BELWIN-MILLS PUBLISHING CORPORATION　11483　1.75
COBB
TEN LITTLE PENGUINS
　　MCA MUSIC　　　　　　　　　　　　　　　　.60
COBB
THIS WAY TO MUSIC
　　BELWIN-MILLS PUBLISHING CORPORATION　11508　1.50
COBB
TWO AND TWENTY CHRISTMAS CAROLS
　　BELWIN-MILLS PUBLISHING CORPORATION　11520　1.25
COBB
VARITY AND SPICE FOR PIANO
　　BELWIN-MILLS PUBLISHING CORPORATION　11525　1.25
COCKSHOTT, G.　　　　　　　　　　　　1-2
DANCE SUITE OF SIX EASY PIECES
　　NOVELLO AND COMPANY, LTD.　　10.0025.10　1.15
COELHO, P.M.R.　　　KASTER　　　　3
FLORES DE MUSICA. WERKE FUR TASTENINSTRUMENTE ODER HARFE --
"PORTUGALIAE MUSICA" -- BK. 1. LIBRO DE TENTOS UND 13 TENTOS IM 1.
TON
　　BARENREITER VERLAG　　　　　　　PM 1
COELHO, P.M.R.　　　KASTER　　　　3
FLORES DE MUSICA. WERKE FUR TASTENINSTRUMENTE ODER HARFE --
"PORTUGALIAE MUSICA" -- BK. 2. KIRCHENMUSIK
　　BARENREITER VERLAG　　　　　　　PM 3
COELHO, P.M.R.　　　KASTNER　　　3
FUNF TIENTOS - RICERCARE
　　SCHOTT　　　　　　　　　　　　2506　　3.50
COELHO, P.M.R.　　　　　　　　　3, 5
PROMENADES ENFANTINES A PARIS, BK. A
　　ALPHONSE LEDUC
COELHO, P.M.R.　　　　　　　　　3, 5
PROMENADES ENFANTINES A PARIS, BK. B
　　ALPHONSE LEDUC
COELHO, P.M.R.
PROMENADES ENFANTINES A PARIS, BK. C
　　ALPHONSE LEDUC
COELHO, P.M.R.　　　KASTNER　　　3-4
VIER SUSANAS UBER 'SUZANNE UN JOUR'
　　SCHOTT　　　　　　　　　　　　4633　　2.25
COHAN　　　　　　　　ZEPP　　　　2-3
THREE ALL AMERICAN SONGS
　　PRO-ART PUBLICATIONS, INC.　　360　　.50
COHEN, M. J.　　　　　　　　　　E
THIRTY TECHNICAL STUDIES, OP. 10
　　C. F. PETERS CORPORATION　　　B13A　　.90
COLE--ED　　　　　　COLE
CZECHOSLOVAKIAN FOLK SONGS
　　EDWARD B. MARKS MUSIC CORPORATION　　01.50
COLERIDGE-TAYLOR, S.
FOUR CHARACTERISTIC WALTZES
　　NOVELLO AND COMPANY, LTD.　10.0026.08　1.25
COLERIDGE-TAYLOR, S.
TWENTY-FOUR NEGRO MELODIES
　　THEODORE PRESSER COMPANY　　　　　　5.00
COLLINS, J.
JUDY COLLINS SONGBOOK, THE
　　MUSIC SALES CORPORATION　　　060016　4.95

CONCONE, G.　　　　DOENHOFF, VON
FIFTEEN STUDIES IN EXPRESSION, OP. 44
　　G. SCHIRMER, INC.　　　　　　L1030　　1.25
CONCONE, G.　　　　OESTERLE
FIFTEEN STUDIES IN STYLE AND EXPRESSION, OP. 25
　　G. SCHIRMER, INC.　　　　　　L141　　1.25
CONCONE, G.　　　　DEIS
FIFTEEN STUDIES IN STYLE, OP. 31
　　G. SCHIRMER, INC.　　　　　　L1374　　1.25
CONCONE, G.　　　　ANSON
THIRTY BRILLIANT PRELUDES OP. 37
　　WILLIS MUSIC COMPANY　　　　　　　　1.00
CONCONE, G.　　　　OESTERLE
THIRTY SELECTED STUDIES
　　G. SCHIRMER, INC.　　　　　　L25　　1.50
CONCONE, G.　　　　OESTERLE
TWENTY STUDIES ON THE SINGING TOUCH, OP. 30
　　G. SCHIRMER, INC.　　　　　　L140　　1.00
CONCONE, G.
TWENTY-FIVE MELODIC STUDIES
　　THEODORE PRESSER COMPANY　　　　　　.75
CONCONE, G.　　　　OESTERLE
TWENTY-FIVE MELODIC STUDIES, OP. 24
　　G. SCHIRMER, INC.　　　　　　L139　　.75
CONCONE, G.
TWENTY-FOUR BRILLIANT PRELUDES
　　THEODORE PRESSER COMPANY　　　　　　.60
CONCONE, G.　　　　OESTERLE
TWENTY-FOUR BRILLIANT PRELUDES IN ALL THE MAJOR AND MINOR KEYS,
OP. 37--FOR SMALL HANDS
　　G. SCHIRMER, INC.　　　　　　L226　　1.00
CONFREY, Z.
EXCITING ERA OF ZEZ CONFREY
　　BELWIN-MILLS PUBLISHING CORPORATION　　2.50
CONSIGLIO
PESCA SUBACQUEA - 9 MELODIOUS PIECES ON 5 NOTES
　　FRANCO COLOMBO PUBLICATIONS　RRR1047　1.50
CONSTANT
PONANT 19
　　FRANCO COLOMBO PUBLICATIONS　A184　　3.00
CONSTANTINIDIS, Y.
GREEK MINIATURES, BK. 1
　　RONGWEN MUSIC, INC.　　　　　　　　02.50
CONSTANTINIDIS, Y.
GREEK MINIATURES, BK. 2
　　RONGWEN MUSIC, INC.　　　　　　　　02.50
CONSTANTINIDIS, Y.
GREEK MINIATURES, BK. 3
　　RONGWEN MUSIC, INC.　　　　　　　　02.50
CONUS, L.
FUNDAMENTALS OF PIANO TECHNIQUE, BK. 2‡ ADVANCED TECHNIQUE
　　SUMMY-BIRCHARD COMPANY　　　　　　　2.00
CONUS, O.
FUNDAMENTALS OF PIANO TECHNIQUE, BK. 1‡ DAILY PROGRESSIVE
EXERCISES
　　SUMMY-BIRCHARD COMPANY　　　　　　　2.00
COOK--ED　　　　　　COOK
GEORGE M. PLAYER PIANO BOOK
　　EDWARD B. MARKS MUSIC CORPORATION　　01.75
COOLS
PIECES INTIMES, OP. 88
　　ASSOCIATED MUSIC PUBLISHERS, INC.　ESC　1.40
COOPER, A.
ALICE COOPER FOLIO
　　THE BIG THREE MUSIC CORPORATION　　03.95
COOPER, J.
THREE BAGATELLES, OP. 13
　　BOOSEY AND HAWKES, INC.　　　　　　1.00
COPE, D.
THREE TWO PART INVENTIONS
　　COMPOSERS AUTOGRAPH PUBLICATIONS　　1.10
COPLAND
FOUR PIANO BLUES
　　BOOSEY AND HAWKES, INC.　　　　　　2.00
COPPIETERS, F.
ANLEITUNG ZUR IMPROVISATION FUR KLAVIER
　　SCHOTT　　　　　　　　　　　5046　　3.00
CORBMAN
FINGER FABLES
　　WILLIS MUSIC COMPANY　　　　　　　1.00
CORBMAN
FINGER FREEDOM
　　WILLIS MUSIC COMPANY　　　　　　　1.50
CORBMAN
FINGERS IN FLIGHT
　　WILLIS MUSIC COMPANY　　　　　　　1.00
CORELLI　　　　　　REINECKE
ALBUM -- 24 PIECES
　　ASSOCIATED MUSIC PUBLISHERS, INC.　B/H　2.00
CORELLI
TWENTY-FOUR PIECES IN 2 VOLUMES - VOL. 1
　　EDWIN F. KALMUS　　　　　　　3311　1.75
CORELLI
TWENTY-FOUR PIECES IN 2 VOLUMES - VOL. 2
　　EDWIN F. KALMUS　　　　　　　3312　1.75
CORNET *　　　　　　HILLEMANN　　2-3
RICERCARE, CANZONEN UND FUGEN DES 17. UND 18. JH. FUR ORGEL ODER
KLAVIER
　　BARENREITER VERLAG　　　　　　NMA 87
CORRADINI　　　　　MOZZATI
FIVE SHORT PIECES
　　FRANCO COLOMBO PUBLICATIONS　130107　1.00
CORY, G. *
CITY BY THE BAY - SHORT SUITE
　　GENERAL MUSIC PUBLISHING COMPANY, INC.　2.00
COULTHARD
AEGEAN SKETCHES
　　ASSOCIATED MUSIC PUBLISHERS, INC.　BER　1.25
COULTHARD
FOUR PIECES
　　ASSOCIATED MUSIC PUBLISHERS, INC.　BER　.75
COUPERIN
COUPERIN PIANO COURSE, BK. 01
　　BOURNE COMPANY　　　　　　　　　2.50
COUPERIN　　　　　　　　　　　INTERMEDIATE
COUPERIN PIANO COURSE, BK. 02
　　BOURNE COMPANY　　　　　　　　　2.50
COUPERIN
COUPERIN PIANO COURSE, BK. 03
　　BOURNE COMPANY　　　　　　　　　2.50
COUPERIN, F.
ALBUM
　　EDWIN F. KALMUS　　　　　　　3316　2.00
COUPERIN, F.　　　　BARTOK
ALBUM -- BK. 1 AND 2
　　KULTURA　　　　　　　　　　　　　EA.

COUPERIN, F.   REINECKE
  ALBUM. SELECTED WORKS
    ASSOCIATED MUSIC PUBLISHERS, INC.   B/H   2.75
COUPERIN, F.   GAT   3-5
  AUSGEWAHLTE STUCKE, BK. 1
    SCHOTT   5921   4.00
COUPERIN, F.
  CLAVICHORD PIECES 1 -- INCLUDING QUATRRE
    EDWIN F. KALMUS   3317   2.75
COUPERIN, F.   MOTCHANE
  GRADED COUPERIN, THE
    BELWIN-MILLS PUBLISHING CORPORATION   2.50
COUPERIN, F.   OESTERLE *
  HARPSICHORD PIECES
    G. SCHIRMER, INC.   L1744   1.50
COUPERIN, F.   HALFORD
  L'ART DE TOUCHER LE CLAVECIN
    ALFRED MUSIC COMPANY   580   3.00
COUPERIN, F.
  L'ART DE TOUCHER LE CLAVECIN
    BROUDE BROTHERS LTD.   25.00
COUPERIN, F.   VRIESLANDER   3
  MUSIK FUR CEMBALO
    BARENREITER VERLAG   NMA 94
COUPERIN, F.
  PIECES DE CLAVECIN
    BROUDE BROTHERS LTD.   80.00
COUPERIN, F.   GAT
  PIECES DE CLAVECIN 1
    BOOSEY AND HAWKES, INC.   8.50
COUPERIN, F.
  PIECES DE CLAVECIN, BK. 1
    ELKAN-VOGEL, INC.   CON   10.75
COUPERIN, F.   GAT
  PIECES DE CLAVECIN, BK. 1
    SCHOTT   6045   4.00
COUPERIN, F.
  PIECES DE CLAVECIN, BK. 2
    ELKAN-VOGEL, INC.   CON   10.75
COUPERIN, F.
  PIECES DE CLAVECIN, BK. 3
    ELKAN-VOGEL, INC.   CON   9.00
COUPERIN, F.
  PIECES DE CLAVECIN, BK. 4
    ELKAN-VOGEL, INC.   CON   9.00
COUPERIN, F.   M-D
  SELECTED KEYBOARD WORKS
    C. F. PETERS CORPORATION   4407C   2.50
COUPERIN, F.   SELVA
  SELECTED PIECES
    FRANCO COLOMBO PUBLICATIONS   SAL   4.00
COUPERIN, F.
  SELECTED PIECES
    EDWARD B. MARKS MUSIC CORPORATION   03.75
COUPERIN, F.   STEINER
  TWENTY-FIVE COUPERIN PIECES
    BELWIN-MILLS PUBLISHING CORPORATION   1517   1.75
COUPERIN, L.   BOUVET
  PIECES DE CLAVECIN, VOL. 2
    ASSOCIATED MUSIC PUBLISHERS, INC.   ESC   2.75
COWELL
  ALBUM OF PIANO MUSIC
    ASSOCIATED MUSIC PUBLISHERS, INC.   AMP   2.50
COWELL
  SIX SONGS--COMPLETE
    ASSOCIATED MUSIC PUBLISHERS, INC.   AMP   1.50
COX,H.
  HUIT PETITES PIECES ENFANTINES
    GERARD BILLAUDOT EDITIONS MUSICALES   2.00
CRAMER, J. *   FERTE   M-D
  ANTHOLOGY, VOL. 5# 14 PIECES BY CRAMER, HUMMEL, ET AL.
    C. F. PETERS CORPORATION   SCH45   2.50
CRAMER, J.
  EIGHTY-FOUR STUDIES, BK. 1
    G. SCHIRMER, INC.   L142   1.50
CRAMER, J.
  EIGHTY-FOUR STUDIES, BK. 2
    G. SCHIRMER, INC.   L143   1.50
CRAMER, J.
  EIGHTY-FOUR STUDIES, BK. 3
    G. SCHIRMER, INC.   L144   1.50
CRAMER, J.
  EIGHTY-FOUR STUDIES, BK. 4
    G. SCHIRMER, INC.   L145   1.50
CRAMER, J.   D
  EIGHTY-FOUR STUDIES, VOL. 1
    C. F. PETERS CORPORATION   184A   2.50
CRAMER, J.   D
  EIGHTY-FOUR STUDIES, VOL. 2
    C. F. PETERS CORPORATION   184B   2.50
CRAMER, J.   D
  EIGHTY-FOUR STUDIES, VOL. 3
    C. F. PETERS CORPORATION   184C   2.50
CRAMER, J.   D
  EIGHTY-FOUR STUDIES, VOL. 4
    C. F. PETERS CORPORATION   184D   2.50
CRAMER, J.   BUELOW
  FIFTY SELECTED STUDIES
    G. SCHIRMER, INC.   L827   2.25
CRAMER, J.
  FIFTY SELECTED STUDIES--IN SPANISH
    G. SCHIRMER, INC.   L1178   2.50
CRAMER, J.
  FIFTY SELECTED STUDIES, BK. 1
    G. SCHIRMER, INC.   L828   1.00
CRAMER, J.
  FIFTY SELECTED STUDIES, BK. 2
    G. SCHIRMER, INC.   L829   1.00
CRAMER, J.
  FIFTY SELECTED STUDIES, BK. 3
    G. SCHIRMER, INC.   L830   1.00
CRAMER, J.
  FIFTY SELECTED STUDIES, BK. 4
    G. SCHIRMER, INC.   L831   1.00
CRAMER, J. *   MUGELLINI *   3
  SIXTY ETUDEN
    BARENREITER VERLAG   CM 12160
CRAMER, J.   BUELOW
  SIXTY SELECTED STUDIES
    FRANCO COLOMBO PUBLICATIONS   ER1520   3.00
CRAMER, J. *   WEINREICH   D
  SIXTY SELECTED STUDIES
    C. F. PETERS CORPORATION   H1492   5.00
CRAMER, J.   BULOW, H.
  SIXTY SELECTED STUDIES -- GERMAN TEXT
    UNIVERSAL EDITION   1304   4.00

CRAMER, J.   MONTANARI, N. AND
  SIXTY STUDI
    EDIZIONI BERBEN   1511   4.50
CRAS
  FOUR DANCES - DANZA MORBIDA, DANZA SCHERZOSA, DANZA TENERA,
  DANZA ANIMATA
    FRANCO COLOMBO PUBLICATIONS   SAL   7.50
CRAS
  IMPROMPTUS
    FRANCO COLOMBO PUBLICATIONS   SAL   4.00
CRAXTON, H.--ED.   CRAXTON, H.
  AIRS AND GRACES
    OXFORD UNIVERSITY PRESS   38.003   1.50
CRAXTON, H.--ED.   CRAXTON, H.
  EASY ELIZABETHANS
    OXFORD UNIVERSITY PRESS   33.701   1.80
CREED   M
  NINE BAGATELLES
    C. F. PETERS CORPORATION   H1492   2.00
CRERIE, E.
  LEDGER LINES AND SPACES THRU CHORD PROGRESSION
    VOLKWEIN BROS.   1.00
CRERIE, E.
  TWELVE LITTLE STEMLESS COMPOSITIONS
    VOLKWEIN BROS.   00.75
CRESTON   ADVANCED
  FIVE DANCES
    SHAWNEE PRESS, INC.   HB-209   3.00
CRESTON
  FIVE LITTLE DANCES, OP. 24
    G. SCHIRMER, INC.   .80
CRESTON
  FIVE TWO-PART INVENTIONS, OP. 14
    G. SCHIRMER, INC.   1.25
CRESTON
  RHYTHMICON, BK. 1
    BELWIN-MILLS PUBLISHING CORPORATION   1.50
CRESTON
  RHYTHMICON, BK. 1 - 29 ELEMENTARY STUDIES
    FRANCO COLOMBO PUBLICATIONS   NY2332   1.50
CRESTON
  RHYTHMICON, BK. 2
    BELWIN-MILLS PUBLISHING CORPORATION   1.50
CRESTON
  RHYTHMICON, BK. 2 - 15 ELEMENTARY STUDIES
    FRANCO COLOMBO PUBLICATIONS   NY2333   1.50
CRESTON
  RHYTHMICON, BK. 3
    BELWIN-MILLS PUBLISHING CORPORATION   1.50
CRESTON
  RHYTHMICON, BK. 3 - 18 EASY STUDIES
    FRANCO COLOMBO PUBLICATIONS   NY2334   1.50
CRESTON
  RHYTHMICON, BK. 4
    BELWIN-MILLS PUBLISHING CORPORATION   1.50
CRESTON
  RHYTHMICON, BK. 4 - 15 LOWER INTERMEDIATE STUDIES
    FRANCO COLOMBO PUBLICATIONS   NY2335   1.75
CRESTON
  RHYTHMICON, BK. 5
    BELWIN-MILLS PUBLISHING CORPORATION   1.50
CRESTON   ADVANCED
  SEVEN THESES FOR PIANO
    SHAWNEE PRESS, INC.   1.25
CRESTON
  SIX PRELUDES, OP. 38
    MCA MUSIC   1.50
CRIST, D. W.--ED.   CRIST, D. W.
  BANNER MELODIES
    VOLKWEIN BROS.   01.00
CRIST, D. W.--ED.   CRIST, D. W.
  CLASSIC MELODIES
    VOLKWEIN BROS.   01.00
CRIST, D. W.--ED.   CRIST, D. W.
  CROWN MELODIES
    VOLKWEIN BROS.   01.00
CRIST, D. W.--ED.   CRIST, D. W.
  CRYSTAL MELODIES
    VOLKWEIN BROS.   01.00
CRIST, D. W.--ED.   CRIST, D. W.
  IMPERIAL MELODIES
    VOLKWEIN BROS.   01.00
CRIST, D. W.--ED.   CRIST, D. W.
  ORGAN MELODIES
    VOLKWEIN BROS.   01.00
CRIST, D. W.--ED.   CRIST, D. W.
  PARLOR MELODIES
    VOLKWEIN BROS.   01.00
CRIST, D. W.--ED.   CRIST, D. W.
  PEERLESS MELODIES
    VOLKWEIN BROS.   01.00
CRIST, D. W.--ED.   CRIST, D. W.
  SILVER MELODIES
    VOLKWEIN BROS.   01.00
CRIST, D. W.--ED.   CRIST, D. W.
  VESPER MELODIES
    VOLKWEIN BROS.   01.00
CROCE, J.
  JIM CROCE SONG BOOK
    THE BIG THREE MUSIC CORPORATION   03.95
CROCKER, D.
  LET'S DISCOVER MUSIC - MY FIRST PIANO BOOK
    WILLIS MUSIC COMPANY   1.25
CROCKER, D.
  LET'S DISCOVER MUSIC - MY FIRST THEORY WORK BOOK
    WILLIS MUSIC COMPANY   1.25
CROCKER, D.
  LET'S DISCOVER MUSIC - MY FIRST WRITING BOOK
    WILLIS MUSIC COMPANY   1.25
CROISEZ, A.   DEIS
  TWENTY-FIVE MELODIOUS ETUDES, OP. 100
    G. SCHIRMER, INC.   L1438   1.50
CUNNINGHAM, M.
  AMERICAN FOLK SONGS
    COMPOSERS AUTOGRAPH PUBLICATIONS   5.28
CUNNINGHAM, M.
  PORTRAITS FOR MODERN DANCE
    COMPOSERS AUTOGRAPH PUBLICATIONS   3.77
CUNNINGHAM, M.
  THREE IMPRESSIONS FOR PIANO
    COMPOSERS AUTOGRAPH PUBLICATIONS   .66
CURCIO
  CATHOLIC CHRISTMAS SONGS FOR THE YOUNG PIANIST
    BELWIN-MILLS PUBLISHING CORPORATION   10004   1.50
CURCIO
  CATHOLIC SONGS FOR THE YOUNG PIANIST
    BELWIN-MILLS PUBLISHING CORPORATION   10005   1.25

CURCIO
LEARN TO FINGER WITHOUT NUMBERS
BOSTON MUSIC COMPANY　　　　　　　　　1.00
CURCIO
MAGIC KEYS, BK. 1
BELWIN-MILLS PUBLISHING CORPORATION　10026　2.00
CURCIO
MAGIC KEYS, BK. 2
BELWIN-MILLS PUBLISHING CORPORATION　10027　2.00
CURCIO
MAGIC KEYS, BK. 3
BELWIN-MILLS PUBLISHING CORPORATION　10028　2.00
CURCIO
SMALL PIECES
SUMMY-BIRCHARD COMPANY　　　　　　　　2.00
CURCIO
SONGS AND DANCES FOR LITTLE PIANISTS
BOSTON MUSIC COMPANY　　　　　　　　　1.50
CURCIO
VERY FIRST PIANO SOLOS - BOOK 1
BOSTON MUSIC COMPANY　　　　　　　　　1.00
CURCIO
VERY FIRST PIANO SOLOS - BOOK 2
BOSTON MUSIC COMPANY　　　　　　　　　1.00
CURCIO--ED　　　　　　CURCIO
CHRISTMAS CAROLS FOR LITTLE PIANISTS
BOSTON MUSIC COMPANY　　　　　　　　　1.25
CURCIO--ED　　　　　　CURCIO
YESTERDAY'S PIANO SOLOS - BOOK 1
BOSTON MUSIC COMPANY　　　　　　　　　2.00
CURCIO--ED　　　　　　CURCIO
YESTERDAY'S PIANO SOLOS - BOOK 2
BOSTON MUSIC COMPANY　　　　　　　　　2.00
CURRIE, E.　　　　　　　　　　　　AI
TWELVE PIECES IN RELATED KEYS, BK. 1
WILLIS MUSIC COMPANY　　　　　　　　　.75
CURRIE, E.
TWELVE PIECES IN RELATED KEYS, BK. 2
WILLIS MUSIC COMPANY　　　　　　　　　.75
CURRIE, E.--ED　　　　CURRIE, E.　　HA
VARIATIONS ON HYMN TUNES
WILLIS MUSIC COMPANY　　　　　　　　　1.25
CURRY
EASY-WAY PIANO -- BEGINNERS METHOD FOR CHILDREN
BELWIN-MILLS PUBLISHING CORPORATION　　　1.50
CURZON, F.
ALBUM OF PIANO PIECES
BOOSEY AND HAWKES, INC.　　　　　　　1.00
CUSTER, A.
FOUR IDEAS FOR PIANO
GENERAL MUSIC PUBLISHING COMPANY, INC.　497　3.00
CZERNY　　　　　　　　　　　　　　　　D
ART OF FINGER DEXTERITY --KUNST DER FINGERFERTIGKEIT--, OP. 740
C. F. PETERS CORPORATION　　2412　5.00
CZERNY　　　　　　　　　　　　　　　　D
ART OF FINGER DEXTERITY --KUNST DER FINGERFERTIGKEIT--, OP. 740,
IN 5 VOLUMES
C. F. PETERS CORPORATION　　2408A-E　2.00
CZERNY　　　　　　　　　BUONAMICI
ART OF FINGER DEXTERITY, OP. 740
FRANCO COLOMBO PUBLICATIONS　ER857　4.50
CZERNY　　　　　　　　　　　　　　　　D
ART OF FINGER DEXTERITY, OP. 740. SELECTION OF 14 STUDIES
C. F. PETERS CORPORATION　　7076　2.00
CZERNY　　　　　　　　　VOGRICH
ART OF FINGER DEXTERITY, OP. 740--50 STUDIES IN BRILLIANT STYLE
G. SCHIRMER, INC.　　　　L154　4.00
CZERNY
ART OF FINGER DEXTERITY, OP. 740--50 STUDIES IN BRILLIANT
STYLE--BK. 1
G. SCHIRMER, INC.　　　　L155　1.25
CZERNY
ART OF FINGER DEXTERITY, OP. 740--50 STUDIES IN BRILLIANT
STYLE--BK. 2
G. SCHIRMER, INC.　　　　L156　1.25
CZERNY
ART OF FINGER DEXTERITY, OP. 740--50 STUDIES IN BRILLIANT
STYLE--BK. 3
G. SCHIRMER, INC.　　　　L157　1.25
CZERNY
ART OF FINGER DEXTERITY, OP. 740--50 STUDIES IN BRILLIANT
STYLE--BK. 4
G. SCHIRMER, INC.　　　　L158　1.25
CZERNY
ART OF FINGER DEXTERITY, OP. 740--50 STUDIES IN BRILLIANT
STYLE--BK. 5
G. SCHIRMER, INC.　　　　L159　1.25
CZERNY
ART OF FINGER DEXTERITY, OP. 740--50 STUDIES IN BRILLIANT
STYLE--BK. 6
G. SCHIRMER, INC.　　　　L160　1.25
CZERNY　　　　　　　　　SCHAUM, J.　　2
CZERNY-SCHAUM, BK.1
BELWIN-MILLS PUBLISHING CORPORATION　　　1.50
CZERNY　　　　　　　　　SCHAUM, J.　　4
CZERNY-SCHAUM, BK.2
BELWIN-MILLS PUBLISHING CORPORATION　　　1.50
CZERNY　　　　　　　　　ECKSTEIN
FACILITY STUDIES FROM CZERNY--90--
CARL FISCHER, INC.　　　O 3811　1.25
CZERNY　　　　　　　　　RAUCH, W.
FIRST BEGINNING -- 100 EASY PIECES
UNIVERSAL EDITION　　　　195　1.80
CZERNY　　　　　　　　　RUTHARDT
FIRST INSTRUCTION IN PIANO-PLAYING--100 RECREATIONS
G. SCHIRMER, INC.　　　　L445　1.25
CZERNY　　　　　　　　　KRAUSE
FIRST INSTRUCTOR IN PIANO PLAYING
ASSOCIATED MUSIC PUBLISHERS, INC.　BRH　1.50
CZERNY
FIRST SCHOOL, OP. 599
UNIVERSAL EDITION　　　　52　1.60
CZERNY　　　　　　　　　BUONAMICI
FORTY DAILY EXERCISES, OP. 337
FRANCO COLOMBO PUBLICATIONS　ER810　2.25
CZERNY　　　　　　　　　　　　　　　　D
FORTY DAILY EXERCISES, OP. 337
C. F. PETERS CORPORATION　　2409　2.50
CZERNY　　　　　　　　　BUONAMICI
FORTY DAILY EXERCISES, OP. 337
G. SCHIRMER, INC.　　　　L149　1.25
CZERNY *　　　　　　　　CESI, S.
FORTY MELODIOUS EXERCISES - TRANSCRIBED FROM WORKS BY CZERNY AND
DIABELLI
FRANCO COLOMBO PUBLICATIONS　ER2350　2.50
CZERNY *
HANON--CZERNY
MUSIC SALES CORPORATION　　020140　1.50

CZERNY *
JAZZ CZERNY
PUGET MUSIC PUBLICATIONS, INC.　P712　4.00
CZERNY　　　　　　　　　CHAUMONT　2, 4
LE PETIT CZERNY, 30 ETUDES
ALPHONSE LEDUC
CZERNY
LITTLE PIANIST, THE--73 EASY PROGRESSIVE EXERCISES--OP. 823
G. SCHIRMER, INC.　　　　L54　1.50
CZERNY
LITTLE PIANIST, THE--73 EASY PROGRESSIVE EXERCISES--OP. 823, BK.
1
G. SCHIRMER, INC.　　　　L55　1.00
CZERNY
LITTLE PIANIST, THE--73 EASY PROGRESSIVE EXERCISES--OP. 823, BK.
2
G. SCHIRMER, INC.　　　　L56　1.00
CZERNY　　　　　　　　　POZZOLI
METHOD FOR BEGINNERS, OP. 599
FRANCO COLOMBO PUBLICATIONS　ER229　1.50
CZERNY
NECESSITY STUDIES FROM OP. 299, IN PROGRESSIVE ORDER
CENTURY MUSIC PUBLISHING COMPANY, INC.　　1.00
CZERNY
NECESSITY STUDIES, OP. 299, BOOKS 1 AND 2 COMBINED
CENTURY MUSIC PUBLISHING COMPANY, INC.　　1.25
CZERNY　　　　　　　　　ROWLEY, A. *
NEW CZERNY, THE, BK. 1
SAM FOX PUBLISHING COMPANY, INC.　　1.25
CZERNY　　　　　　　　　ROWLEY, A. *
NEW CZERNY, THE, BK. 2
SAM FOX PUBLISHING COMPANY, INC.　　1.25
CZERNY　　　　　　　　　ROWLEY, A. *
NEW CZERNY, THE, BK. 3
SAM FOX PUBLISHING COMPANY, INC.　　1.25
CZERNY　　　　　　　　　ROWLEY, A. *
NEW CZERNY, THE, BK. 4
SAM FOX PUBLISHING COMPANY, INC.　　1.25
CZERNY　　　　　　　　　ROWLEY, A. *
NEW CZERNY, THE, BK. 5
SAM FOX PUBLISHING COMPANY, INC.　　1.25
CZERNY　　　　　　　　　BUONAMICI
NEW SCHOOL OF VELOCITY, OP. 834
FRANCO COLOMBO PUBLICATIONS　ER1166　4.00
CZERNY
NEW SCHOOL OF VELOCITY, OP. 834. 2 VOLS
C. F. PETERS CORPORATION　　3085A-B　2.50
CZERNY　　　　　　　　　M-D
OCTAVE STUDIES --6-- OP. 553
C. F. PETERS CORPORATION　　3175　2.00
CZERNY
ON THE PROPER PERFORMANCE OF ALL BEETHOVEN'S WORKS FOR THE PIANO
-- ENGLISH TEXT
UNIVERSAL EDITION　　　　13340E　6.00
CZERNY
ON THE PROPER PERFORMANCE OF ALL BEETHOVEN'S WORKS FOR THE PIANO
-- GERMAN TEXT
UNIVERSAL EDITION　　　　13340　7.20
CZERNY　　　　　　　　　BUONAMICI
ONE HUNDRED AND TEN EASY AND PROGRESSIVE EXERCISES, OP. 453
G. SCHIRMER, INC.　　　　L749　1.75
CZERNY　　　　　　　　　E-M
ONE HUNDRED EASY STUDIES, OP. 139
C. F. PETERS CORPORATION　　2403　2.50
CZERNY
ONE HUNDRED PRACTICAL EXERCISES, OP. 139
UNIVERSAL EDITION　　　　123　1.75
CZERNY　　　　　　　　　BUONAMICI
ONE HUNDRED PROGRESSIVE EXERCISES, OP. 139
FRANCO COLOMBO PUBLICATIONS　ER2285　3.25
CZERNY　　　　　　　　　VOGRICH
ONE HUNDRED PROGRESSIVE STUDIES WITHOUT OCTAVES, OP. 139
G. SCHIRMER, INC.　　　　L153　1.50
CZERNY　　　　　　　　　E-M
ONE HUNDRED RECREATIONS
C. F. PETERS CORPORATION　　2633　2.50
CZERNY　　　　　　　　　RAUCH, W.
ONE HUNDRED RECREATIONS
UNIVERSAL EDITION　　　　260　2.00
CZERNY　　　　　　　　　　　　　　　　D
ONE HUNDRED SIXTY EIGHT-MEASURE EXERCISES, OP. 821
C. F. PETERS CORPORATION　　2405　2.50
CZERNY　　　　　　　　　BUONAMICI
ONE HUNDRED SIXTY EIGHT-MEASURE EXERCISES, OP. 821
G. SCHIRMER, INC.　　　　L147　2.00
CZERNY　　　　　　　　　MARTIENSSEN　M
ONE HUNDRED TWENTY-FIVE EXERCISES FOR
PASSAGE-PLAYING--PASSAGENUEBUNGEN--, OP. 261
C. F. PETERS CORPORATION　　　　2.50
CZERNY　　　　　　　　　BUONAMICI
ONE HUNDRED TWENTY-FIVE EXERCISES IN PASSAGE-PLAYING, OP.
261--ELEMENTARY STUDIES
G. SCHIRMER, INC.　　　　L378　1.25
CZERNY　　　　　　　　　BUONAMICI
ONE HUNDRED TWENTY-FIVE SHORT EXERCISES AND PROGRESSIVE
SONATINAS
FRANCO COLOMBO PUBLICATIONS　ER1236　1.75
CZERNY　　　　　　　　　HERZOG
PERFECTION IN STYLE, OP. 755--25 FINISHING STUDIES
G. SCHIRMER, INC.　　　　L1158　1.75
CZERNY　　　　　　　　　ROLLE
PRACTICAL FINGER EXERCISES, OP. 802
G. SCHIRMER, INC.　　　　L192　1.50
CZERNY　　　　　　　　　E
PRACTICAL METHOD FOR BEGINNERS --ERSTER LEHRMEISTER--, OP. 599
C. F. PETERS CORPORATION　　2402　2.50
CZERNY　　　　　　　　　BUONAMICI
PRACTICAL METHOD FOR BEGINNERS, OP. 599
G. SCHIRMER, INC.　　　　L146　1.00
CZERNY　　　　　　　　　M-D
PRELIMINARY SCHOOL OF FINGER DEXTERITY --VORSCHULE DER
FINGERFERTIGKEIT--, OP. 636
C. F. PETERS CORPORATION　　2407　2.50
CZERNY　　　　　　　　　POZZOLI
PRELIMINARY SCHOOL OF FINGER DEXTERITY, OP. 626
FRANCO COLOMBO PUBLICATIONS　ER230　1.75
CZERNY　　　　　　　　　BUONAMICI
PRELIMINARY SCHOOL OF FINGER DEXTERITY, OP. 636
G. SCHIRMER, INC.　　　　L148　1.00
CZERNY
PREPARATORY SCHOOLS OF FINGER DEXTERITY, OP. 636
CARL FISCHER, INC.　　　L 482　1.00
CZERNY　　　　　　　　　POZZOLI
SCHOOL OF LEGATO AND STACCATO, OP. 335
FRANCO COLOMBO PUBLICATIONS　ER447　4.25
CZERNY　　　　　　　　　BUONAMICI
SCHOOL OF LEGATO AND STACCATO, OP. 335--50 EXERCISES
G. SCHIRMER, INC.　　　　L150　1.75

CZERNY   BUONAMICI
  SCHOOL OF THE LEFT HAND, OP. 399
    FRANCO COLOMBO PUBLICATIONS   ER1040   2.75
CZERNY   D
  SCHOOL OF THE VIRTUOSO --STUDIES IN BRAVURA AND STYLE--, OP. 365
    C. F. PETERS CORPORATION   2410   5.00
CZERNY   BUONAMICI
  SCHOOL OF THE VIRTUOSO, OP. 365
    FRANCO COLOMBO PUBLICATIONS   ER839   5.50
CZERNY   BUONAMICI
  SCHOOL OF THE VIRTUOSO, THE--60 STUDIES IN BRAVURA AND STYLE,
  OP. 365
    G. SCHIRMER, INC.   L383   2.50
CZERNY   PALMER, W. A.
  SCHOOL OF VELOCITY --COMPLETE--
    ALFRED MUSIC COMPANY   612   2.50
CZERNY   M-D
  SCHOOL OF VELOCITY --SCHULE DER GELAEUFIGKEIT--, OP. 299
    C. F. PETERS CORPORATION   2411   3.00
CZERNY   BUONAMICI
  SCHOOL OF VELOCITY, OP. 299
    FRANCO COLOMBO PUBLICATIONS   ER671   1.75
CZERNY
  SCHOOL OF VELOCITY, OP. 299
    UNIVERSAL EDITION   51   4.15
CZERNY
  SCHOOL OF VELOCITY, OP. 299. COMPLETE
    CARL FISCHER, INC.   L 338   2.00
CZERNY   KRAUSE
  SCHOOL OF VELOCITY, OP. 299, BK. 1
    ASSOCIATED MUSIC PUBLISHERS, INC.   BRH   1.00
CZERNY
  SCHOOL OF VELOCITY, OP. 299, BK. 1
    CARL FISCHER, INC.   L 339   1.00
CZERNY   M-D
  SCHOOL OF VELOCITY, OP. 299, BK. 1
    C. F. PETERS CORPORATION   2406A   1.25
CZERNY   KRAUSE
  SCHOOL OF VELOCITY, OP. 299, BK. 2
    ASSOCIATED MUSIC PUBLISHERS, INC.   BRH   1.00
CZERNY   M-D
  SCHOOL OF VELOCITY, OP. 299, BK. 2
    C. F. PETERS CORPORATION   2406B   1.25
CZERNY   KRAUSE
  SCHOOL OF VELOCITY, OP. 299, BK. 3
    ASSOCIATED MUSIC PUBLISHERS, INC.   BRH   1.00
CZERNY   M-D
  SCHOOL OF VELOCITY, OP. 299, BK. 3
    C. F. PETERS CORPORATION   2406C   1.50
CZERNY   M-D   O
  SCHOOL OF VELOCITY, OP. 299, BK. 4
    C. F. PETERS CORPORATION   2406D   1.50
CZERNY   PALMER, W. A.
  SCHOOL OF VELOCITY, PART 1
    ALFRED MUSIC COMPANY   613   1.25
CZERNY   PALMER, W. A.
  SCHOOL OF VELOCITY, PART 2
    ALFRED MUSIC COMPANY   614   1.25
CZERNY   VOGRICH
  SCHOOL OF VELOCITY, THE--40 STUDIES, OP. 299
    G. SCHIRMER, INC.   L161   1.50
CZERNY
  SCHOOL OF VELOCITY, THE--40 STUDIES, OP. 299, BK. 1
    G. SCHIRMER, INC.   L162   1.00
CZERNY
  SCHOOL OF VELOCITY, THE--40 STUDIES, OP. 299, BK. 2
    G. SCHIRMER, INC.   L163   1.00
CZERNY
  SCHOOL OF VELOCITY, THE--40 STUDIES, OP. 299, BK. 3
    G. SCHIRMER, INC.   L164   1.00
CZERNY
  SCHOOL OF VELOCITY, THE--40 STUDIES, OP. 299, BK. 4
    G. SCHIRMER, INC.   L165   1.00
CZERNY *   NICHOLL
  SELECTED PIANO STUDIES - BOOK 1
    BOSTON MUSIC COMPANY   2.75
CZERNY *   NICHOLL
  SELECTED PIANO STUDIES - BOOK 2
    BOSTON MUSIC COMPANY   2.75
CZERNY   CESI
  SELECTED STUDIES, BK. 1 - WITHOUT THUMB PASSAGES
    FRANCO COLOMBO PUBLICATIONS   ER2408   1.00
CZERNY   MUGELLINI
  SELECTED STUDIES, BK. 1 -- 52 STUDIES --
    FRANCO COLOMBO PUBLICATIONS   ER2377   2.50
CZERNY   UPPER ELEMENTARY AND LOWER
  SELECTED STUDIES, BK. 1--170 STUDIES IN THE UPPER ELEMENTARY AND
  LOWER MIDDLE GRADES
    G. SCHIRMER, INC.   L994   3.50
CZERNY   CESI
  SELECTED STUDIES, BK. 2 - FOR THUMB PASSAGES
    FRANCO COLOMBO PUBLICATIONS   99512   1.75
CZERNY   MUGELLINI
  SELECTED STUDIES, BK. 2 -- 44 STUDIES --
    FRANCO COLOMBO PUBLICATIONS   ER2378   3.75
CZERNY   MIDDLE GRADE
  SELECTED STUDIES, BK. 2--92 STUDIES IN THE MIDDLE GRADE
    G. SCHIRMER, INC.   L995   3.50
CZERNY   CESI
  SELECTED STUDIES, BK. 3 - FOR THUMB PASSAGES
    FRANCO COLOMBO PUBLICATIONS   99513   1.75
CZERNY   MUGELLINI
  SELECTED STUDIES, BK. 3 -- 34 STUDIES --
    FRANCO COLOMBO PUBLICATIONS   ER2379   6.50
CZERNY   MUGELLINI
  SELECTED STUDIES, BK. 4 -- 20 STUDIES --
    FRANCO COLOMBO PUBLICATIONS   ER2380   4.00
CZERNY   MARCIANO
  SEVENTY SELECTED AND PROGRESSIVE STUDIES
    FRANCO COLOMBO PUBLICATIONS   ER599   2.25
CZERNY   MARCIANO
  SIGHT READING EXERCISES
    FRANCO COLOMBO PUBLICATIONS   ER598   1.25
CZERNY   SCHULTZ
  SIX OCTAVE-STUDIES IN PROGRESSIVE DIFFICULTY, OP. 553
    G. SCHIRMER, INC.   L402   .75
CZERNY   E
  SIXTY CHILDREN'S EXERCISES
    C. F. PETERS CORPORATION   2667   2.00
CZERNY   BECALLI, F.
  STUDI -- BK. 1, 45 BREVI STUDI FACILI
    EDIZIONI BERBEN   1169   2.10
CZERNY   BECALLI, F.
  STUDI -- BK. 2, 35 STUDI FACILI E PROGRESSIVI
    EDIZIONI BERBEN   1170   2.10
CZERNY   BECALLI, F.
  STUDI -- BK. 3, 25 STUDI
    EDIZIONI BERBEN   1175   3.00

CZERNY   D
  STUDIES FOR THE LEFT HAND, OP. 399
    C. F. PETERS CORPORATION   2842   4.00
CZERNY
  STUDIES IN MECHANISM, OP. 849
    CARL FISCHER, INC.   L 487   1.50
CZERNY   BUONAMICI
  THIRTY NEW STUDIES IN TECHNICS, OP. 849--PREPARATORY TO ''THE
  SCHOOL OF VELOCITY''
    G. SCHIRMER, INC.   L272   1.50
CZERNY   E
  THIRTY NEW STUDIES IN TECHNIQUE--ETUDES DE MECHANISME--, OP.
  849. PREPARATORY TO OP. 299--SCHOOL OF VELOCITY--
    C. F. PETERS CORPORATION   2611   2.50
CZERNY   POZZOLI
  THIRTY STUDIES IN MECHANISM, OP. 849
    FRANCO COLOMBO PUBLICATIONS   ER363   1.50
CZERNY
  THIRTY STUDIES IN MECHANISM, OP. 849
    UNIVERSAL EDITION   143   1.80
CZERNY   BUONAMICI
  TWENTY-FOUR EASY MELODIOUS FIVE-FINGER EXERCISES, OP. 777
    FRANCO COLOMBO PUBLICATIONS   ER1265   1.00
CZERNY   M-D
  TWENTY-FOUR STUDIES FOR THE LEFT HAND, OP. 718
    C. F. PETERS CORPORATION   3244   2.00
CZERNY   SCHARFENBERG
  TWENTY-FOUR STUDIES FOR THE LEFT HAND, OP. 718
    G. SCHIRMER, INC.   L60   1.00
D'ANGLEBERT, J.
  PIECES DE CLAVECIN
    BROUDE BROTHERS LTD.   22.50
D'INDY, V.   8
  TABLEAUX DE VOYAGE, OP. 33
    ALPHONSE LEDUC
DA COSTA DE LISBOA   FERNANDES   3
  TENCAO. AUSGEWAHLTE KONTRAPUNKSTUCKE
    BARENREITER VERLAG   PM 7
DAHLEN--ED   DAHLEN
  GEORGE M. SIMPLIFIED HITS
    EDWARD B. MARKS MUSIC CORPORATION   01.50
DALCROZE
  FIFTY ETUDES MINIATURES DE METRIQUE ET DE RHYTHMIQUE, BK. 1 --
  EASY --
    FRANCO COLOMBO PUBLICATIONS   SAL   4.25
DALCROZE
  FIFTY ETUDES MINIATURES DE METRIQUE ET DE RHYTHMIQUE, BK. 2 --
  FAIRLY EASY --
    FRANCO COLOMBO PUBLICATIONS   SAL   4.25
DALCROZE
  FIFTY ETUDES MINIATURES DE METRIQUE ET DE RHYTHMIQUE, BK. 3 --
  MEDIUM DIFFICULTY --
    FRANCO COLOMBO PUBLICATIONS   SAL   4.25
DALCROZE
  FIFTY ETUDES MINIATURES DE METRIQUE ET DE RHYTHMIQUE, BK. 4 --
  DIFFICULT --
    FRANCO COLOMBO PUBLICATIONS   SAL   4.50
DALCROZE
  MUSIQUE POUR FAIRE DANSER - BK. 1 .. LE MIELLEUX TZIGANE, O
  SWEET ARABELLA, ENTREE DES TROIS CHERS VIEUX GENTLEMEN
    FRANCO COLOMBO PUBLICATIONS   SAL   3.50
DALCROZE
  MUSIQUE POUR FAIRE DANSER - BK. 2 .. LA CUISINIERE BOURGEOISE,
  LOULOU DEBUTE, TCHECOSLOVAQUE
    FRANCO COLOMBO PUBLICATIONS   SAL   3.50
DALCROZE
  THREE PIECES ENFANTINES - MAMAN EST TRISTE, TOUTE PETITE VALSE,
  LA GUERRE
    FRANCO COLOMBO PUBLICATIONS   SAL   1.75
DALCROZE
  THREE PIECES MIGNONNES - PETITE GAVOTTE, PETIT MENUET, RONDE
  VILLAGEOISE
    FRANCO COLOMBO PUBLICATIONS   SAL   3.25
DALLAPICCOLA   4-5
  DREI EPISODEN AUS DEM BALLETT 'MARSIA'
    BARENREITER VERLAG   CM 20869
DALLIN--ED.   DALLIN
  CHRISTMAS CAROLER
    PRO-ART PUBLICATIONS, INC.   1038   1.50
DANDELOT
  ETUDE DU RYTHME, BK. 3 - RYTHMES SIMULTANES
    ALPHONSE LEDUC
DANDELOT
  JARDIN DE MARIE, LE -- EIGHT EASY PIECES
    ASSOCIATED MUSIC PUBLISHERS, INC.   ESC   3.75
DANDRIEU, P.   2-3
  NOELS, HEFT 1 -- 'L'ORGANISTE LITURGIQUE', 12 --
    BARENREITER VERLAG
DANDRIEU, P.   2-3
  NOELS, HEFT 2 -- 'L'ORGANISTE LITURGIQUE', 16 --
    BARENREITER VERLAG
DANDRIEU, P.   2-3
  NOELS, HEFT 3 -- 'L'ORGANISTE LITURGIQUE', 19-20 --
    BARENREITER VERLAG
DANDRIEU, P.   2-3
  NOELS, HEFT 4 -- 'L'ORGANISTE LITURGIQUE', 22
    BARENREITER VERLAG
DANDRIEU, P.   WHITE   3
  WERKE FUR CEMBALO. SUITEN NO. 1, 4 UND 6 IN H, C UND D AUS DEN
  'PIECES DE CLAVECIN'
    BARENREITER VERLAG   PSM 6
DANIEL-LESUR
  THREE NOELS
    FRANCO COLOMBO PUBLICATIONS   A118   .90
DAQUIN, C.
  PREMIER LIVRE DE PIECES DE CLAVECIN
    BROUDE BROTHERS LTD.   40.00
DARMES   3, 4
  PETIT LIVRE DES TENUES, LE
    ALPHONSE LEDUC
DASHER, J.
  CHRISTMAS ECHOES
    WILLIS MUSIC COMPANY   .50
DAVICO
  POEMETTI PASTORALI
    ASSOCIATED MUSIC PUBLISHERS, INC.   DOB   2.50
DAVICO
  SIX NOCTURNES
    ASSOCIATED MUSIC PUBLISHERS, INC.   ESC   4.50
DAVID
  BAGATELLES
    ASSOCIATED MUSIC PUBLISHERS, INC.   DOB   2.50
DAVIES--ED.   DAVIES
  CAROLS FOR CHRISTMAS
    SHAWNEE PRESS, INC.   1.00

DAVIS *
   DOORS INTO MUSIC - BOOK 1
      BOSTON MUSIC COMPANY   1.50
DAVIS *
   DOORS INTO MUSIC - BOOK 2
      BOSTON MUSIC COMPANY   1.50
DAVIS *
   DOORS INTO MUSIC - BOOK 3
      BOSTON MUSIC COMPANY   1.50
DAVIS *
   DOORS INTO MUSIC - BOOK 4
      BOSTON MUSIC COMPANY   1.75
DAVIS *
   DOORS INTO MUSIC THEORY - BOOK 1
      BOSTON MUSIC COMPANY   1.25
DAVIS *
   DOORS INTO MUSIC THEORY - BOOK 2
      BOSTON MUSIC COMPANY   1.25
DAVIS *
   DOORS INTO TECHNIC - BOOK 1
      BOSTON MUSIC COMPANY   1.00
DAVIS *
   DOORS INTO TECHNIC - BOOK 2
      BOSTON MUSIC COMPANY   1.00
DAVIS *
   DOORS INTO TECHNIC - BOOK 3
      BOSTON MUSIC COMPANY   1.00
DAVIS *
   DOORS INTO TECHNIC - BOOK 4
      BOSTON MUSIC COMPANY   1.00
DAVIS
   TRICKS AND TREATS
      PRO-ART PUBLICATIONS, INC.   777   .85
DAVIS, J.
   SLICK TRICKS
      THEODORE PRESSER COMPANY   1.50
DAVIS, J.
   YANKEE DOODLE DOODLES -- A THEME AND TWELVE VARIATIONS FOR THE
   INTERMEDIATE PIANIST
      THEODORE PRESSER COMPANY   1.25
DAVIS, J. R.--ED   DAVIS, J. R.
   GREAT THEMES MADE EASY FOR PIANO
      WARNER BROTHERS PUBLISHERS   1.95
DAVIS, J. R.--ED   DAVIS, J. R.
   HARMS HITS THROUGH THE YEARS MADE EASY
      WARNER BROTHERS PUBLISHERS   1.25
DAVIS, J. R.--ED   DAVIS, J. R.
   IRISH FAVORITES FOR PIANO
      WARNER BROTHERS PUBLISHERS   1.50
DAVIS, J. R.--ED   DAVIS, J. R.
   PETER, PAUL AND MARY, HITS OF, MADE EASY FOR PIANO
      WARNER BROTHERS PUBLISHERS   PPM 24   1.50
DAVIS, M.
   MARILYN K. DAVIS GROUP PIANO METHOD - GROUP ACTIVITIES AT THE
   KEYBOARD, BK. 01
      BOURNE COMPANY   1.25
DAVIS, M.
   MARILYN K. DAVIS GROUP PIANO METHOD - GROUP ACTIVITIES AT THE
   KEYBOARD, BK. 02
      BOURNE COMPANY   1.25
DAVIS, M.--ED   DAVIS, M.
   SINGING FINGERS
      PRO-ART PUBLICATIONS, INC.   1302   1.50
DE ANGELIS VALENTINI
   ANTHOLOGY OF EASY AND PROGRESSIVE EXERCISES AND PIECES
      FRANCO COLOMBO PUBLICATIONS   ER2613   5.00
DE ANGELIS VALENTINI
   CHILDREN'S DREAMS - 10 EASY PIECES
      FRANCO COLOMBO PUBLICATIONS   128518   1.25
DE ANGELIS VALENTINI
   COMPLETE METHOD, BK. 1
      FRANCO COLOMBO PUBLICATIONS   BON.1970   2.50
DE ANGELIS VALENTINI
   COMPLETE METHOD, BK. 2
      FRANCO COLOMBO PUBLICATIONS   BON.1971   2.50
DE ANGELIS VALENTINI
   COMPLETE METHOD, BK. 3
      FRANCO COLOMBO PUBLICATIONS   BON.1972   3.00
DE ANGELIS VALENTINI
   COMPLETE METHOD, BK. 4
      FRANCO COLOMBO PUBLICATIONS   BON.1973   3.00
DE ANGELIS VALENTINI
   COMPLETE METHOD, BK. 5
      FRANCO COLOMBO PUBLICATIONS   BON.1974   3.25
DE ANGELIS VALENTINI
   COMPLETE METHOD, BK. 6
      FRANCO COLOMBO PUBLICATIONS   BON.1975   3.25
DE ANGELIS VALENTINI
   ELEVEN STUDIES IN MODERN TECHNIQUE
      FRANCO COLOMBO PUBLICATIONS   BON.1901   2.25
DE ANGELIS VALENTINI
   FOR THE YOUNG - 3 CONCERT STUDIES
      FRANCO COLOMBO PUBLICATIONS   BON.1881   1.50
DE ANGELIS VALENTINI
   FORTY-ONE DELIGHTFUL LITTLE STUDIES
      FRANCO COLOMBO PUBLICATIONS   ER2451   .90
DE ANGELIS VALENTINI
   FORTY-ONE ELEMENTARY LITTLE STUDIES
      FRANCO COLOMBO PUBLICATIONS   BON.2214   2.25
DE ANGELIS VALENTINI
   WHITE ROSES - 15 VERY EASY PIECES
      FRANCO COLOMBO PUBLICATIONS   129040   1.50
DE CESARE
   FRENCH GAME SONGS -- CHANTS DE JEUX FRANCAIS
      BELWIN-MILLS PUBLISHING CORPORATION   1.00
DE CESARE
   LATIN AMERICAN GAME SONGS
      BELWIN-MILLS PUBLISHING CORPORATION   1.00
DE CESARE
   SONGS FOR THE FRENCH CLASS -- LES CHANSONS POUR LA CLASSE DE
   FRANCAIS
      BELWIN-MILLS PUBLISHING CORPORATION   1.00
DE CESARE
   SONGS FOR THE GERMAN CLASS -- LIEDER FUR DIE DEUTSHE KLASSE
      BELWIN-MILLS PUBLISHING CORPORATION   1.00
DE CESARE
   SONGS FOR THE ITALIAN CLASS -- CANZONI PER LA CLASSE D'ITALIANO
      BELWIN-MILLS PUBLISHING CORPORATION   1.00
DE CESARE
   SONGS FOR THE SPANISH CLASS -- CANCIONES PARA LA CLASE DE ESPANO
      BELWIN-MILLS PUBLISHING CORPORATION   1.00
DE FILIPPI, A.
   DANCE RHYTHMS
      GENERAL MUSIC PUBLISHING COMPANY, INC.   586   2.00
DE FILIPPI, A.
   SEVEN EASY PIECES - ON A 12 TONE ROW-
      GENERAL MUSIC PUBLISHING COMPANY, INC.   585   2.50

DE FILIPPI, A.
   TWELVE SHORT PIECES
      GENERAL MUSIC PUBLISHING COMPANY, INC.   588   2.50
DE FRAGUIER
   THREE PIECES
      FRANCO COLOMBO PUBLICATIONS   SAL   4.00
DE FRANCMESNIL
   TWELVE PIECES ENFANTINES
      FRANCO COLOMBO PUBLICATIONS   SAL   4.00
DE RUBERTIS
   TEN CANTI PAESANI DEL MOLISE
      FRANCO COLOMBO PUBLICATIONS   BON.1403   1.00
DE SABATA
   THREE PIECES
      FRANCO COLOMBO PUBLICATIONS   128603   .75
DE SAINT-LAMBERT, M.
   LES PRINCIPES DU CLAVECIN
      BROUDE BROTHERS LTD.   25.00
DE SAINT-LAMBERT, M.
   NOUVEAU TRAITE DE L'ACCOMPAGNEMENT
      BROUDE BROTHERS LTD.   25.00
DE SANTIS
   DE SANTIS ALBUMS - FOR LITTLE PIANISTS, BK. 1
      FRANCO COLOMBO PUBLICATIONS   DS662   2.75
DE SANTIS
   DE SANTIS ALBUMS - FOR LITTLE PIANISTS, BK. 2
      FRANCO COLOMBO PUBLICATIONS   DS663   2.75
DE SOLIS
   THREE POSITIONS OF HARMONIZED SCALES
      BELWIN-MILLS PUBLISHING CORPORATION   11502   1.50
DE VILLERMONT, D.
   VARIETES PIANISTIQUES, BK. 1
      ELKAN-VOGEL, INC.   LEM   2.75
DE VILLERMONT, D.
   VARIETES PIANISTIQUES, BK. 2
      ELKAN-VOGEL, INC.   LEM   2.75
DE VILLERMONT, D.
   VARIETES PIANISTIQUES, BK. 3
      ELKAN-VOGEL, INC.   LEM   2.75
DE VILLERMONT, D.
   VARIETES PIANISTIQUES, BK. 4
      ELKAN-VOGEL, INC.   LEM   3.50
DE VITO, A.
   CHORD APPROACH TO 'POP' PIANO PLAYING, BK. 1
      KENYON PUBLICATIONS   1.50
DE VITO, A.
   CHORD APPROACH TO 'POP' PIANO PLAYING, BK. 2
      KENYON PUBLICATIONS   1.75
DE VITO, A.
   CHORD APPROACH TO 'POP' PIANO PLAYING, BK. 3
      KENYON PUBLICATIONS   1.75
DE VITO, A.
   CHORD APPROACH TO 'POP' PIANO PLAYING, BK. 4
      KENYON PUBLICATIONS   1.75
DE VITO, A.
   CHORD PIANIST --SUPPLEMENTARY BOOKS TO BE USED WITH CHORD
   APPROACH METHOD--
      KENYON PUBLICATIONS   GR. 5
DE VITO, A.
   NOVELETTES, SEVEN
      KENYON PUBLICATIONS   3.00
DE VITO, A.
   PEDRO DANCES
      BOURNE COMPANY   1.00
DE VITO, A.   GD. 2-3
   TOYS
      KENYON PUBLICATIONS   1.50
DE VITO, A.--ED.   DE VITO, A.
   ALBERT DE VITO PIANO COURSE, BK. 1
      KENYON PUBLICATIONS   1.50
DE VITO, A.--ED.   DE VITO, A.
   CHRISTMAS SONGS
      KENYON PUBLICATIONS   1.00
DE VITO, A.--ED.   DE VITO, A.
   CLASSICAL FAVORITES - BK. B
      KENYON PUBLICATIONS   2.00
DE VITO, A.--ED.   DE VITO, A.
   COUNTRY WESTERN
      KENYON PUBLICATIONS   1.00
DE VITO, A.--ED.   DE VITO, A.
   PATRIOTIC SONGS
      PRO-ART PUBLICATIONS, INC.   683   .75
DE VITO, A.--ED.   DE VITO, A.
   POPULAR PIANO CLASSICS
      KENYON PUBLICATIONS   1.25
DE VITO, A.--ED.   DE VITO, A.
   STANDARD FAVORITES - BK. A
      KENYON PUBLICATIONS   2.00
DEBREVILLE
   EQUISSES - IMPROVISATION, DEDICACE, PRELUDE, CREPUSCULE, DANSE
   D'ESPRITS, THEME, VARIATIONS
      FRANCO COLOMBO PUBLICATIONS   SAL   6.25
DEBREVILLE
   STAMBOUL - STAMBOUL, LE PHANAR, EYOUB, GALATA
      FRANCO COLOMBO PUBLICATIONS   SAL   6.50
DEBRIE
   TWELVE PETITES PIECES, BK. 1
      FRANCO COLOMBO PUBLICATIONS   SAL   2.50
DEBRIE
   TWELVE PETITES PIECES, BK. 2
      FRANCO COLOMBO PUBLICATIONS   SAL   2.50
DEBUSSY
   ALBUM
      EDWIN F. KALMUS   3389   3.00
DEBUSSY
   ALBUM OF FIVE PIECES
      BOSTON MUSIC COMPANY   1.25
DEBUSSY
   ALBUM OF 6 CHOICE PIECES
      ELKAN-VOGEL, INC.   6.00
DEBUSSY
   ARABESQUES NOS. 1 AND 2
      EDWIN F. KALMUS   3370   1.00
DEBUSSY
   CHILDREN'S CORNER
      ELKAN-VOGEL, INC.   5.00
DEBUSSY   DEBUSSY
      ASHLEY DEALERS SERVICE, INC.   HG 03   2.95
DEBUSSY *   PHILLIP
   DEBUSSY AND RAVEL
      CARL FISCHER, INC.   O 4013   2.50
DEBUSSY
   DEBUSSY MASTERPIECES
      EDWARD B. MARKS MUSIC CORPORATION   02.50

DEBUSSY		M	
DEUX ARABESQUES			
C. F. PETERS CORPORATION	7259		1.25
DEBUSSY			
DEUX ARABESQUES COMPLETE			
ASHLEY DEALERS SERVICE, INC.	ES		1.00
DEBUSSY			
ENJOY DEBUSSY			
ASHLEY DEALERS SERVICE, INC.			2.95
DEBUSSY			
ESTAMPES			
ELKAN-VOGEL, INC.			2.00
DEBUSSY			
ESTAMPES, COMPLETE			
EDWIN F. KALMUS	3375		2.25
DEBUSSY			
IMAGES--1ST SERIES			
ELKAN-VOGEL, INC.			2.00
DEBUSSY			
IMAGES--2ND SERIES			
ELKAN-VOGEL, INC.			5.00
DEBUSSY		PHILIPP, I.	
IMAGES, BK. 1			
INTERNATIONAL MUSIC COMPANY			2.00
DEBUSSY			
IMAGES, BK. 1			
EDWIN F. KALMUS	3376		3.00
DEBUSSY			
MASQUES			
EDWIN F. KALMUS	3381		2.00
DEBUSSY		4	
PAGE D'ALBUM			
THEODORE PRESSER COMPANY			.50
DEBUSSY			
PETITE SUITE			
ELKAN-VOGEL, INC.			2.00
DEBUSSY			
PETITE SUITE, COMPLETE			
EDWIN F. KALMUS	3383		2.00
DEBUSSY			
POUR LE PIANO			
EDWIN F. KALMUS	3384		1.75
DEBUSSY			
POUR LE PIANO			
EDWARD B. MARKS MUSIC CORPORATION			01.50
DEBUSSY			
PRELUDES, BK. 1			
ELKAN-VOGEL, INC.			9.00
DEBUSSY			
PRELUDES, BK. 2			
ELKAN-VOGEL, INC.			9.00
DEBUSSY			
SELECTED WORKS			
G. SCHIRMER, INC.	L1813		2.50
DEBUSSY			
SIX EPIGRAPHES ANTIQUES			
ELKAN-VOGEL, INC.			5.00
DEBUSSY			
SUITE BERGAMASQUE			
EDWIN F. KALMUS	3387		2.00
DEBUSSY		M	
SUITE BERGAMASQUE			
C. F. PETERS CORPORATION	7261		1.50
DEBUSSY			
SUITE BERGAMASQUE			
G. SCHIRMER, INC.	L1812		1.50
DEBUSSY			
SUITE POUR LE PIANO			
G. SCHIRMER, INC.	L1795		1.50
DEBUSSY			
TWELVE ETUDES, BK. 1			
ELKAN-VOGEL, INC.			6.75
DEBUSSY			
TWELVE ETUDES, BK. 2			
ELKAN-VOGEL, INC.			6.75
DEBUSSY			
TWO ARABESQUES			
ELKAN-VOGEL, INC.			1.25
DEBUSSY		PHILIPP, I.	
TWO ARABESQUES			
INTERNATIONAL MUSIC COMPANY			1.25
DECESARE			
PIANO GAMES			
EDWARD B. MARKS MUSIC CORPORATION			01.50
DECOLA, F.			
TEN PIECES IN MODERN DANCE RHYTHMS			
G. SCHIRMER, INC.			1.00
DEE, M.			
CHRISTMAS CAROLS			
VOLKWEIN BROS.			00.75
DEE, M.			
FACE THE MUSIC, BOOK 1			
VOLKWEIN BROS.			1.00
DEE, M.			
FACE THE MUSIC, BOOK 2			
VOLKWEIN BROS.			.75
DEE, M.			
JOLLY JINGLES			
VOLKWEIN BROS.			00.75
DEE, M.			
MY PIANO WORKSHOP SERIES, BOOK 1--GET ACQUAINTED BOOK			
VOLKWEIN BROS.			1.25
DEE, M.			
MY PIANO WORKSHOP SERIES, BOOK 2--ON WE GO			
VOLKWEIN BROS.			1.25
DEE, M.			
MY PIANO WORKSHOP SERIES, BOOK 3--MORE TO LEARN			
VOLKWEIN BROS.			1.25
DEE, M.			
MY PIANO WORKSHOP SERIES, BOOK 4--READY TO PLAY			
VOLKWEIN BROS.			1.25
DEE, M.			
NOTEBOOK ASSIGNMENTS			
VOLKWEIN BROS.			.75
DEE, M.			
TIPS FOR JUNIOR PIANISTS			
VOLKWEIN BROS.			1.00
DEE, M.			
TIPS PIANISTS			
VOLKWEIN BROS.			1.25
DEFILIPPI, A.			
FOLK MELODIES FOR PIANO			
GENERAL MUSIC PUBLISHING COMPANY, INC.			2.00
DEFILIPPI, A.			
SEVEN EASY PIECES			
GENERAL MUSIC PUBLISHING COMPANY, INC.			2.50

DEFILIPPI, A.			
TWELVE SHORT PIECES			
GENERAL MUSIC PUBLISHING COMPANY, INC.			2.50
DEFOSSEZ		E	
LES CAPRICES DE MA POUPEE --PETITE SUITE--			
C. F. PETERS CORPORATION	SCH148		2.00
DEGEN		3	
DREI SONATINEN			
BARENREITER VERLAG	SM 1744		
DEGEN		5-6	
DREIZIG KONZERT-ETUDEN, BK. 1			
SCHOTT	3955		3.25
DEGEN		5-6	
DREIZIG KONZERT-ETUDEN, BK. 2			
SCHOTT			3.25
DEGEN		5-6	
DREIZIG KONZERT-ETUDEN, BK. 3			
SCHOTT	3957		3.25
DEGEN		2-3	
SPIELMUSIK. EINE REIHE 15 KLEINER STUCKE FUR KLAVIER			
BARENREITER VERLAG	SM 1101		
DEGEN		1	
TWENTY-FIVE KLEINE KLAVIERSTUCKE FUR KINDER			
BARENREITER VERLAG	SM 1862		
DEGEN		2-3	
WEIHNACHTSBUCH. MUSIK AUS 36 ALTEN WEIHNACHTSLIEDERN FUR KLAVIER, BK. 1 - 7 ALTE WEIHNACHTSLIEDER UND 6 KRIPPENLIEDER			
BARENREITER VERLAG	SM 2101		
DEGEN		2-3	
WEIHNACHTSBUCH. MUSIK AUS 36 ALTEN WEIHNACHTSLIEDERN FUR KLAVIER, BK. 2 - 6 WIEGENLIEDER, 8 HIRTENLIEDER			
BARENREITER VERLAG			
DEGEN		2-3	
WEIHNACHTSBUCH. MUSIK AUS 36 ALTEN WEIHNACHTSLIEDERN FUR KLAVIER, BK. 3 - 2 DREI KONIGE-LIEDER UND 7 WEIHNACHTS-CHORALE			
BARENREITER VERLAG	SM 2103		
DEHNERT			
LEIPZIGER KLAVIERBUCH -- SMALL PIANO WORKS BY DEHNERT, GEISSLER, LOHSE, THIELE AND OTHERS			
ASSOCIATED MUSIC PUBLISHERS, INC.	BRH		3.00
DEHNERT			
TWO SONATINAS			
ASSOCIATED MUSIC PUBLISHERS, INC.	B/H		1.50
DEIS			
FOUR STUDIES WITHOUT WORDS--INTRODUCING TWO AGAINST THREE			
G. SCHIRMER, INC.			.50
DEKOVEN, R.			
MAGNOLIA BLOSSOMS--WALTZES			
G. SCHIRMER, INC.			.75
DEKOVEN, R.			
SELECTIONS FROM ''ROBIN HOOD''			
G. SCHIRMER, INC.			.60
DEL TREDICI			
FANTASY PIECES			
BOOSEY AND HAWKES, INC.			2.00
DEL VALLE			
TWENTY-FIVE SOLFEGGI, BK. 1			
FRANCO COLOMBO PUBLICATIONS	FOR.11401		1.50
DEL VALLE			
TWENTY-FIVE SOLFEGGI, BK. 2			
FRANCO COLOMBO PUBLICATIONS	FOR.11402		1.25
DELA			
TWO IMPROMPTUS			
ASSOCIATED MUSIC PUBLISHERS, INC.	BER		.75
DELACHI			
TWELVE SHORT PIECES			
FRANCO COLOMBO PUBLICATIONS	127593		1.25
DELACHI			
TWENTY PRELUDES IN THE FORM OF CANONS			
FRANCO COLOMBO PUBLICATIONS	ER2192		1.75
DELAMOTTE			
TEN FANTASIEN AM KLAVIER --1968 --			
BARENREITER VERLAG	BA 4137		6.50
DELAMOTTE		5	
ZEHN FANTASIEN AM KLAVIER -- 1968 --			
BARENREITER VERLAG	BA 4137		
DELANNOY			
THIRTEEN DANCES -- WORKS BY DELANNOY, HARSANYI, LOPATNIKOFF, MARTINU, MIGOT, TANSMAN AND OTHERS			
ASSOCIATED MUSIC PUBLISHERS, INC.	ESC		5.50
DELIBES, L.		BANTOCK, G.	
COPPELIA, COMPLETE ILLUSTRATED			
BELWIN-MILLS PUBLISHING CORPORATION	09468		3.00
DELIBES, L.		BANTOCK, G.	
COPPELIA, SELECTIONS FROM			
BELWIN-MILLS PUBLISHING CORPORATION	09469		1.50
DELIUS, F.			
FIVE PIANO PIECES			
BOOSEY AND HAWKES, INC.			1.25
DELIUS, F.			
THREE PRELUDES			
OXFORD UNIVERSITY PRESS	32.401		1.50
DELIUS, F.			
TWO PIECES FOR SMALL ORCHESTRA			
OXFORD UNIVERSITY PRESS	32.701		1.75
DELL'ANNO			
THREE SHORT PIECES			
SAM FOX PUBLISHING COMPANY, INC.			1.25
DELLA CIAIA *		ROSSI	3-4
I CLAVICEMBALISTI ITALIANI. 20 KOMPOSITIONEN			
BARENREITER VERLAG	CM 20092		
DELLO JOIO, N.			
LYRIC PIECES FOR THE YOUNG			
EDWARD B. MARKS MUSIC CORPORATION			01.50
DELLO JOIO, N.			
SUITE FOR THE YOUNG			
EDWARD B. MARKS MUSIC CORPORATION			01.25
DELVINCOURT		6, 9	
BOCCACERIE - 5 PORTRAITS POUR LE DECAMERON			
ALPHONSE LEDUC			
DELVINCOURT		5, 7	
CINQ PIECES			
ALPHONSE LEDUC			
DELVINCOURT		5, 6	
CROQUEMBOUCHES			
ALPHONSE LEDUC			
DELVINCOURT		4, 6	
HEURES JUVENILES			
ALPHONSE LEDUC			
DEMARQUEZ			
SECOND SUPPLEMENT TO THE METHOD BY MARTHE MORHANGE MOTCHANE -- 14 SHORT PIECES --			
FRANCO COLOMBO PUBLICATIONS	SAL		3.25
DEMIERRE			
PAGES ENFANTINES			
FRANCO COLOMBO PUBLICATIONS	SAL		3.00

DEMIERRE
  TWENTY-FOUR PRELUDES IN ALL THE MAJOR AND MINOR KEYS
    FRANCO COLOMBO PUBLICATIONS   SAL   5.25
DENNIS, M.   INTERMEDIATE
  BLUES PIANO STYLES
    MEL BAY PUBLICATIONS, INC.   2.00
DENNIS, M.   INTERMEDIATE
  JAZZ PIANO STYLES
    MEL BAY PUBLICATIONS, INC.   2.00
DENNIS, M.   INTERMEDIATE
  PENSIVE PIANO MOODS
    MEL BAY PUBLICATIONS, INC.   2.00
DENNIS, M.   INTERMEDIATE
  RAGTIME PIANO STYLES
    MEL BAY PUBLICATIONS, INC.   2.00
DENNIS, M.   INTERMEDIATE
  ROCK PIANO STYLES
    MEL BAY PUBLICATIONS, INC.   2.00
DERE   4
  A LA CAMPAGNE, BK. 1
    ALPHONSE LEDUC
DERE   4
  A LA CAMPAGNE, BK. 2
    ALPHONSE LEDUC
DERE   4
  A LA CAMPAGNE, BK. 3
    ALPHONSE LEDUC
DERE   6, 7
  DIX ETUDES DE TECHNIQUE ET DE STYLE
    ALPHONSE LEDUC
DERE   2, 3
  DIX ETUDES FACILES
    ALPHONSE LEDUC
DESCAVES, L.
  CONTEMPORAINS,LES BK.1
    GERARD BILLAUDOT EDITIONS MUSICALES   3.80
DESCAVES, L.
  CONTEMPORAINS,LES BK.2
    GERARD BILLAUDOT EDITIONS MUSICALES   3.80
DESCAVES, L.
  CONTEMPORAINS,LES BK.3
    GERARD BILLAUDOT EDITIONS MUSICALES   3.80
DESCAVES, L.
  CONTEMPORAINS,LES BK.4
    GERARD BILLAUDOT EDITIONS MUSICALES   3.80
DESCAVES, L.
  TECHNIQUE, VOL.1
    GERARD BILLAUDOT EDITIONS MUSICALES   3.80
DESCAVES, L.
  TECHNIQUE, VOL.2
    GERARD BILLAUDOT EDITIONS MUSICALES   3.50
DESSAUX
  PREMIERS CONCERTS
    ALPHONSE LEDUC
DEUTSCH, L.
  FOR SIGHT READING, BK. 1
    ASHLEY DEALERS SERVICE, INC.   1.25
DEUTSCH, L.
  FOR SIGHT READING, BK. 2
    ASHLEY DEALERS SERVICE, INC.   1.50
DEUTSCH, L.   1
  FOR SIGHT READING, VOL. 1
    CENTURY MUSIC PUBLISHING COMPANY, INC.   1.25
DEUTSCH, L.   2-3
  FOR SIGHT READING, VOL. 2
    CENTURY MUSIC PUBLISHING COMPANY, INC.   1.50
DIABELLI   KLEE, L.
  ELEVEN SONATINAS, OP. 151 AND OP. 168
    G. SCHIRMER, INC.   L266   1.25
DIABELLI
  ELEVEN SONATINAS, OP. 151, 168
    EDWIN F. KALMUS   3397   1.75
DIABELLI   KRAUSE
  FOUR SONATINAS, OP. 151
    ASSOCIATED MUSIC PUBLISHERS, INC.   B/H   1.00
DIABELLI   MARCIANO
  SIX SONATINAS, OP. 163
    FRANCO COLOMBO PUBLICATIONS   ER33   1.75
DIABELLI   E
  SONATINAS
    C. F. PETERS CORPORATION   2439   3.00
DIABELLI   MARCIANO
  SONATINAS, OP. 151 AND 168
    FRANCO COLOMBO PUBLICATIONS   ER34   3.00
DIABELLI   CESI
  SONATINAS, OP. 24, 54, 58, 60
    FRANCO COLOMBO PUBLICATIONS   ER29   2.00
DIABELLI   CESI
  THREE SONATAS, OP. 32, 33, 37
    FRANCO COLOMBO PUBLICATIONS   ER30   2.00
DIABELLI *   MARCIANO
  TWENTY LITTLE INSTRUCTIVE PIECES
    FRANCO COLOMBO PUBLICATIONS   ER1237   1.00
DIABELLI   MARCIANO
  TWENTY-EIGHT PIECES ON 5 NOTES, OP. 149
    FRANCO COLOMBO PUBLICATIONS   ER32   1.25
DIABELLI   CESI
  TWO SONATAS, OP. 38 AND 73
    FRANCO COLOMBO PUBLICATIONS   ER31   2.25
DIAMOND, D.
  ALBUM FOR THE YOUNG
    ELKAN-VOGEL, INC.   1.00
DIAMOND, D.
  ALONE AT THE PIANO, BK. 1
    PEER SOUTHERN ORGANIZATION   01.50
DIAMOND, D.
  ALONE AT THE PIANO, BK. 2
    PEER SOUTHERN ORGANIZATION   01.50
DIAMOND, D.
  ALONE AT THE PIANO, BK. 3
    PEER SOUTHERN ORGANIZATION   01.75
DIAMOND, D.
  EIGHT PIANO PIECES
    G. SCHIRMER, INC.   1.00
DIAMOND, D.
  PRIVATE WORLD, A
    PEER SOUTHERN ORGANIZATION   02.00
DIAMOND, D.
  THEN AND NOW
    PEER SOUTHERN ORGANIZATION   01.50
DICHLER
  SIX LITTLE PIECES -- 1953 --
    ASSOCIATED MUSIC PUBLISHERS, INC.   DOB   1.60
DICHLER-SEDLACEK
  HAMPELMANN FANG AN. TWELVE MARCHES
    ASSOCIATED MUSIC PUBLISHERS, INC.   DOB   1.50

DICHLER-SEDLACEK
  MINIATURES -- PIANO PIECES TO DAILY MORNING EXERCISES
    ASSOCIATED MUSIC PUBLISHERS, INC.   DOB   2.25
DICHLER-SEDLACEK
  SKIZZEN -- PIANO PIECES TO DAILY MORNING EXERCISES
    ASSOCIATED MUSIC PUBLISHERS, INC.   DOB   2.25
DICKINSON, P.   4-5
  FIVE DIVERSIONS
    NOVELLO AND COMPANY, LTD.   10.0031.04   1.25
DIEHL--ED   DIEHL
  CHRISTMAS ALBUM -- 14 CHRISTMAS SONGS WITH GERMAN TEXT
    ASSOCIATED MUSIC PUBLISHERS, INC.   BOT   .50
DIET   3, 5
  BABILLAGES
    ALPHONSE LEDUC
DIET   1, 2
  DEUX PIECES
    ALPHONSE LEDUC
DIET   3
  HISTORIETTES
    ALPHONSE LEDUC
DIETRICH--ED.   DIETRICH
  LATERNE, LATERNE, SONNE, MOND UND STERNE
    BARENREITER VERLAG   BA 1003   1.75
DIETRICH--ED.   DIETRICH   1
  LATERNE, LATERNE, SONNE, MOND UND STERNE. 23 VOLKSKINDERLIEDER
  IN GANZ LEICHTEN SATZEN
    BARENREITER VERLAG   BA 1003
DIETRICH--ED.   DIETRICH
  VOLKSLIEDBUCHLEIN
    BARENREITER VERLAG   BA 1499   3.00
DIETRICH--ED.   DIETRICH   2
  VOLKSLIEDBUCHLEIN
    BARENREITER VERLAG   BA 1499
DIEUDONNE
  TWELVE IMAGES EN COURTS PRELUDES
    FRANCO COLOMBO PUBLICATIONS   SAL   4.00
DILLER, A.   GRADE 2
  BAKER'S DOZEN, A--13 PIECES TO READ AT SIGHT--
    G. SCHIRMER, INC.   1.00
DILLER, A.   GRADE 2
  DARING PRINCE AND 9 OTHER PIECES, THE
    G. SCHIRMER, INC.   .75
DILLER, A. *   GRADE 2
  DILLER-PAGE CAROL BOOK, THE
    G. SCHIRMER, INC.   1.00
DILLER, A. *   GRADE 2
  DILLER-PAGE CAROL BOOK= 38E
    G. SCHIRMER, INC.   1.00
DILLER, A. *   GRADE 3
  DILLER-PAGE SONG-BOOKS, THE, VOL. 1
    G. SCHIRMER, INC.   1.25
DILLER, A. *   GRADE 3
  DILLER-PAGE SONG-BOOKS, THE, VOL. 2
    G. SCHIRMER, INC.   1.25
DILLER, A. *   GRADE 2
  FIRST PEDAL-STUDIES--24 PROGRESSIVE EXERCISES AND PIECES
    G. SCHIRMER, INC.   1.00
DILLER, A.   GRADE 3
  KEYBOARD HARMONY COURSE, BK. 1--FEATURING MELODY MAKING
    G. SCHIRMER, INC.   1.25
DILLER, A.   GRADE 4
  KEYBOARD HARMONY COURSE, BK. 2--FEATURING HARMONIC DEVELOPMENT
  AND CHORD VOCABULARY
    G. SCHIRMER, INC.   1.00
DILLER, A.   GRADE 5
  KEYBOARD HARMONY COURSE, BK. 3--FEATURING HARMONIZING MELODIES
  WITH AN ELEMENTARY CHORD VOCABULARY
    G. SCHIRMER, INC.   1.50
DILLER, A.   GRADE 5
  KEYBOARD HARMONY COURSE, BK. 4--FEATURING HARMONIZING MELODIES
  AND ANALYZING ILLUSTRATIVE MATERIAL
    G. SCHIRMER, INC.   2.00
DILLER, A.   GRADE 1
  NINE FIRST-GRADE PIANO SOLOS TO LEARN BY ROTE--EASY TO PLAY BUT
  HARD TO READ--A BOOK FOR TEACHERS
    G. SCHIRMER, INC.   1.25
DILLER, A. *   PRELIMINARY GRADE
  OFF WE GO AGAIN--SECOND BOOK OF POETRY PIECES
    G. SCHIRMER, INC.   1.25
DILLER, A. *   PRELIMINARY GRADE
  OFF WE GO--BOOK OF POETRY PIECES
    G. SCHIRMER, INC.   1.25
DILLER, A. *
  PRE-SCHOOL MUSIC BOOK, A
    G. SCHIRMER, INC.   1.00
DILLER, A. *
  PRE-SCHOOL MUSIC BOOK, A.
    G. SCHIRMER, INC.   1.00
DILLER, A. *   GRADE 1
  SOLO BOOK--1ST
    G. SCHIRMER, INC.   1.00
DILLER, A. *   HOERLER   GRADE 1
  SOLO BOOK--1ST--GERMAN EDITION
    G. SCHIRMER, INC.   .75
DILLER, A. *   GRADE 2
  SOLO BOOK--2ND
    G. SCHIRMER, INC.   1.00
DILLER, A. *   GRADE 3
  SOLO BOOK--3RD
    G. SCHIRMER, INC.   1.00
DILLER, A. *   GRADE 4
  SOLO BOOK--4TH
    G. SCHIRMER, INC.   1.00
DILLER, A. *   GRADE 1
  TWENTY-FIVE FIRST-GRADE PIANO PIECES--COMPANION PIECES TO THE
  ''1ST SOLO BOOK''
    G. SCHIRMER, INC.   1.00
DILLER, A.--ED   DILLER, A.
  NINE FIRST-GRADE PIANO PIECES TO LEARN BY ROTE -- EASY TO PLAY
  BUT HARD TO READ -- A BOOK FOR TEACHERS
    G. SCHIRMER, INC.   1.25
DILLER, A.--ED *   DILLER, A. *   E
  TUNES FROM MANY LANDS
    WILLIS MUSIC COMPANY   1.25
DINSART   E-M
  MNEMONIC PROCESS --FOR THE STUDY OF SCALES AND ARPEGGIO
  FINGERING--
    C. F. PETERS CORPORATION   SCH128   1.50
DIONISI
  FIFTEEN LITTLE COMPOSITIONS FOR LITTLE PIANISTS
    FRANCO COLOMBO PUBLICATIONS   129719   1.00
DISTLER   2-3
  ELF KLEINE KLAVIERSTUCKE FUR DIE JUGEND, OP. 15B
    BARENREITER VERLAG   BA 1803
DITTENHAVER
  MY PIANO SKETCHBOOK, PART 1
    THEODORE PRESSER COMPANY   1.25

DITTENHAVER			
MY PIANO SKETCHBOOK, PART 2			
THEODORE PRESSER COMPANY			1.50
DITTENHAVER			
PICK A TUNE, BK. 1			
BRODT MUSIC COMPANY			1.25
DITTENHAVER			
PICK A TUNE, BK. 2			
BRODT MUSIC COMPANY			1.25
DITTERSDORF, K.D. VON DOEBEREINER			
THREE CADENZAS TO THE CONCERTO IN A			
ASSOCIATED MUSIC PUBLISHERS, INC.		NAG	.60
DOBIAS	3-4		
DREI POETISCHE POLKAS			
BARENREITER VERLAG		AP 555	
DOBRONITCH			
POPULAR YUGOSLAVIAN DANCES			
FRANCO COLOMBO PUBLICATIONS		SAL	7.00
DOBROWEN, I.			
SEVEN PIECES, OP. 13			
UNIVERSAL EDITION		UE 7799	1.95
DOBROWEN, I.			
TWO WALTZES, OP. 6			
UNIVERSAL EDITION		UE 7321	1.10
DOEBEREINER			
THREE CADENZAS TO DITTERSDORF CONCERTO IN A			
ASSOCIATED MUSIC PUBLISHERS, INC.		NAG	.60
DOERFFEL--ED DOERFFEL E			
CHORALBUCH			
C. F. PETERS CORPORATION		1423	2.00
DOERING, C. H.			
EIGHT OCTAVE-STUDIES, OP. 25			
G. SCHIRMER, INC.		L1035	1.00
DOERING, C. H.			
EXERCISES AND STUDIES IN STACCATO OCTAVE-PLAYING, OP. 24			
G. SCHIRMER, INC.		L651	1.00
DOFLEIN--ED. DOFLEIN			
FUGENBUCHLEIN			
BARENREITER VERLAG		BA 1007	1.75
DOFLEIN--ED. DOFLEIN			
ZWANZIG DEUTSCHE VOLKSTANZE			
BARENREITER VERLAG		BA 1145	1.75
DOFLEIN--ED. DOFLEIN 2			
ZWANZIG DEUTSCHE VOLKSTANZE			
BARENREITER VERLAG		BA 1145	
DOHNANYI			
DOHNANYI MASTERPIECES			
EDWARD B. MARKS MUSIC CORPORATION			02.50
DOHNANYI			
ESSENTIAL FINGER EXERCISES			
EDWARD B. MARKS MUSIC CORPORATION			02.50
DOHNANYI			
SELECTED PIANO COMPOSITIONS			
KULTURA			4.00
DOHNANYI			
SIX CONCERT ETUDES, BK. 1 AND 2			
KULTURA			EA.
DOHNANYI			
SIX PIANO PIECES, OP. 41			
BELWIN-MILLS PUBLISHING CORPORATION		20453	1.50
DOHNANYI			
THREE SINGULAR PIECES, OP. 44 -- 1951 --			
ASSOCIATED MUSIC PUBLISHERS, INC.		AMP	2.00
DOHNANYI			
WINTERREIGEN, OP. 13 -- TEN BAGATELLES			
ASSOCIATED MUSIC PUBLISHERS, INC.		DOB	4.00
DONALDSON			
CHILD'S WORLD			
VOLKWEIN BROS.			01.25
DONATH--ED DONATH 3-4			
KLEINMEISTER DER KLASSIK			
SCHOTT		4127	1.75
DONATO, A.			
RECREATIONS			
PEER SOUTHERN ORGANIZATION			01.50
DONATONI, F. 6			
TRE IMPROVVISAZIONI - 1957			
SCHOTT		10657	5.00
DOTRAS-VILA			
THREE SPANISH PIECES			
ASSOCIATED MUSIC PUBLISHERS, INC.		UME	1.25
DOUBRAVA	3		
FUNF BAGATELLEN -- 1953 --			
BARENREITER VERLAG		AP 556	
DOWLAND, R. HUNT 3-4			
VARIETIE OF LUTE LESSONS - 1610. LAUTENTABULATUR FUR KLAVIER			
SCHOTT		10310	5.50
DRAESEL			
NOW HYMNS FOR YOUNG PEOPLE			
EDWARD B. MARKS MUSIC CORPORATION			01.50
DRAGOI			
MINIATURES			
ASSOCIATED MUSIC PUBLISHERS, INC.		SIM	1.50
DRAO--ED DRAO			
LATIN RHYTHMS			
PRO-ART PUBLICATIONS, INC.		933	.85
DRATHS--ED DRATHS 1			
MORGEN KOMMT DER WEIHNACHTSMANN			
SCHOTT		5325	2.25
DRATHS--ED DRATHS 2			
O WUNDER, WAS WILL DAS BEDEUTEN			
SCHOTT		5700	2.25
DRAW			
EARLY KEYBOARD TECHNIC, BK. A			
PRO-ART PUBLICATIONS, INC.		838	1.00
DRAW			
EARLY KEYBOARD TECHNIC, BK. B			
PRO-ART PUBLICATIONS, INC.		839	1.00
DRAW			
EARLY KEYBOARD TECHNIC, BK. C			
PRO-ART PUBLICATIONS, INC.		840	1.00
DRAW			
EARLY KEYBOARD TECHNIC, BK. D			
PRO-ART PUBLICATIONS, INC.		841	1.00
DREISBACH			
CHURCH AND CHAPEL VOLUNTARIES			
G. SCHIRMER, INC.			2.50
DREWS			
PIANO TECHNIQUE, BK. 1			
FRANCO COLOMBO PUBLICATIONS		SIK.490A	8.25
DREWS			
PIANO TECHNIQUE, BK. 2			
FRANCO COLOMBO PUBLICATIONS		SIK.490B	9.75
DRIESSLER	3-4		
APHORISMEN, OP. 7			
BARENREITER VERLAG			

DRIESSLER	2-3		
DREI SONATINEN, OP. 29 NO. 2			
BARENREITER VERLAG		BA 2694	
DRIESSLER	4		
DREI TOCCATEN, OP. 29 NO. 1			
BARENREITER VERLAG		BA 2494	
DRIESSLER			
MUSIC FOR PIANO, OP. 2 NO. I			
BARENREITER VERLAG		BA 2541	2.50
DRIESSLER	4		
MUSIK FUR KLAVIER, OP. 2 NO. 2			
BARENREITER VERLAG		BA 2541	
DRIESSLER			
THREE TOCCATAS, OP. 29 NO. 1			
BARENREITER VERLAG		BA 2494	3.25
DRING			
TWELVE PIECES IN THE FORM OF STUDIES			
EDWARD B. MARKS MUSIC CORPORATION			01.25
DRISCHNER	E-M		
PARTITAS ON TWO CHRISTMAS SONGS			
C. F. PETERS CORPORATION		VP149	2.00
DUBOIS, P. M.	1, 3		
CONTES DE MOURRICES			
ALPHONSE LEDUC			
DUBOIS, P. M.			
DIX ETUDES DE CONCERT			
ALPHONSE LEDUC			
DUBOIS, P. M.	8, 9		
DIX ETUDES DE CONCERT, BK. 1			
ALPHONSE LEDUC			
DUBOIS, P. M.	8, 9		
DIX ETUDES DE CONCERT, BK. 2			
ALPHONSE LEDUC			
DUBOIS, P. M.	3, 5		
ESQUISSES			
ALPHONSE LEDUC			
DUBOIS, P. M.	4, 7		
POUR MA MIEUX AIMEE			
ALPHONSE LEDUC			
DUBOIS, P. M.	8		
TROIS PIECES			
ALPHONSE LEDUC			
DUBOSQC			
MATINES, SARABANDES ET GAILLARDES			
FRANCO COLOMBO PUBLICATIONS		SAL	7.00
DUBSKY	1-2		
TWO LITTLE PIECES			
CENTURY MUSIC PUBLISHING COMPANY, INC.		4377	.40
DUCHIN			
DUCHIN'S, EDDY, PIANORAMA			
WARNER BROTHERS PUBLISHERS			1.50
DUCHIN			
EDDY DUCHIN AT THE PIANO			
THE BIG THREE MUSIC CORPORATION			1.50
DUCHIN			
PETER DUCHIN PIANO SHOWCASE			
CHAPPELL AND COMPANY, INC.		0038026	2.50
DUCKWORTH, G.			
KEYBOARD BUILDER -- BOOK 3			
M-F COMPANY			1.75
DUCKWORTH, G.			
KEYBOARD DISCOVERER -- BOOK 2			
M-F COMPANY			1.75
DUCKWORTH, G.			
KEYBOARD EXPLORER -- BOOK 1			
M-F COMPANY			1.75
DUCKWORTH, G.			
KEYBOARD MUSICIAN -- BOOK 4			
M-F COMPANY			1.75
DUCKWORTH, G.			
KEYBOARD PERFORMER			
M-F COMPANY			1.75
DUHAMEL			
IMPRESSIONS DE BRETAGNE - EN ALLANT AU PARDON, BINIOUS DANS LA LANDE, BAL CHAMPETRE			
FRANCO COLOMBO PUBLICATIONS		SAL	2.00
DUKE, H.	1		
FAVOURITES -- 12 EASY PIECES			
NOVELLO AND COMPANY, LTD.		10.0035.07	1.25
DUKE, H.	1		
FIRST SUITE OF SIX EASY PIECES			
NOVELLO AND COMPANY, LTD.		10.0033.00	1.15
DUKE, H.	1		
SECOND SUITE OF SIX EASY PIECES			
NOVELLO AND COMPANY, LTD.		10.0034.09	1.25
DUKE, H.	1		
SIGHT-READING TESTS, BK. 1			
NOVELLO AND COMPANY, LTD.		11.0015.07	.75
DUKE, H.	2		
SIGHT-READING TESTS, BK. 2			
NOVELLO AND COMPANY, LTD.		11.0016.05	.75
DUKELSKY			
TWO PIECES			
BOOSEY AND HAWKES, INC.			1.50
DUMM			
HOLIDAY FOR THE HACKNEYED			
BELWIN-MILLS PUBLISHING CORPORATION		11587	1.75
DUMM			
MORE PARALLEL BARS			
BELWIN-MILLS PUBLISHING CORPORATION		11318	1.75
DUMM			
PARALLEL BARS			
BELWIN-MILLS PUBLISHING CORPORATION		11373	1.75
DUMM			
PIANO SOUNDINGS			
BELWIN-MILLS PUBLISHING CORPORATION		11383	1.75
DUMM			
PIANO STYLEPRINTS			
BELWIN-MILLS PUBLISHING CORPORATION		11384	1.75
DUNGAN			
COUNTRY TUNES TO SING AND PLAY			
THEODORE PRESSER COMPANY			1.00
DUPONT, J.	5, 6		
SOIRS A JUAN-LES-PINS			
ALPHONSE LEDUC			
DUPONT, J.	6		
TROIS PIECES, OP. 8			
ALPHONSE LEDUC			
DUPRE, M.	5, 7		
QUATRE PIECES, OP. 19			
ALPHONSE LEDUC			
DUPRE, M.	7		
SIX PRELUDES, OP. 12			
ALPHONSE LEDUC			
DURANTE PAUMGARTNER, B. 3			
SEI STUDII E SEI DIVERTIMENTI PER CEMBALO			
BARENREITER VERLAG		BA 340	

```
DURANTE
  SIX SONATAS FOR HARPSICHORD
    BARENREITER VERLAG                              BA 340     3.50
DUSSEK
  SIX SONATINAS, OP. 20
    FRANCO COLOMBO PUBLICATIONS                     128442     2.00
DUSSEK, J.              SYKORA            3
  KLAVIERSONATEN 1 -- 1-7 --
    BARENREITER VERLAG                              MAB 46
DUSSEK, J.              SYKORA            3
  KLAVIERSONATEN 2 -- 8-16 --
    BARENREITER VERLAG                              MAB 53
DUSSEK, J.              SYKORA            3-4
  KLAVIERSONATEN 3 -- 17-23 --
    BARENREITER VERLAG                              MAB 59
DUSSEK, J.              SYKORA            3-4
  KLAVIERSONATEN 4 -- 24-29 --
    BARENREITER VERLAG                              MAB 63
DUSSEK, J.                                D
  PIANO PIECES --8--
    C. F. PETERS CORPORATION                        2748       3.50
DUSSEK, J.              KLEE
  SIX SONATINAS, OP. 20
    G. SCHIRMER, INC.                                          1.25
DUSSEK, J.              RUTHARDT          M
  SONATINAS --6--, OP. 20
    C. F. PETERS CORPORATION                        1302       2.50
DUSSEK, J.
  SONATINAS, OP. 20
    EDWIN F. KALMUS                                 3417       1.25
DUSSEK, J. *           SYKORA            3-4
  TSCHECHISCHE KLASSIKER, BAND 2 - 9 STUCKE
    BARENREITER VERLAG                              MAB 20
DUSSEK, J.             KURZ               3-4
  ZWEI KLAVIERKOMPOSITIONEN -- LES ADIEUX UND LA CONSOLATION, OP.
  62 --
    BARENREITER VERLAG                              AP 561
DUSSEK, J.             SYKORA             3
  ZWOLF MELODISCHE ETUDEN, OP. 16
    BARENREITER VERLAG                              MAB 21
DUSSEK, J.             SYKORA
  ZWOLF MELODISCHE ETUDEN, OP. 16
    BARENREITER VERLAG                              MAB 21
DUTILLEUX                                 5
  AU GRE DES ONDES, 6 PETITES PIECES
    ALPHONSE LEDUC
DUTILLEUX
  LOUP, LE -- BALLET --
    FRANCO COLOMBO PUBLICATIONS                     R1299      5.25
DUVERNOY, J.                              M-D
  ECOLE DU MECANISME, OP. 120 --15 ETUDES--
    C. F. PETERS CORPORATION                        3276       2.00
DUVERNOY, J.
  ECOLE PRIMAIRE, OP. 176--25 ELEMENTARY STUDIES
    G. SCHIRMER, INC.                               L50        .75
DUVERNOY, J.
  ELEMENTARY STUDIES, OP. 176
    CARL FISCHER, INC.                              L 506      1.00
DUVERNOY, J.
  ELEMENTARY STUDIES, OP. 176
    FRANCO COLOMBO PUBLICATIONS                     ER642      1.00
DUVERNOY, J.
  ELEMENTARY STUDIES, OP. 176
    UNIVERSAL EDITION                               2073       1.20
DUVERNOY, J.
  EMULATION, OP. 314 - 20 LITTLE PIECES
    FRANCO COLOMBO PUBLICATIONS                     ER2415     1.50
DUVERNOY, J.
  MODERN SCHOOL, OP. 299
    FRANCO COLOMBO PUBLICATIONS                     ER2234     1.25
DUVERNOY, J.
  PREPARATORY SCHOOL OF VELOCITY, OP. 276
    FRANCO COLOMBO PUBLICATIONS                     ER1210     1.50
DUVERNOY, J.
  PREPARATORY SCHOOL, OP. 276
    UNIVERSAL EDITION                               1530       1.40
DUVERNOY, J.
  SCHOOL OF MECHANISM, OP. 120
    CARL FISCHER, INC.                              L 361      1.00
DUVERNOY, J.
  SCHOOL OF MECHANISM, OP. 120
    FRANCO COLOMBO PUBLICATIONS                     ER641      1.25
DUVERNOY, J.           KLAUSER
  SCHOOL OF MECHANISM, THE--OP. 120--15 STUDIES PREPARATORY TO
  CZERNY'S ''SCHOOL OF VELOCITY''
    G. SCHIRMER, INC.                               L316       1.00
DUVERNOY, J.
  SCHOOL OF MECHANISM, THE--OP. 120--15 STUDIES PREPARATORY TO
  CZERNY'S ''SCHOOL OF VELOCITY''--BK. 1
    G. SCHIRMER, INC.                               L1292      1.00
DUVERNOY, J.           PALMER. W. A.
  TWENTY-FIVE ELEMENTARY STUDIES
    ALFRED MUSIC COMPANY                            636        1.50
DUVERNOY, J.                              E
  TWENTY-FIVE ELEMENTARY STUDIES, OP. 176
    C. F. PETERS CORPORATION                        3277       2.00
DVORAK                 POKORNY            3-4
  BERUHMTE MELODIEN
    BARENREITER VERLAG                              AP 562
DVORAK
  COMPOSITIONS FOR PIANO, OP. 52
    ARTIA                                                      3.25
DVORAK
  DANCES
    ARTIA                                                      2.00
DVORAK                 VINKLAT            3
  DUMKA UND FURIANT, OP. 12 NO. 2
    BARENREITER VERLAG                              AP 564
DVORAK                 KELLER
  EIGHT SLAVONIC DANCES, OP. 46 -- VOL. 1
    ASSOCIATED MUSIC PUBLISHERS, INC.               SIM        1.50
DVORAK                 KELLER
  EIGHT SLAVONIC DANCES, OP. 46 -- VOL. 2
    ASSOCIATED MUSIC PUBLISHERS, INC.               SIM        1.25
DVORAK                 KELLER
  EIGHT SLAVONIC DANCES, OP. 72 -- VOL. 1
    ASSOCIATED MUSIC PUBLISHERS, INC.               SIM        1.50
DVORAK                 KELLER
  EIGHT SLAVONIC DANCES, OP. 72 -- VOL. 2
    ASSOCIATED MUSIC PUBLISHERS, INC.               SIM        1.50
DVORAK
  EIGHT WALTZES, OP. 54 -- VOL. 1
    ASSOCIATED MUSIC PUBLISHERS, INC.               SIM        1.50
DVORAK
  EIGHT WALTZES, OP. 54 -- VOL. 2
    ASSOCIATED MUSIC PUBLISHERS, INC.               SIM        1.50

DVORAK                 SOUREK            3
  HUMORESKEN, OP. 101
    BARENREITER VERLAG                              AP 275
DVORAK                 BURGHAUSER *      3
  IMPROMPTU IN D MINOR UND HUMORESKE IN F SHARP
    BARENREITER VERLAG                              AP 273
DVORAK
  MAZURKAS, OP. 56
    ARTIA                                                      3.00
DVORAK                 MONTANI
  POETIC IMPRESSIONS, OP. 85
    FRANCO COLOMBO PUBLICATIONS                     129198     1.50
DVORAK
  POETIC TONE-PICTURES, OP. 85
    ARTIA                                                      4.25
DVORAK
  POETICAL IMPRESSIONS, OP. 85 -- VOL. 1
    ASSOCIATED MUSIC PUBLISHERS, INC.               SIM        1.75
DVORAK
  POETICAL IMPRESSIONS, OP. 85 -- VOL. 2
    ASSOCIATED MUSIC PUBLISHERS, INC.               SIM        1.75
DVORAK
  POETICAL IMPRESSIONS, OP. 85 -- VOL. 3
    ASSOCIATED MUSIC PUBLISHERS, INC.               SIM        1.75
DVORAK                                    M-D
  SELECTED PIANO PIECES --24--
    C. F. PETERS CORPORATION                        4676       6.00
DVORAK                 BURGHAUSER        3
  SIEBEN MAZURKEN, OP. 56
    BARENREITER VERLAG                              AP 320
DVORAK
  SILHOUETTES, OP. 8
    ARTIA                                                      2.00
DVORAK                 CUBR *            2-3
  SIX KLAVIERSTUCKE, OP. 52
    BARENREITER VERLAG                              AP 328
DVORAK                 SOLC
  SLAVONIC DANCES, OP. 46
    ARTIA                                                      2.50
DVORAK                 SOLC
  SLAVONIC DANCES, OP. 72
    ARTIA                                                      2.50
DVORAK                 HERRMANN          4-5
  SLAWISCHE TANZE AUS OP. 46 UND 72
    SCHOTT                                          4610       1.50
DVORAK                 HERRMANN          4-5
  SLAWISCHE TANZE OP. 46 -- BK. 2
    SCHOTT                                          4607       1.75
DVORAK                 HERRMANN          4-5
  SLAWISCHE TANZE OP. 72 -- BK. 1
    SCHOTT                                          4608       1.75
DVORAK                 HERRMANN          4-5
  SLAWISCHE TANZE OP. 72 -- BK. 2
    SCHOTT                                          4608       1.75
DVORAK                 SOLC              3-4
  SLAWISCHE TANZE, OP. 46
    BARENREITER VERLAG                              AP 575
DVORAK                 SOLC              3-4
  SLAWISCHE TANZE, OP. 72
    BARENREITER VERLAG                              AP 576
DVORAK                 BURGHAUSER *      3
  TANZE -- POLKA IN E, 10 MENUETTE, SCHOTTISCHE TANZE --
    BARENREITER VERLAG                              AP 314
DVORAK                 SOUREK            3-4
  THIRTEEN POETISCHE STIMMUNGBILDER, OP. 85
    BARENREITER VERLAG                              AP 573
DVORAK                 BURGHAUSER        3
  TWELVE SILHOUETTEN, OP. 8
    BARENREITER VERLAG                              AP. 574
DVORAK
  WALTZES, OP. 54
    ARTIA                                                      2.50
DVORAK                 VINKLAT           2-3
  WALZER IN A AND D FLAT, OP. 54 NO. 1
    BARENREITER VERLAG                              AP 582
DVORAK                 POKORNY *         3
  WALZER, OP. 54
    BARENREITER VERLAG                              AP 580
DVORAK                 SOLC              3
  WIEGENLIED UND CAPRICCIO
    BARENREITER VERLAG                              AP 288
DVORAK                 BURGHAUSER        4
  ZWEI FURIANTE, OP. 42
    BARENREITER VERLAG                              AP 1685
DVORAK                 LASKA             2-3
  ZWEI KLEINE PERLEN
    BARENREITER VERLAG                              AP 581
DYLAN                  NEALE, J.
  INSTANT PICTURE CHORD PIANO NO. 2, BOB DYLAN
    WARNER BROTHERS PUBLISHERS                                 1.95
EARHART, L.
  CLASSICS FOR THE CHURCH PIANIST
    THEODORE PRESSER COMPANY                                   3.00
EARLE
  EIGHTEENTH CENTURY DANCES -- HOW TO ADD MELODIC ORNAMENTATION
    LEE ROBERTS MUSIC PUBLICATIONS, INC.                       1.25
EBBENHORST TENGBERGEN                     E
  FIFTY POLYPHONIC PIECES
    C. F. PETERS CORPORATION                        B32A       1.25
ECKARD, W.
  BOY'S FAVORITE SOLO ALBUM
    THEODORE PRESSER COMPANY                                   1.50
ECKARD, W.
  HYMNS TO PLAY AND SING
    THEODORE PRESSER COMPANY                                   1.50
ECKARD, W.
  MUSIC OF FAITH, BK. 2
    THEODORE PRESSER COMPANY                                   1.75
ECKARD, W.             REESER *          3
  OEUVRE COMPLETES POUR LE CLAVECIN OU LE PIANOFORTE. 8 SONATEN,
  OP. 1 NOS. 1-6 UND OP. 2 NOS. 1-2 UND MENUET D'EXAUDET AVEC DES
  VARIATIONS
    BARENREITER VERLAG
ECKARD, W.--ED         ECKARD, W.
  GIRLS' FAVORITE SOLO ALBUM
    THEODORE PRESSER COMPANY                                   1.75
ECKSTEIN
  ECKSTEIN PIANO COURSE - ADULT PIANO, BK. 1 --95--
    CARL FISCHER, INC.                              O 3832     1.75
ECKSTEIN
  ECKSTEIN PIANO COURSE - ADULT PIANO, BK. 2 --65--
    CARL FISCHER, INC.                              O 4205     1.50
ECKSTEIN
  ECKSTEIN PIANO COURSE, BK. 1 --175--
    CARL FISCHER, INC.                              O 3703     1.25
ECKSTEIN
  ECKSTEIN PIANO COURSE, BK. 2 --175--
    CARL FISCHER, INC.                              O 3704     1.25
```

ECKSTEIN
  ECKSTEIN PIANO COURSE, BK. 3 --140--
    CARL FISCHER, INC.   O 3705   1.25
ECKSTEIN
  ECKSTEIN PIANO COURSE, BK. 4 --150--
    CARL FISCHER, INC.   O 3706   1.25
ECKSTEIN
  ECKSTEIN PIANO COURSE, BK. 5 --65--
    CARL FISCHER, INC.   O 3707   1.25
ECKSTEIN
  ECKSTEIN PIANO COURSE, BK. 6 --100--
    CARL FISCHER, INC.   O 3708   1.50
ECKSTEIN
  PICTURE POINTERS
    CARL FISCHER, INC.   O 3451   1.50
ECKSTEIN
  TOUCH, TONE, TECHNIC
    CARL FISCHER, INC.   O 4109   1.25
ECKSTEIN
  WRITE AND PLAY THE SCALES AND CHORDS
    CARL FISCHER, INC.   O 3913   1.50
EDER
  RHYTHMISCHE KLAVIERSTUECKE, OP. 18 -- 1955 --
    ASSOCIATED MUSIC PUBLISHERS, INC.   DOB   2.25
EDER
  ZWEI APHORISMEN UM EIN NACHTSTUCK, OP. 52
    BARENREITER VERLAG   BE 341   3.00
                                     E
EDGINTON
  EIGHT LITTLE NIGHT FANCIES
    C. F. PETERS CORPORATION   H844   1.25
                                     E
EDGINTON
  ENGLISH VILLAGE SUITE
    C. F. PETERS CORPORATION   H732   1.25
                                     E
EDGINTON
  HOPEFUL TRAVELLER, THE --22 PIECES FOR BOYS--
    C. F. PETERS CORPORATION   H1491   1.25
EDMONDS
  SEVEN MUSIGRAMS
    SAM FOX PUBLISHING COMPANY, INC.   1.00
EDWARDS, J.
  JONATHAN EDWARDS
    THE BIG THREE MUSIC CORPORATION   04.95
EHMANN--ED.   EHMANN
  ALTE LIEDSATZE
    BARENREITER VERLAG   BA 1287   3.25
EHMANN--ED.   EHMANN   2-3
  ALTE LIEDSATZE - 19 VOLKSLIEDSATZE AUS TABULATURBUCHERN DES 16.
  JAHRH.
    BARENREITER VERLAG   BA 1287
EINEM, G.
  PIANO PIECES
    UNIVERSAL EDITION   UE 11471   3.75
EISLER
  FOUR PIANO PIECES, OP. 3
    UNIVERSAL EDITION   8436   1.95
EITLER, E.
  PRELUDIO Y CAPRICHO
    PEER SOUTHERN ORGANIZATION   00.85
                                     E
ELDABH
  MEKTA IN THE ART OF KITA. FOR CHILDREN AND ADULTS, VOL. 1
    C. F. PETERS CORPORATION   6184   1.25
                                     M-D
ELDABH
  MEKTA IN THE ART OF KITA. FOR CHILDREN AND ADULTS, VOL. 2
    C. F. PETERS CORPORATION   6185   1.50
                                     3
ELGAR, E.
  SALUT D'AMOUR OP. 12
    SCHOTT   09672-3   1.50
ELLINGTON   NEVIN
  DUKE ELLINGTON'S BEST
    BELWIN-MILLS PUBLISHING CORPORATION   2.00
ELLINGTON
  GREAT MUSIC OF DUKE ELLINGTON
    DOVER PUBLICATIONS, INC.   20757-9   5.95
                                     2-3
ELLIOTT, R.
  THREE LYRIC PIECES
    NOVELLO AND COMPANY, LTD.   10.0044.06   .65
ELWELL, H.
  PIECES FOR PIANO --PRELUDE, CORTEGE, BERCEUSE, DANCE--
    ROCHESTER MUSIC PUBLISHERS, INC.   1.50
ELWELL, H.
  THREE PRELUDES
    ROCHESTER MUSIC PUBLISHERS, INC.   1.50
EMERSON--ED   EMERSON
  MASTERS AND THEIR MELODIES
    WILLIS MUSIC COMPANY   1.00
EMIG, L.
  LET'S LEARN TO COUNT - BOOK 1
    PRO-ART PUBLICATIONS, INC.   682   1.00
EMIG, L.
  LET'S LEARN TO COUNT - BOOK 2
    PRO-ART PUBLICATIONS, INC.   684   1.00
EMONTS, F.
  ERSTES KLAVIERSPIEL. EIN LEHRGANG FUR DEN ANFANGSUNTERRICHT,
  BAND 01
    SCHOTT   4689   2.75
EMONTS, F.
  ERSTES KLAVIERSPIEL. EIN LEHRGANG FUR DEN ANFANGSUNTERRICHT,
  BAND 02
    SCHOTT   4711   2.75
                                     2-3
EMONTS, F.
  POLYPHONES KLAVIERSPIEL, HEFT 01
    SCHOTT   5451   4.25
                                     3
EMONTS, F.
  POLYPHONES KLAVIERSPIEL, HEFT 02
    SCHOTT   5452   4.25
EMONTS, F.--ED   EMONTS, F.   2
  LEICHTE KLAVIERMUSIK DER ROMANTIK UND NACHROMANTIK
    SCHOTT   4748   2.00
EMONTS, F.--ED   EMONTS, F.   2
  LEICHTE KLAVIERMUSIK DES BAROK
    SCHOTT   5096   2.00
EMONTS, F.--ED   EMONTS, F.   2
  LEICHTE KLAVIERSTUCKE VON BACHS SOHNEN BIS BEETHOVEN
    SCHOTT   4747   2.00
EMONTS, F.--ED   EMONTS, F.   1-2
  SPIEL MIT FUNF TONEN. LIEDER UND STUCKE FUR DEN ERSTEN ANFANG
    SCHOTT   5285   2.00
EMONTS, F.--ED   EMONTS, F.   1-2
  VON BARTOK BIS STRAVINSKY
    SCHOTT   4769   2.25
ENGEL--ED *   ENGEL *
  MY HANUKKAH SONG BOOK
    WILLIS MUSIC COMPANY   1.50
ENGEL, S.--ARR.   ENGEL, S.   ADVANCED
  GREAT HYMNS
    SCREEN GEMS - COLUMBIA PUBLICATIONS   F0260P1   3.50

ENGEL, S.--ARR.   ENGEL, S.   ADVANCED
  TWENTY-FOUR CARAT GOLD
    SCREEN GEMS - COLUMBIA PUBLICATIONS   F0200P1   3.95
ENGELS, M. W.
  EXERCISES FOR RHYTHMIC STUDY, BK. 1
    FREDERICK HARRIS MUSIC COMPANY   1.50
ENKE   MARCIANO
  TWELVE MELODIOUS PIECES, OP. 6 AND 8
    FRANCO COLOMBO PUBLICATIONS   ER662   2.25
ENOCH   E
  LET'S MAKE MUSIC --50 PIECES FOR THE PIANO CLASS--
    C. F. PETERS CORPORATION   H1533   2.50
ENRIQUEZ, M.
  A LAPIZ -TRES APUNTES PARA PIANO
    EDICIONES MEXICANAS DE MUSICA, A. C.   01.50
ENRIQUEZ, M.
  PARA ALICIA MUSICA
    PEER SOUTHERN ORGANIZATION   02.50
ERB
  VERY EASIEST FAVORITE SONGS
    BOSTON MUSIC COMPANY   1.25
ERINC, C.
  FOUR TURKISH PIANO PIECES, OP. 9
    UNIVERSAL EDITION   UE 10249   1.10
ESPLA
  LEVANTE. TEN MELODIES AND DANCE THEMES
    ASSOCIATED MUSIC PUBLISHERS, INC.   UME   1.50
ESPLA
  LIRICA ESPANOLA, OP. 54 -- VOL. 2
    ASSOCIATED MUSIC PUBLISHERS, INC.   UME   .60
ESPLA
  LIRICA ESPANOLA, OP. 54 -- VOL. 3 --
    ASSOCIATED MUSIC PUBLISHERS, INC.   UME   .90
ESPLA
  LIRICA ESPANOLA, OP. 54 -- VOL. 4 --
    ASSOCIATED MUSIC PUBLISHERS, INC.   UME   1.25
ESPLA
  THREE MOVEMENTS
    ASSOCIATED MUSIC PUBLISHERS, INC.   UME   1.25
ESPOSITO, M.--ED   ESPOSITO, M.
  EARLY ITALIAN PIANO MUSIC
    THEODORE PRESSER COMPANY   5.00
ESTELLA
  EVERYBODY LIKES THE PIANO, BK. 1
    ASHLEY DEALERS SERVICE, INC.   1.25
ESTELLA
  EVERYBODY LIKES THE PIANO, BK. 2
    ASHLEY DEALERS SERVICE, INC.   1.25
ESTELLA
  EVERYBODY LIKES THE PIANO, BK. 3
    ASHLEY DEALERS SERVICE, INC.   1.25
ESTELLA
  EVERYBODY LIKES THE PIANO, BK. 4
    ASHLEY DEALERS SERVICE, INC.   1.25
ESTELLA
  EVERYBODY LIKES THE PIANO, BK. 5
    ASHLEY DEALERS SERVICE, INC.   1.25
ESTELLA
  EVERYBODY LIKES THE PIANO, PREPARATORY BOOK
    ASHLEY DEALERS SERVICE, INC.   1.25
ETTORE, E.
  SCHERZO AND WALTZ
    COMPOSERS AUTOGRAPH PUBLICATIONS   1.54
                                     1B
ETTS, M.
  LITTLE TREASURY SERIES - PIECETIME
    CENTURY MUSIC PUBLISHING COMPANY, INC.   1.00
                                     1C
ETTS, M.
  LITTLE TREASURY SERIES - PLAYTIME
    CENTURY MUSIC PUBLISHING COMPANY, INC.   1.00
ETTS, M.--ED *   ETTS, M. *
  CLASSICS MADE EASY, BK. 1
    CENTURY MUSIC PUBLISHING COMPANY, INC.   1.25
ETTS, M.--ED   ETTS, M.   1C
  LITTLE TREASURY SERIES -- PIECETIME
    ASHLEY DEALERS SERVICE, INC.   1.00
ETTS, M.--ED   ETTS, M.   1B
  LITTLE TREASURY SERIES -- PLAYTIME
    ASHLEY DEALERS SERVICE, INC.   1.00
EVANS
  BILL EVANS PIANO SOLOS
    TRO SONGWAYS SERVICE, INC.   2.00
EVANS
  BILL EVANS PLAYS
    TRO SONGWAYS SERVICE, INC.   2.95
EYBLER   NEMETZ *
  THREE MINUETS
    ASSOCIATED MUSIC PUBLISHERS, INC.   OBV   .60
EZELL, H.
  SNIPS AND SNAILS - TWELVE PIANO SOLOS FOR BOYS AND TOMBOYS
    BOSTON MUSIC COMPANY   1.00
FAIRCHILD
  FOURTH ROMANESQUE, BKS. 1 AND 2
    ELKAN-VOGEL, INC.   D   7.25
FAIRCHILD
  FOURTH ROMANESQUE, BKS. 3 AND 4
    ELKAN-VOGEL, INC.   D   6.00
FAITH   BEGINNING/INTERMEDIATE
  FINGER PAINTINGS
    SHAWNEE PRESS, INC.   2.00
FAITH   MEDIUM/ADVANCED
  FIVE PRELUDES AND A NOCTURNE
    SHAWNEE PRESS, INC.   2.00
FAITH   GR. 3
  FOUR CAMEOS
    SHAWNEE PRESS, INC.   1.25
FAITH
  TRAVELS
    SHAWNEE PRESS, INC.   1.75
FALCINELLI   3
  HARMONIES ET LIGNES, 8 PETITES PIECES POUR PIANO, OP. 32
    ALPHONSE LEDUC
FALK
  DIX ETUDES ATONALES, DONT 2 DE CONCERT --SELON LA TECHNIQUE DE
  L'ATONALISME INTEGRAL--
    ALPHONSE LEDUC
FALKENBERG   4, 6
  SIX ETUDES-EXERCICES
    ALPHONSE LEDUC
FALLA, M. DE
  PIECES ESPAGNOLES
    ELKAN-VOGEL, INC.   5.00
FALLA, M. DE   HALFFTER
  SIETE CANCIONES POPULARES ESPANOLAS
    ASSOCIATED MUSIC PUBLISHERS, INC.   ESC   7.25
FANENGHI
  EIGHTEEN FAMOUS ARIAS -- TESORO DEL MELODRAMMA --
    FRANCO COLOMBO PUBLICATIONS   127652   1.50

FANENGHI
 MOST BEAUTIFUL LOVE SONGS, THE
  FRANCO COLOMBO PUBLICATIONS 127615 1.50
FANO, G. A.
 FOUR FANTASIES, OP. 6
  FRANCO COLOMBO PUBLICATIONS BON.176 2.25
FANO, G. A.
 STUDY OF THE PIANO, THE, BK. 1 - THE TECHNIQUE OF THE SCALE
  FRANCO COLOMBO PUBLICATIONS ER389 2.75
FANO, G. A.
 STUDY OF THE PIANO, THE, BK. 2 - CHORDS, ARPEGGIOS AND THE PEDAL
  FRANCO COLOMBO PUBLICATIONS ER1323 1.50
FANO, G. A.
 STUDY OF THE PIANO, THE, BK. 3 - POLYPHONIC STYLE, ADVANCED
 TECHNIQUES AND METHODS OF STUDY
  FRANCO COLOMBO PUBLICATIONS ER1597 2.25
FARKAS, F.
 THREE MONOGRAMS
  KULTURA 1.00
FAURE, G.   PHILIPP
 ALBUM OF PIANO PIECES
  G. SCHIRMER, INC. 1.50
FAURE, G.
 BARCAROLLES, IMPROMPTUS, NOCTURNES
  HEUGEL ET CIE. 8.75
FAURE, G.
 EIGHT NOCTURNES
  ELKAN-VOGEL, INC. 9.00
FAURE, G.   PHILIPP, I.
 EIGHT NOCTURNES
  INTERNATIONAL MUSIC COMPANY 3.75
FAURE, G.
 EIGHT PIECES BREVES, OP. 84
  INTERNATIONAL MUSIC COMPANY 2.50
FAURE, G.
 PIECES BREVES, OP. 84
  EDWIN F. KALMUS 3437 2.50
FAURE, G.
 PRELUDES, OP. 103
  HEUGEL ET CIE. 6.00
FAURE, G.
 SIX BARCAROLLES
  INTERNATIONAL MUSIC COMPANY 3.00
FAURE, G.
 SIX BARCAROLLES
  EDWIN F. KALMUS 3433 2.50
FAURE, G.
 SONGS WITHOUT WORDS, OP. 17
  INTERNATIONAL MUSIC COMPANY 1.75
FAURE, G.
 THREE IMPROMPTUS, OP. 25, 31, 34
  INTERNATIONAL MUSIC COMPANY 2.00
FAURE, G.
 THREE IMPROMPTUS, OP. 25, 31, 34
  EDWIN F. KALMUS 3434 2.00
FEATHER   HYMAN, D.
 HI FI SUITE
  BELWIN-MILLS PUBLISHING CORPORATION 2.00
FEINBERG, S.
 THREE PRELUDES, OP. 15
  UNIVERSAL EDITION UE 7343 1.50
FEJARD
 THREE ETUDES
  FRANCO COLOMBO PUBLICATIONS SAL 4.00
FELBER, R.--ED FELBER, R. 4
 SLOWAKISCHE TANZE
  SCHOTT 1285 2.00
FELDMAN   M
 LAST PIECES
  C. F. PETERS CORPORATION 6941 1.50
FELTON, W.
 EVENING MOODS
  THEODORE PRESSER COMPANY 2.00
FELTON, W.
 GROWN-UP BEGINNER'S BOOK
  THEODORE PRESSER COMPANY 2.95
FELTON, W.--ED FELTON, W.
 MELTING POT
  THEODORE PRESSER COMPANY .90
FELTON, W.--ED FELTON, W.
 PLAY WITH PLEASURE -- AN ALBUM FOR THE GROWN-UP PIANO STUDENT
  THEODORE PRESSER COMPANY 2.50
FEMENIA
 MADRID. 5 ESTAMPAS
  ASSOCIATED MUSIC PUBLISHERS, INC. UME 1.50
FENNIMORE
 BITS AND PIECES
  EDWARD B. MARKS MUSIC CORPORATION 01.25
FERGUSON, H.
 FIVE BAGATELLES
  BOOSEY AND HAWKES, INC. 2.75
FERGUSON, H.
 STYLE AND INTERPRETATION, BK. 1
  OXFORD UNIVERSITY PRESS 39.611 3.00
FERGUSON, H.
 STYLE AND INTERPRETATION, BK. 2
  OXFORD UNIVERSITY PRESS 39.612 3.50
FERGUSON, H.
 STYLE AND INTERPRETATION, BK. 3
  OXFORD UNIVERSITY PRESS 39.613 3.00
FERGUSON, H.
 STYLE AND INTERPRETATION, BK. 4
  OXFORD UNIVERSITY PRESS 39.614 3.00
FERGUSON, H.--ED. FERGUSON, H.
 EARLY FRENCH KEYBOARD MUSIC, BK. 1
  OXFORD UNIVERSITY PRESS 39.615 4.00
FERGUSON, H.--ED. FERGUSON, H.
 EARLY FRENCH KEYBOARD MUSIC, BK. 2
  OXFORD UNIVERSITY PRESS 39.616 4.00
FERGUSON, H.--ED. FERGUSON, H.
 EARLY GERMAN KEYBOARD MUSIC, BK. 1
  OXFORD UNIVERSITY PRESS 39.621 4.00
FERGUSON, H.--ED. FERGUSON, H.
 EARLY GERMAN KEYBOARD MUSIC, BK. 2
  OXFORD UNIVERSITY PRESS 39.622 4.00
FERGUSON, H.--ED. FERGUSON, H.
 EARLY ITALIAN KEYBOARD MUSIC, BK. 1
  OXFORD UNIVERSITY PRESS 39.617 4.00
FERGUSON, H.--ED. FERGUSON, H.
 EARLY ITALIAN KEYBOARD MUSIC, BK. 2
  OXFORD UNIVERSITY PRESS 39.618 4.00
FERNANDEZ, O.
 TWO MINIATURES
  PEER SOUTHERN ORGANIZATION 01.00
FERRARI-TRECATE
 CHILDHOOD MEMORIES, SERIES 1
  FRANCO COLOMBO PUBLICATIONS BON.883 .90

FERRARI-TRECATE
 CHILDHOOD MEMORIES, SERIES 2
  FRANCO COLOMBO PUBLICATIONS BON.1557 2.25
FERRARI-TRECATE
 COLLODIANA OR PINOCCHIO AND CO.
  FRANCO COLOMBO PUBLICATIONS BON.2236 1.75
FERRARI-TRECATE
 PICCINO PICCIO - EASY PIECES ON 5 NOTES, SERIES 1
  FRANCO COLOMBO PUBLICATIONS BON.2234 1.50
FERRARI-TRECATE
 PICCINO PICCIO - EASY PIECES ON 5 NOTES, SERIES 2
  FRANCO COLOMBO PUBLICATIONS BON.2236 1.50
FERRARI-TRECATE
 TEATRINO IN MUSICA
  FRANCO COLOMBO PUBLICATIONS BON.1700 2.25
FERROUD, P. O.
 AU PARC MONCEAU - CHAT JOUANT AVEC LES OISEAUX, SUR LE BANC,
 NONCHALANTE, BAMBINS
  FRANCO COLOMBO PUBLICATIONS SAL 5.50
FERROUD, P. O.
 TYPES - VIEUX BEAU, BOURGEOISE DE QUALITE, BUSINESSMAN
  FRANCO COLOMBO PUBLICATIONS SAL 6.50
FERTE   M
 PIANO METHOD
  C. F. PETERS CORPORATION SCH16 3.50
FERTE   M
 PIANO METHOD. FRENCH TEXT
  C. F. PETERS CORPORATION SCH15 3.50
FERTE--ED FERTE E-M
 ANTHOLOGY, VOL. 1# 33 PIECES
  C. F. PETERS CORPORATION SCH41 2.00
FERTE--ED FERTE M
 ANTHOLOGY, VOL. 2. 20 PIECES FOR HARPSICHORD
  C. F. PETERS CORPORATION SCH42 2.00
FERTE--ED FERTE M-D
 ANTHOLOGY, VOL. 3# 16 PIECES FOR HARPSICHORD
  C. F. PETERS CORPORATION SCH43 2.50
FERTE--ED FERTE M
 ANTHOLOGY, VOL. 6# 26 PIECES BY ROMANTIC COMPOSERS
  C. F. PETERS CORPORATION SCH46 2.50
FERTE--ED FERTE E
 PROGRESSIVE STUDIES, VOL. 1
  C. F. PETERS CORPORATION SCH30 2.00
FERTE--ED FERTE E-M
 PROGRESSIVE STUDIES, VOL. 2
  C. F. PETERS CORPORATION SCH31 2.00
FERTE--ED FERTE M
 PROGRESSIVE STUDIES, VOL. 3
  C. F. PETERS CORPORATION SCH32 2.00
FERTE--ED FERTE M
 PROGRESSIVE STUDIES, VOL. 4
  C. F. PETERS CORPORATION SCH33 2.00
FERTE--ED FERTE M
 PROGRESSIVE STUDIES, VOL. 5
  C. F. PETERS CORPORATION SCH34 2.00
FERTE--ED FERTE M
 PROGRESSIVE STUDIES, VOL. 6
  C. F. PETERS CORPORATION SCH35 2.00
FERTE--ED FERTE M-D
 PROGRESSIVE STUDIES, VOL. 7
  C. F. PETERS CORPORATION SCH36 2.00
FERTE--ED FERTE M-D
 PROGRESSIVE STUDIES, VOL. 8
  C. F. PETERS CORPORATION SCH37 2.00
FERTE--ED FERTE E-M
 SELECTED SONATINAS, VOL. 1# 14 SONATINAS
  C. F. PETERS CORPORATION SCH47 2.00
FERTE--ED FERTE M
 SELECTED SONATINAS, VOL. 2# 10 SONATINAS
  C. F. PETERS CORPORATION SCH48 2.00
FERTE--ED FERTE M
 SELECTED SONATINAS, VOL. 3# 8 SONATINAS
  C. F. PETERS CORPORATION SCH49 2.00
FERTE--ED FERTE D
 SPECIAL STUDIES, VOL. 1# 20 STUDIES FOR THE LEFT HAND
  C. F. PETERS CORPORATION SCH38 2.00
FERTE--ED FERTE D
 SPECIAL STUDIES, VOL. 2# 20 STUDIES FOR BOTH HANDS
  C. F. PETERS CORPORATION SCH39 2.00
FERTE--ED FERTE D
 SPECIAL STUDIES, VOL. 3# 20 OCTAVE STUDIES
  C. F. PETERS CORPORATION SCH40 2.00
FEYER, G.
 PIANO ECHOES
  EDWARD B. MARKS MUSIC CORPORATION 01.50
FIBICH, Z.   3
 ALBUM NO. 1 -- 13 STUCKE AUS OP. 41, 44 UND 47 --
  BARENREITER VERLAG AP 588
FIBICH, Z.   2
 ALBUM NO. 2 -- PILGERLIED, MORGENGESPRACHE, FRUHLING UND JUGEND,
 VENETIANISCHES GONDELLIED, LIED OHNE WORTE, ALLEGRETTO, ANDANTE
 INNOCENTE, VIVACE, CAVATINE, VALSE, SONATINE --
  BARENREITER VERLAG AP 589
FIBICH, Z.   3
 ALBUMBLATTER, OP. 2 -- WIDMUNG, FANTASTISCHES STUCK, NORDISCHES
 FISCHERLIED, CAPRICE, EPILOG --
  BARENREITER VERLAG AP 584
FIBICH, Z.   3
 MALERSTUDIEN, OP. 56 -- WALDEINSAMKEIT, DISPUT VON KARNEVAL UND
 FASTEN, TANZ DER GLUCKLICHEN, JO UND JUPITER, GARTENFEST --
  BARENREITER VERLAG AP 587
FIBICH, Z.   4
 MELODRAMEN FUR SPRECHER UND KLAVIER
  BARENREITER VERLAG AP 1694
FIBICH, Z.   3
 STIMMUNGEN, EINDRUCKE UND ERINNERUNGEN, OP. 41, HEFT 1 -- NOS.
 1-44 --
  BARENREITER VERLAG AP 586A
FIBICH, Z.   3
 STIMMUNGEN, EINDRUCKE UND ERINNERUNGEN, OP. 41, HEFT 2 -- NOS.
 45-85 --
  BARENREITER VERLAG AP 586B
FIBICH, Z.   3
 STIMMUNGEN, EINDRUCKE UND ERINNERUNGEN, OP. 41, HEFT 3 -- NOS.
 86-125 --
  BARENREITER VERLAG AP 586C
FIBICH, Z.   3
 STIMMUNGEN, EINDRUCKE UND ERINNERUNGEN, OP. 41, HEFT 4 -- NOS.
 126-171 --
  BARENREITER VERLAG AP 586D
FIBICH, Z.   2-3
 THIRTY-SEVEN UBUNGEN UND ETUDEN -- 2-3 --
  BARENREITER VERLAG AP 594
FIBICH, Z.
 UBUNGEN UND ETUDEN
  BARENREITER VERLAG AP 594

FIBICH, Z.   3
  ZWEI SCHERZI
    BARENREITER VERLAG   AP 593

FICHANDLER, W.
  TEN POLYTONAL COMPOSITIONS FOR PIANO SOLO
    BELWIN-MILLS PUBLISHING CORPORATION   1.25

FICHER
  FIVE PRELUDES, OP. 4
    FRANCO COLOMBO PUBLICATIONS   BA11818   3.25

FIELD, J.   MARCIANO
  EIGHTEEN NOCTURNES
    FRANCO COLOMBO PUBLICATIONS   ER529   3.50

FIELD, J.   LISZT
  EIGHTEEN NOCTURNES
    G. SCHIRMER, INC.   L42   1.75

FIELD, J.
  NINE NOCTURNES
    EDWIN F. KALMUS   3438   1.25

FIELD, J.   M-D
  NOCTURNES, COMPLETE
    C. F. PETERS CORPORATION   491   3.00

FIELDS, I.
  MODERN APPROACH TO POPULAR PLAYING, VOL. 1
    CARL FISCHER, INC.   O 4656   2.00

FIELDS, I.
  MODERN APPROACH TO POPULAR PLAYING, VOL. 2
    CARL FISCHER, INC.   O 4657   2.00

FIEVET, P.
  AU BOIS FLEURI -- 1. CHANTOISEAU, 2. SYLPHIDES
    ELKAN-VOGEL, INC.   CON   2.25

FINE, I.
  MUSIC FOR PIANO
    G. SCHIRMER, INC.   2.00

FINK, M.
  THREE LYRIC PIECES
    E. C. SCHIRMER MUSIC COMPANY   231   01.00

FINKE
  TEN LITTLE PIECES
    ASSOCIATED MUSIC PUBLISHERS, INC.   B/H   2.00

FINLAYSON, W.
  SKETCHES FOR PIANO
    EDWARD B. MARKS MUSIC CORPORATION   01.00

FINNEY   E-M
  THIRTY-TWO PIANO GAMES
    C. F. PETERS CORPORATION   66256   1.50

FIOCCO, J.
  WERKEN VOOR CLAVECIMBEL
    BROUDE BROTHERS LTD.   17.50

FISCHER--ED   FISCHER, HANS *   E-M
  GERMAN KEYBOARD MUSIC OF THE SEVENTEENTH AND EIGHTEENTH
  CENTURIES, VOL. 1 - EASY PIECES OF BOTH CENTURIES
    C. F. PETERS CORPORATION   V120   2.00

FISCHER--ED   FISCHER, HANS *   E-M
  GERMAN KEYBOARD MUSIC OF THE SEVENTEENTH AND EIGHTEENTH
  CENTURIES, VOL. 2 - COMPOSERS OF THE SEVENTEENTH CENTURY
    C. F. PETERS CORPORATION   V121   2.00

FISCHER--ED   FISCHER, HANS *   E-M
  GERMAN KEYBOARD MUSIC OF THE SEVENTEENTH AND EIGHTEENTH
  CENTURIES, VOL. 3# COMPOSERS OF THE EIGHTEENTH CENTURY
    C. F. PETERS CORPORATION   V122   2.00

FISCHER--ED   FISCHER, HANS *   E-M
  GERMAN KEYBOARD MUSIC OF THE SEVENTEENTH AND EIGHTEENTH
  CENTURIES, VOL. 8,9# MUSIC IN BERLIN AT THE TIME OF FREDERICK THE
  GREAT
    C. F. PETERS CORPORATION   V127,V128   2.00

FISCHER, C.
  HARMONIC EXERCISES FOR PIANO
    GWYN PUBLISHING COMPANY   4.50

FISCHER, E.   4
  PITTORESKEN, 4 PIANO-SOLI
    SCHOTT   2523   2.00

FISCHER, E.   4
  SYNKOPEN, 4 PIANO-SOLI
    SCHOTT   2832   2.00

FISCHER, E.   4
  TINTENKLECKSE, 4 PIANO-SOLI
    SCHOTT   2476   2.00

FISCHER, H.   TOWNSEND
  ARIADNE MUSICA --PRELUDES AND FUGUES FOR PIANO OR ORGAN
    SAM FOX PUBLISHING COMPANY, INC.   2.50

FISCHER, H.   E
  EASY PIANO MUSIC OF OLD MASTERS
    C. F. PETERS CORPORATION   V129   2.00

FISCHER, H.
  FISCHER'S FIRST PIANO BOOK, PART 1
    BELWIN-MILLS PUBLISHING CORPORATION   1.25

FISCHER, H.
  FISCHER'S FIRST PIANO BOOK, PART 2
    BELWIN-MILLS PUBLISHING CORPORATION   1.25

FISCHER, J.   DOFLEIN   3
  AUSGEWAHLTE KLAVIERWERKE
    SCHOTT   2479   2.25

FISCHER, J. *   DOFLEIN   2
  FUGENBUCHLEIN. 17 KLEINE FUGEN
    BARENREITER VERLAG   BA 1007

FISCHER, J.   LUDWIG   2
  NOTENBUCHLEIN
    SCHOTT   3770   1.50

FISCHER, J.
  SAEMTLICHE WERKE FUER KLAVIER UND ORGEL
    BROUDE BROTHERS LTD.   25.00

FISHER--ED   FISHER   M
  BIRDS
    C. F. PETERS CORPORATION   H497   1.50

FISHER, A.
  SIX APHORISMS FOR THE PIANO
    COMPOSERS AUTOGRAPH PUBLICATIONS   3.52

FISK
  KEYBOARD FUNDAMENTALS - BOOK 1
    BOSTON MUSIC COMPANY   3.00

FISK
  KEYBOARD FUNDAMENTALS - BOOK 2
    BOSTON MUSIC COMPANY   1.50

FISK
  KEYBOARD FUNDAMENTALS - BOOK 3
    BOSTON MUSIC COMPANY   1.50

FISK
  KEYBOARD FUNDAMENTALS - TEACHER'S MANUAL
    BOSTON MUSIC COMPANY   1.25

FITCH, J.
  OUTSIDE-INSIDE PIECES
    THEODORE PRESSER COMPANY   1.25

FITELBERG
  THREE MAZURKAS
    FRANCO COLOMBO PUBLICATIONS   SAL   3.50

FLAGELLO, N.
  EPISODES
    GENERAL MUSIC PUBLISHING COMPANY, INC.   51   2.00

FLAGELLO, N.
  PETITS PASTELS - SEVEN DRAWINGS FOR THE YOUNG PIANIST
    GENERAL MUSIC PUBLISHING COMPANY, INC.   530   2.00

FLAGELLO, N.
  PETITS PASTELS - SEVEN DRAWINGS FOR YOUNG PIANISTS
    GENERAL MUSIC PUBLISHING COMPANY, INC.   2.00

FLAGELLO, N.
  THREE DANCES
    GENERAL MUSIC PUBLISHING COMPANY, INC.   63   .60

FLAMMER--ED   FLAMMER   GR. 2-3
  BLUE RIBBON PIANO ALBUM
    SHAWNEE PRESS, INC.   1.25

FLAXLAND
  ALBUM DE CORINNE
    FRANCO COLOMBO PUBLICATIONS   SAL   4.25

FLETCHER
  MUSIC LESSONS HAVE BEGUN
    BOSTON MUSIC COMPANY   1.25

FLETCHER
  STREET SCENES
    SUMMY-BIRCHARD COMPANY   1.25

FLETCHER
  THEORY PAPERS - VOLUME 1
    BOSTON MUSIC COMPANY   1.00

FLETCHER
  THEORY PAPERS - VOLUME 2
    BOSTON MUSIC COMPANY   1.00

FLETCHER
  THEORY PAPERS - VOLUME 3
    BOSTON MUSIC COMPANY   1.00

FLETCHER, L.--ED   FLETCHER, L.
  FOX POPULAR SONG FAVORITES
    SAM FOX PUBLISHING COMPANY, INC.   1.25

FLETCHER, S.
  TECHNIC KNACKS
    PEER SOUTHERN ORGANIZATION   01.25

FLOOD
  RELATIVE TALE OF TRIAD AND SCALE, THE, OP. 20
    FRANCO COLOMBO PUBLICATIONS   NY1624   1.00

FLOSSMAN   3
  DREI TSCHECHISCHE TANZE
    BARENREITER VERLAG   AP 595

FLOTHIUS   E
  TEN EASY PIECES
    C. F. PETERS CORPORATION   D206   1.25

FLOYD, C.
  EPISODES, BK. 1
    BOOSEY AND HAWKES, INC.   1.50

FLOYD, C.
  EPISODES, BK. 2
    BOOSEY AND HAWKES, INC.   1.50

FOERSTER   SOLC   3
  ZWEI TANZE AUS DER OPER 'EVA' -- SOUSEDSKA/POLKA -- FUR KLAVIER
  BEARBEITET
    BARENREITER VERLAG   AP 1719

FONRAT
  TRADITIONAL DANCES OF SPAIN
    FRANCO COLOMBO PUBLICATIONS   BA9330   2.50

FONT Y DE ANTA
  ANDALUCIA. SUITE -- VOL. 1
    ASSOCIATED MUSIC PUBLISHERS, INC.   UME   2.00

FONT Y DE ANTA
  ANDALUCIA. SUITE -- VOL. 2
    ASSOCIATED MUSIC PUBLISHERS, INC.   UME   2.00

FONT Y DE ANTA
  ANDALUCIA. SUITE -- VOL. 3
    ASSOCIATED MUSIC PUBLISHERS, INC.   UME   2.00

FONTRIERE, G.
  LITTLE SUITE FOR PIANO
    GENERAL MUSIC PUBLISHING COMPANY, INC.   61   1.50

FORD, T. E.
  POINTER LIBRARY - A TREASURY OF INSPIRATIONAL SONGS
    POINTER PUBLICATIONS   2.95

FORD, T. E.
  TREASURY OF INSPIRATIONAL SONGS
    POINTER PUBLICATIONS   4.95

FORLIVESI
  FIVE CHRISTMAS SONGS
    FRANCO COLOMBO PUBLICATIONS   FOR.12160   1.00

FORNUTO
  JAZZ-ROCK STUDIES -- THE BLOCK-CHORD STYLE
    LEE ROBERTS MUSIC PUBLICATIONS, INC.   1.25

FORNUTO
  TRICKS WITH TRIADS, SET 1
    LEE ROBERTS MUSIC PUBLICATIONS, INC.   1.25

FORNUTO
  TRICKS WITH TRIADS, SET 2
    LEE ROBERTS MUSIC PUBLICATIONS, INC.   1.25

FORNUTO
  TRICKS WITH TRIADS, SET 3 -- A LA MODE
    LEE ROBERTS MUSIC PUBLICATIONS, INC.   2.50

FORTNER, W.   6
  SIEBEN ELEGIEN
    SCHOTT   4191   2.75

FOSTER   MALOOF
  FOSTER MELODIES FOR YOUNG FOLKS
    EDWARD B. MARKS MUSIC CORPORATION   01.00

FOSTER   SCHAUM, J.   1
  STEPHEN FOSTER FAVORITES
    SCHAUM PUBLICATIONS, INC.   1.25

FOSTER   SCHAUM, J.   1
  STEPHEN FOSTER FAVORITES
    SCHAUM PUBLICATIONS, INC.   1.25

FOSTER   SAMMASTINO
  TEN POPULAR SONGS
    FRANCO COLOMBO PUBLICATIONS   BA8815   1.50

FOUTS, M.
  FUN ON THE KEYS--47 EASY PIANO PIECES
    G. SCHIRMER, INC.   1.25

FOX
  DIGEST OF PIANO PIECES FOR LEFT HAND ALONE
    BOSTON MUSIC COMPANY   1.00

FRACKENPOHL, A.
  THREE MINIATURES
    ELKAN-VOGEL, INC.   1.00

FRANCAIX, J.   5
  CINQ 'BIS' -- FUNF ZUGABEN, 1965
    SCHOTT   5826   2.50

FRANCAIX, J.
  FIVE ETUDES
    FRANCO COLOMBO PUBLICATIONS   SAL   4.25

FRANCAIX, J.   5
  FUNF PORTRAITS
    SCHOTT   2483   3.00

FRANCAIX, J.
  MON RECITAL
    FRANCO COLOMBO PUBLICATIONS   SAL   3.25

FRANCAIX, J.
  POLYMELODIE PREPARATOIRE
      FRANCO COLOMBO PUBLICATIONS   SAL   5.75
FRANCESCHI
  FANCIULLEZZA, BK. 1
      FRANCO COLOMBO PUBLICATIONS   FOR.11020   1.50
FRANCESCHI
  FANCIULLEZZA, BK. 2
      FRANCO COLOMBO PUBLICATIONS   FOR.11021   1.50
FRANCESCHI
  SIX SONATINAS
      FRANCO COLOMBO PUBLICATIONS   FOR.12049   1.50
FRANCHETTI
  THREE INVENTIONS
      FRANCO COLOMBO PUBLICATIONS   BON.2399   1.75
FRANCISQUE, A.
  LE TRESOR D'ORPHEE
      BROUDE BROTHERS LTD.   09.00
FRANCK, C.   AGAY, D.
  FORTY-SIX SHORT PIECES FOR PIANO
      THEODORE PRESSER COMPANY   2.50
FRANCK, C.   5
  PRALUDIUM, ARIE UND FINALE
      SCHOTT   08864-5   1.75
FRANCK, C.   WERNER
  SEVEN TRADITIONAL FRENCH NOELS
      G. SCHIRMER, INC.   1.00
FRANCK, C.   E
  SHORT PIECES --18--
      C. F. PETERS CORPORATION   4529   1.25
FRANK--ED.   FRANK
  HITS OF TODAY--EASY PIANO-- SERIES 2
      MCA MUSIC   1.25
FRANK--ED.   FRANK
  HITS OF TODAY--EASY PIANO-- SERIES 3
      MCA MUSIC   1.50
FRANK, R.
  PIANO HYMN CLASSICS NO. 1
      LILLENAS PUBLISHING COMPANY   MB-146   2.50
FRANK, R.
  PIANO HYMN CLASSICS NO. 2
      LILLENAS PUBLISHING COMPANY   MB-147   2.50
FRANKLIN, A.
  READING WITH ACES IS EASY
      THEODORE PRESSER COMPANY   .85
FREDRICH, F.
  FIRST WORKBOOK OF SCALES AND CHORDS
      WILLIS MUSIC COMPANY   1.00
FREDRICH, F.
  MAKING MUSIC AT THE PIANO - BOOK 1
      PRO-ART PUBLICATIONS, INC.   183   .85
FREDRICH, F.
  MAKING MUSIC AT THE PIANO - BOOK 2
      PRO-ART PUBLICATIONS, INC.   184   .85
FREDRICH, F.
  MAKING SURE OF PIANO PLAY
      PRO-ART PUBLICATIONS, INC.   186   .60
FREDRICH, F.
  MUSIC READER - BOOK 1
      PRO-ART PUBLICATIONS, INC.   185   1.00
FREDRICH, F.
  MUSIC READER - BOOK 2
      PRO-ART PUBLICATIONS, INC.   260   .85
FREDRICH, F.
  OCCASIONS
      SUMMY-BIRCHARD COMPANY   1.50
FREDRICH, F.--ED   FREDRICH, F.
  FIRST BOOK OF HYMNS AND CAROLS, A
      WILLIS MUSIC COMPANY   1.00
FREDRICH, F.--ED.
  CAROLS FOR CHRISTMAS
      PRO-ART PUBLICATIONS, INC.   125   1.25
FREED
  FIRST YEAR ESSENTIALS
      CARL FISCHER, INC.   O 2368   1.50
FREED--ED.   FREED
  AMERICAN MUSIC BY DISTINGUISHED COMPOSERS, BK. 1 --EARLY
  GRADES--
      THEODORE PRESSER COMPANY   1.50
FREED--ED.   FREED
  AMERICAN MUSIC BY DISTINGUISHED COMPOSERS, BK. 2 --MEDIUM
  GRADES--
      THEODORE PRESSER COMPANY   2.00
FREED, I.
  FIVE PIECES -- 1928-30 --
      ASSOCIATED MUSIC PUBLISHERS, INC.   ESC   2.75
FREED, I.
  PASTORALES. EIGHT PIECES
      ASSOCIATED MUSIC PUBLISHERS, INC.   ESC   3.75
FREMONT, R.--ED.   FREMONT, R.
  FAVORITE SONGS OF THE NINETIES
      DOVER PUBLICATIONS, INC.   21536-9   5.95
FRESCOBALDI   PICCIOLI
  COMPOSITIONS -- ORGAN --
      FRANCO COLOMBO PUBLICATIONS   BON.1835   3.00
FRESCOBALDI   PIDOUX, P.
  ORGAN AND KEYBOARD WORKS, COMPLETE , BK. 1
      BARENREITER VERLAG   BA 2201   6.50
FRESCOBALDI   PIDOUX, P.
  ORGAN AND KEYBOARD WORKS, COMPLETE , BK. 2
      BARENREITER VERLAG   BA 2202   7.50
FRESCOBALDI   PIDOUX, P.
  ORGAN AND KEYBOARD WORKS, COMPLETE , BK. 3
      BARENREITER VERLAG   BA 2203   7.50
FRESCOBALDI   PIDOUX, P.
  ORGAN AND KEYBOARD WORKS, COMPLETE , BK. 4
      BARENREITER VERLAG   BA 2204   7.5 0
FRESCOBALDI   PIDOUX, P.
  ORGAN AND KEYBOARD WORKS, COMPLETE , BK. 5
      BARENREITER VERLAG   BA 2205   6.5 0
FRESCOBALDI   PIDOUX, P.   3
  ORGEL- UND KLAVIER-WERKE. GESAMTAUSGABE NACH DEM URTEXT, BAND 1
  - 23 FANTASIEN UND CANZONI ALLA FRANCESE
      BARENREITER VERLAG   BA 2201
FRESCOBALDI   PIDOUX, P.   3
  ORGEL- UND KLAVIER-WERKE. GESAMTAUSGABE NACH DEM URTEXT, BAND 2
  - 12 CAPRICCI, 10 RICERCARI UND 5 CANZONI
      BARENREITER VERLAG   BA 2202
FRESCOBALDI   PIDOUX, P.   3
  ORGEL- UND KLAVIER-WERKE. GESAMTAUSGABE NACH DEM URTEXT, BAND 3
  - 12 TOCCATEN, PARTITEN SOPRA L'ARIE DELLA ROMANESCA, DI MONICHA,
  DI RUGGIERO, DI FOLLIA, 4 CORRENTEN, 3 BALLETTI, CENTO PARTITE
      BARENREITER VERLAG   BA 2203
FRESCOBALDI   PIDOUX, P.   3
  ORGEL- UND KLAVIER-WERKE. GESAMTAUSGABE NACH DEM URTEXT, BAND 4
  - 11 TOCCATEN, 6 CANZONEN, 3 HYMNEN, 3 MAGNIFICAT, MADRIGAL VON
  D'ARCADELT, ARIA DETTA BALLETTO, 5 GAGLIARDEN, ARIA DETTA LA
      BARENREITER VERLAG   BA 2204

FRESCOBALDI   PIDOUX, P.   3
  ORGEL- UND KLAVIER-WERKE. GESAMTAUSGABE NACH DEM URTEXT, BAND 5
  - FIORI MUSICALI -- 3 ORGELMESSEN MANUALITER, 'ORBIS FACTOR',
  'CONCTIPOTENS GENITOR DEUS', 'CUM JUBILO' --
      BARENREITER VERLAG   BA 2205
FRESCOBALDI
  PARTITAS, 1, 2
      EDWIN F. KALMUS   3453   3.00
FRESCOBALDI
  TOCCATAS
      EDWIN F. KALMUS   3452   3.00
FRESCOBALDI   GERMANI
  TOCCATAS, BK. 1
      FRANCO COLOMBO PUBLICATIONS   DS451   4.00
FRESCOBALDI   GERMANI
  TOCCATAS, BK. 2
      FRANCO COLOMBO PUBLICATIONS   DS491   4.00
FREY   1
  IM FLUG, BK. 1
      SCHOTT   2510   2.00
FREY   2-3
  IM FLUG, BK. 2
      SCHOTT   2894   2.00
FREY   2
  KLAVIER GESCHICHTEN AM KLAVIER
      SCHOTT   3973   2.00
FREY   E
  RECREATION --12 EASY PIECES--, OP. 77
      C. F. PETERS CORPORATION   3964   2.00
FREY   E
  RECREATION, OP. 78
      C. F. PETERS CORPORATION   4332   2.00
FREY
  SEVEN DANCES
      ASSOCIATED MUSIC PUBLISHERS, INC.   LEU   1.25
FREY--ED   FREY
  AGE OF CHIVALRY, THE -- 29 18TH-CENTURY DANCES
      ASSOCIATED MUSIC PUBLISHERS, INC.   SIM   1.00
FREY--ED   FREY
  CHILDREN'S BOOK
      MUSIC SALES CORPORATION   040008   2.95
FREY--ED   FREY   E-M
  CONTEMPORARIES OF TELEMAN
      C. F. PETERS CORPORATION   4305   2.00
FREY--ED   FREY
  MASTERS OF THE ROCOCO, BK. 1 -- WORKS BY COUPERIN, DANDRIEU,
  DESTOUCHES, LULLY, MARAIS, RAMEAU AND ROYER
      ASSOCIATED MUSIC PUBLISHERS, INC.   SIM   2.00
FREY--ED   FREY
  MASTERS OF THE ROCOCO, BK. 2 -- WORKS BY COUPERIN, DANDRIEU,
  DESTOUCHES, LULLY, MARAIS, RAMEAU AND ROYER
      ASSOCIATED MUSIC PUBLISHERS, INC.   SIM   2.00
FREY--ED   FREY   2
  NEUES SONATINBUCH -- VORSTUFE
      SCHOTT   2891   2.50
FREY--ED   FREY   2-3
  NEUES SONATINENBUCH -- BK. 1
      SCHOTT   2511   4.00
FREY--ED   FREY   2-3
  NEUES SONATINENBUCH -- BK. 2
      SCHOTT   2512   4.00
FREY--ED   FREY
  SIMPLIFIED PIANO PIECES
      MUSIC SALES CORPORATION   040009   2.95
FREY--ED   FREY   3-4
  SONATENBUCH DER VORKLASSIK
      SCHOTT   3975   5.00
FREY--ED   FREY
  WORLD FAMOUS PIANO CLASSICS
      MUSIC SALES CORPORATION   040004   2.95
FREY--ED   FREY
  WORLD FAMOUS PIANO PIECES
      MUSIC SALES CORPORATION   040001   2.95
FRIBOULET
  FOUR PIECES
      FRANCO COLOMBO PUBLICATIONS   SAL   4.00
FRIBOULET
  THREE PIECES BREVES
      FRANCO COLOMBO PUBLICATIONS   SAL   2.75
FRICKER, P.   5
  VIER IMPROMPTUS, OP. 17
      SCHOTT   10246   1.75
FRICKER, P.   6
  ZWOLF STUDIEN, OP. 38
      SCHOTT   10804   4.25
FRICKERT--ED   FRICKERT
  EASY MINIATURES -- 21 PIECES BY FRANCK, SCHUMANN, KABALEVSKY,
  TSCHAIKOVSKY AND OTHERS
      ASSOCIATED MUSIC PUBLISHERS, INC.   SIM   3.00
FRIEDMAN   GARTNER
  SIX VIENNESE DANCES
      UNIVERSAL EDITION   8585   3.65
FRIML, R.   LEVINE
  ALBUM OF RUDOLF FRIML, AN
      G. SCHIRMER, INC.   1.25
FRIML, R.   LANGEY
  FIREFLY WALTZES, THE--''THE FIREFLY''
      G. SCHIRMER, INC.   1.00
FRIML, R.
  MUSICAL ADVENTURES FOR FOUR LITTLE HANDS
      WILLIS MUSIC COMPANY   .80
FRIML, R.
  SELECTIONS FROM ''GLORIANNA''
      G. SCHIRMER, INC.   1.00
FRIML, R.   KIEFERT
  SELECTIONS FROM ''KATINKA''
      G. SCHIRMER, INC.   .75
FRIML, R.   BARTLETT
  SELECTIONS FROM ''THE FIREFLY''
      G. SCHIRMER, INC.   1.50
FRISCH, F. T.
  BY MYSELF, BK. 1
      ASHLEY DEALERS SERVICE, INC.   1.00
FRISCH, F. T.
  BY MYSELF, BK. 2
      ASHLEY DEALERS SERVICE, INC.   1.00
FRISCH, F. T.
  FUN ALL DAY -- INTRODUCTORY BOOK
      ASHLEY DEALERS SERVICE, INC.   1.00
FRISCH, F. T.
  HAPPY PLAYING, BK. 1
      ASHLEY DEALERS SERVICE, INC.   1.00
FRISCH, F. T.
  PLAY ALONG, BK. 3
      ASHLEY DEALERS SERVICE, INC.   1.00
FRISCH, F. T.
  PLAY-WAY TO MUSIC SERIES - BY MYSELF, BOOK 1
      CENTURY MUSIC PUBLISHING COMPANY, INC.   1.00

FRISCH, F. T.
  PLAY-WAY TO MUSIC SERIES - BY MYSELF, BOOK 2
    CENTURY MUSIC PUBLISHING COMPANY, INC.   1.00
FRISCH, F. T.
  PLAY-WAY TO MUSIC SERIES - FUN ALL DAY, INTRODUCTORY BOOK
    CENTURY MUSIC PUBLISHING COMPANY, INC.   1.00
FRISCH, F. T.
  PLAY-WAY TO MUSIC SERIES - HAPPY PLAYING, BOOK 1
    CENTURY MUSIC PUBLISHING COMPANY, INC.   1.00
FRISCH, F. T.
  PLAY-WAY TO MUSIC SERIES - PLAY ALONG, BOOK 3
    CENTURY MUSIC PUBLISHING COMPANY, INC.   1.00
FRISCH, F. T.
  PLAY-WAY TO MUSIC SERIES - SEE AND PLAY, BOOK 4
    CENTURY MUSIC PUBLISHING COMPANY, INC.   1.00
FRISCH, F. T.
  PLAY-WAY TO MUSIC SERIES - SKIP ALONG, BOOK 2
    CENTURY MUSIC PUBLISHING COMPANY, INC.   1.00
FRISCH, F. T.
  SEE AND PLAY, BK. 4
    ASHLEY DEALERS SERVICE, INC.   1.00
FRISCH, F. T.
  SKIP ALONG, BK. 2
    ASHLEY DEALERS SERVICE, INC.   1.00
FRISKIN--ED   FRISKIN
  TWELVE SELECTED SONATAS FOR PIANO, BK. 01
    BELWIN-MILLS PUBLISHING CORPORATION   2.00
FRISKIN--ED   FRISKIN
  TWELVE SELECTED SONATAS FOR PIANO, BK. 02
    BELWIN-MILLS PUBLISHING CORPORATION   2.00
FROBERGER   SCHUBERT   3
  AUSGEWAHLTE KLAVIERWERKE
    SCHOTT   2356   2.25
FROBERGER   DARVAS   E-M
  FIVE SELECTED PIECES
    C. F. PETERS CORPORATION   Z455   2.00
FROBERGER
  NINE PIECES
    EDWIN F. KALMUS   3454   2.50
FROBERGER   M-D
  SELECTED KEYBOARD WORKS
    C. F. PETERS CORPORATION   4407A   2.50
FROST
  ADULT AT THE PIANO, THE - BOOK 1
    BOSTON MUSIC COMPANY   1.25
FROST
  ADULT AT THE PIANO, THE - BOOK 2
    BOSTON MUSIC COMPANY   1.25
FROST
  ADULT AT THE PIANO, THE - BOOK 3
    BOSTON MUSIC COMPANY   1.25
FROST
  AT THE PIANO - BOOK 1
    BOSTON MUSIC COMPANY   1.50
FROST
  AT THE PIANO - BOOK 2
    BOSTON MUSIC COMPANY   2.00
FROST
  AT THE PIANO - BOOK 3
    BOSTON MUSIC COMPANY   2.50
FROST
  AT THE PIANO - BOOK 4
    BOSTON MUSIC COMPANY   2.25
FROST
  BEGINNING AT THE PIANO
    BOSTON MUSIC COMPANY   1.00
FROST
  CHRISTMAS CAROLS
    BELWIN-MILLS PUBLISHING CORPORATION   1.00
FROST
  CLASSICS FOR PIANO, BK. 1
    BELWIN-MILLS PUBLISHING CORPORATION   2.00
FROST
  CLASSICS FOR PIANO, BK. 2
    BELWIN-MILLS PUBLISHING CORPORATION   2.00
FROST
  COMPANION SERIES - BOOK 1
    BOSTON MUSIC COMPANY   1.25
FROST
  COMPANION SERIES - BOOK 2
    BOSTON MUSIC COMPANY   1.50
FROST
  COMPANION SERIES - PREPARATORY
    BOSTON MUSIC COMPANY   1.25
FROST
  FOUR SONATINAS
    BELWIN-MILLS PUBLISHING CORPORATION   1.50
FROST
  PIANO REPERTOIRE
    BELWIN-MILLS PUBLISHING CORPORATION   3.00
FROST
  PLAY THE PIANO
    BELWIN-MILLS PUBLISHING CORPORATION   1.25
FROST
  SIX SONATAS
    BELWIN-MILLS PUBLISHING CORPORATION   1.50
FROST
  SIX SONATAS FOR PIANO
    BELWIN-MILLS PUBLISHING CORPORATION   2.50
FROST
  SOLO TECHNIC BOOK
    BOSTON MUSIC COMPANY   1.00
FROST
  WHERE PLAYING FINGERS BEGIN
    BOSTON MUSIC COMPANY   1.25
FROST--ED   FROST
  TWENTIETH CENTURY PIANO MUSIC, BK. 1A
    BELWIN-MILLS PUBLISHING CORPORATION   1.25
FROST--ED   FROST
  TWENTIETH CENTURY PIANO MUSIC, BK. 1B
    BELWIN-MILLS PUBLISHING CORPORATION   1.25
FROST--ED   FROST
  TWENTIETH CENTURY PIANO MUSIC, BK. 2A
    BELWIN-MILLS PUBLISHING CORPORATION   1.25
FROST--ED   FROST
  TWENTIETH CENTURY PIANO MUSIC, BK. 2B
    BELWIN-MILLS PUBLISHING CORPORATION   1.25
FROST--ED   FROST
  TWENTIETH CENTURY PIANO MUSIC, BK. 3A
    BELWIN-MILLS PUBLISHING CORPORATION   1.25
FROST--ED   FROST
  TWENTIETH CENTURY PIANO MUSIC, BK. 3B
    BELWIN-MILLS PUBLISHING CORPORATION   1.25
FRUGATTA
  TOUCH - EXERCISES ON 5 NOTES, BK. 1
    FRANCO COLOMBO PUBLICATIONS   ER2416   .90

FRUGATTA
  TOUCH - EXERCISES ON 5 NOTES, BK. 2
    FRANCO COLOMBO PUBLICATIONS   ER2417   .75
FRYER, H.--ED   FRYER, H.   1-2
  COURSE OF PIANO STUDIES -- SELECTED AND GRADED BY HERBERT FRYER
  FROM THE WORKS OF BERTINI, BRUNNER, CHOPIN, CLEMENTI, CRAMER,
  CZERNY, DUVERNOY, KALKBRENNER, KOHLER, LEMOINE, MOSCHELES, MOZART
    NOVELLO AND COMPANY, LTD.   11.0017.03 1.25
FRYER, H.--ED   FRYER, H.   5
  COURSE OF PIANO STUDIES -- SELECTED AND GRADED BY HERBERT FRYER
  FROM THE WORKS OF BERTINI, BRUNNER, CHOPIN, CLEMENTI, CRAMER,
  CZERNY, DUVERNOY, KALKBRENNER, KOHLER, LEMOINE, MOSCHELES, MOZART
    NOVELLO AND COMPANY, LTD.   11.0018.01 1.25
FRYER, H.--ED   FRYER, H.   6
  COURSE OF PIANO STUDIES -- SELECTED AND GRADED BY HERBERT FRYER
  FROM THE WORKS OF BERTINI, BRUNNER, CHOPIN, CLEMENTI, CRAMER,
  CZERNY, DUVERNOY, KALKBRENNER, KOHLER, LEMOINE, MOSCHELES, MOZART
    NOVELLO AND COMPANY, LTD.   11.0019.10 1.25
FRYER, H.--ED   FRYER, H.   7
  COURSE OF PIANO STUDIES -- SELECTED AND GRADED BY HERBERT FRYER
  FROM THE WORKS OF BERTINI, BRUNNER, CHOPIN, CLEMENTI, CRAMER,
  CZERNY, DUVERNOY, KALKBRENNER, KOHLER, LEMOINE, MOSCHELES, MOZART
    NOVELLO AND COMPANY, LTD.   11.0020.03 1.25
FRYER, H.--ED   FRYER, H.   7
  COURSE OF PIANO STUDIES -- SELECTED AND GRADED BY HERBERT FRYER
  FROM THE WORKS OF BERTINI, BRUNNER, CHOPIN, CLEMENTI, CRAMER,
  CZERNY, DUVERNOY, KALKBRENNER, KOHLER, LEMOINE, MOSCHELES, MOZART
    NOVELLO AND COMPANY, LTD.   11.0021.01 1.25
FRYER, H.--ED   FRYER, H.   8
  COURSE OF PIANO STUDIES -- SELECTED AND GRADED BY HERBERT FRYER
  FROM THE WORKS OF BERTINI, BRUNNER, CHOPIN, CLEMENTI, CRAMER,
  CZERNY, DUVERNOY, KALKBRENNER, KOHLER, LEMOINE, MOSCHELES, MOZART
    NOVELLO AND COMPANY, LTD.   11.0130.07 1.25
FRYER, H.--ED   FRYER, H.   8
  COURSE OF PIANO STUDIES -- SELECTED AND GRADED BY HERBERT FRYER
  FROM THE WORKS OF BERTINI, BRUNNER, CHOPIN, CLEMENTI, CRAMER,
  CZERNY, DUVERNOY, KALKBRENNER, KOHLER, LEMOINE, MOSCHELES, MOZART
    NOVELLO AND COMPANY, LTD.   11.0131.05 1.25
FUGAZZA
  SIX VERY EASY PIECES
    FRANCO COLOMBO PUBLICATIONS   129132   .90
FULEIHAN, A.
  AROUND THE CLOCK
    PEER SOUTHERN ORGANIZATION   01.25
FULEIHAN, A.
  FIVE TRIBUTES
    PEER SOUTHERN ORGANIZATION   02.00
FULEIHAN, A.
  FIVE VERY SHORT PIECES
    PEER SOUTHERN ORGANIZATION   00.75
FULEIHAN, A.
  FOOT IN THE DOOR, A
    BOSTON MUSIC COMPANY   1.75
FULEIHAN, A.
  FROM THE AEGEAN
    PEER SOUTHERN ORGANIZATION   01.25
FULEIHAN, A.
  NOT FOR SQUARES
    BOSTON MUSIC COMPANY   1.00
FULEIHAN, A.
  SEVEN SUPPLEMENTARY EXERCISES
    PEER SOUTHERN ORGANIZATION   00.85
FULLER *   FULLER-MAITLAND *
  FITZWILLIAM VIRGINAL BOOK, BK. 1
    ASSOCIATED MUSIC PUBLISHERS, INC.   BRH   2.50
FULLER *   FULLER-MAITLAND *
  FITZWILLIAM VIRGINAL BOOK, BK. 2
    ASSOCIATED MUSIC PUBLISHERS, INC.   BRH   2.50
FULLER
  KEYBOARD MODULATIONS
    PRO-ART PUBLICATIONS, INC.   780   3.00
FULLER
  SERVICE INTERLUDES
    PRO-ART PUBLICATIONS, INC.   931   1.25
FULLER-MAITLAND--ED   FULLER-MAITLAND
  FITZWILLIAM VIRGINAL BOOK
    DOVER PUBLICATIONS, INC.   21068-5,   10.00
FUMET
  SIX ETUDES CARACTERISTIQUES DE HAUTE TECHNIQUE MUSICALE
    FRANCO COLOMBO PUBLICATIONS   SAL   6.50
FUX   SCHENK
  THREE PIECES
    ASSOCIATED MUSIC PUBLISHERS, INC.   OBV   .80
FUX   SCHENK
  TWELVE MINUETS
    ASSOCIATED MUSIC PUBLISHERS, INC.   OBV   .70
FUX   RIEDEL   3
  WERKE FUR TASTENINSTRUMENTE -- PARTHIEN IN A MINOR, F, A, G,
  OUVERTURE IN G, CAPRICCIO IN G MINOR, CIACONNA IN D, HARPEGGIO IN
  G, 12 MENUETTE --
    BARENREITER VERLAG
GABRIELI, A.   PIDOUX, P.
  ORGAN AND KEYBOARD WORKS, BK. 1
    BARENREITER VERLAG   BA 1779   4.50
GABRIELI, A.   PIDOUX, P.
  ORGAN AND KEYBOARD WORKS, BK. 2
    BARENREITER VERLAG   BA 1780   4.50
GABRIELI, A.   PIDOUX, P.
  ORGAN AND KEYBOARD WORKS, BK. 3
    BARENREITER VERLAG   BA 1781   4.50
GABRIELI, A.   PIDOUX, P.
  ORGAN AND KEYBOARD WORKS, BK. 4
    BARENREITER VERLAG   BA 1782   4.50
GABRIELI, A.   PIDOUX, P.
  ORGAN AND KEYBOARD WORKS, BK. 5
    BARENREITER VERLAG   BA 1783   4.50
GABRIELI, A.   PIDOUX, P.   3
  ORGEL- UND KLAVIER-WERKE, BAND 1 - INTONATIONEN
    BARENREITER VERLAG   BA 1779
GABRIELI, A.   PIDOUX, P.   1
  ORGEL- UND KLAVIER-WERKE, BAND 2 - 9 RICERCARI
    BARENREITER VERLAG   BA 1780
GABRIELI, A.   PIDOUX, P.   3
  ORGEL- UND KLAVIER-WERKE, BAND 3 - RICERCARI 2
    BARENREITER VERLAG   BA 1781
GABRIELI, A.   PIDOUX, P.   3
  ORGEL- UND KLAVIER-WERKE, BAND 4 - CANZONEN UND RICERCARI ARIOSO
    BARENREITER VERLAG   BA 1782
GABRIELI, A.   PIDOUX, P.   3
  ORGEL- UND KLAVIER-WERKE, BAND 5 - CANZONI ALLA FRANCESE
    BARENREITER VERLAG   BA 1783
GABSCHUSS--ED   GABSCHUSS
  KINDERLIEDER UND VOLKSLIEDER FUR DEN SYSTHEMATISCHEN UNTERRICHT
  AM KLAVIER
    SCHOTT   6150

GAGNEBIN
    NOEL NOEL - 6 PIECES FOR CHILDREN
        FRANCO COLOMBO PUBLICATIONS   129587   1.00
GAGNEUR
    PETIT ALBUM FACILE
        FRANCO COLOMBO PUBLICATIONS   SAL   2.50
GAGNEUR
    TWO POEMES
        FRANCO COLOMBO PUBLICATIONS   SAL   2.75
GAHM--ED.   GAHM
    SACRED PIANO ALBUM
        CARL FISCHER, INC.   O 2618   1.50
GAITO
    ALBUM FOR THE YOUNG, OP. 21, BK. 1
        FRANCO COLOMBO PUBLICATIONS   BA5018   1.50
GAITO
    ALBUM FOR THE YOUNG, OP. 21, BK. 2
        FRANCO COLOMBO PUBLICATIONS   BA5025   1.50
GAITO
    ALBUM FOR THE YOUNG, OP. 21, BK. 3
        FRANCO COLOMBO PUBLICATIONS   BA5026   1.50
GAITO
    CIUDAD DE LAS PUERTAS DE ORO, LA -- BALLET, WITH CHORUS --
        FRANCO COLOMBO PUBLICATIONS   BA9240   3.25
GAITO
    THREE CREOLE DANCES
        FRANCO COLOMBO PUBLICATIONS   BA8069   1.00
GAL, H.
    TWENTY-FOUR PRELUDES, BK. 1, NOS. 1-12
        UNIVERSAL EDITION   UE 12998   3.35
GAL, H.
    TWENTY-FOUR PRELUDES, BK. 2, NOS. 13-24
        UNIVERSAL EDITION   UE 12999   3.35
GALINDO, B.
    CINCO PRELUDIOS
        EDICIONES MEXICANAS DE MUSICA, A. C.   02.50
GALINDO, B.
    SIETE PIEZAS
        EDICIONES MEXICANAS DE MUSICA, A. C.   02.00
GALLON, J.
    TWO ETUDES -- C MAJOR AND A MINOR --
        FRANCO COLOMBO PUBLICATIONS   SAL   2.50
GALLON, J.
    TWO SHORT ETUDES -- F MAJOR AND G MAJOR --
        FRANCO COLOMBO PUBLICATIONS   SAL   2.50
GALLUZZI
    RECREATIONAL PIECES, BK. 2
        FRANCO COLOMBO PUBLICATIONS   ER41   1.50
GALLUZZI
    RECREATIONAL PIECES, BK. 2
        FRANCO COLOMBO PUBLICATIONS   ER519   2.50
GALUPPI   CARNANA   M
    SIX SONATAS FOR HARPSICHORD
        C. F. PETERS CORPORATION   ZA5052   3.50
GALUPPI   BENVENUTI
    TWELVE SONATAS
        FRANCO COLOMBO PUBLICATIONS   BON.1174   6.50
GANZ
    EXERCISES FOR PIANO
        SUMMY-BIRCHARD COMPANY   4.00
GARCIA MORILLO
    CONJUROS
        EDITORIAL COOPERATIVA INTER-AMERICANA   01.45
GARCIA MORILLO
    CUENTOS PARA NINOS TRAVIESOS - SERIES 2
        FRANCO COLOMBO PUBLICATIONS   BA11015   1.50
GARCIA MORILLO
    THREE PIECES, OP. 2
        FRANCO COLOMBO PUBLICATIONS   BA8111   1.50
GARCIA MORILLO
    VARIACIONES
        EDITORIAL COOPERATIVA INTER-AMERICANA   00.85
GARLICK, A.
    THREE PIECES FOR PIANO
        SEESAW MUSIC CORPORATION   4.00
GARRATT   M
    DANCE MINIATURES
        C. F. PETERS CORPORATION   H26   1.25
GARRATT   M
    LONDON MONOLOGUES
        C. F. PETERS CORPORATION   H79   .90
GARROW
    NEW PIECES FOR ME
        SUMMY-BIRCHARD COMPANY   1.25
GARROW
    SEVENTEEN FOLK TUNES FOR PIANO
        BRODT MUSIC COMPANY   1.50
GARROW, L.   2
    SACRED MUSIC
        BELWIN-MILLS PUBLISHING CORPORATION   FDL 323   1.75
GARSCIA
    FAVORITE TUNES FOR PIANO
        EDWARD B. MARKS MUSIC CORPORATION   02.00
GARSCIA
    LITTLE ETUDES
        EDWARD B. MARKS MUSIC CORPORATION   01.50
GARSCIA
    MINIATURES FOR PIANO
        EDWARD B. MARKS MUSIC CORPORATION   02.00
GARSCIA
    VERY EASY PIECES FOR CHILDREN
        EDWARD B. MARKS MUSIC CORPORATION   02.00
GARVELMANN, D.--ED.   GARVELMANN, D.
    THIRTEEN TRANSCRIPTIONS FOR PIANO SOLO OF CHOPIN'S WALTZ IN D
    FLAT, OP. 64 NO. 1
        MUSIC TREASURE PUBLICATIONS   5.00
GASPARINI, F.
    L'ARMONICO PRATICO AL CIMBALO
        BROUDE BROTHERS LTD.   25.00
GASULEAS, S.
    ELEVEN APHORISMS
        UNIVERSAL EDITION   UE 13182   2.25
GAUTIER, L.
    CHARMES DE L'ETUDE, LES -- 12 LITTLE PIECES WITHOUT OCTAVES, FOR
    SMALL HANDS --
        FRANCO COLOMBO PUBLICATIONS   SAL   3.50
GAYNOR
    FIRST PEDAL STUDIES
        THEODORE PRESSER COMPANY   1.00
GAYNOR   BLAKE, D. G.
    THIRTY RHYTHMIC PANTOMIMES
        THEODORE PRESSER COMPANY   1.50
GEBHARD   2-3
    ZWEI SONATINEN, OP. 44A, B IN G UND E MINOR
        BARENREITER VERLAG   SM 1490A/B

GEIRINGER, K.--ED   GEIRINGER, K.
    BACH FAMILY, THE -- 14 PIECES
        THEODORE PRESSER COMPANY   1.50
GEISSLER
    KLAVIERSTUECKE FUR CHARLOTTE
        ASSOCIATED MUSIC PUBLISHERS, INC.   B/H   2.00
GEISSMAR, E.
    INVITATION TO MUSIC -- BEGINNING PIANO FOR TEEN-AGE AND ADULT
    STUDENTS
        PUGET MUSIC PUBLICATIONS, INC.   P714   4.00
GELBRUN, A.
    FOUR PRELUDES
        ISRAEL MUSIC INSTITUTE   3.50
GENZMER   E
    STUDIES, VOL. 1. ELEVEN PIECES
        C. F. PETERS CORPORATION   5929A   2.50
GENZMER   M-D
    STUDIES, VOL. 2. TEN PIECES
        C. F. PETERS CORPORATION   5929B   2.50
GENZMER   D
    TEN PRELUDES
        C. F. PETERS CORPORATION   5960   3.00
GEORGE
    DAY IN THE JUNGLE, A
        SUMMY-BIRCHARD COMPANY   1.50
GEORGE
    KALEIDOSCOPE -- SOLO BOOK 1
        ALFRED MUSIC COMPANY   686   1.25
GEORGE
    KALEIDOSCOPE -- SOLO BOOK 2
        ALFRED MUSIC COMPANY   687   1.25
GEORGE
    KALEIDOSCOPE -- SOLO BOOK 3
        ALFRED MUSIC COMPANY   688   1.25
GEORGE
    KALEIDOSCOPE -- SOLO BOOK 4
        ALFRED MUSIC COMPANY   689   1.25
GEORGE
    KALEIDOSCOPE -- SOLO BOOK 5
        ALFRED MUSIC COMPANY   690   1.25
GEORGE
    MUSICAL MOMENTS, BK. 1
        SCHMITT, HALL AND MCCREARY COMPANY   9979   1.25
GEORGE
    MUSICAL MOMENTS, BK. 2
        SCHMITT, HALL AND MCCREARY COMPANY   9980   1.25
GEORGE
    PLAY TIME ONE
        SUMMY-BIRCHARD COMPANY   1.25
GEORGE
    PLAY TIME TWO
        SUMMY-BIRCHARD COMPANY   1.50
GEORGE
    PLAY TIME 1
        SUMMY-BIRCHARD COMPANY   1.25
GEORGE
    PLAY TIME 2
        SUMMY-BIRCHARD COMPANY   1.50
GEORGE
    STUDENTS' CHOICE, SET 1 --5 PIECES--
        SUMMY-BIRCHARD COMPANY   1.00
GEORGE
    STUDENTS' CHOICE, SET 2 --5 PIECES--
        SUMMY-BIRCHARD COMPANY   1.00
GEORGE
    STUDENTS' CHOICE, SET 3 --4 PIECES--
        SUMMY-BIRCHARD COMPANY   1.00
GEORGE
    STUDENTS' CHOICE, SET 4 --4 PIECES--
        SUMMY-BIRCHARD COMPANY   1.00
GERIG, HANS--ED.   GERIG, HANS
    CONTEMPORARY BULGARIAN PIANO MUSIC, BK. 1
        MCA MUSIC   HG 507   5.00
GERIG, HANS--ED.   GERIG, HANS
    CONTEMPORARY BULGARIAN PIANO MUSIC, BK. 2
        MCA MUSIC   HG 508   5.00
GERIG, HANS--ED.   GERIG, HANS
    CONTEMPORARY CZECHOSLOVAKIAN PIANO MUSIC, BK. 1
        MCA MUSIC   HG 657   5.00
GERIG, HANS--ED.   GERIG, HANS
    CONTEMPORARY CZECHOSLOVAKIAN PIANO MUSIC, BK. 2
        MCA MUSIC   HG 658   5.00
GERIG, HANS--ED.   GERIG, HANS
    CONTEMPORARY GREEK PIANO MUSIC, BK. 1
        MCA MUSIC   HG 590   5.00
GERIG, HANS--ED.   GERIG, HANS
    CONTEMPORARY GREEK PIANO MUSIC, BK. 2
        MCA MUSIC   HG 591   5.00
GERIG, HANS--ED.   GERIG, HANS
    CONTEMPORARY RUMANIAN MUSIC, BK. 1
        MCA MUSIC   HG 775   5.00
GERIG, HANS--ED.   GERIG, HANS
    CONTEMPORARY RUMANIAN MUSIC, BK. 2
        MCA MUSIC   HG 776   5.00
GERIG, HANS--ED.   GERIG, HANS
    CONTEMPORARY SOVIET PIANO MUSIC, BK. 1
        MCA MUSIC   HG 617   5.00
GERIG, HANS--ED.   GERIG, HANS
    CONTEMPORARY SOVIET PIANO MUSIC, BK. 2
        MCA MUSIC   HG 615   5.00
GERIG, HANS--ED.   GERIG, HANS
    CONTEMPORARY YUGOSLAVIAN PIANO MUSIC -- BK. 1
        MCA MUSIC   HG 551   5.00
GERIG, HANS--ED.   GERIG, HANS
    CONTEMPORARY YUGOSLAVIAN PIANO MUSIC, BK. 2
        MCA MUSIC   HG 552   5.00
GERIG, HANS--ED.   GERIG, HANS
    KEYBOARD MUSIC OF THE BAROQUE AND ROCOCO, BK. 1
        MCA MUSIC   AV 138   6.00
GERIG, HANS--ED.   GERIG, HANS
    KEYBOARD MUSIC OF THE BAROQUE AND ROCOCO, BK. 2
        MCA MUSIC   AV 151   6.00
GERIG, HANS--ED.   GERIG, HANS
    KEYBOARD MUSIC OF THE BAROQUE AND ROCOCO, BK. 3
        MCA MUSIC   AV 153   6.00
GERIG, R.--ED   GERIG, R.
    PIANO PRELUDES ON HYMNS AND CHORALES
        HOPE PUBLISHING COMPANY   3.00
GERMAN, E.
    THREE DANCES FROM ''HENRY THE EIGHTH''
        G. SCHIRMER, INC.   L1535   1.00
GERMER, H.
    RHYTHMICAL PROBLEMS
        G. SCHIRMER, INC.   1.25
GERSHWIN
    GERSHWIN AT THE KEYBOARD
        WARNER BROTHERS PUBLISHERS   2.50

GERSHWIN
  MEET GEORGE GERSHWIN AT THE PIANO
        CHAPPELL AND COMPANY, INC.   3718756   2.50
GERSHWIN
  POINTER LIBRARY - THE BEST OF GEORGE GERSHWIN
        POINTER PUBLICATIONS   2.95
GERSHWIN
  PORGY AND BESS
        CHAPPELL AND COMPANY, INC.   4672507   1.50
GERSHWIN
  PORGY AND BESS
        CHAPPELL AND COMPANY, INC.   4672507   1.95
GERSHWIN
  PRELUDES
        WARNER BROTHERS PUBLISHERS   1.50
GERSHWIN   CHAPLIN
  TWO WALTZES IN C
        WARNER BROTHERS PUBLISHERS   1.50
GEST, E.   GRADE 2
  SECOND BOOK OF TONES AND TUNES
        G. SCHIRMER, INC.   1.00
GEST, E.   FROST
  SIX SONATINAS FOR PIANO
        BELWIN-MILLS PUBLISHING CORPORATION   1.50
GHEDINI
  PUERILIA - 4 PIECES ON 5 NOTES
        FRANCO COLOMBO PUBLICATIONS   130291   1.50
GIACCHINO CUSENZA
  THREE PIECES
        FRANCO COLOMBO PUBLICATIONS   124599   1.00
GIACHETTI
  THREE COMPOSITIONS
        FRANCO COLOMBO PUBLICATIONS   FOR.10818   1.25
GIANNEO
  FIVE LITTLE PIECES -- 1938 --
        ASSOCIATED MUSIC PUBLISHERS, INC.   ESC   2.00
GIANNEO
  MUSICA PARA NINOS
        PEER SOUTHERN ORGANIZATION   02.00
GIANNEO
  SIETE PIEZAS INGANTILES
        PEER SOUTHERN ORGANIZATION   01.75
GIANNEO
  TRES DANZAS ARGENTINAS
        PEER SOUTHERN ORGANIZATION   01.50
GIBBONS
  ALBUM
        EDWIN F. KALMUS   3470   1.50
GIBBS   E
  SIX CHARACTERS FROM SHAKESPEARE
        C. F. PETERS CORPORATION   H424   .90
GIGGY, F.
  THREE LULLABIES
        COMPOSERS AUTOGRAPH PUBLICATIONS   1.10
GILARDI
  FOUR PRELUDIOS UNITONALES
        FRANCO COLOMBO PUBLICATIONS   BA12332   1.25
GILLOCK   4
  ACCENT ON ANALYTICAL SONATINAS
        WILLIS MUSIC COMPANY   1.00
GILLOCK   2-3
  ACCENT ON MAJORS
        WILLIS MUSIC COMPANY   1.00
GILLOCK   3-4
  ACCENT ON MAJORS AND MINORS
        WILLIS MUSIC COMPANY   1.00
GILLOCK   3
  ACCENT ON RHYTHM AND STYLE
        WILLIS MUSIC COMPANY   1.00
GILLOCK   1
  ACCENT ON SOLOS
        WILLIS MUSIC COMPANY   .75
GILLOCK   2
  ACCENT ON SOLOS
        WILLIS MUSIC COMPANY   .75
GILLOCK   3
  ACCENT ON SOLOS
        WILLIS MUSIC COMPANY   .75
GILLOCK
  ACCENT ON THE BLACK KEYS
        WILLIS MUSIC COMPANY   1.00
GILLOCK   3
  CHRISTMAS AT THE PIANO
        WILLIS MUSIC COMPANY   1.50
GILLOCK
  FANFARE
        SUMMY-BIRCHARD COMPANY   1.75
GILLOCK   2
  FOLK SONGS AND RHYTHMIC DANCES
        WILLIS MUSIC COMPANY   .75
GILLOCK
  GILLOCK COLLECTION, THE
        SUMMY-BIRCHARD COMPANY   1.25
GILLOCK   4
  HYMNS AT THE PIANO
        WILLIS MUSIC COMPANY   .75
GILLOCK
  LYRIC PRELUDES
        SUMMY-BIRCHARD COMPANY   2.00
GILLOCK
  MORE NEW ORLEANS JAZZ STYLES -- ADVANCING INTERMEDIATE
        WILLIS MUSIC COMPANY   1.00
GILLOCK
  NEW ORLEANS JAZZ STYLES -- ADVANCING INTERMEDIATE
        WILLIS MUSIC COMPANY   1.00
GILLOCK   1A
  PIANO ALL THE WAY -- LEVEL 1A
        WILLIS MUSIC COMPANY   1.00
GILLOCK   1B
  PIANO ALL THE WAY -- LEVEL 1B
        WILLIS MUSIC COMPANY   1.00
GILLOCK   2
  PIANO ALL THE WAY -- LEVEL 2
        WILLIS MUSIC COMPANY   1.25
GILLOCK   3
  PIANO ALL THE WAY -- LEVEL 3
        WILLIS MUSIC COMPANY   1.25
GILLOCK   4
  PIANO ALL THE WAY -- LEVEL 4
        WILLIS MUSIC COMPANY   1.25
GILLOCK
  SOLO REPERTOIRE FOR THE YOUNG PIANIST, BK. 1 -- ELEMENTARY
        WILLIS MUSIC COMPANY   1.25
GILLOCK
  SOLO REPERTOIRE FOR THE YOUNG PIANIST, BK. 2 -- ADVANCING
  ELEMENTARY
        WILLIS MUSIC COMPANY   1.25

GILLOCK
  SOLO REPERTOIRE FOR THE YOUNG PIANIST, BK. 3 -- EARLY
  INTERMEDIATE
        WILLIS MUSIC COMPANY   1.25
GILLOCK
  SOLO REPERTOIRE FOR THE YOUNG PIANIST, BK. 4 -- EARLY
  INTERMEDIATE
        WILLIS MUSIC COMPANY   1.25
GILLOCK
  THREE JAZZ PRELUDES
        WILLIS MUSIC COMPANY   1.00
GILLOCK   1
  YOUNG PIANIST'S FIRST BIG NOTE SOLOS
        WILLIS MUSIC COMPANY   1.00
GILLOCK   2
  YOUNG PIANIST'S FIRST CHRISTMAS
        WILLIS MUSIC COMPANY   1.50
GILLOCK
  YOUNG PIANIST'S FIRST CHRISTMAS
        WILLIS MUSIC COMPANY   1.50
GILLOCK--ED   GILLOCK   AE
  SOLO REPERTOIRE FOR THE YOUNG PIANIST, BK. 1
        WILLIS MUSIC COMPANY   1.50
GILLOCK--ED   GILLOCK   EI
  SOLO REPERTOIRE FOR THE YOUNG PIANIST, BK. 1
        WILLIS MUSIC COMPANY   1.25
GILLOCK--ED   GILLOCK   AE
  SOLO REPERTOIRE FOR THE YOUNG PIANIST, BK. 2
        WILLIS MUSIC COMPANY   1.50
GILLOCK--ED   GILLOCK   EI
  SOLO REPERTOIRE FOR THE YOUNG PIANIST, BK. 2
        WILLIS MUSIC COMPANY   1.25
GINASTERA
  THREE ARGENTINIAN DANCES
        FRANCO COLOMBO PUBLICATIONS   BA9638   1.25
GINASTERA
  THREE PIECES
        FRANCO COLOMBO PUBLICATIONS   BA8009   1.25
GINASTERA
  TWELVE AMERICAN PRELUDES, BK. 1
        CARL FISCHER, INC.   O 3431   1.50
GINASTERA
  TWELVE AMERICAN PRELUDES, BK. 2
        CARL FISCHER, INC.   O 3432   1.50
GIORDANO   DE CRISTOFARO
  ANDREA CHENIER SELECTIONS, BK. 1
        FRANCO COLOMBO PUBLICATIONS   SON.1859   1.25
GIORDANO   DE CRISTOFARO
  ANDREA CHENIER SELECTIONS, BK. 2
        FRANCO COLOMBO PUBLICATIONS   SON.1860   1.25
GIORDANO   DE CHRISTOFARO
  CENA DELLE BEFFE, LA - GRAND FANTASY FROM ACTS 1 AND 2
        FRANCO COLOMBO PUBLICATIONS   SON.2529   1.50
GIORDANO
  FEDORA - SELECTIONS
        FRANCO COLOMBO PUBLICATIONS   SON.1726   1.75
GIORDANO
  FEDORA - SELECTIONS, BK. 1
        FRANCO COLOMBO PUBLICATIONS   SON.1718   .90
GIORDANO
  FEDORA - SELECTIONS, BK. 2
        FRANCO COLOMBO PUBLICATIONS   SON.1719   .90
GIORDANO
  WALTZES
        FRANCO COLOMBO PUBLICATIONS   SON.990   1.25
GIOVANNI
  MY PIANO PLAY BOOK
        BOSTON MUSIC COMPANY   1.25
GIRLAMO, F.
  FIRST LESSONS FOR THE DANCE BAND PIANIST
        BELWIN-MILLS PUBLISHING CORPORATION   2.00
GIRLAMO, F.
  LET'S GO BOOGIE WOOGIE
        BELWIN-MILLS PUBLISHING CORPORATION   2.00
GIRLAMO, F.
  LET'S GO LATIN AMERICAN
        BELWIN-MILLS PUBLISHING CORPORATION   2.00
GIRLAMO, F.
  MUSIC FOR HOLIDAYS
        BELWIN-MILLS PUBLISHING CORPORATION   2.00
GIRLAMO, F.
  MUSIC FOR SPECIAL OCCASIONS
        BELWIN-MILLS PUBLISHING CORPORATION   2.00
GIRLAMO, F.
  PIANO FOR PLEASURE, BK. 1
        BELWIN-MILLS PUBLISHING CORPORATION   2.00
GIRLAMO, F.
  PIANO FOR PLEASURE, BK. 2
        BELWIN-MILLS PUBLISHING CORPORATION   2.00
GIRLAMO, F.
  PIANO FOR PLEASURE, BK. 3
        BELWIN-MILLS PUBLISHING CORPORATION   2.00
GIRLAMO, F.
  PIANO FOR PLEASURE, BK. 4
        BELWIN-MILLS PUBLISHING CORPORATION   2.00
GIRLAMO, F.
  PIANO FOR PLEASURE, BK. 5
        BELWIN-MILLS PUBLISHING CORPORATION   2.00
GIRLAMO, F.
  PIANO FOR PLEASURE, PREP BOOK
        BELWIN-MILLS PUBLISHING CORPORATION   2.00
GLAZOUNOW, A.
  RAYMONDA, OP. 57 --COMPLETE BALLET--
        BOOSEY AND HAWKES, INC.   7.50
GLAZOUNOW, A.
  SEASONS, OP. 67 --COMPLETE BALLET--
        BOOSEY AND HAWKES, INC.   7.50
GLAZOUNOW, A.
  TWO PIECES, OP. 22
        BOOSEY AND HAWKES, INC.   2.00
GLIERE   M
  TWELVE CHILDREN'S PIECES, OP. 31
        C. F. PETERS CORPORATION   4735   3.00
GLOVER, D.   1
  ADULT STUDENT, LEVEL 1
        BELWIN-MILLS PUBLISHING CORPORATION   FDL 458   3.00
GLOVER, D.   2
  ADULT STUDENT, LEVEL 2
        BELWIN-MILLS PUBLISHING CORPORATION   FDL 459   3.00
GLOVER, D.   3
  ADULT STUDENT, LEVEL 3
        BELWIN-MILLS PUBLISHING CORPORATION   FDL 460   3.00
GLOVER, D. *   7
  ADVANCED HYMN PLAYING
        BELWIN-MILLS PUBLISHING CORPORATION   2.00
GLOVER, D. *   8
  ADVANCED HYMN PLAYING
        BELWIN-MILLS PUBLISHING CORPORATION   2.00

GLOVER, D. *
  ADVENTURE IN JAZZ, BK. 1
    BELWIN-MILLS PUBLISHING CORPORATION   FDL 478   2.00
GLOVER, D. *
  ADVENTURE IN JAZZ, BK. 2
    BELWIN-MILLS PUBLISHING CORPORATION   FDL 479   2.00
GLOVER, D. *
  ADVENTURE IN JAZZ, BK. 3
    BELWIN-MILLS PUBLISHING CORPORATION   FDL 480   2.00
GLOVER, D. *
  ADVENTURE IN JAZZ, BK. 4
    BELWIN-MILLS PUBLISHING CORPORATION   FDL 481   2.00
GLOVER, D.
  BOOGIE WOOGIE SCHOOL DAYS
    BELWIN-MILLS PUBLISHING CORPORATION   11061   .85
GLOVER, D.
  CANDLELIGHT ENCORES
    VOLKWEIN BROS.   01.00
GLOVER, D. *   1
  CHORDS AND KEYS
    BELWIN-MILLS PUBLISHING CORPORATION   FDL 338   2.00
GLOVER, D. *   2
  CHORDS AND KEYS
    BELWIN-MILLS PUBLISHING CORPORATION   FDL 389   2.00
GLOVER, D. *   PRIM.
  CHRISTMAS MUSIC
    BELWIN-MILLS PUBLISHING CORPORATION   EL 2218   1.75
GLOVER, D. *   1
  CHRISTMAS MUSIC
    BELWIN-MILLS PUBLISHING CORPORATION   EL 2219   1.75
GLOVER, D. *   1
  CHURCH MUSICIAN, LEVEL 1
    BELWIN-MILLS PUBLISHING CORPORATION   FDL 549   2.00
GLOVER, D. *   2
  CHURCH MUSICIAN, LEVEL 2
    BELWIN-MILLS PUBLISHING CORPORATION   FDL 550   2.00
GLOVER, D. *   3
  CHURCH MUSICIAN, LEVEL 3
    BELWIN-MILLS PUBLISHING CORPORATION   FDL 551   2.00
GLOVER, D. *   4
  CHURCH MUSICIAN, LEVEL 4
    BELWIN-MILLS PUBLISHING CORPORATION   FDL 552   2.00
GLOVER, D. *   5
  CHURCH MUSICIAN, LEVEL 5
    BELWIN-MILLS PUBLISHING CORPORATION   FDL 553   2.00
GLOVER, D. *   6
  CHURCH MUSICIAN, LEVEL 6
    BELWIN-MILLS PUBLISHING CORPORATION   FDL 554   2.00
GLOVER, D. *   PRIM.
  CHURCH MUSICIAN, PRIMER LEVEL
    BELWIN-MILLS PUBLISHING CORPORATION   FDL 548   2.00
GLOVER, D.
  FIVE FINGER BOOGIE
    BELWIN-MILLS PUBLISHING CORPORATION   11171   1.25
GLOVER, D.
  GLOVER'S BEST
    BELWIN-MILLS PUBLISHING CORPORATION   11612   1.75
GLOVER, D. *   7
  KEYBOARD HARMONY
    BELWIN-MILLS PUBLISHING CORPORATION   2.00
GLOVER, D. *   8
  KEYBOARD HARMONY
    BELWIN-MILLS PUBLISHING CORPORATION   2.00
GLOVER, D.
  MY STEP BY STEP HYMN BOOK
    BELWIN-MILLS PUBLISHING CORPORATION   10031   1.25
GLOVER, D. *   4
  PIANO ARPEGGIOS
    BELWIN-MILLS PUBLISHING CORPORATION   FDL 334   2.00
GLOVER, D. *   PRIM.
  PIANO REPERTOIRE
    BELWIN-MILLS PUBLISHING CORPORATION   FDL 313   1.75
GLOVER, D. *   1
  PIANO REPERTOIRE
    BELWIN-MILLS PUBLISHING CORPORATION   FDL 316   1.75
GLOVER, D. *   2
  PIANO REPERTOIRE
    BELWIN-MILLS PUBLISHING CORPORATION   FDL 320   1.75
GLOVER, D. *   3
  PIANO REPERTOIRE
    BELWIN-MILLS PUBLISHING CORPORATION   FDL 326   1.75
GLOVER, D. *   4
  PIANO REPERTOIRE
    BELWIN-MILLS PUBLISHING CORPORATION   FDL 331   1.75
GLOVER, D. *   5
  PIANO REPERTOIRE
    BELWIN-MILLS PUBLISHING CORPORATION   FDL 467   2.00
GLOVER, D. *   PRIM.
  PIANO STUDENT
    BELWIN-MILLS PUBLISHING CORPORATION   FDL 312   2.00
GLOVER, D. *   1
  PIANO STUDENT
    BELWIN-MILLS PUBLISHING CORPORATION   FDL 315   2.00
GLOVER, D. *   2
  PIANO STUDENT
    BELWIN-MILLS PUBLISHING CORPORATION   FDL 319   2.00
GLOVER, D. *   3
  PIANO STUDENT
    BELWIN-MILLS PUBLISHING CORPORATION   FDL 325   2.00
GLOVER, D. *   4
  PIANO STUDENT
    BELWIN-MILLS PUBLISHING CORPORATION   FDL 330   2.00
GLOVER, D.   5
  PIANO STUDENT
    BELWIN-MILLS PUBLISHING CORPORATION   FDL 466   2.00
GLOVER, D.   6
  PIANO STUDENT
    BELWIN-MILLS PUBLISHING CORPORATION   FDL 471   2.00
GLOVER, D.   1
  PIANO TECHNIC
    BELWIN-MILLS PUBLISHING CORPORATION   FDL 318   1.75
GLOVER, D. *   2
  PIANO TECHNIC
    BELWIN-MILLS PUBLISHING CORPORATION   FDL 332   1.75
GLOVER, D. *   3
  PIANO TECHNIC
    BELWIN-MILLS PUBLISHING PRINT CORPORATION   FDL 328   1.75
GLOVER, D. *   4
  PIANO TECHNIC
    BELWIN-MILLS PUBLISHING CORPORATION   FDL 333   1.75
GLOVER, D. *   5
  PIANO TECHNIC
    BELWIN-MILLS PUBLISHING CORPORATION   FDL 470   2.00
GLOVER, D.   6
  PIANO TECHNIC
    BELWIN-MILLS PUBLISHING CORPORATION   FDL 475   2.00

GLOVER, D. *   PRIM.
  PIANO THEORY
    BELWIN-MILLS PUBLISHING CORPORATION   FDL 314   1.75
GLOVER, D. *   1
  PIANO THEORY
    BELWIN-MILLS PUBLISHING CORPORATION   FDL 317   1.75
GLOVER, D. *   2
  PIANO THEORY
    BELWIN-MILLS PUBLISHING CORPORATION   FDL 321   1.75
GLOVER, D. *   3
  PIANO THEORY
    BELWIN-MILLS PUBLISHING CORPORATION   FDL 327   1.75
GLOVER, D. *   4
  PIANO THEORY
    BELWIN-MILLS PUBLISHING CORPORATION   FDL 332   1.75
GLOVER, D. *   4
  PIANO THEORY
    BELWIN-MILLS PUBLISHING CORPORATION   FDL 469   2.00
GLOVER, D. *   5
  PIANO THEORY
    BELWIN-MILLS PUBLISHING CORPORATION   FDL 474   2.00
GLOVER, D.
  TIP TOP TUNES, BK. 1
    BELWIN-MILLS PUBLISHING CORPORATION   11505   1.50
GLOVER, D.
  TIP TOP TUNES, BK. 2
    BELWIN-MILLS PUBLISHING CORPORATION   11506   1.50
GLOVER, D.
  TIP TOP TUNES, BK. 3
    BELWIN-MILLS PUBLISHING CORPORATION   11507   1.50
GLOVER, D.   2
  VACATION BOOGIE
    BELWIN-MILLS PUBLISHING CORPORATION   11523   1.50
GLOVER, D. *   3
  WRITE AND PLAY MAJOR SCALES
    BELWIN-MILLS PUBLISHING CORPORATION   FDL 324   1.75
GLOVER, D. *
  WRITE AND PLAY MINOR SCALES
    BELWIN-MILLS PUBLISHING CORPORATION   FDL 329   1.75
GLUCK *   LONGO
  GOLDEN LIBRARY, BK. 6 - GLUCK, MEYERBEER, WAGNER, WEBER
    FRANCO COLOMBO PUBLICATIONS   112504   5.50
GODARD
  SOUVENIRS DE TAVERNY -- 7 PIECES
    FRANCO COLOMBO PUBLICATIONS   SAL   2.50
GODARD, B.
  EIGHTEEN SELECTED PIECES, BK. 1
    G. SCHIRMER, INC.   L213   1.50
GODARD, B.
  EIGHTEEN SELECTED PIECES, BK. 2
    G. SCHIRMER, INC.   L214   1.50
GODOWSKY, L.   D
  FIFTY-THREE STUDIES BASED ON 26 CHOPIN ETUDES, VOL. 1
    C. F. PETERS CORPORATION   R190   7.50
GODOWSKY, L.   D
  FIFTY-THREE STUDIES BASED ON 26 CHOPIN ETUDES, VOL. 2
    C. F. PETERS CORPORATION   R191   7.50
GODOWSKY, L.   D
  FIFTY-THREE STUDIES BASED ON 26 CHOPIN ETUDES, VOL. 3
    C. F. PETERS CORPORATION   R192   7.50
GODOWSKY, L.   D
  FIFTY-THREE STUDIES BASED ON 26 CHOPIN ETUDES, VOL. 4
    C. F. PETERS CORPORATION   R173   7.50
GODOWSKY, L.   D
  FIFTY-THREE STUDIES BASED ON 26 CHOPIN ETUDES, VOL. 5
    C. F. PETERS CORPORATION   R194   7.50
GOEBELS   GOEBELS, F.
  NEW CEMBALO MUSIC
    BARENREITER VERLAG   BA 3804   7.50
GOEBELS--ED   GOEBELS   3
  DREI PAVANEN UBER DAS GLEICHE THEMA VON BULL, CABEZON, SWEELINCK
  UND SCHEIDT
    SCHOTT   5457   2.00
GOEBELS--ED   GOEBELS
  FOLIES D'ESPAGNE - VARIATIONEN U. D. FOLLIA
    SCHOTT   5775
GOEHR, A.
  THREE PIECES, OP. 18
    SCHOTT   10910   2.75
GOLD
  THREE MINIATURES
    ASSOCIATED MUSIC PUBLISHERS, INC.   SIM   3.25
GOLDBERGER, D.--ED. *   GOLDBERGER, D. *
  ETUDE BOOK 1
    CONSOLIDATED MUSIC PUBLISHERS, INC.   040115   1.25
GOLDBERGER, D.--ED. *   GOLDBERGER, D. *
  ETUDE BOOK 2
    CONSOLIDATED MUSIC PUBLISHERS, INC.   040116   1.25
GOLDBERGER, D.--ED. *   GOLDBERGER, D. *
  ETUDE BOOK 3
    CONSOLIDATED MUSIC PUBLISHERS, INC.   040117   1.25
GOLDBERGER, D.--ED. *   GOLDBERGER, D. *
  FOLK SONG BOOK 1
    CONSOLIDATED MUSIC PUBLISHERS, INC.   040100   1.25
GOLDBERGER, D.--ED. *   GOLDBERGER, D. *
  FOLK SONG BOOK 2
    CONSOLIDATED MUSIC PUBLISHERS, INC.   040101   1.25
GOLDBERGER, D.--ED. *   GOLDBERGER, D. *
  FOLK SONG BOOK 3
    CONSOLIDATED MUSIC PUBLISHERS, INC.   040102   1.25
GOLDBERGER, D.--ED. *   GOLDBERGER, D. *
  SOLO BOOK 1
    CONSOLIDATED MUSIC PUBLISHERS, INC.   040103   1.25
GOLDBERGER, D.--ED. *   GOLDBERGER, D. *
  SOLO BOOK 2
    CONSOLIDATED MUSIC PUBLISHERS, INC.   040104   1.25
GOLDBERGER, D.--ED. *   GOLDBERGER, D. *
  SOLO BOOK 3
    CONSOLIDATED MUSIC PUBLISHERS, INC.   040105   1.25
GOLDBERGER, D.--ED. *   GOLDBERGER, D. *
  SONATINA BOOK 1
    CONSOLIDATED MUSIC PUBLISHERS, INC.   040109   1.25
GOLDBERGER, D.--ED. *   GOLDBERGER, D. *
  SONATINA BOOK 2
    CONSOLIDATED MUSIC PUBLISHERS, INC.   040110   1.25
GOLDBERGER, D.--ED. *   GOLDBERGER, D. *
  SONATINA BOOK 3
    CONSOLIDATED MUSIC PUBLISHERS, INC.   040111   1.25
GOLDMAN--ED. *   GOLDMAN *
  LANDMARKS OF EARLY AMERICAN MUSIC 1760-1800--32 PSALM-TUNES,
  HUMNS, PATRIOTIC SONGS, AND MARCHES
    G. SCHIRMER, INC.   2.00
GOLDMAN, E.
  ALBUM OF 12 MARCHES
    G. SCHIRMER, INC.   1.25
GOLDSTEIN *
  CONTEMPORARY COLLECTION, NO. 1
    SUMMY-BIRCHARD COMPANY   2.00

GOLIO
FIVE LITTLE PIECES
FRANCO COLOMBO PUBLICATIONS   128737   1.00
GONZALEZ AVILA, J.
INVENCIONES
EDICIONES MEXICANAS DE MUSICA, A. C.   02.25
GOODE
PIANO HYMNS FOR THE LITURGICAL YEAR
HOPE PUBLISHING COMPANY   2.50
GOODE   MOD. DIFF.
PIANO VOLUNTARIES ON HYMN TUNES
ABINGDON PRESS   2.00
GOODRICH
FIRST BOOK OF TUNES TO PLAY
NEW ENGLAND CONSERVATORY   1.25
GOODRICH
SECOND PIANO BOOK
NEW ENGLAND CONSERVATORY   1.25
GORDON
ART OF ROCK
BELWIN-MILLS PUBLISHING CORPORATION   1.50
GORDON
JAZZ FOR JUNIOR
EDWARD B. MARKS MUSIC CORPORATION   01.25
GORDON
JUNIOR JAZZ
EDWARD B. MARKS MUSIC CORPORATION   01.25
GORDON, L.
INTRODUCTION TO THE ART OF ROCK
BELWIN-MILLS PUBLISHING CORPORATION   20569
GORINI FALCO
EIGHT BOZZETTI FACILI
FRANCO COLOMBO PUBLICATIONS   BON.2513   1.75
GORNSTON *
PLAYING WITH CHORDS
SAM FOX PUBLISHING COMPANY, INC.   1.75
GOTTSCHALK
ALBUM
EDWIN F. KALMUS   3468   3.00
GOTTSCHALK   LIST, G.
GOTTSCHALK - A COMPENDIUM OF PIANO MUSIC
CARL FISCHER, INC.   O 4818   3.00
GOTTSCHALK   BEHREND, J.
GOTTSCHALK PIANO ALBUM
THEODORE PRESSER COMPANY   3.50
GOULD, M.
AT THE PIANO, BK. 1
CHAPPELL AND COMPANY, INC.   0021287-1801 1.50
GOULD, M.
AT THE PIANO, BK. 2
CHAPPELL AND COMPANY, INC.   0021287-1802 1.50
GOULD, M.
TEN FOR DEBORAH
CHAPPELL AND COMPANY, INC.   0021568   1.50
GOUNOD, C.
FAUST - WALTZES
FRANCO COLOMBO PUBLICATIONS   67691   .90
GOUNOD, C.   CHIESA
FAUST - WALTZES
FRANCO COLOMBO PUBLICATIONS   109091   .50
GRADSTEIN
HOMMAGE A CHOPIN -- 12 ETUDES -- BK. 1
FRANCO COLOMBO PUBLICATIONS   SAL   6.00
GRADSTEIN
HOMMAGE A CHOPIN -- 12 ETUDES -- BK. 2
FRANCO COLOMBO PUBLICATIONS   SAL   6.00
GRADSTEIN
HOMMAGE A CHOPIN -- 12 ETUDES -- BK. 3
FRANCO COLOMBO PUBLICATIONS   SAL   6.00
GRAENER, P.
IMPRESSIONS, 3 PIECES
UNIVERSAL EDITION   UE 3389   1.30
GRAETZER
DANCES OF 7 CENTURIES
FRANCO COLOMBO PUBLICATIONS   BA12190   7.50
GRAHAM
PIANO PEDAL SOLOS
BELWIN-MILLS PUBLISHING CORPORATION   1.25
GRAHAM
SEVENTY-ONE RECITAL PIECES FOR PIANO
BELWIN-MILLS PUBLISHING CORPORATION   2.00
GRAINGER, P.
MUSIC OF PERCY GRAINGER, THE
G. SCHIRMER, INC.   2.50
GRAITZER, G.
FIVE BAGATELLES
PEER SOUTHERN ORGANIZATION   01.50
GRAITZER, G.
TRES TOCATAS
EDITORIAL COOPERATIVA INTER-AMERICANA   01.35
GRAMATGES
DOS DANZAS CUBANAS
PEER SOUTHERN ORGANIZATION   01.50
GRAMATGES
THREE PRELUDES
PAN AMERICAN UNION   01.60
GRANADOS
ALBUM
EDWARD B. MARKS MUSIC CORPORATION   02.50
GRANADOS
AMOR Y LA MUERTE, EL. LOS MAJOS ENAMORADOS -- NOS. 5 AND 6, FROM
GOYESCAS
ASSOCIATED MUSIC PUBLISHERS, INC.   UME   .90
GRANADOS
BOCETOS. COLLECTION OF EASY PIECES
ASSOCIATED MUSIC PUBLISHERS, INC.   UME   1.10
GRANADOS
DANZAS ESPANOLAS, VOL. 1
ASSOCIATED MUSIC PUBLISHERS, INC.   UME   1.50
GRANADOS
DANZAS ESPANOLAS, VOL. 2
ASSOCIATED MUSIC PUBLISHERS, INC.   UME   1.50
GRANADOS
DANZAS ESPANOLAS, VOL. 3
ASSOCIATED MUSIC PUBLISHERS, INC.   UME   1.50
GRANADOS
DANZAS ESPANOLAS, VOL. 4
ASSOCIATED MUSIC PUBLISHERS, INC.   UME   1.50
GRANADOS
ESCENAS POETICAS Y LIBRA DE HORAS
ASSOCIATED MUSIC PUBLISHERS, INC.   UME   .90
GRANADOS
ESCENAS ROMANTICAS
ASSOCIATED MUSIC PUBLISHERS, INC.   UME   1.10
GRANADOS
ESCENAS ROMANTICAS
INTERNATIONAL MUSIC COMPANY   2.00

GRANADOS
GOYESCAS, PART 1
ASSOCIATED MUSIC PUBLISHERS, INC.   UME   3.00
GRANADOS
GOYESCAS, PART 2
ASSOCIATED MUSIC PUBLISHERS, INC.   UME   2.00
GRANADOS
METODO TEORICO PRACTICO
ASSOCIATED MUSIC PUBLISHERS, INC.   UME   1.50
GRANADOS
MORESQUE AND CHANSON ARABE
ASSOCIATED MUSIC PUBLISHERS, INC.   UME   .75
GRANADOS
SIES ESTUDIOS ESPRESIVOS
ASSOCIATED MUSIC PUBLISHERS, INC.   UME   1.25
GRANADOS
SIX PIECES ON SPANISH FOLK SONGS -- COMPLETE
ASSOCIATED MUSIC PUBLISHERS, INC.   UME   3.00
GRANADOS
TWELVE SPANISH DANCES
INTERNATIONAL MUSIC COMPANY   3.50
GRANADOS
TWELVE SPANISH DANCES, BK. 1
EDWIN F. KALMUS   3478   1.50
GRANADOS
TWELVE SPANISH DANCES, BK. 2
EDWIN F. KALMUS   3479   1.50
GRANADOS
TWO DANSES CARACTERISTIQUES .. DANZA GITANA, DANZA ARAGONESA --
POSTHUMOUS WORK, EDITED AND FINGERED BY INFANTE --
FRANCO COLOMBO PUBLICATIONS   SAL   4.00
GRANADOS
TWO IMPROMPTUS
ASSOCIATED MUSIC PUBLISHERS, INC.   UME   1.10
GRANT, L.--ED   GRANT, L.
HYMNS WITH EASY CHORDS
SCHUBERTH CO.   1.95
GRAUPNER   HOFFMAN *
EIGHT PARTITAS
ASSOCIATED MUSIC PUBLISHERS, INC.   B/H   3.60
GRAY, D.
FIVE PIECES
FRANCO COLOMBO PUBLICATIONS   SAL   4.25
GRAY, D.
PRELIMINARY SCALES AND ARPEGGIOS
BOOSEY AND HAWKES, INC.   .90
GRAY, D.
TWO ALBUM LEAVES
BOOSEY AND HAWKES, INC.   .75
GRAY, D.
VERY FIRST CLASSICS, BK. 1
BOOSEY AND HAWKES, INC.   .90
GRAY, D.
VERY FIRST CLASSICS, BK. 3
BOOSEY AND HAWKES, INC.   .90
GREAN
CHRISTMAS TREE, THE
EDWARD B. MARKS MUSIC CORPORATION   01.50
GREEN, R.
PIANO BOOKS FOR YOUNG PIANISTS -- A-BOOK FOR THE EARLIEST
BEGINNER
AMERICAN MUSIC EDITION   .75
GREEN, R.
PIANO BOOKS FOR YOUNG PIANISTS -- B-BOOK FOR THE STUDENT
BEGINNER
AMERICAN MUSIC EDITION   .85
GREEN, R.
PIANO BOOKS FOR YOUNG PIANISTS -- C-BOOK FOR THE YOUNG PIANISTS
AMERICAN MUSIC EDITION   1.00
GREEN, R.
PIANO BOOKS FOR YOUNG PIANISTS -- D-BOOK FOR YOUNG SOLOISTS
AMERICAN MUSIC EDITION   1.00
GREEN, R.
PIANO BOOKS FOR YOUNG PIANISTS -- E-BOOK FOR YOUNG ARTISTS
AMERICAN MUSIC EDITION   1.25
GREEN, R.
PIANO BOOKS FOR YOUNG PIANISTS -- F-BOOK FOR YOUNG MASTERS
AMERICAN MUSIC EDITION   1.25
GREEN, R.
PIANO WORKSHOP FOR YOUNG PIANISTS, BK. 1
AMERICAN MUSIC EDITION   1.00
GREEN, R.
PIANO WORKSHOP FOR YOUNG PIANISTS, BK. 2
AMERICAN MUSIC EDITION   1.25
GREEN, R.
PIANO WORKSHOP FOR YOUNG PIANISTS, BK. 3
AMERICAN MUSIC EDITION   1.50
GREENHILL, H.   3-4
SPRINGTIME IN THE FOREST
NOVELLO AND COMPANY, LTD.   10.0057.08 1.25
GREGH
BERGERS WATTEAU, LES OP. 5
FRANCO COLOMBO PUBLICATIONS   SAL   2.00
GREGH
NUITS ALGERIENNES, OP. 98 - AU CAFE MAURE, ECHOS DU SOIR, DANSE
DES OULED-NAILS
FRANCO COLOMBO PUBLICATIONS   SAL   5.75
GREISSLE, F.--ED.   GREISSLE, F.
INTERNATIONAL LIBRARY OF PIANO MUSIC
INTERNATIONAL LIBRARY OF PIANO MUSIC
GRENZ
ZAUBERLEHRING, DIE -- BALLET --
FRANCO COLOMBO PUBLICATIONS   SIK.331   20.00
GRETCHANINOFF
ALBUM D'ANDRUCHA, OP. 133
ASSOCIATED MUSIC PUBLISHERS, INC.   ESC   1.75
GRETCHANINOFF
ALBUM DE NINA, OP. 144
ASSOCIATED MUSIC PUBLISHERS, INC.   ESC   1.75
GRETCHANINOFF
ARABESQUES, OP. 150 -- TEN EASY MINIATURES
ASSOCIATED MUSIC PUBLISHERS, INC.   ESC   1.75
GRETCHANINOFF
CHILD'S DAY
EDWARD B. MARKS MUSIC CORPORATION   01.00
GRETCHANINOFF
CHILDREN'S ALBUM, OP. 98
INTERNATIONAL MUSIC COMPANY   1.25
GRETCHANINOFF   AGAY, D.
CHILDREN'S ALBUM, OP. 98
MCA MUSIC   1.25
GRETCHANINOFF
CHILDREN'S BOOK, OP. 98
EDWARD B. MARKS MUSIC CORPORATION   01.00
GRETCHANINOFF   2
DAS GROSSVATERBUCH OP. 119
SCHOTT   1467   2.25

GRETCHANINOFF   2
    DAS KINDERBUCH OP. 98
        SCHOTT   1100   2.25
GRETCHANINOFF
    FIVE MINIATURES
        EDWARD B. MARKS MUSIC CORPORATION   01.00
GRETCHANINOFF   2
    GLASPERLEM OP. 123
        SCHOTT   1518   2.25
GRETCHANINOFF   BEGINNER
    GLASS BEADS
        EDWIN F. KALMUS   3499   1.00
GRETCHANINOFF
    GOUCHES - THREE LITTLE PIECES, OP. 189
        MCA MUSIC   .60
GRETCHANINOFF   BEGINNER
    GRANDFATHERS BOOK
        EDWIN F. KALMUS   3500   1.00
GRETCHANINOFF
    GRANDFATHERS BOOK, OP. 119
        EDWARD B. MARKS MUSIC CORPORATION   01.00
GRETCHANINOFF   3, 4
    HISTORIETTES, OP. 118
        ALPHONSE LEDUC
GRETCHANINOFF
    LETTERS TO A FRIEND
        EDWARD B. MARKS MUSIC CORPORATION   01.00
GRETCHANINOFF
    ON HORSEBACK, ON THE LAWN
        MCA MUSIC   .60
GRETCHANINOFF   2, 4
    PROMENADE AU BOIS, OP. 143
        ALPHONSE LEDUC
GRETCHANINOFF   2 - 3
    SUITE MINIATURE, OP. 145
        ALPHONSE LEDUC
GRETCHANINOFF
    TWELVE LITTLE SKETCHES FOR CHILDREN, OP. 182
        INTERNATIONAL MUSIC COMPANY   1.25
GRIEG   THORNE
    ALBUM
        BOOSEY AND HAWKES, INC.   1.50
GRIEG   M-D
    ALBUM LEAVES, OP. 28
        C. F. PETERS CORPORATION   1870   1.25
GRIEG   M
    ALBUM, BK. 1
        C. F. PETERS CORPORATION   3305A   1.50
GRIEG   M
    ALBUM, BK. 2
        C. F. PETERS CORPORATION   3305B   1.50
GRIEG   ANSON, G.   INTERMEDIATE
    ANSON INTRODUCES GRIEG, BK. 1
        WILLIS MUSIC COMPANY   1.50
GRIEG   3-5
    AUSWAHL -- 15 DER BEKANNTESTEN STUCKE
        SCHOTT   505   1.75
GRIEG   SCHAUM, J.   3
    BEST OF GRIEG
        SCHAUM PUBLICATIONS, INC.   1.25
GRIEG
    COMPLETE PIANO WORKS IN 3 VOLS. CLOTH-BOUND
        C. F. PETERS CORPORATION   15.00
GRIEG   M-D
    COMPLETE PIANO WORKS, VOL. 1
        C. F. PETERS CORPORATION   3100A   10.00
GRIEG   M-D
    COMPLETE PIANO WORKS, VOL. 2
        C. F. PETERS CORPORATION   3100B   10.00
GRIEG   M-D
    COMPLETE PIANO WORKS, VOL. 3
        C. F. PETERS CORPORATION   3100C   10.00
GRIEG   M
    CRADLE SONG AND 'I LOVE THEE'
        C. F. PETERS CORPORATION   3129A   .90
GRIEG   M-D
    CRADLE SONG AND SOLVEJG'S SONG
        C. F. PETERS CORPORATION   3515   .90
GRIEG   M-D
    ELEGIAC MELODIES, OP. 34
        C. F. PETERS CORPORATION   2265   1.25
GRIEG   SPIVAK, S.
    FINEST MUSIC SERIES -- GRIEG
        SCHUBERTH CO.   NO. 08   1.50
GRIEG
    FIRST PEER GYNT SUITE, OP. 46
        THEODORE PRESSER COMPANY   .75
GRIEG
    FORTY-FIVE SELECTED COMPOSITIONS, BK. 1
        G. SCHIRMER, INC.   L106   1.50
GRIEG
    FORTY-FIVE SELECTED COMPOSITIONS, BK. 2
        G. SCHIRMER, INC.   L107   1.50
GRIEG   MONTANI
    FORTY-FIVE SELECTED PIECES
        FRANCO COLOMBO PUBLICATIONS   ER2592   5.50
GRIEG   4-5
    GARLAND FOR GRIEG, A, BK. 2
        NOVELLO AND COMPANY, LTD.   10.0059.04 .65
GRIEG
    GRIEG
        ASHLEY DEALERS SERVICE, INC.   HG 01   2.95
GRIEG   ROVENGER
    GRIEG FOR THE YOUNG
        RUBANK, INC.   1.50
GRIEG   LEVINE, H.
    GRIEG--SELECTED WORKS
        ALFRED MUSIC COMPANY   641   3.50
GRIEG   M
    HUMORESQUES, OP. 6
        C. F. PETERS CORPORATION   1139   1.25
GRIEG   M
    I LOVE THEE, OP. 41 NO. 3, AND CRADLE SONG --WIEGENLIED--, OP.
    41 NO. 1
        C. F. PETERS CORPORATION   3129A   .90
GRIEG   M
    LYRIC PIECES FOR THE YOUNG. 7 FAVORITE PIECES
        C. F. PETERS CORPORATION   3305A   1.50
GRIEG   M
    LYRIC PIECES, BK. 01, OP. 12
        C. F. PETERS CORPORATION   1269   1.25
GRIEG   M-D
    LYRIC PIECES, BK. 02, OP. 38
        C. F. PETERS CORPORATION   2150   1.25
GRIEG   M-D
    LYRIC PIECES, BK. 03, OP. 43
        C. F. PETERS CORPORATION   2154   1.25

GRIEG   M-D
    LYRIC PIECES, BK. 04, OP. 47
        C. F. PETERS CORPORATION   2421   1.50
GRIEG   M-D
    LYRIC PIECES, BK. 05, OP. 54
        C. F. PETERS CORPORATION   2651   1.50
GRIEG   M-D
    LYRIC PIECES, BK. 06, OP. 57, VOL. 1
        C. F. PETERS CORPORATION   2657A   1.50
GRIEG   M-D
    LYRIC PIECES, BK. 06, OP. 57, VOL. 2
        C. F. PETERS CORPORATION   2657B   1.50
GRIEG   M-D
    LYRIC PIECES, BK. 07, OP. 62, VOL. 1
        C. F. PETERS CORPORATION   2824A   1.50
GRIEG   M-D
    LYRIC PIECES, BK. 07, OP. 62, VOL. 2
        C. F. PETERS CORPORATION   2824B   1.50
GRIEG   M-D
    LYRIC PIECES, BK. 08, OP. 65, VOL. 1
        C. F. PETERS CORPORATION   2859A   1.50
GRIEG   M-D
    LYRIC PIECES, BK. 08, OP. 65, VOL. 2
        C. F. PETERS CORPORATION   2859B   1.50
GRIEG   M-D
    LYRIC PIECES, BK. 09, OP. 68
        C. F. PETERS CORPORATION   2924   2.00
GRIEG   M-D
    LYRIC PIECES, BK. 10, OP. 71
        C. F. PETERS CORPORATION   2985   2.00
GRIEG   M-D
    LYRIC PIECES, COMPLETE
        C. F. PETERS CORPORATION   3100A   10.00
GRIEG   M-D
    LYRIC PIECES, OP. 12
        FRANCO COLOMBO PUBLICATIONS   129145   1.25
GRIEG
    LYRIC PIECES, OP. 12
        EDWIN F. KALMUS   3480   1.25
GRIEG
    LYRIC PIECES, OP. 38
        EDWIN F. KALMUS   3481   1.25
GRIEG
    LYRIC PIECES, OP. 43
        EDWIN F. KALMUS   3482   1.25
GRIEG
    LYRIC PIECES, OP. 57
        G. SCHIRMER, INC.   L1810   1.00
GRIEG   RUTHARDT
    LYRICAL PIECES, OP. 12
        G. SCHIRMER, INC.   L201   1.00
GRIEG   OESTERLE
    LYRICAL PIECES, OP. 38
        G. SCHIRMER, INC.   L772   1.00
GRIEG   OESTERLE
    LYRICAL PIECES, OP. 43
        G. SCHIRMER, INC.   L773   1.00
GRIEG   OESTERLE
    LYRICAL PIECES, OP. 47
        G. SCHIRMER, INC.   L774   1.00
GRIEG   OESTERLE
    LYRICAL PIECES, OP. 54
        G. SCHIRMER, INC.   L775   1.00
GRIEG   OESTERLE
    LYRICAL PIECES, OP. 68
        G. SCHIRMER, INC.   L779   1.00
GRIEG   M
    MARCHES --4--
        C. F. PETERS CORPORATION   550B   1.50
GRIEG   HUGHES
    MASTER SERIES FOR THE YOUNG, VOL. 11 --GRIEG--
        G. SCHIRMER, INC.   1.25
GRIEG   CHING   EASY
    NEW GRADED CLASSIC ALBUM - GRIEG
        GENERAL WORDS AND MUSIC COMPANY   1.25
GRIEG   E-M
    NORTHERN DANCES AND FOLK TUNES, OP. 17
        C. F. PETERS CORPORATION   1482   2.00
GRIEG   RUTHARDT
    NORTHERN DANCES AND FOLK TUNES, OP. 17
        G. SCHIRMER, INC.   L728   1.00
GRIEG   M-D
    NORWEGIAN DANCES, OP. 35
        C. F. PETERS CORPORATION   2155   2.00
GRIEG   E-M
    NORWEGIAN FOLK TUNES --22 SIMPLIFIED PIECES FROM VARIOUS
    COLLECTIONS--
        C. F. PETERS CORPORATION   550C   1.50
GRIEG   M-D
    NORWEGIAN FOLK TUNES, OP. 66
        C. F. PETERS CORPORATION   2860   2.00
GRIEG   M-D
    NORWEGIAN MELODIES, OP. 63
        C. F. PETERS CORPORATION   2855   2.00
GRIEG   E-M
    NORWEGIAN NOTEBOOK. 16 PIECES FROM NORDIC DANCES AND FOLK TUNES
    --OP. 17, OP. 66--
        C. F. PETERS CORPORATION   4536   .90
GRIEG   M-D
    NORWEGIAN PEASANT DANCES --SLATTER--, OP. 72
        C. F. PETERS CORPORATION   3097   3.50
GRIEG
    NORWEGIAN SKETCHES, OP. 19
        FRANCO COLOMBO PUBLICATIONS   129146   .90
GRIEG   M
    NORWEGIAN SKETCHES, OP. 19
        C. F. PETERS CORPORATION   1270   2.00
GRIEG   M-D
    PEER GYNT SUITE NO. 1, OP. 46
        C. F. PETERS CORPORATION   2420   1.50
GRIEG   M-D
    PEER GYNT SUITE NO. 2, OP. 55
        C. F. PETERS CORPORATION   2653   1.50
GRIEG   SCHAUM, J.   3
    PEER GYNT SUITES
        SCHAUM PUBLICATIONS, INC.   1.50
GRIEG   M-D
    PEER GYNT.
        C. F. PETERS CORPORATION   3709   7.50
GRIEG   M
    PEER GYNT, SELECTIONS
        C. F. PETERS CORPORATION   550D   1.50
GRIEG   4-5
    PEER-GYNT-SUITE 1, OP. 46
        SCHOTT   4692   1.00

GRIEG   4
    PEER-GYNT-SUITE 2 -- SOLVEJGS LIED OP. 55 NO. 4, SOLVEJGS
    WIEGENLIED OP. 23
        SCHOTT   09594 1/2   1.00
GRIEG   4-5
    PEER-GYNT-SUITE 2, OP. 55
        SCHOTT   4693   1.00
                                                     M-D
GRIEG
    POETIC TONE-PICTURES, OP. 3
        C. F. PETERS CORPORATION   1353   1.25
GRIEG
    RADIO CITY ALBUM, BK. 2
        EDWARD B. MARKS MUSIC CORPORATION   01.50
                                                      M
GRIEG
    SELECTED PIECES --22--
        C. F. PETERS CORPORATION   4922   3.50
                                                     M-D
GRIEG
    SIGURD JORSALFAR, OP. 56
        C. F. PETERS CORPORATION   2655   2.00
                            RUTHARDT
GRIEG   \
    SIX POETIC TONE-PICTURES, OP. 3
        G. SCHIRMER, INC.   L198   .75
                                                     M-D
GRIEG
    SOLVEJG'S SONG AND CRADLE SONG
        C. F. PETERS CORPORATION   3515   .90
                            OESTERLE
GRIEG
    TWO ELEGIAC MELODIES, OP. 34
        G. SCHIRMER, INC.   L209   .75
                                                     M-D
GRIEG
    TWO MELODIES, OP. 53
        C. F. PETERS CORPORATION   2650   1.50
                            GRIEG   M
GRIEG
    WALTZ-CAPRICES, OP. 37
        C. F. PETERS CORPORATION   2159   2.50
                                                     E-M
GRIEG
    WALTZES AND DANCES --7--
        C. F. PETERS CORPORATION   550A   1.50
                                                     M-D
GRIEG
    WIEGENLIED, OP. 41 NO. 1, AND 'ICH LIEBE DICH' OP. 41 NO. 3
        C. F. PETERS CORPORATION   3129A   .90
                                                      M
GRIFFES, C.
    THREE PRELUDES
        C. F. PETERS CORPORATION   66120   1.25
GRIMM, C. W.
    NOTE SPELLING BOOK
        THEODORE PRESSER COMPANY   1.00
GRINDEA, C.
    FIRST TEN LESSONS, THE - A MANUAL FOR TEACHERS
        OXFORD UNIVERSITY PRESS   39.609   2.10
GROFE, F.
    MUSIC FOR MODERNS
        THE BIG THREE MUSIC CORPORATION   01.50
GRUENEWALD   RUF
    TWO PARTITAS
        FRANCO COLOMBO PUBLICATIONS   SY636   2.50
GRYCE
    MODERN SOUNDS, BK. 1
        BELWIN-MILLS PUBLISHING CORPORATION   10029   1.50
GRYCE
    MODERN SOUNDS, BK. 2
        BELWIN-MILLS PUBLISHING CORPORATION   10030   1.50
GUARALDI
    COMPLETE PEANUTS KEYBOARD FUN SERIES
        POINTER PUBLICATIONS   6.95
GUARALDI
    PEANUTS KEYBOARD FUN SERIES - A BOY NAMED CHARLIE BROWN
        POINTER PUBLICATIONS   2.95
GUARALDI
    PEANUTS KEYBOARD FUN SERIES - A CHARLIE BROWN CHRISTMAS
        POINTER PUBLICATIONS   2.95
GUARALDI
    PEANUTS KEYBOARD FUN SERIES - CHARLIE BROWN ALL STARS
        POINTER PUBLICATIONS   2.95
GUARALDI
    PEANUTS KEYBOARD FUN SERIES - HE'S YOUR DOG, CHARLIE BROWN
        POINTER PUBLICATIONS   2.95
GUARALDI
    PEANUTS KEYBOARD FUN SERIES - IT WAS A SHORT SUMMER, CHARLIE
    BROWN
        POINTER PUBLICATIONS   2.95
GUARALDI
    PEANUTS KEYBOARD FUN SERIES - IT'S THE GREAT PUMPKIN, CHARLIE
    BROWN
        POINTER PUBLICATIONS   2.95
GUARALDI
    PEANUTS KEYBOARD FUN SERIES - PIANO FUN BOOK
        POINTER PUBLICATIONS   2.95
GUARALDI
    PEANUTS KEYBOARD FUN SERIES - SUPPLEMENTARY SONGS FOR THE PIANO
    FUN BOOK
        POINTER PUBLICATIONS   1.95
GUARALDI
    PEANUTS KEYBOARD FUN SERIES - YOU'RE IN LOVE, CHARLIE BROWN
        POINTER PUBLICATIONS   2.95
GUARNIERI
    FIVE ESTUDIOS
        FRANCO COLOMBO PUBLICATIONS   BA11209   1.50
GUARNIERI
    FIVE PECAS INFANTIS
        FRANCO COLOMBO PUBLICATIONS   BA11296   1.00
GUARNIERI
    PONTEIOS -- PRELUDES -- BK. 2 -- 1-10 --
        FRANCO COLOMBO PUBLICATIONS   BA11210   2.50
GUARNIERI
    PONTEIOS -- PRELUDES -- BK. 2 -- 11-20 --
        FRANCO COLOMBO PUBLICATIONS   BA11211   2.50
GUARNIERI
    PONTEIOS -- PRELUDES -- BK. 3 -- 21-30 --
        FRANCO COLOMBO PUBLICATIONS   BA11354   2.50
GUARNIERI
    PONTEIOS -- PRELUDES -- BK. 4 -- 31-40 --
        FRANCO COLOMBO PUBLICATIONS   BA11622   2.50
GUARNIERI
    PONTEIOS -- PRELUDES -- BK. 5 -- 41-50 --
        FRANCO COLOMBO PUBLICATIONS   BA11895   2.50
GUASTAVINO
    TEN CANTILENAS ARGENTINAS
        FRANCO COLOMBO PUBLICATIONS   BA11684   3.50
GUASTAVINO
    TEN PRELUDES
        FRANCO COLOMBO PUBLICATIONS   BA10584   1.50
GUASTAVINO
    THREE SONATINAS
        FRANCO COLOMBO PUBLICATIONS   BA10301   1.50
GUENTHER--ED   GUENTHER
    CLASSICS FOR ADULTS, BK. 1
        MUSICORD PUBLICATIONS, INC.   1.25

GUENTHER--ED   GUENTHER
    PIANO AND ITS ANCESTORS, THE -- AN ANTHOLOGY OF EARLY KEYBOARD
    MUSIC, 1563-1800
        ASSOCIATED MUSIC PUBLISHERS, INC.   AMP   1.00
GUENTHER--ED   GUENTHER   2
    SWING YOUR PARTNER
        CENTURY MUSIC PUBLISHING COMPANY, INC.   1.00
GUERRINI, G.   FLORIS
    NINETEEN STUDIES
        FRANCO COLOMBO PUBLICATIONS   ER1947   2.25
GUERRINI, G.
    THREE EASY LITTLE PIECES
        FRANCO COLOMBO PUBLICATIONS   BON.653   .90
GUILLOU, R.   6
    ASSISE
        ALPHONSE LEDUC
GUILLOU, R.   5, 6
    DIURNES
        ALPHONSE LEDUC
GUILLOU, R.   6
    PIECES
        ALPHONSE LEDUC
GUILLOU, R.   6, 7
    PLEIN AIR
        ALPHONSE LEDUC
GUILLOU, R.   5, 6
    QUATRE PIECES
        ALPHONSE LEDUC
GUILLOU, R.   5, 6
    SUITE SUR DES MOTIFS DE TERROIR
        ALPHONSE LEDUC
GUION, D.
    ALLEY TUNES--THREE SCENES FROM THE SOUTH
        G. SCHIRMER, INC.   1.25
GURIDI
    DIES MELODIAS VASCAS
        ASSOCIATED MUSIC PUBLISHERS, INC.   UME   2.25
GURIDI
    OCHO APUNTES
        ASSOCIATED MUSIC PUBLISHERS, INC.   UME   1.25
GURIDI
    VASCONIA -- THREE PIECES ON POPULAR BASQUE THEMES
        ASSOCIATED MUSIC PUBLISHERS, INC.   UME   1.50
GURLITT   PALMER, W. A.
    ALBUM FOR THE YOUNG
        ALFRED MUSIC COMPANY   633   1.50
GURLITT
    ALBUM FOR THE YOUNG, OP. 140--20 MELODIOUS PIECES
        G. SCHIRMER, INC.   L325   1.00
GURLITT
    ALBUM-LEAVES FOR THE YOUNG, OP. 101
        G. SCHIRMER, INC.   L309   1.00
GURLITT
    BUDS AND BLOSSOMS, OP. 107--12 MELODIOUS STUDIES
        G. SCHIRMER, INC.   L323   .75
GURLITT   1-2
    DER ERSTE VORTRAG OP. 210
        SCHOTT   196   2.00
GURLITT   REHBERG   1-3
    DER NEUE GURLITT, 64 LEICHTE STUCKE -- BK. 1
        SCHOTT   1583   2.50
GURLITT   REHBERG   1-3
    DER NEUE GURLITT, 64 LEICHTE STUCKE -- BK. 2
        SCHOTT   1584   2.50
GURLITT   1
    DIE ERSTEN SCHRITTE DES JUGEND KLAVIERSPIELERS OP. 82 - BK. 1
        SCHOTT   384   2.00
GURLITT   1
    DIE LEICHTSTEN GELAUFIGKEITSETUDEN OP. 83 - BK. 2
        SCHOTT   387   2.00
GURLITT
    EASIEST STUDIES IN VELOCITY, OP. 83
        G. SCHIRMER, INC.   L536   1.00
GURLITT   BEGINNER
    FIRST BOOK, A
        EDWIN F. KALMUS   3497   1.25
GURLITT   BEGINNER
    FIRST LESSONS, OP. 117
        EDWIN F. KALMUS   3489   1.00
GURLITT
    FIRST LESSONS, THE--TWENTY-FOUR LITTLE MELODIES, OP. 117
        G. SCHIRMER, INC.   L324   .75
GURLITT
    FIRST STEPS OF THE YOUNG PIANIST, THE--100 NEW AND VERY EASY
    PRACTICE PIECES, OP. 82--BK. 1
        G. SCHIRMER, INC.   L534   1.00
GURLITT
    FIRST STEPS OF THE YOUNG PIANIST, THE--100 NEW AND VERY EASY
    PRACTICE PIECES, OP. 82--BK. 2
        G. SCHIRMER, INC.   L535   1.00
GURLITT   E
    FOUR SONATINES, OP. 214
        C. F. PETERS CORPORATION   B427   1.50
GURLITT   1-2
    JUGENDALBUM OP. 62
        SCHOTT   342   2.00
GURLITT   E
    MERRY GURLITT --30 EASY PIECES--
        C. F. PETERS CORPORATION   5374   2.50
GURLITT
    SCHOOL OF VELOCITY, OP. 141--24 SHORT STUDIES FOR BEGINNERS
        G. SCHIRMER, INC.   L326   1.00
GURLITT   5
    SCHWANKE UND IDYLLEN OP. 55
        SCHOTT   1728   2.25
GURLITT   PALMER, W. A.
    SIX SONATINAS
        ALFRED MUSIC COMPANY   571   1.50
GURLITT
    SIX SONATINAS, OP. 54
        G. SCHIRMER, INC.   L1612   1.25
GURLITT
    THIRTY-FIVE EASY STUDIES WITHOUT OCTAVES, OP. 130
        G. SCHIRMER, INC.   L339   1.25
GURLITT
    TWENTY-FOUR EASY MELODIOUS STUDIES, OP. 50
        G. SCHIRMER, INC.   L798   1.00
GURLITT
    TWENTY-FOUR MELODIOUS AND PROGRESSIVE STUDIES, OP. 131
        G. SCHIRMER, INC.   L206   1.50
GURLITT
    TWENTY-FOUR MELODIOUS STUDIES OF MEDUIM DIFFICULTY, OP. 51
        G. SCHIRMER, INC.   L801   1.00
GURLITT
    TWENTY-FOUR OCTAVE-STUDIES, OP. 100
        G. SCHIRMER, INC.   L539   1.00

GURLITT
 TWENTY-FOUR STUDIES ON SCALES AND ARPEGGIOS, OP. 85
  G. SCHIRMER, INC.   L807 1.00
GURLITT   1
 VIER UND FUNFZIG KLAVIUR MEL. ETUDEN OP. 187
  SCHOTT   233 2.00
GUTIERREZ-PONCE
 IMPRESION ANDALUZA. THREE PIECES
  ASSOCIATED MUSIC PUBLISHERS, INC. ESC 2.00
GWILT, D.
 TWO PIECCES
  NOVELLO AND COMPANY, LTD. 10.0060.08 1.15
HAAS
 GOOD HUMOR, OP. 18. HUMORESQUES
  ASSOCIATED MUSIC PUBLISHERS, INC. SIM 1.25
HAAS   3-4
 HAUSMARCHEN OP. 35, 43, 53 - BK. 1
  SCHOTT   2628 2.25
HAAS   3-4
 HAUSMARCHEN OP. 35, 43, 53 - BK. 2
  SCHOTT   2629 2.25
HAAS   3-4
 HAUSMARCHEN OP. 35, 43, 53 - BK. 3
  SCHOTT   2630 2.25
HAAS   4
 KLANGSPIELE OP. 99, BK. 1
  SCHOTT   5273 2.50
HAAS   4
 KLANGSPIELE OP. 99, BK. 2
  SCHOTT   5274 2.50
HAAS   2
 STUCKE FUR DIE JUGEND OP. 69 -- DREI KLEINE SUITEN
  SCHOTT   1405 2.50
HAAS   2
 STUCKE FUR DIE JUGEND OP. 69 -- 7 KLAVIER VOR TRAGSTUCKE
  SCHOTT   1409 2.50
HAAS   4
 VIER SONATINEN OP. 94, BK. 1
  SCHOTT   3873 1.75
HAAS   4
 VIER SONATINEN OP. 94, BK. 2
  SCHOTT   3874 1.75
HABERBIER, E.   RUTHARDT
 ETUDE POESIES, OP. 53 AND OP. 59
  G. SCHIRMER, INC.   L191 1.50
HABERBIER, E.   PARSONS
 MODERN FINGER GYMNASTICS
  G. SCHIRMER, INC.   .75
HABERBIER, E.   POZZOLI
 POETIC STUDIES, OP. 53 AND 59
  FRANCO COLOMBO PUBLICATIONS ER913 2.25
HAESSLER   M
 SIX EASY SONATAS
  C. F. PETERS CORPORATION 1862 2.00
HAESSLER
 TWENTY-FOUR WALTZ ETUDES
  FRANCO COLOMBO PUBLICATIONS SIK.104 1.50
HAGEMAN
 SIX PIANO PICTURES
  SHAWNEE PRESS, INC.   1.50
HAIDMEYER *   MARCKHL
 STYRIAN COMPOSERS, WORKS FOR PIANO -- BK. 2
  ASSOCIATED MUSIC PUBLISHERS, INC. OBV 1.25
HAIEFF, A.
 FOUR JUKE BOX PIECES
  BOOSEY AND HAWKES, INC.   1.50
HAIEFF, A.
 THREE BAGATELLES
  BROUDE BROTHERS LTD.   02.50
HALFFTER, R.
 DOS SONATAS DE EL ESCORIAL -- 1928
  ASSOCIATED MUSIC PUBLISHERS, INC. UME .75
HALFFTER, R.
 ELEVEN BAGATELLES, OP. 19
  ASSOCIATED MUSIC PUBLISHERS, INC. UME 3.00
HALFFTER, R.
 TRES HOJAS DE ALBUM, OP. 22
  ASSOCIATED MUSIC PUBLISHERS, INC. UME 1.50
HALL, F.   FREY   MEDIUM
 WEDDING OF THE WINDS
  SHAWNEE PRESS, INC.   HB-25 .60
HAMILTON, I.   5
 NOCTURNES WITH CADENZAS
  SCHOTT   10882 2.00
HANDEL   M
 ALBUM. 20 FAVORITE PIECES
  C. F. PETERS CORPORATION 1821 2.50
HANDEL   BUONAMICI
 ALBUM--22 FAVORITE PIECES
  G. SCHIRMER, INC.   1.25
HANDEL   ANSON, G. ELEMENTARY
 ANSON INTRODUCES HANDEL, BK. 1
  WILLIS MUSIC COMPANY   .75
HANDEL   ANSON, G. INTERMEDIATE
 ANSON INTRODUCES HANDEL, BK. 2
  WILLIS MUSIC COMPANY   1.00
HANDEL   DOFLEIN   3
 AUSGEWAHLTE KLAVIERWERKE
  SCHOTT   4484 2.25
HANDEL   3-4
 AUSWAHL - 25 VIELGESPIELTE STUCKE
  SCHOTT   506 1.75
HANDEL   3
 AYLESFORDER STUCKE
  SCHOTT   2129 2.25
HANDEL   COIT, L. E. *
 CHILDHOOD DAYS OF FAMOUS COMPOSERS -- CHILD HANDEL
  THEODORE PRESSER COMPANY   1.00
HANDEL   ROWLEY   E-M
 EASIER PIECES FOR PIANO
  C. F. PETERS CORPORATION H3 1.50
HANDEL   E
 EASY DANCES AND PIECES --23--
  C. F. PETERS CORPORATION L5019 1.25
HANDEL   BUELOW *   E-M
 EASY PIECES --12--
  C. F. PETERS CORPORATION 4334 1.50
HANDEL   STEGLICH
 EIGHT LARGE SUITES, THE
  BARENREITER VERLAG BA 4005 5.00
HANDEL   BEGINNER
 FIRST BOOK, A
  EDWIN F. KALMUS   3507 1.25
HANDEL   BRADLEY
 FIRST COMPOSERS - HANDEL
  FRANCO COLOMBO PUBLICATIONS LD204 1.00

HANDEL   RUTHARDT   M
 FIRST STUDIES --14 PIECES IN PROGRESSIVE ORDER.
  C. F. PETERS CORPORATION 2669 2.50
HANDEL   M
 FUGHETTES --6--
  C. F. PETERS CORPORATION 4D 1.25
HANDEL
 FUGHETTES NOS. 5 AND 6
  FREDERICK HARRIS MUSIC COMPANY .40
HANDEL
 FUGUES --6-- AND FUGUETTES --6--. URTEXT.
  C. F. PETERS CORPORATION 4984 3.00
HANDEL   PASQUET
 GEORGE FRIEDRICH HANDEL, BK. 1 -- ADVANCED INTERMEDIATE
  WILLIS MUSIC COMPANY   1.00
HANDEL   PASQUET
 GEORGE FRIEDRICH HANDEL, BK. 2 -- EARLY ADVANCED
  WILLIS MUSIC COMPANY   1.00
HANDEL   SCHOLZ
 HANDEL ALBUM, A - THE EASIEST PIECES
  THEODORE PRESSER COMPANY   1.00
HANDEL   MOORE
 INTRODUCTION TO HANDEL
  CARL FISCHER, INC.   PT 447 1.00
HANDEL   STEGLICH 3-4
 KLAVIERWERKE 1. DIE ACHT GROSSEN SUITEN -- HALLISCHE
 HANDEL-AUSGABE --
  BARENREITER VERLAG BA 4005
HANDEL   M
 LECONS, CHACONNE, PIECES, 6 GRAND FUGUES
  C. F. PETERS CORPORATION 4C 2.50
HANDEL
 LECONS, PIECES, GRAND FUGUES, FUGHETTES
  EDWIN F. KALMUS   3510 2.50
HANDEL   HUGHES
 MASTER SERIES FOR THE YOUNG, VOL. 02--HANDEL--
  G. SCHIRMER, INC.   1.25
HANDEL *   SCHWARZ 3-4
 MEISTERWERKE DER KLAVIERMUSIK, BK. 1 - 27 STUCKE
  BARENREITER VERLAG SM 2117
HANDEL   E
 MELODIES FROM 'MESSIAH'
  C. F. PETERS CORPORATION H272 1.25
HANDEL   CHING   EASY
 NEW EASY GRADED CLASSIC ALBUM - HANDEL
  GENERAL WORDS AND MUSIC COMPANY 1.25
HANDEL   MATTHAEI, K. 3
 ORGELKONZERTE, OP. 4 FUR KLAVIER ODER ORGEL MANUALITER, HEFT 1 -
 G MINOR, B FLAT, G MINOR
  BARENREITER VERLAG BA 1894
HANDEL   MATTHAEI, K. 3
 ORGELKONZERTE, OP. 4 FUR KLAVIER ODER ORGEL MANUALITER, HEFT 2 -
 F, F, B FLAT
  BARENREITER VERLAG BA 1895
HANDEL   E-M
 PIANO BOOK OF THE YOUNG HANDEL --10 PIECES--
  C. F. PETERS CORPORATION 4985 3.00
HANDEL   SERAUKY   M-D
 PIANO WORKS --URTEXT-- IN 5 VOLUMES# VOL.1# 8 SUITES
  C. F. PETERS CORPORATION 4981 4.00
HANDEL   SERAUKY   M-D
 PIANO WORKS --URTEXT-- IN 5 VOLUMES# VOL.2# 6 SUITES, PRELUDE,
 ARIA, AND CHACONNE
  C. F. PETERS CORPORATION 4982 4.00
HANDEL   SERAUKY   M-D
 PIANO WORKS --URTEXT-- IN 5 VOLUMES# VOL.3# 2 SUITES, 10 PIECES
  C. F. PETERS CORPORATION 4983 3.50
HANDEL   GLASENAPP   M
 PIANO WORKS --URTEXT-- IN 5 VOLUMES# VOL.4# 6 FUGUES, 6
 FUGUETTES
  C. F. PETERS CORPORATION 4984 3.00
HANDEL   SERAUKY   E-M
 PIANO WORKS --URTEXT-- IN 5 VOLUMES# VOL.5# PIANO BOOK OF THE
 YOUNG HANDEL --10 PIECES--
  C. F. PETERS CORPORATION 4985 3.00
HANDEL   RUTHARDT   M-D
 PIANO WORKS, VOL. 1
  C. F. PETERS CORPORATION 4A 2.00
HANDEL   RUTHARDT   M-D
 PIANO WORKS, VOL. 2
  C. F. PETERS CORPORATION 4B 2.00
HANDEL   RUTHARDT   M
 PIANO WORKS, VOL. 3
  C. F. PETERS CORPORATION 4C 2.50
HANDEL   RUTHARDT   M
 PIANO WORKS, VOL. 4
  C. F. PETERS CORPORATION 4D 1.25
HANDEL   BRODSZKY
 PIECES FOR HARPSICHORD
  KULTURA   2.25
HANDEL   3
 SECHS FUGHETTEN
  SCHOTT   09627 1/2 1.00
HANDEL   BUONAMICI *
 SELECTED COMPOSITIONS
  FRANCO COLOMBO PUBLICATIONS ER2486 2.00
HANDEL   M
 SELECTED PIECES --7--
  C. F. PETERS CORPORATION 4335 2.00
HANDEL   LONGO
 SIX FUGHETTE
  FRANCO COLOMBO PUBLICATIONS ER418 1.00
HANDEL   M
 SIX FUGUES --VOLUNTARIES-- FOR HARPSICHORD OR ORGAN --'TALLIS TO
 WESLEY' SERIES NO.12--
  C. F. PETERS CORPORATION H1685A 2.50
HANDEL   HERNADI
 SIXTEEN LITTLE PIANO PIECES
  KULTURA   1.00
HANDEL
 SIXTEEN SUITES, BK. 1
  EDWIN F. KALMUS   3508 2.00
HANDEL   BUONAMICI *
 SIXTEEN SUITES, BK. 1 -- 1-8 --
  FRANCO COLOMBO PUBLICATIONS ER1042 2.75
HANDEL
 SIXTEEN SUITES, BK. 2
  EDWIN F. KALMUS   3509 2.00
HANDEL   BUONAMICI *
 SIXTEEN SUITES, BK. 2 -- 9-16 --
  FRANCO COLOMBO PUBLICATIONS ER1043 2.00
HANDEL   M-D
 SUITES, VOL. 1 NOS. 1-8
  C. F. PETERS CORPORATION 4A 2.00
HANDEL   M-D
 SUITES, VOL. 2 NOS. 9-16
  C. F. PETERS CORPORATION 4B 2.00

HANDEL   ZINGEL   2-3
   TEMA CON VARIAZIONI
      SCHOTT   4913   1.75
HANDEL   BUELOW
   TWELVE EASY PIECES
      FRANCO COLOMBO PUBLICATIONS   ER1326   .75
HANDEL   BUELOW
   TWELVE EASY PIECES
      G. SCHIRMER, INC.   L381   1.00
                                          M
HANDEL
   TWELVE FANTASIAS AND 4 PIECES
      C. F. PETERS CORPORATION   A90   2.50
HANDEL   ALDRIDGE, M.
   YOUNG PIANIST'S HANDEL, THE, BK. 1
      OXFORD UNIVERSITY PRESS   38.011   2.25
HANDEL   ALDRIDGE, M.
   YOUNG PIANIST'S HANDEL, THE, BK. 2
      OXFORD UNIVERSITY PRESS   38.012   2.25
HANDEL   M
   ZADOK THE PRIEST, 3 PIECES
      C. F. PETERS CORPORATION   H391   1.25
HANDEL   FREY   2-3
   ZWANZIG KLEINE TANZE
      SCHOTT   2680   1.75
HANKINSON, R.
   POP - GOES THE PIANO, VOL. 1
      GENERAL MUSIC PUBLISHING COMPANY, INC.   2.50
HANKINSON, R.
   POP - GOES THE PIANO, VOL. 2
      GENERAL MUSIC PUBLISHING COMPANY, INC.   2.50
HANKINSON, R.
   POP - GOES THE PIANO, VOL. 3
      GENERAL MUSIC PUBLISHING COMPANY, INC.   2.50
HANKINSON, R.
   POP - GOES THE PIANO, VOL. 4
      GENERAL MUSIC PUBLISHING COMPANY, INC.   2.50
HANKINSON, R.
   POP, GOES THE PIANO, BK. 1
      GENERAL MUSIC PUBLISHING COMPANY, INC.   553   2.50
HANKINSON, R.
   POP, GOES THE PIANO, BK. 2
      GENERAL MUSIC PUBLISHING COMPANY, INC.   554   2.50
HANKINSON, R.
   POP, GOES THE PIANO, BK. 3
      GENERAL MUSIC PUBLISHING COMPANY, INC.   555   2.50
HANKINSON, R.
   POP, GOES THE PIANO, BK. 4
      GENERAL MUSIC PUBLISHING COMPANY, INC.   733   2.50
HANON   ZEPP
   HANON IN ALL KEYS
      PRO-ART PUBLICATIONS, INC.   309   .85
HANON, C.   BRIMHALL, J.
   FIRST BOOK OF HANON
      CHARLES HANSEN   H404   1.50
HANON, C.   BEZDEK
   HANON PREPARATORY BOOK
      WILLIS MUSIC COMPANY   1.25
HANON, C.   BRIMHALL, J.
   HANON THROUGH THE KEYS
      CHARLES HANSEN   H405   1.50
HANON, C.   FROST
   HANON-FROST - BOOK 1
      BOSTON MUSIC COMPANY   1.00
HANON, C.   FROST
   HANON-FROST - BOOK 2
      BOSTON MUSIC COMPANY   1.00
HANON, C.   SCHAUM, J.   1 1/2
   HANON-SCHAUM, BK.1
      BELWIN-MILLS PUBLISHING CORPORATION   1.50
HANON, C.   SCHAUM, J.   2 1/2
   HANON-SCHAUM, BK.2
      BELWIN-MILLS PUBLISHING CORPORATION   1.50
HANON, C.   MONTANARI
   IL PIANISTA VIRTUOSO, 60 ESERCIZI
      EDIZIONI BERBEN   1399   4.50
HANON, C. *
   JAZZ HANON
      PUGET MUSIC PUBLICATIONS, INC.   P713   4.00
HANON, C.   RING
   LITTLE HANON, THE
      SUMMY-BIRCHARD COMPANY   1.50
HANON, C.   BEZDEK
   RHYTHMIC VARIATIONS ON HANON, BK. 1
      WILLIS MUSIC COMPANY   1.50
HANON, C.   BEZDEK
   RHYTHMIC VARIATIONS ON HANON, BK. 2
      WILLIS MUSIC COMPANY   1.50
HANON, C.   LINDQUIST
   TECHNICAL VARIANTS
      SUMMY-BIRCHARD COMPANY   1.75
HANON, C.   THOMPSON, J.   1
   THOMPSON-HANON, BOOK 1
      WILLIS MUSIC COMPANY   1.25
HANON, C.   THOMPSON, J.   3
   THOMPSON-HANON, BOOK 2
      WILLIS MUSIC COMPANY   1.25
HANON, C.
   VIRTUOSO PIANIST IN 60 EXERCISES, THE
      G. SCHIRMER, INC.   L925   2.00
HANON, C.
   VIRTUOSO PIANIST IN 60 EXERSICES, THE--IN SPANISH
      G. SCHIRMER, INC.   L1081   2.00
HANON, C.
   VIRTUOSO PIANIST. COMPLETE
      CARL FISCHER, INC.   L 684   2.50
HANON, C.
   VIRTUOSO PIANIST, BK. 1
      CARL FISCHER, INC.   L 728   1.00
HANON, C.
   VIRTUOSO PIANIST, BK. 2
      CARL FISCHER, INC.   L 729   1.00
HANON, C.
   VIRTUOSO PIANIST, BK. 3
      CARL FISCHER, INC.   L 730   1.00
HANON, C.   WEINREICH   M-D
   VIRTUOSO PIANIST, IN 60 EXERCISES. COMPLETE
      C. F. PETERS CORPORATION   4354   3.50
HANON, C.   FERTE   M-D
   VIRTUOSO PIANIST, IN 60 EXERCISES. COMPLETE
      C. F. PETERS CORPORATION   SCH143   4.00
HANON, C.   SMALL, A.
   VIRTUOSO PIANIST, THE, BK. 1
      ALFRED MUSIC COMPANY   617   1.00
HANON, C.   SMALL, A.
   VIRTUOSO PIANIST, THE, BK. 2
      ALFRED MUSIC COMPANY   682   1.50

HANON, C.
   VIRTUOSO PIANIST, THE, BK. 1
      G. SCHIRMER, INC.   L1071   .85
HANON, C.
   VIRTUOSO PIANIST, THE, BK. 2
      G. SCHIRMER, INC.   L1072   .85
HANON, C.
   VIRTUOSO PIANIST, THE, BK. 3
      G. SCHIRMER, INC.   L1073   .85
HANON, C.   SMALL, A.
   VIRTUOSO PIANIST, THE, COMPLETE
      ALFRED MUSIC COMPANY   616   2.50
HANON, C.   POZZOLI
   VIRTUOSO PIANISTS, THE
      FRANCO COLOMBO PUBLICATIONS   ER381   2.75
HANON, C.   FERTE   E-M
   YOUNG VIRTUOSO PIANIST, IN 40 EXERCISES
      C. F. PETERS CORPORATION   SCH84   3.50
HANSON, H.--ED   HANSON, H.
   NEW SCRIBNER MUSIC LIBRARY, VOL. 01 'EASY PIANO MUSIC BY
      AMERICAN COMPOSERS'
         CHARLES SCRIBNER'S SONS
HANSON, H.--ED   HANSON, H.
   NEW SCRIBNER MUSIC LIBRARY, VOL. 02 'KEYBOARD PANORAMA'
         CHARLES SCRIBNER'S SONS
HANSON, H.--ED   HANSON, H.
   NEW SCRIBNER MUSIC LIBRARY, VOL. 03 'PIANO CLASSICS'
         CHARLES SCRIBNER'S SONS
HANSON, H.--ED   HANSON, H.
   NEW SCRIBNER MUSIC LIBRARY, VOL. 04 'A CENTURY OF PIANO MUSIC'
         CHARLES SCRIBNER'S SONS
HANSON, H.--ED   HANSON, H.
   NEW SCRIBNER MUSIC LIBRARY, VOL. 05 'ALL-TIME PIANO FAVORITES'
         CHARLES SCRIBNER'S SONS
HANSON, H.--ED   HANSON, H.
   NEW SCRIBNER MUSIC LIBRARY, VOL. 07 'AT THE OPERA'
         CHARLES SCRIBNER'S SONS
HANSON, H.--ED   HANSON, H.
   NEW SCRIBNER MUSIC LIBRARY, VOL. 08 'MUSIC FOR THE DANCE'
         CHARLES SCRIBNER'S SONS
HANSON, H.--ED   HANSON, H.
   NEW SCRIBNER MUSIC LIBRARY, VOL. 09 'HOME FAVORITES'
         CHARLES SCRIBNER'S SONS
HANSON, H.--ED   HANSON, H.
   NEW SCRIBNER MUSIC LIBRARY, VOL. 10 'ART SONGS'
         CHARLES SCRIBNER'S SONS
HANSON, H.--ED   HANSON, H.
   NEW SCRIBNER MUSIC LIBRARY, VOL. 11 'REFERENCE VOLUME'
         CHARLES SCRIBNER'S SONS
HANUS, J.   2
   AUGENBLICKE IN DER NATUR. 10 LEICHTE BAGATELLEN, OP. 18
      BARENREITER VERLAG   AP 602
HANUS, J.
   MUSIC OF NATURE, THE
      GENERAL MUSIC PUBLISHING COMPANY, INC.   728   3.00
HARALDSTED--ED.   HARALDSTED
   BALLET MUSIC OF THE ROYAL DANISH BALLET, BK. 1--WILHELM HANSEN
      EDITION
         G. SCHIRMER, INC.   2.50
HARALDSTED--ED.   HARALDSTED
   BALLET MUSIC OF THE ROYAL DANISH BALLET, BK. 2--WILHELM HANSEN
      EDITION
         G. SCHIRMER, INC.   3.50
HARDING, R.
   NURSERY RHYMES FOR TOTS
      WILLIS MUSIC COMPANY   .90
HARDING, R.--ED   HARDING, R.
   CHRISTMAS CAROLS FOR EVERYONE
      WILLIS MUSIC COMPANY   .50
HARMER
   TOY MAKER, THE, AND HOP, SKIP, AND JUMP
      ASSOCIATED MUSIC PUBLISHERS, INC.   BER   .50
HARRIES, D.
   FOUR IMPROMPTUS
      OXFORD UNIVERSITY PRESS   32.156 2.30
HARRISON
   CHORDING THE KEYBOARD
      WARNER BROTHERS PUBLISHERS   2.50
HARRISON, S.--ED   HARRISON, S.
   MASTER TOUCH -- BEETHOVEN, THE
      BELWIN-MILLS PUBLISHING CORPORATION   07057   1.50
HARRISON, S.--ED   HARRISON, S.
   MASTER TOUCH -- CHOPIN, THE
      BELWIN-MILLS PUBLISHING CORPORATION   07058   1.50
HARRISON, S.--ED   HARRISON, S.
   MASTER TOUCH -- MOZART, THE
      BELWIN-MILLS PUBLISHING CORPORATION   07059   1.50
HARSANYI
   FIVE SHORT PRELUDES
      ASSOCIATED MUSIC PUBLISHERS, INC.   ESC   3.00
HARSANYI
   FOUR PIECES - PRELUDE, SERENADE, AIR, DANCE
      FRANCO COLOMBO PUBLICATIONS   SAL   5.50
HARSANYI
   RYTHMES
      FRANCO COLOMBO PUBLICATIONS   SAL   4.00
HARSANYI
   SUITE - PRELUDE, ROMANCE, INTERMEZZO, NOCTURNE
      FRANCO COLOMBO PUBLICATIONS   SAL   4.00
HARSANYI
   SUITE BREVE -- 5 PIECES --
      FRANCO COLOMBO PUBLICATIONS   SAL   4.25
HARSANYI
   TWELVE EASY PIECES
      FRANCO COLOMBO PUBLICATIONS   SAL   5.50
HART, F.
   SONGS OF FREDDIE HART, THE
      THE BIG THREE MUSIC CORPORATION   02.95
HARTMANN
   THREE POEMS, OP. 34
      ASSOCIATED MUSIC PUBLISHERS, INC.   AMP   .75
HARTNESS, R.
   LEARN TO PLAY GOSPEL PIANO
      LILLENAS PUBLISHING COMPANY   MB-063 6.95
HARTZELL
   NINE UNCRITICAL PIECES -- 1968
      ASSOCIATED MUSIC PUBLISHERS, INC.   DOB   3.00
HARVEY, A.
   RHYTHMS AND DANCES FOR PRE-SCHOOL AND KINDEGARTEN
      G. SCHIRMER, INC.   .75
HARVEY, SR. A.
   RHYTHMS AND DANCES FOR PRE-SCHOOL AND KINDERGARTEN
      G. SCHIRMER, INC.   .75
HARVEY, VIVIEN
   BIRDS OF A FEATHER - 10 EASY PIECES
      FRANCO COLOMBO PUBLICATIONS   NY1468 1.00

HARVEY, VIVIEN
  TANGLEWOOD TALES
    BELWIN-MILLS PUBLISHING CORPORATION — 1.50
HARVEY, VIVIEN
  TUNES FOR EVERYBODY - 65 FAMOUS PIECES IN EASY ARRANGEMENTS
    FRANCO COLOMBO PUBLICATIONS — NY1454 — 1.25
HASSE — RUF
  TWO SONATAS
    FRANCO COLOMBO PUBLICATIONS — SY640 — 1.75
HASSLER, J. — 2-3
  TWENTY-FOUR KLEINE ETUDEN IN WALZFORM
    SCHOTT — 2830 — 2.25
HAUBIEL, C. — E
  HOMAGE TO BACH–BOOK 1
    COMPOSERS PRESS, INC. — 3.00
HAUBIEL, C. — E
  HOMAGE TO BACH–BOOK 2
    COMPOSERS PRESS, INC. — 3.00
HAUER, J.
  PIANO PIECES, OP. 3, 9, 10, 16
    UNIVERSAL EDITION — UE 8380 — 1.70
HAUFRECHT
  THREE NOCTURNES -- 1957
    ASSOCIATED MUSIC PUBLISHERS, INC. — AMP — 1.50
HAVENS, R.
  RICHIE HAVENS - ANTHOLOGY
    THE BIG THREE MUSIC CORPORATION — 03.95
HAVILL, L.
  YOU CAN SIGHT READ -- THE PLEASURES OF PIANO SIGHT READING THROUGH KEYBOARD HARMONY AND TECHNIQUE, BK. 1
    THEODORE PRESSER COMPANY — 3.75
HAVILL, L.
  YOU CAN SIGHT READ -- THE PLEASURES OF PIANO SIGHT READING THROUGH KEYBOARD HARMONY AND TECHNIQUE, BK. 2
    THEODORE PRESSER COMPANY — 3.50
HAYDN
  ALBUM
    KULTURA — 2.00
HAYDN — 3-4
  AUSWAHL -- 15 AUSGEWAHLTE KOMPOSITIONEN
    SCHOTT — 501 — 1.75
HAYDN — BADURA-SKODA
  CADENZAS TO THE CONCERTO IN D
    ASSOCIATED MUSIC PUBLISHERS, INC. — DOB — 1.00
HAYDN — LANDON, CHR. *
  COMPLETE SONATAS FOR PIANO, VOL. 1A --NOS. 1-18--
    WIENER URTEXT EDITION — UT 50026 — 7.50
HAYDN — LANDON, CHR. *
  COMPLETE SONATAS FOR PIANO, VOL. 1B --NOS. 19-35--
    WIENER URTEXT EDITION — UT 50027 — 7.50
HAYDN — LANDON, CHR. *
  COMPLETE SONATAS FOR PIANO, VOL. 2 --NOS. 36-52--
    WIENER URTEXT EDITION — UT 50028 — 10.00
HAYDN — LANDON, CHR. *
  COMPLETE SONATAS FOR PIANO, VOL. 3 --NOS. 53-62--
    WIENER URTEXT EDITION — UT 50029 — 7.50
HAYDN — E
  DANCES AND PIECES --14--
    C. F. PETERS CORPORATION — L5004 — 1.50
HAYDN — ZEITLIN *
  DIGEST OF SHORT PIANO WORKS, A
    BOSTON MUSIC COMPANY — 2.00
HAYDN — E
  DIVERTIMENTI --SONATINAS-- 6. URTEXT
    C. F. PETERS CORPORATION — 4443 — 2.00
HAYDN — ROWLEY — M
  EASIEST ORIGINAL PIECES FOR PIANO
    C. F. PETERS CORPORATION — H4 — 1.50
HAYDN — LONGO
  EASY COMPOSITIONS -- WITH MOZART'S EASY COMPOSITIONS --
    FRANCO COLOMBO PUBLICATIONS — ER867 — 2.50
HAYDN
  EIGHT VARIOUS COMPOSITIONS
    EDWIN F. KALMUS — 3534 — 1.50
HAYDN — BEGINNER
  FIRST BOOK
    EDWIN F. KALMUS — 3523 — 1.25
HAYDN
  FIRST HAYDN BOOK, A
    EDWIN F. KALMUS — 3523 — 1.25
HAYDN — 2
  FIRST HAYDN BOOK, THE
    ASHLEY DEALERS SERVICE, INC. — 1.25
HAYDN
  FIRST HAYDN BOOK, THE, MEMORIES OF OLD VIENNA
    CENTURY MUSIC PUBLISHING COMPANY, INC. — 1.25
HAYDN — SCHMID
  FLOETENUHRSTUECKE
    ASSOCIATED MUSIC PUBLISHERS, INC. — NAG — 4.00
HAYDN — SCHMID
  FLOTENUHRSTUCKE
    BARENREITER VERLAG — EN 802 — 4.00
HAYDN — SCHMID — 3
  FLOTENUHRSTUCKE. 32 STUCKE FUR SPIELUHREN, EINGERICHTET FUR KLAVIER
    BARENREITER VERLAG — EN 802
HAYDN — MARTIENSSEN
  FORTY-THREE SONATAS --URTEXT--, COMPLETE IN 4 VOLS.; VOLS. 1 AND 2 BOUND TOGETHER. CLOTH-BOUND
    C. F. PETERS CORPORATION — 12.50
HAYDN — MARTIENSSEN
  FORTY-THREE SONATAS --URTEXT--, COMPLETE IN 4 VOLS.; VOLS. 3 AND 4 BOUND TOGETHER. CLOTH-BOUND
    C. F. PETERS CORPORATION — 12.50
HAYDN — ZILCHER
  FORTY-TWO SONATAS, VOL. 1
    ASSOCIATED MUSIC PUBLISHERS, INC. — B/H — 4.00
HAYDN — ZILCHER
  FORTY-TWO SONATAS, VOL. 2
    ASSOCIATED MUSIC PUBLISHERS, INC. — B/H — 4.00
HAYDN — ZILCHER
  FORTY-TWO SONATAS, VOL. 3
    ASSOCIATED MUSIC PUBLISHERS, INC. — B/H — 4.00
HAYDN — ZILCHER
  FORTY-TWO SONATAS, VOL. 4
    ASSOCIATED MUSIC PUBLISHERS, INC. — B/H — 4.00
HAYDN — VARRO
  FOUR VERY EASY MINUETS
    KULTURA — .75
HAYDN
  HAYDN
    ASHLEY DEALERS SERVICE, INC. — HG 10 — 2.95
HAYDN — SCHAUM, J. — 1 1/2
  HAYDN-SCHAUM, BK. 1
    BELWIN-MILLS PUBLISHING CORPORATION — 1.50
HAYDN — SCHAUM, J. — 4
  HAYDN-SCHAUM, BK. 2
    BELWIN-MILLS PUBLISHING CORPORATION — 1.50

HAYDN — 2
  LEHRER UND SCHULER, HOBOKEN 17A
    SCHOTT — 01052 1/2 — 1.00
HAYDN — FREY * — 2
  LEICHTE TANZE -- HOBOKEN 9-10, NO. 1-12 UND HOBOKEN 9-12, NO. 1-12
    SCHOTT — 2582 — 1.75
HAYDN
  LITTLE DANCES FOR THE YOUNG
    UNIVERSAL EDITION — 10270 — .60
HAYDN — E
  LITTLE PIANO BOOK. SELECTION OF EASIEST PIECES AND DANCES
    C. F. PETERS CORPORATION — L5004 — 1.50
HAYDN — HUGHES
  MASTER SERIES FOR THE YOUNG, VOL. 03--HAYDN
    G. SCHIRMER, INC. — 1.25
HAYDN * — E-M
  MASTERS FOR THE YOUNG. VOL. 1
    C. F. PETERS CORPORATION — 2710 — 2.50
HAYDN — IRMER, VON
  MINIATURES FOR PIANO--MUSIKVERLAG ZUM PELIKAN EDITION
    G. SCHIRMER, INC. — 1.00
HAYDN — CHING — EASY
  NEW EASY GRADED CLASSIC ALBUM - HAYDN
    GENERAL WORDS AND MUSIC COMPANY — 1.25
HAYDN — M-D
  ORIGINAL COMPOSITIONS
    C. F. PETERS CORPORATION — 4392 — 3.00
HAYDN
  OXENMENUET AND GYPSY RONDO
    EDWIN F. KALMUS — 3436 — 1.00
HAYDN
  PIANO PIECES
    G. HENLE MUSIKVERLAG — 224 — 3.10
HAYDN
  PIANO PIECES -- CLOTH
    G. HENLE MUSIKVERLAG — 225 — 6.20
HAYDN — LANDON, C.
  PIANO SONATAS, BK. 1
    UNIVERSAL EDITION — 13337 — 11.25
HAYDN — LANDON, C.
  PIANO SONATAS, BK. 2
    UNIVERSAL EDITION — 13338 — 8.00
HAYDN — LANDON, C.
  PIANO SONATAS, BK. 3
    UNIVERSAL EDITION — 13339 — 7.20
HAYDN — HERRMANN — 2-3
  SAMMLUNG LEICHTER KLAVIERSTUCKE
    SCHOTT — 2829 — 2.25
HAYDN — MAERKER — 3
  SECHS ESTERHAZY-SONATEN -- BK. 1, HOBOKEN 16, 21-23
    SCHOTT — 2357 — 2.25
HAYDN — MAERKER — 3
  SECHS ESTERHAZY-SONATEN -- BK. 2, HOBOKEN 16, 24-26
    SCHOTT — 2358 — 2.25
HAYDN — WOEHL — 2-3
  SECHS SONATINEN -- HOBOKEN 16-4, 7, 8, 9, 10, 11
    SCHOTT — 2333 — 2.50
HAYDN — HERNADI
  SELECTED PIANO SONATAS, BKS. 1 AND 2
    KULTURA — EA.
HAYDN — M
  SHORT PIECES --12--. MOVEMENTS FROM STRING QUARTETS AND SYMPHONIES
    C. F. PETERS CORPORATION — 1120 — 1.25
HAYDN — BEER, L. J.
  SIX FAVORITE MINUETS
    UNIVERSAL EDITION — 11100 — 1.20
HAYDN — PALMER, W. A.
  SIX SONATINAS
    ALFRED MUSIC COMPANY — 618 — 1.50
HAYDN — BRODSZKY
  SIX SONATINAS
    KULTURA — 1.50
HAYDN — CHING
  SONATA NO. 27 IN G
    GENERAL WORDS AND MUSIC COMPANY — .75
HAYDN — CHING
  SONATA NO. 34 IN E MINOR
    GENERAL WORDS AND MUSIC COMPANY — .75
HAYDN — CHING
  SONATA NO. 35 IN C
    GENERAL WORDS AND MUSIC COMPANY — .75
HAYDN — M
  SONATAS --49--, VOL.1; NOS. 1-11
    C. F. PETERS CORPORATION — 713A — 2.50
HAYDN — M
  SONATAS --49--, VOL.2; NOS. 12-23
    C. F. PETERS CORPORATION — 713B — 2.50
HAYDN — M
  SONATAS --49--, VOL.3; NOS. 24-33
    C. F. PETERS CORPORATION — 713C — 2.50
HAYDN — M
  SONATAS --49--, VOL.4; NOS. 34-43
    C. F. PETERS CORPORATION — 713D — 2.50
HAYDN — E
  SONATAS --49--, VOL.5; SONATINAS --DIVERTIMENTI-- 6
    C. F. PETERS CORPORATION — 4443 — 2.00
HAYDN — CURRIE
  SONATAS FOR PIANO, BK. 1 NOS. 1-5
    WILLIS MUSIC COMPANY — 1.50
HAYDN — CURRIE
  SONATAS FOR PIANO, BK. 2 NO. 6-10
    WILLIS MUSIC COMPANY — 1.50
HAYDN
  SONATAS, BK. 1, 1-11
    EDWIN F. KALMUS — 3526 — 2.50
HAYDN
  SONATAS, BK. 2, 12-23
    EDWIN F. KALMUS — 3527 — 2.50
HAYDN
  SONATAS, BK. 3, 24-33
    EDWIN F. KALMUS — 3528 — 2.50
HAYDN
  SONATAS, BK. 4, 34-43
    EDWIN F. KALMUS — 3529 — 2.50
HAYDN
  SONATAS, VOL. 1
    G. HENLE MUSIKVERLAG — 152 — 4.40
HAYDN
  SONATAS, VOL. 2
    G. HENLE MUSIKVERLAG — 153 — 4.40
HAYDN
  SONATAS, VOLS. 1 AND 2 IN ONE VOLUME--CLOTH
    G. HENLE MUSIKVERLAG — 172 — 11.55
HAYDN — DUMM
  SONATINAS
    BOSTON MUSIC COMPANY — 1.25

HAYDN * | KURZ | 2-3
SONATINEN UND RONDI, HEFT 2
  BARENREITER VERLAG | AP 1619
HAYDN | MANSFIELD
STEPS TO THE MASTERS
  BANKS AND SON LTD. | 1.35
HAYDN | ZANON
SYMPHONIES -- SELECTED -- BK. 1
  FRANCO COLOMBO PUBLICATIONS | ER1056 | 4.50
HAYDN | ZANON
SYMPHONIES -- SELECTED -- BK. 2
  FRANCO COLOMBO PUBLICATIONS | ER1057 | 4.50
HAYDN | M
SYMPHONIES --12--
  C. F. PETERS CORPORATION | 197 | 10.00
HAYDN | BEGINNER
TEN GERMAN DANCES
  EDWIN F. KALMUS | 3525 | 1.00
HAYDN | RAUCH, W.
THIRTY-FOUR SONATAS, BK. 1
  UNIVERSAL EDITION | 1 | 3.00
HAYDN | RAUCH, W.
THIRTY-FOUR SONATAS, BK. 2
  UNIVERSAL EDITION | 2 | 3.00
HAYDN | RAUCH, W.
THIRTY-FOUR SONATAS, BK. 4
  UNIVERSAL EDITION | 4 | 3.00
HAYDN | BEGINNER
TWELVE EASY PIECES
  EDWIN F. KALMUS | 3524 | 1.25
HAYDN
TWELVE EASY PIECES
  EDWIN F. KALMUS | 3524 | 1.50
HAYDN | RAUCH, W.
TWELVE EASY PIECES
  UNIVERSAL EDITION | 157 | 1.20
HAYDN | KRIEGER, N.
TWELVE MINUETS
  THEODORE PRESSER COMPANY | 1.50
HAYDN | PALMER, W. A.
TWELVE SHORT PIANO PIECES
  ALFRED MUSIC COMPANY | 627 | 1.25
HAYDN | KLEE *
TWENTY SONATAS, BK. 1
  G. SCHIRMER, INC. | L295 | 2.00
HAYDN | BUONAMICI
TWENTY SONATAS, BK. 1 -- 1-10 --
  FRANCO COLOMBO PUBLICATIONS | ER54 | 3.25
HAYDN | KLEE *
TWENTY SONATAS, BK. 2
  G. SCHIRMER, INC. | L296 | 2.00
HAYDN | MARCIANO
TWENTY SONATAS, BK. 2 -- 11-20 --
  FRANCO COLOMBO PUBLICATIONS | ER55 | 3.50
HAYDN | 5
TWO MENUETS
  LEE ROBERTS MUSIC PUBLICATIONS, INC. | .50
HAYDN | VARRO
TWO VERY EASY SONATAS
  KULTURA | .90
HAYDN--ED. | HAYDN | 3
DEUTSCHLAND-LIED
  SCHOTT | 07150 1/2 | 1.00
HAYDN, M. | M
SIX MINUETS
  C. F. PETERS CORPORATION | N3086 | 1.25
HAYWARD, L.
THREE SHORT PIANO PIECES
  THEODORE PRESSER COMPANY | 1.25
HAZART
DE TOUTES PETITES PIECES
  FRANCO COLOMBO PUBLICATIONS | SAL | 1.75
HAZELLE
TOPICS OF THE TROPICS
  BELWIN-MILLS PUBLISHING CORPORATION | 1.00
HEACOX
KEYBOARD TRAINING IN HARMONY, BK. A
  SUMMY-BIRCHARD COMPANY | 2.00
HEACOX
KEYBOARD TRAINING IN HARMONY, BK. B
  SUMMY-BIRCHARD COMPANY | 2.00
HEAPS, S.
SACRED AND SECULAR PIANO ALBUM, BK. 1
  BELWIN-MILLS PUBLISHING CORPORATION | 1.50
HEAPS, S.
SACRED AND SECULAR PIANO ALBUM, BK. 2
  BELWIN-MILLS PUBLISHING CORPORATION | 1.50
HEAPS, S.--ED | HEAPS, S. | E
PIANO MEDITATIONS FOR CHURCH AND HOME
  WILLIS MUSIC COMPANY | 1.50
HEDGES
FIVE PRELUDES
  NOVELLO AND COMPANY, LTD. | 10.0064.00 | 1.40
HEIDELBERGER, P.
BUSY DAYS, BK. 1
  WILLIS MUSIC COMPANY | 1.00
HEIDELBERGER, P.
BUSY DAYS, BK. 2
  WILLIS MUSIC COMPANY | 1.00
HEIDELBERGER, P.
BUSY DAYS, BK. 3
  WILLIS MUSIC COMPANY | 1.00
HEIDELBERGER, P.
HAPPY DAYS, BK. 1
  WILLIS MUSIC COMPANY | 1.25
HEIDELBERGER, P.
HAPPY DAYS, BK. 2
  WILLIS MUSIC COMPANY | 1.25
HEIDELBERGER, P.
HAPPY DAYS, BK. 3
  WILLIS MUSIC COMPANY | 1.00
HEIDELBERGER, P.
MASTER METHOD PIANO NORMAL AND TEACHERS' MANUAL
  WILLIS MUSIC COMPANY | 1.00
HEIDSIEK
INTERVAL PLAY
  BELWIN-MILLS PUBLISHING CORPORATION | 11243 | 1.25
HEISS
CAPRICCI RITMICI -- 1949/50
  ASSOCIATED MUSIC PUBLISHERS, INC. | B/H | 2.25
HEISS
GYMNASTIK AUF TASTEN -- EXERCISES IN FINGER AND HAND POSITION
  ASSOCIATED MUSIC PUBLISHERS, INC. | BRH | 2.25
HELLER, S | PICCIOLI
TWENTY-FIVE STUDIES FOR RHYTHM AND EXPRESSION, OP. 47
  FRANCO COLOMBO PUBLICATIONS | BON.2157 | 2.25

HELLER, S. | M
ALBUM
  C. F. PETERS CORPORATION | 3565 | 3.00
HELLER, S.
ART OF PHRASING, THE--26 MELODIOUS STUDIES, OP. 16--BK. 1
  G. SCHIRMER, INC. | L179 | 1.25
HELLER, S.
ART OF PHRASING, THE--26 MELODIOUS STUDIES, OP. 16--BK. 2
  G. SCHIRMER, INC. | L180 | 1.25
HELLER, S. | TAGLIAPIETRA
ART OF PHRASING, THE, OP. 16
  FRANCO COLOMBO PUBLICATIONS | ER749 | 3.25
HELLER, S. | OESTERLE
FIFTY SELECTED STUDIES--FROM OP. 45, 46, 47
  G. SCHIRMER, INC. | L24 | 2.00
HELLER, S.
FLOWER-FRUIT-AND-THORN-PIECES, OP. 82--18 CHARACTERISTIC PIECES
  G. SCHIRMER, INC. | L600 | 1.00
HELLER, S.
MELODIOUS EXERCISES, OP. 125 -- BK. 1
  ASSOCIATED MUSIC PUBLISHERS, INC. | B/H | .75
HELLER, S. | STEINER
STEPHEN HELLER ALBUM
  BELWIN-MILLS PUBLISHING CORPORATION | 1329 | 1.75
HELLER, S.
THIRTY PROGRESSIVE STUDIES, OP. 46
  CARL FISCHER, INC. | L 328 | 1.25
HELLER, S. | ANDREOLI
THIRTY PROGRESSIVE STUDIES, OP. 46
  FRANCO COLOMBO PUBLICATIONS | ER702 | 2.50
HELLER, S. | M-D
THIRTY PROGRESSIVE STUDIES, OP. 46
  C. F. PETERS CORPORATION | 3562 | 2.50
HELLER, S. | OESTERLE
THIRTY PROGRESSIVE STUDIES, OP. 46
  G. SCHIRMER, INC. | L177 | 1.25
HELLER, S.
THIRTY PROGRESSIVE STUDIES, OP. 46
  UNIVERSAL EDITION | 5921 | 1.25
HELLER, S. | OESTERLE
THIRTY PROGRESSIVE STUDIES, OP. 46--BK. 1
  G. SCHIRMER, INC. | L1120 | .75
HELLER, S. | OESTERLE
THIRTY-TWO PRELUDES, OP. 119
  G. SCHIRMER, INC. | L748 | 1.25
HELLER, S. | ANDREOLI
TWENTY-FIVE MELODIOUS STUDIES, OP. 45
  FRANCO COLOMBO PUBLICATIONS | ER424 | 2.25
HELLER, S. | PICCIOLI
TWENTY-FIVE MELODIOUS STUDIES, OP. 45
  FRANCO COLOMBO PUBLICATIONS | BON.2159 | 3.00
HELLER, S. | TEICHMUELLER | E-M
TWENTY-FIVE MELODIOUS STUDIES, OP. 45
  C. F. PETERS CORPORATION | 3561A | 2.00
HELLER, S. | OESTERLE
TWENTY-FIVE MELODIOUS STUDIES, OP. 45
  G. SCHIRMER, INC. | L176 | 1.50
HELLER, S.
TWENTY-FIVE MELODIOUS STUDIES, OP. 45
  UNIVERSAL EDITION | 5920 | 1.25
HELLER, S. | OESTERLE
TWENTY-FIVE MELODIOUS STUDIES, OP. 45--BK. 1, NOS. 1-9
  G. SCHIRMER, INC. | L1117 | .75
HELLER, S.
TWENTY-FIVE STUDIES FOR DEVELOPMENT OF RHYTHM AND EXPRESSION, OP. 47
  ASHLEY DEALERS SERVICE, INC. | 1.00
HELLER, S. | ANDREOLI
TWENTY-FIVE STUDIES FOR RHYTHM AND EXPRESSION, OP. 47
  FRANCO COLOMBO PUBLICATIONS | ER426 | 1.50
HELLER, S. | OESTERLE
TWENTY-FIVE STUDIES FOR RHYTHM AND EXPRESSION, OP. 47
  G. SCHIRMER, INC. | L178 | 1.25
HELLER, S. | OESTERLE
TWENTY-FIVE STUDIES FOR RHYTHM AND EXPRESSION, OP. 47--BK. 1
  G. SCHIRMER, INC. | L1123 | 1.00
HELLER, S.
TWENTY-FIVE STUDIES FOR RHYTHM, OP. 47
  UNIVERSAL EDITION | 5922 | 1.25
HELLER, S. | ANDREOLI
TWENTY-FIVE STUDIES FROM OP. 46
  FRANCO COLOMBO PUBLICATIONS | ER425 | 1.75
HELLER, S. | PICCIOLI
TWENTY-FIVE STUDIES FROM OP. 46
  FRANCO COLOMBO PUBLICATIONS | BON.2158 | 2.50
HELLER, S.
TWENTY-FIVE STUDIES OF RHYTHM AND EXPRESSION, OP. 47
  CENTURY MUSIC PUBLISHING COMPANY, INC. | 1.00
HELLER, S. | M-D
TWENTY-FIVE STUDIES, OP. 47
  C. F. PETERS CORPORATION | 3563 | 2.00
HELLER, S. | M
TWENTY-FOUR MELODIOUS STUDIES, OP. 125
  C. F. PETERS CORPORATION | 4364 | 2.50
HELLER, S. | M-D
TWENTY-FOUR PRELUDES, OP. 81
  C. F. PETERS CORPORATION | 4666 | 2.50
HELLER, S.
TWENTY-FOUR PRELUDES, OP. 81
  G. SCHIRMER, INC. | L130 | 1.00
HELLER, S.
TWENTY-FOUR STUDIES FOR EXPRESSION AND RHYTHM, OP. 125
  UNIVERSAL EDITION | 1695 | 1.25
HELLER, S. | TAGLIAPIETRA
TWENTY-FOUR STUDIES FOR RHYTHM AND EXPRESSION, OP. 125
  FRANCO COLOMBO PUBLICATIONS | ER432 | 1.75
HELLER, S. | SCHARFENBERG
TWENTY-FOUR STUDIES FOR RHYTHM AND EXPRESSION, OP. 125
  G. SCHIRMER, INC. | L766 | 1.25
HELM, E.
NEW HORIZONS--12 PIECES FOR PIANO--INTRODUCTION TO CONTEMPORARY
STYLES IN PIANO MUSIC
  G. SCHIRMER, INC. | 1.50
HELPS | D
THREE ETUDES
  C. F. PETERS CORPORATION | 6998 | 1.50
HELYER, M. | 1-2
CAROL TUNES
  NOVELLO AND COMPANY, LTD. | 10.0065.09 | 1.15
HENDERSON
NOTE 'N SPELL, BK. 01
  BELWIN-MILLS PUBLISHING CORPORATION | 1.25
HENDERSON
NOTE 'N SPELL, BK. 02
  BELWIN-MILLS PUBLISHING CORPORATION | 1.25
HENDERSON
REDISCOVERED CLASSICS, BK. 1
  BOOSEY AND HAWKES, INC. | 1.50

HENDERSON
  REDISCOVERED CLASSICS, BK. 2
    BOOSEY AND HAWKES, INC.   1.50
HENDERSON
  REDISCOVERED CLASSICS, BK. 3
    BOOSEY AND HAWKES, INC.   1.50
HENDERSON
  REDISCOVERED CLASSICS, BK. 4
    BOOSEY AND HAWKES, INC.   1.50
HENDERSON, R.
  EASY TO LEARN POPULAR PIANO MUSIC
    BOSTON MUSIC COMPANY   1.50
HENDERSON, R.
  INTRODUCTIONS AND ENDINGS
    BOSTON MUSIC COMPANY   1.50
HENDERSON, R.
  LEFT HAND RHYTHMS
    BOSTON MUSIC COMPANY   1.00
HENDERSON, R.
  PLAY PIANO OR ORGAN BY EAR
    BOSTON MUSIC COMPANY   1.50
HENDERSON, R.
  POPULAR MUSIC PIANO PLAYING
    BOSTON MUSIC COMPANY   1.50
HENDERSON, R.
  RIGHT HAND TREATMENTS
    BOSTON MUSIC COMPANY   1.25
HENGEVELD   E
  OSTINATO
    C. F. PETERS CORPORATION   B830   1.25
HENGEVELD   E-M
  POLYPHONIC STUDIES, VOL. 1
    C. F. PETERS CORPORATION   B804   1.25
HENGEVELD   M-D
  POLYPHONIC STUDIES, VOL. 2
    C. F. PETERS CORPORATION   B815   1.25
HENGEVELD   E-M
  THIRTEEN EASY IMPROVISATIONS
    C. F. PETERS CORPORATION   B831   1.25
HENNES, A.   RITTER
  MELODIC EXERCISES, BK. 1
    ASSOCIATED MUSIC PUBLISHERS, INC.   BRH   1.00
HENRY, C.   ASSEZ FACILE - 4
  LA BOITE A MUSIQUE, BK. 1
    ALPHONSE LEDUC
HENRY, C.   ASSEZ FACILE - 4, 5
  LA BOITE A MUSIQUE, BK. 2
    ALPHONSE LEDUC
HENRY, C.   ASSEZ FACILE - 5
  LA BOITE A MUSIQUE, BK. 3
    ALPHONSE LEDUC
HENSELT, A.   JONAS
  TWELVE CHARACTERISTIC CONCERT STUDIES, OP. 2
    G. SCHIRMER, INC.   L44   1.75
HENZE, H.   5
  SIX ABSENCES POUR LE CLAVECIN, 1961
    SCHOTT   5380   3.00
HERARD   PHILIPP, I.   5, 6, 7
  TWELVE ETUDES PIANISTIQUES POUR LA MAIN GAUCHE, OP. 103
    ALPHONSE LEDUC
HERARD
  VARIATIONS EN FORME DE PETITES ETUDES
    ALPHONSE LEDUC
HERBERT   SAVINO
  SELECTIONS FROM ''SWEETHEARTS''
    G. SCHIRMER, INC.   1.25
HERBERT   STAFFORD
  VICTOR HERBERT FAVORITES
    WARNER BROTHERS PUBLISHERS   1.25
HERMAN
  WOODY HERMAN FIVE BOOGIE WOOGIE AND BLUES SOLOS
    MCA MUSIC   1.00
HERMANN, R.
  SIX PETITES PIECES FACILES
    GERARD BILLAUDOT EDITIONS MUSICALES   1.60
HERMANN, R.
  SIX SHORT PIECES
    FRANCO COLOMBO PUBLICATIONS   SAL   2.00
HERNANDEZ NONCADA, E.
  CINCO PIEZAS BAILABLES
    EDICIONES MEXICANAS DE MUSICA, A. C.   02.00
HERNANDEZ--ED   HERNANDEZ
  FLORES DE ESPANA -- 38 FOLK SONGS WITH SPANISH TEXT
    ASSOCIATED MUSIC PUBLISHERS, INC.   3.50
HERRMANN--ED   HERRMANN   2
  ALT-DRESDNER TANZBUCH -- 18 JAHRHUNDERT
    SCHOTT   3941   1.75
HERRMANN--ED   HERRMANN
  ALT-DRESDNER TANZBUCH --18. JARHUNDERT --
    SCHOTT   3941   1.75
HERRMANN--ED   HERRMANN   2
  ALT-NURNBERGER KLAVIERBUCHLEIN -- 17. UND 18. JH. --
    SCHOTT   3769   1.75
HERRMANN--ED   HERRMANN   2
  CLAVIERBUCH EINER SCHWABISCHEN HERZOGIN
    SCHOTT   3940   1.75
HERRMANN--ED   HERRMANN   2
  DITTER V. DITTERSDORF, 20 ENGLISCHE TANZE
    SCHOTT   3935   1.75
HERRMANN--ED   HERRMANN
  EUROPEAN FOLK DANCES
    ASSOCIATED MUSIC PUBLISHERS, INC.   SIM   1.50
HERRMANN--ED   HERRMANN   2-3
  HANDEL-BUCHLEIN
    SCHOTT   3934   1.75
HERRMANN--ED   HERRMANN   M
  OLD MASTERS OF PIANO MUSIC, VOL. 2# FRENCH
    C. F. PETERS CORPORATION   4641B   5.00
HERRMANN--ED   HERRMANN   3
  SONATENBUCH -- 10 KLASSISCHE SONATEN VON BEETHOVEN, HAYDN UND
  MOZART
    SCHOTT   4450   5.00
HERRMANN--ED   HERRMANN
  TUNES FROM FAR AWAY -- 50 EASY ARRANGEMENTS OF FOLKSONGS FROM
  MANY LANDS
    ASSOCIATED MUSIC PUBLISHERS, INC.   SIM   2.00
HERRMANN--ED.   HERRMANN   2
  ALT-NURNBERGER KLAVIERBUCHLEIN -- 17 UND 18 JR.
    SCHOTT   3769   1.75
HERRMANN, K.
  LIVING PIANO TECHNIQUE, BK. 1
    FRANCO COLOMBO PUBLICATIONS   SIK.197   2.50
HERRMANN, K.
  LIVING PIANO TECHNIQUE, BK. 2
    FRANCO COLOMBO PUBLICATIONS   SIK.198   2.50
HERRMANN, K.
  LIVING PIANO TECHNIQUE, BK. 3
    FRANCO COLOMBO PUBLICATIONS   SIK.199   2.50

HERRMANN, K.
  MIT ZWEEN STIMMEN, BK. 1
    FRANCO COLOMBO PUBLICATIONS   SIK.132A   1.25
HERRMANN, K.
  MIT ZWEEN STIMMEN, BK. 2
    FRANCO COLOMBO PUBLICATIONS   SIK.132B   1.25
HERRMANN, K.--ED   HERRMANN, K.   E
  ETUDES BY GREAT MASTERS --DER GERADE WEG--, VOL. 1
    C. F. PETERS CORPORATION   A108   2.00
HERRMANN, K.--ED   HERRMANN, K.   E-M
  ETUDES BY GREAT MASTERS --DER GERADE WEG--, VOL. 2
    C. F. PETERS CORPORATION   A109   2.00
HERRMANN, K.--ED   HERRMANN, K.   M
  ETUDES BY GREAT MASTERS --DER GERADE WEG--, VOL. 3
    C. F. PETERS CORPORATION   A110   2.00
HERRMANN, K.--ED   HERRMANN, K.   E-M
  HARPSICHORD MUSIC OF THE SEVENTEENTH AND EIGHTEENTH CENTURIES,
  VOL. 1
    C. F. PETERS CORPORATION   A65   2.50
HERRMANN, K.--ED   HERRMANN, K.   E-M
  HARPSICHORD MUSIC OF THE SEVENTEENTH AND EIGHTEENTH CENTURIES,
  VOL. 2
    C. F. PETERS CORPORATION   A66   2.50
HERRMANN, K.--ED   HERRMANN, K.   E-M
  TEACHERS AND PUPILS OF J. S. BACH, VOL. 1
    C. F. PETERS CORPORATION   A119   2.00
HERRMANN, K.--ED   HERRMANN, K.   E-M
  TEACHERS AND PUPILS OF J. S. BACH, VOL. 2
    C. F. PETERS CORPORATION   A120   2.00
HERRMANN, R.--ED.   HERRMANN, R.
  SEVENTEENTH CENTURY MASTERS
    INTERNATIONAL MUSIC COMPANY   2.50
HERZ, H.   TAGLIAPIETRA
  COLLECTION OF EXERCISES AND SCALES
    FRANCO COLOMBO PUBLICATIONS   ER737   1.75
HERZ, H.   M-D
  EXERCISES AND PRELUDES, OP. 21
    C. F. PETERS CORPORATION   291   3.50
HERZ, H.   CESI
  EXERCISES AND SCALES
    FRANCO COLOMBO PUBLICATIONS   ER51   2.25
HERZ, H.
  ONE THOUSAND EXERCISES
    FRANCO COLOMBO PUBLICATIONS   ER2141   3.00
HERZ, H.
  SCALES
    CARL FISCHER, INC.   L 320   1.25
HERZ, H.   GAMMES   D
  SCALES AND EXERCISES
    C. F. PETERS CORPORATION   290   2.50
HERZ, H.   VOGRICH
  SCALES AND EXERCISES
    G. SCHIRMER, INC.   L170   1.25
HERZ, H.
  SCALES AND EXERCISES--IN SPANISH
    G. SCHIRMER, INC.   L1083   1.25
HESS
  TWELVE LITTLE PIECES
    FRANCO COLOMBO PUBLICATIONS   SY82   1.50
HESS--ED.   HESS
  MYRA HESS ALBUM
    BOOSEY AND HAWKES, INC.   2.50
HESSENBERG, K.   3
  KLEINE HAUSMUSIK, OP. 24
    SCHOTT   2834   2.25
HESSENBERG, K.   3
  SIEBEN KLEINE KLAVIERSTUCKE, OP. 12
    SCHOTT   2882   2.50
HESSENBERG, K.   3
  ZEHN KLEINE PRALUDIEN, OP. 35
    SCHOTT   1403   2.75
HEYWOOD, E.
  MODERN PIANO TRANSCRIPTIONS
    THE BIG THREE MUSIC CORPORATION   01.50
HILLEMANN *
  FIRST PIANO BOOK, BK. 1
    BARENREITER VERLAG   EN 804   2.50
HILLEMANN *
  FIRST PIANO BOOK, BK. 2
    BARENREITER VERLAG   EN 805   2.50
HILLEMANN *
  FIRST PIANO BOOK, BK. 3
    BARENREITER VERLAG   EN 806   2.50
HILLEMANN--ED   HILLEMANN
  RICERCARE, CANZONEN UND FUGEN
    BARENREITER VERLAG   NMA 87   5.00
HILLEMANN--ED   HILLEMANN
  RICERCARI, CANZONE AND FUGUES -- WORKS BY GABRIELI, CORNET,
  HASSLER, ERBACH, KERLL, MURSCHHAUSER, KRIEGER, PACHELBEL AND
  WALTHER
    ASSOCIATED MUSIC PUBLISHERS, INC.   NAG   4.50
HILLER   HERRMANN
  EASY DANCE PIECES
    FRANCO COLOMBO PUBLICATIONS   SIK.108   1.50
HILMAR   3
  SIXTEEN POLKAS
    BARENREITER VERLAG   AP 603
HINDEMITH   6
  KLAVIERMUSIK, OP. 37 NO. 1, UBUNG IN DREI STUCKEN
    SCHOTT   1299   2.50
HINDEMITH   6
  KLAVIERMUSIK, OP. 37 NO. 2, REIHE KLEINE STUCKE
    SCHOTT   1300   3.50
HINDEMITH   2-3
  KLEINE KLAVIERMUSIK, OP. 45 NO. 4
    SCHOTT   1466   2.00
HINDEMITH   3-5
  LUDUS TONALIS, 1942
    SCHOTT   3964   5.00
HINDEMITH   4-5
  TANZST, OP. 19
    SCHOTT   1418   2.50
HINDEMITH   2
  WIR BAUEN EINE STADT, KLAVIERSTUCKE FUR KINDER, 1931
    SCHOTT   2200   2.00
HINKLE, N.--ED   HINKLE, N.
  FORTY CHRISTMAS CAROLS FOR VOICE AND PIANO
    THEODORE PRESSER COMPANY   1.50
HINSON, M. *   5
  CONTEMPORARY PIANO REPERTOIRE
    BELWIN-MILLS PUBLISHING CORPORATION   FDL 468   2.00
HINSON, M. *   6
  CONTEMPORARY PIANO REPERTOIRE
    BELWIN-MILLS PUBLISHING CORPORATION   FDL 473   2.00
HIRSCHBERG, D.   1
  I LIKE PIECES, BK. 1
    MUSICORD PUBLICATIONS, INC.   1.00

HIRSCHBERG, D.
MUSIC APPRECIATION IS FUN, BK. 1
MUSICORD PUBLICATIONS, INC.   1.25
HIRSCHBERG, D.
PIANO COURSE FOR JUNIORS - PREPARATORY BOOK
MUSICORD PUBLICATIONS, INC.   1.25
HIRSCHBERG, D.
PIANO COURSE FOR JUNIORS, BK. 1
MUSICORD PUBLICATIONS, INC.   1.25
HIRSCHBERG, D.
PIANO LESSONS ARE FUN, BK. 1
MUSICORD PUBLICATIONS, INC.   1.25
HIRSCHBERG, D.
PIECES ARE FUN, BK. 1
MUSICORD PUBLICATIONS, INC.   1.25
HIRSCHBERG, D.
PIECES ARE FUN, BK. 2
MUSICORD PUBLICATIONS, INC.   1.25
HIRSCHBERG, D.
PIECES ARE FUN, BK. 3
MUSICORD PUBLICATIONS, INC.   1.25
HIRSCHBERG, D.
PIECES FOR ENJOYMENT
MUSICORD PUBLICATIONS, INC.   1.25
HIRSCHBERG, D.
SCALES AND CHORDS ARE FUN - BOOK 1 -- MAJOR
MUSICORD PUBLICATIONS, INC.   1.25
HIRSCHBERG, D.
SCALES AND CHORDS ARE FUN - BOOK 2 -- MINOR
MUSICORD PUBLICATIONS, INC.   1.25
HIRSCHBERG, D.
TECHNIC FOR ADULTS, BK. 1
MUSICORD PUBLICATIONS, INC.   1.25
HIRSCHBERG, D.
TECHNIC IS FUN - PREPARATORY BOOK
MUSICORD PUBLICATIONS, INC.   1.25
HIRSCHBERG, D.
TECHNIC IS FUN, BK. 1
MUSICORD PUBLICATIONS, INC.   1.25
HIRSCHBERG, D.
TECHNIC IS FUN, BK. 2
MUSICORD PUBLICATIONS, INC.   1.25
HIRSCHBERG, D.
TECHNIC IS FUN, BK. 3
MUSICORD PUBLICATIONS, INC.   1.25
HIRSCHBERG, D.
TECHNIC IS FUN, BK. 4
MUSICORD PUBLICATIONS, INC.   1.25
HIRSCHBERG, D.
TECHNIC IS FUN, BK. 5
MUSICORD PUBLICATIONS, INC.   1.25
HIRSCHBERG, D.
THEORY IS FUN, BK. 1
MUSICORD PUBLICATIONS, INC.   1.25
HIRSCHBERG, D.
THEORY IS FUN, BK. 2
MUSICORD PUBLICATIONS, INC.   1.25
HIRSCHBERG, D.--ED   HIRSCHBERG, D.
CLASSICS ARE FUN, BK. 1
MUSICORD PUBLICATIONS, INC.   1.25
HIRSCHBERG, D.--ED   HIRSCHBERG, D.
DAVID HIRSCHBERG PIANO COURSE
MUSICORD PUBLICATIONS, INC.   1.25
HIRSCHBERG, D.--ED   HIRSHBERG, D.   2
GREAT MASTERS
ASHLEY DEALERS SERVICE, INC.   1.25
HIRSCHBERG, D.--ED   HIRSCHBERG, D.   2
GREAT MASTERS
CENTURY MUSIC PUBLISHING COMPANY, INC.   1.25
HIRSCHBERG, D.--ED   HIRSCHBERG, D.
MUSIC FOR HAPPINESS, BK. 1
MUSICORD PUBLICATIONS, INC.   1.25
HIRSCHBERG, D.--ED   HIRSCHBERG, D.
MUSIC FOR HAPPINESS, BK. 2
MUSICORD PUBLICATIONS, INC.   1.25
HOFFMAN--ED   HOFFMAN   AE
EASIEST SONATINA ALBUM
WILLIS MUSIC COMPANY   1.25
HOFMANN   MARTIENSSEN   E-M
TONE PICTURES, OP. 88
C. F. PETERS CORPORATION   4158   2.50
HOFSTAD, M.
A TO G - A VERY FIRST MUSICAL ALPHABET BOK
BOSTON MUSIC COMPANY   .75
HOFSTAD, M.
ENJOY YOUR PIANO WITH CHORDS
BOSTON MUSIC COMPANY   1.25
HOFSTAD, M.
FIRST STEPHEN FOSTER
WILLIS MUSIC COMPANY   .80
HOFSTAD, M.
LITTLE PIANIST
BOSTON MUSIC COMPANY   1.95
HOFSTAD, M.--ED   HOFSTAD, M.
LITTLE RHYMES TO SING AND PLAY -- FIVE-FINGER POSITIONS
THEODORE PRESSER COMPANY   1.00
HOFSTAD, M.--ED   HOFSTAD, M.
VERY FIRST CLASSICS
BOSTON MUSIC COMPANY   1.00
HOFSTAD, M.--ED   HOFSTAD, M.
VERY FIRST FAVORITES--ARRANGED FOR PIANO IN FIVE-FINGER POSITION
G. SCHIRMER, INC.   .85
HOFSTAD, M.--ED   HOFSTAD, M.
VERY FIRST HYMNS
BOSTON MUSIC COMPANY   1.25
HOIBY, L.
FIVE PRELUDES, OP. 7
G. SCHIRMER, INC.   1.25
HOLBROOK, N.--ED   HOLBROOK, N.
SCHOOL AND GYMNASSIUM MARCHES
THEODORE PRESSER COMPANY   2.00
HOLCOMB, L. R.--ED   HOLCOMB, L. R.
HYMNS FOR THE BEGINNING PIANIST
BROADMAN MUSIC   4571-07   2.00
HOLLANDER
INDIAN DRUM-BEATS
BELWIN-MILLS PUBLISHING CORPORATION   1.00
HOLLANDER
MY FAVORITE CHRISTMAS CAROLS
EDWARD B. MARKS MUSIC CORPORATION   01.25
HOLLANDER
MY FIRST CLASSICS
EDWARD B. MARKS MUSIC CORPORATION   01.00
HOLLANDER
ON THE TRAIL
PRO-ART PUBLICATIONS, INC.   525   1.00

HOLLANDER
YOU CAN PLAY PIANO SERIES, LEVEL 1 -- YOU CAN PLAY MARCHES
BOOSEY AND HAWKES, INC.   1.00
HOLLANDER
YOU CAN PLAY PIANO SERIES, LEVEL 1 -- YOU CAN PLAY SUNDAY SCHOOL
HYMNS
BOOSEY AND HAWKES, INC.   1.00
HOLLANDER
YOU CAN PLAY PIANO SERIES, LEVEL 2 -- YOU CAN PLAY CHRISTMAS
CAROLS
BOOSEY AND HAWKES, INC.   1.00
HOLLANDER
YOU CAN PLAY PIANO SERIES, LEVEL 2 -- YOU CAN PLAY FOLK SONGS
BOOSEY AND HAWKES, INC.   1.00
HOLLANDER
YOU CAN PLAY PIANO SERIES, LEVEL 2 -- YOU CAN PLAY WALTZES
BOOSEY AND HAWKES, INC.   1.00
HOLLANDER
YOU CAN PLAY PIANO SERIES, LEVEL 3 -- YOU CAN PLAY DANCE-TIME
MUSIC
BOOSEY AND HAWKES, INC.   1.00
HOLLANDER
YOU CAN PLAY PIANO SERIES, LEVEL 3 -- YOU CAN PLAY FAMILIAR
THEMES
BOOSEY AND HAWKES, INC.   1.00
HOLLANDER
YOU CAN PLAY PIANO SERIES, LEVEL 3 -- YOU CAN PLAY FOLK SONGS
BOOSEY AND HAWKES, INC.   1.00
HOLLANDER
YOU CAN PLAY PIANO SERIES, LEVEL 3 -- YOU CAN PLAY WALTZES
BOOSEY AND HAWKES, INC.   1.00
HOLLIGER, H.   5
ELIS, DREI NACHTSTUCKE, 1961
SCHOTT   5389   2.50
HOLMAN, D.   1-2
EIGHT FRENCH FOLK TUNES
NOVELLO AND COMPANY, LTD.   10.0074.08   1.15
HOLMES *
ANIMAL ALPHABET
THE BIG THREE MUSIC CORPORATION   1.95
HOLST   3 1/2
SPINGTIME SONATINA OP. 48 NO. 3 -- AWAY WITH THE SOUTHWIND,
ALONE IN THE FOREST, MOONLIGHT FANTASIE
VOLKWEIN BROS.   .75
HOLT, H.
CHORD-A-TUNE
THEODORE PRESSER COMPANY   1.50
HOLT, H.--ED   HOLT, H.
CARL FISCHER NOTE SPELLER
CARL FISCHER, INC.   O 3410   1.00
HONEGGER, A.
SEVEN SHORT PIECES
ASSOCIATED MUSIC PUBLISHERS, INC.   ESC   4.00
HONEGGER, A.
THREE PIECES - PRELUDE, HOMMAGE A RAVEL, DANCE
FRANCO COLOMBO PUBLICATIONS   SAL   1.50
HOPKINS, A.   E
FOR TALENTED BEGINNERS, BK. 1
OXFORD UNIVERSITY PRESS   39.006   1.00
HOPKINS, A.   E
FOR TALENTED BEGINNERS, BK. 2
OXFORD UNIVERSITY PRESS   39.007   1.00
HORTON   HORTON
ADULT EDUCATION PIANO METHOD, BK. 1
PRO-ART PUBLICATIONS, INC.   778   1.50
HORTON   HORTON
ADULT EDUCATION PIANO METHOD, BK. 2
PRO-ART PUBLICATIONS, INC.   794   1.50
HOUGHTON, W. E.
PRACTICAL HARMONY AT THE KEYBOARD
BANKS AND SON LTD.   .80
HOVHANESS, A.   M
FIVE VISIONARY LANDSCAPES
C. F. PETERS CORPORATION   66043   1.50
HOVHANESS, A.
MOUNTAIN IDYLLS
ASSOCIATED MUSIC PUBLISHERS, INC.   AMP   .75
HOVHANESS, A.
SLUMBER SONG /SIRIS DANCE
MCA MUSIC   .60
HOVHANESS, A.   M
THREE HAIKUS
C. F. PETERS CORPORATION   66028   .60
HOVHANESS, A.   M
THREE PRELUDES AND FUGUES
C. F. PETERS CORPORATION   6569   1.25
HOVHANESS, A.   M-D
TWELVE ARMENIAN FOLK SONGS
C. F. PETERS CORPORATION   6432   1.25
HOVHANESS, A.   M
TWO GHAZALS
C. F. PETERS CORPORATION   6485   .60
HOWELL--ED   HOWELL
ENJOYING THE PIANO
PRO-ART PUBLICATIONS, INC.   212   1.25
HOWELL--ED   HOWELL
FAVORITE FOLK TUNES
PRO-ART PUBLICATIONS, INC.   107   .75
HOWELL, I.
MY FIRST MUSIC WORKBOOK
PRO-ART PUBLICATIONS, INC.   105   1.25
HOWELL, I.
MY FIRST TRIP TO MUSIC LAND
PRO-ART PUBLICATIONS, INC.   106   1.00
HOWELL, I.
MY SECOND MUSIC WORKBOOK
PRO-ART PUBLICATIONS, INC.   210   1.25
HOWELL, I.
TECHNIQUE BUILDER
PRO-ART PUBLICATIONS, INC.   134   1.00
HOWELL, I.
TUNES FOR TECHNIC
PRO-ART PUBLICATIONS, INC.   367   .85
HOWELLS, H.
HOWELL'S CLAVICHORD, BK. 1
NOVELLO AND COMPANY, LTD.   10.0075.06   2.90
HOWELLS, H.
HOWELL'S CLAVICHORD, BK. 2
NOVELLO AND COMPANY, LTD.   10.0076.04   2.90
HOWELLS, H.
LAMBERTS CLAVICHORD
OXFORD UNIVERSITY PRESS   32.047   2.50
HOY *
KEYWAYS TO MUSIC, BK. 1 --IN PREP--
WESTERN INTERNATIONAL MUSIC, INC.
HRUBY, V.   3
OPERETTEN-RAUSCH, MELODIENFOLGE MIT TEXT
SCHOTT   2.00

HUBLER, E.
    J'ACCOMPAGNE LA DANSE, VOL. 1
        GERARD BILLAUDOT EDITIONS MUSICALES   4.90
HUBLER, E.
    J'ACCOMPAGNE LA DANSE, VOL. 2
        GERARD BILLAUDOT EDITIONS MUSICALES   5.70
HUENTEN   POZZOLI
    NINE RONDOS
        FRANCO COLOMBO PUBLICATIONS   ER605   1.50
HUENTEN   MUGELLINI
    TWENTY-FIVE STUDIES, OP. 114
        FRANCO COLOMBO PUBLICATIONS   ER1438   2.50
HUGHES--ED.   HUGHES
    KEYBOARD MEDLEYS
        LORENZ PUBLISHING COMPANY   2.00
HUGON, G.
    TROIS PIECES EN DO POUR LES JEUNES
        EDITIONS MUSICALES TRANSATLANTIQUES   1.95
HUMBER, L. M.
    MY MERRY MUSIC BOOK -- A METHOD FOR BEGINNERS
        ASSOCIATED MUSIC PUBLISHERS, INC.   BER   1.50
HUMMEL, J. N.   PHILIPP, I.
    EIGHTEEN GRANDES ETUDES POUR L'ENSEIGNEMENT SUPERIEUR DU PIANO
        ALPHONSE LEDUC
HUNEKE--ED   HUNEKE
    BIG NOTE CHRISTMAS CAROLS
        BOSTON MUSIC COMPANY   1.00
HUNTLEY--ED   HUNTLEY
    COWBOY SONGS
        BOSTON MUSIC COMPANY   1.00
HUNTLEY, C.--ED   HUNTLEY, C.
    CHRISTMAS CAROLS FOR CHILDREN
        WILLIS MUSIC COMPANY   1.00
HURLEBUSCH   JAMBOR
    KEYBOARD SONATAS, BK. 1
        ELKAN-VOGEL, INC.   3.00
HURLEBUSCH   JAMBOR
    KEYBOARD SONATAS, BK. 2
        ELKAN-VOGEL, INC.   3.00
HUTCHESON
    ELEMENTS OF PIANO TECHNIQUE, THE
        WILLIS MUSIC COMPANY   1.50
IBERT   5, 6
    ESCALES
        ALPHONSE LEDUC
IBERT   4, 7
    HISTOIRES
        ALPHONSE LEDUC
IDYL *
    THREE INTERLUDES FOR PIANO
        THEODORE PRESSER COMPANY   2.00
ILLIASHENKO
    DANCES -- IN THE FORM OF VARIATIONS ON A RUSSIAN THEME --
        FRANCO COLOMBO PUBLICATIONS   SAL   2.75
INFANTE   7
    POCHADES ANDALOUSES
        ALPHONSE LEDUC
INGHELBRECHT, D. E.   5, 7
    NURSERY, LA
        ALPHONSE LEDUC
INGHELBRECHT, D. E.
    NURSERY, LA - BK. 1
        FRANCO COLOMBO PUBLICATIONS   SAL   3.25
INGHELBRECHT, D. E.
    NURSERY, LA - BK. 2
        FRANCO COLOMBO PUBLICATIONS   SAL   3.25
INGHELBRECHT, D. E.
    NURSERY, LA - BK. 4
        FRANCO COLOMBO PUBLICATIONS   SAL   3.25
INGHELBRECHT, D. E.
    NURSERY, LA - BK. 5
        FRANCO COLOMBO PUBLICATIONS   SAL   3.25
INGHELBRECHT, D. E.
    NURSERY, LA - BK. 6
        FRANCO COLOMBO PUBLICATIONS   SAL   3.25
INGHELBRECHT, D. E.
    SIX DANSES SUEDOISES
        FRANCO COLOMBO PUBLICATIONS   SAL   4.25
IPPOLITOV-IVANOV, M.
    CAUCASIAN SKETCHES, OP. 10
        ASSOCIATED MUSIC PUBLISHERS, INC.   SIM   1.50
IRMER, VON--ED.   IRMER, VON
    MINIATURES FOR PIANO--EARLY FRENCH MASTERS--MUSIKVERLAG ZUM
    PELIKAN EDITION
        G. SCHIRMER, INC.   1.00
IRMER, VON--ED.   IRMER, VON
    MINIATURES FOR PIANO--OLD MASTERS--MUSIKVERLAG ZUM PELIKAN
    EDITION
        G. SCHIRMER, INC.   1.00
IRWIN--ED.   IRWIN
    BILL IRWIN'S MAGIC STUDY SERIES - DIMINISHED CHORD MAGIC
        POINTER PUBLICATIONS   2.50
IRWIN--ED.   IRWIN
    BILL IRWIN'S MAGIC STUDY SERIES - MODERN FILL MAGIC
        POINTER PUBLICATIONS   2.50
IRWIN--ED.   IRWIN
    BILL IRWIN'S MAGIC STUDY SERIES - MODERN MELODY MAGIC
        POINTER PUBLICATIONS   2.50
IRWIN--ED.   IRWIN
    BILL IRWIN'S MAGIC STUDY SERIES -CHORD CONSTRUCTION MAGIC
        POINTER PUBLICATIONS   2.50
IRWIN--ED.   IRWIN
    BILL IRWIN'S MAGIS STUDY SERIES - RHYTHM ACCOMPANIMENT MAGIC
        POINTER PUBLICATIONS   2.50
JACOB, C.   4
    DIX PETITES ETUDES MODERNES
        ALPHONSE LEDUC
JACOB, M.   4, 5
    GUIRLANDE
        ALPHONSE LEDUC
JAMES, S.
    SONGS OF SONNY JAMES
        THE BIG THREE MUSIC CORPORATION   02.95
JAMES, W. G.
    FOUR DANCES FOR YOUNG PIANISTS
        FRANCO COLOMBO PUBLICATIONS   SD1   1.00
JANACEK   3
    AUF VERWACHSENEM PFADE. 15 KLAVIERSTUCKE
        BARENREITER VERLAG   AP 605
JANACEK   3
    FIFTEEN MAHRISCHE VOLKSLIEDER
        BARENREITER VERLAG   AP 613
JANACEK   3-4
    IM NEBEL
        BARENREITER VERLAG   AP 609
JANACEK
    MORAVIAN NATIONAL DANCES
        ARTIA   5.50

JANACEK
    MUSIC FOR GYMNASTICAL EXERCIES
        ARTIA   .90
JANACEK   3
    MUSIK ZUM KEULENSCHWINGEN. 5 KLAVIERSTUCKE
        BARENREITER VERLAG   AP 614
JANACEK   3
    SIX LACHISCHE TANZE
        BARENREITER VERLAG   AP 612
JANACEK   3
    TWENTY-THREE VOLKSTANZE AUS MAHREN
        BARENREITER VERLAG   AP 618
JAQUE, R.
    SUITE, OP. 11
        ASSOCIATED MUSIC PUBLISHERS, INC.   BER   1.25
JAQUE, R.
    TWO TWO-PART INVENTIONS
        ASSOCIATED MUSIC PUBLISHERS, INC.   BER   .50
JAY--ED   JAY   AI
    TIME TO PLAY POLKAS
        WILLIS MUSIC COMPANY   1.00
JEANNERET
    THREE MELODIES
        FRANCO COLOMBO PUBLICATIONS   SAL   2.75
JELINEK, H.
    TWELVE-TONE MUSIC, OP. 15 BK. 1, FOUR 2-PART INVENTIONS
        UNIVERSAL EDITION   UE 11898   2.60
JELINEK, H.
    TWELVE-TONE MUSIC, OP. 15 BK. 2, SIX LITTLE CHARACTERISTIC
    PIECES
        UNIVERSAL EDITION   UE 11899   2.85
JELINEK, H.
    TWELVE-TONE MUSIC, OP. 15 BK. 3, THREE DANCE PIECES
        UNIVERSAL EDITION   UE 11900   2.15
JELINEK, H.
    TWELVE-TONE MUSIC, OP. 15 BK. 4, FOUR TOCCATAS
        UNIVERSAL EDITION   UE 12023   2.35
JELOBINSKY
    SCENES OF CHILDHOOD
        MCA MUSIC   1.25
JENKINS, E.
    ELLA JENKINS SONG BOOK FOR CHILDREN
        OAK PUBLICATIONS   000025   1.95
JENSEN, A.   M-D
    SCENES OF TRAVEL, OP. 17
        C. F. PETERS CORPORATION   1148   3.00
JENSEN, A.   M-D
    STUDIES, OP. 32. VOL. 1, NOS. 1-8
        C. F. PETERS CORPORATION   1317A   2.00
JENSEN, A.   M-D
    STUDIES, OP. 32. VOL. 1, NOS. 9-18
        C. F. PETERS CORPORATION   2.00
JENSEN, A.   M-D
    STUDIES, OP. 32. VOL. 3, NOS. 19-25
        C. F. PETERS CORPORATION   1317C   2.00
JENSEN, A.
    TWENTY-FIVE ETUDES, OP. 32--PRELIMINARY STUDIES TO THE WORKS OF
    THE MODERN SCHOOL--BK. 1
        G. SCHIRMER, INC.   L763   .75
JENSEN, A.
    TWENTY-FIVE ETUDES, OP. 32--PRELIMINARY STUDIES TO THE WORKS OF
    THE MODERN SCHOOL--BK. 2
        G. SCHIRMER, INC.   L764   .75
JENSEN, A.   TAGLIAPIETRA
    TWENTY-FIVE STUDIES, OP. 32, BK. 1 -- 1-8 --
        FRANCO COLOMBO PUBLICATIONS   ER707   1.00
JENSEN, A.   TAGLIAPIETRA
    TWENTY-FIVE STUDIES, OP. 32, BK. 2 -- 9-18 --
        FRANCO COLOMBO PUBLICATIONS   ER708   1.25
JENSEN, A.   TAGLIAPIETRA
    TWENTY-FIVE STUDIES, OP. 32, BK. 3 -- 19-25 --
        FRANCO COLOMBO PUBLICATIONS   ER709   1.25
JENSVOLD, J.--ED   JENSVOLD, J.
    I LOVE CHRISTMAS MUSIC
        WILLIS MUSIC COMPANY   1.00
JENSVOLD, J.--ED   JENSVOLD, J.
    MY HYMNS
        WILLIS MUSIC COMPANY   1.25
JOACHIM, O.
    TWELVE TWELVE-TONE PIECES FOR CHILDREN
        ASSOCIATED MUSIC PUBLISHERS, INC.   BER   1.50
JOBIM   HARNELL
    MUSIC OF ANTONIO CARLOS JOBIM STYLED FOR PIANO BY JOE HARNELL
        TRO SONGWAYS SERVICE, INC.   2.50
JOBSON, V.
    MOTHER GOOSE MELODIES FOR THE YOUNG PIANIST--40 TRADITIONAL
    TUNES ARRANGED IN 5-FINGER POSITION
        G. SCHIRMER, INC.   1.00
JOHNSON--ED.   JOHNSON
    READ AND PLAY SERIES IN 9 VOLS., VOL. 1# BEGINNERS TUNES
        C. F. PETERS CORPORATION   H861   1.25
JOHNSON--ED.   JOHNSON
    READ AND PLAY SERIES IN 9 VOLS., VOL. 2# HANDS TOGETHER
        C. F. PETERS CORPORATION   H862   1.25
JOHNSON--ED.   JOHNSON
    READ AND PLAY SERIES IN 9 VOLS., VOL. 3# MOVING FORWARD
        C. F. PETERS CORPORATION   H863   2.00
JOHNSON--ED.   JOHNSON
    READ AND PLAY SERIES IN 9 VOLS., VOL. 4# MAKING PROGRESS
        C. F. PETERS CORPORATION   H864   2.00
JOHNSON--ED.   JOHNSON
    READ AND PLAY SERIES IN 9 VOLS., VOL.5# MINIATURE MELODIES
        C. F. PETERS CORPORATION   H865   1.25
JOHNSON--ED.   JOHNSON   INTERMEDIATE
    READ AND PLAY SERIES IN 9 VOLS., VOL.6# GAINING GROUND
        C. F. PETERS CORPORATION   H866   1.50
JOHNSON--ED.   JOHNSON   ADVANCED
    READ AND PLAY SERIES IN 9 VOLS., VOL.7# PRESSING ON
        C. F. PETERS CORPORATION   H867   1.50
JOHNSON--ED.   JOHNSON   FINAL
    READ AND PLAY SERIES IN 9 VOLS., VOL.8# NEAR THE TOP
        C. F. PETERS CORPORATION   H868   1950
JOHNSON--ED.   JOHNSON   DIPLOMA
    READ AND PLAY SERIES IN 9 VOLS., VOL.9# AT THE TOP
        C. F. PETERS CORPORATION   H869   1.50
JOHNSON, L.
    TWO SONATINAS, OP. 49
        PUGET MUSIC PUBLICATIONS, INC.   P711   2.50
JOHNSON, M.--ED. *   JOHNSON, M. *
    EARLY AMERICAN SONGS
        ASSOCIATED MUSIC PUBLISHERS, INC.   AMP   .40
JOHNSON, T.   E-M
    RURAL SKETCHES
        C. F. PETERS CORPORATION   H34   1.25
JOHNSTON, R.
    SUITE NO. 1
        ASSOCIATED MUSIC PUBLISHERS, INC.   BER   .60

JOHNSTON, R.
SUITE NO. 2
ASSOCIATED MUSIC PUBLISHERS, INC.　　　BER　　　1.00
JONAS--ED.　　　　　　JONAS
PORTUGUESE AND SPANISH MUSIC OF THE 18TH CENTURY
SUMMY-BIRCHARD COMPANY　　　　　　　　　　3.00
JOOSEN　　　　　　　　　　　　E
THREE EASY SONATINAS
C. F. PETERS CORPORATION　　　B819　　　.90
JOPLIN, S. *　　　　　　BLESH, R.
CLASSIC PIANO RAGS
DOVER PUBLICATIONS, INC.　　　20469-3　　6.00
JOPLIN, S.
COLLECTED PIANO WORKS
BELWIN-MILLS PUBLISHING CORPORATION　　　9.95
JOPLIN, S.　　　　　　　　INTERMEDIATE
MATT DENNIS PLAYS SCOTT JOPLIN
MEL BAY PUBLICATIONS, INC.　　　　　　2.50
JOPLIN, S.　　　　　SCHAUM, J.　　　2 1/2
SCOTT JOPLIN RAGTIME RAGE, BK. 1
SCHAUM PUBLICATIONS, INC.　　　　　　1.75
JOPLIN, S.　　　　　SCHAUM, J.　　　2 1/2
SCOTT JOPLIN RAGTIME RAGE, BK. 2
SCHAUM PUBLICATIONS, INC.　　　　　　1.75
JOSEFFY, R.
SCHOOL OF ADVANCED PIANO PLAYING
G. SCHIRMER, INC.　　　　　　　　　　3.50
JOSEPHS, W.
FOURTEEN STUDIES, BK. 1
OXFORD UNIVERSITY PRESS　　　32.153　　3.85
JOSEPHS, W.
FOURTEEN STUDIES, BK. 2
OXFORD UNIVERSITY PRESS　　　32.154　　3.85
JOYNER, B.
SINGING FIVE FINGERS
WILLIS MUSIC COMPANY　　　　　　　　.80
JOYNER, B.--ED　　　　JOYNER, B.
CHILD'S CHRISTMAS, A
WILLIS MUSIC COMPANY　　　　　　　　1.25
JOYNER, B.--ED　　　　JOYNER, B.
FAVORITE FOLK SONGS
WILLIS MUSIC COMPANY　　　　　　　　1.25
JUAN--ED　　　　　　　JUAN
SEIS HABANERAS TRADICIONALES
ASSOCIATED MUSIC PUBLISHERS, INC.　　UME　　1.00
JUON, P.
KINDERTRAUME, OP. 74--VOL. 2
ASSOCIATED MUSIC PUBLISHERS, INC.　　LEU　　2.75
KABALEVSKY　　　　　　　　E
ALBUM FOR THE YOUNG
C. F. PETERS CORPORATION　　　4764A　　3.00
KABALEVSKY　　　　ANSON, G.　　ELEMENTARY
ANSON INTRODUCES KABALEVSKY, BK. 1
WILLIS MUSIC COMPANY　　　　　　　　1.25
KABALEVSKY　　　　ANSON, G.　　INTERMEDIATE
ANSON INTRODUCES KABALEVSKY, BK. 2
WILLIS MUSIC COMPANY　　　　　　　　1.25
KABALEVSKY　　　　　　　　BEGINNER
BEGINNERS PIECES, OP. 39
EDWIN F. KALMUS　　　3560　　.75
KABALEVSKY　　　　　　　　BEGINNER
EASY PIECES, OP. 27
EDWIN F. KALMUS　　　3559　　1.25
KABALEVSKY
EASY PIECES, OP. 39
EDWARD B. MARKS MUSIC CORPORATION　　01.50
KABALEVSKY
EASY VARIATIONS, OP. 40/1
EDWIN F. KALMUS　　　3574　　1.00
KABALEVSKY　　　　MIROVITCH, A.
FIFTEEN CHILDREN'S PIECES, OP. 27, BK. 1
MCA MUSIC　　　　　　　　　　1.25
KABALEVSKY　　　　MAIER
FIVE SETS OF VARIATIONS, OP. 51
MCA MUSIC　　　　　　　　　　2.00
KABALEVSKY　　　　MAIER
FIVE SETS OF VARIATIONS, OP. 51 - SIX VARIATIONS ON UKRANIAN
FOLK SONG
MCA MUSIC　　　　　　　　　　.85
KABALEVSKY　　　　MAIER
FIVE SETS OF VARIATIONS, OP. 51, BK. 1 - FIVE HAPPY VARIATIONS
ON A RUSSIAN FOLK SONG
MCA MUSIC　　　　　　　　　　.85
KABALEVSKY　　　　MAIER
FIVE SETS OF VARIATIONS, OP. 51, BK. 2 - MERRY DANCE VARIATIONS
ON A RUSSIAN FOLK SONG
MCA MUSIC　　　　　　　　　　.85
KABALEVSKY　　　　MAIER
FIVE SETS OF VARIATIONS, OP. 51, BK. 3 - GRAY DAY VARIATIONS ON
SLOVAKIAN FOLK SONG
MCA MUSIC　　　　　　　　　　.85
KABALEVSKY　　　　MAIER
FIVE SETS OF VARIATIONS, OP. 51, BK. 4 - SEVEN GOOD-HUMOURED
VARIATIONS ON A UKRANIAN FOLK SONG
MCA MUSIC　　　　　　　　　　.85
KABALEVSKY　　　　MIROVITCH, A.
FOUR LITTLE PIECES, OP. 14
MCA MUSIC　　　　　　　　　　1.25
KABALEVSKY
FOUR PRELUDES, OP. 5
MCA MUSIC　　　　　　　　　　1.00
KABALEVSKY
FOUR RONDOS, OP. 60
INTERNATIONAL MUSIC COMPANY　　　　1.50
KABALEVSKY
FOUR RONDOS, OP. 60
MCA MUSIC　　　　　　　　　　1.25
KABALEVSKY　　　　FOLDES
MARCH AND WALTZ FROM --THE　COMEDIANS
MCA MUSIC　　　　　　　　　　.60
KABALEVSKY
PRELUDES AND FUGUES, OP. 61
INTERNATIONAL MUSIC COMPANY　　　　2.00
KABALEVSKY
RONDO FOR PIANO
EDWIN F. KALMUS　　　3563　　1.00
KABALEVSKY　　　　　　　　E-M
SELECTED PIECES FOR CHILDREN, OP. 27 --17--
C. F. PETERS CORPORATION　　　4719　　2.50
KABALEVSKY
SEVENTEEN EASY PIANO PIECES, OP. 27
EDWIN F. KALMUS　　　3559　　2.00
KABALEVSKY
SIX PRELUDES AND FUGUES, OP. 61
MCA MUSIC　　　　　　　　　　2.00
KABALEVSKY
SONATINA, OP. 13 NO. 1
EDWIN F. KALMUS　　　3561　　1.00

KABALEVSKY
SONATINA, OP. 13 NO. 2
EDWIN F. KALMUS　　　3562　　1.00
KABALEVSKY
SPRING GAMES AND DANCES
MCA MUSIC　　　　　　　　　　2.00
KABALEVSKY　　　　MIROVITCH, A.
TEN CHILDREN'S PIECES, OP. 27, BK. 2
MCA MUSIC　　　　　　　　　　1.50
KABALEVSKY
TWELVE EASY PIANO PIECES
BOOSEY AND HAWKES, INC.　　　　　　.85
KABALEVSKY
TWENTY-FOUR LITTLE PIECES FOR CHILDREN　OP. 39
INTERNATIONAL MUSIC COMPANY　　　　1.25
KABALEVSKY
TWENTY-FOUR LITTLE PIECES, OP. 39
MCA MUSIC　　　　　　　　　　1.25
KABALEVSKY　　　　PALMER, W. A.
TWENTY-FOUR PIECES FOR CHILDREN
ALFRED MUSIC COMPANY　　　619　　1.00
KABALEVSKY
TWENTY-FOUR PIECES FOR CHILDREN, OP. 39
G. SCHIRMER, INC.　　　　　　　　.75
KABALEVSKY
TWENTY-FOUR PRELUDES, OP. 38
INTERNATIONAL MUSIC COMPANY　　　　3.00
KABALEVSKY
TWENTY-FOUR PRELUDES, OP. 38
EDWIN F. KALMUS　　　3573　　3.00
KABALEVSKY
TWENTY-FOUR PRELUDES, OP. 38
EDWARD B. MARKS MUSIC CORPORATION　　02.75
KABALEVSKY
TWENTY-FOUR PRELUDES, OP. 38
MCA MUSIC　　　　　　　　　　3.95
KABALEVSKY　　　　　　　　D
TWENTY-FOUR PRELUDES, OP. 38
C. F. PETERS CORPORATION　　　4785　　6.00
KABALEVSKY
TWENTY-TWO PIECES FOR CHILDREN, OP. 27
INTERNATIONAL MUSIC COMPANY　　　　1.75
KABELAC　　　　　　　　3
SIEBEN STUCKE, OP. 14
BARENREITER VERLAG　　　AP 633
KADOSA
FIFTY-FIVE SMALL PIANO PIECES, BK. 1
KULTURA　　　　　　　　　　1.50
KADOSA
FIFTY-FIVE SMALL PIANO PIECES, BK. 2
KULTURA　　　　　　　　　　1.50
KADOSA
FIVE ETUDES, OP. 23C
KULTURA　　　　　　　　　　1.25
KADOSA
FOUR CAPRICHOS, OP. 57
KULTURA　　　　　　　　　　1.50
KADOSA
FOUR PIANO PIECES FOR CHILDREN
KULTURA　　　　　　　　　　.75
KADOSA
TEN BAGATELLES, OP. 51
KULTURA　　　　　　　　　　1.75
KADOSA
THREE VERY EASY SONATINAS, OP. 18A
KULTURA　　　　　　　　　　1.25
KADOSA
TWELVE SHORT CHILDREN'S PIECES, OP. 35B
KULTURA　　　　　　　　　　.90
KADOSA
TWENTY-FOUR EASY TECHNICAL STUDIES
KULTURA　　　　　　　　　　2.00
KAEMPER
SUR LES AILES DE LA CHANSON
ALPHONSE LEDUC
KAEMPER
TECHNIQUES PIANISTIQUES
ALPHONSE LEDUC
KAHL
CHRISTMAS CHIMES
BOSTON MUSIC COMPANY　　　　　　　1.25
KAHL
EASTERTIME
BOSTON MUSIC COMPANY　　　　　　　1.50
KAHL
SACRED MOODS
BOSTON MUSIC COMPANY　　　　　　　1.00
KAHL
SONGS FOR BEGINNERS TO PLAY
BOSTON MUSIC COMPANY　　　　　　　1.50
KAHL--ED　　　　　　　KAHL
CHRISTMAS CAROLS - BOOK 1
BOSTON MUSIC COMPANY　　　　　　　1.50
KAHL--ED　　　　　　　KAHL
CHRISTMAS CAROLS - BOOK 2
BOSTON MUSIC COMPANY　　　　　　　1.50
KAHL--ED　　　　　　　KAHL
CHRISTMAS CAROLS - BOOK 3
BOSTON MUSIC COMPANY　　　　　　　1.50
KAHL--ED　　　　　　　KAHL
JUNIOR HYMNBOOK - BOOK 1
BOSTON MUSIC COMPANY　　　　　　　1.50
KAHL--ED　　　　　　　KAHL
JUNIOR HYMNBOOK - BOOK 2
BOSTON MUSIC COMPANY　　　　　　　1.50
KAHL--ED　　　　　　　KAHL
JUNIOR HYMNBOOK - BOOK 3
BOSTON MUSIC COMPANY　　　　　　　1.75
KAHN
GUIDELINES TO IMPROVISATION - BK. 1
WARNER BROTHERS PUBLISHERS　　　　1.95
KAHN
GUIDELINES TO IMPROVISATION - BK. 2
WARNER BROTHERS PUBLISHERS　　　　1.95
KAHN
GUIDELINES TO IMPROVISATION - BK. 3
WARNER BROTHERS PUBLISHERS　　　　1.95
KAHN, M.
BEGINNER'S GUIDE TO POPULAR PIANO PLAYING
BELWIN-MILLS PUBLISHING CORPORATION　　11508　　1.75
KAHN, M.
BREAKS, FILLER, ENDINGS AND INTRODUCTIONS FOR POPULAR PIANO
PLAYING
BELWIN-MILLS PUBLISHING CORPORATION　　11074　　1.50
KAHN, M.
CHORD CONSTRUCTION AND HINTS FOR POPULAR PIANO PLAYING
BELWIN-MILLS PUBLISHING CORPORATION　　11083　　1.75

KAHN, M.
    EASY CHORDS FOR STANDARD HITS
        BELWIN-MILLS PUBLISHING CORPORATION   11132   1.50
KAHN, M.
    MODERN MELODIES FOR POPULAR PIANO PLAYING
        BELWIN-MILLS PUBLISHING CORPORATION   11304   1.50
KAHN, M.
    MODERN STYLES AND HARMONIC CONSTRUCTION
        BELWIN-MILLS PUBLISHING CORPORATION   11307   1.75
KAHN, M.
    MORE MODERN MELODIES FOR POPULAR PIANO PLAYING
        BELWIN-MILLS PUBLISHING CORPORATION   11316   1.50
KAHN, M.
    NOTE SPELLER AND EAR TRAINING BOOK
        BELWIN-MILLS PUBLISHING CORPORATION   11356   1.50
KAHN, M.
    PIANO MOODS -- ORIGINAL MODERN PIANO SOLOS
        BELWIN-MILLS PUBLISHING CORPORATION   11377   1.50
KAHN, M. *
    POPULAR BEGINNER FOR TEEN-AGERS AND ADULTS
        BELWIN-MILLS PUBLISHING CORPORATION   11394   1.75
KAHN, M. *
    SONG SHINDIG
        BELWIN-MILLS PUBLISHING CORPORATION   2.00
KAHN, M.
    STRICTLY POPULAR
        BELWIN-MILLS PUBLISHING CORPORATION   1.50
KAHN, M.
    YOUVE GOT RHYTHM
        EDWARD B. MARKS MUSIC CORPORATION   01.50
KAHN, M.--ED *   KAHN, M. *
    DISNEY SHOWCASE
        BOURNE COMPANY   1.50
KAHN, M.--ED   KAHN, M.
    MARVIN KAHN'S SONG SHOWCASE
        BOURNE COMPANY   1.50
KAMINSKI
    KLAVIERBUCHLEIN
        BARENREITER VERLAG   BA 886
KAMINSKI   1-2
    KLAVIERBUCHLEIN -- 10 KLEINE UBUNGEN FUR DEN ANFANG --
        BARENREITER VERLAG   BA 886
KAMINSKI
    LITTLE PIANO BOOK
        BARENREITER VERLAG   BA 886   2.75
KANN, H.--ED   KANN, H.
    OLD VIENNESE MASTERS
        UNIVERSAL EDITION   UE 13830   3.40
KANN, H.--ED   KANN, H.
    PIANO MUSIC FROM AUSTRIA
        UNIVERSAL EDITION   UE 13830   3.20
KANN, H.--ED   KANN, H.
    VIENNESE MASTERS -- 14 PIECES FROM THE BAROQUE, CLASSICAL AND
    BIEDERMEIER PERIODS
        UNIVERSAL EDITION   UE 13830E   3.40
KAPP, R.
    SIMPLE ETUDES FOR ADVANCED BEGINNERS
        GENERAL MUSIC PUBLISHING COMPANY, INC.   161   2.50
KAPP, R.
    SIMPLE ETUDES FOR ADVANCED BEGINNERS
        GENERAL MUSIC PUBLISHING COMPANY, INC.   2.50
KAPR   *   3-4
    DAHEIM, HEFT 2
        BARENREITER VERLAG   AP 635
KAPR   3-4
    VIER STUCKE
        BARENREITER VERLAG   AP 636
KARDOS
    THREE PIECES, FROM 'TWELVE PRELUDES'
        KULTURA   1.25
KARJINSKY
    MUSIQUE POUR TITI - APRES LA VODKA, REVE DU CACATOES,
    TITI-MAMAN, DOUDOU LE CHEVALIER
        FRANCO COLOMBO PUBLICATIONS   SAL   2.50
KAROLYI
    FIVE PIANO PIECES
        KULTURA   1.25
KARTUN   6, 7
    FIFTEEN EXERCICES
        ALPHONSE LEDUC
KARTUN
    SYNTHETIC STUDY OF DAILY PIANO TECHNIQUE - 142 EXERCISES
        LES EDITIONS OUVRIERES   7.50
KASEMETS, U.
    ONE PLUS ONE-- 20 STUDIES FOR BEGINNERS
        ASSOCIATED MUSIC PUBLISHERS, INC.   BER   .85
KASEMETS, U.
    ONE PLUS ONE--10 EASY PIECES ON WELL-KNOWN SONGS
        ASSOCIATED MUSIC PUBLISHERS, INC.   BER   1.00
KASEMETS, U.
    TWENTY PIANO STUDIES FOR BEGINNERS, BK. 1
        ASSOCIATED MUSIC PUBLISHERS, INC.   BER   .85
KASSCHAU, H.
    FIRST GRADE PEDAL BOOK
        G. SCHIRMER, INC.   .85
KASSCHAU, H.
    KEYBOARD INTERPRETATION
        G. SCHIRMER, INC.   1.50
KASSCHAU, H.
    NOTE SPELLER
        G. SCHIRMER, INC.   .85
KASSCHAU, H.
    PIANO COURSE--TEACH ME TO PLAY--BK. 1
        G. SCHIRMER, INC.   1.25
KASSCHAU, H.
    PIANO COURSE--TEACH ME TO PLAY--BK. 2
        G. SCHIRMER, INC.   1.25
KASSCHAU, H.
    PIANO COURSE--TEACH ME TO PLAY--BK. 3
        G. SCHIRMER, INC.   1.25
KASSCHAU, H.
    PIANO COURSE--TEACH ME TO PLAY--BK. 4
        G. SCHIRMER, INC.   1.50
KASSCHAU, H.
    PIANO COURSE--TEACH ME TO PLAY--BK. 5
        G. SCHIRMER, INC.   1.50
KASSCHAU, H.
    PIANO COURSE--TEACH ME TO PLAY--PRELIMINARY BK.
        G. SCHIRMER, INC.   .85
KASSCHAU, H.   ADVANCED GRADES
    SELECT PIANO MUSIC FOR ADVANCED GRADES
        G. SCHIRMER, INC.   1.50
KASSCHAU, H.   EARLY GRADES
    SELECT PIANO MUSIC FOR EARLY GRADES
        G. SCHIRMER, INC.   1.00
KASSCHAU, H.   INTERMEDIATE GRADES
    SELECT PIANO MUSIC FOR INTERMEDIATE GRADES
        G. SCHIRMER, INC.   1.50

KASSCHAU, H.   KASSCHAU, H.
    SONGS FOR CHRISTMAS-TIME
        SAM FOX PUBLISHING COMPANY, INC.   1.00
KASSCHAU, H.
    TOUCH AND GO, BK. 1
        SAM FOX PUBLISHING COMPANY, INC.   1.25
KASSCHAU, H.
    TOUCH AND GO, BK. 2
        SAM FOX PUBLISHING COMPANY, INC.   1.25
KASSCHAU, H.
    TOUCH AND GO, BK. 3
        SAM FOX PUBLISHING COMPANY, INC.   1.25
KASSCHAU, H.--ED   KASSCHAU, H.
    ONE HUNDRED AND SIX GREATEST PIANO STUDIES, BK. 1, NOS. 1-62--IN
    PROGRESSIVE ORDER
        G. SCHIRMER, INC.   1.25
KASSCHAU, H.--ED   KASSCHAU, H.
    ONE HUNDRED AND SIX GREATEST PIANO STUDIES, BK. 2, NO.S
    63-106--IN PROGRESSIVE ORDER
        G. SCHIRMER, INC.   1.25
KASSCHAU, H.--ED   KASSCHAU, H.   ADVANCED GRADES
    SCHIRMER'S SELECT PIANO MUSIC--FOR ADVANCED GRADES
        G. SCHIRMER, INC.   1.50
KASSCHAU, H.--ED   KASSCHAU, H.   EARLY GRADES
    SCHIRMER'S SELECT PIANO MUSIC--FOR EARLY GRADES
        G. SCHIRMER, INC.   1.00
KASSCHAU, H.--ED   KASSCHAU, H.   INTERMEDIATE GRADES
    SCHIRMER'S SELECT PIANO MUSIC--FOR INTERMEDIATE GRADES
        G. SCHIRMER, INC.   1.50
KASTNER--ED.   KASTNER   3
    ALTE PORTUGLESISCHE MEISTER -- BK. 1
        SCHOTT   2382   4.25
KASTNER--ED.   KASTNER   3
    ALTE PORTUGLESISCHE MEISTER -- BK. 2
        SCHOTT   4050   4.25
KASTNER--ED.   KASTNER   2-3
    ALTITALIENISCHE VERSETTEN IN ALLEN KIRCHENTONARTEN
        SCHOTT   4926   2.50
KASTNER--ED.   KASTNER   2-3
    ALTITALIENISCHE VERSETTEN IN ALLEN KIRCHENTONARTEN
        SCHOTT   4926   2.00
KASTNER--ED.   KASTNER   3
    CRAVISTAS PORTUGUEZES, BK. 1
        SCHOTT   2382   4.25
KASTNER--ED.   KASTNER   3
    CRAVISTAS PORTUGUEZES, BK. 2
        SCHOTT   4050   1.25
KAUER, F.   KOLZ
    SIX EASY PIECES
        ASSOCIATED MUSIC PUBLISHERS, INC.   DOB   1.00
KAUFMANN, A. *
    FOUR PIECES, OP. 79
        ASSOCIATED MUSIC PUBLISHERS, INC.   DOB   1.50
KAY, U.
    FOUR INVENTIONS FOR PIANO
        MCA MUSIC   1.50
KAY, U.
    TEN SHORT ESSAYS
        MCA MUSIC   1.50
KAY, U.
    TWO SHORT PIECES
        FRANCO COLOMBO PUBLICATIONS   NY2227   1.00
KAYE
    JAZZ FOR THE YOUNG IN HEART
        EDWARD B. MARKS MUSIC CORPORATION   01.00
KAYE, C.
    CAROL KAYE ORIGINAL SONGBOOK
        GWYN PUBLISHING COMPANY   2.50
KAYE, CAROL
    CONTEMPORARY BASS LINES FOR ALL KEYBOARD INSTRUMENTS
        GWYN PUBLISHING COMPANY   2.50
KAYE, E.   EASY
    A LA MODE
        FRANK MUSIC CORPORATION   1.25
KEIGHLEY, T.
    FIRST THEORY LESSONS FOR YOUNG PIANIST, BK. 1
        BANKS AND SON LTD.   .20
KEIGHLEY, T.
    SONATINA SCHOOL, BK. 1
        BANKS AND SON LTD.   .95
KEIGHLEY, T.
    SONATINA SCHOOL, BK. 2
        BANKS AND SON LTD.   .95
KEIGHLEY, T.
    SONATINA SCHOOL, BK. 3
        BANKS AND SON LTD.   .95
KELEMEN   D
    DESSINS COMMENTES --7 PIECES--
        C. F. PETERS CORPORATION   5981   4.00
KELEMEN   E
    DONKEY WALKS ALONG THE BEACH, THE --9 PIECES--
        C. F. PETERS CORPORATION   5813   1.50
KELLER--ED.   KELLER   E-M
    EIGHTY CHORALE PRELUDES OF THE SEVENTEENTH AND EIGHTEENTH
    CENTURIES
        C. F. PETERS CORPORATION   4448   3.50
KELLER--ED.   KELLER   M
    OLD MASTERS OF PIANO MUSIC, VOL. 1* GERMAN
        C. F. PETERS CORPORATION   4641A   5.00
KELLER--ED.   KELLER   M
    OLD MASTERS OF PIANO MUSIC, VOL. 3* ITALIAN
        C. F. PETERS CORPORATION   4641C   5.00
KELLER--ED.   KELLER   M
    OLD MASTERS OF PIANO MUSIC, VOL. 4* ENGLISH
        C. F. PETERS CORPORATION   4641D   5.00
KELLER, G.   E
    KINDERLIEDERQUELL --39 CHILDREN'S SONGS--
        C. F. PETERS CORPORATION   N1271   3.50
KEMPFF
    CADENZAS TO BEETHOVEN PIANO CONCERTI NOS. 1-4
        ASSOCIATED MUSIC PUBLISHERS, INC.   BOT   3.50
KENDALL
    WEDDING TIME
        EDWARD B. MARKS MUSIC CORPORATION   01.75
KENDALL--ED   KENDALL
    SIMPLIFIED SONG GEMS FOR PIANO
        BOURNE COMPANY   1.00
KENNAN, K.
    THREE PRELUDES
        G. SCHIRMER, INC.   .75
KENT
    BEAUTIFUL THAILAND
        BELWIN-MILLS PUBLISHING CORPORATION   1.00
KENTON, S.
    STAN KENTON ORIGINALS FOR PIANO
        THE BIG THREE MUSIC CORPORATION   01.25

KENTON, W.
    FUNDAMENTAL PRINCIPLES OF POPULAR PIANO
        EDWARD B. MARKS MUSIC CORPORATION   01.25
KERN
    HARMONIZATION-TRANSPOSITION AT THE KEYBOARD
        SUMMY-BIRCHARD COMPANY   5.00
KERN, F.
    FIVE ANIMAL PICTURES, OP. 54
        ASSOCIATED MUSIC PUBLISHERS, INC.   OBV   .90
KERN, J.   BRADLEY, R.   EASY
    BRADLEY'S JEROME KERN ALBUM
        SCREEN GEMS - COLUMBIA PUBLICATIONS   F0020P2   1.95
KERN, J.
    POINTER LIBRARY - THE BEST OF JEROME KERN
        POINTER PUBLICATIONS   2.95
KERR, R. N.
    ALL IN ONE
        THEODORE PRESSER COMPANY   1.50
KERR, R. N.
    LITTLE PLAYERS
        THEODORE PRESSER COMPANY   1.10
KERR, R. N.
    LITTLE PLAYERS GROWING UP
        THEODORE PRESSER COMPANY   1.25
KERR, R. N.
    LITTLE PLAYERS HAVE ARRIVED
        THEODORE PRESSER COMPANY   1.25
KERR, R. N.
    TUNES FOR LITTLE PLAYERS
        THEODORE PRESSER COMPANY   1.25
KESSLER   DEIS
    FIFTEEN SELECTED STUDIES, OP. 20
        G. SCHIRMER, INC.   L1416   2.00
KESSLER   MUGELLINI
    TWENTY-FOUR STUDIES, OP. 20
        FRANCO COLOMBO PUBLICATIONS   ER712   5.00
KETTERER, E.
    ADVENTURES IN MUSIC LAND
        THEODORE PRESSER COMPANY   1.50
KETTERER, E.
    ADVENTURES IN PIANO TECHNIC
        THEODORE PRESSER COMPANY   1.50
KETTERER, E.
    BOOK OF PIANO PIECES
        THEODORE PRESSER COMPANY   2.00
KETTERER, E.
    LET'S PLAY
        THEODORE PRESSER COMPANY   .75
KETTERER, E.   1
    TWO VERY FIRST PIECES -- CHURCH BELLS AND LITTLE BROWN BIRD
        THEODORE PRESSER COMPANY   .50
KETTERER, E.--ED.   KETTERER, E.
    SHORT CLASSICS YOUNG PEOPLE LIKE
        THEODORE PRESSER COMPANY   1.25
KEVAN
    THIRTY-ONE FAVORITE CHILDREN'S HYMNS
        EDWARD B. MARKS MUSIC CORPORATION   01.00
KHATCHATURIAN
    ADVENTURES OF IVAN--EIGHT PIECES FOR STUDENTS
        MCA MUSIC   1.25
KHATCHATURIAN   E-M
    CHILDREN'S ALBUM, VOL. 1
        C. F. PETERS CORPORATION   4741   2.50
KHATCHATURIAN   E-M
    CHILDREN'S ALBUM, VOL. 2
        C. F. PETERS CORPORATION   4760   2.00
KHATCHATURIAN   BEGINNER
    CHILDREN'S PIECES
        EDWIN F. KALMUS   3578   1.00
KHATCHATURIAN   M
    THREE DANCES FROM MASKERADE
        C. F. PETERS CORPORATION   4717   2.50
KHATCHATURIAN
    TWO CHARACTERISTIC PIECES
        MCA MUSIC   .60
KHATCHATURIAN   M
    TWO PIANO PIECES
        C. F. PETERS CORPORATION   4737   2.00
KHATCHATURIAN
    TWO PIECES
        EDWIN F. KALMUS   3584   1.75
KHATCHATURIAN
    TWO PIECES -- WALSE CAPRICE, DANSE
        MCA MUSIC   1.00
KINDERMANN   BAUM
    TANZSTUCKE
        BARENREITER VERLAG   HM 61   2.50
KINDERMANN   BAUM   2
    TANZSTUCKE. 14 TANZSATZE FUR KLAVIER
        BARENREITER VERLAG   HM 61
KING
    FIRST JAZZ
        BOSTON MUSIC COMPANY   1.00
KING
    GOOD TIME TUNES
        BOSTON MUSIC COMPANY   1.00
KING
    HERE'S BOOGIE WOOGIE
        CARL FISCHER, INC.   O 3313   1.25
KING
    HERE'S MORE BOOGIE WOOGIE
        CARL FISCHER, INC.   O 3370   1.50
KING
    KEYBOARD BELL
        BOSTON MUSIC COMPANY   1.00
KING
    SONATEENERS
        BOSTON MUSIC COMPANY   1.00
KING
    SYNCO POPS
        BOSTON MUSIC COMPANY   1.00
KING--ED *   KING *   2-3
    TUNEFUL TECHNIC
        CENTURY MUSIC PUBLISHING COMPANY, INC.   1.00
KING, C.   ENGEL, S.   ADVANCED
    CAROLE KING PIANO SOLOS
        SCREEN GEMS - COLUMBIA PUBLICATIONS   F0089P   3.95
KING, S.
    BOY AND HIS PIANO
        BELWIN-MILLS PUBLISHING CORPORATION   11072   1.25
KING, S.
    DIXIELAND JAZZ FOR PIANO
        THEODORE PRESSER COMPANY   1.25
KING, S.
    GIRL AND HER PIANO
        BELWIN-MILLS PUBLISHING CORPORATION   11210   1.50

KING, S.
    GUY FROM CENTRAL HIGH, THE - 20 PIANO PIECES FOR THE TEEN-AGE
    PIANIST
        THEODORE PRESSER COMPANY   1.25
KING, S.
    HIGH SCHOOL HARMONIES
        THEODORE PRESSER COMPANY   1.25
KING, S.
    JUNIOR MISS PLAYS PIANO
        BELWIN-MILLS PUBLISHING CORPORATION   11254   1.50
KING, S.
    JUNIOR MISTER PLAYS PIANO
        BELWIN-MILLS PUBLISHING CORPORATION   11255   1.50
KING, S.
    PIANO PLAYTIME FOR BOYS
        BELWIN-MILLS PUBLISHING CORPORATION   11381   1.50
KING, S.
    PIANO PLAYTIME FOR GIRLS
        BELWIN-MILLS PUBLISHING CORPORATION   11382   1.50
KING, S.
    PROGRESSIVE JAZZ FOR JUNIORS
        THEODORE PRESSER COMPANY   1.25
KING, S.
    SELECTED STUDIES, BK. 1
        BELWIN-MILLS PUBLISHING CORPORATION   11428   1.50
KING, S.
    SELECTED STUDIES, BK. 2
        BELWIN-MILLS PUBLISHING CORPORATION   11429   1.50
KING, S.
    STUDIES ON FAMOUS TUNES
        THEODORE PRESSER COMPANY   1.25
KING, S.
    TUNES WITH THE TEEN-AGE TOUCH
        THEODORE PRESSER COMPANY   1.25
KING, S.--ED.   KING, S.
    HARMONIES DELUXE -- 6 WORLD-FAMOUS MELODIES IN CONTEMPORARY
    STYLE --
        THEODORE PRESSER COMPANY   1.25
KINSCELLA, H.
    STEPS FOR THE YOUNG PIANIST--A COURSE OF INSTRUCTIONS--1ST STEPS
        G. SCHIRMER, INC.   1.00
KINSCELLA, H.
    STEPS FOR THE YOUNG PIANIST--A COURSE OF INSTRUCTIONS--2ND STEPS
        G. SCHIRMER, INC.   1.50
KINSCELLA, H.
    STEPS FOR THE YOUNG PIANIST--A COURSE OF INSTRUCTIONS--3RD STEPS
        G. SCHIRMER, INC.   1.50
KINSCELLA, H.
    STEPS FOR THE YOUNG PIANIST--A COURSE OF INSTRUCTIONS--4TH STEPS
        G. SCHIRMER, INC.   1.50
KIRBY, M. B.
    COMBINATION FLASH CARDS
        FREDERICK HARRIS MUSIC COMPANY   9.00
KIRBY, M. B.
    FLASH CARDS, BK. 1
        FREDERICK HARRIS MUSIC COMPANY   1.90
KIRBY, M. B.
    FLASH CARDS, BK. 2
        FREDERICK HARRIS MUSIC COMPANY   1.90
KIRBY, M. B.
    FLASH CARDS, BK. 3
        FREDERICK HARRIS MUSIC COMPANY   1.90
KIRBY, M. B.
    FLASH CARDS, BK. 4
        FREDERICK HARRIS MUSIC COMPANY   1.90
KIRBY, M. B.
    KEY TO MUSIC TEACHING -- TEACHER'S MANUAL
        FREDERICK HARRIS MUSIC COMPANY   9.00
KIRBY, M. B.
    KINDERGARTEN PIANO METHOD, BK. 1
        FREDERICK HARRIS MUSIC COMPANY   1.50
KIRBY, M. B.
    KINDERGARTEN PIANO METHOD, BK. 2
        FREDERICK HARRIS MUSIC COMPANY   1.50
KIRBY, M. B.
    KINDERGARTEN PIANO METHOD, BK. 3
        FREDERICK HARRIS MUSIC COMPANY   1.50
KIRBY, M. B.
    KINDERGARTEN PIANO METHOD, BK. 4
        FREDERICK HARRIS MUSIC COMPANY   1.50
KIRBY, M. B.
    MUSIC FOR OLDER BEGINNERS, BK. 1
        FREDERICK HARRIS MUSIC COMPANY   1.90
KIRBY, M. B.
    MUSIC FOR OLDER BEGINNERS, BK. 2
        FREDERICK HARRIS MUSIC COMPANY   1.90
KIRBY, M. B.
    SIGHT READING, BK. 1-2
        FREDERICK HARRIS MUSIC COMPANY   1.50
KIRBY, M. B.
    THEORY AND WORK BOOK, BK. 1
        FREDERICK HARRIS MUSIC COMPANY   1.15
KIRBY, M. B.
    THEORY AND WORK BOOK, BK. 2
        FREDERICK HARRIS MUSIC COMPANY   1.15
KIRBY, M. B.
    THEORY AND WORK BOOK, BK. 3
        FREDERICK HARRIS MUSIC COMPANY   1.15
KIRBY, M. B.
    THEORY AND WORK BOOK, BK. 4
        FREDERICK HARRIS MUSIC COMPANY   1.15
KIRBY, M. B.
    THEORY AND WORK BOOK, BK. 5
        FREDERICK HARRIS MUSIC COMPANY   1.15
KIRBY, M. B.
    THEORY AND WORK BOOK, BK. 6
        FREDERICK HARRIS MUSIC COMPANY   1.50
KIRBY, W.
    FAMOUS MELODIES FOR THE YOUNG PIANIST
        G. SCHIRMER, INC.   1.00
KIRBY, W.
    MERRY CHRISTMAS--13 CHRISTMAS CAROLS IN VERY EASY ARRANGEMENTS
        G. SCHIRMER, INC.   .75
KIRBY, W.
    NOEL-NOEL--18 CHRISTMAS CAROLS, ARRANGED FOR PIANO AND VOICE
        G. SCHIRMER, INC.   .75
KIRBY, W.--ED.   KIRBY, W.
    FAMOUS MELODIES FOR THE YOUNG PIANIST
        G. SCHIRMER, INC.   1.00
KIRNBERGER, J. P.   3
    TANZSTUCKE
        SCHOTT   2484   2.25
KITTLER, R.
    SIX PIECES, 1957
        ASSOCIATED MUSIC PUBLISHERS, INC.   DOB   2.00
KLARMAN--ED   KLARMAN
    STUDENT PRINCE, THE, SELECTIONS FROM
        WARNER BROTHERS PUBLISHERS   .85

KLEBE, G.
   FOUR INVENTIONS, OP. 26
      ASSOCIATED MUSIC PUBLISHERS, INC.   BOT   1.50
KLEBE, G.
   THREE ROMANCES, OP. 43
      ASSOCIATED MUSIC PUBLISHERS, INC.   BOT   2.25
KLEINMAN, A.
   MUSIC BOX PIANO ALBUM, THE
      BELWIN-MILLS PUBLISHING CORPORATION   .85
KLEINMICHEL--ED   KLEINMICHEL
   SONATINAS AND RONDOS--32 SONATINAS AND RONDOS
      G. SCHIRMER, INC.   L693   2.50
KLEINMICHEL--ED   KLEINMICHEL   M
   SONATINAS, RONDOS AND PIECES, VOL. 1
      C. F. PETERS CORPORATION   4300A   3.00
KLEINMICHEL--ED   KLEINMICHEL   M
   SONATINAS, RONDOS AND PIECES, VOL. 2
      C. F. PETERS CORPORATION   4300B   3.50
KLEINSINGER, G.
   MUSIC FOR YOUNG POEPLE
      CHAPPELL AND COMPANY, INC.   0016139   1.00
KLENAU, P. V.
   SIX PRELUDES AND FUGUES
      UNIVERSAL EDITION   UE 11130   2.15
KLEPPER
   TWO DANCES
      FRANCO COLOMBO PUBLICATIONS   SAL   3.25
KLUSSMANN
   XENIEN, OP. 27
      FRANCO COLOMBO PUBLICATIONS   SIK.201   1.50
KNAB, A.   3
   LINDEGGER LANDLER
      SCHOTT   2487   2.25
KNAB, A.   1
   MUSIKANTEN, DIE KOMMEN
      BARENREITER VERLAG   BA 1720
KNIPPEL--ED.   KNIPPEL
   WE SING--WE PLAY --HAPPY SONGS FOR LITTLE VOICES
      SHAPIRO, BERNSTEIN ORGANIZATION   1.50
KNORR, E.L. VON   1-3
   KLAVIERMUSIK IN VIER TEILEN, TEIL 1 - 10 STUCKE
      BARENREITER VERLAG   BA 1001
KNORR, E.L. VON   1-3
   KLAVIERMUSIK IN VIER TEILEN, TEIL 1 - 10 STUCKE
      BARENREITER VERLAG   BA 1001
KNORR, E.L. VON   2-3
   KLAVIERMUSIK IN VIER TEILEN, TEIL 2 - 10 STUCKE
      BARENREITER VERLAG   BA 1002
KNORR, E.L. VON   2-3
   KLAVIERMUSIK IN VIER TEILEN, TEIL 2 - 10 STUCKE
      BARENREITER VERLAG   BA 1002
KNORR, E.L. VON   3
   KLAVIERMUSIK IN VIER TEILEN, TEIL 3 - 10 STUCKE
      BARENREITER VERLAG   BA 1011
KNORR, E.L. VON   3
   KLAVIERMUSIK IN VIER TEILEN, TEIL 3 - 10 STUCKE
      BARENREITER VERLAG   BA 1011
KNORR, E.L. VON   3
   KLAVIERMUSIK IN VIER TEILEN, TEIL 4 - 10 STUCKE
      BARENREITER VERLAG   BA 1012
KNORR, E.L. VON   3
   KLAVIERMUSIK IN VIER TEILEN, TEIL 4 - 10 STUCKE
      BARENREITER VERLAG   BA 1012
KNORR, E.L. VON
   MUSIC FOR PIANO, BK. 1
      BARENREITER VERLAG   BA 1001   2.50
KNORR, E.L. VON
   MUSIC FOR PIANO, BK. 2
      BARENREITER VERLAG   BA 1002   2.50
KNORR, E.L. VON
   MUSIC FOR PIANO, BK. 3
      BARENREITER VERLAG   BA 1011   2.50
KNORR, E.L. VON
   MUSIC FOR PIANO, BK. 5
      BARENREITER VERLAG   BA 1012   2.50
KOCH, F.
   BABETTE'S PIANO BOOK - EASY SUITE
      GENERAL MUSIC PUBLISHING COMPANY, INC.   2.00
KOCH, F.
   BABETTES PIANO BOOK
      GENERAL MUSIC PUBLISHING COMPANY, INC.   513   2.00
KOCH, F.
   CAROLS FROM MANY NATIONS
      GENERAL MUSIC PUBLISHING COMPANY, INC.   511   2.00
KOCH, F.
   CAROLS FROM MANY NATIONS
      GENERAL MUSIC PUBLISHING COMPANY, INC.   2.00
KOCH, F.   E
   FIVE PIECES FOR CHILDREN
      COMPOSERS PRESS, INC.   3.00
KOCH, F.
   TWO MINUS ONE - THE 'DO-IT-YOURSELF' COMPOSING BOOK
      GENERAL MUSIC PUBLISHING COMPANY, INC.   596   2.00
KOCH, F.
   TWO MINUS ONE - THE 'DO-IT-YOURSELF' COMPOSING BOOK
      GENERAL MUSIC PUBLISHING COMPANY, INC.   2.00
KOCH, J.
   ANDANTE AND SCHERZO - NO. 2 FROM SUITE FOR PIANO
      GENERAL MUSIC PUBLISHING COMPANY, INC.   1.75
KODALY
   TEN PIECES
      EDWIN F. KALMUS   3587   1.50
KODALY, Z.
   BALLET MUSIC
      UNIVERSAL EDITION   UE 10722   1.35
KODALY, Z.
   CHILDREN'S DANCES
      BOOSEY AND HAWKES, INC.   2.75
KODALY, Z.
   NINE PIANO PIECES, OP. 3
      KULTURA   2.00
KODALY, Z.   AGAY, D.
   NINE PIANO PIECES, OP. 3 AND VALSETTE
      MCA MUSIC   2.50
KODALY, Z.
   TWENTY-FOUR LITTLE CANONS ON THE BLACK KEYS
      BOOSEY AND HAWKES, INC.   .75
KOECHLIN, C.
   PAYSAGES ET MARINES - BK. 1
      FRANCO COLOMBO PUBLICATIONS   SAL   4.25
KOECHLIN, C.
   PAYSAGES ET MARINES - BK. 2
      FRANCO COLOMBO PUBLICATIONS   SAL   4.25
KOECHLIN, C.
   TEN EASY PIECES
      FRANCO COLOMBO PUBLICATIONS   SAL   2.75

KOECHLIN, C.
   TWELVE ESQUISSES - BK. 2
      FRANCO COLOMBO PUBLICATIONS   SAL   4.25
KOECHLIN, C.
   TWELVE ESQUISSES - BK. 1
      FRANCO COLOMBO PUBLICATIONS   SAL   4.25
KOECHLIN, C.
   TWELVE LITTLE PIECES
      FRANCO COLOMBO PUBLICATIONS   SAL   3.00
KOECHLIN, C.
   TWELVE PETITES PIECES FACILES
      HEUGEL ET CIE.   2.60
KOECHLIN, C.
   TWELVE PRELUDES
      FRANCO COLOMBO PUBLICATIONS   SAL   5.50
KOEHLER   BEGINNER
   CHILDREN'S ALBUM, OP. 210
      EDWIN F. KALMUS   3588   1.50
KOEHLER
   CHILDREN'S ALBUM, OP. 210
      G. SCHIRMER, INC.   L436   1.25
KOEHLER   BEGINNER
   CHILDREN'S EXERCISE, OP. 218
      EDWIN F. KALMUS   3591   1.00
KOEHLER
   CHILDREN'S FRIEND, OP. 243, BK. 1
      FRANCO COLOMBO PUBLICATIONS   ER39   1.75
KOEHLER
   CHILDREN'S FRIEND, OP. 243, BK. 2
      FRANCO COLOMBO PUBLICATIONS   ER40   1.75
KOEHLER   BEGINNER
   EASIEST STUDIES, OP. 151
      EDWIN F. KALMUS   3590   1.00
KOEHLER *   ECKSTEIN
   EASY VELOCITY STUDIES FROM KOEHLER-DUVERNOY--65--
      CARL FISCHER, INC.   O 3813   1.25
KOEHLER   MARCIANO
   EXERCISES AND MELODIES FOR CHILDREN, OP. 218
      FRANCO COLOMBO PUBLICATIONS   ER27   .75
KOEHLER
   FIRST ALBUM FOR CHILDREN, OP. 210
      FRANCO COLOMBO PUBLICATIONS   ER16   1.50
KOEHLER   BEGINNER
   FIRST STUDIES, OP. 50
      EDWIN F. KALMUS   3592   1.00
KOEHLER   E
   FIRST STUDIES, OP. 50
      C. F. PETERS CORPORATION   3521   2.50
KOEHLER
   FIRST STUDIES, OP. 50
      G. SCHIRMER, INC.   L317   1.00
KOEHLER
   FORTY CHILDREN'S EXERCISES AND MELODIES, OP. 218
      G. SCHIRMER, INC.   L490   1.00
KOEHLER   PHILIPP
   LA VIRTUOSITE, VOL.1
      GERARD BILLAUDOT EDITIONS MUSICALES   4.40
KOEHLER   PHILIPP
   LA VIRTUOSITE, VOL.2,BK.1--EXERCISES--
      GERARD BILLAUDOT EDITIONS MUSICALES   4.90
KOEHLER   PHILIPP
   LA VIRTUOSITE, VOL.2,BK.2--OCTAVES--
      GERARD BILLAUDOT EDITIONS MUSICALES   4.40
KOEHLER   PHILIPP
   LA VIRTUOSITE, VOL.3,BK.1
      GERARD BILLAUDOT EDITIONS MUSICALES   4.40
KOEHLER   PHILIPP
   LA VIRTUOSITE, VOL.3,BK.2
      GERARD BILLAUDOT EDITIONS MUSICALES   4.90
KOEHLER
   LITTLE PIANISTS, OP. 189 - 40 RECREATIONS
      FRANCO COLOMBO PUBLICATIONS   ER12   1.00
KOEHLER
   METODO PRACTICO, OP. 249, BK. 1--IN SPANISH AND ENGLISH
      G. SCHIRMER, INC.   L1082   1.25
KOEHLER   POZZOLI
   NEW SCHOOL OF VELOCITY, OP. 128
      FRANCO COLOMBO PUBLICATIONS   ER181   1.50
KOEHLER   E-M
   PRACTICAL METHOD FOR PIANO, OP. 300, VOL. 1
      C. F. PETERS CORPORATION   1969A   3.00
KOEHLER   E-M
   PRACTICAL METHOD FOR PIANO, OP. 300, VOL. 2
      C. F. PETERS CORPORATION   1969B   3.00
KOEHLER
   PRACTICAL METHOD FOR THE PIANOFORTE, BK. 1
      BELWIN-MILLS PUBLISHING CORPORATION   1.50
KOEHLER
   PRACTICAL METHOD, OP. 249. BK. 1
      CARL FISCHER, INC.   O 305   1.00
KOEHLER
   PRACTICAL METHOD, OP. 249. BK. 2
      CARL FISCHER, INC.   O 306   1.00
KOEHLER
   PRACTICAL METHOD, OP. 249. BK. 3
      CARL FISCHER, INC.   O 307   1.00
KOEHLER
   PRACTICAL METHOD, OP. 249, BK. 1--IN SPANISH, ENGLISH, AND FRENCH
      G. SCHIRMER, INC.   .75
KOEHLER
   PRACTICAL METHOD, OP. 249, BK. 2--IN SPANISH, ENGLISH, AND FRENCH
      G. SCHIRMER, INC.   .75
KOEHLER
   PRACTICAL METHOD, OP. 249, BK. 3--IN SPANISH, ENGLISH, AND FRENCH
      G. SCHIRMER, INC.   .75
KOEHLER
   PRACTICAL METHOD, OP. 249, BK. 4--IN SPANISH, ENGLISH, AND FRENCH
      G. SCHIRMER, INC.   .75
KOEHLER
   PRACTICAL METHOD, OP. 300, BK. 1
      G. SCHIRMER, INC.   L935   1.50
KOEHLER
   PRACTICAL METHOD, OP. 300, BK. 2
      G. SCHIRMER, INC.   L936   1.50
KOEHLER   M-D
   SCHOOL OF THE LEFT HAND, OP. 302
      C. F. PETERS CORPORATION   2033   6.00
KOEHLER
   SECOND ALBUM FOR CHILDREN, OP. 246
      FRANCO COLOMBO PUBLICATIONS   ER17   1.75
KOEHLER
   SHORT SCHOOL OF VELOCITY WITHOUT OCTAVES, OP. 242
      G. SCHIRMER, INC.   L321   1.00

KOEHLER   M
    SHORT SCHOOL OF VELOCITY, OP. 242
        C. F. PETERS CORPORATION   3526   2.50
KOEHLER
    SIXTEEN ELEMENTARY STUDIES, OP. 163
        G. SCHIRMER, INC.   L196   .75
KOEHLER
    SIXTEEN STUDIES OF MODERATE DIFFICULTY, OP. 224
        FRANCO COLOMBO PUBLICATIONS   ER13
KOEHLER
    SONATINA ALBUM
        CARL FISCHER, INC.   L 509   2.00
KOEHLER
    TWELVE EASIEST STUDIES, OP. 151
        G. SCHIRMER, INC.   L318   1.00
KOEHLER
    TWELVE EASY STUDIES, OP. 157
        G. SCHIRMER, INC.   L425   .75
KOEHLER
    TWELVE LITTLE STUDIES FOR DEVELOPMENT OF VELOCITY, OP. 157
        FRANCO COLOMBO PUBLICATIONS   ER11   1.00
KOEHLER
    TWELVE LITTLE STUDIES, OP. 157
        CARL FISCHER, INC.   L 380   1.00
KOEHLER
    TWENTY EASY STUDIES, OP. 159
        FRANCO COLOMBO PUBLICATIONS   ER743   .75
KOEHLER
    TWENTY STUDIES IN CONTINUOUS SCALE AND CHORD PASSAGES, OP. 60
        G. SCHIRMER, INC.   L543   1.00
KOEHLER
    VELOCITY STUDIES, BK. 3 --21-30--, OP. 173
        FRANCO COLOMBO PUBLICATIONS   ER744   1.50
KOEHLER
    VERY EASIEST EXERCISES, OP. 190
        CARL FISCHER, INC.   L 381   1.00
KOEHLER   BEGINNER
    VERY EASIEST STUDIES, THE, OP. 190
        EDWIN F. KALMUS   3589   1.00
KOEHLER
    VERY EASIEST STUDIES, THE, OP. 190
        G. SCHIRMER, INC.   L480   .75
KOEHLER   POZZOLI
    VERY FIRST STUDIES, OP. 190
        FRANCO COLOMBO PUBLICATIONS   ER536   1.00
KOEHLER--ED   KOEHLER   M
    ETUDES, ALBUM OF, VOL. 1
        C. F. PETERS CORPORATION   1967A   3.50
KOEHLER--ED   KOEHLER   M
    ETUDES, ALBUM OF, VOL. 2
        C. F. PETERS CORPORATION   1967B   3.50
KOEHLER--ED   KOEHLER
    SONATINA ALBUM--30 FAVORITE SONATINAS, RONDOS, AND PIECES
        G. SCHIRMER, INC.   L51   2.00
KOEHLER, L.   GOETSCHIUS, P.
    SONATINA ALBUM
        THEODORE PRESSER COMPANY   3.75
KOERPPEN, A.
    ORPHEUS IN THRAZIEN, SUITE
        ASSOCIATED MUSIC PUBLISHERS, INC.   BRH   3.00
KOHLER, F.
    PIANO METHOD, BK. 1
        VOLKWEIN BROS.   .50
KOHLER, F.
    PIANO METHOD, BK. 2
        VOLKWEIN BROS.   .50
KOHLER, F.
    PIANO METHOD, BK. 3
        VOLKWEIN BROS.   .50
KOHLER, F.   PALMER, W. A.
    SHORT SCHOOL OF VELOCITY
        ALFRED MUSIC COMPANY   628   1.25
KOHLER, F.   PALMER, W. A.
    TWELVE EASY STUDIES
        ALFRED MUSIC COMPANY   567   1.25
KOHLMANN, C.
    CONCERTO TRANSCRIPTIONS OF FAVORITE HYMNS
        THEODORE PRESSER COMPANY   1.25
KOHLMANN, C.
    EIGHTEEN HYMN TRANSCRIPTIONS
        THEODORE PRESSER COMPANY   1.95
KOHLMANN, C.
    MORE CONCERT TRANSCRIPTIONS OF FAVORITE HYMNS
        THEODORE PRESSER COMPANY   1.25
KOLZ, E.
    SIX BAGATELLES
        ASSOCIATED MUSIC PUBLISHERS, INC.   DOB   1.50
KOLZ, E.
    THREE DANCE PIECES, 1959
        ASSOCIATED MUSIC PUBLISHERS, INC.   DOB   1.50
KONOWITZ, B.
    COMPLETE ROCK PIANO METHOD
        ALFRED MUSIC COMPANY   685   4.95
KONOWITZ, B.
    JAZZ FOR PIANO, BK. 1
        LEE ROBERTS MUSIC PUBLICATIONS, INC.   1.50
KONOWITZ, B.
    JAZZ FOR PIANO, BK. 2
        LEE ROBERTS MUSIC PUBLICATIONS, INC.   1.50
KONOWITZ, B.
    JAZZ SCENES -- BLUE NOTE BOOGIE, CHOO CHOO STOMP, LAZY DAZE,
    POUNDIN' THE BEAT
        LEE ROBERTS MUSIC PUBLICATIONS, INC.   1.25
KONSTANTINOFF
    TWO PIECES
        FRANCO COLOMBO PUBLICATIONS   SAL   2.75
KONT, P.
    KLAVIERMUSIK FUR KINDER
        ASSOCIATED MUSIC PUBLISHERS, INC.   DOB   1.10
KONT, P.
    SOPHIE UND SONATINE FUR SCHULE UND HAUS, AN
        ASSOCIATED MUSIC PUBLISHERS, INC.   DOB   1.75
KOPTAGEL, Y.
    FOSSIL SUITE
        ASSOCIATED MUSIC PUBLISHERS, INC.   BOT   .75
KOPTAGEL, Y.
    IMPRESSIONS DE MINORQUE
        ASSOCIATED MUSIC PUBLISHERS, INC.   ESC   3.75
KOPTAGEL, Y.
    THREE PIECES
        ASSOCIATED MUSIC PUBLISHERS, INC.   ESC   3.50
KORANIEVSKY, M.
    AT THE SEA SHORE--8 PIECES WITH WORDS
        G. SCHIRMER, INC.   .75
KORANIEVSKY, M.
    BACK TO SCHOOL--8 PIECES WITH WORDS
        G. SCHIRMER, INC.   .75

KORDA--ED.   KORDA   2
    ALT-WIENER TANZBUCHLEIN
        SCHOTT   3942   1.75
KORDA--ED.   KORDA   2
    ALT-WIENER TANZBUCHLEIN
        SCHOTT   3942   1.75
KOREVAAR   E
    DELFT DANCES
        C. F. PETERS CORPORATION   B80   .60
KORNAUTH, E.
    FIVE PIECES, OP. 44
        ASSOCIATED MUSIC PUBLISHERS, INC.   DOB   2.50
KORNAUTH, E.
    PRELUDE AND PASSACAGLIA, OP. 43
        ASSOCIATED MUSIC PUBLISHERS, INC.   DOB   2.50
KORNAUTH, E.
    THREE CANONS
        ASSOCIATED MUSIC PUBLISHERS, INC.   OBV   1.00
KOSCHINSKY   E
    ADVENT. SEVENTEEN ADVENT SONGS WITH GERMAN TEXT
        C. F. PETERS CORPORATION   N1252   1.25
KOSCHINSKY   E
    CHRISTMAS NIGHTINGALE
        C. F. PETERS CORPORATION   N3194   1.75
KOSMA, J.
    SUITE LANGUEDOCIENNE
        ASSOCIATED MUSIC PUBLISHERS, INC.   ENO   1.25
KOUGELL, A.
    EIGHT PIECES IN THE FORM OF ETUDES
        ASSOCIATED MUSIC PUBLISHERS, INC.   ESC   3.25
KOUNTZ, R.   1
    AT GRANDMA'S HOUSE - BIG CLOCK AND LITTLE CLOCK, SPINNING WHEEL
        THEODORE PRESSER COMPANY   .50
KOZAKIEWICZ
    THIRD GRADE PIECES
        FRANCO COLOMBO PUBLICATIONS   NY1791   1.00
KOZELUCH, L.   3
    FUNF SONATEN
        BARENREITER VERLAG   AP 340
KRAEHENBUEHL
    CALENDAR SCENES
        SCHMITT, HALL AND MCCREARY COMPANY   9965   1.25
KRAFT, L.
    EASY ANIMAL PIECES
        GENERAL MUSIC PUBLISHING COMPANY, INC.   287   2.00
KRAFT, L.
    EASY ANIMAL PIECES
        GENERAL MUSIC PUBLISHING COMPANY, INC.   2.00
KRAUS--ED   KRAUS
    CADENZAS FROM MOZART'S PIANO CONCERTOS
        BELWIN-MILLS PUBLISHING CORPORATION   6.00
KRAUSE, A.
    TEN TRILL STUDIES, OP. 2
        G. SCHIRMER, INC.   L553   .75
KRAWITZ, I. *
    HOW TO TEACH RHYTHMS AND RHYTHM BANDS -- FIFTEEN LESSONS IN
    FUNDAMENTAL RHYTHMIC TRAINING
        G. SCHIRMER, INC.   1.50
KREBS   HERRMANN
    EASY DANCE PIECES
        FRANCO COLOMBO PUBLICATIONS   SIK.109   1.50
KREBS   FRICKERT
    THREE FUGUES
        FRANCO COLOMBO PUBLICATIONS   129234   1.25
KREJCI, I.   3-4
    TRE SCHERZINI
        BARENREITER VERLAG   AP 2104
KREMENLIEV
    SIX MINIATURES
        MCA MUSIC   .75
KRENEK, E.   3-4
    ECHOES FROM AUSTRIA
        BARENREITER VERLAG
KRENEK, E.   A
    EIGHT PIANO PIECES
        THEODORE PRESSER COMPANY   1.00
KRENEK, E.
    EIGHT PIANO PIECES --1946--
        THEODORE PRESSER COMPANY   1.25
KRENEK, E.
    FIVE PIANO PIECES, OP. 39
        UNIVERSAL EDITION   8601   1.70
KRENEK, E.
    SECHS VERMESSENE
        BARENREITER VERLAG   BA 3507   6.00
KRENEK, E.   4
    SECHS VERMESSENE
        BARENREITER VERLAG   BA 3507
KRENEK, E.
    TWELVE SHORT PIANO PIECES, WRITTEN IN THE 12-TONE TECHNIQUE--OP.
    83
        G. SCHIRMER, INC.   1.50
KRENEK, E.
    TWO SUITES, OP. 26
        UNIVERSAL EDITION   7798   3.00
KRENTZLIN, R.--ED   KRENTZLIN, R.   2
    DIE JUGEND TANZT
        SCHOTT   2300   3.00
KRENTZLIN, R.--ED   KRENTZLIN, R.   2
    KLINGENDE MELODIEN, BAND 01
        SCHOTT   2650   3.25
KRENTZLIN, R.--ED   KRENTZLIN, R.   2
    KLINGENDE MELODIEN, BAND 02
        SCHOTT   2895   3.25
KRENTZLIN, R.--ED   KRENTZLIN, R.   2
    KLINGENDE MELODIEN, BAND 03
        SCHOTT   4350   3.25
KRENTZLIN, R.--ED   KRENTZLIN, R.   2
    OPERN UND OPERETTEN, BAND 01
        SCHOTT   2340   2.50
KRENTZLIN, R.--ED   KRENTZLIN, R.   2
    OPERN UND OPERETTEN, BAND 02
        SCHOTT   4175   2.50
KRENTZLIN, R.--ED   KRENTZLIN, R.   2
    ROMANTIKER-BUCH FUR DIE JUGEND
        SCHOTT   2575   2.75
KRENTZLIN, R.--ED   KRENTZLIN, R.   2
    TANZENDES ROKOKO UND DIE ZEIT DER ROMANTIK, BAND 01
        SCHOTT   2503   2.50
KRENTZLIN, R.--ED   KRENTZLIN, R.   2
    TANZENDES ROKOKO UND DIE ZEIT DER ROMANTIK, BAND 02
        SCHOTT   4795   2.50
KRESS--ED.   KRESS   1-2
    KLAVIER-UBUNGEN DES FRANK. DORFSCHULMEISTERS GEORG AD. KRESS
        SCHOTT   3766   1.75

KREUTZ --ED.   KREUTZ
   KLAVIERTANZE
      BARENREITER VERLAG   BA 885   3.25
KREUTZ--ED.   KREUTZ   2
   CLAVIER-SONATINEN DES 18 JAHRHUNDERTS
      SCHOTT   3765   1.75
KREUTZ--ED.   KREUTZ   1-2
   CLAVIERSTUCKE FUR ANFANGER --18 JAHRHUNDERT
      SCHOTT   2572   1.75
KREUTZ--ED.   KREUTZ   2
   KLEINE LEICHTE KLAVIERSTUCKE -- 18 JAHRHUNDERT
      SCHOTT   2425   1.75
KREUTZ--ED.   KREUTZ   2-3
   LEICHTE CLAVIER-SONATEN DES 18 JAHRHUNDERTS
      SCHOTT   2896   2.25
KREUTZER
   FOR A YOUNG PIANIST, BK. 1
      ASHLEY DEALERS SERVICE, INC.   1.00
KREUTZER
   FOR A YOUNG PIANIST, BK. 2
      ASHLEY DEALERS SERVICE, INC.   1.00
KREUTZER
   FOR A YOUNG PIANIST, BOOK 1
      CENTURY MUSIC PUBLISHING COMPANY, INC.   1.00
KREUTZER
   FOR A YOUNG PIANIST, BOOK 2
      CENTURY MUSIC PUBLISHING COMPANY, INC.   1.00
KREUTZER
   LET'S PLAY HYMNS
      ASHLEY DEALERS SERVICE, INC.   1.25
KREUTZER
   NINE LITTLE LYRIC PIECES
      BOSTON MUSIC COMPANY   1.00
KREUTZER
   ORIGINAL AIRS AND DANCES
      BOSTON MUSIC COMPANY   1.00
KREUTZER
   YOUNG PIANIST, BK. 1 - ELEMENTARY
      ASHLEY DEALERS SERVICE, INC.   1.00
KREUTZER
   YOUNG PIANIST, BK. 2 - ELEMENTARY
      ASHLEY DEALERS SERVICE, INC.   1.00
KREUTZER
   YOUNG PIANIST, BK. 3 - ELEMENTARY
      ASHLEY DEALERS SERVICE, INC.   1.00
KREUTZER
   YOUNG PIANIST, BK. 4
      ASHLEY DEALERS SERVICE, INC.   1.25
KREUTZER
   YOUNG PIANIST, BK. 5
      ASHLEY DEALERS SERVICE, INC.   1.25
KREUTZER
   YOUNG PIANIST, BK. 6
      ASHLEY DEALERS SERVICE, INC.   1.25
KREUTZER
   YOUNG PIANIST, THE - BOOK 4
      CENTURY MUSIC PUBLISHING COMPANY, INC.   1.25
KREUTZER
   YOUNG PIANIST, THE - BOOK 5
      CENTURY MUSIC PUBLISHING COMPANY, INC.   1.25
KREUTZER
   YOUNG PIANIST, THE - BOOK 6
      CENTURY MUSIC PUBLISHING COMPANY, INC.   1.25
KREUTZER
   YOUNG PIANIST, THE - ELEMENTARY BOOK 1
      CENTURY MUSIC PUBLISHING COMPANY, INC.   1.00
KREUTZER
   YOUNG PIANIST, THE - ELEMENTARY BOOK 2
      CENTURY MUSIC PUBLISHING COMPANY, INC.   1.00
KREUTZER
   YOUNG PIANIST, THE - ELEMENTARY BOOK 3
      CENTURY MUSIC PUBLISHING COMPANY, INC.   1.25
KREUTZER--ED   KREUTZER
   FROM FAMOUS NOTEBOOKS
      BOSTON MUSIC COMPANY   1.00
KREUTZER--ED   KREUTZER
   HERITAGE HYMN BOOK
      CENTURY MUSIC PUBLISHING COMPANY, INC.   1.00
KREUTZER--ED   KREUTZER
   LET'S PLAY HYMNS
      CENTURY MUSIC PUBLISHING COMPANY, INC.   1.25
KREVIT, W.
   STYLES AND TOUCHES
      BELWIN-MILLS PUBLISHING CORPORATION   11481   1.50
KRICKA   2-3
   ZWEI MARSCHE
      BARENREITER VERLAG   AP 649
KRIEGER   KREUTZ   3
   AUSGEWAHLTE KLAVIERWERKE. 18 STUCKE AUS DEN SECHS MUSIKALISCHEN
   PARTIEN 1697 UND DER ANMUTHIGEN CLAVIER-UBUNG 1699
      BARENREITER VERLAG   BA 1649
KRIEGER   KREUTZ
   SELECTED PIANO WORKS --FROM SECHS MUSIKALISCHEN PARTIEN 1697 AND
   ANMUTHIGEN CLAVIER-UBUNG 1699
      BARENREITER VERLAG   BA 1649   2.00
KROGMANN, C. W.
   ZEPHYRS FROM MELODYLAND, OP. 15
      G. SCHIRMER, INC.   1.25
KROME--ED   KROME   2-3
   LEICHTES TANZBUCH
      SCHOTT   3714   2.50
KUBA   2-3
   TSCHECHISCHE MUSIK IN DOMALICE
      BARENREITER VERLAG   AP 652
KUEHNER, C.   LOWER ELEMENTARY GRADE
   SCHOOL OF ETUDES, BK. 1
      G. SCHIRMER, INC.   L481   1.50
KUEHNER, C.   HIGHER ELEMENTARY GRADE
   SCHOOL OF ETUDES, BK. 2
      G. SCHIRMER, INC.   L482   1.50
KUEHNER, C.   LOWER MEDIUM GRADE
   SCHOOL OF ETUDES, BK. 3
      G. SCHIRMER, INC.   L483   1.50
KUHLAU, F.
   NINETEEN SONATINAS, OP. 44 AND 66
      FRANCO COLOMBO PUBLICATIONS   ER684   2.25
KUHLAU, F.   E-M
   SEVEN SONATINAS, OP. 60 AND OP. 88
      C. F. PETERS CORPORATION   715B   3.00
KUHLAU, F.   POZZOLI
   SEVEN SONATINAS, OP. 60 AND 88
      FRANCO COLOMBO PUBLICATIONS   ER646   4.25
KUHLAU, F.   E-M
   SONATINAS
      C. F. PETERS CORPORATION   1233A   3.00

KUHLAU, F.   E-M
   SONATINAS
      C. F. PETERS CORPORATION   1233B   3.00
KUHLAU, F.   KLEE
   SONATINAS, BK. 1--OP. 20, 55, 59
      G. SCHIRMER, INC.   L52   1.50
KUHLAU, F.   KLEE
   SONATINAS, BK. 2--OP. 60, 88
      G. SCHIRMER, INC.   L53   1.50
KUHLAU, F.
   SONATINAS, VOL. 1
      CARL FISCHER, INC.   L 374   1.50
KUHLAU, F.
   SONATINAS, VOL. 2
      CARL FISCHER, INC.   L 473   1.50
KUHLAU, F.   POZZOLI
   TWELVE SONATINAS, OP. 20, 55 AND 59
      FRANCO COLOMBO PUBLICATIONS   ER592   4.25
KUHLAU, F.
   TWELVE SONATINAS, OP. 20, 55, 59
      UNIVERSAL EDITION   95   2.40
KUHLAU, F.   E-M
   TWELVE SONATINAS+ OP. 20, OP. 55, OP. 59
      C. F. PETERS CORPORATION   715A   3.00
KUHLAU, F.   MORONI   2-3
   ZWOLF SONATINEN, OP. 20 NOS. 1-3, OP. 55 NOS. 1-6, OP. 59 NOS.
   1-3
      BARENREITER VERLAG   CM 20051
KUHNAU, J.   FRICKERT
   EASY SUITE MOVEMENTS
      ASSOCIATED MUSIC PUBLISHERS, INC.   LEU   2.25
KUHNAU, J.   2-3
   PARTITEN UND SONATEN
      SCHOTT   2508   2.25
KUHNAU, J.
   SIX BIBLICAL SONATAS
      BROUDE BROTHERS LTD.   09.00
KUKUCK   1-2
   KLEINE MUSIKANTENSTUCKE
      SCHOTT   4128   1.75
KULLAK, T.   PALMER, W. A.
   ALBUM FOR THE YOUNG
      ALFRED MUSIC COMPANY   568   1.25
KULLAK, T.
   SCENES FROM CHILDHOOD -- COMPLETE
      UNIVERSAL EDITION   3712   1.20
KULLAK, T.   KLAUSER
   SCENES FROM CHILDHOOD--24 CHARACTERISTIC PIECES, OP. 62, 81
      G. SCHIRMER, INC.   L365   1.25
KULLAK, T.   M
   SCENES FROM CHILDHOOD, OP. 62 AND 81
      C. F. PETERS CORPORATION   3369   2900
KULLAK, T.   POZZOLI
   SCHOOL OF OCTAVE PLAYING, BK. 1
      FRANCO COLOMBO PUBLICATIONS   ER700   1.75
KULLAK, T.   POZZOLI
   SCHOOL OF OCTAVE PLAYING, BK. 2
      FRANCO COLOMBO PUBLICATIONS   ER701   1.75
KULLAK, T.   POZZOLI
   SCHOOL OF OCTAVE PLAYING, BK. 3
      FRANCO COLOMBO PUBLICATIONS   ER1214   1.75
KULLAK, T.
   SCHOOL OF OCTAVE-PLAYING, THE--OP. 48--BK. 1, PRELIMINARY SCHOOL
      G. SCHIRMER, INC.   L475   1.00
KULLAK, T.
   SCHOOL OF OCTAVE-PLAYING, THE--OP. 48--BK. 2, SEVEN
   OCTAVE-STUDIES
      G. SCHIRMER, INC.   L476   1.25
KULLAK, T.   SAUER   M-D
   SCHOOL OF OCTAVES, OP. 48. VOL. 1
      C. F. PETERS CORPORATION   3273A   2.75
KULLAK, T.   SAUER   D
   SCHOOL OF OCTAVES, OP. 48. VOL. 2
      C. F. PETERS CORPORATION   3273B   2.75
KULLAK, T.   SAUER   D
   SCHOOL OF OCTAVES, OP. 48. VOL. 3
      C. F. PETERS CORPORATION   3273C   3.00
KUNC, B.
   LITTLE PIECES FOR LITTLE PEOPLE
      RONGWEN MUSIC, INC.   02.00
KUNZ   MARCIANO
   TWO HUNDRED SHORT TWO-PART CANONS, OP. 14
      FRANCO COLOMBO PUBLICATIONS   ER35   1.25
KUNZ   BUELOW
   TWO HUNDRED SHORT 2-PART CANONS FOR THE BEGINNER, OP. 14
      G. SCHIRMER, INC.   L939   1.25
KUPFERMAN, M.
   FOURTEEN CANONIC INVENTIONS FOR YOUNG COMPOSERS
      GENERAL MUSIC PUBLISHING COMPANY, INC.   402   3.00
KUPFERMAN, M.
   FOURTEEN CANONIC INVENTIONS FOR YOUNG COMPOSERS
      GENERAL MUSIC PUBLISHING COMPANY, INC.   3.00
KURANDA, M.--ED   KURANDA, M.
   SIXTEEN MASTERWORKS
      UNIVERSAL EDITION   UE 10440   1.50
KURANDA, M.--ED   KURANDA, M.
   SIXTEEN MASTERWORKS FOR THE PIANO
      THEODORE PRESSER COMPANY   1.50
KURKA, R.
   MIDSUMMER DAY DREAM AND IN A CAVERN
      WEINTRAUB MUSIC COMPANY   070106   .50
KURKA, R.
   MIST ON THE LAKE AND TO THE TOP OF THE MOUNTAIN
      WEINTRAUB MUSIC COMPANY   070105   .50
KURKA, R.
   MOUNTAINTOPS AND FIELDS IN THE MORNING
      WEINTRAUB MUSIC COMPANY   070107   .50
KURKA, R.
   PRAIRIE SNOW AND SHOOTING THE RAPIDS
      WEINTRAUB MUSIC COMPANY   070108   .50
KURKA, R.
   SPRING PLANTING AND SPARKLING WATER
      WEINTRAUB MUSIC COMPANY   070109   .50
KURKA, R.
   WATCHING BREAKERS AND CONVERSATIONS AT SUNDOWN
      WEINTRAUB MUSIC COMPANY   070104   .50
KVAPIL   3
   KLAVIERKOMPOSITIONEN AUS DEM JAHR 1912
      BARENREITER VERLAG   AP 653
LA ROWE, J.
   MEDITATIONS FOR PIANO
      LILLENAS PUBLISHING COMPANY   MB-123   2.50
LABEY
   SIX PIECES
      FRANCO COLOMBO PUBLICATIONS   SAL   2.75

LACK
  METHODE
    ALPHONSE LEDUC
LACK   6
  MURMURE DE LA SOURCE, LE, IDYLLE, OP. 241
    ALPHONSE LEDUC
LACK   3, 4
  TROIS SONATINES, OP. 257
    ALPHONSE LEDUC
LADD, A.
  BALLET MUSIC FOR THE DANCE STUDIO
    THEODORE PRESSER COMPANY   1.50
LAKNER, Y.
  FIVE BIRTHDAYS
    ISRAEL MUSIC INSTITUTE   4.00
LAMB
  RAGTIME TREASURES
    BELWIN-MILLS PUBLISHING CORPORATION   2.95
LAMBARDO
  TWELVE CONTEMPORARY PIECES FOR CHILDREN
    PEER SOUTHERN ORGANIZATION   01.35
LAMBERT--ED.   LAMBERT
  DANCE MUSIC FROM THREE CENTURIES--CURWEN EDITION
    G. SCHIRMER, INC.   1.50
LAMBERT, A.
  PIANO METHOD FOR BEGINNERS
    G. SCHIRMER, INC.   1.50
LAMBERT, C.--ED   LAMBERT, C.   2A
  LITTLE TREASURY SERIES - CLASSICS, BK. 1
    CENTURY MUSIC PUBLISHING COMPANY, INC.   1.00
LAMBERT, C.--ED   LAMBERT, C.   2B
  LITTLE TREASURY SERIES - CLASSICS, BK. 2
    CENTURY MUSIC PUBLISHING COMPANY, INC.   1.00
LAMBERT, C.--ED   LAMBERT, C.   2C
  LITTLE TREASURY SERIES - CLASSICS, BK. 3
    CENTURY MUSIC PUBLISHING COMPANY, INC.   1.00
LAMBERT, C.--ED   LAMBERT, C.   3A
  LITTLE TREASURY SERIES - CLASSICS, BK. 4
    CENTURY MUSIC PUBLISHING COMPANY, INC.   1.00
LAMBERT, C.--ED   LAMBERT, C.   1C
  LITTLE TREASURY SERIES - FOLK SONGS AND DANCES, BK. 1
    CENTURY MUSIC PUBLISHING COMPANY, INC.   1.00
LAMBERT, C.--ED   LAMBERT, C.   2A
  LITTLE TREASURY SERIES - FOLK SONGS AND DANCES, BK. 2
    CENTURY MUSIC PUBLISHING COMPANY, INC.   1.00
LAMBERT, C.--ED   LAMBERT, C.   2A-2B
  LITTLE TREASURY SERIES - POLYPHONICS, BK. 1
    CENTURY MUSIC PUBLISHING COMPANY, INC.   1.00
LAMBERT, C.--ED   LAMBERT, C.   2C-3A
  LITTLE TREASURY SERIES - POLYPHONICS, BK. 2
    CENTURY MUSIC PUBLISHING COMPANY, INC.   1.00
LAMBERT, C.--ED   LAMBERT, C.   2-3
  LITTLE TREASURY SERIES - SONATINAS, BK. 1
    CENTURY MUSIC PUBLISHING COMPANY, INC.   1.00
LAMBERT, C.--ED   LAMBERT, C.   3
  LITTLE TREASURY SERIES - SONATINAS, BK. 2
    CENTURY MUSIC PUBLISHING COMPANY, INC.   1.00
LAMBERT, C.--ED   LAMBERT, C.   1
  LITTLE TREASURY SERIES -- CLASSICS, BK. 1
    ASHLEY DEALERS SERVICE, INC.   1.00
LAMBERT, C.--ED   LAMBERT, C.   2B
  LITTLE TREASURY SERIES -- CLASSICS, BK. 2
    ASHLEY DEALERS SERVICE, INC.   1.00
LAMBERT, C.--ED   LAMBERT, C.   2C
  LITTLE TREASURY SERIES -- CLASSICS, BK. 3
    ASHLEY DEALERS SERVICE, INC.   1.00
LAMBERT, C.--ED   LAMBERT, C.   3A
  LITTLE TREASURY SERIES -- CLASSICS, BK. 4
    ASHLEY DEALERS SERVICE, INC.   1.00
LAMBERT, C.--ED   LAMBERT, C.   1A-1B
  LITTLE TREASURY SERIES -- ETUDES. BK. 1
    ASHLEY DEALERS SERVICE, INC.   1.00
LAMBERT, C.--ED   LAMBERT, C.   2A-3A
  LITTLE TREASURY SERIES -- ETUDES, BK. 2
    ASHLEY DEALERS SERVICE, INC.   1.00
LAMBERT, C.--ED   LAMBERT, C.   1C
  LITTLE TREASURY SERIES -- FOLK SONGS AND DANCES, BK. 1
    ASHLEY DEALERS SERVICE, INC.   1.00
LAMBERT, C.--ED   LAMBERT, C.   2A
  LITTLE TREASURY SERIES -- FOLK SONGS AND DANCES, BK. 2
    ASHLEY DEALERS SERVICE, INC.   1.00
LAMBERT, C.--ED   LAMBERT, C.   2A-2B
  LITTLE TREASURY SERIES -- POLYPHONIC PIECES, BK. 1
    ASHLEY DEALERS SERVICE, INC.   1.00
LAMBERT, C.--ED   LAMBERT, C.   3A-3B
  LITTLE TREASURY SERIES -- POLYPHONIC PIECES, BK. 2
    ASHLEY DEALERS SERVICE, INC.   1.00
LAMBERT, C.--ED   LAMBERT, C.   2A-2B
  LITTLE TREASURY SERIES -- RECITAL CLASSICS, BK. 1
    ASHLEY DEALERS SERVICE, INC.   1.00
LAMBERT, C.--ED   LAMBERT, C.   2C-3A
  LITTLE TREASURY SERIES -- RECITAL CLASSICS, BK. 2
    ASHLEY DEALERS SERVICE, INC.   1.00
LAMBERT, C.--ED   LAMBERT, C.   2-3
  LITTLE TREASURY SERIES -- SONATINAS, BK. 1
    ASHLEY DEALERS SERVICE, INC.   1.00
LAMBERT, C.--ED   LAMBERT, C.   3
  LITTLE TREASURY SERIES -- SONATINAS, BK. 2
    ASHLEY DEALERS SERVICE, INC.   1.00
LAMONTAINE, J.
  CHILD'S PICTURE BOOK, A
    BROUDE BROTHERS LTD.   02.50
LAMONTAINE, J.
  COPYCATS
    SUMMY-BIRCHARD COMPANY   1.50
LAMONTAINE, J.
  SIX DANCE PRELUDES, OP. 18
    BROUDE BROTHERS LTD.   03.75
LAMOTE DE GRIGNON, R.
  ALBORADA--12 SHORT PIECES
    ASSOCIATED MUSIC PUBLISHERS, INC.   UME   .75
LANCEN   E
  MINIATURES. PROGRESSIVE PIECES FOR SMALL HANDS. VOL. 1
    C. F. PETERS CORPORATION   H1905A   1.25
LANCEN   E
  MINIATURES. PROGRESSIVE PIECES FOR SMALL HANDS. VOL. 2
    C. F. PETERS CORPORATION   H1905B   1.25
LANCEN   D
  THREE IMPROMPTUS
    C. F. PETERS CORPORATION   H373   1.25
LANDE
  KAY LANDE'S ABC-123
    THE BIG THREE MUSIC CORPORATION   1.95
LANDRY   2
  POUR NOS BABYS, OP. 236
    ALPHONSE LEDUC

LANE--ED.   LANE
  TEACHER'S PET, BK. 01
    THE BIG THREE MUSIC CORPORATION   1.95
LANE--ED.   LANE
  TEACHER'S PET, BK. 02
    THE BIG THREE MUSIC CORPORATION   1.95
LANE--ED.   LANE
  TEACHER'S PET, BK. 03
    THE BIG THREE MUSIC CORPORATION   1.95
LANE--ED.   LANE
  TEACHER'S PET, BK. 04
    THE BIG THREE MUSIC CORPORATION   1.95
LANE--ED.   LANE
  TEACHER'S PET, BK. 05
    THE BIG THREE MUSIC CORPORATION   1.95
LANE--ED.   LANE
  TEACHER'S PET, BK. 06
    THE BIG THREE MUSIC CORPORATION   1.95
LANE--ED.   LANE
  TEACHER'S PET, BK. 07
    THE BIG THREE MUSIC CORPORATION   1.95
LANE--ED.   LANE
  TEACHER'S PET, BK. 08
    THE BIG THREE MUSIC CORPORATION   1.95
LANE--ED.   LANE
  TEACHER'S PET, BK. 09
    THE BIG THREE MUSIC CORPORATION   1.95
LANE--ED.   LANE
  TEACHER'S PET, BK. 10
    THE BIG THREE MUSIC CORPORATION   1.95
LANE--ED.   LANE
  TEACHER'S PET, BK. 11
    THE BIG THREE MUSIC CORPORATION   1.95
LANE, J.
  CREATIVE PIANO SOLOS, BK. 1
    THE BIG THREE MUSIC CORPORATION   02.95
LANE, J.
  EASY APPROACH TO THE PIANO, BK. 1
    THE BIG THREE MUSIC CORPORATION   02.50
LANE, J.
  EASY APPROACH TO THE PIANO, BK. 2
    THE BIG THREE MUSIC CORPORATION   02.50
LANE, J.
  JOHN LANE SAYS 'KIDS ARE PEOPLE TOO'
    THE BIG THREE MUSIC CORPORATION   02.95
LANE, J.
  TEACHER'S PET NO. 12-16 BIG HITS
    THE BIG THREE MUSIC CORPORATION   01.95
LANE, J.
  TEACHER'S PET NO. 13
    THE BIG THREE MUSIC CORPORATION   01.95
LANE, J.--ED   LANE
  BEST OF JOHN LANE, THE
    THE BIG THREE MUSIC CORPORATION   2.95
LANE, J.--ED   LANE
  JOHN LANE GOES TO NASHVILLE
    THE BIG THREE MUSIC CORPORATION   1.95
LANE, J.--ED   LANE
  JOHN LANE SALUTES THE SEVENTIES
    THE BIG THREE MUSIC CORPORATION   3.95
LANE, J.--ED   LANE
  JOHN LANE'S BEST OF COUNTRY MUSIC
    THE BIG THREE MUSIC CORPORATION   2.95
LANE, J.--ED   LANE
  JOHN LANE'S FAVORITE HYMNS
    THE BIG THREE MUSIC CORPORATION   2.95
LANE, J.--ED   LANE
  JOHN LANE'S HAVE FAITH
    THE BIG THREE MUSIC CORPORATION   2.95
LANE, J.--ED   LANE
  JOHN LANE'S INTERMEDIATE PIANO SOLOS, BK. 1
    THE BIG THREE MUSIC CORPORATION   2.95
LANE, J.--ED   LANE
  JOHN LANE'S INTERMEDIATE PIANO SOLOS, BK. 2
    THE BIG THREE MUSIC CORPORATION   2.95
LANE, J.--ED   LANE
  TEN BIG HITS, EASY TO PLAY, NO. 1
    THE BIG THREE MUSIC CORPORATION   1.25
LANE, J.--ED   LANE
  TEN BIG HITS, EASY TO PLAY, NO. 2
    THE BIG THREE MUSIC CORPORATION   1.25
LANE, J.--ED   LANE
  TEN BIG HITS, EASY TO PLAY, NO. 2
    THE BIG THREE MUSIC CORPORATION   1.25
LANE, J.--ED   LANE
  TEN BIG HITS, EASY TO PLAY, NO. 3
    THE BIG THREE MUSIC CORPORATION   1.25
LANG--ED   LANG   2
  TANZ, TANZ, GRETELEIN
    SCHOTT   3938   1.75
LANG--ED #   LANG #   2-3
  WAS UNSRE KINDER SINGEN
    SCHOTT   600   4.00
LANG, C. S.   3
  SKETCHES FOR PIANO, BK. 1
    NOVELLO AND COMPANY, LTD.   10.0086.01   1.15
LANG, C. S.   3
  SKETCHES FOR PIANO, BK. 2
    NOVELLO AND COMPANY, LTD.   10.0092.06   1.15
LANG, C. S.   4
  SKETCHES FOR PIANO, BK. 3
    NOVELLO AND COMPANY, LTD.   10.0093.04   1.25
LANGE, F.--ED.   LANGE, F.
  LATIN-AMERICAN ART MUSIC--SELECTED FROM THE WORKS OF 12
  CONTEMPORARY COMPOSERS
    G. SCHIRMER, INC.   1.75
LANKFORD--ED.   LANKFORD   EARLY GRADES
  CLASSICS FOR THE YOUNG PIANIST, BK. 1
    G. SCHIRMER, INC.   1.25
LANKFORD--ED.   LANKFORD   INTERMEDIATE GRADES
  CLASSICS FOR THE YOUNG PIANIST, BK. 2
    G. SCHIRMER, INC.   1.25
LANNER, J. F. C.   M
  EIGHT POPULAR WALTZES
    C. F. PETERS CORPORATION   1382A   3.00
LANNING--ED   LANNING
  EARLY ORIGINAL CLASSICS
    MUSICORD PUBLICATIONS, INC.   1.50
LANNING--ED   LANNING   1, 2, 3
  MUSIC BY THE MASTERS
    MUSICORD PUBLICATIONS, INC.   2.00
LANZA
  TWELVE TWO-PART FUGUES
    FRANCO COLOMBO PUBLICATIONS   ER1294   1.25
LAPARRA, R.
  RHYTHMES ESPAGNOLS--7 SPANISH DANCES
    ASSOCIATED MUSIC PUBLISHERS, INC.   ENO   2.75

LAPARRA, R.
    SCENES IBERIENNES--8 SPANISH SCENES
        ASSOCIATED MUSIC PUBLISHERS, INC.   ENO   2.75
LAPORTE, J.
    GUIDE TO IMPROVISATION, A - FOR THE KEYBOARD INSTRUCTOR
        BERKLEE PRESS PUBLICATIONS   B25-T   12.50
LARA, A.
    GRANADA - TEACHING EDITION
        EDITORIAL COOPERATIVA INTER-AMERICANA   00.85
LAST, J.
    ASTRONAUT, THE
        SCHMITT, HALL AND MCCREARY COMPANY   9982   1.50
LAST, J.
    AT THE KEYBOARD, BK. 1
        OXFORD UNIVERSITY PRESS   39.601   1.00
LAST, J.
    AT THE KEYBOARD, BK. 2
        OXFORD UNIVERSITY PRESS   39.602   1.00
LAST, J.
    AT THE KEYBOARD, BK. 3
        OXFORD UNIVERSITY PRESS   39.603   1.25
LAST, J.
    AT THE KEYBOARD, BK. 4
        OXFORD UNIVERSITY PRESS   39.604   1.25
LAST, J.   VE
    KEYBOARD GAMES FOR THE VERY YOUNG PIANIST
        OXFORD UNIVERSITY PRESS   33.913   1.25
LAST, J.   VE
    PARTY PIECES
        OXFORD UNIVERSITY PRESS   33.926   1.20
LAST, J.   VE
    SIGHT READING FOR THE VERY YOUNG PIANIST
        OXFORD UNIVERSITY PRESS   33.914   1.50
LAST, J.
    THREE SEASCAPES
        OXFORD UNIVERSITY PRESS   33.930   .50
LAST, J.
    TUNES AT THE KEYBOARD
        OXFORD UNIVERSITY PRESS   39.608   1.20
LAST, J.
    TWO BAGATELLES
        OXFORD UNIVERSITY PRESS   33.924   1.10
LATROBE, C. I.   STEVENS
    THREE PIANO SONATAS
        BOOSEY AND HAWKES, INC.   3.50
LAUMES, D.
    EIGHT PIECES, SERIES 1
        ASSOCIATED MUSIC PUBLISHERS, INC.   BER   .60
LAUMES, D.
    EIGHT PIECES, SERIES 2
        ASSOCIATED MUSIC PUBLISHERS, INC.   BER   .60
LAVAGNE
    THREE PRELUDES
        FRANCO COLOMBO PUBLICATIONS   SAL   1.75
LAVIN, C.
    SUITE ANDINE
        ASSOCIATED MUSIC PUBLISHERS, INC.   ESC   3.00
LAVIOLETTE, W.
    SEVEN PRELUDES
        ASSOCIATED MUSIC PUBLISHERS, INC.   AMP   1.25
LAVRY
    FIVE COUNTRY DANCES
        MCA MUSIC   1.50
LAWLOR, G.
    RECITAL ETUDES FOR PIANO
        BELWIN-MILLS PUBLISHING CORPORATION   1.25
LAYTON, B.
    THREE STUDIES FOR PIANO, OP. 5
        G. SCHIRMER, INC.   2.00
LAZAR, F.
    PIECES MINUSCULES POUR LES ENFANTS, BK. 1
        ELKAN-VOGEL, INC.   D   2.00
LAZAR, F.
    PIECES MINUSCULES POUR LES ENFANTS, BK. 2
        ELKAN-VOGEL, INC.   D   2.50
LAZARE-LEVY
    SANS OCTAVES -- 12 LITTLE PIECES -- BK. 1
        FRANCO COLOMBO PUBLICATIONS   SAL   2.75
LAZARE-LEVY
    SANS OCTAVES -- 12 LITTLE PIECES -- BK. 2
        FRANCO COLOMBO PUBLICATIONS   SAL   2.75
LAZARE-LEVY
    TWO ETUDES, OP. 10
        FRANCO COLOMBO PUBLICATIONS   SAL   4.00
LAZARE-LEVY
    TWO SONATINAS
        FRANCO COLOMBO PUBLICATIONS   SAL   4.00
LAZARE-LEVY
    WALTZES
        FRANCO COLOMBO PUBLICATIONS   SAL   4.00
LAZARUS
    SIX PIECES
        FRANCO COLOMBO PUBLICATIONS   SAL   4.00
LAZZARI
    TWO MINIATURES - DUETTINO, VALSE MELANCOLIQUE
        FRANCO COLOMBO PUBLICATIONS   SAL   2.50
LE GUILLARD
    TWO SHORT PIECES
        FRANCO COLOMBO PUBLICATIONS   SAL   4.00
LEBERT, S. *
    SCHOOL OF EMBELLISHMENTS, THE--18 ETUDES FROM PART 2 OF THE
    THEORETICAL AND PRACTICAL PIANO-SCHOOL
        G. SCHIRMER, INC.   1.00
LEBERT, S. *
    TEORICA Y PRACTICA ESCUELA DE PIANO, PARTE 1--ESCUELA ELEMENTAL,
    PRIMER GRADO
        G. SCHIRMER, INC.   2.00
LEBERT, S. *
    TEORICA Y PRACTICA ESCUELA DE PIANO, PARTE 2--EJERCICIOS Y
    ESTUDIOS, SEGUNDO GRADO
        G. SCHIRMER, INC.   2.00
LEBERT, S.   MONTANI
    THEORETICAL AND PRACTICAL METHOD - ABRIDGED EDITION IN ONE
    VOLUME
        FRANCO COLOMBO PUBLICATIONS   ER2412   3.00
LEBERT, S.   IVALDI
    THEORETICAL AND PRACTICAL METHOD, BK. 1
        FRANCO COLOMBO PUBLICATIONS   ER130   2.75
LEBERT, S.   IVALDI
    THEORETICAL AND PRACTICAL METHOD, BK. 2
        FRANCO COLOMBO PUBLICATIONS   ER131   2.75
LEBERT, S.   IVALDI
    THEORETICAL AND PRACTICAL METHOD, BK. 3
        FRANCO COLOMBO PUBLICATIONS   ER132   5.50
LEBERT, S. *
    THEORETICAL AND PRACTICAL PIANO-SCHOOL, PART 1--ELEMENTARY
    SCHOOL, FIRST DEGREE
        G. SCHIRMER, INC.   1.75

LEBERT, S. *
    THEORETICAL AND PRACTICAL PIANO-SCHOOL, PART 2--EXERCISES AND
    ETUDES, SECOND DEGREE
        G. SCHIRMER, INC.   2.00
LEBERT, S. *
    THEORETICAL AND PRACTICAL PIANO-SCHOOL, PART 3--EXERCISES AND
    ETUDES, THIRD DEGREE
        G. SCHIRMER, INC.   3.00
LECARPENTIER, A.   GUARINONI
    ELEMENTARY PRACTICAL COURSE, BK. 1 - PRINCIPLES OF MUSIC AND OF
    THE PIANO
        FRANCO COLOMBO PUBLICATIONS   ER1547   2.75
LECARPENTIER, A.   DE GUARINONI
    ELEMENTARY PRACTICAL COURSE, BK. 2 - 25 STUDIES AND 12
    RECREATIONS
        FRANCO COLOMBO PUBLICATIONS   ER1548   2.25
LECARPENTIER, A.
    METHODE DE PIANO POUR LES ENFANTS
        GERARD BILLAUDOT EDITIONS MUSICALES   2.50
LECARPENTIER, A.
    PIANO METHOD FOR CHILDREN, A--SPANISH AND ENGLISH
        G. SCHIRMER, INC.   L1133   1.50
LECHNER--ED   LECHNER   3
    HAUSMUSIK FUR WEIHNACHTEN -- ALTE UND NEUE WEIHNACHTMUSIK
        SCHOTT   4220   2.50
LECHNER--ED   LECHNER   3
    HAUSMUSIK FUR WEIHNACHTEN --ALTE UND NEUE WEIHNACHTSMUSIK
        SCHOTT   4220   2.50
LECHNER--ED   LECHNER   2
    LEICHTES MARSCHBUCH -- ERFOLGREICHE MARSCHE
        SCHOTT   4615   2.50
LECHNER--ED   LECHNER   1-2
    MEIN WEIHNACHTSBUCH -- 33 DER SCHONSTEN WEIHNACHTSLIEDER FUR DEN
    ANFANGER FUR KLAVIER ZU 2 UND 4 HANDEN
        SCHOTT   4220   2.25
LECHNER--ED   LECHNER
    TONLEITERN UND AKKORDE DURCH ALLE DUR-UND MOLL-TONARTEN
        SCHOTT   04312 1/2   1.00
LECOUPPEY, F.   SCHARFENBERG
    ALPHABET, THE--25 VERY EASY STUDIES FOR SMALL HANDS--OP. 17
        G. SCHIRMER, INC.   L430   1.25
LECOUPPEY, F.   KLENGEL
    ALPHABET, THE, OP. 17   25 VERY EASY STUDIES
        ASSOCIATED MUSIC PUBLISHERS, INC.   BRH   1.00
LECOUPPEY, F.
    COURS DE PIANO, NO.1 ABC
        GERARD BILLAUDOT EDITIONS MUSICALES   2.50
LECOUPPEY, F.
    COURS DE PIANO, NO.2 ALPHABET
        GERARD BILLAUDOT EDITIONS MUSICALES   2.50
LECOUPPEY, F.
    COURS DE PIANO, NO.3 LE PROGRES
        GERARD BILLAUDOT EDITIONS MUSICALES   2.50
LECOUPPEY, F.
    COURS DE PIANO, NO.5 AGILITE
        GERARD BILLAUDOT EDITIONS MUSICALES   2.50
LECOUPPEY, F.
    FIFTEEN PREPARATORY STUDIES TO CZERNY'S 'SCHOOL OF
    VELOCITY'--OP. 26
        G. SCHIRMER, INC.   L69   1.00
LECOUPPEY, F.
    FIFTEEN STUDIES, OP. 26
        FRANCO COLOMBO PUBLICATIONS   BA8936   1.50
LECOUPPEY, F.
    L'AGILITE--25 PROGRESSIVE STUDIES FOR MECHANISM AND LIGHT
    TOUCH--OP. 20
        G. SCHIRMER, INC.   L67   1.25
LECUONA
    ANDALUCIA SUITE
        EDWARD B. MARKS MUSIC CORPORATION   02.50
LECUONA
    DANZAS AFRO CUBANAS
        EDWARD B. MARKS MUSIC CORPORATION   02.00
LECUONA
    DANZAS CUBANAS
        EDWARD B. MARKS MUSIC CORPORATION   02.00
LECUONA
    DIARY OF A CHILD
        EDWARD B. MARKS MUSIC CORPORATION   01.50
LECUONA
    LECUONAS BEST MADE EASIER FOR YOU
        EDWARD B. MARKS MUSIC CORPORATION   02.00
LECUONA
    TRES MINIATURAS
        EDWARD B. MARKS MUSIC CORPORATION   01.25
LEDUC, A.
    METHODE ELEMENTAIRE, OP. 130
        ALPHONSE LEDUC
LEDUC, A.   1, 2
    TWENTY-FIVE PETITS ETUDES TRES FACILES, OP. 156
        ALPHONSE LEDUC
LEES, B.
    SIX ORNAMENTAL ETUDES
        BOOSEY AND HAWKES, INC.   1.50
LEEUW, R.   D
    MUSIC FOR PIANO 1
        C. F. PETERS CORPORATION   D373   2.00
LEFEVRE, A.
    TWO PIECES FOR PIANO
        GERARD BILLAUDOT EDITIONS MUSICALES   1.10
LEFLEMING, C.
    SUNDAY MORNING, AND WHISTLING TUNE
        OXFORD UNIVERSITY PRESS   33.067   1.05
LEGINSKA, E.   M-D
    THREE VICTORIAN PORTRAITS
        COMPOSERS PRESS, INC.   3.00
LEHAR   4
    MERRY WIDOW WALTZES, THE
        CENTURY MUSIC PUBLISHING COMPANY, INC.   1310   .40
LEHAR
    MERRY WIDOW, THE
        CHAPPELL AND COMPANY, INC.   3735008   1.95
LEHAR   4
    WALTZES, MERRY WIDOW
        CENTURY MUSIC PUBLISHING COMPANY, INC.   1310   .40
LEHMAN, E.   1, 2
    CROQUIS POUR LA JEUNESSE
        ALPHONSE LEDUC
LEIBOWITZ, R.
    FOUR PIECES FOR PIANO
        UNIVERSAL EDITION   UE 11775   6.00
LEIGHTON
    FIVE STUDIES, OP. 22
        NOVELLO AND COMPANY, LTD.   10.0088.08   2.50
LEIGHTON   3
    PIECES FOR ANGELA, OP. 47
        NOVELLO AND COMPANY, LTD.   10.0089.06   1.65

LELEU   6, 7
    EN ITALIE
        ALPHONSE LEDUC
LELEU   5
    POCHADES
        ALPHONSE LEDUC
LEMELAND, A.
    FIVE EPISODES FOR PIANO
        GERARD BILLAUDOT EDITIONS MUSICALES   3.00
LEMOINE, H.
    ETUDES ENFANTINES, OP. 37
        CARL FISCHER, INC.   L 323   1.50
LEMOINE, H.   E
    ETUDES ENFANTINES, OP. 37
        C. F. PETERS CORPORATION   2213   2.00
LEMOINE, H.   SCHARFENBERG
    ETUDES ENFANTINES, OP. 37
        G. SCHIRMER, INC.   L175   1.25
LEMOINE, H.
    ETUDES ENFANTINES, OP. 37
        UNIVERSAL EDITION   161   2.00
LEMONT, C. W.
    TWELVE MELODIOUS STUDIES
        THEODORE PRESSER COMPANY   .60
LENNON *
    FIFTY BY JOHN LENNON AND PAUL MCCARTNEY, EASY BIG NOTE PIANO
        WARNER BROTHERS PUBLISHERS   3.95
LENNON *
    POINTER LIBRARY - THE BEST OF LENNON AND MCCARTNEY
        POINTER PUBLICATIONS   2.95
LEO, L.   MAFFIOLETTI *   3
    SECHS TOCCATEN
        BARENREITER VERLAG   CM 21452
LEONCAVALLO
    WALTZES FROM 'LA REGINETTA DELLE ROSE'
        FRANCO COLOMBO PUBLICATIONS   SON.6040   1.50
LEONTOVICH
    TWO UKRANIAN FOLK SONGS
        MCA MUSIC   .60
LEOZ, J.G.
    SONATINA
        ASSOCIATED MUSIC PUBLISHERS, INC.   UME   1.75
LEPITRE
    THREE VERY EASY LITTLE PIECES
        FRANCO COLOMBO PUBLICATIONS   SAL   1.50
LERMA, P.
    BOCETOS PIANISTICOS
        ASSOCIATED MUSIC PUBLISHERS, INC.   UME   1.75
LERNER *   KASSCHAU, H.
    BRIGADOON
        SAM FOX PUBLISHING COMPANY, INC.   1.50
LERNER *   LAMONT, V.
    BRIGADOON -- SELECTION
        SAM FOX PUBLISHING COMPANY, INC.   2.50
LEROUX, GASPARD   FULLER   E-M
    COMPLETE WORKS FOR CLAVECIN
        C. F. PETERS CORPORATION   6166   10.00
LESSARD, J.
    LITTLE CONCERT SUITE
        GENERAL MUSIC PUBLISHING COMPANY, INC.   3.00
LESSARD, J.
    NEW WORLDS FOR THE YOUNG PIANIST, BK. 1
        GENERAL MUSIC PUBLISHING COMPANY, INC.   316   2.00
LESSARD, J.
    NEW WORLDS FOR THE YOUNG PIANIST, BK. 2
        GENERAL MUSIC PUBLISHING COMPANY, INC.   317   2.00
LESSARD, J.
    NEW WORLDS FOR THE YOUNG PIANIST, VOL. 1
        GENERAL MUSIC PUBLISHING COMPANY, INC.   2.50
LESSARD, J.
    NEW WORLDS FOR THE YOUNG PIANIST, VOL. 2
        GENERAL MUSIC PUBLISHING COMPANY, INC.   3.50
LEVINE
    FIVE FINGER FAVORITES
        BOSTON MUSIC COMPANY   1.25
LEVINE
    LEVINE'S PIANO COURSE - BOOK 1
        BOSTON MUSIC COMPANY   1.25
LEVINE
    LEVINE'S PIANO COURSE - BOOK 2
        BOSTON MUSIC COMPANY   1.25
LEVINE
    SOUTH AMERICAN PIANO MUSIC
        FRANCO COLOMBO PUBLICATIONS   NY1856   1.00
LEVINE, H.--ED   LEVINE, H.
    MORE THEMES FROM THE GREAT CONCERTOS
        THEODORE PRESSER COMPANY   1.25
LEVINE, H.--ED   LEVINE, H.
    PIANO CLASSICS SIMPLIFIED
        ALFRED MUSIC COMPANY   528   1.50
LEVINE, H.--ED   LEVINE, H.
    THEMES FROM GREAT CHAMBER MUSIC
        THEODORE PRESSER COMPANY   1.50
LEVINE, H.--ED   LEVINE, H.
    THEMES FROM THE GREAT BALLETS
        THEODORE PRESSER COMPANY   1.25
LEVINE, H.--ED   LEVINE, H.
    THEMES FROM THE GREAT ORATORIOS
        THEODORE PRESSER COMPANY   1.75
LEVINE, H.--ED   LEVINE, H.
    THEMES FROM THE GREAT PIANO CONCERTOS
        THEODORE PRESSER COMPANY   1.50
LEVINE, H.--ED   LEVINE, H.
    THEMES FROM THE GREAT SYMPHONIES
        THEODORE PRESSER COMPANY   2.00
LEVINE, H.--ED   LEVINE, H.
    THEMES FROM THE ORCHESTRAL REPERTOIRE
        THEODORE PRESSER COMPANY   1.25
LEVY, E.
    SEVEN PIANO PIECES
        BOOSEY AND HAWKES, INC.   1.50
LEVY, E.
    TWO PIECES HUMORISTIQUE
        FRANCO COLOMBO PUBLICATIONS   SAL   2.75
LEVY, M. D.
    FIVE EASY PIANO PIECES
        BOOSEY AND HAWKES, INC.   1.25
LEWIS, P. T.
    SWEETS FOR PIANO
        THEODORE PRESSER COMPANY   2.00
LIAPUNOFF   D
    ETUDES D'EXECUTION TRANSCENDANTE, OP. 11. VOL. 1
        C. F. PETERS CORPORATION   ZM1172   2.50
LIAPUNOFF   D
    ETUDES D'EXECUTION TRANSCENDANTE, OP. 11. VOL. 2
        C. F. PETERS CORPORATION   ZM1173   2.50

LIAPUNOFF   D
    ETUDES D'EXECUTION TRANSCENDANTE, OP. 11. VOL. 3
        C. F. PETERS CORPORATION   ZM1174   2.50
LIAPUNOFF   D
    ETUDES D'EXECUTION TRANSCENDANTE, OP. 11. VOL. 4
        C. F. PETERS CORPORATION   1175   2.50
LICHNER, H.
    NINE SONATINAS--OP. 4, 49, 66
        G. SCHIRMER, INC.   L989   1.25
LIEBERMAN, F.
    FOUR PIECES FOR PIANO
        E. C. SCHIRMER MUSIC COMPANY   236   01.00
LIEBERSON, G.
    PIANO PIECES FOR ADVANCED CHILDREN OR RETARDED ADULTS 2. SIX
    TECHNICAL STUDIES -- WHICH WILL TEACH YOU NOTHING
        BELWIN-MILLS PUBLISHING CORPORATION   11379   1.75
LIEBERSON, G.
    PIANO PIECES FOR ADVANCED CHILDREN OR RETARDED ADULTS 3. EIGHT
    STUDIES IN MUSICOLOGY -- WHICH WILL TEACH YOU A GREAT DEAL
        BELWIN-MILLS PUBLISHING CORPORATION   11380   1.75
LIEFELD--ED.   LIEFELD
    FAMOUS THEMES IN THE MODERN MANNER
        RUBANK, INC.   1.25
LIFTL, F. J.
    PREPARATORY SCHOOL TO BACH
        THEODORE PRESSER COMPANY   1.25
LIFTL, F. J.
    PREPARATORY SCHOOL TO THE SONATINA
        THEODORE PRESSER COMPANY   1.50
LINDFORS
    KEY RELATIVES
        BELWIN-MILLS PUBLISHING CORPORATION   11256   1.50
LINDFORS, E.
    GUILD MUSICIANSHIP BOOK, PART 1
        SUMMY-BIRCHARD COMPANY   1.75
LINDFORS, E.
    GUILD MUSICIANSHIP BOOK, PART 2
        SUMMY-BIRCHARD COMPANY   2.00
LINDFORS, E.
    MAJORS AND THEIR RELATIVES, THE
        BELWIN-MILLS PUBLISHING CORPORATION   1.50
LINDFORS, E.
    MY FIRST RECORD FOR STUDENT, TEACHER, AND PARENT
        BELWIN-MILLS PUBLISHING CORPORATION   1.00
LINDFORS, E.
    MY MUSIC RECORD
        BELWIN-MILLS PUBLISHING CORPORATION   1.00
LINDFORS, E.
    TONAL MOODS FOR KEYBOARD MUSICIANS
        WILLIS MUSIC COMPANY   1.75
LINDO, S.
    EASY SOLOS FOR PIANO
        OXFORD UNIVERSITY PRESS   38.009   1.40
LINDO, S.
    FOLK SONGS FOR PIANO, BK. 1
        OXFORD UNIVERSITY PRESS   38.010   1.65
LINDO, S.
    FOLK SONGS FOR PIANO, BK. 2
        OXFORD UNIVERSITY PRESS   38.012   2.00
LINDSAY, C. JR.--ED   LINDSAY, C. JR.
    BIG BANDS, THE
        MUSIC SALES CORPORATION   040051   2.95
LINDSAY, C. JR.--ED   LINDSAY, C. JR.
    HAVE FUN PLAYING JAZZ
        MUSIC SALES CORPORATION   040046   2.95
LIPSCOMB--ED.   LIPSCOMB
    FAVORITE FOLKSONGS
        BOSTON MUSIC COMPANY   1.25
LIPSCOMB--ED.   LIPSCOMB
    FORTY-SIX EASY ARRANGEMENTS OF SACRED MELODIES--WITH WORDS
        G. SCHIRMER, INC.   1.00
LIPSCOMB--ED.   LIPSCOMB
    HYMNS TO REMEMBER
        G. SCHIRMER, INC.   1.00
LIST, G.
    MUSIC FOR CHILDREN--8 PIECES
        ASSOCIATED MUSIC PUBLISHERS, INC.   AMP   .90
LISZT
    ALBUM
        KULTURA   2.00
LISZT   D
    ALBUM FOR PIANO
        C. F. PETERS CORPORATION   H89   2.00
LISZT   SAUER   D
    ANNEES DE PELERINAGE
        C. F. PETERS CORPORATION   3603   7.50
LISZT
    ANNEES DE PELERINAGE--DEUXIEME ANNEE 'ITALIE'
        G. SCHIRMER, INC.   L911   2.00
LISZT   JOSEFFY
    ANNEES DE PELERINAGE--PREMIERE ANNEE 'SUISSE'
        G. SCHIRMER, INC.   L910   2.75
LISZT   TAGLIAPIETRA
    ANNEES DE PELERINAGE, 2ND YEAR, ITALY - SONETTI DEL PETRARCA,
    NOS. 47, 104, 123
        FRANCO COLOMBO PUBLICATIONS   ER728   1.25
LISZT   BOGHEN
    ANNEES DE PELERINAGE, 3RD YEAR - 6 CONSOLATIONS
        FRANCO COLOMBO PUBLICATIONS   ER790   .75
LISZT   ANSON, G.
    ANSON INTRODUCES LISZT
        WILLIS MUSIC COMPANY   1.50
LISZT   3-5
    AUSWAHL -- 9 BEL STUCKE
        SCHOTT   507   1.75
LISZT   SAUER   D
    BALLADS
        C. F. PETERS CORPORATION   7201   2950
LISZT   M-D
    CHRISTMAS TREE, VOL. 1
        C. F. PETERS CORPORATION   H88A   2.00
LISZT   D
    CHRISTMAS TREE, VOL. 2
        C. F. PETERS CORPORATION   H88B   2.00
LISZT
    COMPLETE WORKS OF FRANZ LISZT -- VOL. 1 TRANSCENDENTAL ETUDES,
    CLOTH
        BELWIN-MILLS PUBLISHING CORPORATION   10.00
LISZT
    COMPLETE WORKS OF FRANZ LISZT -- VOL. 1 TRANSCENDENTAL ETUDES,
    PAPER
        BELWIN-MILLS PUBLISHING CORPORATION   6.00
LISZT
    COMPLETE WORKS OF FRANZ LISZT -- VOL. 2 ETUDES, CLOTH
        BELWIN-MILLS PUBLISHING CORPORATION   10.00
LISZT
    COMPLETE WORKS OF FRANZ LISZT -- VOL. 2 ETUDES, PAPER
        BELWIN-MILLS PUBLISHING CORPORATION   6.00

LISZT
COMPLETE WORKS OF FRANZ LISZT -- VOL. 3 HUNGARIAN RHAPSODIES,
CLOTH
BELWIN-MILLS PUBLISHING CORPORATION 10.00
LISZT
COMPLETE WORKS OF FRANZ LISZT -- VOL. 3 HUNGARIAN RHAPSODIES,
PAPER
BELWIN-MILLS PUBLISHING CORPORATION 6.00
LISZT   CORTOT
CONCERT ETUDES - FOREST MURMERS, GNOMENREIGEN
FRANCO COLOMBO PUBLICATIONS   SAL   3.00
LISZT   SCHMID-LINDNER
CONSOLATIONS
ASSOCIATED MUSIC PUBLISHERS, INC.   BRH   .60
LISZT   JOSEFFY
CONSOLATIONS AND LIEBESTRAUME
G. SCHIRMER, INC.   L341   1.00
LISZT
DANCES
EDWIN F. KALMUS   3643   2.50
LISZT   LEE   5
DREI SPATE KLAVIERSTUCKE
BARENREITER VERLAG   19104
LISZT
EARLY AND LATE WOEKS
EDWIN F. KALMUS   3642   2.50
LISZT   SCHER, W.   INTERMEDIATE GRADES
EASY LISZT--12 FAMOUS CONCERT PIECES, ARRANGED FOR INTERMEDIATE
GRADES
G. SCHIRMER, INC.   1.00
LISZT   SAUER   D
ETUDES D'EXECUTION TRANSCENDANTE
C. F. PETERS CORPORATION   3600C   4.50
LISZT   CORTOT
ETUDES D'EXECUTION TRANSCENDANTE, BK. 1 -- NOS. 1-4 --
FRANCO COLOMBO PUBLICATIONS   SAL   5.75
LISZT   CORTOT
ETUDES D'EXECUTION TRANSCENDANTE, BK. 2 -- NOS. 5-8 --
FRANCO COLOMBO PUBLICATIONS   SAL   5.00
LISZT   CORTOT
ETUDES D'EXECUTION TRANSCENDANTE, BK. 3 -- NOS. 9-12 --
FRANCO COLOMBO PUBLICATIONS   SAL   5.75
LISZT
ETUDES D'EXECUTION TRANSCENDANTE, VOL. 1
ASSOCIATED MUSIC PUBLISHERS, INC.   BRH   4.00
LISZT
ETUDES D'EXECUTION TRANSCENDANTE, VOL. 1
EDWIN F. KALMUS   3626   1.75
LISZT
ETUDES D'EXECUTION TRANSCENDANTE, VOL. 2
ASSOCIATED MUSIC PUBLISHERS, INC.   BRH   4.00
LISZT
ETUDES D'EXECUTION TRANSCENDANTE, VOL. 2
EDWIN F. KALMUS   3627   1.75
LISZT
ETUDES, BKS. 1 AND 2
KULTURA   EA.
LISZT   SPIVAK, S.
FINEST MUSIC SERIES -- LISZT
SCHUBERTH CO.   NO. 05   1.50
LISZT   WERNER
FIVE LISZT DISCOVERIES--CURWEN EDITION
G. SCHIRMER, INC.   .90
LISZT
FOURTEEN PIECES FOR THE PIANO
EDWARD B. MARKS MUSIC CORPORATION   01.50
LISZT
HARMONIES POETIQUES AND RELIGIEUSES
EDWIN F. KALMUS   3629   3.00
LISZT   SAUER   D
HUNGARIAN RHAPSODIES, VOL. 1
C. F. PETERS CORPORATION   3600A   4.00
LISZT   SAUER   D
HUNGARIAN RHAPSODIES, VOL. 2
C. F. PETERS CORPORATION   3600B   4.00
LISZT   KREUTZER
IN VARIOUS MOODS
BOSTON MUSIC COMPANY   1.25
LISZT
LATE PIANO WORKS
EDWIN F. KALMUS   3641   2.50
LISZT
LIEBESTRAUME AND 3 NOCTURNES
UNIVERSAL EDITION   5881   1.00
LISZT
LISZT
ASHLEY DEALERS SERVICE, INC.   HG 13   2.95
LISZT
LISZT ALBUM, BK. 1
EDWIN F. KALMUS   3621   2.50
LISZT
LISZT ALBUM, BK. 2
EDWIN F. KALMUS   3622   2.50
LISZT   M-D
NINETEEN PIANO PIECES
C. F. PETERS CORPORATION   4667   4.50
LISZT   SAUER   D
OPERA FANTASIES, VOL. 1
C. F. PETERS CORPORATION   3601C   8.50
LISZT   SAUER   D
OPERA FANTASIES, VOL. 2
C. F. PETERS CORPORATION   3601D   8.50
LISZT   SAUER   D
ORIGINAL COMPOSITIONS, VOL. 1
C. F. PETERS CORPORATION   3601A   6.00
LISZT   SAUER   D
ORIGINAL COMPOSITIONS, VOL. 2
C. F. PETERS CORPORATION   3601B   6.00
LISZT   SAUER   D
PAGANINI ETUDES AND FIVE OTHER CONCERT ETUDES
C. F. PETERS CORPORATION   3600D   3.50
LISZT
PAGANINI STUDIES
EDWIN F. KALMUS   3637   1.75
LISZT
PAGANINI-ETUDES
ASSOCIATED MUSIC PUBLISHERS, INC.   BRH   2.25
LISZT   JOSEFFY
RHAPSODIES HONGROISES, BK. 1--NO. 1-8
G. SCHIRMER, INC.   L1033   2.50
LISZT   JOSEFFY
RHAPSODIES HONGROISES, BK. 2--NO. 9-15
G. SCHIRMER, INC.   L1034   2.50
LISZT
ROMANCE OUBLIEE - THREE VERSIONS --1848 TO 1880 SEARLE 169,
309A, 527
MUSICA OBSCURA   3.00

LISZT   GARDONYI AND
SELECTED WORKS
KULTURA   4.00
LISZT   CORTOT
SIX CONSOLATIONS
FRANCO COLOMBO PUBLICATIONS   SAL   3.25
LISZT
SIX CONSOLATIONS
EDWIN F. KALMUS   3625   1.25
LISZT   SAUER   D
SIX CONSOLATIONS AND THREE LIEBESTRAEUME
C. F. PETERS CORPORATION   3604   1.50
LISZT
SIX CONSOLATIONS, NOS. 1 AND 2
FRANCO COLOMBO PUBLICATIONS   128849   .50
LISZT   BRUGNOLI
SIX ETUDES DE CONCERT
FRANCO COLOMBO PUBLICATIONS   ER73   2.75
LISZT *   GALLICO
SIX GRAND ETUDES
G. SCHIRMER, INC.   L835   1.25
LISZT   GALLICO
SIX GRANDES ETUDES AFTER N. PAGANINI
G. SCHIRMER, INC.   L835   1.25
LISZT   BRUGNOLI
SIX GRANDES ETUDES D'APRES PAGANINI
FRANCO COLOMBO PUBLICATIONS   ER105   5.50
LISZT   CORTOT
SIX PAGANINI ETUDES
FRANCO COLOMBO PUBLICATIONS   SAL   7.00
LISZT
SOIREES DE VIENNE
EDWIN F. KALMUS   3638   3.00
LISZT   SAUER   D
SOIREES DE VIENNE
C. F. PETERS CORPORATION   3616   6.50
LISZT   FRIEDHEIM
SOIREES DE VIENNE--VALSES-CAPRICES AFTER SCHUBERT, BK. 1
G. SCHIRMER, INC.   L1369   1.50
LISZT   FRIEDHEIM
SOIREES DE VIENNE--VALSES-CAPRICES AFTER SCHUBERT, BK. 2
G. SCHIRMER, INC.   L1370   1.75
LISZT   SAUER   D
SONG TRANSCRIPTIONS
C. F. PETERS CORPORATION   3602A   10.00
LISZT   SAUER   D
SUPPLEMENT‡ TWO ORIGINAL WORKS, SIX TRANSCRIPTIONS
C. F. PETERS CORPORATION   3602D   7.50
LISZT   ESTEBAN
TECHNICAL EXERCISES --COMPLETE--
ALFRED MUSIC COMPANY   630   6.00
LISZT   WINTERBERGER
TECHNICAL EXERCISES, BK. 01
FRANCO COLOMBO PUBLICATIONS   BA47   1.50
LISZT   WINTERBERGER
TECHNICAL EXERCISES, BK. 02
FRANCO COLOMBO PUBLICATIONS   BA48   1.25
LISZT   WINTERBERGER
TECHNICAL EXERCISES, BK. 03
FRANCO COLOMBO PUBLICATIONS   BA215   1.25
LISZT   WINTERBERGER
TECHNICAL EXERCISES, BK. 04
FRANCO COLOMBO PUBLICATIONS   BA261   1.25
LISZT   WINTERBERGER
TECHNICAL EXERCISES, BK. 05
FRANCO COLOMBO PUBLICATIONS   BA262   1.50
LISZT   WINTERBERGER
TECHNICAL EXERCISES, BK. 06
FRANCO COLOMBO PUBLICATIONS   BA266   1.25
LISZT   WINTERBERGER
TECHNICAL EXERCISES, BK. 07
FRANCO COLOMBO PUBLICATIONS   BA264   1.50
LISZT   WINTERBERGER
TECHNICAL EXERCISES, BK. 08
FRANCO COLOMBO PUBLICATIONS   BA269   1.50
LISZT   WINTERBERGER
TECHNICAL EXERCISES, BK. 09
FRANCO COLOMBO PUBLICATIONS   BA267   1.50
LISZT   WINTERBERGER
TECHNICAL EXERCISES, BK. 10
FRANCO COLOMBO PUBLICATIONS   BA277   2.00
LISZT   WINTERBERGER
TECHNICAL EXERCISES, BK. 11
FRANCO COLOMBO PUBLICATIONS   BA6089   2.00
LISZT   WINTERBERGER
TECHNICAL EXERCISES, BK. 12
FRANCO COLOMBO PUBLICATIONS   BA6090   2.00
LISZT   LEE, R. C.
THREE LATE PIANO PIECES
BARENREITER VERLAG   BA 19104 3.25
LISZT   POZZOLI
THREE LIEBESTRAEUME
FRANCO COLOMBO PUBLICATIONS   ER843   1.00
LISZT   CORTOT
THREE LIEBESTRAEUME
FRANCO COLOMBO PUBLICATIONS   SAL   3.00
LISZT   SAUER   D
TRANSCRIPTIONS
C. F. PETERS CORPORATION   3602B   10.00
LISZT
TROIS ETUDES DE CONCERT -- LAMENTO, LEGIERO, SOSPIRO --
EDWIN F. KALMUS   3628   1.75
LISZT   GALLICO
TWELVE ETUDES D'EXECUTION TRANSCENDANTE
G. SCHIRMER, INC.   L788   2.50
LISZT   SZELENYI
TWELVE ETUDES, OP. 1
KULTURA   2.00
LISZT   HOWAT   D
TWELVE ETUDES, VOL. 1
C. F. PETERS CORPORATION   H1422A   2.00
LISZT   HOWAT   D
TWELVE ETUDES, VOL. 2
C. F. PETERS CORPORATION   H1422B   2.00
LISZT
TWENTY PIANO TRANSCRIPTIONS
THEODORE PRESSER COMPANY   5.00
LISZT   TAGLIAPIETRA
TWENTY RHAPSODIES -- 19 HUNGARIAN AND RHAPSODIE ESPAGNOLE -- BK.
1 -- 1-10 --
FRANCO COLOMBO PUBLICATIONS   ER4   4.50
LISZT   TAGLIAPIETRA
TWENTY RHAPSODIES -- 19 HUNGARIAN AND RHAPSODIE ESPAGNOLE -- BK.
2 -- 11-20 --
FRANCO COLOMBO PUBLICATIONS   ER5   4.50

LISZT *
  TWENTY-FOUR SONG TRANSCRIPTIONS, BK. 1
    G. SCHIRMER, INC.   L128   1.75
LISZT *
  TWENTY-FOUR SONG TRANSCRIPTIONS, BK. 2
    G. SCHIRMER, INC.   L129   1.75
LISZT   CORTOT
  TWO CAPRICES POETIQUES - IL LAMENTO, LA LEGGIEREZZA
    FRANCO COLOMBO PUBLICATIONS   SAL   4.00
LISZT   SAUER   D
  TWO CONCERT ETUDES
    C. F. PETERS CORPORATION   3605   1.50
LISZT   JOSEFFY *
  TWO CONCERT ETUDES AND TWO LEGENDS
    G. SCHIRMER, INC.   L1753   1.50
LISZT   CORTOT
  TWO LEGENDS
    FRANCO COLOMBO PUBLICATIONS   SAL   3.50
LISZT   TAGLIAPIETRA
  TWO POLONAISES
    FRANCO COLOMBO PUBLICATIONS   ER501   1.75
LISZT   CORTOT
  VENEZIA E NAPOLI
    FRANCO COLOMBO PUBLICATIONS   SAL   3.50
LISZT
  VENEZIA E NAPOLI--SUPPLEMENT TO DEUXIEME ANNEE DE PELERINAGE
    G. SCHIRMER, INC.   L917   1.25
LISZT   MAIER, G.
  YOUR LISZT BOOK
    BELWIN-MILLS PUBLISHING CORPORATION   11543   2.50
LITTLE--ED   LITTLE
  WELK, LAWRENCE, FAVORITES FOR HONKY TONK PIANO
    WARNER BROTHERS PUBLISHERS   1.95
LLONGUERAS, J.
  MIA, 6 IMPRESSIONS, NO. 1--MIA PREGA
    ASSOCIATED MUSIC PUBLISHERS, INC.   UME   .25
LLOYD, N.
  EPISODES
    ELKAN-VOGEL, INC.   M   1.25
LOCKE
  SEVEN PIECES
    C. F. PETERS CORPORATION   H1630A   1.50
LOEHLEIN   HERRMANN
  DANCES AND PIECES
    FRANCO COLOMBO PUBLICATIONS   SIK.110   1.50
LOEILLET   E
  CIBEL, MINUET, SARABAND
    C. F. PETERS CORPORATION   H9   1.50
LOEILLET
  WERKEN VOOR CLAVECIMBEL
    BROUDE BROTHERS LTD.   17.50
LOESCHHORN   MARCIANO
  LITTLE STUDIES, OP. 181 BK.1
    FRANCO COLOMBO PUBLICATIONS   ER612   1.25
LOESCHHORN   MARCIANO
  LITTLE STUDIES, OP. 181 BK.1
    FRANCO COLOMBO PUBLICATIONS   ER613   1.25
LOESCHHORN
  STUDIES FOR THE DEVELOPMENT OF TECHNIQUE AND EXPRESSION, OP. 65
    WILLIS MUSIC COMPANY   1.50
LOESCHHORN, A.   E
  CHILDREN'S STUDIES, OP. 181, VOL. 1
    C. F. PETERS CORPORATION   2134A   2.00
LOESCHHORN, A.   E
  CHILDREN'S STUDIES, OP. 181, VOL. 2
    C. F. PETERS CORPORATION   2134B   2.00
LOESCHHORN, A.   D
  MELODIC STUDIES, OP. 38. VOL. 1
    C. F. PETERS CORPORATION   1318A   2.00
LOESCHHORN, A.   D
  MELODIC STUDIES, OP. 38. VOL. 2
    C. F. PETERS CORPORATION   1318B   2.00
LOESCHHORN, A.   D
  MELODIC STUDIES, OP. 38. VOL. 3
    C. F. PETERS CORPORATION   1318C   2.00
LOESCHHORN, A.   M-D
  MELODIC STUDIES, OP. 52. VOL. 1
    C. F. PETERS CORPORATION   1319A   2.00
LOESCHHORN, A.   M-D
  MELODIC STUDIES, OP. 52. VOL. 2
    C. F. PETERS CORPORATION   1319B   2.00
LOESCHHORN, A.   M-D
  MELODIC STUDIES, OP. 52. VOL. 3
    C. F. PETERS CORPORATION   1319C   2.00
LOESCHHORN, A.
  PIANOFORTE TECHNICS--DAILY EXERCISES
    G. SCHIRMER, INC.   L254   1.00
LOESCHHORN, A.   BEGINNERS
  STUDIES FOR THE DEVELOPMENT OF TECHNIQUE AND EXPRESSION--PART 1,
  OP. 65--BEGINNERS
    G. SCHIRMER, INC.   L966   1.50
LOESCHHORN, A.   BEGINNERS
  STUDIES FOR THE DEVELOPMENT OF TECHNIQUE AND EXPRESSION--PART 1,
  OP. 65--BEGINNERS--BK. 1
    G. SCHIRMER, INC.   L310   .85
LOESCHHORN, A.   BEGINNERS
  STUDIES FOR THE DEVELOPMENT OF TECHNIQUE AND EXPRESSION--PART 1,
  OP. 65--BEGINNERS--BK. 2
    G. SCHIRMER, INC.   L311   .85
LOESCHHORN, A.   BEGINNERS
  STUDIES FOR THE DEVELOPMENT OF TECHNIQUE AND EXPRESSION--PART 1,
  OP. 65--BEGINNERS--BK. 3
    G. SCHIRMER, INC.   L312   .85
LOESCHHORN, A.   INTERMEDIATE
  STUDIES FOR THE DEVELOPMENT OF TECHNIQUE AND EXPRESSION--PART 2,
  OP. 66--INTERMEDIATE DEGREE
    G. SCHIRMER, INC.   L967   1.75
LOESCHHORN, A.   INTERMEDIATE
  STUDIES FOR THE DEVELOPMENT OF TECHNIQUE AND EXPRESSION--PART 2,
  OP. 66--INTERMEDIATE DEGREE--BK. 1
    G. SCHIRMER, INC.   L313   .75
LOESCHHORN, A.   INTERMEDIATE
  STUDIES FOR THE DEVELOPMENT OF TECHNIQUE AND EXPRESSION--PART 2,
  OP. 66--INTERMEDIATE DEGREE--BK. 2
    G. SCHIRMER, INC.   L314   .75
LOESCHHORN, A.   INTERMEDIATE
  STUDIES FOR THE DEVELOPMENT OF TECHNIQUE AND EXPRESSION--PART 2,
  OP. 66--INTERMEDIATE DEGREE--BK. 3
    G. SCHIRMER, INC.   L315   .75
LOESCHHORN, A.   ADVANCED
  STUDIES FOR THE DEVELOPMENT OF TECHNIQUE AND EXPRESSION--PART 3,
  OP. 67--ADVANCED
    G. SCHIRMER, INC.   L968   1.75
LOESCHHORN, A.   MARCIANO
  TWELVE MELODIOUS AND CHARACTERISTIC PIECES, OP. 51
    FRANCO COLOMBO PUBLICATIONS   ER38   1.75

LOESCHHORN, A.
  TWENTY MELODIOUS STUDIES, OP. 52
    G. SCHIRMER, INC.   L1616   1.25
LOESCHHORN, A.   PARSONS   MEDIUM GRADE
  UNIVERSAL PIANO STUDIES--OP. 169, 170
    G. SCHIRMER, INC.   L1615   1.50
LOESCHHORN, A.--ED   LOESCHHORN, A.   E-M
  CLASSICAL ALBUM FOR THE YOUNG
    C. F. PETERS CORPORATION   2135A   2.50
LOESSER, F.
  GREENWILLOW
    FRANK MUSIC CORPORATION   1.50
LOESSER, F.
  HOW TO SUCCEED IN BUSINESS WITHOUT REALLY TRYING
    FRANK MUSIC CORPORATION   1.50
LOESSER, F.
  MOST HAPPY FELLA, THE
    FRANK MUSIC CORPORATION   1.25
LOESSER, F.   AGAY, D.   EASY
  SONGS FROM 'GREENWILLOW'
    FRANK MUSIC CORPORATION   1.25
LOESSER, F.   RICHTER   EASY
  SONGS FROM 'HANS CHRISTIAN ANDERSEN'
    FRANK MUSIC CORPORATION   1.25
LOESSER, F.   AGAY, D.   EASY
  SONGS FROM 'HOW TO SUCCEED IN BUSINESS WITHOUT REALLY TRYING'
    FRANK MUSIC CORPORATION   1.25
LOEW, J.   SCHARFENBERG
  OCTAVE-STUDIES, OP. 281
    G. SCHIRMER, INC.   L913   1.00
LOEWE, F. *
  LOEWE AND LERNER
    CHAPPELL AND COMPANY, INC.   0013268   1.50
LOEWE, F.
  MEET FREDERICK LOEWE AT THE PIANO
    CHAPPELL AND COMPANY, INC.   3719051   2.50
LOEWE, F.
  MY FAIR LADY
    CHAPPELL AND COMPANY, INC.   3922507   1.50
LOEWE, F.
  MY FAIR LADY
    CHAPPELL AND COMPANY, INC.   3900507   1.95
LOMBARDO   M
  LAUDA, FUGA, AND CAVATINA
    C. F. PETERS CORPORATION   6243   1.50
LOMBATO, D.
  SEIS DANZAS
    EDICIONES MEXICANAS DE MUSICA, A. C.   05.50
LONG
  SHORT PIANO METHOD
    FRANCO COLOMBO PUBLICATIONS   SAL   10.75
LONGAS
  THREE PETITES PIECES ESPAGNOLES
    FRANCO COLOMBO PUBLICATIONS   SAL   2.50
LONGO--ED.   LONGO
  GOLDEN LIBRARY, BK. 1 - VARIOUS COMPOSERS
    FRANCO COLOMBO PUBLICATIONS   103950   5.50
LONGO--ED.   LONGO
  GOLDEN LIBRARY, BK. 3 - VARIOUS COMPOSERS
    FRANCO COLOMBO PUBLICATIONS   112501   5.50
LONGO, A.
  FORTY MELODIOUS STUDIES FOR SMALL HANDS, OP. 43
    FRANCO COLOMBO PUBLICATIONS   ER460   1.75
LONGO, A.
  SIX OCTAVE STUDIES, OP. 48
    FRANCO COLOMBO PUBLICATIONS   ER461   1.75
LONGO, A.
  SIX STUDIES IN SIXTHS, OP. 42
    FRANCO COLOMBO PUBLICATIONS   ER459   1.50
LONGO, A.
  TWELVE STUDIES IN THIRDS, OP. 35
    FRANCO COLOMBO PUBLICATIONS   ER458   2.50
LONGO, A.
  TWENTY-FOUR LITTLE PIECES, OP. 24
    FRANCO COLOMBO PUBLICATIONS   ER2444   2.00
LONGO, A.
  TWENTY-FOUR LITTLE STUDIES ON ARPEGGIOS IN ALL THE MAJOR AND
  MINOR KEYS, OP. 37
    FRANCO COLOMBO PUBLICATIONS   ER1434   2.25
LORENZ, G.--ED.   LORENZ, G.
  ALL-TIME GOSPEL FAVORITES FOR PIANO
    LORENZ PUBLISHING COMPANY   2.95
LOSZKOWSKI   E-M
  SPANISH DANCES, OP. 12, NOS. 3, 5
    C. F. PETERS CORPORATION   2130B   .90
LOUVIER
  ETUDES POUR AGRESSEURS, BK. 1
    ALPHONSE LEDUC
LOUVIER
  ETUDES POUR AGRESSEURS, BK. 2
    ALPHONSE LEDUC
LOVELL
  SEVEN SHAKESPEARE SKETCHES
    FRANCO COLOMBO PUBLICATIONS   LD365   1.25
LUBIN, E.
  PIANISTS CHORD GUIDE, THE
    MUSIC SALES CORPORATION   020150   2.95
LUBIN, E.
  START AT THE PIANO, A
    MUSIC SALES CORPORATION   020149   2.95
LUCAS--ED.
  SIXTEEN SELECTED ETUDES -- BRAHMS, CRAMER, KULLAK, ETC. --
    FRANCO COLOMBO PUBLICATIONS   SAL   5.00
LUCIUK
  FOUR SONATINAS
    EDWARD B. MARKS MUSIC CORPORATION   03.50
LUCIUK
  IMPROVISATIONS FOR CHILDREN
    EDWARD B. MARKS MUSIC CORPORATION   01.50
LUCKTENBERG *   6
  PIANO REPERTOIRE
    BELWIN-MILLS PUBLISHING CORPORATION   FDL 472   2.00
LUDT   E
  GLIMT FRA BARNAS VERDEN --FROM THE CHILDREN'S WORLD--
    C. F. PETERS CORPORATION   LY166   2.00
LUEBECK   M
  CLAVIERUEBUNG --1728--
    C. F. PETERS CORPORATION   4478   1.50
LUNDE, J.   D
  CAPRICES, VOL. 1
    C. F. PETERS CORPORATION   LY148   1.25
LUNDE, J.   D
  CAPRICES, VOL. 2
    C. F. PETERS CORPORATION   LY301   1.25
LUPI
  SIX STUDIES
    FRANCO COLOMBO PUBLICATIONS   DS696   3.25

LUTECE
    TWENTY-FOUR PRELUDES IN ALL KEYS - BK. 1
        FRANCO COLOMBO PUBLICATIONS   SAL   5.50
LUTECE
    TWENTY-FOUR PRELUDES IN ALL KEYS - BK. 2
        FRANCO COLOMBO PUBLICATIONS   SAL   9.00
LUTOSLAWSKI
    BUCOLICS FOR PIANO
        EDWARD B. MARKS MUSIC CORPORATION   02.00
LUTOSLAWSKI
    FOLK MELODIES FOR PIANO
        EDWARD B. MARKS MUSIC CORPORATION   02.50
LUTOSLAWSKI
    TWO STUDIES FOR PIANO
        EDWARD B. MARKS MUSIC CORPORATION   02.50
LUTTGERS--ED   LUTTGERS   1-2
    DER GUTE FREUND. LEICHTE VOLKS-TANZ- UND OPERNMELODIEN
        BARENREITER VERLAG   SM 80
LUTZ--ED   LUTZ
    AM RHEIN BEIM WEIN
        SCHOTT   4900   3.00
LUTZ--ED   LUTZ
    DER WIMPEL, FAHRTENLIEDER
        SCHOTT   5250   2.50
LUTZ--ED   LUTZ   3
    DIE GROSSE OPER, BAND 01
        SCHOTT   4949   5.00
LUTZ--ED   LUTZ   3-4
    DIE GROSSE OPER, BAND 02
        SCHOTT   4950   5.00
LUTZ--ED   LUTZ   2-3
    FROHE WEIHNACHT
        SCHOTT   4006   2.25
LUTZ--ED   LUTZ   2-3
    ITALIEN IM LIED
        SCHOTT   4825   3.00
LUTZ--ED   LUTZ   1-2
    MEIN KINDERLIEDERBUCH - 60 KINDERLIEDER
        SCHOTT   3000   2.50
LUTZ--ED   LUTZ   2
    MEIN VOLKSLIEDERBUCH
        SCHOTT   4100   2.50
LYALL, M.--ED   LYALL, M.
    FAVORITE HYMNS FOR THE PIANO
        BROADMAN MUSIC   4571-02   2.25
LYALL, M.--ED   LYALL, M.
    HYMN TUNE PRELUDES FOR THE PIANO, NO. 1
        BROADMAN MUSIC   4571-03   2.25
LYALL, M.--ED   LYALL, M.
    HYMN TUNE PRELUDES FOR THE PIANO, NO. 2
        BROADMAN MUSIC   4571-04   2.25
LYKE *
    KEYBOARD MUSICIANSHIP - GROUP PIANO FOR ADULTS, BK. 1, 2ND ED.
    REV.
        STIPES PUBLISHING COMPANY   5.80
LYKE *
    KEYBOARD MUSICIANSHIP - GROUP PIANO FOR ADULTS, BK. 2. 2ND ED.
    REV.
        STIPES PUBLISHING COMPANY   6.80
LYNES
    THREE ANALYTICAL SONATINAS
        SUMMY-BIRCHARD COMPANY   1.50
LYON
    CLASSICS FOR LITTLE FOLK
        BELWIN-MILLS PUBLISHING CORPORATION   1.00
LYON
    LITTLE TUNES FOR LITTLE FOLK
        BELWIN-MILLS PUBLISHING CORPORATION   1.00
LYON
    MY FIRST BOOGIE BOOK
        BELWIN-MILLS PUBLISHING CORPORATION   1.00
LYON
    YOU AND I IN MUSIC LAND
        BELWIN-MILLS PUBLISHING CORPORATION   1.00
MACCARTNEY *
    METER AND TIME VALUES
        WILLIS MUSIC COMPANY   1.50
MACDOWELL   3-4
    AMERIKANISCHE WALDIDYLLEN OP. 51
        SCHOTT   1292   2.25
MACDOWELL
    FOUR LITTLE PIECES, OP. 32
        EDWIN F. KALMUS   3656   1.25
MACDOWELL
    FOUR LITTLE POEMS, OP. 32
        G. SCHIRMER, INC.   L1497   1.00
MACDOWELL
    HEXENTANZ--FANTASIESTUCKE, OP. 17 NO. 2
        G. SCHIRMER, INC.   .70
MACDOWELL   SCHAUM, J.   4
    MACDOWELL MASTERPIECES
        SCHAUM PUBLICATIONS, INC.   2.00
MACDOWELL   3-4
    NEU-ENGLAND-IDYLL OP. 62
        SCHOTT   1765   2.50
MACDOWELL
    SEA PIECES, OP. 55 AND NEW ENGLAND IDYLS, OP. 62
        G. SCHIRMER, INC.   L1811   1.50
MACDOWELL   TAUBMANN
    SECOND INDIAN SUITE
        ASSOCIATED MUSIC PUBLISHERS, INC.   BRH   1.50
MACDOWELL   M-D
    SIXTEEN SELECTED PIECES
        C. F. PETERS CORPORATION   4942   4.00
MACDOWELL
    TWELVE ETUDES, OP. 39
        BOSTON MUSIC COMPANY   2.00
MACDOWELL
    TWELVE ETUDES, OP. 39
        EDWIN F. KALMUS   3659   1.50
MACDOWELL
    TWELVE VIRTUOSO STUDIES, OP. 46
        EDWIN F. KALMUS   3660   2.00
MACDOWELL
    WOODLAND SKETCHES
        ASHLEY DEALERS SERVICE, INC.   1.00
MACDOWELL
    WOODLAND SKETCHES
        BOSTON MUSIC COMPANY   1.00
MACERO
    PIECES OF EIGHT
        EDWARD B. MARKS MUSIC CORPORATION   01.25
MACFARREN, W.
    SCALE AND ARPEGGIO MANUAL
        G. SCHIRMER, INC.   L1037   2.00
MACK, E.
    ADVENTURES IN IMPROVISATION AT THE KEYBOARD
        SUMMY-BIRCHARD COMPANY   4.00

MACMAHON, D.
    MANUSCRIPT BOOK OF ELEMENTARY HARMONY, BK. 1
        BANKS AND SON LTD.   .80
MACMAHON, D.
    MANUSCRIPT BOOK OF ELEMENTARY HARMONY, BK. 2
        BANKS AND SON LTD.   .80
MACMAHON, D.
    MANUSCRIPT BOOK OF RUDIMENTS OF MUSIC, BK. 1
        BANKS AND SON LTD.   .55
MACMAHON, D.
    MANUSCRIPT BOOK OF RUDIMENTS OF MUSIC, BK. 2
        BANKS AND SON LTD.   .55
MACMILLAN, E. *
    GRADED SIGHT READING EXERCISES FOR PIANO, BK. 1
        FREDERICK HARRIS MUSIC COMPANY   .90
MACMILLAN, E. *
    GRADED SIGHT READING EXERCISES FOR PIANO, BK. 2
        FREDERICK HARRIS MUSIC COMPANY   .90
MAGGIONI
    SIX INCA MELODIES
        FRANCO COLOMBO PUBLICATIONS   129301   2.25
MAGONE
    THREE WALTZES
        FRANCO COLOMBO PUBLICATIONS   BON-2347   4.25
MAIER, G.
    PIANO TEACHER'S COMPANION, THE -- CLOTHBOUND EDITION
        BELWIN-MILLS PUBLISHING CORPORATION 90072   9.00
MAIER, G.   CORZILIUS
    PLAYING THE PIANO
        BELWIN-MILLS PUBLISHING CORPORATION   1.50
MAIER, G. *
    READING TIME
        BELWIN-MILLS PUBLISHING CORPORATION 10039   1.50
MAIER, G.   1 1/2 - 2
    SONG CARGO
        SCHAUM PUBLICATIONS, INC.   1.60
MAIER, G.
    THINKING FINGERS, BK. 1
        BELWIN-MILLS PUBLISHING CORPORATION 11493   1.75
MAIER, G.
    THINKING FINGERS, BK. 2
        BELWIN-MILLS PUBLISHING CORPORATION 11494   1.75
MAILLARD   6
    DEUX PIECES
        ALPHONSE LEDUC
MAILLARD   6, 7
    TROIS PRELUDES
        ALPHONSE LEDUC
MAILMAN, M.
    MARTHA'S VINEYARD
        THEODORE PRESSER COMPANY   1.25
MALER, W.   3
    DREI KLEINE KLAVIERSTUCKE
        SCHOTT   2772   1.75
MALER, W.   3
    JAHRESKREIS. KLAVIER INVENTIONEN UBER DEUTSCHE VOLKSLIEDER
        SCHOTT   2363   2.00
MALEZIEUX
    THREE VERY EASY LITTLE PIECES - LA ROSE, LA VIOLETTE, LE LYS
        FRANCO COLOMBO PUBLICATIONS   SAL   2.00
MALIPIERO, G. F.
    HORTUS CONCLUSUS, BK. 1
        FRANCO COLOMBO PUBLICATIONS   127878   1.50
MALIPIERO, G. F.
    THREE PIECES
        FRANCO COLOMBO PUBLICATIONS   Z1922   1.50
MALIPIERO, G. F.--ED   MALIPIERO, G. F.
    EIGHTEENTH CENTURY ITALIAN KEYBOARD MUSIC
        THEODORE PRESSER COMPANY   1.00
MALOOF
    KNOW YOUR MUSIC, BK. 1
        PEER SOUTHERN ORGANIZATION   02.00
MALOOF
    KNOW YOUR MUSIC, BK. 2
        PEER SOUTHERN ORGANIZATION   01.75
MALOOF
    KNOW YOUR MUSIC, BK. 3
        PEER SOUTHERN ORGANIZATION   01.50
MALOOF
    KNOW YOUR MUSIC, BK. 4
        PEER SOUTHERN ORGANIZATION   02.50
MALOOF
    MASTER MELODIES IN MINIATURE
        CARL FISCHER, INC.   O 3317   1.25
MALTZMAN--ED   MALTZMAN
    SONGS EN FRANCAIS
        PRO-ART PUBLICATIONS, INC.   607   .75
MANA-ZUCCA
    PIANO PLAY
        PRO-ART PUBLICATIONS, INC.   673   .60
MANA-ZUCCA
    PIANO SKETCHES
        PRO-ART PUBLICATIONS, INC.   674   .75
MANAS
    DANSES POPULAIRES TURQUES
        FRANCO COLOMBO PUBLICATIONS   SAL   4.00
MANGEOT, A.
    VRAIS DEBUTS DU PIANO, LES
        ASSOCIATED MUSIC PUBLISHERS, INC.   ESC   7.00
MANZINO
    FIVE EASY PIECES
        FRANCO COLOMBO PUBLICATIONS   129727   1.00
MARCEL, G.
    SCHOOL MARCHES, BK. 2
        BANKS AND SON LTD.   .95
MARCEL, L. A.
    LES EXERCISES ET LES JEUX -- 16 PROGRESSIVE PIECES FOR CHILDREN,
    BK. 1
        EDITIONS MUSICALES TRANSATLANTIQUES   5.60
MARCEL, L. A.
    LES EXERCISES ET LES JEUX -- 16 PROGRESSIVE PIECES FOR CHILDREN,
    BK. 2
        EDITIONS MUSICALES TRANSATLANTIQUES   5.60
MARGOLA
    FOUR SONATINAS
        FRANCO COLOMBO PUBLICATIONS   BON-2420   2.50
MARGOLA
    SIX LITTLE PIECES FOR CHILDREN
        FRANCO COLOMBO PUBLICATIONS   BON-2192   2.25
MARGOLA
    THREE PIECES
        FRANCO COLOMBO PUBLICATIONS   BON-2542   3.00
MARLOWE
    HAPPY CHRISTMAS
        BOSTON MUSIC COMPANY   1.25
MARTIN
    FORWARD STEPS
        WILLIS MUSIC COMPANY   1.50

MARTIN
    FUN WITH NEW STEPS AHEAD
        WILLIS MUSIC COMPANY   1.25
MARTIN
    MIDDLE C AND ITS NEAR NEIGHBORS
        SUMMY-BIRCHARD COMPANY   1.75
MARTIN, E.
    SEIS PRELUDIOS
        EDITORIAL COOPERATIVA INTER-AMERICANA   01.00
MARTIN, F.
    EIGHT PRELUDES
        UNIVERSAL EDITION   UE 11973   7.50
MARTIN, G.
    MARTIN'S MAJOR AND MINOR SCALES AND PRINCIPAL CHORDS
        CENTURY MUSIC PUBLISHING COMPANY, INC.   1.25
MARTIN, G.
    MORE REAL COOL PIANO
        THEODORE PRESSER COMPANY   1.25
MARTIN, G.
    ROCK 'N' ROLL PIANO
        THEODORE PRESSER COMPANY   1.25
MARTIN, G.--ED   MARTIN, G.
    DIZZY PIANO
        SAM FOX PUBLISHING COMPANY, INC.   2.00
MARTIN, G.--ED   MARTIN, G.
    ECHOES OF BROADWAY -- WITH WORDS
        SAM FOX PUBLISHING COMPANY, INC.   1.50
MARTIN, G.--ED   MARTIN, G.
    ECHOES OF HOLLYWOOD -- WITH WORDS
        SAM FOX PUBLISHING COMPANY, INC.   1.75
MARTIN, G.--ED   MARTIN, G.
    GALAXY OF GREAT HITS
        SAM FOX PUBLISHING COMPANY, INC.   1.50
MARTIN, G.--ED   MARTIN, G.
    HIT FESTIVAL -- 41 FAMOUS MELODIES WITH WORDS
        SAM FOX PUBLISHING COMPANY, INC.   3.00
MARTIN, H.
    TUNE TIME FOR TWO
        BELWIN-MILLS PUBLISHING CORPORATION   1.25
MARTINI, G.   HOFFMANN-ERBRECHT
    SIX SONATAS
        ASSOCIATED MUSIC PUBLISHERS, INC.   BRH   4.00
MARTINI, G.
    SIX SONATAS
        EDWIN F. KALMUS   3661   2.00
                                    6
MARTINU, B.
    BOROVA, 7 DANSES TCHEQUES
        ALPHONSE LEDUC
MARTINU, B.
    ETUDES AND POLKAS, BK. 1
        BOOSEY AND HAWKES, INC.   3.00
MARTINU, B.
    ETUDES AND POLKAS, BK. 2
        BOOSEY AND HAWKES, INC.   3.00
MARTINU, B.
    ETUDES AND POLKAS, BK. 3
        BOOSEY AND HAWKES, INC.   3.00
                                    2
MARTINU, B.
    FABELN -- 1924 --
        BARENREITER VERLAG   AP 1517
MARTINU, B.
    FANTASY AND TOCCATA, 1940
        ASSOCIATED MUSIC PUBLISHERS, INC.   AMP   4.00
                                    2
MARTINU, B.
    FRUHLING IM GARTEN. 4 KLAVIERSTUCKE FUR KINDER
        BARENREITER VERLAG   AP 1518
                                    2
MARTINU, B.
    MARIONETTEN. KLEINE STUCKE FUR KLAVIER, BK. 1
        BARENREITER VERLAG   AP 1523
                                    2
MARTINU, B.
    MARIONETTEN. KLEINE STUCKE FUR KLAVIER, BK. 2
        BARENREITER VERLAG   AP 1524
                                    2
MARTINU, B.
    MARIONETTEN. KLEINE STUCKE FUR KLAVIER, BK. 3
        BARENREITER VERLAG   AP 1525
                                    7, 8
MARTINU, B.
    PRELUDES
        ALPHONSE LEDUC
MARTINU, B.
    PUPPETS, BK. 1
        ARTIA   1.50
MARTINU, B.
    PUPPETS, BK. 2
        ARTIA   1.50
MARTINU, B.
    PUPPETS, BK. 3
        ARTIA   1.50
MARTINU, B.
    THREE CZECH DANCES, 1926
        ASSOCIATED MUSIC PUBLISHERS, INC.   ESC   5.75
MARTINU, B.
    TROIS ESQUISSES
        ASSOCIATED MUSIC PUBLISHERS, INC.   ESC   4.25
                                    3
MARTINU, B.
    ZWEI TANZE -- VALSE UND POLKA -- AUS 'SPALICEK'
        BARENREITER VERLAG   AP 1536
MARTUCCI
    SELECTED COMPOSITIONS
        FRANCO COLOMBO PUBLICATIONS   ER2181   6.75
MARTUCCI   CESI
    TWENTY LITTLE PIECES
        FRANCO COLOMBO PUBLICATIONS   ER782   3.00
                                    2
MARX
    KLAVIERBUCHLEIN FUR PETER
        BARENREITER VERLAG   BA 1428
                                    3
MARX
    KLAVIERMUSIK NACH VOLKSLIEDERN, BK. 1 - OP. 40
        BARENREITER VERLAG   BA 2079
                                    3
MARX
    KLAVIERMUSIK NACH VOLKSLIEDERN, BK. 2 - OP. 59
        BARENREITER VERLAG   BA 3509
MARX
    LITTLE PIANO BOOK FOR PETER
        BARENREITER VERLAG   BA 1428   1.75
MARX
    PIANO MUSIC ON FOLKSONGS, BK. 1 --OP. 40 --
        BARENREITER VERLAG   BA 2079   4.25
MARX
    PIANO MUSIC ON FOLKSONGS, BK. 2 --OP. 59 --
        BARENREITER VERLAG   BA 3509   3.50
MASCAGNI, P.   DE SIMONE
    CAVALLERIA RUSTICANA - SELECTIONS
        FRANCO COLOMBO PUBLICATIONS   SON.1381   1.75
MASCAGNI, P.
    CAVALLERIA RUSTICANA - SELECTIONS
        FRANCO COLOMBO PUBLICATIONS   SON.1751   1.50

MASETTI
    DEDICATIONS
        FRANCO COLOMBO PUBLICATIONS   BON.1787   1.50
MASETTI
    SEVEN EASY LITTLE PIECES
        FRANCO COLOMBO PUBLICATIONS   BON.2515   1.75
MASON, I.
    ADULT APPROACH TO THE PIANO
        THEODORE PRESSER COMPANY   2.50
MASON, I.
    FLASH CARDS
        THEODORE PRESSER COMPANY   1.50
MASON, I.
    FOLK SONGS AND FAMOUS PICTURES
        THEODORE PRESSER COMPANY   2.25
MASON, I.
    MODERN ART OF PIANO PLAYING, THE, BK. 1
        SHAPIRO, BERNSTEIN ORGANIZATION   1.25
MASON, I.
    PREPARATORY PEDAL EXERCISES FOR YOUNG PIANISTS
        SHAPIRO, BERNSTEIN ORGANIZATION   1.00
MASON, I.   ADVANCED
    SKIDMORE MODERN KEYBOARD SERIES - ENCHANTED ISLE
        SHAPIRO, BERNSTEIN ORGANIZATION   .75
MASON, I.   INTERMEDIATE
    SKIDMORE MODERN KEYBOARD SERIES - PASTELS
        SHAPIRO, BERNSTEIN ORGANIZATION   .75
MASON, I.
    SKIDMORE MODERN KEYBOARD SERIES --INTERMEDIATE --GREEN SERIES
    --CORAL SANDS
        SHAPIRO, BERNSTEIN ORGANIZATION   .75
MASON, I.
    SKIDMORE MODERN KEYBOARD SERIES --INTERMEDIATE --GREEN SERIES
    --KERRY GREEN
        SHAPIRO, BERNSTEIN ORGANIZATION   .75
MASON, I.
    SKIDMORE MODERN KEYBOARD SERIES --SECONDARY --CAMEO
        SHAPIRO, BERNSTEIN ORGANIZATION   .75
MASON, I.   INTERMEDIATE
    SKIDMORE MODERN KEYBOARD SERIES -MALEKULA MOON DANCE
        SHAPIRO, BERNSTEIN ORGANIZATION   .75
MASON, I.
    SKIMORE MODERN KEYBOARD SERIES --ADVANCED --BLUE SERIES
    --NEPTUNE'S FOUNTAIN
        SHAPIRO, BERNSTEIN ORGANIZATION   .75
MASON, I.
    TWELVE TELL-A-TALE TUNES
        BELWIN-MILLS PUBLISHING CORPORATION   11516   1.00
MASON, M. B.
    CHRISTMAS CAROLS MADE EASY TO PLAY AND SING
        THEODORE PRESSER COMPANY   1.00
MATHE, E.
    THREE ETUDES
        ASSOCIATED MUSIC PUBLISHERS, INC.   ESC   2.00
MATHEWS, W.   1
    STANDARD GRADED COURSE OF STUDIES, GRADE 01
        THEODORE PRESSER COMPANY   1.25
MATHEWS, W.   2
    STANDARD GRADED COURSE OF STUDIES, GRADE 02
        THEODORE PRESSER COMPANY   1.50
MATHEWS, W.   3
    STANDARD GRADED COURSE OF STUDIES, GRADE 03
        THEODORE PRESSER COMPANY   1.50
MATHEWS, W.   4
    STANDARD GRADED COURSE OF STUDIES, GRADE 04
        THEODORE PRESSER COMPANY   1.50
MATHEWS, W.   5
    STANDARD GRADED COURSE OF STUDIES, GRADE 05
        THEODORE PRESSER COMPANY   1.25
MATHEWS, W.   6
    STANDARD GRADED COURSE OF STUDIES, GRADE 06
        THEODORE PRESSER COMPANY   2.50
MATHEWS, W.   7
    STANDARD GRADED COURSE OF STUDIES, GRADE 07
        THEODORE PRESSER COMPANY   1.25
MATHEWS, W.   9
    STANDARD GRADED COURSE OF STUDIES, GRADE 09
        THEODORE PRESSER COMPANY   1.50
MATHEWS, W.   10
    STANDARD GRADED COURSE OF STUDIES, GRADE 10
        THEODORE PRESSER COMPANY   1.50
MATHEWS, W.--ED   MATHEWS, W.
    FIRST SONATINAS -- AN INTRODUCTION TO THE CLASSICS
        THEODORE PRESSER COMPANY   2.00
MATTHAY, T. *
    APPROACH TO MUSIC, BK. 1
        BOOSEY AND HAWKES, INC.   1.50
MATTHAY, T. *
    APPROACH TO MUSIC, BK. 4
        BOOSEY AND HAWKES, INC.   1.50
MATTHAY, T. *
    APPROACH TO MUSIC, BK. 5
        BOOSEY AND HAWKES, INC.   1.50
MATTHAY, T. *
    APPROACH TO MUSIC, BK. 6
        BOOSEY AND HAWKES, INC.   1.50
MATTHAY, T. *
    APPROACH TO MUSIC, BK. 7
        BOOSEY AND HAWKES, INC.   1.50
MATTHAY, T.
    FIRST LIGHTS ON PIANO PLAYING
        BOOSEY AND HAWKES, INC.   2.50
MATTHESON, J.
    PIECES DE CLAVECIN
        BROUDE BROTHERS LTD.   22.50
MATTHESON, J.   HOFFMANN-ERBRECHT
    WOHLKLINGENDE FINGERSPRACHE, DIE--FUGUES AND PIECES
        ASSOCIATED MUSIC PUBLISHERS, INC.   BRH   2.00
MATTOS, E.
    AMERICAN FOLK SONGS FOR THE YOUNG PIANIST
        BELWIN-MILLS PUBLISHING CORPORATION   11406   1.50
MATTOS, E.
    SKIDMORE MODERN KEYBOARD SERIES --ADVANCED --BLUE SERIES
    --PINWHEEL
        SHAPIRO, BERNSTEIN ORGANIZATION   .75
MATTOS, E.
    SKIDMORE MODERN KEYBOARD SERIES --SECONDARY --DEMITASSE
        SHAPIRO, BERNSTEIN ORGANIZATION   .75
MAURAT, E.
    PRELUDES--OP. 04 NOS. 06-07--PIEGHEVOLMENTE, SCIOLTAMENTE
        ASSOCIATED MUSIC PUBLISHERS, INC.   ESC   .80
MAURAT, E.
    PRELUDES, OP. 10 NOS. 17-19
        ASSOCIATED MUSIC PUBLISHERS, INC.   ESC   1.75
MAURAT, E.
    PRELUDES, OP. 10 NOS. 20-24
        ASSOCIATED MUSIC PUBLISHERS, INC.   ESC   2.25

MAURAT, E.
  PRELUDES, OP. 10 NOS. 25-26
    ASSOCIATED MUSIC PUBLISHERS, INC.   ESC   1.25
MAURAT, E.
  PRELUDES, OP. 10 NOS. 27-28
    ASSOCIATED MUSIC PUBLISHERS, INC.   ESC   1.25
MAURAT, E.
  PRELUDES, OP. 10 NOS. 29-31
    ASSOCIATED MUSIC PUBLISHERS, INC.   ESC   1.25
MAURAT, E.
  THEME VARIE
    ASSOCIATED MUSIC PUBLISHERS, INC.   ESC   7.00
MAURAT, E.
  VARIATIONS A LOISIR, OP. 25
    ASSOCIATED MUSIC PUBLISHERS, INC.   ESC   3.75
MAURICE, P.   3
  MUSIC-HALL DES MARIONNETTES, LE
    ALPHONSE LEDUC
MAURY, L.
  MAGIC LINES AND SPACES, AN INTRODUCTION
    CORRELATION MUSIC INDUSTRIES   2.00
MAURY, L.
  MAGIC LINES AND SPACES, INSTRUCTION BK. 1
    CORRELATION MUSIC INDUSTRIES   3.00
MAURY, L.
  MAGIC LINES AND SPACES, INSTRUCTION BK. 2
    CORRELATION MUSIC INDUSTRIES   3.00
MAURY, L.
  MAGIC LINES AND SPACES, REPERTOIRE BK. 1
    CORRELATION MUSIC INDUSTRIES   3.00
MAURY, L.
  MAGIC LINES AND SPACES, REPERTOIRE BK. 2
    CORRELATION MUSIC INDUSTRIES   3.00
MAXWELL DAVIES, P.
  FIVE LITTLE PIECES
    BOOSEY AND HAWKES, INC.   1.00
MAYER
  DANCES FROM FAMOUS BALLETS
    FRANCO COLOMBO PUBLICATIONS   NY1464   1.00
MAYER
  DANCES FROM FAMOUS OPERAS
    FRANCO COLOMBO PUBLICATIONS   NY1463   1.00
MAYER *
  DER PRAKTISCHE CZERNY, STUDIEN UND ETUDEN AUS DEM GES. SHAFFEN
  -- BK. 1 VORSTUFE
    SCHOTT   3721   2.25
MAYER *
  DER PRAKTISCHE CZERNY, STUDIEN UND ETUDEN AUS DEM GES. SHAFFEN
  -- BK. 2 UNTERSTUFE
    SCHOTT   3722   2.25
MAYER *
  DER PRAKTISCHE CZERNY, STUDIEN UND ETUDEN AUS DEM GES. SHAFFEN
  -- BK. 3 UNTERE MITTELSTUFE
    SCHOTT   3723   2.25
MAYER *
  DER PRAKTISCHE CZERNY, STUDIEN UND ETUDEN AUS DEM GES. SHAFFEN
  -- BK. 4 MITTELSTUFE
    SCHOTT   33724   2.25
MAYER *
  DER PRAKTISCHE CZERNY, STUDIEN UND ETUDEN AUS DEM GES. SHAFFEN
  -- BK. 5 HOHERE MITTELSTUFE
    SCHOTT   3725   2.25
MAYER
  NATIONAL DANCES OF EUROPE
    FRANCO COLOMBO PUBLICATIONS   BA8902   2.50
MAYER--ED. *   MAYER *
  MUSICAL PIANO TEACHING, BK. 1
    ASSOCIATED MUSIC PUBLISHERS, INC.   SIM   1.50
MAYER--ED. *   MAYER *
  MUSICAL PIANO TEACHING, BK. 2
    ASSOCIATED MUSIC PUBLISHERS, INC.   SIM   1.50
MAYKAPAR
  EIGHTEEN SELECTED PIECES, FOR STUDENTS
    MCA MUSIC   2.50
MAYKAPAR   MIROVITCH, A.
  FIRST STEPS -- EASY DUETS
    MCA MUSIC   1.50
MAYUZUMI
  PIECES FOR PREPARED PIANO AND STRINGS. PIANO SOLO PART.
    C. F. PETERS CORPORATION   6325A   2.00
MCCABE, J.
  THREE IMPROMPTUS
    OXFORD UNIVERSITY PRESS   32.926   1.25
MCCLENNY, A.--ED *   MCCLENNY, A. *
  COLLECTION OF EARLY AMERICAN KEYBOARD MUSIC, A
    WILLIS MUSIC COMPANY   3.00
MCCLENNY, A.--ED *   4
  EARLY AMERICAN MUSIC
    BELWIN-MILLS PUBLISHING CORPORATION   FDL 464   2.00
MCCLUSKY
  PIANO FUN
    PRO-ART PUBLICATIONS, INC.   1252   1.25
MCCLUSKY
  PIANO TALK
    PRO-ART PUBLICATIONS, INC.   1199   1.50
MCCONATHY
  LOOK AND PLAY PIANO COURSE
    CARL FISCHER, INC.   O 2787   1.25
MCDONALD, H.
  EL CAMINO REAL, SUITE
    ASSOCIATED MUSIC PUBLISHERS, INC.   AMP   2.50
MCFARLAND, G.
  GARY MCFARLAND TOUCH, THE
    SAM FOX PUBLISHING COMPANY, INC.   1.75
MCGINLEY
  CHORDS AND MELODIES - CHRISTMAS SONGS TO ARRANGE
    SHAWNEE PRESS, INC.   1.00
MCGINLEY
  CHORDS AND MELODIES - TUNES YOU KNOW
    SHAWNEE PRESS, INC.   1.00
MCGINLEY
  CHORDS AND MELODIES - 20 TUNES TO ARRANGE, SET 1
    SHAWNEE PRESS, INC.   1.50
MCGINLEY
  CHORDS AND MELODIES - 20 TUNES TO ARRANGE, SET 2
    SHAWNEE PRESS, INC.   1.25
MCGINLEY
  CHORDS AND MELODIES - 20 TUNES TO ARRANGE, SET 3
    SHAWNEE PRESS, INC.   1.25
MCGINLEY
  CHORDS AND MELODIES - 20 TUNES TO ARRANGE, SET 4
    SHAWNEE PRESS, INC.   .75
MCGINLEY
  CHORDS AND MELODIES SERIES - ADVANCED LEVEL 1
    SHAWNEE PRESS, INC.   1.50

MCGINLEY
  CHORDS AND MELODIES SERIES - BEGINNER'S LEVEL 1
    SHAWNEE PRESS, INC.   2.50
MCGINLEY
  CHORDS AND MELODIES SERIES - BEGINNER'S LEVEL 2
    SHAWNEE PRESS, INC.   3.00
MCGINLEY
  CHORDS AND MELODIES SERIES - INTERMEDIATE LEVEL 1
    SHAWNEE PRESS, INC.   1.50
MCGINLEY
  CHORDS AND MELODIES SERIES - INTERMEDIATE LEVEL 2
    SHAWNEE PRESS, INC.   2.00
MCGINLEY
  PIANO SESSIONS - KINDERGARTEN SERIES -# MR. AND MRS. MIDDLE
    SHAWNEE PRESS, INC.   1.25
MCGINLEY
  PIANO SESSIONS - KINDERGARTEN SERIES‡ DANCING IN THE SQUARE
  --SUPP. MUSIC FOR MR. AND MRS. MIDDLE--
    SHAWNEE PRESS, INC.   .35
MCGINLEY
  PIANO SESSIONS - KINDERGARTEN SERIES‡ EVERYDAY PIECES FOR TRUDY
  TREBLE --SUPP. MUSIC FOR TRUDY TREBLE AND TOM--
    SHAWNEE PRESS, INC.   .60
MCGINLEY
  PIANO SESSIONS - KINDERGARTEN SERIES‡ FIRST WALTZ --SUPP. MUSIC
  FOR MR. AND MRS. MIDDLE--
    SHAWNEE PRESS, INC.   .35
MCGINLEY
  PIANO SESSIONS - KINDERGARTEN SERIES‡ FUN AT THE FAIR --SUPP.
  MUSIC FOR TRUDY TREBLE AND TOM--
    SHAWNEE PRESS, INC.   .25
MCGINLEY
  PIANO SESSIONS - KINDERGARTEN SERIES‡ LITTLE NOCTURNE --SUPP.
  MUSIC FOR TRUDY TREBLE AND TOM--
    SHAWNEE PRESS, INC.   .25
MCGINLEY
  PIANO SESSIONS - KINDERGARTEN SERIES‡ LONG, LONG AGO --SUPP.
  MUSIC FOR MR. AND MRS. MIDDLE--
    SHAWNEE PRESS, INC.   .35
MCGINLEY
  PIANO SESSIONS - KINDERGARTEN SERIES‡ ON TOP OF OLD SMOKY
  --SUPP. MUSIC FOR MR. AND MRS. MIDDLE--
    SHAWNEE PRESS, INC.   .35
MCGINLEY
  PIANO SESSIONS - KINDERGARTEN SERIES‡ READY TO PLAY
    SHAWNEE PRESS, INC.   .75
MCGINLEY
  PIANO SESSIONS - KINDERGARTEN SERIES‡ RED RIVER VALLEY --SUPP.
  MUSIC FOR MR. AND MRS. MIDDLE--
    SHAWNEE PRESS, INC.   .35
MCGINLEY
  PIANO SESSIONS - KINDERGARTEN SERIES‡ SONGS FOR CHRISTMAS
  --SUPP. MUSIC FOR TRUDY TREBLE AND TOM--
    SHAWNEE PRESS, INC.   .60
MCGINLEY
  PIANO SESSIONS - KINDERGARTEN SERIES‡ STEPPING AND SKIPPING
    SHAWNEE PRESS, INC.   1.00
MCGINLEY
  PIANO SESSIONS - KINDERGARTEN SERIES‡ TRUDY TREBLE AND TOM
    SHAWNEE PRESS, INC.   1.25
MCGINLEY
  PIANO SESSIONS - KINDERGARTEN SERIES‡ TWINKLE, TWINKLE LITTLE
  STAR --SUPP. MUSIC FOR TRUDY TREBLE AND TOM--
    SHAWNEE PRESS, INC.   .25
MCGINLEY
  PIANO SESSIONS - KINDERGARTEN SERIES‡ WALK IN THE WOODS, A
  --SUPP. MUSIC FOR MR. AND MRS. MIDDLE--
    SHAWNEE PRESS, INC.   .35
MCGINLEY
  PIANO SESSIONS BASIC COURSE, BK. 1‡ EXPLORING MUSIC AT THE
  KEYBOARD
    SHAWNEE PRESS, INC.   2.00
MCGINLEY
  PIANO SESSIONS BASIC COURSE, BK. 2‡ ADVENTURES IN READING AND
  PLAYING
    SHAWNEE PRESS, INC.   1.25
MCGINLEY
  PIANO SESSIONS BASIC COURSE, BK. 3‡ KEYS TO CHORDS
    SHAWNEE PRESS, INC.   1.25
MCGINLEY   MCGINLEY
  PIANO SESSIONS BASIC COURSE, SUPP. MATERIAL FOR BK. 2‡ EASIEST
  PIANO CLASSICS, SET 1
    SHAWNEE PRESS, INC.   .75
MCGRAW
  PET SILHOUETTES, BK. 1
    THEODORE PRESSER COMPANY   1.25
MCGRAW
  PET SILHOUETTES, BK. 2
    THEODORE PRESSER COMPANY   2.00
MCGRAW *
  SPARKLERS
    SCHMITT, HALL AND MCCREARY COMPANY   9966   1.25
MCGRAW
  TUNES AROUND THE CLOCK
    EDWARD B. MARKS MUSIC CORPORATION   01.50
MCGRAW--ED   MCGRAW
  FOUR CENTURIES OF KEYBOARD MUSIC - BOOK 1
    BOSTON MUSIC COMPANY   2.00
MCGRAW--ED   MCGRAW
  FOUR CENTURIES OF KEYBOARD MUSIC - BOOK 2
    BOSTON MUSIC COMPANY   2.00
MCGRAW--ED   MCGRAW
  FOUR CENTURIES OF KEYBOARD MUSIC - BOOK 3
    BOSTON MUSIC COMPANY   2.00
MCGRAW--ED   MCGRAW
  FOUR CENTURIES OF KEYBOARD MUSIC - BOOK 4
    BOSTON MUSIC COMPANY   2.00
MCHALE, M.
  TEN TRICKS FOR TEN FINGERS
    BOSTON MUSIC COMPANY   1.00
MCINTOSH
  DISTINCTIVE PROGRAM PIECES
    CARL FISCHER, INC.   O 3310   1.25
MCINTOSH   MCINTOSH
  TEN DESCRIPTIVE SKETCHES
    SHAWNEE PRESS, INC.   1.00
MCKAY, G.
  CACTUS TOWN
    CENTURY MUSIC PUBLISHING COMPANY, INC.   1.00
MCKAY, G.
  EXPLORATIONS, BK. 1
    BELWIN-MILLS PUBLISHING CORPORATION   1.50
MCKAY, G.
  SEVEN OUTDOOR PIECES
    THEODORE PRESSER COMPANY   1.25
MCKINNEY
  HYMN FAVORITES FOR PIANO
    BELWIN-MILLS PUBLISHING CORPORATION   2.00

MCKINNEY
  PIANO VOLUNTARIES
    BELWIN-MILLS PUBLISHING CORPORATION   2.00
MCKUEN   ROGERS, M.
  GRAND TOUR
    POINTER PUBLICATIONS   4.95
MCKUEN   ROGERS, M.
  NEW CAROLS FOR CHRISTMAS
    POINTER PUBLICATIONS   3.95
MCLEAN, D.
  SONGS OF DON MCLEAN, THE
    THE BIG THREE MUSIC CORPORATION   04.95
MCSHANN
  JAY MCSHANN BOOGIE WOOGIE AND BLUES PIANO SOLOS
    MCA MUSIC   1.00
MEAD
  IMPROVISATION ON CHRISTMAS TUNES - SERIES 1
    BOSTON MUSIC COMPANY   .50
MEAD
  IMPROVISATION ON CHRISTMAS TUNES - SERIES 2
    BOSTON MUSIC COMPANY   .50
MEDAU, H.
  RHYTHMIC MUSIC, 10 PIECES, BK. 1
    ASSOCIATED MUSIC PUBLISHERS, INC.   BOT   1.75
MEDAU, H.
  RHYTHMIC MUSIC, 10 PIECES, BK. 2
    ASSOCIATED MUSIC PUBLISHERS, INC.   BOT   1.75
MEDIA VILLA
  TWO SPANISH DANCES
    FRANCO COLOMBO PUBLICATIONS   DS670   3.25
MEDTNER, N.
  ALBUM OF SELECTED PIECES
    INTERNATIONAL MUSIC COMPANY   2.50
MEDTNER, N.   D
  TWO ELEGIES, OP. 59
    C. F. PETERS CORPORATION   ZM1026   1.25
MEHEGAN, J.
  CONTEMPORARY STYLES FOR THE JAZZ PIANIST -- BK. 1
    SAM FOX PUBLISHING COMPANY, INC.   3.00
MEHEGAN, J.
  CONTEMPORARY STYLES FOR THE JAZZ PIANIST -- BK. 2
    SAM FOX PUBLISHING COMPANY, INC.   3.00
MEHEGAN, J.
  CONTEMPORARY STYLES FOR THE JAZZ PIANIST -- BK. 3
    SAM FOX PUBLISHING COMPANY, INC.   3.00
MEHEGAN, J.
  JAZZ IMPROVISATIONS --CONTEMPORARY PIANO STYLES
    MUSIC SALES CORPORATION   040160   5.95
MEHEGAN, J.
  JAZZ IMPROVISATIONS, BK. 3 --SWING AND EARLY PROGRESSIVE PIANO
  STYLES
    MUSIC SALES CORPORATION   040159   5.95
MEHEGAN, J.
  JAZZ PIANIST, THE -- BOOK 1 WITH INSTRUCTION RECORD
    SAM FOX PUBLISHING COMPANY, INC.   6.95
MEHEGAN, J.
  JAZZ PRELUDES
    SAM FOX PUBLISHING COMPANY, INC.   2.50
MEHEGAN, J.
  STUDIES IN JAZZ HARMONY
    SAM FOX PUBLISHING COMPANY, INC.   3.00
MEHEGAN, J.
  STYLES FOR THE JAZZ PIANIST, BK. 1
    SAM FOX PUBLISHING COMPANY, INC.   3.00
MEHEGAN, J.
  STYLES FOR THE JAZZ PIANIST, BK. 3
    SAM FOX PUBLISHING COMPANY, INC.   3.00
MEHEGAN, J.
  TOUCH AND RHYTHM TECHNIQUES FOR THE JAZZ PIANIST
    SAM FOX PUBLISHING COMPANY, INC.   3.00
MELIS, J.
  JOSE MELIS PIANO MOODS
    THE BIG THREE MUSIC CORPORATION   01.25
MELVIN, B.
  PIANO ANTICS IN BOOGIE STYLE
    BELWIN-MILLS PUBLISHING CORPORATION   1.00
MENDELSSOHN
  ALBUM
    KULTURA   2.00
MENDELSSOHN   3-5
  AUSWAHL -- 23 BEKANNTE STUCKE
    SCHOTT   508   1.75
MENDELSSOHN
  CHILDREN'S PIECES, OP. 72
    G. HENLE MUSIKVERLAG   221   1.15
MENDELSSOHN
  CHILDREN'S PIECES, OP. 72
    EDWIN F. KALMUS   3678   1.25
MENDELSSOHN   M-D
  COMPLETE PIANO WORKS, VOL. 1‡ SONGS WITHOUT WORDS
    C. F. PETERS CORPORATION   1704A   3.50
MENDELSSOHN   D
  COMPLETE PIANO WORKS, VOL. 2‡ OP. 5, 7, 14, 16, 33, 72, AND
  ANDANTE CANTABILE E PRESTO AGITATO
    C. F. PETERS CORPORATION   1704B   7.50
MENDELSSOHN   D
  COMPLETE PIANO WORKS, VOL. 3‡ OP. 28, 35, 54, 82, 83, 104,
  SCHERZO IN B MINOR, ETUDE IN F MINOR, AND SCHERZO A CAPRICCIO
    C. F. PETERS CORPORATION   1704C   7.50
MENDELSSOHN   D
  COMPLETE PIANO WORKS, VOL. 4‡ CONCERTI--ARR. PF. SOLO--, OP. 22,
  29, 43
    C. F. PETERS CORPORATION   1704D   7.50
MENDELSSOHN   D
  COMPLETE PIANO WORKS, VOL. 5‡ SUPPLEMENT
    C. F. PETERS CORPORATION   1704E   7.50
MENDELSSOHN
  COMPLETE WORKS, BK. 1
    EDWIN F. KALMUS   3680   5.00
MENDELSSOHN
  COMPLETE WORKS, BK. 2
    EDWIN F. KALMUS   3681   5.00
MENDELSSOHN
  COMPLETE WORKS, BK. 3
    EDWIN F. KALMUS   3682   5.00
MENDELSSOHN   M
  FIVE MARCHES
    C. F. PETERS CORPORATION   1783   2.50
MENDELSSOHN   ROMANIELLO
  FORTY-EIGHT SONGS WITHOUT WORDS
    FRANCO COLOMBO PUBLICATIONS   ER364   5.50
MENDELSSOHN *   LONGO
  GOLDEN LIBRARY, BK. 4 - MENDELSSOHN, SCHUBERT, SCHUMANN
    FRANCO COLOMBO PUBLICATIONS   112502   5.50
MENDELSSOHN   3
  LIEDER OHNE WORTE -- OP. 19 NO. 3 A-DUR -- JAGERLIED UND OP. 19
  NO. 4 A-DUR
    SCHOTT   08752 1/2   1.00

MENDELSSOHN   3
  LIEDER OHNE WORTE -- OP. 19 NO. 6 G-MOLL UND OP. 30 NO. 6
  FIS-MOLL -- 1. UND 2. VENET. GONDELLIED
    SCHOTT   08756 1/2   1.00
MENDELSSOHN   3-4
  LIEDER OHNE WORTE -- OP. 30 NO. 3 E-DUR UND OP. 67 NO. 4 C-DUR
  -- SPINNERLIED
    SCHOTT   08767 1/2   1.00
MENDELSSOHN   3
  LIEDER OHNE WORTE -- OP. 62 NO. 5 A-MOLL -- 3. VENET. GONDELLIED
  UND OP. 62 NO. 6 A-DUR -- FRUHLINGSLIED
    SCHOTT   08765 1/2   1.00
MENDELSSOHN   HUGHES
  MASTER SERIES FOR THE YOUNG, VOL.' 08--MENDELSSOHN
    G. SCHIRMER, INC.   1.25
MENDELSSOHN *   E-M
  MASTERS FOR THE YOUNG. VOL. 3
    C. F. PETERS CORPORATION   2712   2.50
MENDELSSOHN
  MENDELSSOHN
    ASHLEY DEALERS SERVICE, INC.   HG 15   2.95
MENDELSSOHN   SCHAUM, J.   3
  MENDELSSOHN'S SONGS WITHOUT WORDS
    SCHAUM PUBLICATIONS, INC.   1.50
MENDELSSOHN   DEXTER, H.
  MID-SUMMER NIGHTS DREAM
    SAM FOX PUBLISHING COMPANY, INC.   1.00
MENDELSSOHN   KULLAK
  MISCELLANEOUS COMPOSITIONS
    G. SCHIRMER, INC.   L59   3.50
MENDELSSOHN   POZZOLI
  MY FIRST MENDELSSOHN
    FRANCO COLOMBO PUBLICATIONS   ER2447   1.25
MENDELSSOHN   TAGLIAPIETRA
  OVERTURES
    FRANCO COLOMBO PUBLICATIONS   ER498   6.00
MENDELSSOHN   SCHARWENKA, X.
  PRELUDE AND FUGUE, OP. 35 NO. 6
    INTERNATIONAL MUSIC COMPANY   2.50
MENDELSSOHN   ROMANIELLO
  SELECTED COMPOSITIONS, BK. 1 - 48 SONGS WITHOUT WORDS
    FRANCO COLOMBO PUBLICATIONS   ER364   5.50
MENDELSSOHN   ROMANIELLO
  SELECTED COMPOSITIONS, BK. 2 - MISCELLANEOUS WORKS
    FRANCO COLOMBO PUBLICATIONS   ER365   2.75
MENDELSSOHN   ROMANIELLO
  SELECTED COMPOSITIONS, BK. 3 - CAPRICCIOS, FANTASY AND 7
  CHARACTERISTIC PIECES
    FRANCO COLOMBO PUBLICATIONS   ER366   4.00
MENDELSSOHN   M-D
  SIX PIECES FOR CHILDREN, OP. 72
    C. F. PETERS CORPORATION   3347   1.50
MENDELSSOHN   KULLAK
  SIX PIECES FOR CHILDREN, OP. 72
    G. SCHIRMER, INC.   .75
MENDELSSOHN   D
  SIX PRELUDES AND FUGUES, OP. 35
    C. F. PETERS CORPORATION   7159   2.50
MENDELSSOHN
  SIX SONGS WITHOUT WORDS, NOS. 3, 6, 12, 29, 30, 34
    FRANCO COLOMBO PUBLICATIONS   ER893   .60
MENDELSSOHN
  SONGS WITHOUR WORDS, NOS. 25-48
    NOVELLO AND COMPANY, LTD.   10.0061.06   2.15
MENDELSSOHN   LEVINE
  SONGS WITHOUT WORDS
    BOSTON MUSIC COMPANY   1.50
MENDELSSOHN
  SONGS WITHOUT WORDS
    CARL FISCHER, INC.   L 310   2.50
MENDELSSOHN   STERNBERG
  SONGS WITHOUT WORDS
    G. SCHIRMER, INC.   L58   2.50
MENDELSSOHN   CORTOT
  SONGS WITHOUT WORDS -- SELECTIONS --
    FRANCO COLOMBO PUBLICATIONS   SAL   3.25
MENDELSSOHN
  SONGS WITHOUT WORDS AND CHILDREN'S PIECES
    EDWIN F. KALMUS   3679   2.50
MENDELSSOHN
  SONGS WITHOUT WORDS, NOS. 1-24
    NOVELLO AND COMPANY, LTD.   10.0098.05   2.15
MENDELSSOHN
  SONGS WITHOUT WORDS, 11 SELECTED PIECES
    NOVELLO AND COMPANY, LTD.   10.0171.10   1.40
MENDELSSOHN   3-4
  STUDENT'S TREASURY OF MENDELSSOHN, A
    ASHLEY DEALERS SERVICE, INC.   1.25
MENDELSSOHN   3-4
  STUDENT'S TREASURY OF MENDELSSOHN, A
    CENTURY MUSIC PUBLISHING COMPANY, INC.   1.25
MENDELSSOHN
  THIRTY PIANO COMPOSITIONS
    THEODORE PRESSER COMPANY   5.00
MENDELSSOHN
  THREE ETUDES FROM OP. 104 AND SCHERZO A CAPRICCIO
    G. SCHIRMER, INC.   L1523   1.50
MENDELSSOHN   BERGMANN
  THREE ETUDES, OP. 104B
    FRANCO COLOMBO PUBLICATIONS   128440   .75
MENDELSSOHN
  THREE PIECES, POSTHUMOUS
    NOVELLO AND COMPANY, LTD.   10.0099.03   1.15
MENDELSSOHN   D
  THREE PRELUDES, OP. 104
    C. F. PETERS CORPORATION   6054   1.25
MENDELSSOHN   ROMANIELLO
  THREE PRELUDES, OP. 104A
    FRANCO COLOMBO PUBLICATIONS   128329   1.00
MENDELSSOHN   M-D
  TWO SYMPHONIES, NO. 3 AND NO. 4
    C. F. PETERS CORPORATION   1705   4.50
MENDELSSOHN   HUGHES
  VARIATIONS--OP. 54, 82, 83
    G. SCHIRMER, INC.   L1492   1.50
MENDOZA-NAVA, J.
  TRES DANZAS BOLIVIANAS
    RONGWEN MUSIC, INC.   03.25
MENOTTI
  POEMETTI - 12 PIECES
    FRANCO COLOMBO PUBLICATIONS   NY1064   1.50
MERATH, S.   2-3
  TANZ-TYPEN, BAND 01
    SCHOTT   4945   2.50
MERATH, S.   2-3
  TANZ-TYPEN, BAND 02
    SCHOTT   4746   2.50

MERK, G.
  THIRTY-TWO PRELUDES, OP. 25
    ASSOCIATED MUSIC PUBLISHERS, INC.   LEU   3.00
MERKUR
  SOLO SNACKS FOR THE PIANIST
    BELWIN-MILLS PUBLISHING CORPORATION   11595   1.75
MERRILL, M.
  SIGHT READING AT THE PIANO
    BELWIN-MILLS PUBLISHING CORPORATION   11442   1.75
MERULO   PIDOUX   3
  CANZONEN 1592
    BARENREITER VERLAG   BA 1759
MESSIAEN, O.   9
  CATALOGUE D'OISEAUX, BK. 1
    ALPHONSE LEDUC
MESSIAEN, O.   9
  CATALOGUE D'OISEAUX, BK. 2
    ALPHONSE LEDUC
MESSIAEN, O.   9
  CATALOGUE D'OISEAUX, BK. 3
    ALPHONSE LEDUC
MESSIAEN, O.   9
  CATALOGUE D'OISEAUX, BK. 4
    ALPHONSE LEDUC
MESSIAEN, O.   9
  CATALOGUE D'OISEAUX, BK. 5
    ALPHONSE LEDUC
MESSIAEN, O.   9
  CATALOGUE D'OISEAUX, BK. 6
    ALPHONSE LEDUC
MESSIAEN, O.   9
  CATALOGUE D'OISEAUX, BK. 7
    ALPHONSE LEDUC
MESSIAEN, O.
  PRELUDES
    ELKAN-VOGEL, INC.   D   10.25
MESSIAEN, O.
  REVEIL DES OISEAUX
    ELKAN-VOGEL, INC.   D   12.00
MESSIAEN, O.
  TWENTY REGARDS SUR L'ENFANT JESUS
    ELKAN-VOGEL, INC.   D   26.50
METIS
  EASY POP ROCK SKETCHES
    EDWARD B. MARKS MUSIC CORPORATION   01.50
METIS
  EASY TOGETHER
    EDWARD B. MARKS MUSIC CORPORATION   01.50
METIS
  RHYTHM FACTORY
    EDWARD B. MARKS MUSIC CORPORATION   01.75
METIS
  ROCK MODES AND MOODS
    EDWARD B. MARKS MUSIC CORPORATION   01.50
METIS, F.
  ENCHANTED SEA
    VOLKWEIN BROS.   02.00
MIASKOVSKY
  FOUR LITTLE FUGUES, OP. 43--78
    EDWIN F. KALMUS   3683   1.25
MICHEELSEN   1-2
  KLAVIERUBUNG NACH VOLKSLIEDERN, HEFT 1 - 20 STUCKE MIT UBUNGEN
  FUR DEN ANFANG
    BARENREITER VERLAG   BA 1335
MICHEELSEN   1-2
  KLAVIERUBUNG NACH VOLKSLIEDERN, HEFT 1 - 32 STUCKE MIT UBUNGEN
  FUR DEN ANFANG
    BARENREITER VERLAG   BA 1334
MICHEELSEN
  KLAVIERUBUNG NACH VOLKSLIEDERN, HEFT 1 - 32 STUCKE MIT UBUNGEN
  FUR DEN ANFANG
    BARENREITER VERLAG   BA 1334
MICHEELSEN
  KLAVIERUBUNG NACH VOLKSLIEDERN, HEFT 2 - 20 STUCKE MIT UBUNGEN
  FUR DEN ANFANG
    BARENREITER VERLAG   BA 1335
MICHEELSEN   1-2
  KLAVIERUBUNG NACH VOLKSLIEDERN, HEFT 3 - LEICHTE SUITE -- 8
  KINDERLIEDER --
    BARENPEITER VERLAG   BA 1336
MICHEELSEN
  KLAVIERUBUNG NACH VOLKSLIEDERN, HEFT 3 - LEICHTE SUITE -- 8
  KINDERLIEDER --
    BARENREITER VERLAG   BA 1336
MICHEELSEN   2
  KLEINE SPIELMUSIK FUR KLAVIER
    BARENREITER VERLAG   BA 1337
MICHEELSEN
  PIANO STUDIES ON FOLKSONGS, BK. 1
    BARENREITER VERLAG   BA 1334   2.75
MICHEELSEN
  PIANO STUDIES ON FOLKSONGS, BK. 2
    BARENREITER VERLAG   BA 1335   2.75
MICHEELSEN
  PIANO STUDIES ON FOLKSONGS, BK. 3
    BARENREITER VERLAG   BA 1336   2.75
MICHELI AGOSTINI
  EIGHT MUSICAL SCENES
    FRANCO COLOMBO PUBLICATIONS   FOR.12103   1.75
MICHELI AGOSTINI
  MUSICAL IMPRESSIONS - 8 EASY PIECES
    FRANCO COLOMBO PUBLICATIONS   129225   1.00
MIGNONE
  SEVEN PIANO PIECES FOR CHILDREN
    EDWARD B. MARKS MUSIC CORPORATION   01.00
MIGNONE
  SIX PRELUDES
    FRANCO COLOMBO PUBLICATIONS   BA11084   1.50
MIGOT   4, 5
  ADUSUM DELPHINI - BK. 1
    ALPHONSE LEDUC
MIGOT   4, 5
  ADUSUM DELPHINI - BK. 2
    ALPHONSE LEDUC
MIGOT   6
  CALENDRIER DU PETIT BERGER, LE, BK. 1
    ALPHONSE LEDUC
MIGOT   6
  CALENDRIER DU PETIT BERGER, LE, BK. 2
    ALPHONSE LEDUC
MIGOT   9
  CINQ ETUDES POUR LA MAIN DROIT, EN FORME DE SUITE
    ALPHONSE LEDUC
MIGOT   2
  LE LIVRE D'ANNE-MARIE
    ALPHONSE LEDUC

MIGOT   2, 3
  PETIT FABLIER, LE
    ALPHONSE LEDUC
MIGOT   6
  PRELUDE, SALUT ET DANSE
    ALPHONSE LEDUC
MIGOT   6, 7
  PRELUDES, BK. 1
    ALPHONSE LEDUC
MIGOT   6, 7
  PRELUDES, BK. 2
    ALPHONSE LEDUC
MIGOT   8
  QUATRE NOCTURNES
    ALPHONSE LEDUC
MIGOT   5
  TROIS EPIGRAMMES
    ALPHONSE LEDUC
MIGOT   7, 8
  TROIS NOCTURNES DANTESQUES
    ALPHONSE LEDUC
MIGOT   6, 8
  TWELVE PRELUDES
    ALPHONSE LEDUC
MIGOT   7, 8
  ZODIAQUE, LE, 12 ETUDES
    ALPHONSE LEDUC
MIHALOVICI
  CHANSON, PASTORAL, DANSE
    FRANCO COLOMBO PUBLICATIONS   SAL   3.25
MIHALOVICI
  THREE NOCTURNES
    FRANCO COLOMBO PUBLICATIONS   SAL   1.75
MIHALY, A.
  TWO PIECES IN ANTIQUE STYLE
    GENERAL MUSIC PUBLISHING COMPANY, INC.   308   2.50
MIHALY, A.
  TWO PIECES IN ANTIQUE STYLE
    GENERAL MUSIC PUBLISHING COMPANY, INC.   3.00
MILHAUD, D.
  ALBUM DE MADAME BOVARY, L'
    ASSOCIATED MUSIC PUBLISHERS, INC.   ENO   1.25
MILHAUD, D.
  CARAMEL MOU--1921--JAZZ BAND
    ASSOCIATED MUSIC PUBLISHERS, INC.   ESC   2.50
MILHAUD, D.
  FOUR ROMANCES SANS PAROLES
    FRANCO COLOMBO PUBLICATIONS   SAL   2.00
MILHAUD, D.
  HYMNE DE GLORIFICATION--1954
    ASSOCIATED MUSIC PUBLISHERS, INC.   ESC   3.25
MILHAUD, D.
  PRINTEMPS, LE--1919-1920--BK. 1
    ASSOCIATED MUSIC PUBLISHERS, INC.   ESC   3.75
MILHAUD, D.
  PRINTEMPS, LE--1919-1920--BK. 2
    ASSOCIATED MUSIC PUBLISHERS, INC.   ESC   3.00
MILHAUD, D.
  SAUDADES DO BRAZIL--SUITE--BK. 1
    ASSOCIATED MUSIC PUBLISHERS, INC.   ESC   5.50
MILHAUD, D.
  SAUDADES DO BRAZIL--SUITE--BK. 2
    ASSOCIATED MUSIC PUBLISHERS, INC.   ESC   5.50
MILHAUD, D.
  THREE WALTZES
    ASSOCIATED MUSIC PUBLISHERS, INC.   ENO   .60
MILLAN
  RACCONTI DI FRIDA, I - 5 LITTLE TYROLEAN PIECES
    FRANCO COLOMBO PUBLICATIONS   Z4536   1.75
MILLER, M. *
  FINGERS PLAY -- SONGS FOR LITTLE FINGERS
    G. SCHIRMER, INC.   1.25
MILLIGAN
  SCALES, CHORDS AND ARPEGGIOS
    WARNER BROTHERS PUBLISHERS   1.50
MILOIEVITCH
  FOUR MORCEAUX, OP. 23
    FRANCO COLOMBO PUBLICATIONS   SAL   4.00
MININBERG--ED *   MININBERG *   2-3
  GREAT MUSIC
    ASHLEY DEALERS SERVICE, INC.   1.25
MININBERG--ED *   MININBERG *   2-3
  GREAT MUSIC
    CENTURY MUSIC PUBLISHING COMPANY, INC.   1.25
MIRANDOLLE   6
  DEUX PRELUDES
    ALPHONSE LEDUC
MIRANDOLLE   6, 7
  TROIS PIECES
    ALPHONSE LEDUC
MIRANTE
  EIGHT RECITAL ENCORES
    PEER SOUTHERN ORGANIZATION   03.00
MIRANTE--ED.   MIRANTE
  EIGHT RECITAL SOLOS
    PRO-ART PUBLICATIONS, INC.   1042   .85
MIROVITCH, A.
  COMMAND OF THE KEYBOARD - BK. 1 THROUGH BK. 4
    THEODORE PRESSER COMPANY   EA.
MIROVITCH, A.
  EXPRESSIVE DYNAMICS
    BELWIN-MILLS PUBLISHING CORPORATION   1.50
MIROVITCH, A.
  KEYBOARD CHORDS
    BELWIN-MILLS PUBLISHING CORPORATION   1.50
MIROVITCH, A.
  KEYBOARD PHRASING AND SHADING
    BELWIN-MILLS PUBLISHING CORPORATION   1.50
MIROVITCH, A.
  KEYBOARD STACCATO
    BELWIN-MILLS PUBLISHING CORPORATION   1.50
MIROVITCH, A.
  LISTEN TO YOURSELF -- BK. 2-UPPER ELEMENTARY GRADES
    MCA MUSIC   1.00
MIROVITCH, A.
  PEDAL, THE
    BELWIN-MILLS PUBLISHING CORPORATION   1.50
MIROVITCH, A.
  TONE COLORS
    BELWIN-MILLS PUBLISHING CORPORATION   1.50
MIROVITCH, A.--ED   MIROVITCH, A.
  OLD VIENNA DANCES
    EDWARD B. MARKS MUSIC CORPORATION   1.25
MIROVITCH, A.--ED.   MIROVITCH, A.
  EARLY CLASSICS FOR THE PIANO
    G. SCHIRMER, INC.   1.50

MIROVITCH, A.--ED.　　　　MIROVITCH, A.　　EARLY GRADES
　INTRODUCTION TO PIANO CLASSICS, VOL. 1
　　　G. SCHIRMER, INC.　　　　　　　　　　　　　　　1.50
MIROVITCH, A.--ED.　　　　MIROVITCH, A.　　EARLY GRADES
　INTRODUCTION TO PIANO CLASSICS, VOL. 2
　　　G. SCHIRMER, INC.　　　　　　　　　　　　　　　2.00
MIROVITCH, A.--ED.　　　　MIROVITCH, A.　　EARLY GRADES
　INTRODUCTION TO PIANO CLASSICS, VOL. 3
　　　G. SCHIRMER, INC.　　　　　　　　　　　　　　　2.00
MIROVITCH, A.--ED.　　　　MIROVITCH, A.
　INTRODUCTION TO THE ROMANTICS
　　　G. SCHIRMER, INC.　　　　　　　　　　　　　　　1.50
MIROVITCH, A.--ED.
　NEW RECITAL REPERTOIRE BY MASTERS OF THE 17TH, 18TH, AND 19TH
　CENTURIES
　　　ELKAN-VOGEL, INC.　　　　　　　　　　　　　　　2.00
MITTLER
　NEWSREEL SUITE
　　　MUSICORD PUBLICATIONS, INC.　　　　　　　　　1.00
MITTLER
　SUITE IN 3/4 TIME
　　　MUSICORD PUBLICATIONS, INC.　　　　　　　　　1.00
MITTLER--ED　　　　　　　MITTLER　　　2, 3
　GREAT BALLET MUSIC
　　　MUSICORD PUBLICATIONS, INC.　　　　　　　　　1.25
MITTLER--ED　　　　　　　MITTLER　　　2, 3
　GREAT CONCERTO MUSIC
　　　MUSICORD PUBLICATIONS, INC.　　　　　　　　　1.25
MITTLER--ED　　　　　　　MITTLER　　　2, 3
　GREAT OPERA MUSIC
　　　MUSICORD PUBLICATIONS, INC.　　　　　　　　　1.25
MITTLER--ED　　　　　　　MITTLER　　　2, 3
　GREAT SYMPHONY MUSIC
　　　MUSICORD PUBLICATIONS, INC.　　　　　　　　　1.25
MITTLER--ED　　　　　　　MITTLER　　　2, 3
　GREAT WALTZ MUSIC
　　　MUSICORD PUBLICATIONS, INC.　　　　　　　　　1.25
MITTLER--ED　　　　　　　MITTLER　　　2
　MUSIC FOR EVERYBODY
　　　MUSICORD PUBLICATIONS, INC.　　　　　　　　　2.00
MITTLER--ED　　　　　　　MITTLER
　MUSIC IS MY HOBBY
　　　MUSICORD PUBLICATIONS, INC.　　　　　　　　　2.50
MIXA *　　　　　　　　　MARCKHL
　STYRIAN COMPOSERS, WORKS FOR PIANO -- BK. 3
　　　ASSOCIATED MUSIC PUBLISHERS, INC.　　OBV　　1.25
MODONA
　EASY BOOKS, BK. 1
　　　FRANCO COLOMBO PUBLICATIONS　　　FOR.10823　1.50
MODONA
　EASY BOOKS, BK. 2
　　　FRANCO COLOMBO PUBLICATIONS　　　FOR.10824　1.50
MODONA
　EASY BOOKS, BK. 3
　　　FRANCO COLOMBO PUBLICATIONS　　　FOR.11405　1.75
MOLLEDA, J. M.
　CIRCO--SUITE
　　　ASSOCIATED MUSIC PUBLISHERS, INC.　　UME　　1.25
MOMPOU, F.
　CANTS MAGICS, 1919
　　　ASSOCIATED MUSIC PUBLISHERS, INC.　　UME　　1.25
MOMPOU, F.
　CHARMES
　　　ASSOCIATED MUSIC PUBLISHERS, INC.　　ESC　　4.00
MOMPOU, F.
　DIALOGUES
　　　ASSOCIATED MUSIC PUBLISHERS, INC.　　ESC　　2.50
MOMPOU, F.
　FOUR PRELUDES
　　　HEUGEL ET CIE.　　　　　　　　　　　　　　　　2.50
MOMPOU, F.
　IMPRESSIONES INTIMAS--1911-1914
　　　ASSOCIATED MUSIC PUBLISHERS, INC.　　UME　　2.25
MOMPOU, F.
　MUSICA CALLADA -- 9 PIECES --
　　　FRANCO COLOMBO PUBLICATIONS　　　SAL　　　4.25
MOMPOU, F.
　PAYSAGES - LA FONTAINE ET LA CLOCHE, LE LAC
　　　FRANCO COLOMBO PUBLICATIONS　　　SAL　　　3.50
MOMPOU, F.
　SIX PRELUDES
　　　FRANCO COLOMBO PUBLICATIONS　　　SAL　　　1.50
MOMPOU, F.
　THREE VARIATIONS
　　　ASSOCIATED MUSIC PUBLISHERS, INC.　　ESC　　2.75
MONCAYO, J.
　MUROS VERDES
　　　EDICIONES MEXICANAS DE MUSICA, A. C.　　02.25
MONCAYO, J.
　TRES PIEZAS
　　　EDICIONES MEXICANAS DE MUSICA, A. C.　　01.75
MONFRED
　FOUR PRELUDES SYNCOPES
　　　FRANCO COLOMBO PUBLICATIONS　　　SAL　　　4.75
MONFRED
　RECITAL FOR CHILDREN, A
　　　FRANCO COLOMBO PUBLICATIONS　　　SAL　　　3.00
MONFRED
　TWO PRELUDES
　　　FRANCO COLOMBO PUBLICATIONS　　　SAL　　　2.75
MONNIKENDAM
　SIX INVENTIONS
　　　FRANCO COLOMBO PUBLICATIONS　　　SAL　　　4.00
MONSOUR *
　PLAY
　　　EDWARD B. MARKS MUSIC CORPORATION　　　01.50
MONTALBAN--ED　　　　　　MONTALBAN
　CORRO DE LAS NINAS, EL -- 60 SPANISH FOLKSONGS FOR CHILDREN WITH
　SPANISH TEXT
　　　ASSOCIATED MUSIC PUBLISHERS, INC.　　UME　　2.75
MONTANARI
　FOUR EASY PIECES
　　　FRANCO COLOMBO PUBLICATIONS　　　FOR.12047　1.25
MONTANARI--ED *　　　　　MONTANARI *
　ANTOLOGIA DI CLAVICEMBALISTI ITALIANI, BK. 1
　　　EDIZIONI BERBEN　　　　　　　　EB 1668　　4.25
MONTANARI--ED *　　　　　MONTANARI *
　ANTOLOGIA DI CLAVICEMBALISTI ITALIANI, BK. 2
　　　EDIZIONI BERBEN　　　　　　　　EB 1728　　4.25
MONTANARI--ED *　　　　　MONTANARI *
　PIECES FROM THE ITALIAN ROMANTICISTS
　　　EDIZIONI BERBEN　　　　　　　　EB 1382　　6.00
MONTANARO
　ANIME SEMPLICE - 6 PROFILES, OP. 143
　　　FRANCO COLOMBO PUBLICATIONS　　　127796　　1.25

MONTANARO
　FIRST STEPS -- PRIMI PASSI -- 12 VERY EASY PIECES
　　　FRANCO COLOMBO PUBLICATIONS　　　127901　　1.50
MONTANI
　CHARACTERISTIC STUDIES
　　　FRANCO COLOMBO PUBLICATIONS　　　ER 1267　　3.50
MONTANI
　CHARACTERISTIC STUDIES - 3 AMERICAN STUDIES
　　　FRANCO COLOMBO PUBLICATIONS　　　ER1419　　.90
MONTANI
　CHARACTERISTIC STUDIES - 3 HUMOROUS STUDIES
　　　FRANCO COLOMBO PUBLICATIONS　　　ER1945　　.90
MONTANI
　CLAVICEMBALISTI ITALIANI --16 PIECES--
　　　FRANCO COLOMBO PUBLICATIONS　　　FOR.12119　1.50
MONTANI
　COMPOSITIONS BY CONTEMPORARY ITALIAN COMPOSERS, BK. 1
　　　FRANCO COLOMBO PUBLICATIONS　　　128721　　1.50
MONTANI
　COMPOSITIONS BY CONTEMPORARY ITALIAN COMPOSERS, BK. 2
　　　FRANCO COLOMBO PUBLICATIONS　　　129540　　1.75
MONTANI
　COMPOSITIONS BY CONTEMPORARY ITALIAN COMPOSERS, BK. 3
　　　FRANCO COLOMBO PUBLICATIONS　　　130137　　1.50
MONTANI
　FIVE ADVANCED TECHNICAL STUDIES
　　　FRANCO COLOMBO PUBLICATIONS　　　ER2205　　1.50
MONTANI
　MY FIRST HARPSICHORD BOOK
　　　FRANCO COLOMBO PUBLICATIONS　　　ER2605　　1.25
MONTANI
　NINE CHRISTMAS SONGS
　　　FRANCO COLOMBO PUBLICATIONS　　　130078　　1.25
MONTANI
　NINE HARPSICHORD PIECES
　　　FRANCO COLOMBO PUBLICATIONS　　　ER2463　　1.00
MONTANI
　SCALES - MAJOR, MINOR AND CHROMATIC
　　　FRANCO COLOMBO PUBLICATIONS　　　ER2308　　1.50
MONTANI
　SCALES IN THIRDS AND SIXTHS
　　　FRANCO COLOMBO PUBLICATIONS　　　ER2372　　.75
MONTANI
　SIX LITTLE DANCES
　　　FRANCO COLOMBO PUBLICATIONS　　　FOR.11910　1.75
MONTANI
　SIXTEEN LYRIC STUDIES
　　　FRANCO COLOMBO PUBLICATIONS　　　ER2469　　1.25
MONTANI
　TWENTY-FOUR PRELUDES
　　　FRANCO COLOMBO PUBLICATIONS　　　124345　　4.50
MONTANI--ED　　　　　　　MONTANI
　MOST BEAUTIFUL PAGES OF HARPSICHORD MUSIC, THE - BACH FAMILY,
　THE
　　　FRANCO COLOMBO PUBLICATIONS　　　ER2574　　2.00
MONTANI--ED　　　　　　　MONTANI
　MOST BEAUTIFUL PAGES OF HARPSICHORD MUSIC, THE - BELGIAN
　　　FRANCO COLOMBO PUBLICATIONS　　　ER2525　　1.25
MONTANI--ED　　　　　　　MONTANI
　MOST BEAUTIFUL PAGES OF HARPSICHORD MUSIC, THE - DUTCH
　　　FRANCO COLOMBO PUBLICATIONS　　　ER2549　　1.25
MONTANI--ED　　　　　　　MONTANI
　MOST BEAUTIFUL PAGES OF HARPSICHORD MUSIC, THE - ENGLISH
　　　FRANCO COLOMBO PUBLICATIONS　　　ER2666　　3.00
MONTANI--ED　　　　　　　MONTANI
　MOST BEAUTIFUL PAGES OF HARPSICHORD MUSIC, THE - FRENCH
　　　FRANCO COLOMBO PUBLICATIONS　　　ER2511　　1.75
MONTANI--ED　　　　　　　MONTANI
　MOST BEAUTIFUL PAGES OF HARPSICHORD MUSIC, THE - PORTUGUESE
　　　FRANCO COLOMBO PUBLICATIONS　　　ER2670　　1.75
MONTANI--ED *　　　　　　MONTANI *
　MOST BEAUTIFUL PAGES OF HARPSICHORD MUSIC, THE - SPANISH
　　　FRANCO COLOMBO PUBLICATIONS　　　ER2470　　1.50
MONTANI--ED　　　　　　　MONTANI
　MOST BEAUTIFUL PAGES OF HARPSOCHORD MUSIC, THE - GERMAN
　　　FRANCO COLOMBO PUBLICATIONS　　　ER2622　　1.75
MONTBRUN, G.　　　　　　　　　　　4, 6
　MELODIES ET PROVERBES
　　　ALPHONSE LEDUC
MONTBRUN, G.　　　　　　　　　　　5, 7
　MOSAIQUE
　　　ALPHONSE LEDUC
MONTBRUN, G.　　　　　　　　　　　6, 8
　TROIS PIECES
　　　ALPHONSE LEDUC
MONTGOMERY, V.
　MUSIC FUN BOOK
　　　THEODORE PRESSER COMPANY　　　　　　　　1.75
MONTGOMERY, V.
　SECOND MUSIC FUN BOOK
　　　THEODORE PRESSER COMPANY　　　　　　　　1.25
MONTIEL OLVERA, A.
　CUATRO DANZAS MEXICANAS
　　　EDICIONES MEXICANAS DE MUSICA, A. C.　　02.00
MONTSALVATGE, X.
　TRES DIVERTIMENTOS
　　　PEER SOUTHERN ORGANIZATION　　　　　　　01.10
MOORE
　WALTZES
　　　BOSTON MUSIC COMPANY　　　　　　　　　　1.00
MOORE--ED　　　　　　　　MOORE
　BIG NOTE CHRISTMAS FAVORITES
　　　BOSTON MUSIC COMPANY　　　　　　　　　　1.00
MOORE--ED　　　　　　　　MOORE
　CHRISTMAS FAVORITES
　　　BOSTON MUSIC COMPANY　　　　　　　　　　1.00
MOPPER, I.
　ALICE IN WONDERLAND -- PIANO PICTURES
　　　BOSTON MUSIC COMPANY　　　　　　　　　　1.00
MORALES
　LATIN AMERICAN RHYTHMS AND IMPROVISATIONS FOR PIANO
　　　BELWIN-MILLS PUBLISHING CORPORATION　　　2.00
MORATH, M.
　GIANTS OF RAGTIME
　　　EDWARD B. MARKS MUSIC CORPORATION　　　03.50
MORATH, M.--ED.　　　　　MORATH
　MAX MORATH'S GUIDE TO RAGTIME
　　　TRO SONGWAYS SERVICE, INC.　　　　　　　3.95
MORAWECK　　　　　　　　　　　　　GR. 5
　CONTEMPORARY PIANO TECHNIQUE
　　　WESTERN INTERNATIONAL MUSIC, INC.　　AV29　　4.00
MORAWETZ
　SUITE FOR PIANO
　　　MCA MUSIC　　　　　　　　　　　　　　　　2.25
MOREAU　　　　　　　　　　　　　　4, 5
　LITTLE SPORTSMAN, THE
　　　ALPHONSE LEDUC

MORHANGE *
  LITTLE CLAVIER, THE .... SUPPLEMENT 2 - 14 PIECES FOR PIANO SOLO
  BY S. DEMARQUEZ
    FRANCO COLOMBO PUBLICATIONS   SAL   3.25
MORHANGE *
  LITTLE CLAVIER, THE - AN INTRODUCTION TO THE PIANO
    FRANCO COLOMBO PUBLICATIONS   SAL   7.00
MORHANGE *
  PETIT CLASSIQUE, LE
    FRANCO COLOMBO PUBLICATIONS   SAL   3.25
MORHANGE *
  PETIT ROMANTIQUE, LE
    FRANCO COLOMBO PUBLICATIONS   SAL   3.25
MORRIS, C.   E
  SEVEN KEY-MEN
    OXFORD UNIVERSITY PRESS   33.109   .65
MORTARI
  FOR THE LITTLEST
    FRANCO COLOMBO PUBLICATIONS   FOR.11811   1.50
MORTARI
  THREE PIECES FOR CHILDREN
    FRANCO COLOMBO PUBLICATIONS   FOR.11331   1.25
MOSCHELES, I.   D
  THREE CONCERT STUDIES, OP. 51
    C. F. PETERS CORPORATION   1402   2.50
MOSCHELES, I.   MUGELLINI
  TWELVE CHARACTERISTIC STUDIES, OP. 95
    FRANCO COLOMBO PUBLICATIONS   ER1085   2.75
MOSCHELES, I.   ANDREOLI
  TWENTY-FOUR STUDIES FOR PERFECTION, OP. 70
    FRANCO COLOMBO PUBLICATIONS   ER748   3.50
MOSCHELES, I.
  TWENTY-FOUR STUDIES FOR PERFECTION, OP. 70 BK. 1 -- 1-12 --
    FRANCO COLOMBO PUBLICATIONS   ER837   2.25
MOSCHELES, I.
  TWENTY-FOUR STUDIES--FINISHING-LESSONS FOR ADVANCED PERFORMERS,
  OP. 70--BK. 1
    G. SCHIRMER, INC.   L404   1.00
MOSCHELES, I.   PAUER
  TWENTY-FOUR STUDIES--FINISHING-LESSONS FOR ADVANCED PERFORMERS,
  OP. 70--IN SPANISH AND ENGLISH
    G. SCHIRMER, INC.   L403   2.25
MOSZKOWSKI   M
  ANDANTE AND SCHERZO FROM CONCERTO, OP. 59. ABRIDGED PIANO SOLO
  ARR.
    C. F. PETERS CORPORATION   2872A   1.25
MOSZKOWSKI   PHILIPP, I.   6, 7
  ESQUISSES TECHNIQUES, OP. 97
    ALPHONSE LEDUC
MOSZKOWSKI
  FIFTEEN ETUDES DE VIRTUOSITE, OP. 72
    BOOSEY AND HAWKES, INC.   2.00
MOSZKOWSKI
  FIFTEEN ETUDES DE VIRTUOSITE, OP. 72
    FRANCO COLOMBO PUBLICATIONS   BA8778   2.00
MOSZKOWSKI
  FIFTEEN ETUDES DE VIRTUOSITE, OP. 72
    G. SCHIRMER, INC.   L1798   2.00
MOSZKOWSKI
  FIFTEEN STUDIES FOR THE LEFT HAND, OP. 92
    FRANCO COLOMBO PUBLICATIONS   BA8779   2.50
MOSZKOWSKI
  FIVE SPANISH DANCES, OP. 12
    FRANCO COLOMBO PUBLICATIONS   BA8010   2.00
MOSZKOWSKI
  QUINZE ETUDES DE VIRTUOSITE, OP. 72
    ASSOCIATED MUSIC PUBLISHERS, INC.   ENO   2.00
MOSZKOWSKI
  QUINZE ETUDES DE VIRTUOSITE, OP. 72
    ASSOCIATED MUSIC PUBLISHERS, INC.   ENO   6.00
MOSZKOWSKI
  SCHOOL OF DOUBLE NOTES, OP. 64
    FRANCO COLOMBO PUBLICATIONS   BA10312   3.50
MOSZKOWSKI
  SCHOOL OF SCALES AND DOUBLE NOTES, BKS. 1- 4
    BOOSEY AND HAWKES, INC.   EA.
MOSZKOWSKI   LOCATELLI
  SPANISH DANCES, OP. 12
    FRANCO COLOMBO PUBLICATIONS   BA11197   1.50
MOSZKOWSKI   M
  SPANISH DANCES, OP. 12
    C. F. PETERS CORPORATION   2126   1.50
MOSZKOWSKI   ULRICH
  SPANISH DANCES, OP. 12
    G. SCHIRMER, INC.   L280   1.00
MOSZKOWSKI   E-M
  SPANISH DANCES, OP. 12. NOS. 1, 2, 4
    C. F. PETERS CORPORATION   2130A   1.25
MOSZKOWSKI
  THREE CONCERT STUDIES, OP. 24
    FRANCO COLOMBO PUBLICATIONS   BA8143   2.00
MOSZKOWSKI
  TWELVE ETUDES FOR THE LEFT HAND ALONE, OP. 92
    ASSOCIATED MUSIC PUBLISHERS, INC.   ENO   3.00
MOSZKOWSKI   PHILIPP, I.   3, 5
  VINGT PETITES ETUDES, OP. 91 - BK. 1
    ALPHONSE LEDUC
MOSZKOWSKI   PHILIPP, I.   5, 6
  VINGT PETITES ETUDES, OP. 91 - BK. 2
    ALPHONSE LEDUC
MOSZKOWSKI   PHILIPP, I.
  VIRTUOSITY STUDIES 'AD ASPERA', OP. 72
    INTERNATIONAL MUSIC COMPANY   2.50
MOTTU
  DANSES ET CONTREDANSES - BK. 1
    FRANCO COLOMBO PUBLICATIONS   SAL   3.25
MOTTU
  DANSES ET CONTREDANSES - BK. 3
    FRANCO COLOMBO PUBLICATIONS   SAL   4.25
MOTTU
  DANSES ET CONTREDANSES - BK. 4
    FRANCO COLOMBO PUBLICATIONS   SAL   4.25
MOTTU
  DANSES ET CONTREDNASES - BK. 2
    FRANCO COLOMBO PUBLICATIONS   SAL   3.25
MOTTU
  FOUR ETUDES RYTHMIQUES
    FRANCO COLOMBO PUBLICATIONS   SAL   4.25
MOUSSORGSKY   3-5
  AUSWAHL, 9 BEL. STUCKE
    SCHOTT   521   3.00
MOUSSORGSKY   DALLAPICCOLA   5
  BILDER EINER AUSSTELLUNG
    BARENREITER VERLAG   CM 19817
MOUSSORGSKY   M-D
  TWO PIANO PIECES. KINDERSCHERZ, INTERMEZZO
    C. F. PETERS CORPORATION   3727B   2.00

MOY, E.
  SIXTY WRITING LESSONS IN MUSICAL THEORY -- PART 1
    BELWIN-MILLS PUBLISHING CORPORATION   11451   .50
MOY, E.
  SIXTY WRITING LESSONS IN MUSICAL THEORY -- PART 2
    BELWIN-MILLS PUBLISHING CORPORATION   11452   .50
MOZART, L.   KREUTZER
  NANNERL MOZART'S PIANO BOOK
    ASHLEY DEALERS SERVICE, INC.   1.25
MOZART, L.   E
  NANNERL NOTENBUCH --1759--. HARD COVER
    C. F. PETERS CORPORATION   N1277   9.00
MOZART, L.
  NOTEBOOK FOR MARIA ANNA
    CENTURY MUSIC PUBLISHING COMPANY, INC.   1.25
MOZART, L.   SCHUNGELER, H.   2
  NOTENBUCH FUR NANNERL MOZART
    SCHOTT   3772   1.50
MOZART, L.   SCHUNGELER, H.   2
  NOTENBUCH FUR WOLFGANG
    SCHOTT   3718   1.50
MOZART, L.   KELLER   E
  THREE SUITES FROM THE NOTEBOOK FOR WOLFGANG
    C. F. PETERS CORPORATION   5172   2.00
MOZART, W. A.   KLEE
  ADAGIO K540 IN B MINOR, AND GIGUE K574 IN G
    G. SCHIRMER, INC.   .40
MOZART, W. A.
  ALBUM
    KULTURA   2.00
MOZART, W. A.   SCHUENEMANN
  ALBUM--'MOZART ALS ACHTJAHRIGER KOMPONIST'
    ASSOCIATED MUSIC PUBLISHERS, INC.   BRH   2.50
MOZART, W. A.   ANSON, G.   INTERMEDIATE
  ANSON INTRODUCES MOZART, BK. 1
    WILLIS MUSIC COMPANY   1.50
MOZART, W. A.   3-5
  AUSWAHL -- 14 ORIGINAL-KLAVIER-STUCKE
    SCHOTT   509   1.75
MOZART, W. A.   SCHAUM, J.   2 1/2
  BEST OF MOZART
    SCHAUM PUBLICATIONS, INC.   1.25
MOZART, W. A.   M
  CONCERTI K.271, 450, 466, 467, 482, 488, 491, 537
    C. F. PETERS CORPORATION   765   12.00
MOZART, W. A.   SCHUNGELER   2
  DER JUNGE MOZART, 19 ORIGINAL-STUCKE DES 6- UND 8 JAHRIGEN
  MOZART
    SCHOTT   3771   1.50
MOZART, W. A.   REHBERG   2
  DIE WIENER SONATINEN
    SCHOTT   2159   1.50
MOZART, W. A.   1
  DREI GRAZIOSE WALZER -- K.V. 536/586
    SCHOTT   0649 1/2   1.00
MOZART, W. A.   VALENTIN, ERICH   E
  EARLIEST PIANO COMPOSITIONS. HARD COVER
    C. F. PETERS CORPORATION   N1288   9.00
MOZART, W. A.   ROWLEY   E
  EASIEST ORIGINAL PIECES FOR PIANO
    C. F. PETERS CORPORATION   H5   1.50
MOZART, W. A.   BEGINNER
  EASY COMPOSITIONS
    EDWIN F. KALMUS   3710   1.25
MOZART, W. A.   LONGO
  EASY COMPOSITIONS -- WITH HAYDN-EASY COMPOSITIONS --
    FRANCO COLOMBO PUBLICATIONS   ER867   2.50
MOZART, W. A.   DOFLEIN
  EASY PIANO PIECES
    BARENREITER VERLAG   BA 1726   1.75
MOZART, W. A.   PAUMGARTNER, B.
  EIGHT MINUETS WITH TRIOS
    THEODORE PRESSER COMPANY   1.25
MOZART, W. A.
  EIGHT MINUETS WITH TRIOS, K315A
    G. HENLE MUSIKVERLAG   51   1.10
MOZART, W. A.   FISCHER, K. VON
  EIGHT VARIATIONS IN G KV 24 / SEVEN VARIATIONS IN D KV 26
    BARENREITER VERLAG   NMA 226   1.75
MOZART, W. A.   FISCHER
  EIGHT VARIATIONS IN G, K. 24 AND SEVEN VARIATIONS IN D, K. 25
    ASSOCIATED MUSIC PUBLISHERS, INC.   NAG   2.00
MOZART, W. A.   BUONAMICI
  FANTASIAS AND RONDOS
    G. SCHIRMER, INC.   L964   1.50
MOZART, W. A.
  FANTASY AND FUGUE K394, FANTASIES K396AND 397, URTEXT
    EDWIN F. KALMUS   3698   1.25
MOZART, W. A.
  FAVORITE COMPOSITIONS
    THEODORE PRESSER COMPANY   1.25
MOZART, W. A.   BRADLEY
  FIRST COMPOSERS - MOZART
    FRANCO COLOMBO PUBLICATIONS   LD199   1.00
MOZART, W. A.   2
  FIRST THREE COMPOSITIONS, THE
    THEODORE PRESSER COMPANY   .50
MOZART, W. A.   AUCLERT, P.
  FORTY-SIX CADENCES ORIGINALES
    EDITIONS MUSICALES TRANSATLANTIQUES   11.50
MOZART, W. A.   FREY   2
  FUNFZEHN WALZER
    SCHOTT   2504   1.75
MOZART, W. A.   CZERNY   E
  GERMAN DANCES
    C. F. PETERS CORPORATION   4450   .80
MOZART, W. A.   KLEE
  GIGUE K574 IN G, AND ADAGIO K540 IN B MINOR
    G. SCHIRMER, INC.   .40
MOZART, W. A.
  HIS LIFE TOLD IN HIS MUSIC
    EDWARD B. MARKS MUSIC CORPORATION   03.00
MOZART, W. A.   DIACK
  INTRODUCTION TO MOZART
    CARL FISCHER, INC.   PT 2566   1.00
MOZART, W. A.   FISCHER, E.
  KADENZEN ZU DEN KLAVIERKONZERTEN -- K.V. 365, 453, 482, 503, 537
  1. SATZ UND K.V. 466, 491 1. UND 3. SATZ
    SCHOTT   4947   3.25
MOZART, W. A.   DOFLEIN   1
  LEICHTE KLAVIERSTUCKE. 12 STUCKE DES SECHS- UND ACHTJAHRIGEN
  MOZART
    BARENREITER VERLAG   BA 1726
MOZART, W. A.
  LITTLE KNOWN PIECES
    EDWIN F. KALMUS   3696   1.50

MOZART, W. A.   FREY   E
  LITTLE SALZBURG DANCE BOOK
    C. F. PETERS CORPORATION   L5001   1.25
MOZART, W. A.   HUGHES
  MASTER SERIES FOR THE YOUNG, VOL. 04--MOZART
    G. SCHIRMER, INC.   1.25
MOZART, W. A.
  MENUETT FAVORI -- SIEHE BENDEL MUSIKALIKALISCHES WURFELSPIEL
    SCHOTT   4474   2.00
MOZART, W. A.   IRMER, VON
  MINIATURES FOR PIANO--MISIKVERLAG ZUM PELIKAN EDITION
    G. SCHIRMER, INC.   1.00
MOZART, W. A.   MOZART
  MOZART
    ASHLEY DEALERS SERVICE, INC.   HG 05   2.95
MOZART, W. A.   GLASS, P. *
  MOZART AT 8 -- THE CHELSEA NOTEBOOK
    THEODORE PRESSER COMPANY   2.50
MOZART, W. A.   ECKHARDT, F.   1
  MOZART FOR THE YOUNG PIANIST
    CENTURY MUSIC PUBLISHING COMPANY, INC. 3960   .40
MOZART, W. A.   BRODER, N.
  MOZART SONATAS AND FANTASIES -- REVISED EDITION
    THEODORE PRESSER COMPANY   6.00
MOZART, W. A.   SCHAUM, J.   1 1/2
  MOZART-SCHAUM, BK. 1
    BELWIN-MILLS PUBLISHING CORPORATION   1.50
MOZART, W. A.   SCHAUM, J.   3
  MOZART-SCHAUM, BK. 2
    BELWIN-MILLS PUBLISHING CORPORATION   1.50
MOZART, W. A.   3-4
  MOZART, SIX VIENNESE SONATINAS
    ASHLEY DEALERS SERVICE, INC.   1.25
MOZART, W. A.
  MOZART'S BEST KNOWN PIANO SONATAS
    ASHLEY DEALERS SERVICE, INC.   WFS NO. 62   2.95
MOZART, W. A.   2
  MOZART'S FIRST FIVE COMPOSITIONS
    BOSTON MUSIC COMPANY   .50
MOZART, W. A.
  MOZART'S FIRST FIVE COMPOSITIONS
    BOSTON MUSIC COMPANY   .75
MOZART, W. A.   E-M
  MUSIC LOVER'S PIANO BOOK
    C. F. PETERS CORPORATION   4509   1.50
MOZART, W. A.   POZZOLI
  MY FIRST MOZART
    FRANCO COLOMBO PUBLICATIONS   ER1955   1.25
MOZART, W. A.   CHING   EASY
  NEW EASY GRADED CLASSIC ALBUM - MOZART
    GENERAL WORDS AND MUSIC COMPANY   1.25
MOZART, W. A.   EPSTEIN
  NINETEEN SONATAS--SPANISH AND ENGLISH
    G. SCHIRMER, INC.   L1304   4.00
MOZART, W. A.
  NINETEEN SONATAS, BK. 1--1-10--
    G. SCHIRMER, INC.   L1305   2.50
MOZART, W. A.
  NINETEEN SONATAS, BK. 2--11-19--
    G. SCHIRMER, INC.   L1306   2.50
MOZART, W. A.
  PIANO PIECES --SELECTION--
    WIENER URTEXT EDITION   UT 50037   3.50
MOZART, W. A.
  PIANO PIECES IN ONE VOLUME
    G. HENLE MUSIKVERLAG   22   4.95
MOZART, W. A.
  PIANO PIECES IN ONE VOLUME -- CLOTH
    G. HENLE MUSIKVERLAG   23   8.00
MOZART, W. A.   M-D
  PIANO PIECES. COMPLETE
    C. F. PETERS CORPORATION   4240A   4.00
MOZART, W. A.   M-D
  PIANO PIECES. SELECTED
    C. F. PETERS CORPORATION   4240   3.50
MOZART, W. A.
  RADIO CITY ALBUM
    EDWARD B. MARKS MUSIC CORPORATION   01.50
MOZART, W. A.
  RONDOS, FANTASIAS
    UNIVERSAL EDITION   UE 238   7.50
MOZART, W. A.   3
  SECHS DEUTSCHE TANZE — K.V. 536 NO. 6, 600 NO. 1, 2, BK. 2
    SCHOTT   0650   1.00
MOZART, W. A.   2
  SECHS DEUTSCHE TANZE — K.V. 586 NO. 6, 567 NO. 4, 5, BK. 1
    SCHOTT   0650   1.00
MOZART, W. A.   ALATI   3
  SECHS SONATINEN
    BARENREITER VERLAG   CM 21375
MOZART, W. A.
  SELECTED WORKS FOR THE PIANO
    G. HENLE MUSIKVERLAG   133   2.70
MOZART, W. A.   TAUBMANN
  SIX GERMAN DANCES, K. 509
    ASSOCIATED MUSIC PUBLISHERS, INC.   BRH   .75
MOZART, W. A.   MUELLER V. ASOW
  SIX GERMAN DANCES, K. 509
    ASSOCIATED MUSIC PUBLISHERS, INC.   DOB   2.00
MOZART, W. A.   BEGINNER
  SIX MINUETS
    EDWIN F. KALMUS   3695   1.00
MOZART, W. A.
  SIX MINUETS
    EDWIN F. KALMUS   3695   1.25
MOZART, W. A.   M-D
  SIX SYMPHONIES
    C. F. PETERS CORPORATION   198   6.50
MOZART, W. A.   MONTANI
  SIX VARIATIONS IN F, K054
    FRANCO COLOMBO PUBLICATIONS   128626   .60
MOZART, W. A.   3-4
  SIX VIENNESE SONATINAS
    CENTURY MUSIC PUBLISHING COMPANY, INC.   1.25
MOZART, W. A.
  SIX VIENNESE SONATINAS
    INTERNATIONAL MUSIC COMPANY   1.75
MOZART, W. A.   BEGINNER
  SIX VIENNESE SONATINAS
    EDWIN F. KALMUS   3697   1.50
MOZART, W. A.
  SIX VIENNESE SONATINAS
    EDWIN F. KALMUS   3697   1.75
MOZART, W. A.   ROWLEY   E-M
  SIX VIENNESE SONATINAS
    C. F. PETERS CORPORATION   H12   1.50

MOZART, W. A.   PROSTAKOFF
  SIX VIENNESE SONATINAS
    G. SCHIRMER, INC.   L1797   1.50
MOZART, W. A.   CHING
  SONATA K331 IN A
    GENERAL WORDS AND MUSIC COMPANY   .75
MOZART, W. A.   CHING
  SONATA K545 IN C
    GENERAL WORDS AND MUSIC COMPANY   .75
MOZART, W. A.   MARTIENSSEN
  SONATAS --URTEXT--, COMPLETE IN 1 VOL. CLOTH-BOUND
    C. F. PETERS CORPORATION   15.00
MOZART, W. A.   CASELLA
  SONATAS AND FANTASIAS -- ENG.-FR.-IT. -- BK. 1
    FRANCO COLOMBO PUBLICATIONS   ER2623   5.25
MOZART, W. A.   CASELLA
  SONATAS AND FANTASIAS -- ENG.-FR.-IT. -- BK. 2
    FRANCO COLOMBO PUBLICATIONS   ER2624   5.25
MOZART, W. A.   RUDORFF
  SONATAS AND FANTASIES, BK. 1
    ASSOCIATED MUSIC PUBLISHERS, INC.   BRH   2.50
MOZART, W. A.   RUDORFF
  SONATAS AND FANTASIES, BK. 2
    ASSOCIATED MUSIC PUBLISHERS, INC.   BRH   2.50
MOZART, W. A.   RUDORFF
  SONATAS AND FANTASIES, BK. 3
    ASSOCIATED MUSIC PUBLISHERS, INC.   BRH   2.50
MOZART, W. A.   RUDORFF
  SONATAS AND FANTASIES, BK. 4
    ASSOCIATED MUSIC PUBLISHERS, INC.   BRH   2.50
MOZART, W. A.
  SONATAS COMPLETE IN ONE VOLUME -- CLOTH
    G. HENLE MUSIKVERLAG   3   12.70
MOZART, W. A.   FUESSL *
  SONATAS FOR PIANO, VOL. 1
    WIENER URTEXT EDITION   UT 50035   7.50
MOZART, W. A.   FUESSL *
  SONATAS FOR PIANO, VOL. 2
    WIENER URTEXT EDITION   UT 50036   7.50
MOZART, W. A.
  SONATAS URTEXT COMPLETE
    EDWIN F. KALMUS   3690   6.00
MOZART, W. A.
  SONATAS URTEXT, BK. 1A --1-10--
    EDWIN F. KALMUS   3691   2.75
MOZART, W. A.
  SONATAS URTEXT, BK. 1B --11-20--
    EDWIN F. KALMUS   3692   2.75
MOZART, W. A.   BARTOK
  SONATAS, BKS. 1 AND 2
    KULTURA   EA.
MOZART, W. A.   KOEHLER *
  SONATAS, IN 2 VOLS. CLOTH-BOUND
    C. F. PETERS CORPORATION   10.00
MOZART, W. A.
  SONATAS, VOL 2
    G. HENLE MUSIKVERLAG   2   4.85
MOZART, W. A.
  SONATAS, VOL. 1
    G. HENLE MUSIKVERLAG   1   4.85
MOZART, W. A.   KOEHLER *   M
  SONATAS, VOL. 1
    C. F. PETERS CORPORATION   486A   3.00
MOZART, W. A.   MARTIENSSEN   M
  SONATAS, VOL. 1
    C. F. PETERS CORPORATION   1800A   5.00
MOZART, W. A.   KOEHLER *   M
  SONATAS, VOL. 2
    C. F. PETERS CORPORATION   486B   3.00
MOZART, W. A.   MARTIENSSEN   M
  SONATAS, VOL. 2
    C. F. PETERS CORPORATION   1800B   5.00
MOZART, W. A.   MANSFIELD
  STEPS TO THE MASTERS
    BANKS AND SON LTD.   1.35
MOZART, W. A.   ZANON
  SYMPHONIES -- SELECTED -- BK. 1
    FRANCO COLOMBO PUBLICATIONS   ER1772   5.00
MOZART, W. A.   ZANON
  SYMPHONIES -- SELECTED -- BK. 2
    FRANCO COLOMBO PUBLICATIONS   ER1773   5.00
MOZART, W. A.   REHBERG   2
  TANZBUCHLEIN, LES PETITS RIENS
    SCHOTT   2232   2.00
MOZART, W. A.
  THIRTY-SIX CADENZAS TO PIANO CONCERTOS
    EDWIN F. KALMUS   3700   3.00
MOZART, W. A.
  THIRTY-SIX CADENZAS, K. 624
    ASSOCIATED MUSIC PUBLISHERS, INC.   BRH   3.50
MOZART, W. A.   RIEFLING   E
  TOGETHER WITH THE YOUNG MOZART --15 PIECES--
    C. F. PETERS CORPORATION   LY284   1.25
MOZART, W. A.   SCHROEDER, H.
  TWELVE GERMAN DANCES
    THEODORE PRESSER COMPANY   1.25
MOZART, W. A.   E-M
  TWELVE MENUETTOS, VOL. 1
    C. F. PETERS CORPORATION   H81A   1.50
MOZART, W. A.   E-M
  TWELVE MENUETTOS, VOL. 2
    C. F. PETERS CORPORATION   H81B   1.50
MOZART, W. A.   KLEE
  TWELVE PIANO PIECES
    G. SCHIRMER, INC.   L382   1.25
MOZART, W. A.
  TWELVE WALTZES FOR THE YOUNG
    UNIVERSAL EDITION   UE 616   2.25
MOZART, W. A.
  TWENTY PIANO COMPOSITIONS
    THEODORE PRESSER COMPANY   5.00
MOZART, W. A.
  TWENTY PIECES COMPOSED WHEN 4 TO 6 YEARS OLD
    ELKAN-VOGEL, INC.   2.75
MOZART, W. A.   BARTOK
  TWENTY SONATAS
    EDWIN F. KALMUS   3693   6.00
MOZART, W. A.   WERNER
  TWO TWO-PART SONATAS K046--CURWEN EDITION
    G. SCHIRMER, INC.   .85
MOZART, W. A.   FISCHER, VON   4
  VARIATIONEN FUR KLAVIER, K24, 25, 179, 180, 264, 352, 353, 354,
  398, 455, 500, 573, 613 -- NEUE MOZART-AUSGABE --
    BARENREITER VERLAG   BA 4525
MOZART, W. A.
  VARIATIONS
    G. HENLE MUSIKVERLAG   116   5.80

MOZART, W. A.
  VARIATIONS -- CLOTH
    G. HENLE MUSIKVERLAG   117   8.85
MOZART, W. A.
  VARIATIONS -- COMPLETE
    UNIVERSAL EDITION   UE 271   4.80
MOZART, W. A.   FISCHER, K. VON
  VARIATIONS FOR PIANO
    BARENREITER VERLAG   BA 4525   7.50
MOZART, W. A.   MUELLER *
  VARIATIONS FOR PIANO, VOL. 1
    WIENER URTEXT EDITION   UT 50008   4.50
MOZART, W. A.   MUELLER *
  VARIATIONS FOR PIANO, VOL. 2
    WIENER URTEXT EDITION   UT 50009   4.50
MOZART, W. A.   M-D
  VARIATIONS, COMPLETE
    C. F. PETERS CORPORATION   273   3.50
MOZART, W. A.
  VARIOUS PIECES
    EDWIN F. KALMUS   3699   4.00
MOZART, W. A.   ZEITLIN
  YOUNG MOZART FOR THE YOUNG PIANIST, BK. 1
    EDWARD B. MARKS MUSIC CORPORATION   1.25
MOZART, W. A.   ZEITLIN
  YOUNG MOZART FOR THE YOUNG PIANIST, BK. 2
    EDWARD B. MARKS MUSIC CORPORATION   1.25
MOZART, W. A.   MAIER, G.
  YOUR MOZART BOOK
    BELWIN-MILLS PUBLISHING CORPORATION   11544   2.50
MUCZYNSKI, R.
  SIX PRELUDES, OP. 6
    G. SCHIRMER, INC.   1.25
MUELLER, A. E.   M
  CADENZAS TO EIGHT MOZART CONCERTI --K.456, K.459, K.466, K.482,
    K. 488, K.491, K.503, K.537
    C. F. PETERS CORPORATION   4519   2.00
MUFFAT
  COMPONIMENTI MUSICALI
    BROUDE BROTHERS LTD.   27.50
MUFFAT   HERRMANN
  EASY DANCE PIECES
    FRANCO COLOMBO PUBLICATIONS   SIK.111   1.50
MUFFAT   GEORGII, W.   2-3
  PARTITEN UND STUCKE
    SCHOTT   2827   2.25
MUFFAT   UPMEYER   2
  SEVENTY-TWO VERSETL UND 12 TOCCATEN
    BARENREITER VERLAG   BA 1922
MUFFAT   UPMEYER
  SEVENTY-TWO VERSETS AND TWELVE TOCCATAS
    BARENREITER VERLAG   BA 1922   5.00
MUFFAT
  ZWEIZEHN TOCCATEN UND 72 VERSETL
    BROUDE BROTHERS LTD.   25.00
MUGNAINI, D.
  SIXTEEN ESERCIZI SULLA POLIFONIA
    EDIZIONI BERBEN   EB 1816   3.50
MULLER
  ALL AMERICAN SQUARE DANCES
    SHAWNEE PRESS, INC.   2.00
MUNN--ED.   MUNN
  YOUNG RECITALIST, THE--15 PIANO SOLOS FOR THE ADVANCING PIANIST
    G. SCHIRMER, INC.   1.25
MUNN, W.--ED.   MUNN, W.
  JUNIOR RECITAL--FOURTEEN PIANO SOLOS FOR THE YOUNG PIANIST
    G. SCHIRMER, INC.   1.00
MUTHEL, J. G.   HOFFMANN-ERBRECHT
  THREE SONATAS
    ASSOCIATED MUSIC PUBLISHERS, INC.   BRH   5.00
MUTHEL, J. G.   HINNENTHAL
  TWELVE MINUETS
    BARENREITER VERLAG   BA 1008   1.75
MUTHEL, J. G.   HOFFMANN-ERBRECHT
  TWO ARIOSI WITH TWELVE VARIATIONS
    ASSOCIATED MUSIC PUBLISHERS, INC.   BRH   3.00
MUTHEL, J. G.   HINNENTHAL   1
  12 MENUETTE
    BARENREITER VERLAG   BA 1008
NABOKOFF, N.
  SHORT STORIES
    FRANCO COLOMBO PUBLICATIONS   SAL   3.25
NAGY, O. *
  DANCES OF THE BAROQUE ERA, BK. 1
    KULTURA   1.75
NAGY, O.--ED.
  DANCES OF THE BAROQUE ERA, BK. 2
    KULTURA   1.75
NAHUM *
  PIANO FUNDAMENTALS -- BOOK 1-A
    BELWIN-MILLS PUBLISHING CORPORATION   1.00
NAHUM *
  PIANO FUNDAMENTALS -- STUDENT'S ASSIGNMENT BOOK
    BELWIN-MILLS PUBLISHING CORPORATION   .60
NAHUM *
  PIANO FUNDAMENTALS -- TEACHER'S MANUAL
    BELWIN-MILLS PUBLISHING CORPORATION   .60
NAKADA
  INTERVALS - SEVEN STUDIES FOR PIANO, OP. 37
    MCA MUSIC   2.00
NAKADA
  JAPANESE FESTIVAL - SEVENTEEN PIANO PIECES FOR STUDENTS
    MCA MUSIC   2.00
NARVAEZ   TORNER
  COLLECCION DE VIHUELISTAS ESPANOLES DEL SIGLO XVI, BK. 1 -- EL
    DELPHIN DE MUSICA -- LUTE
    ASSOCIATED MUSIC PUBLISHERS, INC.   UME   4.00
NAVARRO, M.
  ESTAMPAS INFANTILES, 1930
    ASSOCIATED MUSIC PUBLISHERS, INC.   ESC   1.75
NAVAS, G.
  COLLECCION DE BAILES ESPANOLAS--16 DANCES
    ASSOCIATED MUSIC PUBLISHERS, INC.   ESC   3.00
NEALE, J.--ED   NEALE, J.
  INSTANT PICTURE CHORD PIANO NO. 1
    WARNER BROTHERS PUBLISHERS   1.95
NEALE, J.--ED   NEALE, J.
  PETER, PAUL AND MARY, MORE MADE EASY FOR PIANO
    WARNER BROTHERS PUBLISHERS   PPM 25   2.00
NELHYBEL, V.
  FOUR PIECES FOR PIANO
    GENERAL MUSIC PUBLISHING COMPANY, INC.   321   2.00
NELHYBEL, V.
  FOUR PIECES FOR PIANO
    GENERAL MUSIC PUBLISHING COMPANY, INC.   3.00
NELHYBEL, V.
  KALEIDOSCOPE - FOR YOUNG PIANISTS, BK. 1
    GENERAL MUSIC PUBLISHING COMPANY, INC.   264   3.00

NELHYBEL, V.
  KALEIDOSCOPE - FOR YOUNG PIANISTS, BK. 1
    GENERAL MUSIC PUBLISHING COMPANY, INC.   3.00
NELHYBEL, V.
  KALEIDOSCOPE - FOR YOUNG PIANISTS, BK. 2
    GENERAL MUSIC PUBLISHING COMPANY, INC.   265   3.00
NELHYBEL, V.
  KALEIDOSCOPE - FOR YOUNG PIANISTS, BK. 2
    GENERAL MUSIC PUBLISHING COMPANY, INC.   3.50
NELHYBEL, V.
  RECITAL PIECES FOR THE YOUNG PIANIST, BK. 1
    BELWIN-MILLS PUBLISHING CORPORATION   1.75
NELHYBEL, V.
  RECITAL PIECES FOR THE YOUNG PIANIST, BK. 2
    BELWIN-MILLS PUBLISHING CORPORATION   1.75
NELSON, O.
  BLUES AND THE ABSTRACT TRUTH
    EDWARD B. MARKS MUSIC CORPORATION   02.00
NERO
  NERO, PETER, AT THE PIANO
    WARNER BROTHERS PUBLISHERS   2.50
NERO
  NERO, PETER, OFF RECORD
    WARNER BROTHERS PUBLISHERS   2.50
NEUGEBOREN
  FIVE SHORT PIECES
    FRANCO COLOMBO PUBLICATIONS   SAL   2.75
NEUGEBOREN
  SIX PRELUDES
    FRANCO COLOMBO PUBLICATIONS   SAL   2.75
NEUPERT, E.
  TWELVE STUDIES
    G. SCHIRMER, INC.   L797   1.00
NEVIN
  ALL AMERICAN BOOGIE
    BELWIN-MILLS PUBLISHING CORPORATION   10001   1.50
NEVIN
  CLASSICS GO BOOGIE, THE
    BELWIN-MILLS PUBLISHING CORPORATION   11093   1.50
NEVIN
  EASY PIANO DUETS --ONE PIANO--
    BELWIN-MILLS PUBLISHING CORPORATION   11613   2.00
NEVIN
  JAZZ JAMBOREE
    BELWIN-MILLS PUBLISHING CORPORATION   10019   1.50
NEVIN
  LOOK, NO FINGER NUMBERS, BK. 1
    BELWIN-MILLS PUBLISHING CORPORATION   10023   1.25
NEVIN
  LOOK, NO FINGER NUMBERS, BK. 2
    BELWIN-MILLS PUBLISHING CORPORATION   10080   1.50
NEVIN
  MARK NEVIN PIANO COURSE, BK. 1
    BELWIN-MILLS PUBLISHING CORPORATION   11335   1.75
NEVIN
  MARK NEVIN PIANO COURSE, BK. 2
    BELWIN-MILLS PUBLISHING CORPORATION   11336   1.75
NEVIN
  MARK NEVIN PIANO COURSE, BK. 3
    BELWIN-MILLS PUBLISHING CORPORATION   11337   1.75
NEVIN
  MARK NEVIN PIANO COURSE, BK. 4
    BELWIN-MILLS PUBLISHING CORPORATION   11338   1.75
NEVIN
  MARK NEVIN PIANO COURSE, BK. 5
    BELWIN-MILLS PUBLISHING CORPORATION   11339   1.75
NEVIN
  MARK NEVIN PIANO COURSE, PREPARATORY BOOK
    BELWIN-MILLS PUBLISHING CORPORATION   11334   1.50
NEVIN
  MILLS PIANO HITS
    BELWIN-MILLS PUBLISHING CORPORATION   11376   1.50
NEVIN
  MODERN MASTERS
    BELWIN-MILLS PUBLISHING CORPORATION   11605   1.75
NEVIN
  MUSIC YOU LOVE BY LEROY ANDERSON -- IN PREP.
    BELWIN-MILLS PUBLISHING CORPORATION   11618   1.75
NEVIN
  PIANO BOOK FOR ADULTS, BK. 1
    EDWARD B. MARKS MUSIC CORPORATION   01.95
NEVIN
  PIANO BOOK FOR ADULTS, BK. 2
    EDWARD B. MARKS MUSIC CORPORATION   01.95
NEVIN
  SACRED SONGS AND SPIRITUALS
    BELWIN-MILLS PUBLISHING CORPORATION   10044   1.50
NEVIN
  SOLO GALLERY
    BELWIN-MILLS PUBLISHING CORPORATION   10050   1.75
NEVIN
  TEN LITTLE FINGERS
    BELWIN-MILLS PUBLISHING CORPORATION   10057   1.50
NEVIN
  TOP POP TUNES
    BELWIN-MILLS PUBLISHING CORPORATION   2.00
NEVIN
  WONDERFUL MUSIC OF CHRISTMAS
    BELWIN-MILLS PUBLISHING CORPORATION   10075   1.50
NEWMAN
  BEGINNER'S OWN BOOK
    CARL FISCHER, INC.   O 1325   2.00
NEWMAN--ED.   NEWMAN
  SIX KEYBOARD SONATAS FROM THE CLASSIC ERA
    SUMMY-BIRCHARD COMPANY   3.50
NEWSOME
  SIX CONTEMPORARY ETCHINGS
    GENERAL WORDS AND MUSIC COMPANY   .75
NICHOLLS, H.
  MORE OF ALL NATIONS TUNES
    BANKS AND SON LTD.   1.10
NICHOLLS, H.
  TUNES OF ALL NATIONS
    BANKS AND SON LTD.   1.10
NICOLOSI SILVESTRI
  MAJOR AND MINOR SCALES
    FRANCO COLOMBO PUBLICATIONS   DS361   3.25
NIELAND, H.   E
  EASY POLYPHONIC STUDIES
    C. F. PETERS CORPORATION   B661   1.25
NIELAND, J.   E
  SIX SONATINAS
    C. F. PETERS CORPORATION   B445   1.50
NIELSEN, C.   D
  THREE PIANO PIECES, OP. 59
    C. F. PETERS CORPORATION   ED12   3.00

NIEMANN		M-D	
ANCIENT CHINA, OP. 62			
C. F. PETERS CORPORATION		3723	.90
NIEMANN		2	
DREI KLEINE SONATINEN			
BARENREITER VERLAG		SM 2158	
NIEMANN		M	
HAMBURG, OP. 107			
C. F. PETERS CORPORATION		3856	3.50
NIEMANN		M	
IN CHILDREN'S LAND, OP. 46			
C. F. PETERS CORPORATION		3507	.90
NIEMANN		M-D	
JANMAATEN --TWO HUMORESQUES FROM THE PORT OF HAMBURG--			
C. F. PETERS CORPORATION		4277	3.50
NIEMANN			
MAGIC BOOK, THE, OP. 76--6 PHANTASMAGORIAS			
ASSOCIATED MUSIC PUBLISHERS, INC.		SIM	1.75
NIEMANN		M	
TWELVE KOCHELER LAENDLER, OP. 135			
C. F. PETERS CORPORATION		4276	2.50
NIEMANN		M	
TWO SONATINAS, OP. 152			
C. F. PETERS CORPORATION		4471	2.50
NIEMANN		E-M	
YULE SLUMBER LILT, OP. 143. SIX EASY CHRISTMAS PIECES			
C. F. PETERS CORPORATION		4279	1.25
NIEMANN			
ZWEI BRASILIANISCHE RHAPSODIEN, OP. 110			
ASSOCIATED MUSIC PUBLISHERS, INC.		LEU	2.25
NILES, J. STICKLES			
JOHN JACOB NILES' SONG BOOK FOR PIANO			
G. SCHIRMER, INC.			1.50
NIN			
CHAIN OF WALTZES, 1927			
ASSOCIATED MUSIC PUBLISHERS, INC.		ESC	7.25
NIN--ED NIN		4	
KLASSISCHE KLAVIERMUSIK ALTER SPANISCHER MEISTER -- BK. 2 17			
SONATEN UND STUCKE			
SCHOTT		2095	13.00
NIN--ED NIN		4	
KLASSISCHE KLAVIERMUSIK ALTER SPNISCHER MEISTER -- BK. 1 16			
SONATEN			
SCHOTT		1779	13.00
NIN--ED NIN			
SEVENTEEN SONATAS OF OLD SPANISH MASTERS -- SONATAS BY V.			
RODRIGUEZ, SOLER, FREIXANET, CASANOVAS, ANGLES, F. RODRIGUEZ AND			
GALLES			
ASSOCIATED MUSIC PUBLISHERS, INC.		ESC	8.00
NIN--ED NIN			
SIXTEEN SONATAS OF OLD SPANISH MASTERS -- SONATAS BY SOLER,			
ALBENIZ, CNATALLOS, SERRANO AND FERRER			
ASSOCIATED MUSIC PUBLISHERS, INC.		ESC	9.00
NIN-CULMELL, J.			
THREE IMPRESSIONES - HABANERA, LAS MOZAS DEL CANTARO, UN JARDIN			
DE TOLEDO			
FRANCO COLOMBO PUBLICATIONS		SAL	4.25
NIN-CULMELL, J.			
TONADAS, BK. 1			
RONGWEN MUSIC, INC.			03.00
NIN-CULMELL, J.			
TONADAS, BK. 2			
RONGWEN MUSIC, INC.			03.00
NIN-CULMELL, J.			
TONADAS, BK. 3			
RONGWEN MUSIC, INC.			03.00
NIN-CULMELL, J.			
TONADAS, BK. 4			
RONGWEN MUSIC, INC.			03.00
NIVERD, L.		3	
PRELUDE, VALSES ET MARCHES			
ALPHONSE LEDUC			
NIVERD, L.			
TOUTE SIMPLEMENT ET PETITE ETUDE MELODIQUE			
GERARD BILLAUDOT EDITIONS MUSICALES			1.30
NIVERD, L.		6, 7	
TROIS MORCEAUX			
ALPHONSE LEDUC			
NOEL, H.			
THREE EASY PIECES IN BLACK AND WHITE			
G. SCHIRMER, INC.			.40
NOEL, P.			
DIALOGUE ET SERENITE			
GERARD BILLAUDOT EDITIONS MUSICALES			1.30
NOEL, P. *			
ETUDES PROGRESSIVES, VOL.1			
GERARD BILLAUDOT EDITIONS MUSICALES			2.50
NOEL, P. *			
ETUDES PROGRESSIVES, VOL.2			
GERARD BILLAUDOT EDITIONS MUSICALES			2.50
NOEL, P. *			
INTERMEZZO ET CAPRICCIO			
GERARD BILLAUDOT EDITIONS MUSICALES			2.50
NOEL, P. *			
LEGENDE ET PASSEGGIATA			
GERARD BILLAUDOT EDITIONS MUSICALES			1.30
NOEL, P. *			
PAQUERETTES ET PRIMEVERES			
GERARD BILLAUDOT EDITIONS MUSICALES			1.30
NOEL, P. *			
PETIT PRINTEMPS ET LA CHANSON DE MARIE-LOUISE			
GERARD BILLAUDOT EDITIONS MUSICALES			1.30
NOEL, P. *			
PRELUDES, BK. 1			
GERARD BILLAUDOT EDITIONS MUSICALES			2.50
NOEL, P. *			
PRELUDES, BK. 2			
GERARD BILLAUDOT EDITIONS MUSICALES			2.70
NOEL, P. *			
SIX RECREATIONS			
GERARD BILLAUDOT EDITIONS MUSICALES			1.30
NOGUERA			
MELODIES POPULAIRES ESPAGNOLES			
FRANCO COLOMBO PUBLICATIONS		SAL	5.00
NOLL, G.			
LIEDERBEGLEITUNG			
SCHOTT		B171	
NOLLET, E.			
FIFTEEN ETUDES MELODIQUES, OP. 43			
THEODORE PRESSER COMPANY			.75
NOLLET, E. HUGHES			
FIFTEEN MELODIOUS STUDIES, OP. 43			
G. SCHIRMER, INC.		L1375	1.25
NORTH, A.			
TWELVE DANCE PRELUDES			
BELWIN-MILLS PUBLISHING CORPORATION		20321	1.50

NOVAK		2-3	
JUGEND. 21 KLAVIERSTUCKE, OP. 55 - BK. 1			
BARENREITER VERLAG		AP 668A	
NOVAK		2-3	
JUGEND. 21 KLAVIERSTUCKE, OP. 55 - BK. 2			
BARENREITER VERLAG		AP 668B	
NOVAK		3	
MEIN MAI. KLAVIERSTUCKE, OP. 20			
BARENREITER VERLAG			
NOVAK		3	
SECHS SONATINEN, OP. 54 - HEFT 1, SONATINEN IN C UND A MINOR			
BARENREITER VERLAG		AP 667A	
NOVAK		3	
SECHS SONATINEN, OP. 54 - HEFT 2, SONATINEN IN F AND E MINOR			
BARENREITER VERLAG		AP 667B	
NOVAK		3	
SECHS SONATINEN, OP. 54 - HEFT 3, SONATINEN IN D MINOR AND G			
BARENREITER VERLAG		AP 667C	
NUNEZ			
PIXIE PIANO BOOK			
WILLIS MUSIC COMPANY			1.50
NUNEZ			
PIXIE PIANO PLAYBOOK, BK. 2			
WILLIS MUSIC COMPANY			1.50
NUNEZ			
PIXIE TUNE SHOP			
WILLIS MUSIC COMPANY			1.75
OBERDORFFER--ED OBERDORFFER		2-3	
TANZE AUS EINEM ALTEN KLAVIERBUCH - 1800'S			
SCHOTT		3761	1.75
OESTEN			
MAYFLOWERS--25 EASY PIECES, OP. 61			
G. SCHIRMER, INC.		L726	.75
OESTERLE		ELEMENTARY AND GRADE 1	
INSTRUCTIVE COURSE OF PIECES, BK. 1--ELEMENTARY AND GRADE 1--48			
PIECES			
G. SCHIRMER, INC.		L1154	1.75
OESTERLE--ED. OESTERLE			
EARLY KEYBOARD MUSIC, BK. 1--W. BYRDE TO A. SCARLATTI			
G. SCHIRMER, INC.		L1559	3.50
OESTERLE--ED. OESTERLE			
EARLY KEYBOARD MUSIC, BK. 2--F. COUPERIN TO J. RAMEAU			
G. SCHIRMER, INC.		L1560	3.50
OESTERLE--ED. OESTERLE			
PIANIST'S ANTHOLOGY, THE--28 FAVORITE PIECES			
G. SCHIRMER, INC.		L1262	2.00
OESTERLE--ED. OESTERLE			
PIANIST'S FIRST AND SECOND YEARS, THE--47 FAVORITE PIECES			
G. SCHIRMER, INC.		L1277	1.50
OESTERLE--ED. OESTERLE			
PIANIST'S SECOND AND THIRD YEARS, THE--41 FAVORITE PIECES			
G. SCHIRMER, INC.		L1265	2.50
OFFENBACH			
RADIO CITY ALBUM			
EDWARD B. MARKS MUSIC CORPORATION			01.50
OFFUTT		GR. 2	
ELECTRIC CUCKOO AND OTHER PIECES			
SHAWNEE PRESS, INC.			1.50
OHANA, M.			
THREE CAPRICES			
GERARD BILLAUDOT EDITIONS MUSICALES			3.15
OLIVIERI *			
MONDO CANE			
EDWARD B. MARKS MUSIC CORPORATION			01.50
OLSEN, P.		M-D	
FIVE INVENTIONS, OP. 38			
C. F. PETERS CORPORATION		EN14	1.50
OLSON			
CIRCUS			
SCHMITT, HALL AND MCCREARY COMPANY		9968	1.50
OLSON			
LIGHT 'N BRIGHT			
SCHMITT, HALL AND MCCREARY COMPANY		9964	1.50
OLSON			
NEAR THE BEGINNING			
CARL FISCHER, INC.		O 4878	1.25
OLSON			
OUR SMALL WORLD			
SCHMITT, HALL AND MCCREARY COMPANY		9977	1.25
OLSON			
ROCK ME EASY			
CARL FISCHER, INC.		O 4887	
OMALLEY		E	
HAUNTED HOUSE, ON THE LAKE, DONKEY RIDE			
C. F. PETERS CORPORATION		H849	.60
ORBAN			
CROQUIS MARITIMES			
FRANCO COLOMBO PUBLICATIONS		SAL	4.25
ORBAN			
POUR LE PIANO - PRELUDE, DIVERTISSEMENTS, NOCTURNE, HUMORESQUE			
FRANCO COLOMBO PUBLICATIONS		SAL	5.50
ORBAN			
SIX PIECES BREVES - LA BASSE-COUR, LE ROUET, LE DEPART POUR LA			
FETE, DANSE, TRISTES SOUVENIRS, LES SORCIERES			
FRANCO COLOMBO PUBLICATIONS		SAL	4.00
ORBAN			
TEN PETITES PIECES ENFANTINES POUR LES JEUNES PIANISTES			
FRANCO COLOMBO PUBLICATIONS		SAL	4.25
ORBON, J.			
PARTITA NO. 1			
PEER SOUTHERN ORGANIZATION			03.00
OREFICE, G.			
TWO STUDI DA CONCERTO			
FRANCO COLOMBO PUBLICATIONS		130153	1.50
ORFF		1	
ORFF-SCHULWERK, JUGENDMUSIK, KLEINES SPIELBUCH			
SCHOTT		3561	1.75
ORGAD, B. Z.			
TWO PRELUDES IN IMPRESSIONISTIC MOOD			
ISRAEL MUSIC INSTITUTE			2.25
ORNSTEIN, L.			
ARABESQUES, OP. 42			
ASSOCIATED MUSIC PUBLISHERS, INC.		AMP	1.50
ORREGO SALAS, J.			
TEN SIMPLE PIECES, OP. 31, BK. 1			
BOOSEY AND HAWKES, INC.			1.00
ORREGO SALAS, J.			
TEN SIMPLE PIECES, OP. 31, BK. 2			
BOOSEY AND HAWKES, INC.			1.00
ORTALI			
SONATA NO. 01 AND SONATA NO. 02			
FRANCO COLOMBO PUBLICATIONS		BON.2439	8.75
ORTHEL		M-D	
DEUX HOMMAGES EN FORME D'ETUDE			
C. F. PETERS CORPORATION		D211	1.25
ORTHEL		M-D	
FIVE ETUDES-CAPRICES			
C. F. PETERS CORPORATION		D210	2.00

ORTHEL	M-D		
THREE PEZZETINI, OP. 42			
C. F. PETERS CORPORATION		D213	1.25
ORTHEL	M-D		
THREE SHORT PIECES			
C. F. PETERS CORPORATION		D212	1.25
OSCHEIT, M.			
FRIEDE AUF ERDEN, OP. 174--A CHRISTMAS POTPOURRI			
ASSOCIATED MUSIC PUBLISHERS, INC.		BOT	.90
OWEN--ED	OWEN		
MODERNE TANZRHYTHMEN			
SCHOTT		6075	2.50
OWENS			
SHORT ROTE SOLOS			
BELWIN-MILLS PUBLISHING CORPORATION			.60
PACE, H.			
CHRISTMAS MUSIC, SECOND COLLECTION			
LEE ROBERTS MUSIC PUBLICATIONS, INC.			1.50
PACE, R.			
CHRISTMAS MUSIC, BK. 1			
LEE ROBERTS MUSIC PUBLICATIONS, INC.			1.50
PACE, R.			
MEET THE PIANO -- TEENAGE AND ADULT BEGINNERS			
THEODORE PRESSER COMPANY			1.25
PACE, R.			
MELODY WORK BOOK -- SUPPLEMENT TO BOOK 1			
THEODORE PRESSER COMPANY			1.25
PACE, R.			
MUSIC FOR PIANO FOR THE OLDER BEGINNER			
LEE ROBERTS MUSIC PUBLICATIONS, INC.			1.75
PACE, R.			
MUSIC FOR PIANO, BK. 1			
LEE ROBERTS MUSIC PUBLICATIONS, INC.			1.75
PACE, R.			
MUSIC FOR PIANO, BK. 2			
LEE ROBERTS MUSIC PUBLICATIONS, INC.			1.75
PACE, R.			
MUSIC FOR PIANO, BK. 3			
LEE ROBERTS MUSIC PUBLICATIONS, INC.			1.75
PACE, R.			
MUSIC FOR PIANO, BK. 4			
LEE ROBERTS MUSIC PUBLICATIONS, INC.			1.75
PACE, R.			
MUSIC FOR PIANO, BK. 5			
LEE ROBERTS MUSIC PUBLICATIONS, INC.			1.75
PACE, R.			
MUSIC FOR PIANO, BK. 6			
LEE ROBERTS MUSIC PUBLICATIONS, INC.			2.00
PACE, R.			
ROBERT PACE PIANO SERIES, BK. 1			
THEODORE PRESSER COMPANY			1.25
PACE, R.			
ROBERT PACE PIANO SERIES, BK. 2			
THEODORE PRESSER COMPANY			1.25
PACE, R.			
ROBERT PACE PIANO SERIES, BK. 3			
THEODORE PRESSER COMPANY			1.25
PACE, R.			
SKILLS AND DRILLS, BK. 1			
LEE ROBERTS MUSIC PUBLICATIONS, INC.			1.75
PACE, R.			
SKILLS AND DRILLS, BK. 2			
LEE ROBERTS MUSIC PUBLICATIONS, INC.			1.75
PACE, R.			
SKILLS AND DRILLS, BK. 3			
LEE ROBERTS MUSIC PUBLICATIONS, INC.			1.75
PACE, R.			
SKILLS AND DRILLS, BK. 4			
LEE ROBERTS MUSIC PUBLICATIONS, INC.			1.75
PACE, R.			
SKILLS AND DRILLS, BK. 5			
LEE ROBERTS MUSIC PUBLICATIONS, INC.			1.75
PACHECO, J. F.			
PEQUENECES--CHILDREN'S ALBUM OF EASY DANCES			
ASSOCIATED MUSIC PUBLISHERS, INC.		UME	1.00
PACHELBEL	DOFLEIN	3	
AUSGEWAHLTE KLAVIERWERKE			
SCHOTT		2349	2.25
PACHELBEL	MOSER, C. *	3	
HEXACHORDUM APOLLINIS, ARIETTE IN F, CIACONEN IN C UND D FUR			
CEMBALO ODER ORGEL			
BARENREITER VERLAG		BA 2818	
PACHELBEL	M-D		
SELECTED KEYBOARD WORKS			
C. F. PETERS CORPORATION		4407B	2.50
PACHELBEL	MATTHAEI		
SEVEN CHORALE PARTITAS FOR HARPSICHORD --PIANO-- OR ORGAN			
BARENREITER VERLAG		BA 1016	4.25
PACHELBEL	MATTHAEI	3	
SIEBEN CHORALPARTITEN FUR CEMBALO -- KLAVIER -- ODER ORGEL			
BARENREITER VERLAG		BA 1016	
PACHELBEL	MOSER, C. *	3	
WERKE FUR ORGEL UND CLAVIER -- GESAMTAUSGABE DER ERHALTENEN			
KOMPOSITIONEN --			
BARENREITER VERLAG		BA 2206	
PACHELBEL	MOSER *		
WORKS FOR ORGAN AND KEYBOARD			
BARENREITER VERLAG		BA 2206	7.50
PACHELBEL	MOSER *		
WORKS FOR PIANO OR ORGAN			
BARENREITER VERLAG		BA 2818	6.00
PAHISSA			
EIGHT POETIC PIECES			
FRANCO COLOMBO PUBLICATIONS		BA10474	1.25
PAHISSA			
SEVEN CHILDREN'S PIECES			
FRANCO COLOMBO PUBLICATIONS		BA8763	1.25
PAHISSA			
TWO DANZAS CATALANAS			
FRANCO COLOMBO PUBLICATIONS		BA9228	1.00
PAHLEN	E		
MELODIES FROM ALL OVER THE WORLD			
C. F. PETERS CORPORATION		A96	1.25
PAIN, E.	VE		
FAVORITE TUNES			
OXFORD UNIVERSITY PRESS		33.027	.75
PAISIELLO, G.	MOLA	3	
SECHS SONATEN			
BARENREITER VERLAG		CM 19845	
PAISIELLO, G.			
SIX SONATAS			
BELWIN-MILLS PUBLISHING CORPORATION		11447	1.75
PALENICEK	4		
SKIZZENBUCH			
BARENREITER VERLAG		AP 1731	
PALESTER, R.			
PRELUDES			
PEER SOUTHERN ORGANIZATION			02.25
PALESTRINA, G.	3		
VIERSTIMMIGE RICERCARE IN DEN ACHT KIRCHENTONARTEN			
SCHOTT		2310	2.75
PALMER			
THREE EPIGRAMS			
PEER SOUTHERN ORGANIZATION			01.35
PALMER			
THREE PRELUDES			
PEER SOUTHERN ORGANIZATION			01.60
PALMER-LETHCO			
CREATING MUSIC AT THE PIANO -- RECITAL BOOK 1			
ALFRED MUSIC COMPANY		557	1.00
PALMER-LETHCO			
CREATING MUSIC AT THE PIANO -- RECITAL BOOK 2			
ALFRED MUSIC COMPANY		558	1.25
PALMER-LETHCO			
CREATING MUSIC AT THE PIANO -- TEACHER'S MANUAL FOR BK. 1			
ALFRED MUSIC COMPANY		564	2.50
PALMER-LETHCO			
CREATING MUSIC AT THE PIANO, BK. 1			
ALFRED MUSIC COMPANY		550	1.95
PALMER-LETHCO			
CREATING MUSIC AT THE PIANO, BK. 2			
ALFRED MUSIC COMPANY		552	1.95
PALMER-LETHCO			
CREATING MUSIC AT THE PIANO, BK. 3			
ALFRED MUSIC COMPANY		553	1.95
PALMER-LETHCO			
CREATING MUSIC AT THE PIANO, BK. 4			
ALFRED MUSIC COMPANY		554	1.95
PALMER, W. A.			
BAROQUE FOLK			
ALFRED MUSIC COMPANY		522	1.25
PALMER, W. A.			
HOW TO PLAY ROCK 'N' ROLL PIANO			
ALFRED MUSIC COMPANY		544	2.95
PALMER, W. A.--ED.	PALMER, W. A.		
FIRST SONATINA BOOK, THE			
ALFRED MUSIC COMPANY		626	1.25
PALMGREN, S.			
ALBUM OF 12 PIECES			
BOSTON MUSIC COMPANY			1.25
PANKOW, E.			
CHAPEL PIANIST NO. 1			
LILLENAS PUBLISHING COMPANY		MB-006	2.50
PANKOW, E.			
CHAPEL PIANIST NO. 2			
LILLENAS PUBLISHING COMPANY		MB-007	2.50
PANKOW, E.			
CHAPEL PIANIST NO. 3			
LILLENAS PUBLISHING COMPANY		MB-008	2.50
PANUFNIK, A.			
SIX MINIATURES STUDIES, BK. 1			
BOOSEY AND HAWKES, INC.			2.50
PANUFNIK, A.			
SIX MINIATURES STUDIES, BK. 2			
BOOSEY AND HAWKES, INC.			2.50
PANZERA, M.			
CHILDREN'S PIANO RECITAL, BK. 1			
EDITIONS MUSICALES TRANSATLANTIQUES			3.50
PAPARELLI	PAPARELLI		
BOOGIE WOOGIE PIANO ARRANGEMENTS, BK. 1 - EASY			
MCA MUSIC			1.00
PAPARELLI	PAPARELLI		
BOOGIE WOOGIE PIANO ARRANGEMENTS, BK. 3 - MEDIUM			
MCA MUSIC			1.50
PAPE, W.			
SCOTCH MELODIES--YE BANKS AND BRAES, BONNIE DUNDEE--OP. 30			
G. SCHIRMER, INC.			.50
PAPINEAU-COUTURE, J.			
SUITE--ARIA AND BAGATELLE NO. 2			
ASSOCIATED MUSIC PUBLISHERS, INC.		BER	.75
PAPINEAU-COUTURE, J.			
SUITE--PRELUDE AND BAGATELLE NO. 1			
ASSOCIATED MUSIC PUBLISHERS, INC.		BER	.75
PAPORISZ, Y.			
DISCOVERIES AT THE PIANO, BK. 1			
PEER SOUTHERN ORGANIZATION			02.00
PAPORISZ, Y.			
DISCOVERIES AT THE PIANO, BK. 2			
PEER SOUTHERN ORGANIZATION			02.00
PAPORISZ, Y.			
DISCOVERIES AT THE PIANO, BK. 3			
PEER SOUTHERN ORGANIZATION			02.00
PAPP, L.			
SIX BAGATELLES			
KULTURA			2.00
PAPP, L.			
THREE RONDOS			
KULTURA			2.00
PARCHMAN, G.			
SIXTEEN SHORT CONTEMPORARY PIECES FOR BEGINNERS			
SEESAW MUSIC CORPORATION			2.00
PARKER, A.--ED.	PARKER, A.		
LETTERS AND NOTES--LAWSON-GOULD EDITION			
G. SCHIRMER, INC.			1.00
PARLOW, E.			
FIRST AND SECOND GRADE STUDY PIECES			
THEODORE PRESSER COMPANY			.75
PARLOW, E.			
THIRTY LITTLE ETUDES			
G. SCHIRMER, INC.		L1251	1.00
PARSONS			
MUSIC OF FAITH, BK. 3			
THEODORE PRESSER COMPANY			2.25
PARSONS			
PIANO TRANSCRIPTIONS OF YOUR FAVORITE CHRISTMAS CAROLS			
THEODORE PRESSER COMPANY			1.50
PARSONS			
PIANO TRANSCRIPTIONS OF YOUR FAVORITE HYMNS			
THEODORE PRESSER COMPANY			1.50
PARSONS			
RHYTHMIC WAY, THE			
THEODORE PRESSER COMPANY			1.25
PASCAL, C.			
LE CAHIER DU LECTEUR OU LA RECREATION PIANISTIQUE, BK. 1			
ELKAN-VOGEL, INC.		D	4.50
PASCAL, C.			
LE CAHIER DU LECTEUR OU LA RECREATION PIANISTIQUE, BK. 2			
ELKAN-VOGEL, INC.		D	3.50
PASCAL, C.			
TWELVE DECHIFFRAGES			
ELKAN-VOGEL, INC.		D	3.50
PASTOR, S.	BERKOWITZ		
SUITE DE FLANDES--GUITAR			
ASSOCIATED MUSIC PUBLISHERS, INC.		UME	2.25

PATORNI *
    FAMOUS PIECES -- WITH HARPSICHORD REGISTRATION -- BK. 1
        FRANCO COLOMBO PUBLICATIONS   SAL   3.25
PATORNI *
    FAMOUS PIECES -- WITH HARPSICHORD REGISTRATION -- BK. 2
        FRANCO COLOMBO PUBLICATIONS   SAL   3.25
PATORNI *
    FAMOUS PIECES -- WITH HARPSICHORD REGISTRATION -- BK. 3
        FRANCO COLOMBO PUBLICATIONS   SAL   3.25
PAUER   M
    FINGER TECHNIQUE STUDIES
        C. F. PETERS CORPORATION   4839   1.50
PAUER   2
    MEIN NOTIZBUCH, HEFT 1 - 6 STUCKE
        BARENREITER VERLAG   AP 676A
PAUER   2
    MEIN NOTIZBUCH, HEFT 2 - 6 STUCKE
        BARENREITER VERLAG   676B
PAUER--ED   PAUER
    OLD MASTERS, BK. 1 -- A COLLECTION OF 17TH AND 18TH CENTURY
    KEYBOARD WORKS
        ASSOCIATED MUSIC PUBLISHERS, INC.   BRH   3.50
PAUER--ED   PAUER
    OLD MASTERS, BK. 2 -- A COLLECTION OF 17TH AND 18TH CENTURY
    KEYBOARD WORKS
        ASSOCIATED MUSIC PUBLISHERS, INC.   BRH   3.50
PAUER--ED   PAUER
    OLD MASTERS, BK. 3 -- A COLLECTION OF 17TH AND 18TH CENTURY
    KEYBOARD WORKS
        ASSOCIATED MUSIC PUBLISHERS, INC.   BRH   3.50
PAUER--ED   PAUER
    OLD MASTERS, BK. 4 -- A COLLECTION OF 17TH AND 18TH CENTURY
    KEYBOARD WORKS
        ASSOCIATED MUSIC PUBLISHERS, INC.   BRH   3.50
PAUER--ED   PAUER
    OLD MASTERS, BK. 5 -- A COLLECTION OF 17TH AND 18TH CENTURY
    KEYBOARD WORKS
        ASSOCIATED MUSIC PUBLISHERS, INC.   BRH   3.50
PAUER--ED   PAUER
    OLD MASTERS, BK. 6 -- A COLLECTION OF 17TH AND 18TH CENTURY
    KEYBOARD WORKS
        ASSOCIATED MUSIC PUBLISHERS, INC.   BRH   3.50
PAULL
    E. T. PAULL'S MARCH FOLIO, NO. 1
        SHAWNEE PRESS, INC.   1.50
PAYNE, W.
    TWELVE HYMN TUNES
        BANKS AND SON LTD.   .70
PEACOCK, K.
    BRIDAL SUITE
        ASSOCIATED MUSIC PUBLISHERS, INC.   BER   1.00
PEDRON
    SIX CHARACTERISTIC STUDIES
        FRANCO COLOMBO PUBLICATIONS   ER2204   1.50
PEERY, R. R.
    CHAPEL MUSINGS
        THEODORE PRESSER COMPANY   1.50
PEERY, R. R.
    ONE-PAGE PIANO VOLUNTARIES
        LORENZ PUBLISHING COMPANY   2.00
PEERY, R. R.
    TIP TOP TUNES
        BOSTON MUSIC COMPANY   1.00
PEERY, R. R.--ED   PEERY, R. R.
    CAROLS OF MANY LANDS
        BOSTON MUSIC COMPANY   1.25
PEERY, R. R.--ED   PEERY, R. R.
    CHAPEL ECHOES
        THEODORE PRESSER COMPANY   1.75
PEERY, R. R.--ED   PEERY   GR. 1
    CHILD'S BOOK OF HYMNS
        LORENZ PUBLISHING COMPANY   2.00
PEERY, R. R.--ED   PEERY, R. R.
    CHRISTMAS CAROL BOOK
        BOSTON MUSIC COMPANY   1.25
PEERY, R. R.--ED   PEERY, R. R.
    FAMOUS SACRED SONGS
        BOSTON MUSIC COMPANY   1.50
PEERY, R. R.--ED   PEERY
    PIANO VOLUNTARIES
        LORENZ PUBLISHING COMPANY   2.50
PEETERS   E-M
    TEN BAGATELLES, OP. 88
        C. F. PETERS CORPORATION   6144   .90
PEETERS   M-D
    TWELVE CHORALE PRELUDES, OP. 114. VOL. 1
        C. F. PETERS CORPORATION   6895A   1.50
PEETERS   M-D
    TWELVE CHORALE PRELUDES, OP. 114. VOL. 2
        C. F. PETERS CORPORATION   6895B   1.50
PELLEGRINI
    STUDENT PIANIST, THE
        FRANCO COLOMBO PUBLICATIONS   FOR.12207 1.25
PELZ
    DANDY CANDY
        PRO-ART PUBLICATIONS, INC.   597   .60
PELZ
    ENCORE STUNTS
        BELWIN-MILLS PUBLISHING CORPORATION   1.00
PENTLAND, B.
    STUDIES IN LINE, 1941
        ASSOCIATED MUSIC PUBLISHERS, INC.   BER   1.20
PEPPING, E.   4
    DREI FUGEN UBER B A C H
        SCHOTT   3959   3.00
PEPPING, E.   3-4
    PHANTASIEN
        BARENREITER VERLAG   BA 2256
PEPPING, E.   4
    TANZWEISEN UND RUNDGESANG
        SCHOTT   3715   3.00
PEPPING, E.   4
    ZUHAUSE -- 4 VARIATIONSSATZE --
        BARENREITER VERLAG   BA 2270
PEPPING, E.   4
    ZWEI ROMANZEN
        SCHOTT   2478   2.00
PERCHERON   2
    JOLIES LEGENDES, LES
        ALPHONSE LEDUC
PERCHERON
    NOUVELLE METHODE
        ALPHONSE LEDUC
PERGOLESI   CAFFARELLI
    SONATAS AND SUITES
        FRANCO COLOMBO PUBLICATIONS   AM   3.00

PERI
    FOUR AMERICAN VARIATIONS ON A THEME BY PAGANINI
        MCA MUSIC   1.25
PERL, H. F.
    CHILD'S WORLD IN MUSIC, A
        THEODORE PRESSER COMPANY   1.75
PERRACHIO
    TWENTY-FIVE PRELUDES
        FRANCO COLOMBO PUBLICATIONS   ER977   1.75
PERRIN   MEDIUM
    LATIN AMERICAN MINIATURES
        SHAWNEE PRESS, INC.   1.25
PERRY, J. H.
    BUSY WORK FOR BEGINNERS
        THEODORE PRESSER COMPANY   1.50
PERRY, J. H.
    MORE BUSY WORK FOR THE YOUNG PIANIST
        THEODORE PRESSER COMPANY   .85
PERRY, J. H.
    MOTHER GOOSE IN NOTELAND
        THEODORE PRESSER COMPANY   .90
PERRY, P.
    MASTER MELODIES FROM THE GREAT SYMPHONIES
        BELWIN-MILLS PUBLISHING CORPORATION   1.25
PERSICHETTI
    POEMS FOR PIANO, BK. 1
        ELKAN-VOGEL, INC.   1.00
PERSICHETTI
    POEMS FOR PIANO, BK. 2
        ELKAN-VOGEL, INC.   1.10
PERSICHETTI
    SIX SONATINAS, BK. 1, NOS. 1-3
        ELKAN-VOGEL, INC.   1.75
PERSICHETTI
    SIX SONATINAS, BK. 2, NOS. 4-6
        ELKAN-VOGEL, INC.   1.25
PESSI
    ART OF THE SUITE
        EDWARD B. MARKS MUSIC CORPORATION   02.50
PETERS--ED   PETERS   AI
    TIME TO PLAY FOLKSONGS
        WILLIS MUSIC COMPANY   1.00
PETERS, W.
    MODERN PIANOFORTE METHOD
        WILLIS MUSIC COMPANY   1.75
PETIT, P.   5
    BOIS DE BOULOGNE
        ALPHONSE LEDUC
PETRALIA
    SONGS FOR THE LITTLEST
        FRANCO COLOMBO PUBLICATIONS   FOR.12337 1.75
PETRONIO   6, 7
    TROIS PRELUDES
        ALPHONSE LEDUC
PETZOLD *   KREUTZ   2-3
    KLAVIERTANZE DER J. S. BACH-ZEITGENOSSEN. 29 TANZSATZE
        BARENREITER VERLAG   BA 885
PEZZE
    SIX BAGATELLES
        FRANCO COLOMBO PUBLICATIONS   BON.2267   1.00
PFEIFFER, A.
    PEDAL STUDIES--SPANISH AND ENGLISH
        G. SCHIRMER, INC.   1.00
PHILIPP, I.   1, 2
    ENFANTINES, LES, OP. 73, BK. 1
        ALPHONSE LEDUC
PHILIPP, I.   1, 2
    ENFANTINES, LES, OP. 73, BK. 2
        ALPHONSE LEDUC
PHILIPP, I.
    EXERCICES DE TENUES
        INTERNATIONAL MUSIC COMPANY   2.50
PHILIPP, I.
    EXERCISES ANALYTIQUES POUR LES OEUVRES DE CHOPIN
        FRANCO COLOMBO PUBLICATIONS   SAL   5.00
PHILIPP, I.
    EXERCISES FOR INDEPENDENCE OF THE FINGERS, BK. 1
        G. SCHIRMER, INC.   1.25
PHILIPP, I.
    EXERCISES FOR INDEPENDENCE OF THE FINGERS, BK. 2
        G. SCHIRMER, INC.   1.25
PHILIPP, I.
    EXERCISES IN VELOCITY
        ASSOCIATED MUSIC PUBLISHERS, INC.   ENO   1.00
PHILIPP, I.
    EXERCISES ON THE BLACK KEYS
        G. SCHIRMER, INC.   L1675   .60
PHILIPP, I.
    FIFTEEN ETUDES MELODIQUES
        FRANCO COLOMBO PUBLICATIONS   SAL   4.25
PHILIPP, I.
    FOURTEEN CAPRICE-ETUDES IN OCTAVES
        ASSOCIATED MUSIC PUBLISHERS, INC.   ENO   2.00
PHILIPP, I.   7, 9
    LE TRILLE
        ALPHONSE LEDUC
PHILIPP, I.   6, 7
    ONE HUNDRED AND SEVENTY-NINE EXERCICES D'EXTENSION
        ALPHONSE LEDUC
PHILIPP, I.
    SCHOOL OF OCTAVE PLAYING, BK. 1--EXERCISES
        G. SCHIRMER, INC.   L1650   1.00
PHILIPP, I.
    SCHOOL OF OCTAVE PLAYING, BK. 2--EXAMPLES FROM MASTERWORKS
        G. SCHIRMER, INC.   L1652   1.75
PHILIPP, I.
    SIX OCTAVE-STUDIES IN THE FORM OF LITTLE FUGUES, OP. 78
        G. SCHIRMER, INC.   L1611   1.00
PHILIPP, I.
    SIXTY NEW PREPARATORY EXERCISES
        ASSOCIATED MUSIC PUBLISHERS, INC.   ESC   3.00
PHILIPP, I.
    TECHNICAL EXERCISES
        INTERNATIONAL MUSIC COMPANY   1.50
PHILIPP, I.--ED.   PHILIPP, I.   MOYENNE DIFFICULTE
    ETUDES CLASSIQUES TIREES DES GRANDS MAITRES, SERIES 1
        ALPHONSE LEDUC
PHILIPP, I.--ED.   PHILIPP, I.   MOYENNE DIFFICULTE
    ETUDES CLASSIQUES TIREES DES GRANDS MAITRES, SERIES 1 BIS
        ALPHONSE LEDUC
PHILIPP, I.--ED.   PHILIPP, I.   ASSEZ DIFFICILE
    ETUDES CLASSIQUES TIREES DES GRANDS MAITRES, SERIES 2
        ALPHONSE LEDUC
PHILIPP, I.--ED.   PHILIPP, I.
    FRENCH AND BELGIAN MASTERS OF THE XVII AND XVIII CENTURIES
        INTERNATIONAL MUSIC COMPANY   2.50

PHILIPP, I.--ED.　　　PHILIPP, I.
ITALIAN MASTERS OF THE XVII AND XVIII CENTURIES
INTERNATIONAL MUSIC COMPANY　　　　　　2.50
PHILIPP, I.--ED.　　　PHILIPP, I.
NOUVEAU GRADUS AD PARNASSUM, BK. 1
ALPHONSE LEDUC
PHILIPP, I.--ED.　　　PHILIPP, I.
PETIT GRADUS AD PARNASSUM, BK. 1
ALPHONSE LEDUC
PHILIPP, I.--ED.　　　PHILIPP, I.
PETIT GRADUS AD PARNASSUM, BK. 2
ALPHONSE LEDUC
PHILIPP, I.--ED.　　　PHILIPP, I.
PETIT GRADUS AD PARNASSUM, BK. 3
ALPHONSE LEDUC
PHILIPP, I.--ED.　　　PHILIPP, I.
PETIT GRADUS AD PARNASSUM, BK. 4
ALPHONSE LEDUC
PHILIPP, I.--ED.　　　PHILIPP, I.
PETIT GRADUS AD PARNASSUM, BK. 5
ALPHONSE LEDUC
PHILLIP, I.
EXERCICES DE TENUES
EDWARD B. MARKS MUSIC CORPORATION　　　　01.50
PHILLIPS, B.
SET OF THREE INFORMALITIES, A--BLUES, SCHERZO, SONATINA
G. SCHIRMER, INC.　　　　　AI
　　　　　　　　　　　　　　1.00
PHIPPEN
TONE SKETCHES AT THE PIANO
WILLIS MUSIC COMPANY　　　　　　　.75
PIAZZA, M.--ED　　　PIAZZA, M.
MARGUERITE PIAZZA'S CHRISTMAS CAROL SING ALONG PARTY
WILLIS MUSIC COMPANY　　　　　　3.95
PICCIOLI
ANTICHI AUTORI BOLOGNESE, BK. 1
FRANCO COLOMBO PUBLICATIONS　　　BON.1836　　1.75
PICCIOLI
ANTICHI AUTORI BOLOGNESE, BK. 2
FRANCO COLOMBO PUBLICATIONS　　　BON.1837　　1.75
PICCIOLI
PREPARATORY EXERCISES FOR THE USE OF THE PEDAL
FRANCO COLOMBO PUBLICATIONS　　　BON.1988　　3.00
PICCIOLI
THREE DANCES IN MINIATURE
FRANCO COLOMBO PUBLICATIONS　　　BON.1772　　1.50
PIECHLER--ED　　　PIECHLER
WIR SINGEN ALLE MIT
SCHOTT　　　　　　5075　　3.00
PIEPER, M.
RHYTHMISCH-STILISTISCHE STUDIEN, BK. 1 -- JAZZ STUDIES
ASSOCIATED MUSIC PUBLISHERS, INC.　　DVM　　3.00
PIER, G.
KAWANA -- 3 PIECES
UNIVERSAL EDITION　　　　UE 12140　　1.30
PIERNE　　　　　　　5
ALBUM POUR MES PETITS AMIS, OP. 14
ALPHONSE LEDUC
PIERNE, P.
PETITES PIECES POMPADOUR
FRANCO COLOMBO PUBLICATIONS　　　SAL　　2.50
PIERNE, P.
SIX EASY PIECES
ASSOCIATED MUSIC PUBLISHERS, INC.　　ESC　　2.50
PIERONI
ALBUM OF LITTLE PIECES
FRANCO COLOMBO PUBLICATIONS　　FOR.11570　　1.25
PIKE, E. F.
EASIEST TUNE BOOK OF SACRED SONGS AND SOLOS, OP. 32
BOOSEY AND HAWKES, INC.　　　　1.00
PILATI
THREE ETUDES
FRANCO COLOMBO PUBLICATIONS　　　ER1598　　1.00
PILLNEY
ESKAPADEN EINES GASSENHAUERS--PARODY VARIATIONS
ASSOCIATED MUSIC PUBLISHERS, INC.　　BRH　　2.50
PILLOIS
TWO PIECES A LA MANIERE DE
FRANCO COLOMBO PUBLICATIONS　　　SAL　　4.00
PINTO, O.
SCENAS INFANTIS
G. SCHIRMER, INC.　　　　　1.00
PISCHNA *
DER GROSSE PISCHNA, 60 PROGRESSIVE TECHNISCHE UBUNGEN MIT
VARIANTEN VON MORONI
BARENREITER VERLAG　　　　CM 18331
PISCHNA　　　　　　WOLFF
FORTY-EIGHT STUDIES - 'THE LITTLE PISCHNA'
FRANCO COLOMBO PUBLICATIONS　　　ER2557　　1.75
PISCHNA　　　　　　WOLFF
LITTLE PISCHNA, THE--48 PRACTICE-PIECES--INTRODUCTION TO
'TECHNICAL STUDIES'
G. SCHIRMER, INC.　　　　L898　　1.00
PISCHNA　　　　　　REHBERG　　　　M-D
SIXTY DAILY EXERCISES
C. F. PETERS CORPORATION　　　Z112　　2.50
PISCHNA　　　　　　SAUER　　　　M-D
SIXTY DAILY EXERCISES
C. F. PETERS CORPORATION　　　3018　　3.00
PISCHNA
SIXTY DAILY STUDIES
CARL FISCHER, INC.　　　　L 484　　2.00
PISCHNA　　　　　　MARCIANO
SIXTY PROGRESSIVE STUDIES
FRANCO COLOMBO PUBLICATIONS　　　ER96　　3.50
PISCHNA　　　　　　WOLFF
TECHNICAL STUDIES--60 PROGRESSIVE EXERCISES, REVISED AND
AUGMENTED WITH ADDITIONAL PRELIMINARY EXERCISES
G. SCHIRMER, INC.　　　　L792　　2.00
PITCHER, G.--ED　　　PITCHER, G.
SING TOGETHER AT CHRISTMAS
WILLIS MUSIC COMPANY　　　　　1.25
PITFIELD
MUSICIANLY SCALE PRACTICE
BOOSEY AND HAWKES, INC.　　　　1.50
PITTALUGA　　　　　6
TROIS PIECES POUR UNE ESPAGNOLADE
ALPHONSE LEDUC
PLAIDY, L.　　　　SAUER　　　M-D
TECHNICAL STUDIES
C. F. PETERS CORPORATION　　　3042　　5.00
PLAIDY, L.　　　　KLAUSER
TECHNICAL STUDIES
G. SCHIRMER, INC.　　　　L304　　1.50
PLAIDY, L.　　　　KLAUSER
TECHNICAL STUDIES, BK. 1--SECTIONS 1-4
G. SCHIRMER, INC.　　　　L1617　　1.25

PLANQUETTE　　　　　3
WALTZES, CHIMES OF NORMANDY
CENTURY MUSIC PUBLISHING COMPANY, INC.　2103　.40
PLATAMONE
THREE DANCES
FRANCO COLOMBO PUBLICATIONS　　　DS830　2.00
PLATTI, G. B.　　　HOFFMANN-ERBRECHT
TWELVE SONATAS, BK. 1
ASSOCIATED MUSIC PUBLISHERS, INC.　　BRH　3.00
PLATTI, G. B.　　　HOFFMANN-ERBRECHT
TWELVE SONATAS, BK. 2
ASSOCIATED MUSIC PUBLISHERS, INC.　　BRH　3.00
PLE
HOMMAGE A CZERNY -- 20 DIVERTISSEMENTS --
FRANCO COLOMBO PUBLICATIONS　　　SAL　5.50
PLE
TEN PRELUDES
FRANCO COLOMBO PUBLICATIONS　　　SAL　5.50
PODESVA, J.
SEVEN LITTLE PIECES
GENERAL MUSIC PUBLISHING COMPANY, INC.　595　2.50
PODESVA, J.
SEVEN LITTLE PIECES WITH COMIC VERSES
GENERAL MUSIC PUBLISHING COMPANY, INC.　　2.50
PODOLSKY, L. *
CHORDS, CADENCES, TRANSPOSITION
BOOSEY AND HAWKES, INC.　　　　1.25
PODOLSKY, L. *
DANCES IN MAJOR AND MINOR
BOOSEY AND HAWKES, INC.　　　　1.25
PODOLSKY, L. *
PILLARS OF PIANO TECHNIC -- THE FIXED HAND, BK. A
BOOSEY AND HAWKES, INC.　　　　1.25
PODOLSKY, L. *
PILLARS OF PIANO TECHNIC -- THE FIXED HAND, BK. B
BOOSEY AND HAWKES, INC.　　　　1.25
PODOLSKY, L. *
PILLARS OF PIANO TECHNIC -- THE FIXED HAND, BK. C, VOL. 1
BOOSEY AND HAWKES, INC.　　　　1.25
PODOLSKY, L. *
PILLARS OF PIANO TECHNIC -- THE FIXED HAND, BK. C, VOL. 2
BOOSEY AND HAWKES, INC.　　　　1.25
PODOLSKY, L. *
PRINCIPLES OF PEDALING
BOOSEY AND HAWKES, INC.　　　　1.25
PODOLSKY, L. *
REPERTOIRE ALBUM -- HIGHER INTERMEDIATE, BK. 1
BOOSEY AND HAWKES, INC.　　　　1.25
PODOLSKY, L. *
REPERTOIRE ALBUM -- INTERMEDIATE
BOOSEY AND HAWKES, INC.　　　　1.25
PODOLSKY, L. *
REPERTOIRE ALBUM -- LOWER ELEMENTARY, BK. 1
BOOSEY AND HAWKES, INC.　　　　1.25
PODOLSKY, L. *
REPERTOIRE ALBUM -- LOWER ELEMENTARY, BK. 2
BOOSEY AND HAWKES, INC.　　　　1.25
PODOLSKY, L. *
REPERTOIRE ALBUM -- LOWER INTERMEDIATE, BK. 1
BOOSEY AND HAWKES, INC.　　　　1.25
PODOLSKY, L. *
REPERTOIRE ALBUM -- LOWER INTERMEDIATE, BK. 2
BOOSEY AND HAWKES, INC.　　　　1.25
PODOLSKY, L. *
REPERTOIRE ALBUM -- UPPER ELEMENTARY, BK. 1
BOOSEY AND HAWKES, INC.　　　　1.25
PODOLSKY, L. *
REPERTOIRE ALBUM -- UPPER ELEMENTARY, BK. 2
BOOSEY AND HAWKES, INC.　　　　1.25
PODOLSKY, L. *
RHYTHMS AND THE I-V7 CHORDS
BOOSEY AND HAWKES, INC.　　　　1.25
PODOLSKY, L.--ED　　　PODOLSKY, L.
CLASSIC SONATAS, VOL. 1 - INTERMEDIATE 'A'
CARL FISCHER, INC.　　　O 4521　1.50
PODOLSKY, L.--ED　　　PODOLSKY, L.
CLASSIC SONATAS, VOL. 2 - INTERMEDIATE 'B'
CARL FISCHER, INC.　　　O 4522　1.50
PODOLSKY, L.--ED　　　PODOLSKY, L.
CLASSIC SONATAS, VOL. 3 - ADVANCING
CARL FISCHER, INC.　　　O 4523　1.50
PODOLSKY, L.--ED　　　PODOLSKY, L.
CLASSIC SONATAS, VOL. 4 - ADVANCING
CARL FISCHER, INC.　　　O 4524　1.50
PODOLSKY, L.--ED　　　PODOLSKY, L.
MORE SELECT SONATINAS, BK. 1
BELWIN-MILLS PUBLISHING CORPORATION　　1.50
PODOLSKY, L.--ED　　　PODOLSKY, L.
MORE SELECT SONATINAS, BK. 2
BELWIN-MILLS PUBLISHING CORPORATION　　1.50
PODOLSKY, L.--ED　　　PODOLSKY, L.
MORE SELECT SONATINAS, BK. 3
BELWIN-MILLS PUBLISHING CORPORATION　　1.50
PODOLSKY, L.--ED　　　PODOLSKY, L.
SELECT SONATINAS FOR PIANO, BK. 1
BELWIN-MILLS PUBLISHING CORPORATION　　1.50
PODOLSKY, L.--ED　　　PODOLSKY, L.
SELECT SONATINAS FOR PIANO, BK. 2
BELWIN-MILLS PUBLISHING CORPORATION　　1.50
PODOLSKY, L.--ED　　　PODOLSKY, L.
SELECT SONATINAS FOR PIANO, BK. 3
BELWIN-MILLS PUBLISHING CORPORATION　　1.50
PODOLSKY, L.--ED　　　PODOLSKY, L.
SELECT SONATINAS FOR PIANO, BK. 4
BELWIN-MILLS PUBLISHING CORPORATION　　1.50
PODOLSKY, L.--ED　　　PODOLSKY, L.
SELECT SONATINAS FOR PIANO, BK. 5
BELWIN-MILLS PUBLISHING CORPORATION　　1.50
POGLIETTI　　　　　NETTLES　　　3-4
CEMBALO-KOMPOSITIONEN
BARENREITER VERLAG　　　PSM 9
POGLIETTI　　　　　D
NIGHTINGALE
C. F. PETERS CORPORATION　　WM57　3.50
POHL, V.--ED *　　　POHL, V. *　　1-2
KINDER SPIELEN ZUR WEIHNACHT. 19 WEIHNACHTSLIEDER FUR KLAVIER
BARENREITER VERLAG　　　EN 803
POLDINI, E.
MUSICAL MOMENTS FOR YOUNG PIANISTS
FRANCO COLOMBO PUBLICATIONS　　128158　.60
POLIVKA
AKKORDE
BARENREITER VERLAG　　　AP 679
POLLA, W.--ED.　　　POLLA, W.
WORLD'S GREATEST MELODIES
SHAWNEE PRESS, INC.　　　　.50

POLLIN, N.   CLASSENS
  LA TROMPETTE CLASSIQUE, VOL. B POUR LE PIANO
    ELKAN-VOGEL, INC.   CON   4.00
POLLINI
  SCALES IN ALL THE KEYS
    FRANCO COLOMBO PUBLICATIONS   101128   .90
PONCE, M.
  CUATRO DANZAS MEXICANAS
    EDITORIAL COOPERATIVA INTER-AMERICANA   01.05
PONCE, M.
  PRELUDIOS ENCADENADOS
    PEER SOUTHERN ORGANIZATION   01.25
PONCE, M.
  TEMA MEXICANO VARIADO
    PEER SOUTHERN ORGANIZATION   00.85
PONCE, M.
  VEINTE PIEZAS FACILES
    PEER SOUTHERN ORGANIZATION   02.00
PONIRIDY
  RYTHMES GRECS
    FRANCO COLOMBO PUBLICATIONS   SAL   5.00
PONIRIDY
  TWO PRELUDES
    FRANCO COLOMBO PUBLICATIONS   SAL   3.25
POOT, M.
  IN ALL DIRECTIONS -- A COLLECTION OF PIECES FOR THE YOUNG
  PIANIST
    UNIVERSAL EDITION   UE 13828E 2.65
POOT, M.
  SIX EASY PIECES
    ASSOCIATED MUSIC PUBLISHERS, INC.   ESC   2.00
POOT, M.
  SIX PETITES PIECES RECREATIVES
    ASSOCIATED MUSIC PUBLISHERS, INC.   ESC   1.50
PORRAS MOYA, V.
  SIX SPANISH DANCES
    ASSOCIATED MUSIC PUBLISHERS, INC.   UME   1.35
PORTER, C.   GLOVER, D.
  COLE PORTER, THE WONDERFUL WORLD OF
    CHAPPELL AND COMPANY, INC.   0010116   2.50
PORTER, C.
  MEET COLE PORTER AT THE PIANO
    CHAPPELL AND COMPANY, INC.   0010074   2.50
PORTER, C.
  POINTER LIBRARY - THE BEST OF COLE PORTER
    POINTER PUBLICATIONS   2.95
PORTNOFF
  PIANO PRANKS
    SUMMY-BIRCHARD COMPANY   1.25
PORTNOFF, M.
  MUSIC OF FAITH, BK. 1
    THEODORE PRESSER COMPANY   1.75
PORTNOFF, M.--ED   PORTNOFF, M.
  DANCE ETUDES
    BOURNE COMPANY   1.00
PORTNOFF, M.--ED   PORTNOFF, M.
  MUSICAL FORMS FROM A TO Z -- CYCLOPEDIA OF MASTERWORKS FOR THE
  STUDENT PIANIST
    THEODORE PRESSER COMPANY   1.50
PORTNOFF, M.--ED   PORTNOFF, M.
  TEN FINGERS IN A FIVE FINGER POSITION
    BOURNE COMPANY   1.00
PORTNOFF, M.--ED   PORTNOFF, M.
  TUNERAMA
    THEODORE PRESSER COMPANY   1.00
POSER
  MUSIC FOR PIANO, OP. 24
    FRANCO COLOMBO PUBLICATIONS   SIK.400   1.75
POSER
  OLD FOLKSONGS IN NEW SETTINGS
    FRANCO COLOMBO PUBLICATIONS   SIK.478   2.25
POST, R.--ED   POST, R.   1
  HOLIDAY BOOK, THE
    ASHLEY DEALERS SERVICE, INC.   1.25
POST, R.--ED   POST, R.
  HOLIDAY BOOK, THE
    CENTURY MUSIC PUBLISHING COMPANY, INC.   1.25
POTTER, H. *
  ALL-IN-ONE BOOGIE WOOGIE
    SHAWNEE PRESS, INC.   .50
POULENC, F.
  FEUILLETS D'ALBUM - ARIETTE, REVE, GIGUE
    FRANCO COLOMBO PUBLICATIONS   SAL   1.75
POULENC, F.
  IMPROVISATIONS, NOS. 1-6
    FRANCO COLOMBO PUBLICATIONS   SAL   2.50
POULENC, F.
  IMPROVISATIONS, NOS. 7-12
    FRANCO COLOMBO PUBLICATIONS   SAL   2.50
POULENC, F.
  NAPOLI - BARCAROLLE, NOCTURNE, CAPRICE ITALIEN
    FRANCO COLOMBO PUBLICATIONS   SAL   2.00
POULENC, F.
  VILLAGEOISES -- EASY PIECES --
    FRANCO COLOMBO PUBLICATIONS   SAL   2.50
POURNY
  DANSE EN FAMILLE -- 20 SHORT AND VERY EASY DANCES --
    FRANCO COLOMBO PUBLICATIONS   SAL   4.00
POWELL
  SUITE SUDISTE
    FRANCO COLOMBO PUBLICATIONS   SAL   5.50
POWERS, M.
  PIANO FUN WITH THEORY
    THEODORE PRESSER COMPANY   .75
POZZOLI
  ALBUM OF 6 PIECES
    FRANCO COLOMBO PUBLICATIONS   ER528   1.00
POZZOLI
  EASY SIGHT-READING STUDIES -- IL SOLFEGGIO AL PIANOFORTE --
    FRANCO COLOMBO PUBLICATIONS   ER2508   1.25
POZZOLI
  EXERCISES AND STUDIES IN THUMB PASSAGES
    FRANCO COLOMBO PUBLICATIONS   ER200   2.00
POZZOLI
  FIFTEEN EASY STUDIES FOR THE SMALL HAND
    FRANCO COLOMBO PUBLICATIONS   ER436   1.50
POZZOLI
  FIRST EXERCISES IN POLYPHONIC STYLE - 50 SHORT CANONS
    FRANCO COLOMBO PUBLICATIONS   ER1748   1.25
POZZOLI
  FIVE SONATINAS IN THE CLASSIC STYLE
    FRANCO COLOMBO PUBLICATIONS   ER2278   2.50
POZZOLI
  IMPRESSIONS, BK. 1
    FRANCO COLOMBO PUBLICATIONS   127900   1.25
POZZOLI
  IMPRESSIONS, BK. 2
    FRANCO COLOMBO PUBLICATIONS   127177   1.00

POZZOLI
  PAGINE MINUSCOLE - 12 SKETCHES
    FRANCO COLOMBO PUBLICATIONS   ER308   1.00
POZZOLI
  PIANISTS' DAILY TECHNIQUE, THE - PART 3
    FRANCO COLOMBO PUBLICATIONS   ER801   2.25
POZZOLI
  PIANISTS' DAILY TECHNIQUE, THE - PARTS 1 AND 2
    FRANCO COLOMBO PUBLICATIONS   ER800   3.00
POZZOLI
  PICCOLE SCINTILLE - 15 EASY PIECES
    FRANCO COLOMBO PUBLICATIONS   129911   2.25
POZZOLI
  PICCOLO 'GRADUS AD PARNASSUM' - 15 STUDIES PREPARATORY TO
  CLEMENTI'S 'GRADUS'
    FRANCO COLOMBO PUBLICATIONS   ER2534   1.75
POZZOLI
  RIFLESSI DEL MARE - 3 CHARACTERISTIC PIECES
    FRANCO COLOMBO PUBLICATIONS   121108   1.50
POZZOLI
  SEVEN LITTLE SKETCHES
    FRANCO COLOMBO PUBLICATIONS   ER2104   1.75
POZZOLI
  SIXTEEN AGILITY STUDIES FOR SMALL HANDS
    FRANCO COLOMBO PUBLICATIONS   ER2230   1.75
POZZOLI
  STUDIES IN VELOCITY
    FRANCO COLOMBO PUBLICATIONS   ER2188   2.50
POZZOLI
  STUDIES OF MEDIUM DIFFICULTY
    FRANCO COLOMBO PUBLICATIONS   ER83   1.75
POZZOLI
  STUDIES ON REPEATED NOTES
    FRANCO COLOMBO PUBLICATIONS   ER1847   1.75
POZZOLI
  SUONO IL PIANOFORTE - 19 LITTLE PIECES
    FRANCO COLOMBO PUBLICATIONS   129754   1.75
POZZOLI
  THIRTY ELEMENTARY STUDIES
    FRANCO COLOMBO PUBLICATIONS   ER46   1.50
POZZOLI
  TWENTY SCALE STUDIES
    FRANCO COLOMBO PUBLICATIONS   ER2128   1.75
POZZOLI
  TWENTY-FOUR EASY AND PROGRESSIVE STUDIES
    FRANCO COLOMBO PUBLICATIONS   ER2067   1.75
POZZOLI
  TWENTY-FOUR EASY STUDIES IN MECHANISM
    FRANCO COLOMBO PUBLICATIONS   ER427   1.75
                                            5, 6
PRESLE
  ALBUM D'IMAGES
    ALPHONSE LEDUC
PRESSER, T.
  SCHOOL FOR THE PIANO PIANOFORTE -- BEGINNER'S BOOK, RED BOOK
    THEODORE PRESSER COMPANY   1.50
PRESSER, T.
  SCHOOL FOR THE PIANO PIANOFORTE -- PLAYER'S BOOK, GREEN BOOK
    THEODORE PRESSER COMPANY   1.75
PRESSER, T.
  SCHOOL FOR THE PIANO PIANOFORTE -- STUDENT'S BOOK, BLUE BOOK
    THEODORE PRESSER COMPANY   1.50
PRESTON *   KOVIKER   3
  SUITEN FUR TASTENINSTRUMENTE AUS 'MELOTHESIA', ACHT SUITEN
    BARENREITER VERLAG   PSM 16
PREVIN, A.
  PLAY PIANO LIKE ANDRE PREVIN, NO. 1
    THE BIG THREE MUSIC CORPORATION   01.50
PREVIN, A.
  PLAY PIANO LIKE ANDRE PREVIN, NO. 2
    THE BIG THREE MUSIC CORPORATION   01.95
PREVIN, A.
  THREE SOUTH AMERICAN SKETCHES
    FRANK MUSIC CORPORATION   1.25
PRICE, F.
  DANCES IN THE CANEBRAKES -- THREE PIECES, 1. NIMBLE FEET 2.
  TROPICAL MOON 3. SILK HAT AND A WALKING CANE
    BELWIN-MILLS PUBLISHING CORPORATION   20490   1.00
PRICE, T.   EASY
  FUN WITH PIANO
    MEL BAY PUBLICATIONS, INC.   1.50
PRIESING *
  LANGUAGE OF THE PIANO
    CARL FISCHER, INC.   O 4131   4.00
PRIGGE, O.
  MEET AND KNOW THE PIANO, BK. 1
    WILLIS MUSIC COMPANY   1.50
PRIGGE, O.
  MEET AND KNOW THE PIANO, BK. 2
    WILLIS MUSIC COMPANY   1.50
PRIGGE, O.
  PLAYING AND SINGING THROUGH THE YEAR
    WILLIS MUSIC COMPANY   1.25
PRIGGE, O.--ED   PRIGGE, O.
  I PLAY CAROLS AT CHRISTMAS TIME
    WILLIS MUSIC COMPANY   1.00
PRISCHING, F.--ED   PRISCHING, F.
  SONATINAS -- PREPARATORY TO CLEMENTI, KUHLAU
    UNIVERSAL EDITION   UE 3778 1.60
PROCTOR
  FUN TO PLAY
    PRO-ART PUBLICATIONS, INC.   205   1.50
PROGRIS, J.
  MODERN METHOD FOR KEYBOARD STUDY, A - COMPLETE SET B-13 THROUGH
  B-16
    BERKLEE PRESS PUBLICATIONS   B-13 - B-16 21.50
PROGRIS, J.
  MODERN METHOD FOR KEYBOARD STUDY, A - VOL. 1
    BERKLEE PRESS PUBLICATIONS   B-13   6.00
PROGRIS, J.
  MODERN METHOD FOR KEYBOARD STUDY, A - VOL. 2
    BERKLEE PRESS PUBLICATIONS   B-14   6.00
PROGRIS, J.
  MODERN METHOD FOR KEYBOARD STUDY, A - VOL. 3
    BERKLEE PRESS PUBLICATIONS   B-15   6.00
PROGRIS, J.
  MODERN METHOD FOR KEYBOARD STUDY, A - VOL. 4
    BERKLEE PRESS PUBLICATIONS   B-16   6.00
PROKOFIEFF
  ALBUM
    EDWIN F. KALMUS   3774   2.50
PROKOFIEFF   BEGINNER
  CHILDREN'S PIECES
    EDWIN F. KALMUS   3772   1.00
PROKOFIEFF   M
  CINDERELLA, OP. 97 --TEN PIECES FROM THE BALLET--
    C. F. PETERS CORPORATION   4782   3.50

PROKOFIEFF
CINDERELLA, TEN PIECES FROM THE BALLET, OP. 97
MCA MUSIC   3.00
PROKOFIEFF   SANDOR
COMPLETE PIANO SONATAS
MCA MUSIC   7.95
PROKOFIEFF
FIVE SARCASMS, OP. 17
EDWIN F. KALMUS   3797   2.00
PROKOFIEFF
FOUR ETUDES, OP. 2
INTERNATIONAL MUSIC COMPANY   1.75
PROKOFIEFF
FOUR ETUDES, OP. 2
EDWIN F. KALMUS   3788   2.00
PROKOFIEFF
FOUR ETUDES, OP. 2
MCA MUSIC   1.00
PROKOFIEFF
FOUR PIECES, OP. 2
INTERNATIONAL MUSIC COMPANY   1.75
PROKOFIEFF   PHILIPP, I.
FOUR PIECES, OP. 32
INTERNATIONAL MUSIC COMPANY   1.75
PROKOFIEFF
FOUR PIECES, OP. 4
EDWIN F. KALMUS   3790   2.00
PROKOFIEFF
FOUR PIECES, OP. 4
MCA MUSIC   1.50
PROKOFIEFF
MUSIC FOR CHILDREN, OP. 65
BOOSEY AND HAWKES, INC.   1.25
PROKOFIEFF
MUSIC FOR CHILDREN, OP. 65
INTERNATIONAL MUSIC COMPANY   1.50
PROKOFIEFF
MUSIC FOR CHILDREN, OP. 65
MCA MUSIC   1.50
PROKOFIEFF
MUSIC FOR CHILDREN, OP. 65--12 EASY PIECES
G. SCHIRMER, INC.   L1772   1.25
PROKOFIEFF   PALMER, W. A.
MUSIC FOR YOUNG PEOPLE
ALFRED MUSIC COMPANY   631   1.50
PROKOFIEFF
NINE SONATAS
INTERNATIONAL MUSIC COMPANY   8.50
PROKOFIEFF
NINE SONATAS
EDWIN F. KALMUS   3773   9.00
PROKOFIEFF   SCHAUM, J.   2
PETER AND THE WOLF
SCHAUM PUBLICATIONS, INC.   1.50
PROKOFIEFF
PETER AND THE WOLF, OP. 67
MCA MUSIC   2.50
PROKOFIEFF *
PKK -- IN 1 BOOK
ASHLEY DEALERS SERVICE, INC.   HG 12   2.95
PROKOFIEFF   AGAY, D.
PROKOFIEFF IS EASY - 12 MELODIOUS PIECES FOR THE YOUNG PIANIST
THEODORE PRESSER COMPANY   1.25
PROKOFIEFF
PROKOFIEFF MASTERPIECES
EDWARD B. MARKS MUSIC CORPORATION   02.50
PROKOFIEFF
ROMEO AND JULIET, OP. 64
MCA MUSIC   12.50
PROKOFIEFF   D
ROMEO AND JULIET, OP. 75 --TEN EXCERPTS--
C. F. PETERS CORPORATION   4790   5.00
PROKOFIEFF
SARCASMS, OP. 17
MCA MUSIC   1.25
PROKOFIEFF   BALOGH
SELECTED WORKS FOR THE PIANO
G. SCHIRMER, INC.   L1766   3.00
PROKOFIEFF
SUR LE BORYSTHENE, OP. 51 - COMPLETE BALLET
BOOSEY AND HAWKES, INC.   5.00
PROKOFIEFF   FOLDES
TALES OF THE OLD GRANDMOTHER, OP. 31
MCA MUSIC   1.00
PROKOFIEFF
TALES OF THE OLD GRANDMOTHER, OP. 31--4 PIECES
ASSOCIATED MUSIC PUBLISHERS, INC.   AMP   1.00
PROKOFIEFF   D
TEN LITTLE PIANO PIECES, OP. 12
C. F. PETERS CORPORATION   F29   3.00
PROKOFIEFF
TEN PIANO PIECES FROM CINDERELLA, OP. 97
EDWIN F. KALMUS   3792   3.00
PROKOFIEFF
TEN PIECES, OP. 12
INTERNATIONAL MUSIC COMPANY   2.50
PROKOFIEFF
TEN PIECES, OP. 12
EDWIN F. KALMUS   3796   2.95
PROKOFIEFF
THREE PIECES, OP. 96
MCA MUSIC   2.00
PROKOFIEFF
THREE WALTZES, OP. 122
EDWIN F. KALMUS   3802   1.50
PROKOFIEFF
TWENTY SKETCHES, OP. 22
EDWIN F. KALMUS   3789   2.00
PROKOFIEFF
TWO PIECES, OP. 3
EDWIN F. KALMUS   3789   1.50
PROKOFIEFF
VISIONS FUGITIVES
EDWARD B. MARKS MUSIC CORPORATION   01.50
PROKOFIEFF
VISIONS FUGITIVES, OP. 22
BOOSEY AND HAWKES, INC.   1.25
PROKOFIEFF   PHILIPP, I.
VISIONS FUGITIVES, OP. 22
INTERNATIONAL MUSIC COMPANY   2.00
PROKOFIEFF
VISIONS FUGITIVES, OP. 22
MCA MUSIC   3.50
PROSTAKOFF--ED.   PROSTAKOFF
NEW MUSIC FOR THE PIANO--LAWSON-GOULD EDITION
G. SCHIRMER, INC.   3.50

PUCCINI   FANANGHI
ALBUM - MELODIE PUCCINIANE - 17 EASY TRANSCRIPTIONS
FRANCO COLOMBO PUBLICATIONS   127651   2.00
PUCCINI   GODFREY, JR.
BOHEME, LA - SELECTION
FRANCO COLOMBO PUBLICATIONS   109358   1.25
PUCHLET--ED   PUCHLET   D
BRAVOURA VARIATIONS --1810-1830--
C. F. PETERS CORPORATION   R198   6.00
PUDELKO, W.   KNABB
MUSIKANTEN, DIE KOMMEN
BARENREITER VERLAG   BA 1720   2.00
PURCELL, H.
CHOICE COLLECTION OF LESSONS
BROUDE BROTHERS LTD.   22.50
PURCELL, H.
EIGHT SUITES AND EIGHT VARIOUS PIECES
EDWIN F. KALMUS   3808   2.00
PURCELL, H.   KELLER   E
EIGHTEEN EASY PIANO PIECES
C. F. PETERS CORPORATION   5071   1.50
PURCELL, H.   OESTERLE *
KEYBOARD SUITES
G. SCHIRMER, INC.   L1743   1.00
PURCELL, H.
SELECTED PIECES
EDWARD B. MARKS MUSIC CORPORATION   02.50
PURCELL, H.
SIX SUITES FOR HARPSICHORD
NOVELLO AND COMPANY, LTD.   10.0106.10   2.15
PURCELL, H.   HILLEMANN   2-3
STUCKE FUR KLAVIER ODER CEMBALO
SCHOTT   4126   1.75
PUTSCHE, T.
SIX PRELUDES FOR PIANO
SEESAW MUSIC CORPORATION   3.00
PUTSCHE, T.
TWELVE STUDIES FOR PIANO
SEESAW MUSIC CORPORATION   3.00
PYLE, H.
UNIVERSITY PIANO SERIES -- A COURSE OF STUDY FOR THE ADULT
STUDENT
CAMPUS PUBLISHERS   2.75
QUAILE, E.   GRADE 1
FIRST BOOK OF TECHNICAL EXERCISES--WITH SPECIAL REFERENCE TO THE
PIECES OF THE DILLER-QUAILE "FIRST SOLO BOOK"
G. SCHIRMER, INC.   1.00
QUAILE, E.
PRE-CZERNY BOOK, A--BK. 1--40 STUDIES
G. SCHIRMER, INC.   1.00
QUAILE, E.
PRE-CZERNY BOOK, A--BK. 2--32 STUDIES
G. SCHIRMER, INC.   1.00
QUAILE, E.   GRADE 3
RHYME AND REASON--MUSICAL TERMS EXPRESSED IN PIANO MUSIC
G. SCHIRMER, INC.   1.00
QUIST
LISTEN TO LEARN
CARL FISCHER, INC.   AH 3   1.25
QUIST
MINDING YOUR P'S AND Q'S - OPUS 1
CARL FISCHER, INC.   AH 4   1.50
QUIST
MINDING YOUR P'S AND Q'S - OPUS 2
CARL FISCHER, INC.   AH 5   1.50
QUIST
MINDING YOUR P'S AND Q'S - OPUS 3
CARL FISCHER, INC.   AH 6   1.50
QUIST
P.Q'S PENCIL QUICKIES
CARL FISCHER, INC.   AH 10   1.50
QUIST
P'S AND Q'S OF PIANO ARTISTRY - BK. 1
CARL FISCHER, INC.   AH 7   1.95
QUIST
P'S AND Q'S OF PIANO ARTISTRY - BK. 2
CARL FISCHER, INC.   AH 8   1.95
QUIST
P'S AND Q'S OF PIANO ARTISTRY - BK. 3
CARL FISCHER, INC.   AH 9   1.95
RABEN
MUSICAL SPEED DRILLS, BK. 1
WILLIS MUSIC COMPANY   .60
RABEN
MUSICAL SPEED DRILLS, BK. 2
WILLIS MUSIC COMPANY   .70
RABEN
MUSICAL SPEED DRILLS, BK. 3
WILLIS MUSIC COMPANY   .80
RABINOFF, S.
MUSICIANSHIP THROUGH IMPROVISATION AT THE KEYBOARD -- BK. 1
HARMONIC FORMS
THEODORE PRESSER COMPANY   3.00
RABINOFF, S.
MUSICIANSHIP THROUGH IMPROVISATION AT THE KEYBOARD -- THE
IMPROVISER, COMPANION TO BK. 1
THEODORE PRESSER COMPANY   2.75
RABINOFF, S.
MUSICIANSHIP THROUGH IMPROVISATION AT THE KEYBOARD -- THE
IMPROVISER'S KEY GUIDEBOOK, COMPANION TO BK. 1
THEODORE PRESSER COMPANY   2.25
RACHMANINOFF
PIANO PIECES, OP. 10, NOS. 1-7
EDWIN F. KALMUS   3822   1.50
RACHMANINOFF, S.
ALBUM
G. SCHIRMER, INC.   1.50
RACHMANINOFF, S.   3-6
AUSWAHL -- 9 BEL. STUCKE
SCHOTT   517   1.75
RACHMANINOFF, S.
ELEVEN PRELUDES, OP. 23 AND OP. 3, NO. 2
INTERNATIONAL MUSIC COMPANY   3.00
RACHMANINOFF, S.
ETUDES-TABLEAUX, OP. 33 , NOS. 3 AND 5
MCA MUSIC   .75
RACHMANINOFF, S.   MIROVITCH, A.
ETUDES-TABLEAUX, OP. 33 AND 39
MCA MUSIC   4.25
RACHMANINOFF, S.
ETUDES-TABLEAUX, OP. 33, COMPLETE
BOOSEY AND HAWKES, INC.   1.50
RACHMANINOFF, S.
NINE ETUDES TABLEAUX, OP. 39
EDWIN F. KALMUS   3821   2.50
RACHMANINOFF, S.
NINE ETUDES-TABLEAUX, OP. 39
INTERNATIONAL MUSIC COMPANY   25.0

RACHMANINOFF, S.			
PRELUDE CIS-MOLL, ERLEICHTART, OP. 2/3			
UNIVERSAL EDITION	8098	1.65	
RACHMANINOFF, S.			
RADIO CITY ALBUM			
EDWARD B. MARKS MUSIC CORPORATION		01.50	
RACHMANINOFF, S. *			
RRR -- IN 1 BOOK			
ASHLEY DEALERS SERVICE, INC.	HG 09	2.95	
RACHMANINOFF, S.			
SIX ETUDES-TABLEAUX, OP. 33			
INTERNATIONAL MUSIC COMPANY		2.00	
RACHMANINOFF, S.			
SIX ETUDES-TABLEAUX, OP.33			
EDWIN F. KALMUS	3817	2.00	
RACHMANINOFF, S.			
SIX MOMENTS MUSICAUX, OP. 16			
INTERNATIONAL MUSIC COMPANY		2.50	
RACHMANINOFF, S.			
SIX MOMENTS MUSICAUX, OP. 16			
EDWIN F. KALMUS	3820	2.50	
RACHMANINOFF, S.			
TEN PRELUDES, OP. 23			
EDWIN F. KALMUS	3818	1.50	
RACHMANINOFF, S.			
TEN PRELUDES, OP. 23			
EDWARD B. MARKS MUSIC CORPORATION		02.50	
RACHMANINOFF, S.			
TEN PRELUDES, OP. 23			
G. SCHIRMER, INC.	L1630	1.50	
RACHMANINOFF, S.			
TEN PRELUDES, OP. 23 --COMPLETE--			
BOOSEY AND HAWKES, INC.		1.75	
RACHMANINOFF, S. PHILIPP, I.			
THIRTEEN PRELUDES, OP. 32			
INTERNATIONAL MUSIC COMPANY		3.00	
RACHMANINOFF, S.			
THIRTEEN PRELUDES, OP. 32			
EDWARD B. MARKS MUSIC CORPORATION		02.50	
RACHMANINOFF, S.			
THIRTEEN PRELUDES, OP. 32			
G. SCHIRMER, INC.	L1631	1.50	
RACHMANINOFF, S.			
THIRTEEN PRELUDES, OP. 32 - COMPLETE			
BOOSEY AND HAWKES, INC.		1.75	
RACHMANINOFF, S. PHILIPP, I.			
TWENTY-FOUR PRELUDES, COMPLETE			
INTERNATIONAL MUSIC COMPANY		6.00	
RAKOV MAIER			
FROM YOUTHFUL DAYS - TEN PIECES FOR STUDENTS			
MCA MUSIC		1.25	
RAMEAU MOTCHANE			
GRADED RAMEAU, THE			
BELWIN-MILLS PUBLISHING CORPORATION		3.00	
RAMEAU			
NOUVELLES SUITES			
BROUDE BROTHERS LTD.		20.00	
RAMEAU JACOBI, W			
PIECES DE CLAVECIN			
BARENREITER VERLAG	BA 3800	17.50	
RAMEAU JACOBI, W. 3-4			
PIECES DE CLAVECIN			
BARENREITER VERLAG	BA 3800		
RAMEAU			
PIECES DE CLAVECIN			
ELKAN-VOGEL, INC.	D	7.70	
RAMEAU			
PIECES DE CLAVECIN			
INTERNATIONAL MUSIC COMPANY		5.00	
RAMEAU			
PIECES DE CLAVECIN - 1731			
BROUDE BROTHERS LTD.		20.00	
RAMEAU JACOBI, W.			
PIECES DE CLAVECIN EN CONCERTS			
BARENREITER VERLAG	BA 3803	16.00	
RAMEAU			
SELECTED PIECES FOR PIANO			
EDWARD B. MARKS MUSIC CORPORATION		03.00	
RAMIREZ, L. A.			
TEN IMPROVISATIONS FOR PIANO			
SEESAW MUSIC CORPORATION		5.00	
RAMSEY, A.			
NOTE GAMES			
THEODORE PRESSER COMPANY		.50	
RANDOLPH, J.--ED RANDOLPH, J.			
SABBATH DAY MUSIC			
THEODORE PRESSER COMPANY		3.75	
RAPHAEL, G. 1-2			
ADVENT- UND WEIHNACHTSLIEDER IN 25 LEICHTEN SATZEN			
BARENREITER VERLAG	SM 2325		
RAPHAEL, G.			
RAPHAEL			
MUSIC SALES CORPORATION	060002	2.95	
RAPHLING			
AMERICAN ALBUM			
THEODORE PRESSER COMPANY		3.00	
RAPHLING			
AMUSEMENT PARK - EASY SUITE			
GENERAL MUSIC PUBLISHING COMPANY, INC.		2.00	
RAPHLING			
CANDID CAMERA - FOR YOUNGEST PIANISTS			
GENERAL MUSIC PUBLISHING COMPANY, INC.	280	2.25	
RAPHLING			
CHILD'S PLAY			
GENERAL MUSIC PUBLISHING COMPANY, INC.	299	2.00	
RAPHLING			
CHILD'S PLAY - TWELVE PIECES FOR THE GROWING PIANIST			
GENERAL MUSIC PUBLISHING COMPANY, INC.		2.00	
RAPHLING			
FIVE FORECASTS FOR PIANO			
MCA MUSIC		.75	
RAPHLING			
FOLKSONG PIANO RECITAL			
MUSIC SALES CORPORATION	040042	2.95	
RAPHLING			
ILLUSTRATED ALPHABET			
GENERAL MUSIC PUBLISHING COMPANY, INC.	278	2.00	
RAPHLING			
ILLUSTRATED ALPHABET - FOR PIANO AND CHILDREN			
GENERAL MUSIC PUBLISHING COMPANY, INC.		2.00	
RAPHLING			
INPUT AND OUTPUT - FOR THE YOUNGEST PIANIST			
GENERAL MUSIC PUBLISHING COMPANY, INC.		1.50	
RAPHLING			
INPUT AND OUTPUT - FOR THE YOUNGEST PIANISTS			
GENERAL MUSIC PUBLISHING COMPANY, INC.	278	1.25	
RAPHLING			
NINE ENCORE PIECES			
BELWIN-MILLS PUBLISHING CORPORATION	11591	2.00	
RAPHLING			
SEVEN MOBILES			
GENERAL MUSIC PUBLISHING COMPANY, INC.	274	2.00	
RAPHLING			
SEVEN PIECES WITHOUT			
GENERAL MUSIC PUBLISHING COMPANY, INC.	275	2.00	
RAPHLING			
SEVEN PIECES WITHOUT			
GENERAL MUSIC PUBLISHING COMPANY, INC.		2.00	
RAPHLING			
SEVENTEEN CONTEMPORARY DANCES			
BELWIN-MILLS PUBLISHING CORPORATION	11584	1.75	
RAPHLING			
SIX INDISCRETIONS			
GENERAL MUSIC PUBLISHING COMPANY, INC.	276	2.00	
RAPHLING			
SIX INDISCRETIONS			
GENERAL MUSIC PUBLISHING COMPANY, INC.		2.00	
RAPHLING			
SIX TINY SONATAS			
GENERAL MUSIC PUBLISHING COMPANY, INC.	604	2.50	
RAPHLING			
SIX TINY SONATAS			
GENERAL MUSIC PUBLISHING COMPANY, INC.		2.50	
RAPHLING			
SOUND TRACKS - SEVEN LITTLE PIECES			
GENERAL MUSIC PUBLISHING COMPANY, INC.		2.00	
RAPHLING			
SOUND TRACKS - 7 LITTLE PIECES			
GENERAL MUSIC PUBLISHING COMPANY, INC.	620	2.00	
RAPHLING			
TIME EXCHANGE - FOR THE YOUNGEST PIANISTS			
GENERAL MUSIC PUBLISHING COMPANY, INC.	283	1.25	
RAPHLING			
TIME-EXCHANGE, THE - FOR THE YOUNGEST PIANIST			
GENERAL MUSIC PUBLISHING COMPANY, INC.		1.25	
RAPHLING			
TWENTY-FOUR ETUDES FOR PIANO, BK. 1			
GENERAL MUSIC PUBLISHING COMPANY, INC.	310	4.00	
RAPHLING			
TWENTY-FOUR ETUDES FOR PIANO, BK. 2			
GENERAL MUSIC PUBLISHING COMPANY, INC.	311	4.00	
RAPHLING			
TWENTY-FOUR ETUDES FOR PIANO, VOL. 1			
GENERAL MUSIC PUBLISHING COMPANY, INC.		5.00	
RAPHLING			
TWENTY-FOUR ETUDES FOR PIANO, VOL. 2			
GENERAL MUSIC PUBLISHING COMPANY, INC.		5.00	
RAPHLING			
TWENTY-SIX CLASSIC DANCES			
BELWIN-MILLS PUBLISHING CORPORATION	11518	1.00	
RAPHLING			
TWENTY-TWO ROMANTIC DANCES			
BELWIN-MILLS PUBLISHING CORPORATION	11519	1.00	
RAPHLING			
TWO ESSAYS FOR PIANO			
GENERAL MUSIC PUBLISHING COMPANY, INC.	295	2.00	
RAPHLING			
TWO ESSAYS FOR PIANO			
GENERAL MUSIC PUBLISHING COMPANY, INC.		3.00	
RAPHLING--ED.			
STUDENT MEETS THE COMPOSER, A			
MUSIC SALES CORPORATION	020108	2.95	
RATHGEBER, V. STEGLICH 2-3			
MUSIKALISCHER ZEITVERTREIB AUF DEM CLAVIER			
BARENREITER VERLAG	NMA 105		
RATHGEBER, V. STEGLICH			
MUSIKALISCHER ZEITVERTREIB--19 PIECES			
ASSOCIATED MUSIC PUBLISHERS, INC.	NAG	1.50	
RAVEL *			
A LA MANIERE DE ... BORODIN, D'INDY, CHABRIER, RAVEL			
FRANCO COLOMBO PUBLICATIONS	SAL	4.00	
RAVEL			
ALBUM			
EDWIN F. KALMUS	3826	2.00	
RAVEL			
GASPARD DE LA NUIT			
ELKAN-VOGEL, INC.		6.00	
RAVEL			
LE TOMBEAU DE COUPERIN			
ELKAN-VOGEL, INC.		6.75	
RAVEL			
MASTERPIECES			
EDWARD B. MARKS MUSIC CORPORATION		02.50	
RAVEL			
MIROIRS			
G. SCHIRMER, INC.	L1586	1.25	
RAVEL 5			
MIROIRS, KOMPLETT			
SCHOTT	1786	8.00	
RAVEL			
MIROIRS, SUITE--COMPLETE			
ASSOCIATED MUSIC PUBLISHERS, INC.	ESC	9.25	
RAVINA, H. 4, 5			
ETUDES MIGNONNES, OP. 60			
ALPHONSE LEDUC			
RAVINA, H.			
HARMONIOUS ETUDES, OP. 50			
G. SCHIRMER, INC.	L1515	1.75	
RAW, W. A. 5-6			
FROM MY SKETCH BOOK, 5 PIECES			
NOVELLO AND COMPANY, LTD.	10.0107.08	1.15	
RAWSTHORNE, A.			
BAGATELLES			
OXFORD UNIVERSITY PRESS	32.808	1.80	
RAWSTHORNE, A.			
FOUR ROMANTIC PIECES			
OXFORD UNIVERSITY PRESS	32.907	1.75	
REBE			
TUNES FROM FAR AND NEAR			
BOSTON MUSIC COMPANY		1.00	
PEBE--ED. REBE			
SIX POLISH CHRISTMAS CAROLS			
G. SCHIRMER, INC.		.60	
REBIKOV ANSON, G. ELEMENTARY			
ANSON INTRODUCES REBIKOV, BK. 1			
WILLIS MUSIC COMPANY		1.00	
REBIKOV			
PICTURES FOR CHILDREN, OP. 37			
INTERNATIONAL MUSIC COMPANY		1.00	
REBIKOV FREY			
SILHOUETTES, OP. 31			
ASSOCIATED MUSIC PUBLISHERS, INC.	ESC	1.00	

REBIKOV　　　　　　　　　DEIS
　　SILHOUETTES, OP. 31--9 CHILDHOOD PICTURES
　　　　G. SCHIRMER, INC.　　　　　　　　　L1474　　　.75
REDA
　　CHORAL-SPIEL-BUCH
　　　　BARENREITER VERLAG　　　　　　　　BA 2064　　6.00
REDA　　　　　　　　　　　　　　　　　2-3
　　CHORAL-SPIEL-BUCH, 30 CHORALSATZE
　　　　BARENREITER VERLAG　　　　　　　　BA 2064
REDA
　　TWELVE MINNELIEDER -- 2 AND 4 HANDS
　　　　BARENREITER VERLAG　　　　　　　　BA 2072　　3.25
REDA　　　　　　　　　　　　　　　　　2
　　ZEHN WEIHNACHTSLIEDER
　　　　BARENREITER VERLAG　　　　　　　　BA 2082
REDA
　　ZEHN WEIHNACHTSLIEDER, AM KLAVIER ZU SINGEN UND ZU SPIELEN
　　　　BARENREITER VERLAG　　　　　　　　BA 2082　　1.25
REDA　　　　　　　　　　　　　　　　　3
　　ZWOLF MINNELIEDER
　　　　BARENREITER VERLAG　　　　　　　　BA 2072
REE-BERNARD
　　SPANISH MUSIC OF THE 15TH AND 16TH CENTURIES FOR THE HARPSICHORD
　　　　C. F. PETERS CORPORATION　　　　　B934　　　2.00
REED, H. O.
　　THREE NATIONALITIES
　　　　BELWIN-MILLS PUBLISHING CORPORATION　20307　　.85
REGER　　　　　　　　　　　　　　　　3-4
　　AQUARELLEN OP. 25, ST.-V.S. 38
　　　　SCHOTT　　　　　　　　　　　　321　　　2.50
REGER
　　AUS MEINEM TAGEBUCH, FROM MY DIARY, OP. 82, BK. 1--12 PIECES
　　　　ASSOCIATED MUSIC PUBLISHERS, INC.　BOT　　　3.75
REGER
　　AUS MEINEM TAGEBUCH, FROM MY DIARY, OP. 82, BK. 2--10 PIECES
　　　　ASSOCIATED MUSIC PUBLISHERS, INC.　BOT　　　3.00
REGER
　　AUS MEINEM TAGEBUCH, FROM MY DIARY, OP. 82, BKS. 3-4
　　　　ASSOCIATED MUSIC PUBLISHERS, INC.　BOT　　　5.00
REGER
　　BLATTER UND BLUTEN, LEAVES AND BLOSSOMS
　　　　ASSOCIATED MUSIC PUBLISHERS, INC.　BRH　　　3.00
REGER　　　　　　　　　　　　　　　　M-D
　　DREAMS AT THE FIRESIDE --TRAEUME AM KAMIN--, OP. 143
　　　　C. F. PETERS CORPORATION　　　　　3992　　　2.00
REGER
　　EIGHT EPISODES, OP. 115
　　　　ASSOCIATED MUSIC PUBLISHERS, INC.　BOT　　　5.00
REGER
　　EIGHT EPISODES, OP. 115, BK. 1
　　　　ASSOCIATED MUSIC PUBLISHERS, INC.　BOT　　　2.25
REGER
　　EIGHT EPISODES, OP. 115, BK. 2
　　　　ASSOCIATED MUSIC PUBLISHERS, INC.　BOT　　　2.25
REGER　　　　　　　　　　　　　　　　D
　　FANTASY PIECES, OP. 26
　　　　C. F. PETERS CORPORATION　　　　　1227　　　4.00
REGER
　　FIVE HUMORESQUES
　　　　UNIVERSAL EDITION　　　　　　　　1173　　　1.95
REGER　　　　　　　　　　　　　　　　3-5
　　IMPROVISATIONEN OP. 18 -- BK. 1, ST.-V.S. 30
　　　　SCHOTT　　　　　　　　　　　　319　　　2.25
REGER　　　　　　　　　　　　　　　　3-5
　　IMPROVISATIONEN OP. 18 -- BK. 2, ST.-V.S. 30
　　　　SCHOTT　　　　　　　　　　　　320　　　2.25
REGER　　　　　　　　　　　　　　　　2-3
　　JUGENDALBUM OP. 17 -- BK. 1 ST.-V.S. 28
　　　　SCHOTT　　　　　　　　　　　　2171　　　2.50
REGER　　　　　　　　　　　　　　　　2-3
　　JUGENDALBUM OP. 17 -- BK. 2 ST.-V.S. 28
　　　　SCHOTT　　　　　　　　　　　　2172　　　2.50
REGER　　　　　　　　　　　　　　　　3-5
　　LOSE BLATTER OP. 13 -- BK. 1 ST.-V.S. 20
　　　　SCHOTT　　　　　　　　　　　　314　　　2.25
REGER　　　　　　　　　　　　　　　　3-5
　　LOSE BLATTER OP. 13 -- BK. 2 ST.-V.S. 20
　　　　SCHOTT　　　　　　　　　　　　315　　　2.25
REGER　　　　　　　　　　　　　　　　3-5
　　SIEBEN WALZER OP. 11 -- BK. 1 ST.-V.S. 18
　　　　SCHOTT　　　　　　　　　　　　312　　　2.50
REGER　　　　　　　　　　　　　　　　3-5
　　SIEBEN WALZER OP. 11 -- BK. 2 ST.-V.S. 18
　　　　SCHOTT　　　　　　　　　　　　313　　　2.50
REGER　　　　　　　　　　　　　　　　D
　　SIX PIANO PIECES, OP. 24
　　　　C. F. PETERS CORPORATION　　　　　1226　　　4.00
REGER
　　SIX PRELUDES AND FUGUES, OP. 99--BK. 1
　　　　ASSOCIATED MUSIC PUBLISHERS, INC.　BOT　　　4.00
REGER
　　SIX PRELUDES AND FUGUES, OP. 99--BK. 2
　　　　ASSOCIATED MUSIC PUBLISHERS, INC.　BOT　　　4.00
REGER
　　TEN PIECES, OP. 79A
　　　　FRANCO COLOMBO PUBLICATIONS　　　SIK.456　3.75
REGER
　　TEN SHORT COMPOSITIONS, OP. 44
　　　　UNIVERSAL EDITION　　　　　　　　1219　　　1.95
REGER　　　　　　　　　PRESSER
　　VARIATIONS AND FUGUE ON A THEME BY BACH, OP. 81
　　　　ASSOCIATED MUSIC PUBLISHERS, INC.　BOT　　　5.00
REGER　　　　　　　　　　　　　　　　4
　　ZWANZIG DEUTSCHE TANZE OP. 10 -- BK. 1 ST.-V.S. 14
　　　　SCHOTT　　　　　　　　　　　　541　　　2.75
REHBERG　　　　　　　　　　　　　　　1-2
　　NEUER ETUDENGANG -- BK. 1
　　　　SCHOTT　　　　　　　　　　　　2351　　　2.50
REHBERG　　　　　　　　　　　　　　　1-2
　　NEUER ETUDENGANG -- BK. 2
　　　　SCHOTT　　　　　　　　　　　　2352　　　2.50
REHBERG--ED.　　　　　REHBERG　　　　　2-3
　　ALTE HAUSMUSIK FUR KLAVIER -- 1550-1780 -- AUS DEUTSCHLAND,
　　ENGLAND, FRANKREICH, UND ITALIEN -- VOL. 1
　　　　SCHOTT　　　　　　　　　　　　2347　　　2.75
REHBERG--ED.　　　　　REHBERG　　　　　2-3
　　ALTE HAUSMUSIK FUR KLAVIER -- 1550-1780 -- AUS DEUTSCHLAND,
　　ENGLAND, FRANKREICH, UND ITALIEN -- VOL. 2
　　　　SCHOTT　　　　　　　　　　　　2348　　　2.75
REHBERG--ED.　　　　　REHBERG　　　　　2-3
　　ALTE HAUSMUSIK FUR KLAVIER -- 1550-1780 AUS DEUTSCHLAND,
　　ENGLAND, FRANKREICH UND ITALIEN, BK. 1
　　　　SCHOTT　　　　　　　　　　　　2347　　　2.75
REHBERG--ED.　　　　　REHBERG　　　　　2-3
　　ALTE HAUSMUSIK FUR KLAVIER -- 1550-1780 AUS DEUTSCHLAND,
　　ENGLAND, FRANKREICH UND ITALIEN, BK. 2
　　　　SCHOTT　　　　　　　　　　　　2348　　　2.75

REHBERG--ED.　　　　　REHBERG　　　　　2-4
　　DAS KLASSIKER-BUCH, BAND 01
　　　　SCHOTT　　　　　　　　　　　　5790　　　3.00
REHBERG--ED.　　　　　REHBERG　　　　　2-4
　　DAS KLASSIKER-BUCH, BAND 02
　　　　SCHOTT　　　　　　　　　　　　5791　　　3.00
REHBERG--ED.　　　　　REHBERG　　　　　2-4
　　DAS KLASSIKERBUCH, KOMPLETT IN LEINEN GEBUNDEN
　　　　SCHOTT　　　　　　　　　　　　　　　　10.00
REHBERG--ED.　　　　　REHBERG　　　　　2-3
　　DIE SOHNE BACH -- ORIGINAL-KLAVIER-WERKE DER 4 SOHNE BACHS
　　　　SCHOTT　　　　　　　　　　　　1519　　　2.75
REHBERG--ED.　　　　　REHBERG
　　NEUER ETUDENGANG, BK. 1
　　　　SCHOTT　　　　　　　　　　　　2351　　　2.50
REHBERG--ED.　　　　　REHBERG
　　NEUER ETUDENGANG, BK. 2
　　　　SCHOTT　　　　　　　　　　　　2352　　　2.50
REHBERG--ED.　　　　　REHBERG　　　　　2
　　VON BACH BIS BEETHOVEN -- 41 LEICHTE ORIG.-STUCKE, BK. 1
　　　　SCHOTT　　　　　　　　　　　　2174　　　1.25
REHBERG--ED.　　　　　REHBERG　　　　　2
　　VON BACH BIS BEETHOVEN -- 41 LEICHTE ORIG.-STUCKE, BK. 2
　　　　SCHOTT　　　　　　　　　　　　2175　　　1.25
REICHA, A.
　　PIANO WORKS
　　　　G. HENLE MUSIKVERLAG　　　　　　254
REIF, P.
　　SEVEN MUSICAL MOMENTS
　　　　GENERAL MUSIC PUBLISHING COMPANY, INC.　419　2.50
REIF, P.
　　SEVEN MUSICAL MOMENTS
　　　　NOVELLO AND COMPANY, LTD.　　　　　　　4.65
REIN　　　　　　　　　　　　　　　　3
　　KLAVIERMUSIK NACH VOLKSLIEDERN
　　　　SCHOTT　　　　　　　　　　　　4619　　　2.00
REIN--ED *　　　　　　REIN *　　　　　2-3
　　DER WUNDERGARTEN
　　　　SCHOTT　　　　　　　　　　　　4501-3　　5.00
REINER　　　　　　　　　　　　　　　4-5
　　DREI KOMPOSITIONEN
　　　　BARENREITER VERLAG　　　　　　　AP 1751
REINER　　　　　　　　　　　　　　　2
　　SIEBEN KLAVIERSTUCKE FUR KINDER
　　　　BARENREITER VERLAG
REINHOLD, H.　　　　　OESTERLE
　　MINIATURES--24 EASY PIECES FOR THE DEVELOPMENT OF MUSICAL
　　STYLE--OP. 39
　　　　G. SCHIRMER, INC.　　　　　　　L700　　　1.00
REINKEN, J. A. *　　　BUCHMAYER
　　EARLY KEYBOARD WORKS -- BK. 4
　　　　ASSOCIATED MUSIC PUBLISHERS, INC.　BRH　　　2.00
REISTRUP, J.　　　　　　　　　　　M-D
　　TOMMELISE -- COMPLETE
　　　　COMPOSERS PRESS, INC.　　　　　　　　　　6.00
REITER, A.
　　TWO SONATINAS
　　　　ASSOCIATED MUSIC PUBLISHERS, INC.　SIM　　　1.25
REIZENSTEIN, F.　　　　　　　　　　ME
　　THREE PIECES
　　　　OXFORD UNIVERSITY PRESS　　　　　33.061　　1.30
REIZENSTEIN, F.　　　　　　　　　　E
　　THREE SHORT STORIES
　　　　OXFORD UNIVERSITY PRESS　　　　　33.062　　1.25
REJCHA　　　　　　　　SETKOVA　　　　3-4
　　L'ART DE VARIER, OP. 57
　　　　BARENREITER VERLAG　　　　　　　MAB 50
REJCHA　　　　　　　　SETKOVA
　　L'ART DE VARIER, OP. 57
　　　　BARENREITER VERLAG　　　　　　　MAB 50
REJCHA　　　　　　　　　　　　　　　3-4
　　ZEHN FUGEN
　　　　BARENREITER VERLAG　　　　　　　AP 684
REMACHA, F.
　　THREE PIECES
　　　　ASSOCIATED MUSIC PUBLISHERS, INC.　UME　　　1.50
REMARK, M.
　　IDEAL PIANO SERIES, BK. 1
　　　　WILLIS MUSIC COMPANY　　　　　　　　　　1.25
REMARK, M.
　　IDEAL PIANO SERIES, BK. 2
　　　　WILLIS MUSIC COMPANY　　　　　　　　　　1.25
REMARK, M.
　　IDEAL WRITING SERIES, BK. 1
　　　　WILLIS MUSIC COMPANY　　　　　　　　　　1.25
REMARK, M.
　　IDEAL WRITING SERIES, BK. 2
　　　　WILLIS MUSIC COMPANY　　　　　　　　　　1.25
RENNICK, E.
　　HYMN TUNES FOR BEGINNERS
　　　　BELWIN-MILLS PUBLISHING CORPORATION　11241　1.50
RENNICK, E.
　　LET'S PLAY TRIOS
　　　　BELWIN-MILLS PUBLISHING CORPORATION　　　1.25
RENZI
　　FIVE PIECES
　　　　FRANCO COLOMBO PUBLICATIONS　　Z4217　　2.00
RESCHOFSKY, A.--ED　　RESCHOFSKY, A.
　　FORTY-FOUR SMALL PIANO PIECES BY NINE HUNGARIAN COMPOSERS, BK. 1
　　　　KULTURA　　　　　　　　　　　　　　　　1.75
RESCHOFSKY, A.--ED　　RESCHOFSKY, A.
　　FORTY-FOUR SMALL PIANO PIECES BY NINE HUNGARIAN COMPOSERS, BK. 2
　　　　KULTURA　　　　　　　　　　　　　　　　1.75
RESPIGHI
　　ANCIENT DANCES AND AIRS - SELECTIONS FROM SUITES 1 AND 2
　　　　FRANCO COLOMBO PUBLICATIONS　　117515　　1.75
RETI, R.
　　MAGIC GATE, THE
　　　　BROUDE BROTHERS LTD.　　　　　　　　　　03.75
RETTENBERG--ED　　　　RETTENBERG
　　CORRIDA -- 10 OF SPAIN'S MOST POPULAR PASODOBLES IN SIMPLIFIED
　　ARRANGEMENTS
　　　　ASSOCIATED MUSIC PUBLISHERS, INC.　AMP　　　.85
REUTTER, H.　　　　　　　　　　　3
　　DIE PASSION IN 9 INVENTIONEN, OP. 25
　　　　SCHOTT　　　　　　　　　　　　2137　　　2.50
REUTTER, H.　　　　　　　　　　　3-4
　　KLEINE KLAVIERSTUCKE, OP. 28
　　　　SCHOTT　　　　　　　　　　　　1415　　　2.00
REVILLE, H.
　　SIX PIECES VILLAGEOISES
　　　　ASSOCIATED MUSIC PUBLISHERS, INC.　ESC　　　3.00
RHENE-BATON
　　ALBUM ROSE, EASY LITTLE PIECES--COMPLETE
　　　　ASSOCIATED MUSIC PUBLISHERS, INC.　ESC　　　2.25
RHENE-BATON
　　EN BRETAGNE, OP. 13 -- COMPLETE
　　　　ELKAN-VOGEL, INC.　　　　　　　　D　　　6.60

RHENE-BATON
  POUR YVONNE, 3 EASY LITTLE PIECES
    ASSOCIATED MUSIC PUBLISHERS, INC.   ESC   1.50
RIBARI, A.
  SIX ETUDES
    GENERAL MUSIC PUBLISHING COMPANY, INC.   3.00
RICHARDSON
  FOR CHILDREN
    BOSTON MUSIC COMPANY   1.00
RICHARDSON, A.
  KIDDY CAROL BOOK
    WILLIS MUSIC COMPANY   .75
RICHARDSON, A.
  SING WE NOW OF CHRISTMAS
    WILLIS MUSIC COMPANY   .50
RICHARTZ   3
  RHEINH. VOLKSTANZE, OP. 69
    SCHOTT   3962   1.50
RICHTER
  ADA RICHTER CHRISTMAS CAROL BOOK, THE
    WARNER BROTHERS PUBLISHERS   AR 20   1.25
RICHTER
  ADA RICHTER PIANO COURSE, BOOK 1
    WARNER BROTHERS PUBLISHERS   AR 3   1.25
RICHTER
  ADA RICHTER PIANO COURSE, BOOK 2
    WARNER BROTHERS PUBLISHERS   AR 4   1.50
RICHTER
  ADA RICHTER PIANO COURSE, BOOK 3
    WARNER BROTHERS PUBLISHERS   AR 5   1.50
RICHTER
  ADA RICHTER PIANO COURSE, BOOK 4
    WARNER BROTHERS PUBLISHERS   AR 6   1.50
RICHTER
  DOWN MEMORY LANE
    WARNER BROTHERS PUBLISHERS   AR 21   1.25
RICHTER
  FIRST LITTLE TUNES
    WARNER BROTHERS PUBLISHERS   AR 23   1.25
RICHTER
  FOLK SONGS OF TODAY
    WARNER BROTHERS PUBLISHERS   AR 24   1.25
RICHTER   2
  JUST FOR ME
    ASHLEY DEALERS SERVICE, INC.   1.00
RICHTER   2
  JUST FOR ME
    CENTURY MUSIC PUBLISHING COMPANY, INC.   1.00
RICHTER
  KINDERGARTEN CLASS BOOK
    THEODORE PRESSER COMPANY   2.00
RICHTER
  LITTLE HYMNAL FOR PIANO, A
    WARNER BROTHERS PUBLISHERS   AR 25   1.50
RICHTER
  MY FIRST NOTE BOOK, BK. 1
    THEODORE PRESSER COMPANY   1.00
RICHTER
  MY FIRST NOTE BOOK, BK. 2
    THEODORE PRESSER COMPANY   1.00
RICHTER
  MY PIANO BOOK, BK. 1
    THEODORE PRESSER COMPANY   1.25
RICHTER
  MY PIANO BOOK, BK. 2
    THEODORE PRESSER COMPANY   1.25
RICHTER
  MY PIANO BOOK, BK. 3
    THEODORE PRESSER COMPANY   1.50
RICHTER
  NUMBER SONGS
    WARNER BROTHERS PUBLISHERS   AR 26   1.25
RICHTER
  OLDER STUDENT, BK. 1
    WARNER BROTHERS PUBLISHERS   AR 7   1.50
RICHTER
  OLDER STUDENT, BK. 2
    WARNER BROTHERS PUBLISHERS   AR 8   1.50
RICHTER
  OLDER STUDENT, BK. 3
    WARNER BROTHERS PUBLISHERS   AR 9   1.50
RICHTER
  PIANO WARM-UPS
    WARNER BROTHERS PUBLISHERS   AR 15   1.25
RICHTER
  PRE-SCHOOL AND KINDERGARTEN BOOK
    WARNER BROTHERS PUBLISHERS   AR 1   1.25
RICHTER
  READ AND PLAY BY PATTERNS
    BOSTON MUSIC COMPANY   2.50
RICHTER
  SING WITH ME -- SONGS OLD AND NEW
    WARNER BROTHERS PUBLISHERS   AR 28   1.25
RICHTER
  SONGS I CAN PLAY -- FOR THE EARLY BEGINNER
    WARNER BROTHERS PUBLISHERS   AR 29   1.50
RICHTER
  SONGS OF AMERICANS
    WARNER BROTHERS PUBLISHERS   AR 30   1.95
RICHTER
  STEPPING STONES TO THE PIANO
    WARNER BROTHERS PUBLISHERS   AR 2   1.25
RICHTER
  TUNE TIME
    WARNER BROTHERS PUBLISHERS   AR 32   1.25
RICHTER
  TWO CHRISTMAS SONGS -- JINGLE BELLS, JOLLY OLD ST. NICHOLAS,
  WITH WORDS
    WARNER BROTHERS PUBLISHERS   .60
RICHTER
  TWO SHORT SUITES FOR YOUNG PIANISTS
    MCA MUSIC   .60
RICHTER
  YOU ADD THE CHORDS - HOW TO HARMONIZE AT THE PIANO
    THEODORE PRESSER COMPANY   2.00
RICHTER
  YOU CAN PLAY THE PIANO, BK. 1
    THEODORE PRESSER COMPANY   1.50
RICHTER
  YOU CAN PLAY THE PIANO, BK. 2
    THEODORE PRESSER COMPANY   1.50
RICHTER
  YOU CAN PLAY THE PIANO, BK. 3
    THEODORE PRESSER COMPANY   1.50
RICHTER--ED   RICHTER
  DISNEY CLASSICS
    BOURNE COMPANY   1.50

RICHTER--ED   RICHTER
  MADE EASY FOR THE PIANO -- COLE PORTER
    WARNER BROTHERS PUBLISHERS   MEZ 7   1.25
RICHTER--ED   RICHTER
  MADE EASY FOR THE PIANO -- GEORGE GERSHWIN, BK. 1
    WARNER BROTHERS PUBLISHERS   MEZ 1   1.25
RICHTER--ED   RICHTER
  MADE EASY FOR THE PIANO -- GEORGE GERSHWIN, BK. 2
    WARNER BROTHERS PUBLISHERS   MEZ 2   1.25
RICHTER--ED   RICHTER
  MADE EASY FOR THE PIANO -- GEORGE GERSHWIN, BK. 3
    WARNER BROTHERS PUBLISHERS   MEZ 3   1.25
RICHTER--ED   RICHTER
  MADE EASY FOR THE PIANO -- SIGMUND ROMBERG, BK. 2
    WARNER BROTHERS PUBLISHERS   MEZ 8   1.25
RICHTER--ED   RICHTER
  MADE EASY FOR THE PIANO -- VICTOR HERBERT, BK. 1
    WARNER BROTHERS PUBLISHERS   MEZ 4   1.25
RICHTER--ED   RICHTER
  MADE EASY FOR THE PIANO -- VICTOR HERBERT, BK. 2
    WARNER BROTHERS PUBLISHERS   MEZ 5   1.25
RICHTER--ED   RICHTER
  MADE EASY FOR THE PIANO -- VICTOR HERBERT, BK. 3
    WARNER BROTHERS PUBLISHERS   MEZ 6   1.25
RICHTER--ED   RICHTER
  MADE EASY FOR THE PIANO -- VINCENT YOUMANS
    WARNER BROTHERS PUBLISHERS   MEZ 11   1.25
RICHTER--ED   RICHTER
  MADE EASY FOR THE PIANO -- 20TH CENTURY HITS, BK. 1
    WARNER BROTHERS PUBLISHERS   MEZ 9   1.25
RICHTER--ED   RICHTER
  MADE EASY FOR THE PIANO -- 20TH CENTURY HITS, BK. 2
    WARNER BROTHERS PUBLISHERS   MEZ 10   1.25
RICHTER--ED   RICHTER
  MY FIRST HYMNAL --FAVORITE CATHOLIC AND OTHER HYMNS--
    SUMMY-BIRCHARD COMPANY   M-1368   1.50
RICHTER--ED   RICHTER
  PIANO CLASSICS OF FOUR CENTURIES
    WARNER BROTHERS PUBLISHERS   AR 27   1.50
RICHTER--ED   RICHTER
  SNOW WHITE AND THE SEVEN DWARFS
    BOURNE COMPANY   1.50
RICHTER, A.
  EXCITING ADVENTURES - SEVEN DESCRIPTIVE PIANO SOLOS
    THEODORE PRESSER COMPANY   1.25
RICHTER, A.
  INTERNATIONAL CHRISTMAS - 139 SONGS ANDCAROLS
    THEODORE PRESSER COMPANY   3.50
RICHTER, A.   1 1/2
  THREE CHRISTMAS SONGS -- JINGLE BELLS, JOLLY OLD SAINT NICHOLAS,
  SILENT NIGHT
    THEODORE PRESSER COMPANY   .50
RICHTER, A.   1 1/2
  THREE YULETIDE MELODIES -- JOY TO THE WORLD, AWAY IN A MANGER
  AND CHRISTMAS
    THEODORE PRESSER COMPANY   .50
RICHTER, A.--ED.   RICHTER, A.
  CHRISTMAS MELODIES IN EASY ARRANGEMENTS
    THEODORE PRESSER COMPANY   1.00
RICHTER, A.--ED.   RICHTER, A.
  MY OWN HYMN BOOK
    THEODORE PRESSER COMPANY   1.50
RICHTER, A.--ED.   RICHTER, A.
  PLAY AND SING
    THEODORE PRESSER COMPANY   1.50
RICHTER, A.--ED.   RICHTER, A.
  SONGS OF MY COUNTRY
    THEODORE PRESSER COMPANY   1.25
RICHTER, A.--ED.   RICHTER, A.
  SONGS OF STEPHEN FOSTER
    THEODORE PRESSER COMPANY   1.25
RICHTER, A.--ED.   RICHTER, A.
  YOUR FAVORITE SONGS
    THEODORE PRESSER COMPANY   1.50
RICHTER, C.--ED   RICHTER, C.
  FIVE FINGERS ON FIVE KEYS, BK. 01
    BOURNE COMPANY   .75
RICHTER, C.--ED   RICHTER, C.
  FIVE FINGERS ON FIVE KEYS, BK. 02
    BOURNE COMPANY   .75
RICHTER, C.--ED   RICHTER, C.
  MERRY CHRISTMAS MUSIC
    BOURNE COMPANY   .75
RICHTER, C.--ED   RICHTER, C.   1
  MUSIC APPRECIATION SERIES, BK. 01
    BOURNE COMPANY   1.25
RICHTER, C.--ED   RICHTER, C.   2
  MUSIC APPRECIATION SERIES, BK. 02
    BOURNE COMPANY   1.25
RICORDI
  RICORDI ALBUMS - ANTOLOGIA DE MUSICA ARGENTINA -- AGUIRRE,
  GAITO, LOPEZ, BUCHARDO, NAPOLITANO, UGARTE, ETC. --
    FRANCO COLOMBO PUBLICATIONS   BA12033   4.00
RICORDI
  RICORDI ALBUMS - AUTORES PERUANOS - 6 SELECTIONS
    FRANCO COLOMBO PUBLICATIONS   BA10692   2.00
RICORDI
  RICORDI ALBUMS - NEW SONGS OF NAPLES
    FRANCO COLOMBO PUBLICATIONS   128620   1.50
RICORDI
  RICORDI ALBUMS - 30 CLASSICAL AND ROMANTIC PIECES
    FRANCO COLOMBO PUBLICATIONS   127450   2.50
RIE, B.   6
  EXERCICES DES CINQ DOIGTS, OP. 32
    ALPHONSE LEDUC
RIE, B.   8
  RYTHME ET ARTICULATION DES DOIGTS, OP. 42
    ALPHONSE LEDUC
RIEG   TAPPER, B.
  PIANO LYRICS AND SHORTER COMPOSITIONS
    THEODORE PRESSER COMPANY   5.00
RIEGGER, W.   M-D
  FOUR TONE PICTURES, OP. 14
    C. F. PETERS CORPORATION   66016   .90
RIETI
  FIVE PIECES FOR YOUNG PIANISTS
    GENERAL MUSIC PUBLISHING COMPANY, INC.   449   2.50
RIETI
  FIVE PIECES FOR YOUNG PIANISTS
    GENERAL MUSIC PUBLISHING COMPANY, INC.   2.50
RIETI
  SIX SHORT PIECES
    NOVELLO AND COMPANY, LTD.   1.90
RIETI
  SIX SHORT PIECES FOR PIANO
    GENERAL MUSIC PUBLISHING COMPANY, INC.   39   2.00

RIETI
 THREE PRELUDES
  FRANCO COLOMBO PUBLICATIONS SAL 4.25
           1-2
RIHOVSKY
 KINDERHERZEN. 35 KLAVIERSTUCKE
  BARENREITER VERLAG AP 685
RIMSKY-KORSAKOFF
 RADIO CITY ALBUM
  EDWARD B. MARKS MUSIC CORPORATION 01.50
RINALDI
 SORRISI DI BIMBA, BK. 1
  FRANCO COLOMBO PUBLICATIONS 104035 1.25
RIOS, DE LOS--ED. RIOS, DE LOS
 SYMPHONIES FOR PIANO
  THE BIG THREE MUSIC CORPORATION 2.95
RITTER, J. C. JACOBI 2
 DREI SONATEN FUR CEMBALO -- 1751 --
  BARENREITER VERLAG DV 8002
RITTER, J. C. JACOBI
 THREE SONATAS--1751--HARPSICHORD
  ASSOCIATED MUSIC PUBLISHERS, INC. DVM 3.50
RIVERA--ED. RIVERA
 GIMNASIA MUSICAL PARA LA ESCUELA -- MUSIC AND DIAGRAMS FOR
 SCHOOL USE
  ASSOCIATED MUSIC PUBLISHERS, INC. UME 1.10
RIVIER, J.
 FIVE MOUVEMENTS BREFS
  FRANCO COLOMBO PUBLICATIONS SAL 4.00
RIVIER, J.
 FOUR FANTASMES
  GERARD BILLAUDOT EDITIONS MUSICALES 3.30
RIVIER, J.
 MUSIQUES POUR PIANO
  FRANCO COLOMBO PUBLICATIONS SAL 5.25
RIVIER, J.
 TORNADES
  FRANCO COLOMBO PUBLICATIONS SAL 3.25
RIVIER, J.
 TROIS POINTES SECHES
  GERARD BILLAUDOT EDITIONS MUSICALES 2.50
ROBBINS--ED ROBBINS AI
 TIME TO PLAY MARCHES
  WILLIS MUSIC COMPANY 1.00
ROBERTS
 FOUR PRELUDES FOR PIANO
  NOVELLO AND COMPANY, LTD. 10.0116.07 1.25
ROBINSON, E. *
 WORK AND PLAY, BK. 1
  BELWIN-MILLS PUBLISHING CORPORATION 10081 1.00
ROBINSON, E. *
 WORK AND PLAY, BK. 2
  BELWIN-MILLS PUBLISHING CORPORATION 10076 1.00
ROBINSON, G. E. *
 MORE ONCE UPON A TIME STORIES OF THE GREAT MUSIC MASTERS
  THEODORE PRESSER COMPANY 1.50
ROBINSON, G. E. SAWYER, H. *
 ONCE UPON A TIME STORIES OF THE GREAT MUSIC MASTERS
  THEODORE PRESSER COMPANY 1.75
ROBYN
 BOYN-GURLITT --EIGHTY-FIVE ETUDES TO DEVELOP SIGHT-READING,
 PEDAL TECHNIC AND RHYTHM--
  THEODORE PRESSER COMPANY 1.50
ROBYN
 BY WAYS IN ETUDE LAND
  THEODORE PRESSER COMPANY 1.25
ROBYN
 HIGHWAYS IN ETUDE LAND
  THEODORE PRESSER COMPANY 1.00
ROBYN
 KEYBOARD TOWN
  THEODORE PRESSER COMPANY 1.25
ROBYN
 ROBYN ROTE-CARDS
  THEODORE PRESSER COMPANY 1.50
ROBYN *
 ROBYN-HANKS HARMONY, BK. 1
  THEODORE PRESSER COMPANY 1.50
ROBYN *
 ROBYN-HANKS HARMONY, BK. 2
  THEODORE PRESSER COMPANY 1.50
ROBYN *
 ROBYN-HANKS HARMONY, BK. 3
  THEODORE PRESSER COMPANY 1.50
ROBYN
 ROBYN-HANON -- TWENTY-FIVE EXERCISES WITH SPECIAL ANNOTATIONS
 AND EXPLANATIONS FOR THE TEACHER --
  THEODORE PRESSER COMPANY 1.25
ROBYN
 SHORT ETUDES WITH ORNAMENTS FOR PIANO
  THEODORE PRESSER COMPANY .90
ROCHBERG, G.
 TWELVE BAGATELLES
  THEODORE PRESSER COMPANY 2.00
ROCHNER
 BEGINNING PIANO STUDY, PT. 1
  FRANCO COLOMBO PUBLICATIONS ER1921 1.25
ROCHNER
 BEGINNING PIANO STUDY, PT. 2
  FRANCO COLOMBO PUBLICATIONS ER1922 1.25
ROCHNER
 BEGINNING PIANO STUDY, PT. 3
  FRANCO COLOMBO PUBLICATIONS ER1923 1.25
ROCHNER
 BEGINNING PIANO STUDY, PT. 4 BK. 1
  FRANCO COLOMBO PUBLICATIONS ER1924 1.75
ROCHNER
 BEGINNING PIANO STUDY, PT. 4 BK. 2
  FRANCO COLOMBO PUBLICATIONS ER1925 1.25
ROCHNER
 BEGINNING PIANO STUDY, PT. 5
  FRANCO COLOMBO PUBLICATIONS ER1926 1.00
RODGERS SIRMAY
 MEET RICHARD RODGERS AT THE PIANO
  MCA MUSIC 2.00
RODGERS * PELS
 RODGERS AND HAMMERSTEIN ALBUM
  MCA MUSIC 2.00
RODGERS * PORTNOFF
 RODGERS AND HAMMERSTEIN PLAY AND SING--SIMPLIFIED PIANO
 COLLECTION
  MCA MUSIC 2.50
RODGERS * GLOVER
 SOUND OF MUSIC SELECTIONS
  MCA MUSIC 2.50
RODGERS, I.
 FIRST PIANO BOOK FOR LITTLE JACKS AND JILLS, A--FOR
 PRE-SCHOOLERS--WITH WORDS AND ILLUSTRATIONS
  G. SCHIRMER, INC. 1.00

RODGERS, I.
 FOURTH PIANO BOOK FOR JACKS AND JILLS, A--ILLUSTRATED
  G. SCHIRMER, INC. 1.00
RODGERS, I.
 MARCHES AND SONGS WE LOVE--WITH WORDS AND ILLUSTRATIONS
  G. SCHIRMER, INC. .80
RODGERS, I.
 MERRY MELODIES FOR LITTLE JACKS AND JILLS--ILLUSTRATED
  G. SCHIRMER, INC. .75
RODGERS, I.
 SECOND PIANO BOOK FOR LITTLE JACKS AND JILLS, A--ILLUSTRATED
  G. SCHIRMER, INC. 1.00
RODGERS, I.
 THIRD PIANO BOOK FOR LITTLE JACKS AND JILLS, A--ILUSTRATED
  G. SCHIRMER, INC. 1.00
RODGERS, I.
 VACATION SCENES
  G. SCHIRMER, INC. 1.00
RODGERS, I.--ED RODGERS, I.
 AT CHRISTMAS TIDE
  WILLIS MUSIC COMPANY .75
RODGERS, I.--ED RODGERS, I.
 CHRISTMAS CAROLS FOR LITTLE BOYS AND GIRLS
  WILLIS MUSIC COMPANY 1.00
RODGERS, I.--ED RODGERS, I.
 JOLLY CHRISTMAS MELODIES
  WILLIS MUSIC COMPANY 1.00
RODIO M
 FIVE RICERCATE, FANTASIA --1575-- FOR HARPSICHORD OR ORGAN
  C. F. PETERS CORPORATION ZA4162 3.50
RODRIGO, J.
 ALBUM DE CECILIA, EL--6 PIECES IN TREBLE CLEF
  ASSOCIATED MUSIC PUBLISHERS, INC. UME 1.50
RODRIGO, J.
 CUATRO ESTAMPAS ANDALUZAS
  ASSOCIATED MUSIC PUBLISHERS, INC. UME 2.25
RODRIGO, J.
 SONATAS DE CASTILLA CON TOCCATA A MODO DE PREGON
  ASSOCIATED MUSIC PUBLISHERS, INC. UME 2.50
RODRIGO, J.
 SUITE POUR PIANO - PRELUDE, SICILIENNE, BOURREE, MENUET,
 RIGAUDON
  FRANCO COLOMBO PUBLICATIONS SAL 4.25
RODRIGUEZ, R.
 SIX PRELUDES--1925
  ASSOCIATED MUSIC PUBLISHERS, INC. ESC 5.00
ROEHR *
 DAS ERSTE KLAVIERBUCH - METHODISCHER LEITFADEN
  BARENREITER VERLAG EN 808
          1-2
ROEHR *
 DAS ERSTE KLAVIERBUCH, HEFT 1 - DER QUINTRAUM
  BARENREITER VERLAG EN 804
ROEHR *
 DAS ERSTE KLAVIERBUCH, HEFT 1 - DER QUINTRAUM
  BARENREITER VERLAG EN 804
          1-2
ROEHR *
 DAS ERSTE KLAVIERBUCH, HEFT 2 - DER DUR-BEREICH
  BARENREITER VERLAG EN 805
ROEHR *
 DAS ERSTE KLAVIERBUCH, HEFT 2 - DER DUR-BEREICH
  BARENREITER VERLAG EN 805
ROEHR HILLEMANN 1-2
 DAS ERSTE KLAVIERBUCH, HEFT 3 - DER MOLL-BEREICH
  BARENREITER VERLAG EN 806
ROEHR *
 DAS ERSTE KLAVIERBUCH, HEFT 3 - DER MOLL-BEREICH
  BARENREITER VERLAG EN 806
ROEHR--ED. * ROEHR *
 ERSTE KLAVIERBUCH, DAS -- BK. 1, FIVE-FINGER POSITION
  ASSOCIATED MUSIC PUBLISHERS, INC. NAG 1.75
ROEHR--ED. * ROEHR *
 ERSTE KLAVIERBUCH, DAS -- BK. 2, MAJOR KEYS
  ASSOCIATED MUSIC PUBLISHERS, INC. NAG 2.50
ROEHR--ED. * ROEHR *
 ERSTE KLAVIERBUCH, DAS -- BK. 3, MINOR KEYS
  ASSOCIATED MUSIC PUBLISHERS, INC. NAG 2.25
ROENTGEN M
 MUZIKALE DIAS --12 CANONS AND 12 FUGHETTAS IN ALL KEYS--
  C. F. PETERS CORPORATION D374 3.00
ROGER-DUCASSE
 BARCAROLLE NO. 01, 2, 3
  ELKAN-VOGEL, INC. D 3.00
ROGER-DUCASSE
 SIX PRELUDES
  ELKAN-VOGEL, INC. D 3.25
ROGERS 2
 FIVE EASY SOLOS
  BOSTON MUSIC COMPANY .70
ROGERS
 MINIATURES
  THEODORE PRESSER COMPANY .90
ROGERS
 PLAYLAND SKETCHES
  PRO-ART PUBLICATIONS, INC. 811 .85
ROGERS 2
 SHORT AND SWEET -- THREE SOLOS
  BOSTON MUSIC COMPANY .50
ROGERS--ED ROGERS
 HYMNS TO PLAY AND SING
  PRO-ART PUBLICATIONS, INC. 527 .75
ROGERS--ED * ROGERS *
 POP GO THE CLASSICS
  PRO-ART PUBLICATIONS, INC. 1045 2.00
ROGERS--ED. ROGERS
 CHRISTMAS AT THE PIANO
  PRO-ART PUBLICATIONS, INC. 526 1.00
ROGERS, E. T. EASY
 BEST OF YOUNG WORLD
  LILLENAS PUBLISHING COMPANY MB-291 2.50
ROGERS, E. T. 1 1/2 - 2
 FAVORITES FROM THE HYMNAL NO. 1
  LILLENAS PUBLISHING COMPANY MB-046 1.50
ROGERS, E. T. 2 1/2 - 3
 FAVORITES FROM THE HYMNAL NO. 2
  LILLENAS PUBLISHING COMPANY MB-047 1.50
ROGERS, E. T. INTERMEDIATE
 FAVORITES FROM YOUNG WORLD
  LILLENAS PUBLISHING COMPANY MB-292 2.50
ROGERS, E. T. 1
 FIRST BOOK OF FAVORITE HYMNS
  LILLENAS PUBLISHING COMPANY MB-050 1.50
ROGERS, J.
 DEVELOPMENT OF VELOCITY, OP. 40, BK. 1--SCALES
  G. SCHIRMER, INC. 1.25
ROGERS, J.
 DEVELOPMENT OF VELOCITY, OP. 40, BK. 2--ARPEGGIOS
  G. SCHIRMER, INC. 1.25

ROGERS, J.
    FIFTEEN EXERCISES AND STUDIES ON BROKEN CHORDS
        G. SCHIRMER, INC.   1.50

ROGERS, S. E.
    FOUR KEYBOARD SETTINGS OF FOLK TUNES
        HOPE PUBLISHING COMPANY   1.95

ROGERS, W. K.
    SIX SHORT PRELUDES ON A TONE ROW
        ASSOCIATED MUSIC PUBLISHERS, INC.   BER   1.00

ROHOZINSKI
    EIGHT LITTLE PIECES
        FRANCO COLOMBO PUBLICATIONS   SAL   4.00

ROHOZINSKI
    PIECES TRISTES
        FRANCO COLOMBO PUBLICATIONS   SAL   2.75

ROMBERG, S.
    SELECTIONS FROM 'MAYTIME'
        G. SCHIRMER, INC.   1.00

ROMERO--ED   ROMERO
    COLLECCION DE CANTOS E BAILES POPULARES ESPANOLES -- 20 POPULAR
    SPANISH SONGS AND DANCES
        ASSOCIATED MUSIC PUBLISHERS, INC.   UME   4.00

ROPARTZ
    CROQUIS D'AUTOMNE
        FRANCO COLOMBO PUBLICATIONS   SAL   4.25

ROPARTZ
    CROQUIS D'ETE
        FRANCO COLOMBO PUBLICATIONS   SAL   5.50

ROPARTZ
    DANS L'OMBRE DE LA MONTAGNE
        ELKAN-VOGEL, INC.   D   6.50

ROPARTZ
    OVERTURE, VARIATIONS AND FINALE
        FRANCO COLOMBO PUBLICATIONS   SAL   6.50

ROREM, N.   E
    THREE BARCAROLLES
        C. F. PETERS CORPORATION   6447   1.25

ROSAS   3
    OVER THE WAVES, WALTZES
        CENTURY MUSIC PUBLISHING COMPANY, INC.   352   .40

ROSCO
    WHIMSEYS
        CARL FISCHER, INC.   O 4841   1.50

ROSEINGRAVE, T.
    EIGHTS SUITES OF LESSONS
        BROUDE BROTHERS LTD.   22.50

ROSEINGRAVE, T.   STEPHENS   3
    KOMPOSITIONEN FUR ORGEL UND CEMBALO
        BARENREITER VERLAG   PSM 2

ROSEMOND, G.
    ART OF MUSIC FOR THE ADULT BEGINNER, THE
        WILLIS MUSIC COMPANY   2.95

ROSEMOND, G.
    FOUNDATION, THE
        WILLIS MUSIC COMPANY   1.00

ROSENTHAL, M.
    EIGHT BAGATELLES
        FRANCO COLOMBO PUBLICATIONS   SAL   4.25

ROSENTHAL, M.
    LES PETITS METIERS, BK. 1
        ELKAN-VOGEL, INC.   J   2.00

ROSENTHAL, M.
    LES PETITS METIERS, BK. 2
        ELKAN-VOGEL, INC.   J   2.00

ROSNER
    TWELVE TRAVEL TUNES
        MUSICORD PUBLICATIONS, INC.   1.25

ROSSI   PONTI   3
    ZWEI TOCCATEN
        BARENREITER VERLAG   CM 21351

ROSSI, N.
    SCHOOL OF DOUBLE NOTES
        FRANCO COLOMBO PUBLICATIONS   ER2166   2.25

ROSSINI, G. *   E-M
    PIANO ALBUM
        C. F. PETERS CORPORATION   6138   1.50

ROSSINI, G.
    SELECTED OVERTURES -- WITH BELLINI-SELECTED OVERTURES --
        FRANCO COLOMBO PUBLICATIONS   ER1163   4.25

ROTHCHILD, F.
    DANNY'S DOZEN--PIECES FOR YOUNG PEOPLE
        ASSOCIATED MUSIC PUBLISHERS, INC.   AMP   1.00

ROUGNON   3
    LA LECTURE MUSICALE AU PIANO, PART 1
        ALPHONSE LEDUC

ROUGNON   3, 4
    LA LECTURE MUSICALE AU PIANO, PART 2
        ALPHONSE LEDUC

ROVENGER--ED.   ROVENGER
    ADULT PROGRAM ALBUM
        RUBANK, INC.   2.50

ROVENGER--ED.   ROVENGER
    CLASSICAL MINIATURES
        RUBANK, INC.   1.25

ROVENGER--ED.   ROVENGER
    LITTLE CLASSICS
        RUBANK, INC.   1.25

ROVENGER--ED.   ROVENGER
    MARCH KINGS ALBUM FOR PIANO
        RUBANK, INC.   1.50

ROWE, D.
    TONE STORIES
        THEODORE PRESSER COMPANY   1.50

ROWLEY   E-M
    EIGHTEEN STUDIES, OP. 42
        C. F. PETERS CORPORATION   4383A   1.50

ROWLEY   E
    ELVES AND FAIRIES, OP. 38
        C. F. PETERS CORPORATION   4324A   1.50

ROWLEY   D
    ETUDES IN TONALITY, OP. 44
        C. F. PETERS CORPORATION   4387   1.50

ROWLEY
    FIFTEEN LITTLE PICTURES
        ELKAN-VOGEL, INC.   LEM   2.00

ROWLEY
    FIVE BY TEN, WORKS BY CONTEMPORARY ENGLISH COMPOSERS -- GRADE 1,
    VERY EASY TO EASY
        BELWIN-MILLS PUBLISHING CORPORATION   05101   2.00

ROWLEY
    FIVE BY TEN, WORKS BY CONTEMPORARY ENGLISH COMPOSERS -- GRADE 2,
    EASY TO MODERATELY EASY
        BELWIN-MILLS PUBLISHING CORPORATION   05102   2.00

ROWLEY
    FIVE BY TEN, WORKS BY CONTEMPORARY ENGLISH COMPOSERS -- GRADE 3,
    MODERATELY EASY TO MODERATE
        BELWIN-MILLS PUBLISHING CORPORATION   05103   2.00

ROWLEY
    FIVE BY TEN, WORKS BY CONTEMPORARY ENGLISH COMPOSERS -- GRADE 4,
    MODERATE TO MODERATELY DIFFICULT
        BELWIN-MILLS PUBLISHING CORPORATION   05104   2.00

ROWLEY
    FIVE BY TEN, WORKS BY CONTEMPORARY ENGLISH COMPOSERS -- GRADE 5,
    MODERATELY DIFFICULT TO DIFFICULT
        BELWIN-MILLS PUBLISHING CORPORATION   05105   2.00

ROWLEY
    FIVE LYRIC STUDIES
        BOOSEY AND HAWKES, INC.   1.25

ROWLEY
    FOUR LITTLE INVENTIONS
        BOOSEY AND HAWKES, INC.   1.00

ROWLEY   E-M
    FROM MY SKETCH BOOK, OP. 39
        C. F. PETERS CORPORATION   4367A   1.50

ROWLEY   M-D
    POLYRHYTHMS, OP. 50
        C. F. PETERS CORPORATION   4389   2.50

ROWLEY   E
    RECREATION, OP. 37
        C. F. PETERS CORPORATION   4323   1.50

ROWLEY
    SKETCHES
        SUMMY-BIRCHARD COMPANY   1.50

ROWLEY
    THREE NOVELETTES
        BOOSEY AND HAWKES, INC.   1.00

ROWLEY
    TWELVE LITTLE FANTASY STUDIES, OP. 13
        BOOSEY AND HAWKES, INC.   1.25

ROWLEY   E-M
    TWELVE STUDIES, OP. 43
        C. F. PETERS CORPORATION   4383B   1.50

ROWLEY   E-M
    TWO SONATINAS, OP. 40 --AUTUMN - WINTER--
        C. F. PETERS CORPORATION   4382B   1.50

ROWLEY   E-M
    TWO SONATINAS, OP. 40 --SPRING - SUMMER--
        C. F. PETERS CORPORATION   4382A   1.50

ROZIN
    LET'S PLAY A JOKE
        BELWIN-MILLS PUBLISHING CORPORATION   1.00

ROZIN
    LET'S PLAY A LIMERICK
        BELWIN-MILLS PUBLISHING CORPORATION   1.00

ROZIN
    LET'S PLAY A RIDDLE
        BELWIN-MILLS PUBLISHING CORPORATION   1.00

ROZIN
    PLAYFUL PIANO --8 EASY SOLOS--
        THEODORE PRESSER COMPANY   1.25

ROZIN
    TWELVE PIANO IMPRESSIONS
        BELWIN-MILLS PUBLISHING CORPORATION   1.00

ROZIN
    TWO COUNTRYSIDE SKETCHES
        SAM FOX PUBLISHING COMPANY, INC.   .50

ROZIN--ED   ROZIN, A.
    FAMOUS MELODIES IN FIVE FINGER POSITION
        SAM FOX PUBLISHING COMPANY, INC.   1.25

ROZIN--ED   ROZIN
    TRADITIONAL HEBREW SONGS
        PRO-ART PUBLICATIONS, INC.   1080   2.00

ROZSA, M.
    KALEIDOSCOPE
        ASSOCIATED MUSIC PUBLISHERS, INC.   AMP   1.50

ROZSA, M.
    SIX BAGATELLES, OP. 12--1932
        ASSOCIATED MUSIC PUBLISHERS, INC.   BRH   2.00

RUBINSTEIN   D
    ALBUM
        C. F. PETERS CORPORATION   3788   5.00

RUBINSTEIN
    DAY IN THE COUNTRY, A
        CARL FISCHER, INC.   O 3389   1.00

RUBINSTEIN
    RADIO CITY ALBUM
        EDWARD B. MARKS MUSIC CORPORATION   01.50

RUBINSTEIN   TAGLIAPIETRA
    SIX ETUDES, OP. 23
        FRANCO COLOMBO PUBLICATIONS   ER471   2.00

RUBINSTEIN   GALLICO
    SIX ETUDES, OP. 23
        G. SCHIRMER, INC.   1.50

RUBINSTEIN   D
    SIX STUDIES, OP. 23
        C. F. PETERS CORPORATION   1009   5.00

RUEFF   2, 4
    VACANCES POUR PIANO, ALBUM 1
        ALPHONSE LEDUC

RUEFF   4, 6
    VACANCES POUR PIANO, ALBUM 2
        ALPHONSE LEDUC

RUMSHINSKY
    SKIDMORE MODERN KEYBOARD SERIES --INTERMEDIATE --GREEN SERIES
    --BAZAARS OF BAGDAD
        SHAPIRO, BERNSTEIN ORGANIZATION   .75

RUSSELL   2
    GUESS AGAIN - FOUR SOLOS
        BOSTON MUSIC COMPANY   .50

RUSSELL
    MY FIRST MUSIC BOOK
        BELWIN-MILLS PUBLISHING CORPORATION   1.00

RUST   D'INDY *
    TWELVE SONATAS
        FRANCO COLOMBO PUBLICATIONS   SAL   8.75

RUTHARDT--ED   RUTHARDT   M-D
    RONDO ALBUM
        C. F. PETERS CORPORATION   2123   3.50

RUTINI   ILLY
    SIX SONATAS, OP. 3
        FRANCO COLOMBO PUBLICATIONS   DS1051   6.50

RUTINI   ILLY
    SIX SONATAS, OP. 5
        FRANCO COLOMBO PUBLICATIONS   DS1063   9.00

RUTINI   ILLY
    SIX SONATAS, OP. 6
        FRANCO COLOMBO PUBLICATIONS   DS1053   6.50

SACCHI
    FOUR EASY LITTLE PIECES
        FRANCO COLOMBO PUBLICATIONS   BON.1955   1.50

SACCO   GR. 1-6
    ANCIENT TO MODERN
        WESTERN INTERNATIONAL MUSIC, INC.   OP124   2.50

SACHSE, H. W.
  SIX BAGATELLES, OP. 76--1964
    ASSOCIATED MUSIC PUBLISHERS, INC.   BRH   2.25
            M-D
SAEVERUD
  PEER GYNT, OP. 28. 11 EXCERPTS
    C. F. PETERS CORPORATION   MH18   2.50
            M
SAEVERUD
  SIX SONATINAS, OP. 30
    C. F. PETERS CORPORATION   MH19   1.50
            M
SAEVERUD
  TUNES AND DANCES FROM SILJUSTOL. VOL. 1. OP. 21
    C. F. PETERS CORPORATION   MH6   1.25
            M
SAEVERUD
  TUNES AND DANCES FROM SILJUSTOL. VOL. 2. OP. 22
    C. F. PETERS CORPORATION   MH7   1.25
            M
SAEVERUD
  TUNES AND DANCES FROM SILJUSTOL. VOL. 3. OP. 24
    C. F. PETERS CORPORATION   MH12   1.25
            M
SAEVERUD
  TUNES AND DANCES FROM SILJUSTOL. VOL. 4. OP. 25
    C. F. PETERS CORPORATION   MH13   1.25
SAINT-SAENS
  ALBUM, OP. 72
    ELKAN-VOGEL, INC.   D   7.50
SAINT-SAENS
  CARNIVAL OF THE
                  ANIMALS
    ELKAN-VOGEL, INC.   4.75
SAINT-SAENS
  SIX BAGATELLES, OP. 3
    ELKAN-VOGEL, INC.   D   3.75
SAINT-SAENS
  SIX ETUDES POUR LE PIANO, BK. 1
    ELKAN-VOGEL, INC.   D   8.00
SAINT-SAENS
  SIX ETUDES, BK. 1, OP. 52
    ELKAN-VOGEL, INC.   7.50
SALTYKOV
  EXERCISE IN F MINOR
    MUSICA OBSCURA   1.00
SALUTRINSKAYA
  SONATINA, HIDE THE STICK, CHRISTMAS TREE
    MCA MUSIC   .60
SALZEDO, C. *
  ART OF MODULATION, THE
    G. SCHIRMER, INC.   3.50
SALZMANN--ED   SALZMANN   2-3
  DER ZUPFGEIGENHANSL
    SCHOTT   4650   9.00
SAMUEL--ED.   SAMUEL
  HUNDRED BEST SHORT CLASSICS, BK. 5
    CARL FISCHER, INC.   PT 185   1.50
SAMUEL--ED.   SAMUEL
  HUNDRED BEST SHORT CLASSICS, BK. 6
    CARL FISCHER, INC.   PT 186   1.50
SAMUEL--ED.   SAMUEL
  HUNDRED BEST SHORT CLASSICS, BK. 7
    CARL FISCHER, INC.   PT 187   1.50
SANBORN, J.--ED   SANBORN, J.
  AMAZING GRACE AND OTHER GOSPEL FAVORITES
    THEODORE PRESSER COMPANY   2.95
SANCAN, P.
  ALBUM FOR SMALL HANDS
    ELKAN-VOGEL, INC.   RR   5.40
SANCAN, P.
  NOUVELLES CADENCES DU CONCERTO EN RE MINEUR DE W. A. MOZART
    ELKAN-VOGEL, INC.   D   1.75
SANCAN, P.
  PIECES ENFANTINES, 1ST DEGREE
    ELKAN-VOGEL, INC.   D   2.75
SANCAN, P.
  PIECES ENFANTINES, 2ND DEGREE
    ELKAN-VOGEL, INC.   D   1.75
SANFORD
  MARCHES
    BOSTON MUSIC COMPANY   1.00
SANFORD
  SQUARE DANCES
    BOSTON MUSIC COMPANY   1.00
SANFORD--ED   SANFORD
  HYMNS
    BOSTON MUSIC COMPANY   1.00
SANGIORGI
  THREE LITTLE PIECES
    FRANCO COLOMBO PUBLICATIONS   FOR.12257   1.25
SANTA CRUZ, D.
  IMAGENES INFANTILES, BK. 1
    PEER SOUTHERN ORGANIZATION   00.85
SANTA CRUZ, D.
  IMAGENES INFANTILES, BK. 2
    PEER SOUTHERN ORGANIZATION   01.00
SANTA MARIA, T. DE   AZPIAZU, J. *
  TWENTY-FIVE FANTASIES FROM ''ARTE DE TANER
  FANTASIA''--PNO/ORG/HP
    ASSOCIATED MUSIC PUBLISHERS, INC.   UME   2.50
SANTISI, R.
  JAZZ ORIGINALS
    BERKLEE PRESS PUBLICATIONS   B-10   2.50
SANTORO, C.
  DANSAS BRASILEIRAS
    PEER SOUTHERN ORGANIZATION   01.00
SARAKATSANNIS
  TWELVE EXCURSIONS FOR THE YOUNG PIANIST
    THEODORE PRESSER COMPANY   1.50
SARASTE   KIRCHNER
  MALAGUENA AND HABANERA, OP. 21 NOS. 1 AND 2
    ASSOCIATED MUSIC PUBLISHERS, INC.   SIM   1.25
SARASTE   KIRCHNER
  SPANISH DANCES, OP. 22 NOS. 1 AND 2
    ASSOCIATED MUSIC PUBLISHERS, INC.   SIM   1.25
SARAUER   3
  MINIATUREN. 8 KLEINE STUCKE
    BARENREITER VERLAG   AP 372
            PRELIM-2
SARSON, M.
  CHILD'S DAY -- 14 PIECES
    NOVELLO AND COMPANY, LTD.   10.0199.01   1.25
            PRELIM-2
SARSON, M.
  CHILD'S DAY, A -- SUITE OF 14 PIECES
    NOVELLO AND COMPANY, LTD.   10.0119.01   1.25
            PRELIM-1
SARSON, M.
  FIRST PIANO LESSONS
    NOVELLO AND COMPANY, LTD.   11.0022.10   1.25
            PRELIM-1
SARSON, M.
  FIRST PIANO LESSONS
    NOVELLO AND COMPANY, LTD.   11.0022.10   1.25

SASLAW, E.
  SONGS AND RHYMES FOR HAPPY TIMES
    WILLIS MUSIC COMPANY   1.50
SASLAW, E.--ED   SASLAW, E.
  FUN WITH FOLK TUNES
    WILLIS MUSIC COMPANY   2.00
SASLAW, E.--ED   SASLAW, E.   AE
  SONGS AND RIMES OF LATIN AMERICA
    WILLIS MUSIC COMPANY   1.50
SATIE, E.
  CHAPITRES TOURNES EN TOUS SENS
    ASSOCIATED MUSIC PUBLISHERS, INC.   ESC   3.50
SATIE, E.
  CROQUIS ET AGACERIES D'UN GROS BONHOMME EN BOIS
    ASSOCIATED MUSIC PUBLISHERS, INC.   ESC   2.75
SATIE, E.
  DESCRIPTIONS AUTOMATIQUES--1913
    ASSOCIATED MUSIC PUBLISHERS, INC.   ESC   3.25
SATIE, E.
  EMBRYONS DESSECHES
    ASSOCIATED MUSIC PUBLISHERS, INC.   ESC   3.50
SATIE, E.
  ENFANTILLAGES PITTORESQUES
    ASSOCIATED MUSIC PUBLISHERS, INC.   ESC   3.00
SATIE, E.
  FOUR PRELUDES
    FRANCO COLOMBO PUBLICATIONS   SAL   2.50
SATIE, E.
  HEURES SECULAIRES ET INSTANTANEES
    ASSOCIATED MUSIC PUBLISHERS, INC.   ESC   2.25
SATIE, E.
  MENUS PROPOS ENFANTINS
    ASSOCIATED MUSIC PUBLISHERS, INC.   ESC   3.00
SATIE, E.
  PAGES MYSTIQUES
    ASSOCIATED MUSIC PUBLISHERS, INC.   ESC   2.75
SATIE, E.
  PECCADILLES IMPORTUNES
    ASSOCIATED MUSIC PUBLISHERS, INC.   ESC   3.00
SATIE, E.
  PIANO MUSIC OF ERIC SATIE--ALBUM OF SELECTED WORKS
    ASSOCIATED MUSIC PUBLISHERS, INC.   AMP   3.00
SATIE, E.
  PIEGE DE MEDUSE, LE -- 7 PIECES --
    FRANCO COLOMBO PUBLICATIONS   SAL   2.50
SATIE, E.
  PRELUDES FLASQUES--POUR UN CHIEN
    ASSOCIATED MUSIC PUBLISHERS, INC.   ESC   3.00
SATIE, E.
  SPORTS ET DIVERTISSEMENTS
    FRANCO COLOMBO PUBLICATIONS   SAL   5.75
SATIE, E.
  THREE VALSES DU PRECIEUX DEGOUTE
    FRANCO COLOMBO PUBLICATIONS   SAL   1.75
SATIE, E.
  VERITABLES PRELUDES FLASQUES--POUR UN CHIEN
    ASSOCIATED MUSIC PUBLISHERS, INC.   ESC   2.50
SATIE, E.
  VIEUX SEQUINS ET VIEILLES CUIRASSES
    ASSOCIATED MUSIC PUBLISHERS, INC.   ESC   2.25
SAUER--ED   SAUER
  CLASSIC KEYBOARD MUSIC
    THEODORE PRESSER COMPANY   3.00
SAUER--ED   SAUER
  GREAT MASTERS, THE
    UNIVERSAL EDITION   UE 10676   4.25
SAUGET
  PIECES POETIQUES, BK. 1
    ASSOCIATED MUSIC PUBLISHERS, INC.   ESC   3.00
SAUGET
  PIECES POETIQUES, BK. 2
    ASSOCIATED MUSIC PUBLISHERS, INC.   ESC   2.00
SAUGUET
  FRANCAISES, BK. 1
    FRANCO COLOMBO PUBLICATIONS   SAL   3.25
SAUGUET
  FRANCAISES, BK. 2 -- NOUVELLES FRANCAISES --
    FRANCO COLOMBO PUBLICATIONS   SAL   3.50
SAUVREZIS
  EN AUTOMNE - BROUILLARDS D'AURORE, CIEL GRIS, ELAN MANITAL, LA
  PLUIE, LES FEUILLES, PROMENADE, LE VENT, PALE SOLEIL MIROITEMENT,
  DERNIERES ROSES, SOIR MAUVE, FETE FORAINE, CIEL ETOILE
    FRANCO COLOMBO PUBLICATIONS   SAL   5.00
SAUVREZIS
  GESTES D'ENFANTS
    FRANCO COLOMBO PUBLICATIONS   SAL   4.00
SAVINO--ED.   SAVINO
  POPULAR SONG CLASSICS FOR PIANO
    THE BIG THREE MUSIC CORPORATION   01.25
SAYGUN, A.
  TEN ETUDES ON AKSAK RHYTHMS
    PEER SOUTHERN ORGANIZATION   04.50
SAYGUN, A.
  TWELVE PRELUDES ON AKSAK RHYTHMS
    PEER SOUTHERN ORGANIZATION   03.50
SCALERO, R.
  SIX ROMANTIC PIECES, OP. 19
    ASSOCIATED MUSIC PUBLISHERS, INC.   BRH   1.25
SCARLATTI, A.   HUBSCH   3
  AUSGEWAHLTE KLAVIERWERKE, BAND 1 - 25 SONATEN
    BARENREITER VERLAG   SM 1497
SCARLATTI, A.   HUBSCH   3
  AUSGEWAHLTE KLAVIERWERKE, BAND 2 - 24 SONATEN UND 'KATZENFUGE'
    BARENREITER VERLAG   SM 1498
SCARLATTI, A.   LONGO
  SELECTED COMPOSITIONS
    FRANCO COLOMBO PUBLICATIONS   ER129   3.75
SCARLATTI, A.   NARDI
  SEVEN TOCCATAS
    BARENREITER VERLAG   BA 341   5.00
SCARLATTI, A.   NARDI   3
  SIEBEN TOCCATEN
    BARENREITER VERLAG   BA 341
SCARLATTI, D.   MARTHE MORHANGE
  ALBUMS - GRADED SCARLATTI, THE - 39 SONATAS COLLECTED AND EDITED
  BY MARTHE MORHANGE MOTCHANE
    FRANCO COLOMBO PUBLICATIONS   NY2054   2.50
SCARLATTI, D.   MONTANI
  ALBUMS - SIX BRILLIANT SONATAS
    FRANCO COLOMBO PUBLICATIONS   FOR.12054   1.50
SCARLATTI, D.   MONTANI
  ALBUMS - 10 BRILLIANT SONATAS
    FRANCO COLOMBO PUBLICATIONS   ER2512   1.25
SCARLATTI, D.   ANSON, G.   INTERMEDIATE
  ANSON INTRODUCES SCARLATTI, BK. 1
    WILLIS MUSIC COMPANY   1.00

SCARLATTI, D.   ANSON, G.   INTERMEDIATE
  ANSON INTRODUCES SCARLATTI, BK. 2
    WILLIS MUSIC COMPANY   1.25
SCARLATTI, D.   LONGO
  COMPLETE WORKS FOR CLAVICEMBALO, BK. 01 -- 1-50 --
    FRANCO COLOMBO PUBLICATIONS   ER541   5.00
SCARLATTI, D.   LONGO
  COMPLETE WORKS FOR CLAVICEMBALO, BK. 02 -- 51-100 --
    FRANCO COLOMBO PUBLICATIONS   ER542   5.00
SCARLATTI, D.   LONGO
  COMPLETE WORKS FOR CLAVICEMBALO, BK. 03 -- 101-150 --
    FRANCO COLOMBO PUBLICATIONS   ER543   5.00
SCARLATTI, D.   LONGO
  COMPLETE WORKS FOR CLAVICEMBALO, BK. 04 -- 151-200 --
    FRANCO COLOMBO PUBLICATIONS   ER544   5.00
SCARLATTI, D.   LONGO
  COMPLETE WORKS FOR CLAVICEMBALO, BK. 05 -- 201-250 --
    FRANCO COLOMBO PUBLICATIONS   ER545   5.00
SCARLATTI, D.   LONGO
  COMPLETE WORKS FOR CLAVICEMBALO, BK. 06 -- 251-300 --
    FRANCO COLOMBO PUBLICATIONS   ER546   5.00
SCARLATTI, D.   LONGO
  COMPLETE WORKS FOR CLAVICEMBALO, BK. 07 -- 301-350 --
    FRANCO COLOMBO PUBLICATIONS   ER547   5.00
SCARLATTI, D.   LONGO
  COMPLETE WORKS FOR CLAVICEMBALO, BK. 08 -- 351-400 --
    FRANCO COLOMBO PUBLICATIONS   ER548   5.00
SCARLATTI, D.   LONGO
  COMPLETE WORKS FOR CLAVICEMBALO, BK. 09 -- 401-450 --
    FRANCO COLOMBO PUBLICATIONS   ER549   5.00
SCARLATTI, D.   LONGO
  COMPLETE WORKS FOR CLAVICEMBALO, BK. 10 -- 451-500 --
    FRANCO COLOMBO PUBLICATIONS   ER550   5.00
SCARLATTI, D.   LONGO
  COMPLETE WORKS FOR CLAVICEMBALO, BK. 11 - THEMATIC INDEX
    FRANCO COLOMBO PUBLICATIONS   ER1912   1.75
SCARLATTI, D.   LONGO
  COMPLETE WORKS FOR CLAVICEMBALO, BK. 11 -- SUPPLEMENT-45
  PIECES--
    FRANCO COLOMBO PUBLICATIONS   ER551   5.00
SCARLATTI, D.   KREUTZER
  FIRST SCARLATTI
    BOSTON MUSIC COMPANY   1.00
SCARLATTI, D.
  FIVE PAIRS OF SONATAS
    E. C. SCHIRMER MUSIC COMPANY   230   02.00
SCARLATTI, D.   RATHAUS, K.
  FOUR STUDIES AFTER DOMENICO SCARLATTI
    THEODORE PRESSER COMPANY   2.00
SCARLATTI, D.   MOTCHANE
  GRADED SCARLATTI, THE
    BELWIN-MILLS PUBLISHING CORPORATION   4.00
SCARLATTI, D.   E
  LITTLE PIANO BOOK
    C. F. PETERS CORPORATION   L5009   1.25
SCARLATTI, D.   CHING   EASY
  NEW EASY GRADED CLASSIC ALBUM - SCARLATTI
    GENERAL WORDS AND MUSIC COMPANY   1.25
SCARLATTI, D.   PHILIPP, I.
  NINE SELECTED SONATAS
    INTERNATIONAL MUSIC COMPANY   1.75
SCARLATTI, D.   AUCLERT
  NINE SONATAS
    FRANCO COLOMBO PUBLICATIONS   R1560   3.00
SCARLATTI, D.   BARTH, H.
  PIANO WORKS, BK. 1 -- 19 SONATAS--
    UNIVERSAL EDITION   450   3.00
SCARLATTI, D.   BARTH, H.
  PIANO WORKS, BK. 2 -- 18 SONATAS--
    UNIVERSAL EDITION   451   3.00
SCARLATTI, D.   PHILIPP, I.
  SIX SELECTED SONATAS
    INTERNATIONAL MUSIC COMPANY   1.75
SCARLATTI, D.   SILVESTRI
  SIXTEEN SONATAS
    FRANCO COLOMBO PUBLICATIONS   ER2095   3.00
SCARLATTI, D.   KIRKPATRICK
  SIXTY SONATAS, BK. 1
    G. SCHIRMER, INC.   L1774   3.00
SCARLATTI, D.   KIRKPATRICK
  SIXTY SONATAS, BK. 2
    G. SCHIRMER, INC.   L1775   3.00
SCARLATTI, D.   KELLER *   M-D
  SONATAS --150-- IN 3 VOLS. VOL. 1
    C. F. PETERS CORPORATION   4692A   10.00
SCARLATTI, D.   KELLER *   M-D
  SONATAS --150-- IN 3 VOLS. VOL. 2
    C. F. PETERS CORPORATION   4692B   10.00
SCARLATTI, D.   KELLER *   M-D
  SONATAS --150-- IN 3 VOLS. VOL. 3
    C. F. PETERS CORPORATION   4692C   10.00
SCARLATTI, D.   LONGO
  THIRTY-FIVE SONATAS, VOL. 1
    CARL FISCHER, INC.   O 3488   3.00
SCARLATTI, D.   LONGO
  THIRTY-FIVE SONATAS, VOL. 2
    CARL FISCHER, INC.   O 3489   3.00
SCARLATTI, D.
  TWELVE EASY SCARLATTI SONATAS
    EDWARD B. MARKS MUSIC CORPORATION   01.50
SCARLATTI, D.
  TWENTY SELECTED SONATAS
    ASSOCIATED MUSIC PUBLISHERS, INC.   BRH   2.75
SCARLATTI, D.   LONGO
  TWENTY-FIVE SONATAS -- NOS. 58, 104, 187, 263, 324, 331, 338,
  345, 375, 381, 413, 422, 424, 429, 430, 433, 465, 475, 486, 490,
  498, 499, SUPPL. 3, SUPPL. 39 --
    FRANCO COLOMBO PUBLICATIONS   NY2393 -- EX 2.50
SCARLATTI, D.
  TWENTY-FOUR PIECES, BK. 1
    ASSOCIATED MUSIC PUBLISHERS, INC.   SIM   2.00
SCARLATTI, D.
  TWENTY-FOUR PIECES, BK. 2
    ASSOCIATED MUSIC PUBLISHERS, INC.   SIM   2.00
SCARLATTI, D.   SAUER   M-D
  TWENTY-FOUR SONATAS
    C. F. PETERS CORPORATION   3245   3.00
SCARLATTI, D.
  TWENTY-SEVEN SELECTED SONATAS
    BOSTON MUSIC COMPANY   3.00
SCARLATTI, D.   GRANADOS
  TWENTY-SIX SONATAS, BK. 1
    ASSOCIATED MUSIC PUBLISHERS, INC.   UME   3.00
SCARLATTI, D.   GRANADOS
  TWENTY-SIX SONATAS, BK. 2
    ASSOCIATED MUSIC PUBLISHERS, INC.   UME   3.00

SCARLATTI, D.   BUONAMICI
  TWENTY-TWO PIECES
    G. SCHIRMER, INC.   L73   2.00
SCARLATTI, D.   ALATI   3-4
  ZWANZIG SONATE BRILLANTI
    BARENREITER VERLAG   CM 21376
SCARMOLIN
  TEN EASY PIANO PIECES
    PRO-ART PUBLICATIONS, INC.   917   .75
SCARMOLIN--ED   SCARMOLIN
  BEST LOVED HYMNS
    PRO-ART PUBLICATIONS, INC.   45   .85
SCARMOLIN--ED   SCARMOLIN
  MELODIES OF THE MASTERS
    PRO-ART PUBLICATIONS, INC.   43   1.00
SCARMOLIN--ED   SCARMOLIN
  SONGS WE LOVE TO PLAY
    PRO-ART PUBLICATIONS, INC.   67   .85
SCELSI
  PRELUDES -- SERIES 1 --
    FRANCO COLOMBO PUBLICATIONS   DS693   3.25
SCHAUB *
  PIANO PROGRESS--BOOK 1-A--LARGE NOTE EDITION
    VOLKWEIN BROS.   4.00
SCHAUB *
  PIANO PROGRESS--BOOK 1-B--LARGE NOTE EDITION
    VOLKWEIN BROS.   4.00
SCHAUB *
  PIANO PROGRESS--BOOK 2-A--LARGE NOTE EDITION
    VOLKWEIN BROS.   4.00
SCHAUB *
  PIANO PROGRESS--BOOK 2-B--LARGE NOTE EDITION
    VOLKWEIN BROS.   4.00
SCHAUB *
  PIANO PROGRESS--BOOK 3-A--LARGE NOTE EDITION
    VOLKWEIN BROS.   4.00
SCHAUB *
  PIANO PROGRESS--BOOK 3-B--LARGE NOTE EDITION
    VOLKWEIN BROS.   4.00
SCHAUB *
  PIANO PROGRESS, BOOK 1
    VOLKWEIN BROS.   1.25
SCHAUB *
  PIANO PROGRESS, BOOK 2
    VOLKWEIN BROS.   1.25
SCHAUB *
  PIANO PROGRESS, BOOK 3
    VOLKWEIN BROS.   1.25
SCHAUB *
  PRIMARY BOOK
    VOLKWEIN BROS.   1.25
SCHAUM, J.   PREP TO 1
  ADULT AT THE PIANO, BK. 1
    SCHAUM PUBLICATIONS, INC.   1.65
SCHAUM, J.   1 - 1 1/2
  ADULT AT THE PIANO, BK. 2
    SCHAUM PUBLICATIONS, INC.   1.50
SCHAUM, J.   2 - 2 1/2
  ADULT AT THE PIANO, BK. 3
    SCHAUM PUBLICATIONS, INC.   1.50
SCHAUM, J.
  ADULT PIANO COURSE, BK. 1
    BELWIN-MILLS PUBLISHING CORPORATION   2.00
SCHAUM, J.
  ADULT PIANO COURSE, BK. 2
    BELWIN-MILLS PUBLISHING CORPORATION   2.00
SCHAUM, J.
  ADULT PIANO COURSE, BK. 3
    BELWIN-MILLS PUBLISHING CORPORATION   2.00
SCHAUM, J.   2 1/2
  AMERICAN FAVORITES
    SCHAUM PUBLICATIONS, INC.   1.75
SCHAUM, J.   2
  AROUND THE WORLD IN ALL KEYS
    SCHAUM PUBLICATIONS, INC.   1.25
SCHAUM, J.   3
  BOOGIE IS MY BEAT
    SCHAUM PUBLICATIONS, INC.   1.50
SCHAUM, J.   PRELIM.
  BOOK 01, PRE-A -- FOR THE EARLIEST BEGINNER
    BELWIN-MILLS PUBLISHING CORPORATION   2.00
SCHAUM, J.   1
  BOOK 02, A -- THE RED BOOK
    BELWIN-MILLS PUBLISHING CORPORATION   2.00
SCHAUM, J.   1 1/2
  BOOK 03, B -- THE BLUE BOOK
    BELWIN-MILLS PUBLISHING CORPORATION   2.00
SCHAUM, J.   2
  BOOK 04, C -- THE PURPLE BOOK
    BELWIN-MILLS PUBLISHING CORPORATION   2.00
SCHAUM, J.   2 1/2
  BOOK 05, D -- THE ORANGE BOOK
    BELWIN-MILLS PUBLISHING CORPORATION   2.00
SCHAUM, J.   3
  BOOK 06, E -- THE VIOLET BOOK
    BELWIN-MILLS PUBLISHING CORPORATION   2.00
SCHAUM, J.   4
  BOOK 07, F -- THE BROWN BOOK
    BELWIN-MILLS PUBLISHING CORPORATION   2.00
SCHAUM, J.   PRE-VIRTUOSO
  BOOK 08, G -- THE AMBER BOOK
    BELWIN-MILLS PUBLISHING CORPORATION   2.00
SCHAUM, J.   VIRTUOSO
  BOOK 09, H -- THE GREY BOOK
    BELWIN-MILLS PUBLISHING CORPORATION   2.00
SCHAUM, J.
  BOOK 10, AFTER H BOOK, BK. 1
    BELWIN-MILLS PUBLISHING CORPORATION   2.00
SCHAUM, J.
  BOOK 10, AFTER H BOOK, BK. 2
    BELWIN-MILLS PUBLISHING CORPORATION   2.00
SCHAUM, J.   2 1/2
  CAMPFIRE SONGS
    SCHAUM PUBLICATIONS, INC.   1.25
SCHAUM, J.   2 1/2
  CONTINENTAL FAVORITES
    SCHAUM PUBLICATIONS, INC.   1.75
SCHAUM, J.   1 1/2
  CZERNY IN ALL KEYS, BK. 1
    SCHAUM PUBLICATIONS, INC.   1.50
SCHAUM, J.   2
  CZERNY IN ALL KEYS, BK. 2
    SCHAUM PUBLICATIONS, INC.   1.50
SCHAUM, J.   1
  DINOSAUR DITTIES
    SCHAUM PUBLICATIONS, INC.   1.25

SCHAUM, J.--ED.   SCHAUM, J.   5
   CONTEMPORARY COMPOSERS
      SCHAUM PUBLICATIONS, INC.   2.00
SCHAUM, J.--ED.   SCHAUM, J.   1
   COWBOY BOOK
      BELWIN-MILLS PUBLISHING CORPORATION   1.50
SCHAUM, J.--ED.   SCHAUM, J.   1
   FOLK AND COUNTRY SONG
      SCHAUM PUBLICATIONS, INC.   1.45
SCHAUM, J.--ED.   SCHAUM, J.   1
   FOLK SONG BOOK
      BELWIN-MILLS PUBLISHING CORPORATION   1.50
SCHAUM, J.--ED.   SCHAUM, J.   PREP
   FOLK SONGS AND DANCES -- MUSIC FOR CHILDREN
      SCHAUM PUBLICATIONS, INC.   1.25
SCHAUM, J.--ED.   SCHAUM, J.   1 1/2
   GAY NINETIES BOOK
      BELWIN-MILLS PUBLISHING CORPORATION   1.50
SCHAUM, J.--ED.   SCHAUM, J.   1 1/2
   GIRLS' BOOK
      BELWIN-MILLS PUBLISHING CORPORATION   1.50
SCHAUM, J.--ED.   SCHAUM, J.   4 1/2
   GOSPEL CAMEOS
      SCHAUM PUBLICATIONS, INC.   1.75
SCHAUM, J.--ED.   SCHAUM, J.   5
   GOSPEL PIANO PROFILES
      SCHAUM PUBLICATIONS, INC.   2.00
SCHAUM, J.--ED.   SCHAUM, J.   5
   GOSPEL PIANO PROFILES
      SCHAUM PUBLICATIONS, INC.   2.00
SCHAUM, J.--ED.   SCHAUM, J.   5
   GOSPEL VIGNETTES
      SCHAUM PUBLICATIONS, INC.   2.00
SCHAUM, J.--ED.   SCHAUM, J.   PREP
   GREAT BALLETS -- CLASSIC MELODIES
      SCHAUM PUBLICATIONS, INC.   1.25
SCHAUM, J.--ED.   SCHAUM, J.   PREP
   GREAT COMPOSERS -- CLASSIC MELODIES
      SCHAUM PUBLICATIONS, INC.   1.25
SCHAUM, J.--ED.   SCHAUM, J.   PREP
   GREAT OPERAS -- CLASSIC MELODIES
      SCHAUM PUBLICATIONS, INC.   1.25
SCHAUM, J.--ED.   SCHAUM, J.   PREP
   GREAT SYMPHONIES -- CLASSIC MELODIES
      SCHAUM PUBLICATIONS, INC.   1.25
SCHAUM, J.--ED.   SCHAUM, J.   2
   HANSEL AND GRETEL
      SCHAUM PUBLICATIONS, INC.   1.50
SCHAUM, J.--ED.   SCHAUM, J.   1 1/2
   HAWAIIAN MUSIC
      SCHAUM PUBLICATIONS, INC.   1.50
SCHAUM, J.--ED.   SCHAUM, J.   1 1/2
   HYMN ALBUM
      BELWIN-MILLS PUBLISHING CORPORATION   1.50
SCHAUM, J.--ED.   SCHAUM, J.   PREP
   HYMN PRIMER
      SCHAUM PUBLICATIONS, INC.   1.25
SCHAUM, J.--ED.   SCHAUM, J.   2 1/2
   HYMNS AND GOSPEL SONGS
      SCHAUM PUBLICATIONS, INC.   1.25
SCHAUM, J.--ED.   SCHAUM, J.   2
   JEWISH FOLK AND HOLIDAY SONGS
      SCHAUM PUBLICATIONS, INC.   1.50
SCHAUM, J.--ED.   SCHAUM, J.
   LATIN AMERICAN MUSIC
      SCHAUM PUBLICATIONS, INC.   1.50
SCHAUM, J.--ED.   SCHAUM, J.   3
   MARCH ALBUM
      BELWIN-MILLS PUBLISHING CORPORATION   1.50
SCHAUM, J.--ED.   SCHAUM, J.   2
   MOUNTAIN BOOK
      BELWIN-MILLS PUBLISHING CORPORATION   1.50
SCHAUM, J.--ED.   SCHAUM, J.   1 1/2
   MUSIC HISTORY PIECES
      BELWIN-MILLS PUBLISHING CORPORATION   1.50
SCHAUM, J.--ED.   SCHAUM, J.   2
   MUSIC OF THE AMERICAN INDIAN
      SCHAUM PUBLICATIONS, INC.   1.50
SCHAUM, J.--ED.   SCHAUM, J.   2
   OPERA BOOK
      BELWIN-MILLS PUBLISHING CORPORATION   1.50
SCHAUM, J.--ED.   SCHAUM, J.   1 1/2
   PARADE BOOK
      BELWIN-MILLS PUBLISHING CORPORATION   1.50
SCHAUM, J.--ED.   SCHAUM, J.   2
   POLKA BOOK
      BELWIN-MILLS PUBLISHING CORPORATION   1.50
SCHAUM, J.--ED.   SCHAUM, J.   2
   POLKA FESTIVAL
      SCHAUM PUBLICATIONS, INC.   1.50
SCHAUM, J.--ED.   SCHAUM, J.   2
   PRELUDES, OFFERTORIES AND POSTLUDES
      BELWIN-MILLS PUBLISHING CORPORATION   1 50
SCHAUM, J.--ED.   SCHAUM, J.   3
   PROGRESSIVE PIANO TECHNIC, BK. 1
      BELWIN-MILLS PUBLISHING CORPORATION   1.50
SCHAUM, J.--ED.   SCHAUM, J.   4 1/2
   PROGRESSIVE PIANO TECHNIC, BK. 2
      BELWIN-MILLS PUBLISHING CORPORATION   1.50
SCHAUM, J.--ED.   SCHAUM, J.   2
   RAGTIME BOOK
      BELWIN-MILLS PUBLISHING CORPORATION   1.50
SCHAUM, J.--ED.   SCHAUM, J.   1
   RECITAL BOOK
      BELWIN-MILLS PUBLISHING CORPORATION   1.50
SCHAUM, J.--ED.   SCHAUM, J.   4
   ROMANTIC CAMEOS
      SCHAUM PUBLICATIONS, INC.   1.50
SCHAUM, J.--ED.   SCHAUM, J.   1
   SACRED BOOK
      BELWIN-MILLS PUBLISHING CORPORATION   1.50
SCHAUM, J.--ED.   SCHAUM, J.   1 1/2
   SCALES AND PIECES IN ALL KEYS, BK. 1
      BELWIN-MILLS PUBLISHING CORPORATION   1.50
SCHAUM, J.--ED.   SCHAUM, J.   4
   SCALES AND PIECES IN ALL KEYS, BK. 2
      BELWIN-MILLS PUBLISHING CORPORATION   1.50
SCHAUM, J.--ED.   SCHAUM, J.   4
   STAR SPANGLED BANNER 'AMERICA' 'AMERICA THE BEAUTIFUL'
      BELWIN-MILLS PUBLISHING CORPORATION   .50
SCHAUM, J.--ED.   SCHAUM, J.   PREP
   SUNDAY SCHOOL HYMNS -- MUSIC FOR CHILDREN
      SCHAUM PUBLICATIONS, INC.   1.25
SCHAUM, J.--ED.   SCHAUM, J.   2
   TECHNIC THROUGH MELODY, BK. 1
      BELWIN-MILLS PUBLISHING CORPORATION   1.50

SCHAUM, J.--ED.   SCHAUM, J.   2 1/2
   TECHNIC THROUGH MELODY, BK. 2
      BELWIN-MILLS PUBLISHING CORPORATION   1.50
SCHAUM, J.--ED.   SCHAUM, J.   1
   TECHNIC TRICKS, BK.1
      BELWIN-MILLS PUBLISHING CORPORATION   1.50
SCHAUM, J.--ED.   SCHAUM, J.   1
   TECHNIC TRICKS, BK.2
      BELWIN-MILLS PUBLISHING CORPORATION   1.50
SCHAUM, J.--ED.   SCHAUM, J.   4
   WALTZ BOOK
      BELWIN-MILLS PUBLISHING CORPORATION   1.50
SCHAUM, J.--ED.   SCHAUM, J.   4
   WEDDING MUSIC
      SCHAUM PUBLICATIONS, INC.   2.00
SCHAUM, J.--ED.   SCHAUM, J.   2 1/2
   WOMEN COMPOSERS OF THE UNITED STATES
      SCHAUM PUBLICATIONS, INC.   1.50
SCHEIDT *   STEGLICH   2-3
   ALTE DEUTSCH WEIHNACHTMUSIK - 11 CHORALE UND VARIATIONEN
      BARENREITER VERLAG   NMA 95
SCHEIDT   DIETRICH   2-3
   DAS GORLITZER TABULATURBUCH. 100 VIERSTIMMIGE CHORALE
      BARENREITER VERLAG   BA 1565
SCHEIDT   M
   FIVE SECULAR SONG VARIATIONS AND DANCE MOVEMENTS
      C. F. PETERS CORPORATION   4393A   2.50
SCHEIDT   E
   GOERLITZ TABULATUR 1650 --100 CHORALES--
      C. F. PETERS CORPORATION   4494   2.50
SCHEIDT   DIETRICH
   GORLITZER TABLATURE BOOK, THE
      BARENREITER VERLAG   BA 1565   5.00
SCHER, W.
   FIFTEEN DESCRIPTIVE MINIATURES
      THEODORE PRESSER COMPANY   .90
SCHER, W.
   FRAGMENTS
      PRO-ART PUBLICATIONS, INC.   1198   1.00
SCHER, W.
   FUN-A-RAMA
      PRO-ART PUBLICATIONS, INC.   1061   .85
SCHER, W.
   JEWISH SONGS AND DANCES--PIANO SETTINGS WITH WORDS AND
   ILLUSTRATIONS
      G. SCHIRMER, INC.   1.00
SCHER, W.
   MELODAYS
      PRO-ART PUBLICATIONS, INC.   677   .75
SCHER, W.
   MINITUNES
      SUMMY-BIRCHARD COMPANY   1.50
SCHER, W.
   PATTERNS, BK. 1
      SUMMY-BIRCHARD COMPANY   1.75
SCHER, W.
   PIANO CAMEOS
      PRO-ART PUBLICATIONS, INC.   562   1.00
SCHER, W.
   PICTURES AT THE PIANO
      PRO-ART PUBLICATIONS, INC.   563   .85
SCHER, W.
   PLAYING FOR PLEASURE
      PRO-ART PUBLICATIONS, INC.   1257   1.00
SCHER, W.
   SPORTS-A-RAMA
      PRO-ART PUBLICATIONS, INC.   923   .75
SCHER, W.
   TEN CHARACTERISTIC DANCES
      BELWIN-MILLS PUBLISHING CORPORATION   11486   1.25
SCHER, W.
   TEN MUSICAL SKETCHES
      BELWIN-MILLS PUBLISHING CORPORATION   11487   1.25
SCHER, W.   EARLY GRADES
   TRAVELOGUES OF MELODY--13 MELODIES FROM 13
   COUNTRIES--ILLUSTRATED
      G. SCHIRMER, INC.   .75
SCHER, W.
   TUNE-A-RAMA
      PRO-ART PUBLICATIONS, INC.   676   .75
SCHER, W.
   TUNELETS
      SUMMY-BIRCHARD COMPANY   1.50
SCHER, W.
   WORLD AROUND
      PRO-ART PUBLICATIONS, INC.   812   .75
SCHER, W.--ED   SCHER
   FAMOUS MELODY ALBUM FOR VERY EARLY GRADES
      G. SCHIRMER, INC.   1.00
SCHER, W.--ED   SCHER, W.
   FAMOUS MELODY ALBUM FOR VERY EARLY GRADES
      G. SCHIRMER, INC.   1.00
SCHER, W.--ED   SCHER, W.
   ISRAELI FAVORITES
      PRO-ART PUBLICATIONS, INC.   932   .85
SCHER, W.--ED   SCHER, W.
   JEWISH SONGS AND DANCES
      G. SCHIRMER, INC.   1.00
SCHER, W.--ED   SCHER, W.
   PIANO SAMPLER
      PRO-ART PUBLICATIONS, INC.   1203   1.00
SCHIBLER--ED   SCHIBLER   E-M
   NOBODY KNOWS, 12 NEGRO SPIRITUALS
      C. F. PETERS CORPORATION   Z247   2.00
SCHILLINGER, J.
   FIVE PIECES, OP. 12
      ASSOCIATED MUSIC PUBLISHERS, INC.   AMP   1.50
SCHININA, L.
   ARPEGGI CONSONANTI E DISSONANTI
      EDIZIONI BERBEN   EB 1535   6.00
SCHIRMER--ED   SCHIRMER
   POPULAR THEMES BY GREAT MASTERS
      BOSTON MUSIC COMPANY   1.00
SCHISKE, K.
   DANCE SUITE, OP. 23--1945
      ASSOCIATED MUSIC PUBLISHERS, INC.   DOB   2.50
SCHISKE, K.
   ETUDENSTUDIE, OP. 36--1951
      ASSOCIATED MUSIC PUBLISHERS, INC.   DOB   1.25
SCHISKE, K.
   LITTLE SUITE, OP. 1--1935
      ASSOCIATED MUSIC PUBLISHERS, INC.   DOB   2.50
SCHISKE, K.
   THEME, 8 VARIATIONS, AND DOUBLE FUGUE, OP. 2--1936
      ASSOCIATED MUSIC PUBLISHERS, INC.   DOB   2.75
SCHISKE, K.
   THREE PIECES ON FOLKTUNES, OP. 35--1951
      ASSOCIATED MUSIC PUBLISHERS, INC.   DOB   .75

SCHMID
   BAYRISCHE LANDLER, OP. 36   4
      SCHOTT   1792   2.00
SCHMID   2-3
   FUR KLEINE HANDE, OP. 95
      SCHOTT   2331   2.00
SCHMID   2-3
   KLEIN. KLAVIERBUCH, OP. 53
      SCHOTT   1406   2.25
SCHMITT
   REFLETS -- BALLET -- BK. 1 .. HEIDELBERG, COBLENTZ, LUEBECK,
   WERDER
      FRANCO COLOMBO PUBLICATIONS   SAL   4.00
SCHMITT
   REFLETS -- BALLET -- BK. 2 .. VIENNA, DRESDEN, NUREMBERG, MUNICH
      FRANCO COLOMBO PUBLICATIONS   SAL   4.00
SCHMITT, A. *   ECKSTEIN
   EARLY TECHNICAL STUDIES FROM SCHMITT-HANON--140--
      CARL FISCHER, INC.   O 3810   1.25
SCHMITT, A.   FRUGATTA
   FIVE FINGER EXERCISES
      FRANCO COLOMBO PUBLICATIONS   ER43   .75
SCHMITT, A.
   FIVE FINGER EXERCISES, OP. 16
      CARL FISCHER, INC.   L 15   1.25
SCHMITT, A.
   PREPARATORY EXERCISES FOR THE PIANO, OP. 16
      WILLIS MUSIC COMPANY   .75
SCHMITT, A.
   PREPARATORY EXERCISES, OP. 16
      FRANCO COLOMBO PUBLICATIONS   ER21   .75
SCHMITT, A.   M
   PREPARATORY EXERCISES, OP. 16
      C. F. PETERS CORPORATION   2467A   1.25
SCHMITT, A.
   SCHMITT'S FIVE FINGER EXERCISES, PART 1
      CENTURY MUSIC PUBLISHING COMPANY, INC.   1207   .40
SCHMITT, A.
   SCHMITT'S FIVE FINGER EXERCISES, PART 2
      CENTURY MUSIC PUBLISHING COMPANY, INC.   1208   .40
SCHMITT, F.
   MUSIQUES INTIMES, BK. 2 OP. 29
      FRANCO COLOMBO PUBLICATIONS   SAL   4.25
SCHMITT, F.
   THREE PRELUDES - PRELUDE TRISTE, OBSESSION, CHANT DE CYGNES
      FRANCO COLOMBO PUBLICATIONS   SAL   3.25
SCHMITT, F.
   THREE VALSE NOCTURNES
      FRANCO COLOMBO PUBLICATIONS   SAL   5.25
SCHMOLL, A.
   NEW PIANO METHOD, BK. 1
      THEODORE PRESSER COMPANY   1.25
SCHMOLL, A.
   NEW PIANO METHOD, BK. 2
      THEODORE PRESSER COMPANY   1.25
SCHNABEL, K.
   MODERN TECHNIQUE OF THE PEDAL
      BELWIN-MILLS PUBLISHING CORPORATION   11308   1.75
SCHOBERLECHNER, A.
   TRIP TO THE WONDERLAND OF MUSIC -- A PIANO SCHOOL FOR ALL AGES,
   BK. 1
      UNIVERSAL EDITION   UE 11940   2.15
SCHOBERLECHNER, A.
   TRIP TO THE WONDERLAND OF MUSIC -- A PIANO SCHOOL FOR ALL AGES,
   BK. 2
      UNIVERSAL EDITION   UE 11941   2.15
SCHOBERLECHNER, A.--ED   SCHOBERLECHNER, A.
   CLASSICAL PIANO ALBUM -- 39 EASY ORIGINAL COMPOSITIONS
      UNIVERSAL EDITION   UE 10850   2.20
SCHOBERLECHNER, A.--ED   SCHOBERLECHNER, A.
   ROMANTIC ALBUM FOR THE YOUNG -- 34 ORIGINAL PIECES OF ROMANCE
   COMPOSERS
      UNIVERSAL EDITION   UE 10930   2.55
SCHOCH   E
   FIFTEEN LITTLE DANCES OF THE 18TH CENTURY
      C. F. PETERS CORPORATION   A30   1.50
SCHOCH   E
   THIRTY MINUETS OF PAST TIMES
      C. F. PETERS CORPORATION   A32   1.50
SCHOENFELD *
   RIDDLES IN SONG
      PRO-ART PUBLICATIONS, INC.   779   .85
SCHOLLUM, R.
   EIGHT LITTLE PIANO PIECES, OP. 54B--1956
      ASSOCIATED MUSIC PUBLISHERS, INC.   DOB   1.75
SCHOLLUM, R.
   FANGT AN ZU MUSIZIEREN--LITTLE PIECES
      ASSOCIATED MUSIC PUBLISHERS, INC.   OBV   2.50
SCHOLLUM, R.
   FANGT AN ZU MUSIZIERIEN--90 LITTLE PIECES FOR THE BEGINNER
      ASSOCIATED MUSIC PUBLISHERS, INC.   OBV   2.50
SCHOLLUM, R.
   KONZERTSTUCKE--''RUCKBLICKE''--OP. 61
      ASSOCIATED MUSIC PUBLISHERS, INC.   DOB   2.50
SCHOLLUM, R.
   WALKS WITH ISOLDE--SPAZIERGANGE MIT ISOOLDE, OP. 70,
   1965-6--HARPSICHORD
      ASSOCIATED MUSIC PUBLISHERS, INC.   DOB   4.00
SCHOLZ
   ABC DER KLAVIERTEACHNIK -- ENG AND GER NOTES -- BK. 1
      ASSOCIATED MUSIC PUBLISHERS, INC.   DOB   3.25
SCHOLZ
   ABC DER KLAVIERTEACHNIK -- ENG AND GER NOTES -- BK. 2
      ASSOCIATED MUSIC PUBLISHERS, INC.   DOB   3.25
SCHOLZ
   ABC DER KLAVIERTEACHNIK -- ENG AND GER NOTES -- BK. 3
      ASSOCIATED MUSIC PUBLISHERS, INC.   DOB   3.25
SCHOLZ
   ADVENTURES IN CONTEMPORARY TECHNIC -- THE MODERN STUDY
      ASSOCIATED MUSIC PUBLISHERS, INC.   AMP   2.00
SCHOLZ
   CALEIDOSCOPE--AMERICAN RHYTHMS, BK. 1
      ASSOCIATED MUSIC PUBLISHERS, INC.   DOB   1.75
SCHOLZ
   CALEIDOSCOPE--AMERICAN RHYTHMS, BK. 2
      ASSOCIATED MUSIC PUBLISHERS, INC.   DOB   1.75
SCHOLZ
   MODERNE STUDIE, DIE -- BK. 1
      ASSOCIATED MUSIC PUBLISHERS, INC.   DOB   3.00
SCHOLZ
   MODERNE STUDIE, DIE -- BK. 2, PART 1
      ASSOCIATED MUSIC PUBLISHERS, INC.   DOB   2.50
SCHOLZ
   MODERNE STUDIE, DIE -- BK. 2, PART 2
      ASSOCIATED MUSIC PUBLISHERS, INC.   DOB   2.50
SCHOLZ
   PIECES FOR CHILDREN
      ASSOCIATED MUSIC PUBLISHERS, INC.   DOB   1.75

SCHOLZ--ED   SCHOLZ
   ALLERERSTEN KLASSIKER UND ROMANTIKER, DIE -- 28 EASY ORIGINAL
   PIECES BY CLASSICAL AND ROMANTIC MASTERS
      ASSOCIATED MUSIC PUBLISHERS, INC.   DOB   2.00
SCHOLZ--ED   SCHOLZ
   KLASSIKER UND ROMANTIKER -- SHORT WORKS BY BACH, BEETHOVEN,
   SCHUBERT, SCHUMANN AND OTHERS
      ASSOCIATED MUSIC PUBLISHERS, INC.   DOB   4.00
SCHONTHAL
   MINIATURES FOR PIANO, VOL. 1
      SHAWNEE PRESS, INC.   1.75
SCHONTHAL
   MINIATURES FOR PIANO, VOL. 2
      SHAWNEE PRESS, INC.   1.75
SCHROEDER, H.   4
   MINNELIEDER
      SCHOTT   3720   2.00
SCHROEDER, H.   3
   SUSANI, ALTE WEIHNACHTSLIEDER
      SCHOTT   3882   2.00
SCHROEDER, H.
   TWO SONATINAS
      ASSOCIATED MUSIC PUBLISHERS, INC.   SIM   2.00
SCHROETER, H.   6
   FUNF ETUDEN, OP. 10
      SCHOTT   4291   2.00
SCHUBERT
   ALBUM
      KULTURA   2.00
SCHUBERT   STEINBRECHER
   ALBUM 'THRO' THE NIGHT ...'
      UNIVERSAL EDITION   10765   3.00
SCHUBERT *   BOHMOVA *   3
   ALBUM BERUHMTER ROMANTIKER, 20 KLAVIERSTUCKE
      BARENREITER VERLAG   AP 1762
SCHUBERT
   ALBUM, BK. 1
      EDWIN F. KALMUS   3886   2.50
SCHUBERT   3-5
   AUSWAHL -- 22 BEL. STUCKE
      SCHOTT   510   1.75
SCHUBERT   KRUG   2
   AVE MARIA, FANTASIE
      SCHOTT   05815 102 1.00
SCHUBERT   FISCHHOF
   BALLET MUSIC - ROSAMUNDE
      UNIVERSAL EDITION   852   .75
SCHUBERT   SCHAUM, J.   2 1/2
   BEST OF SCHUBERT
      SCHAUM PUBLICATIONS, INC.   1.50
SCHUBERT   WEINMANN *
   COMPLETE DANCES FOR PIANO, VOL. 1
      WIENER URTEXT EDITION   UT 50021   8.00
SCHUBERT   WEINMANN *
   COMPLETE DANCES FOR PIANO, VOL. 2
      WIENER URTEXT EDITION   UT 50022   8.00
SCHUBERT   EPSTEIN, J.
   COMPLETE SONATAS FOR PIANOFORTE SOLO
      DOVER PUBLICATIONS, INC.   22647-6   5.00
SCHUBERT   M-D
   COMPOSITIONS. SUPPLEMENT
      C. F. PETERS CORPORATION   718   4.50
SCHUBERT
   DANCE ALBUM
      G. HENLE MUSIKVERLAG   125   2.20
SCHUBERT
   DANCES
      G. SCHIRMER, INC.   L1537   1.50
SCHUBERT
   DANCES -- WALTZES, 'LAENDLER', GERMAN DANCES, ECOSSAISES -- OP.
   9, 18, 33, 49, 50, 67, 77, 91 AND 127
      UNIVERSAL EDITION   33   2.50
SCHUBERT   HERRMANN
   DANCES AND PIECES
      FRANCO COLOMBO PUBLICATIONS   SIK.112   1.50
SCHUBERT
   DANCES AND WALTZES
      EDWIN F. KALMUS   3878   2.50
SCHUBERT   PAUER
   DANCES, BK. 1
      ASSOCIATED MUSIC PUBLISHERS, INC.   BRH   3.00
SCHUBERT   PAUER
   DANCES, BK. 2
      ASSOCIATED MUSIC PUBLISHERS, INC.   BRH   3.00
SCHUBERT
   DANCES, VOL. 1
      G. HENLE MUSIKVERLAG   74   4.95
SCHUBERT
   DANCES, VOL. 2
      G. HENLE MUSIKVERLAG   76   4.95
SCHUBERT   4
   DEUTSCHE TANZE OP. 33
      SCHOTT   0703   1.00
SCHUBERT   ROWLEY   E-M
   EASIEST ORIGINAL PIECES FOR PIANO
      C. F. PETERS CORPORATION   H6   1.50
SCHUBERT   BEGINNER
   EASY ALBUM, AN
      EDWIN F. KALMUS   3876   1.25
SCHUBERT   SEAK
   EIGHT IMPROMPTUS, OP. 90 AND 142
      FRANCO COLOMBO PUBLICATIONS   ER2657   2.75
SCHUBERT   E-M
   EIGHT MINUETS
      C. F. PETERS CORPORATION   4498   2.00
SCHUBERT
   EIGHT VALSE SENTIMENTALES AND WALTZES
      EDWIN F. KALMUS   3882   1.50
SCHUBERT   D
   FANTASIA, IMPROMPTUS, MOMENTS MUSICAUX
      C. F. PETERS CORPORATION   716   3.50
SCHUBERT   BUONAMICI
   FANTASIAS, IMPROMPTUS, MOMENTS MUSICAUX
      G. SCHIRMER, INC.   L75   3.00
SCHUBERT   PAUER
   FANTASIES, IMPROMPTUS, MOMENTS MUSICAUX
      ASSOCIATED MUSIC PUBLISHERS, INC.   BRH   4.00
SCHUBERT   M
   FAVORITE PIECES
      C. F. PETERS CORPORATION   1825A   1.50
SCHUBERT   BRADLEY
   FIRST COMPOSERS - SCHUBERT
      FRANCO COLOMBO PUBLICATIONS   LD205   1.00
SCHUBERT   BUONAMICI
   FOUR IMPROMPTUS, OP. 142
      G. SCHIRMER, INC.   L1126   1.25

SCHUBERT   KROLL
  FOUR IMPROMPTUS, OP. 90
      FRANCO COLOMBO PUBLICATIONS   ER2269   2.00
SCHUBERT   BUONAMICI
  FOUR IMPROMPTUS, OP. 90
      G. SCHIRMER, INC.   L1125   1.25
SCHUBERT   RATZ, E.
  FOURTEEN SONATAS, ACCORDING TO THE AUTOGRAPHS AND IN
  CHRONOLOGICAL ORDER - BK. 1
      UNIVERSAL EDITION   257A   6.75
SCHUBERT   RATZ, E.
  FOURTEEN SONATAS, ACCORDING TO THE AUTOGRAPHS AND IN
  CHRONOLOGICAL ORDER - BK. 2
      UNIVERSAL EDITION   257B   6.75
SCHUBERT   CHING
  IMPROMPTU IN A FLAT, OP. 142 NO. 2
      GENERAL WORDS AND MUSIC COMPANY   .75
SCHUBERT   CHING
  IMPROMPTU IN A FLAT, OP. 90 NO. 4
      GENERAL WORDS AND MUSIC COMPANY   .75
SCHUBERT   M-D
  IMPROMPTUS
      C. F. PETERS CORPORATION   3235A   2.00
SCHUBERT
  IMPROMPTUS - MOMENTS MUSICAUS DREI KLAVIERSTUCKE
      UNIVERSAL EDITION   13307   4.80
SCHUBERT   PAUER
  IMPROMPTUS AND MOMENTS MUSICAUX
      ASSOCIATED MUSIC PUBLISHERS, INC.   BRH   1.75
SCHUBERT
  IMPROMPTUS AND MOMENTS MUSICAUX
      G. HENLE MUSIKVERLAG   4   2.70
SCHUBERT   M-D
  IMPROMPTUS AND MOMENTS MUSICAUX
      C. F. PETERS CORPORATION   3235   2.50
SCHUBERT
  IMPROMPTUS AND MOMENTS MUSICAUX -- CLOTH
      G. HENLE MUSIKVERLAG   138   5.80
SCHUBERT
  IMPROMPTUS, MOMENTS MUSICAUX. CLOTH-BOUND
      C. F. PETERS CORPORATION   10.00
SCHUBERT   BADURA-SKODA
  IMPROMPTUS, MOMENTS MUSICAUX, 3 PIANO PIECES
      WIENER URTEXT EDITION   UT 50001   8.50
SCHUBERT   BAUER
  LANDLER AND OTHER DANCES
      G. SCHIRMER, INC.   1.50
SCHUBERT *   STEINBRECHER
  LEISE FLEHEN MEINE LIEDER -- 23 SCHUBERT MELODIES IN EASY
  ARRANGEMENTS
      UNIVERSAL EDITION   UE 10765   4.25
SCHUBERT   E-M
  LITTLE VIENNESE DANCE BOOK
      C. F. PETERS CORPORATION   L5015   1.25
SCHUBERT   M-D
  MARCHES
      C. F. PETERS CORPORATION   726   4.50
SCHUBERT   HUGHES
  MASTER SERIES FOR THE YOUNG--VOL. 06--SCHUBERT
      G. SCHIRMER, INC.   1.25
SCHUBERT   M-D
  MOMENTS MUSICAUX
      C. F. PETERS CORPORATION   3235B   1.00
SCHUBERT   BADURA-SKODA
  MOMENTS MUSICAUX, D 780 --OP. 94--
      WIENER URTEXT EDITION   UT 50043   2.00
SCHUBERT   LONGO
  MOMENTS MUSICAUX, OP. 94
      FRANCO COLOMBO PUBLICATIONS   ER1549   .60
SCHUBERT   BUONAMICI
  MOMENTS MUSICAUX, OP. 94
      G. SCHIRMER, INC.   L1127   .75
SCHUBERT   POZZOLI
  MY FIRST SCHUBERT
      FRANCO COLOMBO PUBLICATIONS   ER1956   1.00
SCHUBERT   CHING   EASY
  NEW EASY GRADED CLASSIC ALBUM - SCHUBERT
      GENERAL WORDS AND MUSIC COMPANY   1.25
SCHUBERT   M-D
  ONE HUNDRED AND SIXTY-ONE DANCES
      C. F. PETERS CORPORATION   150   2.50
SCHUBERT
  RADIO CITY ALBUM
      EDWARD B. MARKS MUSIC CORPORATION   01.50
SCHUBERT   SCHAUM, J.   2 1/2
  ROMANTIC WALTZES OF FRANZ SCHUBERT
      SCHAUM PUBLICATIONS, INC.   1.60
SCHUBERT   SCHAUM, J.   2 1/2
  ROMANTIC WALTZES OF FRANZ SCHUBERT
      SCHAUM PUBLICATIONS, INC.   1.60
SCHUBERT   M
  ROSAMUNDE. ENTR'ACTES AND BALLET MUSIC
      C. F. PETERS CORPORATION   1310   2.00
SCHUBERT   STEINER   2
  SCHUBERT FESTIVAL, A MEDLEY -- 1. ROSAMUNDE'S LOVE SONG, 2.
  SPRING BREEZES, 3. IN THE MEADOW
      BELWIN-MILLS PUBLISHING CORPORATION   .60
SCHUBERT   ECKHARDT, F.   1
  SCHUBERT FOR THE YOUNG PIANIST
      CENTURY MUSIC PUBLISHING COMPANY, INC.   3961   .40
SCHUBERT   SMALL, A.
  SCHUBERT WALTZ SAMPLER
      ALFRED MUSIC COMPANY   548   1.95
SCHUBERT   VITALI
  SELECTED COMPOSITIONS
      FRANCO COLOMBO PUBLICATIONS   ER47   2.00
SCHUBERT   SPANUTH
  SELECTED PIANO COMPOSITIONS
      THEODORE PRESSER COMPANY   5.00
SCHUBERT
  SEVEN VIENNESE GERMAN DANCES
      EDWIN F. KALMUS   3881   1.50
SCHUBERT   EPSTEIN, J.
  SHORTER WORKS FOR PIANOFORTE SOLO
      DOVER PUBLICATIONS, INC.   22648-4   4.00
SCHUBERT
  SIX GERMAN DANCES OP. POSTH
      UNIVERSAL EDITION   2743   .85
SCHUBERT
  SIX VARIATIONS
      EDITIONS MUSICALES TRANSATLANTIQUES   3.85
SCHUBERT
  SIXTEEN GERMAN DANCES AND TWO ECOSSAISES, OP. 33, D. 783
      G. HENLE MUSIKVERLAG   179   1.15
SCHUBERT   PAUER
  SIXTEEN LITTLE PIECES
      ASSOCIATED MUSIC PUBLISHERS, INC.   BRH   3.00

SCHUBERT   PAUER
  SONATAS, BK. 1
      ASSOCIATED MUSIC PUBLISHERS, INC.   BRH   3.50
SCHUBERT
  SONATAS, BK. 1
      EDWIN F. KALMUS   3883   3.25
SCHUBERT   TAGLIAPIETRA
  SONATAS, BK. 1 -- OP. 42, 53, 120, 122, 143, 147 --
      FRANCO COLOMBO PUBLICATIONS   ER1331   3.75
SCHUBERT   PAUER
  SONATAS, BK. 2
      ASSOCIATED MUSIC PUBLISHERS, INC.   BRH   3.50
SCHUBERT
  SONATAS, BK. 2
      EDWIN F. KALMUS   3884   3.25
SCHUBERT   TAGLIAPIETRA
  SONATAS, BK. 2 -- OP. 164, OP. POSTH. IN C MINOR, A, B-FLAT, G
  --
      FRANCO COLOMBO PUBLICATIONS   ER1332   3.75
SCHUBERT   PAUER
  SONATAS, BK. 3
      ASSOCIATED MUSIC PUBLISHERS, INC.   BRH   4.00
SCHUBERT
  SONATAS, COMPLETE IN 2 VOLS. CLOTH-BOUND
      C. F. PETERS CORPORATION   10.00
SCHUBERT
  SONATAS, VOL. 1
      G. HENLE MUSIKVERLAG   146   5.50
SCHUBERT   M-D
  SONATAS, VOL. 1
      C. F. PETERS CORPORATION   488A   3.00
SCHUBERT
  SONATAS, VOL. 1 -- CLOTH
      G. HENLE MUSIKVERLAG   147   8.50
SCHUBERT
  SONATAS, VOL. 2
      G. HENLE MUSIKVERLAG   148   5.50
SCHUBERT   M-D
  SONATAS, VOL. 2
      C. F. PETERS CORPORATION   488B   3.00
SCHUBERT
  SONATAS, VOL. 2 -- CLOTH
      G. HENLE MUSIKVERLAG   149   8.50
SCHUBERT   MANSFIELD
  STEPS TO THE MASTERS
      BANKS AND SON LTD.   1.35
SCHUBERT   FREY   2-3
  TANZE F. D. JUGEND
      SCHOTT   2792   1.75
SCHUBERT   M-D
  TEN POLONAISES
      C. F. PETERS CORPORATION   1383   2.00
SCHUBERT   BUONAMICI
  TEN SONATAS
      G. SCHIRMER, INC.   L837   4.50
SCHUBERT
  THREE PIANO PIECES -- POSTHUMOUS IMPROMPTUS
      G. HENLE MUSIKVERLAG   66   1.95
SCHUBERT   M-D
  THREE PIANO PIECES, OP. POSTH.
      C. F. PETERS CORPORATION   7091   2.00
SCHUBERT
  THREE WALTZES
      G. SCHIRMER, INC.   .30
SCHUBERT
  THREE WALTZES, OP. 98
      WILLIS MUSIC COMPANY   .25
SCHUBERT
  TWELVE LAENDLER
      EDWIN F. KALMUS   3880   1.50
SCHUBERT   CORTOT
  TWELVE LAENDLER, OP. 171
      FRANCO COLOMBO PUBLICATIONS   SAL   2.50
SCHUBERT *
  TWENTY-FOUR SONG TRANSCRIPTIONS, BK. 1
      G. SCHIRMER, INC.   L128   1.75
SCHUBERT *
  TWENTY-FOUR SONG TRANSCRIPTIONS, BK. 2
      G. SCHIRMER, INC.   L129   1.75
SCHUBERT   KREUTZER
  TWO DOZEN DANCES
      BOSTON MUSIC COMPANY   1.00
SCHUBERT   CORTOT
  TWO IMPROMPTUS, OP. 142 NOS. 2 AND 3
      FRANCO COLOMBO PUBLICATIONS   SAL   2.50
SCHUBERT   CORTOT
  TWO IMPROMPTUS, OP. 90 NOS. 2 AND 4
      FRANCO COLOMBO PUBLICATIONS   SAL   3.25
SCHUBERT
  TWO SCHERZOS, OP. POSTH.
      FRANCO COLOMBO PUBLICATIONS   128022   .60
SCHUBERT   KRENTZLIN   2
  UNSTERBLICHER SCHUBERT, 20 BEKANNTE MELODIEN
      SCHOTT   2424   2.50
SCHUBERT
  VARIOUS PIECES
      EDWIN F. KALMUS   3885   3.00
SCHUBERT   PROKOFIEFF
  WALTZES
      INTERNATIONAL MUSIC COMPANY   1.50
SCHUBERT   2
  WALTZES FROM OP. 9A
      CENTURY MUSIC PUBLISHING COMPANY, INC.   3715   .40
SCHUBERT   MAIER, G.
  WALTZES, SET 1
      BELWIN-MILLS PUBLISHING CORPORATION   1.25
SCHUBERT   MAIER, G.
  WALTZES, SET 2
      BELWIN-MILLS PUBLISHING CORPORATION   1.25
SCHUBERT   MAIER, G.
  WALTZES, SET 3
      BELWIN-MILLS PUBLISHING CORPORATION   1.25
SCHUBERT   MAIER, G.
  WALTZES, SET 4
      BELWIN-MILLS PUBLISHING CORPORATION   1.25
SCHUBERT   MAIER, G.
  WALTZES, SET 5
      BELWIN-MILLS PUBLISHING CORPORATION   1.25
SCHUBERT
  WALZER
      UNIVERSAL EDITION   14930   1.50
SCHUBERT   2-3
  WIENER TANZE UND STUCKE
      SCHOTT   3933   1.75
SCHUBERT   3
  ZWEI SCHERZI B UND DES
      SCHOTT   0708 1/2   1.00

SCHULER, G. S.
  EVANGELISTIC PIANO PLAYING
    THEODORE PRESSER COMPANY   1.50
SCHULTHESS, W.
  DREI KLAVIERSTUCKE, OP. 12
    SCHOTT   1795   3.00
SCHULTHESS, W.
  SECHS KLEINE FANTASIESTUCKE
    SCHOTT   1411   3.00
SCHULTZE
  SONGS FROM THE OPERA SCHWARZER PETER
    FRANCO COLOMBO PUBLICATIONS   SIK.130   2.25
SCHULZ   2
  LIEDER IM VOLKSTON
    SCHOTT   3773   1.75
SCHULZ   HILLEMANN   3
  SECHS STUCKE FUR KLAVIER -- CEMBALO OP. 1
    SCHOTT   2355   2.00
SCHULZ, F. A.
  SCALES AND CHORDS
    CARL FISCHER, INC.   L 176   1.00
SCHULZ, J.   E
  EIGHTEEN POPULAR SONGS
    C. F. PETERS CORPORATION   T18   1.50
SCHUMANN, W.
  VOYAGE - A CYCLE OF FIVE PIECES FOR PIANO
    THEODORE PRESSER COMPANY   2.50
SCHUMANN, C.   M-D
  CADENZAS TO BEETHOVEN CONCERTOS NOS. 3, 4. TO MOZART CONCERTO
  NO. 20--K.466--
    C. F. PETERS CORPORATION   3629   2.00
SCHUMANN, C.   GOEBELS   3-4
  ROMANTISCHE KLAVIERMUSIK - HEFT 1, CLARA SCHUMANN -- DREI
  PRELUDIEN UND FUGEN, OP. 16, VARIATIONEN UBER EIN THEMA VON ROBERT
  SCHUMANN, OP. 20, ROMANZE, OP. 21 NO. 3 --
    BARENREITER VERLAG   SM 2483
SCHUMANN, C.   D
  VARIOUS PIANO PIECES
    C. F. PETERS CORPORATION   WM102   3.50
SCHUMANN, G.
  DURCH DUR UND MOLL, OP. 61, BK. 1
    ASSOCIATED MUSIC PUBLISHERS, INC.   LEU   2.00
SCHUMANN, G.
  DURCH DUR UND MOLL, OP. 61, BK. 2
    ASSOCIATED MUSIC PUBLISHERS, INC.   LEU   2.00
SCHUMANN, G.
  DURCH DUR UND MOLL, OP. 61, BK. 3
    ASSOCIATED MUSIC PUBLISHERS, INC.   LEU   2.00
SCHUMANN, R.   M
  ACCOMPANIMENTS TO BACH'S SIX SOLO VIOLIN SONATAS. VOL. 1
    C. F. PETERS CORPORATION   228C   3.00
SCHUMANN, R.   M
  ACCOMPANIMENTS TO BACH'S SIX SOLO VIOLIN SONATAS. VOL. 2
    C. F. PETERS CORPORATION   228D   3.00
SCHUMANN, R.   M-D
  ACCOMPANIMENTS TO PAGANINI'S CAPRICES, OP. 1. VOL. 1
    C. F. PETERS CORPORATION   4497A   4.00
SCHUMANN, R.   M
  ACCOMPANIMENTS TO PAGANINI'S CAPRICES, OP. 1. VOL. 2
    C. F. PETERS CORPORATION   4497B   4.00
SCHUMANN, R.   PALMER, W. A.
  ALBUM FOR THE YOUNG
    ALFRED MUSIC COMPANY   620   2.00
SCHUMANN, R.   GOLDBERGER, D. *
  ALBUM FOR THE YOUNG
    CONSOLIDATED MUSIC PUBLISHERS, INC. 040119   1.50
SCHUMANN, R.   BEGINNER
  ALBUM FOR THE YOUNG
    EDWIN F. KALMUS   3895   1.25
SCHUMANN, R.
  ALBUM FOR THE YOUNG
    EDWIN F. KALMUS   3895   1.50
SCHUMANN, R.
  ALBUM FOR THE YOUNG WITH SCENES FROM CHILDHOOD, OP. 15
    CARL FISCHER, INC.   L 811   2.00
SCHUMANN, R.   SCHUMANN, C.
  ALBUM FOR THE YOUNG, OP. 68
    ASSOCIATED MUSIC PUBLISHERS, INC.   BRH   1.50
SCHUMANN, R.
  ALBUM FOR THE YOUNG, OP. 68
    CARL FISCHER, INC.   L 811   1.25
SCHUMANN, R.   SAUER   M
  ALBUM FOR THE YOUNG, OP. 68
    C. F. PETERS CORPORATION   1805   1.50
SCHUMANN, R.   BAUER
  ALBUM FOR THE YOUNG, OP. 68
    G. SCHIRMER, INC.   L91   1.25
SCHUMANN, R.
  ALBUM FOR THE YOUNG, OP. 68
    UNIVERSAL EDITION   361   1.80
SCHUMANN, R.   SAUER   E-M
  ALBUM FOR THE YOUNG, OP. 68. THE EASIER PIECES
    C. F. PETERS CORPORATION   1805A   1.25
SCHUMANN, R.   BAUER
  ALBUM FOR THE YOUNG, OP. 68, AND SCENES FROM CHILDHOOD, OP. 15
    G. SCHIRMER, INC.   L90   1.50
SCHUMANN, R.   PAUER, M.   3
  ALBUM FUER DIE JUGEND, AUSWAHL OP. 68
    SCHOTT   0746 1/2   1.00
SCHUMANN, R.   SAUER   M-D
  ALBUM LEAVES, OP. 124
    C. F. PETERS CORPORATION   2302   2.00
SCHUMANN, R.   VOGRICH
  ALBUM--22 PIECES
    G. SCHIRMER, INC.   L100   1.50
SCHUMANN, R.
  ALBUM-LEAVES, OP. 124
    G. HENLE MUSIKVERLAG   82   1.65
SCHUMANN, R.   BAUER
  ALBUM-LEAVES, OP. 124
    G. SCHIRMER, INC.   L1075   1.00
SCHUMANN, R.
  ALBUM, BK. 1
    EDWIN F. KALMUS   3930   2.50
SCHUMANN, R.
  ALBUM, BK. 2
    EDWIN F. KALMUS   3931   2.50
SCHUMANN, R.   PAUER, M.   3
  ALBUMBLAETTER, OP. 124 -- WALZER - SCHLUMMERLIED - ELFE
    SCHOTT   0723 1/2   1.00
SCHUMANN, R.   ANSON, G.   INTERMEDIATE
  ANSON INTRODUCES SCHUMANN, BK. 1
    WILLIS MUSIC COMPANY   1.75
SCHUMANN, R.   BAUER
  ARABESQUE, OP. 18, BLUMENSTUCK, OP. 19, THREE ROMANCES, OP. 28
    G. SCHIRMER, INC.   L1686   1.50

SCHUMANN, R.
  ARABESQUES, BLUMENSTUCKE, OP. 18/19 -- COMPLETE
    UNIVERSAL EDITION   437   1.60
SCHUMANN, R.   PAUER, M.   3-5
  AUSWAHL -- 28 BEK. STUCKE
    SCHOTT   5181   3.00
SCHUMANN, R.   SAUER   M
  BUNTE BLAETTER, OP. 99
    C. F. PETERS CORPORATION   2303   2.50
SCHUMANN, R.   SCHUMANN, C. *
  CARNAVAL, OP. 9
    ASSOCIATED MUSIC PUBLISHERS, INC.   BRH   1.25
SCHUMANN, R.
  COLORED LEAVES, OP. 99
    G. HENLE MUSIKVERLAG   81   1.80
SCHUMANN, R.   BAUER
  COLORED LEAVES, OP. 99
    G. SCHIRMER, INC.   L1275   1.25
SCHUMANN, R.   M-D
  COMPLETE PIANO WORKS IN 5 VOLS. VOL. 1
    C. F. PETERS CORPORATION   2300A   12.00
SCHUMANN, R.   M-D
  COMPLETE PIANO WORKS IN 5 VOLS. VOL. 2
    C. F. PETERS CORPORATION   2300B   12.00
SCHUMANN, R.   D
  COMPLETE PIANO WORKS IN 5 VOLS. VOL. 3
    C. F. PETERS CORPORATION   2300C   12.00
SCHUMANN, R.   M-D
  COMPLETE PIANO WORKS IN 5 VOLS. VOL. 4
    C. F. PETERS CORPORATION   2300D   12.00
SCHUMANN, R.   D
  COMPLETE PIANO WORKS IN 5 VOLS. VOL. 5
    C. F. PETERS CORPORATION   2300E   12.00
SCHUMANN, R.   SAUER
  COMPLETE PIANO WORKS, IN 5 VOLS. CLOTH-BOUND
    C. F. PETERS CORPORATION   15.00
SCHUMANN, R.
  COMPLETE WORKS, BK. 1
    EDWIN F. KALMUS   3923   4.25
SCHUMANN, R.
  COMPLETE WORKS, BK. 2
    EDWIN F. KALMUS   3924   4.25
SCHUMANN, R.
  COMPLETE WORKS, BK. 3
    EDWIN F. KALMUS   3925   4.25
SCHUMANN, R.
  COMPLETE WORKS, BK. 4
    EDWIN F. KALMUS   3926   4.25
SCHUMANN, R.
  COMPLETE WORKS, BK. 5
    EDWIN F. KALMUS   3927   3.00
SCHUMANN, R.
  COMPLETE WORKS, BK. 6
    EDWIN F. KALMUS   3928   3.00
SCHUMANN, R.
  COMPLETE WORKS, BK. 7
    EDWIN F. KALMUS   3929   3.00
SCHUMANN, R.   BAUER
  DAVIDSBUENDLERTAENZE, OP. 6
    G. SCHIRMER, INC.   L1140   .75
SCHUMANN, R.   ROWLEY   M
  EASIEST ORIGINAL PIECES
    C. F. PETERS CORPORATION   H7   1.50
SCHUMANN, R.   SAUER   D
  EIGHT FANTASIESTUECKE, OP. 12
    C. F. PETERS CORPORATION   2309   1.25
SCHUMANN, R.   SCHUMANN, C. *
  FANTASIA IN C, OP. 17
    ASSOCIATED MUSIC PUBLISHERS, INC.   BRH   2.00
SCHUMANN, R.   PAUER, M.   5
  FANTASIESTUCKE OP. 12 NO. 3 AND 4 WARUM UND GRILLEN
    SCHOTT   0738 1/2   1.00
SCHUMANN, R.   SCHUMANN, C. *
  FANTASIESTUCKE, OP. 12
    ASSOCIATED MUSIC PUBLISHERS, INC.   BRH   1.10
SCHUMANN, R.
  FANTASIESTUCKE, OP. 12
    G. HENLE MUSIKVERLAG   91   1.80
SCHUMANN, R.   BAUER
  FANTASIESTUCKE, OP. 12
    G. SCHIRMER, INC.   L92   1.25
SCHUMANN, R.
  FANTASY PIECES, OP. 12
    EDWIN F. KALMUS   3906   1.50
SCHUMANN, R.
  FANTASY PIECES, OP. 12
    UNIVERSAL EDITION   519   1.60
SCHUMANN, R.   SCHUMANN, C.
  FASCHINGSSCHWANK AUS WIEN, OP. 26
    ASSOCIATED MUSIC PUBLISHERS, INC.   BRH   1.00
SCHUMANN, R.
  FIFTY PIANO COMPOSITIONS
    THEODORE PRESSER COMPANY   5.00
SCHUMANN, R.   SCHUMANN, C. *
  FOREST SCENES--WALDSZENEN, OP. 82
    ASSOCIATED MUSIC PUBLISHERS, INC.   BRH   .90
SCHUMANN, R.
  FOREST SCENES, OP. 82
    G. HENLE MUSIKVERLAG   83   1.65
SCHUMANN, R.   SAUER   M
  FOREST SCENES, OP. 82
    C. F. PETERS CORPORATION   2305A   1.00
SCHUMANN, R.   BAUER
  FOREST SCENES, OP. 82
    G. SCHIRMER, INC.   L1690   1.00
SCHUMANN, R.   SAUER   M
  FOUR FUGUES, OP. 72
    C. F. PETERS CORPORATION   2319   3.00
SCHUMANN, R.   BAUER
  FOUR FUGUES, OP. 72, FOUR MARCHES, OP. 76, SEVEN PIECES IN
  FUGHETTA FORM, OP. 126
    G. SCHIRMER, INC.   D   L1716   1.50
SCHUMANN, R.
  FOUR SYMPHONIES
    C. F. PETERS CORPORATION   2332   7.50
SCHUMANN, R.   BAUER
  IMPROMPTUS ON A ROMANCE BY CLARA WIECK, OP. 5
    G. SCHIRMER, INC.   L1164   1.50
SCHUMANN, R.   SAUER   D
  IMPROMPTUS, 12 VARIATIONS, OP. 5
    C. F. PETERS CORPORATION   2318   2.00
SCHUMANN, R.   SAUER   D
  INTERMEZZI, OP. 4
    C. F. PETERS CORPORATION   2317   2.50
SCHUMANN, R.   BAUER
  INTERMEZZI, OP. 4
    G. SCHIRMER, INC.   L1166   1.00

SCHUMANN, R.   THIMAN
    INTRODUCTION TO SCHUMANN
        CARL FISCHER, INC.   PT 449   1.00
SCHUMANN, R.   STEGLICH   2
    KINDERSZENEN
        BARENREITER VERLAG   BA 345
SCHUMANN, R.   GOEBELS   2
    KINDERSZENEN OP. 15
        SCHOTT   5647
SCHUMANN, R.   GOEBELS   2
    KINDERSZENEN OP. 15 -- VIER STUCKE
        SCHOTT   0755   .75
SCHUMANN, R.   SCHUMANN, C. *
    KREISLERIANA, OP. 16
        ASSOCIATED MUSIC PUBLISHERS, INC.   BRH   1.75
SCHUMANN, R.   HUGHES
    MASTER SERIES FOR THE YOUNG--VOL. 09--SCHUMANN
        G. SCHIRMER, INC.   1.25
SCHUMANN, R.   POZZOLI
    MY FIRST SCHUMANN
        FRANCO COLOMBO PUBLICATIONS   ER1957   1.25
SCHUMANN, R.   SAUER   M-D
    NACHTSTUCKE, OP. 23
        C. F. PETERS CORPORATION   2320A   2.00
SCHUMANN, R.   BAUER
    NACHTSTUCKE, OP. 23, AND THREE FANTASIESTUCKE, OP. 111
        G. SCHIRMER, INC.   L94   1.25
SCHUMANN, R.   CHING   EASY
    NEW EASY GRADED CLASSIC ALBUM - SCHUMANN
        GENERAL WORDS AND MUSIC COMPANY   1.25
SCHUMANN, R.   CORTOT
    NOVELETTES, OP. 21
        FRANCO COLOMBO PUBLICATIONS   SAL   8.00
SCHUMANN, R.   BUONAMICI
    NOVELLETTEN, OP. 21
        FRANCO COLOMBO PUBLICATIONS   ER806   3.00
SCHUMANN, R.   SAUER   D
    NOVELLETTEN, OP. 21
        C. F. PETERS CORPORATION   2308   2.50
SCHUMANN, R.   BAUER
    NOVELLETTEN, OP. 21
        G. SCHIRMER, INC.   L98   1.75
SCHUMANN, R.   SCHUMANN, C. *
    NOVELLETTES, OP. 21
        ASSOCIATED MUSIC PUBLISHERS, INC.   BRH   1.75
SCHUMANN, R.
    NOVELLETTEN, OP. 21
        G. HENLE MUSIKVERLAG   88   2.20
SCHUMANN, R.   SCHUMANN, C. *
    PAPILLONS, OP. 2
        ASSOCIATED MUSIC PUBLISHERS, INC.   BRH   .75
SCHUMANN, R.
    PIANO SOLOS, VOL. 1
        G. HENLE MUSIKVERLAG   108   5.50
SCHUMANN, R.
    PIANO SOLOS, VOL. 1 -- CLOTH
        G. HENLE MUSIKVERLAG   109   8.50
SCHUMANN, R.
    PIANO SOLOS, VOL. 2
        G. HENLE MUSIKVERLAG   110   6.75
SCHUMANN, R.
    PIANO SOLOS, VOL. 2 -- CLOTH
        G. HENLE MUSIKVERLAG   111   9.85
SCHUMANN, R.   SCHUMANN, C. *
    PIANO WORKS, BK. 1
        ASSOCIATED MUSIC PUBLISHERS, INC.   BRH   4.00
SCHUMANN, R.   SCHUMANN, C. *
    PIANO WORKS, BK. 2
        ASSOCIATED MUSIC PUBLISHERS, INC.   BRH   3.75
SCHUMANN, R.
    PIANO WORKS, BK. 2, OP. 2, 7, 9 AND 18
        NOVELLO AND COMPANY, LTD.   10.0122.01 1.90
SCHUMANN, R.   SCHUMANN, C. *
    PIANO WORKS, BK. 3
        ASSOCIATED MUSIC PUBLISHERS, INC.   BRH   3.75
SCHUMANN, R.
    PIANO WORKS, BK. 3, DAVIDSBUNDLER DANCES, OP. 6
        NOVELLO AND COMPANY, LTD.   10.0123.10 1.25
SCHUMANN, R.   SCHUMANN, C. *
    PIANO WORKS, BK. 4
        ASSOCIATED MUSIC PUBLISHERS, INC.   BRH   4.00
SCHUMANN, R.   SCHUMANN, C. *
    PIANO WORKS, BK. 5
        ASSOCIATED MUSIC PUBLISHERS, INC.   BRH   3.50
SCHUMANN, R.   SCHUMANN, C. *
    PIANO WORKS, BK. 6
        ASSOCIATED MUSIC PUBLISHERS, INC.   BRH   3.75
SCHUMANN, R.   SCHUMANN, C. *
    PIANO WORKS, BK. 7
        ASSOCIATED MUSIC PUBLISHERS, INC.   BRH   3.75
SCHUMANN, R.   BEGINNER
    SCENES FROM CHILDHOOD
        EDWIN F. KALMUS   3896   .85
SCHUMANN, R.   SCHUMANN, C.
    SCENES FROM CHILDHOOD, OP. 15
        ASSOCIATED MUSIC PUBLISHERS, INC.   BRH   .90
SCHUMANN, R.   SAUER   E-M
    SCENES FROM CHILDHOOD, OP. 15
        C. F. PETERS CORPORATION   2466   1.00
SCHUMANN, R.   BAUER
    SCENES FROM CHILDHOOD, OP. 15
        G. SCHIRMER, INC.   L101   .75
SCHUMANN, R.   GOEBELS
    SCENES FROM CHILDHOOD, OP. 15
        WIENER URTEXT EDITION   UT 50006   1.75
SCHUMANN, R.
    SCENES FROM CHILDHOOD, OP. 15, AND ALBUM FOR THE YOUNG, OP. 68
        G. HENLE MUSIKVERLAG   46   2.35
SCHUMANN, R.   BAUER
    SCENES FROM CHILDHOOD, OP. 15, AND ALBUM FOR THE YOUNG, OP. 68
        G. SCHIRMER, INC.   L90   1.50
SCHUMANN, R.   E-M
    SCHERZO, GIGUE, ROMANCE, FUGHETTE, OP. 32. ALSO CONTAINS OP. 72
        C. F. PETERS CORPORATION   2319   3.00
SCHUMANN, R.
    SCHUMANN
        ASHLEY DEALERS SERVICE, INC.   HG 11   2.95
SCHUMANN, R.   ECKHARDT, F.   1
    SCHUMANN FOR THE YOUNG PIANIST
        CENTURY MUSIC PUBLISHING COMPANY, INC. 3962   .40
SCHUMANN, R.   ECKHARDT, F.   1
    SCHUMANN FOR THE YOUNG PIANIST
        CENTURY MUSIC PUBLISHING COMPANY, INC. 3962   .40
SCHUMANN, R.   SCHAUM, J.   2 1/2
    SCHUMANN-SCHAUM
        BELWIN-MILLS PUBLISHING CORPORATION   1.50

SCHUMANN, R.   SAUER   D
    SIX CONCERT STUDIES AFTER CAPRICES BY PAGANINI, OP. 10
        C. F. PETERS CORPORATION   2324   1.25
SCHUMANN, R.   SCHUMANN, C. *
    SIX CONCERT STUDIES ON CAPRICES OF PAGANINI, OP. 10
        ASSOCIATED MUSIC PUBLISHERS, INC.   BRH   1.25
SCHUMANN, R.   MANSFIELD
    STEPS TO THE MASTERS
        BANKS AND SON LTD.   1.35
SCHUMANN, R.   BAUER
    STUDIES AFTER PAGANINI'S "CAPRICES", OP. 3, AND CONCERT-STUDIES
    AFTER PAGANINI'S "CAPRICES", OP. 10
        G. SCHIRMER, INC.   L1727   1.50
SCHUMANN, R.   SCHUMANN, C. *
    STUDIES ON CAPRICES OF PAGANINI, OP. 3
        ASSOCIATED MUSIC PUBLISHERS, INC.   BRH   1.00
SCHUMANN, R.   SCHUMANN, C.
    SYMPHONIC ETUDES, OP. 13
        ASSOCIATED MUSIC PUBLISHERS, INC.   BRH   1.00
SCHUMANN, R.
    SYMPHONIC ETUDES, OP. 13
        EDWIN F. KALMUS   3916   1.25
SCHUMANN, R.
    THREE FANTASIESTUCKE, OP. 111
        G. HENLE MUSIKVERLAG   89   1.15
SCHUMANN, R.   SAUER   M-D
    THREE FANTASIESTUCKE, OP. 111
        C. F. PETERS CORPORATION   2320B   .90
SCHUMANN, R.   BAUER
    THREE FANTASIESTUCKE, OP. 111, AND FOUR NACHTSTUCKE, OP. 23
        G. SCHIRMER, INC.   L94   1.25
SCHUMANN, R.   BUONAMICI
    THREE ROMANCES, OP. 28
        FRANCO COLOMBO PUBLICATIONS   ER1466   .75
SCHUMANN, R.
    THREE ROMANCES, OP. 28
        G. HENLE MUSIKVERLAG   85   1.40
SCHUMANN, R.
    THREE ROMANCES, OP. 28
        EDWIN F. KALMUS   3911   1.00
SCHUMANN, R.   SAUER   M-D
    THREE ROMANCES, OP. 28
        C. F. PETERS CORPORATION   2305B   2.00
SCHUMANN, R.
    THREE ROMANCES, OP. 28
        UNIVERSAL EDITION   531   1.20
SCHUMANN, R.   SAUER   D
    THREE SONATAS FOR THE YOUNG, OP. 118
        C. F. PETERS CORPORATION   2325   3.00
SCHUMANN, R.   BAUER
    THREE SONATAS FOR YOUNG PEOPLE, OP. 118
        G. SCHIRMER, INC.   L1180   1.50
SCHUMANN, R.
    THREE SONATAS, OP. 118
        EDWIN F. KALMUS   3915   1.75
SCHUMANN, R.
    TRAUMEREI, AND ROMANZE
        G. SCHIRMER, INC.   .40
SCHUMANN, R.   SAUER   D
    TWO SONATAS, OP. 11, 22
        C. F. PETERS CORPORATION   2326   3.50
SCHUNGELER, H.   1-2
    DAS NEUE KINDERLIEDERBUCH
        SCHOTT   3719   2.50
SCHUNGELER, H.   2-3
    DAS NEUE VOLKSLIEDERBUCH
        SCHOTT   3968   2.50
SCHUNGELER, H.
    DAS NEUE WEG. AUSGEWAHLTE ETUDEN UND STUDIEN, HEFT 03
        SCHOTT   4010   2.25
SCHUNGELER, H.   3-5
    DER NEUE GRADUS AD PARNASSUM VON CLEMENTI NEBST ERGANZUNGEN,
    BAND 01
        SCHOTT   2770A   2.50
SCHUNGELER, H.   3-5
    DER NEUE GRADUS AD PARNASSUM VON CLEMENTI NEBST ERGANZUNGEN,
    BAND 02
        SCHOTT   2770B   2.50
SCHUNGELER, H.
    DER NEUE WEG. AUSGEWAHLTE ETUDEN UND STUDIEN, HEFT 01
        SCHOTT   4008   2.25
SCHUNGELER, H.
    DER NEUE WEG. AUSGEWAHLTE ETUDEN UND STUDIEN, HEFT 02
        SCHOTT   4009   2.25
SCHUNGELER, H.
    KLAVIERSCHULE, BAND 01
        SCHOTT   4011   4.00
SCHUNGELER, H.
    KLAVIERSCHULE, BAND 02
        SCHOTT   4012   4.00
SCHUNGELER, H.   2
    NEUES VORTRAGSBUCH, HEFT 01
        SCHOTT   2793   2.75
SCHUNGELER, H.   3-4
    NEUES VORTRAGSBUCH, HEFT 02
        SCHOTT   2794   2.75
SCHUNGELER, H.
    TONLEITERN UND AKKORDE
        SCHOTT   3967   1.75
SCHUNGELER, H.--ED   SCHUNGELER, H.   1-2
    DAS NEUE KINDERLIEDERBUCH
        SCHOTT   3719   2.50
SCHUNGELER, H.--ED   SCHUNGELER, H.   2-3
    DAS NEUE VOLKSLIEDERBUCH
        SCHOTT   3968   2.50
SCHYTTE
    TWENTY-FIVE SHORT AND MELODIOUS STUDIES, OP. 108
        G. SCHIRMER, INC.   L1371   1.00
SCIAMMARELLA
    TEN SHORT PIECES
        FRANCO COLOMBO PUBLICATIONS   BA11260   3.25
SCIONTI
    ROAD TO PIANO ARTISTRY, VOL. 1
        CARL FISCHER, INC.   O 3349   1.25
SCIONTI
    ROAD TO PIANO ARTISTRY, VOL. 2
        CARL FISCHER, INC.   O 3350   1.25
SCIONTI
    ROAD TO PIANO ARTISTRY, VOL. 3
        CARL FISCHER, INC.   O 3351   1.25
SCIONTI
    ROAD TO PIANO ARTISTRY, VOL. 4
        CARL FISCHER, INC.   O 3352   1.25
SCIONTI
    ROAD TO PIANO ARTISTRY, VOL. 5
        CARL FISCHER, INC.   O 3353   1.25

SCIONTI
   ROAD TO PIANO ARTISTRY, VOL. 6
      CARL FISCHER, INC.   O 3354   1.25
SCIONTI
   ROAD TO PIANO ARTISTRY, VOL. 7
      CARL FISCHER, INC.   O 3355   1.25
SCIONTI
   ROAD TO PIANO ARTISTRY, VOL. 8
      CARL FISCHER, INC.   O 3356   1.25
SCIONTI
   ROAD TO PIANO ARTISTRY, VOL. 9
      CARL FISCHER, INC.   O 3357   1.25
SCIORTINO, E.
   AGRESTIES - UNE GARDEUSE, D'OIES QUI PASSE, SUR UNE ROUTE, UN
   SOIR CALME D'ETE, AU TROT D'UN PETIT ANE
      FRANCO COLOMBO PUBLICATIONS   SAL   2.50
SCOTT, C.
   LENTO --2 PIERROT PIECES--
      CARL FISCHER, INC.   P 3060   .60
SCOTT, H.
   HAZEL SCOTT FIVE SOLOS -- BOOGIE WOOGIE TO THE CLASSICS
      MCA MUSIC   1.00
SCRIABINE, A.   PHILIPP, I.
   ALBUM OF 12 SELECTED PRELUDES
      INTERNATIONAL MUSIC COMPANY   2.00
SCRIABINE, A.
   ALBUM OF 6 PIECES
      INTERNATIONAL MUSIC COMPANY   1.75
SCRIABINE, A.
   EIGHT ETUDES, OP. 42
      INTERNATIONAL MUSIC COMPANY   2.50
SCRIABINE, A.
   ETUDES, OP. 42
      EDWIN F. KALMUS   3942   2.50
SCRIABINE, A.
   FIVE PRELUDES, OP. 15
      BOOSEY AND HAWKES, INC.   2.00
SCRIABINE, A.
   FIVE PRELUDES, OP. 16
      BOOSEY AND HAWKES, INC.   3.00
SCRIABINE, A.
   FIVE PRELUDES, OP. 74
      ASSOCIATED MUSIC PUBLISHERS, INC.   SIM   1.50
SCRIABINE, A.
   FIVE PRELUDES, OP. 74
      INTERNATIONAL MUSIC COMPANY   1.75
SCRIABINE, A.
   FOUR PRELUDES, OP. 48
      BOOSEY AND HAWKES, INC.   2.00
SCRIABINE, A.   FREY
   GUIRLANDES AND FLAMMES SOMBRES, OP. 73 NOS. 1 AND 2
      ASSOCIATED MUSIC PUBLISHERS, INC.   SIM   1.50
SCRIABINE, A.
   MASTERPIECES
      EDWARD B. MARKS MUSIC CORPORATION   02.50
SCRIABINE, A.
   NINE MAZURKAS, OP. 25
      BOOSEY AND HAWKES, INC.   3.75
SCRIABINE, A.   FREY
   POEMES, OP. 69 NOS. 1 AND 2
      ASSOCIATED MUSIC PUBLISHERS, INC.   SIM   1.50
SCRIABINE, A.   BAYLOR
   SCRIABIN -- SELECTED WORKS
      ALFRED MUSIC COMPANY   642   3.50
SCRIABINE, A.   PHILIPP, G.   D
   SELECTED PIANO WORKS, VOL. 1‡ ETUDES
      C. F. PETERS CORPORATION   9077A   7.50
SCRIABINE, A.   PHILIPP, G.   D
   SELECTED PIANO WORKS, VOL. 2
      C. F. PETERS CORPORATION   9077B   7.50
SCRIABINE, A.   PHILIPP, G.   D
   SELECTED PIANO WORKS, VOL. 3
      C. F. PETERS CORPORATION   9077C   7.50
SCRIABINE, A.
   SEVEN PRELUDES, OP. 17
      BOOSEY AND HAWKES, INC.   2.75
SCRIABINE, A.
   SIX PRELUDES, OP. 13
      BOOSEY AND HAWKES, INC.   2.00
SCRIABINE, A.   DEIS
   SIXTEEN PRELUDES
      G. SCHIRMER, INC.   L1684   1.00
SCRIABINE, A.
   TEN SONATAS
      MCA MUSIC   8.50
SCRIABINE, A.
   TWELVE ETUDES, OP. 8
      BOOSEY AND HAWKES, INC.   2.75
SCRIABINE, A.   PHILIPP, I.
   TWELVE ETUDES, OP. 8
      INTERNATIONAL MUSIC COMPANY   2.50
SCRIABINE, A.
   TWELVE ETUDES, OP. 8
      EDWARD B. MARKS MUSIC CORPORATION   02.50
SCRIABINE, A.
   TWENTY-FOUR PRELUDES, OP. 11
      BOOSEY AND HAWKES, INC.   3.00
SCRIABINE, A.
   TWENTY-FOUR PRELUDES, OP. 11
      EDWARD B. MARKS MUSIC CORPORATION   02.50
SCRIABINE, A.   PHILIPP, I.
   TWENTY-FOUR PRELUDES, OP.11
      INTERNATIONAL MUSIC COMPANY   2.50
SCRIABINE, A.
   TWO IMPROMPTUS, OP. 12
      BOOSEY AND HAWKES, INC.   2.50
SCRIABINE, A.
   TWO IMPROMPTUS, OP. 14
      BOOSEY AND HAWKES, INC.   2.00
SCRIABINE, A.
   TWO PIECES, OP. 57
      BOOSEY AND HAWKES, INC.   1.00
SCRIABINE, A.
   TWO POEMS, OP. 32
      BOOSEY AND HAWKES, INC.   1.50
SCRIABINE, A.
   TWO POEMS, OP. 32
      INTERNATIONAL MUSIC COMPANY   1.25
SCRIABINE, A.
   TWO POEMS, OP. 71
      ASSOCIATED MUSIC PUBLISHERS, INC.   SIM   1.50
SCRIABINE, A.   FREY
   TWO PRELUDES, OP. 67
      ASSOCIATED MUSIC PUBLISHERS, INC.   SIM   1.50
SCRIABINE, A. *   GARVELMANN, D.
   YOUTHFUL AND EARLY WORKS OF ALEXANDER AND JULIAN SCRIABIN
      MUSIC TREASURE PUBLICATIONS   6.00

SCULTHORPE, P.
   FIVE NIGHT PIECES
      FABER MUSIC, LTD.   F0369
SEBASTIANI, P.
   CUATRO PRELUDIOS NO. 1
      PEER SOUTHERN ORGANIZATION   01.00
SEBASTIANI, P.
   CUATRO PRELUDIOS NO. 2
      PEER SOUTHERN ORGANIZATION   01.00
SEBASTIANI, P.
   CUATRO PRELUDIOS NO. 3
      PEER SOUTHERN ORGANIZATION   00.85
SEBASTIANI, P.
   CUATRO PRELUDIOS NO. 4
      PEER SOUTHERN ORGANIZATION   01.25
SEDERBERG
   TECHNIC BOOK
      WILLIS MUSIC COMPANY   1.50
SEDLAK, A.
   FIVE DANCES
      ASSOCIATED MUSIC PUBLISHERS, INC.   DOB   1.50
SEDLON
   SEDLON PIANO METHOD, BK. 1
      BOOSEY AND HAWKES, INC.   1.25
SEDLON
   SEDLON PIANO METHOD, BK. 2
      BOOSEY AND HAWKES, INC.   1.25
SEIBER, M.   2
   LEICHTE TANZE, HEFT 01
      SCHOTT   2234   2.50
SEIBER, M.   2
   LEICHTE TANZE, HEFT 02
      SCHOTT   2546   2.50
SEIBER, M.   3
   RHYTHMISCHE STUDIEN
      SCHOTT   2.50
SEIDER
   TALES OF SCALES
      WILLIS MUSIC COMPANY   2.50
SEIDER, S.
   SEA-GOING TIME
      ASHLEY DEALERS SERVICE, INC.   1.25
SEIDER, S.
   SEA-GOING TIME
      CENTURY MUSIC PUBLISHING COMPANY, INC.   1.25
SEIXAS   KASTNER   3
   EIGHTY SONATAS PARA INSTRUMENTOS DE TECLA, HEFT 1 -- SONATEN
   1-18 --
      BARENREITER VERLAG   PM 10
SEIXAS   KASTNER   3
   EIGHTY SONATAS PARA INSTRUMENTOS DE TECLA, HEFT 2 -- SONATEN
   19-39 --
      BARENREITER VERLAG   PM 10
SEIXAS   KASTNER   3
   EIGHTY SONATAS PARA INSTRUMENTOS DE TECLA, HEFT 3 -- SONATEN
   40-60 --
      BARENREITER VERLAG   PM 10
SEIXAS   KASTNER   3
   EIGHTY SONATAS PARA INSTRUMENTOS DE TECLA, HEFT 4 -- SONATEN
   61-80 --
      BARENREITER VERLAG   PM 10
SELVA
   ENSEIGNEMENT MUSICAL DE LA TECHNIQUE DU PIANO, L' ....
   PREPARATORY BOOK 1 - PRINCIPES PRIMORDIAUX DU TRAVAIL PIANISTIQUE
      FRANCO COLOMBO PUBLICATIONS   SAL   8.75
SELVA
   ENSEIGNEMENT MUSICAL DE LA TECHNIQUE DU PIANO, L' ....
   PREPARATORY BOOK 2 - PREPARATION DU TOUCHER AU PIANO
      FRANCO COLOMBO PUBLICATIONS   SAL   19.50
SELVA
   ENSEIGNEMENT MUSICAL DE LA TECHNIQUE DU PIANO, L' .... VOL. 1 -
   PRINCIPES DE LA SONORITE AU PIANO, TRAVAIL ELEMENTAIRE DES TOUCHES
   .. STUDENT'S BOOK
      FRANCO COLOMBO PUBLICATIONS   SAL   2.75
SELVA
   ENSEIGNEMENT MUSICAL DE LA TECHNIQUE DU PIANO, L' .... VOL. 1 -
   PRINCIPES DE LA SONORITE AU PIANO, TRAVAIL ELEMENTAIRE DES TOUCHES.
   .. TEACHER'S BOOK
      FRANCO COLOMBO PUBLICATIONS   SAL   10.75
SELVA
   ENSEIGNEMENT MUSICAL DE LA TECHNIQUE DU PIANO, L' .... VOL. 2 -
   LA SIMULTANEITE DES SONS AU PIANO, TRAVAIL ELEMENTAIRE DEA DOUBLE
   NOTES
      FRANCO COLOMBO PUBLICATIONS   SAL   18.00
SELVA
   ENSEIGNEMENT MUSICAL DE LA TECHNIQUE DU PIANO, L' .... VOL. 3 -
   LE TRAIT DEPLOIEMENT RYTHMIQUE DE L'HARMONIE .. PART 1 - DOUBLES
   NOTES, TREMOLOS, TRAITS BRISES, ARPEDES
      FRANCO COLOMBO PUBLICATIONS   SAL   18.00
SELVA
   ENSEIGNEMENT MUSICAL DE LA TECHNIQUE DU PIANO, L' .... VOL. 3 -
   LE TRAIT DEPLOIEMENT RYTHMIQUE DE L'HARMONIE .. PART 2 - GAMMES,
   ARPEGES, TRAITS COMPOSES
      FRANCO COLOMBO PUBLICATIONS   SAL   18.00
SENTIS, J. *
   RAPSODIE ARAGONAISE AND RAPSODIE CATALNE
      ASSOCIATED MUSIC PUBLISHERS, INC.   ESC   2.75
SEROUX
   DANCES
      FRANCO COLOMBO PUBLICATIONS   SAL   2.75
SEROUX
   RONDOS
      FRANCO COLOMBO PUBLICATIONS   SAL   2.75
SERRA, M.
   DELICIAS DEL CAMPO--SUITE
      ASSOCIATED MUSIC PUBLISHERS, INC.   UME   .60
SETCHELL
   CHURCH PIANO MUSIC
      CARL FISCHER, INC.   RB 30   3.00
SEUTIN
   METHOD FOR THE PIANO
      FRANCO COLOMBO PUBLICATIONS   SAL   16.25
SEVERAC
   CERDANA
      FRANCO COLOMBO PUBLICATIONS   SAL   9.00
SEVERAC
   EN LANGUEDOC
      FRANCO COLOMBO PUBLICATIONS   SAL   9.00
SEVERAC
   EN VACANCES, BK. 1
      FRANCO COLOMBO PUBLICATIONS   SAL   4.50
SEVERAC
   EN VACANCES, BK. 2
      FRANCO COLOMBO PUBLICATIONS   SAL   3.50
SHACKLEY--ED.   SHACKLEY
   CHRISTMAS TIDE
      SHAWNEE PRESS, INC.   1.25

SHANKO, S. W.--ED   SHANKO, S. W.
    HYMN TUNE PRELUDES FOR THE PIANO, NO. 3
        BROADMAN MUSIC   4571-05   2.25
SHAW
    EARLY ITALIAN PIANO MUSIC OF THE 17TH CENTURY
        BELWIN-MILLS PUBLISHING CORPORATION   2.00
SHAW, A.
    MOBILES -- 10 GRAPHIC IMPRESSIONS
        THEODORE PRESSER COMPANY   1.25
SHAW, A.
    PLABILES -- 12 SONGS WITHOUT WORDS
        THEODORE PRESSER COMPANY   1.75
SHAW, A.
    STABILES -- 12 IMAGES
        THEODORE PRESSER COMPANY   1.75
SHEARING, G.
    INTERPRETATIONS FOR PIANO, NO. 1
        THE BIG THREE MUSIC CORPORATION   01.50
SHEARING, G.
    INTERPRETATIONS FOR PIANO, NO. 2
        THE BIG THREE MUSIC CORPORATION   01.50
SHEARING, G.
    INTERPRETATIONS FOR PIANO, NO. 3
        THE BIG THREE MUSIC CORPORATION   01.50
SHEARING, G.
    INTERPRETATIONS FOR PIANO, NO. 4
        THE BIG THREE MUSIC CORPORATION   01.50
SHEARING, G.
    INTERPRETATIONS FOR PIANO, NO. 5
        THE BIG THREE MUSIC CORPORATION   01.50
SHEARING, G.
    INTERPRETATIONS FOR PIANO, NO. 6
        THE BIG THREE MUSIC CORPORATION   01.50
SHEARING, G.
    INTERPRETATIONS FOR PIANO, NO. 7
        THE BIG THREE MUSIC CORPORATION   01.50
SHEARING, G.
    PLAY PIANO LIKE GEORGE SHEARING
        THE BIG THREE MUSIC CORPORATION   01.50
SHEBALIN
    THREE SONATINAS, OP. 12
        MCA MUSIC   1.50
SHELDON
    ALL ABOUT MUSIC - COMPLETE BOOK OF MUSICAL THEORY
        BOSTON MUSIC COMPANY   2.00
SHELLEY--ED.   SHELLEY
    MELODIES FOR CHURCH AND HOME
        G. SCHIRMER, INC.   1.50
SHERWOOD
    TOUCH AND TECHNIC
        MUSICA OBSCURA   1.50
SHINN, D.
    HOW TO PLAY CHORD PIANO IN 10 DAYS
        SHINN MUSIC AIDS   3.95
SHINN, D.
    HOW TO PLAY LUSH, MODERN, 'MOOD' PIANO
        SHINN MUSIC AIDS   3.95
SHINN, D.
    HOW TO PLAY PIANO BY EAR
        SHINN MUSIC AIDS   3.95
SHINN, D.
    HOW TO TEACH YOURSELF ALL ABOUT CHORDS
        SHINN MUSIC AIDS   3.95
SHINN, D.
    HOW TO TEACH YOURSELF HARMONY -- INSTANTLY
        SHINN MUSIC AIDS   3.95
SHINN, D.
    SEVEN MAGIC STEPS TO SPEED SIGHT READING
        SHINN MUSIC AIDS   3.95
SHINN, D.
    TWENTY LESSON COURSE IN EVANGELISTIC PIANO PLAYING
        SHINN MUSIC AIDS   6.95
SHLIMOVITZ
    RHYTHM SINGER, THE
        BELWIN-MILLS PUBLISHING CORPORATION   1.00
SHORES
    SWINGIN' TECHNIC
        SUMMY-BIRCHARD COMPANY   1.75
SHOSTAKOVITCH
    ALBUM OF SELECTED PIANO WORKS
        INTERNATIONAL MUSIC COMPANY   2.00
SHOSTAKOVITCH
    ALBUM, BK. 1
        EDWIN F. KALMUS   3958   2.75
SHOSTAKOVITCH
    APHORISMS - TEN PIECES FOR PIANO, OP. 13
        MCA MUSIC   1.75
SHOSTAKOVITCH   E
    CHILDREN'S BOOK
        C. F. PETERS CORPORATION   4749   2.00
SHOSTAKOVITCH
    DANCES OF THE DOLLS. SEVEN PIECES FOR PIANO
        MCA MUSIC   1.50
SHOSTAKOVITCH   E
    DOLL'S DANCES
        C. F. PETERS CORPORATION   4711   2.00
SHOSTAKOVITCH
    FANTASTIC DANCES
        EDWIN F. KALMUS   3968   1.25
SHOSTAKOVITCH
    FIVE PRELUDES
        MCA MUSIC   1.25
SHOSTAKOVITCH
    FOUR PRELUDES, OP. 34, NOS. 13, 16, 17, 24
        EDWIN F. KALMUS   3966   1.00
SHOSTAKOVITCH
    MASTERPIECES
        EDWARD B. MARKS MUSIC CORPORATION   02.50
SHOSTAKOVITCH   AGAY, D.
    SIX CHILDREN'S PIECES
        MCA MUSIC   1.25
SHOSTAKOVITCH
    THREE FANTASTIC DANCES
        INTERNATIONAL MUSIC COMPANY   1.00
SHOSTAKOVITCH
    THREE FANTASTIC DANCES
        EDWARD B. MARKS MUSIC CORPORATION   01.00
SHOSTAKOVITCH
    THREE FANTASTIC DANCES, OP. 5
        MCA MUSIC   1.25
SHOSTAKOVITCH
    TWENTY FOUR PRELUDES
        INTERNATIONAL MUSIC COMPANY   2.25
SHOSTAKOVITCH
    TWENTY-FOUR PRELUDES
        BOSTON MUSIC COMPANY   1.50

SHOSTAKOVITCH   MUSAFIA
    TWENTY-FOUR PRELUDES AND FUGURES, OP. 87
        MCA MUSIC   9.00
SHOSTAKOVITCH   M-D
    TWENTY-FOUR PRELUDES AND FUGUES, OP. 87. VOL. 1
        C. F. PETERS CORPORATION   4716A   6.50
SHOSTAKOVITCH   M-D
    TWENTY-FOUR PRELUDES AND FUGUES, OP. 87. VOL. 2
        C. F. PETERS CORPORATION   4716B   6.50
SHOSTAKOVITCH
    TWENTY-FOUR PRELUDES AND FUGUES, OP.87--BK. 1
        EDWIN F. KALMUS   3962   1.50
SHOSTAKOVITCH
    TWENTY-FOUR PRELUDES AND FUGUES, OP.87--BK. 2
        EDWIN F. KALMUS   3963   1.50
SHOSTAKOVITCH
    TWENTY-FOUR PRELUDES AND FUGUES, OP.87--BK. 3
        EDWIN F. KALMUS   3964   1.50
SHOSTAKOVITCH
    TWENTY-FOUR PRELUDES AND FUGUES, OP.87--BK. 4
        EDWIN F. KALMUS   3965   3.00
SHOSTAKOVITCH
    TWENTY-FOUR PRELUDES, OP. 34
        EDWIN F. KALMUS   3967   2.00
SHOSTAKOVITCH
    TWENTY-FOUR PRELUDES, OP. 34
        MCA MUSIC   3.00
SHOSTAKOVITCH   M-D
    TWENTY-FOUR PRELUDES, OP. 34. VOL. 1
        C. F. PETERS CORPORATION   4773A   3.00
SHOSTAKOVITCH   M-D
    TWENTY-FOUR PRELUDES, OP. 34. VOL. 2
        C. F. PETERS CORPORATION   4773B   3.00
SHOSTAKOVITCH   PHILIPP, I.
    TWO PRELUDES AND FUGUES, OP. 87
        INTERNATIONAL MUSIC COMPANY   1.50
SHOSTAKOVITCH
    TWO PRELUDES, OP. 34 NOS. 14 AND 34
        MCA MUSIC   .60
SHUKEN   GR. 3-5
    EIGHT HARMONIC IMPROVISATIONS
        WESTERN INTERNATIONAL MUSIC, INC.   HP803   1.75
SHULGIN
    TEN CHILDREN'S PIECES
        MCA MUSIC   .75
SHULMAN
    MARCH AND DRIPPING FAUCET
        WEINTRAUB MUSIC COMPANY   070088   .50
SIBELIUS   TAUBMANN
    KING CHRISTIAN SUITE--NOCTURNE AND SERENADE
        ASSOCIATED MUSIC PUBLISHERS, INC.   BRH   1.25
SIBELIUS
    ROMANCE, OP. 24 NO. 4 AND WALTZ, OP. 24 NO. 5
        ASSOCIATED MUSIC PUBLISHERS, INC.   BRH   2.00
SIBELIUS
    SIX FINNISH FOLKSONGS
        ASSOCIATED MUSIC PUBLISHERS, INC.   BRH   1.20
SICILIANI
    THREE DANZAS AMERICANAS
        FRANCO COLOMBO PUBLICATIONS   BA11235   1.25
SICILIANO   M-D
    EIGHT CHILDREN'S MINIATURES
        C. F. PETERS CORPORATION   HD2184   1.50
SICILIANO
    FIGURINE - 6 LITTLE PIECES ON 5 NOTES
        FRANCO COLOMBO PUBLICATIONS   FOR.12211 1.25
SIEGL, O.
    FORM UND AUSDRUCK, 15 POLYPHONIC PIECES, BK. 1
        ASSOCIATED MUSIC PUBLISHERS, INC.   DOB   2.50
SIEGL, O.
    FORM UND AUSDRUCK, 15 POLYPHONIC PIECES, BK. 2
        ASSOCIATED MUSIC PUBLISHERS, INC.   DOB   2.50
SIEGL, O.
    UNTERHALTSAME KLAVIERLEHSTUCKE
        ASSOCIATED MUSIC PUBLISHERS, INC.   DOB   1.75
SIEGMEISTER
    CHILDREN'S DAY- SIX PIECES
        MCA MUSIC   .75
SIEGMEISTER
    FOLK WAYS, U. S. A., BK. 1
        THEODORE PRESSER COMPANY   1.25
SIEGMEISTER
    FOLK WAYS, U. S. A., BK. 2
        THEODORE PRESSER COMPANY   1.25
SIEGMEISTER
    FOLK WAYS, U. S. A., BK. 3
        THEODORE PRESSER COMPANY   1.25
SIEGMEISTER
    FROM MY WINDOW
        CHAPPELL AND COMPANY, INC.   0015172   1.75
SIKORSKI
    SIKORSKI ALBUM - KLINGENDE HEIMAT - FOLKSONGS FROM ALL PARTS
    OF GERMANY ----- CLOTH
        FRANCO COLOMBO PUBLICATIONS   SIK.221   10.00
SIKORSKI
    SIKORSKI ALBUM - KLINGENDE HEIMAT - FOLKSONGS FROM ALL PARTS
    OF GERMANY ----- PAPER
        FRANCO COLOMBO PUBLICATIONS   SIK.221   6.00
SILL, H.
    CHORD SYSTEM PIANO COURSE - BK. 1
        WILLIS MUSIC COMPANY   1.50
SILL, H.
    CHORD SYSTEM PIANO COURSE - BK. 2
        WILLIS MUSIC COMPANY   1.25
SILL, H.
    CHORD SYSTEM PIANO COURSE - BK. 3
        WILLIS MUSIC COMPANY   1.00
SILL, H.
    CHORD SYSTEM PIANO COURSE - BK. 4
        WILLIS MUSIC COMPANY   1.00
SILL, H.
    CHORD SYSTEM PIANO COURSE - BK. 5
        WILLIS MUSIC COMPANY   1.00
SILL, H.
    CHORD SYSTEM PIANO COURSE - BK. 6
        WILLIS MUSIC COMPANY   1.00
SILL, H.
    CHORD SYSTEM PIANO COURSE - STARTER SET, BK. A
        WILLIS MUSIC COMPANY   1.25
SILL, H.
    CHORD SYSTEM PIANO COURSE - STARTER SET, BK. B
        WILLIS MUSIC COMPANY   1.75
SILVESTRI
    EIGHTEEN ITALIAN HARPSICHORD PIECES
        FRANCO COLOMBO PUBLICATIONS   ER1905   2.25
SILVESTRI
    SCALES, THE - BK. 1 -- SIMPLE SCALES --
        FRANCO COLOMBO PUBLICATIONS   ER1759   2.50

SILVESTRI
 SCALES, THE - BK. 2 -- SCALES IN THIRDS AND SIXTHS --
  FRANCO COLOMBO PUBLICATIONS   ER1760   5.50
SIMS
 FIVE PIANO RHAPSODIES
  SHAWNEE PRESS, INC.   D
    2.00
SINDING
 ALBUM FOR PIANO
  C. F. PETERS CORPORATION   2974C   2.50
SINGER, L.--ED   SINGER, L.
 CHAPPELL'S FAMOUS MELODIES
  CHAPPELL AND COMPANY, INC.   0021964-1741 2.00
SINGERY
 POUR UNE PETITE BIEN SAGE
  FRANCO COLOMBO PUBLICATIONS   SAL   2.75
SIRIANNI
 FIVE EASY LITTLE PIECES
  FRANCO COLOMBO PUBLICATIONS   129302   .90
SKALKOTTAS, N.
 TEN PIANO PIECES FROM '32 PIANO PIECES'
  UNIVERSAL EDITION   UE 12958   7.55
SKELLY
 SOLEMN SONG, BUTTINSKI MARCH
  MCA MUSIC   .60
SKJERNE--ED.   SKJERNE, A.
 BABY SCHOOL -- 40 SELECTIONS FOR BEGINNERS' BALLET TRAINING FROM
 THE MASTERS
  G. SCHIRMER, INC.   1.50
SKJERNE--ED.   SKJERNE, A.
 BALLET SCHOOL -- 100 SELECTIONS FROM THE MASTERS FOR DAILY
 TRAINING
  G. SCHIRMER, INC.   1.80
SKJERNE--ED.   SKJERNE
 BALLET SCHOOL--WILHELM HANSEN EDITION
  G. SCHIRMER, INC.   1.80
SKJERNE--ED.   SKJERNE, A.
 CINQ POSITIONS, LES -- 80 SELECTIONS FROM THE MASTERS FOR DAILY
 TRAINING
  G. SCHIRMER, INC.   1.80
SKJERNE--ED.   SKJERNE, A.
 FIRST STEP IN BALLET, THE -- 40 SELECTIONS FROM THE MASTERS FOR
 DAILY TRAINING
  G. SCHIRMER, INC.   3.00
SKJERNE--ED.   SKJERNE
 LES CINQ POSITIONS--WILHELM HANSEN EDITION
  G. SCHIRMER, INC.   1.80
SKORZENY, F.
 MUSIQUETTES--1962
  ASSOCIATED MUSIC PUBLISHERS, INC.   DOB   2.25
SLAVICKY, K.   3-4
 DREI KLAVIERSTUCKE -- BURLESCA, INTERMEZZO, TOCCATA --
  BARENREITER VERLAG   AP 695
SLAVICKY, K.
 ON THE BLACKS AND WHITES
  ARTIA   1.25
SLAVICKY, K.
 THREE PIECES FOR PIANO
  ARTIA   1.75
SLAVICKY, K.
 TWELVE SMALL STUDIES
  ARTIA   1.00
SLAVICKY, K.   KLEINOVA   3-4
 ZWOLF KLEINE ETUDEN
  BARENREITER VERLAG   AP 1766
SLONIMSKY   ADVANCED
 TWO ETUDES
  SHAWNEE PRESS, INC.   .75
SLOTE, G. --ED   SLOTE, G.
 SONGS FOR ALL YEAR LONG AND GOSH, WHAT A WONDERFUL WORLD
  OAK PUBLICATIONS   000090   2.95
SMALL, A.
 ALLAN SMALL PIANO METHOD, THE
  ALFRED MUSIC COMPANY   536   1.25
SMALL, A.
 ARPEGGIO PIANO SOLOS
  ALFRED MUSIC COMPANY   521   1.25
SMALL, A.
 BEGINNER'S ROCK 'N' ROLL PIANO BOOK
  ALFRED MUSIC COMPANY   542   1.00
SMALL, A.
 BLUES AND HOW
  ALFRED MUSIC COMPANY   543   1.95
SMALL, A.
 CHRISTMAS CAROL SONGBOOK, THE
  ALFRED MUSIC COMPANY   662   1.50
SMALL, A.
 CLASSICS, THE
  ALFRED MUSIC COMPANY   523   1.95
SMALL, A.
 COLLECTION OF PIANO SOLOS
  ALFRED MUSIC COMPANY   524   .80
SMALL, A.
 EASIEST CHRISTMAS CAROLS
  ALFRED MUSIC COMPANY   660   1.25
SMALL, A.
 EASY PIANO CHRISTMAS CAROLS
  ALFRED MUSIC COMPANY   661   1.00
SMALL, A.
 ETERNAL HYMNS
  ALFRED MUSIC COMPANY   525   2.95
SMALL, A.
 FAMILIAR MELODIES IN SONATINA STYLE
  ALFRED MUSIC COMPANY   526   1.25
SMALL, A.
 PIANO STUDENTS CHOICE
  ALFRED MUSIC COMPANY   529   1.95
SMALL, A.
 PRE-SONATINA ALBUM
  ALFRED MUSIC COMPANY   530   1.25
SMALL, A.
 ROCK 'N' ROLL PIANIST, THE
  ALFRED MUSIC COMPANY   545   1.50
SMALL, A.
 SHALOM, 72 TRADITIONAL HEBREW MELODIES
  ALFRED MUSIC COMPANY   547   3.50
SMALL, A.
 TEACHER'S CHOICE FOR THE YOUNG PIANIST
  ALFRED MUSIC COMPANY   534   1.95
SMALL, A.
 THIRTY-SIX VERY EASY ALL-TIME FAVORITES
  ALFRED MUSIC COMPANY   535   1.50
SMALL, A.
 VERY FIRST PIANO SOLO BOOK
  ALFRED MUSIC COMPANY   538   1.95
SMALLEY, R.
 PIANO PIECES 1-4
  FABER MUSIC, LTD.   F0191

SMART, D.
 FOUR SEASONAL PRELUDES
  HOPE PUBLISHING COMPANY   1.00
SMETANA   3
 AUS SMETANAS OPERN
  BARENREITER VERLAG   AP 721
SMETANA   2-3
 BAGATELLEN UND IMPROMPTUS
  BARENREITER VERLAG   AP 704
SMETANA
 BAGATELLES AND IMPROMPTUS
  ARTIA   1.50
SMETANA
 BOHEMIAN DANCES
  ARTIA   2.25
SMETANA   STEPAN   4
 BOHMISCHE TANZE
  BARENREITER VERLAG   AP 1677
SMETANA   3-4
 DREI ETUDEN
  BARENREITER VERLAG   AP 709
SMETANA
 DREI ETUDEN
  BARENREITER VERLAG   AP 709
SMETANA   3
 DREI KOMPOSITIONEN AUS DEM REVOLUTIONSJAHR 1848
  BARENREITER VERLAG   AP 708
SMETANA   3
 DREI POLKAS -- E, G MINOR, A --
  BARENREITER VERLAG   AP 711
SMETANA   SOLC   3
 DREI SALONPOLKAS, OP. 7
  BARENREITER VERLAG   AP 700
SMETANA   3
 FOUR POLKAS
  ARTIA   .75
SMETANA
 KLAVIERKOMPOSITIONEN
  BARENREITER VERLAG   AP 714
SMETANA   3-4
 KLAVIERWERKE - 1, DIE ERSTEN ZYKLEN
  BARENREITER VERLAG   AP 323
SMETANA   3-4
 KLAVIERWERKE - 2, STUDIENSTUCKE UND SONATEN AUS DEM JAHRE 1846
  BARENREITER VERLAG   AP 324
SMETANA   3
 MEIN VATERLAND GESAMTAUSGABE
  BARENREITER VERLAG   AP 748
SMETANA   M-D
 POLKAS
  C. F. PETERS CORPORATION   4455   3.00
SMETANA   3
 SECHS ALBUMBLATTER, OP. 2
  BARENREITER VERLAG   AP 697
SMETANA   D
 SELECTED PIECES
  C. F. PETERS CORPORATION   4642   3.50
SMETANA
 SIX BOHEMIAN DANCES
  EDWIN F. KALMUS   3980   3.00
SMETANA   M-D
 SIX BOHEMIAN DANCES
  C. F. PETERS CORPORATION   4435   3.00
SMETANA   3-4
 SIX CHARAKTERISTISCHE KOMPOSITIONEN, OP. 1
  BARENREITER VERLAG   AP 696
SMETANA
 SONATA ALBUM, BK. 1
  EDWIN F. KALMUS   3981   3.50
SMETANA
 SONATA ALBUM, BK. 2
  EDWIN F. KALMUS   3982   3.50
SMETANA
 THREE ETUDES
  ARTIA   1.50
SMETANA
 THREE POLKAS
  ARTIA   1.00
SMETANA   WERNER
 TWO ALBUM LEAVES, OP. 5 NO. 7 AND OP. 5 NO. 22--CURWEN EDITION
  G. SCHIRMER, INC.   .75
SMETANA   3
 VIER POLKAS
  BARENREITER VERLAG   AP 725
SMETANA
 WALTZES
  ARTIA   .75
SMETANA
 WALZER
  BARENREITER VERLAG   AP 726
SMIT, L.
 SEVEN CHARACTERISTIC PIECES
  BROUDE BROTHERS LTD.   03.25
SMITH--ED   SMITH
 TWENTY-NINE VERY EASY FOLK SONGS
  BOSTON MUSIC COMPANY   1.25
SMITH, H.
 FACES OF JAZZ
  EDWARD B. MARKS MUSIC CORPORATION   01.50
SMITH, L.   M
 FOUR ETUDES
  THEODORE PRESSER COMPANY   1.00
SMITH, T.
 CONCERT HYMN TRANSCRIPTIONS
  HOPE PUBLISHING COMPANY   1.50
SMITH, T.
 CRUSADE PIANIST NO. 1
  LILLENAS PUBLISHING COMPANY   MB-030   2.50
SMITH, T.
 CRUSADE PIANIST NO. 2
  LILLENAS PUBLISHING COMPANY   MB-031   2.50
SMITH, T.
 CRUSADE PIANIST NO. 3
  LILLENAS PUBLISHING COMPANY   MB-032   2.50
SMITH, T.
 CRUSADE PIANIST NO. 4
  LILLENAS PUBLISHING COMPANY   MB-235   2.50
SMITH, T.
 FOLK-ROCK IMAGES
  HOPE PUBLISHING COMPANY   2.95
SMITH, T.
 GREAT HYMNS OF THE CHURCH
  HOPE PUBLISHING COMPANY   2.50
SMITH, T.
 SIMPLIFIED PIANO ARRANGEMENTS
  HOPE PUBLISHING COMPANY   2.50

SMITH, T.--ED   SMITH, T.
    PIANO PORTRAITS - SACRED SOLOS
        BROADMAN MUSIC   4571-09   2.75
SNIZKOVA--ED   SNIZKOVA   1-2
    KUTTENBERGER MENUETTBUCHLEIN. 15 MENUETTE AUS DER ANONYMEN
    SAMMLUNG IM WOCEL-ARCHIV IN KUTTENBERG
        BARENREITER VERLAG   MVH 3
SOENSTEVOLD   E-M
    TWO PRELUDES
        C. F. PETERS CORPORATION   LY362   .50
SOEUR SOURIRE   FRANK, M.
    TEN PIECES FROM 'THE SINGING NUN'
        GENERAL MUSIC PUBLISHING COMPANY, INC.   3.00
SOHY
    SIX LITTLE PIECES
        FRANCO COLOMBO PUBLICATIONS   SAL   2.50
                                                      4
SOKOLA
    ZWOLF PRALUDIEN -- 1954 --
        BARENREITER VERLAG   AP 1761
SOLER, A.   DUCK, L.
    SIX SONATAS FOR PIANOFORTE, BK. 1-- NOS. 1, 2 AND 3
        BELWIN-MILLS PUBLISHING CORPORATION   11448   1 .00
SOLER, A.   DUCK, L.
    SIX SONATAS FOR PIANOFORTE, BK. 2 -- NOS. 4, 5 AND 6
        BELWIN-MILLS PUBLISHING CORPORATION   11450   1.00
SOLER, A.   MARVIN, F.
    SONATAS FOR PIANO, BK. 1
        BELWIN-MILLS PUBLISHING CORPORATION   07102   4.00
SOLER, A.   MARVIN, F.
    SONATAS FOR PIANO, BK. 3
        BELWIN-MILLS PUBLISHING CORPORATION   07104   4.00
SOLER, A.   RUBIO
    SONATAS, BK. 1
        ASSOCIATED MUSIC PUBLISHERS, INC.   UME   6.50
SOLER, A.   RUBIO
    SONATAS, BK. 2
        ASSOCIATED MUSIC PUBLISHERS, INC.   UME   5.00
SOLER, A.   RUBIO
    SONATAS, BK. 3
        ASSOCIATED MUSIC PUBLISHERS, INC.   UME   6.00
SOLER, A.   RUBIO
    SONATAS, BK. 4
        ASSOCIATED MUSIC PUBLISHERS, INC.   UME   8.00
SOLER, A.   RUBIO
    SONATAS, BK. 5
        ASSOCIATED MUSIC PUBLISHERS, INC.   UME   6.50
SOLER, A.   RUBIO
    SONATAS, BK. 6
        ASSOCIATED MUSIC PUBLISHERS, INC.   UME   9.00
SOLER, A.
    SONATAS, VOLS. 5 AND 6 IN PREPARATION
        ALEXANDER BROUDE, INC.
SOLER, A.   MARVIN
    SONATAS, VOLUMES 1-4
        ALEXANDER BROUDE, INC.   6.00
SOLER, J.
    TRES PECES PER A PIANO
        PEER SOUTHERN ORGANIZATION   01.00
SOMERS, H.
    THREE SONNETS
        ASSOCIATED MUSIC PUBLISHERS, INC.   BER   1.50
SOMERS, H.
    TWELVE TIME TWELVE--FUGUES FOR PIANO
        ASSOCIATED MUSIC PUBLISHERS, INC.   BER   2.00
SOMERVELL, A.
    MARCH AND DANCE ALBUM
        BOOSEY AND HAWKES, INC.   1.25
SOPRONI, J.
    FOUR BAGATELLES
        KULTURA   1.50
SOPRONI, J.
    SEVEN PIANO PIECES
        KULTURA   1.50
SORESINA
    SIX SONATINAS
        FRANCO COLOMBO PUBLICATIONS   129129   1.50
SOULE
    TUNEFUL TEN
        PRO-ART PUBLICATIONS, INC.   1143   .85
SOUSA
    SOUSA ALBUM
        CARL FISCHER, INC.   O 4006   1.50
SOUSA
    SOUSA ALBUM
        CARL FISCHER, INC.   O 4006   2.00
SOUSA
    SOUSA ALBUM FOR PIANO SOLO
        THEODORE PRESSER COMPANY   1.50
SOUSA   LEVINE, H.
    SOUSA'S FAMOUS MARCHES FOR PIANO SOLO
        THEODORE PRESSER COMPANY   2.00
SOUSA   RICHTER, A.
    STARS AND STRIPES FOREVER -- 9 OTHER WELL-KNOWN FAVORITES
        THEODORE PRESSER COMPANY   1.00
SOUTHAM, A.
    THREE IN BLUE
        ASSOCIATED MUSIC PUBLISHERS, INC.   BER   1.50
SPECKNER--ED.   SPECKNER   2-3
    ALTE ENGLISCHE KONTRATANZE FUR TASTEN-INSTRUMENT
        SCHOTT   5584   2.00
SPECKNER--ED.   SPECKNER   2-3
    ALTE ENGLISCHE KONTRATANZE FUR TASTEN-INSTRUMENT
        SCHOTT   5584   2.00
SPENCER, J.
    FAVORITE CHRISTMAS MELODIES
        VOLKWEIN BROS.   01.00
SPENCER, J.
    FAVORITE MELODIES MADE EASY
        VOLKWEIN BROS.   01.00
SPIES, C.
    THREE INTERMEZZI
        ELKAN-VOGEL, INC.   1.50
SPIES, L.
    KOPENICKER KLAVIERBUCH, BK. 1
        ASSOCIATED MUSIC PUBLISHERS, INC.   BRH   1.50
SPIES, L.
    KOPENICKER KLAVIERBUCH, BK. 2
        ASSOCIATED MUSIC PUBLISHERS, INC.   BRH   1.50
SPIVAK, S.
    BEGINNERS PLAY BOOGIE WOOGIE
        ASHLEY DEALERS SERVICE, INC.   1.25
SPIVAK, S.
    BOOGIE WOOGIE FOR ADULT STUDENTS
        BELWIN-MILLS PUBLISHING CORPORATION   1.00
SPIVAK, S.
    BOOGIE WOOGIE FOR YOUNG STUDENTS
        BELWIN-MILLS PUBLISHING CORPORATION   1.00

SPIVAK, S.
    BOOGIE WOOGIE HOLIDAY
        BELWIN-MILLS PUBLISHING CORPORATION   1.00
SPIVAK, S.
    BOOGIE WOOGIE IN 15 LANGUAGES
        BELWIN-MILLS PUBLISHING CORPORATION   1.00
SPIVAK, S.
    FIFTY-EIGHT TUNEFUL TECHNICAL STUDIES, BK. 1
        ASHLEY DEALERS SERVICE, INC.   1.50
SPIVAK, S.
    FORTY-EIGHT TUNEFUL TECHNICAL STUDIES, BK. 2
        ASHLEY DEALERS SERVICE, INC.   1.50
SPIVAK, S.--ED   SPIVAK, S.
    PLAYING CLASSICS FOR PLEASURE
        SCHUBERTH CO.   1.50
SPIVAK, S.--ED   SPIVAK, S.
    PLAYING PIANO FOR PLEASURE, BK. 1
        SCHUBERTH CO.   1.50
SPIVAK, S.--ED   SPIVAK, S.
    PLAYING PIANO FOR PLEASURE, BK. 2
        SCHUBERTH CO.   1.50
SPIVAK, S.--ED   SPIVAK, S.
    PLAYING PIANO FOR PLEASURE, BK. 3
        SCHUBERTH CO.   1.50
SPRONGL, N.
    FOUR DANCE PIECES, OP. 96
        ASSOCIATED MUSIC PUBLISHERS, INC.   DOB   2.75
SPRONGL, N.
    SIXTEEN LITTLE CONCERT PIECES, OP. 99
        ASSOCIATED MUSIC PUBLISHERS, INC.   DOB   1.75
SPURLING, C.   2-3
    OUR VILLAGE IN WINTER -- SUITE OF 6 PIECES
        NOVELLO AND COMPANY, LTD.   10.0128.00   1.15
                                                      4
SROM
    SIEBEN STUCKE FUR KLAVIER
        BARENREITER VERLAG   AP 730
STAEMPFLI, E.
    SEVEN PIANO PIECES--1954
        ASSOCIATED MUSIC PUBLISHERS, INC.   BOT   2.50
STAEMPFLI, E.
    TOCCATA AND AIR VARIE--HPCHD
        ASSOCIATED MUSIC PUBLISHERS, INC.   BOT   5.00
STAEPS, H. U.
    ATRITONISCHE MUSIK III
        ASSOCIATED MUSIC PUBLISHERS, INC.   SCH   3.00
STAIRS, L.
    BOOK OF EASY PIANO PIECES
        THEODORE PRESSER COMPANY   1.50
STALLAERT, A.
    DEUX CROQUIS - 1. POUR LA MAIN GAUCHE 2. TOCCATA
        EDITIONS MUSICALES TRANSATLANTIQUES   2.00
STALLAERT, A.
    THREE ETUDES
        GERARD BILLAUDOT EDITIONS MUSICALES   3.30
STANDEL--ED   STANDEL
    PIANIST'S DIGEST OF BAROQUE MUSIC
        BOSTON MUSIC COMPANY   1.50
STANDEL--ED   STANDEL
    PIANIST'S DIGEST OF BAROQUE MUSIC
        BOSTON MUSIC COMPANY   1.50
STANDEL--ED   STANDEL
    PIANIST'S DIGEST OF MODERN MUSIC
        BOSTON MUSIC COMPANY   1.00
STANDEL--ED   STANDEL
    PIANIST'S DIGEST OF MODERN MUSIC
        BOSTON MUSIC COMPANY   1.00
STANISLAUS
    LEARNING TO READ, LEARNING TO PLAY
        WILLIS MUSIC COMPANY   1.00
STANZANI, E.
    EIGHT NOVELETTES
        EDIZIONI BERBEN   EB 1508   3.00
STARER
    FIVE CAPRICES
        PEER SOUTHERN ORGANIZATION   01.35
STARER
    FIVE DUETS FOR YOUNG PIANISTS
        MCA MUSIC   1.50
STARER
    FIVE PRELUDES FOR PIANO
        MCA MUSIC   1.75
STARER
    SEVEN VIGNETTES
        MCA MUSIC   .60
STARER
    SKETCHES IN COLOUR-SET 1
        MCA MUSIC   1.50
STARER
    SKETCHES IN COLOUR-SET 2
        MCA MUSIC   1.75
STARER
    THREE ISRAELI SKETCHES
        MCA MUSIC   1.25
STARER
    TWELVE PIECES FOR TEN FINGERS
        SAM FOX PUBLISHING COMPANY, INC.   1.00
STECHER *
    IN THE SPIRIT OF '76
        SCHMITT, HALL AND MCCREARY COMPANY   9950   2.00
STECHER *
    LEARNING TO PLAY, BK. 1
        SUMMY-BIRCHARD COMPANY   2.00
STECHER *
    LEARNING TO PLAY, BK. 2
        SUMMY-BIRCHARD COMPANY   2.00
STECHER *
    LEARNING TO PLAY, BK. 3
        SUMMY-BIRCHARD COMPANY   2.00
STECHER *
    LEARNING TO PLAY, BK. 4
        SUMMY-BIRCHARD COMPANY   2.00
STECHER *
    PLAYING TO LEARN, BK. 1
        SUMMY-BIRCHARD COMPANY   1.25
STECHER *
    PLAYING TO LEARN, BK. 2
        SUMMY-BIRCHARD COMPANY   1.25
STECHER *
    PLAYING TO LEARN, BK. 3
        SUMMY-BIRCHARD COMPANY   1.25
STECHER *
    PLAYING TO LEARN, BK. 4
        SUMMY-BIRCHARD COMPANY   1.25
STECHER *
    ROCK WITH JAZZ, BK. 1
        SCHMITT, HALL AND MCCREARY COMPANY   9981   1.25

STECHER *
    ROCK WITH JAZZ, BK. 2
        SCHMITT, HALL AND MCCREARY COMPANY   9973   1.25
STECHER *
    ROCK WITH JAZZ, BK. 3
        SCHMITT, HALL AND MCCREARY COMPANY   9969   1.25
STECHER *
    ROCK WITH JAZZ, BK. 4
        SCHMITT, HALL AND MCCREARY COMPANY   9970   1.25
STECHER *
    ROCK WITH JAZZ, BK. 5
        SCHMITT, HALL AND MCCREARY COMPANY   9974   1.25
STECHER *
    WE WISH YOU A MERRY CHRISTMAS, BK. 1
        SCHMITT, HALL AND MCCREARY COMPANY   9967   1.00
STECHER *
    WE WISH YOU A MERRY CHRISTMAS, BK. 2
        SCHMITT, HALL AND MCCREARY COMPANY   9978   1.25
STEFFEN, W.
    LES SPIRALES, OP. 36
        ASSOCIATED MUSIC PUBLISHERS, INC.   BOT   5.50
STEFFEN, W.
    REIHENPROPORTIONEN, OP. 25
        ASSOCIATED MUSIC PUBLISHERS, INC.   BOT   4.50
STEGLICH--ED   STEGLICH
    ALTE DEUTSCHE WEIHNACHTSMUSIK
        BARENREITER VERLAG   NMA 95   2.75
STEGLICH--ED   STEGLICH
    OLD GERMAN CHRISTMAS MUSIC -- CHRISTMAS PIECES BY SCHEIDT,
    PACHELBEL, MUFFAT AND OTHERS
        ASSOCIATED MUSIC PUBLISHERS, INC.   NAG   3.75
STEIBELT   SIMONETTI
    SIX SONATINAS, OP. 49
        FRANCO COLOMBO PUBLICATIONS   ER1310   1.50
STEIBELT   TAGLIAPIETRA
    TWENTY-FIVE STUDIES, OP. 78
        FRANCO COLOMBO PUBLICATIONS   3.00
STEINBRECHER
    ALPHABET IN MUSIC, AN
        UNIVERSAL EDITION   UE 10299   3.00
STEINBRECHER--ED   STEINBRECHER
    FORTY FAVORITE PIECES, SIMPLIFIED
        THEODORE PRESSER COMPANY   1.50
STEINBRECHER--ED   STEINBRECHER
    SO SINGT MAN IN WIEN -- 32 FAMOUS VIENNESE SONGS IN EASY
    ARRANGEMENTS
        UNIVERSAL EDITION   UE 10940   2.55
STEINER   2 1/2, 3
    ADVANCING PIANIST PLAYS BOOGIE, THE
        BELWIN-MILLS PUBLISHING CORPORATION   1767   1.75
STEINER   3, 4
    ADVANCING PIANIST PLAYS CONCERTOS, THE
        BELWIN-MILLS PUBLISHING CORPORATION   1766   1.75
STEINER   2 1/2, 3
    ADVANCING PIANIST PLAYS MARCHES, THE
        BELWIN-MILLS PUBLISHING CORPORATION   1750   1.75
STEINER   2 1/2, 3
    ADVANCING PIANIST PLAYS OPERA, THE
        BELWIN-MILLS PUBLISHING CORPORATION   1765   1.75
STEINER   2 1/2, 3
    ADVANCING PIANIST PLAYS RECITAL MUSIC, THE
        BELWIN-MILLS PUBLISHING CORPORATION   1759   1.75
STEINER   3, 4
    ADVANCING PIANIST PLAYS SYMPHONIES, THE
        BELWIN-MILLS PUBLISHING CORPORATION   1928   1.75
STEINER   2 1/2, 3
    ADVANCING PIANIST PLAYS WALTZES, THE
        BELWIN-MILLS PUBLISHING CORPORATION   1743   1.75
STEINER   2
    AMERICAN MUSIC FOR THE YOUNG PIANIST
        BELWIN-MILLS PUBLISHING CORPORATION   1863   1.75
STEINER
    ART OF PHRASING
        BELWIN-MILLS PUBLISHING CORPORATION   1975   1.75
STEINER
    AT EASE IN ALL KEYS, BK. 1
        BELWIN-MILLS PUBLISHING CORPORATION   965   1.50
STEINER
    AT EASE IN ALL KEYS, BK. 2
        BELWIN-MILLS PUBLISHING CORPORATION   967   1.75
STEINER
    BEYER MODERNIZED
        BELWIN-MILLS PUBLISHING CORPORATION   1764   1.75
STEINER   2
    BOOGIE WOOGIE FOR THE YOUNG PIANIST
        BELWIN-MILLS PUBLISHING CORPORATION   1862   1.75
STEINER
    CHORD STUDIES AND PIECES, BK. 1
        BELWIN-MILLS PUBLISHING CORPORATION   1970   1.75
STEINER
    CHORD STUDIES AND PIECES, BK. 2
        BELWIN-MILLS PUBLISHING CORPORATION   1971   1.75
STEINER
    CHORDS FOR PLEASURE -- MARCHES, WALTZES AND DANCES
        BELWIN-MILLS PUBLISHING CORPORATION   11086   1.50
STEINER
    CHRISTMAS AT THE PIANO
        BELWIN-MILLS PUBLISHING CORPORATION   1527   1.75
STEINER
    CHRISTMAS CAROLS -- FOR THE VERY YOUNG
        BELWIN-MILLS PUBLISHING CORPORATION   2210   1.75
STEINER   1 1/2
    CHRISTMAS MEDLEY -- 1. HARK, THE HERALD ANGELS SING, 2. SILENT
    NIGHT, 3. O COME ALL YE FAITHFUL
        BELWIN-MILLS PUBLISHING CORPORATION   .60
STEINER
    CREATIVE INTERVAL STUDIES
        BELWIN-MILLS PUBLISHING CORPORATION   2221   1.75
STEINER
    CUBS AND BROWNIES AT THE PIANO
        BELWIN-MILLS PUBLISHING CORPORATION   1540   1.75
STEINER
    DEVOTIONAL MUSIC
        BELWIN-MILLS PUBLISHING CORPORATION   1541   1.75
STEINER   STEINER   PREPARATORY
    ERIC STEINER PIANO COURSE--JUNIOR APPROACH
        BELWIN-MILLS PUBLISHING CORPORATION   1.25
STEINER   STEINER   PREPARATORY
    ERIC STEINER PIANO COURSE--SENIOR APPROACH
        BELWIN-MILLS PUBLISHING CORPORATION   1.25
STEINER
    EXPRESSION THROUGH MELODY
        BELWIN-MILLS PUBLISHING CORPORATION   1737   1.75
STEINER
    FIFTEEN HUMOROUS PIANO PIECES
        BELWIN-MILLS PUBLISHING CORPORATION   902   1.75

STEINER
    FIRST GRADE SUPPLEMENT
        BELWIN-MILLS PUBLISHING CORPORATION   2220   2.00
STEINER
    HARMONY FOR PIANO, BK. 1
        BELWIN-MILLS PUBLISHING CORPORATION   1844   1.75
STEINER
    HARMONY FOR PIANO, BK. 2
        BELWIN-MILLS PUBLISHING CORPORATION   1845   1.75
STEINER   1, 2
    HYMNS FOR THE YOUNG PIANIST
        BELWIN-MILLS PUBLISHING CORPORATION   1864   1.75
STEINER
    I LIKE TO PLAY THE PIANO
        BELWIN-MILLS PUBLISHING CORPORATION   1295   1.75
STEINER
    JEWISH FOLK SONGS
        BELWIN-MILLS PUBLISHING CORPORATION   11248   1.50
STEINER
    JUNIOR CLASSICS, BK. 1
        BELWIN-MILLS PUBLISHING CORPORATION   1340   2.00
STEINER
    JUNIOR CLASSICS, BK. 2
        BELWIN-MILLS PUBLISHING CORPORATION   1341   2.00
STEINER
    LEGER LINE DRILLS AND PIECES
        BELWIN-MILLS PUBLISHING CORPORATION   2145   2.00
STEINER   1, 2
    LIGHT CLASSICS
        BELWIN-MILLS PUBLISHING CORPORATION   1435   2.00
STEINER
    MARCHES FOR THE YOUNG PIANIST
        BELWIN-MILLS PUBLISHING CORPORATION   1865   1.75
STEINER
    MELODIES IN MINOR
        BELWIN-MILLS PUBLISHING CORPORATION   11290   1.50
STEINER
    MELODY TREASURE, BK. 1
        BELWIN-MILLS PUBLISHING CORPORATION   1567   1.75
STEINER
    MELODY TREASURE, BK. 2
        BELWIN-MILLS PUBLISHING CORPORATION   1568   1.75
STEINER
    MINIATURE ETUDES
        BELWIN-MILLS PUBLISHING CORPORATION   2016   1.75
STEINER
    MORE ONE, FOUR, FIVE
        BELWIN-MILLS PUBLISHING CORPORATION   2354   1.75
STEINER
    MOTHER GOOSE AT THE PIANO, BK. 1
        BELWIN-MILLS PUBLISHING CORPORATION   1330   1.50
STEINER
    MOTHER GOOSE AT THE PIANO, BK. 2
        BELWIN-MILLS PUBLISHING CORPORATION   1331   1.50
STEINER
    MUSIC FROM MAKE-BELIEVE LAND
        BELWIN-MILLS PUBLISHING CORPORATION   1655   1.75
STEINER
    MUSICAL JOURNEY THROUGH EUROPE, A
        BELWIN-MILLS PUBLISHING CORPORATION   1738   1.75
STEINER
    OLD MASTERS FOR YOUNG ARTISTS
        BELWIN-MILLS PUBLISHING CORPORATION   1661   2.00
STEINER
    ONE HAND ONLY
        BELWIN-MILLS PUBLISHING CORPORATION   1934   1.75
STEINER
    ONE, FOUR, FIVE
        BELWIN-MILLS PUBLISHING CORPORATION   11364   1.50
STEINER
    PIANO COURSE -- JUNIOR APPROACH
        BELWIN-MILLS PUBLISHING CORPORATION   2.00
STEINER   1
    PIANO COURSE -- SENIOR APPROACH
        BELWIN-MILLS PUBLISHING CORPORATION   2.00
STEINER   2
    PIANO COURSE, BK. 1
        BELWIN-MILLS PUBLISHING CORPORATION   2.00
STEINER   2 1/2
    PIANO COURSE, BK. 2
        BELWIN-MILLS PUBLISHING CORPORATION   2.00
STEINER   3
    PIANO COURSE, BK. 3
        BELWIN-MILLS PUBLISHING CORPORATION   2.00
STEINER   4-5
    PIANO COURSE, BK. 3
        BELWIN-MILLS PUBLISHING CORPORATION   2.00
STEINER
    PIANO COURSE, BK. 4
        BELWIN-MILLS PUBLISHING CORPORATION   2.00
STEINER
    PLAY AND LISTEN
        BELWIN-MILLS PUBLISHING CORPORATION   1056   1.75
STEINER
    PLAY AND THINK
        BELWIN-MILLS PUBLISHING CORPORATION   924   1.75
STEINER
    PLAYING THROUGH THE HISTORY OF THE PIANO
        BELWIN-MILLS PUBLISHING CORPORATION   1375   2.00
STEINER
    POST GRADUATE COURSE, BK. 1
        BELWIN-MILLS PUBLISHING CORPORATION   2.00
STEINER   2
    POST GRADUATE COURSE, BK. 2
        BELWIN-MILLS PUBLISHING CORPORATION   2.00
STEINER
    RECITAL MUSIC FOR THE YOUNG PIANIST
        BELWIN-MILLS PUBLISHING CORPORATION   1866   1.75
STEINER
    RECREATIONAL PIANO ALBUM, BK. 1
        BELWIN-MILLS PUBLISHING CORPORATION   1519   1.75
STEINER
    RECREATIONAL PIANO ALBUM, BK. 2
        BELWIN-MILLS PUBLISHING CORPORATION   1520   1.75
STEINER
    RELIGIOUS MUSIC OF THE MASTERS
        BELWIN-MILLS PUBLISHING CORPORATION   2146   2.00
STEINER
    REPERTOIRE ALBUM, BK. 1
        BELWIN-MILLS PUBLISHING CORPORATION   1304   2.00
STEINER
    REPERTOIRE ALBUM, BK. 2
        BELWIN-MILLS PUBLISHING CORPORATION   1305   2.00
STEINER
    SCALE MELODIES, BK. 1
        BELWIN-MILLS PUBLISHING CORPORATION   1979   1.75

STEINER
  SIXTEEN MEASURES OF KEYBOARD PLEASURES
    BELWIN-MILLS PUBLISHING CORPORATION   2028   1.75
STEINER
  SIXTEEN STREABBOG PIECES
    BELWIN-MILLS PUBLISHING CORPORATION   1384   1.75
STEINER
  SOLO AND DUET ALBUM
    BELWIN-MILLS PUBLISHING CORPORATION   1414   1.75
STEINER
  THEORY FOR THE PIANO -- A WORKBOOK, BK. 1
    BELWIN-MILLS PUBLISHING CORPORATION   1659   1.75
STEINER
  THEORY FOR THE PIANO -- A WORKBOOK, BK. 2
    BELWIN-MILLS PUBLISHING CORPORATION   1660   1.75
STEINER
  THREE CHORDS IN THREE KEYS
    BELWIN-MILLS PUBLISHING CORPORATION   11501   1.50
STEINER
  TRANSPOSITION FOR PIANO
    BELWIN-MILLS PUBLISHING CORPORATION   1847   2.00
STEINER
  TUNEFUL RHYTHM PATTERNS
    BELWIN-MILLS PUBLISHING CORPORATION   1073   1.75
STEINER
  TWENTY-FOUR MEASURES OF KEYBOARD PLEASURES
    BELWIN-MILLS PUBLISHING CORPORATION   2029   1.75
STEINER
  VARIETY IN TIME SIGNATURES
    BELWIN-MILLS PUBLISHING CORPORATION   1586   2.00
STEINER   1, 2
  WALTZES FOR THE YOUNG PIANIST
    BELWIN-MILLS PUBLISHING CORPORATION   1867   1.75
STEINER
  WORKBOOK IN MUSICAL NOTATION, BK. 1
    BELWIN-MILLS PUBLISHING CORPORATION   1607   1.75
STEINER
  WORKBOOK IN MUSICAL NOTATION, BK. 2
    BELWIN-MILLS PUBLISHING CORPORATION   1608   1.75
STEINER
  YOU'RE THE COMPOSER
    BELWIN-MILLS PUBLISHING CORPORATION   11546   1.50
STEINER
  YOUNG SOLOIST AT THE PIANO, THE, BK. 01
    BELWIN-MILLS PUBLISHING CORPORATION   1652   1.75
STEINER
  YOUNG SOLOIST AT THE PIANO, THE, BK. 02
    BELWIN-MILLS PUBLISHING CORPORATION   1653   1.75
STEINER
  YOUR OWN HARMONIES
    BELWIN-MILLS PUBLISHING CORPORATION   11545   1.50
STEINER--ED.   STEINER   1
  ERIC STEINER PIANO COURSE, BK. 1
    BELWIN-MILLS PUBLISHING CORPORATION   1.50
STEINER--ED.   STEINER   2
  ERIC STEINER PIANO COURSE, BK. 2
    BELWIN-MILLS PUBLISHING CORPORATION   1.50
STEINER--ED.   STEINER   2 1/2
  ERIC STEINER PIANO COURSE, BK. 3
    BELWIN-MILLS PUBLISHING CORPORATION   1.50
STEINER--ED.   STEINER   3
  ERIC STEINER PIANO COURSE, BK. 4
    BELWIN-MILLS PUBLISHING CORPORATION   1.50
STEINER--ED.   STEINER   4
  ERIC STEINER PIANO COURSE, BK. 5
    BELWIN-MILLS PUBLISHING CORPORATION   1.50
STEINER--ED.   STEINER   4-5
  ERIC STEINER PIANO COURSE, POST-GRADUATE COURSE, BK. 1
    BELWIN-MILLS PUBLISHING CORPORATION   1.50
STEINER--ED.   STEINER   5-6
  ERIC STEINER PIANO COURSE, POST-GRADUATE COURSE, BK. 2
    BELWIN-MILLS PUBLISHING CORPORATION   1.50
STEINER--ED.   STEINER
  FUN TIME
    PRO-ART PUBLICATIONS, INC.   1303   1.25
STEINER--ED.   STEINER
  HEBREW SONGS FOR THE YOUNG PIANIST, BK. 1
    BELWIN-MILLS PUBLISHING CORPORATION   11233   1.25
STEINER--ED.   STEINER
  HEBREW SONGS FOR THE YOUNG PIANIST, BK. 2
    BELWIN-MILLS PUBLISHING CORPORATION   11234   1.25
STEINHAUSEN
  ERREURS PHYSIOLOGIQUES ET LA TRANSFORMATION DE LA TECHNIQUE DU
  PIANO, LES
    FRANCO COLOMBO PUBLICATIONS   SAL   4.25
STEINKE, G.
  SIX PIECES FOR PIANO, 1964
    SEESAW MUSIC CORPORATION   5.00
STEPAN   SETKOVA   3
  COMPOSIZIONI PER PIANO, BAND 1 -- 6 DIVERTIMENTI, OP. 1 - 6
  SONATEN, OP. 3 - SONATEN IN E FLAT, B FLAT AND A --
    BARENREITER VERLAG   MAB 64
STEPAN   SETKOVA   3
  COMPOSIZIONI PER PIANO, BAND 2
    BARENREITER VERLAG   MAB 70
STEPAN--ED   STEPAN   4-5
  KLAVIERKOMPOSITIONEN, HEFT 2
    BARENREITER VERLAG   AP 1683
STEPAN--ED   STEPAN   5
  KLAVIERKOMPOSITIONEN, HEFT 3
    BARENREITER VERLAG   AP 1684
STEPHAN *   SETKOVA   3
  BOHMISCHE VARIATIONEN DES 18. JAHRHUNDERTS
    BARENREITER VERLAG   MVH 15
STEVENS
  CHORDS, CADENCES AND ARPEGGIOS
    BELWIN-MILLS PUBLISHING CORPORATION   2.00
STEVENS
  ON THE MARCH
    BELWIN-MILLS PUBLISHING CORPORATION   1.50
STEVENS--ED.   STEVENS
  ALTENGLISCHE KLAVIERMUSIK
    BARENREITER VERLAG   BA 2663   1.75
STEVENS, E.
  PIANO SCENES
    THEODORE PRESSER COMPANY   1.25
STEVENS, E.
  SIX MODAL MINIATURES
    THEODORE PRESSER COMPANY   1.25
STEVENS, H.
  FIVE PORTUGUESE FOLK SONGS
    PEER SOUTHERN ORGANIZATION   01.00
STICKLES--ED
  GEORGE M. COHAN CAVALCADE, BK. 1
    EDWARD B. MARKS MUSIC CORPORATION   01.00
STICKLES--ED
  GEORGE M. COHAN CAVALCADE, BK. 2
    EDWARD B. MARKS MUSIC CORPORATION   01.00

STICKLES--ED   STICKLES
  SCHIRMER'S FAVORITE SACRED SONGS
    G. SCHIRMER, INC.   1.25
STICKLES--ED   STICKLES
  SONGS OF FAITH
    G. SCHIRMER, INC.   1.50
STOKER   E
  FROM AN ARTIST'S SKETCHBOOK
    C. F. PETERS CORPORATION   H422   .90
STONE, D.   2
  TWELVE IMPRESSIONS, NOS. 1-6
    NOVELLO AND COMPANY, LTD.   10.0047.00   1.15
STONE, D.   3
  TWELVE IMPRESSIONS, NOS. 7-12
    NOVELLO AND COMPANY, LTD.   10.0080.02   1.15
STONE, E.--ED   STONE, E.
  CHAPPELL'S FAVORITES
    CHAPPELL AND COMPANY, INC.   0021998   1.00
STORR, S.
  ADVENTURES IN PHRASING
    BELWIN-MILLS PUBLISHING CORPORATION   1.25
STRAUSS, E.
  TROIS ETUDES DE JAZZ, OP. 2
    ASSOCIATED MUSIC PUBLISHERS, INC.   ESC   1.90
STRAUSS, J.
  ALBUM - 8 FAMOUS WALTZES
    FRANCO COLOMBO PUBLICATIONS   127640   2.25
STRAUSS, J.   DEL MAGLIO
  ALBUM - 8 FAMOUS WALTZES
    FRANCO COLOMBO PUBLICATIONS   127641   1.25
STRAUSS, J.
  ALBUM OF WALTZES
    CARL FISCHER, INC.   O 2927   1.50
STRAUSS, J.
  ALBUM OF 28 FAVORITE DANCES, BK. 1
    G. SCHIRMER, INC.   L131   1.50
STRAUSS, J.
  ALBUM OF 28 FAVORITE DANCES, BK. 2
    G. SCHIRMER, INC.   L132   1.50
STRAUSS, J.
  ALBUM OF 28 FAVORITE DANCES, BK. 3
    G. SCHIRMER, INC.   L133   1.50
STRAUSS, J. *
  ALBUM--''SEID UMSCHLNGEN MILLIONEN''
    ASSOCIATED MUSIC PUBLISHERS, INC.   DOB   2.50
STRAUSS, J.
  FAMOUS WALZES
    BOOSEY AND HAWKES, INC.   1.00
STRAUSS, J.   SPIVAK, S.
  FINEST MUSIC SERIES -- STRAUSS
    SCHUBERTH CO.   NO. 09   1.50
STRAUSS, J.   3
  JOHANN STRAUSS
    ASHLEY DEALERS SERVICE, INC.   HG 14   2.95
STRAUSS, J.   3
  MEINE STRAUSS-WALZER, BAND 01
    SCHOTT   1504   2.50
STRAUSS, J.   3
  MEINE STRAUSS-WALZER, BAND 02
    SCHOTT   1564   3.50
STRAUSS, J.
  MEMORIES OF JOHANN STRAUSS
    EDWARD B. MARKS MUSIC CORPORATION   02.00
STRAUSS, J.   ZILCHER   2
  NUR WALZER VON STRAUSS
    SCHOTT   1507   3.00
STRAUSS, J.   M
  SIXTEEN FAVORITE WALTZES, VOL. 1
    C. F. PETERS CORPORATION   4318A   3.00
STRAUSS, J.   M
  SIXTEEN FAVORITE WALTZES, VOL. 2
    C. F. PETERS CORPORATION   4318B   3.00
STRAUSS, J.   KROME   1
  STRAUSS FUR ALLE
    SCHOTT   2840   2.50
STRAUSS, J. *   NOVAK   2-3
  STRAUSS SLOWAKISCHER LIEDER. 12 VOLKSLIEDER
    BARENREITER VERLAG   AP 670
STRAUSS, J.
  STRAUSS WALTZ ALBUM
    MUSIC SALES CORPORATION   020008   2.95
STRAUSS, J.   SCHAUM, J.   3
  STRAUSS WALTZES
    SCHAUM PUBLICATIONS, INC.   1.50
STRAUSS, J.
  TWELVE WALTZES
    FRANCO COLOMBO PUBLICATIONS   SAL   5.50
STRAUSS, J.   DOHNANYI
  TWO WALTZ TRANSCRIPTIONS
    KULTURA   2.50
STRAUSS, J.
  VALSES, BK. 1
    EDWIN F. KALMUS   3986   2.00
STRAUSS, J.
  VALSES, BK. 2
    EDWIN F. KALMUS   3987   2.00
STRAUSS, J.
  WALTZ KING, THE--16 FAVORITE WALTZES
    G. SCHIRMER, INC.   1.50
STRAUSS, R.
  BURGER ALS EDELMANN, OP. 60 - COMPLETE BALLET
    BOOSEY AND HAWKES, INC.   17.50
STRAUSS, R.
  JOSEPHSLEGENDE, OP. 63 -- COMPLETE BALLET
    BOOSEY AND HAWKES, INC.   15.00
STRAVINSKY, I.   PHILIPP, I.
  FOUR ETUDES, OP. 7
    INTERNATIONAL MUSIC COMPANY   1.75
STRAVINSKY, I.
  MASTERPIECES
    EDWARD B. MARKS MUSIC CORPORATION   02.50
STRAVINSKY, I.
  THREE MOVEMENTS, FROM 'PETROUCHKA'
    BOOSEY AND HAWKES, INC.   2.50
STRAVINSKY, S.   M
  ART OF SCALES, 24 PRELUDES
    C. F. PETERS CORPORATION   6139   1.25
STRAVINSKY, S.   M
  ART OF SCALES‡ TWENTY-FOUR PRELUDES
    C. F. PETERS CORPORATION   6139   1.25
STRAVINSKY, S.   M
  EIGHTEEN ORIGINAL CADENZAS AND FOUR FERMATAS TO MOZART CONCERTI
    C. F. PETERS CORPORATION   6021   3.00
STRAVINSKY, S.   M
  EIGHTEEN ORIGINAL CADENZAS AND 4 FERMATAS TO MOZART PIANO
  CONCERTI
    C. F. PETERS CORPORATION   6021   3.00

STRAVINSKY, S.	E			
PIANO MUSIC FOR CHILDREN, VOL. 1				
C. F. PETERS CORPORATION		6127		1.25
STRAVINSKY, S.	E			
PIANO MUSIC FOR CHILDREN, VOL. 2				
C. F. PETERS CORPORATION		6128		1.25
STRAVINSKY, S.				
PIANO VARIATIONS, VOL. 1				
C. F. PETERS CORPORATION		66279A		1.50
STRAVINSKY, S.				
PIANO VARIATIONS, VOL. 2				
C. F. PETERS CORPORATION		66279B		1.50
STRAVINSKY, S.	E			
SIX EASY SONATINAS FOR YOUNG PIANISTS, VOL. 1				
C. F. PETERS CORPORATION		6590A		1.25
STRAVINSKY, S.	E			
SIX EASY SONATINAS FOR YOUNG PIANISTS, VOL. 2				
C. F. PETERS CORPORATION		6590B		1.25
STRAVINSKY, S.	M-D			
THREE INVENTIONS				
C. F. PETERS CORPORATION		6323		1.50
STREABBOG	1-2			
ALBUM				
SCHOTT		250		2.75
STREABBOG * ECKSTEIN				
MELODIOUS TECHNICAL STUDIES FROM STREABBOG-BURGMUELLER--75--				
CARL FISCHER, INC.		O 3812		1.25
STREABBOG				
STREABBOG ALBUM				
ASHLEY DEALERS SERVICE, INC.				1.25
STREABBOG				
STREABBOG ALBUM				
CENTURY MUSIC PUBLISHING COMPANY, INC.				1.25
STREABBOG PALMER, W. A.				
STREABBOG--12 MELODIOUS PIECES, BK. 1				
ALFRED MUSIC COMPANY		621		1.00
STREABBOG PALMER, W. A.				
STREABBOG--12 MELODIOUS PIECES, BK. 2				
ALFRED MUSIC COMPANY		565		1.25
STREABBOG				
TWELVE EASY AND MELODIOUS STUDIES, OP. 64--SECOND DEGREE				
G. SCHIRMER, INC.		L479		1.00
STREABBOG				
TWELVE MELODIOUS STUDIES, OP. 63				
CARL FISCHER, INC.		L 363		.75
STREABBOG				
TWELVE VERY EASY AND MELODIOUS STUDIES, OP. 63				
THEODORE PRESSER COMPANY				1.00
STREABBOG				
TWELVE VERY EASY AND MELODIOUS STUDIES, OP. 63--FIRST DEGREE				
G. SCHIRMER, INC.		L478		1.00
STRIMER				
ALBUM DE MAROUSSIA				
FRANCO COLOMBO PUBLICATIONS		SAL		3.50
STRIMER				
ALBUM DE NATACHA				
FRANCO COLOMBO PUBLICATIONS		SAL		3.50
STRIMER				
ALBUM DE TANIA				
FRANCO COLOMBO PUBLICATIONS		SAL		2.50
STRIMER				
DANS LA FORET				
FRANCO COLOMBO PUBLICATIONS		SAL		2.75
STRIMER				
DANS LA RUE				
FRANCO COLOMBO PUBLICATIONS		SAL		
STRIMER, J.				
ALBUM POUR LES TOUT PETITS				
ASSOCIATED MUSIC PUBLISHERS, INC.		ESC		1.75
STRIMER, J.--ED STRIMER, J.				
MY REPERTOIRE OF FAMOUS COMPOSERS				
PRO-ART PUBLICATIONS, INC.		41		1.00
STRIMER, J.--ED STRIMER, J.				
TWELVE FAVORITES				
PRO-ART PUBLICATIONS, INC.		69		.75
STROHBACH, S.--ED STROHBACH				
WEIHNACHTS LIEDERBUCH, DAS -- 40 CHRISTMAS SONGS WITH GERMAN				
SUPERLINEAR TEXT				
ASSOCIATED MUSIC PUBLISHERS, INC.		BRH		2.00
STRONG *				
POPULAR PIANO CHORD METHOD FOR BEGINNERS				
BELWIN-MILLS PUBLISHING CORPORATION		11395		1.50
STRONG, J. CHOSAK				
POPULAR CHORD METHOD FOR BEGINNERS				
BELWIN-MILLS PUBLISHING CORPORATION				1.25
STUBBLEFIELD				
LITTLE FINGERS MAKE MUSIC				
WILLIS MUSIC COMPANY				1.00
SUDDARDS				
TWENTY-FOUR FAVORITE CAROLS, MADE EASY TO PLAY AND SING				
ELKAN-VOGEL, INC.				1.10
SUFFERN, C.				
CUENTOS DE NINOS				
EDITORIAL COOPERATIVA INTER-AMERICANA				00.95
SUK				
DREI KLAVIERSTUCKE				
BARENREITER VERLAG		AP 736		
SUK	2-3			
LANDLER				
BARENREITER VERLAG		AP 742		
SUK	2-3			
MUTTER, OP. 28				
BARENREITER VERLAG		AP 744		
SUK	3			
SOMMEREINDRUCKE, OP. 22B				
BARENREITER VERLAG		AP 745		
SUK	2-3			
VIER KOMPOSITIONEN AUS DER JUGEND				
BARENREITER VERLAG		AP 741		
SURINACH, C.				
ACROBATS OF GOD--5 DANCES FROM THE BALLET				
ASSOCIATED MUSIC PUBLISHERS, INC.		AMP		2.50
SURINACH, C.				
TALES FROM THE FLAMENCO KINGDOM--1955				
ASSOCIATED MUSIC PUBLISHERS, INC.		AMP		.75
SURINACH, C.				
TROIS CHANSONS ET DANSES ESPAGNOLES				
PEER SOUTHERN ORGANIZATION				01.60
SUTER	D			
DEUX PIECES POUR CLAVECIN --FACSIMILE--				
C. F. PETERS CORPORATION		N6180		3.00
SUTERMEISTER, H.	3			
BERGSOMMER, ACHT KLEINE STUCKE				
SCHOTT		2881		2.25
SUZUKI, S.				
SUZUKI PIANO SCHOOL, VOL. 1				
SUMMY-BIRCHARD COMPANY				2.00

SUZUKI, S.				
SUZUKI PIANO SCHOOL, VOL. 2				
SUMMY-BIRCHARD COMPANY				2.00
SUZUKI, S.				
SUZUKI PIANO SCHOOL, VOL. 3				
SUMMY-BIRCHARD COMPANY				2.00
SUZUKI, S.				
SUZUKI PIANO SCHOOL, VOL. 4				
SUMMY-BIRCHARD COMPANY				2.00
SUZUKI, S.				
SUZUKI PIANO SCHOOL, 12 INCH LP RECORD ALBUM FOR VOLS. 1 AND 2				
SUMMY-BIRCHARD COMPANY				6.00
SUZUKI, S.				
SUZUKI PIANO SCHOOL, 12 INCH LP RECORD ALBUM FOR VOLS. 3 AND 4				
SUMMY-BIRCHARD COMPANY				6.00
SWEELINCK * WUEHRER	3-4			
KLAVIERMUSIK AUS ALTER ZEIT				
BARENREITER VERLAG		SM 1773		
SWEELINCK HELLMANN	M			
SELECTED WORKS				
C. F. PETERS CORPORATION		4645B		2.50
SWEELINCK HELLMANN	M			
SELECTED WORKS, VOL. 1				
C. F. PETERS CORPORATION		4645A		3.00
SWENSON, L.				
MELODY MODES AND MOODS THROUGH ALL THE KEYS				
THEODORE PRESSER COMPANY				1.50
SWENSON, L.				
MELODY PRELUDES THROUGH THE KEYS				
THEODORE PRESSER COMPANY				1.50
SWENSON, L.				
MELODY RHYMES THROUGH ALL THE KEYS				
THEODORE PRESSER COMPANY				1.50
SWENSON, L.				
MORE MELODY RHYMES THROUGH ALL THE KEYS				
THEODORE PRESSER COMPANY				1.50
SWENSON, L.				
PRELUDES AND NOCTURNES				
THEODORE PRESSER COMPANY				1.95
SWIFT, N.				
TWELVE CHILDREN'S PIECES				
G. SCHIRMER, INC.		L823		1.00
SWINSTEAD, F.				
STEP BY STEP SIGHT READING, BK. 1				
BANKS AND SON LTD.				1.35
SWINSTEAD, F.				
STEP BY STEP SIGHT READING, BK. 2				
BANKS AND SON LTD.				1.35
SWINSTEAD, F.				
STEP BY STEP STUDIES, BK. 1				
BANKS AND SON LTD.				1.20
SWINSTEAD, F.				
STEP BY STEP STUDIES, BK. 2				
BANKS AND SON LTD.				1.20
SWINSTEAD, F.				
STEP BY STEP STUDIES, BK. 3				
BANKS AND SON LTD.				1.20
SWINSTEAD, F.				
STEP BY STEP STUDIES, BK. 4				
BANKS AND SON LTD.				1.20
SWINSTEAD, F.				
STEP BY STEP STUDIES, BK. 5				
BANKS AND SON LTD.				1.20
SWINSTEAD, F.				
STEP BY STEP STUDIES, BK. 6				
BANKS AND SON LTD.				1.20
SWINSTEAD, F.				
STEP BY STEP TO THE CLASSICS, BK. 1				
BANKS AND SON LTD.				1.25
SWINSTEAD, F.				
STEP BY STEP TO THE CLASSICS, BK. 2				
BANKS AND SON LTD.				1.25
SWINSTEAD, F.				
STEP BY STEP TO THE CLASSICS, BK. 3				
BANKS AND SON LTD.				1.25
SWINSTEAD, F.				
STEP BY STEP TO THE CLASSICS, BK. 4				
BANKS AND SON LTD.				1.20
SWINSTEAD, F.				
STEP BY STEP TO THE CLASSICS, BK. 5				
BANKS AND SON LTD.				1.20
SWINSTEAD, F.				
STEP BY STEP TO THE CLASSICS, BK. 6				
BANKS AND SON LTD.				1.20
SYMONS				
THREE ANCIENT DANCES				
FRANCO COLOMBO PUBLICATIONS		SAL		2.75
SZARAI--ED. * SZARAI *				
PIANO MUSIC FOR BEGINNERS				
KULTURA				3.00
SZEKERES				
TEN PIECES				
FRANCO COLOMBO PUBLICATIONS		SAL		2.75
SZELENYI	2			
MUSIKALISCHES BILDERBUCH				
SCHOTT		5770		3.25
SZONYI, E.				
FIVE PRELUDES				
KULTURA				1.50
SZYMANOWSKI				
MAZURKAS, OP. 50, BK. 1				
UNIVERSAL EDITION		UE 8592		2.65
SZYMANOWSKI				
MAZURKAS, OP. 50, BK. 2				
UNIVERSAL EDITION		UE 8593		2.65
SZYMANOWSKI				
MAZURKAS, OP. 50, BK. 3				
UNIVERSAL EDITION		UE 8594		2.60
SZYMANOWSKI				
MAZURKAS, OP. 50, BK. 4				
UNIVERSAL EDITION		UE 1342		2.50
SZYMANOWSKI				
MAZURKAS, OP. 50, BK. 5				
UNIVERSAL EDITION		UE 1343		2.60
TAGLIAPIETRA, C.				
CADENZAS FOR CONCERTI BY MOZART AND BEETHOVEN				
FRANCO COLOMBO PUBLICATIONS		Z2131		2.25
TAGLIAPIETRA, C.				
FOR THE YOUNG - 24 BAGATELLES				
FRANCO COLOMBO PUBLICATIONS		Z912		2.25
TAGLIAPIETRA, C.				
THREE PIECES				
FRANCO COLOMBO PUBLICATIONS		Z1890		1.50
TAGLIAPIETRA, C.				
THREE SPECIAL STUDIES FOR THE CROSSING OF THE HANDS				
FRANCO COLOMBO PUBLICATIONS		Z1311		1.25

TAGLIAPIETRA, G.
  ANTHOLOGY OF ANCIENT AND MODERN MUSIC, BK. 1 - MASTERS OF THE
  16TH CENTURY
    FRANCO COLOMBO PUBLICATIONS   ER980   5.00
TAGLIAPIETRA, G.
  ANTHOLOGY OF ANCIENT AND MODERN MUSIC, BK. 2 - MASTERS OF THE
  16TH CENTURY
    FRANCO COLOMBO PUBLICATIONS   ER981   5.00
TAGLIAPIETRA, G.
  FORTY STUDIES FOR PERFECTION, BK. 1
    FRANCO COLOMBO PUBLICATIONS   ER196   2.25
TAGLIAPIETRA, G.
  FORTY STUDIES FOR PERFECTION, BK. 2
    FRANCO COLOMBO PUBLICATIONS   ER197   4.25
TAIT, G. *
  COWBOY DOE -- 14 PIECES FOR BEGINNERS
    NOVELLO AND COMPANY, LTD.   10.0082.09   .75
                                       3-4
TAJCEVIC, M.
  BALKANTANZE
    SCHOTT   4930   2.00
TAJCEVIC, M.
  SERBIAN DANCES
    RONGWEN MUSIC, INC.   02.50
TAJCEVIC, M.
  SONGS FROM MUR ISLAND --SMALL PIANO SOLOS--
    G. HENLE MUSIKVERLAG   166   1.15
TAKACS, J.
  FOR ME--LITTLE RECITAL PIECES, OP. 76
    ASSOCIATED MUSIC PUBLISHERS, INC.   DOB   2.50
TAKACS, J.
  FOUR EPITAPHS, OP. 79
    ASSOCIATED MUSIC PUBLISHERS, INC.   DOB   2.50
TAKACS, J.
  FROM FAR AND WIDE, OP. 37 -- 20 EASY INSTRUCTIVE PIECES
    UNIVERSAL EDITION   UE 10929   1.70
TAKACS, J.
  SOUNDS AND SILENCES, OP. 78
    ASSOCIATED MUSIC PUBLISHERS, INC.   DOB   2.75
TAKACS, J.
  TOCCATA AND FUGUE, OP. 56--LEFT HAND
    ASSOCIATED MUSIC PUBLISHERS, INC.   DOB   2.75
TAL, J.
  DODECAPHONIC EPISODES
    ISRAEL MUSIC INSTITUTE   5.50
TALLIS   M
  COMPLETE KEYBOARD WORKS
    C. F. PETERS CORPORATION   H1585   3.00
TALLIS   E
  FOUR PIECES FROM THE MULLINER BOOK
    C. F. PETERS CORPORATION   H1585B   1.25
TALLIS   E-M
  HYMN VERSES AND ANTIPHONS
    C. F. PETERS CORPORATION   H1585A   1.25
TALMA, L.
  SIX ETUDES
    G. SCHIRMER, INC.   2.00
TAMAS   D
  IMPROVISATIONS --FACSIMILE--
    C. F. PETERS CORPORATION   Z422   3.50
TANSMAN, A.
  DEUX PIECES HEBRAIQUES--1956
    ASSOCIATED MUSIC PUBLISHERS, INC.   ESC   2.75
TANSMAN, A.
  EIGHT CANTILENAS - HOMAGE TO BACH
    MCA MUSIC   1.00
TANSMAN, A.
  ELEVEN INTERLUDES
    ASSOCIATED MUSIC PUBLISHERS, INC.   ESC   4.00
TANSMAN, A.   BARTH
  FIFTEEN MODERATELY EASY PIECES FOR THE YOUNG PIANIST--DANCING
  BEAR, THE--DRESDEN CHINA FIGURES
    ASSOCIATED MUSIC PUBLISHERS, INC.   ESC   .35
TANSMAN, A.   BARTH
  FIFTEEN MODERATELY EASY PIECES FOR THE YOUNG
  PIANIST--MEDITATION, MAZURKA
    ASSOCIATED MUSIC PUBLISHERS, INC.   ESC   .35
TANSMAN, A.   BARTH
  FIFTEEN MODERATELY EASY PIECES FOR THE YOUNG PIANIST--OLD
  BEGGAR, THE--PING-PONG
    ASSOCIATED MUSIC PUBLISHERS, INC.   ESC   .35
TANSMAN, A.   BARTH
  FIFTEEN MODERATELY EASY PIECES FOR THE YOUNG PIANIST--PETITE
  REVERIE, NOEL
    ASSOCIATED MUSIC PUBLISHERS, INC.   ESC   .35
TANSMAN, A.   BARTH
  FIFTEEN MODERATELY EASY PIECES FOR THE YOUNG PIANIST--SCOOTER,
  THE--COQUETTE
    ASSOCIATED MUSIC PUBLISHERS, INC.   ESC   .35
TANSMAN, A.
  FIVE IMPRESSIONS--1934
    ASSOCIATED MUSIC PUBLISHERS, INC.   ESC   3.25
TANSMAN, A.
  FOUR DANSES MINIATURES
    FRANCO COLOMBO PUBLICATIONS   SAL   2.50
TANSMAN, A.
  FOUR NOCTURNES
    UNIVERSAL EDITION   UE 12096   2.50
TANSMAN, A.
  FOUR POLISH DANCES--1931
    ASSOCIATED MUSIC PUBLISHERS, INC.   ESC   2.75
TANSMAN, A.
  HAPPY TIME, BK. 1 - PRIMARY
    MCA MUSIC   1.50
TANSMAN, A.
  HAPPY TIME, BK. 2 - ELEMENTARY
    MCA MUSIC   1.50
TANSMAN, A.
  HAPPY TIME, BK. 3 - INTERMEDIATE
    MCA MUSIC   1.50
TANSMAN, A.
  INTERMEZZI--SERIES 1, NOS. 1-6
    ASSOCIATED MUSIC PUBLISHERS, INC.   ESC   4.50
TANSMAN, A.
  INTERMEZZI--SERIES 2, NOS. 7-12
    ASSOCIATED MUSIC PUBLISHERS, INC.   ESC   5.00
TANSMAN, A.
  INTERMEZZI--SERIES 3, NOS. 13-18
    ASSOCIATED MUSIC PUBLISHERS, INC.   ESC   4.75
TANSMAN, A.
  INTERMEZZI--SERIES 4, NOS. 19-24
    ASSOCIATED MUSIC PUBLISHERS, INC.   ESC   1.50
TANSMAN, A.
  JEUNES AU PIANO, LES--BK. 1--MIREILLE ET LES ANIMAUX''--VERY
  EASY
    ASSOCIATED MUSIC PUBLISHERS, INC.   ESC   2.75

TANSMAN, A.
  JEUNES AU PIANO, LES--BK. 2--MARIANNE DEVANT LE KIOSQUE AUX
  JOURNEAUX--EASY
    ASSOCIATED MUSIC PUBLISHERS, INC.   ESC   3.00
TANSMAN, A.
  JEUNES AU PIANO, LES--BK. 3--L'AUTOBUS IMAGINAIRE--MODERATELY
  DIFFICULT
    ASSOCIATED MUSIC PUBLISHERS, INC.   ESC   2.75
TANSMAN, A.
  JEUNES AU PIANO, LES--BK. 4--AU TELESCOPE--RATHER DIFFICULT
    ASSOCIATED MUSIC PUBLISHERS, INC.   ESC   2.75
TANSMAN, A.
  MAZURKAS, BK. 1
    ASSOCIATED MUSIC PUBLISHERS, INC.   ESC   2.75
TANSMAN, A.
  MAZURKAS, BK. 2
    ASSOCIATED MUSIC PUBLISHERS, INC.   ESC   2.75
TANSMAN, A.
  PIANO IN PROGRESS, BK. 1
    EDWARD B. MARKS MUSIC CORPORATION   01.75
TANSMAN, A.
  PIANO IN PROGRESS, BK. 2
    EDWARD B. MARKS MUSIC CORPORATION   01.75
TANSMAN, A.
  POUR LES ENFANTS, BK. 1
    ASSOCIATED MUSIC PUBLISHERS, INC.   ESC   1.25
TANSMAN, A.
  POUR LES ENFANTS, BK. 2
    ASSOCIATED MUSIC PUBLISHERS, INC.   ESC   1.25
TANSMAN, A.
  POUR LES ENFANTS, BK. 3
    ASSOCIATED MUSIC PUBLISHERS, INC.   ESC   1.25
TANSMAN, A.
  POUR LES ENFANTS, BK. 4
    ASSOCIATED MUSIC PUBLISHERS, INC.   ESC   1.25
TANSMAN, A.
  PRELUDES, BK. 1
    ASSOCIATED MUSIC PUBLISHERS, INC.   ESC   1.25
TANSMAN, A.
  PRELUDES, BK. 2
    ASSOCIATED MUSIC PUBLISHERS, INC.   ESC   1.75
TANSMAN, A.
  RECREATIONS
    SUMMY-BIRCHARD COMPANY   2.00
TANSMAN, A.
  SIX ARABESQUES
    ASSOCIATED MUSIC PUBLISHERS, INC.   ESC   1.75
TANSMAN, A.
  TEN DIVERSIONS FOR THE YOUNG PIANIST--COMPLETE
    ASSOCIATED MUSIC PUBLISHERS, INC.   AMP   1.25
TANSMAN, A.
  THREE ETUDES TRANSCENDANTES
    FRANCO COLOMBO PUBLICATIONS   SAL   2.50
TANSMAN, A.
  TOCCATA AND SOUTH AMERICAN DANCE -- FROM CHILDREN AT PLAY
    MCA MUSIC   .60
TANSMAN, A.
  TOUR DU MONDE EN MINIATURE, LE
    ASSOCIATED MUSIC PUBLISHERS, INC.   ESC   3.00
TANSMAN, A.
  TROIS PRELUDES EN FORME DE BLUES
    ASSOCIATED MUSIC PUBLISHERS, INC.   ESC   3.00
TANSMAN, A.
  TWENTY EASY PIECES BASED ON POPULAR POLISH SONGS
    FRANCO COLOMBO PUBLICATIONS   SAL   3.50
TANSMAN, A.
  VISIT TO ISRAEL
    EDWARD B. MARKS MUSIC CORPORATION   01.50
TARDOS, B.
  FIVE BAGATELLES
    KULTURA   1.25
TATUM, A.
  ART TATUM IMPROVISATIONS, NO. 2
    THE BIG THREE MUSIC CORPORATION   01.50
TAUBERT
  HOFISCHE TANZE
    SCHOTT   5947A   2.25
TAUBERT--ED.   TAUBERT   E
  OLD CONTRADANCES FROM ENGLAND
    C. F. PETERS CORPORATION   RE42   2.50
TAURIELLO, A.
  FOUR SONATINAS
    BOOSEY AND HAWKES, INC.   1.00
TAUSIG   CESI
  DAILY EXERCISES
    FRANCO COLOMBO PUBLICATIONS   ER399   4.00
TAUSIG   EHRLICH
  DAILY STUDIES
    G. SCHIRMER, INC.   L1353   2.50
TAUSIG   D
  TWO CONCERT TRANSCRIPTIONS
    C. F. PETERS CORPORATION   3015   2.00
TAYLOR, C.   2-3
  ANNE-MARIE'S PIANO BOOK -- 4 EASY PIECES FOUNDED ON FRENCH TUNES
    NOVELLO AND COMPANY, LTD.   E   10.0084.05   1.15
TAYLOR, C.
  THREE TRIFLES
    OXFORD UNIVERSITY PRESS   33.069   1.10
TAYLOR, J.
  JAMES TAYLOR
    MUSIC SALES CORPORATION   020638   4.95
TCHEREPNIN
  BAGATELLES OP. 5, 10 NOS.
    HEUGEL ET CIE.   2.40
TCHEREPNIN   PHILIPP, I.
  BAGATELLES, OP. 5
    INTERNATIONAL MUSIC COMPANY   2.00
TCHEREPNIN
  BAGATELLES, OP. 5
    G. SCHIRMER, INC.   1.50
TCHEREPNIN
  BAGATELLES, OP. 5 - TEN PIECES FOR PIANO
    MCA MUSIC   1.50
TCHEREPNIN
  CHINESE BAGATELLES, OP. 51, NO. 3
    HEUGEL ET CIE.   2.75
TCHEREPNIN
  EIGHT PIECES FOR PIANO
    THEODORE PRESSER COMPANY   2.50
TCHEREPNIN
  EIGHT PRELUDES
    HEUGEL ET CIE.   2.75
TCHEREPNIN
  EPISODES, 12 PIECES
    HEUGEL ET CIE.   2.40
TCHEREPNIN
  EXPRESSIONS, OP.81- TEN PIECES FOR PIANO
    MCA MUSIC   1.50

TCHEREPNIN
  NINE INVENTIONS, OP. 13
    ASSOCIATED MUSIC PUBLISHERS, INC.   ESC   2.75
TCHEREPNIN
  PARC D'ATTRACTIONS -- EXPO 1937 -- 14 WORKS BY TCHEREPNIN,
  MARTINU, MOMPOU, RIETI, HONEGGER, HALFFTER, TANSMAN, MIHALOVICI,
  AND HARSANYI
    ASSOCIATED MUSIC PUBLISHERS, INC.   ESC   7.00
TCHEREPNIN
  POUR PETITES GRANDS, BK. 1
    ELKAN-VOGEL, INC.   D   3.10
TCHEREPNIN
  POUR PETITES GRANDS, BK. 2
    ELKAN-VOGEL, INC.   D   4.25
TCHEREPNIN
  QUATRE PRELUDES
    ELKAN-VOGEL, INC.   D   2.50
TCHEREPNIN
  QUATRE ROMANCES OP. 31
    UNIVERSAL EDITION   7350   1.50
TCHEREPNIN
  SEVEN ETUDES, OP. 56
    BOOSEY AND HAWKES, INC.   2.50
TCHEREPNIN
  SIX ETUDES DE TRAVAIL OP. 21
    HEUGEL ET CIE.   D   6.65
TCHEREPNIN
  SONGS WITHOUT WORDS, OP. 82
    C. F. PETERS CORPORATION   6015   1.25
TCHEREPNIN   D
  TECHNICAL STUDIES ON THE PENTATONIC SCALE
    C. F. PETERS CORPORATION   4436   3.50
TCHEREPNIN, I.
  FOUR PIECES FROM BEFORE
    BOOSEY AND HAWKES, INC.   1.00
TCHEREPNIN, N.
  FOUR PIECES IN C
    BOOSEY AND HAWKES, INC.   2.50
TEBOLDI
  TECHNICAL EXERCISES FOR THE INDEPENDENCE OF TOUCH IN POLYPHONIC
  PLAYING
    FRANCO COLOMBO PUBLICATIONS   ER1934   2.50
TEBOLDI
  THREE PIECES FOR CHILDREN
    FRANCO COLOMBO PUBLICATIONS   128108   .60
TEICHMUELLER   M-D
  PIANO TECHNIQUE
    C. F. PETERS CORPORATION   H32   3.00
TELEMANN, G.P.   SEIFFERT   3
  DREI DUTZEND KLAVIERFANTASIEN
    BARENREITER VERLAG   BA 733
TELEMANN, G.P.   KELLER
  EASY CHORALE PRELUDES
    C. F. PETERS CORPORATION   4239   E-M
TELEMANN, G.P.   LANGE
  EASY FUGUES AND LITTLE PIECES
    BARENREITER VERLAG   BA 268   3.50
TELEMANN, G.P.
  EASY FUGUES AND LITTLE PIECES
    EDWIN F. KALMUS   4003   1.50
TELEMANN, G.P.   LANGE
  EASY FUGUES AND SHORT PEICES
    INTERNATIONAL MUSIC COMPANY   1.75
TELEMANN, G.P.   KELLER   M
  FANTASIES
    C. F. PETERS CORPORATION   4681   3.50
TELEMANN, G.P.
  FANTASIES CHOISIES
    EDWARD B. MARKS MUSIC CORPORATION   02.25
TELEMANN, G.P.
  FANTASIES POUR LE CLAVESSIN
    BROUDE BROTHERS LTD.   04.00
TELEMANN, G.P.   FISCHER, HANS *   E-M
  GERMAN KEYBOARD MUSIC OF THE SEVENTEENTH AND EIGHTEENTH
  CENTURIES, VOL. 4# TELEMANN
    C. F. PETERS CORPORATION   V123   2.00
TELEMANN, G.P.   FISCHER, HANS *   E-M
  GERMAN KEYBOARD MUSIC OF THE SEVENTEENTH AND EIGHTEENTH
  CENTURIES, VOL. 5# TELEMANN
    C. F. PETERS CORPORATION   V124   2.00
TELEMANN, G.P.   IRMER, VON   2-3
  KLAVIER-BUCHLEIN
    SCHOTT   4230   1.75
TELEMANN, G.P.   DOFLEIN   3
  KLEINE FANTASIEN
    SCHOTT   2330   2.25
TELEMANN, G.P.   LANGE   3
  LEICHTE FUGEN UND KLEINE STUCKE
    BARENREITER VERLAG   BA 268
TELEMANN, G.P.   FRANKE   E-M
  OVERTURES
    C. F. PETERS CORPORATION   9107   4.00
TELEMANN, G.P.   RUF   3
  SECHS OUVERTUREN FUR CEMBALO
    SCHOTT   5774   2.50
TELEMANN, G.P.
  SIX FANTASIES AND SIX FUGUES
    ASSOCIATED MUSIC PUBLISHERS, INC.   BRH   3.00
TELEMANN, G.P.   RUF   3
  SOLI AUS 'ESSERCIZII MUSICI'
    SCHOTT   5296   2.25
TELEMANN, G.P.   DEGEN
  SPIELSTUCKE FUR KLAVIER
    BARENREITER VERLAG   HM 9   6.00
TELEMANN, G.P.   DEGEN   2-3
  SPIELSTUCKE FUR KLAVIER. 36 STUCKE AUS DEM 'GETREUEN
  MUSIKMEISTER', TEILWEISE FUR LAUTE.
    BARENREITER VERLAG   HM 9
TELEMANN, G.P.   SEIFFERT
  THREE DOZEN FANTASIAS
    BARENREITER VERLAG   BA 733   3.50
TELEMANN, G.P.   UPMEYER
  TWENTY LITTLE FUGUES
    ASSOCIATED MUSIC PUBLISHERS, INC.   NAG   3.50
TELEMANN, G.P.   UPMEYER
  TWENTY LITTLE FUGUES FOR ORGAN OR PIANO
    BARENREITER VERLAG   NMA 13   3.50
TELEMANN, G.P.   UPMEYER   3
  ZWANZIG KLEINE FUGEN FUR ORGEL ODER KLAVIER
    BARENREITER VERLAG   NMA 13
TEMPLETON, A.
  PIANO PORTRAITS -- BK. 1 -- LOWER INTERMEDIATE GRADES
    SAM FOX PUBLISHING COMPANY, INC.   1.00
TEMPLETON, A.
  PIANO PORTRAITS -- BK. 2 -- UPPER INTERMEDIATE GRADES
    SAM FOX PUBLISHING COMPANY, INC.   1.00

TEMPLETON, A.
  SULTRY DAY IN NEW YORK
    THE BIG THREE MUSIC CORPORATION   00.95
TERHUNE, A.
  SCHIRMER'S MUSIC SPELLING-BOOK
    G. SCHIRMER, INC.   1.00
TERRY--ED   TERRY
  HONKY-TONK RAGTIME PIANO
    WARNER BROTHERS PUBLISHERS   1.95
TERRY, F.   SECOND GRADE
  TUNEFUL TASKS FOR PIANO STUDENTS OF THE SECOND GRADE
    G. SCHIRMER, INC.   1.00
THALBERG
  THREE OPERATIC FANTASIES FOR PIANO SOLO
    MUSIC TREASURE PUBLICATIONS   5.00
THALBERG
  TRE GIORNI, AIR DE PERGOLESE
    MUSICAL SCOPE PUBLISHERS   01.25
THALBERG
  TWELVE STUDIES, OP. 26
    FRANCO COLOMBO PUBLICATIONS   ER2237   2.00
THIEFFRY
  EASY PIECES
    FRANCO COLOMBO PUBLICATIONS   SAL   2.50
THIELE, S.
  THREE PIECES
    ASSOCIATED MUSIC PUBLISHERS, INC.   BRH   1.50
THOMAS, A.
  PLAY PEN BOOK, THE
    BANKS AND SON LTD.   .80
THOMAS, C. J.
  FOURTEEN LITTLE PIANO PIECES FOR EARLY GRADES
    BROOT MUSIC COMPANY   1.25
THOMAS, H. T.
  FIRST MOMENTS AT THE PIANO, PART 1
    THEODORE PRESSER COMPANY   1.75
THOMAS, H. T.
  FIRST MOMENTS AT THE PIANO, PART 2
    THEODORE PRESSER COMPANY   1.75
THOMAS, H. T.
  NINE SHORT SOLOS
    THEODORE PRESSER COMPANY   1.25
THOMPSON, J.   3
  ALL ON ONE PAGE
    WILLIS MUSIC COMPANY   1.50
THOMPSON, J.   1
  CHIPS FROM OTHER BLOCKS
    WILLIS MUSIC COMPANY   1.00
THOMPSON, J.
  CHRISTMAS BOOK
    WILLIS MUSIC COMPANY   1.00
THOMPSON, J.   1
  COVERED WAGON SUITE, THE
    WILLIS MUSIC COMPANY   .80
THOMPSON, J.   5
  FIFTH GRADE TECHNIC
    WILLIS MUSIC COMPANY   1.00
THOMPSON, J.   2
  FIFTY SECOND GRADE ETUDES
    WILLIS MUSIC COMPANY   1.50
THOMPSON, J.   1
  FIRST GRADE ETUDES
    WILLIS MUSIC COMPANY   1.00
THOMPSON, J.   1
  FOR LEFT HAND ALONE - BK. 1
    WILLIS MUSIC COMPANY   1.00
THOMPSON, J.   2
  FOR LEFT HAND ALONE - BK. 1
    WILLIS MUSIC COMPANY   1.00
THOMPSON, J.   4
  FOURTH GRADE ETUDES
    WILLIS MUSIC COMPANY   1.75
THOMPSON, J.
  JOHN THOMPSON'S DELUXE BOOK OF CHRISTMAS CAROLS
    WILLIS MUSIC COMPANY   2.00
THOMPSON, J.   3
  KEYBOARD ATTACKS
    WILLIS MUSIC COMPANY   1.75
THOMPSON, J.   3
  LITTLE VIRTUOSO SUITE, A
    WILLIS MUSIC COMPANY   .60
THOMPSON, J.   5
  OCTAVE BOOK
    WILLIS MUSIC COMPANY   1.00
THOMPSON, J.   2
  PILGRIM SUITE, THE
    WILLIS MUSIC COMPANY   1.00
THOMPSON, J. *   PORTNOFF
  PUSS IN BOOKS -- PIANO FOLIO FOR CHILDREN
    MCA MUSIC   1.75
THOMPSON, J.   1
  SYNCOPATION MADE EASY - BOOK 1
    WILLIS MUSIC COMPANY   1.00
THOMPSON, J.   2
  SYNCOPATION MADE EASY - BOOK 2
    WILLIS MUSIC COMPANY   1.00
THOMPSON, J.   1
  TECHNIC FOR THE FIRST YEAR
    WILLIS MUSIC COMPANY   1.25
THOMPSON, J.   3
  THIRD GRADE VELOCITY STUDIES
    WILLIS MUSIC COMPANY   1.25
THOMPSON, J.
  THOMPSON ADULT PREPARATORY BOOK
    WILLIS MUSIC COMPANY   1.50
THOMPSON, J.
  THOMPSON EASIEST PIANO COURSE - PART 1
    WILLIS MUSIC COMPANY   .90
THOMPSON, J.
  THOMPSON EASIEST PIANO COURSE - PART 2
    WILLIS MUSIC COMPANY   1.00
THOMPSON, J.
  THOMPSON EASIEST PIANO COURSE - PART 3
    WILLIS MUSIC COMPANY   1.00
THOMPSON, J.
  THOMPSON EASIEST PIANO COURSE - PART 4
    WILLIS MUSIC COMPANY   1.00
THOMPSON, J.
  THOMPSON EASIEST PIANO COURSE - PART 5
    WILLIS MUSIC COMPANY   1.50
THOMPSON, J.
  THOMPSON EASIEST PIANO COURSE - PART 6
    WILLIS MUSIC COMPANY   1.50
THOMPSON, J.
  THOMPSON EASIEST PIANO COURSE - PART 7
    WILLIS MUSIC COMPANY   1.00

THOMPSON, J.
    THOMPSON EASIEST PIANO COURSE - PART 8
        WILLIS MUSIC COMPANY   1.00
THOMPSON, J.
    THOMPSON MELODY ALL THE WAY - BOOK 1-A
        WILLIS MUSIC COMPANY   1.25
THOMPSON, J.
    THOMPSON MELODY ALL THE WAY - BOOK 1-B
        WILLIS MUSIC COMPANY   1.25
THOMPSON, J.
    THOMPSON MELODY ALL THE WAY - BOOK 2-A
        WILLIS MUSIC COMPANY   1.25
THOMPSON, J.
    THOMPSON MELODY ALL THE WAY - BOOK 2-B
        WILLIS MUSIC COMPANY   1.25
THOMPSON, J.
    THOMPSON MELODY ALL THE WAY - BOOK 3-A
        WILLIS MUSIC COMPANY   1.25
THOMPSON, J.
    THOMPSON MELODY ALL THE WAY - BOOK 3-B
        WILLIS MUSIC COMPANY   1.25
THOMPSON, J.
    THOMPSON MELODY ALL THE WAY - PREPARATORY BOOK
        WILLIS MUSIC COMPANY   .90
THOMPSON, J.
    THOMPSON MODERN COURSE FOR THE PIANO - FIFTH GRADE BOOK
        WILLIS MUSIC COMPANY   1.60
THOMPSON, J.
    THOMPSON MODERN COURSE FOR THE PIANO - FIRST GRADE BOOK
        WILLIS MUSIC COMPANY   1.60
THOMPSON, J.
    THOMPSON MODERN COURSE FOR THE PIANO - FOURTH GRADE BOOK
        WILLIS MUSIC COMPANY   1.60
THOMPSON, J.
    THOMPSON MODERN COURSE FOR THE PIANO - SECOND GRADE BOOK
        WILLIS MUSIC COMPANY   1.60
THOMPSON, J.
    THOMPSON MODERN COURSE FOR THE PIANO - TEACHING LITTLE FINGERS
    TO PLAY
        WILLIS MUSIC COMPANY   .75
THOMPSON, J.
    THOMPSON MODERN COURSE FOR THE PIANO - THIRD GRADE BOOK
        WILLIS MUSIC COMPANY   1.60
THOMPSON, J.   PREPARATORY
    TINY TECHNIC
        WILLIS MUSIC COMPANY   1.00
THOMPSON, J.
    TUNEFUL TASKS
        THEODORE PRESSER COMPANY   1.00
THOMPSON, J.   2
    TUNEFUL TECHNIC - BK. 1
        WILLIS MUSIC COMPANY   .90
THOMPSON, J.   3
    TUNEFUL TECHNIC - BK. 2
        WILLIS MUSIC COMPANY   .90
THOMPSON, J.
    TWENTY-FOUR MINIATURES IN PRELUDE FORM FOR STUDY -- ONE IN EACH
    KEY, OP. 34
        BELWIN-MILLS PUBLISHING CORPORATION   10063   1.00
THOMPSON, J.
    TWENTY-FOUR MINIATURES IN PRELUDE FORM, OP. 34
        BELWIN-MILLS PUBLISHING CORPORATION   1.00
THOMPSON, J.   4
    WRIST AND ARM TECHNIC
        WILLIS MUSIC COMPANY   1.00
THOMPSON, J.--ED   THOMPSON, J.   1
    DEBUT
        WILLIS MUSIC COMPANY   1.00
THOMPSON, J.--ED   THOMPSON, J.   2
    FAVORITE CATHOLIC HYMNS
        WILLIS MUSIC COMPANY   1.00
THOMPSON, J.--ED   THOMPSON, J.   1
    FIRST YEAR CLASSICS
        WILLIS MUSIC COMPANY   1.25
THOMPSON, J.--ED   THOMPSON, J.   1
    FOR GIRLS WHO PLAY
        WILLIS MUSIC COMPANY   1.50
THOMPSON, J.--ED   THOMPSON, J.   2
    GOSPEL HYMNS
        WILLIS MUSIC COMPANY   1.25
THOMPSON, J.--ED   THOMPSON, J.   2
    HYMNS OF FAITH
        WILLIS MUSIC COMPANY   1.00
THOMPSON, J.--ED   THOMPSON, J.   3
    INTRODUCTION TO BACH, AN
        WILLIS MUSIC COMPANY   1.25
THOMPSON, J.--ED   THOMPSON, J.   PREPARATORY
    JOHN THOMPSON'S CHRISTMAS CAROL BOOK
        WILLIS MUSIC COMPANY   1.00
THOMPSON, J.--ED   THOMPSON, J.   1
    JOHN THOMPSON'S CHRISTMAS CAROLS
        WILLIS MUSIC COMPANY   1.00
THOMPSON, J.--ED   THOMPSON, J.   1
    LET'S JOIN THE ARMY
        WILLIS MUSIC COMPANY   1.50
THOMPSON, J.--ED   THOMPSON, J.   3
    NOTES FROM OTHER PENS
        WILLIS MUSIC COMPANY   1.00
THOMPSON, J.--ED   THOMPSON, J.   4
    REPERTOIRE
        WILLIS MUSIC COMPANY   1.25
THOMPSON, J.--ED   THOMPSON, J.   2
    SECOND YEAR PIANO CLASSICS
        WILLIS MUSIC COMPANY   1.00
THOMPSON, J.--ED   THOMPSON, J.   2
    SIX LITTLE RECITAL PIECES
        WILLIS MUSIC COMPANY   1.00
THOMPSON, J.--ED   THOMPSON, J.   4
    SIX PARTY PIECES
        WILLIS MUSIC COMPANY   .80
THOMPSON, J.--ED   THOMPSON, J.   4
    SIX WEDDING MARCHES
        WILLIS MUSIC COMPANY   1.25
THOMPSON, J.--ED   THOMPSON, J.   2
    SPARKS FROM OTHER ANVILS
        WILLIS MUSIC COMPANY   1.00
THOMPSON, J.--ED   THOMPSON, J.   2
    STUDIES IN STYLE
        WILLIS MUSIC COMPANY   1.00
THOMPSON, J.--ED   THOMPSON, J.   4
    THEMES FROM PIANO CONCERTOS
        WILLIS MUSIC COMPANY   1.25
THOMPSON, J.--ED   THOMPSON, J.   2
    WE'RE IN THE NAVY NOW
        WILLIS MUSIC COMPANY   1.50

THOMPSON, J.--ED   THOMPSON, J.   2
    WORLD FAMOUS MELODIES
        WILLIS MUSIC COMPANY   2.00
THOMPSON, J.--ED   THOMPSON, J.   3
    WORLD KNOWN MELODIES
        WILLIS MUSIC COMPANY   1.00
THOMPSON, J.--ED   THOMPSON, J.   3
    YOUNG ARTIST, THE
        WILLIS MUSIC COMPANY   1.00
THOMPSON, J.--ED   THOMPSON, J.   2
    YOUNG RECITALIST, THE
        WILLIS MUSIC COMPANY   1.25
THOMSON, V.
    NINE PORTRAITS
        PEER SOUTHERN ORGANIZATION   02.50
THOMSON, V.
    SYNTHETIC WALTZES -- SET OF 2 COPIES
        ELKAN-VOGEL, INC.   3.50
THOMSON, V.
    TEN EASY PIECES AND A CODA
        PEER SOUTHERN ORGANIZATION   01.75
THORNE
    EIGHT INTROSPECTIONS
        EDWARD B. MARKS MUSIC CORPORATION   01.00
THORNE
    NINE PLAYFUL PLOYS FOR PIANO
        GENERAL MUSIC PUBLISHING COMPANY, INC.   2.50
THORNE
    SHE DOESN'T - TWO PIECES FOR PIANO SOLO
        GENERAL MUSIC PUBLISHING COMPANY, INC.   2.00
THUMER
    THUMERS NEUE ETUDEN-SCHULE - VORBEREITUNGSSCHULE, HEFT 01
        SCHOTT   700A   2.25
THUMER
    THUMERS NEUE ETUDEN-SCHULE - VORBEREITUNGSSCHULE, HEFT 02
        SCHOTT   700B   2.25
THUMER
    THUMERS NEUE ETUDEN-SCHULE - 01 VORST., ELEMENTARSTUFE
        SCHOTT   701   2.25
THUMER
    THUMERS NEUE ETUDEN-SCHULE - 02 VORST., ELEMENTARSTUFE
        SCHOTT   702   2.25
THUMER
    THUMERS NEUE ETUDEN-SCHULE - 03, HOHERE ELEMENTARSTUFE
        SCHOTT   703   2.25
THUMER
    THUMERS NEUE ETUDEN-SCHULE - 04, HOHERE ELEMENTARSTUFE
        SCHOTT   704   2.25
THUMER
    THUMERS NEUE ETUDEN-SCHULE - 05A, UNTER MITTELSTUFE
        SCHOTT   705A   2.25
THUMER
    THUMERS NEUE ETUDEN-SCHULE - 05B, UNTER MITTELSTUFE
        SCHOTT   705B   2.25
TJEKNAVORIAN, L. Z.
    THREE ARMENIAN DANCES, OP. 2--1958
        ASSOCIATED MUSIC PUBLISHERS, INC.   DOB   2.50
TOBLER--ED   TOBLER
    NEUE SCHULE DES KLAVIERSPIELS
        BARENREITER VERLAG   SM 1899
TOCH, E.   5
    BURLESKEN, OP. 31
        SCHOTT   1822   2.50
TOCH, E.   3
    CAPRICCETTI, OP. 36
        SCHOTT   1825   2.25
TOCH, E.
    DIVERSIONS. FIVE PIECES, OP. 78A
        MCA MUSIC   1.00
TOCH, E.
    ETUDEN FUR KLAVIER, 5 TIMES 10 - ZEHN ANFANGS-ETUDEN, OP. 59
        SCHOTT   2196   2.50
TOCH, E.
    ETUDEN FUR KLAVIER, 5 TIMES 10 - ZEHN EINFACHE ETUDEN, OP. 58
        SCHOTT   2197   2.50
TOCH, E.
    ETUDEN FUR KLAVIER, 5 TIMES 10 - ZEHN KONZERT-ETUDEN, OP. 55,
    HEFT 01
        SCHOTT   2161   2.50
TOCH, E.
    ETUDEN FUR KLAVIER, 5 TIMES 10 - ZEHN KONZERT-ETUDEN, OP. 55,
    HEFT 02
        SCHOTT   2162   2.50
TOCH, E.
    ETUDEN FUR KLAVIER, 5 TIMES 10 - ZEHN MITTELSTUFEN-ETUDEN, OP.
    57, HEFT 01
        SCHOTT   2198   2.50
TOCH, E.
    ETUDEN FUR KLAVIER, 5 TIMES 10 - ZEHN MITTELSTUFEN-ETUDEN, OP.
    57, HEFT 02
        SCHOTT   2199   2.50
TOCH, E.
    ETUDEN FUR KLAVIER, 5 TIMES 10 - ZEHN VORTRAGS-ETUDEN, OP. 56,
    HEFT 01
        SCHOTT   2166   2.50
TOCH, E.
    ETUDEN FUR KLAVIER, 5 TIMES 10 - ZEHN VORTRAGS-ETUDEN, OP. 56,
    HEFT 02
        SCHOTT   2167   2.50
TOCH, E.
    IDEAS. FOUR PIECES, OP. 69
        MCA MUSIC   2.00
TOCH, E.   2-3
    KLEINSTADTBILDER, OP. 49
        SCHOTT   2082   2.50
TOCH, E.
    PROFILES, OP. 68
        ASSOCIATED MUSIC PUBLISHERS, INC.   AMP   2.50
TOLSON, P.
    CHRISTMAS AT THE PIANO
        LILLENAS PUBLISHING COMPANY   MC-242   1.95
TOLSON, P.
    REFLECTIONS AT THE PIANO
        LILLENAS PUBLISHING COMPANY   MB-157   1.95
TOLSON, P.
    SPIRITUALS AT THE PIANO
        LILLENAS PUBLISHING COMPANY   MB-202   1.95
TOM, BLIND
    BATTLE OF MANASSAS
        MUSICA OBSCURA   2.50
TOMASEK   POHANKA   3
    TRE DITIRAMBI, OP. 65
        BARENREITER VERLAG   MAB 29
TOMASI, H.   3
    COIN DE CLAUDINET, LE
        ALPHONSE LEDUC

TOMASI, H.   5
    SCENES MUNICIPALES
        ALPHONSE LEDUC
TONON
    FIVE LITTLE PIECES
        FRANCO COLOMBO PUBLICATIONS   Z4796   1.75
TOSATTI
    THREE CONCERT STUDIES
        FRANCO COLOMBO PUBLICATIONS   128879   1.50
TOTZAUER, H.
    TWO PIECES
        ASSOCIATED MUSIC PUBLISHERS, INC. OOB   1.50
TOURBIE--ED.   TOURBIE   M
    SELECTIONS FROM THE CLASSICS
        C. F. PETERS CORPORATION   ZM1750   2.50
TOURNEMIRE, C.
    DOUZE PRELUDES -- POEMES, OP. 58
        HEUGEL ET CIE.   12.00
TOWNSEND
    THIS 'N THAT
        PRO-ART PUBLICATIONS, INC.   608   .60
TRABACI   MISCHIATI   2-3
    COMPOSIZIONI PER ORGANO E CEMBALO, HEFT 1 - 12 RICERCARE
        BARENREITER VERLAG
TRABACI   3
    COMPOSIZIONI PER ORGANO E CEMBALO, HEFT 2 - 7 CANZONI FRANCESI,
    2 CAPRICCI, 4 CANTI FERMI
        BARENREITER VERLAG
TRAPP, M.
    FOUR PIECES, OP. 35
        ASSOCIATED MUSIC PUBLISHERS, INC. LEU   3.00
TRAVAGLIA
    CHRISTMAS ALBUM
        FRANCO COLOMBO PUBLICATIONS   Z1760   1.50
TREBINSKY, A.
    DOUZE PRELUDES
        EDITIONS MUSICALES TRANSATLANTIQUES   4.00
TREBINSKY, A.
    FIVE ETUDES
        FRANCO COLOMBO PUBLICATIONS   SAL   5.75
TREBINSKY, A.
    TWELVE PRELUDES
        FRANCO COLOMBO PUBLICATIONS   SAL   4.25
TREHARNE
    CHILDREN'S PLAYTIME PIECES
        BOSTON MUSIC COMPANY   1.25
TREMER, J.
    LES PETITS ARTISTES
        ELKAN-VOGEL, INC.   D   3.40
TRIGGS
    SIX SURREALIST AFTERLUDES
        BELWIN-MILLS PUBLISHING CORPORATION   1.50
TRIMBLE
    FIVE EPISODES FOR PIANO
        MCA MUSIC   2.50
TROIANI
    TWELVE MELODIES FROM THE MOUNTAINS AND THE PLAINS
        FRANCO COLOMBO PUBLICATIONS   BA9197   2.50
TROJELLI
    PETITES MAINS, LES
        FRANCO COLOMBO PUBLICATIONS   SAL   2.75
TROJELLI
    SIX PIECES MIGNONNES POUR LES PETITES MAINS
        FRANCO COLOMBO PUBLICATIONS   SAL   3.50
TROTTER *   ROGERS, M.
    BABAR COMES TO AMERICA
        POINTER PUBLICATIONS   2.95
TSCHAIKOWSKY
    ALBUM
        KULTURA   2.00
TSCHAIKOWSKY   RUTHARDT   M-D
    ALBUM
        C. F. PETERS CORPORATION   3066   4.00
TSCHAIKOWSKY
    ALBUM D'ENFANTS, OP. 39
        GERARD BILLAUDOT EDITIONS MUSICALES   2.70
TSCHAIKOWSKY
    ALBUM FOR THE YOUNG
        EDWARD B. MARKS MUSIC CORPORATION   01.00
TSCHAIKOWSKY
    ALBUM FOR THE YOUNG, OP. 39
        ASSOCIATED MUSIC PUBLISHERS, INC. BRH   1.00
TSCHAIKOWSKY
    ALBUM FOR THE YOUNG, OP. 39
        CARL FISCHER, INC.   O 4805   1.25
TSCHAIKOWSKY
    ALBUM FOR THE YOUNG, OP. 39
        EDWIN F. KALMUS   4018   1.25
TSCHAIKOWSKY   NIEMANN   E-M
    ALBUM FOR THE YOUNG, OP. 39
        C. F. PETERS CORPORATION   3782   2.00
TSCHAIKOWSKY   RUTHARDT
    ALBUM FOR THE YOUNG, OP. 39--24 EASY PIECES
        G. SCHIRMER, INC.   L816   1.00
TSCHAIKOWSKY   3-5
    AUSWAHL -- 12 AUSGEWAHLTE STUCKE
        SCHOTT   516   1.75
TSCHAIKOWSKY   2
    BEL MELODIEN I. LEICHT. SATZ
        SCHOTT   04097 1/2 1.00
TSCHAIKOWSKY   SCHAUM, J.   2 1/2
    BEST OF TSCHAIKOWSKY
        SCHAUM PUBLICATIONS, INC.   1.25
TSCHAIKOWSKY   DEXTER, H.
    CHILDREN'S TSCHAIKOWSKY
        SAM FOX PUBLISHING COMPANY, INC.   1.00
TSCHAIKOWSKY   HUGHES
    MASTER SERIES FOR THE YOUNG--VOL. 12
        G. SCHIRMER, INC.   1.25
TSCHAIKOWSKY
    MASTERPIECE ALBUM
        FRANCO COLOMBO PUBLICATIONS   SAL   5.00
TSCHAIKOWSKY   POZZOLI
    MY FIRST TSCHAIKOWSKY
        FRANCO COLOMBO PUBLICATIONS   ER2599   1.25
TSCHAIKOWSKY   BANTOCK
    NUTCRACKER -- COMPLETE, ILLUSTRATED
        BELWIN-MILLS PUBLISHING CORPORATION 09470   3.50
TSCHAIKOWSKY   ROVENGER
    NUTCRACKER SUITE
        RUBANK, INC.   1.00
TSCHAIKOWSKY   SCHAUM, J.   2 1/2
    NUTCRACKER SUITE
        SCHAUM PUBLICATIONS, INC.   1.50
TSCHAIKOWSKY
    RADIO CITY ALBUM
        EDWARD B. MARKS MUSIC CORPORATION   01.50

TSCHAIKOWSKY   M
    SEASONS, OP. 37A
        C. F. PETERS CORPORATION   3781   2.50
TSCHAIKOWSKY
    SEASONS, THE, OP. 37A--12 CHARACTERISTIC PIECES
        G. SCHIRMER, INC.   L909   1.50
TSCHAIKOWSKY
    SEASONS, THE, OP. 73B
        ASSOCIATED MUSIC PUBLISHERS, INC. BRH   .90
TSCHAIKOWSKY
    SELECTED COMPOSITIONS
        G. SCHIRMER, INC.   L1634   1.50
TSCHAIKOWSKY   D
    SELECTED PIANO WORKS, VOL. 1
        C. F. PETERS CORPORATION   4652   6.00
TSCHAIKOWSKY   D
    SELECTED PIANO WORKS, VOL. 2
        C. F. PETERS CORPORATION   4653   6.00
TSCHAIKOWSKY   D
    SELECTED PIANO WORKS, VOL. 3
        C. F. PETERS CORPORATION   4654   6.00
TSCHAIKOWSKY   MARCIANO
    SELECTED PIECES
        FRANCO COLOMBO PUBLICATIONS   ER521   3.50
TSCHAIKOWSKY   ROTH
    SLEEPING BEAUTY -- BALLET TOLD IN WORDS AND MUSIC
        BOOSEY AND HAWKES, INC.   1.50
TSCHAIKOWSKY   ROTH
    SWAN LAKE -- BALLET TOLD IN WORDS AND MUSIC
        BOOSEY AND HAWKES, INC.   1.50
TCHAIKOWSKY
    ASHLEY DEALERS SERVICE, INC.   HG 08   2.95
TSCHAIKOWSKY   ROVENGER
    TSCHAIKOWSKY FOR THE YOUNG
        RUBANK, INC.   1.50
TSCHAIKOWSKY   ECKHARDT, F.   1
    TSCHAIKOWSKY FOR THE YOUNG PIANIST
        CENTURY MUSIC PUBLISHING COMPANY, INC. 3963   .40
TSCHAIKOWSKY
    TSCHAIKOWSKY MADE EASY FOR EVERYONE
        MUSICORD PUBLICATIONS, INC.   1.50
TSCHAIKOWSKY   4
    WALZER AUS DER SERENADE FUR STREICHORCHESTER OP. 48 NO. 2
        SCHOTT   07094 1/2 1.00
TUCKMAN
    LATIN AMERICAN FAVORITES
        BELWIN-MILLS PUBLISHING CORPORATION   1.00
TUCKMAN
    TRADITIONAL MUSIC OF ISRAEL
        BELWIN-MILLS PUBLISHING CORPORATION   1.00
TUERK   2
    ANFANGERSTUCKE
        SCHOTT   3763   1.75
TUERK   AUERBACH
    FORTY-NINE PIECES FOR SMALL HANDS
        ASSOCIATED MUSIC PUBLISHERS, INC. NAG   3.00
TUERK   AUERBACH
    KLEINE HANDSTUCKE
        BARENREITER VERLAG   EN 810   3.00
TUERK
    KLEINE HANDSTUCKE FUR ANGEHENDE KLAVIERSPIELER
        BARENREITER VERLAG   EN 810
TUERK   AUERBACH   1-3
    KLEINE HANDSTUCKE FUR ANGEHENDE KLAVIERSPIELER. 50 KLEINE STUCKE
    IN PROGRESSIVER REIHENFOLGE
        BARENREITER VERLAG   EN 810
TUERK   DOFLEIN   2
    LEICHTE STUCKE
        SCHOTT   3943   1.75
TUERK   E
    SIXTY VERY EASY PIECES --IN PROGRESSIVE ORDER--
        C. F. PETERS CORPORATION   L5602   3.00
TUERK   E
    TWELVE PIECES
        C. F. PETERS CORPORATION   L5603   2.00
TURECK, R.
    INTRODUCTION TO THE PERFORMANCE OF BACH, BK. 1
        OXFORD UNIVERSITY PRESS   93.802   2.50
TURECK, R.
    INTRODUCTION TO THE PERFORMANCE OF BACH, BK. 2
        OXFORD UNIVERSITY PRESS   93.803   2.50
TURECK, R.
    INTRODUCTION TO THE PERFORMANCE OF BACH, BK. 3
        OXFORD UNIVERSITY PRESS   93.804   3.00
TUREL
    TWELVE SKETCHES --DOUZE DESSINS
        MCA MUSIC   2.00
TURINA, J.
    ALBUM DE VIAJE
        INTERNATIONAL MUSIC COMPANY   2.00
TURINA, J.
    ALBUM DE VIAJE, OP. 15
        ASSOCIATED MUSIC PUBLISHERS, INC. UME   2.50
TURINA, J.
    BAILETE - ENTRADA, TIRANA, BOLERO, DANZA DE CORTE, FANDANGO
        FRANCO COLOMBO PUBLICATIONS   SAL   2.00
TURINA, J.
    CICLO PIANISTICO--FIVE PRELUDES, OP. 80
        ASSOCIATED MUSIC PUBLISHERS, INC. UME   1.00
TURINA, J.
    CONTES D'ESPAGNE, BK. 1
        FRANCO COLOMBO PUBLICATIONS   SAL   5.50
TURINA, J.
    CONTES D'ESPAGNE, BK. 2
        FRANCO COLOMBO PUBLICATIONS   SAL   5.50
TURINA, J.
    DANSES GITANES, BK. 1 - ZAMBRA, DANZA RITUAL, SACRO-MONTE
        FRANCO COLOMBO PUBLICATIONS   SAL   2.00
TURINA, J.
    DANSES GITANES, BK. 2 - FIESTA DE LA CALDERAS, INVOCATION, DANZA
    RITMICA, SEGUIRIYA
        FRANCO COLOMBO PUBLICATIONS   SAL   2.00
TURINA, J.
    EVOCACIONES, OP. 46
        ASSOCIATED MUSIC PUBLISHERS, INC. UME   1.75
TURINA, J.
    FEMMES D'ESPAGNE, BK. 1 - LA MADRILENE CLASSIQUE, L'ANDALOUSE
    SENTIMENTALE, LA BRAVE COQUETTE
        FRANCO COLOMBO PUBLICATIONS   SAL   2.50
TURINA, J.
    FEMMES D'ESPAGNE, BK. 2 - LA GITANE AMOUREUSE, LA MARCHANDE DE
    FLEURS, LA DANSEUSE MONDAINE, LA BELLE MURCIENNE, LA SEVILLANE
    JOYEUSE
        FRANCO COLOMBO PUBLICATIONS   SAL   2.00

TURINA, J.
    FEMMES DE SEVILLE - LA POTIERE DE TRIANA, JOLIE FILLE, LA
    GRACIEUSE MARCARENA, LA CIGARIERE ESPIEGLE, MANTILLES ET GRANDE
    PEIGNES
        FRANCO COLOMBO PUBLICATIONS   SAL   1.50
                            4
TURINA, J.
    IM SCHUSTERLADEN
        SCHOTT   2231   2.50
TURINA, J.
    JARDINS D'ANDALOUSIE
        FRANCO COLOMBO PUBLICATIONS   SAL   5.50
TURINA, J.
    JARDINS D'ENFANTS - MARCHE, L'ENFANT S'ENDORT, BOITE A MUSIQUE,
    CLOCHES, PETITE DANSE, PETITE FUGUE, JEUX SUR LA PLAGE, FINAL
        FRANCO COLOMBO PUBLICATIONS   SAL   2.50
TURINA, J.
    MALLORCA
        FRANCO COLOMBO PUBLICATIONS   SAL   5.50
                            3
TURINA, J.
    MINIATUREN, ACHT KLEINE STUCKE
        SCHOTT   2106   2.50
TURINA, J.
    NINERIAS, BK. 1
        FRANCO COLOMBO PUBLICATIONS   SAL   5.50
TURINA, J.
    NINERIAS, BK. 2
        FRANCO COLOMBO PUBLICATIONS   SAL   5.50
                            4
TURINA, J.
    POSTKARTEN, FUNF STUCKE
        SCHOTT   2146   2.50
TURINA, J.
    PRELUDE AND PANTOMINE FROM "JARDIN DE ORIENTE"
        ASSOCIATED MUSIC PUBLISHERS, INC.   UME   1.75
TURINA, J.
    SEVILLA, SUITE PITTORESQUE--COMPLETE
        ASSOCIATED MUSIC PUBLISHERS, INC.   ESC   6.00
TURINA, J.
    SILHOUETTES
        FRANCO COLOMBO PUBLICATIONS   SAL   5.50
TURINA, J.
    SOUVENIRS DE L'ANCIENNE ESPAGNE
        FRANCO COLOMBO PUBLICATIONS   SAL   5.50
TURINA, J.
    THREE DANSES ANDALOUSES - PETENERA, TANGO, ZAPATEADO
        FRANCO COLOMBO PUBLICATIONS   SAL   2.00
TWITTENHOFF   3
    KUCKUCK, KUCKUCK. VARIATIONEN UBER 5 BEKANNTE KINDERLIEDER
        BARENREITER VERLAG   SM 899
TWITTENHOFF--ED   TWITTENHOFF   2
    VOLKSTANZBUCHLEIN
        SCHOTT   3774   1.75
UGARTE
    FIVE PRELUDES
        FRANCO COLOMBO PUBLICATIONS   BA9186   2.00
ULEHLA, L.
    FIVE OVER TWELVE - FIVE PRELUDES
        GENERAL MUSIC PUBLISHING COMPANY, INC.   2.50
UNDARRA *   SYKOVA   3
    KLAVIERKOMPOSITIONEN DES ALTEN SPANIEN UND PORTUGAL. 16 TIENTOS,
    HYMNEN, SONATEN, RONDI UND TOCCATEN
        BARENREITER VERLAG   MVH 17
                            3
URBACH, E.
    KNECHT RUPRECHT
        SCHOTT   1.50
URBANNER, E.
    ELEVEN BAGATELLES
        UNIVERSAL EDITION   UE 13165   1.50
VAILLANT, H.
    LE PETIT VIRTUOSE
        GERARD BILLAUDOT EDITIONS MUSICALES   3.30
                            M-D
VALEN
    FOUR PIANO PIECES, OP. 22
        C. F. PETERS CORPORATION   LY154   .90
                            D
VALEN
    GAVOTTE AND MUSETTE, OP. 24
        C. F. PETERS CORPORATION   LY106   .60
                            D
VALEN
    PRELUDE AND FUGUE, OP. 28
        C. F. PETERS CORPORATION   LY142   .60
VANDRE
    CLAP, COUNT, AND PLAY, BK. 1
        PRO-ART PUBLICATIONS, INC.   809   1.25
VANDRE
    CLAP, COUNT, AND PLAY, BK. 2
        PRO-ART PUBLICATIONS, INC.   810   1.25
VANHAL   MILLEROVA   2
    LEICHTE SONATINEN. 16 KLEINE STUCK
        BARENREITER VERLAG   AP 334
VANNORT, I.
    MUSIC LAND--A FIRST PIANO BOOK FOR INDIVIDUAL OR CLASS
    INSTRUCTION
        G. SCHIRMER, INC.   1.25
                            GR. 4-5
VAUGHAN
    SIX PRELUDES
        WESTERN INTERNATIONAL MUSIC, INC.   AV17   1.50
VELLONES, P.
    AU JARDIN DES BETES SAUVAGES, VOL. 1
        ELKAN-VOGEL, INC.   D   5.35
VELLONES, P.
    AU JARDIN DES BETES SAUVAGES, VOL. 2
        ELKAN-VOGEL, INC.   D   5.00
VEON
    KEYBOARD HARMONY AND TRANSPOSITION
        VOLKWEIN BROS.   .75
VEON
    MUSIC MAKER BOOK 1
        VOLKWEIN BROS.   .85
VEON
    MUSIC MAKER BOOK 2
        VOLKWEIN BROS.   .85
VEON
    MUSIC MAKER BOOK 3
        VOLKWEIN BROS.   .85
VERDI
    ALBUMS - OVERTURES AND PRELUDES
        FRANCO COLOMBO PUBLICATIONS   ER1279   3.00
VERDI   FANENGHI
    ALBUMS - 18 FAMOUS ARIAS
        FRANCO COLOMBO PUBLICATIONS   127650   1.00
VERDI   HARRISON
    ALBUMS - 7 MELODIES FROM THE OPERAS
        FRANCO COLOMBO PUBLICATIONS   LD432   1.50
VERDI   ZILCHER   2-3
    DIE VERDI-OPER
        SCHOTT   1565   3.50
VERDI *   SAUER   D
    TWO OPERA FANTASIES+ PARAPHRASES ON RIGOLETTO AND TROVATORE
        C. F. PETERS CORPORATION   3614   2.00

VIERNE
    THREE NOCTURNES
        FRANCO COLOMBO PUBLICATIONS   SAL   4.00
VILLA-LOBOS, H.
    GUIA PRATICO
        PEER SOUTHERN ORGANIZATION   02.00
VILLA-LOBOS, H.
    GUIA PRATICO - BK. 1
        MUSIC SALES CORPORATION   040940   1.25
VILLA-LOBOS, H.
    GUIA PRATICO - BK. 8
        MUSIC SALES CORPORATION   040938   1.25
VILLA-LOBOS, H.
    GUIA PRATICO - BK. 9
        MUSIC SALES CORPORATION   040939   1.25
VILLA-LOBOS, H.
    GUIA PRATICO--2ND ALBUM
        ASSOCIATED MUSIC PUBLISHERS, INC.   ESC   3.25
VILLA-LOBOS, H.
    GUIA PRATICO--3RD ALBUM
        ASSOCIATED MUSIC PUBLISHERS, INC.   ESC   3.00
VILLA-LOBOS, H.
    PROLE DO BEBE
        EDWARD B. MARKS MUSIC CORPORATION   02.50
VILLA-LOBOS, H.
    SAUDADES DAS SELVAS BRASILERIAS
        ASSOCIATED MUSIC PUBLISHERS, INC.   ESC   3.75
VILLA-LOBOS, H.
    SIMPLES COLETANEA
        MUSIC SALES CORPORATION   040948   1.00
VILLA-LOBOS, H.
    SUITE FLORAL, OP. 97
        MUSIC SALES CORPORATION   040949   1.00
VILLA-LOBOS, H.
    THREE MARIES
        CARL FISCHER, INC.   O 4146   1.25
VILLA-LOBOS, H.
    TWICE FIVE PIECES -- EASY
        THEODORE PRESSER COMPANY   2.00
VILLE, M.
    MUSIC MADE EASY, BK. 1
        THEODORE PRESSER COMPANY   1.25
VILLE, M.
    MUSIC MADE EASY, BK. 2
        THEODORE PRESSER COMPANY   1.25
VINCK
    ELEMENTS DE TECHNIQUE --TEXT IN FRENCH-- FOR YOUNG PIANISTS
        DELRIEU ET CIE.   2.75
VITALI--ED.   VITALI
    ANCIENT ITALIAN MASTERS, BK. 1 - FRESCOBALDI, GRIECO, POLLAROLI,
    PASQUINI, ZIPOLI, MARCELLO, PESCETTI, D. SCARLATTI
        FRANCO COLOMBO PUBLICATIONS   ER134   1.75
VITALI--ED.   VITALI
    ANCIENT ITALIAN MASTERS, BK. 2 - RUTINI, DURANTE, GRAZIOLI,
    GALUPPI, TURINI, PORPORA, MARTINI, PARADISI
        FRANCO COLOMBO PUBLICATIONS   ER135   1.75
VITASEK   MILLEROVA   2-3
    DREI VORTRAGSSTUCKE
        BARENREITER VERLAG   MVH 4
VITTADINI
    RELIGIOUS MELODIES - 23 PIECES
        FRANCO COLOMBO PUBLICATIONS   127150   1.00
VOGEL   1-2
    JUGENDALBUM. 20 KLAVIERSTUCKE, OP. 25 IN FORTSCHREITENDER
    REIHENFOLGE
        BARENREITER VERLAG   SM 454
VOGEL--ED   VOGEL
    GREAT FRENCH SONGS FOR LITTLE HANDS
        ASSOCIATED MUSIC PUBLISHERS, INC.   ESC   2.50
VOGT, J.
    TWENTY-FOUR OCTAVE STUDIES OF MEDIUM DIFFICULTY, OP. 145
        G. SCHIRMER, INC.   L965   1.25
VOLGER--ED   VOLGER   E-M
    SONATINA BOOK, VOL. 1
        C. F. PETERS CORPORATION   4680A   4.00
VOLGER--ED   VOLGER   M
    SONATINA BOOK, VOL. 2
        C. F. PETERS CORPORATION   4680B   4.00
VOLKART-SCHLAGER   1
    ARBEITSBUCH FUR KLEINE KLAVIERSPIELER - 23 VOLKSLIEDSATZE --
    'WIR MUSIZIEREN', HEFT 10
        BARENREITER VERLAG   SM 911
VOLKART-SCHLAGER   1
    FUR KLEINE LEUTE. 30 LEICHTE KLAVIERSTUCKE FUR DEN ANFANG
        BARENREITER VERLAG   SM 529
VOLKART-SCHLAGER, K.
    DER TONKREIS - HEFT 01, RUNDHERUM
        SCHOTT   3936   1.75
VOLKART-SCHLAGER, K.   2
    DER TONKREIS - HEFT 02, EIN TAGESLAUF
        SCHOTT   3937   1.75
VOMACKA   3
    ERNEUTE BILDER, OP. 28
        BARENREITER VERLAG   AP 756
VOORMOLEN
    LIVRE DES ENFANTS, LE - BK. 1
        FRANCO COLOMBO PUBLICATIONS   SAL   5.00
VOORMOLEN
    LIVRE DES ENFANTS, LE - BK. 2
        FRANCO COLOMBO PUBLICATIONS   SAL   5.00
VOORMOLEN
    TABLEAUX DES PAYS-BAS. BK. 1
        FRANCO COLOMBO PUBLICATIONS   SAL   3.25
VOORMOLEN
    TABLEAUX DES PAYS-BAS. BK. 2
        FRANCO COLOMBO PUBLICATIONS   SAL   3.50
VORISEK   LOULOVA   3
    KLAVIERSTUCKE
        BARENREITER VERLAG   MAB 52
VORISEK   HELFFERT   3
    SIX IMPROMPTUS, OP. 7
        BARENREITER VERLAG   MAB 1
VOSS, L.
    WORK AND PLAY, BK. 1
        WILLIS MUSIC COMPANY   1.00
VOSS, L.
    WORK AND PLAY, BK. 2
        WILLIS MUSIC COMPANY   1.00
VOSS, L.
    WORK AND PLAY, BK. 3
        WILLIS MUSIC COMPANY   1.00
VOVK   GR. 2
    SKETCHES
        SHAWNEE PRESS, INC.   1.50
VREDENBURG
    SIX PIECES
        FRANCO COLOMBO PUBLICATIONS   SAL   2.75

VUATAZ
    ETUDES FOR PIANO BASED ON FOLKSONGS, BK. 1 - INTRODUCTION
        FRANCO COLOMBO PUBLICATIONS   SAL   4.25
VUATAZ
    ETUDES FOR PIANO BASED ON FOLKSONGS, BK. 2 - ETUDES 1-12
        FRANCO COLOMBO PUBLICATIONS   SAL   4.25
VUATAZ
    ETUDES FOR PIANO BASED ON FOLKSONGS, BK. 3 - ETUDES 13-24
        FRANCO COLOMBO PUBLICATIONS   SAL   5.00
VUATAZ
    ETUDES FOR PIANO BASED ON FOLKSONGS, BK. 4 - ETUDES 25-36
        FRANCO COLOMBO PUBLICATIONS   SAL   5.00
VYCPALEK   3
    ERWACHE, O HERZ. 2 VARIATIONSFANTASIEN UBER GEISTLICHE
    VOLKSLIEDER, OP. 30
        BARENREITER VERLAG   AP 767
VYCPALEK   3
    UNTERWEGS. KLAVIERSTUCKE, OP. 9
        BARENREITER VERLAG   AP 768
WACHS, F.
    LOISIRS DU JEUNE AGE, LES
        FRANCO COLOMBO PUBLICATIONS   SAL
WACHS, P.   2, 3
    FETES DE L'ENFANCE, LES
        ALPHONSE LEDUC
WACHS, P.
    POUR NOS PETITS -- 6 LITTLE PIECES WITH LARGE NOTES --
        FRANCO COLOMBO PUBLICATIONS   SAL   2.75
WAGNER   OESTERLE
    ALBUM--20 PIECES
        G. SCHIRMER, INC.   L1103   2.50
WAGNER   WINDSPERGER
    DAS BUCH DER MOTIVE UND THEMEN AUS SAMTLICHEN OPERN UND
    MUSIKDRAMEN FUR KLAVIER MIT TEXT -- BK. 1
        SCHOTT   300   3.50
WAGNER   WINDSPERGER
    DAS BUCH DER MOTIVE UND THEMEN AUS SAMTLICHEN OPERN UND
    MUSIKDRAMEN FUR KLAVIER MIT TEXT -- BK. 2
        SCHOTT   301   3.50
WAGNER   REGENY, R.
    LITTLE PIANO BOOK
        UNIVERSAL EDITION   11263   1.50
WAGNER
    SUITE FROM THE MONADNOCK REGION
        MCA MUSIC   2.00
WAGNER   REGENY, R.
    TWO DANCES -- PALUCCA
        UNIVERSAL EDITION   11706   1.50
WAGNER   REGENY, R.
    TWO SONATAS
        UNIVERSAL EDITION   11432   2.35
WAGNER   ECKHARDT, F.   1
    WAGNER FOR THE YOUNG PIANIST
        CENTURY MUSIC PUBLISHING COMPANY, INC.   3964   .40
WAGNER *
    WAGNER-LISZT ALBUM--9 TRANSCRIPTIONS FROM WAGNER'S OPERAS
        G. SCHIRMER, INC.   L57   2.50
WAGNER-REGENY, R.
    FIVE FRENCH PIECES
        ASSOCIATED MUSIC PUBLISHERS, INC.   BOT   3.00
WAGNER-REGENY, R.
    SEVEN FUGUES--1953
        ASSOCIATED MUSIC PUBLISHERS, INC.   BOT   3.00
WAGNER, E. D.   CORNELL
    FIRST INSTRUCTION BOOK, BK. 1
        G. SCHIRMER, INC.   1.50
WAGNER, J.
    FOUR LANDSCAPES
        PEER SOUTHERN ORGANIZATION   01.25
WAGNER, J.
    FOUR MINIATURES
        PEER SOUTHERN ORGANIZATION   01.25
WAGNER, J.
    PASTORALE AND TOCCATA
        PEER SOUTHERN ORGANIZATION   01.25
WAGNESS
    FOURTEEN SKETCHES IN STYLE FOR YOUNG ARTISTS
        THEODORE PRESSER COMPANY   1.25
WAGNESS
    PIANO COURSE, BK. 1
        THEODORE PRESSER COMPANY   1.95
WAGNESS
    PIANO COURSE, BK. 2
        THEODORE PRESSER COMPANY   2.95
WAGNESS
    PIANO COURSE, BK. 3
        THEODORE PRESSER COMPANY   3.75
WAGNESS
    PIANO COURSE, PREPARATORY BOOK
        THEODORE PRESSER COMPANY   1.25
WAGNESS   WAGNESS
    WAGNESS ADULT PIANO COURSE, VOL. 1
        RUBANK, INC.   2.00
WAGNESS   WAGNESS
    WAGNESS ADULT PIANO COURSE, VOL. 2
        RUBANK, INC.   2.50
WAGNESS--ED.   WAGNESS
    CHRISTMAS CAROLS TO PLAY AND SING
        SHAWNEE PRESS, INC.   1.00
WAGNESS--ED.   WAGNESS
    I PLEDGE ALLEGIANCE -- A PATRIOTIC ALBUM FOR ALL AMERICANS
        RUBANK, INC.   .90
WAGNESS--ED.   WAGNESS   GR. 2 - 3
    ORIGINAL CLASSICS, VOL. 1
        SHAWNEE PRESS, INC.   1.00
WAGNESS--ED.   WAGNESS   GR. 2 - 3
    ORIGINAL CLASSICS, VOL. 2
        SHAWNEE PRESS, INC.   1.00
WAGNESS--ED.   WAGNESS
    WAGNESS PIANO COURSE, BK. 4
        SHAWNEE PRESS, INC.   2.00
WALDTEUFEL, E.   SCHAUM, J.   1 1/2
    DOLORES, WALTZ
        BELWIN-MILLS PUBLISHING CORPORATION   .50
WALDTEUFEL, E.
    FIFTEEN FAVORITE WALTZES
        FRANCO COLOMBO PUBLICATIONS   BA9105   3.50
WALDTEUFEL, E.   SAMMARTINO
    TEN FAMOUS WALTZES
        FRANCO COLOMBO PUBLICATIONS   BA9100   2.00
WALDTEUFEL, E.
    TEN VALSES CELEBRES, BK. 1
        ELKAN-VOGEL, INC.   D   6.25
WALDTEUFEL, E.
    TEN VALSES CELEBRES, BK. 2
        ELKAN-VOGEL, INC.   D   4.50

WALDTEUFEL, E.   E-M
    WALTZES, VOL. 1
        C. F. PETERS CORPORATION   5125A   3.00
WALDTEUFEL, E.   E-M
    WALTZES, VOL. 2
        C. F. PETERS CORPORATION   5125B   3.00
WALLIS
    MUSIC
        WILLIS MUSIC COMPANY   1.75
WALLIS
    MUSIC THE WHOLE WORLD LOVES
        WILLIS MUSIC COMPANY   1.25
WALLIS--ED   WALLIS
    BOSTON MUSIC CO.'S CHRISTMAS CAROL BOOK
        BOSTON MUSIC COMPANY   1.25
WALLIS--ED   WALLIS
    SIX CHRISTMAS CAROLS
        BOSTON MUSIC COMPANY   .50
WALTON, W.   ME
    MUSIC FOR CHILDREN, BK. 1
        OXFORD UNIVERSITY PRESS   33.100   1.50
WALTON, W.   ME
    MUSIC FOR CHILDREN, BK. 2
        OXFORD UNIVERSITY PRESS   33.101   1.50
WARD
    FOURTEEN KEYS
        BOSTON MUSIC COMPANY   1.00
WARD
    JIBBIDY F AND A-C-E
        BOSTON MUSIC COMPANY   1.00
WARD
    PIANO PLEASURE
        PRO-ART PUBLICATIONS, INC.   879   .75
WARD
    TIME TO PLAY
        PRO-ART PUBLICATIONS, INC.   681   .75
WARD--ED   WARD
    HYMNS FOR YOU TO PLAY AND SING
        BOSTON MUSIC COMPANY   1.00
WARD--ED   WARD
    STUDENT CLASSICS - BOOK 1
        PRO-ART PUBLICATIONS, INC.   880   .75
WARD--ED   WARD
    STUDENT CLASSICS - BOOK 2
        PRO-ART PUBLICATIONS, INC.   881   .75
WARD-STEINMAN, D.
    THREE IMPROVISATIONS ON A THEME OF DARIUS MILHAUD
        FRANCO COLOMBO PUBLICATIONS   SAL   3.50
WARD-STEINMAN, D.   5
    THREE MINIATURES
        LEE ROBERTS MUSIC PUBLICATIONS, INC.   .85
WARD-STEINMAN, D.--ED
    LATTER-DAY LULLABIES
        EDWARD B. MARKS MUSIC CORPORATION   01.75
WARD, J.   ELEMENTARY
    ARPEGGIO ETUDES - D1
        PRO-ART PUBLICATIONS, INC.   D1   .75
WARD, J.   LOWER INTERMEDIATE
    ARPEGGIO ETUDES - D2
        PRO-ART PUBLICATIONS, INC.   D2   1.00
WARD, J.   UPPER INTERMEDIATE
    ARPEGGIO ETUDES - D3
        PRO-ART PUBLICATIONS, INC.   D3   1.25
WARD, J.   ADVANCED
    ARPEGGIO ETUDES - D4
        PRO-ART PUBLICATIONS, INC.   D4   1.50
WARD, J.   ELEMENTARY
    BROKEN CHORD ETUDES - B1
        PRO-ART PUBLICATIONS, INC.   B1   .75
WARD, J.   LOWER INTERMEDIATE
    BROKEN CHORD ETUDES - B2
        PRO-ART PUBLICATIONS, INC.   B2   1.00
WARD, J.   UPPER INTERMEDIATE
    BROKEN CHORD ETUDES - B3
        PRO-ART PUBLICATIONS, INC.   B3   1.25
WARD, J.   ADVANCED
    BROKEN CHORD ETUDES - B4
        PRO-ART PUBLICATIONS, INC.   B4   1.50
WARD, J.   ELEMENTARY
    BROKEN INTERVAL ETUDES - E1
        PRO-ART PUBLICATIONS, INC.   E1   .75
WARD, J.   LOWER INTERMEDIATE
    BROKEN INTERVAL ETUDES - E2
        PRO-ART PUBLICATIONS, INC.   E2   1.00
WARD, J.   UPPER INTERMEDIATE
    BROKEN INTERVAL ETUDES - E3
        PRO-ART PUBLICATIONS, INC.   E3   1.25
WARD, J.   ADVANCED
    BROKEN INTERVAL ETUDES - E4
        PRO-ART PUBLICATIONS, INC.   E4   1.50
WARD, J.   ELEMENTARY
    CHORD ETUDES - K1
        PRO-ART PUBLICATIONS, INC.   K1   .75
WARD, J.   LOWER INTERMEDIATE
    CHORD ETUDES - K2
        PRO-ART PUBLICATIONS, INC.   K2   1.00
WARD, J.   UPPER INTERMEDIATE
    CHORD ETUDES - K3
        PRO-ART PUBLICATIONS, INC.   K3   1.25
WARD, J.   ADVANCED
    CHORD ETUDES - K4
        PRO-ART PUBLICATIONS, INC.   K4   1.50
WARD, J.   ELEMENTARY
    CROSS HAND ETUDES - F1
        PRO-ART PUBLICATIONS, INC.   F1   .75
WARD, J.   LOWER INTERMEDIATE
    CROSS HAND ETUDES - F2
        PRO-ART PUBLICATIONS, INC.   F2   1.00
WARD, J.   UPPER INTERMEDIATE
    CROSS HAND ETUDES - F3
        PRO-ART PUBLICATIONS, INC.   F3   1.25
WARD, J.   ADVANCED
    CROSS HAND ETUDES - F4
        PRO-ART PUBLICATIONS, INC.   F4   1.50
WARD, J.   ELEMENTARY
    DOUBLE NOTE ETUDES - H1
        PRO-ART PUBLICATIONS, INC.   H1   .75
WARD, J.   LOWER INTERMEDIATE
    DOUBLE NOTE ETUDES - H2
        PRO-ART PUBLICATIONS, INC.   H2   1.00
WARD, J.   UPPER INTERMEDIATE
    DOUBLE NOTE ETUDES - H3
        PRO-ART PUBLICATIONS, INC.   H3   1.25
WARD, J.   ADVANCED
    DOUBLE NOTE ETUDES - H4
        PRO-ART PUBLICATIONS, INC.   H4   1.50

WARD, J.　　　　　　　　　　　　　　　　　　　ELEMENTARY
　　EMBELLISHMENT ETUDES - G1
　　　　PRO-ART PUBLICATIONS, INC.　　　　　　　G1　　　.75
WARD, J.　　　　　　　　　　　　　　　　　　　LOWER INTERMEDIATE
　　EMBELLISHMENT ETUDES - G2
　　　　PRO-ART PUBLICATIONS, INC.　　　　　　　G2　　　1.00
WARD, J.　　　　　　　　　　　　　　　　　　　UPPER INTERMEDIATE
　　EMBELLISHMENT ETUDES - G3
　　　　PRO-ART PUBLICATIONS, INC.　　　　　　　G3　　　1.25
WARD, J.　　　　　　　　　　　　　　　　　　　ADVANCED
　　EMBELLISHMENT ETUDES - G4
　　　　PRO-ART PUBLICATIONS, INC.　　　　　　　G4　　　1.50
WARD, J.　　　　　　　　　　　　　　　　　　　ELEMENTARY
　　OCTAVE ETUDES - J1
　　　　PRO-ART PUBLICATIONS, INC.　　　　　　　J1　　　.75
WARD, J.　　　　　　　　　　　　　　　　　　　LOWER INTERMEDIATE
　　OCTAVE ETUDES - J2
　　　　PRO-ART PUBLICATIONS, INC.　　　　　　　J2　　　1.00
WARD, J.　　　　　　　　　　　　　　　　　　　UPPER INTERMEDIATE
　　OCTAVE ETUDES - J3
　　　　PRO-ART PUBLICATIONS, INC.　　　　　　　J3　　　1.25
WARD, J.　　　　　　　　　　　　　　　　　　　ADVANCED
　　OCTAVE ETUDES - J4
　　　　PRO-ART PUBLICATIONS, INC.　　　　　　　J4　　　1.50
WARD, J.　　　　　　　　　　　　　　　　　　　ELEMENTARY
　　PASSAGE ETUDES - C1
　　　　PRO-ART PUBLICATIONS, INC.　　　　　　　C1　　　.75
WARD, J.　　　　　　　　　　　　　　　　　　　LOWER INTERMEDIATE
　　PASSAGE ETUDES - C2
　　　　PRO-ART PUBLICATIONS, INC.　　　　　　　C2　　　1.00
WARD, J.　　　　　　　　　　　　　　　　　　　UPPER INTERMEDIATE
　　PASSAGE ETUDES - C3
　　　　PRO-ART PUBLICATIONS, INC.　　　　　　　C3　　　1.25
WARD, J.　　　　　　　　　　　　　　　　　　　ADVANCED
　　PASSAGE ETUDES - C4
　　　　PRO-ART PUBLICATIONS, INC.　　　　　　　C4　　　1.50
WARD, J.　　　　　　　　　　　　　　　　　　　ELEMENTARY
　　SCALE ETUDES - A1
　　　　PRO-ART PUBLICATIONS, INC.　　　　　　　A1　　　.75
WARD, J.　　　　　　　　　　　　　　　　　　　LOWER INTERMEDIATE
　　SCALE ETUDES - A2
　　　　PRO-ART PUBLICATIONS, INC.　　　　　　　A2　　　1.00
WARD, J.　　　　　　　　　　　　　　　　　　　UPPER INTERMEDIATE
　　SCALE ETUDES - A3
　　　　PRO-ART PUBLICATIONS, INC.　　　　　　　A3　　　1.25
WARD, J.　　　　　　　　　　　　　　　　　　　ADVANCED
　　SCALE ETUDES - A4
　　　　PRO-ART PUBLICATIONS, INC.　　　　　　　A4　　　1.50
WARD, J.　　　　　　　　　　　　　　　　　　　ELEMENTARY
　　SELECTED ETUDES - L1
　　　　PRO-ART PUBLICATIONS, INC.　　　　　　　L1　　　.75
WARD, J.　　　　　　　　　　　　　　　　　　　LOWER INTERMEDIATE
　　SELECTED ETUDES - L2
　　　　PRO-ART PUBLICATIONS, INC.　　　　　　　L2　　　1.00
WARD, J.　　　　　　　　　　　　　　　　　　　UPPER INTERMEDIATE
　　SELECTED ETUDES - L3
　　　　PRO-ART PUBLICATIONS, INC.　　　　　　　3　　　1.25
WARD, J.　　　　　　　　　　　　　　　　　　　ADVANCED
　　SELECTED ETUDES - L4
　　　　PRO-ART PUBLICATIONS, INC.　　　　　　　L4　　　1.50
WATERMAN *
　　FIRST YEAR PIANO LESSONS
　　　　FABER MUSIC, LTD.　　　　　　　　　　　F0024
WATERMAN *
　　FIRST YEAR PIANO LESSONS
　　　　MCA MUSIC　　　　　　　　　　　　　　　　　2.00
WATERMAN *
　　REPERTOIRE FOR FIRST YEAR PIANISTS
　　　　MCA MUSIC　　　　　　　　　　　　　　　　　1.75
WATERMAN *
　　REPERTOIRE FOR SECOND YEAR PIANISTS
　　　　MCA MUSIC　　　　　　　　　　　　　　　　　1.75
WATERMAN *
　　SECOND YEAR PIANO LESSONS
　　　　FABER MUSIC, LTD.　　　　　　　　　　　F0211
WATERMAN *
　　SECOND YEAR PIANO LESSONS
　　　　MCA MUSIC　　　　　　　　　　　　　　　　　2.00
WATERMAN *
　　THIRD YEAR PIANO LESSONS
　　　　FABER MUSIC, LTD.　　　　　　　　　　　F0311
WATERMAN *
　　YOUNG PIANIST'S REPERTOIRE, BK. 1
　　　　FABER MUSIC, LTD.　　　　　　　　　　　F0210
WATERMAN *
　　YOUNG PIANIST'S REPERTOIRE, BK. 2
　　　　FABER MUSIC, LTD.　　　　　　　　　　　F0366
WATSON
　　HOW TO PLAY LIKE A PLAYER PIANO
　　　　BELWIN-MILLS PUBLISHING CORPORATION　　　　2.00
WATSON
　　THEMES FOR PIANO
　　　　BELWIN-MILLS PUBLISHING CORPORATION　　　　1.50
WATSON--ED.　　　　　WATSON
　　CHRISTMAS CAROLS --WITH WORDS--
　　　　CARL FISCHER, INC.　　　　　　　　　RB 33　　1.25
WATSON--ED.　　　　　WATSON
　　FAVORITE HYMNS, EASY TO READ, PLAY, SING
　　　　CARL FISCHER, INC.　　　　　　　　　RB 37　　1.25
WATSON--ED.　　　　　WATSON
　　LET'S PLAY PLAYER-PIANO STYLE
　　　　WARNER BROTHERS PUBLISHERS　　　　　　　　1.95
WAXMAN
　　TWO LITTLE SHOES -- FROM THE CHARM BRACELET
　　　　MCA MUSIC　　　　　　　　　　　　　　　　　.60
WEBBER--ED.　　　　　WEBBER
　　PIANO HOUR, BK. 1 --175--
　　　　CARL FISCHER, INC.　　　　　　　　　　　　1.50
WEBBER--ED.　　　　　WEBBER
　　PIANO HOUR, BK. 2 --25--
　　　　CARL FISCHER, INC.　　　　　　　　　　　　1.50
WEBER, A.　　　　　　　　　　　　　　　　　2, 4
　　MODES ENFANTINES, SEPT PIECES FACILES
　　　　ALPHONSE LEDUC
WEBER, B.
　　THREE PIECES, OP. 23
　　　　ASSOCIATED MUSIC PUBLISHERS, INC.　　BMP　　1.50
WEBER, VON　　　　　　　　　　　　　　　　　D
　　COMPLETE PIANO WORKS, VOL. 1‡ SONATAS
　　　　C. F. PETERS CORPORATION　　　　　　717A　　5.00
WEBER, VON　　　　　　　　　　　　　　　　　D
　　COMPLETE PIANO WORKS, VOL. 2‡ PIANO PIECES
　　　　C. F. PETERS CORPORATION　　　　　　717B　　5.00
WEBER, VON　　　　　　　　　　　　　　　　　D
　　COMPLETE PIANO WORKS, VOL. 3‡ VARIATIONS AND CONCERTOS
　　　　C. F. PETERS CORPORATION　　　　　　717C　　6.50

WEBER, VON　　　　　　　FREY　　　　　　3
　　DEUTSCHE TANZE OP. 4
　　　　SCHOTT　　　　　　　　　　　　08797 1/2　1.00
WEBER, VON　　　　　　　HUGHES
　　MASTER SERIES FOR THE YOUNG--VOL. 06--WEBER
　　　　G. SCHIRMER, INC.　　　　　　　　　　　　1.25
WEBER, VON *　　　　　　　　　　　　E-M
　　MASTERS FOR THE YOUNG. VOL. 5
　　　　C. F. PETERS CORPORATION　　　　　2776　　2.50
WEBER, VON　　　　　　　HALE *
　　MISCELLANEOUS COMPOSITIONS
　　　　G. SCHIRMER, INC.　　　　　　　　L1667　　1.50
WEBER, VON
　　PERPETUUM MOBILE--ORIGINAL AND ARRANGEMENTS BY BRAHMS AND
　　TSCHAIKOVSKY
　　　　ASSOCIATED MUSIC PUBLISHERS, INC.　　SIM　　4.00
WEBER, VON　　　　　　　WERNER
　　SEVEN ECOSSAISES--CURWEN EDITION
　　　　G. SCHIRMER, INC.　　　　　　　　　　　　.75
WEBER, VON　　　　　　　TAGLIAPIETRA
　　SONATAS, OP. 24, 39, 49, 70
　　　　FRANCO COLOMBO PUBLICATIONS　　　　ER918　5.50
WEBER, VON　　　　　　　WOLTERS　　　2-3
　　TANZBUCHLEIN FUR KLAVIER
　　　　SCHOTT　　　　　　　　　　　　　4778　　1.75
WEBER, VON　　　　　　　FRICKERT　　　E
　　TWENTY EASY DANCES
　　　　C. F. PETERS CORPORATION　　　　　5638　　2.00
WEBER, VON *　　　　　　　　　　　　D
　　TWO STUDIES --PERPETUUM MOBILE--
　　　　C. F. PETERS CORPORATION　　　　　4831　　2.00
WECKMANN, M.　　　　　　BUCHMAYER
　　EARLY KEYBOARD WORKS -- BK. 1
　　　　ASSOCIATED MUSIC PUBLISHERS, INC.　　BRH　　1.75
WECKMANN, M. *　　　　　BUCHMAYER
　　EARLY KEYBOARD WORKS -- BK. 2
　　　　ASSOCIATED MUSIC PUBLISHERS, INC.　　BRH　　2.50
WECKMANN, M. *　　　　　BUCHMAYER
　　EARLY KEYBOARD WORKS -- BK. 3
　　　　ASSOCIATED MUSIC PUBLISHERS, INC.　　BRH　　2.00
WEILL, K.
　　KURT WEILL
　　　　CHAPPELL AND COMPANY, INC.　　　0017855　1.50
WEILL, K.
　　MEET KURT WEILL AT THE PIANO
　　　　CHAPPELL AND COMPANY, INC.　　　3719408　2.50
WEINER
　　THIRTY-ONE HUNGARIAN PEASANT SONGS, BK. 1
　　　　GENERAL MUSIC PUBLISHING COMPANY, INC.　187　4.00
WEINER
　　THIRTY-ONE HUNGARIAN PEASANT SONGS, BK. 2
　　　　GENERAL MUSIC PUBLISHING COMPANY, INC.　188　4.00
WEINER
　　THIRTY-ONE HUNGARIAN PEASANT SONGS, VOL. 1
　　　　GENERAL MUSIC PUBLISHING COMPANY, INC.　　4.00
WEINER
　　THIRTY-ONE HUNGARIAN PEASANT SONGS, VOL. 2
　　　　GENERAL MUSIC PUBLISHING COMPANY, INC.　3　4.00
WEISMANN, J.
　　ACHTZEHN INVENTIONEN, OP. 101
　　　　BARENREITER VERLAG　　　　　　　SM 559
WEISMANN, J.
　　TEN LITTLE WALTZES, OP. 59
　　　　ASSOCIATED MUSIC PUBLISHERS, INC.　　LEU　　2.50
WEISS, E.
　　KLAVIERMUSIK NACH VOLKSLIEDERN--16 PIECES BASED ON FOLK SONGS
　　　　ASSOCIATED MUSIC PUBLISHERS, INC.　　BRH　　3.00
WELLESZ, E.
　　STUDIEN IN GRAU, OP. 106
　　　　ASSOCIATED MUSIC PUBLISHERS, INC.　　DOB　　2.75
WELLESZ, E.
　　THREE SKETCHES, OP. 6
　　　　ASSOCIATED MUSIC PUBLISHERS, INC.　　DOB　　1.75
WELLESZ, E.
　　TRIPTYCHON, OP. 98
　　　　ASSOCIATED MUSIC PUBLISHERS, INC.　　DOB　　3.00
WELLESZ, E.
　　TWO STUDIES, OP. 29
　　　　ASSOCIATED MUSIC PUBLISHERS, INC.　　DOB　　1.75
WERNER--ED.　　　　　　WERNER
　　UNKNOWN CLASSICS FOR THE PIANO--CURWEN EDITION
　　　　G. SCHIRMER, INC.　　　　　　　　　　　　1.00
WERNER, F.--ED.　　　　WERNER, F.　　　E
　　WIR SPIELEN ZUR WEIHNACHT, OP. 43. 26 OLD CHRISTMAS SONGS
　　　　C. F. PETERS CORPORATION　　　　　V138　　2.00
WERNER, J.　　　　　　　　　　　　　E
　　AT THE FAIR
　　　　C. F. PETERS CORPORATION　　　　　H614　　.90
WERNER, J.
　　PIECES A MARYJANE
　　　　ASSOCIATED MUSIC PUBLISHERS, INC.　　ESC　　1.50
WESTERVELT, M.　　　　　　　　　　FOR BEGINNERS
　　CHILD'S BOOK OF FOLK-TUNES, A--SUPPLEMENTARY READING MATERIAL
　　FOR THE BEGINNER--WITH WORDS
　　　　G. SCHIRMER, INC.　　　　　　　　　　　　1.00
WESTERVELT, M.--ED　　　WESTERVELT, M.
　　AMERICAN TRAVELER -- FOLK SONGS WITH WORDS
　　　　THEODORE PRESSER COMPANY　　　　　　　　1.00
WESTERVELT, M.--ED　　　WESTERVELT, M.
　　CHRISTMAS IN MEXICO -- WITH WORDS
　　　　THEODORE PRESSER COMPANY　　　　　　　　1.00
WESTERVELT, M.--ED　　　WESTERVELT, M.
　　CHRISTMAS IN THE SOUTH -- WITH WORDS
　　　　THEODORE PRESSER COMPANY　　　　　　　　1.00
WESTERVELT, M.--ED　　　WESTERVELT, M.
　　MARDI GRAS -- WITH WORDS
　　　　THEODORE PRESSER COMPANY　　　　　　　　1.00
WESTERVELT, M.--ED　　　WESTERVELT, M.
　　RODEO -- WITH WORDS
　　　　THEODORE PRESSER COMPANY　　　　　　　　1.00
WESTMORELAND-KAHN
　　WESTMORELAND-KAHN PIANO COURSE, BK. 1, STUDENT'S EDITION
　　　　BELWIN-MILLS PUBLISHING CORPORATION　11122　1.75
WESTMORELAND-KAHN
　　WESTMORELAND-KAHN PIANO COURSE, BK. 1, TEACHER'S EDITION
　　　　BELWIN-MILLS PUBLISHING CORPORATION　11124　3.00
WESTMORELAND-KAHN
　　WESTMORELAND-KAHN PIANO COURSE, BK. 2, STUDENT'S EDITION
　　　　BELWIN-MILLS PUBLISHING CORPORATION　11123　1.75
WESTMORELAND-KAHN
　　WESTMORELAND-KAHN PIANO COURSE, BK. 2, TEACHER'S EDITION
　　　　BELWIN-MILLS PUBLISHING CORPORATION　11125　3.00
WESTMORELAND-KAHN
　　WESTMORELAND-KAHN PIANO COURSE, BK. 3, STUDENT'S EDITION
　　　　BELWIN-MILLS PUBLISHING CORPORATION　11597　1.75
WESTMORELAND-KAHN
　　WESTMORELAND-KAHN PIANO COURSE, BK. 3, TEACHER'S EDITION
　　　　BELWIN-MILLS PUBLISHING CORPORATION　11598　3.00

WHITEMORE--ED. WHITEMORE			
HUNDRED BEST SHORT CLASSICS, BK. 3			
CARL FISCHER, INC.		PT 183	1.50
WHITEMORE--ED. WHITEMORE			
HUNDRED BEST SHORT CLASSICS, BK. 4			
CARL FISCHER, INC.		PT 184	1.50
WHITFORD			
FILL-INS FOR THE PIANIST			
ROBERT WHITFORD PUBLICATIONS			1.00
WHITFORD			
ROBERT WHITFORD BREAK SHEET BOOK FOR PIANO			
ROBERT WHITFORD PUBLICATIONS			2.50
WHITFORD			
ROBERT WHITFORD CHORD CHART FOR THE MODERN PIANIST			
ROBERT WHITFORD PUBLICATIONS			1.50
WHITFORD			
ROBERT WHITFORD MODERN PIANO EFFECTS			
ROBERT WHITFORD PUBLICATIONS			2.00
WHITFORD			
ROBERT WHITFORD TECHNIC FOR PIANISTS, BK. 1			
ROBERT WHITFORD PUBLICATIONS			1.25
WHITFORD			
ROBERT WHITFORD TECHNIC FOR PIANISTS, BK. 2			
ROBERT WHITFORD PUBLICATIONS			1.25
WHITFORD			
ROBERT WHITFORD TECHNIC FOR PIANISTS, BK. 3			
ROBERT WHITFORD PUBLICATIONS			1.25
WHITFORD			
ROBERT WHITFORD TECHNIC FOR PIANISTS, BK. 4			
ROBERT WHITFORD PUBLICATIONS			1.50
WHITFORD			
ROBERT WHITFORD TECHNIC FOR PIANISTS, BK. 5			
ROBERT WHITFORD PUBLICATIONS			1.50
WHITFORD			
ROBERT WHITFORD TECHNIC FOR PIANISTS, BK. 6			
ROBERT WHITFORD PUBLICATIONS			1.50
WHITFORD--ED. WHITFORD	GR. 2-3		
CLASSIC COLLECTION NO. 1			
ROBERT WHITFORD PUBLICATIONS			.60
WHITFORD--ED. WHITFORD	GR. 1 1/2 - 2 1/2		
FAVORITES FOR THE PIANIST, HYMNS NO. 1			
ROBERT WHITFORD PUBLICATIONS			.60
WHITFORD--ED. WHITFORD	GR. 1 1/2 - 2 1/2		
FAVORITES FOR THE PIANIST, NO. 01			
ROBERT WHITFORD PUBLICATIONS			.60
WHITFORD--ED. WHITFORD	GR. 1 1/2 - 2 1/2		
FAVORITES FOR THE PIANIST, NO. 02			
ROBERT WHITFORD PUBLICATIONS			.60
WHITFORD--ED. WHITFORD	GR. 1 1/2 - 2 1/2		
FAVORITES FOR THE PIANIST, NO. 03			
ROBERT WHITFORD PUBLICATIONS			.60
WHITFORD--ED. WHITFORD	GR. 1 1/2 - 2 1/2		
FAVORITES FOR THE PIANIST, NO. 04			
ROBERT WHITFORD PUBLICATIONS			.60
WHITFORD--ED. WHITFORD	GR. 1 1/2 - 2 1/2		
FAVORITES FOR THE PIANIST, NO. 05			
ROBERT WHITFORD PUBLICATIONS			.60
WHITFORD--ED. WHITFORD	GR. 1 1/2 - 2 1/2		
FAVORITES FOR THE PIANIST, NO. 06			
ROBERT WHITFORD PUBLICATIONS			.60
WHITFORD--ED. WHITFORD	GR. 1 1/2 - 2 1/2		
FAVORITES FOR THE PIANIST, NO. 07			
ROBERT WHITFORD PUBLICATIONS			.60
WHITFORD--ED. WHITFORD	GR. 1 1/2 - 2 1/2		
FAVORITES FOR THE PIANIST, NO. 08			
ROBERT WHITFORD PUBLICATIONS			.60
WHITFORD--ED. WHITFORD	GR. 1 1/2 - 2 1/2		
FAVORITES FOR THE PIANIST, NO. 09			
ROBERT WHITFORD PUBLICATIONS			.60
WHITFORD--ED. WHITFORD	GR. 1 1/2 - 2 1/2		
FAVORITES FOR THE PIANIST, NO. 10			
ROBERT WHITFORD PUBLICATIONS			.60
WHITFORD--ED. WHITFORD	GR. 1 1/2 - 2 1/2		
FAVORITES FOR THE PIANIST, NO. 11			
ROBERT WHITFORD PUBLICATIONS			.60
WHITFORD--ED. WHITFORD	GR. 1 1/2 - 2 1/2		
FAVORITES FOR THE PIANIST, NO. 12			
ROBERT WHITFORD PUBLICATIONS			.60
WHITFORD--ED. WHITFORD	GR. 1 1/2 - 2 1/2		
FAVORITES FOR THE PIANIST, NO. 13			
ROBERT WHITFORD PUBLICATIONS			.60
WHITFORD--ED. WHITFORD	GR. 1 1/2 - 2 1/2		
FAVORITES FOR THE PIANIST, NO. 14			
ROBERT WHITFORD PUBLICATIONS			.60
WHITFORD--ED. WHITFORD	GR. 1 1/2 - 2 1/2		
FAVORITES FOR THE PIANIST, NO. 15			
ROBERT WHITFORD PUBLICATIONS			.60
WHITFORD--ED. WHITFORD	GR. 1 1/2 - 2 1/2		
FAVORITES FOR THE PIANIST, NO. 16			
ROBERT WHITFORD PUBLICATIONS			.60
WHITFORD--ED. WHITFORD	GR. 1 1/2 - 2 1/2		
FAVORITES FOR THE PIANIST, NO. 17			
ROBERT WHITFORD PUBLICATIONS			.60
WHITFORD--ED. WHITFORD	GR. 1 1/2 - 2 1/2		
FAVORITES FOR THE PIANIST, NO. 18			
ROBERT WHITFORD PUBLICATIONS			.60
WHITFORD--ED. WHITFORD	GR. 1 1/2 - 2 1/2		
FAVORITES FOR THE PIANIST, NO. 19			
ROBERT WHITFORD PUBLICATIONS			.60
WHITFORD--ED. WHITFORD	GR. 1 1/2 - 2 1/2		
FAVORITES FOR THE PIANIST, NO. 20			
ROBERT WHITFORD PUBLICATIONS			.60
WHITFORD--ED. WHITFORD			
ROBERT WHITFORD CLASSIC PIANO METHOD, BK. 01			
ROBERT WHITFORD PUBLICATIONS			1.60
WHITFORD--ED. WHITFORD			
ROBERT WHITFORD CLASSIC PIANO METHOD, BK. 02			
ROBERT WHITFORD PUBLICATIONS			1.60
WHITFORD--ED. WHITFORD			
ROBERT WHITFORD CLASSIC PIANO METHOD, BK. 03			
ROBERT WHITFORD PUBLICATIONS			1.80
WHITFORD--ED. WHITFORD			
ROBERT WHITFORD CLASSIC PIANO METHOD, BK. 04			
ROBERT WHITFORD PUBLICATIONS			1.80
WHITFORD--ED. WHITFORD			
ROBERT WHITFORD CLASSIC PIANO METHOD, BK. 05			
ROBERT WHITFORD PUBLICATIONS			1.80
WHITFORD--ED. WHITFORD			
ROBERT WHITFORD CLASSIC PIANO METHOD, BK. 06			
ROBERT WHITFORD PUBLICATIONS			1.80
WHITFORD--ED. WHITFORD			
ROBERT WHITFORD CLASSIC PIANO METHOD, BK. 07			
ROBERT WHITFORD PUBLICATIONS			2.00
WHITFORD--ED. WHITFORD			
ROBERT WHITFORD CLASSIC PIANO METHOD, BK. 08			
ROBERT WHITFORD PUBLICATIONS			2.00

WHITFORD--ED. WHITFORD			
ROBERT WHITFORD CLASSIC PIANO METHOD, BK. 09			
ROBERT WHITFORD PUBLICATIONS			2.00
WHITFORD--ED. WHITFORD			
ROBERT WHITFORD CLASSIC PIANO METHOD, BK. 10			
ROBERT WHITFORD PUBLICATIONS			2.00
WHITFORD--ED. WHITFORD			
ROBERT WHITFORD MODERN PIANO METHOD, BK. 1			
ROBERT WHITFORD PUBLICATIONS			2.50
WHITFORD--ED. WHITFORD			
ROBERT WHITFORD MODERN PIANO METHOD, BK. 2			
ROBERT WHITFORD PUBLICATIONS			2.50
WHITFORD--ED. WHITFORD			
ROBERT WHITFORD MODERN PIANO METHOD, BK. 3			
ROBERT WHITFORD PUBLICATIONS			2.50
WHITFORD--ED. WHITFORD			
ROBERT WHITFORD MODERN PIANO METHOD, BK. 4			
ROBERT WHITFORD PUBLICATIONS			2.50
WHITFORD--ED. WHITFORD	GR. 1		
TUNES FOR THE PIANIST, NO. 1			
ROBERT WHITFORD PUBLICATIONS			.60
WHITFORD--ED. WHITFORD	GR. 1		
TUNES FOR THE PIANIST, NO. 2			
ROBERT WHITFORD PUBLICATIONS			.60
WHITFORD--ED. WHITFORD	GR. 1		
TUNES FOR THE PIANIST, NO. 3			
ROBERT WHITFORD PUBLICATIONS			.60
WHITFORD--ED. WHITFORD	GR. 1		
TUNES FOR THE PIANIST, NO. 4			
ROBERT WHITFORD PUBLICATIONS			.60
WIECK	M-D		
PIANO STUDIES			
C. F. PETERS CORPORATION		375	1.50
WIECK			
STUDIES			
G. SCHIRMER, INC.		L66	1.00
WIEHMAYER, T.			
SCHOOL OF ARPEGGIOS -- GER AND FR NOTES			
ASSOCIATED MUSIC PUBLISHERS, INC.		BRH	.50
WIEHMAYER, T.			
SCHOOL OF SCALES -- ENG AND GER NOTES			
ASSOCIATED MUSIC PUBLISHERS, INC.		BRH	1.80
WIERNSBERGER, J.			
METHODE THEORIQUE ET PRATIQUE DE PIANO, PART 1			
GERARD BILLAUDOT EDITIONS MUSICALES			3.30
WILDER, A.			
PIECES FOR YOUNG PIANISTS			
SAM FOX PUBLISHING COMPANY, INC.		W 106	1.50
WILDER, A.			
TWELVE MOSAICS			
THEODORE PRESSER COMPANY			1.25
WILDMAN			
SWEDISH RHAPSODY			
MCA MUSIC			1.50
WILKS, N.			
CONSERVATORY SONATINA ALBUMS, BK. 1			
FREDERICK HARRIS MUSIC COMPANY			1.15
WILKS, N.			
CONSERVATORY SONATINA ALBUMS, BK. 2			
FREDERICK HARRIS MUSIC COMPANY			1.15
WILLAN			
CHILDREN'S FAVORITE CHRISTMAS CAROLS			
FREDERICK HARRIS MUSIC COMPANY			.75
WILLAN			
THREE CHARACTER SKETCHES OF OLD LONDON			
FREDERICK HARRIS MUSIC COMPANY			.90
WILLERT-ORFF, G.	2-3		
KLEINE KLAVIERSTUCKE, HEFT 01			
SCHOTT		4520	1.75
WILLERT-ORFF, G.	2-3		
KLEINE KLAVIERSTUCKE, HEFT 02			
SCHOTT		4521	1.75
WILLERT-ORFF, G.			
KLEINE KLAVIERSTUCKE, HEFT 03			
SCHOTT		4855	1.75
WILLERT-ORFF, G.			
KLEINE KLAVIERSTUCKE, HEFT 04			
SCHOTT		4896	1.75
WILLIAMS--ED. WILLIAMS			
FAVORITE SACRED CLASSICS			
PRO-ART PUBLICATIONS, INC.		314	1.50
WILLIAMS, D. M.			
INSPIRATIONS FROM THE PIANO			
LILLENAS PUBLISHING COMPANY		MB-306	2.50
WILLIAMS, F.--ED. WILLIAMS, F.			
TEN CHRISTMAS CAROLS			
SHAWNEE PRESS, INC.			1.10
WILLIAMS, J.			
ADVANCED FIRST GRADE BOOK			
BOSTON MUSIC COMPANY			1.50
WILLIAMS, J.			
BOOK FOR OLDER BEGINNERS -- OLD EDITION			
THEODORE PRESSER COMPANY			1.75
WILLIAMS, J.			
CHILD'S FIRST MUSIC BOOK			
G. SCHIRMER, INC.			1.25
WILLIAMS, J.			
EL PRIMER LIBRO MUSICAL DEL NINO--SPANISH EDITION OF 'CHILD'S			
FIRST MUSIC BOOK'			
G. SCHIRMER, INC.			1.25
WILLIAMS, J.			
FAVORITE MELODIES FOR THE ADULT			
BOSTON MUSIC COMPANY			1.50
WILLIAMS, J.			
FIFTH GRADE PIANO BOOK			
BOSTON MUSIC COMPANY			2.50
WILLIAMS, J.			
FIRST BOOK FOR THE ADULT BEGINNER			
BOSTON MUSIC COMPANY			1.75
WILLIAMS, J.			
FIRST GRADE PIANO BOOK			
BOSTON MUSIC COMPANY			1.50
WILLIAMS, J.			
FIRST YEAR -- COMPLETE, NEW EDITION			
THEODORE PRESSER COMPANY			3.25
WILLIAMS, J.			
FIRST YEAR -- PART 1			
THEODORE PRESSER COMPANY			1.00
WILLIAMS, J.			
FOURTH GRADE PIANO BOOK			
BOSTON MUSIC COMPANY			1.50
WILLIAMS, J.			
FOURTH YEAR			
THEODORE PRESSER COMPANY			2.25
WILLIAMS, J.			
HAPPY HOUR BOOK			
BOSTON MUSIC COMPANY			3.25

WILLIAMS, J.
LIBRO PRELIMINAR DE PIANO PARA NINOS - SPANISH EDITION
BOSTON MUSIC COMPANY   1.50
WILLIAMS, J.
NOTHING EASIER--ILLUSTRATED
G. SCHIRMER, INC.   1.00
WILLIAMS, J.
OLDER BEGINNER'S PIANO BOOK -- NEW EDITION
THEODORE PRESSER COMPANY   3.50
WILLIAMS, J.
PIANO PIECES FOR PLEASURE
THEODORE PRESSER COMPANY   1.25
WILLIAMS, J.
SECOND GRADE PIANO BOOK
BOSTON MUSIC COMPANY   1.50
WILLIAMS, J.
SECOND YEAR
THEODORE PRESSER COMPANY   2.25
WILLIAMS, J.
THIRD GRADE PIANO BOOK
BOSTON MUSIC COMPANY   1.75
WILLIAMS, J.
THIRD YEAR
THEODORE PRESSER COMPANY   2.25
WILLIAMS, J.
VERY FIRST PIANO BOOK
BOSTON MUSIC COMPANY   1.50
WILLIAMS, L. R.--ED   WILLIAMS, L. R.
FAVORITE HYMNS TO PLAY AND SING IN EASY PIANO ARRANGEMENTS
BROADMAN MUSIC   4571-01   1.50
WILLIAMS, LOU.
MARY LOU WILLIAMS FIVE BARRELHOUSE BOOGIE WOOGIE AND BLUES
SOLOS
MCA MUSIC   1.00
WILLIAMS, R.
MEET ROGER WILLIAMS
THE BIG THREE MUSIC CORPORATION   02.95
WILLIAMS, R.
PIANO INTERPRETATIONS, NO. 1
THE BIG THREE MUSIC CORPORATION   01.95
WILLIAMS, R.
PIANO INTERPRETATIONS, NO. 2
THE BIG THREE MUSIC CORPORATION   01.95
WILLIAMS, R.
PIANO INTERPRETATIONS, NO. 3
THE BIG THREE MUSIC CORPORATION   01.95
WILLIAMS, R.
RECORDED PIANO INTERPRETATIONS
THE BIG THREE MUSIC CORPORATION   02.00
WILLIAMS, R.
THIS IS ROGER WILLIAMS
THE BIG THREE MUSIC CORPORATION   02.95
WILLIS *   CURRIE, E.
SIX SONATINAS, OP. 36
WILLIS MUSIC COMPANY   1.50
WILLNER, A.
NOVEL INSTRUCTION BOOK, OP. 66 -- 10 MELODIOUS PIECES FOR THE
YOUNG
UNIVERSAL EDITION   UE 10433A   1.10
WILLSON, M.
MUSIC MAN, THE
FRANK MUSIC CORPORATION   1.25
WILLSON, M.   AGAY, D.   EASY
SONGS FROM 'THE MUSIC MAN'
FRANK MUSIC CORPORATION   1.25
WILLSON, M.   AGAY, D.   EASY
SONGS FROM 'THE UNSINKABLE MOLLY BROWN'
FRANK MUSIC CORPORATION   1.25
WILLSON, M.
UNSINKABLE MOLLY BROWN, THE
FRANK MUSIC CORPORATION   1.25
WILM, N. VON
SCHNEEFLOCKEN, OP. 8, 6 PIECES--BK. 1
ASSOCIATED MUSIC PUBLISHERS, INC.   LEU   1.50
WILM, N. VON
SCHNEEFLOCKEN, OP. 8, 6 PIECES--BK. 2
ASSOCIATED MUSIC PUBLISHERS, INC.   LEU   1.50
WILM, N. VON   E
TWENTY-FOUR EASY PIECES, OP. 81 VOL. 1
C. F. PETERS CORPORATION   2482A   1.50
WILM, N. VON   E
TWENTY-FOUR EASY PIECES, OP. 81 VOL. 2
C. F. PETERS CORPORATION   2482B   1.50
WILSON   AI
LEAVES FROM MY NOTEBOOK
WILLIS MUSIC COMPANY   1.00
WILSON, J. F.
FAMILIAR HYMNS FOR THE PIANO
HOPE PUBLISHING COMPANY   2.50
WILSON, S.
SO EASY
ASHLEY DEALERS SERVICE, INC.   1.00
WILSON, S.   ELEMENTARY
SO EASY
CENTURY MUSIC PUBLISHING COMPANY, INC.   1.00
WILSON, T.
TEDDY WILSON, PIANO PATTERNS
THE BIG THREE MUSIC CORPORATION   01.50
WINANS, W. L.
WORSHIP HYMNS FOR PIANO
LILLENAS PUBLISHING COMPANY   MB-228   2.50
WINROTH, G.--ED   WINROTH, G.
CATHEDRAL CHIMES
WILLIS MUSIC COMPANY   .60
WINWOOD, S.
STEVIE WINWOOD AND FRIENDS
MUSIC SALES CORPORATION   090004   2.95
WISSMER, P.
THREE ETUDES
GERARD BILLAUDOT EDITIONS MUSICALES   3.30
WOLFE
THREE CHILDREN'S PROFILES
MCA MUSIC   .60
WOLFE, W.   ETTS, M.
CLASSICS MADE EASY, ONE
ASHLEY DEALERS SERVICE, INC.   1.25
WOLFF, B.
THREE PIECES MAROCAINES
FRANCO COLOMBO PUBLICATIONS   SAL   4.00
WOLFF, B.
TWELVE SHORT OCTAVE-STUDIES, OP. 118
G. SCHIRMER, INC.   L1099   .75
WOLFF, B. C.
LITTLE PISCHNA
CARL FISCHER, INC.   L 475   1.00
WOLFRAM   E
FIFTY MEISTERCHORAELE
C. F. PETERS CORPORATION   2180   3.00

WOLFRAM   E
PRAELUDIEN-ALBUM, OP. 6
C. F. PETERS CORPORATION   2086   3.00
WOLFRAM--ED   WOLFRAM   E
MEISTERCHORAELE --50--
C. F. PETERS CORPORATION   2180   3.00
WOLFSON, J.
PARAPHRASES ON OLD HEBREW FOLK SONGS, BK. 1
UNIVERSAL EDITION   UE 6931   1.80
WOLFSON, J.
PARAPHRASES ON OLD HEBREW FOLK SONGS, BK. 2
UNIVERSAL EDITION   UE 6932   1.80
WOLLENHAUPT
FIVE MORCEAUX CARACTERISTIQUE EN FORME D'ETUDES, OP. 22
G. SCHIRMER, INC.   .90
WOOD, H.
THREE PIANO PIECES
UNIVERSAL EDITION   UE 12978   2.75
WOODFORD-FINDEN
FOUR INDIAN LOVE LYRICS
BOOSEY AND HAWKES, INC.   1.50
WOOLLETT
CROQUIS DE ROUTE -- 12 PIECES --
FRANCO COLOMBO PUBLICATIONS   SAL   4.00
WOOLLETT
PRELUDES AND WALTZES
FRANCO COLOMBO PUBLICATIONS   SAL   4.00
WRIGHT, N.
PIECES FOR THE DEVELOPMENT OF TECHNIC
THEODORE PRESSER COMPANY   .75
WRIGHT, N.
TWELVE PRELUDES, OP. 25
G. SCHIRMER, INC.   1.25
WRIGHT, R. *
KISMET
FRANK MUSIC CORPORATION   1.25
WRIGHT, R. *   RICHTER   EASY
NEW SONGS FROM THE MOTION PICTURE 'SONG OF NORWAY'
FRANK MUSIC CORPORATION   1.25
WRIGHT, R. *   RICHTER   EASY
SONGS FROM 'KISMET'
FRANK MUSIC CORPORATION   1.25
WUEHRER   4
ACHTZEHN STUDIEN ZU CHOPINS ETUDEN 'IN MOTU CONTRARIO'
BARENREITER VERLAG   SM 2000
WUEHRER
CADENZAS TO MOZART CONCERTO IN C MINOR, K. 491
ASSOCIATED MUSIC PUBLISHERS, INC.   DOB   1.00
WUEHRER
CADENZAS TO MOZART CONCERTO IN C, K. 467
ASSOCIATED MUSIC PUBLISHERS, INC.   DOB   1.25
WUEHRER   D
EIGHTEEN STUDIES TO CHOPIN ETUDES, OP. 10 AND 25 --UN MOTU
CONTRARIO--
C. F. PETERS CORPORATION   WM110   3.50
WUENSCH
TWELVE GLIMPSES INTO 20TH CENTURY IDIOMS
MCA MUSIC   3.50
WURMSER, L.
DIX PETITES ETUDES
GERARD BILLAUDOT EDITIONS MUSICALES   2.50
WURMSER, L.
THREE PRELUDES
FRANCO COLOMBO PUBLICATIONS   SAL   2.50
XAVERIA, S.
MUSIC AND GUIDE BOOK
WILLIS MUSIC COMPANY   1.00
XAVERIA, S.
MY MUSIC COLOR BOOK
WILLIS MUSIC COMPANY   1.00
XAVERIA, S.
MY MUSIC LETTER BOOK
WILLIS MUSIC COMPANY   1.00
XAVERIA, S.
MY MUSIC NOTE BOOK
WILLIS MUSIC COMPANY   1.25
XAVERIA, S.
MY MUSIC PICTURE BOOK
WILLIS MUSIC COMPANY   1.00
YGOUW
CAUCASIAN SCENES, BK. 1
FRANCO COLOMBO PUBLICATIONS   SAL   4.00
YGOUW
CAUCASIAN SCENES, BK. 2 -- NEW CAUCASIAN SCENES --
FRANCO COLOMBO PUBLICATIONS   SAL   4.00
YOUNG, G.
CHRISTMAS SUITE, A
HOPE PUBLISHING COMPANY   1.95
YOUNG, I.--ED.   YOUNG, I.
THIRTY-SIX FAVORITE FOLK SONGS FOR THE PIANO
G. SCHIRMER, INC.   1.25
YOUNG, I.--ED.   YOUNG, I.
THIRTY-SIX FAVORITE FOLK SONGS FOR THE PIANO
G. SCHIRMER, INC.   1.25
YOUNG, I.--ED.   YOUNG, I.
THIRTY-SIX FAVORITE MELODIES FOR THE PIANO
G. SCHIRMER, INC.   1.25
YOUNG, I.--ED.   YOUNG, I.
THIRTY-SIX FAVORITE MELODIES FOR THE PIANO
G. SCHIRMER, INC.   1.25
YOUNG, I.--ED.   YOUNG, I.
THIRTY-THREE TRADITIONAL AMERICAN SONGS
G. SCHIRMER, INC.   1.25
YUN, I.
FIVE PIECES--1958
ASSOCIATED MUSIC PUBLISHERS, INC.   BOT   3.25
ZACHOW, F. W.   LOHMANN
GESAMMELTE WERKE--PNO/ORG/HPCHD
ASSOCIATED MUSIC PUBLISHERS, INC.   BRH   6.75
ZAJAN, P. *
FINGER PLAY
G. SCHIRMER, INC.   1.25
ZANDSTRA   E
PASTELS, VOL. 1
C. F. PETERS CORPORATION   B839   1.25
ZANDSTRA   E
PASTELS, VOL. 2
C. F. PETERS CORPORATION   B844   1.25
ZEISL, E.
PIECES FOR BARBARA
ASSOCIATED MUSIC PUBLISHERS, INC.   OBV   1.50
ZEITLIN--ED
FRENCH BAROQUE MUSIC FOR THE YOUNG PIANIST
EDWARD B. MARKS MUSIC CORPORATION   02.00
ZEITLIN--ED   ZEITLIN *
RUSSIAN MUSIC FOR THE YOUNG PIANIST -- BOOK 1
MCA MUSIC   1.75

ZEITLIN--ED　　　　　ZEITLIN *			
RUSSIAN MUSIC FOR THE YOUNG PIANIST -- BOOK 2			
MCA MUSIC			1.75
ZEITLIN--ED　　　　　ZEITLIN *			
RUSSIAN MUSIC FOR THE YOUNG PIANIST -- BOOK 3			
MCA MUSIC			1.75
ZEITLIN--ED　　　　　ZEITLIN *			
RUSSIAN MUSIC FOR THE YOUNG PIANIST -- BOOK 4			
MCA MUSIC			1.75
ZEITLIN--ED　　　　　ZEITLIN *			
RUSSIAN MUSIC FOR THE YOUNG PIANIST -- BOOK 5			
MCA MUSIC			1.75
ZEITLIN--ED　　　　　ZEITLIN *			
RUSSIAN MUSIC FOR THE YOUNG PIANIST -- BOOK 6			
MCA MUSIC			1.75
ZENDER, H.			
THREE NOCTURNES--1963--HPCHD			
ASSOCIATED MUSIC PUBLISHERS, INC.		BOT	4.50
ZEPP			
FUN WITH FOUR CHORDS			
PRO-ART PUBLICATIONS, INC.		424	1.25
ZEPP			
FUN WITH THREE CHORDS - BOOK 1			
PRO-ART PUBLICATIONS, INC.		257	1.00
ZEPP			
FUN WITH THREE CHORDS - BOOK 2			
PRO-ART PUBLICATIONS, INC.		357	1.00
ZEPP			
JUST WRITE			
PRO-ART PUBLICATIONS, INC.		926	1.25
ZEPP			
LET'S COMPOSE A SONG			
PRO-ART PUBLICATIONS, INC.		535	1.00
ZEPP			
LET'S GET TECHNICAL			
PRO-ART PUBLICATIONS, INC.		557	1.00
ZEPP			
LET'S IMPROVISE - BOOK 1			
PRO-ART PUBLICATIONS, INC.		353	1.25
ZEPP			
LET'S IMPROVISE - BOOK 2			
PRO-ART PUBLICATIONS, INC.		353	1.50
ZEPP			
LET'S LEARN CHORDS - BOOK 1			
PRO-ART PUBLICATIONS, INC.		355	1.50
ZEPP			
LET'S LEARN CHORDS - BOOK 2			
PRO-ART PUBLICATIONS, INC.		423	1.50
ZEPP			
LET'S TRANSPOSE			
PRO-ART PUBLICATIONS, INC.		534	1.25
ZEPP			
LITTLE SONGS AND SOLOS			
PRO-ART PUBLICATIONS, INC.		883	1.00
ZEPP			
ON MY COLOR T. V.			
PRO-ART PUBLICATIONS, INC.		384	1.00
ZEPP			
SIX MORE SWINGY SOLOS			
PRO-ART PUBLICATIONS, INC.		383	.85
ZEPP			
SIX SWINGY SOLOS			
PRO-ART PUBLICATIONS, INC.		305	.85
ZEPP			
SKYSCRAPERS AND HARPS			
PRO-ART PUBLICATIONS, INC.		347	1.00
ZEPP			
TECHNIC INDISPENSABLES			
PRO-ART PUBLICATIONS, INC.		1022	1.00
ZEPP			
TECHNIC PATTERNS - BOOK 1			
PRO-ART PUBLICATIONS, INC.		884	1.25
ZEPP			
TECHNIC PATTERNS - BOOK 2			
PRO-ART PUBLICATIONS, INC.		1217	1.50
ZEPP			
TECHNIC PATTERNS - BOOK 3			
PRO-ART PUBLICATIONS, INC.		1218	1.50
ZEPP			
TEN TECHNIC TUNES			
PRO-ART PUBLICATIONS, INC.		1000	1.00
ZEPP			
ZEPP PIANO COURSE - BOOK 1			
PRO-ART PUBLICATIONS, INC.		925	1.50
ZEPP			
ZEPP PIANO COURSE - BOOK 2			
PRO-ART PUBLICATIONS, INC.		956	1.50
ZEPP			
ZEPP PIANO COURSE - BOOK 3			
PRO-ART PUBLICATIONS, INC.		1011	1.50
ZEPP			
ZEPP PIANO COURSE - BOOK 4			
PRO-ART PUBLICATIONS, INC.		1058	1.50
ZEPP			
ZEPP PIANO COURSE - BOOK 5			
PRO-ART PUBLICATIONS, INC.		1216	1.75
ZEPP			
ZEPP PIANO COURSE - PREPARATORY BOOK			
PRO-ART PUBLICATIONS, INC.		915	1.50
ZEPP--ED　　　　　ZEPP			
CAROLS FOR DECEMBER			
PRO-ART PUBLICATIONS, INC.		1220	1.00
ZEPP--ED　　　　　ZEPP			
CHRISTMAS SONGS AND SOLOS			
PRO-ART PUBLICATIONS, INC.		717	1.00
ZEPP--ED　　　　　ZEPP			
EVERLASTING HYMNS			
PRO-ART PUBLICATIONS, INC.		808	1.25
ZEPP--ED　　　　　ZEPP			
FUN WITH FIVE FAVORITE SONGS			
PRO-ART PUBLICATIONS, INC.		606	1.00
ZEPP--ED　　　　　ZEPP			
LET'S ARRANGE CHRISTMAS SONGS			
PRO-ART PUBLICATIONS, INC.		482	.75
ZEPP--ED　　　　　ZEPP			
LET'S PLAY CHRISTMAS CAROLS			
PRO-ART PUBLICATIONS, INC.		715	1.00
ZEPP--ED　　　　　ZEPP			
LET'S PLAY CHRISTMAS FAVORITES			
PRO-ART PUBLICATIONS, INC.		716	1.00
ZEPP--ED　　　　　ZEPP			
LET'S PLAY FAVORITES			
PRO-ART PUBLICATIONS, INC.		603	1.00
ZEPP--ED　　　　　ZEPP			
LET'S PLAY HYMNS			
PRO-ART PUBLICATIONS, INC.		488	1.25

ZEPP--ED　　　　　ZEPP			
LET'S PLAY MORE FAVORITES			
PRO-ART PUBLICATIONS, INC.		604	.85
ZEPP--ED　　　　　ZEPP			
SACRED SONGS AND HYMNS			
PRO-ART PUBLICATIONS, INC.		1157	1.00
ZEPP--ED　　　　　ZEPP			
SEVEN ALL TIME HITS			
PRO-ART PUBLICATIONS, INC.		807	.85
ZEPP--ED　　　　　ZEPP			
SONG AND SOLO HIGHLIGHTS			
PRO-ART PUBLICATIONS, INC.		1158	1.25
ZEPP--ED　　　　　ZEPP　　4			
THREE PATRIOTIC SONGS			
PRO-ART PUBLICATIONS, INC.		110	.50
ZEPP--ED　　　　　ZEPP			
TIDINGS OF CHRISTMAS			
PRO-ART PUBLICATIONS, INC.		483	1.00
ZIEHRER　　　　　　4			
VIENNA BEAUTIES, WALTZES			
CENTURY MUSIC PUBLISHING COMPANY, INC.		893	.40
ZILCHER　　　　　　1			
DEBUT DU PIANO, LE			
ALPHONSE LEDUC			
ZILCHER　　　　　　1-3			
DIE ERSTE ZEIT AM KLAVIER, OP. 50			
SCHOTT		408	2.50
ZILCHER			
FOUR EASY PIECES, OP. 105			
ASSOCIATED MUSIC PUBLISHERS, INC.		LEU	2.00
ZILCHER　　　　　　2			
FOUR EASY PIECES, OP. 218			
ASSOCIATED MUSIC PUBLISHERS, INC.		LEU	1.75
ZILCHER			
PETIT ALBUM POUR LA JEUNESSE			
ALPHONSE LEDUC			
ZILCHER　　　　　　2			
SIX EASY PIECES, OP. 139			
ASSOCIATED MUSIC PUBLISHERS, INC.		LEU	1.75
ZILCHER　　　　　　5-6			
WEIHNACHTS-ALBUM			
SCHOTT		421	2.50
ZIMMERMAN　　　　　2			
ENCHIRIDION, KLEINE STUCKE			
SCHOTT		4214	2.50
ZIMMERMAN			
KONFIGURATIONEN			
SCHOTT		4942	2.50
ZIPOLI　　　　　　M			
CEMBALO WORKS --SONATA D'INTAVOLATURA, 1716--			
C. F. PETERS CORPORATION		WM20	6.00
ZIPOLI　　　　　　FRICKERT			
PIECES			
ASSOCIATED MUSIC PUBLISHERS, INC.		LEU	2.50
ZIPOLI　　　　　　RUF			
SELECTED WORKS			
FRANCO COLOMBO PUBLICATIONS		SY587	1.75
ZIPOLI　　　　　　TAGLIAVINI　　3			
WERKE FUR ORGEL UND CEMBALO, BK. 2 - CEMBALO			
BARENREITER VERLAG		SM 2204	
ZIPP			
LITTLE CHRISTMAS BOOK FOR ROSWITHA			
BARENREITER VERLAG		26666	1.75
ZIPP　　　　　　M			
TWO INTERMEZZI, OP. 28			
C. F. PETERS CORPORATION		N3306	1.25
ZIPP　　　　　　1			
WEIHNACHTSBUCHLEIN FUR ROSWITHA			
BARENREITER VERLAG		BA 2666	
ZUSCHNEID, K.			
THEORETISCH-PRAKT. KLAVIERSCHULE, TEIL 01			
SCHOTT		4680	4.25
ZUSCHNEID, K.			
THEORETISCH-PRAKT. KLAVIERSCHULE, TEIL 02			
SCHOTT		4681	6.00
ZUSCHNEID, K.--ED　　　ZUSCHNEID, K.　　2-4			
SONATINEN UND STUCKE FUR DEN KLAVIERUNTERRICHT, HEFT 01			
SCHOTT		4682	2.50
ZUSCHNEID, K.--ED　　　ZUSCHNEID, K.　　2-4			
SONATINEN UND STUCKE FUR DEN KLAVIERUNTERRICHT, HEFT 02			
SCHOTT		4683	2.50
ZUSCHNEID, K.--ED　　　ZUSCHNEID, K.　　2-4			
SONATINEN UND STUCKE FUR DEN KLAVIERUNTERRICHT, HEFT 03			
SCHOTT		4684	2.75
ZUSCHNEID, K.--ED　　　ZUSCHNEID, K.　　2-4			
SONATINEN UND STUCKE FUR DEN KLAVIERUNTERRICHT, HEFT 04			
SCHOTT		4685	2.75
ZYKAN, O. M.			
SIX CHANSONS			
ASSOCIATED MUSIC PUBLISHERS, INC.		DOB	2.50

**Collections, Anthologies and Instructional Systems or Methods:
Composer/Editor/Arranger Unlisted—Works Alphabetized by Title**

A L'EXPOSITION .. MUSICAL ILLUSTRATIONS -- AURIC, IBERT, MILHAUD, POULENC, ETC. --			
FRANCO COLOMBO PUBLICATIONS		SAL	1.50
ACADEMY AWARD WINNER AND OTHER BIG HITS, THE			
THE BIG THREE MUSIC CORPORATION			02.95
ACCENT NO. 1 - NINE 'POP' NOVELTY SOLOS BY VARIOUS COMPOSERS			
GENERAL MUSIC PUBLISHING COMPANY, INC.			2.50
ACCENT NO. 1 - NINE SOLOS BY VARIOUS DUTCH COMPOSERS			
GENERAL MUSIC PUBLISHING COMPANY, INC.		28	2.00
ACCENT NO. 2 - EIGHT 'POP' NOVELTY SOLOS BY VARIOUS COMPOSERS			
GENERAL MUSIC PUBLISHING COMPANY, INC.			2.50
ACCENT NO. 2 - EIGHT SOLOS BY VARIOUS DUTCH COMPOSERS			
GENERAL MUSIC PUBLISHING COMPANY, INC.		30	2.00
ADULT ACTIVITIES AT THE KEYBOARD			
BOURNE COMPANY			1.50

ADVENTURELAND
  EDWARD B. MARKS MUSIC CORPORATION   01.25

ALBUM OF PROGRESSIVE PIANO CLASSICS
  G. SCHIRMER, INC.   L1314   1.50

ALBUM OF 25 PIANO CLASSICS
  G. SCHIRMER, INC.   L1315   1.75

2

ALTE DEUTSCHE VOLKSTANZE
  SCHOTT   04032 1/2   1.00

AMERICAN COMPOSERS OF TODAY
  EDWARD B. MARKS MUSIC CORPORATION   02.50

AMERICAN FESTIVAL, BK. 1. PRIMARY --ENLARGED ED.--
  SUMMY-BIRCHARD COMPANY   2.00

AMERICAN FESTIVAL, BK. 2. EARLY GRADE --ENLARGED ED.--
  SUMMY-BIRCHARD COMPANY   2.00

AMERICAN FESTIVAL, BK. 4. ADVANCED
  SUMMY-BIRCHARD COMPANY   1.50

E-M

BACH'S SONS
  C. F. PETERS CORPORATION   H8   1.50

E

BACH'S SONS
  C. F. PETERS CORPORATION   L5011   1.25

BALLET MUSIC
  MUSIC SALES CORPORATION   020089   2.95

EASY

BAROQUE PIANO MUSIC
  MEL BAY PUBLICATIONS, INC.   2.00

BELAFONTE FOLK SONG BOOK, THE
  MUSIC SALES CORPORATION   040165   2.95

BELLS ARE RINGING
  CHAPPELL AND COMPANY, INC.   0430009-176   1.50

BELLS ARE RINGING
  CHAPPELL AND COMPANY, INC.   0430009-171   1.95

BERRY BASKET, THE, BK. 1
  BELWIN-MILLS PUBLISHING CORPORATION   1.25

BERRY BASKET, THE, BK. 2
  BELWIN-MILLS PUBLISHING CORPORATION   1.25

BEST OF ALL, THE
  MUSIC SALES CORPORATION   060003   2.95

BIG NOTE CARNIVAL--100--
  CARL FISCHER, INC.   O 4267   1.00

BIG NOTE PARADE--150--
  CARL FISCHER, INC.   O 3632   1.25

BIG SEVENTY-FIVE SONG BOOK, THE - EASY BIG NOTE PIANO
  WARNER BROTHERS PUBLISHERS   3.95

BIG 3'S BEST IN POPS
  THE BIG THREE MUSIC CORPORATION   02.95

BIG 3'S 20 BIG HITS OF TODAY
  THE BIG THREE MUSIC CORPORATION   02.95

BIG-NOTE BOOK
  BELWIN-MILLS PUBLISHING CORPORATION   1.00

BLOOD, SWEAT, AND TEARS
  MUSIC SALES CORPORATION   02065   4.95

BLOOMER GIRL
  CHAPPELL AND COMPANY, INC.   0517508   1.95

BLUESMEN, THE
  MUSIC SALES CORPORATION   000096   3.95

BOY FRIEND, THE
  CHAPPELL AND COMPANY, INC.   0577502   1.95

2 - 3

BOYS' BOOK OF PIECES
  BOSTON MUSIC COMPANY   1.50

3

BRILLIANT PIANO SOLOS
  BOSTON MUSIC COMPANY   1.50

CAMELOT
  CHAPPELL AND COMPANY, INC.   0690008   1.50

CAMELOT
  CHAPPELL AND COMPANY, INC.   0690008   1.95

CAN-CAN
  CHAPPELL AND COMPANY, INC.   0695015   1.50

CAN-CAN
  CHAPPELL AND COMPANY, INC.   0695015   1.95

CANADIAN FESTIVAL ALBUM -- FAVORITE WORKS FOR STUDENTS BY
CANADIAN COMPOSERS, BK. 1 -- 10 PIECES
  ASSOCIATED MUSIC PUBLISHERS, INC.   BER   1.00

CANADIAN FESTIVAL ALBUM -- FAVORITE WORKS FOR STUDENTS BY
CANADIAN COMPOSERS, BK. 2 -- 12 PIECES
  ASSOCIATED MUSIC PUBLISHERS, INC.   BER   1.25

CHAPPEL'S EASYPLAY PIANO SERIES -- THE BEST OF COUNTRY ANN
WESTERN
  CHAPPELL AND COMPANY, INC.   0020958   1.95

CHAPPEL'S EASYPLAY PIANO SERIES, BK. 1 -- FILM THEMES
  CHAPPELL AND COMPANY, INC.   0025114-174   1.95

CHAPPELL'S EASYPLAY PIANO SERIES, BK. 2 -- LOVE THEMES
  CHAPPELL AND COMPANY, INC.   0025122   1.95

CHAPPELL'S EASYPLAY PIANO SERIES, BK. 3 -- SHOWSTOPPERS
  CHAPPELL AND COMPANY, INC.   0025130   1.95

CHAPPELL'S SACRED SONG FAVORITES
  CHAPPELL AND COMPANY, INC.   0016501   1.50

CHILDREN'S PIANO PIECES
  ASHLEY DEALERS SERVICE, INC.   WFS NO. 1   2.95

CHILDREN'S PIANO PIECES BY SOVIET COMPOSERS
  MCA MUSIC   1.50

CHILDREN'S PIANO PIECES THE WHOLE WORLD PLAYS
  MUSIC SALES CORPORATION   010001   2.95

CHILDREN'S TV WONDERLAND SONG BOOK
  THE BIG THREE MUSIC CORPORATION   1.95

CHILDREN'S VERY FIRST PIANO PIECES
  ASHLEY DEALERS SERVICE, INC.   1.50

CHITTY CHITTY BANG BANG
  THE BIG THREE MUSIC CORPORATION   1.95

E

CHRISTMAS ALBUM. VIOLIN AND V'CELLO AD LIB.
  C. F. PETERS CORPORATION   2800A   2.50

M

CHRISTMAS MUSIC
  C. F. PETERS CORPORATION   4610   2.50

CHURCH PIANIST, THE. NOS 1 AND 3
  LORENZ PUBLISHING COMPANY   2.50

CHURCH PIANIST'S HYMNAL, THE
  LORENZ PUBLISHING COMPANY   2.50

CINERAMA HOLIDAY
  CHAPPELL AND COMPANY, INC.   0021253   1.00

EASY

CLASSIC ERA PIANO MUSIC
  MEL BAY PUBLICATIONS, INC.   2.00

CLASSIC TO CONTEMPORARY PIANO MUSIC
  ASHLEY DEALERS SERVICE, INC.   WFS NO. 13   2.95

CLASSICAL ALBUM OF ORIGINAL PIANO PIECES FOR EARLY GRADES
  BOSTON MUSIC COMPANY   1.00

CLASSICAL THEMES FOR PEOPLE WHO HATE CLASSICAL MUSIC
  MUSIC SALES CORPORATION   020100   2.95

CLASSICS
  BOSTON MUSIC COMPANY   1.50

CLASSICS TO MODERNS IN THE INTERMEDIATE GRADES
  MUSIC SALES CORPORATION   040037   2.95

CLAVECINISTES FRANCAIS -- COLLECTION OF PIECES BY EARLY FRENCH
COMPOSERS, BK. 1
  ELKAN-VOGEL, INC.   D   13.25

CLAVECINISTES FRANCAIS -- COLLECTION OF PIECES BY EARLY FRENCH
COMPOSERS, BK. 2
  ELKAN-VOGEL, INC.   D   6.60

CLAVECINISTES FRANCAIS -- COLLECTION OF PIECES BY EARLY FRENCH
COMPOSERS, BK. 3
  ELKAN-VOGEL, INC.   D   7.00

CLAVECINISTES FRANCAIS -- COLLECTION OF PIECES BY EARLY FRENCH
COMPOSERS, BK. 4
  ELKAN-VOGEL, INC.   D   4.00

COCO
  CHAPPELL AND COMPANY, INC.   0906255   1.50

COLLECTION MODERNE, BK. 2
  EDWARD B. MARKS MUSIC CORPORATION   02.50

COMPENDIUM OF PIANO TECHNIQUE, BK. 1
  EDWARD B. MARKS MUSIC CORPORATION   08.00

COMPLETE COURSE OF POINTER SYSTEM FOR PIANO
  POINTER PUBLICATIONS   9.95

BEGINNER

CONTEMPORARIES OF BACH
  EDWIN F. KALMUS   3068   1.25

E-M

CONTEMPORARIES OF PURCELL
  C. F. PETERS CORPORATION   H9   1.50

COWBOY TIME --BIG NOTE-- --175--
  CARL FISCHER, INC.   O 3662   1.25

CRUSADE, PIANO STYLINGS
  LORENZ PUBLISHING COMPANY   2.50

DANZAS ET MELODIES ANCIENNES, BK. 1
  EDWARD B. MARKS MUSIC CORPORATION   02.50

DANZAS ET MELODIES ANCIENNES, BK. 2
  EDWARD B. MARKS MUSIC CORPORATION   03.50

2-3

DAS FROHE RHEINLIEDER-BUCH, BAND 01
  SCHOTT   2500   3.75

2-3

DAS FROHE RHEINLIEDER-BUCH, BAND 02
  SCHOTT   4775   1.75

3

DAS GOLDENE MARSCH-BUCH, BAND 01
  SCHOTT   373   3.75

3

DAS GOLDENE MARSCH-BUCH, BAND 02
  SCHOTT   374   3.75

3

DAS KLINGENDE BUCH, BAND 1
  SCHOTT   2400   5.00

3

DAS KLINGENDE BUCH, BAND 2
  SCHOTT   2545   5.00

3

DAS KLINGENDE BUCH, BAND 3
  SCHOTT   2800   5.00

3

DAS LIEBSTE LIED, BAND 01
  SCHOTT   3799   3.75

3

DAS LIEBSTE LIED, BAND 02
  SCHOTT   4000   3.75

2-3

DAS NEUE KLAVIERBUCH, BAND 1
  SCHOTT   6010   3.75

2-3

DAS NEUE KLAVIERBUCH, BAND 2 SCHOTT	6011 3	3.75	
DAS NEUE OPERETTEN-BUCH, BAND 01 SCHOTT	2525 3	4.00	
DAS NEUE OPERETTEN-BUCH, BAND 02 SCHOTT	2850 3	4.00	
DAS NEUE OPERETTEN-BUCH, BAND 03 SCHOTT	3700 3	4.00	
DAS NEUE OPERETTEN-BUCH, BAND 04 SCHOTT	4300 3	4.00	
DAS NEUE OPERETTEN-BUCH, BAND 05 SCHOTT	4500	4.00	
DEEP PURPLE SONG BOOK THE BIG THREE MUSIC CORPORATION	3	03.95	
DER LANGSAME WALZER SCHOTT	3798	3.50	
DESTRY RIDES AGAIN CHAPPELL AND COMPANY, INC.	1157502 3	1.95	
DIE OPER IM HEIM, BAND 1 SCHOTT	2777 3	5.00	
DIE OPER IM HEIM, BAND 2 SCHOTT	2778	5.00	
DOCTOR DOOLITTLE THE BIG THREE MUSIC CORPORATION	M-D	1.95	
DUTCH PIANO ALBUM NO. 2 C. F. PETERS CORPORATION	B33 M-D	3.00	
DUTCH PIANO ALBUM NO. 3 C. F. PETERS CORPORATION	B34	3.00	
EARLY ADVANCED CLASSICS TO MODERNS MUSIC SALES CORPORATION	040047	2.95	
EASY CLASSICS TO MODERNS MUSIC SALES CORPORATION	040017	2.95	
EASY DOES IT FOR PIANO - NO. 1 WARNER BROTHERS PUBLISHERS	EZ 1	1.95	
EASY DOES IT FOR PIANO - NO. 2 WARNER BROTHERS PUBLISHERS	EZ 2	1.95	
EASY DOES IT FOR PIANO - NO. 3 WARNER BROTHERS PUBLISHERS	EZ 3	1.95	
EASY DOES IT FOR PIANO - NO. 4 WARNER BROTHERS PUBLISHERS	EZ 4 EASY	1.95	
EASY PIANO HYMN PIECES LORENZ PUBLISHING COMPANY		2.00	
EASY PIANO PIECES MUSIC SALES CORPORATION	040003	2.95	
EASY PIECES FOR PIANO ASHLEY DEALERS SERVICE, INC.	WFS NO. 44	2.95	
EASY PIECES FOR PIANO AND ORGAN CENTURY MUSIC PUBLISHING COMPANY, INC.	MPS VOL. 4	1.95	
EASY TO PLAY HITS THROUGH THE YEARS - VOL. 1 WARNER BROTHERS PUBLISHERS		1.25	
EASY TO PLAY HITS THROUGH THE YEARS - VOL. 2 WARNER BROTHERS PUBLISHERS		1.25	
EASY TO PLAY PIANO PIECES ASHLEY DEALERS SERVICE, INC.	WFS NO. 7 EASY	2.95	
EASY WEDDING MUSIC NO. 1 LORENZ PUBLISHING COMPANY		2.00	
EASY-BEAT BIG NOTE PIANO WARNER BROTHERS PUBLISHERS		2.95	
EL CID -- MUSICAL HIGHLIGHTS THE BIG THREE MUSIC CORPORATION		2.00	
ELEMENTARY PIANO PIECES MUSIC SALES CORPORATION	020052 BEGINNER	2.95	
ENGLISH TUNES AND DANCES EDWIN F. KALMUS	3428	1.25	
EVERYBODY'S FAVORITE PIANO PIECES MUSIC SALES CORPORATION	020002	2.95	
EXCURSIONS--130-- CARL FISCHER, INC.	O 4867	1.50	
EXODUS CHAPPELL AND COMPANY, INC.	1405000	1.95	
FAMILY MUSIC BOOK, THE G. SCHIRMER, INC.		9.95	
FAMOUS PIANO PIECES MUSIC SALES CORPORATION	020090	2.95	
FANNY CHAPPELL AND COMPANY, INC.	1435007	1.95	
FANTASTICKS, THE CHAPPELL AND COMPANY, INC.	1442508	1.50	
FANTASTICKS, THE CHAPPELL AND COMPANY, INC.	1442508	1.95	
FANTASY LAND EDWARD B. MARKS MUSIC CORPORATION	3	01.25	
FAVORITE CHRISTMAS MELODIES BELWIN-MILLS PUBLISHING CORPORATION	577	.60	

FAVORITE HYMNS MADE EASY --BIG NOTE-- --200-- CARL FISCHER, INC.	3	O 4045	1.25
FAVORITE REELS AND JIGS BELWIN-MILLS PUBLISHING CORPORATION		546	.60
FERRANTE AND TEICHER INTERPRETATIONS FOR SOLO PIANO THE BIG THREE MUSIC CORPORATION			02.95
FIFTEEN MEDIUM GRADE PIANO SOLOS BELWIN-MILLS PUBLISHING CORPORATION	AI		1.50
FIFTY-FIVE AND ONE-HALF PIANO SOLOS WILLIS MUSIC COMPANY			1.95
FIFTY-FIVE PIANO CLASSICS WARNER BROTHERS PUBLISHERS		MFE 16	1.95
FIFTY-FIVE PIANO CLASSICS - PAST AND PRESENT WARNER BROTHERS PUBLISHERS		MFE 32	1.95
FIFTY-FIVE POPULAR PIANO TEACHING PIECES WARNER BROTHERS PUBLISHERS			3.95
FIFTY-FOUR FAMOUS MARCHES FOR PIANO WARNER BROTHERS PUBLISHERS		MFE 17	2.50
FIFTY-NINE FAMOUS PIANO SOLOS WARNER BROTHERS PUBLISHERS		MFE 1	2.95
FIFTY-NINE PIANO SOLOS YOU LIKE TO PLAY G. SCHIRMER, INC.			1.75
FIFTY-ONE PIANO PIECES FROM THE MODERN REPERTOIRE G. SCHIRMER, INC.			2.00
FIFTY-SEVEN PIANO PIECES CHILDREN LIKE TO PLAY G. SCHIRMER, INC.			1.75
FIFTY-SIX PIANO CLASSICS THE BIG THREE MUSIC CORPORATION			02.50
FIFTY-THREE PIANO SOLOS IN THE EARLY GRADES G. SCHIRMER, INC.			1.75
FIFTY-TWO GREAT ROCK AND ROLL HITS THE BIG THREE MUSIC CORPORATION			03.95
FINIAN'S RAINBOW CHAPPELL AND COMPANY, INC.		1480003	1.50
FINIAN'S RAINBOW CHAPPELL AND COMPANY, INC.		1480003	1.95
FIRST CLASSIC COLLECTION BELWIN-MILLS PUBLISHING CORPORATION			2.50
FIRST FAVORITES EDWARD B. MARKS MUSIC CORPORATION	1		01.50
FIRST TIME AROUND BOURNE COMPANY			1.50
FITZWILLIAM VIRGINAL BOOK, THE BROUDE BROTHERS LTD.			22.50
FLAIR STYLINGS FOR PIANO OF DAYS OF WINE AND ROSES WARNER BROTHERS PUBLISHERS			1.95
FOLK BLUES MUSIC SALES CORPORATION		000113	4.95
FOR ME AND MY PIANO, BK. 1 SUMMY-BIRCHARD COMPANY			2.00
FOR ME AND MY PIANO, BK. 2 SUMMY-BIRCHARD COMPANY			2.00
FOR ME AND MY PIANO, BK. 3 SUMMY-BIRCHARD COMPANY			2.00
FORTY HITS OF OUR TIMES-POPULAR SONGS IN BIG NOTES FOR PIANO MCA MUSIC			3.50
FORTY PIANO SELECTIONS BY MODERN COMPOSERS THE BIG THREE MUSIC CORPORATION			02.50
FORTY-SIX CONTEMPORARY PIANO SOLOS WARNER BROTHERS PUBLISHERS		MFE 33	2.95
FORTY-SIX ORIGINAL PIANO CLASSICS WARNER BROTHERS PUBLISHERS		MFE 35	2.95
FOUR MAGIC CHORDS FOR PIANO WARNER BROTHERS PUBLISHERS			2.50
FOURTEEN LARGE-NOTE PIECES FOR THE PIANO G. SCHIRMER, INC.			.75
FOURTEEN PIANO PIECES BY CANADIAN COMPOSERS FREDERICK HARRIS MUSIC COMPANY			2.25
FRANK ZAPPA SONG BOOK, BK. 1 THE BIG THREE MUSIC CORPORATION			05.95
FROM BACH TO BROADWAY WARNER BROTHERS PUBLISHERS	M-D	MFE 37	2.50
FROM RAMEAU TO GRIEG C. F. PETERS CORPORATION		4300B	3.50
FROSTY THE SNOW MAN AND OTHER CHRISTMAS SONGS THE BIG THREE MUSIC CORPORATION	1		02.95
FUN AT THE PIANO BOSTON MUSIC COMPANY			1.50
FUNNY GIRL CHAPPELL AND COMPANY, INC.		1622505	1.50
FUNNY GIRL CHAPPELL AND COMPANY, INC.		1622505 BEGINNER	1.95
GERMAN MASTERS OF THE 17TH AND 18TH CENTURIES EDWIN F. KALMUS		3469	1.25
GIGI CHAPPELL AND COMPANY, INC.		1680008	1.50

GIGI		
CHAPPELL AND COMPANY, INC.	1680008	1.95
GIRL AT THE PIANO		
BOSTON MUSIC COMPANY		1.25
GOSPEL HYMN PIANIST		
LORENZ PUBLISHING COMPANY		2.50
GRADED PIANO PIECES		
MUSIC SALES CORPORATION	020031	2.95
GRANDPA'S DANCE ALBUM		
BELWIN-MILLS PUBLISHING CORPORATION		1.25
GREAT PIANO MUSIC		
ASHLEY DEALERS SERVICE, INC.	WFS NO. 48	2.95
GREAT SONGS OF THE YEAR - 1973 EDITION		
THE BIG THREE MUSIC CORPORATION		04.95
GYPSY		
CHAPPELL AND COMPANY, INC.	1847508	1.50
GYPSY		
CHAPPELL AND COMPANY, INC.	1847508	1.95
HAPPINESS IS		
BELWIN-MILLS PUBLISHING CORPORATION		2.00
HAPPY HUNTING		
CHAPPELL AND COMPANY, INC.	1892504	1.95
HAPPY SONGS FOR CHILDREN		
THE BIG THREE MUSIC CORPORATION		01.95
HARMS HITS THROUGH THE YEARS FOR PIANO		
WARNER BROTHERS PUBLISHERS		1.95
HAYDN TO GRIEG, FROM		
C. F. PETERS CORPORATION	H101	1.50
HEART OF THE OPERETTA, THE		
CENTURY MUSIC PUBLISHING COMPANY, INC.		1.50
HERE'S BOOGIE WOOGIE		
CARL FISCHER, INC.	O 3313	1.25
HOW THE WEST WAS WON		
THE BIG THREE MUSIC CORPORATION		1.25
HYMN TUNES FOR PIANO--110--		
CARL FISCHER, INC.	O 3775	1.50
HYMN VARIATIONS FOR PIANO		
ASHLEY DEALERS SERVICE, INC.	WFS NO. 63	2.95
HYMNS OF NATIONS --15--		
C. F. PETERS CORPORATION	ZM1310	1.25
HYMNS WE LOVE		
THE BIG THREE MUSIC CORPORATION		3.95
I DO, I DO		
CHAPPELL AND COMPANY, INC.	2192508	1.50
IMPRESSIONIST ERA PIANO MUSIC		
MEL BAY PUBLICATIONS, INC.		2.00
INCREDIBLE STRING BAND, THE		
MUSIC SALES CORPORATION	060009	2.95
INSTANT MODULATOR		
LILLENAS PUBLISHING COMPANY	MU-14	2.50
INSTANT PIANO PHASE 1		
SIGHT AND SOUND SYSTEMS, INC.	31-101	12.00
INSTANT PIANO PHASE 2		
SIGHT AND SOUND SYSTEMS, INC.	31-102	12.00
INSTRUMENTAL GREATS		
SCREEN GEMS - COLUMBIA PUBLICATIONS	F0186P	3.95
IT'S EASY TO PLAY PIANO THE THREE CHORD WAY		
MUSIC SALES CORPORATION	040041	2.95
ITALIAN MASTERS, BK. 1		
EDWIN F. KALMUS	3555	1.50
ITALIAN MASTERS, BK. 2		
EDWIN F. KALMUS	3556	1.50
JEFFERSON AIRPLANE, THE		
MUSIC SALES CORPORATION	060001	2.95
JESUS SONGS		
MEL BAY PUBLICATIONS, INC.		1.50
JUST FOR GIRLS		
BELWIN-MILLS PUBLISHING CORPORATION		1.00
KALEIDOSCOPE		
CHAPPELL AND COMPANY, INC.	0024299	3.95
KEYBOARD ARTS PIANO REPERTOIRE SERIES, BK. 1		
NATIONAL KEYBOARD ARTS ASSOCIATES		2.00
KEYBOARD ARTS PIANO REPERTOIRE SERIES, BK. 2		
NATIONAL KEYBOARD ARTS ASSOCIATES		2.00
KEYBOARD ARTS PIANO REPERTOIRE SERIES, BK. 3		
NATIONAL KEYBOARD ARTS ASSOCIATES		2.00
KEYBOARD ARTS PIANO REPERTOIRE SERIES, BK. 4		
NATIONAL KEYBOARD ARTS ASSOCIATES		2.00
KEYBOARD ARTS PIANO REPERTOIRE SERIES, BK. 5		
NATIONAL KEYBOARD ARTS ASSOCIATES		2.00
KEYBOARD ARTS PIANO REPERTOIRE SERIES, BK. 6		
NATIONAL KEYBOARD ARTS ASSOCIATES		2.00
KEYBOARD CAMEOS--100--		
CARL FISCHER, INC.	O 4789	1.25

Marginal level markings (left column): M (near HAYDN TO GRIEG), E (near HYMNS OF NATIONS), EASY (near I DO, I DO), INTERMEDIATE (near INSTRUMENTAL GREATS)

KEYBOARD CAVALCADE--50--		
CARL FISCHER, INC.	O 4281	1.50
KEYBOARD HIT-KIT, THE		
WARNER BROTHERS PUBLISHERS		1.50
KEYBOARD KALEIDOSCOPE, BK. 1 --100--		
CARL FISCHER, INC.	O 4737	1.25
KEYBOARD KALEIDOSCOPE, BK. 2 --125--		
CARL FISCHER, INC.	O 4738	1.25
KINDER SPIELEN ZUR WEIHNACHT -- 19 CHRISTMAS SONGS WITH GERMAN TEXT		
ASSOCIATED MUSIC PUBLISHERS, INC.	NAG	1.75
KLASSISCHE LIEBLINGSSTUCKE		
SCHOTT	04020 1/2	1.00
LARGE NOTE PIANO PIECES		
MUSIC SALES CORPORATION	020084	2.95
LARGE NOTE PIANO SOLOS FOR READING AND RHYTHM		
BELWIN-MILLS PUBLISHING CORPORATION		1.25
LEFT FOOT, RIGHT FOOT MARCH FOLIO		
VOLKWEIN BROS.		01.50
LEIPZIG PIANO MUSIC - PAST AND PRESENT		
C. F. PETERS CORPORATION	9047	5.00
LET US HAVE MUSIC SERIES - CHRISTMAS		
CARL FISCHER, INC.	O 3507	1.50
LET US HAVE MUSIC SERIES - MARCHING		
CARL FISCHER, INC.	O 3613	1.50
LET US HAVE MUSIC SERIES - PIANO, JUNIOR --125--		
CARL FISCHER, INC.	O 4105	1.25
LET US HAVE MUSIC SERIES - PIANO, VOL. 1 --86--		
CARL FISCHER, INC.	O 2942	1.95
LET US HAVE MUSIC SERIES - PIANO, VOL. 2 --48--		
CARL FISCHER, INC.	O 3127	1.95
LET US HAVE MUSIC SERIES - YOUNG PEOPLE --PIANO WITH WORDS--		
CARL FISCHER, INC.	O 4234	1.75
LITTLE CLASSICS. 67 EASY PIECES SELECTED FROM THE WORKS OF GREAT COMPOSERS--EDITED BY EMINENT MASTERS--BK. 1		
G. SCHIRMER, INC.	L1240	1.75
LITTLE CLASSICS. 67 EASY PIECES SELECTED FROM THE WORKS OF GREAT COMPOSERS--EDITED BY EMINENT MASTERS--BK. 2		
G. SCHIRMER, INC.	L1241	1.75
LITTLE PIANO BOOKS, VOL. 1+ PRE-BACH MASTERS		
C. F. PETERS CORPORATION	4451	3.00
LITTLE PIANO BOOKS, VOL. 2+ CONTEMPORARIES OF BACH		
C. F. PETERS CORPORATION	4452	3.00
LITTLE PIANO BOOKS, VOL. 3+ THE CLASSICAL PERIOD		
C. F. PETERS CORPORATION	4453	3.00
LITTLE PIANO BOOKS, VOL. 4+ THE ROMANTIC PERIOD		
C. F. PETERS CORPORATION	4454	3.00
LITTLE SONGS THAT TEACH		
THE BIG THREE MUSIC CORPORATION		03.95
LITTLE TREASURY SERIES - RECITAL CLASSICS, BK. 1		
CENTURY MUSIC PUBLISHING COMPANY, INC.		1.00
LITTLE TREASURY SERIES - RECITAL CLASSICS, BK. 2		
CENTURY MUSIC PUBLISHING COMPANY, INC.		1.00
LOVE FROM BROADWAYS		
CHAPPELL AND COMPANY, INC.	0015826	1.95
MANO SINISTRA --SIX PIECES FOR LEFT HAND ONLY BY DUTCH COMPOSERS--		
C. F. PETERS CORPORATION	D320	3.00
MARDI GRAS		
CHAPPELL AND COMPANY, INC.	0016014	1.00
MASTER MELODIES --100--		
CARL FISCHER, INC.	P 4665	1.25
MASTERPIECES OF PIANO MUSIC --17--		
CARL FISCHER, INC.	O 3619	10.00
MASTERS OF OUR DAY --70--		
CARL FISCHER, INC.	O 4361	1.75
MASTERS OF THE 17TH CENTURY		
EDWIN F. KALMUS	3662	1.50
MASTERS OF THE 17TH CENTURY		
EDWIN F. KALMUS	3662	1.50
MEET MODERN MUSIC, BK. 1		
THEODORE PRESSER COMPANY		1.00
MEET MODERN MUSIC, BK. 2		
THEODORE PRESSER COMPANY		1.25
MEET THE KEYS --100--		
CARL FISCHER, INC.	O 4448	1.25
MEIN HEIMATLAND		
SCHOTT	2222	5.00
MEISTERBUCH. A COLLECTION OF FIFTY-FIVE CELEBRATED PIANO PIECES OF THREE CENTURIES.		
C. F. PETERS CORPORATION	4901	7.50
MELODIEN-SCHATZ, FUNF LEICHTE KLAVIERSTUCKE, HEFT 2		
BARENREITER VERLAG	AP 1697	
MELODY JOYS FOR GIRLS AND BOYS		
THEODORE PRESSER COMPANY		2.00
MERRY CHRISTMAS - THE HILLSIDE SINGERS		
THE BIG THREE MUSIC CORPORATION		02.95

Marginal level markings (right column): 2-3 (near KINDER SPIELEN), E-M (near LEFT FOOT), M (near LITTLE PIANO BOOKS entries), 2A-2B (near LITTLE TREASURY BK.1), 2C-3A (near LITTLE TREASURY BK.2), D (near LOVE FROM BROADWAYS), 2-3 (near MEET THE KEYS), M-D (near MEISTERBUCH), 1-2 (near MELODIEN-SCHATZ), 2 (near MERRY CHRISTMAS)

MERRY TUNES FOR PIANO BOSTON MUSIC COMPANY		1.50
MODERN PIANIST SERIES - CHRISTMAS SKETCHES POINTER PUBLICATIONS		1.95
MODERN PIANIST SERIES - CZERNY FOR THE MODERN PIANIST POINTER PUBLICATIONS		1.95
MODERN PIANIST SERIES - GUIDE TO THE MODERN PIANIST --TEACHING OUTLINE-- POINTER PUBLICATIONS		FREE
MODERN PIANIST SERIES - MINIATURE CLASSICS POINTER PUBLICATIONS		1.95
MODERN PIANIST SERIES - SONGS OF FAITH POINTER PUBLICATIONS		1.95
MODERN PIANIST SERIES - SUPPLEMENTARY SONGS, BK. 1 POINTER PUBLICATIONS		2.50
MODERN PIANIST SERIES - SUPPLEMENTARY SONGS, BK. 2 POINTER PUBLICATIONS		2.50
MODERN PIANIST SERIES - SUPPLEMENTARY SONGS, BK. 3 POINTER PUBLICATIONS		2.50
MODERN PIANIST SERIES - SUPPLEMENTARY SONGS, BK. 4 POINTER PUBLICATIONS		2.50
MODERN PIANIST SERIES, BK. 1 POINTER PUBLICATIONS		2.50
MODERN PIANIST SERIES, BK. 2 POINTER PUBLICATIONS		2.50
MODERN PIANIST SERIES, BK. 3 POINTER PUBLICATIONS		2.50
MODERN PIANIST SERIES, BK. 4 POINTER PUBLICATIONS		2.50
MODERN PIANO PIECES MUSIC SALES CORPORATION	020014	2.95
MODERN RUSSIAN PIANO MUSIC -- AKIMENKO TO KORESTCHENKO, BK. 1 THEODORE PRESSER COMPANY		5.00
MORE EASY CLASSICS TO MODERNS MUSIC SALES CORPORATION	040027	2.95
MORRISON HOTEL -- THE DOORS MUSIC SALES CORPORATION	060008	2.95
MOST POPULAR SERIES - VOL. 1, PIANO PIECES CENTURY MUSIC PUBLISHING COMPANY, INC.		1.95
MOST POPULAR SERIES - VOL. 2, PIANO PIECES IN SIMPLIFIED FORM CENTURY MUSIC PUBLISHING COMPANY, INC.		1.95
MOST POPULAR SERIES - VOL. 3A, TUNES YOU LIKE TO PLAY CENTURY MUSIC PUBLISHING COMPANY, INC.		1.95
MOST POPULAR SERIES - VOL. 3B, TUNES YOU LIKE TO PLAY CENTURY MUSIC PUBLISHING COMPANY, INC.		1.95
MOST POPULAR SERIES - VOL. 4, EASY PIECES FOR PIANO AND ALL ORGANS CENTURY MUSIC PUBLISHING COMPANY, INC.		1.95
MOST POPULAR SERIES - VOL. 5, MUSIC FROM THE MASTERS TO THE MINORS CENTURY MUSIC PUBLISHING COMPANY, INC.		1.95
MOST POPULAR SERIES - VOL. 7, NINETY-THREE SHORT CLASSICS CENTURY MUSIC PUBLISHING COMPANY, INC.		1.95
MUSIC EDUCATION SUPPLEMENT - COMPLETE SET B-17 THROUGH B-20 BERKLEE PRESS PUBLICATIONS	COMPLETE SET	17.50
MUSIC EDUCATION SUPPLEMENT - VOL. 1 BERKLEE PRESS PUBLICATIONS	B-17	5.00
MUSIC EDUCATION SUPPLEMENT - VOL. 2 BERKLEE PRESS PUBLICATIONS	B-18	5.00
MUSIC EDUCATION SUPPLEMENT - VOL. 3 BERKLEE PRESS PUBLICATIONS	B-19	5.00
MUSIC EDUCATION SUPPLEMENT - VOL. 4 BERKLEE PRESS PUBLICATIONS	B-20	5.00
MUSIC FOR THE WEDDING CARL FISCHER, INC.	P 2452	1.25
MUSIC FROM THE MASTERS TO THE MINORS CENTURY MUSIC PUBLISHING COMPANY, INC.	MPS VOL. 5	1.95
MUSIC IS A WORLD OF JOY THE BIG THREE MUSIC CORPORATION		02.95
MUSIC STUDY FOR ADULTS CARL FISCHER, INC.	O 2960	1.50
MUSICAL ADVENTURES IN MARKSLAND EDWARD B. MARKS MUSIC CORPORATION		02.50
MUSICAL CHRISTMAS CARDS --SIX PIECES-- C. F. PETERS CORPORATION	M H400A	1.25
MUSICAL SELF-PORTRAITS --FOURTEEN PIECES BY DUTCH COMPOSERS-- C. F. PETERS CORPORATION	M-D AL11	3.00
MUSICAL VISIT WITH THE MASTERS, A -- 16 CLASSICAL COMPOSITIONS IN SIMPLIFIED ARRANGEMENTS THEODORE PRESSER COMPANY		1.25
MUSICLAND EDWARD B. MARKS MUSIC CORPORATION		01.25
MY FAVORITE PROGRAM ALBUM --54-- CARL FISCHER, INC.	O 3198	2.00
MY FAVORITE REPERTOIRE ALBUM --25-- CARL FISCHER, INC.	O 3252	2.00

MY FAVORITE SOLO ALBUM CARL FISCHER, INC.	O 3223	2.95
	2	
NEUE WEIHNACHTSLIEDER BARENREITER VERLAG	BA 1371	
NEW ENGLAND CONSERVATORY PIANO COURSE - ALBUM OF SONATINAS AND SONATAS NEW ENGLAND CONSERVATORY		2.50
NEW ENGLAND CONSERVATORY PIANO COURSE - FIRST GRADE NEW ENGLAND CONSERVATORY		1.75
NEW ENGLAND CONSERVATORY PIANO COURSE - SECOND GRADE NEW ENGLAND CONSERVATORY		2.00
NEW ENGLAND CONSERVATORY PIANO COURSE - SELECTED PIECES, BOOK 1 NEW ENGLAND CONSERVATORY		1.50
NEW ENGLAND CONSERVATORY PIANO COURSE - SELECTED PIECES, BOOK 2 NEW ENGLAND CONSERVATORY		1.50
NEW ENGLAND CONSERVATORY PIANO COURSE - THIRD GRADE NEW ENGLAND CONSERVATORY		2.75
NEW ENGLAND CONSERVATORY PIANO COURSE - THIRTY-FIVE EASY PIECES NEW ENGLAND CONSERVATORY		1.25
NEW INSTRUCTIONS FOR PLAYING THE HARPSICHORD, PIANO-FORTE, OR SPINNET BROUDE BROTHERS LTD.		20.00
NEW MUSIC FOR THE PIANO, A COMPILATION OF 22 CONTEMPORARY COMPOSERS LAWSON-GOULD MUSIC PUBLISHERS, INC.		
NINETY GAY NINETIES FAVORITES THE BIG THREE MUSIC CORPORATION		02.95
NINETY TRI-CHORD TUNES CENTURY MUSIC PUBLISHING COMPANY, INC.	MPS VOL. 8	1.95
NINETY-FIVE EASY PIANO CLASSICS WARNER BROTHERS PUBLISHERS	MFE 3	2.95
NINETY-FIVE FOLK SONGS AND DANCES FOR PIANO WARNER BROTHERS PUBLISHERS	MFE 28	1.95
NINETY-THREE SHORT CLASSICS CENTURY MUSIC PUBLISHING COMPANY, INC.	MPS VOL. 7	1.95
NOTENMAPPE DES KLAVIERSCHULERS - TEIL 01 ELEMENTARSTUFE, HEFT 2 SCHOTT	718B	2.25
NOTENMAPPE DES KLAVIERSCHULERS - TEIL 02 HOHERE ELEMENTARSTUFE, HEFT 1 SCHOTT	719A	2.25
NOTENMAPPE DES KLAVIERSCHULERS - TEIL 03 UNTERE MITTELSTUFE, HEFT 01 SCHOTT	720A	2.25
NOTENMAPPE DES KLAVIERSCHULERS - TEIL 03 UNTERE MITTELSTUFE, HEFT 02 SCHOTT	720B	2.25
NOTENMAPPE DES KLAVIERSCHULERS - VORSTUFE, HEFT 01 SCHOTT	717A	2.25
NOTENMAPPE DES KLAVIERSCHULERS - VORSTUFE, HEFT 02 SCHOTT	717B	2.25
	E-M	
OLD MASTERS FROM THE SIXTEENTH TO EIGHTEENTH CENTURIES, VOL. 1 C. F. PETERS CORPORATION	4527A	2.50
	M	
OLD MASTERS FROM THE SIXTEENTH TO EIGHTEENTH CENTURIES, VOL. 2 C. F. PETERS CORPORATION	4527B	2.50
	E-M	
OLD MASTERS OF THE PIANO C. F. PETERS CORPORATION	L5618	2.00
	M-D	
OLD MASTERS OF THE SEVENTEENTH AND EIGHTEENTH CENTURIES, VOL. 1 C. F. PETERS CORPORATION	3173A	2.00
	M-D	
OLD MASTERS OF THE SEVENTEENTH AND EIGHTEENTH CENTURIES, VOL. 2 C. F. PETERS CORPORATION	3173B	2.00
	M-D	
OLD MASTERS OF THE SEVENTEENTH AND EIGHTEENTH CENTURIES, VOL. 3 C. F. PETERS CORPORATION	3173C	2.00
OLD MASTERS OF THE 16TH - 18TH CENTURIES EDWIN F. KALMUS	3750	4.00
OLZEN'S SCANDINAVIAN DANCE ALBUMS, BK. 1 --ACCORDION OR PIANO-- SUMMY-BIRCHARD COMPANY		1.50
ON A CLEAR DAY YOU CAN SEE FOREVER CHAPPELL AND COMPANY, INC.	4322509	1.50
ON A CLEAR DAY YOU CAN SEE FOREVER CHAPPELL AND COMPANY, INC.	4322509	1.95
ONE HUNDRED AND SEVEN EASY-TO-PLAY HYMNS CENTURY MUSIC PUBLISHING COMPANY, INC.	MPS VOL. 9	1.95
ONE HUNDRED FIVE EASY PIANO PIECES THE BIG THREE MUSIC CORPORATION		02.95
ONE HUNDRED NINETY CHILDREN'S SONGS THE BIG THREE MUSIC CORPORATION		02.95
ONE HUNDRED OF THE GREATEST ROCK AND ROLL HITS THE BIG THREE MUSIC CORPORATION		05.95
ONE HUNDRED SEVENTY CHRISTMAS SONGS AND CAROLS THE BIG THREE MUSIC CORPORATION		04.95
ONE HUNDRED TWENTY AMERICAN SONGS THE BIG THREE MUSIC CORPORATION		02.50
ONE WAY SONGBOOK MEL BAY PUBLICATIONS, INC.	3-6	1.50
OUVERTUREN-ALBUM, BAND 01 SCHOTT	354 3-6	4.25

OUVERTUREN-ALBUM, BAND 02		
SCHOTT	355	4.25
3-6		
OUVERTUREN-ALBUM, BAND 03		
SCHOTT	356	4.25
M		
OVERTURES, VOL. 1		
C. F. PETERS CORPORATION	1946	4.50
M		
OVERTURES, VOL. 2		
C. F. PETERS CORPORATION	1947	4.50
M		
OVERTURES, VOL. 3		
C. F. PETERS CORPORATION	1948	4.50
M		
OVERTURES, VOL. 4		
C. F. PETERS CORPORATION	1949	4.50
M		
OVERTURES, VOL. 5		
C. F. PETERS CORPORATION	4940	4.50
PAINT YOUR WAGON		
CHAPPELL AND COMPANY, INC.	4480000	1.50
PAINT YOUR WAGON		
CHAPPELL AND COMPANY, INC.	4480000	1.95
PAL JOEY		
CHAPPELL AND COMPANY, INC.	4482501	1.95
PETER, PAUL AND MOMMY, EASY BIG NOTE PIANO		
WARNER BROTHERS PUBLISHERS	PPM 26	1.95
PETITS VIETUOSES, LES - SIXTY SHORT TRANSCRIPTIONS IN 4 BKS, BK. 2		
FRANCO COLOMBO PUBLICATIONS	SAL	1.50
PETITS VIRTUOSES, LES - SIXTY SHORT TRANSCRIPTIONS IN 4 BKS, BK. 1		
FRANCO COLOMBO PUBLICATIONS	SAL	1.50
PETITS VIRTUOSES, LES - SIXTY SHORT TRANSCRIPTIONS IN 4 BKS, BK. 3		
FRANCO COLOMBO PUBLICATIONS	SAL	1.50
PETITS VIRTUOSES, LES - SIXTY SHORT TRANSCRIPTIONS IN 4 BKS, BK. 4		
FRANCO COLOMBO PUBLICATIONS	SAL	1.50
PIANISTES DE L'AVENIR, LES - 36 SHORT TRANSCRIPTIONS IN 3 BKS, BK. 1		
FRANCO COLOMBO PUBLICATIONS	SAL	1.50
PIANISTES DE L'AVENIR, LES - 36 SHORT TRANSCRIPTIONS IN 3 BKS, BK. 2		
FRANCO COLOMBO PUBLICATIONS	SAL	1.50
PIANISTES DE L'AVENIR, LES - 36 SHORT TRANSCRIPTIONS IN 3 BKS, BK. 3		
FRANCO COLOMBO PUBLICATIONS	SAL	1.50
PIANO CLASSIC COLLECTION OF PIECES FOR THE INTERMEDIATE GRADES		
BELWIN-MILLS PUBLISHING CORPORATION		3.00
PIANO HYMN VOLUNTARIES. NOS 1, 2, AND 3		
LORENZ PUBLISHING COMPANY		2.50
PIANO MASTERPIECES		
BELWIN-MILLS PUBLISHING CORPORATION		2.50
PIANO PIECES		
ASHLEY DEALERS SERVICE, INC.	WFS NO. 2	2.95
PIANO PIECES		
CENTURY MUSIC PUBLISHING COMPANY, INC.	MPS VOL. 1	1.95
PIANO PIECES -- SIMP.		
CENTURY MUSIC PUBLISHING COMPANY, INC.	MPS VOL. 2	1.95
PIANO PIECES FOR CHILDREN		
MUSIC SALES CORPORATION	020003	2.95
PIANO PIECES FOR THE ADULT STUDENT		
MUSIC SALES CORPORATION	020004	2.95
PIANO PIECES FOR THE YOUNG STUDENT		
MUSIC SALES CORPORATION	020080	2.95
PIANO PIECES THE WHOLE WORLD PLAYS		
MUSIC SALES CORPORATION	010000	2.95
PIANO PLAYTIME		
SUMMY-BIRCHARD COMPANY		2.50
PIANO PLAYTIME		
SUMMY-BIRCHARD COMPANY		2.50
PIANO PLAYTIME		
SUMMY-BIRCHARD COMPANY		1.75
E		
PIANO PLAYTIME, BK A		
WILLIS MUSIC COMPANY		.80
AE		
PIANO PLAYTIME, BK B		
WILLIS MUSIC COMPANY		.80
AI		
PIANO PLAYTIME, BK C		
WILLIS MUSIC COMPANY		.80
AI		
PIANO PLAYTIME, BK D		
WILLIS MUSIC COMPANY		.80
A		
PIANO PLAYTIME, BK E		
WILLIS MUSIC COMPANY		.80
PIANO SOLOS		
ASHLEY DEALERS SERVICE, INC.	WFS NO. 49	2.95
PIANO SOLOS FROM 'THE EDDY DUCHIN STORY' --TO LOVE AGAIN AND CHOPSTICKS RHAPSODY		
SHAPIRO, BERNSTEIN ORGANIZATION		.95
PIANOLAND		
EDWARD B. MARKS MUSIC CORPORATION		01.25
PIANOTIME FAVORITES --BIG NOTE-- --120--		
CARL FISCHER, INC.	O 3837	1.00

PINEAPPLE POLL BALLET		
CHAPPELL AND COMPANY, INC.	4602504	1.95
PLAIN AND FANCY		
CHAPPELL AND COMPANY, INC.	4620001	1.95
PLAY IT NOW --BIG NOTE-- --150--		
CARL FISCHER, INC.	O 4001	1.00
PLAY THEM RAGS		
BELWIN-MILLS PUBLISHING CORPORATION		2.00
PLAYING PLEASURE		
EDWARD B. MARKS MUSIC CORPORATION		01.25
POINTER LIBRARY - CAVALCADE OF POPS		
POINTER PUBLICATIONS		2.95
POINTER LIBRARY - FAMOUS HYMNS		
POINTER PUBLICATIONS		2.95
POINTER LIBRARY - GOLDEN POPS		
POINTER PUBLICATIONS		2.95
POINTER LIBRARY - HITS, HITS, HITS, VOL. 1		
POINTER PUBLICATIONS		2.95
POINTER LIBRARY - HITS, HITS, HITS, VOL. 2		
POINTER PUBLICATIONS		2.95
POINTER LIBRARY - MEMORIES OF CHRISTMAS		
POINTER PUBLICATIONS		2.95
POINTER LIBRARY - PARADE OF POPS, VOL. 1		
POINTER PUBLICATIONS		2.95
POINTER LIBRARY - PARADE OF POPS, VOL. 2		
POINTER PUBLICATIONS		2.95
POINTER LIBRARY - POP PROMENADE		
POINTER PUBLICATIONS		2.95
POINTER LIBRARY - POPS FOR PLEASURE		
POINTER PUBLICATIONS		2.95
POINTER LIBRARY - POPS OF THE 60'S		
POINTER PUBLICATIONS		2.95
POINTER LIBRARY - POPS OF YESTERYEAR		
POINTER PUBLICATIONS		2.95
POINTER LIBRARY - ROMANTIC OPERETTA		
POINTER PUBLICATIONS		2.95
POINTER LIBRARY - THE NEW POPS		
POINTER PUBLICATIONS		2.95
POINTER LIBRARY - THEMES FROM THE CLASSICS		
POINTER PUBLICATIONS		2.95
POINTER SYSTEM - CAROLS		
POINTER PUBLICATIONS		1.50
POINTER SYSTEM - CLASSICS		
POINTER PUBLICATIONS		1.50
POINTER SYSTEM - FAVORITE SONGS		
POINTER PUBLICATIONS		1.50
POINTER SYSTEM - FOLK SONGS		
POINTER PUBLICATIONS		1.50
POINTER SYSTEM - GAY NINETIES		
POINTER PUBLICATIONS		1.50
POINTER SYSTEM - HOLIDAYS IN SONG		
POINTER PUBLICATIONS		1.50
POINTER SYSTEM - HYMNS		
POINTER PUBLICATIONS		1.50
POINTER SYSTEM - LATIN MOODS		
POINTER PUBLICATIONS		1.50
POINTER SYSTEM - SONG MEMORIES		
POINTER PUBLICATIONS		1.50
POINTER SYSTEM - SONGS OF MANY LANDS		
POINTER PUBLICATIONS		1.50
POINTER SYSTEM - SONGS THAT LIVE FOREVER		
POINTER PUBLICATIONS		1.50
POINTER SYSTEM - WALTZES		
POINTER PUBLICATIONS		1.50
POINTER SYSTEM - WALTZES OF VIENNA		
POINTER PUBLICATIONS		1.50
POINTER SYSTEM FOR PIANO, BK. 1		
POINTER PUBLICATIONS		2.50
POINTER SYSTEM FOR PIANO, BK. 2		
POINTER PUBLICATIONS		2.50
POINTER SYSTEM FOR PIANO, BK. 3		
POINTER PUBLICATIONS		2.50
POINTER SYSTEM FOR PIANO, BK. 4		
POINTER PUBLICATIONS		2.50
POINTER SYSTEM FOR PIANO, BK. 5		
POINTER PUBLICATIONS		2.50
POLISH CONTEMPORARY PIANO MINIATURES		
EDWARD B. MARKS MUSIC CORPORATION		08.50
POLKA LAND		
EDWARD B. MARKS MUSIC CORPORATION		02.00
POPULAR CLASSICS FOR PIANO		
ASHLEY DEALERS SERVICE, INC.	WFS NO. 69	2.95
POPULAR CLASSICS FOR PIANO		
BELWIN-MILLS PUBLISHING CORPORATION		3.00
POPULAR CLASSICS IN BIG NOTES --100--		
CARL FISCHER, INC.	O 4446	1.25

PRECEPTOR, THE
  BROUDE BROTHERS LTD.   20.00

PREDECESSORS OF BACH
  EDWIN F. KALMUS   3115   1.25

PRELUDES, OFFERTORIES AND POSTLUDES FOR THE PIANO, BK. 1
  ASHLEY DEALERS SERVICE, INC.   WFS NO. 70   2.95

PROGRAM PIECES FOR THE YOUNGER CHILD, BK. 1
  SUMMY-BIRCHARD COMPANY   1.50

PROGRESSIVE PIANO PIECES
  MUSIC SALES CORPORATION   020068   2.95

PUPPET SONGS FROM ''CARNIVAL''
  THE BIG THREE MUSIC CORPORATION   1.00

RAGGEDY ANN SONG BOOK, A
  THE BIG THREE MUSIC CORPORATION   2.50

RAGTIME PIANO
  BELWIN-MILLS PUBLISHING CORPORATION   2.50

RECITAL PIECES, BK. 1
  SUMMY-BIRCHARD COMPANY   1.75

RECITAL PIECES, BK. 2
  SUMMY-BIRCHARD COMPANY   1.95

RECORDED FAVORITES OF NINA SIMONE
  SAM FOX PUBLISHING COMPANY, INC.   1975

RED SHOES BALLET, THE
  CHAPPELL AND COMPANY, INC.   4810008   1.95

RELIGIOUS SONGS
  SCHUBERTH CO.   NO. 10   1.50

REVERIE ALBUM
  THEODORE PRESSER COMPANY   2.00

ROBBINS FOLIO OF POPULAR MARCHES, THE
  THE BIG THREE MUSIC CORPORATION   01.95
                                                 EASY
ROMANTIC ERA PIANO MUSIC
  MEL BAY PUBLICATIONS, INC.   2.00
                                                 E
ROMANTIC MASTERS
  C. F. PETERS CORPORATION   L5033   1.25
                                                 1
ROYAL CONSERVATORY OF MUSIC, UNIVERSITY OF TORONTO -- PIANOFORTE
EXAMINATION, GRADE 01
  FREDERICK HARRIS MUSIC COMPANY   1.60
                                                 2
ROYAL CONSERVATORY OF MUSIC, UNIVERSITY OF TORONTO -- PIANOFORTE
EXAMINATION, GRADE 02
  FREDERICK HARRIS MUSIC COMPANY   1.60
                                                 3
ROYAL CONSERVATORY OF MUSIC, UNIVERSITY OF TORONTO -- PIANOFORTE
EXAMINATION, GRADE 03
  FREDERICK HARRIS MUSIC COMPANY   1.60
                                                 4
ROYAL CONSERVATORY OF MUSIC, UNIVERSITY OF TORONTO -- PIANOFORTE
EXAMINATION, GRADE 04
  FREDERICK HARRIS MUSIC COMPANY   1.60
                                                 5
ROYAL CONSERVATORY OF MUSIC, UNIVERSITY OF TORONTO -- PIANOFORTE
EXAMINATION, GRADE 05
  FREDERICK HARRIS MUSIC COMPANY   1.60
                                                 6
ROYAL CONSERVATORY OF MUSIC, UNIVERSITY OF TORONTO -- PIANOFORTE
EXAMINATION, GRADE 06
  FREDERICK HARRIS MUSIC COMPANY   1.60
                                                 7
ROYAL CONSERVATORY OF MUSIC, UNIVERSITY OF TORONTO -- PIANOFORTE
EXAMINATION, GRADE 07
  FREDERICK HARRIS MUSIC COMPANY   2.60
                                                 8
ROYAL CONSERVATORY OF MUSIC, UNIVERSITY OF TORONTO -- PIANOFORTE
EXAMINATION, GRADE 08
  FREDERICK HARRIS MUSIC COMPANY   2.60
                                                 9
ROYAL CONSERVATORY OF MUSIC, UNIVERSITY OF TORONTO -- PIANOFORTE
EXAMINATION, GRADE 09
  FREDERICK HARRIS MUSIC COMPANY   2.10
                                                 10
ROYAL CONSERVATORY OF MUSIC, UNIVERSITY OF TORONTO -- PIANOFORTE
EXAMINATION, GRADE 10
  FREDERICK HARRIS MUSIC COMPANY   2.10
                                                 E
RUSSIAN PIANO MUSIC
  C. F. PETERS CORPORATION   4798   3.00
                                                 EASY
SACRED PIANIST
  MEL BAY PUBLICATIONS, INC.   1.50
                                            ROVENGER
SACRED REFLECTIONS FOR PIANO SOLO
  RUBANK, INC.   1.50

SAIL AWAY
  CHAPPELL AND COMPANY, INC.   4960001   1.95

SCALES, CHORDS, ARPEGGIOS AND OCTAVES FOR PIANO
  SHAPIRO, BERNSTEIN ORGANIZATION   2.00
                                                 M-D
SCARLATTI TO ALBENIZ
  C. F. PETERS CORPORATION   B733   1.50

SELECTED PIANO MUSIC
  MUSIC SALES CORPORATION   020022   2.95
                                              ELEMENTARY
SELECTED PIANO SOLOS BY ROMANTIC COMPOSERS, BK. 1--ELEMENTARY
  G. SCHIRMER, INC.   L1718   1.75
                                              INTERMEDIATE
SELECTED PIANO SOLOS BY ROMANTIC COMPOSERS, BK. 2--INTERMEDIATE
  G. SCHIRMER, INC.   L1719   1.50
                                           LOWER ADVANCED
SELECTED PIANO SOLOS BY ROMANTIC COMPOSERS, BK. 3--LOWER
ADVANCED
  G. SCHIRMER, INC.   L1720   1.75

SELECTED SONATAS FOR PIANO
  MUSIC SALES CORPORATION   020073   2.95
                                              ELEMENTARY
SELECTED SONATINAS, BK. 1--ELEMENTARY
  G. SCHIRMER, INC.   L1594   1.25
                                              INTERMEDIATE

SELECTED SONATINAS, BK. 2--INTERMEDIATE
  G. SCHIRMER, INC.   L1595   1.25
                                           LOWER ADVANCED
SELECTED SONATINAS, BK. 3--LOWER ADVANCED
  G. SCHIRMER, INC.   L1596   1.25

SELECTIONS FROM 'HAIR'
  THE BIG THREE MUSIC CORPORATION   2.50

SELECTIONS FROM SIX FAVORITE OPERAS
  G. SCHIRMER, INC.   L1638   4.00

SENSATIONAL 70 FOR THE 70'S, THE
  SCREEN GEMS - COLUMBIA PUBLICATIONS   F0050P1   5.95

SEVENTY-FIVE FAMOUS PIANO PIECES
  THE BIG THREE MUSIC CORPORATION   02.95

SIGNS SHALL FOLLOW SONGBOOK
  MEL BAY PUBLICATIONS, INC.   1.50

SILK STOCKINGS
  CHAPPELL AND COMPANY, INC.   5160015   1.95

SINGING KEYS, BK. 1
  SUMMY-BIRCHARD COMPANY   2.25

SINGING KEYS, BK. 2
  SUMMY-BIRCHARD COMPANY   2.50

SINGING KEYS, BK. 3
  SUMMY-BIRCHARD COMPANY   2.00

SINGING KEYS, BK. 4
  SUMMY-BIRCHARD COMPANY   2.25

SINGING MELODIES
  THEODORE PRESSER COMPANY   1.25

SIXTY PROGRESSIVE PIANO PIECES YOU LIKE TO PLAY
  G. SCHIRMER, INC.   1.75

SIXTY-EIGHT GREATEST COUNTRY HITS, MAMMOTH COLLECTION NO. 27
  THE BIG THREE MUSIC CORPORATION   04.95

SIXTY-FIVE WORLD FAMOUS WALTZES
  THE BIG THREE MUSIC CORPORATION   02.50

SIXTY-ONE EASY TO PLAY HYMNS FOR PIANO
  ASHLEY DEALERS SERVICE, INC.   1.50

SIXTY-ONE GEMS FOR PIANO
  ASHLEY DEALERS SERVICE, INC.   WFS NO. 61   2.95
                                                 M-D
SLAVIC PIANO MUSIC, VOL. 1
  C. F. PETERS CORPORATION   ZM1325   2.50
                                                 M-D
SLAVIC PIANO MUSIC, VOL. 2
  C. F. PETERS CORPORATION   ZM1326   2.50

SOLO TIME U. S. A. --100--
  CARL FISCHER, INC.   O 4469   1.75

SONATA ALBUM
  BELWIN-MILLS PUBLISHING CORPORATION   3.00

SONATA ALBUM --2 VOLS. BOUND TOGETHER--. CLOTH-BOUND
  C. F. PETERS CORPORATION   12.50

SONATES PRECLASSIQUES CHOISIES
  EDWARD B. MARKS MUSIC CORPORATION   04.00

SONATINA ALBUM--ABRIDGED--15 FAVORITE SONATINAS
  G. SCHIRMER, INC.   L265   1.50
                                                 E-M
SONATINA ALBUM, VOL. 1
  C. F. PETERS CORPORATION   1233A   3.00
                                                 E-M
SONATINA ALBUM, VOL. 2
  C. F. PETERS CORPORATION   1233B   3.00

SONATINA AND SALON ALBUM--15 SONATINAS AND 15 MISCELLANEOUS
PIECES
  G. SCHIRMER, INC.   L305   1.75
                                                 E
SONATINEN VORSTUFE --PREPARATORY SONATINA ALBUM--, VOL. 1
  C. F. PETERS CORPORATION   3195A   3.00
                                                 E
SONATINEN VORSTUFE --PREPARATORY SONATINA ALBUM--, VOL. 2
  C. F. PETERS CORPORATION   3195B   3.00

SONG OF NORWAY
  CHAPPELL AND COMPANY, INC.   536003   1.95

SONGS FROM 'THE WORLD IS A GHETTO'
  THE BIG THREE MUSIC CORPORATION   03.50

SONGS OF HOPE AND INSPIRATION
  THE BIG THREE MUSIC CORPORATION   01.50

SONGS OF THE SPIRIT - EASY HYMN ARRANGEMENTS FOR PIANO
  LORENZ PUBLISHING COMPANY   2.00

SPAIN ON PARADE
  EDWARD B. MARKS MUSIC CORPORATION   01.50

SPANISH AND LATIN AMERICAN SONGS AND DANCES
  MUSIC SALES CORPORATION   020093   2.95
                                                 1
SPIELBUCHLEIN FUR DEN ERSTEN ANFANG
  SCHOTT   2696   1.75

SPIRIT FILLED SONGS
  MEL BAY PUBLICATIONS, INC.   1.50

STAR - EASY PIANO
  WARNER BROTHERS PUBLISHERS   1.95

SUCCESSFUL PIANO SOLOS--SUITABLE FOR TEACHING, RECITAL AND
GENERAL USE
  G. SCHIRMER, INC.   1.75

SUNDAY PIANO MUSIC
  BOSTON MUSIC COMPANY   1.50

SWEET CHARITY
  THE BIG THREE MUSIC CORPORATION   1.95
                                                 3

SWING LOW, 21 SONGS UND EVERGREENS FUR KLAVIER UND GESANG
SCHOTT   4820   3.75

TEACHER'S CHOICE, BK. 1
SUMMY-BIRCHARD COMPANY   2.00

TEACHER'S CHOICE, BK. 2
SUMMY-BIRCHARD COMPANY   2.00

TEACHER'S CHOICE, BK. 3
SUMMY-BIRCHARD COMPANY   2.00

THEMELODIES FOR PIANO --70--
CARL FISCHER, INC.   O 3204   1925

THEMES FOR THE SABBATH DAY--FOR THE PIANO, REED-ORGAN OR HAMMOND ORGAN
G. SCHIRMER, INC.   1.25

THEMES FROM FAMOUS OVERTURES --100--
CARL FISCHER, INC.   O 3562   1.25

THEY ALL PLAYED RAGTIME
MUSIC SALES CORPORATION   000091   4.45

THOSE WONDERFUL YEARS 1900-1920
THE BIG THREE MUSIC CORPORATION   05.95

TODAY'S BIG COUNTRY HITS, BK. 5
THE BIG THREE MUSIC CORPORATION   02.50

TODAY'S POP SCENE, BK. 1
THE BIG THREE MUSIC CORPORATION   02.95

TOMPALL AND THE GLAZER BROTHERS
THE BIG THREE MUSIC CORPORATION   02.95

TOP HITS OF 1972
THE BIG THREE MUSIC CORPORATION   03.50

TOP TUNES IN BIG NOTES --150--
CARL FISCHER, INC.   O 3818   1.00

TREASURY OF EASY CLASSICS, A   2-3
ASHLEY DEALERS SERVICE, INC.   1.50

TREASURY OF EASY CLASSICS, A   2-3
CENTURY MUSIC PUBLISHING COMPANY, INC.   1.50

TREASURY OF POPULAR CLASSICS
MUSIC SALES CORPORATION   020096   2.95

TREASURY OF THE PIANO SONATA, A
CENTURY MUSIC PUBLISHING COMPANY, INC.   1.50

TUNES YOU LIKE TO PLAY
CENTURY MUSIC PUBLISHING COMPANY, INC.   MPS VOL. 3A   1.95

TUNES YOU LIKE TO PLAY
CENTURY MUSIC PUBLISHING COMPANY, INC.   MPS VOL. 3B   1.95

TWELVE EASY RECREATIONS
THEODORE PRESSER COMPANY   1.75
                   EASY

TWENTIETH CENTURY ERA PIANO MUSIC
MEL BAY PUBLICATIONS, INC.   2.00

TWENTY EASY RECREATIONS
THEODORE PRESSER COMPANY   1.75

TWENTY-ONE BIGGEST HITS OF TODAY
THE BIG THREE MUSIC CORPORATION   02.95

TWO HUNDRED JIGS, REELS AND COUNTRY DANCES
THE BIG THREE MUSIC CORPORATION   01.50

TWO SONGS FOR CHRISTMAS --SILENT NIGHT AND ADESTE FIDELIS--
CARL FISCHER, INC.   P 2239   .50

U.S.A. VOL. 1
MCA MUSIC   2.50

UNSER LIEDERBUCH
SCHOTT   5.00
          3

UNSTERBLICHE OPERETTEN
SCHOTT   1508   3.25
          3

UNSTERBLICHE WALZER, BAND 01
SCHOTT   364   4.00
          3

UNSTERBLICHE WALZER, BAND 02
SCHOTT   367   4.00
          3

UNSTERBLICHE WALZER, BAND 03
SCHOTT   576   4.00

VIRGINALISTS, THE
EDWARD B. MARKS MUSIC CORPORATION   03.50

WALTZ, THE --70--
CARL FISCHER, INC.   O 3631   2.50

WAR- - ALL DAY MUSIC
THE BIG THREE MUSIC CORPORATION   02.95

WEDDING MUSIC FOR PIANO SOLO
ASHLEY DEALERS SERVICE, INC.   WFS NO. 72   2.95

WEDDING SONGS --225--
CARL FISCHER, INC.   O 4133   1.00
          2

WEIHNACHTSLIEDER FUR KLAVIER. DIE 40 WEIHNACHTSLIEDER DES QUEMPAS-HEFTES IN LEICHTEN KLAVIERSATZEN ALTER UND ZEITGENOSSISCHER MEISTER
BARENREITER VERLAG   BA 825
          2-3

WEIHNACHTSLIEDER. KLAVIERAUSGABE ZUM QUEMPAS-BUCH. DIE 97 SCHONSTEN ALTEN UND NEUEN LIEDER FUR DEN WEIHNACHTSFESTKREIS
BARENREITER VERLAG   BA 3500
          1

WESTERN ONTARIO CONSERVATORY OF MUSIC -- GRADED EXAMINATION REPERTOIRE, PIANO, GRADE 1
FREDERICK HARRIS MUSIC COMPANY   1.50
          2

WESTERN ONTARIO CONSERVATORY OF MUSIC -- GRADED EXAMINATION REPERTOIRE, PIANO, GRADE 2
FREDERICK HARRIS MUSIC COMPANY   1.50
          3

WESTERN ONTARIO CONSERVATORY OF MUSIC -- GRADED EXAMINATION REPERTOIRE, PIANO, GRADE 3
FREDERICK HARRIS MUSIC COMPANY   1.60
          4

WESTERN ONTARIO CONSERVATORY OF MUSIC -- GRADED EXAMINATION REPERTOIRE, PIANO, GRADE 4
FREDERICK HARRIS MUSIC COMPANY   1.60
          5

WESTERN ONTARIO CONSERVATORY OF MUSIC -- GRADED EXAMINATION REPERTOIRE, PIANO, GRADE 5
FREDERICK HARRIS MUSIC COMPANY   1.60
          6

WESTERN ONTARIO CONSERVATORY OF MUSIC -- GRADED EXAMINATION REPERTOIRE, PIANO, GRADE 6
FREDERICK HARRIS MUSIC COMPANY   1.90
          7

WESTERN ONTARIO CONSERVATORY OF MUSIC -- GRADED EXAMINATION REPERTOIRE, PIANO, GRADE 7
FREDERICK HARRIS MUSIC COMPANY   2.25
          8

WESTERN ONTARIO CONSERVATORY OF MUSIC -- GRADED EXAMINATION REPERTOIRE, PIANO, GRADE 8
FREDERICK HARRIS MUSIC COMPANY   2.25
          3

WIEN, WIEN NUR DU ALLEIN
SCHOTT   2601   3.75
          E

WILLIS ROADWAY BIG NOTE PIECES
WILLIS MUSIC COMPANY   1.75
          AE

WILLIS ROADWAY PIANO BOOK FOR CHILDREN
WILLIS MUSIC COMPANY   1.75
          AI

WILLIS ROADWAY TO CLASSICS
WILLIS MUSIC COMPANY   1.75

WISH YOU WERE HERE
CHAPPELL AND COMPANY, INC.   6702500   1.95

WIZARD OF OZ, THE
THE BIG THREE MUSIC CORPORATION   1.95

WONDERFUL TOWN
CHAPPELL AND COMPANY, INC.   6742506   1.95

WONDERFUL WORLD OF BROADWAY, BK. 1
CHAPPELL AND COMPANY, INC.   0021501   1.95

WONDERFUL WORLD OF BROADWAY, BK. 2
CHAPPELL AND COMPANY, INC.   0015818   1.95

WONDERFUL WORLD OF BROADWAY, BK. 3
CHAPPELL AND COMPANY, INC.   0017541   1.95

WONDERFUL WORLD OF BROADWAY, BK. 4
CHAPPELL AND COMPANY, INC.   0020321   1.95

WONDERFUL WORLD OF BROADWAY, BK. 5
CHAPPELL AND COMPANY, INC.   0018994   1.95

WORLD FAMOUS MARCH ALBUM
FREDERICK HARRIS MUSIC COMPANY   1.15

WORLD FAMOUS PIANO PIECES
FREDERICK HARRIS MUSIC COMPANY   2.25

WORLD FAMOUS SONGS
THE BIG THREE MUSIC CORPORATION   02.95

WORLD FAMOUS WALTZ ALBUM
FREDERICK HARRIS MUSIC COMPANY   1.50
          AGAY, D.

WORLD OF MODERN PIANO MUSIC, THE.
MCA MUSIC   2.95

WORLD OF OPERA, THE
MUSIC SALES CORPORATION   020018   2.95

YOUR FAVORITE NEGRO SPIRITUALS
SHAWNEE PRESS, INC.   2.00

YOUR FAVORITE NEGRO SPIRITUALS
SHAWNEE PRESS, INC.   2.00

YOUR PIANO PIECES GRADED FOR YOU
WILLIS MUSIC COMPANY   1.50

YOUTH AND BEAUTY--BOOK 4
VOLKWEIN BROS.   01.00

One Piano, Four Hands
(Original and Arranged)

AARON, M.	RIEGGER, W.	EASY	
DANCE OF THE DWARFS			
SHAWNEE PRESS, INC.		HC-5011	.60
AARON, M.			
MICHAEL AARON DUET BOOK			
BELWIN-MILLS PUBLISHING CORPORATION		11009	1.25
AARON, M.			
PIANO DUET BOOK			
BELWIN-MILLS PUBLISHING CORPORATION		11009	1.50
ADAM, A.	KLEINMICHEL		
SI J'ETAIS ROI - OVERTURE			
FRANCO COLOMBO PUBLICATIONS		BA9063	1.00
ADAMS, B.		4	
ALMA MATER			
BELWIN-MILLS PUBLISHING CORPORATION			.60
ADAMS, B.		4	
ALMA MATER			
BELWIN-MILLS PUBLISHING CORPORATION			.60
ADAMS, B.		5	
FASCINATION			
BELWIN-MILLS PUBLISHING CORPORATION			.60
AGAY, D.--ED	AGAY, D.	A	
BROADWAY CLASSICS FOR PIANO DUETS, BK. 1			
WARNER BROTHERS PUBLISHERS		YPL 11	1.50
AGAY, D.--ED	AGAY, D.	B	
BROADWAY CLASSICS FOR PIANO DUETS, BK. 2			
WARNER BROTHERS PUBLISHERS		YPL 11	1.50
AGAY, D.--ED	AGAY, D.	C	
BROADWAY CLASSICS FOR PIANO DUETS, BK. 3			
WARNER BROTHERS PUBLISHERS		YPL 11	1.50
AGAY, D.--ED	AGAY, D.	A	
DUET RECITAL BOOK, BK. 1			
WARNER BROTHERS PUBLISHERS		YPL 6	1.50
AGAY, D.--ED	AGAY, D.	B	
DUET RECITAL BOOK, BK. 2			
WARNER BROTHERS PUBLISHERS		YPL 6	1.50
AGAY, D.--ED	AGAY, D.	C	
DUET RECITAL BOOK, BK. 3			
WARNER BROTHERS PUBLISHERS		YPL 6	1.50
AGAY, D.--ED	AGAY, D.		
FIRST DUETS, THE			
MUSIC SALES CORPORATION		080062	.85
AGAY, D.--ED	AGAY, D.		
HIGHLIGHTS OF FAMILIAR MUSIC FOR PIANO DUET --39 MELODIES IN			
EASY ARRANGEMENTS--			
THEODORE PRESSER COMPANY			2.95
AGAY, D.--ED	AGAY, D.		
JAZZ DUETS			
MUSIC SALES CORPORATION		080059	.85
AGAY, D.--ED	AGAY, D.		
JOY OF PIANO DUETS, THE			
MUSIC SALES CORPORATION		080008	1.75
AGAY, D.--ED	AGAY, D.	C	
SOLO PIECES OF TODAY, BK. 3			
WARNER BROTHERS PUBLISHERS		YPL 7	1.50
AGAY, D.			
DANCE TOCCATA			
SOUTHERN MUSIC COMPANY			1.50
AGUILA--ED	AGUILA		
VILLANCICOS DE ESPANA -- 15 VILLANCICOS WITH SPANISH SUPERLINEAR			
TEXT			
ASSOCIATED MUSIC PUBLISHERS, INC.		UME	1.50
AGUILAR			
PITUSINES -- 4 EASY PIECES			
ASSOCIATED MUSIC PUBLISHERS, INC.		UME	.75
AITKEN, H.			
FOUR PIECES FOR ONE PIANO FOUR HANDS			
ELKAN-VOGEL, INC.			.60
AKIMENKO			
SIX PIECES UKRAINIENNES, OP. 71			
FRANCO COLOMBO PUBLICATIONS		SAL	7.50
ALBENIZ, I.	SAMAZEUILH		
PEPITA JIMENEZ -- INTERLUDE			
ASSOCIATED MUSIC PUBLISHERS, INC.		ESC	1.50
ALBENIZ, I.	MILICI		
SEVILLA			
FRANCO COLOMBO PUBLICATIONS		BA10075	.75
ALBENIZ, I.			
SEVILLA			
EDWARD B. MARKS MUSIC CORPORATION			01.25
ALBENIZ, I.	MILICI		
TANGO			
FRANCO COLOMBO PUBLICATIONS		BA10076	.75
ALETTER, W.		4	
RENDEZVOUS -- INTERMEZZO ROCOCO			
BELWIN-MILLS PUBLISHING CORPORATION			.60
ALETTER	MELVIN, B.	3	
ROCOCO-INTERMEZZO			
PRO-ART PUBLICATIONS, INC.		289	.50
ALFORD, K.	SEARS		
COLONEL BOGEY			
BOOSEY AND HAWKES, INC.			.75
ALKAN			
BOMBARDO-CARILLON			
GERARD BILLAUDOT EDITIONS MUSICALES			3.00
ALKAN			
FINALE			
GERARD BILLAUDOT EDITIONS MUSICALES			2.00
ALKAN			
MARCH, OP. 40 NO. 1			
THE BIG THREE MUSIC CORPORATION			2.00
ALKAN			
MARCH, OP. 40 NO. 2			
GERARD BILLAUDOT EDITIONS MUSICALES			3.00
ALKAN			
MARCH, OP. 40 NO. 3			
GERARD BILLAUDOT EDITIONS MUSICALES			2.50
ALKAN	MOTTA, J. DA		
NEUF PRELUDES, OP. 66			
GERARD BILLAUDOT EDITIONS MUSICALES			6.90
ALT, H.			
SECONDO SCALES			
SUMMY-BIRCHARD COMPANY			1.50
ANDERSON, L.			
BLUE TANGO			
BELWIN-MILLS PUBLISHING CORPORATION		26502	1.00
ANDERSON, L.			
FIDDLE-FADDLE			
BELWIN-MILLS PUBLISHING CORPORATION		26537	1.00
ANDERSON, L.			
PROMENADE			
BELWIN-MILLS PUBLISHING CORPORATION		26517	1.00

ANDERSON, L.			
SARABAND			
BELWIN-MILLS PUBLISHING CORPORATION		26514	1.00
ANDERSON, L. *			
SLEIGH RIDE			
BELWIN-MILLS PUBLISHING CORPORATION		26544	1.00
ANDERSON, L.			
SYNCOPATED CLOCK, THE			
BELWIN-MILLS PUBLISHING CORPORATION		26528	1.00
ANDRE		E-M	
DIVERTIMENTO IN A MINOR			
C. F. PETERS CORPORATION		6059	.90
ANDRIESSEN, J.		E	
KATHENKA'S MUSIC BOOK			
C. F. PETERS CORPORATION		8647	1.25
ANSON, G.		2 1/2	
WHEN THE SUN GOES DOWN			
WILLIS MUSIC COMPANY			.95
ANSON, G.		2	
WHIRLING DERVISH			
WILLIS MUSIC COMPANY			.95
ANTHONY, B. R.		3	
SALUTE TO THE COLORS			
THEODORE PRESSER COMPANY			.60
ANTHONY, G. W.--ED	ANTHONY, G. W.		
YOUR FAVORITE DUETS			
THEODORE PRESSER COMPANY			1.50
ANTIGA			
LET'S PLAY TOGETHER, 3 VOLS. 18 SHORT, EASY AND MELODIOUS			
PIECES, WITH LARGE NOTATION			
DELRIEU ET CIE.			2.50
APPLEBAUM			
MUSICAL MINIATURES			
CHAPPELL AND COMPANY, INC.		0016147	1.00
ARCHER--ED	ARCHER		
TEN FOLK SONGS FOR FOUR HANDS, BK. 1 -- MELODIES TYPICAL OF			
QUEBEC			
ASSOCIATED MUSIC PUBLISHERS, INC.		BER	1.50
ARCHER--ED	ARCHER		
TEN FOLK SONGS FOR FOUR HANDS, BK. 2 -- MELODIES TYPICAL OF NOVA			
SCOTIA			
ASSOCIATED MUSIC PUBLISHERS, INC.		DOB	1.50
ARENSKY, A.	PHILIPP, I.		
SIX CHILDREN'S PIECES, OP. 34			
INTERNATIONAL MUSIC COMPANY			2.00
ARNDT			
NOLA			
SOUTHERN MUSIC COMPANY			1.25
ARNELL		E	
TWO SIMPLE PIANO DUETS			
C. F. PETERS CORPORATION		H725	1.25
ARRIEU			
SUITE POUR MELODYNE			
FRANCO COLOMBO PUBLICATIONS		A123	1.25
AUBEL, D'		2, 3	
MORCEAUX A 4 OU A 3 MAINS			
ALPHONSE LEDUC			
AUBER *		M	
OVERTURES, IN 5 VOLS* VOL. 1			
C. F. PETERS CORPORATION		1950	6.50
AURIC			
OVERTURE FROM THE FIVE BAGATELLES			
HEUGEL ET CIE.			2.05
AURIC			
PETITE MARCHE FROM THE FIVE BAGATELLES			
HEUGEL ET CIE.			1.90
AURIC			
RETRAITE FROM THE FIVE BAGATELLES			
HEUGEL ET CIE.			2.05
AURIC			
REVERIE FROM THE FIVE BAGATELLES			
HEUGEL ET CIE.			1.25
AURIC			
VALSE FROM THE FIVE BAGATELLES			
HEUGEL ET CIE.			1.75
BACH, J.S.			
ADAGIO FROM ORGAN TOCCATA IN C MAJOR			
ELKAN-VOGEL, INC.			.50
BACH, J.S.			
ADAGIO FROM ORGAN TOCCATA IN C MAJOR			
ELKAN-VOGEL, INC.			.50
BACH, J.S.			
ART OF THE FUGUE, THE			
ASSOCIATED MUSIC PUBLISHERS, INC.		BRH	6.75
BACH, J.S. *	LUCKTENBERG *	4	
BACH FOR PIANO ENSEMBLE			
BELWIN-MILLS PUBLISHING CORPORATION		FDL 463	1.75
BACH, J.S.	HIRSCHBERG, D.		
BACH IS FUN			
MUSICORD PUBLICATIONS, INC.			1.25
BACH, J.S.	REGER		
BRANDENBURG CONCERTOS, BK. 1			
INTERNATIONAL MUSIC COMPANY			3.50
BACH, J.S.			
BRANDENBURG CONCERTOS, BK. 1			
EDWIN F. KALMUS		3027	3.50
BACH, J.S.	REGER		
BRANDENBURG CONCERTOS, BK. 2			
INTERNATIONAL MUSIC COMPANY			4.00
BACH, J.S.			
BRANDENBURG CONCERTOS, BK. 2			
EDWIN F. KALMUS		3028	4.00
BACH, J.S.	REGER	D	
BRANDENBURG CONCERTOS, VOL. 1			
C. F. PETERS CORPORATION		3108A	6.00
BACH, J.S.	REGER	D	
BRANDENBURG CONCERTOS, VOL. 2			
C. F. PETERS CORPORATION		3108B	6.00
BACH, J.S.	REGER	D	
BRANDENBURG CONCERTO NO. 1 IN F			
C. F. PETERS CORPORATION		3108AA	2.00
BACH, J.S.	REGER	D	
BRANDENBURG CONCERTO NO. 2 IN F			
C. F. PETERS CORPORATION		3108BB	2.00
BACH, J.S.	REGER	D	
BRANDENBURG CONCERTO NO. 3 IN G			
C. F. PETERS CORPORATION		3108C	2.00
BACH, J.S.	REGER	D	
BRANDENBURG CONCERTO NO. 4 IN G			
C. F. PETERS CORPORATION		3108D	2.00
BACH, J.S.	REGER	D	
BRANDENBURG CONCERTO NO. 5 IN D			
C. F. PETERS CORPORATION		3108E	2.00
BACH, J.S.	REGER	D	
BRANDENBURG CONCERTO NO. 6 IN B FLAT			
C. F. PETERS CORPORATION		3108F	2.00

BACH, J.S.   HUTCHERSON, R.
FIVE BACH DUETS
        BELWIN-MILLS PUBLISHING CORPORATION   11170   1.25
BACH, J.S.   SOLDAN
FOUR DUETS -- URTEXT --
        C. F. PETERS CORPORATION   4465   1.25
BACH, J.S.   REGER
FOUR ORCHESTRAL SUITES
        INTERNATIONAL MUSIC COMPANY   3.00
BACH, J.S. *   M-D
FOUR SUITES, ARR. REGER. COMPLETE
        C. F. PETERS CORPORATION   3181   3.50
BACH, J.S.   SIMKINS   M-D
FUGUE A LA GIGUE --BWV577--
        C. F. PETERS CORPORATION   H1541   1.50
BACH, J.S.   HESS
JESU, JOY OF MAN'S DESIRING
        OXFORD UNIVERSITY PRESS   34.009   1.50
BACH, J.S.   DUCK   M
JESU, MAN'S DESIRE
        C. F. PETERS CORPORATION   H688   1.25
BACH, J.S.   GLEICHAUF   M-D
ORGAN COMPOSITIONS IN 2 VOLS., VOL. 1
        C. F. PETERS CORPORATION   224   6.00
BACH, J.S.   GLEICHAUF   M-D
ORGAN COMPOSITIONS IN 2 VOLS., VOL. 2
        C. F. PETERS CORPORATION   225   6.00
BACH, J.S.   GLEICHAUF
ORGAN WORKS, BK. 1
        INTERNATIONAL MUSIC COMPANY   4.50
BACH, J.S.   GLEICHAUF
ORGAN WORKS, BK. 2
        INTERNATIONAL MUSIC COMPANY   4.50
BACH, J.S.   HOWE
RICERCAR A 6 VOCI --MUSICAL OFFERING--
        C. F. PETERS CORPORATION   219A   1.25
BACH, J.S.   DUCK   M
SHEEP MAY SAFELY GRAZE
        OXFORD UNIVERSITY PRESS   34.002   1.50
BACH, J.S.   DUCK   M
SHEEP THAT SAFELY GRAZE
        C. F. PETERS CORPORATION   H689   1.25
BACH, J.S.   DUCK   M
SLEEPERS, AWAKE
        C. F. PETERS CORPORATION   H690   1.25
BACH, J.S.   COHEN
SLEEPERS, WAKE
        OXFORD UNIVERSITY PRESS   34.023   1.50
BACH, J.S.
SUITES
        EDWIN F. KALMUS   3026   3.00
BACH, J. CHRISTIAN   2
RONDO F-DUR
        SCHOTT   08308 1/2 1.00
BACH, J. CHRISTIAN KUESTER   3
SONATA IN A, OP. 18 NO. 5
        BARENREITER VERLAG   NMA 115
BACH, J. CHRISTIAN KUESTER
SONATA IN A
        INTERNATIONAL MUSIC COMPANY   1.50
BACH, J. CHRISTIAN KUSTER
SONATA IN C
        ASSOCIATED MUSIC PUBLISHERS, INC.   NAG   2.50
BACH, J. CHRISTIAN HOCKNER
SONATA IN C
        ASSOCIATED MUSIC PUBLISHERS, INC.   SIM   2.00
BACH, J. CHRISTIAN KUESTER   3
SONATA IN C
        BARENREITER VERLAG   NMA 4
BACH, J. CHRISTIAN KUSTER
SONATA IN C
        BARENREITER VERLAG   NMA 4   3.50
BACH, J. CHRISTIAN KUESTER
SONATA IN C
        INTERNATIONAL MUSIC COMPANY   1.50
BACHMANN, G.   4
LES SYLPHES, VALSE
        CENTURY MUSIC PUBLISHING COMPANY, INC.   933   .60
BACON, E.
JERICHO FOR TWO PIANOS OR ONE PIANO FOUR HANDS
        AMERICAN MUSIC EDITION   1.50
BACON, E.
RIVER QUEEN FOR TWO PIANOS OR ONE PIANO FOUR HANDS
        AMERICAN MUSIC EDITION   1.50
BACON, E.
SASSAFRAS--LAWSON-GOULD EDITION
        G. SCHIRMER, INC.   1.00
BADINGS   1-2
ARCADIA - HEFT 04, ZEHN KLEINE STUCKE
        SCHOTT   4179   2.00
BADINGS   1-2
ARCADIA - HEFT 05, ZEHN KLEINE STUCKE
        SCHOTT   4180   2.00
BAINES, W.   2 1/2
CAMEL TRAIN -- DESCRIPTIVE
        THEODORE PRESSER COMPANY   .60
BAINES, W.   2 1/2
KING'S REVIEW, THE
        THEODORE PRESSER COMPANY   .60
BAKER, F. T.   3
DANSE ECOSSAISE
        THEODORE PRESSER COMPANY   .75
BALOGH--ED   BALOGH
EIGHTEEN ORIGINAL PIANO DUETS BY BIZET, DVORAK, FAURE, GLIERE,
MUSSORGSKY, RACHMANINOFF, SAINT-SAENS, STRAVINSKY
        G. SCHIRMER, INC.   L1764   2.50
BARBER, S.
SOUVENIRS, OP. 28
        G. SCHIRMER, INC.   3.00
BARLOW
SAD LITTLE SPINNER
        BOOSEY AND HAWKES, INC.   .60
BARTOK   SUCHOFF
BARTOK FOR TWO
        EDWARD B. MARKS MUSIC CORPORATION   01.00
BARTOK
MIRACULOUS MANDARIN
        BOOSEY AND HAWKES, INC.   7.50
BARTOK   SUCHOFF
PIECES AND SUITES
        SOUTHERN MUSIC COMPANY   1.50
BASTIEN
DUETS FOR FUN, BK. 1
        NEIL A. KJOS MUSIC COMPANY   22   1.00
BASTIEN
DUETS FOR FUN, BK. 2
        NEIL A. KJOS MUSIC COMPANY   43   1.25

BATH
CORNISH RHAPSODY
        SOUTHERN MUSIC COMPANY   1.00
BAUER, M.--ED   BAUER, M.
CLASSICS AS DUETS, BK. 1
        ASHLEY DEALERS SERVICE, INC.   1.00
BAUER, M.--ED   BAUER, M.   2A
CLASSICS AS DUETS, BK. 1
        CENTURY MUSIC PUBLISHING COMPANY, INC.   1.00
BAUER, M.--ED   BAUER, M.
CLASSICS AS DUETS, BK. 2
        ASHLEY DEALERS SERVICE, INC.   1.00
BAUER, M.--ED   BAUER, M.   2B-C
CLASSICS AS DUETS, BK. 2
        CENTURY MUSIC PUBLISHING COMPANY, INC.   1.00
BECHTER, K.   2
JOLLY MINSTRELS
        THEODORE PRESSER COMPANY   .60
BECUCCI
SORRISI
        FRANCO COLOMBO PUBLICATIONS   104628   .60
BEEBE
TWENTY FINGERS - DUETS
        PRO-ART PUBLICATIONS, INC.   1062   1.00
BEER, L. J.--ED
EASY PIANO DUETS ARRANGED FROM MUSIC OF THE 17TH AND 18TH
CENTURIES
        THEODORE PRESSER COMPANY   1.60
BEER, L. J.--ED
EASY PIANO DUETS
        UNIVERSAL EDITION   UE 11003 3.75
BEER, L. J.--ED   BEER, L. J.
TUNES FOR FOUR HANDS -- ORIGINAL COMPOSITIONS FROM MOZART TO
SCHUBERT, BK. 1
        THEODORE PRESSER COMPANY   1.50
BEER, L. J.--ED   BEER, L. J.
TUNES FOR FOUR HANDS -- ORIGINAL COMPOSITIONS FROM WEBER TO
REGER, BK. 2
        THEODORE PRESSER COMPANY   2.00
BEESON, J.
ROUND AND ROUND
        OXFORD UNIVERSITY PRESS   93.404   1.50
BEETHOVEN
ALL ORIGINAL COMPOSITIONS, COMPLETE
        INTERNATIONAL MUSIC COMPANY   2.50
BEETHOVEN   CZERNY
BEETHOVEN'S 'ADELAIDE' OP. 176, FOUR HANDS
        MUSICA OBSCURA   2.50
BEETHOVEN   HIRSCHBERG, D.
BEETHOVEN IS FUN
        MUSICORD PUBLICATIONS, INC.   1.25
BEETHOVEN   2
CONGRATULATIONS MINUET
        CENTURY MUSIC PUBLISHING COMPANY, INC.   4044   .60
BEETHOVEN   3
CONTRA DANCE
        THEODORE PRESSER COMPANY   .60
BEETHOVEN   BEER, L. J.
FIFTEEN LITTLE DANCES
        THEODORE PRESSER COMPANY   1.50
BEETHOVEN   BITTNER   E
GERMAN DANCES, ORIGINAL
        C. F. PETERS CORPORATION   4399   1.25
BEETHOVEN   MACGREGOR   2
MARCH FROM 'RUINS OF ATHENS'
        BOSTON MUSIC COMPANY   .60
BEETHOVEN *   E-M
MASTERS FOR THE YOUNG, IN 3 VOLS‡ VOL. 2
        C. F. PETERS CORPORATION   2753   2.00
BEETHOVEN   3
MINUET IN G
        CENTURY MUSIC PUBLISHING COMPANY, INC.   2407   .60
BEETHOVEN   FUSSEL
ORIGINAL COMPOSITIONS FOR PIANO, 4 HANDS
        UNIVERSAL EDITION   13303   2.20
BEETHOVEN   M
ORIGINAL COMPOSITIONS IN 1 VOL.
        C. F. PETERS CORPORATION   285   3.00
BEETHOVEN   M
ORIGINAL COMPOSITIONS IN 2 VOLS., VOL. 1
        C. F. PETERS CORPORATION   285A   2.00
BEETHOVEN   M
ORIGINAL COMPOSITIONS IN 2 VOLS., VOL. 2
        C. F. PETERS CORPORATION   285B   2.00
BEETHOVEN *   M
OVERTURES, IN 5 VOLS‡ VOL. 2
        C. F. PETERS CORPORATION   1951   6.50
BEETHOVEN *   M
PIANOFORTE ALBUM, IN 2 VOLS‡ VOL. 1. ORIGINAL WORKS
        C. F. PETERS CORPORATION   1978A   4.50
BEETHOVEN *   M
PIANOFORTE ALBUM, IN 2 VOLS‡ VOL. 2. ARRANGEMENTS
        C. F. PETERS CORPORATION   1978B   4.50
BEETHOVEN   3
POLONAISE, OP. 42
        THEODORE PRESSER COMPANY   .60
BEETHOVEN   M-D
SEPTET IN E FLAT, OP. 20
        C. F. PETERS CORPORATION   11   2.00
BEETHOVEN   MARCHI, G.
SONATA NO. 07 IN D, OP. 10 NO. 3
        EDIZIONI BERBEN   1315   2.10
BEETHOVEN   2
SONATE FACILE D-DUR OP. 6
        SCHOTT   01048 1/2 1.00
BEETHOVEN
STRING QUARTETS, BK. 1
        ELKAN-VOGEL, INC.   D   6.25
BEETHOVEN
SYMPHONIES, BK. 1--NOS. 1-5
        G. SCHIRMER, INC.   L10   4.00
BEETHOVEN   CASELLA
SYMPHONIES, BK. 1 -- 1-3 --
        FRANCO COLOMBO PUBLICATIONS   ER481   6.00
BEETHOVEN
SYMPHONIES, BK. 2--NOS. 6-9
        G. SCHIRMER, INC.   L11   4.00
BEETHOVEN   CASELLA
SYMPHONIES, BK. 2 -- 4-6 --
        FRANCO COLOMBO PUBLICATIONS   ER482   7.00
BEETHOVEN   CASELLA
SYMPHONIES, BK. 3 -- 7-9 --
        FRANCO COLOMBO PUBLICATIONS   ER483   8.00
BEETHOVEN   M-D
SYMPHONIES IN 2 VOLS., VOL. 1
        C. F. PETERS CORPORATION   9   7.50

BEETHOVEN　　　　　　　　　　　　　　　　　　M-D
SYMPHONIES IN 2 VOLS., VOL. 2
C. F. PETERS CORPORATION　　　　　　10　　7.50
BEETHOVEN
SYMPHONY NO. 05 IN D MINOR, OP. 67
G. SCHIRMER, INC.　　　　　　L285　　1.25
BEETHOVEN　　　　　WALLIS　　　2
THEME FROM THE FIRST MOVEMENT OF THE 'MOONLIGHT SONATA'
BOSTON MUSIC COMPANY　　　　　　　　.60
BEETHOVEN　　　　　KIRCHNER　　　E
TWENTY-THREE DANCES
C. F. PETERS CORPORATION　　　　3530　　2.50
BEHR, F.
SNOW DROPS -- EASY DANCE WITHIN THE COMPASS OF 5 NOTES, OP. 451
NO. 4 -- GALOP
G. SCHIRMER, INC.　　　　　　　　　.50
BELLETTI
SIX LITTLE CHARACTERISTIC PIECES
FRANCO COLOMBO PUBLICATIONS　　BON.1148　　2.25
BELLINI　　　　　TENAGLIA
NORMA - OVERTURE
FRANCO COLOMBO PUBLICATIONS　　97407　　1.00
BELLINI *　　　　　　　　　　M
OVERTURES
C. F. PETERS CORPORATION　　　　141　　6.00
BELLINI *　　　　　TENAGLIA
SELECTED OVERTURES
FRANCO COLOMBO PUBLICATIONS　　129787　　5.00
BELLISARIO, A.
ACQUARIO
EDIZIONI BERBEN　　　　　EB 1788　　3.00
BENJAMIN　　　　　TRIMBLE
JAMAICAN RUMBA
BOOSEY AND HAWKES, INC.　　　　　　.75
BENNETT, R.
CAPRICCIO FOR PIANO DUET
UNIVERSAL EDITION　　　　UE 14645　　4.25
BERENS, H.　　　　　　　　　　E-M
MELODIOUS EXERCISES, OP. 62
C. F. PETERS CORPORATION　　　　3349　　2.50
BERENS, H.
MELODIOUS EXERCISES, OP.62
EDWIN F. KALMUS　　　　　3207　　1.50
BERLIN, B.
OUR FIRST DUETS FOR THE PIANO
FREDERICK HARRIS MUSIC COMPANY　　　.90
BERLIOZ　　　　　　　　　　　M-D
FANTASTIC SYMPHONY, OP. 14
C. F. PETERS CORPORATION　　　　3107A　　6.00
BERLIOZ　　　　　　　　　　　M-D
SYMPHONY 'ROMEO AND JULIET', OP. 17
C. F. PETERS CORPORATION　　　　3107B　　6.00
BERMONT, G.　　　　KING, S.　　　EASY
WALTZ OF THE TOYS
SHAWNEE PRESS, INC.　　　　HC-5018　　.45
BERNSTEIN, L.　　　FERRANTE *
TONIGHT--FROM 'WEST SIDE STORY'
G. SCHIRMER, INC.　　　　　　　　1.00
BESTHOFF, M.
BASS SINGER, THE
BELWIN-MILLS PUBLISHING CORPORATION　　26531　　.50
BESTHOFF, M.
CHOIR SINGER, THE
BELWIN-MILLS PUBLISHING CORPORATION　　26534　　.50
BESTHOFF, M.
DAINTY TOES
BELWIN-MILLS PUBLISHING CORPORATION　　26535　　.50
BESTHOFF, M.
DANCING DOLORES
BELWIN-MILLS PUBLISHING CORPORATION　　26536　　.50
BESTHOFF, M.
HAPPY HOP TOADS
BELWIN-MILLS PUBLISHING CORPORATION　　26540　　.50
BESTHOFF, M.
ON THE WAY TO DREAMTOWN
BELWIN-MILLS PUBLISHING CORPORATION　　26541　　.50
BESTHOFF, M.
TIRED HIKERS
BELWIN-MILLS PUBLISHING CORPORATION　　26549　　.50
BESTHOFF, M.
YOUNG PIANO PRODIGY, THE
BELWIN-MILLS PUBLISHING CORPORATION　　26550　　.50
BEYER, F.
SERENADE SUR LES DERNIERES VALSES D'UN FOU
FRANCO COLOMBO PUBLICATIONS　　SAL　　2.75
BEYER, F.　　　　　　　　　2
UNE TOUTE PETITE MATINEE
ALPHONSE LEDUC
BEYER, F.　　　　　　　　　3
UNE TOUTE PETITE SOUREE
ALPHONSE LEDUC
BHATIA, V.　　　　　　　　　5-6
INDIAN NURSERY
NOVELLO AND COMPANY, LTD.　　10.0113.02　　2.15
BIEDERMANN, A. J.
LITTLE JEWEL, A--OP. 87
G. SCHIRMER, INC.　　　　　　　.50
BILBRO, M.　　　　　　　　　2
AT THE CIRCUS
WILLIS MUSIC COMPANY　　　　　　.35
BILBRO, M.　　　　　　　　　2
FLAME VINE
WILLIS MUSIC COMPANY　　　　　　.50
BILBRO, M.　　　　　　　　　3
MARCHE MILITAIRE
WILLIS MUSIC COMPANY　　　　　　.60
BILBRO, M.
OUR FIRST DUET BOOK
THEODORE PRESSER COMPANY　　　　1.50
BILLI
CHILDREN'S PARADISE - 6 EASY PIECES
FRANCO COLOMBO PUBLICATIONS　　117450　　1.50
BILLI
FESTA DELLA MAMMA, LA
FRANCO COLOMBO PUBLICATIONS　　FOR.11424　　.75
BILLI
HAPPY AGE, THE - 1. THE LITTLE SHARPSHOOTER
FRANCO COLOMBO PUBLICATIONS　　115503　　.90
BILLI
HAPPY AGE, THE - 2. WITH FULL SAILS
FRANCO COLOMBO PUBLICATIONS　　115504　　.90
BILLI
HAPPY AGE, THE - 3. ON GREEN MEADOWS
FRANCO COLOMBO PUBLICATIONS　　115505　　.90
BILLI
HAPPY AGE, THE - 4. VILLAGE BELLS
FRANCO COLOMBO PUBLICATIONS　　115506　　.75

BILLI
HAPPY AGE, THE - 5. THE FIRST SORROW
FRANCO COLOMBO PUBLICATIONS　　115507　　.75
BILLI
HAPPY AGE, THE - 6. THE LITTLE GEISHA
FRANCO COLOMBO PUBLICATIONS　　115508　　.75
BILLI
PATTAGLIA GIAPPONESE
FRANCO COLOMBO PUBLICATIONS　　FOR.9320　　1.00
BISHOP
FOLK HOLIDAY
CARL FISCHER, INC.　　　　O 4135　　1.50
BISHOP　　　　　BRUGUIER　　　2
HOME SWEET HOME, RONDO
CENTURY MUSIC PUBLISHING COMPANY, INC.　　927　　.60
BITSCH　　　　　　　　　2, 3
PASTOURELLES, BK. 1
ALPHONSE LEDUC
BITSCH　　　　　　　　　3, 4
PASTOURELLES, BK. 2
ALPHONSE LEDUC
BIZET, G.　　　　　　　　　M
ARLESIENNE SUITE NOS. 1 AND 2
C. F. PETERS CORPORATION　　　3199　　5.00
BIZET, G.　　　　　　　　　3
CARMEN, ENTR'ACTE
CENTURY MUSIC PUBLISHING COMPANY, INC.　　3924　　.60
BIZET, G.　　　　　MARLIN　　　3
HABANERA
PRO-ART PUBLICATIONS, INC.　　15　　.60
BIZET, G.　　　　　PHILIPP, I.
JEUX D'ENFANTS, OP. 22
INTERNATIONAL MUSIC COMPANY　　　2.50
BIZET, G.　　　　　　　　　M
JEUX D'ENFANTS --CHILDREN AT PLAY--, OP. 22
C. F. PETERS CORPORATION　　　A5　　3.50
BIZET, G.　　　　　　　　　M
JEUX D'ENFANTS -- CHILDREN AT PLAY--, OP. 22. 6 PIECES
C. F. PETERS CORPORATION　　　9008　　3.50
BIZET, G.
JEUX D'ENFANTS
ELKAN-VOGEL, INC.　　　　　　4.00
BIZET, G.　　　　　VILBAC
L'ARLESIENNE--TWO CONCERT SUITES
G. SCHIRMER, INC.　　　　L358　　1.50
BIZET, G.　　　　　　　　　3
MARSCH AUS, JEUX D'ENFANTS
SCHOTT　　　　09193 1/2　　1.00
BIZET, G. *　　　　　　　　M
OVERTURES, IN 5 VOLS* VOL. 4
C. F. PETERS CORPORATION　　　1953　　6.50
BIZET, G. *　　　　　　　　E-M
PIANOFORTE ALBUM, IN 2 VOLS* VOL. 2
C. F. PETERS CORPORATION　　　H388A　　2.00
BLAKE, D.　　　　　　　　　1
CAMEL, THE
WILLIS MUSIC COMPANY　　　　　.40
BLAKE, D.　　　　　　　　　1
CHRISTMAS CHIMES
WILLIS MUSIC COMPANY　　　　　.40
BLAKE, D.　　　　　　　　　1
CLOCK MAN
WILLIS MUSIC COMPANY　　　　　.35
BLAKE, D.　　　　　　　　　1
DOWN THE RIVER
WILLIS MUSIC COMPANY　　　　　.40
BLAKE, D.　　　　　　　　　1
INDIAN BRAVES
WILLIS MUSIC COMPANY　　　　　.25
BLAKE, D.　　　　　　　　　2
IN SEVILLE
WILLIS MUSIC COMPANY　　　　　.40
BLAKE, D.　　　　　　　　　1
MAID IN GREEN, THE
WILLIS MUSIC COMPANY　　　　　.30
BLAKE, D.　　　　　　　　　1
MY CLOCK
WILLIS MUSIC COMPANY　　　　　.25
BLAKE, D.　　　　　　　　　1
OLD TIME FIDDLER, THE
WILLIS MUSIC COMPANY　　　　　.35
BLAKE, D.　　　　　　　　　1
OUR REPUBLIC
WILLIS MUSIC COMPANY　　　　　.40
BLAKE, D.　　　　　　　　　1
QUICK STEP
WILLIS MUSIC COMPANY　　　　　.35
BLAKE, D.　　　　　　　　　1
ROW, BROTHER, ROW
WILLIS MUSIC COMPANY　　　　　.35
BLAKE, D.　　　　　　　　　1
SPRING DANCE
WILLIS MUSIC COMPANY　　　　　.40
BLAKE, D.　　　　　　　　　1
SUNRISE TRAIL
WILLIS MUSIC COMPANY　　　　　.35
BLAKE, D.　　　　　　　　　2
WOODEN SHOE DANCE
WILLIS MUSIC COMPANY　　　　　.40
BLAKE, J. *
CHRISTMAS CAROLS FOR BEGINNERS
BOOSEY AND HAWKES, INC.　　　　1.00
BLAKE, J.
EIGHT DUETS FOR BEGINNERS
BOOSEY AND HAWKES, INC.　　　　.90
BLAKE
TOUR DE FRANCE
FRANCO COLOMBO PUBLICATIONS　　SAL　　2.50
BLEY
CHAMPAGNE
FRANCO COLOMBO PUBLICATIONS　　SAL　　2.75
BLOOM　　　　　POTTER, H.
SOLILOQUY
BELWIN-MILLS PUBLISHING CORPORATION　　26521　　1.00
BLOOM　　　　　MERKUR
SPRING FEVER
BELWIN-MILLS PUBLISHING CORPORATION　　26525　　1.00
BOCCOSI, BIO
TARANTELLA
EDIZIONI BERBEN　　　　EB 1310　　1.50
BOELLMANN, L.
SCENES DU MOYEN-AGE.. RONDE DE NUIT, LA VEILLEE, LE TOURNOI
FRANCO COLOMBO PUBLICATIONS　　SAL　　2.50
BOELLMANN, L.　　　BENFELD, A.
SUITE GOTHIQUE
ELKAN-VOGEL, INC.　　　　D　　4.60

BOHM   4
    ATTACK OF THE UHLANS
        CENTURY MUSIC PUBLISHING COMPANY, INC.   1041   .60
BOHM
    ATTAQUE DES UHLANS -- GALOP
        G. SCHIRMER, INC.   .75
BOHM   4
    CHARGE OF THE UHLANS, OP. 213
        CENTURY MUSIC PUBLISHING COMPANY, INC.   1641   .60
BOHM   3
    GRACE, LA
        CENTURY MUSIC PUBLISHING COMPANY, INC.   932   .60
BOHM   3
    GRACE WALTZ, OP. 207
        CENTURY MUSIC PUBLISHING COMPANY, INC.   911   .60
BOHM   4
    INTERMEZZO, BIRTHDAY SUITE
        CENTURY MUSIC PUBLISHING COMPANY, INC.   1986   .60
BOHM   4
    MARCH, BIRTHDAY SUITE
        CENTURY MUSIC PUBLISHING COMPANY, INC.   1985   .60
BOHM   3
    SILVER STARS, MAZURKA
        CENTURY MUSIC PUBLISHING COMPANY, INC.   1475   .60
BOND   3
    PERFECT DAY, A
        BOSTON MUSIC COMPANY   .60
BORDES
    EUSKAL HERRIA
        FRANCO COLOMBO PUBLICATIONS   SAL   6.50
BORODIN, A.
    IN THE STEPPES OF CENTRAL ASIA
        BOOSEY AND HAWKES, INC.   2.50
BORODIN, A.   7
    PETITE SUITE
        ALPHONSE LEDUC
BORODIN, A.   SOKOLOFF
    PRINCE IGOR OVERTURE
        BOOSEY AND HAWKES, INC.   3.00
BORODIN, A.   BLUMENFELD
    QUARTET NO. 2
        BOOSEY AND HAWKES, INC.   4.75
BORODIN, A.   7
    SYMPHONIE NO. 01 EN MI FLAT
        ALPHONSE LEDUC
BORODIN, A.   7
    SYMPHONIE NO. 02 EN SI MINEUR
        ALPHONSE LEDUC
BORTKIEWICZ
    RUSSIAN MELODIES AND DANCES, OP. 31
        ASSOCIATED MUSIC PUBLISHERS, INC.   SIM   3.00
BOUD, R.
    CAROLS AND HYMNS FOR FOUR HANDS
        HOPE PUBLISHING COMPANY   2.50
BOUTRY
    TABATIERE A MUSIQUE
        FRANCO COLOMBO PUBLICATIONS   SAL   1.50
BRADLEY, R.--ARR.   BRADLEY, R.   EASY
    BRADLEY'S DOUBLE JOY - PIANO DUETS
        SCREEN GEMS - COLUMBIA PUBLICATIONS   F0241P5   1.75
BRADLEY, R.--ARR.   BRADLEY, R.
    BRADLEY PIANO DUETS - BLESS THE BEASTS AND CHILDREN
        SCREEN GEMS - COLUMBIA PUBLICATIONS   4710BP5   1.00
BRADLEY, R.--ARR.   BRADLEY, R.
    BRADLEY PIANO DUETS - BORN FREE
        SCREEN GEMS - COLUMBIA PUBLICATIONS   4701BP5   1.00
BRADLEY, R.--ARR.   BRADLEY, R.
    BRADLEY PIANO DUETS - BRIAN'S SONG
        SCREEN GEMS - COLUMBIA PUBLICATIONS   5707BP5   1.00
BRADLEY, R.--ARR.   BRADLEY, R.
    BRADLEY PIANO DUETS - CANDY MAN, THE
        SCREEN GEMS - COLUMBIA PUBLICATIONS   0007CP5   1.00
BRADLEY, R.--ARR.   BRADLEY, R.
    BRADLEY PIANO DUETS - IF
        SCREEN GEMS - COLUMBIA PUBLICATIONS   1702IP5   1.00
BRADLEY, R.--ARR.   BRADLEY, R.
    BRADLEY PIANO DUETS - JOY TO THE WORLD
        SCREEN GEMS - COLUMBIA PUBLICATIONS   4703JP5   1.00
BRADLEY, R.--ARR.   BRADLEY, R.
    BRADLEY PIANO DUETS - MISTY
        SCREEN GEMS - COLUMBIA PUBLICATIONS   2728MP5   1.00
BRADLEY, R.--ARR.   BRADLEY, R.
    BRADLEY PIANO DUETS - MORNING AFTER, THE
        SCREEN GEMS - COLUMBIA PUBLICATIONS   4723MP2   1.00
BRADLEY, R.--ARR.   BRADLEY, R.
    BRADLEY PIANO DUETS - WAY WE WERE, THE
        SCREEN GEMS - COLUMBIA PUBLICATIONS   0055WP5   1.00
BRAHAM   LEVINE
    LIMEHOUSE BLUES
        WARNER BROTHERS PUBLISHERS   1.00
BRAHMS *   JONAS
    BRAHMS AND DVORAK FOR TWO
        SUMMY-BIRCHARD COMPANY   1.50
BRAHMS   LEVINE, H.
    BRAHMS DUETS SIMPLIFIED
        ALFRED MUSIC COMPANY   527   1.50
BRAHMS   MARCHI, G.
    DANZA UNGHERESA NO. 5
        EDIZIONI BERBEN   1269   1.20
BRAHMS   LEVINE, H.
    DUETS
        ALFRED MUSIC COMPANY   681   1.50
BRAHMS
    EIGHTEEN LOVE SONG WALTZES, OP. 52 -- SATB AD LIB
        ASSOCIATED MUSIC PUBLISHERS, INC.   SIM   1.75
BRAHMS
    EIGHTEEN LOVE SONG WALTZES, OP. 52 -- SATB AD LIB
        ASSOCIATED MUSIC PUBLISHERS, INC.   BRH   2.25
BRAHMS   MELVIN, B.   4
    FIVE BRAHMS WALTZES - NO. 1 AND 2
        PRO-ART PUBLICATIONS, INC.   301   .60
BRAHMS   MELVIN, B.   4
    FIVE BRAHMS WALTZES - NO. 3
        PRO-ART PUBLICATIONS, INC.   302   .60
BRAHMS   MELVIN, B.   5
    FIVE BRAHMS WALTZES - NO. 4
        PRO-ART PUBLICATIONS, INC.   303   .60
BRAHMS   MELVIN, B.   4
    FIVE BRAHMS WALTZES - NO. 5
        PRO-ART PUBLICATIONS, INC.   304   .60
BRAHMS
    FOURTEEN NEW LOVE SONG WALTZES, OP. 65A -- SATB AD LIB
        ASSOCIATED MUSIC PUBLISHERS, INC.   SIM   2.00
BRAHMS
    FOURTEEN NEW LOVE SONG WALTZES, OP. 65A -- SATB AD LIB
        ASSOCIATED MUSIC PUBLISHERS, INC.   BRH   2.25

BRAHMS   M
    HAYDN VARIATIONS, OP. 56B --ST. ANTHONY CHORALE AND 4
    VARIATIONS--
        C. F. PETERS CORPORATION   7099   1.25
BRAHMS
    HUNGARIAN DANCES, BK. 1--NOS. 01-10
        G. SCHIRMER, INC.   L257   1.50
BRAHMS
    HUNGARIAN DANCES, BK. 1
        ASSOCIATED MUSIC PUBLISHERS, INC.   BRH   2.50
BRAHMS
    HUNGARIAN DANCES, BK. 1
        INTERNATIONAL MUSIC COMPANY   2.50
BRAHMS
    HUNGARIAN DANCES, BK. 2--NOS. 11-21
        G. SCHIRMER, INC.   L439   1.50
BRAHMS
    HUNGARIAN DANCES, BK. 2
        ASSOCIATED MUSIC PUBLISHERS, INC.   BRH   2.50
BRAHMS
    HUNGARIAN DANCES, BK. 2
        INTERNATIONAL MUSIC COMPANY   2.50
BRAHMS
    HUNGARIAN DANCES, NOS. 1-21
        G. HENLE MUSIKVERLAG   68   3.85
BRAHMS   SINGER   M-D
    HUNGARIAN DANCES IN 2 VOLS., VOL.1
        C. F. PETERS CORPORATION   2100A   2.50
BRAHMS   SINGER   M-D
    HUNGARIAN DANCES IN 2 VOLS., VOL.2
        C. F. PETERS CORPORATION   2100B   2.50
BRAHMS   4
    HUNGARIAN DANCE NO. 05
        CENTURY MUSIC PUBLISHING COMPANY, INC.   3739   .60
BRAHMS   WALLIS   4
    HUNGARIAN DANCE NO. 05
        WILLIS MUSIC COMPANY   .40
BRAHMS   5
    HUNGARIAN DANCE NO. 07
        THEODORE PRESSER COMPANY   .50
BRAHMS
    LIEBESLIEDER, OP. 52 -- CHORUS AD LIB
        ASSOCIATED MUSIC PUBLISHERS, INC.   BRH   3.75
BRAHMS   M
    LIEBESLIEDER WALTZES OP. 52 AND NEW LIEBESLIEDER WALTZES OP. 65.
    WITH 1-4 VOICES AD LIB
        C. F. PETERS CORPORATION   3912   3.00
BRAHMS   SCHAUM, J.   3
    PAGANINI VARIATIONS
        BELWIN-MILLS PUBLISHING CORPORATION   .50
BRAHMS *   E-M
    ROMANTIC MASTERS
        C. F. PETERS CORPORATION   4531   2.50
BRAHMS
    SIXTEEN WALTZES, OP. 39
        ASSOCIATED MUSIC PUBLISHERS, INC.   BRH   1.00
BRAHMS   M-D
    SYMPHONIES, COMPLETE IN 2 VOLS., VOL. 1
        C. F. PETERS CORPORATION   3043A   6.50
BRAHMS   M-D
    SYMPHONIES, COMPLETE IN 2 VOLS., VOL. 2
        C. F. PETERS CORPORATION   3043B   6.50
BRAHMS
    SYMPHONIES
        G. SCHIRMER, INC.   L258   5.00
BRAHMS
    SYMPHONY NO. 01 IN C MINOR, OP. 68
        G. SCHIRMER, INC.   L267   2.00
BRAHMS
    SYMPHONY NO. 02 IN D, OP. 73
        G. SCHIRMER, INC.   L268   2.00
BRAHMS
    SYMPHONY NO. 03 IN F, OP. 90
        G. SCHIRMER, INC.   L269   2.00
BRAHMS   4
    UNGARISCHER TANZ NO. 05
        SCHOTT   07575 1/2   1.00
BRAHMS   4
    UNGARISCHER TANZ NO. 06
        SCHOTT   07576 1/2   1.00
BRAHMS   KELLER
    VARIATIONS ON A THEME BY HAYDN, OP. 56B
        ASSOCIATED MUSIC PUBLISHERS, INC.   SIM   2.25
BRAHMS
    VARIATIONS ON A THEME BY ROBERT SCHUMANN, OP. 23
        ASSOCIATED MUSIC PUBLISHERS, INC.   BRH   3.00
BRAHMS
    VARIATIONS ON A THEME BY SCHUMANN, OP. 23
        INTERNATIONAL MUSIC COMPANY   2.00
BRAHMS   D
    VARIATIONS ON A THEME BY SCHUMANN, OP. 23
        C. F. PETERS CORPORATION   3659   1.50
BRAHMS
    WALTZES, OP. 39
        G. HENLE MUSIKVERLAG   67   1.65
BRAHMS
    WALTZES, OP. 39
        INTERNATIONAL MUSIC COMPANY   1.25
BRAHMS
    WALTZES, OP. 39
        G. SCHIRMER, INC.   L1843   1.25
BRAHMS   4
    WALZER OP. 39
        SCHOTT   1656   1.50
BRAHMS   M
    WALZES, OP. 39
        C. F. PETERS CORPORATION   3665   1.50
BREVILLE
    PROCESSION
        FRANCO COLOMBO PUBLICATIONS   SAL   2.00
BROWN, M.
    NURSERY RHYMES DUETS
        BANKS AND SON LTD.   .80
BROWN
    VARIATIONS --IN PREP--
        WESTERN INTERNATIONAL MUSIC, INC.
BRUCKNER   E
    QUADRILLE
        C. F. PETERS CORPORATION   N186   1.25
BRUCKNER   M-D
    SYMPHONIES, COMPLETE IN 3 VOLS., VOL. 1
        C. F. PETERS CORPORATION   3800A   12.00
BRUCKNER   M-D
    SYMPHONIES, COMPLETE IN 3 VOLS., VOL. 2
        C. F. PETERS CORPORATION   3800B   12.00

BRUCKNER	M-D		
SYMPHONIES, COMPLETE IN 3 VOLS., VOL. 3			
C. F. PETERS CORPORATION	3800C	12.00	
BRUCKNER			
SYMPHONY NO. 04			
EDWIN F. KALMUS	3267	5.00	
BRUCKNER			
SYMPHONY NO. 04			
EDWIN F. KALMUS	3268	5.00	
BRUCKNER WERNER			
THREE LITTLE PIECES			
OXFORD UNIVERSITY PRESS	34.712	1.15	
BUGBEE, L. A.	1		
DANCE OF THE FAIRY QUEEN			
THEODORE PRESSER COMPANY		.50	
BULL			
AU CLAIR DE LA LUNE			
FRANCO COLOMBO PUBLICATIONS	SAL	2.50	
BURNAM	1		
CHANGING PLACES			
WILLIS MUSIC COMPANY		.50	
BURNAM	1		
CHIAPANECAS -- MEXICAN HAT DANCE			
WILLIS MUSIC COMPANY		.50	
BURNAM			
DOZEN PIANO DUETS, BK. 1			
WILLIS MUSIC COMPANY		1.00	
BURNAM			
DOZEN PIANO DUETS, BK. 3			
WILLIS MUSIC COMPANY		1.50	
BURNAM			
ROUNDS FOR READING			
WILLIS MUSIC COMPANY		.75	
BURNS	3		
FLOWERS IN THE FOREST			
WILLIS MUSIC COMPANY		.50	
BURROWS	4		
FIRST ROUNDS FOR PIANO -- FOR 2 PLAYERS			
CENTURY MUSIC PUBLISHING COMPANY, INC.	3896	.40	
BURROWS	1		
FIRST ROUNDS			
CENTURY MUSIC PUBLISHING COMPANY, INC.	3896	.60	
BUSCHBAUM *			
KINDER SPIELEN ZUR WEIHNACHT			
BARENREITER VERLAG	EN 803	2.50	
BUSONI	E-M		
FINNISH FOLK TUNES, OP. 27			
C. F. PETERS CORPORATION	2448	2.00	
BUTCHER--ARR. BUTCHER	E		
TWO FRENCH TUNES. PIANO, SIX HANDS			
C. F. PETERS CORPORATION	H306	1.25	
CADMAN, C.	3		
DANCE OF THE SUNBEAMS, OP. 34 NO. 8			
THEODORE PRESSER COMPANY		.75	
CALVINI, A.	3		
CHASE AUX GAZELLES, LA, OP. 11			
THEODORE PRESSER COMPANY		.60	
CAMPBELL			
FIRST PIANO DUETS			
BELWIN-MILLS PUBLISHING CORPORATION		1.25	
CAPLET, D.			
UNE PETITE BARCAROLLE			
ELKAN-VOGEL, INC.	D	2.25	
CAPLET, D.			
UNE PETITE BERCEUSE			
ELKAN-VOGEL, INC.	D	2.25	
CAPLET, D.			
UNE PETITE DANSE SLOVAQUE			
ELKAN-VOGEL, INC.	D	2.25	
CAPLET, D.			
UNE PETITE MARCHE BIEN FRANCAISE			
ELKAN-VOGEL, INC.	D	3.00	
CAPLET, D.			
UN PETIT TRUC EMBETANT			
ELKAN-VOGEL, INC.	D	2.25	
CAPLET, D.			
UN PETIT TRUC EMBETANT			
ELKAN-VOGEL, INC.	D	2.25	
CARMAN			
SABOTIERE			
FRANCO COLOMBO PUBLICATIONS	SAL	2.00	
CASSADO			
NISPANIA			
FRANCO COLOMBO PUBLICATIONS	SAL	8.75	
CHABRIER			
SOUBENIRS DE MUNICH -- FANTASY IN FOR OF QUADRILLES, ON THEMES			
OF R. WAGNER'S TRISTAN AND ISOLDE			
EDITIONS MUSICALES TRANSATLANTIQUES		2.80	
CHADWICK, G.			
CRICKET AND THE BUMBLE BEE			
BELWIN-MILLS PUBLISHING CORPORATION	28075	.50	
CHAMINADE	4		
FLATTERER, THE			
CENTURY MUSIC PUBLISHING COMPANY, INC.	1473	.60	
CHANDLER * MERKUR			
CANADIAN CAPERS			
WARNER BROTHERS PUBLISHERS		1.50	
CHAUNCEY, R. G.	3 1/2		
CARNIVAL DANCERS			
THEODORE PRESSER COMPANY		.60	
CHAUSSON			
STRING QUARTET, OP. 30			
FRANCO COLOMBO PUBLICATIONS	SAL	10.75	
CHAUSSON			
SYMPHONY IN B-FLAT MAJOR			
FRANCO COLOMBO PUBLICATIONS	SAL	10.75	
CHOPIN			
CONCERTOS			
EDWARD B. MARKS MUSIC CORPORATION		07.50	
CHOPIN			
ETUDES			
EDWARD B. MARKS MUSIC CORPORATION		05.00	
CHOPIN			
FANTASIA, BERCEUSE, BARCAROLLE			
EDWARD B. MARKS MUSIC CORPORATION		03.00	
CHOPIN	3		
FUNERAL MARCH			
CENTURY MUSIC PUBLISHING COMPANY, INC.	2024	.60	
CHOPIN			
IMPROMPTUS			
EDWARD B. MARKS MUSIC CORPORATION		03.00	
CHOPIN	3		
MARCH FUNEBRE			
CENTURY MUSIC PUBLISHING COMPANY, INC.	2024	.60	
CHOPIN			
MAZURKAS			
EDWARD B. MARKS MUSIC CORPORATION		07.00	

CHOPIN			
MINOR WORKS			
EDWARD B. MARKS MUSIC CORPORATION		05.00	
CHOPIN			
NOCTURNES			
EDWARD B. MARKS MUSIC CORPORATION		05.00	
CHOPIN WALLIS			
PIANO DUETS			
BOSTON MUSIC COMPANY		1.00	
CHOPIN	3		
POLONAISE, OP. 53			
CENTURY MUSIC PUBLISHING COMPANY, INC.	3923	.60	
CHOPIN			
POLONAISES			
EDWARD B. MARKS MUSIC CORPORATION		05.00	
CHOPIN HORN M-D			
POLONAISES			
C. F. PETERS CORPORATION	1923	3.00	
CHOPIN	4		
POLONAISE IN C MINOR			
CENTURY MUSIC PUBLISHING COMPANY, INC.	3970	.60	
CHOPIN	5		
POLONAISE MILITAIRE			
CENTURY MUSIC PUBLISHING COMPANY, INC.	3740	.60	
CHOPIN			
POLONAISE MILITAIRE			
CARL FISCHER, INC.	P 3068	1.00	
CHOPIN MITTLER 3A			
POLONAISE			
MUSICORD PUBLICATIONS, INC.		.45	
CHOPIN			
PRELUDES			
EDWARD B. MARKS MUSIC CORPORATION		03.00	
CHOPIN			
RONDOS			
EDWARD B. MARKS MUSIC CORPORATION		05.00	
CHOPIN			
SCHERZOS			
EDWARD B. MARKS MUSIC CORPORATION		05.00	
CHOPIN SCHER, W.			
SIX FAMOUS WALTZES			
G. SCHIRMER, INC.		1.50	
CHOPIN			
SONATAS			
EDWARD B. MARKS MUSIC CORPORATION		05.00	
CHOPIN			
SONGS			
EDWARD B. MARKS MUSIC CORPORATION		06.00	
CHOPIN			
VARIATIONS IN D --ON A THEME BY THOMAS MORE			
EDWARD B. MARKS MUSIC CORPORATION		02.00	
CHOPIN M			
WALTZES, EIGHT			
C. F. PETERS CORPORATION	1921	3.00	
CHOPIN M			
WALTZES, THREE			
C. F. PETERS CORPORATION	H1921	2.50	
CHOPIN			
WALTZES			
EDWARD B. MARKS MUSIC CORPORATION		05.00	
CHOPIN			
WORKS FOR PIANO AND ORCHESTRA			
EDWARD B. MARKS MUSIC CORPORATION		07.50	
CHOPIN			
WORKS FOR PIANO AND ORCHESTRA			
EDWARD B. MARKS MUSIC CORPORATION		11.00	
CHRETIEN			
PASTELS, BK. 2			
FRANCO COLOMBO PUBLICATIONS	SAL	3.25	
CLARK, H. A.			
LIVELY DANCE, A			
FREDERICK HARRIS MUSIC COMPANY		.90	
CLARK, M. E.--ED CLARK, M. E. 3			
BELL DOTH TOLL, THE			
BELWIN-MILLS PUBLISHING CORPORATION		.60	
CLARK, M. E.	3		
KOOKABURRA -- AUSTRALIAN ROUND			
BELWIN-MILLS PUBLISHING CORPORATION		.60	
CLEMENTI *	E-M		
PIANOFORTE ALBUM, IN 2 VOLS: VOL. 1			
C. F. PETERS CORPORATION	H378A	2.00	
CLEMENTI ZEITLIN *			
SIX SONATAS			
G. SCHIRMER, INC.	L1796	2.50	
CLEMENTI M			
SONATAS --4--			
C. F. PETERS CORPORATION	1323	3.50	
CLEMENTI			
SONATAS			
EDWIN F. KALMUS	3307	3.50	
CLEMENTI	E-M		
SONATINAS, OP. 36			
C. F. PETERS CORPORATION	1979	3.50	
CLEMENTI SPADA, P.			
TRE PEZZI -- DAI 'DUETTINI'			
EDIZIONI BERBEN	EB 1589	5.70	
COBB			
PIANO DUETS			
SUMMY-BIRCHARD COMPANY		1.75	
COBB	3		
SPIRIT OF THE U. S. A.			
WILLIS MUSIC COMPANY		.50	
COLOMER, B.			
ECOLE PROGRESSIVE FOR PIANO 4 HANDS, BK.1, PREFACE			
GERARD BILLAUDOT EDITIONS MUSICALES		2.50	
COLOMER, B.			
ECOLE PROGRESSIVE FOR PIANO 4 HANDS, BK.2, DO, RE, MI, FA, SOL			
GERARD BILLAUDOT EDITIONS MUSICALES		3.30	
COLOMER, B.			
ECOLE PROGRESSIVE FOR PIANO 4 HANDS, BK.3, VIGNETTES MUSICALES			
GERARD BILLAUDOT EDITIONS MUSICALES		2.45	
COLOMER, B.			
ECOLE PROGRESSIVE FOR PIANO 4 HANDS, BK.4, DE DO A SI			
GERARD BILLAUDOT EDITIONS MUSICALES		3.30	
COLOMER, B.			
ECOLE PROGRESSIVE FOR PIANO 4 HANDS, DEBUT LE PETIT ENSEMBLE			
GERARD BILLAUDOT EDITIONS MUSICALES		3.80	
COOTE	3		
PRINCE IMPERIAL GALOP			
CENTURY MUSIC PUBLISHING COMPANY, INC.	3506	.60	
COSTA	3		
A FRANGESA, MARCH			
CENTURY MUSIC PUBLISHING COMPANY, INC.	921	.60	
COUPERIN, F. HART, F. 4			
SARABANDE			
LEE ROBERTS MUSIC PUBLICATIONS, INC.		.60	

CRAS
  AMES D'ENFANTS
    FRANCO COLOMBO PUBLICATIONS   SAL   5.75
CRAS
  STRING QUARTET NO. 1
    FRANCO COLOMBO PUBLICATIONS   SAL   13.00
CRAWFORD, C.
  ON THE ICE AT SWEET BRIAR
    BELWIN-MILLS PUBLISHING CORPORATION   28076   .75
CRIST, D. W.--ED.   CRIST, D. W.
  DUET MELODIES
    VOLKWEIN BROS.   01.00
CRIST, D. W.--ED.   CRIST, D. W.
  FOUR HAND MELODIES
    VOLKWEIN BROS.   01.00
CROISEZ, A.
  HIRONDELLE ET LE PRISONNIER, L'
    FRANCO COLOMBO PUBLICATIONS   SAL   2.50
CROISEZ, A.
  MARIEE DU MOULIN, LA
    FRANCO COLOMBO PUBLICATIONS   SAL   2.50
CROISEZ, A.
  VOUAGE D'UNE HIRONDELLE
    FRANCO COLOMBO PUBLICATIONS   SAL   2.50
CROSBY, M.   2
  WALTZ OF THE FLOWER FAIRIES
    THEODORE PRESSER COMPANY   .75
CUMMINGS, R.
  HOLIDAYS
    BOOSEY AND HAWKES, INC.   1.00
CURCIO--ED   CURCIO
  YESTERDAY'S PIANO SOLOS
    BOSTON MUSIC COMPANY   2.00
CZERNY
  PETIT PIANIST - LE PETIT WOHLFAHRT-CZERNY, BK. 1
    DELRIEU ET CIE.   2.75
CZERNY
  PETIT PIANIST - LE PETIT WOHLFAHRT-CZERNY, BK. 2
    DELRIEU ET CIE.   3.50
CZERNY   SCHULTZE
  PRACTICAL METHOD FOR PLAYING IN CORRECT TIME, OP. 824
    G. SCHIRMER, INC.   L916   1.50
CZERNY   TOWNSEND
  SONATINE BRILLANTE
    SOUTHERN MUSIC COMPANY   1.50
CZIBULKA   WEYBRIGHT   1 1/2
  AFTER THE DANCE
    BELWIN-MILLS PUBLISHING CORPORATION   .60
D'INDY, V.
  DIPTYQUE MEDITERRANEEN
    FRANCO COLOMBO PUBLICATIONS   SAL   6.50
D'INDY, V.
  POEME DES RIVAGES
    FRANCO COLOMBO PUBLICATIONS   SAL   10.75
D'INDY, V.
  QUESTE DE DIEU, LA
    FRANCO COLOMBO PUBLICATIONS   SAL   5.00
D'INDY, V.
  SEVEN CHANTS DE TERROIR
    FRANCO COLOMBO PUBLICATIONS   SAL   6.50
D'INDY, V.
  SYMPHONY NO. 03
    FRANCO COLOMBO PUBLICATIONS   SAL   10.75
D'INDY, V.
  TRIPLE CONCERTO, OP. 89
    FRANCO COLOMBO PUBLICATIONS   SAL   8.25
DANDELOT
  SIX CHANTS POPULAIRES BRETONS
    FRANCO COLOMBO PUBLICATIONS   SAL   3.00
DARION   AGAY, D.
  IMPOSSIBLE DREAM, THE -- FROM 'MAN OF LA MANCHA'
    SOUTHERN MUSIC COMPANY   1.25
DAVICO
  THREE LITTLE PIECES - BARCAROLLE, SERENADE, PASTORALE
    FRANCO COLOMBO PUBLICATIONS   SAL   3.25
DAVIES, E. J.   3
  IN HANGING GARDENS
    WILLIS MUSIC COMPANY   .50
DAVIS, M.
  ARBUTUS -- INTERMEZZO
    BELWIN-MILLS PUBLISHING CORPORATION   28054   .50
DEBUSSY
  BALLADE
    ELKAN-VOGEL, INC.   J   2.00
DEBUSSY
  BALLET
    ELKAN-VOGEL, INC.   D   3.00
DEBUSSY   CURCIO   4
  CLAIR DE LUNE
    BOSTON MUSIC COMPANY   1.00
DEBUSSY   RICHTER
  CLAIR DE LUNE
    ELKAN-VOGEL, INC.   1.00
DEBUSSY
  CORTEGE -- DE PETITE SUITE
    ELKAN-VOGEL, INC.   D   2.50
DEBUSSY
  DANSES 1. DANSE SACREE, 2. DANSE PROFANE
    ELKAN-VOGEL, INC.   D   4.25
DEBUSSY
  DANSEUSES DE PELPHES
    ELKAN-VOGEL, INC.   D   1.70
DEBUSSY
  DANSE
    ELKAN-VOGEL, INC.   J   3.00
DEBUSSY
  EN BATEAU -- DE PETITE SUITE
    ELKAN-VOGEL, INC.   D   2.75
DEBUSSY
  FIRST ARABESQUE
    ELKAN-VOGEL, INC.   2.50
DEBUSSY
  GIGUES -- IMAGES POUR ORCHESTRE, NO. 1
    ELKAN-VOGEL, INC.   D   3.10
DEBUSSY
  GOLLIWOGG'S CAKE-WALK
    ELKAN-VOGEL, INC.   2.50
DEBUSSY
  JARDINS SOUS LA PLUIE
    ELKAN-VOGEL, INC.   D   4.25
DEBUSSY
  LA CATHEDRALE ENGLOUTIE
    ELKAN-VOGEL, INC.   D   2.50
DEBUSSY
  LA FILLE AUX CHEVEAUX DE LIN
    ELKAN-VOGEL, INC.   D   1.75

DEBUSSY
  LA MER
    ELKAN-VOGEL, INC.   D   7.50
DEBUSSY
  LA PLUS QUE LENTE
    ELKAN-VOGEL, INC.   2.50
DEBUSSY
  LE PETIT NEGRE
    ELKAN-VOGEL, INC.   LED   3.00
DEBUSSY
  MARCHE ECOSSAISE
    ELKAN-VOGEL, INC.   J   3.00
DEBUSSY
  MENUET -- DE PETITE SUITE
    ELKAN-VOGEL, INC.   D   2.25
DEBUSSY
  NOCTURNES -- FETES
    ELKAN-VOGEL, INC.   J   6.00
DEBUSSY
  NOCTURNES -- NAUGES
    ELKAN-VOGEL, INC.   J   3.00
DEBUSSY
  NOCTURNES -- SIRENES
    ELKAN-VOGEL, INC.   J   4.00
DEBUSSY
  PETITE SUITE
    ELKAN-VOGEL, INC.   2.00
DEBUSSY   PHILIPP, I.
  PETITE SUITE
    INTERNATIONAL MUSIC COMPANY   2.00
DEBUSSY
  PETITE SUITE
    EDWARD B. MARKS MUSIC CORPORATION   02.00
DEBUSSY   M
  PETITE SUITE
    C. F. PETERS CORPORATION   7262   2.00
DEBUSSY
  PREMIER QUATUOR
    ELKAN-VOGEL, INC.   D   7.00
DEBUSSY
  PRINTEMPS
    ELKAN-VOGEL, INC.   D   6.25
DEBUSSY
  REVERIE
    ELKAN-VOGEL, INC.   J   3.00
DEBUSSY   STANLEY, A. H.   M
  REVERIE
    THEODORE PRESSER COMPANY   .75
DEBUSSY
  RONDES DE PRINTEMPS
    ELKAN-VOGEL, INC.   D   6.25
DEBUSSY
  SECOND ARABESQUE
    ELKAN-VOGEL, INC.   2.50
DEBUSSY
  SIX EPIGRAPHES ANTIQUES
    ELKAN-VOGEL, INC.   6.00
DEBUSSY
  SUITE BERGAMASQUE -- 1. PRELUDE
    ELKAN-VOGEL, INC.   J   3.50
DEBUSSY
  SUITE BERGAMASQUE -- 2. MENUET
    ELKAN-VOGEL, INC.   J   3.50
DEBUSSY
  SUITE BERGAMASQUE -- 3. CLAIR DE LUNE
    ELKAN-VOGEL, INC.   J   3.50
DEBUSSY   M
  TRIOMPHE DE BACCHUS --ARR. BY COMPOSER--
    C. F. PETERS CORPORATION   C352   3.50
DECOURSEY, R.
  BLUE PAGODA, THE
    G. SCHIRMER, INC.   .60
DEDIEU-PETERS
  THREE LITTLE PRELUDES
    FRANCO COLOMBO PUBLICATIONS   SAL   4.00
DELANNOY
  BOURREE, FROM L'EVENTAIL DE JEANNE
    HEUGEL ET CIE.   2.40
DELIBES, L.
  PIZZICATI--FROM 'SYLVIA'
    G. SCHIRMER, INC.   .50
DELIBES, L.   WEYBRIGHT   3 1/2
  VALSE LENTE FROM ''SYLVIA''
    BELWIN-MILLS PUBLISHING CORPORATION   .60
DELLO JOIO, N.
  CHRISTMAS MUSIC FOR DUET
    EDWARD B. MARKS MUSIC CORPORATION   01.50
DELLO JOIO, N.
  FAMILY ALBUM
    EDWARD B. MARKS MUSIC CORPORATION   01.25
DELLO JOIO, N.
  FIVE IMAGES
    EDWARD B. MARKS MUSIC CORPORATION   01.50
DELVINCOURT   3, 5
  IMAGES POUR LES CONTES DU TEMPS PASSEE
    ALPHONSE LEDUC
DEMARQUEZ
  TWENTY LITTLE PIECES -- SUPPLEMENT NO. 1 TO 'LE PETIT CLAVIER'
  BY MORHANGE-MOTCHANE --
    FRANCO COLOMBO PUBLICATIONS   SAL   4.00
DENZA *   SCARMOLIN   3
  NAPOLI - MEDLEY OF FUNICULI FUNICULA AND O SOLE MIO
    PRO-ART PUBLICATIONS, INC.   41   .60
DEPRET, M.   3
  APRIL SMILES, WALTZ, OP. 11
    CENTURY MUSIC PUBLISHING COMPANY, INC.   922   .60
DESORMES
  EN REVENANT DE LA REVEU
    FRANCO COLOMBO PUBLICATIONS   SAL   2.00
DESSAUX
  DERBY, LE
    FRANCO COLOMBO PUBLICATIONS   SAL   2.00
DESSAUX
  FLEUR D'ETE
    FRANCO COLOMBO PUBLICATIONS   SAL   1.75
DESSAUX   2
  PETIT BAISER, LE, VALSE MIGNONNE
    ALPHONSE LEDUC
DEXTER, H.
  PIANO DUET ALBUM OF BALLET FROM THE 'MELODY-WAY' SERIES
    BELWIN-MILLS PUBLISHING CORPORATION   11375   .60
DE LA TOMBELLE
  FOUR MAINS DU PREMIER AGE, LE - BERCEUSE LOINTAIN
    FRANCO COLOMBO PUBLICATIONS   SAL   1.50
DE LA TOMBELLE
  FOUR MAINS DU PREMIER AGE, LE - DEPART POUR LE CHAMPS
    FRANCO COLOMBO PUBLICATIONS   SAL   1.50

DE LA TOMBELLE
    FOUR MAINS DU PREMIER AGE, LE
        FRANCO COLOMBO PUBLICATIONS   SAL   6.00
DE LULLI, A.   1
    CHOPSTICKS, WALTZ
        CENTURY MUSIC PUBLISHING COMPANY, INC.   924   .60
DIABELLI   STEINER   3
    DIABELLI MARCH
        BELWIN-MILLS PUBLISHING CORPORATION   .60
DIABELLI   KLEE
    FIVE SONATINAS -- OP. 24 NOS. 1-2, OP. 54, 58, 60
        G. SCHIRMER, INC.   L187   1.50
DIABELLI   E-M
    FIVE SONATINAS
        C. F. PETERS CORPORATION   2440 A   2.00
DIABELLI   KRAUSE
    JUGENDFREUDEN, OP. 163
        ASSOCIATED MUSIC PUBLISHERS, INC.   BRH   1.25
DIABELLI   KRAUSE
    MELODIOUS EXERCISES, OP. 149
        ASSOCIATED MUSIC PUBLISHERS, INC.   BRH   1.25
DIABELLI
    MELODIOUS EXERCISES, OP. 149
        UNIVERSAL EDITION   35   2.30
DIABELLI
    MELODIOUS PIECES, OP. 149
        EDWIN F. KALMUS   3402   1.75
DIABELLI   E
    MELODIOUS PIECES, OP. 149
        C. F. PETERS CORPORATION   2442   1.50
DIABELLI   3
    MILITARY RONDO
        CENTURY MUSIC PUBLISHING COMPANY, INC.   1651   .60
DIABELLI   E
    PLEASURES OF YOUTH, OP. 163
        C. F. PETERS CORPORATION   2440B   2.00
DIABELLI
    PLEASURES OF YOUTH, OP. 163
        UNIVERSAL EDITION   115   2.30
DIABELLI   KLEE
    PLEASURES OF YOUTH -- 6 SONATINAS ON 5 NOTES, OP. 163
        G. SCHIRMER, INC.   L188   1.50
DIABELLI
    PLEASURES OF YOUTH
        EDWIN F. KALMUS   3398   2.00
DIABELLI
    RONDEAU MILITAIRE
        EDWIN F. KALMUS   3403   1.25
DIABELLI   3
    RONDO MILITAIRE
        CENTURY MUSIC PUBLISHING COMPANY, INC.   1651   .60
DIABELLI
    SONATAS, OP. 32, 33, 37
        EDWIN F. KALMUS   3400   2.50
DIABELLI
    SONATAS, OP. 38 , 73
        EDWIN F. KALMUS   3401   2.00
DIABELLI   E-M
    SONATAS OP. 38 AND 73
        C. F. PETERS CORPORATION   2443B   3.00
DIABELLI   E
    SONATES MIGNONNES, OP. 150 AND RONDEAU MILITAIRE, OP. 152
        C. F. PETERS CORPORATION   2441   1.50
DIABELLI
    SONATINAS, OP. 150 AND 152
        ASSOCIATED MUSIC PUBLISHERS, INC.   BRH   2.00
DIABELLI
    SONATINAS, OP. 24 NOS. 54, 58, 60
        EDWIN F. KALMUS   3399   1.75
DIABELLI   ELKAN
    THREE SONATAS, OP. 32, 33 AND 37
        SOUTHERN MUSIC COMPANY   1.75
DIABELLI   E-M
    THREE SONATAS
        C. F. PETERS CORPORATION   2443A   2.50
DIABELLI   KLEE
    TWENTY-EIGHT MELODIOUS PIECES ON 5 NOTES, OP. 149
        G. SCHIRMER, INC.   L186   1.25
DICAPUA   WEYBRIGHT   2
    O SOLO MIO
        BELWIN-MILLS PUBLISHING CORPORATION   .60
DICHLER
    KINDERSZENEN -- 1950
        ASSOCIATED MUSIC PUBLISHERS, INC.   DOB   2.00
DICKINSON, P.
    FIVE FORGERIES
        NOVELLO AND COMPANY, LTD.   10.0114.00   1.65
DIENY, A.
    HISTOIRE DE MES POUPEES, L' -- LITTLE SUITE
        ASSOCIATED MUSIC PUBLISHERS, INC.   ESC   2.50
DILLER, A. *   GRADE 2
    DILLER-PAGE CAROL BOOK, THE
        G. SCHIRMER, INC.   1.00
DILLER, A. *   GRADE 2
    DILLER-PAGE CAROL BOOK= 38E
        G. SCHIRMER, INC.   1.00
DILLER, A. *   GRADE 1
    DUET ALBUMS FOR 2 BEGINNERS, BK. 1--THE GREEN DUET BOOK
        G. SCHIRMER, INC.   1.25
DILLER, A. *   GRADE 2
    DUET ALBUMS FOR 2 BEGINNERS, BK. 2--THE BROWN DUET BOOK
        G. SCHIRMER, INC.   1.25
DILLER, A. *   HOERLER   GRADE 1
    FIRST DUET BOOK--GERMAN EDITION
        G. SCHIRMER, INC.   1.25
DILLER, A. *   GRADE 1
    FIRST DUET BOOK--50 DUETS
        G. SCHIRMER, INC.   1.25
DILLER, A. *   GRADE 2
    SECOND DUET BOOK--33 DUETS
        G. SCHIRMER, INC.   1.25
DILLER, A. *   GRADE 3
    THIRD DUET BOOK--23 DUETS
        G. SCHIRMER, INC.   1.25
DITTENHAVER   1
    CHILDREN'S PARADE, THE
        THE WILLIS MUSIC COMPANY   .40
DITTENHAVER
    LET'S PLAY DUETS
        THEODORE PRESSER COMPANY   1.50
DOIGE
    SEVEN UP-DUETS
        PRO-ART PUBLICATIONS, INC.   882   .85
DONALDSON, M.
    PIANO PARTNERS -- THE YOUNG PIANIST OR ADULT BEGINNER WITH THE
    ADVANCED PIANIST
        THEODORE PRESSER COMPANY   .90

DOROLLE, A.
    ANCIENT DANCES, BK. 1
        BOOSEY AND HAWKES, INC.   1.50
DOROLLE, A.
    ANCIENT DANCES, BK. 2
        BOOSEY AND HAWKES, INC.   1.50
DOUGLAS   2
    DAN, THE PICCOLO MAN
        BELWIN-MILLS PUBLISHING CORPORATION   .60
DRESSER   ZEPP   2-3
    ON THE BANKS OF THE WABASH
        PRO-ART PUBLICATIONS, INC.   230   .50
DRIGO, R.   MELVIN, B.   2-3
    LES MILLIONS D'ARLEQUIN
        PRO-ART PUBLICATIONS, INC.   283   .50
DRIGO, R.   WEYBRIGHT   2 1/2
    SERENADE
        BELWIN-MILLS PUBLISHING CORPORATION   .60
DRIGO, R.   4
    SERENADE
        CENTURY MUSIC PUBLISHING COMPANY, INC.   2420   .60
DRING
    THREE FOR TWO
        EDWARD B. MARKS MUSIC CORPORATION   02.25
DRISCHNER   M
    NORDIC CANZONAS, IN 2 VOLS., VOL. 1
        C. F. PETERS CORPORATION   VP155   3.50
DRISCHNER   M
    NORDIC CANZONAS, IN 2 VOLS., VOL. 2
        C. F. PETERS CORPORATION   VP156   3.50
DRISCHNER   M
    PASSACAGLIA IN E --SUN HYMN--
        C. F. PETERS CORPORATION   VP150   3.00
DRUMHELLER   4
    BEAUTIFUL STAR OF HEAVEN
        VOLKWEIN BROS.   .60
DUCELLE, P.
    MUSICAL MEMORIES, OP. 16--LITTLE GAZELLE, NO. 3
        G. SCHIRMER, INC.   .40
DUCELLE, P.
    MUSICAL MEMORIES, OP. 16--QUEEN OF DROWSY-LAND, NO. 2
        G. SCHIRMER, INC.   .45
DUKAS, P.
    SYMPHONY IN C MAJOR
        FRANCO COLOMBO PUBLICATIONS   SAL   10.75
DUNGAN   2
    DANCE OF THE FLEAS
        THEODORE PRESSER COMPANY   .60
DUNGAN   2 1/2
    DANCING ON SKATES
        THEODORE PRESSER COMPANY   .50
DUNGAN   2
    RED-NOSED CLOWN
        THEODORE PRESSER COMPANY   .50
DUPARC, H.
    AUX ETOILES
        FRANCO COLOMBO PUBLICATIONS   SAL   1.75
DUPARC, H.
    LENORE -- SYMPHONIC POEM --
        FRANCO COLOMBO PUBLICATIONS   SAL   4.25
DURAND, A.   4
    VALSE
        WILLIS MUSIC COMPANY   1.00
DURAND DE CRAU
    CLOCHETTES, LES
        FRANCO COLOMBO PUBLICATIONS   SAL   2.50
DURAND DE CRAU
    CORRICOLO, IL
        FRANCO COLOMBO PUBLICATIONS   SAL   2.50
DUSSEK, J. *   KLEINOVA *   2-3
    ALBUM VIERHANDIGER KLAVIERKOMPOSITIONEN ALTER TSCHECHISCHER
    MEISTER, 19 STUCKE
        BARENREITER VERLAG   AP 1715
DUSSEK, J.   POLDI ZEITLIN,
    SONATAS FOR 1 PIANO 4 HANDS
        ELKAN-VOGEL, INC.   2.50
DU PLESIS, H.
    PRELUDE, FUGUE AND POSTLUDE
        NOVELLO AND COMPANY, LTD.   10.0115.09   1.65
DU PLESIS, H.
    SONATA, OP. 10
        NOVELLO AND COMPANY, LTD.   10.0126.04   2.40
DVORAK   CUBR   3-4
    AUS DEM BOHMERWALDE, OP. 68
        BARENREITER VERLAG   AP 269
DVORAK   MARCHI, G.
    DANZA SLAVA, OP. 72, NO. 2
        EDIZIONI BERBEN   1274   1.20
DVORAK
    FIVE BAGATELLES, OP. 47
        ASSOCIATED MUSIC PUBLISHERS, INC.   SIM   1.75
DVORAK
    FROM THE BOHEMIAN FOREST, OP. 68
        ARTIA   1.75
DVORAK   3
    HUMORESKE
        CENTURY MUSIC PUBLISHING COMPANY, INC.   1743   .60
DVORAK   BARTOS, J. *   3-4
    LEGENDEN, OP. 59
        BARENREITER VERLAG   AP 769
DVORAK
    LEGENDS, OP. 59 -- BK. 1
        ASSOCIATED MUSIC PUBLISHERS, INC.   SIM   2.25
DVORAK
    LEGENDS, OP. 59 -- BK. 2
        ASSOCIATED MUSIC PUBLISHERS, INC.   SIM   2.25
DVORAK   M
    POLONAISE IN E FLAT
        C. F. PETERS CORPORATION   2649   2.00
DVORAK   M
    SELECTED PIECES
        C. F. PETERS CORPORATION   4935   6.50
DVORAK   VON DOENHOFF
    SLAVIC DANCES, OP. 46 -- BK. 1, NOS. 1-8
        G. SCHIRMER, INC.   L1028   1.75
DVORAK
    SLAVIC DANCES, OP. 72 -- BK. 2, NOS. 9-16
        G. SCHIRMER, INC.   L1029   2.00
DVORAK
    SLAVONIC DANCES, OP. 46 -- BK. 1
        ASSOCIATED MUSIC PUBLISHERS, INC.   SIM   2.00
DVORAK
    SLAVONIC DANCES, OP. 46 -- BK. 1
        ASSOCIATED MUSIC PUBLISHERS, INC.   SIM   2.00
DVORAK
    SLAVONIC DANCES, OP. 46
        ARTIA   2.75

DVORAK				
SLAVONIC DANCES, OP. 46				
INTERNATIONAL MUSIC COMPANY				3.50
DVORAK				
SLAVONIC DANCES, OP. 72 -- BK. 1				
ASSOCIATED MUSIC PUBLISHERS, INC.			SIM	2.00
DVORAK				
SLAVONIC DANCES, OP. 72 -- BK. 1				
ASSOCIATED MUSIC PUBLISHERS, INC.			SIM	2.00
DVORAK				
SLAVONIC DANCES, OP. 72				
ARTIA				2.75
DVORAK	BURGHAUSER	3-4		
SLAWISCHE TANZE, OP. 46				
BARENREITER VERLAG			AP 770	
DVORAK	HERRMANN	4-5		
SLAWISCHE TANZE OP. 46 -- BK. 1				
SCHOTT			4606	1.75
DVORINE		1		
BUGLES AND DRUMS				
CENTURY MUSIC PUBLISHING COMPANY, INC.			4043	.60
DVORINE		1		
FLAGSHIP, THE				
CENTURY MUSIC PUBLISHING COMPANY, INC.			4042	.60
DVORINE		1-2		
HAYSEED				
CENTURY MUSIC PUBLISHING COMPANY, INC.			4041	.60
DVORKIN, J.		E		
TWO PAIRS OF SHOES				
THEODORE PRESSER COMPANY				.50
ECKARD, W.--ED	ECKARD, W.			
FORTY-FOUR ORIGINAL PIANO DUETS -- HAYDN TO STRAVINSKY				
THEODORE PRESSER COMPANY				2.50
ECKSTEIN--ED.	ECKSTEIN			
MY FAVORITE DUET ALBUM				
CARL FISCHER, INC.			O 3253	2.50
ECKSTEIN				
BY A BLUE LAGOON				
CARL FISCHER, INC.			P 3085	.75
ECKSTEIN		EASY		
DREAMS OF YESTERDAY				
SHAWNEE PRESS, INC.				.45
ECKSTEIN				
FIRST DUET BOOK				
CARL FISCHER, INC.			O 3426	2.00
ECKSTEIN	RIEGGER, W.	EASY		
GINGERSNAP BRIGADE, THE				
SHAWNEE PRESS, INC.			HC-5022	.80
EDWARDS, C.				
ANGELS WE HAVE HEARD ON HIGH				
WILLIS MUSIC COMPANY				.40
EDWARDS, C.				
MARCH OF THE MAGI KINGS				
WILLIS MUSIC COMPANY				.40
EICHHORN, H. W.				
THREE OLE'UNS -- CINDY-SHENANDOAH-JOSHUA				
BRODT MUSIC COMPANY				1.50
EILENBERG				
REGIMENT QUI PASSE, LE				
FRANCO COLOMBO PUBLICATIONS			SAL	2.50
ELGAR, E.	SCHMID			
POMP AND CIRCUMSTANCE MARCH NO . 1 IN D				
BOOSEY AND HAWKES, INC.				1.00
ELGAR, E.				
SERENADE IN E MINOR, OP. 20				
ASSOCIATED MUSIC PUBLISHERS, INC.			BRH	1.75
ELGAR, E.				
VARIATIONS, OP. 36, 'ENIGMA'				
NOVELLO AND COMPANY, LTD.			10.0130.02	4.00
ELLIOTT, R.		6-7		
FANTASIE SUP UN MOTIF DE SARABANDE				
NOVELLO AND COMPANY, LTD.			10.0131.00	.90
EMONTS, F.--ED	EMONTS, F.	1-2		
VIERHANDIGES SPIELBUCH				
SCHOTT			4793	2.25
EMONTS, F.		1-2		
FROHLICHE TANZE NACH ALTEN WEISEN				
SCHOTT			5176	2.25
EMONTS, F.		1-2		
VIERHANDIGES SPIELBUCH FUR DEN ERSTEN ANFANG				
SCHOTT			4793	2.25
ENGELMANN, H. U.		3		
FLOATING ZEPHYRS				
WILLIS MUSIC COMPANY				.50
ENGELMANN, H. U.		3 1/2		
MELODY OF LOVE, OP. 600				
THEODORE PRESSER COMPANY				.75
ENGELMANN, H. U.		3 1/2		
OVER HILL AND DALE, OP. 270				
THEODORE PRESSER COMPANY				.95
ENGELMANN, H. U.		3		
PIFF-PAFF				
THEODORE PRESSER COMPANY				.50
ENGELMANN, H. U.		2 1/2		
UNDER THE MISTLETOE				
THEODORE PRESSER COMPANY				.60
EVANS				
LADY OF SPAIN				
SOUTHERN MUSIC COMPANY				1.25
EVERETT--ED	EVERETT			
DUETS OF WELL-KNOWN TUNES				
BOSTON MUSIC COMPANY				1.00
EVERETT--ED	EVERETT			
DUETS OF WELL-KNOWN TUNES				
BOSTON MUSIC COMPANY				1.00
EWING, M.		3 1/2		
AMID THE TULIPS				
THEODORE PRESSER COMPANY				.50
EZELL, H.				
WE TWO				
BOSTON MUSIC COMPANY				1.25
FALLA, M. DE	SAMAZEUILH			
VIE BREVE, LA -- SPANISH DANCE NO. 1				
ASSOCIATED MUSIC PUBLISHERS, INC.			ESC	3.00
FALLA, M. DE	SAMAZEUILH			
VIE BREVE, LA -- SPANISH DANCE NO. 2				
ASSOCIATED MUSIC PUBLISHERS, INC.			ESC	3.50
FARJALL				
CAUSERIE BADINE				
FRANCO COLOMBO PUBLICATIONS			SAL	2.75
FAURE, G.				
BALLAD				
ELKAN-VOGEL, INC.			HAM	6.00
FAURE, G.	PHILIPP, I.			
DOLLY - SET OF SIX ORIGINAL PIECES, OP. 56				
INTERNATIONAL MUSIC COMPANY				2.50

FAURE, G.				
DOLLY SUITE, OP. 56				
ELKAN-VOGEL, INC.				5.00
FAURE, G.				
MASQUES ET BERGAMASQUES				
ELKAN-VOGEL, INC.			D	5.10
FEDERER, R.		4		
LONELY DANCER				
THEODORE PRESSER COMPANY				.60
FEDERER, R.		3 1/2		
SCARLET CAPE, THE				
THEODORE PRESSER COMPANY				1.00
FELBER, R.		3		
SLOWAKISCHE TANZE, BAND 01				
SCHOTT			1174	1.75
FERGUSON, H.		2		
BRITISH FOLK SONG AND COUNTRY DANCE				
LEE ROBERTS MUSIC PUBLICATIONS, INC.				.75
FERGUSON, H.		2		
TWO FRENCH SONGS AND I SAW THREE SHIPS				
LEE ROBERTS MUSIC PUBLICATIONS, INC.				.85
FERNANDEZ, O.				
FANTASTIC HORSEMAN, THE				
PEER SOUTHERN ORGANIZATION				00.95
FERROUD, P. O.				
MARCHE FROM L'EVENTAIL DE JEANNE				
HEUGEL ET CIE.				2.40
FERROUD, P. O.				
SERENADE				
ELKAN-VOGEL, INC.			D	4.10
FERTE		E		
DIALOGUES. 4 PIECES				
C. F. PETERS CORPORATION			SCH29	2.50
FIALA				
DANCE				
ASSOCIATED MUSIC PUBLISHERS, INC.			BER	.50
FIBICH, Z.		3		
POEM				
CENTURY MUSIC PUBLISHING COMPANY, INC.			3505	.60
FICHANDLER, W.				
SIX DUETS				
CHAPPELL AND COMPANY, INC.			0016683	2.50
FICHER				
TRES DANZAS HEBRAICAS				
PEER SOUTHERN ORGANIZATION				05.00
FIEVET, P.				
JOURNEE D'UN PETIT ENFANT BIEN SAGE, LA -- 6 LITTLE PIECES				
ASSOCIATED MUSIC PUBLISHERS, INC.			ESC	2.00
FINKBEINER				
DREI ZAHME KLAVIERSTUCKCHEN				
ASSOCIATED MUSIC PUBLISHERS, INC.			BRH	1.75
FINKE				
TEN PIECES FOR TEACHERS AND STUDENTS				
ASSOCIATED MUSIC PUBLISHERS, INC.			BRH	1.75
FISCHER		4		
A TRAVERS BOIS				
ALPHONSE LEDUC				
FISCHER		4		
HOP HOP				
ALPHONSE LEDUC				
FISHER, L.		4		
ROBINS RETURN CAPRICE				
CENTURY MUSIC PUBLISHING COMPANY, INC.			2430	.60
FLETCHER, L.		EASY		
WATER SPRITES				
SHAWNEE PRESS, INC.				.40
FLORENTINE, S.		2		
SUNBEAM FROLIC				
WILLIS MUSIC COMPANY				.50
FLOTHIUS		M		
VALSES NOBLES, OP. 52				
C. F. PETERS CORPORATION			D47	1.50
FLOTOW		2		
MARTHA, SELECTIONS				
CENTURY MUSIC PUBLISHING COMPANY, INC.			1472	.60
FLOTOW *		M		
OVERTURES, IN 5 VOLS+ VOL. 5				
C. F. PETERS CORPORATION			1954	6.50
FOERSTER	VESELY	3		
FESTOUVERTURE, OP. 70				
BARENREITER VERLAG			AP 773	
FOERSTER		3		
LEGENDE VOM GLUCK, OP. 83				
BARENREITER VERLAG			AP 774	
FOERSTER		3		
SHAKESPEARE-SUITE, OP. 76				
BARENREITER VERLAG			AP 775	
FOERSTER		3-4		
SINFONIE NO. 02, OP. 29 IN F				
BARENREITER VERLAG			AP 776	
FOSTER		2		
OLD FOLKS AT HOME				
THEODORE PRESSER COMPANY				.50
FRAEMCKE--ED	FRAEMCKE			
POPULAR DUETS, BK. 1 -- 26 PIECES, GRADE 1-2				
G. SCHIRMER, INC.				1.50
FRANCAIX, A.				
NOS VIELLES CHANSONS				
FRANCO COLOMBO PUBLICATIONS			SAL	3.00
FRANCAIX, J.				
NAPOLEON SUITE				
EDITIONS MUSICALES TRANSATLANTIQUES				6.15
FRANCK, C.				
SYMPHONY IN D MINOR				
G. SCHIRMER, INC.			L1571	3.00
FRANCMESNIL				
FOUR LITTLE PIECES - BERCEUSE SOUVENIR				
FRANCO COLOMBO PUBLICATIONS			SAL	1.75
FRANCMESNIL				
FOUR LITTLE PIECES - LE BON VIEUX TEMPS				
FRANCO COLOMBO PUBLICATIONS			SAL	1.75
FRANCMESNIL				
FOUR LITTLE PIECES - PRELUDE				
FRANCO COLOMBO PUBLICATIONS			SAL	1.75
FRANGIPANE--ED	FRANGIPANE	2		
HE'S GOT THE WHOLE WORLD IN HIS HANDS				
CENTURY MUSIC PUBLISHING COMPANY, INC.			4296	.60
FRANGIPANE--ED	FRANGIPANE	2		
WHEN THE SAINTS GO MARCHING IN				
CENTURY MUSIC PUBLISHING COMPANY, INC.			4297	.60
FRANKE, T.		3		
RUSSIAN INTERMEZZO				
THEODORE PRESSER COMPANY				.50
FREY--ED	FREY			
EASY PIANO DUETS				
MUSIC SALES CORPORATION			040007	2.95

FRICKERT--ED	FRICKERT	3	
SONATEN FUR LIEBHABER			
SCHOTT		5460	3.00
FRID, G.			
KERMESSE A CHARLEROI			
PEER SOUTHERN ORGANIZATION			01.50
FRIML, R.		1	
BLUE FAIRY			
WILLIS MUSIC COMPANY			.40
FRIML, R.		1	
CHATTERBOX			
WILLIS MUSIC COMPANY			.40
FRIML, R. *	STEINER		
DONKEY SERENADE, THE--FROM 'THE FIREFLY'			
G. SCHIRMER, INC.			.60
FRIML, R.	STEINER		
GIANNINA MIA--FROM 'THE FIREFLY'			
G. SCHIRMER, INC.			.50
FRIML, R.	STONE		
INDIAN LOVE CALL			
WARNER BROTHERS PUBLISHERS			1.25
FRIML, R.		4	
MOON DAWN			
THEODORE PRESSER COMPANY			.70
FRIML, R.	STEINER		
SYMPATHY--FROM 'THE FIREFLY'			
G. SCHIRMER, INC.			.50
FROST			
TWO PLAYERS AT THE PIANO - BOOK 1			
BOSTON MUSIC COMPANY			1.25
FROST			
TWO PLAYERS AT THE PIANO - PREPARATORY BOOK			
BOSTON MUSIC COMPANY			1.25
FUCHS, R.			
VIENNESE WALTZES, OP. 42 -- BK. 1			
ASSOCIATED MUSIC PUBLISHERS, INC.		SIM	1.50
FUCHS, R.			
VIENNESE WALTZES, OP. 42 -- BK. 2			
ASSOCIATED MUSIC PUBLISHERS, INC.		SIM	1.50
FUCIK			
ENTRANCE OF THE GLADIATORS			
FRANCO COLOMBO PUBLICATIONS		SAL	2.50
FULTON, N.		E	
DANCE MINIATURES, SET 1. MINUET AND HORNPIPE			
OXFORD UNIVERSITY PRESS		34.714	1.40
FULTON, N.		E	
DANCE MINIATURES, SET 2. TARANTELLA AND RHUMBA			
OXFORD UNIVERSITY PRESS		34.715	1.40
FULTON, N.		E	
DANCE MINIATURES, SET 3. POLONAISE AND TANGO			
OXFORD UNIVERSITY PRESS		34.716	1.40
FULTON, N.		E	
DANCE MINIATURES, SET 4. WALTZ AND HUNGARIAN DANCE			
OXFORD UNIVERSITY PRESS		34.717	1.40
GADE, N.	STONE		
JALOUSIE			
WARNER BROTHERS PUBLISHERS			1.25
GALINDO, B.			
SECOND CONCERTO			
EDICIONES MEXICANAS DE MUSICA, A. C.			06.75
GALOS		4	
LAC DE COME, LE			
ALPHONSE LEDUC			
GANNE		4	
CZARINE, LA, MAZURKA RUSSE			
CENTURY MUSIC PUBLISHING COMPANY, INC.		931	.60
GANSCHALS			
FOR THE HOME - BOOK 1			
BOSTON MUSIC COMPANY			1.00
GANSCHALS			
FOR THE HOME - BOOK 2			
BOSTON MUSIC COMPANY			1.00
GANZ		4	
QUI VIVE, GRAND GALOP DE CON.			
CENTURY MUSIC PUBLISHING COMPANY, INC.		943	.60
GANZ			
QUI VIVE, OP. 12 -- GRAND GALOP DE CONCERT			
G. SCHIRMER, INC.			.90
GARROW, L.		2 1/2	
CARIBBEAN MOONLIGHT			
BELWIN-MILLS PUBLISHING CORPORATION			.60
GARROW, L.		2 1/2	
MARCH OF THE ANIMALS			
BELWIN-MILLS PUBLISHING CORPORATION			.60
GARSCIA			
LETS PLAY A PIANO DUET, BK. 1			
EDWARD B. MARKS MUSIC CORPORATION			02.00
GARSCIA			
LETS PLAY A PIANO DUET, BK. 2			
EDWARD B. MARKS MUSIC CORPORATION			02.00
GAUTIER, L.			
SOUS L'OMBRAGE			
FRANCO COLOMBO PUBLICATIONS		SAL	2.00
GAYNOR		2	
MARCH OF THE WEE FOLK			
THEODORE PRESSER COMPANY			.50
GAYNOR			
MINIATURE DUETS --FOR TEACHER AND PUPIL--			
THEODORE PRESSER COMPANY			1.25
GENZMER		M-D	
SONATA IN D			
C. F. PETERS CORPORATION		5020	3.50
GENZMER		2-3	
SPIELBUCH, HEFT 01			
SCHOTT		2758	2.50
GENZMER		2-3	
SPIELBUCH, HEFT 02			
SCHOTT		2759	2.50
GEORGE			
COWBOY SONG			
SUMMY-BIRCHARD COMPANY			.50
GEORGE			
KALEIDOSCOPE -- DUET BOOK 1			
ALFRED MUSIC COMPANY		691	1.25
GEORGE			
KALEIDOSCOPE -- DUET BOOK 2			
ALFRED MUSIC COMPANY		692	1.25
GEORGE			
KALEIDOSCOPE -- DUET BOOK 2			
ALFRED MUSIC COMPANY		698	1.25
GEORGE			
KALEIDOSCOPE -- DUET BOOK 3			
ALFRED MUSIC COMPANY		693	1.25
GEORGE			
KALEIDOSCOPE -- DUET BOOK 4			
ALFRED MUSIC COMPANY		697	1.25

GEORGE			
TWO AT ONE PIANO, BK. 2			
SUMMY-BIRCHARD COMPANY			1.25
GEORGE			
TWO AT ONE PIANO			
SUMMY-BIRCHARD COMPANY			1.25
GEORGE			
TWO AT ONE PIANO			
SUMMY-BIRCHARD COMPANY			1.25
GERMAN, E.		6	
MORRIS DANCE FROM 'HENRY VIII'			
NOVELLO AND COMPANY, LTD.		10.0133.07	1.15
GERMAN, E.			
THREE DANCES FROM 'HENRY VIII'			
NOVELLO AND COMPANY, LTD.		10.0132.09	2.00
GERSHWIN			
CUBAN OVERTURE			
WARNER BROTHERS PUBLISHERS			3.50
GERSHWIN	STONE		
FASCINATING RHYTHM			
WARNER BROTHERS PUBLISHERS			1.50
GERSHWIN			
GEORGE GERSHWIN ALBUM			
CHAPPELL AND COMPANY, INC.		0021659	2.50
GERSHWIN	STONE		
I GOT RHYTHM - IMPROMPTU VARIATIONS			
WARNER BROTHERS PUBLISHERS			1.50
GERSHWIN	LEVINE		
LIZA			
WARNER BROTHERS PUBLISHERS			1.25
GERSHWIN	MERKUR		
MAN I LOVE, THE			
WARNER BROTHERS PUBLISHERS			1.25
GERSHWIN	STONE		
PRELUDES			
WARNER BROTHERS PUBLISHERS			3.00
GERSHWIN	KLARMAN	EASY	
RHAPSODY IN BLUE, THEME FROM			
WARNER BROTHERS PUBLISHERS			1.00
GERSHWIN	LEVINE		
RHAPSODY IN BLUE			
WARNER BROTHERS PUBLISHERS			5.00
GHYS		3	
AMARYLLIS, GAVOTTE DE LOUIS XIII			
CENTURY MUSIC PUBLISHING COMPANY, INC.		1984	.60
GHYS	MELVIN, B.	3	
AMARYLLIS			
PRO-ART PUBLICATIONS, INC.		134	.60
GIASSON, P.			
CARRIAGE TRADE, THE			
GENERAL MUSIC PUBLISHING COMPANY, INC.			2.00
GIASSON, P.			
CARRIAGE TRADE, THE			
GENERAL MUSIC PUBLISHING COMPANY, INC.		45	1.25
GIASSON, P.			
CUCKOO BIRD, THE			
GENERAL MUSIC PUBLISHING COMPANY, INC.			2.00
GIASSON, P.			
CUCKOO BIRD, THE			
GENERAL MUSIC PUBLISHING COMPANY, INC.		46	1.25
GIASSON, P.		MEDIUM	
DANCE OF THE CHRISTMAS GOOSE			
SHAWNEE PRESS, INC.			.45
GIASSON, P.			
GYPSY DREAMS			
SHAWNEE PRESS, INC.			.45
GIASSON, P.			
SLEIGH-BELL SERENADE, A			
GENERAL MUSIC PUBLISHING COMPANY, INC.			1.25
GIASSON, P.			
SLEIGH BELL SERENADE			
GENERAL MUSIC PUBLISHING COMPANY, INC.		411	1.25
GIASSON, P.			
THREE PLAY-FULL DUETS			
GENERAL MUSIC PUBLISHING COMPANY, INC.			2.50
GIASSON, P.			
THREE PLAY-FULL DUETS			
GENERAL MUSIC PUBLISHING COMPANY, INC.		528	2.50
GILLOCK			
YOUNG PIANIST'S FIRST CHRISTMAS			
WILLIS MUSIC COMPANY			1.50
GLIERE		4	
DANCE FROM RED POPPY			
CENTURY MUSIC PUBLISHING COMPANY, INC.		3971	.60
GLOVER, D. *		7	
ADVANCED SACRED MUSIC DUETS			
BELWIN-MILLS PUBLISHING CORPORATION			2.00
GLOVER, D. *		8	
ADVANCED SACRED MUSIC DUETS			
BELWIN-MILLS PUBLISHING CORPORATION			2.00
GLOVER, D.			
BLOW THAT BUGLE			
BELWIN-MILLS PUBLISHING CORPORATION		26532	.60
GLOVER, D.		2 1/2	
CLOWNS			
BELWIN-MILLS PUBLISHING CORPORATION			.60
GLOVER, D.		2 1/2	
DONKEY WITH A SOMBRERO			
BELWIN-MILLS PUBLISHING CORPORATION			.60
GLOVER, D. *		1	
PIANO DUETS			
BELWIN-MILLS PUBLISHING CORPORATION		FDL 461	1.75
GLOVER, D. *		2	
PIANO DUETS			
BELWIN-MILLS PUBLISHING CORPORATION		FDL 462	1.75
GLOVER, D.		3	
PIANO DUETS			
BELWIN-MILLS PUBLISHING CORPORATION		FDL 476	1.75
GLOVER, D.		4	
PIANO DUETS			
BELWIN-MILLS PUBLISHING CORPORATION		FDL 477	2.00
GLOVER, D.		2 1/2	
SLEIGH BELLS			
BELWIN-MILLS PUBLISHING CORPORATION			.60
GLOVER, D.		2 1/2	
WALTZ			
BELWIN-MILLS PUBLISHING CORPORATION			.60
GODARD, B.			
MAZURKA NO. 01			
FRANCO COLOMBO PUBLICATIONS		SAL	2.00
GODARD, B.		4	
SECOND VALSE, OP. 56			
THEODORE PRESSER COMPANY			.70
GODARD, B.			
WALTZ NO. 01			
FRANCO COLOMBO PUBLICATIONS		SAL	2.00

GOEPDELER, R.
   YULETIDE BELLS
      BOSTON MUSIC COMPANY   .60
GOETSCHY
   ESPOIR DU RETOUR, L'
      FRANCO COLOMBO PUBLICATIONS   SAL   2.50
GOLDBERGER, D.--ED. *   GOLDBERGER, D. *
   DUET BOOK 1
      CONSOLIDATED MUSIC PUBLISHERS, INC.   040112   1.25
GOLDBERGER, D.--ED. *   GOLDBERGER, D. *
   DUET BOOK 2
      CONSOLIDATED MUSIC PUBLISHERS, INC.   040113   1.25
GOLDBERGER, D.--ED. *   GOLDBERGER, D. *
   DUET BOOK 3
      CONSOLIDATED MUSIC PUBLISHERS, INC.   040114   1.25
GOLDBERGER, D.--ED. *   GOLDBERGER, D. *
   EASY ORIGINAL PIANO DUETS
      MUSIC SALES CORPORATION   040023   2.95
GOLDBERGER, D.--ED. *   GOLDBERGER, D. *
   FOLK SONG BOOK 1
      CONSOLIDATED MUSIC PUBLISHERS, INC.   040100   1.25
GOLDBERGER, D.--ED. *   GOLDBERGER, D. *
   FOLK SONG BOOK 2
      CONSOLIDATED MUSIC PUBLISHERS, INC.   040101   1.25
GOLDBERGER, D.--ED. *   GOLDBERGER, D. *
   FOLK SONG BOOK 3
      CONSOLIDATED MUSIC PUBLISHERS, INC.   040102   1.25
GOLDEN
   TOYMAKERS DREAM
      EDWARD B. MARKS MUSIC CORPORATION   01.00
GOULD, M.--ED.   GOULD, M.
   STAR DUST
      BELWIN-MILLS PUBLISHING CORPORATION   26547   1.00
GOULD, M.
   PAVANNE
      BELWIN-MILLS PUBLISHING CORPORATION   26516   1.00
GOULD, M.
   SOPHISTICATED LADY
      BELWIN-MILLS PUBLISHING CORPORATION   26523   1.00
GOUNOD, C.   5
   L'ANGELUS, IMPROMPTU
      ALPHONSE LEDUC
GRAHAM, R.   1 1/2
   FIDDLE TUNE
      ELKAN-VOGEL, INC.   .50
GRAHAM, R.   1 1/2 - 2
   MAVERICK TRAIL
      ELKAN-VOGEL, INC.   .50
GRAHAM, R.
   SHEPHERD'S SUITE
      ELKAN-VOGEL, INC.   1.00
GRAINGER, P.--ED   GRAINGER, P.
   COUNTRY GARDENS -- ENGLISH MORRIS-DANCE TUNE
      G. SCHIRMER, INC.   .60
GRAVES, J.   PRELIM.
   SPRINGTIME PIECES
      NOVELLO AND COMPANY, LTD.   10.0134.05   1.25
GRAY, D.
   CLASSICAL DUETS, BK. 1
      BOOSEY AND HAWKES, INC.   1.00
GRAY, D.
   CLASSICAL DUETS, BK. 2
      BOOSEY AND HAWKES, INC.   1.00
GRAY, D.
   OVER THE HILLS
      BOOSEY AND HAWKES, INC.   1.25
GREEN, R.
   HYMN TUNE SET
      AMERICAN MUSIC EDITION   1.50
GREEN, R.
   JIG FOR A CONCERT
      AMERICAN MUSIC EDITION   2.00
GREEN, R.
   SCOTCH, SONATINA
      AMERICAN MUSIC EDITION   1.50
GREENWALD, M.   2
   DANCERS, THE
      CENTURY MUSIC PUBLISHING COMPANY, INC.   3085   .60
GREENWALD, M.   2
   MARCH MILITAIRE
      CENTURY MUSIC PUBLISHING COMPANY, INC.   3083   .60
GREENWALD, M.   1
   PRETTY SUNSHINE, WALTZ
      CENTURY MUSIC PUBLISHING COMPANY, INC.   3081   .60
GREGH
   BERGERETTE, OP. 23
      FRANCO COLOMBO PUBLICATIONS   SAL   2.50
GREGH
   BERGERS WATTEAU, LES OP. 5
      FRANCO COLOMBO PUBLICATIONS   SAL   2.50
GREGH
   COQUETTERIE, OP. 30
      FRANCO COLOMBO PUBLICATIONS   SAL   2.50
GREGH
   JOYEUSE AUBADE, OP. 54
      FRANCO COLOMBO PUBLICATIONS   SAL   2.50
GREGH
   JOYEUX PAPILLONS, LES OP. 8
      FRANCO COLOMBO PUBLICATIONS   SAL   2.50
GREGH
   LONG DE LA ROUTE, LE OP. 89
      FRANCO COLOMBO PUBLICATIONS   SAL   2.50
GREGH
   PASTORALE LOUIS XV, OP. 12
      FRANCO COLOMBO PUBLICATIONS   SAL   2.50
GREGH
   RETOUR DES MOISSONNEURS, LE OP. 13
      FRANCO COLOMBO PUBLICATIONS   SAL   2.50
GREGH
   SALTARELLE, OP. 49
      FRANCO COLOMBO PUBLICATIONS   SAL   2.50
GREIM
   DUTCH DANCE
      CARL FISCHER, INC.   P 2011   .50
GREIM
   TWILIGHT
      CARL FISCHER, INC.   P 2012   .50
GRETCHANINOFF   REHBERG   2
   AUSWAHL -- 12 LEICHTE STUCKE
      SCHOTT   1171   2.25
GRETCHANINOFF   1-2
   IM GRUNEN OP. 99
      SCHOTT   1172   2.25
GRIEG   4
   ANITRA'S DANCE, PEER GYNT
      CENTURY MUSIC PUBLISHING COMPANY, INC.   3738   .60

GRIEG   M
   ARABIAN DANCE, OP. 55 NO. 2 --PEER GYNT SUITE NO. 2--
      C. F. PETERS CORPORATION   2659   2.00
GRIEG   WALLIS   2
   BY THE CRADLE
      BOSTON MUSIC COMPANY   .60
GRIEG
   DANCE OF ANITRA, OP. 46 NO. 3
      G. SCHIRMER, INC.   .40
GRIEG   MARCHI, G.
   DANZA NORVEGESE, OP. 35, NO. 2
      EDIZIONI BERBEN   1272   1.20
GRIEG   JOHNSON   E
   FIVE LYRIC PIECES FROM OP. 12
      C. F. PETERS CORPORATION   H1539A   1.25
GRIEG   E
   IN AUTUMN, CONCERT OVERTURE, OP. 11
      C. F. PETERS CORPORATION   2430   1.25
GRIEG   E
   LULLABY, OP. 38 NO. 1
      C. F. PETERS CORPORATION   2426B   1.25
GRIEG   M-D
   MORNING MOOD --PEER GYNT SUITE NO. 1--
      C. F. PETERS CORPORATION   2432A   .90
GRIEG   M-D
   NORWEGIAN BRIDAL PROCESSION, OP. 19 NO. 2
      C. F. PETERS CORPORATION   2719   1.25
GRIEG   M
   NORWEGIAN DANCE, OP. 35 NO. 2
      C. F. PETERS CORPORATION   2056B   .60
GRIEG   M
   NORWEGIAN DANCE, OP. 35 NO. 3
      G. SCHIRMER, INC.   .40
GRIEG   M
   NORWEGIAN DANCE, OP. 35 NO. 4
      C. F. PETERS CORPORATION   2056D   1.25
GRIEG   M
   NORWEGIAN DANCES, OP. 35 NOS. 1 TO 4
      C. F. PETERS CORPORATION   2056   2.00
GRIFG   3
   NORWEGIAN TANZE OP. 35
      SCHOTT   4695   2.25
GRIEG   OESTERLE
   PEER GYNT SUITE NO. 1, OP. 46--ARRANGED BY COMPOSER
      G. SCHIRMER, INC.   L203   1.25
GRIEG   M-D
   PEER GYNT SUITE NO. 1, OP. 46
      C. F. PETERS CORPORATION   2432   2.00
GRIEG   M-D
   PEER GYNT SUITE NO. 2, OP. 55
      C. F. PETERS CORPORATION   2663   2.00
GRIEG   KLEINMICHEL   D
   PIANO CONCERTO IN A MINOR, OP. 16. ABRIDGED
      C. F. PETERS CORPORATION   2505A   2.00
GRIEG   KLEINMICHEL   D
   PIANO CONCERTO IN A MINOR, OP. 16
      C. F. PETERS CORPORATION   2505   3.50
GRIEG   LEVINE, H.
   PIANO CONCERTO
      ALFRED MUSIC COMPANY   640   2.50
GRIEG   M
   SIGURD JORSALFAR, OP. 56. THREE PIECES
      C. F. PETERS CORPORATION   2697   2.50
GRIEG   M-D
   STRING QUARTET IN G MINOR, OP. 27
      C. F. PETERS CORPORATION   2700   5.00
GRIEG   M-D
   SYMPHONIC DANCES, OP. 64 --ARR. BY COMPOSER--
      C. F. PETERS CORPORATION   2857   3.50
GRIEG   M-D
   SYMPHONIC PIECES, OP. 14
      C. F. PETERS CORPORATION   1439   1.50
GRIEG   WALLIS   3
   THEME FROM THE FIRST MOVEMENT OF PIANO CONCERTO IN A MINOR
      BOSTON MUSIC COMPANY   .60
GRIEG   M
   TRIUMPHAL MARCH, OP. 56 NO. 3
      C. F. PETERS CORPORATION   2698   1.25
GRIEG   M-D
   WALTZ-CAPRICES, OP. 37
      C. F. PETERS CORPORATION   2156   2.00
GRIEG   M
   WEDDING DAY AT TROLDHAUGEN, OP. 65 NO. 6
      C. F. PETERS CORPORATION   3306   1.25
GROTON, F.   3 1/2
   CHARMANTE, OP. 67
      THEODORE PRESSER COMPANY   .75
GURLITT   2
   ALBUMBLAETTER, OP. 147, BK. 1
      SCHOTT   467   2.00
GURLITT   1-2
   DER ANFANGER OP. 211
      SCHOTT   197   2.00
GWYNN, F.   KING, S.   EASY
   PENNY WHISTLE
      SHAWNEE PRESS, INC.   HC-5006   .60
HALL, F.   FRANGIPANE   2
   WEDDING OF THE WINDS
      CENTURY MUSIC PUBLISHING COMPANY, INC.   4318   .60
HANDEL   E
   ARRIVAL OF THE QUEEN OF SHEBA
      C. F. PETERS CORPORATION   H107   1.25
HANDEL   2
   BERUHMTES LARGO
      SCHOTT   02118 1/2   1.00
HANDEL
   ORGAN CONCERTOS, BK. 1
      INTERNATIONAL MUSIC COMPANY   4.50
HANDEL
   ORGAN CONCERTOS, BK. 2
      INTERNATIONAL MUSIC COMPANY   4.50
HANDEL   RICHARDSON
   SUITE FROM THE WATER MUSIC
      OXFORD UNIVERSITY PRESS   34.706   1.00
HANDEL   M-D
   TWELVE ORGAN CONCERTI IN 2 VOLS‡ VOL. 1
      C. F. PETERS CORPORATION   2591A   5.00
HANDEL   M-D
   TWELVE ORGAN CONCERTI IN 2 VOLS‡ VOL. 2
      C. F. PETERS CORPORATION   2591B   5.00
HANDEL   E-M
   WATER MUSIC SUITE
      C. F. PETERS CORPORATION   H46   2.00
HANDEL   E
   ZADOK THE PRIEST‡ THREE PIECES
      C. F. PETERS CORPORATION   H392   1.50

HANSON, H.--ED   HANSON, H.
    NEW SCRIBNER MUSIC LIBRARY, VOL. 06 "PIANO MUSIC FOR TWO"
        CHARLES SCRIBNER'S SONS   3
HARRIS, W. H.
    WINDSOR DANCES, THE
        NOVELLO AND COMPANY, LTD.   10.0135.03   1.40
HARTECK   M
    TWENTY FINGERS --LITTLE MOSAIC--
        C. F. PETERS CORPORATION   Z246   1.50
HAUER, J. M.
    ZWOLFTONSPIEL -- APRIL, 1956
        ASSOCIATED MUSIC PUBLISHERS, INC.   DOB   1.25
HAUER, J.
    LABYRINTH DANCE
        UNIVERSAL EDITION   UE 12166   1.80
HAUPT, L. VON
    VERY FIRST DUETS
        CARL FISCHER, INC.   O 2021   1.00
HAYDN *   E-M
    MASTERS FOR THE YOUNG, IN 3 VOLS# VOL. 1
        C. F. PETERS CORPORATION   2752   2.00
HAYDN   JOHNSON   E
    SERENADE FROM STRING QUARTET, OP. 3 NO. 5
        C. F. PETERS CORPORATION   H808   1.25
HAYDN   ULRICH
    TWELVE SYMPHONIES, BK. 1
        G. SCHIRMER, INC.   L189   3.50
HAYDN   ULRICH
    TWELVE SYMPHONIES, BK. 2
        G. SCHIRMER, INC.   L190   3.50
HAYDN   M
    TWENTY-FOUR SYMPHONIES, IN 4 VOLS# VOL. 1
        C. F. PETERS CORPORATION   186A   5.00
HAYDN   M
    TWENTY-FOUR SYMPHONIES, IN 4 VOLS# VOL. 2
        C. F. PETERS CORPORATION   186B   6.00
HAYDN   M
    TWENTY-FOUR SYMPHONIES, IN 4 VOLS# VOL. 3
        C. F. PETERS CORPORATION   186C   6.50
HAYDN   M
    TWENTY-FOUR SYMPHONIES, IN 4 VOLS# VOL. 4
        C. F. PETERS CORPORATION   186D   6.50
HAYDN   E
    WIENER HOFBALL MINUETS
        C. F. PETERS CORPORATION   N3847   1.50
HEIDEN
    SONATA -- 1946
        ASSOCIATED MUSIC PUBLISHERS, INC.   AMP   2.50
HEINS   LOWENSTEIN   2
    MUSICAL CLOCK
        BOSTON MUSIC COMPANY   .60
HELLER, S.   1-2
    BLACKSMITH, THE
        CENTURY MUSIC PUBLISHING COMPANY, INC. 4161   .60
HELPS
    SACCADE
        C. F. PETERS CORPORATION   66282   1.50
HELYER, M.
    HOLIDAY SKETCHES
        NOVELLO AND COMPANY, LTD.   10.0137.10   4-5
HELYER, M.   1
    NIMBLE FINGERS -- 14 PIECES
        NOVELLO AND COMPANY, LTD.   10.0138.08   1.25
HELYER, M.   2
    TWO'S COMPANY
        NOVELLO AND COMPANY, LTD.   10.0139.06   .90
HENGEVELD   E-M
    TEN FOLK AND RHYTHMICAL DANCES
        C. F. PETERS CORPORATION   B756   1.50
HENGEVELD   E-M
    TEN RHYTHMICAL DANCES
        C. F. PETERS CORPORATION   B444   1.50
HENZE, H.
    ARIOSI FUR SOPRAN, VIOLINE UND GRISSES ORCHESTER, KLAVIERAUSZUG
    MIT UBERL. SOLOSTIM.
        SCHOTT   5454   10.00
HERBERT   STEINER   3
    BECAUSE YOU'RE YOU
        BELWIN-MILLS PUBLISHING CORPORATION   .60
HERBERT   MERKUR
    ITALIAN STREET SONG
        WARNER BROTHERS PUBLISHERS   1.25
HEROLD   5
    ZAMPA, OVERTURE
        CENTURY MUSIC PUBLISHING COMPANY, INC.   949   .60
HEROLD
    ZAMPA OVERTURE
        G. SCHIRMER, INC.   .85
HERRMANN--ED *   HERRMANN *   3-4
    VIERHANDIGES KLAVIERBUCH -- LEICHTE BIS MITTELSCHWERE
    ORIGINALKOMPOSITIONEN VON BEETHOVEN BIS DVORAK
        SCHOTT   4550   4.00
HERRMANN   E
    DANCE SKETCHES
        C. F. PETERS CORPORATION   A95   2.00
HERZER, R.   3
    HOCH HEIDECKSBURG, OP. 10, MARSCH
        SCHOTT   1.50
HESSENBERG, K.   4
    SONATA IN C MINOR, OP. 34 NO. 1
        SCHOTT   1404   2.75
HINDEMITH   4
    SINFONIE "MATHIS DER MALER", 1934 - KLAVIERAUSZUG
        SCHOTT   3286   4.50
HINDEMITH   5
    SINFONIE IN E FLAT, 1940 - KLAVIERAUSZUG
        SCHOTT   3952   6.00
HINDEMITH   5
    SINFONISCHE TANZE, 1937 - KLAVIERAUSZUG
        SCHOTT   3717   4.00
HINDEMITH   5
    SONATA, 1938
        SCHOTT   3716   4.00
HIRSCHBERG, D.--ED   HIRSCHBERG, D.
    I LIKE DUETS, BK. 1
        MUSICORD PUBLICATIONS, INC.   1.00
HIRSCHBERG, D.
    DUETS ARE FUN, BK. 1
        MUSICORD PUBLICATIONS, INC.   1.25
HIRSCHBERG, D.
    DUETS ARE FUN, BK. 2
        MUSICORD PUBLICATIONS, INC.   1.25
HOELLER   E
    LITTLE SONATA IN B MINOR, OP. 32 NO. 1
        C. F. PETERS CORPORATION   5023   3.50

HOELLER   E
    LITTLE SONATA IN G, OP. 32 NO. 2
        C. F. PETERS CORPORATION   5024   3.50
HOKANSON, M.   1
    ON THE MOUNTAIN
        WILLIS MUSIC COMPANY   .50
HOLLANDER
    MY FIRST DUETS, BK. 1
        EDWARD B. MARKS MUSIC CORPORATION   01.00
HONEGGER, A.
    CHANT DE JOIE
        FRANCO COLOMBO PUBLICATIONS   SAL   4.25
HONEGGER, A.
    CHANT DE NIGAMON, LE
        FRANCO COLOMBO PUBLICATIONS   SAL   5.25
HONEGGER, A.
    HORACE VICTORIEUX
        FRANCO COLOMBO PUBLICATIONS   SAL   6.00
HONEGGER, A.
    PACIFIC 231
        FRANCO COLOMBO PUBLICATIONS   SAL   4.25
HONEGGER, A.
    PASTORALE D'ETE
        FRANCO COLOMBO PUBLICATIONS   SAL   4.00
HONEGGER, A.
    PRELUDE POUR LA TEMPETE
        FRANCO COLOMBO PUBLICATIONS   SAL   4.75
HOPKINS, H.   1-2
    FIRST ROSE OF SPRING WALTZ
        CENTURY MUSIC PUBLISHING COMPANY, INC. 2933   .60
HOPKINS, H.   1-2
    GOLDEN BUTTERFLY, MEDITATION
        CENTURY MUSIC PUBLISHING COMPANY, INC. 2935   .60
HOPKINS, H.   1 1/2
    LITTLE BROWN BUNNY
        THEODORE PRESSER COMPANY   .50
HOPKINS, H.   2
    OLD MOSS COVERED CHURCH
        CENTURY MUSIC PUBLISHING COMPANY, INC. 3500   .60
HOPKINS, H.   1-2
    RACING PONIES, CAPRICE
        CENTURY MUSIC PUBLISHING COMPANY, INC. 2936   .60
HOPKINS, H.   1-2
    SI, SENORA, SPANISH SERENADE
        CENTURY MUSIC PUBLISHING COMPANY, INC. 2934   .60
HOPSON, E.   KING, S.   EASY
    MARCH OF THE CANDY SOLDIERS
        SHAWNEE PRESS, INC.   HC-5002   .60
HORDER   E
    THREE OPEN-AIR WALTZES
        C. F. PETERS CORPORATION   H655   1.50
HORDER   E
    TRAVELOGUE, SUITE --7 PIECES--
        C. F. PETERS CORPORATION   H420A   1.50
HORDER   E
    TRAVELOGUE 2, ANOTHER SUITE --7 PIECES--
        C. F. PETERS CORPORATION   H420B   1.50
HOVHANESS, A.   M-D
    CHILD IN THE GARDEN, OP. 168
        C. F. PETERS CORPORATION   6291   .90
HOWELL, C. R.   2
    RUSTIC DANCE
        CENTURY MUSIC PUBLISHING COMPANY, INC. 3501   .60
HOWELL, C. R.   3
    RUSTIC DANCE
        THEODORE PRESSER COMPANY   .60
HOWELL, I.--ED   HOWELL, I.
    LET'S DO DUETS
        PRO-ART PUBLICATIONS, INC.   213   1.25
HOWELL   2 1/2
    INTERMEZZO
        VOLKWEIN BROS.   .40
HUDSON
    COMMENCEMENT GRAND MARCH
        SOUTHERN MUSIC COMPANY   1.00
HUE, G.
    EMOTIONS
        FRANCO COLOMBO PUBLICATIONS   SAL   5.50
HULL, A.
    ANCIENT BALLAD
        OXFORD UNIVERSITY PRESS   93.402   .40
HUMBERT, G.   1
    ZU ZWEIEN
        SCHOTT   3776   2.00
HUMMEL, J. N.   CHAGY   3
    FAVORITLANDLERWALZER
        PRO-ART PUBLICATIONS, INC.   461   .75
HUMMEL, J. N. *   HLUCHAN   2
    WIR SPIELEN VIERHANDIG, 12 LEICHTE VORTRAGSSTUCKE
        BARENREITER VERLAG   AP 1721
HUNTLEY, C.--ED   HUNTLEY, C.
    CHRISTMAS CAROLS FOR CHILDREN
        WILLIS MUSIC COMPANY   1.00
HUSA, K.   3
    ACHT BOHM DUETTE
        SCHOTT   4779   2.50
IBBERSON--ED   IBBERSON
    SACRED CHRISTMAS DUETS
        PRO-ART PUBLICATIONS, INC.   1101   1.00
IBBERSON--ED   IBBERSON
    SECULAR CHRISTMAS DUETS
        PRO-ART PUBLICATIONS, INC.   1102   1.00
IBERT   8
    BALLADE DE LA GEOLE DE READING
        ALPHONSE LEDUC
ILJYNSKY   BRUSSELS, I.   3
    LULLABY
        BOSTON MUSIC COMPANY   .60
INDY, V. D'
    DEUXIEME SYMPHONIE
        ELKAN-VOGEL, INC.   D   5.75
INGHELBRECHT, D. E.
    NURSERY, LA BK. 1 - PETIT PAPA, UNE SOURIS VERTE, EGLOGUE, J'AI
    DESCENDU DANS MON JARDIN, BERCEUSE POUR UNE POUPEE MALADE,
    AM-STRAM-GRAM
        FRANCO COLOMBO PUBLICATIONS   SAL   4.25
INGHELBRECHT, D. E.
    NURSERY, LA BK. 2 - OU VAS-TU P'TITE BOITEUSE, LE PETIT HOMME
    GRIS, BALLADE DU PETIT JEAN, LA BERGERE, LES CHEVALIERS DU ROY, UNE
    POULE SUR UN MUR
        FRANCO COLOMBO PUBLICATIONS   SAL   4.25
INGHELBRECHT, D. E.
    NURSERY, LA BK. 4 - LA BONNE AVENTURE, LA BOULANGERE, A MON BEAU
    CHATEAU, J'AI FAIT VOLER MON CERFVOLANT, LE FORET, SU' L'PONT DU
    NORD
        FRANCO COLOMBO PUBLICATIONS   SAL   4.25

INGHELBRECHT, D. E.
NURSERY, LA BK. 5 - BONJOUR MA TANTE, BIQUETTE, DERRIERE CHEZ
MON PERE, UN OISEAU CHANTAIT, LE PETIT BOSSU, MON ANE MALBROUGH
FRANCO COLOMBO PUBLICATIONS   SAL   4.25
INGHELBRECHT, D. E.
NURSERY, LA BK. 6 - LE PETIT CHRISTOPHE, QUAND J'ETAIS PETITE
FILLE, A MA MAIN DROITE, J'AI UN ROSIER, DANSEZ BAMBOULA, JEAN DE
LA LUNE, LE P'TIT MARCHAND D'ALLUMETTES
FRANCO COLOMBO PUBLICATIONS   4 SAL   4.25
INGHELBRECHT, D. E.
NURSERY, LE
ALPHONSE LEDUC
INGHELBRECHT, D. E.
POUR LE JOUR DE LA PREMIERE NEIGE AU VIEUX JAPON
FRANCO COLOMBO PUBLICATIONS   SAL   5.25
INGHELBRECHT, D. E.
RHAPSODIE DE PRINTEMPS
FRANCO COLOMBO PUBLICATIONS   4 SAL   5.00
IVEY
PARADE
LEE ROBERTS MUSIC PUBLICATIONS, INC.   1.25
JAMBOR, A.
THREE PIECES FOR ONE PIANO FOUR HANDS
ELKAN-VOGEL, INC.   .75
JAMES, M.--ED   JAMES, M.   4
TWO GUITARS
CENTURY MUSIC PUBLISHING COMPANY, INC. 3742   .60
JENKINS, C.   2
DOWN THE SHADY PATH
WILLIS MUSIC COMPANY   .50
JENKINS, C.   2
IN THE MORNING EARLY
WILLIS MUSIC COMPANY   .50
JENKINS, C.   2
STROLLING PLAYERS, THE
WILLIS MUSIC COMPANY   .50
JESSEL
PARADE OF THE WOODEN SOLDIERS
EDWARD B. MARKS MUSIC CORPORATION   01.00
JESSEL
PARADE OF THE WOODEN SOLDIERS
EDWARD B. MARKS MUSIC CORPORATION   01.00
JOHNSON--ED.   JOHNSON   PRIMARY
READ AND PLAY SERIES --PARTNERS--, IN 3 VOLS# VOL. 1. YOU AND I
C. F. PETERS CORPORATION   H883   1.50
JOHNSON--ED.   JOHNSON   ELEM.
READ AND PLAY SERIES --PARTNERS--, IN 3 VOLS# VOL. 2. TOGETHER
WE PLAY
C. F. PETERS CORPORATION   H884   1.50
JOHNSON--ED.   JOHNSON   TRANSITIONAL
READ AND PLAY SERIES --PARTNERS--, IN 3 VOLS# VOL. 3. MELODY
MAKING FOR TWO
C. F. PETERS CORPORATION   H885   2.00
JOHNSON   E
FIFTEEN CAROLS FOR TWO
C. F. PETERS CORPORATION   H881   1.25
JOHNSON   E
FOURTEEN TRADITIONAL AIRS
C. F. PETERS CORPORATION   H649   1.50
JOUBERT, J.
DIVERTIMENTO -- 5 PIECES
NOVELLO AND COMPANY, LTD.   10.0140.10 1.65
JOYNER, B.   1
IN SUNNY FIELDS
WILLIS MUSIC COMPANY   .35
JUST, J. A.   HILLEMANN   2
ZWEI KLEINE SONATEN
SCHOTT   3939   1.75
KABALEVSKY   JOHNSON   E
VARIATIONS IN D, OP. 40 NO. 1. 12 EASY VARIATIONS ON A NURSERY
TUNE
C. F. PETERS CORPORATION   4707C   1.50
KABALEVSKY   MONTANDON   3
WALTZ -- FROM 'THE COMEDIANS'
WILLIS MUSIC COMPANY   .60
KABELAC   3-4
KLEINE SUITE, OP. 42
BARENREITER VERLAG   AP 1711
KADOSA
LITTLE SUITE
KULTURA   2.00
KADOSA
SIX BAGATELLES
KULTURA   1.25
KAESTNER--ED *   KAESTNER *   2
VIERHANDIGES TANZBUCHLEIN
SCHOTT   2695   1.75
KAHL--ED   KAHL
CHRISTMAS DUETS
BOSTON MUSIC COMPANY   1.25
KAHL
DUETS IN 3/4 TIME
BOSTON MUSIC COMPANY   1.00
KAHL
DUETS IN 4/4 TIME
BOSTON MUSIC COMPANY   1.00
KAHN, M.
TWO FOR THE SHOW
BELWIN-MILLS PUBLISHING CORPORATION 11521 1.25
KALLIWODA   E
TWO GRAND WALTZES, OP. 27, 129
C. F. PETERS CORPORATION   1062   2.50
KARP, D.   4
NIGHTFALL
LEE ROBERTS MUSIC PUBLICATIONS, INC.   .85
KARP, D.   5
POLLY WOLLY SWINGS
LEE ROBERTS MUSIC PUBLICATIONS, INC.   .75
KARP   2-3
CLOUDS
PRO-ART PUBLICATIONS, INC.   619   .75
KARP   2
FUN FOR TWO
PRO-ART PUBLICATIONS, INC.   503   .75
KARP   1
HOLIDAY POLKA
PRO-ART PUBLICATIONS, INC.   552   .60
KARP   2-3
ISRAELI DANCE
PRO-ART PUBLICATIONS, INC.   534   .50
KARP   2
ISRAELI DANCE
LEE ROBERTS MUSIC PUBLICATIONS, INC.   .85
KARP
JUNIOR DUETS FOR YOUNG PIANISTS
PRO-ART PUBLICATIONS, INC.   1250   1.25

KARP   2-3
MERRY MERRY DANCE
PRO-ART PUBLICATIONS, INC.   598   .75
KARP   2
PERKY PANDA
PRO-ART PUBLICATIONS, INC.   589   .75
KARP   2-3
ROCKY MOUNTAIN DANCE
PRO-ART PUBLICATIONS, INC.   564   .75
KARP   2-3
TRUMPET PARADE
PRO-ART PUBLICATIONS, INC.   568   .75
KASSCHAU, H.
SUPPLEMENTARY PIANO MATERIAL--ENSEMBLE BOOK FOR 'TEACH ME TO
PLAY'
G. SCHIRMER, INC.   .75
KASSLER, M.
PRELUDE, WALTZ AND MARCH
ELKAN-VOGEL, INC.   .60
KEATS, F.   3
DANCE OF THE ROSEBUDS
THEODORE PRESSER COMPANY   .60
KEENAN
OFF TO DONEGAL AND BACK
CARL FISCHER, INC.   P 2003   .50
KELBERENE--ED   KELBERENE   5
DEEP RIVER
THEODORE PRESSER COMPANY   .50
KELER BELA   4
LUSTSPIEL, OVERTURE
CENTURY MUSIC PUBLISHING COMPANY, INC. 1366   .60
KENNAWAY   M
DOWNSTREAM, INTERRUPTED SERENADE
C. F. PETERS CORPORATION   H418   1.50
KENNEDY, A.   3
STAR OF HOPE
CENTURY MUSIC PUBLISHING COMPANY, INC. 2182   .60
KETTERER, E.
PARTNERS AT THE KEYBOARD
THEODORE PRESSER COMPANY   .90
KETTERER, E.
SHARE THE FUN
THEODORE PRESSER COMPANY   1.25
KETTERER, E.
SIDE BY SIDE
THEODORE PRESSER COMPANY   1.25
KEVAN   1 1/2
OLD FASHIONED BALLROOM, AN
PRO-ART PUBLICATIONS, INC.   56   .50
KEVAN   2-3
PEG LEG PETE
PRO-ART PUBLICATIONS, INC.   253   .60
KEVAN   2
TINKLING BELLS
PRO-ART PUBLICATIONS, INC.   254   .60
KEYS   1
HAPPY AND GAY
WILLIS MUSIC COMPANY   .35
KEYS   1
PARADE
WILLIS MUSIC COMPANY   .35
KEYS   1
PIXIES' DANCE
WILLIS MUSIC COMPANY   .35
KHATCHATURIAN   MONTANDON   3
GALOP -- FROM 'MASQUERADE SUITE'
WILLIS MUSIC COMPANY   .60
KHATCHATURIAN   D
SABRE DANCE --FROM GAYNE--
C. F. PETERS CORPORATION   4740   2.00
KING, S.--ED.   KING, S.
COUNTRY GARDENS
SHAWNEE PRESS, INC.   HC-5004   .60
KING, S.   EASY
SWISS WALTZ
SHAWNEE PRESS, INC.   HC-5013   .60
KINGMAN   GR. 2-3
FOUR MINIATURES FOR YOUNG PIANISTS
WESTERN INTERNATIONAL MUSIC, INC.   AV30   1.00
KING
SONG OF THE ISLANDS
EDWARD B. MARKS MUSIC CORPORATION   01.25
KINKEL, C.   3
MOUNTAIN BELLE, SCHOTTISCHE
CENTURY MUSIC PUBLISHING COMPANY, INC. 2991   .60
KIRBY, M. B.
TRIPPING LIGHTLY
FREDERICK HARRIS MUSIC COMPANY   .60
KOCH, F.   3
GOLLIWOG'S DANCE
BOSTON MUSIC COMPANY   .60
KOCH, F.
IT TAKES TWO - SIX PIECES -
GENERAL MUSIC PUBLISHING COMPANY, INC. 512   2.00
KOCH, F.
IT TAKES TWO - SIX PIECES FOR YOUNG PIANISTS
GENERAL MUSIC PUBLISHING COMPANY, INC.   2.00
KOELLING   4
HUNGARY, RAPSODIE MIGNONNE
THEODORE PRESSER COMPANY   .85
KOHLMANN, C.
TWENTY PIANO DUET TRANSCRIPTIONS OF FAVORITE HYMNS
THEODORE PRESSER COMPANY   1.75
KOHN
CASTLES AND KINGS
CARL FISCHER, INC.   O 4453   1.75
KOLINSKI, M.
FIRST PIANO DUETS--SEVEN EASY PIECES
G. SCHIRMER, INC.   1.00
KOLINSKY
AROUND THE MAYPOLE
CARL FISCHER, INC.   P 2796   .50
KOPELENT   1-2
ZEHN KURZE VORTRAGSSTUCKE FUR DIE JUGEND
BARENREITER VERLAG   AP 184
KORDA--ED   KORDA
AUS OSTERREICH -- AUSTRIAN FOLK DANCES
ASSOCIATED MUSIC PUBLISHERS, INC.   DOB   2.00
KOUNTZ, R.
SLEIGH, THE--A LA RUSSE
G. SCHIRMER, INC.   .60
KRAEHENBUEHL--ARR.   KRAEHENBUEHL
WHEN JOHNNY COMES MARCHING HOME
SUMMY-BIRCHARD COMPANY   .75
KRAEHENBUEHL
BUGLERS' HOLIDAY
SUMMY-BIRCHARD COMPANY   .75

KRAEHENBUEHL
    CHRISTMAS CANZONA
        NATIONAL KEYBOARD ARTS ASSOCIATES   1.25
KRAEHENBUEHL
    GRAND MARCH
        SUMMY-BIRCHARD COMPANY   .50
KRAEHENBUEHL
    LOWLANDS
        NATIONAL KEYBOARD ARTS ASSOCIATES   .90
KRAEHENBUEHL
    RODENT REEL
        SUMMY-BIRCHARD COMPANY   .75
KRAEMER, C.   1
    ETTA WALTZ
        WILLIS MUSIC COMPANY   .35
KRAFT   1
    BALLAD
        CENTURY MUSIC PUBLISHING COMPANY, INC.   3965   .60
KRAFT   1
    FOREST ELF, THE
        CENTURY MUSIC PUBLISHING COMPANY, INC.   3966   .60
KRAFT   1-2
    FUN FOR TWO
        CENTURY MUSIC PUBLISHING COMPANY, INC.   3967   .60
KRAFT   1
    MARCH
        CENTURY MUSIC PUBLISHING COMPANY, INC.   3968   .60
KRAFT   1
    WALTZ
        CENTURY MUSIC PUBLISHING COMPANY, INC.   3969   .60
KREISLER   BERKOWITZ
    CAPRICE VIENNOIS
        CARL FISCHER, INC.   F 2351   1.00
KREISLER   EICHORN
    LIEBESFREUD
        CARL FISCHER, INC.   F 2352   1.00
KREISLER   EICHORN
    LIEBESLEID
        CARL FISCHER, INC.   F 2356   1.00
KREISLER   LAMBERT
    MIDNIGHT BELLS
        CARL FISCHER, INC.   F 2354   1.00
KREISLER   LAMBERT
    RONDINO ON A THEME OF BEETHOVEN
        CARL FISCHER, INC.   F 2353   1.00
KREISLER   EICHORN
    SCHON ROSMARIN
        CARL FISCHER, INC.   F 2357   1.00
KRENEK, E.   4
    HAUSMUSIK. 7 STUCKE FUR DIE 7 TAGE DER WOCHE
        BARENREITER VERLAG   BA 3478
KRENEK, E.
    HAUSMUSIK -- SEVEN PIECES FOR THE SEVEN DAYS OF THE WEEK
        BARENREITER VERLAG   BA 3478   6.00
KRENTZLIN, R.--ED   KRENTZLIN, R.   2
    DIE JUGEND TANZT
        SCHOTT   2502   3.50
KRENTZLIN, R.--ED   KRENTZLIN, R.   1-2
    OPERN UND OPERETTEN, BAND 01
        SCHOTT   2586   3.00
KRENTZLIN, R.--ED   KRENTZLIN, R.   1-2
    OPERN UND OPERETTEN, BAND 02
        SCHOTT   4483   3.00
KRENTZLIN, R.   3
    IN SCHUBERT'S DAY, OP. 109
        THEODORE PRESSER COMPANY   .60
KREUTZ--ED.   KREUTZ   2-3
    ZWEI STUCKE FUR VIER HANDE -- E. W. WOLF -- SONATE, W. F. E.
    BACH -- ANDANTE
        SCHOTT   2571   1.75
KREUTZER--ED   KREUTZER
    LET'S PLAY HYMNS
        CENTURY MUSIC PUBLISHING COMPANY, INC.   1.25
KREUTZ   2
    VERMISCHTE HANDSTUCKE -- 18 JH.
        SCHOTT   2699   1.75
KROGMANN, C. W.
    LITTLE PATRIOT, OP. 15 NO. 7
        G. SCHIRMER, INC.   .50
KROGMANN, C. W.
    LITTLE PRINCE, OP. 15 NO. 1
        G. SCHIRMER, INC.   .50
KROGMANN, C. W.
    MERRY BOBOLINK, OP. 15 NO. 10
        G. SCHIRMER, INC.   .50
KROGMANN, C. W.
    ROBIN'S LULLABY, OP. 15 NO. 12
        G. SCHIRMER, INC.   .50
KROGMANN, C. W.
    ZEPHYRS FROM MELODYLAND, OP. 15
        G. SCHIRMER, INC.   1.50
KUHLAU, F.   M
    SONATINAS, OP. 44, 66
        C. F. PETERS CORPORATION   728   4.00
KURKA, R.
    DANCE SUITE
        WEINTRAUB MUSIC COMPANY   070112   3.50
LABEY *
    FOUR EASY PIECES FOR TEACHER AND STUDENT - POUR MONIQUE, POUR
    ELAINE, POUR PHILIPPE, POUR FRANCE
        FRANCO COLOMBO PUBLICATIONS   SAL   3.25
LABITZKY, A.   3-4
    DREAM OF THE SHEPHERDESS
        CENTURY MUSIC PUBLISHING COMPANY, INC.   2419   .60
LADMIRAULT   6, 7
    RHAPSODIE GAELIQUE
        ALPHONSE LEDUC
LADMIRAULT
    SUITE BRETONNE - CHANSON POPULAIRE
        FRANCO COLOMBO PUBLICATIONS   SAL   3.25
LADMIRAULT
    SUITE BRETONNE - CHANT DES BUGALE-NOZ
        FRANCO COLOMBO PUBLICATIONS   SAL   3.25
LAIS--ED   LAIS   3
    TURKEY IN THE STRAW
        PRO-ART PUBLICATIONS, INC.   38   .60
LAMBERT, C.
    TROIS PIECES NEGRES
        OXFORD UNIVERSITY PRESS   34.001   2.25
LAMBERT   LAIS   3
    WHEN JOHNNY COMES MARCHING HOME
        PRO-ART PUBLICATIONS, INC.   40   .60
LAMONTAINE
    SONATA FOR ONE PIANO FOUR HANDS, OP. 25
        ELKAN-VOGEL, INC.   3.00

LANDRY
    APRES LA MOISSON
        FRANCO COLOMBO PUBLICATIONS   SAL   2.50
LANDRY
    MARCHE PERSANE
        FRANCO COLOMBO PUBLICATIONS   SAL   2.50
LANDRY   4
    MARIEE DE VILLAGE, FETE PAYSANNE, OP. 216
        ALPHONSE LEDUC
LANDRY
    SOUVENIR DU TYROL
        FRANCO COLOMBO PUBLICATIONS   SAL   1.75
LANE, J.--ED   LANE
    JOHN LANE'S EASY PIANO DUETS, NO. 1
        THE BIG THREE MUSIC CORPORATION   1.95
LANE, J.--ED   LANE
    JOHN LANE'S EASY PIANO DUETS, NO. 2
        THE BIG THREE MUSIC CORPORATION   1.95
LANGE, G.   3
    EDELWEISS, PURE AS SNOW
        CENTURY MUSIC PUBLISHING COMPANY, INC.   1468   .60
LANGE, G.   3
    FLOWER SONG, OP. 39
        CENTURY MUSIC PUBLISHING COMPANY, INC.   2418   .60
LANNER, J. F. C.   E-M
    ALBUM --5 WALTZES--
        C. F. PETERS CORPORATION   1382B   3.50
LARA, A.
    GRANADA
        PEER SOUTHERN ORGANIZATION   01.25
LAST, J.   VE
    TWO AND A PIANO, BK. 1
        OXFORD UNIVERSITY PRESS   34.707   1.10
LAST, J.   VE
    TWO AND A PIANO, BK. 2
        OXFORD UNIVERSITY PRESS   34.708   1.10
LAST, J.   VE
    TWO AND A PIANO, BK. 3
        OXFORD UNIVERSITY PRESS   34.709   1.10
LAST, J.   VE
    TWO AND A PIANO, BK. 4
        OXFORD UNIVERSITY PRESS   34.710   1.10
LAST, J.   VE
    TWO AND A PIANO, BK. 5
        OXFORD UNIVERSITY PRESS   34.711   1.10
LATOUR
    LAME D'ARGENT
        SPRATT MUSIC PUBLISHERS   .90
LAZARUS
    MARCHE FUNEBRE
        FRANCO COLOMBO PUBLICATIONS   SAL   2.75
LAZZARI
    STRING QUARTET IN A MINOR, OP. 17
        FRANCO COLOMBO PUBLICATIONS   SAL   10.75
LECHNER--ED   LECHNER   1-2
    MEIN WEIHNACHTSBUCH -- 33 DER SCHONSTEN WEIHNACHTSLIEDER FUR DEN
    ANFANGER FUR KLAVIER ZU 2 UND 4 HANDEN
        SCHOTT   4220   2.25
LECUONA
    ANDALUCIA
        EDWARD B. MARKS MUSIC CORPORATION   01.25
LECUONA
    COMPARSA, LA
        EDWARD B. MARKS MUSIC CORPORATION   01.00
LECUONA
    CORDOBA
        EDWARD B. MARKS MUSIC CORPORATION   01.00
LECUONA
    DANZA LUCUMI
        EDWARD B. MARKS MUSIC CORPORATION   01.50
LECUONA
    DOLLS HAVE A PARTY, THE
        EDWARD B. MARKS MUSIC CORPORATION   01.25
LECUONA
    GITANERIAS
        EDWARD B. MARKS MUSIC CORPORATION   01.25
LECUONA   FRANK
    GOOD MORNING
        EDWARD B. MARKS MUSIC CORPORATION   01.00
LECUONA
    MALAGUENA
        EDWARD B. MARKS MUSIC CORPORATION   01.00
LECUONA
    MALAGUENA
        EDWARD B. MARKS MUSIC CORPORATION   01.50
LECUONA   FRANK
    MERRY-GO-ROUND WHIRL
        EDWARD B. MARKS MUSIC CORPORATION   01.00
LECUONA   FRANK
    MOON LIGHTS UP, THE
        EDWARD B. MARKS MUSIC CORPORATION   01.00
LECUONA   FRANK
    PUPPETS DANCE, THE
        EDWARD B. MARKS MUSIC CORPORATION   01.00
LEE, E. M.   E
    ALICE IN WONDERLAND, BK. 1
        OXFORD UNIVERSITY PRESS   34.020   1.50
LEE, E. M.   E
    ALICE IN WONDERLAND, BK. 2
        OXFORD UNIVERSITY PRESS   34.021   1.50
LEFEBVRE
    BALLADE
        FRANCO COLOMBO PUBLICATIONS   SAL   1.75
LEHAR
    FRASQUITA SERENADE
        EDWARD B. MARKS MUSIC CORPORATION   01.25
LEHAR   2
    MERRY WIDOW WALTZ
        CENTURY MUSIC PUBLISHING COMPANY, INC.   3499   .60
LEKEU
    FANTASIE SUR 2 AIRS ANGEVINS
        FRANCO COLOMBO PUBLICATIONS   SAL   6.50
LEONI, F.
    CHRYSANTHEMUMS
        G. SCHIRMER, INC.   .40
LEONI, F.
    DAISIES
        G. SCHIRMER, INC.   .30
LEONI, F.
    PANSIES
        G. SCHIRMER, INC.   .30
LEONI, F.
    PINKS
        G. SCHIRMER, INC.   .30
LEONI, F.
    WILD ROSES
        G. SCHIRMER, INC.   .30

LESTER, I.   4
  CRIMSON BLUSHES
    CENTURY MUSIC PUBLISHING COMPANY, INC.   2181   .60
LEVITZKI, M.   LEVINE
  VALSE, OP. 2
    G. SCHIRMER, INC.   .60
LE GRAND
  THREE PETITES ESQUISSES - CAUSERIE MATINALE, PETITE RETRAITE,
  BERCEUSE
    FRANCO COLOMBO PUBLICATIONS   SAL   1.75
LIGHT, F. M.   2
  BETTY'S WOODEN SHOE DANCE
    THEODORE PRESSER COMPANY   .60
LINCKE, P.   FRANGIPANE   2
  GLOW WORM, THE
    CENTURY MUSIC PUBLISHING COMPANY, INC.   4295   .60
LINCKE, P.
  GLOW WORM
    EDWARD B. MARKS MUSIC CORPORATION   01.00
LINCKE, P.
  GLOW WORM
    EDWARD B. MARKS MUSIC CORPORATION   01.00
LINCOLN, H.
  REPASZ BAND
    BELWIN-MILLS PUBLISHING CORPORATION   26519   1.00
LIPSCOMB--ED.   LIPSCOMB
  EIGHTEEN HYMN DUETS--11 HAVE DESCANTS FOR FLUTE, RECORDER OR
  VIOLIN
    G. SCHIRMER, INC.   1.00
LISZT   BENDEL   5
  HUNGARIAN RHAPSODY NO. 02
    CENTURY MUSIC PUBLISHING COMPANY, INC.   2099   .60
LISZT   MERO   4
  LOVE'S DREAM, NO. 3
    THEODORE PRESSER COMPANY   .75
LISZT
  PRELUDES, LES -- SYMPHONIC POEM -- ARR. BY THE COMPOSER
    G. SCHIRMER, INC.   L783   1.25
LISZT   BENDEL
  RHAPSODIE HONGROISE NO. 02
    G. SCHIRMER, INC.   1.10
LISZT   3
  UNGARISCHE RHAPSODIE NO. 02
    SCHOTT   06524-5 1/2 1.75
LOEFFLER, C. M.   LABEY
  MORT DE TINTAGILES, LA -- POEME DRAMATIQUE POUR GRAND ORCHESTRE
  ET VIOLE D'AMOUR
    G. SCHIRMER, INC.   2.00
LOESCHHORN, A.   E
  TONE PICTURES, OP. 51. TWELVE PIECES FOR BEGINNERS
    C. F. PETERS CORPORATION   1011   3.50
LOESCHORN, A.
  BEGINNERS PIECES, OP. 51
    EDWIN F. KALMUS   3646   1.75
LOEW, J.
  TEACHER AND PUPIL, A PRACTICAL COURSE OF 4-HAND PIANO PLAYING --
  BK. 1
    G. SCHIRMER, INC.   L472   1.25
LOEW, J.
  TEACHER AND PUPIL, A PRACTICAL COURSE OF 4-HAND PIANO PLAYING --
  BK. 2
    G. SCHIRMER, INC.   L472   1.25
LOEW, J.
  TEACHER AND PUPIL, BK. 1
    EDWIN F. KALMUS   3647   1.50
LOEW, J.
  TEACHER AND PUPIL, BK. 2
    EDWIN F. KALMUS   3648   1.50
LOEWE, F.
  MY FAIR LADY SELECTION
    CHAPPELL AND COMPANY, INC.   3922507   2.50
LOTH, L.
  SPRINGTIME DANCE
    G. SCHIRMER, INC.   .40
LOUIS XIII   KING, S.
  AMARYLLIS
    SHAWNEE PRESS, INC.   HC-5012   .45
LOUMEY, A.   3-4
  SHADOWS ON THE WATER
    CENTURY MUSIC PUBLISHING COMPANY, INC.   3129   .60
LUDOVIC, G.   3
  ORANGE BLOSSOMS
    THEODORE PRESSER COMPANY   .50
LUIGINI
  BALLET EGYPTIEN
    ELKAN-VOGEL, INC.   LEM   4.60
LUTZ--ED   LUTZ   1-2
  MEIN KINDERLIEDERBUCH - 60 KINDERLIEDER, AUSWAHL FUR KLAVIER ZU
  VIER HANDEN
    SCHOTT   4400   3.00
LUTZ--ED   LUTZ   1-2
  MEIN KINDERLIEDERBUCH
    SCHOTT   4400   3.00
LUTZ--ED   LUTZ   2
  MEIN VOLKSLIEDERBUCH - AUSWAHL FUR KLAVIER ZU VIER HANDEN
    SCHOTT   4325   3.00
LUTZ--ED   LUTZ   2
  MEIN VOLKSLIEDERBUCH
    SCHOTT   4325   3.00
LYBBERT   D
  MOVEMENT
    C. F. PETERS CORPORATION   66015   2.00
LYKE--ED.   LYKE
  ENSEMBLE MUSIC FOR GROUP PIANO
    STIPES PUBLISHING COMPANY   4.00
LYKE *
  KEYBOARD MUSICIANSHIP - GROUP PIANO FOR ADULTS, BK. 1, 2ND ED.
  REV.
    STIPES PUBLISHING COMPANY   5.80
LYKE *
  KEYBOARD MUSICIANSHIP - GROUP PIANO FOR ADULTS, BK. 2. 2ND ED.
  REV.
    STIPES PUBLISHING COMPANY   6.80
MACDOWELL
  MOON-PICTURES, OP. 21 -- AFTER H. C. ANDERSON'S "PICTURE-BOOK
  -- WITHOUT PICTURES"
    G. SCHIRMER, INC.   1.10
MACDOWELL   LEVINE   3
  TO A WATER LILY
    BOSTON MUSIC COMPANY   .60
MACDOWELL   2
  TO A WATER LILY
    CENTURY MUSIC PUBLISHING COMPANY, INC.   4097   .60
MACDOWELL   LEVINE   2
  TO A WILD ROSE
    BOSTON MUSIC COMPANY   .60

MACDOWELL   2
  TO A WILD ROSE
    CENTURY MUSIC PUBLISHING COMPANY, INC.   4096   .60
MACDOWELL   5
  WITCHES' DANCE, OP. 17, NO. 2
    THEODORE PRESSER COMPANY   1.00
MACGREGOR, H.   2
  SINGING IN THE MOONLIGHT
    WILLIS MUSIC COMPANY   .35
MACGREGOR   1
  SINGING IN THE MOONLIGHT
    WILLIS MUSIC COMPANY   .25
MACK, E.   3
  GENERAL GRANT'S MARCH
    CENTURY MUSIC PUBLISHING COMPANY, INC.   3504   .60
MACLACHLAN, T.   KING, S.
  CLIMBING
    SHAWNEE PRESS, INC.   HC-5007   .45
MACLACHLAN, T.   KING, S.
  VIENNESE WALTZ
    SHAWNEE PRESS, INC.   HC-5024   .45
MADELINE
  POUR MES PETITS AMIS
    FRANCO COLOMBO PUBLICATIONS   SAL   2.25
MAGNARD
  CHANT FUNEBRE, OP. 9
    FRANCO COLOMBO PUBLICATIONS   SAL   4.25
MAGNARD
  HYMNE A LA JUSTICE, OP. 14
    FRANCO COLOMBO PUBLICATIONS   SAL   6.50
MAGNARD
  HYMNE A VENUS, OP. 17
    FRANCO COLOMBO PUBLICATIONS   SAL   5.50
MAGNARD
  OVERTURE, OP. 10
    FRANCO COLOMBO PUBLICATIONS   SAL   5.50
MAGNARD
  SYMPHONY NO. 01
    FRANCO COLOMBO PUBLICATIONS   SAL   8.75
MAGNARD
  SYMPHONY NO. 02
    FRANCO COLOMBO PUBLICATIONS   SAL   10.75
MAGNARD
  SYMPHONY NO. 04
    FRANCO COLOMBO PUBLICATIONS   SAL   10.75
MAHLER
  ADAGIO FROM SYMPHONIE NO. 10
    UNIVERSAL EDITION   13879   9.00
MAHLER
  SYMPHONY NO. 01
    EDWIN F. KALMUS   3657   5.00
MAHLER
  SYMPHONY NO. 02
    EDWIN F. KALMUS   3658   5.00
MAHLER   WOSS
  SYMPHONY NO. 03
    UNIVERSAL EDITION   UE 951   9.35
MAHLER
  SYMPHONY NO. 04
    EDWIN F. KALMUS   3673   5.00
MAHLER
  SYMPHONY NO. 05
    EDWIN F. KALMUS   3673   5.00
MAHLER   SINGER   D
  SYMPHONY NO. 05
    C. F. PETERS CORPORATION   3081   7.50
MAHLER   WOSS
  SYMPHONY NO. 09
    UNIVERSAL EDITION   UE 3397   10.00
MAIER, G. *
  TWO OF US
    SUMMY-BIRCHARD COMPANY   1.50
MALIPIERO, G. F.
  ARMENIA
    FRANCO COLOMBO PUBLICATIONS   SAL   4.00
MALIPIERO, G. F.
  IMPRESSIONI DAL VERO NO. 1
    FRANCO COLOMBO PUBLICATIONS   SAL   4.25
MALOTTE, A.   STEINER
  LORD'S PRAYER, THE
    G. SCHIRMER, INC.   .85
MAMLOK, U. L.   1 1/2
  BELLS
    THEODORE PRESSER COMPANY   .50
MANA-ZUCCA
  FOUR HAND FANCIES
    THEODORE PRESSER COMPANY   2.50
MANA-ZUCCA
  JOKING
    G. SCHIRMER, INC.   .35
MANA-ZUCCA
  THREE LITTLE DUCKS
    G. SCHIRMER, INC.   .35
MARGIS, A.   4
  VALSE BLEUE
    CENTURY MUSIC PUBLISHING COMPANY, INC.   948   .60
MARGIS, A.   WEYBRIGHT   2
  VALSE BLUE
    BELWIN-MILLS PUBLISHING CORPORATION   .60
MARIE
  KLEIS
    FRANCO COLOMBO PUBLICATIONS   SAL   3.50
MARIE
  MARCHE FUNEBRE D'UNE MOUSME
    FRANCO COLOMBO PUBLICATIONS   SAL   2.50
MARTIN, G.   2
  AT THE COUNTY FAIR, MARCH
    CENTURY MUSIC PUBLISHING COMPANY, INC.   3084   .60
MARTIN, G.   1-2
  BETTY'S WALTZ
    CENTURY MUSIC PUBLISHING COMPANY, INC.   2986   .60
MARTIN, G.   1
  BUNCH OF DAISIES, A, VALSE
    CENTURY MUSIC PUBLISHING COMPANY, INC.   3079   .60
MARTIN, G.   2
  DANSE POLONAISE, MAZURKA
    CENTURY MUSIC PUBLISHING COMPANY, INC.   3087   .60
MARTIN, G.   1
  DREAMING OF SANTA CLAUS
    CENTURY MUSIC PUBLISHING COMPANY, INC.   3080   .60
MARTIN, G.   1
  ELIZABETH WALTZ
    CENTURY MUSIC PUBLISHING COMPANY, INC.   3078   .60
MARTIN, G.   1-2
  MARCH OF THE BOY SCOUTS
    CENTURY MUSIC PUBLISHING COMPANY, INC.   2987   .60

MARTIN, G.   2
  MEADOW BROOK, THE
    CENTURY MUSIC PUBLISHING COMPANY, INC.   3086   .60
MARTIN, G.   1
  ON A VISIT, MARCH
    CENTURY MUSIC PUBLISHING COMPANY, INC.   3082   .60
MARTIN, H.
  PEPPERMINT POLKA
    BELWIN-MILLS PUBLISHING CORPORATION   26539   .50
MARTIN, H.
  PINEAPPLE POLKA
    BELWIN-MILLS PUBLISHING CORPORATION   26543   .60
MARTIN, H.
  TANGO MODERNE
    BELWIN-MILLS PUBLISHING CORPORATION   26526   .75
MARTIN, H.
  TUNE TIME FOR TWO
    BELWIN-MILLS PUBLISHING CORPORATION   11512   1.25
MARTINI, G.   HART, F.   4
  GAVOTTE
    LEE ROBERTS MUSIC PUBLICATIONS, INC.   .85
MARWICK, M. *
  DUETS FOR CHRISTMAS
    LEE ROBERTS MUSIC PUBLICATIONS, INC.   1.25
MARX
  SONATINA IN E, OP. 48 NO. 5
    BARENREITER VERLAG   BA 1985   4.25
MARX   3-4
  SONATINE IN E, OP. 48 NO. 5
    BARENREITER VERLAG   BA 1985
MASCAGNI, P.   4
  CAVALLERIA RUSTICANA, INTERMEZZO
    CENTURY MUSIC PUBLISHING COMPANY, INC.   923   .60
MASCAGNI, P.   4
  CAVALLERIA RUSTICANA
    CENTURY MUSIC PUBLISHING COMPANY, INC.   923   .60
MASSENET, J.   3
  ARAGONAISE, LE CID
    CENTURY MUSIC PUBLISHING COMPANY, INC.   3503   .60
MASSENET, J.
  ARAGONAISE -- FROM THE BALLET-MUSIC FROM ''LE CID''
    G. SCHIRMER, INC.   .50
MASSEUS   M
  ZOOLOGICAL IMPRESSIONS
    C. F. PETERS CORPORATION   D57   2.00
MCCLENNY, A.--ED *   4
  DUETS OF EARLY AMERICAN MUSIC
    BELWIN-MILLS PUBLISHING CORPORATION   FDL 465   2.00
MCGRAW   3
  TWO PIECES FOR PIANO DUET
    BOSTON MUSIC COMPANY   .60
MCINTYRE, E.   MACKAYE   2
  CIRCUS DAY
    WILLIS MUSIC COMPANY   .50
MCINTYRE, E.   3
  MARCHING ON
    WILLIS MUSIC COMPANY   .50
MCINTYRE, E.   2
  MEADOW LARK, THE
    WILLIS MUSIC COMPANY   .50
MCINTYRE, E.   2
  SUMMER HOLIDAYS
    WILLIS MUSIC COMPANY   .50
MCSWEEN, F. W.   2-3
  MY SHADOW
    PRO-ART PUBLICATIONS, INC.   216   .60
MEACHAM, F.   KING, S.
  AMERICAN PATROL MARCH
    SHAWNEE PRESS, INC.   HC-5015   .45
MEACHAM, F.
  AMERICAN PATROL
    EDWARD B. MARKS MUSIC CORPORATION   01.25
MEACHAM, F.
  DANCE OF THE FAIRIES
    EDWARD B. MARKS MUSIC CORPORATION   01.25
MEHEGAN, J.
  JAZZ CAPER
    SOUTHERN MUSIC COMPANY   1.25
MEHEGAN, J.
  VIENNA WOODSHED -- JAZZ WALTZ
    SOUTHERN MUSIC COMPANY   1.25
MELVIN, B.--ED   MELVIN, B.   2
  ANCIENT AYRE - GREENSLEEVES
    PRO-ART PUBLICATIONS, INC.   290   .60
MENDELSSOHN
  ALL ORIGINAL COMPOSITIONS, COMPLETE
    INTERNATIONAL MUSIC COMPANY   2.50
MENDELSSOHN   M
  MARCHES, FIVE
    C. F. PETERS CORPORATION   1784   3.50
MENDELSSOHN   4
  MARCH OF THE PRIESTS
    CENTURY MUSIC PUBLISHING COMPANY, INC.   1929   .60
MENDELSSOHN *   E-M
  MASTERS FOR THE YOUNG, IN 3 VOLS* VOL. 3
    C. F. PETERS CORPORATION   2754   3.00
MENDELSSOHN   SMITH, S.   5
  MIDSUMMER NIGHT'S DREAM, OP. 76
    THEODORE PRESSER COMPANY   1.00
MENDELSSOHN
  ORIGINAL COMPOSITIONS FOR PIANO, 4-HANDS
    G. SCHIRMER, INC.   L1732   1.50
MENDELSSOHN   M-D
  ORIGINAL COMPOSITIONS
    C. F. PETERS CORPORATION   1715   3.00
MENDELSSOHN   4
  PRIESTS' MARCH, ATHALIA
    CENTURY MUSIC PUBLISHING COMPANY, INC.   1929   .60
MENDELSSOHN   3
  SPRING SONG, OP. 62 NO. 6
    CENTURY MUSIC PUBLISHING COMPANY, INC.   2027   .60
MENDELSSOHN
  WAR MARCH OF THE PRIESTS -- FROM ''ATHALIA''
    G. SCHIRMER, INC.   .60
MERKUR--ED   MERKUR
  HAVAH NAGILAH
    BELWIN-MILLS PUBLISHING CORPORATION   1.00
MERKUR--ED   MERKUR
  JAZZ LEGATO
    BELWIN-MILLS PUBLISHING CORPORATION   26509   1.00
MERKUR--ED   MERKUR
  JAZZ PIZZICATO
    BELWIN-MILLS PUBLISHING CORPORATION   26510   1.00
MERKUR--ED   MERKUR
  MARCH OF THE BLUES
    BELWIN-MILLS PUBLISHING CORPORATION   26512   1.00

MERKUR--ED   MERKUR
  SOLITUDE
    BELWIN-MILLS PUBLISHING CORPORATION   26522   1.00
MERKUR--ED   MERKUR
  SOPHISTICATED SWING
    BELWIN-MILLS PUBLISHING CORPORATION   26524   1.00
MERKUR--ED   MERKUR
  STROLLING
    BELWIN-MILLS PUBLISHING CORPORATION   26527   1.00
MERKUR
  ONE MORNING IN MAY
    BELWIN-MILLS PUBLISHING CORPORATION   26515   1.00
MERKUR
  OPALS -- TANGO
    BELWIN-MILLS PUBLISHING CORPORATION   26542   1.00
MERKUR
  ORIENTAL TEA GARDEN
    BELWIN-MILLS PUBLISHING CORPORATION   26555   .75
MERKUR
  REGIMENTAL SONG
    BELWIN-MILLS PUBLISHING CORPORATION   26518   1.00
METIS
  POP-ROCK SKETCHES FOR PIANO DUET
    EDWARD B. MARKS MUSIC CORPORATION   01.50
MEYERBEER, G.   3
  CORONATION MARCH, PROPHET
    CENTURY MUSIC PUBLISHING COMPANY, INC.   1827   .60
MEYERBEER, G.
  CORONATION MARCH -- FROM ''LE PROPHETE''
    G. SCHIRMER, INC.   .70
MEYERBEER, G.   3
  MARCH, PROPHET
    CENTURY MUSIC PUBLISHING COMPANY, INC.   1827   .60
MICHIELS   4
  CZARDAS, DANSE STYRIENNE
    CENTURY MUSIC PUBLISHING COMPANY, INC.   1927   .60
MICHIELS   4
  HUNGARIAN DANCE
    CENTURY MUSIC PUBLISHING COMPANY, INC.   1927   .60
MILES
  SPARKLETS
    SOUTHERN MUSIC COMPANY   1.25
MILES
  WATER BUG, THE
    SOUTHERN MUSIC COMPANY   1.00
MILHAUD, D.
  BOEUF SUR LE TOIT, LE
    ASSOCIATED MUSIC PUBLISHERS, INC.   ESC   10.75
MILHAUD, D.
  CREATION DU MONDE, LE -- BALLET
    ASSOCIATED MUSIC PUBLISHERS, INC.   ESC   6.50
MILHAUD, D.
  ENFANTINES
    ASSOCIATED MUSIC PUBLISHERS, INC.   ESC   4.00
MILHAUD, D.
  STRING QUARTET NO. 4
    FRANCO COLOMBO PUBLICATIONS   SAL   4.25
MILHAUD, D.
  STRING QUARTET NO. 5
    FRANCO COLOMBO PUBLICATIONS   SAL   6.00
MILHAUD, D.
  SUITE SYMPHONIQUE NO. 1 -- ORCH
    ASSOCIATED MUSIC PUBLISHERS, INC.   ESC   6.00
MITTLER--ED   MITTLER   2
  DUETS FOR EVERYBODY
    MUSICORD PUBLICATIONS, INC.   2.00
MONIOT
  CREPUSCULE, LE
    FRANCO COLOMBO PUBLICATIONS   SAL   2.50
MORHANGE *
  LITTLE CLAVIER, THE .... SUPPLEMENT 1 - 20 SHORT PIECES FOR
  PIANO 4 HANDS BY S. DEMARQUEZ
    FRANCO COLOMBO PUBLICATIONS   SAL   4.00
MOSS, L.
  OMAGGIO
    ELKAN-VOGEL, INC.   2.00
MOSSMAN, T.
  GIRL OF MY DREAMS-- SIMP.
    BELWIN-MILLS PUBLISHING CORPORATION   26507   .50
MOSZKOWSKI
  FIVE SPANISH DANCES, OP. 12 -- COMPLETE
    G. SCHIRMER, INC.   L255   1.50
MOSZKOWSKI
  FIVE SPANISH DANCES, OP. 12 -- NO. 1 IN C
    G. SCHIRMER, INC.   .50
MOSZKOWSKI
  FIVE SPANISH DANCES, OP. 12 -- NO. 5 IN D -- BOLERO
    G. SCHIRMER, INC.   .60
MOSZKOWSKI
  FIVE WALTZES, OP. 8 AND FROM FOREIGN PARTS, OP. 23
    G. SCHIRMER, INC.   L330   1.50
MOSZKOWSKI   CURRIE, E.   3
  FROM FIVE WALTZES, OP. 8 NO. 01
    WILLIS MUSIC COMPANY   .60
MOSZKOWSKI   CURRIE, E.   3
  FROM FIVE WALTZES, OP. 8 NO. 02
    WILLIS MUSIC COMPANY   .60
MOSZKOWSKI   CURRIE, E.   3
  FROM FIVE WALTZES, OP. 8 NO. 03
    WILLIS MUSIC COMPANY   .60
MOSZKOWSKI   CURRIE, E.   3
  FROM FIVE WALTZES, OP. 8 NO. 04
    WILLIS MUSIC COMPANY   .60
MOSZKOWSKI   M
  NEW SPANISH DANCES, OP. 65
    C. F. PETERS CORPORATION   2992   3.50
MOSZKOWSKI   M
  POLISH FOLK DANCES, OP. 55
    C. F. PETERS CORPORATION   2777   2.00
MOSZKOWSKI   E-M
  SPANISH DANCE, OP. 12 NO. 1 FLAMENCA --GYPSY DANCE--
    C. F. PETERS CORPORATION   2125F   .90
MOSZKOWSKI   4
  SPANISH DANCE, OP. 12 NO. 1
    CENTURY MUSIC PUBLISHING COMPANY, INC.   945   .60
MOSZKOWSKI   E-M
  SPANISH DANCE, OP. 12 NO. 2 ROMANCE IN CORDOVA
    C. F. PETERS CORPORATION   2125D   1.25
MOSZKOWSKI   E-M
  SPANISH DANCE, OP. 12 NO. 3 JUANA --ANDALUSIAN VITO--
    C. F. PETERS CORPORATION   2125G   .90
MOSZKOWSKI   E
  SPANISH DANCE, OP. 12 NO. 5 BOLERO --SIMPLIFIED--
    C. F. PETERS CORPORATION   2130B   .90
MOSZKOWSKI   E-M
  SPANISH DANCE, OP. 12 NO. 5 BOLERO
    C. F. PETERS CORPORATION   2125H   .90

MOSZKOWSKI   4
  SPANISH DANCE, OP. 12 NO. 5
    THEODORE PRESSER COMPANY   .50
MOSZKOWSKI   E-M
  SPANISH DANCES, OP. 12
    C. F. PETERS CORPORATION   2125   2.00
MOSZKOWSKI   3
  SPANISH DANCE NO. 02
    CENTURY MUSIC PUBLISHING COMPANY, INC.   946   .60
MOSZKOWSKI   M
  TORCH DANCE --FACKELTANZ--, OP. 51
    C. F. PETERS CORPORATION   2748   2.50
MOSZKOWSKI   M
  WALTZES, OP. 8
    C. F. PETERS CORPORATION   2465   3.00
MOYER, E.   2
  ANGELUS, THE
    WILLIS MUSIC COMPANY   .50
MOZART, W. A.
  ALL ORIGINAL COMPOSITIONS, COMPLETE
    INTERNATIONAL MUSIC COMPANY   4.00
MOZART, W. A.   KRIEGER
  DANCES AND MARCHES
    UNIVERSAL EDITION   10915   1.80
MOZART, W. A.
  EINE KLEINE NACHTMUSIK, K525 -- SONDERAUSSTATTUNG
    SCHOTT   5196   1.75
MOZART, W. A.
  EINE KLEINE NACHTMUSIK, K525
    G. SCHIRMER, INC.   L1842   1.25
MOZART, W. A.   3
  EINE KLEINE NACHTMUSIK, K525
    SCHOTT   2505   1.50
MOZART, W. A.
  FIGARO'S WEDDING, OVERTURE
    CARL FISCHER, INC.   P 2404   1.00
MOZART, W. A.
  ORIGINAL COMPOSITIONS -- CLOTH
    G. HENLE MUSIKVERLAG   93   8.85
MOZART, W. A.
  ORIGINAL COMPOSITIONS FOR ONE PIANO, 4-HANDS
    G. SCHIRMER, INC.   L1735   4.00
MOZART, W. A.
  ORIGINAL COMPOSITIONS
    G. HENLE MUSIKVERLAG   92   5.80
MOZART, W. A.   M
  ORIGINAL COMPOSITIONS
    C. F. PETERS CORPORATION   12   3.00
MOZART, W. A. *   M
  OVERTURES, IN 5 VOLS* VOL. 3
    C. F. PETERS CORPORATION   1952   6.50
MOZART, W. A.   BURCHARD
  RONDO ALLA TURCA -- FROM SONATA K331 IN A
    G. SCHIRMER, INC.   .70
MOZART, W. A.   2
  RONDO A LA TURQUE
    BOSTON MUSIC COMPANY   .60
MOZART, W. A.   DIETRICH, F.   2
  SECHS LANDLERISCHE TANZE, K606
    BARENREITER VERLAG   BA 1615
MOZART, W. A.   3
  SERENADE, FROM 'DON GIOVANNI'
    THEODORE PRESSER COMPANY   .50
MOZART, W. A.   STEINER   3
  SERENADE -- DON GIOVANNI
    BELWIN-MILLS PUBLISHING CORPORATION   .60
MOZART, W. A.
  SERENADE 'EINE KLEINE NACHT MUSIK'
    INTERNATIONAL MUSIC COMPANY   1.50
MOZART, W. A.   M
  SERENADE IN G, K525 --KLEINE NACHTMUSIK--
    C. F. PETERS CORPORATION   3078   1.50
MOZART, W. A.   M
  SEVEN OVERTURES
    C. F. PETERS CORPORATION   135A   2.50
MOZART, W. A.   DIETRICH
  SIX LANDLER DANCES, K606
    BARENREITER VERLAG   BA 1615   7.00
MOZART, W. A.   JOHNSON   E-M
  SIX VIENNESE SONATINAS
    C. F. PETERS CORPORATION   7017   3.00
MOZART, W. A.   FERGUSON, H.
  SONATA K019D IN C
    OXFORD UNIVERSITY PRESS   34.040   2.50
MOZART, W. A.   4
  SONATA K358 IN B
    ASHLEY DEALERS SERVICE, INC.   1.25
MOZART, W. A.   4
  SONATA K381 IN D
    ASHLEY DEALERS SERVICE, INC.   1.25
MOZART, W. A.   D
  SONATINAS --AFTER K213, 240--
    C. F. PETERS CORPORATION   4456   1.25
MOZART, W. A.   M
  SYMPHONIES AND SERENADES --12--, IN 2 VOLS* VOL. 1
    C. F. PETERS CORPORATION   187A   7.50
MOZART, W. A.   M
  SYMPHONIES AND SERENADES --12--, IN 2 VOLS* VOL. 2
    C. F. PETERS CORPORATION   187B   7.50
MOZART, W. A.
  TEN CELEBRATED OVERTURES
    INTERNATIONAL MUSIC COMPANY   3.50
MOZART, W. A.   STEINER   1 1/2
  THEME FROM SYMPHONY NO. 15
    BELWIN-MILLS PUBLISHING CORPORATION   .60
MOZART, W. A.
  TWELVE SYMPHONIES, BK. 1
    G. SCHIRMER, INC.   L71   4.00
MOZART, W. A.
  TWELVE SYMPHONIES, BK. 2
    G. SCHIRMER, INC.   L72   4.00
MOZART, W. A.   REHM   3-4
  WERKE FUR KLAVIER ZU VIER HANDEN, K190, 381, 358, 497, 501, 521,
  357 -- NEUE MOZART-AUSGABE --
    BARENREITER VERLAG   BA 4503
MOZART, W. A.   LANDON, C.
  WORKS FOR PIANO, 4 HANDS --VIENNA URTEXT ED.--
    UNIVERSAL EDITION   13304   5.80
MOZART, W. A.
  WORKS FOR PIANO FOUR HANDS
    BARENREITER VERLAG   BA 2072   7.00
MUCZYNSKI, R.--ED   MUCZYNSKI, R.
  AMERICAN SONGS, BK. 1
    ASSOCIATED MUSIC PUBLISHERS, INC.   AMP   1.25
MUCZYNSKI, R.--ED   MUCZYNSKI, R.
  AMERICAN SONGS, BK. 1
    ASSOCIATED MUSIC PUBLISHERS, INC.   AMP   1.25

MUCZYNSKI, R.--ED
  AMERICAN SONGS, BK. 1
    ASSOCIATED MUSIC PUBLISHERS, INC.   AMP   1.50
MUCZYNSKI, R.--ED
  AMERICAN SONGS, BK. 2
    ASSOCIATED MUSIC PUBLISHERS, INC.   AMP   1.25
MUNN, W.   1
  MARCH OF THE TINY SOLDIERS
    WILLIS MUSIC COMPANY   .35
MURRAY   3
  THEME AND VARIATIONS
    LEE ROBERTS MUSIC PUBLICATIONS, INC.   1.00
NAGAN, Z.
  SEVEN PIECES
    ISRAEL MUSIC INSTITUTE   3.00
NAGY, M.   5
  DANZA ESPANA
    LEE ROBERTS MUSIC PUBLICATIONS, INC.   1.00
NAGY, M.   4
  DOUBLE EXPOSURE
    LEE ROBERTS MUSIC PUBLICATIONS, INC.   .85
NAGY, M.   3
  FINGER PUPPETS
    LEE ROBERTS MUSIC PUBLICATIONS, INC.   .60
NAGY, M.   1
  FOLK TALES FOR TWO
    LEE ROBERTS MUSIC PUBLICATIONS, INC.   1.00
NAGY, M.   4
  FROM THE COLOR WHEEL
    LEE ROBERTS MUSIC PUBLICATIONS, INC.   .75
NAGY, M.   4
  HEY PEDRO
    LEE ROBERTS MUSIC PUBLICATIONS, INC.   .85
NAGY, M.   3
  MAGIC MANDARINS
    LEE ROBERTS MUSIC PUBLICATIONS, INC.   .75
NAGY, M.   3
  PARTY POLKA
    LEE ROBERTS MUSIC PUBLICATIONS, INC.   .85
NAGY, M.   2
  TWO BITS O'SCOTCH
    LEE ROBERTS MUSIC PUBLICATIONS, INC.   .85
NELSON
  THAT THING
    SUMMY-BIRCHARD COMPANY   .40 PER
NEUMANN, F.
  DUETS FOR BEGINNERS, OP. 1 -- BK. 1
    ASSOCIATED MUSIC PUBLISHERS, INC.   BRH   1.00
NEUSTEDT
  GAVOTTE FAVORITE DE MARIE-ANTOINETTE
    FRANCO COLOMBO PUBLICATIONS   SAL   2.50
NEVIN   3
  BARCHETTA
    BOSTON MUSIC COMPANY   .60
NEVIN   4
  GONDOLIERI
    THEODORE PRESSER COMPANY   .75
NEVIN
  LITTLE MAJORETTE
    BELWIN-MILLS PUBLISHING CORPORATION   28110   .75
NEVIN
  MARK NEVIN'S EASY PIANO DUETS
    BELWIN-MILLS PUBLISHING CORPORATION   11613   1.75
NEVIN   3
  NARCISSUS
    BOSTON MUSIC COMPANY   .60
NEVIN   3-4
  NARCISSUS
    CENTURY MUSIC PUBLISHING COMPANY, INC.   4091   .60
NEVIN   3
  ROSARY, THE
    BOSTON MUSIC COMPANY   .60
NEVIN   M
  THREE JAZZ DUETS
    BELWIN-MILLS PUBLISHING CORPORATION   28217   1.00
NIEMANN
  TWELVE KOCHELER LAENDLER, OP. 136
    C. F. PETERS CORPORATION   4281   1.50
NILES, J.--ED   NILES, J.
  AMERICAN CAROLS IN EASY ARRANGEMENTS -- CAROL OF THE ANGELS, THE
    G. SCHIRMER, INC.   .60
NILES, J.--ED   NILES, J.
  AMERICAN CAROLS IN EASY ARRANGEMENTS -- I WONDER AS I WANDER
    G. SCHIRMER, INC.   .75
NILES, J.--ED   NILES, J.
  AMERICAN CAROLS IN EASY ARRANGEMENTS -- JESUS, JESUS, REST YOUR
  HEAD
    G. SCHIRMER, INC.   .60
NILES, J.--ED   NILES, J.
  AMERICAN CAROLS IN EASY ARRANGEMENTS -- JESUS, THE CHRIST, IS
  BORN
    G. SCHIRMER, INC.   .60
NOACK, K.   3
  HEINZELMANNCHENS WACHTPARADE, OP. 5
    SCHOTT   1.50
NOEL, H.   4
  PARE -- STOP
    LEE ROBERTS MUSIC PUBLICATIONS, INC.   .85
NOEL   2
  CADENCIA
    PRO-ART PUBLICATIONS, INC.   455   .75
NOFKA, R.   1
  BOBOLINK
    WILLIS MUSIC COMPANY   .50
NOFKA, R.   1
  HOME DREAMS
    WILLIS MUSIC COMPANY   .40
NOONA, W.   6
  EL DIABLO COJUELO -- THE LIMPING DEVIL
    BELWIN-MILLS PUBLISHING CORPORATION   .60
NOONA, W.   4
  STAMP ON IT
    BELWIN-MILLS PUBLISHING CORPORATION   .60
NOONA, W.   3
  WALTZ SIMPLICE
    BELWIN-MILLS PUBLISHING CORPORATION   .60
NOVAK   VESELY   3
  VON EWIGER SEHNSUCHT, OP. 33
    BARENREITER VERLAG   AP 779
OCHS   2-3
  S KOMMT EIN VOGEL GEFLOGEN. IM STILE ALTERER UND NEUERER MEISTER
  HUMORISTISCH BEARBEITET
    BARENREITER VERLAG   SM 960
OESTEN   2-3
  DOLL'S DREAM, OP. 202 NO. 4
    CENTURY MUSIC PUBLISHING COMPANY, INC.   2989   .60

OESTERLE--ED　　　　　　OESTERLE
　RECITAL PIECES -- 15 ORIGINAL PIECES
　　G. SCHIRMER, INC.　　　　　　　　　　　　L1143　　　2.25
OESTERLE
　FOUR-HAND COLLECTION -- 42 MELODIOUS AND INSTRUCTIVE PIANO DUETS
　　FOR ELEMENTARY AND FIRST GRADES
　　G. SCHIRMER, INC.　　　　　　　　　　　　L1148　　　1.75
OFFENBACH　　　　　　　　　　　　　　　　3
　TALES OF HOFFMAN, BARCAROLLE
　　CENTURY MUSIC PUBLISHING COMPANY, INC.　1826　　　.60
OGLE, L.　　　　　　　　　　　　　　　　3
　ON A BRIGHT DAY
　　CENTURY MUSIC PUBLISHING COMPANY, INC.　4275　　　.40
OLDENBURG, E.　　　　　　　　　　　　　1
　CUCKOO, CUCKOO
　　BOSTON MUSIC COMPANY　　　　　　　　　　　　　　.60
OLDENBURG, E.　　　　　　　　　　　　　2
　WOODLAND FROLIC
　　BOSTON MUSIC COMPANY　　　　　　　　　　　　　　.60
OLIVIERO *
　MORE
　　EDWARD B. MARKS MUSIC CORPORATION　　　　　　　01.00
OLSON--ED.　　　　　　　OLSON
　ASH GROVE
　　CARL FISCHER, INC.　　　　　　　　　　P 3193　　.75
ORBAN
　POUR LES PETITS -- 6 EASY PIECES --
　　FRANCO COLOMBO PUBLICATIONS　　　　　　SAL　　　3.25
OSBORNE, E.
　SECOND CONCORD DUET BOOK
　　E. C. SCHIRMER MUSIC COMPANY　　　　　609　　　01.50
　　　　　　　　　　　　　　　　　　3 1/2
OVERLADE, A. R.
　SWAYING DAFFODILS
　　THEODORE PRESSER COMPANY　　　　　　　　　　　.80
PACE, R.--ED　　　　　PACE, R.　　　1
　DUETS FOR PIANO, SET 1
　　LEE ROBERTS MUSIC PUBLICATIONS, INC.　　　　　.75
PACE, R.--ED　　　　　PACE, R.　　　2
　DUETS FOR PIANO, SET 2
　　LEE ROBERTS MUSIC PUBLICATIONS, INC.　　　　　.75
PADEREWSKI, I. J.　　　　KING, S.
　MINUET
　　SHAWNEE PRESS, INC.　　　　　　　　　HC-5005　　.60
PALMER
　SONATA FOR PIANO
　　PEER SOUTHERN ORGANIZATION　　　　　　　　　　05.50
PAPINEAU-COUTURE, J.
　RONDO FOR PIANO
　　PEER SOUTHERN ORGANIZATION　　　　　　　　　　01.50
PAUER
　CASCADE, LA
　　FRANCO COLOMBO PUBLICATIONS　　　　　　SAL　　　2.75
　　　　　　　　　　　　　　　　　　3
PAULL
　BEN HUR CHARIOT RACE
　　CENTURY MUSIC PUBLISHING COMPANY, INC.　4333　　　.60
PELS, W.--ED.　　　　　PELS, W.
　FAMOUS MOVEMENTS FROM GREAT SYMPHONIES
　　G. SCHIRMER, INC.　　　　　　　　　　　　　　2.25
PELS, W.　　　　　　　　　　　　　　　1
　THREE HANDS AT THE PIANO
　　CENTURY MUSIC PUBLISHING COMPANY, INC.　4317　　　.40
PELS, W.　　　　　　　　　　　　　　　1, 2
　TUNES TWO CAN PLAY
　　MUSICORD PUBLICATIONS, INC.　　　　　　　　　　1.25
PENNY, M.--ED　　　　　PENNY, M.
　TWO 18TH CENTURY DANCES
　　OXFORD UNIVERSITY PRESS　　　　　　　34.004　　1.40
PENTLAND, B.
　PUPPET-SHOW
　　ASSOCIATED MUSIC PUBLISHERS, INC.　　　BER　　　.75
PERSICHETTI
　CONCERTO
　　ELKAN-VOGEL, INC.　　　　　　　　　　　　　　7.50
PERSICHETTI
　SERENADE NO. 08
　　ELKAN-VOGEL, INC.　　　　　　　　　　　　　　1.25
PESSARD　　　　　　　　　　　　　　　6
　ANDALOUSE, OP. 20
　　ALPHONSE LEDUC
PESTALOZZA　　　　　WEYBRIGHT　　　3
　CIRIBIRIBIN
　　BELWIN-MILLS PUBLISHING CORPORATION　　　　　.60
PETIT, P.
　SIX PETITS PIECES
　　GERARD BILLAUDOT EDITIONS MUSICALES　　　　　2.50
　　　　　　　　　　　　　　　　　　E
PFEIFFER, A.
　IL MAESTRO E SCOLARE --SONATA--
　　C. F. PETERS CORPORATION　　　　　　　EH311　　1.25
PFEIFFER, A.
　MAZURKA DE SALON NO. 4
　　FRANCO COLOMBO PUBLICATIONS　　　　　　SAL　　　2.75
PFEIFFER, A.
　MUSETTE
　　FRANCO COLOMBO PUBLICATIONS　　　　　　SAL　　　2.50
PHILLIPS, B.
　SERENADE FOR PIANO
　　PEER SOUTHERN ORGANIZATION　　　　　　　　　　02.00
PHOENIX　　　　　　　　　　　　　　　1-2
　ARGUMENT OF THE KATYDIDS
　　CENTURY MUSIC PUBLISHING COMPANY, INC.　4162　　　.60
PIERNE
　DIVERTISSEMENT ON A PASTORAL THEME
　　FRANCO COLOMBO PUBLICATIONS　　　　　　SAL　　　5.75
　　　　　　　　　　　　　　　　　　5
PIERNE
　MARCHE DES PETITS SOLDATS DE PLOMB
　　ALPHONSE LEDUC
PILLNEY--ED　　　　　PILLNEY
　WEIHNACHTLICHE HAUSMUSIK -- ELABORATIONS OF 5 CHRISTMAS SONGS
　　WITH GERMAN TEXT
　　ASSOCIATED MUSIC PUBLISHERS, INC.　　　BRH　　　1.75
　　　　　　　　　　　　　　　　　　E-M
PLEYEL
　SONATA IN G MINOR
　　C. F. PETERS CORPORATION　　　　　　　6058　　　.90
PODOLSKY, L.
　DUET PLAYING, BK. 1
　　BELWIN-MILLS PUBLISHING CORPORATION　　　　　1.50
PODOLSKY, L.
　DUET PLAYING, BK. 2
　　BELWIN-MILLS PUBLISHING CORPORATION　　　　　1.50
PODOLSKY, L.
　DUET PLAYING, BK. 3
　　BELWIN-MILLS PUBLISHING CORPORATION　　　　　1.50
PODOLSKY, L.
　DUET PLAYING, BK. 4
　　BELWIN-MILLS PUBLISHING CORPORATION　　　　　1.50
PODOLSKY, L.
　DUET PLAYING, BK. 5
　　BELWIN-MILLS PUBLISHING CORPORATION　　　　　1.50

POHL, V.--ED *　　　　　POHL *　　　1-2
　KINDER SPIELEN ZUR WEIHNACHT
　　BARENREITER VERLAG　　　　　　　　　EN 803
POLDINI, E.　　　　　SAMMARTINO
　POUPEE VALSANTE
　　FRANCO COLOMBO PUBLICATIONS　　　　　　BA9219　　.75
POLLA, W.--ED　　　　　POLLA, W.
　FLAPPERETTE
　　BELWIN-MILLS PUBLISHING CORPORATION　　26506　　1.00
POLLA, W.--ED　　　　　POLLA, W.
　KITTEN ON THE KEYS
　　BELWIN-MILLS PUBLISHING CORPORATION　　26511　　1.00
POLONIO
　SOUVENIR DU BRESIL
　　FRANCO COLOMBO PUBLICATIONS　　　　　　SAL　　　2.75
PONCHIELLI
　GIOCONDA, LA - DANCE OF THE HOURS
　　FRANCO COLOMBO PUBLICATIONS　　　　　　44862　　1.50
POOL, K.
　TEN DUETS FOR PIANO ON RHYMES FROM MOTHER GOOSE
　　BRODT MUSIC COMPANY　　　　　　　　　　　　　1.00
　　　　　　　　　　　　　　　　　　1
POOLE, C.
　CLAPPING SONG
　　WILLIS MUSIC COMPANY　　　　　　　　　　　　.40
　　　　　　　　　　　　　　　　　　1
POOLE, C.
　CONGA IN G
　　WILLIS MUSIC COMPANY　　　　　　　　　　　　.50
POOLE, C.
　HIPPOPOTAMUS HORNPIPE
　　FREDERICK HARRIS MUSIC COMPANY　　　　　　　　.60
　　　　　　　　　　　　　　　　　　3
POOLE, C.
　WALTZ
　　WILLIS MUSIC COMPANY　　　　　　　　　　　　.50
PORTER, C.　　　　　STONE
　BEGIN THE BEGUINE
　　WARNER BROTHERS PUBLISHERS　　　　　　　　　　1.50
PORTER, C.
　COLE PORTER ALBUM
　　CHAPPELL AND COMPANY, INC.　　　　　　001　　　2.50
PORTER, C.　　　　　MERKUR
　NIGHT AND DAY
　　WARNER BROTHERS PUBLISHERS　　　　　　　　　　1.25
PORTER, C.　　　　　SAWYER　　　　EASY
　NIGHT AND DAY
　　WARNER BROTHERS PUBLISHERS　　　　　　　　　　1.00
POSER
　LITTLE SUITE, OP. 13 NO. 1
　　FRANCO COLOMBO PUBLICATIONS　　　　　　SIK.122　1.50
POSER
　SONATA, OP. 17
　　FRANCO COLOMBO PUBLICATIONS　　　　　　SIK.127　4.25
POTTER, H.
　DIZZY FINGERS
　　BELWIN-MILLS PUBLISHING CORPORATION　　26504　　1.00
POTTER, H.
　FARMERETTE
　　BELWIN-MILLS PUBLISHING CORPORATION　　26505　　1.00
POZZOLI
　SORRISI INFANTILI - 25 LITTLE PIECES ON 5 NOTES
　　FRANCO COLOMBO PUBLICATIONS　　　　　　129544　2.75
POZZOLI
　TEN LITTLE CHARACTERISTIC PIECES
　　FRANCO COLOMBO PUBLICATIONS　　　　　　129752　2.00
PRESTON, M. L.　　　　　　　　　　1 1/2
　TOMMY'S NEW DRUM
　　THEODORE PRESSER COMPANY　　　　　　　　　　　.50
PROCTER, A.　　　　　　　　　　　1 1/2
　FUN FOR TWO -- A BOOK OF PIANO DUETS
　　ELKAN-VOGEL, INC.　　　　　　　　　　　　　　1.25
PROCTER, A.　　　　　　　　　　　E
　HAPPY GO LUCKY
　　OXFORD UNIVERSITY PRESS　　　　　　　93.401　　.40
PROCTER, A.　　　　　　　　　　　1 1/2
　HOLIDAY BELLS
　　ELKAN-VOGEL, INC.　　　　　　　　　　　　　　.60
PROCTER, A.　　　　　　　　　　　1-2
　LULLABY
　　ELKAN-VOGEL, INC.　　　　　　　　　　　　　　.50
PROCTER, A.　　　　　　　　　　　2
　MARCH OF THE MOON MEN
　　ELKAN-VOGEL, INC.　　　　　　　　　　　　　　.50
PROCTER, A.　　　　　　　　　　　1 1/2
　ON THE ROAD
　　ELKAN-VOGEL, INC.　　　　　　　　　　　　　　.60
PROCTER, A.　　　　　　　　　　　E
　SQUARES TONIGHT
　　ELKAN-VOGEL, INC.　　　　　　　　　　　　　　.50
PROCTER, A.　　　　　　　　　　　E
　SWING TUNE
　　ELKAN-VOGEL, INC.　　　　　　　　　　　　　　.50
PROCTER, A.　　　　　　　　　　　1 1/2
　VILLAGE DANCE
　　ELKAN-VOGEL, INC.　　　　　　　　　　　　　　.50
PROKOFIEFF　　　　　MONTANDON　　3
　GAVOTTE, OP. 32 NO. 3
　　WILLIS MUSIC COMPANY　　　　　　　　　　　　.60
PROKOFIEFF
　TRIUMPHAL MARCH--PETER AND THE WOLF
　　EDWARD B. MARKS MUSIC CORPORATION　　　　　　01.25
PURCELL, H.
　OLD BACHELOR, THE
　　OXFORD UNIVERSITY PRESS　　　　　　　34.700　　1.50
PURCELL, H.　　　　　GEEHL
　TRUMPET VOLUNTARY
　　BOOSEY AND HAWKES, INC.　　　　　　　　　　　.75
PURCELL, H.
　VIRTUOUS WIFE, THE
　　OXFORD UNIVERSITY PRESS　　　　　　　34.028　　1.25
RACHMANINOFF, S.
　BARCAROLLE, OP. 11 NO. 1
　　BOOSEY AND HAWKES, INC.　　　　　　　　　　　1.50
RACHMANINOFF, S.
　ISLE OF THE DEAD, OP. 29
　　BOOSEY AND HAWKES, INC.　　　　　　　　　　　2.50
RACHMANINOFF, S.
　ITALIAN POLKA
　　BELWIN-MILLS PUBLISHING CORPORATION　　　　　1.50
RACHMANINOFF, S.
　ROMANCE, OP. 11 NO. 5
　　BOOSEY AND HAWKES, INC.　　　　　　　　　　　1.50
RACHMANINOFF, S.　　　　　PHILIPP, I.
　RUSSIAN THEME, OP.11 NO. 3
　　INTERNATIONAL MUSIC COMPANY　　　　　　　　　1.00
RACHMANINOFF, S.
　SCHERZO, OP. 11 NO. 2
　　BOOSEY AND HAWKES, INC.　　　　　　　　　　　1.50

RACHMANINOFF, S.   PHILIPP, I.
    SIX ORIGINAL PIECES, OP. 11
        INTERNATIONAL MUSIC COMPANY   3.00
RACHMANINOFF, S.
    SLAVA, OP. 11 NO. 6
        BOOSEY AND HAWKES, INC.   1.50
RACHMANINOFF, S.
    THEME RUSSE, OP. 11 NO. 3
        BOOSEY AND HAWKES, INC.   1.50
RACHMANINOFF, S.
    VALSE, OP. 11 NO. 4
        BOOSEY AND HAWKES, INC.   1.50
RAMEAU   ROQUES, L.
    DARDANUS -- AIRS DE BALLET, SUITE 1
        ELKAN-VOGEL, INC.   D   4.00
RAMEAU   ROQUES, L.
    DARDANUS -- AIRS DE BALLET, SUITE 2
        ELKAN-VOGEL, INC.   D   3.50
RAPHLING
    FOUR-HAND SONATA FOR PIANO
        GENERAL MUSIC PUBLISHING COMPANY, INC.   3.00
RAPHLING
    SONATA
        GENERAL MUSIC PUBLISHING COMPANY, INC.   575   3.00
RAPHLING
    TWO PLUS TWO - TWELVE LITTLE PIECES
        GENERAL MUSIC PUBLISHING COMPANY, INC.   2.00
RAPHLING
    TWO PLUS TWO - TWELVE LITTLE PIECES
        GENERAL MUSIC PUBLISHING COMPANY, INC.   472   2.00
RASBACH, O.   STEINER
    TREES
        G. SCHIRMER, INC.   .60
RAVEL
    BERCEUSE SUR LE NOM DE FAURE
        ELKAN-VOGEL, INC.   D   2.10
RAVEL
    BOLERO
        ELKAN-VOGEL, INC.   5.00
RAVEL
    DAPHNIS ET CHLOE
        ELKAN-VOGEL, INC.   D   8.00
RAVEL
    FANFARE, FROM L'EVENTAIL DE JEANNE
        HEUGEL ET CIE.   1.30
RAVEL
    INTRODUCTION ET ALLEGRO
        ELKAN-VOGEL, INC.   D   5.35
RAVEL
    L'ENFANT ET LES SORTILEGES -- FIVE O'CLOCK FOX-TROT
        ELKAN-VOGEL, INC.   D   2.50
RAVEL
    LA VALSE
        ELKAN-VOGEL, INC.   D   4.80
RAVEL
    LA VALSE
        ELKAN-VOGEL, INC.   6.75
RAVEL
    LE TOMBEAU DE COUPERIN
        ELKAN-VOGEL, INC.   D   6.00
RAVEL   ROQUES, L.
    MENUET -- DE LA SONATINE
        ELKAN-VOGEL, INC.   D   1.75
RAVEL
    MENUET SUR LE NOM D'HAYDN
        ELKAN-VOGEL, INC.   D   2.10
RAVEL   JEMAIN
    MIROIRS -- NO. 1, NOCTUELLES
        ASSOCIATED MUSIC PUBLISHERS, INC.   ESC   2.50
RAVEL   JEMAIN
    MIROIRS -- NO. 2, OISEAUX TRISTES
        ASSOCIATED MUSIC PUBLISHERS, INC.   ESC   2.00
RAVEL   JEMAIN
    MIROIRS -- NO. 4, ALBORADA DEL GRACIOSO
        ASSOCIATED MUSIC PUBLISHERS, INC.   ESC   3.50
RAVEL   JEMAIN
    MIROIRS -- NO. 5, LA VALLEE DES CLOCHES
        ASSOCIATED MUSIC PUBLISHERS, INC.   ESC   2.25
RAVEL
    MOTHER GOOSE SUITE
        ELKAN-VOGEL, INC.   6.00
RAVEL   JEMAIN
    PAVANE POUR UNE INFANTE DEFUNTE
        ASSOCIATED MUSIC PUBLISHERS, INC.   ESC   2.25
RAVEL   3
    PAVANE
        CENTURY MUSIC PUBLISHING COMPANY, INC.   3922   .60
RAVEL
    QUATUOR
        ELKAN-VOGEL, INC.   D   7.00
RAVEL
    RAPSODIE ESPAGNOLE
        ELKAN-VOGEL, INC.   6.00
RAVEL   GARBAN, L.
    VALSES NOBLES ET SENTIMENTALES
        ELKAN-VOGEL, INC.   D   6.20
RAWICZ
    SNOW-FLAKES
        BELWIN-MILLS PUBLISHING CORPORATION   26520   1.00
RAWSTHORNE, A.
    CREEL, THE
        OXFORD UNIVERSITY PRESS   34.008   1.25
RAYMOND, J.
    HAVING FUN
        BELWIN-MILLS PUBLISHING CORPORATION   26538   1.00
READ, E.   2
    WILD ROSE WALTZ
        WILLIS MUSIC COMPANY   .50
READ, G.
    LITTLE SOLDIERS, THE
        BELWIN-MILLS PUBLISHING CORPORATION   1.00
READ, G.
    TOY PARADE, THE
        BELWIN-MILLS PUBLISHING CORPORATION   .75
REBE   1
    SALUTE TO AMERICA
        WILLIS MUSIC COMPANY   .50
REDA
    TWELVE MINNELIEDER -- 2 AND 4 HANDS
        BARENREITER VERLAG   BA 2072   3.25
REDA   3
    ZWOLF MINNELIEDER
        BARENREITER VERLAG   BA 2072
REGER   4
    DEUTSCHE TANZE OP. 10 NO. 7 UND 17, ST.-V.S. 14/17
        SCHOTT   08974 1/2   1.00

REGER   D
    MOZART VARIATIONS AND FUGUE, OP. 132
        C. F. PETERS CORPORATION   3974   5.00
REGER   D
    SIX BURLESQUES, OP. 58
        C. F. PETERS CORPORATION   3949   3.50
REGER   D
    SIX PIECES, OP. 94
        C. F. PETERS CORPORATION   3111   3.50
REGER
    SIX WALTZES, OP. 22
        UNIVERSAL EDITION   1175   2.60
REGER   REGER   4
    WEIHNACHTSTRAUM OP. 17 NO. 9 ST.-V.S. 29
        SCHOTT   1.50
REHBERG--ED.   REHBERG   2-3
    VIERHANDIGES KLASSIKERBUCH -- LEICHTE BIS MITTELSCHWERE ORIGINAL
    STUCKE VON BACH BIS BRAHMS
        SCHOTT   2528   4.00
RESPIGHI
    SIX LITTLE PIECES
        ASSOCIATED MUSIC PUBLISHERS, INC.   SIM   1.75
RICHARDS, B.   1
    GOLDEN SUNSET WALTZ -- SOLO - DUET
        VOLKWEIN BROS.   .25
RICHARDS, B.   1
    GOLDEN SUNSET WALTZ
        VOLKWEIN BROS.   .25
RICHARDS, B.   1
    SILVER MOONBEAMS -- SOLO OR DUET
        VOLKWEIN BROS.   .25
RICHARDS, B.   1
    SILVER MOONBEAMS
        VOLKWEIN BROS.   .25
RICHARDSON, A.
    IMPROVISATION ON A NURSERY TUNE
        BOOSEY AND HAWKES, INC.   .60
RICHMOND
    DANCE OF THE HONEYBEES
        EDWARD B. MARKS MUSIC CORPORATION   01.50
RICHTER, A.--ED.   RICHTER, A.
    HANON FOR TWO
        WARNER BROTHERS PUBLISHERS   1.50
RICHTER, A.
    CHRISTMAS CAROLS IN VERY EASY ARRANGEMENTS FOR PIANO DUET
        THEODORE PRESSER COMPANY   1.00
RICHTER, A.
    FAVORITE HYMNS IN EASY ARRANGEMENTS FOR PIANO DUET
        THEODORE PRESSER COMPANY   1.25
RICHTER, C.--ED   RICHTER, C.
    CARL RICHTER PIANO DUETS, BK. 02
        BOURNE COMPANY   .75
RICHTER
    ENSEMBLE BOOK -- EASY DUETS
        WARNER BROTHERS PUBLISHERS   AR 22   1.25
RICHTER
    TRICKS FOR TWO -- EASY DUETS
        WARNER BROTHERS PUBLISHERS   AR 31   1.50
RIEGGER, W.--ED.   RIEGGER, W.   EASY
    GALWAY PIPER, THE
        SHAWNEE PRESS, INC.   HC-5001   .60
RIEGGER, W.--ED.   RIEGGER, W.
    HAROLD FLAMMER DUET ALBUM
        SHAWNEE PRESS, INC.   1.00
RIEGGER, W.--ED.   RIEGGER, W.   EASY
    SKIP TO MY LOU
        SHAWNEE PRESS, INC.   HC-5003   .60
RIEGGER, W.
    CRY, THE
        PEER SOUTHERN ORGANIZATION   01.25
RIEGGER, W.
    EVOCATION
        PEER SOUTHERN ORGANIZATION   01.50
RIEGGER, W.   EASY
    GARDEN FLOWERS
        SHAWNEE PRESS, INC.   .60
RIMSKY-KORSAKOFF
    CAPRICCIO ESPAGNOL, OP. 34
        BOOSEY AND HAWKES, INC.   4.50
RIMSKY-KORSAKOFF   BLUMENFELD
    RUSSIAN EASTER FESTIVAL, OP. 36
        BOOSEY AND HAWKES, INC.   3.75
RIMSKY-KORSAKOFF   GILSON
    SCHEHERAZADE, OP. 35
        BOOSEY AND HAWKES, INC.   5.00
RIMSKY-KORSAKOFF   STERNBERG
    SHEHERAZADE, OP. 35 -- SYMPHONIC SUITE, ARR. BY THE COMPOSER
        G. SCHIRMER, INC.   L1349   2.75
RIMSKY-KORSAKOFF   4
    SONG OF INDIA
        CENTURY MUSIC PUBLISHING COMPANY, INC.   3741   .60
ROBINSON, A.   1
    LITTLE CLOG DANCE
        WILLIS MUSIC COMPANY   .40
ROBINSON, A.   1
    LITTLE MARCH
        WILLIS MUSIC COMPANY   .40
ROBINSON, A.   1
    LULLABY
        WILLIS MUSIC COMPANY   .40
ROBINSON, A.   1
    POLKA PETITE
        WILLIS MUSIC COMPANY   .40
ROBINSON, A.   1
    WALTZING
        WILLIS MUSIC COMPANY   .40
ROBINSON, W. E.   2 1/2
    OOMPAH POLKA
        BELWIN-MILLS PUBLISHING CORPORATION   .60
ROBINSON, W. E.   3
    RONDO IN A
        WILLIS MUSIC COMPANY   .50
ROBINSON   1-2
    JOYOUS BELLS
        CENTURY MUSIC PUBLISHING COMPANY, INC.   4219   .60
ROBLES
    CONDOR PASA, EL
        EDWARD B. MARKS MUSIC CORPORATION   01.25
RODGERS, I.
    FIRST DUET BOOK FOR LITTLE JACKS AND JILLS, A
        G. SCHIRMER, INC.   1.00
RODGERS, I.
    SECOND DUET BOOK FOR LITTLE JACKS AND JILLS, A
        G. SCHIRMER, INC.   1.00
RODGERS   MERKUR
    WITH A SONG IN MY HEART
        WARNER BROTHERS PUBLISHERS   1.25

RODRIGO, J.
  GRAN MARCHA DE LOS SUBSECRETARIOS
    ASSOCIATED MUSIC PUBLISHERS, INC.   SIM   1.75
ROGER-DUCASSE
  PASTORALE
    ELKAN-VOGEL, INC.   D   2.00
ROGERS--ED *   ROGERS *
  THREE WAY DUETS
    PRO-ART PUBLICATIONS, INC.   1003   1.50
ROGERS, E. T.   3 1/2 - 4
  DUETS FROM THE HYMNAL
    LILLENAS PUBLISHING COMPANY   MB-043   2.50
ROGERS, E. T.   2-2 1/2
  HYMNS FOR TWO
    LILLENAS PUBLISHING COMPANY   MB-081   2.50
ROGERS, E.   1C
  ADVENTURES OF PRIMO AND SECONDO, THE
    ASHLEY DEALERS SERVICE, INC.   1.00
ROGERS, E.   1C
  ADVENTURES OF PRIMO AND SECONDO
    CENTURY MUSIC PUBLISHING COMPANY, INC.   1.00
ROGERS, E.
  ONE PLUS ONE
    ASHLEY DEALERS SERVICE, INC.   1.00
ROGERS, E.
  ONE PLUS ONE
    CENTURY MUSIC PUBLISHING COMPANY, INC.   1.00
ROGERS   2
  ALPINE SONG
    WILLIS MUSIC COMPANY   .50
ROLFE, W.   2
  AMERICA FIRST
    THEODORE PRESSER COMPANY   .50
ROLFE, W.   KING, S.   EASY
  SPRING FLOWERS
    SHAWNEE PRESS, INC.   HC-5008   .60
ROMBERG, S.   LEVINE
  DESERT SONG
    WARNER BROTHERS PUBLISHERS   1.25
ROMBERG, S.   NEWES
  SIGMUND ROMBERG 'EASY TO PLAY' PIANO DUETS
    WARNER BROTHERS PUBLISHERS   1.50
ROPARTZ
  CLOCHE DES MORTS
    FRANCO COLOMBO PUBLICATIONS   SAL   2.50
ROPARTZ
  INTIMITE
    FRANCO COLOMBO PUBLICATIONS   SAL   1.50
ROPARTZ
  LITTLE PIECES - CHORAL
    FRANCO COLOMBO PUBLICATIONS   SAL   1.50
ROPARTZ
  LITTLE PIECES - CLOCHES DU SOIR
    FRANCO COLOMBO PUBLICATIONS   SAL   1.50
ROPARTZ
  LITTLE PIECES - L'ANGELUS
    FRANCO COLOMBO PUBLICATIONS   SAL   1.50
ROPARTZ
  LITTLE PIECES - LE GLAS
    FRANCO COLOMBO PUBLICATIONS   SAL   1.50
ROPARTZ
  LITTLE PIECES - PAR LES CHAMPS
    FRANCO COLOMBO PUBLICATIONS   SAL   1.50
ROPARTZ
  LITTLE PIECES - POUR GAUD
    FRANCO COLOMBO PUBLICATIONS   SAL   1.50
ROPARTZ
  LITTLE PIECES - TRISTESSE
    FRANCO COLOMBO PUBLICATIONS   SAL   1.50
ROPARTZ
  SERENADE FOR STRING QUARTET
    FRANCO COLOMBO PUBLICATIONS   SAL   2.50
ROPARTZ
  SYMPHONY NO. 01
    FRANCO COLOMBO PUBLICATIONS   SAL   10.75
ROSAS   3
  OVER THE WAVES, MEXICAN WALTZES
    CENTURY MUSIC PUBLISHING COMPANY, INC.   1471   .60
ROSAS   VILAFRANC
  OVER THE WAVES
    FRANCO COLOMBO PUBLICATIONS   BA8861   1.00
ROSSINI, G.
  BARBIERE DI SIVIGLIA, IL - OVERTURE
    FRANCO COLOMBO PUBLICATIONS   97464   1.25
ROSSINI, G.
  GAZZA LADRA, LA - OVERTURE
    FRANCO COLOMBO PUBLICATIONS   97465   1.25
ROSSINI, G.
  ITALIANA IN ALGERI, L' - OVERTURE
    FRANCO COLOMBO PUBLICATIONS   97467   1.25
ROSSINI, G.   STREABBOG
  MOSE - PRAYER
    FRANCO COLOMBO PUBLICATIONS   BA1762   .75
ROSSINI, G. *   M
  OVERTURES
    C. F. PETERS CORPORATION   141   6.00
ROSSINI, G.   TENAGLIA
  SELECTED OVERTURES -- WITH BELLINI .... SELECTED OVERTURES --
    FRANCO COLOMBO PUBLICATIONS   129787   5.00
ROSSINI, G.
  WILLIAM TELL OVERTURE
    G. SCHIRMER, INC.   1.10
ROUGNON
  COUCOU
    FRANCO COLOMBO PUBLICATIONS   SAL   1.75
ROUGNON
  DANSEZ, FILLETTES
    FRANCO COLOMBO PUBLICATIONS   SAL   1.75
ROUGNON
  EN PROMENADE
    FRANCO COLOMBO PUBLICATIONS   SAL   1.75
ROUSSEL, A.
  SARABANDE FROM L'EVENTAIL DE JEANNE
    HEUGEL ET CIE.   1.95
ROUSSEL, A.
  SYMPHONY IN D MINOR -- POEME DE LA FORET --
    FRANCO COLOMBO PUBLICATIONS   SAL   10.75
ROVENGER--ED.   ROVENGER
  SIDE BY SIDE AT THE PIANO
    RUBANK, INC.   1.75
ROWLEY
  PASTORALE
    BOOSEY AND HAWKES, INC.   .60
ROWLEY
  SEVEN MARCHES, OP. 47
    C. F. PETERS CORPORATION   4386   2.50

ROWLEY   E
  SIX SHORT DANCE IMPRESSIONS, OP. 41
    C. F. PETERS CORPORATION   4381   2.50
ROZIN
  LITTLE CONCERTO
    BRODT MUSIC COMPANY   1.25
RUBINSTEIN   4
  MELODY IN F
    THEODORE PRESSER COMPANY   .50
RUIZ DEL PORTAL
  RETRAITE ESPAGNOLE
    FRANCO COLOMBO PUBLICATIONS   SAL   2.50
RUSSELL
  FANTASY ON 'IN DULCI JUBILO'
    BOSTON MUSIC COMPANY   .60
RUSSELL   3
  IN DULCI JUBILO
    BOSTON MUSIC COMPANY   .60
RUSSELL
  PLACES - SUITE
    GENERAL MUSIC PUBLISHING COMPANY, INC.   4.00
RUSSELL
  SUITE FOR PIANO
    NOVELLO AND COMPANY, LTD.   7.50
RUSSELL
  TURNABOUT DUETS
    PRO-ART PUBLICATIONS, INC.   885   .85
RUTHARDT   E-M
  TEACHER AND PUPIL --40 PIECES--
    C. F. PETERS CORPORATION   2720   2.50
RUTHARDT
  TEACHER AND PUPIL
    EDWIN F. KALMUS   3844   2.00
SAINT-SAENS
  CAPRICE-VALSE FROM 'WEDDING CAKE'
    ELKAN-VOGEL, INC.   D   4.25
SAINT-SAENS
  CARNIVAL OF THE ANIMALS
    ELKAN-VOGEL, INC.   7.75
SAINT-SAENS
  DANSE MACABRE
    ELKAN-VOGEL, INC.   4.10
SAINT-SAENS
  LE CYGNE -- THE SWAN
    ELKAN-VOGEL, INC.   D   1.60
SAINT-SAENS
  MARCHE HEROIQUE, OP. 34
    ELKAN-VOGEL, INC.   D   6.00
SALTER, L.
  GREY DAY AND OUT IN THE SUN
    BOOSEY AND HAWKES, INC.   .75
SAMMARTINO
  GATO
    FRANCO COLOMBO PUBLICATIONS   BA9220   .75
SAMMARTINO
  HUELLA
    FRANCO COLOMBO PUBLICATIONS   BA10286   .75
SAMMARTINO
  MILONGA
    FRANCO COLOMBO PUBLICATIONS   BA10287   .75
SAMMARTINO
  PERICON
    FRANCO COLOMBO PUBLICATIONS   BA10288   .75
SAMMARTINO
  SELECTED CLASSICAL AND MODERN WORKS, BK. 1
    FRANCO COLOMBO PUBLICATIONS   BA11372   1.25
SAMMARTINO
  SELECTED CLASSICAL AND MODERN WORKS, BK. 2
    FRANCO COLOMBO PUBLICATIONS   BA11373   1.25
SAMMARTINO
  TRIUNFO, EL
    FRANCO COLOMBO PUBLICATIONS   BA10289   .75
SAMMARTINO
  ZAMBA DE VARGAS
    FRANCO COLOMBO PUBLICATIONS   BA10290   .75
SARASATE   SCARMOLIN   3
  GYPSY DANCE
    PRO-ART PUBLICATIONS, INC.   12   .60
SATIE, E.
  APERCUS DESAGREABLES
    ASSOCIATED MUSIC PUBLISHERS, INC.   ESC   3.75
SATIE, E.
  CINEMA
    FRANCO COLOMBO PUBLICATIONS   SAL   6.50
SATIE, E.
  EN HABIT DE CHEVAL
    FRANCO COLOMBO PUBLICATIONS   SAL   3.25
SATIE, E.
  PARADE -- BALLET --
    FRANCO COLOMBO PUBLICATIONS   SAL   5.50
SATIE, E.
  THREE MORCEAUX EN FORME DE POIRE
    FRANCO COLOMBO PUBLICATIONS   SAL   5.75
SATIE, E.
  TROIS PETITES PIECES MONTEES
    ASSOCIATED MUSIC PUBLISHERS, INC.   ESC   4.00
SAUVREZIS
  FRESQUE MARINE
    FRANCO COLOMBO PUBLICATIONS   SAL   4.00
SAUVREZIS
  PETITES FEUILLES
    FRANCO COLOMBO PUBLICATIONS   SAL   4.00
SAUVREZIS
  THREE LITTLE PIECES
    FRANCO COLOMBO PUBLICATIONS   SAL   2.25
SCARMOLIN--ED   SCARMOLIN   3
  SHORT*NIN' BREAD
    PRO-ART PUBLICATIONS, INC.   14   .60
SCARMOLIN   3
  ARKANSAS TRAVELER
    PRO-ART PUBLICATIONS, INC.   13   .60
SCARMOLIN   3
  AY, AY, AY
    PRO-ART PUBLICATIONS, INC.   37   .50
SCARMOLIN   3
  DRINK TO ME ONLY WITH THINE EYES
    PRO-ART PUBLICATIONS, INC.   39   .50
SCHAEFER, R.
  VOLKS-UND KINDERLIEDER
    ASSOCIATED MUSIC PUBLISHERS, INC.   DOB   1.75
SCHARWENKA, X.   4
  POLISH DANCE, NO. 01
    CENTURY MUSIC PUBLISHING COMPANY, INC.   942   .60
SCHARWENKA, X.
  POLISH DANCE IN E FLAT MINOR, OP. 3 NO. 1
    G. SCHIRMER, INC.   .60
SCHAUM, J.--ED.   SCHAUM, J.   3
  BLUE BOOGIE
    BELWIN-MILLS PUBLISHING CORPORATION   .50

SCHAUM, J.--ED.   SCHAUM, J.   1
  CHOP STICKS
          BELWIN-MILLS PUBLISHING CORPORATION   .50
SCHAUM, J.--ED.   SCHAUM, J.   1
  CHRISTMAS ALBUM -- PIANO DUET
          BELWIN-MILLS PUBLISHING CORPORATION   1.25
SCHAUM, J.--ED.   SCHAUM, J.   1
  CHRISTMAS ALBUM
          BELWIN-MILLS PUBLISHING CORPORATION   1.50
SCHAUM, J.--ED.   SCHAUM, J.   2
  CHRISTMAS MORNING
          BELWIN-MILLS PUBLISHING CORPORATION   .50
SCHAUM, J.--ED.   SCHAUM, J.   1
  DUET ALBUM, BK. 1
          BELWIN-MILLS PUBLISHING CORPORATION   1.50
SCHAUM, J.--ED.   SCHAUM, J.   2
  DUET ALBUM, BK. 2
          BELWIN-MILLS PUBLISHING CORPORATION   1.50
SCHAUM, J.--ED.   SCHAUM, J.   3
  DUET ALBUM, BK. 3
          BELWIN-MILLS PUBLISHING CORPORATION   1.50
SCHAUM, J.--ED.   SCHAUM, J.   1
  EGGS PERT HEN, THE
          BELWIN-MILLS PUBLISHING CORPORATION   .50
SCHAUM, J.--ED.   SCHAUM, J.   1
  HYMN DUETS FOR CHILDREN
          SCHAUM PUBLICATIONS, INC.   1.50
SCHAUM, J.--ED.   SCHAUM, J.   4
  ORIGINAL PIANO DUETS BY AMERICAN COMPOSERS
          SCHAUM PUBLICATIONS, INC.   2.00
SCHAUM, J.--ED.   SCHAUM, J.   1
  PIANO ACCOMPANIMENTS TO THE 'A' BOOK
          BELWIN-MILLS PUBLISHING CORPORATION   1.50
SCHAUM, J.
  PRE A EMSEMBLE BOOK
          BELWIN-MILLS PUBLISHING CORPORATION   1.50
SCHAUM, J.   1
  TUNES FOR TWO, BK. 1
          SCHAUM PUBLICATIONS, INC.   1.50
SCHAUM, J.   1
  TUNES FOR TWO, BK. 1
          SCHAUM PUBLICATIONS, INC.   1.50
SCHAUM, J.   2
  TUNES FOR TWO, BK. 2
          SCHAUM PUBLICATIONS, INC.   1.50
SCHAUM, J.   2
  TUNES FOR TWO, BK. 2
          SCHAUM PUBLICATIONS, INC.   1.25
SCHELB   3
  KLEINE SONATE
          BARENREITER VERLAG   SM 13998
SCHER, W.--ED   SCHER, W.
  FOURTEEN PIANO DUETS FOR THE EARLY GRADES
          G. SCHIRMER, INC.   1.25
SCHER, W.--ED   SCHER, W.
  TRAVELOGUES OF MELODY -- 13 MELODIES FROM 13 COUNTRIES
          G. SCHIRMER, INC.   1.00
SCHER, W.--ED   SCHER, W.
  TWENTY PIANO DUETS -- FOR THE INTERMEDIATE GRADES
          G. SCHIRMER, INC.   1.50
SCHER, W.   1-2
  ARABIAN DANCE
          PRO-ART PUBLICATIONS, INC.   174   .60
SCHER, W.   3
  BLUE CANDLELIGHT
          PRO-ART PUBLICATIONS, INC.   510   .60
SCHER, W.   1-2
  CHINESE FAIRY TALE, A
          PRO-ART PUBLICATIONS, INC.   169   .50
SCHER, W.
  CZARDAS RHAPSODY
          CARL FISCHER, INC.   RS 402   .75
SCHER, W.   1-2
  DANCING MOSQUITOES
          PRO-ART PUBLICATIONS, INC.   172   .50
SCHER, W.   2 1/2
  DANCING PUPPETS
          THEODORE PRESSER COMPANY   .50
SCHER, W.
  FOLK SONGS OF ISRAEL
          PRO-ART PUBLICATIONS, INC.   924   .85
SCHER, W.
  FOR FOUR HANDS
          PRO-ART PUBLICATIONS, INC.   601   .85
SCHER, W.
  HAPPY GO LUCKY
          CARL FISCHER, INC.   P 2996   .60
SCHER, W.   2
  HOBBY HORSE
          PRO-ART PUBLICATIONS, INC.   511   .50
SCHER, W.   4
  HUNGARIAN WEDDING SCENE
          BELWIN-MILLS PUBLISHING CORPORATION   .60
SCHER, W.   2
  JOLLY LITTLE CHINAMAN
          BOSTON MUSIC COMPANY   .60
SCHER, W.
  LITTLE COSSACKS
          SOUTHERN MUSIC COMPANY   1.75
SCHER, W.   2
  MARCH OF THE GREEN BERETS
          PRO-ART PUBLICATIONS, INC.   546   .60
SCHER, W.
  MOVIE MYSTERY, A
          SOUTHERN MUSIC COMPANY   .75
SCHER, W.   1-2
  PEASANT DANCE
          PRO-ART PUBLICATIONS, INC.   173   .75
SCHER, W.   2-3
  POLKA DOT POLKA
          PRO-ART PUBLICATIONS, INC.   509   .50
SCHER, W.   2
  RHAPSODY FOR TWO
          PRO-ART PUBLICATIONS, INC.   250   .60
SCHER, W.
  ROCKING HORSE POLKA
          SOUTHERN MUSIC COMPANY   .75
SCHER, W.   1-2
  SCOOTER RACE
          PRO-ART PUBLICATIONS, INC.   170   .50
SCHER, W.   1-2
  WALTZING PEACOCK
          PRO-ART PUBLICATIONS, INC.   171   .60
SCHICKELE, P.
  OVERTURE TO THE CIVILIAN BARBER
          ELKAN-VOGEL, INC.   1.00

SCHILLER, F.   1
  PEACOCK, SONG WITHOUT WORDS
          CENTURY MUSIC PUBLISHING COMPANY, INC. 1389   .60
SCHILLIO, E. J.   3
  MORNING IN MADRID
          THEODORE PRESSER COMPANY   .50
SCHMID   4
  BAYRISCHE LANDLER, OP. 36
          SCHOTT   1853   2.25
SCHMITT, F.
  FEUILLETS DE VOYAGE, BK. 1
          ELKAN-VOGEL, INC.   D   8.60
SCHMITT, F.
  FEUILLETS DE VOYAGE, BK. 2
          ELKAN-VOGEL, INC.   D   5.00
SCHMITT, F.
  KERMESSE VALSE FROM L'EVENTAIL DE JEANNE
          HEUGEL ET CIE.   3.75
SCHMITT, F.
  UNE SEMAINE DU PETIT ELFE FERME-L'OEIL -- OR LES SONGES DE
  HIALMAR
          ELKAN-VOGEL, INC.   D   8.00
SCHMITT
  EASY TUNES FOR TWO
          BOSTON MUSIC COMPANY   1.00
SCHMITT
  REFLETS D'ALLEMAGNE, BK. 1 - HEIDELBERG, COBLENTZ, LUEBECK,
  WERDER
          FRANCO COLOMBO PUBLICATIONS   SAL   6.00
SCHMITT
  REFLETS D'ALLEMAGNE, BK. 2 - VIENNA, DRESDEN, NUREMBERG, MUNICH
          FRANCO COLOMBO PUBLICATIONS   SAL   7.25
SCHOENBERG   JALOWETZ, H.
  PELLEAS UND MELISANDE, SYMPHONIC POEM FOR ORCHESTRA OP. 5 ARR.
  FOR PIANO -- FOUR HANDS
          UNIVERSAL EDITION   UE 7269   7.20
SCHOLZ--ED   SCHOLZ
  ALLERERSTEN KLASSIKER UND ROMANTIKER, DIE -- LITTLE WORKS BY
  BEETHOVEN, BRAHMS, BRUCKNER, DIABELLI, SCHUBERT AND OTHERS
          ASSOCIATED MUSIC PUBLISHERS, INC.   DOB   3.00
SCHROEDER, H.   3
  FUNF DEUTSCHE WEIHNACHTSLIEDER
          SCHOTT   2509   2.50
SCHUBERT, C.--ED   SCHUBERT, C.
  OUVERTURES CELEBRES
          ELKAN-VOGEL, INC.   D   2.50
SCHUBERT   3
  BALLET MUSIC, ROSAMUND
          CENTURY MUSIC PUBLISHING COMPANY, INC. 1983   .60
SCHUBERT
  CHILDREN'S MARCH
          G. SCHIRMER, INC.   .30
SCHUBERT   2-3
  DANCES
          ASHLEY DEALERS SERVICE, INC.   1.25
SCHUBERT   2-3
  DANCES
          CENTURY MUSIC PUBLISHING COMPANY, INC.   1.25
SCHUBERT   M-D
  EIGHTEEN MARCHES
          C. F. PETERS CORPORATION   749   5.00
SCHUBERT
  FANTAISIE, OP. 103
          G. SCHIRMER, INC.   L1841   1.25
SCHUBERT
  FANTASIE IN F MINOR, OP. 103 -- D. 940
          G. HENLE MUSIKVERLAG   180   1.95
SCHUBERT   CURWEN *
  GERMAN DANCE IN E MAJOR
          G. SCHIRMER, INC.   .75
SCHUBERT   CURWEN *
  GERMAN DANCE IN G MAJOR
          G. SCHIRMER, INC.   .90
SCHUBERT   2-3
  LANDLER UND KINDERMARSCH
          SCHOTT   08798 1/2   1.00
SCHUBERT   MARCIANO
  MARCHE MILITAIRE, OP. 51 NO. 1
          FRANCO COLOMBO PUBLICATIONS   100793   .75
SCHUBERT   3
  MARCH MILITAIRE
          CENTURY MUSIC PUBLISHING COMPANY, INC. 1640   .60
SCHUBERT   MARCHI, G.
  MARCIA DI FANCIULLI, 4 LANDLER, MARCIA MILITARE
          EDIZIONI BERBEN   1503   2.40
SCHUBERT   ROSATI, G.
  MARCIA EROICA, OP. 27 NO. 3
          EDIZIONI BERBEN   EB 1771   2.50
SCHUBERT   3
  MILITARMARSCH D-DUR OP. 51 NO. 1
          SCHOTT   01031 1/2   1.00
SCHUBERT
  MILITARY MARCH --MARCHE MILITAIRE--, OP. 51 NO. 1
          CARL FISCHER, INC.   P 3047   .75
SCHUBERT
  MILITARY MARCH IN D, OP. 51 NO. 1
          G. SCHIRMER, INC.   .50
SCHUBERT   DIETRICH, F.   3
  MULLERLIED-VARIATIONEN -- UBER 'IHR BLUMLEIN ALLE' --
          BARENREITER VERLAG   BA 1652
SCHUBERT   M-D
  ORIGINAL COMPOSITIONS, COMPLETE IN 4 VOLS* VOL. 1
          C. F. PETERS CORPORATION   155A   3.50
SCHUBERT   M-D
  ORIGINAL COMPOSITIONS, COMPLETE IN 4 VOLS* VOL. 2
          C. F. PETERS CORPORATION   155B   3.50
SCHUBERT   M-D
  ORIGINAL COMPOSITIONS, COMPLETE IN 4 VOLS* VOL. 3
          C. F. PETERS CORPORATION   155C   3.50
SCHUBERT   M
  ORIGINAL COMPOSITIONS, COMPLETE IN 4 VOLS* VOL. 4
          C. F. PETERS CORPORATION   155D   2.00
SCHUBERT
  ORIGINAL COMPOSITIONS, VOL. 1-- CLOTH
          G. HENLE MUSIKVERLAG   95   9.25
SCHUBERT
  ORIGINAL COMPOSITIONS, VOL. 1
          G. HENLE MUSIKVERLAG   94   6.20
SCHUBERT
  ORIGINAL COMPOSITIONS, VOL. 2 -- CLOTH
          G. HENLE MUSIKVERLAG   97   10.40
SCHUBERT
  ORIGINAL COMPOSITIONS, VOL. 2
          G. HENLE MUSIKVERLAG   96   7.35
SCHUBERT
  ORIGINAL COMPOSITIONS, VOL. 3 -- CLOTH
          G. HENLE MUSIKVERLAG   99   7.35

SCHUBERT
    ORIGINAL COMPOSITIONS, VOL. 3
        G. HENLE MUSIKVERLAG   98   4.25
SCHUBERT   WOSS
    ORIGINAL COMPOSITIONS
        UNIVERSAL EDITION   466   2.50
SCHUBERT   ROSATI, G.
    POLACCA, OP. 61 NO. 1
        EDIZIONI BERBEN   EB 1595   1.50
SCHUBERT   3
    ROSAMUND, BALLET MUSIC
        CENTURY MUSIC PUBLISHING COMPANY, INC.   1983   .60
SCHUBERT   3
    SECHS LANDLER UND 11 V. BRAHMS VIERHANDIG GESTZTE LANDLER
        SCHOTT   2338   2.25
SCHUBERT
    SELECTED ORIGINAL COMPOSITIONS FOR PIANO, FOUR HANDS -- BK. 1
        G. SCHIRMER, INC.   L1778   3.00
SCHUBERT
    SELECTED ORIGINAL COMPOSITIONS FOR PIANO, FOUR HANDS -- BK. 2
        G. SCHIRMER, INC.   L1779   3.00
SCHUBERT
    SELECTED ORIGINAL COMPOSITIONS
        INTERNATIONAL MUSIC COMPANY   3.75
SCHUBERT   3
    SERENADE -- STAENOCHEN --
        CENTURY MUSIC PUBLISHING COMPANY, INC.   1828   .60
SCHUBERT   3
    SINFONIE H-MOLL -- UNVOLLENDETE KLAVIERAUSZUG
        SCHOTT   129   1.75
SCHUBERT
    SONATA IN C, OP. 140
        INTERNATIONAL MUSIC COMPANY   2.50
SCHUBERT   ULRICH   M
    SYMPHONIES --4--
        C. F. PETERS CORPORATION   1892   9.00
SCHUBERT   DEIS
    SYMPHONY NO. 08 IN B MINOR, ''UNFINISHED''
        G. SCHIRMER, INC.   L1409   1.25
SCHUBERT   M
    SYMPHONY NO. 08 IN B MINOR --'UNFINISHED'--
        C. F. PETERS CORPORATION   768   2.00
SCHULHOFF
    VALSE BRILLANTE NO. 2 IN D-FLAT MAJOR, OP. 20
        FRANCO COLOMBO PUBLICATIONS   SAL   2.75
SCHUMANN, R.   MARCHI, G.
    ALLA FONTANA, OP. 85 NO. 9
        EDIZIONI BERBEN   EB 1628   2.70
SCHUMANN, R.
    ALL ORIGINAL COMPOSITIONS
        INTERNATIONAL MUSIC COMPANY   5.00
SCHUMANN, R.
    COMPLETE OVERTURES
        UNIVERSAL EDITION   678   2.75
SCHUMANN, R.   1
    GEBURTSTAGSMARSCH OP. 85 NO. 1
        SCHOTT   01046   .75
SCHUMANN, R.   MARCHI, G.
    GIORNO DI FESTA MARCIA, OP. 85, NO. 1, CANTO DELLA SERA, OP. 85,
    NO. 12, VALZER, OP. 130, NO. 2
        EDIZIONI BERBEN   1267   1.20
SCHUMANN, R.
    IMPRESSIONE D'ORIENTE, OP. 66 NO. 1
        EDIZIONI BERBEN   EB 1772   2.75
SCHUMANN, R.   3
    JOYOUS PEASANT, OP. 68 NO. 10
        THEODORE PRESSER COMPANY   .50
SCHUMANN, R.   M
    ORIGINAL COMPOSITIONS
        C. F. PETERS CORPORATION   2347   4.50
SCHUMANN, R.
    OVERTURE, SCHERZO, FINALE
        UNIVERSAL EDITION   907   1.65
SCHUMANN, R.   BRISSLER
    OVERTURES
        ASSOCIATED MUSIC PUBLISHERS, INC.   BRH   1.75
SCHUMANN, R.
    PETIT PIANIST - LE PETIT SCHUMANN
        DELRIEU ET CIE.   2.75
SCHUMANN, R.   M
    PICTURES FROM THE EAST, OP. 66
        C. F. PETERS CORPORATION   2347A   1.50
SCHUMANN, R.   4
    PICTURES FROM THE EAST
        ASHLEY DEALERS SERVICE, INC.   1.25
SCHUMANN, R.
    PICTURES FROM THE EAST
        CENTURY MUSIC PUBLISHING COMPANY, INC.   1.25
SCHUMANN, R.   E-M
    SCENES FROM CHILDHOOD, OP. 15
        C. F. PETERS CORPORATION   2356   1.50
SCHUMANN, R.
    SIX ETUDES, OP. 56
        ELKAN-VOGEL, INC.   2.75
SCHUMANN, R.   KIRCHNER   M-D
    SYMPHONIES, OP. 38, 61, 97, 120. COMPLETE
        C. F. PETERS CORPORATION   2348   10.00
SCHUMANN, R.   OESTERLE
    TWELVE FOUR-HAND PIANO PIECES, OP. 85
        G. SCHIRMER, INC.   L825   1.50
SCHUMANN, R.   STEINER   1
    TWO HAPPY FARMERS
        BELWIN-MILLS PUBLISHING CORPORATION   .60
SCHUNGELER, H.--ED   SCHUNGELER, H.   2
    DAS NEUE KINDERLIEDERBUCH, AUSWAHL FUR KLAVIER ZU VIER HANDEN
        SCHOTT   2831   2.25
SCHUNGELER, H.--ED   SCHUNGELER, H.   2
    DAS NEUE KINDERLIEDERBUCH
        SCHOTT   2831   2.75
SCHUNGELER, H.--ED   SCHUNGELER, H.   2-4
    VIERHANDIGES VORTRAGSBUCH, BAND 01
        SCHOTT   2892   3.00
SCHUNGELER, H.--ED   SCHUNGELER, H.   2-4
    VIERHANDIGES VORTRAGSBUCH, BAND 02
        SCHOTT   2893   2.50
SCHWALM, R.
    YOUNG MUSICIANS, THE VERY EASIEST OF PIECES
        EDWIN F. KALMUS   3939   1.50
SCHWALM, R.
    YOUNG MUSICIANS -- THE VERY EASIEST CHILDREN'S PIECES WITHIN THE
    COMPASS OF A FIFTH -- 30 FOLK-SONGS AND SHORT MELODIOUS
    TONE-PICTURES IN PROGRESSIVE ORDER
        G. SCHIRMER, INC.   L174   1.25
SCOTT, J.   4
    AT THE DONNYBROOK FAIR
        THEODORE PRESSER COMPANY   .60

SEDLACK. A.--ED   SEDLACK, A.
    PIANO MUSIC FOR FOUR HANDS, BK. 1 -- CHILDREN- AND FOLKSONGS
        ASSOCIATED MUSIC PUBLISHERS, INC.   DOB   2.25
SEDLACK. A.--ED   SEDLACK, A.
    PIANO MUSIC FOR FOUR HANDS, BK. 2 FOLKSONGS AND DANCES
        ASSOCIATED MUSIC PUBLISHERS, INC.   DOB   1.60
SEIBER, M.   2
    LEICHTE TENZE
        SCHOTT   2529   2.75
SELLENICK   5
    MARCHE INDIENNE
        ALPHONSE LEDUC
SEVERAC
    DANSE DES TREILLES
        FRANCO COLOMBO PUBLICATIONS   SAL   3.25
SEVERAC
    EN VACANCES - INVOCATION A SCHUMANN
        FRANCO COLOMBO PUBLICATIONS   SAL   2.00
SEVERAC *
    EN VACANCES - LES CARESSES DE GRAND'MAMAN
        FRANCO COLOMBO PUBLICATIONS   SAL   2.00
SEVERAC
    EN VACANCES - LES PETITES VOISINES EN VISITE
        FRANCO COLOMBO PUBLICATIONS   SAL   2.00
SEVERAC
    EN VACANCES - RONDE DANS LE PARC
        FRANCO COLOMBO PUBLICATIONS   SAL   2.00
SEVERAC
    EN VACANCES - TOTO DEGUISE EN SUISSE D'EGLISE AND MIMI SE
    DEGUISE EN MARQUISE
        FRANCO COLOMBO PUBLICATIONS   SAL   2.00
SEVERAC
    EN VACANCES - VALSE ROMANTIQUE
        FRANCO COLOMBO PUBLICATIONS   SAL   2.00
SEVERAC
    EN VACANCES - VIELLES BOITE A MUSIQUE
        FRANCO COLOMBO PUBLICATIONS   SAL   2.00
SEVERAC
    EN VACANCES
        FRANCO COLOMBO PUBLICATIONS   SAL   6.50
SEVERAC
    SOLDAT DE PLOMB, LE
        FRANCO COLOMBO PUBLICATIONS   SAL   4.25
SHAW, C.   5
    THIRD STREET RHUMBA
        THEODORE PRESSER COMPANY   .60
SHAW, G.   3-5
    SIX BLACK KEY DUETS
        NOVELLO AND COMPANY, LTD.   10.0141.08   1.40
SHAW, G.   4
    SIX TRADITIONAL MELODIES
        NOVELLO AND COMPANY, LTD.   10.0143.04   1.40
SHIFRIN   M-D
    MODERN TEMPER, THE. A DANCE
        C. F. PETERS CORPORATION   5877   3.50
SHOSTAKOVITCH
    SYMPHONY NO. 01, OP. 10
        INTERNATIONAL MUSIC COMPANY   2.50
SIBELIUS   TAUBMANN
    SWAN OF TUONELA, THE, OP. 22 NO. 3 -- ORCH
        ASSOCIATED MUSIC PUBLISHERS, INC.   BRH   1.25
SIBELIUS   WALLIS   2
    THEME FROM FINLANDIA
        BOSTON MUSIC COMPANY   .60
SIBELIUS   TAUBMANN
    VALSE TRISTE, OP. 44 -- ORCH
        ASSOCIATED MUSIC PUBLISHERS, INC.   BRH   2.50
SIBELIUS   WALLIS   2
    VALSE TRISTE
        BOSTON MUSIC COMPANY   .60
SIEGL, O.
    THREE POLYPHONIC PIECES
        ASSOCIATED MUSIC PUBLISHERS, INC.   DOB   2.00
SINDING   M
    RUSTLE OF SPRING, OP. 32 NO. 3
        C. F. PETERS CORPORATION   2870F   1.25
SMALL, A.
    TWENTY FAVORITES FOR TWO PIANISTS
        ALFRED MUSIC COMPANY   540   1.25
SMALL, A.
    VERY FIRST DUET BOOK
        ALFRED MUSIC COMPANY   539   1.00
SMETANA   3
    MEINE VATERLAND -- ORIGINAL-BEARBEITUNG DES KOMPONISTEN -- HEFT
    1, VYSEHRAD
        BARENREITER VERLAG   AP 781A
SMETANA   3
    MEIN VATERLAND -- ORIGINAL-BEARBEITUNG DES KOMPONISTEN -- HEFT
    2, DIE MOLDAU
        BARENREITER VERLAG   AP 781B
SMETANA   3
    MEIN VATERLAND -- ORIGINAL-BEARBEITUNG DES KOMPONISTEN -- HEFT
    3, SARKA
        BARENREITER VERLAG   AP 781C
SMETANA   3
    MEIN VATERLAND -- ORIGINAL-BEARBEITUNG DES KOMPONISTEN -- HEFT
    4, AUS BOHMENS HAIN UND FLUR
        BARENREITER VERLAG   AP 781D
SMETANA   3
    MEIN VATERLAND -- ORIGINAL-BEARBEITUNG DES KOMPONISTEN -- HEFT
    5, TABOR
        BARENREITER VERLAG   AP 781F
SMETANA   3
    MEIN VATERLAND -- ORIGINAL-BEARBEITUNG DES KOMPONISTEN -- HEFT
    6, BLANIK
        BARENREITER VERLAG   AP 781F
SMETANA
    OUVERTURE ZUR VERKAUFTEN BRAUT -- FAKSIMILE DER
    ORIGINALUBERTRAGUNG SMETANAS --
        BARENREITER VERLAG   AP 780
SMETANA *   3
    PRAGER KARNEVAL
        BARENREITER VERLAG   AP 782
SMETANA   VESELY   3
    STRING QUARTET NO. 2 IN D MINOR
        BARENREITER VERLAG   AP 783
SMETANA   MELVIN, B.   2-3
    THEME FROM 'MOLDAU'
        PRO-ART PUBLICATIONS, INC.   522   .85
SMITH--ED   SMITH   2
    STAR SPANGLED BANNER, THE
        BOSTON MUSIC COMPANY   .60
SMITH, H.   1
    ON PARADE
        WILLIS MUSIC COMPANY   .50
SMITH, J.
    FLOWER DUETS, THE, BK. 1
        BANKS AND SON LTD.   .95

SMITH, T.
  KEYBOARD DUETS NO. 1
    LILLENAS PUBLISHING COMPANY   MB-098   2.50
SMITH, T.
  KEYBOARD DUETS NO. 2
    LILLENAS PUBLISHING COMPANY   MB-239   2.50
SMITH, T.
  SACRED CLASSICS FOR FOUR HANDS-ONE PIANO
    HOPE PUBLISHING COMPANY   2.50
SMITH   3
  DANCE OF THE GOBLINS
    VOLKWEIN BROS.   .50
SMOLANOFF
  PAGES FROM A SUMMER JOURNAL
    SEESAW MUSIC CORPORATION   3.00
SOLTERS
  FIRST PIECES FOR FOUR HANDS
    BARENREITER VERLAG   BA 3508   3.25
SOUBEYRAN
  LIVRE BLEU, LE
    FRANCO COLOMBO PUBLICATIONS   SAL   5.00
SOUBEYRAN
  POUR 2 PETITS AMIS
    FRANCO COLOMBO PUBLICATIONS   SAL   3.25
SOUSA   3 1/2
  EL CAPITAN
    THEODORE PRESSER COMPANY   .75
SOUSA   2
  HARMONICA WIZARD --MARCH--
    THEODORE PRESSER COMPANY   .60
SOUSA   3
  HARMONICA WIZARD
    THEODORE PRESSER COMPANY   .60
SOUSA   MELVIN, B.   3
  SEMPRE FIDELIS
    PRO-ART PUBLICATIONS, INC.   291   .60
SOUSA   MELVIN, B.   3
  STARS AND STRIPES FOREVER
    PRO-ART PUBLICATIONS, INC.   133   .60
SOUSA   3
  STARS AND STRIPES FOREVER
    THEODORE PRESSER COMPANY   .70
SPAULDING, G. L.   1
  AIRY FAIRIES
    THEODORE PRESSER COMPANY   .50
SPAULDING, G. L.
  JUST WE TWO
    THEODORE PRESSER COMPANY   1.50
SPAULDING, G. L.
  YOU AND I
    THEODORE PRESSER COMPANY   2.25
SPEAKS, O.   STEINER
  ON THE ROAD TO MANDALAY
    G. SCHIRMER, INC.   .80
SPENCER, R.   3
  FIREFLIES FROLIC
    WILLIS MUSIC COMPANY   .50
SPIVAK, S.--ED   SPIVAK, S.
  PLAYING OPERATIC DUETS FOR PLEASURE, BK. 1 -- SIMP.
    SCHUBERTH CO.   1.50
SPIVAK, S.--ED   SPIVAK, S.
  PLAYING OPERATIC DUETS FOR PLEASURE, BK. 2 -- SIMP.
    SCHUBERTH CO.   1.50
SPIVAK, S.   3
  BOOGIE WOOGIE NOCTURNE
    BELWIN-MILLS PUBLISHING CORPORATION   .60
STECHER *
  WE WISH YOU A MERRY CHRISTMAS, BK. 1
    SCHMITT, HALL AND MCCREARY COMPANY   9967   1.00
STECHER *
  WE WISH YOU A MERRY CHRISTMAS, BK. 2
    SCHMITT, HALL AND MCCREARY COMPANY   9978   1.25
STEEL
  SCALA PIANO DUET ALBUM
    FRANCO COLOMBO PUBLICATIONS   LD425   1.25
STEINER--ED.   STEINER   1
  SOMEBODY'S KNOCKING AT YOUR DOOR
    BELWIN-MILLS PUBLISHING CORPORATION   .60
STEINER   2 1/2, 3, 4
  ADVANCING PIANIST PLAYS DUETS, THE
    BELWIN-MILLS PUBLISHING CORPORATION 1927   1.75
STEINER
  CHORD DUETS
    BELWIN-MILLS PUBLISHING CORPORATION 2030   1.75
STEINER   JR. APPR.
  FOUR IN A ROWBOAT
    BELWIN-MILLS PUBLISHING CORPORATION   .60
STEINER
  SOLO AND DUET ALBUM
    BELWIN-MILLS PUBLISHING CORPORATION 1414   1.75
STEINER
  STARTING TOGETHER
    BELWIN-MILLS PUBLISHING CORPORATION 1972   1.75
STEINER
  TWO PIANISTS AT ONE PIANO, BK. 1
    BELWIN-MILLS PUBLISHING CORPORATION 1690   1.75
STEINER
  TWO PIANISTS AT ONE PIANO, BK. 2
    BELWIN-MILLS PUBLISHING CORPORATION 1691   1.75
STEVENS, E.   1 - 1 1/2
  SUGARLOAF MOUNTAIN
    ELKAN-VOGEL, INC.   .50
STRATEGIER   M
  SUITE
    C. F. PETERS CORPORATION   D41   2.00
STRAUSS, J.   GUENTHER, F.   M
  AFTER YOU, MR. STRAUSS
    THEODORE PRESSER COMPANY   .50
STRAUSS, J.   2
  BLUE DANUBE
    VOLKWEIN BROS.   .50
STRAUSS, J.   3
  MEINE STRAUSS-WALZER
    SCHOTT   1534   4.00
STRAUSS, J.   3 1/2
  ON THE BEAUTIFUL BLUE DANUBE
    THEODORE PRESSER COMPANY   .50
STRAUSS, J.   MARLIN   2-3
  PIZZICATO POLKA
    PRO-ART PUBLICATIONS, INC.   16   .60
STRAUSS, J.   WEYBRIGHT   2
  ROSES FROM THE SOUTH
    BELWIN-MILLS PUBLISHING CORPORATION   .60
STRAUSS, J.   BISHOP
  SERENADE, OP. 17
    CARL FISCHER, INC.   P 3147   2.00

STRAUSS, J.   RICHTER, C.
  STRAUSS WALTZES
    BOURNE COMPANY   1.25
STRAUSS, J.   WEYBRIGHT   1 1/2
  SWEETHEART WALTZ
    BELWIN-MILLS PUBLISHING CORPORATION   .60
STRAUSS, J.   KING, S.
  TALES FROM THE VIENNA WOODS
    SHAWNEE PRESS, INC.   HC-5010   .45
STRAUSS, J.   3
  TALES OF THE VIENNA WOODS
    CENTURY MUSIC PUBLISHING COMPANY, INC. 3507   .60
STRAUSS, R.   SINGER
  ALPENSINFONIE, EINE, OP. 64
    ASSOCIATED MUSIC PUBLISHERS, INC.   LEU   7.50
STRAUSS, R.   D
  AUS ITALIEN, OP. 16. SYMPHONIC POEM
    C. F. PETERS CORPORATION   4194A   6.50
STRAUSS, R.   SINGER
  CONCERT WALTZ, FROM 'DER ROSENKAVALIER'
    BOOSEY AND HAWKES, INC.   3.00
STRAUSS, R.   D
  DEATH AND TRANSFIGURATION, OP. 24. SYMPHONIC POEM
    C. F. PETERS CORPORATION   4194D   6.50
STRAUSS, R.   SINGER
  HELDENLEBEN, EIN, OP. 40 -- ORCH
    ASSOCIATED MUSIC PUBLISHERS, INC.   LEU   6.00
STRAUSS, R.
  IN SILENT FORESTS, OP. 9 -- STIMMUNGSBILDER, BK. 1
    UNIVERSAL EDITION   UE 1416   1.50
STRAUSS, R.
  IN SILENT FORESTS, OP. 9 -- STIMMUNGSBILDER, BK. 2
    UNIVERSAL EDITION   UE 1417   1.50
STRAUSS, R.
  IN SILENT FORESTS, OP. 9 -- STIMMUNGSBILDER, BK. 3
    UNIVERSAL EDITION   UE 1418   1.50
STRAUSS, R.
  IN SILENT FORESTS, OP. 9 -- STIMMUNGSBILDER, BK. 4
    UNIVERSAL EDITION   UE 1419   1.50
STRAUSS, R.
  IN SILENT FORESTS, OP. 9 -- STIMMUNGSBILDER, BK. 5
    UNIVERSAL EDITION   UE 1420   1.75
STRAUSS, R.   D
  MACBETH, OP. 23. SYMPHONIC POEM
    C. F. PETERS CORPORATION   4194C   6.50
STRAUSS, R.   D
  THUS SPAKE ZARATHUSTRA, OP. 30. SYMPHONIC POEM
    C. F. PETERS CORPORATION   4194F   6.50
STRAVINSKY, I.
  DANCE RUSSE --PETROUCHKA
    EDWARD B. MARKS MUSIC CORPORATION   01.50
STRAVINSKY, I.
  FIVE EASY PIECES
    INTERNATIONAL MUSIC COMPANY   2.00
STRAVINSKY, I.
  FIVE EASY PIECES
    SOUTHERN MUSIC COMPANY   1.50
STRAVINSKY, I.
  PETROUCHKA - REVISED 1947 VERSION
    BOOSEY AND HAWKES, INC.   8.50
STRAVINSKY, I.
  RITE OF SPRING
    BOOSEY AND HAWKES, INC.   7.50
STRAVINSKY, I.
  THREE EASY PIECES
    INTERNATIONAL MUSIC COMPANY   1.25
STRAVINSKY, I.
  THREE EASY PIECES
    SOUTHERN MUSIC COMPANY   1.50
STREABBOG   2
  ADONIS, GALOP
    CENTURY MUSIC PUBLISHING COMPANY, INC. 920   .60
STREABBOG   2 1/2
  DEPARTURE, OP. 100, NO. 7
    THEODORE PRESSER COMPANY   .50
STREABBOG
  EIGHT EASY PIECES
    FRANCO COLOMBO PUBLICATIONS   BA8816   2.50
STREABBOG   2
  GOLDEN STAR WALTZ
    CENTURY MUSIC PUBLISHING COMPANY, INC. 925   .60
STREABBOG   2
  GUARDS' MARCH
    CENTURY MUSIC PUBLISHING COMPANY, INC. 926   .60
STREABBOG   1
  HONEY BELL POLKA
    CENTURY MUSIC PUBLISHING COMPANY, INC. 928   .60
STREABBOG   2
  IDA POLKA MAZURKA
    CENTURY MUSIC PUBLISHING COMPANY, INC. 929   .60
STREABBOG   1
  LILY POLKA
    CENTURY MUSIC PUBLISHING COMPANY, INC. 934   .60
STREABBOG   2
  LITTLE FAIRY MARCH
    CENTURY MUSIC PUBLISHING COMPANY, INC. 938   .60
STREABBOG   2
  LITTLE FAIRY SCHOTTISCHE
    CENTURY MUSIC PUBLISHING COMPANY, INC. 936   .60
STREABBOG   2
  LITTLE FAIRY WALTZ
    CENTURY MUSIC PUBLISHING COMPANY, INC. 937   .60
STREABBOG   2
  MARCH MILITAIRE
    CENTURY MUSIC PUBLISHING COMPANY, INC. 939   .60
STREABBOG   2
  MORNING PRAYER, NO. 130
    CENTURY MUSIC PUBLISHING COMPANY, INC. 2421   .60
STREABBOG   LOWENSTEIN   2
  SILVER BELLS
    BOSTON MUSIC COMPANY   .60
STRIMER, J.--ED   STRIMER, J.
  FORTY PIANO PARTNERS - ELEMENTARY DUETS
    PRO-ART PUBLICATIONS, INC.   40   .85
STRIMER, J.--ED   STRIMER, J.   3
  THIRTY-TWO PIANO PARTNERS - GRADE 3 - DUETS
    PRO-ART PUBLICATIONS, INC.   32   1.25
SUGARMAN--ED
  FIRST YEAR IN MUSIC DUETS, BK. 1
    EDWARD B. MARKS MUSIC CORPORATION   01.25
SUGARMAN--ED
  FIRST YEAR IN MUSIC DUETS, BK. 2
    EDWARD B. MARKS MUSIC CORPORATION   01.25
SUGARMAN--ED
  FIRST YEAR IN MUSIC DUETS, BK. 3
    EDWARD B. MARKS MUSIC CORPORATION   01.25

SUGARMAN--ED
   FIRST YEAR IN MUSIC DUETS, BK. 4
      EDWARD B. MARKS MUSIC CORPORATION   01.25
SUGARMAN
   TAKES TWO TO DUET
      EDWARD B. MARKS MUSIC CORPORATION   02.00
SUK   3
   PRAGA. SYMPHONISCHE DICHTUNG, OP. 26 -- KLAVIERAUSZUG --
      BARENREITER VERLAG   AP 784
SUPINO   M
   TIC TAC
      FRANCO COLOMBO PUBLICATIONS   BON.2227   .90
SUPPE, F.
   OVERTURES, --6--
      C. F. PETERS CORPORATION   1395   5.00
SUPPE, F.   4
   POET AND PEASANT, OVERTURE
      CENTURY MUSIC PUBLISHING COMPANY, INC.   941   .60
SUPPE, F.
   POET AND PEASANT OVERTURE
      G. SCHIRMER, INC.   1.10
SUPPUS, P.A.
   POLONAISE E FLAT , FOUR HANDS
      MUSICA OBSCURA   1.00
SVENDSEN   M-D
   NORWEGIAN CARNIVAL, OP. 14
      C. F. PETERS CORPORATION   2076   2.00
SWANDER, D.
   DEEP IN THE HEART OF TEXAS
      PEER SOUTHERN ORGANIZATION   01.00
SWINSTEAD, F.
   LIGHT HEART
      BOOSEY AND HAWKES, INC.   .75
SZONYI, E.
   SMALL CHAMBER MUSIC
      KULTURA   2.00
TANSMAN, A.
   JARDIN DU PARADIS, LE -- LA DANSE DE LA SORCIERE
      ASSOCIATED MUSIC PUBLISHERS, INC.   ESC   2.00
TANSMAN, A.
   JEUNES AU PIANO, LES -- BK. 1, EN TOURNANT LA T.S.F. -- VERY
   EASY
      ASSOCIATED MUSIC PUBLISHERS, INC.   ESC   2.75
TANSMAN, A.
   JEUNES AU PIANO, LES -- BK. 2, PIECES DE FANTAISIE -- FAIRLY
   EASY
      ASSOCIATED MUSIC PUBLISHERS, INC.   ESC   2.50
TANSMAN, A.
   JEUNES AU PIANO, LES -- BK. 3, FEUILLETS'ALBUM -- LESS DIFFICULT
      ASSOCIATED MUSIC PUBLISHERS, INC.   ESC   2.25
TANSMAN, A.
   JEUNES AU PIANO, LES -- BK. 4, QUATRE PIECES FUGUEES -- FAIRLY
   DIFFICULT
      ASSOCIATED MUSIC PUBLISHERS, INC.   ESC   2.00
TANSMAN, A.
   NOUS JOUONS POUR MAMAN, NO. 01 -- NOEL
      ASSOCIATED MUSIC PUBLISHERS, INC.   ESC   .75
TANSMAN, A.
   NOUS JOUONS POUR MAMAN, NO. 02 -- AIR SOLENNEL
      ASSOCIATED MUSIC PUBLISHERS, INC.   ESC   .75
TANSMAN, A.
   NOUS JOUONS POUR MAMAN, NO. 03 -- REVERIE
      ASSOCIATED MUSIC PUBLISHERS, INC.   ESC   .75
TANSMAN, A.
   NOUS JOUONS POUR MAMAN, NO. 04 -- AIR A BERCER
      ASSOCIATED MUSIC PUBLISHERS, INC.   ESC   .75
TANSMAN, A.
   NOUS JOUONS POUR MAMAN, NO. 05 -- CHORAL
      ASSOCIATED MUSIC PUBLISHERS, INC.   ESC   .75
TANSMAN, A.
   NOUS JOUONS POUR MAMAN, NO. 06 -- VALSE
      ASSOCIATED MUSIC PUBLISHERS, INC.   ESC   .75
TANSMAN, A.
   NOUS JOUONS POUR MAMAN, NO. 07 -- CHANSON
      ASSOCIATED MUSIC PUBLISHERS, INC.   ESC   .75
TANSMAN, A.
   NOUS JOUONS POUR MAMAN, NO. 08 -- ARIETTA
      ASSOCIATED MUSIC PUBLISHERS, INC.   ESC   .75
TANSMAN, A.
   NOUS JOUONS POUR MAMAN, NO. 09 -- TEMPO DI MINUETTO
      ASSOCIATED MUSIC PUBLISHERS, INC.   ESC   .75
TANSMAN, A.
   NOUS JOUONS POUR MAMAN, NO. 10 -- AIR POPULAIRE
      ASSOCIATED MUSIC PUBLISHERS, INC.   ESC   .75
TANSMAN, A.
   NOUS JOUONS POUR MAMAN, NO. 11 -- FINAL
      ASSOCIATED MUSIC PUBLISHERS, INC.   ESC   .75
TANSMAN, A.
   NOUS JOUONS POUR MAMAN, NO. 11 -- PETITE CONTE
      ASSOCIATED MUSIC PUBLISHERS, INC.   ESC   .75
TATE, P.   VE
   FIFTEEN FINGERS
      OXFORD UNIVERSITY PRESS   33=#52   1.25
TATE, P.   E
   LETS PLAY DUETS
      OXFORD UNIVERSITY PRESS   34.033   1.50
TCHEREPNIN
   PARAPHRASES ON 'CHOPSTICKS'
      BOOSEY AND HAWKES, INC.   4.00
THOMAS, A.
   MIGNON OVERTURE
      G. SCHIRMER, INC.   .85
THOMPSON, J.   2
   FIVE FOR FOUR
      WILLIS MUSIC COMPANY   1.00
THOMPSON, J.
   MODERN COURSE FOR THE PIANO - A TUNEFUL DUET ALBUM FOR THE FIRST
   YEAR
      WILLIS MUSIC COMPANY   1.25
THOMPSON, J.
   SECOND PIANO ACCOMPANIMENTS TO FIVE TWO-PART BACH INVENTIONS
      WILLIS MUSIC COMPANY   1.00
THOMPSON, J.   1
   SIX ALL TIME FAVORITES
      WILLIS MUSIC COMPANY   1.50
THOMPSON, J.
   THOMPSON MELODY ALL THE WAY - ACCOMPANIMENTS TO THE PREPARATORY
   BOOK
      WILLIS MUSIC COMPANY   1.00
THOMPSON, J.
   THOMPSON MODERN COURSE FOR THE PIANO - TEACHING LITTLE FINGERS
   TO PLAY -- DUET ACCOMPANIMENTS
      WILLIS MUSIC COMPANY   1.00
THURM--ED.   THURM   E
   EUROPEAN FOLK SONGS
      C. F. PETERS CORPORATION   5336   3.00

TOCH, E.
   SONATA, OP. 87
      BELWIN-MILLS PUBLISHING CORPORATION   26530   2.50
TOSELLI   WALLIS   3
   SERENADE
      BOSTON MUSIC COMPANY   .60
TOURS
   ROMANCE
      G. SCHIRMER, INC.   .40
TOWNSEND   E-M
   FOUR FANTASIES ON AMERICAN FOLK SONGS, OP. 4
      C. F. PETERS CORPORATION   6040   2.00
TOWSEND, D.--ED *   TOWSEND, D. *
   PIANO DUETS OF THE CLASSICAL PERIOD
      THEODORE PRESSER COMPANY   1.75
TSCHAIKOWSKY   3
   CHANT SANS PAROLES
      CENTURY MUSIC PUBLISHING COMPANY, INC.   1928   .60
TSCHAIKOWSKY   STRIMER   3
   CHINESE DANCE
      BOSTON MUSIC COMPANY   .60
TSCHAIKOWSKY   WALLIS   3
   DANCE OF THE CANDY FAIRY
      BOSTON MUSIC COMPANY   .60
TSCHAIKOWSKY   STRIMER   3
   DANCE OF THE SUGAR PLUM FAIRY
      BOSTON MUSIC COMPANY   .60
TSCHAIKOWSKY
   FIFTY RUSSIAN FOLK SONGS
      INTERNATIONAL MUSIC COMPANY   2.50
TSCHAIKOWSKY
   MARCHE SLAVE, OP. 31
      G. SCHIRMER, INC.   1.25
TSCHAIKOWSKY   5
   MARCH SLAVE, OP. 31
      THEODORE PRESSER COMPANY   .70
TSCHAIKOWSKY   LANGER *
   NUTCRACKER SUITE, THE, OP. 71A
      G. SCHIRMER, INC.   L1359   2.00
TSCHAIKOWSKY   E
   PIANO CONCERTO IN B FLAT MINOR, OP. 23
      C. F. PETERS CORPORATION   37758   2.00
TSCHAIKOWSKY
   RUSSIAN FOLK SONGS, IN PROGRESSIVE ORDER. NOS. 1, 2, 9 TO 14
      C. F. PETERS CORPORATION   4493A   1.25
TSCHAIKOWSKY   3
   SONG WITHOUT WORDS
      CENTURY MUSIC PUBLISHING COMPANY, INC.   1928   .60
TSCHAIKOWSKY   M-D
   SYMPHONY NO. 04 IN F MINOR, OP. 36
      C. F. PETERS CORPORATION   4307   6.00
TSCHAIKOWSKY   M-D
   SYMPHONY NO. 05 IN E MINOR, OP. 64
      C. F. PETERS CORPORATION   3778   6.00
TSCHAIKOWSKY   TANEEFF
   SYMPHONY NO. 05 IN E MINOR, OP. 64
      G. SCHIRMER, INC.   L862   2.50
TSCHAIKOWSKY   M-D
   SYMPHONY NO. 06 IN B MINOR, OP. 74 --'PATHETIQUE'--
      C. F. PETERS CORPORATION   3779   6.00
TSCHAIKOWSKY
   SYMPHONY NO. 06 IN B MINOR, OP. 74 -- ''PATHETIQUE'' -- ARR. BY
   THE COMPOSER
      G. SCHIRMER, INC.   L784   2.50
TSCHAIKOWSKY   E
   THIRTY-SIX RUSSIAN FOLK SONGS, IN PROGRESSIVE ORDER
      C. F. PETERS CORPORATION   4493   2.50
TSCHAIKOWSKY   4
   TROIKA RIDE
      CENTURY MUSIC PUBLISHING COMPANY, INC.   3926   .60
TSCHAIKOWSKY   WEYBRIGHT   2
   WALTZ, FROM 'SLEEPING BEAUTY'
      BELWIN-MILLS PUBLISHING CORPORATION   .60
TSCHAIKOWSKY   4
   WALTZ OF THE FLOWERS
      CENTURY MUSIC PUBLISHING COMPANY, INC.   3743   .60
TSCHAIKOWSKY   4
   WALTZ OF THE FLOWERS
      THEODORE PRESSER COMPANY   .75
TUERK   SERAUKY   E
   THIRTY PIECES FOR BEGINNERS
      C. F. PETERS CORPORATION   5607   2.50
TUERK   DOFLEIN   2-3
   TONSTUCKE FUR VIER HANDE, HEFT 01
      SCHOTT   2296   2.50
TUERK   DOFLEIN   2-3
   TONSTUCKE FUR VIER HANDE, HEFT 02
      SCHOTT   2297   2.50
TURINA, J.
   PROCESSION DU ROSIO, LA
      FRANCO COLOMBO PUBLICATIONS   SAL   5.50
TURNER, J.   3
   FAIRY WEDDING WALTZ
      CENTURY MUSIC PUBLISHING COMPANY, INC.   2990   .60
TWINN, S.
   FIRST YEAR DUETS
      BELWIN-MILLS PUBLISHING CORPORATION   1.00
TWINN, S.
   FIRST YEAR DUETS
      BELWIN-MILLS PUBLISHING CORPORATION   11169   1.00
VANHAL   FRICKERT   3
   SECHS LEICHTE STUCKE
      BARENREITER VERLAG   BA 4369
VANHAL   FRICKERT
   SIX EASY PIECES
      BARENREITER VERLAG   BA 4369   1.75
VAN ALSTYNE, E.   STEINER   2
   CHEYENNE
      BELWIN-MILLS PUBLISHING CORPORATION   .60
VAN GAEL, H.
   WALTZ-LULLABY, OP. 89
      ASSOCIATED MUSIC PUBLISHERS, INC.   .50
VAN SLYCK, N.
   WITH TWENTY FINGERS, VOL. 1
      GENERAL MUSIC PUBLISHING COMPANY, INC.   2.50
VAN SLYCK, N.
   WITH TWENTY FINGERS, VOL. 2
      GENERAL MUSIC PUBLISHING COMPANY, INC.   3.00
VAN SLYCK, N.
   WITH TWENTY FINGERS, VOL. 3
      GENERAL MUSIC PUBLISHING COMPANY, INC.   3.50
VASSEUR
   AIR FAVORI DE LA REINE MARIE LECZINSKA
      FRANCO COLOMBO PUBLICATIONS   SAL   1.75
VAUGHAN WILLIAMS, R.
   GREENSLEEVES
      OXFORD UNIVERSITY PRESS   34.010   1.55

VELLONES, P.
    INVITATION A LA MUSIQUE
        ASSOCIATED MUSIC PUBLISHERS, INC.   ESC   1.95
VELLONES, P.
    UNE AVENTURE DE BABAR
        ELKAN-VOGEL, INC.   LEM   2.55
VERDI   2
    IL TROVATORE, SELECTION
        CENTURY MUSIC PUBLISHING COMPANY, INC.   1469   .60
VERDI   4
    QUARTET FROM RIGOLETTO
        THEODORE PRESSER COMPANY   .50
VERDI
    TRAVIATA, LA - PRELUDE TO ACT I
        FRANCO COLOMBO PUBLICATIONS   97480   .75
VERNE   2
    DUETS ON FOUR BRAZILIAN SONGS
        LEE ROBERTS MUSIC PUBLICATIONS, INC.   1.25
VILBRE   3
    HEAVENWARD MARCH
        CENTURY MUSIC PUBLISHING COMPANY, INC.   1676   .60
VILLA-LOBOS, H.   LEVINE
    LITTLE TRAIN OF THE CAIPIRA, THE - FROM BACHIANAS BRASILEIRES
    NO. 2
        FRANCO COLOMBO PUBLICATIONS   NY2244   1.00
VOLKART-SCHLAGER, K.   2
    DER SPIELGARTEN
        SCHOTT   3775   1.75
VOLKART-SCHLAGER, K.   2-3
    MOHRENTANZ UND MUMMENSCHANZ
        SCHOTT   4895   2.00
VOLKART-SCHLAGER   1-2
    ZU ZWEIT MEHR FREUD. KLEINE STUCKE ZUM ANFANG, ERSTE FOLGE - 26
    STUCKE
        BARENREITER VERLAG   SM 527
VOLKART-SCHLAGER   2
    ZU ZWEIT MEHR FREUD. KLEINE STUCKE ZUM ANFANG, ZWEITE FOLGE - 20
    STUCKE
        BARENREITER VERLAG   SM 902
VOLKART, H.
    CRUISE ON THE RIVER, A
        BELWIN-MILLS PUBLISHING CORPORATION   26552   .85
VOLKART, H.
    RIDIN' ALONG
        BELWIN-MILLS PUBLISHING CORPORATION   26551   .50
VORLOVA, S.
    HAPPY INTERVALS - CHILDREN'S STUDIES
        GENERAL MUSIC PUBLISHING COMPANY, INC.   3.00
VORLOVA, S.
    HAPPY INTERVALS - CHILDREN'S STUDIES
        GENERAL MUSIC PUBLISHING COMPANY, INC.   286   2.50
WACHS, P.   3 1/2
    MARCH OF THE FLOWER GIRLS
        THEODORE PRESSER COMPANY   .60
WACHS, P.   4
    SHOWERS OF STARS
        THEODORE PRESSER COMPANY   .60
WACHS
    MES PETITS CONCERTS - APRES LE CONCERT
        FRANCO COLOMBO PUBLICATIONS   SAL   1.50
WACHS
    MES PETITS CONCERTS - BERTRAND ET RATON
        FRANCO COLOMBO PUBLICATIONS   SAL   1.50
WACHS
    MES PETITS CONCERTS - BLANCHE ET VERMEILLE
        FRANCO COLOMBO PUBLICATIONS   SAL   1.50
WACHS
    MES PETITS CONCERTS - LE RENDEZ-VOUS DE CHASSE
        FRANCO COLOMBO PUBLICATIONS   SAL   1.50
WACHS
    MES PETITS CONCERTS - MENUET DE LA POUPEE
        FRANCO COLOMBO PUBLICATIONS   SAL   1.50
WACHS
    MES PETITS CONCERTS - PROMENADE EN BARQUE
        FRANCO COLOMBO PUBLICATIONS   SAL   1.50
WAGNER   4
    MARCH, LOHENGRIN
        CENTURY MUSIC PUBLISHING COMPANY, INC.   938   .60
WAGNER   4
    MEISTERSINGER -- VORSPIEL
        SCHOTT   012 1/2   1.00
WAGNER   4
    POLONAISE
        CENTURY MUSIC PUBLISHING COMPANY, INC.   3925   .60
WAGNER   M
    SIEGFRIED IDYLL
        C. F. PETERS CORPORATION   3436   2.00
WAGNER
    TRISTAN AND ISOLE -- PRELUDE
        G. SCHIRMER, INC.   .60
WALDTEUFEL, E.   SAMMARTINO
    AMOUR ET PRINTEMPS
        FRANCO COLOMBO PUBLICATIONS   BA10069   .75
WALDTEUFEL, E.   SAMMARTINO
    DOLORES
        FRANCO COLOMBO PUBLICATIONS   BA10070   .75
WALDTEUFEL, E.   LUDOVICI
    ESTUDIANTINA
        FRANCO COLOMBO PUBLICATIONS   BA11161   .75
WALDTEUFEL, E.   SAMMARTINO
    ETINCELLES
        FRANCO COLOMBO PUBLICATIONS   BA10071   .75
WALDTEUFEL, E.   SAMMARTINO
    PATINEURS, LES
        FRANCO COLOMBO PUBLICATIONS   BA10072   .75
WALDTEUFEL, E.   WEYBRIGHT   1 1/2
    SKATERS' WALTZ
        BELWIN-MILLS PUBLISHING CORPORATION   .60
WALDTEUFEL, E.   2
    SKATERS WALTZ
        CENTURY MUSIC PUBLISHING COMPANY, INC.   3502   .60
WALDTEUFEL, E.   SAMMARTINO
    TRES JOLIE
        FRANCO COLOMBO PUBLICATIONS   BA10073   .75
WALLIS--ED   WALLIS
    CHRISTMAS CAROLS
        BOSTON MUSIC COMPANY   1.00
WALLIS--ED   WALLIS
    MUSIC
        WILLIS MUSIC COMPANY   1.50
WALLIS--ED   WALLIS
    PIANO DUETS THE WHOLE WORLD LOVES
        WILLIS MUSIC COMPANY   1.00
WALLIS   2
    COUNTRY GARDENS
        BOSTON MUSIC COMPANY   .60

WALLIS
    MUSIC LOVERS' DUETS - BOOK 1
        BOSTON MUSIC COMPANY   1.25
WALLIS
    MUSIC LOVERS' DUETS - BOOK 2
        BOSTON MUSIC COMPANY   1.25
WALSH, M.   3
    BLACK HAWK WALTZ
        CENTURY MUSIC PUBLISHING COMPANY, INC.   2988   .60
WALSH, M.   2
    BLACK HAWK WALTZ
        WILLIS MUSIC COMPANY   .50
WALTON, W.
    DUETS FOR CHILDREN, BK. 1
        OXFORD UNIVERSITY PRESS   34.012   2.00
WALTON, W.
    DUETS FOR CHILDREN, BK. 2
        OXFORD UNIVERSITY PRESS   34.013   1.75
WALTON, W.
    FACADE EXCERPTS -- POPULAR SONG
        OXFORD UNIVERSITY PRESS   34.044   1.55
WALTON, W.
    FACADE EXCERPTS -- SWISS YODELLING SONG
        OXFORD UNIVERSITY PRESS   34.041   1.55
WALTON, W.
    FACADE EXCERPTS -- TANGO
        OXFORD UNIVERSITY PRESS   34.043   1.55
WARD--ED   WARD
    HYMNS FOR TWO
        BOSTON MUSIC COMPANY   1.00
WARD--ED   WARD
    HYMNS FOR TWO
        BOSTON MUSIC COMPANY   1.00
WARD   SCHAUM, J.   2
    BAND PLAYED ON, THE
        BELWIN-MILLS PUBLISHING CORPORATION   .50
WARD
    TWENTY FINGERS - BOOK 1
        BOSTON MUSIC COMPANY   1.00
WARD
    TWENTY FINGERS - BOOK 2
        BOSTON MUSIC COMPANY   1.00
WEBER, E.   3
    SLAVISCHE TANZWEISEN MIT VARIATIONEN
        SCHOTT   4495   2.00
WEBER, VON
    ALL ORIGINAL COMPOSITIONS
        INTERNATIONAL MUSIC COMPANY   3.50
WEBER, VON   2-3
    ANDANTE CON VARIAZIONI
        SCHOTT   09581 1/2   1.00
WEBER, VON   3
    AUFFORDERUNG ZUM TANZ, OP. 65
        SCHOTT   01064 1/2   1.00
WEBER, VON   ANDREOLI
    COMPOSITIONS, OP. 3, 10, 60
        FRANCO COLOMBO PUBLICATIONS   ER1212   2.75
WEBER, VON
    INVITATION A LA VALSE, OP. 65
        G. SCHIRMER, INC.   1.00
WEBER, VON   5
    INVITATION TO THE DANCE, OP. 65
        CENTURY MUSIC PUBLISHING COMPANY, INC.   930   .60
WEBER, VON
    INVITATION TO THE DANCE, OP. 65
        CARL FISCHER, INC.   P 2841   1.25
WEBER, VON
    INVITATION TO THE DANCE, OP. 65
        FRANCO COLOMBO PUBLICATIONS   32403   1.25
WEBER, VON   CARPER
    MARCH -- FROM KONZERTSTUCK IN F MINOR
        G. SCHIRMER, INC.   .75
WEBER, VON   3-4
    MODERATO, OP. 10 NO. 1
        SCHOTT   09582 1/2   1.00
WEBER, VON   M
    ORIGINAL COMPOSITIONS
        C. F. PETERS CORPORATION   188A   3.00
WEBER, VON   M-D
    SELECTED COMPOSITIONS
        C. F. PETERS CORPORATION   188B   3.50
WEBER, VON   MARCHI, G.
    SONATINA DA 6 PEZZI, OP. 3
        EDIZIONI BERBEN   EB 1268   1.20
WEBER, VON   KINDERMANN
    TWELVE EASY PIECES, OP. 3 AND OP. 10
        BARENREITER VERLAG   BA19501   7.00
WEINER
    SUITE, OP. 18
        KULTURA   3.75
WEINER
    VARIATIONS ON THE BASE OF HUNGARIAN FOLK SONG, OP. 32
        KULTURA   2.50
WERNER, F.--ED.   WERNER, F.   E
    WIR SPIELEN ZUR WEIHNACHT, OP. 43. 26 OLD CHRISTMAS SONGS
        C. F. PETERS CORPORATION   V138   2.00
WERNER, J.
    LA BOITE A JEUX -- PIECES ENFANTINES
        EDITIONS MUSICALES TRANSATLANTIQUES   2.00
WESLEY, S.   RAMSEY, B.   3
    MARCH
        NOVELLO AND COMPANY, LTD.   10.0144.02   .90
WEYBRIGHT--ED.   WEYBRIGHT   1 1/2
    ALPHABET SONG
        BELWIN-MILLS PUBLISHING CORPORATION   .60
WEYBRIGHT--ED.   WEYBRIGHT   2
    ERIE CANAL, THE
        BELWIN-MILLS PUBLISHING CORPORATION   .60
WEYBRIGHT--ED.   WEYBRIGHT   2
    I WISH I WUZ A MOLE
        BELWIN-MILLS PUBLISHING CORPORATION   .60
WEYBRIGHT--ED.   WEYBRIGHT   2
    MADDALENA
        BELWIN-MILLS PUBLISHING CORPORATION   .60
WEYBRIGHT--ED.   WEYBRIGHT   2
    SANTA LUCIA
        BELWIN-MILLS PUBLISHING CORPORATION   .60
WEYBRIGHT--ED.   WEYBRIGHT   1
    WE'LL GO FISHIN' IN A CRAWDAD HOLE
        BELWIN-MILLS PUBLISHING CORPORATION   .60
WEYBRIGHT
    ANOTHER DUET BOOK
        BELWIN-MILLS PUBLISHING CORPORATION   1.75
WEYBRIGHT
    DOUBLE PLAY
        BELWIN-MILLS PUBLISHING CORPORATION   11128   1.00

WEYBRIGHT		2	
DOUBLE PLAY			
BELWIN-MILLS PUBLISHING CORPORATION			1.25
WEYBRIGHT		1	
DOZEN DUETS FOR PIANO			
WILLIS MUSIC COMPANY			1.25
WEYBRIGHT		2	
IN THE SADDLE			
BELWIN-MILLS PUBLISHING CORPORATION			.60
WEYBRIGHT		2	
WEYBRIGHT DUET BOOK			
BELWIN-MILLS PUBLISHING CORPORATION			1.75
WEYBRIGHT		2	
WEYBRIGHT DUET BOOK			
BELWIN-MILLS PUBLISHING CORPORATION			1.25
WHITEFIELD			
BOOGIE WOOGIE FOR FOUR HANDS			
BOSTON MUSIC COMPANY			1.00
WHITEFIELD			
EASY BOOGIE WOOGIE DUETS			
BOSTON MUSIC COMPANY			1.00
WHITFORD			
SEVEN PIECES FOR FOUR HANDS			
BOSTON MUSIC COMPANY			1.50
WHITSON *			
LET ME CALL YOU SWEETHEART			
SHAPIRO, BERNSTEIN ORGANIZATION			1.00
WHITSON * MURKER	EASY		
LET ME CALL YOU SWEETHEART			
SHAWNEE PRESS, INC.			1.00
WILHELM, C.		1	
GERMAN NATIONAL SONG			
THEODORE PRESSER COMPANY			.50
WILKINSON, P.		4-5	
TWO COUNTRY SKETCHES			
NOVELLO AND COMPANY, LTD.		10.0145.00	1.15
WILLFORT, E. S.			
DUETS FOR EVERYONE, BK. 1			
ASSOCIATED MUSIC PUBLISHERS, INC.		OBV	1.50
WILLFORT, E. S.			
DUETS FOR EVERYONE, BK. 2			
ASSOCIATED MUSIC PUBLISHERS, INC.		OBV	1.50
WILLFORT, E. S.			
IN THE WOODS -- SUITE			
ASSOCIATED MUSIC PUBLISHERS, INC.		OBV	1.10
WILLIAMS, C.			
THEME FROM 'THE APARTMENT'			
BELWIN-MILLS PUBLISHING CORPORATION		26553	1.00
WILLIAMS, J.		3	
COUNTRY GARDENS			
BOSTON MUSIC COMPANY			.60
WILMANS--ED WILMANS		3	
FOUR-HAND RECREATIONS			
THEODORE PRESSER COMPANY			1.25
WILSON, M.		3	
SHEPHERD BOY, THE			
CENTURY MUSIC PUBLISHING COMPANY, INC.		1470	.60
WILSON, S.			
FIVE DUETS FOR TWENTY FINGERS			
BELWIN-MILLS PUBLISHING CORPORATION		10015	.75
WILSON, S.			
LET'S PLAY DUETS, BK. 1			
BELWIN-MILLS PUBLISHING CORPORATION		10086	1.00
WILSON, S.			
LET'S PLAY DUETS, BK. 2			
BELWIN-MILLS PUBLISHING CORPORATION		10022	1.00
WILSON			
EASY FOR ME TO PLAY AND SING			
BOSTON MUSIC COMPANY			1.00
WILSON			
FOR ME AND MY TEACHER			
CARL FISCHER, INC.		RS 378	1.00
WILSON			
FUN TUNE DUETS			
BOSTON MUSIC COMPANY			1.00
WOHLFAHRT	E		
CHILDREN'S FRIEND, OP. 87. 50 EASY AND MELODIOUS PIECES IN			
PROGRESSIVE ORDER			
C. F. PETERS CORPORATION		1330	2.00
WOHLFAHRT			
CHILDREN'S FRIEND, THE OP. 87			
FRANCO COLOMBO PUBLICATIONS		ER20	1.25
WOHLFAHRT			
EASY FOUR HAND PIECES FOR CHILDREN, OP. 87			
EDWIN F. KALMUS		4039	2.00
WOHLFAHRT			
MUSICAL CHILDREN'S FRIEND, THE, OP. 87 -- 50 MELODIOUS PIECES			
FOR BEGINNERS			
G. SCHIRMER, INC.			1.50
WOLFE, J. KING, S.	EASY		
SHORT'NIN' BREAD			
SHAWNEE PRESS, INC.		HC-5009	.60
WOLTERS			
ERSTES SPIEL ZU VIER HANDEN. 34 ALTE VOLKSLIEDER IN SEHR			
LEICHTEN SATZEN FUR KLAVIER			
BARENREITER VERLAG		BA 3508	
WOLTERS		1	
ERSTES SPIEL ZU VIER HANDEN. 34 ALTE VOLKSLIEDER IN SEHR			
LEICHTEN SATZEN			
BARENREITER VERLAG		BA 3508	
WOOLEN, R.			
SONATA FOR PIANO 4 HANDS			
PAN AMERICAN UNION			03.00
WOOLLETT			
EN BARQUE			
FRANCO COLOMBO PUBLICATIONS		SAL	2.75
WRIGHT--ED WRIGHT			
EIGHTEENTH CENTURY MUSIC OF COLONIAL AMERICA			
BOSTON MUSIC COMPANY			1.00
WRIGHT, L. LOWENSTEIN		2	
BANJO PICKER			
WILLIS MUSIC COMPANY			.50
WRIGHT, N.		3 1/2	
ECHOES OF VIENNA			
THEODORE PRESSER COMPANY			.60
WUORINEN			
MAKING ENDS MEET --IN PREPARATION--			
C. F. PETERS CORPORATION		66372	
YOUMANS MERKUR			
TEA FOR TWO			
WARNER BROTHERS PUBLISHERS			1.25
YOUNG		2	
MERRY DANCE, A			
BOSTON MUSIC COMPANY			.60
YUNG			
REVERIES DE MARGUERITE			
FRANCO COLOMBO PUBLICATIONS		SAL	2.00

ZAMECNIK			
CHINA DOLL PARADE			
SOUTHERN MUSIC COMPANY			1.00
ZAMECNIK			
CHINA DOLL PARADE			
SOUTHERN MUSIC COMPANY			1.50
ZANINELLI SOKOLOFF			
LEXICON OF BEASTIES, A			
SHAWNEE PRESS, INC.			2.50
ZECCHI			
BELLA ADDORMENTATA, LA			
FRANCO COLOMBO PUBLICATIONS		BON.2286	1.75
ZEITLIN--ED * ZEITLIN *			
ELEVEN PIANO DUETS BY THE MASTERS -- INTERMEDIATE GRADES			
G. SCHIRMER, INC.			2.50
ZEITLIN--ED * ZEITLIN *	INTERMEDIATE GRADES		
ELEVEN PIANO DUETS BY THE MASTERS			
G. SCHIRMER, INC.			2.50
ZEPP--ED ZEPP			
DUET FUN WITH THREE CHORDS			
PRO-ART PUBLICATIONS, INC.		356	.85
ZEPP--ED ZEPP			
LET'S PLAY CHRISTMAS DUETS			
PRO-ART PUBLICATIONS, INC.		605	1.00
ZIPP		3	
CANZONA E SONATA, OP. 22			
SCHOTT		3972	2.25
ZUCCARO			
DANCE OF THE DEMON			
FRANCO COLOMBO PUBLICATIONS		52209	.75

One Piano, Four Hands (Original and Arranged):
Composer/Editor/Arranger Unlisted—Works Alphabetized by Title

ALICE BLUE GOWN			
THE BIG THREE MUSIC CORPORATION			01.50
ALICE BLUE GOWN			
THE BIG THREE MUSIC CORPORATION			01.25
ALICE BLUE			
THE BIG THREE MUSIC CORPORATION			01.50
ALL THE THINGS YOU ARE			
CIMINO PUBLICATIONS, INC.		H	1.25
ANCHORS AWEIGH			
THE BIG THREE MUSIC CORPORATION			01.50
BEAUTY AND GRACE			
THE BIG THREE MUSIC CORPORATION			01.50
BEAUTY AND GRACE			
THE BIG THREE MUSIC CORPORATION			01.25
BLUE MOON			
THE BIG THREE MUSIC CORPORATION			01.50
CAMELOT SELECTION			
CHAPPELL AND COMPANY, INC.		0690008-175	2.50
CANADIAN SUNSET			
CIMINO PUBLICATIONS, INC.		V	1.25
CHINA BOY			
THE BIG THREE MUSIC CORPORATION			01.50
CLASSICAL ALBUM--TWELVE ORIGINAL PIECES			
G. SCHIRMER, INC.		L371	2.00
COUNTRY GARDENS	3		
CENTURY MUSIC PUBLISHING COMPANY, INC.		3124	.60
CZECH FOLK DANCES AND SONGS	E		
C. F. PETERS CORPORATION		4902	3.00
DEEP PURPLE			
THE BIG THREE MUSIC CORPORATION			01.25
DEEP PURPLE			
THE BIG THREE MUSIC CORPORATION			01.50
DOLL DANCE			
THE BIG THREE MUSIC CORPORATION			01.50
DUETS FOR YOUNG PIANISTS			
MUSIC SALES CORPORATION		020092	2.95
EASY DUETS FOR PIANO			
CENTURY MUSIC PUBLISHING COMPANY, INC.		MPS VOL. 6	1.95
EASY PIANO DUETS IN FIVE FINGER POSITION			
THE BIG THREE MUSIC CORPORATION			2.50
EASY TO PLAY PIANO DUETS			
ASHLEY DEALERS SERVICE, INC.		WFS NO. 4	2.95
EBB TIDE			
THE BIG THREE MUSIC CORPORATION			01.25
EBB TIDE			
THE BIG THREE MUSIC CORPORATION			01.50
FOREVER AND EVER			
THE BIG THREE MUSIC CORPORATION			01.25
FORTY-EIGHT EASY PIANO DUETS			
WARNER BROTHERS PUBLISHERS		MFE 6	2.95
FOUR HANDS AT THE KEYBOARD			
CARL FISCHER, INC.		O 4459	1.50
	1-2		
FROHLICH LASST UNS MUSIZIEREN			
SCHOTT		2697	1.75
GAYETY			
THE BIG THREE MUSIC CORPORATION			01.50
GOOD NIGHT SWEETHEART			
THE BIG THREE MUSIC CORPORATION			01.25

GREEN LEAVES OF SUMMER
   THE BIG THREE MUSIC CORPORATION   01.25

HI-LILI, HI-LO
   THE BIG THREE MUSIC CORPORATION   01.50

IN A MIST
   THE BIG THREE MUSIC CORPORATION   01.50

LARA'S THEME - DOCTOR ZHIVAGO
   THE BIG THREE MUSIC CORPORATION   01.25

LAZY RHAPSODY
   THE BIG THREE MUSIC CORPORATION   01.50

LONDONDERRY AIR -- FREE TRANSCRIPTION
   ELKAN-VOGEL, INC.   .50

LOVE IS A MANY-SPLENDORED THING
   THE BIG THREE MUSIC CORPORATION   01.25

LOVE MAKES THE WORLD GO 'ROUND
   THE BIG THREE MUSIC CORPORATION   01.25

MANHATTAN SERENADE
   THE BIG THREE MUSIC CORPORATION   01.50

MANZANILLO
   THE BIG THREE MUSIC CORPORATION   01.50

MODERN PIANIST SERIES - CHRISTMAS DUETS
   POINTER PUBLICATIONS   1.95
                    E-M
MODERN PIANIST SERIES - ONE PIANO, FOUR HANDS
   POINTER PUBLICATIONS   1.95

MOONLIGHT MOOD
   THE BIG THREE MUSIC CORPORATION   01.50

MORE THAN YOU KNOW
   THE BIG THREE MUSIC CORPORATION   01.25

MOST POPULAR SERIES - VOL. 6, EASY DUETS FOR PIANO
   CENTURY MUSIC PUBLISHING COMPANY, INC.   1.95

MY BLUE HEAVEN
   THE BIG THREE MUSIC CORPORATION   01.25

MY FAVORITE DUET ALBUM --28--
   CARL FISCHER, INC.   O 3253   2.95

NINETY-ONE EASY PIANO DUETS
   WARNER BROTHERS PUBLISHERS   MFE 15   2.50
                  2
NOTENMAPPE DES KLAVIERSCHULERS, HEFT 01
   SCHOTT   721A   2.25

ONE PIANO FOUR HANDS
   MUSIC SALES CORPORATION   020129   2.95

ON THE TRAIL
   THE BIG THREE MUSIC CORPORATION   01.50

OVER THE RAINBOW
   THE BIG THREE MUSIC CORPORATION   01.25

OVER THE RAINBOW
   THE BIG THREE MUSIC CORPORATION   01.50

PIANINO COLLECTION
   DELRIEU ET CIE.

PIANO DUETS FOR CHILDREN
   MUSIC SALES CORPORATION   020021   2.95

PIANO DUETS
   ASHLEY DEALERS SERVICE, INC.   WFS NO. 5   2.95

PIANO DUETS
   MUSIC SALES CORPORATION   02007   2.95

PIANO PIECES FOR THE YOUNG STUDENT
   MUSIC SALES CORPORATION   020080   2.95

PLAYING TOGETHER
   THEODORE PRESSER COMPANY   1.50

RAG DOLL
   THE BIG THREE MUSIC CORPORATION   01.50

RECITAL DUOS. COMPILATION
   SUMMY-BIRCHARD COMPANY   1.75

RUBY
   THE BIG THREE MUSIC CORPORATION   01.25

SACRED PIANO DUETS
   LORENZ PUBLISHING COMPANY   2.50
                ROVENGER
SACRED REFLECTIONS FOR PIANO DUET
   RUBANK, INC.   1.50

SACRED TRANSCRIPTIONS FOR PIANO
   LILLENAS PUBLISHING COMPANY   MB-181   2.50

SANTA CLAUS IS COMIN' TO TOWN
   THE BIG THREE MUSIC CORPORATION   01.25

SERENADE FOR A WEALTHY WIDOW
   THE BIG THREE MUSIC CORPORATION   01.50

SHADOW OF YOUR SMILE, THE
   THE BIG THREE MUSIC CORPORATION   01.25

SIBONEY
   THE BIG THREE MUSIC CORPORATION   01.50

SIXTY PIANO DUETS --PROGRESSIVE GRADED
   THE BIG THREE MUSIC CORPORATION   02.50

SONG OF LOVE
   THE BIG THREE MUSIC CORPORATION   01.25

SONG OF LOVE
   THE BIG THREE MUSIC CORPORATION   01.50

SONG OF THE BAYOU
   THE BIG THREE MUSIC CORPORATION   01.50
                  1
SPIELBUCHLEIN FUR DEN ERSTEN ANFANG
   SCHOTT   2696   1.75
                  1
SPIELBUCHLEIN FUR DEN ERSTEN ANFANG
   SCHOTT   2696   1.75

STAR OF THE SEA
   THE BIG THREE MUSIC CORPORATION   01.50

STOMPING AT THE SAVOY
   THE BIG THREE MUSIC CORPORATION   01.50

THREE O'CLOCK IN THE MORNING
   THE BIG THREE MUSIC CORPORATION   01.25

TIGER RAG
   THE BIG THREE MUSIC CORPORATION   01.50

TIME ON MY HANDS
   THE BIG THREE MUSIC CORPORATION   01.25

TWENTY-FOUR PROGRESSIVE PIANO DUETS YOU LIKE TO PLAY
   G. SCHIRMER, INC.   1.75

TWICE TOLD THEMES, BK. 1 --COMPILATION--
   SUMMY-BIRCHARD COMPANY   1.75

TWICE TOLD THEMES, BK. 2 --COMPILATION--
   SUMMY-BIRCHARD COMPANY   2.00

TWO LITTLE PLAYERS - FORTY-EIGHT SELECTIONS
   BOSTON MUSIC COMPANY   1.50

VERY FIRST DUET BOOK
   THEODORE PRESSER COMPANY   2.25

WALTZ YOU SAVED FOR ME
   THE BIG THREE MUSIC CORPORATION   01.25

WEDDING OF THE PAINTED DOLL
   THE BIG THREE MUSIC CORPORATION   01.50

WHEN IT'S SPRINGTIME IN THE ROCKIES
   THE BIG THREE MUSIC CORPORATION   01.25

WHEN I GROW TOO OLD TO DREAM
   THE BIG THREE MUSIC CORPORATION   01.25

WHEN I GROW TOO OLD TO DREAM
   THE BIG THREE MUSIC CORPORATION   01.50

WHEN YOU WORE A TULIP
   THE BIG THREE MUSIC CORPORATION   01.25

WHISPERING
   THE BIG THREE MUSIC CORPORATION   01.25

Two Piano, Four Hands
(Original and Arranged-includes Concertos)

AARON, M.   BOWEN   MEDIUM
  DANCE OF THE DWARFS
    SHAWNEE PRESS, INC.   .45
ADAIR, M.   2
  SUMMER SONG
    WILLIS MUSIC COMPANY   .35
ADAMS
  ALBUM OF PIANO DUOS -- 9 PIECES OF MEDIUM DIFFICULTY
    G. SCHIRMER, INC.   1.50
AGUIRRE   LASALA
  CANCION NO. 3
    FRANCO COLOMBO PUBLICATIONS   BA10343   .75
AGUIRRE
  GATO
    FRANCO COLOMBO PUBLICATIONS   BA9674   1.00
AGUIRRE
  HUELLA
    FRANCO COLOMBO PUBLICATIONS   BA9675   .75
ALBENIZ, I.   GRAETZER
  CASTILLA
    FRANCO COLOMBO PUBLICATIONS   BA9691   1.00
ALBENIZ, I.
  RAPSODIA ESPANOLA, OP. 70
    INTERNATIONAL MUSIC COMPANY   2.50
ALBENIZ, I.   HALFFTER, C.
  RAPSODIA ESPANOLA
    ASSOCIATED MUSIC PUBLISHERS, INC.   UME   3.50
ALBENIZ, I.   DUNGAN   3
  TANGO IN D
    BOSTON MUSIC COMPANY   1.00
ALBENIZ, I.   MILLER
  TRIANA -- SET
    G. SCHIRMER, INC.   2.00
ALBERT, E. D'
  CONCERTO NO. 02 IN E, OP. 12
    ASSOCIATED MUSIC PUBLISHERS, INC.   BOT   10.25
ALFORD, K.   SAMUELSON
  COLONEL BOGEY
    BOOSEY AND HAWKES, INC.   1.25
ALKAN
  FIRST CONCERTO DA CAMERA ADAGIO MOVEMENT
    MUSICA OBSCURA   1.50
ALKAN
  FIRST CONCERTO DA CAMERA IN A MINOR, OP. 10 NO. 1
    MUSICA OBSCURA   4.00
ALKAN
  FIRST CONCERTO DA CAMERA IN A MINOR, OP. 10
    GERARD BILLAUDOT EDITIONS MUSICALES   4.10
ALKAN
  SECOND CONCERTO DA CAMERA, OP. 10 NO. 2 IN C SHARP MINOR
    MUSICA OBSCURA   3.00
ALKAN
  SECOND CONCERTO DA CAMERA IN C SHARP MINOR, OP. 10
    GERARD BILLAUDOT EDITIONS MUSICALES   3.30
ALKAN
  TUTTI DE CONCERTO, DANS LE GENRE ANCIEN OP. 63, NO. 15
    MUSICA OBSCURA   1.00
ANDERSON, G.
  CONCERTINO FOR PIANO AND ORCHESTRA
    AMERICAN MUSIC EDITION   4.00
ANDREWS
  GALLITO QUE CANTA, EL
    SUMMY-BIRCHARD COMPANY   2.50
ANDREWS
  PEACH-PICKERS' FROLIC
    SUMMY-BIRCHARD COMPANY   1.50
ANDRIESSEN, J.   M-D
  CONCERTO SENZA ORCHESTRA
    C. F. PETERS CORPORATION   D48   3.00
ANGERER
  CONCERTO
    ASSOCIATED MUSIC PUBLISHERS, INC.   DOB   4.25
ANSON, G.
  CONCERTO
    NOVELLO AND COMPANY, LTD.   10.0146.09   2.50
ANSON, G.   3
  KID CONCERTO
    WILLIS MUSIC COMPANY   1.75
ANSON, G.   1
  KID KONCERTO
    WILLIS MUSIC COMPANY   1.75
ANSON, G.
  MINIATURE CONCERTO
    SOUTHERN MUSIC COMPANY   1.75
ANSON, G.
  POLKA DOTS
    SOUTHERN MUSIC COMPANY   .75
ANSON, G.
  SIESTA TIME
    BELWIN-MILLS PUBLISHING CORPORATION   27037   .60
ANSON, G.
  TWO'S COMPANY -- A FIRST 2-PIANO BOOK
    ELKAN-VOGEL, INC.   1.50
ANTONIOU   4
  CONCERTINO, OP. 21 FUR KLAVIER, 9 BLASER UND SCHLAGZEUG
    BARENREITER VERLAG   BA 4377
ANTONIOU   4
  KONZERTINO, OP. 16B FUR KLAVIER, STREICHER UND SCHLAGZEUG
    BARENREITER VERLAG   BA 4378
APOSTEL
  CONCERTO, OP. 30
    UNIVERSAL EDITION   13174   5.75
ARENSKY, A.   SCHAUM, J.   3
  ARENSKY WALTZ, THE
    BELWIN-MILLS PUBLISHING CORPORATION   .50
ARENSKY, A.   PHILIPP, I.
  POLONAISE, OP. 65 NO. 8
    INTERNATIONAL MUSIC COMPANY   1.50
ARENSKY, A.   D
  SILHOUETTES, OP. 23
    C. F. PETERS CORPORATION   F25   3.00
ARENSKY, A.   OESTERLE
  SUITE, OP. 15 -- SET
    G. SCHIRMER, INC.   L1300   1.25
ARENSKY, A.
  SUITE, OP. 15
    BOOSEY AND HAWKES, INC.   2.50
ARENSKY, A.   BABIN
  SUITE, OP. 15
    INTERNATIONAL MUSIC COMPANY   2.50
ARENSKY, A.
  SUITE IN CANON-FORM, OP. 65 -- SET
    G. SCHIRMER, INC.   L1482   2.00

ARENSKY, A.   OESTERLE
  VALSE FROM THE SUITE, OP. 15 -- SET
    G. SCHIRMER, INC.   .90
ARENSKY, A.   BABIN
  WALTZE FROM SUITE, OP. 15
    INTERNATIONAL MUSIC COMPANY   1.50
ARGENTO, D.
  DIVERTIMENTO FOR PIANO AND STRINGS
    BOOSEY AND HAWKES, INC.   4.00
ARMA, P.
  SEPT TRANSPARENCES
    ELKAN-VOGEL, INC.   LEM   8.75
ARNDT
  NOLA
    SOUTHERN MUSIC COMPANY   1.50
ARNE   2
  KONZERT NO. 05 IN G MINOR
    BARENREITER VERLAG   NMA 210
AUBERT
  FANTAISIE, OP. 8
    ELKAN-VOGEL, INC.   D   8.40
AUBERT
  SUITE BREVE
    ELKAN-VOGEL, INC.   D   6.00
AURIC
  PARTITA -- SET
    ASSOCIATED MUSIC PUBLISHERS, INC.   ESC   8.25
AURIC
  WALTZ, A -- 1949 -- SET
    ASSOCIATED MUSIC PUBLISHERS, INC.   ESC   6.00
AVERY, R.   3 1/2
  CONCERTINO ON FAMILIAR TUNES
    THEODORE PRESSER COMPANY   1.25
BABIN
  CONCERTO NO. 02 FOR TWO PIANOS
    BOOSEY AND HAWKES, INC.   12.50
BABIN
  ETUDE NO. 1 - TEMPO GIUSTO
    BOOSEY AND HAWKES, INC.   1.25
BABIN
  ETUDE NO. 2 - ADAGIETTO CANTABILE
    BOOSEY AND HAWKES, INC.   1.25
BABIN
  ETUDE NO. 3 - VELOCE
    BOOSEY AND HAWKES, INC.   1.50
BABIN
  ETUDE NO. 4 - VIVACE
    BOOSEY AND HAWKES, INC.   1.50
BABIN
  THREE MARCH RHYTHMS
    BOOSEY AND HAWKES, INC.   2.50
BACH, C.P.E.   M-D
  CONCERTO FOR 2 PIANOS --WITH ORCH. ACC. IN PIANO 3--
    C. F. PETERS CORPORATION   Z450   4.50
BACH, C.P.E.   WERTHEIM
  CONCERTO IN D MINOR
    ASSOCIATED MUSIC PUBLISHERS, INC.   BRH   3.75
BACH, C.P.E.   DARVAS
  CONCERTO IN D MINOR
    KULTURA   4.50
BACH, C.P.E.   LANDSHOFF   D
  CONCERTO IN D
    C. F. PETERS CORPORATION   N1178   7.50
BACH, C.P.E.   JACOBI   3-4
  DOPPELKONZERT IN E FLAT FUR KLAVIER, CEMBALO UND KAMMERORCHESTER
    BARENREITER VERLAG   BA 2043
BACH, C.P.E.   OBERDORFFER   3
  KONZERT IN F FUR CEMBALO UND STREICHER
    BARENREITER VERLAG   BA 2004
BACH, C.P.E.   OBERDORFFER   3
  KONZERT IN G MINOR FUR CEMBALO UND STREICHER
    BARENREITER VERLAG   BA 2005
BACH, C.P.E.   OBERDORFFER   3
  SONATINE IN D MINOR FUR CEMBALO, 2 QUERFLOTEN UND STREICHER
    BARENREITER VERLAG   BA 2006
BACH, C.P.E.   OBERDORFFER   3
  SONATINE IN E FLAT FUR CEMBALO, 2 QUERFLOTEN UND STREICHER
    BARENREITER VERLAG   BA 2007
BACH, J.S.   STEINER
  ADAGIO IN A MINOR
    BELWIN-MILLS PUBLISHING CORPORATION   1.25
BACH, J.S.
  AIR IN D MAJOR -- AIR FOR THE G STRING
    BELWIN-MILLS PUBLISHING CORPORATION   1.25
BACH, J.S.   MOORE
  AIR ON THE G STRING
    BOOSEY AND HAWKES, INC.   1.25
BACH, J.S. *   HINMAN   4
  AIR
    WILLIS MUSIC COMPANY   .30
BACH, J.S.   MAIER, G.
  ALLEGRO FROM TRIO IN D MINOR
    BELWIN-MILLS PUBLISHING CORPORATION   1.25
BACH, J.S.   ANSON, G.
  ANSON INTRODUCES BACH - THE PIANO PARTNER
    WILLIS MUSIC COMPANY   1.25
BACH, J.S.   HARRIS, W. H.
  AN WASSERFLUSSEN BABYLON -- BY THE WATERS OF BABYLON
    NOVELLO AND COMPANY, LTD.   10.0150.07   1.25
BACH, J.S. *   HINMAN   3
  AVE MARIA
    WILLIS MUSIC COMPANY   .50
BACH, J.S.   STORR, S.   3
  BADINERIE
    BOSTON MUSIC COMPANY   .75
BACH, J.S.   WEYBRIGHT   4
  BIST DU BEI MIR -- FROM THE NOTENBUCHLEIN OF A. M. BACH
    BELWIN-MILLS PUBLISHING CORPORATION   .60
BACH, J.S.   GRAINGER, P.
  BLITHE BELLS -- ARIA, ''SHEEP MAY GRAZE IN SAFETY'' FROM CANTATA
    208 -- SET
    G. SCHIRMER, INC.   1.25
BACH, J.S.   STEINER
  BOURREE IN D FROM SUITE NO. 3 FOR ORCH -- TRANSCRIBED IN THE
    EARLY GRADES -- SET
    G. SCHIRMER, INC.   .60
BACH, J.S.   REGER   D
  BRANDENBURG CONCERTOS, VOL. 1
    C. F. PETERS CORPORATION   3108A   6.00
BACH, J.S.   REGER   D
  BRANDENBURG CONCERTOS, VOL. 2
    C. F. PETERS CORPORATION   3108B   6.00
BACH, J.S.   ZANON
  BRANDENBURG CONCERTO NO. 1 IN F
    FRANCO COLOMBO PUBLICATIONS   ER2491   1.75

BACH, J.S.   REGER   D
BRANDENBURG CONCERTO NO. 1 IN F
    C. F. PETERS CORPORATION   3108AA   2.00
BACH, J.S.   M
BRANDENBURG CONCERTO NO. 1
    C. F. PETERS CORPORATION   H304   1.25
BACH, J.S.   ZANON
BRANDENBURG CONCERTO NO. 2 IN F
    FRANCO COLOMBO PUBLICATIONS   ER2492   1.75
BACH, J.S.   REGER   D
BRANDENBURG CONCERTO NO. 2 IN F
    C. F. PETERS CORPORATION   3108BB   2.00
BACH, J.S.   ZANON
BRANDENBURG CONCERTO NO. 3 IN G
    FRANCO COLOMBO PUBLICATIONS   ER2493   1.75
BACH, J.S.   REGER   D
BRANDENBURG CONCERTO NO. 3 IN G
    C. F. PETERS CORPORATION   3108C   2.00
BACH, J.S.   D
BRANDENBURG CONCERTO NO. 3
    C. F. PETERS CORPORATION   H305   2.00
BACH, J.S.   ZANON
BRANDENBURG CONCERTO NO. 4 IN G
    FRANCO COLOMBO PUBLICATIONS   ER2494   2.25
BACH, J.S.   REGER   D
BRANDENBURG CONCERTO NO. 4 IN G
    C. F. PETERS CORPORATION   3108D   2.00
BACH, J.S.   WENZINGER
BRANDENBURG CONCERTO NO. 5 IN D
    BARENREITER VERLAG
BACH, J.S.   ZANON
BRANDENBURG CONCERTO NO. 5 IN D
    FRANCO COLOMBO PUBLICATIONS   ER2495   2.25
BACH, J.S.   REGER   D
BRANDENBURG CONCERTO NO. 5 IN D
    C. F. PETERS CORPORATION   3108E   2.00
BACH, J.S.   ZANON
BRANDENBURG CONCERTO NO. 6 IN B-FLAT
    FRANCO COLOMBO PUBLICATIONS   ER2496   2.25
BACH, J.S.   REGER   D
BRANDENBURG CONCERTO NO. 6 IN B FLAT
    C. F. PETERS CORPORATION   3108F   2.00
BACH, J.S.   GEST
CHORALE -- JESUS BLEIBET MEINE FREUDE FROM CANTATA 147 -- SET
    G. SCHIRMER, INC.   1.00
BACH, J.S.   PHILIPP
CHORALE BY BACH, A
    FRANCO COLOMBO PUBLICATIONS   SAL   1.75
BACH, J.S.   M-D
CONCERTI AFTER OTHER COMPOSERS. 16 CONCERTI IN 3 VOLUMES. VOL.1
    C. F. PETERS CORPORATION   217A   3.00
BACH, J.S.   M-D
CONCERTI AFTER OTHER COMPOSERS. 16 CONCERTI IN 3 VOLUMES. VOL.2
    C. F. PETERS CORPORATION   217B   3.00
BACH, J.S.   M-D
CONCERTI AFTER OTHER COMPOSERS. 16 CONCERTI IN 3 VOLUMES. VOL.3
    C. F. PETERS CORPORATION   217C   1.50
BACH, J.S.   SEAK
CONCERTO AFTER VIVALDI -- OP. 3 NO. 9
    FRANCO COLOMBO PUBLICATIONS   129578   .90
BACH, J.S.
CONCERTO IN A, SCH NO. 1055
    ASSOCIATED MUSIC PUBLISHERS, INC.   BRH   1.00
BACH, J.S.   M-D
CONCERTO IN A --URTEXT--
    C. F. PETERS CORPORATION   4467   1.50
BACH, J.S.
CONCERTO IN A MINOR FOR 4 PIANOS, SCH NO.1065
    ASSOCIATED MUSIC PUBLISHERS, INC.   BRH   1.00
BACH, J.S.   M-D
CONCERTO IN C FOR 2 PIANOS --2 COPIES--
    C. F. PETERS CORPORATION   2200A   2.50
BACH, J.S.
CONCERTO IN C FOR 2 PIANOS
    INTERNATIONAL MUSIC COMPANY   3.00
BACH, J.S.   M-D
CONCERTO IN C MINOR FOR 2 PIANOS --2 COPIES--
    C. F. PETERS CORPORATION   2200B   2.50
BACH, J.S.
CONCERTO IN C MINOR FOR 2 PIANOS
    INTERNATIONAL MUSIC COMPANY   3.00
BACH, J.S.   BAUER
CONCERTO IN C MINOR
    G. SCHIRMER, INC.   1.25
BACH, J.S.   BAUER
CONCERTO IN C MINOR
    G. SCHIRMER, INC.   1.25
BACH, J.S.
CONCERTO IN D, SCH NO. 1054
    ASSOCIATED MUSIC PUBLISHERS, INC.   BRH   1.00
BACH, J.S.   M-D
CONCERTO IN D MINOR, AFTER MARCELLO OBOE CONCERTO
    C. F. PETERS CORPORATION   217D   1.50
BACH, J.S.   BUSONI
CONCERTO IN D MINOR, SCH NO. 1052
    ASSOCIATED MUSIC PUBLISHERS, INC.   BRH   1.50
BACH, J.S.   TAGLIAPIETRA
CONCERTO IN D MINOR
    FRANCO COLOMBO PUBLICATIONS   ER1432   1.75
BACH, J.S.   M-D
CONCERTO IN D MINOR
    C. F. PETERS CORPORATION   2912   1.50
BACH, J.S.   HUGHES
CONCERTO IN D MINOR
    G. SCHIRMER, INC.   L1527   2.00
BACH, J.S.   HUGHES
CONCERTO IN D MINOR
    G. SCHIRMER, INC.   L1527   2.00
BACH, J.S.   RONTGEN
CONCERTO IN D MINOR
    UNIVERSAL EDITION   625   2.40
BACH, J.S.
CONCERTO IN E, SCH. NO. 1053
    ASSOCIATED MUSIC PUBLISHERS, INC.   BRH   1.00
BACH, J.S.   M-D
CONCERTO IN E --URTEXT--
    C. F. PETERS CORPORATION   4469   2.50
BACH, J.S.
CONCERTO IN F MINOR, SCH NO. 1056
    ASSOCIATED MUSIC PUBLISHERS, INC.   BRH   1.00
BACH, J.S.   TEICHMUELLER   M-D
CONCERTO IN F MINOR --URTEXT--
    C. F. PETERS CORPORATION   3830   1.50
BACH, J.S.   TAGLIAPIETRA
CONCERTO IN F MINOR
    FRANCO COLOMBO PUBLICATIONS   ER2434   1.25

BACH, J.S.   FISCHER, E.
CONCERTO IN F MINOR
    INTERNATIONAL MUSIC COMPANY   2.00
BACH, J.S.
CONCERTO IN G MINOR, SCH NO. 1058
    ASSOCIATED MUSIC PUBLISHERS, INC.   BRH   1.00
BACH, J.S.   GOEDICKE *
CONCERTO IN G MINOR
    INTERNATIONAL MUSIC COMPANY   2.00
BACH, J.S.   RALSTON
CONCERTO IN THE ITALIAN STYLE
    G. SCHIRMER, INC.   L1806   1.50
BACH, J.S.
CONCERTO NO. 01 IN C MINOR FOR 2 PIANOS, SCH NO. 1060
    ASSOCIATED MUSIC PUBLISHERS, INC.   BRH   1.00
BACH, J.S.
CONCERTO NO. 01 IN D MINOR FOR 3 PIANOS, SCH NO. 1063
    ASSOCIATED MUSIC PUBLISHERS, INC.   BRH   1.00
BACH, J.S.
CONCERTO NO. 02 IN C FOR 2 PIANOS, SCH NO. 1061
    ASSOCIATED MUSIC PUBLISHERS, INC.   BRH   1.00
BACH, J.S.
CONCERTO NO. 02 IN C FOR 3 PIANOS, SCH NO. 1064
    ASSOCIATED MUSIC PUBLISHERS, INC.   BRH   1.00
BACH, J.S.
CONCERTO NO. 03 IN C MINOR FOR 2 PIANOS, SCH NO. 1062
    ASSOCIATED MUSIC PUBLISHERS, INC.   BRH   1.00
BACH, J.S.   DUNCAN
ELEVEN CHORALE PRELUDES FROM THE LITTLE ORGAN BOOK -- SET
    G. SCHIRMER, INC.   L1724   1.75
BACH, J.S.   MARLOWE, R. *   4
ESURIENTES FROM THE MAGNIFICAT
    THEODORE PRESSER COMPANY   1.50
BACH, J.S.   HUTCHERSON, R.
FIVE BACH DUETS
    BELWIN-MILLS PUBLISHING CORPORATION   11170   1.25
BACH, J.S.   HUTCHERSON, R.
FIVE DUETS
    BELWIN-MILLS PUBLISHING CORPORATION   1.25
BACH, J.S.   M
FOUR CHORALE PRELUDES
    C. F. PETERS CORPORATION   H335   2.00
BACH, J.S.   SPENCER
FOUR COURTLY DANCES -- SET
    G. SCHIRMER, INC.   1.10
BACH, J.S.   LEE
FOUR DANCE MEASURES
    OXFORD UNIVERSITY PRESS   35.501   1.55
BACH, J.S.   BRAGDON
FUGHETTAS -- 18 LITTLE PRELUDES AND FUGUES FOR TWO PIANOS, FOUR
HANDS
    BELWIN-MILLS PUBLISHING CORPORATION   2.00
BACH, J.S.   SAMUELSON
FUGHETTA
    BELWIN-MILLS PUBLISHING CORPORATION   1.00
BACH, J.S.   SCIONTI
FUGUE IN G MINOR 'THE LITTLE'
    FRANCO COLOMBO PUBLICATIONS   NY1208   .75
BACH, J.S.   KRAMER   3-4
FUGUE IN G MINOR
    PRO-ART PUBLICATIONS, INC.   10   1.50
BACH, J.S.   SAMUELSON
GAVOTTE IN G MAJOR
    BELWIN-MILLS PUBLISHING CORPORATION   .75
BACH, J.S.   STEINER
GIGUE IN D FROM SUITE NO. 3 FOR ORCH -- TRANSCRIBED IN THE EARLY
GRADES -- SET
    G. SCHIRMER, INC.   .75
BACH, J.S.   SCIONTI
GONE IS SORROW, GONE IS SADNESS
    FRANCO COLOMBO PUBLICATIONS   NY1209   .75
BACH, J.S.   HARRIS, W. H.
HERR JESU CHRIST, DICH ZU UNS WEND -- LORD CHRIST, REVEAL THY
HOLY FACE
    NOVELLO AND COMPANY, LTD.   10.0151.05   1.50
BACH, J.S.   BAUER
ITALIAN CONCERTO--ARR. IN HARPSICHORD STYLE
    G. SCHIRMER, INC.   3.00
BACH, J.S.   BAUER
ITALIAN CONCERTO, ARR. IN HARPSICHORD STYLE -- SET
    G. SCHIRMER, INC.   3.00
BACH, J.S.   BISCHOFF
ITALIAN CONCERTO
    INTERNATIONAL MUSIC COMPANY   1.50
BACH, J.S.   RONTGEN
ITALIAN CONCERTO
    UNIVERSAL EDITION   330   1.30
BACH, J.S.   KREUTZ   5
ITALIENISCHES KONZERT -- BWV 971
    SCHOTT   0876 1/2   1.00
BACH, J.S.   BABIN   3
JESU, JOY OF MAN'S DESIRING
    BOSTON MUSIC COMPANY   1.25
BACH, J.S.   HESS
JESU, JOY OF MAN'S DESIRING
    OXFORD UNIVERSITY PRESS   35.018   1.60
BACH, J.S.   EMERY
JESUS CHRISTUS UNSER HEILAND -- JESUS CHRIST, OUR SAVIOUR
    NOVELLO AND COMPANY, LTD.   10.0147.07   1.40
BACH, J.S.   HOWE
KOMM SUESSER TOD
    FRANCO COLOMBO PUBLICATIONS   NY1276   .75
BACH, J.S.   WILLIANS   E-M
LITTLE G MINOR ORGAN FUGUE
    C. F. PETERS CORPORATION   H65   1.50
BACH, J.S.   STEINER
MINUET IN D FROM SUITE NO. 4 FOR ORCH -- TRANSCRIBED IN THE
EARLY GRADES -- SET
    G. SCHIRMER, INC.   .75
BACH, J.S.   HAUPT, L. VON
MUSETTE
    BELWIN-MILLS PUBLISHING CORPORATION   27035   .60
BACH, J.S.   LUBOSHUTZ
NOW COMES THE GENTLE SAVIOR
    BELWIN-MILLS PUBLISHING CORPORATION   1.50
BACH, J.S.   BURMEISTER, R.
ORGAN FANTASIA AND FUGUE IN G MINOR
    INTERNATIONAL MUSIC COMPANY   2.50
BACH, J.S.   DUPARC, H.
ORGAN PRELUDE AND FUGUE IN E MINOR
    INTERNATIONAL MUSIC COMPANY   2.00
BACH, J.S.   MILLER
ORGAN PRELUDE IN C MINOR
    NOVELLO AND COMPANY, LTD.   10.0153.01   1.90
BACH, J.S.   BRAGGIOTTI, M.
ORGAN TOCCATA AND FUGUE IN D MINOR -- SET
    G. SCHIRMER, INC.   2.00

BACH, J.S.   CHASINS, A.
PASSACAGLIA IN C MINOR
          BELWIN-MILLS PUBLISHING CORPORATION   2.50
BACH, J.S.   TAGLIAPIETRA
PASSACAGLIA IN C MINOR
          FRANCO COLOMBO PUBLICATIONS   RE2475   2.75
BACH, J.S.   MAIER, G.
PASTORALE
          BELWIN-MILLS PUBLISHING CORPORATION   1.25
BACH, J.S.   ODOM *
PASTORAL SYMPHONY FROM THE CHRISTMAS ORATORIO -- SET
          G. SCHIRMER, INC.   1.25
BACH, J.S.
PIANO CONCERTO FOR TWO PIANOS IN C MINOR
          EDWIN F. KALMUS   3032   2.50
BACH, J.S.
PIANO CONCERTO FOR TWO PIANOS IN C
          EDWIN F. KALMUS   3031   2.50
BACH, J.S.
PIANO CONCERTO IN D MINOR
          EDWIN F. KALMUS   3029   2.50
BACH, J.S.
PIANO CONCERTO IN F MINOR
          EDWIN F. KALMUS   3030   1.50
BACH, J.S.   SCIONTI
PRELUDE AND FUGUE IN G
          FRANCO COLOMBO PUBLICATIONS   NY1293   1.00
BACH, J.S.
PRELUDIO
          BELWIN-MILLS PUBLISHING CORPORATION   1.00
BACH, J.S.   SCIONTI
REJOICE, BELOVED CHRISTIANS
          FRANCO COLOMBO PUBLICATIONS   NY1260   .75
BACH, J.S.   STEINER
RONDO IN B MINOR FROM SUITE NO. 2 FOR ORCH -- TRANSCRIBED IN THE
EARLY GRADES -- SET
          G. SCHIRMER, INC.   .75
BACH, J.S.   BABIN   3
SHEEP MAY SAFELY GRAZE
          BOSTON MUSIC COMPANY   1.25
BACH, J.S.   HOWE
SHEEP MAY SAFELY GRAZE
          OXFORD UNIVERSITY PRESS   35.025   1.75
BACH, J.S.   MAIER, G.
SICILIENNE
          BELWIN-MILLS PUBLISHING CORPORATION   1.25
BACH, J.S.   M
SINFONIA --FROM CHRISTMAS ORATORIO, PART 2--
          C. F. PETERS CORPORATION   N967   1.50
BACH, J.S.   EMERY
SINFONIA FROM CANTATA 75
          NOVELLO AND COMPANY, LTD.   10.0149.03   1.25
BACH, J.S.   EMERY
SINFONIA NO. 1 FROM CANTATA 35
          NOVELLO AND COMPANY, LTD.   10.0148.05   1.90
BACH, J.S.   LEUCHTER
SIX CONCERTOS AFTER VIVALDI -- OP. 3, NOS. 3, 9, 12. OP. 4, NOS.
1, 6. OP. 7, NO. 2
          FRANCO COLOMBO PUBLICATIONS   BA12114   4.00
BACH, J.S.   WHITTAKER
SLEEPERS, WAKE
          OXFORD UNIVERSITY PRESS   35.303   1.90
BACH, J.S.   VAN HULSE, C.   4
SOLFEGGIETO
          WILLIS MUSIC COMPANY   .60
BACH, J.S.   KEENEY
SONATINA -- PRELUDE TO THE CANTATA ''GOD'S TIME IS THE BEST'' --
SET
          G. SCHIRMER, INC.   .75
BACH, J.S. *   WHITFORD   MEDIUM/ADVANCED
TEN PIECES FOR PIANO AND ORGAN
          SHAWNEE PRESS, INC.   2.50
BACH, J.S.   HOIBY
THREE ORGAN CHORALE PRELUDES
          BOOSEY AND HAWKES, INC.   2.25
BACH, J.S. *
THREE PIECES BY J. S. BACH
          BOOSEY AND HAWKES, INC.   2.50
BACH, J.S.   SCIONTI
TOCCATA AND FUGUE IN D MINOR
          BELWIN-MILLS PUBLISHING CORPORATION   1.00
BACH, J.S.   SCIONTI
TOCCATA AND FUGUE IN D MINOR
          FRANCO COLOMBO PUBLICATIONS   NY1259   1.00
BACH, J.S.   HARRIS, W. H.
TOCCATA IN THE DORIAN MODE
          NOVELLO AND COMPANY, LTD.   10.0152.03   1.90
BACH, J.S.   MAIER, G.
TWO-PART INVENTIONS
          BELWIN-MILLS PUBLISHING CORPORATION   2.25
BACH, J.S.   BENOIST   3
TWO MENUETS -- G MAJOR NO. 1, G MINOR NO. 2
          VOLKWEIN BROS.   1.00
BACH, J.S.
TWO MIRROR FUGUES --CONTRAPUNCTUS 13--. ART OF THE FUGUE
          C. F. PETERS CORPORATION   218A   1.50
BACH, J.S. *   VOLKART-SCHLAGER   2-3
WIR MUSIZIEREN AN ZWEI KLAVIEREN. 12 KLEINE STUCKE
          BARENREITER VERLAG   SM 567
BACH, J. C. F.   SEILER
CONCERTO FOR PIANO AND VIOLA OBBLIGATO -- 2-PNO RED. WITH VIOLA
PART
          ASSOCIATED MUSIC PUBLISHERS, INC.   BOT   11.00
BACH, J. CHRISTIAN   DOEBEREINER   M
CONCERTO, OP. 7, NO. 5
          C. F. PETERS CORPORATION   3873   2.50
BACH, J. CHRISTIAN
CONCERTO IN A FUR CEMBALO -- KLAVIER UND STREICH-ORCHESTER,
KLAVIERAUSZUG
          SCHOTT   2320   3.50
BACH, J. CHRISTIAN   LANDSHOFF   E-M
CONCERTO IN B FLAT, OP. 13, NO. 4
          C. F. PETERS CORPORATION   4329   1.50
BACH, J. CHRISTIAN
CONCERTO IN G FUR CEMBALO -- KLAVIER UND STREICH-ORCHESTER,
KLAVIERAUSZUG
          SCHOTT   3703   2.50
BACH, J. CHRISTIAN   LANDSHOFF   E-M
CONCERTO OP.13, NO.2 IN D,URTEXT
          C. F. PETERS CORPORATION   4262   1.50
BACH, J. CHRISTIAN   MARTINI, G.   3-4
KONZERT IN F MINOR FUR CEMBALO -- KLAVIER -- UND STREICHER
          BARENREITER VERLAG   NMA 170
BACH, J. CHRISTIAN   M
QUARTET, OP. 8 NO. 2 --2 HARPSICHORDS# 1 CONCERTANTE, 2
RIPIENO--
          C. F. PETERS CORPORATION   WM70   3.00

BACH, J. CHRISTIAN   JANETZKY   3
QUARTETT IN E FLAT, OP. 8 NO. 2 ''ACCOMODATO PER DUE CEMBALI'
          BARENREITER VERLAG   SM 2201
BACH, J. CHRISTIAN
SONATA IN C
          EDWIN F. KALMUS   3087   1.50
BACH, J. CHRISTIAN   CASSISA *
SONATA IN G
          FRANCO COLOMBO PUBLICATIONS   130062   1.75
BACH, J. CHRISTIAN   HUDNIK *
SONATA IN G
          INTERNATIONAL MUSIC COMPANY   2.50
BACH, J. CHRISTIAN
SONATE G-DUR
          SCHOTT   2445   2.75
BACH, W.F.
KONZERT FUR 2 KLAVIERE F-DUR
          SCHOTT   10159   2.50
BACH, W.F.
PIANO CONCERTO IN A MINOR
          EDWIN F. KALMUS   3109   3.00
BACH, W.F.
PIANO CONCERTO IN E MINOR
          EDWIN F. KALMUS   3108   3.00
BACH, W.F.   BRAHMS   M
SONATA IN F FOR 2 PIANOS--1 COPY--
          C. F. PETERS CORPORATION   4284   1.25
BACH, W.F.
SONATA IN F
          INTERNATIONAL MUSIC COMPANY   2.50
BACH, W.F.   BRAHMS   M
SONATA IN F
          C. F. PETERS CORPORATION   4284   1.25
BACON, E.
JERICHO FOR TWO PIANOS OR ONE PIANO FOUR HANDS
          AMERICAN MUSIC EDITION   1.50
BACON, E.
RIVER QUEEN FOR TWO PIANOS OR ONE PIANO FOUR HANDS
          AMERICAN MUSIC EDITION   1.50
BADURA-SKODA
CADENZAS TO HAYDN CONCERTO IN D
          ASSOCIATED MUSIC PUBLISHERS, INC.   DOB   1.25
BADURA-SKODA
CADENZAS TO MOZART CONCERTO IN D MINOR, K. 466
          ASSOCIATED MUSIC PUBLISHERS, INC.   DOB   1.25
BADURA-SKODA
CADENZAS TO MOZART CONCERTO IN E FLAT, K. 482
          ASSOCIATED MUSIC PUBLISHERS, INC.   DOB   1.25
BADURA-SKODA
CADENZA AND INTRODUCTIONS TO MOZART CONCERTO IN C MINOR, K. 491
          ASSOCIATED MUSIC PUBLISHERS, INC.   DOB   1.25
BADURA-SKODA
CADENZA TO MOZART CONCERTO IN C, K. 503
          ASSOCIATED MUSIC PUBLISHERS, INC.   DOB   1.25
BAIRD *
CAT TAILS
          CARL FISCHER, INC.   P 2540   .75
BARBER, S.
PIANO CONCERTO, OP. 38
          G. SCHIRMER, INC.   4.00
BARBER, S.
PIANO CONCERTO, OP. 38
          G. SCHIRMER, INC.   4.00
BARBER, S.   GOLD *
SOUVENIRS -- SET
          G. SCHIRMER, INC.   4.00
BARROZO NETTO   BRITAIN
MINHA TERRA
          FRANCO COLOMBO PUBLICATIONS   BR2142   1.00
BARTA   4
KONZERT FUR KLAVIER UND ORCHESTER
          BARENREITER VERLAG   CHF 5227
BARTLETT, E.
ELIZABETHAN SUITE
          OXFORD UNIVERSITY PRESS   35.207   2.25
BARTOK
CONCERTO NO. 01
          BOOSEY AND HAWKES, INC.   7.50
BARTOK
CONCERTO NO. 02
          BOOSEY AND HAWKES, INC.   7.50
BARTOK
CONCERTO NO. 03
          BOOSEY AND HAWKES, INC.   7.50
BARTOK
RHAPSODY, OP. 1
          KULTURA   4.00
BARTOK
SCHERZO FUR ORCHESTER UND KLAVIER, KLAVIERAUSZUG
          SCHOTT   4811   6.00
BARTOK
SEVEN PIECES, FROM 'MIKROKOSMOS'
          BOOSEY AND HAWKES, INC.   5.00
BARTOK
SONATA FOR TWO PIANOS AND PERCUSSION --COMPLETE--
          BOOSEY AND HAWKES, INC.   20.00
BARTOK
SONATA FOR TWO PIANOS AND PERCUSSION --PERCUSSION PART--
          BOOSEY AND HAWKES, INC.   EA.
BARTOK
SONATA FOR TWO PIANOS AND PERCUSSION --PIANO PART--
          BOOSEY AND HAWKES, INC.   EA.
BARTOK
SUITE, OP. 4B
          BOOSEY AND HAWKES, INC.   5.00
BAUER, M.
AMERICAN YOUTH CONCERTO
          G. SCHIRMER, INC.   1.50
BAUER, M.
AMERICAN YOUTH CONCERTO
          G. SCHIRMER, INC.   1.50
BAUERNFEIND
FESTIVE PIECE
          ASSOCIATED MUSIC PUBLISHERS, INC.   OBV   1.25
BAUR
KONZERTANTE MUSIK -- 1958
          ASSOCIATED MUSIC PUBLISHERS, INC.   BRH   5.00
BAZELAIRE   7
CHASSE, SCHERZO, OP. 103
          ALPHONSE LEDUC
BECK, C.   5
CONCERTINO FUR KLAVIER UND ORCHESTER, KLAVIERAUSZUG
          SCHOTT   2068   3.75
BECK
SONATINA FUR ZWEI KLAVIER
          SCHOTT   4909   3.00

BEETHOVEN	STUMM	3	
ADIEU TO THE PIANO			
BOSTON MUSIC COMPANY			2.00
BEETHOVEN	KEMPFF		
CADENZAS TO CONCERTI NOS. 1-4			
ASSOCIATED MUSIC PUBLISHERS, INC.		DOB	3.50
BEETHOVEN			
CADENZA TO CONCERTO NO. 02 IN B FLAT, OP. 19			
ASSOCIATED MUSIC PUBLISHERS, INC.		DOB	1.00
BEETHOVEN			
CADENZA TO CONCERTO NO. 03 IN C MINOR, OP. 37			
ASSOCIATED MUSIC PUBLISHERS, INC.		DOB	1.25
BEETHOVEN			
CADENZA TO CONCERTO NO. 04 IN G, OP. 58			
ASSOCIATED MUSIC PUBLISHERS, INC.		DOB	1.25
BEETHOVEN			
CADENZA TO MOZART CONCERTO IN D MINOR, K. 466			
ASSOCIATED MUSIC PUBLISHERS, INC.		DOB	1.00
BEETHOVEN	ALBERT, E. D'		
CONCERTO NO. 01 IN C, OP. 15			
ASSOCIATED MUSIC PUBLISHERS, INC.		BRH	3.00
BEETHOVEN	MONTANI		
CONCERTO NO. 01 IN C, OP. 15			
FRANCO COLOMBO PUBLICATIONS		ER2427	2.25
BEETHOVEN	PAUER	D	
CONCERTO NO. 01 IN C, OP. 15			
C. F. PETERS CORPORATION		2894A	1.50
BEETHOVEN	KULLAK, T.		
CONCERTO NO. 01 IN C, OP. 15			
G. SCHIRMER, INC.		L621	1.50
BEETHOVEN	KULLAK		
CONCERTO NO. 01 IN C MAJOR, OP. 1			
G. SCHIRMER, INC.		L621	1.50
BEETHOVEN	ALBERT, E. D' *		
CONCERTO NO. 02 IN B FLAT, OP. 19			
ASSOCIATED MUSIC PUBLISHERS, INC.		BRH	3.00
BEETHOVEN	TAGLIAPIETRA		
CONCERTO NO. 02 IN B FLAT, OP. 19			
FRANCO COLOMBO PUBLICATIONS		ER1413	1.75
BEETHOVEN	PAUER	D	
CONCERTO NO. 02 IN B FLAT, OP. 19			
C. F. PETERS CORPORATION		2894B	1.50
BEETHOVEN	KULLAK, T.		
CONCERTO NO. 02 IN B FLAT, OP. 19			
G. SCHIRMER, INC.		L622	1.25
BEETHOVEN	KULLAK		
CONCERTO NO. 02 IN B FLAT MAJOR, OP. 19			
G. SCHIRMER, INC.		L622	1.50
BEETHOVEN	PAUER	M	
CONCERTO NO. 03 IN C MINOR, OP. 37. ABRIDGED PIANO SOLO			
ARRANGEMENT.			
C. F. PETERS CORPORATION		2894CC	1.25
BEETHOVEN			
CONCERTO NO. 03 IN C MINOR, OP. 37 - CADENZA FOR THE FIRST			
MOVEMENT			
FRANCO COLOMBO PUBLICATIONS		ER2645	.60
BEETHOVEN	ALBERT, E. D'		
CONCERTO NO. 03 IN C MINOR, OP. 37			
ASSOCIATED MUSIC PUBLISHERS, INC.		BRH	3.00
BEETHOVEN	TAGLIAPIETRA		
CONCERTO NO. 03 IN C MINOR, OP. 37			
FRANCO COLOMBO PUBLICATIONS		ER1414	2.25
BEETHOVEN	ALKAN		
CONCERTO NO. 03 IN C MINOR, OP. 37			
GERARD BILLAUDOT EDITIONS MUSICALES			2.50
BEETHOVEN	PAUER	D	
CONCERTO NO. 03 IN C MINOR, OP. 37			
C. F. PETERS CORPORATION		2894C	1.50
BEETHOVEN	KULLAK, T.		
CONCERTO NO. 03 IN C MINOR, OP. 37			
G. SCHIRMER, INC.		L623	1.50
BEETHOVEN	KULLAK		
CONCERTO NO. 03 IN C MINOR, OP. 37			
G. SCHIRMER, INC.		L623	1.50
BEETHOVEN	PAUER	M	
CONCERTO NO. 04 IN G, OP. 58. ABRIDGED PIANO SOLO ARRANGEMENT			
C. F. PETERS CORPORATION		2894DD	1.25
BEETHOVEN	ALBERT, E. D'		
CONCERTO NO. 04 IN G, OP. 58			
ASSOCIATED MUSIC PUBLISHERS, INC.		BRH	1.50
BEETHOVEN	TAGLIAPIETRA		
CONCERTO NO. 04 IN G, OP. 58			
FRANCO COLOMBO PUBLICATIONS		ER1415	3.50
BEETHOVEN	PAUER	D	
CONCERTO NO. 04 IN G, OP. 58			
C. F. PETERS CORPORATION		2894D	1.50
BEETHOVEN	KULLAK, T.		
CONCERTO NO. 04 IN G, OP. 58			
G. SCHIRMER, INC.		L624	1.50
BEETHOVEN	SAUER		
CONCERTO NO. 04 IN G, OP. 58			
UNIVERSAL EDITION		304	2.40
BEETHOVEN	KULLAK		
CONCERTO NO. 04 IN G MAJOR, OP. 58			
G. SCHIRMER, INC.		L624	1.50
BEETHOVEN	PAUER	M	
CONCERTO NO. 05 IN E FLAT,-OP. 73 --EMPEROR--. ABRIDGED PIANO			
SOLO ARRANGEMENT			
C. F. PETERS CORPORATION		2894EE	1.25
BEETHOVEN	PAUER	D	
CONCERTO NO. 05 IN E FLAT, OP. 73 --EMPEROR--			
C. F. PETERS CORPORATION		2894E	1.50
BEETHOVEN	ALBERT, E. D'		
CONCERTO NO. 05 IN E FLAT, OP. 73 -- ''EMPEROR''			
ASSOCIATED MUSIC PUBLISHERS, INC.		BRH	3.00
BEETHOVEN	KULLAK, T.		
CONCERTO NO. 05 IN E FLAT, OP. 73 -- ''EMPEROR''			
G. SCHIRMER, INC.		L625	1.50
BEETHOVEN	TAGLIAPIETRA		
CONCERTO NO. 05 IN E FLAT, OP. 73 'EMPEROR'			
FRANCO COLOMBO PUBLICATIONS		ER1416	3.75
BEETHOVEN	SAUER		
CONCERTO NO. 05 IN E FLAT, OP. 73			
UNIVERSAL EDITION			2.80
BEETHOVEN	KULLAK		
CONCERTO NO. 05 IN E FLAT MAJOR--OP. 73-- 'EMPEROR'			
G. SCHIRMER, INC.		L625	1.00
BEETHOVEN	SAAR		
CONTRE DANCE NO. 1			
BELWIN-MILLS PUBLISHING CORPORATION			1.50
BEETHOVEN		D	
FIVE CONCERTI AND CHORAL FANTASY, OP. 80			
C. F. PETERS CORPORATION		144	10.00
BEETHOVEN	HESS	3	
KONZERT IN E FLAT -- 1784 -- FUR KLAVIER UND KAMMERORCHESTER			
BARENREITER VERLAG		AE 218	

BEETHOVEN	DUNGAN	3	
MOONLIGHT SONATA - FIRST MOVEMENT			
BOSTON MUSIC COMPANY			1.00
BEETHOVEN			
ORIGINAL CADENZAS TO THE PIANO CONCERTI			
ASSOCIATED MUSIC PUBLISHERS, INC.		B/H	2.75
BEETHOVEN			
ORIGINAL COMPOSITIONS FOR TWO PIANOS, FOUR HANDS			
EDWIN F. KALMUS		3165	2.50
BEETHOVEN			
PIANO CONCERTO IN D FROM THE VIOLIN CONCERTO IN D, OP. 61 --			
ORIGINAL ARR. BY BEETHOVEN -- 1807			
ASSOCIATED MUSIC PUBLISHERS, INC.		BRH	5.50
BEETHOVEN			
PIANO CONCERTO NO. 01			
EDWIN F. KALMUS		3160	2.00
BEETHOVEN			
PIANO CONCERTO NO. 02			
EDWIN F. KALMUS		3161	2.00
BEETHOVEN			
PIANO CONCERTO NO. 03			
EDWIN F. KALMUS		3162	2.00
BEETHOVEN			
PIANO CONCERTO NO. 04			
EDWIN F. KALMUS		3163	2.00
BEETHOVEN			
PIANO CONCERTO NO. 05			
EDWIN F. KALMUS		3164	2.00
BEETHOVEN	STEINER		
SCHERZO IN G FROM STRING QUARTET, OP. 18 NO. 2 -- TRANSCRIBED IN			
THE EARLY GRADES -- SET			
G. SCHIRMER, INC.			1.10
BEETHOVEN	RUTHARDT	M	
SEPTET, OP. 20			
C. F. PETERS CORPORATION		2951	3.00
BEETHOVEN	PODOLSKY		
SONATINA IN G MAJOR			
VOLKWEIN BROS.			
BEETHOVEN		M	
SYMPHONY NO. 02 IN D, OP. 36			
C. F. PETERS CORPORATION		3033B	8.50
BEETHOVEN		M	
SYMPHONY NO. 03 IN E FLAT, OP. 55. 'EROICA'			
C. F. PETERS CORPORATION		3033C	8.50
BEETHOVEN		M	
SYMPHONY NO. 05 IN C MINOR, OP. 67			
C. F. PETERS CORPORATION		3033E	8.50
BEETHOVEN		M	
SYMPHONY NO. 09 IN D MINOR, OP. 125			
C. F. PETERS CORPORATION		3033I	10.00
BEETHOVEN	THERN		
TURKISH MARCH FROM ''THE RUINS OF ATHENS'' -- SET			
G. SCHIRMER, INC.			.60
BEETHOVEN	OMIZZOLO		
TURKISH MARCH FROM 'RUINS OF ATHENS'			
FRANCO COLOMBO PUBLICATIONS		129003	.75
BEETHOVEN	PHILIPP		
VARIATIONS BY BEETHOVEN			
FRANCO COLOMBO PUBLICATIONS		SAL	2.50
BEN-HAIM			
CAPRICCIO FOR PIANO AND ORCHESTRA --SCORE AND PARTS ON RENTAL--			
ALEXANDER BROUDE, INC.			6.30
BENDA, R.	BETHAN	3	
KONZERT IN G FUR CEMBALO UND STREICHORCHESTER			
BARENREITER VERLAG		NMA 144	
BENDA, R.	RACEK	3	
KONZERT IN C MINOR FUR CEMBALO UND STREICHORCHESTER			
BARENREITER VERLAG		MAB 10	
BENJAMIN			
CARIBBEAN DANCE			
BOOSEY AND HAWKES, INC.			2.50
BENJAMIN			
CONCERTO QUASI UNA FANTASIA			
BOOSEY AND HAWKES, INC.			5.00
BENJAMIN			
FROM SAN DOMINGO			
BOOSEY AND HAWKES, INC.			1.75
BENJAMIN			
JAMAICALYPSO			
BOOSEY AND HAWKES, INC.			1.00
BENJAMIN			
JAMAICAN RUMBA			
BOOSEY AND HAWKES, INC.			1.00
BENJAMIN			
TWO JAMAICAN STREET SONGS			
BOOSEY AND HAWKES, INC.			2.50
BENNETT, R.			
PARTY PIECES FOR YOUNG PLAYERS, 2 PNO. SCORE			
UNIVERSAL EDITION		15425	4.70
BENNETT, R.			
PARTY PIECE FOR YOUNG PLAYERS			
UNIVERSAL EDITION		UE 15425	4.70
BENNETT, R.			
PIANO CONCERTO			
UNIVERSAL EDITION		UE 14655	15.30
BENOIST, A.		5	
THEME AND VARIATIONS IN ROCOCO STYLE			
VOLKWEIN BROS.			01.00
BENTLEY			
MISCHIEVOUS ELF			
BELWIN-MILLS PUBLISHING CORPORATION			1.25
BERGER			
CARIBBEAN CRUISE			
BROUDE BROTHERS LTD.			08.00
BERGGRUN, J.			
CHORALE AND FUGUE ON A THEME BY J. S. BACH			
BRODT MUSIC COMPANY			.85
BERNSTEIN, L.	SMITH		
AGE OF ANXIETY, THE -- SYMPHONY NO. 2 FOR PIANO AND ORCHESTRA --			
AFTER W. H. AUDEN -- REVISED EDITION			
G. SCHIRMER, INC.			3.50
BESLEY, M.	SAMUELSON		
SECOND MINUET			
BOOSEY AND HAWKES, INC.			.75
BILBRO, M.		1	
AT THE PARTY			
WILLIS MUSIC COMPANY			.35
BILBRO, M.		3	
MARCH MILITAIRE			
WILLIS MUSIC COMPANY			.75
BILBRO, M.		2	
ROSE GARDEN			
WILLIS MUSIC COMPANY			.50
BILBRO, M.		2	
WITH HOUND AND HORN			
WILLIS MUSIC COMPANY			.45

BILOTTI 3-4
  SCHERZO
    PRO-ART PUBLICATIONS, INC.   30   1.25
BIZET, G.
  CHILDREN'S GAMES
    EDWIN F. KALMUS   3222   2.50
BIZET, G.
  JEUX D'ENFANTS
    EDWIN F. KALMUS   3223   2.50
BLACHER
  CONCERTO, OP. 28
    ASSOCIATED MUSIC PUBLISHERS, INC.   BOT   9.00
BLACHER
  VARIATIONS ON A THEME BY CLEMENTI, OP. 61
    ASSOCIATED MUSIC PUBLISHERS, INC.   BOT   6.00
BLAKE, D. 2
  COTTON BLOSSOM TIME
    WILLIS MUSIC COMPANY   .40
BLAKE, D. 2
  FOREST VOICES
    WILLIS MUSIC COMPANY   .50
BLAKE, D. 2
  HOLLYHOCK AND HONEY BEE
    WILLIS MUSIC COMPANY   .60
BLAKE, D. 4
  IRISH DANCE
    WILLIS MUSIC COMPANY   .50
BLAKE, D. 2
  SONG OF THE RAIN
    WILLIS MUSIC COMPANY   .35
BLAKE, D. 1
  YE MERRIE WINTER
    WILLIS MUSIC COMPANY   .50
BLANCHET
  BALLADE, OP. 57
    ASSOCIATED MUSIC PUBLISHERS, INC.   ESC   6.75
BLANCO   KASTNER
  CONCIERTO DE DOS ORGANOS ODER FUR 2 HARFEN ODER 2
  TASTEN-INSTRUMENTE
    SCHOTT   4809   2.50
BLISS, A.
  BARAZA
    NOVELLO AND COMPANY, LTD.   10.0154.10   1.40
BLISS, A.
  CONCERTO FOR TWO PIANOS AND ORCHESTRA -- THREE PIANO SCORE --
    OXFORD UNIVERSITY PRESS   35.605   3.35
BLISS, A.
  PIANO CONCERTO -- WITH ACCOMPANIMENT ARRANGED FOR SECOND PIANO
    NOVELLO AND COMPANY, LTD.   10.0009.08   7.50
BLISS, A.
  PIANO CONCERTO
    NOVELLO AND COMPANY, LTD.   10.0009.08   7.50
BLOCH, E.
  CONCERTO SYMPHONIQUE
    BOOSEY AND HAWKES, INC.   6.00
BLOCH, E.
  EVOCATIONS -- TRS. BY THE COMPOSER FROM THE SYMPHONIC SUITE --
  SET
    G. SCHIRMER, INC.   2.50
BLOCH, E.
  SCHERZO FANTASTIQUE -- ORCH. PART ARR. FOR SECOND PIANO BY THE
  COMPOSER
    G. SCHIRMER, INC.   2.50
BLOCH, W.
  CONCERTO NO. 02
    ASSOCIATED MUSIC PUBLISHERS, INC.   DOB   7.50
BOCCHERINI   LENTZ
  MENUET
    ELKAN-VOGEL, INC.   LEM   1.00
BOCCOSI, BIO
  TARANTELLA
    EDIZIONI BERBEN   EB 1271   1.50
BOELLMANN, L.   BENFELD, A.
  SUITE GOTHIQUE
    ELKAN-VOGEL, INC.   D   6.25
BOISMORTIER, J. B. DE   LUBOSHUTZ
  LES REVERANCES NUPTIALES
    BELWIN-MILLS PUBLISHING CORPORATION   1.00
BORDES
  RHAPSODIE BASQUE
    FRANCO COLOMBO PUBLICATIONS   SAL   6.50
BORKOVEC 4
  CONCERTO GROSSO FUR 2 VIOLINEN, VIOLONCELLO, ORCHESTER UND
  OBLIGATES CEMBALO
    BARENREITER VERLAG   AP 1300
BORKOVEC 4
  KLAVIERKONZERT NO. 02
    BARENREITER VERLAG   CHF 5324
BOSSI, R.
  PINOCCHIO, OP. 29
    FRANCO COLOMBO PUBLICATIONS   BON.1786   3.00
BOUCOURECHLIEV
  PAGES D'ANARCHIPEL # ARCHIPEL 5D
    ALPHONSE LEDUC
BOULEZ
  STRUCTURES
    UNIVERSAL EDITION   12267   7.50
BOUTRY
  TRASNE
    FRANCO COLOMBO PUBLICATIONS   SAL   5.75
BOWLES, P.
  NIGHT WALTZ FOR TWO PIANOS
    AMERICAN MUSIC EDITION   1.50
BOWLES, P.
  SONATA -- SET
    G. SCHIRMER, INC.   1.50
BOYCE, W.   CRAXTON
  TEMPO DI GAVOTTA
    OXFORD UNIVERSITY PRESS   35.900   1.35
BOZZA 8
  SONATA
    ALPHONSE LEDUC
BRAGGIOTTI, M.
  VARIATIONS ON YANKEE DOODLE IN THE MANNER OF BACH, BEETHOVEN,
  CHOPIN, DEBUSSY AND GERSHWIN -- SET
    G. SCHIRMER, INC.   2.00
BRAHMS   MACKINNON
  CHORALE PRELUDES -- A ROSE BREAKS INTO BLOOM, OP. 122 NO. 8 --
  SET
    G. SCHIRMER, INC.   .50
BRAHMS   MACKINNON
  CHORALE PRELUDES -- O GOD, THOU HOLY GOD, OP. 122 NO. 7 -- SET
    G. SCHIRMER, INC.   .75
BRAHMS   HUGHES
  CONCERTO IN B FLAT MAJOR, OP. 83
    G. SCHIRMER, INC.   L1465   3.00

BRAHMS   HUGHES
  CONCERTO IN D MINOR, OP. 15
    G. SCHIRMER, INC.   L1429   3.50
BRAHMS
  CONCERTO NO. 01 IN D MINOR, OP. 15
    ASSOCIATED MUSIC PUBLISHERS, INC.   BRH   2.50
BRAHMS
  CONCERTO NO. 01 IN D MINOR, OP. 15
    INTERNATIONAL MUSIC COMPANY   3.75
BRAHMS   SAUER   D
  CONCERTO NO. 01 IN D MINOR, OP. 15
    C. F. PETERS CORPORATION   3655   2.50
BRAHMS   HUGHES
  CONCERTO NO. 01 IN D MINOR, OP. 15
    G. SCHIRMER, INC.   L1429   3.50
BRAHMS
  CONCERTO NO. 02 IN B FLAT, OP. 83
    ASSOCIATED MUSIC PUBLISHERS, INC.   BRH   3.00
BRAHMS
  CONCERTO NO. 02 IN B FLAT, OP. 83
    INTERNATIONAL MUSIC COMPANY   3.75
BRAHMS   SAUER   D
  CONCERTO NO. 02 IN B FLAT, OP. 83
    C. F. PETERS CORPORATION   3895   2.50
BRAHMS   HUGHES
  CONCERTO NO. 02 IN B FLAT, OP. 83
    G. SCHIRMER, INC.   L1465   3.00
BRAHMS   M-D
  FIVE WALTZES FROM OP. 39, TRANSCRIBED BY THE COMPOSER
    C. F. PETERS CORPORATION   3667   1.25
BRAHMS   M-D
  HAYDN VARIATIONS, OP. 56B --2 COPIES--
    C. F. PETERS CORPORATION   3892   2.00
BRAHMS *
  HAYDN VARIATIONS, OP. 56B
    EDWIN F. KALMUS   3248   2.00
BRAHMS   M-D
  HAYDN VARIATIONS, OP. 56B
    C. F. PETERS CORPORATION   3892   2.00
BRAHMS   KRAMER   4
  HOW LOVELY ARE THY DWELLINGS
    PRO-ART PUBLICATIONS, INC.   9   1.50
BRAHMS   GRAETZER
  HUNGARIAN DANCE NO. 05
    FRANCO COLOMBO PUBLICATIONS   BA9700   .50
BRAHMS   DUNGAN   2
  LULLABY
    BOSTON MUSIC COMPANY   .75
BRAHMS   MAIER, G.
  SIX WALTZES -- LIEBESLIEDER, SET 1
    BELWIN-MILLS PUBLISHING CORPORATION   2.50
BRAHMS   D
  SONATA, OP. 34 BIS --F MINOR--. AFTER THE PIANO QUINTET--
    C. F. PETERS CORPORATION   3662   2.25
BRAHMS
  SONATA IN F MINOR, OP. 34B
    ASSOCIATED MUSIC PUBLISHERS, INC.   BRH   5.00
BRAHMS
  SONATA IN F MINOR, OP. 34
    INTERNATIONAL MUSIC COMPANY   5.00
BRAHMS   KELLER
  VARIATIONS ON A THEME BY HAYDN, OP. 56B
    ASSOCIATED MUSIC PUBLISHERS, INC.   SIM   2.25
BRAHMS   KELLER
  VARIATIONS ON A THEME BY HAYDN, OP. 56B
    ASSOCIATED MUSIC PUBLISHERS, INC.   BRH   2.00
BRAHMS   HUGHES
  VARIATIONS ON A THEME BY HAYDN, OP. 56B
    G. SCHIRMER, INC.   L1496   1.25
BRAHMS
  VARIATIONS ON A THEME BY HAYDN
    INTERNATIONAL MUSIC COMPANY   3.00
BRAHMS   SILVESTRI
  VARIATIONS ON A THEME OF PAGANINI, OP. 35
    FRANCO COLOMBO PUBLICATIONS   ER2467   1.75
BRAHMS   HAUPT, L. VON
  WALTZ, OP. 39 NO. 3
    BELWIN-MILLS PUBLISHING CORPORATION   27041   .50
BRAHMS
  WALTZES, OP. 39
    EDWIN F. KALMUS   3262   1.50
BRAHMS   HUGHES
  WALTZES, OP. 39
    G. SCHIRMER, INC.   L1530   1.00
BRENDEL, T.
  CADENZAS TO MOZART CONCERTO IN D MINOR, K. 466
    ASSOCIATED MUSIC PUBLISHERS, INC.   DOB   1.00
BRENET, T.
  CONCERTO POUR UN POEM INCONNU -- PIANO, STRING ORCH. AND ONDES
  MARTENONT, PIANO SCORE
    ELKAN-VOGEL, INC.   RR   10.50
BRESGEN 4
  KONZERT FUR ZWEI KLAVIERE
    BARENREITER VERLAG   SM 1008A
BRESGEN 4
  SINFONISCHES KONZERT, OP. 21
    BARENREITER VERLAG   SM 1144
BRESGEN 4
  TOTENTANZ. TOCCATA NACH HOLBEIN FUR KLAVIER UND KLEINES
  ORCHESTER
    BARENREITER VERLAG   BA 3502
BREWER, A. H.   SAMUELSON
  FAIRY PIPERS
    BOOSEY AND HAWKES, INC.   .75
BRIMHALL, J.--ED.   BRIMHALL, J.
  PLAY BY TWOS BK. 1
    CHARLES HANSEN   H530   1.25
BRIMHALL, J.--ED.   BRIMHALL, J.
  PLAY BY TWOS BK. 2
    CHARLES HANSEN   H531   1.25
BRIMHALL, J.--ED.   BRIMHALL, J.
  SELECTIONS FROM LOVE STORY
    CHARLES HANSEN   F51860   3.00
BRITTEN, B.
  CONCERTO, OP. 13
    BOOSEY AND HAWKES, INC.   7.50
BRITTEN, B.
  DIVERSIONS FOR PIANO -- LEFT HAND, OP. 21
    BOOSEY AND HAWKES, INC.   6.50
BRITTEN, B.
  INTRODUCTION AND RONDO ALLA BURLESCA, OP. 23 NO. 1
    BOOSEY AND HAWKES, INC.   4.50
BRITTEN, B.
  MAZURKA ELEGIACA, OP. 23 NO. 2
    BOOSEY AND HAWKES, INC.   1.25
BRITTEN, B.
  SCOTTISH BALLAD, OP. 25 FOR TWO PIANOS AND ORCHESTRA
    BOOSEY AND HAWKES, INC.   5.00

BROWN, E.
    CORROBOREE FOR 2 OR 3 PIANOS
        UNIVERSAL EDITION   15308   5.25
BROWN
    CONCERTO FOR TWO PIANOS, BRASS AND PERCUSSION --IN PREP--
        WESTERN INTERNATIONAL MUSIC, INC.
BRUCKNER   D
    SYMPHONY NO. 05 IN B FLAT
        C. F. PETERS CORPORATION   3841E   10.00
BRUNNER
    PARTITA FOR PIANO AND ORCHESTRA
        BARENREITER VERLAG   BA 2024A   7.50
BRUNNER   4
    PARTITA FUR KLAVIER UND ORCHESTER
        BARENREITER VERLAG   BA 2024A
BRUNNER   4
    PARTITA FUR KLAVIER UND ORCHESTER
        BARENREITER VERLAG   BA 2024A
BUCALOSSI   SAMUELSON
    GRASSHOPPERS' DANCE
        BOOSEY AND HAWKES, INC.   1.00
BUCCHI
    CONCERTO IN RONDO -- 1957 --
        FRANCO COLOMBO PUBLICATIONS   FOR.12373   7.75
BUECHTGER   3
    CONCERTINO NO. 02 FUR KLAVIER UND KLEINES ORCHESTER
        BARENREITER VERLAG   BE 312
BUELOW
    CADENZAS TO BEETHOVEN CONCERTO IV
        MUSICA OBSCURA   2.50
BURGMUELLER   BUTLER   4
    TWENTY-FIVE EASY AND PROGRESSIVE STUDIES, OP. 100
        BOSTON MUSIC COMPANY   1.25
BURKHARD, W.   4
    CONCERTINO, OP. 94, FUR 2 QUERFLOTEN, CEMBALO UND STREICHER
        BARENREITER VERLAG   BA 2489
BURT, F.
    MUSIC, OP. 4
        ASSOCIATED MUSIC PUBLISHERS, INC. BOT   4.00
BUSCHBAUM *
    KINDER SPIELEN ZUR WEIHNACHT
        BARENREITER VERLAG   EN 803   6.00
BUSH
    WHYDAH VARIATIONS
        NOVELLO AND COMPANY, LTD.   10.0156.06 2.40
BUSONI
    DUETTO CONCERTANTE, AFTER MOZART -- SET
        ASSOCIATED MUSIC PUBLISHERS, INC. BRH   3.75
BUSONI
    FANTASIA CONTRAPPUNTISTICA -- COMPLETE ORIGINAL
        ASSOCIATED MUSIC PUBLISHERS, INC. BRH   6.00
BUSONI
    IMPROVISATION ON THE BACH CHORALE ''WIE WOHL IST MIR, O FREUND
    DER SEELE,'' S. 517
        ASSOCIATED MUSIC PUBLISHERS, INC. BRH   5.50
BUSSOTTI
    TABLEAUX VIVANTS - FROM 'LA PASSION SELON SADE'
        FRANCO COLOMBO PUBLICATIONS   130962   4.50
BUXTEHUDE   HARRIS, W. H.
    CIACONA
        NOVELLO AND COMPANY, LTD.   10.0157.04 1.65
CAGE   D
    CONCERTO FOR PIANO AND ORCHESTRA
        C. F. PETERS CORPORATION   6705   20.00
CAMARATA
    RUMBALERO
        BELWIN-MILLS PUBLISHING CORPORATION 27030   4.00
CAMBINI   BARBLAN
    CONCERTO IN B-FLAT, OP. 15 NO. 1
        FRANCO COLOMBO PUBLICATIONS   130484   4.00
CAMBINI   BARBLAN
    CONCERTO IN G, OP. 15 NO. 3
        FRANCO COLOMBO PUBLICATIONS   129856   2.75
CAMMAROTA
    CONCERTO
        FRANCO COLOMBO PUBLICATIONS   Z4297   5.75
CAMMAROTA
    TWELVE STUDI DA CONCERTO
        FRANCO COLOMBO PUBLICATIONS   BON. 2510   4.25
CANNON, P.
    CALOP PARISIEN
        NOVELLO AND COMPANY, LTD.   10.0159.00 2.00
CANNON, P.
    CONCERTINO FOR PIANO AND STRINGS
        NOVELLO AND COMPANY, LTD.   10.0158.02 2.15
CARDEW
    TWO BOOKS OF STUDY FOR PIANISTS. COMPLETE
        C. F. PETERS CORPORATION   H822   7.50
CARPENTER, J.
    CONCERTINO IN B MINOR
        G. SCHIRMER, INC.   2.50
CARPENTER, J.
    CONCERTINO
        G. SCHIRMER, INC.   2.50
CARRE
    WHITECAPS
        BELWIN-MILLS PUBLISHING CORPORATION   1.50
CARTER
    CONCERTO -- 1964-65
        ASSOCIATED MUSIC PUBLISHERS, INC. AMP   7.50
CASADESUS, R.
    CONCERTO, OP. 37
        ELKAN-VOGEL, INC.   D   16.50
CASADESUS, R.
    SIX PIECES
        ELKAN-VOGEL, INC.   D   14.00
CASANOVA, A.
    CONCERTINO POUR PIANO ET ORCHESTRE DE CHAMBRE
        ELKAN-VOGEL, INC.   J   7.90
CASELLA, A.
    SCARLATTIANA
        UNIVERSAL EDITION   UE 9530   6.80
CASTELNUOVO-TEDESCO
    ALT WIEN
        FRANCO COLOMBO PUBLICATIONS   FOR.11426   7.25
CASTELNUOVO-TEDESCO
    CONCERTO NO. 02
        FRANCO COLOMBO PUBLICATIONS   FOR.12374   9.50
CASTELNUOVO-TEDESCO
    DUO PIANISM
        FRANCO COLOMBO PUBLICATIONS   FOR.12350   1.50
CASTERA
    CONCERTO
        FRANCO COLOMBO PUBLICATIONS   SAL   13.00
CASTERA
    JOUR DE FETE AU PAYS BASQUE
        FRANCO COLOMBO PUBLICATIONS   SAL   13.00

CASTEREDE, J.
    CONCERTO FOR PIANO AND STRING ORCHESTRA
        FRANCO COLOMBO PUBLICATIONS   SAL   10.75
CAZDEN, N.
    STONY HOLLOW
        SPRATT MUSIC PUBLISHERS   2.00
CHABRIER
    ESPANA RHAPSODY
        BELWIN-MILLS PUBLISHING CORPORATION   2.00
CHABRIER
    ESPANA
        BOOSEY AND HAWKES, INC.   3.00
CHABRIER   PHILIPP, I.
    VALSE ROMANTIQUE NO. 2
        INTERNATIONAL MUSIC COMPANY   1.75
CHAMBERS, J.
    ALL AMERICAN, IN FOUR MOVEMENTS
        BELWIN-MILLS PUBLISHING CORPORATION 27002   3.50
CHAMINADE   ADAMS
    ANDANTE, OP. 59
        G. SCHIRMER, INC.   .50
CHAMINADE
    MATIN
        BOOSEY AND HAWKES, INC.   1.50
CHANCE, J. B.
    INTRODUCTION AND CAPRICCIO
        BOOSEY AND HAWKES, INC.   2.00
CHANDLER *
    CANADIAN CAPERS
        WARNER BROTHERS PUBLISHERS   2.00
CHARLES-HENRY
    OSMOSE
        FRANCO COLOMBO PUBLICATIONS   SAL   13.00
CHARPENTIER, G.
    NAPOLI FROM 'IMPRESSIONS OF ITALY'
        HEUGEL ET CIE.   12.00
CHASINS, A.   7
    FLEDERMAUS FANTASY
        THEODORE PRESSER COMPANY   1.25
CHASINS, A.
    RUSH HOUR IN HONG KONG
        BELWIN-MILLS PUBLISHING CORPORATION   2.00
CHAUSSON
    CONCERTO FOR VIOLIN, PIANO AND STRING QUARTET
        FRANCO COLOMBO PUBLICATIONS   SAL   10.00
CHAUSSON
    STRING QUARTET IN A MAJOR
        FRANCO COLOMBO PUBLICATIONS   SAL   10.75
CHAUSSON
    SYMPHONY NO. 01
        FRANCO COLOMBO PUBLICATIONS   SAL   8.75
CHAVEZ, C.
    CONCERTO FOR PIANO AND ORCHESTRA
        G. SCHIRMER, INC.   3.00
CHAVEZ, C.
    CONCERTO FOR PIANO AND ORCHESTRA
        G. SCHIRMER, INC.   3.00
CHISHOLM, E.
    KONZERT NO. 02 NACH HINDUSTAN, KLAVIERAUSZUG
        SCHOTT   10180   12.00
CHOPIN
    CONCERTOS
        EDWARD B. MARKS MUSIC CORPORATION   07.50
CHOPIN   FRIEDMAN
    CONCERTO NO. 01 IN E MINOR, OP. 11
        ASSOCIATED MUSIC PUBLISHERS, INC. BRH   2.75
CHOPIN
    CONCERTO NO. 01 IN E MINOR, OP. 11
        EDWARD B. MARKS MUSIC CORPORATION   07.50
CHOPIN   POZNIAK   D
    CONCERTO NO. 01 IN E MINOR, OP. 11
        C. F. PETERS CORPORATION   2895A   3.00
CHOPIN   M
    CONCERTO NO. 01 IN E MINOR, OP. 11
        C. F. PETERS CORPORATION   2895AA   1.25
CHOPIN   JOSEFFY, R.
    CONCERTO NO. 01 IN E MINOR, OP. 11
        G. SCHIRMER, INC.   L1350   1.75
CHOPIN   JOSEFFY
    CONCERTO NO. 01 IN E MINOR, OP. 11
        G. SCHIRMER, INC.   L1350   1.75
CHOPIN   MIKULI
    CONCERTO NO. 01 IN E MINOR, OP. 11
        G. SCHIRMER, INC.   L1558   1.50
CHOPIN   FRIEDMAN
    CONCERTO NO. 02 IN F MINOR, OP. 21
        ASSOCIATED MUSIC PUBLISHERS, INC. BRH   2.75
CHOPIN
    CONCERTO NO. 02 IN F MINOR, OP. 21
        EDWARD B. MARKS MUSIC CORPORATION   06.50
CHOPIN   POZNIAK   D
    CONCERTO NO. 02 IN F MINOR, OP. 21
        C. F. PETERS CORPORATION   28958   3.00
CHOPIN   JOSEFFY, R.
    CONCERTO NO. 02 IN F MINOR, OP. 21
        G. SCHIRMER, INC.   L1351   1.75
CHOPIN   JOSEFFY
    CONCERTO NO. 02 IN F MINOR, OP. 21
        G. SCHIRMER, INC.   L1351   1.75
CHOPIN   MIKULI
    CONCERTO NO. 02 IN F MINOR, OP. 21
        G. SCHIRMER, INC.   L1557   1.50
CHOPIN
    CONCERT ALLEGRO
        EDWARD B. MARKS MUSIC CORPORATION   04.00
CHOPIN   JOSEFFY, R.
    FOUR CONCERT PIECES -- 2ND PIANO PART ONLY, TO BE USED WITH
    LIBRARY VOL. 38
        G. SCHIRMER, INC.   L1352   1.25
CHOPIN   D
    GRANDE POLONAISE BRILLANTE, PRECEDED BY AN ANDANTE SPIANATO, OP.
    22
        C. F. PETERS CORPORATION   2968   1.25
CHOPIN   STEINER
    MILITARY POLONAISE
        BELWIN-MILLS PUBLISHING CORPORATION   1.25
CHOPIN   HUGHES
    RONDO, OP. 73
        G. SCHIRMER, INC.   L1508   1.50
CHOPIN   D
    RONDO IN C, OP. 73
        C. F. PETERS CORPORATION   1914   1.25
CHOPIN   MAIER, G.
    TWO ETUDES IN G FLAT
        BELWIN-MILLS PUBLISHING CORPORATION   1.50

CHOPIN   SAMUELSON
    VALSE IN D FLAT
       BELWIN-MILLS PUBLISHING CORPORATION   .75
CHOPIN   BAMPTON, R.   3
    WALTZ, OP. 64 NO. 1
       BOSTON MUSIC COMPANY   .75
CHOPIN   STUMM   4
    WALTZ IN A FLAT, OP. 64 NO. 3
       BOSTON MUSIC COMPANY   1.25
CHOPIN   PENNARIO
    WALTZ IN D FLAT, OP. 64 -- MINUTE WALTZ
       BELWIN-MILLS PUBLISHING CORPORATION   27042   1.25
CHRISTIANSEN, L.
    CONTRASTS FOR TWO PIANOS
       COMPOSERS AUTOGRAPH PUBLICATIONS   .88
CILENSEK, J.
    CONCERTO -- 1950
       ASSOCIATED MUSIC PUBLISHERS, INC.   BRH   4.00
CLEMENTI   FASANO *
    CONCERTO IN C
       FRANCO COLOMBO PUBLICATIONS   130491   5.50
CLEMENTI   ROSATI, G.
    DUE SONATE
       EDIZIONI BERBEN   EB 1594   5.70
CLEMENTI   WOODWORTH, M. *
    SONATINAS OP. 36 NO. 3 AND 5
       VOLKWEIN BROS.   2.25
CLEMENTI   VAN HULSE, C.   3
    SONATINA NO. 01, OP. 36
       WILLIS MUSIC COMPANY   1.00
CLEMENTI   VAN HULSE, C.   3
    SONATINA NO. 02, OP. 36
       WILLIS MUSIC COMPANY   1.00
CLEMENTI   WOODWORTH, M. *
    SONATINA OP. 36 NO. 1
       VOLKWEIN BROS.   1.75
CLEMENTI   M-D
    TWO SONATAS IN B FLAT
       C. F. PETERS CORPORATION   1982   3.00
CLEMENTI   HUGHES
    TWO SONATAS
       G. SCHIRMER, INC.   L1532   1.50
COKELY, C.
    MISTER LITTLE TOAD
       BELWIN-MILLS PUBLISHING CORPORATION   1.00
COPLAND
    BILLY THE KID
       BOOSEY AND HAWKES, INC.   3.75
COPLAND
    CONCERTO
       BOOSEY AND HAWKES, INC.   2.00
COPLAND
    DANCE OF THE ADOLESCENT
       BOOSEY AND HAWKES, INC.   3.50
COPLAND
    DANZA DE JALISCO
       BOOSEY AND HAWKES, INC.   3.00
COPLAND
    DANZON CUBANO
       BOOSEY AND HAWKES, INC.   3.00
COPLAND   BERNSTEIN, L.
    EL SALON MEXICO
       BOOSEY AND HAWKES, INC.   3.75
COPLAND   GOLD *
    HOE DOWN AND SATURDAY NIGHT WALTZ, FROM 'RODEO'
       BOOSEY AND HAWKES, INC.   1.75
COPPOLA, P.
    POEME
       ASSOCIATED MUSIC PUBLISHERS, INC.   ESC   5.00
CORDERO, R.
    DUO - 1954
       PEER SOUTHERN ORGANIZATION   04.00
CORIGLIANO, J.
    KALEIDOSCOPE -- SET
       G. SCHIRMER, INC.   2.50
CORRETTE   RUF   3
    KONZERT IN D MINOR FUR CEMBALO ODER ORGEL, QUERFLOTE UND
    STREICHER, OP. 26 NO. 6
       BARENREITER VERLAG   NMA 201
COSAN, M.   WOOD
    WALTZING MATILDA
       OXFORD UNIVERSITY PRESS   35.410   2.00
COUPERIN, F.   DIEMER
    ALLEMANDE
       ELKAN-VOGEL, INC.   D   2.10
COUPERIN, F.   GEST
    LITTLE WINDMILLS, THE -- SET
       G. SCHIRMER, INC.   .75
COURSEY, R. DE   2
    WALTZ FOR TWO PIANOS
       CENTURY MUSIC PUBLISHING COMPANY, INC.   4394   .60
COURSEY, R. DE   2
    WALTZ FOR TWO PIANOS
       CENTURY MUSIC PUBLISHING COMPANY, INC.   4394   .40
COWAN *
    WALTZING MATILDA
       CARL FISCHER, INC.   P 2982   1.25
CRAS
    CONCERTO
       FRANCO COLOMBO PUBLICATIONS   SAL   8.75
CRAWFORD, C.
    ON THE ICE AT SWEET BRIAR
       BELWIN-MILLS PUBLISHING CORPORATION   28071   1.00
CUI, C.   GEST, E.
    ORIENTALE
       ELKAN-VOGEL, INC.   .60
CZERNY
    CONCERTINO IN C, OP. 210, PIANO SCORE
       MUSICA OBSCURA   3.50
CZERNY
    CONCERTINO IN C, OP. 210, SET OF PARTS
       MUSICA OBSCURA   6.50
D'INDY, V.
    TRIPLE CONCERTO, OP. 89
       FRANCO COLOMBO PUBLICATIONS   SAL   8.25
DALLAPICCOLA
    PICCOLO CONCERTO PER MURIEL COUVREUX FUR KLAVIER UND ORCHESTER
       BARENREITER VERLAG   CM 20218
DALLAPICCOLA   4-5
    PICCOLO CONCERTO PER MURIEL COUVREUX FUR KLAVIER UND ORCHESTER
       BARENREITER VERLAG   CM 20218
DAMASE, J. M.
    COMPLIMENT D'ANNIVERSAIRE
       EDITIONS MUSICALES TRANSATLANTIQUES   3.85
DAMASE, J. M.
    CONCERTO NO. 02
       EDITIONS MUSICALES TRANSATLANTIQUES   12.25

DAMASE, J. M.
    CONCERTO
       FRANCO COLOMBO PUBLICATIONS   SAL   10.75
DAMASE, J. M.
    RHAPSODIE DE PRINTEMPS -- PIANO SOLO, WITH ORCHESTRA REDUCED FOR
    SECOND PIANO
       EDITIONS MUSICALES TRANSATLANTIQUES   8.80
DAMASE, J. M.
    VARIATIONS ON A THEME BY RAMEAU FOR CLAVECIN AND STRING
    ORCHESTRA
       EDITIONS MUSICALES TRANSATLANTIQUES   7.70
CANDELOT
    CONCERTO -- 1932
       ASSOCIATED MUSIC PUBLISHERS, INC.   ESC   6.00
DAWSON   1
    SING AND PLAY TOGETHER
       WILLIS MUSIC COMPANY   1.25
DAY, R. E.   3
    COLORED WINDMILLS
       BELWIN-MILLS PUBLISHING CORPORATION   .60
DAY, R. E.   3
    LITTLE FRENCH MUSIC BOX
       BELWIN-MILLS PUBLISHING CORPORATION   .60
DEBUSSY
    ARABESQUE NO. 1
       ELKAN-VOGEL, INC.   3.40
DEBUSSY
    ARABESQUE NO. 2
       ELKAN-VOGEL, INC.   4.10
DEBUSSY   SCHROTH
    CLAIR DE LUNE
       BELWIN-MILLS PUBLISHING CORPORATION   1.50
DEBUSSY
    CLAIR DE LUNE
       ELKAN-VOGEL, INC.   3.10
DEBUSSY
    DANSES
       ELKAN-VOGEL, INC.   6.00
DEBUSSY
    DR. GRADUS AD PARNASSUM
       ELKAN-VOGEL, INC.   D   2.75
DEBUSSY
    EN BLANC ET NOIR
       ELKAN-VOGEL, INC.   9.50
DEBUSSY
    FANTAISIE
       ELKAN-VOGEL, INC.   J   11.80
DEBUSSY   RAVEL
    FETES
       ELKAN-VOGEL, INC.   6.50
DEBUSSY
    GIGUES -- IMAGES POUR ORCHESTRE, NO. 1
       ELKAN-VOGEL, INC.   D   6.00
DEBUSSY
    GOLLIWOGG'S CAKE-WALK
       ELKAN-VOGEL, INC.   4.10
DEBUSSY
    IBERIA -- IMAGES POUR ORCHESTRE, NO. 2
       ELKAN-VOGEL, INC.   D   9.50
DEBUSSY
    LA MER
       ELKAN-VOGEL, INC.   14.00
DEBUSSY
    LE PETIT NEGRE
       ELKAN-VOGEL, INC.   LED   3.00
DEBUSSY
    LINDARAJA
       ELKAN-VOGEL, INC.   J   2.55
DEBUSSY   RAVEL
    NOCTURNES -- 1. NUAGES, 2. FETES
       ELKAN-VOGEL, INC.   J   11.25
DEBUSSY
    NUAGES
       ELKAN-VOGEL, INC.   4.00
DEBUSSY
    PETITE SUITE
       ELKAN-VOGEL, INC.   7.50
DEBUSSY
    PRELUDE TO ''THE AFTERNOON OF A FAUN'' -- SET
       G. SCHIRMER, INC.   1.50
DEBUSSY
    PRELUDE TO THE AFTERNOON OF A FAUN
       ELKAN-VOGEL, INC.   5.50
DEBUSSY
    RONDES DE PRINTEMPS -- IMAGES POUR ORCHESTRE, NO. 3
       ELKAN-VOGEL, INC.   D   6.20
DELANNOY
    BALLADE CONCERTANTE, OP. 59
       ASSOCIATED MUSIC PUBLISHERS, INC.   ESC   8.00
DELANNOY
    CONCERTO DE MAI, OP. 50 -- 1949-50
       ASSOCIATED MUSIC PUBLISHERS, INC.   ESC   7.50
DELIBES, L.   SAMUELSON
    COPPELIA BALLET -- VALSE LENTE
       BELWIN-MILLS PUBLISHING CORPORATION   .60
DELIUS, F.   TRIMBLE
    CALINDA, FROM 'KOANGA'
       BOOSEY AND HAWKES, INC.   2.75
DELIUS, F.
    DANCE RHAPSODY, A
       UNIVERSAL EDITION   UE 7142   3.80
DELIUS, F.   BARTLETT, H.
    FANTASTIC DANCE
       BOOSEY AND HAWKES, INC.   1.50
DELLO JOIO, N.
    ARIA AND TOCCATA
       CARL FISCHER, INC.   O 3943   2.00
DELLO JOIO, N.
    SUITE FROM BALLET ''ON STAGE'' -- SET
       G. SCHIRMER, INC.   2.50
DEMARQUEZ
    BARCAROLLE
       FRANCO COLOMBO PUBLICATIONS   SAL   8.75
DIABELLI   STEINER
    DIABELLI SCHERZO
       BELWIN-MILLS PUBLISHING CORPORATION   1.25
DIAMOND, D.
    CONCERTO FOR 2 SOLO PIANOS
       PEER SOUTHERN ORGANIZATION   05.50
DIERCKS
    VARIATIONS ON A FLOWER DRUM SONG -- TWO PREPARED PIANOS --
       COMPOSERS AUTOGRAPH PUBLICATIONS   .88
DILLER, A.
    SECOND PIANO PARTS TO 1ST SOLO BOOK PIECES BY DILLER AND QUAILE
       G. SCHIRMER, INC.   1.00

DISTLER
  KONZERTSTUCK FUR KLAVIER UND ORCHESTER -- OP. POSTH. --   4
  KLAVIERAUSZUG
      BARENREITER VERLAG   BA 2783A
DISTLER   4
  KONZERTSTUCK FUR KLAVIER UND ORCHESTER -- OP. POSTH. --
      BARENREITER VERLAG   BA 2783
DISTLER   4
  KONZERTSTUCK
      BARENREITER VERLAG   BA 1877
DISTLER   4
  KONZERT FUR CEMBALO UND STREICHORCHESTER, OP. 14
      BARENREITER VERLAG   BA 1000
DITTERHAVER
  STREET FAIR
      CARL FISCHER, INC.   P 2905   .75
DITTERSDORF, K.D. VON *   3
  KONZERT IN A FUR CEMBALO -- KLAVIER -- UND STREICHER
      BARENREITER VERLAG   NMA 41
DITTERSDORF, K.D. VON   DOEBEREINER
  THREE CADENZAS TO THE CONCERTO IN A
      ASSOCIATED MUSIC PUBLISHERS, INC.   NAG   .60
DOBIAS   4
  SONATA FUR KLAVIER, 5 BLASER, PAUKEN UND STREICHER
      BARENREITER VERLAG   CHF 5002
DOEBEREINER
  THREE CADENZAS TO DITTERSDORF CONCERTO IN A
      ASSOCIATED MUSIC PUBLISHERS, INC.   NAG   .60
DOHNANYI
  CONCERTO IN E MINOR, OP. 5
      ASSOCIATED MUSIC PUBLISHERS, INC.   DOB   9.00
DOHNANYI
  VARIATIONS ON A NURSERY RHYME, OP. 25
      ASSOCIATED MUSIC PUBLISHERS, INC.   SIM   4.00
DOUGHERTY, C.
  MUSIC FROM SEAS AND SHIPS -- SET
      G. SCHIRMER, INC.   3.00
DREYSCHOCK
  CADENZA TO BEETHOVEN CONCERTO III
      MUSICA OBSCURA   2.50
DRIESSLER   4
  KONZERT FUR KLAVIER UND ORCHESTER, OP. 27
      BARENREITER VERLAG   BA 2782
DUBOIS, P. M.   8
  DIVERTIMENTO
      ALPHONSE LEDUC
DUCHIN
  EDDY DUCHIN'S PIANO TECHNIQUE
      THE BIG THREE MUSIC CORPORATION   02.95
DUKAS, P.
  L'APPRENTI SORCIER
      ELKAN-VOGEL, INC.   D   5.90
DUKAS, P.
  SYMPHONY NO. 01
      FRANCO COLOMBO PUBLICATIONS   SAL   13.00
DUKELSKY
  CONCERTO IN C
      HEUGEL ET CIE.   12.00
DUNGAN   3
  ARKANSAS TRAVELER
      BOSTON MUSIC COMPANY   1.50
DUNGAN   2
  DONKEY RIDE
      BOSTON MUSIC COMPANY   .75
DUNGAN   1
  IN THE WOODS
      BOSTON MUSIC COMPANY   1.50
DUNGAN   1
  PANDA PARADES
      BOSTON MUSIC COMPANY   1.50
DUNYON   RAYMOND, J.   2
  BAND CONCERT, THE
      BOSTON MUSIC COMPANY   1.50
DUPARC, H.
  LENORE -- SYMPHONIC POEM --
      FRANCO COLOMBO PUBLICATIONS   SAL   6.50
DUPONT, J.
  CONCERT, POUR PIANO ET ORCHESTRE, OP. 2
      ALPHONSE LEDUC
DUPONT
  FANTASY FOR PIANO AND ORCHESTRA
      FRANCO COLOMBO PUBLICATIONS   SAL   12.50
DUPONT
  LA ROSITA
      SOUTHERN MUSIC COMPANY   1.50
DUSSEK, J.   3-4
  KONZERT FUR KLAVIER UND ORCHESTER, OP. 26
      BARENREITER VERLAG   CHF 5170
DUSSEK, J.   3-4
  KONZERT FUR 2 KLAVIERE UND ORCHESTER
      BARENREITER VERLAG   CHF 5030
DUSSEK, J.
  SONATE F-DUR OP. 26
      SCHOTT   10507   3.25
DUVERNOY, J.   FOX
  FEU ROLLANT
      EDWARD B. MARKS MUSIC CORPORATION   01.50
DVORAK
  CONCERTO IN G MINOR, OP. 33
      BOOSEY AND HAWKES, INC.   11.00
DVORAK   BERKOVEC *   4
  KONZERT FUR KLAVIER UND ORCHESTER IN G MINOR, OP. 33,
  KLAVIERAUSZUG
      BARENREITER VERLAG   AP 786
DVORAK   BERKOVEC *   4
  KONZERT FUR KLAVIER UND ORCHESTER IN G MINOR, OP. 33
      BARENREITER VERLAG   AP 145
DVORAK   4
  KONZERT IN G MINOR FUR KLAVIER UND ORCHESTER, OP. 33
      BARENREITER VERLAG   AP 786
DVORAK   HAUPT, L. VON
  LARGO
      BELWIN-MILLS PUBLISHING CORPORATION   27033   .60
DVORAK   STEINER
  SLAVONIC DANCE IN E MINOR
      BELWIN-MILLS PUBLISHING CORPORATION   1.25
DVORAK   GRAETZER
  SLAVONIC DANCE NO. 9
      FRANCO COLOMBO PUBLICATIONS   BA9701   1.00
DYSON, G.
  CONCERTO LEGGIERO
      NOVELLO AND COMPANY, LTD.   10.0160.04   3.25
EBEN   4
  KONZERT FUR KLAVIER UND ORCHESTER
      BARENREITER VERLAG
ECKSTEIN
  BY A BLUE LAGOON
      CARL FISCHER, INC.   P 3086   1.00

ECKSTEIN
  CONCERTO FOR YOUNG AMERICANS
      CARL FISCHER, INC.   O 3923   2.00
EDER   4
  CONCERTO SEMISERIO FUR 2 KLAVIERE UND ORCHESTER
      BARENREITER VERLAG   BA 4310
EGGE   D
  CONCERTO NO. 02, OP. 21
      C. F. PETERS CORPORATION   LY156A   5.00
EINEM, G.
  CONCERTO, OP. 20
      ASSOCIATED MUSIC PUBLISHERS, INC.   BOT   11.00
ELGAR, E.   SAMUELSON
  POMP AND CIRCUMSTANCE MARCH NO. 1
      BOOSEY AND HAWKES, INC.   1.25
ELGAR, E.   MCNAUGHT
  VARIATIONS, OP. 36, 'ENIGMA'
      NOVELLO AND COMPANY, LTD.   10.0161.02   4.75
ELLINGTON
  DUKE ELLINGTON AT THE PIANO
      THE BIG THREE MUSIC CORPORATION   01.95
ENDERS, H.
  RUSSIAN PICNIC -- SET
      G. SCHIRMER, INC.   1.25
ENOCH   E
  LET'S MAKE MUSIC --50 PIECES FOR THE PIANO CLASS--
      C. F. PETERS CORPORATION   H1533   2.50
ERBSE
  SONATA, OP. 3 -- 1951
      ASSOCIATED MUSIC PUBLISHERS, INC.   BOT   3.00
EVETT   D
  CONCERTO FOR HARPSICHORD. POCKET SCORE
      C. F. PETERS CORPORATION   6504   5.00
FALLA, M. DE
  CONCERTO FOR HARPSICHORD
      ASSOCIATED MUSIC PUBLISHERS, INC.   ESC   4.50
FALLA, M. DE
  NIGHTS IN THE GARDENS OF SPAIN -- SOLO AND PIANO, 4 HANDS
      ASSOCIATED MUSIC PUBLISHERS, INC.   ESC   10.75
FALLA, M. DE
  NIGHTS IN THE GARDENS OF SPAIN
      ASSOCIATED MUSIC PUBLISHERS, INC.   ESC   7.25
FALLA, M. DE   KOVACS
  VIE BREVE, LA -- SPANISH DANCE NO. 1 -- SET
      ASSOCIATED MUSIC PUBLISHERS, INC.   AMP   2.00
FANO, G. A.
  ANDANTE AND ALLEGRO CON FUOCO
      FRANCO COLOMBO PUBLICATIONS   Z4371   5.00
FARKAS, F.
  CONCERTINO
      KULTURA   2.50
FAURE, G.   PHILIPP, I.
  BALLADE FOR PIANO AND ORCHESTRA, OP. 19
      INTERNATIONAL MUSIC COMPANY   3.00
FAURE, G.
  FANTAISIE, OP. 111
      ELKAN-VOGEL, INC.   D   12.75
FAURE, G.   STORR, S.   3
  PAVANE
      BOSTON MUSIC COMPANY   1.00
FEDERER, R.   6
  RHAPSODY IN D MINOR FOR SOLO PIANO AND ORCH.
      THEODORE PRESSER COMPANY   1.25
FEDERER, R.   D
  RHAPSODY IN D MINOR
      THEODORE PRESSER COMPANY   1.25
FERGUSON, H.
  CONCERTO
      BOOSEY AND HAWKES, INC.   3.00
FERGUSON, H.
  PARTITA
      BOOSEY AND HAWKES, INC.   3.75
FERNEYHOUGH   D
  SONATA
      C. F. PETERS CORPORATION   7120   6.00
FICHANDLER, W.
  FUN FOR FOUR HANDS
      WILLIS MUSIC COMPANY   1.00
FINKE
  CAPRICCIO IN E FLAT ON A POLISH FOLKSONG -- 1953
      ASSOCIATED MUSIC PUBLISHERS, INC.   BRH   3.50
FINNEY
  CONCERTO IN E
      C. F. PETERS CORPORATION   66115   RENTAL
FINZI, G.
  GRAND FANTASIA AND TOCCATA
      BOOSEY AND HAWKES, INC.   3.00
FISCHER, E.
  GLATTEIS, PERPETUUM MOBILE
      SCHOTT   2443   3.00
FISCHER, E.
  TANZENDE MASKEN, MARABU
      SCHOTT   2579   2.50
FORTNER, W.   6
  MOUVEMENTS FUR KLAVIER UND ORCHESTER, KLAVIERAUSZUG
      SCHOTT   4544   3.50
FOSS, L.
  CONCERTINO -- SET
      G. SCHIRMER, INC.   1.25
FRANCAIX, J.   5
  CONCERTINO FUR KLAVIER UND KLEINES ORCHESTER, KLAVIERAUSZUG
      SCHOTT   3288   4.00
FRANCAIX, J.
  CONCERTO POUR CLAVECIN ET ENSEMBLES INSTRUMENTALES
      SCHOTT   RENTAL
FRANCAIX, J.
  HUIT DANSES EXOTIQUES
      SCHOTT   4984   3.50
FRANCAIX, J.   5
  KONZERT FUR KLAVIER UND ORCHESTER, KLAVIERAUSZUG
      SCHOTT   3670   5.00
FRANCK, C.
  CANTABILE
      ELKAN-VOGEL, INC.   D   2.25
FRANCK, C.
  GRANDE PIECE SYMPHONIQUE
      ELKAN-VOGEL, INC.   D   4.00
FRANCK, C.
  PIECE HEROIQUE
      ELKAN-VOGEL, INC.   D   3.25
FRANCK, C.   SILVESTRI
  PRELUDE, ARIA AND FINALE
      FRANCO COLOMBO PUBLICATIONS   ER2586   2.25
FRANCK, C.
  PRELUDE, FUGUE AND VARIATIONS
      ELKAN-VOGEL, INC.   4.10

FRANCK, C.   D
    SYMPHONIC VARIATIONS --2 COPIES--
        C. F. PETERS CORPORATION   3741   2.50
FRANCK, C.   MONTES
    SYMPHONIC VARIATIONS
        FRANCO COLOMBO PUBLICATIONS   BA8968   2.50
FRANCK, C.   WEBSTER, B.
    SYMPHONIC VARIATIONS
        INTERNATIONAL MUSIC COMPANY   2.50
FRANCK, C.
    SYMPHONIC VARIATIONS
        EDWIN F. KALMUS   3442   2.00
FRANCK, C.
    TROIS CHORALS NO. 01
        ELKAN-VOGEL, INC.   D   6.00
FRANCK, C.
    TROIS CHORALS NO. 02
        ELKAN-VOGEL, INC.   D   6.00
FRANCK, C.
    TROIS CHORALS NO. 03
        ELKAN-VOGEL, INC.   D   6.00
FRANCK, C.   PHILIPP, I.
    VARIATIONS SYMPHONIQUES
        G. SCHIRMER, INC.   L1407   1.50
FRANCK, C.   PHILIPP
    VARIATIONS SYMPHONIQUES
        G. SCHIRMER, INC.   L1407   1.50
FREED   6
    CARNIVAL
        THEODORE PRESSER COMPANY   1.50
FREED   6
    HARD TIMES - PARAPHRASE ON A FOLK THEME
        THEODORE PRESSER COMPANY   1.00
FRICKER, P.   6
    KONZERT FUR KLAVIER UND ORCHESTER, OP. 19, KLAVIERAUSZUG
        SCHOTT   10396   5.00
FRICKER, P.
    NOCTURNE UND SCHERZO, OP. 23
        SCHOTT   10650   3.50
FRICKER, P.   6
    TOCCATA FUR KLAVIER UND ORCHESTER, OP. 33, KLAVIERAUSZUG
        SCHOTT   10654   5.00
FRICKER, P.
    VIER FUGHETTEN, OP. 2
        SCHOTT   10124   2.50
FRID, G.
    PRELUDE AND FUGUE
        PEER SOUTHERN ORGANIZATION   04.50
FRIML, R. *   COBURN
    DONKEY SERENADE, THE -- SET
        G. SCHIRMER, INC.   1.50
FROST
    CART WHEELS
        BELWIN-MILLS PUBLISHING CORPORATION   1.00
FUCHS, R.   4
    KONZERT FUR CEMBALO UND STREICHORCHESTER
        BARENREITER VERLAG   BA 2488
FUGA
    TOCCATA
        FRANCO COLOMBO PUBLICATIONS   128919   5.00
FULEIHAN, A.
    CONCERTO NO. 02 FOR PIANO AND ORCHESTRA
        G. SCHIRMER, INC.   3.00
FULEIHAN, A.
    CONCERTO NO. 02
        G. SCHIRMER, INC.   3.00
FULEIHAN, A.
    EPITHALAMIUM -- VARIATIONS FOR PIANO AND STRING ORCHESTRA
        G. SCHIRMER, INC.   2.00
FULEIHAN, A.
    EPITHALAMIUM -- VARIATIONS FOR PIANO AND STRING ORCHESTRA
        G. SCHIRMER, INC.   2.00
FULEIHAN, A.
    TOCCATA FOR 2 PIANOS
        PEER SOUTHERN ORGANIZATION   05.50
FURTWANGLER   4
    SYMPHONISCHES KONZERT FUR KLAVIER UND ORCHESTER
        BARENREITER VERLAG   AE 285
GABAYE   8
    RECITAL EXPRESS
        ALPHONSE LEDUC
GABRIEL, M.
    BUFFOON DANCE
        SOUTHERN MUSIC COMPANY   1.00
GABRIELI, G.   E
    SONATA PIAN E FORTE, FOR DOUBLE BRASS CHOIR. REDUCTION FOR 2
    KEYBOARD INSTRUMENTS INCLUDED IN FULL SCORE
        C. F. PETERS CORPORATION   4267   3.00
GAERTNER   2, 3
    CONCERTINO
        ALPHONSE LEDUC
GAGNEBIN
    CONCERTO
        FRANCO COLOMBO PUBLICATIONS   129293   3.50
GAILLARD
    IMAGES D'EPINAL -- 1939
        ASSOCIATED MUSIC PUBLISHERS, INC.   ESC   3.75
GAILLARD   D
    TOMBEAU ROMANTIQUE
        C. F. PETERS CORPORATION   C256   3.50
GAITO   MONTES
    PAMPEANITA
        FRANCO COLOMBO PUBLICATIONS   BA9687   .75
GAL, H.
    CONCERTINO, OP. 43
        ASSOCIATED MUSIC PUBLISHERS, INC.   SIM   2.50
GALINDO, B.   2
    SECOND CONCERTO
        EDICIONES MEXICANAS DE MUSICA, A. C.   06.75
GAYNOR   2
    GUITAR SERENADE
        THEODORE PRESSER COMPANY   .75
GAYNOR   2
    MARCH OF THE WEE FOLK
        THEODORE PRESSER COMPANY   .60
GENZMER   D
    CONCERTINO NO. 2
        C. F. PETERS CORPORATION   5973A   4.00
GENZMER   4-5
    KONZERT FUR KLAVIER UND ORCHESTER, KLAVIERAUSZUG
        SCHOTT   5278   5.00
GENZMER
    SONATA FUR ZWEI KLAVIER
        SCHOTT   4332   3.00
GERSHWIN   STONE
    AMERICAN IN PARIS, AN
        WARNER BROTHERS PUBLISHERS   6.00

GERSHWIN   DAVIS, J. R.
    CONCERTO IN F, SECOND MOVEMENT
        WARNER BROTHERS PUBLISHERS   1.00
GERSHWIN   CASTAGNETTA
    CONCERTO IN F - CONCERT TRANSCRIPTION
        WARNER BROTHERS PUBLISHERS   5.00
GERSHWIN
    CONCERTO IN F
        WARNER BROTHERS PUBLISHERS   5.00
GERSHWIN   STONE
    CUBAN OVERTURE
        WARNER BROTHERS PUBLISHERS   6.00
GERSHWIN
    I GOT RHYTHM - VARIATIONS
        WARNER BROTHERS PUBLISHERS   3.50
GERSHWIN   STONE
    PRELUDES
        WARNER BROTHERS PUBLISHERS   4.00
GERSHWIN   KLARMAN
    RHAPSODY IN BLUE, 'LITTLE'
        WARNER BROTHERS PUBLISHERS   1.00
GERSHWIN   WASSERMAN
    RHAPSODY IN BLUE, MODIFIED
        WARNER BROTHERS PUBLISHERS   3.50
GERSHWIN   LEVINE
    RHAPSODY IN BLUE, THEME FROM
        WARNER BROTHERS PUBLISHERS   1.00
GERSHWIN   RICHTER   FIRST YEAR
    RHAPSODY IN BLUE, THEME FROM
        WARNER BROTHERS PUBLISHERS   .75
GERSHWIN
    RHAPSODY IN BLUE
        WARNER BROTHERS PUBLISHERS   5.00
GERSHWIN
    RHAPSODY IN BLUE
        WARNER BROTHERS PUBLISHERS   4.00
GERSHWIN
    SECOND RHAPSODY
        WARNER BROTHERS PUBLISHERS   4.00
GEST, E.
    FRERE JACQUES' CONCERT
        BELWIN-MILLS PUBLISHING CORPORATION   1.25
GEST, E.
    SNOW BIRD
        BELWIN-MILLS PUBLISHING CORPORATION   1.25
GIDEON, M.   M
    HOMMAGE A MA JEUNESSE
        THEODORE PRESSER COMPANY   3.00
GILBERT AND SULLIVAN   STEINER
    THREE CHEERS FOR THE SAILOR'S BRIDE
        BELWIN-MILLS PUBLISHING CORPORATION   1.25
GILLOCK   4
    ON A PARIS BOULEVARD
        WILLIS MUSIC COMPANY   .60
GILLOCK   2
    ON A PARIS BOULEVARD
        WILLIS MUSIC COMPANY   .60
GINASTERA
    CONCERTO NO. 01
        BOOSEY AND HAWKES, INC.   7.00
GIORDANI   CASTAGNONE *
    CONCERTO NO. 03 IN C
        FRANCO COLOMBO PUBLICATIONS   130483   2.50
GIORDANI   CASTAGNONE *
    CONCERTO NO. 05 IN D
        FRANCO COLOMBO PUBLICATIONS   130477   2.75
GIORDANI   BITTNER   3
    KONZERT IN C FUR KLAVIER UND STREICHER
        BARENREITER VERLAG   NMA 157
GIRNATIS
    CONCERT RETROSPECTIF
        FRANCO COLOMBO PUBLICATIONS   SIK.327   21.00
GIRNATIS   4-5
    RONDO-BOLERO FUR KLAVIER UND ORCHESTER
        BARENREITER VERLAG   SM 1928
GLAZOUNOW, A.
    CONCERTO NO. 01, OP. 92
        BOOSEY AND HAWKES, INC.   5.00
GLAZOUNOW, A.
    CONCERTO NO. 02, OP. 100
        BOOSEY AND HAWKES, INC.   6.00
GLIERE   STONE
    DANCE OF THE RUSSIAN SAILORS
        EDWARD B. MARKS MUSIC CORPORATION   01.50
GLIERE   PHILIPP, I.
    SIX ORIGINAL PIECES, OP. 41
        INTERNATIONAL MUSIC COMPANY   2.50
GLINKA   LUBOSHUTZ
    LARK, THE
        BELWIN-MILLS PUBLISHING CORPORATION   1.50
GLUCK   HAUPT, L. VON
    DANCE OF THE SPIRITS FROM 'ORPHEUS'
        BELWIN-MILLS PUBLISHING CORPORATION   27032   .60
GODOWSKY, L.
    ALT-WIEN -- OLD VIENNA -- SET
        G. SCHIRMER, INC.   1.00
GOLDMAN, R.
    LE BOBINO
        PEER SOUTHERN ORGANIZATION   02.00
GOTTSCHALK   MOROSS
    BANJO, THE -- SET
        G. SCHIRMER, INC.   1.50
GOTTSCHALK   KAY
    GRAND TARANTELLE
        BOOSEY AND HAWKES, INC.   3.00
GOULD--ED.   GOULD   MEDIUM
    LA CUCARACHA
        SHAWNEE PRESS, INC.   1.25
GOULD, M.
    BOOGIE WOOGIE ETUDE
        BELWIN-MILLS PUBLISHING CORPORATION   27003   1.50
GOULD, M.
    INTERPLAY-- AMERICAN CONCERTETTE IN FOUR MOVEMENTS
        BELWIN-MILLS PUBLISHING CORPORATION   27016   3.50
GOULD, M.
    PAVANNE
        BELWIN-MILLS PUBLISHING CORPORATION   27024   2.00
GOUNOD, C.   BONAWITZ
    FAUST -- DUO
        G. SCHIRMER, INC.   1.00
GOUNOD, C.   BURT   3
    MARCH PONTIFICAL
        WILLIS MUSIC COMPANY   1.00
GOUNOD, C.   PIERNE   6, 7
    SUITE CONCERTANTE
        ALPHONSE LEDUC

GRABNER 4
CONCERTINO FUR EIN TASTENINSTRUMENT UND STREICHER, OP. 60
BARENREITER VERLAG   BA 3141
GRAINGER, P.
SPOON RIVER, AMERICAN FOLKDANCE -- SET
G. SCHIRMER, INC.   1.00
GRAUN   M-D
CONCERTO IN F. SCORE, HARPSICHORD SOLO PART
C. F. PETERS CORPORATION   WM1   5.00
GRAUN   RUF   3
KONZERT IN F FUR CEMBALO -- ORGEL -- UND STREICHER -- 'BANCHETTO
MUSICALE' --
BARENREITER VERLAG   SM 1103
GREEN, R.
DANCE SONATA FOR TWO PIANOS
AMERICAN MUSIC EDITION   2.50
GRENZ
CAPRICCIO
FRANCO COLOMBO PUBLICATIONS   SIK.330   12.00
GRETCHANINOFF   GEST, E.
CHANSON MILITAIRE
BELWIN-MILLS PUBLISHING CORPORATION   1.00
GRIEG   DEIS
ACCOMPANIMENTS FOR A 2ND PIANO FOR FANTASIA K475 AND SONATA K457
BY MOZART
G. SCHIRMER, INC.   L1443   2.25
GRIEG   DEIS
ACCOMPANIMENTS FOR A 2ND PIANO FOR SONATA K283 IN G BY MOZART
G. SCHIRMER, INC.   L144   1.25
GRIEG   DEIS
ACCOMPANIMENTS FOR A 2ND PIANO FOR SONATA K533 --K594-- IN F BY
MOZART
G. SCHIRMER, INC.   L1441   1.50
GRIEG   DEIS
ACCOMPANIMENTS FOR A 2ND PIANO FOR SONATA K545 IN C BY MOZART
G. SCHIRMER, INC.   L1440   1.00
GRIEG   D
CONCERTO IN A MINOR, OP. 16
C. F. PETERS CORPORATION   2164   2.00
GRIEG   M
CONCERTO IN A MINOR, OP. 16
C. F. PETERS CORPORATION   2164B   1.25
GRIEG   D
CONCERTO IN A MINOR, OP. 16
C. F. PETERS CORPORATION   2164   2.00
GRIEG   GRAINGER, P.
CONCERTO IN A MINOR, OP. 16
G. SCHIRMER, INC.   L1399   2.50
GRIEG   GRAINGER, P.
CONCERTO IN A MINOR, OP. 16
G. SCHIRMER, INC.   L1399   2.50
GRIEG   3
ELFIN DANCE, OP. 12, NO. 4
THEODORE PRESSER COMPANY   .50
GRIEG   M-D
OLD NORWEGIAN ROMANCE WITH VARIATIONS, OP. 51
C. F. PETERS CORPORATION   2494   3.00
GRIEG   KLEINMICHEL   D
PIANO CONCERTO IN A MINOR, OP. 16. ABRIDGED
C. F. PETERS CORPORATION   2505A   2.00
GRIEG   KLEINMICHEL   D
PIANO CONCERTO IN A MINOR, OP. 16
C. F. PETERS CORPORATION   2505   3.50
GRIEG
PIANO CONCERTO
EDWIN F. KALMUS   3487   3.00
GRIEG   M
SECOND PIANO ACCOMPANIMENT TO MOZART'S SONATA IN C --K545--
C. F. PETERS CORPORATION   2490C   1.50
GRIEG   M
TRIUMPHAL MARCH --SIGURD JORSALFAR--, OP. 56, NO. 3
C. F. PETERS CORPORATION   2656A   1.50
GRIEG   MARLOWE, J. * 4
WEDDING DAY AT TROLDHAUGEN
THEODORE PRESSER COMPANY   2.50
GRIFFIS, E.   M
TANGO ESPANOL FOR 2 PIANOS
COMPOSERS PRESS, INC.   5.00
GROSS   4
KONZERT FUR KAMMERORCHESTER MIT OBLIGATEM KLAVIER
BARENREITER VERLAG   AE 234
GRUNENWALD
CONCERTO
FRANCO COLOMBO PUBLICATIONS   SAL   8.75
GRUNENWALD
CONCERT D'ETE, FOR PIANO AND STRING ORCHESTRA
FRANCO COLOMBO PUBLICATIONS   SAL   8.00
GUARNIERI
CONCERTO NO. 02 -- 1946
ASSOCIATED MUSIC PUBLISHERS, INC.   AMP   3.75
GUASTAVINO
BAILECITO
FRANCO COLOMBO PUBLICATIONS   BA9897   .75
GUASTAVINO
GATO
FRANCO COLOMBO PUBLICATIONS   BA9898   1.00
GUASTAVINO
LLANURA
FRANCO COLOMBO PUBLICATIONS   BA10992   1.00
GUASTAVINO
ROMANCE DE SANTA FE
FRANCO COLOMBO PUBLICATIONS   BA11194   2.50
GUASTAVINO
SE EQUIVOCO LA PALOMA
FRANCO COLOMBO PUBLICATIONS   BA10993   .75
GUERRINI, G.
TEMPI DI CONCERTO
FRANCO COLOMBO PUBLICATIONS   124035   1.75
GUERRINI, G.
THEME AND VARIATIONS
FRANCO COLOMBO PUBLICATIONS   128757   2.25
GUION, D.
HARMONICA-PLAYER, THE -- FROM ''ALLEY TUNES -- 3 SCENES FROM THE
SOUTH'' -- SET
G. SCHIRMER, INC.   1.00
GUION, D.
SHEEP AND GOAT WALKIN' TO THE PASTURE, COWBOYS' AND OLD
FIDDLERS' BREAKDOWN -- SET
G. SCHIRMER, INC.   1.00
GULDA
CADENZA TO MOZART CONCERTO IN C, K. 503
ASSOCIATED MUSIC PUBLISHERS, INC.   DOB   .75
GULDA
CADENZA TO MOZART CONCERTO IN D, K. 537 -- CORONATION --
ASSOCIATED MUSIC PUBLISHERS, INC.   DOB   .75

GURLITT
EIGHT MELODIOUS PIECES, OP. 174 -- SET
G. SCHIRMER, INC.   L1619   1.25
GURLITT
RONDO IN D, OP. 175 NO. 1 -- SET
G. SCHIRMER, INC.   L739   .75
GURLITT
RONDO IN E FLAT, OP. 175 NO. 2 -- SET
G. SCHIRMER, INC.   L740   .75
GURLITT
RONDO IN E MINOR, OP. 175 NO. 3 -- SET
G. SCHIRMER, INC.   L741   1.00
GUYONNET, J.
POLYPHONIE II
UNIVERSAL EDITION   UE 13549   2.15
HAIEFF, A.
CONCERTO
BOOSEY AND HAWKES, INC.   6.00
HALFFTER, E.
RAPSODIA PORTUGUESA
ASSOCIATED MUSIC PUBLISHERS, INC.   ESC   7.00
HAMPTON
CATCH-UP. TAPE RECORDER AND 2 PIANOS --OR 4 PIANOS--
C. F. PETERS CORPORATION   66175   2.00
HAMPTON
TRIPLE PLAY. ONDES MARTENOT AND 2 PIANOS, 4 HANDS
C. F. PETERS CORPORATION   66176   2.00
HANDEL   EASDALE
ARRIVAL OF THE QUEEN OF SHEBA
OXFORD UNIVERSITY PRESS   35.300   2.15
HANDEL   BEECHAM
CONCERTO IN A MAJOR FOR PIANOFORTE AND ORCHESTRA IN FOUR
MOVEMENTS, 2-PIANO VERSION
BELWIN-MILLS PUBLISHING CORPORATION 27006   3.00
HANDEL   BEECHAM
CONCERTO IN A MAJOR FOR PIANOFORTE AND ORCHESTRA IN FOUR
MOVEMENTS -- 2-PIANO VERSION
BELWIN-MILLS PUBLISHING CORPORATION 27006   3.00
HANDEL   M
CONCERTO IN B FLAT, OP. 4, NO. 6. SCORE/HARPSICHORD SOLO PART
C. F. PETERS CORPORATION   V11A   4.00
HANDEL   EASDALE
HARMONIOUS BLACKSMITH
OXFORD UNIVERSITY PRESS   35.002   2.50
HANDEL   LANDOWSKA, W.
KEYBOARD CONCERTO IN B FLAT, OP.4 NO. 6 -- SECOND MVT
BROUDE BROTHERS LTD.   01.75
HANDEL   BRUSOTTI
KONZERT G-DUR FUR KLAVIER -- CEMBALO UND STREICHORCHESTER --
HOBOKEN 18-9 KLAVIER-AUSZUG
SCHOTT   5313   3.75
HANDEL   HILLEMANN   3
KONZERT IN B FLAT, OP. 4 NO. 6 FUR KLAVIER -- ORGEL, CEMBALO --
UND STREICHORCHESTER
BARENREITER VERLAG   NMA 136
HANDEL   PHILIPP
MINUET BY HANDEL, A
FRANCO COLOMBO PUBLICATIONS   SAL   1.75
HANDEL   MATTHAEI, K.
ORGAN CONCERTI, OP. 4 BK. 1
BARENREITER VERLAG   BA 1894   3.25
HANDEL   MATTHAEI, K.
ORGAN CONCERTI, OP. 4 BK. 2
BARENREITER VERLAG   BA 1895   3.25
HANDEL
ORGAN CONCERTOS, BK. 1
INTERNATIONAL MUSIC COMPANY   4.50
HANDEL
ORGAN CONCERTOS, BK. 2
INTERNATIONAL MUSIC COMPANY   4.50
HANDEL   MATTHAEI   3-4
ORGELKONZERTE, OP. 4 NO. 1 IN G MINOR -- 'HALLISCHE
HANDEL-AUSGABE' --
BARENREITER VERLAG   BA 4006
HANDEL   MATTHAEI   3-4
ORGELKONZERTE, OP. 4 NO. 2 IN B FLAT -- 'HALLISCHE
HANDEL-AUSGABE' --
BARENREITER VERLAG   BA 359
HANDEL   MATTHAEI   3-4
ORGELKONZERTE, OP. 4 NO. 3 IN G MINOR -- 'HALLISCHE
HANDEL-AUSGABE' --
BARENREITER VERLAG   BA 360
HANDEL   MATTHAEI   3-4
ORGELKONZERTE, OP. 4 NO. 4 IN F -- 'HALLISCHE HANDEL-AUSGABE' --
BARENREITER VERLAG   BA 362
HANDEL   MATTHAEI   3-4
ORGELKONZERTE, OP. 4 NO. 5 IN F -- 'HALLISCHE HANDEL-AUSGABE' --
BARENREITER VERLAG   BA 363
HANDEL   MATTHAEI   3-4
ORGELKONZERTE, OP. 4 NO. 6 IN B FLAT -- 'HALLISCHE
HANDEL-AUSGABE' --
BARENREITER VERLAG   BA 364
HANDEL   DART
SUITE A DEUX CLAVECINS
OXFORD UNIVERSITY PRESS   35.028   1.75
HANDEL   TATE
SUITE FROM THE WATER MUSIC
OXFORD UNIVERSITY PRESS   35.503   2.25
HANDEL   BILOTTI   3
THEME AND VARIATIONS
PRO-ART PUBLICATIONS, INC.   31   1.25
HANDEL   M-D
TWELVE ORGAN CONCERTI IN 2 VOLS# VOL. 1
C. F. PETERS CORPORATION   2591A   5.00
HANDEL   M-D
TWELVE ORGAN CONCERTI IN 2 VOLS# VOL. 2
C. F. PETERS CORPORATION   2591B   5.00
HANDEL   NEVIN
WHERE'ER YOU WALK
BELWIN-MILLS PUBLISHING CORPORATION   .60
HARSANYI
CONCERTSTUECK
FRANCO COLOMBO PUBLICATIONS   SAL   5.50
HARSANYI
PIECE
FRANCO COLOMBO PUBLICATIONS   SAL   4.25
HARTLEY, W.--ED   HARTLEY, W.
BALLET MUSIC FOR ORCHESTRA ARR. FOR TWO PIANO-FOUR HANDS
FEMA MUSIC PUBLICATIONS   4.50
HARTLEY, W.
CONCERTO FOR PIANO AND ORCHESTRA ARR. FOR TWO PIANO FOUR HANDS
FEMA MUSIC PUBLICATIONS   6.00
HATTORI, KOH-ICHI
CONCERTINO FOR SMALL HANDS
BOOSEY AND HAWKES, INC.   1.50
HAUBENSTOCK-RAMATI, R.
CATCH 2
UNIVERSAL EDITION   UE 14881   11.00

IRVING
   CAROUSEL AND FERRIS WHEEL --PIANO SOLO OR 2 PIANOS, 4 HANDS--
      SUMMY-BIRCHARD COMPANY   1.00
IVES, C.   D
   THREE QUARTER-TONE PIECES --PAPPASTAVROU--
      C. F. PETERS CORPORATION   66285   3.00
JACHINO
   CONCERTO NO. 02
      FRANCO COLOMBO PUBLICATIONS   130621   10.00
JACOB, G.
   CONCERTO NO. 01
      OXFORD UNIVERSITY PRESS   32.906   3.00
JIRKO   4
   KONZERT FUR KLAVIER UND ORCHESTER
      BARENREITER VERLAG   CHF 5102
JOLIVET, A.
   CONCERTO
      HEUGEL ET CIE.   12.00
JOLIVET, A.
   HOPI SNAKE DANCE
      GERARD BILLAUDOT EDITIONS MUSICALES   6.30
JONGEN, J.
   CONCERTO
      ELKAN-VOGEL, INC.   LEM   15.00
JOUBERT, J.
   PIANO CONCERTO
      NOVELLO AND COMPANY, LTD.   10.0078.00 5.25
JOUBERT, J.
   PIANO CONCERTO
      NOVELLO AND COMPANY, LTD.   10.0078.00 5.25
JOYNER, B.   1 1/2
   ONE SUNNY DAY
      THEODORE PRESSER COMPANY   .60
JUON, P.
   KINDERTRAUME, OP. 74--VOL. 1
      ASSOCIATED MUSIC PUBLISHERS, INC. LEU   2.75
JUROWSKY   4
   SYMPHONIE NO. 1 FUR KONZERTANTES KLAVIER UND STREICHORCHESTER
      BARENREITER VERLAG   CHF 5221
KABALEVSKY
   CONCERTO NO. 03, OP. 50
      INTERNATIONAL MUSIC COMPANY   3.75
KABALEVSKY
   CONCERTO NO. 03
      EDWIN F. KALMUS   3569   3.50
KABALEVSKY
   PIANO CONCERTO NO. 03, OP. 50 --'YOUTH'
      MCA MUSIC   3.75
KABALEVSKY
   RHAPSODY ON THE THEME OF THE SONG 'SCHOOL YEAR'
      MCA MUSIC   5.75
KADOSA
   CONCERTINO
      KULTURA   2.50
KADOSA
   CONCERTO NO. 03, OP. 47
      KULTURA   3.50
KADOSA
   SONATA FOR TWO PIANOS
      KULTURA   2.50
KALABIS   4
   KONZERT FUR KLAVIER UND ORCHESTER
      BARENREITER VERLAG   CHF 5106
KARKOSCHKA   4
   POLYPHONE STUDIEN FUR ORCHESTER UND OBLIGATES KLAVIER
      BARENREITER VERLAG   BA 3579
KASSCHAU, H.
   CANDLELIGHT CONCERTO
      SOUTHERN MUSIC COMPANY   1.00
KASSCHAU, H.
   LEGEND OF SLEEPY HOLLOW, THE -- A PROGRAM CONCERTO -- SET
      G. SCHIRMER, INC.   2.50
KASSCHAU, H.
   SUPPLEMENTARY PIANO MATERIAL--ENSEMBLE BOOK FOR 'TEACH ME TO
   PLAY'
      G. SCHIRMER, INC.   .75
KASSERN, T. Z.
   TEEN-AGE CONCERTO
      G. SCHIRMER, INC.   1.00
KATTNIGG, R.   4-5
   KONZERT FUR KLAVIER UND KLEINES ORCHESTER, OP. 15
      BARENREITER VERLAG   SM 1159
KAYLIN, S.   4.84
   FANTASY ON SOUSA'S STARS AND STRIPES
      COMPOSERS AUTOGRAPH PUBLICATIONS
KEATS, F.   4
   DANCE OF THE ROSEBUDS
      THEODORE PRESSER COMPANY   1.00
KEENAN
   COUNTRY DANCE
      CARL FISCHER, INC.   P 2016   .75
KEENAN   2
   WOODEN SHOES
      BOSTON MUSIC COMPANY   .75
KEENEY, W.   GEARHART
   MOUNTAIN TUNE -- SET
      G. SCHIRMER, INC.   1.25
KELTERBORN   4
   CONCERTINO FUR KLAVIER, SCHLAGZEUG UND STREICHORCHESTER
      BARENREITER VERLAG   BA 3909
KELTERBORN
   SONATA
      BARENREITER VERLAG   BA 3505   7.00
KELTERBORN   4
   SONATE
      BARENREITER VERLAG   BA 3505
KENNAN   2
   PADDY THE FIDDLER
      BOSTON MUSIC COMPANY   .75
KETTERER, E.   1 1/2
   AT THE DANCE
      THEODORE PRESSER COMPANY   .60
KEYS   1
   NINE LITTLE PLAYTIME DUETS
      WILLIS MUSIC COMPANY   .75
KHATCHATURIAN
   CONCERTO -- 1936
      ASSOCIATED MUSIC PUBLISHERS, INC. BRH   6.25
KHATCHATURIAN
   CONCERTO IN D FLAT
      INTERNATIONAL MUSIC COMPANY   3.75
KHATCHATURIAN
   PIANO CONCERTO
      EDWIN F. KALMUS   3577   3.50
KHATCHATURIAN
   THREE PIECES
      EDWIN F. KALMUS   3585   2.00

KHATCHATURIAN   D
   THREE PIECES
      C. F. PETERS CORPORATION   4738   6.50
KIMES, K.
   YOUNG DAYS
      BELWIN-MILLS PUBLISHING CORPORATION   1.50
KING   SUGARMAN
   SONG OF THE ISLANDS
      EDWARD B. MARKS MUSIC CORPORATION   01.25
KIRCHNER, T.   E-M
   SEVEN WALTZES, OP. 86
      C. F. PETERS CORPORATION   2468   3.50
KLEBE, G.   4
   CONCERTO A CINQUE, OP. 50
      BARENREITER VERLAG   BA 4467
KLEIN, J.
   JIG WALTZ -- SET
      ASSOCIATED MUSIC PUBLISHERS, INC. AMP   1.50
KLEIN, J.
   STOOP DANCE -- SET
      ASSOCIATED MUSIC PUBLISHERS, INC. AMP   1.25
KOCH, F.
   TWO IMPRESSIONS FOR TWO PIANOS
      SEESAW MUSIC CORPORATION   5.00
KOELLING   4
   HUNGARY
      THEODORE PRESSER COMPANY   1.00
KOUNTZ, R.
   SLEIGH, THE -- ARR. BY THE COMPOSER -- SET
      G. SCHIRMER, INC.   .80
KOZELUCH, L.   MEYLAN
   CONCERTO IN D
      ASSOCIATED MUSIC PUBLISHERS, INC. BRH   7.00
KREBS   KLEINE   4
   KONZERT IN A MINOR FUR ZWEI CEMBALI
      BARENREITER VERLAG   DV 8102
KREISLER   WEYBRIGHT
   CAPRICE VIENNOIS --STUDENT EDITION--
      CARL FISCHER, INC.   F 2311   1.25
KREISLER   MILLER
   CAPRICE VIENNOIS
      CARL FISCHER, INC.   F 2301   2.50
KREISLER   MAIER
   LIEBESFREUD --STUDENT EDITION--
      CARL FISCHER, INC.   F 2304   1.00
KREISLER   RITTER
   LIEBESFREUD
      CARL FISCHER, INC.   F 2306   2.00
KREISLER   MAIER
   LIEBESLEID --STUDENT EDITION--
      CARL FISCHER, INC.   F 2305   1.00
KREISLER   HEUBERGER *
   MIDNIGHT BELLS --STUDENT EDITION--
      CARL FISCHER, INC.   F 2316   1.00
KREISLER   BRANT
   MINIATURE VIENNESE MARCH --STUDENT EDITION--
      CARL FISCHER, INC.   F 2322   1.00
KREISLER   LAMPERT
   OLD REFRAIN, THE --STUDENT EDITION--
      CARL FISCHER, INC.   F 2309   1.00
KREISLER   LAMPERT
   SCHON ROSMARIN --STUDENT EDITION--
      CARL FISCHER, INC.   F 2308   1.00
KREISLER   GOULD, M.
   SCHON ROSMARIN
      CARL FISCHER, INC.   F 2313   2.00
KREISLER   FLETCHER
   TAMBOURIN CHINOIS --STUDENT EDITION--
      CARL FISCHER, INC.   F 2320   1.25
KREISLER   BRANT
   TOY SOLDIERS MARCH --STUDENT EDITION--
      CARL FISCHER, INC.   F 2321   1.00
KRENEK, E.   4
   BASLER MASSARBEIT
      BARENREITER VERLAG   BA 3510
KRENEK, E.
   BASLER MASSARBEIT
      BARENREITER VERLAG   BA 3510   6.00
KRENEK, E.   4
   KLAVIERKONZERT NO. 04
      BARENREITER VERLAG   BA 3498
KRENEK, E.   4
   KONZERT FUR 2 KLAVIERE UND ORCHESTER
      BARENREITER VERLAG   BA 4331
KUHLAU, F. *   M
   SONATINAS, WITH 2ND PIANO ACC. BY RIEDEL, IN 2 VOLS# VOL. 1
      C. F. PETERS CORPORATION   3874A   1.50
KUHLAU, F. *   M
   SONATINAS, WITH 2ND PIANO ACC. BY RIEDEL, IN 2 VOLS# VOL. 2
      C. F. PETERS CORPORATION   3874B   1.50
KUHLAU, F.   KOVALOV *
   SONATINA OP. 20 NO. 1
      VOLKWEIN BROS.   2.00
KULLMANN
   POEME CONCERTANT
      FRANCO COLOMBO PUBLICATIONS   SAL   5.75
KUNC, B.   4
   HURDY-GURDY
      RONGWEN MUSIC, INC.   03.00
LACK, T.   ROQUES *
   CABALETTA, OP. 83
      G. SCHIRMER, INC.   .50
LADMIRAULT
   BROCELIANDE AU MATIN
      FRANCO COLOMBO PUBLICATIONS   SAL   4.25
LADMIRAULT
   SUITE BRETONNE - DANSE DE 1 EPEE
      FRANCO COLOMBO PUBLICATIONS   SAL   3.25
LADMIRAULT
   SUITE BRETONNE - RONDO
      FRANCO COLOMBO PUBLICATIONS   SAL   3.25
LADMIRAULT
   SUITE BRETONNE - SCHERZO
      FRANCO COLOMBO PUBLICATIONS   SAL   3.25
LALO, E.
   SYMPHONIE ESPAGNOLE, OP. 21
      ELKAN-VOGEL, INC.   D   14.00
LANDOWSKI   D
   CONCERTO NO. 02
      C. F. PETERS CORPORATION   C402   3.00
LANDRY
   APRES LA MOISSON
      FRANCO COLOMBO PUBLICATIONS   SAL   2.50
LANDRY
   SOUVENIR DU TYROL
      FRANCO COLOMBO PUBLICATIONS   SAL   2.75

LANG
　　VALSE ESPAGNOLE
　　　　FRANCO COLOMBO PUBLICATIONS　　　　　　SY2003　　1.25
LANNER, J. F. C.　　　　　DOUGHERTY *
　　VINDOBONA, INTRODUCTION AND WALTZES -- SET
　　　　ASSOCIATED MUSIC PUBLISHERS, INC.　　　AMP　　　　3.00
LANZA, A.
　　PLECTROS I -- 1962-II, FOR ONE OR TWO PIANOS
　　　　BOOSEY AND HAWKES, INC.　　　　　　　　　　　　　1.00
LASALA
　　DANZA DE LA CHINA QUERENDONA
　　　　FRANCO COLOMBO PUBLICATIONS　　　　　　BA10344　　.75
LASALA
　　PAYADA
　　　　FRANCO COLOMBO PUBLICATIONS　　　　　　BA10928　1.00
LECUONA　　　　　　　　　NASH
　　ANDALUCIA
　　　　EDWARD B. MARKS MUSIC CORPORATION　　　　　　01.75
LECUONA　　　　　　　　　SUGARMAN
　　ANTE EL ESCORIAL
　　　　EDWARD B. MARKS MUSIC CORPORATION　　　　　　01.25
LECUONA　　　　　　　　　NASH
　　COMPARSA, LA
　　　　EDWARD B. MARKS MUSIC CORPORATION　　　　　　01.25
LECUONA　　　　　　　　　CABIATI *
　　DANZA LUCUMI
　　　　EDWARD B. MARKS MUSIC CORPORATION　　　　　　01.50
LECUONA
　　GITANERIAS
　　　　EDWARD B. MARKS MUSIC CORPORATION　　　　　　01.50
LECUONA　　　　　　　　　NASH
　　MALAGUENA
　　　　EDWARD B. MARKS MUSIC CORPORATION　　　　　　02.00
LECUONA　　　　　　　　　SUGARMAN
　　SAN FRANCISCO EL GRANDE
　　　　EDWARD B. MARKS MUSIC CORPORATION　　　　　　01.50
LEES, B.
　　SONATA
　　　　BOOSEY AND HAWKES, INC.　　　　　　　　　　　　5.00
LEEUW　　　　　　　　　　　　　　　　　　M-D
　　SONATA
　　　　C. F. PETERS CORPORATION　　　　　　　D218　　3.00
LEHNER　　　　　　　　　　　　　　　　　　3
　　KLEINES KONZERT FUR KLAVIER, STREICHER UND SCHLAGZEUG
　　　　BARENREITER VERLAG　　　　　　　　　　BE 303
LELEU　　　　　　　　　　　　　　　　　　7
　　SUITE SYMPHONIQUE
　　　　ALPHONSE LEDUC
LEMONT, C. W. *
　　ORGANIST, THE
　　　　CARL FISCHER, INC.　　　　　　　　　　P 2539　　1.00
LEONI, F.　　　　　　　　SAMUELSON
　　BROWNIES
　　　　BOOSEY AND HAWKES, INC.　　　　　　　　　　　　.75
LESUR, D.
　　FANTASY
　　　　FRANCO COLOMBO PUBLICATIONS　　　　　　R2201　　5.50
LESUR, D.
　　PASSACAILLE
　　　　GERARD BILLAUDOT EDITIONS MUSICALES　　　　　3.80
LEVITZKI, M.　　　　　　　BERKOWITZ
　　VALSE -- SET
　　　　G. SCHIRMER, INC.　　　　　　　　　　　　　　　.90
LIAPUNOFF　　　　　　　　　　　　　　　　　D
　　RHAPSODY ON UKRAINIAN THEMES, OP. 28
　　　　C. F. PETERS CORPORATION　　　　　　　ZM1714　　3.50
LINEK　　　　　　　　　　　　　　　　　　M
　　CONCERTO IN F
　　　　C. F. PETERS CORPORATION　　　　　　　N6109　　6.00
LIPATTI, D.
　　CONCERTINO CLASSIQUE
　　　　UNIVERSAL EDITION　　　　　　　　　　　UE 11546　10.00
LIPATTI, D.
　　DANSES ROUMAINES
　　　　FRANCO COLOMBO PUBLICATIONS　　　　　　SAL　　14.50
LISZT
　　CADENZA TO BEETHOVEN CONCERTO III
　　　　MUSICA OBSCURA　　　　　　　　　　　　　　　　1.50
LISZT　　　　　　　　　　SAUER　　　　D
　　CONCERTI AND OTHER WORKS WITH ORCHESTRA
　　　　C. F. PETERS CORPORATION　　　　　　　3602C　10.00
LISZT　　　　　　　　　　MONTES
　　CONCERTO NO. 01 IN E FLAT
　　　　FRANCO COLOMBO PUBLICATIONS　　　　　　BA10067　3.25
LISZT　　　　　　　　　　SAUER　　　　D
　　CONCERTO NO. 01 IN E FLAT
　　　　C. F. PETERS CORPORATION　　　　　　　3606　　2.00
LISZT　　　　　　　　　　JOSEFFY, R.
　　CONCERTO NO. 01 IN E FLAT
　　　　G. SCHIRMER, INC.　　　　　　　　　　　L1057　　1.75
LISZT　　　　　　　　　　JOSEFFY
　　CONCERTO NO. 01 IN E FLAT
　　　　G. SCHIRMER, INC.　　　　　　　　　　　L1057　　1.75
LISZT　　　　　　　　　　MONTES
　　CONCERTO NO. 02 IN A
　　　　FRANCO COLOMBO PUBLICATIONS　　　　　　BA11778　4.00
LISZT　　　　　　　　　　SAUER　　　　D
　　CONCERTO NO. 02 IN A
　　　　C. F. PETERS CORPORATION　　　　　　　3607　　2.50
LISZT　　　　　　　　　　JOSEFFY, R.
　　CONCERTO NO. 02 IN A
　　　　G. SCHIRMER, INC.　　　　　　　　　　　L1058　　2.50
LISZT　　　　　　　　　　JOSEFFY
　　CONCERTO NO. 02 IN A
　　　　G. SCHIRMER, INC.　　　　　　　　　　　L1058　　2.50
LISZT　　　　　　　　　　HUGHES
　　CONCERTO PATHETIQUE IN E MINOR
　　　　G. SCHIRMER, INC.　　　　　　　　　　　L1534　　1.50
LISZT　　　　　　　　　　HUGHES
　　CONCERTO PATHETIQUE IN E MINOR
　　　　G. SCHIRMER, INC.　　　　　　　　　　　L1534　　1.50
LISZT　　　　　　　　　　SAUER　　　　D
　　HUNGARIAN FANTASY
　　　　C. F. PETERS CORPORATION　　　　　　　3612　　2.00
LISZT　　　　　　　　　　JOSEFFY, R.
　　HUNGARIAN FANTASY
　　　　G. SCHIRMER, INC.　　　　　　　　　　　L1056　　1.25
LISZT　　　　　　　　　　JOSEFFY
　　HUNGARIAN FANTASY
　　　　G. SCHIRMER, INC.　　　　　　　　　　　L1056　　1.25
LISZT
　　HUNGARIAN FANTASY
　　　　UNIVERSAL EDITION　　　　　　　　　　　5945　　1.60
LISZT　　　　　　　　　　KLEINMICHEL
　　HUNGARIAN RHAPSODY NO. 02 -- SET
　　　　G. SCHIRMER, INC.　　　　　　　　　　　L1568　　1.75

LISZT　　　　　　　　　　RICHARDSON, T.
　　MALEDICTION FOR PIANO AND STRINGS --SEARLE 121--
　　　　MUSICA OBSCURA　　　　　　　　　　　　　　　　7.50
LISZT
　　PIANO CONCERTO NO. 01 IN E FLAT
　　　　EDWIN F. KALMUS　　　　　　　　　　　　3613　　2.00
LISZT
　　PIANO CONCERTO NO. 02 IN A
　　　　EDWIN F. KALMUS　　　　　　　　　　　　3614　　2.50
LISZT　　　　　　　　　　SINGER　　　D
　　PRELUDES, LES
　　　　C. F. PETERS CORPORATION　　　　　　　3621　　7.50
LISZT　　　　　　　　　　BUSONI
　　SPANISH RHAPSODY--ARRANGED FOR PIANO AND ORCHESTRA
　　　　G. SCHIRMER, INC.　　　　　　　　　　　L1252　　2.50
LISZT　　　　　　　　　　BUSONI
　　SPANISH RHAPSODY
　　　　G. SCHIRMER, INC.　　　　　　　　　　　L1252　　2.50
LITER, M.
　　PRELUDE ESPAGNOLE
　　　　BOOSEY AND HAWKES, INC.　　　　　　　　　　　2.2P
LITOLFF
　　CONCERTO SYMPHONIQUE NO. 3, OP. 45 AND SCHERZO FROM CONCERTO
　　SYMPHONIQUE NO. 4, OP. 102
　　　　MUSIC TREASURE PUBLICATIONS　　　　　　　　　5.00
LITOLFF
　　CONCERTO SYMPHONIQUE
　　　　EDWIN F. KALMUS　　　　　　　　　　　　3604　　5.00
LONGAS
　　ARAGON
　　　　EDWARD B. MARKS MUSIC CORPORATION　　　　　　02.00
LONGAS
　　JOTA ARAGONESA
　　　　FRANCO COLOMBO PUBLICATIONS　　　　　　BA9723　　1.00
LONGO, A.
　　VARIATIONS ON 'AH, VOUS DIRAI-JE, MAMAN' OP. 39 NO. 1
　　　　FRANCO COLOMBO PUBLICATIONS　　　　　　ER325　　1.50
LOPATNIKOFF
　　CONCERTO FOR TWO PIANOS AND ORCHESTRA, OP. 33 -- INCLUDES TWO
　　PARTS
　　　　MCA MUSIC　　　　　　　　　　　　　　　　　　5.00
LOPATNIKOFF
　　KONZERT FUR KLAVIER UND ORCHESTER, OP. 15, KLAVIERAUSZUG
　　　　SCHOTT　　　　　　　　　　　　　　　　　2138　　5.00
LOPEZ BUCHARDO　　　　　MONTES
　　BAILECITO
　　　　FRANCO COLOMBO PUBLICATIONS　　　　　　BA9688　　1.00
LOPEZ BUCHARDO　　　　　LASALA
　　DANZON
　　　　FRANCO COLOMBO PUBLICATIONS　　　　　　BA10318　1.00
LOPEZ BUCHARDO　　　　　LASALA
　　NOCTURNE
　　　　FRANCO COLOMBO PUBLICATIONS　　　　　　BA10337　.75
LUCCHINETTI, G. B.　　　EWERHART
　　CONCERTO -- 2 PNO/ORG/HPCHD
　　　　ASSOCIATED MUSIC PUBLISHERS, INC.　　　DOB　　2.75
LUTECE
　　RHAPSODY IN SWING
　　　　FRANCO COLOMBO PUBLICATIONS　　　　　　SAL　　14.50
LUTOSLAWSKI
　　VARIATIONS ON A THEME BY PAGANINI
　　　　EDWARD B. MARKS MUSIC CORPORATION　　　　　　02.00
LUTYENS, E.
　　SYMPHONIES FUR SOLOKLAVIER, BLASER, HARFE, UND SCHLAGZEUG,
　　KLAVIERAUSZUG
　　　　SCHOTT　　　　　　　　　　　　　　　　　10907　　6.25
LYKE--ED.　　　　　　　　LYKE
　　ENSEMBLE MUSIC FOR GROUP PIANO
　　　　STIPES PUBLISHING COMPANY　　　　　　　　　　4.00
MACDOWELL
　　CONCERTO NO. 01 IN A MINOR, OP. 15
　　　　ASSOCIATED MUSIC PUBLISHERS, INC.　　　BRH　　2.25
MACDOWELL　　　　　　　　HUGHES
　　CONCERTO NO. 02, OP. 23
　　　　G. SCHIRMER, INC.　　　　　　　　　　　L1462　　2.50
MACDOWELL　　　　　　　　HUGHES
　　CONCERTO NO. 02 IN D MINOR, OP. 23
　　　　G. SCHIRMER, INC.　　　　　　　　　　　L1462　　2.50
MACDOWELL　　　　　　　　GRUEN
　　POLONAISE, OP. 46 NO. 12 -- SET
　　　　ASSOCIATED MUSIC PUBLISHERS, INC.　　　AMP　　1.50
MACERO
　　ONE-THREE QUARTERS. PICC, FL, VN, VC, TRB, TBA, 2 PIANOS, 4
　　HANDS
　　　　C. F. PETERS CORPORATION　　　　　　　66178　　7.50
MAHLER　　　　　　　　　　WOSS
　　SYMPHONY NO. 03
　　　　UNIVERSAL EDITION　　　　　　　　　　　UE 951　　7.35
MAHLER　　　　　　　　　　STRADAL　　　D
　　SYMPHONY NO. 05
　　　　C. F. PETERS CORPORATION　　　　　　　3761　　8.50
MALIPIERO, G. F.
　　DIALOGHI NO. 1 - 'CON MANUEL DE FALLA'
　　　　FRANCO COLOMBO PUBLICATIONS　　　　　　129401　1.50
MALIPIERO, G. F.
　　DIALOGHI NO. 2 - 'BETWEEN TWO PIANOS'
　　　　FRANCO COLOMBO PUBLICATIONS　　　　　　129402　1.75
MALIPIERO, G. F.
　　DIALOGHI NO. 3 - 'CON JACOPONE DA TODI' -- FOR VOICE AND 2
　　PIANOS --
　　　　FRANCO COLOMBO PUBLICATIONS　　　　　　129403　1.50
MALOTTE, A.　　　　　　　DEIS
　　LORD'S PRAYER, THE -- SET
　　　　G. SCHIRMER, INC.　　　　　　　　　　　　　　1.00
MANA-ZUCCA　　　　　　　　IHRER
　　VALSE BRILLANTE -- SET
　　　　G. SCHIRMER, INC.　　　　　　　　　　　　　　1.25
MANNES, L. D.
　　PETITE SUITE
　　　　FRANCO COLOMBO PUBLICATIONS　　　　　　SAL　　5.00
MANNINO, V.
　　CONCERTO
　　　　FRANCO COLOMBO PUBLICATIONS　　　　　　DS935　　6.50
MANNINO, V.
　　SERIE
　　　　FRANCO COLOMBO PUBLICATIONS　　　　　　130904　3.50
MARCELLO *　　　　　　　　　　　　　　　　M
　　CONCERTO IN D MINOR
　　　　C. F. PETERS CORPORATION　　　　　　　217D　　1.50
MARGOLA
　　GINEVRINA, LA
　　　　FRANCO COLOMBO PUBLICATIONS　　　　　　BON.2337　7.00
MARGOLA
　　KINDERKONZERT
　　　　FRANCO COLOMBO PUBLICATIONS　　　　　　128918　2.75

MARIE
    LE TOMBEAU DE CARRILLO
        ELKAN-VOGEL, INC.   J   d.25
MARTIN, E.   SAMUELSON
    COME TO THE FAIR
        BOOSEY AND HAWKES, INC.   1   1.00
MARTIN, E.
    GRASSHOPPERS' DANCE
        WILLIS MUSIC COMPANY   1   .35
MARTIN, E.
    MEADOW LARK
        WILLIS MUSIC COMPANY   .40
MARTIN, F.
    BALLADE
        UNIVERSAL EDITION   UE 11556   10.25
MARTIN, F.
    CONCERT FOR CLAVECIN
        UNIVERSAL EDITION   UE 12364   7.00
MARTIN, F.
    ETUDES FOR 2 PIANOS
        UNIVERSAL EDITION   UE 13012   6.00
MARTINO
    CONCERTO FOR PIANO AND ORCHESTRA
        E. C. SCHIRMER MUSIC COMPANY   1441   02.50
MARTINU, B.   4
    CONCERTINO FUR KLAVIERTRIO UND STREICHORCHESTER
        BARENREITER VERLAG   CHF 5178
MARTINU, B.   4
    CONCERTINO FUR KLAVIER -- LINKE HAND -- UND ORCHESTER
        BARENREITER VERLAG   CHF 5200
MARTINU, B.   4
    CONCERTINO FUR KLAVIER UND ORCHESTER
        BARENREITER VERLAG   CHF 5191
MARTINU, B.
    CONCERTO FOR 2 PIANOS
        ASSOCIATED MUSIC PUBLISHERS, INC.   AMP   4.00
MARTINU, B.
    CONCERTO NO. 02
        ARTIA   6.00
MARTINU, B.
    CONCERTO NO. 03
        ARTIA   8.00
MARTINU, B.
    FANTASY -- SET
        ASSOCIATED MUSIC PUBLISHERS, INC.   ESC   16.00
MARTINU, B.   4
    INCANTATIONS. KONZERT NO. 4 FUR KLAVIER UND ORCHESTER
        BARENREITER VERLAG   BA 4318
MARTINU, B.   5
    KLAVIERKONZERT NO. 01
        BARENREITER VERLAG   AP 1733
MARTINU, B.   4
    KLAVIERKONZERT NO. 02 - KLAVIERAUSZUG
        BARENREITER VERLAG   AP 1511
MARTINU, B.   4
    KLAVIERKONZERT NO. 02
        BARENREITER VERLAG   CHF 5190
MARTINU, B.   4
    KLAVIERKONZERT NO. 02
        BARENREITER VERLAG   AP 1511
MARTINU, B.   4
    KLAVIERKONZERT NO. 03 - KLAVIERAUSZUG
        BARENREITER VERLAG   AP 1512
MARTINU, B.   4
    KLAVIERKONZERT NO. 03
        BARENREITER VERLAG   CHF 5209
MARTINU, B.   4
    KLAVIERKONZERT NO. 03
        BARENREITER VERLAG   AP 1512
MARTINU, B.
    SINFONIETTA GIOCOSA
        BOOSEY AND HAWKES, INC.   5.00
MARTINU, B.
    THREE CZECH DANCES -- SET
        ASSOCIATED MUSIC PUBLISHERS, INC.   ESC   14.00
MARTIN *
    DANCE OF THE PUPPETS
        CARL FISCHER, INC.   P 2538   .75
MATHIAS, W.
    CONCERTO NO. 02
        OXFORD UNIVERSITY PRESS   35.106   6.20
MATTHESON, J.   CANNON, B.C.   M-D
    SONATA A DUF CEMBALI IN G MINOR
        C. F. PETERS CORPORATION   H311A   2.00
MATTHESON, J.   CANNON, B.C.   M-D
    SUITE FOR 2 CEMBALI IN G MINOR
        C. F. PETERS CORPORATION   H311B   2.00
MAYER
    OCTAGON
        MCA MUSIC   6.95
MCKAY, G.
    DANCING IN A DREAM
        MCA MUSIC   1.00
MCPHEE, C.
    CONCERTO FOR PIANO AND WIND OCTET ACCOMPANIMENT -- SET
        ASSOCIATED MUSIC PUBLISHERS, INC.   AMP   6.50
MEDTNER, N.   D
    CONCERTO NO. 02, OP. 50
        C. F. PETERS CORPORATION   ZM1002   6.00
MEDTNER, N.   D
    CONCERTO NO. 03, OP. 60
        C. F. PETERS CORPORATION   ZM1003   6.00
MELLICHAMP, N.   1
    THREE CLOCKS
        CENTURY MUSIC PUBLISHING COMPANY, INC.   4092   .60
MENDELSSOHN   D
    CAPRICCIO BRILLANTE, OP. 22
        C. F. PETERS CORPORATION   2942   1.25
MENDELSSOHN   STERNBERG
    CAPRICCIO BRILLANTE, OP. 22
        G. SCHIRMER, INC.   L1187   1.25
MENDELSSOHN   STERNBERG
    CAPRICCIO BRILLANTE
        G. SCHIRMER, INC.   L1187   1.25
MENDELSSOHN
    CONCERTO IN D MINOR FOR PIANO, VIOLIN AND STRING ORCHESTRA
        ASSOCIATED MUSIC PUBLISHERS, INC.   DVM   9.00
MENDELSSOHN
    CONCERTO IN E FOR 2 PIANOS AND ORCHESTRA
        ASSOCIATED MUSIC PUBLISHERS, INC.   DVM   5.00
MENDELSSOHN
    CONCERTO NO. 01, OP. 25
        EDWIN F. KALMUS   3672   2.00
MENDELSSOHN   D
    CONCERTO NO. 01 IN G MINOR, OP. 25
        C. F. PETERS CORPORATION   2896A   1.50
MENDELSSOHN   RUTHARDT
    CONCERTO NO. 01 IN G MINOR, OP. 25
        G. SCHIRMER, INC.   L61   1.25
MENDELSSOHN   RUTHARDT
    CONCERTO NO. 01 IN G MINOR, OP. 25
        G. SCHIRMER, INC.   L61   1.25
MENDELSSOHN   D
    CONCERTO NO. 02 IN D MINOR, OP. 40
        C. F. PETERS CORPORATION   2896B   3.00
MENDELSSOHN   RUTHARDT
    CONCERTO NO. 02 IN D MINOR, OP. 40
        G. SCHIRMER, INC.   L62   1.50
MENDELSSOHN   RUTHARDT
    CONCERTO NO. 02 IN D MINOR, OP. 40
        G. SCHIRMER, INC.   L62   1.50
MENDELSSOHN
    ON WINGS OF SONG
        ASSOCIATED MUSIC PUBLISHERS, INC.   AMP   2.00
MENDELSSOHN
    OP. 83A, OP. 92
        EDWIN F. KALMUS   3671   2.50
MENDELSSOHN   LONG, K.
    ORGAN SONATA NO. 03 -- FIRST MOVEMENT
        NOVELLO AND COMPANY, LTD.   10.0164.07   2.40
MENDELSSOHN   STERNBERG
    RONDO BRILLANTE, OP. 29
        G. SCHIRMER, INC.   L1188   1.25
MENDELSSOHN   STERNBERG
    RONDO BRILLANTE, OP. 29
        G. SCHIRMER, INC.   L1188   1.25
MENDELSSOHN   D
    RONDO BRILLANT IN E FLAT, OP. 29
        C. F. PETERS CORPORATION   3491   2.50
MENDELSSOHN   BEACH
    RONDO CAPRICCIOSO -- SET
        G. SCHIRMER, INC.   L1659   1.50
MENDELSSOHN   PALMER   4
    SPRING SONG
        WILLIS MUSIC COMPANY   .40
MENOTTI
    CONCERTO IN F
        FRANCO COLOMBO PUBLICATIONS   127655   4.00
MERKUR--ED   MERKUR
    DREAM OF A DOLL
        BELWIN-MILLS PUBLISHING CORPORATION   27010   1.50
MERKUR--ED   MERKUR
    HAVAH NAGILAH
        BELWIN-MILLS PUBLISHING CORPORATION   27046   1.50
MERKUR--ED   MERKUR
    KITTEN ON THE KEYS
        BELWIN-MILLS PUBLISHING CORPORATION   27018   1.50
MERKUR--ED   MERKUR
    LA CUCARACHA
        BELWIN-MILLS PUBLISHING CORPORATION   27019   1.50
MERKUR--ED   MERKUR
    SOPHISTICATED LADY
        BELWIN-MILLS PUBLISHING CORPORATION   27027   1.50
MERKUR--ED   MERKUR
    STAR DUST
        BELWIN-MILLS PUBLISHING CORPORATION   27038   1.50
MERKUR
    CLEAR TRACK AHEAD
        BELWIN-MILLS PUBLISHING CORPORATION   1.00
MERKUR
    NEW HORIZONS
        BELWIN-MILLS PUBLISHING CORPORATION   1.50
MERLET   8
    MUSIQUE POUR DEUX PIANOS
        ALPHONSE LEDUC
MESSIAEN, O.   9
    COULEURS DE LA CITE CELESTE
        ALPHONSE LEDUC
MESSIAEN, O.   9
    SEPT HAIKAI
        ALPHONSE LEDUC
METIS, F.   INTERMEDIATE
    AFRICASIAN AFFAIR--2, 3, OR 4 PIANOS
        VOLKWEIN BROS.   3.00
METIS, F.   EASY
    HAPPINESS HILL--2, 3, OR 4 PIANOS
        VOLKWEIN BROS.   1.50
METIS, F.   INTERMEDIATE
    PARISIAN POLKA--2, 3, OR 4 PIANOS
        VOLKWEIN BROS.   3.00
METIS, F.   INTERMEDIATE
    WICKED WORLD WALTZ--2, 3, OR 4 PIANOS
        VOLKWEIN BROS.   3.00
MEYEROWITZ
    HOMAGE TO HIERONYMOUS BOSCH
        RONGWEN MUSIC, INC.   10.00
MICHALSKY
    SONATA --IN PREP--
        WESTERN INTERNATIONAL MUSIC, INC.   AV186
MIEG, P.
    CONCERTO FOR HARPSICHORD -- 1954
        ASSOCIATED MUSIC PUBLISHERS, INC.   BOT   6.00
MIGOT   7
    SUITE EN 3 PARTIES
        ALPHONSE LEDUC
MIHALOVICI
    CANTUS FIRMUS
        HEUGEL ET CIE.   2.90
MILFORD   M
    FISHING BY MOONLIGHT
        C. F. PETERS CORPORATION   H303   2.00
MILHAUD, D.
    CARNIVAL D'AIX
        HEUGEL ET CIE.   18.50
MILHAUD, D.
    CONCERTO FOR 2 PIANOS AND ORCHESTRA -- PIANO SCORE
        ELKAN-VOGEL, INC.   16.00
MILHAUD, D.
    CONCERTO NO. 03
        ASSOCIATED MUSIC PUBLISHERS, INC.   AMP   3.25
MILHAUD, D.
    CONCERTO NO. 04
        HEUGEL ET CIE.   13.70
MILHAUD, D.
    CONCERTO NO. 05
        ASSOCIATED MUSIC PUBLISHERS, INC.   ESC   8.25
MILHAUD, D.
    CONCERTO
        FRANCO COLOMBO PUBLICATIONS   SAL   10.75
MILHAUD, D.   BABIN
    DIVERTISSEMENTS -- SET
        ASSOCIATED MUSIC PUBLISHERS, INC.   ESC   9.50

MILHAUD, D.
 FANTASIE PASTORALE
  FRANCO COLOMBO PUBLICATIONS SAL 8.25
MILHAUD, D.
 SCARAMOUCHE
  FRANCO COLOMBO PUBLICATIONS SAL 7.00
MILHAUD, D.
 SUITE CONCERTANTE -- SET
  ASSOCIATED MUSIC PUBLISHERS, INC. ESC 9.00
MILLER, C.   5
 CUBANAISE
  THEODORE PRESSER COMPANY 1.50
MILLER, J.
 SOUTH OF THE RIO GRANDE
  BELWIN-MILLS PUBLISHING CORPORATION 2.00
MITTLER--ED MITTLER INTERMEDIATE
 JUNIOR AMERICAN PIANO CONCEERTO
  MUSICORD PUBLICATIONS, INC. 1.00
MOESCHINGER
 KONZERT NO. 02 FUR KLAVIER UND KAMMERORCHESTER, OP. 23,
 CLAVIERAUSZUG
  SCHOTT 3275 3.75
MOHAUPT, R.
 CONCERTO -- 1938, REV. 1942
  ASSOCIATED MUSIC PUBLISHERS, INC. AMP 3.25
MONTANI
 CONCERTINO IN E
  FRANCO COLOMBO PUBLICATIONS 124916 2.75
MONTGOMERY, B.
 CONCERT WALTZ
  NOVELLO AND COMPANY, LTD. 10.0165.05 1.90
MONTI, V. *
 CZARDAS
  CARL FISCHER, INC. P 2005 1.25
MONTSALVATGE, X.
 CONCERTO BREVE FOR PIANO AND ORCHESTRA
  PEER SOUTHERN ORGANIZATION 05.50
MORAWETZ
 PIANO CONCERTO NO. 01
  MCA MUSIC 4.00
MORGAN--ED. * MORGAN *
 KITTEN ON THE KEYS
  BELWIN-MILLS PUBLISHING CORPORATION 27017 1.50
MORLEY *   MEDIUM
 BABY BOOGIE
  SHAWNEE PRESS, INC. 2.00
MORTARI
 FANTASIA
  FRANCO COLOMBO PUBLICATIONS FOR.11977 6.00
MOSCHELES, I.
 PIANO CONCERTO NO. 03 IN G MINOR, OP. 58
  MUSIC TREASURE PUBLICATIONS 5.00
MOSZKOWSKI KRAMER 4
 BOLERO, OP. 12 NO. 5
  BOSTON MUSIC COMPANY 1.50
MOSZKOWSKI   D
 CONCERTO IN E, OP. 59
  C. F. PETERS CORPORATION 2872 3.50
MOSZKOWSKI WOLFF, B.
 FIVE SPANISH DANCES, OP. 12 -- SET
  G. SCHIRMER, INC. L1777 1.50
MOUSSORGSKY PATTISON
 CORONATION SCENE -- FROM ''BORIS GODOUNOFF'' -- SET
  G. SCHIRMER, INC. 1.75
MOUSSORGSKY GRAETZER
 GOPAK
  FRANCO COLOMBO PUBLICATIONS BA9702 .75
MOZART, W. A. OMIZZOLO
 ADAGIO AND ALLEGRO FOR MECHANICAL ORGAN, K594
  FRANCO COLOMBO PUBLICATIONS 128761 1.00
MOZART, W. A. BADURA-SKODA
 ALLEGRETTO AND ALLEGRO IN E FLAT -- SET
  G. SCHIRMER, INC. L1840 1.75
MOZART, W. A. MAIER
 ALLEGRO, FROM SONATINA IN B FLAT FOR PIANO AND VIOLIN
  CARL FISCHER, INC. P 1969 1.00
MOZART, W. A. MAIER
 ANDANTE AND MINUET, FROM SONATINA IN F FOR PIANO AND VIOLIN
  CARL FISCHER, INC. P 1970 1.00
MOZART, W. A. STEINER
 ANDANTE FROM SYMPHONY NO. 39
  BELWIN-MILLS PUBLISHING CORPORATION 1.25
MOZART, W. A.
 CADENZAS FOR K365
  INTERNATIONAL MUSIC COMPANY 1.00
MOZART, W. A. LANDOWSKA, W.
 CADENZA - CONCERTO K271 IN E FLAT
  BROUDE BROTHERS LTD. 01.75
MOZART, W. A. LANDOWSKA, W.
 CADENZA - CONCERTO K413 IN F
  BROUDE BROTHERS LTD. 01.75
MOZART, W. A. LANDOWSKA, W.
 CADENZA - CONCERTO K414 IN A
  BROUDE BROTHERS LTD. 01.75
MOZART, W. A. LANDOWSKA, W.
 CADENZA - CONCERTO K466 IN D MINOR
  BROUDE BROTHERS LTD. 02.00
MOZART, W. A. LANDOWSKA, W.
 CADENZA - CONCERTO K482 IN E FLAT
  BROUDE BROTHERS LTD. 02.00
MOZART, W. A. LANDOWSKA, W.
 CADENZA - CONCERTO K537 IN D
  BROUDE BROTHERS LTD. 02.00
MOZART, W. A.   M
 CONCERTI K.271, 450, 466, 467, 482, 488, 491, 537
  C. F. PETERS CORPORATION 765 12.00
MOZART, W. A.
 CONCERTO IN E FLAT, K365 FOR 2 PIANOS AND ORCHESTRA
  INTERNATIONAL MUSIC COMPANY 3.75
MOZART, W. A. BALSAM
 CONCERTO K037 IN F
  OXFORD UNIVERSITY PRESS 32.143 3.30
MOZART, W. A. BALSAM
 CONCERTO K039 IN B FLAT
  OXFORD UNIVERSITY PRESS 32.144 3.30
MOZART, W. A. BALSAM
 CONCERTO K041 IN G
  OXFORD UNIVERSITY PRESS 32.146 3.30
MOZART, W. A. BALSAM
 CONCERTO K043 IN D
  OXFORD UNIVERSITY PRESS 32.145 3.30
MOZART, W. A.
 CONCERTO K175 IN D --ORCH RED--
  ASSOCIATED MUSIC PUBLISHERS, INC. BRH 1.50
MOZART, W. A.
 CONCERTO K175 IN D --SOLO ONLY--
  ASSOCIATED MUSIC PUBLISHERS, INC. BRH 1.50

MOZART, W. A.   M
 CONCERTO K175 IN D MAJOR --CADENZA BY S. STRAVINSKY--
  C. F. PETERS CORPORATION 6391 2.00
MOZART, W. A.   M
 CONCERTO K238 IN B FLAT --CADENZA BY S. STRAVINSKY--
  C. F. PETERS CORPORATION 6392 2.00
MOZART, W. A.
 CONCERTO K238 IN B FLAT --ORCH RED--
  ASSOCIATED MUSIC PUBLISHERS, INC. BRH 1.50
MOZART, W. A.
 CONCERTO K238 IN B FLAT --SOLO ONLY--
  ASSOCIATED MUSIC PUBLISHERS, INC. BRH 1.50
MOZART, W. A.
 CONCERTO K246 IN C --ORCH RED--
  ASSOCIATED MUSIC PUBLISHERS, INC. BRH 1.50
MOZART, W. A.
 CONCERTO K246 IN C --SOLO ONLY--
  ASSOCIATED MUSIC PUBLISHERS, INC. BRH 1.50
MOZART, W. A. PHILIPP, I.
 CONCERTO K246 IN C
  G. SCHIRMER, INC. L1791 1.50
MOZART, W. A. PHILIPP
 CONCERTO K246 IN C
  G. SCHIRMER, INC. L1791 1.50
MOZART, W. A.
 CONCERTO K271 IN E FLAT
  INTERNATIONAL MUSIC COMPANY 2.50
MOZART, W. A.
 CONCERTO K271 IN E FLAT
  EDWIN F. KALMUS 3712 2.00
MOZART, W. A.   M
 CONCERTO K271 IN E FLAT
  C. F. PETERS CORPORATION 3309F 1.50
MOZART, W. A. PHILIPP, I.
 CONCERTO K271 IN E FLAT
  G. SCHIRMER, INC. L1734 1.50
MOZART, W. A. PHILIPP
 CONCERTO K271 IN E FLAT
  G. SCHIRMER, INC. L1704 1.50
MOZART, W. A.
 CONCERTO K365 IN E FLAT, FOR TWO PIANOS
  EDWIN F. KALMUS 3702 3.00
MOZART, W. A.   M
 CONCERTO K365 IN E FLAT --TWO COPIES--
  C. F. PETERS CORPORATION 2212 3.00
MOZART, W. A.
 CONCERTO K382 IN D
  INTERNATIONAL MUSIC COMPANY 1.50
MOZART, W. A.
 CONCERTO K413 IN F --ORCH RED--
  ASSOCIATED MUSIC PUBLISHERS, INC. BRH 1.50
MOZART, W. A.
 CONCERTO K413 IN F --SOLO ONLY--
  ASSOCIATED MUSIC PUBLISHERS, INC. BRH 1.50
MOZART, W. A. HINZE * M
 CONCERTO K413 IN F
  C. F. PETERS CORPORATION 9046 4.50
MOZART, W. A. PHILIPP, I.
 CONCERTO K413 IN F
  G. SCHIRMER, INC. L1788 1.50
MOZART, W. A. PHILIPP
 CONCERTO K413 IN F
  G. SCHIRMER, INC. L1788 1.50
MOZART, W. A.
 CONCERTO K414 IN A
  INTERNATIONAL MUSIC COMPANY 2.00
MOZART, W. A.
 CONCERTO K414 IN A
  EDWIN F. KALMUS 3713 2.00
MOZART, W. A. HINZE * M
 CONCERTO K414 IN A
  C. F. PETERS CORPORATION 9028 4.50
MOZART, W. A. PHILIPP, I.
 CONCERTO K414 IN A
  G. SCHIRMER, INC. L1731 1.50
MOZART, W. A. PHILIPP
 CONCERTO K414 IN A
  G. SCHIRMER, INC. L1731 1.50
MOZART, W. A.
 CONCERTO K415 IN C --ORCH RED--
  ASSOCIATED MUSIC PUBLISHERS, INC. BRH 1.50
MOZART, W. A.
 CONCERTO K415 IN C --SOLO ONLY--
  ASSOCIATED MUSIC PUBLISHERS, INC. BRH 1.50
MOZART, W. A. HINZE * M
 CONCERTO K415 IN C
  C. F. PETERS CORPORATION 9080 4.50
MOZART, W. A. PHILIPP
 CONCERTO K415 IN C
  G. SCHIRMER, INC. L1789 1.50
MOZART, W. A. PHILIPP, I.
 CONCERTO K415 IN G
  G. SCHIRMER, INC. L1789 1.50
MOZART, W. A.
 CONCERTO K449 IN E FLAT
  INTERNATIONAL MUSIC COMPANY 2.00
MOZART, W. A. HINZE * M
 CONCERTO K449 IN E FLAT
  C. F. PETERS CORPORATION 4601 1.50
MOZART, W. A. PHILIPP, I.
 CONCERTO K449 IN E FLAT
  G. SCHIRMER, INC. L1756 1.25
MOZART, W. A. PHILIPP
 CONCERTO K449 IN E FLAT
  G. SCHIRMER, INC. L1756 1.25
MOZART, W. A.
 CONCERTO K450 IN B FLAT --ORCH RED--
  ASSOCIATED MUSIC PUBLISHERS, INC. BRH 1.50
MOZART, W. A.
 CONCERTO K450 IN B FLAT --SOLO ONLY--
  ASSOCIATED MUSIC PUBLISHERS, INC. BRH 1.50
MOZART, W. A.
 CONCERTO K450 IN B FLAT
  INTERNATIONAL MUSIC COMPANY 2.00
MOZART, W. A.
 CONCERTO K450 IN B FLAT
  EDWIN F. KALMUS 3714 2.00
MOZART, W. A.   M
 CONCERTO K450 IN B FLAT
  C. F. PETERS CORPORATION 3309G 1.50
MOZART, W. A. PHILIPP, I.
 CONCERTO K450 IN B FLAT
  G. SCHIRMER, INC. L1746 1.50
MOZART, W. A. PHILIPP
 CONCERTO K450 IN B FLAT
  G. SCHIRMER, INC. L1746 1.50

MOZART, W. A.
    CONCERTO K451 IN D --ORCH RED--
        ASSOCIATED MUSIC PUBLISHERS, INC.   BRH   1.50
MOZART, W. A.
    CONCERTO K451 IN D --SOLO ONLY--
        ASSOCIATED MUSIC PUBLISHERS, INC.   BRH   1.50
MOZART, W. A.
    CONCERTO K453 IN G --ORCH RED--
        ASSOCIATED MUSIC PUBLISHERS, INC.   BRH   1.50
MOZART, W. A.
    CONCERTO K453 IN G --SOLO ONLY--
        ASSOCIATED MUSIC PUBLISHERS, INC.   BRH   1.50
MOZART, W. A.
    CONCERTO K453 IN G
        INTERNATIONAL MUSIC COMPANY   2.00
MOZART, W. A.   PHILIPP, I.
    CONCERTO K453 IN G
        G. SCHIRMER, INC.   L1734   1.75
MOZART, W. A.   PHILIPP
    CONCERTO K453 IN G
        G. SCHIRMER, INC.   M-D L1734   1.75
MOZART, W. A.
    CONCERTO K456 IN B FLAT --CADENZAS BY MOZART AND MUELLER--
        C. F. PETERS CORPORATION   H707   2.50
MOZART, W. A.   PHILIPP, I.
    CONCERTO K456 IN B FLAT
        INTERNATIONAL MUSIC COMPANY   2.50
MOZART, W. A.   PHILIPP, I.
    CONCERTO K456 IN B FLAT
        G. SCHIRMER, INC.   L1823   2.50
MOZART, W. A.   HINZE *
    CONCERTO K459 IN F --ORCH RED--
        ASSOCIATED MUSIC PUBLISHERS, INC.   BRH   1.50
MOZART, W. A.   HINZE *
    CONCERTO K459 IN F --SET--
        ASSOCIATED MUSIC PUBLISHERS, INC.   BRH   3.50
MOZART, W. A.   HINZE *
    CONCERTO K459 IN F --SOLO ONLY--
        ASSOCIATED MUSIC PUBLISHERS, INC.   BRH   1.50
MOZART, W. A.   PHILIPP, I.
    CONCERTO K459 IN F
        G. SCHIRMER, INC.   L1701   2.00
MOZART, W. A.   PHILIPP
    CONCERTO K459 IN F
        G. SCHIRMER, INC.   L1701   2.00
MOZART, W. A.   MONTANI
    CONCERTO K465 IN C
        FRANCO COLOMBO PUBLICATIONS   ER2458   1.75
MOZART, W. A.   BECK
    CONCERTO K466 IN A - PIANO REDUCTION
        BARENREITER VERLAG   BA 4740A 4.50
MOZART, W. A.
    CONCERTO K466 IN D MINOR --ORCH RED--
        ASSOCIATED MUSIC PUBLISHERS, INC.   BRH   1.00
MOZART, W. A.
    CONCERTO K466 IN D MINOR --SOLO ONLY--
        ASSOCIATED MUSIC PUBLISHERS, INC.   BRH   1.00
MOZART, W. A.   MONTANI
    CONCERTO K466 IN D MINOR
        FRANCO COLOMBO PUBLICATIONS   ER2460   2.50
MOZART, W. A.
    CONCERTO K466 IN D MINOR
        INTERNATIONAL MUSIC COMPANY   2.50
MOZART, W. A.
    CONCERTO K466 IN D MINOR
        EDWIN F. KALMUS   3715   2.00
MOZART, W. A.   M
    CONCERTO K466 IN D MINOR
        C. F. PETERS CORPORATION   2897D   1.50
MOZART, W. A.   KULLAK, T.
    CONCERTO K466 IN D MINOR
        G. SCHIRMER, INC.   L661   1.50
MOZART, W. A.   KULLAK, T.
    CONCERTO K466 IN D MINOR
        G. SCHIRMER, INC.   L661   1.50
MOZART, W. A.
    CONCERTO K467 IN C --ORCH RED--
        ASSOCIATED MUSIC PUBLISHERS, INC.   BRH   1.50
MOZART, W. A.
    CONCERTO K467 IN C --SOLO ONLY--
        ASSOCIATED MUSIC PUBLISHERS, INC.   BRH   1.50
MOZART, W. A.
    CONCERTO K467 IN C
        EDWIN F. KALMUS   3716   2.00
MOZART, W. A.   M
    CONCERTO K467 IN C
        C. F. PETERS CORPORATION   2897E   1.50
MOZART, W. A.   BISCHOFF
    CONCERTO K467 IN C
        G. SCHIRMER, INC.   L661   1.75
MOZART, W. A.   BISCHOFF
    CONCERTO K467 IN C
        G. SCHIRMER, INC.   L662   1.75
MOZART, W. A.
    CONCERTO K482 IN E FLAT --ORCH RED--
        ASSOCIATED MUSIC PUBLISHERS, INC.   BRH   1.50
MOZART, W. A.
    CONCERTO K482 IN E FLAT --SOLO ONLY--
        ASSOCIATED MUSIC PUBLISHERS, INC.   BRH   2.00
MOZART, W. A.   M
    CONCERTO K482 IN E FLAT --W. HUMMEL CADENZAS--
        C. F. PETERS CORPORATION   3826   1.50
MOZART, W. A.
    CONCERTO K482 IN E FLAT
        EDWIN F. KALMUS   3717   2.00
MOZART, W. A.   BISCHOFF
    CONCERTO K482 IN E FLAT
        G. SCHIRMER, INC.   L663   1.50
MOZART, W. A.   BISCHOFF
    CONCERTO K482 IN E FLAT
        G. SCHIRMER, INC.   L663   1.50
MOZART, W. A.   MONTANI
    CONCERTO K488 IN A
        FRANCO COLOMBO PUBLICATIONS   ER2459   2.25
MOZART, W. A.
    CONCERTO K488 IN A
        EDWIN F. KALMUS   3718   2.00
MOZART, W. A.   M
    CONCERTO K488 IN A
        C. F. PETERS CORPORATION   3309E   1.50
MOZART, W. A.   M
    CONCERTO K488 IN A
        C. F. PETERS CORPORATION   3309EE   1.25
MOZART, W. A.   YORK
    CONCERTO K488 IN A
        G. SCHIRMER, INC.   L1584   1.50

MOZART, W. A.   YORK
    CONCERTO K488 IN A
        G. SCHIRMER, INC.   L1584   1.50
MOZART, W. A.
    CONCERTO K491 IN C MINOR --ORCH RED--
        ASSOCIATED MUSIC PUBLISHERS, INC.   BRH   1.50
MOZART, W. A.
    CONCERTO K491 IN C MINOR --SOLO ONLY--
        ASSOCIATED MUSIC PUBLISHERS, INC.   BRH   1.50
MOZART, W. A.   BECK
    CONCERTO K491 IN C MINOR - PIANO REDUCTION
        BARENREITER VERLAG   BA 4741A 4.50
MOZART, W. A.
    CONCERTO K491 IN C MINOR
        EDWIN F. KALMUS   3719   2.00
MOZART, W. A.   M
    CONCERTO K491 IN C MINOR
        C. F. PETERS CORPORATION   3309H   1.50
MOZART, W. A.   BISCHOFF
    CONCERTO K491 IN C MINOR
        G. SCHIRMER, INC.   L664   1.50
MOZART, W. A.   BISCHOFF
    CONCERTO K491 IN C MINOR
        G. SCHIRMER, INC.   L664   1.50
MOZART, W. A.   KING, A. H.   M
    CONCERTO K503 IN C --W. PH. K. HOFFMANN CADENZA--
        C. F. PETERS CORPORATION   H683   2.50
MOZART, W. A.   BECK
    CONCERTO K503 IN C - PIANO REDUCTION
        BARENREITER VERLAG   BA 4742A 6.00
MOZART, W. A.
    CONCERTO K503 IN C
        INTERNATIONAL MUSIC COMPANY   2.50
MOZART, W. A.   PHILIPP, I.
    CONCERTO K503 IN C
        G. SCHIRMER, INC.   L1786   1.75
MOZART, W. A.   PHILIPP
    CONCERTO K503 IN C
        G. SCHIRMER, INC.   L1786   1.75
MOZART, W. A.   REHBERG
    CONCERTO K537 IN D--'CORONATION'
        G. SCHIRMER, INC.   L665   1.50
MOZART, W. A.   REHBERG
    CONCERTO K537 IN D -- ''CORONATION''
        G. SCHIRMER, INC.   L665   1.50
MOZART, W. A.
    CONCERTO K537 IN D 'CORONATION' --ORCH RED--
        ASSOCIATED MUSIC PUBLISHERS, INC.   BRH   1.50
MOZART, W. A.
    CONCERTO K537 IN D 'CORONATION' --SOLO ONLY--
        ASSOCIATED MUSIC PUBLISHERS, INC.   BRH   1.50
MOZART, W. A.
    CONCERTO K537 IN D
        EDWIN F. KALMUS   3720   2.00
MOZART, W. A.   M
    CONCERTO K537 IN D
        C. F. PETERS CORPORATION   2897F   1.50
MOZART, W. A.
    CONCERTO K595 IN B FLAT --ORCH RED--
        ASSOCIATED MUSIC PUBLISHERS, INC.   BRH   1.50
MOZART, W. A.
    CONCERTO K595 IN B FLAT --SOLO ONLY--
        ASSOCIATED MUSIC PUBLISHERS, INC.   BRH   1.50
MOZART, W. A.
    CONCERTO K595 IN B FLAT
        ASSOCIATED MUSIC PUBLISHERS, INC.   BRH   3.50
MOZART, W. A.
    CONCERTO K595 IN B FLAT
        INTERNATIONAL MUSIC COMPANY   2.50
MOZART, W. A.   PHILIPP, I.
    CONCERTO K595 IN B FLAT
        G. SCHIRMER, INC.   L1721   2.00
MOZART, W. A.   PHILIPP
    CONCERTO K595 IN B FLAT
        G. SCHIRMER, INC.   L1721   2.00
MOZART, W. A.
    CONCERT RONDO, K382
        ASSOCIATED MUSIC PUBLISHERS, INC.   BRH   2.25
MOZART, W. A.   FISHERMAN, M.
    CONCERT RONDO IN D, K382
        G. SCHIRMER, INC.   1.00
MOZART, W. A.   SAAR
    DOUBLE CONCERTO IN E FLAT, K365
        G. SCHIRMER, INC.   3.50
MOZART, W. A.   SAAR
    DOUBLE CONCERTO K365 IN E FLAT
        G. SCHIRMER, INC.   3.50
MOZART, W. A.   BUSONI
    FANTASIA FOR MUSICAL CLOCKWORK
        INTEPNATIONAL MUSIC COMPANY   2.50
MOZART, W. A.   MILLER, R.
    FANTASIA IN F MINOR
        NOVELLO AND COMPANY, LTD.   10.0166.03 2.00
MOZART, W. A.   BUSONI
    FANTASY FOR A MUSICAL CLOCK, K608
        ASSOCIATED MUSIC PUBLISHERS, INC.   BRH   1.50
MOZART, W. A.   MARCHI, G.
    FUGA IN DO MINORE, K426
        EDIZIONI BERBEN   1502   2.40
MOZART, W. A.   KRAUSE, A.
    FUGUE IN C MINOR, K426 AND SONATA K448 IN D
        ASSOCIATED MUSIC PUBLISHERS, INC.   BRH   2.50
MOZART, W. A.   ROBYN   3 1/2
    KINDER CONCERTO
        THEODORE PRESSER COMPANY   1.25
MOZART, W. A.   BECK   4
    KLAVIERKONZERT IN A, K488, KLAVIERAUSZUG
        BARENREITER VERLAG   BA 4740A
MOZART, W. A.   BECK   4
    KLAVIERKONZERT IN A, K488
        BARENREITER VERLAG   BA 4740
MOZART, W. A.   BECK   4
    KLAVIERKONZERT IN A, K488
        BARENREITER VERLAG   BA 4740A
MOZART, W. A.   BECK   4
    KLAVIERKONZERT IN C, K503, KLAVIERAUSZUG
        BARENREITER VERLAG   BA 4742A
MOZART, W. A.   BECK   4
    KLAVIERKONZERT IN C, K503
        BARENREITER VERLAG   BA 4742
MOZART, W. A.   BECK   4
    KLAVIERKONZERT IN C, K503
        BARENREITER VERLAG   BA 4742A
MOZART, W. A.   BECK   4
    KLAVIERKONZERT IN C MINOR, K491, KLAVIERAUSZUG
        BARENREITER VERLAG   BA 4741A

MOZART, W. A.   BECK   4
KLAVIERKONZERT IN C MINOR, K491
    BARENREITER VERLAG   BA 4741
MOZART, W. A.   BECK   4
KLAVIERKONZERT IN C MINOR, K491
    BARENREITER VERLAG   BA 4741A
MOZART, W. A.
KONZERT-RONDO A-DUR, K.V. 386 FUR KLAVIER UND ORCHESTER,
KLAVIERAUSZUG
    SCHOTT   5187   2.25
MOZART, W. A.   BADURA-SKODA *
KONZERT-RONDO A-DUR -- K.V. 386 FUR KLAVIER UND ORCHESTER,
KLAVIERAUSZUG
    SCHOTT   5187   2.25
MOZART, W. A.   WOLLHEIM
KONZERT FUR CEMBALO MIT STREICH-ORCHESTER -- K.V. 107 D-DUR
    SCHOTT   1601   3.25
MOZART, W. A.   WOLLHEIM
KONZERT FUR CEMBALO MIT STREICH-ORCHESTER ES-DUR
    SCHOTT   1603   3.25
MOZART, W. A.   WOLLHEIM
KONZERT FUR CEMBALO MIT STREICH-ORCHESTER G-DUR
    SCHOTT   1602   3.25
MOZART, W. A.   CROLL, G.
LARGHETTO AND ALLEGRO IN E FLAT
    BARENREITER VERLAG   BA 4754   3.50
MOZART, W. A.   CROLL, G.   3
LARGHETTO UND ALLEGRO IN E FLAT FUR 2 KLAVIERE -- OHNE KV-NUMMER
--
    BARENREITER VERLAG   BA 4754
MOZART, W. A.   WAGNER
LODRON CONCERTO K242 --SET--
    G. SCHIRMER, INC.   L1578   1.50
MOZART, W. A.   WAGNER
LODRON CONCERTO K242
    G. SCHIRMER, INC.   L1578   1.50
MOZART, W. A.   BUSONI
MAGIC FLUTE, THE -- OVERTURE
    ASSOCIATED MUSIC PUBLISHERS, INC.   BRH   1.00
MOZART, W. A.   E
MASONIC FUNERAL MUSIC, K477
    C. F. PETERS CORPORATION   N964   1.25
MOZART, W. A.   PHILIPP
MINUET BY MOZART, A
    FRANCO COLOMBO PUBLICATIONS   SAL   1.75
MOZART, W. A.   DUNGAN   3
MINUET FROM 'DON GIOVANNI'
    BOSTON MUSIC COMPANY   .75
MOZART, W. A.   HAUPT, L. VON
MINUET FROM 'DON GIOVANNI'
    BELWIN-MILLS PUBLISHING CORPORATION 27034   .50
MOZART, W. A.   STEINER   EASY
MINUET FROM SERENADE IN G
    ELKAN-VOGEL, INC.   .70
MOZART, W. A.   E-M
MUSICAL JOKE, K522
    C. F. PETERS CORPORATION   N965   2.00
MOZART, W. A.
ORIGINAL COMPOSITIONS FOR TWO PIANOS, FOUR HANDS
    EDWIN F. KALMUS   3722   3.50
MOZART, W. A.   BUSONI
OVERTURE, 'THE MAGIC FLUTE'
    INTERNATIONAL MUSIC COMPANY   2.50
MOZART, W. A.
ROMANCE FROM 'A LITTLE NIGHT MUSIC'
    OXFORD UNIVERSITY PRESS   35.400   2.00
MOZART, W. A.   EINSTEIN, A.
RONDO IN A, K386
    UNIVERSAL EDITION   10776   2.60
MOZART, W. A.
SONATA AND FUGUE, K448 AND K426
    INTERNATIONAL MUSIC COMPANY   3.50
MOZART, W. A.   M
SONATA AND FUGUE --K448, 426--, WITH ADAGIO --K546--
    C. F. PETERS CORPORATION   1327   2.00
MOZART, W. A.   KRAUSE, A.
SONATA K448 IN D AND FUGUE IN C MINOR, K426 --SET--
    ASSOCIATED MUSIC PUBLISHERS, INC.   BRH   3.50
MOZART, W. A.   HUGHES
SONATA K448 IN D AND FUGUE IN C MINOR, K426 --SET--
    G. SCHIRMER, INC.   L1504   3.50
MOZART, W. A. *
SONATA K545 IN C
    EDWIN F. KALMUS   3721   1.25
MOZART, W. A.   M
SYMPHONY NO. 41 IN C, K551
    C. F. PETERS CORPORATION   3467A   7.50
MOZART, W. A.   RHEINBERGER
THEME AND VARIATIONS IN F, K613 --SET--
    ASSOCIATED MUSIC PUBLISHERS, INC.   LEU   8.25
MOZART, W. A.   SCHMID   3-4
WERKE FUR 2 KLAVIERE, K488 UND 426 -- NEUE MOZART-AUSGABE --
    BARENREITER VERLAG   BA 4501
MOZART, W. A.
WORKS FOR 2 PIANOS KV 448 AND 426
    BARENREITER VERLAG   BA 4501   10.00
MUTHEL, J. G.   KREUTZ
SONATA IN E FLAT -- ''DUETTO''
    ASSOCIATED MUSIC PUBLISHERS, INC.   NAG   3.25
MUTHEL, J. G.   KREUTZ
SONATA
    BARENREITER VERLAG   NMA 176   6.00
MUTHEL, J. G.   KREUTZ   3-4
SONATE -- DUETTO --
    BARENREITER VERLAG   NMA 176
MYSLIVECEK   FENDLER
CONCERTO NO. 02
    BOOSEY AND HAWKES, INC.   1.75
NAGY, M.   4
CAPRICE
    LEE ROBERTS MUSIC PUBLICATIONS, INC.   1.00
NAGY, M.   5
FANFARE AND MARCH
    LEE ROBERTS MUSIC PUBLICATIONS, INC.   .85
NAGY, M.   5
WALTZ
    LEE ROBERTS MUSIC PUBLICATIONS, INC.   .50
NAPOLITANO
HUELLA
    FRANCO COLOMBO PUBLICATIONS   BA10898   1.50
NAT, Y.
CONCERTO FOR PIANO AND ORCH. -- PNO. SOLO
    EDITIONS MUSICALES TRANSATLANTIQUES   12.00
NAT, Y.
CONCERTO
    EDITIONS MUSICALES TRANSATLANTIQUES   12.00

NEVIN--ED.   NEVIN
VOICES OF SPRING
    BELWIN-MILLS PUBLISHING CORPORATION 28134   1.00
NEVIN
ALL AMERICAN MEDLEY
    BELWIN-MILLS PUBLISHING CORPORATION 28099   1.00
NEVIN
ALL AMERICAN MEDLEY
    BELWIN-MILLS PUBLISHING CORPORATION 28099   1.00
NEVIN   3 1/2
BUONA NOTTE, FROM 'DAY IN VENICE'
    THEODORE PRESSER COMPANY   1.25
NEVIN   4
COUNTRY DANCE
    BOSTON MUSIC COMPANY   .90
NEVIN
FUN WITH A FUGUE
    BELWIN-MILLS PUBLISHING CORPORATION 28098   1.00
NEVIN   3 1/2
GONDOLIERS, OP. 25, NO. 2 FROM 'A DAY IN VENICE SUITE'
    THEODORE PRESSER COMPANY   1.25
NEVIN   E
HOPAK -- SECOND PIANO PART
    BELWIN-MILLS PUBLISHING CORPORATION 28136   .60
NEVIN   E
JOLLY FINGERS -- SECOND PIANO PART
    BELWIN-MILLS PUBLISHING CORPORATION 28123   .60
NEVIN   E
KRISS KROSS KAPERS -- SECOND PIANO PART
    BELWIN-MILLS PUBLISHING CORPORATION 28142   .60
NEVIN
LITTLE MAJORETTE
    BELWIN-MILLS PUBLISHING CORPORATION 28110   .75
NEVIN
MOZART MINUET
    BELWIN-MILLS PUBLISHING CORPORATION 28124   .85
NEVIN   HULL *   4
NARCISSUS
    BOSTON MUSIC COMPANY   1.50
NEVIN   HULL *   4
ROSARY, THE
    BOSTON MUSIC COMPANY   .75
NEVIN
TAP DANCE
    BELWIN-MILLS PUBLISHING CORPORATION 3-4 28125 .85
NICHELMANN   BITTNER   3-4
KONZERT IN A FUR CEMBALO -- KLAVIER -- UND STREICHER
    BARENREITER VERLAG   NMA 145
NICHOLS, J. H.
ROUNDELAY -- SET
    G. SCHIRMER, INC.   1.00
NIELSEN, R.   M-D
SONATA
    FRANCO COLOMBO PUBLICATIONS   BON.2376 5.25
NIEMANN
CHAMBER CONCERTO NO. 1 IN C, OP. 153
    C. F. PETERS CORPORATION   4477   6.00
NIEMANN   STONE
SINGING FOUNTAIN, THE OP. 30
    EDWARD B. MARKS MUSIC CORPORATION   01.75
NILES, J.
MY LITTLE MOHEE, A FAMILY FOLKSONG -- KENTUCKY -- SET
    G. SCHIRMER, INC.   .75
NIN-CULMELL, J.
CONCERTO
    ASSOCIATED MUSIC PUBLISHERS, INC.   ESC   9.00
NORDMAN--ED.   NORDMAN
MODERN PIANIST DUO-PIANO SERIES
    POINTER PUBLICATIONS   1.95
NOVAK   4
KONZERT FUR 2 KLAVIERE UND ORCHESTER
    BARENREITER VERLAG   CHF 5087
OBOUSSIER   4
KONZERT FUR KLAVIER UND ORCHESTER
    BARENREITER VERLAG   BA 2470
OERTZEN, R. VON
CONCERT LYRIQUE FOR HARPSICHORD
    ASSOCIATED MUSIC PUBLISHERS, INC.   SIM   2.75
OLIVIERO *
MORE
    EDWARD B. MARKS MUSIC CORPORATION   02.00
OMIZZOLO
FANTASIA
    FRANCO COLOMBO PUBLICATIONS   128696   1.25
OTAKA, H.
MIDARE
    ONGAKU NO TOMO SHA   4.50
PADEREWSKI, I. J.
CONCERTO IN A MINOR, OP. 17
    ASSOCIATED MUSIC PUBLISHERS, INC.   BOT   5.00
PADEREWSKI, I. J.   PALMER   4
MINUET
    WILLIS MUSIC COMPANY   .75
PADEREWSKI, I. J.
POLISH FANTASY, OP. 19
    ASSOCIATED MUSIC PUBLISHERS, INC.   BOT   10.75
PAISIELLO, G.   TINTORI
CONCERTO IN F
    FRANCO COLOMBO PUBLICATIONS   130482   2.75
PALMER
SONATA FOR 2 PIANOS
    PEER SOUTHERN ORGANIZATION   04.50
PANIZZA
THEME AND VARIATIONS
    FRANCO COLOMBO PUBLICATIONS   BA9334   4.00
PANUFNIK, A.
CONCERTO
    BOOSEY AND HAWKES, INC.   5.00
PARCHMAN, G.
CONCERTO FOR PIANO 4-HANDS AND ORCHESTRA
    SEESAW MUSIC CORPORATION   22.00
PARCHMAN, G.
ELEGY FOR TWO PIANOS, 1963
    SEESAW MUSIC CORPORATION   3.00
PASQUINI   CANINO, B.
SONATA NO. 10 IN E MINOR
    EDIZIONI BERBEN   EB 1312   1.20
PASQUINI
SONATA
    NOVELLO AND COMPANY, LTD.   10.0167.01 1.40
PATTISON
ARKANSAS TRAVELER, THE -- OLD FIDDLER'S TUNE, FREELY ARR.
    G. SCHIRMER, INC.   .90
PEDROLLO
CASTELLI DI GIULIETTA E ROMEO
    FRANCO COLOMBO PUBLICATIONS   Z4363   5.25

PEPPING, E.   4
   KONZERT FUR KLAVIER UND ORCHESTER
      BARENREITER VERLAG   BA 2278
PERAGALLO, M.
   CONCERTO
      UNIVERSAL EDITION   UE 12049   6.80
PERSICHETTI
   PIANO CONCERTO, OP. 90
      ELKAN-VOGEL, INC.   6.00
PETYREK, F.
   SIX CONCERTO ETUDES
      EDIZIONI BERBEN   EB 10251   3.40
PETYREK, F.
   TOCCATA AND FUGUE
      UNIVERSAL EDITION   UE 10275   3.40
PFEIFFER, A.   STEGLICH   2-3
   KONZERT FUR CEMBALO -- KLAVIER -- UND STREICHER
      BARENREITER VERLAG   NMA 79
PFITZER, H.   3
   SPANISH DANCE
      WILLIS MUSIC COMPANY   .75
PFITZNER, H.
   CONCERTO IN E FLAT, OP. 31
      BOOSEY AND HAWKES, INC.   5.00
PHILIPP, I.
   FEUX-FOLLETS -- JACK O'LANTERNS -- OP. 24 NO. 3 -- SET
      G. SCHIRMER, INC.   1.00
PHILLIPS, D.
   CONCERTO IN JAZZ
      BELWIN-MILLS PUBLISHING CORPORATION   3.50
PHILLIPS, D.
   CONCERTO IN JAZZ
      BELWIN-MILLS PUBLISHING CORPORATION   27005   3.50
PHILLIPS, R.
   CHACONNE AND TOCCATA FOR TWO PIANOS
      SEESAW MUSIC CORPORATION   4.00
PHILLIPS, R.
   SONATINA FOR TWO PIANOS
      SEESAW MUSIC CORPORATION   5.00
PICCIOLI
   CONCERTANTE
      UNIVERSAL EDITION   11879   5.25
PIERNE   8
   CONCERTO EN UT MINEUR
      ALPHONSE LEDUC
PIERNE   RIEGGER, W.   EASY
   MARCH OF THE LITTLE LEAD SOLDIERS
      SHAWNEE PRESS, INC.   1.25
PIJPER   D
   CONCERTO
      C. F. PETERS CORPORATION   D415   3.50
PIJPER   D
   SONATA
      C. F. PETERS CORPORATION   D9   2.50
PIKLER
   FIRST NOEL, THE
      BOSTON MUSIC COMPANY   .75
PINTO, O.
   SCENAS INFANTIS -- MEMORIES OF CHILDHOOD
      G. SCHIRMER, INC.   1.25
PISK
   MY PRETTY LITTLE PINK -- A MERRY FUGUE ON A SOUTHERN FOLK TUNE
   -- INCLUDES TWO PARTS
      MCA MUSIC   2.00
PISTON, W.
   CONCERTINO -- 1937
      ASSOCIATED MUSIC PUBLISHERS, INC.   AMP   3.00
PISTON, W.
   CONCERTO FOR 2 PIANOS AND ORCHESTRA -- 3 PNO RED
      ASSOCIATED MUSIC PUBLISHERS, INC.   AMP   4.50
PITFIELD   M-D
   CONCERTO NO. 02 --THE STUDENT--
      C. F. PETERS CORPORATION   H715   2.50
PIZZETTI   ZANON
   CANTI DELLA STAGIONE ALTA
      FRANCO COLOMBO PUBLICATIONS   122911   3.75
PLATT, R.   5
   PASTORALE
      THEODORE PRESSER COMPANY   .90
POLDINI, E.   SAMUELSON
   DANCING DOLL, THE
      BELWIN-MILLS PUBLISHING CORPORATION   1.00
POLDINI, E.   COBURN
   MARCHE MIGNONNE, OP. 15 NO. 2 -- SET
      G. SCHIRMER, INC.   1.00
PONCE, M.
   IDILIO MEXICANO FOR 2 PIANOS
      PEER SOUTHERN ORGANIZATION   02.00
POOT, M.
   CONCERTO
      ASSOCIATED MUSIC PUBLISHERS, INC.   ESC   10.00
POOT, M.
   LEGENDE EPIQUE -- SET
      ASSOCIATED MUSIC PUBLISHERS, INC.   ESC   5.00
PORTNOFF
   SENTIMENTAL PARTING
      BELWIN-MILLS PUBLISHING CORPORATION   1.50
POULENC, F.
   AUBADE
      FRANCO COLOMBO PUBLICATIONS   SAL   8.75
POULENC, F.
   CAPRICCIO
      FRANCO COLOMBO PUBLICATIONS   SAL   8.75
POULENC, F.
   CONCERTO -- 1949 --
      FRANCO COLOMBO PUBLICATIONS   SAL   9.00
POULENC, F.
   CONCERTO IN D MINOR FOR 2 PIANOS AND ORCHESTRA -- SOLO PARTS --
      FRANCO COLOMBO PUBLICATIONS   SAL   6.50
POULENC, F.
   CONCERT CHAMPETRE
      FRANCO COLOMBO PUBLICATIONS   SAL   9.50
POULENC, F.
   ELEGIE, 1959 -- SET
      ASSOCIATED MUSIC PUBLISHERS, INC.   ESC   8.50
POULENC, F.
   EMBARQUEMENT POUR CYTHERE, L' -- VALSE-MUSETTE -- SET
      ASSOCIATED MUSIC PUBLISHERS, INC.   ESC   9.50
POULENC, F.
   SONATA, 1953 -- SET
      ASSOCIATED MUSIC PUBLISHERS, INC.   ESC   14.50
POWELL, J.
   RHAPSODIE NEGRE
      G. SCHIRMER, INC.   3.00
POZZOLI
   ALLEGRO DI CONCERTO
      FRANCO COLOMBO PUBLICATIONS   129804   2.25

POZZOLI
   TARANTELLA
      FRANCO COLOMBO PUBLICATIONS   120087   1.00
PREDIERI, G.
   CHRISTMAS CONCERTO IN G. SCORE/HARPSICHORD SOLO PART
      C. F. PETERS CORPORATION   V154   4.00
PROKOFIEFF   D
   CONCERTO NO. 01, OP. 10
      C. F. PETERS CORPORATION   F26   5.00
PROKOFIEFF   WEBSTER, B.
   CONCERTO NO. 01 IN D FLAT, OP. 10
      INTERNATIONAL MUSIC COMPANY   3.75
PROKOFIEFF
   CONCERTO NO. 02, OP. 16
      BOOSEY AND HAWKES, INC.   3.75
PROKOFIEFF   WEBSTER, B.
   CONCERTO NO. 02 IN G MINOR, OP. 16
      INTERNATIONAL MUSIC COMPANY   3.75
PROKOFIEFF
   CONCERTO NO. 03, OP. 26
      BOOSEY AND HAWKES, INC.   3.75
PROKOFIEFF   PHILIPP, I.
   CONCERTO NO. 03 IN C, OP. 26
      INTERNATIONAL MUSIC COMPANY   3.75
PROKOFIEFF
   CONCERTO NO. 04 FOR THE LEFT HAND, OP. 53
      INTERNATIONAL MUSIC COMPANY   3.75
PROKOFIEFF
   CONCERTO NO. 05, OP. 55
      BOOSEY AND HAWKES, INC.   3.75
PROKOFIEFF
   CONCERTO NO. 05 IN G, OP. 55
      INTERNATIONAL MUSIC COMPANY   3.75
PROKOFIEFF   BAMPTON, R.   3
   GAVOTTE FROM 'CLASSICAL SYMPHONY'
      BOSTON MUSIC COMPANY   1.50
PROKOFIEFF   GUENTHER
   MARCH --LOVE OF THREE ORANGES
      EDWARD B. MARKS MUSIC CORPORATION   01.25
PROKOFIEFF
   PIANO CONCERTO NO. 03
      EDWIN F. KALMUS   3771   3.50
PUCCINI, D.V.M.   ABBADO *
   CONCERTO IN B-FLAT
      FRANCO COLOMBO PUBLICATIONS   130467   2.25
PURCELL, H.   GEEHL
   TRUMPET VOLUNTARY
      BOOSEY AND HAWKES, INC.   .90
PURCELL, H.   DICKINSON
   TWO BOURREES -- SET
      G. SCHIRMER, INC.   1.00
RACHMANINOFF, S.
   CONCERTO NO. 01, OP. 1
      BOOSEY AND HAWKES, INC.   2.00
RACHMANINOFF, S.
   CONCERTO NO. 01, OP. 2
      EDWIN F. KALMUS   3814   2.50
RACHMANINOFF, S.
   CONCERTO NO. 01 IN F SHARP MINOR, OP. 1
      INTERNATIONAL MUSIC COMPANY   3.50
RACHMANINOFF, S.
   CONCERTO NO. 01 IN F SHARP MINOR, OP. 1
      G. SCHIRMER, INC.   L1655   2.00
RACHMANINOFF, S.
   CONCERTO NO. 01 IN F SHARP MINOR, OP. 1
      G. SCHIRMER, INC.   L1655   2.00
RACHMANINOFF, S.
   CONCERTO NO. 02, OP. 18
      BOOSEY AND HAWKES, INC.   2.00
RACHMANINOFF, S.
   CONCERTO NO. 02, OP. 18
      EDWIN F. KALMUS   3815   2.50
RACHMANINOFF, S.   ECKSTEIN
   CONCERTO NO. 02, THEMES FROM ALL 3 MVTS.
      CARL FISCHER, INC.   P 2889   1.00
RACHMANINOFF, S.   ECKSTEIN
   CONCERTO NO. 02, THEME FROM 1ST MOVEMENT
      CARL FISCHER, INC.   S 2313   .50
RACHMANINOFF, S.
   CONCERTO NO. 02 IN C MINOR, OP. 18
      G. SCHIRMER, INC.   L1576   2.00
RACHMANINOFF, S.
   CONCERTO NO. 02 IN C MINOR, OP. 18
      G. SCHIRMER, INC.   L1576   2.00
RACHMANINOFF, S.   PHILIPP, I.
   CONCERTO NO. 02 IN C MINOR, OP. 18
      INTERNATIONAL MUSIC COMPANY   3.50
RACHMANINOFF, S.
   CONCERTO NO. 03, OP. 30
      BOOSEY AND HAWKES, INC.   2.50
RACHMANINOFF, S.
   CONCERTO NO. 03, OP. 30
      EDWIN F. KALMUS   3816   2.50
RACHMANINOFF, S.
   CONCERTO NO. 03 IN D MINOR, OP. 30
      INTERNATIONAL MUSIC COMPANY   3.75
RACHMANINOFF, S.
   CONCERTO NO. 03 IN D MINOR, OP. 30
      G. SCHIRMER, INC.   L1610   2.50
RACHMANINOFF, S.
   CONCERTO NO. 03 IN D MINOR, OP. 30
      G. SCHIRMER, INC.   L1610   2.50
RACHMANINOFF, S.
   CONCERTO NO. 04, OP. 40
      BELWIN-MILLS PUBLISHING CORPORATION   5.00
RACHMANINOFF, S.
   EIGHTEENTH VARIATION -- FROM RAPSODIE ON A THEME BY PAGANINI
      BELWIN-MILLS PUBLISHING CORPORATION   2.00
RACHMANINOFF, S.
   FANTAISIE, OP. 5
      BOOSEY AND HAWKES, INC.   4.50
RACHMANINOFF, S.
   FANTASY -SUITE NO. 1- ,OP. 5
      INTERNATIONAL MUSIC COMPANY   6.00
RACHMANINOFF, S.   BABIN
   FLOODS OF SPRING
      BOOSEY AND HAWKES, INC.   2.00
RACHMANINOFF, S.   BABIN
   IT'S LOVELY HERE
      BOOSEY AND HAWKES, INC.   1.50
RACHMANINOFF, S.   BRANT
   ITALIAN POLKA
      BELWIN-MILLS PUBLISHING CORPORATION   2.00
RACHMANINOFF, S.
   PRELUDE AND GIGUE
      BELWIN-MILLS PUBLISHING CORPORATION   3.00

RACHMANINOFF, S.
    PRELUDE IN C MINOR, WALTZ FROM SUITE, OP. 17, ROMANCE FROM SUITE
    OP. 17, CONCERTO NO. 2, OP. 18
        BELWIN-MILLS PUBLISHING CORPORATION   3.00
RACHMANINOFF, S.
    PRELUDE IN C MINOR
        BELWIN-MILLS PUBLISHING CORPORATION   2.00
RACHMANINOFF, S.   LAMBERT
    RAPSODIE, OP. 43 ON A THEME BY PAGANINI -- ABRIDGED ARRANGEMENT
        BELWIN-MILLS PUBLISHING CORPORATION   2.50
RACHMANINOFF, S.
    RAPSODIE, OP. 43 ON A THEME BY PAGANINI
        BELWIN-MILLS PUBLISHING CORPORATION   4.00
RACHMANINOFF, S.
    SUITE NO. 2, OP. 17
        BOOSEY AND HAWKES, INC.   3.50
RACHMANINOFF, S.
    SYMPHONIC DANCES, OP. 45
        BELWIN-MILLS PUBLISHING CORPORATION   5.00
RACHMANINOFF, S.   GEARHART   ADVANCED
TEARS
        SHAWNEE PRESS, INC.   2.00
RACHMANINOFF, S.   ECKSTEIN
    THEME FROM SECOND PIANO CONCERTO, OP. 18
        CARL FISCHER, INC.   S 2313   .50
RACHMANINOFF, S.   BABIN
VOCALISE
        BOOSEY AND HAWKES, INC.   1.50
RAFF, J.   PESCIO *
GAVOTTE AND MUSETTE--FROM SUITE OP. 200
        G. SCHIRMER, INC.   L1543   1.50
RAFF, J.   PESCIO *
GAVOTTE AND MUSETTE -- FROM THE SUITE, OP. 200 -- SET
        G. SCHIRMER, INC.   L1543   1.50
RAFF, J.   PESCIO, A.
GAVOTTE AND MUSETTE FROM THE SUITE, OP. 200 -- SET
        G. SCHIRMER, INC.   L1543   1.50
RAMEAU   LUBOSHUTZ
GAY MELODY
        BELWIN-MILLS PUBLISHING CORPORATION   1.50
RANDS, B.
ESPRESSIONE IV
        UNIVERSAL EDITION   UE 14156   4.00
RAPHAEL, G.   4
TOCCATA FUR 2 KLAVIERE
        BARENREITER VERLAG   SM 1613
RAPHLING
BAGATELLE CUBANA
        SOUTHERN MUSIC COMPANY   1.00
RAPHLING
ISRAEL RHAPSODY
        SOUTHERN MUSIC COMPANY   5.00
RAPHLING   MD
SQUARE DANCE FROM 'AMERICAN ALBUM'
        THEODORE PRESSER COMPANY   1.25
RAVEL
BOLERO
        ELKAN-VOGEL, INC.   9.25
RAVEL
CONCERTO FOR THE LEFT HAND
        ELKAN-VOGEL, INC.   14.50
RAVEL
CONCERTO IN G
        ELKAN-VOGEL, INC.   7.50
RAVEL
CONCERTO IN G
        ELKAN-VOGEL, INC.   15.00
RAVEL   GARBAN, L.
DAPHNIS AND CHLOE
        ELKAN-VOGEL, INC.   D   15.60
RAVEL   ROQUES, L.
DAPHNIS ET CHLOE
        ELKAN-VOGEL, INC.   D   7.00
RAVEL
INTRODUCTION ET ALLEGRO
        ELKAN-VOGEL, INC.   D   6.25
RAVEL
LA VALSE
        ELKAN-VOGEL, INC.   15.50
RAVEL
MOTHER GOOSE SUITE
        ELKAN-VOGEL, INC.   13.00
RAVEL   CASTELNUOVO-TEDESCO
PAVANE POUR UNE ENFANTE -- INCLUDES TWO PARTS
        MCA MUSIC   2.00
RAVEL
RAPSODIE ESPAGNOLE
        ELKAN-VOGEL, INC.   11.50
RAVINI, E.   SAMUELSON
RAVINI'S SERENADE
        BOOSEY AND HAWKES, INC.   .75
RAWSTHORNE, A.
CONCERTO NO. 01
        OXFORD UNIVERSITY PRESS   32.807   6.25
RAWSTHORNE, A.
CONCERTO NO. 02
        OXFORD UNIVERSITY PRESS   32.807   6.85
RAYMOND, J.
HAVING FUN
        BELWIN-MILLS PUBLISHING CORPORATION   26538   1.00
READ, G.
SONATA DA CHIESA FOR TWO PIANOS
        SEESAW MUSIC CORPORATION   8.00
REBIKOV   REEDER
SIX PIECES FROM ''SILHOUETTES'', OP. 31 -- SET
        G. SCHIRMER, INC.   L1790   1.25
REGER
CONCERTO IN F MINOR, OP. 114
        ASSOCIATED MUSIC PUBLISHERS, INC.   BOT   9.00
REGER
INTRODUCTION, PASSACAGLIA AND FUGUE, OP. 96
        ASSOCIATED MUSIC PUBLISHERS, INC.   BOT   6.50
REGER   D
MOZART VARIATIONS AND FUGUE, OP. 132A
        C. F. PETERS CORPORATION   3976   3.50
REGER   PRESSER, T.
VARIATIONS AND FUGUE ON A THEME OF BEETHOVEN, OP. 86
        ASSOCIATED MUSIC PUBLISHERS, INC.   BOT   7.25
REINECKE
CADENZAS FOR MOZART K365
        INTERNATIONAL MUSIC COMPANY   1.50
REINECKE
IMPROMPTU IN A, OP. 66 -- SET
        ASSOCIATED MUSIC PUBLISHERS, INC.   BRH   1.80
RENNARD   1
FUN IN THE SNOW - OPTIONAL 2ND PIANO PART
        BOSTON MUSIC COMPANY   .50

RESPIGHI
CONCERTO IN THE MIXOLYDIAN MODE
        ASSOCIATED MUSIC PUBLISHERS, INC.   BOT   11.00
RESPIGHI   MESSINA
TOCCATA
        FRANCO COLOMBO PUBLICATIONS   121014   3.50
REUTTER, H.
CAPRICCIO, ARIA UND FINALE, 1963, FUR KLAVIER UND ORCHESTER -
KLAVIERAUSZUG
        SCHOTT   5396   6.00
RICHMOND   NASH
DANCE OF THE HONEYBEES
        EDWARD B. MARKS MUSIC CORPORATION   01.25
RIDKY   4
KONZERT FUR KLAVIER UND ORCHESTER, KLAVIERAUSZUG
        BARENREITER VERLAG   AP 290
RIDKY   4
KONZERT FUR KLAVIER UND ORCHESTER, OP. 46
        BARENREITER VERLAG   AP 290
RIDKY   4
KONZERT FUR KLAVIER UND ORCHESTER, OP. 46
        BARENREITER VERLAG   AP 290
RIDKY   4
KONZERT FUR KLAVIER UND ORCHESTER
        BARENREITER VERLAG   CHF 5343
RIEDE   3-4
CAPRICCIO FUR KLAVIER UND ORCHESTER, OP. 19
        BARENREITER VERLAG   AE 301
RIEGGER, W.
CRY, THE
        PEER SOUTHERN ORGANIZATION   02.50
RIEGGER, W.
EVOCATION
        PEER SOUTHERN ORGANIZATION   02.50
RIEGGER, W.
NEW DANCE
        ASSOCIATED MUSIC PUBLISHERS, INC.   AMP   1.25
RIEGGER, W.
SCHERZO
        PEER SOUTHERN ORGANIZATION   03.00
RIEGGER, W.
VARIATIONS, OP. 54A -- 1954
        ASSOCIATED MUSIC PUBLISHERS, INC.   AMP   3.75
RIES
CONCERTO NO. 03 IN C SHARP MINOR, PIANO SOLO SCORE
        MUSICA OBSCURA   5.00
RIETI
CHESS-SERENADE, 1945 -- SET
        ASSOCIATED MUSIC PUBLISHERS, INC.   AMP   6.00
RIETI
CHORALE, VARIATIONS AND FINALE
        GENERAL MUSIC PUBLISHING COMPANY, INC.   10.00
RIETI
CHORALE, VARIATIONS AND FINALE
        GENERAL MUSIC PUBLISHING COMPANY, INC.   615   10.00
RIETI
CONCERTO
        UNIVERSAL EDITION   UE 8799   5.10
RIETI
NEW WALTZES, 1965/7
        ASSOCIATED MUSIC PUBLISHERS, INC.   AMP   8.00
RIETI
SECOND AVENUE WALTZES, 1942 -- SET
        ASSOCIATED MUSIC PUBLISHERS, INC.   AMP   4.00
RIETI
SUITE CHAMPETRE, 1948 -- SET
        ASSOCIATED MUSIC PUBLISHERS, INC.   AMP   6.00
RIETI
THREE VAUDEVILLE MARCHES
        GENERAL MUSIC PUBLISHING COMPANY, INC.   7.50
RIETI
THREE VAUDEVILLE MARCHES
        GENERAL MUSIC PUBLISHING COMPANY, INC.   613   7.50
RIETI
VALSE FUGITIVE
        GENERAL MUSIC PUBLISHING COMPANY, INC.   3.00
RIETI
VALSE FUGITIVE
        GENERAL MUSIC PUBLISHING COMPANY, INC.   614   3.00
RIMSKY-KORSAKOFF
CONCERTO, OP. 30
        BOOSEY AND HAWKES, INC.   3.00
RIMSKY-KORSAKOFF
CONCERTO IN C SHARP MINOR, OP. 30
        INTERNATIONAL MUSIC COMPANY   2.50
RIMSKY-KORSAKOFF   BERCKMAN
DANCE OF THE TUMBLERS -- FROM ''THE SNOW MAIDEN'' -- SET
        G. SCHIRMER, INC.   L1683   1.50
RIMSKY-KORSAKOFF   BRAGGIOTTI, M.
FLIGHT OF THE BUMBLE BEE -- FROM ''TSAR SALTAN'' -- SET
        G. SCHIRMER, INC.   1.00
RIMSKY-KORSAKOFF   GEARHART   ADVANCED
FLIGHT OF THE BUMBLE BEE
        SHAWNEE PRESS, INC.   2.00
ROBBONE
TWO MOUVEMENTS
        FRANCO COLOMBO PUBLICATIONS   BON.2377   3.00
ROBERTS
TWO CHORALES
        NOVELLO AND COMPANY, LTD.   10.0168.10   1.40
ROBERTS
VARIATIONS ON AN ORIGINAL THEME
        NOVELLO AND COMPANY, LTD.   10.0169.08   4.15
ROBINSON, S.
RONDO
        BOOSEY AND HAWKES, INC.   1.25
RODGERS *   RITTMAN
MARCH OF THE SIAMESE CHILDREN
        MCA MUSIC   1.50
RODGERS *   WHITTEMORE *
WONDERFUL GUY, A
        MCA MUSIC   1.25
ROGER-ROGER
JAZZ CONCERTO NO. 2
        FRANCO COLOMBO PUBLICATIONS   SAL   10.00
ROPARTZ
FANTASY IN D MAJOR
        FRANCO COLOMBO PUBLICATIONS   SAL   10.75
ROPARTZ
SYMPHONY NO. 02 IN F MINOR
        FRANCO COLOMBO PUBLICATIONS   SAL   10.75
ROREM, N.
SICILIENNE FOR 2 PIANOS
        PEER SOUTHERN ORGANIZATION   02.00
ROSSINI, G.   OMIZZOLO
DANZA, LA
        FRANCO COLOMBO PUBLICATIONS   128762   1.00

ROSSINI, G.   RUSSELL
    DANZA, LA
        SUMMY-BIRCHARD COMPANY   2.00
ROSZA
    SPELLBOUND CONCERTO
        CHAPPELL AND COMPANY, INC.   0023341-1501   1.25
ROUSSEL, A.
    CONCERTO FOR PIANO AND ORCH., PIANO RED.
        ELKAN-VOGEL, INC.   D   8.00
ROWLEY
    CONCERTO IN D, OP. 49
        C. F. PETERS CORPORATION   H24   2.00
ROWLEY
    MINIATURE CONCERTO
        BOOSEY AND HAWKES, INC.   1.50
ROZIN
    LITTLE CONCERTO
        BRODT MUSIC COMPANY   1.25
ROZSA, M.
    CONCERTO, OP. 31
        ASSOCIATED MUSIC PUBLISHERS, INC.   BRH   9.75
RUBINSTEIN   JOSEFFY, R.
    CONCERTO NO. 04 IN D MINOR, OP. 70
        G. SCHIRMER, INC.   L1047   3.00
RUBINSTEIN   JOSEFFY
    CONCERTO NO. 04 IN D MINOR, OP. 70
        G. SCHIRMER, INC.   L1047   3.00
RUBINSTEIN   BERIOT *
    MELODY IN F, OP. 3
        G. SCHIRMER, INC.   .60
RUFTY, H.   GEST
    HOBBY ON THE GREEN -- SET
        G. SCHIRMER, INC.   1.00
SAAR
    SECOND-PIANO PART TO THE 15 TWO-PART INVENTIONS OF J.S. BACH
        G. SCHIRMER, INC.   1.25
SAINT-SAENS
    AFRICA, OP. 89
        ELKAN-VOGEL, INC.   D   7.00
SAINT-SAENS
    AFRICA, OP. 89
        ELKAN-VOGEL, INC.   6.75
SAINT-SAENS   BENFELD, A.
    CAPRICE ARABE
        ELKAN-VOGEL, INC.   D   5.00
SAINT-SAENS
    CAPRICE HEROIQUE, OP. 106
        ELKAN-VOGEL, INC.   D   6.00
SAINT-SAENS
    CARNIVAL OF THE ANIMALS
        ELKAN-VOGEL, INC.   11.00
SAINT-SAENS
    CONCERTO NO. 01, OP. 17
        ELKAN-VOGEL, INC.   D   16.00
SAINT-SAENS
    CONCERTO NO. 02, OP. 22
        ELKAN-VOGEL, INC.   D   21.00
SAINT-SAENS   PHILIPP, I.
    CONCERTO NO. 02 IN G MINOR, OP. 22
        G. SCHIRMER, INC.   L1405   3.50
SAINT-SAENS   PHILIPP
    CONCERTO NO. 02 IN G MINOR, OP. 22
        G. SCHIRMER, INC.   L1405   3.50
SAINT-SAENS
    CONCERTO NO. 04, OP. 44
        ELKAN-VOGEL, INC.   D   20.50
SAINT-SAENS   PHILIPP, I.
    CONCERTO NO. 04 IN C MINOR, OP. 44
        G. SCHIRMER, INC.   L1486   3.50
SAINT-SAENS   PHILIPP
    CONCERTO NO. 04 IN C MINOR, OP. 44
        G. SCHIRMER, INC.   L1486   3.50
SAINT-SAENS
    CONCERTO NO. 05, OP. 103
        ELKAN-VOGEL, INC.   D   23.00
SAINT-SAENS
    CONCERTO NO. 05, OP. 103
        ELKAN-VOGEL, INC.   4.00
SAINT-SAENS   DIEMER
    CONCERTO NO. 05 IN F, OP. 103
        G. SCHIRMER, INC.   L1838   3.00
SAINT-SAENS
    CONCERTO NO. 05 IN F, OP. 103
        G. SCHIRMER, INC.   L1838   3.00
SAINT-SAENS
    DANSE MACABRE, OP. 40
        ELKAN-VOGEL, INC.   6.00
SAINT-SAENS
    DEUXIEME CONCERTO, EDITION A
        ELKAN-VOGEL, INC.   D   10.50
SAINT-SAENS
    DEUXIEME CONCERTO, EDITION B
        ELKAN-VOGEL, INC.   D   5.75
SAINT-SAENS
    ETUDE EN TIERCES MAJEURES CHROMATIQUES
        ELKAN-VOGEL, INC.   D   2.25
SAINT-SAENS   BABIN *
    INTRODUCTION AND RONDO CAPRICCIOSO, OP. 28
        INTERNATIONAL MUSIC COMPANY   2.50
SAINT-SAENS
    LE CYGNE -- THE SWAN
        ELKAN-VOGEL, INC.   D   3.10
SAINT-SAENS
    LE ROUET D'OMPHALE, OP. 31
        ELKAN-VOGEL, INC.   D   7.00
SAINT-SAENS
    MARCHE HEROIQUE, OP. 34
        ELKAN-VOGEL, INC.   D   4.50
SAINT-SAENS
    MENUET ET GAVOTTE DU SEPTUOR, OP. 65
        ELKAN-VOGEL, INC.   D   3.00
SAINT-SAENS
    MINUET AND GAVOTTE, OP. 65
        INTERNATIONAL MUSIC COMPANY   1.75
SAINT-SAENS
    PIANO CONCERTO NO. 02, OP. 22
        ELKAN-VOGEL, INC.   5.50
SAINT-SAENS
    PIANO CONCERTO NO. 02, OP. 22
        EDWIN F. KALMUS   3854   3.50
SAINT-SAENS
    PIANO CONCERTO NO. 04, OP. 44
        ELKAN-VOGEL, INC.   10.00
SAINT-SAENS
    PIANO CONCERTO NO. 05, OP. 103
        ELKAN-VOGEL, INC.   11.00

SAINT-SAENS
    POLONAISE, OP. 77
        ELKAN-VOGEL, INC.   D   6.25
SAINT-SAENS
    PREMIER CONCERTO POUR PIANO
        ELKAN-VOGEL, INC.   D   7.50
SAINT-SAENS
    QUATRIEME CONCERTO, OP. 44
        ELKAN-VOGEL, INC.   D   10.50
SAINT-SAENS
    RHAPSODIE D'AUVERGNE, OP. 73
        ELKAN-VOGEL, INC.   D   6.10
SAINT-SAENS
    SCHERZO, OP. 87
        ELKAN-VOGEL, INC.   6.00
SAINT-SAENS
    SCHERZO, OP. 87
        INTERNATIONAL MUSIC COMPANY   3.00
SAINT-SAENS
    SUITE ALGERIENNE, OP. 60
        ELKAN-VOGEL, INC.   7.00
SAINT-SAENS
    TROISIEME CONCERTO, OP. 29
        ELKAN-VOGEL, INC.   D   7.50
SAINT-SAENS
    VARIATIONS ON A THEME BY BEETHOVEN, OP. 35
        INTERNATIONAL MUSIC COMPANY   3.00
SAINT-SAENS   HUGHES
    VARIATIONS ON A THEME BY BEETHOVEN, OP. 35
        G. SCHIRMER, INC.   L1449   1.50
SAINT-SAENS
    VARIATIONS ON A THEME OF BEETHOVEN, OP. 35
        ELKAN-VOGEL, INC.   7.50
SALMON, K.
    SUITE ON GREEK THEMES
        ISRAEL MUSIC INSTITUTE   7.50
SANCAN, P.
    CONCERTO
        ELKAN-VOGEL, INC.   D   4.50
SANTORO, C.
    CONCERTO NO. 01
        FRANCO COLOMBO PUBLICATIONS   SAL   4.00
SAUGUET
    CONCERTO NO. 01 IN A MINOR
        ASSOCIATED MUSIC PUBLISHERS, INC.   ESC   8.50
SAUGUET
    CONCERT DES MONDES SOUTERRAINS -- NO. 3 --
        FRANCO COLOMBO PUBLICATIONS   SAL   14.50
SAUGUET
    VALSE BREVE, 1949 -- SET
        ASSOCIATED MUSIC PUBLISHERS, INC.   ESC   5.50
SCARLATTI, D.   GOBBI
    ALLEGRO IN F
        INTERNATIONAL MUSIC COMPANY   1.75
SCARLATTI, D.   DOEBBER
    PASTORAL AND CAPRICCIO
        INTERNATIONAL MUSIC COMPANY   1.75
SCARLATTI, D.   GEST, E.
    SONATA ALLEGRO IN G MINOR
        ELKAN-VOGEL, INC.   D   1.25
SCARLATTI, D.   MILLER *
    SONATA IN A -- SET
        G. SCHIRMER, INC.   1.25
SCARLATTI, D.   SWINSTEAD, F.
    SUITE
        NOVELLO AND COMPANY, LTD.   10.0170.01   2.15
SCHAEFER   3
    CONCERTO FUR QUERFLOTE, V, TROMP, KLAVIER, SCHLAGZEUG UND
    STREICHER
        BARENREITER VERLAG   BE 314
SCHAEFER   4-5
    KLAVIERKONZERT, OP. 37
        BARENREITER VERLAG   SM 1378
SCHARWENKA, X.
    PIANO CONCERTO NO. 01 IN B FLAT MINOR, OP. 32
        MUSIC TREASURE PUBLICATIONS   5   5.00
SCHARWENKA, X.
    POLISH DANCE, A
        THEODORE PRESSER COMPANY   1.20
SCHARWENKA, X.   DUNGAN   3
    POLISH DANCE
        BOSTON MUSIC COMPANY   .75
SCHAUM, J.--ED.   SCHAUM, J.   1
    PIANO ACCOMPANIMENTS TO THE 'A' BOOK
        BELWIN-MILLS PUBLISHING CORPORATION   1.50
SCHAUM, J.
    MOUNTAIN CONCERTO
        BELWIN-MILLS PUBLISHING CORPORATION   2.50
SCHELLING, E.
    IMPRESSIONS FROM AN ARTIST'S LIFE
        ASSOCIATED MUSIC PUBLISHERS, INC.   LEU   11.50
SCHER, W.
    SEA FANTASY
        CARL FISCHER, INC.   RS 408   2.00
SCHMEID, A.   1
    LORELEI
        WILLIS MUSIC COMPANY   .35
SCHMEID, A.   1
    MUST I GO
        WILLIS MUSIC COMPANY   .35
SCHMEID, A.   1
    ON TIPTOES
        WILLIS MUSIC COMPANY   .35
SCHMITT, F.
    TROIS RHAPSODIES -- 1. FRANCAISE, 2. POLONAISE, 3. VIENNOISE
        ELKAN-VOGEL, INC.   D   12.75
SCHOENBERG   STEUERMANN, E.
    CONCERTO, OP. 42
        G. SCHIRMER, INC.   3.50
SCHOENBERG   STEUERMANN, E.
    CONCERTO, OP. 42
        G. SCHIRMER, INC.   3.50
SCHOENBERG   WEBERN   D
    FIVE PIECES FOR ORCHESTRA, OP. 16
        C. F. PETERS CORPORATION   3378   7.50
SCHOENBERG   DOUTHERTY
    VARIATIONS ON A RECITATIVE
        BELWIN-MILLS PUBLISHING CORPORATION   3.00
SCHROEDER
    CONCERTO, OP. 42
        MCA MUSIC   3.50
SCHROETER, H.
    BAGATELLEN, OP. 9
        SCHOTT   4290   3.00
SCHROTER, J. S.   SCHULTZ *   2-3
    KONZERT IN C FUR KLAVIER UND STREICHORCHESTER, KLAVIERAUSZUG
        SCHOTT   4974   3.00

SCHUBERT, H. — 4
AMBROSIANISCHES KLAVIERKONZERT
BARENREITER VERLAG — AE 219

SCHUBERT * — JOSEFFY, R.
FANTASIA, OP. 15
G. SCHIRMER, INC. — L1046 — 1.50

SCHUBERT — LISZT *
FANTASIA IN C, OP. 15
G. SCHIRMER, INC. — L1046 — 1.50

SCHUBERT — BAUER
FANTASIA IN F MINOR, OP. 103
G. SCHIRMER, INC. — 2.00

SCHUBERT — STEINER
HUNGARIAN MARCH
BELWIN-MILLS PUBLISHING CORPORATION — 1.25

SCHUBERT — DOUGHERTY *
LANDLERISCHE TANZE -- SET
G. SCHIRMER, INC. — .90

SCHUBERT — BAUER
MARCHE MILITAIRE, OP. 51 NO. 1 -- SET
G. SCHIRMER, INC. — 1.50

SCHUBERT — GRAETZER
MARCHE MILITAIRE, OP. 51 NO. 1
FRANCO COLOMBO PUBLICATIONS — BA9703 — .75

SCHUBERT — OLSON
MENUETTO -- FROM SYMPHONY NO. 3 -- SET
G. SCHIRMER, INC. — 1.00

SCHUBERT — STEINER
MINUET -- FROM SYMPHONY NO. 5 IN B FLAT -- SET
G. SCHIRMER, INC. — .75

SCHUBERT — PHILIPP, I.
MOMENT MUSICAL, OP. 94 NO.3
INTERNATIONAL MUSIC COMPANY — 1.75

SCHUBERT — PIKLER — 3
MOMENT MUSICAL
BOSTON MUSIC COMPANY — 1.00

SCHUBERT
ORIGINAL COMPOSITIONS, BK. 1
EDWIN F. KALMUS — 3889 — 3.50

SCHUBERT
ORIGINAL COMPOSITIONS, BK. 1
EDWIN F. KALMUS — 3890 — 3.50

SCHUBERT
ORIGINAL COMPOSITIONS, BK. 3
EDWIN F. KALMUS — 3891 — 3.50

SCHUBERT
ORIGINAL COMPOSITIONS, BK. 4
EDWIN F. KALMUS — 3892 — 3.50

SCHUBERT
ORIGINAL COMPOSITIONS, BK. 5
EDWIN F. KALMUS — 3893 — 3.50

SCHUBERT — BAUER
RONDO BRILLANTE, OP. 84 NO. 2
G. SCHIRMER, INC. — 1.50

SCHUBERT — HAUPT, L. VON
SERENADE
BELWIN-MILLS PUBLISHING CORPORATION — 27036 — .60

SCHUBERT
TROUT, THE
OXFORD UNIVERSITY PRESS — 35.104 — 2.75

SCHUBERT — HAUPT, L. VON
VALSE NOBLE, OP. 77 NO. 9
BELWIN-MILLS PUBLISHING CORPORATION — 27040 — .60

SCHUETT
IMPROMPTU-ROCOCO, OP. 58 NO. 2 -- SET
ASSOCIATED MUSIC PUBLISHERS, INC. — SIM — 3.00

SCHULHOFF — 4
DOPPELKONZERT FUR KLAVIER UND QUERFLOTE, 2 OB UND STREICHER
BARENREITER VERLAG — CHF 5292

SCHULLER, G.
CONCERTO -- 1962
ASSOCIATED MUSIC PUBLISHERS, INC. — AMP — 11.00

SCHULLER, G.
KONZERT FUR KLAVIER UND ORCHESTER, KLAVIERAUSZUG
SCHOTT — 10895 — 14.00

SCHUMAN, W.
CONCERTO FOR PIANO AND SMALL ORCHESTRA
G. SCHIRMER, INC. — 3.00

SCHUMAN, W.
CONCERTO FOR PIANO AND SMALL ORCHESTRA
G. SCHIRMER, INC. — 3.00

SCHUMANN, R. — HUGHES
ANDANTE AND VARIATIONS, OP. 46
G. SCHIRMER, INC. — L1489 — 1.50

SCHUMANN, R. — SAUER — D
ANDANTE AND VARIATIONS IN B FLAT, OP. 46
C. F. PETERS CORPORATION — 2362 — 2.50

SCHUMANN, R. — M
CONCERTO IN A MINOR, OP. 54. ABRIDGED
C. F. PETERS CORPORATION — 2898A — 1.25

SCHUMANN, R. — SAUER — D
CONCERTO IN A MINOR, OP. 54
C. F. PETERS CORPORATION — 2898 — 2.50

SCHUMANN, R. — HUGHES
CONCERTO IN A MINOR, OP. 54
G. SCHIRMER, INC. — L1358 — 1.75

SCHUMANN, R. — FRYER, H.
CONCERTO IN A MINOR -- WITH ACCOMPANIMENT ARRANGED FOR SECOND PIANO
NOVELLO AND COMPANY, LTD. — 10.0124.08 — 2.00

SCHUMANN, R. — FRYER, H.
CONCERTO IN A MINOR
NOVELLO AND COMPANY, LTD. — 10.0124.08 — 2.00

SCHUMANN, R. — HUGHES
CONCERTO IN A MINOR
G. SCHIRMER, INC. — L1358 — 1.75

SCHUMANN, R. — BAUER
CONCERT ALLEGRO WITH INTRODUCTION, OP. 134, INTRODUCTION AND ALLEGRO APPASSIONATA, OP. 92
G. SCHIRMER, INC. — L1707 — 2.00

SCHUMANN, R. — PIKLER — 2
ECHOES FROM THE THEATER
WILLIS MUSIC COMPANY — .50

SCHUMANN, R. — DICKIE — 2
HAPPY FARMER, THE
BOSTON MUSIC COMPANY — 1.50

SCHUMANN, R. — PIKLER — 3
HORSEMAN, THE
WILLIS MUSIC COMPANY — .50

SCHUMANN, R. — BAUER
INTRODUCTION AND ALLEGRO APPASSIONATA, OP. 92, CONCERT ALLEGRO WITH INTRODUCTION, OP. 134
G. SCHIRMER, INC. — L1707 — 2.00

SCHUMANN, R. — BAUER
INTRODUCTION AND ALLEGRO APPASSIONATO, OP. 92 AND CONCERT ALLEGRO WITH INTRODUCTION, OP. 34
G. SCHIRMER, INC. — L1707 — 2.00

SCHUMANN, R.
ORIGINAL COMPOSITIONS FOR TWO PIANOS - FOUR HANDS, BK. 1
EDWIN F. KALMUS — 3921 — 2.25

SCHUMANN, R.
ORIGINAL COMPOSITIONS FOR TWO PIANOS - FOUR HANDS, BK. 2
EDWIN F. KALMUS — 3922 — 2.25

SCHUMANN, R.
PIANO CONCERTO, OP. 54
EDWIN F. KALMUS — 3897 — 2.50

SCHUMANN, R. — PIKLER — 2
SAILORS SONG
WILLIS MUSIC COMPANY — .60

SCHUMANN, R. — DEBUSSY *
SIX CANONIC ETUDES, OP. 56
INTERNATIONAL MUSIC COMPANY — 3.00

SCHUMANN, R. — DEBUSSY
SIX ETUDES IN CANON FORM
ELKAN-VOGEL, INC. — D — 8.50

SCIONTI
REJOICE, BELOVED CHRISTIANS
BELWIN-MILLS PUBLISHING CORPORATION — .75

SCOTT, C. — GRAINGER, P.
DREI SINFONISCHE TANZE
SCHOTT — 1855 — 4.00

SCOTT, C.
EARLY ONE MORNING -- 1962 VERSION
BOOSEY AND HAWKES, INC. — 2.75

SCOTT, C. — ARNOLD
LENTO
BOOSEY AND HAWKES, INC. — .90

SCRIABINE, A.
CONCERTO, OP. 20
BOOSEY AND HAWKES, INC. — 5.00

SEARLE, H.
KONZERT NO. 02 FUR KLAVIER UND ORCHESTER, OP. 27
SCHOTT — 10397 — 4.00

SESSIONS, R.
CONCERTO FOR PIANO AND ORCHESTRA
EDWARD B. MARKS MUSIC CORPORATION — 06.00

SEUEL-HOLST, M.
IN ELFLAND
SUMMY-BIRCHARD COMPANY — 1.50

SEUEL * — PODOLSKY — 4
SPRINGTIME SONATINA
VOLKWEIN BROS. — 1.00

SHOSTAKOVITCH
CONCERTO, OP. 35 FOR PIANO, TRUMPET, STRINGS
MCA MUSIC — 3.00

SHOSTAKOVITCH
CONCERTO NO. 01 IN C MINOR, OP. 35
INTERNATIONAL MUSIC COMPANY — 3.50

SHOSTAKOVITCH
CONCERTO NO. 02, OP. 102
MCA MUSIC — 4.50

SHOSTAKOVITCH
CONCERTO NO. 02, OP. 102 — D
C. F. PETERS CORPORATION — 4772 — 6.50

SHOSTAKOVITCH
CONCERTO NO. 02 IN F, OP. 102
INTERNATIONAL MUSIC COMPANY — 3.75

SHOSTAKOVITCH
FESTIVAL OVERTURE
EDWIN F. KALMUS — 3867 — 2.00

SHOSTAKOVITCH
PIANO CONCERTO NO. 02, OP. 102
EDWIN F. KALMUS — 3969 — 3.50

SHOSTAKOVITCH
POLKA -- FROM BALLET L'AGE D'OR
BELWIN-MILLS PUBLISHING CORPORATION — 1.50

SHOSTAKOVITCH — LUBOSHUTZ
WALTZ, OP. 30 FROM 'GOLDEN MOUNTAIN'
MCA MUSIC — 2.50

SIBELIUS — SCHAUM, J.
FINLANDIA
BELWIN-MILLS PUBLISHING CORPORATION — 2.00

SIEGL, O.
CHAMBER CONCERTO
ASSOCIATED MUSIC PUBLISHERS, INC. — DOB — 6.50

SIMMONS, H.
GRYPHON AND THE MOCK TURTLE
BELWIN-MILLS PUBLISHING CORPORATION — 1.25

SIMMONS, H.
SCHERZINO
BELWIN-MILLS PUBLISHING CORPORATION — 2.00

SKALKOTTAS, N.
CONCERTINO FOR 2 PIANOS AND ORCHESTRA
UNIVERSAL EDITION — UE 14296 — 5.10

SLONIMSKY — MEDIUM
MY TOY BALLOON
SHAWNEE PRESS, INC. — 2.00

SMETANA — KRAMER — 4-5
BARTERED BRIDE OVERTURE
PRO-ART PUBLICATIONS, INC. — 8 — 2.00

SMETANA — M-D
QUARTET IN E MINOR --FROM MY LIFE--
C. F. PETERS CORPORATION — N968 — 2.50

SMITH--ED — SMITH — 2
STAR SPANGLED BANNER
BOSTON MUSIC COMPANY — .75

SMITH, J. — 5
AMERICAN DANCE SUITE
THEODORE PRESSER COMPANY — 3.00

SMITH, J. — D
CONCERTO FOR PIANO AND ORCHESTRA
THEODORE PRESSER COMPANY — 6.50

SMITH, J. — BAUER
STAR-SPANGLED BANNER, THE -- SET
G. SCHIRMER, INC. — .45

SMITH — 2
CRISS CROSS
BOSTON MUSIC COMPANY — .75

SOLER, A. — MARCHI, G.
FIRST CONCERTO IN C MAJOR
EDIZIONI BERBEN — EB 1381 — 2.50

SOLER, A. — RUBIO
SIX CONCERTI FOR 2 KEYBOARD INSTRUMENTS -- COMPLETE
ASSOCIATED MUSIC PUBLISHERS, INC. — UME — 10.00

SOLER, A. — RUBIO
SIX CONCERTI FOR 2 KEYBOARD INSTRUMENTS -- NO. 1 IN C
ASSOCIATED MUSIC PUBLISHERS, INC. — UME — 2.00

SOLER, A. — RUBIO
SIX CONCERTI FOR 2 KEYBOARD INSTRUMENTS -- NO. 2 IN A MINOR
ASSOCIATED MUSIC PUBLISHERS, INC. — UME — 2.50

SOLER, A. — RUBIO
SIX CONCERTI FOR 2 KEYBOARD INSTRUMENTS -- NO. 3 IN G
ASSOCIATED MUSIC PUBLISHERS, INC. — UME — 2.00

SOLER, A.   RUBIO
  SIX CONCERTI FOR 2 KEYBOARD INSTRUMENTS -- NO. 4 IN F
      ASSOCIATED MUSIC PUBLISHERS, INC.   UME   2.00
SOLER, A.   RUBIO
  SIX CONCERTI FOR 2 KEYBOARD INSTRUMENTS -- NO. 5 IN A
      ASSOCIATED MUSIC PUBLISHERS, INC.   UME   2.50
SOLER, A.   RUBIO
  SIX CONCERTI FOR 2 KEYBOARD INSTRUMENTS -- NO. 6 IN D
      ASSOCIATED MUSIC PUBLISHERS, INC.   UME   3.00
SPAULDING, G. L.   1
  AIRY FAIRIES
      THEODORE PRESSER COMPANY   .75
SPINKS   D
  VARIATIONS ON A GREEK FOLK SONG, OP. 6
      C. F. PETERS CORPORATION   H35   2.00
SPITZMULLER, A.
  CONCERTO, OP. 39
      UNIVERSAL EDITION   UE 12151 4.25
SPITZMULLER, A.
  PRAELUDIUM AND FUGUE
      UNIVERSAL EDITION   UE 12151 4.25
STAEMPFLI, E.   4-5
  CONCERTINO FUR KLAVIER UND KAMMERORCHESTER
      BARENREITER VERLAG   SM 2249
STAMITZ, K.
  CONCERTO IN F
      ASSOCIATED MUSIC PUBLISHERS, INC.   BRH   5.00
STARER
  CONCERTO NO. 02 FOR PIANO AND ORCHESTRA -- OR WIND ENSEMBLE
      MCA MUSIC   5.00
STARER   5
  FRINGES OF A BALL -- WALTZ VARIATIONS ON A THEME BY W. SCHUMAN
      THEODORE PRESSER COMPANY   2.50
STAUB, V.
  SOUS BOIS, OP. 6
      ELKAN-VOGEL, INC.   D   4.15
STEFFE --ED   ECKSTEIN
  BATTLE HYMN OF THE REPUBLIC
      CARL FISCHER, INC.   P 2974   .75
STEIBELT
  CONCERTO NO. 03, OP. 33 'THE STORM'
      MUSICA OBSCURA   5.00
STEINER, G.
  CONCERTO FOR PIANO AND ORCHESTRA, 1967
      SEESAW MUSIC CORPORATION   28.00
STEINER
  WINNING DANCE TEAM
      BELWIN-MILLS PUBLISHING CORPORATION   1.25
STERKEL, F. X.   KAUL
  ERSTES KLAVIERKONZERT IN C, OP. 20 - KLAVIER-EINRICHTUNG
      SCHOTT   5760
STEVENS, E.
  JO-JO THE JUGGLER
      BELWIN-MILLS PUBLISHING CORPORATION   1.25
STEWART, R.
  RONDEAU FOR TWO PIANOS
      COMPOSERS AUTOGRAPH PUBLICATIONS   5.72
STOUGHTON, R. S.   3
  PROMENADE
      THEODORE PRESSER COMPANY   .85
STRAUSS, J.   CHASINS, A.
  ARTIST'S LIFE
      BELWIN-MILLS PUBLISHING CORPORATION   3.00
STRAUSS, J.   CHASINS, A.
  BLUE DANUBE WALTZ
      BELWIN-MILLS PUBLISHING CORPORATION   2.50
STRAUSS, J.   WALLIS   3
  TALES FROM THE VIENNA WOODS
      BOSTON MUSIC COMPANY   1.00
STRAUSS, R.   SINGER
  ALPENSINFONIE, EINE, OP. 64
      ASSOCIATED MUSIC PUBLISHERS, INC.   LEU   6.00
STRAUSS, R.
  BURLESKE
      EDWARD B. MARKS MUSIC CORPORATION   01.50
STRAUSS, R.   PHILIPP, I.
  BURLESQUE
      INTERNATIONAL MUSIC COMPANY   2.50
STRAUSS, R.
  BURLESQUE
      EDWIN F. KALMUS   4010   2.50
STRAUSS, R.   SINGER
  CONCERT WALTZ, FROM 'DER ROSENKAVALIER'
      BOOSEY AND HAWKES, INC.   2.50
STRAUSS, R.   SINGER
  DANCE OF THE SEVEN VEILS, FROM 'SALOME'
      BOOSEY AND HAWKES, INC.   2.50
STRAUSS, R.
  PANATHENAENZUG, OP. 74 FOR LEFT HAND
      BOOSEY AND HAWKES, INC.   4.50
STRAUSS, R.
  PARERGON ZUR SINFONIA DOMESTICA, OP. 73 FOR LEFT HAND
      BOOSEY AND HAWKES, INC.   3.75
STRAVINSKY, I.
  AGON
      BOOSEY AND HAWKES, INC.   5.00
STRAVINSKY, I.
  CAPRICCIO - REVISED 1949 VERSION
      BOOSEY AND HAWKES, INC.   4.00
STRAVINSKY, I.
  CAPRICCIO
      INTERNATIONAL MUSIC COMPANY   3.00
STRAVINSKY, I.
  CIRCUS-POLKA F. ORCHESTER, KLAVIERAUSZUG
      SCHOTT   4283   4.75
STRAVINSKY, I.
  CONCERTO FOR PIANO AND WINDS
      BOOSEY AND HAWKES, INC.   6.50
STRAVINSKY, I.
  CONCERTO IN ES, DUMBARTON OAKS FUR KAMMERORCHESTER,
  KLAVIERAUSZUG
      SCHOTT   2791   7.50
STRAVINSKY, I.
  CONCERTO PER DUE PIANO FORTI SOLI
      SCHOTT   2520   7.50
STRAVINSKY, I.   ALBERT *
  DANSE RUSSE
      EDWARD B. MARKS MUSIC CORPORATION   01.50
STRAVINSKY, I.
  MADRID
      BOOSEY AND HAWKES, INC.   1.75
STRAVINSKY, I.
  MOVEMENTS
      BOOSEY AND HAWKES, INC.   2.00
STRAVINSKY, I.
  SCHERZO A LA RUSSE, 1944 -- ORCH -- SET
      ASSOCIATED MUSIC PUBLISHERS, INC.   AMP   2.50

STRAVINSKY, I.
  SCHERZO A LA RUSSE FUR ORCHESTER, KLAVIERAUSZUG
      SCHOTT   10646   4.25
STRAVINSKY, I.
  SEPTET
      BOOSEY AND HAWKES, INC.   3.75
STRAVINSKY, I.
  SONATA
      SCHOTT   4015   4.00
STRAVINSKY, I.   BABIN
  TANGO
      SCHOTT   4720   2.50
STRAVINSKY, I.   BABIN   MD
  TANGO
      THEODORE PRESSER COMPANY   2.00
STRAVINSKY, I.   BABIN
  THREE MOVEMENTS, FROM 'PETROUCHKA' -- NO. 1 RUSSIAN DANCE
      BOOSEY AND HAWKES, INC.   1.75
STRAVINSKY, I.   BABIN
  THREE MOVEMENTS, FROM 'PETROUCHKA' -- NO. 2 CHEZ PETROUCHKA
      BOOSEY AND HAWKES, INC.   2.75
STRAVINSKY, I.   BABIN
  THREE MOVEMENTS, FROM 'PETROUCHKA' -- NO. 3 SHROVE - TIDE FAIR
      BOOSEY AND HAWKES, INC.   2.75
STUDER   4
  KAMMERKONZERT FUR KLAVIER UND KLEINES ORCHESTER
      BARENREITER VERLAG   BA 2020
STUDER   4
  KLEINES KONZERT FUR STREICHER, KLAVIER ZU 4 HANDEN UND 2
  QUERFLOTEN
      BARENREITER VERLAG   BA 1914
STUPP   4
  DIVISIONS ON A GROUND BASS
      BOSTON MUSIC COMPANY   1.80
SUBOTNICK
  PRELUDE NO. 03 FOR PIANO AND ELECTRONIC SOUNDS --1964 --INCLUDES
  TAPE
      MCA MUSIC   8.00
SUBOTNICK
  PRELUDE NO. 04 FOR PIANO AND ELECTRONIC SOUNDS --1966 --INCLUDES
  TAPE
      MCA MUSIC   7.50
SURINACH, C.   5
  FLAMENQUERAS, 1952 -- SET
      ASSOCIATED MUSIC PUBLISHERS, INC.   AMP   3.00
SUTERMEISTER, H.   5
  KONZERT FUR KLAVIER UND ORCHESTER, KLAVIERAUSZUG
      SCHOTT   3669   6.00
SUTERMEISTER, H.   5
  KONZERT NO. 02 FUR KLAVIER UND ORCHESTER, KLAVIERAUSZUG
      SCHOTT   4548   5.00
SUTERMEISTER, H.   5-6
  KONZERT NO. 03 FUR KLAVIER UND ORCHESTER, KLAVIERAUSZUG
      SCHOTT   4819   9.00
SZYMANOWSKI
  HARNASIE, OP. 55 -- BALLET IN 3 ACTS
      ASSOCIATED MUSIC PUBLISHERS, INC.   ESC   4.30
SZYMANOWSKI
  SYMPHONIE CONCERTANTE, OP. 60
      ASSOCIATED MUSIC PUBLISHERS, INC.   ESC   9.00
TAILLEFERRE, G.
  JEUX DE PLEIN AIR
      ELKAN-VOGEL, INC.   D   8.00
TAILLEFERRE, G.
  PIANO CONCERTO
      HEUGEL ET CIE.   13.50
TAILLEFERRE, G.
  TWO VALSES
      ELKAN-VOGEL, INC.   D   5.00
TANSMAN, A.
  CONCERTINO -- 1931
      ASSOCIATED MUSIC PUBLISHERS, INC.   ESC   5.75
TANSMAN, A.
  CONCERTO FOR 2 PIANOS AND ORCHESTRA
      ASSOCIATED MUSIC PUBLISHERS, INC.   ESC   10.75
TANSMAN, A.
  CONCERTO NO. 01
      ASSOCIATED MUSIC PUBLISHERS, INC.   ESC   6.50
TANSMAN, A.
  CONCERTO NO. 02
      ASSOCIATED MUSIC PUBLISHERS, INC.   ESC   2.50
TANSMAN, A.
  FANTAISIE SUR LES VALSES DE JOHANN STRAUSS -- SET
      ASSOCIATED MUSIC PUBLISHERS, INC.   ESC   7.50
TANSMAN, A.
  FANTASY -- 1937
      ASSOCIATED MUSIC PUBLISHERS, INC.   ESC   4.00
TANSMAN, A.
  GRANDE VILLE, LA -- 1935 -- BALLET IN 3 TABLEAUX
      ASSOCIATED MUSIC PUBLISHERS, INC.   ESC   4.00
TANSMAN, A.
  LES HABITS NEUF DE ROI -- THE KING'S NEW CLOTHES
      UNIVERSAL EDITION   UE 13147 4.50
TANSMAN, A.   7
  SONATINE TRANSATLANTIQUE
      ALPHONSE LEDUC
TAYLOR, C.
  THREE IMPROMPTUS, COMPLETE
      BELWIN-MILLS PUBLISHING CORPORATION   27022   1.25
TAYLOR, DEEMS   WHITAKER
  THROUGH THE LOOKING GLASS
      FRANCO COLOMBO PUBLICATIONS   NY5096   3.00
TAYLOR, E.
  TWO PIANO PORTRAITS
      SAM FOX PUBLISHING COMPANY, INC.   .50
TAYLOR   3
  SPRING DANCE
      BOSTON MUSIC COMPANY   .75
TCHEREPNIN
  CONCERTO NO. 02
      HEUGEL ET CIE.   13.40
TCHEREPNIN
  CONCERTO NO. 05, OP. 96
      BOOSEY AND HAWKES, INC.   7.50
TCHEREPNIN
  CONCERTO NO. 06, OP. 99
      BOOSEY AND HAWKES, INC.   D   4.75
TCHEREPNIN
  FANTAISIE FOR PIANO AND ORCHESTRA
      C. F. PETERS CORPORATION   H68   3.00
TCHEREPNIN   M-D
  RONDO, OP. 87A
      C. F. PETERS CORPORATION   6074   2.00
TCHEREPNIN
  SUITE GEORGIENNE, OP. 57
      ASSOCIATED MUSIC PUBLISHERS, INC.   ESC   11.00

TELEMANN, G.P. *　　　　　　　　　　　　　　M-D
　　CONCERTO IN G MINOR
　　　　C. F. PETERS CORPORATION　　　　　　2178　　3.00
TELEMANN, G.P.　　　　　　BABIN
　　FANTASIA
　　　　BOOSEY AND HAWKES, INC.　　　　　　　　　2.00
THALBERG
　　ANDANTE FINALE DE LUCIA DI LA MMERMOOR --DONIZETTI OP. 44, FOUR
　　HANDS
　　　　MUSICA OBSCURA　　　　　　　　　　　　　3.00
THARICHEN, W.
　　CONCERTO, OP. 39
　　　　ASSOCIATED MUSIC PUBLISHERS, INC.　　BOT　　7.50
THIEME　　　　　　4
　　MASCHERATA PICCOLA. CONCERTINO GIOCOSO FUR KLAVIER UND
　　KAMMERORCHESTER
　　　　BARENREITER VERLAG　　　　　　　　　SM 2086
THIRNE
　　BROADWAY AND 52ND
　　　　FRANCO COLOMBO PUBLICATIONS　　　FOR.12362　　6.00
THOMPSON, J.--ED　　　THOMPSON, J.　　4
　　THEMES FROM PIANO CONCERTOS
　　　　WILLIS MUSIC COMPANY　　　　　　　　　1.25
THOMPSON, J.　　　　　　　　　5
　　BOLERO
　　　　WILLIS MUSIC COMPANY　　　　　　　　　1.50
THOMPSON, J.　　　　　　　　　2
　　CONCERTINA
　　　　WILLIS MUSIC COMPANY　　　　　　　　　1.75
THOMPSON, J.　　　　　　　　　2
　　CONCERTINA
　　　　WILLIS MUSIC COMPANY　　　　　　　　　1.75
THOMPSON, J.　　　　　　　　　3
　　CONCERTO AMERICANA
　　　　WILLIS MUSIC COMPANY　　　　　　　　　1.75
THOMPSON, J.　　　　　　　　　4
　　CONCERTO IN D MINOR
　　　　WILLIS MUSIC COMPANY　　　　　　　　　1.25
THOMPSON, J.
　　FIRST GRADE ETUDES - SECOND PIANO ACCOMPANIMENTS
　　　　WILLIS MUSIC COMPANY　　　　　　　　　1.00
THOMPSON, J.
　　MODERN COURSE FOR PIANO - SECOND PIANO ACCOMPANIMENTS FOR FIRST
　　GRADE BOOK
　　　　WILLIS MUSIC COMPANY　　　　　　　　　1.50
THOMPSON, J.
　　STUDIES IN STYLE - SECOND PIANO ACCOMPANIMENTS FOR SECOND GRADE
　　BOOK
　　　　WILLIS MUSIC COMPANY　　　　　　　　　1.50
THOMPSON, J.
　　TWO-PIANO ALBUM FOR THE FIRST YEAR
　　　　WILLIS MUSIC COMPANY　　　　　　　　　1.50
THOMSON, V.
　　SYNTHETIC WALTZES -- SET OF 2 COPIES
　　　　ELKAN-VOGEL, INC.　　　　　　　　　　3.50
THOMSON, V.
　　WALKING SONG -- SET
　　　　G. SCHIRMER, INC.　　　　　　　　　　.75
TIMM, H. C.
　　SECOND PIANO PARTS TO 6 SONATINAS, OP. 36 BY CLEMENTI -- BK. 1,
　　NO. 1,C, NO. 2,G, NO. 4, F
　　　　G. SCHIRMER, INC.　　　　　　　　　　.90
TIMM, H. C.
　　SECOND PIANO PARTS TO 6 SONATINAS, OP. 36 BY CLEMENTI -- BK. 2,
　　NO. 3, NO. 5, G, NO. 6, D
　　　　G. SCHIRMER, INC.　　　　　　　　　　.90
TOCCHI
　　THREE FAVOLETTE
　　　　FRANCO COLOMBO PUBLICATIONS　　　DS474　　3.25
TOCH, E.　　　　　　6
　　KONZERT FUR KLAVIER UND ORCHESTER, OP. 38 - KLAVIERAUSZUG
　　　　SCHOTT　　　　　　　　　　　　　1859
TOCH, E.　　　　　　6
　　SYMPHONIE FUR KLAVIER UND ORCHESTER, OP. 61 - KLAVIERAUSZUG
　　　　SCHOTT　　　　　　　　　　　　　3277　　6.00
TODD
　　SWISS VILLAGE
　　　　BELWIN-MILLS PUBLISHING CORPORATION　　　1.25
TONSING
　　CONCERTO FOR A YOUNG PIANIST --SOLO AND 2ND PIANO--
　　　　ROCHESTER MUSIC PUBLISHERS, INC.　　　　3.00
TOSELLI　　　　　HULL *　　3
　　SERENADE
　　　　BOSTON MUSIC COMPANY　　　　　　　　.75
TRIMBLE
　　BARD OF LISGOLLE
　　　　BOOSEY AND HAWKES, INC.　　　　　　　1.25
TRIMBLE
　　SONATINA
　　　　BOOSEY AND HAWKES, INC.　　　　　　　2.00
TRUXELL, E.　　　　　　　　4
　　SILVER ANNIVERSARY WALTZ
　　　　VOLKWEIN BROS.　　　　　　　　　　01.00
TRUXELL, E.　　　　　　　　4
　　SPRINGTIME IN THE AIR
　　　　VOLKWEIN BROS.　　　　　　　　　　01.00
TRUXELL, E.　　　　　　　　4
　　TANGO
　　　　VOLKWEIN BROS.　　　　　　　　　　01.00
TRUXELL, E.　　　　　　　　4
　　VALSE CHANTEE
　　　　VOLKWEIN BROS.　　　　　　　　　　01.00
TSCHAIKOWSKY
　　CHANT SANS PAROLES, OP. 2 NO. 3
　　　　GERARD BILLAUDOT EDITIONS MUSICALES　　　1.10
TSCHAIKOWSKY
　　CONCERTO, OP. 23
　　　　EDWIN F. KALMUS　　　　　　　　4015　　3.00
TSCHAIKOWSKY　　　　WHITFORD　　GR. 2 1/2
　　CONCERTO IN B FLAT MINOR
　　　　ROBERT WHITFORD PUBLICATIONS　　　　　.40
TSCHAIKOWSKY　　　　　　　　M
　　CONCERTO NO. 01 IN B FLAT MINOR, OP. 23 ABRIDGED
　　　　C. F. PETERS CORPORATION　　　　3775A　　1.25
TSCHAIKOWSKY
　　CONCERTO NO. 01 IN B FLAT MINOR, OP. 23
　　　　INTERNATIONAL MUSIC COMPANY　　　　　3.00
TSCHAIKOWSKY　　　　　　　　D
　　CONCERTO NO. 01 IN B FLAT MINOR, OP. 23
　　　　C. F. PETERS CORPORATION　　　　3775　　3.00
TSCHAIKOWSKY　　　　JOSEFFY, R.
　　CONCERTO NO. 01 IN B FLAT MINOR, OP. 23
　　　　G. SCHIRMER, INC.　　　　　　　L1045　　3.00
TSCHAIKOWSKY　　　　JOSEFFY
　　CONCERTO NO. 01 IN B FLAT MINOR, OP. 23
　　　　G. SCHIRMER, INC.　　　　　　　L1045　　3.00

TSCHAIKOWSKY　　　　　　　　D
　　CONCERTO NO. 02 IN G, OP. 44
　　　　C. F. PETERS CORPORATION　　　　4644　　5.00
TSCHAIKOWSKY　　　　　　4
　　KLAVIERKONZERT NO. 02 IN G
　　　　BARENREITER VERLAG　　　　　　AE 241
TSCHAIKOWSKY　　　　KELBERINE
　　LULLABY
　　　　BELWIN-MILLS PUBLISHING CORPORATION　　　1.25
TSCHAIKOWSKY　　　　PHILIPP, I.
　　MARCH MINIATURE, OP. 43
　　　　INTERNATIONAL MUSIC COMPANY　　　　　1.50
TSCHAIKOWSKY　　　　HESSELBERG
　　NUTCRACKER SUITE DE BALLET, THE -- CASSE-NOISETTE -- MINIATURE
　　OVERTURE
　　　　G. SCHIRMER, INC.　　　　　　　　　1.25
TSCHAIKOWSKY　　　　HESSELBERG
　　NUTCRACKER SUITE DE BALLET -- CASSE-NOISETTE -- CHINESE DANCE
　　　　G. SCHIRMER, INC.　　　　　　　　　.60
TSCHAIKOWSKY　　　　HESSELBERG
　　NUTCRACKER SUITE DE BALLET -- CASSE-NOISETTE -- DANCE OF THE
　　ORANGE TARTS, DANSE DES MIRLITONS
　　　　G. SCHIRMER, INC.　　　　　　　　　.75
TSCHAIKOWSKY　　　　HESSELBERG
　　NUTCRACKER SUITE DE BALLET -- CASSE-NOISETTE -- FLOWER WALTZ
　　　　G. SCHIRMER, INC.　　　　　　　　　1.50
TSCHAIKOWSKY　　　　HESSELBERG
　　NUTCRACKER SUITE DE BALLET -- CASSE-NOISETTE -- MARCH
　　　　G. SCHIRMER, INC.　　　　　　　　　.90
TSCHAIKOWSKY　　　　HESSELBERG
　　NUTCRACKER SUITE DE BALLET -- CASSE-NOISETTE -- TREPAK, RUSSIAN
　　DANCE
　　　　G. SCHIRMER, INC.　　　　　　　　　.60
TSCHAIKOWSKY　　　　HESSELBERG
　　NUTCRACKER SUITE DE BALLET -- CASSE NOISETTE -- DANCE OF THE
　　CANDY-FAIRY, DANSE DE LA FEE DRAGELET -- CASSE NOISETTE -- DANCE OF
　　THE CANDY-FAIRY, DANSE DE LA FEE DRAGE
　　　　G. SCHIRMER, INC.　　　　　　　　　.60
TSCHAIKOWSKY
　　RUSSIAN FOLK SONGS -- EASY-
　　　　EDWIN F. KALMUS　　　　　　　　4090　　2.50
TSCHAIKOWSKY　　　　DOUGHERTY
　　SLEEPING BEAUTY --EXCERPTS--
　　　　CARL FISCHER, INC.　　　　　　　P 2971　　2.00
TSCHAIKOWSKY　　　　ECKSTEIN
　　THEME FROM PIANO CONCERTO NO. 1 IN B FLAT
　　　　CARL FISCHER, INC.　　　　　　　S 2281　　.50
TSCHAIKOWSKY　　　　ECKSTEIN
　　THEME FROM PIANO CONCERTO NO. 1 IN B FLAT
　　　　CARL FISCHER, INC.　　　　　　　S 2282　　.50
TSCHAIKOWSKY　　　　BABIN
　　VALSE SENTIMENTALE
　　　　BOOSEY AND HAWKES, INC.　　　　　　1.50
TSCHAIKOWSKY　　　　BABIN
　　WALTZES -- EUGENE ONEGIN, SERENADE FOR STRINGS, SWAN LAKE AND
　　VALSE DES FLEURS
　　　　BOOSEY AND HAWKES, INC.　　　　　　EA.
TSCHAIKOWSKY　　　　BERKOWITZ
　　WALTZ FROM THE SLEEPING BEAUTY
　　　　ELKAN-VOGEL, INC.　　　　　　　　1.60
TURINA, J.
　　RAPSODIA SINFONICA
　　　　ASSOCIATED MUSIC PUBLISHERS, INC.　　UME　　2.75
TUTTLE, T. K.
　　UNBRELLA IN THE WIND
　　　　BELWIN-MILLS PUBLISHING CORPORATION　　　1.25
URBANNER, E.
　　DIALOGUE -- 1965
　　　　ASSOCIATED MUSIC PUBLISHERS, INC.　　DOB　　6.75
VALEN　　　　　　　　D
　　CONCERTO, OP. 44. SCORE --DOUBLING AS PIANO PART--
　　　　C. F. PETERS CORPORATION　　　　LY583A　　5.00
VAN DYKE　　　　　　3-4
　　BARCAROLE
　　　　PRO-ART PUBLICATIONS, INC.　　　　4　　.60
VAUGHAN WILLIAMS, R.
　　GREENSLEEVES
　　　　OXFORD UNIVERSITY PRESS　　　　35.301　　1.80
VAUGHAN WILLIAMS, R.
　　INTRODUCTION AND FUGUE
　　　　OXFORD UNIVERSITY PRESS　　　　35.021　　3.00
VERHAAR　　　　　　　　M-D
　　MUZIEK. HARPSICHORD, STRING ORCHESTRA. POCKET SCORE
　　　　C. F. PETERS CORPORATION　　　　D464　　3.50
VILLA-LOBOS, H.
　　BACHIANAS BRASILEIRAS NO. 3
　　　　FRANCO COLOMBO PUBLICATIONS　　　NY1945　　3.00
VILLA-LOBOS, H.
　　LITTLE PAPER DOLL, THE -- SET
　　　　ASSOCIATED MUSIC PUBLISHERS, INC.　　AMP　　2.00
VILLA-LOBOS, H.
　　MOMO PRECOCE -- 1929
　　　　ASSOCIATED MUSIC PUBLISHERS, INC.　　ESC　　10.00
VIOTTI　　　　　　GIAZOTTO *
　　CONCERTO IN G MINOR
　　　　FRANCO COLOMBO PUBLICATIONS　　　130171　　2.75
VIOZZI, G.
　　TEMPO DI SAMBA
　　　　EDIZIONI BERBEN　　　　　　　EB 1393　　2.40
VIOZZI, G.
　　THRENODY
　　　　FRANCO COLOMBO PUBLICATIONS　　　129037　　1.00
VIOZZI, G.
　　TOCCATA
　　　　EDIZIONI BERBEN　　　　　　　EB 1726　　5.50
VIVALDI *　　　　　　7
　　CONCERTI IN G AND A MINOR
　　　　C. F. PETERS CORPORATION　　　　4510　　2.50
VIVALDI
　　CONCERTO IN B MINOR -- FREE TRANSCRIPTION BY TAMBURINI AFTER
　　VERSION BY BACH --
　　　　FRANCO COLOMBO PUBLICATIONS　　　ER2039　　1.75
VIVALDI　　　　STEINER
　　LARGO IN E FLAT FROM "L'INVERNO" -- CONCERTO
　　　　ELKAN-VOGEL, INC.　　　　　　　　　.80
VIVALDI *　　　　STRADAL
　　ORGAN CONCERTO IN D MINOR
　　　　INTERNATIONAL MUSIC COMPANY　　　　　2.00
VOGLER, G. J.
　　VARIATIONEN UND CAPRICCIO UBER "MARLBROUGH S'EN VA-T-EN GUERRE"
　　FUR KLAVIER UND KAMMERORCHESTER, SOLOSTIMME
　　　　SCHOTT　　　　　　　　　　　4161　　3.00
VOGT　　　　　　　　4
　　CONCERTINO FUR KLAVIER, 9 BLASER UND SCHLAGZEUG
　　　　BARENREITER VERLAG　　　　　　AE 134
VOGT　　　　　　　　4
　　KONZERT FUR KLAVIER UND ORCHESTER
　　　　BARENREITER VERLAG　　　　　　AE 288

WAGNER, J.
    CONCERTINO IN G MINOR FOR PIANO AND ORCHESTRA, TWO PIANO
    REDUCTION
        SEESAW MUSIC CORPORATION   8.00

WALDENMAIER   4
    SKIZZEN FUR KLAVIER UND KAMMERORCHESTER, OP. 19
        BARENREITER VERLAG   AE 305

WALKER, G.
    SONATA FOR TWO PIANOS
        COMPOSERS AUTOGRAPH PUBLICATIONS   8.36

WALLERSTEIN, A.   SAMUELSON
    JENNY LIND POLKA
        BELWIN-MILLS PUBLISHING CORPORATION   .75

WALTON, W.
    FACADE EXCERPTS -- POPULAR SONG
        OXFORD UNIVERSITY PRESS   35.023   1.50

WALTON, W.
    FACADE EXCERPTS -- VALSE
        OXFORD UNIVERSITY PRESS   35.022   1.90

WALTON, W.
    SINFONIA CONCERTANTE
        OXFORD UNIVERSITY PRESS   35.020   4.25

WARD, S. A.   SCHAUM, J.   4
    AMERICA THE BEAUTIFUL
        BELWIN-MILLS PUBLISHING CORPORATION   .50

WARRACK, G.
    FURIANT
        BOOSEY AND HAWKES, INC.   1.75

WARRACK, G.
    POLKA FUGATA
        BOOSEY AND HAWKES, INC.   1.75

WARRACK, G.
    PRELUDE
        BOOSEY AND HAWKES, INC.   1.75

WEBER, VON   D
    COMPLETE PIANO WORKS, VOL. 3* VARIATIONS AND CONCERTOS
        C. F. PETERS CORPORATION   717C   6.50

WEBER, VON   STERNBERG
    CONCERTSTUCK, OP. 79
        G. SCHIRMER, INC.   L1189   1.00

WEBER, VON   STERNBERG
    CONCERTSTUCK IN F MINOR, OP. 79
        G. SCHIRMER, INC.   L1189   1.00

WEBER, VON   D
    CONCERT PIECE IN F MINOR, OP. 79
        C. F. PETERS CORPORATION   2899   2.00

WEBER, VON   D
    CONCERT PIECE IN F MINOR, OP. 79
        C. F. PETERS CORPORATION   2899   2.00

WEBER, VON   GRAETZER
    INVITATION TO THE DANCE, OP. 65
        FRANCO COLOMBO PUBLICATIONS   BA9692   1.00

WEBER, VON   MILICI
    INVITATION TO THE DANCE, OP. 65
        FRANCO COLOMBO PUBLICATIONS   BA8333   .75

WEBER, VON   WEINGARTNER
    INVITATION TO THE DANCE
        BOOSEY AND HAWKES, INC.   2.75

WEBER, VON
    KONZERTSTUCK IN F MINOR, OP. 79
        ASSOCIATED MUSIC PUBLISHERS, INC.   BRH   1.50

WEBER, VON   CARPER
    MARCH -- FROM CONCERTSTUCK IN F MINOR, OP. 79 -- SET
        G. SCHIRMER, INC.   .75

WEBER, VON *   SPENCER
    POLONAISE BRILLANTE, OP. 72
        G. SCHIRMER, INC.   L1382   1.25

WEBER, VON *   SPENCER
    POLONAISE BRILLANTE, OP. 72
        G. SCHIRMER, INC.   L1382   1.25

WEBER, VON   STEINER
    SONATINA IN C
        BELWIN-MILLS PUBLISHING CORPORATION   1.25

WEINBERGER, J.
    SHVANDA -- POLKA AND FUGUE -- SET
        ASSOCIATED MUSIC PUBLISHERS, INC.   AMP   2.50

WEINER
    SONATA FOR PIANO, OP. 5
        MCA MUSIC   3.95

WEISGALL, H.   MD
    FUGUE AND ROMANCE
        THEODORE PRESSER COMPANY   1.75

WEISMANN, J.   4-5
    KLAVIERKONZERT, OP. 33
        BARENREITER VERLAG   SM 1215

WEISMANN, J.   4
    SUITE FUR KLAVIER UND ORCHESTER, OP. 97
        BARENREITER VERLAG   SM 460

WERNER   SCHMID   2-3
    PASTORELLA IN D FUR ORGEL -- KLAVIER -- UND STREICHER
        BARENREITER VERLAG   BA 1557

WERNER   SCHMID   2-3
    PASTORELLA ZUR WEIHNACHT IN G FUR ORGEL -- KLAVIER -- UND
    STREICHER
        BARENREITER VERLAG   BA 953

WESLEY, C.   FINZI   M
    CONCERTO NO. 04 IN C. HARPSICHORD SOLO PART
        C. F. PETERS CORPORATION   H290A   1.50

WEYBRIGHT--ED.   WEYBRIGHT   1
    DOZEN DUETS FOR PIANO, A
        WILLIS MUSIC COMPANY   1.25

WEYBRIGHT   3
    BRAZILIANA
        BELWIN-MILLS PUBLISHING CORPORATION   .60

WEYBRIGHT   1
    SHEPHERD'S HEY
        WILLIS MUSIC COMPANY   .40

WEYBRIGHT   1
    TUMBLE-TOWN CAKEWALK
        WILLIS MUSIC COMPANY   .50

WEYBRIGHT   1
    TUMBLE-TOWN WATERFALL
        WILLIS MUSIC COMPANY   .50

WEYBRIGHT   1
    TURKEY IN THE STRAW
        WILLIS MUSIC COMPANY   .35

WHITHORNE
    SOONER AND LATER
        FRANCO COLOMBO PUBLICATIONS   SAL   14.50

WIDOR, CH.   PHILIPP, I.
    FANTAISIE POUR PIANO ET ORCHESTRE
        ELKAN-VOGEL, INC.   D   5.25

WIDOR, CH.   PHILIPP, I.
    TOCCATA FROM THE FIFTH SYMPHONY FOR ORGAN
        G. SCHIRMER, INC.   L1660   1.00

WIGHAM, M.
    CONCERTO FOR TWO PIANOS
        CARL FISCHER, INC.   RS 399   3.00

WILLIAMS, C.
    THEME FROM 'THE APARTMENT'
        BELWIN-MILLS PUBLISHING CORPORATION   27043   1.50

WILLIAMSON, E.   MD
    SONATA FOR 2 PIANOS
        THEODORE PRESSER COMPANY   3.00

WILLIAMS   LEONARD
    DREAM OF OL'WEN, THE
        BELWIN-MILLS PUBLISHING CORPORATION   27011   2.00

WILLIAMS   LEONARD
    DREAM OF OLWEN, THE
        BELWIN-MILLS PUBLISHING CORPORATION   27011   2.00

WILM, N. VON
    VARIATIONS, OP. 64 -- SET
        ASSOCIATED MUSIC PUBLISHERS, INC.   LEU   6.00

WILM, N. VON
    WALTZ -- SET
        ASSOCIATED MUSIC PUBLISHERS, INC.   LEU   4.50

WISSE
    CRISTALLI
        IMPERO-VERLAG   2.50

WISSE   M-D
    CRISTALLI
        C. F. PETERS CORPORATION   D219   2.00

WITKOWSKY
    MON LAC
        FRANCO COLOMBO PUBLICATIONS   SAL   10.00

WOHLFAHPT
    PASSION DES PROMETHEUS, DIE -- MARCH
        ASSOCIATED MUSIC PUBLISHERS, INC.   BOT   1.50

WOLF, W.
    CONCERTO, OP. 13
        BOOSEY AND HAWKES, INC.   7.50

WOOD, H.
    CONCERTO IN D MINOR
        BOOSEY AND HAWKES, INC.   4.00

WOZENCRAFT, M.
    TWO EASY TWIN PIECES WHICH CAN BE PLAYED SEPARATELY AS SOLOS OR
    TOGETHER AT TWO PIANOS--WALTZ ME AROUND, AND WALTZ ME AROUND, TOO
        G. SCHIRMER, INC.   .40

WRIGHT, N.
    BUTTERFLY, THE -- FROM ''IN SPRINGTIME,'' OP. 36 NO. 4 -- WITH
    SUPPLEMENTARY PIANO II PART BY WEYBRIGHT -- SET
        G. SCHIRMER, INC.   .70

WYTTENBACH, J.
    NACHSPIEL IN DREI TEILEN
        SCHOTT   AV 87   3.00

YON, P. A.   FROST
    GESU BAMBINO
        BELWIN-MILLS PUBLISHING CORPORATION   1.50

YOUMANS   MERKUR
    TEA FOR TWO
        WARNER BROTHERS PUBLISHERS   2.00

YOUNG   M
    FUGAL CONCERTO IN G MINOR
        C. F. PETERS CORPORATION   H205   2.50

ZACH   GOTTRON   3-4
    KONZERT FUR CEMBALO -- KLAVIER -- UND STREICHER
        BARENREITER VERLAG   NMA 165

ZAFRED   AMISANO
    CONCERTO
        FRANCO COLOMBO PUBLICATIONS   129923   3.50

ZAFRED
    VARIAZIONI CONCERTANTI
        FRANCO COLOMBO PUBLICATIONS   130835   6.75

ZAMECNIK
    POLLY
        SOUTHERN MUSIC COMPANY   1.50

ZBINDEN, J. F.
    CONCERTO DE CAMERA, OP. 16
        ASSOCIATED MUSIC PUBLISHERS, INC.   BRH   3.75

ZIMMER   4
    CONCERTINO FUR KLAVIER UND STREICHORCHESTER
        BARENREITER VERLAG   CHF 5132

Two Piano, Four Hands (Original and Arranged):
Composer/Editor/Arranger Unlisted—Works Alphabetized by Title

ALAMEIN CONCERTO
    CHAPPELL AND COMPANY, INC.   0014258-1501   1.25

ALICE BLUE
    THE BIG THREE MUSIC CORPORATION   02.00

ANCHORS AWEIGH
    THE BIG THREE MUSIC CORPORATION   02.00

CHICKEN REEL
    THE BIG THREE MUSIC CORPORATION   02.00

DAINTY MISS
    THE BIG THREE MUSIC CORPORATION   02.00

DEEP PURPLE
    THE BIG THREE MUSIC CORPORATION   02.00

DODGING A DIVORCEE
    THE BIG THREE MUSIC CORPORATION   02.00

DOLL DANCE
    THE BIG THREE MUSIC CORPORATION   02.00

ENSEMBLE AT TWO PIANOS. COMPILATION
    SUMMY-BIRCHARD COMPANY   1   3.50

FAMILIAR TUNES FOR FOUR SMALL HANDS
    WILLIS MUSIC COMPANY   .80

FOUR HAND RECREATIONS, BK. 1
    WILLIS MUSIC COMPANY   1.00

FOUR HAND RECREATIONS, BK. 2
    WILLIS MUSIC COMPANY   1.00

GAYETY
    THE BIG THREE MUSIC CORPORATION   02.00

HOLIDAY
    THE BIG THREE MUSIC CORPORATION   02.00

IN A MIST
    THE BIG THREE MUSIC CORPORATION   02.00

JOSEPHINE
    THE BIG THREE MUSIC CORPORATION   02.00

LAZY RHAPSODY
    THE BIG THREE MUSIC CORPORATION   02.00

MODERN PIANIST SERIES - DUO-CLASSICS
    POINTER PUBLICATIONS   1.95

MODERN PIANIST SERIES - DUO-FAVORITES
    POINTER PUBLICATIONS   1.95

MODERN PIANIST SERIES - DUO-MODS
    POINTER PUBLICATIONS   2.50

MODERN PIANIST SERIES - DUO-POPS
    POINTER PUBLICATIONS   2.50

MOONLIGHT MOOD
    THE BIG THREE MUSIC CORPORATION   02.00

ON THE TRAIL
    THE BIG THREE MUSIC CORPORATION   02.00

PEARLS ON VELVET
    THE BIG THREE MUSIC CORPORATION   02.00

ROYAL BLUE
    THE BIG THREE MUSIC CORPORATION   02.00

SERENADE FOR A WEALTHY WIDOW
    THE BIG THREE MUSIC CORPORATION   02.00

SONG OF THE BAYOU
    THE BIG THREE MUSIC CORPORATION   02.00

STREET SCENE
    THE BIG THREE MUSIC CORPORATION   02.00

TEMPTATION
    THE BIG THREE MUSIC CORPORATION   02.00

WILLIS ROADWAY TO PIANO DUETS
    WILLIS MUSIC COMPANY   1.75

Concertos

ABEL   E
CONCERTINO IN E FLAT. WITH TWO VIOLINS, V'CELLO
    C. F. PETERS CORPORATION   4409A   3.50

ADDINSELL
WARSAW CONCERTO -- THEME EASY
    CHAPPELL AND COMPANY, INC.   0017798-1503   .95

ADDINSELL
WARSAW CONCERTO -- THEME
    CHAPPELL AND COMPANY, INC.   0017780-1502   .95

ADDINSELL
WARSAW CONCERTO
    CHAPPELL AND COMPANY, INC.   0017780-1501   1.25

ADDINSELL   LIBERACE
WARSAW CONCERTO
    CHAPPELL AND COMPANY, INC.   0021592-1504   1.00

ALBENIZ, I.   GODOWSKY   5
TANGO NO. 2. KONZERTTRANSKRIPTION
    SCHOTT   1705   1.75

ALBERT, E. D'
CONCERTO NO. 02 IN E, OP. 12
    ASSOCIATED MUSIC PUBLISHERS, INC.   BOT   10.25

ALKAN
FIRST CONCERTO DA CAMERA ADAGIO MOVEMENT
    MUSICA OBSCURA   1.50

ALKAN
FIRST CONCERTO DA CAMERA IN A MINOR, OP. 10 NO. 1
    MUSICA OBSCURA   4.00

ALKAN
FIRST CONCERTO DA CAMERA IN A MINOR, OP. 10
    GERARD BILLAUDOT EDITIONS MUSICALES   4.10

ALKAN
SECOND CONCERTO DA CAMERA, OP. 10 NO. 2 IN C SHARP MINOR
    MUSICA OBSCURA   3.00

ALKAN
SECOND CONCERTO DA CAMERA IN C SHARP MINOR, OP. 10
    GERARD BILLAUDOT EDITIONS MUSICALES   3.30

ALKAN
TUTTI DE CONCERTO, DANS LE GENRE ANCIEN OP. 63, NO. 15
    MUSICA OBSCURA   1.00

ALKAN
TWELVE ETUDES IN MINOR KEYS, NO. 08, CONCERTO-ALLEGRO ASSAI--G SHARP MINOR--
    GERARD BILLAUDOT EDITIONS MUSICALES   5.70

ALKAN
TWELVE ETUDES IN MINOR KEYS, NO. 09, CONCERTO-ADAGIO--C SHARP MINOR--
    GERARD BILLAUDOT EDITIONS MUSICALES   3.00

ANDERSON, G.
CONCERTINO FOR PIANO AND ORCHESTRA
    AMERICAN MUSIC EDITION   4.00

ANDRIESSEN, J.   M-D
CONCERTO SENZA ORCHESTRA
    C. F. PETERS CORPORATION   D48   3.00

ANGERER
CONCERTO
    ASSOCIATED MUSIC PUBLISHERS, INC.   DOB   4.25

ANSON, G.
CONCERTO
    NOVELLO AND COMPANY, LTD.   10.0146.09   2.50

ANSON, G.   3
KID CONCERTO
    WILLIS MUSIC COMPANY   1.75

ANSON, G.
MINIATURE CONCERTO
    SOUTHERN MUSIC COMPANY   1.75

ANTONIOU   4
CONCERTINO, OP. 21 FUR KLAVIER, 9 BLASER UND SCHLAGZEUG
    BARENREITER VERLAG   BA 4377

ANTONIOU   4
KONZERTINO, OP. 16B FUR KLAVIER, STREICHER UND SCHLAGZEUG
    BARENREITER VERLAG   BA 4378

APOSTEL
CONCERTO, OP. 30
    UNIVERSAL EDITION   13174   5.75

ARNE   2
KONZERT NO. 05 IN G MINOR
    BARENREITER VERLAG   NMA 210

AVERY, R.   3 1/2
CONCERTINO ON FAMILIAR TUNES
    THEODORE PRESSER COMPANY   1.25

BABIN
CONCERTO NO. 02 FOR TWO PIANOS
    BOOSEY AND HAWKES, INC.   12.50

BACH, C.P.E.   M
CONCERTO FOR 2 PIANOS --WITH ORCH. ACC. IN PIANO THREE--. THREE PIANOS, SIX HANDS
    C. F. PETERS CORPORATION   Z450   4.50

BACH, C.P.E.   M-D
CONCERTO FOR 2 PIANOS --WITH ORCH. ACC. IN PIANO 3--
    C. F. PETERS CORPORATION   Z450   4.50

BACH, C.P.E.   WERTHEIM
CONCERTO IN D MINOR
    ASSOCIATED MUSIC PUBLISHERS, INC.   BRH   3.75

BACH, C.P.E.   DARVAS
CONCERTO IN D MINOR
    KULTURA   4.50

BACH, C.P.E.   LANDSHOFF   D
CONCERTO IN D
    C. F. PETERS CORPORATION   N1178   7.50

BACH, C.P.E.   JACOBI   3-4
DOPPELKONZERT IN E FLAT FUR KLAVIER, CEMBALO UND KAMMERORCHESTER
    BARENREITER VERLAG   BA 2043

BACH, C.P.E.   OBERDORFFER   3
KONZERT IN F FUR CEMBALO UND STREICHER
    BARENREITER VERLAG   BA 2004

BACH, C.P.E.   OBERDORFFER   3
KONZERT IN G MINOR FUR CEMBALO UND STREICHER
    BARENREITER VERLAG   BA 2005

BACH, J.S.   REGER
BRANDENBURG CONCERTOS, BK. 1
    INTERNATIONAL MUSIC COMPANY   3.50

BACH, J.S.
BRANDENBURG CONCERTOS, BK. 1
    EDWIN F. KALMUS   3027   3.50

BACH, J.S.   REGER
BRANDENBURG CONCERTOS, BK. 2
    INTERNATIONAL MUSIC COMPANY   4.00

BACH, J.S.
BRANDENBURG CONCERTOS, BK. 2
    EDWIN F. KALMUS   3028   4.00

BACH, J.S.   REGER   D
BRANDENBURG CONCERTOS, VOL. 1
    C. F. PETERS CORPORATION   3108A   6.00

BACH, J.S.   REGER   D
BRANDENBURG CONCERTOS, VOL. 2
    C. F. PETERS CORPORATION   3108B   6.00

BACH, J.S.   ZANON
BRANDENBURG CONCERTO NO. 1 IN F
    FRANCO COLOMBO PUBLICATIONS   ER2491   1.75

BACH, J.S.   REGER   D
BRANDENBURG CONCERTO NO. 1 IN F
    C. F. PETERS CORPORATION   3108AA   2.00

BACH, J.S.   M
BRANDENBURG CONCERTO NO. 1
    C. F. PETERS CORPORATION   H304   1.25

BACH, J.S.   ZANON
BRANDENBURG CONCERTO NO. 2 IN F
    FRANCO COLOMBO PUBLICATIONS   ER2492   1.75

BACH, J.S.   REGER   D
BRANDENBURG CONCERTO NO. 2 IN F
    C. F. PETERS CORPORATION   3108BB   2.00

BACH, J.S.   ZANON
BRANDENBURG CONCERTO NO. 3 IN G
    FRANCO COLOMBO PUBLICATIONS   ER2493   1.75

BACH, J.S.   REGER   D
BRANDENBURG CONCERTO NO. 3 IN G
    C. F. PETERS CORPORATION   3108C   2.00

BACH, J.S.   D
BRANDENBURG CONCERTO NO. 3
    C. F. PETERS CORPORATION   H305   2.00

BACH, J.S.   ZANON
BRANDENBURG CONCERTO NO. 4 IN G
    FRANCO COLOMBO PUBLICATIONS   ER2494   2.25

BACH, J.S.   REGER   D
BRANDENBURG CONCERTO NO. 4 IN G
    C. F. PETERS CORPORATION   3108D   2.00

BACH, J.S.   WENZINGER
BRANDENBURG CONCERTO NO. 5 IN D
    BARENREITER VERLAG

BACH, J.S.   ZANON
BRANDENBURG CONCERTO NO. 5 IN D
    FRANCO COLOMBO PUBLICATIONS   ER2495   2.25

BACH, J.S.   REGER   D
BRANDENBURG CONCERTO NO. 5 IN D
    C. F. PETERS CORPORATION   3108E   2.00

BACH, J.S.   ZANON
BRANDENBURG CONCERTO NO. 6 IN B-FLAT
    FRANCO COLOMBO PUBLICATIONS   ER2496   2.25

BACH, J.S.   REGER   D
BRANDENBURG CONCERTO NO. 6 IN B FLAT
    C. F. PETERS CORPORATION   3108F   2.00

BACH, J.S.   BUELOW
CHROMATIC FANTASY AND FUGUE, CONCERTO IN THE ITALIAN STYLE, FANTASY IN C MINOR, PRELUDE AND FUGUE IN A MINOR
    G. SCHIRMER, INC.   L22   1.25

BACH, J.S.   M-D
CONCERTI AFTER OTHER COMPOSERS. 16 CONCERTI IN 3 VOLUMES. VOL.1
    C. F. PETERS CORPORATION   217A   3.00

BACH, J.S.   M-D
CONCERTI AFTER OTHER COMPOSERS. 16 CONCERTI IN 3 VOLUMES. VOL.2
    C. F. PETERS CORPORATION   217B   3.00

BACH, J.S.   M-D
CONCERTI AFTER OTHER COMPOSERS. 16 CONCERTI IN 3 VOLUMES. VOL.3
    C. F. PETERS CORPORATION   217C   1.50

BACH, J.S.   SEAK
CONCERTO AFTER VIVALDI -- OP. 3 NO. 9
    FRANCO COLOMBO PUBLICATIONS   129578   .90

BACH, J.S.
CONCERTO IN A, SCH NO. 1055
    ASSOCIATED MUSIC PUBLISHERS, INC.   BRH   1.00

BACH, J.S.   M-D
CONCERTO IN A --URTEXT--
    C. F. PETERS CORPORATION   4467   1.50

BACH, J.S.
CONCERTO IN A MINOR FOR 4 PIANOS, SCH NO.1065
    ASSOCIATED MUSIC PUBLISHERS, INC.   BRH   1.00

BACH, J.S.   BAUER
CONCERTO IN C -- 6-HANDS
    G. SCHIRMER, INC.   1.25

BACH, J.S.   M-D
CONCERTO IN C FOR 2 PIANOS --2 COPIES--
    C. F. PETERS CORPORATION   2200A   2.50

BACH, J.S.
CONCERTO IN C FOR 2 PIANOS
    INTERNATIONAL MUSIC COMPANY   3.00

BACH, J.S.   M-D
CONCERTO IN C MINOR FOR 2 PIANOS --2 COPIES--
    C. F. PETERS CORPORATION   2200B   2.50

BACH, J.S.
CONCERTO IN C MINOR FOR 2 PIANOS
    INTERNATIONAL MUSIC COMPANY   3.00

BACH, J.S.   BAUER
CONCERTO IN C MINOR
    G. SCHIRMER, INC.   1.25

BACH, J.S.   BAUER
CONCERTO IN C MINOR
    G. SCHIRMER, INC.   1.25

BACH, J.S.
CONCERTO IN D, SCH NO. 1054
    ASSOCIATED MUSIC PUBLISHERS, INC.   BRH   1.00

BACH, J.S.   M-D
CONCERTO IN D MINOR, AFTER MARCELLO OBOE CONCERTO
    C. F. PETERS CORPORATION   217D   1.50

BACH, J.S.   BUSONI
CONCERTO IN D MINOR, SCH NO. 1052
    ASSOCIATED MUSIC PUBLISHERS, INC.   BRH   1.50

BACH, J.S.   TAGLIAPIETRA
CONCERTO IN D MINOR
    FRANCO COLOMBO PUBLICATIONS   ER1432   1.75

BACH, J.S.   M-D
CONCERTO IN D MINOR
    C. F. PETERS CORPORATION   2912   1.50

BACH, J.S.   HUGHES
CONCERTO IN D MINOR
    G. SCHIRMER, INC.   L1527   2.00

BACH, J.S.   HUGHES
CONCERTO IN D MINOR
    G. SCHIRMER, INC.   L1527   2.00

BACH, J.S.   RONTGEN
CONCERTO IN D MINOR
    UNIVERSAL EDITION   625   2.40

BACH, J.S.
CONCERTO IN E, SCH. NO. 1053
    ASSOCIATED MUSIC PUBLISHERS, INC.   BRH   1.00

BACH, J.S.   M-D
CONCERTO IN E --URTEXT--
    C. F. PETERS CORPORATION   4469   2.50

BACH, J.S.
CONCERTO IN F MINOR, SCH NO. 1056
    ASSOCIATED MUSIC PUBLISHERS, INC.   BRH   1.00

BACH, J.S. TEICHMUELLER M-D
CONCERTO IN F MINOR --URTEXT--
 C. F. PETERS CORPORATION 3830 1.50
BACH, J.S. TAGLIAPIETRA
CONCERTO IN F MINOR
 FRANCO COLOMBO PUBLICATIONS ER2434 1.25
BACH, J.S. FISCHER, E.
CONCERTO IN F MINOR
 INTERNATIONAL MUSIC COMPANY 2.00
BACH, J.S.
CONCERTO IN G MINOR, SCH NO. 1058
 ASSOCIATED MUSIC PUBLISHERS, INC. BRH 1.00
BACH, J.S. GOEDICKE *
CONCERTO IN G MINOR
 INTERNATIONAL MUSIC COMPANY 2.00
BACH, J.S. BUELOW *
CONCERTO IN THE ITALIAN STYLE
 FRANCO COLOMBO PUBLICATIONS ER2631 .90
BACH, J.S. RALSTON
CONCERTO IN THE ITALIAN STYLE
 G. SCHIRMER, INC. L1806 1.50
BACH, J.S. BUELOW
CONCERTO IN THE ITALIAN STYLE
 G. SCHIRMER, INC. .90
BACH, J.S.
CONCERTO NO. 01 IN C MINOR FOR 2 PIANOS, SCH NO. 1060
 ASSOCIATED MUSIC PUBLISHERS, INC. BRH 1.00
BACH, J.S.
CONCERTO NO. 01 IN D MINOR FOR 3 PIANOS, SCH NO. 1063
 ASSOCIATED MUSIC PUBLISHERS, INC. BRH 1.00
BACH, J.S.
CONCERTO NO. 02 IN C FOR 2 PIANOS, SCH NO. 1061
 ASSOCIATED MUSIC PUBLISHERS, INC. BRH 1.00
BACH, J.S.
CONCERTO NO. 02 IN C FOR 3 PIANOS, SCH NO. 1064
 ASSOCIATED MUSIC PUBLISHERS, INC. BRH 1.00
BACH, J.S.
CONCERTO NO. 03 IN C MINOR FOR 2 PIANOS, SCH NO. 1062
 ASSOCIATED MUSIC PUBLISHERS, INC. BRH 1.00
BACH, J.S. D
FANTASIA IN C MINOR, PRELUDIO CON FUGA IN A MINOR, ITALIAN
CONCERTO IN F, FANTASIA CROMATICA CON FUGA IN D MINOR
 C. F. PETERS CORPORATION 207 3.00
BACH, J.S. M-D
FRENCH OVERTURE AND ITALIAN CONCERTO, URTEXT
 C. F. PETERS CORPORATION 4594 2.00
BACH, J.S. BAUER
ITALIAN CONCERTO--ARR. IN HARPSICHORD STYLE
 G. SCHIRMER, INC. 3.00
BACH, J.S. BAUER
ITALIAN CONCERTO, ARR. IN HARPSICHORD STYLE -- SET
 G. SCHIRMER, INC. 3.00
BACH, J.S. PETRI
ITALIAN CONCERTO, S. 971, AND PARTITA IN B MINOR, S. 831
 ASSOCIATED MUSIC PUBLISHERS, INC. B/H 2.25
BACH, J.S. M-D
ITALIAN CONCERTO AND FRENCH OVERTURE--URTEXT--
 C. F. PETERS CORPORATION 4464 2.00
BACH, J.S. SOLDAN
ITALIAN CONCERTO AND FRENCH OVERTURE -- URTEXT --
 C. F. PETERS CORPORATION 4464 2.00
BACH, J.S. PALMER, W. A.
ITALIAN CONCERTO
 ALFRED MUSIC COMPANY 573 2.00
BACH, J.S.
ITALIAN CONCERTO,
 G. HENLE MUSIKVERLAG 160 1.15
BACH, J.S. BISCHOFF
ITALIAN CONCERTO
 INTERNATIONAL MUSIC COMPANY 1.50
BACH, J.S. BISCHOFF
ITALIAN CONCERTO
 EDWIN F. KALMUS 3100 1.00
BACH, J.S. RONTGEN
ITALIAN CONCERTO
 UNIVERSAL EDITION 330 1.30
BACH, J.S. KREUTZ 5
ITALIENISCHES KONZERT -- BWV 971
 SCHOTT 0876 1/2 1.00
BACH, J.S. M-D
KLAVIERUEBUNG --URTEXT--. PART 2: ITALIAN CONCERTO AND FRENCH
OVERTURE
 C. F. PETERS CORPORATION 4464 2.00
BACH, J.S. KEMPFF
LARGO FROM THE CLAVIER CONCERTO IN F MINOR
 ASSOCIATED MUSIC PUBLISHERS, INC. B/B .90
BACH, J.S. M
MENUETTO, POLACCA, 2 TRIOS --FROM BRANDENBURG CONCERTO NO.1--
 C. F. PETERS CORPORATION H304 1.25
BACH, J.S. PETRI
PARTITA IN B MINOR, S. 831, AND ITALIAN CONCERTO, S. 971
 ASSOCIATED MUSIC PUBLISHERS, INC. B/H 2.00
BACH, J.S.
PIANO CONCERTO FOR TWO PIANOS IN C MINOR
 EDWIN F. KALMUS 3032 2.50
BACH, J.S.
PIANO CONCERTO FOR TWO PIANOS IN C
 EDWIN F. KALMUS 3031 2.50
BACH, J.S.
PIANO CONCERTO IN D MINOR
 EDWIN F. KALMUS 3029 2.50
BACH, J.S.
PIANO CONCERTO IN F MINOR
 EDWIN F. KALMUS 3030 1.50
BACH, J.S. LEUCHTER
SIX CONCERTOS AFTER VIVALDI -- OP. 3, NOS. 3, 9, 12. OP. 4, NOS.
1, 6. OP. 7, NO. 2
 FRANCO COLOMBO PUBLICATIONS BA12114 4.00
BACH, J.S. BUSONI *
THREE SONATAS, CONCERTO IN C MINOR, AND MISCELLANEOUS PIECES
 ASSOCIATED MUSIC PUBLISHERS, INC. B/H 2.25
BACH, J. C. F. SEILER
CONCERTO FOR PIANO AND VIOLA OBBLIGATO -- 2-PNO RED. WITH VIOLA
PART
 ASSOCIATED MUSIC PUBLISHERS, INC. BOT 11.00
BACH, J. CHRISTIAN DOEBEREINER M
CONCERTO, OP. 7, NO. 5
 C. F. PETERS CORPORATION 3873 2.50
BACH, J. CHRISTIAN
CONCERTO IN A FUR CEMBALO -- KLAVIER UND STREICH-ORCHESTER,
KLAVIERAUSZUG
 SCHOTT 2320 3.50
BACH, J. CHRISTIAN LANDSHOFF E-M
CONCERTO IN B FLAT, OP. 13, NO. 4
 C. F. PETERS CORPORATION 4329 1.50

BACH, J. CHRISTIAN
CONCERTO IN G FUR CEMBALO -- KLAVIER UND STREICH-ORCHESTER,
KLAVIERAUSZUG
 SCHOTT 3703 2.50
BACH, J. CHRISTIAN LANDSHOFF E-M
CONCERTO OP.13, NO.2 IN D, URTEXT
 C. F. PETERS CORPORATION 4262 1.50
BACH, J. CHRISTIAN MARTINI, G. 3-4
KONZERT IN F MINOR FUR CEMBALO -- KLAVIER -- UND STREICHER
 BARENREITER VERLAG NMA 170
BACH, W.F.
KONZERT FUR 2 KLAVIERE F-DUR
 SCHOTT 10159 2.50
BACH, W.F.
PIANO CONCERTO IN A MINOR
 EDWIN F. KALMUS 3109 3.00
BACH, W.F.
PIANO CONCERTO IN E MINOR
 EDWIN F. KALMUS 3108 3.00
BADURA-SKODA
CADENZAS TO HAYDN CONCERTO IN D
 ASSOCIATED MUSIC PUBLISHERS, INC. DOB 1.25
BADURA-SKODA
CADENZAS TO MOZART'S PIANO CONCERTI
 BARENREITER VERLAG BA 4461 10.00
BADURA-SKODA
CADENZAS TO MOZART CONCERTO IN D MINOR, K. 466
 ASSOCIATED MUSIC PUBLISHERS, INC. DOB 1.25
BADURA-SKODA
CADENZAS TO MOZART CONCERTO IN E FLAT, K. 482
 ASSOCIATED MUSIC PUBLISHERS, INC. DOB 1.25
BADURA-SKODA
CADENZA AND INTRODUCTIONS TO MOZART CONCERTO IN C MINOR, K. 491
 ASSOCIATED MUSIC PUBLISHERS, INC. DOB 1.25
BADURA-SKODA
CADENZA TO MOZART CONCERTO IN C, K. 503
 ASSOCIATED MUSIC PUBLISHERS, INC. DOB 1.25
BADURA-SKODA 4-5
KADENZEN ZU MOZARTS KLAVIERKONZERTEN K175, 238, 415, 449, 453,
456, 467, 482, 491, 503, 537, AND 595
 BARENREITER VERLAG BA 4461
BARBER, S.
PIANO CONCERTO, OP. 38
 G. SCHIRMER, INC. 4.00
BARBER, S.
PIANO CONCERTO, OP. 38
 G. SCHIRMER, INC. 4.00
BARTA 4
KONZERT FUR KLAVIER UND ORCHESTER
 BARENREITER VERLAG CHF 5227
BARTOK
CONCERTO NO. 01
 BOOSEY AND HAWKES, INC. 7.50
BARTOK
CONCERTO NO. 02
 BOOSEY AND HAWKES, INC. 7.50
BARTOK
CONCERTO NO. 03
 BOOSEY AND HAWKES, INC. 7.50
BAUER, M.
AMERICAN YOUTH CONCERTO
 G. SCHIRMER, INC. 1.50
BAUER, M.
AMERICAN YOUTH CONCERTO
 G. SCHIRMER, INC. 1.50
BAUR
KONZERTANTE MUSIK -- 1958
 ASSOCIATED MUSIC PUBLISHERS, INC. BRH 5.00
BECK, C. 5
CONCERTINO FUR KLAVIER UND ORCHESTER, KLAVIERAUSZUG
 SCHOTT 2068 3.75
BEETHOVEN KEMPFF
CADENZAS TO CONCERTI NOS. 1-4
 ASSOCIATED MUSIC PUBLISHERS, INC. DOB 3.50
BEETHOVEN BUSONI D
CADENZAS TO CONCERTOS 1, 3, 4
 C. F. PETERS CORPORATION N798 2.00
BEETHOVEN
CADENZAS TO PIANO CONCERTOS BY BEETHOVEN HIMSELF
 EDWIN F. KALMUS 3195 2.00
BEETHOVEN
CADENZA TO CONCERTO NO. 02 IN B FLAT, OP. 19
 ASSOCIATED MUSIC PUBLISHERS, INC. DOB 1.00
BEETHOVEN
CADENZA TO CONCERTO NO. 03 IN C MINOR, OP. 37
 ASSOCIATED MUSIC PUBLISHERS, INC. DOB 1.25
BEETHOVEN
CADENZA TO CONCERTO NO. 04 IN G, OP. 58
 ASSOCIATED MUSIC PUBLISHERS, INC. DOB 1.25
BEETHOVEN
CADENZA TO MOZART CONCERTO IN D MINOR, K. 466
 ASSOCIATED MUSIC PUBLISHERS, INC. DOB 1.00
BEETHOVEN REINECKE
CADENZA TO THE CONCERTO NO. 3 IN C MINOR, OP. 37--FIRST MOVEMENT
 G. SCHIRMER, INC. .70
BEETHOVEN HESS D
CONCERTO IN E FLAT. JUGENDKONZERT
 C. F. PETERS CORPORATION Z454 4.70
BEETHOVEN ALBERT, E. D'
CONCERTO NO. 01 IN C, OP. 15
 ASSOCIATED MUSIC PUBLISHERS, INC. BRH 3.00
BEETHOVEN MONTANI
CONCERTO NO. 01 IN C, OP. 15
 FRANCO COLOMBO PUBLICATIONS ER2427 2.25
BEETHOVEN PAUER D
CONCERTO NO. 01 IN C, OP. 15
 C. F. PETERS CORPORATION 2894A 1.50
BEETHOVEN KULLAK, T.
CONCERTO NO. 01 IN C, OP. 15
 G. SCHIRMER, INC. L621 1.50
BEETHOVEN KULLAK
CONCERTO NO. 01 IN C MAJOR, OP. 1
 G. SCHIRMER, INC. L621 1.50
BEETHOVEN ALBERT, E. D' *
CONCERTO NO. 02 IN B FLAT, OP. 19
 ASSOCIATED MUSIC PUBLISHERS, INC. BRH 3.00
BEETHOVEN TAGLIAPIETRA
CONCERTO NO. 02 IN B FLAT, OP. 19
 FRANCO COLOMBO PUBLICATIONS ER1413 1.75
BEETHOVEN PAUER D
CONCERTO NO. 02 IN B FLAT, OP. 19
 C. F. PETERS CORPORATION 2894B 1.50
BEETHOVEN KULLAK, T.
CONCERTO NO. 02 IN B FLAT, OP. 19
 G. SCHIRMER, INC. L622 1.25
BEETHOVEN KULLAK
CONCERTO NO. 02 IN B FLAT MAJOR, OP. 19
 G. SCHIRMER, INC. L622 1.50

BEETHOVEN   PAUER   M
CONCERTO NO. 03 IN C MINOR, OP. 37. ABRIDGED PIANO SOLO
ARRANGEMENT.
    C. F. PETERS CORPORATION   2894CC   1.25
BEETHOVEN
CONCERTO NO. 03 IN C MINOR, OP. 37 - CADENZA FOR THE FIRST
MOVEMENT
    FRANCO COLOMBO PUBLICATIONS   ER2645   .60
BEETHOVEN   ALBERT, E. D'
CONCERTO NO. 03 IN C MINOR, OP. 37
    ASSOCIATED MUSIC PUBLISHERS, INC.   BRH   3.00
BEETHOVEN   TAGLIAPIETRA
CONCERTO NO. 03 IN C MINOR, OP. 37
    FRANCO COLOMBO PUBLICATIONS   ER1414   2.25
BEETHOVEN   ALKAN
CONCERTO NO. 03 IN C MINOR, OP. 37
    GERARD BILLAUDOT EDITIONS MUSICALES   2.50
BEETHOVEN   PAUER   D
CONCERTO NO. 03 IN C MINOR, OP. 37
    C. F. PETERS CORPORATION   2894C   1.50
BEETHOVEN   KULLAK, T.
CONCERTO NO. 03 IN C MINOR, OP. 37
    G. SCHIRMER, INC.   L623   1.50
BEETHOVEN   KULLAK
CONCERTO NO. 03 IN C MINOR, OP. 37
    G. SCHIRMER, INC.   L623   1.50
BEETHOVEN   PAUER   M
CONCERTO NO. 04 IN G, OP. 58. ABRIDGED PIANO SOLO ARRANGEMENT
    C. F. PETERS CORPORATION   2894DD   1.25
BEETHOVEN   ALBERT, E. D'
CONCERTO NO. 04 IN G, OP. 58
    ASSOCIATED MUSIC PUBLISHERS, INC.   BRH   1.50
BEETHOVEN   TAGLIAPIETRA
CONCERTO NO. 04 IN G, OP. 58
    FRANCO COLOMBO PUBLICATIONS   ER1415   3.50
BEETHOVEN   PAUER   D
CONCERTO NO. 04 IN G, OP. 58
    C. F. PETERS CORPORATION   2894D   1.50
BEETHOVEN   KULLAK, T.
CONCERTO NO. 04 IN G, OP. 58
    G. SCHIRMER, INC.   L624   1.50
BEETHOVEN   SAUER
CONCERTO NO. 04 IN G, OP. 58
    UNIVERSAL EDITION   304   2.40
BEETHOVEN   KULLAK
CONCERTO NO. 04 IN G MAJOR, OP. 58
    G. SCHIRMER, INC.   L624   1.50
BEETHOVEN   PAUER   M
CONCERTO NO. 05 IN E FLAT, OP. 73 --EMPEROR--. ABRIDGED PIANO
SOLO ARRANGEMENT
    C. F. PETERS CORPORATION   2894EE   1.25
BEETHOVEN   PAUER   D
CONCERTO NO. 05 IN E FLAT, OP. 73 --EMPEROR--
    C. F. PETERS CORPORATION   2894E   1.50
BEETHOVEN   ALBERT, E. D'
CONCERTO NO. 05 IN E FLAT, OP. 73 -- ''EMPEROR''
    ASSOCIATED MUSIC PUBLISHERS, INC.   BRH   3.00
BEETHOVEN   KULLAK, T.
CONCERTO NO. 05 IN E FLAT, OP. 73 -- ''EMPEROR''
    G. SCHIRMER, INC.   L625   1.50
BEETHOVEN   TAGLIAPIETRA
CONCERTO NO. 05 IN E FLAT, OP. 73 'EMPEROR'
    FRANCO COLOMBO PUBLICATIONS   ER1416   3.75
BEETHOVEN   SAUER
CONCERTO NO. 05 IN E FLAT, OP. 73
    UNIVERSAL EDITION   2.80
BEETHOVEN   KULLAK
CONCERTO NO. 05 IN E FLAT MAJOR--OP. 73-- 'EMPEROR'
    G. SCHIRMER, INC.   L625   1.00
BEETHOVEN   D
FIVE CONCERTI AND CHORAL FANTASY, OP. 80
    C. F. PETERS CORPORATION   144   10.00
BEETHOVEN   FISCHER, E.
KADENZEN ZU DEN KLAVIERKONZERTEN OP. 15 U. 58--1. SATZ, U. OP.
37
    SCHOTT   4946   2.50
BEETHOVEN   HESS   3
KONZERT IN E FLAT -- 1784 -- FUR KLAVIER UND KAMMERORCHESTER
    BARENREITER VERLAG   AE 218
BEETHOVEN
ORIGINAL CADENZAS TO THE PIANO CONCERTI
    ASSOCIATED MUSIC PUBLISHERS, INC.   B/H   2.75
BEETHOVEN
PIANO CONCERTO IN D FROM THE VIOLIN CONCERTO IN D, OP. 61 --
ORIGINAL ARR. BY BEETHOVEN -- 1807
    ASSOCIATED MUSIC PUBLISHERS, INC.   BRH   5.50
BEETHOVEN
PIANO CONCERTO NO. 01
    EDWIN F. KALMUS   3160   2.00
BEETHOVEN
PIANO CONCERTO NO. 02
    EDWIN F. KALMUS   3161   2.00
BEETHOVEN
PIANO CONCERTO NO. 03
    EDWIN F. KALMUS   3162   2.00
BEETHOVEN
PIANO CONCERTO NO. 04
    EDWIN F. KALMUS   3163   2.00
BEETHOVEN
PIANO CONCERTO NO. 05
    EDWIN F. KALMUS   3164   2.00
BEETHOVEN   HARDING, R.   3
RONDO FROM FIFTH CONCERTO
    WILLIS MUSIC COMPANY   .35
BEETHOVEN   M
VIOLIN CONCERTO, OP. 61. ABRIDGED PIANO SOLO ARRANGEMENT
    C. F. PETERS CORPORATION   189B   1.50
BENDA, R.   BETHAN   3
KONZERT IN G FUR CEMBALO UND STREICHORCHESTER
    BARENREITER VERLAG   NMA 144
BENDA, R.   RACEK   3
KONZERT IN G MINOR FUR CEMBALO UND STREICHORCHESTER
    BARENREITER VERLAG   MAB 10
BENJAMIN
CONCERTO QUASI UNA FANTASIA
    BOOSEY AND HAWKES, INC.   5.00
BENNETT, R.
PIANO CONCERTO
    UNIVERSAL EDITION   UE 14656   5.50
BENNETT, R.
PIANO CONCERTO
    UNIVERSAL EDITION   UE 14655   15.30
BETTINELLI
CONCERTO FOR 2 PIANOS -- 3 PIANOS, 6 HANDS --
    FRANCO COLOMBO PUBLICATIONS   130516   6.75

BILLEMA
CHILDREN'S CONCERTO, OP. 68 -- 1 PIANO 6 HANDS --
    FRANCO COLOMBO PUBLICATIONS   BA8542   1.25
BLACHER
CONCERTO, OP. 28
    ASSOCIATED MUSIC PUBLISHERS, INC.   BOT   9.00
BLISS, A.
CONCERTO FOR TWO PIANOS AND ORCHESTRA -- THREE PIANO SCORE --
    OXFORD UNIVERSITY PRESS   35.605   3.35
BLISS, A.
PIANO CONCERTO -- WITH ACCOMPANIMENT ARRANGED FOR SECOND PIANO
    NOVELLO AND COMPANY, LTD.   10.0009.08   7.50
BLISS, A.
PIANO CONCERTO
    NOVELLO AND COMPANY, LTD.   10.0009.08   7.50
BLOCH, E.
CONCERTO SYMPHONIQUE
    BOOSEY AND HAWKES, INC.   6.00
BLOCH, W.
CONCERTO NO. 02
    ASSOCIATED MUSIC PUBLISHERS, INC.   DOB   7.50
BORKOVEC   4
CONCERTO GROSSO FUR 2 VIOLINEN, VIOLONCELLO, ORCHESTER UND
OBLIGATES CEMBALO
    BARENREITER VERLAG   AP 1300
BORKOVEC   4
KLAVIERKONZERT NO. 02
    BARENREITER VERLAG   CHF 5324
BOWLES, P.
CONCERTO FOR TWO PIANOS, WINDS AND PERCUSSION
    AMERICAN MUSIC EDITION   1.50
BRAHMS   HUGHES
CONCERTO IN B FLAT MAJOR, OP. 83
    G. SCHIRMER, INC.   L1465   3.00
BRAHMS   HUGHES
CONCERTO IN D MINOR, OP. 15
    G. SCHIRMER, INC.   L1429   3.50
BRAHMS
CONCERTO NO. 01 IN D MINOR, OP. 15
    ASSOCIATED MUSIC PUBLISHERS, INC.   BRH   2.50
BRAHMS
CONCERTO NO. 01 IN D MINOR, OP. 15
    INTERNATIONAL MUSIC COMPANY   3.75
BRAHMS   SAUER   D
CONCERTO NO. 01 IN D MINOR, OP. 15
    C. F. PETERS CORPORATION   3655   2.50
BRAHMS   HUGHES
CONCERTO NO. 01 IN D MINOR, OP. 15
    G. SCHIRMER, INC.   L1429   3.50
BRAHMS
CONCERTO NO. 02 IN B FLAT, OP. 83
    ASSOCIATED MUSIC PUBLISHERS, INC.   BRH   3.00
BRAHMS
CONCERTO NO. 02 IN B FLAT, OP. 83
    INTERNATIONAL MUSIC COMPANY   3.75
BRAHMS   SAUER   D
CONCERTO NO. 02 IN B FLAT, OP. 83
    C. F. PETERS CORPORATION   3895   2.50
BRAHMS   HUGHES
CONCERTO NO. 02 IN B FLAT, OP. 83
    G. SCHIRMER, INC.   L1465   3.00
BRAHMS
PIANO WORKS, BK. 3 -- 2 PIANO CONCERTI, PAGANINI VARIATIONS,
WALTZES
    EDWIN F. KALMUS   3256   6.00
BRENDEL
CADENZAS TO MOZART CONCERTO IN D MINOR, K. 466
    ASSOCIATED MUSIC PUBLISHERS, INC.   DOB   1.00
BRENET, T.
CONCERTO POUR UN POEM INCONNU -- PIANO, STRING ORCH. AND ONDES
MARTENONT, PIANO SCORE
    ELKAN-VOGEL, INC.   RR   10.50
BRESGEN   4
KONZERT FUR ZWEI KLAVIERE
    BARENREITER VERLAG   SM 1008A
BRESGEN   4
SINFONISCHES KONZERT, OP. 21
    BARENREITER VERLAG   SM 1144
BRITTEN, B.
CONCERTO, OP. 13
    BOOSEY AND HAWKES, INC.   7.50
BROWN
CONCERTO FOR TWO PIANOS, BRASS AND PERCUSSION --IN PREP--
    WESTERN INTERNATIONAL MUSIC, INC.
BUCCHI
CONCERTO IN RONDO -- 1957 --
    FRANCO COLOMBO PUBLICATIONS   FOR.12373   7.75
BUECHTGER   3
CONCERTINO NO. 02 FUR KLAVIER UND KLEINES ORCHESTER
    BARENREITER VERLAG   BE 312
BUELOW
CADENZAS TO BEETHOVEN CONCERTO IV
    MUSICA OBSCURA   2.50
BURKHARD, W.   4
CONCERTINO, OP. 94, FUR 2 QUERFLOTEN, CEMBALO UND STREICHER
    BARENREITER VERLAG   BA 2489
CACAVAS   1
CONCERTO PETITE
    WILLIS MUSIC COMPANY   .50
CAGE   D
CONCERTO FOR PIANO AND ORCHESTRA
    C. F. PETERS CORPORATION   6705   20.00
CAMBINI   BARBLAN
CONCERTO IN B-FLAT, OP. 15 NO. 1
    FRANCO COLOMBO PUBLICATIONS   130484   4.00
CAMBINI   BARBLAN
CONCERTO IN G, OP. 15 NO. 3
    FRANCO COLOMBO PUBLICATIONS   129856   2.75
CAMMAROTA
CONCERTO
    FRANCO COLOMBO PUBLICATIONS   Z4297   5.75
CAMMAROTA
TWELVE STUDI DA CONCERTO
    FRANCO COLOMBO PUBLICATIONS   BON. 2510   4.25
CANNON, P.
CONCERTINO FOR PIANO AND STRINGS
    NOVELLO AND COMPANY, LTD.   10.0158.02   2.15
CARPENTER, J.
CONCERTINO IN B MINOR
    G. SCHIRMER, INC.   2.50
CARPENTER, J.
CONCERTINO
    G. SCHIRMER, INC.   2.50
CARTER
CONCERTO -- 1964-65
    ASSOCIATED MUSIC PUBLISHERS, INC.   AMP   7.50

CASADESUS, R.
CADENZAS FOR 3 CONCERTI -- BEETHOVEN, MOZART --
    FRANCO COLOMBO PUBLICATIONS   SAL   4.00
CASADESUS, R.
CADENZAS TO MOZART'S CONCERTO NO. 22 IN E FLAT
    INTERNATIONAL MUSIC COMPANY   1.00
CASADESUS, R.
CONCERTO, OP. 37
    ELKAN-VOGEL, INC.   D   16.50
CASADESUS, R.
CONCERTO POUR TROIS PIANOS ET ORCHESTRE A CORDES, FOR 3 PIANOS 6 HANDS
    ELKAN-VOGEL, INC.   D   30.00
CASANOVA, A.
CONCERTINO POUR PIANO ET ORCHESTRE DE CHAMBRE
    ELKAN-VOGEL, INC.   J   7.90
CASTELNUOVO-TEDESCO
CONCERTO NO. 02
    FRANCO COLOMBO PUBLICATIONS   FOR.12374   9.50
CASTERA
CONCERTO
    FRANCO COLOMBO PUBLICATIONS   SAL   13.00
CASTEREDE, J.
CONCERTO FOR PIANO AND STRING ORCHESTRA
    FRANCO COLOMBO PUBLICATIONS   SAL   10.75
CHAUSSON
CONCERTO FOR VIOLIN, PIANO AND STRING QUARTET
    FRANCO COLOMBO PUBLICATIONS   SAL   10.00
CHAVEZ, C.
CONCERTO FOR PIANO AND ORCHESTRA
    G. SCHIRMER, INC.   3.00
CHAVEZ, C.
CONCERTO FOR PIANO AND ORCHESTRA
    G. SCHIRMER, INC.   3.00
CHISHOLM, E.
KONZERT NO. 02 NACH HINDUSTAN, KLAVIERAUSZUG
    SCHOTT   10180   12.00
CHOPIN
CONCERTOS
    EDWARD B. MARKS MUSIC CORPORATION   07.50
CHOPIN   FRIEDMAN
CONCERTO NO. 01 IN E MINOR, OP. 11
    ASSOCIATED MUSIC PUBLISHERS, INC.   BRH   2.75
CHOPIN
CONCERTO NO. 01 IN E MINOR, OP. 11
    EDWARD B. MARKS MUSIC CORPORATION   07.50
CHOPIN   POZNIAK   D
CONCERTO NO. 01 IN E MINOR, OP. 11
    C. F. PETERS CORPORATION   2895A   3.00
CHOPIN   M
CONCERTO NO. 01 IN E MINOR, OP. 11
    C. F. PETERS CORPORATION   2895AA   1.25
CHOPIN   JOSEFFY, R.
CONCERTO NO. 01 IN E MINOR, OP. 11
    G. SCHIRMER, INC.   L1350   1.75
CHOPIN   JOSEFFY
CONCERTO NO. 01 IN E MINOR, OP. 11
    G. SCHIRMER, INC.   L1350   1.75
CHOPIN   MIKULI
CONCERTO NO. 01 IN E MINOR, OP. 11
    G. SCHIRMER, INC.   L1558   1.50
CHOPIN   FRIEDMAN
CONCERTO NO. 02 IN F MINOR, OP. 21
    ASSOCIATED MUSIC PUBLISHERS, INC.   BRH   2.75
CHOPIN
CONCERTO NO. 02 IN F MINOR, OP. 21
    EDWARD B. MARKS MUSIC CORPORATION   06.50
CHOPIN   POZNIAK   D
CONCERTO NO. 02 IN F MINOR, OP. 21
    C. F. PETERS CORPORATION   2895B   3.00
CHOPIN   JOSEFFY, R.
CONCERTO NO. 02 IN F MINOR, OP. 21
    G. SCHIRMER, INC.   L1351   1.75
CHOPIN   JOSEFFY
CONCERTO NO. 02 IN F MINOR, OP. 21
    G. SCHIRMER, INC.   L1351   1.75
CHOPIN   MIKULI
CONCERTO NO. 02 IN F MINOR, OP. 21
    G. SCHIRMER, INC.   L1557   1.50
CILENSEK, J.
CONCERTO -- 1950
    ASSOCIATED MUSIC PUBLISHERS, INC.   BRH   4.00
CLEMENTI   FASANO *
CONCERTO IN C
    FRANCO COLOMBO PUBLICATIONS   130491   5.50
COPLAND
CONCERTO
    BOOSEY AND HAWKES, INC.   2.00
CORELLI   WEYBRIGHT   4
PASTORAL FROM 'CONCERTO GROSSO NO. 8'
    BELWIN-MILLS PUBLISHING CORPORATION   .60
CORRETTE   RUF   3
KONZERT IN D MINOR FUR CEMBALO ODER ORGEL, QUERFLOTE UND STREICHER, OP. 26 NO. 6
    BARENREITER VERLAG   NMA 201
CRAS
CONCERTO
    FRANCO COLOMBO PUBLICATIONS   SAL   8.75
CZERNY
CONCERTINO IN C, OP. 210, PIANO SCORE
    MUSICA OBSCURA   3.50
CZERNY
CONCERTINO IN C, OP. 210, SET OF PARTS
    MUSICA OBSCURA   6.50
D'INDY, V.
TRIPLE CONCERTO, OP. 89
    FRANCO COLOMBO PUBLICATIONS   SAL   8.25
DALLAPICCOLA
PICCOLO CONCERTO PER MURIEL COUVREUX FUR KLAVIER UND ORCHESTER
    BARENREITER VERLAG   CM 20218
DALLAPICCOLA   4-5
PICCOLO CONCERTO PER MURIEL COUVREUX FUR KLAVIER UND ORCHESTER
    BARENREITER VERLAG   CM 20218
DAMASE, J. M.
CONCERTO NO. 02
    EDITIONS MUSICALES TRANSATLANTIQUES   12.25
DAMASE, J. M.
CONCERTO
    FRANCO COLOMBO PUBLICATIONS   SAL   10.75
DAMASE, J. M.
DEUXIEME CONCERTO
    EDITIONS MUSICALES TRANSATLANTIQUES   12.25
DANDELOT
CONCERTO -- 1932
    ASSOCIATED MUSIC PUBLISHERS, INC.   ESC   6.00

DEGEN   5-6
DREIZIG KONZERT-ETUDEN, BK. 1
    SCHOTT   3955   3.25
DEGEN   5-6
DREIZIG KONZERT-ETUDEN, BK. 2
    SCHOTT   3.25
DEGEN   5-6
DREIZIG KONZERT-ETUDEN, BK. 3
    SCHOTT   3957   3.25
DELANNOY
CONCERTO DE MAI, OP. 50 -- 1949-50
    ASSOCIATED MUSIC PUBLISHERS, INC.   ESC   7.50
DIAMOND, D.
CONCERTO FOR 2 SOLO PIANOS
    PEER SOUTHERN ORGANIZATION   05.50
DISTLER   4
KONZERTSTUCK FUR KLAVIER UND ORCHESTER -- OP. POSTH. -- KLAVIERAUSZUG
    BARENREITER VERLAG   BA 2783A
DISTLER   4
KONZERTSTUCK FUR KLAVIER UND ORCHESTER -- OP. POSTH. --
    BARENREITER VERLAG   BA 2783
DISTLER   4
KONZERTSTUCK
    BARENREITER VERLAG   BA 1877
DISTLER   4
KONZERT FUR CEMBALO UND STREICHORCHESTER, OP. 14
    BARENREITER VERLAG   BA 1000
DITTERSDORF, K.D. VON *   3
KONZERT IN A FUR CEMBALO -- KLAVIER -- UND STREICHER
    BARENREITER VERLAG   NMA 41
DITTERSDORF, K.D. VON   DOEBEREINER
THREE CADENZAS TO THE CONCERTO IN A
    ASSOCIATED MUSIC PUBLISHERS, INC.   NAG   .60
DOEBEREINER
THREE CADENZAS TO DITTERSDORF CONCERTO IN A
    ASSOCIATED MUSIC PUBLISHERS, INC.   NAG   .60
DOHNANYI
CONCERTO IN E MINOR, OP. 5
    ASSOCIATED MUSIC PUBLISHERS, INC.   DOB   9.00
DONENFELD, J.   3-4
CONCERTINO
    PRO-ART PUBLICATIONS, INC.   478   .50
DREYSCHOCK
CADENZA TO BEETHOVEN CONCERTO III
    MUSICA OBSCURA   2.50
DRIESSLER   4
KONZERT FUR KLAVIER UND ORCHESTER, OP. 27
    BARENREITER VERLAG   BA 2782
DUKELSKY
CONCERTO IN C
    HEUGEL ET CIE.   12.00
DUSSEK, J.   3-4
KONZERT FUR KLAVIER UND ORCHESTER, OP. 26
    BARENREITER VERLAG   CHF 5170
DUSSEK, J.   3-4
KONZERT FUR 2 KLAVIERE UND ORCHESTER
    BARENREITER VERLAG   CHF 5030
DVORAK
CONCERTO IN G MINOR, OP. 33
    BOOSEY AND HAWKES, INC.   11.00
DVORAK   BERKOVEC *   4
KONZERT FUR KLAVIER UND ORCHESTER IN G MINOR, OP. 33, KLAVIERAUSZUG
    BARENREITER VERLAG   AP 786
DVORAK   BERKOVEC *   4
KONZERT FUR KLAVIER UND ORCHESTER IN G MINOR, OP. 33
    BARENREITER VERLAG   AP 145
DVORAK   4
KONZERT IN G MINOR FUR KLAVIER UND ORCHESTER, OP. 33
    BARENREITER VERLAG   AP 786
DYSON, G.
CONCERTO LEGGIERO
    NOVELLO AND COMPANY, LTD.   10.0160.04   3.25
EBEN   4
KONZERT FUR KLAVIER UND ORCHESTER
    BARENREITER VERLAG
ECKSTEIN
CONCERTO FOR YOUNG AMERICANS
    CARL FISCHER, INC.   O 3923   2.00
EDER   4
CONCERTO SEMISERIO FUR 2 KLAVIERE UND ORCHESTER
    BARENREITER VERLAG   BA 4310
EGGE   D
CONCERTO NO. 02, OP. 21
    C. F. PETERS CORPORATION   LY156A   5.00
EINEM, G.
CONCERTO, OP. 20
    ASSOCIATED MUSIC PUBLISHERS, INC.   BOT   11.00
ELLSTEIN, A.
NEGEV CONCERTO
    BELWIN-MILLS PUBLISHING CORPORATION   20336   2.00
EVETT   D
CONCERTO FOR HARPSICHORD. POCKET SCORE
    C. F. PETERS CORPORATION   6504   5.00
FALLA, M. DE
CONCERTO FOR HARPSICHORD
    ASSOCIATED MUSIC PUBLISHERS, INC.   ESC   4.50
FARKAS, F.
CONCERTINO
    KULTURA   2.50
FERGUSON, H.
CONCERTO
    BOOSEY AND HAWKES, INC.   3.00
FINNEY
CONCERTO IN E
    C. F. PETERS CORPORATION   66115   RENTAL
FOLDES   4
KADENZA ZU KLAVIERKONZERT IN C, K467 BY W. A. MOZART
    BARENREITER VERLAG   BA 3823
FOLDES   4
KADENZA ZU KLAVIERKONZERT IN C, K503 BY W. A. MOZART
    BARENREITER VERLAG   BA 3822
FOLDES   4
KADENZA ZU KLAVIERKONZERT IN E FLAT, K482 BY W. A. MOZART
    BARENREITER VERLAG   BA 3908
FOLDES   4
KADENZA ZU KLAVIERKONZERT IN G, K453 BY W. A. MOZART
    BARENREITER VERLAG   BA 3821
FOSS, L.
CONCERTINO -- SET
    G. SCHIRMER, INC.   1.25
FRANCAIX, J.   5
CONCERTINO FUR KLAVIER UND KLEINES ORCHESTER, KLAVIERAUSZUG
    SCHOTT   3288   4.00

FRANCAIX, J.
  CONCERTO POUR CLAVECIN ET ENSEMBLES INSTRUMENTALES
    SCHOTT   RENTAL
FRANCAIX, J.   5
  KONZERT FUR KLAVIER UND ORCHESTER, KLAVIERAUSZUG
    SCHOTT   3670   5.00
FRICKER, P.   6
  KONZERT FUR KLAVIER UND ORCHESTER, OP. 19, KLAVIERAUSZUG
    SCHOTT   10396   5.00
FUCHS, R.   4
  KONZERT FUR CEMBALO UND STREICHORCHESTER
    BARENREITER VERLAG   BA 2488
FULEIHAN, A.
  CONCERTO NO. 02 FOR PIANO AND ORCHESTRA
    G. SCHIRMER, INC.   3.00
FULEIHAN, A.
  CONCERTO NO. 02
    G. SCHIRMER, INC.   3.00
FURTWANGLER   4
  SYMPHONISCHES KONZERT FUR KLAVIER UND ORCHESTER
    BARENREITER VERLAG   AE 285
GAERTNER   2, 3
  CONCERTINO
    ALPHONSE LEDUC
GAGNEBIN
  CONCERTO
    FRANCO COLOMBO PUBLICATIONS   129293   3.50
GAL, H.
  CONCERTINO, OP. 43
    ASSOCIATED MUSIC PUBLISHERS, INC.   SIM   2.50
GALINDO, B.
  SECOND CONCERTO
    EDICIONES MEXICANAS DE MUSICA, A. C.   06.75
GARLICK, A.
  CONCERTO GROSSO FOR ORGAN AND PIANO
    SEESAW MUSIC CORPORATION   D   18.00
GENZMER
  CONCERTINO NO. 2
    C. F. PETERS CORPORATION   5973A   4.00
GENZMER   4-5
  KONZERT FUR KLAVIER UND ORCHESTER, KLAVIERAUSZUG
    SCHOTT   5278   5.00
GERARD, J.
  MUSIC BOX CONCERTO, THE
    FREDERICK HARRIS MUSIC COMPANY   .60
GERSHWIN   DAVIS, J. R.
  CONCERTO IN F, SECOND MOVEMENT
    WARNER BROTHERS PUBLISHERS   1.00
GERSHWIN   CASTAGNETTA
  CONCERTO IN F - CONCERT TRANSCRIPTION
    WARNER BROTHERS PUBLISHERS   5.00
GERSHWIN
  CONCERTO IN F
    WARNER BROTHERS PUBLISHERS   5.00
GINASTERA
  CONCERTO NO. 01
    BOOSEY AND HAWKES, INC.   7.00
GIORDANI   CASTAGNONE *
  CONCERTO NO. 03 IN C
    FRANCO COLOMBO PUBLICATIONS   130483   2.50
GIORDANI   CASTAGNONE *
  CONCERTO NO. 05 IN D
    FRANCO COLOMBO PUBLICATIONS   130477   2.75
GIORDANI   BITTNER   3
  KONZERT IN C FUR KLAVIER UND STREICHER
    BARENREITER VERLAG   NMA 157
GLAZOUNOW, A.
  CONCERTO NO. 01, OP. 92
    BOOSEY AND HAWKES, INC.   5.00
GLAZOUNOW, A.
  CONCERTO NO. 02, OP. 100
    BOOSEY AND HAWKES, INC.   6.00
GLAZOUNOW, A.   FREDERICKS
  CONCERTO THEME FROM PIANO CONCERTO, OP. 92
    MCA MUSIC   .75
GLOVER, D.   3
  EVENING CONCERTO, NO. 1
    BELWIN-MILLS PUBLISHING CORPORATION   .60
GRABNER   4
  CONCERTINO FUR EIN TASTENINSTRUMENT UND STREICHER, OP. 60
    BARENREITER VERLAG   BA 3141
GRAINGER, P.
  GRIEG'S PIANO CONCERTO, FIRST MOVEMENT--CONCERT TRANSCRIPTION OF
    MAIN THEMES AND EPISODES--
    G. SCHIRMER, INC.   .80
GRAINGER, P.
  RACHMANINOFF'S PIANO CONCERTO NO. 2 IN C MINOR, OP. 18, THIRD
    MOVEMENT--CONCERT TRANSCRIPTION OF MAIN THEMES AND EPISODES--
    G. SCHIRMER, INC.   1.00
GRAINGER, P.
  SCHUMANN'S PIANO CONCERTO, FIRST MOVEMENT--CONCERT TRANSCRIPTION
    OF MAIN THEMES AND EPISODES--
    G. SCHIRMER, INC.   1.25
GRAUN   M-D
  CONCERTO IN F. SCORE, HARPSICHORD SOLO PART
    C. F. PETERS CORPORATION   WM1   5.00
GRAUN   RUF   3
  KONZERT IN F FUR CEMBALO -- ORGEL -- UND STREICHER -- 'BANCHETTO
    MUSICALE' --
    BARENREITER VERLAG   SM 1103
GRIEG   GRAINGER, P.
  CONCERTO, FIRST MOVEMENT--CONCERT TRANSCRIPTION OF MAIN THEMES
    AND EPISODES
    G. SCHIRMER, INC.   .80
GRIEG   4
  CONCERTO, THEME
    CENTURY MUSIC PUBLISHING COMPANY, INC.   3533   .40
GRIEG   M
  CONCERTO IN A MINOR, OP. 16. ABRIDGED PIANO SOLO ARRANGEMENT
    C. F. PETERS CORPORATION   2164B   1.25
GRIEG   D
  CONCERTO IN A MINOR, OP. 16
    C. F. PETERS CORPORATION   2164   2.00
GRIEG   M
  CONCERTO IN A MINOR, OP. 16
    C. F. PETERS CORPORATION   2164B   1.25
GRIEG   D
  CONCERTO IN A MINOR, OP. 16
    C. F. PETERS CORPORATION   2164   2.00
GRIEG   GRAINGER, P.
  CONCERTO IN A MINOR, OP. 16
    G. SCHIRMER, INC.   L1399   2.50
GRIEG   GRAINGER, P.
  CONCERTO IN A MINOR, OP. 16
    G. SCHIRMER, INC.   L1399   2.50

GRIEG
  CONCERTO IN A MINOR -- OPENING THEME
    ASHLEY DEALERS SERVICE, INC.   ES   .95
GRIEG
  CONCERTO IN A MINOR
    ASHLEY DEALERS SERVICE, INC.   1.95
GRIEG   NIELSON
  CONCERTO IN A MINOR
    BOOSEY AND HAWKES, INC.   1.50
GRIEG   THOMPSON, J.   2
  CONCERTO IN A MINOR
    WILLIS MUSIC COMPANY   .35
GRIEG   MITTLER   3B
  GRIEG CONCERTO
    MUSICORD PUBLICATIONS, INC.   .45
GRIEG   SCHAUM, J.   4 1/2
  NORWEGIAN CONCERTO
    BELWIN-MILLS PUBLISHING CORPORATION   .50
GRIEG   KLEINMICHEL   D
  PIANO CONCERTO IN A MINOR, OP. 16. ABRIDGED
    C. F. PETERS CORPORATION   2505A   2.00
GRIEG   KLEINMICHEL   D
  PIANO CONCERTO IN A MINOR, OP. 16. TWO PIANOS, EIGHT HANDS
    C. F. PETERS CORPORATION   H2164D   3.00
GRIEG   KLEINMICHEL   D
  PIANO CONCERTO IN A MINOR, OP. 16
    C. F. PETERS CORPORATION   2505   3.50
GRIEG   4
  PIANO CONCERTO IN A MINOR, THEME
    CENTURY MUSIC PUBLISHING COMPANY, INC.   3533   .40
GRIEG   MOSSMAN
  PIANO CONCERTO IN A MINOR -- FIRST MOVEMENT
    BELWIN-MILLS PUBLISHING CORPORATION   26089   .60
GRIEG   LEVINE, H.
  PIANO CONCERTO
    ALFRED MUSIC COMPANY   640   2.50
GRIEG   FREY, H.
  PIANO CONCERTO
    THE BIG THREE MUSIC CORPORATION   00.75
GRIEG
  PIANO CONCERTO
    EDWIN F. KALMUS   3487   3.00
GRIEG   LEVINE   5
  THEME, FROM PIANO CONCERTO IN A MINOR
    THEODORE PRESSER COMPANY   .50
GRIEG   TRUXELL, E.   3 1/2
  THEMES FROM PIANO CONCERTO
    VOLKWEIN BROS.   00.40
GRIEG   ECKSTEIN
  THEME FROM PIANO CONCERTO, OP. 16
    CARL FISCHER, INC.   S 2295   .50
GRIEG   4
  THEME FROM THE FIRST MOVEMENT OF PIANO CONCERTO IN A MINOR
    BOSTON MUSIC COMPANY   .50
GRIEG   WALLIS   2
  THEME FROM THE FIRST MOVEMENT OF PIANO CONCERTO IN A MINOR
    BOSTON MUSIC COMPANY   .50
GRIEG   WALLIS   3
  THEME FROM THE FIRST MOVEMENT OF PIANO CONCERTO IN A MINOR
    BOSTON MUSIC COMPANY   .60
GROSS   4
  KONZERT FUR KAMMERORCHESTER MIT OBLIGATEM KLAVIER
    BARENREITER VERLAG   AE 234
GRUNENWALD
  CONCERTO
    FRANCO COLOMBO PUBLICATIONS   SAL   8.75
GUARNIERI
  CONCERTO NO. 02 -- 1946
    ASSOCIATED MUSIC PUBLISHERS, INC.   AMP   3.75
GUERRINI, G.
  TEMPI DI CONCERTO
    FRANCO COLOMBO PUBLICATIONS   124035   1.75
GULDA
  CADENZA TO MOZART CONCERTO IN C, K. 503
    ASSOCIATED MUSIC PUBLISHERS, INC.   DOB   .75
GULDA
  CADENZA TO MOZART CONCERTO IN D, K. 537 -- CORONATION --
    ASSOCIATED MUSIC PUBLISHERS, INC.   DOB   .75
HAIEFF, A.
  CONCERTO
    BOOSEY AND HAWKES, INC.   6.00
HANDEL   BEARD
  AIR VARIE FROM CONCERTO GROSSO NO. 2
    ELKAN-VOGEL, INC.   .50
HANDEL   BEECHAM
  CONCERTO IN A MAJOR FOR PIANOFORTE AND ORCHESTRA IN FOUR
    MOVEMENTS, 2-PIANO VERSION
    BELWIN-MILLS PUBLISHING CORPORATION   27006   3.00
HANDEL   BEECHAM
  CONCERTO IN A MAJOR FOR PIANOFORTE AND ORCHESTRA IN FOUR
    MOVEMENTS -- 2-PIANO VERSION
    BELWIN-MILLS PUBLISHING CORPORATION   27006   3.00
HANDEL   M
  CONCERTO IN B FLAT, OP. 4, NO. 6. SCORE/HARPSICHORD SOLO PART
    C. F. PETERS CORPORATION   V11A   4.00
HANDEL   LANDOWSKA, W.
  KEYBOARD CONCERTO IN B FLAT, OP.4 NO. 6 -- SECOND MVT
    BROUDE BROTHERS LTD.   01.75
HANDEL   BRUSOTTI
  KONZERT G-DUR FUR KLAVIER -- CEMBALO UND STREICHORCHESTER --
    HOBOKEN 18-9 KLAVIER-AUSZUG
    SCHOTT   5313   3.75
HANDEL   HILLEMANN   3
  KONZERT IN B FLAT, OP. 4 NO. 6 FUR KLAVIER -- ORGEL, CEMBALO --
    UND STREICHORCHESTER
    BARENREITER VERLAG   NMA 136
HANDEL   MATTHAEI, K.
  ORGAN CONCERTI, OP. 4 BK. 1
    BARENREITER VERLAG   BA 1894   3.25
HANDEL   MATTHAEI, K.
  ORGAN CONCERTI, OP. 4 BK. 2
    BARENREITER VERLAG   BA 1895   3.25
HANDEL
  ORGAN CONCERTOS, BK. 1
    INTERNATIONAL MUSIC COMPANY   4.50
HANDEL
  ORGAN CONCERTOS, BK. 2
    INTERNATIONAL MUSIC COMPANY   4.50
HANDEL   MATTHAEI, K.   3
  ORGELKONZERTE, OP. 4 FUR KLAVIER ODER ORGEL MANUALITER, HEFT 1 -
    G MINOR, B FLAT, G MINOR
    BARENREITER VERLAG   BA 1894
HANDEL   MATTHAEI, K.   3
  ORGELKONZERTE, OP. 4 FUR KLAVIER ODER ORGEL MANUALITER, HEFT 2 -
    F, F, B FLAT
    BARENREITER VERLAG   BA 1895

HANDEL   MATTHAEI   3-4
ORGELKONZERTE, OP. 4 NO. 1 IN G MINOR -- 'HALLISCHE
HANDEL-AUSGABE' --
    BARENREITER VERLAG   BA 4006

HANDEL   MATTHAEI   3-4
ORGELKONZERTE, OP. 4 NO. 2 IN B FLAT -- 'HALLISCHE
HANDEL-AUSGABE' --
    BARENREITER VERLAG   BA 359

HANDEL   MATTHAEI   3-4
ORGELKONZERTE, OP. 4 NO. 3 IN G MINOR -- 'HALLISCHE
HANDEL-AUSGABE' --
    BARENREITER VERLAG   BA 360

HANDEL   MATTHAEI   3-4
ORGELKONZERTE, OP. 4 NO. 4 IN F -- 'HALLISCHE HANDEL-AUSGABE' --
    BARENREITER VERLAG   BA 362

HANDEL   MATTHAEI   3-4
ORGELKONZERTE, OP. 4 NO. 5 IN F -- 'HALLISCHE HANDEL-AUSGABE' --
    BARENREITER VERLAG   BA 363

HANDEL   MATTHAEI   3-4
ORGELKONZERTE, OP. 4 NO. 6 IN B FLAT -- 'HALLISCHE
HANDEL-AUSGABE' --
    BARENREITER VERLAG   BA 364

HANDEL   M-D
TWELVE ORGAN CONCERTI IN 2 VOLS* VOL. 1
    C. F. PETERS CORPORATION   2591A   5.00

HANDEL   M-D
TWELVE ORGAN CONCERTI IN 2 VOLS* VOL. 2
    C. F. PETERS CORPORATION   2591B   5.00

HARTLEY, W.
CONCERTO FOR PIANO AND ORCHESTRA ARR. FOR TWO PIANO FOUR HANDS
    FEMA MUSIC PUBLICATIONS   6.00

HATTORI, KOH-ICHI
CONCERTINO FOR SMALL HANDS
    BOOSEY AND HAWKES, INC.   1.50

HAYDN   BADURA-SKODA
CADENZAS TO THE CONCERTO IN D
    ASSOCIATED MUSIC PUBLISHERS, INC.   DOB   1.00

HAYDN   LANDOWSKA, W.
CADENZA - CONCERTO IN D, OP. 21
    BROUDE BROTHERS LTD.   02.00

HAYDN   WERNER
CHILDREN'S CONCERTO--CURWEN EDITION
    G. SCHIRMER, INC.   .75

HAYDN   E
CONCERTINO --DIVERTIMENTO-- IN C. WITH 2 VIOLINS, V'CELLO
    C. F. PETERS CORPORATION   4611   1.50

HAYDN   ANSON   E
CONCERTINO --DIVERTIMENTO IN C
    C. F. PETERS CORPORATION   6282   1.50

HAYDN   LASSEN   4
CONCERTO F-DUR FUR KLAVIER--CEMBALO UND ORCHESTER MIT KADENZEN
VON H. SCHROTER, KLAVIER-AUSZUG, HOBOKEN 18, 3
    SCHOTT   4959   3.00

HAYDN   SCHNEIDER
CONCERTO IN C
    ASSOCIATED MUSIC PUBLISHERS, INC.   BRH   3.00

HAYDN   WERTHEIM
CONCERTO IN C
    BOOSEY AND HAWKES, INC.   1.50

HAYDN   E-M
CONCERTO IN D --WITH HAYDN CADENZAS--
    C. F. PETERS CORPORATION   4353   1.50

HAYDN   GANZ
CONCERTO IN D MAJOR
    G. SCHIRMER, INC.   L1700   1.75

HAYDN   MONTANI
CONCERTO IN D
    FRANCO COLOMBO PUBLICATIONS   ER2429   2.00

HAYDN   MERTKE, E. *
CONCERTO IN D
    INTERNATIONAL MUSIC COMPANY   2.00

HAYDN   MERTKE *
CONCERTO IN D
    INTERNATIONAL MUSIC COMPANY   2.00

HAYDN   GANZ
CONCERTO IN D
    G. SCHIRMER, INC.   L1700   1.75

HAYDN
CONCERTO IN F
    INTERNATIONAL MUSIC COMPANY   2.00

HAYDN   HINZE *   M
CONCERTO IN G --WITH CADENZAS--
    C. F. PETERS CORPORATION   4643   3.00

HAYDN   CASTAGNONE
CONCERTO IN G
    FRANCO COLOMBO PUBLICATIONS   ER2589   2.25

HAYDN
CONCERTO IN G
    INTERNATIONAL MUSIC COMPANY   2.00

HAYDN   ROBYN   3 1/2
KINDER CONCERTO
    THEODORE PRESSER COMPANY   1.25

HAYDN   GOEBELS *   3
KLEINES KONZERT IN F FUR CEMBALO UND KLEINES ORCHESTER -- HOB.
DEEST --
    BARENREITER VERLAG   SM 1325

HAYDN
KONZERT F-DUR FUR KLAVIER -- CEMBALO UND ORCHESTER -- HOBOKEN
18- 3 KLAVIER AUSZUG
    SCHOTT   4959   3.00

HAYDN
KONZERT G-DUR FUR KLAVIER -- CEMBALO, 2 VIOL. UND BASS, HOBOKEN
18-9, KLAVIERZUSZUG
    SCHOTT   5313   3.75

HAYDN   HEUSSNER   2-3
KONZERT IN C FUR KLAVIER -- CEMBALO -- UND STREICHER -- HOB. 18,
5 --
    BARENREITER VERLAG   NMA 200

HAYDN   SCHULTZ   3-4
KONZERT IN F FUR VIOLINE, CEMBALO UND STREICHER -- DOPPELKONZERT
-- HOB. 18, 6
    BARENREITER VERLAG   BA 3839

HAYDN   SCHUBERT   4
KONZERT NO. 02 IN G FUR CEMBALO -- KLAVIER -- UND STREICHER,
HOB. 18, 4
    BARENREITER VERLAG   NMA 86

HAYDN   KREUTZER   3
LITTLE CONCERTO
    BOSTON MUSIC COMPANY   2.00

HEIM, E.
KLAVIERKONZERT IN G FUR KLAVIER UND ORCHESTER, KLAVIERAUSZUG
    SCHOTT   4289   5.00

HELM, E.
CONCERTO NO. 02
    ASSOCIATED MUSIC PUBLISHERS, INC.   BOT   4.50

HELM, E.   6
KONZERT IN G FUR KLAVIER UND ORCHESTER, KLAVIERAUSZUG
    SCHOTT   4289   5.00

HELPS
PIANO CONCERTO
    C. F. PETERS CORPORATION   6608   RENTAL

HENSELT, A.
PIANO CONCERTO IN F MINOR, OP. 16
    MUSIC TREASURE PUBLICATIONS   5.00

HENSELT, A.
PIANO CONCERTO
    MUSICAL SCOPE PUBLISHERS   01.25

HENZE, H.   6
KONZERT NO. 01 FUR KLAVIER UND ORCHESTER, 1950, KLAVIERAUSZUG
    SCHOTT   4931   7.50

HENZE, H.   5 - 6
KONZERT NO. 02 FUR KLAVIER UND ORCHESTER IN EINEN SATZ, 1967 -
KLAVIERAUSZUG
    SCHOTT   5957   15.00

HILLER   PUCHELT   4
KONZERT IN F SHARP MINOR FUR KLAVIER UND ORCHESTER
    BARENREITER VERLAG   BA 3849

HINDEMITH
KAMMERMUSIK NO. 02, KLAVIER-KONZERT, OP. 36 NO. 1 -
KLAVIERAUSZUG
    SCHOTT   1857   7.50

HINDEMITH
KONZERTMUSIK FUR KLAVIER, BLECHBL. UND HARFEN, OP. 49 -
KLAVIERAUSZUG
    SCHOTT   3248   10.00

HINDEMITH
KONZERT FUR KLAVIER UND ORCHESTER, 1945 -- KLAVIERAUSZUG
    SCHOTT   3838   6.00

HODDINOTT, A.
CONCERTO NO. 02
    OXFORD UNIVERSITY PRESS   32.152   7.35

HODDINOTT, A.
CONCERTO NO. 03
    OXFORD UNIVERSITY PRESS   32.148   7.35

HOFFMANN, PH. K.   M
CADENZA TO MOZART CONCERTO K.467
    C. F. PETERS CORPORATION   H1756A   2.00

HOFFMANN, PH. K.   M
CADENZA TO MOZART CONCERTO K.482
    C. F. PETERS CORPORATION   H1756B   2.00

HOFFMANN, PH. K.   M
CADENZA TO MOZART CONCERTO K.488
    C. F. PETERS CORPORATION   H1756C   2.00

HOFFMANN, PH. K.   M
CADENZA TO MOZART CONCERTO K.491
    C. F. PETERS CORPORATION   H1756D   2.00

HOFFMANN, PH. K.   M
CADENZA TO MOZART CONCERTO K.503
    C. F. PETERS CORPORATION   H1756E   2.00

HOFFMANN, PH. K.   M
CADENZA TO MOZART CONCERTO K.595
    C. F. PETERS CORPORATION   H1756F   2.00

HOFFMEISTER   M
CONCERTO, OP. 24
    C. F. PETERS CORPORATION   K36   3.00

HONEGGER, A.
CONCERTINO
    FRANCO COLOMBO PUBLICATIONS   SAL   9.00

HOSSEIN, A.
CONCERTO NO. 02 -- PIANO SOLO, WITH ORCHESTRA REDUCED FOR SECOND
PIANO
    EDITIONS MUSICALES TRANSATLANTIQUES   4.80

HOSSEIN, A.
CONCERTO NO. 02
    EDITIONS MUSICALES TRANSATLANTIQUES   4.80

HOUDY   7
CONCERTO FOR PIANO
    ALPHONSE LEDUC

HUMMEL, J. N.   D
CONCERTO, OP. 85
    C. F. PETERS CORPORATION   2952   5.00

JACHINO
CONCERTO NO. 02
    FRANCO COLOMBO PUBLICATIONS   130621   10.00

JACOB, G.
CONCERTO NO. 01
    OXFORD UNIVERSITY PRESS   32.906   3.00

JIRKO   4
KONZERT FUR KLAVIER UND ORCHESTER
    BARENREITER VERLAG   CHF 5102

JOLIVET, A.
CONCERTO
    HEUGEL ET CIE.   12.00

JONGEN, J.
CONCERTO
    ELKAN-VOGEL, INC.   LEM   15.00

JOUBERT, J.
PIANO CONCERTO
    NOVELLO AND COMPANY, LTD.   10.0078.00   5.25

JOUBERT, J.
PIANO CONCERTO
    NOVELLO AND COMPANY, LTD.   10.0078.00   5.25

JUROWSKY   4
SYMPHONIE NO. 1 FUR KONZERTANTES KLAVIER UND STREICHORCHESTER
    BARENREITER VERLAG   CHF 5221

KABALEVSKY
CONCERTO NO. 03, OP. 50
    INTERNATIONAL MUSIC COMPANY   3.75

KABALEVSKY
CONCERTO NO. 03
    EDWIN F. KALMUS   3569   3.50

KABALEVSKY
PIANO CONCERTO NO. 03, OP. 50 --'YOUTH'
    MCA MUSIC   3.75

KADOSA
CONCERTINO
    KULTURA   2.50

KADOSA
CONCERTO NO. 03, OP. 47
    KULTURA   3.50

KALABIS   4
KONZERT FUR KLAVIER UND ORCHESTER
    BARENREITER VERLAG   CHF 5106

KASSCHAU, H.
CANDLELIGHT CONCERTO
    SOUTHERN MUSIC COMPANY   1.00

KASSCHAU, H.
LEGEND OF SLEEPY HOLLOW, THE -- A PROGRAM CONCERTO -- SET
    G. SCHIRMER, INC.   2.50

KASSERN, T. Z.
TEEN-AGE CONCERTO
    G. SCHIRMER, INC.   1.00

KATTNIGG, R.   4-5
    KONZERT FUR KLAVIER UND KLEINES ORCHESTER, OP. 15
        BARENREITER VERLAG   SM 1159
KELTERBORN   4
    CONCERTINO FUR KLAVIER, SCHLAGZEUG UND STREICHORCHESTER
        BARENREITER VERLAG   BA 3909
KEMPFF
    CADENZAS TO BEETHOVEN PIANO CONCERTI NOS. 1-4
        ASSOCIATED MUSIC PUBLISHERS, INC.   BOT   3.50
KHATCHATURIAN
    CONCERTO -- 1936
        ASSOCIATED MUSIC PUBLISHERS, INC.   BRH   6.25
KHATCHATURIAN
    CONCERTO IN D FLAT
        INTERNATIONAL MUSIC COMPANY   3.75
KHATCHATURIAN
    PIANO CONCERTO
        EDWIN F. KALMUS   3577   3.50
KLEBE, G.   4
    CONCERTO A CINQUE, OP. 50
        BARENREITER VERLAG   BA 4467
KOHLMANN, C.
    CONCERTO TRANSCRIPTIONS OF FAVORITE HYMNS
        THEODORE PRESSER COMPANY   1.25
KOZELUCH, L.   MEYLAN
    CONCERTO IN D
        ASSOCIATED MUSIC PUBLISHERS, INC.   BRH   7.00
KRAUS--ED   KRAUS
    CADENZAS FROM MOZART'S PIANO CONCERTOS
        BELWIN-MILLS PUBLISHING CORPORATION   6.00
KREBS   KLEINE   4
    KONZERT IN A MINOR FUR ZWEI CEMBALI
        BARENREITER VERLAG   DV 8102
KRENEK, E.   4
    KLAVIERKONZERT NO. 04
        BARENREITER VERLAG   BA 3498
KRENEK, E.   4
    KONZERT FUR 2 KLAVIERE UND ORCHESTER
        BARENREITER VERLAG   BA 4331
LANCEN   M-D
    CONCERTINO FOR PIANO
        C. F. PETERS CORPORATION   H371   2.00
LANDOWSKI   D
    CONCERTO NO. 02
        C. F. PETERS CORPORATION   C402   3.00
LEHNER   3
    KLEINES KONZERT FUR KLAVIER, STREICHER UND SCHLAGZEUG
        BARENREITER VERLAG   BE 303
LEVINE, H.--ED   LEVINE, H.
    MORE THEMES FROM THE GREAT CONCERTOS
        THEODORE PRESSER COMPANY   1.25
LEVINE, H.--ED   LEVINE, H.
    THEMES FROM THE GREAT PIANO CONCERTOS
        THEODORE PRESSER COMPANY   1.50
LINEK   M
    CONCERTO IN F
        C. F. PETERS CORPORATION   N6109   6.00
LIPATTI, D.
    CONCERTINO CLASSIQUE
        UNIVERSAL EDITION   UE 11546 10.00
LISZT
    CADENZA TO BEETHOVEN CONCERTO III
        MUSICA OBSCURA   1.50
LISZT   SAUER   D
    CONCERTI AND OTHER WORKS WITH ORCHESTRA
        C. F. PETERS CORPORATION   3602C   10.00
LISZT   MONTES
    CONCERTO NO. 01 IN E FLAT
        FRANCO COLOMBO PUBLICATIONS   BA10067   3.25
LISZT   SAUER   D
    CONCERTO NO. 01 IN E FLAT
        C. F. PETERS CORPORATION   3606   2.00
LISZT   JOSEFFY, R.
    CONCERTO NO. 01 IN E FLAT
        G. SCHIRMER, INC.   L1057   1.75
LISZT   JOSEFFY
    CONCERTO NO. 01 IN E FLAT
        G. SCHIRMER, INC.   L1057   1.75
LISZT   MONTES
    CONCERTO NO. 02 IN A
        FRANCO COLOMBO PUBLICATIONS   BA11778   4.00
LISZT   SAUER   D
    CONCERTO NO. 02 IN A
        C. F. PETERS CORPORATION   3607   2.50
LISZT   JOSEFFY, R.
    CONCERTO NO. 02 IN A
        G. SCHIRMER, INC.   L1058   2.50
LISZT   JOSEFFY
    CONCERTO NO. 02 IN A
        G. SCHIRMER, INC.   L1058   2.50
LISZT   HUGHES
    CONCERTO PATHETIQUE IN E MINOR
        G. SCHIRMER, INC.   L1534   1.50
LISZT   HUGHES
    CONCERTO PATHETIQUE IN E MINOR
        G. SCHIRMER, INC.   L1534   1.50
LISZT   5
    KONZERT-ETUDE - GNOMENREIGEN
        SCHOTT   06455 1/2 1.00
LISZT   5
    KONZERT-ETUDE - UN SOSPIRO
        SCHOTT   06779 1/2 1.00
LISZT   5
    KONZERT-ETUDE - WALDESRAUSCHEN
        SCHOTT   06454 1/2 1.00
LISZT
    PIANO CONCERTO NO. 01 IN E FLAT
        EDWIN F. KALMUS   3613   2.00
LISZT
    PIANO CONCERTO NO. 02 IN A
        EDWIN F. KALMUS   3614   2.50
LITOLFF
    CONCERTO SYMPHONIQUE NO. 3, OP. 45 AND SCHERZO FROM CONCERTO
    SYMPHONIQUE NO. 4, OP. 102
        MUSIC TREASURE PUBLICATIONS   5.00
LITOLFF
    CONCERTO SYMPHONIQUE
        EDWIN F. KALMUS   3604   5.00
LITOLFF   CURZON
    SCHERZO CONCERTO
        BOOSEY AND HAWKES, INC.   1.25
LITOLFF   JOHNSON   M
    SCHERZO --FROM CONCERTO SYMPHONIQUE NO. 4--
        C. F. PETERS CORPORATION   H1462   1.25
LOPATNIKOFF
    CONCERTO FOR TWO PIANOS AND ORCHESTRA, OP. 33 -- INCLUDES TWO
    PARTS
        MCA MUSIC   5.00

LOPATNIKOFF
    KONZERT FUR KLAVIER UND ORCHESTER, OP. 15, KLAVIERAUSZUG
        SCHOTT   2138   5.00
LUCCHINETTI, G. B.   EWERHART
    CONCERTO -- 2 PNO/ORG/HPCHD
        ASSOCIATED MUSIC PUBLISHERS, INC.   DOB   2.75
MACDOWELL
    CONCERTO NO. 01 IN A MINOR, OP. 15
        ASSOCIATED MUSIC PUBLISHERS, INC.   BRH   2.25
MACDOWELL   HUGHES
    CONCERTO NO. 02, OP. 23
        G. SCHIRMER, INC.   L1462   2.50
MACDOWELL   HUGHES
    CONCERTO NO. 02 IN D MINOR, OP. 23
        G. SCHIRMER, INC.   L1462   2.50
MANNINO, V.
    CONCERTO
        FRANCO COLOMBO PUBLICATIONS   DS935   6.50
MARCELLO *   M
    CONCERTO IN D MINOR
        C. F. PETERS CORPORATION   217D   1.50
MARGOLA
    KINDERKONZERT
        FRANCO COLOMBO PUBLICATIONS   128918   2.75
MARTELLI, M.   D
    CONCERTO, OP. 56
        C. F. PETERS CORPORATION   C404   3.00
MARTINO
    CONCERTO FOR PIANO AND ORCHESTRA
        E. C. SCHIRMER MUSIC COMPANY   1441   02.50
MARTINU, B.   4
    CONCERTINO FUR KLAVIERTRIO UND STREICHORCHESTER
        BARENREITER VERLAG   CHF 5178
MARTINU, B.   4
    CONCERTINO FUR KLAVIER -- LINKE HAND -- UND ORCHESTER
        BARENREITER VERLAG   CHF 5200
MARTINU, B.   4
    CONCERTINO FUR KLAVIER UND ORCHESTER
        BARENREITER VERLAG   CHF 5191
MARTINU, B.
    CONCERTO FOR 2 PIANOS
        ASSOCIATED MUSIC PUBLISHERS, INC.   AMP   4.00
MARTINU, B.
    CONCERTO NO. 02
        ARTIA   6.00
MARTINU, B.
    CONCERTO NO. 03
        ARTIA   8.00
MARTINU, B.   4
    INCANTATIONS. KONZERT NO. 4 FUR KLAVIER UND ORCHESTER
        BARENREITER VERLAG   BA 4318
MARTINU, B.   5
    KLAVIERKONZERT NO. 01
        BARENREITER VERLAG   AP 1733
MARTINU, B.   4
    KLAVIERKONZERT NO. 02 - KLAVIERAUSZUG
        BARENREITER VERLAG   AP 1511
MARTINU, B.   4
    KLAVIERKONZERT NO. 02
        BARENREITER VERLAG   CHF 5190
MARTINU, B.   4
    KLAVIERKONZERT NO. 02
        BARENREITER VERLAG   AP 1511
MARTINU, B.   4
    KLAVIERKONZERT NO. 03 - KLAVIERAUSZUG
        BARENREITER VERLAG   AP 1512
MARTINU, B.   4
    KLAVIERKONZERT NO. 03
        BARENREITER VERLAG   CHF 5209
MARTINU, B.   4
    KLAVIERKONZERT NO. 03
        BARENREITER VERLAG   AP 1512
MARTUCCI
    STUDIO DI CONCERTO, OP. 9
        FRANCO COLOMBO PUBLICATIONS   44526   1.25
MATHIAS, W.
    CONCERTO NO. 02
        OXFORD UNIVERSITY PRESS   35.106   6.20
MCPHEE, C.
    CONCERTO FOR PIANO AND WIND OCTET ACCOMPANIMENT -- SET
        ASSOCIATED MUSIC PUBLISHERS, INC.   AMP   6.50
MEDTNER, N.   D
    CONCERTO NO. 02, OP. 50
        C. F. PETERS CORPORATION   ZM1002   6.00
MEDTNER, N.   D
    CONCERTO NO. 03, OP. 60
        C. F. PETERS CORPORATION   ZM1003   6.00
MENDELSSOHN   3
    ANDANTE CANTABILE, VIOLIN CONCERTO
        CENTURY MUSIC PUBLISHING COMPANY, INC.   1916   .40
MENDELSSOHN   D
    COMPLETE PIANO WORKS, VOL. 4# CONCERTI--ARR. PF. SOLO--, OP. 22,
    29, 43
        C. F. PETERS CORPORATION   1704D   7.50
MENDELSSOHN
    CONCERTO IN D MINOR FOR PIANO, VIOLIN AND STRING ORCHESTRA
        ASSOCIATED MUSIC PUBLISHERS, INC.   DVM   9.00
MENDELSSOHN
    CONCERTO IN E FOR 2 PIANOS AND ORCHESTRA
        ASSOCIATED MUSIC PUBLISHERS, INC.   DVM   5.00
MENDELSSOHN
    CONCERTO NO. 01, OP. 25
        EDWIN F. KALMUS   3672   2.00
MENDELSSOHN   D
    CONCERTO NO. 01 IN G MINOR, OP. 25
        C. F. PETERS CORPORATION   2896A   1.50
MENDELSSOHN   RUTHARDT
    CONCERTO NO. 01 IN G MINOR, OP. 25
        G. SCHIRMER, INC.   L61   1.25
MENDELSSOHN   RUTHARDT
    CONCERTO NO. 01 IN G MINOR, OP. 25
        G. SCHIRMER, INC.   L61   1.25
MENDELSSOHN   D
    CONCERTO NO. 02 IN D MINOR, OP. 40
        C. F. PETERS CORPORATION   2896B   3.00
MENDELSSOHN   RUTHARDT
    CONCERTO NO. 02 IN D MINOR, OP. 40
        G. SCHIRMER, INC.   L62   1.50
MENDELSSOHN   RUTHARDT
    CONCERTO NO. 02 IN D MINOR, OP. 40
        G. SCHIRMER, INC.   L62   1.50
MENDELSSOHN   M
    VIOLIN CONCERTO, OP. 64. ABRIDGED PIANO SOLO ARR.
        C. F. PETERS CORPORATION   1731B   1.50
MENOTTI
    CONCERTO IN F
        FRANCO COLOMBO PUBLICATIONS   127655   4.00

MIEG, P.
        CONCERTO FOR HARPSICHORD -- 1954
                ASSOCIATED MUSIC PUBLISHERS, INC.   BOT   6.00
MILHAUD, D.
        CONCERTO FOR 2 PIANOS AND ORCHESTRA -- PIANO SCORE
                ELKAN-VOGEL, INC.   16.00
MILHAUD, D.
        CONCERTO NO. 02 FOR 2 PIANOS AND PERCUSSION -- PIANO SCORE
                ASSOCIATED MUSIC PUBLISHERS, INC.   ESC   12.00
MILHAUD, D.
        CONCERTO NO. 02 FOR 2 PIANOS AND PERCUSSION -- 4 PERCUSSION
PARTS
                ASSOCIATED MUSIC PUBLISHERS, INC.   ESC   6.00
MILHAUD, D.
        CONCERTO NO. 03
                ASSOCIATED MUSIC PUBLISHERS, INC.   AMP   3.25
MILHAUD, D.
        CONCERTO NO. 04
                HEUGEL ET CIE.   13.70
MILHAUD, D.
        CONCERTO NO. 05
                ASSOCIATED MUSIC PUBLISHERS, INC.   ESC   8.25
MILHAUD, D.
        CONCERTO
                FRANCO COLOMBO PUBLICATIONS   SAL   10.75
MITTLER--ED   MITTLER   2, 3
        GREAT CONCERTO MUSIC
                MUSICORD PUBLICATIONS, INC.   1.25
MOESCHINGER
        KONZERT NO. 02 FUR KLAVIER UND KAMMERORCHESTER, OP. 23,
        CLAVIERAUSZUG
                SCHOTT   3275   3.75
MOHAUPT, R.
        CONCERTO -- 1938, REV. 1942
                ASSOCIATED MUSIC PUBLISHERS, INC.   AMP   3.25
MOHLER   4-5
        KONZERTSTUCKE, OP. 21
                BARENREITER VERLAG   SM 1705
MONTANI
        CONCERTINO IN E
                FRANCO COLOMBO PUBLICATIONS   124916   2.75
MONTSALVATGE, X.
        CONCERTO BREVE FOR PIANO AND ORCHESTRA
                PEER SOUTHERN ORGANIZATION   05.50
MORAWETZ
        PIANO CONCERTO NO. 01
                MCA MUSIC   4.00
MOSCHELES, I.
        PIANO CONCERTO NO. 03 IN G MINOR, OP. 58
                MUSIC TREASURE PUBLICATIONS   5.00
MOSZKOWSKI   M
        ANDANTE AND SCHERZO FROM CONCERTO, OP. 59. ABRIDGED PIANO SOLO
ARR.
                C. F. PETERS CORPORATION   2872A   1.25
MOSZKOWSKI   D
        CONCERTO IN E, OP. 59
                C. F. PETERS CORPORATION   2872   3.50
MOZART, W. A.   BUSONI
        ANDANTINO FROM PIANO CONCERTO K271
                ASSOCIATED MUSIC PUBLISHERS, INC.   BRH   1.20
MOZART, W. A.   LANDOWSKA, W.
        CADENZA - CONCERTO K271 IN E FLAT
                BROUDE BROTHERS LTD.   01.75
MOZART, W. A.   LANDOWSKA, W.
        CADENZA - CONCERTO K413 IN F
                BROUDE BROTHERS LTD.   01.75
MOZART, W. A.   LANDOWSKA, W.
        CADENZA - CONCERTO K414 IN A
                BROUDE BROTHERS LTD.   01.75
MOZART, W. A.   LANDOWSKA, W.
        CADENZA - CONCERTO K466 IN D MINOR
                BROUDE BROTHERS LTD.   02.00
MOZART, W. A.   LANDOWSKA, W.
        CADENZA - CONCERTO K482 IN E FLAT
                BROUDE BROTHERS LTD.   02.00
MOZART, W. A.   LANDOWSKA, W.
        CADENZA - CONCERTO K537 IN D
                BROUDE BROTHERS LTD.   02.00
MOZART, W. A.   M
        CONCERTI K.271, 450, 466, 467, 482, 488, 491, 537
                C. F. PETERS CORPORATION   765   12.00
MOZART, W. A.
        CONCERTO IN C MAJOR, NO. 21 -- THEME FROM 'ELVIRA MADIGAN'
                ASHLEY DEALERS SERVICE, INC.   1.00
MOZART, W. A.
        CONCERTO IN E FLAT, K365 FOR 2 PIANOS AND ORCHESTRA
                INTERNATIONAL MUSIC COMPANY   3.75
MOZART, W. A.   BALSAM
        CONCERTO K037 IN F
                OXFORD UNIVERSITY PRESS   32.143   3.30
MOZART, W. A.   BALSAM
        CONCERTO K039 IN B FLAT
                OXFORD UNIVERSITY PRESS   32.144   3.30
MOZART, W. A.   BALSAM
        CONCERTO K041 IN G
                OXFORD UNIVERSITY PRESS   32.146   3.30
MOZART, W. A.   BALSAM
        CONCERTO K043 IN D
                OXFORD UNIVERSITY PRESS   32.145   3.30
MOZART, W. A.
        CONCERTO K175 IN D --ORCH RED--
                ASSOCIATED MUSIC PUBLISHERS, INC.   BRH   1.50
MOZART, W. A.
        CONCERTO K175 IN D --SOLO ONLY--
                ASSOCIATED MUSIC PUBLISHERS, INC.   BRH   1.50
MOZART, W. A.   M
        CONCERTO K175 IN D MAJOR --CADENZA BY S. STRAVINSKY--
                C. F. PETERS CORPORATION   6391   2.00
MOZART, W. A.   M
        CONCERTO K238 IN B FLAT --CADENZA BY S. STRAVINSKY--
                C. F. PETERS CORPORATION   6392   2.00
MOZART, W. A.
        CONCERTO K238 IN B FLAT --ORCH RED--
                ASSOCIATED MUSIC PUBLISHERS, INC.   BRH   1.50
MOZART, W. A.
        CONCERTO K238 IN B FLAT --SOLO ONLY--
                ASSOCIATED MUSIC PUBLISHERS, INC.   BRH   1.50
MOZART, W. A.
        CONCERTO K246 IN C --ORCH RED--
                ASSOCIATED MUSIC PUBLISHERS, INC.   BRH   1.50
MOZART, W. A.
        CONCERTO K246 IN C --SOLO ONLY--
                ASSOCIATED MUSIC PUBLISHERS, INC.   BRH   1.50
MOZART, W. A.   PHILIPP, I.
        CONCERTO K246 IN C
                G. SCHIRMER, INC.   L1791   1.50

MOZART, W. A.   PHILIPP
        CONCERTO K246 IN C
                G. SCHIRMER, INC.   L1791   1.50
MOZART, W. A.
        CONCERTO K271 IN E FLAT
                INTERNATIONAL MUSIC COMPANY   2.50
MOZART, W. A.
        CONCERTO K271 IN E FLAT
                EDWIN F. KALMUS   M   3712   2.00
MOZART, W. A.
        CONCERTO K271 IN E FLAT
                C. F. PETERS CORPORATION   3309F   1.50
MOZART, W. A.   PHILIPP, I.
        CONCERTO K271 IN E FLAT
                G. SCHIRMER, INC.   L1734   1.50
MOZART, W. A.   PHILIPP
        CONCERTO K271 IN E FLAT
                G. SCHIRMER, INC.   L1704   1.50
MOZART, W. A.
        CONCERTO K365 IN E FLAT, FOR TWO PIANOS
                EDWIN F. KALMUS   M   3702   3.00
MOZART, W. A.
        CONCERTO K365 IN E FLAT --TWO COPIES--
                C. F. PETERS CORPORATION   2212   3.00
MOZART, W. A.
        CONCERTO K382 IN D
                INTERNATIONAL MUSIC COMPANY   1.50
MOZART, W. A.
        CONCERTO K413 IN F --ORCH RED--
                ASSOCIATED MUSIC PUBLISHERS, INC.   BRH   1.50
MOZART, W. A.
        CONCERTO K413 IN F --SOLO ONLY--
                ASSOCIATED MUSIC PUBLISHERS, INC.   BRH   1.50
MOZART, W. A.   HINZE *   M
        CONCERTO K413 IN F
                C. F. PETERS CORPORATION   9046   4.50
MOZART, W. A.   PHILIPP, I.
        CONCERTO K413 IN F
                G. SCHIRMER, INC.   L1788   1.50
MOZART, W. A.   PHILIPP
        CONCERTO K413 IN F
                G. SCHIRMER, INC.   L1788   1.50
MOZART, W. A.
        CONCERTO K414 IN A
                INTERNATIONAL MUSIC COMPANY   2.00
MOZART, W. A.
        CONCERTO K414 IN A
                EDWIN F. KALMUS   M   3713   2.00
MOZART, W. A.   HINZE *   M
        CONCERTO K414 IN A
                C. F. PETERS CORPORATION   9028   4.50
MOZART, W. A.   PHILIPP, I.
        CONCERTO K414 IN A
                G. SCHIRMER, INC.   L1731   1.50
MOZART, W. A.   PHILIPP
        CONCERTO K414 IN A
                G. SCHIRMER, INC.   L1731   1.50
MOZART, W. A.
        CONCERTO K415 IN C --ORCH RED--
                ASSOCIATED MUSIC PUBLISHERS, INC.   BRH   1.50
MOZART, W. A.
        CONCERTO K415 IN C --SOLO ONLY--
                ASSOCIATED MUSIC PUBLISHERS, INC.   BRH   1.50
MOZART, W. A.   HINZE *   M
        CONCERTO K415 IN C
                C. F. PETERS CORPORATION   9080   4.50
MOZART, W. A.   PHILIPP
        CONCERTO K415 IN C
                G. SCHIRMER, INC.   L1789   1.50
MOZART, W. A.   PHILIPP, I.
        CONCERTO K415 IN G
                G. SCHIRMER, INC.   L1789   1.50
MOZART, W. A.
        CONCERTO K449 IN E FLAT
                INTERNATIONAL MUSIC COMPANY   2.00
MOZART, W. A.   HINZE *   M
        CONCERTO K449 IN E FLAT
                C. F. PETERS CORPORATION   4601   1.50
MOZART, W. A.   PHILIPP, I.
        CONCERTO K449 IN E FLAT
                G. SCHIRMER, INC.   L1756   1.25
MOZART, W. A.   PHILIPP
        CONCERTO K449 IN E FLAT
                G. SCHIRMER, INC.   L1756   1.25
MOZART, W. A.
        CONCERTO K450 IN B FLAT --ORCH RED--
                ASSOCIATED MUSIC PUBLISHERS, INC.   BRH   1.50
MOZART, W. A.
        CONCERTO K450 IN B FLAT --SOLO ONLY--
                ASSOCIATED MUSIC PUBLISHERS, INC.   BRH   1.50
MOZART, W. A.
        CONCERTO K450 IN B FLAT
                INTERNATIONAL MUSIC COMPANY   2.00
MOZART, W. A.
        CONCERTO K450 IN B FLAT
                EDWIN F. KALMUS   M   3714   2.00
MOZART, W. A.
        CONCERTO K450 IN B FLAT
                C. F. PETERS CORPORATION   3309G   1.50
MOZART, W. A.   PHILIPP, I.
        CONCERTO K450 IN B FLAT
                G. SCHIRMER, INC.   L1746   1.50
MOZART, W. A.   PHILIPP
        CONCERTO K450 IN B FLAT
                G. SCHIRMER, INC.   L1746   1.50
MOZART, W. A.
        CONCERTO K451 IN D --ORCH RED--
                ASSOCIATED MUSIC PUBLISHERS, INC.   BRH   1.50
MOZART, W. A.
        CONCERTO K451 IN D --SOLO ONLY--
                ASSOCIATED MUSIC PUBLISHERS, INC.   BRH   1.50
MOZART, W. A.
        CONCERTO K453 IN G --ORCH RED--
                ASSOCIATED MUSIC PUBLISHERS, INC.   BRH   1.50
MOZART, W. A.
        CONCERTO K453 IN G --SOLO ONLY--
                ASSOCIATED MUSIC PUBLISHERS, INC.   BRH   1.50
MOZART, W. A.
        CONCERTO K453 IN G
                INTERNATIONAL MUSIC COMPANY   2.00
MOZART, W. A.   PHILIPP, I.
        CONCERTO K453 IN G
                G. SCHIRMER, INC.   L1734   1.75
MOZART, W. A.   PHILIPP
        CONCERTO K453 IN G
                G. SCHIRMER, INC.   L1734   1.75

MOZART, W. A.　　　　　　　　　　　　　　M-D
　CONCERTO K456 IN B FLAT --CADENZAS BY MOZART AND MUELLER--
　　　C. F. PETERS CORPORATION　　　　　H707　　　2.50
MOZART, W. A.　　　　PHILIPP, I.
　CONCERTO K456 IN B FLAT
　　　INTERNATIONAL MUSIC COMPANY　　　　　　　2.50
MOZART, W. A.　　　　PHILIPP, I.
　CONCERTO K456 IN B FLAT
　　　G. SCHIRMER, INC.　　　　　　　　L1823　　2.50
MOZART, W. A.　　　　HINZE *
　CONCERTO K459 IN F --ORCH RED--
　　　ASSOCIATED MUSIC PUBLISHERS, INC.　BRH　　1.50
MOZART, W. A.　　　　HINZE *
　CONCERTO K459 IN F --SET--
　　　ASSOCIATED MUSIC PUBLISHERS, INC.　BRH　　3.50
MOZART, W. A.　　　　HINZE *
　CONCERTO K459 IN F --SOLO ONLY--
　　　ASSOCIATED MUSIC PUBLISHERS, INC.　BRH　　1.50
MOZART, W. A.　　　　PHILIPP, I.
　CONCERTO K459 IN F
　　　G. SCHIRMER, INC.　　　　　　　　L1701　　2.00
MOZART, W. A.　　　　PHILIPP
　CONCERTO K459 IN F
　　　G. SCHIRMER, INC.　　　　　　　　L1701　　2.00
MOZART, W. A.　　　　MONTANI
　CONCERTO K465 IN C
　　　FRANCO COLOMBO PUBLICATIONS　　　ER2458　1.75
MOZART, W. A.　　　　BECK
　CONCERTO K466 IN A - PIANO REDUCTION
　　　BARENREITER VERLAG　　　　　　　BA 4740A　4.50
MOZART, W. A.
　CONCERTO K466 IN D MINOR --ORCH RED--
　　　ASSOCIATED MUSIC PUBLISHERS, INC.　BRH　　1.00
MOZART, W. A.
　CONCERTO K466 IN D MINOR --SOLO ONLY--
　　　ASSOCIATED MUSIC PUBLISHERS, INC.　BRH　　1.00
MOZART, W. A.　　　　MONTANI
　CONCERTO K466 IN D MINOR
　　　FRANCO COLOMBO PUBLICATIONS　　　ER2460　2.50
MOZART, W. A.
　CONCERTO K466 IN D MINOR
　　　INTERNATIONAL MUSIC COMPANY　　　　　　　2.50
MOZART, W. A.
　CONCERTO K466 IN D MINOR
　　　EDWIN F. KALMUS　　　　　　　　　3715　　2.00
MOZART, W. A.　　　　　　　　　　　　M
　CONCERTO K466 IN D MINOR
　　　C. F. PETERS CORPORATION　　　　2897D　　1.50
MOZART, W. A.　　　　KULLAK, T.
　CONCERTO K466 IN D MINOR
　　　G. SCHIRMER, INC.　　　　　　　　L661　　1.50
MOZART, W. A.　　　　KULLAK, T.
　CONCERTO K466 IN D MINOR
　　　G. SCHIRMER, INC.　　　　　　　　L661　　1.50
MOZART, W. A.
　CONCERTO K467 IN C --ORCH RED--
　　　ASSOCIATED MUSIC PUBLISHERS, INC.　BRH　　1.50
MOZART, W. A.
　CONCERTO K467 IN C --SOLO ONLY--
　　　ASSOCIATED MUSIC PUBLISHERS, INC.　BRH　　1.50
MOZART, W. A.
　CONCERTO K467 IN C
　　　EDWIN F. KALMUS　　　　　　　　　3716　　2.00
MOZART, W. A.　　　　　　　　　　　　M
　CONCERTO K467 IN C
　　　C. F. PETERS CORPORATION　　　　2897E　　1.50
MOZART, W. A.　　　　BISCHOFF
　CONCERTO K467 IN C
　　　G. SCHIRMER, INC.　　　　　　　　L661　　1.75
MOZART, W. A.　　　　BISCHOFF
　CONCERTO K467 IN C
　　　G. SCHIRMER, INC.　　　　　　　　L662　　1.75
MOZART, W. A.
　CONCERTO K482 IN E FLAT --ORCH RED--
　　　ASSOCIATED MUSIC PUBLISHERS, INC.　BRH　　1.50
MOZART, W. A.
　CONCERTO K482 IN E FLAT --SOLO ONLY--
　　　ASSOCIATED MUSIC PUBLISHERS, INC.　BRH　　2.00
MOZART, W. A.　　　　　　　　　　　　M
　CONCERTO K482 IN E FLAT --W. HUMMEL CADENZAS--
　　　C. F. PETERS CORPORATION　　　　3826　　1.50
MOZART, W. A.
　CONCERTO K482 IN E FLAT
　　　EDWIN F. KALMUS　　　　　　　　　3717　　2.00
MOZART, W. A.　　　　BISCHOFF
　CONCERTO K482 IN E FLAT
　　　G. SCHIRMER, INC.　　　　　　　　L663　　1.50
MOZART, W. A.　　　　BISCHOFF
　CONCERTO K482 IN E FLAT
　　　G. SCHIRMER, INC.　　　　　　　　L663　　1.50
MOZART, W. A.　　　　MONTANI
　CONCERTO K488 IN A
　　　FRANCO COLOMBO PUBLICATIONS　　　ER2459　2.25
MOZART, W. A.
　CONCERTO K488 IN A
　　　EDWIN F. KALMUS　　　　　　　　　3718　　2.00
MOZART, W. A.　　　　　　　　　　　　M
　CONCERTO K488 IN A
　　　C. F. PETERS CORPORATION　　　　3309E　　1.50
MOZART, W. A.　　　　　　　　　　　　M
　CONCERTO K488 IN A
　　　C. F. PETERS CORPORATION　　　　3309EE　1.25
MOZART, W. A.　　　　YORK
　CONCERTO K488 IN A
　　　G. SCHIRMER, INC.　　　　　　　　L1584　　1.50
MOZART, W. A.　　　　YORK
　CONCERTO K488 IN A
　　　G. SCHIRMER, INC.　　　　　　　　L1584　　1.50
MOZART, W. A.
　CONCERTO K491 IN C MINOR --ORCH RED--
　　　ASSOCIATED MUSIC PUBLISHERS, INC.　BRH　　1.50
MOZART, W. A.
　CONCERTO K491 IN C MINOR --SOLO ONLY--
　　　ASSOCIATED MUSIC PUBLISHERS, INC.　BRH　　1.50
MOZART, W. A.　　　　BECK
　CONCERTO K491 IN C MINOR - PIANO REDUCTION
　　　BARENREITER VERLAG　　　　　　　BA 4741A　4.50
MOZART, W. A.
　CONCERTO K491 IN C MINOR
　　　EDWIN F. KALMUS　　　　　　　　　3719　　2.00
MOZART, W. A.　　　　　　　　　　　　M
　CONCERTO K491 IN C MINOR
　　　C. F. PETERS CORPORATION　　　　3309H　　1.50
MOZART, W. A.　　　　BISCHOFF
　CONCERTO K491 IN C MINOR
　　　G. SCHIRMER, INC.　　　　　　　　L664　　1.50

MOZART, W. A.　　　　BISCHOFF
　CONCERTO K491 IN C MINOR
　　　G. SCHIRMER, INC.　　　　　　　　L664　　1.50
MOZART, W. A.　　　　KING, A. H.　　　M
　CONCERTO K503 IN C --W. PH. K. HOFFMANN CADENZA--
　　　C. F. PETERS CORPORATION　　　　H683　　2.50
MOZART, W. A.　　　　BECK
　CONCERTO K503 IN C - PIANO REDUCTION
　　　BARENREITER VERLAG　　　　　　　BA 4742A　6.00
MOZART, W. A.
　CONCERTO K503 IN C
　　　INTERNATIONAL MUSIC COMPANY　　　　　　　2.50
MOZART, W. A.　　　　PHILIPP, I.
　CONCERTO K503 IN C
　　　G. SCHIRMER, INC.　　　　　　　　L1786　　1.75
MOZART, W. A.　　　　PHILIPP
　CONCERTO K503 IN C
　　　G. SCHIRMER, INC.　　　　　　　　L1786　　1.75
MOZART, W. A.　　　　REHBERG
　CONCERTO K537 IN D --'CORONATION'
　　　G. SCHIRMER, INC.　　　　　　　　L665　　1.50
MOZART, W. A.　　　　REHBERG
　CONCERTO K537 IN D -- ''CORONATION''
　　　G. SCHIRMER, INC.　　　　　　　　L665　　1.50
MOZART, W. A.
　CONCERTO K537 IN D 'CORONATION' --ORCH RED--
　　　ASSOCIATED MUSIC PUBLISHERS, INC.　BRH　　1.50
MOZART, W. A.
　CONCERTO K537 IN D 'CORONATION' --SOLO ONLY--
　　　ASSOCIATED MUSIC PUBLISHERS, INC.　BRH　　1.50
MOZART, W. A.
　CONCERTO K537 IN D
　　　EDWIN F. KALMUS　　　　　　　　　3720　　2.00
MOZART, W. A.　　　　　　　　　　　　M
　CONCERTO K537 IN D
　　　C. F. PETERS CORPORATION　　　　2897F　　1.50
MOZART, W. A.
　CONCERTO K595 IN B FLAT --ORCH RED--
　　　ASSOCIATED MUSIC PUBLISHERS, INC.　BRH　　1.50
MOZART, W. A.
　CONCERTO K595 IN B FLAT --SOLO ONLY--
　　　ASSOCIATED MUSIC PUBLISHERS, INC.　BRH　　1.50
MOZART, W. A.
　CONCERTO K595 IN B FLAT
　　　ASSOCIATED MUSIC PUBLISHERS, INC.　BRH　　3.50
MOZART, W. A.
　CONCERTO K595 IN B FLAT
　　　INTERNATIONAL MUSIC COMPANY　　　　　　　2.50
MOZART, W. A.　　　　PHILIPP, I.
　CONCERTO K595 IN B FLAT
　　　G. SCHIRMER, INC.　　　　　　　　L1721　　2.00
MOZART, W. A.　　　　PHILIPP
　CONCERTO K595 IN B FLAT
　　　G. SCHIRMER, INC.　　　　　　　　L1721　　2.00
MOZART, W. A.　　　　SAAR
　DOUBLE CONCERTO IN E FLAT, K365
　　　G. SCHIRMER, INC.　　　　　　　　　　　3.50
MOZART, W. A.　　　　SAAR
　DOUBLE CONCERTO K365 IN E FLAT
　　　G. SCHIRMER, INC.　　　　　　　　　　　3.50
MOZART, W. A.　　　　FISCHER, E.
　KADENZEN ZU DEN KLAVIERKONZERTEN -- K.V. 365, 453, 482, 503, 537
　1. SATZ UND K.V. 466, 491 1. UND 3. SATZ
　　　SCHOTT　　　　　　　　　　　　　4947　　3.25
MOZART, W. A.　　　　ROBYN　　　　　　3 1/2
　KINDER CONCERTO
　　　THEODORE PRESSER COMPANY　　　　　　　　1.25
MOZART, W. A.　　　　BECK　　　　　　　4
　KLAVIERKONZERT IN A, K488, KLAVIERAUSZUG
　　　BARENREITER VERLAG　　　　　　　BA 4740A
MOZART, W. A.　　　　BECK　　　　　　　4
　KLAVIERKONZERT IN A, K488
　　　BARENREITER VERLAG　　　　　　　BA 4740
MOZART, W. A.　　　　BECK　　　　　　　4
　KLAVIERKONZERT IN A, K488
　　　BARENREITER VERLAG　　　　　　　BA 4740A
MOZART, W. A.　　　　BECK　　　　　　　4
　KLAVIERKONZERT IN C, K503, KLAVIERAUSZUG
　　　BARENREITER VERLAG　　　　　　　BA 4742A
MOZART, W. A.　　　　BECK　　　　　　　4
　KLAVIERKONZERT IN C, K503
　　　BARENREITER VERLAG　　　　　　　BA 4742
MOZART, W. A.　　　　BECK　　　　　　　4
　KLAVIERKONZERT IN C, K503
　　　BARENREITER VERLAG　　　　　　　BA 4742A
MOZART, W. A.　　　　BECK　　　　　　　4
　KLAVIERKONZERT IN C MINOR, K491, KLAVIERAUSZUG
　　　BARENREITER VERLAG　　　　　　　BA 4741A
MOZART, W. A.　　　　BECK　　　　　　　4
　KLAVIERKONZERT IN C MINOR, K491
　　　BARENREITER VERLAG　　　　　　　BA 4741
MOZART, W. A.　　　　BECK　　　　　　　4
　KLAVIERKONZERT IN C MINOR, K491
　　　BARENREITER VERLAG　　　　　　　BA 4741A
MOZART, W. A.
　KONZERT-RONDO A-DUR, K.V. 386 FUR KLAVIER UND ORCHESTER,
　KLAVIERAUSZUG
　　　SCHOTT　　　　　　　　　　　　　5187　　2.25
MOZART, W. A.　　　　BADURA-SKODA *
　KONZERT-RONDO A-DUR -- K.V. 386 FUR KLAVIER UND ORCHESTER,
　KLAVIERAUSZUG
　　　SCHOTT　　　　　　　　　　　　　5187　　2.25
MOZART, W. A.　　　　WOLLHEIM
　KONZERT FUR CEMBALO MIT STREICH-ORCHESTER -- K.V. 107 D-DUR
　　　SCHOTT　　　　　　　　　　　　　1601　　3.25
MOZART, W. A.　　　　WOLLHEIM
　KONZERT FUR CEMBALO MIT STREICH-ORCHESTER ES-DUR
　　　SCHOTT　　　　　　　　　　　　　1603　　3.25
MOZART, W. A.　　　　WOLLHEIM
　KONZERT FUR CEMBALO MIT STREICH-ORCHESTER G-DUR
　　　SCHOTT　　　　　　　　　　　　　1602　　3.25
MOZART, W. A.　　　　WAGNER
　LODRON CONCERTO K242 --SET--
　　　G. SCHIRMER, INC.　　　　　　　　L1578　　1.50
MOZART, W. A.　　　　WAGNER
　LODRON CONCERTO K242
　　　G. SCHIRMER, INC.　　　　　　　　L1578　　1.50
MOZART, W. A.
　THIRTY-SIX CADENZAS TO PIANO CONCERTOS
　　　EDWIN F. KALMUS　　　　　　　　　3700　　3.00
MUELLER, A. E.　　　　　　　　　　　　M
　CADENZAS TO EIGHT MOZART CONCERTI --K.456, K.459, K.466, K.482,
　K. 488, K.491, K.503, K.537
　　　C. F. PETERS CORPORATION　　　　4519　　2.00
MYSLIVECEK　　　　　　FENDLER
　CONCERTO NO. 02
　　　BOOSEY AND HAWKES, INC.　　　　　　　　1.75

RACHMANINOFF, S.   TRUXELL, E.   3 1/2
    THEMES FROM PIANO CONCERTO
      VOLKWEIN BROS.   00.40
RACHMANINOFF, S.   ECKSTEIN
    THEME FROM SECOND PIANO CONCERTO, OP. 18
      CARL FISCHER, INC.   S 2313   .50
RAVEL
    CONCERTO FOR THE LEFT HAND--SOLO PART
      ELKAN-VOGEL, INC.   6.75
RAVEL
    CONCERTO FOR THE LEFT HAND
      ELKAN-VOGEL, INC.   14.50
RAVEL
    CONCERTO IN G
      ELKAN-VOGEL, INC.   7.50
RAVEL
    CONCERTO IN G
      ELKAN-VOGEL, INC.   15.00
RAWSTHORNE, A.
    CONCERTO NO. 01
      OXFORD UNIVERSITY PRESS   32.807   6.25
RAWSTHORNE, A.
    CONCERTO NO. 02
      OXFORD UNIVERSITY PRESS   32.807   6.85
REGER
    CONCERTO IN F MINOR, OP. 114
      ASSOCIATED MUSIC PUBLISHERS, INC.   BOT   9.00
REINECKE   HUGHES
    CADENZA TO THE BEETHOVEN CONCERTO IN CM, OP. 37, FIRST
    MOVEMENT--OP. 87 NO. 3
      G. SCHIRMER, INC.   .70
RESPIGHI
    CONCERTO IN THE MIXOLYDIAN MODE
      ASSOCIATED MUSIC PUBLISHERS, INC.   BOT   11.00
RIDKY   4
    KONZERT FUR KLAVIER UND ORCHESTER, KLAVIERAUSZUG
      BARENREITER VERLAG   AP 290
RIDKY   4
    KONZERT FUR KLAVIER UND ORCHESTER, OP. 46
      BARENREITER VERLAG   AP 290
RIDKY   4
    KONZERT FUR KLAVIER UND ORCHESTER, OP. 46
      BARENREITER VERLAG   AP 290
RIDKY   4
    KONZERT FUR KLAVIER UND ORCHESTER
      BARENREITER VERLAG   CHF 5343
RIES
    CONCERTO NO. 03 IN C SHARP MINOR, PIANO SOLO SCORE
      MUSICA OBSCURA   5.00
RIETI
    CONCERTO
      UNIVERSAL EDITION   UE 8799   5.10
RIMSKY-KORSAKOFF
    CONCERTO, OP. 30
      BOOSEY AND HAWKES, INC.   3.00
RIMSKY-KORSAKOFF
    CONCERTO IN C SHARP MINOR, OP. 30
      INTERNATIONAL MUSIC COMPANY   2.50
ROGER-ROGER
    JAZZ CONCERTO NO. 2
      FRANCO COLOMBO PUBLICATIONS   SAL   10.00
ROSZA
    SPELLBOUND CONCERTO -- THEME
      CHAPPELL AND COMPANY, INC.   0023341-1502 .95
ROSZA
    SPELLBOUND CONCERTO
      CHAPPELL AND COMPANY, INC.   0023341-1501 1.25
ROUSSEL, A.
    CONCERTO FOR PIANO AND ORCH. , PIANO RED.
      ELKAN-VOGEL, INC.   D   8.00
ROWLEY   D
    CONCERTO IN D, OP. 49
      C. F. PETERS CORPORATION   H24   2.00
ROWLEY
    MINIATURE CONCERTO
      BOOSEY AND HAWKES, INC.   1.50
ROZIN
    LITTLE CONCERTO
      BRODT MUSIC COMPANY   1.25
ROZSA, M.
    CONCERTO, OP. 31
      ASSOCIATED MUSIC PUBLISHERS, INC.   BRH   9.75
RUBINSTEIN   JOSEFFY, R.
    CONCERTO NO. 04 IN D MINOR, OP. 70
      G. SCHIRMER, INC.   L1047   3.00
RUBINSTEIN   JOSEFFY
    CONCERTO NO. 04 IN D MINOR, OP. 70
      G. SCHIRMER, INC.   L1047   3.00
SAINT-SAENS
    CONCERTO NO. 01, OP. 17
      ELKAN-VOGEL, INC.   D   16.00
SAINT-SAENS
    CONCERTO NO. 02, OP. 22
      ELKAN-VOGEL, INC.   D   21.00
SAINT-SAENS   PHILIPP, I.
    CONCERTO NO. 02 IN G MINOR, OP. 22
      G. SCHIRMER, INC.   L1405   3.50
SAINT-SAENS   PHILIPP
    CONCERTO NO. 02 IN G MINOR, OP. 22
      G. SCHIRMER, INC.   L1405   3.50
SAINT-SAENS
    CONCERTO NO. 04, OP. 44
      ELKAN-VOGEL, INC.   D   20.50
SAINT-SAENS   PHILIPP, I.
    CONCERTO NO. 04 IN C MINOR, OP. 44
      G. SCHIRMER, INC.   L1486   3.50
SAINT-SAENS   PHILIPP
    CONCERTO NO. 04 IN C MINOR, OP. 44
      G. SCHIRMER, INC.   L1486   3.50
SAINT-SAENS
    CONCERTO NO. 05, OP. 103
      ELKAN-VOGEL, INC.   D   23.00
SAINT-SAENS
    CONCERTO NO. 05, OP. 103
      ELKAN-VOGEL, INC.   4.00
SAINT-SAENS   DIEMER
    CONCERTO NO. 05 IN F, OP. 103
      G. SCHIRMER, INC.   L1838   3.00
SAINT-SAENS
    CONCERTO NO. 05 IN F, OP. 103
      G. SCHIRMER, INC.   L1838   3.00
SAINT-SAENS
    DEUXIEME CONCERTO, EDITION A
      ELKAN-VOGEL, INC.   D   10.50
SAINT-SAENS
    DEUXIEME CONCERTO, EDITION B
      ELKAN-VOGEL, INC.   D   5.75

SAINT-SAENS
    PIANO CONCERTO NO. 02, OP. 22
      ELKAN-VOGEL, INC.   5.50
SAINT-SAENS
    PIANO CONCERTO NO. 02, OP. 22
      EDWIN F. KALMUS   3854   3.50
SAINT-SAENS
    PIANO CONCERTO NO. 04, OP. 44
      ELKAN-VOGEL, INC.   10.00
SAINT-SAENS
    PIANO CONCERTO NO. 05, OP. 103
      ELKAN-VOGEL, INC.   11.00
SAINT-SAENS
    PREMIER CONCERTO POUR PIANO
      ELKAN-VOGEL, INC.   D   7.50
SAINT-SAENS
    QUATRIEME CONCERTO, OP. 44
      ELKAN-VOGEL, INC.   D   10.50
SAINT-SAENS
    SIX ETUDES POUR LE PIANO, BK. 2, NO. 06 -- TOCCATA D'APRES LE
    CINQUIEME CONCERTO
      ELKAN-VOGEL, INC.   D   3.00
SAINT-SAENS
    TROISIEME CONCERTO, OP. 29
      ELKAN-VOGEL, INC.   D   7.50
SANCAN, P.
    CONCERTO
      ELKAN-VOGEL, INC.   D   4.50
SANCAN, P.
    NOUVELLES CADENCES DU CONCERTO EN RE MINEUR DE W. A. MOZART
      ELKAN-VOGEL, INC.   D   1.75
SANTORO, C.
    CONCERTO NO. 01
      FRANCO COLOMBO PUBLICATIONS   SAL   4.00
SAUER   5
    KONZERT-ETUDE -- COUPLET SANS PAROLES
      SCHOTT   1.50
SAUER   5
    KONZERT-ETUDE -- NO. 26 PREGHIERA
      SCHOTT   1.50
SAUER   5
    KONZERT-ETUDE -- NO. 6 FRISSON DE FEUILLES
      SCHOTT   1.50
SAUGUET
    CONCERTO NO. 01 IN A MINOR
      ASSOCIATED MUSIC PUBLISHERS, INC.   ESC   8.50
SCHAEFER   3
    CONCERTO FUR QUERFLOTE, V, TROMP, KLAVIER, SCHLAGZEUG UND
    STREICHER
      BARENREITER VERLAG   BE 314
SCHAEFER   4-5
    KLAVIERKONZERT, OP. 37
      BARENREITER VERLAG   SM 1378
SCHARWENKA, X.
    PIANO CONCERTO NO. 01 IN B FLAT MINOR, OP. 32
      MUSIC TREASURE PUBLICATIONS   5.00
SCHAUM, J.
    MOUNTAIN CONCERTO
      BELWIN-MILLS PUBLISHING CORPORATION   2.50
SCHOENBERG   STEUERMANN, E.
    CONCERTO, OP. 42
      G. SCHIRMER, INC.   3.50
SCHOENBERG   STEUERMANN, E.
    CONCERTO, OP. 42
      G. SCHIRMER, INC.   3.50
SCHOLLUM, R.
    KONZERTSTUCKE--''RUCKBLICKE''--OP. 61
      ASSOCIATED MUSIC PUBLISHERS, INC.   DOB   2.50
SCHROEDER
    CONCERTO, OP. 42
      MCA MUSIC   3.50
SCHROTER, J. S.   SCHULTZ *   2-3
    KONZERT IN C FUR KLAVIER UND STREICHORCHESTER, KLAVIERAUSZUG
      SCHOTT   4974   3.00
SCHUBERT, H.   4
    AMBROSIANISCHES KLAVIERKONZERT
      BARENREITER VERLAG   AE 219
SCHULHOFF   4
    DOPPELKONZERT FUR KLAVIER UND QUERFLOTE, 2 OB UND STREICHER
      BARENREITER VERLAG   CHF 5292
SCHULLER, G.
    CONCERTO -- 1962
      ASSOCIATED MUSIC PUBLISHERS, INC.   AMP   11.00
SCHULLER, G.
    KONZERT FUR KLAVIER UND ORCHESTER, KLAVIERAUSZUG
      SCHOTT   10895   14.00
SCHUMAN, W.
    CONCERTO FOR PIANO AND SMALL ORCHESTRA
      G. SCHIRMER, INC.   3.00
SCHUMAN, W.
    CONCERTO FOR PIANO AND SMALL ORCHESTRA
      G. SCHIRMER, INC.   3.00
SCHUMANN, C.   M-D
    CADENZAS TO BEETHOVEN CONCERTOS NOS. 3, 4. TO MOZART CONCERTO
    NO. 20--K.466--
      C. F. PETERS CORPORATION   3629   2.00
SCHUMANN, R.   GRAINGER
    CONCERTO, FIRST MOVEMENT--CONCERT TRANSCRIPTION
      G. SCHIRMER, INC.   1.25
SCHUMANN, R.   M
    CONCERTO IN A MINOR, OP. 54. ABRIDGED
      C. F. PETERS CORPORATION   2898A   1.25
SCHUMANN, R.   SAUER   D
    CONCERTO IN A MINOR, OP. 54
      C. F. PETERS CORPORATION   2898   2.50
SCHUMANN, R.   HUGHES
    CONCERTO IN A MINOR, OP. 54
      G. SCHIRMER, INC.   L1358   1.75
SCHUMANN, R.   FRYER, H.
    CONCERTO IN A MINOR -- WITH ACCOMPANIMENT ARRANGED FOR SECOND
    PIANO
      NOVELLO AND COMPANY, LTD.   10.0124.08   2.00
SCHUMANN, R.   FRYER, H.
    CONCERTO IN A MINOR
      NOVELLO AND COMPANY, LTD.   10.0124.08   2.00
SCHUMANN, R.   HUGHES
    CONCERTO IN A MINOR
      G. SCHIRMER, INC.   L1358   1.75
SCHUMANN, R.
    PIANO CONCERTO, OP. 54
      EDWIN F. KALMUS   3897   2.50
SCRIABINE, A.
    CONCERTO, OP. 20
      BOOSEY AND HAWKES, INC.   5.00
SEARLE, H.
    KONZERT NO. 02 FUR KLAVIER UND ORCHESTER, OP. 27
      SCHOTT   10397   4.00

SESSIONS, R.
  CONCERTO FOR PIANO AND ORCHESTRA
    EDWARD B. MARKS MUSIC CORPORATION   06.00
SGAMBATI   6
  KONZERT-ETUDE FIS-MOLL OP. 10 NO. 2
    SCHOTT   1.25
SHOSTAKOVITCH
  CONCERTO, OP. 35 FOR PIANO, TRUMPET, STRINGS
    MCA MUSIC   3.00
SHOSTAKOVITCH
  CONCERTO NO. 01 IN C MINOR, OP. 35
    INTERNATIONAL MUSIC COMPANY   3.50
SHOSTAKOVITCH
  CONCERTO NO. 02, OP. 102
    MCA MUSIC   4.50
SHOSTAKOVITCH   D
  CONCERTO NO. 02, OP. 102
    C. F. PETERS CORPORATION   4772   6.50
SHOSTAKOVITCH
  CONCERTO NO. 02 IN F, OP. 102
    INTERNATIONAL MUSIC COMPANY   3.75
SHOSTAKOVITCH
  PIANO CONCERTO NO. 02, OP. 102
    EDWIN F. KALMUS   3969   3.50
SIEGL, O.
  CHAMBER CONCERTO
    ASSOCIATED MUSIC PUBLISHERS, INC.   DOB   6.50
SKALKOTTAS, N.
  CONCERTINO FOR 2 PIANOS AND ORCHESTRA
    UNIVERSAL EDITION   UE 14296   5.10
SMETANA   3-4
  AM MEERESSTRAND. KONZERTETUDE, OP. 17
    BARENREITER VERLAG   AP 701
SMITH, J.   D
  CONCERTO FOR PIANO AND ORCHESTRA
    THEODORE PRESSER COMPANY   6.50
SMOLANOFF
  CONCERTO FOR PIANO 4-HANDS, STRINGS, PERCUSSIONS
    SEESAW MUSIC CORPORATION   18.00
SOLER, A.   MARCHI, G.
  FIRST CONCERTO IN C MAJOR
    EDIZIONI BERBEN   EB 1381   2.50
SOLER, A.   RUBIO
  SIX CONCERTI FOR 2 KEYBOARD INSTRUMENTS -- COMPLETE
    ASSOCIATED MUSIC PUBLISHERS, INC.   UME   10.00
SOLER, A.   RUBIO
  SIX CONCERTI FOR 2 KEYBOARD INSTRUMENTS -- NO. 1 IN C
    ASSOCIATED MUSIC PUBLISHERS, INC.   UME   2.00
SOLER, A.   RUBIO
  SIX CONCERTI FOR 2 KEYBOARD INSTRUMENTS -- NO. 2 IN A MINOR
    ASSOCIATED MUSIC PUBLISHERS, INC.   UME   2.50
SOLER, A.   RUBIO
  SIX CONCERTI FOR 2 KEYBOARD INSTRUMENTS -- NO. 3 IN G
    ASSOCIATED MUSIC PUBLISHERS, INC.   UME   2.00
SOLER, A.   RUBIO
  SIX CONCERTI FOR 2 KEYBOARD INSTRUMENTS -- NO. 4 IN F
    ASSOCIATED MUSIC PUBLISHERS, INC.   UME   2.00
SOLER, A.   RUBIO
  SIX CONCERTI FOR 2 KEYBOARD INSTRUMENTS -- NO. 5 IN A
    ASSOCIATED MUSIC PUBLISHERS, INC.   UME   2.50
SOLER, A.   RUBIO
  SIX CONCERTI FOR 2 KEYBOARD INSTRUMENTS -- NO. 6 IN D
    ASSOCIATED MUSIC PUBLISHERS, INC.   UME   3.00
SPITZMULLER, A.
  CONCERTO, OP. 39
    UNIVERSAL EDITION   UE 12151   4.25
STAEMPFLI, E.   4-5
  CONCERTINO FUR KLAVIER UND KAMMERORCHESTER
    BARENREITER VERLAG   SM 2249
STAMITZ, K.
  CONCERTO IN F
    ASSOCIATED MUSIC PUBLISHERS, INC.   BRH   5.00
STARER
  CONCERTO NO. 02 FOR PIANO AND ORCHESTRA -- OR WIND ENSEMBLE
    MCA MUSIC   5.00
STEIBELT
  CONCERTO NO. 03, OP. 33 'THE STORM'
    MUSICA OBSCURA   5.00
STEINER, G.
  CONCERTO FOR PIANO AND ORCHESTRA, 1967
    SEESAW MUSIC CORPORATION   28.00
STEINER   3, 4
  ADVANCING PIANIST PLAYS CONCERTOS, THE
    BELWIN-MILLS PUBLISHING CORPORATION   1766   1.75
STERKEL, F. X.   KAUL
  ERSTES KLAVIERKONZERT IN C, OP. 20 - KLAVIER-EINRICHTUNG
    SCHOTT   5760
STRAUSS, J. *   6
  ROSEN AUS DEM SUDEN, KONZERTWALZER
    SCHOTT   3712   2.00
STRAVINSKY, I.
  CONCERTO FOR PIANO AND WINDS
    BOOSEY AND HAWKES, INC.   6.50
STRAVINSKY, I.
  CONCERTO IN ES, DUMBARTON OAKS FUR KAMMERORCHESTER,
  KLAVIERAUSZUG
    SCHOTT   2791   7.50
STRAVINSKY, I.
  CONCERTO PER DUE PIANO FORTI SOLI
    SCHOTT   2520   7.50
STRAVINSKY, S.   M
  EIGHTEEN ORIGINAL CADENZAS AND FOUR FERMATAS TO MOZART CONCERTI
    C. F. PETERS CORPORATION   6021   3.00
STRAVINSKY, S.   M
  EIGHTEEN ORIGINAL CADENZAS AND 4 FERMATAS TO MOZART PIANO
  CONCERTI
    C. F. PETERS CORPORATION   6021   3.00
STUDER   4
  KAMMERKONZERT FUR KLAVIER UND KLEINES ORCHESTER
    BARENREITER VERLAG   BA 2020
STUDER   4
  KLEINES KONZERT FUR STREICHER, KLAVIER ZU 4 HANDEN UND 2
  QUERFLOTEN
    BARENREITER VERLAG   BA 1914
SUTERMEISTER, H.   5
  KONZERT FUR KLAVIER UND ORCHESTER, KLAVIERAUSZUG
    SCHOTT   3669   6.00
SUTERMEISTER, H.   5
  KONZERT NO. 02 FUR KLAVIER UND ORCHESTER, KLAVIERAUSZUG
    SCHOTT   4548   5.00
SUTERMEISTER, H.   5-6
  KONZERT NO. 03 FUR KLAVIER UND ORCHESTER, KLAVIERAUSZUG
    SCHOTT   4819   9.00
SYDEMAN, W.
  CONCERTINO FOR OBOE, PIANO AND STRINGS
    SEESAW MUSIC CORPORATION   13.00

TAGLIAPIETRA, C.
  CADENZAS FOR CONCERTI BY MOZART AND BEETHOVEN
    FRANCO COLOMBO PUBLICATIONS   Z2131   2.25
TAILLEFERRE, G.
  PIANO CONCERTO
    HEUGEL ET CIE.   13.50
TANSMAN, A.
  CONCERTINO -- 1931
    ASSOCIATED MUSIC PUBLISHERS, INC.   ESC   5.75
TANSMAN, A.
  CONCERTO FOR 2 PIANOS AND ORCHESTRA
    ASSOCIATED MUSIC PUBLISHERS, INC.   ESC   10.75
TANSMAN, A.
  CONCERTO NO. 01
    ASSOCIATED MUSIC PUBLISHERS, INC.   ESC   6.50
TANSMAN, A.
  CONCERTO NO. 02
    ASSOCIATED MUSIC PUBLISHERS, INC.   ESC   2.50
TCHEREPNIN
  CONCERTO NO. 02
    HEUGEL ET CIE.   13.40
TCHEREPNIN
  CONCERTO NO. 05, OP. 96
    BOOSEY AND HAWKES, INC.   7.50
TCHEREPNIN
  CONCERTO NO. 06, OP. 99
    BOOSEY AND HAWKES, INC.   4.75
TCHEREPNIN   5
  FUNF KONZERT-ETUDEN OP. 52 -- DIE LAUTE
    SCHOTT   4278   1.25
TCHEREPNIN   5
  FUNF KONZERT-ETUDEN OP. 52 -- KASPERLSPIEL
    SCHOTT   4280   1.25
TCHEREPNIN   5
  FUNF KONZERT-ETUDEN OP. 52 -- LOBGES
    SCHOTT   4281   1.25
TCHEREPNIN   5
  FUNF KONZERT-ETUDEN OP. 52 -- SCHATTENSPIIEL
    SCHOTT   4277   1.25
TCHEREPNIN   5
  FUNF KONZERT-ETUDEN OP. 52 -- WIDMUNG AN CHINA
    SCHOTT   4279   1.25
TELEMANN, G.P. *   M-D
  CONCERTO IN G MINOR
    C. F. PETERS CORPORATION   217B   3.00
THARICHEN, W.
  CONCERTO, OP. 39
    ASSOCIATED MUSIC PUBLISHERS, INC.   BOT   7.50
THIEME   4
  MASCHERATA PICCOLA. CONCERTINO GIOCOSO FUR KLAVIER UND
  KAMMERORCHESTER
    BARENREITER VERLAG   SM 2086
THOMPSON, J.--ED   THOMPSON, J.   4
  THEMES FROM PIANO CONCERTOS
    WILLIS MUSIC COMPANY   1.25
THOMPSON, J.   3
  ANDANTINO FROM CONCERTO IN D MINOR
    WILLIS MUSIC COMPANY   .40
THOMPSON, J.   2
  CONCERTINA
    WILLIS MUSIC COMPANY   1.75
THOMPSON, J.   2
  CONCERTINA
    WILLIS MUSIC COMPANY   1.75
THOMPSON, J.   3
  CONCERTO AMERICANA
    WILLIS MUSIC COMPANY   1.75
THOMPSON, J.   4
  CONCERTO IN D MINOR
    WILLIS MUSIC COMPANY   1.25
TOCH, E.
  ETUDEN FUR KLAVIER, 5 TIMES 10 - ZEHN KONZERT-ETUDEN, OP. 55,
  HEFT 01
    SCHOTT   2161   2.50
TOCH, E.
  ETUDEN FUR KLAVIER, 5 TIMES 10 - ZEHN KONZERT-ETUDEN, OP. 55,
  HEFT 02
    SCHOTT   2162   2.50
TOCH, E.   6
  KONZERT FUR KLAVIER UND ORCHESTER, OP. 38 - KLAVIERAUSZUG
    SCHOTT   1859
TONSING
  CONCERTO FOR A YOUNG PIANIST --SOLO AND 2ND PIANO--
    ROCHESTER MUSIC PUBLISHERS, INC.   3.00
TOSATTI
  ALLEGRO DA CONCERTO
    FRANCO COLOMBO PUBLICATIONS   128878   .90
TSCHAIKOWSKY
  CONCERTO, OP. 23
    EDWIN F. KALMUS   4015   3.00
TSCHAIKOWSKY   WHITFORD   GR. 2 1/2
  CONCERTO IN B FLAT MINOR
    ROBERT WHITFORD PUBLICATIONS   .40
TSCHAIKOWSKY   SCHIEFELBEIN   2 1/2
  CONCERTO NO. 01 -- OPENING THEME
    VOLKWEIN BROS.   .25
TSCHAIKOWSKY   M
  CONCERTO NO. 01 IN B FLAT MINOR, OP. 23   ABRIDGED
    C. F. PETERS CORPORATION   3775A   1.25
TSCHAIKOWSKY   5
  CONCERTO NO. 01 IN B FLAT MINOR, OP. 23
    INTERNATIONAL MUSIC COMPANY   3.00
TSCHAIKOWSKY   D
  CONCERTO NO. 01 IN B FLAT MINOR, OP. 23
    C. F. PETERS CORPORATION   3775   3.00
TSCHAIKOWSKY   JOSEFFY, R.
  CONCERTO NO. 01 IN B FLAT MINOR, OP. 23
    G. SCHIRMER, INC.   L1045   3.00
TSCHAIKOWSKY   JOSEFFY
  CONCERTO NO. 01 IN B FLAT MINOR, OP. 23
    G. SCHIRMER, INC.   L1045   3.00
TSCHAIKOWSKY
  CONCERTO NO. 01 IN B FLAT MINOR
    ASHLEY DEALERS SERVICE, INC.   1.95
TSCHAIKOWSKY   4
  CONCERTO NO. 01 IN B FLAT MINOR
    CENTURY MUSIC PUBLISHING COMPANY, INC.   3530   .40
TSCHAIKOWSKY   D
  CONCERTO NO. 02 IN G, OP. 44
    C. F. PETERS CORPORATION   4644   5.00
TSCHAIKOWSKY   FREY, H.
  CONCERTO NO. 02
    THE BIG THREE MUSIC CORPORATION   00.75
TSCHAIKOWSKY   4
  KLAVIERKONZERT NO. 02 IN G
    BARENREITER VERLAG   AE 241

TSCHAIKOWSKY   DEIS
   OPENING THEME OF THE B FLAT MINOR PIANO CONCERTO
      G. SCHIRMER, INC.   .40
TSCHAIKOWSKY   GRAINGER
   OPENING THEME OF THE B FLAT MINOR PIANO CONCERTO
      G. SCHIRMER, INC.   .50
TSCHAIKOWSKY
   PIANO CONCERTO, THEME FROM FIRST MOVEMENT
      ASHLEY DEALERS SERVICE, INC.   ES   .95
TSCHAIKOWSKY   SINGER
   PIANO CONCERTO IN B FLAT -- THEME AND VARIATION
      MCA MUSIC   .60
TSCHAIKOWSKY
   PIANO CONCERTO IN B FLAT MINOR, OP. 23
      C. F. PETERS CORPORATION   37758   2.00
TSCHAIKOWSKY   4
   PIANO CONCERTO IN B FLAT MINOR, THEME
      CENTURY MUSIC PUBLISHING COMPANY, INC. 3530   .40
TSCHAIKOWSKY   2
   PIANO CONCERTO NO. 01, EASY
      CENTURY MUSIC PUBLISHING COMPANY, INC. 3557   .40
TSCHAIKOWSKY   ECKSTEIN
   THEME FROM PIANO CONCERTO NO. 1 IN B FLAT
      CARL FISCHER, INC.   S 2281   .50
TSCHAIKOWSKY   ECKSTEIN
   THEME FROM PIANO CONCERTO NO. 1 IN B FLAT
      CARL FISCHER, INC.   S 2282   .50
TSCHAIKOWSKY   WALLIS   2
   THEME FROM THE FIRST MOVEMENT OF PIANO CONCERTO NO. 1
      BOSTON MUSIC COMPANY   .50
TSCHAIKOWSKY   MITTLER   2B
   TSCHAIKOWSKY CONCERTO
      MUSICORD PUBLICATIONS, INC.   .45
TSCHAIKOWSKY   2
   VIOLIN CONCERTO, THEME
      CENTURY MUSIC PUBLISHING COMPANY, INC. 3847   .40
TURINA, J.
   CICLO PIANISTICO--CONCERTO WITHOUT ORCHESTRA, OP. 88
      ASSOCIATED MUSIC PUBLISHERS, INC.   UME   1.00
VALEN   D
   CONCERTO, OP. 44. SCORE --DOUBLING AS PIANO PART--
      C. F. PETERS CORPORATION   LY583A   5.00
VIOTTI   GIAZOTTO *
   CONCERTO IN G MINOR
      FRANCO COLOMBO PUBLICATIONS   130171 2.75
VIVALDI *   7
   CONCERTI IN G AND A MINOR
      C. F. PETERS CORPORATION   4510   2.50
VIVALDI
   CONCERTO IN B MINOR -- FREE TRANSCRIPTION BY TAMBURINI AFTER
   VERSION BY BACH --
      FRANCO COLOMBO PUBLICATIONS   ER2039 1.75
VIVALDI   STEINER
   LARGO IN E FLAT FROM 'L'INVERNO' -- CONCERTO
      ELKAN-VOGEL, INC.   .80
VIVALDI *   STRADAL
   ORGAN CONCERTO IN D MINOR
      INTERNATIONAL MUSIC COMPANY   2.00
VOGT   4
   CONCERTINO FUR KLAVIER, 9 BLASER UND SCHLAGZEUG
      BARENREITER VERLAG   AE 134
VOGT   4
   KONZERT FUR KLAVIER UND ORCHESTER
      BARENREITER VERLAG   AE 288
WAGNER, J.
   CONCERTINO IN G MINOR FOR PIANO AND ORCHESTRA, TWO PIANO
   REDUCTION
      SEESAW MUSIC CORPORATION   8.00
WAGNER
   CONCERTO IN G MINOR
      MCA MUSIC   3.00
WEBER, VON   D
   COMPLETE PIANO WORKS, VOL. 3: VARIATIONS AND CONCERTOS
      C. F. PETERS CORPORATION   717C   6.50

WEBER, VON
   KONZERTSTUCK IN F MINOR, OP. 79
      ASSOCIATED MUSIC PUBLISHERS, INC. BRH   1.50
WEBER, VON   CARPER
   MARCH -- FROM KONZERTSTUCK IN F MINOR
      G. SCHIRMER, INC.   .75
WEISMANN, J.   4-5
   KLAVIERKONZERT, OP. 33
      BARENREITER VERLAG   SM 1215
WESLEY, C.   FINZI   M
   CONCERTO NO. 04 IN C. HARPSICHORD SOLO PART
      C. F. PETERS CORPORATION   H290A   1.50
WIGHAM, M.
   CONCERTO FOR TWO PIANOS
      CARL FISCHER, INC.   RS 399   3.00
WILDMAN
   STOCKHOLM CONCERTO
      MCA MUSIC   1.00
WOLF, W.
   CONCERTO, OP. 13
      BOOSEY AND HAWKES, INC.   7.50
WOOD, H.
   CONCERTO IN D MINOR
      BOOSEY AND HAWKES, INC.   4.00
WRIGHT, L.   M
   CONCERTO WALTZ
      COMPOSERS PRESS, INC.   1.50
WUEHRER
   CADENZAS TO MOZART CONCERTO IN C, K. 467
      ASSOCIATED MUSIC PUBLISHERS, INC. DOB   1.25
WUEHRER
   CADENZAS TO MOZART CONCERTO IN C MINOR, K. 491
      ASSOCIATED MUSIC PUBLISHERS, INC. DOB   1.00
YOUNG   M
   FUGAL CONCERTO IN G MINOR
      C. F. PETERS CORPORATION   H205   2.50
ZACH   GOTTRON   3-4
   KONZERT FUR CEMBALO -- KLAVIER -- UND STREICHER
      BARENREITER VERLAG   NMA 165
ZAFRED
   CONCERTO FOR 2 PIANOS -- 3 PIANOS, 6 HANDS --
      FRANCO COLOMBO PUBLICATIONS   130303 8.00
ZAFRED   AMTSANO
   CONCERTO
      FRANCO COLOMBO PUBLICATIONS   129923 3.50
ZBINDEN, J. F.
   CONCERTO DE CAMERA, OP. 16
      ASSOCIATED MUSIC PUBLISHERS, INC. BRH   3.75
ZIMMER   4
   CONCERTINO FUR KLAVIER UND STREICHORCHESTER
      BARENREITER VERLAG   CHF 5132

Concertos:
Composer/Editor/Arranger Unlisted—Works Alphabetized by Title

ALAMEIN CONCERTO -- THEME
      CHAPPELL AND COMPANY, INC.   0014258-1502 .95

ALAMEIN CONCERTO
      CHAPPELL AND COMPANY, INC.   0014258-1501 1.25

MEDITERRANEAN CONCERTO -- THEMES
      CHAPPELL AND COMPANY, INC.   3717501-1502 .95

MEDITERRANEAN CONCERTO
      CHAPPELL AND COMPANY, INC.   3717501-1501 1.25

TAP DANCE CONCERTO
      CHAPPELL AND COMPANY, INC.   5695002   2.50

Other Piano Ensembles

ABEL   E
   CONCERTINO IN E FLAT. WITH TWO VIOLINS, V'CELLO
     C. F. PETERS CORPORATION   4409A   3.50
ALT, H.
   CAT SAT ON A CHAIR OF GOLD, THE -- FOR 1 OR MORE PIANOS, SIX
   HANDS
     THEODORE PRESSER COMPANY   .50
ANSON, G.
   IN THE TOY SHOP -- ONE PIANO, SIX HANDS
     SOUTHERN MUSIC COMPANY   1.00
ANTHONY, B. R.   3
   SALUTE TO THE COLORS
     THEODORE PRESSER COMPANY   1.50
BACH, C.P.E.   M
   CONCERTO FOR 2 PIANOS --WITH ORCH. ACC. IN PIANO THREE--. THREE
   PIANOS, SIX HANDS
     C. F. PETERS CORPORATION   Z450   4.50
BACH, J.S.
   CONCERTO IN A MINOR FOR 4 PIANOS, SCH NO.1065
     ASSOCIATED MUSIC PUBLISHERS, INC.   BRH   1.00
BACH, J.S.   BAUER
   CONCERTO IN C -- 6-HANDS
     G. SCHIRMER, INC.   1.25
BACH, J.S.   M-D
   CONCERTO IN C FOR 2 PIANOS --2 COPIES--
     C. F. PETERS CORPORATION   2200A   2.50
BACH, J.S.   M-D
   CONCERTO IN C MINOR FOR 2 PIANOS --2 COPIES--
     C. F. PETERS CORPORATION   2200B   2.50
BACH, J.S.
   CONCERTO NO. 01 IN D MINOR FOR 3 PIANOS, SCH NO. 1063
     ASSOCIATED MUSIC PUBLISHERS, INC.   BRH   1.00
BACH, J.S.
   CONCERTO NO. 02 IN C FOR 3 PIANOS, SCH NO. 1064
     ASSOCIATED MUSIC PUBLISHERS, INC.   BRH   1.00
BACH, J.S.   CONNOR
   FIVE CHORALES -- 8-HANDS, SET
     G. SCHIRMER, INC.   1.00
BACH, J.S.   GRAINGER, P.
   FUGUE IN A MINOR, NO. 20 OF ''THE WELL-TEMPERED CLAVICHORD'',
   BK. 1 -- ARR. FOR 4 OR ANY MULTIPLE OF 4 PIANISTS
     G. SCHIRMER, INC.   1.00
BACH, J.S. *
   MUSETTE --2 PIANOS, 8 HANDS--
     CARL FISCHER, INC.   P 2015   .75
BACH, J.S.   LANDSHOFF   D
   MUSICAL OFFERING--URTEXT--. COMPLETE SCORE IN ORIGINAL CLEFS,
   PLUS SUPPLEMENT OF COMPLETE SCORE IN MODERN CLEFS
     C. F. PETERS CORPORATION   4202   10.00
BACH, J.S.   LANDSHOFF
   MUSICAL OFFERING
     C. F. PETERS CORPORATION   4202A   3.50
BAINES, W.   2 1/2
   KING'S REVIEW, THE, FOR ONE PIANO SIX HANDS
     THEODORE PRESSER COMPANY   .75
BALKIN
   SIX FOR EIGHT--PIANO QUARTETTE--
     NEIL A. KJOS MUSIC COMPANY   501   1.50
BARATI   D
   QUARTET FOR HARPSICHORD, FLUTE, OBOE, BASS
     C. F. PETERS CORPORATION   66112   3.50
BARRETT--ED.   BARRETT
   TWO FOLK TUNES FOR 8 HANDS AT 2 PIANOS
     SCHMITT, HALL AND MCCREARY COMPANY   9983   1.25
BASTIEN   BASTIEN
   CHRISTMAS CAROLS FOR MULTIPLE PIANOS
     NEIL A. KJOS MUSIC COMPANY   42   1.25
BAVICCHI, J.
   TRIO NO. 3 -- PIANO AND TWO PERCUSSIONISTS
     SEESAW MUSIC CORPORATION   15.00
BEETHOVEN   SARTORIO   3
   ADIEU TO THE PIANO - TWO PIANOS, EIGHT HANDS
     WILLIS MUSIC COMPANY   .75
BEETHOVEN   E
   EGMONT OVERTURE, OP. 84. TWO PIANOS, EIGHT HANDS
     C. F. PETERS CORPORATION   L617   2.00
BEETHOVEN   E-M
   FIDELIO OVERTURE, OP. 72B. TWO PIANOS, EIGHT HANDS
     C. F. PETERS CORPORATION   L618   2.00
BEETHOVEN   2-3
   MINUET IN G -- ONE PIANO, SIX HANDS --
     CENTURY MUSIC PUBLISHING COMPANY, INC.   2755   .60
BEETHOVEN   METIS
   ODE TO JOY
     EDWARD B. MARKS MUSIC CORPORATION   01.75
BEETHOVEN   MACGREGOR
   THEMES FROM RONDO A CAPRICCIO, OP. 129 -- 8-HANDS, SET
     G. SCHIRMER, INC.   .80
BEHR, F.
   FESTIVAL MARCH -- 6-HANDS
     G. SCHIRMER, INC.   .75
BENSON, E.   2
   CIRCUS DAY - TWO PIANOS, EIGHT HANDS
     WILLIS MUSIC COMPANY   .40
BENSON, E.   2
   GAY BUTTERFLIES - TWO PIANOS, EIGHT HANDS
     WILLIS MUSIC COMPANY   .40
BENSON, E.   1
   SPRING BREEZES, ONE PIANO - SIX HANDS
     WILLIS MUSIC COMPANY   .25
BERLIOZ   E-M
   TROJANS AT CARTHAGE. FANTASY ON THEMES FROM THE OPERA. TWO
   PIANOS, EIGHT HANDS
     C. F. PETERS CORPORATION   C214   4.00
BETTINELLI
   CONCERTO FOR 2 PIANOS -- 3 PIANOS, 6 HANDS --
     FRANCO COLOMBO PUBLICATIONS   130516   6.75
BILBRO, M.
   FORWARD, MARCH -- 6-HANDS
     G. SCHIRMER, INC.   .50
BILBRO, M.   1
   MARCH OF THE JUMPING JACKS -- FOR ONE PIANO, SIX HANDS
     WILLIS MUSIC COMPANY   .35
BILBRO, M.
   SPRING VIOLETS -- 6-HANDS
     G. SCHIRMER, INC.   .60
BILLEMA
   CHILDREN'S CONCERTO, OP. 68 -- 1 PIANO 6 HANDS --
     FRANCO COLOMBO PUBLICATIONS   BA8542   1.25
BILLI   TUCCI
   SORRETO -- 1 PIANO 6 HANDS --
     FRANCO COLOMBO PUBLICATIONS   129867   1.00
BIZET, G.   E
   CARMEN. FANTASY. TWO PIANOS, EIGHT HANDS
     C. F. PETERS CORPORATION   C217   4.00

BIZET, G.   3
   CARMEN OVERTURE -- FOR ONE PIANO, SIX HANDS
     WILLIS MUSIC COMPANY   .75
BIZET, H. C.   TIMM, H. C.
   HABANERA FROM ''CARMEN'' -- 8-HANDS, SET
     G. SCHIRMER, INC.   .80
BIZET, G.   M
   L'ARLESIENNE. FANTASY. TWO PIANOS, EIGHT HANDS
     C. F. PETERS CORPORATION   C215   4.00
BIZET, G.   E
   L'ARLESIENNE. FIRST MINUET. TWO PIANOS, EIGHT HANDS
     C. F. PETERS CORPORATION   C216   4.00
BIZET, G.   TIMM, H. C.
   TOREADOR'S SONG FROM ''CARMEN'' -- 8-HANDS, SET
     G. SCHIRMER, INC.   1.00
BLISS, P.   2
   CONQUERORS, ONE PIANO - SIX HANDS
     WILLIS MUSIC COMPANY   .75
BLISS, P.   1
   DREAMS, ONE PIANO - SIX HANDS
     WILLIS MUSIC COMPANY   .75
BOWLES, P.
   CONCERTO FOR TWO PIANOS, WINDS AND PERCUSSION
     AMERICAN MUSIC EDITION   1.50
BRAHMS   3 1/2
   HUNGARIAN DANCE NO. 06 FOR TWO PIANOS, EIGHT HANDS
     THEODORE PRESSER COMPANY   1.00
BRAHMS   CARPER
   SAINT ANTHONY CHORALE FROM VARIATIONS ON A THEME BY HAYDN --
   8-HANDS, SET
     G. SCHIRMER, INC.   .50
BRANT, A.
   FOUR SQUARE MARCH FOR FOUR PIANOS -- COMPLETE
     AMERICAN MUSIC EDITION   2.00
BRATTON   2
   HEBF, ONE PIANO - SIX HANDS
     WILLIS MUSIC COMPANY   .40
BROWN
   CONCERTO FOR TWO PIANOS, BRASS AND PERCUSSION --IN PREP--
     WESTERN INTERNATIONAL MUSIC, INC.
BURROWS
   FIRST ROUNDS FOR PIANO -- FOR 3 AND 4 PLAYERS
     CENTURY MUSIC PUBLISHING COMPANY, INC.   3897   .40
BURROWS   1
   FIRST ROUNDS FOR PIANO -- ONE PIANO, SIX HANDS --
     CENTURY MUSIC PUBLISHING COMPANY, INC.   3897   .60
CAGE   D
   AMORES. TWO PIECES FOR PREPARED PIANO --AND TWO PERCUSSION
   PIECES
     C. F. PETERS CORPORATION   6264   5.00
CASADESUS, R.
   CONCERTO POUR TROIS PIANOS ET ORCHESTRE A CORDES, FOR 3 PIANOS 6
   HANDS
     ELKAN-VOGEL, INC.   D   30.00
CHURCHILL--ED   CHURCHILL   3
   LOVE SOMEBODY, YES I DO- WITH 'SOUND THE FLUTE' FOR TWO PIANOS,
   EIGHT HANDS
     BOSTON MUSIC COMPANY   .75
CHURCHILL--ED   CHURCHILL   3
   PARTNER QUARTET - 'CAPTAIN JINKS' WITH 'PUSH THE BUSINESS ON'
   FOR TWO PIANOS, EIGHT HANDS
     BOSTON MUSIC COMPANY   .75
CHURCHILL--ED   CHURCHILL   3
   PARTNER QUARTET - 'THE GALWAY PIPER' WITH 'SKIP TO MY LOU' FOR
   TWO PIANOS, EIGHT HANDS
     BOSTON MUSIC COMPANY   .75
CITATI-BRACCI
   SHALL WE PLAY A TRIO -- 1 PIANO 6 HANDS --
     FRANCO COLOMBO PUBLICATIONS   128751   1.00
CITATI-BRACCI
   THREE CHILDREN AT ONE KEYBOARD -- 1 PIANO 6 HANDS --
     FRANCO COLOMBO PUBLICATIONS   129181   1.00
CLARK, A.   3
   MARCHE AUX FLAMBEAUS, OP. 32 FOR ONE PIANO, SIX HANDS
     THEODORE PRESSER COMPANY   .80
COHAN   METIS
   YOU'RE A GRAND OLD FLAG
     EDWARD B. MARKS MUSIC CORPORATION   03.00
CRAMMOND, C. C.   2 1/2
   COMMENCEMENT DAY, OP. 190 FOR ONE PIANO, SIX HANDS
     THEODORE PRESSER COMPANY   .50
CRAS
   AMES D'ENFANTS
     FRANCO COLOMBO PUBLICATIONS   SAL   6.00
CROISEZ, A.
   VOYAGE D'UNE HIRONDELLE
     FRANCO COLOMBO PUBLICATIONS   SAL   2.50
CZERNY   GURLITT
   AIR DE CHASSE -- 6-HANDS
     G. SCHIRMER, INC.   .50
DAHL   M
   QUODLIBET ON AMERICAN FOLK TUNES. TWO PIANOS, EIGHT HANDS
     C. F. PETERS CORPORATION   6004   3.00
DALE, R.
   RACING SLEIGHS, THE -- 6-HANDS
     G. SCHIRMER, INC.   .50
DALLAPICCOLA   INNI   3
   MUSICA PER TRE PIANOFORTI -- 1935 --
     BARENREITER VERLAG   CM 18633
DAVIDOVSKY
   SYNCHRONISMS NO. 6
     EDWARD B. MARKS MUSIC CORPORATION   15.00
DAY, R. E.   2
   FRIENDLY FROLICS -- FOR 2 PIANOS 8 HANDS
     BELWIN-MILLS PUBLISHING CORPORATION   .60
DAY, R.   1
   FLUTTERING BUTTERFLIES - TWO PIANOS, EIGHT HANDS
     WILLIS MUSIC COMPANY   .35
DAY, R.   2
   HAPPY DANCERS - TWO PIANOS, EIGHT HANDS
     WILLIS MUSIC COMPANY   .60
DEBUSSY
   FIRST ARABESQUE, FOR 2 PIANOS 8 HANDS
     ELKAN-VOGEL, INC.   D   4.25
DEBUSSY
   PETITE SUITE, FOR 2 PIANOS 8 HANDS
     ELKAN-VOGEL, INC.   D   7.50
DEBUSSY
   SECOND ARABESQUE, FOR 2 PIANOS 8 HANDS
     ELKAN-VOGEL, INC.   D   4.25
DE BERADINIS, J.
   MUSIC FOR PERCUSSION AND PIANO, 1971
     SEESAW MUSIC CORPORATION   10.00
DE PUE
   KNIGHT WALTZ, A--PIANO QUARTETTE--
     NEIL A. KJOS MUSIC COMPANY   532   2.00

DE PUE
SIXTEEN PAWNS--PIANO QUARTETTE--
NEIL A. KJOS MUSIC COMPANY 500 1.50
DUCELLE, P.
MUSICAL MEMORIES, OP. 16 -- NO. 01, DANCING STARS -- WALTZ -- 6 HANDS
G. SCHIRMER, INC. .75
DUCELLE, P.
MUSICAL MEMORIES, OP. 16 -- NO. 02, LILLIPUTIAN PARADE -- 6 HANDS
G. SCHIRMER, INC. .60
DUCELLE, P.
MUSICAL MEMORIES, OP. 16 -- NO. 04, DANCE OF THE DEWDROPS --6 HANDS--
G. SCHIRMER, INC. .50
DUCELLE, P.
MUSICAL MEMOPIES, OP. 16 -- NO. 07, NITA, SPANISH DANCE -- 6-HANDS
G. SCHIRMER, INC. .75
DUCELLE, P.
MUSICAL MEMORIES, OP. 16 -- 11, ALPINE SONG -- 6-HANDS
G. SCHIRMER, INC. .50
DURAND, A.
CHACONNE, OP. 62, FOR 2 PIANOS 8 HANDS
ELKAN-VOGEL, INC. D 2.50
DVORAK KRAEHENBUEHL
ECOSSAISES, OP. 41 --2 PIANOS, 8 HANDS--
SUMMY-BIRCHARD COMPANY 1.25
DVORAK 3
HUMORESKE, OP. 101 NO. 7 -- ONE PIANO, SIX HANDS --
CENTURY MUSIC PUBLISHING COMPANY, INC. 2754 .60
ECKSTEIN
CORNISH MAY DANCE --2 PIANOS, 8 HANDS--
CARL FISCHER, INC. P 2065 1.00
EDGINTON E
GAY MARCH. TWO PIANOS, TWELVE HANDS
C. F. PETERS CORPORATION H845A 1.25
ELDABH M
MOSAIC NO. 1. PIANO AND PERCUSSION
C. F. PETERS CORPORATION 6994 2.00
ELDABH M
TABLA DANCE. PIANO, PERCUSSION ENSEMBLE
C. F. PETERS CORPORATION 6194 2.00
ELGAR, E. CARPER
POMP AND CIRCUMSTANCE MARCH --8 HANDS--
G. SCHIRMER, INC. 1.50
EMERY
FAIRY LULLABY -- 6-HANDS
G. SCHIRMER, INC. .50
EZELL, H. 1
TOY SHOP BAND -- FOR ONE PIANO, SIX HANDS
WILLIS MUSIC COMPANY .40
FICHTER MCWHERTOR
CAUSE IT'S CHRISTMAS -- VOCAL EDITION
VOLKWEIN BROS. .75
FLOTOW E
MARTHA. FANTASY. TWO PIANOS, EIGHT HANDS
C. F. PETERS CORPORATION C219 4.00
FLOTOW E
MARTHA. OVERTURE. TWO PIANOS, EIGHT HANDS
C. F. PETERS CORPORATION C220 4.00
FLOTOW
MARTHA, FOR TWO PIANOS, EIGHT HANDS
THEODORE PRESSER COMPANY 1.50
GARLICK, A.
CONCERTO GROSSO FOR ORGAN AND PIANO
SEESAW MUSIC CORPORATION 18.00
GAUTIER, L. 3
LE SECRET, INTERMEZZO PIZZICATO FOR ONE PIANO, SIX HANDS
THEODORE PRESSER COMPANY .60
GAUTIER, L. GURLITT
SECRET, LE -- INTERMEZZO -- 6-HANDS
G. SCHIRMER, INC. .60
GEORGE
TWINKLE, TWINKLE, LITTLE STAR -- ONE PIANO, SIX HANDS --
SUMMY-BIRCHARD COMPANY .40
GLUCK 3
AIR FROM 'ORPHEUS' FOR ONE PIANO, SIX HANDS
THEODORE PRESSER COMPANY .50
GOUNOD, C. E
FAUST. SOLDIERS' CHORUS. TWO PIANOS, EIGHT HANDS
C. F. PETERS CORPORATION C222 4.00
GOUNOD, C. E
FAUST. VALSE. TWO PIANOS, EIGHT HANDS
C. F. PETERS CORPORATION C223 4.00
GOUNOD, C. E
PHILEMON AND BAUCIS. FANTASY. TWO PIANOS, EIGHT HANDS
C. F. PETERS CORPORATION C224 4.00
GOUNOD, C. E
QUEEN OF SHEBA. FANTASY. TWO PIANOS, EIGHT HANDS
C. F. PETERS CORPORATION C225 4.00
GOUNOD, C. E
SAPHO. FANTASY. TWO PIANOS, EIGHT HANDS
C. F. PETERS CORPORATION C227 4.00
GOUNOD, C. TIMM, H. C.
WALTZ AND CHORUS FROM ''FAUST'' -- 8-HANDS, SET
G. SCHIRMER, INC. 1.00
GRAINGER, P.--ED GRAINGER, P.
COUNTRY GARDENS -- ENGLISH MORRIS-DANCE TUNE -- 8-HANDS
G. SCHIRMER, INC. 1.00
GREENWALD, M. 2
BARBARA, WALTZ -- ONE PIANO, SIX HANDS --
CENTURY MUSIC PUBLISHING COMPANY, INC. 3096 .60
GREENWALD, M. 3
HOME GUARD, THE -- ONE PIANO, SIX HANDS --
CENTURY MUSIC PUBLISHING COMPANY, INC. 2756 .60
GREGH
BERGERS WATTEAU, LES OP. 5
FRANCO COLOMBO PUBLICATIONS SAL 2.75
GREGH
RETOUR DES MOISSINNEURS, LE OP. 13
FRANCO COLOMBO PUBLICATIONS SAL 2.75
GREGH
SALTARELLO, OP. 49
FRANCO COLOMBO PUBLICATIONS SAL 2.75
GREIM
GOBLINS --PIANO, 6 HANDS--
CARL FISCHER, INC. P 2042 .50
GREIM
MARCH OF THE LEAD SOLDIERS --PIANO, 6 HANDS--
CARL FISCHER, INC. P 2082 .60
GRIEG THRESHER 2
DANCE OF THE ELVES, ONE PIANO - SIX HANDS
WILLIS MUSIC COMPANY .40
GRIEG 6
NORWEGIAN BRIDAL PROCESSION FOR TWO PIANOS, EIGHT HANDS
THEODORE PRESSER COMPANY 1.25
GRIEG E
PEER GYNT SUITE NO. 1, OP. 46. VOL. 1# MORNING MOOD. TWO PIANOS, EIGHT HANDS
C. F. PETERS CORPORATION 2832A 2.00
GRIEG E
PEER GYNT SUITE NO. 1, OP. 46. VOL. 2# DEATH OF ASE, ANITRA'S DANCE. TWO PIANOS, EIGHT HANDS
C. F. PETERS CORPORATION 2832B 2.00
GRIEG E
PEER GYNT SUITE NO. 1, OP. 46. VOL. 3# IN THE HALL OF THE MOUNTAIN KING. TWO PIANOS, EIGHT HANDS
C. F. PETERS CORPORATION 2832C 2.00
GRIEG D
PIANO CONCERTO IN A MINOR, OP. 16. TWO PIANOS, EIGHT HANDS
C. F. PETERS CORPORATION H2164D 3.00
GUIRAUD, E. STEIGER, C.
CARNAVAL, FOR 2 PIANOS 8 HANDS
ELKAN-VOGEL, INC. D 3.25
HAMPTON
CATCH-UP. TAPE RECORDER AND 2 PIANOS --OR 4 PIANOS--
C. F. PETERS CORPORATION 66175 2.00
HAMPTON
TRIPLE PLAY. ONDES MARTENOT AND 2 PIANOS, 4 HANDS
C. F. PETERS CORPORATION 66176 2.00
HANDEL CARPER
ALLEGRO DECISO -- FROM ''THE WATER MUSIC'' -- 8-HANDS, SET
G. SCHIRMER, INC. 1.25
HANDEL CARPER
TWO MINUETS -- FROM ''MUSIC FOR THE ROYAL FIREWORKS -- 8-HANDS, SET
G. SCHIRMER, INC. 1.25
HAYDN KRAEHENBUEHL
MINUETTO --2 PIANOS, 8 HANDS--
SUMMY-BIRCHARD COMPANY 1.00
HAYDN REHBERG 3
SERENADE AUS DEM STREICHQUARTETT IN F -- HOBOKEN 3-17
SCHOTT 0505 1/2 1.00
HAYS, D.
IF -- TWO PIANOS AND PRE-RECORDED TAPE
SEESAW MUSIC CORPORATION 2.00
HOLST 3
DIANA -- FOR TWO PIANOS, EIGHT HANDS
WILLIS MUSIC COMPANY 1.00
HOPKINS, H. 1
BIG BASS FIDDLE HUMORESQUE -- ONE PIANO, 6 HANDS --
CENTURY MUSIC PUBLISHING COMPANY, INC. 3088 .60
HOPKINS, H. 2
BIG DRUM MAJOR, THE, MARCH -- ONE PIANO, 6 HANDS --
CENTURY MUSIC PUBLISHING COMPANY, INC. 3071 .60
HOPKINS, H. 1
GOLDEN ROD WALTZ -- ONE PIANO, SIX HANDS --
CENTURY MUSIC PUBLISHING COMPANY, INC. 3070 .60
HOPKINS, H. 1
LITTLE FRENCH DOLL -- ONE PIANO, SIX HANDS --
CENTURY MUSIC PUBLISHING COMPANY, INC. 3089 .60
HOPKINS, H. 2
SUNSHINE WALTZ -- ONE PIANO, SIX HANDS --
CENTURY MUSIC PUBLISHING COMPANY, INC. 3072 .60
HOPKINS, H. 1
SWEET MOMENTS, REVERIE -- ONE PIANO, SIX HANDS
CENTURY MUSIC PUBLISHING COMPANY, INC. 3069 .60
HOVHANESS, A. M
DUET. VIOLIN AND HARPSICHORD
C. F. PETERS CORPORATION 6439 1.50
HUBICKI, M.
DOUBLE DUETS, EASY ARRANGEMENTS -- 8-HANDS, SET
G. SCHIRMER, INC. 1.25
HYSON--ED. HYSON
FANTASY ON THREE ENGLISH FOLKSONGS--PIANO QUARTETTE--
NEIL A. KJOS MUSIC COMPANY 503 2.00
HYSON
EIGHT LIGHT HEARTED VARIATIONS ON THE JOLLY MILLER-- PIANO QUARTETTE--
NEIL A. KJOS MUSIC COMPANY 504 1.00
JESSEL GLOVER
PARADE OF THE WOODEN SOLDIERS
EDWARD B. MARKS MUSIC CORPORATION 03.00
JOHNSON, T. CURWEN
SCHERZO -- 6-HANDS
G. SCHIRMER, INC. .50
KASEMETS, U.
FIFTH ROOT OF FIVE -- 2 PNO AND PERC, SET OF 4 SCORES
ASSOCIATED MUSIC PUBLISHERS, INC. BER 4.50
KEATS, F. 3
DANCE OF THE ROSEBUDS
THEODORE PRESSER COMPANY .75
KEENAN
KILTIES ARE COMING --PIANO, 6 HANDS--
CARL FISCHER, INC. P 2094 .60
KENNEDY, A. 3
STAR OF HOPE -- ONE PIANO, SIX HANDS --
CENTURY MUSIC PUBLISHING COMPANY, INC. 2757 .60
KOELLING 4 1/2
HUNGARY FOR TWO PIANOS, EIGHT HANDS
THEODORE PRESSER COMPANY 1.25
KRAEHENBUEHL--ARR. KRAEHENBUEHL
TEN LITTLE INDIANS --1 PIANO, 8 HANDS--
SUMMY-BIRCHARD COMPANY 1.00
KRAEHENBUEHL
DRUNKEN SAILOR, THE -- ONE PIANO, EIGHT HANDS--
SUMMY-BIRCHARD COMPANY .60
KRAEHENBUEHL
TEN LITTLE INDIANS -- ONE PIANO, EIGHT HANDS --
SUMMY-BIRCHARD COMPANY 1.00
KRAEHENBUEHL
THERE AND BACK --A STRANGE PROCESSION-- 2 PIANOS, 8 HANDS
NATIONAL KEYBOARD ARTS ASSOCIATES 2.50
KRAEHENBUEHL
WAYFARING STRANGER, THE -- ONE PIANO, SIX HANDS --
SUMMY-BIRCHARD COMPANY .60
KRAMER
POLONAISE, OP. 7 --PIANO, 6 HANDS--
CARL FISCHER, INC. S 2758 .50
KRAWITZ, I. *
HOW TO TEACH RHYTHMS AND RHYTHM BANDS
G. SCHIRMER, INC. 1.50
KROGMANN, C. W.
ZEPHYRS FROM MELODYLAND, OP. 15 -- NO. 01, LITTLE PRINCE -- 6-HANDS
G. SCHIRMER, INC. .50
KROGMANN, C. W.
ZEPHYRS FROM MELODYLAND, OP. 15 -- NO. 07, LITTLE PATRIOT -- 6-HANDS
G. SCHIRMER, INC. .50
KROGMANN, C. W.
ZEPHYRS FROM MELODYLAND, OP. 15 -- NO. 12, ROBIN'S LULLABY -- 6-HANDS
G. SCHIRMER, INC. .60

LANGDON, C.   2
    GRACE AND FAVOR - TWO PIANOS, EIGHT HANDS
        WILLIS MUSIC COMPANY   .50
LANGDON, C.   2
    HALL OF MIRRORS, ONE PIANO - SIX HANDS
        WILLIS MUSIC COMPANY   .40
LANGDON, C.   2
    HALL OF MIRRORS - TWO PIANOS, EIGHT HANDS
        WILLIS MUSIC COMPANY   .50
LEPRE, P.   2
    MARCH DE AVIATEURS, ONE PIANO - SIX HANDS
        WILLIS MUSIC COMPANY   .60
LICHNER, P.
    IDLE MOMENTS, WALTZ -- ONE PIANO, SIX HANDS --
        CENTURY MUSIC PUBLISHING COMPANY, INC.   3095   .60
LISZT   KLEINMICHEL
    HUNGARIAN RHAPSODY NO. 02 -- 8-HANDS, SET
        G. SCHIRMER, INC.   L1570   3.25
LYBBERT
    LINES FOR THE FALLEN, SOPRANO AND 2 PIANOS, 4 HANDS
        C. F. PETERS CORPORATION   66174   2.00
MACBRIDE, D.
    ILLEGAL TENDER -- PREPARED PIANO AND BASSOON
        SEESAW MUSIC CORPORATION   1.00
MACERO
    ONE-THREE QUARTERS. PICC, FL, VN, VC, TR8, TBA, 2 PIANOS, 4
    HANDS
        C. F. PETERS CORPORATION   66178   7.50
MACGREGOR   2
    DOUBLE MELODIES, ONE PIANO - SIX HANDS
        WILLIS MUSIC COMPANY   .50
MACGREGOR   1
    FOLLOW ME, ONE PIANO - SIX HANDS
        WILLIS MUSIC COMPANY   .40
MACGREGOR   2
    HUMORESQUE, ONE PIANO - SIX HANDS
        WILLIS MUSIC COMPANY   .40
MACGREGOR
    ITALIAN DANCE -- 8-HANDS
        G. SCHIRMER, INC.   .40
MACGREGOR   1
    LAZY MARY AND OH DEAR, ONE PIANO - SIX HANDS
        WILLIS MUSIC COMPANY   .40
MACGREGOR   2
    OLD FOLKS AT HOME, ONE PIANO - SIX HANDS
        WILLIS MUSIC COMPANY   .40
MACGREGOR
    PIJE KUBA, BOHEMIAN DANCE -- 8-HANDS, SET
        G. SCHIRMER, INC.   .40
MACGREGOR   2
    ROW, ROW, ROW, ONE PIANO - SIX HANDS
        WILLIS MUSIC COMPANY   .35
MACGREGOR   1
    SO MERRILY DANCING AND POOR LITTLE AUGUSTINE, ONE PIANO - SIX
    HANDS
        WILLIS MUSIC COMPANY   .25
MACGREGOR
    SPINNING SONG -- DUTCH BRIDE'S DANCE -- 12-HANDS, SET
        G. SCHIRMER, INC.   .50
MACGREGOR   2
    THREE BLIND MICE, ONE PIANO - SIX HANDS
        WILLIS MUSIC COMPANY   .40
MACGREGOR   2
    TUNES OF THE U. S. A., ONE PIANO SIX HANDS
        WILLIS MUSIC COMPANY   .35
MANGDON, C.   2
    GRACE AND FAVOR, ONE PIANO - SIX HANDS
        WILLIS MUSIC COMPANY   .50
MARTIN, G.   1
    BETTY'S WALTZ -- ONE PIANO, 6 HANDS --
        CENTURY MUSIC PUBLISHING COMPANY, INC.   2752   .60
MARTIN, G.   2
    CUCKOO SONG -- ONE PIANO, SIX HANDS --
        CENTURY MUSIC PUBLISHING COMPANY, INC.   3097   .60
MARTIN, G.   2
    FLORAL PARADE, THE, VALSE -- ONE PIANO, SIX HANDS --
        CENTURY MUSIC PUBLISHING COMPANY, INC.   3094   .60
MATTINGLY, J.   1
    DANCING FAIRIES, ONE PIANO - SIX HANDS
        WILLIS MUSIC COMPANY   .50
MATTINGLY, J.   2
    JACK FROST, ONE PIANO - SIX HANDS
        WILLIS MUSIC COMPANY   .50
MATTINGLY, J.   2
    MERRY MAKERS, ONE PIANO - SIX HANDS
        WILLIS MUSIC COMPANY   .50
MAYUZUMI
    PIECES FOR PREPARED PIANO AND STRINGS. SCORE ALONE.
        C. F. PETERS CORPORATION   6325   3.00
MAYUZUMI   D
    PIECES FOR PREPARED PIANO AND STRINGS. SCORE AND PARTS --INCL.
    PIANO SOLO PART--
        C. F. PETERS CORPORATION   6325B   10.00
MELLICHAMP, N.   1
    THREE CLOCKS -- ONE PIANO, SIX HANDS --
        CENTURY MUSIC PUBLISHING COMPANY, INC.   4092   .60
MELLNAES
    CAPRICORN FLAKES. FOR PIANO, HARPSICHORD,
    VIBRAPHONE/GLOCKENSPIEL --THREE COPIES NEEDED FOR PERFORMANCE--
        C. F. PETERS CORPORATION   66353   3.00
MENDELSSOHN   2 1/2
    CHILDREN'S PIECE, OP. 72 NO. 5 - FOR TWO PIANOS, EIGHT HANDS
        THEODORE PRESSER COMPANY   1.10
MERKUR
    NEW HORIZONS FOR TWO PIANOS, EIGHT HANDS
        BELWIN-MILLS PUBLISHING CORPORATION   27029   1.50
MESTRES-QUADRENY
    SUITE BUFFA -- OPERA FOR MALE PIANIST, SOPRANO AND DANCER
        SEESAW MUSIC CORPORATION   12.00
MESTRES-QUADRENY
    THREE CANONS IN HOMAGE TO GALILEO FOR PIANO AND THREE TAPE
    RECORDERS, WITH PERCUSSION AND ONDES MARTENOT
        SEESAW MUSIC CORPORATION   7.00
MESTRES-QUADRENY
    THREE CANONS IN HOMAGE TO GALILEO FOR PIANO AND THREE TAPE
    RECORDERS
        SEESAW MUSIC CORPORATION   3.00
METIS, F.   INTERMEDIATE
    AFRICASIAN AFFAIR--2, 3, OR 4 PIANOS
        VOLKWEIN BROS.   3.00
METIS, F.   EASY
    HAPPINESS HILL--2, 3, OR 4 PIANOS
        VOLKWEIN BROS.   1.50
METIS, F.   INTERMEDIATE
    PARISIAN POLKA--2, 3, OR 4 PIANOS
        VOLKWEIN BROS.   3.00

METIS, F.   INTERMEDIATE
    WICKED WORLD WALTZ--2, 3, OR 4 PIANOS
        VOLKWEIN BROS.   3.00
METIS
    GOOD 'N' GROOVY
        EDWARD B. MARKS MUSIC CORPORATION   01.75
METIS
    KIDS 'N' KEYBOARDS
        EDWARD B. MARKS MUSIC CORPORATION   01.75
METIS
    ROCK MODES AND MOODS
        EDWARD B. MARKS MUSIC CORPORATION   01.50
METIS
    SCARBOROUGH FAIR
        EDWARD B. MARKS MUSIC CORPORATION   03.00
MEYERBEER, G.   KRAMER
    CORONATION MARCH -- FROM "LE PROPHETE" -- 6-HANDS
        G. SCHIRMER, INC.   .75
MEYERBEER, G.   SARTORIO   4
    CORONATION WALTZ - TWO PIANOS, EIGHT HANDS
        WILLIS MUSIC COMPANY   .75
MILHAUD, D.
    CONCERTO NO. 02 FOR 2 PIANOS AND PERCUSSION -- PIANO SCORE
        ASSOCIATED MUSIC PUBLISHERS, INC.   ESC   12.00
MILHAUD, D.
    CONCERTO NO. 02 FOR 2 PIANOS AND PERCUSSION -- 4 PERCUSSION
    PARTS
        ASSOCIATED MUSIC PUBLISHERS, INC.   ESC   6.00
MILHAUD, D.
    PARIS, SUITE FOR 4 PIANOS -- SET
        ASSOCIATED MUSIC PUBLISHERS, INC.   ESC   10.00
MONTANI
    THREE WALTZES -- 1 PIANO 6 HANDS --
        FRANCO COLOMBO PUBLICATIONS   129300   .90
MOSZKOWSKI   E
    SPANISH DANCE, OP. 12, NO. 1. TWO PIANOS, EIGHT HANDS
        C. F. PETERS CORPORATION   H3313A   2.00
MOSZKOWSKI   GURLITT
    VALSE BRILLANTE IN A FLAT -- 8-HANDS, SET
        G. SCHIRMER, INC.   L197   1.25
MOUSSORGSKY
    OX-CART, THE --2 PIANOS, 8 HANDS--
        NATIONAL KEYBOARD ARTS ASSOCIATES   2.50
MOZART, W. A.   E
    DON GIOVANNI. OVERTURE. TWO PIANOS, EIGHT HANDS
        C. F. PETERS CORPORATION   L620   2.00
MOZART, W. A.
    MENUET FROM SYMPHONY IN E FLAT --PIANO, 6 HANDS--
        CARL FISCHER, INC.   P 2556   1.00
MOZART, W. A.   3
    MINUET IN E FLAT, FOR ONE PIANO, SIX HANDS
        THEODORE PRESSER COMPANY   .60
MOZART, W. A.
    VEDRAI CARINO -- FROM "DON GIOVANNI" -- 8-HANDS, SET
        G. SCHIRMER, INC.   .75
NEVIN   TREHARNE   3
    ROSARY, THE - FOR ONE PIANO, SIX HANDS
        BOSTON MUSIC COMPANY   .75
NICOLAI   E
    MERRY WIVES OF WINDSOR. OVERTURE. TWO PIANOS, EIGHT HANDS
        C. F. PETERS CORPORATION   C228   4.00
NOEL, H.   BENFORD
    MARCH -- 6-HANDS
        G. SCHIRMER, INC.   .75
NOEL, H.   BENFORD
    WALTZ -- 6-HANDS
        G. SCHIRMER, INC.   .75
OFFENBACH   E
    FILLE DU TAMBOUR-MAJOR. FANTASY. TWO PIANOS, EIGHT HANDS
        C. F. PETERS CORPORATION   C230   4.00
OFFENBACH   E
    TALES OF HOFFMANN. FANTASY. TWO PIANOS, EIGHT HANDS
        C. F. PETERS CORPORATION   C229   4.00
OLDENBURG, E.
    FORWARD MARCH -- 6-HANDS
        G. SCHIRMER, INC.   .50
OLIVIERO *
    MORE
        EDWARD B. MARKS MUSIC CORPORATION   02.00
PACE, R.
    JIG FROM 'WEST SUITE', FOR 2 PIANOS 8 HANDS
        BELWIN-MILLS PUBLISHING CORPORATION   1.25
PACE, R.
    RHUMBA --2 PIANOS, 8 HANDS--
        CARL FISCHER, INC.   P 2816   1.50
PARCHMAN, G.
    CONCERTO FOR PIANO 4-HANDS AND ORCHESTRA
        SEESAW MUSIC CORPORATION   22.00
PARCHMAN, G.
    SECOND CONCERTO FOR 2 PIANOS AND ORCHESTRA
        SEESAW MUSIC CORPORATION   22.00
PARCHMAN, G.
    TWELVE VARIATIONS ON AN ORIGINAL THEME FOR TWO PIANOS AND
    ORCHESTRA
        SEESAW MUSIC CORPORATION   18.00
PESSE
    DEUX PIECES ORIGINALES -- 1. SOUS LE BRILLANT SOLEIL DE MAI, FOR
    2 PIANOS 8 HANDS
        ELKAN-VOGEL, INC.   D   3.40
PESSE
    DEUX PIECES ORIGINALES -- 2. MARCHE TRIOMPHALE, FOR 2 PIANOS 8
    HANDS
        ELKAN-VOGEL, INC.   D   3.10
PHILIPP, I.
    CONCERTINO FOR 3 PIANOS -- WITHOUT ORCHESTRA --
        FRANCO COLOMBO PUBLICATIONS   SAL   10.75
PHILLIPS, R.
    THREE PIECES FOR TWO LEFT HANDS
        SEESAW MUSIC CORPORATION   4.00
POWELL, J.
    DIRGE, OP. 26 -- 12-HANDS, SET
        G. SCHIRMER, INC.   1.25
POWELL, J.
    IN THE HAMMOCK -- SCENE SENTIMENTALE, OP. 19 -- 8-HANDS, SET
        G. SCHIRMER, INC.   1.50
PROKOFIEFF
    HUMOROUS SKETCH --2 PIANOS, 8 HANDS--
        NATIONAL KEYBOARD ARTS ASSOCIATES   2.50
RACHMANINOFF, S.   REBNER
    PRELUDE IN G MINOR, OP. 23 NO. 5 -- 8-HANDS, SET
        G. SCHIRMER, INC.   L1583   1.50
RACHMANINOFF, S.   BURGESS
    ROMANCE --ONE PIANO-SIX HANDS
        MCA MUSIC   1.25
REID   1
    THREE PALS - FOR ONE PIANO, SIX HANDS
        PRO-ART PUBLICATIONS, INC.   210   .50

RENNICK, E.
LET'S PLAY TRIOS FOR ONE PIANO -- SIX HANDS
    BELWIN-MILLS PUBLISHING CORPORATION   11272   .85
RODGERS, I. *
SIX LITTLE HANDS AT ONE KEYBOARD -- A PREPARATORY BOOK OF
ENSEMBLE-PLAYING AND A FIRST APPROACH TO SIGHT-READING
    G. SCHIRMER, INC.   1.00
ROWLEY   CURWEN
BELLS -- 6-HANDS
    G. SCHIRMER, INC.   .35
ROWLEY   CURWEN
TAMBOURIN -- 6-HANDS
    G. SCHIRMER, INC.   .50
ROY   5
FORTY BARS FOR FORTY FINGERS, FOR 2 PIANOS AND 8 HANDS
    LEE ROBERTS MUSIC PUBLICATIONS, INC.   .75
SAINT-SAENS
DANSE MACABRE, FOR 2 PIANOS 8 HANDS
    ELKAN-VOGEL, INC.   D   10.75
SAINT-SAENS   ROQUES, L.
LE ROUET D'OMPHALE, OP. 31, FOR 2 PIANOS 8 HANDS
    ELKAN-VOGEL, INC.   D   6.00
SAINT-SAENS
SUITE ALGERIENNE, OP. 60, FOR 2 PIANOS 8 HANDS
    ELKAN-VOGEL, INC.   D   7.00
SCHAUM, J.--ED.   SCHAUM, J.   2 1/2
BATTLE HYMN OF THE REPUBLIC--TWO PIANOS-EIGHT HANDS--
    BELWIN-MILLS PUBLISHING CORPORATION   .50
SCHAUM, J.--ED.   SCHAUM, J.   1
FOUR BELLS AND ALL'S WELL--ONE PIANO-EIGHT HANDS--
    BELWIN-MILLS PUBLISHING CORPORATION   .50
SCHAUM, J.--ED.   SCHAUM, J.   1
MEXICAN 'CLAP HANDS' DANCE--TWO PIANOS-EIGHT HANDS--
    BELWIN-MILLS PUBLISHING CORPORATION   .50
SCHAUM, J.--ED.   SCHAUM, J.   1
THREE BLIND MICE--ONE PIANO-SIX HANDS--
    BELWIN-MILLS PUBLISHING CORPORATION   .50
SCHAUM, J.--ED.   SCHAUM, J.   1
THREE KITTENS--ONE PIANO-SIX HANDS--
    BELWIN-MILLS PUBLISHING CORPORATION   .50
SCHAUM, J.--ED.   SCHAUM, J.   1
THREE MUSKETEERS, THE--PIANO TRIO--
    BELWIN-MILLS PUBLISHING CORPORATION   .50
SCHER, W.   2 1/2
DANCING PUPPETS, FOR ONE PIANO, SIX HANDS
    THEODORE PRESSER COMPANY   .50
SCHILLER, F.   2
HUMMING BIRD, WALTZ -- ONE PIANO, SIX HANDS --
    CENTURY MUSIC PUBLISHING COMPANY, INC.   3093   .60
SCHUBERT
FOUR COUNTRY DANCES--2 PIANOS, 8 HANDS--
    NATIONAL KEYBOARD ARTS ASSOCIATES   2.50
SCHUBERT   HORVATH, G.
MARCHE MILITAIRE, OP. 51 NO. 1 -- 6 HANDS
    G. SCHIRMER, INC.   .70
SCHUBERT
MILITARY MARCH, OP. 51 NO. 1 -- ARR FOR TWO PIANOS, EIGHT HANDS
    EDWIN F. KALMUS   3877   3.00
SCHUBERT
MILITARY MARCH, OP. 51 NO. 1 -- 8-HANDS, SET
    G. SCHIRMER, INC.   .90
SCHUBERT   JELLY
MINUET, ARR. FOR 3 OR 4 PARTS -- OPTIONAL PART FOR TEACHER
REQUIRES A 2ND PIANO
    G. SCHIRMER, INC.   .50
SCHUMANN, R.   2 1/2
KNIGHT RUPERT, FOR TWO PIANOS, EIGHT HANDS
    THEODORE PRESSER COMPANY   1.25
SCHUMANN, R.
SKETCH --2 PIANOS, 8 HANDS--
    NATIONAL KEYBOARD ARTS ASSOCIATES   2.50
SCHUMANN, R.
SYMPHONY NO. 04 IN D MINOR, OP. 120 -- HORN -- 8 HANDS, SET
    ASSOCIATED MUSIC PUBLISHERS, INC.   BRH   2.00
SCHUMANN, R.   SARTORIO   4
TRAVELER'S SONG -- TWO PIANOS, EIGHT HANDS
    WILLIS MUSIC COMPANY   .75
SEBASTIAN
SANTA AND HIS SLEIGH - FOR PIANO, SIX HANDS
    BOSTON MUSIC COMPANY   .60
SMETANA   E
RONDO IN C. TWO PIANOS, EIGHT HANDS
    C. F. PETERS CORPORATION   4479   1.50
SMETANA   3
RONDO IN C FOR 2 PIANOS, 8 HANDS
    BARENREITER VERLAG   AP 790
SMETANA   M
SONATA IN E MINOR. TWO PIANOS, EIGHT HANDS
    C. F. PETERS CORPORATION   H19   3.00
SMETANA
SONATA IN ONE MOVEMENT FOR TWO PIANOS -- EIGHT HAND
    ARTIA   1.25
SMETANA   3
SONATE IN F MINOR FOR 2 PIANOS, 8 HANDS
    BARENREITER VERLAG   AP 791
SMITH--ED   CARPENTER, J.   2
STAR SPANGLED BANNER, THE FOR TWO PIANOS, EIGHT HANDS
    BOSTON MUSIC COMPANY   .75
SMITH, STUART
GESTURES, I, II AND III FOR PREPARED PIANO
    SEESAW MUSIC CORPORATION   2.00
SMOLANOFF
CONCERTO FOR PIANO 4-HANDS, STRINGS, PERCUSSIONS
    SEESAW MUSIC CORPORATION   18.00
SOUSA   3
STARS AND STRIPES FOREVER --ONE PIANO, SIX HANDS--
    THEODORE PRESSER COMPANY   1.00
SPAULDING, G. L.   1 1/2
CONTENTED FAIRY, THE, FOR ONE PIANO SIX HANDS
    THEODORE PRESSER COMPANY   .50
SPAULDING, G. L.   3
MARCHE HEROQUE
    THEODORE PRESSER COMPANY   .60
STEINER, G.
TRIO, 1969 -- PIANO AND TWO PERCUSSIONISTS
    SEESAW MUSIC CORPORATION   12.00
STEINER   1
CHOPSTICKS FOR THREE -- FOR 1 PIANO 6 HANDS
    BELWIN-MILLS PUBLISHING CORPORATION   .60
STRAUSS, R.   M-D
DEATH AND TRANSFIGURATION, OP. 24. TWO PIANOS, EIGHT HANDS
    C. F. PETERS CORPORATION   4196B   10.00

STRAUSS, R.   M-D
DON JUAN, OP. 20. TWO PIANOS, EIGHT HANDS
    C. F. PETERS CORPORATION   4196A   10.00
STRAUSS, R.   M-D
THUS SPAKE ZARATHUSTRA, OP. 30. TWO PIANOS, EIGHT HANDS
    C. F. PETERS CORPORATION   4196D   10.00
STRAUSS, R.   M-D
TILL EULENSPIEGEL'S MERRY PRANKS, OP. 28. TWO PIANOS, EIGHT
HANDS
    C. F. PETERS CORPORATION   4196C   10.00
STREABBOG   2
FAST MAIL GALOP, FOR TWO PIANOS, EIGHT HANDS
    THEODORE PRESSER COMPANY   .90
STREABBOG   2
VALSE, OP. 100 NO. 2, FOR ONE PIANO, SIX HANDS
    THEODORE PRESSER COMPANY   .60
STREABBOG
WALTZ, OP. 100 NO. 2 -- 6-HANDS
    G. SCHIRMER, INC.   .50
SUPPE, F.   RIEDEL
LIGHT CAVALRY -- OVERTURE -- 8-HANDS, SET
    G. SCHIRMER, INC.   1.10
SYDEMAN, W.
THREE PIECES AND A FINALE FOR PIANO AND TAPE
    SEESAW MUSIC CORPORATION   3.00
TCHEREPNIN
LOST FLUTE, THE. WITH NARRATOR AND PERCUSSION OR ORCHESTRA
    SHAWNEE PRESS, INC.   2.50
TORRA
VIDALITA -- 1 PIANO 6 HANDS --
    FRANCO COLOMBO PUBLICATIONS   BA11592   .75
TRIMBLE   D
FOUR FRAGMENTS FROM THE CANTERBURY TALES. FOR HARPSICHORD,
SOPRANO, FLUTE, CLARINET
    C. F. PETERS CORPORATION   66068   5.00
TSCHAIKOWSKY   LANGER
MARCHE SLAVE, OP. 31 -- 8-HANDS, SET
    G. SCHIRMER, INC.   3.00
VANDEVERE, J. L.
GAY GONDOLIERES -- BARCAROLE -- 6-HANDS
    G. SCHIRMER, INC.   .60
VANDEVERE   1
WE FOLLOW THE BAND - FOR ONE PIANO, SIX HANDS
    BOSTON MUSIC COMPANY   .60
VANDEVERE   1
WE GO HIKING - FOR ONE PIANO, SIX HANDS
    BOSTON MUSIC COMPANY   .60
VANDEVERE   1
WE GO SAILING - FOR ONE PIANO, SIX HANDS
    BOSTON MUSIC COMPANY   .60
VANDEVERE   1
WE WALTZ - FOR ONE PIANO, SIX HANDS
    BOSTON MUSIC COMPANY   .60
WAGNER
OUVERTURE DE TANNHAUSER, FOR 2 PIANOS 8 HANDS
    ELKAN-VOGEL, INC.   D   4.25
WATTS *
EIGHT HANDS AT TWO PIANOS, BK. 1
    SUMMY-BIRCHARD COMPANY   3.50
WEBER, VON   E-M
INVITATION TO THE DANCE, OP. 65. TWO PIANOS, EIGHT HANDS
    C. F. PETERS CORPORATION   L1567   2.00
WERNER, F.--ED.   WERNER, F.   E
WIR SPIELEN ZUR WEIHNACHT, OP. 43. SOPRANO RECORDER PART
    C. F. PETERS CORPORATION   V138A   .50
WEYBRIGHT--ED.   WEYBRIGHT   1 1/2
YANKEE DOODLE -- PIANO TRIO
    BELWIN-MILLS PUBLISHING CORPORATION   .60
WEYBRIGHT   2
BOOK OF TRIOS, FOR ONE PIANO, SIX HANDS
    BELWIN-MILLS PUBLISHING CORPORATION   1.75
WEYBRIGHT   2
BOOK OF TRIOS -- ONE PIANO, SIX HANDS
    BELWIN-MILLS PUBLISHING CORPORATION   1.25
WEYBRIGHT   1 1/2
MARY'S OTHER LAMBS, FOR 1 PIANO 6 HANDS
    BELWIN-MILLS PUBLISHING CORPORATION   .60
WEYBRIGHT   1 1/2
THREE ON ONE -- PIANO TRIO
    BELWIN-MILLS PUBLISHING CORPORATION   .60
WILLIAMS, M.   1
OH DEAR, WHAT CAN THE MATTER BE, ONE PIANO - SIX HANDS
    WILLIS MUSIC COMPANY   .35
WILLIAMS   1
OH DEAR, WHAT CAN THE MATTER BE -- FOR ONE PIANO, SIX HANDS
    WILLIS MUSIC COMPANY   .35
WILLIAMS
TWINKLE, TWINKLE, LITTLE STAR -- FOR ONE PIANO, SIX HANDS
    WILLIS MUSIC COMPANY   .35
WILSON, M.   3
AT THE PHOTOGRAPHERS, OP. 98 NO. 1 -- TWO PIANOS, EIGHT HANDS --
    CENTURY MUSIC PUBLISHING COMPANY, INC.   2717   .60
WILSON, M.   2
AUNT SUSANNAH, OP. 98 NO. 3 -- TWO PIANOS, EIGHT HANDS --
    CENTURY MUSIC PUBLISHING COMPANY, INC.   2719   .60
WILSON, M.   2
GRANDMA AND GRANDPA, OP. 98 NO. 2 -- ONE PIANO, EIGHT HANDS --
    CENTURY MUSIC PUBLISHING COMPANY, INC.   2720   .60
WILSON, M.   MELLICHAMP, N.   1
SOLDIERS MARCH -- ONE PIANO, EIGHT HANDS --
    CENTURY MUSIC PUBLISHING COMPANY, INC.   4556   .60
WOLPE
LAZY ANDY ANT -- TWO PIANOS AND VOICE
    SEESAW MUSIC CORPORATION   10.00
ZAFRED
CONCERTO FOR 2 PIANOS -- 3 PIANOS, 6 HANDS --
    FRANCO COLOMBO PUBLICATIONS   130303   8.00
ZILCHER
AT THE BALL -- 8-HANDS, SET
    G. SCHIRMER, INC.   .75
ZILCHER
ON PARADE -- 8-HANDS, SET
    G. SCHIRMER, INC.   .50

Other Piano Ensembles:
Composer/Editor/Arranger Unlisted—Works Alphabetized by Title

CHRISTMAS ALBUM. VIOLIN AND V'CELLO AD LIB.
    C. F. PETERS CORPORATION   2800A   2.50

Technical Material

AARON, M.
  PIANO TECHNIC, BK. 1
    BELWIN-MILLS PUBLISHING CORPORATION   11011   1.50
AARON, M.
  PIANO TECHNIC, BK. 2
    BELWIN-MILLS PUBLISHING CORPORATION   11010   1.50
ABSIL, J.
  ETUDES, BK. 1
    ELKAN-VOGEL, INC.   LEM   2.50
ABSIL, J.
  ETUDES, BK. 2
    ELKAN-VOGEL, INC.   LEM   2.50
ADLER, S.
  GRADUS, BK. 1
    OXFORD UNIVERSITY PRESS   93.808   3.00
ADLER, S.
  GRADUS, BK. 2
    OXFORD UNIVERSITY PRESS   93.809   3.00
AGAY, D.--ED   AGAY, D.   A
  TECHNIC TREASURY, BK. 1
    WARNER BROTHERS PUBLISHERS   YPL 8   1.50
AGAY, D.--ED   AGAY, D.   B
  TECHNIC TREASURY, BK. 2   *
    WARNER BROTHERS PUBLISHERS   YPL 8   1.50
AGAY, D.--ED   AGAY, D.   C
  TECHNIC TREASURY, BK. 3
    WARNER BROTHERS PUBLISHERS   YPL 8   1.50
ALKAN
  PERPETUUM MOBILE
    GERARD BILLAUDOT EDITIONS MUSICALES   1.60
ALKAN
  THREE ETUDES DE BRAVOURE, OP. 16--SCHERZI--
    GERARD BILLAUDOT EDITIONS MUSICALES   3.80
ALKAN
  THREE ETUDES DE BRAVOURE, OP.12--IMPROVISATIONS--
    GERARD BILLAUDOT EDITIONS MUSICALES   3.00
ALKAN
  THREE GRANDES ETUDES, OP. 76, NO. 1, FANTAISIE IN A FLAT--LEFT
  HAND ONLY--
    GERARD BILLAUDOT EDITIONS MUSICALES   2.50
ALKAN
  THREE GRANDES ETUDES, OP. 76, NO. 2, INTRODUCTION, VARIATION,
  FINALE--RIGHT HAND ONLY--
    GERARD BILLAUDOT EDITIONS MUSICALES   3.30
ALKAN
  THREE GRANDES ETUDES, OP. 76, NO. 3, MOUVEMENT SEMBLABLE ET
  PERPETUEL--BOTH HANDS--
    GERARD BILLAUDOT EDITIONS MUSICALES   3.30
ALKAN
  TWELVE ETUDES IN MINOR KEYS, NO. 01, COMME LE VENT--A MINOR--
    GERARD BILLAUDOT EDITIONS MUSICALES   3.30
ALKAN
  TWELVE ETUDES IN MINOR KEYS, NO. 02, RYTHME MOLOSSIQUE--D
  MINOR--
    GERARD BILLAUDOT EDITIONS MUSICALES   3.00
ALKAN
  TWELVE ETUDES IN MINOR KEYS, NO. 03, SCHERZO DIABOLICO--G
  MINOR--
    GERARD BILLAUDOT EDITIONS MUSICALES   2.50
ALKAN
  TWELVE ETUDES IN MINOR KEYS, NO. 04, ALLEGRO MODERATO--C MINOR--
    GERARD BILLAUDOT EDITIONS MUSICALES   3.00
ALKAN
  TWELVE ETUDES IN MINOR KEYS, NO. 05, MARCHE FUNEBRE--F MINOR--
    GERARD BILLAUDOT EDITIONS MUSICALES   1.60
ALKAN
  TWELVE ETUDES IN MINOR KEYS, NO. 06, MENUET--B FLAT MINOR--
    GERARD BILLAUDOT EDITIONS MUSICALES   2.50
ALKAN
  TWELVE ETUDES IN MINOR KEYS, NO. 07, FINALE--E FLAT MINOR--
    GERARD BILLAUDOT EDITIONS MUSICALES   3.00
ALKAN
  TWELVE ETUDES IN MINOR KEYS, NO. 08, CONCERTO-ALLEGRO ASSAI--G
  SHARP MINOR--
    GERARD BILLAUDOT EDITIONS MUSICALES   5.70
ALKAN
  TWELVE ETUDES IN MINOR KEYS, NO. 09, CONCERTO-ADAGIO--C SHARP
  MINOR--
    GERARD BILLAUDOT EDITIONS MUSICALES   3.00
ALKAN
  TWELVE ETUDES IN MINOR KEYS, NO. 10, ALLEGRO ALA BARBARESCA--F
  SHARP MINOR--
    GERARD BILLAUDOT EDITIONS MUSICALES   4.40
ALKAN
  TWELVE ETUDES IN MINOR KEYS, NO. 11, OUVERTURE--B MINOR--
    GERARD BILLAUDOT EDITIONS MUSICALES   4.10
ARMOUR   2
  AFTER THE GAME, F MAJOR
    CENTURY MUSIC PUBLISHING COMPANY, INC.   3409   .40
ATHERTON, F. P.
  EXTENSION STUDIES FOR SMALL HANDS, OP. 166
    THEODORE PRESSER COMPANY   .60
BACCIGALUPI
  SCALES FOR THE STUDY OF PIANO
    EDIZIONI BERBEN   EB 1574   5.40
BACH, J. CHRISTIAN *
  METHODE OU RECUEIL DE CONNOISANCES ELEMENTAIRES POUR LE
  FORTEPIANO OU CLAVECIN
    BROUDE BROTHERS LTD.   27.50
BARESEL, A.   E
  ONE HUNDRED PEDAL EXERCISES WITH ELEMENTARY PEDAL MANUAL
    C. F. PETERS CORPORATION   ZM1246   2.00
BARRAINE, E.
  BOITE DE PANDORE, LA
    GERARD BILLAUDOT EDITIONS MUSICALES   6.90
BARTH, H.
  TECHNIC, BK. 1
    BELWIN-MILLS PUBLISHING CORPORATION   2.00
BARTH, H.
  TECHNIC, BK. 2
    BELWIN-MILLS PUBLISHING CORPORATION   2.00
BARTH, H.
  TECHNIC, BK. 3
    BELWIN-MILLS PUBLISHING CORPORATION   2.00
BARTH, H.
  TECHNIC
    BELWIN-MILLS PUBLISHING CORPORATION   1.50
BASTIEN--ED.   BASTIEN
  CZERNY AND HANON FOR THE INTERMEDIATE GRADES
    NEIL A. KJOS MUSIC COMPANY   30   1.95
BASTIEN--ED.   BASTIEN
  MAJOR SCALES AND PIECES
    NEIL A. KJOS MUSIC COMPANY   11   1.50

BASTIEN--ED.   BASTIEN
  MINOR SCALES AND PIECES
    NEIL A. KJOS MUSIC COMPANY   12   1.50
BASTIEN
  MAGIC FINGER TECHNIQUE, BK. 1
    NEIL A. KJOS MUSIC COMPANY   13   1.25
BASTIEN
  MAGIC FINGER TECHNIQUE, BK. 2
    NEIL A. KJOS MUSIC COMPANY   14   1.25
BASTIEN
  MAGIC FINGER TECHNIQUE, BK. 3
    NEIL A. KJOS MUSIC COMPANY   15   1.25
BELAUBRE, L.
  POETIQUE DU PIANO, VOL.1
    GERARD BILLAUDOT EDITIONS MUSICALES   3.30
BELAUBRE, L.
  POETIQUE DU PIANO, VOL.2
    GERARD BILLAUDOT EDITIONS MUSICALES   3.80
BELLAIRS
  ELEMENTS OF PIANO TECHNIQUE ARRANGED ON A RHYTHMIC BASIS
    BOOSEY AND HAWKES, INC.   1.00
BERENS, H.   PHILIPP, I.   6-7
  EXERCISES ET ETUDES POUR LA MAIN GAUCHE SEULE, OP. 89
    ALPHONSE LEDUC
BERENS, H.   E-M
  MELODIOUS EXERCISES, OP. 62
    C. F. PETERS CORPORATION   3349   2.50
BERENS, H.
  MELODIOUS EXERCISES, OP.62
    EDWIN F. KALMUS   3207   1.50
BERENS, H.
  NEW SCHOOL OF VELOCITY, BK. 1 -- 1-14 --
    FRANCO COLOMBO PUBLICATIONS   ER733   1.50
BERENS, H.
  NEW SCHOOL OF VELOCITY, BK. 2 -- 15-26 --
    FRANCO COLOMBO PUBLICATIONS   ER734   1.25
BERENS, H.
  NEW SCHOOL OF VELOCITY, BK. 3 -- 27-33 --
    FRANCO COLOMBO PUBLICATIONS   ER735   1.25
BERENS, H.
  NEW SCHOOL OF VELOCITY, OP. 61 - 40 EXERCISES, COMPLETE
    FRANCO COLOMBO PUBLICATIONS   ER456   2.50
BERENS, H.
  SCHOOL OF SCALES, CHORDS AND EMBELLISHMENTS, THE--28 PROGRESSIVE
  STUDIES, OP. 88
    G. SCHIRMER, INC.   L526   1.00
BERENS, H.
  SCHOOL OF VELOCITY--40 STUDIES, OP. 61--COMPLETE
    G. SCHIRMER, INC.   L1070   1.75
BERENS, H.
  SCHOOL OF VELOCITY, OP. 61, BK. 1
    G. SCHIRMER, INC.   L259   .75
BERENS, H.
  SCHOOL OF VELOCITY, OP. 61, BK. 2
    G. SCHIRMER, INC.   L260   1.00
BERENS, H.
  SCHOOL OF VELOCITY, OP. 61, BK. 3
    G. SCHIRMER, INC.   L262   .75
BERENS, H.   M-D
  SCHOOL OF VELOCITY, VOL. 1# NOS. 1-14
    C. F. PETERS CORPORATION   3187A   1.25
BERENS, H.   M-D
  SCHOOL OF VELOCITY, VOL. 2# NOS. 15-26
    C. F. PETERS CORPORATION   3187B   1.25
BERENS, H.   M-D
  SCHOOL OF VELOCITY, VOL. 3# NOS. 27-33
    C. F. PETERS CORPORATION   3187C   1.50
BERENS, H.   M-D
  SCHOOL OF VELOCITY, VOL. 4# NOS. 34-40
    C. F. PETERS CORPORATION   3187D   1.50
BERENS, H.
  TRAINING OF THE LEFT HAND--46 EXERCISES AND 25 STUDIES FOR THE
  LEFT HAND ALONE, OP. 89
    G. SCHIRMER, INC.   L1031   1.00
BERENS, H.   M-D
  TRAINING OF THE LEFT HAND, OP. 89
    C. F. PETERS CORPORATION   3188   2.50
BERENS, H.
  TWENTY CHILDREN-STUDIES WITHOUT OCTAVES, OP. 79
    G. SCHIRMER, INC.   L508   1.00
BERINGER, O. *   BRIMHALL, J.
  DAILY PIANOFORTE EXERCISES
    CHARLES HANSEN   H413   .99
BERKOWITZ
  SCALES AND ARPEGGIOS
    ELKAN-VOGEL, INC.   .65
BERTINI   GERMER
  FIFTY SELECTED STUDIES, FROM OP. 29, 32, 100
    G. SCHIRMER, INC.   L795   1.50
BERTINI
  FORTY-EIGHT STUDIES, OP. 29 - BK. 1
    UNIVERSAL EDITION   129   1.40
BERTINI
  FORTY-EIGHT STUDIES, OP. 32 - BK. 2
    UNIVERSAL EDITION   130   1.40
BERTINI   VOGRICH *
  TWENTY-FIVE EASY STUDIES WITHOUT OCTAVES, OP. 100
    G. SCHIRMER, INC.   L136   1.00
BERTINI   E
  TWENTY-FIVE EASY STUDIES WITHOUT OCTAVES, OP.100
    C. F. PETERS CORPORATION   181B   2.00
BERTINI   OESTERLE
  TWENTY-FIVE PRIMARY ETUDES, OP. 166
    G. SCHIRMER, INC.   L691   1.00
BERTINI
  TWENTY-FIVE STUDIES FOR SMALL HANDS, OP. 100
    UNIVERSAL EDITION   132   1.20
BERTINI   M
  TWENTY-FOUR STUDIES, OP. 29 --PREPARATORY SONATINAS TO CRAMER,
  PART 1--
    C. F. PETERS CORPORATION   182A   2.00
BERTINI   M
  TWENTY-FOUR STUDIES, OP. 29 --PREPARATORY SONATINAS TO CRAMER,
  PART 1--
    C. F. PETERS CORPORATION   182B   2.50
BERTINI   VOGRICH *
  TWENTY-FOUR STUDIES, OP. 29 --PREPARATORY TO THE CRAMER
  STUDIES--
    G. SCHIRMER, INC.   L137   1.00
BERTINI   VOGRICH *
  TWENTY-FOUR STUDIES, OP. 32 --SEQUEL TO OP. 29--
    G. SCHIRMER, INC.   L138   1.00
BEYER, F.   E
  ELEMENTARY INSTRUCTION BOOK, OP. 101
    C. F. PETERS CORPORATION   2721   2.50

BEYER, F.
ELEMENTARY METHOD
CARL FISCHER, INC. O 70 1.00

BIEHL, A.
TWENTY-FIVE EASY AND PROGRESSIVE STUDIES WITH SPECIAL REFERENCES TO THE LEFT HAND, OP. 44, BK. 1
G. SCHIRMER, INC. L497 1.00

BIEHL, A.
TWENTY-FIVE EASY AND PROGRESSIVE STUDIES WITH SPECIAL REFERENCES TO THE LEFT HAND, OP. 44, BK. 2
G. SCHIRMER, INC. L498 1.00

BIEHL, A.
TWENTY-FIVE EASY AND PROGRESSIVE STUDIES WITH SPECIAL REFERENCES TO THE LEFT HAND, OP. 44, BK. 3
G. SCHIRMER, INC. L499 1.00

BILBRO, M.
FUN IN SCALE PLAYING
WILLIS MUSIC COMPANY .80

BILBRO, M.
LITTLE ETUDES FOR LITTLE FINGERS, BK. 1
WILLIS MUSIC COMPANY .75

BILBRO, M.
LITTLE ETUDES FOR LITTLE FINGERS, BK. 2
WILLIS MUSIC COMPANY .90

BISHOP
CHORDS IN ACTION
CARL FISCHER, INC. O 4007 1.75

BLANCARD
ELEMENTARY PRINCIPLES OF PIANO TECHNIQUE
FRANCO COLOMBO PUBLICATIONS SAL 3.25

BLANCHET
MODERN PIANO TECHNIQUE -- FR.-E. --
FRANCO COLOMBO PUBLICATIONS SAL 8.00

BLUMENFELD
ETUDE FOR THE LEFT HAND, OP. 36
BOOSEY AND HAWKES, INC. 1.75

BRAHMS
COMPLETE PIANO TRANSCRIPTIONS, CADENZAS, AND EXERCISES
DOVER PUBLICATIONS, INC. 22652-2 4.00

BRAHMS
FIFTY-ONE ETUDES
EDWIN F. KALMUS 3261 1.50

BRAHMS POZZOLI
FIFTY-ONE EXERCISES, OP. POSTH. BK. 1
FRANCO COLOMBO PUBLICATIONS ER2126 2.00

BRAHMS POZZOLI
FIFTY-ONE EXERCISES, OP. POSTH. BK. 2
FRANCO COLOMBO PUBLICATIONS ER2163 1.75

BRAHMS
FIFTY-ONE EXERCISES
INTERNATIONAL MUSIC COMPANY 2.00

BRAHMS
FIFTY-ONE EXERCISES
G. SCHIRMER, INC. L1600 1.25

BRAHMS
FIFTY-ONE STUDIES
ASSOCIATED MUSIC PUBLISHERS, INC. B/H 2.00

BRAUER, F.
TWELVE STUDIES FOR DEVELOPMENT OF VELOCITY, OP. 15 --PREPARATION TO CZERNY'S SCHOOL OF VELOCITY--
G. SCHIRMER, INC. L494 1.00

BREE, M.
GROUNDWORK OF THE LESCHETIZKY METHOD, THE
G. SCHIRMER, INC. 3.50

BRESGEN
STUDIES 1. EASY STUDIES FOR CHILDREN
ASSOCIATED MUSIC PUBLISHERS, INC. DOB 2.25

BRIMHALL, J.--ED. BRIMHALL, J.
BRIMHALL'S ENCYCLOPEDIA OF SCALES AND ARPEGGIOS
CHARLES HANSEN T81 1.50

BRIMHALL, J.--ED. BRIMHALL, J. 2
CHILDREN'S PIANO PIECES -- POPULAR EDITION
CHARLES HANSEN H361 1.50

BRIMHALL, J.--ED. BRIMHALL, J.
EASY POPULAR PIANO TEACHING PIECES, ISSUE NO. 1
CHARLES HANSEN H390 1.50

BRIMHALL, J.--ED. BRIMHALL, J.
EASY POPULAR PIANO TEACHING PIECES, ISSUE NO. 2
CHARLES HANSEN H391 1.50

BRIMHALL, J.--ED. BRIMHALL, J.
FIRST FUN AT THE PIANO
CHARLES HANSEN T2 1.95

BRIMHALL, J.--ED. BRIMHALL, J.
HOW TO PLAY POPULAR MUSIC
CHARLES HANSEN K192 1.95

BRIMHALL, J.--ED. BRIMHALL, J.
JOHN BRIMHALL'S ENO TEACHING PIECES, ISSUE NO. 3
CHARLES HANSEN H414 1.50

BRIMHALL, J.--ED. BRIMHALL, J.
JOHN BRIMHALL'S ENO TEACHING PIECES, ISSUE NO. 4
CHARLES HANSEN H415 1.50

BRIMHALL, J.--ED. BRIMHALL, J.
JOHN BRIMHALL'S EXERCISES IN RHYTHM
CHARLES HANSEN T82 1.50

BRIMHALL, J.--ED. BRIMHALL, J.
JOHN BRIMHALL'S PIANO POWER
CHARLES HANSEN D113 3.95

BRIMHALL, J.--ED. BRIMHALL, J.
JOHN BRIMHALL'S 62 CHILDREN'S PIANO PIECES
CHARLES HANSEN O188 2.95

BRIMHALL, J.--ED. BRIMHALL, J.
JOHN BRIMHALL PIANO METHOD, BK. 1
CHARLES HANSEN T101 1.75

BRIMHALL, J.--ED. BRIMHALL, J.
JOHN BRIMHALL PIANO METHOD, BK. 2
CHARLES HANSEN T401 2.00

BRIMHALL, J.--ED. BRIMHALL, J.
JOHN BRIMHALL PIANO METHOD, BK. 2
CHARLES HANSEN T102 1.50

BRIMHALL, J.--ED. BRIMHALL, J.
JOHN BRIMHALL PIANO METHOD, BK. 3
CHARLES HANSEN T103 1.50

BRIMHALL, J.--ED. BRIMHALL, J.
JOHN BRIMHALL PIANO METHOD, BK. 4
CHARLES HANSEN T104 1.75

BRIMHALL, J.--ED. BRIMHALL, J.
JOHN BRIMHALL PIANO METHOD, BK. 5
CHARLES HANSEN T105 1.95

BRIMHALL, J.--ED. BRIMHALL, J.
JOHN BRIMHALL PIANO METHOD, THE PRIMER
CHARLES HANSEN T100 1.50

BRIMHALL, J.--ED. BRIMHALL, J.
JOHN BRIMHALL PIANO METHOD - IN FRENCH, PRIMER
CHARLES HANSEN T451 1.50

BRIMHALL, J.--ED. BRIMHALL, J.
JOHN BRIMHALL PIANO METHOD - IN SPANISH, BK. 1
CHARLES HANSEN T100 2.00

BRIMHALL, J.--ED. BRIMHALL, J. 1
MY FAVORITE CLASSICS
CHARLES HANSEN O114 2.95

BRIMHALL, J.--ED. BRIMHALL, J.
PLAY BY TWOS BK. 1
CHARLES HANSEN H530 1.25

BRIMHALL, J.--ED. BRIMHALL, J.
PLAY BY TWOS BK. 2
CHARLES HANSEN H531 1.25

BRIMHALL, J.--ED. BRIMHALL, J.
POPULAR CHORD INSTRUCTOR
CHARLES HANSEN T59 1.75

BRIMHALL, J.--ED. BRIMHALL, J.
STANDARD MUSIC OF TODAY
CHARLES HANSEN T68 1.50

BRIMHALL, J.--ED. BRIMHALL, J.
TEACHING FINGERS HOW TO PLAY POPS, ISSUE 1
CHARLES HANSEN H525 1.25

BRIMHALL, J.--ED. BRIMHALL, J.
TEACHING FINGERS HOW TO PLAY POPS, ISSUE 2
CHARLES HANSEN H526 1.25

BRIMHALL, J.--ED. BRIMHALL, J.
TEACHING FINGERS HOW TO PLAY POPS, ISSUE 3
CHARLES HANSEN H527 1.25

BRIMHALL, J.--ED. BRIMHALL, J.
TEACHING FINGERS HOW TO PLAY POPS, ISSUE 4
CHARLES HANSEN H528 1.25

BRIMHALL, J.--ED. BRIMHALL, J.
TEACHING FINGERS HOW TO PLAY SONGS FOR LITTLE NEIGHBORS, ISSUE 7
CHARLES HANSEN H612 1.25

BUOGO
TECHNIC OF THE ARPEGGIO, BK. 1
FRANCO COLOMBO PUBLICATIONS ER1764 2.00

BURDICK--ED
HANON VIRTUOSO PIANIST, PART 1
CENTURY MUSIC PUBLISHING COMPANY, INC. 2379 .40

BURDICK--ED
HANON VIRTUOSO PIANIST, PART 2
CENTURY MUSIC PUBLISHING COMPANY, INC. 2380 .40

BURGMUELLER GERMER 3-4
ACHTZEHN GENRE-ETUDEN OP. 109
SCHOTT 175 2.50

BURGMUELLER
BALLADE, OP. 100
WILLIS MUSIC COMPANY .80

BURGMUELLER SCHAUM, J. 2 1/2
BURGMUELLER-SCHAUM, BK. 1
BELWIN-MILLS PUBLISHING CORPORATION 1.25

BURGMUELLER SCHAUM, J. 5
BURGMUELLER SCHAUM, BK. 2
BELWIN-MILLS PUBLISHING CORPORATION 1.25

BURGMUELLER
EASY AND PROGRESSIVE STUDIES, OP. 100
THEODORE PRESSER COMPANY 1.25

BURGMUELLER M-D
EIGHTEEN CHARACTERISTIC STUDIES, OP. 109
C. F. PETERS CORPORATION 3103 1.50

BURGMUELLER OESTERLE
EIGHTEEN CHARACTERISTIC STUDIES, OP. 109
G. SCHIRMER, INC. L752 1.00

BURGMUELLER
EIGHTEEN STUDIES, OP. 109
FRANCO COLOMBO PUBLICATIONS ER419 .75

BURGMUELLER GERMER 1-2
FUNF UND ZWANZIG LEICHTE ETUDEN OP. 100
SCHOTT 173 2.50

BURGMUELLER OESTERLE
TWELVE BRILLIANT AND MELODIOUS STUDIES, OP. 105
G. SCHIRMER, INC. L755 1.00

BURGMUELLER
TWELVE BRILLIANT STUDIES, OP. 105
FRANCO COLOMBO PUBLICATIONS ER815 .75

BURGMUELLER M-D
TWELVE STUDIES, OP. 105
C. F. PETERS CORPORATION 3102 2.00

BURGMUELLER
TWENTY-FIVE EASY AND PROGRESSIVE STUDIES, OP. 100--BK. 1
G. SCHIRMER, INC. L977 .75

BURGMUELLER
TWENTY-FIVE EASY AND PROGRESSIVE STUDIES, OP. 100--BK. 2
G. SCHIRMER, INC. L978 .75

BURGMUELLER E
TWENTY-FIVE EASY AND PROGRESSIVE STUDIES, OP. 100
C. F. PETERS CORPORATION 3101 2.00

BURGMUELLER OESTERLE
TWENTY-FIVE EASY AND PROGRESSIVE STUDIES, OP. 100
G. SCHIRMER, INC. L500 .85

BURGMUELLER
TWENTY-FIVE EASY ETUDES, OP. 100
CARL FISCHER, INC. L 324 1.00

BURGMUELLER
TWENTY-FIVE EASY STUDIES, OP. 100
CENTURY MUSIC PUBLISHING COMPANY, INC. 1.25

BURGMUELLER
TWENTY-FIVE STUDIES, OP. 100
BANKS AND SON LTD. 1.50

BURGMUELLER
TWENTY-FIVE STUDIES, OP. 100
FRANCO COLOMBO PUBLICATIONS ER429 1.75

BURGMUELLER GERMER 3-4
ZWOLF ETUDEN OP. 105
SCHOTT 174 2.50

BURLEY
GENTLEMEN, START YOUR ENGINES
NEIL A. KJOS MUSIC COMPANY 134 1.75

BURNAM
DOZEN A DAY PIANO BOOKS, BK. 1 -- ELEMENTARY
WILLIS MUSIC COMPANY 1.00

BURNAM
DOZEN A DAY PIANO BOOKS, BK. 2 -- TRANSITIONAL
WILLIS MUSIC COMPANY 1.00

BURNAM
DOZEN A DAY PIANO BOOKS, BK. 3 -- LOWER-HIGHER
WILLIS MUSIC COMPANY 1.25

BURNAM
DOZEN A DAY PIANO BOOKS, BK. 4 -- HIGHER
WILLIS MUSIC COMPANY 1.50

BURNAM
DOZEN A DAY PIANO BOOKS, PREPARATORY -- PRIMARY
WILLIS MUSIC COMPANY 1.00

BUSONI GOEBELS
NEW BUSONI. EXERCISES AND STUDIES FROM THE 'KLAVIERUEBUNG', VOL. 1
ASSOCIATED MUSIC PUBLISHERS, INC. B/H 4.00

BUSONI GOEBELS
NEW BUSONI, THE. EXERCISES AND STUDIES FROM THE 'KLAVIERUEBUNG', VOL. 2
ASSOCIATED MUSIC PUBLISHERS, INC. B/H 4.00

BUSONI	GOEBELS		
NEW BUSONI, THE--EXERCISES AND STUDIES FROM ''KLAVIERUBUNG''--BK. 1			
ASSOCIATED MUSIC PUBLISHERS, INC.		BRH	4.00
BUSONI	GOEBELS		
NEW BUSONI, THE--EXERCISES AND STUDIES FROM ''KLAVIERUBUNG''--BK. 2			
ASSOCIATED MUSIC PUBLISHERS, INC.		BRH	4.00
CAMBISSA, G.			
SEVEN LITTLE STUDIES			
EDIZIONI BERBEN		EB 1443	3.00
CAVALHO, R.			
SCALE PATTERNS FOR YOUNG PIANISTS			
ASSOCIATED MUSIC PUBLISHERS, INC.		BER	1.50
CESI, B.			
PRACTICAL THEORETICAL METHOD, BK. 01. ELEMENTS AND 20 EXERCISES			
FRANCO COLOMBO PUBLICATIONS		ER2351	.75
CESI, B.			
PRACTICAL THEORETICAL METHOD, BK. 02. EXERCISES AND SCALES			
FRANCO COLOMBO PUBLICATIONS		ER2352	2.25
CESI, B.			
PRACTICAL THEORETICAL METHOD, BK. 03. ARPEGGIOS			
FRANCO COLOMBO PUBLICATIONS		ER2353	2.25
CESI, B.			
PRACTICAL THEORETICAL METHOD, BK. 04. EQUALIZATION OF THE HANDS			
FRANCO COLOMBO PUBLICATIONS		ER2354	2.25
CESI, B.			
PRACTICAL THEORETICAL METHOD, BK. 05. REPEATED NOTES			
FRANCO COLOMBO PUBLICATIONS		ER2355	3.25
CESI, B.			
PRACTICAL THEORETICAL METHOD, BK. 06. WRIST MOVEMENT			
FRANCO COLOMBO PUBLICATIONS		ER2356	1.50
CESI, B.			
PRACTICAL THEORETICAL METHOD, BK. 07. OCTAVE TECHNIQUE			
FRANCO COLOMBO PUBLICATIONS		ER2357	3.75
CESI, B.			
PRACTICAL THEORETICAL METHOD, BK. 08. LEGATO			
FRANCO COLOMBO PUBLICATIONS		ER2358	1.50
CESI, B.			
PRACTICAL THEORETICAL METHOD, BK. 09. THIRDS--LEGATO--			
FRANCO COLOMBO PUBLICATIONS		ER2359	2.00
CESI, B.			
PRACTICAL THEORETICAL METHOD, BK. 10. DOUBLE NOTES			
FRANCO COLOMBO PUBLICATIONS		ER2360	1.75
CESI, B.			
PRACTICAL THEORETICAL METHOD, BK. 11. SIXTHS			
FRANCO COLOMBO PUBLICATIONS		ER2361	1.75
CESI, B.			
PRACTICAL THEORETICAL METHOD, BK. 12. ADVANCED MECHANISM			
FRANCO COLOMBO PUBLICATIONS		ER2362	4.00
CHILDE, M.			
TECHNICAL AIDS TO THE PLAYING OF SCALES, BROKEN CHORDS, AND ARPEGGIOS, BK. 1			
OXFORD UNIVERSITY PRESS		39.605	.80
CHILDE, M.			
TECHNICAL AIDS TO THE PLAYING OF SCALES, BROKEN CHORDS, AND ARPEGGIOS, BK. 2			
OXFORD UNIVERSITY PRESS		39.606	.80
CHILDE, M.			
TECHNICAL AIDS TO THE PLAYING OF SCALES, BROKEN CHORDS, AND ARPEGGIOS, BK. 3			
OXFORD UNIVERSITY PRESS		39.607	.80
CHING			
NEW GRADED PEDALLING, BK. 1			
GENERAL WORDS AND MUSIC COMPANY			1.25
CHING			
NEW GRADED PEDALLING, BK. 2			
GENERAL WORDS AND MUSIC COMPANY			1.25
CHING			
NEW GRADED SIGHT-READING, BK. 1			
GENERAL WORDS AND MUSIC COMPANY			1.25
CHING			
NEW GRADED SIGHT-READING, BK. 2			
GENERAL WORDS AND MUSIC COMPANY			1.25
CHING			
NEW GRADED STUDIES, BK. 1			
GENERAL WORDS AND MUSIC COMPANY			1.25
CHING			
NEW GRADED STUDIES, BK. 2			
GENERAL WORDS AND MUSIC COMPANY			1.25
CHING			
NEW GRADED STUDIES, BK. 3			
GENERAL WORDS AND MUSIC COMPANY			1.25
CHING			
NEW GRADED STUDIES, BK. 4			
GENERAL WORDS AND MUSIC COMPANY			1.25
CHING			
NEW GRADED STUDIES, BK. 5			
GENERAL WORDS AND MUSIC COMPANY			1.25
CHING			
NEW GRADED TIME EXERCISES			
GENERAL WORDS AND MUSIC COMPANY			1.25
CHING			
SCALE AND ARPEGGIO BOOK			
GENERAL WORDS AND MUSIC COMPANY			1.25
CHOPIN	BADURA-SKODA		
ETUDES, OP. 10			
WIENER URTEXT EDITION		UT 50030	3.50
CHOPIN	BADURA-SKODA		
ETUDES, OP. 25			
WIENER URTEXT EDITION		UT 50031	3.50
CHOPIN	SCHOLTZ	D	
ETUDES --27-- COMPLETE			
C. F. PETERS CORPORATION		1907	2.50
CHOPIN		9	
ETUDE IN G FLAT, OP. 10 NO. 5			
THEODORE PRESSER COMPANY			.50
CHOPIN	PUGNO		
TWENTY-FIVE ETUDES			
UNIVERSAL EDITION		347	4.50
CINTOLESI			
TWO STUDIES FOR REPEATED NOTES			
FRANCO COLOMBO PUBLICATIONS		FOR.12127	.90
CLARK, F.--ED.	CLARK, F.		
PIANO TECHNIC, BK. 1			
SUMMY-BIRCHARD COMPANY			2.50
CLARK, F.--ED.	CLARK, F.		
PIANO TECHNIC, BK. 2			
SUMMY-BIRCHARD COMPANY			2.25
CLARK, F.--ED.	CLARK, F.		
PIANO TECHNIC, BK. 3			
SUMMY-BIRCHARD COMPANY			2.25
CLARK, F.--ED.	CLARK, F.		
PIANO TECHNIC, BK. 4			
SUMMY-BIRCHARD COMPANY			2.25

CLARK, F.--ED.	CLARK, F.		
PIANO TECHNIC, BK. 5			
SUMMY-BIRCHARD COMPANY			2.50
CLARK, F.--ED.	CLARK, F.		
PIANO TECHNIC, BK. 6			
SUMMY-BIRCHARD COMPANY			1.50
CLARK, F.--ED.	CLARK, F.		
TECHNIC TIME - PART A			
SUMMY-BIRCHARD COMPANY			2.50
CLARK, F.--ED.	CLARK, F.		
TECHNIC TIME - PART B			
SUMMY-BIRCHARD COMPANY			2.50
CLEMENTI	SCHUNGELER	3-5	
DER NEUE GRADUS AD PARNASSUM, BK. 1			
SCHOTT		2770A	2.50
CLEMENTI	SCHUNGELER	3-5	
DER NEUE GRADUS AD PARNASSUM, BK. 2			
SCHOTT		2770B	2.50
CLEMENTI	TAUSIG		
FIVE FUNDAMENTAL STUDIES FOR DAILY EXERCISE, FROM ''GRADUS AD PARNASSUM''			
G. SCHIRMER, INC.			.60
CLEMENTI	TAUSIG	D	
GRADUS AD PARNASSUM. 29 SELECTED STUDIES			
C. F. PETERS CORPORATION		3013	4.50
CLEMENTI	VOGRICH		
GRADUS AD PARNASSUM--100 EXERCISES, BK. 1			
G. SCHIRMER, INC.		L167	2.50
CLEMENTI	VOGRICH		
GRADUS AD PARNASSUM--100 EXERCISES, BK. 2			
G. SCHIRMER, INC.		L168	2.50
CLEMENTI	TAUSIG		
GRADUS AD PARNASSUM--29 SELECTED STUDIES, PLUS SCALES IN ALL MAJOR AND MINOR KEYS--IN SPANISH, FRENCH, AND ENGLISH			
G. SCHIRMER, INC.		L1112	2.00
CLEMENTI	TAUSIG		
GRADUS AD PARNASSUM--29 SELECTED STUDIES, PLUS SCALES IN ALL MAJOR AND MINOR KEYS			
G. SCHIRMER, INC.		L780	2.25
CLEMENTI	VOGRICH		
PRELUDES AND EXERCISES IN ALL THE MAJOR AND MINOR KEYS--SCHOOL OF SCALES			
G. SCHIRMER, INC.		L376	1.75
CLEMENTI	MUGELLINI		
PRELUDES AND EXERCISES			
FRANCO COLOMBO PUBLICATIONS		ER590	1.75
CLEMENTI	BUSTINI		
TWENTY-THREE STUDIES FROM 'GRADUS AD PARNASSUM'			
FRANCO COLOMBO PUBLICATIONS		DS445	3.25
CLEMENTI	MONTANI		
TWENTY-THREE STUDIES FROM 'GRADUS AD PARNASSUM'			
FRANCO COLOMBO PUBLICATIONS		ER2317	2.75
COBB			
TECHNIQUE BUILDERS			
BELWIN-MILLS PUBLISHING CORPORATION			1.50
COBB			
TECHNIQUE BUILDERS			
BELWIN-MILLS PUBLISHING CORPORATION		11483	1.75
COHEN, M. J.		E	
THIRTY TECHNICAL STUDIES, OP. 10			
C. F. PETERS CORPORATION		B13A	.90
CONCONE, G.	DEIS		
FIFTEEN STUDIES IN STYLE, OP. 31			
G. SCHIRMER, INC.		L1374	1.25
CONCONE, G.	OESTERLE		
FIFTEEN STUDIES IN STYLE AND EXPRESSION, OP. 25			
G. SCHIRMER, INC.		L141	1.25
CONCONE, G.	OESTERLE		
THIRTY SELECTED STUDIES			
G. SCHIRMER, INC.		L25	1.50
CONCONE, G.	OESTERLE		
TWENTY-FIVE MELODIC STUDIES, OP. 24			
G. SCHIRMER, INC.		L139	.75
CONCONE, G.	OESTERLE		
TWENTY STUDIES ON THE SINGING TOUCH, OP. 30			
G. SCHIRMER, INC.		L140	1.00
CONUS, L.			
FUNDAMENTALS OF PIANO TECHNIQUE, BK. 2: ADVANCED TECHNIQUE			
SUMMY-BIRCHARD COMPANY			2.00
CONUS, D.			
FUNDAMENTALS OF PIANO TECHNIQUE, BK. 1: DAILY PROGRESSIVE EXERCISES			
SUMMY-BIRCHARD COMPANY			2.00
COOKE, J. F.			
MASTERING THE SCALES AND ARPEGGIOS			
THEODORE PRESSER COMPANY			4.00
CORTOT			
MUSICAL EXERCISES			
FRANCO COLOMBO PUBLICATIONS		SAL	5.00
CORTOT			
RATIONAL PRINCIPLES OF PIANOFORTE TECHNIQUE -- E. --			
FRANCO COLOMBO PUBLICATIONS		SAL	10.50
CORTOT			
RATIONAL PRINCIPLES OF PIANOFORTE TECHNIQUE -- FR. --			
FRANCO COLOMBO PUBLICATIONS		SAL	10.50
CORTOT			
RATIONAL PRINCIPLES OF PIANOFORTE TECHNIQUE -- GER. --			
FRANCO COLOMBO PUBLICATIONS		SAL	10.50
CRAMER, J.			
EIGHTY-FOUR STUDIES, BK. 1			
G. SCHIRMER, INC.		L142	1.50
CRAMER, J.			
EIGHTY-FOUR STUDIES, BK. 2			
G. SCHIRMER, INC.		L143	1.50
CRAMER, J.			
EIGHTY-FOUR STUDIES, BK. 3			
G. SCHIRMER, INC.		L144	1.50
CRAMER, J.			
EIGHTY-FOUR STUDIES, BK. 4			
G. SCHIRMER, INC.		L145	1.50
CRAMER, J.		D	
EIGHTY-FOUR STUDIES, VOL. 1			
C. F. PETERS CORPORATION		184A	2.50
CRAMER, J.		D	
EIGHTY-FOUR STUDIES, VOL. 2			
C. F. PETERS CORPORATION		184B	2.50
CRAMER, J.		D	
EIGHTY-FOUR STUDIES, VOL. 3			
C. F. PETERS CORPORATION		184C	2.50
CRAMER, J.		D	
EIGHTY-FOUR STUDIES, VOL. 4			
C. F. PETERS CORPORATION		184D	2.50
CRAMER, J.			
FIFTY SELECTED STUDIES--IN SPANISH			
G. SCHIRMER, INC.		L1178	2.50
CRAMER, J.			
FIFTY SELECTED STUDIES, BK. 1			
G. SCHIRMER, INC.		L828	1.00

CZERNY   KRAUSE
SCHOOL OF VELOCITY, OP. 299, BK. 2
    ASSOCIATED MUSIC PUBLISHERS, INC.   BRH   1.00
                 M-D
CZERNY
SCHOOL OF VELOCITY, OP. 299, BK. 2
    C. F. PETERS CORPORATION   2406B   1.25
CZERNY   KRAUSE
SCHOOL OF VELOCITY, OP. 299, BK. 3
    ASSOCIATED MUSIC PUBLISHERS, INC.   BRH   1.00
                 M-D
CZERNY
SCHOOL OF VELOCITY, OP. 299, BK. 3
    C. F. PETERS CORPORATION   2406C   1.50
                 M-D
CZERNY   O
SCHOOL OF VELOCITY, OP. 299, BK. 4
    C. F. PETERS CORPORATION   2406D   1.50
CZERNY
SCHOOL OF VELOCITY, OP. 299, BKS. 1 AND 2
    ASHLEY DEALERS SERVICE, INC.   1.25
CZERNY
SCHOOL OF VELOCITY, OP. 299
    ASHLEY DEALERS SERVICE, INC.   1.00
CZERNY   BUONAMICI
SCHOOL OF VELOCITY, OP. 299
    FRANCO COLOMBO PUBLICATIONS   ER671   1.75
CZERNY
SCHOOL OF VELOCITY, OP. 299
    UNIVERSAL EDITION   51   4.15
CZERNY
SCHOOL OF VELOCITY, OP. 299
    WILLIS MUSIC COMPANY   1.50
CZERNY   PALMER, W. A.
SCHOOL OF VELOCITY, PART 1
    ALFRED MUSIC COMPANY   613   1.25
CZERNY   PALMER, W. A.
SCHOOL OF VELOCITY, PART 2
    ALFRED MUSIC COMPANY   614   1.25
CZERNY
SCHOOL OF VELOCITY, THE--40 STUDIES, OP. 299, BK. 1
    G. SCHIRMER, INC.   L162   1.00
CZERNY
SCHOOL OF VELOCITY, THE--40 STUDIES, OP. 299, BK. 2
    G. SCHIRMER, INC.   L163   1.00
CZERNY
SCHOOL OF VELOCITY, THE--40 STUDIES, OP. 299, BK. 3
    G. SCHIRMER, INC.   L164   1.00
CZERNY
SCHOOL OF VELOCITY, THE--40 STUDIES, OP. 299, BK. 4
    G. SCHIRMER, INC.   L165   1.00
CZERNY   VOGRICH
SCHOOL OF VELOCITY, THE--40 STUDIES, OP. 299
    G. SCHIRMER, INC.   L161   1.50
CZERNY   PALMER, W. A.
SCHOOL OF VELOCITY --COMPLETE--
    ALFRED MUSIC COMPANY   612   2.50
                 M-D
CZERNY
SCHOOL OF VELOCITY --SCHULE DER GELAEUFIGKEIT--, OP. 299
    C. F. PETERS CORPORATION   2411   3.00
CZERNY   NICHOLL
SELECTED PIANO STUDIES - BOOK 1
    BOSTON MUSIC COMPANY   2.75
CZERNY *   NICHOLL
SELECTED PIANO STUDIES - BOOK 2
    BOSTON MUSIC COMPANY   2.75
CZERNY   UPPER ELEMENTARY AND LOWER
SELECTED STUDIES, BK. 1--170 STUDIES IN THE UPPER ELEMENTARY AND
LOWER MIDDLE GRADES
    G. SCHIRMER, INC.   L994   3.50
CZERNY   MUGELLINI
SELECTED STUDIES, BK. 1 -- 52 STUDIES --
    FRANCO COLOMBO PUBLICATIONS   ER2377   2.50
CZERNY   CESI
SELECTED STUDIES, BK. 1 - WITHOUT THUMB PASSAGES
    FRANCO COLOMBO PUBLICATIONS   ER2408   1.00
CZERNY   LIEBLING
SELECTED STUDIES, BK. 1
    THEODORE PRESSER COMPANY   1.50
CZERNY   MIDDLE GRADE
SELECTED STUDIES, BK. 2--92 STUDIES IN THE MIDDLE GRADE
    G. SCHIRMER, INC.   L995   3.50
CZERNY   MUGELLINI
SELECTED STUDIES, BK. 2 -- 44 STUDIES --
    FRANCO COLOMBO PUBLICATIONS   ER2378   3.75
CZERNY   CESI
SELECTED STUDIES, BK. 2 - FOR THUMB PASSAGES
    FRANCO COLOMBO PUBLICATIONS   99512   1.75
CZERNY   LIEBLING
SELECTED STUDIES, BK. 2
    THEODORE PRESSER COMPANY   1.50
CZERNY   MUGELLINI
SELECTED STUDIES, BK. 3 -- 34 STUDIES --
    FRANCO COLOMBO PUBLICATIONS   ER2379   6.50
CZERNY   CESI
SELECTED STUDIES, BK. 3 - FOR THUMB PASSAGES
    FRANCO COLOMBO PUBLICATIONS   99513   1.75
CZERNY   LIEBLING
SELECTED STUDIES, BK. 3
    THEODORE PRESSER COMPANY   2.00
CZERNY   MUGELLINI
SELECTED STUDIES, BK. 4 -- 20 STUDIES --
    FRANCO COLOMBO PUBLICATIONS   ER2380   4.00
CZERNY   MARCIANO
SEVENTY SELECTED AND PROGRESSIVE STUDIES
    FRANCO COLOMBO PUBLICATIONS   ER599   2.25
CZERNY   MARCIANO
SIGHT READING EXERCISES
    FRANCO COLOMBO PUBLICATIONS   ER598   1.25
CZERNY   E
SIXTY CHILDREN'S EXERCISES
    C. F. PETERS CORPORATION   2667   2.00
CZERNY   SCHULTZ
SIX OCTAVE-STUDIES IN PROGRESSIVE DIFFICULTY, OP. 553
    G. SCHIRMER, INC.   L402   .75
CZERNY   D
STUDIES FOR THE LEFT HAND, OP. 399
    C. F. PETERS CORPORATION   2842   4.00
CZERNY
STUDIES IN MECHANISM, OP. 849
    CARL FISCHER, INC.   L 487   1.50
CZERNY   BUONAMICI
THIRTY NEW STUDIES IN TECHNICS, OP. 849--PREPARATORY TO ''THE
SCHOOL OF VELOCITY''
    G. SCHIRMER, INC.   L272   1.50
CZERNY   E
THIRTY NEW STUDIES IN TECHNIQUE--ETUDES DE MECHANISME--, OP.
849. PREPARATORY TO OP. 299--SCHOOL OF VELOCITY--
    C. F. PETERS CORPORATION   2611   2.50

CZERNY   POZZOLI
THIRTY STUDIES IN MECHANISM, OP. 849
    FRANCO COLOMBO PUBLICATIONS   ER363   1.50
CZERNY
THIRTY STUDIES IN MECHANISM, OP. 849
    UNIVERSAL EDITION   143   1.80
CZERNY   BUONAMICI
TWENTY-FOUR EASY MELODIOUS FIVE-FINGER EXERCISES, OP. 777
    FRANCO COLOMBO PUBLICATIONS   ER1265   1.00
                 M-D
CZERNY
TWENTY-FOUR STUDIES FOR THE LEFT HAND, OP. 718
    C. F. PETERS CORPORATION   3244   2.00
CZERNY   SCHARFENBERG
TWENTY-FOUR STUDIES FOR THE LEFT HAND, OP. 718
    G. SCHIRMER, INC.   L60   1.00
DAMM, G.   PEARCE
METHOD FOR THE PIANO FORTE
    G. SCHIRMER, INC.   4.00
DEBUSSY
DR. GRADUS AD PARNASSUM
    THEODORE PRESSER COMPANY   1.25
DEE, M.
CREATIVE TECHNIQUE FOR PIANO
    VOLKWEIN BROS.   1.50
DEE, M.
TOUCH TECHNIQUE FOR EVERY PIANIST
    VOLKWEIN BROS.   1.25
DESCAVES, L. *
NOUVELLE METHODE, LE COUPPEY
    GERARD BILLAUDOT EDITIONS MUSICALES   3.50
DESCAVES, L.
TECHNIQUE, VOL.1
    GERARD BILLAUDOT EDITIONS MUSICALES   3.80
DESCAVES, L.
TECHNIQUE, VOL.2
    GERARD BILLAUDOT EDITIONS MUSICALES   3.50
DE ANGELIS VALENTINI
ANTHOLOGY OF EASY AND PROGRESSIVE EXERCISES AND PIECES
    FRANCO COLOMBO PUBLICATIONS   ER2613   5.00
DE ANGELIS VALENTINI
COMPLETE METHOD, BK. 1
    FRANCO COLOMBO PUBLICATIONS   BON.1970   2.50
DE ANGELIS VALENTINI
COMPLETE METHOD, BK. 2
    FRANCO COLOMBO PUBLICATIONS   BON.1971   2.50
DE ANGELIS VALENTINI
COMPLETE METHOD, BK. 3
    FRANCO COLOMBO PUBLICATIONS   BON.1972   3.00
DE ANGELIS VALENTINI
COMPLETE METHOD, BK. 4
    FRANCO COLOMBO PUBLICATIONS   BON.1973   3.00
DE ANGELIS VALENTINI
COMPLETE METHOD, BK. 5
    FRANCO COLOMBO PUBLICATIONS   BON.1974   3.25
DE ANGELIS VALENTINI
COMPLETE METHOD, BK. 6
    FRANCO COLOMBO PUBLICATIONS   BON.1975   3.25
DE ANGELIS VALENTINI
FORTY-ONE DELIGHTFUL LITTLE STUDIES
    FRANCO COLOMBO PUBLICATIONS   ER2451   .90
DE ANGELIS VALENTINI
FORTY-ONE ELEMENTARY LITTLE STUDIES
    FRANCO COLOMBO PUBLICATIONS   BON.2214   2.25
DE FILIPPI, A.
DANCE RHYTHMS
    GENERAL MUSIC PUBLISHING COMPANY, INC.   586   2.00
DE FILIPPI, A.
SEVEN EASY PIECES - ON A 12 TONE ROW-
    GENERAL MUSIC PUBLISHING COMPANY, INC.   585   2.50
DE FILIPPI, A.
TWELVE SHORT PIECES
    GENERAL MUSIC PUBLISHING COMPANY, INC.   588   2.50
DE SAINT-LAMBERT, M.
LES PRINCIPES DU CLAVECIN
    BROUDE BROTHERS LTD.   25.00
DE SOLIS
THREE POSITIONS OF HARMONIZED SCALES
    BELWIN-MILLS PUBLISHING CORPORATION   11502   1.50
DICKS, E. A.
SCALES AND CHORDS FOR THE PIANO
    FREDERICK HARRIS MUSIC COMPANY   .75
DINSART   E-M
MNEMONIC PROCESS --FOR THE STUDY OF SCALES AND ARPEGGIO
FINGERING--
    C. F. PETERS CORPORATION   SCH128   1.50
DOERING, C. H.
EIGHT OCTAVE-STUDIES, OP. 25
    G. SCHIRMER, INC.   L1035   1.00
DOERING, C. H.
EXERCISES AND STUDIES IN STACCATO OCTAVE-PLAYING, OP. 24
    G. SCHIRMER, INC.   L651   1.00
DOHNANYI
DAILY FINGER EXERCISES, BK. 1
    BELWIN-MILLS PUBLISHING CORPORATION   11113   2.75
DOHNANYI
DAILY FINGER EXERCISES, BK. 2
    BELWIN-MILLS PUBLISHING CORPORATION   11114   2.75
DOHNANYI
DAILY FINGER EXERCISES, BK. 3
    BELWIN-MILLS PUBLISHING CORPORATION   11115   2.75
DOHNANYI
ESSENTIAL FINGER EXERCISES
    EDWARD B. MARKS MUSIC CORPORATION   02.50
DRAW
EARLY KEYBOARD TECHNIC, BK. A
    PRO-ART PUBLICATIONS, INC.   838   1.00
DRAW
EARLY KEYBOARD TECHNIC, BK. B
    PRO-ART PUBLICATIONS, INC.   839   1.00
DRAW
EARLY KEYBOARD TECHNIC, BK. C
    PRO-ART PUBLICATIONS, INC.   840   1.00
DRAW
EARLY KEYBOARD TECHNIC, BK. D
    PRO-ART PUBLICATIONS, INC.   841   1.00
DREWS
PIANO TECHNIQUE, BK. 1
    FRANCO COLOMBO PUBLICATIONS   SIK.490A   8.25
DREWS
PIANO TECHNIQUE, BK. 2
    FRANCO COLOMBO PUBLICATIONS   SIK.490B   9.75
DUCHIN
EDDY DUCHIN'S PIANO TECHNIQUE
    THE BIG THREE MUSIC CORPORATION   02.95
DUVERNOY, J.   M-D
ECOLE DU MECANISME, OP. 120 --15 ETUDES--
    C. F. PETERS CORPORATION   3276   2.00

DUVERNOY, J.
　ECOLE PRIMAIRE, OP. 176--25 ELEMENTARY STUDIES
　　G. SCHIRMER, INC.　　　　　　　　　L50　　　　.75
DUVERNOY, J.
　ECOLE PRIMAIRE, OP. 176 --TWENTY-FIVE EASY AND PROGRESSIVE
　STUDIES--
　　THEODORE PRESSER COMPANY　　　　　　　　　　.75
DUVERNOY, J.
　ELEMENTARY STUDIES, OP. 176
　　CARL FISCHER, INC.　　　　　　　　　L 506　　　1.00
DUVERNOY, J.
　ELEMENTARY STUDIES, OP. 176
　　FRANCO COLOMBO PUBLICATIONS　　　　ER642　　　1.00
DUVERNOY, J.
　PREPARATORY SCHOOL OF VELOCITY, OP. 276
　　FRANCO COLOMBO PUBLICATIONS　　　　ER1210　　1.50
DUVERNOY, J.
　RAPID FIRE, OP. 256--ETUDE
　　G. SCHIRMER, INC.　　　　　　　　　　　　　.40
DUVERNOY, J.
　SCHOOL OF MECHANISM, OP. 120
　　CARL FISCHER, INC.　　　　　　　　　L 361　　　1.00
DUVERNOY, J.
　SCHOOL OF MECHANISM, OP. 120
　　FRANCO COLOMBO PUBLICATIONS　　　　ER641　　　1.25
DUVERNOY, J.
　SCHOOL OF MECHANISM, THE--OP. 120--15 STUDIES PREPARATORY TO
　CZERNY'S ''SCHOOL OF VELOCITY''--BK. 1
　　G. SCHIRMER, INC.　　　　　　　　　L1292　　　1.00
DUVERNOY, J.　　　　　KLAUSER
　SCHOOL OF MECHANISM, THE--OP. 120--15 STUDIES PREPARATORY TO
　CZERNY'S ''SCHOOL OF VELOCITY''
　　G. SCHIRMER, INC.　　　　　　　　　L316　　　1.00
DUVERNOY, J.
　SCHOOL OF MECHANISM OP. 120
　　WILLIS MUSIC COMPANY　　　　　　　　　　　.80
DUVERNOY, J.　　　　　　　　E
　TWENTY-FIVE ELEMENTARY STUDIES, OP. 176
　　C. F. PETERS CORPORATION　　　　　3277　　　2.00
DUVERNOY, J.　　　　　PALMER. W. A.
　TWENTY-FIVE ELEMENTARY STUDIES
　　ALFRED MUSIC COMPANY　　　　　　　636　　　1.50
ECKSTEIN
　PICTURE POINTERS
　　CARL FISCHER, INC.　　　　　　　　O 3451　　1.50
ECKSTEIN
　TOUCH, TONE, TECHNIC
　　CARL FISCHER, INC.　　　　　　　　O 4109　　1.25
ECKSTEIN
　WRITE AND PLAY THE SCALES AND CHORDS
　　CARL FISCHER, INC.　　　　　　　　O 3913　　1.50
FALK
　DIX ETUDES ATONALES, DONT 2 DE CONCERT --SELON LA TECHNIQUE DE
　L'ATONALISME INTEGRAL--
　　ALPHONSE LEDUC
FANO, G. A.
　STUDY OF THE PIANO, THE, BK. 1 - THE TECHNIQUE OF THE SCALE
　　FRANCO COLOMBO PUBLICATIONS　　　ER389　　2.75
FANO, G. A.
　STUDY OF THE PIANO, THE, BK. 2 - CHORDS, ARPEGGIOS AND THE PEDAL
　　FRANCO COLOMBO PUBLICATIONS　　　ER1323　　1.50
FANO, G. A.
　STUDY OF THE PIANO, THE, BK. 3 - POLYPHONIC STYLE, ADVANCED
　TECHNIQUES AND METHODS OF STUDY
　　FRANCO COLOMBO PUBLICATIONS　　　ER1597　　2.25
FAY, AMY
　DEPPE FINGER EXERCISES FOR RAPIDLY DEVELOPING AN ARTISTIC TOUCH
　IN PIANO FORTE PLAYING
　　MUSICA OBSCURA　　　　　　　　　　　　　2.50
FERGUSON, H.
　STYLE AND INTERPRETATION, BK. 1
　　OXFORD UNIVERSITY PRESS　　　　　39.611　　3.00
FERGUSON, H.
　STYLE AND INTERPRETATION, BK. 2
　　OXFORD UNIVERSITY PRESS　　　　　39.612　　3.50
FERGUSON, H.
　STYLE AND INTERPRETATION, BK. 3
　　OXFORD UNIVERSITY PRESS　　　　　39.613　　3.00
FERGUSON, H.
　STYLE AND INTERPRETATION, BK. 4
　　OXFORD UNIVERSITY PRESS　　　　　39.614　　3.00
FERTE--ED　　　　　FERTE　　　E
　PROGRESSIVE STUDIES, VOL. 1
　　C. F. PETERS CORPORATION　　　　SCH30　　2.00
FERTE--ED　　　　　FERTE　　　E-M
　PROGRESSIVE STUDIES, VOL. 2
　　C. F. PETERS CORPORATION　　　　SCH31　　2.00
FERTE--ED　　　　　FERTE　　　M
　PROGRESSIVE STUDIES, VOL. 3
　　C. F. PETERS CORPORATION　　　　SCH32　　2.00
FERTE--ED　　　　　FERTE　　　M
　PROGRESSIVE STUDIES, VOL. 4
　　C. F. PETERS CORPORATION　　　　SCH33　　2.00
FERTE--ED　　　　　FERTE　　　M
　PROGRESSIVE STUDIES, VOL. 5
　　C. F. PETERS CORPORATION　　　　SCH34　　2.00
FERTE--ED　　　　　FERTE　　　M
　PROGRESSIVE STUDIES, VOL. 6
　　C. F. PETERS CORPORATION　　　　SCH35　　2.00
FERTE--ED　　　　　FERTE　　　M-D
　PROGRESSIVE STUDIES, VOL. 7
　　C. F. PETERS CORPORATION　　　　SCH36　　2.00
FERTE--ED　　　　　FERTE　　　M-D
　PROGRESSIVE STUDIES, VOL. 8
　　C. F. PETERS CORPORATION　　　　SCH37　　2.00
FERTE--ED　　　　　FERTE　　　D
　SPECIAL STUDIES, VOL. 1# 20 STUDIES FOR THE LEFT HAND
　　C. F. PETERS CORPORATION　　　　SCH38　　2.00
FERTE--ED　　　　　FERTE　　　D
　SPECIAL STUDIES, VOL. 2# 20 STUDIES FOR BOTH HANDS
　　C. F. PETERS CORPORATION　　　　SCH39　　2.00
FERTE--ED　　　　　FERTE　　　D
　SPECIAL STUDIES, VOL. 3# 20 OCTAVE STUDIES
　　C. F. PETERS CORPORATION　　　　SCH40　　2.00
FERTE　　　　　　　　　　M
　PIANO METHOD. FRENCH TEXT
　　C. F. PETERS CORPORATION　　　　SCH15　　3.50
FERTE　　　　　　　　　　M
　PIANO METHOD
　　C. F. PETERS CORPORATION　　　　SCH16　　3.50
FLAGELLO, N.
　EPISODES
　　GENERAL MUSIC PUBLISHING COMPANY, INC.　51　　2.00
FLAGELLO, N.
　PETITS PASTELS - SEVEN DRAWINGS FOR THE YOUNG PIANIST
　　GENERAL MUSIC PUBLISHING COMPANY, INC.　530　　2.00

FLETCHER, S.
　TECHNIC KNACKS
　　PEER SOUTHERN ORGANIZATION　　　　　　01.25
FLOOD
　RELATIVE TALE OF TRIAD AND SCALE, THE, OP. 20
　　FRANCO COLOMBO PUBLICATIONS　　　NY1624　　1.00
FONTRIEPE, G.
　LITTLE SUITE FOR PIANO
　　GENERAL MUSIC PUBLISHING COMPANY, INC.　61　　1.50
FRUGATTA
　TOUCH - EXERCISES ON 5 NOTES, BK. 1
　　FRANCO COLOMBO PUBLICATIONS　　　ER2416　　.90
FRUGATTA
　TOUCH - EXERCISES ON 5 NOTES, BK. 2
　　FRANCO COLOMBO PUBLICATIONS　　　ER2417　　.75
FULEIHAN, A.
　SEVEN SUPPLEMENTARY EXERCISES
　　PEER SOUTHERN ORGANIZATION　　　　　　00.85
FUSSL, K.
　FIVE TONES, FIVE FINGERS
　　UNIVERSAL EDITION　　　　　　　UE 13679E　3.50
GANZ
　EXERCISES FOR PIANO
　　SUMMY-BIRCHARD COMPANY　　　　　　　　4.00
GARTENLAUB, O.
　PETITE ETUDE POUR LES MAINS ALTERNEES
　　ELKAN-VOGEL, INC.　　　　　　　　RR　　1.20
GARTENLAUB, O.
　PETITE ETUDE POUR LES TIERCES
　　ELKAN-VOGEL, INC.　　　　　　　　RR　　1.20
GENZMER　　　　　　　　　　E
　STUDIES, VOL. 1. ELEVEN PIECES
　　C. F. PETERS CORPORATION　　　　5929A　　2.50
GENZMER　　　　　　　　　　M-D
　STUDIES, VOL. 2. TEN PIECES
　　C. F. PETERS CORPORATION　　　　5929B　　2.50
GLOVER, D. *　　　　　1
　CHORDS AND KEYS
　　BELWIN-MILLS PUBLISHING CORPORATION　FDL 338　2.00
GLOVER, D. *　　　　　2
　CHORDS AND KEYS
　　BELWIN-MILLS PUBLISHING CORPORATION　FDL 389　2.00
GLOVER, D. *　　　　　4
　PIANO APPEGGIOS
　　BELWIN-MILLS PUBLISHING CORPORATION　FDL 334　2.00
GLOVER, D. *　　　　　1
　PIANO TECHNIC
　　BELWIN-MILLS PUBLISHING CORPORATION　FDL 318　1.75
GLOVER, D. *　　　　　2
　PIANO TECHNIC
　　BELWIN-MILLS PUBLISHING CORPORATION　FDL 332　1.75
GLOVER, D. *　　　　　3
　PIANO TECHNIC
　　BELWIN-MILLS PUBLISHING CORPORATION　FDL 328　1.75
GLOVER, D.　　　　　　4
　PIANO TECHNIC
　　BELWIN-MILLS PUBLISHING CORPORATION　FDL 333　1.75
GLOVER, D.　　　　　　5
　PIANO TECHNIC
　　BELWIN-MILLS PUBLISHING CORPORATION　FDL 470　2.00
GLOVER, D.　　　　　　6
　PIANO TECHNIC
　　BELWIN-MILLS PUBLISHING CORPORATION　FDL 475　2.00
GLOVER, D. *　　　　　2
　WRITE AND PLAY MAJOR SCALES
　　BELWIN-MILLS PUBLISHING CORPORATION　FDL 324　1.75
GLOVER, D. *　　　　　3
　WRITE AND PLAY MINOR SCALES
　　BELWIN-MILLS PUBLISHING CORPORATION　FDL 329　1.75
GODOWSKY, L.　　　　　　D
　FIFTY-THREE STUDIES BASED ON 26 CHOPIN ETUDES, VOL. 1
　　C. F. PETERS CORPORATION　　　　R190　　7.50
GODOWSKY, L.　　　　　　D
　FIFTY-THREE STUDIES BASED ON 26 CHOPIN ETUDES, VOL. 2
　　C. F. PETERS CORPORATION　　　　R191　　7.50
GODOWSKY, L.　　　　　　D
　FIFTY-THREE STUDIES BASED ON 26 CHOPIN ETUDES, VOL. 3
　　C. F. PETERS CORPORATION　　　　R192　　7.50
GODOWSKY, L.　　　　　　D
　FIFTY-THREE STUDIES BASED ON 26 CHOPIN ETUDES, VOL. 4
　　C. F. PETERS CORPORATION　　　　R173　　7.50
GODOWSKY, L.　　　　　　D
　FIFTY-THREE STUDIES BASED ON 26 CHOPIN ETUDES, VOL. 5
　　C. F. PETERS CORPORATION　　　　R194　　7.50
GOLDBERGER, D.--ED. *　　GOLDBERGER, D. *
　ETUDE BOOK 1
　　CONSOLIDATED MUSIC PUBLISHERS, INC.　040115　1.25
GOLDBERGER, D.--ED. *　　GOLDBERGER, D. *
　ETUDE BOOK 2
　　CONSOLIDATED MUSIC PUBLISHERS, INC.　040116　1.25
GOLDBERGER, D.--ED. *　　GOLDBERGER, D. *
　ETUDE BOOK 3
　　CONSOLIDATED MUSIC PUBLISHERS, INC.　040117　1.25
GOLDMAN, R.
　ETUDE ON WHITE KEYS
　　THEODORE PRESSER COMPANY　　　　　　MD
GRINDEA, C.
　FIRST TEN LESSONS, THE - A MANUAL FOR TEACHERS
　　OXFORD UNIVERSITY PRESS　　　　39.609　　2.10
GUARALDI
　PEANUTS KEYBOARD FUN SERIES - CHARLIE BROWN ALL STARS
　　POINTER PUBLICATIONS　　　　　　　　2.95
GUARALDI
　PEANUTS KEYBOARD FUN SERIES - IT'S THE GREAT PUMPKIN, CHARLIE
　BROWN
　　POINTER PUBLICATIONS　　　　　　　　2.95
GUAPALDI
　PEANUTS KEYBOARD FUN SERIES - IT WAS A SHORT SUMMER, CHARLIE
　BROWN
　　POINTER PUBLICATIONS　　　　　　　　2.95
GUARALDI
　PEANUTS KEYBOARD FUN SERIES - YOU'RE IN LOVE, CHARLIE BROWN
　　POINTER PUBLICATIONS　　　　　　　　2.95
GUERRINI, G.　　　　　FLORIS
　NINETEEN STUDIES
　　FRANCO COLOMBO PUBLICATIONS　　　ER1947　　2.25
GURLITT
　BUDS AND BLOSSOMS, OP. 107--12 MELODIOUS STUDIES
　　G. SCHIRMER, INC.　　　　　　　　L323　　.75
GURLITT
　EASIEST STUDIES IN VELOCITY, OP. 83
　　G. SCHIRMER, INC.　　　　　　　　L536　　1.00
GURLITT
　SCHOOL OF VELOCITY, OP. 141--24 SHORT STUDIES FOR BEGINNERS
　　G. SCHIRMER, INC.　　　　　　　　L326　　1.00

GURLITT
THIRTY-FIVE EASY STUDIES WITHOUT OCTAVES, OP. 130
G. SCHIRMER, INC.　　　　　L339　　1.25

GURLITT
TWENTY-FOUR EASY MELODIOUS STUDIES, OP. 50
G. SCHIRMER, INC.　　　　　L798　　1.00

GURLITT
TWENTY-FOUR MELODIOUS AND PROGRESSIVE STUDIES, OP. 131
G. SCHIRMER, INC.　　　　　L206　　1.50

GURLITT
TWENTY-FOUR MELODIOUS STUDIES OF MEDUIM DIFFICULTY, OP. 51
G. SCHIRMER, INC.　　　　　L801　　1.00

GURLITT
TWENTY-FOUR OCTAVE-STUDIES, OP. 100
G. SCHIRMER, INC.　　　　　L539　　1.00

GURLITT
TWENTY-FOUR STUDIES ON SCALES AND ARPEGGIOS, OP. 85
G. SCHIRMER, INC.　　　　　L807　　1.00

GURLITT　　　　　　　　　　　　　　　　　1
VIER UND FUNFZIG KLAVIUR MEL. ETUDEN OP. 187
SCHOTT　　　　　　　　　　　233　　2.00

HABERBIER, E.　　　　PARSONS
MODERN FINGER GYMNASTICS
G. SCHIRMER, INC.　　　　　　　　　.75

HALL　　　　　　　　　　　　　　　　D
ETUDE FOR PIANO
C. F. PETERS CORPORATION　　H273　　1.25

HANKINSON, R.
POP, GOES THE PIANO, BK. 1
GENERAL MUSIC PUBLISHING COMPANY, INC.　553　2.50

HANKINSON, R.
POP, GOES THE PIANO, BK. 2
GENERAL MUSIC PUBLISHING COMPANY, INC.　554　2.50

HANKINSON, R.
POP, GOES THE PIANO, BK. 3
GENERAL MUSIC PUBLISHING COMPANY, INC.　555　2.50

HANKINSON, R.
POP, GOES THE PIANO, BK. 4
GENERAL MUSIC PUBLISHING COMPANY, INC.　733　2.50

HANON, C.　　　　　　BRIMHALL, J.
FIRST BOOK OF HANON
CHARLES HANSEN　　　　　H404　　1.50

HANON, C.　　　　　　SCHAUM, J.　　1 1/2
HANON-SCHAUM, BK.1
BELWIN-MILLS PUBLISHING CORPORATION　　1.50

HANON, C.　　　　　　SCHAUM, J.　　2 1/2
HANON-SCHAUM, BK.2
BELWIN-MILLS PUBLISHING CORPORATION　　1.50

HANON, C.　　　　　　BEZDEK
HANON PREPARATORY BOOK
WILLIS MUSIC COMPANY　　　　　1.25

HANON, C.　　　　　　BRIMHALL, J.
HANON THROUGH THE KEYS
CHARLES HANSEN　　　　　H405　　1.50

HANON, C.　　　　　　MONTANARI
IL PIANISTA VIRTUOSO, 60 ESERCIZI
EDIZIONI BERBEN　　　　　1399　　4.50

HANON, C.　　　　　　SMALL, A.
JUNIOR HANON
ALFRED MUSIC COMPANY　　　518　　1.25

HANON, C.　　　　　　STEINER
JUNIOR HANON
BELWIN-MILLS PUBLISHING CORPORATION　1693　1.75

HANON, C.　　　　　　RING
LITTLE HANON, THE
SUMMY-BIRCHARD COMPANY　　　　1.50

HANON, C.　　　　　　BEZDEK
RHYTHMIC VARIATIONS ON HANON, BK. 1
WILLIS MUSIC COMPANY　　　　　1.50

HANON, C.　　　　　　BEZDEK
RHYTHMIC VARIATIONS ON HANON, BK. 2
WILLIS MUSIC COMPANY　　　　　1.50

HANON, C.　　　　　　LINDQUIST
TECHNICAL VARIANTS
SUMMY-BIRCHARD COMPANY　　　　1.75

HANON, C.
VIRTUOSO PIANIST. COMPLETE
CARL FISCHER, INC.　　　　L 684　　2.50

HANON, C.
VIRTUOSO PIANIST, BK. 1
CARL FISCHER, INC.　　　　L 728　　1.00

HANON, C.
VIRTUOSO PIANIST, BK. 2
CARL FISCHER, INC.　　　　L 729　　1.00

HANON, C.
VIRTUOSO PIANIST, BK. 3
CARL FISCHER, INC.　　　　L 730　　1.00

HANON, C.　　　　　　WEINREICH　　M-D
VIRTUOSO PIANIST, IN 60 EXERCISES. COMPLETE
C. F. PETERS CORPORATION　　4354　　3.50

HANON, C.　　　　　　FERTE　　M-D
VIRTUOSO PIANIST, IN 60 EXERCISES. COMPLETE
C. F. PETERS CORPORATION　　SCH143　4.00

HANON, C.　　　　　　SMALL, A.
VIRTUOSO PIANIST, THE, BK. 1
ALFRED MUSIC COMPANY　　　617　　1.00

HANON, C.　　　　　　SMALL, A.
VIRTUOSO PIANIST, THE, BK. 2
ALFRED MUSIC COMPANY　　　682　　1.50

HANON, C.
VIRTUOSO PIANIST, THE, BK. 1
BELWIN-MILLS PUBLISHING CORPORATION　　1.00

HANON, C.
VIRTUOSO PIANIST, THE, BK. 1
G. SCHIRMER, INC.　　　　L1071　　.85

HANON, C.
VIRTUOSO PIANIST, THE, BK. 1
THEODORE PRESSER COMPANY　　　1.00

HANON, C.
VIRTUOSO PIANIST, THE, BK. 2
G. SCHIRMER, INC.　　　　L1072　　.85

HANON, C.
VIRTUOSO PIANIST, THE, BK. 3
G. SCHIRMER, INC.　　　　L1073　　.85

HANON, C.
VIRTUOSO PIANIST, THE, BK. 3
THEODORE PRESSER COMPANY　　　.75

HANON, C.　　　　　　SMALL, A.
VIRTUOSO PIANIST, THE, COMPLETE
ALFRED MUSIC COMPANY　　　616　　2.50

HANON, C.
VIRTUOSO PIANIST, THE --COMPLETE--
THEODORE PRESSER COMPANY　　　2.00

HANON, C.　　　　　　POZZOLI
VIRTUOSO PIANISTS, THE
FRANCO COLOMBO PUBLICATIONS　ER381　2.75

HANON, C.
VIRTUOSO PIANIST IN SEVENTEEN EXERCISES, BK. 3
WILLIS MUSIC COMPANY　　　　.85

HANON, C.
VIRTUOSO PIANIST IN SIXTY EXERCISES, COMPLETE
WILLIS MUSIC COMPANY　　　　2.00

HANON, C.
VIRTUOSO PIANIST IN TWENTY-TWO EXERCISES, BK. 2
WILLIS MUSIC COMPANY　　　　.85

HANON, C.
VIRTUOSO PIANIST IN TWENTY EXERCISES, BK. 1
WILLIS MUSIC COMPANY　　　　.85

HANON, C.
VIRTUOSO PIANIST IN 60 EXERCISES, THE
G. SCHIRMER, INC.　　　　L925　　2.00

HANON, C.
VIRTUOSO PIANIST IN 60 EXERSICES, THE--IN SPANISH
G. SCHIRMER, INC.　　　　L1081　　2.00

HANON, C.　　　　　　FERTE　　E-M
YOUNG VIRTUOSO PIANIST, IN 40 EXERCISES
C. F. PETERS CORPORATION　　SCH84　　3.50

HANON　　　　　　　　ZEPP
HANON IN ALL KEYS
PRO-ART PUBLICATIONS, INC.　　309　　.85

HANUS, J.
MUSIC OF NATURE, THE
GENERAL MUSIC PUBLISHING COMPANY, INC.　728　3.00

HAUER, J.
STUDIES, OP. 22, BK. 1
UNIVERSAL EDITION　　　UE 8381A　3.25

HAUER, J.
STUDIES, OP. 22, BK. 2
UNIVERSAL EDITION　　　UE 8381B　3.75

HEISS
GYMNASTIK AUF TASTEN -- EXERCISES IN FINGER AND HAND POSITION
ASSOCIATED MUSIC PUBLISHERS, INC.　BRH　2.25

HELLER, S.
ART OF PHRASING, THE--26 MELODIOUS STUDIES, OP. 16--BK. 1
G. SCHIRMER, INC.　　　　L179　　1.25

HELLER, S.
ART OF PHRASING, THE--26 MELODIOUS STUDIES, OP. 16--BK. 2
G. SCHIRMER, INC.　　　　L180　　1.25

HELLER, S.　　　　　　OESTERLE
FIFTY SELECTED STUDIES--FROM OP. 45, 46, 47
G. SCHIRMER, INC.　　　　L24　　2.00

HELLER, S.　　　　　　OESTERLE
THIRTY PROGRESSIVE STUDIES, OP. 46--BK. 1
G. SCHIRMER, INC.　　　　L1120　　.75

HELLER, S.　　　　　　ANDREOLI
THIRTY PROGRESSIVE STUDIES, OP. 46
FRANCO COLOMBO PUBLICATIONS　ER702　2.50

HELLER, S.　　　　　　　　　　M-D
THIRTY PROGRESSIVE STUDIES, OP. 46
C. F. PETERS CORPORATION　　3562　　2.50

HELLER, S.　　　　　　OESTERLE
THIRTY PROGRESSIVE STUDIES, OP. 46
G. SCHIRMER, INC.　　　　L177　　1.25

HELLER, S.　　　　　　OESTERLE
TWENTY-FIVE MELODIOUS STUDIES, OP. 45--BK. 1, NOS. 1-9
G. SCHIRMER, INC.　　　　L1117　　.75

HELLER, S.　　　　　　TEICHMUELLER　E-M
TWENTY-FIVE MELODIOUS STUDIES, OP. 45
C. F. PETERS CORPORATION　　3561A　　2.00

HELLER, S.　　　　　　OESTERLE
TWENTY-FIVE MELODIOUS STUDIES, OP. 45
G. SCHIRMER, INC.　　　　L176　　1.50

HELLER, S.　　　　　　　　　　M-D
TWENTY-FIVE STUDIES, OP. 47
C. F. PETERS CORPORATION　　3563　　2.00

HELLER, S.
TWENTY-FIVE STUDIES, OP. 47
THEODORE PRESSER COMPANY　　　1.00

HELLER, S.　　　　　　OESTERLE
TWENTY-FIVE STUDIES FOR RHYTHM AND EXPRESSION, OP. 47--BK. 1
G. SCHIRMER, INC.　　　　L1123　　1.00

HELLER, S.　　　　　　ANDREOLI
TWENTY-FIVE STUDIES FOR RHYTHM AND EXPRESSION, OP. 47
FRANCO COLOMBO PUBLICATIONS　ER426　1.50

HELLER, S.　　　　　　OESTERLE
TWENTY-FIVE STUDIES FOR RHYTHM AND EXPRESSION, OP. 47
G. SCHIRMER, INC.　　　　L178　　1.25

HELLER, S.　　　　　　ANDREOLI
TWENTY-FIVE STUDIES FROM OP. 46
FRANCO COLOMBO PUBLICATIONS　ER425　1.75

HELLER, S.　　　　　　PICCIOLI
TWENTY-FIVE STUDIES FROM OP. 46
FRANCO COLOMBO PUBLICATIONS　BON.2158　2.50

HELLER, S.　　　　　　　　　　M
TWENTY-FIVE STUDIES OF RHYTHM AND EXPRESSION, OP. 47
CENTURY MUSIC PUBLISHING COMPANY, INC.　1.00

HELLER, S.
TWENTY-FOUR MELODIOUS STUDIES, OP. 125
C. F. PETERS CORPORATION　　4364　　2.50

HELLER, S.　　　　　　TAGLIAPIETRA
TWENTY-FOUR STUDIES FOR RHYTHM AND EXPRESSION, OP. 125
FRANCO COLOMBO PUBLICATIONS　ER432　1.75

HELLER, S.　　　　　　SCHARFENBERG
TWENTY-FOUR STUDIES FOR RHYTHM AND EXPRESSION, OP. 125
G. SCHIRMER, INC.　　　　L766　　1.25

HELLER, S　　　　　　PICCIOLI
TWENTY-FIVE STUDIES FOR RHYTHM AND EXPRESSION, OP. 47
FRANCO COLOMBO PUBLICATIONS　BON.2157　2.25

HELPS　　　　　　　　　　　　　　D
THREE ETUDES
C. F. PETERS CORPORATION　　6998　　1.50

HENDERSON, R.
TRANSPOSITION CHART - MAJOR KEYS
BOSTON MUSIC COMPANY　　　　.60

HENDERSON, R.
TRANSPOSITION CHART - MINOR KEYS
BOSTON MUSIC COMPANY　　　　.60

HENNES, A.　　　　　　RITTER
MELODIC EXERCISES, BK. 1
ASSOCIATED MUSIC PUBLISHERS, INC.　BRH　1.00

HENSELT, A.　　　　　　JONAS
TWELVE CHARACTERISTIC CONCERT STUDIES, OP. 2
G. SCHIRMER, INC.　　　　L44　　1.75

HERRMANN, K.--ED　　　HERRMANN, K.　　E
ETUDES BY GREAT MASTERS --DER GERADE WEG--, VOL. 1
C. F. PETERS CORPORATION　　A108　　2.00

HERRMANN, K.--ED　　　HERRMANN, K.　　E-M
ÉTUDES BY GREAT MASTERS --DER GERADE WEG--, VOL. 2
C. F. PETERS CORPORATION　　A109　　2.00

HERRMANN, K.--ED　　　HERRMANN, K.　　M
ETUDES BY GREAT MASTERS --DER GERADE WEG--, VOL. 3
C. F. PETERS CORPORATION　　A110　　2.00

HERRMANN, K.
LIVING PIANO TECHNIQUE, BK. 1
FRANCO COLOMBO PUBLICATIONS   SIK.197   2.50
HERRMANN, K.
LIVING PIANO TECHNIQUE, BK. 2
FRANCO COLOMBO PUBLICATIONS   SIK.198   2.50
HERRMANN, K.
LIVING PIANO TECHNIQUE, BK. 3
FRANCO COLOMBO PUBLICATIONS   SIK.199   2.50
HERZ, H.   TAGLIAPIETRA
COLLECTION OF EXERCISES AND SCALES
FRANCO COLOMBO PUBLICATIONS   ER737   1.75
HERZ, H.   M-D
EXERCISES AND PRELUDES, OP. 21
C. F. PETERS CORPORATION   291   3.50
HERZ, H.   CESI
EXERCISES AND SCALES
FRANCO COLOMBO PUBLICATIONS   ER51   2.25
HERZ, H.
ONE THOUSAND EXERCISES
FRANCO COLOMBO PUBLICATIONS   ER2141   3.00
HERZ, H.
SCALES AND EXERCIES
UNIVERSAL EDITION   UE 689   1.40
HERZ, H.
SCALES AND EXERCISES--IN SPANISH
G. SCHIRMER, INC.   L1083   1.25
HERZ, H.   GAMMES   D
SCALES AND EXERCISES
C. F. PETERS CORPORATION   290   2.50
HERZ, H.   VOGRICH
SCALES AND EXERCISES
G. SCHIRMER, INC.   L170   1.25
HERZ, H.
SCALES
CARL FISCHER, INC.   L 320   1.25
HILLEMANN *
FIRST PIANO BOOK, BK. 1
BARENREITER VERLAG   EN 804   2.50
HILLEMANN *
FIRST PIANO BOOK, BK. 2
BARENREITER VERLAG   EN 805   2.50
HILLEMANN *
FIRST PIANO BOOK, BK. 3
BARENREITER VERLAG   EN 806   2.50
HIRSCHBERG, D.
MY ARPEGGIO BOOK
MUSICORD PUBLICATIONS, INC.   1.25
HIRSCHBERG, D.
MY SCALE BOOK
MUSICORD PUBLICATIONS, INC.   1.00
HIRSCHBERG, D.
PIANO COURSE FOR JUNIORS, BK. 1
MUSICORD PUBLICATIONS, INC.   1.25
HIRSCHBERG, D.
PIANO COURSE FOR JUNIORS - PREPARATORY BOOK
MUSICORD PUBLICATIONS, INC.   1.25
HIRSCHBERG, D.
PIANO LESSONS ARE FUN, BK. 1
MUSICORD PUBLICATIONS, INC.   1.25
HIRSCHBERG, D.
SCALES AND CHORDS ARE FUN - BOOK 1 -- MAJOR
MUSICORD PUBLICATIONS, INC.   1.25
HIRSCHBERG, D.
SCALES AND CHORDS ARE FUN - BOOK 2 -- MINOR
MUSICORD PUBLICATIONS, INC.   1.25
HIRSCHBERG, D.   1B
SCALES FOR JUNIORS - PART 1 MAJOR
MUSICORD PUBLICATIONS, INC.   .45
HIRSCHBERG, D.   1B
SCALES FOR JUNIORS - PART 2 MINOR
MUSICORD PUBLICATIONS, INC.   .45
HIRSCHBERG, D.
TECHNIC FOR ADULTS, BK. 1
MUSICORD PUBLICATIONS, INC.   1.25
HIRSCHBERG, D.
TECHNIC IS FUN, BK. 1
MUSICORD PUBLICATIONS, INC.   1.25
HIRSCHBERG, D.
TECHNIC IS FUN, BK. 2
MUSICORD PUBLICATIONS, INC.   1.25
HIRSCHBERG, D.
TECHNIC IS FUN, BK. 3
MUSICORD PUBLICATIONS, INC.   1.25
HIRSCHBERG, D.
TECHNIC IS FUN, BK. 4
MUSICORD PUBLICATIONS, INC.   1.25
HIRSCHBERG, D.
TECHNIC IS FUN, BK. 5
MUSICORD PUBLICATIONS, INC.   1.25
HIRSCHBERG, D.
TECHNIC IS FUN - PREPARATORY BOOK
MUSICORD PUBLICATIONS, INC.   1.25
HOLT, H.--ED   HOLT, H.
CARL FISCHER NOTE SPELLER
CARL FISCHER, INC.   O 3410   1.00
HOPKINS, A.   E
FOR TALENTED BEGINNERS, BK. 1
OXFORD UNIVERSITY PRESS   39.006   1.00
HOPKINS, A.   E
FOR TALENTED BEGINNERS, BK. 2
OXFORD UNIVERSITY PRESS   39.007   1.00
HORVATH, G.
FIRST VELOCITY STUDIES
THEODORE PRESSER COMPANY   .75
HUENTEN   MUGELLINI
TWENTY-FIVE STUDIES, OP. 114
FRANCO COLOMBO PUBLICATIONS   ER1438   2.50
HUGOUNENC
MECANISME ET VIRTUOSITE DU PIANISTE
FRANCO COLOMBO PUBLICATIONS   SAL   5.75
HURE
PIANO TECHNIQUE
FRANCO COLOMBO PUBLICATIONS   SAL   4.00
IRWIN--ED.   IRWIN
BILL IRWIN'S MAGIC STUDY SERIES - DIMINISHED CHORD MAGIC
POINTER PUBLICATIONS   2.50
IRWIN--ED.   IRWIN
BILL IRWIN'S MAGIC STUDY SERIES - MODERN FILL MAGIC
POINTER PUBLICATIONS   2.50
IRWIN--ED.   IRWIN
BILL IRWIN'S MAGIC STUDY SERIES - MODERN MELODY MAGIC
POINTER PUBLICATIONS   2.50
IRWIN--ED.   IRWIN
BILL IRWIN'S MAGIS STUDY SERIES - RHYTHM ACCOMPANIMENT MAGIC
POINTER PUBLICATIONS   2.50

JENSEN, A.   M-D
STUDIES, OP. 32, VOL. 1, NOS. 1-8
C. F. PETERS CORPORATION   1317A   2.00
JENSEN, A.   M-D
STUDIES, OP. 32, VOL. 1, NOS. 9-18
C. F. PETERS CORPORATION   2.00
JENSEN, A.   M-D
STUDIES, OP. 32, VOL. 3, NOS. 19-25
C. F. PETERS CORPORATION   1317C   2.00
JENSEN, A.
TWENTY-FIVE ETUDES, OP. 32--PRELIMINARY STUDIES TO THE WORKS OF
THE MODERN SCHOOL--BK. 1
G. SCHIRMER, INC.   L763   .75
JENSEN, A.
TWENTY-FIVE ETUDES, OP. 32--PRELIMINARY STUDIES TO THE WORKS OF
THE MODERN SCHOOL--BK. 2
G. SCHIRMER, INC.   L764   .75
JENSEN, A.   TAGLIAPIETRA
TWENTY-FIVE STUDIES, OP. 32, BK. 1 -- 1-8 --
FRANCO COLOMBO PUBLICATIONS   ER707   1.00
JENSEN, A.   TAGLIAPIETRA
TWENTY-FIVE STUDIES, OP. 32, BK. 2 -- 9-18 --
FRANCO COLOMBO PUBLICATIONS   ER708   1.25
JENSEN, A.   TAGLIAPIETRA
TWENTY-FIVE STUDIES, OP. 32, BK. 3 -- 19-25 --
FRANCO COLOMBO PUBLICATIONS   ER709   1.25
JOSEFFY, R.
SCHOOL OF ADVANCED PIANO PLAYING
G. SCHIRMER, INC.   3.50
JOSEPHS, W.
FOURTEEN STUDIES, BK. 1
OXFORD UNIVERSITY PRESS   32.153   3.85
JOSEPHS, W.
FOURTEEN STUDIES, BK. 2
OXFORD UNIVERSITY PRESS   32.154   3.85
KABALEVSKY   MIROVITCH, A.
ETUDE, OP. 27
MCA MUSIC   .60
KADOSA
TWENTY-FOUR EASY TECHNICAL STUDIES
KULTURA   2.00
KAPP, R.
SIMPLE ETUDES FOR ADVANCED BEGINNERS
GENERAL MUSIC PUBLISHING COMPANY, INC.   161   2.50
KAPP, R.
SIMPLE ETUDES FOR ADVANCED BEGINNERS
NOVELLO AND COMPANY, LTD.   2.00
KARTUN
SYNTHETIC STUDY OF DAILY PIANO TECHNIQUE - 142 EXERCISES
LES EDITIONS OUVRIERES   7.50
KASEMETS, U.
ONE PLUS ONE-- 20 STUDIES FOR BEGINNERS
ASSOCIATED MUSIC PUBLISHERS, INC.   BER   .85
KASEMETS, U.
TWENTY PIANO STUDIES FOR BEGINNERS, BK. 1
ASSOCIATED MUSIC PUBLISHERS, INC.   BER   .85
KASSCHAU, H.--ED.   KASSCHAU, H.
ONE HUNDRED AND SIX GREATEST PIANO STUDIES, BK. 1, NOS. 1-62--IN
PROGRESSIVE ORDER
G. SCHIRMER, INC.   1.25
KASSCHAU, H.--ED.   KASSCHAU, H.
ONE HUNDRED AND SIX GREATEST PIANO STUDIES, BK. 2, NO.S
63-106--IN PROGRESSIVE ORDER
G. SCHIRMER, INC.   1.25
KESSLER   DEIS
FIFTEEN SELECTED STUDIES, OP. 20
G. SCHIRMER, INC.   L1416   2.00
KESSLER   MUGELLINI
TWENTY-FOUR STUDIES, OP. 20
FRANCO COLOMBO PUBLICATIONS   ER712   5.00
KETTERER, E.
TWENTY-EIGHT MINIATURE ETUDES
THEODORE PRESSER COMPANY   1.50
KETTERER, E.
TWENTY-EIGHT PLEASING STUDIES FOR EQUALIZATION OF THE HANDS
THEODORE PRESSER COMPANY   1.25
KING, S.
MASTER STUDIES IN MODERN STYLE
THEODORE PRESSER COMPANY   1.25
KING, S.
TEEN-AGE TECHNIC
THEODORE PRESSER COMPANY   1.25
KING *   2-3
TUNEFUL TECHNIC
ASHLEY DEALERS SERVICE, INC.   1.00
KOCH, F.
BABETTES PIANO BOOK
GENERAL MUSIC PUBLISHING COMPANY, INC.   513   2.00
KOCH, F.
TWO MINUS ONE - THE 'DO-IT-YOURSELF' COMPOSING BOOK
GENERAL MUSIC PUBLISHING COMPANY, INC.   596   2.00
KOEHLER--ED   KOEHLER   M
ETUDES, ALBUM OF, VOL. 1
C. F. PETERS CORPORATION   1967A   3.50
KOEHLER--ED   KOEHLER   M
ETUDES, ALBUM OF, VOL. 2
C. F. PETERS CORPORATION   1967B   3.50
KOEHLER   BEGINNER
CHILDREN'S EXERCISE, OP. 218
EDWIN F. KALMUS   3591   1.00
KOEHLER   BEGINNER
EASIEST STUDIES, OP. 151
EDWIN F. KALMUS   3590   1.00
KOEHLER *   ECKSTEIN
EASY VELOCITY STUDIES FROM KOEHLER-DUVERNOY--65--
CARL FISCHER, INC.   O 3813   1.25
KOEHLER   MARCIANO
EXERCISES AND MELODIES FOR CHILDREN, OP. 218
FRANCO COLOMBO PUBLICATIONS   ER27   .75
KOEHLER   BEGINNER
FIRST STUDIES, OP. 50
EDWIN F. KALMUS   3592   1.00
KOEHLER   E
FIRST STUDIES, OP. 50
C. F. PETERS CORPORATION   3521   2.50
KOEHLER
FIRST STUDIES, OP. 50
G. SCHIRMER, INC.   L317   1.00
KOEHLER
FORTY CHILDREN'S EXERCISES AND MELODIES, OP. 218
G. SCHIRMER, INC.   L490   1.00
KOEHLER   PHILIPP
LA VIRTUOSITE, VOL.1
GERARD BILLAUDOT EDITIONS MUSICALES   4.40
KOEHLER   PHILIPP
LA VIRTUOSITE, VOL.2,BK.1--EXERCISES--
GERARD BILLAUDOT EDITIONS MUSICALES   4.90

KOEHLER   PHILIPP
   LA VIRTUOSITE, VOL.2,BK.2--OCTAVES--
      GERARD BILLAUDOT EDITIONS MUSICALES   4.40
KOEHLER   PHILIPP
   LA VIRTUOSITE, VOL.3,BK.1
      GERARD BILLAUDOT EDITIONS MUSICALES   4.40
KOEHLER   PHILIPP
   LA VIRTUOSITE, VOL.3,BK.2
      GERARD BILLAUDOT EDITIONS MUSICALES   4.90
KOEHLER
   LITTLE PIANISTS, OP. 189 - 40 RECREATIONS
      FRANCO COLOMBO PUBLICATIONS   ER12   1.00
KOEHLER
   METODO PRACTICO, OP. 249, BK. 1--IN SPANISH AND ENGLISH
      G. SCHIRMER, INC.   L1082   1.25
KOEHLER   POZZOLI
   NEW SCHOOL OF VELOCITY, OP. 128
      FRANCO COLOMBO PUBLICATIONS   ER181   1.50
KOEHLER
   PRACTICAL METHOD, OP. 249. BK. 1
      CARL FISCHER, INC.   O 305   1.00
KOEHLER
   PRACTICAL METHOD, OP. 249. BK. 2
      CARL FISCHER, INC.   O 306   1.00
KOEHLER
   PRACTICAL METHOD, OP. 249. BK. 3
      CARL FISCHER, INC.   O 307   1.00
KOEHLER
   PRACTICAL METHOD, OP. 249. BK. 1--IN SPANISH, ENGLISH, AND
   FRENCH
      G. SCHIRMER, INC.   .75
KOEHLER
   PRACTICAL METHOD, OP. 249. BK. 2--IN SPANISH, ENGLISH, AND
   FRENCH
      G. SCHIRMER, INC.   .75
KOEHLER
   PRACTICAL METHOD, OP. 249. BK. 3--IN SPANISH, ENGLISH, AND
   FRENCH
      G. SCHIRMER, INC.   .75
KOEHLER
   PRACTICAL METHOD, OP. 249. BK. 4--IN SPANISH, ENGLISH, AND
   FRENCH
      G. SCHIRMER, INC.   .75
KOEHLER
   PRACTICAL METHOD, OP. 300, BK. 1
      G. SCHIRMER, INC.   L935   1.50
KOEHLER
   PRACTICAL METHOD, OP. 300, BK. 2
      G. SCHIRMER, INC.   L936   1.50
KOEHLER   E-M
   PRACTICAL METHOD FOR PIANO, OP. 300, VOL. 1
      C. F. PETERS CORPORATION   1969A   3.00
KOEHLER   E-M
   PRACTICAL METHOD FOR PIANO, OP. 300, VOL. 2
      C. F. PETERS CORPORATION   1969B   3.00
KOEHLER   M-D
   SCHOOL OF THE LEFT HAND, OP. 302
      C. F. PETERS CORPORATION   2033   6.00
KOEHLER   M
   SHORT SCHOOL OF VELOCITY, OP. 242
      C. F. PETERS CORPORATION   3526   2.50
KOEHLER
   SHORT SCHOOL OF VELOCITY WITHOUT OCTAVES, OP. 242
      G. SCHIRMER, INC.   L321   1.00
KOEHLER
   SIXTEEN ELEMENTARY STUDIES, OP. 163
      G. SCHIRMER, INC.   L196   .75
KOEHLER
   SIXTEEN STUDIES OF MODERATE DIFFICULTY, OP. 224
      FRANCO COLOMBO PUBLICATIONS   ER13
KOEHLER
   TWELVE EASIEST STUDIES, OP. 151
      G. SCHIRMER, INC.   L318   1.00
KOEHLER
   TWELVE EASY STUDIES, OP. 157
      G. SCHIRMER, INC.   L425   .75
KOEHLER
   TWELVE EASY STUDIES OP. 157
      WILLIS MUSIC COMPANY   .60
KOEHLER
   TWELVE LITTLE STUDIES, OP. 157
      CARL FISCHER, INC.   L 380   1.00
KOEHLER
   TWELVE LITTLE STUDIES FOR DEVELOPMENT OF VELOCITY, OP. 157
      FRANCO COLOMBO PUBLICATIONS   ER11   1.00
KOEHLER
   TWENTY EASY STUDIES, OP. 159
      FRANCO COLOMBO PUBLICATIONS   ER743   .75
KOEHLER
   TWENTY STUDIES IN CONTINUOUS SCALE AND CHORD PASSAGES, OP. 60
      G. SCHIRMER, INC.   L543   1.00
KOEHLER
   VELOCITY STUDIES, BK. 3 --21-30--, OP. 173
      FRANCO COLOMBO PUBLICATIONS   ER744   1.50
KOEHLER
   VERY EASIEST EXERCISES, OP. 190
      CARL FISCHER, INC.   L 381   1.00
KOEHLER   BEGINNER
   VERY EASIEST STUDIES, THE, OP. 190
      EDWIN F. KALMUS   3589   1.00
KOEHLER
   VERY EASIEST STUDIES, THE, OP. 190
      G. SCHIRMER, INC.   L480   .75
KOEHLER   POZZOLI
   VERY FIRST STUDIES, OP. 190
      FRANCO COLOMBO PUBLICATIONS   ER536   1.00
KOHLER, F.   2
   KOHLER'S SCALES AND CHORDS
      CENTURY MUSIC PUBLISHING COMPANY, INC. 1312   .40
KOHLER, F.
   SCALES AND CHORDS
      VOLKWEIN BROS.   .35
KOHLER, F.   PALMER, W. A.
   SHORT SCHOOL OF VELOCITY
      ALFRED MUSIC COMPANY   628   1.25
KOUGELL, A.
   EIGHT PIECES IN THE FORM OF ETUDES
      ASSOCIATED MUSIC PUBLISHERS, INC.   ESC   3.25
KRAUSE, A.
   TEN TRILL STUDIES, OP. 2
      G. SCHIRMER, INC.   L553   .75
KRAWITZ, I. *
   HOW TO TEACH RHYTHMS AND RHYTHM BANDS -- FIFTEEN LESSONS IN
   FUNDAMENTAL RHYTHMIC TRAINING
      G. SCHIRMER, INC.   1.50

KUEHNER, C.   LOWER ELEMENTARY GRADE
   SCHOOL OF ETUDES, BK. 1
      G. SCHIRMER, INC.   L481   1.50
KUEHNER, C.   HIGHER ELEMENTARY GRADE
   SCHOOL OF ETUDES, BK. 2
      G. SCHIRMER, INC.   L482   1.50
KUEHNER, C.   LOWER MEDIUM GRADE
   SCHOOL OF ETUDES, BK. 3
      G. SCHIRMER, INC.   L483   1.50
KULLAK, T.
   SCHOOL OF OCTAVE-PLAYING, THE--OP. 48--BK. 1, PRELIMINARY SCHOOL
      G. SCHIRMER, INC.   L475   1.00
KULLAK, T.
   SCHOOL OF OCTAVE-PLAYING, THE--OP. 48--BK. 2, SEVEN
   OCTAVE-STUDIES
      G. SCHIRMER, INC.   L476   1.25
KULLAK, T.   SAUER   M-D
   SCHOOL OF OCTAVES, OP. 48. VOL. 1
      C. F. PETERS CORPORATION   3273A   2.75
KULLAK, T.   SAUER   D
   SCHOOL OF OCTAVES, OP. 48. VOL. 2
      C. F. PETERS CORPORATION   3273B   2.75
KULLAK, T.   SAUER   D
   SCHOOL OF OCTAVES, OP. 48. VOL. 3
      C. F. PETERS CORPORATION   3273C   3.00
KULLAK, T.   POZZOLI
   SCHOOL OF OCTAVE PLAYING, BK. 1
      FRANCO COLOMBO PUBLICATIONS   ER700   1.75
KULLAK, T.   POZZOLI
   SCHOOL OF OCTAVE PLAYING, BK. 2
      FRANCO COLOMBO PUBLICATIONS   ER701   1.75
KULLAK, T.   POZZOLI
   SCHOOL OF OCTAVE PLAYING, BK. 3
      FRANCO COLOMBO PUBLICATIONS   ER1214   1.75
LAKE
   DAILY DOZEN - BOOK 1
      BOSTON MUSIC COMPANY   1.25
LAKE
   DAILY DOZEN - BOOK 2
      BOSTON MUSIC COMPANY   1.25
LANE, J.
   EASY APPROACH TO THE PIANO, BK. 1
      THE BIG THREE MUSIC CORPORATION   02.50
LANE, J.
   EASY APPROACH TO THE PIANO, BK. 2
      THE BIG THREE MUSIC CORPORATION   02.50
LAST, J.
   AT THE KEYBOARD, BK. 1
      OXFORD UNIVERSITY PRESS   39.601   1.00
LAST, J.
   AT THE KEYBOARD, BK. 2
      OXFORD UNIVERSITY PRESS   39.602   1.00
LAST, J.
   AT THE KEYBOARD, BK. 3
      OXFORD UNIVERSITY PRESS   39.603   1.25
LAST, J.
   AT THE KEYBOARD, BK. 4
      OXFORD UNIVERSITY PRESS   39.604   1.25
LAURENT
   JAZZ PIANO TECHNIQUE
      FRANCO COLOMBO PUBLICATIONS   SAL   5.00
LAYTON, B.
   THREE STUDIES FOR PIANO, OP. 5
      G. SCHIRMER, INC.   2.00
LEBERT, S. *
   TEORICA Y PRACTICA ESCUELA DE PIANO, PARTE 2--EJERCICIOS Y
   ESTUDIOS, SEGUNDO GRADO
      G. SCHIRMER, INC.   2.00
LEBERT, S.   IVALDI
   THEORETICAL AND PRACTICAL METHOD, BK. 1
      FRANCO COLOMBO PUBLICATIONS   ER130   2.75
LEBERT, S.   IVALDI
   THEORETICAL AND PRACTICAL METHOD, BK. 2
      FRANCO COLOMBO PUBLICATIONS   ER131   2.75
LEBERT, S.   IVALDI
   THEORETICAL AND PRACTICAL METHOD, BK. 3
      FRANCO COLOMBO PUBLICATIONS   ER132   5.50
LEBERT, S.   MONTANI
   THEORETICAL AND PRACTICAL METHOD - ABRIDGED EDITION IN ONE
   VOLUME
      FRANCO COLOMBO PUBLICATIONS   ER2412   3.00
LEBERT, S. *
   THEORETICAL AND PRACTICAL PIANO-SCHOOL, PART 2--EXERCISES AND
   ETUDES, SECOND DEGREE
      G. SCHIRMER, INC.   2.00
LEBERT, S. *
   THEORETICAL AND PRACTICAL PIANO-SCHOOL, PART 3--EXERCISES AND
   ETUDES, THIRD DEGREE
      G. SCHIRMER, INC.   3.00
LECARPENTIER, A.   GUARINONI
   ELEMENTARY PRACTICAL COURSE, BK. 1 - PRINCIPLES OF MUSIC AND OF
   THE PIANO
      FRANCO COLOMBO PUBLICATIONS   ER1547   2.75
LECARPENTIER, A.   DE GUARINONI
   ELEMENTARY PRACTICAL COURSE, BK. 2 - 25 STUDIES AND 12
   RECREATIONS
      FRANCO COLOMBO PUBLICATIONS   ER1548   2.25
LECARPENTIER, A.
   METHODE DE PIANO POUR LES ENFANTS
      GERARD BILLAUDOT EDITIONS MUSICALES   2.50
LECOUPPEY, F.   SCHARFENBERG
   ALPHABET, THE--25 VERY EASY STUDIES FOR SMALL HANDS--OP. 17
      G. SCHIRMER, INC.   L430   1.25
LECOUPPEY, F.   KLENGEL
   ALPHABET, THE, OP. 17   25 VERY EASY STUDIES
      ASSOCIATED MUSIC PUBLISHERS, INC.   BRH   1.00
LECOUPPEY, F.
   FIFTEEN PREPARATORY STUDIES TO CZERNY'S 'SCHOOL OF
   VELOCITY'--OP. 26
      G. SCHIRMER, INC.   L69   1.00
LECOUPPEY, F.
   FIFTEEN STUDIES, OP. 26
      FRANCO COLOMBO PUBLICATIONS   BA8936   1.50
LECOUPPEY, F.
   L'AGILITE--25 PROGRESSIVE STUDIES FOR MECHANISM AND LIGHT
   TOUCH--OP. 20
      G. SCHIRMER, INC.   L67   1.25
LEMOINE, H.
   ETUDES ENFANTINES, OP. 37
      CARL FISCHER, INC.   L 323   1.50
LEMOINE, H.   E
   ETUDES ENFANTINES, OP. 37
      C. F. PETERS CORPORATION   2213   2.00
LEMOINE, H.   SCHARFENBERG
   ETUDES ENFANTINES, OP. 37
      G. SCHIRMER, INC.   L175   1.25

```
LESSARD, J.
   NEW WORLDS FOR THE YOUNG PIANIST, BK. 1
      GENERAL MUSIC PUBLISHING COMPANY, INC.    316        2.00
LESSARD, J.
   NEW WORLDS FOR THE YOUNG PIANIST, BK. 2
      GENERAL MUSIC PUBLISHING COMPANY, INC.    317        2.00
LEVINE
   KNOW YOUR SCALES
      BOSTON MUSIC COMPANY                                 1.25
LIAPUNOFF                              D
   ETUDES D'EXECUTION TRANSCENDANTE, OP. 11. VOL. 1
      C. F. PETERS CORPORATION                  ZM1172     2.50
LIAPUNOFF                              D
   ETUDES D'EXECUTION TRANSCENDANTE, OP. 11. VOL. 2
      C. F. PETERS CORPORATION                  ZM1173     2.50
LIAPUNOFF                              D
   ETUDES D'EXECUTION TRANSCENDANTE, OP. 11. VOL. 3
      C. F. PETERS CORPORATION                  ZM1174     2.50
LIAPUNOFF                              D
   ETUDES D'EXECUTION TRANSCENDANTE, OP. 11. VOL. 4
      C. F. PETERS CORPORATION                  1175       2.50
LIEBERSON, G.
   PIANO PIECES FOR ADVANCED CHILDREN OR RETARDED ADULTS 2. SIX
   TECHNICAL STUDIES -- WHICH WILL TEACH YOU NOTHING
      BELWIN-MILLS PUBLISHING CORPORATION       11379      1.75
LISZT                  BUSONI-DA MOTTA
   CONCERT ETUDE NO. 3 IN D FLAT
      ASSOCIATED MUSIC PUBLISHERS, INC.         BRH        .75
LISZT
   ETUDES D'EXECUTION TRANSCENDANTE, VOL. 1
      ASSOCIATED MUSIC PUBLISHERS, INC.         BRH        4.00
LISZT
   ETUDES D'EXECUTION TRANSCENDANTE, VOL. 1
      EDWIN F. KALMUS                           3626       1.75
LISZT
   ETUDES D'EXECUTION TRANSCENDANTE, VOL. 2
      ASSOCIATED MUSIC PUBLISHERS, INC.         BRH        4.00
LISZT
   ETUDES D'EXECUTION TRANSCENDANTE, VOL. 2
      EDWIN F. KALMUS                           3627       1.75
LISZT                  SAUER            D
   ETUDES D'EXECUTION TRANSCENDANTE
      C. F. PETERS CORPORATION                  3600C      4.50
LISZT
   ETUDE NO. 02 IN A MINOR
      ASSOCIATED MUSIC PUBLISHERS, INC.         BRH        .50
LISZT
   ETUDE NO. 12 IN B FLAT MINOR--'CHASSE NEIGE'
      ASSOCIATED MUSIC PUBLISHERS, INC.         BRH        .60
LISZT                  BUSONI-DA MOTTA
   GNOMENREIGEN--CONCERT ETUDE
      ASSOCIATED MUSIC PUBLISHERS, INC.         BRH        .75
LISZT
   PAGANINI-ETUDES--NO. 2 IN E FLAT
      ASSOCIATED MUSIC PUBLISHERS, INC.         BRH        .50
LISZT                  BUSONI
   PAGANINI-ETUDES--NO. 3 IN G-SHARP MINOR--CONCERT TRANSCRIPTION
      ASSOCIATED MUSIC PUBLISHERS, INC.         BRH        .75
LISZT
   PAGANINI-ETUDES--NO. 3 IN G-SHARP MINOR-- LA CAMPANELLA
      ASSOCIATED MUSIC PUBLISHERS, INC.         BRH        .75
LISZT
   PAGANINI-ETUDES--NO. 4 IN E
      ASSOCIATED MUSIC PUBLISHERS, INC.         BRH        .50
LISZT
   PAGANINI-ETUDES
      ASSOCIATED MUSIC PUBLISHERS, INC.         BRH        2.25
LISZT                  SAUER            D
   PAGANINI ETUDES AND FIVE OTHER CONCERT ETUDES
      C. F. PETERS CORPORATION                  3600D      3.50
LISZT
   PAGANINI STUDIES
      EDWIN F. KALMUS                           3637       1.75
LISZT
   PAYSAGE--ETUDE NO. 3
      ASSOCIATED MUSIC PUBLISHERS, INC.         BRH        .60
LISZT                  WINTERBERGER
   TECHNICAL EXERCISES, BK. 01
      FRANCO COLOMBO PUBLICATIONS               BA47       1.50
LISZT                  WINTERBERGER
   TECHNICAL EXERCISES, BK. 02
      FRANCO COLOMBO PUBLICATIONS               BA48       1.25
LISZT                  WINTERBERGER
   TECHNICAL EXERCISES, BK. 03
      FRANCO COLOMBO PUBLICATIONS               BA215      1.25
LISZT                  WINTERBERGER
   TECHNICAL EXERCISES, BK. 04
      FRANCO COLOMBO PUBLICATIONS               BA261      1.25
LISZT                  WINTERBERGER
   TECHNICAL EXERCISES, BK. 05
      FRANCO COLOMBO PUBLICATIONS               BA262      1.50
LISZT                  WINTERBERGER
   TECHNICAL EXERCISES, BK. 06
      FRANCO COLOMBO PUBLICATIONS               BA266      1.25
LISZT                  WINTERBERGER
   TECHNICAL EXERCISES, BK. 07
      FRANCO COLOMBO PUBLICATIONS               BA264      1.50
LISZT                  WINTERBERGER
   TECHNICAL EXERCISES, BK. 08
      FRANCO COLOMBO PUBLICATIONS               BA269      1.50
LISZT                  WINTERBERGER
   TECHNICAL EXERCISES, BK. 09
      FRANCO COLOMBO PUBLICATIONS               BA267      1.50
LISZT                  WINTERBERGER
   TECHNICAL EXERCISES, BK. 10
      FRANCO COLOMBO PUBLICATIONS               BA277      2.00
LISZT                  WINTERBERGER
   TECHNICAL EXERCISES, BK. 11
      FRANCO COLOMBO PUBLICATIONS               BA6089     2.00
LISZT                  WINTERBERGER
   TECHNICAL EXERCISES, BK. 12
      FRANCO COLOMBO PUBLICATIONS               BA6090     2.00
LISZT                  ESTEBAN
   TECHNICAL EXERCISES --COMPLETE--
      ALFRED MUSIC COMPANY                      630        6.00
LISZT                  HOWAT            D
   TWELVE ETUDES, VOL. 1
      C. F. PETERS CORPORATION                  H1422A     2.00
LISZT                  HOWAT            D
   TWELVE ETUDES, VOL. 2
      C. F. PETERS CORPORATION                  H1422B     2.00
LISZT                  GALLICO
   TWELVE ETUDES D'EXECUTION TRANSCENDANTE
      G. SCHIRMER, INC.                         L788       2.50
LOESCHHORN, A.                         E
   CHILDREN'S STUDIES, OP. 181, VOL. 1
      C. F. PETERS CORPORATION                  2134A      2.00

LOESCHHORN, A.                         E
   CHILDREN'S STUDIES, OP. 181, VOL. 2
      C. F. PETERS CORPORATION                  2134B      2.00
LOESCHHORN, A.                         D
   MELODIC STUDIES, OP. 38. VOL. 1
      C. F. PETERS CORPORATION                  1318A      2.00
LOESCHHORN, A.                         D
   MELODIC STUDIES, OP. 38. VOL. 2
      C. F. PETERS CORPORATION                  1318B      2.00
LOESCHHORN, A.                         D
   MELODIC STUDIES, OP. 38. VOL. 3
      C. F. PETERS CORPORATION                  1318C      2.00
LOESCHHORN, A.                         M-D
   MELODIC STUDIES, OP. 52. VOL. 1
      C. F. PETERS CORPORATION                  1319A      2.00
LOESCHHORN, A.                         M-D
   MELODIC STUDIES, OP. 52. VOL. 2
      C. F. PETERS CORPORATION                  1319B      2.00
LOESCHHORN, A.                         M-D
   MELODIC STUDIES, OP. 52. VOL. 3
      C. F. PETERS CORPORATION                  1319C      2.00
LOESCHHORN, A.
   PIANOFORTE TECHNICS--DAILY EXERCISES
      G. SCHIRMER, INC.                         L254       1.00
LOESCHHORN, A.                         BEGINNERS
   STUDIES FOR THE DEVELOPMENT OF TECHNIQUE AND EXPRESSION--PART 1,
   OP. 65--BEGINNERS--BK. 1
      G. SCHIRMER, INC.                         L310       .85
LOESCHHORN, A.                         BEGINNERS
   STUDIES FOR THE DEVELOPMENT OF TECHNIQUE AND EXPRESSION--PART 1,
   OP. 65--BEGINNERS--BK. 2
      G. SCHIRMER, INC.                         L311       .85
LOESCHHORN, A.                         BEGINNERS
   STUDIES FOR THE DEVELOPMENT OF TECHNIQUE AND EXPRESSION--PART 1,
   OP. 65--BEGINNERS--BK. 3
      G. SCHIRMER, INC.                         L312       .85
LOESCHHORN, A.                         BEGINNERS
   STUDIES FOR THE DEVELOPMENT OF TECHNIQUE AND EXPRESSION--PART 1,
   OP. 65--BEGINNERS
      G. SCHIRMER, INC.                         L966       1.50
LOESCHHORN, A.                         INTERMEDIATE
   STUDIES FOR THE DEVELOPMENT OF TECHNIQUE AND EXPRESSION--PART 2,
   OP. 66--INTERMEDIATE DEGREE--BK. 1
      G. SCHIRMER, INC.                         L313       .75
LOESCHHORN, A.                         INTERMEDIATE
   STUDIES FOR THE DEVELOPMENT OF TECHNIQUE AND EXPRESSION--PART 2,
   OP. 66--INTERMEDIATE DEGREE--BK. 2
      G. SCHIRMER, INC.                         L314       .75
LOESCHHORN, A.                         INTERMEDIATE
   STUDIES FOR THE DEVELOPMENT OF TECHNIQUE AND EXPRESSION--PART 2,
   OP. 66--INTERMEDIATE DEGREE--BK. 3
      G. SCHIRMER, INC.                         L315       .75
LOESCHHORN, A.                         INTERMEDIATE
   STUDIES FOR THE DEVELOPMENT OF TECHNIQUE AND EXPRESSION--PART 2,
   OP. 66--INTERMEDIATE DEGREE
      G. SCHIRMER, INC.                         L967       1.75
LOESCHHORN, A.                         ADVANCED
   STUDIES FOR THE DEVELOPMENT OF TECHNIQUE AND EXPRESSION--PART 3,
   OP. 67--ADVANCED
      G. SCHIRMER, INC.                         L968       1.75
LOESCHHORN, A.
   TWENTY MELODIOUS STUDIES, OP. 52
      G. SCHIRMER, INC.                         L1616      1.25
LOESCHHORN, A.         PARSONS          MEDIUM GRADE
   UNIVERSAL PIANO STUDIES--OP. 169, 170
      G. SCHIRMER, INC.                         L1615      1.50
LOESCHORN, A.
   BEGINNERS PIECES, OP. 51
      EDWIN F. KALMUS                           3646       1.75
LOEW, J.               SCHARFENBERG
   OCTAVE-STUDIES, OP. 281
      G. SCHIRMER, INC.                         L913       1.00
LOEW, J.
   TEACHER AND PUPIL, BK. 1
      EDWIN F. KALMUS                           3647       1.50
LOEW, J.
   TEACHER AND PUPIL, BK. 2
      EDWIN F. KALMUS                           3648       1.50
LONGO, A.
   FORTY MELODIOUS STUDIES FOR SMALL HANDS, OP. 43
      FRANCO COLOMBO PUBLICATIONS               ER460      1.75
LONGO, A.
   SIX OCTAVE STUDIES, OP. 48
      FRANCO COLOMBO PUBLICATIONS               ER461      1.75
LONGO, A.
   SIX STUDIES IN SIXTHS, OP. 42
      FRANCO COLOMBO PUBLICATIONS               ER459      1.50
LONGO, A.
   TWELVE STUDIES IN THIRDS, OP. 35
      FRANCO COLOMBO PUBLICATIONS               ER458      2.50
LONGO, A.
   TWENTY-FOUR LITTLE STUDIES ON ARPEGGIOS IN ALL THE MAJOR AND
   MINOR KEYS, OP. 37
      FRANCO COLOMBO PUBLICATIONS               ER1434     2.25
LONG
   PIANO TECHNIQUE -- 'LE PIANO' --
      FRANCO COLOMBO PUBLICATIONS               SAL        18.00
LOVELOCK, W.
   BEGINNERS' SCALES AND ARPEGGIOS
      BANKS AND SON LTD.                                   .80
LUBIN, E.
   START AT THE PIANO, A
      MUSIC SALES CORPORATION                   020149     2.95
LYKE *
   KEYBOARD MUSICIANSHIP - GROUP PIANO FOR ADULTS, BK. 1, 2ND ED.
   REV.
      STIPES PUBLISHING COMPANY                            5.80
LYKE *
   KEYBOARD MUSICIANSHIP - GROUP PIANO FOR ADULTS, BK. 2. 2ND ED.
   REV.
      STIPES PUBLISHING COMPANY                            6.80
MACDOWELL
   TWELVE ETUDES, OP. 39
      EDWIN F. KALMUS                           3659       1.50
MACDOWELL
   TWELVE VIRTUOSO STUDIES, OP. 46--NO. 1,    NOVELETTE
      ASSOCIATED MUSIC PUBLISHERS, INC.         AMP        .60
MACDOWELL
   TWELVE VIRTUOSO STUDIES, OP. 46--NO. 10,   MARCH WIND
      ASSOCIATED MUSIC PUBLISHERS, INC.         AMP        .60
MACDOWELL
   TWELVE VIRTUOSO STUDIES, OP. 46--NO. 11,   IMPROMPTU
      ASSOCIATED MUSIC PUBLISHERS, INC.         AMP        .60
MACDOWELL
   TWELVE VIRTUOSO STUDIES, OP. 46--NO. 12,   POLONAISE
      ASSOCIATED MUSIC PUBLISHERS, INC.         AMP        .60
```

MACDOWELL
    TWELVE VIRTUOSO STUDIES, OP. 46--NO. 2,   MOTO PERPETUO
        ASSOCIATED MUSIC PUBLISHERS, INC.   AMP   .60
MACDOWELL
    TWELVE VIRTUOSO STUDIES, OP. 46--NO. 4,   IMPROVISATION
        ASSOCIATED MUSIC PUBLISHERS, INC.   AMP   .60
MACDOWELL
    TWELVE VIRTUOSO STUDIES, OP. 46--NO. 7,   BURLESQUE
        ASSOCIATED MUSIC PUBLISHERS, INC.   AMP   .60
MACDOWELL
    TWELVE VIRTUOSO STUDIES, OP. 46
        EDWIN F. KALMUS   3660   2.00
MACFARREN, W.
    SCALE AND ARPEGGIO MANUAL
        G. SCHIRMER, INC.   L1037   2.00
MAIER, G. *
    CHILDREN'S TECHNIC BOOK
        THEODORE PRESSER COMPANY   1.00
MALOOF
    KNOW YOUR MUSIC, BK. 1
        PEER SOUTHERN ORGANIZATION   02.00
MALOOF
    KNOW YOUR MUSIC, BK. 2
        PEER SOUTHERN ORGANIZATION   01.75
MALOOF
    KNOW YOUR MUSIC, BK. 3
        PEER SOUTHERN ORGANIZATION   01.50
MALOOF
    KNOW YOUR MUSIC, BK. 4
        PEER SOUTHERN ORGANIZATION   02.50
MARTIN, G.
    MARTIN'S MAJOR AND MINOR SCALES AND PRINCIPAL CHORDS
        CENTURY MUSIC PUBLISHING COMPANY, INC.   1.25
MARTIN
    MARTIN'S MAJOR AND MINOR SCALES AND PRINCIPAL CHORDS
        ASHLEY DEALERS SERVICE, INC.   1.25
MAYER *
    DER PRAKTISCHE CZERNY, STUDIEN UND ETUDEN AUS DEM GES. SHAFFEN
    -- BK. 1 VORSTUFE
        SCHOTT   3721   2.25
MAYER *
    DER PRAKTISCHE CZERNY, STUDIEN UND ETUDEN AUS DEM GES. SHAFFEN
    -- BK. 2 UNTERSTUFE
        SCHOTT   3722   2.25
MAYER *
    DER PRAKTISCHE CZERNY, STUDIEN UND ETUDEN AUS DEM GES. SHAFFEN
    -- BK. 3 UNTERE MITTELSTUFE
        SCHOTT   3723   2.25
MAYER *
    DER PRAKTISCHE CZERNY, STUDIEN UND ETUDEN AUS DEM GES. SHAFFEN
    -- BK. 4 MITTELSTUFE
        SCHOTT   33724   2.25
MAYER *
    DER PRAKTISCHE CZERNY, STUDIEN UND ETUDEN AUS DEM GES. SHAFFEN
    -- BK. 5 HOHERE MITTELSTUFE
        SCHOTT   3725   2.25
MCGINLEY
    CHORDS AND MELODIES - CHRISTMAS SONGS TO ARRANGE
        SHAWNEE PRESS, INC.   1.00
MCGINLEY
    CHORDS AND MELODIES - TUNES YOU KNOW
        SHAWNEE PRESS, INC.   1.00
MCGINLEY
    CHORDS AND MELODIES - 20 TUNES TO ARRANGE, SET 1
        SHAWNEE PRESS, INC.   1.50
MCGINLEY
    CHORDS AND MELODIES - 20 TUNES TO ARRANGE, SET 2
        SHAWNEE PRESS, INC.   1.25
MCGINLEY
    CHORDS AND MELODIES - 20 TUNES TO ARRANGE, SET 3
        SHAWNEE PRESS, INC.   1.25
MCGINLEY
    CHORDS AND MELODIES - 20 TUNES TO ARRANGE, SET 4
        SHAWNEE PRESS, INC.   .75
MCGINLEY
    CHORDS AND MELODIES SERIES - ADVANCED LEVEL 1
        SHAWNEE PRESS, INC.   1.50
MCGINLEY
    CHORDS AND MELODIES SERIES - BEGINNER'S LEVEL 1
        SHAWNEE PRESS, INC.   2.50
MCGINLEY
    CHORDS AND MELODIES SERIES - BEGINNER'S LEVEL 2
        SHAWNEE PRESS, INC.   3.00
MCGINLEY
    CHORDS AND MELODIES SERIES - INTERMEDIATE LEVEL 1
        SHAWNEE PRESS, INC.   1.50
MCGINLEY
    CHORDS AND MELODIES SERIES - INTERMEDIATE LEVEL 2
        SHAWNEE PRESS, INC.   2.00
MCGINLEY
    PIANO SESSIONS BASIC COURSE, BK. 1# EXPLORING MUSIC AT THE
    KEYBOARD
        SHAWNEE PRESS, INC.   2.00
MCGINLEY
    PIANO SESSIONS BASIC COURSE, BK. 2# ADVENTURES IN READING AND
    PLAYING
        SHAWNEE PRESS, INC.   1.25
MCGINLEY
    PIANO SESSIONS BASIC COURSE, BK. 3# KEYS TO CHORDS
        SHAWNEE PRESS, INC.   1.25
MCINTOSH   MCINTOSH
    TEN DESCRIPTIVE SKETCHES
        SHAWNEE PRESS, INC.   1.00
MENOZZI, J.   CARILLO
    METODO TEORICO-PRACTICO DE LECTURA MUSICAL--IN SPANISH
        G. SCHIRMER, INC.   L843   1.50
METIS
    RHYTHM FACTORY
        EDWARD B. MARKS MUSIC CORPORATION   01.75
METIS
    ROCK MODES AND MOODS
        EDWARD B. MARKS MUSIC CORPORATION   01.50
METZGER
    HAPPY LITTLE FINGERS
        BELWIN-MILLS PUBLISHING CORPORATION   1.00
MILLIGAN
    SCALES, CHORDS AND ARPEGGIOS
        WARNER BROTHERS PUBLISHERS   1.50
MIROVITCH, A.
    LEGATO AND NON LEGATO
        BELWIN-MILLS PUBLISHING CORPORATION   1.50
MONTANI
    FIVE ADVANCED TECHNICAL STUDIES
        FRANCO COLOMBO PUBLICATIONS   ER2205   1.50
MONTANI
    SCALES - MAJOR, MINOR AND CHROMATIC
        FRANCO COLOMBO PUBLICATIONS   ER2308   1.50

MONTANI
    SCALES IN THIRDS AND SIXTHS
        FRANCO COLOMBO PUBLICATIONS   ER2372   .75
MORAWECK   GR. 5
    CONTEMPORARY PIANO TECHNIQUE
        WESTERN INTERNATIONAL MUSIC, INC.   AV29   4.00
MORHANGE *
    LITTLE CLAVIER, THE - AN INTRODUCTION TO THE PIANO
        FRANCO COLOMBO PUBLICATIONS   SAL   7.00
MOSCHELES, I.   D
    THREE CONCERT STUDIES, OP. 51
        C. F. PETERS CORPORATION   1402   2.50
MOSCHELES, I.
    TWENTY-FOUR STUDIES--FINISHING-LESSONS FOR ADVANCED PERFORMERS,
    OP. 70--BK. 1
        G. SCHIRMER, INC.   L404   1.00
MOSCHELES, I.   PAUER
    TWENTY-FOUR STUDIES--FINISHING-LESSONS FOR ADVANCED PERFORMERS,
    OP. 70--IN SPANISH AND ENGLISH
        G. SCHIRMER, INC.   L403   2.25
MOSCHELES, I.
    TWENTY-FOUR STUDIES FOR PERFECTION, OP. 70 BK. 1 -- 1-12 --
        FRANCO COLOMBO PUBLICATIONS   ER837   2.25
MOSCHELES, I.   ANDREOLI
    TWENTY-FOUR STUDIES FOR PERFECTION, OP. 70
        FRANCO COLOMBO PUBLICATIONS   ER748   3.50
MOSZKOWSKI
    ETUDE IN D, OP. 32 NO. 2
        G. SCHIRMER, INC.   .50
MOSZKOWSKI
    ETUDE IN G, OP. 18 NO. 3
        G. SCHIRMER, INC.   .50
MOSZKOWSKI
    FIFTEEN ETUDES DE VIRTUOSITE, OP. 72
        BOOSEY AND HAWKES, INC.   2.00
MOSZKOWSKI
    FIFTEEN ETUDES DE VIRTUOSITE, OP. 72
        G. SCHIRMER, INC.   L1798   2.00
MOSZKOWSKI
    FIFTEEN STUDIES FOR THE LEFT HAND, OP. 92
        FRANCO COLOMBO PUBLICATIONS   BA8779   2.50
MOSZKOWSKI
    QUINZE ETUDES DE VIRTUOSITE, OP. 72
        ASSOCIATED MUSIC PUBLISHERS, INC.   ENO   2.00
MOSZKOWSKI
    QUINZE ETUDES DE VIRTUOSITE, OP. 72
        ASSOCIATED MUSIC PUBLISHERS, INC.   ENO   6.00
MOSZKOWSKI
    SCHOOL OF DOUBLE NOTES, OP. 64
        FRANCO COLOMBO PUBLICATIONS   BA10312   3.50
MOSZKOWSKI
    SCHOOL OF SCALES AND DOUBLE NOTES, BKS. 1- 4
        BOOSEY AND HAWKES, INC.   EA.
MOSZKOWSKI
    TWELVE ETUDES FOR THE LEFT HAND ALONE, OP. 92
        ASSOCIATED MUSIC PUBLISHERS, INC.   ENO   3.00
MOSZKOWSKI   PHILIPP, I.
    VIRTUOSITY STUDIES 'AD ASPERA', OP. 72
        INTERNATIONAL MUSIC COMPANY   2.50
MUNN, S.
    PLAYING THE PIANO, PART 2, FINGERS
        NOVELLO AND COMPANY, LTD.   63.0177.07   1.75
MUSAFIA
    ART OF FINGERING IN PIANO PLAYING, THE
        MCA MUSIC   6.95
NELHYBEL, V.
    KALEIDOSCOPE - FOR YOUNG PIANISTS, BK. 1
        GENERAL MUSIC PUBLISHING COMPANY, INC.   264   3.00
NELHYBEL, V.
    KALEIDOSCOPE - FOR YOUNG PIANISTS, BK. 2
        GENERAL MUSIC PUBLISHING COMPANY, INC.   265   3.00
NEUPERT, E.
    TWELVE STUDIES
        G. SCHIRMER, INC.   L797   1.00
NEVIN
    PIANO BOOK FOR ADULTS, BK. 1
        EDWARD B. MARKS MUSIC CORPORATION   01.95
NEVIN
    PIANO BOOK FOR ADULTS, BK. 2
        EDWARD B. MARKS MUSIC CORPORATION   01.95
NICOLOSI SILVESTRI
    MAJOR AND MINOR SCALES
        FRANCO COLOMBO PUBLICATIONS   DS361   3.25
NOEL, P. *
    ETUDES PROGRESSIVES, VOL.1
        GERARD BILLAUDOT EDITIONS MUSICALES   2.50
NOEL, P. *
    ETUDES PROGRESSIVES, VOL.2
        GERARD BILLAUDOT EDITIONS MUSICALES   2.50
NOLLET, E.   HUGHES
    FIFTEEN MELODIOUS STUDIES, OP. 43
        G. SCHIRMER, INC.   L1375   1.25
OETTING, H.   4
    MEDITATION -- A PEDAL STUDY
        VOLKWEIN BROS.   .40
OLDENBURG, E.   2-3
    MINIATURES--THIRTY SHORT STUDIES
        VOLKWEIN BROS.   1.25
OLDENBURG, E.
    TWELVE PLAYTIME PIECES
        VOLKWEIN BROS.   .85
OREM, P. W.
    CHORDS AND APPEGGIOS
        THEODORE PRESSER COMPANY   1.00
PAPORISZ, Y.
    DISCOVERIES AT THE PIANO, BK. 1
        PEER SOUTHERN ORGANIZATION   02.00
PAPORISZ, Y.
    DISCOVERIES AT THE PIANO, BK. 2
        PEER SOUTHERN ORGANIZATION   02.00
PAPORISZ, Y.
    DISCOVERIES AT THE PIANO, BK. 3
        PEER SOUTHERN ORGANIZATION   02.00
PARLOW, E.
    THIRTY LITTLE ETUDES
        G. SCHIRMER, INC.   L1251   1.00
PATORNI *
    HARPSICHORD TECHNIQUE
        FRANCO COLOMBO PUBLICATIONS   SAL   3.25
PAUER   M
    FINGER TECHNIQUE STUDIES
        C. F. PETERS CORPORATION   4839   1.50
PELLEGRINI
    STUDENT PIANIST, THE
        FRANCO COLOMBO PUBLICATIONS   FOR.12207   1.25

PFEIFFER, A.
 PEDAL STUDIES--SPANISH AND ENGLISH
  G. SCHIRMER, INC.   1.00
PHILIPP, I.--ED.   PHILIPP, I.
 EXERCICES PREPARATORIES DE AD. HENSELT
  HEUGEL ET CIE.   11.10
PHILIPP, I.--ED.   PHILIPP, I.
 EXERCICES PROGRESSIFS DE J. PISCHNA
  HEUGEL ET CIE.   3.75
PHILIPP, I.
 COMPLETE SCHOOL OF TECHNIC
  THEODORE PRESSER COMPANY   2.75
PHILIPP, I.
 EXERCICES DE TENUES
  INTERNATIONAL MUSIC COMPANY   2.50
PHILIPP, I.
 EXERCICES ET ETUDES TECHNIQUES DE PIANO POUR LA MAIN GAUCHE
 SEULE
  ELKAN-VOGEL, INC.   D   7.50
PHILIPP, I.
 EXERCICES PRATIQUES POUR LE PIANO, OP. 9
  ELKAN-VOGEL, INC.   D   8.00
PHILIPP, I.
 EXERCISES FOR INDEPENDENCE OF THE FINGERS, BK. 1
  G. SCHIRMER, INC.   1.25
PHILIPP, I.
 EXERCISES FOR INDEPENDENCE OF THE FINGERS, BK. 2
  G. SCHIRMER, INC.   1.25
PHILIPP, I.
 EXERCISES IN VELOCITY
  ASSOCIATED MUSIC PUBLISHERS, INC.   ENO   1.00
PHILIPP, I.
 EXERCISES ON THE BLACK KEYS
  G. SCHIRMER, INC.   L1675   .60
PHILIPP, I.
 FOURTEEN CAPRICE-ETUDES IN OCTAVES
  ASSOCIATED MUSIC PUBLISHERS, INC.   ENO   2.00
PHILIPP, I.
 NEW GRADUS AD PARNASSUM, THE -- HANDS TOGETHER--
  THEODORE PRESSER COMPANY   .90
PHILIPP, I.
 OCTAVES AND CHORDS
  THEODORE PRESSER COMPANY   .90
PHILIPP, I.
 SCHOOL OF OCTAVE PLAYING, BK. 1--EXERCISES
  G. SCHIRMER, INC.   L1650   1.00
PHILIPP, I.
 SCHOOL OF OCTAVE PLAYING, BK. 2--EXAMPLES FROM MASTERWORKS
  G. SCHIRMER, INC.   L1652   1.75
PHILIPP, I.
 SIXTY NEW PREPARATORY EXERCISES
  ASSOCIATED MUSIC PUBLISHERS, INC.   ESC   3.00
PHILIPP, I.
 SIX OCTAVE-STUDIES IN THE FORM OF LITTLE FUGUES, OP. 78
  G. SCHIRMER, INC.   L1611   1.00
PHILIPP, I.
 TECHNICAL EXERCISES
  INTERNATIONAL MUSIC COMPANY   1.50
PHILIPP, I.
 TRILL, THE
  THEODORE PRESSER COMPANY   .90
PHILLIP, I.
 EXERCICES DE TENUES
  EDWARD B. MARKS MUSIC CORPORATION   01.50
PHILLIP, I.
 PIANO STUDY--APPLICATION AND TECHNIQUE
  MCA MUSIC   6.95
PICCIOLI
 PREPARATORY EXERCISES FOR THE USE OF THE PEDAL
  FRANCO COLOMBO PUBLICATIONS   BON.1988   3.00
PIEPER, M.
 RHYTHMISCH-STILISTISCHE STUDIEN, BK. 1 -- JAZZ STUDIES
  ASSOCIATED MUSIC PUBLISHERS, INC.   DVM   3.00
PISCHNA   WOLFF
 LITTLE PISCHNA, THE--48 PRACTICE-PIECES--INTRODUCTION TO
 'TECHNICAL STUDIES'
  G. SCHIRMER, INC.   L898   1.00
PISCHNA   BRISMAN, H.
 PISCHNA--TECHNICAL STUDIES
  ALFRED MUSIC COMPANY   637   3.00
PISCHNA   REHBERG   M-D
 SIXTY DAILY EXERCISES
  C. F. PETERS CORPORATION   Z112   2.50
PISCHNA   SAUER   M-D
 SIXTY DAILY EXERCISES
  C. F. PETERS CORPORATION   3018   3.00
PISCHNA
 SIXTY DAILY STUDIES
  CARL FISCHER, INC.   L 484   2.00
PISCHNA   MARCIANO
 SIXTY PROGRESSIVE STUDIES
  FRANCO COLOMBO PUBLICATIONS   ER96   3.50
PISCHNA   WOLFF
 TECHNICAL STUDIES--60 PROGRESSIVE EXERCISES, REVISED AND
 AUGMENTED WITH ADDITIONAL PRELIMINARY EXERCISES
  G. SCHIRMER, INC.   L792   2.00
PLAIDY, L.   KLAUSER
 TECHNICAL STUDIES, BK. 1--SECTIONS 1-4
  G. SCHIRMER, INC.   L1617   1.25
PLAIDY, L.   SAUER   M-D
 TECHNICAL STUDIES
  C. F. PETERS CORPORATION   3042   5.00
PLAIDY, L.   KLAUSER
 TECHNICAL STUDIES
  G. SCHIRMER, INC.   L304   1.50
PODOLSKY, L. *
 PILLARS OF PIANO TECHNIC -- THE MOVING HAND
  BOOSEY AND HAWKES, INC.   1.25
PODOLSKY, L. *
 PILLARS OF PIANO TECHNIC -- THE STATIONARY HAND, BK. A
  BOOSEY AND HAWKES, INC.   1.25
PODOLSKY, L. *
 PILLARS OF PIANO TECHNIC -- THE STATIONARY HAND, BK. B
  BOOSEY AND HAWKES, INC.   1.25
PODOLSKY, L. *
 TECHNIC FOR THIRDS, SIXTHS AND OCTAVES
  BOOSEY AND HAWKES, INC.   1.25
POLLINI
 SCALES IN ALL THE KEYS
  FRANCO COLOMBO PUBLICATIONS   101128   .90
POOT, M.
 ETUDE--1951
  ASSOCIATED MUSIC PUBLISHERS, INC.   ESC   3.00
POZZOLI
 EXERCISES AND STUDIES IN THUMB PASSAGES
  FRANCO COLOMBO PUBLICATIONS   ER200   2.00

POZZOLI
 FIFTEEN EASY STUDIES FOR THE SMALL HAND
  FRANCO COLOMBO PUBLICATIONS   ER436   1.50
POZZOLI
 FIRST EXERCISES IN POLYPHONIC STYLE - 50 SHORT CANONS
  FRANCO COLOMBO PUBLICATIONS   ER1748   1.25
POZZOLI
 PIANISTS' DAILY TECHNIQUE, THE - PARTS 1 AND 2
  FRANCO COLOMBO PUBLICATIONS   ER800   3.00
POZZOLI
 PIANISTS' DAILY TECHNIQUE, THE - PART 3
  FRANCO COLOMBO PUBLICATIONS   ER801   2.25
POZZOLI
 PICCOLO 'GRADUS AD PARNASSUM' - 15 STUDIES PREPARATORY TO
 CLEMENTI'S 'GRADUS'
  FRANCO COLOMBO PUBLICATIONS   ER2534   1.75
POZZOLI
 SIXTEEN AGILITY STUDIES FOR SMALL HANDS
  FRANCO COLOMBO PUBLICATIONS   ER2230   1.75
POZZOLI
 STUDIES IN VELOCITY
  FRANCO COLOMBO PUBLICATIONS   ER2188   2.50
POZZOLI
 STUDIES OF MEDIUM DIFFICULTY
  FRANCO COLOMBO PUBLICATIONS   ER83   1.75
POZZOLI
 STUDIES ON REPEATED NOTES
  FRANCO COLOMBO PUBLICATIONS   ER1847   1.75
POZZOLI
 THIRTY ELEMENTARY STUDIES
  FRANCO COLOMBO PUBLICATIONS   ER46   1.50
POZZOLI
 TWENTY-FOUR EASY AND PROGRESSIVE STUDIES
  FRANCO COLOMBO PUBLICATIONS   ER2067   1.75
POZZOLI
 TWENTY-FOUR EASY STUDIES IN MECHANISM
  FRANCO COLOMBO PUBLICATIONS   ER427   1.75
POZZOLI
 TWENTY SCALE STUDIES
  FRANCO COLOMBO PUBLICATIONS   ER2128   1.75
PRESSER, T.
 SCALES AND CADENCES
  THEODORE PRESSER COMPANY   1.00
PROGRIS, J.
 MODERN METHOD FOR KEYBOARD STUDY, A - COMPLETE SET B-13 THROUGH
 B-16
  BERKLEE PRESS PUBLICATIONS   B-13 - B-16   21.50
PROGRIS, J.
 MODERN METHOD FOR KEYBOARD STUDY, A - VOL. 1
  BERKLEE PRESS PUBLICATIONS   B-13   6.00
PROGRIS, J.
 MODERN METHOD FOR KEYBOARD STUDY, A - VOL. 2
  BERKLEE PRESS PUBLICATIONS   B-14   6.00
PROGRIS, J.
 MODERN METHOD FOR KEYBOARD STUDY, A - VOL. 3
  BERKLEE PRESS PUBLICATIONS   B-15   6.00
PROGRIS, J.
 MODERN METHOD FOR KEYBOARD STUDY, A - VOL. 4
  BERKLEE PRESS PUBLICATIONS   B-16   6.00
PROKOFIEFF   D
 ETUDE OP. 2 NO. 1
  C. F. PETERS CORPORATION   F62   1.25
PROKOFIEFF   D
 ETUDE OP. 2 NO. 2
  C. F. PETERS CORPORATION   F63   1.25
PROKOFIEFF   D
 ETUDE OP. 2 NO. 3
  C. F. PETERS CORPORATION   F64   1.25
PROKOFIEFF   D
 ETUDE OP. 2 NO. 4
  C. F. PETERS CORPORATION   F65   1.25
PROKOFIEFF
 FOUR ETUDES, OP. 2
  MCA MUSIC   1.00
QUAILE, E.   GRADE 1
 FIRST BOOK OF TECHNICAL EXERCISES--WITH SPECIAL REFERENCE TO THE
 PIECES OF THE DILLER-QUAILE 'FIRST SOLO BOOK'
  G. SCHIRMER, INC.   1.00
QUAILE, E.
 PRE-CZERNY BOOK, A--BK. 1--40 STUDIES
  G. SCHIRMER, INC.   1.00
QUAILE, E.
 PRE-CZERNY BOOK, A--BK. 2--32 STUDIES
  G. SCHIRMER, INC.   1.00
RACHMANINOFF, S.
 ETUDES-TABLEAUX, OP. 33 , NOS. 3 AND 5
  MCA MUSIC   .75
RACHMANINOFF, S.   MIROVITCH, A.
 ETUDES-TABLEAUX, OP. 33 AND 39
  MCA MUSIC   4.25
RAPHLING
 CANDID CAMERA - FOR YOUNGEST PIANISTS
  GENERAL MUSIC PUBLISHING COMPANY, INC. 280   2.25
RAPHLING
 ILLUSTRATED ALPHABET
  GENERAL MUSIC PUBLISHING COMPANY, INC. 278   2.00
RAPHLING
 INPUT AND OUTPUT - FOR THE YOUNGEST PIANISTS
  GENERAL MUSIC PUBLISHING COMPANY, INC. 278   1.25
RAPHLING
 TIME EXCHANGE - FOR THE YOUNGEST PIANISTS
  GENERAL MUSIC PUBLISHING COMPANY, INC. 283   1.25
RAVINA, H.
 HARMONIOUS ETUDES, OP. 50
  G. SCHIRMER, INC.   L1515   1.75
REBE
 TECHNIC TUNES
  WILLIS MUSIC COMPANY   1.00
REHBERG   1-2
 NEUER ETUDENGANG -- BK. 1
  SCHOTT   2351   2.50
REHBERG   1-2
 NEUER ETUDENGANG -- BK. 2
  SCHOTT   2352   2.50
RICHTER
 ADVENTURES AT THE KEYBOARD
  WARNER BROTHERS PUBLISHERS   AR 10   1.50
RICHTER
 KEYBOARD GAMES
  WARNER BROTHERS PUBLISHERS   AR 11   1.50
RICHTER
 KEYBOARD TECHNIC, MORE, FOR THE OLDER STUDENT
  WARNER BROTHERS PUBLISHERS   AR 13   1.25
RICHTER
 KEYBOARD TECHNIC FOR THE OLDER STUDENT
  WARNER BROTHERS PUBLISHERS   AR 12   1.50

RICHTER
KNOW YOUR SCALES AND ARPEGGIOS
WARNER BROTHERS PUBLISHERS   AR 14   1.50

RISHER, A. P.
TECHNIC FOR BEGINNERS
THEODORE PRESSER COMPANY   1.25

ROBYN
TECHNIC TALES, BK. 1
THEODORE PRESSER COMPANY   1.25

ROBYN
TECHNIC TALES, BK. 2
THEODORE PRESSER COMPANY   1.25

ROBYN
TECHNIC TALES, BK. 3
THEODORE PRESSER COMPANY   1.50

ROGER-DUCASSE
EXERCISES DE VIRTUOSITE, BK. 1
ELKAN-VOGEL, INC.   D   3.50

ROGER-DUCASSE
EXERCISES DE VIRTUOSITE, BK. 2
ELKAN-VOGEL, INC.   D   3.25

ROGERS, J.
DEVELOPMENT OF VELOCITY, OP. 40, BK. 1--SCALES
G. SCHIRMER, INC.   1.25

ROGERS, J.
DEVELOPMENT OF VELOCITY, OP. 40, BK, 2--ARPEGGIOS
G. SCHIRMER, INC.   1.25

ROGERS, J.
FIFTEEN EXERCISES AND STUDIES ON BROKEN CHORDS
G. SCHIRMER, INC.   1.50

ROGERS
OCTAVES VELOCITY
THEODORE PRESSER COMPANY   1.00

ROSSI, N.
SCHOOL OF DOUBLE NOTES
FRANCO COLOMBO PUBLICATIONS   ER2166   2.25

ROWLEY   E-M
EIGHTEEN STUDIES, OP. 42
C. F. PETERS CORPORATION   4383A   1.50

ROWLEY   D
ETUDES IN TONALITY, OP. 44
C. F. PETERS CORPORATION   4387   1.50

ROWLEY   E-M
TWELVE STUDIES, OP. 43
C. F. PETERS CORPORATION   4383B   1.50

RUBINSTEIN   GALLICO
SIX ETUDES, OP. 23
G. SCHIRMER, INC.   1.50

RUBINSTEIN   D
SIX STUDIES, OP. 23
C. F. PETERS CORPORATION   1009   5.00

RUMMO
FUNCTIONAL PIANO
VOLKWEIN BROS.   4.00

RUTHARDT
TEACHER AND PUPIL
EDWIN F. KALMUS   3844   2.00

SAINT-SAENS
ETUDE EN TIERCES MAJEURES CHROMATIQUES
ELKAN-VOGEL, INC.   D   2.25

SAINT-SAENS
SIX ETUDES POUR LA MAIN GAUCHE SEULE, OP. 135 -- BOUREE
ELKAN-VOGEL, INC.   D   3.25

SAINT-SAENS
SIX ETUDES POUR LA MAIN GAUCHE SEULE, OP. 135 -- ELEGIE
ELKAN-VOGEL, INC.   D   2.00

SAINT-SAENS
SIX ETUDES POUR LA MAIN GAUCHE SEULE, OP. 135 -- MOTO PERPETUO
ELKAN-VOGEL, INC.   D   1.05

SAINT-SAENS
SIX ETUDES POUR LA MAIN GAUCHE SEULE, OP. 135
ELKAN-VOGEL, INC.   D   8.00

SAYGUN, A.
TEN ETUDES ON AKSAK RHYTHMS
PEER SOUTHERN ORGANIZATION   04.50

SAYGUN, A.
TWELVE PRELUDES ON AKSAK RHYTHMS
PEER SOUTHERN ORGANIZATION   03.50

SCHAUM, J.--ED.   SCHAUM, J.   2 1/2
APPEGGIOS AND PIECES IN ALL KEYS, BK. 1
BELWIN-MILLS PUBLISHING CORPORATION   1.25

SCHAUM, J.--ED.   SCHAUM, J.   4 1/2 - 5
ARPEGGIOS AND PIECES IN ALL KEYS, BK. 2
BELWIN-MILLS PUBLISHING CORPORATION   1.25

SCHAUM, J.--ED.   SCHAUM, J.   3
PROGRESSIVE PIANO TECHNIC, BK. 1
BELWIN-MILLS PUBLISHING CORPORATION   1.50

SCHAUM, J.--ED.   SCHAUM, J.   4 1/2
PROGRESSIVE PIANO TECHNIC, BK. 2
BELWIN-MILLS PUBLISHING CORPORATION   1.50

SCHAUM, J.--ED.   SCHAUM, J.   2
TECHNIC THROUGH MELODY, BK. 1
BELWIN-MILLS PUBLISHING CORPORATION   1.50

SCHAUM, J.--ED.   SCHAUM, J.   2 1/2
TECHNIC THROUGH MELODY, BK. 2
BELWIN-MILLS PUBLISHING CORPORATION   1.50

SCHAUM, J.--ED.   SCHAUM, J.   1
TECHNIC TRICKS, BK.1
BELWIN-MILLS PUBLISHING CORPORATION   1.50

SCHAUM, J.--ED.   SCHAUM, J.   1
TECHNIC TRICKS, BK.2
BELWIN-MILLS PUBLISHING CORPORATION   1.50

SCHAUM, J.   2
AROUND THE WORLD IN ALL KEYS
SCHAUM PUBLICATIONS, INC.   1.25

SCHAUM, J.   1 1/2
CZERNY IN ALL KEYS, BK. 1
SCHAUM PUBLICATIONS, INC.   1.50

SCHAUM, J.   2
CZERNY IN ALL KEYS, BK. 2
SCHAUM PUBLICATIONS, INC.   1.50

SCHAUM, J.   1
FINGERPOWER, BK. 1
SCHAUM PUBLICATIONS, INC.   1.45

SCHAUM, J.   1 1/2
FINGERPOWER, BK. 2
SCHAUM PUBLICATIONS, INC.   1.25

SCHAUM, J.   2
FINGERPOWER, BK. 3
SCHAUM PUBLICATIONS, INC.   1.25

SCHAUM, J.   2 1/2
FINGERPOWER, BK. 4
SCHAUM PUBLICATIONS, INC.   1.50

SCHAUM, J.   3
FINGERPOWER, BK. 5
SCHAUM PUBLICATIONS, INC.   1.50

SCHAUM, J.   4
FINGERPOWER, BK. 6
SCHAUM PUBLICATIONS, INC.   1.50

SCHAUM, J.   PREP
FINGERPOWER, PREP BOOK
SCHAUM PUBLICATIONS, INC.   1.25

SCHAUM, J.   2 1/2
GAYNOR-SCHAUM PEDAL STUDIES
SCHAUM PUBLICATIONS, INC.   1.25

SCHAUM, J.   1 1/2
LEFT HAND STUDIES, BK. 1
BELWIN-MILLS PUBLISHING CORPORATION   1.50

SCHAUM, J.   2 1/2
LEFT HAND STUDIES, BK. 2
BELWIN-MILLS PUBLISHING CORPORATION   1.50

SCHAUM, J.   3
OCTAVE STUDIES, BK. 1
BELWIN-MILLS PUBLISHING CORPORATION   1.50

SCHAUM, J.   4
OCTAVE STUDIES, BK. 2
BELWIN-MILLS PUBLISHING CORPORATION   1.50

SCHER, W.
FIFTEEN RECREATIVE ETUDES
THEODORE PRESSER COMPANY   .90

SCHININA, L.
TUTTI LE SCALE PER PIANOFORTE, BK. 1
EDIZIONI BERBEN   EB 1336   3.60

SCHININA, L.
TUTTI LE SCALE PER PIANOFORTE, BK. 2
EDIZIONI BERBEN   EB 1380   3.60

SCHISKE, K.
ETUDENSTUDIE, OP. 36--1951
ASSOCIATED MUSIC PUBLISHERS, INC. DOB   1.25

SCHMITT, A. *   ECKSTEIN
EARLY TECHNICAL STUDIES FROM SCHMITT-HANON--140--
CARL FISCHER, INC.   O 3810   1.25

SCHMITT, A.
FIVE FINGER EXERCISES, OP. 16
CARL FISCHER, INC.   L 15   1.25

SCHMITT, A.   1
FIVE FINGER EXERCISES, PART 1
CENTURY MUSIC PUBLISHING COMPANY, INC. 1207   .40

SCHMITT, A.   1
FIVE FINGER EXERCISES, PART 2
CENTURY MUSIC PUBLISHING COMPANY, INC. 1208   .40

SCHMITT, A.   FRUGATTA
FIVE FINGER EXERCISES
FRANCO COLOMBO PUBLICATIONS   ER43   .75

SCHMITT, A.   KNECHT
PREPARATORY EXERCISES. 5-FINGER EXERCISES. OP. 16
G. SCHIRMER, INC.   L434   .85

SCHMITT, A.
PREPARATORY EXERCISES, OP. 16A
THEODORE PRESSER COMPANY   1.75

SCHMITT, A.
PREPARATORY EXERCISES, OP. 16
FRANCO COLOMBO PUBLICATIONS   ER21   .75

SCHMITT, A.   M
PREPARATORY EXERCISES, OP. 16
C. F. PETERS CORPORATION   2467A   1.25

SCHMITT, A.
PREPARATORY EXERCISES, OP. 16
UNIVERSAL EDITION   UE 278   .80

SCHMITT, A.
PREPARATORY EXERCISES
BANKS AND SON LTD.   .95

SCHMITT, F.
PREPARATORY EXERCISES FOR THE PIANO
BELWIN-MILLS PUBLISHING CORPORATION   1.00

SCHOLZ
ABC DER KLAVIERTEACHNIK -- ENG AND GER NOTES -- BK. 1
ASSOCIATED MUSIC PUBLISHERS, INC. DOB   3.25

SCHOLZ
ABC DER KLAVIERTEACHNIK -- ENG AND GER NOTES -- BK. 2
ASSOCIATED MUSIC PUBLISHERS, INC. DOB   3.25

SCHOLZ
ABC DER KLAVIERTEACHNIK -- ENG AND GER NOTES -- BK. 3
ASSOCIATED MUSIC PUBLISHERS, INC. DOB   3.25

SCHOLZ
ADVENTURES IN CONTEMPORARY TECHNIC -- THE MODERN STUDY
ASSOCIATED MUSIC PUBLISHERS, INC. AMP   2.00

SCHOLZ
MODERNE STUDIE, DIE -- BK. 1
ASSOCIATED MUSIC PUBLISHERS, INC. DOB   3.00

SCHOLZ
MODERNE STUDIE, DIE -- BK. 2, PART 1
ASSOCIATED MUSIC PUBLISHERS, INC. DOB   2.50

SCHOLZ
MODERNE STUDIE, DIE -- BK. 2, PART 2
ASSOCIATED MUSIC PUBLISHERS, INC. DOB   2.50

SCHULZ, F. A.
SCALES AND CHORDS -- ALL THE MAJOR AND MINOR KEYS
THEODORE PRESSER COMPANY   1.00

SCHULZ, F. A.
SCALES AND CHORDS IN ALL THE MAJOR AND MINOR KEYS
G. SCHIRMER, INC.   L392   .75

SCHULZ, F. A.
SCALES AND CHORDS
CARL FISCHER, INC.   L 176   1.00

SCHUNGELER, H.
DAS NEUE WEG. AUSGEWAHLTE ETUDEN UND STUDIEN, HEFT 03
SCHOTT   4010   2.25

SCHUNGELER, H.
DER NEUE WEG. AUSGEWAHLTE ETUDEN UND STUDIEN, HEFT 01
SCHOTT   4008   2.25

SCHUNGELER, H.
DER NEUE WEG. AUSGEWAHLTE ETUDEN UND STUDIEN, HEFT 02
SCHOTT   4009   2.25

SCHWALM, R.
DAILY EXERCISES
G. SCHIRMER, INC.   L796   1.25

SCHWALM, R.
YOUNG MUSICIANS, THE VERY EASIEST OF PIECES
EDWIN F. KALMUS   3939   1.50

SCHYTTE
ETUDE IN B MINOR, OP. 15 NO. 12--'GHOST'
G. SCHIRMER, INC.   .40

SCHYTTE
TWENTY-FIVE SHORT AND MELODIOUS STUDIES, OP. 108
G. SCHIRMER, INC.   L1371   1.00

SCRIABINE, A.   D
ETUDE, OP. 2 NO. 1
C. F. PETERS CORPORATION   F61   .90

SCRIABINE, A.   D
ETUDE IN B FLAT, OP. 65 NO. 1
C. F. PETERS CORPORATION   F50   1.25

SCRIABINE, A.   D
ETUDE IN C SHARP, OP. 65 NO. 2
    C. F. PETERS CORPORATION   F51   1.25
SCRIABINE, A.
ETUDE IN C SHARP MINOR, OP. 2 NO. 1
    G. SCHIRMER, INC.   .40
SCRIABINE, A.   FRIEDHEIM
ETUDE IN D SHARP MINOR, OP. 8 NO. 12
    G. SCHIRMER, INC.   .50
SCRIABINE, A.   D
ETUDE IN G, OP. 65 NO. 3
    C. F. PETERS CORPORATION   F52   1.25
SCRIABINE, A.   PHILIPP, G.   D
SELECTED PIANO WORKS, VOL. 1# ETUDES
    C. F. PETERS CORPORATION   9077A   7.50
SELVA
ENSEIGNEMENT MUSICAL DE LA TECHNIQUE DU PIANO, L' ....
PREPARATORY BOOK 1 - PRINCIPES PRIMORDIAUX DU TRAVAIL PIANISTIQUE
    FRANCO COLOMBO PUBLICATIONS   SAL   8.75
SELVA
ENSEIGNEMENT MUSICAL DE LA TECHNIQUE DU PIANO, L' ....
PREPAPATORY BOOK 2 - PREPARATION DU TOUCHER AU PIANO
    FRANCO COLOMBO PUBLICATIONS   SAL   19.50
SELVA
ENSEIGNEMENT MUSICAL DE LA TECHNIQUE DU PIANO, L' .... VOL. 1 -
PRINCIPES DE LA SONORITE AU PIANO, TRAVAIL ELEMENTAIRE DES TOUCHES.
.. TEACHER'S BOOK
    FRANCO COLOMBO PUBLICATIONS   SAL   10.75
SELVA
ENSEIGNEMENT MUSICAL DE LA TECHNIQUE DU PIANO, L' .... VOL. 1 -
PRINCIPES DE LA SONORITE AU PIANO, TRAVAIL ELEMENTAIRE DES TOUCHES
.. STUDENT'S BOOK
    FRANCO COLOMBO PUBLICATIONS   SAL   2.75
SELVA
ENSEIGNEMENT MUSICAL DE LA TECHNIQUE DU PIANO, L' .... VOL. 2 -
LA SIMULTANEITE DES SONS AU PIANO, TRAVAIL ELEMENTAIRE DEA DOUBLE
NOTES
    FRANCO COLOMBO PUBLICATIONS   SAL   18.00
SELVA
ENSEIGNEMENT MUSICAL DE LA TECHNIQUE DU PIANO, L' .... VOL. 3 -
LE TRAIT DEPLOIEMENT RYTHMIQUE DE L'HARMONIE .. PART 1 - DOUBLES
NOTES, TREMOLOS, TRAITS BRISES, ARPEDES
    FRANCO COLOMBO PUBLICATIONS   SAL   18.00
SELVA
ENSEIGNEMENT MUSICAL DE LA TECHNIQUE DU PIANO, L' .... VOL. 3 -
LE TRAIT DEPLOIEMENT RYTHMIQUE DE L'HARMONIE .. PART 2 - GAMMES,
ARPEGES, TRAITS COMPOSES
    FRANCO COLOMBO PUBLICATIONS   SAL   18.00
SHAW, G.   3-5
SIX BLACK KEY DUETS
    NOVELLO AND COMPANY, LTD.   10.0141.08 1.40
SHORES
SWINGIN' TECHNIC
    SUMMY-BIRCHARD COMPANY   1.75
SILVESTRI
SCALES, THE - BK. 1 -- SIMPLE SCALES --
    FRANCO COLOMBO PUBLICATIONS   ER1759   2.50
SILVESTRI
SCALES, THE - BK. 2 -- SCALES IN THIRDS AND SIXTHS --
    FRANCO COLOMBO PUBLICATIONS   ER1760   5.50
SLONIMSKY   ADVANCED
TWO ETUDES
    SHAWNEE PRESS, INC.   .75
SMALL, A.
BASIC TIMING FOR PIANIST
    ALFRED MUSIC COMPANY   517   1.00
SMALL, A.
TECHNIQUE AND MELODY IN ALL KEYS
    ALFRED MUSIC COMPANY   519   1.95
SMITH, L.   M
FOUR ETUDES
    THEODORE PRESSER COMPANY   1.00
SMITH, W. G.
THEMATIC OCTAVE STUDIES -- IN THE FORM OF VARIATIONS ON AN
ORIGINAL THEME FOR PIANO
    THEODORE PRESSER COMPANY   1.50
SPIVAK, S.
FIFTY-EIGHT TUNEFUL TECHNICAL STUDIES, BK. 1
    ASHLEY DEALERS SERVICE, INC.   1.50
SPIVAK, S.
FORTY-EIGHT TUNEFUL TECHNICAL STUDIES, BK. 2
    ASHLEY DEALERS SERVICE, INC.   1.50
STALLAERT, A.
THREE ETUDES
    GERARD BILLAUDOT EDITIONS MUSICALES   3.30
STAMATY, C.
RHYTHMIC TRAINING FOR THE FINGERS, OP. 3--IN SPANISH AND ENGLISH
    G. SCHIRMER, INC.   L1136   2.00
STAMATY, C.
SINGING TOUCH AND TECHNIQUE--25 EASY STUDIES FOR SMALL HANDS,
OP. 37
    G. SCHIRMER, INC.   L858   1.50
STEIBELT   TAGLIAPIETRA
TWENTY-FIVE STUDIES, OP. 78
    FRANCO COLOMBO PUBLICATIONS   3.00
STEINER
MINIATURE ETUDES
    BELWIN-MILLS PUBLISHING CORPORATION 2016   1.75
STEINER
PRE-SCALE BOOK
    BELWIN-MILLS PUBLISHING CORPORATION 2017   1.75
STEINER   2
RUNNING SMOOTHLY -- 24 PIECES EMBRACING TECHNICAL PROBLEMS FOR
THE STUDENT IN SECOND GRADE
    ELKAN-VOGEL, INC.   1.00
STEINER
SIXTY ETUDES, BK. 1
    BELWIN-MILLS PUBLISHING CORPORATION 1589   1.75
STEINER
SIXTY ETUDES, BK. 2
    BELWIN-MILLS PUBLISHING CORPORATION 1590   1.75
STEINER
SKILLS IN PIANO TECHNIC, BK. 1
    BELWIN-MILLS PUBLISHING CORPORATION 1648   1.75
STEINER
SKILLS IN PIANO TECHNIC, BK. 2
    BELWIN-MILLS PUBLISHING CORPORATION 1649   1.75
STEINER
SKILLS IN SCALES, BK. 1
    BELWIN-MILLS PUBLISHING CORPORATION 1209   1.75
STEINER
SKILLS IN SCALES, BK. 2
    BELWIN-MILLS PUBLISHING CORPORATION 1210   1.75
STEINER
TECHNIC FROM THE MASTERS
    BELWIN-MILLS PUBLISHING CORPORATION 1967   2.00

STEINHAUSEN
ERREUPS PHYSIOLOGIQUES ET LA TRANSFORMATION DE LA TECHNIQUE DU
PIANO, LES
    FRANCO COLOMBO PUBLICATIONS   SAL   4.25
STRAVINSKY, S.   M
ART OF SCALES, 24 PRELUDES
    C. F. PETERS CORPORATION   6139   1.25
STREABBOG *   ECKSTEIN
MELODIOUS TECHNICAL STUDIES FROM STREABBOG-BURGMUELLER--75--
    CARL FISCHER, INC.   O 3812   1.25
STREABBOG
STREABBOG ALBUM
    CENTURY MUSIC PUBLISHING COMPANY, INC.   1.25
STREABBOG
TWELVE EASY AND MELODIOUS STUDIES, OP. 64--SECOND DEGREE
    G. SCHIRMER, INC.   L479   1.00
STREABBOG
TWELVE MELODIOUS STUDIES, OP. 63
    CARL FISCHER, INC.   L 363   .75
STREABBOG
TWELVE MELODIOUS STUDIES, OP. 63
    WILLIS MUSIC COMPANY   .75
STREABBOG
TWELVE VERY EASY AND MELODIOUS STUDIES, OP. 63--FIRST DEGREE
    G. SCHIRMER, INC.   L478   1.00
TAGLIAPIETRA, C.
THREE SPECIAL STUDIES FOR THE CROSSING OF THE HANDS
    FRANCO COLOMBO PUBLICATIONS   Z1311   1.25
TAGLIAPIETRA, G.
FORTY STUDIES FOR PERFECTION, BK. 1
    FRANCO COLOMBO PUBLICATIONS   ER196   2.25
TAGLIAPIETRA, G.
FORTY STUDIES FOR PERFECTION, BK. 2
    FRANCO COLOMBO PUBLICATIONS   ER197   4.25
TAKACS, J.
DOUBLE DOZEN FOR SMALL FINGERS
    UNIVERSAL EDITION   UE 13030E   3.50
TALMA, L.
SIX ETUDES
    G. SCHIRMER, INC.   2.00
TANSMAN, A.
ETUDE
    ASSOCIATED MUSIC PUBLISHERS, INC. ESC   4.00
TANSMAN, A.
PIANO IN PROGRESS, BK. 1
    EDWARD B. MARKS MUSIC CORPORATION   01.75
TANSMAN, A.
PIANO IN PROGRESS, BK. 2
    EDWARD B. MARKS MUSIC CORPORATION   01.75
TAUSIG   CESI
DAILY EXERCISES
    FRANCO COLOMBO PUBLICATIONS   ER399   4.00
TAUSIG   EHRLICH
DAILY STUDIES
    G. SCHIRMER, INC.   L1353   2.50
TCHEREPNIN   D
TECHNICAL STUDIES ON THE PENTATONIC SCALE
    C. F. PETERS CORPORATION   4436   3.50
TEBOLDI
TECHNICAL EXERCISES FOR THE INDEPENDENCE OF TOUCH IN POLYPHONIC
PLAYING
    FRANCO COLOMBO PUBLICATIONS   ER1934   2.50
TEICHMUELLER   M-D
PIANO TECHNIQUE
    C. F. PETERS CORPORATION   H32   3.00
TERRY, F.
SCALES AND ARPEGGIOS AT PLAY
    BOSTON MUSIC COMPANY   1.00
THOMPSON, J.
THOMPSON EASIEST PIANO COURSE - PART 1
    WILLIS MUSIC COMPANY   .90
THOMPSON, J.
THOMPSON EASIEST PIANO COURSE - PART 2
    WILLIS MUSIC COMPANY   1.00
THOMPSON, J.
THOMPSON EASIEST PIANO COURSE - PART 3
    WILLIS MUSIC COMPANY   1.00
THOMPSON, J.
THOMPSON EASIEST PIANO COURSE - PART 4
    WILLIS MUSIC COMPANY   1.00
THOMPSON, J.
THOMPSON EASIEST PIANO COURSE - PART 5
    WILLIS MUSIC COMPANY   1.50
THOMPSON, J.
THOMPSON EASIEST PIANO COURSE - PART 6
    WILLIS MUSIC COMPANY   1.50
THOMPSON, J.
THOMPSON EASIEST PIANO COURSE - PART 7
    WILLIS MUSIC COMPANY   1.00
THOMPSON, J.
THOMPSON EASIEST PIANO COURSE - PART 8
    WILLIS MUSIC COMPANY   1.00
TUERK   AUERBACH
KLEINE HANDSTUCKE
    BARENREITER VERLAG   EN 810   3.00
VAILLANT, H.
LE PETIT VIRTUOSE
    GERARD BILLAUDOT EDITIONS MUSICALES   3.30
VEON
BASIC PIANO TECHNIQUE BOOK 1
    VOLKWEIN BROS.   *   .85
VEON
BASIC PIANO TECHNIQUE BOOK 2
    VOLKWEIN BROS.   .85
VEON
SUPPLEMENTARY PIANO STUDIES
    VOLKWEIN BROS.   .85
VINCK
ELEMENTS DE TECHNIQUE --TEXT IN FRENCH-- FOR YOUNG PIANISTS
    DELRIEU ET CIE.   2.75
VOGT, J.
TWENTY-FOUR OCTAVE STUDIES OF MEDIUM DIFFICULTY, OP. 145
    G. SCHIRMER, INC.   L965   1.25
VORLOVA, S.
HAPPY INTERVALS - CHILDREN'S STUDIES
    GENERAL MUSIC PUBLISHING COMPANY, INC. 286 2.50
WAGNESS--ED.   WAGNESS
WAGNESS PIANO COURSE, BK. 4
    SHAWNEE PRESS, INC.   2.00
WARD, J.   ELEMENTARY
ARPEGGIO ETUDES - D1
    PRO-ART PUBLICATIONS, INC.   D1   .75
WARD, J.   LOWER INTERMEDIATE
ARPEGGIO ETUDES - D2
    PRO-ART PUBLICATIONS, INC.   D2   1.00
WARD, J.   UPPER INTERMEDIATE
ARPEGGIO ETUDES - D3
    PRO-ART PUBLICATIONS, INC.   D3   1.25

WARD, J.
    ARPEGGIO ETUDES - D4
        PRO-ART PUBLICATIONS, INC.
                                          ADVANCED
                                            D4   1.50
WARD, J.   ELEMENTARY
    BROKEN CHORD ETUDES - B1
        PRO-ART PUBLICATIONS, INC.   B1   .75
WARD, J.   LOWER INTERMEDIATE
    BROKEN CHORD ETUDES - B2
        PRO-ART PUBLICATIONS, INC.   B2   1.00
WARD, J.   UPPER INTERMEDIATE
    BROKEN CHORD ETUDES - B3
        PRO-ART PUBLICATIONS, INC.   B3   1.25
WARD, J.   ADVANCED
    BROKEN CHORD ETUDES - B4
        PRO-ART PUBLICATIONS, INC.   B4   1.50
WARD, J.   ELEMENTARY
    BROKEN INTERVAL ETUDES - E1
        PRO-ART PUBLICATIONS, INC.   E1   .75
WARD, J.   LOWER INTERMEDIATE
    BROKEN INTERVAL ETUDES - E2
        PRO-ART PUBLICATIONS, INC.   E2   1.00
WARD, J.   UPPER INTERMEDIATE
    BROKEN INTERVAL ETUDES - E3
        PRO-ART PUBLICATIONS, INC.   E3   1.25
WARD, J.   ADVANCED
    BROKEN INTERVAL ETUDES - E4
        PRO-ART PUBLICATIONS, INC.   E4   1.50
WARD, J.   ELEMENTARY
    CHORD ETUDES - K1
        PRO-ART PUBLICATIONS, INC.   K1   .75
WARD, J.   LOWER INTERMEDIATE
    CHORD ETUDES - K2
        PRO-ART PUBLICATIONS, INC.   K2   1.00
WARD, J.   UPPER INTERMEDIATE
    CHORD ETUDES - K3
        PRO-ART PUBLICATIONS, INC.   K3   1.25
WARD, J.   ADVANCED
    CHORD ETUDES - K4
        PRO-ART PUBLICATIONS, INC.   K4   1.50
WARD, J.   ELEMENTARY
    CROSS HAND ETUDES - F1
        PRO-ART PUBLICATIONS, INC.   F1   .75
WARD, J.   LOWER INTERMEDIATE
    CROSS HAND ETUDES - F2
        PRO-ART PUBLICATIONS, INC.   F2   1.00
WARD, J.   UPPER INTERMEDIATE
    CROSS HAND ETUDES - F3
        PRO-ART PUBLICATIONS, INC.   F3   1.25
WARD, J.   ADVANCED
    CROSS HAND ETUDES - F4
        PRO-ART PUBLICATIONS, INC.   F4   1.50
WARD, J.   ELEMENTARY
    DOUBLE NOTE ETUDES - H1
        PRO-ART PUBLICATIONS, INC.   H1   .75
WARD, J.   LOWER INTERMEDIATE
    DOUBLE NOTE ETUDES - H2
        PRO-ART PUBLICATIONS, INC.   H2   1.00
WARD, J.   UPPER INTERMEDIATE
    DOUBLE NOTE ETUDES - H3
        PRO-ART PUBLICATIONS, INC.   H3   1.25
WARD, J.   ADVANCED
    DOUBLE NOTE ETUDES - H4
        PRO-ART PUBLICATIONS, INC.   H4   1.50
WARD, J.   ELEMENTARY
    EMBELLISHMENT ETUDES - G1
        PRO-ART PUBLICATIONS, INC.   G1   .75
WARD, J.   LOWER INTERMEDIATE
    EMBELLISHMENT ETUDES - G2
        PRO-ART PUBLICATIONS, INC.   G2   1.00
WARD, J.   UPPER INTERMEDIATE
    EMBELLISHMENT ETUDES - G3
        PRO-ART PUBLICATIONS, INC.   G3   1.25
WARD, J.   ADVANCED
    EMBELLISHMENT ETUDES - G4
        PRO-ART PUBLICATIONS, INC.   G4   1.50
WARD, J.   ELEMENTARY
    OCTAVE ETUDES - J1
        PRO-ART PUBLICATIONS, INC.   J1   .75
WARD, J.   LOWER INTERMEDIATE
    OCTAVE ETUDES - J2
        PRO-ART PUBLICATIONS, INC.   J2   1.00
WARD, J.   UPPER INTERMEDIATE
    OCTAVE ETUDES - J3
        PRO-ART PUBLICATIONS, INC.   J3   1.25
WARD, J.   ADVANCED
    OCTAVE ETUDES - J4
        PRO-ART PUBLICATIONS, INC.   J4   1.50
WARD, J.   ELEMENTARY
    PASSAGE ETUDES - C1
        PRO-ART PUBLICATIONS, INC.   C1   .75
WARD, J.   LOWER INTERMEDIATE
    PASSAGE ETUDES - C2
        PRO-ART PUBLICATIONS, INC.   C2   1.00
WARD, J.   UPPER INTERMEDIATE
    PASSAGE ETUDES - C3
        PRO-ART PUBLICATIONS, INC.   C3   1.25
WARD, J.   ADVANCED
    PASSAGE ETUDES - C4
        PRO-ART PUBLICATIONS, INC.   C4   1.50
WARD, J.   ELEMENTARY
    SCALE ETUDES - A1
        PRO-ART PUBLICATIONS, INC.   A1   .75
WARD, J.   LOWER INTERMEDIATE
    SCALE ETUDES - A2
        PRO-ART PUBLICATIONS, INC.   A2   1.00
WARD, J.   UPPER INTERMEDIATE
    SCALE ETUDES - A3
        PRO-ART PUBLICATIONS, INC.   A3   1.25
WARD, J.   ADVANCED
    SCALE ETUDES - A4
        PRO-ART PUBLICATIONS, INC.   A4   1.50
WARD, J.   ELEMENTARY
    SELECTED ETUDES - L1
        PRO-ART PUBLICATIONS, INC.   L1   .75
WARD, J.   LOWER INTERMEDIATE
    SELECTED ETUDES - L2
        PRO-ART PUBLICATIONS, INC.   L2   1.00
WARD, J.   UPPER INTERMEDIATE
    SELECTED ETUDES - L3
        PRO-ART PUBLICATIONS, INC.   3   1.25
WARD, J.   ADVANCED
    SELECTED ETUDES - L4
        PRO-ART PUBLICATIONS, INC.   L4   1.50
WEBER, A.
    ETUDES ACROSTICHES EN FORME DE VARIATIONS
        ALPHONSE LEDUC

WEYBRIGHT   2 1/2
    ETUDES FOR PIANISTS, BK. 1
        BELWIN-MILLS PUBLISHING CORPORATION   1.25
WEYBRIGHT   3
    ETUDES FOR PIANISTS, BK. 2
        BELWIN-MILLS PUBLISHING CORPORATION   1.25
WEYBRIGHT   2
    TECHNIC FOR PIANISTS, BK. 1
        BELWIN-MILLS PUBLISHING CORPORATION   1.25
WEYBRIGHT   2 1/2
    TECHNIC FOR PIANISTS, BK. 2
        BELWIN-MILLS PUBLISHING CORPORATION   1.25
WHITFORD--ED.   WHITFORD
    ROBERT WHITFORD CLASSIC PIANO METHOD, BK. 01
        ROBERT WHITFORD PUBLICATIONS   1.60
WHITFORD--ED.   WHITFORD
    ROBERT WHITFORD CLASSIC PIANO METHOD, BK. 02
        ROBERT WHITFORD PUBLICATIONS   1.60
WHITFORD--ED.   WHITFORD
    ROBERT WHITFORD CLASSIC PIANO METHOD, BK. 03
        ROBERT WHITFORD PUBLICATIONS   1.80
WHITFORD--ED.   WHITFORD
    ROBERT WHITFORD CLASSIC PIANO METHOD, BK. 04
        ROBERT WHITFORD PUBLICATIONS   1.80
WHITFORD--ED.   WHITFORD
    ROBERT WHITFORD CLASSIC PIANO METHOD, BK. 05
        ROBERT WHITFORD PUBLICATIONS   1.80
WHITFORD--ED.   WHITFORD
    ROBERT WHITFORD CLASSIC PIANO METHOD, BK. 06
        ROBERT WHITFORD PUBLICATIONS   1.80
WHITFORD--ED.   WHITFORD
    ROBERT WHITFORD CLASSIC PIANO METHOD, BK. 07
        ROBERT WHITFORD PUBLICATIONS   2.00
WHITFORD--ED.   WHITFORD
    ROBERT WHITFORD CLASSIC PIANO METHOD, BK. 08
        ROBERT WHITFORD PUBLICATIONS   2.00
WHITFORD--ED.   WHITFORD
    ROBERT WHITFORD CLASSIC PIANO METHOD, BK. 09
        ROBERT WHITFORD PUBLICATIONS   2.00
WHITFORD--ED.   WHITFORD
    ROBERT WHITFORD CLASSIC PIANO METHOD, BK. 10
        ROBERT WHITFORD PUBLICATIONS   2.00
WHITFORD--ED.   WHITFORD
    ROBERT WHITFORD MODERN PIANO METHOD, BK. 1
        ROBERT WHITFORD PUBLICATIONS   2.50
WHITFORD--ED.   WHITFORD
    ROBERT WHITFORD MODERN PIANO METHOD, BK. 2
        ROBERT WHITFORD PUBLICATIONS   2.50
WHITFORD--ED.   WHITFORD
    ROBERT WHITFORD MODERN PIANO METHOD, BK. 3
        ROBERT WHITFORD PUBLICATIONS   2.50
WHITFORD--ED.   WHITFORD
    ROBERT WHITFORD MODERN PIANO METHOD, BK. 4
        ROBERT WHITFORD PUBLICATIONS   2.50
WHITFORD
    FILL-INS FOR THE PIANIST
        ROBERT WHITFORD PUBLICATIONS   1.00
WHITFORD
    ROBERT WHITFORD BREAK SHEET BOOK FOR PIANO
        ROBERT WHITFORD PUBLICATIONS   2.50
WHITFORD
    ROBERT WHITFORD CHORD CHART FOR THE MODERN PIANIST
        ROBERT WHITFORD PUBLICATIONS   1.50
WHITFORD
    ROBERT WHITFORD MODERN PIANO EFFECTS
        ROBERT WHITFORD PUBLICATIONS   2.00
WHITFORD
    ROBERT WHITFORD TECHNIC FOR PIANISTS, BK. 1
        ROBERT WHITFORD PUBLICATIONS   1.25
WHITFORD
    ROBERT WHITFORD TECHNIC FOR PIANISTS, BK. 2
        ROBERT WHITFORD PUBLICATIONS   1.25
WHITFORD
    ROBERT WHITFORD TECHNIC FOR PIANISTS, BK. 3
        ROBERT WHITFORD PUBLICATIONS   1.25
WHITFORD
    ROBERT WHITFORD TECHNIC FOR PIANISTS, BK. 4
        ROBERT WHITFORD PUBLICATIONS   1.50
WHITFORD
    ROBERT WHITFORD TECHNIC FOR PIANISTS, BK. 5
        ROBERT WHITFORD PUBLICATIONS   1.50
WHITFORD
    ROBERT WHITFORD TECHNIC FOR PIANISTS, BK. 6
        ROBERT WHITFORD PUBLICATIONS   1.50
WIECK   M-D
    PIANO STUDIES
        C. F. PETERS CORPORATION   375   1.50
WIECK
    STUDIES
        G. SCHIRMER, INC.   L66   1.00
WIEHMAYER, T.
    SCHOOL OF ARPEGGIOS -- GER AND FR NOTES
        ASSOCIATED MUSIC PUBLISHERS, INC. BRH   .50
WIEHMAYER, T.
    SCHOOL OF SCALES -- ENG AND GER NOTES
        ASSOCIATED MUSIC PUBLISHERS, INC. BRH   1.80
WIERNSBERGER, J.
    METHODE THEORIQUE ET PRATIQUE DE PIANO, PART 1
        GERARD BILLAUDOT EDITIONS MUSICALES   3.30
WILDGANS, F.
    ETUDE--1949
        ASSOCIATED MUSIC PUBLISHERS, INC. DOB   1.50
WISSMER, P.
    THREE ETUDES
        GERARD BILLAUDOT EDITIONS MUSICALES   3.30
WITTGENSTEIN, P.
    SCHOOL FOR THE LEFT HAND, BK. 1, EXERCISES
        UNIVERSAL EDITION   UE 12327   3.25
WITTGENSTEIN, P.
    SCHOOL FOR THE LEFT HAND, BK. 2, STUDIES
        UNIVERSAL EDITION   UE 12328   2.50
WITTGENSTEIN, P.
    SCHOOL FOR THE LEFT HAND, BK. 3, TRANSCRIPTIONS
        UNIVERSAL EDITION   UE 12329   3.35
WOHLFAHRT
    EASY FOUR HAND PIECES FOR CHILDREN, OP. 87
        EDWIN F. KALMUS   4039   2.00
WOLFF, B. C.
    LITTLE PISCHNA
        CARL FISCHER, INC.   L 475   1.00
WOLFF, B.
    TWELVE SHORT OCTAVE-STUDIES, OP. 118
        G. SCHIRMER, INC.   L1099   .75
WRIGHT, N.
    PIECES FOR THE DEVELOPMENT OF TECHNIC
        THEODORE PRESSER COMPANY   .75

WUEHRER   D
    EIGHTEEN STUDIES TO CHOPIN ETUDES, OP. 10 AND 25 --UN MOTU
    CONTRARIO--
        C. F. PETERS CORPORATION   WM110   3.50
WURMSER, L.
    GRADUS MODERNE, LE--NO. 1, MOUVEMENT
        ASSOCIATED MUSIC PUBLISHERS, INC.   ESC   1.00
WURMSER, L.
    GRADUS MODERNE, LE--NO. 2, MAIN GAUCHE SEULE
        ASSOCIATED MUSIC PUBLISHERS, INC.   ESC   1.50
WURMSER, L.
    GRADUS MODERNE, LE--NO. 3, PAPILLONS BLANCS
        ASSOCIATED MUSIC PUBLISHERS, INC.   ESC   1.50
WURMSER, L.
    GRADUS MODERNE, LE--NO. 4, PETITE TOCCATA
        ASSOCIATED MUSIC PUBLISHERS, INC.   ESC   1.50
WURMSER, L.
    GRADUS MODERNE, LE--NO. 5, L'ENJOUEE
        ASSOCIATED MUSIC PUBLISHERS, INC.   ESC   1.50
WURMSER, L.
    GRADUS MODERNE, LE--NO. 6, ARABESQUES
        ASSOCIATED MUSIC PUBLISHERS, INC.   ESC   1.50
WURMSER, L.
    QUELQUES EXERCISES POUR LE PIANO
        FRANCO COLOMBO PUBLICATIONS   SAL   2.25
ZEPP
    DEVELOPING TECHNIC AND MUSICIANSHIP
        PRO-ART PUBLICATIONS, INC.   1219   1.25
ZEPP
    LET'S GET TECHNICAL
        PRO-ART PUBLICATIONS, INC.   557   1.00
ZEPP
    LET'S LEARN MAJOR SCALES AND CHORDS
        PRO-ART PUBLICATIONS, INC.   385   1.00
ZEPP
    LET'S LEARN MINOR SCALES AND CHORDS
        PRO-ART PUBLICATIONS, INC.   934   1.00

Technical Material:
Composer/Editor/Arranger Unlisted—Works Alphabetized by Title

    GRADED SIGHT-READING - BOOK 1
        BOSTON MUSIC COMPANY   1.75

    GRADED SIGHT-READING - BOOK 2
        BOSTON MUSIC COMPANY   1.75

    GRADED SIGHT-READING - BOOK 3
        BOSTON MUSIC COMPANY   1.75

    GRADED SIGHT-READING - BOOK 4
        BOSTON MUSIC COMPANY   1.75

    IT'S EASY TO PLAY PIANO THE THREE CHORD WAY
        MUSIC SALES CORPORATION   040041   2.95

    MAJOR SCALES - BOOK 1
        BOSTON MUSIC COMPANY   1.95

    MAJOR SCALES - BOOK 2
        BOSTON MUSIC COMPANY   1.25

    MUSIC EDUCATION SUPPLEMENT - COMPLETE SET B-17 THROUGH B-20
        BERKLEE PRESS PUBLICATIONS   COMPLETE SET   17.50

    MUSIC EDUCATION SUPPLEMENT - VOL. 1
        BERKLEE PRESS PUBLICATIONS   B-17   5.00

    MUSIC EDUCATION SUPPLEMENT - VOL. 2
        BERKLEE PRESS PUBLICATIONS   B-18   5.00

    MUSIC EDUCATION SUPPLEMENT - VOL. 3
        BERKLEE PRESS PUBLICATIONS   B-19   5.00

    MUSIC EDUCATION SUPPLEMENT - VOL. 4
        BERKLEE PRESS PUBLICATIONS   B-20   5.00

    NEW INSTRUCTIONS FOR PLAYING THE HARPSICHORD, PIANO-FORTE, OR
    SPINNET
        BROUDE BROTHERS LTD.   20.00

    ROYAL CONSERVATORY OF MUSIC, UNIVERSITY OF TORONTO -- SCALES,
    CHORDS AND ARPEGGIOS FOR PIANO
        FREDERICK HARRIS MUSIC COMPANY   1.40

    ROYAL CONSERVATORY OF MUSIC, UNIVERSITY OF TORONTO -- STUDIES,
    GRADES 7 AND 8
        FREDERICK HARRIS MUSIC COMPANY   2.60

    ROYAL CONSERVATORY OF MUSIC, UNIVERSITY OF TORONTO -- STUDIES,
    GRADES 9 AND 10
        FREDERICK HARRIS MUSIC COMPANY   2.10

    ROYAL CONSERVATORY OF MUSIC, UNIVERSITY OF TORONTO -- TECHNICAL
    REQUIREMENTS HANDBOOK FOR PIANOFORTE, GRADES 1 TO ASSOCIATESHIP
        FREDERICK HARRIS MUSIC COMPANY   1.80

    WESTERN ONTARIO CONSERVATORY OF MUSIC -- TECHNICAL REQUIREMENTS,
    BK. 1, GRADES 1, 2 AND 3
        FREDERICK HARRIS MUSIC COMPANY   .70

    WESTERN ONTARIO CONSERVATORY OF MUSIC -- TECHNICAL REQUIREMENTS,
    BK. 2, GRADES 4 AND 5
        FREDERICK HARRIS MUSIC COMPANY   .70

Simplified Versions

ADAM, A.   STEINER
    CANTIQUE DE NOEL
        G. SCHIRMER, INC.   .50
ADAMS, R. G.   SPENCER, J.   2
    O HOLY NIGHT
        VOLKWEIN BROS.   .30
ADAMS, S.   3
    HOLY CITY
        BOSTON MUSIC COMPANY   .50
ADLER, R. *   EASY
    HITS FROM 'DAMN YANKEES'
        FRANK MUSIC CORPORATION   1.25
ADLER, R. *   PACE, R.   EASY
    SONGS FROM 'THE PAJAMA GAME'
        FRANK MUSIC CORPORATION   1.25
AGAY, D.--ED   AGAY, D.   EASY
    MATINEE MELODIES
        FRANK MUSIC CORPORATION   1.50
AGAY, D.--ED   AGAY, D.
    POPULAR MASTERPIECES
        MUSIC SALES CORPORATION   080055   .85
ALBENIZ, I.
    MALAGUENA
        EDWARD B. MARKS MUSIC CORPORATION   01.00
ALFASSY, L.--ED   ALFASSY, L.
    CHILDREN'S JAZZ PIECES
        MUSIC SALES CORPORATION   040056   2.95
ALFORD, K.
    COLONEL BOGEY
        BOOSEY AND HAWKES, INC.   .60
ANDERSON, L.   KING, S.
    SYNCOPATED CLOCK, THE -- SIMP.
        BELWIN-MILLS PUBLISHING CORPORATION 26037   .75
ARNDT
    NOLA -- SIMPLIFIED
        SOUTHERN MUSIC COMPANY   1.00
ARNDT
    NOLA
        SAM FOX PUBLISHING COMPANY, INC.   1.00
AULD, W. J.
    PIANO HYMNSCRIPTIONS NO. 1
        LILLENAS PUBLISHING COMPANY   MB-148   2.50
AULD, W. J.
    PIANO HYMNSCRIPTIONS NO. 2
        LILLENAS PUBLISHING COMPANY   MB-149   2.50
BACH, J.S.   BARTH, H.
    ALLEMANDE IN A MINOR
        BELWIN-MILLS PUBLISHING CORPORATION 20370   .50
BACH, J.S.   SCHAUM, J.   2 1/2
    BACH-SCHAUM, BK. 1
        BELWIN-MILLS PUBLISHING CORPORATION   1.25
BACH, J.S.   SCHAUM, J.   3-4
    BACH-SCHAUM, BK. 2
        BELWIN-MILLS PUBLISHING CORPORATION   1.25
BACH, J.S.   LIPSCOMB
    JESU, JOY OF MAN'S DESIRING
        G. SCHIRMER, INC.   .60
BACHMANN, G.   ROLFE, W.   3
    SYLPHES, LES, EASY
        CENTURY MUSIC PUBLISHING COMPANY, INC. 3365   .40
BART   GREEN
    OLIVER - EASY PIANO
        TRO SONGWAYS SERVICE, INC.   1.95
BEAUMONT, P.   2
    WITH MY LOVE, EASY
        CENTURY MUSIC PUBLISHING COMPANY, INC. 2589   .40
BEETHOVEN   ECKHARDT, F.   1
    BEETHOVEN FOR THE YOUNG PIANIST
        CENTURY MUSIC PUBLISHING COMPANY, INC. 3957   .40
BEETHOVEN   ROVENGER
    BEETHOVEN FOR THE YOUNG
        RUBANK, INC.   1.50
BEETHOVEN   MITTLER   2B
    FIFTH SYMPHONY
        MUSICORD PUBLICATIONS, INC.   .45
BEETHOVEN   DEIS
    GAVOTTE IN F MAJOR
        G. SCHIRMER, INC.   .50
BEETHOVEN   ECKSTEIN
    MOONLIGHT SONATA, FIRST MVT.
        CARL FISCHER, INC.   S 2311   .50
BEETHOVEN   MITTLER   2B
    MOONLIGHT SONATA
        MUSICORD PUBLICATIONS, INC.   .45
BEETHOVEN   PODOLSKY, J.
    SONATA NO. 08 IN C MINOR, OP. 13
        VOLKWEIN BROS.   1.00
BELL, W.--ARR.   BELL, W.   EASY
    JUST FOR FUN - HIT TUNES EVERYBODY KNOWS
        SCREEN GEMS - COLUMBIA PUBLICATIONS F0126P4   1.95
BELL, W.--ARR.   BELL. W.   EASY
    JUST FOR FUN - MELODIES EVERYBODY KNOWS
        SCREEN GEMS - COLUMBIA PUBLICATIONS F0125P4   1.95
BELL, W.--ARR.   BELL, W.   EASY
    JUST FOR FUN - POPS EVERYBODY KNOWS
        SCREEN GEMS - COLUMBIA PUBLICATIONS F0081P4   1.50
BELL, W.--ARR.   BELL, W.   EASY
    JUST FOR FUN - SHOW TUNES EVERYBODY KNOWS
        SCREEN GEMS - COLUMBIA PUBLICATIONS F0107P4   1.95
BELLINI   PALMERI
    CANTO NAPOLETANO
        G. SCHIRMER, INC.   .50
BELLINI   DEL MAGLIO
    DOLENTE IMAGINE
        FRANCO COLOMBO PUBLICATIONS   128122   .50
BELLINI   BURGMUELLER   2
    MARCH, NORMA
        CENTURY MUSIC PUBLISHING COMPANY, INC. 647   .40
BELLINI   KRUG   2
    NORMA, EASY TRANSCRIPTION
        CENTURY MUSIC PUBLISHING COMPANY, INC. 525   .40
BELLINI   DEL MAGLIO
    NORMA - CASTA DIVA
        FRANCO COLOMBO PUBLICATIONS   128139   .50
BELLINI   DEL MAGLIO
    NORMA - DELL'AURA TUA PROFETICA
        FRANCO COLOMBO PUBLICATIONS   124708   .60
BERMONT, H.--ED   BERMONT, H.
    ALL-AMERICAN FOLK SONGS, BK. 1
        MUSICORD PUBLICATIONS, INC.   1.50
BERMONT, H.--ED   BERMONT, H.
    ALL-AMERICAN FOLK SONGS, BK. 2
        MUSICORD PUBLICATIONS, INC.   1.50

BERMONT, H.--ED   BERMONT, H.
    LETS PLAY CAROLS
        MUSICORD PUBLICATIONS, INC.   1.00
BERMONT, H.--ED   BERMONT, H.
    TUNEFUL VARIETIES, BK. 1
        MUSICORD PUBLICATIONS, INC.   1.25
BERMONT, H.--ED   BERMONT, H.
    TUNEFUL VARIETIES, BK. 2
        MUSICORD PUBLICATIONS, INC.   1.25
BERMONT, H.--ED   BERMONT, H.
    TWENTY-EIGHT STAR MELODIES, BK. 1
        MUSICORD PUBLICATIONS, INC.   1.25
BERMONT, H.--ED   BERMONT, H.
    YOUR HIT TUNES - GREEN BOOK
        MUSICORD PUBLICATIONS, INC.   1.25
BERMONT, H.--ED   BERMONT, H.
    YOUR HIT TUNES - RED BOOK
        MUSICORD PUBLICATIONS, INC.   1.25
BERNSTEIN, L.   STICKLES
    WEST SIDE STORY, SELECTIONS FROM
        G. SCHIRMER, INC.   1.25
BIZET, G.   E
    CARMEN. COMPLETE.
        C. F. PETERS CORPORATION   H639   2.00
BIZET, G.   LOEW, J.   3
    MARCH, CARMEN
        CENTURY MUSIC PUBLISHING COMPANY, INC. 1632   .40
BLACK, M.
    PAPER DOLL
        EDWARD B. MARKS MUSIC CORPORATION   01.00
BLAKE--ED   BLAKE
    TALES AND TUNES FROM GRAND OPERA
        WILLIS MUSIC COMPANY   1.50
BOCCHERINI   CHIESA
    FAMOUS MINUET - FROM QUINTET, OP. 13 NO. 5
        FRANCO COLOMBO PUBLICATIONS   107478   .60
BOCCHERINI   DEL MAGLIO
    SECOND FAMOUS MINUET
        FRANCO COLOMBO PUBLICATIONS   128151   .50
BOHM   ROLFE, W.   3
    ZINGANA, LA, EASY
        CENTURY MUSIC PUBLISHING COMPANY, INC. 3363   .40
BOLZONI   DEL MAGLIO
    MINUETTO
        FRANCO COLOMBO PUBLICATIONS   127752   .50
BORODIN, A.   ZEPP   4
    MELODIC THEME FROM POLOVETZIAN DANCE
        PRO-ART PUBLICATIONS, INC.   163   .50
BORODIN, A.   POST   1-2
    POLOVETSIAN DANCE, PRINCE IGOR
        CENTURY MUSIC PUBLISHING COMPANY, INC. 4159   .40
BRADLEY, R.--ARR.   BRADLEY, R.   EASY
    ABRAHAM, MARTIN AND JOHN
        SCREEN GEMS - COLUMBIA PUBLICATIONS 0403AP2   .85
BRADLEY, R.--ARR.   BRADLEY, R.   EASY
    ALLEY CAT
        SCREEN GEMS - COLUMBIA PUBLICATIONS 3733AP2   .85
BRADLEY, R.--ARR.   BRADLEY, R.   BIG NOTE EASY
    AMAZING GRACE - AND - HE'S GOT THE WHOLE WORLD IN HIS HANDS
        SCREEN GEMS - COLUMBIA PUBLICATIONS C0019P3   1.00
BRADLEY, R.--ARR.   BRADLEY, R.   EASY
    AM I LOSING YOU
        SCREEN GEMS - COLUMBIA PUBLICATIONS 4002AP2   .85
BRADLEY, R.--ARR.   BRADLEY, R.   EASY
    ARE YOU LONESOME TONIGHT
        SCREEN GEMS - COLUMBIA PUBLICATIONS 5703AP2   .85
BRADLEY, R.--ARR.   BRADLEY, R.   EASY
    AUBREY
        SCREEN GEMS - COLUMBIA PUBLICATIONS 6704AP2   .85
BRADLEY, R.--ARR.   BRADLEY, R.   EASY
    BABY DON'T GET HOOKED ON ME
        SCREEN GEMS - COLUMBIA PUBLICATIONS 0010BP2   .85
BRADLEY, R.--ARR.   BRADLEY, R.   EASY
    BABY I'M-A WANT YOU
        SCREEN GEMS - COLUMBIA PUBLICATIONS 0003BP2   .85
BRADLEY, R.--ARR.   BRADLEY, R.   EASY
    BACK TO CALIFORNIA
        SCREEN GEMS - COLUMBIA PUBLICATIONS 0004BP2   .85
BRADLEY, R.--ARR.   BRADLEY, R.   EASY
    BEAUTIFUL CITY
        SCREEN GEMS - COLUMBIA PUBLICATIONS 1430BP2   .85
BRADLEY, R.--ARR.   BRADLEY, R.   EASY
    BEEN TO CANAAN
        SCREEN GEMS - COLUMBIA PUBLICATIONS 1423BP2   .85
BRADLEY, R.--ARR.   BRADLEY, R.   EASY
    BEN
        SCREEN GEMS - COLUMBIA PUBLICATIONS 1443BP2   .85
BRADLEY, R.--ARR.   BRADLEY, R.   BIG NOTE EASY
    BLACK AND WHITE - AND - BRIAN'S SONG
        SCREEN GEMS - COLUMBIA PUBLICATIONS C0015P3   1.00
BRADLEY, R.--ARR.   BRADLEY, R.   EASY
    BLACK AND WHITE
        SCREEN GEMS - COLUMBIA PUBLICATIONS 3712BP2   .85
BRADLEY, R.--ARR.   BRADLEY, R.   EASY
    BLESS THE BEASTS AND CHILDREN
        SCREEN GEMS - COLUMBIA PUBLICATIONS 3702BP2   .85
BRADLEY, R.--ARR.   BRADLEY, R.   BIG NOTE EASY
    BORN FREE
        SCREEN GEMS - COLUMBIA PUBLICATIONS 4701BP3   .85
BRADLEY, R.--ARR.   BRADLEY, R.   EASY
    BORN FREE
        SCREEN GEMS - COLUMBIA PUBLICATIONS 4701BP2   .85
BRADLEY, R.--ARR.   BRADLEY, R.   EASY
    BRADLEY'S BEST OF THE BEST - BREAD
        SCREEN GEMS - COLUMBIA PUBLICATIONS F0108P2   1.75
BRADLEY, R.--ARR.   BRADLEY, R.   EASY
    BRADLEY'S BEST OF THE BEST - BROADWAY
        SCREEN GEMS - COLUMBIA PUBLICATIONS F0077P2   1.75
BRADLEY, R.--ARR.   BRADLEY, R.   EASY
    BRADLEY'S BEST OF THE BEST - CAROLE KING
        SCREEN GEMS - COLUMBIA PUBLICATIONS F0027P2A   1.75
BRADLEY, R.--ARR.   BRADLEY, R.   EASY
    BRADLEY'S BEST OF THE BEST - CHRISTMAS CAROLS
        SCREEN GEMS - COLUMBIA PUBLICATIONS F0211P2   1.75
BRADLEY, R.--ARR.   BRADLEY, R.   EASY
    BRADLEY'S BEST OF THE BEST - COUNTRY HITS
        SCREEN GEMS - COLUMBIA PUBLICATIONS F0029P2   1.50
BRADLEY, R.--ARR.   BRADLEY, R.   EASY
    BRADLEY'S BEST OF THE BEST - MOTION PICTURE HITS
        SCREEN GEMS - COLUMBIA PUBLICATIONS F0037P2   1.50
BRADLEY, R.--ARR.   BRADLEY, R.   EASY
    BRADLEY'S BEST OF THE BEST - POPULAR SACRED SONGS
        SCREEN GEMS - COLUMBIA PUBLICATIONS F0135P2   1.50
BRADLEY, R.--ARR.   BRADLEY, R.   EASY
    BRADLEY'S BEST OF THE BEST - POP TEACHING PIECES
        SCREEN GEMS - COLUMBIA PUBLICATIONS F0230P2   1.75

BRADLEY, R.--ARR.   BRADLEY, R.   BIG NOTE EASY
 BRADLEY'S BIG NOTE BLOCKBUSTERS
        SCREEN GEMS - COLUMBIA PUBLICATIONS   F0233P3   2.95
BRADLEY, R.--ARR.   BRADLEY, R.   EASY
 BRADLEY'S CHRISTMAS JOY - ISSUE NO. 1
        SCREEN GEMS - COLUMBIA PUBLICATIONS   F0213P2   1.75
BRADLEY, R.--ARR.   BRADLEY, R.   EASY
 BRADLEY'S COUNTRY JOY - ISSUE NO. 1
        SCREEN GEMS - COLUMBIA PUBLICATIONS   F0189P2   1.50
BRADLEY, R.--ARR.   BRADLEY, R.   EASY
 BRADLEY'S HYMN JOY - ISSUE NO. 1
        SCREEN GEMS - COLUMBIA PUBLICATIONS   F0275P2   1.50
BRADLEY, R.--ARR.   BRADLEY, R.   EASY
 BRADLEY'S POPULAR JOY - ISSUE NO. 1
        SCREEN GEMS - COLUMBIA PUBLICATIONS   F0128P2   1.50
BRADLEY, R.--ARR.   BRADLEY, R.   EASY
 BRADLEY'S POPULAR JOY - ISSUE NO. 2
        SCREEN GEMS - COLUMBIA PUBLICATIONS   F0187P2   1.50
BRADLEY, R.--ARR.   BRADLEY, R.   EASY
 BRADLEY'S POPULAR JOY - ISSUE NO. 3
        SCREEN GEMS - COLUMBIA PUBLICATIONS   F0216P2   1.50
BRADLEY, P.--ARR.   BRADLEY, R.   EASY
 BRADLEY'S POPULAR JOY - ISSUE NO. 4
        SCREEN GEMS - COLUMBIA PUBLICATIONS   F0261P2   1.50
BRADLEY, R.--ARR.   BRADLEY, R.   EASY
 BRADLEY'S SUPERSTARS
        SCREEN GEMS - COLUMBIA PUBLICATIONS   F0223P2   2.50
BRADLEY, R.--ARR.   BRADLEY, R.   EASY
 BRADLEY'S SUPER POPULAR MUSIC
        SCREEN GEMS - COLUMBIA PUBLICATIONS   F0016P2   2.50
BRADLEY, R.--ARR.   BRADLEY, R.   EASY
 BRADLEY - LIKE IT IS TODAY - EASY PIANO HIT PARADE NO. 1
        SCREEN GEMS - COLUMBIA PUBLICATIONS   F0025P2   1.25
BRADLEY, R.--ARR.   BRADLEY, R.   EASY
 BRADLEY - LIKE IT IS TODAY - EASY PIANO HIT PARADE NO. 2
        SCREEN GEMS - COLUMBIA PUBLICATIONS   F0051P2   1.50
BRADLEY, R.--ARR.   BRADLEY, R.   EASY
 BRADLEY - LIKE IT IS TODAY - EASY PIANO HIT PARADE NO. 3
        SCREEN GEMS - COLUMBIA PUBLICATIONS   F0075P2   1.75
BRADLEY, R.--ARR.   BRADLEY, R.   EASY
 BRADLEY - LIKE IT IS TODAY - EASY PIANO HIT PARADE NO. 4
        SCREEN GEMS - COLUMBIA PUBLICATIONS   F0100P2   1.75
BRADLEY, R.--ARR.   BRADLEY, R.   EASY
 BREAKING UP IS HARD TO DO
        SCREEN GEMS - COLUMBIA PUBLICATIONS   5701BP2   .85
BRADLEY, R.--ARR.   BRADLEY, R.   BIG NOTE EASY
 BRIAN'S SONG
        SCREEN GEMS - COLUMBIA PUBLICATIONS   5707BP3   .85
BRADLEY, R.--ARR.   BRADLEY, R.   EASY
 BRIAN'S SONG
        SCREEN GEMS - COLUMBIA PUBLICATIONS   5707BP2   .85
BRADLEY, R.--ARR.   BRADLEY, R.   EASY
 BY THE TIME I GET TO PHOENIX
        SCREEN GEMS - COLUMBIA PUBLICATIONS   8002BP2   .85
BRADLEY, R.--ARR.   BRADLEY, R.   BIG NOTE EASY
 CANDY MAN, THE - AND - BORN FREE
        SCREEN GEMS - COLUMBIA PUBLICATIONS   C0016P3   1.00
BRADLEY, R.--ARR.   BRADLEY, R.   BIG NOTE EASY
 CANDY MAN, THE
        SCREEN GEMS - COLUMBIA PUBLICATIONS   0007CP3   .85
BRADLEY, R.--ARR.   BRADLEY, R.   EASY
 CANDY MAN, THE
        SCREEN GEMS - COLUMBIA PUBLICATIONS   0007CP2   .85
BRADLEY, R.--ARR.   BRADLEY, R.   EASY
 CHERISH
        SCREEN GEMS - COLUMBIA PUBLICATIONS   2406CP2   .85
BRADLEY, R.--ARR.   BRADLEY, R.   EASY
 CLOUDS
        SCREEN GEMS - COLUMBIA PUBLICATIONS   3709CP2   .85
BRADLEY, R.--ARR.   BRADLEY, R.   EASY
 COUNTRY POPS
        SCREEN GEMS - COLUMBIA PUBLICATIONS   F0244P2   2.95
BRADLEY, R.--ARR.   BRADLEY, R.   EASY
 DAY BY DAY
        SCREEN GEMS - COLUMBIA PUBLICATIONS   0014DP2   .85
BRADLEY, R.--ARR.   BRADLEY, R.   EASY
 DIARY
        SCREEN GEMS - COLUMBIA PUBLICATIONS   2705DP2   .85
BRADLEY, R.--ARR.   BRADLEY, R.   EASY
 DON'T IT MAKE YOU WANTA GO HOME
        SCREEN GEMS - COLUMBIA PUBLICATIONS   4706DP2   .85
BRADLEY, R.--ARR.   BRADLEY, R.   EASY
 EVERYTHING I OWN
        SCREEN GEMS - COLUMBIA PUBLICATIONS   7007EP2   .85
BRADLEY, R.--ARR.   BRADLEY, R.   EASY
 FIRST TIME EVER I SAW YOUR FACE, THE
        SCREEN GEMS - COLUMBIA PUBLICATIONS   2703FP2   .85
BRADLEY, R.--ARR.   BRADLEY, R.   EASY
 FOR ONCE IN MY LIFE
        SCREEN GEMS - COLUMBIA PUBLICATIONS   4717FP2   .85
BRADLEY, R.--ARR.   BRADLEY, R.   EASY
 FUNNY FACE
        SCREEN GEMS - COLUMBIA PUBLICATIONS   6706FP2   .85
BRADLEY, R.--ARR.   BRADLEY, R.   EASY
 GOING OUT OF MY HEAD
        SCREEN GEMS - COLUMBIA PUBLICATIONS   4717GP2   .85
BRADLEY, R.--ARR.   BRADLEY, R.   EASY
 GO AWAY LITTLE GIRL
        SCREEN GEMS - COLUMBIA PUBLICATIONS   4702GP2   .85
BRADLEY, R.--ARR.   BRADLEY, R.   EASY
 GREEN GREEN GRASS OF HOME
        SCREEN GEMS - COLUMBIA PUBLICATIONS   5702GP2   .85
BRADLEY, R.--ARR.   BRADLEY, R.   EASY
 GUITAR MAN, THE
        SCREEN GEMS - COLUMBIA PUBLICATIONS   6704GP2   .85
BRADLEY, R.--ARR.   BRADLEY, R.   EASY
 HANDS OF TIME, THE
        SCREEN GEMS - COLUMBIA PUBLICATIONS   0011HP2   .85
BRADLEY, R.--ARR.   BRADLEY, R.   EASY
 HAPPIEST GIRL IN THE WHOLE U.S.A., THE
        SCREEN GEMS - COLUMBIA PUBLICATIONS   0014HP2   .85
BRADLEY, R.--ARR.   BRADLEY, R.   EASY
 HAVA NAGILA
        SCREEN GEMS - COLUMBIA PUBLICATIONS   0026HP2   .85
BRADLEY, R.--ARR.   BRADLEY, R.   EASY
 HEY, GIRL
        SCREEN GEMS - COLUMBIA PUBLICATIONS   1402HP2   .85
BRADLEY, R.--ARR.   BRADLEY, R.   EASY
 HI-DE-HO --THAT OLD SWEET ROLL--
        SCREEN GEMS - COLUMBIA PUBLICATIONS   2701HP2   .85
BRADLEY, R.--ARR.   BRADLEY, R.   EASY
 HOLLY JOLLY CHRISTMAS, A
        SCREEN GEMS - COLUMBIA PUBLICATIONS   4714HP2   .85
BRADLEY, R.--ARR.   BRADLEY, R.   EASY
 HOME AGAIN
        SCREEN GEMS - COLUMBIA PUBLICATIONS   4703HP2   .85

BRADLEY, R.--ARR.   BRADLEY, R.   EASY
 HOUSE OF THE RISING SUN, THE
        SCREEN GEMS - COLUMBIA PUBLICATIONS   4701HP2   .85
BRADLEY, R.--ARR.   BRADLEY, R.   EASY
 HURTING EACH OTHER
        SCREEN GEMS - COLUMBIA PUBLICATIONS   6704HP2   .85
BRADLEY, R.--ARR.   BRADLEY, R.   EASY
 IF
        SCREEN GEMS - COLUMBIA PUBLICATIONS   1702IP2   .85
BRADLEY, R.--ARR.   BRADLEY, R.   EASY
 IN TUNE WITH THE TIMES
        SCREEN GEMS - COLUMBIA PUBLICATIONS   F0145P2   2.95
BRADLEY, R.--ARR.   BRADLEY, R.   EASY
 IT'S GOING TO TAKE SOME TIME
        SCREEN GEMS - COLUMBIA PUBLICATIONS   6415IP2   .85
BRADLEY, R.--ARR.   BRADLEY, R.   EASY
 IT'S ONE OF THOSE NIGHTS --YES LOVE--
        SCREEN GEMS - COLUMBIA PUBLICATIONS   6414IP2   .85
BRADLEY, R.--ARR.   BRADLEY, R.   EASY
 I BELIEVE IN MUSIC
        SCREEN GEMS - COLUMBIA PUBLICATIONS   0402IP2   .85
BRADLEY, R.--ARR.   BRADLEY, R.   EASY
 I GOT A NAME
        SCREEN GEMS - COLUMBIA PUBLICATIONS   2004IP2   .85
BRADLEY, R.--ARR.   BRADLEY, R.   EASY
 I KNEW YOU WHEN
        SCREEN GEMS - COLUMBIA PUBLICATIONS   3401IP2   .85
BRADLEY, R.--ARR.   BRADLEY, R.   EASY
 I NEVER PROMISED YOU A ROSE GARDEN
        SCREEN GEMS - COLUMBIA PUBLICATIONS   4702RP2   .85
BRADLEY, R.--ARR.   BRADLEY, R.   EASY
 I WILL WAIT FOR YOU
        SCREEN GEMS - COLUMBIA PUBLICATIONS   7408IP2   .85
BRADLEY, R.--ARR.   BRADLEY, R.   EASY
 I WOKE UP IN LOVE THIS MORNING
        SCREEN GEMS - COLUMBIA PUBLICATIONS   7402IP2   .85
BRADLEY, R.--ARR.   BRADLEY, R.   EASY
 JEAN
        SCREEN GEMS - COLUMBIA PUBLICATIONS   1417JP2   .85
BRADLEY, R.--ARR.   BRADLEY, R.   BIG NOTE EASY
 JINGLE BELLS
        SCREEN GEMS - COLUMBIA PUBLICATIONS   2703JP2   .85
BRADLEY, R.--ARR.   BRADLEY, R.   BIG NOTE EASY
 JOY TO THE WORLD
        SCREEN GEMS - COLUMBIA PUBLICATIONS   4703JP3   .85
BRADLEY, R.--ARR.   BRADLEY, R.   EASY
 JOY TO THE WORLD
        SCREEN GEMS - COLUMBIA PUBLICATIONS   4703JP2   .85
BRADLEY, R.--ARR.   BRADLEY, R.   EASY
 JOY
        SCREEN GEMS - COLUMBIA PUBLICATIONS   4706JP2   .85
BRADLEY, R.--ARR.   BRADLEY, R.   EASY
 KNOCKIN' ON HEAVEN'S DOOR
        SCREEN GEMS - COLUMBIA PUBLICATIONS   4703KP2   .85
BRADLEY, R.--ARR.   BRADLEY, R.   EASY
 L-O-V-E
        SCREEN GEMS - COLUMBIA PUBLICATIONS   4704LP2   .85
BRADLEY, R.--ARR.   BRADLEY, R.   EASY
 LAST TIME I SAW HIM
        SCREEN GEMS - COLUMBIA PUBLICATIONS   0042LP2   .85
BRADLEY, R.--ARR.   BRADLEY, R.   EASY
 LITTLE PEOPLE AMERICA
        SCREEN GEMS - COLUMBIA PUBLICATIONS   2703LP2   .85
BRADLEY, R.--ARR.   BRADLEY, R.   BIG NOTE EASY
 LIVING TOGETHER, GROWING TOGETHER - AND - QUESTION ME AN ANSWER
        SCREEN GEMS - COLUMBIA PUBLICATIONS   C0030P3   1.00
BRADLEY, R.--ARR.   BRADLEY, R.   EASY
 LIVING TOGETHER, GROWING TOGETHER
        SCREEN GEMS - COLUMBIA PUBLICATIONS   2715LP2   .85
BRADLEY, R.--ARR.   BRADLEY, R.   EASY
 LONG-HAIRED LOVER FROM LIVERPOOL
        SCREEN GEMS - COLUMBIA PUBLICATIONS   4728LP2   .85
BRADLEY, R.--ARR.   BRADLEY, R.   EASY
 LOOK OF LOVE, THE
        SCREEN GEMS - COLUMBIA PUBLICATIONS   4703LP2   .85
BRADLEY, R.--ARR.   BRADLEY, R.   EASY
 LOST HORIZON
        SCREEN GEMS - COLUMBIA PUBLICATIONS   F0158P2   2.50
BRADLEY, R.--ARR.   BRADLEY, R.   EASY
 MISTY
        SCREEN GEMS - COLUMBIA PUBLICATIONS   2728MP2   .85
BRADLEY, R.--ARR.   BRADLEY, R.   EASY
 MORE 24 CARAT GOLD
        SCREEN GEMS - COLUMBIA PUBLICATIONS   F0268P2   3.95
BRADLEY, R.--ARR.   BRADLEY, R.   EASY
 MORE 24 CARAT GOLD
        SCREEN GEMS - COLUMBIA PUBLICATIONS   F0268P2   3.95
BRADLEY, R.--ARR.   BRADLEY, R.   EASY
 MORNING AFTER, THE
        SCREEN GEMS - COLUMBIA PUBLICATIONS   4723MP2   .85
BRADLEY, R.--ARR.   BRADLEY, R.   EASY
 MOST BEAUTIFUL GIRL, THE
        SCREEN GEMS - COLUMBIA PUBLICATIONS   4722MP2   .85
BRADLEY, R.--ARR.   BRADLEY, R.   EASY
 MOVIE POPS
        SCREEN GEMS - COLUMBIA PUBLICATIONS   F0259P2   2.50
BRADLEY, R.--ARR.   BRADLEY, R.   EASY
 MUSIC
        SCREEN GEMS - COLUMBIA PUBLICATIONS   6701MP2   .85
BRADLEY, R.--ARR.   BRADLEY, R.   EASY
 NEVER BEEN TO SPAIN
        SCREEN GEMS - COLUMBIA PUBLICATIONS   1403NP2   .85
BRADLEY, R.--ARR.   BRADLEY, R.   EASY
 NEVER CAN SAY GOODBYE
        SCREEN GEMS - COLUMBIA PUBLICATIONS   1413NP2   .85
BRADLEY, R.--ARR.   BRADLEY, R.   EASY
 ONE TIN SOLDIER
        SCREEN GEMS - COLUMBIA PUBLICATIONS   4438OP2   .85
BRADLEY, R.--ARR.   BRADLEY, R.   EASY
 PAPER ROSES
        SCREEN GEMS - COLUMBIA PUBLICATIONS   0015PP2   .85
BRADLEY, R.--ARR.   BRADLEY, R.   EASY
 PARTRIDGE FAMILY, THE - AT HOME WITH THEIR GREATEST HITS
        SCREEN GEMS - COLUMBIA PUBLICATIONS   P0036P2   2.50
BRADLEY, R.--ARR.   BRADLEY, R.   EASY
 POPCORN
        SCREEN GEMS - COLUMBIA PUBLICATIONS   4709PP2   .85
BRADLEY, R.--ARR.   BRADLEY, R.   EASY
 POPS MADE EASY FOR PIANO
        SCREEN GEMS - COLUMBIA PUBLICATIONS   F0167P2   2.95
BRADLEY, R.--ARR.   BRADLEY, R.   EASY
 POPULAR TEACHER'S CHOICE
        SCREEN GEMS - COLUMBIA PUBLICATIONS   F0112P2i   3.95
BRADLEY, R.--ARR.   BRADLEY, R.   EASY
 ROCKIN' AROUND THE CHRISTMAS TREE
        SCREEN GEMS - COLUMBIA PUBLICATIONS   4711RP2   .85

CHOPIN   ECKHARDT, F.   2
    CHOPIN FOR THE YOUNG PIANIST
        CENTURY MUSIC PUBLISHING COMPANY, INC.   3959   .40
CHOPIN   ROVENGER
    CHOPIN FOR THE YOUNG
        RUBANK, INC.   1.50
CHOPIN   TREHARNE
    CHOPIN SIMPLIFIED
        BOSTON MUSIC COMPANY   1.00
CHOPIN   M
    CONCERTO NO. 01 IN E MINOR, OP. 11
        C. F. PETERS CORPORATION   2895AA   1.25
CHOPIN   DEL MAGLIO
    ECOSSAISE, OP. 72, NO. 3
        FRANCO COLOMBO PUBLICATIONS   127141   .50
CHOPIN   DEL MAGLIO
    ETUDE IN C MINOR, OP. 10 NO. 12
        FRANCO COLOMBO PUBLICATIONS   127142   .50
CHOPIN   DEL MAGLIO
    ETUDE IN E, OP. 10 NO. 3
        FRANCO COLOMBO PUBLICATIONS   127484   .60
CHOPIN   MOSSMAN
    ETUDE IN E MAJOR
        BELWIN-MILLS PUBLISHING CORPORATION   26065   .60
CHOPIN   DEL MAGLIO
    FUNERAL MARCH - FROM SONATA, OP. 35
        FRANCO COLOMBO PUBLICATIONS   129099   .60
CHOPIN   DEL MAGLIO
    MAZURKA, OP. 7 NO. 1
        FRANCO COLOMBO PUBLICATIONS   129100   .60
CHOPIN   2
    MILITARY POLONAISE, EASY
        CENTURY MUSIC PUBLISHING COMPANY, INC.   1825   .40
CHOPIN   DEL MAGLIO
    NOCTURNE, OP. 55 NO. 1
        FRANCO COLOMBO PUBLICATIONS   124715   .60
CHOPIN   DEL MAGLIO
    NOCTURNE IN E FLAT, OP. 9 NO. 2
        FRANCO COLOMBO PUBLICATIONS   124714   .75
CHOPIN   DEL MAGLIO
    POLONAISE, OP. 53 'HEROIC'
        FRANCO COLOMBO PUBLICATIONS   129101   .60
CHOPIN   WALLIS   3
    POLONAISE, OP. 53
        BOSTON MUSIC COMPANY   .50
CHOPIN   BALLATORE
    POLONAISE IN A, OP. 40 NO. 1
        G. SCHIRMER, INC.   .40
CHOPIN   ROLFE, W.   2
    POLONAISE MILITAIRE, EASY
        CENTURY MUSIC PUBLISHING COMPANY, INC.   3221   .40
CHOPIN   ROLFE, W.   2
    RAINDROP, THE, EASY
        CENTURY MUSIC PUBLISHING COMPANY, INC.   3659   .40
CHOPIN   DEIS
    TWO PRELUDES - OP. 28 NOS. 7 AND 20
        G. SCHIRMER, INC.   .50
CHOPIN   2
    VALSE, OP. 64 NO. 1, EASY
        CENTURY MUSIC PUBLISHING COMPANY, INC.   2160   .40
CHOPIN   CHIESA
    WALTZ, OP. 18 IN E FLAT
        FRANCO COLOMBO PUBLICATIONS   107479   .60
CHOPIN   DEL MAGLIO
    WALTZ, OP. 34 NO. 1 IN A FLAT
        FRANCO COLOMBO PUBLICATIONS   127143   .60
CHOPIN   DEL MAGLIO
    WALTZ, OP. 34 NO. 2 IN A MINOR
        FRANCO COLOMBO PUBLICATIONS   129104   .60
CHOPIN   DEL MAGLIO
    WALTZ, OP. 64 NO. 1 IN D FLAT
        FRANCO COLOMBO PUBLICATIONS   127144   .60
CHOPIN   DEL MAGLIO
    WALTZ, OP. 64 NO. 2 IN C SHARP
        FRANCO COLOMBO PUBLICATIONS   129105   .60
CHOPIN   DEL MAGLIO
    WALTZ, OP. 69 NO. 1 IN A FLAT
        FRANCO COLOMBO PUBLICATIONS   127147   .60
CHOPIN   JORDA
    WALTZ IN E FLAT MAJOR, OP. 18--GRANDE VALSE BRILLIANTE
        G. SCHIRMER, INC.   .50
COHAN, G. M.
    GIVE MY REGARDS TO BROADWAY
        EDWARD B. MARKS MUSIC CORPORATION   00.60
COHAN, G. M.
    HARRIGAN
        EDWARD B. MARKS MUSIC CORPORATION   00.60
COHAN, G. M.
    MARY'S A GRAND OLD NAME
        EDWARD B. MARKS MUSIC CORPORATION   00.60
COHAN   ZEPP   2-3
    THREE ALL AMERICAN SONGS
        PRO-ART PUBLICATIONS, INC.   360   .50
COHAN
    YANKEE DOODLE BOY
        EDWARD B. MARKS MUSIC CORPORATION   00.60
COHAN
    YOU'RE A GRAND OLD FLAG
        EDWARD B. MARKS MUSIC CORPORATION   00.60
COTTRAU   DEL MAGLIO
    ADDIO A NAPOLI
        FRANCO COLOMBO PUBLICATIONS   127756   .50
CRAWFORD   ECKSTEIN
    U. S. AIR FORCE
        CARL FISCHER, INC.   P 2290   .75
CROISEZ, A.
    VOYAGE D'UNE HIRONDELLE
        FRANCO COLOMBO PUBLICATIONS   SAL   1.50
CURRIER
    SLEIGH RIDE -- SIMP.
        BELWIN-MILLS PUBLISHING CORPORATION   90114   1.00
D'HARDELOT
    BECAUSE
        CHAPPELL AND COMPANY, INC.   0420000-170   .60
DAVIS, J. R.--ED   DAVIS, J. R.
    GREAT THEMES MADE EASY FOR PIANO
        WARNER BROTHERS PUBLISHERS   1.95
DAVIS, J. R.--ED   DAVIS, J. R.
    HARMS HITS THROUGH THE YEARS MADE EASY
        WARNER BROTHERS PUBLISHERS   1.25
DAVIS, J. R.--ED   DAVIS, J. R.
    PETER, PAUL AND MARY, HITS OF, MADE EASY FOR PIANO
        WARNER BROTHERS PUBLISHERS   PPM 24   1.50
DAVIS, K. *
    LITTLE DRUMMER BOY, THE -- SIMP.
        BELWIN-MILLS PUBLISHING CORPORATION   26071   .50

DEBUSSY   4
    AFTERNOON OF A FAUN, E MAJOR
        CENTURY MUSIC PUBLISHING COMPANY, INC.   3721   .40
DEBUSSY   MITTLER   2B
    AFTERNOON OF A FAUN
        MUSICORD PUBLICATIONS, INC.   .45
DEBUSSY
    CLAIR DE LUNE
        ASHLEY DEALERS SERVICE, INC.   ES   .95
DEBUSSY   RICHTER
    CLAIR DE LUNE
        ELKAN-VOGEL, INC.   .60
DEBUSSY   RICHTER   1
    CLAIR DE LUNE
        ELKAN-VOGEL, INC.   .50
DEBUSSY   MOSSMAN, T.
    REVERIE -- SIMP.
        BELWIN-MILLS PUBLISHING CORPORATION   26094   .50
DEKOVEN, R.   STEINER
    OH, PROMISE ME
        G. SCHIRMER, INC.   .50
DELIBES, L.   BANTOCK, G.
    COPPELIA, COMPLETE ILLUSTRATED
        BELWIN-MILLS PUBLISHING CORPORATION   09468   3.00
DELIBES, L.   BANTOCK, G.
    COPPELIA, SELECTIONS FROM
        BELWIN-MILLS PUBLISHING CORPORATION   09469   1.50
DELIBES, L.   ROLFE, W.   2
    VALSE LENTE, NAILA, EASY
        CENTURY MUSIC PUBLISHING COMPANY, INC.   3547   .40
DENZA   DEL MAGLIO
    FUNICULI-FUNICULA
        FRANCO COLOMBO PUBLICATIONS   124716   .60
DENZA   CLAUSETTI
    FUNICULI-FUNICULA
        FRANCO COLOMBO PUBLICATIONS   47171   .60
DENZA   DEL MAGLIO
    SE
        FRANCO COLOMBO PUBLICATIONS   128138   .50
DESORMES
    EN REVANT DE LA REVEU
        FRANCO COLOMBO PUBLICATIONS   SAL   1.50
DESSAUX   2
    BIJOUX CHERIS, PETITE VALSE -- SIMPLIFIED VERSION
        ALPHONSE LEDUC
DESSAUX   3
    BUCEPHALE, PREMIER GALOP -- SIMPLIFIED VERSION
        ALPHONSE LEDUC
DESSAUX   1
    LE PETIT BAISER, VALSE MIGNONNE -- SIMPLIFIED VERSION
        ALPHONSE LEDUC
DEUTSCH
    PLAY FIDDLE PLAY
        EDWARD B. MARKS MUSIC CORPORATION   01.00
DE NARDIS   DEL MAGLIO
    SALTARELLO ABRUZZESE
        FRANCO COLOMBO PUBLICATIONS   127758   .60
DE VITO, A.
    PEDRO DANCES
        BOURNE COMPANY   1.00
DICAPUA   ROGERS   2
    O SOLE MIO, SIMPLIFIED
        BELWIN-MILLS PUBLISHING CORPORATION   709   .60
DICHIARI   JETSON, I. H.   2
    LA SPAGNOLA
        VOLKWEIN BROS.   .35
DIETRICH--ED.   DIETRICH   1
    LATERNE, LATERNE, SONNE, MOND UND STERNE. 23 VOLKSKINDERLIEDER
    IN GANZ LEICHTEN SATZEN
        BARENREITER VERLAG   BA 1003
DILLER, A.   SMITH   GRADE 2
    STAR-SPANGLED BANNER, THE--ARR. IN G
        G. SCHIRMER, INC.   .40
DOHNANYI   BLASSER
    WEDDING-WALTZ FROM ''DER SCHLEIER DER PIERETTE'' -- SIMPLIFIED
    VERSION
        ASSOCIATED MUSIC PUBLISHERS, INC.   DOB   1.25
DONIZETTI   DEL MAGLIO
    ELISIR D'AMORE, L' - FURTIVA LAGRIMA, UNA
        FRANCO COLOMBO PUBLICATIONS   128146   .60
DONIZETTI   DEL MAGLIO
    LUCIA DI LAMMERMOOR - VERRANNO A TE AND TU CHE A DIO
        FRANCO COLOMBO PUBLICATIONS   128120   .50
DONIZETTI   2
    SEXTETTE, LUCIA, EASY
        CENTURY MUSIC PUBLISHING COMPANY, INC.   2512   .40
DONIZETTI   JESTON, I. H.   4
    SEXTET -- LUCIA DI LAMMERMOOR
        VOLKWEIN BROS.   .35
DRATHS--ED   DRATHS   1
    MORGEN KOMMT DER WEIHNACHTSMANN
        SCHOTT   5325   2.25
DRIGO, R.   2-3
    HARLEQUIN SERENADE, EASY
        CENTURY MUSIC PUBLISHING COMPANY, INC   2468   .40
DRIGO, R.   GROOMS   2
    MILLIONS OF HARLEQUIN, EASY
        CENTURY MUSIC PUBLISHING COMPANY, INC.   2468   .40
DURAND, A.   3
    VALSE, NO. 02, EASY
        CENTURY MUSIC PUBLISHING COMPANY, INC.   2520   .40
DVORAK   LECHNER   2-3
    HUMORESKE OP. 101 NO. 7
        SCHOTT   03694   .75
DVORAK   DEL MAGLIO
    HUMORESQUE, OP. 101, NO. 7
        FRANCO COLOMBO PUBLICATIONS   129079   .60
DVORAK   COWDREY   3
    LARGO FROM THE 'NEW WORLD SYMPHONY'
        BOSTON MUSIC COMPANY   .50
DVORAK   ROLFE, W.   2
    NEW WORLD SYMPHONY, LARGO, EASY
        CENTURY MUSIC PUBLISHING COMPANY, INC.   3392   .40
DVORAK   2
    SLAVONIC DANCE NO. 6, EASY
        CENTURY MUSIC PUBLISHING COMPANY, INC.   3978   .40
DYLAN   NEALE, J.
    INSTANT PICTURE CHORD PIANO NO. 2, BOB DYLAN
        WARNER BROTHERS PUBLISHERS   1.95
ELGAR, E.   VALBER
    LAND OF HOPE AND GLORY
        BOOSEY AND HAWKES, INC.   .60
ELGAR, E.   ZEPP   3
    POMP AND CIRCUMSTANCE - SMALL CHORD VERSION
        PRO-ART PUBLICATIONS, INC.   148   .50

ELGAR, E.   BELLAIRS
  POMP AND CIRCUMSTANCE MARCH NO. 1 IN D
    BOOSEY AND HAWKES, INC.   .75
ELGAR, E.   ZEPP   2
  POMP AND CIRCUMSTANCE
    PRO-ART PUBLICATIONS, INC.   147   .50
ELGAR, E.   PALMERI
  SALUT D'AMOUR, OP. 12
    G. SCHIRMER, INC.   .50
ELLINGTON   MOSSMAN, R.
  MOOD INDIGO, SIMP.
    BELWIN-MILLS PUBLISHING CORPORATION   .60
ETTS, M.--ED *   ETTS, M. *
  CLASSICS MADE EASY, BK. 1
    CENTURY MUSIC PUBLISHING COMPANY, INC.   1.25
EVANS   KLICKMANN
  LADY OF SPAIN -- SIMPLIFIED
    SOUTHERN MUSIC COMPANY   .50
EVANS   KLICKMANN
  LADY OF SPAIN
    SAM FOX PUBLISHING COMPANY, INC.   .50
FANENGHI
  EIGHTEEN FAMOUS ARIAS -- TESORO DEL MELODRAMMA --
    FRANCO COLOMBO PUBLICATIONS   127652   1.50
FANENGHI
  MOST BEAUTIFUL LOVE SONGS, THE
    FRANCO COLOMBO PUBLICATIONS   127615   1.50
FERNANDEZ   DEL MAGLIO
  CIELITO LINDO
    FRANCO COLOMBO PUBLICATIONS   129115   .60
FIBICH, Z.   DEL MAGLIO
  POEM, OP. 41, NO. 14
    FRANCO COLOMBO PUBLICATIONS   128847   .60
FIBICH, Z.   2-3
  POEM -- ERLEICHTERT -- UND FRUHLING UND JUGEND
    BARENREITER VERLAG   AP 591
FICHTER   MCWHERTOR   2
  CAUSE IT'S CHRISTMAS
    VOLKWEIN BROS.   .50
FIELD, J.   DEL MAGLIO
  NOCTURNE NO. 01 IN E FLAT
    FRANCO COLOMBO PUBLICATIONS   129080   .50
FLOTOW   KRUG   2
  MARTHA, EASY TRANSCRIPTION
    CENTURY MUSIC PUBLISHING COMPANY, INC.   524   .40
FOSTER   SCHIEFELBEIN, F. 2
  COME WHERE MY LOVE LIES DREAMING
    VOLKWEIN BROS.   .25
FOSTER   SCHIEFELBEIN, F. 2
  GENTLE ANNIE
    VOLKWEIN BROS.   .25
FOSTER   SCHIEFELBEIN, F. 2
  HARD TIMES COME AGAIN NO MORE
    VOLKWEIN BROS.   .25
FOSTER   SCHIEFELBEIN, F. 2
  MASSA'S IN THE COLD, COLD GROUND
    VOLKWEIN BROS.   .25
FOSTER   SCHIEFELBEIN, F. 2
  MY OLD KENTUCKY HOME
    VOLKWEIN BROS.   .25
FOSTER   SPENCER, J.   2
  MY OLD KENTUCKY HOME
    VOLKWEIN BROS.   .25
FOSTER   SCHIEFELBEIN, F. 2
  OH SUSANNA
    VOLKWEIN BROS.   .25
FOSTER   SCHIEFELBEIN, F. 2
  OLD BLACK JOE
    VOLKWEIN BROS.   .25
FOSTER   SPENCER, J.   1
  OLD BLACK JOE
    VOLKWEIN BROS.   .25
FOSTER   SCHIEFELBEIN, F. 2
  OLD DOG TRAY
    VOLKWEIN BROS.   .25
FOSTER   SCHIEFELBEIN, F. 2
  OLD FOLKS AT HOME
    VOLKWEIN BROS.   .25
FOSTER   SPENCER, J.   2
  OLD FOLKS AT HOME
    VOLKWEIN BROS.   .25
FOSTER   SCHIEFELBEIN, F. 2
  UNCLE NED
    VOLKWEIN BROS.   00.25
FOSTER   SCHIEFELBEIN, F. 2
  WILLIE WE HAVE MISSED YOU
    VOLKWEIN BROS.   00.25
FRANCK, C.   M
  SYMPHONIC VARIATIONS
    C. F. PETERS CORPORATION   3741A   1.25
FREDERICKS   2
  COUNTRY GARDENS -- EASY
    VOLKWEIN BROS.   .30
FREY--ED   FREY
  SIMPLIFIED PIANO PIECES
    MUSIC SALES CORPORATION   040009   2.95
FRIML, R.   STEINER
  ALLAH'S HOLIDAY--''KATINKA''
    G. SCHIRMER, INC.   .40
FRIML, R.   LEVINE
  ALLAH'S HOLIDAY--''KATINKA''
    G. SCHIRMER, INC.   .50
FRIML, R.   WHITE
  DONKEY SERENADE, THE
    G. SCHIRMER, INC.   .50
FRIML, R.   PALMERI
  GIANNINA MIA--''THE FIREFLY''
    G. SCHIRMER, INC.   .50
FRIML, R.   PALMERI
  SYMPATHY WALTZ--''THE FIREFLY''
    G. SCHIRMER, INC.   .35
FRIML, R.   LEVINE
  VALSE LUCILLE, OP. 85 BIS, NO. 1
    G. SCHIRMER, INC.   .50
GABRIEL, M.   2
  GOLDEN WEDDING, EASY
    CENTURY MUSIC PUBLISHING COMPANY, INC.   2596   .40
GANNE   2
  LA CZARINE, MAZURKA, EASY
    CENTURY MUSIC PUBLISHING COMPANY, INC.   2138   .40
GARLAND   HARING
  IN THE MOOD
    SHAPIRO, BERNSTEIN ORGANIZATION   .95
GAUTIER, L.   ROLFE, W.   2
  SECRET, THE, EASY
    CENTURY MUSIC PUBLISHING COMPANY, INC.   3364   .40

GERSHWIN
  GERSHWIN, THE BEST OF HOLLYWOOD
    CHAPPELL AND COMPANY, INC.   0021675   1.50
GERSHWIN
  PORGY AND BESS
    CHAPPELL AND COMPANY, INC.   4672507   1.50
GERSHWIN
  SUMMERTIME
    CHAPPELL AND COMPANY, INC.   5565023   .60
GIORDANI   DEL MAGLIO
  CARO MIO BEN
    FRANCO COLOMBO PUBLICATIONS   128119   .50
GIORDANO   DE CHRISTOFARO
  CENA DELLE BEFFE, LA - GRAND FANTASY FROM ACTS 1 AND 2
    FRANCO COLOMBO PUBLICATIONS   SON.2529   1.50
GIORZA   DEL MAGLIO
  DAGHELA AVANTI UN PASSO
    FRANCO COLOMBO PUBLICATIONS   127837   .50
GLUCK   DEL MAGLIO
  ORFEO - CHE FARO SENZA EURIDICE
    FRANCO COLOMBO PUBLICATIONS   128123   .60
GODARD, B.   ROLFE, W.   2
  FIFTH WALTZ, EASY
    CENTURY MUSIC PUBLISHING COMPANY, INC.   3555   .40
GODARD, B.   3
  JOCELYN, BERCEUSE, EASY
    CENTURY MUSIC PUBLISHING COMPANY, INC.   2518   .40
GODARD, B.   3
  LULLABY, JOCELYN, EASY
    CENTURY MUSIC PUBLISHING COMPANY, INC.   2518   .40
GODARD, B.   3
  VALSE NO. 02, EASY
    CENTURY MUSIC PUBLISHING COMPANY, INC.   2592   .40
GODOWSKY, L.   STEINER
  ALT-WIEN--FROM TRIAKONTAMERON
    G. SCHIRMER, INC.   .50
GOETSCHY
  ESPOIR DU RETOUR, L' -- CAPRICE --
    FRANCO COLOMBO PUBLICATIONS   SAL   1.50
GOTTSCHALK   REEG, G. A.   3
  LAST HOPE
    VOLKWEIN BROS.   .35
GOUNOD, C.   CHIESA
  FAUST - WALTZES
    FRANCO COLOMBO PUBLICATIONS   109091   .50
GOUNOD, C.   BURGMUELLER
  FAUST - WALTZES
    FRANCO COLOMBO PUBLICATIONS   64451   .75
GOUNOD, C.   MILICI
  FAUST - WALTZ
    FRANCO COLOMBO PUBLICATIONS   BA8329   .75
GOUNOD, C.   M
  FAUST
    C. F. PETERS CORPORATION   H640   2.00
GOUNOD, C.   RICHARDS, B.   4
  MARCH, FAUST
    CENTURY MUSIC PUBLISHING COMPANY, INC.   1544   .40
GOUNOD, C.
  MEDITATION ON THE FIRST PRELUDE BY J. S. BACH
    G. SCHIRMER, INC.   .40
GOUNOD, C.   DEL MAGLIO
  SERENADE
    FRANCO COLOMBO PUBLICATIONS   124717   .50
GRAINGER, P.
  COUNTRY GARDENS--EASY VERSION--
    G. SCHIRMER, INC.   .60
GRAINGER, P.
  COUNTRY GARDENS--ESPECIALLY EASY VERSION--
    G. SCHIRMER, INC.   .50
GRIEG   M
  ALBUM, BK. 1
    C. F. PETERS CORPORATION   3305A   1.50
GRIEG   M
  ALBUM, BK. 2
    C. F. PETERS CORPORATION   3305B   1.50
GRIEG   M
  CONCERTO IN A MINOR, OP. 16. ABRIDGED PIANO SOLO ARRANGEMENT
    C. F. PETERS CORPORATION   2164B   1.25
GRIEG   M
  CONCERTO IN A MINOR, OP. 16
    C. F. PETERS CORPORATION   2164B   1.25
GRIEG
  CONCERTO IN A MINOR -- OPENING THEME
    ASHLEY DEALERS SERVICE, INC.   ES   .95
GRIEG   MITTLER   3B
  GRIEG CONCERTO
    MUSICORD PUBLICATIONS, INC.   .45
GRIEG   ROVENGER
  GRIEG FOR THE YOUNG
    RUBANK, INC.   1.50
GRIEG   M
  LYRIC PIECES FOR THE YOUNG. 7 FAVORITE PIECES
    C. F. PETERS CORPORATION   3305A   1.50
GRIEG   KING, S.
  MORNING MOOD
    SHAWNEE PRESS, INC.   HB-5033   .40
GRIEG   M
  PEER GYNT, SELECTIONS
    C. F. PETERS CORPORATION   550D   1.50
GRIEG   SCHAUM, J.   3
  PEER GYNT SUITES
    SCHAUM PUBLICATIONS, INC.   1.50
GRIEG   MOSSMAN
  PIANO CONCERTO IN A MINOR -- FIRST MOVEMENT
    BELWIN-MILLS PUBLISHING CORPORATION   26089   .60
GRIEG   TRUXELL, E.   3 1/2
  THEMES FROM PIANO CONCERTO
    VOLKWEIN BROS.   00.40
GRIEG   WALLIS   2
  THEME FROM THE FIRST MOVEMENT OF PIANO CONCERTO IN A MINOR
    BOSTON MUSIC COMPANY   .50
GRIEG   E
  TO SPRING, OP. 43 NO. 6
    C. F. PETERS CORPORATION   2422A   .90
GRIEG   MOSSMAN
  TO SPRING
    BELWIN-MILLS PUBLISHING CORPORATION   26101   .60
GRIEG   ROLFE, W.   2
  TROLDTOG, EASY
    CENTURY MUSIC PUBLISHING COMPANY, INC.   3657   .40
GRIEG   E-M
  WEDDING DAY AT TROLDHAUGEN, OP. 65 NO. 6
    C. F. PETERS CORPORATION   2922A   .80
GRUBER, F.   SPENCER, J.   2
  SILENT NIGHT
    VOLKWEIN BROS.   .35

GUENTHER--ED   GUENTHER
    CLASSICS FOR ADULTS, BK. 1
        MUSICORD PUBLICATIONS, INC.   1.25
GUTHRIE
    THIS LAND IS YOUR LAND
        TRO SONGWAYS SERVICE, INC.   2082   .85
HAMMERSTEIN *   GLOVER
    CLIMB EV'RY MOUNTAIN
        MCA MUSIC   .85
HAMMERSTEIN *   GLOVER
    EDELWEISS
        MCA MUSIC   .85
HAMMERSTEIN *   SIRMAY
    IT'S A GRAND NIGHT FOR SINGING
        MCA MUSIC   .85
HAMMERSTEIN *   PORTNOFF
    I WHISTLE A HAPPY TUNE
        MCA MUSIC   .85
HAMMERSTEIN *   SIRMAY
    MARCH OF THE SIAMESE CHILDREN
        MCA MUSIC   .85
HAMMERSTEIN *   SIRMAY
    OH, WHAT A BEAUTIFUL MORNIN'
        MCA MUSIC   .85
HAMMERSTEIN *   PORTNOFF
    SOME ENCHANTED EVENING
        MCA MUSIC   .85
HAMMERSTEIN *   GLOVER
    SOUND OF MUSIC, THE.
        MCA MUSIC   .85
HAMMERSTEIN *   SIRMAY
    SURREY WITH THE FRINGE ON TOP
        MCA MUSIC   .85
HANDEL   SHELDON
    HALLELUJAH CHORUS -- FROM 'MESSIAH'
        BELWIN-MILLS PUBLISHING CORPORATION   20121   .60
HANDEL   SCHAUM, J.   3
    HANDEL'S MESSIAH
        SCHAUM PUBLICATIONS, INC.   1.50
HANDEL   DEL MAGLIO
    LARGO FROM 'SERSE'
        FRANCO COLOMBO PUBLICATIONS   124718   .60
HANDEL   DEIS
    LARGO FROM 'XERXES'
        G. SCHIRMER, INC.   .35
HANDEL   2
    XERXES, LARGO, EASY
        CENTURY MUSIC PUBLISHING COMPANY, INC.   2465   .40
HART, F. *
    MANHATTAN
        EDWARD B. MARKS MUSIC CORPORATION   01.00
HEINS, C.   ROLFE, W.   2
    SENNERS TRAUM, EASY
        CENTURY MUSIC PUBLISHING COMPANY, INC.   3370   .40
HERBERT   GAMSE   1
    MARCH OF THE TOYS, SIMPLIFIED
        CENTURY MUSIC PUBLISHING COMPANY, INC.   4416   .40
HERBERT
    MARCH OF THE TOYS -- SIMP.
        ASHLEY DEALERS SERVICE, INC.   ES   .95
HEROLD   3
    OVERTURE, ZAMPA, EASY
        CENTURY MUSIC PUBLISHING COMPANY, INC.   2121   .40
HERZER, R.   2
    HOCH HEIDECKSBURG, MARSCH - OP. 10, ERLEICHTERT
        SCHOTT   1.25
HOLCOMB, L. R.--ED   HOLCOMB, L. R.
    HYMNS FOR THE BEGINNING PIANIST
        BROADMAN MUSIC   4571-07   2.00
HOLLANDER
    MY FAVORITE CHRISTMAS CAROLS
        EDWARD B. MARKS MUSIC CORPORATION   01.25
HOLLANDER
    MY FIRST CLASSICS
        EDWARD B. MARKS MUSIC CORPORATION   01.00
HYDE *   SINGER
    LITTLE GIRL
        MCA MUSIC   .60
ILJINSKY, A.   MOSSMAN, T.
    BERCEUSE, OP. 13 NO. 7
        BELWIN-MILLS PUBLISHING CORPORATION   26105   .50
INFANTE
    VITO, EL -- EDITION B - SIMPLIFIED --
        FRANCO COLOMBO PUBLICATIONS   SAL   2.75
IPPOLITOV-IVANOV, M.   MOSSMAN
    PROCESSION OF THE SARDAR -- FROM 'CAUCASIAN SKETCHES'
        BELWIN-MILLS PUBLISHING CORPORATION   26093   .60
IVANOVICI, J.   MOSSMAN
    WAVES OF THE DANUBE -- BOOGIE WOOGIE
        BELWIN-MILLS PUBLISHING CORPORATION   26061   .90
IVANOVICI, J.   JESTON, I. H.   2
    WAVES OF THE DANUBE WALTZ
        VOLKWEIN BROS.   00.35
IVANOVICI, J.   CHIESA
    WAVES OF THE DANUBE
        FRANCO COLOMBO PUBLICATIONS   107481   .50
IVANOW   2
    MARCH OF THE SARDAR, EASY
        CENTURY MUSIC PUBLISHING COMPANY, INC.   3384   .40
IVANOW   ROLFE, W.   2
    PROCESSION OF THE SARDAR, EASY
        CENTURY MUSIC PUBLISHING COMPANY, INC.   3384   .40
JEFFRIES *   SINGER
    CANDY STORE BLUES
        MCA MUSIC   .60
JESSEL
    PARADE OF THE WOODEN SOLDIERS -- SIMP.
        ASHLEY DEALERS SERVICE, INC.   ES   .95
JESSEL
    PARADE OF THE WOODEN SOLDIERS
        EDWARD B. MARKS MUSIC CORPORATION   01.00
JOUBERTI
    BAL CHEZ LE MINISTRE, UN -- MAZURKA --
        FRANCO COLOMBO PUBLICATIONS   SAL   1.50
KAHN, M.--ED *   KAHN, M. *
    DISNEY SHOWCASE
        BOURNE COMPANY   1.50
KAHN, M.--ED   KAHN, M.
    DOES YOUR CHEWING GUM LOSE ITS FLAVOR ON THE BEDPOST OVERNIGHT
    -- SIMP.
        BELWIN-MILLS PUBLISHING CORPORATION   26074   .50
KAHN, M.--ED   KAHN, M.
    I WAS KAISER BILL'S BATMAN -- SIMP.
        BELWIN-MILLS PUBLISHING CORPORATION   26121   .50
KAHN, M.--ED   KAHN, M.
    MARVIN KAHN'S SONG SHOWCASE
        BOURNE COMPANY   1.50

KAIHAN *
    NOW IS THE HOUR
        MCA MUSIC   .60
KELER BELA   4
    OVERTURE, LUSTSPIEL
        CENTURY MUSIC PUBLISHING COMPANY, INC.   642   .40
KENDALL--ED   KENDALL
    SIMPLIFIED SONG GEMS FOR PIANO
        BOURNE COMPANY   1.00
KERN, J.   BRADLEY, R.   EASY
    BRADLEY'S JEROME KERN ALBUM
        SCREEN GEMS - COLUMBIA PUBLICATIONS   F0020P2   1.95
KHATCHATURIAN
    SABRE DANCE -- SIMP.
        ASHLEY DEALERS SERVICE, INC.   ES   .95
KHATCHATURIAN   KING, S.
    SWORD DANCE -- FROM BALLET 'GAYNE'
        BELWIN-MILLS PUBLISHING CORPORATION   26054   .60
KING, S.--ED.   KING, S.
    DOWN BY THE STATION -- SIMP.
        BELWIN-MILLS PUBLISHING CORPORATION   26063   .50
KING, S.--ED.   KING, S.
    RED ROSES FOR A BLUE LADY --SIMP.
        BELWIN-MILLS PUBLISHING CORPORATION   26064   .50
KING, S.--ED.   KING, S.
    SLEIGH RIDE -- SIMP.
        BELWIN-MILLS PUBLISHING CORPORATION   26047   .50
KING, S.--ED.   KING, S.
    THAT'S MY DESIRE -- SIMP.
        BELWIN-MILLS PUBLISHING CORPORATION   26056   .50
KING, S.
    FIDDLE-FADDLE -- SIMP.
        BELWIN-MILLS PUBLISHING CORPORATION   26013   .50
KIRBY, W.
    MERRY CHRISTMAS--13 CHRISTMAS CAROLS IN VERY EASY ARRANGEMENTS
        G. SCHIRMER, INC.   .75
KOWALSKI, H.   2
    HUNGARIAN MARCH, EASY
        CENTURY MUSIC PUBLISHING COMPANY, INC.   2133   .40
KREISLER   MAIER
    CAPRICE VIENNOIS --STUDENT EDITION--
        CARL FISCHER, INC.   F 2057   .65
KREISLER   MAIER
    LIEBESFREUD --STUDENT EDITION--
        CARL FISCHER, INC.   F 2055   .65
KREISLER   FLETCHER
    LIEBESLIED --STUDENT EDITION--
        CARL FISCHER, INC.   F 2315   .65
KREISLER   MAIER
    MIDNIGHT BELLS --STUDENT EDITION--
        CARL FISCHER, INC.   F 2056   .65
KREISLER   FLETCHER
    SCHON ROSMARIN
        CARL FISCHER, INC.   F 2061   .65
KREISLER   MAIER
    SHEPHERD'S MADRIGAL
        CARL FISCHER, INC.   F 2054   .65
KRENTZLIN, R.--ED   KRENTZLIN, R.   2
    OPERN UND OPERETTEN, BAND 01
        SCHOTT   2340   2.50
KRENTZLIN, R.--ED   KRENTZLIN, R.   2
    OPERN UND OPERETTEN, BAND 02
        SCHOTT   4175   2.50
LABITZKY, A.   2-3
    SHEPHERDESS' DREAM, EASY
        CENTURY MUSIC PUBLISHING COMPANY, INC.   2515   .40
LANE, J.--ED.   LANE, J.
    ALICE BLUE GOWN
        THE BIG THREE MUSIC CORPORATION   00.70
LANE, J.--ED.   LANE, J.
    AMERICAN PIE
        THE BIG THREE MUSIC CORPORATION   00.70
LANE, J.--ED.   LANE, J.
    ANCHORS AWEIGH
        THE BIG THREE MUSIC CORPORATION   00.70
LANE, J.--ED.   LANE, J.
    ANY TIME
        THE BIG THREE MUSIC CORPORATION   00.70
LANE, J.--ED.   LANE, J.
    APRIL LOVE
        THE BIG THREE MUSIC CORPORATION   00.70
LANE, J.--ED.   LANE, J.
    AQUARIUS
        THE BIG THREE MUSIC CORPORATION   00.70
LANE, J.--ED.   LANE, J.
    ARRIVEDERCI, ROMA
        THE BIG THREE MUSIC CORPORATION   00.70
LANE, J.--ED.   LANE, J.
    AT SUNDOWN
        THE BIG THREE MUSIC CORPORATION   00.70
LANE, J.--ED.   LANE, J.
    BATMAN THEME
        THE BIG THREE MUSIC CORPORATION   00.70
LANE, J.--ED.   LANE, J.
    BECAUSE YOU'RE MINE
        THE BIG THREE MUSIC CORPORATION   00.70
LANE, J.--ED.   LANE, J.
    BEYOND THE SUNSET
        THE BIG THREE MUSIC CORPORATION   00.70
LANE, J.--ED.   LANE, J.
    BIG SPENDER
        THE BIG THREE MUSIC CORPORATION   00.70
LANE, J.--ED.   LANE, J.
    BLUE MOON
        THE BIG THREE MUSIC CORPORATION   00.70
LANE, J.--ED.   LANE, J.
    CANDIDA
        THE BIG THREE MUSIC CORPORATION   00.70
LANE, J.--ED.   LANE, J.
    CERTAIN SMILE, A
        THE BIG THREE MUSIC CORPORATION   00.70
LANE, J.--ED.   LANE, J.
    CHARMAINE
        THE BIG THREE MUSIC CORPORATION   00.70
LANE, J.--ED.   LANE, J.
    CHATTANOOGA CHOO CHOO
        THE BIG THREE MUSIC CORPORATION   00.70
LANE, J.--ED.   LANE, J.
    CHILDREN'S MARCHING SONG
        THE BIG THREE MUSIC CORPORATION   00.70
LANE, J.--ED.   LANE, J.
    CHITTY CHITTY BANG BANG
        THE BIG THREE MUSIC CORPORATION   00.70
LANE, J.--ED.   LANE, J.
    CIRCUS WORLD
        THE BIG THREE MUSIC CORPORATION   00.70

LUTZ--ED   LUTZ   3
  DIE GROSSE OPER, BAND 01
    SCHOTT   4949   5.00
LUTZ--ED   LUTZ   3-4
  DIE GROSSE OPER, BAND 02
    SCHOTT   4950   5.00
LYALL, M.--ED   LYALL, M.
  FAVORITE HYMNS FOR THE PIANO
    BROADMAN MUSIC   4571-02   2.25
LYALL, M.--ED   LYALL, M.
  HYMN TUNE PRELUDES FOR THE PIANO, NO. 1
    BROADMAN MUSIC   4571-03   2.25
LYALL, M.--ED   LYALL, M.
  HYMN TUNE PRELUDES FOR THE PIANO, NO. 2
    BROADMAN MUSIC   4571-04   2.25
MACDOWELL   ROLFE, W.   3
  HEXENTANZ, EASY
    CENTURY MUSIC PUBLISHING COMPANY, INC. 3372   .40
MACDOWELL   ECKSTEIN
  TO A WILD ROSE
    CARL FISCHER, INC.   P 2777   .50
MACDOWELL   BERMONT, H.   2A
  TO A WILD ROSE
    MUSICORD PUBLICATIONS, INC.   .45
MACK, E.   SCHIEFELBEIN, F. 3
  GENERAL GRANT'S GRAND MARCH
    VOLKWEIN BROS.   .25
MALOTTE, A.   DEWS
  LORD'S PRAYER, THE
    G. SCHIRMER, INC.   .60
MALOTTE, A.   LEVINE
  LORD'S PRAYER, THE
    G. SCHIRMER, INC.   .50
MANNING   SINGER
  PUSSY CAT SONG
    MCA MUSIC   .60
MARCHETTI, F.
  FASCINATION -- SIMP.
    ASHLEY DEALERS SERVICE, INC.   ES   .95
MARGIS, A.
  VALSE BLANCHE
    FRANCO COLOMBO PUBLICATIONS   SAL   1.50
MARSCHALL   LOEPKE   3
  STARLIGHT
    VOLKWEIN BROS.   .35
MARTIN, G. B.   DEL MAGLIO
  GAVOTTE
    FRANCO COLOMBO PUBLICATIONS   129093   .60
MASCAGNI, P.   AZZONI
  AMICO FRITZ, L' - INTERMEZZO
    FRANCO COLOMBO PUBLICATIONS   SON.620   .90
MASCAGNI, P.
  CAVALLERIA RUSTICANA - GRAND FANTASY
    FRANCO COLOMBO PUBLICATIONS   SON.1764   1.50
MASCAGNI, P.   DE SIMONE
  CAVALLERIA RUSTICANA - INTERMEZZO
    FRANCO COLOMBO PUBLICATIONS   SON.1348   .90
MASSENET, J.   DEL MAGLIO
  CID, LE - ARAGONAISE
    FRANCO COLOMBO PUBLICATIONS   BA10206   .75
MASSENET, J.   JETSON, I. H.   4
  ELEGY
    VOLKWEIN BROS.   .35
MASSENET, J.   KING, S.
  MEDITATION -- FROM 'THAIS'
    BELWIN-MILLS PUBLISHING CORPORATION 26029   .60
MASSENET, J.   DEL MAGLIO
  THAIS - MEDITATION
    FRANCO COLOMBO PUBLICATIONS   BA10205   .75
MATOS RODRIGUEZ   DEL MAGLIO
  CUMPARSITA, LA
    FRANCO COLOMBO PUBLICATIONS   127204   .60
MATTEI   3
  TOURBILLON, VALSE DE CONCERT, EASY
    CENTURY MUSIC PUBLISHING COMPANY, INC. 2516   .40
MAYR   DEL MAGLIO
  BIONDA IN GONDOLETTA, LA
    FRANCO COLOMBO PUBLICATIONS   129081   .60
MCGINLEY
  PIANO SESSIONS - KINDERGARTEN SERIES‡ SONGS FOR CHRISTMAS
  --SUPP. MUSIC FOR TRUDY TREBLE AND TOM--
    SHAWNEE PRESS, INC.   .60
MEACHAM, F.   ECISTEIN
  AMERICAN PATROL MARCH --SIMPLIFIED--
    CARL FISCHER, INC.   P 2960   .50
MEACHAM, F.   MITTLER   2A
  AMERICAN PATROL MARCH
    MUSICORD PUBLICATIONS, INC.   .45
MEACHAM, F.   MESSINA, J.   1
  AMERICAN PATROL
    VOLKWEIN BROS.   .35
MENDELSSOHN   2-3
  FRUEHLINGSLIED, EASY
    CENTURY MUSIC PUBLISHING COMPANY, INC. 2158   .40
MENDELSSOHN   4
  MARCH OF THE PRIESTS, ATHALIA
    CENTURY MUSIC PUBLISHING COMPANY, INC. 1531   .40
MENDELSSOHN   ROLFE, W.   3
  MARCH OF THE PRIESTS, EASY
    CENTURY MUSIC PUBLISHING COMPANY, INC. 3395   .40
MENDELSSOHN   SCHAUM, J.   3
  MENDELSSOHN'S SONGS WITHOUT WORDS
    SCHAUM PUBLICATIONS, INC.   1.50
MENDELSSOHN   CHIESA
  MIDSUMMER NIGHT'S DREAM, A - WEDDING MARCH
    FRANCO COLOMBO PUBLICATIONS   107507   .60
MENDELSSOHN   DEL MAGLIO
  ON WINGS OF SONG
    FRANCO COLOMBO PUBLICATIONS   129092   .60
MENDELSSOHN   DEL MAGLIO
  SPRING SONG, OP. 62 NO. 6
    FRANCO COLOMBO PUBLICATIONS   128844   .60
MENDELSSOHN   JETSON, I. H.   2
  SPRING SONG
    VOLKWEIN BROS.   .35
MENDELSSOHN   DEL MAGLIO
  VENETIAN BOAT SONG, OP. 19 NO. 6
    FRANCO COLOMBO PUBLICATIONS   124719   .60
MENDELSSOHN   DEL MAGLIO
  VENETIAN BOAT SONG, OP. 30 NO. 6
    FRANCO COLOMBO PUBLICATIONS   124720   .60
MENDELSSOHN   ROLFE, W.   3
  WAR MARCH OF THE PRIESTS, EASY
    CENTURY MUSIC PUBLISHING COMPANY, INC. 3395   .40
MERKEL, G.   ROLFE, W.   2
  PAPILLON, EASY
    CENTURY MUSIC PUBLISHING COMPANY, INC. 3357   .40

METRA   DEL MAGLIO
  SERENATA
    FRANCO COLOMBO PUBLICATIONS   129107   .60
METRA   2
  VALSE SERENADE, EASY
    CENTURY MUSIC PUBLISHING COMPANY, INC. 2141   .40
MEYER-LUTZ
  PAS DE QUATRE
    FRANCO COLOMBO PUBLICATIONS   SAL   1.50
MEYERBEER, G.   2
  PROPHETE, CORONATION MARCH, EASY
    CENTURY MUSIC PUBLISHING COMPANY, INC. 3760   .40
MITTLER--ED   MITTLER   2, 3
  GREAT BALLET MUSIC
    MUSICORD PUBLICATIONS, INC.   1.25
MITTLER--ED   MITTLER   2, 3
  GREAT CONCERTO MUSIC
    MUSICORD PUBLICATIONS, INC.   1.25
MITTLER--ED   MITTLER   2, 3
  GREAT OPERA MUSIC
    MUSICORD PUBLICATIONS, INC.   1.25
MITTLER--ED   MITTLER   2, 3
  GREAT SYMPHONY MUSIC
    MUSICORD PUBLICATIONS, INC.   1.25
MITTLER--ED   MITTLER   2, 3
  GREAT WALTZ MUSIC
    MUSICORD PUBLICATIONS, INC.   1.25
MITTLER--ED   MITTLER
  MUSIC IS MY HOBBY
    MUSICORD PUBLICATIONS, INC.   2.50
MOLLER *
  HAPPY WANDERER, THE -- SIMP. VERSION
    SOUTHERN MUSIC COMPANY   .50
MOLLER *
  HAPPY WANDERER, THE
    SAM FOX PUBLISHING COMPANY, INC.   .50
MOLLOY, J. L.--ED   MOLLOY, J. L.   3
  LOVE'S OLD SWEET SONG
    CENTURY MUSIC PUBLISHING COMPANY, INC. 2438   .40
MOLLOY, J. L.--ED   MOLLOY, J. L.   2
  LOVE'S OLD SWEET SONG
    CENTURY MUSIC PUBLISHING COMPANY, INC. 2061   .40
MONRI, V.   DEL MAGLIO
  CZARDAS NO. 1
    FRANCO COLOMBO PUBLICATIONS   127211   .60
MOSSMAN, T.--ED   MOSSMAN, T.
  HANDS ACROSS THE TABLE, SIMPLIFIED
    BELWIN-MILLS PUBLISHING CORPORATION   .60
MOSSMAN, T.--ED   MOSSMAN, T.
  KITTEN ON THE KEYS -- SIMP.
    BELWIN-MILLS PUBLISHING CORPORATION 26023   .50
MOSSMAN, T.--ED   MOSSMAN, T.
  ORGAN GRINDER'S SWING -- SIMP.
    BELWIN-MILLS PUBLISHING CORPORATION 26068   .50
MOSSMAN, T.--ED   MOSSMAN, T.
  PAVANNE -- SIMP.
    BELWIN-MILLS PUBLISHING CORPORATION 26036   .50
MOSSMAN, T.--ED   MOSSMAN, T.
  SERENADE IN THE NIGHT -- SIMP.
    BELWIN-MILLS PUBLISHING CORPORATION 26092   .50
MOSSMAN, T.--ED   MOSSMAN, T.
  SHEIK OF ARABY, THE -- SIMP.
    BELWIN-MILLS PUBLISHING CORPORATION   .50
MOSSMAN, T.--ED   MOSSMAN, T.
  SWEET LORRAINE -- SIMP.
    BELWIN-MILLS PUBLISHING CORPORATION 26052   .50
MOSSMAN, T.--ED   MOSSMAN, T.
  SWEET ROSIE O'GRADY SIMP.
    BELWIN-MILLS PUBLISHING CORPORATION 26053   .50
MOSSMAN, T.--ED   MOSSMAN, T.
  TAKE ME IN YOUR ARMS -- SIMP.
    BELWIN-MILLS PUBLISHING CORPORATION 26055   .50
MOSSMAN, T.--ED   MOSSMAN, T.
  WHEN IT'S SLEEPY TIME DOWN SOUTH -- SIMP.
    BELWIN-MILLS PUBLISHING CORPORATION 26062   .50
MOSSMAN, T.
  AT A GEORGIA CAMP MEETING -- SIMP.
    BELWIN-MILLS PUBLISHING CORPORATION 26004   .50
MOSSMAN, T.
  BELLS OF AVALON, THE -- SIMP.
    BELWIN-MILLS PUBLISHING CORPORATION 26066   .50
MOSSMAN, T.
  COMPOSING A RONDO WITH BEETHOVEN -- SIMP.
    BELWIN-MILLS PUBLISHING CORPORATION 26079   .50
MOSSMAN, T.
  FOR ME AND MY GAL -- SIMP.
    BELWIN-MILLS PUBLISHING CORPORATION 26075   .50
MOSSMAN, T.
  HANDS ACROSS THE TABLE -- SIMP.
    BELWIN-MILLS PUBLISHING CORPORATION 26069   .50
MOSSMAN, T.
  HAYDN GOES HUNTING -- SIMP.
    BELWIN-MILLS PUBLISHING CORPORATION 26018   .50
MOSSMAN, T.
  HOME -- SIMP.
    BELWIN-MILLS PUBLISHING CORPORATION 26020   .50
MOSSMAN, T.
  IN SUNNY SOUTH AMERICAN -- SIMP.
    BELWIN-MILLS PUBLISHING CORPORATION 26078   .50
MOSSMAN, T.
  I CAN'T GIVE YOU ANYTHING BUT LOVE -- SIMP.
    BELWIN-MILLS PUBLISHING CORPORATION 26021   .50
MOSSMAN, T.
  ONE MORNING IN MAY -- SIMP.
    BELWIN-MILLS PUBLISHING CORPORATION 26035   .50
MOSSMAN, T.
  REPASZ BAND -- SIMP.
    BELWIN-MILLS PUBLISHING CORPORATION 26041   .50
MOSSMAN, T.
  SCHOOL DAYS -- SIMP.
    BELWIN-MILLS PUBLISHING CORPORATION 26042   .50
MOSSMAN, T.
  SIMPLIFIED BOOGIE WOOGIE
    BELWIN-MILLS PUBLISHING CORPORATION   1.25
MOSSMAN, T.
  SOLITUDE -- SIMP.
    BELWIN-MILLS PUBLISHING CORPORATION 26049   .50
MOSSMAN, T.
  SOPHISTICATED LADY -- SIMP.
    BELWIN-MILLS PUBLISHING CORPORATION 26050   .50
MOSSMAN, T.
  WALTZING WITH STRAUSS
    BELWIN-MILLS PUBLISHING CORPORATION 26059   .50
MOSZKOWSKI   M
  CAPRICE ESPAGNOL
    C. F. PETERS CORPORATION   2218A   .90

MOSZKOWSKI   E
  GUITAR, OP. 45 NO. 2
    C. F. PETERS CORPORATION   2223A   .90
MOSZKOWSKI   E-M
  SPANISH DANCES, OP. 12. NOS. 1, 2, 4
    C. F. PETERS CORPORATION   2130A   1.25
MOUSSORGSKY   MOSSMAN, T.
  GOPAK FROM 'THE FAIR AT SOROCHINSK' -- SIMP.
    BELWIN-MILLS PUBLISHING CORPORATION   26080   .50
MOZART, W. A.   DEL MAGLIO
  ANDANTE FROM SONATA NO. 15
    FRANCO COLOMBO PUBLICATIONS   124724   .50
MOZART, W. A.   DEL MAGLIO
  DON GIOVANNI - DEH VIENI ALLA FINESTRA
    FRANCO COLOMBO PUBLICATIONS   124722   .50
MOZART, W. A.   3
  MAGIC FLUTE, PRIESTS' MARCH
    CENTURY MUSIC PUBLISHING COMPANY, INC.   454   .40
MOZART, W. A.   1
  MINUETTO 'DON GIOVANNI', SIMPLIFIED
    BELWIN-MILLS PUBLISHING CORPORATION   527   .60
MOZART, W. A.   ECKHARDT, F.   1
  MOZART FOR THE YOUNG PIANIST
    CENTURY MUSIC PUBLISHING COMPANY, INC.   3960   .40
MOZART, W. A.   CHIESA
  RONDO ALLA TURCA FROM SONATA NO. 11
    FRANCO COLOMBO PUBLICATIONS   107488   .60
MULE   MORINI
  LARGO
    FRANCO COLOMBO PUBLICATIONS   BON.2030   .90
NEALE, J.--ED   NEALE, J.
  INSTANT PICTURE CHORD PIANO NO. 1
    WARNER BROTHERS PUBLISHERS   1.95
NEALE, J.--ED   NEALE, J.
  PETER, PAUL AND MARY, MORE MADE EASY FOR PIANO
    WARNER BROTHERS PUBLISHERS   PPM 25   2.00
NEIDLINGER, W. H.   STEINER
  BIRTHDAY OF A KING, THE
    G. SCHIRMER, INC.   .35
NEVIN   LEVINE   3
  GONDOLIERS
    BOSTON MUSIC COMPANY   .50
NEVIN   LEVINE   2
  MIGHTY LAK' A ROSE
    BOSTON MUSIC COMPANY   .50
NEVIN   DEL MAGLIO
  NARCISSUS, OP. 13 NO. 4
    FRANCO COLOMBO PUBLICATIONS   128846   .60
NOVARO   DEL MAGLIO
  INNO DI MAMELI -- WITH WORDS --
    FRANCO COLOMBO PUBLICATIONS   127212   .60
OFFENBACH   1
  TALES OF HOFFMANN - BARCAROLLE, SIMP.
    BELWIN-MILLS PUBLISHING CORPORATION   514   .60
OLIVIERI   DEL MAGLIO
  GARIBALDI HYMN -- WITH WORDS --
    FRANCO COLOMBO PUBLICATIONS   127213   .50
OLIVIERO *
  MORE
    EDWARD B. MARKS MUSIC CORPORATION   01.00
PADEREWSKI, I. J.   2
  MENUET, SIMPLIFIED
    BELWIN-MILLS PUBLISHING CORPORATION   710   .60
PAGANINI, N.   CHIESA
  CARNIVAL OF VENICE
    FRANCO COLOMBO PUBLICATIONS   107490   .60
PANELLA, L.   2
  IN COMMAND -- SIMPLIFIED
    VOLKWEIN BROS.   .30
PANELLA, L.   2
  LOVE TOKENS -- SIMPLIFIED
    VOLKWEIN BROS.   .40
PERGOLESI   DEL MAGLIO
  SE TU M'AMI
    FRANCO COLOMBO PUBLICATIONS   128124   .50
POLDINI, E.   ROLFE, W.   2
  WALTZING DOLL, EASY
    CENTURY MUSIC PUBLISHING COMPANY, INC.   3543   .40
PONCHIELLI   CHIESA
  GIOCONDA, LA - DANCE OF THE HOURS
    FRANCO COLOMBO PUBLICATIONS   109093   .60
PORTNOFF, M.--ED   PORTNOFF, M.
  DANCE ETUDES
    BOURNE COMPANY   1.00
PORTNOFF, M.--ED   PORTNOFF, M.
  TEN FINGERS IN A FIVE FINGER POSITION
    BOURNE COMPANY   1.00
PRESS
  WEDDING DANCE
    WEINTRAUB MUSIC COMPANY   070101   .60
PROKOFIEFF   SINGER
  MARCH FROM 'PETER AND THE WOLF'
    MCA MUSIC   .60
PROKOFIEFF   4
  MARCH FROM 'THE LOVE OF THREE ORANGES', OP. 33
    BOSTON MUSIC COMPANY   .50
PROKOFIEFF   WALLIS   3
  PETER AND THE WOLF
    BOSTON MUSIC COMPANY   1.00
PROKOFIEFF   HIRSCHBERG, D.   3A
  PETER AND THE WOLF
    MUSICORD PUBLICATIONS, INC.   .45
PROKOFIEFF   SCHAUM, J.   2
  PETER AND THE WOLF
    SCHAUM PUBLICATIONS, INC.   1.50
PROKOFIEFF   E-M
  WALTZ FROM CINDERELLA BALLET
    C. F. PETERS CORPORATION   4774   2.00
PUCCINI   MARCIANO
  BOHEME, LA - CHE GELIDA MANINA
    FRANCO COLOMBO PUBLICATIONS   99747   .90
PUCCINI   RICHTER
  BOHEME, LA - CHE GELIDA MANINA
    FRANCO COLOMBO PUBLICATIONS   NY1530   .60
PUCCINI   ALASSIO
  BOHEME, LA - MUSETTA'S WALTZ SONG
    FRANCO COLOMBO PUBLICATIONS   99483   .60
PUCCINI   RICHTER
  BOHEME, LA - MUSETTA'S WALTZ SONG
    FRANCO COLOMBO PUBLICATIONS   NY1529   .60
PUCCINI   MARCIANO
  BOHEME, LA - SI, MI CHIAMANO MIMI
    FRANCO COLOMBO PUBLICATIONS   99748   .60
PUCCINI   ALASSIO
  BOHEME, LA - SI, MI CHIAMANO MIMI
    FRANCO COLOMBO PUBLICATIONS   99482   .50

PUCCINI   DEL MAGLIO
  E L'UCCELLINO - BERCEUSE
    FRANCO COLOMBO PUBLICATIONS   124726   .50
PUCCINI   DEL MAGLIO
  GIANNI SCHICCHI - O MIO BABBINO CARO
    FRANCO COLOMBO PUBLICATIONS   127760   .60
PUCCINI   DEL MAGLIO
  MANON LESCAUT - IN QUELLE TRINE MORBIDE
    FRANCO COLOMBO PUBLICATIONS   127761   .60
PUCCINI   3
  MUSETTA'S WALTZ, LA BOHEME
    CENTURY MUSIC PUBLISHING COMPANY, INC.   4085   .40
PUCCINI   ALASSIO
  TOSCA - O DOLCI BACI
    FRANCO COLOMBO PUBLICATIONS   103325   .60
RACHMANINOFF, S.   3
  PIANO CONCERTO, THEME
    CENTURY MUSIC PUBLISHING COMPANY, INC.   3764   .40
RACHMANINOFF, S.   MOSSMAN
  PIANO CONCERTO NO. 02 IN C MINOR -- THIRD MOVEMENT
    BELWIN-MILLS PUBLISHING CORPORATION   26090   .60
RACHMANINOFF, S.   ECKSTEIN
  PRELUDE IN C SHARP MINOR, OP. 3 NO. 2
    CARL FISCHER, INC.   S 2319   .50
RACHMANINOFF, S.   DEL MAGLIO
  PRELUDE IN C SHARP MINOR, OP. 3 NO. 2
    FRANCO COLOMBO PUBLICATIONS   129082   .60
RACHMANINOFF, S.   MITTLER   3B
  PRELUDE IN C SHARP MINOR
    MUSICORD PUBLICATIONS, INC.   .45
RACHMANINOFF, S.   PALMERI
  PRELUDE IN G MINOR
    G. SCHIRMER, INC.   .40
RACHMANINOFF, S.   ROLFE, W.   3
  PUNCHINELLO, OP. 3 NO. 4, EASY
    CENTURY MUSIC PUBLISHING COMPANY, INC.   3394   .40
RACHMANINOFF, S.   MITTLER   3A
  RACHMANINOFF CONCERTO
    MUSICORD PUBLICATIONS, INC.   .45
RACHMANINOFF, S.   TRUXELL, E.   3 1/2
  THEMES FROM PIANO CONCERTO
    VOLKWEIN BROS.   00.40
RAMOS, E.   HARRIS   3-4
  PAQUITA MIA
    VOLKWEIN BROS.   .30
RASBACH, O.   DEIS
  TREES
    G. SCHIRMER, INC.   .50
REED, H.   SINGER
  GYPSY, THE
    MCA MUSIC   .60
RETTENBERG--ED   RETTENBERG
  CORRIDA -- 10 OF SPAIN'S MOST POPULAR PASODOBLES IN SIMPLIFIED
  ARRANGEMENTS
    ASSOCIATED MUSIC PUBLISHERS, INC.   AMP   .85
RICHTER--ED   RICHTER
  DISNEY CLASSICS
    BOURNE COMPANY   1.50
RICHTER--ED   RICHTER
  SNOW WHITE AND THE SEVEN DWARFS
    BOURNE COMPANY   1.50
RICHTER, C.--ED   RICHTER, C.
  FIVE FINGERS ON FIVE KEYS, BK. 01
    BOURNE COMPANY   .75
RICHTER, C.--ED   RICHTER, C.
  FIVE FINGERS ON FIVE KEYS, BK. 02
    BOURNE COMPANY   .75
RICHTER, C.--ED   RICHTER, C.
  MERRY CHRISTMAS MUSIC
    BOURNE COMPANY   .75
RICHTER, C.--ED   RICHTER, C.   1
  MUSIC APPRECIATION SERIES, BK. 01
    BOURNE COMPANY   1.25
RICHTER, C.--ED   RICHTER, C.   2
  MUSIC APPRECIATION SERIES, BK. 02
    BOURNE COMPANY   1.25
RIMSKY-KORSAKOFF
  FLIGHT OF THE BUMBLE BEE
    EDWARD B. MARKS MUSIC CORPORATION   01.00
RIMSKY-KORSAKOFF   MOSSMAN
  SCHEHERAZADE
    BELWIN-MILLS PUBLISHING CORPORATION   26097   .60
RIMSKY-KORSAKOFF   4
  SCHEHEREZADE, FESTIVAL AT BAGDAD
    CENTURY MUSIC PUBLISHING COMPANY, INC.   3722   .40
RIMSKY-KORSAKOFF   3
  SONG OF INDIA, A
    CENTURY MUSIC PUBLISHING COMPANY, INC.   3626   .40
RIMSKY-KORSAKOFF   MOSSMAN
  SONG OF INDIA
    BELWIN-MILLS PUBLISHING CORPORATION   26098   .60
ROIG
  YOURS --QUIEREME MUCHO
    EDWARD B. MARKS MUSIC CORPORATION   01.00
ROMBERG, S.   DEIS
  WILL YOU REMEMBER--FROM 'MAYTIME'
    G. SCHIRMER, INC.   .40
ROMBERG, S.   LEVINE
  WILL YOU REMEMBER--FROM 'MAYTIME'
    G. SCHIRMER, INC.   .50
ROSAS   CHIESA
  OVER THE WAVES
    FRANCO COLOMBO PUBLICATIONS   109199   .60
ROSAS   2
  SOBRE LAS OLAS, VALSE, EASY
    CENTURY MUSIC PUBLISHING COMPANY, INC.   2137   .40
ROSSINI, G.   CHIESA
  BARBIERE DI SIVIGLIA, IL - CAVATINA - UNA VOCE POCO FA
    FRANCO COLOMBO PUBLICATIONS   107483   .60
ROSSINI, G.   DEL MAGLIO
  DANZA, LA
    FRANCO COLOMBO PUBLICATIONS   124727   .60
ROSSINI, G.   DEL MAGLIO
  GUILLAUME TELL - PASTORALE FROM THE OVERTURE
    FRANCO COLOMBO PUBLICATIONS   128145   .50
ROSSINI, G.   DEL MAGLIO
  MOSE - DAL TUO STELLATO SOGLIO
    FRANCO COLOMBO PUBLICATIONS   124728   .60
ROSSINI, G.   3
  OVERTURE, WILLIAM TELL, EASY
    CENTURY MUSIC PUBLISHING COMPANY, INC.   2513   .40
ROSSINI, G.   BERMONT, H.   1B
  WILLIAM TELL -- FANFARE
    MUSICORD PUBLICATIONS, INC.   .45
ROSSINI, G.   KRUG   2
  WILLIAM TELL OVERTURE, EASY
    CENTURY MUSIC PUBLISHING COMPANY, INC.   532   .40

ROSSINI, G.   ZEPP   2-3
    WILLIAM TELL
        PRO-ART PUBLICATIONS, INC.   325   .50
ROSSI   4
    SPIN, SPIN, ESTHONIAN FOLK SONG
        CENTURY MUSIC PUBLISHING COMPANY, INC.   2288   .40
RUBINSTEIN   DEL MAGLIO
    MELODY IN F, OP. 3 NO. 1
        FRANCO COLOMBO PUBLICATIONS   127354   .50
RUBINSTEIN   2
    MELODY IN F -- SIMPLIFIED
        VOLKWEIN BROS.   .25
RUBINSTEIN   JESTON, I. H.   3
    MELODY IN F
        VOLKWEIN BROS.   .35
RUBINSTEIN   DEL MAGLIO
    ROMANCE IN E FLAT, OP. 44
        FRANCO COLOMBO PUBLICATIONS   127355   .50
SAINT-SAENS   PALMERI
    SWAN, THE--FROM 'CARNAVAL DES ANIMAUX'
        G. SCHIRMER, INC.   .35
SAINT-SAENS   LEVINE
    SWAN, THE--FROM 'CARNAVAL DES ANIMAUX'
        G. SCHIRMER, INC.   .50
SCHAUM, J.--ED   SCHAUM, J.   2
    HANSEL AND GRETEL
        SCHAUM PUBLICATIONS, INC.   1.50
SCHAUM, J.--ED   SCHAUM, J.
    LATIN AMERICAN MUSIC
        SCHAUM PUBLICATIONS, INC.   1.50
SCHAUM, J.--ED   SCHAUM, J.   PREP
    SUNDAY SCHOOL HYMNS -- MUSIC FOR CHILDREN
        SCHAUM PUBLICATIONS, INC.   1.25
SCHIEFELBEIN, F.   2
    JINGLE BELLS
        VOLKWEIN BROS.   .35
SCHIEFELBEIN, F.   2
    LEFT FOOT, RIGHT FOOT -- SIMPLIFIED
        VOLKWEIN BROS.   .30
SCHUBERT   DEL MAGLIO
    AN DEN MOND
        FRANCO COLOMBO PUBLICATIONS   128143   .50
SCHUBERT   DEL MAGLIO
    AVE MARIA, OP. 52 NO. 6
        FRANCO COLOMBO PUBLICATIONS   128149   .60
SCHUBERT   DEL MAGLIO
    FORELLE, DIE
        FRANCO COLOMBO PUBLICATIONS   128142   .50
SCHUBERT   DEL MAGLIO
    HEIDENROESLEIN, OP. 3 NO. 3
        FRANCO COLOMBO PUBLICATIONS   128125   .50
SCHUBERT   3
    IMPROMPTU G-DUR, OP. 90
        SCHOTT   0688 102   1.00
SCHUBERT   DEL MAGLIO
    IMPROMPTU IN G FLAT, OP. 90 NO. 3
        FRANCO COLOMBO PUBLICATIONS   124730   .50
SCHUBERT   DEL MAGLIO
    MARCHE MILITAIRE, OP. 51 NO. 1
        FRANCO COLOMBO PUBLICATIONS   124731   .60
SCHUBERT   KRENTZLIN   2
    MILITARMARSCH D-DUR OP. 51 NO. 1
        SCHOTT   08260 1/2 1.00
SCHUBERT   ROLFE, W.   2
    MILITARY MARCH, EASY
        CENTURY MUSIC PUBLISHING COMPANY, INC.   3176   .40
SCHUBERT   DEL MAGLIO
    MOMENT MUSICAL, OP. 94 NO. 3
        FRANCO COLOMBO PUBLICATIONS   124732   .50
SCHUBERT   SCHAUM, J.   2 1/2
    ROMANTIC WALTZES OF FRANZ SCHUBERT
        SCHAUM PUBLICATIONS, INC.   1.60
SCHUBERT   ECKHARDT, F.   1
    SCHUBERT FOR THE YOUNG PIANIST
        CENTURY MUSIC PUBLISHING COMPANY, INC.   3961   .40
SCHUBERT   DEL MAGLIO
    SERENADE
        FRANCO COLOMBO PUBLICATIONS   128150   .60
SCHUBERT   JESTON, I. H.   3
    SERENADE
        VOLKWEIN BROS.   .35
SCHUBERT   DEL MAGLIO
    SYMPHONY IN B MINOR 'UNFINISHED' -- THEMES IN EASY TRANSCR. --
        FRANCO COLOMBO PUBLICATIONS   128144   .50
SCHUBERT   DEL MAGLIO
    WOHIN OP. 25 NO. 2
        FRANCO COLOMBO PUBLICATIONS   128126   .50
SCHULTZE
    LILLI MARLENE
        EDWARD B. MARKS MUSIC CORPORATION   01.00
SCHUMANN, R.   DEL MAGLIO
    ABENDLIED, OP. 85 NO. 12
        FRANCO COLOMBO PUBLICATIONS   128845   .60
SCHUMANN, R.   DEL MAGLIO
    ALBUMBLAETTER, OP. 124 NO. 16
        FRANCO COLOMBO PUBLICATIONS   129084   .60
SCHUMANN, R.   DEL MAGLIO
    ALBUM FUER DIE JUGEND -- ALBUM FOR THE YOUNG --, OP. 68 NO. 10 -
    THE HAPPY FARMER
        FRANCO COLOMBO PUBLICATIONS   .60
SCHUMANN, R.   DEL MAGLIO
    KINDERSCENEN -- SCENES FROM CHILDHOOD --, OP. 15 NO. 7 -
    TRAEUMEREI
        FRANCO COLOMBO PUBLICATIONS   128129   .60
SCHUMANN, R.   ECKHARDT, F.   1
    SCHUMANN FOR THE YOUNG PIANIST
        CENTURY MUSIC PUBLISHING COMPANY, INC.   3962   .40
SERRADELL   3
    LA GOLONDRINA -- THE SWALLOW, EASY
        CENTURY MUSIC PUBLISHING COMPANY, INC.   3569   .40
SHANKO, S. W.--ED   SHANKO, S. W.
    HYMN TUNE PRELUDES FOR THE PIANO, NO. 3
        BROADMAN MUSIC   4571-05   2.25
SHINN, D.
    POPULAR PIANO PLAYING SIMPLIFIED
        SHINN MUSIC AIDS   1.95
SIBELIUS   WALLIS   2
    THEME FROM FINLANDIA
        BOSTON MUSIC COMPANY   .50
SIMONETTI   DEL MAGLIO
    MADRIGAL
        FRANCO COLOMBO PUBLICATIONS   124733   .50
SIMONS
    PEANUT VENDOR, THE
        EDWARD B. MARKS MUSIC CORPORATION   01.00

SINDING   3
    FRUEHLINGSRAUCHEN, EASY
        CENTURY MUSIC PUBLISHING COMPANY, INC.   2134   .40
SINDING   E
    RUSTLE OF SPRING, OP. 32 NO. 3
        C. F. PETERS CORPORATION   2870AA   .60
SINDING   3
    RUSTLE OF SPRING
        VOLKWEIN BROS.   .25
SMITH, J.   DILLER
    STAR-SPANGLED BANNER, THE
        G. SCHIRMER, INC.   .40
SOUSA   PELS, W.   1B
    STARS AND STRIPES FOREVER -- FINALE THEME
        MUSICORD PUBLICATIONS, INC.   .45
SOUSA   ZEPP   2
    STARS AND STRIPES FOREVER
        PRO-ART PUBLICATIONS, INC.   144   .50
SOUSA   1 1/2
    STARS AND STRIPES FOREVER
        WILLIS MUSIC COMPANY   .40
SOUSA   3
    WASHINGTON POST, THE
        BOSTON MUSIC COMPANY   .50
SPAULDING, G. L.--ED   SPAULDING, G. L.
    BELLS OF ST. MARY'S, WALTZ
        CHAPPELL AND COMPANY, INC.   0437509-1503 .95
SPENCER, J.
    FAVORITE CHRISTMAS MELODIES
        VOLKWEIN BROS.   01.00
SPENCER, J.
    FAVORITE MELODIES MADE EASY
        VOLKWEIN BROS.   01.00
SPENCER, J.   1
    STAR SPANGLED BANNER
        VOLKWEIN BROS.   .30
STEINER--ED.   STEINER
    FORGOTTEN DREAMS -- SIMP.
        BELWIN-MILLS PUBLISHING CORPORATION   26070   .50
STEINER--ED.   STEINER
    HEY, MR. BANJO
        BELWIN-MILLS PUBLISHING CORPORATION   25092   .50
STEINER--ED.   STEINER
    SLEIGH RIDE -- CHILDREN'S EDITION
        BELWIN-MILLS PUBLISHING CORPORATION   25133   .50
STEINER--ED.   STEINER
    WALTZING CAT, THE
        BELWIN-MILLS PUBLISHING CORPORATION   25135   .50
STRADELLA   DEL MAGLIO
    PRAYER
        FRANCO COLOMBO PUBLICATIONS   128141   .50
STRAUSS, J.   DEL MAGLIO
    ACCELERATIONS, OP. 234
        FRANCO COLOMBO PUBLICATIONS   124734   .50
STRAUSS, J.   DEL MAGLIO
    ALBUM - 8 FAMOUS WALTZES
        FRANCO COLOMBO PUBLICATIONS   127641   1.25
STRAUSS, J.   DEL MAGLIO
    ARTIST'S LIFE, OP. 316
        FRANCO COLOMBO PUBLICATIONS   124737   .60
STRAUSS, J.   DEL MAGLIO
    BEAUTIFUL MAY, OP. 375
        FRANCO COLOMBO PUBLICATIONS   124742   .60
STRAUSS, J.
    BLUE DANUBE WALTZ --SIMPLIFIED--
        CARL FISCHER, INC.   S 1120   .60
STRAUSS, J.   MITTLER   2B
    BLUE DANUBE WALTZ
        MUSICORD PUBLICATIONS, INC.   .45
STRAUSS, J.
    BLUE DANUBE
        FRANCO COLOMBO PUBLICATIONS   SAL   1.50
STRAUSS, J.   TRUXELL, E.   1 1/2
    BLUE DANUBE
        VOLKWEIN BROS.   .30
STRAUSS, J.   STEINER
    DRINKING SONG -- FROM 'DIE FLEDERMAUS'
        BELWIN-MILLS PUBLISHING CORPORATION   26012   .60
STRAUSS, J.   DEL MAGLIO
    EMPEROR WALTZ, OP. 437
        FRANCO COLOMBO PUBLICATIONS   124748   .60
STRAUSS, J.   DEL MAGLIO
    KISS WALTZ, OP. 411
        FRANCO COLOMBO PUBLICATIONS   124744   .60
STRAUSS, J.   DEL MAGLIO
    LAGOON WALTZ, OP. 411
        FRANCO COLOMBO PUBLICATIONS   124746   .60
STRAUSS, J.   STEINER
    LAUGHING SONG -- FROM 'DIE FLEDERMAUS'
        BELWIN-MILLS PUBLISHING CORPORATION   26025   .60
STRAUSS, J.   DEL MAGLIO
    MORNING PAPERS, OP. 279
        FRANCO COLOMBO PUBLICATIONS   .60
STRAUSS, J.   ZILCHER   2
    NUR WALZER VON STRAUSS
        SCHOTT   1507   3.00
STRAUSS, J.
    ON THE BEAUTIFUL BLUE DANUBE, OP. 314
        FRANCO COLOMBO PUBLICATIONS   40967   .60
STRAUSS, J.   DEL MAGLIO
    ON THE BEAUTIFUL BLUE DANUBE, OP. 314
        FRANCO COLOMBO PUBLICATIONS   124736   .60
STRAUSS, J.   DEIS *
    ON THE BEAUTIFUL BLUE DANUBE
        G. SCHIRMER, INC.   .60
STRAUSS, J.   STEINER
    PRINCE ORLOFSKY'S SONG -- FROM 'DIE FLEDERMAUS'
        BELWIN-MILLS PUBLISHING CORPORATION   26039   .60
STRAUSS, J.   DEL MAGLIO
    ROSES FROM THE SOUTH, OP. 388
        FRANCO COLOMBO PUBLICATIONS   124743   .60
STRAUSS, J.   SCHAUM, J.   3
    STRAUSS WALTZES
        SCHAUM PUBLICATIONS, INC.   1.50
STRAUSS, J.   DEL MAGLIO
    TALES FROM THE VIENNA WOODS, OP. 325
        FRANCO COLOMBO PUBLICATIONS   .60
STRAUSS, J.   TRUXELL, E.   3
    TALES FROM THE VIENNA WOODS WALTZ
        VOLKWEIN BROS.   00.50
STRAUSS, J.   FLETCHER   2
    TALES FROM THE VIENNA WOODS
        BOSTON MUSIC COMPANY   .50
STRAUSS, J.   WALLIS   3
    TALES FROM THE VIENNA WOODS
        BOSTON MUSIC COMPANY   .50

STRAUSS, J.   MITTLER   2B
  TALES FROM THE VIENNA WOODS
    MUSICORD PUBLICATIONS, INC.   .45
STRAUSS, J.   TRUXELL, E.   2
  TALES FROM THE VIENNA WOODS
    VOLKWEIN BROS.   00.40
STRAUSS, J.   DEL MAGLIO
  TREASURE WALTZ, OP. 418
    FRANCO COLOMBO PUBLICATIONS   124747   .60
STRAUSS, J.   DEL MAGLIO
  VIENNA BLOOD, OP. 354
    FRANCO COLOMBO PUBLICATIONS   124740   .60
STRAUSS, J.   DEL MAGLIO
  VOICES OF SPRING, OP. 410
    FRANCO COLOMBO PUBLICATIONS   124745   .60
STRAUSS, J.   DEL MAGLIO
  WINE, WOMEN AND SONG, OP. 333
    FRANCO COLOMBO PUBLICATIONS   124739   .50
STRAUSS, J.
  YOU AND YOU FROM 'FLEDERMAUS'
    FRANCO COLOMBO PUBLICATIONS   124741   .60
SUPPE, F.   5
  OVERTURE, LIGHT CAVALRY
    CENTURY MUSIC PUBLISHING COMPANY, INC. 1528   .40
SUPPE, F.   2
  OVERTURE, LIGHT CAVALRY
    CENTURY MUSIC PUBLISHING COMPANY, INC. 3668   .40
SUPPE, F.   3
  OVERTURE, POET AND PEASANT, EASY
    CENTURY MUSIC PUBLISHING COMPANY, INC. 2123   .40
SUPPE, F.   DEL MAGLIO
  POET AND PEASANT OVERTURE
    FRANCO COLOMBO PUBLICATIONS   128675   .60
THOMAS, A.   3
  MIGNON, GAVOTTE
    CENTURY MUSIC PUBLISHING COMPANY, INC. 1941   .40
THOMAS, A.   3
  OVERTURE, RAYMOND, EASY
    CENTURY MUSIC PUBLISHING COMPANY, INC. 2095   .40
THOMAS, J. J.   JESTON, I. H.   3
  RAYMOND FANTASIA
    VOLKWEIN BROS.   .35
THOMPSON, J.
  THOMPSON MELODY ALL THE WAY - BOOK 1-A
    WILLIS MUSIC COMPANY   1.25
THOMPSON, J.
  THOMPSON MELODY ALL THE WAY - BOOK 1-B
    WILLIS MUSIC COMPANY   1.25
THOMPSON, J.
  THOMPSON MELODY ALL THE WAY - BOOK 2-A
    WILLIS MUSIC COMPANY   1.25
THOMPSON, J.
  THOMPSON MELODY ALL THE WAY - BOOK 2-B
    WILLIS MUSIC COMPANY   1.25
THOMPSON, J.
  THOMPSON MELODY ALL THE WAY - BOOK 3-A
    WILLIS MUSIC COMPANY   1.25
THOMPSON, J.
  THOMPSON MELODY ALL THE WAY - BOOK 3-B
    WILLIS MUSIC COMPANY   1.25
THOMPSON, J.
  THOMPSON MELODY ALL THE WAY - PREPARATORY BOOK
    WILLIS MUSIC COMPANY   .90
THUILLIER   2
  FRILEUSE, LA, VALSE
    ALPHONSE LEDUC
TIRINDELLI   DEL MAGLIO
  O PRIMAVERA
    FRANCO COLOMBO PUBLICATIONS   127762   .50
TOBANI
  HEARTS AND FLOWERS
    ASHLEY DEALERS SERVICE, INC.   ES   .95
TOBANI   WOODE   1
  HEARTS AND FLOWERS
    BOSTON MUSIC COMPANY   .50
TOSTI   DEL MAGLIO
  IDEALE
    FRANCO COLOMBO PUBLICATIONS   124749   .50
TOSTI   DEL MAGLIO
  MALIA
    FRANCO COLOMBO PUBLICATIONS   124750   .50
TOSTI   DEL MAGLIO
  MARECHIARE
    FRANCO COLOMBO PUBLICATIONS   124751   .60
TOSTI   DEL MAGLIO
  NON T'AMO PIU
    FRANCO COLOMBO PUBLICATIONS   128148   .50
TOSTI
  VORREI
    FRANCO COLOMBO PUBLICATIONS   128137   .50
TRUXELL, E.   1
  STAR SPANGLED BANNER
    VOLKWEIN BROS.   .30
TSCHAIKOWSKY   3
  LOVE THEME, ROMEO AND JULIET
    CENTURY MUSIC PUBLISHING COMPANY, INC. 3431   .40
TSCHAIKOWSKY   DEL MAGLIO
  NONE BUT THE LONELY HEART, OP. 6 NO. 6
    FRANCO COLOMBO PUBLICATIONS   127114   .60
TSCHAIKOWSKY   MOSSMAN
  NONE BUT THE LONELY HEART
    BELWIN-MILLS PUBLISHING CORPORATION   26086   .60
TSCHAIKOWSKY   2
  NUTCRACKER SUITE, OP. 71A - CHINESE DANCE, EASY
    CENTURY MUSIC PUBLISHING COMPANY, INC. 4083   .40
TSCHAIKOWSKY   2
  NUTCRACKER SUITE, OP. 71A - MARCH, EASY
    CENTURY MUSIC PUBLISHING COMPANY, INC. 3828   .40
TSCHAIKOWSKY   2
  NUTCRACKER SUITE, OP. 71A - TREPAK, EASY
    CENTURY MUSIC PUBLISHING COMPANY, INC. 3673   .40
TSCHAIKOWSKY   2
  NUTCRACKER SUITE, OP. 71A - WALTZ OF THE FLOWERS, EASY
    CENTURY MUSIC PUBLISHING COMPANY, INC. 3227   .40
TSCHAIKOWSKY   2
  NUTCRACKER SUITE, OP. 71A - DANCE OF THE REED FLUTES
    CENTURY MUSIC PUBLISHING COMPANY, INC. 4084   .40
TSCHAIKOWSKY   SCHAUM, J.   2 1/2
  NUTCRACKER SUITE
    SCHAUM PUBLICATIONS, INC.   1.50
TSCHAIKOWSKY   3-4
  OVERTURE 1812, THEMES
    CENTURY MUSIC PUBLISHING COMPANY, INC. 3561   .40
TSCHAIKOWSKY   3
  PATHETIQUE SYMPHONY, THEME
    CENTURY MUSIC PUBLISHING COMPANY, INC. 3349   .40

TSCHAIKOWSKY   4
  PIANO CONCERTO IN B FLAT MINOR, THEME
    CENTURY MUSIC PUBLISHING COMPANY, INC. 3530   .40
TSCHAIKOWSKY   2
  PIANO CONCERTO NO. 01, EASY
    CENTURY MUSIC PUBLISHING COMPANY, INC. 3557   .40
TSCHAIKOWSKY   DEL MAGLIO
  ROMANCE, OP. 5
    FRANCO COLOMBO PUBLICATIONS   129098   .60
TSCHAIKOWSKY   ARMAND   3
  SLEEPING BEAUTY WALTZ, THE
    BOSTON MUSIC COMPANY   .75
TSCHAIKOWSKY   WALLIS   2
  SLEEPING BEAUTY WALTZ, THE
    BOSTON MUSIC COMPANY   .50
TSCHAIKOWSKY   DEL MAGLIO
  SONG WITHOUT WORDS, OP. 2 NO. 3
    FRANCO COLOMBO PUBLICATIONS   129097   .60
TSCHAIKOWSKY   BANTOCK, G.
  SWAN LAKE, SEVEN EXCERPTS
    BELWIN-MILLS PUBLISHING CORPORATION   09473   1.50
TSCHAIKOWSKY   MITTLER   3B
  SWAN LAKE BALLET
    MUSICORD PUBLICATIONS, INC.   .45
TSCHAIKOWSKY   ROLFE, W.   2
  SYMPHONY NO. 05, THEME EASY
    CENTURY MUSIC PUBLISHING COMPANY, INC. 3382   .40
TSCHAIKOWSKY   ECKSTEIN
  THEME FROM PIANO CONCERTO NO. 1 IN B FLAT
    CARL FISCHER, INC.   S 2282   .50
TSCHAIKOWSKY   WALLIS   2
  THEME FROM THE FIRST MOVEMENT OF PIANO CONCERTO NO. 1
    BOSTON MUSIC COMPANY   .50
TSCHAIKOWSKY   MITTLER   2B
  TSCHAIKOWSKY CONCERTO
    MUSICORD PUBLICATIONS, INC.   .45
TSCHAIKOWSKY   ECKHARDT, F.   1
  TSCHAIKOWSKY FOR THE YOUNG PIANIST
    CENTURY MUSIC PUBLISHING COMPANY, INC. 3963   .40
TSCHAIKOWSKY   ROVENGER
  TSCHAIKOWSKY FOR THE YOUNG
    RUBANK, INC.   1.50
TSCHAIKOWSKY
  TSCHAIKOWSKY MADE EASY FOR EVERYONE
    MUSICORD PUBLICATIONS, INC.   1.50
TSCHAIKOWSKY   DEL MAGLIO
  WALTZ OF THE FLOWERS FROM 'NUTCRACKER'
    FRANCO COLOMBO PUBLICATIONS   127115   .60
TSCHAIKOWSKY   TRUXELL, E.   2
  WALTZ OF THE FLOWERS
    VOLKWEIN BROS.   00.40
TSCHAIKOWSKY   TRUXELL, E.   2 1/2
  WALTZ OF THE FLOWERS
    VOLKWEIN BROS.   00.50
VERDI   ZILCHER   2-3
  DIE VERDI-OPER
    SCHOTT   1565   3.50
VERDI   DEL MAGLIO
  FORZA DEL DESTINO, LA - VERGINE DEGLI ANGELI, LA
    FRANCO COLOMBO PUBLICATIONS   124754   .90
VERDI   2
  IL TROVATORE, ANVIL CHORUS, EASY
    CENTURY MUSIC PUBLISHING COMPANY, INC. 3654   .40
VERDI   2
  IL TROVATORE, MISERERE, EASY
    CENTURY MUSIC PUBLISHING COMPANY, INC. 2153   .40
VERDI   DEL MAGLIO
  LOMBARDI, I - O SIGNORE DAL TETTO NATIO
    FRANCO COLOMBO PUBLICATIONS   124755   .60
VERDI   3
  MARCH, AIDA
    CENTURY MUSIC PUBLISHING COMPANY, INC. 4707   .40
VERDI   2
  MISERERE, IL TROVATORE, EASY
    CENTURY MUSIC PUBLISHING COMPANY, INC. 2153   .40
VERDI   4
  PRELUDE, TRAVIATA
    CENTURY MUSIC PUBLISHING COMPANY, INC. 3784   .40
VERDI   2
  RIGOLETTO, DONNA E MOBILE, EASY
    CENTURY MUSIC PUBLISHING COMPANY, INC. 2156   .40
VERDI   KRUG   2
  TRAVIATA, EASY TRANSCRIPTION
    CENTURY MUSIC PUBLISHING COMPANY, INC. 2145   .40
VERDI   ROLFE, W.   2
  TROVATORE, IL, ANVIL CHORUS, EASY
    CENTURY MUSIC PUBLISHING COMPANY, INC. 3654   .40
VERDI   KRUG   2
  TROVATORE, IL, EASY TRANSCRIPTION
    CENTURY MUSIC PUBLISHING COMPANY, INC. 530   .40
VITTADINI
  RELIGIOUS MELODIES - 23 PIECES
    FRANCO COLOMBO PUBLICATIONS   127150   1.00
WAGNER   DEL MAGLIO
  LOHENGRIN - WEDDING MARCH
    FRANCO COLOMBO PUBLICATIONS   128118   .50
WAGNER   LANGE, G.   5
  LOVE SONG, WALKUERE
    CENTURY MUSIC PUBLISHING COMPANY, INC. 1192   .40
WAGNER   SPINDLER   4
  MARCH, TANNHAUSER
    CENTURY MUSIC PUBLISHING COMPANY, INC. 313   .40
WAGNER   3
  PARSIFAL, GOOD FRIDAY SPELL
    CENTURY MUSIC PUBLISHING COMPANY, INC. 3642   .40
WAGNER   LANGE, E.   5
  PILGRIMS' CHORUS, TANNHAUSER
    CENTURY MUSIC PUBLISHING COMPANY, INC. 1027   .40
WAGNER   2
  PRELUDE, ACT 3, LOHENGRIN
    CENTURY MUSIC PUBLISHING COMPANY, INC. 2039   .40
WAGNER   DEL MAGLIO
  TANNHAEUSER - MARCH
    FRANCO COLOMBO PUBLICATIONS   128140   .50
WAGNER   DEL MAGLIO
  TANNHAEUSER - PILGRIMS' CHORUS
    FRANCO COLOMBO PUBLICATIONS   128147   .60
WAGNER   ECKHARDT, F.   1
  WAGNER FOR THE YOUNG PIANIST
    CENTURY MUSIC PUBLISHING COMPANY, INC. 3964   .40
WALDTEUFEL, E.   ROLFE, W.   2
  PATINEURS, LES, EASY
    CENTURY MUSIC PUBLISHING COMPANY, INC. 3191   .40
WALDTEUFEL, E.   WEYBRIGHT
  SKATER'S WALTZ, THE
    BELWIN-MILLS PUBLISHING CORPORATION   26046   .60

WALDTEUFEL, E.   MITTLER   28
  SKATERS WALTZ
    MUSICORD PUBLICATIONS, INC.   .45
WALDTEUFEL, E.   2
  SPANISH STUDENTS, WALTZES, EASY
    CENTURY MUSIC PUBLISHING COMPANY, INC.   3666   .40
WALDTEUFEL, E.   SAMMARTINO
  TEN FAMOUS WALTZES
    FRANCO COLOMBO PUBLICATIONS   BA9100   2.00
WEBER, VON   DEL MAGLIO
  INVITATION TO THE DANCE, OP. 65
    FRANCO COLOMBO PUBLICATIONS   124756   .50
WEILL, K.
  KURT WEILL
    CHAPPELL AND COMPANY, INC.   0017855   1.50
WERNER, F.   SCHIEFELBEIN, F.   2
  HEDGE ROSE
    VOLKWEIN BROS.   .30
WESTERHOUT   DEL MAGLIO
  MA BELLE QUI DANSE
    FRANCO COLOMBO PUBLICATIONS   127763   .50
WESTERHOUT   DEL MAGLIO
  RONDE D'AMOUR
    FRANCO COLOMBO PUBLICATIONS   127764   .50
WILLIAMS, C.   NEVIN
  THEME FROM 'THE APARTMENT' -- SIMP.
    BELWIN-MILLS PUBLISHING CORPORATION   26108   .50
WILLIAMS, L. R.--ED   WILLIAMS, L. R.
  FAVORITE HYMNS TO PLAY AND SING IN EASY PIANO ARRANGEMENTS
    BROADMAN MUSIC   4571-01   1.50
WILLSON, M.   RICHTER   2 1/2 - 3
  SEVENTY SIX TROMBONES
    FRANK MUSIC CORPORATION   .75
WILLSON, M.   AGAY, D.   EASY
  SONGS FROM 'THE MUSIC MAN'
    FRANK MUSIC CORPORATION   1.25
WILLSON, M.   AGAY, D.   EASY
  SONGS FROM 'THE UNSINKABLE MOLLY BROWN'
    FRANK MUSIC CORPORATION   1.25
WILLSON, M.   RICHTER   2 1/2 - 3
  TILL THERE WAS YOU
    FRANK MUSIC CORPORATION   .75
WOLFE, W.   ETTS, M.
  CLASSICS MADE EASY, ONE
    ASHLEY DEALERS SERVICE, INC.   1.25
WRIGHT, R. *   RICHTER   EASY
  NEW SONGS FROM THE MOTION PICTURE 'SONG OF NORWAY'
    FRANK MUSIC CORPORATION   1.25
WRIGHT, R. *   RICHTER   EASY
  SONGS FROM 'KISMET'
    FRANK MUSIC CORPORATION   1.25
YOUNG, I.--ED.   YOUNG, I.
  THIRTY-SIX FAVORITE MELODIES FOR THE PIANO
    G. SCHIRMER, INC.   1.25
YRADIER   2
  DOVE, THE -- LA PALOMA, EASY
    CENTURY MUSIC PUBLISHING COMPANY, INC.   2139   .40
YRADIER   CHIESA
  PALOMA, LA
    FRANCO COLOMBO PUBLICATIONS   107485   .60
ZAMECNIK   KLICKMANN
  NEAPOLITAN NIGHTS -- SIMPLIFIED
    SOUTHERN MUSIC COMPANY   .50
ZAMECNIK   KLICKMANN
  NEAPOLITAN NIGHTS
    SAM FOX PUBLISHING COMPANY, INC.   .50
ZEPP--ED   ZEPP   2
  HAVA NAGILA
    PRO-ART PUBLICATIONS, INC.   362   .50
ZEPP--ED   ZEPP   2
  JOSHUA FIT DE BATTLE OF JERICHO
    PRO-ART PUBLICATIONS, INC.   262   .50
ZEPP--ED   ZEPP   4
  THREE PATRIOTIC SONGS
    PRO-ART PUBLICATIONS, INC.   110   .50

Simplified Versions:
Composer/Editor/Arranger Unlisted—Works Alphabetized by Title

ALAMEIN CONCERTO -- THEME
  CHAPPELL AND COMPANY, INC.   0014258-1502   .95
BELLS ARE RINGING
  CHAPPELL AND COMPANY, INC.   0430009-176   1.50
BELLS OF ST. MARY'S
  CHAPPELL AND COMPANY, INC.   0437509   .60
BIG SEVENTY-FIVE SONG BOOK, THE - EASY BIG NOTE PIANO
  WARNER BROTHERS PUBLISHERS   3.95
CAMELOT
  CHAPPELL AND COMPANY, INC.   0690008   1.50
CAN-CAN
  CHAPPELL AND COMPANY, INC.   0695015   1.50
CARDINAL STAY WITH ME, THE
  CHAPPELL AND COMPANY, INC.   5490008   .60
CHAPPEL'S EASYPLAY PIANO SERIES, BK. 1 -- FILM THEMES
  CHAPPELL AND COMPANY, INC.   0025114-174   1.95
CHAPPEL'S EASYPLAY PIANO SERIES, BK. 2 -- LOVE THEMES
  CHAPPELL AND COMPANY, INC.   0025122   1.95
CHAPPEL'S EASYPLAY PIANO SERIES, BK. 3 -- SHOWSTOPPERS
  CHAPPELL AND COMPANY, INC.   0025130   1.95
COCO
  CHAPPELL AND COMPANY, INC.   0906255   1.50
DAS NEUE OPERETTEN-BUCH, BAND 01   3
  SCHOTT   2525   4.00
DAS NEUE OPERETTEN-BUCH, BAND 02   3
  SCHOTT   2850   4.00

3
DAS NEUE OPERETTEN-BUCH, BAND 03   3
  SCHOTT   3700   4.00
DAS NEUE OPERETTEN-BUCH, BAND 04   3
  SCHOTT   4300   4.00
DAS NEUE OPERETTEN-BUCH, BAND 05   3
  SCHOTT   4500   4.00
DIE OPER IM HEIM, BAND 1   3
  SCHOTT   2777   5.00
DIE OPER IM HEIM, BAND 2   3
  SCHOTT   2778   5.00
FALLING IN LOVE WITH LOVE
  CHAPPELL AND COMPANY, INC.   1427509   .60
FANTASTICKS, THE
  CHAPPELL AND COMPANY, INC.   1442508   1.50
FINIAN'S RAINBOW   1
  CHAPPELL AND COMPANY, INC.   1480003   1.50
FIRST TIME AROUND
  BOURNE COMPANY   1.50
FUNNY GIRL
  CHAPPELL AND COMPANY, INC.   1622505   1.50
GEORGY GIRL
  CHAPPELL AND COMPANY, INC.   1662501   .60
GIGI
  CHAPPELL AND COMPANY, INC.   1680008   1.50
HAPPY SONGS FOR CHILDREN
  THE BIG THREE MUSIC CORPORATION   01.95
HARBOR LIGHTS
  CHAPPELL AND COMPANY, INC.   1900000   .60
HOW ARE THINGS IN GLOCCA MORRA
  CHAPPELL AND COMPANY, INC.   20600002   .60
I DO, I DO
  CHAPPELL AND COMPANY, INC.   2192508   1.50
I GOT PLENTY O' NUTTIN'
  CHAPPELL AND COMPANY, INC.   2230027   .60
    LANE, J.
JINGLE BELL ROCK
  THE BIG THREE MUSIC CORPORATION   00.70
    LANE, J.
KNOCK THREE TIMES
  THE BIG THREE MUSIC CORPORATION   00.70
LEFT FOOT, RIGHT FOOT MARCH FOLIO
  VOLKWEIN BROS.   01.50
MUSICAL VISIT WITH THE MASTERS, A -- 16 CLASSICAL COMPOSITIONS
IN SIMPLIFIED ARRANGEMENTS
  THEODORE PRESSER COMPANY   1.25
MY BEAUTIFUL LADY
  CHAPPELL AND COMPANY, INC.   3905007   .60
NIGHT THEY INVENTED CHAMPAGNE, THE
  CHAPPELL AND COMPANY, INC.   4090007   .60
ON A CLEAR DAY YOU CAN SEE FOREVER
  CHAPPELL AND COMPANY, INC.   4322509   1.50
OUVERTUREN-ALBUM, BAND 01   3-6
  SCHOTT   354   4.25
OUVERTUREN-ALBUM, BAND 02   3-6
  SCHOTT   355   4.25
OUVERTUREN-ALBUM, BAND 03   3-6
  SCHOTT   356   4.25
PAINT YOUR WAGON
  CHAPPELL AND COMPANY, INC.   4480000   1.50
PETER, PAUL AND MOMMY, EASY BIG NOTE PIANO
  WARNER BROTHERS PUBLISHERS   PPM 26   1.95
PIANO PIECES -- SIMP.
  CENTURY MUSIC PUBLISHING COMPANY, INC.   MPS VOL. 2   1.95
PLAYING PLEASURE
  EDWARD B. MARKS MUSIC CORPORATION   01.25
SEPTEMBER SONG
  CHAPPELL AND COMPANY, INC.   5060009   .60
SLEEPY LAGOON
  CHAPPELL AND COMPANY, INC.   5225008   .60
SONGS OF HOPE AND INSPIRATION
  THE BIG THREE MUSIC CORPORATION   01.50
STAR - EASY PIANO
  WARNER BROTHERS PUBLISHERS   1.95
STRANGE MUSIC
  CHAPPELL AND COMPANY, INC.   5520002   .60
THANK HEAVEN FOR LITTLE GIRLS
  CHAPPELL AND COMPANY, INC.   5740006   .60
THEY CALL THE WIND MARIA
  CHAPPELL AND COMPANY, INC.   5930003   .75
TRUE LOVE
  CHAPPELL AND COMPANY, INC.   6165005   .60
UNSTERBLICHE OPERETTEN   3
  SCHOTT   1508   3.25

Arrangements and Transcriptions

ADAM, A.
GISELLE -- BALLET-PANTOMINE IN 2 ACTS
ASSOCIATED MUSIC PUBLISHERS, INC.   ESC   12.75
ADAM, A.   HESS   5
O HOLY NIGHT
THEODORE PRESSER COMPANY   .60
ADAM, A.   PEERY   4
O HOLY NIGHT
THEODORE PRESSER COMPANY   .60
ADAMS, R. G.   SPENCER, J.   2
O HOLY NIGHT
VOLKWEIN BROS.   .30
ADAMS, S.   GODFREY
HOLY CITY
BOOSEY AND HAWKES, INC.   .75
ADAMS, S.   PERRY
HOLY CITY
BOOSEY AND HAWKES, INC.   .50
ADDINSELL   LIBERACE
WARSAW CONCERTO
CHAPPELL AND COMPANY, INC.   0021592-1504 1.00
ADDRISI   NEALE, J.   EASY
NEVER MY LOVE
WARNER BROTHERS PUBLISHERS   .75
ADLER, R. *   EASY
HITS FROM 'DAMN YANKEES'
FRANK MUSIC CORPORATION   1.25
ADLER, R. *
PAJAMA GAME, THE
FRANK MUSIC CORPORATION   1.25
ADLER, R. *   PACE, R.   EASY
SONGS FROM 'THE PAJAMA GAME'
FRANK MUSIC CORPORATION   1.25
AGAY, D.--ED   AGAY, D.
BOOGIE AND BLUES
MUSIC SALES CORPORATION   080056   .85
AGAY, D.--ED   AGAY, D.
CHRISTMAS RECITAL
MUSIC SALES CORPORATION   08006   .85
AGAY, D.--ED   AGAY, D.
CURTAIN TIME - MELODIES FROM THE MODERN THEATRE
FRANK MUSIC CORPORATION   2.00
AGAY, D.--ED   AGAY, D.
DANCING KEYBOARD, THE
WARNER BROTHERS PUBLISHERS   1.25
AGAY, D.--ED   AGAY, D.
FIESTA
MUSIC SALES CORPORATION   080057   .85
AGAY, D.--ED   AGAY, D.
JAZZ SOLOS
MUSIC SALES CORPORATION   080058   .85
AGAY, D.--ED   AGAY, D.
JOY OF BOOGIE AND BLUES, THE
MUSIC SALES CORPORATION   080010   1.75
AGAY, D.--ED   AGAY, D.
JOY OF CLASSICS, THE
MUSIC SALES CORPORATION   080005   1.75
AGAY, D.--ED   AGAY, D.
JOY OF FOLK SONGS, THE
MUSIC SALES CORPORATION   080006   1.75
AGAY, D.--ED   AGAY, D.
JOY OF JAZZ, THE
MUSIC SALES CORPORATION   080004   1.75
AGAY, D.--ED   AGAY, D.
JOY OF PIANO
MUSIC SALES CORPORATION   080002   1.75
AGAY, D.--ED   AGAY, D.   EASY
MATINEE MELODIES
FRANK MUSIC CORPORATION   1.50
AGAY, D.--ED   AGAY, D.
POPULAR MASTERPIECES
MUSIC SALES CORPORATION   080055   .85
AGAY, D.--ED   AGAY, D.
POP CONCERT
MUSIC SALES CORPORATION   080053   .85
AGAY, D.--ED   AGAY, D.
ROMANCING KEYBOARD, THE
WARNER BROTHERS PUBLISHERS   1.25
AGAY, D.--ED   AGAY, D.
SMILING KEYBOARD, THE
WARNER BROTHERS PUBLISHERS   1.25
AGAY, D.--ED   AGAY, D.
THIRTY-THREE HITS FROM BROADWAY
FRANK MUSIC CORPORATION   2.50
AGAY, D.--ED   AGAY, D.
THIRTY-TWO MORE HITS FROM BROADWAY
FRANK MUSIC CORPORATION   2.50
AGAY, D.--ED   AGAY, D.
WELL-PAMPERED PIANIST, THE
WARNER BROTHERS PUBLISHERS   1.25
AHRENS
KLEINES SPIELBUCH
BARENREITER VERLAG   BA 1725   1.75
AISBERG, D. S.
DEUX ETUDES DE CONCERT EN OCTAVES -- D'APRES LES ETUDES EN LA
MINEUR ET DO MINEUR DE CHOPIN
ELKAN-VOGEL, INC.   1.60
ALABIEFF   LISZT   6
NIGHTINGALE, THE, FROM LE ROSSIGNOL
CENTURY MUSIC PUBLISHING COMPANY, INC.   3342   .40
ALABIEFF *   6
NIGHTINGALE, THE
CENTURY MUSIC PUBLISHING COMPANY, INC.   3342   .40
ALABIEFF *   TAGLIAPIETRA
NIGHTINGALE, THE
FRANCO COLOMBO PUBLICATIONS   ER24   .60
ALABIEFF *   DEIS
NIGHTINGALE, THE
G. SCHIRMER, INC.   .50
ALBENIZ, I.   GODOWSKY   5
TANGO NO. 2. KONZERTTRANSKRIPTION
SCHOTT   1705   1.75
ALBENIZ, I.   OBERSTADT   3
TANGO NO. 2. TRANSCRIPTION
SCHOTT   2077   1.25
ALFASSY, L.--ED   ALFASSY, L.
CHILDREN'S JAZZ PIECES
MUSIC SALES CORPORATION   040056   2.95
ALFASSY, L.--ED   ALFASSY, L.
JUST BLUES
MUSIC SALES CORPORATION   040055   2.95

ALFORD, K.
COLONEL BOGEY
BOOSEY AND HAWKES, INC.   .60
ALFORD, K.   WATTERS
VOICE OF THE GUNS
BOOSEY AND HAWKES, INC.   .75
ALLISON, I.--ED   ALLISON, I.
IRL ALLISON PIANO LIBRARY -- ELEMENTARY A, PRG 01
WILLIS MUSIC COMPANY   9568   1.25
ALLISON, I.--ED   ALLISON, I.
IRL ALLISON PIANO LIBRARY -- ELEMENTARY A, PRG 02
WILLIS MUSIC COMPANY   9569   1.25
ALLISON, I.--ED   ALLISON, I.
IRL ALLISON PIANO LIBRARY -- ELEMENTARY B
WILLIS MUSIC COMPANY   9570   1.25
ALLISON, I.--ED   ALLISON, I.
IRL ALLISON PIANO LIBRARY -- ELEMENTARY C
WILLIS MUSIC COMPANY   9571   1.25
ALLISON, I.--ED   ALLISON, I.
IRL ALLISON PIANO LIBRARY -- ELEMENTARY D
WILLIS MUSIC COMPANY   9572   1.25
ALLISON, I.--ED   ALLISON, I.
IRL ALLISON PIANO LIBRARY -- INTERMEDIATE A, PRG 01
WILLIS MUSIC COMPANY   9548   1.50
ALLISON, I.--ED   ALLISON, I.
IRL ALLISON PIANO LIBRARY -- INTERMEDIATE A, PRG 02
WILLIS MUSIC COMPANY   9549   1.50
ALLISON, I.--ED   ALLISON, I.
IRL ALLISON PIANO LIBRARY -- INTERMEDIATE B, PRG 01
WILLIS MUSIC COMPANY   9550   1.50
ALLISON, I.--ED   ALLISON, I.
IRL ALLISON PIANO LIBRARY -- INTERMEDIATE B, PRG 02
WILLIS MUSIC COMPANY   9551   1.50
ALLISON, I.--ED   ALLISON, I.
IRL ALLISON PIANO LIBRARY -- INTERMEDIATE C, PRG 01
WILLIS MUSIC COMPANY   9552   1.50
ALLISON, I.--ED   ALLISON, I.
IRL ALLISON PIANO LIBRARY -- INTERMEDIATE C, PRG 02
WILLIS MUSIC COMPANY   9553   1.50
ALLISON, I.--ED   ALLISON, I.
IRL ALLISON PIANO LIBRARY -- INTERMEDIATE D, PRG 01
WILLIS MUSIC COMPANY   9554   1.50
ALLISON, I.--ED   ALLISON, I.
IRL ALLISON PIANO LIBRARY -- INTERMEDIATE D, PRG 02
WILLIS MUSIC COMPANY   9555   1.50
ALLISON, I.--ED   ALLISON, I.
IRL ALLISON PIANO LIBRARY -- INTERMEDIATE E, PRG 01
WILLIS MUSIC COMPANY   9556   1.50
ALLISON, I.--ED   ALLISON, I.
IRL ALLISON PIANO LIBRARY -- INTERMEDIATE E, PRG 02
WILLIS MUSIC COMPANY   9557   1.50
ALLISON, I.--ED   ALLISON, I.
IRL ALLISON PIANO LIBRARY -- INTERMEDIATE F, PRG 01
WILLIS MUSIC COMPANY   9558   1.50
ALLISON, I.--ED   ALLISON, I.
IRL ALLISON PIANO LIBRARY -- INTERMEDIATE F, PRG 02
WILLIS MUSIC COMPANY   9559   1.50
ALLISON, I.--ED   ALLISON, I.
IRL ALLISON PIANO LIBRARY -- PREPARATORY A, PRG 01
WILLIS MUSIC COMPANY   9560   1.75
ALLISON, I.--ED   ALLISON, I.
IRL ALLISON PIANO LIBRARY -- PREPARATORY A, PRG 02
WILLIS MUSIC COMPANY   9561   1.75
ALLISON, I.--ED   ALLISON, I.
IRL ALLISON PIANO LIBRARY -- PREPARATORY B, PRG 01
WILLIS MUSIC COMPANY   9562   1.75
ALLISON, I.--ED   ALLISON, I.
IRL ALLISON PIANO LIBRARY -- PREPARATORY B, PRG 02
WILLIS MUSIC COMPANY   9563   1.75
ALLISON, I.--ED   ALLISON, I.
IRL ALLISON PIANO LIBRARY -- PREPARATORY C, PRG 01
WILLIS MUSIC COMPANY   9564   1.75
ALLISON, I.--ED   ALLISON, I.
IRL ALLISON PIANO LIBRARY -- PREPARATORY C, PRG 02
WILLIS MUSIC COMPANY   9565   1.75
ALLISON, I.--ED   ALLISON, I.
IRL ALLISON PIANO LIBRARY -- PREPARATORY D, PRG 01
WILLIS MUSIC COMPANY   9566   1.75
ALLISON, I.--ED   ALLISON, I.
IRL ALLISON PIANO LIBRARY -- PREPARATORY D, PRG 02
WILLIS MUSIC COMPANY   9567   1.75
ALLISON, I.--ED   ALLISON, I.
MY VERY FIRST PIANO PROGRAM
WILLIS MUSIC COMPANY   1.25
ALLISON, I.
LET'S LEARN ALL THE NOTES AND READ BETTER
WILLIS MUSIC COMPANY   1.25
ALT, H.--ED   ALT, H.
SONGS OF A SWISS SUMMER
WILLIS MUSIC COMPANY   1.50
ALTER, L.
CANDLE IN THE WIND
THE BIG THREE MUSIC CORPORATION   00.95
ALTER, L.
MANHATTAN NOONLIGHT
THE BIG THREE MUSIC CORPORATION   00.95
ALTER, L.
MANHATTAN SERENADE
THE BIG THREE MUSIC CORPORATION   00.95
ALTER, L.
METROPOLITAN NOCTURNE
THE BIG THREE MUSIC CORPORATION   00.95
AMRAM
THEMES FROM 'J.B.'
FRANK MUSIC CORPORATION   .95
ANDERSON, L.   GLOVER, D.
SLEIGH RIDE
BELWIN-MILLS PUBLISHING CORPORATION   .60
ANDERSON, L.   KING
SYNCOPATED CLOCK, THE, SIMP.
BELWIN-MILLS PUBLISHING CORPORATION   .60
ANDREWS--ED   ANDREWS   AI
TIME TO PLAY WALTZES
WILLIS MUSIC COMPANY   1.00
ANSON, G.--ED   ANSON, G.
ANSON INTRODUCES THE SONATA SAMPLER, BK. 1
WILLIS MUSIC COMPANY   1.50
ANSON, G.--ED   ANSON, G.
ANSON INTRODUCES THE SONATA SAMPLER, BK. 2
WILLIS MUSIC COMPANY   1.25
ANSON, G.--ED   ANSON, G.
ANSON INTRODUCES THE SONATA SAMPLER, BK. 3
WILLIS MUSIC COMPANY   2.00
ANSON, G.--ED   ANSON, G.   ELEMENTARY
HAPPY HOLIDAY
WILLIS MUSIC COMPANY   1.00

ANSON, G.--ED   ANSON, G.
    NEW DIRECTIONS
        WILLIS MUSIC COMPANY   1.25
ANSON, G.--ED   ANSON, G.
    NIGHT MUSIC
        WILLIS MUSIC COMPANY   1.50
ANSON, G.--ED   ANSON, G.
    THIRTY PIECES IN THIRTY KEYS, BK. 1
        WILLIS MUSIC COMPANY   1.00
ANSON, G.--ED   ANSON, G.
    THIRTY PIECES IN THIRTY KEYS, BK. 2
        WILLIS MUSIC COMPANY   1.00
ANTHONY, G. W.--ED   ANTHONY, G. W.
    EASY ALBUM FOR BOYS
        THEODORE PRESSER COMPANY   1.25
ANTHONY, G. W.--ED   ANTHONY, G. W.
    HIGHLIGHTS OF FAMILIAR HYMNS IN TRANSCRIPTION
        THEODORE PRESSER COMPANY   2.95
ANTHONY, G. W.--ED   ANTHONY, G. W.
    HIGHLIGHTS OF FAMILIAR MUSIC, BK. 1, INTERNATIONAL EDITION
        THEODORE PRESSER COMPANY   1.50
ANTHONY, G. W.--ED   ANTHONY, G. W.
    HIGHLIGHTS OF FAMILIAR SACRED MUSIC
        THEODORE PRESSER COMPANY   2.95
ANTHONY, G. W.--ED   ANTHONY, G. W.
    PIANO DIVERSIONS, BK. 1
        THEODORE PRESSER COMPANY   1.25
ANTHONY, G. W.--ED   ANTHONY, G. W.
    PIANO DIVERSIONS, BK. 2
        THEODORE PRESSER COMPANY   1.25
ANTHONY, G. W.--ED   ANTHONY, G. W.
    YOUR FAVORITE SOLOS FOR ADVANCED PIANISTS
        THEODORE PRESSER COMPANY   1.50
ANTHONY, G. W.--ED   ANTHONY, G. W.
    YOUR FAVORITE SOLOS
        THEODORE PRESSER COMPANY   2.00
ANTHONY, G. W.--ED   ANTHONY, G. W.
    YOUR VERY FIRST FAVORITE SOLOS
        THEODORE PRESSER COMPANY   1.50
ARANY--ED   ARANY
    HAVE FUN PLAYING PIANO
        MUSIC SALES CORPORATION   040033   2.95
ARDITI   WEYBRIGHT   2
    IL BACIO
        BELWIN-MILLS PUBLISHING CORPORATION   .60
ARLEN, H.   WALTER
    BLUES IN THE NIGHT
        WARNER BROTHERS PUBLISHERS   1.00
ARLEN, H.   RICHTER   FIRST YEAR
    I LOVE A PARADE
        WARNER BROTHERS PUBLISHERS   .75
ARLEN *
    OVER THE RAINBOW
        THE BIG THREE MUSIC CORPORATION   00.95
ARMBRUSTER
    NATIONAL VELVET - THEME
        THE BIG THREE MUSIC CORPORATION   00.95
ARMOUR--ED   ARMOUR   1
    POLLY WOLLY DOODLE
        CENTURY MUSIC PUBLISHING COMPANY, INC.   3466   .40
ARMOUR--ED   ARMOUR   2
    STAR SPANGLED BANNER
        CENTURY MUSIC PUBLISHING COMPANY, INC.   3472   .40
ARMOUR   2
    MY BONNIE LIES OVER THE OCEAN
        CENTURY MUSIC PUBLISHING COMPANY, INC.   3471   .40
ARNDT   KLICKMANN
    NOLA -- EASY ARR.
        SOUTHERN MUSIC COMPANY   .50
ARNDT   KLICKMANN
    NOLA
        SAM FOX PUBLISHING COMPANY, INC.   .50
AULD, W. J.
    PIANO HYMNSCRIPTIONS NO. 1
        LILLENAS PUBLISHING COMPANY   MB-148   2.50
AULD, W. J.
    PIANO HYMNSCRIPTIONS NO. 2
        LILLENAS PUBLISHING COMPANY   MB-149   2.50
AULD, W. J.
    SACRED TRANSCRIPTIONS -- PIANO NO. 1
        LILLENAS PUBLISHING COMPANY   MB-178   2.95
AULD, W. J.
    SACRED TRANSCRIPTIONS -- PIANO NO. 2
        LILLENAS PUBLISHING COMPANY   MB-179   2.95
AULD, W. J.
    SACRED TRANSCRIPTIONS -- PIANO NO. 3
        LILLENAS PUBLISHING COMPANY   MB-180   2.95
AURIC
    FACHOUX, LES -- BALLET -- .. LES JOUEURS DE BOULES
        FRANCO COLOMBO PUBLICATIONS   SAL   1.75
AURIC
    FACHOUX, LES -- BALLET -- .. LE MAITRE A DANSER
        FRANCO COLOMBO PUBLICATIONS   SAL   1.75
AURIC
    FACHOUX, LES -- BALLET -- .. NOCTURNE
        FRANCO COLOMBO PUBLICATIONS   SAL   1.75
AURIC
    FACHOUX, LES -- BALLET --
        FRANCO COLOMBO PUBLICATIONS   SAL   10.75
AURIC
    PEINTRE ET SON MODELE, LE -- BALLET --
        FRANCO COLOMBO PUBLICATIONS   SAL   6.25
BACH, C.P.E.   VRIESLANDER
    LITTLE KEYBOARD PIECES
        BARENREITER VERLAG   NMA 65   3.00
BACH, C.P.E.   POTAMKIN
    SOLFEGGIETTO
        ELKAN-VOGEL, INC.   .50
BACH, J.S.   HESS
    ADAGIO, FROM ORGAN TOCCATA NO. 1
        OXFORD UNIVERSITY PRESS   32.039   1.10
BACH, J.S.   JOHNSON
    AIR ON THE G STRING, FROM ORCHESTRA SUITE NO. 3
        C. F. PETERS CORPORATION   7110   .60
BACH, J.S.   HEINZE   E-M
    ALBUM, 21 FAVORITE PIECES FROM SUITES, PARTITAS, ETC.
        C. F. PETERS CORPORATION   1820   2.00
BACH, J.S.   ANSON, G.   INTERMEDIATE
    ANSON INTRODUCES BACH - DANCE FORMS FROM THE SUITES
        WILLIS MUSIC COMPANY   1.25
BACH, J.S.   ANSON, G.
    ANSON INTRODUCES BACH - SELECTIONS FROM THE ANNA MAGDALENA BACH
    NOTEBOOK
        WILLIS MUSIC COMPANY   1.00
BACH, J.S.   ANSON, G.   INTERMEDIATE
    ANSON INTRODUCES BACH - TWELVE LITTLE PRELUDES
        WILLIS MUSIC COMPANY   1.25

BACH, J.S.
    ARIOSO --FROM THE CANTATA NO. 156--
        CARL FISCHER, INC.   S 2316   .50
BACH, J.S.   BILOTTI   4-5
    ARIOSO
        PRO-ART PUBLICATIONS, INC.   6   .50
BACH, J.S.   ZEPP   4
    ARIOSO
        PRO-ART PUBLICATIONS, INC.   265   .50
BACH, J.S.   TOVEY, D.
    ART OF THE FUGUE
        OXFORD UNIVERSITY PRESS   32.064   5.00
BACH, J.S. *   3
    AVE MARIA
        BELWIN-MILLS PUBLISHING CORPORATION   530   .60
BACH, J.S. *   3
    AVE MARIA
        CENTURY MUSIC PUBLISHING COMPANY, INC. 3707   .40
BACH, J.S. *   ZEPP   4
    AVE MARIA
        PRO-ART PUBLICATIONS, INC.   577   .50
BACH, J.S. *   SPENCER, J.   1
    AVE MARIA
        VOLKWEIN BROS.   .25
BACH, J.S.   PALMER, W. A.
    BACH--AN INTRODUCTION TO HIS PIANO WORKS
        ALFRED MUSIC COMPANY   638   2.50
BACH, J.S.   HIRSCHBERG, D.
    BACH IS FUN
        MUSICORD PUBLICATIONS, INC.   1.25
BACH, J.S.   HARRIS, R.
    BACH ORGAN PRELUDES
        BELWIN-MILLS PUBLISHING CORPORATION   20023   1.25
BACH, J.S.   SCHAUM, J.   2 1/2
    BEST OF BACH
        SCHAUM PUBLICATIONS, INC.   1.25
BACH, J.S.   WEYBRIGHT   4
    BIST DU BEI MIR
        BELWIN-MILLS PUBLISHING CORPORATION   .60
BACH, J.S.   HARRIS
    BIST DU BEI MIR
        OXFORD UNIVERSITY PRESS   32.105   .95
BACH, J.S.   BRADLEY, R.
    BRADLEY CLASSICAL SERIES - PRELUDE NO. 1 IN C FROM THE
    WELL-TEMPERED CLAVIER
        SCREEN GEMS - COLUMBIA PUBLICATIONS   5713PP2   .85
BACH, J.S.   BRADLEY, R.
    BRADLEY CLASSICAL SERIES - TWO-PART INVENTION NO. 1 IN C
        SCREEN GEMS - COLUMBIA PUBLICATIONS   7407TP2   .85
BACH, J.S.   BRADLEY, R.
    BRADLEY CLASSICAL SERIES - TWO-PART INVENTION NO. 8 IN F
        SCREEN GEMS - COLUMBIA PUBLICATIONS   7408TP2   .85
BACH, J.S.   BRADLEY, R.
    BRADLEY CLASSICAL SERIES - TWO MINUETS IN G
        SCREEN GEMS - COLUMBIA PUBLICATIONS   C0020TP2   .85
BACH, J.S.   FRISKIN   3
    CAPRICCIO ON THE DEPARTURE OF A BELOVED BROTHER
        BELWIN-MILLS PUBLISHING CORPORATION   1.00
BACH, J.S.   FOGWELL
    CHORALE FROM CANTATA 147
        BANKS AND SON LTD.   .55
BACH, J.S.   KELBERINE
    COME, SWEET DEATH
        ELKAN-VOGEL, INC.   .50
BACH, J.S.   ARMA, P.
    EIGHT LITTLE PRELUDES AND FUGUES FOR ORGAN
        EDITIONS MUSICALES TRANSATLANTIQUES   2.80
BACH, J.S. *   BOGHEN
    FANTASIA AND FUGUE IN G MINOR FOR ORGAN
        FRANCO COLOMBO PUBLICATIONS   ER2371   1.25
BACH, J.S. *   BOGHEN
    FANTASIA AND FUGUE IN G MINOR FOR ORGAN
        FRANCO COLOMBO PUBLICATIONS   ER2371   1.25
BACH, J.S.   CLOUGH *
    FIRST STEPS IN BACH
        BOSTON MUSIC COMPANY   1.00
BACH, J.S.   2-3
    FRUEHLINGSERWACHEN, EASY
        CENTURY MUSIC PUBLISHING COMPANY, INC. 2161   .40
BACH, J.S.   SAINT-SAENS
    GAVOTTE IN B MINOR
        WILLIS MUSIC COMPANY   .35
BACH, J.S.   NIELAND   E-M
    JESU, JOY OF MAN'S DESIRE --FROM CANTATA NO. 147--
        C. F. PETERS CORPORATION   B14   .90
BACH, J.S.   MANSFIELD   E-M
    JESU, JOY OF MAN'S DESIRE --FROM CANTATA NO. 147--
        C. F. PETERS CORPORATION   2648   .80
BACH, J.S.   FREED
    JESU, JOY OF MAN'S DESIRING --CHORALE FROM CANTATA NO. 147--
        CARL FISCHER, INC.   P 2075   .60
BACH, J.S.   ELAINE   1
    JESU, JOY OF MAN'S DESIRING -- CHORALE FROM CANTATA NO. 147
        WILLIS MUSIC COMPANY   .40
BACH, J.S.
    JESU, JOY OF MAN'S DESIRING
        ASHLEY DEALERS SERVICE, INC.   1.00
BACH, J.S.   HESS
    JESU, JOY OF MAN'S DESIRING
        OXFORD UNIVERSITY PRESS   32.049   1.25
BACH, J.S.   KARTUN
    JESU, JOY OF MAN'S DESIRING
        LES EDITIONS OUVRIERES   2.00
BACH, J.S.   ZEPP   3-4
    JESU JOY OF MAN'S DESIRING
        PRO-ART PUBLICATIONS, INC.   559   .75
BACH, J.S.   PARKER, T.
    JOY
        THE BIG THREE MUSIC CORPORATION   00.95
BACH, J.S.   M
    KLAVIERUEBUNG --URTEXT--. PART 3# 4 DUETS --FOR PIANO SOLO--
        C. F. PETERS CORPORATION   4465   1.25
BACH, J.S.   WEYBRIGHT   3
    MARCH, FROM A COLLECTION OF 'PIECES FOR KLAVIER' EDITED FOR SOLO
    PIANO
        BELWIN-MILLS PUBLISHING CORPORATION   .60
BACH, J.S.   SCHAUM, J.   2 1/2
    MINUET MEDLEY
        SCHAUM PUBLICATIONS, INC.   .50
BACH, J.S.   ZEPP   3-4
    MINUET
        PRO-ART PUBLICATIONS, INC.   231   .50
BACH, J.S.   BUSONI
    ORGAN CHORAL PRELUDES, BK. 1
        CARL FISCHER, INC.   O 3496   1.50

BACH, J.S.　　　　　　　　BUSONI
ORGAN CHORAL PRELUDES, BK. 2
　　CARL FISCHER, INC.　　　　　　　　　　　　O 3508　　1.50
BACH, J.S.　　　　　　　　SAUER　　　　　　D
ORGAN COMPOSITIONS TRANSCRIBED FOR PIANO BY LISZT. VOL. 1,
PRELUDES AND FUGUES NOS. 1-3--A MINOR, C, C MINOR--
　　C. F. PETERS CORPORATION　　　　　　　222　　2.50
BACH, J.S.　　　　　　　　SAUER　　　　　　D
ORGAN COMPOSITIONS TRANSCRIBED FOR PIANO BY LISZT. VOL. 2,
PRELUDES AND FUGUES NOS. 4-6--C, E MINOR, BMINOR--
　　C. F. PETERS CORPORATION　　　　　　　223　　2.50
BACH, J.S. *　　　　　　　HUGHES
ORGAN FANTASIE AND FUGUE IN G MINOR
　　G. SCHIRMER, INC.　　　　　　　　　　L1494　　.75
BACH, J.S.　　　　　　　　SAMAROFF
ORGAN FUGUE IN G MINOR--THE LITTLE
　　ELKAN-VOGEL, INC.
　　　　　　　　　　　　　　　　　　　　　　　　.60
BACH, J.S.　　　　　　　　SILOTI
ORGAN PRELUDE IN E MINOR
　　CARL FISCHER, INC.　　　　　　　　　P 1323　　.60
BACH, J.S.　　　　　　　　SILOTI
ORGAN PRELUDE IN G MINOR --AFTER SZANTO--
　　CARL FISCHER, INC.　　　　　　　　　P 1397　　.75
BACH, J.S.　　　　　　　　KARTUN
OVERTURE, CANTATA NO. 29
　　LES EDITIONS OUVRIERES
　　　　　　　　　　　　　　　　　　　　　　　2.25
BACH, J.S.　　　　　　　　BENJAMIN
PASSEPIED
　　BOOSEY AND HAWKES, INC.
　　　　　　　　　　　　　　　　　　　　　　　　.60
BACH, J.S.　　　　　　　　BAMPTON, R.　　　3
PASTORALE FROM 'CHRISTMAS ORATORIO'
　　BOSTON MUSIC COMPANY
　　　　　　　　　　　　　　　　　　　　　　　　.50
BACH, J.S.　　　　　　　　ASHBY
PIANISTS BOOK OF BACH CHORALES
　　OXFORD UNIVERSITY PRESS　　　　　33.055　　2.75
BACH, J.S. *　　　　　　　MONTANI
PRELUDE AND FUGUE IN A MINOR FOR ORGAN
　　FRANCO COLOMBO PUBLICATIONS　　128426　　1.00
BACH, J.S. *　　　　　　　MONTANI
PRELUDE AND FUGUE IN A MINOR FOR ORGAN
　　FRANCO COLOMBO PUBLICATIONS　　128426　　1.00
BACH, J.S. *　　　　　　　HUGHES
PRELUDE AND FUGUE IN A MINOR
　　G. SCHIRMER, INC.　　　　　　　　　L1475　　1.00
BACH, J.S.　　　　　　　　HARRIS, R.
PRELUDE AND FUGUE
　　BELWIN-MILLS PUBLISHING CORPORATION　20210　　1.75
BACH, J.S.　　　　　　　　FRISKIN
PRELUDE FROM CANTATA 'GOTTES ZEIT IST DIE ALLERBESTE ZEIT'
　　BELWIN-MILLS PUBLISHING CORPORATION　　　4　　.60
BACH, J.S.　　　　　　　　ZEPP　　　　　　4
PRELUDE IN C
　　PRO-ART PUBLICATIONS, INC.　　　　516　　.60
BACH, J.S.　　　　　　　　M
PRELUDE IN E -- VIOLIN PARTITA NO.3--
　　C. F. PETERS CORPORATION　　　　　H253　　1.25
BACH, J.S.　　　　　　　　TURECK, R.
SARABANDE IN C MINOR
　　OXFORD UNIVERSITY PRESS　　　　32.924　　.90
BACH, J.S.　　　　　　　　PETRI
SHEEP MAY SAFELY GRAZE
　　BOOSEY AND HAWKES, INC.
　　　　　　　　　　　　　　　　　　　　　　　　.60
BACH, J.S.　　　　　　　　WHITFORD　　　　3
SHEEP MAY SAFELY GRAZE
　　BOSTON MUSIC COMPANY
　　　　　　　　　　　　　　　　　　　　　　　　.50
BACH, J.S.　　　　　　　　HOWE
SHEEP MAY SAFELY GRAZE
　　OXFORD UNIVERSITY PRESS　　　　32.110　　1.20
BACH, J.S.　　　　　　　　ANSON, G.
SHORT PRELUDES AND FUGUES
　　WILLIS MUSIC COMPANY
　　　　　　　　　　　　　　　　　　　　　　　1.00
BACH, J.S.　　　　　　　　HUGHES, E.
SICILIANO--FROM SONATA NO. 2 FOR FLUTE AND HARPSICHORD
　　G. SCHIRMER, INC.
　　　　　　　　　　　　　　　　　　　　　　　　.50
BACH, J.S.　　　　　　　　M
SICILIANO --FROM FLUTE SONATA NO.2--
　　C. F. PETERS CORPORATION　　　　　B15　　.90
BACH, J.S.　　　　　　　　ALKAN
SICILIANO FROM E FLAT SONATA FOR FLUTE AND CEMBALO S. 1031
　　MUSICA OBSCURA
　　　　　　　　　　　　　　　　　　　　　　　1.00
BACH, J.S.　　　　　　　　WEYBRIGHT　　　　4 1/2
SICILIENNA FROM 'FLUTE AND PIANO SONATA'
　　BELWIN-MILLS PUBLISHING CORPORATION
　　　　　　　　　　　　　　　　　　　　　　　　.60
BACH, J.S.　　　　　　　　HESS
SLEEPERS, WAKE
　　OXFORD UNIVERSITY PRESS　　　　32.201　　1.25
BACH, J.S.　　　　　　　　ZEPP　　　　　　4
SOLFEGGIETTO
　　PRO-ART PUBLICATIONS, INC.　　　　405　　.50
BACH, J.S.　　　　　　　　CLOUGH *　　　　3
SOLFEGIETTO IN C MINOR
　　BOSTON MUSIC COMPANY
　　　　　　　　　　　　　　　　　　　　　　　　.50
BACH, J.S.　　　　　　　　BARTOK
SONATA NO. 06
　　KULTURA
　　　　　　　　　　　　　　　　　　　　　　　1.75
BACH, J.S.　　　　　　　　MANSFIELD
STEPS TO THE MASTERS
　　BANKS AND SON LTD.
　　　　　　　　　　　　　　　　　　　　　　　1.35
BACH, J.S.　　　　　　　　RACHMANINOFF, S.
SUITE FROM THE PARTITA IN E MAJOR FOR VIOLIN --
PRELUDIO-GAVOTTE-GIGUE
　　BELWIN-MILLS PUBLISHING CORPORATION
　　　　　　　　　　　　　　　　　　　　　　　2.00
BACH, J.S.　　　　　　　　MAIER, G.
TWENTY PIECES FROM BACH'S BOOK FOR HIS SON FRIEDMANN
　　BELWIN-MILLS PUBLISHING CORPORATION
　　　　　　　　　　　　　　　　　　　　　　　1.50
BACH, J.S.　　　　　　　　ANSON, G.
TWO-PART INVENTIONS
　　WILLIS MUSIC COMPANY
　　　　　　　　　　　　　　　　　　　　　　　1.25
BACH, J.S.　　　　　　　　THOMPSON, J.　　　4
TWO-PART INVENTIONS
　　WILLIS MUSIC COMPANY
　　　　　　　　　　　　　　　　　　　　　　　3.00
BACH, J.S.　　　　　　　　DUMM
TWO MINUETS
　　BELWIN-MILLS PUBLISHING CORPORATION　26120　　.60
BACH, J.S.　　　　　　　　DAVIES
YOUNG PIANIST'S BACH, THE
　　OXFORD UNIVERSITY PRESS　　　　33.005　　1.90
BACH, W.F.　　　　　　　　STEINER　　　　　2
BEDTIME STORY -- LULLABY
　　BELWIN-MILLS PUBLISHING CORPORATION
　　　　　　　　　　　　　　　　　　　　　　　　.60
BACH, W.F.　　　　　　　　FEDTKE　　　　　M
EIGHT FUGUES FOR ORGAN OR CLAVIER, 3 THREE-PART FUGUES FOR
ORGAN--2 STAVES--
　　C. F. PETERS CORPORATION　　　　　8010A　　3.50
BACH, W. F.　　　　　　　　DUMM
RECITAL REFRESHER SERIES -- LAMENTO IN E MINOR
　　BELWIN-MILLS PUBLISHING CORPORATION　26109　　.60

BACHMANN, G.　　　　　　ROLFE, W.　　　　3
SYLPHES, LES, EASY
　　CENTURY MUSIC PUBLISHING COMPANY, INC.　3365　　.40
BACON, E.--ED　　　　　　BACON, E.
PATRIOTIC AMERICAN MELODIES
　　THEODORE PRESSER COMPANY
　　　　　　　　　　　　　　　　　　　　　　　1.25
BADARZEWSKA, T.　　　　　STEINER　　　　　3
MAIDEN'S PRAYER, THE
　　BELWIN-MILLS PUBLISHING CORPORATION
　　　　　　　　　　　　　　　　　　　　　　　　.60
BAEZ, J.
AMERICAN BALLADS AND FOLKSONGS
　　MUSIC SALES CORPORATION　　　　040974　　2.95
BAEZ, J.
BRITISH BALLADS AND FOLK SONGS
　　MUSIC SALES CORPORATION　　　　040975　　2.95
BAEZ, J.
JOAN BAEZ SONGBOOK, THE
　　MUSIC SALES CORPORATION　　　　040973　　4.95
BAEZ, J.
NOEL
　　MUSIC SALES CORPORATION　　　　040976　　2.95
BAEZ, J.
SONGS FOR OUR TIMES
　　MUSIC SALES CORPORATION　　　　040972　　2.95
BAGLEY, E.
NATIONAL EMBLEM MARCH
　　THE BIG THREE MUSIC CORPORATION
　　　　　　　　　　　　　　　　　　　　　　00.95
BAGLEY, E.　　　　　　　　STEINER　　　　　2
NATIONAL EMBLEM MARCH
　　BELWIN-MILLS PUBLISHING CORPORATION
　　　　　　　　　　　　　　　　　　　　　　　　.60
BAGLEY, E.　　　　　　　　SCHAUM, J.　　　　2
NATIONAL EMBLEM MARCH
　　SCHAUM PUBLICATIONS, INC.
　　　　　　　　　　　　　　　　　　　　　　　　.50
BALAKIREV
L'ALOUETTE--GLINKA
　　G. SCHIRMER, INC.
　　　　　　　　　　　　　　　　　　　　　　　　.50
BARNES, B.
DAINTY DOLL
　　THE BIG THREE MUSIC CORPORATION
　　　　　　　　　　　　　　　　　　　　　　00.95
BARNES, B.
DAINTY MISS
　　THE BIG THREE MUSIC CORPORATION
　　　　　　　　　　　　　　　　　　　　　　00.95
BARRY
THEME FROM THE PERSUADERS
　　WARNER BROTHERS PUBLISHERS
　　　　　　　　　　　　　　　　　　　　　　　1.00
BARTOK　　　　　　　　　ANSON, G.　　　ELEMENTARY
ANSON INTRODUCES BARTOK, BK. 1
　　WILLIS MUSIC COMPANY
　　　　　　　　　　　　　　　　　　　　　　　1.00
BARTOK　　　　　　　　　ANSON, G.　　　INTERMEDIATE
ANSON INTRODUCES BARTOK, BK. 2
　　WILLIS MUSIC COMPANY
　　　　　　　　　　　　　　　　　　　　　　　1.00
BARTOK
PETITE SUITE, FROM 'FORTY-FOUR DUOS FOR TWO VIOLINS'
　　BOOSEY AND HAWKES, INC.
　　　　　　　　　　　　　　　　　　　　　　　1.00
BART　　　　　　　　　　GREEN
OLIVER - EASY PIANO
　　TRO SONGWAYS SERVICE, INC.
　　　　　　　　　　　　　　　　　　　　　　　1.95
BART　　　　　　　　　　GREEN
OLIVER - PIANO SELECTIONS
　　TRO SONGWAYS SERVICE, INC.
　　　　　　　　　　　　　　　　　　　　　　　1.95
BASIE
ONE O'CLOCK JUMP
　　THE BIG THREE MUSIC CORPORATION
　　　　　　　　　　　　　　　　　　　　　　00.95
BAUDUC *
SOUTH RAMPART STREET PARADE
　　THE BIG THREE MUSIC CORPORATION
　　　　　　　　　　　　　　　　　　　　　　00.95
BAUM--ED. *　　　　　　BAUM *　　　　　2
BRUDER SINGER. 270 LIEDER UNSERES VOLKES IN LEICHTEN
KLAVIERSATZEN
　　BARENREITER VERLAG　　　　　　BA 2999
BAUM--ED. *　　　　　　BAUM *
BRUDER SINGER
　　BARENREITER VERLAG　　　　　　BA 2999　　7.00
BAUM--ED *　　　　　　BAUM *　　　　　2-3
KLAVIERCHORALBUCH. 206 KLAVIERSATZE ZUM EVANGELISCHEN
KIRCHENGESANGBUCH
　　BARENREITER VERLAG　　　　　　BA 3499
BEAUMONT, P.　　　　　　　　　　　　　2
WITH MY LOVE, EASY
　　CENTURY MUSIC PUBLISHING COMPANY, INC.　2589　　.40
BECAUD　　　　　　　　　DAVIS, J. R.　　FIRST YEAR
WHAT NOW MY LOVE
　　WARNER BROTHERS PUBLISHERS
　　　　　　　　　　　　　　　　　　　　　　　　.75
BECAUD *　　　　　　　　NEALE, J.　　　EASY
WHAT NOW MY LOVE
　　WARNER BROTHERS PUBLISHERS
　　　　　　　　　　　　　　　　　　　　　　　　.75
BECUCCI
ALI DORATE
　　FRANCO COLOMBO PUBLICATIONS　　127751　　.50
BECUCCI
TESORO MIO
　　FRANCO COLOMBO PUBLICATIONS　　111077　　.60
BECUCCI　　　　　　　　　DEL MAGLIO
TESORO MIO
　　FRANCO COLOMBO PUBLICATIONS　　127110　　.60
BEER, L. J.--ED　　　　　BEER, L. J.
SIXTEEN MASTERWORKS FOR PIANO
　　THEODORE PRESSER COMPANY
　　　　　　　　　　　　　　　　　　　　　　　1.50
BEETHOVEN　　　　　　　　DEL MAGLIO
ADAGIO CANTABILE-FROM SONATA, OP. 13
　　FRANCO COLOMBO PUBLICATIONS　　124704　　.75
BEETHOVEN　　　　　　　　FICHANDLER, W.　　3
ADAGIO FROM STRING TRIO, OP. 8
　　BELWIN-MILLS PUBLISHING CORPORATION
　　　　　　　　　　　　　　　　　　　　　　　　.60
BEETHOVEN　　　　　　　　DEL MAGLIO
ADAGIO SOSTENUTO-FROM SONATA, OP. 27 NO. 2
　　FRANCO COLOMBO PUBLICATIONS　　124705　　.60
BEETHOVEN　　　　　　　　THORNE
BEETHOVEN FOR EVERYBODY
　　BOOSEY AND HAWKES, INC.
　　　　　　　　　　　　　　　　　　　　　　　1.75
BEETHOVEN　　　　　　　　ECKHARDT, F.　　1
BEETHOVEN FOR THE YOUNG PIANIST
　　CENTURY MUSIC PUBLISHING COMPANY, INC.　3957　　.40
BEETHOVEN　　　　　　　　HIRSCHBERG, D.
BEETHOVEN IS FUN
　　MUSICORD PUBLICATIONS, INC.
　　　　　　　　　　　　　　　　　　　　　　　1.25
BEETHOVEN
BEETHOVEN OVERTURES, THE -- EGMONT, CORIOLANUS, LEONORE NO. 3 --
　　CENTURY MUSIC PUBLISHING COMPANY, INC.
　　　　　　　　　　　　　　　　　　　　　　　1.25
BEETHOVEN　　　　　　　　SCHAUM, J.　　　2 1/2
BEST OF BEETHOVEN
　　SCHAUM PUBLICATIONS, INC.
　　　　　　　　　　　　　　　　　　　　　　　1.50
BEETHOVEN　　　　　　　　BRADLEY, R.
BRADLEY CLASSICAL SERIES - ECCOSSAISES
　　SCREEN GEMS - COLUMBIA PUBLICATIONS　0702EP2　　.85
BEETHOVEN　　　　　　　　BRADLEY, R.
BRADLEY CLASSICAL SERIES - FUR ELISE
　　SCREEN GEMS - COLUMBIA PUBLICATIONS　6707FP2　　.85

BEETHOVEN   BRADLEY, R.
BRADLEY CLASSICAL SERIES - MOONLIGHT SONATA
    SCREEN GEMS - COLUMBIA PUBLICATIONS   4715MP2   .85
BEETHOVEN   BRADLEY, R.
BRADLEY CLASSICAL SERIES - SONATINA NO. 01 IN G
    SCREEN GEMS - COLUMBIA PUBLICATIONS   4742SP2   .85
BEETHOVEN   ALKAN
CAVATINA FROM THE THIRTEENTH QUARTET OP. 130
    MUSICA OBSCURA   1.50
BEETHOVEN   SEISS
CONTRA DANCES
    CARL FISCHER, INC.   P 2865   1.00
BEETHOVEN   STEINER   1 1/2
DUKE AND DUCHESS
    BELWIN-MILLS PUBLISHING CORPORATION   .60
BEETHOVEN   DEL MAGLIO
FAREWELL TO THE PIANO
    FRANCO COLOMBO PUBLICATIONS   129091   .60
BEETHOVEN   MITTLER   2B
FIFTH SYMPHONY
    MUSICORD PUBLICATIONS, INC.   .45
BEETHOVEN   D
FIVE CONCERTI AND CHORAL FANTASY, OP. 80
    C. F. PETERS CORPORATION   144   10.00
BEETHOVEN   CHIESA
FUNERAL MARCH, OP. 26
    FRANCO COLOMBO PUBLICATIONS   128121   .50
BEETHOVEN   DEL MAGLIO
FUR ELISE
    FRANCO COLOMBO PUBLICATIONS   128112   .60
BEETHOVEN   SCHAUM, J.   2 1/2
FUR ELISE
    SCHAUM PUBLICATIONS, INC.   .60
BEETHOVEN   WHITFORD   GR. 2 1/2
FUR ELISE
    ROBERT WHITFORD PUBLICATIONS   .40
BEETHOVEN   ZEPP   4
GERMAN DANCE
    PRO-ART PUBLICATIONS, INC.   379   .50
BEETHOVEN   CHIESA
MARCHE A LA TURQUE-FROM 'THE RUINS OF ATHENS'
    FRANCO COLOMBO PUBLICATIONS   107506   .50
BEETHOVEN   3
MENUET, FROM SONATA OP. 49 NO. 2
    BELWIN-MILLS PUBLISHING CORPORATION   22   .60
BEETHOVEN   1
MENUET IN G, EASY
    CENTURY MUSIC PUBLISHING COMPANY, INC.   3822   .40
BEETHOVEN   DEL MAGLIO
MINUET FROM SONATA, OP. 49 NO. 2
    FRANCO COLOMBO PUBLICATIONS   124706   .60
BEETHOVEN   BARTH, H.
MINUET IN C
    BELWIN-MILLS PUBLISHING CORPORATION   20168   .60
BEETHOVEN   BARTH, H.
MINUET IN E FLAT
    BELWIN-MILLS PUBLISHING CORPORATION   20399   .60
BEETHOVEN   WEYBRIGHT   2 1/2
MINUET IN G
    BELWIN-MILLS PUBLISHING CORPORATION   .60
BEETHOVEN   2
MINUET IN G
    CENTURY MUSIC PUBLISHING COMPANY, INC.   3498   .60
BEETHOVEN   DEL MAGLIO
MINUET IN G
    FRANCO COLOMBO PUBLICATIONS   124707   .60
BEETHOVEN   ECKSTEIN
MOONLIGHT SONATA, FIRST MVT.
    CARL FISCHER, INC.   S 2292   .50
BEETHOVEN   ECKSTEIN
MOONLIGHT SONATA, FIRST MVT.
    CARL FISCHER, INC.   S 2311   .50
BEETHOVEN   WALLIS   2
MOONLIGHT SONATA THEME
    WILLIS MUSIC COMPANY   .35
BEETHOVEN   MITTLER   2B
MOONLIGHT SONATA
    MUSICORD PUBLICATIONS, INC.   .45
BEETHOVEN   ZEPP   5
MOONLIGHT SONATA
    PRO-ART PUBLICATIONS, INC.   457   .60
BEETHOVEN   THOMPSON, J.   1
NINTH SYMPHONY
    WILLIS MUSIC COMPANY   .35
BEETHOVEN
ODE TO JOY
    ASHLEY DEALERS SERVICE, INC.   1.00
BEETHOVEN   DUMM
RECITAL REFRESHER SERIES -- CLAVIERSTUECK
    BELWIN-MILLS PUBLISHING CORPORATION   26115   .60
BEETHOVEN   HARDING, R.   3
RONDO FROM FIFTH CONCERTO
    WILLIS MUSIC COMPANY   .35
BEETHOVEN   RUBINSTEIN   5
RUINS OF ATHENS, TURKISH MARCH
    CENTURY MUSIC PUBLISHING COMPANY, INC.   2406   .40
BEETHOVEN   MIROVITCH
SCHERZO AND MENUET
    ELKAN-VOGEL, INC.   .70
BEETHOVEN   SINGER   M-D
SEPTET, OP. 20
    C. F. PETERS CORPORATION   490   2.50
BEETHOVEN   HARDING, R.   3
SEVENTH SYMPHONY
    WILLIS MUSIC COMPANY   .35
BEETHOVEN   DEL MAGLIO
SIX ECOSSAISES
    FRANCO COLOMBO PUBLICATIONS   127111   .60
BEETHOVEN   VAN DYCK
SONATINA IN C--FOR MANDOLIN AND CEMBALO, TRANSCRIBED FOR PIANO
    G. SCHIRMER, INC.   .75
BEETHOVEN   SCHAUM, J.   1
SONG OF JOY
    SCHAUM PUBLICATIONS, INC.   .60
BEETHOVEN   MANSFIELD
STEPS TO THE MASTERS
    BANKS AND SON LTD.   1.35
BEETHOVEN   SINGER
SYMPHONIES, BK. 1--NOS. 1-5
    G. SCHIRMER, INC.   L1562   4.50
BEETHOVEN   SINGER
SYMPHONIES, BK. 2--NOS. 6-9
    G. SCHIRMER, INC.   L1563   4.50
BEETHOVEN   POZZOLI
SYMPHONIES BK. 1 — 1-5 --
    FRANCO COLOMBO PUBLICATIONS   ER401   5.00

BEETHOVEN   POZZOLI
SYMPHONIES BK. 2 -- 6-9 --
    FRANCO COLOMBO PUBLICATIONS   ER402   5.00
BEETHOVEN
SYMPHONY NO. 01 IN C, OP. 21
    FRANCO COLOMBO PUBLICATIONS   ER403   1.25
BEETHOVEN
SYMPHONY NO. 03 IN E FLAT, OP. 55 'EROICA'
    FRANCO COLOMBO PUBLICATIONS   ER405   1.75
BEETHOVEN   3
SYMPHONY NO. 05, ALLEGRO CON BRIO
    CENTURY MUSIC PUBLISHING COMPANY, INC.   3532   .40
BEETHOVEN   2
SYMPHONY NO. 05, ANDANTE CON MOTO
    CENTURY MUSIC PUBLISHING COMPANY, INC.   3428   .40
BEETHOVEN   3
SYMPHONY NO. 05, VICTORY THEME
    CENTURY MUSIC PUBLISHING COMPANY, INC.   3532   .40
BEETHOVEN
SYMPHONY NO. 05 IN C MINOR, OP. 67
    FRANCO COLOMBO PUBLICATIONS   130181   2.75
BEETHOVEN
SYMPHONY NO. 05 IN C MINOR
    ASHLEY DEALERS SERVICE, INC.   1.95
BEETHOVEN   GOETSCHIUS, P.
SYMPHONY NO. 05 IN C MINOR
    THEODORE PRESSER COMPANY   1.75
BEETHOVEN
SYMPHONY NO. 06 IN F, OP. 68 'PASTORAL'
    FRANCO COLOMBO PUBLICATIONS   130306   2.25
BEETHOVEN   4
SYMPHONY NO. 07, ALLEGRETTO
    CENTURY MUSIC PUBLISHING COMPANY, INC.   129   .40
BEETHOVEN
SYMPHONY NO. 07 IN A, OP. 92
    FRANCO COLOMBO PUBLICATIONS   ER409   1.50
BEETHOVEN   4
SYMPHONY NO. 08, ALLEGRETTO SCHERZANDO
    CENTURY MUSIC PUBLISHING COMPANY, INC.   3643   .40
BEETHOVEN
SYMPHONY NO. 09 IN D MINOR, OP. 125 'CHORAL'
    FRANCO COLOMBO PUBLICATIONS   129761   3.25
BEETHOVEN   HOLLANDER
THEMES I'LL REMEMBER
    BOOSEY AND HAWKES, INC.   .75
BEETHOVEN   WALLIS   2
THEME -- FIRST MOVEMENT -- FROM 'MOONLIGHT SONATA'
    BOSTON MUSIC COMPANY   .50
BEETHOVEN   ECKSTEIN
THEME FROM FIFTH SYMPHONY --FIRST MVT.--
    CARL FISCHER, INC.   S 2283   .50
BEETHOVEN   THOMPSON, J.   2
THEME FROM FIFTH SYMPHONY
    WILLIS MUSIC COMPANY   .40
BEETHOVEN   RUSSELL   2
THEME FROM SONATA IN E FLAT, OP. 27 NO. 1
    BOSTON MUSIC COMPANY   .50
BEETHOVEN   HARDING, R.   3
THEME WITH VARIATIONS FROM OP. 26
    WILLIS MUSIC COMPANY   .35
BEETHOVEN   M
VIOLIN CONCERTO, OP. 61. ABRIDGED PIANO SOLO ARRANGEMENT
    C. F. PETERS CORPORATION   189B   1.50
BEHR, F.   HIRSCHBERG, D.   2A
CAMP OF THE GYPSIES
    MUSICORD PUBLICATIONS, INC.   .45
BEIDERBECKE, B.
DAVENPORT BLUES
    THE BIG THREE MUSIC CORPORATION   00.95
BEIDERBECKE, B.
IN A MIST
    THE BIG THREE MUSIC CORPORATION   00.95
BELL, W.--ARR.   BELL, W.   EASY
JUST FOR FUN - HIT TUNES EVERYBODY KNOWS
    SCREEN GEMS - COLUMBIA PUBLICATIONS   F0126P4   1.95
BELL, W.--ARR.   BELL, W.   EASY
JUST FOR FUN - MELODIES EVERYBODY KNOWS
    SCREEN GEMS - COLUMBIA PUBLICATIONS   F0125P4   1.95
BELL, W.--ARR.   BELL, W.   EASY
JUST FOR FUN - POPS EVERYBODY KNOWS
    SCREEN GEMS - COLUMBIA PUBLICATIONS   F0081P4   1.50
BELL, W.--ARR.   BELL, W.   EASY
JUST FOR FUN - SHOW TUNES EVERYBODY KNOWS
    SCREEN GEMS - COLUMBIA PUBLICATIONS   F0107P4   1.95
BELLINI   DEL MAGLIO
DOLENTE IMAGINE
    FRANCO COLOMBO PUBLICATIONS   128122   .50
BELLINI   BURGMUELLER   2
MARCH, NORMA
    CENTURY MUSIC PUBLISHING COMPANY, INC.   647   .40
BELLINI   KRUG   2
NORMA, EASY TRANSCRIPTION
    CENTURY MUSIC PUBLISHING COMPANY, INC.   525   .40
BELLINI
NORMA -- COMPLETE OPERA --
    FRANCO COLOMBO PUBLICATIONS   41007   5.00
BELLINI
NORMA - CASTA DIVA
    FRANCO COLOMBO PUBLICATIONS   123380   .60
BELLINI   DEL MAGLIO
NORMA - CASTA DIVA
    FRANCO COLOMBO PUBLICATIONS   128139   .50
BELLINI   DEL MAGLIO
NORMA - DELL'AURA TUA PROFETICA
    FRANCO COLOMBO PUBLICATIONS   124708   .60
BELLINI   CHIESA
NORMA - EASY FANTASIA
    FRANCO COLOMBO PUBLICATIONS   107494   .50
BELLINI
NORMA - OVERTURE
    FRANCO COLOMBO PUBLICATIONS   128370   1.00
BELLINI   CHIESA
PURITANI, I - EASY FANTASIA
    FRANCO COLOMBO PUBLICATIONS   107492   .60
BELLINI
SELECTED OVERTURES -- WITH ROSSINI - SELECTED OVERTURES --
    FRANCO COLOMBO PUBLICATIONS   ER1163   4.25
BELLINI   CHIESA
SONNAMBULA, LA - EASY FANTASIA
    FRANCO COLOMBO PUBLICATIONS   107493   .60
BENEDICT   MENDEL, S.   1 1/2
CARNIVAL OF VENICE
    WILLIS MUSIC COMPANY   .40
BENFORD--ED   BENFORD
MEET THE MASTERS
    PRO-ART PUBLICATIONS, INC.   989   1.00

BENNETT, R.			FOUR FREEDOMS SYMPHONY	THE BIG THREE MUSIC CORPORATION		03.00
BERLIOZ *		6	RAKOCZY MARCH	CENTURY MUSIC PUBLISHING COMPANY, INC.	370	.40
BERMONT, H.--ED	BERMONT, H.		ALL-AMERICAN FOLK SONGS, BK. 1	MUSICORD PUBLICATIONS, INC.		1.50
BERMONT, H.--ED	BERMONT, H.		ALL-AMERICAN FOLK SONGS, BK. 2	MUSICORD PUBLICATIONS, INC.		1.50
BERMONT, H.--ED	BERMONT, H.		HYMNS WE LOVE	MUSICORD PUBLICATIONS, INC.		1.25
BERMONT, H.--ED	BERMONT, H.		LETS PLAY CAROLS	MUSICORD PUBLICATIONS, INC.		1.00
BERMONT, H.--ED	BERMONT, H.		PLAY THAT TUNE, BK. 1	MUSICORD PUBLICATIONS, INC.		1.25
BERMONT, H.--ED	BERMONT, H.		PLAY THAT TUNE, BK. 2	MUSICORD PUBLICATIONS, INC.		1.25
BERMONT, H.--ED	BERMONT, H.		PLAY THAT TUNE, BK. 3	MUSICORD PUBLICATIONS, INC.		1.25
BERMONT, H.--ED	BERMONT, H.		PLAY THAT TUNE, BK. 4	MUSICORD PUBLICATIONS, INC.		1.25
BERMONT, H.--ED	BERMONT, H.		TUNEFUL VARIETIES, BK. 1	MUSICORD PUBLICATIONS, INC.		1.25
BERMONT, H.--ED	BERMONT, H.		TUNEFUL VARIETIES, BK. 2	MUSICORD PUBLICATIONS, INC.		1.25
BERMONT, H.--ED	BERMONT, H.		TWENTY-EIGHT STAR MELODIES, BK. 1	MUSICORD PUBLICATIONS, INC.		1.25
BERMONT, H.--ED	BERMONT, H.		YOUR HIT TUNES - GREEN BOOK	MUSICORD PUBLICATIONS, INC.		1.25
BERMONT, H.--ED	BERMONT, H.		YOUR HIT TUNES - RED BOOK	MUSICORD PUBLICATIONS, INC.		1.25
BERMONT, H.			ANYONE CAN PLAY PIANO	MUSICORD PUBLICATIONS, INC.		2.00
BERNSTEIN, E.			FROM THE TERRACE	THE BIG THREE MUSIC CORPORATION		00.95
BERRILL, R.			LOVE MAKES THE WORLD GO 'ROUND	THE BIG THREE MUSIC CORPORATION		00.95
BERTRAND, C.	BROWN	2	ITZY BITZY SPIDER	WILLIS MUSIC COMPANY		.30
BESTHOFF, M.			MERRY CHRISTMAS CAROLS TO SING AND PLAY	BELWIN-MILLS PUBLISHING CORPORATION		1.00
BEYER, F.--ED	BEYER, F.	4	MARSEILLAISE, THE	CENTURY MUSIC PUBLISHING COMPANY, INC.	635	.40
BIGELOW, F.			OUR DIRECTOR MARCH	THE BIG THREE MUSIC CORPORATION		00.95
BIVENS *			JOSEPHINE	THE BIG THREE MUSIC CORPORATION		00.95
BIZET, G.		3	ARLESIENNE SUITE, INTERMEZZO	CENTURY MUSIC PUBLISHING COMPANY, INC.	3562	.40
BIZET, G.		E	CARMEN. COMPLETE.	C. F. PETERS CORPORATION	H639	2.00
BIZET, G.		M	CARMEN. COMPLETE OPERA IN PIANO SOLO ARRANGEMENT	C. F. PETERS CORPORATION	C339	7.50
BIZET, G.	KRUG	2	CARMEN, EASY TRANS.	CENTURY MUSIC PUBLISHING COMPANY, INC.	2146	.40
BIZET, G.		2	CARMEN, HABANERA	CENTURY MUSIC PUBLISHING COMPANY, INC.	2336	.40
BIZET, G.	LOEW, J.	3	CARMEN, MARCH	CENTURY MUSIC PUBLISHING COMPANY, INC.	1632	.40
BIZET, G.		3	CARMEN, TOREADOR SONG	CENTURY MUSIC PUBLISHING COMPANY, INC.	1577	.40
BIZET, G.	LANGE, G.	4	HABANERA, FROM 'CARMEN'	CENTURY MUSIC PUBLISHING COMPANY, INC.	2336	.40
BIZET, G.		3	L'ARLESIENNE, INTERMEZZO	CENTURY MUSIC PUBLISHING COMPANY, INC.	3562	.40
BIZET, G.		3	L'ARLESIENNE, INTERMEZZO	CENTURY MUSIC PUBLISHING COMPANY, INC.	3562	.40
BIZET, G.		4	L'ARLESIENNE, MINUETTO	CENTURY MUSIC PUBLISHING COMPANY, INC.	3977	.40
BIZET, G.	LOEW, J.	3	MARCH, CARMEN	CENTURY MUSIC PUBLISHING COMPANY, INC.	1632	.40
BIZET, G.	WEYBRIGHT	3	MARCH OF THE TOREADORS	BELWIN-MILLS PUBLISHING CORPORATION		.60
BIZET, G.		4	MINUETTO, L'ARLESIENNE	CENTURY MUSIC PUBLISHING COMPANY, INC.	3977	.40
BIZET, G.		3	TOREADOR SONG, CARMEN	CENTURY MUSIC PUBLISHING COMPANY, INC.	1577	.40
BIZET, G.	WEINGARTNER	D	VARIATIONS CHROMATIQUES, OP. 3 --CONCERT EDITION--	C. F. PETERS CORPORATION	C436	3.50
BIZZELLI			MADONNA PURITA -- BALLET --	FRANCO COLOMBO PUBLICATIONS	DS374	6.50
BLACHER			CHIARINA, OP. 33 -- BALLET IN ONE ACT	ASSOCIATED MUSIC PUBLISHERS, INC.	BOT	5.00
BLACHER			DEMETER -- 1963 -- BALLET IN 4 SCENES	ASSOCIATED MUSIC PUBLISHERS, INC.	BOT	10.00
BLACHER			FEST IM SUEDEN, OP. 6 -- DANCE-DRAMA IN ONE ACT	ASSOCIATED MUSIC PUBLISHERS, INC.	BOT	6.00
BLACHER			HAMLET, OP. 35 -- CHORAL BALLET IN ONE PROLOGUE AND 3 TABLEAUX	ASSOCIATED MUSIC PUBLISHERS, INC.	BOT	6.00
BLACHER			LYSISTRATA, OP. 34 -- BALLET IN 3 TABLEAUX	ASSOCIATED MUSIC PUBLISHERS, INC.	BOT	7.50
BLACHER			TRISTAN -- 1965 -- BALLET IN 7 SCENES	ASSOCIATED MUSIC PUBLISHERS, INC.	BOT	12.00
BLAKE--ED	BLAKE		COMPANIONS AT THE KEYBOARD	WILLIS MUSIC COMPANY		.90
BLAKE--ED	BLAKE		TALES AND TUNES FROM GRAND OPERA	WILLIS MUSIC COMPANY		1.50
BLAKE, C.	WALLIS	3	CLAYTON'S GRAND MARCH	WILLIS MUSIC COMPANY		.50
BLAKE	SCHAUM, J.	2	MEMORIES OF YOU	SCHAUM PUBLICATIONS, INC.		.75
BLISS, A.			BALLET 'ADAM ZERO', PIANO SCORE	NOVELLO AND COMPANY, LTD.	10.0005.05	4.90
BLISS, A.			BALLET 'CHECKMATE', PIANO SCORE	NOVELLO AND COMPANY, LTD.	10.0007.01	6.25
BLISS, A.			BALLET 'MIRACLE IN THE GORBALS', PIANO SCORE	NOVELLO AND COMPANY, LTD.	10.0006.03	3.65
BLISS, A.			LADY OF SHALOTT, THE -- EXCERP FROM THE BALLET	NOVELLO AND COMPANY, LTD.	10.0008.10	.90
BLOCK--ED	BLOCK	2-3	JARABE TAPATIO, HAT DANCE	CENTURY MUSIC PUBLISHING COMPANY, INC.	3647	.40
BOCCHERINI			FAMOUS MINUET - FROM QUINTET, OP. 13 NO. 5	FRANCO COLOMBO PUBLICATIONS	45917	.60
BOCCHERINI	CHIESA		FAMOUS MINUET - FROM QUINTET, OP. 13 NO. 5	FRANCO COLOMBO PUBLICATIONS	107478	.60
BOCCHERINI	DEL MAGLIO		SECOND FAMOUS MINUET	FRANCO COLOMBO PUBLICATIONS	128151	.50
BOCK, F.--ED	BOCK, F.		HOW GREAT THOU ART	THEODORE PRESSER COMPANY		2.95
BOCK, F.			SACRED SONGS FOR THE PIANO	BROADMAN MUSIC	4571-08	2.50
BOCK, F.			YOUNG WORLD PIANIST	LILLENAS PUBLISHING COMPANY	MB-260	2.50
BOCK, J.	SCHAUM, J.	2 1/2	FIDDLER ON THE ROOF	SCHAUM PUBLICATIONS, INC.		.75
BOCK, J.	SCHAUM, J.	1 1/2	IF I WERE A RICH MAN	SCHAUM PUBLICATIONS, INC.		.75
BOCK, J.	SCHAUM, J.	2	MATCHMAKER	SCHAUM PUBLICATIONS, INC.		.75
BOCK, J.	SCHAUM, J.	1	SUNRISE, SUNSET	SCHAUM PUBLICATIONS, INC.		.75
BOEHME	WEYBRIGHT	2	AMERICAN EAGLE MARCH	BELWIN-MILLS PUBLISHING CORPORATION		.60
BOHME--ED	BOHME	2-3	WEIHNACHTSMUSIK FUR KLAVIER	SCHOTT	5450	2.25
BOHM	ROLFE, W.	2	FOUNTAIN, THE, EASY	CENTURY MUSIC PUBLISHING COMPANY, INC.	3545	.40
BOHM	ROLFE, W.	3	ZINGANA, LA, EASY	CENTURY MUSIC PUBLISHING COMPANY, INC.	3363	.40
BOITO	CHIESA		MEFISTOFELE - EASY FANTASIA	FRANCO COLOMBO PUBLICATIONS	109092	.50
BONNEL *			TURKEY IN THE STRAW	THE BIG THREE MUSIC CORPORATION		00.95
BONO	NEALE, J.	EASY	BEAT GOES ON, THE	WARNER BROTHERS PUBLISHERS		.75
BORODIN, A.	JADOUL		IN THE STEPPES OF CENTRAL ASIA	BOOSEY AND HAWKES, INC.		2.50
BORODIN, A.	ZEPP	4	MELODIC THEME FROM POLOVETZIAN DANCE	PRO-ART PUBLICATIONS, INC.	163	.50
BORODIN, A.	COOMBS		NOCTURNE, FROM 'SECOND QUARTET'	BOOSEY AND HAWKES, INC.		.60
BORODIN, A.	POST	1-2	POLOVETSIAN DANCE, PRINCE IGOR	CENTURY MUSIC PUBLISHING COMPANY, INC.	4159	.40
BORODIN, A.			POLOVETSIAN DANCES, FROM 'PRINCE IGOR'	BOOSEY AND HAWKES, INC.		3.00
BORODIN, A.	BLUMENFELD		PRINCE IGOR OVERTURE	BOOSEY AND HAWKES, INC.		2.00
BOTSFORD, G.			BLACK AND WHITE RAG	WARNER BROTHERS PUBLISHERS		1.00
BOUD, R.			RON BOUD PIANO STYLINGS	HOPE PUBLISHING COMPANY		2.00
BRADLEY, R.--ARR.	BRADLEY, R.	EASY	ABRAHAM, MARTIN AND JOHN	SCREEN GEMS - COLUMBIA PUBLICATIONS	0403AP2	.85
BRADLEY, R.--ARR.	BRADLEY, R.	EASY	ALLEY CAT	SCREEN GEMS - COLUMBIA PUBLICATIONS	3733AP2	.85
BRADLEY, R.--ARR.	BRADLEY, R.	BIG NOTE EASY	AMAZING GRACE - AND - HE'S GOT THE WHOLE WORLD IN HIS HANDS	SCREEN GEMS - COLUMBIA PUBLICATIONS	C0019P3	1.00
BRADLEY, R.--ARR.	BRADLEY, R.	EASY	AM I LOSING YOU	SCREEN GEMS - COLUMBIA PUBLICATIONS	4002AP2	.85

BRADLEY, R.--ARR. BRADLEY, R. EASY
ARE YOU LONESOME TONIGHT
SCREEN GEMS - COLUMBIA PUBLICATIONS 5703AP2 .85

BRADLEY, R.--ARR. BRADLEY, R. EASY
AUBREY
SCREEN GEMS - COLUMBIA PUBLICATIONS 6704AP2 .85

BRADLEY, R.--ARR. BRADLEY, R. EASY
BABY DON'T GET HOOKED ON ME
SCREEN GEMS - COLUMBIA PUBLICATIONS 0010BP2 .85

BRADLEY, R.--ARR. BRADLEY, R. EASY
BABY I'M-A WANT YOU
SCREEN GEMS - COLUMBIA PUBLICATIONS 0003BP2 .85

BRADLEY, R.--ARR. BRADLEY, R. EASY
BACK TO CALIFORNIA
SCREEN GEMS - COLUMBIA PUBLICATIONS 0004BP2 .85

BRADLEY, R.--ARR. BRADLEY, R. EASY
BEAUTIFUL CITY
SCREEN GEMS - COLUMBIA PUBLICATIONS 1430BP2 .85

BRADLEY, R.--ARR. BRADLEY, R. EASY
BEEN TO CANAAN
SCREEN GEMS - COLUMBIA PUBLICATIONS 1423BP2 .85

BRADLEY, R.--ARR. BRADLEY, R. EASY
BEN
SCREEN GEMS - COLUMBIA PUBLICATIONS 1443BP2 .85

BRADLEY, R.--ARR. BRADLEY, R. BIG NOTE EASY
BLACK AND WHITE - AND - BRIAN'S SONG
SCREEN GEMS - COLUMBIA PUBLICATIONS C0015P3 1.00

BRADLEY, R.--ARR. BRADLEY, R. EASY
BLACK AND WHITE
SCREEN GEMS - COLUMBIA PUBLICATIONS 3712BP2 .85

BRADLEY, R.--ARR. BRADLEY, R. EASY
BLESS THE BEASTS AND CHILDREN
SCREEN GEMS - COLUMBIA PUBLICATIONS 3702BP2 .85

BRADLEY, R.--ARR. BRADLEY, R. EASY
BORN FREE
SCREEN GEMS - COLUMBIA PUBLICATIONS 4701BP2 .85

BRADLEY, R.--ARR. BRADLEY, R. BIG NOTE EASY
BORN FREE
SCREEN GEMS - COLUMBIA PUBLICATIONS 4701BP3 .85

BRADLEY, R.--ARR. BRADLEY, R. INTERMEDIATE
BORN FREE
SCREEN GEMS - COLUMBIA PUBLICATIONS 4701BP 1.00

BRADLEY, R.--ARR. BRADLEY, R. EASY
BRADLEY'S BEST OF THE BEST - BREAD
SCREEN GEMS - COLUMBIA PUBLICATIONS F0108P2 1.75

BRADLEY, R.--ARR. BRADLEY, R. EASY
BRADLEY'S BEST OF THE BEST - BROADWAY
SCREEN GEMS - COLUMBIA PUBLICATIONS F0077P2 1.75

BRADLEY, R.--ARR. BRADLEY, R. EASY
BRADLEY'S BEST OF THE BEST - CAROLE KING
SCREEN GEMS - COLUMBIA PUBLICATIONS F0027P2A 1.75

BRADLEY, R.--ARR. BRADLEY, R. EASY
BRADLEY'S BEST OF THE BEST - CHRISTMAS CAROLS
SCREEN GEMS - COLUMBIA PUBLICATIONS F0211P2 1.75

BRADLEY, R.--ARR. BRADLEY, R. EASY
BRADLEY'S BEST OF THE BEST - COUNTRY HITS
SCREEN GEMS - COLUMBIA PUBLICATIONS F0029P2 1.50

BRADLEY, R.--ARR. BRADLEY, R. EASY
BRADLEY'S BEST OF THE BEST - MOTION PICTURE HITS
SCREEN GEMS - COLUMBIA PUBLICATIONS F0037P2 1.50

BRADLEY, R.--ARR. BRADLEY, R. EASY
BRADLEY'S BEST OF THE BEST - POPULAR SACRED SONGS
SCREEN GEMS - COLUMBIA PUBLICATIONS F0135P2 1.50

BRADLEY, R.--ARR. BRADLEY, R. EASY
BRADLEY'S BEST OF THE BEST - POP TEACHING PIECES
SCREEN GEMS - COLUMBIA PUBLICATIONS F0230P2 1.75

BRADLEY, R.--ARR. BRADLEY, R. BIG NOTE EASY
BRADLEY'S BIG NOTE BLOCKBUSTERS
SCREEN GEMS - COLUMBIA PUBLICATIONS F0233P3 2.95

BRADLEY, R.--ARR. BRADLEY, R. EASY
BRADLEY'S CHRISTMAS JOY - ISSUE NO. 1
SCREEN GEMS - COLUMBIA PUBLICATIONS F0213P2 1.75

BRADLEY, R.--ARR. BRADLEY, R. EASY
BRADLEY'S COUNTRY JOY - ISSUE NO. 1
SCREEN GEMS - COLUMBIA PUBLICATIONS F0189P2 1.50

BRADLEY, R.--ARR. BRADLEY, R. EASY
BRADLEY'S HYMN JOY - ISSUE NO. 1
SCREEN GEMS - COLUMBIA PUBLICATIONS F0275P2 1.50

BRADLEY, R.--ARR. BRADLEY, R. EASY
BRADLEY'S POPULAR JOY - ISSUE NO. 1
SCREEN GEMS - COLUMBIA PUBLICATIONS F0128P2 1.50

BRADLEY, R.--ARR. BRADLEY, R. EASY
BRADLEY'S POPULAR JOY - ISSUE NO. 2
SCREEN GEMS - COLUMBIA PUBLICATIONS F0187P2 1.50

BRADLEY, R.--ARR. BRADLEY, R. EASY
BRADLEY'S POPULAR JOY - ISSUE NO. 3
SCREEN GEMS - COLUMBIA PUBLICATIONS F0216P2 1.50

BRADLEY, R.--ARR. BRADLEY, R. EASY
BRADLEY'S POPULAR JOY - ISSUE NO. 4
SCREEN GEMS - COLUMBIA PUBLICATIONS F0261P2 1.50

BRADLEY, R.--ARR. BRADLEY, R. EASY
BRADLEY'S SUPERSTARS
SCREEN GEMS - COLUMBIA PUBLICATIONS F0223P2 2.50

BRADLEY, R.--ARR. BRADLEY, R. EASY
BRADLEY'S SUPER POPULAR MUSIC
SCREEN GEMS - COLUMBIA PUBLICATIONS F0016P2 2.50

BRADLEY, R.--ARR. BRADLEY, R. INTERMEDIATE
BRADLEY'S TODAY'S SOUND PIANO SOLOS
SCREEN GEMS - COLUMBIA PUBLICATIONS F0035P 2.95

BRADLEY, R.--ARR. BRADLEY, R. EASY
BRADLEY - LIKE IT IS TODAY - EASY PIANO HIT PARADE NO. 1
SCREEN GEMS - COLUMBIA PUBLICATIONS F0025P2 1.25

BRADLEY, R.--ARR. BRADLEY, R. EASY
BRADLEY - LIKE IT IS TODAY - EASY PIANO HIT PARADE NO. 2
SCREEN GEMS - COLUMBIA PUBLICATIONS F0051P2 1.50

BRADLEY, R.--ARR. BRADLEY, R. EASY
BRADLEY - LIKE IT IS TODAY - EASY PIANO HIT PARADE NO. 3
SCREEN GEMS - COLUMBIA PUBLICATIONS F0075P2 1.75

BRADLEY, R.--ARR. BRADLEY, R. EASY
BRADLEY - LIKE IT IS TODAY - EASY PIANO HIT PARADE NO. 4
SCREEN GEMS - COLUMBIA PUBLICATIONS F0100P2 1.75

BRADLEY, R.--ARR. BRADLEY, R. EASY
BREAKING UP IS HARD TO DO
SCREEN GEMS - COLUMBIA PUBLICATIONS 5701BP2 .85

BRADLEY, R.--ARR. BRADLEY, R. EASY
BRIAN'S SONG
SCREEN GEMS - COLUMBIA PUBLICATIONS 5707BP2 .85

BRADLEY, R.--ARR. BRADLEY, R. BIG NOTE EASY
BRIAN'S SONG
SCREEN GEMS - COLUMBIA PUBLICATIONS 5707BP3 .85

BRADLEY, R.--ARR. BRADLEY, R. EASY
BY THE TIME I GET TO PHOENIX
SCREEN GEMS - COLUMBIA PUBLICATIONS 8002BP2 .85

BRADLEY, R.--ARR. BRADLEY, R. BIG NOTE EASY
CANDY MAN, THE - AND - BORN FREE
SCREEN GEMS - COLUMBIA PUBLICATIONS C0016P3 1.00

BRADLEY, R.--ARR. BRADLEY, R. EASY
CANDY MAN, THE
SCREEN GEMS - COLUMBIA PUBLICATIONS 0007CP2 .85

BRADLEY, R.--ARR. BRADLEY, R. BIG NOTE EASY
CANDY MAN, THE
SCREEN GEMS - COLUMBIA PUBLICATIONS 0007CP3 .85

BRADLEY, R.--ARR. BRADLEY, R. EASY
CHERISH
SCREEN GEMS - COLUMBIA PUBLICATIONS 2406CP2 .85

BRADLEY, R.--ARR. BRADLEY, R. EASY
CLOUDS
SCREEN GEMS - COLUMBIA PUBLICATIONS 3709CP2 .85

BRADLEY, R.--ARR. BRADLEY, R. EASY
COUNTRY POPS
SCREEN GEMS - COLUMBIA PUBLICATIONS F0244P2 2.95

BRADLEY, R.--ARR. BRADLEY, R. EASY
DAY BY DAY
SCREEN GEMS - COLUMBIA PUBLICATIONS 0014DP2 .85

BRADLEY, R.--ARR. BRADLEY, R. EASY
DIARY
SCREEN GEMS - COLUMBIA PUBLICATIONS 2705DP2 .85

BRADLEY, R.--ARR. BRADLEY, R. EASY
DON'T IT MAKE YOU WANTA GO HOME
SCREEN GEMS - COLUMBIA PUBLICATIONS 4706DP2 .85

BRADLEY, R.--ARR. BRADLEY, R. EASY
EVERYTHING I OWN
SCREEN GEMS - COLUMBIA PUBLICATIONS 7007EP2 .85

BRADLEY, R.--ARR. BRADLEY, R. EASY
FIRST TIME EVER I SAW YOUR FACE, THE
SCREEN GEMS - COLUMBIA PUBLICATIONS 2703FP2 .85

BRADLEY, R.--ARR. BRADLEY, R. EASY
FOR ONCE IN MY LIFE
SCREEN GEMS - COLUMBIA PUBLICATIONS 4717FP2 .85

BRADLEY, R.--ARR. BRADLEY, R. EASY
FUNNY FACE
SCREEN GEMS - COLUMBIA PUBLICATIONS 6706FP2 .85

BRADLEY, R.--ARR. BRADLEY, R. EASY
GOING OUT OF MY HEAD
SCREEN GEMS - COLUMBIA PUBLICATIONS 4717GP2 .85

BRADLEY, R.--ARR. BRADLEY, R. EASY
GO AWAY LITTLE GIRL
SCREEN GEMS - COLUMBIA PUBLICATIONS 4702GP2 .85

BRADLEY, R.--ARR. BRADLEY, R. EASY
GREEN GREEN GRASS OF HOME
SCREEN GEMS - COLUMBIA PUBLICATIONS 5702GP2 .85

BRADLEY, R.--ARR. BRADLEY, R. EASY
GUITAR MAN, THE
SCREEN GEMS - COLUMBIA PUBLICATIONS 6704GP2 .85

BRADLEY, R.--ARR. BRADLEY, R. EASY
HANDS OF TIME, THE
SCREEN GEMS - COLUMBIA PUBLICATIONS 0011HP2 .85

BRADLEY, R.--ARR. BRADLEY, R. EASY
HAPPIEST GIRL IN THE WHOLE U.S.A., THE
SCREEN GEMS - COLUMBIA PUBLICATIONS 0014HP2 .85

BRADLEY, R.--ARR. BRADLEY, R. EASY
HAVA NAGILA
SCREEN GEMS - COLUMBIA PUBLICATIONS 0026HP2 .85

BRADLEY, R.--ARR. BRADLEY, R. EASY
HEY, GIRL
SCREEN GEMS - COLUMBIA PUBLICATIONS 1402HP2 .85

BRADLEY, R.--ARR. BRADLEY, R. EASY
HI-DE-HO --THAT OLD SWEET ROLL--
SCREEN GEMS - COLUMBIA PUBLICATIONS 2701HP2 .85

BRADLEY, R.--ARR. BRADLEY, R. EASY
HOLLY JOLLY CHRISTMAS, A
SCREEN GEMS - COLUMBIA PUBLICATIONS 4714HP2 .85

BRADLEY, R.--ARR. BRADLEY, R. EASY
HOME AGAIN
SCREEN GEMS - COLUMBIA PUBLICATIONS 4703HP2 .85

BRADLEY, R.--ARR. BRADLEY, R. EASY
HOUSE OF THE RISING SUN, THE
SCREEN GEMS - COLUMBIA PUBLICATIONS 4701HP2 .85

BRADLEY, R.--ARR. BRADLEY, R. EASY
HURTING EACH OTHER
SCREEN GEMS - COLUMBIA PUBLICATIONS 6704HP2 .85

BRADLEY, R.--ARR. BRADLEY, R. EASY
IF
SCREEN GEMS - COLUMBIA PUBLICATIONS 1702IP2 .85

BRADLEY, R.--ARR. BRADLEY, R. EASY
IN TUNE WITH THE TIMES
SCREEN GEMS - COLUMBIA PUBLICATIONS F0145P2 2.95

BRADLEY, R.--ARR. BRADLEY, R. EASY
IT'S GOING TO TAKE SOME TIME
SCREEN GEMS - COLUMBIA PUBLICATIONS 6415IP2 .85

BRADLEY, R.--ARR. BRADLEY, R. EASY
IT'S ONE OF THOSE NIGHTS --YES LOVE--
SCREEN GEMS - COLUMBIA PUBLICATIONS 6414IP2 .85

BRADLEY, R.--ARR. BRADLEY, R. INTERMEDIATE
IT'S TOO LATE
SCREEN GEMS - COLUMBIA PUBLICATIONS 6403IP 1.00

BRADLEY, R.--ARR. BRADLEY, R. EASY
I BELIEVE IN MUSIC
SCREEN GEMS - COLUMBIA PUBLICATIONS 0402IP2 .85

BRADLEY, R.--ARR. BRADLEY, R. EASY
I GOT A NAME
SCREEN GEMS - COLUMBIA PUBLICATIONS 2004IP2 .85

BRADLEY, R.--ARR. BRADLEY, R. EASY
I KNEW YOU WHEN
SCREEN GEMS - COLUMBIA PUBLICATIONS 3401IP2 .85

BRADLEY, R.--ARR. BRADLEY, R. EASY
I NEVER PROMISED YOU A ROSE GARDEN
SCREEN GEMS - COLUMBIA PUBLICATIONS 4702RP2 .85

BRADLEY, R.--ARR. BRADLEY, R. EASY
I WILL WAIT FOR YOU
SCREEN GEMS - COLUMBIA PUBLICATIONS 7408IP2 .85

BRADLEY, R.--ARR. BRADLEY,R. EASY
I WOKE UP IN LOVE THIS MORNING
SCREEN GEMS - COLUMBIA PUBLICATIONS 7402IP2 .85

BRADLEY, R.--ARR. BRADLEY, R. EASY
JEAN
SCREEN GEMS - COLUMBIA PUBLICATIONS 1417JP2 .85

BRADLEY, R.--ARR. BRADLEY, R. BIG NOTE EASY
JINGLE BELLS
SCREEN GEMS - COLUMBIA PUBLICATIONS 2703JP2 .85

BRADLEY, R.--ARR. BRADLEY, R. EASY
JOY TO THE WORLD
SCREEN GEMS - COLUMBIA PUBLICATIONS 4703JP2 .85

BRADLEY, R.--ARR. BRADLEY, R. BIG NOTE EASY
JOY TO THE WORLD
SCREEN GEMS - COLUMBIA PUBLICATIONS 4703JP3 .85

BRADLEY, R.--ARR. BRADLEY, R. EASY
JOY
SCREEN GEMS - COLUMBIA PUBLICATIONS 4706JP2 .85

BRADLEY, R.--ARR. BRADLEY, R. EASY
KNOCKIN' ON HEAVEN'S DOOR
SCREEN GEMS - COLUMBIA PUBLICATIONS 4703KP2 .85

BRADLEY, R.--ARR.   BRADLEY, R.   EASY
L-O-V-E
    SCREEN GEMS - COLUMBIA PUBLICATIONS   4704LP2   .85
BRADLEY, R.--ARR.   BRADLEY, R.   EASY
LAST TIME I SAW HIM
    SCREEN GEMS - COLUMBIA PUBLICATIONS   0042LP2   .85
BRADLEY, R.--ARR.   BRADLEY, R.   EASY
LITTLE PEOPLE AMERICA
    SCREEN GEMS - COLUMBIA PUBLICATIONS   2703LP2   .85
BRADLEY, R.--ARR.   BRADLEY, R.   BIG NOTE EASY
LIVING TOGETHER, GROWING TOGETHER - AND - QUESTION ME AN ANSWER
    SCREEN GEMS - COLUMBIA PUBLICATIONS   C0030P3   1.00
BRADLEY, R.--ARR.   BRADLEY, R.   EASY
LIVING TOGETHER, GROWING TOGETHER
    SCREEN GEMS - COLUMBIA PUBLICATIONS   2715LP2   .85
BRADLEY, R.--ARR.   BRADLEY, R.   EASY
LONG-HAIRED LOVER FROM LIVERPOOL
    SCREEN GEMS - COLUMBIA PUBLICATIONS   4728LP2   .85
BRADLEY, R.--ARR.   BRADLEY, R.   EASY
LOOK OF LOVE, THE
    SCREEN GEMS - COLUMBIA PUBLICATIONS   4703LP2   .85
BRADLEY, R.--ARR.   BRADLEY, R.   EASY
LOST HORIZON
    SCREEN GEMS - COLUMBIA PUBLICATIONS   F0158P2   2.50
BRADLEY, R.--ARR.   BRADLEY, R.   INTERMEDIATE
LOVE MEANS --YOU NEVER HAVE TO SAY YOU'RE SORRY--
    SCREEN GEMS - COLUMBIA PUBLICATIONS   4717LP   1.00
BRADLEY, R.--ARR.   BRADLEY, R.   EASY
MISTY
    SCREEN GEMS - COLUMBIA PUBLICATIONS   2728MP2   .85
BRADLEY, R.--ARR.   BRADLEY, R.   EASY
MORE 24 CARAT GOLD
    SCREEN GEMS - COLUMBIA PUBLICATIONS   F0268P2   3.95
BRADLEY, R.--ARR.   BRADLEY, R.   EASY
MORE 24 CARAT GOLD
    SCREEN GEMS - COLUMBIA PUBLICATIONS   F0268P2   3.95
BRADLEY, R.--ARR.   BRADLEY, R.   EASY
MORNING AFTER, THE
    SCREEN GEMS - COLUMBIA PUBLICATIONS   4723MP2   .85
BRADLEY, R.--ARR.   BRADLEY, R.   EASY
MOST BEAUTIFUL GIRL, THE
    SCREEN GEMS - COLUMBIA PUBLICATIONS   4722MP2   .85
BRADLEY, R.--ARR.   BRADLEY, R.   EASY
MOVIE POPS
    SCREEN GEMS - COLUMBIA PUBLICATIONS   F0259P2   2.50
BRADLEY, R.--ARR.   BRADLEY, R.   EASY
MUSIC
    SCREEN GEMS - COLUMBIA PUBLICATIONS   6701MP2   .85
BRADLEY, R.--ARR.   BRADLEY, R.   EASY
NEVER BEEN TO SPAIN
    SCREEN GEMS - COLUMBIA PUBLICATIONS   1403NP2   .85
BRADLEY, R.--ARR.   BRADLEY, R.   EASY
NEVER CAN SAY GOODBYE
    SCREEN GEMS - COLUMBIA PUBLICATIONS   1413NP2   .85
BRADLEY, R.--ARR.   BRADLEY, R.   EASY
ONE TIN SOLDIER
    SCREEN GEMS - COLUMBIA PUBLICATIONS   4438OP2   .85
BRADLEY, R.--ARR.   BRADLEY, R.   EASY
PAPER ROSES
    SCREEN GEMS - COLUMBIA PUBLICATIONS   0015PP2   .85
BRADLEY, R.--ARR.   BRADLEY, R.   EASY
PARTRIDGE FAMILY, THE - AT HOME WITH THEIR GREATEST HITS
    SCREEN GEMS - COLUMBIA PUBLICATIONS   P0036P2   2.50
BRADLEY, R.--ARR.   BRADLEY, R.   EASY
POPCORN
    SCREEN GEMS - COLUMBIA PUBLICATIONS   4709PP2   .85
BRADLEY, R.--ARR.   BRADLEY, R.   EASY
POPS MADE EASY FOR PIANO
    SCREEN GEMS - COLUMBIA PUBLICATIONS   F0167P2   2.95
BRADLEY, R.--ARR.   BRADLEY, R.   EASY
POPULAR TEACHER'S CHOICE
    SCREEN GEMS - COLUMBIA PUBLICATIONS   F0112P21   3.95
BRADLEY, R.--ARR.   BRADLEY, R.   EASY
ROCKIN' AROUND THE CHRISTMAS TREE
    SCREEN GEMS - COLUMBIA PUBLICATIONS   4711RP2   .85
BRADLEY, R.--ARR.   BRADLEY, R.   EASY
ROCK AND ROLL LULLABY
    SCREEN GEMS - COLUMBIA PUBLICATIONS   4705RP2   .85
BRADLEY, R.--ARR.   BRADLEY, R.   BIG NOTE EASY
RUDOLPH THE RED-NOSED REINDEER
    SCREEN GEMS - COLUMBIA PUBLICATIONS   6706RP3   .85
BRADLEY, R.--ARR.   BRADLEY, R.   EASY
RUN RUN RUN
    SCREEN GEMS - COLUMBIA PUBLICATIONS   6706RP2   .85
BRADLEY, R.--ARR.   BRADLEY, R.   EASY
SEATTLE
    SCREEN GEMS - COLUMBIA PUBLICATIONS   1401SP2   .85
BRADLEY, R.--ARR.   BRADLEY, R.   EASY
SEE YOU IN SEPTEMBER
    SCREEN GEMS - COLUMBIA PUBLICATIONS   1407SP2   .85
BRADLEY, R.--ARR.   BRADLEY, R.   EASY
SENSATIONAL 70 FOR THE 70'S
    SCREEN GEMS - COLUMBIA PUBLICATIONS   F0050P2A   4.95
BRADLEY, R.--ARR.   BRADLEY, R.   BIG NOTE EASY
SILENT NIGHT
    SCREEN GEMS - COLUMBIA PUBLICATIONS   2706SP3   .85
BRADLEY, R.--ARR.   BRADLEY, R.   EASY
SIMON AND GARFUNKEL'S GREATEST HITS
    SCREEN GEMS - COLUMBIA PUBLICATIONS   P0037P2   2.50
BRADLEY, R.--ARR.   BRADLEY, R.   BIG NOTE EASY
SIMPLY BRADLEY - CHRISTMAS CAROLS
    SCREEN GEMS - COLUMBIA PUBLICATIONS   F0105P3   1.50
BRADLEY, R.--ARR.   BRADLEY, R.   BIG NOTE EASY
SIMPLY BRADLEY - FOLK BOOK
    SCREEN GEMS - COLUMBIA PUBLICATIONS   F0054P3   1.50
BRADLEY, R.--ARR.   BRADLEY, R.   BIG NOTE EASY
SIMPLY BRADLEY - HYMN BOOK
    SCREEN GEMS - COLUMBIA PUBLICATIONS   F0048P3   1.50
BRADLEY, R.--ARR.   BRADLEY, R.   BIG NOTE EASY
SIMPLY BRADLEY - MOVIE BOOK
    SCREEN GEMS - COLUMBIA PUBLICATIONS   F0095P3   1.50
BRADLEY, R.--ARR.   BRADLEY, R.   BIG NOTE EASY
SIMPLY BRADLEY - POP BOOK
    SCREEN GEMS - COLUMBIA PUBLICATIONS   F0188P3   1.50
BRADLEY, R.--ARR.   BRADLEY, R.   BIG NOTE EASY
SIMPLY BRADLEY - RUDOLPH THE RED-NOSED REINDEER AND OTHER
CHRISTMAS FAVORITES
    SCREEN GEMS - COLUMBIA PUBLICATIONS   F0111P3   1.50
BRADLEY, R.--ARR.   BRADLEY, R.   BIG NOTE EASY
SIMPLY BRADLEY - SECOND POP BOOK, THE
    SCREEN GEMS - COLUMBIA PUBLICATIONS   F0269P3   1.50
BRADLEY, R.--ARR.   BRADLEY, R.   BIG NOTE EASY
SIMPLY BRADLEY - THE PARTRIDGE FAMILY
    SCREEN GEMS - COLUMBIA PUBLICATIONS   P0018P3   1.50
BRADLEY, R.--ARR.   BRADLEY, R.   EASY
SIXTY-SEVEN BRADLEY POP TEACHING PIECES FOR PIANO
    SCREEN GEMS - COLUMBIA PUBLICATIONS   F0245P2   4.95

BRADLEY, R.--ARR.   BRADLEY, R.   EASY
SMILE - HAVE A HAPPY DAY
    SCREEN GEMS - COLUMBIA PUBLICATIONS   4002SP2   .85
BRADLEY, R.--ARR.   BRADLEY, R.   EASY
SNOOPY'S CHRISTMAS
    SCREEN GEMS - COLUMBIA PUBLICATIONS   4405SP2   .85
BRADLEY, R.--ARR.   BRADLEY, R.   EASY
SOME KIND OF WONDERFUL
    SCREEN GEMS - COLUMBIA PUBLICATIONS   4702SP2   .85
BRADLEY, R.--ARR.   BRADLEY, R.   EASY
SONG OF LONG AGO
    SCREEN GEMS - COLUMBIA PUBLICATIONS   4712SP2   .85
BRADLEY, R.--ARR.   BRADLEY, R.   EASY
SO FAR AWAY
    SCREEN GEMS - COLUMBIA PUBLICATIONS   4703SP2   .85
BRADLEY, R.--ARR.   BRADLEY, R.   EASY
SPANISH EYES
    SCREEN GEMS - COLUMBIA PUBLICATIONS   5002SP2   .85
BRADLEY, R.--ARR.   BRADLEY, R.   EASY
SUPER POPULAR MUSIC
    SCREEN GEMS - COLUMBIA PUBLICATIONS   F0042P2   2.50
BRADLEY, R.--ARR.   BRADLEY, R.   EASY
SUPER 77, THE
    SCREEN GEMS - COLUMBIA PUBLICATIONS   F0199P2   4.95
BRADLEY, R.--ARR.   BRADLEY, R.   EASY
SWEET SEASONS
    SCREEN GEMS - COLUMBIA PUBLICATIONS   7406SP2   .85
BRADLEY, R.--ARR.   BRADLEY, R.   EASY
SWEET SURRENDER
    SCREEN GEMS - COLUMBIA PUBLICATIONS   7420SP2   .85
BRADLEY, R.--ARR.   BRADLEY, R.   EASY
TAPESTRY
    SCREEN GEMS - COLUMBIA PUBLICATIONS   003TP2   .85
BRADLEY, R.--ARR.   BRADLEY, R.   EASY
THEME FROM NICHOLAS AND ALEXANDRA
    SCREEN GEMS - COLUMBIA PUBLICATIONS   2701NP2   .85
BRADLEY, R.--ARR.   BRADLEY, R.   EASY
THEME FROM SHAFT
    SCREEN GEMS - COLUMBIA PUBLICATIONS   2422SP2   .85
BRADLEY, R.--ARR.   BRADLEY, R.   EASY
TOO YOUNG
    SCREEN GEMS - COLUMBIA PUBLICATIONS   4716TP2   .85
BRADLEY, R.--ARR.   BRADLEY, R.   EASY
TOUCH ME IN THE MORNING
    SCREEN GEMS - COLUMBIA PUBLICATIONS   4738TP2   .85
BRADLEY, R.--ARR.   BRADLEY, R.   EASY
TRACES
    SCREEN GEMS - COLUMBIA PUBLICATIONS   5701TP2   .85
BRADLEY, R.--ARR.   BRADLEY, R.   EASY
TWENTY-FOUR CARAT GOLD
    SCREEN GEMS - COLUMBIA PUBLICATIONS   F0257P2   3.95
BRADLEY, R.--ARR.   BRADLEY, R.   EASY
UP, UP AND AWAY
    SCREEN GEMS - COLUMBIA PUBLICATIONS   5002UP2   .85
BRADLEY, R.--ARR.   BRADLEY, R.   EASY
WALK A MILE IN MY SHOES
    SCREEN GEMS - COLUMBIA PUBLICATIONS   0005WP2   .85
BRADLEY, R.--ARR.   BRADLEY, R.   EASY
WAY WE WERE, THE
    SCREEN GEMS - COLUMBIA PUBLICATIONS   0055WP2   .85
BRADLEY, R.--ARR.   BRADLEY, R.   BIG NOTE EASY
WAY WE WERE, THE
    SCREEN GEMS - COLUMBIA PUBLICATIONS   0055WP3   .85
BRADLEY, R.--ARR.   BRADLEY, R.   INTERMEDIATE
WAY WE WERE, THE
    SCREEN GEMS - COLUMBIA PUBLICATIONS   0055WP   1.00
BRADLEY, R.--ARR.   BRADLEY, R.   EASY
WHEN YOU SAY LOVE
    SCREEN GEMS - COLUMBIA PUBLICATIONS   2437WP2   .85
BRADLEY, R.--ARR.   BRADLEY, R.   EASY
WHERE IS THE LOVE
    SCREEN GEMS - COLUMBIA PUBLICATIONS   2435WP2   .85
BRADLEY, R.--ARR.   BRADLEY, R.   EASY
WINTER WONDERLAND
    SCREEN GEMS - COLUMBIA PUBLICATIONS   2722WP2   .85
BRADLEY, R.--ARR.   BRADLEY, R.   BIG NOTE EASY
WINTER WONDERLAND
    SCREEN GEMS - COLUMBIA PUBLICATIONS   2722WP3   .85
BRADLEY, R.--ARR.   BRADLEY, R.   BIG NOTE EASY
WORLD IS A CIRCLE, THE - AND - REFLECTIONS
    SCREEN GEMS - COLUMBIA PUBLICATIONS   C0031P3   1.00
BRADLEY, R.--ARR.   BRADLEY, R.   EASY
WORLD IS A CIRCLE, THE
    SCREEN GEMS - COLUMBIA PUBLICATIONS   4717WP2   .85
BRADLEY, R.--ARR.   BRADLEY, R.   EASY
YOU'VE GOT A FRIEND
    SCREEN GEMS - COLUMBIA PUBLICATIONS   4702YP2   .85
BRADLEY, R.--ARR.   BRADLEY, R.   INTERMEDIATE
YOU'VE GOT A FRIEND
    SCREEN GEMS - COLUMBIA PUBLICATIONS   4702YP   1.00
BRADLEY, R.--ARR.   BRADLEY, R.   EASY
YOUNG LOVE
    SCREEN GEMS - COLUMBIA PUBLICATIONS   4756YP2   .85
BRADLEY, R.--ARR.   BRADLEY, R.   EASY
YO YO
    SCREEN GEMS - COLUMBIA PUBLICATIONS   4704YP2   .85
BRADY--ED   BRADY
CAROLS FOR CHRISTMAS
    BOSTON MUSIC COMPANY   1.50
BRAGA   WEYBRIGHT   1 1/2
ANGEL'S SERENADE
    BELWIN-MILLS PUBLISHING CORPORATION   .60
BRAHMS   MAIER, G.   3
BLACKSMITH, THE
    BELWIN-MILLS PUBLISHING CORPORATION   .60
BRAHMS   2
BRAHMS AT THE PIANO
    CENTURY MUSIC PUBLISHING COMPANY, INC.   1.00
BRAHMS   ECKHARDT, F.   1
BRAHMS FOR THE YOUNG PIANIST
    CENTURY MUSIC PUBLISHING COMPANY, INC.   3958   .40
BRAHMS   LEVINE, H.
BRAHMS WALTZES SIMPLIFIED
    ALFRED MUSIC COMPANY   546   1.25
BRAHMS   ROLFE, W.   2
CRADLE SONG
    CENTURY MUSIC PUBLISHING COMPANY, INC.   3243   .40
BRAHMS   SPENCER, J.   2
CRADLE SONG
    VOLKWEIN BROS.   .30
BRAHMS   MAIER, G.   3
DISAPPOINTED SERENADER, THE
    BELWIN-MILLS PUBLISHING CORPORATION   .60
BRAHMS   LEVINE, H.
FAVORITE BRAHMS HUNGARIAN DANCES
    ALFRED MUSIC COMPANY   684   1.50

BRUCKNER   SINGER   D
SELECTED MOVEMENTS FROM THE SYMPHONIES NOS. 1, 2, 3, 4, 7
C. F. PETERS CORPORATION   3847   3.50
BRUNS, V.
NEUE ODYSSEE -- BALLET IN 5 TABLEAUX
ASSOCIATED MUSIC PUBLISHERS, INC.   BRH   12.50
BRUNS, V.
RECHT DES HERRN, DAS -- BALLET IN 2 TABLEAUX
ASSOCIATED MUSIC PUBLISHERS, INC.   BRH   4.80
BRYANT   NEALE, J.   EASY
ALL I HAVE TO DO IS DREAM
WARNER BROTHERS PUBLISHERS   .75
BURKE *   NEALE, J.   EASY
TIP-TOE THRU' THE TULIPS WITH ME
WARNER BROTHERS PUBLISHERS   .75
BURNAM--ED   BURNAM   2
DANNY BOY
WILLIS MUSIC COMPANY   .40
BURNAM--ED   BURNAM   2
GREENSLEEVES
WILLIS MUSIC COMPANY   .40
BURNAM--ED   BURNAM   1
HE'S GOT THE WHOLE WORLD IN HIS HANDS
WILLIS MUSIC COMPANY   .40
BURNAM
FOR YOU ALONE
WILLIS MUSIC COMPANY   .90
BUSCHBAUM *
KINDER SPIELEN ZUR WEIHNACHT
BARENREITER VERLAG   EN 803   6.00
BUTTERFIELD   2
WHEN YOU AND I WERE YOUNG MAGGIE
CENTURY MUSIC PUBLISHING COMPANY, INC.   2439   .40
BUXTEHUDE   PROKOFIEFF
ORGAN PRELUDE AND FUGUE IN D MINOR
MCA MUSIC   .60
BUXTEHUDE   PROKOFIEFF
PRELUDE AND FUGUE IN D MINOR
INTERNATIONAL MUSIC COMPANY   1.00
BYRD, W.   BARTH, H.
CARMAN'S WHISTLE, THE
BELWIN-MILLS PUBLISHING CORPORATION   20359   .50
CAHN *
THREE COINS IN A FOUNTAIN
THE BIG THREE MUSIC CORPORATION   00.95
CAMEO--ED   CAMEO   4
GREENSLEEVES
SCHAUM PUBLICATIONS, INC.   .60
CAMEO--ED   CAMEO   4
JINGLE BELLS JUBILEE
SCHAUM PUBLICATIONS, INC.   .60
CAREY, H.   WALLIS *   1
MY COUNTRY 'TIS OF THEE
WILLIS MUSIC COMPANY   .30
CARMICHAEL   MOSSMAN, T.
STAR DUST -- SIMP.
BELWIN-MILLS PUBLISHING CORPORATION   26077   .50
CARMICHAEL   MALTBY
STAR DUST MAMBO
BELWIN-MILLS PUBLISHING CORPORATION   20278   .85
CARMICHAEL   GLOVER, D.
STAR DUST
BELWIN-MILLS PUBLISHING CORPORATION   .60
CARMICHAEL   KRENZ, B.
STAR DUST
BELWIN-MILLS PUBLISHING CORPORATION   20352   .85
CARMICHAEL   MATTE, J.
STAR DUST
BELWIN-MILLS PUBLISHING CORPORATION   20354   .85
CARMICHAEL   DESOLIS
STAR DUST
BELWIN-MILLS PUBLISHING CORPORATION   20468   1.00
CAROL--ED.   CAROL   EASY
TWO AMERICAN CHRISTMAS CAROLS
DELRIEU ET CIE.   .85
CARROLL   SCHAUM, J.   1 1/2
BY THE BEAUTIFUL SEA
SCHAUM PUBLICATIONS, INC.   .75
CARROLL *
I'M ALWAYS CHASING RAINBOWS
THE BIG THREE MUSIC CORPORATION   00.95
CARVER--ED   CARVER
CHAPPELL'S FAMOUS MELODIES
CHAPPELL AND COMPANY, INC.   0021964   1.00
CASELLA, A.
LA GIARA -- DER GROSSE KRUG
UNIVERSAL EDITION   UE 7715   14.00
CASHMAN *
FOLIO
THE BIG THREE MUSIC CORPORATION   03.95
CASSIDY, D.
ROCK ME BABY
THE BIG THREE MUSIC CORPORATION   03.95
CAVALLARO
CAVALLARO'S KEYBOARD CREATIONS
WARNER BROTHERS PUBLISHERS   1.95
CHAMBONNIERES, J. *   SETKOVA   2-3
ALTE TANZE DES 17. UND 18. JAHRHUNDERTS, 27 STUCKE
BARENREITER VERLAG   AP 1728
CHAMINADE   3
LA LISONJERA, EASY
CENTURY MUSIC PUBLISHING COMPANY, INC.   2508   .40
CHARPENTIER, G.
LOUISE
HEUGEL ET CIE.   21.70
CHATHAM, B. J.--ED   CHATHAM, B. J.
GOSPEL SONG FAVORITES FOR THE PIANO
BROADMAN MUSIC   4571-06   2.25
CHEDEVILLE, E. P.   MOFFAT   5
TAMBOURIN CHINOIS
NOVELLO AND COMPANY, LTD.   55.0046.10 .40
CHIATRI   JESTON, I. H.   2
LA SPAGNOLA
VOLKWEIN BROS.   .35
CHIESA *
MUSICAL PEARLS - EASY TRANSCRIPTION OF FAMOUS PIECES, BK. 1
FRANCO COLOMBO PUBLICATIONS   127548   1.75
CHIESA *
MUSICAL PEARLS - EASY TRANSCRIPTION OF FAMOUS PIECES, BK. 2
FRANCO COLOMBO PUBLICATIONS   127549   1.75
CHOPIN   ANSON, G.
ANSON INTRODUCES CHOPIN
WILLIS MUSIC COMPANY   1.50
CHOPIN   SCHAUM, J.   3
BEST OF CHOPIN
SCHAUM PUBLICATIONS, INC.   1.50

CHOPIN   BRADLEY, R.
BRADLEY CLASSICAL SERIES - MINUTE WALTZ, OP. 64 NO. 1
SCREEN GEMS - COLUMBIA PUBLICATIONS   2718MP2   .85
CHOPIN   BRADLEY, R.
BRADLEY CLASSICAL SERIES - NOCTURNE IN E FLAT, OP. 9 NO. 2
SCREEN GEMS - COLUMBIA PUBLICATIONS   4721NP2   .85
CHOPIN   BRADLEY, R.
BRADLEY CLASSICAL SERIES - PRELUDE IN A - AND - PRELUDE IN C MINOR
SCREEN GEMS - COLUMBIA PUBLICATIONS   5715PP2   .85
CHOPIN   BRADLEY, R.
BRADLEY CLASSICAL SERIES - PRELUDE IN E MINOR, OP. 28 NO. 4
SCREEN GEMS - COLUMBIA PUBLICATIONS   5714PP2   .85
CHOPIN *   JOSEFFY
CHANT POLONAIS, OP. 74 NO. 5
G. SCHIRMER, INC.   .50
CHOPIN   THORNE
CHOPIN FOR EVERYBODY
BOOSEY AND HAWKES, INC.   1.50
CHOPIN   ECKHARDT, F.   2
CHOPIN FOR THE YOUNG PIANIST
CENTURY MUSIC PUBLISHING COMPANY, INC.   3959   .40
CHOPIN   SMALL, A.
CHOPIN SAMPLER
ALFRED MUSIC COMPANY   520   3.95
CHOPIN   TREHARNE
CHOPIN SIMPLIFIED
BOSTON MUSIC COMPANY   1.00
CHOPIN   M
CONCERTO NO. 01 IN E MINOR, OP. 11
C. F. PETERS CORPORATION   2895AA   1.25
CHOPIN   D
CONCERT PIECES, OP. 2, 13, 14, 22 --ARR. FOR PIANO SOLO--
C. F. PETERS CORPORATION   1912   6.00
CHOPIN   DEL MAGLIO
ECOSSAISE, OP. 72, NO. 3
FRANCO COLOMBO PUBLICATIONS   127141   .50
CHOPIN   ESTEBAN
ETUDES, OP. 10
ALFRED MUSIC COMPANY   576   3.00
CHOPIN
ETUDES
EDWARD B. MARKS MUSIC CORPORATION   05.00
CHOPIN   DEL MAGLIO
ETUDE IN C MINOR, OP. 10 NO. 12
FRANCO COLOMBO PUBLICATIONS   127142   .50
CHOPIN   DEL MAGLIO
ETUDE IN E, OP. 10 NO. 3
FRANCO COLOMBO PUBLICATIONS   127484   .60
CHOPIN   MOSSMAN
ETUDE IN E MAJOR
BELWIN-MILLS PUBLISHING CORPORATION   26065   .60
CHOPIN   SCHAUM, J.   3
ETUDE IN E MAJOR
SCHAUM PUBLICATIONS, INC.   .60
CHOPIN
FANTASIA, BERCEUSE, BARCAROLLE
EDWARD B. MARKS MUSIC CORPORATION   03.00
CHOPIN   WEYBRIGHT   1
FAVORITE THEME, A -- FROM FANTASIE IMPROMPTU
BELWIN-MILLS PUBLISHING CORPORATION   .60
CHOPIN *
FOUR ETUDES TRANSCRIBED FOR THE LEFT HAND
FRANCO COLOMBO PUBLICATIONS   SAL   4.25
CHOPIN   STEINER   2 1/2
FRENCH RIVER BOAT, ADAPTED FROM THE NOCTURNE OP. 37 NO. 2
BELWIN-MILLS PUBLISHING CORPORATION   .60
CHOPIN   DEL MAGLIO
FUNERAL MARCH - FROM SONATA, OP. 35
FRANCO COLOMBO PUBLICATIONS   129099   .60
CHOPIN
IMPROMPTUS
EDWARD B. MARKS MUSIC CORPORATION   03.00
CHOPIN *   4
MAIDEN'S WISH, THE
CENTURY MUSIC PUBLISHING COMPANY, INC.   3339   .40
CHOPIN   LONG, L.   2
MAIDEN'S WISH, THE
WILLIS MUSIC COMPANY   .35
CHOPIN *
MAIDEN'S WISH
G. SCHIRMER, INC.   .60
CHOPIN   DEL MAGLIO
MAZURKA, OP. 7 NO. 1
FRANCO COLOMBO PUBLICATIONS   129100   .60
CHOPIN
MAZURKAS
EDWARD B. MARKS MUSIC CORPORATION   07.00
CHOPIN   ZEPP   3
MELODY AND PRELUDE
PRO-ART PUBLICATIONS, INC.   150   .50
CHOPIN   2
MILITARY POLONAISE, EASY
CENTURY MUSIC PUBLISHING COMPANY, INC.   1825   .40
CHOPIN
MINOR WORKS
EDWARD B. MARKS MUSIC CORPORATION   05.00
CHOPIN   2
MINUTE WALTZ, EASY
CENTURY MUSIC PUBLISHING COMPANY, INC.   2160   .40
CHOPIN   THOMPSON, J.   4
NOCTURNE, OP. 15 NO. 2
WILLIS MUSIC COMPANY   .60
CHOPIN   THOMPSON, J.   3
NOCTURNE, OP. 37 NO. 2
WILLIS MUSIC COMPANY   .60
CHOPIN   THOMPSON, J.   3
NOCTURNE, OP. 48 NO. 1
WILLIS MUSIC COMPANY   .60
CHOPIN   DEL MAGLIO
NOCTURNE, OP. 55 NO. 1
FRANCO COLOMBO PUBLICATIONS   124715   .60
CHOPIN
NOCTURNES
EDWARD B. MARKS MUSIC CORPORATION   05.00
CHOPIN   DEL MAGLIO
NOCTURNE IN E FLAT, OP. 9 NO. 2
FRANCO COLOMBO PUBLICATIONS   124714   .75
CHOPIN   EDWARDS, C.
NOCTURNE IN E FLAT
BELWIN-MILLS PUBLISHING CORPORATION   26034   .60
CHOPIN   WHITFORD   GR. 2 1/2
NOCTURNE IN F SHARP
ROBERT WHITFORD PUBLICATIONS   .40
CHOPIN   DEL MAGLIO
POLONAISE, OP. 53 "HEROIC"
FRANCO COLOMBO PUBLICATIONS   129101   .60

CHOPIN   FREY, H.
  POLONAISE, OP. 53
    THE BIG THREE MUSIC CORPORATION   00.75
CHOPIN   CAVALLARO, C.
  POLONAISE, OP. 53
    THE BIG THREE MUSIC CORPORATION   00.95
CHOPIN   THOMPSON, J.   3
  POLONAISE, OP. 53
    WILLIS MUSIC COMPANY   .60
CHOPIN
  POLONAISES
    EDWARD B. MARKS MUSIC CORPORATION   05.00
CHOPIN   ROLFE, W.   2
  POLONAISE MILITAIRE, EASY
    CENTURY MUSIC PUBLISHING COMPANY, INC.   3221   .40
CHOPIN
  PRELUDES
    EDWARD B. MARKS MUSIC CORPORATION   03.00
CHOPIN   THOMPSON, J.   3
  PRELUDE IN C MINOR
    WILLIS MUSIC COMPANY   .60
CHOPIN   ROLFE, W.   2
  RAINDROP, THE, EASY
    CENTURY MUSIC PUBLISHING COMPANY, INC.   3659   .40
CHOPIN   STEINER   3
  ROMANTIC ETUDE, OP. 10 NO. 3
    BELWIN-MILLS PUBLISHING CORPORATION   .60
CHOPIN
  RONDOS
    EDWARD B. MARKS MUSIC CORPORATION   05.00
CHOPIN
  SCHERZOS
    EDWARD B. MARKS MUSIC CORPORATION   05.00
CHOPIN   THOMPSON, J.   4
  SIX CHOPIN ETUDES
    WILLIS MUSIC COMPANY   1.00
CHOPIN *   TAGLIAPIETRA
  SIX POLISH SONGS
    FRANCO COLOMBO PUBLICATIONS   ER941   1.00
CHOPIN *   TAGLIAPIETRA
  SIX POLISH SONGS
    FRANCO COLOMBO PUBLICATIONS   ER941   1.00
CHOPIN
  SONATAS
    EDWARD B. MARKS MUSIC CORPORATION   05.00
CHOPIN
  SONGS
    EDWARD B. MARKS MUSIC CORPORATION   06.00
CHOPIN   MANSFIELD
  STEPS TO THE MASTERS
    BANKS AND SON LTD.   1.50
CHOPIN   HALL
  SYLPHIDES
    BOOSEY AND HAWKES, INC.   1.50
CHOPIN   ZEPP   4
  THEME FROM ETUDE IN E
    PRO-ART PUBLICATIONS, INC.   68   .50
CHOPIN   THOMPSON, J.   2
  VALSE, OP. 18
    WILLIS MUSIC COMPANY   .60
CHOPIN   2
  VALSE, OP. 64 NO. 1, EASY
    CENTURY MUSIC PUBLISHING COMPANY, INC.   2160   .40
CHOPIN   THOMPSON, J.   3 1/2
  VALSE, OP. 64 NO. 2
    WILLIS MUSIC COMPANY   .60
CHOPIN   CHIESA
  WALTZ, OP. 18 IN E FLAT
    FRANCO COLOMBO PUBLICATIONS   107479   .60
CHOPIN   DEL MAGLIO
  WALTZ, OP. 34 NO. 1 IN A FLAT
    FRANCO COLOMBO PUBLICATIONS   127143   .60
CHOPIN   DEL MAGLIO
  WALTZ, OP. 34 NO. 2 IN A MINOR
    FRANCO COLOMBO PUBLICATIONS   129104   .60
CHOPIN   DEL MAGLIO
  WALTZ, OP. 64 NO. 1 IN D FLAT
    FRANCO COLOMBO PUBLICATIONS   127144   .60
CHOPIN   DEL MAGLIO
  WALTZ, OP. 64 NO. 2 IN C SHARP
    FRANCO COLOMBO PUBLICATIONS   129105   .60
CHOPIN   WHITFORD   GR. 2
  WALTZ, OP. 64 NO. 2
    ROBERT WHITFORD PUBLICATIONS   .40
CHOPIN   DEL MAGLIO
  WALTZ, OP. 69 NO. 1 IN A FLAT
    FRANCO COLOMBO PUBLICATIONS   127147   .60
CHOPIN
  WALTZES
    EDWARD B. MARKS MUSIC CORPORATION   05.00
CILEA
  ADRIANA LECOUVREUR - INTERMEZZO FROM ACT II
    FRANCO COLOMBO PUBLICATIONS   SON.1110   .90
CILEA
  ARLESIANA, L' - LAMENTO DI FEDERICO
    FRANCO COLOMBO PUBLICATIONS   SON.2875   .90
CLEMENTS--ED.   CLEMENTS   INTERMEDIATE
  HANS BRINKER, OR THE SILVER SKATES
    POINTER PUBLICATIONS   2.95
COATES, E.   SCHAUM, J.   2
  SLEEPY LAGOON
    SCHAUM PUBLICATIONS, INC.   .50
COBURN *
  WHISPERING
    THE BIG THREE MUSIC CORPORATION   00.95
COFFEY, J. R.
  SCORPIO
    WARNER BROTHERS PUBLISHERS   1.00
COHAN   WEYBRIGHT   2
  GIVE MY REGARDS TO BROADWAY
    BELWIN-MILLS PUBLISHING CORPORATION   .60
COHAN   SCHAUM, J.   2
  GIVE MY REGARDS TO BROADWAY
    SCHAUM PUBLICATIONS, INC.   .60
COHAN   STEINER   2 1/2
  SO LONG MARY
    BELWIN-MILLS PUBLISHING CORPORATION   .60
COHAN   ZEPP   2-3
  THREE ALL AMERICAN SONGS
    PRO-ART PUBLICATIONS, INC.   360   .50
COHAN   SCHAUM, J.   2
  YANKEE DOODLE DANDY
    SCHAUM PUBLICATIONS, INC.   .50
COHAN   STEINER   2
  YOU'RE A GRAND OLD FLAG
    BELWIN-MILLS PUBLISHING CORPORATION   .60

COHAN   SCHAUM, J.   2
  YOU'RE A GRAND OLD FLAG
    SCHAUM PUBLICATIONS, INC.   .60
COLE--ED   COLE
  CZECHOSLOVAKIAN FOLK SONGS
    EDWARD B. MARKS MUSIC CORPORATION   01.50
COLERIDGE-TAYLOR, S.
  TWENTY-FOUR NEGRO MELODIES
    THEODORE PRESSER COMPANY   5.00
COLLET
  TOREROS, LOS -- BALLET PANTOMIME --
    FRANCO COLOMBO PUBLICATIONS   SAL   6.50
COLLINS, J.
  JUDY COLLINS SONGBOOK, THE
    MUSIC SALES CORPORATION   060016   4.95
CONFREY, Z.   SCHAUM, J.   4 1/2
  AFTER THEATER TANGO
    SCHAUM PUBLICATIONS, INC.   .60
CONFREY, Z.
  STUMBLING
    THE BIG THREE MUSIC CORPORATION   00.95
COOPER, A.
  ALICE COOPER FOLIO
    THE BIG THREE MUSIC CORPORATION   03.95
COPLAND   FOSS
  BILLY THE KID
    BOOSEY AND HAWKES, INC.   1.50
COPLAND   SMIT
  DANZON CUBANO
    BOOSEY AND HAWKES, INC.   1.25
CORELLI   WEYBRIGHT   4
  PASTORAL FROM 'CONCERTO GROSSO NO. 8'
    BELWIN-MILLS PUBLISHING CORPORATION   .60
COTTRAU   DEL MAGLIO
  ADDIO A NAPOLI
    FRANCO COLOMBO PUBLICATIONS   127756   .50
COUPERIN, F.   MOTCHANE
  GRADED COUPERIN, THE
    BELWIN-MILLS PUBLISHING CORPORATION   2.50
COUPERIN, F.   HALFORD
  L'ART DE TOUCHER LE CLAVECIN
    ALFRED MUSIC COMPANY   580   3.00
COUPERIN
  COUPERIN PIANO COURSE, BK. 01
    BOURNE COMPANY   2.50
COUPERIN   INTERMEDIATE
  COUPERIN PIANO COURSE, BK. 02
    BOURNE COMPANY   2.50
COUPERIN
  COUPERIN PIANO COURSE, BK. 03
    BOURNE COMPANY   2.50
COWARD   MACLACHLAN   FIRST YEAR
  ZIGEUNER
    WARNER BROTHERS PUBLISHERS   .75
CRAIG, P.--ED   CRIAG, P.   2
  THANKSGIVING SCENE
    SCHAUM PUBLICATIONS, INC.   .60
CRAMER, J. *   MUGELLINI *   3
  SIXTY ETUDEN
    BARENREITER VERLAG   CM 12160
CRAXTON, H.--ED.   CRAXTON, H.
  AIRS AND GRACES
    OXFORD UNIVERSITY PRESS   38.003   1.50
CRAXTON, H.--ED.   CRAXTON, H.
  EASY ELIZABETHANS
    OXFORD UNIVERSITY PRESS   33.701   1.80
CRERIE, E.   SCHIEFELBEIN, F.   4
  SILENT NIGHT VARIATIONS
    VOLKWEIN BROS.   00.50
CRIST, D. W.--ED.   CRIST, D. W.
  CLASSIC MELODIES
    VOLKWEIN BROS.   01.00
CROCE, J.
  JIM CROCE SONG BOOK
    THE BIG THREE MUSIC CORPORATION   03.95
CUI, C.   THOMPSON, J.   2
  ORIENTALE
    WILLIS MUSIC COMPANY   .40
CUNNINGHAM, M.
  AMERICAN FOLK SONGS
    COMPOSERS AUTOGRAPH PUBLICATIONS   5.28
CURCIO--ED   CURCIO
  CHRISTMAS CAROLS FOR LITTLE PIANISTS
    BOSTON MUSIC COMPANY   1.25
CURCIO--ED   CURCIO
  YESTERDAY'S PIANO SOLOS - BOOK 1
    BOSTON MUSIC COMPANY   2.00
CURCIO--ED   CURCIO
  YESTERDAY'S PIANO SOLOS - BOOK 2
    BOSTON MUSIC COMPANY   2.00
CURRIE, E.--ED   CURRIE, E.   HA
  VARIATIONS ON HYMN TUNES
    WILLIS MUSIC COMPANY   1.25
CZERNY   STEINER   2
  HARVEST IN BOHEMIA
    BELWIN-MILLS PUBLISHING CORPORATION   .60
CZERNY   STEINER
  JUNIOR CZERNY
    BELWIN-MILLS PUBLISHING CORPORATION   1969   1.75
D'HARDELOT   4
  BECAUSE, A FLAT MAJOR
    CENTURY MUSIC PUBLISHING COMPANY, INC.   4276   .40
DACRE   MENDEL, S.   1
  BICYCLE BUILT FOR TWO, A
    WILLIS MUSIC COMPANY   .40
DALLAPICCOLA   4-5
  DREI EPISODEN AUS DEM BALLETT 'MARSIA'
    BARENREITER VERLAG   CM 20869
DANFORD, A.   SCHAUM, J.   1
  BLUE GNU
    SCHAUM PUBLICATIONS, INC.   .50
DANKS   3
  SILVER THREADS AMONG THE GOLD
    CENTURY MUSIC PUBLISHING COMPANY, INC.   2618   .40
DAQUIN, C.   ECKSTEIN
  COUCOU, LE --RONDEAU--
    CARL FISCHER, INC.   S 316   .50
DARDENELLE, L.
  CHRISTMAS CHIMES
    WILLIS MUSIC COMPANY   .50
DARION *
  IMPOSSIBLE DREAM, THE -- FROM 'MAN OF LA MANCHA'
    SOUTHERN MUSIC COMPANY   1.25
DARION *   AGAY, D.
  IMPOSSIBLE DREAM, THE -- FROM 'MAN OF LA MANCHA'
    SOUTHERN MUSIC COMPANY   1.00

DASHER, J.
YULETIDE MEDLEY
WILLIS MUSIC COMPANY .50
DAVIES--ED. DAVIES
CAROLS FOR CHRISTMAS
SHAWNEE PRESS, INC. 1.00
DAVIS, J. R.--ED DAVIS, J. R.
GREAT THEMES MADE EASY FOR PIANO
WARNER BROTHERS PUBLISHERS 1.95
DAVIS, J. R.--ED DAVIS, J. R.
HARMS HITS THROUGH THE YEARS MADE EASY
WARNER BROTHERS PUBLISHERS 1.25
DAVIS, J. R.--ED DAVIS, J. R.
IRISH FAVORITES FOR PIANO
WARNER BROTHERS PUBLISHERS 1.50
DAVIS, J. R.--ED DAVIS, J. R.
PETER, PAUL AND MARY, HITS OF, MADE EASY FOR PIANO
WARNER BROTHERS PUBLISHERS PPM 24 1.50
DAVIS, J. GLOVER, D.
I'LL BE THERE
BELWIN-MILLS PUBLISHING CORPORATION .60
DAVIS, M.--ED DAVIS, M.
SINGING FINGERS
PRO-ART PUBLICATIONS, INC. 1302 1.50
DAVIS, M.
MARILYN K. DAVIS GROUP PIANO METHOD - GROUP ACTIVITIES AT THE
KEYBOARD, BK. 01
BOURNE COMPANY 1.25
DAVIS, M.
MARILYN K. DAVIS GROUP PIANO METHOD - GROUP ACTIVITIES AT THE
KEYBOARD, BK. 02
BOURNE COMPANY 1.25
DEBUSSY
AFTERNOON OF A FAUN
ASHLEY DEALERS SERVICE, INC. ES 1.00
DEBUSSY MITTLER 2B
AFTERNOON OF A FAUN
MUSICORD PUBLICATIONS, INC. .45
DEBUSSY
CLAIR DE LUNE
ASHLEY DEALERS SERVICE, INC. ES .95
DEBUSSY ECKSTEIN
CLAIR DE LUNE
CARL FISCHER, INC. P 3025 .50
DEBUSSY WATSON
CLAIR DE LUNE
CARL FISCHER, INC. RS 384 .50
DEBUSSY ZEPP 5
CLAIR DE LUNE
PRO-ART PUBLICATIONS, INC. 361 .75
DEBUSSY SCHAUM, J. 4
CLAIR DE LUNE
SCHAUM PUBLICATIONS, INC. .60
DEBUSSY DAVIS, J. R. FIRST YEAR
CLAIR DE LUNE
WARNER BROTHERS PUBLISHERS .75
DEBUSSY ANSON, G. 5
CLAIR DE LUNE
WILLIS MUSIC COMPANY .75
DEBUSSY 4
L'APRES-MIDI D'UN FAUNE
CENTURY MUSIC PUBLISHING COMPANY, INC. 3721 .40
DEE, M.
CHRISTMAS CAROLS
VOLKWEIN BROS. 00.75
DEFILIPPI, A.
FOLK MELODIES FOR PIANO
GENERAL MUSIC PUBLISHING COMPANY, INC. 2.00
DEGEN 2-3
WEIHNACHTSBUCH. MUSIK AUS 36 ALTEN WEIHNACHTSLIEDERN FUR
KLAVIER, BK. 1 - 7 ALTE WEIHNACHTSLIEDER UND 6 KRIPPENLIEDER
BARENREITER VERLAG SM 2101
DEGEN 2-3
WEIHNACHTSBUCH. MUSIK AUS 36 ALTEN WEIHNACHTSLIEDERN FUR
KLAVIER, BK. 2 - 6 WIEGENLIEDER, 8 HIRTENLIEDER
BARENREITER VERLAG
DEGEN 2-3
WEIHNACHTSBUCH. MUSIK AUS 36 ALTEN WEIHNACHTSLIEDERN FUR
KLAVIER, BK. 3 - 2 DREI KONIGE-LIEDER UND 7 WEIHNACHTS-CHORALE
BARENREITER VERLAG SM 2103
DELANNOY
CENDRILLON -- CINDERELLA -- BALLET
ASSOCIATED MUSIC PUBLISHERS, INC. ESC 6.00
DELANNOY
LE FOU DE LA DAME -- SARABANDE
HEUGEL ET CIE. 8.05
DELANNOY
LE MARCHAND DE LUNETTES
HEUGEL ET CIE. 3.25
DELANNOY
NOCES FANTASTIQUES, LES -- BALLET IN 2 ACTS
ASSOCIATED MUSIC PUBLISHERS, INC. ESC 12.00
DELIBES, L. BANTOCK, G.
COPPELIA, COMPLETE ILLUSTRATED
BELWIN-MILLS PUBLISHING CORPORATION 09468 3.00
DELIBES, L. BANTOCK, G.
COPPELIA, SELECTIONS FROM
BELWIN-MILLS PUBLISHING CORPORATION 09469 1.50
DELIBES, L. 4
COPPELIA, VALSE LENTE
CENTURY MUSIC PUBLISHING COMPANY, INC. 591 .40
DELIBES, L.
COPPELIA
HEUGEL ET CIE. 15.25
DELIBES, L.
LA SOURCE
HEUGEL ET CIE. 16.75
DELIBES, L. ROLFE, W. 2
NAILA WALTZ, EASY
CENTURY MUSIC PUBLISHING COMPANY, INC. 3547 .40
DELIBES, L. 4
PAS DES FLEURS, NAILA
CENTURY MUSIC PUBLISHING COMPANY, INC. 1514 .40
DELIBES, L. MENDEL, S. 2
PIZZICATI
WILLIS MUSIC COMPANY .40
DELIBES, L. 2
SYLVIA, PIZZICATO, EASY
CENTURY MUSIC PUBLISHING COMPANY, INC. 2142 .40
DELIBES, L. DEXGER, H.
SYLVIA BALLET
SAM FOX PUBLISHING COMPANY, INC. 1.00
DELIBES, L. 4
VALSE LENTE, COPPELIA
CENTURY MUSIC PUBLISHING COMPANY, INC. 591 .40
DELIBES, L. ROLFE, W. 2
VALSE LENTE, NAILA, EASY
CENTURY MUSIC PUBLISHING COMPANY, INC. 3547 .40

DELIUS, F. FENBY
AIR AND DANCE
BOOSEY AND HAWKES, INC. .60
DELIUS, F. PERRY
CALINDA, FROM 'KOANGA'
BOOSEY AND HAWKES, INC. 1.00
DELIUS, F. FENBY
IRMELIN PRELUDE
BOOSEY AND HAWKES, INC. 1.00
DELIUS, F.
SERENADE, FROM 'HASSAN'
BOOSEY AND HAWKES, INC. .50
DELIUS, F.
WALK TO THE PARADISE GARDEN, FROM 'A VILLAGE ROMEO AND JULIET'
BOOSEY AND HAWKES, INC. .60
DELLA CIAIA * ROSSI 3-4
I CLAVICEMBALISTI ITALIANI. 20 KOMPOSITIONEN
BARENREITER VERLAG CM 20092
DENZA WEYBRIGHT
FUNICULI-FUNICULA -- SIMP.
BELWIN-MILLS PUBLISHING CORPORATION 26015 .50
DENZA CLAUSETTI
FUNICULI-FUNICULA
FRANCO COLOMBO PUBLICATIONS 47171 .60
DENZA DEL MAGLIO
FUNICULI-FUNICULA
FRANCO COLOMBO PUBLICATIONS 124716 .60
DENZA DEL MAGLIO
SE
FRANCO COLOMBO PUBLICATIONS 128138 .50
DESREZ 7
ETOILE, POEME SYMPHONIQUE
ALPHONSE LEDUC
DESREZ 8
L'APPEL DU PRINTEMPS, SYMPHONIE
ALPHONSE LEDUC
DESSAUX 2
BIJOUX CHERIS, PETITE VALSE -- SIMPLIFIED VERSION
ALPHONSE LEDUC
DESSAUX 3
BUCEPHALE, PREMIER GALOP -- SIMPLIFIED VERSION
ALPHONSE LEDUC
DESSAUX 1
LE PETIT BAISER, VALSE MIGNONNE -- SIMPLIFIED VERSION
ALPHONSE LEDUC
DEUTSCH, L. 1
FOR SIGHT READING, VOL. 1
CENTURY MUSIC PUBLISHING COMPANY, INC. 1.25
DEUTSCH, L. 2-3
FOR SIGHT READING, VOL. 2
CENTURY MUSIC PUBLISHING COMPANY, INC. 1.50
DEUTSCH *
HI-LILI, HI-LO
THE BIG THREE MUSIC CORPORATION 00.95
DE CESARE
FRENCH GAME SONGS -- CHANTS DE JEUX FRANCAIS
BELWIN-MILLS PUBLISHING CORPORATION 1.00
DE CESARE
SONGS FOR THE FRENCH CLASS -- LES CHANSONS POUR LA CLASSE DE
FRANCAIS
BELWIN-MILLS PUBLISHING CORPORATION 1.00
DE CESARE
SONGS FOR THE GERMAN CLASS -- LIEDER FUR DIE DEUTSHE KLASSE
BELWIN-MILLS PUBLISHING CORPORATION 1.00
DE CESARE
SONGS FOR THE ITALIAN CLASS -- CANZONI PER LA CLASSE D'ITALIANO
BELWIN-MILLS PUBLISHING CORPORATION 1.00
DE CESARE
SONGS FOR THE SPANISH CLASS -- CANCIONES PARA LA CLASE DE ESPANO
BELWIN-MILLS PUBLISHING CORPORATION 1.00
DE LULLI, A. 1
CHOP STICKS
WILLIS MUSIC COMPANY .35
DE NARDIS DEL MAGLIO
SALTARELLO ABRUZZESE
FRANCO COLOMBO PUBLICATIONS 127758 .60
DE ROSE, P.
AMERICAN WALTZ
THE BIG THREE MUSIC CORPORATION 00.95
DE ROSE, P.
AUTUMN SERENADE
THE BIG THREE MUSIC CORPORATION 00.95
DE ROSE, P.
DEEP PURPLE
THE BIG THREE MUSIC CORPORATION 00.95
DE ROSE, P.
FOUNTAIN IN CENTRAL PARK
THE BIG THREE MUSIC CORPORATION 00.95
DE ROSE, P. SCHAUM, J. 2 1/2
HAVE YOU EVER BEEN LONELY
SCHAUM PUBLICATIONS, INC. .75
DE ROSE, P.
MOONLIGHT MOOD
THE BIG THREE MUSIC CORPORATION 00.95
DE ROSE, P.
MUSIC BOX IN BLUE
THE BIG THREE MUSIC CORPORATION 00.95
DE ROSE, P.
WHITE ORCHIDS
THE BIG THREE MUSIC CORPORATION 00.95
DE VITO, A.--ED. DE VITO, A.
CHRISTMAS SONGS
KENYON PUBLICATIONS 1.00
DE VITO, A.--ED. DE VITO, A.
COUNTRY WESTERN
KENYON PUBLICATIONS 1.00
DE VITO, A.--ED. DE VITO, A.
PATRIOTIC SONGS
PRO-ART PUBLICATIONS, INC. 683 .75
DE VITO, A.--ED. DE VITO, A.
POPULAR PIANO CLASSICS
KENYON PUBLICATIONS 1.25
DE VITO, A.
PEDRO DANCES
BOURNE COMPANY 1.00
DICAPUA ZEPP 4
MY LOVE FOR YOU
PRO-ART PUBLICATIONS, INC. 109 .50
DICAPUA 3
O, SOLE MIO
CENTURY MUSIC PUBLISHING COMPANY, INC. 1807 .40
DICAPUA 3
O, SOLE MIO
CENTURY MUSIC PUBLISHING COMPANY, INC. 3701 .40
DICAPUA ROGERS 2
O SOLE MIO, SIMPLIFIED
BELWIN-MILLS PUBLISHING CORPORATION 709 .60

DICAPUA   KALBERT   2
  O SOLE MIO
    BOSTON MUSIC COMPANY   .50
DICHIARI   JETSON, I. H.   2
  LA SPAGNOLA
    VOLKWEIN BROS.   .35
DIETRICH--ED.   DIETRICH   1
  LATERNE, LATERNE, SONNE, MOND UND STERNE. 23 VOLKSKINDERLIEDER
  IN GANZ LEICHTEN SATZEN
    BARENREITER VERLAG   BA 1003
DIETRICH--ED.   DIETRICH   2
  VOLKSLIEDBUCHLEIN
    BARENREITER VERLAG   BA 1499
DIETRICH--ED.   DIETRICH
  VOLKSLIEDBUCHLEIN
    BARENREITER VERLAG   BA 1499   3.00
DIETZ *   LEVINE
  LOUISIANA HAYRIDE
    WARNER BROTHERS PUBLISHERS   1.00
DILLER, A.--ED *   DILLER, A. *   E
  TUNES FROM MANY LANDS
    WILLIS MUSIC COMPANY   1.25
DILLER, A. *   GRADE 2
  DILLER-PAGE CAROL BOOK, THE
    G. SCHIRMER, INC.   1.00
DOFLEIN--ED.   DOFLEIN   2
  ZWANZIG DEUTSCHE VOLKSTANZE
    BARENREITER VERLAG   BA 1145
DOFLEIN--ED.   DOFLEIN
  ZWANZIG DEUTSCHE VOLKSTANZE
    BARENREITER VERLAG   BA 1145   1.75
DONIDA   HASTINGS
  AL DI LA
    WARNER BROTHERS PUBLISHERS   1.00
DONIDA   SAMPIETRO   FIRST YEAR
  AL DI LA
    WARNER BROTHERS PUBLISHERS   .75
DONIDA *   NEALE, J.   EASY
  AL DI LA
    WARNER BROTHERS PUBLISHERS   .75
DONIZETTI
  DON PASQUALE, OVERTURE
    FRANCO COLOMBO PUBLICATIONS   128623   1.00
DONIZETTI   CHIESA
  ELISIR D'AMORE, L', EASY FANTASIA
    FRANCO COLOMBO PUBLICATIONS   107496   .50
DONIZETTI
  ELISIR D'AMORE, L' - FURTIVA LAGRIMA, UNA
    FRANCO COLOMBO PUBLICATIONS   125429   .60
DONIZETTI   DEL MAGLIO
  ELISIR D'AMORE, L' - FURTIVA LAGRIMA, UNA
    FRANCO COLOMBO PUBLICATIONS   128146   .60
DONIZETTI   CHIESA
  FAVORITA, LA - EASY FANTASIA
    FRANCO COLOMBO PUBLICATIONS   107508   .50
DONIZETTI   CHIESA
  LINDA DI CHAMONIX - EASY FANTASIA
    FRANCO COLOMBO PUBLICATIONS   107504   .50
DONIZETTI   BOHM   3
  LUCIA, SEXTETTE
    CENTURY MUSIC PUBLISHING COMPANY, INC.   1183   .40
DONIZETTI *   REISER, V.   6
  LUCIA DI LAMMERMOOR, SEXTETTE
    CENTURY MUSIC PUBLISHING COMPANY, INC.   1860   .40
DONIZETTI   CHIESA
  LUCIA DI LAMMERMOOR - EASY FANTASIA
    FRANCO COLOMBO PUBLICATIONS   107495   .50
DONIZETTI   DEL MAGLIO
  LUCIA DI LAMMERMOOR - VERRANNO A TE AND TU CHE A DIO
    FRANCO COLOMBO PUBLICATIONS   128120   .50
DONIZETTI   LEYBACH, I.   5
  LUCIA DI LAMMERMOOR
    CENTURY MUSIC PUBLISHING COMPANY, INC.   1178   .40
DONIZETTI   KRUG   2
  LUCIA DI LAMMERMOOR
    CENTURY MUSIC PUBLISHING COMPANY, INC.   523   .40
DONIZETTI   2
  SEXTETTE, LUCIA, EASY
    CENTURY MUSIC PUBLISHING COMPANY, INC.   2512   .40
DONIZETTI   BOHM   3
  SEXTETTE, LUCIA
    CENTURY MUSIC PUBLISHING COMPANY, INC.   1183   .40
DONIZETTI   JESTON, I. H.   4
  SEXTET -- LUCIA DI LAMMERMOOR
    VOLKWEIN BROS.   .35
DOWLAND, R.   HUNT   3-4
  VARIETIE OF LUTE LESSONS - 1610. LAUTENTABULATUR FUR KLAVIER
    SCHOTT   10310   5.50
DRAESEL
  NOW HYMNS FOR YOUNG PEOPLE
    EDWARD B. MARKS MUSIC CORPORATION   01.50
DRAKE *   SCHAUM, J.   2 1/2
  I BELIEVE
    SCHAUM PUBLICATIONS, INC.   .75
DRATHS--ED   DRATHS   1
  MORGEN KOMMT DER WEIHNACHTSMANN
    SCHOTT   5325   2.25
DRATHS--ED   DRATHS   2
  O WUNDER, WAS WILL DAS BEDEUTEN
    SCHOTT   5700   2.25
DRESSER   ZEPP   2-3
  ON THE BANKS OF THE WABASH
    PRO-ART PUBLICATIONS, INC.   230   .50
DRIGO, R.   WEYBRIGHT   2
  DRIGO SERENADE
    BELWIN-MILLS PUBLISHING CORPORATION   .60
DRIGO, R.   2-3
  HARLEQUIN SERENADE, EASY
    CENTURY MUSIC PUBLISHING COMPANY, INC.   2468   .40
DRIGO, R.   GROOMS   2
  MILLIONS OF HARLEQUIN, EASY
    CENTURY MUSIC PUBLISHING COMPANY, INC.   2468   .40
DRIGO, R.   3
  VALSE BLUETTE, AIR DE BALLET
    CENTURY MUSIC PUBLISHING COMPANY, INC.   2002   .40
DRIGO, R.   THOMPSON, J.   5
  VALSE BLUETTE
    WILLIS MUSIC COMPANY   .50
DUCLOS, P.   DESCOMBEY, M.
  LE RENDEZ-VOUS BALLET
    EDITIONS MUSICALES TRANSATLANTIQUES   2.80
DUCLOS, P.
  LE RENDEZVOUS
    EDITIONS MUSICALES TRANSATLANTIQUES   2.80
DUKAS, P.   4
  SORCERER'S APPRENTICE
    CENTURY MUSIC PUBLISHING COMPANY, INC.   3799   .40

DUKE, V.
  NEW YORK NOCTURNE
    THE BIG THREE MUSIC CORPORATION   00.95
DUKE   WHITNEY
  APRIL IN PARIS
    WARNER BROTHERS PUBLISHERS   1.00
DUKE   RICHTER   FIRST YEAR
  APRIL IN PARIS
    WARNER BROTHERS PUBLISHERS   .75
DUKE   WHITNEY
  AUTUMN IN NEW YORK
    WARNER BROTHERS PUBLISHERS   1.00
DUNGAN   GORE, G.
  BLUE GRAPES
    BELWIN-MILLS PUBLISHING CORPORATION   .60
DUNGAN   GORE, G.
  CARROT TALKS, THE
    BELWIN-MILLS PUBLISHING CORPORATION   .60
DUNGAN   GORE, G.
  GROWING PEANUTS
    BELWIN-MILLS PUBLISHING CORPORATION   .60
DUNGAN   GORE, G.
  STRAWBERRY TALKS, THE
    BELWIN-MILLS PUBLISHING CORPORATION   .60
DUNGAN   GORE, G.
  THREE FAMOUS BEARS
    BELWIN-MILLS PUBLISHING CORPORATION   .60
DUNGAN   GORE, G.
  VITAMINS PLUS
    BELWIN-MILLS PUBLISHING CORPORATION   .60
DUNYON   SCHAUM, J.   1
  LEGER LINE CIRCUS
    SCHAUM PUBLICATIONS, INC.   .50
DUPONT, J.
  CONCERT, POUR PIANO ET ORCHESTRE, OP. 2
    ALPHONSE LEDUC
DURAND, A.   3
  VALSE, NO. 02, EASY
    CENTURY MUSIC PUBLISHING COMPANY, INC.   2520   .40
DUROCHER, L.   SCHAUM, J.   1 1/2
  ABOMINABLE SNOWMAN
    SCHAUM PUBLICATIONS, INC.   .50
DUTILLEUX
  LOUP, LE -- BALLET --
    FRANCO COLOMBO PUBLICATIONS   R1299   5.25
DVORAK   POKORNY   3-4
  BERUHMTE MELODIEN
    BARENREITER VERLAG   AP 562
DVORAK   LECHNER   2-3
  HUMORESKE OP. 101 NO. 7
    SCHOTT   03694   .75
DVORAK   POKORNY
  HUMORESQUE, OP. 101, NO. 7
    ARTIA   .50
DVORAK   DEL MAGLIO
  HUMORESQUE, OP. 101, NO. 7
    FRANCO COLOMBO PUBLICATIONS   129079   .60
DVORAK   SCHAUM, J.   4 1/2
  HUMORESQUE
    SCHAUM PUBLICATIONS, INC.   .60
DVORAK   3
  LARGO -- NEVER MORE TO ROAM --
    CENTURY MUSIC PUBLISHING COMPANY, INC.   3624   .40
DVORAK   COWDREY   3
  LARGO FROM THE 'NEW WORLD SYMPHONY'
    BOSTON MUSIC COMPANY   .50
DVORAK   STEINER   1
  LARGO FROM THE 'NEW WORLD SYMPHONY'
    BELWIN-MILLS PUBLISHING CORPORATION   .60
DVORAK   WEYBRIGHT   1 1/2
  LARGO FROM THE 'NEW WORLD SYMPHONY'
    BELWIN-MILLS PUBLISHING CORPORATION   .60
DVORAK   6
  LARGO FROM THE NEW WORLD SYMPHONY
    CENTURY MUSIC PUBLISHING COMPANY, INC.   2198   .40
DVORAK   ROLFE, W.   2
  NEW WORLD SYMPHONY, LARGO, EASY
    CENTURY MUSIC PUBLISHING COMPANY, INC.   3392   .40
DVORAK   6
  NEW WORLD SYMPHONY, LARGO
    CENTURY MUSIC PUBLISHING COMPANY, INC.   2198   .40
DVORAK   SOLC   3-4
  SINFONIE NO. 08 IN G, OP. 88
    BARENREITER VERLAG   AP 286
DVORAK   LASKA   2-3
  SINFONIE NO. 09 IN E MINOR, OP. 95, 'AUS DER NEUEN WELT' --
  LARGO --
    BARENREITER VERLAG   AP 570
DVORAK   SOLC   3
  SINFONIE NO. 09 IN E MINOR, OP. 95, 'AUS DER NEUEN WELT'
    BARENREITER VERLAG   AP 577
DVORAK   SOLC
  SLAVONIC DANCES, OP. 46
    ARTIA   2.50
DVORAK   SOLC
  SLAVONIC DANCES, OP. 72
    ARTIA   2.50
DVORAK   2
  SLAVONIC DANCE NO. 6, EASY
    CENTURY MUSIC PUBLISHING COMPANY, INC.   3978   .40
DVORAK   3
  SONGS MY MOTHER TAUGHT ME
    CENTURY MUSIC PUBLISHING COMPANY, INC.   2499   .40
DVORAK   3
  SONGS MY MOTHER TAUGHT ME
    CENTURY MUSIC PUBLISHING COMPANY, INC.   3477   .40
DVORAK
  SYMPHONY NO. 09 IN E MINOR, OP. 95 FROM 'THE NEW WORLD'
    ARTIA   1.75
DYKES   WEYBRIGHT   2
  HOLY, HOLY, HOLY
    BELWIN-MILLS PUBLISHING CORPORATION   .60
DYLAN   NEALE, J.   EASY
  BLOWIN' IN THE WIND
    WARNER BROTHERS PUBLISHERS   .75
DYLAN   NEALE, J.
  INSTANT PICTURE CHORD PIANO NO. 2, BOB DYLAN
    WARNER BROTHERS PUBLISHERS   1.95
EARL   SCHAUM, J.   1 1/2
  BEAUTIFUL OHIO
    SCHAUM PUBLICATIONS, INC.   .75
ECKARD, W.--ED   ECKARD, W.
  GIRLS' FAVORITE SOLO ALBUM
    THEODORE PRESSER COMPANY   1.75
ECKHARDT, F.--ED   ECKHARDT, F.   3
  HEAV'N, HEAV'N
    CENTURY MUSIC PUBLISHING COMPANY, INC.   3786   .40

ECKSTEIN--ARR.   ECKSTEIN
  DOWN IN THE VALLEY
    CARL FISCHER, INC.   P 2857   .50
EDWARDS, C.   ZEPP   2
  IN MY MERRY OLDSMOBILE
    PRO-ART PUBLICATIONS, INC.   380   .50
EDWARDS, G.   SCHAUM, J.   1
  IN MY MERRY OLDSMOBILE
    SCHAUM PUBLICATIONS, INC.   .50
EDWARDS, G.   SCHAUM, J.   1
  SCHOOL DAYS
    SCHAUM PUBLICATIONS, INC.   .75
EDWARDS, J.
  JONATHAN EDWARDS
    THE BIG THREE MUSIC CORPORATION   04.95
EHMANN--ED.   EHMANN   2-3
  ALTE LIEDSATZE - 19 VOLKSLIEDSATZE AUS TABULATURBUCHERN DES 16.
  JAHRH.
    BARENREITER VERLAG   BA 1287
EINEM, G.
  PRINZESSIN TURANDOT, OP. 1 -- BALLET IN 2 TABLEAUX
    ASSOCIATED MUSIC PUBLISHERS, INC.   BOT   7.50
EINEM, G.
  RONDO VOM GOLDENEN KALB, OP. 13 -- BALLET IN 3 SCENES
    ASSOCIATED MUSIC PUBLISHERS, INC.   BOT   6.00
ELGAR, E.   VALBER
  LAND OF HOPE AND GLORY
    BOOSEY AND HAWKES, INC.   .60
ELGAR, E.   WATTERS
  LAND OF HOPE AND GLORY
    BOOSEY AND HAWKES, INC.   .60
ELGAR, E.   4
  LOVE'S GREETING
    CENTURY MUSIC PUBLISHING COMPANY, INC.   1229   .40
ELGAR, E.   ECKSTEIN
  POMP AND CIRCUMSTANCE --THEME--
    CARL FISCHER, INC.   P 2924   .50
ELGAR, E.   ZEPP   4
  POMP AND CIRCUMSTANCE - FULL CHORD VERSION
    PRO-ART PUBLICATIONS, INC.   149   .50
ELGAR, E.   ZEPP   3
  POMP AND CIRCUMSTANCE - SMALL CHORD VERSION
    PRO-ART PUBLICATIONS, INC.   148   .50
ELGAR, E.   BELLAIRS
  POMP AND CIRCUMSTANCE MARCH NO. 1 IN D
    BOOSEY AND HAWKES, INC.   .75
ELGAR, E.   SCHMID
  POMP AND CIRCUMSTANCE MARCH NO. 1 IN D
    BOOSEY AND HAWKES, INC.   .75
ELGAR, E.   SCHMID
  POMP AND CIRCUMSTANCE MARCH NO. 4 IN G
    BOOSEY AND HAWKES, INC.   1.25
ELGAR, E.   ZEPP   2
  POMP AND CIRCUMSTANCE
    PRO-ART PUBLICATIONS, INC.   147   .50
ELGAR, E.   THOMPSON, J.   3
  POMP AND CIRCUMSTANCE
    WILLIS MUSIC COMPANY   .50
ELGAR, E.   WEYBRIGHT   1
  SALUT D'AMOUR -- LOVE'S GREETING
    BELWIN-MILLS PUBLISHING CORPORATION   .60
ELGAR, E.
  VARIATIONS, OP. 36, 'ENIGMA'
    NOVELLO AND COMPANY, LTD.   10.0042.10 3.25
ELISCU *
  WITHOUT A SONG
    THE BIG THREE MUSIC CORPORATION   00.95
ELLINGTON
  BIRD OF PARADISE
    THE BIG THREE MUSIC CORPORATION   00.95
ELLINGTON   NEVIN
  DUKE ELLINGTON'S BEST
    BELWIN-MILLS PUBLISHING CORPORATION   2.00
ELLINGTON   MOSSMAN, R.
  MOOD INDIGO, SIMP.
    BELWIN-MILLS PUBLISHING CORPORATION   .60
ELLIS, E.   PAULL   ADVANCED
  NAPOLEON'S LAST CHARGE
    SHAWNEE PRESS, INC.   HB-61   .60
EMERSON--ED   EMERSON
  MASTERS AND THEIR MELODIES
    WILLIS MUSIC COMPANY   1.00
EMMETT   ARMOUR   2
  DIXIE
    CENTURY MUSIC PUBLISHING COMPANY, INC.   3469   .40
EMMETT   ZEPP   2-3
  DIXIE
    PRO-ART PUBLICATIONS, INC.   197   .50
ENGEL--ED *   ENGEL *
  MY HANUKKAH SONG BOOK
    WILLIS MUSIC COMPANY   1.50
ENGEL, S.--ARR.   ENGEL, S.   ADVANCED
  GREAT HYMNS
    SCREEN GEMS - COLUMBIA PUBLICATIONS   F0260P1   3.50
ENGEL, S.--ARR.   ENGEL, S.   ADVANCED
  TWENTY-FOUR CARAT GOLD
    SCREEN GEMS - COLUMBIA PUBLICATIONS   F0200P1   3.95
ENGELMANN, H. U.   CARLETON, B.   1 1/2
  MELODY OF LOVE
    THEODORE PRESSER COMPANY   .50
ENGELMANN, H. U.   SINGER   5
  MELODY OF LOVE
    THEODORE PRESSER COMPANY   .60
ENGELMANN, H. U.   RICHTER   FIRST YEAR
  MELODY OF LOVE
    WARNER BROTHERS PUBLISHERS   .75
ENGELMANN, H. U.   BURNAM   2
  MELODY OF LOVE
    WILLIS MUSIC COMPANY   .40
ENGELMANN, H. U.
  NIGHT BEFORE CHRISTMAS, THE
    BOSTON MUSIC COMPANY   .50
ENGLEMANN, H. U.   2
  MELODY OF LOVE - CARY
    CENTURY MUSIC PUBLISHING COMPANY, INC.   4289   .40
EPPEL *   SCHAUM, J.
  MISSOURI WALTZ
    BELWIN-MILLS PUBLISHING CORPORATION   .60
ERBSE
  RUTH, OP. 16 -- BALLET IN 2 ACTS
    ASSOCIATED MUSIC PUBLISHERS, INC.   BOT   9.00
ERB
  VERY EASIEST FAVORITE SONGS
    BOSTON MUSIC COMPANY   1.25
ETTS, M.--ED *   ETTS, M. *
  CLASSICS MADE EASY, BK. 1
    CENTURY MUSIC PUBLISHING COMPANY, INC.   1.25

EVANS   KLICKMANN
  LADY OF SPAIN -- SIMPLIFIED
    SOUTHERN MUSIC COMPANY   .50
FABER   WEYBRIGHT   2
  FAITH OF OUR FATHERS, A HYMN
    BELWIN-MILLS PUBLISHING CORPORATION   .60
FAHNESTOCK   SCHAUM, J.   2
  NIGHT FLIGHT
    SCHAUM PUBLICATIONS, INC.   .50
FAIN *
  APRIL LOVE
    THE BIG THREE MUSIC CORPORATION   00.95
FAIN *
  LOVE IS A MANY-SPLENDORED THING
    THE BIG THREE MUSIC CORPORATION   00.95
FAIN   HASTINGS
  SECRET LOVE
    WARNER BROTHERS PUBLISHERS   1.00
FAIRCHILD   3
  IRISH MEDLEY
    VOLKWEIN BROS.   00.50
FAIRCHILD   3
  IRISH MEDLEY
    VOLKWEIN BROS.   .25
FAITH *
  SWEDISH RHAPSODY
    TRO SONGWAYS SERVICE, INC.   2054
FANENGHI
  EIGHTEEN FAMOUS ARIAS -- TESORO DEL MELODRAMMA --
    FRANCO COLOMBO PUBLICATIONS   127652   1.50
FANENGHI
  MOST BEAUTIFUL LOVE SONGS, THE
    FRANCO COLOMBO PUBLICATIONS   127615   1.50
FAURE, G.   FREEMAN   4
  PALMS, THE
    CENTURY MUSIC PUBLISHING COMPANY, INC.   594   .40
FAURE, J.   LEYBACH   5
  PALMS, THE, TRANS.
    CENTURY MUSIC PUBLISHING COMPANY, INC.   526   .40
FAURE, J.   FREEMAN   4
  PALMS, THE, VAR.
    CENTURY MUSIC PUBLISHING COMPANY, INC.   594   .40
FAWCETT   WEYBRIGHT   1 1/2
  BLEST BE THE TIE THAT BINDS -- HYMN
    BELWIN-MILLS PUBLISHING CORPORATION   .60
FEARIS, J. S.   STEINER   1
  BEAUTIFUL ISLE OF SOMEWHERE
    BELWIN-MILLS PUBLISHING CORPORATION   .60
FEATHER   HYMAN, D.
  HI FI SUITE
    BELWIN-MILLS PUBLISHING CORPORATION   2.00
FELBER, R.--ED   FELBER, R.   4
  SLOWAKISCHE TANZE
    SCHOTT   1285   2.00
FERNANDEZ   DEL MAGLIO
  CIELITO LINDO
    FRANCO COLOMBO PUBLICATIONS   129115   .60
FIBICH, Z.   OSTRAL   3
  AM ABEND, OP. 39
    BARENREITER VERLAG   AP 585A
FIBICH, Z.   DEL MAGLIO
  POEM, OP. 41, NO. 14
    FRANCO COLOMBO PUBLICATIONS   128847   .60
FIBICH, Z.   2-3
  POEM -- ERLEICHTERT -- UND FRUHLING UND JUGEND
    BARENREITER VERLAG   AP 591
FICHANDLER, W.   3
  NOCTURNE FROM 'SECOND STRING QUARTET'
    BELWIN-MILLS PUBLISHING CORPORATION   .60
FICHTER   MCWHERTOR   2
  CAUSE IT'S CHRISTMAS
    VOLKWEIN BROS.   .50
FIELD, J.   DEL MAGLIO
  NOCTURNE NO. 01 IN E FLAT
    FRANCO COLOMBO PUBLICATIONS   129080   .50
FISHER--ED   FISHER   M
  BIRDS
    C. F. PETERS CORPORATION   H497   1.50
FLOTOW   KRUG   2
  MARTHA, EASY TRANSCRIPTION
    CENTURY MUSIC PUBLISHING COMPANY, INC.   524   .40
FLOTOW   DORN   4
  MARTHA, FANTASIE, OP. 39
    CENTURY MUSIC PUBLISHING COMPANY, INC.   306   .40
FOERSTER   SOLC   3
  ZWEI TANZE AUS DER OPER 'EVA' -- SOUSEDSKA/POLKA -- FUR KLAVIER
  BEARBEITET
    BARENREITER VERLAG   AP 1719
FONRAT
  TRADITIONAL DANCES OF SPAIN
    FRANCO COLOMBO PUBLICATIONS   BA9330   2.50
FORD, T. E.
  TREASURY OF INSPIRATIONAL SONGS
    POINTER PUBLICATIONS   4.95
FOSTER   SCHIEFELBEIN, F. 2
  BEAUTIFUL DREAMER
    VOLKWEIN BROS.   .25
FOSTER   SCHIEFELBEIN, F. 2
  COME WHERE MY LOVE LIES DREAMING
    VOLKWEIN BROS.   .25
FOSTER   WEYBRIGHT   1
  DE CAMPTOWN RACES
    BELWIN-MILLS PUBLISHING CORPORATION   .60
FOSTER   MALOOF
  FOSTER MELODIES FOR YOUNG FOLKS
    EDWARD B. MARKS MUSIC CORPORATION   01.00
FOSTER   SCHIEFELBEIN, F. 2
  GENTLE ANNIE
    VOLKWEIN BROS.   .25
FOSTER   WEYBRIGHT   2
  GLENDY BURKE, THE
    BELWIN-MILLS PUBLISHING CORPORATION   .60
FOSTER   SCHIEFELBEIN, F. 2
  HARD TIMES COME AGAIN NO MORE
    VOLKWEIN BROS.   .25
FOSTER   WEYBRIGHT   2
  JEANNIE WITH THE LIGHT BROWN HAIR
    BELWIN-MILLS PUBLISHING CORPORATION   .60
FOSTER   BERLIN, B.
  JEANNIE WITH THE LIGHT BROWN HAIR
    FREDERICK HARRIS MUSIC COMPANY   .30
FOSTER   ZEPP   4
  JEANNIE WITH THE LIGHT BROWN HAIR
    PRO-ART PUBLICATIONS, INC.   152   .50
FOSTER   BERLIN, B.
  MASSA'S IN DE COLD, COLD GROUND
    FREDERICK HARRIS MUSIC COMPANY   .30

FOSTER   SCHIEFELBEIN, F.   2
MASSA'S IN THE COLD, COLD GROUND
VOLKWEIN BROS.   .25

FOSTER   SCHIEFELBEIN, F.   2
MY OLD KENTUCKY HOME
VOLKWEIN BROS.   .25

FOSTER   SPENCER, J.   2
MY OLD KENTUCKY HOME
VOLKWEIN BROS.   .25

FOSTER   ARMOUR   1
OH SUSANNA
CENTURY MUSIC PUBLISHING COMPANY, INC.   3464   .40

FOSTER   SCHIEFELBEIN, F.   2
OH SUSANNA
VOLKWEIN BROS.   .25

FOSTER   SCHIEFELBEIN, F.   2
OLD BLACK JOE
VOLKWEIN BROS.   .25

FOSTER   SPENCER, J.   1
OLD BLACK JOE
VOLKWEIN BROS.   .25

FOSTER   SCHIEFELBEIN, F.   2
OLD DOG TRAY
VOLKWEIN BROS.   .25

FOSTER   ARMOUR   1
OLD FOLKS AT HOME
CENTURY MUSIC PUBLISHING COMPANY, INC.   3465   .40

FOSTER   MEACHAM, F.   4
OLD FOLKS AT HOME
CENTURY MUSIC PUBLISHING COMPANY, INC.   1046   .40

FOSTER   SCHIEFELBEIN, F.   2
OLD FOLKS AT HOME
VOLKWEIN BROS.   .25

FOSTER   SPENCER, J.   2
OLD FOLKS AT HOME
VOLKWEIN BROS.   .25

FOSTER   SCHAUM, J.   1
STEPHEN FOSTER FAVORITES
SCHAUM PUBLICATIONS, INC.   1.25

FOSTER   ZEPP   3-4
SWANEE MOOD
PRO-ART PUBLICATIONS, INC.   151   .50

FOSTER   SCHIEFELBEIN, F.   2
UNCLE NED
VOLKWEIN BROS.   00.25

FOSTER   MEACHAM, F.   4
WAY DOWN UPON THE SWANEE RIVER
CENTURY MUSIC PUBLISHING COMPANY, INC.   1046   .40

FOSTER   SCHIEFELBEIN, F.   2
WILLIE WE HAVE MISSED YOU
VOLKWEIN BROS.   00.25

FRANCAIX, J.
LA DAME DANS LA LUNE
EDITIONS MUSICALES TRANSATLANTIQUES   8.00

FRANCAIX *
LADY L - THEME
THE BIG THREE MUSIC CORPORATION   00.95

FRANCISQUE, A.
LE TRESOR D'ORPHEE
BROUDE BROTHERS LTD.   09.00

FRANCK, C.   BAUER
PRELUDE, FUGUE AND VARIATIONS
ELKAN-VOGEL, INC.   3.00

FRANCK, C.   DUMM
RECITAL REFRESHER SERIES -- THE DOLL'S COMPLAINT
BELWIN-MILLS PUBLISHING CORPORATION   26116   .60

FRANCK, C.   JEMAIN
REDEMPTION - MORCEAU SYMPHONIQUE
HEUGEL ET CIE.   2.40

FRANCK, C.   SCHAUM, J.   4 1/2
SYMPHONIC RHAPSODY
SCHAUM PUBLICATIONS, INC.   .50

FRANCK, C.   M
SYMPHONIC VARIATIONS
C. F. PETERS CORPORATION   3741A   1.25

FRANCK, C.   3
THEME FROM SYMPHONY IN D MINOR
CENTURY MUSIC PUBLISHING COMPANY, INC.   3612   .40

FRANGIPANE--ED   2
WHEN THE SAINTS GO MARCHING
CENTURY MUSIC PUBLISHING COMPANY, INC.   4299   .40

FRANK, R.
PIANO HYMN CLASSICS NO. 1
LILLENAS PUBLISHING COMPANY   MB-146   2.50

FRANK, R.
PIANO HYMN CLASSICS NO. 2
LILLENAS PUBLISHING COMPANY   MB-147   2.50

FRANTZ, C.   SCHAUM, J.   1
TUMBLEWEED TRAIL
SCHAUM PUBLICATIONS, INC.   .60

FRANTZEN   WEYBRIGHT   2
COLLEGE LIFE, MARCH
BELWIN-MILLS PUBLISHING CORPORATION   .60

FREDRICH, F.--ED   FREDRICH, F.
FIRST BOOK OF HYMNS AND CAROLS, A
WILLIS MUSIC COMPANY   1.00

FREEMAN--ED.   FREEMAN   4
LEAD, KINDLY LIGHT
CENTURY MUSIC PUBLISHING COMPANY, INC.   637   .40

FREEMAN--ED.   FREEMAN   3
OLD KENTUCKY HOME
CENTURY MUSIC PUBLISHING COMPANY, INC.   835   .40

FREEMAN   FREEMAN   4
CALVARY, TRANSCRIPTION
CENTURY MUSIC PUBLISHING COMPANY, INC.   683   .40

FREEMAN   FREEMAN   4
EASTER HYMN, TRANS.
CENTURY MUSIC PUBLISHING COMPANY, INC.   623   .40

FREEMAN   3
KATHLEEN MAVOURNEEN, TRANS.
CENTURY MUSIC PUBLISHING COMPANY, INC.   809   .40

FREEMAN   3
MY OLD KENTUCKY HOME
CENTURY MUSIC PUBLISHING COMPANY, INC.   835   .40

FREEMAN   4
NEARER, MY GOD, TO THEE
CENTURY MUSIC PUBLISHING COMPANY, INC.   646   .40

FRESCOBALDI   PICCIOLI
COMPOSITIONS -- ORGAN --
FRANCO COLOMBO PUBLICATIONS   BON.1835   3.00

FRESCOBALDI   RESPIGHI
PASSACAGLIA -- ORGAN --
FRANCO COLOMBO PUBLICATIONS   117143   .90

FRESCOBALDI   RESPIGHI
PRELUDE AND FUGUE IN G MINOR -- ORGAN --
FRANCO COLOMBO PUBLICATIONS   117144   .75

FRESCOBALDI   BRUGNOLI
TOCCATA AND FUGUE IN A MINOR -- ORGAN --
FRANCO COLOMBO PUBLICATIONS   ER413   1.00

FRESCOBALDI   RESPIGHI
TOCCATA AND FUGUE IN A MINOR -- ORGAN --
FRANCO COLOMBO PUBLICATIONS   117145   1.00

FRIEDMAN   GARTNER
SIX VIENNESE DANCES
UNIVERSAL EDITION   8585   3.65

FRIEDMAN   GARTNER
VIENNESE DANCE, NO. 4
UNIVERSAL EDITION   8312   1.30

FRIEDMAN   GARTNER
VIENNESE DANCE, NO. 5
UNIVERSAL EDITION   8313   1.30

FRIEDMAN   GARTNER
VIENNESE DANCE, NO. 6
UNIVERSAL EDITION   9904   1.30

FRIML, R.   MOKREJS
INDIAN LOVE CALL
WARNER BROTHERS PUBLISHERS   1.00

FRIML, R.   WHITNEY
INDIAN LOVE CALL
WARNER BROTHERS PUBLISHERS   1.00

FRIML, R.   RIEGGER
ROSE MARIE
WARNER BROTHERS PUBLISHERS   1.00

FRONTIERE, D.
HANG 'EM HIGH
THE BIG THREE MUSIC CORPORATION   00.95

FRONTIERE, D.
LA CHAMADE
THE BIG THREE MUSIC CORPORATION   00.95

FRONTIERE, D.
TWELVE O'CLOCK HIGH - THEME
THE BIG THREE MUSIC CORPORATION   00.95

FRONTINI   MARTIN
LITTLE MUSICIANS
BOOSEY AND HAWKES, INC.   .60

FUERST, P. W.
DORIAN GRAY -- BALLET IN 6 SCENES
ASSOCIATED MUSIC PUBLISHERS, INC.   DOB   10.00

GABRIEL, M.   2
GOLDEN WEDDING, EASY
CENTURY MUSIC PUBLISHING COMPANY, INC.   2596   .40

GABSCHUSS--ED   GABSCHUSS
KINDERLIEDER UND VOLKSLIEDER FUR DEN SYSTHEMATISCHEN UNTERRICHT
AM KLAVIER
SCHOTT   6150

GAIL   RICHTER
FOR MY DOLLY
BELWIN-MILLS PUBLISHING CORPORATION   .60

GAIL   RICHTER
SCHOOL BAND, THE
BELWIN-MILLS PUBLISHING CORPORATION   .60

GAITO
CIUDAD DE LAS PUERTAS DE ORO, LA -- BALLET, WITH CHORUS --
FRANCO COLOMBO PUBLICATIONS   BA9240   3.25

GALUPPI   GALLON, N.
SONATE EN RE
ELKAN-VOGEL, INC.   CON   1.75

GAMBETTI   3
ROYAL MARCH OF ITALY
CENTURY MUSIC PUBLISHING COMPANY, INC.   1677   .40

GANNE   WEYBRIGHT   3 1/2
LA CZARINA -- MAZURKA
BELWIN-MILLS PUBLISHING CORPORATION   .60

GANNE   2
LA CZARINE, MAZURKA, EASY
CENTURY MUSIC PUBLISHING COMPANY, INC.   2138   .40

GANNE   4
RUSSIAN MARCH
CENTURY MUSIC PUBLISHING COMPANY, INC.   1938   .40

GARLAND   HARING
IN THE MOOD
SHAPIRO, BERNSTEIN ORGANIZATION   .95

GARLAND   SCHAUM, J.   2
IN THE MOOD
SCHAUM PUBLICATIONS, INC.   .75

GARVELMANN, D.--ED.   GARVELMANN, D.
THIRTEEN TRANSCRIPTIONS FOR PIANO SOLO OF CHOPIN'S WALTZ IN D
FLAT, OP. 64 NO. 1
MUSIC TREASURE PUBLICATIONS   5.00

GAUTIER, L.   ROLFE, W.   2
SECRET, THE, EASY
CENTURY MUSIC PUBLISHING COMPANY, INC.   3364   .40

GAYNOR   BLAKE, D. G.
THIRTY RHYTHMIC PANTOMIMES
THEODORE PRESSER COMPANY   1.50

GAY *   E-M
BEGGAR'S OPERA, ABRIDGED.
C. F. PETERS CORPORATION   H1728   1.50

GEIBEL *   ZEPP   2-3
KENTUCKY BABE
PRO-ART PUBLICATIONS, INC.   195   .50

GEISSLER
PIGMENT -- BALLET IN 5 TABLEAUX
ASSOCIATED MUSIC PUBLISHERS, INC.   BRH   10.00

GELLAR *   NEVIN
ABERGAVENNY
BELWIN-MILLS PUBLISHING CORPORATION   .60

GERIG, R.--ED   GERIG, R.
PIANO PRELUDES ON HYMNS AND CHORALES
HOPE PUBLISHING COMPANY   3.00

GERSHWIN   WHITNEY
AMERICAN IN PARIS, AN - IN MINIATURE
WARNER BROTHERS PUBLISHERS   1.50

GERSHWIN   DALY
AMERICAN IN PARIS, AN
WARNER BROTHERS PUBLISHERS   4.00

GERSHWIN   LEVINE
EMBRACEABLE YOU
WARNER BROTHERS PUBLISHERS   1.00

GERSHWIN   WALTER
EMBRACEABLE YOU
WARNER BROTHERS PUBLISHERS   1.00

GERSHWIN   RICHTER   FIRST YEAR
EMBRACEABLE YOU
WARNER BROTHERS PUBLISHERS   .75

GERSHWIN   STONE
FASCINATING RHYTHM
WARNER BROTHERS PUBLISHERS   1.00

GERSHWIN
GERSHWIN AT THE KEYBOARD
WARNER BROTHERS PUBLISHERS   2.50

GERSHWIN   LEVINE
  I GOT RHYTHM
        WARNER BROTHERS PUBLISHERS   1.00
GERSHWIN   LEVINE
  LIZA
        WARNER BROTHERS PUBLISHERS   1.00
GERSHWIN   LEVINE
  MAN I LOVE, THE
        WARNER BROTHERS PUBLISHERS   1.00
GERSHWIN   GRAINGER, P.
  MAN I LOVE, THE
        WARNER BROTHERS PUBLISHERS   1.00
GERSHWIN   RICHTER   FIRST YEAR
  MAN I LOVE, THE
        WARNER BROTHERS PUBLISHERS   .75
GERSHWIN   LEVINE
  OH, LADY BE GOOD
        WARNER BROTHERS PUBLISHERS   1.00
GERSHWIN   RICHTER   FIRST YEAR
  SOMEONE TO WATCH OVER ME
        WARNER BROTHERS PUBLISHERS   .75
GERSHWIN   LEVINE
  SOMEONE TO WATCH OVER ME
        WARNER BROTHERS PUBLISHERS   1.00
GERSHWIN   WHITNEY
  SOMEONE TO WATCH OVER ME
        WARNER BROTHERS PUBLISHERS   1.00
GERSHWIN   LEVINE
  STRIKE UP THE BAND
        WARNER BROTHERS PUBLISHERS   1.00
GERSHWIN   CHAPLIN
  TWO WALTZES IN C
        WARNER BROTHERS PUBLISHERS   1.50
GEST, E.   FROST
  SIX SONATINAS FOR PIANO
        BELWIN-MILLS PUBLISHING CORPORATION   1.50
GILBERT AND SULLIVAN   STEINER   1
  PIRATE KING, THE
        BELWIN-MILLS PUBLISHING CORPORATION   .60
GILBERT *   STEINER   2
  I'VE GOT A LITTLE LIST
        BELWIN-MILLS PUBLISHING CORPORATION   .60
GILLOCK--ED   GILLOCK   AE
  SOLO REPERTOIRE FOR THE YOUNG PIANIST, BK. 1
        WILLIS MUSIC COMPANY   1.50
GILLOCK--ED   GILLOCK   EI
  SOLO REPERTOIRE FOR THE YOUNG PIANIST, BK. 1
        WILLIS MUSIC COMPANY   1.25
GILLOCK--ED   GILLOCK   AE
  SOLO REPERTOIRE FOR THE YOUNG PIANIST, BK. 2
        WILLIS MUSIC COMPANY   1.50
GILLOCK--ED   GILLOCK   EI
  SOLO REPERTOIRE FOR THE YOUNG PIANIST, BK. 2
        WILLIS MUSIC COMPANY   1.25
GINASTERA
  PEQUENA DANZA, FROM 'ESTANCIA'
        BOOSEY AND HAWKES, INC.   .75
GIORDANI   DEL MAGLIO
  CARO MIO BEN
        FRANCO COLOMBO PUBLICATIONS   128119   .50
GIORDANO   MARCIANO
  ANDREA CHENIER - MADDALENA'S ARIA
        FRANCO COLOMBO PUBLICATIONS   SON.936   .90
GIORDANO   DE CRISTOFARO
  ANDREA CHENIER SELECTIONS, BK. 1
        FRANCO COLOMBO PUBLICATIONS   SON.1859   1.25
GIORDANO   DE CRISTOFARO
  ANDREA CHENIER SELECTIONS, BK. 2
        FRANCO COLOMBO PUBLICATIONS   SON.1860   1.25
GIORDANO *
  ANNA
        TRO SONGWAYS SERVICE, INC.   2003
GIORDANO   DE CHRISTOFARO
  CENA DELLE BEFFE, LA - GRAND FANTASY FROM ACTS 1 AND 2
        FRANCO COLOMBO PUBLICATIONS   SON.2529   1.50
GIORDANO
  FEDORA - INTERLUDIO
        FRANCO COLOMBO PUBLICATIONS   SON.994   .90
GIORDANO
  FEDORA - SELECTIONS, BK. 1
        FRANCO COLOMBO PUBLICATIONS   SON.1718   .90
GIORDANO
  FEDORA - SELECTIONS, BK. 2
        FRANCO COLOMBO PUBLICATIONS   SON.1719   .90
GIORDANO   DE CHRISTOFARO
  FEDORA - SELECTIONS
        FRANCO COLOMBO PUBLICATIONS   SON.1726   1.75
GIORDANO
  SIBERIA - DANCE OF THE BALALAIKAS
        FRANCO COLOMBO PUBLICATIONS   SON.1921   .90
GIORZA   DEL MAGLIO
  DAGHELA AVANTI UN PASSO
        FRANCO COLOMBO PUBLICATIONS   127837   .50
GLAZOUNOW, A.
  AUTUMN, FROM 'THE SEASONS'
        BOOSEY AND HAWKES, INC.   3.25
GLAZOUNOW, A.   FREDERICKS
  CONCERTO THEME FROM PIANO CONCERTO, OP. 92
        MCA MUSIC   .75
GLAZOUNOW, A.
  PIZZICATO, FROM 'RAYMONDA'
        BOOSEY AND HAWKES, INC.   1.25
GLIERE   5
  RED POPPY BALLET, DANCE
        CENTURY MUSIC PUBLISHING COMPANY, INC.   3482   .40
GLINKA   BALAKIREV   5
  L'ALOUETTE TRANSKRIPTION
        SCHOTT   10392   .75
GLINKA   BALAKIREV   9
  LARK, THE
        THEODORE PRESSER COMPANY   .50
GLINKA
  RUSSLAN AND LUDMILLA
        CENTURY MUSIC PUBLISHING COMPANY, INC.   1.25
GLUCK   WEYBRIGHT   4
  ALCESTE BALLET MUSIC FROM OPERA
        BELWIN-MILLS PUBLISHING CORPORATION   .60
GLUCK
  CAPRICE BY SAINT-SAENS, ON AIRS FROM 'ALCESTE'
        G. SCHIRMER, INC.   1.10
GLUCK   DEL MAGLIO
  ORFEO - CHE FARO SENZA EURIDICE
        FRANCO COLOMBO PUBLICATIONS   128123   .60
GODARD, B.   ROLFE, W.   2
  CHROMATIC WALTZ, EASY
        CENTURY MUSIC PUBLISHING COMPANY, INC.   3555   .40

GODARD, B.   ROLFE, W.   2
  FIFTH WALTZ, EASY
        CENTURY MUSIC PUBLISHING COMPANY, INC.   3555   .40
GODARD, B.   3
  JOCELYN, BERCEUSE, EASY
        CENTURY MUSIC PUBLISHING COMPANY, INC.   2518   .40
GODARD, B.   3
  LULLABY, JOCELYN, EASY
        CENTURY MUSIC PUBLISHING COMPANY, INC.   2518   .40
GODARD, B.   5
  LULLABY, JOCELYN
        CENTURY MUSIC PUBLISHING COMPANY, INC.   1322   .40
GODARD, B.   3
  VALSE NO. 02, EASY
        CENTURY MUSIC PUBLISHING COMPANY, INC.   2592   .40
GODOWSKY, L.
  MENUET FROM L'ARLESIENNE --BIZET
        MUSICA OBSCURA   2.00
GODOWSKY, L.
  TRANSCRIPTION OF HENSELT'S 'SI OISEAU J'ETAIS' OP. 2 NO. 6
        MUSICA OBSCURA   2.50
GOLDBERGER, D.--ED. *   GOLDBERGER, D. *
  FOLK SONG BOOK 1
        CONSOLIDATED MUSIC PUBLISHERS, INC.   040100   1.25
GOLDBERGER, D.--ED. *   GOLDBERGER, D. *
  FOLK SONG BOOK 2
        CONSOLIDATED MUSIC PUBLISHERS, INC.   040101   1.25
GOLDBERGER, D.--ED. *   GOLDBERGER, D. *
  FOLK SONG BOOK 3
        CONSOLIDATED MUSIC PUBLISHERS, INC.   040102   1.25
GOLDBERGER, D.--ED. *   GOLDBERGER, D. *
  SOLO BOOK 1
        CONSOLIDATED MUSIC PUBLISHERS, INC.   040103   1.25
GOLDBERGER, D.--ED. *   GOLDBERGER, D. *
  SOLO BOOK 2
        CONSOLIDATED MUSIC PUBLISHERS, INC.   040104   1.25
GOLDBERGER, D.--ED. *   GOLDBERGER, D. *
  SOLO BOOK 3
        CONSOLIDATED MUSIC PUBLISHERS, INC.   040105   1.25
GOLDSMITH, J.
  BLUE MAX, THE
        THE BIG THREE MUSIC CORPORATION   00.95
GOLDSMITH, J.
  LILA'S THEME - THE STRIPPER
        THE BIG THREE MUSIC CORPORATION   00.95
GOLDSMITH, J.
  MAN FROM U.N.C.L.E. - THEME
        THE BIG THREE MUSIC CORPORATION   00.95
GOLDSMITH, J.
  OUR MAN FLINT
        THE BIG THREE MUSIC CORPORATION   00.95
GOLDSMITH, J.
  VON RYAN MARCH
        THE BIG THREE MUSIC CORPORATION   00.95
GOMES
  GUARANY, IL - OVERTURE
        FRANCO COLOMBO PUBLICATIONS   127730   1.00
GOODMAN *
  STOMPING AT THE SAVOY
        THE BIG THREE MUSIC CORPORATION   00.95
GOODWIN, R.
  OF HUMAN BONDAGE - THEME
        THE BIG THREE MUSIC CORPORATION   00.95
GOTTSCHALK   REEG, G. A.   3
  LAST HOPE
        VOLKWEIN BROS.   .35
GOULD, M.
  GUARACHA, THIRD MOV'T FROM LATIN-AMERICAN SYMPHONETTE
        BELWIN-MILLS PUBLISHING CORPORATION   20118   .85
GOUNOD, C.   3
  BALLET NO. 1, FAUST
        CENTURY MUSIC PUBLISHING COMPANY, INC.   2052   .40
GOUNOD, C. *
  FAUST, VALSE
        G. SCHIRMER, INC.   1.10
GOUNOD, C.   CHIESA
  FAUST - EASY FANTASIA
        FRANCO COLOMBO PUBLICATIONS   109094   .50
GOUNOD, C.
  FAUST - WALTZES
        FRANCO COLOMBO PUBLICATIONS   67691   .90
GOUNOD, C.   CHIESA
  FAUST - WALTZES
        FRANCO COLOMBO PUBLICATIONS   109091   .50
GOUNOD, C.   BURGMUELLER
  FAUST - WALTZES
        FRANCO COLOMBO PUBLICATIONS   64451   .75
GOUNOD, C.   MILICI
  FAUST - WALTZ
        FRANCO COLOMBO PUBLICATIONS   BA8329   .75
GOUNOD, C.   3
  FAUST BALLET, NO. 1
        CENTURY MUSIC PUBLISHING COMPANY, INC.   2052   .40
GOUNOD, C.   3
  FAUST BALLET, NO. 6
        CENTURY MUSIC PUBLISHING COMPANY, INC.   2054   .40
GOUNOD, C.   M
  FAUST
        C. F. PETERS CORPORATION   H640   2.00
GOUNOD, C.   SCHAUM, J.   2 1/2
  FUNERAL MARCH OF A MARIONETTE
        SCHAUM PUBLICATIONS, INC.   .60
GOUNOD, C.   RICHARDS, B.   4
  MARCH, FAUST
        CENTURY MUSIC PUBLISHING COMPANY, INC.   1544   .40
GOUNOD, C.   2
  MIREILLE, WALTZ SONG
        CENTURY MUSIC PUBLISHING COMPANY, INC.   2040   .40
GOUNOD, C.   2
  ROMEO AND JULIET, WALTZ
        CENTURY MUSIC PUBLISHING COMPANY, INC.   2044   .40
GOUNOD, C.   WEYBRIGHT   2
  SEND OUT THY LIGHT -- ANTHEM
        BELWIN-MILLS PUBLISHING CORPORATION   .60
GOUNOD, C.   DEL MAGLIO
  SERENADE
        FRANCO COLOMBO PUBLICATIONS   124717   .50
GOUNOD, C. *
  VALSE--'FAUST'
        G. SCHIRMER, INC.   1.10
GOUNOD, C.   LANGE
  WALTZ FROM 'FAUST', OP. 196 NO. 1
        BELWIN-MILLS PUBLISHING CORPORATION   28159   .70
GRAETZER
  DANCES OF 7 CENTURIES
        FRANCO COLOMBO PUBLICATIONS   BA12190   7.50

GRANADOS   MARCHI, G.
    ANDALUZA FROM 'DANZAS ESPANOLAS'
        EDIZIONI BERBEN   1264   1.20
GRANADOS   MARCHI, G.
    ORIENTAL FROM 'DANZAS ESPANOLAS'
        EDIZIONI BERBEN   1265   1.20
GREENWALD, M.--ED   GREENWALD, M.   4
    OPERATIC GEMS OVERTURE
        CENTURY MUSIC PUBLISHING COMPANY, INC.   1384   .40
GREENWALD, M.--ED   GREENWALD, M.   3
    RUSSIAN FOLK SONG
        CENTURY MUSIC PUBLISHING COMPANY, INC.   1903   .40
GREENWALD, M.--ED   GREENWALD, M.   3
    SONG OF THE VOLGA BOATMAN
        CENTURY MUSIC PUBLISHING COMPANY, INC.   1903   .40
GREENWALD, M.--ED   GREENWALD, M.   3
    VOLGA BOAT SONG
        CENTURY MUSIC PUBLISHING COMPANY, INC.   1903   .40
GREENWALD, M.
    CHAPEL CHIMES
        THE BIG THREE MUSIC CORPORATION   00.95
GREEN   LEVINE
    BODY AND SOUL
        WARNER BROTHERS PUBLISHERS   1.00
GREEN   WALTER
    BODY AND SOUL
        WARNER BROTHERS PUBLISHERS   1.00
GREEN *
    COQUETTE
        THE BIG THREE MUSIC CORPORATION   00.95
GRENZ
    ZAUBERLEHRING, DIE -- BALLET --
        FRANCO COLOMBO PUBLICATIONS   SIK.331   20.00
GRIEG   THORNE
    ALBUM
        BOOSEY AND HAWKES, INC.   1.50
GRIEG   THOMPSON, J.   3
    ANITRA'S DANCE
        WILLIS MUSIC COMPANY   .40
GRIEG   ANSON, G.   INTERMEDIATE
    ANSON INTRODUCES GRIEG, BK. 1
        WILLIS MUSIC COMPANY   1.50
GRIEG   ROLFE, W.   3
    AN DEN FRUEHLING, EASY
        CENTURY MUSIC PUBLISHING COMPANY, INC.   3225   .60
GRIEG   SCHAUM, J.   3
    BEST OF GRIEG
        SCHAUM PUBLICATIONS, INC.   1.25
GRIEG   4
    CONCERTO, THEME
        CENTURY MUSIC PUBLISHING COMPANY, INC.   3533   .40
GRIEG
    CONCERTO IN A MINOR, OP. 16. ABRIDGED PIANO SOLO ARRANGEMENT
        C. F. PETERS CORPORATION   2164B   1.25
GRIEG   M
    CONCERTO IN A MINOR, OP. 16
        C. F. PETERS CORPORATION   2164B   1.25
GRIEG
    CONCERTO IN A MINOR -- OPENING THEME
        ASHLEY DEALERS SERVICE, INC.   ES   .95
GRIEG
    CONCERTO IN A MINOR
        ASHLEY DEALERS SERVICE, INC.   1.95
GRIEG   NIELSON
    CONCERTO IN A MINOR
        BOOSEY AND HAWKES, INC.   1.50
GRIEG   THOMPSON, J.   2
    CONCERTO IN A MINOR
        WILLIS MUSIC COMPANY   .35
GRIEG   MITTLER   3B
    GRIEG CONCERTO
        MUSICORD PUBLICATIONS, INC.   .45
GRIEG   ZEPP   5
    ICH LIEBE DICH
        PRO-ART PUBLICATIONS, INC.   434   .50
GRIEG   KING, S.
    IN THE HALL OF THE MOUNTAIN KING --A STUDY IN STACCATO--
        SHAWNEE PRESS, INC.   HB-5040   .40
GRIEG
    I LOVE THEE, OP. 41 NO. 3
        G. SCHIRMER, INC.   .40
GRIEG   KING, S.
    MORNING MOOD
        SHAWNEE PRESS, INC.   HB-5033   .40
GRIEG   WEYBRIGHT   2 1/2
    NATIONAL SONG
        BELWIN-MILLS PUBLISHING CORPORATION   .60
GRIEG   SCHAUM, J.   3
    PEER GYNT SUITES
        SCHAUM PUBLICATIONS, INC.   1.50
GRIEG   RICHTER, A.
    PEER GYNT SUITE - A STORY WITH
        THEODORE PRESSER COMPANY   1.25
GRIEG
    PEER GYNT SUITE 1
        EDWIN F. KALMUS   3483   1.25
GRIEG   MOSSMAN
    PIANO CONCERTO IN A MINOR -- FIRST MOVEMENT
        BELWIN-MILLS PUBLISHING CORPORATION   26089   .60
GRIEG   FREY, H.
    PIANO CONCERTO
        THE BIG THREE MUSIC CORPORATION   00.75
GRIEG   DUMM
    RECITAL REFRESHER SERIES -- FOLK SONG
        BELWIN-MILLS PUBLISHING CORPORATION   26117   .60
GRIEG   M-D
    SIGURD JORSALFAR, OP. 56
        C. F. PETERS CORPORATION   2655   2.00
GRIEG
    SOLVEJG'S SONG, OP. 52 NO. 4
        G. SCHIRMER, INC.   .35
GRIEG   LEVINE   5
    THEME, FROM PIANO CONCERTO IN A MINOR
        THEODORE PRESSER COMPANY   .50
GRIEG   TRUXELL, E.   3 1/2
    THEMES FROM PIANO CONCERTO
        VOLKWEIN BROS.   00.40
GRIEG   ECKSTEIN
    THEME FROM PIANO CONCERTO, OP. 16
        CARL FISCHER, INC.   S 2295   .50
GRIEG   4
    THEME FROM THE FIRST MOVEMENT OF PIANO CONCERTO IN A MINOR
        BOSTON MUSIC COMPANY   .50
GRIEG   WALLIS   2
    THEME FROM THE FIRST MOVEMENT OF PIANO CONCERTO IN A MINOR
        BOSTON MUSIC COMPANY   .50

GRIEG   D
    TRIUMPHAL MARCH --SIGURD JORSALFAR--, OP. 56 NO. 3
        C. F. PETERS CORPORATION   2656   1.25
GRIEG   ROLFE, W.   2
    TROLDTOG, EASY
        CENTURY MUSIC PUBLISHING COMPANY, INC.   3657   .40
GRIEG   GRIEG   M
    WALTZ-CAPRICES, OP. 37
        C. F. PETERS CORPORATION   2159   2.50
GRIEG   BARTH, H.   3
    WALTZ IN A MINOR
        BELWIN-MILLS PUBLISHING CORPORATION   .60
GRISELLE, T.
    TWO AMERICAN SKETCHES
        THE BIG THREE MUSIC CORPORATION   01.25
GROFE, F.
    ALICE BLUE
        THE BIG THREE MUSIC CORPORATION   00.95
GROFE, F.
    AVIATION SUITE
        THE BIG THREE MUSIC CORPORATION   03.00
GROFE, F.
    BLACK SAPPHIRE
        THE BIG THREE MUSIC CORPORATION   00.95
GROFE, F.
    BROADWAY AT NIGHT
        THE BIG THREE MUSIC CORPORATION   01.25
GROFE, F.
    CHRISTMAS EVE
        THE BIG THREE MUSIC CORPORATION   00.95
GROFE, F.
    FATHER OF WATERS
        THE BIG THREE MUSIC CORPORATION   00.95
GROFE, F.
    FESTIVIANA
        THE BIG THREE MUSIC CORPORATION   01.25
GROFE, F.
    FREE AIR
        THE BIG THREE MUSIC CORPORATION   00.95
GROFE, F.
    GRAND CANYON SUITE
        THE BIG THREE MUSIC CORPORATION   03.00
GROFE, F.
    KILLARNEY
        THE BIG THREE MUSIC CORPORATION   01.25
GROFE, F.
    KNUTE ROCKNE
        THE BIG THREE MUSIC CORPORATION   01.25
GROFE, F.
    MARCH FOR AMERICANS
        THE BIG THREE MUSIC CORPORATION   00.95
GROFE, F.
    MARDI GRAS
        THE BIG THREE MUSIC CORPORATION   00.95
GROFE, F.
    MISSISSIPPI SUITE
        THE BIG THREE MUSIC CORPORATION   02.50
GROFE, F.
    ON THE TRAIL
        THE BIG THREE MUSIC CORPORATION   00.95
GROFE, F.
    SERENADE
        THE BIG THREE MUSIC CORPORATION   00.95
GROFE, F.
    SYMPHONY IN STEEL
        THE BIG THREE MUSIC CORPORATION   01.25
GROFE, F.
    TABLOID
        THE BIG THREE MUSIC CORPORATION   03.00
GROFE, F.
    WHEELS
        THE BIG THREE MUSIC CORPORATION   03.00
GROFE, F.
    WORLD'S FAIR SUITE
        THE BIG THREE MUSIC CORPORATION   03.00
GROOMS--ED   GROOMS   3
    AY, AY, AY, TRANS.
        CENTURY MUSIC PUBLISHING COMPANY, INC.   2542   .40
GROOMS--ED   GROOMS   3
    DARK EYES
        CENTURY MUSIC PUBLISHING COMPANY, INC.   2671   .40
GROOMS--ED   GROOMS   3
    DEEP RIVER, TRANS.
        CENTURY MUSIC PUBLISHING COMPANY, INC.   2541   .40
GROOMS--ED   GROOMS   3
    IN THE GLOAMING, TRANS.
        CENTURY MUSIC PUBLISHING COMPANY, INC.   2536   .40
GROOMS--ED   GROOMS   3
    LAST ROSE OF SUMMER
        CENTURY MUSIC PUBLISHING COMPANY, INC.   2539   .40
GROOMS--ED   GROOMS   3
    LONDONDERRY AIR
        CENTURY MUSIC PUBLISHING COMPANY, INC.   2535   .40
GROOMS--ED   GROOMS   3
    MINSTREL BOY, THE
        CENTURY MUSIC PUBLISHING COMPANY, INC.   2538   .40
GROOMS--ED   GROOMS   3
    TURKEY IN THE STRAW
        CENTURY MUSIC PUBLISHING COMPANY, INC.   2496   .40
GROOMS--ED   GROOMS   3
    TWO GUITARS
        CENTURY MUSIC PUBLISHING COMPANY, INC.   2670   .40
GROOMS   3
    ANNIE LAURIE, TRANS.
        CENTURY MUSIC PUBLISHING COMPANY, INC.   2537   .60
GROOMS   3
    NOBODY KNOWS DE TROUBLE I SEE
        CENTURY MUSIC PUBLISHING COMPANY, INC.   2579   .40
GRUBER, F.   KRUG   3
    HOLY NIGHT, SILENT NIGHT
        CENTURY MUSIC PUBLISHING COMPANY, INC.   1633   .40
GRUBER, F.   HENLEIN
    HOLY NIGHT
        WILLIS MUSIC COMPANY   .30
GRUBER, F.   KRUG   3
    SILENT NIGHT, HOLY NIGHT
        CENTURY MUSIC PUBLISHING COMPANY, INC.   1633   .40
GRUBER, F.   ADLER, M.   1 1/2
    SILENT NIGHT, HOLY NIGHT
        THEODORE PRESSER COMPANY   .50
GRUBER, F.   HARVEY   2
    SILENT NIGHT -- CHRISTMAS MEDLEY
        VOLKWEIN BROS.   .25
GRUBER, F.   KOHLMANN, C.   5
    SILENT NIGHT
        THEODORE PRESSER COMPANY   .60

GRUBER, F.   SPENCER, J.   2
  SILENT NIGHT
    VOLKWEIN BROS.   .35
GRUBER, F.   RICHTER   FIRST YEAR
  SILENT NIGHT
    WARNER BROTHERS PUBLISHERS   .75
GRUBER, F.   WOODE
  SILENT NIGHT
    WILLIS MUSIC COMPANY   .30
GUENTHER--ED   GUENTHER
  CLASSICS FOR ADULTS, BK. 1
    MUSICORD PUBLICATIONS, INC.   1.25
GUENTHER--ED   GUENTHER   2
  SWING YOUR PARTNER
    CENTURY MUSIC PUBLISHING COMPANY, INC.   1.00
GUENTHER   GRIEG   3-4
  DREAM, A
    CENTURY MUSIC PUBLISHING COMPANY, INC.   3916   .40
GUION, D.
  ARKANSAS TRAVELER--OLD FIDDLER'S BREAKDOWN
    G. SCHIRMER, INC.   .75
GUION, D.
  SHEEP AND GOAT WALKIN' TO THE PASTURE--COWBOYS' AND OLD FIDDLERS
  BREAKDOWN
    G. SCHIRMER, INC.   .50
GUTHRIE
  THIS LAND IS YOUR LAND
    TRO SONGWAYS SERVICE, INC.   2082   .85
HABERBIER, E.   RIVE-KING, JULIE
  CONCERT TRANSCRIPTIONS FROM HER REPERTOIRE -- PRELUDE AND FUGUE
  IN D
    MUSICA OBSCURA   2.50
HABERBIER, E.   KING, JULIE RIVE
  PRELUDE AND FUGUE IN D, TRANSCRIBED BY JULIE RIVE-KING
    MUSICA OBSCURA   2.50
HALFFTER, E.
  SONATINA -- BALLET IN ONE ACT
    ASSOCIATED MUSIC PUBLISHERS, INC.   ESC   9.00
HALL *
  JOHNSON RAG
    THE BIG THREE MUSIC CORPORATION   00.95
HAMPTON, L.
  HAMPS BOOGIE-WOOGIE
    THE BIG THREE MUSIC CORPORATION   00.95
HANDEL   BEARD
  AIR VARIE FROM CONCERTO GROSSO NO. 2
    ELKAN-VOGEL, INC.   .50
HANDEL   ANSON, G.   ELEMENTARY
  ANSON INTRODUCES HANDEL, BK. 1
    WILLIS MUSIC COMPANY   .75
HANDEL   ANSON, G.   INTERMEDIATE
  ANSON INTRODUCES HANDEL, BK. 2
    WILLIS MUSIC COMPANY   1.00
HANDEL   M
  ARRIVAL OF THE QUEEN OF SHEBA, FROM 'SOLOMON'. CONCERT VERSION.
    C. F. PETERS CORPORATION   H375   1.25
HANDEL   2
  BERUHMTES LARGO -- ERLEICHTERT
    SCHOTT   06667   .75
HANDEL   BARTH, H.
  BOURREE
    BELWIN-MILLS PUBLISHING CORPORATION   .60
HANDEL *
  CHOEUR DES PRETRES DE DAGON, FROM SAMSON
    MUSICA OBSCURA   1.50
HANDEL   4
  HALLELUJAH CHORUS, FROM MESSIAH
    CENTURY MUSIC PUBLISHING COMPANY, INC.   3723   .40
HANDEL   SHELDON
  HALLELUJAH CHORUS -- FROM 'MESSIAH'
    BELWIN-MILLS PUBLISHING CORPORATION   20121   .60
HANDEL   ZEPP   4
  HALLELUJAH CHORUS
    PRO-ART PUBLICATIONS, INC.   359   .50
HANDEL   SCHAUM, J.   3
  HALLELUJAH CHORUS
    SCHAUM PUBLICATIONS, INC.   .60
HANDEL   SCHAUM, J.   3
  HANDEL'S MESSIAH
    SCHAUM PUBLICATIONS, INC.   1.50
HANDEL   5
  HARMONIOUS BLACKSMITH
    CENTURY MUSIC PUBLISHING COMPANY, INC.   1172   .40
HANDEL   DEL MAGLIO
  LARGO FROM 'SERSE'
    FRANCO COLOMBO PUBLICATIONS   124718   .60
HANDEL   3
  LARGO
    CENTURY MUSIC PUBLISHING COMPANY, INC.   272   .40
HANDEL   E
  MELODIES FROM 'MESSIAH'
    C. F. PETERS CORPORATION   H272   1.25
HANDEL   4
  MESSIAH, THE, HALLELUJAH CHORUS
    CENTURY MUSIC PUBLISHING COMPANY, INC.   3723   .40
HANDEL   PHILLIPS, D.
  MINUET IN G MINOR
    BELWIN-MILLS PUBLISHING CORPORATION   .60
HANDEL   PHILLIPS, D.   3
  MINUET IN G MINOR
    BELWIN-MILLS PUBLISHING CORPORATION   .60
HANDEL   SHAW, W.
  OVERTURE 'MESSIAH'
    NOVELLO AND COMPANY, LTD.   01.0078.01   .50
HANDEL   DUMM
  RECITAL REFRESHER SERIES -- FANFARE
    BELWIN-MILLS PUBLISHING CORPORATION   26113   .60
HANDEL
  SARABANDE WITH VARIATIONS, SUITE 11, WATER MUSIC
    CENTURY MUSIC PUBLISHING COMPANY, INC.   3746   .40
HANDEL   BAUER, M.   MEDIUM
  SIX LITTLE FUGUES
    SHAWNEE PRESS, INC.   HB-203   1.25
HANDEL   3
  WATER MUSIC, ADAGIO-BOURREE
    CENTURY MUSIC PUBLISHING COMPANY, INC.   3913   .40
HANDEL   3
  WATER MUSIC, ANDANTE-HORNPIPE
    CENTURY MUSIC PUBLISHING COMPANY, INC.   3915   .40
HANDEL   2
  XERXES, LARGO, EASY
    CENTURY MUSIC PUBLISHING COMPANY, INC.   2465   .40
HANDEL   ALDRIDGE, M.
  YOUNG PIANIST'S HANDEL, THE, BK. 1
    OXFORD UNIVERSITY PRESS   38.011   2.25
HANDEL   ALDRIDGE, M.
  YOUNG PIANIST'S HANDEL, THE, BK. 2
    OXFORD UNIVERSITY PRESS   38.012   2.25

HANLEY, J.   SCHAUM, J.   2
  BACK HOME AGAIN IN INDIANA
    SCHAUM PUBLICATIONS, INC.   .75
HANLEY, J.   SCHAUM, J.   2 1/2
  SECOND HAND ROSE
    SCHAUM PUBLICATIONS, INC.   .75
HANON, C.   STEINER
  JUNIOR HANON
    BELWIN-MILLS PUBLISHING CORPORATION   1693   1.75
HANON   ZEPP
  HANON IN ALL KEYS
    PRO-ART PUBLICATIONS, INC.   309   .85
HANSON, H.--ED   HANSON, H.
  NEW SCRIBNER MUSIC LIBRARY, VOL. 07 'AT THE OPERA'
    CHARLES SCRIBNER'S SONS
HANSON, H.--ED   HANSON, H.
  NEW SCRIBNER MUSIC LIBRARY, VOL. 09 'HOME FAVORITES'
    CHARLES SCRIBNER'S SONS
HARDING, R.--ED   HARDING, R.
  CHRISTMAS CAROLS FOR EVERYONE
    WILLIS MUSIC COMPANY   .50
HARDING, R.
  HARK THE HERALD ANGELS SING
    WILLIS MUSIC COMPANY   .30
HARDING, R.
  NURSERY RHYMES FOR TOTS
    WILLIS MUSIC COMPANY   .90
HARDING, R.
  O LITTLE TOWN OF BETHLEHEM
    WILLIS MUSIC COMPANY   .35
HARRIS   HASTINGS
  FOOTPRINTS ON THE MOON
    WARNER BROTHERS PUBLISHERS   1.00
HART, F.
  SONGS OF FREDDIE HART, THE
    THE BIG THREE MUSIC CORPORATION   02.95
HARTIG
  SCHWARZE SONNE, OP. 31 -- BALLET IN 9 TABLEAUX
    ASSOCIATED MUSIC PUBLISHERS, INC.   BOT   7.50
HART *
  BLUE MOON
    THE BIG THREE MUSIC CORPORATION   00.95
HART *
  SPRING IS HERE
    THE BIG THREE MUSIC CORPORATION   00.95
HARVEY, VIVIEN
  TUNES FOR EVERYBODY - 65 FAMOUS PIECES IN EASY ARRANGEMENTS
    FRANCO COLOMBO PUBLICATIONS   NY1454   1.25
HARVEY   2
  JINGLE BELLS MARCH
    VOLKWEIN BROS.   00.25
HARVEY   3
  JINGLE BELLS MARCH
    VOLKWEIN BROS.   .25
HAUBIEL, C.   E
  HOMAGE TO BACH-BOOK 1
    COMPOSERS PRESS, INC.   3.00
HAUBIEL, C.   E
  HOMAGE TO BACH-BOOK 2
    COMPOSERS PRESS, INC.   3.00
HAUPT, L. VON
  HANSEL AND GRETEL--ADAPTED FROM HUMPERDINCK AS A CHILDREN'S
  OPERA-STORY
    G. SCHIRMER, INC.   .75
HAUSER   THOMPSON, J.   4
  HUNGARIAN
    WILLIS MUSIC COMPANY   .40
HAVENS, R.
  RICHIE HAVENS - ANTHOLOGY
    THE BIG THREE MUSIC CORPORATION   03.95
HAWTHORNE, A.   BURNAM   1 1/2
  WHISPERING HOPE
    WILLIS MUSIC COMPANY   .35
HAYDN   DELIOUX
  ANDANTE FROM ''SURPRISE'' SYMPHONY IN G MAJOR
    G. SCHIRMER, INC.   .60
HAYDN   SCHMID
  FLOTENUHRSTUCKE
    BARENREITER VERLAG   EN 802   4.00
HAYDN   BARTH, H.
  MINUETTO GIOCOSO
    BELWIN-MILLS PUBLISHING CORPORATION   20169   .60
HAYDN   WEYBRIGHT   2
  O WORSHIP THE KING -- A HYMN
    BELWIN-MILLS PUBLISHING CORPORATION   .60
HAYDN   STEINER   2 1/2
  PERPETUUM MOBILE, OP. 64 NO. 5 -- PERPETUAL MOTION
    BELWIN-MILLS PUBLISHING CORPORATION   .60
HAYDN   M
  SHORT PIECES --12--. MOVEMENTS FROM STRING QUARTETS AND
  SYMPHONIES
    C. F. PETERS CORPORATION   1120   1.25
HAYDN   MANSFIELD
  STEPS TO THE MASTERS
    BANKS AND SON LTD.   1.35
HAYDN   THOMPSON, J.   1
  SURPRISE SYMPHONY, THE
    WILLIS MUSIC COMPANY   .35
HAYDN   ZANON
  SYMPHONIES -- SELECTED -- BK. 1
    FRANCO COLOMBO PUBLICATIONS   ER1056   4.50
HAYDN   ZANON
  SYMPHONIES -- SELECTED -- BK. 2
    FRANCO COLOMBO PUBLICATIONS   ER1057   4.50
HAYDN   M
  SYMPHONIES --12--
    C. F. PETERS CORPORATION   197   10.00
HAYDN   GOETSCHIUS, P.
  SYMPHONY NO. 16 IN G MAJOR
    THEODORE PRESSER COMPANY   .75
HAYDN   1
  THEME FROM SURPRISE SYMPHONY
    CENTURY MUSIC PUBLISHING COMPANY, INC.   3606   .40
HEAPS, S.--ED   HEAPS, S.   E
  PIANO MEDITATIONS FOR CHURCH AND HOME
    WILLIS MUSIC COMPANY   1.50
HEFTI, N.
  BATMAN THEME
    THE BIG THREE MUSIC CORPORATION   00.95
HEIM, J.   SCHAUM, J.   PREP
  PENGUINS AT PLAY
    SCHAUM PUBLICATIONS, INC.   .50
HEINS, C.   ROLFE, W.   2
  SENNERS TRAUM, EASY
    CENTURY MUSIC PUBLISHING COMPANY, INC.   3370   .40
HEISER-DAILY   STEINER   1
  DREAMING
    BELWIN-MILLS PUBLISHING CORPORATION   .60

HELYER, M. 1-2
 CAROL TUNES
  NOVELLO AND COMPANY, LTD. 10.0065.09 1.15
HENDERSON WALTER
 BIRTH OF THE BLUES, THE
  WARNER BROTHERS PUBLISHERS 1.00
HENDERSON MACLACHLAN FIRST YEAR
 BIRTH OF THE BLUES, THE
  WARNER BROTHERS PUBLISHERS .75
HENDRICKS *
 DESAFINADO
  TRO SONGWAYS SERVICE, INC. 2019
HENSELT, A. GODOWSKY, L.
 SI OISEAU J'ETAIS, OP. 2 NO. 6
  MUSICA OBSCURA 2.50
HENZE, H. 5
 LUCY ESCOTT VARIATIONS FOR HARPSICHORD, 1963 - KLAVIERFASSUNG
  SCHOTT 5453 3.50
HERBERT WEYBRIGHT 3
 AL FRESCO
  BELWIN-MILLS PUBLISHING CORPORATION .60
HERBERT MENDEL, S. 1 1-2
 GYPSY LOVE SONG
  WILLIS MUSIC COMPANY .40
HERBERT STEINER 1 1/2
 IN OLD NEW YORK, FROM "THE RED MILL"
  BELWIN-MILLS PUBLISHING CORPORATION .60
HERBERT STEINER 1
 IN THE LAND OF THE EMIR
  BELWIN-MILLS PUBLISHING CORPORATION .60
HERBERT SCHAUM, J. 4
 KISS ME AGAIN
  SCHAUM PUBLICATIONS, INC. .60
HERBERT GAMSE 1
 MARCH OF THE TOYS, SIMPLIFIED
  CENTURY MUSIC PUBLISHING COMPANY, INC. 4416 .40
HERBERT 3
 MARCH OF THE TOYS
  CENTURY MUSIC PUBLISHING COMPANY, INC. 4415 .40
HERBERT SCHAUM, J. 4
 MARCH OF THE TOYS
  SCHAUM PUBLICATIONS, INC. .60
HERBERT STEINER 3
 TOYLAND
  BELWIN-MILLS PUBLISHING CORPORATION .60
HERBERT ZEPP 2
 TOYLAND
  PRO-ART PUBLICATIONS, INC. 228 .50
HERBERT SCHAUM, J. 4
 TOYLAND
  SCHAUM PUBLICATIONS, INC. .60
HERBERT STAFFORD
 VICTOR HERBERT FAVORITES
  WARNER BROTHERS PUBLISHERS 1.25
HEROLD 3
 OVERTURE, ZAMPA, EASY
  CENTURY MUSIC PUBLISHING COMPANY, INC. 2121 .40
HEROLD
 ZAMPA OVERTURE
  FRANCO COLOMBO PUBLICATIONS 28625 1.00
HERRMANN--ED HERRMANN
 TUNES FROM FAR AWAY -- 50 EASY ARRANGEMENTS OF FOLKSONGS FROM
 MANY LANDS
  ASSOCIATED MUSIC PUBLISHERS, INC. SIM 2.00
HERZER, R. 2
 HOCH HEIDECKSBURG, MARSCH - OP. 10, ERLEICHTERT
  SCHOTT 1.25
HEYWOOD, E.
 MODERN PIANO TRANSCRIPTIONS
  THE BIG THREE MUSIC CORPORATION 01.50
HILL, B. SCHAUM, J. 2 1/2
 GLORY OF LOVE
  SCHAUM PUBLICATIONS, INC. .75
HILLER GLOVER, D.
 UNITED WE STAND
  BELWIN-MILLS PUBLISHING CORPORATION .60
HINDEMITH
 KONZERT FUR KLAVIER UND ORCHESTER, 1945 -- KLAVIERAUSZUG
  SCHOTT 3838 6.00
HINKLE, N.--ED HINKLE, N.
 FORTY CHRISTMAS CAROLS FOR VOICE AND PIANO
  THEODORE PRESSER COMPANY 1.50
HIRSCHBERG, D.--ED HIRSCHBERG, D.
 DAVID HIRSCHBERG PIANO COURSE
  MUSICORD PUBLICATIONS, INC. 1.25
HITZ, F.
 LA SERENATA--TRANSCRIPTION AFTER MELODY BY BRAGA
  G. SCHIRMER, INC. .40
HITZEL--ED HITZEL 2
 LAST ROSE OF SUMMER
  CENTURY MUSIC PUBLISHING COMPANY, INC. 2045 .40
HOFFMAN--ED HOFFMAN AE
 EASIEST SONATINA ALBUM
  WILLIS MUSIC COMPANY 1.25
HOFSTAD, M.--ED HOFSTAD, M.
 VERY FIRST HYMNS
  BOSTON MUSIC COMPANY 1.25
HOLCOMB, L. R.--ED HOLCOMB, L. R.
 HYMNS FOR THE BEGINNING PIANIST
  BROADMAN MUSIC 4571-07 2.00
HOLLINS, A. CHAMBERS, H. A.
 SPRING SONG
  NOVELLO AND COMPANY, LTD. 10.0073.10 1.15
HOLZMANN, A.
 BLAZE AWAY
  THE BIG THREE MUSIC CORPORATION 00.95
HONEGGER, A.
 LE CANTIQUE DES CANTIQUES -- BALLET CHANTE
  HEUGEL ET CIE. 8.90
HOPKINS, K.
 HUSTLER, THE -THEME
  THE BIG THREE MUSIC CORPORATION 00.95
HOTCHKISS, J.
 WALTZ OF THE TOREADORS, THE
  BELWIN-MILLS PUBLISHING CORPORATION 20459 .85
HOWARD, J. SCHAUM, J. 2
 GOODBY MY LADY LOVE
  SCHAUM PUBLICATIONS, INC. .50
HOWARD
 FLY ME TO THE MOON --BOSSA NOVA--
  TRO SONGWAYS SERVICE, INC. 2024
HOWELLS, H.
 LAMBERTS CLAVICHORD
  OXFORD UNIVERSITY PRESS 32.047 2.50
HOWE STEFFE * 2
 BATTLE HYMN OF THE REPUBLIC, THE
  WILLIS MUSIC COMPANY .35

HOWE STEFFE *
 BATTLE HYMN OF THE REPUBLIC
  CARL FISCHER, INC. P 2973 .50
HOWE STEFFE * 4
 BATTLE HYMN OF THE REPUBLIC
  PRO-ART PUBLICATIONS, INC. 579 .50
HOWE STEFFE * 1
 BATTLE HYMN OF THE REPUBLIC
  WILLIS MUSIC COMPANY .30
HRUBY, V. 3
 OPERETTEN-RAUSCH, MELODIENFOLGE MIT TEXT
  SCHOTT 2.00
HUBBELL WHITNEY
 POOR BUTTERFLY
  WARNER BROTHERS PUBLISHERS 1.00
HUGHES--ED. HUGHES
 KEYBOARD MEDLEYS
  LORENZ PUBLISHING COMPANY 2.00
HUMPERDINCK, E. STEINER APPR.
 CHILDREN'S DANCE FROM "HANSEL AND GRETEL"
  BELWIN-MILLS PUBLISHING CORPORATION .60
HUMPERDINCK, E. WEYBRIGHT 1 1/2
 CHILDREN'S PRAYER, THE -- FROM HANSEL AND GRETEL
  BELWIN-MILLS PUBLISHING CORPORATION .60
HUMPERDINCK, E.
 EVENING PRAYER, FROM "HANSEL AND GRETEL"
  CENTURY MUSIC PUBLISHING COMPANY, INC. 3402 .40
HUMPERDINCK, E. HAUPT, L. VON
 HANSEL AND GRETEL--ADAPTED AS A CHILDREN'S OPERA-STORY
  G. SCHIRMER, INC. .75
HUMPERDINCK, E. 2
 HANSEL AND GRETEL, PRAYER
  CENTURY MUSIC PUBLISHING COMPANY, INC. 3402 .40
HUMPERDINCK, E. 3
 HANSEL AND GRETEL, SUSY LITTLE SUSY
  CENTURY MUSIC PUBLISHING COMPANY, INC. 3433 .40
HUMPERDINCK, E. 3
 HANSEL AND GRETEL, THE LITTLE MAN
  CENTURY MUSIC PUBLISHING COMPANY, INC. 3435 .40
HUMPERDINCK, E. 4
 HANSEL UND GRETEL -- ABENDSEGEN UND ENGELREIGEN
  SCHOTT 1.50
HUMPERDINCK, E. 4
 HANSEL UND GRETEL -- KNUSPERWALZER
  SCHOTT 1.50
HUMPERDINCK, E. 5
 HANSEL UND GRETEL -- VORSPIEL
  SCHOTT 1.75
HUMPERDINCK, E. 3
 LITTLE MAN, THE, HANSEL AND GRETEL
  CENTURY MUSIC PUBLISHING COMPANY, INC. 3435 .40
HUMPERDINCK, E. 2
 PRAYER, HANSEL AND GRETEL
  CENTURY MUSIC PUBLISHING COMPANY, INC. 3402 .40
HUMPERDINCK, E. WEYBRIGHT 1 1/2
 SUSY, LITTLE SUSY -- GERMAN FOLK SONG, USED IN THE OPERA "HANSEL
 AND GRETEL"
  BELWIN-MILLS PUBLISHING CORPORATION .60
HUMPERDINCK, E. 3
 SUSY LITTLE SUSY, HANSEL AND GRETEL
  CENTURY MUSIC PUBLISHING COMPANY, INC. 3433 .40
HUNEKE--ED HUNEKE
 BIG NOTE CHRISTMAS CAROLS
  BOSTON MUSIC COMPANY 1.00
HUNTLEY--ED HUNTLEY
 COWBOY SONGS
  BOSTON MUSIC COMPANY 1.00
HUNTLEY, C.--ED HUNTLEY, C.
 CHRISTMAS CAROLS FOR CHILDREN
  WILLIS MUSIC COMPANY 1.00
IBERT
 AMOURS DE JUPITER, LES -- BALLET --
  FRANCO COLOMBO PUBLICATIONS SAL 7.25
IBERT 5, 6
 ESCALES
  ALPHONSE LEDUC
IBERT 7
 FERRIQUE
  ALPHONSE LEDUC
INGHELBRECHT, D. E.
 LE DIABLE DANS LE BEFROI
  HEUGEL ET CIE. 7.30
INGHELBRECHT, D. E.
 METAMORPHOSE D'EVE -- BALLET --
  FRANCO COLOMBO PUBLICATIONS SAL 7.00
INGLE NEALE, J. EASY
 IN-A-GADDA-DA-VIDA
  WARNER BROTHERS PUBLISHERS .75
IPPOLITOV-IVANOV, M.
 PROCESSION OF THE SARDAR -- FROM "CAUCASIAN SKETCHES"
  BELWIN-MILLS PUBLISHING CORPORATION 26093 .60
ITURBI, J.
 THREE BLIND MICE - 3 INTERPRETATIONS
  THE BIG THREE MUSIC CORPORATION 00.95
IVANOVICI, J. MOSSMAN
 WAVES OF THE DANUBE -- BOOGIE WOOGIE
  BELWIN-MILLS PUBLISHING CORPORATION 26061 .90
IVANOVICI, J. JESTON, I. H. 2
 WAVES OF THE DANUBE WALTZ
  VOLKWEIN BROS. 00.35
IVANOVICI, J. CHIESA
 WAVES OF THE DANUBE
  FRANCO COLOMBO PUBLICATIONS 107481 .50
IVANOVICI, J. CARLETON 1 1/2
 WAVES OF THE DANUBE
  THEODORE PRESSER COMPANY .50
IVANOW 2
 MARCH OF THE SARDAR, EASY
  CENTURY MUSIC PUBLISHING COMPANY, INC. 3384 .40
IVANOW ROLFE, W. 2
 PROCESSION OF THE SARDAR, EASY
  CENTURY MUSIC PUBLISHING COMPANY, INC. 3384 .40
IVANOW 5-6
 PROCESSION OF THE SARDAR
  CENTURY MUSIC PUBLISHING COMPANY, INC. 3182 .40
IVES, C. KIRKPATRICK D
 VARIED AIR AND VARIATIONS
  THEODORE PRESSER COMPANY 2.50
JACOBS * ZEPP 2
 I LOVE YOU TRULY
  PRO-ART PUBLICATIONS, INC. 229 .50
JAMES, S.
 SONGS OF SONNY JAMES
  THE BIG THREE MUSIC CORPORATION 02.95
JANACEK 3
 TWENTY-THREE VOLKSTANZE AUS MAHREN
  BARENREITER VERLAG AP 618

JARRE, M.
  GRAND PRIX - THEME
    THE BIG THREE MUSIC CORPORATION   00.95
JARRE, M.
  LARA'S THEME - 'DOCTOR ZHIVAGO'
    THE BIG THREE MUSIC CORPORATION   00.95
JAY--ED   JAY   AI
  TIME TO PLAY POLKAS
    WILLIS MUSIC COMPANY   1.00
JENSVOLD, J.--ED   JENSVOLD, J.
  I LOVE CHRISTMAS MUSIC
    WILLIS MUSIC COMPANY   1.00
JENSVOLD, J.--ED   JENSVOLD, J.
  MY HYMNS
    WILLIS MUSIC COMPANY   1.25
JESSEL   SCHAUM, J.   1 1/2
  PARADE OF THE TOY SOLDIERS
    SCHAUM PUBLICATIONS, INC.   .50
JESSEL   ZEPP   2
  WOODEN SOLDIERS ON PARADE
    PRO-ART PUBLICATIONS, INC.   322   .50
JOBIM   HARNELL
  MUSIC OF ANTONIO CARLOS JOBIM STYLED FOR PIANO BY JOE HARNELL
    TRO SONGWAYS SERVICE, INC.   2.50
JOBSON, V.
  MOTHER GOOSE MELODIES FOR THE YOUNG PIANIST--40 TRADITIONAL
  TUNES ARRANGED IN 5-FINGER POSITION
    G. SCHIRMER, INC.   1.00
JOHNSON, J. R.   SCHAUM, J.   2
  LIFT EV'RY VOICE AND SING
    SCHAUM PUBLICATIONS, INC.   .60
JOHNSON, R.   STEINER   4
  LAZY MOON -- PIANO SOLO WITH WORDS
    BELWIN-MILLS PUBLISHING CORPORATION   .60
JOLIVET, A.
  GUIGNOL ET PANDORE -- BALLET IN ONE ACT
    ASSOCIATED MUSIC PUBLISHERS, INC.   ESC   5.40
JOLSON *   SCHAUM, J.   1
  ANNIVERSARY SONG
    SCHAUM PUBLICATIONS, INC.   .75
JONES, S.   STEINER   2
  GEISHA, THE
    BELWIN-MILLS PUBLISHING CORPORATION   .60
JONES *
  CHRISTMAS CAROLS ROCK
    ALFRED MUSIC COMPANY   644   1.50
JONSON   ZEPP   4
  DRINK TO ME ONLY WITH THINE EYES
    PRO-ART PUBLICATIONS, INC.   234   .50
JOPLIN
  MAPLE LEAF RAG
    THE BIG THREE MUSIC CORPORATION   00.95
JOPLIN, S.   ZEPP   4-5
  MAPLE LEAF RAG
    PRO-ART PUBLICATIONS, INC.   328   .50
JORDA, L.
  CARNIVAL OF VENICE
    G. SCHIRMER, INC.   .35
JORDA, L.
  DANCE FROM BALLET-MUSIC FOR 'ROSAMUNDE'
    G. SCHIRMER, INC.   .35
JORDAN, J.
  LITTLE RED MONKEY
    THE BIG THREE MUSIC CORPORATION   00.95
JOSEFFY, R.
  ARIETTA DI BALLETTO--GLUCK
    G. SCHIRMER, INC.   .50
JOYNER, B.--ED   JOYNER, B.
  CHILD'S CHRISTMAS, A
    WILLIS MUSIC COMPANY   1.25
JOYNER, B.--ED   JOYNER, B.
  FAVORITE FOLK SONGS
    WILLIS MUSIC COMPANY   1.25
KABALEVSKY   ANSON, G.   ELEMENTARY
  ANSON INTRODUCES KABALEVSKY, BK. 1
    WILLIS MUSIC COMPANY   1.25
KABALEVSKY   ANSON, G.   INTERMEDIATE
  ANSON INTRODUCES KABALEVSKY, BK. 2
    WILLIS MUSIC COMPANY   1.25
KAHL--ED   KAHL
  CHRISTMAS CAROLS - BOOK 1
    BOSTON MUSIC COMPANY   1.50
KAHL--ED   KAHL
  CHRISTMAS CAROLS - BOOK 2
    BOSTON MUSIC COMPANY   1.50
KAHL--ED   KAHL
  CHRISTMAS CAROLS - BOOK 3
    BOSTON MUSIC COMPANY   1.50
KAHL--ED   KAHL
  JUNIOR HYMNBOOK - BOOK 1
    BOSTON MUSIC COMPANY   1.50
KAHL--ED   KAHL
  JUNIOR HYMNBOOK - BOOK 2
    BOSTON MUSIC COMPANY   1.50
KAHL--ED   KAHL
  JUNIOR HYMNBOOK - BOOK 3
    BOSTON MUSIC COMPANY   1.75
KAHL   SCHAUM, J.   2 1/2
  CARAVAN
    SCHAUM PUBLICATIONS, INC.   .60
KAHN, M.--ED *   KAHN, M. *
  DISNEY SHOWCASE
    BOURNE COMPANY   1.50
KAHN, M.--ED   KAHN, M.
  DOES YOUR CHEWING GUM LOSE ITS FLAVOR ON THE BEDPOST OVERNIGHT
  -- SIMP.
    BELWIN-MILLS PUBLISHING CORPORATION   26074   .50
KAHN, M.--ED   KAHN, M.
  I WAS KAISER BILL'S BATMAN -- SIMP.
    BELWIN-MILLS PUBLISHING CORPORATION   26121   .50
KAHN, M.--ED   KAHN, M.
  MARVIN KAHN'S SONG SHOWCASE
    BOURNE COMPANY   1.50
KAISER   3
  NATIONAL AIRS, MEDLEY MARCH
    CENTURY MUSIC PUBLISHING COMPANY, INC.   978   .40
KALMAN   SIRMAY
  PLAY GYPSIES - DANCE GYPSIES
    WARNER BROTHERS PUBLISHERS   1.00
KALMAN   RICHTER   FIRST YEAR
  PLAY GYPSIES - DANCE GYPSIES
    WARNER BROTHERS PUBLISHERS   .75
KAPER, B.
  CONFETTI
    THE BIG THREE MUSIC CORPORATION   00.95
KAPER, B.
  INVITATION
    THE BIG THREE MUSIC CORPORATION   00.95

KAPER, B.
  MUTINY ON THE BOUNTY
    THE BIG THREE MUSIC CORPORATION   00.95
KAPER, B.
  TWO LOVES - THEME
    THE BIG THREE MUSIC CORPORATION   00.95
KARDOS
  THREE PIECES, FROM 'TWELVE PRELUDES'
    KULTURA   1.25
KASTLER, A.   SCHAUM, J.   3
  CANDY CANE LANE
    SCHAUM PUBLICATIONS, INC.   .60
KATCHER   RICHTER   FIRST YEAR
  WHEN DAY IS DONE
    WARNER BROTHERS PUBLISHERS   .75
KEISER   4
  FLOWERS AND FERNS, TONE POEM
    CENTURY MUSIC PUBLISHING COMPANY, INC.   1070   .40
KEISER   4
  FLOWERS AND FERNS
    CENTURY MUSIC PUBLISHING COMPANY, INC.   2179   .60
KELER BELA   4
  OVERTURE, LUSTSPIEL
    CENTURY MUSIC PUBLISHING COMPANY, INC.   642   .40
KENDALL--ED   KENDALL
  SIMPLIFIED SONG GEMS FOR PIANO
    BOURNE COMPANY   1.00
KENNEDY *   SCHAUM, J.   2
  SOUTH OF THE BORDER
    SCHAUM PUBLICATIONS, INC.   .75
KERN, J.   BRADLEY, R.   EASY
  BRADLEY'S JEROME KERN ALBUM
    SCREEN GEMS - COLUMBIA PUBLICATIONS   F0020P2   1.95
KETELBEY, A.   RICHTER   FIRST YEAR
  IN A MONASTERY GARDEN
    WARNER BROTHERS PUBLISHERS   .75
KETELBEY, A.   SCHAUM, J.
  SANCTUARY OF THE HEART
    BELWIN-MILLS PUBLISHING CORPORATION   .60
KHATCHATURIAN   LEVINE
  SABRE DANCE FROM 'GAYNE BALLET'
    G. SCHIRMER, INC.   .50
KHATCHATURIAN
  SABRE DANCE
    EDWIN F. KALMUS   3579   .90
KHATCHATURIAN   KING, S.
  SWORD DANCE -- FROM BALLET 'GAYNE'
    BELWIN-MILLS PUBLISHING CORPORATION   26054   .60
KING, C.   ENGEL, S.   ADVANCED
  CAROLE KING PIANO SOLOS
    SCREEN GEMS - COLUMBIA PUBLICATIONS   F0089P   3.95
KING, C.   BRADLEY, R.   EASY
  GOLD, UPDATED
    SCREEN GEMS - COLUMBIA PUBLICATIONS   P0086P2   2.95
KING, C.   BRADLEY, R.   EASY
  TAPESTRY
    SCREEN GEMS - COLUMBIA PUBLICATIONS   P0039P2   2.50
KING, S.--ED.   KING, S.   EASY
  COUNTRY GARDENS
    SHAWNEE PRESS, INC.   HB-5029   .60
KING, S.--ED.   KING, S.
  DOWN BY THE STATION -- SIMP.
    BELWIN-MILLS PUBLISHING CORPORATION   26063   .50
KING, S.--ED.   KING, S.
  HARMONIES DELUXE -- 6 WORLD-FAMOUS MELODIES IN CONTEMPORARY
  STYLE
    THEODORE PRESSER COMPANY   1.25
KING, S.--ED.   KING, S.
  RED ROSES FOR A BLUE LADY --SIMP.
    BELWIN-MILLS PUBLISHING CORPORATION   26064   .50
KING, S.--ED.   KING, S.
  SLEIGH RIDE -- SIMP.
    BELWIN-MILLS PUBLISHING CORPORATION   26047   .50
KING, S.--ED.   KING, S.
  THAT'S MY DESIRE -- SIMP.
    BELWIN-MILLS PUBLISHING CORPORATION   26056   .50
KING, S.--ED.   KING, S.
  THAT OLD TIME BEAT
    THEODORE PRESSER COMPANY   1.25
KING, S.
  FIDDLE-FADDLE -- SIMP.
    BELWIN-MILLS PUBLISHING CORPORATION   26013   .50
KING
  FIRST JAZZ
    BOSTON MUSIC COMPANY   1.00
KIRBY, W.
  FAMOUS MELODIES FOR THE YOUNG PIANIST
    G. SCHIRMER, INC.   1.00
KIRBY, W.
  NOEL-NOEL--18 CHRISTMAS CAROLS, ARRANGED FOR PIANO AND VOICE
    G. SCHIRMER, INC.   .75
KLARMAN--ED   KLARMAN
  STUDENT PRINCE, THE, SELECTIONS FROM
    WARNER BROTHERS PUBLISHERS   .85
KLEBE, G.
  MENAGERIE, OP. 31 -- BALLET IN 5 TABLEAUX
    ASSOCIATED MUSIC PUBLISHERS, INC.   BOT   6.00
KOCH, F.
  CAROLS FROM MANY NATIONS
    GENERAL MUSIC PUBLISHING COMPANY, INC.   2.00
KODALY, Z.   FOLDES, A.
  SONG FROM 'HARY JANOS'
    UNIVERSAL EDITION   UE 12192   1.00
KODALY, Z.   FOLDES, A.
  VIENNESE CLOCK FROM 'HARY JANOS'
    UNIVERSAL EDITION   UE 10671   3.00
KOHLMANN, C.
  EIGHTEEN HYMN TRANSCRIPTIONS
    THEODORE PRESSER COMPANY   1.95
KOHLMANN, C.
  MORE CONCERT TRANSCRIPTIONS OF FAVORITE HYMNS
    THEODORE PRESSER COMPANY   1.25
KOVACS, S.
  FLEDERMAUS PARAPHRASE--ON AIRS FROM 'THE BAT' BY J. STRAUSS
    G. SCHIRMER, INC.   .90
KOWALSKI, H.   2
  HUNGARIAN MARCH, EASY
    CENTURY MUSIC PUBLISHING COMPANY, INC.   2133   .40
KRAUS--ED   KRAUS
  CADENZAS FROM MOZART'S PIANO CONCERTOS
    BELWIN-MILLS PUBLISHING CORPORATION   6.00
KREISLER   4
  IM PARADIES-WIENER VOLKSLIED
    SCHOTT   1.75
KREISLER   RACHMANINOFF, S.
  LIEBESFREUD
    BELWIN-MILLS PUBLISHING CORPORATION   1.50

KREISLER   RACHMANINOFF, S.
  LIEBESLIED
    BELWIN-MILLS PUBLISHING CORPORATION   1.50
KREISLER   FLETCHER
  SCHON ROSMARIN
    CARL FISCHER, INC.   F 2061   .65
KRENTZLIN, R.--ED   KRENTZLIN, R.   2
  DIE JUGEND TANZT
    SCHOTT   2300   3.00
KRENTZLIN, R.--ED   KRENTZLIN, R.   2
  OPERN UND OPERETTEN, BAND 01
    SCHOTT   2340   2.50
KRENTZLIN, R.--ED   KRENTZLIN, R.   2
  OPERN UND OPERETTEN, BAND 02
    SCHOTT   4175   2.50
KRENTZLIN, R.--ED   KRENTZLIN, R.   2
  TANZENDES ROKOKO UND DIE ZEIT DER ROMANTIK, BAND 01
    SCHOTT   2503   2.50
KRENTZLIN, R.--ED   KRENTZLIN, R.   2
  TANZENDES ROKOKO UND DIE ZEIT DER ROMANTIK, BAND 02
    SCHOTT   4795   2.50
KREUTZER--ED   KREUTZER
  HERITAGE HYMN BOOK
    CENTURY MUSIC PUBLISHING COMPANY, INC.   1.00
KREUTZER--ED   KREUTZER
  LET'S PLAY HYMNS
    CENTURY MUSIC PUBLISHING COMPANY, INC.   1.25
KROEGER, E. R.   STEINER   2
  CIRCUS ELEPHANTS
    BELWIN-MILLS PUBLISHING CORPORATION   .60
KROME--ED   KROME   2-3
  LEICHTES TANZBUCH
    SCHOTT   3714   2.50
KURANDA, M.--ED   KURANDA, M.
  SIXTEEN MASTERWORKS FOR THE PIANO
    THEODORE PRESSER COMPANY   1.50
LABITZKY, A.   2-3
  SHEPHERDESS' DREAM, EASY
    CENTURY MUSIC PUBLISHING COMPANY, INC.   2515   .40
LAI, F.
  LIVE FOR LIFE
    THE BIG THREE MUSIC CORPORATION   00.95
LAMBERT--ED.   LAMBERT   2
  ON TOP OF OLD SMOKY
    CENTURY MUSIC PUBLISHING COMPANY, INC.   4026   .40
LAMBERT, C.--ED   LAMBERT, C.   2A-2B
  LITTLE TREASURY SERIES - POLYPHONICS, BK. 1
    CENTURY MUSIC PUBLISHING COMPANY, INC.   1.00
LAMBERT, C.--ED   LAMBERT, C.   2C-3A
  LITTLE TREASURY SERIES - POLYPHONICS, BK. 2
    CENTURY MUSIC PUBLISHING COMPANY, INC.   1.00
LANE, J.--ED.   LANE, J.
  ALICE BLUE GOWN
    THE BIG THREE MUSIC CORPORATION   00.70
LANE, J.--ED.   LANE, J.
  ALL I EVER NEED IS YOU
    THE BIG THREE MUSIC CORPORATION   00.85
LANE, J.--ED.   LANE, J.
  AMERICAN PIE
    THE BIG THREE MUSIC CORPORATION   00.70
LANE, J.--ED.   LANE, J.
  ANCHORS AWEIGH
    THE BIG THREE MUSIC CORPORATION   00.70
LANE, J.--ED.   LANE, J.
  ANY TIME
    THE BIG THREE MUSIC CORPORATION   00.70
LANE, J.--ED.   LANE, J.
  APRIL LOVE
    THE BIG THREE MUSIC CORPORATION   00.70
LANE, J.--ED.   LANE, J.
  AQUARIUS
    THE BIG THREE MUSIC CORPORATION   00.70
LANE, J.--ED.   LANE, J.
  ARRIVEDERCI, ROMA
    THE BIG THREE MUSIC CORPORATION   00.70
LANE, J.--ED.   LANE, J.
  AT SUNDOWN
    THE BIG THREE MUSIC CORPORATION   00.70
LANE, J.--ED.   LANE, J.
  BATMAN THEME
    THE BIG THREE MUSIC CORPORATION   00.70
LANE, J.--ED.   LANE, J.
  BEAUTIFUL SUNDAY
    THE BIG THREE MUSIC CORPORATION   00.85
LANE, J.--ED.   LANE, J.
  BECAUSE YOU'RE MINE
    THE BIG THREE MUSIC CORPORATION   00.70
LANE, J.--ED.   LANE, J.
  BEYOND THE SUNSET
    THE BIG THREE MUSIC CORPORATION   00.70
LANE, J.--ED.   LANE, J.
  BIG SPENDER
    THE BIG THREE MUSIC CORPORATION   00.70
LANE, J.--ED.   LANE, J.
  BLUE MOON
    THE BIG THREE MUSIC CORPORATION   00.70
LANE, J.--ED.   LANE, J.
  CANDIDA
    THE BIG THREE MUSIC CORPORATION   00.70
LANE, J.--ED.   LANE, J.
  CERTAIN SMILE, A
    THE BIG THREE MUSIC CORPORATION   00.70
LANE, J.--ED.   LANE, J.
  CHARMAINE
    THE BIG THREE MUSIC CORPORATION   00.70
LANE, J.--ED.   LANE, J.
  CHATTANOOGA CHOO CHOO
    THE BIG THREE MUSIC CORPORATION   00.70
LANE, J.--ED.   LANE, J.
  CHILDREN'S MARCHING SONG
    THE BIG THREE MUSIC CORPORATION   00.70
LANE, J.--ED.   LANE, J.
  CHITTY CHITTY BANG BANG
    THE BIG THREE MUSIC CORPORATION   00.70
LANE, J.--ED.   LANE, J.
  CIRCUS WORLD
    THE BIG THREE MUSIC CORPORATION   00.70
LANE, J.--ED.   LANE, J.
  CRYING IN THE CHAPEL
    THE BIG THREE MUSIC CORPORATION   00.70
LANE, J.--ED.   LANE, J.
  DARKTOWN STRUTTERS' BALL
    THE BIG THREE MUSIC CORPORATION   00.70
LANE, J.--ED.   LANE, J.
  DAY IN THE LIFE OF A FOOL, A
    THE BIG THREE MUSIC CORPORATION   .70

LANE, J.--ED.   LANE, J.
  DEEP PURPLE
    THE BIG THREE MUSIC CORPORATION   00.70
LANE, J.--ED.   LANE, J.
  DELILAH
    THE BIG THREE MUSIC CORPORATION   00.85
LANE, J.--ED.   LANE, J.
  DELILAH
    THE BIG THREE MUSIC CORPORATION   00.85
LANE, J.--ED.   LANE, J.
  DIAMONDS ARE FOREVER
    THE BIG THREE MUSIC CORPORATION   00.70
LANE, J.--ED.   LANE, J.
  DIANE
    THE BIG THREE MUSIC CORPORATION   00.70
LANE, J.--ED.   LANE, J.
  DOLL DANCE
    THE BIG THREE MUSIC CORPORATION   00.70
LANE, J.--ED.   LANE, J.
  DON'T BLAME ME
    THE BIG THREE MUSIC CORPORATION   00.70
LANE, J.--ED.   LANE, J.
  DR. KILDARE THEME
    THE BIG THREE MUSIC CORPORATION   00.70
LANE, J.--ED.   LANE, J.
  EBB TIDE
    THE BIG THREE MUSIC CORPORATION   00.70
LANE, J.--ED.   LANE, J.
  ELMER'S TUNE
    THE BIG THREE MUSIC CORPORATION   00.70
LANE, J.--ED.   LANE, J.
  EVERY DAY OF MY LIFE
    THE BIG THREE MUSIC CORPORATION   00.70
LANE, J.--ED.   LANE, J.
  FLIPPER
    THE BIG THREE MUSIC CORPORATION   00.70
LANE, J.--ED.   LANE, J.
  FOREVER AND EVER
    THE BIG THREE MUSIC CORPORATION   00.70
LANE, J.--ED.   LANE, J.
  FORGET DOMANI
    THE BIG THREE MUSIC CORPORATION   00.70
LANE, J.--ED.   LANE, J.
  FRIENDLY PERSUASION
    THE BIG THREE MUSIC CORPORATION   00.70
LANE, J.--ED.   LANE, J.
  FROSTY THE SNOWMAN
    THE BIG THREE MUSIC CORPORATION   00.70
LANE, J.--ED.   LANE, J.
  GANG THAT SANG 'HEART OF MY HEART'
    THE BIG THREE MUSIC CORPORATION   .70
LANE, J.--ED.   LANE, J.
  GENTLE ON MY MIND
    THE BIG THREE MUSIC CORPORATION   00.70
LANE, J.--ED.   LANE, J.
  GOOD MORNING, STARSHINE
    THE BIG THREE MUSIC CORPORATION   00.70
LANE, J.--ED.   LANE, J.
  GOOD NIGHT SWEETHEART
    THE BIG THREE MUSIC CORPORATION   00.70
LANE, J.--ED.   LANE, J.
  GREEN LEAVES OF SUMMER
    THE BIG THREE MUSIC CORPORATION   00.70
LANE, J.--ED.   LANE, J.
  HAPPY HEART
    THE BIG THREE MUSIC CORPORATION   00.70
LANE, J.--ED.   LANE, J.
  HAVE YOURSELF A MERRY LITTLE CHRISTMAS
    THE BIG THREE MUSIC CORPORATION   .70
LANE, J.--ED.   LANE, J.
  HERE COMES SANTA CLAUS
    THE BIG THREE MUSIC CORPORATION   00.70
LANE, J.--ED.   LANE, J.
  HE
    THE BIG THREE MUSIC CORPORATION   00.70
LANE, J.--ED.   LANE, J.
  HE
    THE BIG THREE MUSIC CORPORATION   01.25
LANE, J.--ED.   LANE, J.
  HI-LILI, HI-LO
    THE BIG THREE MUSIC CORPORATION   00.70
LANE, J.--ED.   LANE, J.
  HOME IN THE MEADOW
    THE BIG THREE MUSIC CORPORATION   00.70
LANE, J.--ED.   LANE, J.
  HONEY
    THE BIG THREE MUSIC CORPORATION   00.70
LANE, J.--ED.   LANE, J.
  HOW THE WEST WAS WON
    THE BIG THREE MUSIC CORPORATION   00.70
LANE, J.--ED.   LANE, J.
  HUSH...HUSH, SWEET CHARLOTTE
    THE BIG THREE MUSIC CORPORATION   00.70
LANE, J.--ED.   LANE, J.
  I'D LIKE TO TEACH THE WORLD TO SING
    THE BIG THREE MUSIC CORPORATION   .70
LANE, J.--ED.   LANE, J.
  I'LL SEE YOU IN MY DREAMS
    THE BIG THREE MUSIC CORPORATION   00.70
LANE, J.--ED.   LANE, J.
  I'M ALWAYS CHASING RAINBOWS
    THE BIG THREE MUSIC CORPORATION   00.70
LANE, J.--ED.   LANE, J.
  I'M HENRY THE EIGHTH, I AM
    THE BIG THREE MUSIC CORPORATION   00.70
LANE, J.--ED.   LANE, J.
  I'M IN THE MOOD FOR LOVE
    THE BIG THREE MUSIC CORPORATION   00.70
LANE, J.--ED.   LANE, J.
  I'M SITTING ON TOP OF THE WORLD
    THE BIG THREE MUSIC CORPORATION   .70
LANE, J.--ED.   LANE, J.
  IF I GIVE MY HEART TO YOU
    THE BIG THREE MUSIC CORPORATION   00.70
LANE, J.--ED.   LANE, J.
  IF MY FRIENDS COULD SEE ME NOW
    THE BIG THREE MUSIC CORPORATION   .70
LANE, J.--ED.   LANE, J.
  IF WE ONLY HAVE LOVE
    THE BIG THREE MUSIC CORPORATION   00.70
LANE, J.--ED.   LANE, J.
  IN A LITTLE SPANISH TOWN
    THE BIG THREE MUSIC CORPORATION   00.70
LANE, J.--ED.   LANE, J.
  IN THE GARDEN
    THE BIG THREE MUSIC CORPORATION   00.70

LANE, J.--ED. LANE, J.		
IT NEVER RAINS IN SOUTHERN CALIFORNIA		
THE BIG THREE MUSIC CORPORATION		.85
LANE, J.--ED. LANE, J.		
IT WAS A GOOD TIME		
THE BIG THREE MUSIC CORPORATION		00.70
LANE, J.--ED. LANE, J.		
I CAN SEE CLEARLY NOW		
THE BIG THREE MUSIC CORPORATION		00.85
LANE, J.--ED. LANE, J.		
I DON'T WANT TO SET THE WORLD ON FIRE		
THE BIG THREE MUSIC CORPORATION		.70
LANE, J.--ED. LANE, J.		
I NEED YOU NOW		
THE BIG THREE MUSIC CORPORATION		00.70
LANE, J.--ED. LANE, J.		
I WILL NEVER PASS THIS WAY AGAIN		
THE BIG THREE MUSIC CORPORATION		.85
LANE, J.--ED. LANE, J.		
JEANNINE		
THE BIG THREE MUSIC CORPORATION		00.70
LANE, J.--ED. LANE, J.		
JOSEPHINE		
THE BIG THREE MUSIC CORPORATION		00.70
LANE, J.--ED. LANE, J.		
JOY		
THE BIG THREE MUSIC CORPORATION		00.70
LANE, J.--ED. LANE, J.		
JUNE NIGHT		
THE BIG THREE MUSIC CORPORATION		00.70
LANE, J.--ED. LANE, J.		
KISS AN ANGEL GOOD MORNING		
THE BIG THREE MUSIC CORPORATION		00.85
LANE, J.--ED. LANE, J.		
L'IL LIZA JANE		
THE BIG THREE MUSIC CORPORATION		00.70
LANE, J.--ED. LANE, J.		
LAURA		
THE BIG THREE MUSIC CORPORATION		00.70
LANE, J.--ED. LANE, J.		
LET THE SUNSHINE IN		
THE BIG THREE MUSIC CORPORATION		00.70
LANE, J.--ED. LANE, J.		
LITTLE RED MONKEY		
THE BIG THREE MUSIC CORPORATION		00.70
LANE, J.--ED. LANE, J.		
LITTLE WOODEN SOLDIER		
THE BIG THREE MUSIC CORPORATION		00.70
LANE, J.--ED. LANE, J.		
LORD'S PRAYER		
THE BIG THREE MUSIC CORPORATION		00.70
LANE, J.--ED. LANE, J.		
LOVELIEST NIGHT OF THE YEAR		
THE BIG THREE MUSIC CORPORATION		00.70
LANE, J.--ED. LANE, J.		
LOVE IS A MANY-SPLENDORED THING		
THE BIG THREE MUSIC CORPORATION		.70
LANE, J.--ED. LANE, J.		
LOVE MAKES THE WORLD GO 'ROUND		
THE BIG THREE MUSIC CORPORATION		.70
LANE, J.--ED. LANE, J.		
LULLABY OF BIRDLAND		
THE BIG THREE MUSIC CORPORATION		00.70
LANE, J.--ED. LANE, J.		
M-I-S-S-I-P-P-I		
THE BIG THREE MUSIC CORPORATION		00.70
LANE, J.--ED. LANE, J.		
M-O-T-H-E-R		
THE BIG THREE MUSIC CORPORATION		00.70
LANE, J.--ED. LANE, J.		
MAMSELLE		
THE BIG THREE MUSIC CORPORATION		00.70
LANE, J.--ED. LANE, J.		
MANSION OVER THE HILLTOP		
THE BIG THREE MUSIC CORPORATION		00.70
LANE, J.--ED. LANE, J.		
MARCHING ALONG TOGETHER		
THE BIG THREE MUSIC CORPORATION		00.70
LANE, J.--ED. LANE, J.		
MAY YOU ALWAYS		
THE BIG THREE MUSIC CORPORATION		00.70
LANE, J.--ED. LANE, J.		
MOONLIGHT AND ROSES		
THE BIG THREE MUSIC CORPORATION		00.70
LANE, J.--ED. LANE, J.		
MUTINY ON THE BOUNTY-LOVE THEME		
THE BIG THREE MUSIC CORPORATION		.70
LANE, J.--ED. LANE, J.		
MY BLUE HEAVEN		
THE BIG THREE MUSIC CORPORATION		00.70
LANE, J.--ED. LANE, J.		
MY GOD IS REAL		
THE BIG THREE MUSIC CORPORATION		00.70
LANE, J.--ED. LANE, J.		
NUTTIN FOR CHRISTMAS		
THE BIG THREE MUSIC CORPORATION		00.70
LANE, J.--ED. LANE, J.		
OH HAPPY DAY		
THE BIG THREE MUSIC CORPORATION		00.70
LANE, J.--ED. LANE, J.		
OLD RUGGED CROSS, THE		
THE BIG THREE MUSIC CORPORATION		00.70
LANE, J.--ED. LANE, J.		
ONCE IN A WHILE		
THE BIG THREE MUSIC CORPORATION		00.70
LANE, J.--ED. LANE, J.		
OVER THE RAINBOW		
THE BIG THREE MUSIC CORPORATION		00.70
LANE, J.--ED. LANE, J.		
PAGAN LOVE SONG		
THE BIG THREE MUSIC CORPORATION		00.70
LANE, J.--ED. LANE, J.		
PEACE IN THE VALLEY		
THE BIG THREE MUSIC CORPORATION		00.70
LANE, J.--ED. LANE, J.		
PEGGY O'NEIL		
THE BIG THREE MUSIC CORPORATION		00.70
LANE, J.--ED. LANE, J.		
PEG O' MY HEART		
THE BIG THREE MUSIC CORPORATION		00.70
LANE, J.--ED. LANE, J.		
PETTICOAT POLKA		
THE BIG THREE MUSIC CORPORATION		00.70
LANE, J.--ED. LANE, J.		
PIECES OF DREAMS		
THE BIG THREE MUSIC CORPORATION		00.70
LANE, J.--ED. LANE, J.		
PUSHBIKE SONG, THE		
THE BIG THREE MUSIC CORPORATION		00.70
LANE, J.--ED. LANE, J.		
RAMONA		
THE BIG THREE MUSIC CORPORATION		00.70
LANE, J.--ED. LANE, J.		
RELEASE ME		
THE BIG THREE MUSIC CORPORATION		00.70
LANE, J.--ED. LANE, J.		
ROCKIN ROBBIN		
THE BIG THREE MUSIC CORPORATION		00.85
LANE, J.--ED. LANE, J.		
RUBY		
THE BIG THREE MUSIC CORPORATION		00.70
LANE, J.--ED. LANE, J.		
SANTA CLAUS IS COMING TO TOWN		
THE BIG THREE MUSIC CORPORATION		.70
LANE, J.--ED. LANE, J.		
SEALED WITH A KISS		
THE BIG THREE MUSIC CORPORATION		00.85
LANE, J.--ED. LANE, J.		
SECOND TIME AROUND		
THE BIG THREE MUSIC CORPORATION		00.70
LANE, J.--ED. LANE, J.		
SHADOW OF YOUR SMILE		
THE BIG THREE MUSIC CORPORATION		00.70
LANE, J.--ED. LANE, J.		
SHANGRI-LA		
THE BIG THREE MUSIC CORPORATION		.70
LANE, J.--ED. LANE, J.		
SIBONEY		
THE BIG THREE MUSIC CORPORATION		00.70
LANE, J.--ED. LANE, J.		
SINGING IN THE RAIN		
THE BIG THREE MUSIC CORPORATION		00.70
LANE, J.--ED. LANE, J.		
SLEEPY TOWN EXPRESS		
THE BIG THREE MUSIC CORPORATION		00.70
LANE, J.--ED. LANE, J.		
SOLFEGGIO		
THE BIG THREE MUSIC CORPORATION		00.70
LANE, J.--ED. LANE, J.		
SOMETHING IN YOUR SMILE		
THE BIG THREE MUSIC CORPORATION		00.70
LANE, J.--ED. LANE, J.		
SOMEWHERE, MY LOVE		
THE BIG THREE MUSIC CORPORATION		00.70
LANE, J.--ED. LANE, J.		
SONG OF 'THE BIBLE'		
THE BIG THREE MUSIC CORPORATION		00.70
LANE, J.--ED. LANE, J.		
SONG OF JOY, A		
THE BIG THREE MUSIC CORPORATION		00.70
LANE, J.--ED. LANE, J.		
SONG OF JOY, THE		
THE BIG THREE MUSIC CORPORATION		01.25
LANE, J.--ED. LANE, J.		
SONG OF LOVE		
THE BIG THREE MUSIC CORPORATION		00.70
LANE, J.--ED. LANE, J.		
SO RARE		
THE BIG THREE MUSIC CORPORATION		00.70
LANE, J.--ED. LANE, J.		
STAIRWAY TO THE STARS		
THE BIG THREE MUSIC CORPORATION		00.70
LANE, J.--ED. LANE, J.		
STEP TO THE REAR		
THE BIG THREE MUSIC CORPORATION		00.70
LANE, J.--ED. LANE, J.		
STUMBLING		
THE BIG THREE MUSIC CORPORATION		00.70
LANE, J.--ED. LANE, J.		
SUMMER SAND		
THE BIG THREE MUSIC CORPORATION		00.70
LANE, J.--ED. LANE, J.		
SUNNY		
THE BIG THREE MUSIC CORPORATION		00.70
LANE, J.--ED. LANE, J.		
SWEET AND LOVELY		
THE BIG THREE MUSIC CORPORATION		00.70
LANE, J.--ED. LANE, J.		
SWINGIN' SHEPHERD BLUES		
THE BIG THREE MUSIC CORPORATION		00.70
LANE, J.--ED. LANE, J.		
TALK TO THE ANIMALS		
THE BIG THREE MUSIC CORPORATION		00.70
LANE, J.--ED. LANE, J.		
THERE'S A KIND OF HUSH		
THE BIG THREE MUSIC CORPORATION		00.70
LANE, J.--ED. LANE, J.		
THIRTY-TWO FEET AND EIGHT LITTLE TAILS		
THE BIG THREE MUSIC CORPORATION		.70
LANE, J.--ED. LANE, J.		
THOSE MAGNIFICENT MEN IN THEIR FLYING MACHINES		
THE BIG THREE MUSIC CORPORATION		00.70
LANE, J.--ED. LANE, J.		
THREE COINS IN THE FOUNTAIN		
THE BIG THREE MUSIC CORPORATION		00.70
LANE, J.--ED. LANE, J.		
THREE O'CLOCK IN THE MORNING		
THE BIG THREE MUSIC CORPORATION		00.70
LANE, J.--ED. LANE, J.		
TIME ON MY HANDS		
THE BIG THREE MUSIC CORPORATION		00.70
LANE, J.--ED. LANE, J.		
TODAY		
THE BIG THREE MUSIC CORPORATION		00.70
LANE, J.--ED. LANE, J.		
VINCENT		
THE BIG THREE MUSIC CORPORATION		00.85
LANE, J.--ED. LANE, J.		
VOLARE		
THE BIG THREE MUSIC CORPORATION		00.70
LANE, J.--ED. LANE, J.		
WALTZ YOU SAVED FOR ME		
THE BIG THREE MUSIC CORPORATION		00.70
LANE, J.--ED. LANE, J.		
WEDDING OF JACK AND JILL		
THE BIG THREE MUSIC CORPORATION		00.70
LANE, J.--ED. LANE, J.		
WEDDING OF THE PAINTED DOLL		
THE BIG THREE MUSIC CORPORATION		00.70
LANE, J.--ED. LANE, J.		
WE ARE TOGETHER		
THE BIG THREE MUSIC CORPORATION		00.70

LANE, J.--ED.	LANE, J.					
WHAT ARE YOU DOING THE REST OF YOUR LIFE						
THE BIG THREE MUSIC CORPORATION						00.70
LANE, J.--ED.	LANE, J.					
WHEN IT'S SPRINGTIME IN THE ROCKIES						
THE BIG THREE MUSIC CORPORATION						00.70
LANE, J.--ED.	LANE, J.					
WHEN I GROW TOO OLD TO DREAM						
THE BIG THREE MUSIC CORPORATION						00.70
LANE, J.--ED.	LANE, J.					
WHEN THE MOON COMES OVER THE MOUNTAIN						
THE BIG THREE MUSIC CORPORATION						00.70
LANE, J.--ED.	LANE, J.					
WHEN YOU WORE A TULIP						
THE BIG THREE MUSIC CORPORATION						00.70
LANE, J.--ED.	LANE, J.					
WHISPERING						
THE BIG THREE MUSIC CORPORATION						00.70
LANE, J.--ED.	LANE, J.					
WHITHER THOU GOEST						
THE BIG THREE MUSIC CORPORATION						00.70
LANE, J.--ED.	LANE, J.					
WINDMILLS OF YOUR MIND, THE						
THE BIG THREE MUSIC CORPORATION						01.25
LANE, J.--ED.	LANE, J.					
WINDMILLS OF YOUR MIND						
THE BIG THREE MUSIC CORPORATION						00.70
LANE, J.--ED.	LANE, J.					
WONDERFUL ONE						
THE BIG THREE MUSIC CORPORATION						00.70
LANE, J.--ED.	LANE, J.					
YOU DON'T MESS AROUND WITH JIM						
THE BIG THREE MUSIC CORPORATION						.85
LANE, J.--ED.	LANE, J.					
YOU WERE MEANT FOR ME						
THE BIG THREE MUSIC CORPORATION						00.70
LANE, J.--ED.	LANE, J.					
ZIP A DEE DO DAH						
THE BIG THREE MUSIC CORPORATION						00.70
LANE, J.--ED.	LANE, J.					
ZORBA THE GREEK - THEME						
THE BIG THREE MUSIC CORPORATION						00.70
LANE, J.						
JOHN LANE PLAYS BIG MOVIE HITS						
THE BIG THREE MUSIC CORPORATION						03.95
LANE, J.						
TEACHER'S PET NO. 12-16 BIG HITS						
THE BIG THREE MUSIC CORPORATION						01.95
LANE, J.						
TEACHER'S PET NO. 13						
THE BIG THREE MUSIC CORPORATION						01.95
LANG--ED	LANG	2				
TANZ, TANZ, GRETELEIN						
SCHOTT				3938		1.75
LANG--ED *	LANG *	2-3				
WAS UNSRE KINDER SINGEN						
SCHOTT				600		4.00
LANGE, G.						
EDELWEISS, EASY						
CENTURY MUSIC PUBLISHING COMPANY, INC.				2778		.40
LANGE, G.	STEINER	1				
FLOWER SONG						
BELWIN-MILLS PUBLISHING CORPORATION						.60
LARA, A.						
GRANADA - SIMPLIFIED						
EDITORIAL COOPERATIVA INTER-AMERICANA						00.85
LARA, A.						
GRANADA - TEACHING EDITION						
EDITORIAL COOPERATIVA INTER-AMERICANA						00.85
LASSON, P.	ZEPP	4				
CRESCENDO						
PRO-ART PUBLICATIONS, INC.				458		.50
LAUDER, H.	SCHAUM, J.	2				
I LOVE A LASSIE						
SCHAUM PUBLICATIONS, INC.						.50
LAVALLEE, C.	ROLFE, W.	3				
PAPILLON, EASY						
CENTURY MUSIC PUBLISHING COMPANY, INC.				3215		.40
LAWLOR, G. *	CURCIO	1				
SIDEWALKS OF NEW YORK, THE						
BOSTON MUSIC COMPANY						.50
LA ROCCA *						
AT THE JAZZ BAND BALL						
THE BIG THREE MUSIC CORPORATION						00.95
LA ROWE, J.						
MEDITATIONS FOR PIANO						
LILLENAS PUBLISHING COMPANY				MB-123		2.50
LECUONA						
LECUONAS BEST MADE EASIER FOR YOU						
EDWARD B. MARKS MUSIC CORPORATION						02.00
LECUONA						
SIBONEY						
THE BIG THREE MUSIC CORPORATION						00.95
LEE *	SCHAUM, J.	1				
PENNSYLVANIA POLKA						
SCHAUM PUBLICATIONS, INC.						.75
LEGRAND *	BALL	EASY				
SUMMER KNOWS, THE						
WARNER BROTHERS PUBLISHERS						.75
LEGRAND	TERRY					
THEME FROM SUMMER OF '42						
WARNER BROTHERS PUBLISHERS						1.00
LEHAR	WEYBRIGHT	1 1/2				
GOLD AND SILVER WALTZ						
BELWIN-MILLS PUBLISHING CORPORATION						.60
LEHAR		3				
MERRY WIDOW, VILIA						
CENTURY MUSIC PUBLISHING COMPANY, INC.				3350		.40
LEHAR	ROGERS	2				
MERRY WIDOW WALTZ, SIMPLIFIED						
BELWIN-MILLS PUBLISHING CORPORATION				717		.60
LEHAR		4				
MERRY WIDOW WALTZES, THE						
CENTURY MUSIC PUBLISHING COMPANY, INC.				1310		.40
LEHAR	WALLIS	2				
MERRY WIDOW WALTZ						
BOSTON MUSIC COMPANY						.50
LEHAR		3				
MERRY WIDOW WALTZ						
CENTURY MUSIC PUBLISHING COMPANY, INC.				3621		.40
LEHAR	MITTLER	2A				
MERRY WIDOW WALTZ						
MUSICORD PUBLICATIONS, INC.						.45
LEHAR	STEINER	1				
ROYAL BALLET						
BELWIN-MILLS PUBLISHING CORPORATION						.60

LEHAR		4				
WALTZES, MERRY WIDOW						
CENTURY MUSIC PUBLISHING COMPANY, INC.				1310		.40
LELEU		7				
SUITE SYMPHONIQUE						
ALPHONSE LEDUC						
LELEU		7				
TRANSPARENCES, NO. 2, MIROUR D'EAU						
ALPHONSE LEDUC						
LEMARE, E.	ARMOUR	3				
ANDANTINO						
CENTURY MUSIC PUBLISHING COMPANY, INC.				3627		.60
LEMARE, E.	WALDO, J.	1				
THEME FROM ANDANTINO						
WILLIS MUSIC COMPANY						.30
LENNON *	NEALE, J.	EASY				
ALL TOGETHER NOW						
WARNER BROTHERS PUBLISHERS						.75
LENNON *	NEALE, J.	EASY				
ALL YOU NEED IS LOVE						
WARNER BROTHERS PUBLISHERS						.75
LENNON *						
FIFTY BY JOHN LENNON AND PAUL MCCARTNEY, EASY BIG NOTE PIANO						
WARNER BROTHERS PUBLISHERS						3.95
LENNON *	NEALE, J.	EASY				
HEY JUDE						
WARNER BROTHERS PUBLISHERS						.75
LENNON *	NEALE, J.	EASY				
LET IT BE						
WARNER BROTHERS PUBLISHERS						.75
LENNON *	NEALE, J.	EASY				
LONG AND WINDING ROAD, THE						
WARNER BROTHERS PUBLISHERS						.75
LENNON *	NEALE, J.	EASY				
MICHELLE						
WARNER BROTHERS PUBLISHERS						.75
LENNON *	NEALE, J.	EASY				
YESTERDAY						
WARNER BROTHERS PUBLISHERS						.75
LEO, L.	MCCLANAHAN, R.					
GIGA -- HARMONIC STUDY EDITION						
BELWIN-MILLS PUBLISHING CORPORATION				20341		.85
LEO, L.	MCCLANAHAN, R.					
SONATA PER CEMBALO, HARMONIC STUDY EDITION -- WITH OPTIONAL						
SECOND PIANO						
BELWIN-MILLS PUBLISHING CORPORATION				20263		.85
LEONCAVALLO	CORONARO					
BOHEME, LA - IO NON CHE UNA POVERA STANZETTA						
FRANCO COLOMBO PUBLICATIONS				SON.970		.90
LEONCAVALLO	ZEPP	4				
IT REALLY CAN HAPPEN						
PRO-ART PUBLICATIONS, INC.				407		.50
LEONCAVALLO	BALLATORE, P.	2				
LA MATTINATA						
PRO-ART PUBLICATIONS, INC.				395		.50
LEONCAVALLO						
PAGLIACCI -- COMPLETE OPERA --						
FRANCO COLOMBO PUBLICATIONS				SON.656		8.75
LEONCAVALLO						
PAGLIACCI - ARIOSO						
FRANCO COLOMBO PUBLICATIONS				SON.1908		.90
LEONCAVALLO	DE CRISTOFARO					
PAGLIACCI - INTERMEZZO AND UN TAL GIOCO						
FRANCO COLOMBO PUBLICATIONS				SON.1845		1.00
LEONCAVALLO						
PAGLIACCI - INTERMEZZO						
FRANCO COLOMBO PUBLICATIONS				SON.732		.90
LEONCAVALLO	DE CRISTOFARO					
PAGLIACCI - MINUET AND SERENATA						
FRANCO COLOMBO PUBLICATIONS				SON.1844		1.00
LEONCAVALLO						
PAGLIACCI - PROLOGUE						
FRANCO COLOMBO PUBLICATIONS				SON.1902		1.25
LESCHETIZKY						
ANDANTE FINALE DE 'LUCIA DI LAMMERMOOR'--FOR THE LEFT HAND						
ALONE--OP. 13						
G. SCHIRMER, INC.						.60
LESTRANGE--ED	LESTRANGE					
BELLS OF ST. MARY'S, WALTZ						
CHAPPELL AND COMPANY, INC.				0437509-1501		.95
LEVINE, H.--ED	LEVINE, H.					
MORE THEMES FROM THE GREAT CONCERTOS						
THEODORE PRESSER COMPANY						1.25
LEVINE, H.--ED	LEVINE, H.					
PIANO CLASSICS SIMPLIFIED						
ALFRED MUSIC COMPANY				528		1.50
LEVINE, H.--ED	LEVINE, H.					
THEMES FROM GREAT CHAMBER MUSIC						
THEODORE PRESSER COMPANY						1.50
LEVINE, H.--ED	LEVINE, H.					
THEMES FROM THE GREAT BALLETS						
THEODORE PRESSER COMPANY						1.25
LEVINE, H.--ED	LEVINE, H.					
THEMES FROM THE GREAT ORATORIOS						
THEODORE PRESSER COMPANY						1.75
LEVINE, H.--ED	LEVINE, H.					
THEMES FROM THE GREAT PIANO CONCERTOS						
THEODORE PRESSER COMPANY						1.50
LEVINE, H.--ED	LEVINE, H.					
THEMES FROM THE GREAT SYMPHONIES						
THEODORE PRESSER COMPANY						2.00
LEVINE, H.--ED	LEVINE, H.					
THEMES FROM THE ORCHESTRAL REPERTOIRE						
THEODORE PRESSER COMPANY						1.25
LEVY, S.	SCHAUM, J.					
NAUGHTY WALTZ, THAT						
BELWIN-MILLS PUBLISHING CORPORATION						.60
LEYBACH, I.		2-3				
NOCTURNE, NO. 05, EASY						
CENTURY MUSIC PUBLISHING COMPANY, INC.				2507		.40
LIBERACE--ED	LIBERACE					
SEPTEMBER SONG						
CHAPPELL AND COMPANY, INC.				5060009-1502		.95
LIDDLE, S.	PERRY					
ABIDE WITH ME						
BOOSEY AND HAWKES, INC.						.50
LIGHTFOOT	NEALE, J.	EASY				
IF YOU COULD READ MY MIND						
WARNER BROTHERS PUBLISHERS						.75
LINCKE, P.	ZEPP	3-4				
GLOW WORM, THE						
PRO-ART PUBLICATIONS, INC.				199		.50
LINCKE, P.	RICHTER	FIRST YEAR				
GLOW WORM						
WARNER BROTHERS PUBLISHERS						.75

LINCKE, P.	SCHAUM, J.	1		
SPRING, SWEET SPRING				
SCHAUM PUBLICATIONS, INC.				.50
LINCOLN, H.	PAULL	ADVANCED		
MIDNIGHT FIRE ALARM				
SHAWNEE PRESS, INC.			HB-58	.60
LINDSAY, C. JR.--ED	LINDSAY, C. JR.			
BIG BANDS, THE				
MUSIC SALES CORPORATION			040051	2.95
LINDSAY, C. JR.--ED	LINDSAY, C. JR.			
HAVE FUN PLAYING JAZZ				
MUSIC SALES CORPORATION			040046	2.95
LIPSCOMB--ED	LIPSCOMB			
FAVORITE FOLKSONGS				
BOSTON MUSIC COMPANY				1.25
LIPSCOMB--ED	LIPSCOMB			
FORTY-SIX EASY ARRANGEMENTS OF SACRED MELODIES--WITH WORDS				
G. SCHIRMER, INC.				1.00
LIPSCOMB--ED	LIPSCOMB			
HYMNS TO REMEMBER				
G. SCHIRMER, INC.				1.00
LISZT	ANSON, G.			
ANSON INTRODUCES LISZT				
WILLIS MUSIC COMPANY				1.50
LISZT	PLANTE, FR.	8		
CELEBRE MELODIE HONGROISE EN SI FLAT				
ALPHONSE LEDUC				
LISZT	RIVE-KING, JULIE			
CONCERT TRANSCRIPTION OF HUNGARIAN RHAPSODY NO. 21				
MUSICA OBSCURA				2.50
LISZT	ECKSTEIN			
DREAMS OF LOVE NO. 3 IN A FLAT --LIEBESTRAUME--				
CARL FISCHER, INC.			S 802	.50
LISZT	GROOMS	3		
DREAM OF LOVE, EASY				
CENTURY MUSIC PUBLISHING COMPANY, INC.			2467	.40
LISZT	THOMPSON, J.	5		
DREAM OF LOVE				
WILLIS MUSIC COMPANY				.50
LISZT	SCHER, W.	INTERMEDIATE GRADES		
EASY LISZT--12 FAMOUS CONCERT PIECES, ARRANGED FOR INTERMEDIATE GRADES				
G. SCHIRMER, INC.				1.00
LISZT	SCHAUM, J.	4		
FORGOTTEN WALTZ				
SCHAUM PUBLICATIONS, INC.				.60
LISZT	SAUER	M		
HUNGARIAN FANTASY				
C. F. PETERS CORPORATION			3612A	1.25
LISZT	KRENZ			
HUNGARIAN RHAPSODY NO. 02				
BELWIN-MILLS PUBLISHING CORPORATION			20127	.95
LISZT	KREUTZER			
IN VARIOUS MOODS				
BOSTON MUSIC COMPANY				1.25
LISZT *	GALLICO			
LA CAMPANELLA				
G. SCHIRMER, INC.				.80
LISZT *	GALLICO			
LA CAMPANELLA				
G. SCHIRMER, INC.				.80
LISZT		6		
LA REGATTA VENETIANA				
CENTURY MUSIC PUBLISHING COMPANY, INC.			1480	.40
LISZT *				
LEISE FLEHEN				
G. SCHIRMER, INC.				.75
LISZT	STRADAL			
LES PRELUDES--SYMPHONIC POEM NO. 3				
ASSOCIATED MUSIC PUBLISHERS, INC.			BRH	2.00
LISZT	WEYBRIGHT	2		
LIEBESTRAUME				
BELWIN-MILLS PUBLISHING CORPORATION				.60
LISZT	MITTLER	2B		
LIEBESTRAUM				
MUSICORD PUBLICATIONS, INC.				.45
LISZT	ZEPP	4-5		
LIEBESTRAUM				
PRO-ART PUBLICATIONS, INC.			358	.50
LISZT	HODSON	3 1/2		
LIEBESTRAUM				
THEODORE PRESSER COMPANY				.50
LISZT	WHITFORD	GR. 2		
LIEBESTRAUM				
ROBERT WHITFORD PUBLICATIONS				.40
LISZT *	TAGLIAPIETRA			
NIGHTINGALE, THE				
FRANCO COLOMBO PUBLICATIONS			ER24	.60
LISZT	THOMPSON, J.	3		
RAKOCZY MARCH				
WILLIS MUSIC COMPANY				.60
LISZT *				
REGATA VENEZIANA, LA				
FRANCO COLOMBO PUBLICATIONS			128857	.90
LISZT *		6		
REGATA VENETIANA				
CENTURY MUSIC PUBLISHING COMPANY, INC.			1480	.40
LISZT	BENDEL			
RHAPSODIES HONGROISES NO. 02				
G. SCHIRMER, INC.				.90
LISZT	BENDEL			
RHAPSODIE NO. 02				
FRANCO COLOMBO PUBLICATIONS			108077	1.25
LISZT	DEL MAGLIO			
RHAPSODIE NO. 02				
FRANCO COLOMBO PUBLICATIONS			129106	.90
LISZT	BENDEL	4		
SECOND HUNGARIAN RHAPSODY				
CENTURY MUSIC PUBLISHING COMPANY, INC.			1645	.40
LISZT	MITTLER	3B		
SECOND HUNGARIAN RHAPSODY				
MUSICORD PUBLICATIONS, INC.				.45
LISZT	DEL MAGLIO			
SIX CONSOLATIONS, NO. 3				
FRANCO COLOMBO PUBLICATIONS			127149	.60
LISZT *				
SPRING NIGHT				
FRANCO COLOMBO PUBLICATIONS			128430	.50
LISZT	ECKSTEIN			
THEME FROM HUNGARIAN RHAPSODY NO. 2				
CARL FISCHER, INC.			S 2303	.50
LISZT	ECKSTEIN			
THEME FROM LIEBESTRAUME				
CARL FISCHER, INC.			S 2286	.50
LISZT	THOMPSON, J.	2		
THEME FROM LIEBESTRAUME				
WILLIS MUSIC COMPANY				.35
LISZT	DEL MAGLIO			
THREE LIEBESTRAEUME - NO. 3				
FRANCO COLOMBO PUBLICATIONS			127203	.60
LISZT	SZELENYI			
TWELVE ETUDES, OP. 1				
KULTURA				2.00
LISZT *				
TWENTY-FOUR SONG TRANSCRIPTIONS, BK. 1				
G. SCHIRMER, INC.			L128	1.75
LISZT *				
TWENTY-FOUR SONG TRANSCRIPTIONS, BK. 2				
G. SCHIRMER, INC.			L129	1.75
LISZT				
TWENTY PIANO TRANSCRIPTIONS				
THEODORE PRESSER COMPANY				5.00
LISZT	BENDEL	3		
UNGARISCHE RHAPSODIEN NO. 02, M. D. BER. KADENZ				
SCHOTT			06435 1/2	1.00
LITTLE--ED	LITTLE			
WELK, LAWRENCE, FAVORITES FOR HONKY TONK PIANO				
WARNER BROTHERS PUBLISHERS				1.95
LITTLEWOOD, R.	SCHAUM, J.	1 1/2		
POPPO THE PORPOISE				
SCHAUM PUBLICATIONS, INC.				.60
LOESSER, F.	RICHTER	2 1/2 - 3		
ADELAIDE'S LAMENT				
FRANK MUSIC CORPORATION				.75
LOESSER, F.				
GREENWILLOW				
FRANK MUSIC CORPORATION				1.50
LOESSER, F.				
HOW TO SUCCEED IN BUSINESS WITHOUT REALLY TRYING				
FRANK MUSIC CORPORATION				1.50
LOESSER, F.				
MOST HAPPY FELLA, THE				
FRANK MUSIC CORPORATION				1.25
LOESSER, F.				
ON A SLOW BOAT TO CHINA				
FRANK MUSIC CORPORATION				.75
LOESSER, F.	AGAY, D.	EASY		
SONGS FROM 'GREENWILLOW'				
FRANK MUSIC CORPORATION				1.25
LOESSER, F.	RICHTER	EASY		
SONGS FROM 'HANS CHRISTIAN ANDERSEN'				
FRANK MUSIC CORPORATION				1.25
LOESSER, F.	AGAY, D.	EASY		
SONGS FROM 'HOW TO SUCCEED IN BUSINESS WITHOUT REALLY TRYING'				
FRANK MUSIC CORPORATION				1.25
LOSEY	WEYBRIGHT	2 1/2		
GLORIA, MARCH				
BELWIN-MILLS PUBLISHING CORPORATION				.60
LUBOFF, N.	RICHTER	2 1/2 - 3		
YELLOW BIRD				
FRANK MUSIC CORPORATION				.75
LUBOFF, N.	TERRY, F.			
YELLOW BIRD				
FRANK MUSIC CORPORATION				.95
LUTTGERS--ED	LUTTGERS	1-2		
DER GUTE FREUND. LEICHTE VOLKS-TANZ- UND OPERNMELODIEN				
BARENREITER VERLAG			SM 80	
LUTZ--ED	LUTZ			
AM RHEIN BEIM WEIN				
SCHOTT			4900	3.00
LUTZ--ED	LUTZ			
DER WIMPEL, FAHRTENLIEDER				
SCHOTT			5250	2.50
LUTZ--ED	LUTZ	3		
DIE GROSSE OPER, BAND 01				
SCHOTT			4949	5.00
LUTZ--ED	LUTZ	3-4		
DIE GROSSE OPER, BAND 02				
SCHOTT			4950	5.00
LUTZ--ED	LUTZ	2-3		
FROHE WEIHNACHT				
SCHOTT			4006	2.25
LUTZ--ED	LUTZ	2-3		
ITALIEN IM LIED				
SCHOTT			4825	3.00
LUTZ--ED	LUTZ	1-2		
MEIN KINDERLIEDERBUCH - 60 KINDERLIEDER				
SCHOTT			3000	2.50
LUTZ--ED	LUTZ	2		
MEIN VOLKSLIEDERBUCH				
SCHOTT			4100	2.50
LYALL, M.--ED	LYALL, M.			
FAVORITE HYMNS FOR THE PIANO				
BROADMAN MUSIC			4571-02	2.25
LYALL, M.--ED	LYALL, M.			
HYMN TUNE PRELUDES FOR THE PIANO, NO. 1				
BROADMAN MUSIC			4571-03	2.25
LYALL, M.--ED	LYALL, M.			
HYMN TUNE PRELUDES FOR THE PIANO, NO. 2				
BROADMAN MUSIC			4571-04	2.25
MACDOWELL	ROLFE, W.	3		
HEXENTANZ, EASY				
CENTURY MUSIC PUBLISHING COMPANY, INC.			3372	.40
MACDOWELL	SCHAUM, J.	4		
MACDOWELL MASTERPIECES				
SCHAUM PUBLICATIONS, INC.				2.00
MACDOWELL	DUMM			
RECITAL REFRESHER SERIES -- TO A HUMMING BIRD				
BELWIN-MILLS PUBLISHING CORPORATION			26110	.60
MACDOWELL	ECKSTEIN			
TO A WILD ROSE				
CARL FISCHER, INC.			P 2777	.50
MACDOWELL	BERMONT, H.	2A		
TO A WILD ROSE				
MUSICORD PUBLICATIONS, INC.				.45
MACDOWELL	WHITFORD	GR. 2		
TO A WILD ROSE				
ROBERT WHITFORD PUBLICATIONS				.40
MACK, E.	SCHIEFELBEIN, F.	3		
GENERAL GRANT'S GRAND MARCH				
VOLKWEIN BROS.				.25
MAGNARD				
SYMPHONY NO. 03				
FRANCO COLOMBO PUBLICATIONS			SAL	6.50
MAHLER	SINGER	D		
SYMPHONY NO. 05				
C. F. PETERS CORPORATION			3760	6.00
MAIER, G.	CORZILIUS			
PLAYING THE PIANO				
BELWIN-MILLS PUBLISHING CORPORATION				1.50
MALER, W.		3		
JAHRESKREIS. KLAVIER INVENTIONEN UBER DEUTSCHE VOLKSLIEDER				
SCHOTT			2363	2.00

MALNECK *
    DREAM STREET
        THE BIG THREE MUSIC CORPORATION   00.95
MALNECK *
    PARK AVENUE FANTASY
        THE BIG THREE MUSIC CORPORATION   00.95
MALTZMAN--ED   MALTZMAN
    SONGS EN FRANCAIS
        PRO-ART PUBLICATIONS, INC.   607   .75
MANCINI   HASTINGS
    DAYS OF WINE AND ROSES
        WARNER BROTHERS PUBLISHERS   1.00
MANCINI   DAVIS, J. R.   FIRST YEAR
    DAYS OF WINE AND ROSES
        WARNER BROTHERS PUBLISHERS   .75
MANCINI *   NEALE, J.   EASY
    DAYS OF WINE AND ROSES
        WARNER BROTHERS PUBLISHERS   .75
MANCINI
    HIGH TIME
        THE BIG THREE MUSIC CORPORATION   00.95
MANCINI
    MR. HOBBS THEME
        THE BIG THREE MUSIC CORPORATION   00.95
MARCHETTI, F.   SCHAUM, J.   2
    FASCINATION WALTZ
        SCHAUM PUBLICATIONS, INC.   .60
MARCHETTI, F.   ZEPP   4
    FASCINATION
        PRO-ART PUBLICATIONS, INC.   264   .50
MARCHETTI, F.   RICHTER   FIRST YEAR
    FASCINATION
        WARNER BROTHERS PUBLISHERS   .75
MARENCO   CHIESA
    EXCELSIOR - EASY FANTASY
        FRANCO COLOMBO PUBLICATIONS   109098   .60
MARIE   WEYBRIGHT   2
    CINQUANTAINE, LA
        BELWIN-MILLS PUBLISHING CORPORATION   .60
MARIE   WEYBRIGHT   2 1/2
    PETITE GAVOTTE
        BELWIN-MILLS PUBLISHING CORPORATION   .60
MARKOWITZ, R.
    HONDO
        THE BIG THREE MUSIC CORPORATION   00.95
MARSCHALL   LOEPKE   3
    STARLIGHT
        VOLKWEIN BROS.   .35
MARTIN, E.   SEDLON
    COME TO THE FAIR
        BOOSEY AND HAWKES, INC.   .40
MARTIN, G. B.   DEL MAGLIO
    GAVOTTE
        FRANCO COLOMBO PUBLICATIONS   129093   .60
MASCAGNI, P.   DE CRISTOFARO
    AMICO FRITZ, L' - CHERRY DUET
        FRANCO COLOMBO PUBLICATIONS   SON.1727   1.00
MASCAGNI, P.   DE CRISTOFARO
    AMICO FRITZ, L' - INTERMEZZO -- FINGERED --
        FRANCO COLOMBO PUBLICATIONS   SON.1816   .90
MASCAGNI, P.
    AMICO FRITZ, L' - INTERMEZZO -- ORIGINAL --
        FRANCO COLOMBO PUBLICATIONS   SON.703   .90
MASCAGNI, P.   AZZONI
    AMICO FRITZ, L' - INTERMEZZO
        FRANCO COLOMBO PUBLICATIONS   SON.620   .90
MASCAGNI, P.   3
    CAVALLERIA RUSTICANA, INTERMEZZO
        CENTURY MUSIC PUBLISHING COMPANY, INC. 158   .40
MASCAGNI, P.
    CAVALLERIA RUSTICANA -- COMPLETE OPERA --
        FRANCO COLOMBO PUBLICATIONS   SON.493   8.75
MASCAGNI, P.
    CAVALLERIA RUSTICANA - GRAND FANTASY
        FRANCO COLOMBO PUBLICATIONS   SON.1764   1.50
MASCAGNI, P.
    CAVALLERIA RUSTICANA - INTERMEZZO -- ORIGINAL --
        FRANCO COLOMBO PUBLICATIONS   SON.509   .90
MASCAGNI, P.   FUMAGALLI
    CAVALLERIA RUSTICANA - INTERMEZZO
        FRANCO COLOMBO PUBLICATIONS   SON.522   .90
MASCAGNI, P.   DE SIMONE
    CAVALLERIA RUSTICANA - INTERMEZZO
        FRANCO COLOMBO PUBLICATIONS   SON.1348   .90
MASCAGNI, P.
    CAVALLERIA RUSTICANA - PRELUDE
        FRANCO COLOMBO PUBLICATIONS   SON.613   1.00
MASCAGNI, P.   DE SIMONE
    CAVALLERIA RUSTICANA - SELECTIONS
        FRANCO COLOMBO PUBLICATIONS   SON.1381   1.75
MASCAGNI, P.   3
    CAVALLERIA RUSTICANA 'INTERMEZZO'
        BELWIN-MILLS PUBLISHING CORPORATION   245   .60
MASCAGNI, P.   GALLI
    GUGLIELMO RATCLIFF - DREAM OF RATCLIFF
        FRANCO COLOMBO PUBLICATIONS   SON.902   .90
MASCAGNI, P.   3
    INTERMEZZO, CAV. RUSTICANA
        CENTURY MUSIC PUBLISHING COMPANY, INC. 158   .40
MASCAGNI, P.   2
    INTERMEZZO, CAV. RUSTICANA
        CENTURY MUSIC PUBLISHING COMPANY, INC. 1784   .40
MASCAGNI, P.   CHIESA
    IRIS - EASY FANTASIA
        FRANCO COLOMBO PUBLICATIONS   111262   .50
MASCAGNI, P.
    IRIS - HYMN TO THE SUN
        FRANCO COLOMBO PUBLICATIONS   102335   1.00
MASCAGNI, P.
    ISABEAU -- COMPLETE OPERA --
        FRANCO COLOMBO PUBLICATIONS   SON.1644   11.50
MASCAGNI, P.
    LODOLETTA -- COMPLETE OPERA --
        FRANCO COLOMBO PUBLICATIONS   SON.2032   11.50
MASCAGNI, P.   MIRRI
    LODOLETTA - SERENATA
        FRANCO COLOMBO PUBLICATIONS   SON.2105   .90
MASCAGNI, P.
    MASCHERE, LE - OVERTURE
        FRANCO COLOMBO PUBLICATIONS   SON.1933   1.25
MASCAGNI, P.
    MASCHERE, LE - PRELUDIETTO TO ACT II
        FRANCO COLOMBO PUBLICATIONS   SON.1938   .90
MASCAGNI, P.
    PICCOLI MARAT, IL -- COMPLETE OPERA --
        FRANCO COLOMBO PUBLICATIONS   SON.2206   11.50

MASCAGNI, P.   BUMMERI
    SILVANO - EASY FANTASY NO. 1
        FRANCO COLOMBO PUBLICATIONS   SON.1707   .90
MASCAGNI, P.   BUCCERI
    SILVANO - EASY FANTASY NO. 2
        FRANCO COLOMBO PUBLICATIONS   SON.1708   .90
MASCAGNI, P.
    SILVANO - NOCTURNE
        FRANCO COLOMBO PUBLICATIONS   SON.2796   .90
MASON, L.   STEINER   APP.
    FATHER, IN THY MYSTERIOUS PRESENCE KNEELING
        BELWIN-MILLS PUBLISHING CORPORATION   .60
MASON, W.
    GAVOTTE IN D FROM THE 6TH 'CELLO-SONATA OF BACH
        G. SCHIRMER, INC.   .50
MASSENET, J.
    ARAGONAISE, FROM LE CID
        CARL FISCHER, INC.   S 94   .50
MASSENET, J.   BARTH, H.   3
    ARAGONAISE
        BELWIN-MILLS PUBLISHING CORPORATION   .60
MASSENET, J.   HOFFMAN   4
    ARGONAISE
        WILLIS MUSIC COMPANY   .35
MASSENET, J.
    CID, LE - ARAGONAISE
        FRANCO COLOMBO PUBLICATIONS   BA6481   .75
MASSENET, J.   DEL MAGLIO
    CID, LE - ARAGONAISE
        FRANCO COLOMBO PUBLICATIONS   BA10206   .75
MASSENET, J.   4
    DERNIER SOMMEIL DE LA VIERGE, LE
        CENTURY MUSIC PUBLISHING COMPANY, INC. 2352   .40
MASSENET, J.   JETSON, I. H.   4
    ELEGY
        VOLKWEIN BROS.   .35
MASSENET, J.
    GAVOTTE FROM 'MANON'
        HEUGEL ET CIE.   1.95
MASSENET, J.
    HERODIADE -- BALLET EXTRACT
        HEUGEL ET CIE.   2.40
MASSENET, J.
    LE CID -- BALLET EXTRACT
        HEUGEL ET CIE.   3.75
MASSENET, J.
    LE GRILLON DU FOYER
        HEUGEL ET CIE.   3.25
MASSENET, J.
    MANON
        HEUGEL ET CIE.   11.00
MASSENET, J.   KING, S.
    MEDITATION -- FROM 'THAIS'
        BELWIN-MILLS PUBLISHING CORPORATION   26029   .60
MASSENET, J.
    MEDITATION 'THAIS'
        ASHLEY DEALERS SERVICE, INC.   ES   .95
MASSENET, J.   3
    MEDITATION FROM 'THAIS'
        BOSTON MUSIC COMPANY   .60
MASSENET, J.
    MEDITATION FROM 'THAIS'
        HEUGEL ET CIE.   1.45
MASSENET, J.
    MEDITATION FROM THAIS
        CARL FISCHER, INC.   P 2294   .75
MASSENET, J.   3
    THAIS, MEDITATION
        CENTURY MUSIC PUBLISHING COMPANY, INC. 4004   .40
MASSENET, J.
    THAIS - MEDITATION
        FRANCO COLOMBO PUBLICATIONS   BA6476   .75
MASSENET, J.   DEL MAGLIO
    THAIS - MEDITATION
        FRANCO COLOMBO PUBLICATIONS   BA10205   .75
MASSENET, J.
    THAIS
        HEUGEL ET CIE.   9.75
MASSENET, J.
    WERTHER
        HEUGEL ET CIE.   8.75
MATHESON   RICHTER
    CHICKADEE, THE
        BELWIN-MILLS PUBLISHING CORPORATION   .60
MATOS RODRIGUEZ   DEL MAGLIO
    CUMPARSITA, LA
        FRANCO COLOMBO PUBLICATIONS   127204   .60
MATTEI   3
    TOURBILLON, VALSE DE CONCERT, EASY
        CENTURY MUSIC PUBLISHING COMPANY, INC. 2516   .40
MAXIM, F.   SCHAUM, J.   1 1/2
    GRANDFATHER'S CLOCK
        SCHAUM PUBLICATIONS, INC.   .50
MAXWELL
    EBB TIDE
        THE BIG THREE MUSIC CORPORATION   00.95
MAYER
    DANCES FROM FAMOUS BALLETS
        FRANCO COLOMBO PUBLICATIONS   NY1464   1.00
MAYER
    DANCES FROM FAMOUS OPERAS
        FRANCO COLOMBO PUBLICATIONS   NY1463   1.00
MAYER
    NATIONAL DANCES OF EUROPE
        FRANCO COLOMBO PUBLICATIONS   BA8902   2.50
MAYER   HASTINGS
    SUMMER WIND
        WARNER BROTHERS PUBLISHERS   1.00
MAYOR   3
    MOTHER'S LOVE, MELODY
        CENTURY MUSIC PUBLISHING COMPANY, INC. 1894   .40
MAYR   DEL MAGLIO
    BIONDA IN GONDOLETTA, LA
        FRANCO COLOMBO PUBLICATIONS   129081   .60
MAYUZUMI
    BIBLE, THE
        THE BIG THREE MUSIC CORPORATION   00.95
MCCARTHY *
    IRENE
        THE BIG THREE MUSIC CORPORATION   01.50
MCCLENNY, A.--ED *   MCCLENNY, A. *
    COLLECTION OF EARLY AMERICAN KEYBOARD MUSIC, A
        WILLIS MUSIC COMPANY   3.00
MCCREARY, D.   SCHAUM, J.   1
    PONY RIDE
        SCHAUM PUBLICATIONS, INC.   .50

```
MCHUGH              SCHAUM, J.        2
  EXACTLY LIKE YOU
    SCHAUM PUBLICATIONS, INC.                           .75
MCHUGH              SCHAUM, J.        2 1/2
  ON THE SUNNY SIDE OF THE STREET
    SCHAUM PUBLICATIONS, INC.                           .75
MCKINNEY
  HYMN FAVORITES FOR PIANO
    BELWIN-MILLS PUBLISHING CORPORATION               2.00
MCKUEN             ROGERS, M.
  GRAND TOUR
    POINTER PUBLICATIONS                              4.95
MCKUEN             ROGERS, M.
  NEW CAROLS FOR CHRISTMAS
    POINTER PUBLICATIONS                              3.95
MCLEAN, D.
  AMERICAN PIE
    THE BIG THREE MUSIC CORPORATION                  00.95
MCLEAN, D.
  SONGS OF DON MCLEAN, THE
    THE BIG THREE MUSIC CORPORATION                  04.95
MEACHAM, F.--ED    MEACHAM, F.       3
  MARCHING THRU GEORGIA
    CENTURY MUSIC PUBLISHING COMPANY, INC.   1263     .40
MEACHAM, F.--ED    MEACHAM, F.       4
  OLD BLACK JOE, VARIATIONS
    CENTURY MUSIC PUBLISHING COMPANY, INC.   1045     .40
MEACHAM, F.--ED    MEACHAM, F.       4
  OLD OAKEN BUCKET, THE
    CENTURY MUSIC PUBLISHING COMPANY, INC.   1062     .40
MEACHAM, F.        MITTLER          2A
  AMERICAN PATROL MARCH
    MUSICORD PUBLICATIONS, INC.                        .45
MEACHAM, F.        WALLIS           2
  AMERICAN PATROL
    WILLIS MUSIC COMPANY                               .40
MEACHAM, F.                         4
  LISTEN TO THE MOCKING BIRD
    CENTURY MUSIC PUBLISHING COMPANY, INC.   1060     .40
MEAD
  IMPROVISATION ON CHRISTMAS TUNES - SERIES 1
    BOSTON MUSIC COMPANY                               .50
MEAD
  IMPROVISATION ON CHRISTMAS TUNES - SERIES 2
    BOSTON MUSIC COMPANY                               .50
MELECCI, A.        BERLIN, B.
  MAGIC PIANO IN ORCHESTRA LAND, THE
    FREDERICK HARRIS MUSIC COMPANY                    1.50
MELIS, J.
  JOSE MELIS PIANO MOODS
    THE BIG THREE MUSIC CORPORATION                  01.25
MELIS, J.
  VOLARE
    THE BIG THREE MUSIC CORPORATION                  00.95
MENDEL, S.--ED     MENDEL, S.        2
  AFTER THE BALL IS OVER
    WILLIS MUSIC COMPANY                               .40
MENDELSSOHN                          3
  ANDANTE CANTABILE, VIOLIN CONCERTO
    CENTURY MUSIC PUBLISHING COMPANY, INC.   1916     .40
MENDELSSOHN        ROLFE, W.         3
  ATHALIA, PRIESTS' MARCH, EASY
    CENTURY MUSIC PUBLISHING COMPANY, INC.   3395     .40
MENDELSSOHN
  FINGAL'S CAVE -- THE HEBRIDES -- OVERTURE
    CENTURY MUSIC PUBLISHING COMPANY, INC.    M      1.25
MENDELSSOHN
  FIVE MARCHES
    C. F. PETERS CORPORATION                 1783    2.50
MENDELSSOHN                         2-3
  FRUEHLINGSLIED, EASY
    CENTURY MUSIC PUBLISHING COMPANY, INC.   2158     .40
MENDELSSOHN        GOERDELER         4
  HARK THE HERALD ANGELS SING
    THEODORE PRESSER COMPANY                           .50
MENDELSSOHN *
  MAID OF GANGES, THE
    G. SCHIRMER, INC.                                  .60
MENDELSSOHN *
  MAID OF THE GANGES, THE
    G. SCHIRMER, INC.                                  .60
MENDELSSOHN                          4
  MARCH OF THE PRIESTS, ATHALIA
    CENTURY MUSIC PUBLISHING COMPANY, INC.   1531     .40
MENDELSSOHN        ROLFE, W.         3
  MARCH OF THE PRIESTS, EASY
    CENTURY MUSIC PUBLISHING COMPANY, INC.   3395     .40
MENDELSSOHN        SCHAUM, J.        3
  MENDELSSOHN'S SONGS WITHOUT WORDS
    SCHAUM PUBLICATIONS, INC.                         1.50
MENDELSSOHN        TAGLIAPIETRA
  MIDSUMMER NIGHT'S DREAM, A - OVERTURE
    FRANCO COLOMBO PUBLICATIONS             ER1002    1.00
MENDELSSOHN
  MIDSUMMER NIGHT'S DREAM, A - WEDDING MARCH
    FRANCO COLOMBO PUBLICATIONS             128358    1.00
MENDELSSOHN        CHIESA
  MIDSUMMER NIGHT'S DREAM, A - WEDDING MARCH
    FRANCO COLOMBO PUBLICATIONS             107507     .60
MENDELSSOHN        KLAUSER
  MIDSUMMER NIGHT'S DREAM, A - WEDDING MARCH
    G. SCHIRMER, INC.                                  .50
MENDELSSOHN        ROLFE            3
  MIDSUMMER NIGHT'S DREAM, NOCTURNE
    CENTURY MUSIC PUBLISHING COMPANY, INC.   4160     .40
MENDELSSOHN        SMITH            5
  MIDSUMMER NIGHT'S DREAM, OP. 76 - PARAPHRASE DE CONCERT
    THEODORE PRESSER COMPANY                           .60
MENDELSSOHN        SMITH            5
  MIDSUMMER NIGHT'S DREAM
    CENTURY MUSIC PUBLISHING COMPANY, INC.   1332     .40
MENDELSSOHN        STEINER          3
  MOMENTS WITH MENDELSSOHN
    BELWIN-MILLS PUBLISHING CORPORATION                .60
MENDELSSOHN        ROLFE, W.         3
  NOCTURNE, MIDSUMMER NIGHT'S DREAM
    CENTURY MUSIC PUBLISHING COMPANY, INC.   4160     .40
MENDELSSOHN *      TAGLIAPIETRA
  ON WINGS OF SONGS
    FRANCO COLOMBO PUBLICATIONS             127926     .90
MENDELSSOHN *                       5
  ON WINGS OF SONG
    CENTURY MUSIC PUBLISHING COMPANY, INC.   2434     .40
MENDELSSOHN *      TAGLIAPIETRA
  ON WINGS OF SONG
    FRANCO COLOMBO PUBLICATIONS             127926     .90

MENDELSSOHN        DEL MAGLIO
  ON WINGS OF SONG
    FRANCO COLOMBO PUBLICATIONS             129092     .60
MENDELSSOHN *      TAGLIAPIETRA
  ON WINGS OF SONG
    FRANCO COLOMBO PUBLICATIONS             127926     .90
MENDELSSOHN        THOMPSON, J.      5
  ON WINGS OF SONG
    WILLIS MUSIC COMPANY                               .40
MENDELSSOHN        TAGLIAPIETRA
  OVERTURES
    FRANCO COLOMBO PUBLICATIONS              ER498    6.00
MENDELSSOHN        RACHMANINOFF, S.
  SCHERZO, FROM A MIDSUMMER NIGHT'S DREAM
    BELWIN-MILLS PUBLISHING CORPORATION               1.50
MENDELSSOHN        STEINER          1
  SPRING'S GREETING
    BELWIN-MILLS PUBLISHING CORPORATION                .60
MENDELSSOHN        DEL MAGLIO
  SPRING SONG, OP. 62 NO. 6
    FRANCO COLOMBO PUBLICATIONS             128844     .60
MENDELSSOHN        GOETSCHIUS, P.
  SYMPHONY NO. 04 IN A MAJOR
    THEODORE PRESSER COMPANY                          1.25
MENDELSSOHN        DEL MAGLIO
  VENETIAN BOAT SONG, OP. 19 NO. 6
    FRANCO COLOMBO PUBLICATIONS             124719     .60
MENDELSSOHN        DEL MAGLIO
  VENETIAN BOAT SONG, OP. 30 NO. 6
    FRANCO COLOMBO PUBLICATIONS             124720     .60
MENDELSSOHN                          M
  VIOLIN CONCERTO, OP. 64. ABRIDGED PIANO SOLO ARR.
    C. F. PETERS CORPORATION                1731B     1.50
MENDELSSOHN        ROLFE, W.         3
  WAR MARCH OF THE PRIESTS, EASY
    CENTURY MUSIC PUBLISHING COMPANY, INC.   3395     .40
MENDELSSOHN        PAUER
  WAR MARCH OF THE PRIESTS, FROM 'ATHALIA'
    G. SCHIRMER, INC.                                  .60
MENDELSSOHN
  WAR MARCH OF THE PRIESTS FROM 'ATHALIA', OP. 74
    CARL FISCHER, INC.                      S 1773     .50
MENDELSSOHN                          4
  WAR MARCH OF THE PRIESTS
    CENTURY MUSIC PUBLISHING COMPANY, INC.   1531     .40
MENDELSSOHN                          4
  WAR MARCH OF THE PRIETS 'ATHALIA'
    BELWIN-MILLS PUBLISHING CORPORATION      251       .60
MENDELSSOHN        WEYBRIGHT
  WEDDING MARCH, FROM 'MID-SUMMER NIGHT'S DREAM'
    BELWIN-MILLS PUBLISHING CORPORATION                .60
MENDELSSOHN
  WEDDING MARCH
    ASHLEY DEALERS SERVICE, INC.             ES        .95
MENOTTI            LEVINE, H.
  BARCAROLLE, FROM THE BALLET 'SEBASTIAN'
    BELWIN-MILLS PUBLISHING CORPORATION                .60
MENOTTI            LEVINE
  BARCAROLLE FROM THE BALLET 'SEBASTIAN'
    FRANCO COLOMBO PUBLICATIONS             NY2056     .75
MENOTTI            LEVINE
  BARCAROLLE FROM THE BALLET 'SEBASTIAN'
    FRANCO COLOMBO PUBLICATIONS             NY2055     .50
MERATH, S.                         2-3
  TANZ-TYPEN, BAND 01
    SCHOTT                                  4945      2.50
MERATH, S.                         2-3
  TANZ-TYPEN, BAND 02
    SCHOTT                                  4746      2.50
MERKEL, G.         ROLFE, W.         2
  PAPILLON, EASY
    CENTURY MUSIC PUBLISHING COMPANY, INC.   3357     .40
MERRILL, B.
  CARNIVAL
    THE BIG THREE MUSIC CORPORATION                  01.50
METIS
  EASY POP ROCK SKETCHES
    EDWARD B. MARKS MUSIC CORPORATION                01.50
METRA              DEL MAGLIO
  SERENATA
    FRANCO COLOMBO PUBLICATIONS             129107     .60
METRA                              2
  VALSE SERENADE, EASY
    CENTURY MUSIC PUBLISHING COMPANY, INC.   2141     .40
MEYERBEER, G.      SMITH            5
  HUGENOTS, FANTASIE
    CENTURY MUSIC PUBLISHING COMPANY, INC.   1171     .40
MEYERBEER, G.                      4
  HUGENOTS, THE, PAGE'S SONG
    CENTURY MUSIC PUBLISHING COMPANY, INC.   2215     .40
MEYERBEER, G.                      2
  PROPHETE, CORONATION MARCH, EASY
    CENTURY MUSIC PUBLISHING COMPANY, INC.   3760     .40
MEYERBEER, G.                      4
  PROPHETE, CORONATION MARCH
    CENTURY MUSIC PUBLISHING COMPANY, INC.   1650     .40
MEYER *            WALTER
  CRAZY RHYTHM
    WARNER BROTHERS PUBLISHERS                        1.00
MICHEELSEN                         1-2
  KLAVIERUBUNG NACH VOLKSLIEDERN, HEFT 1 - 20 STUCKE MIT UBUNGEN
  FUR DEN ANFANG
    BARENREITER VERLAG                      BA 1335
MICHEELSEN                         1-2
  KLAVIERUBUNG NACH VOLKSLIEDERN, HEFT 1 - 32 STUCKE MIT UBUNGEN
  FUR DEN ANFANG
    BARENREITER VERLAG                      BA 1334
MICHEELSEN                         1-2
  KLAVIERUBUNG NACH VOLKSLIEDERN, HEFT 3 - LEICHTE SUITE -- 8
  KINDERLIEDER --
    BARENREITER VERLAG                      BA 1336
MIHALOVICI
  ALTERNAMENTI -- BALLET --
    FRANCO COLOMBO PUBLICATIONS              R1591    9.00
MILES *
  ANCHORS AWEIGH
    THE BIG THREE MUSIC CORPORATION                  00.95
MILHAUD, D.
  ADAME MIROIR
    HEUGEL ET CIE.                                   2.75
MILHAUD, D.                         MD
  ALAMEDA FROM 'FOUR SKETCHES'
    THEODORE PRESSER COMPANY                           .60
MILHAUD, D.
  CARAMEL MOU--1921--JAZZ BAND
    ASSOCIATED MUSIC PUBLISHERS, INC.       ESC      2.50
```

MILHAUD, D.
  LE TRAIN BLEU
    HEUGEL ET CIE.   14.70
MILHAUD, D.
  SALADE -- BALLET CHANTE
    HEUGEL ET CIE.   14.60
MILHAUD, D.
  SONGES, LES -- BALLET --
    FRANCO COLOMBO PUBLICATIONS   SAL   6.00
MILLER *
  MOONLIGHT SERENADE
    THE BIG THREE MUSIC CORPORATION   00.95
MILLER   GLOVER, D.
  PLACE IN THE SUN, A
    BELWIN-MILLS PUBLISHING CORPORATION   .60
MILLIGAN   RICHTER
  ALIDA'S DANCE
    BELWIN-MILLS PUBLISHING CORPORATION   .60
MILLWARD   4
  ROCK OF AGES, TRANSCRIPTION
    CENTURY MUSIC PUBLISHING COMPANY, INC.   654   .40
MININBERG--ED   MININBERG *   2-3
  GREAT MUSIC
    CENTURY MUSIC PUBLISHING COMPANY, INC.   1.25
MITTLER--ED   MITTLER   2A
  COUNTRY GARDENS
    MUSICORD PUBLICATIONS, INC.   .45
MITTLER--ED   MITTLER   2, 3
  GREAT BALLET MUSIC
    MUSICORD PUBLICATIONS, INC.   1.25
MITTLER--ED   MITTLER   2, 3
  GREAT CONCERTO MUSIC
    MUSICORD PUBLICATIONS, INC.   1.25
MITTLER--ED   MITTLER   2, 3
  GREAT OPERA MUSIC
    MUSICORD PUBLICATIONS, INC.   1.25
MITTLER--ED   MITTLER   2, 3
  GREAT SYMPHONY MUSIC
    MUSICORD PUBLICATIONS, INC.   1.25
MITTLER--ED   MITTLER   2, 3
  GREAT WALTZ MUSIC
    MUSICORD PUBLICATIONS, INC.   1.25
MITTLER--ED   MITTLER   1B
  MARINES' HYMN
    MUSICORD PUBLICATIONS, INC.   .45
MITTLER--ED   MITTLER   2
  MUSIC FOR EVERYBODY
    MUSICORD PUBLICATIONS, INC.   2.00
MITTLER--ED   MITTLER
  MUSIC IS MY HOBBY
    MUSICORD PUBLICATIONS, INC.   2.50
MITTLER--ED   MITTLER   2B
  TWO GUITARS
    MUSICORD PUBLICATIONS, INC.   .45
MOFFAT--ED   7
  VAUDEVILLE A DANSER
    NOVELLO AND COMPANY, LTD.   55.0015.10   .40
MOHAUPT, R.
  MAX AND MORITZ -- A MUSICAL STORY
    ASSOCIATED MUSIC PUBLISHERS, INC.   AMP   3.25
MOLLER *
  HAPPY WANDERER, THE -- TRANSCRIPTION
    SOUTHERN MUSIC COMPANY   .75
MOLLER *
  HAPPY WANDERER, THE
    SAM FOX PUBLISHING COMPANY, INC.   .75
MOLLOY, J. L.--ED   MOLLOY, J. L.   3
  LOVE'S OLD SWEET SONG
    CENTURY MUSIC PUBLISHING COMPANY, INC. 2438   .40
MOLLOY, J. L.--ED   MOLLOY, J. L.   2
  LOVE'S OLD SWEET SONG
    CENTURY MUSIC PUBLISHING COMPANY, INC. 2061   .40
MOLLOY, J. L.   STEINER   1 1/2
  OH, THE DAYS OF THE KERRY DANCING
    BELWIN-MILLS PUBLISHING CORPORATION   .60
MONRI, V.   DEL MAGLIO
  CZARDAS NO. 1
    FRANCO COLOMBO PUBLICATIONS   127211   .60
MONTANI--ED   MONTANI
  MOST BEAUTIFUL PAGES OF HARPSICHORD MUSIC, THE - BACH FAMILY,
  THE
    FRANCO COLOMBO PUBLICATIONS   ER2574   2.00
MONTANI--ED   MONTANI
  MOST BEAUTIFUL PAGES OF HARPSICHORD MUSIC, THE - BELGIAN
    FRANCO COLOMBO PUBLICATIONS   ER2525   1.25
MONTANI--ED   MONTANI
  MOST BEAUTIFUL PAGES OF HARPSICHORD MUSIC, THE - DUTCH
    FRANCO COLOMBO PUBLICATIONS   ER2549   1.25
MONTANI--ED   MONTANI
  MOST BEAUTIFUL PAGES OF HARPSICHORD MUSIC, THE - ENGLISH
    FRANCO COLOMBO PUBLICATIONS   ER2666   3.00
MONTANI--ED   MONTANI
  MOST BEAUTIFUL PAGES OF HARPSICHORD MUSIC, THE - FRENCH
    FRANCO COLOMBO PUBLICATIONS   ER2511   1.75
MONTANI--ED   MONTANI
  MOST BEAUTIFUL PAGES OF HARPSICHORD MUSIC, THE - PORTUGUESE
    FRANCO COLOMBO PUBLICATIONS   ER2670   1.75
MONTANI--ED *   MONTANI *
  MOST BEAUTIFUL PAGES OF HARPSICHORD MUSIC, THE - SPANISH
    FRANCO COLOMBO PUBLICATIONS   ER2470   1.50
MONTANI--ED   MONTANI
  MOST BEAUTIFUL PAGES OF HARPSOCHORD MUSIC, THE - GERMAN
    FRANCO COLOMBO PUBLICATIONS   ER2622   1.75
MONTANI
  CLAVICEMBALISTI ITALIANI --16 PIECES--
    FRANCO COLOMBO PUBLICATIONS   FOR.12119   1.50
MONTANI
  MY FIRST HARPSICHORD BOOK
    FRANCO COLOMBO PUBLICATIONS   ER2605   1.25
MONTANI
  NINE HARPSICHORD PIECES
    FRANCO COLOMBO PUBLICATIONS   ER2463   1.00
MOORE--ED   MOORE
  BIG NOTE CHRISTMAS FAVORITES
    BOSTON MUSIC COMPANY   1.00
MOORE--ED   MOORE
  CHRISTMAS FAVORITES
    BOSTON MUSIC COMPANY   1.00
MOORE   SCHAUM, J.   4
  CHRISTMAS FANTASY
    SCHAUM PUBLICATIONS, INC.   .60
MORRICONE, E.
  GOOD, THE BAD, AND THE UGLY, THE
    THE BIG THREE MUSIC CORPORATION   00.95
MOSSMAN, T.--ED   MOSSMAN, T.
  HANDS ACROSS THE TABLE, SIMPLIFIED
    BELWIN-MILLS PUBLISHING CORPORATION   .60

MOSSMAN, T.--ED   MOSSMAN, T.
  KITTEN ON THE KEYS -- SIMP.
    BELWIN-MILLS PUBLISHING CORPORATION   26023   .50
MOSSMAN, T.--ED   MOSSMAN, T.
  ORGAN GRINDER'S SWING -- SIMP.
    BELWIN-MILLS PUBLISHING CORPORATION   26068   .50
MOSSMAN, T.--ED   MOSSMAN, T.
  PAVANNE -- SIMP.
    BELWIN-MILLS PUBLISHING CORPORATION   26036   .50
MOSSMAN, T.--ED   MOSSMAN, T.
  SERENADE IN THE NIGHT -- SIMP.
    BELWIN-MILLS PUBLISHING CORPORATION   26092   .50
MOSSMAN, T.--ED   MOSSMAN, T.
  SHEIK OF ARABY, THE -- SIMP.
    BELWIN-MILLS PUBLISHING CORPORATION   .50
MOSSMAN, T.--ED   MOSSMAN, T.
  SWEET LORRAINE -- SIMP.
    BELWIN-MILLS PUBLISHING CORPORATION   26052   .50
MOSSMAN, T.--ED   MOSSMAN, T.
  SWEET ROSIE O'GRADY SIMP.
    BELWIN-MILLS PUBLISHING CORPORATION   26053   .50
MOSSMAN, T.--ED   MOSSMAN, T.
  TAKE ME IN YOUR ARMS -- SIMP.
    BELWIN-MILLS PUBLISHING CORPORATION   26055   .50
MOSSMAN, T.--ED   MOSSMAN, T.
  WHEN IT'S SLEEPY TIME DOWN SOUTH -- SIMP.
    BELWIN-MILLS PUBLISHING CORPORATION   26062   .50
MOSSMAN, T.
  BUGLE CALL RAG -- SIMP.
    BELWIN-MILLS PUBLISHING CORPORATION   26072   .50
MOSSMAN, T.
  CENTRAL PARK ROMANCE
    THE BIG THREE MUSIC CORPORATION   00.95
MOSSMAN, T.
  FOR ME AND MY GAL -- SIMP.
    BELWIN-MILLS PUBLISHING CORPORATION   26075   .50
MOSSMAN, T.
  HANDS ACROSS THE TABLE -- SIMP.
    BELWIN-MILLS PUBLISHING CORPORATION   26069   .50
MOSSMAN, T.
  ODE TO GERSHWIN
    THE BIG THREE MUSIC CORPORATION   00.95
MOSSMAN, T.
  SOPHISTICATED LADY -- SIMP.
    BELWIN-MILLS PUBLISHING CORPORATION   26050   .50
MOSZKOWSKI   M
  ANDANTE AND SCHERZO FROM CONCERTO, OP. 59. ABRIDGED PIANO SOLO
  ARR.
    C. F. PETERS CORPORATION   2872A   1.25
MOUSSORGSKY   DALLAPICCOLA   5
  BILDER EINER AUSSTELLUNG
    BARENREITER VERLAG   CM 19817
MOUSSORGSKY   MOSSMAN, T.
  GOPAK FROM 'THE FAIR AT SOROCHINSK' -- SIMP.
    BELWIN-MILLS PUBLISHING CORPORATION   26080   .50
MOUSSORGSKY   RACHMANINOFF, S.
  HOPAK
    BELWIN-MILLS PUBLISHING CORPORATION   1.00
MOUSSORGSKY   DANIEL, R. M.
  TABLEAUX D'UNE EXPOSITION
    ELKAN-VOGEL, INC.   CON   3.50
MOUSSORGSKY   GRATIA, L. E.
  TABLEAUX D'UNE EXPOSITION
    ELKAN-VOGEL, INC.   CON   2.75
MOZART, L.   KREUTZER
  NANNERL MOZART'S PIANO BOOK
    ASHLEY DEALERS SERVICE, INC.   1.25
MOZART, L.   STEINER   2 1/2
  POLONAISE IN C
    BELWIN-MILLS PUBLISHING CORPORATION   .60
MOZART, W. A.   STEINER   1
  AIR OF THE SHEPHERDESS
    BELWIN-MILLS PUBLISHING CORPORATION   .60
MOZART, W. A.   DEL MAGLIO
  ANDANTE FROM SONATA NO. 15
    FRANCO COLOMBO PUBLICATIONS   124724   .50
MOZART, W. A.   BUSONI
  ANDANTINO FROM PIANO CONCERTO K271
    ASSOCIATED MUSIC PUBLISHERS, INC.   BRH   1.20
MOZART, W. A.   ANSON, G.   INTERMEDIATE
  ANSON INTRODUCES MOZART, BK. 1
    WILLIS MUSIC COMPANY   1.50
MOZART, W. A.   SCHAUM, J.   2 1/2
  BEST OF MOZART
    SCHAUM PUBLICATIONS, INC.   1.25
MOZART, W. A.   POTAMKIN
  BREAD AND BUTTER WALTZ
    ELKAN-VOGEL, INC.   .50
MOZART, W. A.   M
  CONCERTI K.271, 450, 466, 467, 482, 488, 491, 537
    C. F. PETERS CORPORATION   765   12.00
MOZART, W. A.
  CONCERTO IN C MAJOR, NO. 21 -- THEME FROM 'ELVIRA MADIGAN'
    ASHLEY DEALERS SERVICE, INC.   1.00
MOZART, W. A.   M
  CONCERTO K488 IN A
    C. F. PETERS CORPORATION   3309EE   1.25
MOZART, W. A.   PIETSCH
  CRADLE SONG
    G. SCHIRMER, INC.   .35
MOZART, W. A.   STEINER   2
  DAINTY DANCE
    BELWIN-MILLS PUBLISHING CORPORATION   .60
MOZART, W. A.   DEL MAGLIO
  DON GIOVANNI - DEH VIENI ALLA FINESTRA
    FRANCO COLOMBO PUBLICATIONS   124722   .50
MOZART, W. A.   CHIESA
  DON GIOVANNI - EASY FANTASIA
    FRANCO COLOMBO PUBLICATIONS   107486   .50
MOZART, W. A.   M
  DON GIOVANNI
    C. F. PETERS CORPORATION   H631   2.00
MOZART, W. A.   STARK
  EINE KLEINE NACHTMUSIK--SERENADE--K525
    ASSOCIATED MUSIC PUBLISHERS, INC.   BRH   .90
MOZART, W. A.   CLASSENS
  EINE KLEINE NACHTMUSIK, A LITTLE NIGHT MUSIC
    ELKAN-VOGEL, INC.   1.60
MOZART, W. A.   ZANON
  EINE KLEINE NACHTMUSIK, K525
    FRANCO COLOMBO PUBLICATIONS   ER2270   1.25
MOZART, W. A.   E-M
  EINE KLEINE NACHTMUSIK, K525
    C. F. PETERS CORPORATION   3957   1.50
MOZART, W. A.   PODOLSKY, L.
  GERMAN DANCE NO. 2
    FREDERICK HARRIS MUSIC COMPANY   .60

MOZART, W. A.   STEINER   2
  HAPPY HARVEST
    BELWIN-MILLS PUBLISHING CORPORATION   .60
MOZART, W. A.   ROLFE, W.   EASY
  HARPSICHORD PLAYER, THE --SONATA IN C--
    SHAWNEE PRESS, INC.   HB-5006   .60
MOZART, W. A.
  LE PETITS RIEN
    HEUGEL ET CIE.   5.65
MOZART, W. A.   M
  MAGIC FLUTE. ABRIDGED
    C. F. PETERS CORPORATION   H633   2.00
MOZART, W. A.   3
  MAGIC FLUTE, PRIESTS' MARCH
    CENTURY MUSIC PUBLISHING COMPANY, INC. 454   .40
MOZART, W. A.   3
  MARCH OF THE PRIESTS, MAGIC FLUTE
    CENTURY MUSIC PUBLISHING COMPANY, INC. 454   .40
MOZART, W. A.   M
  MARRIAGE OF FIGARO. ABRIDGED
    C. F. PETERS CORPORATION   H632   2.00
MOZART, W. A.   3
  MENUETT AUS D. ES-DUR-SYMPHONIE -- K.V. 543
    SCHOTT   07782   .75
MOZART, W. A.   4
  MENUET AND TRIO, SYMPHONY NO. 39 IN E FLAT
    CENTURY MUSIC PUBLISHING COMPANY, INC. 2334   .40
MOZART, W. A.
  MENUET FROM SYMPHONY IN E FLAT
    CARL FISCHER, INC.   S 88   .50
MOZART, W. A.   DEIS
  MINUET--FROM DIVERTIMENTO K334 IN D
    G. SCHIRMER, INC.   .40
MOZART, W. A.   SCHULHOFF
  MINUET--FROM SYMPHONY K543 IN E FLAT
    G. SCHIRMER, INC.   .40
MOZART, W. A.   1
  MINUETTO 'DON GIOVANNI', SIMPLIFIED
    BELWIN-MILLS PUBLISHING CORPORATION   527   .60
MOZART, W. A.   SCHULHOFF
  MINUET AND TRIO FROM SYMPHONY IN E FLAT
    BELWIN-MILLS PUBLISHING CORPORATION   28160   .60
MOZART, W. A.   2
  MINUET FROM DON GIOVANNI
    CENTURY MUSIC PUBLISHING COMPANY, INC. 1813   .40
MOZART, W. A.   POTAMKIN
  MINUET FROM DON JUAN
    ELKAN-VOGEL, INC.   .50
MOZART, W. A.   SCHULHOFF
  MINUET FROM SYMPHONY NO. 39
    ASSOCIATED MUSIC PUBLISHERS, INC.   LEU   .75
MOZART, W. A.   CHIESA
  MINUET FROM SYMPHONY NO. 39
    FRANCO COLOMBO PUBLICATIONS   107487   .60
MOZART, W. A.   GLASS, P. *
  MOZART AT 8 -- THE CHELSEA NOTEBOOK
    THEODORE PRESSER COMPANY   2.50
MOZART, W. A.   ECKHARDT, F.   1
  MOZART FOR THE YOUNG PIANIST
    CENTURY MUSIC PUBLISHING COMPANY, INC. 3960   .40
MOZART, W. A.
  NOZZE DI FIGARO, LE - OVERTURE
    FRANCO COLOMBO PUBLICATIONS   128009   1.00
MOZART, W. A.   CHIESA
  RONDO ALLA TURCA FROM SONATA NO. 11
    FRANCO COLOMBO PUBLICATIONS   107488   .60
MOZART, W. A.   BACKHAUS
  SERENADE--'DON GIOVANNI'
    G. SCHIRMER, INC.   .50
MOZART, W. A.   M-D
  SIX SYMPHONIES
    C. F. PETERS CORPORATION   198   6.50
MOZART, W. A.   WHITFORD   GR. 3
  SONATA IN C
    ROBERT WHITFORD PUBLICATIONS   .40
MOZART, W. A.   MANSFIELD
  STEPS TO THE MASTERS
    BANKS AND SON LTD.   1.35
MOZART, W. A.   ZANON
  SYMPHONIES -- SELECTED -- BK. 1
    FRANCO COLOMBO PUBLICATIONS   ER1772   5.00
MOZART, W. A.   ZANON
  SYMPHONIES -- SELECTED -- BK. 2
    FRANCO COLOMBO PUBLICATIONS   ER1773   5.00
MOZART, W. A.   4
  SYMPHONY IN E FLAT, MINUET
    CENTURY MUSIC PUBLISHING COMPANY, INC. 317   .40
MOZART, W. A.   3
  SYMPHONY IN E FLAT, MINUET
    CENTURY MUSIC PUBLISHING COMPANY, INC. 2334   .40
MOZART, W. A.   GOETSCHIUS, P.
  SYMPHONY NO. 38 IN D -- WITHOUT MINUET
    THEODORE PRESSER COMPANY   .75
MOZART, W. A.   SCHAUM, J.   2
  SYMPHONY NO. 40 -- FIRST THEME
    SCHAUM PUBLICATIONS, INC.   .50
MOZART, W. A.   DE LOS RIOS
  SYMPHONY NO. 40 - THEMES
    THE BIG THREE MUSIC CORPORATION   00.95
MOZART, W. A.   RUSSELL   2
  THEME FROM 'DON JUAN'
    BOSTON MUSIC COMPANY   .50
MOZART, W. A.   ECKSTEIN
  THEME FROM SONATA IN C, FIRST MVT.
    CARL FISCHER, INC.   S 2291   .50
MOZART, W. A.   ROLFE, W.   2
  TURKISH MARCH, EASY
    CENTURY MUSIC PUBLISHING COMPANY, INC. 3653   .40
MOZART, W. A.   SCHAUM, J.   2 1/2
  TURKISH MARCH
    SCHAUM PUBLICATIONS, INC.   .60
MOZART, W. A.   SCHROEDER, H.
  TWELVE GERMAN DANCES
    THEODORE PRESSER COMPANY   1.25
MOZART, W. A.   POTAMKIN
  VALSE FAVORITE
    ELKAN-VOGEL, INC.   .50
MOZART, W. A.   STEINER   2
  VIENNESE MINUET
    BELWIN-MILLS PUBLISHING CORPORATION   .60
MUELLER, C.   STEINER   JR. APPR.
  AWAY IN A MANGER
    BELWIN-MILLS PUBLISHING CORPORATION   .60
MULE   MORINI
  LARGO
    FRANCO COLOMBO PUBLICATIONS   BON.2030   .90

MYDDLETON   SCHAUM, J.   3
  COTTON PICKIN' BOOGIE
    SCHAUM PUBLICATIONS, INC.   .50
NAPOLITANO   RICHTER
  GATO, OP. 8 NO. 3
    FRANCO COLOMBO PUBLICATIONS   NY1571   .40
NARVAEZ   TORNER
  COLLECCION DE VIHUELISTAS ESPANOLES DEL SIGLO XVI, BK. 1 -- EL
  DELPHIN DE MUSICA -- LUTE
    ASSOCIATED MUSIC PUBLISHERS, INC.   UME   4.00
NASCIMBENE
  FRANCIS OF ASSISI - THEME
    THE BIG THREE MUSIC CORPORATION   00.95
NASH, J.
  I CAN SEE CLEARLY NOW
    THE BIG THREE MUSIC CORPORATION   02.95
NEALE, J.--ED   NEALE, J.
  INSTANT PICTURE CHORD PIANO NO. 1
    WARNER BROTHERS PUBLISHERS   1.95
NEALE, J.--ED   NEALE, J.
  PETER, PAUL AND MARY, MORE MADE EASY FOR PIANO
    WARNER BROTHERS PUBLISHERS   PPM 25   2.00
NEIDLINGER, W. H.   ZEPP   4-5
  BIRTHDAY TO A KING
    PRO-ART PUBLICATIONS, INC.   508   .50
NERO
  NERO, PETER, AT THE PIANO
    WARNER BROTHERS PUBLISHERS   2.50
NERO
  NERO, PETER, OFF RECORD
    WARNER BROTHERS PUBLISHERS   2.50
NEVIN   RICHTER, A.
  DAY IN VENICE, A --VENEZIA--
    THEODORE PRESSER COMPANY   1.50
NEVIN   DEL MAGLIO
  NARCISSUS, OP. 13 NO. 4
    FRANCO COLOMBO PUBLICATIONS   128846   .60
NEVIN   WEYBRIGHT   2
  NARCISSUS, THEME
    BELWIN-MILLS PUBLISHING CORPORATION   .60
NEWMAN, A.
  STREET SCENE
    THE BIG THREE MUSIC CORPORATION   00.95
NEWMAN, L.
  HONG KONG
    THE BIG THREE MUSIC CORPORATION   00.95
NEWMAN, W.   SCHAUM, J.   1 1/2
  SEAGULL
    SCHAUM PUBLICATIONS, INC.   .50
NIN-CULMELL, J.
  TROMPEUR DE SEVILLE, LE -- BALLET IN ONE ACT
    ASSOCIATED MUSIC PUBLISHERS, INC.   ESC   10.75
NOBLE   SCHAUM, J.   2
  CHEROKEE
    SCHAUM PUBLICATIONS, INC.   .75
NOBLITT, K. M.   SCHAUM, J.   1
  WINDSHIELD WIPER ROCK
    SCHAUM PUBLICATIONS, INC.   .60
NORTH, A.
  ANTONY AND CLEOPATRA THEME
    THE BIG THREE MUSIC CORPORATION   00.95
NORTH, A.
  CAESAR AND CLEOPATRA THEME
    THE BIG THREE MUSIC CORPORATION   00.95
NORTH, A.
  OUTRAGE, THE - THEME
    THE BIG THREE MUSIC CORPORATION   00.95
NORTH, A.
  RECONCILIATION
    THE BIG THREE MUSIC CORPORATION   00.95
NORTH, A.
  SHOES OF THE FISHERMAN, THE
    THE BIG THREE MUSIC CORPORATION   00.95
NOVARO   DEL MAGLIO
  INNO DI MAMELI -- WITH WORDS --
    FRANCO COLOMBO PUBLICATIONS   127212   .60
OAKLAND, B.
  VALSE MODERNE
    THE BIG THREE MUSIC CORPORATION   00.95
OBERDORFFER--ED   OBERDORFFER   2-3
  TANZE AUS EINEM ALTEN KLAVIERBUCH - 1800'S
    SCHOTT   3761   1.75
OFFENBACH   SEIDT   4
  BACAROLLE -- TALES OF HOFFMAN
    VOLKWEIN BROS.   .35
OFFENBACH
  BARBE-BLEUE
    HEUGEL ET CIE.   12.00
OFFENBACH   3
  BARCAROLLE, BEAUTIFUL NIGHT
    CENTURY MUSIC PUBLISHING COMPANY, INC. 3623   .40
OFFENBACH   3
  BARCAROLLE, TALES OF HOFFMANN
    CENTURY MUSIC PUBLISHING COMPANY, INC. 1321   .40
OFFENBACH   WEYBRIGHT   2 1/2
  BARCAROLLE
    BELWIN-MILLS PUBLISHING CORPORATION   .60
OFFENBACH
  LA BELLE HELENE
    HEUGEL ET CIE.   9.75
OFFENBACH
  LA CHANSON DE FORTUNIO
    HEUGEL ET CIE.   7.30
OFFENBACH
  LES CONTES D'HOFFMANN--BARCAROLLE. INTERMEZZO
    G. SCHIRMER, INC.   .35
OFFENBACH   SPINDLER
  LES CONTES D'HOFFMANN--BARCAROLLE. O BELLE NUIT
    G. SCHIRMER, INC.   .60
OFFENBACH
  ORPHEE AUX ENFERS
    HEUGEL ET CIE.   24.00
OFFENBACH *
  ORPHEUS IN THE UNDERWORLD -- QUADRILLE
    HEUGEL ET CIE.   2.05
OFFENBACH   2
  TALES OF HOFFMAN, BARCAROLLE
    CENTURY MUSIC PUBLISHING COMPANY, INC. 2505   .40
OFFENBACH   SAMMARTINO
  TALES OF HOFFMANN - BARCAROLLE
    FRANCO COLOMBO PUBLICATIONS   BA9218   .75
OFFENBACH   SEAK
  TALES OF HOFFMAN - BARCAROLLE
    FRANCO COLOMBO PUBLICATIONS   129189   .50
OLCOTT   CURCIO   1
  MY WILD IRISH ROSE
    BOSTON MUSIC COMPANY   .50

OLIVIERI   DEL MAGLIO
  GARIBALDI HYMN -- WITH WORDS --
      FRANCO COLOMBO PUBLICATIONS   127213   .50
OLLONE, M. D'
  LE TEMPLE ABANDONNE
      HEUGEL ET CIE.   5.00
ORTOLANI
  ELOISE
      THE BIG THREE MUSIC CORPORATION   00.95
ORTOLANI
  MAE
      THE BIG THREE MUSIC CORPORATION   00.95
ORTOLANI
  MAYA
      THE BIG THREE MUSIC CORPORATION   00.95
ORTOLANI
  YELLOW ROLLS-ROYCE - THEME
      THE BIG THREE MUSIC CORPORATION   00.95
OWEN--ED   OWEN
  MODERNE TANZRHYTHMEN
      SCHOTT   6075   2.50
PACHELBEL   DOFLEIN   3
  AUSGEWAHLTE KLAVIERWERKE
      SCHOTT   2349   2.25
PADEREWSKI, I. J. MASON, W.   6
  MENUET A L'ANTIQUE, OP. 14 NO. 1
      THEODORE PRESSER COMPANY   .75
PADEREWSKI, I. J. KING, S.   EASY
  MINUET
      SHAWNEE PRESS, INC.   HB-5034   .40
PAGANINI, N.   CHIESA
  CARNIVAL OF VENICE
      FRANCO COLOMBO PUBLICATIONS   107490   .60
PALESTRINA, G.   3
  VIERSTIMMIGE RICERCARE IN DEN ACHT KIRCHENTONARTEN
      SCHOTT   2310   2.75
PARISH, M. *   GLOVER, D.
  SYNCOPATED CLOCK
      BELWIN-MILLS PUBLISHING CORPORATION   .60
PARNES *   GLOVER, D.
  HAPPINESS IS
      BELWIN-MILLS PUBLISHING CORPORATION   .60
PARSONS
  PIANO TRANSCRIPTIONS OF YOUR FAVORITE CHRISTMAS CAROLS
      THEODORE PRESSER COMPANY   1.50
PASCAL, C.
  LE DOUX SOMMEIL DES FEES -- FROM 'L'ALBUM DE LISETTE ET POULOT'
      ELKAN-VOGEL, INC.   D   .80
PASTOR, S.   BERKOWITZ
  SUITE DE FLANDES--GUITAR
      ASSOCIATED MUSIC PUBLISHERS, INC.   UME   2.25
PAULL   MENDEL, S.   2 1/2
  BEN HUR CHARIOT RACE
      WILLIS MUSIC COMPANY   .40
PEERY, R. R.--ED   PEERY, R. R.
  CAROLS OF MANY LANDS
      BOSTON MUSIC COMPANY   1.25
PEERY, R. R.--ED   PEERY   GR. 1
  CHILD'S BOOK OF HYMNS
      LORENZ PUBLISHING COMPANY   2.00
PEERY, R. R.--ED   PEERY, R. R.
  CHRISTMAS CAROL BOOK
      BOSTON MUSIC COMPANY   1.25
PEERY, R. R.--ED   PEERY, R. R.
  FAMOUS SACRED SONGS
      BOSTON MUSIC COMPANY   1.50
PEERY, R. R.--ED   PEERY
  PIANO VOLUNTARIES
      LORENZ PUBLISHING COMPANY   2.50
PEPUSCH   E-M
  BEGGAR'S OPERA, ABRIDGED
      C. F. PETERS CORPORATION   H1728   1.50
PERGOLESI   DEL MAGLIO
  SE TU M'AMI
      FRANCO COLOMBO PUBLICATIONS   128124   .50
PERI
  FOUR AMERICAN VARIATIONS ON A THEME BY PAGANINI
      MCA MUSIC   1.25
PERRY, P.
  MASTER MELODIES FROM THE GREAT SYMPHONIES
      BELWIN-MILLS PUBLISHING CORPORATION   1.25
PETERS--ED   PETERS   AI
  TIME TO PLAY FOLKSONGS
      WILLIS MUSIC COMPANY   1.00
PETRASSI
  RITRATTO DI DON CHISCIOTTE
      UNIVERSAL EDITION   UE 11841   4.05
PETRIE-WINGATE   STEINER   2 1/2
  BACKYARD BOOGIE
      BELWIN-MILLS PUBLISHING CORPORATION   .60
PHILIPP, I.--ED.   PHILIPP, I.
  QUATRE PIECES DE CONCERT, NO. 1, TARTINI--DANCE
      ASSOCIATED MUSIC PUBLISHERS, INC.   ESC   .85
PHILIPP, I.--ED.   PHILIPP, I.
  QUATRE PIECES DE CONCERT, NO. 2, TARTINI--BALLET
      ASSOCIATED MUSIC PUBLISHERS, INC.   ESC   .85
PHILIPP, I.--ED.   PHILIPP, I.
  QUATRE PIECES DE CONCERT, NO. 3, VERACINI--DIVERTISSEMENT
      ASSOCIATED MUSIC PUBLISHERS, INC.   ESC   1.00
PHILIPP, I.--ED.   PHILIPP, I.
  QUATRE PIECES DE CONCERT, NO. 4, VERACINI--DANSE VILLAGEOISE
      ASSOCIATED MUSIC PUBLISHERS, INC.   ESC   .65
PHILIPP, I.
  TWO OLD ITALIAN AIRS
      G. SCHIRMER, INC.   .50
PHIPPEN   AI
  TONE SKETCHES AT THE PIANO
      WILLIS MUSIC COMPANY   .75
PIAZZA, M.--ED   PIAZZA, M.
  MARGUERITE PIAZZA'S CHRISTMAS CAROL SING ALONG PARTY
      WILLIS MUSIC COMPANY   3.95
PICK-MANGIAGALLI
  CARILLON MAGICO, IL -- BALLET --
      FRANCO COLOMBO PUBLICATIONS   4.50
PIECHLER--ED   PIECHLER
  WIR SINGEN ALLE MIT
      SCHOTT   5075   3.00
PISCHNA *
  DER GROSSE PISCHNA, 60 PROGRESSIVE TECHNISCHE UBUNGEN MIT
  VARIANTEN VON MORONI
      BARENREITER VERLAG   CM 18331
PITCHER, G.--ED   PITCHER, G.
  SING TOGETHER AT CHRISTMAS
      WILLIS MUSIC COMPANY   1.25
PITTALUGA
  CUCKOLD'S FAIR, THE -- LA ROMERIA DE LOS CORNUDOS -- BALLET IN
  ONE ACT
      ASSOCIATED MUSIC PUBLISHERS, INC.   UME   2.00

PLANK, E.   SCHAUM, J.   1
  CHEERLEADER, THE
      SCHAUM PUBLICATIONS, INC.   .60
POHL, V.--ED *   POHL, V. *   1-2
  KINDER SPIELEN ZUR WEIHNACHT. 19 WEIHNACHTSLIEDER FUR KLAVIER
      BARENREITER VERLAG   EN 803
POLDINI, E.   MENDEL, S.   2
  DANCING DOLL
      WILLIS MUSIC COMPANY   .40
POLDINI, E.   ROLFE, W.   2
  POUPEE VALSANTE
      CENTURY MUSIC PUBLISHING COMPANY, INC.   3543   .40
POLDINI, E.   ROLFE, W.   2
  WALTZING DOLL, EASY
      CENTURY MUSIC PUBLISHING COMPANY, INC.   3543   .40
POLDINI, E.   4
  WALTZING DOLL
      CENTURY MUSIC PUBLISHING COMPANY, INC.   1697   .40
POLLA, W.--ED.   POLLA, W.
  WORLD'S GREATEST MELODIES
      SHAWNEE PRESS, INC.   .50
POLLA, W.--ED   POLLA, W.   5
  TWO GUITARS
      BELWIN-MILLS PUBLISHING CORPORATION   473   .60
POLLACK *
  DIANE
      THE BIG THREE MUSIC CORPORATION   00.95
PONCE, E.
  HOLIDAY
      THE BIG THREE MUSIC CORPORATION   00.95
PONCE, M.   ROLFE, W.   3
  ESTRELLITA
      CENTURY MUSIC PUBLISHING COMPANY, INC.   3630   .40
PONCHIELLI
  DANCE OF THE HOURS--BALLET FROM 'LA GIOCCONDA'
      G. SCHIRMER, INC.   L1396   1.00
PONCHIELLI   ZEPP   3-4
  DANCE OF THE HOURS - FROM THE OPERA 'LA GIOCANDA'
      PRO-ART PUBLICATIONS, INC.   404   .50
PONCHIELLI   MENDEL, S.   1 1/2
  DANCE OF THE HOURS
      WILLIS MUSIC COMPANY   .40
PONCHIELLI
  GIOCONDA, LA - DANCE OF THE HOURS
      FRANCO COLOMBO PUBLICATIONS   44836   .75
PONCHIELLI   CHIESA
  GIOCONDA, LA - DANCE OF THE HOURS
      FRANCO COLOMBO PUBLICATIONS   109093   .60
PONCHIELLI   DEL MAGLIO
  GIOCONDA, LA - DANCE OF THE HOURS
      FRANCO COLOMBO PUBLICATIONS   45389   .60
PONCHIELLI   CHIESA
  GIOCONDA, LA - EASY FANTASIA
      FRANCO COLOMBO PUBLICATIONS   109097   .50
PONCHIELLI   TAVAN
  GIOCONDA, LA - FANTASIA
      FRANCO COLOMBO PUBLICATIONS   128785   1.00
PONCHIELLI   4
  LA GIOCONDA, DANCE OF HOURS
      CENTURY MUSIC PUBLISHING COMPANY, INC.   1902   .40
PORRINO
  MONDO-TONDO -- BALLET --
      FRANCO COLOMBO PUBLICATIONS   126085   4.50
PORTER, C.   LEVINE
  BEGIN THE BEGUINE
      WARNER BROTHERS PUBLISHERS   1.00
PORTER, C.   WALTER
  BEGIN THE BEGUINE
      WARNER BROTHERS PUBLISHERS   1.00
PORTER, C.   HEYWOOD
  BEGIN THE BEGUINE
      WARNER BROTHERS PUBLISHERS   1.00
PORTER, C.   RICHTER   FIRST YEAR
  BEGIN THE BEGUINE
      WARNER BROTHERS PUBLISHERS   .75
PORTER, C.   GLOVER, D.
  COLE PORTER, THE WONDERFUL WORLD OF
      CHAPPELL AND COMPANY, INC.   0010116   2.50
PORTER, C.   HASTINGS
  NIGHT AND DAY
      WARNER BROTHERS PUBLISHERS   1.00
PORTER, C.   MACLACHLAN   FIRST YEAR
  NIGHT AND DAY
      WARNER BROTHERS PUBLISHERS   .75
PORTNOFF, M.--ED   PORTNOFF, M.
  DANCE ETUDES
      BOURNE COMPANY   1.00
PORTNOFF, M.--ED   PORTNOFF, M.
  TEN FINGERS IN A FIVE FINGER POSITION
      BOURNE COMPANY   1.00
POST--ED   POST   1-2
  THANKSGIVING HYMN
      CENTURY MUSIC PUBLISHING COMPANY, INC.   4158   .40
POST--ED   POST   1-2
  WE GATHER TOGETHER
      CENTURY MUSIC PUBLISHING COMPANY, INC.   4158   .40
POST, R.--ED   POST, R.   1
  HOLIDAY BOOK, THE
      ASHLEY DEALERS SERVICE, INC.   1.25
POST, R.--ED   POST, R.
  HOLIDAY BOOK, THE
      CENTURY MUSIC PUBLISHING COMPANY, INC.   1.25
POTTER, H. *
  ALL-IN-ONE BOOGIE WOOGIE
      SHAWNEE PRESS, INC.   .50
POULENC, F.
  ANIMAUX MODELES, LES -- BALLET IN ONE ACT
      ASSOCIATED MUSIC PUBLISHERS, INC.   ESC   12.50
POULENC, F.
  AUBADE -- PIANO REDUCTION --
      FRANCO COLOMBO PUBLICATIONS   SAL   8.75
POULENC, F.
  LES BICHES -- COMPLETE
      HEUGEL ET CIE.   22.00
POULENC, F.   4 1/2
  PASTOURELLE, FROM THE BALLET 'L'EVENTAIL DE JEANNE'
      THEODORE PRESSER COMPANY   .50
PREVIN, A.
  LIKE BLUE
      THE BIG THREE MUSIC CORPORATION   00.95
PREVIN, A.
  LIKE YOUNG
      THE BIG THREE MUSIC CORPORATION   00.95
PREVIN, A.
  PLAY PIANO LIKE ANDRE PREVIN, NO. 1
      THE BIG THREE MUSIC CORPORATION   01.50
PREVIN, A.
  PLAY PIANO LIKE ANDRE PREVIN, NO. 2
      THE BIG THREE MUSIC CORPORATION   01.95

RACHMANINOFF, S. THORNE
 THEME, FROM "CONCERTO NO. 02"
  BOOSEY AND HAWKES, INC.   .60
RACHMANINOFF, S. TRUXELL, E. 3 1/2
 THEMES FROM PIANO CONCERTO
  VOLKWEIN BROS.   00.40
RACHMANINOFF, S. ECKSTEIN
 THEME FROM SECOND PIANO CONCERTO, OP. 18
  CARL FISCHER, INC.   S 2313 .50
RACHMANINOFF, S. RICHARDSON
 VOCALISE, OP. 34 NO. 14
  BOOSEY AND HAWKES, INC.   .75
RAFF, J. *
 TRANSCRIPTION OF RAFF'S 'LA FILEUSE' OP. 157, NO. 02
  MUSICA OBSCURA   2.00
RAGAS *
 CLARINET MARMALADE
  THE BIG THREE MUSIC CORPORATION 00.95
RAKSIN, D.
 BAD AND THE BEAUTIFUL, THE
  THE BIG THREE MUSIC CORPORATION 00.95
RAMEAU GODOWSKY, L.
 ELEGY
  SHAWNEE PRESS, INC.   HB-235 .75
RAMEAU MOTCHANE
 GRADED RAMEAU, THE
  BELWIN-MILLS PUBLISHING CORPORATION 3.00
RAMEAU MOFFAT 6
 LA BOURREE DE VINCENT
  NOVELLO AND COMPANY, LTD. 55.0016.08 .40
RAMEAU THOMPSON, J. 1
 LE TAMBORIN
  WILLIS MUSIC COMPANY   .35
RAMEAU   4
 POULE, LA -- THE HEN --
  CENTURY MUSIC PUBLISHING COMPANY, INC. 3907 .40
RAMEAU DUMM
 RECITAL REFRESHER SERIES -- MINUET
  BELWIN-MILLS PUBLISHING CORPORATION 26118 .60
RAMOS, E. HARRIS 3-4
 PAQUITA MIA
  VOLKWEIN BROS.   .30
RAMOS, E. HARRIS 4
 YOLANDA
  VOLKWEIN BROS.   00.30
RAPHAEL, G.
 RAPHAEL
  MUSIC SALES CORPORATION 060002 2.95
RASBACH, O. RASBACH, O.
 TREES
  G. SCHIRMER, INC.   .50
RASBACH, O. DEIS
 TREES
  G. SCHIRMER, INC.   .50
RASKIN, D.
 LAURA
  THE BIG THREE MUSIC CORPORATION 00.95
RAVEL
 KADDISCH -- MELODIE HEBRAIQUE
  ELKAN-VOGEL, INC.   D 2.25
RAVEL DUMESNIL, M. 6
 PIECE EN FORME DE HABANERA
  ALPHONSE LEDUC
READING, H.--ED READING, H.
 ADESTE FIDELIS
  WILLIS MUSIC COMPANY   .30
REBIKOV ANSON, G. ELEMENTARY
 ANSON INTRODUCES REBIKOV, BK. 1
  WILLIS MUSIC COMPANY   1.00
REDA   2
 ZEHN WEIHNACHTSLIEDER
  BARENREITER VERLAG   BA 2082
REEL WEYBRIGHT 2 1/2
 IRISH WASHERWOMAN
  BELWIN-MILLS PUBLISHING CORPORATION .60
REGER
 VIRGIN'S SLUMBER SONG, THE, MARIA WIEGENLIED, OP. 76 NO. 52
  ASSOCIATED MUSIC PUBLISHERS, INC. BOT 1.00
REICH, M. SCHAUM, J. PREP
 PLAYFUL POODLE
  SCHAUM PUBLICATIONS, INC.   .50
REID--ED REID 1
 JESUS LOVES ME, THIS I KNOW
  BELWIN-MILLS PUBLISHING CORPORATION .60
REIN--ED * REIN * 2-3
 DER WUNDERGARTEN
  SCHOTT   4501-3 5.00
REIN   3
 KLAVIERMUSIK NACH VOLKSLIEDERN
  SCHOTT   4619 2.00
REISER, V.   1-2
 GLOW WORM
  CENTURY MUSIC PUBLISHING COMPANY, INC. 4291 .40
REISER, V.   1-2
 MELODY OF LOVE
  CENTURY MUSIC PUBLISHING COMPANY, INC. 4289 .40
REISFELD--ED REISFELD 2
 DEEP RIVER
  CENTURY MUSIC PUBLISHING COMPANY, INC. 3830 .40
REISFELD--ED REISFELD 2
 ROLL, JORDAN, ROLL
  CENTURY MUSIC PUBLISHING COMPANY, INC. 3832 .40
REISFELD--ED REISFELD 2
 STANDIN' IN THE NEED OF PRAYER
  CENTURY MUSIC PUBLISHING COMPANY, INC. 3835 .40
REISFELD   2
 NOBODY KNOWS DE TROUBLE I'VE SEEN
  CENTURY MUSIC PUBLISHING COMPANY, INC. 3831 .40
RICHARTZ   3
 RHEINH. VOLKSTANZE, OP. 69
  SCHOTT   3962 1.50
RICHTER--ED RICHTER
 DISNEY CLASSICS
  BOURNE COMPANY   1.50
RICHTER--ED RICHTER
 MADE EASY FOR THE PIANO -- COLE PORTER
  WARNER BROTHERS PUBLISHERS MEZ 7 1.25
RICHTER--ED RICHTER
 MADE EASY FOR THE PIANO -- GEORGE GERSHWIN, BK. 1
  WARNER BROTHERS PUBLISHERS MEZ 1 1.25
RICHTER--ED RICHTER
 MADE EASY FOR THE PIANO -- GEORGE GERSHWIN, BK. 2
  WARNER BROTHERS PUBLISHERS MEZ 2 1.25
RICHTER--ED RICHTER
 MADE EASY FOR THE PIANO -- GEORGE GERSHWIN, BK. 3
  WARNER BROTHERS PUBLISHERS MEZ 3 1.25

RICHTER--ED RICHTER
 MADE EASY FOR THE PIANO -- SIGMUND ROMBERG, BK. 2
  WARNER BROTHERS PUBLISHERS MEZ 8 1.25
RICHTER--ED RICHTER
 MADE EASY FOR THE PIANO -- VICTOR HERBERT, BK. 1
  WARNER BROTHERS PUBLISHERS MEZ 4 1.25
RICHTER--ED RICHTER
 MADE EASY FOR THE PIANO -- VICTOR HERBERT, BK. 2
  WARNER BROTHERS PUBLISHERS MEZ 5 1.25
RICHTER--ED RICHTER
 MADE EASY FOR THE PIANO -- VICTOR HERBERT, BK. 3
  WARNER BROTHERS PUBLISHERS MEZ 6 1.25
RICHTER--ED RICHTER
 MADE EASY FOR THE PIANO -- VINCENT YOUMANS
  WARNER BROTHERS PUBLISHERS MEZ 11 1.25
RICHTER--ED RICHTER
 MADE EASY FOR THE PIANO -- 20TH CENTURY HITS, BK. 1
  WARNER BROTHERS PUBLISHERS MEZ 9 1.25
RICHTER--ED RICHTER
 MADE EASY FOR THE PIANO -- 20TH CENTURY HITS, BK. 2
  WARNER BROTHERS PUBLISHERS MEZ 10 1.25
RICHTER--ED RICHTER
 SNOW WHITE AND THE SEVEN DWARFS
  BOURNE COMPANY   1.50
RICHTER, A.--ED. RICHTER, A.
 CHRISTMAS MELODIES IN EASY ARRANGEMENTS
  THEODORE PRESSER COMPANY   1.00
RICHTER, A.--ED. RICHTER, A.
 MY EVERYDAY HYMN BOOK
  THEODORE PRESSER COMPANY   1.25
RICHTER, A.--ED. RICHTER, A.
 MY OWN HYMN BOOK
  THEODORE PRESSER COMPANY   1.50
RICHTER, A.--ED. RICHTER, A.
 SONGS OF MY COUNTRY
  THEODORE PRESSER COMPANY   1.25
RICHTER, A.--ED. RICHTER, A.
 SONGS OF STEPHEN FOSTER
  THEODORE PRESSER COMPANY   1.25
RICHTER, A.--ED. RICHTER, A.
 YOUR FAVORITE SONGS
  THEODORE PRESSER COMPANY   1.50
RICHTER, A.
 INTERNATIONAL CHRISTMAS - 139 SONGS ANDCAROLS
  THEODORE PRESSER COMPANY   3.50
RICHTER, C.--ED RICHTER, C.
 FIVE FINGERS ON FIVE KEYS, BK. 01
  BOURNE COMPANY   .75
RICHTER, C.--ED RICHTER, C.
 FIVE FINGERS ON FIVE KEYS, BK. 02
  BOURNE COMPANY   .75
RICHTER, C.--ED RICHTER, C.
 MERRY CHRISTMAS MUSIC
  BOURNE COMPANY   .75
RICHTER, C.--ED RICHTER, C. 1
 MUSIC APPRECIATION SERIES, BK. 01
  BOURNE COMPANY   1.25
RICHTER, C.--ED RICHTER, C. 2
 MUSIC APPRECIATION SERIES, BK. 02
  BOURNE COMPANY   1.25
RIDDLE, N.
 THEME FROM 'THE UNTOUCHABLES'
  FRANK MUSIC CORPORATION   .95
RIEMANN, A.
 STOFFRESTE -- BALLET IN ONE ACT
  ASSOCIATED MUSIC PUBLISHERS, INC. BOT 7.50
RIMSKY-KORSAKOFF BUSH 2-3
 CELEBRATIONS IN THE SACRED FOREST
  PRO-ART PUBLICATIONS, INC. 22 .50
RIMSKY-KORSAKOFF   6
 COQ D'OR, HYMN TO SUN
  CENTURY MUSIC PUBLISHING COMPANY, INC. 2299 .40
RIMSKY-KORSAKOFF   4
 FESTIVAL AT BAGDAD, SCHEHEREZADE
  CENTURY MUSIC PUBLISHING COMPANY, INC. 3722 .40
RIMSKY-KORSAKOFF   5
 FLIGHT OF THE BUMBLE BEE
  CENTURY MUSIC PUBLISHING COMPANY, INC. 3184 .40
RIMSKY-KORSAKOFF ECKSTEIN
 FLIGHT OF THE BUMBLE BEE
  CARL FISCHER, INC.   S 2278 .50
RIMSKY-KORSAKOFF FELTON, W. 5
 FLIGHT OF THE BUMBLE BEE
  THEODORE PRESSER COMPANY   .50
RIMSKY-KORSAKOFF GILSON
 SCHEHERAZADE, OP. 35
  BOOSEY AND HAWKES, INC.   3.50
RIMSKY-KORSAKOFF MOSSMAN
 SCHEHERAZADE
  BELWIN-MILLS PUBLISHING CORPORATION 26097 .60
RIMSKY-KORSAKOFF   4
 SCHEHEREZADE, FESTIVAL AT BAGDAD
  CENTURY MUSIC PUBLISHING COMPANY, INC. 3722 .40
RIMSKY-KORSAKOFF GILSON *
 SHEHERAZADE--SYMPHONIC SUITE, OP. 35
  G. SCHIRMER, INC.   L1348 1.50
RIMSKY-KORSAKOFF DEIS
 SONG OF INDIA--FROM 'SADKO'
  G. SCHIRMER, INC.   .50
RIMSKY-KORSAKOFF   3
 SONG OF INDIA, A
  CENTURY MUSIC PUBLISHING COMPANY, INC. 3626 .40
RIMSKY-KORSAKOFF
 SONG OF INDIA -- SIMP.
  BOOSEY AND HAWKES, INC.   .60
RIMSKY-KORSAKOFF TCHEREPNIN
 SONG OF INDIA
  BOOSEY AND HAWKES, INC.   .75
RIMSKY-KORSAKOFF MOSSMAN
 SONG OF INDIA
  BELWIN-MILLS PUBLISHING CORPORATION 26098 .60
RIMSKY-KORSAKOFF THOMPSON, J. 3
 YOUNG PRINCE AND PRINCESS, THE
  WILLIS MUSIC COMPANY   .35
RITCHIE--ED RITCHIE 3
 CLAIR DE LUNE
  CENTURY MUSIC PUBLISHING COMPANY, INC. 4330 .40
RITTMAN--ED RITTMAN
 YESTERDAYS
  CIMINO PUBLICATIONS, INC. H 1.25
RIVE-KING *
 CONCERT TRANSCRIPTION OF HUNGARIAN RHAPSODY NO. 19
  MUSICA OBSCURA   2.50
ROBBINS--ED ROBBINS AI
 TIME TO PLAY MARCHES
  WILLIS MUSIC COMPANY   1.00

ROBINSON, G. E.　　　SAWYER, H. *
ONCE UPON A TIME STORIES OF THE GREAT MUSIC MASTERS
THEODORE PRESSER COMPANY　　　　　　　1.75
ROBYN, A.
MANZANILLO
THE BIG THREE MUSIC CORPORATION　　　　00.95
RODGERS, I.--ED　　　RODGERS, I.
AT CHRISTMAS TIDE
WILLIS MUSIC COMPANY　　　　　　　.75
RODGERS, I.--ED　　　RODGERS, I.
CHRISTMAS CAROLS FOR LITTLE BOYS AND GIRLS
WILLIS MUSIC COMPANY　　　　　　　1.00
RODGERS, I.--ED　　　RODGERS, I.
JOLLY CHRISTMAS MELODIES
WILLIS MUSIC COMPANY　　　　　　　1.00
RODGERS　　　MACLACHLAN　　　FIRST YEAR
BLUE ROOM, THE
WARNER BROTHERS PUBLISHERS　　　　　.75
RODGERS　　　LIBERACE
SLAUGHTER ON TENTH AVENUE
CHAPPELL AND COMPANY, INC.　　0017764-1502 1.00
RODGERS　　　RICHTER　　　FIRST YEAR
WITH A SONG IN MY HEART
WARNER BROTHERS PUBLISHERS　　　　　.75
ROFF　　　ROFF
SACRED SONGS IN THE CATHOLIC HOME
SAM FOX PUBLISHING COMPANY, INC.　　1.25
ROGERS--ED　　　ROGERS
HYMNS TO PLAY AND SING
PRO-ART PUBLICATIONS, INC.　　527　　.75
ROGERS--ED *　　　ROGERS *
POP GO THE CLASSICS
PRO-ART PUBLICATIONS, INC.　　1045　　2.00
ROGERS, E. T.　　　EASY
BEST OF YOUNG WORLD
LILLENAS PUBLISHING COMPANY　　MB-291　　2.50
ROGERS, E. T.　　　INTERMEDIATE
FAVORITES FROM YOUNG WORLD
LILLENAS PUBLISHING COMPANY　　MB-292　　2.50
ROGERS, E. T.　　　1
FIRST BOOK OF FAVORITE HYMNS
LILLENAS PUBLISHING COMPANY　　MB-050　　1.50
ROGERS, S. E.
FOUR KEYBOARD SETTINGS OF FOLK TUNES
HOPE PUBLISHING COMPANY　　　　　1.95
ROLAND *
L'ECRAN DES JEUNES FILLES
HEUGEL ET CIE.　　　　　　　8.10
ROLAND *
LE TOURNOI SINGULIER
HEUGEL ET CIE.　　　　　　　2.75
ROLFE, W.--ED　　　ROLFE, W.　　　2
AY, AY, AY
CENTURY MUSIC PUBLISHING COMPANY, INC.　3575　　.40
ROLFE, W.--ED　　　ROLFE, W.　　　3
BRITISH GRENADIERS
CENTURY MUSIC PUBLISHING COMPANY, INC.　3616　　.40
ROLFE, W.--ED　　　ROLFE, W.　　　2
CHRISTMAS CAROLS
CENTURY MUSIC PUBLISHING COMPANY, INC.　3724　　.40
ROLFE, W.--ED　　　ROLFE, W.　　　2
CHRISTMAS HYMNS
CENTURY MUSIC PUBLISHING COMPANY, INC.　3725　　.40
ROLFE, W.--ED　　　ROLFE, W.　　　2
DEEP RIVER
CENTURY MUSIC PUBLISHING COMPANY, INC.　3476　　.40
ROLFE, W.--ED　　　ROLFE, W.　　　2
GOD BE WITH YOU TILL WE MEET AGAIN
CENTURY MUSIC PUBLISHING COMPANY, INC.　3699　　.40
ROLFE, W.--ED　　　ROLFE, W.　　　3
HOME ON THE RANGE
CENTURY MUSIC PUBLISHING COMPANY, INC.　3475　　.40
ROLFE, W.--ED　　　ROLFE, W.　　　2
KERRY DANCE, THE
CENTURY MUSIC PUBLISHING COMPANY, INC.　3572　　.40
ROLFE, W.--ED　　　ROLFE, W.　　　2
LOCH LOMMOND
CENTURY MUSIC PUBLISHING COMPANY, INC.　3765　　.40
ROLFE, W.--ED　　　ROLFE, W.　　　2
LONDONDERRY AIR
CENTURY MUSIC PUBLISHING COMPANY, INC.　3474　　.40
ROLFE, W.--ED　　　ROLFE, W.　　　1
MOTHER HUBBARD AND SONG OF SIXPENCE
CENTURY MUSIC PUBLISHING COMPANY, INC.　3209　　.40
ROLFE, W.--ED　　　ROLFE, W.　　　2
OLD VIENNESE MELODY
CENTURY MUSIC PUBLISHING COMPANY, INC.　3574　　.40
ROLFE, W.--ED　　　ROLFE, W.　　　1
POLLY PUT THE KETTLE ON
CENTURY MUSIC PUBLISHING COMPANY, INC.　3210　　.40
ROLFE, W.--ED　　　ROLFE, W.　　　3
RED RIVER VALLEY
CENTURY MUSIC PUBLISHING COMPANY, INC.　3571　　.40
ROLFE, W.--ED　　　ROLFE, W.　　　1
ROCK-A-BYE BABY
CENTURY MUSIC PUBLISHING COMPANY, INC.　3208　　.40
ROLFE, W.--ED　　　ROLFE, W.　　　3
SHORTNIN' BREAD
CENTURY MUSIC PUBLISHING COMPANY, INC.　3573　　.40
ROLFE, W.--ED　　　ROLFE, W.　　　3
SONG OF THE VOLGA BOATMAN
CENTURY MUSIC PUBLISHING COMPANY, INC.　3634　　.40
ROLFE, W.　　　BEETHOVEN　　　2
CHICADEE FROM BEETHOVEN'S SYMPHONY NO. 8
CENTURY MUSIC PUBLISHING COMPANY, INC.　3179　　.40
ROLFE, W.　　　CHOPIN　　　2
DANCING THE MENUET FROM CHOPIN'S PRELUDE, OP. 28
CENTURY MUSIC PUBLISHING COMPANY, INC.　3170　　.40
ROLFE, W.　　　CHOPIN　　　2
EVENING SHADOWS FROM CHOPIN'S NOCTURNE
CENTURY MUSIC PUBLISHING COMPANY, INC.　3174　　.40
ROLFE, W.　　　CHOPIN　　　2
LACES AND FRILLS FROM CHOPIN'S MAZURKA
CENTURY MUSIC PUBLISHING COMPANY, INC.　3173　　.40
ROLFE, W.　　　CHOPIN　　　2
LITTLE BALLAD FROM CHOPIN'S OP. 47
CENTURY MUSIC PUBLISHING COMPANY, INC.　3171　　.40
ROLFE, W.　　　　　　1
PETER, PETER AND HUMPTY DUMPTY
CENTURY MUSIC PUBLISHING COMPANY, INC.　3202　　.40
ROLFE, W.　　　　　　1
POOR DOG BRIGHT AND HEY DIDDLE
CENTURY MUSIC PUBLISHING COMPANY, INC.　3201　　.40
ROLFE, W.　　　BEETHOVEN　　　2
PRAYER FROM BEETHOVEN'S SYMPHONY NO. 2, A
CENTURY MUSIC PUBLISHING COMPANY, INC.　3180　　.40

ROLFE, W.　　　　　　1
SING A SONG OF SIXPENCE
CENTURY MUSIC PUBLISHING COMPANY, INC.　3209　　.40
ROLFE, W.　　　BEETHOVEN　　　2
STOP, STOP, PRETTY WATER FROM BEETHOVEN'S SONATA, OP. 49 NO. 1
CENTURY MUSIC PUBLISHING COMPANY, INC.　3181　　.40
ROLFE, W.　　　CHOPIN　　　2
VALSE TRISTE FROM CHOPIN'S OP. 34 NO. 2
CENTURY MUSIC PUBLISHING COMPANY, INC.　3172　　.40
ROLFE, W.　　　MOZART, W.A.　　　2
VIOLET FROM MOZART'S SONATA NO. 12, THE
CENTURY MUSIC PUBLISHING COMPANY, INC.　3177　　.40
ROLFE, W.　　　BEETHOVEN　　　2
WISH FROM BEETHOVEN'S SYMPHONY NO. 3, A
CENTURY MUSIC PUBLISHING COMPANY, INC.　3178　　.40
ROMBERG, S.
BLOSSOM TIME
THE BIG THREE MUSIC CORPORATION　　　01.50
ROMBERG, S.　　　RICHTER　　　FIRST YEAR
DESERT SONG, THE
WARNER BROTHERS PUBLISHERS　　　　　.75
ROMBERG, S.
SELECTIONS FROM 'MAYTIME'
G. SCHIRMER, INC.　　　　　　　1.00
ROMBERG, S.　　　RICHTER　　　FIRST YEAR
SERENADE
WARNER BROTHERS PUBLISHERS　　　　　.75
ROMBERG, S.　　　RIEGGER
SERENADE
WARNER BROTHERS PUBLISHERS　　　　　1.00
ROMBERG, S.　　　RICHTER　　　FIRST YEAR
STOUTHEARTED MEN
WARNER BROTHERS PUBLISHERS　　　　　.75
RONNEFELD, P.
PETER SCHLEMIHL
UNIVERSAL EDITION　　UE 12475　　8.10
ROSAS　　　JESTON, I. H.　　　2
OVER THE WAVES WALTZ
VOLKWEIN BROS.　　　　　　　.35
ROSAS　　　CHIESA
OVER THE WAVES
FRANCO COLOMBO PUBLICATIONS　　109199　　.60
ROSAS　　　　　　2
SOBRE LAS OLAS, VALSE, EASY
CENTURY MUSIC PUBLISHING COMPANY, INC.　2137　　.40
ROSE, D.
HOMBRE
THE BIG THREE MUSIC CORPORATION　　　00.95
ROSE, E.　　　STEINER　　　2
GEORGIA MINSTREL BAND
BELWIN-MILLS PUBLISHING CORPORATION　　.60
ROSEMOND, G.
FOUNDATION, THE
WILLIS MUSIC COMPANY　　　　　　1.00
ROSENTHAL, L.
COMEDIANS, THE
THE BIG THREE MUSIC CORPORATION　　　00.95
ROSSELLINI
RACCONTO D'INVERNO -- WINTER TALE -- -- BALLET --
FRANCO COLOMBO PUBLICATIONS　　128607　　2.25
ROSSINI, G.
ASSEDIO DI CORINTO, L' - OVERTURE
FRANCO COLOMBO PUBLICATIONS　　127768　　1.00
ROSSINI, G.　　　　　　E-M
BARBER OF SEVILLE, ABRIDGED
C. F. PETERS CORPORATION　　H638　　2.00
ROSSINI, G.　　　KRUG　　　2
BARBER OF SEVILLE, TRANS.
CENTURY MUSIC PUBLISHING COMPANY, INC.　513　　.40
ROSSINI, G.
BARBIERE DI SIVIGLIA, IL -- COMPLETE OPERA --
FRANCO COLOMBO PUBLICATIONS　　124061　　6.00
ROSSINI, G.　　　CHIESA
BARBIERE DI SIVIGLIA, IL - CAVATINA - UNA VOCE POCO FA
FRANCO COLOMBO PUBLICATIONS　　107483　　.60
ROSSINI, G.
BARBIERE DI SIVIGLIA, IL - OVERTURE
FRANCO COLOMBO PUBLICATIONS　　127659　　1.00
ROSSINI, G.　　　　　　5
CUJUS ANIMAM FROM STABAT MATER
CENTURY MUSIC PUBLISHING COMPANY, INC.　182　　.40
ROSSINI, G.　　　DEL MAGLIO
DANZA, LA
FRANCO COLOMBO PUBLICATIONS　　124727　　.60
ROSSINI, G. *
DANZA, LA
FRANCO COLOMBO PUBLICATIONS　　128321　　1.00
ROSSINI, G.　　　ECKSTEIN
FANFARE FROM 'WILLIAM TELL'
CARL FISCHER, INC.　　S 2288　　.50
ROSSINI, G.
GAZZA LADRA, LA - OVERTURE
FRANCO COLOMBO PUBLICATIONS　　127997　　1.25
ROSSINI, G.　　　CHIESA
GUILLAUME TELL - EASY FANTASIA
FRANCO COLOMBO PUBLICATIONS　　107499　　.50
ROSSINI, G.
GUILLAUME TELL - OVERTURE
FRANCO COLOMBO PUBLICATIONS　　128081　　1.00
ROSSINI, G.　　　DEL MAGLIO
GUILLAUME TELL - PASTORALE FROM THE OVERTURE
FRANCO COLOMBO PUBLICATIONS　　128145　　.50
ROSSINI, G.
ITALIANA IN ALGERI, L' - OVERTURE
FRANCO COLOMBO PUBLICATIONS　　127585　　1.00
ROSSINI, G.　　　SCHAUM, J.　　　4
LA DANZA
SCHAUM PUBLICATIONS, INC.　　　　　.60
ROSSINI, G.　　　PERONI
MATILDE DI SHABRAN - OVERTURE
FRANCO COLOMBO PUBLICATIONS　　129243　　1.00
ROSSINI, G.
MOSE - DAL TUO STELLATO SOGLIO
FRANCO COLOMBO PUBLICATIONS　　42195　　.60
ROSSINI, G.　　　DEL MAGLIO
MOSE - DAL TUO STELLATO SOGLIO
FRANCO COLOMBO PUBLICATIONS　　124728　　.60
ROSSINI, G.　　　　　　3
OVERTURE, WILLIAM TELL, EASY
CENTURY MUSIC PUBLISHING COMPANY, INC.　2513　　.40
ROSSINI, G.　　　　　　5
OVERTURE, WILLIAM TELL
CENTURY MUSIC PUBLISHING COMPANY, INC.　1529　　.40
ROSSINI, G.　　　ROLFE, W.　　　2
OVERTURE, WILLIAM TELL
CENTURY MUSIC PUBLISHING COMPANY, INC.　3401　　.40

ROSSINI, G.
  OVERTURE FROM 'WILLIAM TELL'
      G. SCHIRMER, INC.   .80
ROSSINI, G.   TOMEKKERI
  PETIT MESSE SOLENNELLE - PRELUDIO RELIGIOSO
      FRANCO COLOMBO PUBLICATIONS   129033   .75
ROSSINI, G.
  SCALA DI SETA, LA - OVERTURE
      FRANCO COLOMBO PUBLICATIONS   127769   1.00
ROSSINI, G.
  SELECTED OVERTURES -- WITH BELLINI-SELECTED OVERTURES --
      FRANCO COLOMBO PUBLICATIONS   ER1163   4.25
ROSSINI, G.
  SEMIRAMIDE - OVERTURE
      FRANCO COLOMBO PUBLICATIONS   128645   .75
ROSSINI, G.   5
  STABAT MATER, CUJUS ANIMaM
      CENTURY MUSIC PUBLISHING COMPANY, INC.   182   .40
ROSSINI, G.
  TANCREDI - OVERTURE
      FRANCO COLOMBO PUBLICATIONS   127904   .60
ROSSINI, G.   BERMONT, H.   1B
  WILLIAM TELL -- FANFARE
      MUSICORD PUBLICATIONS, INC.   .45
ROSSINI, G.   KRUG   2
  WILLIAM TELL OVERTURE, EASY
      CENTURY MUSIC PUBLISHING COMPANY, INC.   532   .40
ROSSINI, G.   ZEPP   2-3
  WILLIAM TELL
      PRO-ART PUBLICATIONS, INC.   325   .50
ROSSINI *
  DANZA, LA
      FRANCO COLOMBO PUBLICATIONS   128321   1.00
ROSSINI *
  REGATA VENEZIANA, LA
      FRANCO COLOMBO PUBLICATIONS   128857   .90
ROSSI   4
  SPIN, SPIN, ESTHONIAN FOLK SONG
      CENTURY MUSIC PUBLISHING COMPANY, INC.   2288   .40
ROSZA
  BEAUTY AND GRACE
      THE BIG THREE MUSIC CORPORATION   00.95
ROSZA
  BEN-HUR
      THE BIG THREE MUSIC CORPORATION   00.95
ROSZA
  KING OF KINGS, THE
      THE BIG THREE MUSIC CORPORATION   00.95
ROTSCHER, K.
  VENEZIANISCHER KARNEVAL, OP. 21 -- BALLET IN 7 PARTS ON THEMES
  OF D'ALBERT
      ASSOCIATED MUSIC PUBLISHERS, INC.   BOT   7.50
ROYAL--ED   ROYAL   3
  CAISSON SONG
      CENTURY MUSIC PUBLISHING COMPANY, INC.   3727   .40
ROYAL--ED   ROYAL   3
  FIELD ARTILLERY SONG
      CENTURY MUSIC PUBLISHING COMPANY, INC.   3727   .40
ROZIN--ED   ROZIN
  TRADITIONAL HEBREW SONGS
      PRO-ART PUBLICATIONS, INC.   1080   2.00
RUBINSTEIN--ED   RUBINSTEIN
  BESS YOU IS MY WOMAN
      CHAPPELL AND COMPANY, INC.   0447524   1.00
RUBINSTEIN--ED   RUBINSTEIN
  I GOT PLENTY O' NUTTIN'
      CHAPPELL AND COMPANY, INC.   2230027-1502 .95
RUBINSTEIN--ED   RUBINSTEIN
  SUMMERTIME, RUBENSTEIN CONCERT ARR.
      CHAPPELL AND COMPANY, INC.   5565023-1503 1.00
RUBINSTEIN   WEYBRIGHT   1 1/2
  KAMENNOI-OSTROW
      BELWIN-MILLS PUBLISHING CORPORATION   .60
RUBINSTEIN   DEL MAGLIO
  MELODY IN F, OP. 3 NO. 1
      FRANCO COLOMBO PUBLICATIONS   127354   .50
RUBINSTEIN   SCHAUM, J.   2 1/2
  MELODY IN F
      SCHAUM PUBLICATIONS, INC.   .60
RUBINSTEIN   JESTON, I. H.   3
  MELODY IN F
      VOLKWEIN BROS.   .35
RUBINSTEIN   DEL MAGLIO
  ROMANCE IN E FLAT, OP. 44
      FRANCO COLOMBO PUBLICATIONS   127355   .50
RUBINSTEIN
  TURKISH MARCH FROM 'THE RUINS OF ATHENS'--BEETHOVEN
      G. SCHIRMER, INC.   .60
RUSSELL   STEINER   4
  BOOGIE ON THE SHANNON RIVER
      BELWIN-MILLS PUBLISHING CORPORATION   .60
RUSSELL   SCHAUM, J.   2 1/2
  WHERE THE RIVER SHANNON FLOWS
      SCHAUM PUBLICATIONS, INC.   .60
SAINT-SAENS   BIZET
  ALLEGRO SCHERZANDO, OP. 22
      ELKAN-VOGEL, INC.   D   2.75
SAINT-SAENS   BENFELD, A.
  CAPRICE-VALSE -- FROM 'WEDDING CAKE', OP. 76
      ELKAN-VOGEL, INC.   D   4.00
SAINT-SAENS   4
  CYGNE, LE
      CENTURY MUSIC PUBLISHING COMPANY, INC.   1693   .40
SAINT-SAENS   2
  CYGNE, LE
      CENTURY MUSIC PUBLISHING COMPANY, INC.   2140   .40
SAINT-SAENS   3
  DANCE MACABRE
      CENTURY MUSIC PUBLISHING COMPANY, INC.   3330   .40
SAINT-SAENS   CRAMER, J.
  DANSE MACABRE, OP. 40
      ELKAN-VOGEL, INC.   D   3.00
SAINT-SAENS   CRAMER
  DANSE MACABRE, OP. 40
      ELKAN-VOGEL, INC.   2.75
SAINT-SAENS   LISZT
  DANSE MACABRE
      ELKAN-VOGEL, INC.   D   5.35
SAINT-SAENS   LISZT
  DANSE MACABRE
      ELKAN-VOGEL, INC.   4.00
SAINT-SAENS   SCHAUM, J.   3
  DANSE MACABRE
      SCHAUM PUBLICATIONS, INC.   .50
SAINT-SAENS   ECKSTEIN
  EXCERPT FROM 'DANSE MACABRE'
      CARL FISCHER, INC.   S 2290   .50

SAINT-SAENS   LEVY
  GAVOTTE IN B MINOR FROM VIOLIN SONATA NO. 2--BACH
      G. SCHIRMER, INC.   .50
SAINT-SAENS
  GAVOTTE IN E FROM VIOLIN SONATA NO. 6--BACH
      G. SCHIRMER, INC.   .40
SAINT-SAENS   3
  MY HEART AT THY SWEET VOICE
      CENTURY MUSIC PUBLISHING COMPANY, INC.   2013   .40
SAINT-SAENS   DURAND, A.
  REVERIE DU SOIR DE LA SUITE ALGERIENNE, OP. 60
      ELKAN-VOGEL, INC.   D   1.70
SAINT-SAENS   3
  SAMSON AND DELILA, MY HEART
      CENTURY MUSIC PUBLISHING COMPANY, INC.   2013   .40
SAINT-SAENS   PALMERI
  SWAN, THE--FROM 'CARNAVAL DES ANIMAUX'
      G. SCHIRMER, INC.   .35
SAINT-SAENS   LEVINE
  SWAN, THE--FROM 'CARNAVAL DES ANIMAUX'
      G. SCHIRMER, INC.   .50
SAINT-SAENS   HOSKIER
  SWAN, THE--MELODY FROM THE 'CARNAVAL DES ANIMAUX'
      G. SCHIRMER, INC.   .50
SAINT-SAENS   ZEPP   4
  SWAN, THE
      PRO-ART PUBLICATIONS, INC.   382   .50
SAINT-SAENS   THOMPSON, J.   1
  SWAN, THE
      WILLIS MUSIC COMPANY   .40
SALZMANN--ED   SALZMANN   2-3
  DER ZUPFGEIGENHANSL
      SCHOTT   4650   9.00
SAMINSKY
  GAILLARDE D'UNE PESTE JOYEUSE -- OPERA-BALLET --
      FRANCO COLOMBO PUBLICATIONS   SAL   7.00
SANFORD--ED   SANFORD
  HYMNS
      BOSTON MUSIC COMPANY   1.00
SANTA MARIA, T. DE   AZPIAZU, J. *
  TWENTY-FIVE FANTASIES FROM "ARTE DE TANER
  FANTASIA"--PNO/ORG/HP
      ASSOCIATED MUSIC PUBLISHERS, INC.   UME   2.50
SANTLY   3-4
  DRIFTING ON, FOX TROT
      CENTURY MUSIC PUBLISHING COMPANY, INC.   2555   .40
SARASATE
  GIPSY AIRS, OP. 20
      G. SCHIRMER, INC.   .70
SASLAW, E.--ED   SASLAW, E.
  FUN WITH FOLK TUNES
      WILLIS MUSIC COMPANY   2.00
SASLAW, E.--ED   SASLAW, E.   AE
  SONGS AND RIMES OF LATIN AMERICA
      WILLIS MUSIC COMPANY   1.50
SATIE, E.   MILHAUD, D.
  FIVE GRIMACES, OP. POSTH.
      UNIVERSAL EDITION   UE 9915   3.75
SATIE, E.
  RELACHE -- BALLET --
      FRANCO COLOMBO PUBLICATIONS   SAL   11.50
SAUER--ED   SAUER
  GREAT MASTERS, THE
      UNIVERSAL EDITION   UE 10676   4.25
SAUGUET
  CHATTE, LA -- BALLET -- .. HYMNE FINAL
      FRANCO COLOMBO PUBLICATIONS   SAL   1.75
SAUGUET
  CHATTE, LA -- BALLET --
      FRANCO COLOMBO PUBLICATIONS   SAL   7.50
SAUGUET
  DAVID -- BALLET --
      FRANCO COLOMBO PUBLICATIONS   SAL   9.00
SAUGUET
  FORAINS, LES -- BALLET --
      FRANCO COLOMBO PUBLICATIONS   SAL   10.75
SAUGUET
  LES CINQ ETAGES
      HEUGEL ET CIE.   3.00
SAUGUET
  LE RECONTRE
      HEUGEL ET CIE.   6.00
SAUGUET
  MIRAGES, LES -- BALLET --
      FRANCO COLOMBO PUBLICATIONS   SAL   7.25
SAUGUET
  NUIT, LA -- BALLET --
      FRANCO COLOMBO PUBLICATIONS   SAL   4.25
SAVAGNONE
  DRAGO ROSSO, IL -- BALLET --
      FRANCO COLOMBO PUBLICATIONS   DS423   5.00
SAVINIO
  VITA DELL'UOMO -- BALLET --
      FRANCO COLOMBO PUBLICATIONS   128135   5.00
SAVINO--ED.   SAVINO
  CHIAPANECAS
      THE BIG THREE MUSIC CORPORATION   00.75
SAVINO--ED.   SAVINO
  POPULAR SONG CLASSICS FOR PIANO
      THE BIG THREE MUSIC CORPORATION   01.25
SAVINO--ED.   SAVINO
  WALTZ YOU SAVED FOR ME
      THE BIG THREE MUSIC CORPORATION   00.95
SAVINO--ED.   SAVINO
  WONDERFUL ONE
      THE BIG THREE MUSIC CORPORATION   00.95
SAVINO
  STUDY IN BLUE
      THE BIG THREE MUSIC CORPORATION   00.95
SAWTELL, P.
  VOYAGE TO THE BOTTOM OF THE SEA
      THE BIG THREE MUSIC CORPORATION   00.95
SCARLATTI, A.   BARTH, H.
  PASTORAL SONATA
      BELWIN-MILLS PUBLISHING CORPORATION   20373   .60
SCARLATTI, D.   ANSON, G.   INTERMEDIATE
  ANSON INTRODUCES SCARLATTI, BK. 1
      WILLIS MUSIC COMPANY   1.00
SCARLATTI, D.   ANSON, G.   INTERMEDIATE
  ANSON INTRODUCES SCARLATTI, BK. 2
      WILLIS MUSIC COMPANY   1.25
SCARL'ATTI, D.   TAUSIG
  CAPRICCIO IN E, LONGO 10--TRANSCRIBED FOR CONCERT-USE
      G. SCHIRMER, INC.   .40
SCARLATTI, D.   RATHAUS, K.
  FOUR STUDIES AFTER DOMENICO SCARLATTI
      THEODORE PRESSER COMPANY   2.00

SCARLATTI, D. MOTCHANE			
GRADED SCARLATTI, THE			
BELWIN-MILLS PUBLISHING CORPORATION			4.00
SCARLATTI, D. TAUSIG			
PASTORALE, LONGO 413--ARRANGED FOR CONCERT-USE			
G. SCHIRMER, INC.			.40
SCARLATTI, D. WURMSER, L.			
TOCCATA DI BRAVURA			
ELKAN-VOGEL, INC.		CON	3.75
SCARMOLIN--ED SCARMOLIN			
MELODIES OF THE MASTERS			
PRO-ART PUBLICATIONS, INC.		43	1.00
SCARMOLIN--ED SCARMOLIN			
SONGS WE LOVE TO PLAY			
PRO-ART PUBLICATIONS, INC.		67	.85
SCHARWENKA, X. HILL 5			
POLISH DANCE			
CENTURY MUSIC PUBLISHING COMPANY, INC.		363	.40
SCHAUM, J.--ED. SCHAUM, J. 5			
AMERICAN COMPOSERS OF THE TWENTIETH CENTURY			
SCHAUM PUBLICATIONS, INC.			2.00
SCHAUM, J.--ED. SCHAUM, J. 3			
AMERICAN SONATINAS			
SCHAUM PUBLICATIONS, INC.			1.50
SCHAUM, J.--ED. SCHAUM, J. 2			
CATHOLIC HYMNS			
SCHAUM PUBLICATIONS, INC.			1.50
SCHAUM, J.--ED. SCHAUM, J. 2 1/2			
CLASSICS OF RENOWN, BK. 1			
SCHAUM PUBLICATIONS, INC.			1.50
SCHAUM, J.--ED. SCHAUM, J. 3 1/2			
CLASSICS OF RENOWN, BK. 2			
SCHAUM PUBLICATIONS, INC.			1.50
SCHAUM, J.--ED. SCHAUM, J. 5			
COMPOSER-PIANISTS			
SCHAUM PUBLICATIONS, INC.			2.00
SCHAUM, J.--ED. SCHAUM, J. 5			
CONTEMPORARY COMPOSERS			
SCHAUM PUBLICATIONS, INC.			2.00
SCHAUM, J.--ED. SCHAUM, J. 4 1/2			
GOSPEL CAMEOS			
SCHAUM PUBLICATIONS, INC.			1.75
SCHAUM, J.--ED. SCHAUM, J. 5			
GOSPEL PIANO PROFILES			
SCHAUM PUBLICATIONS, INC.			2.00
SCHAUM, J.--ED. SCHAUM, J. PREP			
GREAT BALLETS -- CLASSIC MELODIES			
SCHAUM PUBLICATIONS, INC.			1.25
SCHAUM, J.--ED. SCHAUM, J. PREP			
GREAT COMPOSERS -- CLASSIC MELODIES			
SCHAUM PUBLICATIONS, INC.			1.25
SCHAUM, J.--ED. SCHAUM, J. PREP			
GREAT OPERAS -- CLASSIC MELODIES			
SCHAUM PUBLICATIONS, INC.			1.25
SCHAUM, J.--ED. SCHAUM, J. PREP			
GREAT SYMPHONIES -- CLASSIC MELODIES			
SCHAUM PUBLICATIONS, INC.			1.25
SCHAUM, J.--ED. SCHAUM, J. 2			
HANSEL AND GRETEL			
SCHAUM PUBLICATIONS, INC.			1.50
SCHAUM, J.--ED. SCHAUM, J. 1 1/2			
HAWAIIAN MUSIC			
SCHAUM PUBLICATIONS, INC.			1.50
SCHAUM, J.--ED. SCHAUM, J. 1 1/2			
HAWAIIAN WARRIOR'S DANCE			
SCHAUM PUBLICATIONS, INC.			.50
SCHAUM, J.--ED. SCHAUM, J.			
LATIN AMERICAN MUSIC			
SCHAUM PUBLICATIONS, INC.			1.50
SCHAUM, J.--ED. SCHAUM, J. 4 1/2			
MEXICAN HAT DANCE			
SCHAUM PUBLICATIONS, INC.			.60
SCHAUM, J.--ED. SCHAUM, J. 2			
MUSIC OF THE AMERICAN INDIAN			
SCHAUM PUBLICATIONS, INC.			1.50
SCHAUM, J.--ED. SCHAUM, J. 4			
ROMANTIC CAMEOS			
SCHAUM PUBLICATIONS, INC.			1.50
SCHAUM, J.--ED. SCHAUM, J. 1 1/2			
WABASH CANNON BALL			
SCHAUM PUBLICATIONS, INC.			.50
SCHAUM, J.--ED. SCHAUM, J. 4			
WEDDING MUSIC			
SCHAUM PUBLICATIONS, INC.			2.00
SCHAUM, J.--ED. SCHAUM, J. 2 1/2			
WOMEN COMPOSERS OF THE UNITED STATES			
SCHAUM PUBLICATIONS, INC.			1.50
SCHAUM, J. 2 1/2			
AMERICAN FAVORITES			
SCHAUM PUBLICATIONS, INC.			1.75
SCHAUM, J. 3			
BOOGIE IS MY BEAT			
SCHAUM PUBLICATIONS, INC.			1.50
SCHAUM, J. 2 1/2			
CONTINENTAL FAVORITES			
SCHAUM PUBLICATIONS, INC.			1.75
SCHAUM, J. PREP TO 1			
FESTIVAL OF SOLOS			
SCHAUM PUBLICATIONS, INC.			1.25
SCHAUM, J. 3			
FIFTY SONGS -- FIFTY STATES			
SCHAUM PUBLICATIONS, INC.			3.50
SCHAUM, J. 2 1/2			
GOOD TIMES SONGS			
SCHAUM PUBLICATIONS, INC.			1.25
SCHAUM, J. 2 1/2			
HOUSE PARTY TUNES			
SCHAUM PUBLICATIONS, INC.			1.50
SCHAUM, J. 1			
MARINES' HYMN, THE			
BOSTON MUSIC COMPANY			.50
SCHAUM, J. 2			
PARADE OF MARCHES			
SCHAUM PUBLICATIONS, INC.			1.25
SCHAUM, J. PREP			
PATRIOTIC PRIMER			
SCHAUM PUBLICATIONS, INC.			1.25
SCHAUM, J. 1 1/2			
PIANO FUN FARE			
SCHAUM PUBLICATIONS, INC.			1.25
SCHAUM, J. 4 1/2			
PRESTIGE PIANO SOLOS -- SCHAUM REPERTOIRE			
SCHAUM PUBLICATIONS, INC.			1.75
SCHAUM, W.--ED SCHAUU, W. 1			
TWELVE DAYS OF CHRISTMAS			
SCHAUM PUBLICATIONS, INC.			.50

SCHAUM, W.--ED SCHAUM, W. 1			
WHAT CHILD IS THIS			
SCHAUM PUBLICATIONS, INC.			.50
SCHER, W.--ED SCHER, W.			
FAMOUS MELODY ALBUM FOR VERY EARLY GRADES			
G. SCHIRMER, INC.			1.00
SCHER, W.--ED SCHER, W.			
ISRAELI FAVORITES			
PRO-ART PUBLICATIONS, INC.		932	.85
SCHER, W.--ED SCHER, W.			
JEWISH SONGS AND DANCES			
G. SCHIRMER, INC.			1.00
SCHER, W.--ED SCHER, W.			
PIANO SAMPLER			
PRO-ART PUBLICATIONS, INC.		1203	1.00
SCHER, W.			
JEWISH SONGS AND DANCES--PIANO SETTINGS WITH WORDS AND			
ILLUSTRATIONS			
G. SCHIRMER, INC.			1.00
SCHIEFELBEIN, F. 2			
JINGLE BELLS			
VOLKWEIN BROS.			.35
SCHIFRIN, L.			
HAUNTING			
THE BIG THREE MUSIC CORPORATION			00.95
SCHIFRIN, L.			
RHINO - THEME			
THE BIG THREE MUSIC CORPORATION			00.95
SCHIFRIN HASTINGS			
BULLITT, THEME FROM			
WARNER BROTHERS PUBLISHERS			1.00
SCHIFRIN			
FOX, THE, THEME FROM			
WARNER BROTHERS PUBLISHERS			1.00
SCHIRMER--ED SCHIRMER			
POPULAR THEMES BY GREAT MASTERS			
BOSTON MUSIC COMPANY			1.00
SCHMID 4			
BAYRISCHE LANDLER, OP. 36			
SCHOTT		1792	2.00
SCHMITT			
REFLETS -- BALLET -- BK. 1 .. HEIDELBERG, COBLENTZ, LUEBECK,			
WERDER			
FRANCO COLOMBO PUBLICATIONS		SAL	4.00
SCHMITT			
REFLETS -- BALLET -- BK. 2 .. VIENNA, DRESDEN, NUREMBERG, MUNICH			
FRANCO COLOMBO PUBLICATIONS		SAL	4.00
SCHROEDER, H. 4			
MINNELIEDER			
SCHOTT		3720	2.00
SCHROEDER, H. 3			
SUSANI, ALTE WEIHNACHTSLIEDER			
SCHOTT		3882	2.00
SCHUBERT DEL MAGLIO			
AN DEN MOND			
FRANCO COLOMBO PUBLICATIONS		128143	.50
SCHUBERT DEL MAGLIO			
AVE MARIA, OP. 52 NO. 6			
FRANCO COLOMBO PUBLICATIONS		128149	.60
SCHUBERT 4			
AVE MARIA, WORDS			
CENTURY MUSIC PUBLISHING COMPANY, INC.		3185	.40
SCHUBERT *			
AVE MARIA			
ELKAN-VOGEL, INC.		D	.50
SCHUBERT			
AVE MARIA			
G. SCHIRMER, INC.			.60
SCHUBERT *			
AVE MARIA			
G. SCHIRMER, INC.			.60
SCHUBERT SCHAUM, J. 4			
AVE MARIA			
SCHAUM PUBLICATIONS, INC.			.60
SCHUBERT 4			
BALLET MUSIC, ROSAMUND			
CENTURY MUSIC PUBLISHING COMPANY, INC.		2003	.40
SCHUBERT FISCHHOF			
BALLET MUSIC - ROSAMUNDE			
UNIVERSAL EDITION		852	.75
SCHUBERT FISCHHOF *			
BALLET MUSIC FROM 'ROSAMUNDE', OP. 26			
G. SCHIRMER, INC. SCHAUM, J. 2 1/2		L1146	.75
SCHUBERT			
BEST OF SCHUBERT			
SCHAUM PUBLICATIONS, INC.			1.50
SCHUBERT MILLER 4			
BY THE SEA			
CENTURY MUSIC PUBLISHING COMPANY, INC.		133	.40
SCHUBERT STEINER 2			
CHARM OF CHAMBER MUSIC			
BELWIN-MILLS PUBLISHING CORPORATION			.60
SCHUBERT *			
DU BIST DIE RUH'			
G. SCHIRMER, INC.			.50
SCHUBERT *			
DU BIST DIE RUH'			
G. SCHIRMER, INC.			.50
SCHUBERT *			
ERLKING			
G. SCHIRMER, INC.			.60
SCHUBERT *			
ERLKING			
G. SCHIRMER, INC.			.60
SCHUBERT * 6			
ERL KING, THE			
CENTURY MUSIC PUBLISHING COMPANY, INC.		1193	.40
SCHUBERT * 6			
ERL KING, THE			
CENTURY MUSIC PUBLISHING COMPANY, INC.		1193	.40
SCHUBERT DEL MAGLIO			
FORELLE, DIE			
FRANCO COLOMBO PUBLICATIONS		128142	.50
SCHUBERT * PARSONS			
HARK, HARK, THE LARK			
G. SCHIRMER, INC.			.60
SCHUBERT * PARSONS			
HARK, HARK, THE LARK			
G. SCHIRMER, INC.			.60
SCHUBERT *			
HARK, HARK, THE LARK			
WILLIS MUSIC COMPANY			.50
SCHUBERT * 6			
HARK, HARK THE LARK			
CENTURY MUSIC PUBLISHING COMPANY, INC.		1335	.40

SCHUBERT *   6
   HARK, HARK THE LARK
     CENTURY MUSIC PUBLISHING COMPANY, INC.   1335   .40
SCHUBERT   DEL MAGLIO
   HEIDENROESLEIN, OP. 3 NO. 3
     FRANCO COLOMBO PUBLICATIONS   128125   .50
SCHUBERT   3
   IMPROMPTU G-DUR, OP. 90
     SCHOTT   0688 102   1.00
SCHUBERT   DEL MAGLIO
   IMPROMPTU IN G FLAT, OP. 90 NO. 3
     FRANCO COLOMBO PUBLICATIONS   124730   .50
SCHUBERT *
   LEISE FLEHEN--SERENADE
     G. SCHIRMER, INC.   .   .75
SCHUBERT   DEL MAGLIO
   MARCHE MILITAIRE, OP. 51 NO. 1
     FRANCO COLOMBO PUBLICATIONS   124731   .60
SCHUBERT *
   MARGUERITE AU ROUET
     ELKAN-VOGEL, INC.   D   .50
SCHUBERT   KRENTZLIN   2
   MILITARMARSCH D-DUR OP. 51 NO. 1
     SCHOTT   08260 1/2   1.00
SCHUBERT   ROLFE, W.   2
   MILITARY MARCH, EASY
     CENTURY MUSIC PUBLISHING COMPANY, INC.   3176   .40
SCHUBERT   3
   MILITARY MARCH, NO. 1
     CENTURY MUSIC PUBLISHING COMPANY, INC.   1648   .40
SCHUBERT   DEL MAGLIO
   MOMENT MUSICAL, OP. 94 NO. 3
     FRANCO COLOMBO PUBLICATIONS   124732   .50
SCHUBERT   SCHAUM, J.   2 1/2
   MOMENT MUSICAL
     SCHAUM PUBLICATIONS, INC.   .50
SCHUBERT   M-D
   QUINTET, OP. 114 'TROUT'
     C. F. PETERS CORPORATION   1307A   2.50
SCHUBERT   SCHAUM, J.   2 1/2
   ROMANTIC WALTZES OF FRANZ SCHUBERT
     SCHAUM PUBLICATIONS, INC.   1.60
SCHUBERT   SCHAUM, J.   2 1/2
   ROMANTIC WALTZES OF FRANZ SCHUBERT
     SCHAUM PUBLICATIONS, INC.   1.60
SCHUBERT   3
   ROSAMUND, BALLET MUSIC
     CENTURY MUSIC PUBLISHING COMPANY, INC.   2003   .40
SCHUBERT   M
   ROSAMUNDE. ENTR'ACTES AND BALLET MUSIC
     C. F. PETERS CORPORATION   1310   2.00
SCHUBERT   STEINER   2
   SCHUBERT FESTIVAL, A MEDLEY -- 1. ROSAMUNDE'S LOVE SONG, 2.
   SPRING BREEZES, 3. IN THE MEADOW
     BELWIN-MILLS PUBLISHING CORPORATION   .60
SCHUBERT   ECKHARDT, F.   1
   SCHUBERT FOR THE YOUNG PIANIST
     CENTURY MUSIC PUBLISHING COMPANY, INC.   3961   .40
SCHUBERT   SMALL, A.
   SCHUBERT WALTZ SAMPLER
     ALFRED MUSIC COMPANY   548   1.95
SCHUBERT   LISZT   6
   SERENADE
     CENTURY MUSIC PUBLISHING COMPANY, INC.   696   .40
SCHUBERT   DEL MAGLIO
   SERENADE
     FRANCO COLOMBO PUBLICATIONS   128150   .60
SCHUBERT   DEL MAGLIO
   SERENADE
     FRANCO COLOMBO PUBLICATIONS   43123   .90
SCHUBERT   JESTON, I. H.   3
   SERENADE
     VOLKWEIN BROS.   .35
SCHUBERT   WHITFORD   GR. 2
   SERENADE
     ROBERT WHITFORD PUBLICATIONS   .40
SCHUBERT   MAIER   4
   STARS, THE
     THEODORE PRESSER COMPANY   .50
SCHUBERT   MANSFIELD
   STEPS TO THE MASTERS
     BANKS AND SON LTD.   1.35
SCHUBERT   5
   SYMPHONIE H-MOLL -- UNVOLL.
     SCHOTT   128   1.50
SCHUBERT   3
   SYMPHONY, UNFINISHED, THEME
     CENTURY MUSIC PUBLISHING COMPANY, INC.   3434   .40
SCHUBERT   DEIS
   SYMPHONY IN B MINOR, NO. 8--'UNFINISHED'
     G. SCHIRMER, INC.   L1408   1.00
SCHUBERT   DEL MAGLIO
   SYMPHONY IN B MINOR 'UNFINISHED' -- THEMES IN EASY TRANSCR. --
     FRANCO COLOMBO PUBLICATIONS   128144   .50
SCHUBERT   TAGLIAPIETRA
   SYMPHONY IN B MINOR 'UNFINISHED'
     FRANCO COLOMBO PUBLICATIONS   ER617   .75
SCHUBERT   GOETSCHIUS, P.
   SYMPHONY NO. 10 IN C MAJOR
     THEODORE PRESSER COMPANY   1.25
SCHUBERT   ECKSTEIN
   THEME FROM 'UNFINISHED SYMPHONY'
     CARL FISCHER, INC.   S 2287   .50
SCHUBERT   RUSSELL   2
   THEME FROM RONDO IN D, OP. 53 NO. 2
     BOSTON MUSIC COMPANY   .50
SCHUBERT *
   TWENTY-FOUR SONG TRANSCRIPTIONS, BK. 1
     G. SCHIRMER, INC.   L128   1.75
SCHUBERT *
   TWENTY-FOUR SONG TRANSCRIPTIONS, BK. 2
     G. SCHIRMER, INC.   L129   1.75
SCHUBERT   3
   UNFINISHED SYMPHONY, 2 THEMES
     CENTURY MUSIC PUBLISHING COMPANY, INC.   3434   .40
SCHUBERT   MAIER, G.
   WALTZES, SET 1
     BELWIN-MILLS PUBLISHING CORPORATION   1.25
SCHUBERT   MAIER, G.
   WALTZES, SET 2
     BELWIN-MILLS PUBLISHING CORPORATION   1.25
SCHUBERT   MAIER, G.
   WALTZES, SET 3
     BELWIN-MILLS PUBLISHING CORPORATION   1.25
SCHUBERT   MAIER, G.
   WALTZES, SET 4
     BELWIN-MILLS PUBLISHING CORPORATION   1.25

SCHUBERT   MAIER, G.
   WALTZES, SET 5
     BELWIN-MILLS PUBLISHING CORPORATION   1.25
SCHUBERT   DEL MAGLIO
   WOHIN OP. 25 NO. 2
     FRANCO COLOMBO PUBLICATIONS   128126   .50
SCHUETT   3
   LOVE WALTZ, OP. 59 NO. 2 - EASY
     CENTURY MUSIC PUBLISHING COMPANY, INC.   2521   .40
SCHULZ-EVLER   GALLICO
   BY THE BEAUTIFUL BLUE DANUBE--J. STRAUSS--CONCERT ARABESQUE
     G. SCHIRMER, INC.   .90
SCHUMANN, R. *
   WIDMUNG
     FRANCO COLOMBO PUBLICATIONS   127908   .50
SCHUMANN, R.   DEL MAGLIO
   ABENDLIED, OP. 85 NO. 12
     FRANCO COLOMBO PUBLICATIONS   128845   .60
SCHUMANN, R.   DEL MAGLIO
   ALBUMBLAETTER, OP. 124 NO. 16
     FRANCO COLOMBO PUBLICATIONS   129084   .60
SCHUMANN, R.   DEL MAGLIO
   ALBUM FUER DIE JUGEND -- ALBUM FOR THE YOUNG --, OP. 68 NO. 10 -
   THE HAPPY FARMER
     FRANCO COLOMBO PUBLICATIONS   .60
SCHUMANN, R.   ANSON, G.   INTERMEDIATE
   ANSON INTRODUCES SCHUMANN, BK. 1
     WILLIS MUSIC COMPANY   1.75
SCHUMANN, R.   BRADLEY, R.
   BRADLEY CLASSICAL SERIES - HAPPY FARMER, THE
     SCREEN GEMS - COLUMBIA PUBLICATIONS   0027HP2   .85
SCHUMANN, R.   BRADLEY, R.
   BRADLEY CLASSICAL SERIES - HUNTING SONG
     SCREEN GEMS - COLUMBIA PUBLICATIONS   6707HP2   .85
SCHUMANN, R.   BRADLEY, R.
   BRADLEY CLASSICAL SERIES - SOLDIER'S MARCH
     SCREEN GEMS - COLUMBIA PUBLICATIONS   4749SP2   .85
SCHUMANN, R.   BRADLEY, R.
   BRADLEY CLASSICAL SERIES - WILD HORSEMAN, THE
     SCREEN GEMS - COLUMBIA PUBLICATIONS   2716WP2   .85
SCHUMANN, R.   GRAINGER
   CONCERTO, FIRST MOVEMENT--CONCERT TRANSCRIPTION
     G. SCHIRMER, INC.   1.25
SCHUMANN, R.   M
   CONCERTO IN A MINOR, OP. 54. ABRIDGED
     C. F. PETERS CORPORATION   2898A   1.25
SCHUMANN, R. *
   DEDICATION
     G. SCHIRMER, INC.   .70
SCHUMANN, R. *
   DEDICATION
     G. SCHIRMER, INC.   .70
SCHUMANN, R.   D
   FOUR SYMPHONIES
     C. F. PETERS CORPORATION   2332   7.50
SCHUMANN, R.   STEINER   2 1/2
   HE, THE NOBLIEST OF ALL
     BELWIN-MILLS PUBLISHING CORPORATION   .60
SCHUMANN, R.   7
   INN, THE, FROM 'FOREST SCENES'
     NOVELLO AND COMPANY, LTD.   55.0035.04   .25
SCHUMANN, R.   HARTL   4
   JOYFUL PEASANT
     CENTURY MUSIC PUBLISHING COMPANY, INC.   2116   .40
SCHUMANN, R.   DEL MAGLIO
   KINDERSCENEN -- SCENES FROM CHILDHOOD --, OP. 15 NO. 7 -
   TRAEUMEREI
     FRANCO COLOMBO PUBLICATIONS   128129   .60
SCHUMANN, R.   6
   LONELY FLOWERS, FROM 'FOREST SCENES'
     NOVELLO AND COMPANY, LTD.   55.0019.02   .40
SCHUMANN, R.   ECKHARDT, F.   1
   SCHUMANN FOR THE YOUNG PIANIST
     CENTURY MUSIC PUBLISHING COMPANY, INC.   3962   .40
SCHUMANN, R.   ECKHARDT, F.   1
   SCHUMANN FOR THE YOUNG PIANIST
     CENTURY MUSIC PUBLISHING COMPANY, INC.   3962   .40
SCHUMANN, R. *
   SPRING NIGHT
     FRANCO COLOMBO PUBLICATIONS   128430   .50
SCHUMANN, R.   MANSFIELD
   STEPS TO THE MASTERS
     BANKS AND SON LTD.   1.35
SCHUMANN, R.   PHILLIPS, M.
   VALSE MODERATO, OP. 124 NO. 10
     BELWIN-MILLS PUBLISHING CORPORATION   .60
SCHUMANN, R.   LISZT
   WIDMUNG -- DEDICATION --, OP. 25 NO. 1
     FRANCO COLOMBO PUBLICATIONS   127908   .50
SCHUMANN, R. *
   WIDMUNG
     FRANCO COLOMBO PUBLICATIONS   127908   .50
SCHUNGELER, H.--ED   SCHUNGELER, H.   1-2
   DAS NEUE KINDERLIEDERBUCH
     SCHOTT   3719   2.50
SCHUNGELER, H.--ED   SCHUNGELER, H.   2-3
   DAS NEUE VOLKSLIEDERBUCH
     SCHOTT   3968   2.50
SCHUNGELER, H.   2-3
   DAS NEUE VOLKSLIEDERBUCH
     SCHOTT   3968   2.50
SCHWARTZ, S.   SCHAUM, J.   1 1/2
   DAY BY DAY
     SCHAUM PUBLICATIONS, INC.   .75
SCOTT, C.   ARNOLD
   LENTO
     BOOSEY AND HAWKES, INC.   .35
SCOTT, C.   SCHAUM, J.   4
   LENTO
     SCHAUM PUBLICATIONS, INC.   .60
SCOTT, C.   ZEPP   5
   LOTUS LAND
     PRO-ART PUBLICATIONS, INC.   459   .60
SCOTT, C.   SCHAUM, J.   4 1/2
   LOTUS LAND
     SCHAUM PUBLICATIONS, INC.   .60
SEGAL, J.   GLOVER, D.
   SCARLET RIBBONS
     BELWIN-MILLS PUBLISHING CORPORATION   .60
SERRADELL   3
   LA GOLONDRINA -- THE SWALLOW, EASY
     CENTURY MUSIC PUBLISHING COMPANY, INC.   3569   .40
SERRADELL   3
   SWALLOW, THE -- LA GOLONDRINA --
     CENTURY MUSIC PUBLISHING COMPANY, INC.   2097   .40
SERRADELL   3
   SWALLOW, THE -- LA GOLONDRINA --
     CENTURY MUSIC PUBLISHING COMPANY, INC.   3569   .40

SINGER, L.--ED   SINGER, L.
  MY FUNNY VALENTINE
    CHAPPELL AND COMPANY, INC.   3930005   .95
SINGER, L.--ED   SINGER, L.
  MY SHIP
    CHAPPELL AND COMPANY, INC.   3995008   .95
SINGER, L.--ED   SINGER, L.
  NEVERTHELESS
    CHAPPELL   4060000   .95
SINGER, L.--ED   SINGER, L.
  NICE WORK IF YOU CAN GET IT
    CHAPPELL AND COMPANY, INC.   4082525   .95
SINGER, L.--ED   SINGER, L.
  OLD DEVIL MOON
    CHAPPELL AND COMPANY, INC.   4297503   .95
SINGER, L.--ED   SINGER, L.
  ON THE STREET WHERE YOU LIVE
    CHAPPELL AND COMPANY, INC   4350005   .95
SINGER, L.--ED   SINGER, L.
  PARTY'S OVER, THE
    CHAPPELL AND COMPANY, INC.   4523759   .95
SINGER, L.--ED   SINGER, L.
  PEOPLE
    CHAPPELL AND COMPANY, INC.   4562500   .95
SINGER, L.--ED   SINGER, L.
  ROSALIE
    CHAPPELL AND COMPANY, INC.   4907507   .95
SINGER, L.--ED   SINGER, L.
  SEAL IT WITH A KISS
    CHAPPELL AND COMPANY, INC.   0019448   .95
SINGER, L.--ED   SINGER, L.
  SEPTEMBER SONG
    CHAPPELL AND COMPANY, INC.   5060009   .95
SINGER, L.--ED   SINGER, L.
  SMALL WORLD
    CHAPPELL AND COMPANY, INC.   5235007   .95
SINGER, L.--ED   SINGER, L.
  SPEAK LOW
    CHAPPELL AND COMPANY, INC.   5412507   .95
SINGER, L.--ED   SINGER, L.
  STRANGE MUSIC
    CHAPPELL AND COMPANY, INC.   5520002   .95
SINGER, L.--ED   SINGER, L.
  STRING OF PEARLS, A
    CHAPPELL AND COMPANY, INC.   5537501   .95
SINGER, L.--ED   SINGER, L.
  THERE'S A SMALL HOTEL
    CHAPPELL AND COMPANY, INC.   5875000   .95
SINGER, L.--ED   SINGER, L.
  THEY CAN'T TAKE THAT AWAY FROM ME
    CHAPPELL AND COMPANY, INC.   5932520   .95
SINGER, L.--ED   SINGER, L.
  THIS CAN'T BE LOVE
    CHAPPELL AND COMPANY, INC.   5955000   .95
SINGER, L.--ED   SINGER, L.
  TILL
    CHAPPELL AND COMPANY, INC.   6057509   .95
SINGER, L.--ED   SINGER, L.
  TRUE LOVE
    CHAPPELL AND COMPANY, INC.   6165005   .95
SINGER, L.--ED   SINGER, L.
  TRY TO REMEMBER
    CHAPPELL AND COMPANY, INC.   6175004   .95
SINGER, L.--ED   SINGER, L.
  WISH YOU WERE HERE
    CHAPPELL AND COMPANY, INC.   6702518   .95
SINGER, L.--ED   SINGER, L.
  WORLD IS WAITING FOR THE SUNRISE, THE
    CHAPPELL AND COMPANY, INC.   6755003   .95
SINGER, L.--ED   SINGER, L.
  WOULDN'T BE LOVERLY
    CHAPPELL AND COMPANY, INC.   6767503   .95
SINGER, L.--ED   SINGER, L.
  YOU'D BE SO NICE TO COME HOME TO
    CHAPPELL AND COMPANY, INC.   6915508   .95
SINGER   WILLIAMS, J.
  YOUNG AND WARM AND WONDERFUL
    FRANK MUSIC CORPORATION   .95
SLOTE, G. --ED   SLOTE, G.
  SONGS FOR ALL YEAR LONG AND GOSH, WHAT A WONDERFUL WORLD
    OAK PUBLICATIONS   000090   2.95
SMALL, A.
  SHALOM, 72 TRADITIONAL HEBREW MELODIES
    ALFRED MUSIC COMPANY   547   3.50
SMETANA   2-3
  DALIBOR. POTPOURRI AUS DER OPER
    BARENREITER VERLAG   AP 707
SMETANA   KAAN   3
  MEIN VATERLAND, HEFT 1 - VYSEHRAD
    BARENREITER VERLAG   AP 717A
SMETANA   KAAN   3
  MEIN VATERLAND, HEFT 2 - DIE MOLDAU
    BARENREITER VERLAG   AP 717B
SMETANA   PEK   3
  MEIN VATERLAND, HEFT 3 - SARKA
    BARENREITER VERLAG   AP 717C
SMETANA   PEK   3
  MEIN VATERLAND, HEFT 4 - AUS BOHMENS HAIN UND FLUR
    BARENREITER VERLAG   AP 717D
SMETANA   PEK   3
  MEIN VATERLAND, HEFT 5 - TABOR
    BARENREITER VERLAG   AP 717E
SMETANA   PEK   3
  MEIN VATERLAND, HEFT 6 - BLANIK
    BARENREITER VERLAG   AP 717F
SMETANA   4
  MOLDAU, THE -- THEME
    CENTURY MUSIC PUBLISHING COMPANY, INC.   3846   .40
SMETANA   KLUSSMANN
  MOLDAU, THE
    FRANCO COLOMBO PUBLICATIONS   SIK.192   2.00
SMETANA   4
  POLKA, BARTERED BRIDE
    CENTURY MUSIC PUBLISHING COMPANY, INC.   3719   .40
SMETANA   SIN   2-3
  POLKA AUS DER OPER 'DIE VERKAUFTE BRAUT'
    BARENREITER VERLAG   AP 294
SMETANA   DUMM
  RECITAL REFRESHER SERIES -- FABLE, OP. 2 NO. 2
    BELWIN-MILLS PUBLISHING CORPORATION 26114   .60
SMITH--ED   SMITH   2
  STAR SPANGLED BANNER
    BOSTON MUSIC COMPANY   .50
SMITH--ED   SMITH
  TWENTY-NINE VERY EASY FOLK SONGS
    BOSTON MUSIC COMPANY   1.25

SMITH, SYDNEY   ROLFE, W.   2
  CHANSON RUSSE, EASY
    CENTURY MUSIC PUBLISHING COMPANY, INC.   3396   .40
SMITH, SYDNEY   4
  RUSSIAN SONG, OP. 31
    CENTURY MUSIC PUBLISHING COMPANY, INC.   2192   .40
SMITH, T.--ED   SMITH, T.
  PIANO PORTRAITS - SACRED SOLOS
    BROADMAN MUSIC   4571-09   2.75
SMITH, T.
  CONCERT HYMN TRANSCRIPTIONS
    HOPE PUBLISHING COMPANY   1.50
SMITH, T.
  CRUSADE PIANIST NO. 1
    LILLENAS PUBLISHING COMPANY   MB-030   2.50
SMITH, T.
  CRUSADE PIANIST NO. 2
    LILLENAS PUBLISHING COMPANY   MB-031   2.50
SMITH, T.
  CRUSADE PIANIST NO. 3
    LILLENAS PUBLISHING COMPANY   MB-032   2.50
SMITH, T.
  CRUSADE PIANIST NO. 4
    LILLENAS PUBLISHING COMPANY   MB-235   2.50
SMITH, T.
  SIMPLIFIED PIANO ARRANGEMENTS
    HOPE PUBLISHING COMPANY   2.50
SOCHTING   GILLOCK   1 1/2
  CUCKOO'S CALL
    WILLIS MUSIC COMPANY   .40
SOSNIK, H.
  GAYETY
    THE BIG THREE MUSIC CORPORATION   00.95
SOUSA   WEYBRIGHT   2
  LIBERTY BELL, THE, MARCH
    BELWIN-MILLS PUBLISHING CORPORATION   .60
SOUSA   LEVINE, H.
  SOUSA'S FAMOUS MARCHES FOR PIANO SOLO
    THEODORE PRESSER COMPANY   2.00
SOUSA   CARLETON   1 1/2
  STARS AND STRIPES FOREVER --TRIO THEME--
    THEODORE PRESSER COMPANY   .50
SOUSA   PELS, W.   1B
  STARS AND STRIPES FOREVER -- FINALE THEME
    MUSICORD PUBLICATIONS, INC.   .45
SOUSA   RICHTER, A.
  STARS AND STRIPES FOREVER -- 9 OTHER WELL-KNOWN FAVORITES
    THEODORE PRESSER COMPANY   1.00
SOUSA   ZEPP   2
  STARS AND STRIPES FOREVER
    PRO-ART PUBLICATIONS, INC.   144   .50
SOUSA   ZEPP   4
  STARS AND STRIPES FOREVER
    PRO-ART PUBLICATIONS, INC.   145   .50
SOUSA   RICHTER   2
  STARS AND STRIPES FOREVER
    THEODORE PRESSER COMPANY   .50
SOUSA   SCHAUM   2 1/2
  STARS AND STRIPES FOREVER
    THEODORE PRESSER COMPANY   .50
SOUSA   3
  WASHINGTON POST, THE
    BOSTON MUSIC COMPANY   .50
SOUSA   THOMPSON, J.   1
  WASHINGTON POST MARCH
    WILLIS MUSIC COMPANY   .35
SPAULDING, G. L.--ED   SPAULDING, G. L.
  BELLS OF ST. MARY'S, WALTZ
    CHAPPELL AND COMPANY, INC.   0437509-1503 .95
SPAULDING, G. L.   SCHAUM, J.   2
  SING, ROBIN SING
    SCHAUM PUBLICATIONS, INC.   .50
SPENCER, J.
  FAVORITE CHRISTMAS MELODIES
    VOLKWEIN BROS.   01.00
SPENCER, J.
  FAVORITE MELODIES MADE EASY
    VOLKWEIN BROS.   01.00
SPENCER, J.   1
  HOME ON THE RANGE -- AMERICAN COWBOY
    VOLKWEIN BROS.   .30
SPITZMULLER, A.
  CONSTRUCTION HUMAINE, OP. 49 -- ABSTRACT BALLET
    ASSOCIATED MUSIC PUBLISHERS, INC.   BOT   7.50
ST. QUENTIN--ED   ST. QUENTIN
  BELLS OF ST. MARY'S, WALTZ
    CHAPPELL AND COMPANY, INC.   0437509-1502 .95
STANLEY--ED   STANLEY   3
  AULD LANG SYNE
    CENTURY MUSIC PUBLISHING COMPANY, INC.   3769   .40
STANLEY--ED   STENLEY   3
  COMIN' THRU THE RYE
    CENTURY MUSIC PUBLISHING COMPANY, INC.   3770   .40
STANLEY--ED   STANLEY   3
  GOODNIGHT LADIES
    CENTURY MUSIC PUBLISHING COMPANY, INC.   3769   .40
STANLEY--ED   STANLEY   3
  HAND ME DOWN MY WALKIN' CANE
    CENTURY MUSIC PUBLISHING COMPANY, INC.   3771   .40
STANLEY--ED   STANLEY   3
  LITTLE BROWN JUG
    CENTURY MUSIC PUBLISHING COMPANY, INC.   3768   .40
STANLEY--ED   STANLEY   3
  OLD GRAY MARE, THE
    CENTURY MUSIC PUBLISHING COMPANY, INC.   3768   .40
STANLEY--ED   STANLEY   3
  OLD MACDONALD HAD A FARM
    CENTURY MUSIC PUBLISHING COMPANY, INC.   3772   .40
STANLEY--ED   STANLEY   3
  SHE'LL BE COMIN' ROUND THE MOUNTAIN
    CENTURY MUSIC PUBLISHING COMPANY, INC.   3771   .40
STARR   STEINER   1 1/2
  STARR SONG -- SOMEBODY LOVES ME
    BELWIN-MILLS PUBLISHING CORPORATION   .60
STECHER *
  IN THE SPIRIT OF '76
    SCHMITT, HALL AND MCCREARY COMPANY 9950   2.00
STECHER *
  WE WISH YOU A MERRY CHRISTMAS, BK. 1
    SCHMITT, HALL AND MCCREARY COMPANY 9967   1.00
STECHER *
  WE WISH YOU A MERRY CHRISTMAS, BK. 2
    SCHMITT, HALL AND MCCREARY COMPANY 9978   1.25
STEINBRECHER--ED   STEINBRECHER
  SO SINGT MAN IN WIEN -- 32 FAMOUS VIENNESE SONGS IN EASY
  ARRANGEMENTS
    UNIVERSAL EDITION   UE 10940   2.55

STEINER--ED.   STEINER   1 1/2
  ALPINE YODEL, FOLK MELODY
    BELWIN-MILLS PUBLISHING CORPORATION   .60
STEINER--ED.   STEINER
  FORGOTTEN DREAMS -- SIMP.
    BELWIN-MILLS PUBLISHING CORPORATION   26070   .50
STEINER--ED.   STEINER
  FUN TIME
    PRO-ART PUBLICATIONS, INC.   1303   1.25
STEINER--ED.   STEINER   2
  GIVE ME THAT OLD-TIME RELIGION -- SPIRITUAL
    BELWIN-MILLS PUBLISHING CORPORATION   .60
STEINER--ED.   STEINER
  HEY, MR. BANJO
    BELWIN-MILLS PUBLISHING CORPORATION   25092   .50
STEINER--ED.   STEINER
  SLEIGH RIDE -- CHILDREN'S EDITION
    BELWIN-MILLS PUBLISHING CORPORATION   25133   .50
STEINER--ED.   STEINER
  WALTZING CAT, THE
    BELWIN-MILLS PUBLISHING CORPORATION   25135   .50
STEINER   3, 4
  ADVANCING PIANIST PLAYS CONCERTOS, THE
    BELWIN-MILLS PUBLISHING CORPORATION   1766   1.75
STEINER   2 1/2, 3
  ADVANCING PIANIST PLAYS MARCHES, THE
    BELWIN-MILLS PUBLISHING CORPORATION   1750   1.75
STEINER   2 1/2, 3
  ADVANCING PIANIST PLAYS OPERA, THE
    BELWIN-MILLS PUBLISHING CORPORATION   1765   1.75
STEINER   2 1/2, 3
  ADVANCING PIANIST PLAYS RECITAL MUSIC, THE
    BELWIN-MILLS PUBLISHING CORPORATION   1759   1.75
STEINER   3, 4
  ADVANCING PIANIST PLAYS SYMPHONIES, THE
    BELWIN-MILLS PUBLISHING CORPORATION   1928   1.75
STEINER   2
  AMERICAN MUSIC FOR THE YOUNG PIANIST
    BELWIN-MILLS PUBLISHING CORPORATION   1863   1.75
STEINER   2
  BOOGIE WOOGIE FOR THE YOUNG PIANIST
    BELWIN-MILLS PUBLISHING CORPORATION   1862   1.75
STEINER   2
  HAWAIIAN DELIGHT -- FOLK MELODIES
    BELWIN-MILLS PUBLISHING CORPORATION   .60
STEINER   2
  HOLIDAY IN LISBON, FOLK DANCE
    BELWIN-MILLS PUBLISHING CORPORATION   .60
STEINER   2
  LIFE ON THE OCEAN WAVE, A -- SAILORS' MARCH
    BELWIN-MILLS PUBLISHING CORPORATION   .60
STEINER   1, 2
  MARCHES FOR THE YOUNG PIANIST
    BELWIN-MILLS PUBLISHING CORPORATION   1865   1.75
STEINER   2
  RECITAL MUSIC FOR THE YOUNG PIANIST
    BELWIN-MILLS PUBLISHING CORPORATION   1866   1.75
STEINER *   NEALE, J.   EASY
  SUMMER PLACE, A, THEME FROM
    WARNER BROTHERS PUBLISHERS   .75
STEINER   FREEMAN
  TARA THEME
    WARNER BROTHERS PUBLISHERS   1.00
STICKLES--ED   STICKLES
  SCHIRMER'S FAVORITE SACRED SONGS
    G. SCHIRMER, INC.   1.25
STICKLES--ED   STICKLES
  SONGS OF FAITH
    G. SCHIRMER, INC.   1.50
STONE, E.--ED   STONE, E.
  CHAPPELL'S FAVORITES
    CHAPPELL AND COMPANY, INC.   0021998   1.00
STONE, E.--ED   STONE, E.
  I GOT PLENTY O' NUTTIN'
    CHAPPELL AND COMPANY, INC.   2230027-1501 .95
STONE, E.--ED   STONE, E.
  SUMMERTIME, STONE CONCERT ARR.
    CHAPPELL AND COMPANY, INC.   5565023-502 1.00
STONE, E.--ED   STONE, E.
  SUMMERTIME
    CHAPPELL AND COMPANY, INC.   5565023   .95
STONE, E.--ED   STONE, E.
  YESTERDAYS
    CIMINO PUBLICATIONS, INC.   H   1.25
STRADELLA   DEL MAGLIO
  PRAYER
    FRANCO COLOMBO PUBLICATIONS   128141   .50
STRAUSS, J.   DEL MAGLIO
  ACCELERATIONS, OP. 234
    FRANCO COLOMBO PUBLICATIONS   124734   .50
STRAUSS, J.   DEL MAGLIO
  ALBUM - 8 FAMOUS WALTZES
    FRANCO COLOMBO PUBLICATIONS   127641   1.25
STRAUSS, J.   DEL MAGLIO
  ARTIST'S LIFE, OP. 316
    FRANCO COLOMBO PUBLICATIONS   124737   .60
STRAUSS, J.   DEL MAGLIO
  BEAUTIFUL MAY, OP. 375
    FRANCO COLOMBO PUBLICATIONS   124742   .60
STRAUSS, J.   ZEPP   2-3
  BLUE DANUBE WALTZ, THE
    PRO-ART PUBLICATIONS, INC.   194   .50
STRAUSS, J.   STREABBOG   2
  BLUE DANUBE WALTZ
    CENTURY MUSIC PUBLISHING COMPANY, INC.   3242   .40
STRAUSS, J.   ECKSTEIN
  BLUE DANUBE WALTZ
    CARL FISCHER, INC.   S 2285   .50
STRAUSS, J.   MITTLER   2B
  BLUE DANUBE WALTZ
    MUSICORD PUBLICATIONS, INC.   .45
STRAUSS, J.   SCHAUM, J.   3
  BLUE DANUBE
    SCHAUM PUBLICATIONS, INC.   .60
STRAUSS, J.   TRUXELL, E.   1 1/2
  BLUE DANUBE
    VOLKWEIN BROS.   .30
STRAUSS, J.   STEINER
  DRINKING SONG -- FROM 'DIE FLEDERMAUS'
    BELWIN-MILLS PUBLISHING CORPORATION   26012   .60
STRAUSS, J.   4
  DU UND DU -- FLEDERMAUS WALTZ
    CENTURY MUSIC PUBLISHING COMPANY, INC.   3426   .40
STRAUSS, J.   DEL MAGLIO
  EMPEROR WALTZ, OP. 437
    FRANCO COLOMBO PUBLICATIONS   124748   .60

STRAUSS, J.   PENNARIO
  EMPEROR WALTZ
    BELWIN-MILLS PUBLISHING CORPORATION   20078   1.50
STRAUSS, J.   ZEPP   3
  EMPEROR WALTZ
    PRO-ART PUBLICATIONS, INC.   196   .50
STRAUSS, J.   WEYBRIGHT   2 1/2
  FLEDERMAUS, DIE
    BELWIN-MILLS PUBLISHING CORPORATION   .60
STRAUSS, J.   KOVACS, S.
  FLEDERMAUS PARAPHRASE--ON AIRS FROM 'THE BAT'
    G. SCHIRMER, INC.   .90
STRAUSS, J.   DORATI
  GRADUATION BALL
    BELWIN-MILLS PUBLISHING CORPORATION   07047   4.00
STRAUSS, J.   STEINER   2
  GYPSY BARON POLKA
    BELWIN-MILLS PUBLISHING CORPORATION   .60
STRAUSS, J.   DEL MAGLIO
  KISS WALTZ, OP. 411
    FRANCO COLOMBO PUBLICATIONS   124744   .60
STRAUSS, J.   DEL MAGLIO
  LAGOON WALTZ, OP. 411
    FRANCO COLOMBO PUBLICATIONS   124746   .60
STRAUSS, J.   STEINER
  LAUGHING SONG -- FROM 'DIE FLEDERMAUS'
    BELWIN-MILLS PUBLISHING CORPORATION   26025   .60
STRAUSS, J.   3
  MEINE STRAUSS-WALZER, BAND 01
    SCHOTT   1504   2.50
STRAUSS, J.   3
  MEINE STRAUSS-WALZER, BAND 02
    SCHOTT   1564   3.50
STRAUSS, J.   DEL MAGLIO
  MORNING PAPERS, OP. 279
    FRANCO COLOMBO PUBLICATIONS   .60
STRAUSS, J.   4
  NIGHT IN VENICE, WALTZES
    CENTURY MUSIC PUBLISHING COMPANY, INC.   3342   .40
STRAUSS, J.   ZILCHER   2
  NUR WALZER VON STRAUSS
    SCHOTT   1507   3.00
STRAUSS, J.   SCHULZ-EVLER
  ON THE BEAUTIFUL BLUE DANUBE--CONCERT ARABESQUE
    G. SCHIRMER, INC.   .90
STRAUSS, J.   DEL MAGLIO
  ON THE BEAUTIFUL BLUE DANUBE, OP. 314
    FRANCO COLOMBO PUBLICATIONS   124736   .60
STRAUSS, J.   STEINER
  PRINCE ORLOFSKY'S SONG -- FROM 'DIE FLEDERMAUS'
    BELWIN-MILLS PUBLISHING CORPORATION   26039   .60
STRAUSS, J.   DEL MAGLIO
  ROSES FROM THE SOUTH, OP. 388
    FRANCO COLOMBO PUBLICATIONS   124743   .60
STRAUSS, J.   KROME   1
  STRAUSS FUR ALLE
    SCHOTT   2840   2.50
STRAUSS, J.   SCHAUM, J.   3
  STRAUSS WALTZES
    SCHAUM PUBLICATIONS, INC.   1.50
STRAUSS, J.   DEL MAGLIO
  TALES FROM THE VIENNA WOODS, OP. 325
    FRANCO COLOMBO PUBLICATIONS   .60
STRAUSS, J.   ECKSTEIN
  TALES FROM THE VIENNA WOODS WALTZ
    CARL FISCHER, INC.   S 2284   .50
STRAUSS, J.   TRUXELL, E.   3
  TALES FROM THE VIENNA WOODS WALTZ
    VOLKWEIN BROS.   00.50
STRAUSS, J.   FLETCHER   2
  TALES FROM THE VIENNA WOODS
    BOSTON MUSIC COMPANY   .50
STRAUSS, J.   WALLIS   3
  TALES FROM THE VIENNA WOODS
    BOSTON MUSIC COMPANY   .50
STRAUSS, J.   MITTLER   2B
  TALES FROM THE VIENNA WOODS
    MUSICORD PUBLICATIONS, INC.   .45
STRAUSS, J.   TRUXELL, E.   2
  TALES FROM THE VIENNA WOODS
    VOLKWEIN BROS.   00.40
STRAUSS, J.   BOHM   2
  TALES FROM VIENNA WOODS
    CENTURY MUSIC PUBLISHING COMPANY, INC.   894   .40
STRAUSS, J.   3
  TALES FROM VIENNA WOODS
    CENTURY MUSIC PUBLISHING COMPANY, INC.   3703   .40
STRAUSS, J.   DEL MAGLIO
  TREASURE WALTZ, OP. 418
    FRANCO COLOMBO PUBLICATIONS   124747   .60
STRAUSS, J.   DOHNANYI
  TWO WALTZ TRANSCRIPTIONS
    KULTURA   2.50
STRAUSS, J.   DEL MAGLIO
  VIENNA BLOOD, OP. 354
    FRANCO COLOMBO PUBLICATIONS   124740   .60
STRAUSS, J.   THOMPSON, J.   5
  VIENNA LIFE
    WILLIS MUSIC COMPANY   .40
STRAUSS, J.   DEL MAGLIO
  VOICES OF SPRING, OP. 410
    FRANCO COLOMBO PUBLICATIONS   124745   .60
STRAUSS, J.
  WALDMEISTER--OVERTURE
    ASSOCIATED MUSIC PUBLISHERS, INC.   DOB   .90
STRAUSS, J.   TAUSIG
  WALTZ CAPRICE
    UNIVERSAL EDITION   3340   .60
STRAUSS, J.   STEINER   2 1/2
  WEDDING CAKE
    BELWIN-MILLS PUBLISHING CORPORATION   .60
STRAUSS, J.   DEL MAGLIO
  WINE, WOMEN AND SONG, OP. 333
    FRANCO COLOMBO PUBLICATIONS   124739   .50
STRAUSS, J.   RASBACH, O.
  YOU AND YOU--WALTZES FROM 'THE BAT'
    G. SCHIRMER, INC.   .50
STRAUSS, J.   DEL MAGLIO
  YOU AND YOU FROM 'FLEDERMAUS'
    FRANCO COLOMBO PUBLICATIONS   124741   .60
STRAUSS, R.   SINGER
  ALPENSINFONIE, EINE, OP. 64
    ASSOCIATED MUSIC PUBLISHERS, INC.   LEU   6.00
STRAUSS, R.   PHILIPP, I.
  BURLESQUE
    INTERNATIONAL MUSIC COMPANY   2.50

STRAUSS, R.   SINGER
     CONCERT WALTZ, FROM 'DER ROSENKAVALIER'
          BOOSEY AND HAWKES, INC.   1.50
STRAUSS, R.   SINGER
     DANCE OF THE SEVEN VEILS, FROM 'SALOME'
          BOOSEY AND HAWKES, INC.   3.50
STRAUSS, R.   4
     FLEDERMAUS, DIE, WALTZ
          CENTURY MUSIC PUBLISHING COMPANY, INC.   3426   .40
STRAUSS, R.   GIESEKING
     SERENADE, OP. 17, NO. 2
          BOOSEY AND HAWKES, INC.   .60
STRAUSS, R.
     SUITE FROM ''DER BURGER ALS EDELMANN''--ORCH
          ASSOCIATED MUSIC PUBLISHERS, INC.   LEU   5.00
STRAVINSKY, I.   4
     FIREBIRD, RONDE DES PRINCESSES
          CENTURY MUSIC PUBLISHING COMPANY, INC.   3563   .40
STRAVINSKY, I.   LOURIE
     OCTET FOR WIND INSTRUMENTS
          BOOSEY AND HAWKES, INC.   2.50
STRAVINSKY, I.   STRAVINSKY, I.
     PETROUCHKA - 3 MOVEMENTS -
          INTERNATIONAL MUSIC COMPANY   2.50
STRAVINSKY, I.
     PETRUSHKA, DANSE RUSSE
          CENTURY MUSIC PUBLISHING COMPANY, INC.   3720   .40
STRAVINSKY, I.
     THREE MOVEMENTS, FROM 'PETROUCHKA'
          BOOSEY AND HAWKES, INC.   2.50
STREABBOG   PALMER, W. A.
     STREABBOG--12 MELODIOUS PIECES, BK. 1
          ALFRED MUSIC COMPANY   621   1.00
STREABBOG   PALMER, W. A.
     STREABBOG--12 MELODIOUS PIECES, BK. 2
          ALFRED MUSIC COMPANY   565   1.25
STRIMER, J.--ED   STRIMER, J.
     MY REPERTOIRE OF FAMOUS COMPOSERS
          PRO-ART PUBLICATIONS, INC.   41   1.00
STRIMER, J.--ED   STRIMER, J.
     TWELVE FAVORITES
          PRO-ART PUBLICATIONS, INC.   69   .75
SUDDARDS   RICHTER
     HAPPY HUFF, THE
          BELWIN-MILLS PUBLISHING CORPORATION   .60
SUDDARDS   RICHTER
     SQUIRREL CHASE
          BELWIN-MILLS PUBLISHING CORPORATION   .60
SUKMAN, H.
     ELEVENTH HOUR
          THE BIG THREE MUSIC CORPORATION   00.95
SULLIVAN, A.   3
     LOST CHORD, THE
          CENTURY MUSIC PUBLISHING COMPANY, INC.   2065   .40
SULLIVAN, A.   PERRY
     LOST CHORD
          BOOSEY AND HAWKES, INC.   .50
SULLIVAN, A.   3
     MIKADO, THE, TIT WILLOW
          CENTURY MUSIC PUBLISHING COMPANY, INC.   3706   .40
SULLIVAN, A.   3
     TIT WILLOW, THE MIKADO
          CENTURY MUSIC PUBLISHING COMPANY, INC.   3706   .40
SULLIVAN, J.
     LITTLE ROCK GETAWAY
          THE BIG THREE MUSIC CORPORATION   00.95
SULLIVAN, J.   STEINER   2
     OLD HAT BOOGIE
          BELWIN-MILLS PUBLISHING CORPORATION   .60
SUPPE. F.   MENDEL, S.   2
     POET AND PEASANT OVERTURE
          WILLIS MUSIC COMPANY   .40
SUPPE, F.   2
     DICHTER UND BAUER, EASY
          CENTURY MUSIC PUBLISHING COMPANY, INC.   2123   .40
SUPPE, F.   5
     OVERTURE, LIGHT CAVALRY
          CENTURY MUSIC PUBLISHING COMPANY, INC.   1528   .40
SUPPE, F.   2
     OVERTURE, LIGHT CAVALRY
          CENTURY MUSIC PUBLISHING COMPANY, INC.   3668   .40
SUPPE, F.   3
     OVERTURE, POET AND PEASANT, EASY
          CENTURY MUSIC PUBLISHING COMPANY, INC.   2123   .40
SUPPE, F.   4
     OVERTURE, POET AND PEASANT
          CENTURY MUSIC PUBLISHING COMPANY, INC.   361   .40
SUPPE, F.   DEL MAGLIO
     POET AND PEASANT OVERTURE
          FRANCO COLOMBO PUBLICATIONS   128675 .60
SURINACH, C.
     ACROBATS OF GOD--5 DANCES FROM THE BALLET
          ASSOCIATED MUSIC. PUBLISHERS, INC.   AMP   2.50
SURINACH, C.
     ACROBATS OF GOD -- 5 DANCES FROM THE BALLET
          ASSOCIATED MUSIC PUBLISHERS, INC.   AMP   2.50
TAILLEFERRE, G.
     MARCHAND DES OISEAUX
          HEUGEL ET CIE.   2.25
TANSMAN, A.
     BRIC-A-BRAC -- 1935 -- BALLET
          ASSOCIATED MUSIC PUBLISHERS, INC.   ESC   4.00
TANSMAN, A.
     OUVERTURE SYMPHONIQUE--ORCH
          ASSOCIATED MUSIC PUBLISHERS, INC.   ESC   2.00
TANSMAN, A.
     RESSURECTION -- BALLET
          ASSOCIATED MUSIC PUBLISHERS, INC.   ESC   9.00
TANSMAN, A.
     SEXTUOR -- 1923 -- BALLET-BOUFFE
          ASSOCIATED MUSIC PUBLISHERS, INC.   ESC   2.50
TANSMAN, A.
     TEMPO AMERICANO FROM ''SYMPHONIE CONCERTANTE''
          ASSOCIATED MUSIC PUBLISHERS, INC.   ESC   2.50
TATUM, A.
     ART TATUM IMPROVISATIONS, NO. 2
          THE BIG THREE MUSIC CORPORATION   01.50
TAUBERT
     HOFISCHE TANZE
          SCHOTT   5947A   2.25
TAYLOR, C.   2-3
     ANNE-MARIE'S PIANO BOOK -- 4 EASY PIECES FOUNDED ON FRENCH TUNES
          NOVELLO AND COMPANY, LTD.   10.0084.05 1.15
TAYLOR, J.
     JAMES TAYLOR
          MUSIC SALES CORPORATION   020638 4.95

TCHEREPNIN
     BAGATELLES OP. 5, 10 NOS.
          HEUGEL ET CIE.   2.40
TCHEREPNIN   PHILIPP, I.
     FEUILLES LIBRES
          ELKAN-VOGEL, INC.   D   1.90
TELEMANN, G.P.   RUF   3
     SECHS OUVERTUREN FUR CEMBALO
          SCHOTT   5774   2.50
TELEMANN, G.P.   RUF   3
     SOLI AUS 'ESSERCIZII MUSICI'
          SCHOTT   5296   2.25
TEMPLETON, A.
     MENDELSSOHN MOWS 'EM DOWN
          THE BIG THREE MUSIC CORPORATION   00.95
TERRY--ED   TERRY
     HONKY-TONK RAGTIME PIANO
          WARNER BROTHERS PUBLISHERS   1.95
THALBERG
     THREE OPERATIC FANTASIES FOR PIANO SOLO
          MUSIC TREASURE PUBLICATIONS   5.00
THEODORAKIS, M.
     ZORBA THE GREEK - THEME
          THE BIG THREE MUSIC CORPORATION   00.95
THOMAS, A.--ED.   THOMAS, A.   3
     O SANCTISSIMA - SICILIAN MARINERS' HYMN
          THEODORE PRESSER COMPANY   .50
THOMAS, A.   3
     GAVOTTE, MIGNON
          CENTURY MUSIC PUBLISHING COMPANY, INC.   1941   .40
THOMAS, A.   WEYBRIGHT   2 1/2
     GAVOTTE 'MIGNON'
          BELWIN-MILLS PUBLISHING CORPORATION   .60
THOMAS, A.
     HAMLET -- LA FETE DU PRINTEMPS
          HEUGEL ET CIE.   4.40
THOMAS, A.
     HAMLET
          HEUGEL ET CIE.   11.00
THOMAS, A.   3
     MIGNON, GAVOTTE
          CENTURY MUSIC PUBLISHING COMPANY, INC.   1941   .40
THOMAS, A.
     MIGNON
          HEUGEL ET CIE.   11.00
THOMAS, A.   3
     OVERTURE, RAYMOND, EASY
          CENTURY MUSIC PUBLISHING COMPANY, INC.   2095   .40
THOMAS, A.   5
     OVERTURE, RAYMOND
          CENTURY MUSIC PUBLISHING COMPANY, INC.   1579   .40
THOMAS, A.   5
     RAYMOND OVERTURE
          CENTURY MUSIC PUBLISHING COMPANY, INC.   1579   .40
THOMAS, J. J.   JESTON, I. H.   3
     RAYMOND FANTASIA
          VOLKWEIN BROS.   .35
THOMPSON, J.--ED   THOMPSON, J.   3
     CIELITO LINDO
          WILLIS MUSIC COMPANY   .35
THOMPSON, J.--ED   THOMPSON, J.   1
     DEBUT
          WILLIS MUSIC COMPANY   1.00
THOMPSON, J.--ED   THOMPSON, J.   2
     FAVORITE CATHOLIC HYMNS
          WILLIS MUSIC COMPANY   1.00
THOMPSON, J.--ED   THOMPSON, J.   1
     FIRST YEAR CLASSICS
          WILLIS MUSIC COMPANY   1.25
THOMPSON, J.--ED   THOMPSON, J.   2
     FOR GIRLS WHO PLAY
          WILLIS MUSIC COMPANY   1.50
THOMPSON, J.--ED   THOMPSON, J.   2
     GOSPEL HYMNS
          WILLIS MUSIC COMPANY   1.25
THOMPSON, J.--ED   THOMPSON, J.   2
     HE'S GOT THE WHOLE WORLD IN HIS HANDS
          WILLIS MUSIC COMPANY   .40
THOMPSON, J.--ED   THOMPSON, J.   2
     HYMNS OF FAITH
          WILLIS MUSIC COMPANY   1.00
THOMPSON, J.--ED   THOMPSON, J.   3
     INTRODUCTION TO BACH, AN
          WILLIS MUSIC COMPANY   1.25
THOMPSON, J.--ED   THOMPSON, J.   1
     JOHN THOMPSON'S CHRISTMAS CAROLS
          WILLIS MUSIC COMPANY   1.00
THOMPSON, J.--ED   PREPARATORY
     JOHN THOMPSON'S CHRISTMAS CAROL BOOK
          WILLIS MUSIC COMPANY   1.00
THOMPSON, J.--ED   THOMPSON, J.   1
     LET'S JOIN THE ARMY
          WILLIS MUSIC COMPANY   1.50
THOMPSON, J.--ED   THOMPSON, J.   3
     NOTES FROM OTHER PENS
          WILLIS MUSIC COMPANY   1.00
THOMPSON, J.--ED   THOMPSON, J.   3
     RECOLLECTIONS OF JOHANN STRAUSS
          WILLIS MUSIC COMPANY   .60
THOMPSON, J.--ED   THOMPSON, J.   4
     REPERTOIRE
          WILLIS MUSIC COMPANY   1.25
THOMPSON, J.--ED   THOMPSON, J.   2
     SECOND YEAR PIANO CLASSICS
          WILLIS MUSIC COMPANY   1.00
THOMPSON, J.--ED   THOMPSON, J.   2
     SIX LITTLE RECITAL PIECES
          WILLIS MUSIC COMPANY   1.00
THOMPSON, J.--ED   THOMPSON, J.   4
     SIX PARTY PIECES
          WILLIS MUSIC COMPANY   .80
THOMPSON, J.--ED   THOMPSON, J.   4
     SIX WEDDING MARCHES
          WILLIS MUSIC COMPANY   1.25
THOMPSON, J.--ED   THOMPSON, J.   2
     SPARKS FROM OTHER ANVILS
          WILLIS MUSIC COMPANY   1.00
THOMPSON, J.--ED   THOMPSON, J.   2
     STAR-SPANGLED BANNER, THE
          WILLIS MUSIC COMPANY   .35
THOMPSON, J.--ED   THOMPSON, J.   2
     STUDIES IN STYLE
          WILLIS MUSIC COMPANY   1.00
THOMPSON, J.--ED   THOMPSON, J.   4
     THEMES FROM PIANO CONCERTOS
          WILLIS MUSIC COMPANY   1.25

THOMPSON, J.--ED   THOMPSON, J.   2
  WE'RE IN THE NAVY NOW
    WILLIS MUSIC COMPANY   1.50
THOMPSON, J.--ED   THOMPSON, J.   2
  WORLD FAMOUS MELODIES
    WILLIS MUSIC COMPANY   2.00
THOMPSON, J.--ED   THOMPSON, J.   3
  WORLD KNOWN MELODIES
    WILLIS MUSIC COMPANY   1.00
THOMPSON, J.--ED   THOMPSON, J.   3
  YOUNG ARTIST, THE
    WILLIS MUSIC COMPANY   1.00
THOMPSON, J.--ED   THOMPSON, J.   2
  YOUNG RECITALIST, THE
    WILLIS MUSIC COMPANY   1.25
THOMPSON, J.   5
  BLACK EYES
    WILLIS MUSIC COMPANY   .50
THOMPSON, J.
  CHRISTMAS BOOK
    WILLIS MUSIC COMPANY   1.00
THOMPSON, J.   3
  HOME ON THE RANGE
    WILLIS MUSIC COMPANY   .35
THOMPSON, J.
  JOHN THOMPSON'S DELUXE BOOK OF CHRISTMAS CAROLS
    WILLIS MUSIC COMPANY   2.00
THOMPSON, J.
  THOMPSON ADULT PREPARATORY BOOK
    WILLIS MUSIC COMPANY   1.50
THOMPSON, J.
  THOMPSON EASIEST PIANO COURSE - PART 1
    WILLIS MUSIC COMPANY   .90
THOMPSON, J.
  THOMPSON EASIEST PIANO COURSE - PART 2
    WILLIS MUSIC COMPANY   1.00
THOMPSON, J.
  THOMPSON EASIEST PIANO COURSE - PART 3
    WILLIS MUSIC COMPANY   1.00
THOMPSON, J.
  THOMPSON EASIEST PIANO COURSE - PART 4
    WILLIS MUSIC COMPANY   1.00
THOMPSON, J.
  THOMPSON EASIEST PIANO COURSE - PART 5
    WILLIS MUSIC COMPANY   1.50
THOMPSON, J.
  THOMPSON EASIEST PIANO COURSE - PART 6
    WILLIS MUSIC COMPANY   1.50
THOMPSON, J.
  THOMPSON EASIEST PIANO COURSE - PART 7
    WILLIS MUSIC COMPANY   1.00
THOMPSON, J.
  THOMPSON EASIEST PIANO COURSE - PART 8
    WILLIS MUSIC COMPANY   1.00
THOMPSON, J.
  THOMPSON MELODY ALL THE WAY - BOOK 1-A
    WILLIS MUSIC COMPANY   1.25
THOMPSON, J.
  THOMPSON MELODY ALL THE WAY - BOOK 1-B
    WILLIS MUSIC COMPANY   1.25
THOMPSON, J.
  THOMPSON MELODY ALL THE WAY - BOOK 2-A
    WILLIS MUSIC COMPANY   1.25
THOMPSON, J.
  THOMPSON MELODY ALL THE WAY - BOOK 2-B
    WILLIS MUSIC COMPANY   1.25
THOMPSON, J.
  THOMPSON MELODY ALL THE WAY - BOOK 3-A
    WILLIS MUSIC COMPANY   1.25
THOMPSON, J.
  THOMPSON MELODY ALL THE WAY - BOOK 3-B
    WILLIS MUSIC COMPANY   1.25
THOMPSON, J.
  THOMPSON MELODY ALL THE WAY - PREPARATORY BOOK
    WILLIS MUSIC COMPANY   .90
THOMPSON, J.
  THOMPSON MODERN COURSE FOR THE PIANO - FIFTH GRADE BOOK
    WILLIS MUSIC COMPANY   1.60
THOMPSON, J.
  THOMPSON MODERN COURSE FOR THE PIANO - FIRST GRADE BOOK
    WILLIS MUSIC COMPANY   1.60
THOMPSON, J.
  THOMPSON MODERN COURSE FOR THE PIANO - FOURTH GRADE BOOK
    WILLIS MUSIC COMPANY   1.60
THOMPSON, J.
  THOMPSON MODERN COURSE FOR THE PIANO - SECOND GRADE BOOK
    WILLIS MUSIC COMPANY   1.60
THOMPSON, J.
  THOMPSON MODERN COURSE FOR THE PIANO - TEACHING LITTLE FINGERS
  TO PLAY
    WILLIS MUSIC COMPANY   .75
THOMPSON, J.
  THOMPSON MODERN COURSE FOR THE PIANO - THIRD GRADE BOOK
    WILLIS MUSIC COMPANY   1.60
THORNTON   STEINER   1
  MAN IN THE MOON, THE
    BELWIN-MILLS PUBLISHING CORPORATION   .60
THORNTON   ZEPP   2
  MY SWEETHEART'S THE MAN IN THE MOON
    PRO-ART PUBLICATIONS, INC.   324   .50
THUILLIER   2
  FRILEUSE, LA, VALSE
    ALPHONSE LEDUC
TIOMKIN, D.
  GREEN LEAVES OF SUMMER, THE
    THE BIG THREE MUSIC CORPORATION   00.95
TIOMKIN, D.   RICHTER   FIRST YEAR
  HIGH AND THE MIGHTY, THE
    WARNER BROTHERS PUBLISHERS   .75
TIRINDELLI   DEL MAGLIO
  O PRIMAVERA
    FRANCO COLOMBO PUBLICATIONS   127762   .50
TOBANI   MENDEL, S.   2
  HEARTS AND FLOWERS
    WILLIS MUSIC COMPANY   .40
TOLSON, P.
  CHRISTMAS AT THE PIANO
    LILLENAS PUBLISHING COMPANY   MC-242   1.95
TOLSON, P.
  REFLECTIONS AT THE PIANO
    LILLENAS PUBLISHING COMPANY   MB-157   1.95
TOLSON, P.
  SPIRITUALS AT THE PIANO
    LILLENAS PUBLISHING COMPANY   MB-202   1.95
TOMASI, H.
  LA GRISI
    HEUGEL ET CIE.   2.75

TOSELLI   SCHAUM, J.   3
  NEAPOLITAN SERENADE
    SCHAUM PUBLICATIONS, INC.   .60
TOSTI   DEL MAGLIO
  IDEALE
    FRANCO COLOMBO PUBLICATIONS   124749   .50
TOSTI   DEL MAGLIO
  MALIA
    FRANCO COLOMBO PUBLICATIONS   124750   .50
TOSTI   DEL MAGLIO
  MARECHIARE
    FRANCO COLOMBO PUBLICATIONS   124751   .60
TOSTI   DEL MAGLIO
  NON T'AMO PIU
    FRANCO COLOMBO PUBLICATIONS   128148   .50
TOSTI   DEL MAGLIO
  VORREI
    FRANCO COLOMBO PUBLICATIONS   128137   .50
TREHDE--ED   TREHDE   4
  DOVE, THE -- LA PALOMA
    CENTURY MUSIC PUBLISHING COMPANY, INC.   687   .40
TROJE-MILLER--ED   TROJE-MILLER   2 1/2
  LET'S GO TO THE SYMPHONY
    BELWIN-MILLS PUBLISHING CORPORATION   .60
TROTTER *   ROGERS, M.
  BABAR COMES TO AMERICA
    POINTER PUBLICATIONS   2.95
TSCHAIKOWSKY   ANDERTON
  ANDANTE --FROM THE FIFTH SYMPHONY--
    BELWIN-MILLS PUBLISHING CORPORATION   28147   .60
TSCHAIKOWSKY   KLINDWORTH
  ANDANTE CANTABILE IN B FLAT--FROM THE STRING QUARTET, OP. 11
    G. SCHIRMER, INC.   .50
TSCHAIKOWSKY   4-5
  ARAB DANCE, G MINOR FROM NUTCRACKER SUITE
    CENTURY MUSIC PUBLISHING COMPANY, INC.   2664   .40
TSCHAIKOWSKY   5
  ARAB DANCE FROM 'NUTCRACKER SUITE'
    BELWIN-MILLS PUBLISHING CORPORATION   498   .60
TSCHAIKOWSKY
  BALLET -- LE LAC DES CYGNES
    NOVELLO AND COMPANY, LTD.   10.0085.03   7.50
TSCHAIKOWSKY   SCHAUM, J.   2 1/2
  BEST OF TSCHAIKOWSKY
    SCHAUM PUBLICATIONS, INC.   1.25
TSCHAIKOWSKY   MIKELA   4-5
  CAPRICCIO ITALIEN
    BARENREITER VERLAG   AP 1701
TSCHAIKOWSKY   4
  CHINESE DANCE IN B FLAT FROM NUTCRACKER SUITE
    CENTURY MUSIC PUBLISHING COMPANY, INC.   2365   .40
TSCHAIKOWSKY   M
  CONCERTO NO. 01 IN B FLAT MINOR, OP. 23 ABRIDGED
    C. F. PETERS CORPORATION   3775A   1.25
TSCHAIKOWSKY
  CONCERTO NO. 01 IN B FLAT MINOR
    ASHLEY DEALERS SERVICE, INC.   1.95
TSCHAIKOWSKY   4
  CONCERTO NO. 01 IN B FLAT MINOR
    CENTURY MUSIC PUBLISHING COMPANY, INC.   3530   .40
TSCHAIKOWSKY   FREY, H.
  CONCERTO NO. 02
    THE BIG THREE MUSIC CORPORATION   00.75
TSCHAIKOWSKY   4-5
  DANCE OF THE REED FLUTES IN D FROM NUTCRACKER SUITE
    CENTURY MUSIC PUBLISHING COMPANY, INC.   2365   .40
TSCHAIKOWSKY   4-5
  DANCE OF THE SUGAR PLUM FAIRY, E MINOR FROM NUTCRACKER SUITE
    CENTURY MUSIC PUBLISHING COMPANY, INC.   2362   .40
TSCHAIKOWSKY   STEINER   3 1/2
  DANCE OF THE SUGAR PLUM FAIRY -- FROM 'THE NUTCRACKER SUITE'
    BELWIN-MILLS PUBLISHING CORPORATION   .60
TSCHAIKOWSKY *
  EUGEN ONEGIN--POLONAISE
    ASSOCIATED MUSIC PUBLISHERS, INC.   DDB   .90
TSCHAIKOWSKY   LISZT
  EUGEN ONEGIN--POLONAISE
    ASSOCIATED MUSIC PUBLISHERS, INC.   SIM   1.10
TSCHAIKOWSKY   ZEPP   3-4
  FAREWELL TO A HERO
    PRO-ART PUBLICATIONS, INC.   525   .50
TSCHAIKOWSKY   4
  JUNE, BARCAROLLE
    CENTURY MUSIC PUBLISHING COMPANY, INC.   748   .40
TSCHAIKOWSKY   3
  LOVE THEME, ROMEO AND JULIET
    CENTURY MUSIC PUBLISHING COMPANY, INC.   3431   .40
TSCHAIKOWSKY   RACHMANINOFF, S.
  LULLABY
    BELWIN-MILLS PUBLISHING CORPORATION   1.00
TSCHAIKOWSKY   4
  MARCH IN G FROM NUTCRACKER SUITE
    CENTURY MUSIC PUBLISHING COMPANY, INC.   2366   .40
TSCHAIKOWSKY   2
  MARCH OF THE TOY SOLDIERS
    CENTURY MUSIC PUBLISHING COMPANY, INC.   2451   .40
TSCHAIKOWSKY   DEL MAGLIO
  NONE BUT THE LONELY HEART, OP. 6 NO. 6
    FRANCO COLOMBO PUBLICATIONS   127114   .60
TSCHAIKOWSKY   MOSSMAN
  NONE BUT THE LONELY HEART
    BELWIN-MILLS PUBLISHING CORPORATION   26086   .60
TSCHAIKOWSKY   NESTLER
  NUTCRACKER SUITE, OP. 71A--WALTZ OF THE FLOWERS
    ASSOCIATED MUSIC PUBLISHERS, INC.   SIM   .60
TSCHAIKOWSKY   4
  NUTCRACKER SUITE, OP. 71A - ARAB DANCE
    CENTURY MUSIC PUBLISHING COMPANY, INC.   2364   .40
TSCHAIKOWSKY   2
  NUTCRACKER SUITE, OP. 71A - CHINESE DANCE, EASY
    CENTURY MUSIC PUBLISHING COMPANY, INC.   4083   .40
TSCHAIKOWSKY   2
  NUTCRACKER SUITE, OP. 71A - MARCH, EASY
    CENTURY MUSIC PUBLISHING COMPANY, INC.   3828   .40
TSCHAIKOWSKY   4
  NUTCRACKER SUITE, OP. 71A - MARCH
    CENTURY MUSIC PUBLISHING COMPANY, INC.   2366   .40
TSCHAIKOWSKY   2
  NUTCRACKER SUITE, OP. 71A - TREPAK, EASY
    CENTURY MUSIC PUBLISHING COMPANY, INC.   3673   .40
TSCHAIKOWSKY   2
  NUTCRACKER SUITE, OP. 71A - WALTZ OF THE FLOWERS, EASY
    CENTURY MUSIC PUBLISHING COMPANY, INC.   3227   .40
TSCHAIKOWSKY   2
  NUTCRACKER SUITE, OP. 71A - DANCE OF THE REED FLUTES
    CENTURY MUSIC PUBLISHING COMPANY, INC.   4084   .40

TSCHAIKOWSKY   DEIS *
NUTCRACKER SUITE, THE, OP. 71A
     G. SCHIRMER, INC.   L1447   1.00
TSCHAIKOWSKY   PALMERI
NUTCRACKER SUITE, THE, OP. 71A
     G. SCHIRMER, INC.   .50
TSCHAIKOWSKY   RICHTER, A.
NUTCRACKER SUITE -- A STORY WITH MUSIC
     THEODORE PRESSER COMPANY   1.25
TSCHAIKOWSKY   BANTOCK, G.
NUTCRACKER SUITE
     BELWIN-MILLS PUBLISHING CORPORATION   09471   2.00
TSCHAIKOWSKY
NUTCRACKER SUITE
     EDWIN F. KALMUS   4316   1.50
TSCHAIKOWSKY   SCHAUM, J.   2 1/2
NUTCRACKER SUITE
     SCHAUM PUBLICATIONS, INC.   1.50
TSCHAIKOWSKY   DEIS
OPENING THEME OF THE B FLAT MINOR PIANO CONCERTO
     G. SCHIRMER, INC.   .40
TSCHAIKOWSKY   GRAINGER
OPENING THEME OF THE B FLAT MINOR PIANO CONCERTO
     G. SCHIRMER, INC.   .50
TSCHAIKOWSKY   3-4
OVERTURE 1812, THEMES
     CENTURY MUSIC PUBLISHING COMPANY, INC.   3561   .40
TSCHAIKOWSKY   3
PATHETIQUE SYMPHONY, THEME
     CENTURY MUSIC PUBLISHING COMPANY, INC.   3349   .40
TSCHAIKOWSKY
PIANO CONCERTO, THEME FROM FIRST MOVEMENT
     ASHLEY DEALERS SERVICE, INC.   ES   .95
TSCHAIKOWSKY   2
PIANO CONCERTO NO. 01, EASY
     CENTURY MUSIC PUBLISHING COMPANY, INC.   3557   .40
TSCHAIKOWSKY   DEL MAGLIO
ROMANCE, OP. 5
     FRANCO COLOMBO PUBLICATIONS   129098   .60
TSCHAIKOWSKY   3
ROMEO AND JULIET, LOVE THEME
     CENTURY MUSIC PUBLISHING COMPANY, INC.   3431   .40
TSCHAIKOWSKY   4
RUSSIAN DANCE, TREPAK, FROM NUTCRACKER SUITE
     CENTURY MUSIC PUBLISHING COMPANY, INC.   2363   .40
TSCHAIKOWSKY   STEINER   2 1/2
RUSTIC POLKA
     BELWIN-MILLS PUBLISHING CORPORATION   .60
TSCHAIKOWSKY   KIRCHNER
SLEEPING BEAUTY--WALTZ
     ASSOCIATED MUSIC PUBLISHERS, INC.   SIM   .75
TSCHAIKOWSKY   4
SLEEPING BEAUTY, VALSE LENTE
     CENTURY MUSIC PUBLISHING COMPANY, INC.   3183   .40
TSCHAIKOWSKY   ROTH
SLEEPING BEAUTY -- BALLET TOLD IN WORDS AND MUSIC
     BOOSEY AND HAWKES, INC.   1.50
TSCHAIKOWSKY   BANTOCK, G.
SLEEPING BEAUTY -- PRINCESS, EXCERPTS
     BELWIN-MILLS PUBLISHING CORPORATION   09472   3.00
TSCHAIKOWSKY   ARMAND   3
SLEEPING BEAUTY WALTZ, THE
     BOSTON MUSIC COMPANY   .75
TSCHAIKOWSKY   WALLIS   2
SLEEPING BEAUTY WALTZ, THE
     BOSTON MUSIC COMPANY   .50
TSCHAIKOWSKY   3
SONG OF THE LARK, THE
     CENTURY MUSIC PUBLISHING COMPANY, INC.   2149   .40
TSCHAIKOWSKY   DEL MAGLIO
SONG WITHOUT WORDS, OP. 2 NO. 3
     FRANCO COLOMBO PUBLICATIONS   129097   .60
TSCHAIKOWSKY   3-4
STRING QUARTET, ANDANTE CANTABILE
     CENTURY MUSIC PUBLISHING COMPANY, INC.   3248   .40
TSCHAIKOWSKY   BANTOCK, G.
SWAN LAKE, SEVEN EXCERPTS
     BELWIN-MILLS PUBLISHING CORPORATION   09473   1.50
TSCHAIKOWSKY   BANTOCK, G.
SWAN LAKE, TWELVE EXCERPTS, ILLUSTRATED
     BELWIN-MILLS PUBLISHING CORPORATION   09474   3.00
TSCHAIKOWSKY   DEXTER, H.
SWAN LAKE BALLET
     SAM FOX PUBLISHING COMPANY, INC.   1.00
TSCHAIKOWSKY   MITTLER   3B
SWAN LAKE BALLET
     MUSICORD PUBLICATIONS, INC.   .45
TSCHAIKOWSKY   GRAETZER
SWAN LAKE SUITE
     FRANCO COLOMBO PUBLICATIONS   BA9180   2.00
TSCHAIKOWSKY   5
SYMPHONY NO. 05, ANDANTE CANTABILE
     CENTURY MUSIC PUBLISHING COMPANY, INC.   3187   .40
TSCHAIKOWSKY   ROLFE, W.   2
SYMPHONY NO. 05, THEME EASY
     CENTURY MUSIC PUBLISHING COMPANY, INC.   3382   .40
TSCHAIKOWSKY   SINGER
SYMPHONY NO. 05
     ASSOCIATED MUSIC PUBLISHERS, INC.   SIM   3.25
TSCHAIKOWSKY   BERGMANN
SYMPHONY NO. 06, OP. 74 'PATHETIQUE'
     FRANCO COLOMBO PUBLICATIONS   129094   3.00
TSCHAIKOWSKY   3
SYMPHONY PATHETIQUE, THEME
     CENTURY MUSIC PUBLISHING COMPANY, INC.   3349   .40
TSCHAIKOWSKY   ECKSTEIN
THEME FROM MELODY IN E FLAT
     CARL FISCHER, INC.   S 2293   .50
TSCHAIKOWSKY   ECKSTEIN
THEME FROM PIANO CONCERTO NO. 1 IN B FLAT
     CARL FISCHER, INC.   S 2281   .50
TSCHAIKOWSKY   ECKSTEIN
THEME FROM PIANO CONCERTO NO. 1 IN B FLAT
     CARL FISCHER, INC.   S 2282   .50
TSCHAIKOWSKY   ECKSTEIN
THEME FROM ROMEO AND JULIET
     CARL FISCHER, INC.   S 2289   .50
TSCHAIKOWSKY   ECKSTEIN
THEME FROM SYMPHONY NO. 5 --2ND MVT. - ANDANTE CANT.--
     CARL FISCHER, INC.   S 2320   .50
TSCHAIKOWSKY   ECKSTEIN
THEME FROM SYMPHONY NO. 6 --PATHETIQUE--
     CARL FISCHER, INC.   S 2299   .50
TSCHAIKOWSKY   WALLIS   2
THEME FROM THE FIRST MOVEMENT OF PIANO CONCERTO NO. 1
     BOSTON MUSIC COMPANY   .50

TSCHAIKOWSKY   5
THEME FROM THE SECOND MOVEMENT OF THE 'FIFTH SYMPHONY'
     BELWIN-MILLS PUBLISHING CORPORATION   132   .60
TSCHAIKOWSKY   4
TREPAK, NUTCRACKER SUITE
     CENTURY MUSIC PUBLISHING COMPANY, INC.   2363   .40
TSCHAIKOWSKY   MITTLER   2B
TSCHAIKOWSKY CONCERTO
     MUSICORD PUBLICATIONS, INC.   .45
TSCHAIKOWSKY   ECKHARDT, F.   1
TSCHAIKOWSKY FOR THE YOUNG PIANIST
     CENTURY MUSIC PUBLISHING COMPANY, INC.   3963   .40
TSCHAIKOWSKY
TSCHAIKOWSKY MADE EASY FOR EVERYONE
     MUSICORD PUBLICATIONS, INC.   1.50
TSCHAIKOWSKY   4
VALSE LENTE FROM THE SLEEPING BEAUTY BALLET
     CENTURY MUSIC PUBLISHING COMPANY, INC.   3183   .40
TSCHAIKOWSKY   2
VIOLIN CONCERTO, THEME
     CENTURY MUSIC PUBLISHING COMPANY, INC.   3847   .40
TSCHAIKOWSKY   5
WALTZ FROM SERENADE FOR STRINGS
     CENTURY MUSIC PUBLISHING COMPANY, INC.   3559   .40
TSCHAIKOWSKY   WEYBRIGHT   1 1/2
WALTZ FROM THE BALLET 'THE SLEEPING BEAUTY'
     BELWIN-MILLS PUBLISHING CORPORATION   .60
TSCHAIKOWSKY
WALTZ OF THE FLOWERS FROM 'NUTCRACKER'
     FRANCO COLOMBO PUBLICATIONS   127072   .75
TSCHAIKOWSKY   DEL MAGLIO
WALTZ OF THE FLOWERS FROM 'NUTCRACKER'
     FRANCO COLOMBO PUBLICATIONS   127115   .60
TSCHAIKOWSKY   ECKSTEIN
WALTZ OF THE FLOWERS FROM THE 'NUTCRACKER SUITE'
     CARL FISCHER, INC.   S 2300   .50
TSCHAIKOWSKY   4
WALTZ OF THE FLOWERS IN D FROM NUTCRACKER SUITE
     CENTURY MUSIC PUBLISHING COMPANY, INC.   2367   .40
TSCHAIKOWSKY   TRUXELL, E.   2
WALTZ OF THE FLOWERS
     VOLKWEIN BROS.   00.40
TSCHAIKOWSKY   TRUXELL, E.   2 1/2
WALTZ OF THE FLOWERS
     VOLKWEIN BROS.   00.50
TSCHAIKOWSKY   4
WALZER AUS DER SERENADE FUR STREICHORCHESTER OP. 48 NO. 2
     SCHOTT   07094 1/2   1.00
TUCKER *   3
SWEET GENEVIEVE, TRANSCRIPTION
     CENTURY MUSIC PUBLISHING COMPANY, INC.   2470   .40
TURINA, J.
NAVIDAD -- MIRACLE PANTOMINE IN 2 ACTS
     ASSOCIATED MUSIC PUBLISHERS, INC.   UME   1.00
TURINA, J.
RITMOS -- FANTASIA COREOGRAFICA
     ASSOCIATED MUSIC PUBLISHERS, INC.   UME   1.00
TWITCHELL--ED   TWITCHELL   4
DOVE, THE -- LA PALOMA
     CENTURY MUSIC PUBLISHING COMPANY, INC.   270   .40
TWITTENHOFF--ED   TWITTENHOFF   2
VOLKSTANZBUCHLEIN
     SCHOTT   3774   1.75
TYERS, W.
PANAMA
     THE BIG THREE MUSIC CORPORATION   00.95
UNDARRA *   SYKOVA   3
KLAVIERKOMPOSITIONEN DES ALTEN SPANIEN UND PORTUGAL. 16 TIENTOS,
HYMNEN, SONATEN, RONDI UND TOCCATEN
     BARENREITER VERLAG   MVH 17
VANHALL, J. B.   PODOLSKY, L.
MINUET IN G
     FREDERICK HARRIS MUSIC COMPANY   .60
VAN ALSTYNE, E.   STEINER   2 1/2
IN THE SHADE OF THE OLD APPLE TREE
     BELWIN-MILLS PUBLISHING CORPORATION   .60
VAN ALSTYNE, E.   STEINER   1 1/2
WON'T YOU COME OVER TO MY HOUSE
     BELWIN-MILLS PUBLISHING CORPORATION   .60
VAN HEUSEN, J.   SCHAUM, J.   2 1/2
DARN THAT DREAM
     SCHAUM PUBLICATIONS, INC.   .75
VAUGHAN WILLIAMS, R. MULLINAR
ENGLISH FOLK SONG SUITE
     BOOSEY AND HAWKES, INC.   1.50
VAUGHAN WILLIAMS, R. PERRY, P.
LINDEN LEA
     BOOSEY AND HAWKES, INC.   .50
VERDI   E-M
AIDA. ABRIDGED
     C. F. PETERS CORPORATION   H634   2.00
VERDI   TAVAN   6
AIDA, FANTAISIE
     ALPHONSE LEDUC
VERDI
AIDA -- COMPLETE OPERA --
     FRANCO COLOMBO PUBLICATIONS   44551   5.00
VERDI   CHIESA
AIDA -- EASY FANTASIA
     FRANCO COLOMBO PUBLICATIONS   109085   .60
VERDI   TAVAN
AIDA - FANTASIA
     FRANCO COLOMBO PUBLICATIONS   128789   1.00
VERDI
AIDA - HYMN AND TRIUMPHAL MARCH
     FRANCO COLOMBO PUBLICATIONS   42519   .60
VERDI   AUBEL, D'   6
AIDA - MARCHE DES TROMPETTES
     ALPHONSE LEDUC
VERDI   BATTMANN   4
AIDA - MARCHE DES TROMPETTES
     ALPHONSE LEDUC
VERDI
ALBUMS - OVERTURES AND PRELUDES
     FRANCO COLOMBO PUBLICATIONS   ER1279   3.00
VERDI   FANENGHI
ALBUMS - 18 FAMOUS ARIAS
     FRANCO COLOMBO PUBLICATIONS   127650   1.00
VERDI   HARRISON
ALBUMS - 7 MELODIES FROM THE OPERAS
     FRANCO COLOMBO PUBLICATIONS   LD432   1.50
VERDI   3
ANVIL CHORUS FROM 'IL TROVATORE'
     CENTURY MUSIC PUBLISHING COMPANY, INC.   511   .40
VERDI   CHIESA
BALLO IN MASCHERA, UN - EASY FANTASIA
     FRANCO COLOMBO PUBLICATIONS   109083   .60

VERDI   SMITH
  BRILLIANT FANTASIA FROM 'IL TROVATORE'
    G. SCHIRMER, INC.   .85
VERDI *
  CONCERT PARAPHRASE ON 'RIGOLETTO'
    FRANCO COLOMBO PUBLICATIONS   35588   .75
VERDI *
  CONCERT PARAPHRASE ON 'RIGOLETTO'
    FRANCO COLOMBO PUBLICATIONS   35588   .75
VERDI   ZILCHER   2-3
  DIE VERDI-OPER
    SCHOTT   1565   3.50
VERDI   2
  DONNA E MOBILE, RIGOLETTO
    CENTURY MUSIC PUBLISHING COMPANY, INC.   2041   .40
VERDI   CHIESA
  ERNANI - EASY FANTASIA
    FRANCO COLOMBO PUBLICATIONS   109088   .50
VERDI   DORN
  FANTASIA FROM 'IL TROVATORE'
    G. SCHIRMER, INC.   .60
VERDI   DORN
  FANTASIA FROM 'RIGOLETTO'
    G. SCHIRMER, INC.   .70
VERDI
  FORZA DEL DESTINO, LA - OVERTURE
    FRANCO COLOMBO PUBLICATIONS   128333   .75
VERDI   DEL MAGLIO
  FORZA DEL DESTINO, LA - VERGINE DEGLI ANGELI, LA
    FRANCO COLOMBO PUBLICATIONS   124754   .90
VERDI   2
  GYPSY SONG, FROM 'IL TROVATORE'
    CENTURY MUSIC PUBLISHING COMPANY, INC.   1566   .40
VERDI   2
  IL TROVATORE, ANVIL CHORUS, EASY
    CENTURY MUSIC PUBLISHING COMPANY, INC.   3654   .40
VERDI   KRUG   2
  IL TROVATORE, EASY TRANS.
    CENTURY MUSIC PUBLISHING COMPANY, INC.   530   .40
VERDI   5
  IL TROVATORE, FANTASIE
    BELWIN-MILLS PUBLISHING CORPORATION   84   .60
VERDI   DORN   4
  IL TROVATORE, FANTASIE
    CENTURY MUSIC PUBLISHING COMPANY, INC.   253   .40
VERDI   SMITH   5
  IL TROVATORE, FANTASIE
    CENTURY MUSIC PUBLISHING COMPANY, INC.   1168   .40
VERDI   2
  IL TROVATORE, GYPSY SONG
    CENTURY MUSIC PUBLISHING COMPANY, INC.   1566   .40
VERDI   3
  IL TROVATORE, HOME TO OUR MOUNTAINS
    CENTURY MUSIC PUBLISHING COMPANY, INC.   1566   .40
VERDI   2
  IL TROVATORE, MISERERE, EASY
    CENTURY MUSIC PUBLISHING COMPANY, INC.   2153   .40
VERDI   TZORR   3
  IL TROVATORE, MISERERE
    CENTURY MUSIC PUBLISHING COMPANY, INC.   1530   .40
VERDI   SMITH   5
  LA TRAVIATA, FANTASIE
    CENTURY MUSIC PUBLISHING COMPANY, INC.   1169   .40
VERDI   4
  LA TRAVIATA, PRELUDE
    CENTURY MUSIC PUBLISHING COMPANY, INC.   1784   .40
VERDI   DEL MAGLIO
  LOMBARDI, I - O SIGNORE DAL TETTO NATIO
    FRANCO COLOMBO PUBLICATIONS   124755   .60
VERDI   3
  MARCH, AIDA
    CENTURY MUSIC PUBLISHING COMPANY, INC.   4707   .40
VERDI   2
  MISERERE, IL TROVATORE, EASY
    CENTURY MUSIC PUBLISHING COMPANY, INC.   2153   .40
VERDI   CHIESA
  NABUCCO - EASY FANTASIA
    FRANCO COLOMBO PUBLICATIONS   109089   .60
VERDI   CHIESA
  NABUCCO - VA, PENSIERO
    FRANCO COLOMBO PUBLICATIONS   13894   .60
VERDI   CHIESA
  OTELLO - EASY FANTASIA
    FRANCO COLOMBO PUBLICATIONS   111265   .75
VERDI   4
  PRELUDE, TRAVIATA
    CENTURY MUSIC PUBLISHING COMPANY, INC.   3784   .40
VERDI   SPINDLER   4
  QUARTET, RIGOLETTO
    CENTURY MUSIC PUBLISHING COMPANY, INC.   1634   .40
VERDI   E-M
  RIGOLETTO. ABRIDGED
    C. F. PETERS CORPORATION   H635   2.00
VERDI *   DEIS
  RIGOLETTO--PARAPHRASE
    G. SCHIRMER, INC.   .80
VERDI   2
  RIGOLETTO, DONNA E MOBILE, EASY
    CENTURY MUSIC PUBLISHING COMPANY, INC.   2156   .40
VERDI   2
  RIGOLETTO, DONNA E MOBILE
    CENTURY MUSIC PUBLISHING COMPANY, INC.   2041   .40
VERDI *   7
  RIGOLETTO, PARAPHRASE
    CENTURY MUSIC PUBLISHING COMPANY, INC.   1201   .40
VERDI *   DEIS
  RIGOLETTO, PARAPHRASE
    G. SCHIRMER, INC.   .80
VERDI   SPINDLER   4
  RIGOLETTO, QUARTETTE
    CENTURY MUSIC PUBLISHING COMPANY, INC.   1634   .40
VERDI
  RIGOLETTO -- COMPLETE OPERA --
    FRANCO COLOMBO PUBLICATIONS   42221   5.00
VERDI   LISZT
  RIGOLETTO - CONCERT PARAPHRASE
    FRANCO COLOMBO PUBLICATIONS   35588   .75
VERDI   CHIESA
  RIGOLETTO - EASY FANTASIA
    FRANCO COLOMBO PUBLICATIONS   109087   .60
VERDI   TAVAN
  RIGOLETTO - FANTASIA
    FRANCO COLOMBO PUBLICATIONS   127845   1.00
VERDI   THOMPSON, J.   2
  THEME FROM 'IL TROVATORE'
    WILLIS MUSIC COMPANY   .40

VERDI   STEINER   3
  THREE WITCHES, FROM 'MACBETH'
    BELWIN-MILLS PUBLISHING CORPORATION   .60
VERDI   E-M
  TRAVIATA. ABRIDGED
    C. F. PETERS CORPORATION   H636   2.00
VERDI   KRUG   2
  TRAVIATA, EASY TRANSCRIPTION
    CENTURY MUSIC PUBLISHING COMPANY, INC.   2145   .40
VERDI   SMITH   5
  TRAVIATA, FANTASIE
    CENTURY MUSIC PUBLISHING COMPANY, INC.   1169   .40
VERDI   4
  TRAVIATA, LA, PRELUDE
    CENTURY MUSIC PUBLISHING COMPANY, INC.   3784   .40
VERDI
  TRAVIATA, LA -- COMPLETE OPERA --
    FRANCO COLOMBO PUBLICATIONS   42222   5.00
VERDI   MENOZZI
  TRAVIATA, LA - BRINDISI
    FRANCO COLOMBO PUBLICATIONS   52554   .60
VERDI   CHIESA
  TRAVIATA, LA - EASY FANTASIA
    FRANCO COLOMBO PUBLICATIONS   109086   .60
VERDI   TAVAN
  TRAVIATA, LA - FANTASIA
    FRANCO COLOMBO PUBLICATIONS   127488   1.00
VERDI
  TRAVIATA, LA - PRELUDE TO ACT III AND ADDIO, DEL PASSATO
    FRANCO COLOMBO PUBLICATIONS   25122   .75
VERDI
  TRAVIATA, LA - PRELUDE TO ACT I
    FRANCO COLOMBO PUBLICATIONS   25121   .60
VERDI
  TRIUMPHAL MARCH FROM 'AIDA'
    G. SCHIRMER, INC.   .60
VERDI   ROBBINS   3
  TRIUMPHAL MARCH FROM 'AIDA'
    WILLIS MUSIC COMPANY   .35
VERDI   E-M
  TROVATORE. ABRIDGED
    C. F. PETERS CORPORATION   H637   2.00
VERDI   ROLFE, W.   2
  TROVATORE, IL, ANVIL CHORUS, EASY
    CENTURY MUSIC PUBLISHING COMPANY, INC.   3654   .40
VERDI   3
  TROVATORE, IL, ANVIL CHORUS
    CENTURY MUSIC PUBLISHING COMPANY, INC.   511   .40
VERDI   KRUG   2
  TROVATORE, IL, EASY TRANSCRIPTION
    CENTURY MUSIC PUBLISHING COMPANY, INC.   530   .40
VERDI   DORN   4
  TROVATORE, IL, FANTASIE
    CENTURY MUSIC PUBLISHING COMPANY, INC.   253   .40
VERDI   SMITH   5
  TROVATORE, IL, FANTASIE
    CENTURY MUSIC PUBLISHING COMPANY, INC.   1168   .40
VERDI   2
  TROVATORE, IL, GYPSY SONG
    CENTURY MUSIC PUBLISHING COMPANY, INC.   1566   .40
VERDI   3
  TROVATORE, IL, HOME TO OUR MOUNTAINS
    CENTURY MUSIC PUBLISHING COMPANY, INC.   1568   .40
VERDI   TZORR   3
  TROVATORE, IL, MISERERE
    CENTURY MUSIC PUBLISHING COMPANY, INC.   1530   .40
VERDI
  TROVATORE, IL -- COMPLETE OPERA --
    FRANCO COLOMBO PUBLICATIONS   128790   5.00
VERDI   CHIESA
  TROVATORE, IL - EASY FANTASIA
    FRANCO COLOMBO PUBLICATIONS   109084   .60
VERDI   TAVAN
  TROVATORE, IL - FANTASIA
    FRANCO COLOMBO PUBLICATIONS   128790   1.00
VERDI
  TROVATORE, IL - MISERERE
    FRANCO COLOMBO PUBLICATIONS   128942   .75
VERDI   CHIESA
  VESPRI SICILIANI, I - OVERTURE
    FRANCO COLOMBO PUBLICATIONS   127999   .75
VERETTI
  GALANTE TIRATORE, IL -- BALLET --
    FRANCO COLOMBO PUBLICATIONS   4.50
VILLA-LOBOS, H.
  CHOROS NO. 5--ALMA BRASILEIRA
    ASSOCIATED MUSIC PUBLISHERS, INC.   ESC   4.75
VILLA-LOBOS, H.   BRANDAO
  FIVE PRELUDES FOR GUITAR--NO. 1
    ASSOCIATED MUSIC PUBLISHERS, INC.   ESC   3.25
VILLA-LOBOS, H.   BRANDAO
  FIVE PRELUDES FOR GUITAR--NO. 2
    ASSOCIATED MUSIC PUBLISHERS, INC.   ESC   3.25
VILLA-LOBOS, H.   BRANDAO
  FIVE PRELUDES FOR GUITAR--NO. 5
    ASSOCIATED MUSIC PUBLISHERS, INC.   ESC   3.25
VILLA-LOBOS, H.   BRANDAO
  FIVE PRELUDES FOR GUITAR
    ASSOCIATED MUSIC PUBLISHERS, INC.   ESC   3.25
VILLA-LOBOS, H.   LEVINE
  LITTLE TRAIN OF CAIPIRA, THE - TOCCATA FROM 'BACHIANAS
  BRASILEIRAS NO. 2'
    FRANCO COLOMBO PUBLICATIONS   NY2066   .75
VILLA-LOBOS, H.   LEVINE, H.
  LITTLE TRAIN OF THE CAIPIRA, THE -- TOCCATA, FROM 'BACHIANAS
  BRASILERIRAS' NO. 2
    BELWIN-MILLS PUBLISHING CORPORATION   .75
VIVALDI   FARINA
  FOUR SEASONS, THE
    FRANCO COLOMBO PUBLICATIONS   129190   2.25
VLAD   TERRY
  ROMEO AND JULIET SUITE
    FRANCO COLOMBO PUBLICATIONS   NY1731   1.25
VOGEL--ED   VOGEL
  GREAT FRENCH SONGS FOR LITTLE HANDS
    ASSOCIATED MUSIC PUBLISHERS, INC.   ESC   2.50
VOLKART-SCHLAGER   1
  ARBEITSBUCH FUR KLEINE KLAVIERSPIELER - 23 VOLKSLIEDSATZE --
  'WIR MUSIZIEREN', HEFT 10
    BARENREITER VERLAG   SM 911
WAGNER   GODDEN
  ALBUM-LEAF, AN--CONCERT TRANSCRIPTION
    ASSOCIATED MUSIC PUBLISHERS, INC.   BER   .75
WAGNER   LOEW
  BRIDAL CHORUS, WEDDING MARCH--FROM 'LOHENGRIN'
    G. SCHIRMER, INC.   .50

WAGNER   2
    BRIDAL CHORUS, LOHENGRIN, E FLAT MAJOR
        CENTURY MUSIC PUBLISHING COMPANY, INC.   1563   .40
WAGNER
    BRIDAL CHORUS FROM 'LOHENGRIN'
        ASHLEY DEALERS SERVICE, INC.   ES   .95
WAGNER
    BRIDAL CHORUS FROM LOHENGRIN
        CARL FISCHER, INC.   S 207   .50
WAGNER   WEYBRIGHT   2
    BRIDAL SONG FROM 'LOHENGRIN'
        BELWIN-MILLS PUBLISHING CORPORATION   .60
WAGNER   5
    BY SILENT HEARTH, FROM "MEISTERSINGER"
        CENTURY MUSIC PUBLISHING COMPANY, INC.   1097   .40
WAGNER   WINDSPERGER
    DAS BUCH DER MOTIVE UND THEMEN AUS SAMTLICHEN OPERN UND
    MUSIKDRAMEN FUR KLAVIER MIT TEXT -- BK. 1
        SCHOTT   300   3.50
WAGNER   WINDSPERGER
    DAS BUCH DER MOTIVE UND THEMEN AUS SAMTLICHEN OPERN UND
    MUSIKDRAMEN FUR KLAVIER MIT TEXT -- BK. 2
        SCHOTT   301   3.50
WAGNER   3
    EVENING STAR -- TANNHAUSER
        CENTURY MUSIC PUBLISHING COMPANY, INC.   1817   .40
WAGNER   3
    EVENING STAR -- TANNHAUSER
        CENTURY MUSIC PUBLISHING COMPANY, INC.   1564   .40
WAGNER *   6
    EVENING STAR -- TANNHAUSER
        CENTURY MUSIC PUBLISHING COMPANY, INC.   692   .40
WAGNER   4
    EVENING STAR 'TANNHAUSER'
        BELWIN-MILLS PUBLISHING CORPORATION   382   .60
WAGNER *   6
    EVENING STAR
        CENTURY MUSIC PUBLISHING COMPANY, INC.   692   .40
WAGNER
    GOTTERDAMMERUNG -- GER AND ENG SUPERLINEAR TEXT
        ASSOCIATED MUSIC PUBLISHERS, INC.   BRH   4.50
WAGNER   REGENY, R.
    LITTLE PIANO BOOK
        UNIVERSAL EDITION   11263   1.50
WAGNER   2
    LOHENGRIN, BRIDAL CHORUS
        CENTURY MUSIC PUBLISHING COMPANY, INC.   2155   .40
WAGNER   3
    LOHENGRIN, BRIDAL CHORUS
        CENTURY MUSIC PUBLISHING COMPANY, INC.   1563   .40
WAGNER   3
    LOHENGRIN, BRIDAL CHORUS
        CENTURY MUSIC PUBLISHING COMPANY, INC.   516   .40
WAGNER   2
    LOHENGRIN, PRELUDE, ACT 3
        CENTURY MUSIC PUBLISHING COMPANY, INC.   2039   .40
WAGNER *   TAGLIAPIETRA
    LOHENGRIN - CHORUS AND WEDDING MARCH
        FRANCO COLOMBO PUBLICATIONS   ER318   1.00
WAGNER   CHIESA
    LOHENGRIN - EASY FANTASIA
        FRANCO COLOMBO PUBLICATIONS   109090   .60
WAGNER
    LOHENGRIN - WEDDING MARCH
        FRANCO COLOMBO PUBLICATIONS   128425   .60
WAGNER   DEL MAGLIO
    LOHENGRIN - WEDDING MARCH
        FRANCO COLOMBO PUBLICATIONS   128118   .50
WAGNER   LANGE, G.   5
    LOVE SONG, WALKUERE
        CENTURY MUSIC PUBLISHING COMPANY, INC.   1192   .40
WAGNER   SPINDLER   4
    MARCH, TANNHAUSER
        CENTURY MUSIC PUBLISHING COMPANY, INC.   313   .40
WAGNER
    MEISTERSINGER, DIE -- GER AND ENG SUPERLINEAR TEXT
        ASSOCIATED MUSIC PUBLISHERS, INC.   BRH   2.50
WAGNER   3
    PARSIFAL, GOOD FRIDAY SPELL
        CENTURY MUSIC PUBLISHING COMPANY, INC.   3642   .40
WAGNER   LANGE, G.   5
    PILGRIM'S CHORUS, FROM 'TANNHAUSER'
        THEODORE PRESSER COMPANY   .50
WAGNER   3
    PILGRIMS' CHORUS, TANNHAUSER
        CENTURY MUSIC PUBLISHING COMPANY, INC.   1574   .40
WAGNER   LANGE, E.   5
    PILGRIMS' CHORUS, TANNHAUSER
        CENTURY MUSIC PUBLISHING COMPANY, INC.   1027   .40
WAGNER   2
    PRELUDE, ACT 3, LOHENGRIN
        CENTURY MUSIC PUBLISHING COMPANY, INC.   2039   .40
WAGNER
    RHEINGOLD, DAS -- GER AND ENG SUPERLINEAR TEXT
        ASSOCIATED MUSIC PUBLISHERS, INC.   BRH   2.50
WAGNER
    RIENZI -- GER AND ENG SUPERLINEAR TEXT
        ASSOCIATED MUSIC PUBLISHERS, INC.   BRH   3.00
WAGNER
    SIEGFRIED -- GER AND ENG SUPERLINEAR TEXT
        ASSOCIATED MUSIC PUBLISHERS, INC.   BRH   2.50
WAGNER
    TANNHAEUSER - MARCH
        FRANCO COLOMBO PUBLICATIONS   92219   1.00
WAGNER   DEL MAGLIO
    TANNHAEUSER - MARCH
        FRANCO COLOMBO PUBLICATIONS   128140   .50
WAGNER   TAGLIAPIETRA *
    TANNHAEUSER - OVERTURE
        FRANCO COLOMBO PUBLICATIONS   ER314   1.25
WAGNER *   TAGLIAPIETRA
    TANNHAEUSER - PILGRIMS' CHORUS
        FRANCO COLOMBO PUBLICATIONS   128792   .50
WAGNER   DEL MAGLIO
    TANNHAEUSER - PILGRIMS' CHORUS
        FRANCO COLOMBO PUBLICATIONS   128147   .60
WAGNER *
    TANNHAUSER--MARCH. ENTRANCE OF THE GUESTS INTO THE WARTBURG
        G. SCHIRMER, INC.   1.00
WAGNER *
    TANNHAUSER--MARCH. ENTRANCE OF THE GUESTS INTO THE WARTBURG
        G. SCHIRMER, INC.   1.00
WAGNER   4
    TANNHAUSER, FANTASIE
        CENTURY MUSIC PUBLISHING COMPANY, INC.   1907   .40

WAGNER   LANGE   4
    TANNHAUSER, MARCH AND CHORUS
        CENTURY MUSIC PUBLISHING COMPANY, INC.   1199   .40
WAGNER   LANGE   5
    TANNHAUSER, PILGRIMS' CHORUS
        CENTURY MUSIC PUBLISHING COMPANY, INC.   1027   .40
WAGNER   4
    TANNHAUSER MARCH AND CHORUS
        BELWIN-MILLS PUBLISHING CORPORATION   611   .60
WAGNER   LOEW
    TO THE EVENING STAR--FROM 'TANNHAUSER'
        G. SCHIRMER, INC.   .35
WAGNER *
    TRISTAN AND ISOLDE--ISOLDE'S LOVE-DEATH
        G. SCHIRMER, INC.   .60
WAGNER *
    TRISTAN UND ISOLDE--ISOLDE'S LOVE-DEATH
        G. SCHIRMER, INC.   .60
WAGNER
    TRISTAN UND ISOLDE -- GER SUPERLINEAR TEXT
        ASSOCIATED MUSIC PUBLISHERS, INC.   BRH   2.50
WAGNER   TAGLIAPIETRA
    TRISTAN UND ISOLDE - LIEBESTOD
        FRANCO COLOMBO PUBLICATIONS   127795   1.00
WAGNER   REGENY, R.
    TWO DANCES -- PALUCCA
        UNIVERSAL EDITION   11706   1.50
WAGNER   REGENY, R.
    TWO SONATAS
        UNIVERSAL EDITION   11432   2.35
WAGNER *
    WAGNER-LISZT ALBUM--9 TRANSCRIPTIONS FROM WAGNER'S OPERAS
        G. SCHIRMER, INC.   L57   2.50
WAGNER   ECKHARDT, F.   1
    WAGNER FOR THE YOUNG PIANIST
        CENTURY MUSIC PUBLISHING COMPANY, INC.   3964   .40
WAGNER   ALASSIO
    WALKUERE, DIE - RIDE OF THE VALKYRIES
        FRANCO COLOMBO PUBLICATIONS   101004   .90
WAGNER   DEL MAGLIO
    WALKUERE, DIE - SIEGMUND'S SPRING SONG
        FRANCO COLOMBO PUBLICATIONS   128128   .50
WAGNER   PAUER
    WEDDING MARCH FROM 'LOHENGRIN'
        G. SCHIRMER, INC.   .60
WAGNESS--ED.   WAGNESS
    CHRISTMAS CAROLS TO PLAY AND SING
        SHAWNEE PRESS, INC.   1.00
WALDTEUFEL, E.   ROLFE, W.   2
    PATINEURS, LES, EASY
        CENTURY MUSIC PUBLISHING COMPANY, INC.   3191   .40
WALDTEUFEL, E.   4
    PATINEURS, LES -- SKATERS --
        CENTURY MUSIC PUBLISHING COMPANY, INC.   390   .40
WALDTEUFEL, E.   WEYBRIGHT
    SKATER'S WALTZ, THE
        BELWIN-MILLS PUBLISHING CORPORATION   26046   .60
WALDTEUFEL, E.   4
    SKATERS' WALTZ
        CENTURY MUSIC PUBLISHING COMPANY, INC.   390   .40
WALDTEUFEL, E.   MITTLER   2B
    SKATERS WALTZ
        MUSICORD PUBLICATIONS, INC.   .45
WALDTEUFEL, E.   2
    SPANISH STUDENTS, WALTZES, EASY
        CENTURY MUSIC PUBLISHING COMPANY, INC.   3666   .40
WALDTEUFEL, E.   3
    SPANISH STUDENTS, WALTZES
        CENTURY MUSIC PUBLISHING COMPANY, INC.   1482   .40
WALDTEUFEL, E.   SAMMARTINO
    TEN FAMOUS WALTZES
        FRANCO COLOMBO PUBLICATIONS   BA9100   2.00
WALKER   NEALE, J.   EASY
    MR. BOJANGLES
        WARNER BROTHERS PUBLISHERS   .75
WALLER, T.
    JITTERBUG WALTZ
        THE BIG THREE MUSIC CORPORATION   00.95
WALLIS--ED   WALLIS
    ADESTE FIDELES
        BOSTON MUSIC COMPANY   .50
WALLIS--ED   WALLIS
    BOSTON MUSIC CO.'S CHRISTMAS CAROL BOOK
        BOSTON MUSIC COMPANY   1.25
WALLIS--ED   WALLIS
    FIRST NOEL, THE
        BOSTON MUSIC COMPANY   .50
WALLIS--ED   WALLIS
    SIX CHRISTMAS CAROLS
        BOSTON MUSIC COMPANY   .50
WALLIS   WEBER, H.   1
    STAR-SPANGLED BANNER, THE
        WILLIS MUSIC COMPANY   .30
WARD--ED   WARD
    HYMNS FOR YOU TO PLAY AND SING
        BOSTON MUSIC COMPANY   1.00
WARD--ED   WARD
    STUDENT CLASSICS - BOOK 1
        PRO-ART PUBLICATIONS, INC.   880   .75
WARD--ED   WARD
    STUDENT CLASSICS - BOOK 2
        PRO-ART PUBLICATIONS, INC.   881   .75
WARFEL, P.   SCHAUM, J.   2
    SKI SLOPE
        SCHAUM PUBLICATIONS, INC.   .60
WATSON--ED.   WATSON
    LET'S PLAY PLAYER-PIANO STYLE
        WARNER BROTHERS PUBLISHERS   1.95
WATSON
    THEMES FOR PIANO
        BELWIN-MILLS PUBLISHING CORPORATION   1.50
WEBER, VON   GEORGII, W.   3
    AUFFORDERUNG ZUM TANZ -- C-DUR OP. 65
        SCHOTT   0794   1.00
WEBER, VON   2
    BARCAROLLE, OBERON
        CENTURY MUSIC PUBLISHING COMPANY, INC.   1788   .40
WEBER, VON   BARNET   4
    BARCAROLLE, OBERON
        CENTURY MUSIC PUBLISHING COMPANY, INC.   2585   .40
WEBER, VON *
    CHOEUR-BARCAROLLE D'OBERON
        MUSICA OBSCURA   1.00
WEBER, VON   WEBSTER, B.
    CONCERTPIECE IN F MINOR OP. 79
        INTERNATIONAL MUSIC COMPANY   2.50

WEBER, VON   5
  DER FREIZCHUTZ, TRANS.
    CENTURY MUSIC PUBLISHING COMPANY, INC.   2295   .40
WEBER, VON   LEYBACH, I.   5
  FREISCHUTZ, FANTASIE
    CENTURY MUSIC PUBLISHING COMPANY, INC.   793   .40
WEBER, VON   5
  FREISCHUTZ, PRAYER
    CENTURY MUSIC PUBLISHING COMPANY, INC.   2295   .40
WEBER, VON   DEL MAGLIO
  INVITATION TO THE DANCE, OP. 65
    FRANCO COLOMBO PUBLICATIONS   124756   .50
WEBER, VON   2
  OBERON, BARCAROLLE
    CENTURY MUSIC PUBLISHING COMPANY, INC.   1788   .40
WEBER, VON   BARNET   4
  OBERON, BARCAROLLE
    CENTURY MUSIC PUBLISHING COMPANY, INC.   2585   .40
WEBER, VON
  PERPETUUM MOBILE--ORIGINAL AND ARRANGEMENTS BY BRAHMS AND
  TSCHAIKOVSKY
    ASSOCIATED MUSIC PUBLISHERS, INC.   SIM   4.00
WEBER, VON   5
  PRAYER, DER FREISCHUTZ
    CENTURY MUSIC PUBLISHING COMPANY, INC.   2295   .40
WEBER, VON   ALKAN,
  SCHERZO FROM   TRIO OP. 63
    MUSICA OBSCURA   1.60
WEBSTER   SAMPIETRO   FIRST YEAR
  SECRET LOVE
    WARNER BROTHERS PUBLISHERS   .75
WEBSTER   3
  SWEET BYE AND BYE, THE
    CENTURY MUSIC PUBLISHING COMPANY, INC.   1660   .40
WEBSTER   STIER   3
  SWEET BY AND BY, THE
    THEODORE PRESSER COMPANY   .60
WEILL, K.   RICHTER   FIRST YEAR
  MACK THE KNIFE
    WARNER BROTHERS PUBLISHERS   .75
WERNER, F.   SCHIEFELBEIN, F.   2
  HEDGE ROSE
    VOLKWEIN BROS.   .30
WESTERHOUT   DEL MAGLIO
  MA BELLE QUI DANSE
    FRANCO COLOMBO PUBLICATIONS   127763   .50
WESTERHOUT   DEL MAGLIO
  RONDE D'AMOUR
    FRANCO COLOMBO PUBLICATIONS   127764   .50
WESTERVELT, M.--ED   WESTERVELT, M.
  MARDI GRAS -- WITH WORDS
    THEODORE PRESSER COMPANY   1.00
WESTERVELT, M.   FOR BEGINNERS
  CHILD'S BOOK OF FOLK-TUNES, A--SUPPLEMENTARY READING MATERIAL
  FOR THE BEGINNER--WITH WORDS
    G. SCHIRMER, INC.   1.00
WESTON, L.   SCHAUM, J.   3
  HAWAIIAN NOCTURNE
    SCHAUM PUBLICATIONS, INC.   .60
WEYBRIGHT--ED.   WEYBRIGHT   2
  FOGGY DEW, THE -- AN IRISH FOLK SONG
    BELWIN-MILLS PUBLISHING CORPORATION   .60
WEYBRIGHT--ED.   WEYBRIGHT   1 1/2
  FOLK FROM THE VILLAGE, THE -- A GERMAN FOLK TUNE FOR SOLO PIANO
    BELWIN-MILLS PUBLISHING CORPORATION   .60
WEYBRIGHT--ED.   WEYBRIGHT   1 1/2
  GERMAN 'CLAP HANDS' DANCE
    BELWIN-MILLS PUBLISHING CORPORATION   .60
WEYBRIGHT--ED.   WEYBRIGHT   1 1/2
  TWO STEPHEN FOSTER SONGS -- NELLY BLY AND BEAUTIFUL DREAMER
    BELWIN-MILLS PUBLISHING CORPORATION   .60
WEYBRIGHT   1 1/2
  COSSACK DANCE, A FOLK SONG
    BELWIN-MILLS PUBLISHING CORPORATION   .60
WEYBRIGHT   2
  CRUSADER'S HYMN -- A SILESIAN FOLK MELODY
    BELWIN-MILLS PUBLISHING CORPORATION   .60
WEYBRIGHT   1
  FARMER IN THE DELL, THE -- AN ENGLISH SINGING GAME
    BELWIN-MILLS PUBLISHING CORPORATION   .60
WEYBRIGHT   2
  FARM MEDLEY, A -- OLD MACDONALD AND ZIP COON
    BELWIN-MILLS PUBLISHING CORPORATION   .60
WEYBRIGHT   1 1/2
  FREDERIKA -- A GERMAN FOLK SONG
    BELWIN-MILLS PUBLISHING CORPORATION   .60
WEYBRIGHT   1 1/2
  LITTLE MAZURKA -- A CZECHOSLAVAKIAN FOLK TUNE
    BELWIN-MILLS PUBLISHING CORPORATION   .60
WEYBRIGHT   3
  MEXICANA -- A MEXICAN FOLK SONG
    BELWIN-MILLS PUBLISHING CORPORATION   .60
WEYBRIGHT   1 1/2
  PERCIA -- A CHILEAN FOLK SONG
    BELWIN-MILLS PUBLISHING CORPORATION   .60
WEYBRIGHT   1 1/2
  PLAY-PARTY MEDLEY, A -- TUNES FROM CHILDHOOD
    BELWIN-MILLS PUBLISHING CORPORATION   .60
WEYBRIGHT   1
  POP GOES THE WEASEL -- AMERICAN GAME SONG
    BELWIN-MILLS PUBLISHING CORPORATION   .60
WEYBRIGHT   1 1/2
  ROSA -- A FLEMISH FOLK SONG
    BELWIN-MILLS PUBLISHING CORPORATION   .60
WEYBRIGHT   2
  SOLDIER, SOLDIER, SOLDIER -- A FRENCH FOLK SONG
    BELWIN-MILLS PUBLISHING CORPORATION   .60
WEYBRIGHT   2
  SWISS MOUNTAIN SONG -- SWISS FOLK SONG
    BELWIN-MILLS PUBLISHING CORPORATION   .60
WEYBRIGHT   1 1/2
  TWO FAMILIAR HYMNS -- 1. THE DOXOLOGY, 2. NOW THANK WE ALL OUR
  GOD
    BELWIN-MILLS PUBLISHING CORPORATION   .60
WEYBRIGHT   1 1/2
  TWO FAMILIAR THEMES
    BELWIN-MILLS PUBLISHING CORPORATION   .60
WEYBRIGHT   3
  WORRIED MAN BLUES, THE -- AN EARLY AMERICAN TUNE
    BELWIN-MILLS PUBLISHING CORPORATION   .60
WHITEFIELD--ED   WHITEFIELD
  BARNARD WHITEFIELDS'SAMERICAN FOLK SONG ALBUM
    CENTURY MUSIC PUBLISHING COMPANY, INC.   1.00
WHITFORD--ED.   WHITFORD   GR. 3
  BADINAGE
    ROBERT WHITFORD PUBLICATIONS   .40

WHITFORD--ED.   WHITFORD   GR. 2-3
  CLASSIC COLLECTION NO. 1
    ROBERT WHITFORD PUBLICATIONS   .60
WHITFORD--ED.   WHITFORD   GR. 2 1/2
  DANCE OF THE FLOWERS
    ROBERT WHITFORD PUBLICATIONS   .40
WHITFORD--ED.   WHITFORD   GR. 2 1/2
  EVENING STAR
    ROBERT WHITFORD PUBLICATIONS   .40
WHITFORD--ED.   WHITFORD   GR. 1 1/2 - 2 1/2
  FAVORITES FOR THE PIANIST, HYMNS NO. 1
    ROBERT WHITFORD PUBLICATIONS   .60
WHITFORD--ED.   WHITFORD   GR. 1 1/2 - 2 1/2
  FAVORITES FOR THE PIANIST, NO. 01
    ROBERT WHITFORD PUBLICATIONS   .60
WHITFORD--ED.   WHITFORD   GR. 1 1/2 - 2 1/2
  FAVORITES FOR THE PIANIST, NO. 02
    ROBERT WHITFORD PUBLICATIONS   .60
WHITFORD--ED.   WHITFORD   GR. 1 1/2 - 2 1/2
  FAVORITES FOR THE PIANIST, NO. 03
    ROBERT WHITFORD PUBLICATIONS   .60
WHITFORD--ED.   WHITFORD   GR. 1 1/2 - 2 1/2
  FAVORITES FOR THE PIANIST, NO. 04
    ROBERT WHITFORD PUBLICATIONS   .60
WHITFORD--ED.   WHITFORD   GR. 1 1/2 - 2 1/2
  FAVORITES FOR THE PIANIST, NO. 05
    ROBERT WHITFORD PUBLICATIONS   .60
WHITFORD--ED.   WHITFORD   GR. 1 1/2 - 2 1/2
  FAVORITES FOR THE PIANIST, NO. 06
    ROBERT WHITFORD PUBLICATIONS   .60
WHITFORD--ED.   WHITFORD   GR. 1 1/2 - 2 1/2
  FAVORITES FOR THE PIANIST, NO. 07
    ROBERT WHITFORD PUBLICATIONS   .60
WHITFORD--ED.   WHITFORD   GR. 1 1/2 - 2 1/2
  FAVORITES FOR THE PIANIST, NO. 08
    ROBERT WHITFORD PUBLICATIONS   .60
WHITFORD--ED.   WHITFORD   GR. 1 1/2 - 2 1/2
  FAVORITES FOR THE PIANIST, NO. 09
    ROBERT WHITFORD PUBLICATIONS   .60
WHITFORD--ED.   WHITFORD   GR. 1 1/2 - 2 1/2
  FAVORITES FOR THE PIANIST, NO. 10
    ROBERT WHITFORD PUBLICATIONS   .60
WHITFORD--ED.   WHITFORD   GR. 1 1/2 - 2 1/2
  FAVORITES FOR THE PIANIST, NO. 11
    ROBERT WHITFORD PUBLICATIONS   .60
WHITFORD--ED.   WHITFORD   GR. 1 1/2 - 2 1/2
  FAVORITES FOR THE PIANIST, NO. 12
    ROBERT WHITFORD PUBLICATIONS   .60
WHITFORD--ED.   WHITFORD   GR. 1 1/2 - 2 1/2
  FAVORITES FOR THE PIANIST, NO. 13
    ROBERT WHITFORD PUBLICATIONS   .60
WHITFORD--ED.   WHITFORD   GR. 1 1/2 - 2 1/2
  FAVORITES FOR THE PIANIST, NO. 14
    ROBERT WHITFORD PUBLICATIONS   .60
WHITFORD--ED.   WHITFORD   GR. 1 1/2 - 2 1/2
  FAVORITES FOR THE PIANIST, NO. 15
    ROBERT WHITFORD PUBLICATIONS   .60
WHITFORD--ED.   WHITFORD   GR. 1 1/2 - 2 1/2
  FAVORITES FOR THE PIANIST, NO. 16
    ROBERT WHITFORD PUBLICATIONS   .60
WHITFORD--ED.   WHITFORD   GR. 1 1/2 - 2 1/2
  FAVORITES FOR THE PIANIST, NO. 17
    ROBERT WHITFORD PUBLICATIONS   .60
WHITFORD--ED.   WHITFORD   GR. 1 1/2 - 2 1/2
  FAVORITES FOR THE PIANIST, NO. 18
    ROBERT WHITFORD PUBLICATIONS   .60
WHITFORD--ED.   WHITFORD   GR. 1 1/2 - 2 1/2
  FAVORITES FOR THE PIANIST, NO. 19
    ROBERT WHITFORD PUBLICATIONS   .60
WHITFORD--ED.   WHITFORD   GR. 1 1/2 - 2 1/2
  FAVORITES FOR THE PIANIST, NO. 20
    ROBERT WHITFORD PUBLICATIONS   .60
WHITFORD--ED.   WHITFORD   GR. 3
  FRANKIE AND JOHNNY BOOGIE
    ROBERT WHITFORD PUBLICATIONS   .40
WHITFORD--ED.   WHITFORD   GR. 4
  IDA --JAZZ ARR.--
    ROBERT WHITFORD PUBLICATIONS   .40
WHITFORD--ED.   WHITFORD   GR. 2
  MARINES' HYMN
    ROBERT WHITFORD PUBLICATIONS   .40
WHITFORD--ED.   WHITFORD   GR. 2
  SWANEE RIVER BOOGIE
    ROBERT WHITFORD PUBLICATIONS   .40
WHITFORD--ED.   WHITFORD   GR. 1
  TUNES FOR THE PIANIST, NO. 1
    ROBERT WHITFORD PUBLICATIONS   .60
WHITFORD--ED.   WHITFORD   GR. 1
  TUNES FOR THE PIANIST, NO. 2
    ROBERT WHITFORD PUBLICATIONS   .60
WHITFORD--ED.   WHITFORD   GR. 1
  TUNES FOR THE PIANIST, NO. 3
    ROBERT WHITFORD PUBLICATIONS   .60
WHITFORD--ED.   WHITFORD   GR. 1
  TUNES FOR THE PIANIST, NO. 4
    ROBERT WHITFORD PUBLICATIONS   .60
WHITSON *   KLICKMANN   EASY
  LET ME CALL YOU SWEETHEART --LARGE NOTE--
    SHAWNEE PRESS, INC.   HB-53   .85
WIDOR, CH.
  CONTE D'AVRIL
    HEUGEL ET CIE.   10.00
WIDOR, CH.
  LA KORRIGANE
    HEUGEL ET CIE.   13.00
WIENIAWSKI   4
  POLISH NATIONAL DANCE
    CENTURY MUSIC PUBLISHING COMPANY, INC.   1709   .40
WILLIAMS, C.   SCHAUM, J.   4
  JOURNEY TO BETHLEHEM
    SCHAUM PUBLICATIONS, INC.   .60
WILLIAMS, C.   NEVIN
  THEME FROM 'THE APARTMENT' -- SIMP.
    BELWIN-MILLS PUBLISHING CORPORATION   26108   .50
WILLIAMS, C.   GLOVER, D.
  THEME FROM 'THE APARTMENT
    BELWIN-MILLS PUBLISHING CORPORATION   .60
WILLIAMS, D. M.
  INSPIRATIONS FROM THE PIANO
    LILLENAS PUBLISHING COMPANY   MB-306   2.50
WILLIAMS, F.--ED.   WILLIAMS, F.
  TEN CHRISTMAS CAROLS
    SHAWNEE PRESS, INC.   1.10
WILLIAMS, H.   SCHAUM, J.   2
  RED SAILS IN THE SUNSET
    SCHAUM PUBLICATIONS, INC.   .75

WILLIAMS, L. R.--ED   WILLIAMS, L. R.
  FAVORITE HYMNS TO PLAY AND SING IN EASY PIANO ARRANGEMENTS
        BROADMAN MUSIC   4571-01   1.50
WILLIAMS, R.--ED.   WILLIAMS, R.
  AFFAIR TO REMEMBER, AN
        THE BIG THREE MUSIC CORPORATION   1.25
WILLIAMS, R.--ED.   WILLIAMS, R.
  ANASTASIA
        THE BIG THREE MUSIC CORPORATION   01.25
WILLIAMS, R.--ED.   WILLIAMS, R.
  ARRIVEDERCI, ROMA
        THE BIG THREE MUSIC CORPORATION   01.25
WILLIAMS, R.--ED.   WILLIAMS, R.
  DAY IN THE LIFE OF A FOOL, A
        THE BIG THREE MUSIC CORPORATION   1.25
WILLIAMS, R.--ED.   WILLIAMS, R.
  DEEP PURPLE
        THE BIG THREE MUSIC CORPORATION   01.25
WILLIAMS, R.--ED.   WILLIAMS, R.
  GENTLE ON MY MIND
        THE BIG THREE MUSIC CORPORATION   01.25
WILLIAMS, R.--ED.   WILLIAMS, R.
  GREEN LEAVES OF SUMMER
        THE BIG THREE MUSIC CORPORATION   1.25
WILLIAMS, R.--ED.   WILLIAMS, R.
  LARA'S THEME - DOCTOR ZHIVAGO
        THE BIG THREE MUSIC CORPORATION   1.25
WILLIAMS, R.--ED.   WILLIAMS, R.
  LOVE MAKES THE WORLD GO 'ROUND
        THE BIG THREE MUSIC CORPORATION   1.25
WILLIAMS, R.--ED.   WILLIAMS, R.
  MOONLIGHT AND ROSES
        THE BIG THREE MUSIC CORPORATION   01.25
WILLIAMS, R.--ED.   WILLIAMS, R.
  MORE THAN A MIRACLE
        THE BIG THREE MUSIC CORPORATION   01.25
WILLIAMS, R.--ED.   WILLIAMS, R.
  ON THE TRAIL
        THE BIG THREE MUSIC CORPORATION   01.25
WILLIAMS, R.--ED.   WILLIAMS, R.
  OVER THE RAINBOW
        THE BIG THREE MUSIC CORPORATION   01.25
WILLIAMS, R.--ED.   WILLIAMS, R.
  SHADOW OF YOUR SMILE
        THE BIG THREE MUSIC CORPORATION   1.25
WILLIAMS, R.--ED.   WILLIAMS, R.
  SUNNY
        THE BIG THREE MUSIC CORPORATION   01.25
WILLIAMS, R.--ED   WILLIAMS, R.
  TILL
        CHAPPELL AND COMPANY, INC.   6057509   .95
WILLIAMS, R.
  MEET ROGER WILLIAMS
        THE BIG THREE MUSIC CORPORATION   02.95
WILLIAMS, R.
  PIANO INTERPRETATIONS, NO. 1
        THE BIG THREE MUSIC CORPORATION   01.95
WILLIAMS, R.
  PIANO INTERPRETATIONS, NO. 2
        THE BIG THREE MUSIC CORPORATION   01.95
WILLIAMS, R.
  PIANO INTERPRETATIONS, NO. 3
        THE BIG THREE MUSIC CORPORATION   01.95
WILLIAMS, R.
  RECORDED PIANO INTERPRETATIONS
        THE BIG THREE MUSIC CORPORATION   02.00
WILLIAMS, R.
  THIS IS ROGER WILLIAMS
        THE BIG THREE MUSIC CORPORATION   02.95
WILLIAMS, T.   STEINER   JR. OR SR. APPR.
  LIFT UP YOUR HEADS
        BELWIN-MILLS PUBLISHING CORPORATION   .60
WILLSON, M.
  I AIN'T DOWN YET
        FRANK MUSIC CORPORATION   .95
WILLSON, M.
  MUSIC MAN, THE
        FRANK MUSIC CORPORATION   1.25
WILLSON, M.
  O.O.MCINTYRE SUITE
        THE BIG THREE MUSIC CORPORATION   01.50
WILLSON, M.   RICHTER   2 1/2 - 3
  SEVENTY SIX TROMBONES
        FRANK MUSIC CORPORATION   .75
WILLSON, M.   AGAY, D.   EASY
  SONGS FROM 'THE MUSIC MAN'
        FRANK MUSIC CORPORATION   1.25
WILLSON, M.   AGAY, D.   EASY
  SONGS FROM 'THE UNSINKABLE MOLLY BROWN'
        FRANK MUSIC CORPORATION   1.25
WILLSON, M.   RICHTER   2 1/2 - 3
  TILL THERE WAS YOU
        FRANK MUSIC CORPORATION   .75
WILLSON, M.
  UNSINKABLE MOLLY BROWN, THE
        FRANK MUSIC CORPORATION   1.25
WILSON, J. F.
  FAMILIAR HYMNS FOR THE PIANO
        HOPE PUBLISHING COMPANY   2.50
WILSON, M.   1 1/2
  IT'S BEGINNING TO LOOK LIKE CHRISTMAS
        SCHAUM PUBLICATIONS, INC.   .75
WILSON, T.
  TEDDY WILSON, PIANO PATTERNS
        THE BIG THREE MUSIC CORPORATION   01.50
WINANS, W. L.
  WORSHIP HYMNS FOR PIANO
        LILLENAS PUBLISHING COMPANY   MB-228   2.50
WINROTH, G.--ED   WINROTH, G.
  CATHEDRAL CHIMES
        WILLIS MUSIC COMPANY   .60
WINWOOD, S.
  STEVIE WINWOOD AND FRIENDS
        MUSIC SALES CORPORATION   090004   2.95
WOLCOTT, C.
  CAT ON A HOT TIN ROOF
        THE BIG THREE MUSIC CORPORATION   00.95
WOLF-FERRARI, E.
  INQUISITIVE WOMEN--PIANO SCORE WITH SUPERLINEAR TEXT
        G. SCHIRMER, INC.   3.00
WOLF-FERRARI, E.   FOLK
  SUZANNE'S SECRET--PIANO SCORE WITH SUPERLINEAR GERMAN TEXT
        G. SCHIRMER, INC.   2.00
WOLFSON, J.
  PARAPHRASES ON OLD HEBREW FOLK SONGS, BK. 1
        UNIVERSAL EDITION   UE 6931   1.80

WOLFSON, J.
  PARAPHRASES ON OLD HEBREW FOLK SONGS, BK. 2
        UNIVERSAL EDITION   UE 6932   1.80
WOODS, H.   SCHAUM, J.   2
  SIDE BY SIDE
        SCHAUM PUBLICATIONS, INC.   .75
WRIGHT, R. *
  KISMET
        FRANK MUSIC CORPORATION   1.25
WRIGHT, R. *   RICHTER   EASY
  NEW SONGS FROM THE MOTION PICTURE 'SONG OF NORWAY'
        FRANK MUSIC CORPORATION   1.25
WRIGHT, R. *   RICHTER   EASY
  SONGS FROM 'KISMET'
        FRANK MUSIC CORPORATION   1.25
YARROW   NEALE, J.   EASY
  DAY IS DONE
        WARNER BROTHERS PUBLISHERS   .75
YARROW *   DAVIS, J. R.   FIRST YEAR
  PUFF, THE MAGIC DRAGON
        WARNER BROTHERS PUBLISHERS   .75
YARROW *   NEALE, J.   EASY
  PUFF, THE MAGIC DRAGON
        WARNER BROTHERS PUBLISHERS   .75
YORKE, P.
  MISTY VALLEY
        THE BIG THREE MUSIC CORPORATION   00.95
YOUMANS   LEVINE
  TEA FOR TWO
        WARNER BROTHERS PUBLISHERS   1.00
YOUMANS   WALTER
  TEA FOR TWO
        WARNER BROTHERS PUBLISHERS   1.00
YOUMANS   RICHTER   FIRST YEAR
  TEA FOR TWO
        WILLIS MUSIC COMPANY   .75
YOUNG, G.
  CHRISTMAS SUITE, A
        HOPE PUBLISHING COMPANY   1.95
YOUNG, V.   SCHAUM, J.   1 1/2
  SWEET SUE - JUST YOU
        SCHAUM PUBLICATIONS, INC.   .75
YRADIER   2
  DOVE, THE — LA PALOMA, EASY
        CENTURY MUSIC PUBLISHING COMPANY, INC.   2139   .40
YRADIER   TWITCHELL   4
  LA PALOMA
        CENTURY MUSIC PUBLISHING COMPANY, INC.   270   .40
YRADIER   CHIESA
  PALOMA, LA
        FRANCO COLOMBO PUBLICATIONS   105260   .60
YRADIER   CHIESA
  PALOMA, LA
        FRANCO COLOMBO PUBLICATIONS   107485   .60
ZANINELLI
  ENCHANTED LAKE -- BALLET --
        FRANCO COLOMBO PUBLICATIONS   NY1702   1.50
ZEPP--ED   ZEPP   2
  AMERICAN PATROL
        PRO-ART PUBLICATIONS, INC.   323   .50
ZEPP--ED   ZEPP   2
  ARKANSAS TRAVELER, THE
        PRO-ART PUBLICATIONS, INC.   192   .50
ZEPP--ED   ZEPP   2-3
  DIXIE BOOGIE
        PRO-ART PUBLICATIONS, INC.   108   .50
ZEPP--ED   ZEPP
  FUN WITH FIVE FAVORITE SONGS
        PRO-ART PUBLICATIONS, INC.   606   1.00
ZEPP--ED   ZEPP   4
  GO DOWN MOSES
        PRO-ART PUBLICATIONS, INC.   233   .50
ZEPP--ED   ZEPP   3
  GREENSLEEVES - WHAT CHILD IS THIS
        PRO-ART PUBLICATIONS, INC.   198   .50
ZEPP--ED   ZEPP   2
  HAVA NAGILA
        PRO-ART PUBLICATIONS, INC.   362   .50
ZEPP--ED   ZEPP   4
  HAVA NAGILA
        PRO-ART PUBLICATIONS, INC.   363   .50
ZEPP--ED   ZEPP   3-4
  HE'S GOT THE WHOLE WORLD IN HIS HANDS
        PRO-ART PUBLICATIONS, INC.   326   .50
ZEPP--ED   ZEPP   4
  JOSHUA FIT DE BATTLE OF JERICHO
        PRO-ART PUBLICATIONS, INC.   200   .50
ZEPP--ED   ZEPP   2
  JOSHUA FIT DE BATTLE OF JERICHO
        PRO-ART PUBLICATIONS, INC.   262   .50
ZEPP--ED   ZEPP   3
  JUGGLE BOOGIE - LITTLE BROWN JUG
        PRO-ART PUBLICATIONS, INC.   69   .50
ZEPP--ED   ZEPP
  LET'S ARRANGE CHRISTMAS SONGS
        PRO-ART PUBLICATIONS, INC.   482   .75
ZEPP--ED   ZEPP
  LET'S PLAY CHRISTMAS CAROLS
        PRO-ART PUBLICATIONS, INC.   715   1.00
ZEPP--ED   ZEPP
  LET'S PLAY CHRISTMAS FAVORITES
        PRO-ART PUBLICATIONS, INC.   716   1.00
ZEPP--ED   ZEPP
  LET'S PLAY FAVORITES
        PRO-ART PUBLICATIONS, INC.   603   1.00
ZEPP--ED   ZEPP
  LET'S PLAY HYMNS
        PRO-ART PUBLICATIONS, INC.   488   1.25
ZEPP--ED   ZEPP   3-4
  LET'S PLAY MORE FAVORITES
        PRO-ART PUBLICATIONS, INC.   604   .85
ZEPP--ED   ZEPP   1-2
  LONDONDERRY AIR
        PRO-ART PUBLICATIONS, INC.   232   .50
ZEPP--ED   ZEPP   1-2
  MARINES' HYMN, THE
        PRO-ART PUBLICATIONS, INC.   226   .50
ZEPP--ED   ZEPP   2
  OH, DEAR - WHAT CAN THE MATTER BE
        PRO-ART PUBLICATIONS, INC.   227   .50
ZEPP--ED   ZEPP   2
  OVER THE RIVER AND THROUGH THE WOODS - THANKSGIVING SONG
        PRO-ART PUBLICATIONS, INC.   191   .50
ZEPP--ED   ZEPP   3-4
  POOR WAYFARING STRANGER
        PRO-ART PUBLICATIONS, INC.   266   .50

ZEPP--ED ZEPP			
SACRED SONGS AND HYMNS			
PRO-ART PUBLICATIONS, INC.		1157	1.00
ZEPP--ED ZEPP	4		
SCARBOROUGH FAIR			
PRO-ART PUBLICATIONS, INC.		526	.50
ZEPP--ED ZEPP			
SEVEN ALL TIME HITS			
PRO-ART PUBLICATIONS, INC.		807	.85
ZEPP--ED ZEPP	4		
SHENANDOAH			
PRO-ART PUBLICATIONS, INC.		527	.50
ZEPP--ED ZEPP	3		
SHINE BOOGIE			
PRO-ART PUBLICATIONS, INC.		57	.50
ZEPP--ED ZEPP	1		
SHORT 'NIN' BREAD			
PRO-ART PUBLICATIONS, INC.		60	.50
ZEPP--ED ZEPP			
SONG AND SOLO HIGHLIGHTS			
PRO-ART PUBLICATIONS, INC.		1158	1.25
ZEPP--ED ZEPP	4		
SPACE BOOGIE			
PRO-ART PUBLICATIONS, INC.		153	.50
ZEPP--ED ZEPP	4		
TARANTELLA			
PRO-ART PUBLICATIONS, INC.		327	.50
ZEPP--ED ZEPP	4		
THREE PATRIOTIC SONGS			
PRO-ART PUBLICATIONS, INC.		110	.50
ZEPP--ED ZEPP			
TIDINGS OF CHRISTMAS			
PRO-ART PUBLICATIONS, INC.		483	1.00
ZEPP--ED ZEPP	3		
UPSIDE DOWN CAKE			
PRO-ART PUBLICATIONS, INC.		70	.50
ZEPP--ED ZEPP	2		
WHERE ARE THOSE PIRATES BOLD			
PRO-ART PUBLICATIONS, INC.		146	.50
ZEPP--ED ZEPP	3-4		
YOUNG MACDONALD HAD A FARM			
PRO-ART PUBLICATIONS, INC.		59	.50
ZEPP	4		
FARMER BOOGIE - BASED ON THE HAPPY FARMER OF SCHUMANN			
PRO-ART PUBLICATIONS, INC.		406	.50
ZIPP			
LITTLE CHRISTMAS BOOK FOR ROSWITHA			
BARENREITER VERLAG		26666	1.75

Arrangements and Transcriptions:
Composer/Editor/Arranger Unlisted—Works Alphabetized by Title

ACADEMY AWARD WINNER AND OTHER BIG HITS, THE			
THE BIG THREE MUSIC CORPORATION			02.95
	2		
ALTE DEUTSCHE VOLKSTANZE			
SCHOTT		04032 1/2	1.00
BALLET MUSIC			
MUSIC SALES CORPORATION		020089	2.95
	EASY		
BAROQUE PIANO MUSIC			
MEL BAY PUBLICATIONS, INC.			2.00
BELAFONTE FOLK SONG BOOK, THE			
MUSIC SALES CORPORATION		040165	2.95
BEST OF ALL, THE			
MUSIC SALES CORPORATION		060003	2.95
BIG SEVENTY-FIVE SONG BOOK, THE - EASY BIG NOTE PIANO			
WARNER BROTHERS PUBLISHERS			3.95
BIG 3'S BEST IN POPS			
THE BIG THREE MUSIC CORPORATION			02.95
BIG 3'S 20 BIG HITS OF TODAY			
THE BIG THREE MUSIC CORPORATION			02.95
BLOOD, SWEAT, AND TEARS			
MUSIC SALES CORPORATION		02065	4.95
BLUESMEN, THE			
MUSIC SALES CORPORATION		000096	3.95
CLASSICAL THEMES FOR PEOPLE WHO HATE CLASSICAL MUSIC			
MUSIC SALES CORPORATION		020100	2.95
CRUSADE, PIANO STYLINGS			
LORENZ PUBLISHING COMPANY			2.50
	2-3		
DAS FROHE RHEINLIEDER-BUCH, BAND 01			
SCHOTT		2500	3.75
	2-3		
DAS FROHE RHEINLIEDER-BUCH, BAND 02			
SCHOTT		4775	1.75
	3		
DAS GOLDENE MARSCH-BUCH, BAND 01			
SCHOTT		373	3.75
	3		
DAS GOLDENE MARSCH-BUCH, BAND 02			
SCHOTT		374	3.75
	3		
DAS LIEBSTE LIED, BAND 01			
SCHOTT		3799	3.75
	3		
DAS LIEBSTE LIED, BAND 02			
SCHOTT		4000	3.75
	3		
DAS NEUE OPERETTEN-BUCH, BAND 01			
SCHOTT		2525	4.00
	3		
DAS NEUE OPERETTEN-BUCH, BAND 02			
SCHOTT		2850	4.00
	3		
DAS NEUE OPERETTEN-BUCH, BAND 03			
SCHOTT		3700	4.00
	3		
DAS NEUE OPERETTEN-BUCH, BAND 04			
SCHOTT		4300	4.00
	3		
DAS NEUE OPERETTEN-BUCH, BAND 05			
SCHOTT		4500	4.00

DEEP PURPLE SONG BOOK			
THE BIG THREE MUSIC CORPORATION			03.95
	3		
DER LANGSAME WALZER			
SCHOTT		3798	3.50
	3		
DIE OPER IM HEIM, BAND 1			
SCHOTT		2777	5.00
	3		
DIE OPER IM HEIM, BAND 2			
SCHOTT		2778	5.00
EASY-BEAT BIG NOTE PIANO			
WARNER BROTHERS PUBLISHERS			2.95
EASY DOES IT FOR PIANO - NO. 1			
WARNER BROTHERS PUBLISHERS		EZ 1	1.95
EASY DOES IT FOR PIANO - NO. 2			
WARNER BROTHERS PUBLISHERS		EZ 2	1.95
EASY DOES IT FOR PIANO - NO. 3			
WARNER BROTHERS PUBLISHERS		EZ 3	1.95
EASY DOES IT FOR PIANO - NO. 4			
WARNER BROTHERS PUBLISHERS		EZ 4	1.95
	EASY		
EASY PIANO HYMN PIECES			
LORENZ PUBLISHING COMPANY			2.00
EASY TO PLAY HITS THROUGH THE YEARS - VOL. 1			
WARNER BROTHERS PUBLISHERS			1.25
EASY TO PLAY HITS THROUGH THE YEARS - VOL. 2			
WARNER BROTHERS PUBLISHERS			1.25
	EASY		
EASY WEDDING MUSIC NO. 1			
LORENZ PUBLISHING COMPANY			2.00
ELEMENTARY PIANO PIECES			
MUSIC SALES CORPORATION		020052	2.95
FAMOUS PIANO PIECES			
MUSIC SALES CORPORATION		020090	2.95
FERRANTE AND TEICHER INTERPRETATIONS FOR SOLO PIANO			
THE BIG THREE MUSIC CORPORATION			02.95
	AI		
FIFTY-FIVE AND ONE-HALF PIANO SOLOS			
WILLIS MUSIC COMPANY			1.95
FIFTY-FIVE PIANO CLASSICS - PAST AND PRESENT			
WARNER BROTHERS PUBLISHERS		MFE 32	1.95
FIFTY-FIVE PIANO CLASSICS			
WARNER BROTHERS PUBLISHERS		MFE 16	1.95
FIFTY-FIVE POPULAR PIANO TEACHING PIECES			
WARNER BROTHERS PUBLISHERS			3.95
FIFTY-FOUR FAMOUS MARCHES FOR PIANO			
WARNER BROTHERS PUBLISHERS		MFE 17	2.50
FIFTY-NINE FAMOUS PIANO SOLOS			
WARNER BROTHERS PUBLISHERS		MFE 1	2.95
FIFTY-TWO GREAT ROCK AND ROLL HITS			
THE BIG THREE MUSIC CORPORATION			03.95
FIRST FAVORITES			
EDWARD B. MARKS MUSIC CORPORATION			01.50
	1		
FIRST TIME AROUND			
BOURNE COMPANY			1.50
FLAIR STYLINGS FOR PIANO OF DAYS OF WINE AND ROSES			
WARNER BROTHERS PUBLISHERS			1.95
FOLK BLUES			
MUSIC SALES CORPORATION		000113	4.95
FORTY-SIX CONTEMPORARY PIANO SOLOS			
WARNER BROTHERS PUBLISHERS		MFE 33	2.95
FORTY-SIX ORIGINAL PIANO CLASSICS			
WARNER BROTHERS PUBLISHERS		MFE 35	2.95
FOUR MAGIC CHORDS FOR PIANO			
WARNER BROTHERS PUBLISHERS			2.50
FRANK ZAPPA SONG BOOK, BK. 1			
THE BIG THREE MUSIC CORPORATION			05.95
FROM BACH TO BROADWAY			
WARNER BROTHERS PUBLISHERS		MFE 37	2.50
FROSTY THE SNOW MAN AND OTHER CHRISTMAS SONGS			
THE BIG THREE MUSIC CORPORATION			02.95
GOSPEL HYMN PIANIST			
LORENZ PUBLISHING COMPANY			2.50
GREAT SONGS OF THE YEAR - 1973 EDITION			
THE BIG THREE MUSIC CORPORATION			04.95
GYPSY			
CHAPPELL AND COMPANY, INC.		1847508	1.50
HARMS HITS THROUGH THE YEARS FOR PIANO			
WARNER BROTHERS PUBLISHERS			1.95
HEART OF THE OPERETTA, THE			
CENTURY MUSIC PUBLISHING COMPANY, INC.			1.50
	EASY		
IMPRESSIONIST ERA PIANO MUSIC			
MEL BAY PUBLICATIONS, INC.			2.00
	1		
IM VIOLINSCHLUSSEL -- FIFTEEN LEICHTE STUCKE			
SCHOTT		2604	2.00
INCREDIBLE STRING BAND, THE			
MUSIC SALES CORPORATION		060009	2.95
INSTANT PIANO PHASE 1			
SIGHT AND SOUND SYSTEMS, INC.		31-101	12.00
INSTANT PIANO PHASE 2			
SIGHT AND SOUND SYSTEMS, INC.		31-102	12.00
	INTERMEDIATE		

INSTRUMENTAL GREATS
SCREEN GEMS - COLUMBIA PUBLICATIONS   F0186P   3.95

IT'S EASY TO PLAY PIANO THE THREE CHORD WAY
MUSIC SALES CORPORATION   040041   2.95

JEFFERSON AIRPLANE, THE
MUSIC SALES CORPORATION   060001   2.95
LANE, J.
JINGLE BELL ROCK
THE BIG THREE MUSIC CORPORATION   00.70

KEYBOARD HIT-KIT, THE
WARNER BROTHERS PUBLISHERS   1.50
2-3
KLASSISCHE LIEBLINGSSTUCKE
SCHOTT   04020 1/2   1.00
LANE, J.
KNOCK THREE TIMES
THE BIG THREE MUSIC CORPORATION   00.70

LARGE NOTE PIANO PIECES
MUSIC SALES CORPORATION   020084   2.95

LEFT FOOT, RIGHT FOOT MARCH FOLIO
VOLKWEIN BROS.   01.50
2-3
MEIN HEIMATLAND
SCHOTT   2222   5.00

MERRY CHRISTMAS - THE HILLSIDE SINGERS
THE BIG THREE MUSIC CORPORATION   02.95

MEXICAN HAT DANCE
EDWARD B. MARKS MUSIC CORPORATION   01.00

MORRISON HOTEL -- THE DOORS
MUSIC SALES CORPORATION   060008   2.95

MUSICAL VISIT WITH THE MASTERS, A -- 16 CLASSICAL COMPOSITIONS
IN SIMPLIFIED ARRANGEMENTS
THEODORE PRESSER COMPANY   1.25

MUSIC IS A WORLD OF JOY
THE BIG THREE MUSIC CORPORATION   02.95
2
NEUE WEIHNACHTSLIEDER
BARENREITER VERLAG   BA 1371

NINETY-FIVE EASY PIANO CLASSICS
WARNER BROTHERS PUBLISHERS   MFE 3   2.95

NINETY-FIVE FOLK SONGS AND DANCES FOR PIANO
WARNER BROTHERS PUBLISHERS   MFE 28   1.95

ONE HUNDRED FIVE EASY PIANO PIECES
THE BIG THREE MUSIC CORPORATION   02.95

ONE HUNDRED NINETY CHILDREN'S SONGS
THE BIG THREE MUSIC CORPORATION   02.95

ONE HUNDRED OF THE GREATEST ROCK AND ROLL HITS
THE BIG THREE MUSIC CORPORATION   05.95

ONE HUNDRED SEVENTY CHRISTMAS SONGS AND CAROLS
THE BIG THREE MUSIC CORPORATION   04.95
3-6
OUVERTUREN-ALBUM, BAND 01
SCHOTT   354   4.25
3-6
OUVERTUREN-ALBUM, BAND 02
SCHOTT   355   4.25
3-6
OUVERTUREN-ALBUM, BAND 03
SCHOTT   356   4.25
M
OVERTURES, VOL. 1
C. F. PETERS CORPORATION   1946   4.50
M
OVERTURES, VOL. 2
C. F. PETERS CORPORATION   1947   4.50
M
OVERTURES, VOL. 3
C. F. PETERS CORPORATION   1948   4.50
M
OVERTURES, VOL. 4
C. F. PETERS CORPORATION   1949   4.50
M
OVERTURES, VOL. 5
C. F. PETERS CORPORATION   4940   4.50

PETER, PAUL AND MOMMY, EASY BIG NOTE PIANO
WARNER BROTHERS PUBLISHERS   PPM 26   1.95

PETITS VIETUOSES, LES - SIXTY SHORT TRANSCRIPTIONS IN 4 BKS, BK.
2
FRANCO COLOMBO PUBLICATIONS   SAL   1.50

PETITS VIRTUOSES, LES - SIXTY SHORT TRANSCRIPTIONS IN 4 BKS, BK.
1
FRANCO COLOMBO PUBLICATIONS   SAL   1.50

PETITS VIRTUOSES, LES - SIXTY SHORT TRANSCRIPTIONS IN 4 BKS, BK.
3
FRANCO COLOMBO PUBLICATIONS   SAL   1.50

PETITS VIRTUOSES, LES - SIXTY SHORT TRANSCRIPTIONS IN 4 BKS, BK.
4
FRANCO COLOMBO PUBLICATIONS   SAL   1.50

PIANISTES DE L'AVENIR, LES - 36 SHORT TRANSCRIPTIONS IN 3 BKS,
BK. 1
FRANCO COLOMBO PUBLICATIONS   SAL   1.50

PIANISTES DE L'AVENIR, LES - 36 SHORT TRANSCRIPTIONS IN 3 BKS,
BK. 2
FRANCO COLOMBO PUBLICATIONS   SAL   1.50

PIANISTES DE L'AVENIR, LES - 36 SHORT TRANSCRIPTIONS IN 3 BKS,
BK. 3
FRANCO COLOMBO PUBLICATIONS   SAL   1.50

PIANO HYMN VOLUNTARIES. NOS 1, 2, AND 3
LORENZ PUBLISHING COMPANY   2.50

PIANO PIECES FOR THE YOUNG STUDENT
MUSIC SALES CORPORATION   020080   2.95

PIANO PIECES THE WHOLE WORLD PLAYS
MUSIC SALES CORPORATION   010000   2.95
E
PIANO PLAYTIME, BK A
WILLIS MUSIC COMPANY   .80
AE
PIANO PLAYTIME, BK B
WILLIS MUSIC COMPANY   .80
AI
PIANO PLAYTIME, BK C
WILLIS MUSIC COMPANY   .80
AI
PIANO PLAYTIME, BK D
WILLIS MUSIC COMPANY   .80
A
PIANO PLAYTIME, BK E
WILLIS MUSIC COMPANY   .80

PLAYING PLEASURE
EDWARD B. MARKS MUSIC CORPORATION   01.25

POINTER LIBRARY - MEMORIES OF CHRISTMAS
POINTER PUBLICATIONS   2.95

POINTER SYSTEM - CAROLS
POINTER PUBLICATIONS   1.50

POINTER SYSTEM - FAVORITE SONGS
POINTER PUBLICATIONS   1.50

POINTER SYSTEM - FOLK SONGS
POINTER PUBLICATIONS   1.50

POINTER SYSTEM - GAY NINETIES
POINTER PUBLICATIONS   1.50

POINTER SYSTEM - HOLIDAYS IN SONG
POINTER PUBLICATIONS   1.50

POINTER SYSTEM - HYMNS
POINTER PUBLICATIONS   1.50

POINTER SYSTEM - LATIN MOODS
POINTER PUBLICATIONS   1.50

POINTER SYSTEM - SONGS OF MANY LANDS
POINTER PUBLICATIONS   1.50

POINTER SYSTEM - SONGS THAT LIVE FOREVER
POINTER PUBLICATIONS   1.50

POINTER SYSTEM - SONG MEMORIES
POINTER PUBLICATIONS   1.50

PROGRESSIVE PIANO PIECES
MUSIC SALES CORPORATION   020068   2.95
ALKAN,
RIGAUDONS DES PETITS VIOLONS ET HARTBOIS DE LOUIS XIV
MUSICA OBSCURA   1.50

ROBBINS FOLIO OF POPULAR MARCHES,THE
THE BIG THREE MUSIC CORPORATION   01.95
EASY
ROMANTIC ERA PIANO MUSIC
MEL BAY PUBLICATIONS, INC.   2.00

SELECTED SONATAS FOR PIANO
MUSIC SALES CORPORATION   020073   2.95

SELECTIONS FROM SIX FAVORITE OPERAS
G. SCHIRMER, INC.   L1638   4.00

SENSATIONAL 70 FOR THE 70'S, THE
SCREEN GEMS - COLUMBIA PUBLICATIONS   F0050P1   5.95

SEVENTY-FIVE FAMOUS PIANO PIECES
THE BIG THREE MUSIC CORPORATION   02.95

SIXTY-EIGHT GREATEST COUNTRY HITS, MAMMOTH COLLECTION NO. 27
THE BIG THREE MUSIC CORPORATION   04.95
2
SOMEBODY'S KNOCKIN' AT YOUR DOOR
CENTURY MUSIC PUBLISHING COMPANY, INC.   3833   .40
2
SOMETIMES I FEEL LIKE A MOTHERLESS CHILD
CENTURY MUSIC PUBLISHING COMPANY, INC.   3834   .40
LANE, J.
SONGMAN
THE BIG THREE MUSIC CORPORATION   00.85

SONGS FROM 'THE WORLD IS A GHETTO'
THE BIG THREE MUSIC CORPORATION   03.50

SONGS OF HOPE AND INSPIRATION
THE BIG THREE MUSIC CORPORATION   01.50

SONGS OF THE SPIRIT - EASY HYMN ARRANGEMENTS FOR PIANO
LORENZ PUBLISHING COMPANY   2.00

SPANISH AND LATIN AMERICAN SONGS AND DANCES
MUSIC SALES CORPORATION   020093   2.95

STAR - EASY PIANO
WARNER BROTHERS PUBLISHERS   1.95
3
SWING LOW, 21 SONGS UND EVERGREENS FUR KLAVIER UND GESANG
SCHOTT   4820   3.75

THOSE WONDERFUL YEARS 1900-1920
THE BIG THREE MUSIC CORPORATION   05.95

TIGER RAG
THE BIG THREE MUSIC CORPORATION   00.95

TODAY'S BIG COUNTRY HITS, BK. 5
THE BIG THREE MUSIC CORPORATION   02.50

TODAY'S POP SCENE, BK. 1
THE BIG THREE MUSIC CORPORATION   02.95

TOMPALL AND THE GLAZER BROTHERS
THE BIG THREE MUSIC CORPORATION   02.95

TOP HITS OF 1972
THE BIG THREE MUSIC CORPORATION   03.50

TRACY'S THEME
TRO SONGWAYS SERVICE, INC.   2057

Popular Music

ADAMSON *				
AS THE GIRLS GO				
SAM FOX PUBLISHING COMPANY, INC.				1.50
ADAMS				
FOLK ROCK				
BELWIN-MILLS PUBLISHING CORPORATION				1.25
ADDRISI	NEALE, J.	EASY		
NEVER MY LOVE				
WARNER BROTHERS PUBLISHERS				.75
ADLER, R. *		EASY		
HITS FROM 'DAMN YANKEES'				
FRANK MUSIC CORPORATION				1.25
ADLER, R. *				
PAJAMA GAME, THE				
FRANK MUSIC CORPORATION				1.25
ADLER, R. *	PACE, R.	EASY		
SONGS FROM 'THE PAJAMA GAME'				
FRANK MUSIC CORPORATION				1.25
AGAY, D.--ED	AGAY, D.			
BOOGIE AND BLUES				
MUSIC SALES CORPORATION			080056	.85
AGAY, D.--ED	AGAY, D.	A		
BROADWAY CLASSICS FOR PIANO, BK. 1				
WARNER BROTHERS PUBLISHERS			YPL 3	1.50
AGAY, D.--ED	AGAY, D.	B		
BROADWAY CLASSICS FOR PIANO, BK. 2				
WARNER BROTHERS PUBLISHERS			YPL 3	1.50
AGAY, D.--ED	AGAY, D.	C		
BROADWAY CLASSICS FOR PIANO, BK. 3				
WARNER BROTHERS PUBLISHERS			YPL 3	1.50
AGAY, D.--ED	AGAY, D.	A		
BROADWAY SHOWCASE OF FAMOUS MELODIES, BK. 1				
WARNER BROTHERS PUBLISHERS			YPL 9	1.50
AGAY, D.--ED	AGAY, D.	B		
BROADWAY SHOWCASE OF FAMOUS MELODIES, BK. 2				
WARNER BROTHERS PUBLISHERS			YPL 9	1.50
AGAY, D.--ED	AGAY, D.	C		
BROADWAY SHOWCASE OF FAMOUS MELODIES, BK. 3				
WARNER BROTHERS PUBLISHERS			YPL 9	1.50
AGAY, D.--ED	AGAY, D.			
CURTAIN TIME - MELODIES FROM THE MODERN THEATRE				
FRANK MUSIC CORPORATION				2.00
AGAY, D.--ED	AGAY, D.			
FROM RAGTIME TO ROCK AND ROLL				
SAM FOX PUBLISHING COMPANY, INC.				1.50
AGAY, D.--ED	AGAY, D.			
JAZZ SOLOS				
MUSIC SALES CORPORATION			080058	.85
AGAY, D.--ED	AGAY, D.			
JOY OF BOOGIE AND BLUES, THE				
MUSIC SALES CORPORATION			080010	1.75
AGAY, D.--ED	AGAY, D.	EASY		
MATINEE MELODIES				
FRANK MUSIC CORPORATION				1.50
AGAY, D.--ED	AGAY, D.			
POPULAR CHOICE -- PIANO TEACHING PIECES				
MCA MUSIC				3.95
AGAY, D.--ED	AGAY, D.	A		
POPULAR RECITAL PIECES FOR PIANO, BK. 1				
WARNER BROTHERS PUBLISHERS			YPL 4	1.50
AGAY, D.--ED	AGAY, D.			
POPULAR RECITAL PIECES FOR PIANO, BK. 2				
WARNER BROTHERS PUBLISHERS			YPL 4	1.50
AGAY, D.--ED	AGAY, D.	C		
POPULAR RECITAL PIECES FOR PIANO, BK. 3				
WARNER BROTHERS PUBLISHERS			YPL 3	1.50
AGAY, D.--ED	AGAY, D.			
POP CONCERT				
MUSIC SALES CORPORATION			080053	.85
AGAY, D.--ED	AGAY, D.			
PRESSER PIANO 'POPS' -- FAVORITE HIT MELODIES OLD AND NEW NO. 1				
THEODORE PRESSER COMPANY				1.00
AGAY, D.--ED	AGAY, D.			
PRESSER PIANO 'POPS' -- FAVORITE HIT MELODIES OLD AND NEW NO. 2				
THEODORE PRESSER COMPANY				1.00
AGAY, D.--ED.	AGAY, D.			
PRESSER PIANO 'POPS' -- FAVORITE HIT MELODIES OLD AND NEW NO. 3				
THEODORE PRESSER COMPANY				1.00
AGAY, D.--ED	AGAY, D.			
PRESSER PIANO 'POPS' -- FAVORITE HIT MELODIES OLD AND NEW NO. 4				
THEODORE PRESSER COMPANY				1.00
AGAY, D.--ED	AGAY, D.			
PRESSER PIANO 'POPS' -- FAVORITE HIT MELODIES OLD AND NEW NO. 5				
THEODORE PRESSER COMPANY				1.00
AGAY, D.--ED	AGAY, D.			
THIRTY-THREE HITS FROM BROADWAY				
FRANK MUSIC CORPORATION				2.50
AGAY, D.--ED	AGAY, D.			
THIRTY-TWO MORE HITS FROM BROADWAY				
FRANK MUSIC CORPORATION				2.50
AKST *				
WHO SAID DREAMS DON'T COME TRUE				
MCA MUSIC				1.00
ALBAM				
JAZZ MAG RAG, THE.				
MCA MUSIC				1.00
ALLEN				
SIESTA AT THE FIESTA				
MCA MUSIC				1.00
ALTER, L.				
CANDLE IN THE WIND				
THE BIG THREE MUSIC CORPORATION				00.95
ALTER, L.				
MANHATTAN NOONLIGHT				
THE BIG THREE MUSIC CORPORATION				00.95
ALTER, L.				
MANHATTAN SERENADE				
THE BIG THREE MUSIC CORPORATION				00.95
ALTER, L.				
METROPOLITAN NOCTURNE				
THE BIG THREE MUSIC CORPORATION				00.95
AMMONS				
BASS GONE CRAZY				
MCA MUSIC				1.00
AMMONS				
BLUEBIRD BOOGIE WOOGIE				
MCA MUSIC				1.00
AMMONS				
BLUEBIRD BOOGIE WOOGIE				
MCA MUSIC				1.00

AMMONS				
BOOGIE WOOGIE STOMP				
MCA MUSIC				1.00
AMMONS				
CHICAGO ON MY MIND				
MCA MUSIC				1.00
AMMONS				
FIVE BOOGIE WOOGIE PIANO SOLOS				
MCA MUSIC				1.00
AMMONS *				
MOVIN' THE BOOGIE				
MCA MUSIC				1.00
AMMONS *				
PINE CREEK				
MCA MUSIC				1.00
AMMONS *				
SIXTH AVENUE EXPRESS				
MCA MUSIC				1.00
AMMONS *				
SIXTH AVENUE EXPRESS				
MCA MUSIC				1.00
AMMONS *				
WALKIN' THE BOOGIE				
MCA MUSIC				1.00
AMRAM				
THEMES FROM 'J.B.'				
FRANK MUSIC CORPORATION				.95
ANDERSON, L.	KING, S.			
SYNCOPATED CLOCK, THE -- SIMP.				
BELWIN-MILLS PUBLISHING CORPORATION			26037	.75
ANDERSON *				
HOOTIE'S IGNORANT OIL				
MCA MUSIC				1.00
ARLEN, H.	WALTER			
BLUES IN THE NIGHT				
WARNER BROTHERS PUBLISHERS				1.00
ARLEN, H.	RICHTER	FIRST YEAR		
I LOVE A PARADE				
WARNER BROTHERS PUBLISHERS				.75
ARLEN *				
OVER THE RAINBOW				
THE BIG THREE MUSIC CORPORATION				00.95
ARMBRUSTER				
NATIONAL VELVET - THEME				
THE BIG THREE MUSIC CORPORATION				00.95
ARNOLD *				
RIVER KWAI MARCH, THE				
SHAPIRO, BERNSTEIN ORGANIZATION				.95
ATKINS	MAXTED			
HEELIE JEEBIE				
MCA MUSIC				1.00
ATKINS	MAXTED			
I WANT A BIG BUTTER AND EGG MAN				
MCA MUSIC				1.00
BACH, J.S.	PARKER, T.			
JOY				
THE BIG THREE MUSIC CORPORATION				00.95
BAEZ, J.				
AMERICAN BALLADS AND FOLKSONGS				
MUSIC SALES CORPORATION			040974	2.95
BAEZ, J.				
BRITISH BALLADS AND FOLK SONGS				
MUSIC SALES CORPORATION			040975	2.95
BAEZ, J.				
JOAN BAEZ SONGBOOK, THE				
MUSIC SALES CORPORATION			040973	4.95
BAEZ, J.				
NOEL				
MUSIC SALES CORPORATION			040976	2.95
BAEZ, J.				
SONGS FOR OUR TIMES				
MUSIC SALES CORPORATION			040972	2.95
BAGLEY, E.				
NATIONAL EMBLEM MARCH				
THE BIG THREE MUSIC CORPORATION				00.95
BALKE, C.				
BLUE CLASSIQUE				
MCA MUSIC				1.00
BARNES, B.				
DAINTY DOLL				
THE BIG THREE MUSIC CORPORATION				00.95
BARNES, B.				
DAINTY MISS				
THE BIG THREE MUSIC CORPORATION				00.95
BARRY				
LOVE THEME FROM 'MARY, QUEEN OF SCOTS'				
MCA MUSIC				1.00
BARRY				
MAN ALONE, A				
MCA MUSIC				1.00
BARRY				
THEME FROM THE PERSUADERS				
WARNER BROTHERS PUBLISHERS				1.00
BART	GREEN			
OLIVER - EASY PIANO				
TRO SONGWAYS SERVICE, INC.				1.95
BART	GREEN			
OLIVER - PIANO SELECTIONS				
TRO SONGWAYS SERVICE, INC.				1.95
BASIE				
ONE O'CLOCK JUMP				
THE BIG THREE MUSIC CORPORATION				00.95
BASTIEN--ED.	BASTIEN			
POP, ROCK 'N BLUES, BK. 1				
NEIL A. KJOS MUSIC COMPANY			37	1.25
BASTIEN--ED.	BASTIEN			
POP, ROCK 'N BLUES, BK. 2				
NEIL A. KJOS MUSIC COMPANY			38	1.25
BASTIEN--ED.	BASTIEN			
POP, ROCK 'N BLUES, BK. 3				
NEIL A. KJOS MUSIC COMPANY			39	1.25
BASTIEN--ED.	BASTIEN			
ROCK 'N BLUES FOR FUN				
NEIL A. KJOS MUSIC COMPANY			56	1.25
BAUDUC *				
SOUTH RAMPART STREET PARADE				
THE BIG THREE MUSIC CORPORATION				00.95
BEAULIEU				
JUNGLE RHUMBA				
MCA MUSIC				1.00
BECAUD *	NEALE, J.	EASY		
WHAT NOW MY LOVE				
WARNER BROTHERS PUBLISHERS				.75
BECAUD	DAVIS, J. R.	FIRST YEAR		
WHAT NOW MY LOVE				
WARNER BROTHERS PUBLISHERS				.75

BECHET
  PAY OFF, THE
    MCA MUSIC   1.00
BEIDERBECKE, B.
  DAVENPORT BLUES
    THE BIG THREE MUSIC CORPORATION   00.95
BEIDERBECKE, B.
  IN A MIST
    THE BIG THREE MUSIC CORPORATION   00.95
BELL, W.--ARR.   BELL, W.   EASY
  JUST FOR FUN - HIT TUNES EVERYBODY KNOWS
    SCREEN GEMS - COLUMBIA PUBLICATIONS   F0126P4   1.95
BELL, W.--ARR.   BELL, W.   EASY
  JUST FOR FUN - POPS EVERYBODY KNOWS
    SCREEN GEMS - COLUMBIA PUBLICATIONS   F0081P4   1.50
BELL, W.--ARR.   BELL, W.   EASY
  JUST FOR FUN - SHOW TUNES EVERYBODY KNOWS
    SCREEN GEMS - COLUMBIA PUBLICATIONS   F0107P4   1.95
BERLIN, I.
  POINTER LIBRARY - WORDS AND MUSIC BY IRVING BERLIN, VOL. 1
    POINTER PUBLICATIONS   2.95
BERLIN, I.
  POINTER LIBRARY - WORDS AND MUSIC BY IRVING BERLIN, VOL. 2
    POINTER PUBLICATIONS   2.95
BERMONT, H.--ED   BERMONT, H.
  TUNEFUL VARIETIES, BK. 1
    MUSICORD PUBLICATIONS, INC.   1.25
BERMONT, H.--ED   BERMONT, H.
  TUNEFUL VARIETIES, BK. 2
    MUSICORD PUBLICATIONS, INC.   1.25
BERMONT, H.--ED   BERMONT, H.
  TWENTY-EIGHT STAR MELODIES, BK. 1
    MUSICORD PUBLICATIONS, INC.   1.25
BERMONT, H.--ED   BERMONT, H.
  YOUR HIT TUNES - GREEN BOOK
    MUSICORD PUBLICATIONS, INC.   1.25
BERMONT, H.--ED   BERMONT, H.
  YOUR HIT TUNES - RED BOOK
    MUSICORD PUBLICATIONS, INC.   1.25
BERMONT, H.
  ANYONE CAN PLAY PIANO
    MUSICORD PUBLICATIONS, INC.   2.00
BERMONT, H.
  PLAY POPULAR - BE POPULAR
    MUSICORD PUBLICATIONS, INC.   2.00
BERNSTEIN, E.
  FROM THE TERRACE
    THE BIG THREE MUSIC CORPORATION   00.95
BERNSTEIN, L.   SINGER
  MARIA, FROM 'WEST SIDE STORY'
    G. SCHIRMER, INC.   .60
BERNSTEIN, L.   SINGER
  TONIGHT, FROM 'WEST SIDE STORY'
    G. SCHIRMER, INC.   .60
BERNSTEIN, L.
  WEST SIDE STORY, SELECTIONS FROM
    G. SCHIRMER, INC.   1.50
BERNSTEIN, L.   STICKLES
  WEST SIDE STORY, SELECTIONS FROM
    G. SCHIRMER, INC.   1.25
BERRILL, R.
  LOVE MAKES THE WORLD GO 'ROUND
    THE BIG THREE MUSIC CORPORATION   00.95
BIGELOW, F.
  OUR DIRECTOR MARCH
    THE BIG THREE MUSIC CORPORATION   00.95
BINKLEY
  BOOGIE ETUDE
    SAM FOX PUBLISHING COMPANY, INC.   .50
BISHOP *
  WOODCHOPPER'S BALL
    MCA MUSIC   1.00
BIVENS *
  JOSEPHINE
    THE BIG THREE MUSIC CORPORATION   00.95
BLANC
  STALACTITE
    MCA MUSIC   1.00
BOCAGE *   MAXTED
  MAM'S GONE, GOODBYE
    MCA MUSIC   1.00
BOLCOM, W.
  SEABISCUITS
    EDWARD B. MARKS MUSIC CORPORATION   01.25
BONNEL *
  TURKEY IN THE STRAW
    THE BIG THREE MUSIC CORPORATION   00.95
BONO   NEALE, J.   EASY
  BEAT GOES ON, THE
    WARNER BROTHERS PUBLISHERS   .75
BOTSFORD, G.
  BLACK AND WHITE RAG
    WARNER BROTHERS PUBLISHERS   1.00
BOWMAN *
  TWELFTH STREET RAG
    SHAPIRO, BERNSTEIN ORGANIZATION   .95
BOWMAN *
  TWELFTH STREET RAG
    SHAPIRO, BERNSTEIN ORGANIZATION   .95
BOWMAN *
  TWELFTH STREET RAG
    SHAPIRO, BERNSTEIN ORGANIZATION   .95
BOWMAN *
  TWELFTH STREET RAG
    SHAPIRO, BERNSTEIN ORGANIZATION   .95
BOWN
  G'WON TRAIN
    MCA MUSIC   1.00
BOWN
  HEAD SHAKIN'
    MCA MUSIC   1.00
BRADLEY, R.--ARR.   BRADLEY, R.   EASY
  ABRAHAM, MARTIN AND JOHN
    SCREEN GEMS - COLUMBIA PUBLICATIONS   0403AP2   .85
BRADLEY, R.--ARR.   BRADLEY, R.   EASY
  ALLEY CAT
    SCREEN GEMS - COLUMBIA PUBLICATIONS   3733AP2   .85
BRADLEY, R.--ARR.   BRADLEY, R.   BIG NOTE EASY
  AMAZING GRACE - AND - HE'S GOT THE WHOLE WORLD IN HIS HANDS
    SCREEN GEMS - COLUMBIA PUBLICATIONS   C0019P3   1.00
BRADLEY, R.--ARR.   BRADLEY, R.   EASY
  AM I LOSING YOU
    SCREEN GEMS - COLUMBIA PUBLICATIONS   4002AP2   .85
BRADLEY, R.--ARR.   BRADLEY, R.   EASY
  ARE YOU LONESOME TONIGHT
    SCREEN GEMS - COLUMBIA PUBLICATIONS   5703AP2   .85

BRADLEY, R.--ARR.   BRADLEY, R.   EASY
  AUBREY
    SCREEN GEMS - COLUMBIA PUBLICATIONS   6704AP2   .85
BRADLEY, R.--ARR.   BRADLEY, R.   EASY
  BABY DON'T GET HOOKED ON ME
    SCREEN GEMS - COLUMBIA PUBLICATIONS   0010BP2   .85
BRADLEY, R.--ARR.   BRADLEY, R.   EASY
  BABY I'M-A WANT YOU
    SCREEN GEMS - COLUMBIA PUBLICATIONS   0003BP2   .85
BRADLEY, R.--ARR.   BRADLEY, R.   EASY
  BACK TO CALIFORNIA
    SCREEN GEMS - COLUMBIA PUBLICATIONS   0004BP2   .85
BRADLEY, R.--ARR.   BRADLEY, R.   EASY
  BEAUTIFUL CITY
    SCREEN GEMS - COLUMBIA PUBLICATIONS   1430BP2   .85
BRADLEY, R.--ARR.   BRADLEY, R.   EASY
  BEEN TO CANAAN
    SCREEN GEMS - COLUMBIA PUBLICATIONS   1423BP2   .85
BRADLEY, R.--ARR.   BRADLEY, R.   EASY
  BEN
    SCREEN GEMS - COLUMBIA PUBLICATIONS   1443BP2   .85
BRADLEY, R.--ARR.   BRADLEY, R.   BIG NOTE EASY
  BLACK AND WHITE - AND - BRIAN'S SONG
    SCREEN GEMS - COLUMBIA PUBLICATIONS   C0015P3   1.00
BRADLEY, R.--ARR.   BRADLEY, R.   EASY
  BLACK AND WHITE
    SCREEN GEMS - COLUMBIA PUBLICATIONS   3712BP2   .85
BRADLEY, R.--ARR.   BRADLEY, R.   EASY
  BLESS THE BEASTS AND CHILDREN
    SCREEN GEMS - COLUMBIA PUBLICATIONS   3702BP2   .85
BRADLEY, R.--ARR.   BRADLEY, R.   BIG NOTE EASY
  BORN FREE
    SCREEN GEMS - COLUMBIA PUBLICATIONS   4701BP3   .85
BRADLEY, R.--ARR.   BRADLEY, R.   INTERMEDIATE
  BORN FREE
    SCREEN GEMS - COLUMBIA PUBLICATIONS   4701BP   1.00
BRADLEY, R.--ARR.   BRADLEY, R.   EASY
  BORN FREE
    SCREEN GEMS - COLUMBIA PUBLICATIONS   4701BP2   .85
BRADLEY, R.--ARR.   BRADLEY, R.   EASY
  BRADLEY'S BEST OF THE BEST - BREAD
    SCREEN GEMS - COLUMBIA PUBLICATIONS   F0108P2   1.75
BRADLEY, R.--ARR.   BRADLEY, R.   EASY
  BRADLEY'S BEST OF THE BEST - BROADWAY
    SCREEN GEMS - COLUMBIA PUBLICATIONS   F0077P2   1.75
BRADLEY, R.--ARR.   BRADLEY, R.   EASY
  BRADLEY'S BEST OF THE BEST - CAROLE KING
    SCREEN GEMS - COLUMBIA PUBLICATIONS   F0027P2A   1.75
BRADLEY, R.--ARR.   BRADLEY, R.   EASY
  BRADLEY'S BEST OF THE BEST - COUNTRY HITS
    SCREEN GEMS - COLUMBIA PUBLICATIONS   F0029P2   1.50
BRADLEY, R.--ARR.   BRADLEY, R.   EASY
  BRADLEY'S BEST OF THE BEST - MOTION PICTURE HITS
    SCREEN GEMS - COLUMBIA PUBLICATIONS   F0037P2   1.50
BRADLEY, R.--ARR.   BRADLEY, R.   EASY
  BRADLEY'S BEST OF THE BEST - POP TEACHING PIECES
    SCREEN GEMS - COLUMBIA PUBLICATIONS   F0230P2   1.75
BRADLEY, R.--ARR.   BRADLEY, R.   EASY
  BRADLEY'S COUNTRY JOY - ISSUE NO. 1
    SCREEN GEMS - COLUMBIA PUBLICATIONS   F0189P2   1.50
BRADLEY, R.--ARR.   BRADLEY, R.   EASY
  BRADLEY'S POPULAR JOY - ISSUE NO. 1
    SCREEN GEMS - COLUMBIA PUBLICATIONS   F0128P2   1.50
BRADLEY, R.--ARR.   BRADLEY, R.   EASY
  BRADLEY'S POPULAR JOY - ISSUE NO. 2
    SCREEN GEMS - COLUMBIA PUBLICATIONS   F0187P2   1.50
BRADLEY, R.--ARR.   BRADLEY, R.   EASY
  BRADLEY'S POPULAR JOY - ISSUE NO. 3
    SCREEN GEMS - COLUMBIA PUBLICATIONS   F0216P2   1.50
BRADLEY, R.--ARR.   BRADLEY, R.   EASY
  BRADLEY'S POPULAR JOY - ISSUE NO. 4
    SCREEN GEMS - COLUMBIA PUBLICATIONS   F0261P2   1.50
BRADLEY, R.--ARR.   BRADLEY, R.   EASY
  BRADLEY'S SUPERSTARS
    SCREEN GEMS - COLUMBIA PUBLICATIONS   F0223P2   2.50
BRADLEY, R.--ARR.   BRADLEY, R.   EASY
  BRADLEY'S SUPER POPULAR MUSIC
    SCREEN GEMS - COLUMBIA PUBLICATIONS   F0016P2   2.50
BRADLEY, R.--ARR.   BRADLEY, R.   EASY
  BRADLEY - LIKE IT IS TODAY - EASY PIANO HIT PARADE NO. 1
    SCREEN GEMS - COLUMBIA PUBLICATIONS   F0025P2   1.25
BRADLEY, R.--ARR.   BRADLEY, R.   EASY
  BRADLEY - LIKE IT IS TODAY - EASY PIANO HIT PARADE NO. 2
    SCREEN GEMS - COLUMBIA PUBLICATIONS   F0051P2   1.50
BRADLEY, R.--ARR.   BRADLEY, R.   EASY
  BRADLEY - LIKE IT IS TODAY - EASY PIANO HIT PARADE NO. 3
    SCREEN GEMS - COLUMBIA PUBLICATIONS   F0075P2   1.75
BRADLEY, R.--ARR.   BRADLEY, R.   EASY
  BRADLEY - LIKE IT IS TODAY - EASY PIANO HIT PARADE NO. 4
    SCREEN GEMS - COLUMBIA PUBLICATIONS   F0100P2   1.75
BRADLEY, R.--ARR.   BRADLEY, R.   BIG NOTE EASY
  BREAKING UP IS HARD TO DO
    SCREEN GEMS - COLUMBIA PUBLICATIONS   5701BP2   .85
BRADLEY, R.--ARR.   BRADLEY, R.   EASY
  BRIAN'S SONG
    SCREEN GEMS - COLUMBIA PUBLICATIONS   5707BP3   .85
BRADLEY, R.--ARR.   BRADLEY, R.   EASY
  BRIAN'S SONG
    SCREEN GEMS - COLUMBIA PUBLICATIONS   5707BP2   .85
BRADLEY, R.--ARR.   BRADLEY, R.   BIG NOTE EASY
  BY THE TIME I GET TO PHOENIX
    SCREEN GEMS - COLUMBIA PUBLICATIONS   8002BP2   .85
BRADLEY, R.--ARR.   BRADLEY, R.   BIG NOTE EASY
  CANDY MAN, THE - AND - BORN FREE
    SCREEN GEMS - COLUMBIA PUBLICATIONS   C0016P3   1.00
BRADLEY, R.--ARR.   BRADLEY, R.   BIG NOTE EASY
  CANDY MAN, THE
    SCREEN GEMS - COLUMBIA PUBLICATIONS   0007CP3   .85
BRADLEY, R.--ARR.   BRADLEY, R.   EASY
  CANDY MAN, THE
    SCREEN GEMS - COLUMBIA PUBLICATIONS   0007CP2   .85
BRADLEY, R.--ARR.   BRADLEY, R.   EASY
  CHERISH
    SCREEN GEMS - COLUMBIA PUBLICATIONS   2406CP2   .85
BRADLEY, R.--ARR.   BRADLEY, R.   EASY
  CLOUDS
    SCREEN GEMS - COLUMBIA PUBLICATIONS   3709CP2   .85
BRADLEY, R.--ARR.   BRADLEY, R.   EASY
  COUNTRY POPS
    SCREEN GEMS - COLUMBIA PUBLICATIONS   F0244P2   2.95
BRADLEY, R.--ARR.   BRADLEY, R.   EASY
  DAY BY DAY
    SCREEN GEMS - COLUMBIA PUBLICATIONS   0014DP2   .85
BRADLEY, R.--ARR.   BRADLEY, R.   EASY
  DIARY
    SCREEN GEMS - COLUMBIA PUBLICATIONS   2705DP2   .85

BRADLEY, R.--ARR.   BRADLEY, R.   EASY
  DON'T IT MAKE YOU WANTA GO HOME
        SCREEN GEMS - COLUMBIA PUBLICATIONS   4706DP2   .85
BRADLEY, R.--ARR.   BRADLEY, R.   EASY
  EVERYTHING I OWN
        SCREEN GEMS - COLUMBIA PUBLICATIONS   7007EP2   .85
BRADLEY, R.--ARR.   BRADLEY, R.   EASY
  FIRST TIME EVER I SAW YOUR FACE, THE
        SCREEN GEMS - COLUMBIA PUBLICATIONS   2703FP2   .85
BRADLEY, R.--ARR.   BRADLEY, R.   EASY
  FOR ONCE IN MY LIFE
        SCREEN GEMS - COLUMBIA PUBLICATIONS   4717FP2   .85
BRADLEY, R.--ARR.   BRADLEY, R.   EASY
  FUNNY FACE
        SCREEN GEMS - COLUMBIA PUBLICATIONS   6706FP2   .85
BRADLEY, R.--ARR.   BRADLEY, R.   EASY
  GOING OUT OF MY HEAD
        SCREEN GEMS - COLUMBIA PUBLICATIONS   4717GP2   .85
BRADLEY, R.--ARR.   BRADLEY, R.   EASY
  GO AWAY LITTLE GIRL
        SCREEN GEMS - COLUMBIA PUBLICATIONS   4702GP2   .85
BRADLEY, R.--ARR.   BRADLEY, R.   EASY
  GREEN GREEN GRASS OF HOME
        SCREEN GEMS - COLUMBIA PUBLICATIONS   5702GP2   .85
BRADLEY, R.--ARR.   BRADLEY, R.   EASY
  GUITAR MAN, THE
        SCREEN GEMS - COLUMBIA PUBLICATIONS   6704GP2   .85
BRADLEY, R.--ARR.   BRADLEY, R.   EASY
  HANDS OF TIME, THE
        SCREEN GEMS - COLUMBIA PUBLICATIONS   0011HP2   .85
BRADLEY, R.--ARR.   BRADLEY, R.   EASY
  HAPPIEST GIRL IN THE WHOLE U.S.A., THE
        SCREEN GEMS - COLUMBIA PUBLICATIONS   0014HP2   .85
BRADLEY, R.--ARR.   BRADLEY, R.   EASY
  HAVA NAGILA
        SCREEN GEMS - COLUMBIA PUBLICATIONS   0026HP2   .85
BRADLEY, R.--ARR.   BRADLEY, R.   EASY
  HEY, GIRL
        SCREEN GEMS - COLUMBIA PUBLICATIONS   1402HP2   .85
BRADLEY, R.--ARR.   BRADLEY, R.   EASY
  HI-DE-HO --THAT OLD SWEET ROLL--
        SCREEN GEMS - COLUMBIA PUBLICATIONS   2701HP2   .85
BRADLEY, R.--ARR.   BRADLEY, R.   EASY
  HOME AGAIN
        SCREEN GEMS - COLUMBIA PUBLICATIONS   4703HP2   .85
BRADLEY, R.--ARR.   BRADLEY, R.   EASY
  HOUSE OF THE RISING SUN, THE
        SCREEN GEMS - COLUMBIA PUBLICATIONS   4701HP2   .85
BRADLEY, R.--ARR.   BRADLEY, R.   EASY
  HURTING EACH OTHER
        SCREEN GEMS - COLUMBIA PUBLICATIONS   6704HP2   .85
BRADLEY, R.--ARR.   BRADLEY, R.   EASY
  IF
        SCREEN GEMS - COLUMBIA PUBLICATIONS   1702IP2   .85
BRADLEY, R.--ARR.   BRADLEY, R.   EASY
  IN TUNE WITH THE TIMES
        SCREEN GEMS - COLUMBIA PUBLICATIONS   F0145P2   2.95
BRADLEY, R.--ARR.   BRADLEY, R.   EASY
  IT'S GOING TO TAKE SOME TIME
        SCREEN GEMS - COLUMBIA PUBLICATIONS   6415IP2   .85
BRADLEY, R.--ARR.   BRADLEY, R.   EASY
  IT'S ONE OF THOSE NIGHTS --YES LOVE--
        SCREEN GEMS - COLUMBIA PUBLICATIONS   6414IP2   .85
BRADLEY, R.--ARR.   BRADLEY, R.   INTERMEDIATE
  IT'S TOO LATE
        SCREEN GEMS - COLUMBIA PUBLICATIONS   64031P   1.00
BRADLEY, R.--ARR.   BRADLEY, R.   EASY
  I BELIEVE IN MUSIC
        SCREEN GEMS - COLUMBIA PUBLICATIONS   0402IP2   .85
BRADLEY, R.--ARR.   BRADLEY, R.   EASY
  I GOT A NAME
        SCREEN GEMS - COLUMBIA PUBLICATIONS   2004IP2   .85
BRADLEY, R.--ARR.   BRADLEY, R.   EASY
  I KNEW YOU WHEN
        SCREEN GEMS - COLUMBIA PUBLICATIONS   3401IP2   .85
BRADLEY, R.--ARR.   BRADLEY, R.   EASY
  I NEVER PROMISED YOU A ROSE GARDEN
        SCREEN GEMS - COLUMBIA PUBLICATIONS   4702RP2   .85
BRADLEY, R.--ARR.   BRADLEY, R.   EASY
  I WILL WAIT FOR YOU
        SCREEN GEMS - COLUMBIA PUBLICATIONS   7408IP2   .85
BRADLEY, R.--ARR.   BRADLEY, R.   EASY
  I WOKE UP IN LOVE THIS MORNING
        SCREEN GEMS - COLUMBIA PUBLICATIONS   7402IP2   .85
BRADLEY, R.--ARR.   BRADLEY, R.   EASY
  JEAN
        SCREEN GEMS - COLUMBIA PUBLICATIONS   1417JP2   .85
BRADLEY, R.--ARR.   BRADLEY, R.   BIG NOTE EASY
  JINGLE BELLS
        SCREEN GEMS - COLUMBIA PUBLICATIONS   2703JP2   .85
BRADLEY, R.--ARR.   BRADLEY, R.   EASY
  JOY TO THE WORLD
        SCREEN GEMS - COLUMBIA PUBLICATIONS   4703JP2   .85
BRADLEY, R.--ARR.   BRADLEY, R.   EASY
  JOY
        SCREEN GEMS - COLUMBIA PUBLICATIONS   4706JP2   .85
BRADLEY, R.--ARR.   BRADLEY, R.   EASY
  KNOCKIN' ON HEAVEN'S DOOR
        SCREEN GEMS - COLUMBIA PUBLICATIONS   4703KP2   .85
BRADLEY, R.--ARR.   BRADLEY, R.   EASY
  L-O-V-E
        SCREEN GEMS - COLUMBIA PUBLICATIONS   4704LP2   .85
BRADLEY, R.--ARR.   BRADLEY, R.   EASY
  LAST TIME I SAW HIM
        SCREEN GEMS - COLUMBIA PUBLICATIONS   0042LP2   .85
BRADLEY, R.--ARR.   BRADLEY, R.   EASY
  LITTLE PEOPLE AMERICA
        SCREEN GEMS - COLUMBIA PUBLICATIONS   2703LP2   .85
BRADLEY, R.--ARR.   BRADLEY, R.   BIG NOTE EASY
  LIVING TOGETHER, GROWING TOGETHER - AND - QUESTION ME AN ANSWER
        SCREEN GEMS - COLUMBIA PUBLICATIONS   C0030P3   1.00
BRADLEY, R.--ARR.   BRADLEY, R.   EASY
  LIVING TOGETHER, GROWING TOGETHER
        SCREEN GEMS - COLUMBIA PUBLICATIONS   2715LP2   .85
BRADLEY, R.--ARR.   BRADLEY, R.   EASY
  LONG-HAIRED LOVER FROM LIVERPOOL
        SCREEN GEMS - COLUMBIA PUBLICATIONS   4728LP2   .85
BRADLEY, R.--ARR.   BRADLEY, R.   EASY
  LOOK OF LOVE, THE
        SCREEN GEMS - COLUMBIA PUBLICATIONS   4703LP2   .85
BRADLEY, R.--ARR.   BRADLEY, R.   INTERMEDIATE
  LOVE MEANS --YOU NEVER HAVE TO SAY YOU'RE SORRY--
        SCREEN GEMS - COLUMBIA PUBLICATIONS   4717LP   1.00
BRADLEY, R.--ARR.   BRADLEY, R.   EASY
  MISTY
        SCREEN GEMS - COLUMBIA PUBLICATIONS   2728MP2   .85

BRADLEY, R.--ARR.   BRADLEY, R.   EASY
  MORNING AFTER, THE
        SCREEN GEMS - COLUMBIA PUBLICATIONS   4723MP2   .85
BRADLEY, R.--ARR.   BRADLEY, R.   EASY
  MOST BEAUTIFUL GIRL, THE
        SCREEN GEMS - COLUMBIA PUBLICATIONS   4722MP2   .85
BRADLEY, R.--ARR.   BRADLEY, R.   EASY
  MOVIE POPS
        SCREEN GEMS - COLUMBIA PUBLICATIONS   F0259P2   2.50
BRADLEY, R.--ARR.   BRADLEY, R.   EASY
  MUSIC
        SCREEN GEMS - COLUMBIA PUBLICATIONS   6701MP2   .85
BRADLEY, R.--ARR.   BRADLEY, R.   EASY
  NEVER BEEN TO SPAIN
        SCREEN GEMS - COLUMBIA PUBLICATIONS   1403NP2   .85
BRADLEY, R.--ARR.   BRADLEY, R.   EASY
  NEVER CAN SAY GOODBYE
        SCREEN GEMS - COLUMBIA PUBLICATIONS   1413NP2   .85
BRADLEY, R.--ARR.   BRADLEY, R.   EASY
  ONE TIN SOLDIER
        SCREEN GEMS - COLUMBIA PUBLICATIONS   4438OP2   .85
BRADLEY, R.--ARR.   BRADLEY, R.   EASY
  PAPER ROSES
        SCREEN GEMS - COLUMBIA PUBLICATIONS   0015PP2   .85
BRADLEY, R.--ARR.   BRADLEY, R.   EASY
  PARTRIDGE FAMILY, THE - AT HOME WITH THEIR GREATEST HITS
        SCREEN GEMS - COLUMBIA PUBLICATIONS   P0036P2   2.50
BRADLEY, R.--ARR.   BRADLEY, R.   EASY
  POPCORN
        SCREEN GEMS - COLUMBIA PUBLICATIONS   4709PP2   .85
BRADLEY, R.--ARR.   BRADLEY, R.   EASY
  POPS MADE EASY FOR PIANO
        SCREEN GEMS - COLUMBIA PUBLICATIONS   F0167P2   2.95
BRADLEY, R.--ARR.   BRADLEY, R.   EASY
  ROCKIN' AROUND THE CHRISTMAS TREE
        SCREEN GEMS - COLUMBIA PUBLICATIONS   4711RP2   .85
BRADLEY, R.--ARR.   BRADLEY, R.   EASY
  ROCK AND ROLL LULLABY
        SCREEN GEMS - COLUMBIA PUBLICATIONS   4705RP2   .85
BRADLEY, R.--ARR.   BRADLEY, R.   EASY
  RUN RUN RUN
        SCREEN GEMS - COLUMBIA PUBLICATIONS   6706RP2   .85
BRADLEY, R.--ARR.   BRADLEY, R.   EASY
  SEATTLE
        SCREEN GEMS - COLUMBIA PUBLICATIONS   1401SP2   .85
BRADLEY, R.--ARR.   BRADLEY, R.   EASY
  SEE YOU IN SEPTEMBER
        SCREEN GEMS - COLUMBIA PUBLICATIONS   1407SP2   .85
BRADLEY, R.--ARR.   BRADLEY, R.   EASY
  SENSATIONAL 70 FOR THE 70'S
        SCREEN GEMS - COLUMBIA PUBLICATIONS   F0050P2A   4.95
BRADLEY, R.--ARR.   BRADLEY, R.   EASY
  SIMON AND GARFUNKEL'S GREATEST HITS
        SCREEN GEMS - COLUMBIA PUBLICATIONS   P0037P2   2.50
BRADLEY, R.--ARR.   BRADLEY, R.   BIG NOTE EASY
  SIMPLY BRADLEY - MOVIE BOOK
        SCREEN GEMS - COLUMBIA PUBLICATIONS   F0095P3   1.50
BRADLEY, R.--ARR.   BRADLEY, R.   BIG NOTE EASY
  SIMPLY BRADLEY - POP BOOK
        SCREEN GEMS - COLUMBIA PUBLICATIONS   F0188P3   1.50
BRADLEY, R.--ARR.   BRADLEY, R.   BIG NOTE EASY
  SIMPLY BRADLEY - SECOND POP BOOK, THE
        SCREEN GEMS - COLUMBIA PUBLICATIONS   F0269P3   1.50
BRADLEY, R.--ARR.   BRADLEY, R.   EASY
  SIMPLY BRADLEY - THE PARTRIDGE FAMILY
        SCREEN GEMS - COLUMBIA PUBLICATIONS   P0018P3   1.50
BRADLEY, R.--ARR.   BRADLEY, R.   EASY
  SIXTY-SEVEN BRADLEY POP TEACHING PIECES FOR PIANO
        SCREEN GEMS - COLUMBIA PUBLICATIONS   F0245P2   4.95
BRADLEY, R.--ARR.   BRADLEY, R.   EASY
  SMILE - HAVE A HAPPY DAY
        SCREEN GEMS - COLUMBIA PUBLICATIONS   4002SP2   .85
BRADLEY, R.--ARR.   BRADLEY, R.   EASY
  SNOOPY'S CHRISTMAS
        SCREEN GEMS - COLUMBIA PUBLICATIONS   4405SP2   .85
BRADLEY, R.--ARR.   BRADLEY, R.   EASY
  SOME KIND OF WONDERFUL
        SCREEN GEMS - COLUMBIA PUBLICATIONS   4702SP2   .85
BRADLEY, R.--ARR.   BRADLEY, R.   EASY
  SONG OF LONG AGO
        SCREEN GEMS - COLUMBIA PUBLICATIONS   4712SP2   .85
BRADLEY, R.--ARR.   BRADLEY, R.   EASY
  SO FAR AWAY
        SCREEN GEMS - COLUMBIA PUBLICATIONS   4703SP2   .85
BRADLEY, R.--ARR.   BRADLEY, R.   EASY
  SPANISH EYES
        SCREEN GEMS - COLUMBIA PUBLICATIONS   5002SP2   .85
BRADLEY, R.--ARR.   BRADLEY, R.   EASY
  SUPER POPULAR MUSIC
        SCREEN GEMS - COLUMBIA PUBLICATIONS   F0042P2   2.50
BRADLEY, R.--ARR.   BRADLEY, R.   EASY
  SUPER 77, THE
        SCREEN GEMS - COLUMBIA PUBLICATIONS   F0199P2   4.95
BRADLEY, R.--ARR.   BRADLEY, R.   EASY
  SWEET SEASONS
        SCREEN GEMS - COLUMBIA PUBLICATIONS   7406SP2   .85
BRADLEY, R.--ARR.   BRADLEY, R.   EASY
  SWEET SURRENDER
        SCREEN GEMS - COLUMBIA PUBLICATIONS   7420SP2   .85
BRADLEY, R.--ARR.   BRADLEY, R.   EASY
  TAPESTRY
        SCREEN GEMS - COLUMBIA PUBLICATIONS   003TP2   .85
BRADLEY, R.--ARR.   BRADLEY, R.   EASY
  THEME FROM NICHOLAS AND ALEXANDRA
        SCREEN GEMS - COLUMBIA PUBLICATIONS   2701NP2   .85
BRADLEY, R.--ARR.   BRADLEY, R.   EASY
  THEME FROM SHAFT
        SCREEN GEMS - COLUMBIA PUBLICATIONS   2422SP2   .85
BRADLEY, R.--ARR.   BRADLEY, R.   EASY
  TOO YOUNG
        SCREEN GEMS - COLUMBIA PUBLICATIONS   4716TP2   .85
BRADLEY, R.--ARR.   BRADLEY, R.   EASY
  TOUCH ME IN THE MORNING
        SCREEN GEMS - COLUMBIA PUBLICATIONS   4738TP2   .85
BRADLEY, R.--ARR.   BRADLEY, R.   EASY
  TRACES
        SCREEN GEMS - COLUMBIA PUBLICATIONS   5701TP2   .85
BRADLEY, R.--ARR.   BRADLEY, R.   EASY
  UP, UP AND AWAY
        SCREEN GEMS - COLUMBIA PUBLICATIONS   5002UP2   .85
BRADLEY, R.--ARR.   BRADLEY, R.   EASY
  WALK A MILE IN MY SHOES
        SCREEN GEMS - COLUMBIA PUBLICATIONS   0005WP2   .85
BRADLEY, R.--ARR.   BRADLEY, R.   EASY
  WAY WE WERE, THE
        SCREEN GEMS - COLUMBIA PUBLICATIONS   0055WP2   .85

BRADLEY, R.--ARR. BRADLEY, R. INTERMEDIATE			
WAY WE WERE, THE			
SCREEN GEMS - COLUMBIA PUBLICATIONS	0055WP	1.00	
BRADLEY, R.--ARR. BRADLEY, R. BIG NOTE EASY			
WAY WE WERE, THE			
SCREEN GEMS - COLUMBIA PUBLICATIONS	0055WP3	.85	
BRADLEY, R.--ARR. BRADLEY, R. EASY			
WHEN YOU SAY LOVE			
SCREEN GEMS - COLUMBIA PUBLICATIONS	2437WP2	.85	
BRADLEY, R.--ARR. BRADLEY, R. EASY			
WHERE IS THE LOVE			
SCREEN GEMS - COLUMBIA PUBLICATIONS	2435WP2	.85	
BRADLEY, R.--ARR. BRADLEY, R. EASY			
WINTER WONDERLAND			
SCREEN GEMS - COLUMBIA PUBLICATIONS	2722WP2	.85	
BRADLEY, R.--ARR. BRADLEY, R. BIG NOTE EASY			
WORLD IS A CIRCLE, THE - AND - REFLECTIONS			
SCREEN GEMS - COLUMBIA PUBLICATIONS	C0031P3	1.00	
BRADLEY, R.--ARR. BRADLEY, R. EASY			
WORLD IS A CIRCLE, THE			
SCREEN GEMS - COLUMBIA PUBLICATIONS	4717WP2	.85	
BRADLEY, R.--ARR. BRADLEY, R. INTERMEDIATE			
YOU'VE GOT A FRIEND			
SCREEN GEMS - COLUMBIA PUBLICATIONS	4702YP	1.00	
BRADLEY, R.--ARR. BRADLEY, R. EASY			
YOU'VE GOT A FRIEND			
SCREEN GEMS - COLUMBIA PUBLICATIONS	4702YP2	.85	
BRADLEY, R.--ARR. BRADLEY, R. EASY			
YOUNG LOVE			
SCREEN GEMS - COLUMBIA PUBLICATIONS	4756YP2	.85	
BRADLEY, R.--ARR. BRADLEY, R. EASY			
YO YO			
SCREEN GEMS - COLUMBIA PUBLICATIONS	4704YP2	.85	
BRAND *			
MIDNIGHT IN MOSCOW --YOU CAN'T KEEP ME FROM LOVING YOU--			
TRO SONGWAYS SERVICE, INC.	2042		
BRATTON			
TEDDY BEARS' PICNIC, THE			
WARNER BROTHERS PUBLISHERS		1.00	
BRATTON MACLACHLAN FIRST YEAR			
TEDDY BEARS' PICNIC, THE			
WARNER BROTHERS PUBLISHERS		.75	
BRICUSSE *			
STOP THE WORLD - I WANT TO GET OFF --EASY PIANO--			
TRO SONGWAYS SERVICE, INC.		1.50	
BRIMHALL, J.--ED. BRIMHALL, J.			
ABRAHAM, MARTIN AND JOHN			
CHARLES HANSEN	35960	.85	
BRIMHALL, J.--ED. BRIMHALL, J.			
ALFIE			
CHARLES HANSEN	F30001	.85	
BRIMHALL, J.--ED. BRIMHALL, J.			
ALL KINDS OF PEOPLE			
CHARLES HANSEN	X30114	.85	
BRIMHALL, J.--ED. BRIMHALL, J.			
ALSO SPRACH ZARATHUSTRA			
CHARLES HANSEN	35979	.85	
BRIMHALL, J.--ED. BRIMHALL, J.			
AMAZING GRACE/HE'S GOT THE WHOLE WORLD IN HIS HANDS			
CHARLES HANSEN	35866	.85	
BRIMHALL, J.--ED. BRIMHALL, J.			
APPLAUSE			
CHARLES HANSEN		.85	
BRIMHALL, J.--ED. BRIMHALL, J.			
AROUND THE WORLD			
CHARLES HANSEN	35912	.85	
BRIMHALL, J.--ED. BRIMHALL, J.			
AUTUMN LEAVES			
CHARLES HANSEN	E32018	.85	
BRIMHALL, J.--ED. BRIMHALL, J.			
BABY ELEPHANT WALK			
CHARLES HANSEN	F30066	.85	
BRIMHALL, J.--ED. BRIMHALL, J.			
BACHARACH AND DAVID'S TOP TEN			
CHARLES HANSEN	K401	1.95	
BRIMHALL, J.--ED. BRIMHALL, J.			
BEGINNINGS			
CHARLES HANSEN	35883	.85	
BRIMHALL, J.--ED. BRIMHALL, J.			
BEST OF BRIMHALL, BK. 1			
CHARLES HANSEN	0171	2.95	
BRIMHALL, J.--ED. BRIMHALL, J.			
BEST OF BRIMHALL, BK. 2			
CHARLES HANSEN	0170	2.95	
BRIMHALL, J.--ED. BRIMHALL, J.			
BEST OF BRIMHALL, BK. 3			
CHARLES HANSEN	0171	2.95	
BRIMHALL, J.--ED. BRIMHALL, J.			
BIBLE TELLS ME SO, THE			
CHARLES HANSEN	F30069	.85	
BRIMHALL, J.--ED. BRIMHALL, J.			
BLACK AND WHITE			
CHARLES HANSEN	35943	.85	
BRIMHALL, J.--ED. BRIMHALL, J.			
BRIGADOON			
CHARLES HANSEN	T95	1.50	
BRIMHALL, J.--ED. BRIMHALL, J.			
BRIMHALL'S LOVE THEMES FROM THE GODFATHER AND OTHER POPULAR			
PIANO PIECES			
CHARLES HANSEN	M429	2.95	
BRIMHALL, J.--ED. BRIMHALL, J.			
BRIMHALL'S 62 EASY-TO-PLAY POP PIANO PIECES			
CHARLES HANSEN	0191	3.45	
BRIMHALL, J.--ED. BRIMHALL, J.			
BRIMHALL'S 64 POPULAR PIANO TEACHING PIECES			
CHARLES HANSEN	0335	3.95	
BRIMHALL, J.--ED. BRIMHALL, J.			
BRIMHALL ISSUE NO. 01			
CHARLES HANSEN	H003	1.50	
BRIMHALL, J.--ED. BRIMHALL, J.			
BRIMHALL ISSUE NO. 02			
CHARLES HANSEN	H004	1.50	
BRIMHALL, J.--ED. BRIMHALL, J.			
BRIMHALL ISSUE NO. 03			
CHARLES HANSEN	H005	1.50	
BRIMHALL, J.--ED. BRIMHALL, J.			
BRIMHALL ISSUE NO. 04			
CHARLES HANSEN	H006	1.50	
BRIMHALL, J.--ED. BRIMHALL, J.			
BRIMHALL ISSUE NO. 05			
CHARLES HANSEN	H028	1.50	
BRIMHALL, J.--ED. BRIMHALL, J.			
BRIMHALL ISSUE NO. 06			
CHARLES HANSEN	H321	1.50	
BRIMHALL, J.--ED. BRIMHALL, J.			
BRIMHALL ISSUE NO. 07			
CHARLES HANSEN	H356	1.50	

BRIMHALL, J.--ED. BRIMHALL, J.			
BRIMHALL ISSUE NO. 08			
CHARLES HANSEN	H362	1.50	
BRIMHALL, J.--ED. BRIMHALL, J.			
BRIMHALL ISSUE NO. 09			
CHARLES HANSEN	H402	1.50	
BRIMHALL, J.--ED. BRIMHALL, J.			
BRIMHALL ISSUE NO. 10			
CHARLES HANSEN	H386	1.50	
BRIMHALL, J.--ED. BRIMHALL, J.			
BRIMHALL ISSUE NO. 11			
CHARLES HANSEN	H460	1.50	
BRIMHALL, J.--ED. BRIMHALL, J.			
BRIMHALL ISSUE NO. 12			
CHARLES HANSEN	H470	1.50	
BRIMHALL, J.--ED. BRIMHALL, J.			
BRIMHALL ISSUE NO. 14			
CHARLES HANSEN	H458	1.95	
BRIMHALL, J.--ED. BRIMHALL, J.			
BRIMHALL ISSUE NO. 15			
CHARLES HANSEN	H514	1.95	
BRIMHALL, J.--ED. BRIMHALL, J.			
BRIMHALL ISSUE NO. 16			
CHARLES HANSEN	H517	1.95	
BRIMHALL, J.--ED. BRIMHALL, J.			
BRIMHALL ISSUE NO. 17			
CHARLES HANSEN	H520	1.95	
BRIMHALL, J.--ED. BRIMHALL, J.			
BRIMHALL ISSUE NO. 18 AN APPLE FOR THE TEACHER			
CHARLES HANSEN	H540	1.50	
BRIMHALL, J.--ED. BRIMHALL, J.			
BRIMHALL ISSUE NO. 20			
CHARLES HANSEN	H587	1.50	
BRIMHALL, J.--ED. BRIMHALL, J.			
BY THE TIME I GET TO PHOENIX			
CHARLES HANSEN	35163	.85	
BRIMHALL, J.--ED. BRIMHALL, J.			
CANDY MAN, THE			
CHARLES HANSEN	35929	.85	
BRIMHALL, J.--ED. BRIMHALL, J.			
CAROL OF THE BELLS			
CHARLES HANSEN		.85	
BRIMHALL, J.--ED. BRIMHALL, J.			
CHERISH			
CHARLES HANSEN	35906	.85	
BRIMHALL, J.--ED. BRIMHALL, J.			
CHIM CHIM CHER-EE			
CHARLES HANSEN	30007	.85	
BRIMHALL, J.--ED. BRIMHALL, J.			
CHRISTMAS SONG, THE			
CHARLES HANSEN		.85	
BRIMHALL, J.--ED. BRIMHALL, J.			
CINDERELLA			
CHARLES HANSEN	T61	1.50	
BRIMHALL, J.--ED. BRIMHALL, J.			
CLASSICAL GAS			
CHARLES HANSEN	35402	.85	
BRIMHALL, J.--ED. BRIMHALL, J.			
CLOSE TO YOU			
CHARLES HANSEN	X30110	.85	
BRIMHALL, J.--ED. BRIMHALL, J.			
CLOSE YOUR EYES			
CHARLES HANSEN	35978	.85	
BRIMHALL, J.--ED. BRIMHALL, J.			
COLOUR MY WORLD			
CHARLES HANSEN	35882	.85	
BRIMHALL, J.--ED. BRIMHALL, J.			
COME SATURDAY MORNING			
CHARLES HANSEN	F30064	.85	
BRIMHALL, J.--ED. BRIMHALL, J.			
CRACKLIN ROSIE			
CHARLES HANSEN	35845	.85	
BRIMHALL, J.--ED. BRIMHALL, J.			
CRAZY HORSES			
CHARLES HANSEN	35961	.85	
BRIMHALL, J.--ED. BRIMHALL, J.			
DEAR WORLD			
CHARLES HANSEN	E32002	.85	
BRIMHALL, J.--ED. BRIMHALL, J.			
DELUXE WALT DISNEY SONGBOOK			
CHARLES HANSEN	E052	5.95	
BRIMHALL, J.--ED. BRIMHALL, J.			
DIDN'T WE			
CHARLES HANSEN	35408	.85	
BRIMHALL, J.--ED. BRIMHALL, J.			
DIZZY			
CHARLES HANSEN	35573	.85	
BRIMHALL, J.--ED. BRIMHALL, J.			
DOWNTOWN			
CHARLES HANSEN	35888	.85	
BRIMHALL, J.--ED. BRIMHALL, J.			
DOWN BY THE LAZY RIVER			
CHARLES HANSEN	35914	.85	
BRIMHALL, J.--ED. BRIMHALL, J.			
DO YOU KNOW THE WAY TO SAN JOSE			
CHARLES HANSEN	X30102	.85	
BRIMHALL, J.--ED. BRIMHALL, J.			
DUELING BANJO			
CHARLES HANSEN	35966	.85	
BRIMHALL, J.--ED. BRIMHALL, J.			
EVERYTHING IS BEAUTIFUL			
CHARLES HANSEN	35817	.85	
BRIMHALL, J.--ED. BRIMHALL, J.			
FASCINATION			
CHARLES HANSEN	32262	.85	
BRIMHALL, J.--ED. BRIMHALL, J.			
FIFTY POPULAR BIGNOTE PIANO TEACHING PIECES, BK. 1			
CHARLES HANSEN	030	2.95	
BRIMHALL, J.--ED. BRIMHALL, J.			
FIFTY POPULAR BIGNOTE PIANO TEACHING PIECES, BK. 2			
CHARLES HANSEN	0173	2.95	
BRIMHALL, J.--ED. BRIMHALL, J.			
FIFTY POPULAR TEACHING PIECES FOR EASY PIANO			
CHARLES HANSEN	0236	3.45	
BRIMHALL, J.--ED. BRIMHALL, J.			
FIRST POPULAR PIANO PIECES, NO. 1			
CHARLES HANSEN	H164	1.50	
BRIMHALL, J.--ED. BRIMHALL, J.			
FIRST POPULAR PIANO PIECES, NO. 2			
CHARLES HANSEN	L117	1.50	
BRIMHALL, J.--ED. BRIMHALL, J.			
FIRST POPULAR PIANO PIECES, NO. 3			
CHARLES HANSEN	H538	1.50	
BRIMHALL, J.--ED. BRIMHALL, J.			
FORTY-EIGHT BRIMHALL WORLD FAMOUS 3-CHORD PIANO SONGS			
CHARLES HANSEN	0117	2.95	

BRIMHALL, J.--ED.   BRIMHALL, J.
MY WAY
        CHARLES HANSEN   35697   .85
BRIMHALL, J.--ED.   BRIMHALL, J.
MY YIDDISCHE MOMMA
        CHARLES HANSEN   35920   .85
BRIMHALL, J.--ED.   BRIMHALL, J.
NEVER ON SUNDAY
        CHARLES HANSEN   30026   .85
BRIMHALL, J.--ED.   BRIMHALL, J.
NIGHT THEY DROVE OLD DIXIE DOWN, THE
        CHARLES HANSEN   35898   .85
BRIMHALL, J.--ED.   BRIMHALL, J.
NINETY-NINE POPULAR PIANO TEACHING PIECES
        CHARLES HANSEN   M480   3.45
BRIMHALL, J.--ED.   BRIMHALL, J.
NOLA
        CHARLES HANSEN   30394   .85
BRIMHALL, J.--ED.   BRIMHALL, J.
ONE BAD APPLE
        CHARLES HANSEN   35860   .85
BRIMHALL, J.--ED.   BRIMHALL, J.
ONE LESS BELL TO ANSWER
        CHARLES HANSEN   X30113   .85
BRIMHALL, J.--ED.   BRIMHALL, J.
ONE NOTE SAMBA
        CHARLES HANSEN   35892   .85
BRIMHALL, J.--ED.   BRIMHALL, J.
ONE OF THOSE SONGS
        CHARLES HANSEN   35907   .85
BRIMHALL, J.--ED.   BRIMHALL, J.
ON THE STREET WHERE YOU LIVE
        CHARLES HANSEN   35921   .85
BRIMHALL, J.--ED.   BRIMHALL, J.
OTHER MAN'S GRASS IS ALWAYS GREENER, THE
        CHARLES HANSEN   35908   .85
BRIMHALL, J.--ED.   BRIMHALL, J.
OVERTURE FROM 'TOMY'
        CHARLES HANSEN   35829   .85
BRIMHALL, J.--ED.   BRIMHALL, J.
O HOLY NIGHT
        CHARLES HANSEN   .85
BRIMHALL, J.--ED.   BRIMHALL, J.
PEACEFUL
        CHARLES HANSEN   35977   .85
BRIMHALL, J.--ED.   BRIMHALL, J.
PETER PAN
        CHARLES HANSEN   T63   1.50
BRIMHALL, J.--ED.   BRIMHALL, J.
PETER RABBIT AND THE TALES OF BEATRIX PORTER
        CHARLES HANSEN   T318   1.50
BRIMHALL, J.--ED.   BRIMHALL, J.
PINBALL WIZARD
        CHARLES HANSEN   35965   .85
BRIMHALL, J.--ED.   BRIMHALL, J.
POPS OF THE 70'S
        CHARLES HANSEN   M368   4.95
BRIMHALL, J.--ED.   BRIMHALL, J.
POPULAR MUSIC OF TODAY, NO. 1
        CHARLES HANSEN   T390   1.75
BRIMHALL, J.--ED.   BRIMHALL, J.
POPULAR MUSIC OF TODAY, NO. 2
        CHARLES HANSEN   T391   1.75
BRIMHALL, J.--ED.   BRIMHALL, J.
PROMISES, PROMISES
        CHARLES HANSEN   E32017   .85
BRIMHALL, J.--ED.   BRIMHALL, J.
PROUD MARY
        CHARLES HANSEN   35855   .85
BRIMHALL, J.--ED.   BRIMHALL, J.
PUT YOUR HAND IN THE HAND
        CHARLES HANSEN   35869   .85
BRIMHALL, J.--ED.   BRIMHALL, J.
QUIET NIGHTS OF QUIET STARS
        CHARLES HANSEN   35893   .85
BRIMHALL, J.--ED.   BRIMHALL, J.
RAINDROPS KEEP FALLIN' ON MY HEAD
        CHARLES HANSEN   X30105   .85
BRIMHALL, J.--ED.   BRIMHALL, J.
RAIN IN SPAIN, THE
        CHARLES HANSEN   35924   .85
BRIMHALL, J.--ED.   BRIMHALL, J.
RUBBER DUCKIE
        CHARLES HANSEN   35836   .85
BRIMHALL, J.--ED.   BRIMHALL, J.
SATURDAY IN THE PARK
        CHARLES HANSEN   35936   .85
BRIMHALL, J.--ED.   BRIMHALL, J.
SCARBOROUGH FAIR
        CHARLES HANSEN   35490   .85
BRIMHALL, J.--ED.   BRIMHALL, J.
SELECTIONS FROM MAN OF LA MANCHA
        CHARLES HANSEN   T83   1.50
BRIMHALL, J.--ED.   BRIMHALL, J.
SEPARATE WAYS
        CHARLES HANSEN   35962   .85
BRIMHALL, J.--ED.   BRIMHALL, J.
SILVER BELLS
        CHARLES HANSEN   F30070   .85
BRIMHALL, J.--ED.   BRIMHALL, J.
SIXTY-THREE BEST OF THE YEAR -- BRIMHALL EASY PIANO --
        CHARLES HANSEN   D122   3.95
BRIMHALL, J.--ED.   BRIMHALL, J.
SIXTY-TWO POPULAR TEACHING PIECES
        CHARLES HANSEN   0197   3.95
BRIMHALL, J.--ED.   BRIMHALL, J.
SNOWBIRD
        CHARLES HANSEN   35848   .85
BRIMHALL, J.--ED.   BRIMHALL, J.
SOMEDAY NEVER COMES
        CHARLES HANSEN   35928   .85
BRIMHALL, J.--ED.   BRIMHALL, J.
SOMETHING STUPID
        CHARLES HANSEN   30070   .85
BRIMHALL, J.--ED.   BRIMHALL, J.
SOMETHING
        CHARLES HANSEN   35821   .85
BRIMHALL, J.--ED.   BRIMHALL, J.
SONG FROM MASH
        CHARLES HANSEN   T31024   .85
BRIMHALL, J.--ED.   BRIMHALL, J.
SONG SUNG BLUE
        CHARLES HANSEN   35927   .85
BRIMHALL, J.--ED.   BRIMHALL, J.
SOUNDS OF THE SEVENTIES
        CHARLES HANSEN   D71   3.95

BRIMHALL, J.--ED.   BRIMHALL, J.
SOUND OF MUSIC, THE
        CHARLES HANSEN   35974   .85
BRIMHALL, J.--ED.   BRIMHALL, J.
SO NICE
        CHARLES HANSEN   35891   .85
BRIMHALL, J.--ED.   BRIMHALL, J.
SPANISH FLEA
        CHARLES HANSEN   30033   .85
BRIMHALL, J.--ED.   BRIMHALL, J.
SPEAK SOFTLY LOVE--THE GODFATHER--
        CHARLES HANSEN   F30081   .85
BRIMHALL, J.--ED.   BRIMHALL, J.
STRANGERS IN THE NIGHT
        CHARLES HANSEN   35889   .85
BRIMHALL, J.--ED.   BRIMHALL, J.
SWEET CAROLINE
        CHARLES HANSEN   35792   .85
BRIMHALL, J.--ED.   BRIMHALL, J.
SWEET HITCH-HIKER
        CHARLES HANSEN   .85
BRIMHALL, J.--ED.   BRIMHALL, J.
TAMMY
        CHARLES HANSEN   35900   .85
BRIMHALL, J.--ED.   BRIMHALL, J.
TASTE OF HONEY, A
        CHARLES HANSEN   30060   .85
BRIMHALL, J.--ED.   BRIMHALL, J.
TEACHING FINGERS HOW TO PLAY POPS, ISSUE 1
        CHARLES HANSEN   H525   1.25
BRIMHALL, J.--ED.   BRIMHALL, J.
TEACHING FINGERS HOW TO PLAY POPS, ISSUE 2
        CHARLES HANSEN   H526   1.25
BRIMHALL, J.--ED.   BRIMHALL, J.
TEACHING FINGERS HOW TO PLAY POPS, ISSUE 3
        CHARLES HANSEN   H527   1.25
BRIMHALL, J.--ED.   BRIMHALL, J.
TEACHING FINGERS HOW TO PLAY POPS, ISSUE 4
        CHARLES HANSEN   H528   1.25
BRIMHALL, J.--ED.   BRIMHALL, J.
TEACHING FINGERS HOW TO PLAY SONGS FOR LITTLE NEIGHBORS, ISSUE 7
        CHARLES HANSEN   H612   1.25
BRIMHALL, J.--ED.   BRIMHALL, J.
TENDERLY
        CHARLES HANSEN   E32008   .85
BRIMHALL, J.--ED.   BRIMHALL, J.
THEME FROM LOVE STORY
        CHARLES HANSEN   F30072   .85
BRIMHALL, J.--ED.   BRIMHALL, J.
THIS GUY'S IN LOVE WITH YOU
        CHARLES HANSEN   X30103   .85
BRIMHALL, J.--ED.   BRIMHALL, J.
THIS IS MY COUNTRY
        CHARLES HANSEN   35815   .85
BRIMHALL, J.--ED.   BRIMHALL, J.
THIS IS MY SONG
        CHARLES HANSEN   35909   .85
BRIMHALL, J.--ED.   BRIMHALL, J.
THOROUGHLY MODERN MILLIE
        CHARLES HANSEN   35910   .85
BRIMHALL, J.--ED.   BRIMHALL, J.
TIAJUANA TAXI
        CHARLES HANSEN   30037   .85
BRIMHALL, J.--ED.   BRIMHALL, J.
TIE ME KANGAROO DOWN
        CHARLES HANSEN   35932   .85
BRIMHALL, J.--ED.   BRIMHALL, J.
TIME FOR US, A   --ROMEO AND JULIET --
        CHARLES HANSEN   F30071   .85
BRIMHALL, J.--ED.   BRIMHALL, J.
TOP TEN BRIMHALL KIDDIE SHEETS ARRANGEMENTS
        CHARLES HANSEN   T374   1.95
BRIMHALL, J.--ED.   BRIMHALL, J.
UNDER PARIS SKIES
        CHARLES HANSEN   35902   .85
BRIMHALL, J.--ED.   BRIMHALL, J.
UP, UP AND AWAY
        CHARLES HANSEN   34042   .85
BRIMHALL, J.--ED.   BRIMHALL, J.
UP AROUND THE BEND
        CHARLES HANSEN   .85
BRIMHALL, J.--ED.   BRIMHALL, J.
WALT DISNEY'S BAMBI
        CHARLES HANSEN   T62   1.50
BRIMHALL, J.--ED.   BRIMHALL, J.
WALT DISNEY'S MARY POPPINS
        CHARLES HANSEN   H29   1.25
BRIMHALL, J.--ED.   BRIMHALL, J.
WALT DISNEY'S PIANO CLASSICS, NO. 1 MICKEY MOUSE
        CHARLES HANSEN   G018   .75
BRIMHALL, J.--ED.   BRIMHALL, J.
WALT DISNEY'S PIANO CLASSICS, NO. 2 PETER PAN
        CHARLES HANSEN   G019   .75
BRIMHALL, J.--ED.   BRIMHALL, J.
WALT DISNEY'S PIANO CLASSICS, NO. 3 ALICE IN WONDERLAND
        CHARLES HANSEN   G020   .75
BRIMHALL, J.--ED.   BRIMHALL, J.
WALT DISNEY'S PIANO CLASSICS, NO. 4 BABES IN TOYLAND
        CHARLES HANSEN   G021   .75
BRIMHALL, J.--ED.   BRIMHALL, J.
WALT DISNEY'S PIANO CLASSICS, NO. 5 CINDERELLA
        CHARLES HANSEN   G022   .75
BRIMHALL, J.--ED.   BRIMHALL, J.
WALT DISNEY'S PIANO CLASSICS, NO. 6 LADY AND THE TRAMP
        CHARLES HANSEN   G023   .75
BRIMHALL, J.--ED.   BRIMHALL, J.
WALT DISNEY 50 HAPPY YEARS, 50 HAPPY HITS
        CHARLES HANSEN   D229   3.95
BRIMHALL, J.--ED.   BRIMHALL, J.
WEDDING SONG
        CHARLES HANSEN   35897   .85
BRIMHALL, J.--ED.   BRIMHALL, J.
WE NEED A LITTLE CHRISTMAS
        CHARLES HANSEN   .85
BRIMHALL, J.--ED.   BRIMHALL, J.
WHAT IS A YOUTH --ROMEO AND JULIET --
        CHARLES HANSEN   35747   .85
BRIMHALL, J.--ED.   BRIMHALL, J.
WHAT THE WORLD NEEDS NOW IS LOVE
        CHARLES HANSEN   X30104   .85
BRIMHALL, J.--ED.   BRIMHALL, J.
WHERE DO I BEGIN --LOVE STORY --
        CHARLES HANSEN   F30073   .85
BRIMHALL, J.--ED.   BRIMHALL, J.
WHY
        CHARLES HANSEN   35939   .85

BRIMHALL, J.--ED.	BRIMHALL, J.			
WINDY				
CHARLES HANSEN		34041		.85
BRIMHALL, J.--ED.	BRIMHALL, J.			
WINTER WONDERLAND				
CHARLES HANSEN		T31021		.85
BRIMHALL, J.--ED.	BRIMHALL, J.			
WITCHCRAFT				
CHARLES HANSEN		E32027		.85
BRIMHALL, J.--ED.	BRIMHALL, J.			
WITHOUT YOU				
CHARLES HANSEN		35915		.85
BRIMHALL, J.--ED.	BRIMHALL, J.			
WORLDS GREATEST DIXIELAND PIANO SOLOS				
CHARLES HANSEN		D208		3.95
BRIMHALL, J.--ED.	BRIMHALL, J.			
WORLDS GREATEST HITS FOR CHORD PLAYING				
CHARLES HANSEN		D152		5.95
BRIMHALL, J.--ED.	BRIMHALL, J.			
WORLDS GREATEST HITS FROM 1900-1919				
CHARLES HANSEN		D201		3.95
BRIMHALL, J.--ED.	BRIMHALL, J.			
WORLDS GREATEST HITS OF COUNTRY MUSIC				
CHARLES HANSEN		D214		3.95
BRIMHALL, J.--ED.	BRIMHALL, J.			
WORLDS GREATEST HITS OF POPULAR CHORALS				
CHARLES HANSEN		D204		2.95
BRIMHALL, J.--ED.	BRIMHALL, J.			
WORLDS GREATEST JAZZ PIANO SOLOS AND SONGS				
CHARLES HANSEN		D206		3.95
BRIMHALL, J.--ED.	BRIMHALL, J.			
YOURE SO VAIN				
CHARLES HANSEN		35959		.85
BROWN, N. H.				
DOLL DANCE				
THE BIG THREE MUSIC CORPORATION				00.95
BROWN, N. H.				
RAG DOLL				
THE BIG THREE MUSIC CORPORATION				00.95
BROWN *				
BEER BARREL POLKA				
SHAPIRO, BERNSTEIN ORGANIZATION				.95
BROWN *				
BEER BARREL POLKA				
SHAPIRO, BERNSTEIN ORGANIZATION				.95
BRUBECK	ADVANCED			
BRUBECK, VOL. 1				
SHAWNEE PRESS, INC.				2.00
BRUBECK	ADVANCED			
BRUBECK, VOL. 2				
SHAWNEE PRESS, INC.				2.00
BRUBECK	ADVANCED			
JAZZ IMPRESSIONS OF JAPAN				
SHAWNEE PRESS, INC.				2.50
BRUBECK	EASY			
THEMES FROM EURASIA				
SHAWNEE PRESS, INC.				2.00
BRUBECK	ADVANCED			
TIME CHANGES				
SHAWNEE PRESS, INC.				2.50
BRYANT	NEALE, J.	EASY		
ALL I HAVE TO DO IS DREAM				
WARNER BROTHERS PUBLISHERS				.75
BURHARD *				
OH -- MY PA-PA				
SHAPIRO, BERNSTEIN ORGANIZATION				.95
BURKE *	NEALE, J.	EASY		
TIP-TOE THRU' THE TULIPS WITH ME				
WARNER BROTHERS PUBLISHERS				.75
BURNETT				
STEAMBOAT RAG				
MCA MUSIC				1.00
CABLE *				
LITTLEST CLOWN , THE.				
MCA MUSIC				2.50
CABLE *	PORTNOFF			
THIEF OF BAGDAD				
MCA MUSIC				1.75
CABLE *				
THIEF OF BAGDAD				
MCA MUSIC				2.50
CAHAN				
MULE DRIVER, THE. --EL MULETERO				
MCA MUSIC				1.00
CAHN				
BASIC TECHNIQUE FOR JAZZ PIANO				
BELWIN-MILLS PUBLISHING CORPORATION				1.50
CAHN				
BASIC TECHNIQUE FOR POPULAR PIANO				
BELWIN-MILLS PUBLISHING CORPORATION				1.50
CAHN *				
THREE COINS IN A FOUNTAIN				
THE BIG THREE MUSIC CORPORATION				00.95
CARLE, F				
CARLE BOOGIE				
SHAPIRO, BERNSTEIN ORGANIZATION				.95
CARMICHAEL	MOSSMAN, T.			
STAR DUST -- SIMP.				
BELWIN-MILLS PUBLISHING CORPORATION		26077		.50
CAROSONE				
ICICLE WING-DING				
MCA MUSIC				1.00
CARROLL *				
I'M ALWAYS CHASING RAINBOWS				
THE BIG THREE MUSIC CORPORATION				00.95
CARTER, P.				
PAUL CARTER POPULAR PIANO COURSE, BK. 1				
SAM FOX PUBLISHING COMPANY, INC.				1.75
CARTER, P.				
PAUL CARTER POPULAR PIANO COURSE, BK. 2				
SAM FOX PUBLISHING COMPANY, INC.				1.75
CARTER, P.				
PAUL CARTER POPULAR PIANO COURSE, BK. 3				
SAM FOX PUBLISHING COMPANY, INC.				1.75
CASHMAN *				
FOLIO				
THE BIG THREE MUSIC CORPORATION				03.95
CASSIDY, D.				
ROCK ME BABY				
THE BIG THREE MUSIC CORPORATION				03.95
CAVALLARO				
CAVALLARO'S KEYBOARD CREATIONS				
WARNER BROTHERS PUBLISHERS				1.95
CELE				
PENNY WHISTLE BLUE -- MAGIC GARDENS, THE.				
MCA MUSIC				1.00

CHANDLER *				
CANADIAN CAPERS				
WARNER BROTHERS PUBLISHERS				1.00
CHAPLIN				
MY STAR				
MCA MUSIC				1.00
CHAPLIN	KERR, R.N.			
THIS IS MY SONG				
MCA MUSIC				1.00
CHOPIN	SCHOEGEL			
CHOPIN'S POLONAISE IN BOOGIE				
MCA MUSIC				1.00
CIOFFI				
STAIRWAY TO THE SEA --SCALINATELLA				
MCA MUSIC				1.00
CLEMENTS--ED.	CLEMENTS	INTERMEDIATE		
HANS BRINKER, OR THE SILVER SKATES				
POINTER PUBLICATIONS				2.95
COBEN	MAXTED			
OLD PIANO ROLL BLUES, THE				
MCA MUSIC				1.00
COFFEY, J. R.				
SCORPIO				
WARNER BROTHERS PUBLISHERS				1.00
COHAN, G. M.				
MARY'S A GRAND OLD NAME				
EDWARD B. MARKS MUSIC CORPORATION				00.60
COHAN				
YANKEE DOODLE BOY				
EDWARD B. MARKS MUSIC CORPORATION				00.60
COHAN				
YOU'RE A GRAND OLD FLAG				
EDWARD B. MARKS MUSIC CORPORATION				00.60
COLLINS, J.				
JUDY COLLINS SONGBOOK, THE				
MUSIC SALES CORPORATION		060016		4.95
CONFREY, Z.				
STUMBLING				
THE BIG THREE MUSIC CORPORATION				00.95
COOPER, A.				
ALICE COOPER FOLIO				
THE BIG THREE MUSIC CORPORATION				03.95
COUPERIN				
COUPERIN PIANO COURSE, BK. 01				
BOURNE COMPANY				2.50
COWARD	MACLACHLAN	FIRST YEAR		
ZIGEUNER				
WARNER BROTHERS PUBLISHERS				.75
CROCE, J.				
JIM CROCE SONG BOOK				
THE BIG THREE MUSIC CORPORATION				03.95
CURRIER				
SLEIGH RIDE -- SIMP.				
BELWIN-MILLS PUBLISHING CORPORATION		90114		1.00
CURTIS *	KERR, R.N.			
LET IT BE ME				
MCA MUSIC				1.00
DAHLEN				
SUMMER SOUNDS AND OTHER BIG SONG HITS				
BELWIN-MILLS PUBLISHING CORPORATION				2.00
DARION *	AGAY, D.			
IMPOSSIBLE DREAM, THE. --FROM 'MAN OF LA MANCHA'				
SAM FOX PUBLISHING COMPANY, INC.				1.00
DARION				
IMPOSSIBLE DREAM, THE. -- FROM 'MAN OF LA MANCHA'				
SAM FOX PUBLISHING COMPANY, INC.				1.25
DARION *	AGAY, D.			
MAN OF LA MANCHA				
SAM FOX PUBLISHING COMPANY, INC.				2.50
DAVIS, J. R.--ED	DAVIS, J. R.			
HARMS HITS THROUGH THE YEARS MADE EASY				
WARNER BROTHERS PUBLISHERS				1.25
DAVIS, J. R.--ED	DAVIS, J. R.			
IRISH FAVORITES FOR PIANO				
WARNER BROTHERS PUBLISHERS				1.50
DAVIS, J. R.--ED	DAVIS, J. R.			
PETER, PAUL AND MARY, HITS OF, MADE EASY FOR PIANO				
WARNER BROTHERS PUBLISHERS		PPM 24		1.50
DAVIS, K. *				
LITTLE DRUMMER BOY, THE -- SIMP.				
BELWIN-MILLS PUBLISHING CORPORATION		26071		.50
DAWES				
MELODY				
WARNER BROTHERS PUBLISHERS				1.00
DEBUSSY	DAVIS, J. R.	FIRST YEAR		
CLAIR DE LUNE				
WARNER BROTHERS PUBLISHERS				.75
DELUGG *				
FRANTIC FOR FIVE				
MCA MUSIC				1.00
DENNIS, M.	INTERMEDIATE			
BLUES PIANO STYLES				
MEL BAY PUBLICATIONS, INC.				2.00
DENNIS, M.	INTERMEDIATE			
JAZZ PIANO STYLES				
MEL BAY PUBLICATIONS, INC.				2.00
DENNIS, M.	INTERMEDIATE			
PENSIVE PIANO MOODS				
MEL BAY PUBLICATIONS, INC.				2.00
DENNIS, M.	INTERMEDIATE			
RAGTIME PIANO STYLES				
MEL BAY PUBLICATIONS, INC.				2.00
DENNIS, M.	INTERMEDIATE			
ROCK PIANO STYLES				
MEL BAY PUBLICATIONS, INC.				2.00
DEUTSCH *				
HI-LILI, HI-LO				
THE BIG THREE MUSIC CORPORATION				00.95
DE ROSE, P.				
AMERICAN WALTZ				
THE BIG THREE MUSIC CORPORATION				00.95
DE ROSE, P.				
AUTUMN SERENADE				
THE BIG THREE MUSIC CORPORATION				00.95
DE ROSE, P.				
DEEP PURPLE				
THE BIG THREE MUSIC CORPORATION				00.95
DE ROSE, P.				
FOUNTAIN IN CENTRAL PARK				
THE BIG THREE MUSIC CORPORATION				00.95
DE ROSE, P.				
MOONLIGHT MOOD				
THE BIG THREE MUSIC CORPORATION				00.95
DE ROSE, P.				
MUSIC BOX IN BLUE				
THE BIG THREE MUSIC CORPORATION				00.95

DE ROSE, P.
  WHITE ORCHIDS
    THE BIG THREE MUSIC CORPORATION   00.95
DE ROSE *
  NOCTURNAL RHAPSODY
    SHAPIRO, BERNSTEIN ORGANIZATION   .95
DE VITO, A.--ED.   DE VITO, A.
  ALBERT DE VITO PIANO COURSE, BK. 1
    KENYON PUBLICATIONS   1.50
DE VITO, A.--ED.   DE VITO, A.
  COUNTRY WESTERN
    KENYON PUBLICATIONS   1.00
DE VITO, A.--ED.   DE VITO, A.
  STANDARD FAVORITES - BK. A
    KENYON PUBLICATIONS   2.00
DE VITO, A.
  PEDRO DANCES
    BOURNE COMPANY   1.00
DIETZ *   LEVINE
  LOUISIANA HAYRIDE
    WARNER BROTHERS PUBLISHERS   1.00
DONIDA   HASTINGS
  AL DI LA
    WARNER BROTHERS PUBLISHERS   1.00
DONIDA *   NEALE, J.   EASY
  AL DI LA
    WARNER BROTHERS PUBLISHERS   .75
DONIDA   SAMPIETRO   FIRST YEAR
  AL DI LA
    WARNER BROTHERS PUBLISHERS   .75
DRAKE *
  TORNADO
    MCA MUSIC   1.00
DUCHIN
  DUCHIN'S, EDDY, PIANORAMA
    WARNER BROTHERS PUBLISHERS   1.50
DUKE, V.
  NEW YORK NOCTURNE
    THE BIG THREE MUSIC CORPORATION   00.95
DUKE   WHITNEY
  APRIL IN PARIS
    WARNER BROTHERS PUBLISHERS   1.00
DUKE   RICHTER   FIRST YEAR
  APRIL IN PARIS
    WARNER BROTHERS PUBLISHERS   .75
DUKE   WHITNEY
  AUTUMN IN NEW YORK
    WARNER BROTHERS PUBLISHERS   1.00
DURAND, A.
  BAKER STREET SKETCHES
    MCA MUSIC   1.00
DURING *
  PICNIC
    SHAPIRO, BERNSTEIN ORGANIZATION   .95
DYLAN   NEALE, J.   EASY
  BLOWIN' IN THE WIND
    WARNER BROTHERS PUBLISHERS   .75
DYLAN   NEALE, J.
  INSTANT PICTURE CHORD PIANO NO. 2, BOB DYLAN
    WARNER BROTHERS PUBLISHERS   1.95
EARL *
  BEAUTIFUL OHIO --FOX TROT
    SHAPIRO, BERNSTEIN ORGANIZATION   .95
EDWARDS, J.
  JONATHAN EDWARDS
    THE BIG THREE MUSIC CORPORATION   04.95
ELISCU *
  WITHOUT A SONG
    THE BIG THREE MUSIC CORPORATION   00.95
ELLINGTON
  BIRD OF PARADISE
    THE BIG THREE MUSIC CORPORATION   00.95
ENGEL, S.--ARR.   ENGEL, S.   ADVANCED
  TWENTY-FOUR CARAT GOLD
    SCREEN GEMS - COLUMBIA PUBLICATIONS   F0200P1   3.95
ENGELMANN, H. U.   RICHTER   FIRST YEAR
  MELODY OF LOVE
    WARNER BROTHERS PUBLISHERS   .75
EVANS
  BILL EVANS PIANO SOLOS
    TRO SONGWAYS SERVICE, INC.   2.00
EVANS
  BILL EVANS PLAYS
    TRO SONGWAYS SERVICE, INC.   2.95
FAIN *
  APRIL LOVE
    THE BIG THREE MUSIC CORPORATION   00.95
FAIN *
  LOVE IS A MANY-SPLENDORED THING
    THE BIG THREE MUSIC CORPORATION   00.95
FAIN   HASTINGS
  SECRET LOVE
    WARNER BROTHERS PUBLISHERS   1.00
FAIRCHILD   3
  IRISH MEDLEY
    VOLKWEIN BROS.   00.50
FAITH *
  SWEDISH RHAPSODY
    TRO SONGWAYS SERVICE, INC.   2054
FAYE
  ONLY YESTERDAY
    MCA MUSIC   1.00
FIEDEL
  TEN WEST
    MCA MUSIC   1.00
FIELDS, I.
  MODERN APPROACH TO POPULAR PLAYING, VOL. 1
    CARL FISCHER, INC.   O 4656   2.00
FIELDS, I.
  MODERN APPROACH TO POPULAR PLAYING, VOL. 2
    CARL FISCHER, INC.   O 4657   2.00
FIELDS *
  ON THE SUNNY SIDE OF THE STREET
    SHAPIRO, BERNSTEIN ORGANIZATION   .95
FLETCHER, L.--ED   FLETCHER, L.
  FOX POPULAR SONG FAVORITES
    SAM FOX PUBLISHING COMPANY, INC.   1.25
FLETCHER *
  SUGAR BLUES
    MCA MUSIC   1.00
FORD, T. E.
  POINTER LIBRARY - A TREASURY OF INSPIRATIONAL SONGS
    POINTER PUBLICATIONS   2.95
FORD, T. E.
  TREASURY OF INSPIRATIONAL SONGS
    POINTER PUBLICATIONS   4.95

FORESYTHE, R.
  SERENADE FOR A WEALTHY WIDOW
    THE BIG THREE MUSIC CORPORATION   00.95
FORNUTO
  JAZZ-ROCK STUDIES -- THE BLOCK-CHORD STYLE
    LEE ROBERTS MUSIC PUBLICATIONS, INC.   1.25
FOSTER   SAMMASTINO
  TEN POPULAR SONGS
    FRANCO COLOMBO PUBLICATIONS   8A8815   1.50
FOUNTAIN *
  OH DIDN'T HE RAMBLE
    MCA MUSIC   1.00
FRANCAIX *
  LADY L - THEME
    THE BIG THREE MUSIC CORPORATION   00.95
FRANK--ED.   FRANK
  HITS OF TODAY--EASY PIANO-- SERIES 1
    MCA MUSIC   1.25
FRANK--ED.   FRANK
  HITS OF TODAY--EASY PIANO-- SERIES 2
    MCA MUSIC   1.25
FRANK--ED.   FRANK
  HITS OF TODAY--EASY PIANO-- SERIES 3
    MCA MUSIC   1.50
FREUNDORFER
  SINGING ZITHER, THE
    MCA MUSIC   1.00
FRIML, R.   MOKREJS
  INDIAN LOVE CALL
    WARNER BROTHERS PUBLISHERS   1.00
FRIML, R.   WHITNEY
  INDIAN LOVE CALL
    WARNER BROTHERS PUBLISHERS   1.00
FRIML, R.   RIEGGER
  ROSE MARIE
    WARNER BROTHERS PUBLISHERS   1.00
FRONTIERE, D.
  HANG 'EM HIGH
    THE BIG THREE MUSIC CORPORATION   00.95
FRONTIERE, D.
  LA CHAMADE
    THE BIG THREE MUSIC CORPORATION   00.95
FRONTIERE, D.
  TWELVE O'CLOCK HIGH - THEME
    THE BIG THREE MUSIC CORPORATION   00.95
FULLER
  SCATTER SHIELD
    MCA MUSIC   1.00
FULLER
  WAIKIKI RUN
    MCA MUSIC   1.00
GALDIERI *
  LOVE THEME FROM 'LA STRADA'
    MCA MUSIC   1.00
GARLAND *
  IN THE MOOD
    SHAPIRO, BERNSTEIN ORGANIZATION   .95
GARLAND   HARING
  IN THE MOOD
    SHAPIRO, BERNSTEIN ORGANIZATION   .95
GERSHWIN   WHITNEY
  AMERICAN IN PARIS, AN - IN MINIATURE
    WARNER BROTHERS PUBLISHERS   1.50
GERSHWIN   DALY
  AMERICAN IN PARIS, AN
    WARNER BROTHERS PUBLISHERS   4.00
GERSHWIN   LEVINE
  EMBRACEABLE YOU
    WARNER BROTHERS PUBLISHERS   1.00
GERSHWIN   WALTER
  EMBRACEABLE YOU
    WARNER BROTHERS PUBLISHERS   1.00
GERSHWIN   RICHTER   FIRST YEAR
  EMBRACEABLE YOU
    WARNER BROTHERS PUBLISHERS   .75
GERSHWIN   STONE
  FASCINATING RHYTHM
    WARNER BROTHERS PUBLISHERS   1.00
GERSHWIN
  GERSHWIN, THE BEST OF HOLLYWOOD
    CHAPPELL AND COMPANY, INC.   0021675   1.50
GERSHWIN
  GERSHWIN AT THE KEYBOARD
    WARNER BROTHERS PUBLISHERS   2.50
GERSHWIN   LEVINE
  I GOT RHYTHM
    WARNER BROTHERS PUBLISHERS   1.00
GERSHWIN   LEVINE
  LIZA
    WARNER BROTHERS PUBLISHERS   1.00
GERSHWIN   LEVINE
  MAN I LOVE, THE
    WARNER BROTHERS PUBLISHERS   1.00
GERSHWIN   GRAINGER, P.
  MAN I LOVE, THE
    WARNER BROTHERS PUBLISHERS   1.00
GERSHWIN   RICHTER   FIRST YEAR
  MAN I LOVE, THE
    WARNER BROTHERS PUBLISHERS   .75
GERSHWIN   LEVINE
  OH, LADY BE GOOD
    WARNER BROTHERS PUBLISHERS   1.00
GERSHWIN
  POINTER LIBRARY - THE BEST OF GEORGE GERSHWIN
    POINTER PUBLICATIONS   2.95
GERSHWIN
  PORGY AND BESS
    CHAPPELL AND COMPANY, INC.   4672507   1.50
GERSHWIN
  PORGY AND BESS
    CHAPPELL AND COMPANY, INC.   4672507   1.95
GERSHWIN   LEVINE
  SOMEONE TO WATCH OVER ME
    WARNER BROTHERS PUBLISHERS   1.00
GERSHWIN   WHITNEY
  SOMEONE TO WATCH OVER ME
    WARNER BROTHERS PUBLISHERS   1.00
GERSHWIN   RICHTER   FIRST YEAR
  SOMEONE TO WATCH OVER ME
    WARNER BROTHERS PUBLISHERS   .75
GERSHWIN   LEVINE
  STRIKE UP THE BAND
    WARNER BROTHERS PUBLISHERS   1.00
GERSHWIN
  SUMMERTIME
    CHAPPELL AND COMPANY, INC.   5565023   .60

GIACOBETTI *
    PICORDATE MARCELLINO
        MCA MUSIC   1.00
GILLOCK
    MORE NEW ORLEANS JAZZ STYLES -- ADVANCING INTERMEDIATE
        WILLIS MUSIC COMPANY   1.00
GILLOCK
    NEW ORLEANS JAZZ STYLES -- ADVANCING INTERMEDIATE
        WILLIS MUSIC COMPANY   1.00
GILLOCK
    THREE JAZZ PRELUDES
        WILLIS MUSIC COMPANY   1.00
GIMBEL *
    BLUESETTE
        MCA MUSIC   1.00
GIMBEL *   KERR, R. N.
    BLUESETTE
        MCA MUSIC   1.00
GIMBEL *   KERR, R.N.
    GIRL FROM IPANEMA
        MCA MUSIC   1.00
GIMBEL *   KERR, R.N.
    HOW INSENSITIVE
        MCA MUSIC   1.00
GIORDANO *
    ANNA
        TRO SONGWAYS SERVICE, INC.   2003
GIRAUD
    UNDER PARIS SKIES
        MCA MUSIC   1.00
GIRLAMO, F.
    LET'S GO BOOGIE WOOGIE
        BELWIN-MILLS PUBLISHING CORPORATION   2.00
GLOVER, D. *
    ADVENTURE IN JAZZ, BK. 1
        BELWIN-MILLS PUBLISHING CORPORATION   FDL 478   2.00
GLOVER, D. *
    ADVENTURE IN JAZZ, BK. 2
        BELWIN-MILLS PUBLISHING CORPORATION   FDL 479   2.00
GLOVER, D. *
    ADVENTURE IN JAZZ, BK. 3
        BELWIN-MILLS PUBLISHING CORPORATION   FDL 480   2.00
GLOVER, D. *
    ADVENTURE IN JAZZ, BK. 4
        BELWIN-MILLS PUBLISHING CORPORATION   FDL 481   2.00
GOLDSMITH, J.
    BLUE MAX, THE
        THE BIG THREE MUSIC CORPORATION   00.95
GOLDSMITH, J.
    LILA'S THEME - THE STRIPPER
        THE BIG THREE MUSIC CORPORATION   00.95
GOLDSMITH, J.
    MAN FROM U.N.C.L.E. - THEME
        THE BIG THREE MUSIC CORPORATION   00.95
GOLDSMITH, J.
    OUR MAN FLINT
        THE BIG THREE MUSIC CORPORATION   00.95
GOLDSMITH, J.
    PRIZE, THE
        THE BIG THREE MUSIC CORPORATION   00.95
GOLDSMITH, J.
    VON RYAN MARCH
        THE BIG THREE MUSIC CORPORATION   00.95
GOODMAN *
    STOMPING AT THE SAVOY
        THE BIG THREE MUSIC CORPORATION   00.95
GOODWIN, R.
    OF HUMAN BONDAGE - THEME
        THE BIG THREE MUSIC CORPORATION   00.95
GORDON
    ART OF ROCK
        BELWIN-MILLS PUBLISHING CORPORATION   1.50
GREEN   LEVINE
    BODY AND SOUL
        WARNER BROTHERS PUBLISHERS   1.00
GREEN   WALTER
    BODY AND SOUL
        WARNER BROTHERS PUBLISHERS   1.00
GREEN *
    COQUETTE
        THE BIG THREE MUSIC CORPORATION   00.95
GREEN
    JOHN AND JULIE
        MCA MUSIC   1.00
GRIEG   FREY, H.
    PIANO CONCERTO
        THE BIG THREE MUSIC CORPORATION   00.75
GRISELLE, T.
    TWO AMERICAN SKETCHES
        THE BIG THREE MUSIC CORPORATION   01.25
GROFE, F.
    ALICE BLUE
        THE BIG THREE MUSIC CORPORATION   00.95
GROFE, F.
    BLACK SAPPHIRE
        THE BIG THREE MUSIC CORPORATION   00.95
GROFE, F.
    BROADWAY AT NIGHT
        THE BIG THREE MUSIC CORPORATION   01.25
GROFE, F.
    FATHER OF WATERS
        THE BIG THREE MUSIC CORPORATION   00.95
GROFE, F.
    FESTIVIANA
        THE BIG THREE MUSIC CORPORATION   01.25
GROFE, F.
    FREE AIR
        THE BIG THREE MUSIC CORPORATION   00.95
GROFE, F.
    KILLARNEY
        THE BIG THREE MUSIC CORPORATION   01.25
GROFE, F.
    KNUTE ROCKNE
        THE BIG THREE MUSIC CORPORATION   01.25
GROFE, F.
    MARCH FOR AMERICANS
        THE BIG THREE MUSIC CORPORATION   00.95
GROFE, F.
    MARDI GRAS
        THE BIG THREE MUSIC CORPORATION   00.95
GROFE, F.
    ON THE TRAIL
        THE BIG THREE MUSIC CORPORATION   00.95
GROFE, F.
    SERENADE
        THE BIG THREE MUSIC CORPORATION   00.95

GRUSIN
    CALIFORNIA MONTAGE
        MCA MUSIC   1.00
GRUSIN
    IT'S NOT UNUSUAL
        MCA MUSIC   1.00
GRUSIN
    IT TAKES A THIEF
        MCA MUSIC   1.00
GRUSIN
    NAME OF THE GAME, THE
        MCA MUSIC   1.00
GUARALDI
    COMPLETE PEANUTS KEYBOARD FUN SERIES
        POINTER PUBLICATIONS   6.95
GUARALDI
    PEANUTS KEYBOARD FUN SERIES - A BOY NAMED CHARLIE BROWN
        POINTER PUBLICATIONS   2.95
GUARALDI
    PEANUTS KEYBOARD FUN SERIES - A CHARLIE BROWN CHRISTMAS
        POINTER PUBLICATIONS   2.95
GUARALDI
    PEANUTS KEYBOARD FUN SERIES - HE'S YOUR DOG, CHARLIE BROWN
        POINTER PUBLICATIONS   2.95
GUARALDI
    PEANUTS KEYBOARD FUN SERIES - PIANO FUN BOOK
        POINTER PUBLICATIONS   2.95
GUARALDI
    PEANUTS KEYBOARD FUN SERIES - SUPPLEMENTARY SONGS FOR THE PIANO
    FUN BOOK
        POINTER PUBLICATIONS   1.95
GUTHRIE
    THIS LAND IS YOUR LAND
        TRO SONGWAYS SERVICE, INC.   2082   .85
HAGEN *
    HAPLEM NOCTURNE
        SHAPIRO, BERNSTEIN ORGANIZATION   .95
HALL *
    JOHNSON RAG
        THE BIG THREE MUSIC CORPORATION   00.95
HAMILTON *
    MAIDS OF MADRID, THE.
        MCA MUSIC   1.00
HAMMERSTEIN *   SINGER
    BALI HA'I
        MCA MUSIC   1.00
HAMMERSTEIN *
    CINDERELLA MARCH
        MCA MUSIC   1.00
HAMMERSTEIN *
    CINDERELLA WALTZ
        MCA MUSIC   1.00
HAMMERSTEIN *
    CINDERELLA
        MCA MUSIC   2.50
HAMMERSTEIN *   PORTNOFF
    CINDERELLA
        MCA MUSIC   1.50
HAMMERSTEIN *   SINGER
    CLIMB EV'RY MOUNTAIN
        MCA MUSIC   1.00
HAMMERSTEIN *   SINGER
    DO-RE-MI
        MCA MUSIC   1.00
HAMMERSTEIN *   SINGER
    DO I LOVE YOU -- BECAUSE YOU'RE BEAUTIFUL
        MCA MUSIC   1.00
HAMMERSTEIN *
    FLOWER DRUM SONG
        MCA MUSIC   2.50
HAMMERSTEIN *   PORTNOFF
    FLOWER DRUM SONG
        MCA MUSIC   1.50
HAMMERSTEIN *   RITTMAN
    GETTING TO KNOW YOU
        MCA MUSIC   1.00
HAMMERSTEIN *   RITTMAN
    HELLO, YOUNG LOVERS
        MCA MUSIC   1.00
HAMMERSTEIN *   SINGER
    IT'S A GRAND NIGHT FOR SINGING
        MCA MUSIC   1.00
HAMMERSTEIN *   RITTMAN
    IT MIGHT AS WELL BE SPRING
        MCA MUSIC   1.00
HAMMERSTEIN *
    IT MIGHT AS WELL BE SPRING
        MCA MUSIC   1.00
HAMMERSTEIN *   RITTMAN
    I WHISTLE A HAPPY TUNE
        MCA MUSIC   1.00
HAMMERSTEIN *   STICKLES
    KING AND I, THE
        MCA MUSIC   1.50
HAMMERSTEIN *
    KING AND I, THE
        MCA MUSIC   2.50
HAMMERSTEIN *
    MARCH OF THE SIAMESE CHILDREN, THE
        MCA MUSIC   1.00
HAMMERSTEIN *
    ME AND JULIET
        MCA MUSIC   1.00
HAMMERSTEIN *   SINGER
    MY FAVORITE THINGS
        MCA MUSIC   1.00
HAMMERSTEIN *   RITTMAN
    MY FAVORITE THINGS
        MCA MUSIC   1.00
HAMMERSTEIN *   SIRMAY
    NO OTHER LOVE
        MCA MUSIC   1.00
HAMMERSTEIN *   RITTMAN
    OH WHAT A BEAUTIFUL MORNIN'
        MCA MUSIC   1.00
HAMMERSTEIN *   STICKLES
    OKLAHOMA
        MCA MUSIC   1.50
HAMMERSTEIN *
    OKLAHOMA
        MCA MUSIC   2.50
HAMMERSTEIN *   RITTMAN
    OUT OF MY DREAMS
        MCA MUSIC   1.00
HAMMERSTEIN *   RITTMAN
    PEOPLE WILL SAY WE'RE IN LOVE
        MCA MUSIC   1.00

HAMMERSTEIN *
   PIPE DREAM
      MCA MUSIC   2.50
HAMMERSTEIN *   RITTMAN
   SOME ENCHANTED EVENING
      MCA MUSIC   1.00
HAMMERSTEIN *   SINGER
   SOUND OF MUSIC, THE.
      MCA MUSIC   1.00
HAMMERSTEIN *
   SOUND OF MUSIC, THE.
      MCA MUSIC   2.50
HAMMERSTEIN *   NEVIN
   SOUND OF MUSIC, THE -- BEGINNERS PIANO BOOK
      MCA MUSIC   1.50
HAMMERSTEIN *   PORTNOFF
   SOUND OF MUSIC, THE.
      MCA MUSIC   1.50
HAMMERSTEIN *   STICKLES
   SOUTH PACIFIC
      MCA MUSIC   1.50
HAMMERSTEIN *
   SOUTH PACIFIC
      MCA MUSIC   2.50
HAMMERSTEIN *
   STATE FAIR
      MCA MUSIC   2.50
HAMMERSTEIN *   STICKLES
   STATE FAIR
      MCA MUSIC   1.50
HAMMERSTEIN *   SINGER
   STRANGE MUSIC
      MCA MUSIC   1.00
HAMMERSTEIN *
   SURREY WITH THE FRINGE ON TOP
      MCA MUSIC   1.00
HAMMERSTEIN *
   WALTZ FOR A BALL
      MCA MUSIC   1.00
HAMMERSTEIN *   RITTMAN
   WE KISS IN A SHADOW
      MCA MUSIC   1.00
HAMMERSTEIN *
   WHERE IS CINDERELLA
      MCA MUSIC   1.00
HAMMERSTEIN *   RITTMAN
   WONDERFUL GUY, THE
      MCA MUSIC   1.00
HAMMERSTEIN *   RITTMAN
   YOUNGER THAN SPRINGTIME
      MCA MUSIC   1.00
HAMMERSTEIN *
   YOU ARE BEAUTIFUL
      MCA MUSIC   1.00
HAMMERSTEIN *   SINGER
   YOU ARE BEAUTIFUL
      MCA MUSIC   1.00
HAMPTON, L.
   HAMPS BOOGIE-WOOGIE
      THE BIG THREE MUSIC CORPORATION   00.95
HARRIS   HASTINGS
   FOOTPRINTS ON THE MOON
      WARNER BROTHERS PUBLISHERS   1.00
HART, F.
   SONGS OF FREDDIE HART, THE
      THE BIG THREE MUSIC CORPORATION   02.95
HART *
   BLUE MOON
      THE BIG THREE MUSIC CORPORATION   00.95
HART *
   SPRING IS HERE
      THE BIG THREE MUSIC CORPORATION   00.95
HATCH   KERR, R. N.
   CALL ME
      MCA MUSIC   1.00
HATCH   KERR, R. N.
   DOWNTOWN
      MCA MUSIC   1.00
HATCH   KERR, R.N.
   SIGN OF THE TIMES, THE.
      MCA MUSIC   1.00
HAVENS, R.
   RICHIE HAVENS - ANTHOLOGY
      THE BIG THREE MUSIC CORPORATION   03.95
HEFTI, N.
   BATMAN THEME
      THE BIG THREE MUSIC CORPORATION   00.95
HENDERSON, R.
   EASY TO LEARN POPULAR PIANO MUSIC
      BOSTON MUSIC COMPANY   1.50
HENDERSON, R.
   POPULAR MUSIC PIANO PLAYING
      BOSTON MUSIC COMPANY   1.50
HENDERSON   WALTER
   BIRTH OF THE BLUES, THE
      WARNER BROTHERS PUBLISHERS   1.00
HENDERSON   MACLACHLAN   FIRST YEAR
   BIRTH OF THE BLUES, THE
      WARNER BROTHERS PUBLISHERS   .75
HENDRICKS *
   DESAFINADO
      TRO SONGWAYS SERVICE, INC.   2019
HERBERT   STAFFORD
   VICTOR HERBERT FAVORITES
      WARNER BROTHERS PUBLISHERS   1.25
HERMAN
   WOODY HERMAN FIVE BOOGIE WOOGIE AND BLUES SOLOS
      MCA MUSIC   1.00
HEYNE
   PETITE GAVOTTE, LA
      MCA MUSIC   1.00
HEYNE
   PETITE WALTZ, THE
      MCA MUSIC   1.00
HEYWOOD, E.
   MODERN PIANO TRANSCRIPTIONS
      THE BIG THREE MUSIC CORPORATION   01.50
HOLT *   KERR, R.N.
   ONE OF THOSE SONGS
      MCA MUSIC   1.00
HOLZMANN, A.
   BLAZE AWAY
      THE BIG THREE MUSIC CORPORATION   00.95
HOPKINS, K.
   HUSTLER, THE -THEME
      THE BIG THREE MUSIC CORPORATION   00.95

HOWARD
   FLY ME TO THE MOON --BOSSA NOVA--
      TRO SONGWAYS SERVICE, INC.   2024
HUBBELL   WHITNEY
   POOR BUTTERFLY
      WARNER BROTHERS PUBLISHERS   1.00
ICINI
   SUMMERTIME IN VENICE
      MCA MUSIC   1.00
INGLE   NEALE, J.   EASY
   IN-A-GADDA-DA-VIDA
      WARNER BROTHERS PUBLISHERS   .75
ITURBI, J.
   THREE BLIND MICE - 3 INTERPRETATIONS
      THE BIG THREE MUSIC CORPORATION   00.95
JAMES, S.
   SONGS OF SONNY JAMES
      THE BIG THREE MUSIC CORPORATION   02.95
JARRE, M.
   GRAND PRIX - THEME
      THE BIG THREE MUSIC CORPORATION   00.95
JARRE, M.
   LARA'S THEME - 'DOCTOR ZHIVAGO'
      THE BIG THREE MUSIC CORPORATION   00.95
JAY *
   VIENNESE LANTERN WALTZ
      MCA MUSIC   1.00
JENKINS, M.
   KALEIDOSCOPE
      MCA MUSIC   1.00
JENKINS, M.
   LOVE THEME FROM 'MANHATTAN TOWER'
      MCA MUSIC   1.00
JOBIM   HARNELL
   MUSIC OF ANTONIO CARLOS JOBIM STYLED FOR PIANO BY JOE HARNELL
      TRO SONGWAYS SERVICE, INC.   2.50
JOHNSON, S. *
   BABY LOOK AT YOU
      MCA MUSIC   1.00
JOHNSON, S.
   BOOGIN' ON THE DOWNBEAT
      MCA MUSIC   1.00
JOHNSON, S.
   CENTRAL AVENUE DRAG
      MCA MUSIC   1.00
JOHNSON, S.
   CHERRY RED
      MCA MUSIC   1.00
JOHNSON, S.
   CLIMBIN' AND SCREAMIN'
      MCA MUSIC   1.00
JOHNSON, S.
   DEATH RAY BOOGIE
      MCA MUSIC   1.00
JOHNSON, S. *
   DEATH RAY BOOGIE
      MCA MUSIC   1.00
JOHNSON, S.
   GOING AWAY BLUES
      MCA MUSIC   1.00
JOHNSON, S.
   HOLLYWOOD BOOGIE
      MCA MUSIC   1.00
JOHNSON, S. *
   IT'S A LOW DOWN DIRTY SHAME
      MCA MUSIC   1.00
JOHNSON, S.
   KANSAS CITY FAREWELL
      MCA MUSIC   1.00
JOHNSON, S. *
   LAST GOODBYE BLUES
      MCA MUSIC   1.00
JOHNSON, S. *
   OH WEE BABY BLUES
      MCA MUSIC   1.00
JOHNSON, S.
   OVER THE BARS
      MCA MUSIC   1.00
JOHNSON, S.
   PETE'S MIXTURE
      MCA MUSIC   1.00
JOHNSON, S.
   ROLL'EM PETE
      MCA MUSIC   1.00
JONES
   IRONSIDE
      MCA MUSIC   1.00
JOPLIN, S.
   COLLECTED PIANO WORKS
      BELWIN-MILLS PUBLISHING CORPORATION   9.95
JOPLIN, S.   SCHAUM, J.   2 1/2
   ENTERTAINER, THE
      SCHAUM PUBLICATIONS, INC.   .75
JOPLIN, S.
   MAPLE LEAF RAG
      ASHLEY DEALERS SERVICE, INC.   ES   .95
JOPLIN, S.
   MAPLE LEAF RAG
      THE BIG THREE MUSIC CORPORATION   00.95
JOPLIN, S.
   MAPLE LEAF RAG
      EDWARD B. MARKS MUSIC CORPORATION   01.00
JOPLIN, S.   INTERMEDIATE
   MATT DENNIS PLAYS SCOTT JOPLIN
      MEL BAY PUBLICATIONS, INC.   2.50
JOPLIN, S.
   NEW RAG
      EDWARD B. MARKS MUSIC CORPORATION   01.00
JOPLIN, S.   SCHAUM, J.   2 1/2
   SCOTT JOPLIN RAGTIME RAGE, BK. 1
      SCHAUM PUBLICATIONS, INC.   1.75
JOPLIN, S.   SCHAUM, J.   2 1/2
   SCOTT JOPLIN RAGTIME RAGE, BK. 2
      SCHAUM PUBLICATIONS, INC.   1.75
JOPLIN *
   CRAZY ORGAN RAG
      SHAPIRO, BERNSTEIN ORGANIZATION   .95
JORDAN, J.
   LITTLE RED MONKEY
      THE BIG THREE MUSIC CORPORATION   00.95
JUNAYEVSKY *
   SNOWFLAKES
      MCA MUSIC   1.00
KAHAL *   RITTMAN
   I'LL BE SEEING YOU
      MCA MUSIC   1.00

KAHAL *   LIBERACE
  I'LL BE SEEING YOU
        MCA MUSIC   1.00
KAHAL *   SINGER
  I'LL BE SEEING YOU
        MCA MUSIC   1.00
KAHN, M.--ED *   KAHN, M. *
  DISNEY SHOWCASE
        BOURNE COMPANY   1.50
KAHN, M.--ED   KAHN, M.
  DOES YOUR CHEWING GUM LOSE ITS FLAVOR ON THE BEDPOST OVERNIGHT
  -- SIMP.
        BELWIN-MILLS PUBLISHING CORPORATION   26074   .50
KAHN, M.--ED   KAHN, M.
  I WAS KAISER BILL'S BATMAN -- SIMP.
        BELWIN-MILLS PUBLISHING CORPORATION   26121   .50
KAHN, M.--ED   KAHN, M.
  MARVIN KAHN'S SONG SHOWCASE
        BOURNE COMPANY   1.50
KAHN, M.
  BEGINNER'S GUIDE TO POPULAR PIANO PLAYING
        BELWIN-MILLS PUBLISHING CORPORATION   11508   1.75
KAHN, M.
  EASY CHORDS FOR STANDARD HITS
        BELWIN-MILLS PUBLISHING CORPORATION   11132   1.50
KAHN, M.
  MODERN MELODIES FOR POPULAR PIANO PLAYING
        BELWIN-MILLS PUBLISHING CORPORATION   11304   1.50
KAHN, M.
  MORE MODERN MELODIES FOR POPULAR PIANO PLAYING
        BELWIN-MILLS PUBLISHING CORPORATION   11316   1.50
KAHN, M.
  POPULAR BEGINNER FOR TEEN-AGERS AND ADULTS
        BELWIN-MILLS PUBLISHING CORPORATION   11394   1.75
KAHN, M.
  STRICTLY POPULAR
        BELWIN-MILLS PUBLISHING CORPORATION   1.50
KAIHAN *
  NOW IS THE HOUR
        MCA MUSIC   1.00
KALMAN   SIRMAY
  PLAY GYPSIES - DANCE GYPSIES
        WARNER BROTHERS PUBLISHERS   1.00
KALMAN   RICHTER   FIRST YEAR
  PLAY GYPSIES - DANCE GYPSIES
        WARNER BROTHERS PUBLISHERS   .75
KAPER, B.
  CONFETTI
        THE BIG THREE MUSIC CORPORATION   00.95
KAPER, B.
  INVITATION
        THE BIG THREE MUSIC CORPORATION   00.95
KAPER, B.
  MUTINY ON THE BOUNTY
        THE BIG THREE MUSIC CORPORATION   00.95
KATCHER   RICHTER   FIRST YEAR
  WHEN DAY IS DONE
        WARNER BROTHERS PUBLISHERS   .75
KENDALL--ED   KENDALL
  SIMPLIFIED SONG GEMS FOR PIANO
        BOURNE COMPANY   1.00
KERN, J.   BRADLEY, R.   EASY
  BRADLEY'S JEROME KERN ALBUM
        SCREEN GEMS - COLUMBIA PUBLICATIONS   F0020P2   1.95
KERN, J.
  POINTER LIBRARY - THE BEST OF JEROME KERN
        POINTER PUBLICATIONS   2.95
KERSEY
  BOOGIE WOOGIE COCKTAIL
        MCA MUSIC   1.00
KHATCHATURIAN
  SABRE DANCE BOOGIE
        MCA MUSIC   1.00
KING, C.   ENGEL, S.   ADVANCED
  CAROLE KING PIANO SOLOS
        SCREEN GEMS - COLUMBIA PUBLICATIONS   F0089P   3.95
KING, C.   BRADLEY, R.   EASY
  GOLD, UPDATED
        SCREEN GEMS - COLUMBIA PUBLICATIONS   P0086P2   2.95
KING, C.   BRADLEY, R.   EASY
  TAPESTRY
        SCREEN GEMS - COLUMBIA PUBLICATIONS   P0039P2   2.50
KING, S.--ED   KING, S.
  BLUE TANGO -- SIMP.
        BELWIN-MILLS PUBLISHING CORPORATION   26067   .50
KING, S.--ED   KING, S.
  DOWN BY THE STATION -- SIMP.
        BELWIN-MILLS PUBLISHING CORPORATION   26063   .50
KING, S.--ED   KING, S.
  RED ROSES FOR A BLUE LADY --SIMP.
        BELWIN-MILLS PUBLISHING CORPORATION   26064   .50
KING, S.--ED   KING, S.
  SLEIGH RIDE -- SIMP.
        BELWIN-MILLS PUBLISHING CORPORATION   26047   .50
KING, S.--ED   KING, S.
  THAT'S MY DESIRE -- SIMP.
        BELWIN-MILLS PUBLISHING CORPORATION   26056   .50
KING, S.
  DIXIELAND JAZZ FOR PIANO
        THEODORE PRESSER COMPANY   1.25
KING, S.
  FIDDLE-FADDLE -- SIMP.
        BELWIN-MILLS PUBLISHING CORPORATION   26013   .50
KING, S.
  PROGRESSIVE JAZZ FOR JUNIORS
        THEODORE PRESSER COMPANY   1.25
KING *
  BEATNIK FLY
        MCA MUSIC   1.00
KING
  FIRST JAZZ
        BOSTON MUSIC COMPANY   1.00
KING
  HERE'S BOOGIE WOOGIE
        CARL FISCHER, INC.   O 3313   1.25
KING
  HERE'S MORE BOOGIE WOOGIE
        CARL FISCHER, INC.   O 3370   1.50
KING
  RUNNYMEDE RHAPSODY --WHERE THE WATERLILIES DREAM
        MCA MUSIC   1.00
KING
  SYNCO POPS
        BOSTON MUSIC COMPANY   1.00
KIRK
  PETITE BOLERO
        MCA MUSIC   1.00

KNAUER
  MONTREAL
        MCA MUSIC   1.00
KNIGHT   KERR, R.N.
  WONDER OF YOU, THE
        MCA MUSIC   1.00
KONOWITZ, B.
  COMPLETE ROCK PIANO METHOD
        ALFRED MUSIC COMPANY   685   4.95
KONOWITZ, B.
  JAZZ FOR PIANO, BK. 1
        LEE ROBERTS MUSIC PUBLICATIONS, INC.   1.50
KONOWITZ, B.
  JAZZ FOR PIANO, BK. 2
        LEE ROBERTS MUSIC PUBLICATIONS, INC.   1.50
KONOWITZ, B.
  JAZZ SCENES -- BLUE NOTE BOOGIE, CHOO CHOO STOMP, LAZY DAZE,
  POUNDIN' THE BEAT
        LEE ROBERTS MUSIC PUBLICATIONS, INC.   1.25
KONOWITZ, B.
  JAZZ SPOOKS
        LEE ROBERTS MUSIC PUBLICATIONS, INC.   .50
KONOWITZ, B.
  JAZZ WALTZ
        LEE ROBERTS MUSIC PUBLICATIONS, INC.   .50
KONOWITZ, B.
  RAGA ROCK
        LEE ROBERTS MUSIC PUBLICATIONS, INC.   .50
KONOWITZ, B.
  SURF SWING
        LEE ROBERTS MUSIC PUBLICATIONS, INC.   .50
KONOWITZ, B.
  TIME CHANGES
        LEE ROBERTS MUSIC PUBLICATIONS, INC.   .50
LAI, F.
  LIVE FOR LIFE
        THE BIG THREE MUSIC CORPORATION   00.95
LAMB
  RAGTIME TREASURES
        BELWIN-MILLS PUBLISHING CORPORATION   2.95
LAMPERT *
  DOODLIN' DRUMMER, THE.
        MCA MUSIC   1.00
LANE, J.--ED.   LANE, J.
  ALICE BLUE GOWN
        THE BIG THREE MUSIC CORPORATION   00.70
LANE, J.--ED.   LANE, J.
  ALL I EVER NEED IS YOU
        THE BIG THREE MUSIC CORPORATION   00.85
LANE, J.--ED.   LANE, J.
  AMERICAN PIE
        THE BIG THREE MUSIC CORPORATION   00.70
LANE, J.--ED.   LANE, J.
  ANCHORS AWEIGH
        THE BIG THREE MUSIC CORPORATION   00.70
LANE, J.--ED.   LANE, J.
  ANY TIME
        THE BIG THREE MUSIC CORPORATION   00.70
LANE, J.--ED.   LANE, J.
  APRIL LOVE
        THE BIG THREE MUSIC CORPORATION   00.70
LANE, J.--ED.   LANE, J.
  AQUARIUS
        THE BIG THREE MUSIC CORPORATION   00.70
LANE, J.--ED.   LANE, J.
  ARRIVEDERCI, ROMA
        THE BIG THREE MUSIC CORPORATION   00.70
LANE, J.--ED.   LANE, J.
  AT SUNDOWN
        THE BIG THREE MUSIC CORPORATION   00.70
LANE, J.--ED.   LANE, J.
  BATMAN THEME
        THE BIG THREE MUSIC CORPORATION   00.70
LANE, J.--ED.   LANE, J.
  BEAUTIFUL SUNDAY
        THE BIG THREE MUSIC CORPORATION   00.85
LANE, J.--ED.   LANE, J.
  BECAUSE YOU'RE MINE
        THE BIG THREE MUSIC CORPORATION   00.70
LANE, J.--ED.   LANE, J.
  BEYOND THE SUNSET
        THE BIG THREE MUSIC CORPORATION   00.70
LANE, J.--ED.   LANE, J.
  BIG SPENDER
        THE BIG THREE MUSIC CORPORATION   00.70
LANE, J.--ED.   LANE, J.
  BLUE MOON
        THE BIG THREE MUSIC CORPORATION   00.70
LANE, J.--ED.   LANE, J.
  CANDIDA
        THE BIG THREE MUSIC CORPORATION   00.70
LANE, J.--ED.   LANE, J.
  CERTAIN SMILE, A
        THE BIG THREE MUSIC CORPORATION   00.70
LANE, J.--ED.   LANE, J.
  CHARMAINE
        THE BIG THREE MUSIC CORPORATION   00.70
LANE, J.--ED.   LANE, J.
  CHATTANOOGA CHOO CHOO
        THE BIG THREE MUSIC CORPORATION   00.70
LANE, J.--ED.   LANE, J.
  CHILDREN'S MARCHING SONG
        THE BIG THREE MUSIC CORPORATION   00.70
LANE, J.--ED.   LANE, J.
  CHITTY CHITTY BANG BANG
        THE BIG THREE MUSIC CORPORATION   00.70
LANE, J.--ED.   LANE, J.
  CIRCUS WORLD
        THE BIG THREE MUSIC CORPORATION   00.70
LANE, J.--ED.   LANE, J.
  CRYING IN THE CHAPEL
        THE BIG THREE MUSIC CORPORATION   00.70
LANE, J.--ED.   LANE, J.
  DARKTOWN STRUTTERS' BALL
        THE BIG THREE MUSIC CORPORATION   00.70
LANE, J.--ED.   LANE, J.
  DAY IN THE LIFE OF A FOOL, A
        THE BIG THREE MUSIC CORPORATION   .70
LANE, J.--ED.   LANE, J.
  DEEP PURPLE
        THE BIG THREE MUSIC CORPORATION   00.70
LANE, J.--ED.   LANE, J.
  DELILAH
        THE BIG THREE MUSIC CORPORATION   00.85
LANE, J.--ED.   LANE, J.
  DELILAH
        THE BIG THREE MUSIC CORPORATION   00.85

LANE, J.--ED.	LANE, J.	
DIAMONDS ARE FOREVER		
	THE BIG THREE MUSIC CORPORATION	00.70
LANE, J.--ED.	LANE, J.	
DIANE		
	THE BIG THREE MUSIC CORPORATION	00.70
LANE, J.--ED.	LANE, J.	
DOLL DANCE		
	THE BIG THREE MUSIC CORPORATION	00.70
LANE, J.--ED.	LANE, J.	
DON'T BLAME ME		
	THE BIG THREE MUSIC CORPORATION	00.70
LANE, J.--ED.	LANE, J.	
DR. KILDARE THEME		
	THE BIG THREE MUSIC CORPORATION	00.70
LANE, J.--ED.	LANE, J.	
EBB TIDE		
	THE BIG THREE MUSIC CORPORATION	00.70
LANE, J.--ED.	LANE, J.	
ELMER'S TUNE		
	THE BIG THREE MUSIC CORPORATION	00.70
LANE, J.--ED.	LANE, J.	
EVERY DAY OF MY LIFE		
	THE BIG THREE MUSIC CORPORATION	00.70
LANE, J.--ED.	LANE, J.	
FLIPPER		
	THE BIG THREE MUSIC CORPORATION	00.70
LANE, J.--ED.	LANE, J.	
FOREVER AND EVER		
	THE BIG THREE MUSIC CORPORATION	00.70
LANE, J.--ED.	LANE, J.	
FORGET DOMANI		
	THE BIG THREE MUSIC CORPORATION	00.70
LANE, J.--ED.	LANE, J.	
FRIENDLY PERSUASION		
	THE BIG THREE MUSIC CORPORATION	00.70
LANE, J.--ED.	LANE, J.	
GANG THAT SANG 'HEART OF MY HEART'		
	THE BIG THREE MUSIC CORPORATION	.70
LANE, J.--ED.	LANE, J.	
GENTLE ON MY MIND		
	THE BIG THREE MUSIC CORPORATION	00.70
LANE, J.--ED.	LANE, J.	
GOOD MORNING, STARSHINE		
	THE BIG THREE MUSIC CORPORATION	00.70
LANE, J.--ED.	LANE, J.	
GOOD NIGHT SWEETHEART		
	THE BIG THREE MUSIC CORPORATION	00.70
LANE, J.--ED.	LANE, J.	
GREEN LEAVES OF SUMMER		
	THE BIG THREE MUSIC CORPORATION	00.70
LANE, J.--ED.	LANE, J.	
HAPPY HEART		
	THE BIG THREE MUSIC CORPORATION	00.70
	HE	
	THE BIG THREE MUSIC CORPORATION	00.70
LANE, J.--ED.	LANE, J.	
HI-LILI, HI-LO		
	THE BIG THREE MUSIC CORPORATION	00.70
LANE, J.--ED.	LANE, J.	
HOME IN THE MEADOW		
	THE BIG THREE MUSIC CORPORATION	00.70
	HONEY	
	THE BIG THREE MUSIC CORPORATION	00.70
LANE, J.--ED.	LANE, J.	
HOW THE WEST WAS WON		
	THE BIG THREE MUSIC CORPORATION	00.70
LANE, J.--ED.	LANE, J.	
HUSH...HUSH, SWEET CHARLOTTE		
	THE BIG THREE MUSIC CORPORATION	00.70
LANE, J.--ED.	LANE, J.	
I'D LIKE TO TEACH THE WORLD TO SING		
	THE BIG THREE MUSIC CORPORATION	.70
LANE, J.--ED.	LANE, J.	
I'LL SEE YOU IN MY DREAMS		
	THE BIG THREE MUSIC CORPORATION	00.70
LANE, J.--ED.	LANE, J.	
I'M ALWAYS CHASING RAINBOWS		
	THE BIG THREE MUSIC CORPORATION	00.70
LANE, J.--ED.	LANE, J.	
I'M HENRY THE EIGHTH, I AM		
	THE BIG THREE MUSIC CORPORATION	00.70
LANE, J.--ED.	LANE, J.	
I'M IN THE MOOD FOR LOVE		
	THE BIG THREE MUSIC CORPORATION	00.70
LANE, J.--ED.	LANE, J.	
I'M SITTING ON TOP OF THE WORLD		
	THE BIG THREE MUSIC CORPORATION	.70
LANE, J.--ED.	LANE, J.	
IF I GIVE MY HEART TO YOU		
	THE BIG THREE MUSIC CORPORATION	00.70
LANE, J.--ED.	LANE, J.	
IF MY FRIENDS COULD SEE ME NOW		
	THE BIG THREE MUSIC CORPORATION	.70
LANE, J.--ED.	LANE, J.	
IF WE ONLY HAVE LOVE		
	THE BIG THREE MUSIC CORPORATION	00.70
LANE, J.--ED.	LANE, J.	
IN A LITTLE SPANISH TOWN		
	THE BIG THREE MUSIC CORPORATION	00.70
LANE, J.--ED.	LANE, J.	
IN THE GARDEN		
	THE BIG THREE MUSIC CORPORATION	00.70
LANE, J.--ED.	LANE, J.	
IT NEVER RAINS IN SOUTHERN CALIFORNIA		
	THE BIG THREE MUSIC CORPORATION	.85
LANE, J.--ED.	LANE, J.	
IT WAS A GOOD TIME		
	THE BIG THREE MUSIC CORPORATION	00.70
LANE, J.--ED.	LANE, J.	
I CAN SEE CLEARLY NOW		
	THE BIG THREE MUSIC CORPORATION	00.85
LANE, J.--ED.	LANE, J.	
I DON'T WANT TO SET THE WORLD ON FIRE		
	THE BIG THREE MUSIC CORPORATION	.70
LANE, J.--ED.	LANE, J.	
I NEED YOU NOW		
	THE BIG THREE MUSIC CORPORATION	00.70
LANE, J.--ED.	LANE, J.	
I WILL NEVER PASS THIS WAY AGAIN		
	THE BIG THREE MUSIC CORPORATION	.85
LANE, J.--ED.	LANE, J.	
JEANNINE		
	THE BIG THREE MUSIC CORPORATION	00.70

LANE, J.--ED.	LANE, J.	
JOSEPHINE		
	THE BIG THREE MUSIC CORPORATION	00.70
LANE, J.--ED.	LANE, J.	
JOY		
	THE BIG THREE MUSIC CORPORATION	00.70
LANE, J.--ED.	LANE, J.	
JUNE NIGHT		
	THE BIG THREE MUSIC CORPORATION	00.70
LANE, J.--ED.	LANE, J.	
KISS AN ANGEL GOOD MORNING		
	THE BIG THREE MUSIC CORPORATION	00.85
LANE, J.--ED.	LANE, J.	
L'IL LIZA JANE		
	THE BIG THREE MUSIC CORPORATION	00.70
LANE, J.--ED.	LANE, J.	
LAURA		
	THE BIG THREE MUSIC CORPORATION	00.70
LANE, J.--ED.	LANE, J.	
LET THE SUNSHINE IN		
	THE BIG THREE MUSIC CORPORATION	00.70
LANE, J.--ED.	LANE, J.	
LITTLE RED MONKEY		
	THE BIG THREE MUSIC CORPORATION	00.70
LANE, J.--ED.	LANE, J.	
LITTLE WOODEN SOLDIER		
	THE BIG THREE MUSIC CORPORATION	00.70
LANE, J.--ED.	LANE, J.	
LORD'S PRAYER		
	THE BIG THREE MUSIC CORPORATION	00.70
LANE, J.--ED.	LANE, J.	
LOVELIEST NIGHT OF THE YEAR		
	THE BIG THREE MUSIC CORPORATION	00.70
LANE, J.--ED.	LANE, J.	
LOVE IS A MANY-SPLENDORED THING		
	THE BIG THREE MUSIC CORPORATION	.70
LANE, J.--ED.	LANE, J.	
LOVE MAKES THE WORLD GO 'ROUND		
	THE BIG THREE MUSIC CORPORATION	.70
LANE, J.--ED.	LANE, J.	
LULLABY OF BIRDLAND		
	THE BIG THREE MUSIC CORPORATION	00.70
LANE, J.--ED.	LANE, J.	
M-I-S-S-I-P-P-I		
	THE BIG THREE MUSIC CORPORATION	00.70
LANE, J.--ED.	LANE, J.	
M-O-T-H-E-R		
	THE BIG THREE MUSIC CORPORATION	00.70
LANE, J.--ED.	LANE, J.	
MAMSELLE		
	THE BIG THREE MUSIC CORPORATION	00.70
LANE, J.--ED.	LANE, J.	
MANSION OVER THE HILLTOP		
	THE BIG THREE MUSIC CORPORATION	00.70
LANE, J.--ED.	LANE, J.	
MARCHING ALONG TOGETHER		
	THE BIG THREE MUSIC CORPORATION	00.70
LANE, J.--ED.	LANE, J.	
MAY YOU ALWAYS		
	THE BIG THREE MUSIC CORPORATION	00.70
LANE, J.--ED.	LANE, J.	
MOONLIGHT AND ROSES		
	THE BIG THREE MUSIC CORPORATION	00.70
LANE, J.--ED.	LANE, J.	
MUTINY ON THE BOUNTY-LOVE THEME		
	THE BIG THREE MUSIC CORPORATION	.70
LANE, J.--ED.	LANE, J.	
MY BLUE HEAVEN		
	THE BIG THREE MUSIC CORPORATION	00.70
LANE, J.--ED.	LANE, J.	
MY GOD IS REAL		
	THE BIG THREE MUSIC CORPORATION	00.70
LANE, J.--ED.	LANE, J.	
NUTTIN FOR CHRISTMAS		
	THE BIG THREE MUSIC CORPORATION	00.70
LANE, J.--ED.	LANE, J.	
OH HAPPY DAY		
	THE BIG THREE MUSIC CORPORATION	00.70
LANE, J.--ED.	LANE, J.	
ONCE IN A WHILE		
	THE BIG THREE MUSIC CORPORATION	00.70
LANE, J.--ED.	LANE, J.	
OVER THE RAINBOW		
	THE BIG THREE MUSIC CORPORATION	00.70
LANE, J.--ED.	LANE, J.	
PAGAN LOVE SONG		
	THE BIG THREE MUSIC CORPORATION	00.70
LANE, J.--ED.	LANE, J.	
PEACE IN THE VALLEY		
	THE BIG THREE MUSIC CORPORATION	00.70
LANE, J.--ED.	LANE, J.	
PEGGY O'NEIL		
	THE BIG THREE MUSIC CORPORATION	00.70
LANE, J.--ED.	LANE, J.	
PEG O' MY HEART		
	THE BIG THREE MUSIC CORPORATION	00.70
LANE, J.--ED.	LANE, J.	
PETTICOAT POLKA		
	THE BIG THREE MUSIC CORPORATION	00.70
LANE, J.--ED.	LANE, J.	
PIECES OF DREAMS		
	THE BIG THREE MUSIC CORPORATION	00.70
LANE, J.--ED.	LANE, J.	
PUSHBIKE SONG, THE		
	THE BIG THREE MUSIC CORPORATION	00.70
LANE, J.--ED.	LANE, J.	
RAMONA		
	THE BIG THREE MUSIC CORPORATION	00.70
LANE, J.--ED.	LANE, J.	
RELEASE ME		
	THE BIG THREE MUSIC CORPORATION	00.70
LANE, J.--ED.	LANE, J.	
ROCKIN ROBBIN		
	THE BIG THREE MUSIC CORPORATION	00.85
LANE, J.--ED.	LANE, J.	
RUBY		
	THE BIG THREE MUSIC CORPORATION	00.70
LANE, J.--ED.	LANE, J.	
SEALED WITH A KISS		
	THE BIG THREE MUSIC CORPORATION	00.85
LANE, J.--ED.	LANE, J.	
SECOND TIME AROUND		
	THE BIG THREE MUSIC CORPORATION	00.70
LANE, J.--ED.	LANE, J.	
SHADOW OF YOUR SMILE		
	THE BIG THREE MUSIC CORPORATION	00.70

LANE, J.--ED.	LANE, J.			
SHANGRI-LA				
THE BIG THREE MUSIC CORPORATION				.70
LANE, J.--ED.	LANE, J.			
SIBONEY				
THE BIG THREE MUSIC CORPORATION				00.70
LANE, J.--ED.	LANE, J.			
SINGING IN THE RAIN				
THE BIG THREE MUSIC CORPORATION				00.70
LANE, J.--ED.	LANE, J.			
SOMETHING IN YOUR SMILE				
THE BIG THREE MUSIC CORPORATION				00.70
LANE, J.--ED.	LANE, J.			
SOMEWHERE, MY LOVE				
THE BIG THREE MUSIC CORPORATION				00.70
LANE, J.--ED.	LANE, J.			
SONG OF 'THE BIBLE'				
THE BIG THREE MUSIC CORPORATION				00.70
LANE, J.--ED.	LANE, J.			
SONG OF JOY, A				
THE BIG THREE MUSIC CORPORATION				00.70
LANE, J.--ED.	LANE, J.			
SONG OF LOVE				
THE BIG THREE MUSIC CORPORATION				00.70
LANE, J.--ED.	LANE, J.			
SO RARE				
THE BIG THREE MUSIC CORPORATION				00.70
LANE, J.--ED.	LANE, J.			
STAIRWAY TO THE STARS				
THE BIG THREE MUSIC CORPORATION				00.70
LANE, J.--ED.	LANE, J.			
STEP TO THE REAR				
THE BIG THREE MUSIC CORPORATION				00.70
LANE, J.--ED.	LANE, J.			
STUMBLING				
THE BIG THREE MUSIC CORPORATION				00.70
LANE, J.--ED.	LANE, J.			
SUMMER SAND				
THE BIG THREE MUSIC CORPORATION				00.70
LANE, J.--ED.	LANE, J.			
SUNNY				
THE BIG THREE MUSIC CORPORATION				00.70
LANE, J.--ED.	LANE, J.			
SWEET AND LOVELY				
THE BIG THREE MUSIC CORPORATION				00.70
LANE, J.--ED.	LANE, J.			
SWINGIN' SHEPHERD BLUES				
THE BIG THREE MUSIC CORPORATION				00.70
LANE, J.--ED.	LANE, J.			
TALK TO THE ANIMALS				
THE BIG THREE MUSIC CORPORATION				00.70
LANE, J.--ED.	LANE, J.			
THERE'S A KIND OF HUSH				
THE BIG THREE MUSIC CORPORATION				00.70
LANE, J.--ED.	LANE, J.			
THOSE MAGNIFICENT MEN IN THEIR FLYING MACHINES				
THE BIG THREE MUSIC CORPORATION				00.70
LANE, J.--ED.	LANE, J.			
THREE COINS IN THE FOUNTAIN				
THE BIG THREE MUSIC CORPORATION				00.70
LANE, J.--ED.	LANE, J.			
THREE O'CLOCK IN THE MORNING				
THE BIG THREE MUSIC CORPORATION				00.70
LANE, J.--ED.	LANE, J.			
TIME ON MY HANDS				
THE BIG THREE MUSIC CORPORATION				00.70
LANE, J.--ED.	LANE, J.			
TODAY				
THE BIG THREE MUSIC CORPORATION				00.70
LANE, J.--ED.	LANE, J.			
VINCENT				
THE BIG THREE MUSIC CORPORATION				00.85
LANE, J.--ED.	LANE, J.			
VOLARE				
THE BIG THREE MUSIC CORPORATION				00.70
LANE, J.--ED.	LANE, J.			
WALTZ YOU SAVED FOR ME				
THE BIG THREE MUSIC CORPORATION				00.70
LANE, J.--ED.	LANE, J.			
WEDDING OF JACK AND JILL				
THE BIG THREE MUSIC CORPORATION				00.70
LANE, J.--ED.	LANE, J.			
WEDDING OF THE PAINTED DOLL				
THE BIG THREE MUSIC CORPORATION				00.70
LANE, J.--ED.	LANE, J.			
WE ARE TOGETHER				
THE BIG THREE MUSIC CORPORATION				00.70
LANE, J.--ED.	LANE, J.			
WHAT ARE YOU DOING THE REST OF YOUR LIFE				
THE BIG THREE MUSIC CORPORATION				00.70
LANE, J.--ED.	LANE, J.			
WHEN IT'S SPRINGTIME IN THE ROCKIES				
THE BIG THREE MUSIC CORPORATION				00.70
LANE, J.--ED.	LANE, J.			
WHEN I GROW TOO OLD TO DREAM				
THE BIG THREE MUSIC CORPORATION				00.70
LANE, J.--ED.	LANE, J.			
WHEN THE MOON COMES OVER THE MOUNTAIN				
THE BIG THREE MUSIC CORPORATION				00.70
LANE, J.--ED.	LANE, J.			
WHEN YOU WORE A TULIP				
THE BIG THREE MUSIC CORPORATION				00.70
LANE, J.--ED.	LANE, J.			
WHISPERING				
THE BIG THREE MUSIC CORPORATION				00.70
LANE, J.--ED.	LANE, J.			
WHITHER THOU GOEST				
THE BIG THREE MUSIC CORPORATION				00.70
LANE, J.--ED.	LANE, J.			
WINDMILLS OF YOUR MIND, THE				
THE BIG THREE MUSIC CORPORATION				01.25
LANE, J.--ED.	LANE, J.			
WINDMILLS OF YOUR MIND				
THE BIG THREE MUSIC CORPORATION				00.70
LANE, J.--ED.	LANE, J.			
WONDERFUL ONE				
THE BIG THREE MUSIC CORPORATION				00.70
LANE, J.--ED.	LANE, J.			
YOU DON'T MESS AROUND WITH JIM				
THE BIG THREE MUSIC CORPORATION				.85
LANE, J.--ED.	LANE, J.			
YOU WERE MEANT FOR ME				
THE BIG THREE MUSIC CORPORATION				00.70
LANE, J.--ED.	LANE, J.			
ZIP A DEE DO DAH				
THE BIG THREE MUSIC CORPORATION				00.70

LANE, J.--ED.	LANE, J.				
ZORBA THE GREEK - THEME					
THE BIG THREE MUSIC CORPORATION					00.70
LANE, J.					
JOHN LANE PLAYS BIG MOVIE HITS					
THE BIG THREE MUSIC CORPORATION					03.95
LANE, J.					
TEACHER'S PET NO. 12-16 BIG HITS					
THE BIG THREE MUSIC CORPORATION					01.95
LANE, J.					
TEACHER'S PET NO. 13					
THE BIG THREE MUSIC CORPORATION					01.95
LAWLOR, G. *	CURCIO	1			
SIDEWALKS OF NEW YORK, THE					
BOSTON MUSIC COMPANY					.50
LAWRENCE *	SHEARING				
ALL OF NOTHING AT ALL					
MCA MUSIC					1.00
LA ROCCA *					
AT THE JAZZ BAND BALL					
THE BIG THREE MUSIC CORPORATION					00.95
LEANDER *	KERR, R.N.				
EARLY IN THE MORNING					
MCA MUSIC					1.00
LECUONA					
SIBONEY					
THE BIG THREE MUSIC CORPORATION					00.95
LEEMANS					
MARCH OF THE BELGIAN PARATROOPS					
MCA MUSIC					1.00
LEES *	KERR, R.N.				
QUIET NIGHTS OF QUIET STARS					
MCA MUSIC					1.00
LEGRAND *	BALL	EASY			
SUMMER KNOWS, THE					
WARNER BROTHERS PUBLISHERS					.75
LEGRAND	TERRY				
THEME FROM SUMMER OF '42					
WARNER BROTHERS PUBLISHERS					1.00
LEHAR					
MERRY WIDOW, THE					
CHAPPELL AND COMPANY, INC.			3735008		1.95
LENNON *	NEALE, J.	EASY			
ALL TOGETHER NOW					
WARNER BROTHERS PUBLISHERS					.75
LENNON *	NEALE, J.	EASY			
ALL YOU NEED IS LOVE					
WARNER BROTHERS PUBLISHERS					.75
LENNON *					
FIFTY BY JOHN LENNON AND PAUL MCCARTNEY, EASY BIG NOTE PIANO					
WARNER BROTHERS PUBLISHERS					3.95
LENNON *	NEALE, J.	EASY			
HEY JUDE					
WARNER BROTHERS PUBLISHERS					.75
LENNON *	NEALE, J.	EASY			
LET IT BE					
WARNER BROTHERS PUBLISHERS					.75
LENNON *	NEALE, J.	EASY			
LONG AND WINDING ROAD, THE					
WARNER BROTHERS PUBLISHERS					.75
LENNON *	NEALE, J.	EASY			
MICHELLE					
WARNER BROTHERS PUBLISHERS					.75
LENNON *					
POINTER LIBRARY - THE BEST OF LENNON AND MCCARTNEY					
POINTER PUBLICATIONS					2.95
LENNON *	NEALE, J.	EASY			
YESTERDAY					
WARNER BROTHERS PUBLISHERS					.75
LEWIS *					
ANSWER TO THE PRAYER					
MCA MUSIC					1.00
LEWIS					
BASS ON TOP					
MCA MUSIC					1.00
LEWIS					
BEARCAT CRAWL					
MCA MUSIC					1.00
LEWIS *					
BOOGIE WOOGIE PRAYER					
MCA MUSIC					1.00
LEWIS *					
CAGE SOCIETY RAG					
MCA MUSIC					1.00
LEWIS *					
HONKY TONK TRAIN					
SHAPIRO, BERNSTEIN ORGANIZATION					.95
LEWIS					
ROCKIN' LITTLE TALE, A					
LEE ROBERTS MUSIC PUBLICATIONS, INC.					.75
LEWIS					
SIX WHEEL CHASER					
MCA MUSIC					1.00
LEWIS					
TANGANA					
LEE ROBERTS MUSIC PUBLICATIONS, INC.					1.00
LEWIS *					
YANCEY SPECIAL					
SHAPIRO, BERNSTEIN ORGANIZATION					.95
LIGHTFOOT	NEALE, J.	EASY			
IF YOU COULD READ MY MIND					
WARNER BROTHERS PUBLISHERS					.75
LINCKE, P.	RICHTER	FIRST YEAR			
GLOW WORM					
WARNER BROTHERS PUBLISHERS					.75
LIPPMAN					
CATCHY TUNE, A.					
MCA MUSIC					1.00
LIPPMAN					
CUTE LITTLE FIGURE, THE					
MCA MUSIC					1.00
LITTLE--ED	LITTLE				
WELK, LAWRENCE, FAVORITES FOR HONKY TONK PIANO					
WARNER BROTHERS PUBLISHERS					1.95
LOBO *					
REZA					
MCA MUSIC					1.00
LOCKYER					
FIDDLERS BOOGIE, THE					
MCA MUSIC					1.00
LOESSER, F.	RICHTER	2 1/2 - 3			
ADELAIDE'S LAMENT					
FRANK MUSIC CORPORATION					.75
LOESSER, F.					
GREENWILLOW					
FRANK MUSIC CORPORATION					1.50

LOESSER, F.
HOW TO SUCCEED IN BUSINESS WITHOUT REALLY TRYING
FRANK MUSIC CORPORATION 1.50
LOESSER, F.
MOST HAPPY FELLA, THE
FRANK MUSIC CORPORATION 1.25
LOESSER, F.
ON A SLOW BOAT TO CHINA
FRANK MUSIC CORPORATION .75
LOESSER, F. AGAY, D. EASY
SONGS FROM 'GREENWILLOW'
FRANK MUSIC CORPORATION 1.25
LOESSER, F. RICHTER EASY
SONGS FROM 'HANS CHRISTIAN ANDERSEN'
FRANK MUSIC CORPORATION 1.25
LOESSER, F. AGAY, D. EASY
SONGS FROM 'HOW TO SUCCEED IN BUSINESS WITHOUT REALLY TRYING'
FRANK MUSIC CORPORATION 1.25
LOEWE, F. *
LOEWE AND LERNER
CHAPPELL AND COMPANY, INC. 0013268 1.50
LOEWE, F.
MY FAIR LADY
CHAPPELL AND COMPANY, INC. 3922507 1.50
LOEWE, F.
MY FAIR LADY
CHAPPELL AND COMPANY, INC. 3900507 1.95
LOGIS *
HAPPY WALTZ, THE
MCA MUSIC 1.00
LOWE SHEARING
I'LL NEVER SMILE AGAIN
MCA MUSIC 1.00
LUBOFF, N. TERRY, F.
YELLOW BIRD
FRANK MUSIC CORPORATION .95
LUBOFF, N. RICHTER 2 1/2 - 3
YELLOW BIRD
FRANK MUSIC CORPORATION .75
LUDWIG
BLUE SCARECROW, THE
MCA MUSIC 1.00
LYONS *
SPAGHETTI RAG
SHAPIRO, BERNSTEIN ORGANIZATION .95
LYON
MY FIRST BOOGIE BOOK
BELWIN-MILLS PUBLISHING CORPORATION 1.00
MACDONALD *
INDIANA
SHAPIRO, BERNSTEIN ORGANIZATION .95
MACKAY
SHOEMAKER'S HOLIDAY, THE
MCA MUSIC 1.00
MALNECK *
DREAM STREET
THE BIG THREE MUSIC CORPORATION 00.95
MALNECK *
PARK AVENUE FANTASY
THE BIG THREE MUSIC CORPORATION 00.95
MALTZMAN--ED MALTZMAN
SONGS EN FRANCAIS
PRO-ART PUBLICATIONS, INC. 607 .75
MANCINI HASTINGS
DAYS OF WINE AND ROSES
WARNER BROTHERS PUBLISHERS 1.00
MANCINI DAVIS, J. R. FIRST YEAR
DAYS OF WINE AND ROSES
WARNER BROTHERS PUBLISHERS .75
MANCINI * NEALE, J. EASY
DAYS OF WINE AND ROSES
WARNER BROTHERS PUBLISHERS .75
MANCINI
HIGH TIME
THE BIG THREE MUSIC CORPORATION 00.95
MANCINI
LOVE THEME FROM 'THE GLENN MILLER STORY'
MCA MUSIC 1.00
MANCINI
MR. HOBBS THEME
THE BIG THREE MUSIC CORPORATION 00.95
MANCINI
MYSTERY MOVIE THEME
MCA MUSIC 1.00
MANCINI
PINK PANTHER
CIMINO PUBLICATIONS, INC. NOR 1.00
MANCINI
PINK PANTHER
CIMINO PUBLICATIONS, INC. NOR 1.25
MANCINI
TANGO AMERICANO
MCA MUSIC 1.00
MANCINI *
TOY TIGER
MCA MUSIC 1.00
MANTOVANI
SERENATA D'AMORE
THE BIG THREE MUSIC CORPORATION 00.95
MARCHETTI, F. RICHTER FIRST YEAR
FASCINATION
WARNER BROTHERS PUBLISHERS .75
MARKOWITZ, R.
HONDO
THE BIG THREE MUSIC CORPORATION 00.95
MARSHALL KERR, R.N.
HAWAIIAN WEDDING SONG
MCA MUSIC 1.00
MARSHALL
THUNDER ROAD CHASE
MCA MUSIC 1.00
MARTIN, G.--ED MARTIN, G.
GALAXY OF GREAT HITS
SAM FOX PUBLISHING COMPANY, INC. 1.50
MARTIN, G.--ED MARTIN, G.
JAZZ GALLERY
SAM FOX PUBLISHING COMPANY, INC. 2.50
MARTIN, G.
ROCK 'N' ROLL PIANO
THEODORE PRESSER COMPANY 1.25
MARTIN
BLUE VIOLINS
MCA MUSIC 1.00
MARTIN
DANCING BELLS
MCA MUSIC 1.00

MARWICK, M. *
ON THE OTHER HAND
LEE ROBERTS MUSIC PUBLICATIONS, INC. .85
MARWICK, M. *
SUMP'N SWEET
LEE ROBERTS MUSIC PUBLICATIONS, INC. .85
MASON, I.
SKIDMORE MODERN KEYBOARD SERIES --INTERMEDIATE --GREEN SERIES
--BAROQUE
SHAPIRO, BERNSTEIN ORGANIZATION .75
MASON, I.
SKIDMORE MODERN KEYBOARD SERIES --INTERMEDIATE --GREEN SERIES
--CORAL SANDS
SHAPIRO, BERNSTEIN ORGANIZATION .75
MASON, I.
SKIDMORE MODERN KEYBOARD SERIES --INTERMEDIATE --GREEN SERIES
--KERRY GREEN
SHAPIRO, BERNSTEIN ORGANIZATION .75
MASON, I. INTERMEDIATE
SKIDMORE MODERN KEYBOARD SERIES --MALEKULA MOON DANCE
SHAPIRO, BERNSTEIN ORGANIZATION .75
MASON, I. ADVANCED
SKIDMORE MODERN KEYBOARD SERIES - ENCHANTED ISLE
SHAPIRO, BERNSTEIN ORGANIZATION .75
MASON, I. INTERMEDIATE
SKIDMORE MODERN KEYBOARD SERIES - PASTELS
SHAPIRO, BERNSTEIN ORGANIZATION .75
MASON, I.
SKIMORE MODERN KEYBOARD SERIES --ADVANCED --BLUE SERIES
--NEPTUNE'S FOUNTAIN
SHAPIRO, BERNSTEIN ORGANIZATION .75
MAXWELL
EBB TIDE
THE BIG THREE MUSIC CORPORATION 00.95
MAXWELL *
SHANGRI-LA
THE BIG THREE MUSIC CORPORATION 00.95
MAYER HASTINGS
SUMMER WIND
WARNER BROTHERS PUBLISHERS 1.00
MAYUZUMI
BIBLE, THE
THE BIG THREE MUSIC CORPORATION 00.95
MCCARTHY *
IRENE
THE BIG THREE MUSIC CORPORATION 01.50
MCKUEN ROGERS, M.
GRAND TOUR
POINTER PUBLICATIONS 4.95
MCKUEN
MIDNIGHT PETE
MCA MUSIC 1.00
MCKUEN ROGERS, M.
NEW CAROLS FOR CHRISTMAS
POINTER PUBLICATIONS 3.95
MCLEAN, D.
AMERICAN PIE
THE BIG THREE MUSIC CORPORATION 00.95
MCLEAN, D.
SONGS OF DON MCLEAN, THE
THE BIG THREE MUSIC CORPORATION 04.95
MCSHANN
JAY MCSHANN BOOGIE WOOGIE AND BLUES PIANO SOLOS
MCA MUSIC 1.00
MCSHANN
DEXTER BLUES
MCA MUSIC 1.00
MCSHANN *
HOOTIE BLUES
MCA MUSIC 1.00
MCSHANN *
SWINGMATISH
MCA MUSIC 1.00
MCSHANN
VINE STREET BOOGIE
MCA MUSIC 1.00
MEHEGAN, J.
CONTEMPORARY STYLES FOR THE JAZZ PIANIST -- BK. 1
SAM FOX PUBLISHING COMPANY, INC. 3.00
MEHEGAN, J.
CONTEMPORARY STYLES FOR THE JAZZ PIANIST -- BK. 2
SAM FOX PUBLISHING COMPANY, INC. 3.00
MEHEGAN, J.
CONTEMPORARY STYLES FOR THE JAZZ PIANIST -- BK. 3
SAM FOX PUBLISHING COMPANY, INC. 3.00
MEHEGAN, J.
JAZZ BOURREE
SAM FOX PUBLISHING COMPANY, INC. .75
MEHEGAN, J.
JAZZ PIANIST, THE -- BK. 1
SAM FOX PUBLISHING COMPANY, INC. 2.50
MEHEGAN, J.
JAZZ PIANIST, THE -- BK. 2
SAM FOX PUBLISHING COMPANY, INC. 2.50
MEHEGAN, J.
JAZZ PIANIST, THE -- BK. 3
SAM FOX PUBLISHING COMPANY, INC. 2.50
MEHEGAN, J.
JAZZ PIANIST, THE -- BOOK 1 WITH INSTRUCTION RECORD
SAM FOX PUBLISHING COMPANY, INC. 6.95
MEHEGAN, J.
JAZZ PRELUDES
SAM FOX PUBLISHING COMPANY, INC. 2.50
MELIS, J.
JOSE MELIS PIANO MOODS
THE BIG THREE MUSIC CORPORATION 01.25
MELIS, J.
VOLARE
THE BIG THREE MUSIC CORPORATION 00.95
MERRILL, B.
CARNIVAL
THE BIG THREE MUSIC CORPORATION 01.50
METIS--ED. METIS
SOUNDS OF HOLLYWOOD
MCA MUSIC 1.50
METIS--ED. METIS
SOUNDS OF HOLLYWOOD
MCA MUSIC 1.50
METIS
RHYTHM FACTORY
EDWARD B. MARKS MUSIC CORPORATION 01.75
METIS
ROCK MODES AND MOODS
EDWARD B. MARKS MUSIC CORPORATION 01.50
MEYER * WALTER
CRAZY RHYTHM
WARNER BROTHERS PUBLISHERS 1.00

MILES *
    ANCHORS AWEIGH
        .HE BIG THREE MUSIC CORPORATION   00.95
MILLER *
    MOONLIGHT SERENADE
        THE BIG THREE MUSIC CORPORATION   00.95
MILLS *   KERR, R.N.
    IT'S NOT UNUSUAL
        MCA MUSIC   1.00
MOONEY
    SWAMP-FIRE
        MCA MUSIC   1.00
MOORE
    RED SQUARE
        MCA MUSIC   1.00
MOORE
    SHOO-SHOO BABY
        MCA MUSIC   1.00
MORALES   SINGER
    JUNGLE FANTASY
        MCA MUSIC   1.00
MORATH, M.--ED.   MORATH
    MAX MORATH'S GUIDE TO RAGTIME
        TRO SONGWAYS SERVICE, INC.   3.95
MORRICONE, E.
    GOOD, THE BAD, AND THE UGLY, THE
        THE BIG THREE MUSIC CORPORATION   00.95
MORRIS, C.
    PLAY THE THING
        MCA MUSIC   1.00
MOSSMAN, T.--ED   MOSSMAN, T.
    KITTEN ON THE KEYS -- SIMP.
        BELWIN-MILLS PUBLISHING CORPORATION   26023   .50
MOSSMAN, T.--ED   MOSSMAN, T.
    ORGAN GRINDER'S SWING -- SIMP.
        BELWIN-MILLS PUBLISHING CORPORATION   26068   .50
MOSSMAN, T.--ED   MOSSMAN, T.
    PAVANNE -- SIMP.
        BELWIN-MILLS PUBLISHING CORPORATION   26036   .50
MOSSMAN, T.--ED   MOSSMAN, T.
    SERENADE IN THE NIGHT -- SIMP.
        BELWIN-MILLS PUBLISHING CORPORATION   26092   .50
MOSSMAN, T.--ED   MOSSMAN, T.
    SHEIK OF ARABY, THE -- SIMP.
        BELWIN-MILLS PUBLISHING CORPORATION   .50
MOSSMAN, T.--ED   MOSSMAN, T.
    SWEET LORRAINE -- SIMP.
        BELWIN-MILLS PUBLISHING CORPORATION   26052   .50
MOSSMAN, T.--ED   MOSSMAN, T.
    SWEET ROSIE O'GRADY SIMP.
        BELWIN-MILLS PUBLISHING CORPORATION   26053   .50
MOSSMAN, T.--ED   MOSSMAN, T.
    TAKE ME IN YOUR ARMS -- SIMP.
        BELWIN-MILLS PUBLISHING CORPORATION   26055   .50
MOSSMAN, T.--ED   MOSSMAN, T.
    WHEN IT'S SLEEPY TIME DOWN SOUTH -- SIMP.
        BELWIN-MILLS PUBLISHING CORPORATION   26062   .50
MOSSMAN, T.
    AIN'T MISBEHAVIN' -- SIMP.
        BELWIN-MILLS PUBLISHING CORPORATION   26003   .50
MOSSMAN, T.
    BUGLE CALL RAG -- SIMP.
        BELWIN-MILLS PUBLISHING CORPORATION   26072   .50
MOSSMAN, T.
    CENTRAL PARK ROMANCE
        THE BIG THREE MUSIC CORPORATION   00.95
MOSSMAN, T.
    FOR ME AND MY GAL -- SIMP.
        BELWIN-MILLS PUBLISHING CORPORATION   26075   .50
MOSSMAN, T.
    I CAN'T GIVE YOU ANYTHING BUT LOVE -- SIMP.
        BELWIN-MILLS PUBLISHING CORPORATION   26021   .50
MOSSMAN, T.
    ODE TO GERSHWIN
        THE BIG THREE MUSIC CORPORATION   00.95
MOSSMAN, T.
    SCHOOL DAYS -- SIMP.
        BELWIN-MILLS PUBLISHING CORPORATION   26042   .50
MOSSMAN, T.
    SIMPLIFIED BOOGIE WOOGIE
        BELWIN-MILLS PUBLISHING CORPORATION   1.25
MOSSMAN, T.
    SOLITUDE -- SIMP.
        BELWIN-MILLS PUBLISHING CORPORATION   26049   .50
MOSSMAN, T.
    SOPHISTICATED LADY -- SIMP.
        BELWIN-MILLS PUBLISHING CORPORATION   26050   .50
MOULIN
    CHARLESTON PARISIEN
        MCA MUSIC   1.00
MSARURGWA *
    SKOKIAAN
        SHAPIRO, BERNSTEIN ORGANIZATION   .95
MULLER
    ALL AMERICAN SQUARE DANCES
        SHAWNEE PRESS, INC.   2.00
MYROW
    AUTUMN NOCTURNE
        WARNER BROTHERS PUBLISHERS   1.00
NASCIMBENE
    FRANCIS OF ASSISI - THEME
        THE BIG THREE MUSIC CORPORATION   00.95
NASCIMBENE
    ROMANOFF AND JULIET
        MCA MUSIC   1.00
NASH, J.
    I CAN SEE CLEARLY NOW
        THE BIG THREE MUSIC CORPORATION   02.95
NEALE, J.--ED   NEALE, J.
    INSTANT PICTURE CHORD PIANO NO. 1
        WARNER BROTHERS PUBLISHERS   1.95
NEALE, J.--ED   NEALE, J.
    PETER, PAUL AND MARY, MORE MADE EASY FOR PIANO
        WARNER BROTHERS PUBLISHERS   PPM 25   2.00
NERO
    HOT CANARY, THE
        MCA MUSIC   1.00
NERO
    NERO, PETER, AT THE PIANO
        WARNER BROTHERS PUBLISHERS   2.50
NERO
    NERO, PETER, OFF RECORD
        WARNER BROTHERS PUBLISHERS   2.50
NEVIN
    MILLS PIANO HITS
        BELWIN-MILLS PUBLISHING CORPORATION   11376   1.50

NEVIN
    TOP POP TUNES
        BELWIN-MILLS PUBLISHING CORPORATION   2.00
NEWMAN, A.
    STREET SCENE
        THE BIG THREE MUSIC CORPORATION   00.95
NEWMAN, L.
    HONG KONG
        THE BIG THREE MUSIC CORPORATION   00.95
NIEDT *
    UNDER THE LINDEN TREE
        MCA MUSIC   1.00
NOBLE *
    CHEROKEE
        SHAPIRO, BERNSTEIN ORGANIZATION   .95
NORMAN *
    FANFARE TANGO
        MCA MUSIC   1.00
NORMAN
    FOREIGN INTRIGUE CONCERTO
        MCA MUSIC   1.00
NORMAN *
    LONELY WHISTLER, THE
        MCA MUSIC   1.00
NORMAN
    THEME FROM FOREIGN INTRIGUE CONCERTO -- SIMPLIFIED EDITION
        MCA MUSIC   1.00
NORTH, A.
    ANTONY AND CLEOPATRA THEME
        THE BIG THREE MUSIC CORPORATION   00.95
NORTH, A.
    CAESAR AND CLEOPATRA THEME
        THE BIG THREE MUSIC CORPORATION   00.95
NORTH, A.
    OUTRAGE, THE - THEME
        THE BIG THREE MUSIC CORPORATION   00.95
NORTH, A.
    RECONCILIATION
        THE BIG THREE MUSIC CORPORATION   00.95
NORTH, A.
    SHOES OF THE FISHERMAN, THE
        THE BIG THREE MUSIC CORPORATION   00.95
OLIVER *
    EASY DOES IT
        MCA MUSIC   1.00
OLIVIERO *
    MORE
        EDWARD B. MARKS MUSIC CORPORATION   01.00
OLIVIERO *
    MORE
        EDWARD B. MARKS MUSIC CORPORATION   01.00
ORTOLANI
    ELOISE
        THE BIG THREE MUSIC CORPORATION   00.95
ORTOLANI
    MAE
        THE BIG THREE MUSIC CORPORATION   00.95
ORTOLANI
    MAYA
        THE BIG THREE MUSIC CORPORATION   00.95
ORTOLANI
    YELLOW ROLLS-ROYCE - THEME
        THE BIG THREE MUSIC CORPORATION   00.95
OSBORNE *
    BETWEEN 18TH AND 19TH ON CHESTNUT STREET
        MCA MUSIC   1.00
OSSER *
    KATHY'S THEME
        MCA MUSIC   1.00
PALMER, W. A.
    BAROQUE FOLK
        ALFRED MUSIC COMPANY   522   1.25
PALMER, W. A.
    HOW TO PLAY ROCK 'N' ROLL PIANO
        ALFRED MUSIC COMPANY   544   2.95
PALMER *
    SERENADE TO AN EMPTY ROOM
        MCA MUSIC   1.00
PAPARELLI   PAPARELLI
    BOOGIE WOOGIE PIANO ARRANGEMENTS, BK. 1 - EASY
        MCA MUSIC   1.00
PAPARELLI   PAPARELLI
    BOOGIE WOOGIE PIANO ARRANGEMENTS, BK. 3 - MEDIUM
        MCA MUSIC   1.50
PAPARELLI
    NEWTON'S BOOGIE WOOGIE
        MCA MUSIC   1.00
PIAF *
    MORE, MORE, AND MORE -- UN GRAND AMOUR
        MCA MUSIC   1.00
POLLACK *
    DIANE
        THE BIG THREE MUSIC CORPORATION   00.95
PONCE, E.
    HOLIDAY
        THE BIG THREE MUSIC CORPORATION   00.95
POPP *
    PORTUGUESE WASHERWOMEN, THE
        WARNER BROTHERS PUBLISHERS   1.00
PORTER, C.   LEVINE
    BEGIN THE BEGUINE
        WARNER BROTHERS PUBLISHERS   1.00
PORTER, C.   WALTER
    BEGIN THE BEGUINE
        WARNER BROTHERS PUBLISHERS   1.00
PORTER, C.   HEYWOOD
    BEGIN THE BEGUINE
        WARNER BROTHERS PUBLISHERS   1.00
PORTER, C.   RICHTER   FIRST YEAR
    BEGIN THE BEGUINE
        WARNER BROTHERS PUBLISHERS   .75
PORTER, C.
    MEET COLE PORTER AT THE PIANO
        CHAPPELL AND COMPANY, INC.   0010074   2.50
PORTER, C.   HASTINGS
    NIGHT AND DAY
        WARNER BROTHERS PUBLISHERS   1.00
PORTER, C.   MACLACHLAN   FIRST YEAR
    NIGHT AND DAY
        WARNER BROTHERS PUBLISHERS   .75
PORTER, C.
    POINTER LIBRARY - THE BEST OF COLE PORTER
        POINTER PUBLICATIONS   2.95
PORTER, C.
    SO IN LOVE
        CIMINO PUBLICATIONS, INC.   H   1.25

POTTER, H. *
ALL-IN-ONE BOOGIE WOOGIE
SHAWNEE PRESS, INC. .50
PREVIN, A.
LIKE BLUE
THE BIG THREE MUSIC CORPORATION 00.95
PREVIN, A.
LIKE YOUNG
THE BIG THREE MUSIC CORPORATION 00.95
PREVIN, A.
LONG DAY'S JOURNEY INTO NIGHT, THEME FROM
MCA MUSIC 1.00
PREVIN, A.
PLAY PIANO LIKE ANDRE PREVIN, NO. 1
THE BIG THREE MUSIC CORPORATION 01.50
PREVIN, A.
PLAY PIANO LIKE ANDRE PREVIN, NO. 2
THE BIG THREE MUSIC CORPORATION 01.95
RAGAS *
CLARINET MARMALADE
THE BIG THREE MUSIC CORPORATION 00.95
RAKSIN, D.
BAD AND THE BEAUTIFUL, THE
THE BIG THREE MUSIC CORPORATION 00.95
RAMEY *
SO YOU WON'T JUMP
MCA MUSIC 1.00
RAPHAEL, G.
RAPHAEL
MUSIC SALES CORPORATION 060002 2.95
RASKIN, D.
LAURA
THE BIG THREE MUSIC CORPORATION 00.95
RAYE *
COW-COW BOOGIE
MCA MUSIC 1.00
RAYE
DOWN THE ROAD A PIECE
MCA MUSIC 1.00
RAYE
DOWN THE ROAD A PIECE
MCA MUSIC 1.00
RAYE *
MISTER FIVE BY FIVE
MCA MUSIC 1.00
RAYE *
RHUMBOOGIE
MCA MUSIC 1.00
RAYE
SCRUB ME MAMA --WITH A BOOGIE BEAT--
MCA MUSIC 1.00
RAYE *
STRUTTIN' WITH SOME BARBECUE
MCA MUSIC 1.00
REISMAN
FRONT ROW CENTER
SHAPIRO, BERNSTEIN ORGANIZATION .95
REISMAN *
JOEY'S SONG
SHAPIRO, BERNSTEIN ORGANIZATION .95
RICE *   KERR, R.N.
I DON'T KNOW HOW TO LOVE HIM
MCA MUSIC 1.00
RICE *   AGAY, D.
JESUS CHRIST SUPERSTAR
MCA MUSIC 1.50
RICHARDSON, A.
RUNNING OFF THE RAILS --A LOCO-MOTIF
MCA MUSIC 1.00
RICHTER--ED   RICHTER
DISNEY CLASSICS
BOURNE COMPANY 1.50
RICHTER--ED   RICHTER
MADE EASY FOR THE PIANO -- 20TH CENTURY HITS, BK. 1
WARNER BROTHERS PUBLISHERS MEZ 9 1.25
RICHTER--ED   RICHTER
MADE EASY FOR THE PIANO -- 20TH CENTURY HITS, BK. 2
WARNER BROTHERS PUBLISHERS MEZ 10 1.25
RICHTER--ED   RICHTER
SNOW WHITE AND THE SEVEN DWARFS
BOURNE COMPANY 1.50
RIDDLE, N.
THEME FROM 'THE UNTOUCHABLES'
FRANK MUSIC CORPORATION .95
RITTMAN--ED   RITTMAN
YESTERDAYS
CIMINO PUBLICATIONS, INC. H 1.25
RIXNER
PAGAMUFFIN
MCA MUSIC 1.00
ROBIN *   SHEARING
UNDECIDED
MCA MUSIC 1.00
ROBIN *
UNDECIDED
MCA MUSIC 1.00
ROBISION
TREE TOP SERENADE
MCA MUSIC 1.00
ROBYN, A.
MANZANILLO
THE BIG THREE MUSIC CORPORATION 00.95
RODGERS   MACLACHLAN   FIRST YEAR
BLUE ROOM, THE
WARNER BROTHERS PUBLISHERS .75
RODGERS
GREAT ADVENTURE, THE
MCA MUSIC 1.00
RODGERS
GUADALCANAL MARCH
MCA MUSIC 1.00
RODGERS   SIRMAY
MEET RICHARD RODGERS AT THE PIANO
MCA MUSIC 2.00
RODGERS   PORTNOFF
NO STRINGS
MCA MUSIC 1.50
RODGERS
NO STRINGS
MCA MUSIC 2.50
RODGERS
REGENTS MARCH, THE. --SALIANT YEARS, MAIN THEME, THE.
MCA MUSIC 1.00
RODGERS *   PORTNOFF
RODGERS AND HAMMERSTEIN PLAY AND SING--SIMPLIFIED PIANO
COLLECTION
MCA MUSIC 2.50

RODGERS   SINGER
SWEETEST SOUNDS, THE
MCA MUSIC 1.00
RODGERS *   MILLER, M.
TWO BY TWO
MCA MUSIC 1.50
RODGERS
VALIENT YEARS, THE. --REGENT MARCH
MCA MUSIC 1.00
RODGERS
VICTORY AT SEA --THEME
MCA MUSIC 1.00
RODGERS
VICTORY AT SEA
MCA MUSIC 1.25
RODGERS   RICHTER   FIRST YEAR
WITH A SONG IN MY HEART
WARNER BROTHERS PUBLISHERS .75
RODGERS   GLOVER
WONDERFUL WORLD OF RICHARD RODGERS, THE. -- EASYPLAY PIANO SOLOS
MCA MUSIC 2.50
ROEMHELD, H.
RUBY
THE BIG THREE MUSIC CORPORATION 00.95
ROIG
YOURS --QUIEREME MUCHO
EDWARD B. MARKS MUSIC CORPORATION 01.00
ROMBERG, S.
BLOSSOM TIME
THE BIG THREE MUSIC CORPORATION 01.50
ROMBERG, S.   RICHTER   FIRST YEAR
DESERT SONG, THE
WARNER BROTHERS PUBLISHERS .75
ROMBERG, S.
SELECTIONS FROM 'MAYTIME'
G. SCHIRMER, INC. 1.00
ROMBERG, S.   RIEGGER
SERENADE
WARNER BROTHERS PUBLISHERS 1.00
ROMBERG, S.   RICHTER   FIRST YEAR
SERENADE
WARNER BROTHERS PUBLISHERS .75
ROMBERG, S.   RICHTER   FIRST YEAR
STOUTHEARTED MEN
WARNER BROTHERS PUBLISHERS .75
ROMBERG, S. *
UP IN CENTRAL PARK
MCA MUSIC 2.50
ROMBERG, S.   KAPLAN
WILL YOU REMEMBER--FROM 'MAYTIME'
G. SCHIRMER, INC. .50
ROMBERG, S.   DEIS
WILL YOU REMEMBER--FROM 'MAYTIME'
G. SCHIRMER, INC. .40
ROMBERG, S.   LEVINE
WILL YOU REMEMBER--FROM 'MAYTIME'
G. SCHIRMER, INC. .50
ROMBERG, S.   LEVINE
WILL YOU REMEMBER--FROM 'MAYTIME'
G. SCHIRMER, INC. .50
ROME *
ON GUARD MARCH
MCA MUSIC 1.00
ROSE, D.
HOMBRE
THE BIG THREE MUSIC CORPORATION 00.95
ROSENTHAL, L.
COMEDIANS, THE
THE BIG THREE MUSIC CORPORATION 00.95
ROSS
MAGIC HORN, THE
MCA MUSIC 1.00
ROSZA
BEAUTY AND GRACE
THE BIG THREE MUSIC CORPORATION 00.95
ROSZA
BEN-HUR
THE BIG THREE MUSIC CORPORATION 00.95
ROSZA
KING OF KINGS, THE
THE BIG THREE MUSIC CORPORATION 00.95
ROTA *
ZAMPANO
MCA MUSIC 1.00
RUBINSTEIN
KAMENNOI-OSTROW
MCA MUSIC 1.00
RUMSHINSKY
SKIDMORE MODERN KEYBOARD SERIES --INTERMEDIATE --GREEN SERIES
--BAZAARS OF BAGDAD
SHAPIRO, BERNSTEIN ORGANIZATION .75
SAINTON
DEPARTURE OF THE PEQUOD, THE
MCA MUSIC 1.00
SALVADOR
AVA
MCA MUSIC 1.00
SANTISI, R.
JAZZ ORIGINALS
BERKLEE PRESS PUBLICATIONS B-10 2.50
SAVINO--ED.   SAVINO
POPULAR SONG CLASSICS FOR PIANO
THE BIG THREE MUSIC CORPORATION 01.25
SAVINO--ED.   SAVINO
WALTZ YOU SAVED FOR ME
THE BIG THREE MUSIC CORPORATION 00.95
SAVINO--ED.   SAVINO
WONDERFUL ONE
THE BIG THREE MUSIC CORPORATION 00.95
SAVINO
STUDY IN BLUE
THE BIG THREE MUSIC CORPORATION 00.95
SAWTELL, P.
VOYAGE TO THE BOTTOM OF THE SEA
THE BIG THREE MUSIC CORPORATION 00.95
SCHAUM, J.
POP PIANO COURSE, BK. 1
BELWIN-MILLS PUBLISHING CORPORATION 2.00
SCHAUM, J.
POP PIANO COURSE, BK. 2
BELWIN-MILLS PUBLISHING CORPORATION 2.00
SCHAUM, J.
POP PIANO COURSE, BK. 3
BELWIN-MILLS PUBLISHING CORPORATION 2.00
SCHAUM, J.
POP PIANO COURSE, BK. 4
BELWIN-MILLS PUBLISHING CORPORATION 2.00

SCHAUM, J.   1 1/2
   RHYTHM AND BLUES, BK. 1
      SCHAUM PUBLICATIONS, INC.   1.25
SCHAUM, J.   2
   RHYTHM AND BLUES, BK. 2
      SCHAUM PUBLICATIONS, INC.   1.25
SCHAUM, J.   2 1/2
   RHYTHM AND BLUES, BK. 3
      SCHAUM PUBLICATIONS, INC.   1.25
SCHIFRIN, L.
   HAUNTING
      THE BIG THREE MUSIC CORPORATION   00.95
SCHIFRIN, L.
   RHINO - THEME
      THE BIG THREE MUSIC CORPORATION   00.95
SCHIFRIN   HASTINGS
   BULLITT, THEME FROM
      WARNER BROTHERS PUBLISHERS   1.00
SCHIFRIN
   FOX, THE, THEME FROM
      WARNER BROTHERS PUBLISHERS   1.00
SCHOEN
   MY POEM
      MCA MUSIC   1.00
SCHULTZE   COLE
   LILLI MARLENE
      EDWARD B. MARKS MUSIC CORPORATION   01.00
SCHULTZE
   LILLI MARLENE
      EDWARD B. MARKS MUSIC CORPORATION   01.00
SCHULZ, J.   E
   EIGHTEEN POPULAR SONGS
      C. F. PETERS CORPORATION   T18   1.50
SCOTT, H.
   HAZEL'S BOOGIE WOOGIE
      MCA MUSIC   1.00
SCOTT, H.
   HAZEL SCOTT FIVE SOLOS -- BOOGIE WOOGIE TO THE CLASSICS
      MCA MUSIC   1.00
SEDORES   SINGER
   CHINA NIGHTS -- SHINA NO YORU
      MCA MUSIC   1.00
SERLY
   FOX TROT
      MCA MUSIC   1.00
SHARPLES
   CAROUSEL CALLIOPE
      MCA MUSIC   1.00
SHAW
   PASTEL BLUES
      MCA MUSIC   1.00
SHEARING, G.
   INTERPRETATIONS FOR PIANO, NO. 1
      THE BIG THREE MUSIC CORPORATION   01.50
SHEARING, G.
   INTERPRETATIONS FOR PIANO, NO. 2
      THE BIG THREE MUSIC CORPORATION   01.50
SHEARING, G.
   INTERPRETATIONS FOR PIANO, NO. 3
      THE BIG THREE MUSIC CORPORATION   01.50
SHEARING, G.
   INTERPRETATIONS FOR PIANO, NO. 4
      THE BIG THREE MUSIC CORPORATION   01.50
SHEARING, G.
   INTERPRETATIONS FOR PIANO, NO. 5
      THE BIG THREE MUSIC CORPORATION   01.50
SHEARING, G.
   INTERPRETATIONS FOR PIANO, NO. 6
      THE BIG THREE MUSIC CORPORATION   01.50
SHEARING, G.
   INTERPRETATIONS FOR PIANO, NO. 7
      THE BIG THREE MUSIC CORPORATION   01.50
SHEARING, G.
   PLAY PIANO LIKE GEORGE SHEARING
      THE BIG THREE MUSIC CORPORATION   01.50
SHINN, D.
   HOW TO PLAY LUSH, MODERN, 'MOOD' PIANO
      SHINN MUSIC AIDS   3.95
SHINN, D.
   POPULAR PIANO PLAYING SIMPLIFIED
      SHINN MUSIC AIDS   1.95
SIEGMEISTER
   BOOGIE
      SAM FOX PUBLISHING COMPANY, INC.   .50
SILVERS   RIEGGER
   APRIL SHOWERS
      WARNER BROTHERS PUBLISHERS   1.00
SILVERS   RICHTER   FIRST YEAR
   APRIL SHOWERS
      WARNER BROTHERS PUBLISHERS   .75
SILVERS *
   INTERLUDE
      MCA MUSIC   1.00
SIMMS
   ROCK'EM BOOGIE
      SAM FOX PUBLISHING COMPANY, INC.   .50
SIMMS
   ROLL'EM BOOGIE
      SAM FOX PUBLISHING COMPANY, INC.   .50
SIMON
   AMBER
      MCA MUSIC   1.00
SIMON *
   DAFFY DAFFODIL
      MCA MUSIC   1.00
SIMON
   DIAMONDS
      MCA MUSIC   1.00
SIMON
   EMERALDS
      MCA MUSIC   1.00
SIMON
   MOONSTONES
      MCA MUSIC   1.00
SIMON
   RUBIES
      MCA MUSIC   1.00
SIMON
   SAPPHIRES
      MCA MUSIC   1.00
SIMPSON
   LAUGHING TROMBONE POLKA
      MCA MUSIC   1.00
SINATRA, R.
   BOOGIE-WOOGIE IN THE KITCHEN
      THE BIG THREE MUSIC CORPORATION   00.95

SINATRA, R.
   BOOGIE-WOOGIE IN THE PARLOR
      THE BIG THREE MUSIC CORPORATION   00.95
SINGER, L.--ED   SINGER, L.
   ALL OF YOU
      CHAPPELL AND COMPANY, INC.   0160002-151   .95
SINGER, L.--ED   SINGER, L.
   AMONG MY SOUVENIRS
      CHAPPELL AND COMPANY, INC.   0212506   .95
SINGER, L.--ED   SINGER, L.
   APRIL IN PORTUGAL
      CHAPPELL AND COMPANY, INC.   0028008   .95
SINGER, L.--ED   SINGER, L.
   BEWITCHED
      CHAPPELL AND COMPANY, INC.   0460006   .95
SINGER, L.--ED   SINGER, L.
   COME RAIN OR COME SHINE
      CHAPPELL AND COMPANY, INC.   0942508   .95
SINGER, L.--ED   SINGER, L.
   EVERYTHING'S COMING UP ROSES
      CHAPPELL AND COMPANY, INC.   1397512   .95
SINGER, L.--ED   SINGER, L.
   FALLING IN LOVE WITH LOVE
      CHAPPELL AND COMPANY, INC.   1427509   .95
SINGER, L.--ED   SINGER, L.
   FOGGY DAY, A
      CHAPPELL AND COMPANY, INC.   1520030   .95
SINGER, L.--ED   SINGER, L.
   FROM THIS MOMENT ON
      CHAPPELL AND COMPANY, INC.   1620004   .95
SINGER, L.--ED   SINGER, L.
   GIGI
      CHAPPELL AND COMPANY, INC.   1680016   .95
SINGER, L.--ED   SINGER, L.
   HARBOR LIGHTS
      CHAPPELL AND COMPANY, INC.   1900000   .95
SINGER, L.--ED   SINGER, L.
   HOW ARE THINGS IN GLOCCA MORRA
      CHAPPELL AND COMPANY, INC.   2060002   .95
SINGER, L.--ED   SINGER, L.
   HOW HIGH THE MOON
      CHAPPELL AND COMPANY, INC.   2085009   .95
SINGER, L.--ED   SINGER, L.
   I'LL FOLLOW MY SECRET HEART
      CHAPPELL AND COMPANY, INC.   2656502   .95
SINGER, L.--ED   SINGER, L.
   I'VE GOT YOU UNDER MY SKIN
      CHAPPELL AND COMPANY, INC.   2875508   .95
SINGER, L.--ED   SINGER, L.
   I'VE GROWN ACCUSTOMED TO HER FACE
      CHAPPELL AND COMPANY, INC.   2877504   .95
SINGER, L.--ED   SINGER, L.
   IF EVER I WOULD LEAVE YOU
      CHAPPELL AND COMPANY, INC.   2577500   .95
SINGER, L.--ED   SINGER, L.
   IN THE STILL OF THE NIGHT
      CHAPPELL AND COMPANY, INC.   2720001   .95
SINGER, L.--ED   SINGER, L.
   IT'S ALL RIGHT WITH ME
      CHAPPELL AND COMPANY, INC.   2838001   .95
SINGER, L.--ED   SINGER, L.
   IT'S DE-LOVELY
      CHAPPELL AND COMPANY, INC.   2842508   .95
SINGER, L.--ED   SINGER, L.
   I CAN'T GET STARTED
      CHAPPELL AND COMPANY, INC.   2167500   .95
SINGER, L.--ED   SINGER, L.
   I CAN DREAM, CAN'T I
      CHAPPELL AND COMPANY, INC.   2150001   .95
SINGER, L.--ED   SINGER, L.
   I CONCENTRATE ON YOU
      CHAPPELL AND COMPANY, INC.   2175008   .60
SINGER, L.--ED   SINGER, L.
   I COULD HAVE DANCED ALL NIGHT
      CHAPPELL AND COMPANY, INC.   2180008   .95
SINGER, L.--ED   SINGER, L.
   I DIDN'T KNOW WHAT TIME IT WAS
      CHAPPELL AND COMPANY, INC.   2190007   .95
SINGER, L.--ED   SINGER, L.
   I HEARD A FOREST PRAYING
      CHAPPELL AND COMPANY, INC.   0015560   .95
SINGER, L.--ED   SINGER, L.
   I LOVE PARIS
      CHAPPELL AND COMPANY, INC.   2330009   .95
SINGER, L.--ED   SINGER, L.
   I LOVE YOU
      CHAPPELL AND COMPANY, INC.   2340008   .95
SINGER, L.--ED   SINGER, L.
   I SEE YOUR FACE BEFORE ME
      CHAPPELL AND COMPANY, INC.   2457505   .95
SINGER, L.--ED   SINGER, L.
   I WAS DOING ALL RIGHT
      CHAPPELL AND COMPANY, INC.   2512507   .95
SINGER, L.--ED   SINGER, L.
   JUST IN TIME
      CHAPPELL AND COMPANY, INC.   3027505   .95
SINGER, L.--ED   SINGER, L.
   LAZY AFTERNOON
      CHAPPELL AND COMPANY, INC.   3167509   .95
SINGER, L.--ED   SINGER, L.
   LONG AGO -- AND FAR AWAY
      CHAPPELL AND COMPANY, INC.   3410008   .95
SINGER, L.--ED   SINGER, L.
   LOVE WALKED IN
      CHAPPELL AND COMPANY, INC.   3515004   .95
SINGER, L.--ED   SINGER, L.
   MAKE SOMEONE HAPPY
      CHAPPELL AND COMPANY, INC.   3600004   .95
SINGER, L.--ED   SINGER, L.
   MY FUNNY VALENTINE
      CHAPPELL AND COMPANY, INC.   3930005   .95
SINGER, L.--ED   SINGER, L.
   MY SHIP
      CHAPPELL AND COMPANY, INC.   3995008   .95
SINGER, L.--ED   SINGER, L.
   NEVERTHELESS
      CHAPPELL AND COMPANY, INC.   4060000   .95
SINGER, L.--ED   SINGER, L.
   NICE WORK IF YOU CAN GET IT
      CHAPPELL AND COMPANY, INC.   4082525   .95
SINGER, L.--ED   SINGER, L.
   OLD DEVIL MOON
      CHAPPELL AND COMPANY, INC.   4297503   .95
SINGER, L.--ED   SINGER, L.
   ON THE STREET WHERE YOU LIVE
      CHAPPELL AND COMPANY, INC.   4350005   .95

SINGER, L.--ED SINGER, L.			
PARTY'S OVER, THE			
CHAPPELL AND COMPANY, INC.		4523759	.95
SINGER, L.--ED SINGER, L.			
PEOPLE			
CHAPPELL AND COMPANY, INC.		4562500	.95
SINGER, L.--ED SINGER, L.			
ROSALIE			
CHAPPELL AND COMPANY, INC.		4907507	.95
SINGER, L.--ED SINGER, L.			
SEAL IT WITH A KISS			
CHAPPELL AND COMPANY, INC.		0019448	.95
SINGER, L.--ED SINGER, L.			
SEPTEMBER SONG			
CHAPPELL AND COMPANY, INC.		5060009	.95
SINGER, L.--ED SINGER, L.			
SMALL WORLD			
CHAPPELL AND COMPANY, INC.		5235007	.95
SINGER, L.--ED SINGER, L.			
SPEAK LOW			
CHAPPELL AND COMPANY, INC.		5412507	.95
SINGER, L.--ED SINGER, L.			
STRANGE MUSIC			
CHAPPELL AND COMPANY, INC.		5520002	.95
SINGER, L.--ED SINGER, L.			
STRING OF PEARLS, A			
CHAPPELL AND COMPANY, INC.		5537501	.95
SINGER, L.--ED SINGER, L.			
THERE'S A SMALL HOTEL			
CHAPPELL AND COMPANY, INC.		5875000	.95
SINGER, L.--ED SINGER, L.			
THEY CAN'T TAKE THAT AWAY FROM ME			
CHAPPELL AND COMPANY, INC.		5932520	.95
SINGER, L.--ED SINGER, L.			
THIS CAN'T BE LOVE			
CHAPPELL AND COMPANY, INC.		5955000	.95
SINGER, L.--ED SINGER, L.			
TILL			
CHAPPELL AND COMPANY, INC.		6057509	.95
SINGER, L.--ED SINGER, L.			
TRUE LOVE			
CHAPPELL AND COMPANY, INC.		6165005	.95
SINGER, L.--ED SINGER, L.			
TRY TO REMEMBER			
CHAPPELL AND COMPANY, INC.		6175004	.95
SINGER, L.--ED SINGER, L.			
WISH YOU WERE HERE			
CHAPPELL AND COMPANY, INC.		6702518	.95
SINGER, L.--ED SINGER, L.			
WORLD IS WAITING FOR THE SUNRISE, THE			
CHAPPELL AND COMPANY, INC.		6755003	.95
SINGER, L.--ED SINGER, L.			
WOULDN'T BE LOVERLY			
CHAPPELL AND COMPANY, INC.		6767503	.95
SINGER, L.--ED SINGER, L.			
YOU'D BE SO NICE TO COME HOME TO			
CHAPPELL AND COMPANY, INC.		6915508	.95
SINGER			
NIGHT WHISPERS			
MCA MUSIC			1.00
SINGER			
PETITE BALLERINA			
MCA MUSIC			1.00
SINGER			
TIC-TAC-TOE			
MCA MUSIC			1.00
SINGER WILLIAMS, J.			
YOUNG AND WARM AND WONDERFUL			
FRANK MUSIC CORPORATION			.95
SINGLETON * KERR, R.N.			
STRANGERS IN THE NIGHT			
MCA MUSIC			1.00
SLACK			
BOLERO ON THE MOON			
MCA MUSIC			1.00
SMALL, A.			
BEGINNER'S ROCK 'N' ROLL PIANO BOOK			
ALFRED MUSIC COMPANY		542	1.00
SMALL, A.			
BLUES AND HOW			
ALFRED MUSIC COMPANY		543	1.95
SMALL, A.			
ROCK 'N' ROLL PIANIST, THE			
ALFRED MUSIC COMPANY		545	1.50
SMITH *			
GUITAR BOOGIE SHUFFLE			
SHAPIRO, BERNSTEIN ORGANIZATION			.95
SMITH			
MINUET IN SWING			
MCA MUSIC			1.00
SMITH			
PINETOP'S BLUES			
MCA MUSIC			1.00
SNYDER, W.			
FASCINATION -- VARIATIONS ON THE THEME FOR PIANO			
ASHLEY DEALERS SERVICE, INC.			1.00
SNYDER, W.			
GREENSLEEVES -- VARIATIONS ON THE THEME FOR PIANO			
ASHLEY DEALERS SERVICE, INC.			1.00
SNYDER, W.			
ON THE TOP OF OLD SMOKY -- IMPROVISATIONS FOR PIANO			
ASHLEY DEALERS SERVICE, INC.			1.00
SOSNIK, H.			
GAYETY			
THE BIG THREE MUSIC CORPORATION			00.95
SPIELER			
FLASHING PEARLS			
MCA MUSIC			1.00
STECHER *			
ROCK WITH JAZZ, BK. 1			
SCHMITT, HALL AND MCCREARY COMPANY		9981	1.25
STECHER *			
ROCK WITH JAZZ, BK. 2			
SCHMITT, HALL AND MCCREARY COMPANY		9973	1.25
STECHER *			
ROCK WITH JAZZ, BK. 3			
SCHMITT, HALL AND MCCREARY COMPANY		9969	1.25
STECHER *			
ROCK WITH JAZZ, BK. 4			
SCHMITT, HALL AND MCCREARY COMPANY		9970	1.25
STECHER *			
ROCK WITH JAZZ, BK. 5			
SCHMITT, HALL AND MCCREARY COMPANY		9974	1.25
STEINER--ED. STEINER			
FORGOTTEN DREAMS -- SIMP.			
BELWIN-MILLS PUBLISHING CORPORATION		26070	.50

STEINER--ED. STEINER			
HEY, MR. BANJO			
BELWIN-MILLS PUBLISHING CORPORATION		25092	.50
STEINER--ED. STEINER			
SLEIGH RIDE -- CHILDREN'S EDITION			
BELWIN-MILLS PUBLISHING CORPORATION		25133	.50
STEINER--ED. STEINER			
SYNCOPATED CLOCK, THE -- CHILDREN'S EDITION			
BELWIN-MILLS PUBLISHING CORPORATION		25134	.50
STEINER--ED. STEINER			
WALTZING CAT, THE			
BELWIN-MILLS PUBLISHING CORPORATION		25135	.50
STEINER 2 1/2, 3			
ADVANCING PIANIST PLAYS BOOGIE, THE			
BELWIN-MILLS PUBLISHING CORPORATION		1767	1.75
STEINER * NEALE, J. EASY			
SUMMER PLACE, A, THEME FROM			
WARNER BROTHERS PUBLISHERS			.75
STEINER FREEMAN			
TARA THEME			
WARNER BROTHERS PUBLISHERS			1.00
STEWART			
ECHO TANGO			
MCA MUSIC			1.00
STOLZ			
HARBOR ROMANCE			
MCA MUSIC			1.00
STONE, E.--ED STONE, E.			
YESTERDAYS			
CIMINO PUBLICATIONS, INC.		H	1.25
STRONG, J. CHOSAK			
POPULAR CHORD METHOD FOR BEGINNERS			
BELWIN-MILLS PUBLISHING CORPORATION			1.25
SUKMAN, H.			
ELEVENTH HOUR			
THE BIG THREE MUSIC CORPORATION			00.95
SULLIVAN, J.			
LITTLE ROCK GETAWAY			
THE BIG THREE MUSIC CORPORATION			00.95
SUNSHINE *			
ENLLORO -- VOODOO- MOON			
MCA MUSIC			1.00
SURFARIS			
POINT PANIC			
MCA MUSIC			1.00
SWAN *			
CHIN CHI CHA			
MCA MUSIC			1.00
SWAN *			
DIXIELAND CHA CHA CHA			
MCA MUSIC			1.00
SWAN *			
MUCHACHACHA			
MCA MUSIC			1.00
SWAN *			
ROCK AND ROLL CHA CHA CHA			
MCA MUSIC			1.00
SWEATMAN, W.			
DOWN HOME RAG			
SHAPIRO, BERNSTEIN ORGANIZATION			.95
TATUM, A.			
ART TATUM IMPROVISATIONS, NO. 2			
THE BIG THREE MUSIC CORPORATION			01.50
TAYLOR, J.			
JAMES TAYLOR			
MUSIC SALES CORPORATION		020638	4.95
TEMPLETON, A.			
MENDELSSOHN MOWS 'EM DOWN			
THE BIG THREE MUSIC CORPORATION			00.95
TERRY--ED TERRY			
HONKY-TONK RAGTIME PIANO			
WARNER BROTHERS PUBLISHERS			1.95
THEODORAKIS, M.			
ZORBA THE GREEK - THEME			
THE BIG THREE MUSIC CORPORATION			00.95
THIELMANS			
BIRDS N'BEES			
MCA MUSIC			1.00
THIELMANS			
VALSE JOLIE, LA. --PRETTY WALTZ, THE.			
MCA MUSIC			1.00
THOMPSON, J. * PORTNOFF			
PUSS IN BOOKS -- PIANO FOLIO FOR CHILDREN			
MCA MUSIC			1.75
TIOMKIN, D.			
GREEN LEAVES OF SUMMER, THE			
THE BIG THREE MUSIC CORPORATION			00.95
TIOMKIN, D.			
GUNS OF NAVARONE, THE			
SHAPIRO, BERNSTEIN ORGANIZATION			.95
TIOMKIN, D. RICHTER FIRST YEAR			
HIGH AND THE MIGHTY, THE			
WARNER BROTHERS PUBLISHERS			.75
TOBIAS *			
OLD LAMP LIGHTER, THE.			
SHAPIRO, BERNSTEIN ORGANIZATION			.95
TROTTER * ROGERS, M.			
BABAR COMES TO AMERICA			
POINTER PUBLICATIONS			2.95
TSCHAIKOWSKY FREY, H.			
CONCERTO NO. 02			
THE BIG THREE MUSIC CORPORATION			00.75
TYERS, W.			
PANAMA			
THE BIG THREE MUSIC CORPORATION			00.95
VALSEN *			
SNOWFLOWER			
MCA MUSIC			1.00
VAUGHN			
CUMBERLAND COUNTY FEUD			
MCA MUSIC			1.00
WALDRON			
REFLECTIONS IN MODERN JAZZ			
SAM FOX PUBLISHING COMPANY, INC.			1.75
WALKER NEALE, J. EASY			
MR. BOJANGLES			
WARNER BROTHERS PUBLISHERS			.75
WALLER, T.			
JITTERBUG WALTZ			
THE BIG THREE MUSIC CORPORATION			00.95
WALLINGTON, G.			
POPULAR PIANO COLLECTIONS -- GEORGE WALLINGTON PRESENTS ORIGINAL			
PIANO COMPOSITIONS			
BELWIN-MILLS PUBLISHING CORPORATION		11207	1.00
WARREN			
THAT HAPPY FEELING			
MCA MUSIC			1.00

WATSON--ED.   WATSON
   LET'S PLAY PLAYER-PIANO STYLE
      WARNER BROTHERS PUBLISHERS   1.95
WEBSTER, J. *
   AIRPORT LOVE THEME
      MCA MUSIC   1.00
WEBSTEP, J. *   KERR, R. N.
   AIRPORT LOVE THEME
      MCA MUSIC   1.00
WEBSTER   SAMPIETRO   FIRST YEAR
   SECRET LOVE
      WARNER BROTHERS PUBLISHERS   .75
WEILL, K.
   KURT WEILL
      CHAPPELL AND COMPANY, INC.   0017855   1.50
WEILL, K.   RICHTER   FIRST YEAR
   MACK THE KNIFE
      WARNER BROTHERS PUBLISHERS   .75
WEILL, K.
   MEET KURT WEILL AT THE PIANO
      CHAPPELL AND COMPANY, INC.   3719408   2.50
WELK, L.
   LAWRENCE WELK'S AROUND THE WORLD --NO. 3
      MCA MUSIC   1.25
WELK, L.
   LAWRENCE WELK'S POLKA FOLIOS --NO. 1
      MCA MUSIC   2.00
WEYBRIGHT
   POPULAR PIANO COLLECTIONS -- ALL AMERICAN MARCH FOLIO
      BELWIN-MILLS PUBLISHING CORPORATION   11030   1.00
WEYBRIGHT
   POPULAR PIANO COLLECTIONS -- DUKES OF DIXIELAND, DIXIELAND
   HOOTNANNY
      BELWIN-MILLS PUBLISHING CORPORATION   11131   2.00
WEYBRIGHT
   POPULAR PIANO COLLECTIONS -- EXCITING ERA OF ZEZ CONFREY
      BELWIN-MILLS PUBLISHING CORPORATION   11154   2.50
WEYBRIGHT
   POPULAR PIANO COLLECTIONS -- FOLK ROCK FOR STUDENT PIANISTS -
   AUL ADAMS
      BELWIN-MILLS PUBLISHING CORPORATION   11600   1.50
WEYBRIGHT
   POPULAR PIANO COLLECTIONS -- FRANKIE CARLE'S PIANO CONCEPTIONS
      BELWIN-MILLS PUBLISHING CORPORATION   11196   1.00
WEYBRIGHT
   POPULAR PIANO COLLECTIONS -- FRANKIE CARLE'S PIANO STYLINGS OF
   FAVORITE SONGS
      BELWIN-MILLS PUBLISHING CORPORATION   11197   1.00
WEYBRIGHT
   POPULAR PIANO COLLECTIONS -- HAPPINESS IS
      BELWIN-MILLS PUBLISHING CORPORATION   11561   2.00
WEYBRIGHT
   POPULAR PIANO COLLECTIONS -- HOW TO PLAY LIKE A PLAYER PIANO
      BELWIN-MILLS PUBLISHING CORPORATION   11583   2.00
WEYBRIGHT
   POPULAR PIANO COLLECTIONS -- LATIN-AMERICAN MELODIES SIMPLIFIED
   FOR PIANO
      BELWIN-MILLS PUBLISHING CORPORATION   11261   1.00
WEYBRIGHT
   POPULAR PIANO COLLECTIONS -- MILLS SONG SHINDIG
      BELWIN-MILLS PUBLISHING CORPORATION   11559   2.00
WEYBRIGHT
   POPULAR PIANO COLLECTIONS -- MILLS SUMMER SOUNDS AND OTHER BIG
   HITS
      BELWIN-MILLS PUBLISHING CORPORATION   11558   2.00
WEYBRIGHT
   POPULAR PIANO COLLECTIONS -- PLAY THEM RAGS
      BELWIN-MILLS PUBLISHING CORPORATION   11388   1.75
WEYBRIGHT
   POPULAR PIANO COLLECTIONS -- RAGTIME TREASURES, JOSEPH LAMB
      BELWIN-MILLS PUBLISHING CORPORATION   11415   2.50
WEYBRIGHT
   POPULAR PIANO COLLECTIONS -- TED MOSSMAN'S SIMPLIFIED BOOGIE
   WOOGIE CONCEPTIONS OF MILLS FAVORITES
      BELWIN-MILLS PUBLISHING CORPORATION   11323   1.50
WEYBRIGHT
   POPULAR PIANO COLLECTION -- RAGTIME PIANO
      BELWIN-MILLS PUBLISHING CORPORATION   11414   2.50
WHITEFIELD
   BEGINNER'S BOOGIE WOOGIE
      BOSTON MUSIC COMPANY   1.00
WHITEFIELD
   BOOGIE WOOGIE FOR ADVANCED BEGINNERS
      BOSTON MUSIC COMPANY   1.25
WHITEFIELD
   BOOGIE WOOGIE FOR GOOD PLAYERS
      BOSTON MUSIC COMPANY   1.25
WHITFORD--ED.   WHITFORD   GR. 1 1/2 - 2 1/2
   FAVORITES FOR THE PIANIST, NO. 01
      ROBERT WHITFORD PUBLICATIONS   .60
WHITFORD--ED.   WHITFORD   GR. 1 1/2 - 2 1/2
   FAVORITES FOR THE PIANIST, NO. 02
      ROBERT WHITFORD PUBLICATIONS   .60
WHITFORD--ED.   WHITFORD   GR. 1 1/2 - 2 1/2
   FAVORITES FOR THE PIANIST, NO. 03
      ROBERT WHITFORD PUBLICATIONS   .60
WHITFORD--ED.   WHITFORD   GR. 1 1/2 - 2 1/2
   FAVORITES FOR THE PIANIST, NO. 04
      ROBERT WHITFORD PUBLICATIONS   .60
WHITFORD--ED.   WHITFORD   GR. 1 1/2 - 2 1/2
   FAVORITES FOR THE PIANIST, NO. 05
      ROBERT WHITFORD PUBLICATIONS   .60
WHITFORD--ED.   WHITFORD   GR. 1 1/2 - 2 1/2
   FAVORITES FOR THE PIANIST, NO. 06
      ROBERT WHITFORD PUBLICATIONS   .60
WHITFORD--ED.   WHITFORD   GR. 1 1/2 - 2 1/2
   FAVORITES FOR THE PIANIST, NO. 07
      ROBERT WHITFORD PUBLICATIONS   .60
WHITFORD--ED.   WHITFORD   GR. 1 1/2 - 2 1/2
   FAVORITES FOR THE PIANIST, NO. 08
      ROBERT WHITFORD PUBLICATIONS   .60
WHITFORD--ED.   WHITFORD   GR. 1 1/2 - 2 1/2
   FAVORITES FOR THE PIANIST, NO. 09
      ROBERT WHITFORD PUBLICATIONS   .60
WHITFORD--ED.   WHITFORD   GR. 1 1/2 - 2 1/2
   FAVORITES FOR THE PIANIST, NO. 10
      ROBERT WHITFORD PUBLICATIONS   .60
WHITFORD--ED.   WHITFORD   GR. 1 1/2 - 2 1/2
   FAVORITES FOR THE PIANIST, NO. 11
      ROBERT WHITFORD PUBLICATIONS   .60
WHITFORD--ED.   WHITFORD   GR. 1 1/2 - 2 1/2
   FAVORITES FOR THE PIANIST, NO. 12
      ROBERT WHITFORD PUBLICATIONS   .60
WHITFORD--ED.   WHITFORD   GR. 1 1/2 - 2 1/2
   FAVORITES FOR THE PIANIST, NO. 13
      ROBERT WHITFORD PUBLICATIONS   .60

WHITFORD--ED.   WHITFORD   GR. 1 1/2 - 2 1/2
   FAVORITES FOR THE PIANIST, NO. 14
      ROBERT WHITFORD PUBLICATIONS   .60
WHITFORD--ED.   WHITFORD   GR. 1 1/2 - 2 1/2
   FAVORITES FOR THE PIANIST, NO. 15
      ROBERT WHITFORD PUBLICATIONS   .60
WHITFORD--ED.   WHITFORD   GR. 1 1/2 - 2 1/2
   FAVORITES FOR THE PIANIST, NO. 16
      ROBERT WHITFORD PUBLICATIONS   .60
WHITFORD--ED.   WHITFORD   GR. 1 1/2 - 2 1/2
   FAVORITES FOR THE PIANIST, NO. 17
      ROBERT WHITFORD PUBLICATIONS   .60
WHITFORD--ED.   WHITFORD   GR. 1 1/2 - 2 1/2
   FAVORITES FOR THE PIANIST, NO. 18
      ROBERT WHITFORD PUBLICATIONS   .60
WHITFORD--ED.   WHITFORD   GR. 1 1/2 - 2 1/2
   FAVORITES FOR THE PIANIST, NO. 19
      ROBERT WHITFORD PUBLICATIONS   .60
WHITFORD--ED.   WHITFORD   GR. 1 1/2 - 2 1/2
   FAVORITES FOR THE PIANIST, NO. 20
      ROBERT WHITFORD PUBLICATIONS   .60
WHITFORD--ED.   WHITFORD   GR. 3
   FRANKIE AND JOHNNY BOOGIE
      ROBERT WHITFORD PUBLICATIONS   .40
WHITFORD--ED.   WHITFORD   GR. 4
   IDA --JAZZ ARR.--
      ROBERT WHITFORD PUBLICATIONS   .40
WHITFORD--ED.   WHITFORD   GR. 1
   TUNES FOR THE PIANIST, NO. 1
      ROBERT WHITFORD PUBLICATIONS   .60
WHITFORD--ED.   WHITFORD   GR. 1
   TUNES FOR THE PIANIST, NO. 2
      ROBERT WHITFORD PUBLICATIONS   .60
WHITFORD--ED.   WHITFORD   GR. 1
   TUNES FOR THE PIANIST, NO. 3
      ROBERT WHITFORD PUBLICATIONS   .60
WHITFORD--ED.   WHITFORD   GR. 1
   TUNES FOR THE PIANIST, NO. 4
      ROBERT WHITFORD PUBLICATIONS   .60
WHITFORD
   FILL-INS FOR THE PIANIST
      ROBERT WHITFORD PUBLICATIONS   1.00
WHITFORD   GR. 3 1/2
   PERRY SQUARE BOOGIE --MODERN RHYTHMIC CLASSICS--
      ROBERT WHITFORD PUBLICATIONS   .40
WHITFORD
   ROBERT WHITFORD BREAK SHEET BOOK FOR PIANO
      ROBERT WHITFORD PUBLICATIONS   2.50
WHITFORD
   ROBERT WHITFORD CHORD CHART FOR THE MODERN PIANIST
      ROBERT WHITFORD PUBLICATIONS   1.50
WHITFORD
   ROBERT WHITFORD MODERN PIANO EFFECTS
      ROBERT WHITFORD PUBLICATIONS   2.00
WHITFORD   GR. 3 1/2
   TEASIN' THE IVORIES --MODERN RHYTHMIC CLASSICS--
      ROBERT WHITFORD PUBLICATIONS   .40
WHITSON *   KLICKMANN   EASY
   LET ME CALL YOU SWEETHEART --LARGE NOTE--
      SHAWNEE PRESS, INC.   HB-53   .85
WILDMAN
   CRAZY VIOLINS
      MCA MUSIC   1.00
WILDMAN
   LOVE THEME FROM 'MADAME X,' -- SWEDISH RHAPSODY
      MCA MUSIC   1.00
WILDMAN
   STOCKHOLM CONCERTO
      MCA MUSIC   1.00
WILDMAN
   SWEDISH RHAPSODY --THEME
      MCA MUSIC   1.00
WILDMAN
   SWEDISH RHAPSODY
      MCA MUSIC   1.50
WILDMAN *
   TANGO PICASSO
      MCA MUSIC   1.00
WILLIAMS, C.   NEVIN
   THEME FROM 'THE APARTMENT' -- SIMP.
      BELWIN-MILLS PUBLISHING CORPORATION   26108   .50
WILLIAMS, C.
   THEME FROM 'THE APARTMENT'
      BELWIN-MILLS PUBLISHING CORPORATION   20413   .85
WILLIAMS, LOU.
   MARY LOU WILLIAMS FIVE BARRELHOUSE BOOGIE WOOGIE AND BLUES
   SOLOS
      MCA MUSIC   1.00
WILLIAMS, R.--ED.   WILLIAMS, R.
   AFFAIR TO REMEMBER, AN
      THE BIG THREE MUSIC CORPORATION   1.25
WILLIAMS, R.--ED.   WILLIAMS, R.
   ANASTASIA
      THE BIG THREE MUSIC CORPORATION   01.25
WILLIAMS, R.--ED.   WILLIAMS, R.
   ARRIVEDERCI, ROMA
      THE BIG THREE MUSIC CORPORATION   01.25
WILLIAMS, R.--ED.   WILLIAMS, R.
   DAY IN THE LIFE OF A FOOL, A
      THE BIG THREE MUSIC CORPORATION   1.25
WILLIAMS, R.--ED.   WILLIAMS, R.
   DEEP PURPLE
      THE BIG THREE MUSIC CORPORATION   01.25
WILLIAMS, R.--ED.   WILLIAMS, R.
   GENTLE ON MY MIND
      THE BIG THREE MUSIC CORPORATION   01.25
WILLIAMS, R.--ED.   WILLIAMS, R.
   GREEN LEAVES OF SUMMER
      THE BIG THREE MUSIC CORPORATION   1.25
WILLIAMS, R.--ED.   WILLIAMS, R.
   LARA'S THEME - DOCTOR ZHIVAGO
      THE BIG THREE MUSIC CORPORATION   1.25
WILLIAMS, R.--ED.   WILLIAMS, R.
   LOVE MAKES THE WORLD GO 'ROUND
      THE BIG THREE MUSIC CORPORATION   1.25
WILLIAMS, R.--ED.   WILLIAMS, R.
   MOONLIGHT AND ROSES
      THE BIG THREE MUSIC CORPORATION   01.25
WILLIAMS, R.--ED.   WILLIAMS, R.
   MORE THAN A MIRACLE
      THE BIG THREE MUSIC CORPORATION   01.25
WILLIAMS, R.--ED.   WILLIAMS, R.
   ON THE TRAIL
      THE BIG THREE MUSIC CORPORATION   01.25
WILLIAMS, R.--ED.   WILLIAMS, R.
   OVER THE RAINBOW
      THE BIG THREE MUSIC CORPORATION   01.25

WILLIAMS, R.--ED.   WILLIAMS, R.
  SHADOW OF YOUR SMILE
    THE BIG THREE MUSIC CORPORATION   1.25
WILLIAMS, R.--ED.   WILLIAMS, R.
  SUNNY
    THE BIG THREE MUSIC CORPORATION   01.25
WILLIAMS, R.
  MEET ROGER WILLIAMS
    THE BIG THREE MUSIC CORPORATION   02.95
WILLIAMS, R.
  PIANO INTERPRETATIONS, NO. 1
    THE BIG THREE MUSIC CORPORATION   01.95
WILLIAMS, R.
  PIANO INTERPRETATIONS, NO. 2
    THE BIG THREE MUSIC CORPORATION   01.95
WILLIAMS, R.
  PIANO INTERPRETATIONS, NO. 3
    THE BIG THREE MUSIC CORPORATION   01.95
WILLIAMS, R.
  RECORDED PIANO INTERPRETATIONS
    THE BIG THREE MUSIC CORPORATION   02.00
WILLIAMS, R.
  THIS IS ROGER WILLIAMS
    THE BIG THREE MUSIC CORPORATION   02.95
WILLIAMS *
  RED SAILS IN THE SUNSET
    SHAPIRO, BERNSTEIN ORGANIZATION   .95
WILLIAMS
  SECRET WAYS, THE
    MCA MUSIC   1.00
WILLSON, M.
  I AIN'T DOWN YET
    FRANK MUSIC CORPORATION   .95
WILLSON, M.
  MUSIC MAN, THE
    FRANK MUSIC CORPORATION   1.25
WILLSON, M.   RICHTER   2 1/2 - 3
  SEVENTY SIX TROMBONES
    FRANK MUSIC CORPORATION   .75
WILLSON, M.   AGAY, D.   EASY
  SONGS FROM 'THE MUSIC MAN'
    FRANK MUSIC CORPORATION   1.25
WILLSON, M.   AGAY, D.   EASY
  SONGS FROM 'THE UNSINKABLE MOLLY BROWN'
    FRANK MUSIC CORPORATION   1.25
WILLSON, M.   RICHTER   2 1/2 - 3
  TILL THERE WAS YOU
    FRANK MUSIC CORPORATION   .75
WILLSON, M.
  UNSINKABLE MOLLY BROWN, THE
    FRANK MUSIC CORPORATION   1.25
WILSON, T.
  TEDDY WILSON, PIANO PATTERNS
    THE BIG THREE MUSIC CORPORATION   01.50
WINWOOD, S.
  STEVIE WINWOOD AND FRIENDS
    MUSIC SALES CORPORATION   090004   2.95
WOLCOTT, C.
  CAT ON A HOT TIN ROOF
    THE BIG THREE MUSIC CORPORATION   00.95
WOLCOTT, C.
  RUBY-DUBY-DU
    THE BIG THREE MUSIC CORPORATION   00.95
WRAGG
  PHANTOM FOUNTAIN, THE
    MCA MUSIC   1.00
WRIGHT, R. *
  KISMET
    FRANK MUSIC CORPORATION   1.25
WRIGHT, R. *   RICHTER   EASY
  NEW SONGS FROM THE MOTION PICTURE 'SONG OF NORWAY'
    FRANK MUSIC CORPORATION   1.25
WRIGHT, R. *   RICHTER   EASY
  SONGS FROM 'KISMET'
    FRANK MUSIC CORPORATION   1.25
WUHRER *
  POPULAR PIANO FOR PLEASURE, BK. 1
    MCA MUSIC   1.95
WUHRER *
  POPULAR PIANO FOR PLEASURE, BK. 2
    MCA MUSIC   3.95
WUHRER *
  POPULAR PIANO FOR PLEASURE, BK. 3
    MCA MUSIC   3.95
YARROW   NEALE, J.   EASY
  DAY IS DONE
    WARNER BROTHERS PUBLISHERS   .75
YARROW *   NEALE, J.   EASY
  PUFF, THE MAGIC DRAGON
    WARNER BROTHERS PUBLISHERS   .75
YARROW *   DAVIS, J. R. FIRST YEAR
  PUFF, THE MAGIC DRAGON
    WARNER BROTHERS PUBLISHERS   .75
YORKE, P.
  MISTY VALLEY
    THE BIG THREE MUSIC CORPORATION   00.95
YOUMANS   LEVINE
  TEA FOR TWO
    WARNER BROTHERS PUBLISHERS   1.00
YOUMANS   WALTER
  TEA FOR TWO
    WARNER BROTHERS PUBLISHERS   1.00
YOUMANS   RICHTER   FIRST YEAR
  TEA FOR TWO
    WILLIS MUSIC COMPANY   .75
YOUNG, V.
  PEARLS ON VELVET
    THE BIG THREE MUSIC CORPORATION   00.95
YVOIRE
  SKI-HIGH --FROM THE ST. MORITZ SUITE
    MCA MUSIC   1.00
ZACHARIAS
  INNOCENTS ABROAD
    MCA MUSIC   1.00

Popular Music:
Composer/Editor/Arranger Unlisted—Works Alphabetized by Title

    ACADEMY AWARD WINNER AND OTHER BIG HITS, THE
      THE BIG THREE MUSIC CORPORATION   02.95

    ACCENT NO. 1 - NINE 'POP' NOVELTY SOLOS BY VARIOUS COMPOSERS
      GENERAL MUSIC PUBLISHING COMPANY, INC.   2.50

ACCENT NO. 2 - EIGHT 'POP' NOVELTY SOLOS BY VARIOUS COMPOSERS
  GENERAL MUSIC PUBLISHING COMPANY, INC.   2.50
ADDIO, SIGNORA
  MUSIC SALES CORPORATION   040988   1.00
ALL THE THINGS YOU ARE -- SHOWCASE
  CIMINO PUBLICATIONS, INC.   H   1.25
ALL THE THINGS YOU ARE
  CIMINO PUBLICATIONS, INC.   H   1.25
AMAZING GRACE
  MUSIC SALES CORPORATION   060999   .95
APPLES AND BANANAS
  CIMINO PUBLICATIONS, INC.   B   1.25
APRIL IN PORTUGAL
  CHAPPELL AND COMPANY, INC.   0028008   .95
ARABESQUE
  CIMINO PUBLICATIONS, INC.   SOU   1.25
AREN'T YOU GLAD YOU'RE YOU
  MUSIC SALES CORPORATION   050999   .95
A CANZONE'E NAPULE
  MUSIC SALES CORPORATION   040987   1.00
A TAZZA,' CAFE
  MUSIC SALES CORPORATION   040990   1.00
BABY, BABY ALL THE TIME
  MUSIC SALES CORPORATION   010990   .95
BALLAD OF THE GREEN BERETS
  CIMINO PUBLICATIONS, INC.   MM   1.00
BELAFONTE FOLK SONG BOOK, THE
  MUSIC SALES CORPORATION   040165   2.95
BELLS ARE RINGING
  CHAPPELL AND COMPANY, INC.   0430009-171 1.95
BELLS ARE RINGING
  CHAPPELL AND COMPANY, INC.   0430009-176 1.50
BEST OF ALL, THE
  MUSIC SALES CORPORATION   060003   2.95
BEYOND THE SEA
  CIMINO PUBLICATIONS, INC.   H   1.25
BIG SEVENTY-FIVE SONG BOOK, THE - EASY BIG NOTE PIANO
  WARNER BROTHERS PUBLISHERS   3.95
BIG 3'S BEST IN POPS
  THE BIG THREE MUSIC CORPORATION   02.95
BIG 3'S 20 BIG HITS OF TODAY
  THE BIG THREE MUSIC CORPORATION   02.95
BILL
  CIMINO PUBLICATIONS, INC.   H   1.25
BLOOMER GIRL
  CHAPPELL AND COMPANY, INC.   0517508   1.95
BLUE CHRISTMAS
  CIMINO PUBLICATIONS, INC.   B   1.00
BLUE VELVET
  CIMINO PUBLICATIONS, INC.   V   1.00
BLUE VELVET
  CIMINO PUBLICATIONS, INC.   V   1.25
BOY FRIEND, THE
  CHAPPELL AND COMPANY, INC.   0577502   1.95
BRAZILIAN SLEIGH BELLS
  CIMINO PUBLICATIONS, INC.   LT   1.25
BUT BEAUTIFUL
  MUSIC SALES CORPORATION   050998   .95
BYE, BYE BABY
  MUSIC SALES CORPORATION   040998   .95
CAMELOT
  CHAPPELL AND COMPANY, INC.   0690008   1.95
CAMELOT
  CHAPPELL AND COMPANY, INC.   0690008   1.50
CAN-CAN
  CHAPPELL AND COMPANY, INC.   0695015   1.95
CAN-CAN
  CHAPPELL AND COMPANY, INC.   0695015   1.50
CAN'T HELP LOVIN' DAT MAN -- SHOWCASE
  CIMINO PUBLICATIONS, INC.   H   1.25
CANADIAN SUNSET
  CIMINO PUBLICATIONS, INC.   V   1.00
CANADIAN SUNSET
  CIMINO PUBLICATIONS, INC.   V   1.25
CARIOCA -- SHOWCASE
  CIMINO PUBLICATIONS, INC.   H   1.25
CARIOCA
  CIMINO PUBLICATIONS, INC.   H   1.25
CAROLINA ON MY MIND
  MUSIC SALES CORPORATION   060998   .95
CAROUSEL WALTZ
  CIMINO PUBLICATIONS, INC.   H   1.50
CHARADE
  CIMINO PUBLICATIONS, INC.   SOU   1.25
CINERAMA HOLIDAY
  CHAPPELL AND COMPANY, INC.   0021253   1.00

COCO
    CHAPPELL AND COMPANY, INC.   0906255   1.50

COME PIOVEVA
    MUSIC SALES CORPORATION   040979   1.00

COUNTRY ROAD
    MUSIC SALES CORPORATION   060997   .95

COUNTRY STYLE
    MUSIC SALES CORPORATION   050997   .95

COUNT BASIE BOOGIE WOOGIE BLUES
    MCA MUSIC   1.00

CUTE
    CIMINO PUBLICATIONS, INC.   NH   1.25

DEAR HEART
    CIMINO PUBLICATIONS, INC.   NOR   1.00

DEAR HEART
    CIMINO PUBLICATIONS, INC.   NOR   1.25

DEEP PURPLE SONG BOOK
    THE BIG THREE MUSIC CORPORATION   03.95

DESTRY RIDES AGAIN
    CHAPPELL AND COMPANY, INC.   1157502   1.95

DIAMONDS ARE A GIRL'S BEST FRIEND
    MUSIC SALES CORPORATION   040997   .95

DICITENCELLO VUIE
    MUSIC SALES CORPORATION   040977   1.00

DON'T EVER LEAVE ME -- SHOWCASE
    CIMINO PUBLICATIONS, INC.   H   1.25

DOWNBEAT'S 88 KEYS TO FAME
    MCA MUSIC   1.00

EASY TO PLAY HITS THROUGH THE YEARS - VOL. 1
    WARNER BROTHERS PUBLISHERS   1.25

EASY TO PLAY HITS THROUGH THE YEARS - VOL. 2
    WARNER BROTHERS PUBLISHERS   1.25

EL MEXICANITO
    CIMINO PUBLICATIONS, INC.   CP   1.25

EN MI VIEJO SAN JUAN
    MUSIC SALES CORPORATION   050996   .95

EVERYTHING HAPPENS TO ME
    MUSIC SALES CORPORATION   050995   .95

EXODUS
    CHAPPELL AND COMPANY, INC.   1405000   1.95

EXPERIMENT IN TERROR
    CIMINO PUBLICATIONS, INC.   SOU   1.25

FALLING IN LOVE WITH LOVE
    CHAPPELL AND COMPANY, INC.   1427509   .60

FANNY
    CHAPPELL AND COMPANY, INC.   1435007   1.95

FANTASTICKS, THE
    CHAPPELL AND COMPANY, INC.   1442508   1.50

FANTASTICKS, THE
    CHAPPELL AND COMPANY, INC.   1442508   1.95

FERRANTE AND TEICHER INTERPRETATIONS FOR SOLO PIANO
    THE BIG THREE MUSIC CORPORATION   02.95

FIFTY-FIVE POPULAR PIANO TEACHING PIECES
    WARNER BROTHERS PUBLISHERS   3.95

FIFTY-TWO GREAT ROCK AND ROLL HITS
    THE BIG THREE MUSIC CORPORATION   03.95

FINIAN'S RAINBOW
    CHAPPELL AND COMPANY, INC.   1480003   1.50

FINIAN'S RAINBOW
    CHAPPELL AND COMPANY, INC.   1480003   1.95

FIRE AND RAIN
    MUSIC SALES CORPORATION   060996   .95

FIRST FAVORITES
    EDWARD B. MARKS MUSIC CORPORATION   01.50
        1

FIRST TIME AROUND
    BOURNE COMPANY   1.50

FLAIR STYLINGS FOR PIANO OF DAYS OF WINE AND ROSES
    WARNER BROTHERS PUBLISHERS   1.95

FORTY HITS OF OUR TIMES-POPULAR SONGS IN BIG NOTES FOR PIANO
    MCA MUSIC   3.50

FRANK ZAPPA SONG BOOK, BK. 1
    THE BIG THREE MUSIC CORPORATION   05.95

FROM BACH TO BROADWAY
    WARNER BROTHERS PUBLISHERS   MFE 37   2.50

FUNNY GIRL
    CHAPPELL AND COMPANY, INC.   1622505   1.50

FUNNY GIRL
    CHAPPELL AND COMPANY, INC.   1622505   1.95

GEORGY GIRL
    CHAPPELL AND COMPANY, INC.   1662501   .60

GIGI
    CHAPPELL AND COMPANY, INC.   1680008   1.50

GIGI
    CHAPPELL AND COMPANY, INC.   1680008   1.95

GOIN' OUT OF MY HEAD
    CIMINO PUBLICATIONS, INC.   V   1.25

GOIN' OUT OF MY HEAD
    CIMINO PUBLICATIONS, INC.   V   1.25

GOING MY WAY
    MUSIC SALES CORPORATION   050994   .95

GREAT IMPOSTER, THE
    CIMINO PUBLICATIONS, INC.   SOU   1.25

GREAT SONGS FROM THOROUGHLY MODERN MILLIE
    MCA MUSIC   2.50

GREAT SONGS FROM THOROUGHLY MODERN MILLIE
    MCA MUSIC   1.25

GREAT SONGS OF THE YEAR - 1973 EDITION
    THE BIG THREE MUSIC CORPORATION   04.95

GYPSY
    CHAPPELL AND COMPANY, INC.   1847508   1.50

GYPSY
    CHAPPELL AND COMPANY, INC.   1847508   1.95

HAPPY BAREFOOT BOY
    CIMINO PUBLICATIONS, INC.   NOR   1.25

HAPPY HUNTING
    CHAPPELL AND COMPANY, INC.   1892504   1.95

HAPPY ORGAN
    MUSIC SALES CORPORATION   010999   .95

HARBOR LIGHTS
    CHAPPELL AND COMPANY, INC.   1900000   .60

HARMS HITS THROUGH THE YEARS FOR PIANO
    WARNER BROTHERS PUBLISHERS   1.95

HERE'S BOOGIE WOOGIE
    CARL FISCHER, INC.   O 3313   1.25

HERE'S THAT RAINY DAY
    MUSIC SALES CORPORATION   050993   .95

HOCUS POCUS
    CIMINO PUBLICATIONS, INC.   RAD   1.25

HOW ARE THINGS IN GLOCCA MORRA
    CHAPPELL AND COMPANY, INC.   20600002   .60

I'VE TOLD EV'RY LITTLE STAR
    CIMINO PUBLICATIONS, INC.   H   1.25

I'VE TOLD EV'RY LITTLE STAR
    CIMINO PUBLICATIONS, INC.   H   1.25

IF I LOVED YOU
    CIMINO PUBLICATIONS, INC.   H   1.25

IL SILENZIO
    MUSIC SALES CORPORATION   010996   .95

IMAGINATION
    MUSIC SALES CORPORATION   050992   .95

INCREDIBLE STRING BAND, THE
    MUSIC SALES CORPORATION   060009   2.95

INSTANT PIANO PHASE 1
    SIGHT AND SOUND SYSTEMS, INC.   31-101   12.00

INSTANT PIANO PHASE 2
    SIGHT AND SOUND SYSTEMS, INC.   31-102   12.00
                                INTERMEDIATE

INSTRUMENTAL GREATS
    SCREEN GEMS - COLUMBIA PUBLICATIONS   F0186P   3.95

ISLE OF CAPRI
    CIMINO PUBLICATIONS, INC.   H   1.25

IT'S DELIGHTFUL DOWN IN CHILE
    MUSIC SALES CORPORATION   040996   .95

IT'S IMPOSSIBLE
    CIMINO PUBLICATIONS, INC.   SU   1.00

IT STARTED ALL OVER AGAIN
    MUSIC SALES CORPORATION   010995   .95

I DO, I DO
    CHAPPELL AND COMPANY, INC.   2192508   1.50

I DREAM OF YOU
    MUSIC SALES CORPORATION   010998   .95

I GOT PLENTY O' NUTTIN'
    CHAPPELL AND COMPANY, INC.   2230027   .60

I THINK OF YOU
    MUSIC SALES CORPORATION   010997   .95

I WANT A GIRL
    CIMINO PUBLICATIONS, INC.   B   1.25

I WILL WAIT FOR YOU
    CIMINO PUBLICATIONS, INC.   V   1.25

I WILL WAIT FOR YOU
    CIMINO PUBLICATIONS, INC.   V   1.25

JAZZ ME BLUES
    EDWARD B. MARKS MUSIC CORPORATION   01.00

JEFFERSON AIRPLANE, THE
    MUSIC SALES CORPORATION   060001   2.95

JOEY
    MUSIC SALES CORPORATION   010994   .95

JUST AS THOUGH YOU WERE HERE
    MUSIC SALES CORPORATION   050991   .95

JUST A KISS APART
    MUSIC SALES CORPORATION   040995   .95

KEYBOARD HIT-KIT, THE
    WARNER BROTHERS PUBLISHERS   1.50

KID FROM RED BANK			
CIMINO PUBLICATIONS, INC.		NH	1.25
LANE, J.			
KNOCK THREE TIMES			
THE BIG THREE MUSIC CORPORATION			00.70
LAND OF DREAMS			
CIMINO PUBLICATIONS, INC.		V	1.25
LANGUAGE, THE			
MUSIC SALES CORPORATION		050972	.95
LET'S GET AWAY FROM IT ALL			
MUSIC SALES CORPORATION		050990	.95
LI'L DARLIN'			
CIMINO PUBLICATIONS, INC.		NH	1.25
LIES			
CIMINO PUBLICATIONS, INC.		V	1.25
LIGHT MY FIRE			
MUSIC SALES CORPORATION		060995	.95
LIKE SOMEONE IN LOVE			
MUSIC SALES CORPORATION		050989	.95
LITTLE GIRL BLUE -- SHOWCASE			
CIMINO PUBLICATIONS, INC.		H	1.25
LITTLE GIRL FROM LITTLE ROCK, A			
MUSIC SALES CORPORATION		040994	.95
LONG AGO AND FAR AWAY -- SHOWCASE			
CIMINO PUBLICATIONS, INC.		8	1.25
LOOK FOR THE SILVER LINING -- SHOWCASE			
CIMINO PUBLICATIONS, INC.		H	1.25
LORELEI, THE			
MUSIC SALES CORPORATION		050988	.95
LOSS OF LOVE			
CIMINO PUBLICATIONS, INC.		NOR	1.25
LOST LOVE			
CIMINO PUBLICATIONS, INC.		V	1.25
LOVE HER MADLY			
MUSIC SALES CORPORATION		060994	.95
MAKE BELIEVE			
CIMINO PUBLICATIONS, INC.		H	1.25
MAKE BELIEVE			
CIMINO PUBLICATIONS, INC.		H	1.00
MAKE BELIEVE			
CIMINO PUBLICATIONS, INC.		H	1.25
MANCINI GENERATION			
CIMINO PUBLICATIONS, INC.		LSM	1.25
MAY I NEVER LOVE AGAIN			
MUSIC SALES CORPORATION		050987	.95
MELANCHOLY SERENADE			
CIMINO PUBLICATIONS, INC.		SS	1.25
MODERN JAZZ QUARTET, THE --MJQ RELEASE			
SAM FOX PUBLISHING COMPANY, INC.			2.50
MOONLIGHT SONATA			
CIMINO PUBLICATIONS, INC.		SOU	1.25
MORRISON HOTEL -- THE DOORS			
MUSIC SALES CORPORATION		060008	2.95
MOST BEAUTIFUL GIRL IN THE WORLD			
CIMINO PUBLICATIONS, INC.		H	1.25
MR. LUCKY			
CIMINO PUBLICATIONS, INC.		SOU	1.25
MUNASTERIO'E SANTA CHIARA			
MUSIC SALES CORPORATION		040986	1.00
MUSIC IS A WORLD OF JOY			
THE BIG THREE MUSIC CORPORATION			02.95
MY BEAUTIFUL LADY			
CHAPPELL AND COMPANY, INC.		3905007	.60
MY ROMANCE			
CIMINO PUBLICATIONS, INC.		H	1.25
NA SERA'E MAGGIO			
MUSIC SALES CORPORATION		040981	1.00
NEVADA			
MUSIC SALES CORPORATION		050986	.95
NIGHTY NIGHT			
MUSIC SALES CORPORATION		050984	.95
NIGHT THEY INVENTED CHAMPAGNE, THE			
CHAPPELL AND COMPANY, INC.		4090007	.60
NIGHT WAS MADE FOR LOVE -- SHOWCASE			
CIMINO PUBLICATIONS, INC.		8	1.25
NIGHT WE CALLED IT A DAY			
MUSIC SALES CORPORATION		050985	.95
NINETY GAY NINETIES FAVORITES			
THE BIG THREE MUSIC CORPORATION			02.95
OH, YOU CRAZY MOON			
MUSIC SALES CORPORATION		050983	.95
OL' MAN RIVER			
CIMINO PUBLICATIONS, INC.		H	1.00
OL' MAN RIVER			
CIMINO PUBLICATIONS, INC.		H	1.25
OLZEN'S SCANDINAVIAN DANCE ALBUMS, BK. 1 --ACCORDION OR PIANO--			
SUMMY-BIRCHARD COMPANY			1.50

ONE HUNDRED OF THE GREATEST ROCK AND ROLL HITS			
THE BIG THREE MUSIC CORPORATION			05.95
ON A CLEAR DAY YOU CAN SEE FOREVER			
CHAPPELL AND COMPANY, INC.		4322509	1.50
ON A CLEAR DAY YOU CAN SEE FOREVER			
CHAPPELL AND COMPANY, INC.		4322509	1.95
OPUS ONE			
MUSIC SALES CORPORATION		010993	.95
ORCHIDS IN THE MOONLIGHT -- SHOWCASE			
CIMINO PUBLICATIONS, INC.			1.25
ORCHIDS IN THE MOONLIGHT			
CIMINO PUBLICATIONS, INC.		H	1.25
O PAESE D'O SOLE			
MUSIC SALES CORPORATION		040991	1.00
PAINT YOUR WAGON			
CHAPPELL AND COMPANY, INC.		4480000	1.50
PAINT YOUR WAGON			
CHAPPELL AND COMPANY, INC.		4480000	1.95
PAL JOEY			
CHAPPELL AND COMPANY, INC.		4482501	1.95
PERRY MASON THEME			
CIMINO PUBLICATIONS, INC.		B	1.25
PERSONALITY			
MUSIC SALES CORPORATION		050982	.95
PETER, PAUL AND MOMMY, EASY BIG NOTE PIANO			
WARNER BROTHERS PUBLISHERS		PPM 26	1.95
PETER GUNN			
CIMINO PUBLICATIONS, INC.		NOR	1.25
PIANO PIECES THE WHOLE WORLD PLAYS			
MUSIC SALES CORPORATION		010000	2.95
PIANO SOLOS FROM 'THE EDDY DUCHIN STORY' --TO LOVE AGAIN AND CHOPSTICKS RHAPSODY			
SHAPIRO, BERNSTEIN ORGANIZATION			.95
PINEAPPLE POLL BALLET			
CHAPPELL AND COMPANY, INC.		4602504	1.95
PLAIN AND FANCY			
CHAPPELL AND COMPANY, INC.		4620001	1.95
PLAYING PLEASURE			
EDWARD B. MARKS MUSIC CORPORATION			01.25
POINTER LIBRARY - CAVALCADE OF POPS			
POINTER PUBLICATIONS			2.95
POINTER LIBRARY - GOLDEN POPS			
POINTER PUBLICATIONS			2.95
POINTER LIBRARY - HITS, HITS, HITS, VOL. 1			
POINTER PUBLICATIONS			2.95
POINTER LIBRARY - HITS, HITS, HITS, VOL. 2			
POINTER PUBLICATIONS			2.95
POINTER LIBRARY - MEMORIES OF CHRISTMAS			
POINTER PUBLICATIONS			2.95
POINTER LIBRARY - PARADE OF POPS, VOL. 1			
POINTER PUBLICATIONS			2.95
POINTER LIBRARY - PARADE OF POPS, VOL. 2			
POINTER PUBLICATIONS			2.95
POINTER LIBRARY - POPS FOR PLEASURE			
POINTER PUBLICATIONS			2.95
POINTER LIBRARY - POPS OF THE 60'S			
POINTER PUBLICATIONS			2.95
POINTER LIBRARY - POPS OF YESTERYEAR			
POINTER PUBLICATIONS			2.95
POINTER LIBRARY - POP PROMENADE			
POINTER PUBLICATIONS			2.95
POINTER LIBRARY - ROMANTIC OPERETTA			
POINTER PUBLICATIONS			2.95
POINTER LIBRARY - THEMES FROM THE CLASSICS			
POINTER PUBLICATIONS			2.95
POINTER LIBRARY - THE NEW POPS			
POINTER PUBLICATIONS			2.95
POINTER SYSTEM - FAVORITE SONGS			
POINTER PUBLICATIONS			1.50
POINTER SYSTEM - GAY NINETIES			
POINTER PUBLICATIONS			1.50
POINTER SYSTEM - SONGS THAT LIVE FOREVER			
POINTER PUBLICATIONS			1.50
POLKA DOTS AND MOONBEAMS			
MUSIC SALES CORPORATION		050981	.95
POPULAR CLASSICS IN BIG NOTES --100--			
CARL FISCHER, INC.		O 4446	1.25
POWDERED WIG			
CIMINO PUBLICATIONS, INC.		SOU	1.25
PRESIDENT KENNEDY MARCH			
CIMINO PUBLICATIONS, INC.		B	1.25
RAGTIME PIANO			
BELWIN-MILLS PUBLISHING CORPORATION			2.50
RED SHOES BALLET, THE			
CHAPPELL AND COMPANY, INC.		4810008	1.95

SAIL AWAY			
CHAPPELL AND COMPANY, INC.		4960001	1.95
SCALINATELLA			
MUSIC SALES CORPORATION		040978	1.00
SCARBOROUGH FAIR			
MUSIC SALES CORPORATION		060992	.95
SENSATIONAL 70 FOR THE 70'S, THE			
SCREEN GEMS - COLUMBIA PUBLICATIONS		F0050P1	5.95
SENZA NISCIUNO			
MUSIC SALES CORPORATION		040983	1.00
SEPTEMBER SONG			
CHAPPELL AND COMPANY, INC.		5060009	.60
SHE DIDN'T SAY YES -- SHOWCASE			
CIMINO PUBLICATIONS, INC.		H	1.25
SHOE SHINE BOY			
MUSIC SALES CORPORATION		050980	.95
SHOT IN THE DARK			
CIMINO PUBLICATIONS, INC.		TWI	1.25
SILENZIO CANTATORE			
MUSIC SALES CORPORATION		040985	1.00
SILK STOCKINGS			
CHAPPELL AND COMPANY, INC.		5160015	1.95
SIXTY-EIGHT GREATEST COUNTRY HITS, MAMMOTH COLLECTION NO. 27			
THE BIG THREE MUSIC CORPORATION			04.95
SLEEPY LAGOON			
CHAPPELL AND COMPANY, INC.		5225008	.60
SMOKE GETS IN YOUR EYES -- SHOWCASE			
CIMINO PUBLICATIONS, INC.		H	1.25
SMOKE GETS IN YOUR EYES			
CIMINO PUBLICATIONS, INC.		H	1.25
SMOKE GETS IN YOUR EYES			
CIMINO PUBLICATIONS, INC.		H	1.25
SMOKE GETS IN YOUR EYES			
CIMINO PUBLICATIONS, INC.		H	1.25
SMOKE RINGS			
MUSIC SALES CORPORATION		050979	.95
SOLDIER IN THE RAIN			
CIMINO PUBLICATIONS, INC.		EAS	1.25
LANE, J.			
SONGMAN			
THE BIG THREE MUSIC CORPORATION			00.85
SONGS FROM 'THE WORLD IS A GHETTO'			
THE BIG THREE MUSIC CORPORATION			03.50
SONG IS YOU			
CIMINO PUBLICATIONS, INC.		H	1.25
SONG OF NORWAY			
CHAPPELL AND COMPANY, INC.		536003	1.95
SOUL MAKOSSA			
CIMINO PUBLICATIONS, INC.		RA	1.25
SPY WITH A COLD NOSE			
CIMINO PUBLICATIONS, INC.		JEL	1.25
STRANGE MUSIC			
CHAPPELL AND COMPANY, INC.		5520002	.60
STRIPPER, THE			
CIMINO PUBLICATIONS, INC.		DR	1.25
STUDY IN BROWN			
CIMINO PUBLICATIONS, INC.		SOU	1.25
SUNDAY, MONDAY OR ALWAYS			
MUSIC SALES CORPORATION		050978	.95
SUNRISE SERENADE -- PIANO SOLO			
MUSIC SALES CORPORATION		050976	.95
SUNRISE SERENADE			
MUSIC SALES CORPORATION		050977	.95
SWEETHEART TREE			
CIMINO PUBLICATIONS, INC.		EAS	1.25
SWEET BABY JAMES			
MUSIC SALES CORPORATION		060993	.95
SWINGING ON A STAR			
MUSIC SALES CORPORATION		050975	.95
TAKE HER TO JAMAICA			
MUSIC SALES CORPORATION		040993	.95
THANK HEAVEN FOR LITTLE GIRLS			
CHAPPELL AND COMPANY, INC.		5740006	.60
THEME FROM 'LION IN WINTER'			
CIMINO PUBLICATIONS, INC.		JEL	1.25
THEME FROM 'THE DEADLY TRAP'			
CIMINO PUBLICATIONS, INC.		H	1.25
THEME FROM 'Z'			
CIMINO PUBLICATIONS, INC.		BL	1.25
THERE ARE SUCH THINGS			
MUSIC SALES CORPORATION		050974	.95
THEY CALL THE WIND MARIA			
CHAPPELL AND COMPANY, INC.		5930003	.75

THEY DIDN'T BELIEVE ME			
CIMINO PUBLICATIONS, INC.		H	1.25
THIS LOVE OF MINE			
MUSIC SALES CORPORATION		010992	.95
THOSE WONDERFUL YEARS 1900-1920			
THE BIG THREE MUSIC CORPORATION			05.95
TIGER RAG			
THE BIG THREE MUSIC CORPORATION			00.95
TODAY'S BIG COUNTRY HITS, BK. 5			
THE BIG THREE MUSIC CORPORATION			02.50
TODAY'S POP SCENE, BK. 1			
THE BIG THREE MUSIC CORPORATION			02.95
TOMPALL AND THE GLAZER BROTHERS			
THE BIG THREE MUSIC CORPORATION			02.95
TOP HITS OF 1972			
THE BIG THREE MUSIC CORPORATION			03.50
TOP TUNES IN BIG NOTES --150--			
CARL FISCHER, INC.		O 3818	1.00
TORNA AL PAESELLO			
MUSIC SALES CORPORATION		040982	1.00
TOUCH OF YOUR HAND			
CIMINO PUBLICATIONS, INC.		H	1.25
TRACY'S THEME			
TRO SONGWAYS SERVICE, INC.		2057	
TRUE LOVE			
CHAPPELL AND COMPANY, INC.		6165005	.60
TU, CA NUN CHIAGNE			
MUSIC SALES CORPORATION		040984	1.00
TWENTY-ONE BIGGEST HITS OF TODAY			
THE BIG THREE MUSIC CORPORATION			02.95
VANESSA			
CIMINO PUBLICATIONS, INC.		V	1.25
VARCA NAPULITANA			
MUSIC SALES CORPORATION		040989	1.00
VERADERO			
CIMINO PUBLICATIONS, INC.		V	1.25
VIENNA ECHOES			
CIMINO PUBLICATIONS, INC.		B	1.25
VIOLETS FOR YOUR FURS			
MUSIC SALES CORPORATION		050973	.95
VURRIA			
MUSIC SALES CORPORATION		040980	1.00
WAR-- ALL DAY MUSIC			
THE BIG THREE MUSIC CORPORATION			02.95
WATCH WHAT HAPPENS			
CIMINO PUBLICATIONS, INC.		V	1.00
WATCH WHAT HAPPENS			
CIMINO PUBLICATIONS, INC.		V	1.25
WATUSI TRUMPETS			
CIMINO PUBLICATIONS, INC.		MP	1.25
WAYWARD WIND			
CIMINO PUBLICATIONS, INC.		V	1.00
WHAT HAVE THEY DONE TO MY SONG, MA			
CIMINO PUBLICATIONS, INC.		KR	1.00
WHO			
CIMINO PUBLICATIONS, INC.		H	1.25
WHY DO I LOVE YOU			
CIMINO PUBLICATIONS, INC.		H	1.25
WHY TRY TO CHANGE ME NOW			
MUSIC SALES CORPORATION		040992	.95
WHY WAS I BORN			
CIMINO PUBLICATIONS, INC.		H	1.25
WILL YOU STILL BE MINE			
MUSIC SALES CORPORATION		050972	.95
WISH YOU WERE HERE			
CHAPPELL AND COMPANY, INC.		6702500	1.95
WONDERFUL TOWN			
CHAPPELL AND COMPANY, INC.		6742506	1.95
WORLD FAMOUS SONGS			
THE BIG THREE MUSIC CORPORATION			02.95
WUNDERBAR -- SHOWCASE			
CIMINO PUBLICATIONS, INC.		H	1.25
YES INDEED			
MUSIC SALES CORPORATION		010991	.95
YOU'LL NEVER WALK ALONE -- SHOWCASE			
CIMINO PUBLICATIONS, INC.		H	1.25
YOU'LL NEVER WALK ALONE			
CIMINO PUBLICATIONS, INC.		H	1.00
YOU'LL NEVER WALK ALONE			
CIMINO PUBLICATIONS, INC.		H	1.25
YOU'LL NEVER WALK ALONE			
CIMINO PUBLICATIONS, INC.		H	1.25
YOU DON'T HAVE TO KNOW			
MUSIC SALES CORPORATION		050972	.95

Folk Music

AGAY, D.--ED   AGAY, D.
  FIESTA
    MUSIC SALES CORPORATION   080057   .85
AGAY, D.--ED   AGAY, D.   A
  FOLK SONGS AND FOLK DANCES, BK. 1
    WARNER BROTHERS PUBLISHERS   YPL 5   1.50
AGAY, D.--ED   AGAY, D.   B
  FOLK SONGS AND FOLK DANCES, BK. 2
    WARNER BROTHERS PUBLISHERS   YPL 5   1.50
AGAY, D.--ED   AGAY, D.   C
  FOLK SONGS AND FOLK DANCES, BK. 3
    WARNER BROTHERS PUBLISHERS   YPL 5   1.50
AGAY, D.--ED   AGAY, D.
  JOY OF FOLK SONGS, THE
    MUSIC SALES CORPORATION   080006   1.75
BACON, E.
  BYWAYS
    G. SCHIRMER, INC.   1.50
BARTOK
  FOR CHILDREN--EIGHTY-FIVE PIECES WITHOUT OCTAVES FOR
  BEGINNERS--VOL. 1
    G. SCHIRMER, INC.   L1780   1.50
BARTOK
  FOR CHILDREN--EIGHTY-FIVE PIECES WITHOUT OCTAVES FOR
  BEGINNERS--VOL. 2
    G. SCHIRMER, INC.   L1781   1.50
BASTIEN--ED.   BASTIEN
  FOLK TUNES FOR FUN
    NEIL A. KJOS MUSIC COMPANY   21   1.25
BASTIEN--ED.   BASTIEN
  MORE FOLK TUNES FOR FUN
    NEIL A. KJOS MUSIC COMPANY   26   1.25
BAUM--ED. *   BAUM   2
  BRUDER SINGER. 270 LIEDER UNSERES VOLKES IN LEICHTEN
  KLAVIERSATZEN
    BARENREITER VERLAG   BA 2999
BENDA, R.
  DARK EYES
    G. SCHIRMER, INC.   .50
BERMONT, H.--ED   BERMONT, H.
  ALL-AMERICAN FOLK SONGS, BK. 1
    MUSICORD PUBLICATIONS, INC.   1.50
BERMONT, H.--ED   BERMONT, H.
  ALL-AMERICAN FOLK SONGS, BK. 2
    MUSICORD PUBLICATIONS, INC.   1.50
BERMONT, H.--ED   BERMONT, H.
  TWENTY-EIGHT STAR MELODIES, BK. 1
    MUSICORD PUBLICATIONS, INC.   1.25
BERMONT, H.
  ANYONE CAN PLAY PIANO
    MUSICORD PUBLICATIONS, INC.   2.00
BRADLEY, R.--ARR.   BRADLEY, R.   BIG NOTE EASY
  SIMPLY BRADLEY - FOLK BOOK
    SCREEN GEMS - COLUMBIA PUBLICATIONS   F0054P3   1.50
BROUTMAN--ED   BROUTMAN   3
  KUM BAH YAH - AFRICAN FOLK SONG
    PRO-ART PUBLICATIONS, INC.   448   .50
BROWN, L.   2
  OLD FOLK SONG, AN
    THEODORE PRESSER COMPANY   .50
BURCHENAL, E.
  AMERICAN COUNTRY-DANCES
    G. SCHIRMER, INC.   3.00
BURCHENAL, E.
  DANCES OF THE PEOPLE
    G. SCHIRMER, INC.   3.50
BURCHENAL, E.
  FOLK-DANCES AND SINGING GAMES
    G. SCHIRMER, INC.   3.50
BURCHENAL, E.
  FOLK-DANCES FROM OLD HOMELANDS
    G. SCHIRMER, INC.   3.50
BURCHENAL, E. *
  FOLK-DANCE MUSIC --ADAPTED FOR USE IN PHYSICAL EDUCATION AND
  PLAY--
    G. SCHIRMER, INC.   1.75
BURKARD, J. A.   1-2
  NEUE ANLEITUNG FUR DAS KLAVIERSPIEL, BEIHEFT 01,
  VOLKSLIEDBUCHLEIN
    SCHOTT   2692   1.75
BURNAM
  DOZEN FOLK TUNES FROM VARIOUS LANDS, A
    WILLIS MUSIC COMPANY   1.00
CAZDEN, N.
  AMERICAN FOLK SONGS FOR PIANO --64 SONGS--
    SPRATT MUSIC PUBLISHERS   1.75
COBURN *
  WHISPERING
    THE BIG THREE MUSIC CORPORATION   00.95
COLE--ED   COLE
  CZECHOSLOVAKIAN FOLK SONGS
    EDWARD B. MARKS MUSIC CORPORATION   01.50
CUNNINGHAM, M.
  AMERICAN FOLK SONGS
    COMPOSERS AUTOGRAPH PUBLICATIONS   5.28
DAVIS, M.
  MARILYN K. DAVIS GROUP PIANO METHOD - GROUP ACTIVITIES AT THE
  KEYBOARD, BK. 01
    BOURNE COMPANY   1.25
DAVIS, M.
  MARILYN K. DAVIS GROUP PIANO METHOD - GROUP ACTIVITIES AT THE
  KEYBOARD, BK. 02
    BOURNE COMPANY   1.25
DEFILIPPI, A.
  FOLK MELODIES FOR PIANO
    GENERAL MUSIC PUBLISHING COMPANY, INC.   2.00
DEUTSCH, L.   1
  FOR SIGHT READING, VOL. 1
    CENTURY MUSIC PUBLISHING COMPANY, INC.   1.25
DEUTSCH, L.   2-3
  FOR SIGHT READING, VOL. 2
    CENTURY MUSIC PUBLISHING COMPANY, INC.   1.50
DIETRICH--ED.   DIETRICH
  LATERNE, LATERNE, SONNE, MOND UND STERNE. 23 VOLKSKINDERLIEDER
  IN GANZ LEICHTEN SATZEN
    BARENREITER VERLAG   BA 1003
DIETRICH--ED.   DIETRICH   2
  VOLKSLIEDBUCHLEIN
    BARENREITER VERLAG   BA 1499
DILLER, A.--ED *   DILLER, A. *   E
  TUNES FROM MANY LANDS
    WILLIS MUSIC COMPANY   1.25
DILLER, A. *   GRADE 3
  DILLER-PAGE SONG-BOOKS, THE, VOL. 1
    G. SCHIRMER, INC.   1.25

DILLER, A. *   GRADE 3
  DILLER-PAGE SONG-BOOKS, THE, VOL. 2
    G. SCHIRMER, INC.   1.25
DILLER, A.   GRADE 1
  IN DAYS OF OLD--AUGUSTIN
    G. SCHIRMER, INC.   .40
DILLER, A.   GRADE 1
  IN DAYS OF OLD--GOSSIP JOAN
    G. SCHIRMER, INC.   .40
DILLER, A.   GRADE 1
  IN DAYS OF OLD--REAP THE FLAX
    G. SCHIRMER, INC.   .35
DILLER, A.   GRADE 1
  IN DAYS OF OLD--THE JUDGE'S DANCE
    G. SCHIRMER, INC.   .35
DOFLEIN--ED.   DOFLEIN   2
  ZWANZIG DEUTSCHE VOLKSTANZE
    BARENREITER VERLAG   BA 1145
ECKSTEIN--ARR.   ECKSTEIN
  DOWN IN THE VALLEY
    CARL FISCHER, INC.   P 2857   .50
EHMANN--ED.   EHMANN   2-3
  ALTE LIEDSATZE - 19 VOLKSLIEDSATZE AUS TABULATURBUCHERN DES 16.
  JAHRH.
    BARENREITER VERLAG   BA 1287
FAIRCHILD   3
  IRISH MEDLEY
    VOLKWEIN BROS.   .25
FAIRCHILD   3
  IRISH MEDLEY
    VOLKWEIN BROS.   00.50
FELBER, R.--ED   FELBER, R.   4
  SLOWAKISCHE TANZE
    SCHOTT   1285   2.00
FORD, T. E.
  TREASURY OF INSPIRATIONAL SONGS
    POINTER PUBLICATIONS   4.95
FOSTER   SCHAUM, J.   1
  STEPHEN FOSTER FAVORITES
    SCHAUM PUBLICATIONS, INC.   1.25
FOSTER   SCHAUM, J.   1
  STEPHEN FOSTER FAVORITES
    SCHAUM PUBLICATIONS, INC.   1.25
FRANK, M.
  PIANO WITH A LATIN BEAT
    SAM FOX PUBLISHING COMPANY, INC.   1.50
GABSCHUSS--ED   GABSCHUSS
  KINDERLIEDER UND VOLKSLIEDER FUR DEN SYSTEMATISCHEN UNTERRICHT
  AM KLAVIER
    SCHOTT   6150
GARROW
  SEVENTEEN FOLK TUNES FOR PIANO
    BRODT MUSIC COMPANY   1.50
GOLDBERGER, D.--ED. *   GOLDBERGER, D. *
  FOLK SONG BOOK 1
    CONSOLIDATED MUSIC PUBLISHERS, INC.   040100   1.25
GOLDBERGER, D.--ED. *   GOLDBERGER, D. *
  FOLK SONG BOOK 2
    CONSOLIDATED MUSIC PUBLISHERS, INC.   040101   1.25
GOLDBERGER, D.--ED. *   GOLDBERGER, D. *
  FOLK SONG BOOK 3
    CONSOLIDATED MUSIC PUBLISHERS, INC.   040102   1.25
GRIEG   RUTHARDT
  NORTHERN DANCES AND FOLK TUNES, OP. 17
    G. SCHIRMER, INC.   L728   1.00
GRIEG   M-D
  NORWEGIAN DANCES, OP. 35
    C. F. PETERS CORPORATION   2155   2.00
GRIEG   M-D
  NORWEGIAN FOLK TUNES, OP. 66
    C. F. PETERS CORPORATION   2860   2.00
GRIEG   E-M
  NORWEGIAN FOLK TUNES --22 SIMPLIFIED PIECES FROM VARIOUS
  COLLECTIONS--
    C. F. PETERS CORPORATION   550C   1.50
GRIEG   M-D
  NORWEGIAN MELODIES, OP. 63
    C. F. PETERS CORPORATION   2855   2.00
GRIEG   E-M
  NORWEGIAN NOTEBOOK. 16 PIECES FROM NORDIC DANCES AND FOLK TUNES
  --OP. 17, OP. 66--
    C. F. PETERS CORPORATION   4536   .90
GRIEG   M-D
  NORWEGIAN PEASANT DANCES --SLATTER--, OP. 72
    C. F. PETERS CORPORATION   3097   3.50
GUENTHER--ED   GUENTHER   2
  SWING YOUR PARTNER
    CENTURY MUSIC PUBLISHING COMPANY, INC.   1.00
HANSON, H.--ED   HANSON, H.
  NEW SCRIBNER MUSIC LIBRARY, VOL. 09 'HOME FAVORITES'
    CHARLES SCRIBNER'S SONS
HERNANDEZ--ED   HERNANDEZ
  FLORES DE ESPANA -- 38 FOLK SONGS WITH SPANISH TEXT
    ASSOCIATED MUSIC PUBLISHERS, INC.   3.50
HERRMANN--ED   HERRMANN
  EUROPEAN FOLK DANCES
    ASSOCIATED MUSIC PUBLISHERS, INC.   SIM   1.50
HERRMANN--ED   HERRMANN
  TUNES FROM FAR AWAY -- 50 EASY ARRANGEMENTS OF FOLKSONGS FROM
  MANY LANDS
    ASSOCIATED MUSIC PUBLISHERS, INC.   SIM   2.00
HOLLANDER
  YOU CAN PLAY PIANO SERIES, LEVEL 3 -- YOU CAN PLAY FOLK SONGS
    BOOSEY AND HAWKES, INC.   1.00
HOLMAN, D.   1-2
  EIGHT FRENCH FOLK TUNES
    NOVELLO AND COMPANY, LTD.   10.0074.08   1.15
HOVHANESS, A.   M
  MACEDONIAN MOUNTAIN DANCE
    C. F. PETERS CORPORATION   6199   .90
HOWELL--ED.   HOWELL
  ENJOYING THE PIANO
    PRO-ART PUBLICATIONS, INC.   212   1.25
HOWELL--ED.   HOWELL
  FAVORITE FOLK TUNES
    PRO-ART PUBLICATIONS, INC.   107   .75
JANACEK   3
  TWENTY-THREE VOLKSTANZE AUS MAHREN
    BARENREITER VERLAG   AP 618
JOYNER, B.--ED   JOYNER, B.
  FAVORITE FOLK SONGS
    WILLIS MUSIC COMPANY   1.25
JUAN--ED   JUAN
  SEIS HABANERAS TRADICIONALES
    ASSOCIATED MUSIC PUBLISHERS, INC.   UME   1.00

KASSCHAU, H.--ED.   KASSCHAU, H.
    FOLK TUNE TIME
        SAM FOX PUBLISHING COMPANY, INC.   1.25
KREISLER   4
    IM PARADIES-WIENER VOLKSLIED
        SCHOTT   1.75
LAMBERT, C.--ED   LAMBERT, C.   1C
    LITTLE TREASURY SERIES - FOLK SONGS AND DANCES, BK. 1
        CENTURY MUSIC PUBLISHING COMPANY, INC.   1.00
LAMBERT, C.--ED   LAMBERT, C.   2A
    LITTLE TREASURY SERIES - FOLK SONGS AND DANCES, BK. 2
        CENTURY MUSIC PUBLISHING COMPANY, INC.   1.00
LIPSCOMB--ED.   LIPSCOMB
    FAVORITE FOLKSONGS
        BOSTON MUSIC COMPANY   1.25
LUTOSLAWSKI
    FOLK MELODIES FOR PIANO
        EDWARD B. MARKS MUSIC CORPORATION   02.50
LUTTGERS--ED   LUTTGERS   1-2
    DER GUTE FREUND. LEICHTE VOLKS-TANZ- UND OPERNMELODIEN
        BARENREITER VERLAG   SM 80
LUTZ--ED   LUTZ
    AM RHEIN BEIM WEIN
        SCHOTT   4900   3.00
LUTZ--ED   LUTZ   2
    MEIN VOLKSLIEDERBUCH
        SCHOTT   4100   2.50
MALER, W.   3
    JAHRESKREIS. KLAVIER INVENTIONEN UBER DEUTSCHE VOLKSLIEDER
        SCHOTT   2363   2.00
MALTZMAN--ED   MALTZMAN
    SONGS EN FRANCAIS
        PRO-ART PUBLICATIONS, INC.   607   .75
MCGINLEY
    PIANO SESSIONS - KINDERGARTEN SERIES‡ ON TOP OF OLD SMOKY
    --SUPP. MUSIC FOR MR. AND MRS. MIDDLE--
        SHAWNEE PRESS, INC.   .35
MCGINLEY
    PIANO SESSIONS - KINDERGARTEN SERIES‡ RED RIVER VALLEY --SUPP.
    MUSIC FOR MR. AND MRS. MIDDLE--
        SHAWNEE PRESS, INC.   .35
MICHEELSEN   1-2
    KLAVIERUBUNG NACH VOLKSLIEDERN, HEFT 1 - 20 STUCKE MIT UBUNGEN
    FUR DEN ANFANG
        BARENREITER VERLAG   BA 1335
MICHEELSEN   1-2
    KLAVIERUBUNG NACH VOLKSLIEDERN, HEFT 1 - 32 STUCKE MIT UBUNGEN
    FUR DEN ANFANG
        BARENREITER VERLAG   BA 1334
MICHEELSEN   1-2
    KLAVIERUBUNG NACH VOLKSLIEDERN, HEFT 3 - LEICHTE SUITE -- 8
    KINDERLIEDER --
        BARENREITER VERLAG   BA 1336
MONTALBAN--ED   MONTALBAN
    CORRO DE LAS NINAS, EL -- 60 SPANISH FOLKSONGS FOR CHILDREN WITH
    SPANISH TEXT
        ASSOCIATED MUSIC PUBLISHERS, INC.   UME   2.75
NILES, J.
    I WONDER AS I WANDER--APPALACHIAN FOLK CAROL
        G. SCHIRMER, INC.   .35
PACHER, J. A.
    MEI HERZIGES DIRNDL--AUSTRIAN FOLK-SONG, OP. 69 NO. 1
        G. SCHIRMER, INC.   .60
PETERS--ED   PETERS   AI
    TIME TO PLAY FOLKSONGS
        WILLIS MUSIC COMPANY   1.00
PORTNOFF, M.--ED   PORTNOFF, M.
    DANCE ETUDES
        BOURNE COMPANY   1.00
POSER
    OLD FOLKSONGS IN NEW SETTINGS
        FRANCO COLOMBO PUBLICATIONS   SIK.478   2.25
RASBACH, O.   ELEMENTARY GRADE
    EARLY CALIFORNIA
        G. SCHIRMER, INC.   .80
RASBACH, O.   INTERMEDIATE GRADE
    FROM DIXIELAND
        G. SCHIRMER, INC.   .80
RASBACH, O.   LOWER ADVANCED GRADE
    IN COLONIAL DAYS
        G. SCHIRMER, INC.   .90
REIN--ED *   REIN *   2-3
    DER WUNDERGARTEN
        SCHOTT   4501-3   5.00
REIN   3
    KLAVIERMUSIK NACH VOLKSLIEDERN
        SCHOTT   4619   2.00
RICHARTZ   3
    RHEINH. VOLKSTANZE, OP. 69
        SCHOTT   3962   1.50
RICHTER, A.--ED.   RICHTER, A.
    SONGS OF STEPHEN FOSTER
        THEODORE PRESSER COMPANY   1.25
RICHTER
    FOLK SONGS OF TODAY
        WARNER BROTHERS PUBLISHERS   AR 24   1.25
ROSEMOND, G.
    FOUNDATION, THE
        WILLIS MUSIC COMPANY   1.00
ROSSI   4
    SPIN, SPIN, ESTHONIAN FOLK SONG
        CENTURY MUSIC PUBLISHING COMPANY, INC. 2288   .40
ROZIN--ED   ROZIN
    TRADITIONAL HEBREW SONGS
        PRO-ART PUBLICATIONS, INC.   1080   2.00
SALZMANN--ED   SALZMANN   2-3
    DER ZUPFGEIGENHANSL
        SCHOTT   4650   9.00
SASLAW, E.--ED   SASLAW, E.
    FUN WITH FOLK TUNES
        WILLIS MUSIC COMPANY   2.00
SAVINO--ED.   SAVINO
    CHIAPANECAS
        THE BIG THREE MUSIC CORPORATION   00.75
SCARMOLIN--ED   SCARMOLIN
    SONGS WE LOVE TO PLAY
        PRO-ART PUBLICATIONS, INC.   67   .85
SCHAUM, J.--ED.   SCHAUM, J.   1
    FOLK AND COUNTRY SONG
        SCHAUM PUBLICATIONS, INC.   1.45
SCHAUM, J.--ED.   SCHAUM, J.   PREP
    FOLK SONGS AND DANCES -- MUSIC FOR CHILDREN
        SCHAUM PUBLICATIONS, INC.   1.25
SCHAUM, J.--ED.   SCHAUM, J.   1
    FOLK SONG BOOK
        BELWIN-MILLS PUBLISHING CORPORATION   1.50

SCHAUM, J.--ED.   SCHAUM, J.   2
    MUSIC OF THE AMERICAN INDIAN
        SCHAUM PUBLICATIONS, INC.   1.50
SCHAUM, J.--ED.   SCHAUM, J.   2
    POLKA FESTIVAL
        SCHAUM PUBLICATIONS, INC.   1.50
SCHAUM, J.--ED.   SCHAUM, J.   1
    THIS OLD MAN
        BELWIN-MILLS PUBLISHING CORPORATION   .50
SCHAUM, J.   2 1/2
    CAMPFIRE SONGS
        SCHAUM PUBLICATIONS, INC.   1.25
SCHAUM, J.   2
    FOLK FESTIVAL
        SCHAUM PUBLICATIONS, INC.   1.25
SCHAUM, J.   3
    FOLK SONGS OF THE NORTH
        SCHAUM PUBLICATIONS, INC.   1.50
SCHAUM, J.   3
    FOLK SONGS OF THE SOUTH
        SCHAUM PUBLICATIONS, INC.   1.50
SCHER, W.--ED   SCHER, W.
    JEWISH SONGS AND DANCES
        G. SCHIRMER, INC.   1.00
SCHMID   4
    BAYRISCHE LANDLER, OP. 36
        SCHOTT   1792   2.00
SCHROEDER, H.   4
    MINNELIEDER
        SCHOTT   3720   2.00
SCHUNGELER, H.--ED   SCHUNGELER, H.   2-3
    DAS NEUE VOLKSLIEDERBUCH
        SCHOTT   3968   2.50
SCHUNGELER, H.   2-3
    DAS NEUE VOLKSLIEDERBUCH
        SCHOTT   3968   2.50
SIKORSKI
    SIKORSKI ALBUM - KLINGENDE HEIMAT - FOLKSONGS FROM ALL PARTS
    OF GERMANY ----- CLOTH
        FRANCO COLOMBO PUBLICATIONS   SIK.221   10.00
SIKORSKI
    SIKORSKI ALBUM - KLINGENDE HEIMAT - FOLKSONGS FROM ALL PARTS
    OF GERMANY ----- PAPER
        FRANCO COLOMBO PUBLICATIONS   SIK.221   6.00
SMITH--ED   SMITH
    TWENTY-NINE VERY EASY FOLK SONGS
        BOSTON MUSIC COMPANY   1.25
SPENCER, J.   1
    HOME ON THE RANGE -- AMERICAN COWBOY
        VOLKWEIN BROS.   .30
STEINER
    JEWISH FOLK SONGS
        BELWIN-MILLS PUBLISHING CORPORATION   11248   1.50
TRUXELL, E.   2
    POP GOES THE WEASEL
        VOLKWEIN BROS.   .40
TWITTENHOFF--ED   TWITTENHOFF   2
    VOLKSTANZBUCHLEIN
        SCHOTT   3774   1.75
VOLKART-SCHLAGER   1
    ARBEITSBUCH FUR KLEINE KLAVIERSPIELER - 23 VOLKSLIEDSATZE --
    'WIR MUSIZIEREN', HEFT 10
        BARENREITER VERLAG   SM 911
VUATAZ
    ETUDES FOR PIANO BASED ON FOLKSONGS, BK. 1 - INTRODUCTION
        FRANCO COLOMBO PUBLICATIONS   SAL   4.25
VUATAZ
    ETUDES FOR PIANO BASED ON FOLKSONGS, BK. 2 - ETUDES 1-12
        FRANCO COLOMBO PUBLICATIONS   SAL   4.25
VUATAZ
    ETUDES FOR PIANO BASED ON FOLKSONGS, BK. 3 - ETUDES 13-24
        FRANCO COLOMBO PUBLICATIONS   SAL   5.00
VUATAZ
    ETUDES FOR PIANO BASED ON FOLKSONGS, BK. 4 - ETUDES 25-36
        FRANCO COLOMBO PUBLICATIONS   SAL   5.00
WESTERVELT, M.   FOR BEGINNERS
    CHILD'S BOOK OF FOLK-TUNES, A--SUPPLEMENTARY READING MATERIAL
    FOR THE BEGINNER--WITH WORDS
        G. SCHIRMER, INC.   1.00
WEYBRIGHT--ED.   WEYBRIGHT   3
    ALOUETTE
        BELWIN-MILLS PUBLISHING CORPORATION   .50
WEYBRIGHT--ED.   WEYBRIGHT   1 1/2
    ALPHABET SONG
        BELWIN-MILLS PUBLISHING CORPORATION   .50
WEYBRIGHT--ED.   WEYBRIGHT   2
    AROUND THE MULBERRY BUSH
        BELWIN-MILLS PUBLISHING CORPORATION   .50
WEYBRIGHT--ED.   WEYBRIGHT   2
    BANJO SONG
        BELWIN-MILLS PUBLISHING CORPORATION   .50
WEYBRIGHT--ED.   WEYBRIGHT   2
    CARA NINA
        BELWIN-MILLS PUBLISHING CORPORATION   .50
WEYBRIGHT--ED.   WEYBRIGHT   2
    CHILEAN FOLK SONG
        BELWIN-MILLS PUBLISHING CORPORATION   .50
WEYBRIGHT--ED.   WEYBRIGHT   2
    FOGGY DEW
        BELWIN-MILLS PUBLISHING CORPORATION   .50
WEYBRIGHT--ED.   WEYBRIGHT   1 1/2
    FOLK FROM THE VILLAGE, THE
        BELWIN-MILLS PUBLISHING CORPORATION   .50
WEYBRIGHT--ED.   WEYBRIGHT   1 1/2
    FREDERIKA
        BELWIN-MILLS PUBLISHING CORPORATION   .50
WEYBRIGHT--ED.   WEYBRIGHT   1 1/2
    FUN WITH MY LOU
        BELWIN-MILLS PUBLISHING CORPORATION   .50
WEYBRIGHT--ED.   WEYBRIGHT   1 1/2
    GAILY THEY DANCE
        BELWIN-MILLS PUBLISHING CORPORATION   .50
WEYBRIGHT--ED.   WEYBRIGHT   1 1/2
    HOP, HOP, HOP
        BELWIN-MILLS PUBLISHING CORPORATION   .50
WEYBRIGHT--ED.   WEYBRIGHT   3
    ISLAND FLOWER
        BELWIN-MILLS PUBLISHING CORPORATION   .50
WEYBRIGHT--ED.   WEYBRIGHT   1 1/2
    JOHNNY GET YOUR HAIR CUT
        BELWIN-MILLS PUBLISHING CORPORATION   .50
WHITEFIELD--ED   WHITEFIELD   2
    BARNARD WHITEFIELDS'SAMERICAN FOLK SONG ALBUM
        CENTURY MUSIC PUBLISHING COMPANY, INC.   1.00
WHITEFIELD   2
    BERNARD WHITEFELD'S AMERICAN FOLK SONG ALBUM
        ASHLEY DEALERS SERVICE, INC.   1.00

WOLFSON, J.
   PARAPHRASES ON OLD HEBREW FOLK SONGS, BK. 1
      UNIVERSAL EDITION   UE 6931   1.80
WOLFSON, J.
   PARAPHRASES ON OLD HEBREW FOLK SONGS, BK. 2
      UNIVERSAL EDITION   UE 6932   1.80
YOUNG, I.--ED.   YOUNG, I.
   THIRTY-SIX FAVORITE FOLK SONGS FOR THE PIANO
      G. SCHIRMER, INC.   1.25
YOUNG, I.--ED.   YOUNG, I.
   THIRTY-SIX FAVORITE FOLK SONGS FOR THE PIANO
      G. SCHIRMER, INC.   1.25

Folk Music:
Composer/Editor/Arranger Unlisted—Works Alphabetized by Title

   ALTE DEUTSCHE VOLKSTANZE   2
      SCHOTT   04032 1/2   1.00

   BLUESMEN, THE
      MUSIC SALES COPPORATION   000096   3.95

   CHRISTMAS MUSIC   M
      C. F. PETERS CORPORATION   4610   2.50

   EARLY ONE MORNING
      FREDERICK HARRIS MUSIC COMPANY   .60

FOLK BLUES
   MUSIC SALES CORPORATION   000113   4.95

LONDON BRIDGE IS FALLING DOWN
   FREDERICK HARRIS MUSIC COMPANY   .60

MEIN HEIMATLAND   2-3
   SCHOTT   2222   5.00

MEXICAN HAT DANCE
   EDWARD B. MARKS MUSIC CORPORATION   01.00

NINETY-FIVE FOLK SONGS AND DANCES FOR PIANO
   WARNER BROTHERS PUBLISHERS   MFE 28   1.95

POINTER SYSTEM - FOLK SONGS
   POINTER PUBLICATIONS   1.50

POINTER SYSTEM - LATIN MOODS
   POINTER PUBLICATIONS   1.50

POINTER SYSTEM - SONG MEMORIES
   POINTER PUBLICATIONS   1.50

TWO HUNDRED JIGS, REELS AND COUNTRY DANCES
   THE BIG THREE MUSIC CORPORATION   01.50

YOUR FAVORITE NEGRO SPIRITUALS
   SHAWNEE PRESS, INC.   2.00

YOUR FAVORITE NEGRO SPIRITUALS
   SHAWNEE PRESS, INC.   2.00

Church Music

ADAMS, G.   1 1/2
    STAR OF BETHLEHEM
        BELWIN-MILLS PUBLISHING CORPORATION   .50
AGAY, D.--ED   AGAY, D.   1 1/2
    HE'S GOT THE WHOLE WORLD IN HIS HANDS
        THEODORE PRESSER COMPANY   .50
ARNO--ED.   ARNO
    SACRED HOUR AT THE PIANO
        CARL FISCHER, INC.   O 3255   2.00
ASHFORD
    PIANO VOLUNTARIES NO. 1
        LORENZ PUBLISHING COMPANY   2.50
AULD, W. J.
    HANDBOOK FOR CHURCH PIANIST
        LILLENAS PUBLISHING COMPANY   MB-061   1.50
AULD, W. J.
    PIANO HYMNSCRIPTIONS NO. 1
        LILLENAS PUBLISHING COMPANY   MB-148   2.50
AULD, W. J.
    PIANO HYMNSCRIPTIONS NO. 2
        LILLENAS PUBLISHING COMPANY   MB-149   2.50
AULD, W. J.
    SACRED TRANSCRIPTIONS -- PIANO NO. 1
        LILLENAS PUBLISHING COMPANY   MB-178   2.95
AULD, W. J.
    SACRED TRANSCRIPTIONS -- PIANO NO. 2
        LILLENAS PUBLISHING COMPANY   MB-179   2.95
AULD, W. J.
    SACRED TRANSCRIPTIONS -- PIANO NO. 3
        LILLENAS PUBLISHING COMPANY   MB-180   2.95
BACH, J.S. *   SPENCER, J.   1
    AVE MARIA
        VOLKWEIN BROS.   .25
BACH, J.S.   BAUER
    COME, SWEET DEATH--KOMM' SUSSER TOD
        G. SCHIRMER, INC.   .50
BACH, J.S.   LIPSCOMB
    JESU, JOY OF MAN'S DESIRING
        G. SCHIRMER, INC.   .60
BACH, J.S.   BAUER
    JESUS, JOY OF MAN'S DESIRE--JESUS BLEIBET MEINE FREUDE--FROM
    CHURCH CANTATA 147
        G. SCHIRMER, INC.   .60
BACH, J.S.   RIEMENSCHNEIDER
    THREE HUNDRED AND SEVENTY ONE HARMONIZED CHORALES AND 69 CHORALE
    MELODIES WITH FIGURED BASS
        G. SCHIRMER, INC.   3.50
BASTIEN--ED.   BASTIEN
    HYMNS FOR PIANO, BK. 1
        NEIL A. KJOS MUSIC COMPANY   24   1.00
BASTIEN--ED.   BASTIEN
    HYMNS FOR PIANO, BK. 2
        NEIL A. KJOS MUSIC COMPANY   25   1.25
BAUM--ED *   BAUM *   2-3
    KLAVIERCHORALBUCH. 206 KLAVIERSATZE ZUM EVANGELISCHEN
    KIRCHENGESANGBUCH
        BARENREITER VERLAG   BA 3499
BENDER   2
    KLEINE CHORALVORSPIELE ZUM GOTTESDIENSTLICHEN GEBRAUCH, HEFT 1 -
    30 CHORALVORSPIELE
        BARENREITER VERLAG   BA 2431
BENDER   2
    KLEINE CHORALVORSPIELE ZUM GOTTESDIENSTLICHEN GEBRAUCH, HEFT 2 -
    30 CHORALVORSPIELE
        BARENREITER VERLAG   BA 2434
BENDER   2
    KLEINE CHORALVORSPIELE ZUM GOTTESDIENSTLICHEN GEBRAUCH, HEFT 3 -
    30 CHORALVORSPIELE
        BARENREITER VERLAG   BA 2429
BENDER   MOD. EASY
    THIRTEEN SERVICE PIECES FOR THE CHURCH PIANIST
        ABINGDON PRESS   1.50
BENDER   MOD. DIFF.
    THIRTEEN VOLUNTARIES FOR THE CHURCH PIANIST
        ABINGDON PRESS   3.00
BOCK, F.
    SACRED SONGS FOR THE PIANO
        BROADMAN MUSIC   4571-08   2.50
BOCK, F.
    YOUNG WORLD PIANIST
        LILLENAS PUBLISHING COMPANY   MB-260   2.50
BOHM *   BAUM   2-3
    ALTE WEIHNACHTSMUSIK - 13 WEIHNACHTSCHORALE UND
    CHORALVARIATIONEN
        BARENREITER VERLAG   BA 826
BORNEFELD   1-2
    BEGLEITSATZE -- DAS CHORALWERK -- HEFT 1, 25 SATZE ZU ADVENT,
    WEIHNACHTEN, JAHRESSCHLUSS UND ERSCHEINUNGSFEST
        BARENREITER VERLAG   BA 2212
BORNEFELD   1-2
    BEGLEITSATZE -- DAS CHORALWERK -- HEFT 2, 28 SATZE ZU PASSION,
    OSTERN, HIMMELFAHRT, PFINGSTEN UND DREIEINIGKEIT
        BARENREITER VERLAG   BA 2213
BORNEFELD   1-2
    BEGLEITSATZE -- DAS CHORALWERK -- HEFT 3, 31 SATZE, KIRCHE,
    WORT, SAKRAMENT
        BARENREITER VERLAG   BA 2214
BORNEFELD   1-2
    BEGLEITSATZE -- DAS CHORALWERK -- HEFT 4, 29 SATZE, PSALMEN,
    GEBETE
        BARENREITER VERLAG   BA 2215
BORNEFELD   1-2
    BEGLEITSATZE -- DAS CHORALWERK -- HEFT 5, 30 SATZE, LOB UND
    DANK, GLAUBE
        BARENREITER VERLAG   BA 2216
BORNEFELD   1-2
    BEGLEITSATZE -- DAS CHORALWERK -- HEFT 6, 32 SATZE ZU MORGEN,
    ABEND, BERUF, TOD UND EWIGKEIT
        BARENREITER VERLAG   BA 2217
BOUD, R.
    RON BOUD PIANO STYLINGS
        HOPE PUBLISHING COMPANY   2.00
BRADLEY, R.--ARR.   BRADLEY, R.   BIG NOTE EASY
    AMAZING GRACE - AND - HE'S GOT THE WHOLE WORLD IN HIS HANDS
        SCREEN GEMS - COLUMBIA PUBLICATIONS C0019P3   1.00
BRADLEY, R.--ARR.   BRADLEY, R.   EASY
    BRADLEY'S BEST OF THE BEST - POPULAR SACRED SONGS
        SCREEN GEMS - COLUMBIA PUBLICATIONS F0135P2   1.50
BRADLEY, R.--ARR.   BRADLEY, R.   EASY
    BRADLEY'S HYMN JOY - ISSUE NO. 1
        SCREEN GEMS - COLUMBIA PUBLICATIONS F0275P2   1.50
BRADLEY, R.--ARR.   BRADLEY, R.   BIG NOTE EASY
    SIMPLY BRADLEY - HYMN BOOK
        SCREEN GEMS - COLUMBIA PUBLICATIONS F0048P3   1.50

BRIMHALL, J.--ED.   BRIMHALL, J.
    AMAZING GRACE/HE'S GOT THE WHOLE WORLD IN HIS HANDS
        CHARLES HANSEN   35866   .85
BRIMHALL, J.--ED.   BRIMHALL, J.
    BEST OF SACRED MUSIC
        CHARLES HANSEN   H446   1.50
BRIMHALL, J.--ED.   BRIMHALL, J.
    BIBLE TELLS ME SO, THE
        CHARLES HANSEN   F30069   .85
BRIMHALL, J.--ED.   BRIMHALL, J.
    BRIMHALL'S SACRED MUSIC OF TODAY
        CHARLES HANSEN   T329   1.50
BRIMHALL, J.--ED.   BRIMHALL, J.
    LET THERE BE PEACE ON EARTH
        CHARLES HANSEN   30046   .85
BRIMHALL, J.--ED.   BRIMHALL, J.
    MAY THE GOOD LORD BLESS AND KEEP YOU
        CHARLES HANSEN   35901   .85
BRIMHALL, J.--ED.   BRIMHALL, J.
    PUT YOUR HAND IN THE HAND
        CHARLES HANSEN   35869   .85
BURNAM--ED   BURNAM   1
    HE'S GOT THE WHOLE WORLD IN HIS HANDS
        WILLIS MUSIC COMPANY   .40
BURNAM
    FAMILY HYMN BOOK, THE
        WILLIS MUSIC COMPANY   1.00
CHATHAM, B. J.--ED   CHATHAM, B. J.
    GOSPEL SONG FAVORITES FOR THE PIANO
        BROADMAN MUSIC   4571-06   2.25
COELHO, P.M.R.   KASTER   3
    FLORES DE MUSICA. WERKE FUR TASTENINSTRUMENTE ODER HARFE --
    'PORTUGALIAE MUSICA' -- BK. 2. KIRCHENMUSIK
        BARENREITER VERLAG   PM 3
CRIST, D. W.--ED.   CRIST, D. W.
    VESPER MELODIES
        VOLKWEIN BROS.   01.00
CURCIO
    CATHOLIC SONGS FOR THE YOUNG PIANIST
        BELWIN-MILLS PUBLISHING CORPORATION 10005   1.25
CURRIE, E.--ED   CURRIE, E.   HA
    VARIATIONS ON HYMN TUNES
        WILLIS MUSIC COMPANY   1.25
DANDRIEU, P.   2-3
    NOELS, HEFT 1 -- 'L'ORGANISTE LITURGIQUE', 12 --
        BARENREITER VERLAG
DANDRIEU, P.   2-3
    NOELS, HEFT 2 -- 'L'ORGANISTE LITURGIQUE', 16 --
        BARENREITER VERLAG
DANDRIEU, P.   2-3
    NOELS, HEFT 3 -- 'L'ORGANISTE LITURGIQUE', 19-20 --
        BARENREITER VERLAG
DANDRIEU, P.   2-3
    NOELS, HEFT 4 -- 'L'ORGANISTE LITURGIQUE', 22
        BARENREITER VERLAG
DEGEN   2-3
    WEIHNACHTSBUCH. MUSIK AUS 36 ALTEN WEIHNACHTSLIEDERN FUR
    KLAVIER, BK. 1 - 7 ALTE WEIHNACHTSLIEDER UND 6 KRIPPENLIEDER
        BARENREITER VERLAG   SM 2101
DEGEN   2-3
    WEIHNACHTSBUCH. MUSIK AUS 36 ALTEN WEIHNACHTSLIEDERN FUR
    KLAVIER, BK. 2 - 6 WIEGENLIEDER, 8 HIRTENLIEDER
        BARENREITER VERLAG
DEGEN   2-3
    WEIHNACHTSBUCH. MUSIK AUS 36 ALTEN WEIHNACHTSLIEDERN FUR
    KLAVIER, BK. 3 - 2 DREI KONIGE-LIEDER UND 7 WEIHNACHTS-CHORALE
        BARENREITER VERLAG   SM 2103
DOERFFEL--ED   DOERFFEL   E
    CHORALBUCH
        C. F. PETERS CORPORATION   1423   2.00
DRAESEL
    NOW HYMNS FOR YOUNG PEOPLE
        EDWARD B. MARKS MUSIC CORPORATION   01.50
ECKARD, W.
    HYMNS TO PLAY AND SING
        THEODORE PRESSER COMPANY   1.50
ECKARD, W.
    MUSIC OF FAITH, BK. 2
        THEODORE PRESSER COMPANY   1.75
ENGEL, S.--ARR.   ENGEL, S.   ADVANCED
    GREAT HYMNS
        SCREEN GEMS - COLUMBIA PUBLICATIONS F0260P1 3.50
FORD, T. E.
    POINTER LIBRARY - A TREASURY OF INSPIRATIONAL SONGS
        POINTER PUBLICATIONS   2.95
FRANK, R.
    PIANO HYMN CLASSICS NO. 1
        LILLENAS PUBLISHING COMPANY   MB-146   2.50
FRANK, R.
    PIANO HYMN CLASSICS NO. 2
        LILLENAS PUBLISHING COMPANY   MB-147   2.50
FREDRICH, F.--ED   FREDRICH, F.
    FIRST BOOK OF HYMNS AND CAROLS, A
        WILLIS MUSIC COMPANY   1.00
FREEMAN--ED.   FREEMAN   4
    ABIDE WITH ME, G MAJOR
        CENTURY MUSIC PUBLISHING COMPANY, INC. 614   .40
FREEMAN--ED.   FREEMAN   4
    LEAD, KINDLY LIGHT
        CENTURY MUSIC PUBLISHING COMPANY, INC. 637   .40
FULLER
    SERVICE INTERLUDES
        PRO-ART PUBLICATIONS, INC.   931   1.25
GAHM--ED.   GAHM
    SACRED PIANO ALBUM
        CARL FISCHER, INC.   O 2618   1.50
GARROW, L.   2
    SACRED MUSIC
        BELWIN-MILLS PUBLISHING CORPORATION FDL 323 1.75
GERIG, R.--ED   GERIG, R.
    PIANO PRELUDES ON HYMNS AND CHORALES
        HOPE PUBLISHING COMPANY   3.00
GILLOCK   4
    HYMNS AT THE PIANO
        WILLIS MUSIC COMPANY   .75
GLOVER, D. *   7
    ADVANCED HYMN PLAYING
        BELWIN-MILLS PUBLISHING CORPORATION   2.00
GLOVER, D. *   8
    ADVANCED HYMN PLAYING
        BELWIN-MILLS PUBLISHING CORPORATION   2.00
GLOVER, D. *   1
    CHURCH MUSICIAN, LEVEL 1
        BELWIN-MILLS PUBLISHING CORPORATION FDL 549 2.00
GLOVER, D. *   2
    CHURCH MUSICIAN, LEVEL 2
        BELWIN-MILLS PUBLISHING CORPORATION FDL 550 2.00

GLOVER, D. *   3
  CHURCH MUSICIAN, LEVEL 3
    BELWIN-MILLS PUBLISHING CORPORATION   FDL 551   2.00
GLOVER, D. *   4
  CHURCH MUSICIAN, LEVEL 4
    BELWIN-MILLS PUBLISHING CORPORATION   FDL 552   2.00
GLOVER, D. *   5
  CHURCH MUSICIAN, LEVEL 5
    BELWIN-MILLS PUBLISHING CORPORATION   FDL 553   2.00
GLOVER, D. *   6
  CHURCH MUSICIAN, LEVEL 6
    BELWIN-MILLS PUBLISHING CORPORATION   FDL 554   2.00
GLOVER, D. *   PRIM.
  CHURCH MUSICIAN, PRIMER LEVEL
    BELWIN-MILLS PUBLISHING CORPORATION   FDL 548   2.00
GLOVER, D.
  MY STEP BY STEP HYMN BOOK
    BELWIN-MILLS PUBLISHING CORPORATION   10031   1.25
GOODE
  PIANO HYMNS FOR THE LITURGICAL YEAR
    HOPE PUBLISHING COMPANY   2.50
GOODE   MOD. DIFF.
  PIANO VOLUNTARIES ON HYMN TUNES
    ABINGDON PRESS   2.00
HANSON, H.--ED   HANSON, H.
  NEW SCRIBNER MUSIC LIBRARY, VOL. 09 'HOME FAVORITES'
    CHARLES SCRIBNER'S SONS
HARTNESS, R.
  LEARN TO PLAY GOSPEL PIANO
    LILLENAS PUBLISHING COMPANY   MB-063   6.95
HAWTHORNE, A.   BURNAM   1 1/2
  WHISPERING HOPE
    WILLIS MUSIC COMPANY   .35
HEAPS, S.--ED   HEAPS, S.   E
  PIANO MEDITATIONS FOR CHURCH AND HOME
    WILLIS MUSIC COMPANY   1.50
HOFSTAD, M.--ED   HOFSTAD, M.
  VERY FIRST HYMNS
    BOSTON MUSIC COMPANY   1.25
HOLCOMB, L. R.--ED   HOLCOMB, L. R.
  HYMNS FOR THE BEGINNING PIANIST
    BROADMAN MUSIC   4571-07   2.00
HUGHES--ED.   HUGHES
  KEYBOARD MEDLEYS
    LORENZ PUBLISHING COMPANY   2.00
JENSVOLD, J.--ED   JENSVOLD, J.
  MY HYMNS
    WILLIS MUSIC COMPANY   1.25
KAHL--ED   KAHL
  JUNIOR HYMNBOOK - BOOK 1
    BOSTON MUSIC COMPANY   1.50
KAHL--ED   KAHL
  JUNIOR HYMNBOOK - BOOK 2
    BOSTON MUSIC COMPANY   1.50
KAHL--ED   KAHL
  JUNIOR HYMNBOOK - BOOK 3
    BOSTON MUSIC COMPANY   1.75
KAHL
  SACRED MOODS
    BOSTON MUSIC COMPANY   1.00
KELLER--ED.   KELLER   E-M
  EIGHTY CHORALE PRELUDES OF THE SEVENTEENTH AND EIGHTEENTH
  CENTURIES
    C. F. PETERS CORPORATION   4448   3.50
KEVAN
  THIRTY-ONE FAVORITE CHILDREN'S HYMNS
    EDWARD B. MARKS MUSIC CORPORATION   01.00
KOHLMANN, C.
  CONCERTO TRANSCRIPTIONS OF FAVORITE HYMNS
    THEODORE PRESSER COMPANY   1.25
KOHLMANN, C.
  EIGHTEEN HYMN TRANSCRIPTIONS
    THEODORE PRESSER COMPANY   1.95
KOHLMANN, C.
  MORE CONCERT TRANSCRIPTIONS OF FAVORITE HYMNS
    THEODORE PRESSER COMPANY   1.25
KREUTZER--ED   KREUTZER
  HERITAGE HYMN BOOK
    CENTURY MUSIC PUBLISHING COMPANY, INC.   1.00
KREUTZER--ED   KREUTZER
  LET'S PLAY HYMNS
    CENTURY MUSIC PUBLISHING COMPANY, INC.   1.25
KREUTZER
  LET'S PLAY HYMNS
    ASHLEY DEALERS SERVICE, INC.   1.25
LANE, J.--ED.   LANE, J.   HE
  THE BIG THREE MUSIC CORPORATION   01.25
LANE, J.--ED.   LANE, J.
  OLD RUGGED CROSS, THE
    THE BIG THREE MUSIC CORPORATION   00.70
LANE, J.--ED   LANE
  JOHN LANE'S FAVORITE HYMNS
    THE BIG THREE MUSIC CORPORATION   2.95
LANE, J.--ED   LANE
  JOHN LANE'S HAVE FAITH
    THE BIG THREE MUSIC CORPORATION   2.95
LA ROWE, J.
  MEDITATIONS FOR PIANO
    LILLENAS PUBLISHING COMPANY   MB-123   2.50
LIPSCOMB--ED.   LIPSCOMB
  FORTY-SIX EASY ARRANGEMENTS OF SACRED MELODIES--WITH WORDS
    G. SCHIRMER, INC.   1.00
LIPSCOMB--ED.   LIPSCOMB
  HYMNS TO REMEMBER
    G. SCHIRMER, INC.   1.00
LORENZ, G.--ED.   LORENZ, G.
  ALL-TIME GOSPEL FAVORITES FOR PIANO
    LORENZ PUBLISHING COMPANY   2.95
LOUKA, M.   3
  HOUR OF PRAYER
    VOLKWEIN BROS.   .40
LYALL, M.--ED   LYALL, M.
  FAVORITE HYMNS FOR THE PIANO
    BROADMAN MUSIC   4571-02   2.25
LYALL, M.--ED   LYALL, M.
  HYMN TUNE PRELUDES FOR THE PIANO, NO. 1
    BROADMAN MUSIC   4571-03   2.25
LYALL, M.--ED   LYALL, M.
  HYMN TUNE PRELUDES FOR THE PIANO, NO. 2
    BROADMAN MUSIC   4571-04   2.25
MCHALE, M.   2
  SCARED SPOOK, THE
    THEODORE PRESSER COMPANY   .50
MCKINNEY
  HYMN FAVORITES FOR PIANO
    BELWIN-MILLS PUBLISHING CORPORATION   2.00

MONK--ED.   MONK   3
  ABIDE WITH ME, C MAJOR
    CENTURY MUSIC PUBLISHING COMPANY, INC.   3619   .40
NEVIN
  SACRED SONGS AND SPIRITUALS
    BELWIN-MILLS PUBLISHING CORPORATION   10044   1.50
PACHELBEL   MATTHAEI   3
  SIEBEN CHORALPARTITEN FUR CEMBALO -- KLAVIER -- ODER ORGEL
    BARENREITER VERLAG   BA 1016
PACHELBEL   MOSER, C. *   3
  WERKE FUR ORGEL UND CLAVIER -- GESAMTAUSGABE DER ERHALTENEN
  KOMPOSITIONEN --
    BARENREITER VERLAG   BA 2206
PANKOW, E.
  CHAPEL PIANIST NO. 1
    LILLENAS PUBLISHING COMPANY   MB-006   2.50
PANKOW, E.
  CHAPEL PIANIST NO. 2
    LILLENAS PUBLISHING COMPANY   MB-007   2.50
PANKOW, E.
  CHAPEL PIANIST NO. 3
    LILLENAS PUBLISHING COMPANY   MB-008   2.50
PARSONS
  MUSIC OF FAITH, BK. 3
    THEODORE PRESSER COMPANY   2.25
PAYNE, W.
  TWELVE HYMN TUNES
    BANKS AND SON LTD.   .70
PEERY, R. R.--ED   PEERY   GR. 1
  CHILD'S BOOK OF HYMNS
    LORENZ PUBLISHING COMPANY   2.00
PEERY, R. R.--ED   PEERY, R. R.
  FAMOUS SACRED SONGS
    BOSTON MUSIC COMPANY   1.50
PEERY, R. R.--ED   PEERY
  PIANO VOLUNTARIES
    LORENZ PUBLISHING COMPANY   2.50
PEERY, R. R.
  CHAPEL MUSINGS
    THEODORE PRESSER COMPANY   1.50
PEERY, R. R.
  ONE-PAGE PIANO VOLUNTARIES
    LORENZ PUBLISHING COMPANY   2.00
PIKE, E. F.
  EASIEST TUNE BOOK OF SACRED SONGS AND SOLOS, OP. 32
    BOOSEY AND HAWKES, INC.   1.00
PORTNOFF, M.
  MUSIC OF FAITH, BK. 1
    THEODORE PRESSER COMPANY   1.75
POST--ED   POST   1-2
  THANKSGIVING HYMN
    CENTURY MUSIC PUBLISHING COMPANY, INC.   4158   .40
RAPHAEL, G.   1-2
  ADVENT- UND WEIHNACHTSLIEDER IN 25 LEICHTEN SATZEN
    BARENREITER VERLAG   SM 2325
REDA   2-3
  CHORAL-SPIEL-BUCH. 30 CHORALSATZE
    BARENREITER VERLAG   BA 2064
REISFELD--ED   REISFELD   2
  STANDIN' IN THE NEED OF PRAYER
    CENTURY MUSIC PUBLISHING COMPANY, INC.   3835   .40
RICHTER--ED   RICHTER
  MY FIRST HYMNAL --FAVORITE CATHOLIC AND OTHER HYMNS--
    SUMMY-BIRCHARD COMPANY   M-1368   1.50
RICHTER, A.--ED.   RICHTER, A.
  MY EVERYDAY HYMN BOOK
    THEODORE PRESSER COMPANY   1.25
RICHTER, A.--ED.   RICHTER, A.
  MY OWN HYMN BOOK
    THEODORE PRESSER COMPANY   1.50
RICHTER, C.--ED   RICHTER, C.
  MERRY CHRISTMAS MUSIC
    BOURNE COMPANY   .75
RICHTER
  LITTLE HYMNAL FOR PIANO, A
    WARNER BROTHERS PUBLISHERS   AR 25   1.50
ROGERS--ED   ROGERS
  HYMNS TO PLAY AND SING
    PRO-ART PUBLICATIONS, INC.   527   .75
ROGERS, E. T.   EASY
  BEST OF YOUNG WORLD
    LILLENAS PUBLISHING COMPANY   MB-291   2.50
ROGERS, E. T.   1 1/2 - 2
  FAVORITES FROM THE HYMNAL NO. 1
    LILLENAS PUBLISHING COMPANY   MB-046   1.50
ROGERS, E. T.   2 1/2 - 3
  FAVORITES FROM THE HYMNAL NO. 2
    LILLENAS PUBLISHING COMPANY   MB-047   1.50
ROGERS, E. T.   INTERMEDIATE
  FAVORITES FROM YOUNG WORLD
    LILLENAS PUBLISHING COMPANY   MB-292   2.50
ROGERS, E. T.   1
  FIRST BOOK OF FAVORITE HYMNS
    LILLENAS PUBLISHING COMPANY   MB-050   1.50
SANBORN, J.--ED   SANBORN, J.
  AMAZING GRACE AND OTHER GOSPEL FAVORITES
    THEODORE PRESSER COMPANY   2.95
SANFORD--ED   SANFORD
  HYMNS
    BOSTON MUSIC COMPANY   1.00
SCARMOLIN--ED   SCARMOLIN
  BEST LOVED HYMNS
    PRO-ART PUBLICATIONS, INC.   45   .85
SCHAUM, J.--ED.   SCHAUM, J.   2
  CATHOLIC HYMNS
    SCHAUM PUBLICATIONS, INC.   1.50
SCHAUM, J.--ED.   SCHAUM, J.   5
  GOSPEL PIANO PROFILES
    SCHAUM PUBLICATIONS, INC.   2.00
SCHAUM, J.--ED.   SCHAUM, J.   5
  GOSPEL PIANO PROFILES
    SCHAUM PUBLICATIONS, INC.   2.00
SCHAUM, J.--ED.   SCHAUM, J.   2 1/2
  GOSPEL VIGNETTES
    SCHAUM PUBLICATIONS, INC.   2.00
SCHAUM, J.--ED.   SCHAUM, J.   PREP
  HYMNS AND GOSPEL SONGS
    SCHAUM PUBLICATIONS, INC.   1.25
SCHAUM, J.--ED.   SCHAUM, J.   2
  HYMN PRIMER
    SCHAUM PUBLICATIONS, INC.   1.25
SCHAUM, J.--ED.   SCHAUM, J.
  JEWISH FOLK AND HOLIDAY SONGS
    SCHAUM PUBLICATIONS, INC.   1.50
SCHAUM, J.--ED.   SCHAUM, J.
  PRELUDES, OFFERTORIES AND POSTLUDES
    BELWIN-MILLS PUBLISHING CORPORATION   1.50

SCHAUM, J.--ED.   SCHAUM, J.   PREP
    SUNDAY SCHOOL HYMNS -- MUSIC FOR CHILDREN
        SCHAUM PUBLICATIONS, INC.   1.25
SCHAUM, J.--ED.   SCHAUM, J.   2
    TWELVE DAYS OF CHRISTMAS
        BELWIN-MILLS PUBLISHING CORPORATION   .50
SCHAUM, J.   SCHAUM, J.   2
    HYMNS OF FAITH
        SCHAUM PUBLICATIONS, INC.   1.50
SCHEIDT *   STEGLICH   2-3
    ALTE DEUTSCH WEIHNACHTMUSIK - 11 CHORALE UND VARIATIONEN
        BARENREITER VERLAG   NMA 95
SCHEIDT   DIETRICH   2-3
    DAS GORLITZER TABULATURBUCH. 100 VIERSTIMMIGE CHORALE
        BARENREITER VERLAG   BA 1565
SCHIBLER--ED   SCHIBLER   E-M
    NOBODY KNOWS, 12 NEGRO SPIRITUALS
        C. F. PETERS CORPORATION   Z247   2.00
SCHIEFELBEIN, F.   2
    SANCTISSIMA
        VOLKWEIN BROS.   .25
SCHROEDER, H.   3
    SUSANI, ALTE WEIHNACHTSLIEDER
        SCHOTT   3882   2.00
SETCHELL
    CHURCH PIANO MUSIC
        CARL FISCHER, INC.   RB 30   3.00
SHANKO, S. W.--ED   SHANKO, S. W.
    HYMN TUNE PRELUDES FOR THE PIANO, NO. 3
        BROADMAN MUSIC   4571-05   2.25
SHELLEY--ED.   SHELLEY
    MELODIES FOR CHURCH AND HOME
        G. SCHIRMER, INC.   1.50
SHINN, D.
    TWENTY LESSON COURSE IN EVANGELISTIC PIANO PLAYING
        SHINN MUSIC AIDS   6.95
SMALL, A.
    ETERNAL HYMNS
        ALFRED MUSIC COMPANY   525   2.95
SMITH, T.--ED   SMITH, T.
    PIANO PORTRAITS - SACRED SOLOS
        BROADMAN MUSIC   4571-09   2.75
SMITH, T.
    CONCERT HYMN TRANSCRIPTIONS
        HOPE PUBLISHING COMPANY   1.50
SMITH, T.
    CRUSADE PIANIST NO. 1
        LILLENAS PUBLISHING COMPANY   MB-030   2.50
SMITH, T.
    CRUSADE PIANIST NO. 2
        LILLENAS PUBLISHING COMPANY   MB-031   2.50
SMITH, T.
    CRUSADE PIANIST NO. 3
        LILLENAS PUBLISHING COMPANY   MB-032   2.50
SMITH, T.
    CRUSADE PIANIST NO. 4
        LILLENAS PUBLISHING COMPANY   MB-235   2.50
SMITH, T.
    FOLK-ROCK IMAGES
        HOPE PUBLISHING COMPANY   2.95
SMITH, T.
    GREAT HYMNS OF THE CHURCH
        HOPE PUBLISHING COMPANY   2.50
SMITH, T.
    SIMPLIFIED PIANO ARRANGEMENTS
        HOPE PUBLISHING COMPANY   2.50
STEINER--ED.   STEINER   1
    BEAUTIFUL ISLE OF SOMEWHERE
        BELWIN-MILLS PUBLISHING CORPORATION   .50
STEINER--ED.   STEINER   PREPARATORY
    BEAUTIFUL SAVIOUR
        BELWIN-MILLS PUBLISHING CORPORATION   .50
STEINER   1, 2
    HYMNS FOR THE YOUNG PIANIST
        BELWIN-MILLS PUBLISHING CORPORATION   1864   1.75
STICKLES--ED   STICKLES
    SCHIRMER'S FAVORITE SACRED SONGS
        G. SCHIRMER, INC.   1.25
STICKLES--ED   STICKLES
    SONGS OF FAITH
        G. SCHIRMER, INC.   1.50
TELEMANN, G.P.   KELLER
    EASY CHORALE PRELUDES
        C. F. PETERS CORPORATION   4239   E-M
THOMAS, A.--ED.   THOMAS, A.   3
    O SANCTISSIMA - SICILIAN MARINERS' HYMN
        THEODORE PRESSER COMPANY   .50
THOMPSON, J.--ED   THOMPSON, J.   2
    FAVORITE CATHOLIC HYMNS
        WILLIS MUSIC COMPANY   1.00
THOMPSON, J.--ED   THOMPSON, J.   2
    GOSPEL HYMNS
        WILLIS MUSIC COMPANY   1.25
THOMPSON, J.--ED   THOMPSON, J.   2
    HYMNS OF FAITH
        WILLIS MUSIC COMPANY   1.00
TOLSON, P.
    REFLECTIONS AT THE PIANO
        LILLENAS PUBLISHING COMPANY   MB-157   1.95
TOLSON, P.
    SPIRITUALS AT THE PIANO
        LILLENAS PUBLISHING COMPANY   MB-202   1.95
WARD--ED   WARD
    HYMNS FOR YOU TO PLAY AND SING
        BOSTON MUSIC COMPANY   1.00
WATSON--ED.   WATSON
    FAVORITE HYMNS, EASY TO READ, PLAY, SING
        CARL FISCHER, INC.   RB 37   1.25
WHITFORD--ED.   WHITFORD   GR. 1 1/2 - 2 1/2
    FAVORITES FOR THE PIANIST, HYMNS NO. 1
        ROBERT WHITFORD PUBLICATIONS   .60
WILLIAMS--ED.   WILLIAMS
    FAVORITE SACRED CLASSICS
        PRO-ART PUBLICATIONS, INC.   314   1.50
WILLIAMS, D. M.
    INSPIRATIONS FROM THE PIANO
        LILLENAS PUBLISHING COMPANY   MB-306   2.50
WILLIAMS, L. R.--ED   WILLIAMS, L. R.
    FAVORITE HYMNS TO PLAY AND SING IN EASY PIANO ARRANGEMENTS
        BROADMAN MUSIC   4571-01   1.50

WILSON, J. F.
    FAMILIAR HYMNS FOR THE PIANO
        HOPE PUBLISHING COMPANY   2.50
WINANS, W. L.
    WORSHIP HYMNS FOR PIANO
        LILLENAS PUBLISHING COMPANY   MB-228   2.50
WOLFRAM   E
    FIFTY MEISTERCHORAELE
        C. F. PETERS CORPORATION   2180   3.00
ZEPP--ED   ZEPP
    EVERLASTING HYMNS
        PRO-ART PUBLICATIONS, INC.   808   1.25
ZEPP--ED   ZEPP
    LET'S PLAY HYMNS
        PRO-ART PUBLICATIONS, INC.   488   1.25
ZEPP--ED   ZEPP
    SACRED SONGS AND HYMNS
        PRO-ART PUBLICATIONS, INC.   1157   1.00

Church Music:
Composer/Editor/Arranger Unlisted—Works Alphabetized by Title

AMAZING GRACE
    MUSIC SALES CORPORATION   060999   .95
CHAPPELL'S SACRED SONG FAVORITES
    CHAPPELL AND COMPANY, INC.   0016501   1.50
                                        M
CHRISTMAS MUSIC
    C. F. PETERS CORPORATION   4610   2.50
CHURCH PIANIST, THE. NOS 1 AND 3
    LORENZ PUBLISHING COMPANY   2.50
CHURCH PIANIST'S HYMNAL, THE
    LORENZ PUBLISHING COMPANY   2.50
CRUSADE, PIANO STYLINGS
    LORENZ PUBLISHING COMPANY   2.50
                                        EASY
EASY PIANO HYMN PIECES
    LORENZ PUBLISHING COMPANY   2.00
                                        EASY
EASY WEDDING MUSIC NO. 1
    LORENZ PUBLISHING COMPANY   2.00
FAVORITE HYMNS MADE EASY --BIG NOTE-- --200--
    CARL FISCHER, INC.   O 4045   1.25
GOSPEL HYMN PIANIST
    LORENZ PUBLISHING COMPANY   2.50
HYMNS WE LOVE
    THE BIG THREE MUSIC CORPORATION   3.95
HYMN TUNES FOR PIANO--110--
    CARL FISCHER, INC.   O 3775   1.50
HYMN VARIATIONS FOR PIANO
    ASHLEY DEALERS SERVICE, INC.   WFS NO. 63 2.95
JESUS SONGS
    MEL BAY PUBLICATIONS, INC.   1.50
MODERN PIANIST SERIES - SONGS OF FAITH
    POINTER PUBLICATIONS   1.95
MUSIC FOR THE WEDDING
    CARL FISCHER, INC.   P 2452   1.25
ONE HUNDRED AND SEVEN EASY-TO-PLAY HYMNS
    CENTURY MUSIC PUBLISHING COMPANY, INC.   MPS VOL. 9   1.95
ONE WAY SONGBOOK
    MEL BAY PUBLICATIONS, INC.   1.50
PIANO HYMN VOLUNTARIES. NOS 1, 2, AND 3
    LORENZ PUBLISHING COMPANY   2.50
POINTER LIBRARY - FAMOUS HYMNS
    POINTER PUBLICATIONS   2.95
POINTER SYSTEM - HYMNS
    POINTER PUBLICATIONS   1.50
                                        EASY
SACRED PIANIST
    MEL BAY PUBLICATIONS, INC.   1.50
                        ROVENGER
SACRED REFLECTIONS FOR PIANO SOLO
    RUBANK, INC.   1.50
SIGNS SHALL FOLLOW SONGBOOK
    MEL BAY PUBLICATIONS, INC.   1.50
SIXTY-ONE EASY TO PLAY HYMNS FOR PIANO
    ASHLEY DEALERS SERVICE, INC.   1.50
SONGS OF HOPE AND INSPIRATION
    THE BIG THREE MUSIC CORPORATION   01.50
SONGS OF THE SPIRIT - EASY HYMN ARRANGEMENTS FOR PIANO
    LORENZ PUBLISHING COMPANY   2.00
SPIRIT FILLED SONGS
    MEL BAY PUBLICATIONS, INC.   1.50
THEMES FOR THE SABBATH DAY--FOR THE PIANO, REED-ORGAN OR HAMMOND
ORGAN
    G. SCHIRMER, INC.   1.25
WEDDING SONGS --225--
    CARL FISCHER, INC.   O 4133   1.00
YOUR FAVORITE NEGRO SPIRITUALS
    SHAWNEE PRESS, INC.   2.00

Christmas Music

ADAM, A. STEINER
 CANTIQUE DE NOEL
  G. SCHIRMER, INC.   .50
ADAM, A.   2
 O HOLY NIGHT
  CENTURY MUSIC PUBLISHING COMPANY, INC. 3785 .40
ADAM, A. PEERY   4
 O HOLY NIGHT
  THEODORE PRESSER COMPANY   .60
ADAM, A. HESS   5
 O HOLY NIGHT
  THEODORE PRESSER COMPANY   .60
ADAMS, R. G. SPENCER, J. 2
 O HOLY NIGHT
  VOLKWEIN BROS.   .30
ADAMS, S.   3
 HOLY CITY, THE
  CENTURY MUSIC PUBLISHING COMPANY, INC. 3576 .40
ADAMS, S. GODFREY
 HOLY CITY
  BOOSEY AND HAWKES, INC.   .75
ADAMS, S. PERRY
 HOLY CITY
  BOOSEY AND HAWKES, INC.   .50
AGAY, D.--ED AGAY, D.
 CHRISTMAS RECITAL
  MUSIC SALES CORPORATION 08006 .85
ANSON, G.--ED ANSON, G. ELEMENTARY
 HAPPY HOLIDAY
  WILLIS MUSIC COMPANY   1.00
ARCHER, I.   1
 ON CHRISTMAS EVE
  CENTURY MUSIC PUBLISHING COMPANY, INC. 4147 .40
AUBERGE, A. D'
 CHRISTMAS CAROL, A
  ALFRED MUSIC COMPANY 657 .85
AUBERGE, A. D'
 IT'S CHRISTMAS TIME
  ALFRED MUSIC COMPANY 659 .85
AULD, W. J.
 CHRISTMAS TRANSCRIPTIONS FOR PIANO
  LILLENAS PUBLISHING COMPANY MC-203 1.95
BARTOS, J.   2
 WEIHNACHTEN — 6 LEICHTE KLAVIERSTUCKE, OP. 20
  BARENREITER VERLAG AP 513
BASTIEN--ED. BASTIEN
 MERRY CHRISTMAS, BK.1
  NEIL A. KJOS MUSIC COMPANY 8 .95
BASTIEN--ED. BASTIEN
 MERRY CHRISTMAS, BK.2
  NEIL A. KJOS MUSIC COMPANY 17 1.00
BASTIEN--ED. BASTIEN
 MERRY CHRISTMAS, BK.3
  NEIL A. KJOS MUSIC COMPANY 41 1.25
BAUM--ED. BAUM
 ALTE WEIHNACHTSMUSIK
  BARENREITER VERLAG BA 826 2.75
BAUM--ED. BAUM
 NEW CHRISTMAS MUSIC
  BARENREITER VERLAG BA 1371 2.75
BENTLEY   4
 CHRISTMAS CAROL
  THEODORE PRESSER COMPANY .60
BERLIN, B.
 WORLD FAMOUS CHRISTMAS CAROLS
  FREDERICK HARRIS MUSIC COMPANY .90
BERMONT, H.--ED BERMONT, H.
 LETS PLAY CAROLS
  MUSICORD PUBLICATIONS, INC. 1.00
BERMONT, H.
 JOY TO THE WORLD
  ALFRED MUSIC COMPANY 643 1.25
BESTHOFF, M.
 MERRY CHRISTMAS CAROLS TO SING AND PLAY
  BELWIN-MILLS PUBLISHING CORPORATION 1.00
BOHME--ED BOHME 2-3
 WEIHNACHTSMUSIK FUR KLAVIER
  SCHOTT 5450 2.25
BOHM * BAUM 2-3
 ALTE WEIHNACHTSMUSIK — 13 WEIHNACHTSCHORALE UND
 CHORALVARIATIONEN
  BARENREITER VERLAG BA 826
BORNEFELD * BAUM 2-3
 NEUE WEIHNACHTSMUSIK. 18 WEIHNACHTSLIEDER IN 24 SATZEN
  BARENREITER VERLAG BA 908
BRADLEY, R.--ARR. BRADLEY, R. EASY
 BRADLEY'S BEST OF THE BEST - CHRISTMAS CAROLS
  SCREEN GEMS - COLUMBIA PUBLICATIONS F0211P2 1.75
BRADLEY, R.--ARR. BRADLEY, R. EASY
 BRADLEY'S CHRISTMAS JOY - ISSUE NO. 1
  SCREEN GEMS - COLUMBIA PUBLICATIONS F0213P2 1.75
BRADLEY, R.--ARR. BRADLEY, R. EASY
 HOLLY JOLLY CHRISTMAS, A
  SCREEN GEMS - COLUMBIA PUBLICATIONS 4714HP2 .85
BRADLEY, R.--ARR. BRADLEY, R. BIG NOTE EASY
 JOY TO THE WORLD
  SCREEN GEMS - COLUMBIA PUBLICATIONS 4703JP3 .85
BRADLEY, R.--ARR. BRADLEY, R. EASY
 ROCKIN' AROUND THE CHRISTMAS TREE
  SCREEN GEMS - COLUMBIA PUBLICATIONS 4711RP2 .85
BRADLEY, R.--ARR. BRADLEY, R. BIG NOTE EASY
 RUDOLPH THE RED-NOSED REINDEER
  SCREEN GEMS - COLUMBIA PUBLICATIONS 6706RP3 .85
BRADLEY, R.--ARR. BRADLEY, R. BIG NOTE EASY
 SILENT NIGHT
  SCREEN GEMS - COLUMBIA PUBLICATIONS 2706SP3 .85
BRADLEY, R.--ARR. BRADLEY, R. BIG NOTE EASY
 SIMPLY BRADLEY - CHRISTMAS CAROLS
  SCREEN GEMS - COLUMBIA PUBLICATIONS F0105P3 1.50
BRADLEY, R.--ARR. BRADLEY, R. BIG NOTE EASY
 SIMPLY BRADLEY - RUDOLPH THE RED-NOSED REINDEER AND OTHER
 CHRISTMAS FAVORITES
  SCREEN GEMS - COLUMBIA PUBLICATIONS F0111P3 1.50
BRADLEY, R.--ARR. BRADLEY, R. EASY
 SNOOPY'S CHRISTMAS
  SCREEN GEMS - COLUMBIA PUBLICATIONS 4405SP2 .85
BRADLEY, R.--ARR. BRADLEY, R. BIG NOTE EASY
 WINTER WONDERLAND
  SCREEN GEMS - COLUMBIA PUBLICATIONS 2722WP3 .85
BRADY--ED BRADY
 CAROLS FOR CHRISTMAS
  BOSTON MUSIC COMPANY 1.50

BRAGDON WILLIAMS, J.
 PICKING HOLLY
  BOSTON MUSIC COMPANY .50
BRIMHALL, J.--ED. BRIMHALL, J.
 CAROL OF THE BELLS
  CHARLES HANSEN .85
BRIMHALL, J.--ED. BRIMHALL, J.
 CHRISTMAS SONG, THE
  CHARLES HANSEN .85
BRIMHALL, J.--ED. BRIMHALL, J.
 GREENSLEEVES
  CHARLES HANSEN 35856 .85
BRIMHALL, J.--ED. BRIMHALL, J.
 I'LL BE HOME FOR CHRISTMAS
  CHARLES HANSEN .85
BRIMHALL, J.--ED. BRIMHALL, J.
 LET IT SNOW, LET IT SNOW
  CHARLES HANSEN .85
BRIMHALL, J.--ED. BRIMHALL, J.
 MERRY CHRISTMAS FROM JOHN BRIMHALL
  CHARLES HANSEN .85
BRIMHALL, J.--ED. BRIMHALL, J.
 O HOLY NIGHT
  CHARLES HANSEN .85
BRIMHALL, J.--ED. BRIMHALL, J.
 SILENT NIGHT
  CHARLES HANSEN .85
BRIMHALL, J.--ED. BRIMHALL, J.
 SILVER BELLS
  CHARLES HANSEN F30070 .85
BRIMHALL, J.--ED. BRIMHALL, J.
 TWELVE DAYS OF CHRISTMAS
  CHARLES HANSEN .85
BRIMHALL, J.--ED. BRIMHALL, J.
 WE NEED A LITTLE CHRISTMAS
  CHARLES HANSEN .85
BRIMHALL, J.--ED. BRIMHALL, J.
 WINTER WONDERLAND
  CHARLES HANSEN T31021 .85
BURKHARD, W.   1
 WAS DIE HIRTEN ALLES ERLEBTEN -- WEIHNACHTSMUSIK FUR URSULA --
  BARENREITER VERLAG BA 1875
BURKHARD, W.
 WAS DIE HIRTEN ALLES ERLEBTEN
  BARENREITER VERLAG BA 1875 1.75
BURKHARD, W.   2
 WEIHNACHTSSONATINE, OP. 71 NO. 1
  BARENREITER VERLAG BA 2074
BURKHARD, W.
 WEIHNACHTSSONATINE, OP. 71
  BARENREITER VERLAG BA 2074 2.25
BURNAM ADAM
 CANTIQUE DE NOEL -- O HOLY NIGHT
  WILLIS MUSIC COMPANY .35
CAROL--ED. CAROL EASY
 TWO AMERICAN CHRISTMAS CAROLS
  DELRIEU ET CIE. .85
COBB
 TWO AND TWENTY CHRISTMAS CAROLS
  BELWIN-MILLS PUBLISHING CORPORATION 11520 1.25
CRERIE, E. *   4
 SILENT NIGHT -- VARIATIONS
  VOLKWEIN BROS. .40
CRERIE, E. SCHIEFELBEIN, F. 4
 SILENT NIGHT VARIATIONS
  VOLKWEIN BROS. 00.50
CURCIO--ED CURCIO
 CHRISTMAS CAROLS FOR LITTLE PIANISTS
  BOSTON MUSIC COMPANY 1.25
CURCIO
 CATHOLIC CHRISTMAS SONGS FOR THE YOUNG PIANIST
  BELWIN-MILLS PUBLISHING CORPORATION 10004 1.50
DALLIN--ED. DALLIN
 CHRISTMAS CAROLER
  PRO-ART PUBLICATIONS, INC. 1038 1.50
DARDENELLE, L.
 CHRISTMAS CHIMES
  WILLIS MUSIC COMPANY .50
DASHER, J.
 CHRISTMAS ECHOES
  WILLIS MUSIC COMPANY .50
DASHER, J.
 CHRISTMAS LULLABY
  WILLIS MUSIC COMPANY .50
DASHER, J.
 CHRISTMAS MEDLEY
  WILLIS MUSIC COMPANY .50
DASHER, J.
 YULETIDE MEDLEY
  WILLIS MUSIC COMPANY .50
DAVIES--ED. DAVIES
 CAROLS FOR CHRISTMAS
  SHAWNEE PRESS, INC. 1.00
DEE, M.
 CHRISTMAS CAROLS
  VOLKWEIN BROS. 00.75
DEGEN   2-3
 WEIHNACHTSBUCH. MUSIK AUS 36 ALTEN WEIHNACHTSLIEDERN FUR
 KLAVIER, BK. 1 - 7 ALTE WEIHNACHTSLIEDER UND 6 KRIPPENLIEDER
  BARENREITER VERLAG SM 2101
DEGEN   2-3
 WEIHNACHTSBUCH. MUSIK AUS 36 ALTEN WEIHNACHTSLIEDERN FUR
 KLAVIER, BK. 2 - 6 WIEGENLIEDER, 8 HIRTENLIEDER
  BARENREITER VERLAG
DEGEN   2-3
 WEIHNACHTSBUCH. MUSIK AUS 36 ALTEN WEIHNACHTSLIEDERN FUR
 KLAVIER, BK. 3 - 2 DREI KONIGE-LIEDER UND 7 WEIHNACHTS-CHORALE
  BARENREITER VERLAG SM 2103
DE VITO, A.--ED. DE VITO, A.
 CHRISTMAS SONGS
  KENYON PUBLICATIONS 1.00
DIEHL--ED DIEHL
 CHRISTMAS ALBUM -- 14 CHRISTMAS SONGS WITH GERMAN TEXT
  ASSOCIATED MUSIC PUBLISHERS, INC. BOT .50
DILLER, A. *   GRADE 2
 DILLER-PAGE CAROL BOOK, THE
  G. SCHIRMER, INC. 1.00
DILLER, A. *   GRADE 2
 DILLER-PAGE CAROL BOOK= 38E
  G. SCHIRMER, INC. 1.00
DRATHS--ED DRATHS 1
 MORGEN KOMMT DER WEIHNACHTSMANN
  SCHOTT 5325 2.25
DRATHS--ED DRATHS 2
 O WUNDER, WAS WILL DAS BEDEUTEN
  SCHOTT 5700 2.25

DRISCHNER   E-M
   PARTITAS ON TWO CHRISTMAS SONGS
      C. F. PETERS CORPORATION   VP149   2.00
DUMM
   CAROLING KEYS
      BOSTON MUSIC COMPANY   1.25
ENGELMANN, H. U.
   NIGHT BEFORE CHRISTMAS, THE
      BOSTON MUSIC COMPANY   .50
FORLIVESI
   FIVE CHRISTMAS SONGS
      FRANCO COLOMBO PUBLICATIONS   FOR.12160   1.00
FREDERICKS   1
   ADESTE FIDELIS
      VOLKWEIN BROS.   .25
FREDERICKS   1
   SILENT NIGHT, HOLY NIGHT
      VOLKWEIN BROS.   .25
FREDRICH, F.--ED.
   CAROLS FOR CHRISTMAS
      PRO-ART PUBLICATIONS, INC.   125   1.25
FREDRICH, F.--ED   FREDRICH, F.
   FIRST BOOK OF HYMNS AND CAROLS, A
      WILLIS MUSIC COMPANY   1.00
FREEMAN--ED.   FREEMAN   4
   ADESTE FIDELIS, A FLAT MAJOR
      CENTURY MUSIC PUBLISHING COMPANY, INC.   615   .40
FROST
   CHRISTMAS CAROLS
      BELWIN-MILLS PUBLISHING CORPORATION   1.00
GILLOCK   3
   CHRISTMAS AT THE PIANO
      WILLIS MUSIC COMPANY   1.50
GILLOCK   2
   YOUNG PIANIST'S FIRST CHRISTMAS
      WILLIS MUSIC COMPANY   1.50
GILLOCK
   YOUNG PIANIST'S FIRST CHRISTMAS
      WILLIS MUSIC COMPANY   1.50
GLOVER, D. *   PRIM.
   CHRISTMAS MUSIC
      BELWIN-MILLS PUBLISHING CORPORATION   EL 2218   1.75
GLOVER, D. *   1
   CHRISTMAS MUSIC
      BELWIN-MILLS PUBLISHING CORPORATION   EL 2219   1.75
GOERDELER, R.   4
   CHRISTMAS CHIMES
      THEODORE PRESSER COMPANY   .50
GOERDELER, R.
   YULETIDE BELLS
      BOSTON MUSIC COMPANY   .50
GREENWALD, M.
   CHAPEL CHIMES
      THE BIG THREE MUSIC CORPORATION   00.95
GROFE, F.
   CHRISTMAS EVE
      THE BIG THREE MUSIC CORPORATION   00.95
GRUBER, F.   HENLEIN
   HOLY NIGHT
      WILLIS MUSIC COMPANY   .30
GRUBER, F.   2
   SILENT NIGHT, HOLY NIGHT
      CENTURY MUSIC PUBLISHING COMPANY, INC.   2159   .40
GRUBER, F.   ADLER, M.   1 1/2
   SILENT NIGHT, HOLY NIGHT
      THEODORE PRESSER COMPANY   .50
GRUBER, F.   WEBER, H.
   SILENT NIGHT, HOLY NIGHT
      WILLIS MUSIC COMPANY   .35
GRUBER, F.   HARVEY   2
   SILENT NIGHT -- CHRISTMAS MEDLEY
      VOLKWEIN BROS.   .25
GRUBER, F.   KOHLMANN, C.   5
   SILENT NIGHT
      THEODORE PRESSER COMPANY   .60
GRUBER, F.   SPENCER, J.   2
   SILENT NIGHT
      VOLKWEIN BROS.   .35
GRUBER, F.   RICHTER   FIRST YEAR
   SILENT NIGHT
      WARNER BROTHERS PUBLISHERS   .75
GRUBER, F.   WOODE
   SILENT NIGHT
      WILLIS MUSIC COMPANY   .30
GUARALDI
   PEANUTS KEYBOARD FUN SERIES - A CHARLIE BROWN CHRISTMAS
      POINTER PUBLICATIONS   2.95
HALLSTROM *
   TINIEST ANGEL, THE
      WILLIS MUSIC COMPANY   .40
HANSON, H.--ED   HANSON, H.
   NEW SCRIBNER MUSIC LIBRARY, VOL. 09 'HOME FAVORITES'
      CHARLES SCRIBNER'S SONS
HARDING, R.--ED   HARDING, R.
   CHRISTMAS CAROLS FOR EVERYONE
      WILLIS MUSIC COMPANY   .50
HARDING, R.
   HARK THE HERALD ANGELS SING
      WILLIS MUSIC COMPANY   .30
HARDING, R.
   I SAW THREE SHIPS
      WILLIS MUSIC COMPANY   .25
HARDING, R.
   O LITTLE TOWN OF BETHLEHEM
      WILLIS MUSIC COMPANY   .35
HARVEY   3
   JINGLE BELLS MARCH
      VOLKWEIN BROS.   .25
HARVEY   2
   JINGLE BELLS MARCH
      VOLKWEIN BROS.   00.25
HEINS, C.   4
   CHRISTMAS EVE
      THEODORE PRESSER COMPANY   .60
HELTMAN   2
   MERRY CHRISTMAS MARCH
      VOLKWEIN BROS.   00.25
HILL
   CHRISTMAS BELLS WALTZ
      VOLKWEIN BROS.   .35
HINKLE, N.--ED   HINKLE, N.
   FORTY CHRISTMAS CAROLS FOR VOICE AND PIANO
      THEODORE PRESSER COMPANY   1.50
HOLLANDER
   MY FAVORITE CHRISTMAS CAROLS
      EDWARD B. MARKS MUSIC CORPORATION   01.25

HOLLANDER
   YOU CAN PLAY PIANO SERIES, LEVEL 2 -- YOU CAN PLAY CHRISTMAS
   CAROLS
      BOOSEY AND HAWKES, INC.   1.00
HUNEKE--ED   HUNEKE
   BIG NOTE CHRISTMAS CAROLS
      BOSTON MUSIC COMPANY   1.00
HUNTLEY, C.--ED   HUNTLEY, C.
   CHRISTMAS CAROLS FOR CHILDREN
      WILLIS MUSIC COMPANY   1.00
JENSVOLD, J.--ED   JENSVOLD, J.
   I LOVE CHRISTMAS MUSIC
      WILLIS MUSIC COMPANY   1.00
JONES *
   CHRISTMAS CAROLS ROCK
      ALFRED MUSIC COMPANY   644   1.50
JOYNER, B.--ED   JOYNER, B.
   CHILD'S CHRISTMAS, A
      WILLIS MUSIC COMPANY   1.25
JOYNER, B.
   DEAR SANTA
      WILLIS MUSIC COMPANY   .35
KAHL--ED   KAHL
   CHRISTMAS CAROLS - BOOK 1
      BOSTON MUSIC COMPANY   1.50
KAHL--ED   KAHL
   CHRISTMAS CAROLS - BOOK 2
      BOSTON MUSIC COMPANY   1.50
KAHL--ED   KAHL
   CHRISTMAS CAROLS - BOOK 3
      BOSTON MUSIC COMPANY   1.50
KAHL
   CHRISTMAS CHIMES
      BOSTON MUSIC COMPANY   1.25
KENNEDY, A.
   STAR OF THE SEA
      THE BIG THREE MUSIC CORPORATION   00.50
KETELBEY, A.
   DREAM OF CHRISTMAS, A
      BELWIN-MILLS PUBLISHING CORPORATION   .75
KING
   KEYBOARD BELL
      BOSTON MUSIC COMPANY   1.00
KIRBY, W.
   MERRY CHRISTMAS--13 CHRISTMAS CAROLS IN VERY EASY ARRANGEMENTS
      G. SCHIRMER, INC.   .75
KIRBY, W.
   NOEL-NOEL--18 CHRISTMAS CAROLS, ARRANGED FOR PIANO AND VOICE
      G. SCHIRMER, INC.   .75
KOCH, F.
   CAROLS FROM MANY NATIONS
      GENERAL MUSIC PUBLISHING COMPANY, INC.   511   2.00
KOCH, F.
   CAROLS FROM MANY NATIONS
      GENERAL MUSIC PUBLISHING COMPANY, INC.   2.00
KOSCHINSKY   E
   ADVENT. SEVENTEEN ADVENT SONGS WITH GERMAN TEXT
      C. F. PETERS CORPORATION   N1252   1.25
KOSCHINSKY   E
   CHRISTMAS NIGHTINGALE
      C. F. PETERS CORPORATION   N3194   1.75
KROGMANN, C. W.
   CHRISTMAS SONG
      WILLIS MUSIC COMPANY   .40
LAMONT   4
   CHRISTMAS TREE FAIRY
      THEODORE PRESSER COMPANY   .50
LANE, J.--ED.   LANE, J.
   FROSTY THE SNOWMAN
      THE BIG THREE MUSIC CORPORATION   00.70
LANE, J.--ED.   LANE, J.
   HAVE YOURSELF A MERRY LITTLE CHRISTMAS
      THE BIG THREE MUSIC CORPORATION   .70
LANE, J.--ED.   LANE, J.
   HERE COMES SANTA CLAUS
      THE BIG THREE MUSIC CORPORATION   00.70
LANE, J.--ED.   LANE, J.
   SANTA CLAUS IS COMING TO TOWN
      THE BIG THREE MUSIC CORPORATION   .70
LANE, J.--ED.   LANE, J.
   THIRTY-TWO FEET AND EIGHT LITTLE TAILS
      THE BIG THREE MUSIC CORPORATION   .70
LEBEGUE   2
   NOELS VARIES -- VARIATIONEN UBER WEIHNACHTSSTUCKE --
      BARENREITER VERLAG
LECHNER--ED   LECHNER   3
   HAUSMUSIK FUR WEIHNACHTEN -- ALTE UND NEUE WEIHNACHTMUSIK
      SCHOTT   4220   2.50
LECHNER--ED   LECHNER   1-2
   MEIN WEIHNACHTSBUCH -- 33 DER SCHONSTEN WEIHNACHTSLIEDER FUR DEN
   ANFANGER FUR KLAVIER ZU 2 UND 4 HANDEN
      SCHOTT   4220   2.25
LISZT   M-D
   CHRISTMAS TREE, VOL. 1
      C. F. PETERS CORPORATION   H88A   2.00
LISZT   D
   CHRISTMAS TREE, VOL. 2
      C. F. PETERS CORPORATION   H88B   2.00
LISZT   M
   CHRISTMAS TREE
      THEODORE PRESSER COMPANY   1.25
LUTZ--ED   LUTZ   2-3
   FROHE WEIHNACHT
      SCHOTT   4006   2.25
MARLOWE
   HAPPY CHRISTMAS
      BOSTON MUSIC COMPANY   1.25
MASON, M. B.
   CHRISTMAS CAROLS MADE EASY TO PLAY AND SING
      THEODORE PRESSER COMPANY   1.00
MCGINLEY
   PIANO SESSIONS - KINDERGARTEN SERIES‡ SONGS FOR CHRISTMAS
   --SUPP. MUSIC FOR TRUDY TREBLE AND TOM--
      SHAWNEE PRESS, INC.   .60
MCKUEN   ROGERS, M.
   NEW CAROLS FOR CHRISTMAS
      POINTER PUBLICATIONS   3.95
MEAD
   IMPROVISATION ON CHRISTMAS TUNES - SERIES 1
      BOSTON MUSIC COMPANY   .50
MEAD
   IMPROVISATION ON CHRISTMAS TUNES - SERIES 2
      BOSTON MUSIC COMPANY   .50
MENDELSSOHN   GOERDELER   4
   HARK THE HERALD ANGELS SING
      THEODORE PRESSER COMPANY   .50

MONTANI
  NINE CHRISTMAS SONGS
    FRANCO COLOMBO PUBLICATIONS   130078   1.25
MOORE--ED   MOORE
  BIG NOTE CHRISTMAS FAVORITES
    BOSTON MUSIC COMPANY   1.00
MOORE--ED   MOORE
  CHRISTMAS FAVORITES
    BOSTON MUSIC COMPANY   1.00
MUELLER, C.   STEINER   PREPARATORY
  AWAY IN A MANGER
    BELWIN-MILLS PUBLISHING CORPORATION   .50
MUELLER, C.   4
  CHRISTMAS FASTASIA
    THEODORE PRESSER COMPANY   .60
NEIDLINGER, W. H.   STEINER
  BIRTHDAY OF A KING, THE
    G. SCHIRMER, INC.   .35
NEVIN
  WONDERFUL MUSIC OF CHRISTMAS
    BELWIN-MILLS PUBLISHING CORPORATION   10075   1.50
NIEMANN   E-M
  CHRISTMAS BELLS, OP. 129
    C. F. PETERS CORPORATION   4272A   1.50
NIEMANN   E-M
  YULE SLUMBER LILT, OP. 143. SIX EASY CHRISTMAS PIECES
    C. F. PETERS CORPORATION   4279   1.25
NILES, J.
  I WONDER AS I WANDER--APPALACHIAN FOLK CAROL
    G. SCHIRMER, INC.   .35
NORMAN
  CHILDREN'S CHRISTMAS
    BOSTON MUSIC COMPANY   1.00
OSCHEIT, M.
  FRIEDE AUF ERDEN, OP. 174--A CHRISTMAS POTPOURRI
    ASSOCIATED MUSIC PUBLISHERS, INC.   BOT   .90
PACE, H.
  CHRISTMAS MUSIC, SECOND COLLECTION
    LEE ROBERTS MUSIC PUBLICATIONS, INC.   1.50
PACE, R.
  CHRISTMAS MUSIC, BK. 1
    LEE ROBERTS MUSIC PUBLICATIONS, INC.   1.50
PALMER, W. A.
  CHRISTMAS HOLIDAY
    ALFRED MUSIC COMPANY   658   1.25
PARSONS
  PIANO TRANSCRIPTIONS OF YOUR FAVORITE CHRISTMAS CAROLS
    THEODORE PRESSER COMPANY   1.50
PEERY, R. R.--ED   PEERY, R. R.
  CAROLS OF MANY LANDS
    BOSTON MUSIC COMPANY   1.25
PEERY, R. R.--ED   PEERY, R. R.
  CHRISTMAS CAROL BOOK
    BOSTON MUSIC COMPANY   1.25
PIAZZA, M.--ED   PIAZZA, M.
  MARGUERITE PIAZZA'S CHRISTMAS CAROL SING ALONG PARTY
    WILLIS MUSIC COMPANY   3.95
PITCHER, G.--ED   PITCHER, G.
  SING TOGETHER AT CHRISTMAS
    WILLIS MUSIC COMPANY   1.25
POHL, V.--ED *   POHL, V. *   1-2
  KINDER SPIELEN ZUR WEIHNACHT. 19 WEIHNACHTSLIEDER FUR KLAVIER
    BARENREITER VERLAG   EN 803
PRIGGE, O.--ED   PRIGGE, O.
  I PLAY CAROLS AT CHRISTMAS TIME
    WILLIS MUSIC COMPANY   1.00
RAPHAEL, G.   1-2
  ADVENT- UND WEIHNACHTSLIEDER IN 25 LEICHTEN SATZEN
    BARENREITER VERLAG   SM 2325
READING, H.--ED   READING, H.
  ADESTE FIDELIS
    WILLIS MUSIC COMPANY   .30
REBE--ED.   REBE
  SIX POLISH CHRISTMAS CAROLS
    G. SCHIRMER, INC.   .60
REDA
  ZEHN WEIHNACHTSLIEDER, AM KLAVIER ZU SINGEN UND ZU SPIELEN
    BARENREITER VERLAG   BA 2082   1.25
REDA   2
  ZEHN WEIHNACHTSLIEDER
    BARENREITER VERLAG   BA 2082
RICHARDS, B.   2
  O COME ALL FAITHFUL -- SANTA CLAUS
    VOLKWEIN BROS.   .30
RICHARDS, B.   2
  SANTA CLAUS MARCH AND O COME ALL
    VOLKWEIN BROS.   .25
RICHARDSON, A.
  KIDDY CAROL BOOK
    WILLIS MUSIC COMPANY   .75
RICHARDSON, A.
  SING WE NOW OF CHRISTMAS
    WILLIS MUSIC COMPANY   .50
RICHTER, A.--ED.   RICHTER, A.
  CHRISTMAS MELODIES IN EASY ARRANGEMENTS
    THEODORE PRESSER COMPANY   1.00
RICHTER, A.
  CHRISTMAS TREE
    THEODORE PRESSER COMPANY   .50
RICHTER, A.
  FIRST CHRISTMAS - A STORY WITH MUSIC
    THEODORE PRESSER COMPANY   1.25
RICHTER, A.   1 1/2
  JINGLE BELLS FROM THE THREE CHRISTMAS SONGS
    THEODORE PRESSER COMPANY   .50
RICHTER, A.   1 1/2
  JOLLY OLD SAINT NICHOLAS FROM THE THREE CHRISTMAS SONGS
    THEODORE PRESSER COMPANY   .50
RICHTER, A.   1 1/2
  JOY TO THE WORLD FROM THE THREE YULETIDE MELODIES
    THEODORE PRESSER COMPANY   .50
RICHTER, A.   1 1/2
  OLD CHRISTMAS TREE
    THEODORE PRESSER COMPANY   .50
RICHTER, A.   2 1/2
  SILENT NIGHT
    THEODORE PRESSER COMPANY   .50
RICHTER, A.   1 1/2
  THREE CHRISTMAS SONGS -- JINGLE BELLS, JOLLY OLD SAINT NICHOLAS, SILENT NIGHT
    THEODORE PRESSER COMPANY   .50
RICHTER, A.   1 1/2
  THREE YULETIDE MELODIES -- JOY TO THE WORLD, AWAY IN A MANGER AND CHRISTMAS
    THEODORE PRESSER COMPANY   .50
RICHTER
  ADA RICHTER CHRISTMAS CAROL BOOK, THE
    WARNER BROTHERS PUBLISHERS   AR 20   1.25

RICHTER
  TWO CHRISTMAS SONGS -- JINGLE BELLS, JOLLY OLD ST. NICHOLAS, WITH WORDS
    WARNER BROTHERS PUBLISHERS   .60
RODGERS, I.--ED   RODGERS, I.
  AT CHRISTMAS TIDE
    WILLIS MUSIC COMPANY   .75
RODGERS, I.--ED   RODGERS, I.
  CHRISTMAS CAROLS FOR LITTLE BOYS AND GIRLS
    WILLIS MUSIC COMPANY   1.00
RODGERS, I.--ED   RODGERS, I.
  JOLLY CHRISTMAS MELODIES
    WILLIS MUSIC COMPANY   1.00
ROGERS--ED.   ROGERS
  CHRISTMAS AT THE PIANO
    PRO-ART PUBLICATIONS, INC.   526   1.00
SCHAUM, J.--ED   SCHAUM, J.   1
  CHRISTMAS ALBUM
    BELWIN-MILLS PUBLISHING CORPORATION   1.25
SCHAUM, J.--ED   SCHAUM, J.   1
  CHRISTMAS ALBUM
    BELWIN-MILLS PUBLISHING CORPORATION   1.50
SCHAUM, J.--ED   SCHAUM, J.   5
  CHRISTMAS RHAPSODY
    BELWIN-MILLS PUBLISHING CORPORATION   .50
SCHAUM, J.--ED   SCHAUM, J.
  FATHER CHRISTMAS
    BELWIN-MILLS PUBLISHING CORPORATION   .50
SCHEIDT *   STEGLICH   2-3
  ALTE DEUTSCH WEIHNACHTMUSIK - 11 CHORALE UND VARIATIONEN
    BARENREITER VERLAG   NMA 95
SCHIEFELBEIN, F.   2
  JINGLE BELLS
    VOLKWEIN BROS.   .35
SCHIEFELBEIN, F.   2
  JINGLE BELLS
    VOLKWEIN BROS.   00.40
SCHIEFELBEIN, F.   2
  SILENT NIGHT, HOLY NIGHT
    VOLKWEIN BROS.   00.40
SCHIEFELBEIN, F.   2
  SILENT NIGHT, HOLY NIGHT
    VOLKWEIN BROS.   .25
SHACKLEY--ED.   SHACKLEY
  CHRISTMAS TIDE
    SHAWNEE PRESS, INC.   1.25
SMALL, A.
  CHRISTMAS CAROL SONGBOOK, THE
    ALFRED MUSIC COMPANY   662   1.50
SMALL, A.
  EASIEST CHRISTMAS CAROLS
    ALFRED MUSIC COMPANY   660   1.25
SMALL, A.
  EASY PIANO CHRISTMAS CAROLS
    ALFRED MUSIC COMPANY   661   1.00
SPENCER, J.   2
  ADESTE FIDELIS AND FIRST NOEL
    VOLKWEIN BROS.   .30
SPENCER, J.   2
  ADESTE FIDELIS AND SANTA CLAUS MARCH
    VOLKWEIN BROS.   .35
SPENCER, J.   2
  COME ALL YE FAITHFUL AND FIRST NOEL
    VOLKWEIN BROS.   .30
SPENCER, J.   2
  COME ALL YE FAITHFUL AND SANTA CLAUS
    VOLKWEIN BROS.   .35
SPENCER, J.   2
  FAVORITE CHRISTMAS MELODIES
    VOLKWEIN BROS.   01.00
SPENCER, J.   2
  FIRST NOEL AND COME ALL YE FAITHFUL
    VOLKWEIN BROS.   .30
SPENCER, J.   2
  O COME ALL FAITHFUL -- FIRST NOEL
    VOLKWEIN BROS.   .30
STECHER *
  WE WISH YOU A MERRY CHRISTMAS, BK. 1
    SCHMITT, HALL AND MCCREARY COMPANY   9967   1.00
STECHER *
  WE WISH YOU A MERRY CHRISTMAS, BK. 2
    SCHMITT, HALL AND MCCREARY COMPANY   9978   1.25
STEGLICH--ED   STEGLICH
  ALTE DEUTSCHE WEIHNACHTSMUSIK
    BARENREITER VERLAG   NMA 95   2.75
STEGLICH--ED   STEGLICH
  OLD GERMAN CHRISTMAS MUSIC -- CHRISTMAS PIECES BY SCHEIDT, PACHELBEL, MUFFAT AND OTHERS
    ASSOCIATED MUSIC PUBLISHERS, INC.   NAG   3.75
STEINER
  CHRISTMAS AT THE PIANO
    BELWIN-MILLS PUBLISHING CORPORATION   1527   1.75
STEINER
  CHRISTMAS CAROLS -- FOR THE VERY YOUNG
    BELWIN-MILLS PUBLISHING CORPORATION   2210   1.75
STEINER   1 1/2
  CHRISTMAS MEDLEY -- 1. HARK, THE HERALD ANGELS SING, 2. SILENT NIGHT, 3. O COME ALL YE FAITHFUL
    BELWIN-MILLS PUBLISHING CORPORATION   .60
STROHBACH, S.--ED   STROHBACH
  WEIHNACHTS LIEDERBUCH, DAS -- 40 CHRISTMAS SONGS WITH GERMAN SUPERLINEAR TEXT
    ASSOCIATED MUSIC PUBLISHERS, INC.   BRH   2.00
SUDDARDS
  TWENTY-FOUR FAVORITE CAROLS, MADE EASY TO PLAY AND SING
    ELKAN-VOGEL, INC.   1.10
THOMPSON, J.--ED   THOMPSON, J.   1
  JOHN THOMPSON'S CHRISTMAS CAROLS
    WILLIS MUSIC COMPANY   1.00
THOMPSON, J.--ED   THOMPSON, J.   PREPARATORY
  JOHN THOMPSON'S CHRISTMAS CAROL BOOK
    WILLIS MUSIC COMPANY   1.00
THOMPSON, J.
  CHRISTMAS BOOK
    WILLIS MUSIC COMPANY   1.00
THOMPSON, J.
  JOHN THOMPSON'S DELUXE BOOK OF CHRISTMAS CAROLS
    WILLIS MUSIC COMPANY   2.00
TOLSON, P.
  CHRISTMAS AT THE PIANO
    LILLENAS PUBLISHING COMPANY   MC-242   1.95
TRAVAGLIA
  CHRISTMAS ALBUM
    FRANCO COLOMBO PUBLICATIONS   Z1760   1.50
WAGNESS--ED.   WAGNESS
  CHRISTMAS CAROLS TO PLAY AND SING
    SHAWNEE PRESS, INC.   1.00

WALLIS--ED	WALLIS		
ADESTE FIDELES			
BOSTON MUSIC COMPANY			.50
WALLIS--ED	WALLIS		
BOSTON MUSIC CO.'S CHRISTMAS CAROL BOOK			
BOSTON MUSIC COMPANY			1.25
WALLIS--ED	WALLIS		
FIRST NOEL, THE			
BOSTON MUSIC COMPANY			.50
WALLIS--ED	WALLIS		
SIX CHRISTMAS CAROLS			
BOSTON MUSIC COMPANY			.50
WALLIS			
GOOD KING WENCESLAS			
WILLIS MUSIC COMPANY			.25
WALLIS			
JOY TO THE WORLD			
WILLIS MUSIC COMPANY			.30
WATSON--ED.	WATSON		
CHRISTMAS CAROLS --WITH WORDS--			
CARL FISCHER, INC.		RB 33	1.25
WEBER, H.			
ADESTE FIDELIS			
WILLIS MUSIC COMPANY			.30
WERNER, F.--ED.	WERNER, F.	E	
WIR SPIELEN ZUR WEIHNACHT, OP. 43. 26 OLD CHRISTMAS SONGS			
C. F. PETERS CORPORATION		V138	2.00
WESTERVELT, M.--ED	WESTERVELT, M.		
CHRISTMAS IN MEXICO -- WITH WORDS			
THEODORE PRESSER COMPANY			1.00
WESTERVELT, M.--ED	WESTERVELT, M.		
CHRISTMAS IN THE SOUTH -- WITH WORDS			
THEODORE PRESSER COMPANY			1.00
WEYBRIGHT--ED.	WEYBRIGHT	2 1/2 - 3	
CHRISTMAS MUSIC, BK. 1 --SECULAR--			
BELWIN-MILLS PUBLISHING CORPORATION			1.25
WEYBRIGHT--ED.	WEYBRIGHT	2 1/2 - 3	
CHRISTMAS MUSIC, BK. 2 --SACRED--			
BELWIN-MILLS PUBLISHING CORPORATION			1.25
WEYBRIGHT--ED.	WEYBRIGHT	1	
MY FIRST CHRISTMAS BOOK			
BELWIN-MILLS PUBLISHING CORPORATION			1.25
WEYBRIGHT--ED.	WEYBRIGHT	3	
RUDOLPH'S CHRISTMAS ALBUM			
BELWIN-MILLS PUBLISHING CORPORATION			1.25
WEYBRIGHT		2 1/2 - 3	
CHRISTMAS MUSIC, BK. 1 -- SECULAR			
BELWIN-MILLS PUBLISHING CORPORATION			1.75
WEYBRIGHT		2 1/2 - 3	
CHRISTMAS MUSIC, BK. 2 -- SACRED			
BELWIN-MILLS PUBLISHING CORPORATION			1.75
WEYBRIGHT			
COURSE FOR PIANISTS, CHRISTMAS MUSIC-- SECULAR, BK. 1			
BELWIN-MILLS PUBLISHING CORPORATION		11089	1.50
WEYBRIGHT			
COURSE FOR PIANISTS, CHRISTMAS MUSIC -- SACRED, BK. 2			
BELWIN-MILLS PUBLISHING CORPORATION			1.50
WEYBRIGHT		1	
MY FIRST CHRISTMAS BOOK			
BELWIN-MILLS PUBLISHING CORPORATION			1.75
WEYBRIGHT		3	
RUDOLPH'S CHRISTMAS ALBUM			
BELWIN-MILLS PUBLISHING CORPORATION			1.75
WILLAN			
CHILDREN'S FAVORITE CHRISTMAS CAROLS			
FREDERICK HARRIS MUSIC COMPANY			.75
WILLIAMS, F.--ED.	WILLIAMS, F.		
TEN CHRISTMAS CAROLS			
SHAWNEE PRESS, INC.			1.10
WINROTH, G.--ED	WINROTH, G.		
CATHEDRAL CHIMES			
WILLIS MUSIC COMPANY			.60
WYMAN, A.		4	
CHRISTMAS BELLS MARCH, OP. 17			
THEODORE PRESSER COMPANY			.60
WYMAN, A.			
CHRISTMAS BELLS MARCH, OP. 17			
VOLKWEIN BROS.			.25
YOUNG, G.			
CHRISTMAS SUITE, A			
HOPE PUBLISHING COMPANY			1.95
ZEPP--ED	ZEPP		
CAROLS FOR DECEMBER			
PRO-ART PUBLICATIONS, INC.		1220	1.00

ZEPP--ED	ZEPP		
CHRISTMAS SONGS AND SOLOS			
PRO-ART PUBLICATIONS, INC.		717	1.00
ZEPP--ED	ZEPP		
LET'S ARRANGE CHRISTMAS SONGS			
PRO-ART PUBLICATIONS, INC.		482	.75
ZEPP--ED	ZEPP		
LET'S PLAY CHRISTMAS CAROLS			
PRO-ART PUBLICATIONS, INC.		715	1.00
ZEPP--ED	ZEPP		
LET'S PLAY CHRISTMAS FAVORITES			
PRO-ART PUBLICATIONS, INC.		716	1.00
ZEPP--ED	ZEPP		
TIDINGS OF CHRISTMAS			
PRO-ART PUBLICATIONS, INC.		483	1.00
ZILCHER		2	
WEIHNACHTS-ALBUM			
SCHOTT		421	2.50
ZIPP			
LITTLE CHRISTMAS BOOK FOR ROSWITHA			
BARENREITER VERLAG		26666	1.75
ZIPP		1	
WEIHNACHTSBUCHLEIN FUR ROSWITHA			
BARENREITER VERLAG		BA 2666	

Christmas Music:
Composer/Editor/Arranger Unlisted—Works Alphabetized by Title

FROSTY THE SNOW MAN AND OTHER CHRISTMAS SONGS		
THE BIG THREE MUSIC CORPORATION		02.95
HOME FOR CHRISTMAS		
CHAPPELL AND COMPANY, INC.	0021436	.95
LANE, J.		
JINGLE BELL ROCK		
THE BIG THREE MUSIC CORPORATION		00.70
KINDER SPIELEN ZUR WEIHNACHT -- 19 CHRISTMAS SONGS WITH GERMAN TEXT		
ASSOCIATED MUSIC PUBLISHERS, INC.	NAG	1.75
LET US HAVE MUSIC SERIES - CHRISTMAS		
CARL FISCHER, INC.	O 3507	1.50
MERRY CHRISTMAS - THE HILLSIDE SINGERS		
THE BIG THREE MUSIC CORPORATION		02.95
MODERN PIANIST SERIES - CHRISTMAS SKETCHES		
POINTER PUBLICATIONS		1.95
	M	
MUSICAL CHRISTMAS CARDS --SIX PIECES--		
C. F. PETERS CORPORATION	H400A	1.25
	2	
NEUE WEIHNACHTSLIEDER		
BARENREITER VERLAG	BA 1371	
ONE HUNDRED SEVENTY CHRISTMAS SONGS AND CAROLS		
THE BIG THREE MUSIC CORPORATION		04.95
POINTER LIBRARY - MEMORIES OF CHRISTMAS		
POINTER PUBLICATIONS		2.95
POINTER SYSTEM - CAROLS		
POINTER PUBLICATIONS		1.50
TWO SONGS FOR CHRISTMAS --SILENT NIGHT AND ADESTE FIDELIS--		
CARL FISCHER, INC.	P 2239	.50
	2-3	
WEIHNACHTSLIEDER. KLAVIERAUSGABE ZUM QUEMPAS-BUCH. DIE 97 SCHONSTEN ALTEN UND NEUEN LIEDER FUR DEN WEIHNACHTSFESTKREIS		
BARENREITER VERLAG	BA 3500	
	2	
WEIHNACHTSLIEDER FUR KLAVIER. DIE 40 WEIHNACHTSLIEDER DES QUEMPAS-HEFTES IN LEICHTEN KLAVIERSATZEN ALTER UND ZEITGENOSSISCHER MEISTER		
BARENREITER VERLAG	BA 825	

Title	Composer
A-RUB-A-DUB	ERB
AANDANTE, WOO 57, F MAJOR	BEETHOVEN
AARDY THE AARDVARK	RICKER
ABBY VARIATIONS	
ABC DER KLAVIERTEACHNIK -- ENG AND GER NOTES -- BK. 1	SCHOLZ
ABC DER KLAVIERTEACHNIK -- ENG AND GER NOTES -- BK. 2	SCHOLZ
ABC DER KLAVIERTEACHNIK -- ENG AND GER NOTES -- BK. 3	SCHOLZ
ABC OF PIANO PLAYING, BK. 1	BERLIN, B.
ABC OF PIANO PLAYING, BK. 2	BERLIN, B.
ABC OF PIANO PLAYING, BK. 3	BERLIN, B.
ABC WALTZ, THE	ANDRE
ABEGG VARIATIONS, OP. 1	SCHUMANN, R.
ABEGG VARIATIONS	SCHUMANN, R.
ABENDLIED, OP. 85 NO. 12	SCHUMANN, R.
ABERGAVENNY	GELLAR *
ABERRATIONS N. VII FOR PIANO	LUCAS, T.
ABIDE WITH ME, C MAJOR	MONK--ED.
ABIDE WITH ME, G MAJOR	FREEMAN--ED.
ABIDE WITH ME	LIDDLE, S.
ABOARD THE SANTE FE	DITTENHAVER
ABOMINABLE SNOWMAN	DUROCHER, L.
ABOVE THE CLOUDS	WEYBRIGHT
ABOVE THE CLOUDS	WEYBRIGHT
ABRAHAM, MARTIN AND JOHN	BRADLEY,
ABRAHAM, MARTIN AND JOHN	BRIMHALL,
ABSCHNITT 37	KANN, H.
ABYSS --DER ABGRUND--. BALLET AFTER A NOVEL BY L.	TCHEREPNIN
ACADEMY AWARD WINNER AND OTHER BIG HITS, THE	
ACALANT - FROM 'SUITE IV CENTENARIO'	GUARNIERI
ACCELERATIONS, OP. 234	STRAUSS, J.
ACCELERATIONS, OP. 234	STRAUSS, J.
ACCELERATION WALTZ	STRAUSS, J.
ACCELERATION WALTZ	STRAUSS, J.
ACCENT NO. 1 - NINE 'POP' NOVELTY SOLOS BY VARIOUS	
ACCENT NO. 1 - NINE SOLOS BY VARIOUS DUTCH COMPOSERS	
ACCENT NO. 2 - EIGHT 'POP' NOVELTY SOLOS BY VARIOUS	
ACCENT NO. 2 - EIGHT SOLOS BY VARIOUS DUTCH COMPOSERS	
ACCENT ON ANALYTICAL SONATINAS	GILLOCK
ACCENT ON MAJORS AND MINORS	GILLOCK
ACCENT ON MAJORS	GILLOCK
ACCENT ON RHYTHM --MODERN RHYTHMIC CLASSICS--	WHITFORD
ACCENT ON RHYTHM AND STYLE	GILLOCK
ACCENT ON SOLOS	GILLOCK
ACCENT ON SOLOS	GILLOCK
ACCENT ON THE BLACK KEYS	GILLOCK
ACCOMPANIMENTS FOR A 2ND PIANO FOR FANTASIA K475 AND	GRIEG
ACCOMPANIMENTS FOR A 2ND PIANO FOR SONATA K283 IN G BY	GRIEG
ACCOMPANIMENTS FOR A 2ND PIANO FOR SONATA K533	GRIEG
ACCOMPANIMENTS FOR A 2ND PIANO FOR SONATA K545 IN C BY	GRIEG
ACCOMPANIMENTS TO BACH'S SIX SOLO VIOLIN SONATAS. VOL.	SCHUMANN, R.
ACCOMPANIMENTS TO BACH'S SIX SOLO VIOLIN SONATAS. VOL.	SCHUMANN, R.
ACCOMPANIMENTS TO PAGANINI'S CAPRICES, OP. 1. VOL. 1	SCHUMANN, R.
ACCOMPANIMENTS TO PAGANINI'S CAPRICES, OP. 1. VOL. 2	SCHUMANN, R.
ACCUEIL AMICAL	MILHAUD, D.
ACHTAMAR	HOVHANESS, A.
ACHTZEHN GENRE-ETUDEN OP. 109	BURGMUELLER
ACHTZEHN INVENTIONEN, OP. 101	WEISMANN, J.
ACHTZEHN STUDIEN ZU CHOPINS ETUDEN 'IN MOTU CONTRARIO'	WUEHRER
ACHT BAGATELLEN, OP. 3	BARTOS, J.
ACHT BOHM DUETTE	HUSA, K.
ACHT ETUDEN VON CRAMER	BUSONI
ACHT KLAVIERSTUCKE, OP. 3	KURTAG, G.
ACHT KOMPOSITIONEN FUR JUNGE PIANISTEN	BARTA
ACHT LEICHTE KLAVIERSTUCKE	BURKHARD, W.
ACQUARIO	BELLISARIO, A.
ACROBAT, THE, G MAJOR	HAYES
ACROBATICS	CANFIELD, J.
ACROBATS OF GOD--5 DANCES FROM THE BALLET	SURINACH, C.
ACROBATS OF GOD -- 5 DANCES FROM THE BALLET	SURINACH, C.
ACROBATS	SCHER, W.
ACROBAT	ANDRE
ACROSS AN AZURE SKY, F MAJOR	RUNGEE
ACROSS THE BORDER	RICHARDSON
ADAGIO--FROM SONATA FOR VIOLIN AND CONTINUO, OP. 5 NO.	CORELLI
ADAGIO--1966	URBANNER, E.
ADAGIO, BOUREE	HANDEL
ADAGIO, FROM ORGAN TOCCATA NO. 1	BACH, J.S.
ADAGIO --7TH SYMPHONY--	BRUCKNER
ADAGIO AND ALLEGRO FOR MECHANICAL ORGAN, K594	MOZART, W. A.
ADAGIO AND PASTORALE	ALDROVANDINI
ADAGIO AUS DER SYMPHONIE NO. 07	BRUCKNER
ADAGIO CANTABILE--FROM SONATA, OP. 13	BEETHOVEN
ADAGIO DE LA SONATA NO. 6	MOZART, W. A.
ADAGIO ESOTICO	GILLOCK
ADAGIO ESOTICO	GILLOCK
ADAGIO FOR PIANOFORTE, B MINOR, K540	MOZART, W. A.
ADAGIO FROM ORGAN TOCCATA IN C MAJOR	BACH, J.S.
ADAGIO FROM ORGAN TOCCATA IN C MAJOR	BACH, J.S.
ADAGIO FROM STRING TRIO, OP. 8	BEETHOVEN
ADAGIO FROM SYMPHONIE NO. 10	MAHLER
ADAGIO IN A MINOR	BACH, J.S.
ADAGIO IN G MINOR	ALBINONI
ADAGIO K540 IN B MINOR, AND GIGUE K574 IN G	MOZART, W. A.
ADAGIO SOSTENUTO--FROM SONATA, OP. 27 NO. 2	BEETHOVEN
ADAGIO SOSTENUTO--FROM SONATA, OP. 27 NO. 2	BEETHOVEN
ADAGIO	MARCELLO
ADAGIO	NARDINI
ADAGIO	RAVEL
ADAME MIROIR	MILHAUD, D.
ADA RICHTER CHRISTMAS CAROL BOOK, THE	RICHTER
ADA RICHTER PIANO COURSE, BOOK 1	RICHTER
ADA RICHTER PIANO COURSE, BOOK 2	RICHTER
ADA RICHTER PIANO COURSE, BOOK 3	RICHTER
ADA RICHTER PIANO COURSE, BOOK 4	RICHTER
ADDIO, SIGNORA	
ADDIO A NAPOLI	COTTRAU
ADELAIDE'S LAMENT	LOESSER, F.
ADESTE FIDELES	WALLIS--ED
ADESTE FIDELIS, A FLAT MAJOR	FREEMAN--ED.
ADESTE FIDELIS AND FIRST NOEL	SPENCER, J.
ADESTE FIDELIS AND SANTA CLAUS MARCH	SPENCER, J.
ADESTE FIDELIS	FREDERICKS
ADESTE FIDELIS	READING, H.--ED
ADESTE FIDELIS	SCHIEFELBEIN, F.
ADESTE FIDELIS	WEBER, H.
ADIEU TO THE PIANO - TWO PIANOS, EIGHT HANDS	BEETHOVEN
ADIEU TO THE PIANO	BEETHOVEN
ADIEU TO THE PIANO	BEETHOVEN
ADIEU TO THE PIANO	BEETHOVEN
ADIEU	ELGAR, E.
ADIEU	ELGAR, E.
ADONIS, GALOP	STREABBOG
ADONIS GALOP, G MAJOR	STREABBOG
ADORATION	WHITFORD
ADRIANA LECOUVREUR - INTERMEZZO FROM ACT II	CILEA
ADULT ACTIVITIES AT THE KEYBOARD	
ADULT APPROACH TO THE PIANO	MASON, I.
ADULT AT THE PIANO, BK. 1	SCHAUM, J.
ADULT AT THE PIANO, BK. 2	SCHAUM, J.
ADULT AT THE PIANO, BK. 3	SCHAUM, J.
ADULT AT THE PIANO, THE - BOOK 1	FROST
ADULT AT THE PIANO, THE - BOOK 2	FROST
ADULT AT THE PIANO, THE - BOOK 3	FROST
ADULT EDUCATION PIANO METHOD, BK. 1	HORTON
ADULT EDUCATION PIANO METHOD, BK. 2	HORTON
ADULT EXPLORER AT THE PIANO, THE	BURROWS *
ADULT PIANO COURSE, BK. 1	AARON, M.
ADULT PIANO COURSE, BK. 1	SCHAUM, J.
ADULT PIANO COURSE, BK. 2	AARON, M.
ADULT PIANO COURSE, BK. 2	SCHAUM, J.
ADULT PIANO COURSE, BK. 3	SCHAUM, J.
ADULT PROGRAM ALBUM	ROVENGER--ED.
ADULT STUDENT, LEVEL 1	GLOVER, D.
ADULT STUDENT, LEVEL 2	GLOVER, D.
ADULT STUDENT, LEVEL 3	GLOVER, D.
ADUSUM DELPHINI - BK. 1	MIGOT
ADUSUM DELPHINI - BK. 2	MIGOT
ADVANCED FIRST GRADE BOOK	WILLIAMS, J.
ADVANCED HYMN PLAYING	GLOVER, D. *
ADVANCED HYMN PLAYING	GLOVER, D. *
ADVANCED SACRED MUSIC DUETS	GLOVER, D. *
ADVANCED SACRED MUSIC DUETS	GLOVER, D. *
ADVANCING PIANIST PLAYS BOOGIE, THE	STEINER
ADVANCING PIANIST PLAYS CONCERTOS, THE	STEINER
ADVANCING PIANIST PLAYS DUETS, THE	STEINER
ADVANCING PIANIST PLAYS MARCHES, THE	STEINER
ADVANCING PIANIST PLAYS OPERA, THE	STEINER
ADVANCING PIANIST PLAYS RECITAL MUSIC, THE	STEINER
ADVANCING PIANIST PLAYS SYMPHONIES, THE	STEINER
ADVANCING PIANIST PLAYS WALTZES, THE	STEINER
ADVENT. SEVENTEEN ADVENT SONGS WITH GERMAN TEXT	KOSCHINSKY
ADVENT- UND WEIHNACHTSLIEDER IN 25 LEICHTEN SATZEN	RAPHAEL, G.
ADVENTURELAND	HORNE
ADVENTURELAND	
ADVENTURES AT THE KEYBOARD	RICHTER
ADVENTURES IN CONTEMPORARY TECHNIC -- THE MODERN STUDY	SCHOLZ
ADVENTURES IN IMPROVISATION AT THE KEYBOARD	MACK, E.
ADVENTURES IN MUSIC LAND	KETTERER, E.
ADVENTURES IN PHRASING	STORR, S.
ADVENTURES IN PIANO TECHNIC	KETTERER, E.
ADVENTURES IN STYLE	BLAKE
ADVENTURES IN THE PARK --SUITE	CLAWSON
ADVENTURES OF A GHOST	GARROW, L.
ADVENTURES OF A TRITONE	HANNA
ADVENTURES OF CHANTICLEER AND PARTLET, THE	SPENCER, C.
ADVENTURES OF IVAN--EIGHT PIECES FOR STUDENTS	KHATCHATURIAN
ADVENTURES OF PRIMO AND SECONDO, THE	ROGERS, E.
ADVENTURES OF PRIMO AND SECONDO	ROGERS, E.
ADVENTURE IN JAZZ, BK. 1	GLOVER, D. *
ADVENTURE IN JAZZ, BK. 2	GLOVER, D. *
ADVENTURE IN JAZZ, BK. 3	GLOVER, D. *
ADVENTURE IN JAZZ, BK. 4	GLOVER, D. *
ADVENTURE	DONOVAN, R.
ADVICE TO DOLLY, G MAJOR	ARNOLD, H.
AEGEAN SKETCHES	COULTHARD
AEOLIAN HARP, E FLAT MAJOR	SMITH, SYDNEY
AEOLIAN HARP, THE, A FLAT MAJOR, OP. 25	KRUGER
AEOLIAN HARP	GILLOCK
AEROPLANE STUNTS	WILLIAMS, M.
AERO FLIGHT	ECKSTEIN
AFFAIR TO REMEMBER, AN	WILLIAMS,
AFRICA, OP. 89 -- FANTASIE FOR PIANO AND ORCH., PIANO	SAINT-SAENS
AFRICA, OP. 89	SAINT-SAENS
AFRICA, OP. 89	SAINT-SAENS
AFRICAN SAFARI	BEHR, F.
AFRICASIAN AFFAIR--2, 3, OR 4 PIANOS	METIS, F.
AFTERNOONS -- 14 EARLY-GRADE PIANO PIECES BASED ON THE	ALT, H.
AFTERNOON OF A FAUN, E MAJOR	DEBUSSY
AFTERNOON OF A FAUN	DEBUSSY
AFTERNOON OF A FAUN	DEBUSSY
AFTERNOON OF A FAUN	DEBUSSY
AFTER A SUMMER RAIN, F MAJOR	MILNES
AFTER DARK IN OLD JAPAN	MUNN, W.
AFTER DARK	GIASSON, P.
AFTER DARK	PECHMAN
AFTER DARK	PECHMAN
AFTER SCHOOL --SUITE--	NELSON
AFTER THEATER TANGO	CONFREY, Z.
AFTER THE BALL, F MAJOR	HARRIS, C. K.
AFTER THE BALL IS OVER	MENDEL, S.--ED
AFTER THE BALL	HARRIS, C. K.
AFTER THE BALL	HARRIS
AFTER THE DANCE	CZIBULKA
AFTER THE DANCE	SWINSTEAD, F.
AFTER THE GAME, F MAJOR	ARMOUR
AFTER THE SHOWER	TAYLOR, EDNA
AFTER YOU, MR. STRAUSS	STRAUSS, J.
AGE OF ANXIETY, THE -- SYMPHONY NO. 2 FOR PIANO AND	BERNSTEIN, L.
AGE OF CHIVALRY, THE -- 29 18TH-CENTURY DANCES	FREY--ED
AGILITE, L', OP. 20	LECOUPPEY, F.
AGON	STRAVINSKY, I.
AGRESTIES - UNE GARDEUSE, D'OIES QUI PASSE, SUR UNE	SCIORTINO, E.
AGYPTEN	SCOTT, C.
AH, SWEET MYSTERY OF LIFE	HERBERT
AHI VIENE EL CHINO	LECUONA
AIDA, ABRIDGED	VERDI
AIDA, FANTAISIE	VERDI
AIDA -- COMPLETE OPERA --	VERDI
AIDA -- GRAND MARCH -- EASY, G MAJOR	VERDI
AIDA -- GRAND MARCH -- F MAJOR	VERDI
AIDA - EASY FANTASIA	VERDI
AIDA - FANTASIA	VERDI
AIDA - HYMN AND TRIUMPHAL MARCH	VERDI
AIDA - MARCHE DES TROMPETTES	VERDI
AIDA - MARCHE DES TROMPETTES	VERDI
AIN'T MISBEHAVIN' -- SIMP.	MOSSMAN, T.
AIR--FROM ORCHESTRA SUITE, D MAJOR	BACH, J.S.
AIR--GAVOTTE--	LOUIS XIII
AIRES REGIONALES -- FOUR EASY PIECES IN TREBLE CLEF	AGUILAR
AIRE DE MILONGA	LUZZATTI
AIRPLANES	STAIRS, L.
AIRPLANE FLIGHT, AN, C MAJOR	WILSON, M.
AIRPLANE RIDE, AN, D MAJOR	RICHTER
AIRPLANE RIDE, AN	KAHL
AIRPORT LOVE THEME	WEBSTER, J. *
AIRPORT LOVE THEME	WEBSTER, J. *
AIRS AND DANCES FROM HARPSICHORD PERIOD	DOROLLE, A.
AIRS AND GRACES	COULTER, G.
AIRS AND GRACES	CRAXTON, H.--ED.
AIRY FAIRIES	SPAULDING, G. L.
AIRY FAIRIES	SPAULDING, G. L.
AIRY FAIRIES	SPAULDING, G. L.

AIR ANCIEN	BERNHEIM
AIR AND DANCE	DELIUS, F.
AIR AND FUGUE ON WHITE KEYS	FULEIHAN, A.
AIR AND VARIATIONS--HARMONIOUS BLACKSMITH	HANDEL
AIR AND VARIATIONS FROM SUITE NO. 5	HANDEL
AIR DE BALLET -- CALLIRHOE -- G MAJOR	CHAMINADE
AIR DE BALLET -- PAS DES AMORPHES -- B FLAT MAJOR	CHAMINADE
AIR DE BALLET IN G MINOR, OP. 36 NO. 5	MOSZKOWSKI
AIR DE BALLET NO. 1, OP. 30	CHAMINADE
AIR DE BALLET	DEPRET, M.
AIR DE BALLET	FERGUSON, J.
AIR DE BALLET	HURE
AIR DE BALLET	THOMPSON, J.
AIR DE BALLET	WRIGHT, N.
AIR DE CHASSE -- 6-HANDS	CZERNY
AIR FAVORI DE LA REINE MARIE LECZINSKA	VASSEUR
AIR FAVORI DE LA REINE MARIE LECZINSKA	VASSEUR
AIR FOR THE G STRING, C MAJOR	BACH, J.S.
AIR FROM 'ORPHEUS' FOR ONE PIANO, SIX HANDS	GLUCK
AIR IN D MAJOR -- AIR FOR THE G STRING	BACH, J.S.
AIR IN G MAJOR, SUITE 14	HANDEL
AIR OF LOUIS XIII, C MAJOR	GHYS
AIR OF LOUIS XIII, E MAJOR	GHYS
AIR OF THE SHEPHERDESS	MOZART, W. A.
AIR OF THE SHEPHERDESS	MOZART, W. A.
AIR ON THE G STRING, FROM ORCHESTRA SUITE NO. 3	BACH, J.S.
AIR ON THE G STRING	BACH, J.S.
AIR ON THE G STRING	BACH, J.S.
AIR VARIE FROM CONCERTO GROSSO NO. 2	HANDEL
AIR WITH CANON	FRACKENPOHL, A.
AIR	BACH, J.S. *
AIR	HANDEL
AIR	HAYDN
AIR	MATTHESON, J.
AI VAN 1	TON-THAT, T.
AKKORDE -- ETUDENWERK --	POLIVKA
AKKORDE	POLIVKA
ALADDINS LAMP	BERMONT, G.
ALADDIN	KOEHLER
ALAMEDA FROM 'FOUR SKETCHES'	MILHAUD, D.
ALAMEIN CONCERTO -- THEME	
ALAMEIN CONCERTO	
ALASKAN CRUISE	BURNAM
ALASKAN TWILIGHT, F MAJOR	SAROLA
ALBAICIN, EL -- FROM IBERIA	ALBENIZ, I.
ALBA BRUMOSA	CASTELLINI
ALBENIZ MASTERPIECES	ALBENIZ, I.
ALBERT DE VITO PIANO COURSE, BK. 1	DE VITO, A.--ED.
ALBORADA--12 SHORT PIECES	LAMOTE DE
ALBORADA -- FROM RECUERDOS DE VIAJE	ALBENIZ, I.
ALBORADA -- NO. 3, FROM RECUERDOS DE VIAJE	ALBENIZ, I.
ALBORADA DEL GRACIOSO, FROM MIROIRS	RAVEL
ALBORADA DEL GRACIOSO, FROM MIROIRS	RAVEL
ALBORADA DEL GRACIOSO, FROM MIROIRS	RAVEL
ALBORADA DEL GRACIOSO	RAVEL
ALBORADA	WATSON
ALBUM. SELECTED WORKS	COUPERIN, F.
ALBUM. 20 FAVORITE PIECES	HANDEL
ALBUM. 32 FAVORITE PIECES	CHOPIN
ALBUM--''SEID UMSCHLNGEN MILLIONEN''	STRAUSS, J. *
ALBUM--'MOZART ALS ACHTJAHRIGER KOMPONIST'	MOZART, W. A.
ALBUM--TWENTY-ONE FAVORITE PIECES	BACH, J.S.
ALBUM--20 PIECES	WAGNER
ALBUM--22 FAVORITE PIECES	HANDEL
ALBUM--22 PIECES	SCHUMANN, R.
ALBUM--33 FAVORITE COMPOSITIONS	CHOPIN
ALBUM-LEAF, AN--CONCERT TRANSCRIPTION	WAGNER
ALBUM-LEAF IN E MINOR, OP. 12, NO. 7	GRIEG
ALBUM-LEAVES, OP. 124	SCHUMANN, R.
ALBUM-LEAVES, OP. 124	SCHUMANN, R.
ALBUM-LEAVES, OP. 28	GRIEG
ALBUM-LEAVES FOR THE YOUNG, OP. 101	GURLITT
ALBUM, BK. 1	BARTOK
ALBUM, BK. 1	GRIEG
ALBUM, BK. 1	SCHUBERT
ALBUM, BK. 1	SCHUMANN, R.
ALBUM, BK. 1	SHOSTAKOVITCH
ALBUM, BK. 2	BARTOK
ALBUM, BK. 2	GRIEG
ALBUM, BK. 2	SCHUMANN, R.
ALBUM, BKS. 1 AND 2	BEETHOVEN
ALBUM, OP. 72 NO. 1 -- PRELUDE	SAINT-SAENS
ALBUM, OP. 72 NO. 2 -- CARILLON	SAINT-SAENS
ALBUM, OP. 72 NO. 3 -- TOCCATA	SAINT-SAENS
ALBUM, OP. 72 NO. 4 -- VALSE	SAINT-SAENS
ALBUM, OP. 72 NO. 5 -- CHANSON NAPOLITAINE	SAINT-SAENS
ALBUM, OP. 72 NO. 6 -- FINAL	SAINT-SAENS
ALBUM, OP. 72	
ALBUM, VOL. 1	CHOPIN
ALBUM, VOL. 1	CHOPIN
ALBUM, VOL. 2	CHOPIN
ALBUM, VOL. 2	CHOPIN
ALBUM, 21 FAVORITE PIECES FROM SUITES, PARTITAS, ETC.	BACH, J.S.
ALBUMBLAETTER, OP. 124 -- WALZER - SCHLUMMERLIED -	SCHUMANN, R.
ALBUMBLAETTER, OP. 124 NO. 16	SCHUMANN, R.
ALBUMBLAETTER, OP. 124	SCHUMANN, R.
ALBUMBLAETTER, OP. 147, BK. 1	GURLITT
ALBUMBLATT--FUR ELISE	BEETHOVEN
ALBUMBLATT, WO O 59, A MINOR 'FOR ELISE'	BEETHOVEN
ALBUMBLATTER, OP. 2 -- WIDMUNG, FANTASTISCHES STUCK,	FIBICH, Z.
ALBUMBLATT -- FUR ELISE	BEETHOVEN
ALBUMBLATT C --1861	WAGNER
ALBUMBLATT D FLAT 'LEGE WOHL'	ABNHEIM, JOSEPH
ALBUMLEAF IN A FLAT--CURWEN EDITION	MEYERBEER, G.
ALBUMSONATE FUR MATHILDE WESENDONCK	WAGNER
ALBUMS - GRADED SCARLATTI, THE - 39 SONATAS COLLECTED	SCARLATTI, D.
ALBUMS - OVERTURES AND PRELUDES	VERDI
ALBUMS - SIX BRILLIANT SONATAS	SCARLATTI, D.
ALBUMS - 10 BRILLIANT SONATAS	SCARLATTI, D.
ALBUMS - 18 FAMOUS ARIAS	VERDI
ALBUMS - 7 MELODIES FROM THE OPERAS	VERDI
ALBUM -- BK. 1 AND 2	COUPERIN, F.
ALBUM -- 24 PIECES	CORELLI
ALBUM --5 WALTZES--	LANNER, J. F. C.
ALBUM - MELODIE PUCCINIANE - 17 EASY TRANSCRIPTIONS	PUCCINI
ALBUM - 8 FAMOUS WALTZES	STRAUSS, J.
ALBUM - 8 FAMOUS WALTZES	STRAUSS, J.
ALBUM 'THRO' THE NIGHT ....'	SCHUBERT
ALBUM ALTER MEISTER - 24 TANZE UND KLEINE STUCKE	CLARKE *
ALBUM BERUHMTER ROMANTIKER, 20 KLAVIERSTUCKE	SCHUBERT *
ALBUM D'ANDRUCHA, OP. 133	GRETCHANINOFF
ALBUM D'ENFANTS, OP. 39	TSCHAIKOWSKY
ALBUM D'IMAGES	PRESLE
ALBUM DES 'SIX' --THE FRENCH SIX--	AURIC *
ALBUM DE CECILIA, EL--6 PIECES IN TREBLE CLEF	RODRIGO, J.
ALBUM DE CORINNE - FLANERIE	FLAXLAND
ALBUM DE CORINNE - WALZETTA	FLAXLAND

ALBUM DE CORINNE	FLAXLAND
ALBUM DE CORRINE - ANDANTE	FLAXLAND
ALBUM DE CORRINE - AU COUVENT	FLAXLAND
ALBUM DE CORRINE - CAPRICE SICILIEN AU BAL	FLAXLAND
ALBUM DE CORRINE - CHANSON ESPAGNOL	FLAXLAND
ALBUM DE CORRINE - LA PROCESSION	FLAXLAND
ALBUM DE CORRINE - PRINTEMPS	FLAXLAND
ALBUM DE CORRINE - RETRAITE MILITAIRE	FLAXLAND
ALBUM DE LA JEUNESSE	CHAUMONT
ALBUM DE MADAME BOVARY, L'	MILHAUD, D.
ALBUM DE MAROUSSIA - AU CINEMA	STRIMER
ALBUM DE MAROUSSIA - CASTAGNETTES	STRIMER
ALBUM DE MAROUSSIA - JAVA	STRIMER
ALBUM DE MAROUSSIA - JOURS D'AUTREFOIS	STRIMER
ALBUM DE MAROUSSIA - LATENDRE EMMA	STRIMER
ALBUM DE MAROUSSIA - LE PETIT SAVANT	STRIMER
ALBUM DE MAROUSSIA - MARIONNETTES	STRIMER
ALBUM DE MAROUSSIA - PETITS POUSSINS	STRIMER
ALBUM DE MAROUSSIA - PROCESSION	STRIMER
ALBUM DE MAROUSSIA - ROSEE MATINALE	STRIMER
ALBUM DE MAROUSSIA - TOURMENT	STRIMER
ALBUM DE MAROUSSIA - VALSE DE MAROUSSIA	STRIMER
ALBUM DE MAROUSSIA	STRIMER
ALBUM DE NATACHA - AU PRINTEMPS	STRIMER
ALBUM DE NATACHA - CARILLON	STRIMER
ALBUM DE NATACHA - DANSE DE LA MOUCHE	STRIMER
ALBUM DE NATACHA - DOUMKA AND HOPAK	STRIMER
ALBUM DE NATACHA - EN VALSANT	STRIMER
ALBUM DE NATACHA - PROMENADE	STRIMER
ALBUM DE NATACHA - TANGO ARGENTIN	STRIMER
ALBUM DE NATACHA - TENDRESSE AND SOUVENIR LOINTAIN	STRIMER
ALBUM DE NATACHA - VALSE DE NATACHA	STRIMER
ALBUM DE NATACHA	STRIMER
ALBUM DE NINA, OP. 144	GRETCHANINOFF
ALBUM DE TANIA - AMUSETTE	STRIMER
ALBUM DE TANIA - IN A MINOR	STRIMER
ALBUM DE TANIA - LA PETITE VIENNOISE	STRIMER
ALBUM DE TANIA - PAYS LOINTAIN	STRIMER
ALBUM DE TANIA - PLAINTE	STRIMER
ALBUM DE TANIA - RONDE JOYEUSE	STRIMER
ALBUM DE TANIA	STRIMER
ALBUM DE VIAJE, OP. 15	TURINA, J.
ALBUM DE VIAJE	TURINA, J.
ALBUM FOR PIANO	LISZT
ALBUM FOR PIANO	SINDING
ALBUM FOR SMALL HANDS	SANCAN, P.
ALBUM FOR THE YOUNG, OP. 140--20 MELODIOUS PIECES	GURLITT
ALBUM FOR THE YOUNG, OP. 21, BK. 1	GAITO
ALBUM FOR THE YOUNG, OP. 21, BK. 2	GAITO
ALBUM FOR THE YOUNG, OP. 21, BK. 3	GAITO
ALBUM FOR THE YOUNG, OP. 39--24 EASY PIECES	TSCHAIKOWSKY
ALBUM FOR THE YOUNG, OP. 39	TSCHAIKOWSKY
ALBUM FOR THE YOUNG, OP. 39	TSCHAIKOWSKY
ALBUM FOR THE YOUNG, OP. 39	TSCHAIKOWSKY
ALBUM FOR THE YOUNG, OP. 39	TSCHAIKOWSKY
ALBUM FOR THE YOUNG, OP. 68, THE EASIER PIECES	SCHUMANN, R.
ALBUM FOR THE YOUNG, OP. 68, AND SCENES FROM	SCHUMANN, R.
ALBUM FOR THE YOUNG, OP. 68	SCHUMANN, R.
ALBUM FOR THE YOUNG, OP. 68	SCHUMANN, R.
ALBUM FOR THE YOUNG, OP. 68	SCHUMANN, R.
ALBUM FOR THE YOUNG, OP. 68	SCHUMANN, R.
ALBUM FOR THE YOUNG WITH SCENES FROM CHILDHOOD, OP. 15	SCHUMANN, R.
ALBUM FOR THE YOUNG	DIAMOND, D.
ALBUM FOR THE YOUNG	GURLITT
ALBUM FOR THE YOUNG	KABALEVSKY
ALBUM FOR THE YOUNG	KULLAK, T.
ALBUM FOR THE YOUNG	SCHUMANN, R.
ALBUM FOR THE YOUNG	SCHUMANN, R.
ALBUM FOR THE YOUNG	SCHUMANN, R.
ALBUM FOR THE YOUNG	SCHUMANN, R.
ALBUM FOR THE YOUNG	TSCHAIKOWSKY
ALBUM FUER DIE JUGEND, AUSWAHL OP. 68	SCHUMANN, R.
ALBUM FUER DIE JUGEND -- ALBUM FOR THE YOUNG --, OP.	SCHUMANN, R.
ALBUM FUER DIE JUGEND -- ALBUM FOR THE YOUNG --, OP.	SCHUMANN, R.
ALBUM FUER DIE JUGEND -- ALBUM FOR THE YOUNG --, OP.	SCHUMANN, R.
ALBUM LEAF --PAGE D'ALBUM--	DEBUSSY
ALBUM LEAF -- ALBUMBLATT -- E MINOR	GRIEG
ALBUM LEAF IN A MINOR	KOELLING
ALBUM LEAF	GRIEG
ALBUM LEAVES, OP. 124	SCHUMANN, R.
ALBUM LEAVES, OP. 124	SCHUMANN, R.
ALBUM LEAVES, OP. 124	SCHUMANN, R.
ALBUM LEAVES, OP. 28	GRIEG
ALBUM MODERNER TSCHECHISCHER KOMPONISTEN 1947 - BAND	BARTOS, J. *
ALBUM MODERNER TSCHECHISCHER KOMPONISTEN 1947 - BAND	AXMANN *
ALBUM NO. 1 -- 13 STUCKE AUS OP. 41, 44 UND 47	FIBICH, Z.
ALBUM NO. 2 -- PILGERLIED, MORGENGESPRACHE, FRUHLING	FIBICH, Z.
ALBUM OF EASY PIECES BY MODERN COMPOSERS, AN	BARTOK *
ALBUM OF FAVORITE PIECES	BRAHMS
ALBUM OF FIVE PIECES	DEBUSSY
ALBUM OF LITTLE PIECES	PIERONI
ALBUM OF PIANO DUOS -- 9 PIECES OF MEDIUM DIFFICULTY	ADAMS
ALBUM OF PIANO MUSIC	COWELL
ALBUM OF PIANO PIECES	COATES, E.
ALBUM OF PIANO PIECES	CURZON, F.
ALBUM OF PIANO PIECES	FAURE, G.
ALBUM OF PROGRESSIVE PIANO CLASSICS	
ALBUM OF RUDOLF FRIML, AN	FRIML, R.
ALBUM OF SELECTED PIANO WORKS	SHOSTAKOVITCH
ALBUM OF SELECTED PIECES	MEDTNER, N.
ALBUM OF WALTZES	STRAUSS, J.
ALBUM OF 12 MARCHES	GOLDMAN, E.
ALBUM OF 12 PIECES	PALMGREN, S.
ALBUM OF 12 SELECTED PIECES	CHOPIN
ALBUM OF 12 SELECTED PRELUDES	SCRIABINE, A.
ALBUM OF 25 PIANO CLASSICS	
ALBUM OF 28 FAVORITE DANCES, BK. 1	STRAUSS, J.
ALBUM OF 28 FAVORITE DANCES, BK. 2	STRAUSS, J.
ALBUM OF 28 FAVORITE DANCES, BK. 3	STRAUSS, J.
ALBUM OF 6 CHOICE PIECES	DEBUSSY
ALBUM OF 6 PIECES	POZZOLI
ALBUM OF 6 PIECES	SCRIABINE, A.
ALBUM PER DANIELA, OP. 15	SULPIZI, F.
ALBUM POUR LES TOUT PETITS	STRIMER, J.
ALBUM POUR MES PETITS AMIS, OP. 14	PIERNE
ALBUM ROSE, EASY LITTLE PIECES--COMPLETE	RHENE-BATON
ALBUM ROSE, EASY LITTLE PIECES, NO. 1--PETITE MELODIE	RHENE-BATON
ALBUM ROSE, EASY LITTLE PIECES, NO. 2--BLUETTE	RHENE-BATON
ALBUM ROSE, EASY LITTLE PIECES, NO. 3--INTERMEZZO	RHENE-BATON
ALBUM ROSE, EASY LITTLE PIECES, NO. 4--PETIT CHORAL	RHENE-BATON
ALBUM ROSE, EASY LITTLE PIECES, NO. 5--VIEILLE ROMANCE	RHENE-BATON
ALBUM ROSE, EASY LITTLE PIECES, NO. 6--MUSETTE	RHENE-BATON
ALBUM VIERHANDIGER KLAVIERKOMPOSITIONEN ALTER	DUSSEK, J. *
ALBUM	BRAHMS
ALBUM	CHOPIN

ALBUM	COUPERIN, F.
ALBUM	DEBUSSY
ALBUM	GIBBONS
ALBUM	GOTTSCHALK
ALBUM	GRANADOS
ALBUM	GRIEG
ALBUM	HAYDN
ALBUM	HELLER, S.
ALBUM	LISZT
ALBUM	MENDELSSOHN
ALBUM	MOZART, W. A.
ALBUM	PROKOFIEFF
ALBUM	RACHMANINOFF, S.
ALBUM	RAVEL
ALBUM	ROSSE, F.
ALBUM	RUBINSTEIN
ALBUM	SCHUBERT
ALBUM	STREABBOG
ALBUM	TSCHAIKOWSKY
ALBUM	TSCHAIKOWSKY
ALCESTE -- BALLET MUSIC	GLUCK
ALCESTE BALLET MUSIC FROM OPERA	GLUCK
ALEGRIAS. PASO DOBLE FLAMENCO	VALVERDE, J.
ALFIE	BRIMHALL,
ALGHE	CASTELNUOVO-TEDE
ALHAMBRA	LECUONA
ALHAMBRA	STERN
ALICANTE	WACHS, P.
ALICE, C MAJOR	ASCHER
ALICE AU PAYS DES MERVEILLES	MASSIAS, G.
ALICE BLUE GOWN	LANE, J.--ED.
ALICE BLUE GOWN	
ALICE BLUE GOWN	
ALICE BLUE	GROFE, F.
ALICE BLUE	
ALICE COOPER FOLIO	COOPER, A.
ALICE IN WONDERLAND, BK. 1	LEE, E. M.
ALICE IN WONDERLAND, BK. 2	LEE, E. M.
ALICE IN WONDERLAND -- PIANO PICTURES	MOPPER, I.
ALICE WALTZ	STREABBOG
ALICIA'S DANCE	JEVONS
ALIDA'S DANCE	MILLIGAN
ALIDA'S DANCE	MILLIGAN
ALIES, LES -- VALSE DE SALON --	CHAVAGNAT
ALI DORATE	BECUCCI
ALL-AMERICAN FOLK SONGS, BK. 1	BERMONT, H.--ED
ALL-AMERICAN FOLK SONGS, BK. 2	BERMONT, H.--ED
ALL-IN-ONE BOOGIE WOOGIE	POTTER, H. *
ALL-TIME GOSPEL FAVORITES FOR PIANO	LORENZ, G.--ED.
ALL'ITALIA	BUSONI
ALL' ANTICA - SUITE	RIBARI, A.
ALLAH'S HOLIDAY--''KATINKA''--FOX-TROT	FRIML, R.
ALLAH'S HOLIDAY--''KATINKA''	FRIML, R.
ALLAH'S HOLIDAY--''KATINKA''	FRIML, R.
ALLAH'S HOLIDAY--''KATINKA''	FRIML, R.
ALLAN SMALL PIANO METHOD, THE	SMALL, A.
ALLA FONTANA, OP. 85 NO. 9	SCHUMANN, R.
ALLA INGHARESE --RAGE OVER THE LOST PENNY--, OP. 129	BEETHOVEN
ALLA INGHARESE QUASI UN CAPRICCIO --THE RAGE OVER THE	BEETHOVEN
ALLA SERA	RICHARDS
ALLA TARANTELLA	MACDOWELL
ALLA TARANTELLA	MACDOWELL
ALLA TURCA, A MINOR, FROM THE SONATA IN A	MOZART, W. A.
ALLA TURCA, A MINOR, FROM THE SONATA IN A MINOR	MOZART, W. A.
ALLA TURCA RONDO	MOZART, W. A.
ALLA TURCA	JANKE, G.
ALLEE JONCHEE DE ROSES, L'	GUENIFFEY
ALLEGIANCE TO THE U. S. A.	NIRELLA, D.
ALLEGRETTO, A MINOR, FROM THE SEVENTH SYMPHONY -- EASY	BEETHOVEN
ALLEGRETTO, A MINOR, FROM THE SEVENTH SYMPHONY	BEETHOVEN
ALLEGRETTO, FROM '7TH SYMPHONY IN A MAJOR'	BEETHOVEN
ALLEGRETTO, OP. 72 NO. 3	MENDELSSOHN
ALLEGRETTO AND ALLEGRO IN E FLAT -- SET	MOZART, W. A.
ALLEGRETTO IN B FLAT MAJOR	HAYDN
ALLEGRETTO IN B MINOR--CURWEN EDITION	BEETHOVEN
ALLEGRETTO IN C MINOR	SCHUBERT
ALLEGRETTO IN C	DIABELLI
ALLEGRETTO SCHERZANDO, B FLAT MAJOR, FROM THE EIGHTH	BEETHOVEN
ALLEGRETTO	HAYDN
ALLEGRO, FROM 'TWO PIERROT PIECES'	SCOTT, C.
ALLEGRO, FROM SONATA, OP. 118 NO. 1	SCHUMANN, R.
ALLEGRO, FROM SONATINA IN B FLAT FOR PIANO AND VIOLIN	MOZART, W. A.
ALLEGRO, OP. 8	SCHUMANN, R.
ALLEGRO APPASSIONATO, OP. 4	SCRIABINE, A.
ALLEGRO APPASSIONATO, OP. 70	SAINT-SAENS
ALLEGRO APPASSIONATO, OP. 70	SAINT-SAENS
ALLEGRO ASSAI	MENDELSSOHN
ALLEGRO BARBARO	ALKAN
ALLEGRO BARBARO	BARTOK
ALLEGRO BARBARO	BARTOK
ALLEGRO BRILLANTE	CARSON
ALLEGRO DA CONCERTO	TOSATTI
ALLEGRO DECISO -- FROM ''THE WATER MUSIC'' -- 8-HANDS,	HANDEL
ALLEGRO DE CONCERT	CHARPENTIER, J.
ALLEGRO DE CONCIERTO	GRANADOS
ALLEGRO DE CONCIERTO	GRANADOS
ALLEGRO DI CONCERTO	POZZOLI
ALLEGRO FROM TRIO IN D MINOR	BACH, J.S.
ALLEGRO IN A MAJOR, OP. 88 NO. 3	KUHLAU, F.
ALLEGRO IN B FLAT MAJOR	MOZART, W. A.
ALLEGRO IN C	HANDEL
ALLEGRO IN D MINOR	HANDEL
ALLEGRO IN F MAJOR	MOZART, W. A.
ALLEGRO IN F MINOR	BACH, C.P.E.
ALLEGRO IN F	HAYDN
ALLEGRO IN F	SCARLATTI, D.
ALLEGRO IN G MAJOR, FROM SUITE NO. 14	HANDEL
ALLEGRO IN G MINOR	HANDEL
ALLEGRO IN G MINOR	HANDEL
ALLEGRO SCHERZANDO, OP. 22	SAINT-SAENS
ALLEGRO VITO	BOLCK, O.
ALLEGRO VIVACE	KUHLAU, F.
ALLEGRO	BACH, J.S.
ALLEGRO	COUTURE
ALLEGRO	MONTBRUN, G.
ALLEGRO	TELEMANN, G.P. *
ALLELUIA, OP. 25	ALKAN
ALLELUIA, OP. 25	ALKAN
ALLELUIA DES OISEAUX	MICHEUZ, G.
ALLEMANDES, WALTZES, SONGS	BEETHOVEN
ALLEMANDE IN A MINOR	BACH, J.S.
ALLEMANDE	BEETHOVEN
ALLEMANDE	COUPERIN, F.
ALLERERSTEN KLASSIKER UND ROMANTIKER, DIE -- LITTLE	SCHOLZ--ED
ALLERERSTEN KLASSIKER UND ROMANTIKER, DIE -- 28 EASY	SCHOLZ--ED
ALLERLEI SPIELZEUG	HUMBERT, G.

ALLEY CAT	BRADLEY,
ALLEY TUNES--THREE SCENES FROM THE SOUTH	GUION, D.
ALLEZ-VOUS EN, GO AWAY	
ALL ABOARD, G MAJOR	RICHTER
ALL ABOARD	AARON, M.
ALL ABOUT FUN	BUTLER, J.
ALL ABOUT MUSIC - COMPLETE BOOK OF MUSICAL THEORY	SHELDON
ALL AMERICAN, IN FOUR MOVEMENTS	CHAMBERS, J.
ALL AMERICAN BOOGIE	NEVIN
ALL AMERICAN MEDLEY	NEVIN
ALL AMERICAN MEDLEY	NEVIN
ALL AMERICAN SQUARE DANCES	MULLER
ALL ANTICA - SUITE	RIBARI, A.
ALL BY MYSELF	NOONA, W.
ALL DRESSED UP, D MAJOR	COWELL
ALL HAIL THE POWER	TEMPLETON, S.
ALL IN ONE	KERR, R. N.
ALL I EVER NEED IS YOU	LANE, J.--ED.
ALL I HAVE TO DO IS DREAM	BRYANT
ALL KINDS OF PEOPLE	BRIMHALL,
ALL NIGHT LONG	CLARK, M. E.
ALL OF NOTHING AT ALL	LAWRENCE *
ALL OF YOU	SINGER, L.--ED
ALL ON A CIRCUS DAY	RAEZER, C.
ALL ON ONE PAGE	THOMPSON, J.
ALL ORIGINAL COMPOSITIONS, COMPLETE	BEETHOVEN
ALL ORIGINAL COMPOSITIONS, COMPLETE	MENDELSSOHN
ALL ORIGINAL COMPOSITIONS, COMPLETE	MOZART, W. A.
ALL ORIGINAL COMPOSITIONS	SCHUMANN, R.
ALL ORIGINAL COMPOSITIONS	WEBER, VON
ALL OVER THE KEYBOARD	COBB
ALL THE THINGS YOU ARE -- SHOWCASE	
ALL THE THINGS YOU ARE	
ALL THE THINGS YOU ARE	
ALL THE THINGS YOU ARE	
ALL THE YEAR ROUND	BROOM, P.
ALL TOGETHER NOW	LENNON *
ALL YOU NEED IS LOVE	LENNON *
ALL	OLIVIERO
ALMA ANDALUZA, NO. 1--EN LA FERIA	MARIANI, L. L.
ALMA ANDALUZA, NO. 2--LA MACARENA	MARIANI, L. L.
ALMA ANDALUZA, NO. 3--EL FLORERO	MARIANI, L. L.
ALMA ANDALUZA, NO. 4--ZAPATEADO	MARIANI, L. L.
ALMA ANDALUZA, NO. 5--SERENATA	MARIANI, L. L.
ALMA BRASILEIRA - CHOROS NO. 5	VILLA-LOBOS, H.
ALMA MATER	ADAMS, B.
ALMA MATER	ADAMS, B.
ALMERIA -- FROM IBERIA	ALBENIZ, I.
ALMOST AS TALL	WEYBRIGHT
ALMOST AS TALL	WEYBRIGHT
ALNILAM	VILLA-LOBOS, H.
ALNITAH	VILLA-LOBOS, H.
ALOHA OE, G MAJOR	WOOD, W.
ALOHA OE	LILIUOKALANI
ALONE AT THE PIANO, BK. 1	DIAMOND, D.
ALONE AT THE PIANO, BK. 2	DIAMOND, D.
ALONE AT THE PIANO, BK. 3	DIAMOND, D.
ALONG THE MOHAWK TRAIL	BERMONT, H.
ALONG THE WAY	BRES, D. J.
ALOUETTE, G MAJOR	MOSHER
ALOUETTE	WEYBRIGHT--ED.
ALOUETTE	WEYBRIGHT
ALP-MAID'S DREAM, THE--OP. 45	LABITZKY, A.
ALPENSINFONIE, EINE, OP. 64	STRAUSS, R.
ALPENSINFONIE, EINE, OP. 64	STRAUSS, R.
ALPENSINFONIE, EINE, OP. 64	STRAUSS, R.
ALPHABET, THE--25 VERY EASY STUDIES FOR SMALL	LECOUPPEY, F.
ALPHABET, THE, OP. 17 25 VERY EASY STUDIES	LECOUPPEY, F.
ALPHABET IN MUSIC, AN	STEINBRECHER
ALPHABET SONG, THE	WEYBRIGHT
ALPHABET SONG	WEYBRIGHT--ED.
ALPHABET SONG	WEYBRIGHT--ED.
ALPHABET WALTZ	NEVIN
ALPINE BOOGIE	KENT, A.
ALPINE FLOWER, F MAJOR, OP. 279 NO. 1	BOHM
ALPINE FLOWER	BOHM
ALPINE GLOW	OESTEN
ALPINE HOLIDAY	AARON, M.
ALPINE HUT	LANGE, G.
ALPINE MELODY	BEHR, F.
ALPINE SONG	ROGERS
ALPINE SPINNING WHEEL	REBE
ALPINE WALTZ	VOLZ, H.
ALPINE YODEL, FOLK MELODY	STEINER--ED.
ALPINE YODEL	STEINER
ALSO SPRACH ZARATHUSTRA	BRIMHALL,
ALT-DRESDNER TANZBUCH -- 18 JAHRHUNDERT	HERRMANN--ED
ALT-DRESDNER TANZBUCH --18. JARHUNDERT --	HERRMANN--ED
ALT-NURNBERGER KLAVIERBUCHLEIN -- 17. UND 18. JH. --	HERRMANN--ED
ALT-NURNBERGER KLAVIERBUCHLEIN -- 17 UND 18 JR.	HERRMANN--ED.
ALT-WIEN--FROM TRIAKONTAMERON	GODOWSKY, L.
ALT-WIEN--FROM TRIAKONTAMERON	GODOWSKY, L.
ALT-WIENER TANZBUCHLEIN	KORDA--ED.
ALT-WIENER TANZBUCHLEIN	KORDA--ED.
ALT-WIENER TANZWEISEN, LIEBESFREUD	KREISLER
ALT-WIENER TANZWEISEN, LIEBESLIED	KREISLER
ALT-WIENER TANZWEISEN, SCHON ROSMARIN	KREISLER
ALT-WIENER TANZWEISEN, TRANSKRIPTION -- RACHMANINOFF	KREISLER
ALT-WIENER TANZWEISEN, TRANSKRIPTION -- RACHMANINOFF	KREISLER
ALT-WIEN -- OLD VIENNA -- SET	GODOWSKY, L.
ALTD. WIEGENLIED, OP. 66	RICHARTZ
ALTENGLISCHE KLAVIERMUSIK - 14 STUCKE	ALLWOOD *
ALTENGLISCHE KLAVIERMUSIK	STEVENS--ED.
ALTERNAMENTI -- BALLET --	MIHALOVICI
ALTER REFRAIN -- DU ALTER STEPHANSTURM	KREISLER
ALTE DEUTSCHE VOLKSTANZE	
ALTE DEUTSCHE WEIHNACHTSMUSIK	STEGLICH--ED
ALTE DEUTSCH WEIHNACHTSMUSIK -- 11 CHORALE UND	SCHEIDT *
ALTE ENGLISCHE KONTRATANZE FUR TASTEN-INSTRUMENT	SPECKNER--ED.
ALTE ENGLISCHE KONTRATANZE FUR TASTEN-INSTRUMENT	SPECKNER--ED.
ALTE HAUSMUSIK FUR KLAVIER -- 1550-1780 -- AUS	REHBERG--ED.
ALTE HAUSMUSIK FUR KLAVIER -- 1550-1780 -- AUS	REHBERG--ED.
ALTE HAUSMUSIK FUR KLAVIER -- 1550-1780 AUS	REHBERG--ED.
ALTE HAUSMUSIK FUR KLAVIER -- 1550-1780 AUS	REHBERG--ED.
ALTE LIEDSATZE - 19 VOLKSLIEDSATZE AUS	EHMANN--ED.
ALTE LIEDSATZE	EHMANN--ED.
ALTE PORTUGLESISCHE MEISTER -- BK. 1	KASTNER--ED.
ALTE PORTUGLESISCHE MEISTER -- BK. 2	KASTNER--ED.
ALTE TANZE DES 17. UND 18. JAHRHUNDERTS, 27 STUCKE	CHAMBONNIERES,
ALTE UNNENNB. TAGE OP. 42	HAAS
ALTE WEIHNACHTSMUSIK - 13 WEIHNACHTSCHORALE UND	BOHM *
ALTE WEIHNACHTSMUSIK	BAUM--ED.
ALTITALIENISCHE VERSETTEN IN ALLEN KIRCHENTONARTEN	KASTNER--ED.
ALTITALIENISCHE VERSETTEN IN ALLEN KIRCHENTONARTEN	KASTNER--ED.
ALTRI TEMPI	BALEANI, V.
ALT WIEN NO. 1 WALTZ	CASTELNUOVO-TEDE
ALT WIEN NO. 2 NOCTURNE	CASTELNUOVO-TEDE

ALT WIEN NO. 3 FOX TROT	CASTELNUOVO-TEDE
ALT WIEN	CASTELNUOVO-TEDE
ALT WIEN	CASTELNUOVO-TEDE
AL DI LA	DONIDA
AL DI LA	DONIDA
AL DI LA	DONIDA *
AL FRESCO, OP. 11A	KADOSA
AL FRESCO	HERBERT
AL FRESCO	HERBERT
AL PIE DE LA REJA, OP. 33	MARIANI, L. L.
AMAMI, MAMMA	DE CRESCENZO
AMANCAY	NESCI
AMAPOLA	LACALLE
AMARYLLIS, AIR DE LOUIS XIII	GHYS
AMARYLLIS, GAVOTTE DE LOUIS XIII	GHYS
AMARYLLIS	GHYS
AMARYLLIS	GHYS
AMARYLLIS	GHYS
AMARYLLIS	LOUIS XIII
AMAZING GRACE/HE'S GOT THE WHOLE WORLD IN HIS HANDS	BRIMHALL,
AMAZING GRACE - AND - HE'S GOT THE WHOLE WORLD IN HIS	BRADLEY,
AMAZING GRACE AND OTHER GOSPEL FAVORITES	SANBORN, J.--ED
AMAZING GRACE	
AMAZING GRACE	
AMAZONAS--BRAZILIAN TONE POEM	VILLA-LOBOS, H.
AMBER	SIMON
AMBIANCE	DELACROIX, R.
AMBITIOUS GOOSE, THE	ERB
AMBROSIANISCHES KLAVIERKONZERT	SCHUBERT, H.
AMERI-CONGA, THE	SCHAUM, J.--ED.
AMERICAN ALBUM	RAPHLING
AMERICAN BALLADS AND FOLKSONGS	BAEZ, J.
AMERICAN CAKE WALK	ALLEN, C.
AMERICAN CAROLS IN EASY ARRANGEMENTS -- CAROL OF THE	NILES, J.--ED
AMERICAN CAROLS IN EASY ARRANGEMENTS -- I WONDER AS I	NILES, J.--ED
AMERICAN CAROLS IN EASY ARRANGEMENTS -- JESUS, JESUS,	NILES, J.--ED
AMERICAN CAROLS IN EASY ARRANGEMENTS -- JESUS, THE	NILES, J.--ED
AMERICAN CIVIL WAR BATTLE PIECE -- THE BATTLE OF	BECKEL
AMERICAN COMPOSERS OF THE TWENTIETH CENTURY	SCHAUM, J.--ED.
AMERICAN COMPOSERS OF TODAY	
AMERICAN COUNTRY-DANCES	BURCHENAL, E.
AMERICAN DANCE SUITE	SMITH, J.
AMERICAN EAGLE MARCH	BOEHME
AMERICAN EAGLE MARCH	BOEHME
AMERICAN FAVORITES	SCHAUM, J.
AMERICAN FESTIVAL, BK. 1. PRIMARY --ENLARGED ED.--	
AMERICAN FESTIVAL, BK. 2. EARLY GRADE --ENLARGED ED.--	
AMERICAN FESTIVAL, BK. 4. ADVANCED	
AMERICAN FOLK SONGS FOR PIANO --64 SONGS--	CAZDEN, N.
AMERICAN FOLK SONGS FOR THE YOUNG PIANIST	MATTOS, E.
AMERICAN FOLK SONGS	CUNNINGHAM, M.
AMERICAN FOLK TUNE, AN	STAIRS, L.
AMERICAN INDIAN RHAPSODY	OREM, P. W.
AMERICAN IN PARIS, AN - IN MINIATURE	GERSHWIN
AMERICAN IN PARIS, AN	GERSHWIN
AMERICAN IN PARIS, AN	GERSHWIN
AMERICAN IN VENICE	NEVIN
AMERICAN KALEIDOSCOPE	SIEGMEISTER
AMERICAN MEDLEY	GROBE
AMERICAN MUSIC BY DISTINGUISHED COMPOSERS, BK. 1	FREED--ED.
AMERICAN MUSIC BY DISTINGUISHED COMPOSERS, BK. 2	FREED--ED.
AMERICAN MUSIC FOR THE YOUNG PIANIST	STEINER
AMERICAN PATROL MARCH --SIMPLIFIED--	MEACHAM, F.
AMERICAN PATROL MARCH	MEACHAM, F.
AMERICAN PATROL MARCH	MEACHAM, F.
AMERICAN PATROL MARCH	MEACHAM, F.
AMERICAN PATROL MARCH	MEACHAM, F.
AMERICAN PATROL MARCH	MEACHAM, F.
AMERICAN PATROL	MEACHAM, F.
AMERICAN PATROL	MEACHAM, F.
AMERICAN PATROL	MEACHAM, F.
AMERICAN PATROL	MEACHAM, F.
AMERICAN PATROL	MEACHAM, F.
AMERICAN PATROL	MEACHAM, F.
AMERICAN PATROL	ZEPP--ED
AMERICAN PIE	LANE, J.--ED.
AMERICAN PIE	MCLEAN, D.
AMERICAN RHAPSODIE	HAUBIEL, C.
AMERICAN RHAPSODY	WHITFORD
AMERICAN SONATINAS	SCHAUM, J.--ED.
AMERICAN SONGS, BK. 1	MUCZYNSKI,
AMERICAN SONGS, BK. 1	MUCZYNSKI,
AMERICAN SONGS, BK. 1	MUCZYNSKI,
AMERICAN SONGS, BK. 2	MUCZYNSKI,
AMERICAN SYMPHONETTE NO. 1 -- FIRST MOV'T	GOULD, M.
AMERICAN SYMPHONETTE NO. 1 -- THIRD MOV'T	GOULD, M.
AMERICAN SYMPHONETTE NO. 2 -- FIRST MOV'T	GOULD, M.
AMERICAN SYMPHONETTE NO. 2 -- THIRD MOV'T	GOULD, M.
AMERICAN SYMPHONETTE NO. 3 -- FIRST MOV'T	GOULD, M.
AMERICAN TRAVELER -- FOLK SONGS WITH WORDS	WESTERVELT,
AMERICAN WALTZ FOR PIANO SOLO	HEMMER, E.
AMERICAN WALTZ	DE ROSE, P.
AMERICAN YOUTH CONCERTO	BAUER, M.
AMERICAN YOUTH CONCERTO	BAUER, M.
AMERICA FIRST	ROLFE, W.
AMERICA THE BEAUTIFUL	WALLIS
AMERICA THE BEAUTIFUL	WARD, S. A.
AMERICA THE BEAUTIFUL	WARD
AMERICA	CAREY, H.
AMERICA	SPENCER, J.
AMERIKANISCHE WALDIDYLLEN OP. 51	MACDOWELL
AMES D'ENFANTS	CRAS
AMES D'ENFANTS	CRAS
AMICO FRITZ, L' - CHERRY DUET	MASCAGNI, P.
AMICO FRITZ, L' - INTERMEZZO -- FINGERED --	MASCAGNI, P.
AMICO FRITZ, L' - INTERMEZZO -- ORIGINAL --	MASCAGNI, P.
AMICO FRITZ, L' - INTERMEZZO	MASCAGNI, P.
AMID THE TULIPS	EWING, M.
AMMERSEE-SUITE, OP. 85	TRUNK, R.
AMONG MY SOUVENIRS	SINGER, L.--ED
AMORES. TWO PIECES FOR PREPARED PIANO --AND TWO	CAGE
AMOROSA	LECUONA
AMOR Y LA MUERTE, EL. LOS MAJOS ENAMORADOS -- NOS. 5	GRANADOS
AMOS	SUDDAROS
AMOUREUSE - WALTZ	BERGER
AMOUREUSE	BERGER
AMOURS DE JUPITER, LES -- BALLET --	IBERT
AMOUR COQUET	FRIML, R.
AMOUR ET PRINTEMPS	WALDTEUFEL, E.
AMUSANTE HISTOIRE, L'	PESSE
AMUSEMENT PARK - EASY SUITE	RAPHLING
AMUSEMENT PARK - SUITE	RAPHLING
AMUSETTE, POLKA MAZURKA	D'ORSO
AM ABEND, OP. 39	FIBICH, Z.
AM I LOSING YOU	BRADLEY,

AM MEERESSTRAND. KONZERTETUDE, OP. 17	SMETANA
AM RHEIN BEIM WEIN	LUTZ--ED
AM WEIHNACHTSABEND, OP. 43	HEINS, C.
ANADOLU DAN	SAYGUN, A.
ANASTASIA	WILLIAMS,
ANCHORED, MARCH	FOLSOM
ANCHORS AWEIGH	LANE, J.--ED.
ANCHORS AWEIGH	MILES *
ANCHORS AWEIGH	
ANCHORS AWEIGH	
ANCIENT AYRE - GREENSLEEVES	MELVIN, B.--ED
ANCIENT BALLAD	HULL, A.
ANCIENT CHARIOT RACE	STEINER
ANCIENT CHARIOT RACE	STEINER
ANCIENT CHINA, OP. 62	NIEMANN
ANCIENT DANCE, AN	READ, G.
ANCIENT DANCES, BK. 1	DOROLLE, A.
ANCIENT DANCES, BK. 2	DOROLLE, A.
ANCIENT DANCES AND AIRS - SELECTIONS FROM SUITES 1 AND	RESPIGHI
ANCIENT ITALIAN MASTERS, BK. 1 - FRESCOBALDI, GRIECO,	VITALI--ED.
ANCIENT ITALIAN MASTERS, BK. 2 - RUTINI, DURANTE,	VITALI--ED.
ANCIENT TO MODERN	SACCO
ANDALOUSE, OP. 20	PESSARD
ANDALOUSE	PESSARD
ANDALUCIA. SUITE -- VOL. 1	FONT Y DE ANTA
ANDALUCIA. SUITE -- VOL. 2	FONT Y DE ANTA
ANDALUCIA. SUITE -- VOL. 3	FONT Y DE ANTA
ANDALUCIA SUITE	LECUONA
ANDALUCIA	LECUONA
ANDALUCIA	LECUONA
ANDALUCIA	LECUONA
ANDALUCIA	LECUONA
ANDALUCIA	LECUONA
ANDALUSIAN DANCE	ROWLEY
ANDALUSIAN SERENADE - FROM SEVEN FLOWERS FROM A	GIASSON, P.
ANDALUSIAN SERENADE	GIASSON, P.
ANDALUZA FROM 'DANZAS ESPANOLAS'	GRANADOS
ANDALUZA FROM PIECES ESPAGNOLES	FALLA, M. DE
ANDANTE--FROM THE EIGHTH QUARTET--	MOZART, W. A. *
ANDANTE, HORNPIPE	HANDEL
ANDANTE, OP. 59	CHAMINADE
ANDANTE --FROM THE FIFTH SYMPHONY--	TSCHAIKOWSKY
ANDANTE AND ALLEGRO CON FUOCO	FANO, G. A.
ANDANTE AND MINUET, FROM SONATINA IN F FOR PIANO AND	MOZART, W. A.
ANDANTE AND RONDO CAPRICCIOSO, OP. 14	MENDELSSOHN
ANDANTE AND RONDO CAPRICCIOSO	MENDELSSOHN
ANDANTE AND SCHERZO - NO. 2 FROM SUITE FOR PIANO	KOCH, J.
ANDANTE AND SCHERZO FROM CONCERTO, OP. 59. ABRIDGED	MOSZKOWSKI
ANDANTE AND SCHERZO	KOCH, J.
ANDANTE AND VARIATIONS, OP. 46	SCHUMANN, R.
ANDANTE AND VARIATIONS IN B FLAT, OP. 46	SCHUMANN, R.
ANDANTE CANTABILE, EXCERPT	TSCHAIKOWSKY
ANDANTE CANTABILE, VIOLIN CONCERTO	MENDELSSOHN
ANDANTE CANTABILE IN B FLAT--FROM THE STRING QUARTET,	TSCHAIKOWSKY
ANDANTE CON VARIAZIONI, K501	MOZART, W. A.
ANDANTE CON VARIAZIONI IN F MINOR	HAYDN
ANDANTE CON VARIAZIONI	WEBER, VON
ANDANTE F-DUR	BEETHOVEN
ANDANTE FAVORI IN F	BEETHOVEN
ANDANTE FESTIVO	SIBELIUS
ANDANTE FINALE DE 'LUCIA DI LAMMERMOOR'--FOR THE LEFT	LESCHETIZKY
ANDANTE FINALE DE LUCIA DI LA MMERMOOR --DONIZETTI OP.	THALBERG
ANDANTE FINALE FROM ''LUCIA DI LAMMERMOOR''--FOR LEFT	DONIZETTI
ANDANTE FOR A SMALL MECHANICAL ORGAN, K616	MOZART, W. A.
ANDANTE FROM ''SURPRISE'' SYMPHONY IN G MAJOR	HAYDN
ANDANTE FROM SONATA NO. 15	MOZART, W. A.
ANDANTE FROM SYMPHONY NO. 39	MOZART, W. A.
ANDANTE FROM THE ''SURPRISE'' SYMPHONY -- TRANSCRIBED	HAYDN
ANDANTE FUNEBRE	OLSEN, S.
ANDANTE IN F MAJOR	BEETHOVEN
ANDANTE	COUTURE
ANDANTINO, K236	MOZART, W. A.
ANDANTINO AND ALLEGRO	ROSSI, M. A.
ANDANTINO FROM CONCERTO IN D MINOR	THOMPSON, J.
ANDANTINO FROM PIANO CONCERTO K271	MOZART, W. A.
ANDANTINO IM STILE VON P. MARTINI	KREISLER
ANDANTINO IN D FLAT -- SIMP.	LEMARE, E.
ANDANTINO	LEMARE, E.
ANDANTINO	LEMARE, E.
ANDANTINO	LEMARE, E.
ANDREA CHENIER - MADDALENA'S ARIA	GIORDANO
ANDREA CHENIER SELECTIONS, BK. 1	GIORDANO
ANDREA CHENIER SELECTIONS, BK. 2	GIORDANO
AND AWAY WE GO	DITTENHAVER
AND AWAY WE GO	MERKUR
AND THE BAND PLAYED ON	RICHTER, A.
AND WITH HIS STRIPES WE ARE HEALED -- MESSIAH CHORUS	HANDEL
ANFANGERSTUCKE	TUERK
ANGEL'S DREAM, OP. 44	LUDOVIC, G.
ANGEL'S DREAM	D'ORSO
ANGEL'S DREAM	LANGE, G.
ANGEL'S SERENADE, THE	BRAGA
ANGEL'S SERENADE	BRAGA
ANGEL'S SERENADE	BRAGA
ANGEL'S SERENADE	BRAGA
ANGEL'S SERENADE	SMITH
ANGELICA	DONENFELD, J.
ANGELINA, NOCTURNE	GREENWALD, M.
ANGELS WE HAVE HEARD ON HIGH	EDWARDS, C.
ANGELUS, THE	GODARD, C.
ANGELUS, THE	MOYER, E.
ANGEL CHIMES -- EASY INTER.	BRITAIN
ANGEL OF LOVE, WALTZES	WALDTEUFEL, E.
ANGEL VOICES EVER NEAR	SWEET, A.
ANIMAL ALPHABET	HOLMES *
ANIMAL CHARACTERS	LONGMIRE
ANIMAL CRACKERS WALTZ	ROLFE, W.
ANIMAL CRACKERS	STAIRS, L.
ANIMAL LAND -- SQUIRRELS, LITTLE MOUNTAIN BURRO,	RICKER, E.
ANIMAL PARADE	STEVENS, E.
ANIMATIONS	KURTZ, E.
ANIMAUX MODELES, LES -- BALLET IN ONE ACT	POULENC, F.
ANIME SEMPLICE - 6 PROFILES, OP. 143	MONTANARO
ANITRA'S DANCE, PEER GYNT	GRIEG
ANITRA'S DANCE --PEER GYNT SUITE NO.1--	GRIEG
ANITRA'S DANCE -- FROM PEER GYNT SUITE	GRIEG
ANITRA'S DANCE FROM 'FIRST PEER GYNT SUITE'	GRIEG
ANITRA'S DANCE FROM THE PEER GYNT SUITE, OP. 46	GRIEG
ANITRA'S DANCE	GRIEG
ANITRA'S DANCE	GRIEG
ANLEITUNG ZUR IMPROVISATION FUR KLAVIER	COPPIETERS, F.
ANNA MAGDALENA BACH'S MUSIC BOOK--20 PIECES--	BACH, J.S.
ANNA MAGDALENA BACH'S MUSIC BOOK, COMPLETE, URTEXT.	BACH, J.S.
ANNA MAGDALENA BACH'S MUSIC BOOK -- URTEXT --	BACH, J.S.
ANNA	GIORDANO *
ANNE-MARIE'S PIANO BOOK -- 4 EASY PIECES FOUNDED ON	TAYLOR, C.
ANNEES DE PELERINAGE--DEUXIEME ANNEE 'ITALIE'	LISZT

Title	Composer
ANNEES OF PELERINAGE--PREMIERE ANNEE 'SUISSE'	LISZT
ANNEES DE PELERINAGE, 1ST YEAR, SWITZERLAND - AU BORD	LISZT
ANNEES DE PELERINAGE, 1ST YEAR, SWITZERLAND - CHAPELLE	LISZT
ANNEES DE PELERINAGE, 1ST YEAR, SWITZERLAND - CLOCHES	LISZT
ANNEES DE PELERINAGE, 1ST YEAR, SWITZERLAND - EGLOGUE	LISZT
ANNEES DE PELERINAGE, 2ND YEAR, ITALY - GONDOLIERA	LISZT
ANNEES DE PELERINAGE, 2ND YEAR, ITALY - SONETTI DEL	LISZT
ANNEES DE PELERINAGE, 2ND YEAR, ITALY - SPOSALIZIO	LISZT
ANNEES DE PELERINAGE, 2ND YEAR, ITALY - SUPPLEMENT,	LISZT
ANNEES DE PELERINAGE, 3RD YEAR - BALLADE NO. 1	LISZT
ANNEES DE PELERINAGE, 3RD YEAR - JEUX D'EAUX A LA	LISZT
ANNEES DE PELERINAGE, 3RD YEAR - 6 CONSOLATIONS	LISZT
ANNEES DE PELERINAGE -- AU BORD D'UNE SOURCE	LISZT
ANNEES DE PELERINAGE -- LES JEUX D'EAUX A LA VILLA	LISZT
ANNEES DE PELERINAGE	LISZT
ANNEN POLKA	STRAUSS, J.
ANNIE LAURIE, TRANS.	GROOMS
ANNIE LAURIE	SPENCER, J.
ANNIVERSAIRE	FOURDRAIN
ANNIVERSARY SONG	BRYANT--ED.
ANNIVERSARY SONG	JOLSON *
ANNIVERSARY TOCCATA	KOCH, F.
ANORANZA -- NO. 1, FROM SIX PIECES ON SPANISH FOLK	GRANADOS
ANOTHER DUET BOOK	WEYBRIGHT
ANOUREUSE	BERGER
ANSON INTRODUCES BACH - DANCE FORMS FROM THE SUITES	BACH, J.S.
ANSON INTRODUCES BACH - SELECTIONS FROM THE ANNA	BACH, J.S.
ANSON INTRODUCES BACH - THE PIANO PARTNER	BACH, J.S.
ANSON INTRODUCES BACH - TWELVE LITTLE PRELUDES	BACH, J.S.
ANSON INTRODUCES BARTOK, BK. 1	BARTOK
ANSON INTRODUCES BARTOK, BK. 2	BARTOK
ANSON INTRODUCES CHOPIN	CHOPIN
ANSON INTRODUCES GRIEG, BK. 1	GRIEG
ANSON INTRODUCES HANDEL, BK. 1	HANDEL
ANSON INTRODUCES HANDEL, BK. 2	HANDEL
ANSON INTRODUCES KABALEVSKY, BK. 1	KABALEVSKY
ANSON INTRODUCES KABALEVSKY, BK. 2	KABALEVSKY
ANSON INTRODUCES LISZT	LISZT
ANSON INTRODUCES MOZART, BK. 1	MOZART, W. A.
ANSON INTRODUCES REBIKOV, BK. 1	REBIKOV
ANSON INTRODUCES SCARLATTI, BK. 1	SCARLATTI, D.
ANSON INTRODUCES SCARLATTI, BK. 2	SCARLATTI, D.
ANSON INTRODUCES SCHUMANN, BK. 1	SCHUMANN, R.
ANSON INTRODUCES THE SONATA SAMPLER, BK. 1	ANSON, G.--ED
ANSON INTRODUCES THE SONATA SAMPLER, BK. 2	ANSON, G.--ED
ANSON INTRODUCES THE SONATA SAMPLER, BK. 3	ANSON, G.--ED
ANSWER TO THE PRAYER	LEWIS *
ANSWER	ROBYN
ANTELOPE ANTICS	VOLZ, H.
ANTE EL ESCORIAL	LECUONA
ANTE EL ESCORIAL	LECUONA
ANTE EL ESCORIAL	LECUONA
ANTHOLOGY, VOL. 1‡ 33 PIECES	FERTE--ED
ANTHOLOGY, VOL. 2. 20 PIECES FOR HARPSICHORD	FERTE--ED
ANTHOLOGY, VOL. 3‡ 16 PIECES FOR HARPSICHORD	FERTE--ED
ANTHOLOGY, VOL. 4‡ 15 PIECES BY MOZART AND BEETHOVEN	BEETHOVEN *
ANTHOLOGY, VOL. 5‡ 14 PIECES BY CRAMER, HUMMEL, ET AL.	CRAMER, J. *
ANTHOLOGY, VOL. 6‡ 26 PIECES BY ROMANTIC COMPOSERS	FERTE--ED
ANTHOLOGY OF ANCIENT AND MODERN MUSIC, BK. 1 - MASTERS	TAGLIAPIETRA, G.
ANTHOLOGY OF ANCIENT AND MODERN MUSIC, BK. 2 - MASTERS	TAGLIAPIETRA, G.
ANTHOLOGY OF EASY AND PROGRESSIVE EXERCISES AND PIECES	DE ANGELIS
ANTHOLOGY OF PIANO MUSIC, BK. 1 THE BAROQUE PERIOD	AGAY, D.--ED
ANTHOLOGY OF PIANO MUSIC, BK. 2 THE CLASSICAL PERIOD	AGAY, D.--ED
ANTHOLOGY OF PIANO MUSIC, BK. 3 THE ROMANTIC PERIOD	AGAY, D.--ED
ANTHOLOGY OF PIANO MUSIC, BK. 4 THE TWENTIETH CENTURY	AGAY, D.--ED
ANTI-ABOLITIONIST RIOTS	IVES, C.
ANTICHI AUTORI BOLOGNESI, BK. 1	PICCIOLI
ANTICHI AUTORI BOLOGNESI, BK. 2	PICCIOLI
ANTIGUA VALLADOLID	BERNAL, J.
ANTIQUE SNUFFBOX, THE	MCGRAW
ANTIQUE SNUFFBOX, THE	MCGRAW
ANTIQUE	WILSON, M.
ANTOLOGIA DI CLAVICEMBALISTI ITALIANI, BK. 1	MONTANARI--ED *
ANTOLOGIA DI CLAVICEMBALISTI ITALIANI, BK. 2	MONTANARI--ED *
ANTOLOGIA PIANISTICA	CASELLA, A.
ANTONY AND CLEOPATRA THEME	NORTH, A.
ANVIL CHORUS FROM 'IL TROVATORE'	VERDI
ANXIOUS TULIP, THE	STAIRS, L.
ANYONE CAN PLAY PIANO	BERMONT, H.
ANY TIME	LANE, J.--ED.
AN DEN FRUEHLING, EASY	GRIEG
AN DEN FRUEHLING -- TO SPRING	GRIEG
AN DEN MOND	SCHUBERT
AN WASSERFLUSSEN BABYLON -- BY THE WATERS OF BABYLON	BACH, J.S.
APACHE DANCE	KEVAN
APACHE DANCE	OFFENBACH
APACHE INDIAN DANCE	SCHAUM, J.--ED.
APARICION	GRANADOS
APERCUS DESAGREABLES	SATIE, E.
APHORISMEN. TWELVE PIECES	BAUR
APHORISMEN, OP. 7	DRIESSLER
APHORISMS - TEN PIECES FOR PIANO, OP. 13	SHOSTAKOVITCH
APOLLON MUSAGETE	STRAVINSKY, I.
APOLLO ETUDE	RUBINSTEIN
APOSTROPHE ET SIX REFLECTIONS	POUSSEUR, H.
APPALACHIAN DANCE	NORDOFF, P.
APPALACHIAN REVERIE	DITTENHAVER
APPALACHIAN SONG	MCGRAW
APPALACHIA	WORK
APPLAUSE	BRIMHALL,
APPLES AND BANANAS	
APPLE BLOSSOMS	BARILI, E. C.
APPROACH TO MUSIC, BK. 1	MATTHAY, T. *
APPROACH TO MUSIC, BK. 4	MATTHAY, T. *
APPROACH TO MUSIC, BK. 5	MATTHAY, T. *
APPROACH TO MUSIC, BK. 6	MATTHAY, T. *
APPROACH TO MUSIC, BK. 7	MATTHAY, T. *
APRES LA CLASSE	MARTIN, R. C.
APRES LA MOISSON -- TWO RUSTIC SKETCHES --	LANDRY
APRES LA MOISSON	LANDRY
APRES LA MOISSON	LANDRY
APRES LES DEVOIRS	MARTIN, R. C.
APRES LE BAL	WALTER
APRES UNE LECTURE DU DANTE	LISZT
APRIL DAYS	THORNTON
APRIL ENCHANTMENT	LANE, J.
APRIL FLOWERS	STEVENS, M.
APRIL HEYDAY	QUINCKE, W.
APRIL IN PARIS	DUKE
APRIL IN PARIS	DUKE
APRIL IN PORTUGAL	SINGER, L.--ED
APRIL IN PORTUGAL	
APRIL LOVE	FAIN *
APRIL LOVE	LANE, J.--ED.
APRIL MOOD	KING, S.
APRIL RAIN -- LARGE NOTES	LAKE
APRIL SHOWERS	SILVERS
APRIL SHOWERS	SILVERS
APRIL SMILES, WALTZ, OP. 11	DEPRET, M.
APRIL	EZELL, H.
AQUARELLEN OP. 25, ST.-V.S. 38	REGER
AQUARELLES, OP. 19	GADE, N.
AQUARELLES	ROWLEY
AQUARIUS	LANE, J.--ED.
ARABESKE OP. 18	SCHUMANN, R.
ARABESKE	MACDOWELL
ARABESQUE, OP. 17 NO. 1	GILBERT, G. V.
ARABESQUE, OP. 18, BLUMENSTUCK, OP. 19, THREE	SCHUMANN, R.
ARABESQUE, OP. 18	SCHUMANN, R.
ARABESQUE, OP. 18	SCHUMANN, R.
ARABESQUE, OP. 18	SCHUMANN, R.
ARABESQUE, OP. 18	SCHUMANN, R.
ARABESQUE, OP. 18	SCHUMANN, R.
ARABESQUE, OP. 18	SCHUMANN, R.
ARABESQUES, BLUMENSTUCKE, OP. 18/19 -- COMPLETE	SCHUMANN, R.
ARABESQUES, OP. 150 -- TEN EASY MINIATURES	GRETCHANINOFF
ARABESQUES, OP. 42	ORNSTEIN, L.
ARABESQUES NOS. 1 AND 2	DEBUSSY
ARABESQUES	MAMEN, C.
ARABESQUE EN FORME D'ETUDE, OP. 45 NO. 1	LESCHETIZKY
ARABESQUE IN C, OP. 18	SCHUMANN, R.
ARABESQUE NO. 1	DEBUSSY
ARABESQUE NO. 1	DEBUSSY
ARABESQUE NO. 1	DEBUSSY
ARABESQUE NO. 1	DEBUSSY
ARABESQUE NO. 2	DEBUSSY
ARABESQUE NO. 2	DEBUSSY
ARABESQUE NO. 2	DEBUSSY
ARABESQUE NO. 2	DEBUSSY
ARABESQUE NOS. 1 AND 2	DEBUSSY
ARABESQUE	BUTLER, J.
ARABESQUE	DRIVER, P.
ARABESQUE	GUERRINI, G.
ARABESQUE	PASQUET, J.
ARABESQUE	RIETI
ARABIAN CAMPFIRE	MCHALE, M.
ARABIAN DANCE, FROM ''THE NUTCRACKER SUITE''	TSCHAIKOWSKY
ARABIAN DANCE, OP. 55 NO. 2 --PEER GYNT SUITE NO. 2--	GRIEG
ARABIAN DANCE --PEER GYNT SUITE NO.2--	GRIEG
ARABIAN DANCE	SCHER, W.
ARABIAN NIGHT--ROMANCE	MILDENBERG, A.
ARAB DANCE, G MINOR FROM NUTCRACKER SUITE	TSCHAIKOWSKY
ARAB DANCE FROM 'NUTCRACKER SUITE'	TSCHAIKOWSKY
ARAB DANCE	CARRE
ARAB DANCE	CARRE
ARAB HORSEMEN, THE	COBB
ARAB RIDERS	EZELL, H.
ARAGON. FANTASIA -- NO. 6, FROM SUITE ESPANOLA NO. 1	ALBENIZ, I.
ARAGONAISE--FROM THE BALLET 'LE CID'	MASSENET, J.
ARAGONAISE, FROM LE CID	MASSENET, J.
ARAGONAISE, LE CID	MASSENET, J.
ARAGONAISE, LE CID	MASSENET, J.
ARAGONAISE, VALSE	THOME, F.
ARAGONAISE -- FROM THE BALLET-MUSIC FROM ''LE CID''	MASSENET, J.
ARAGONAISE 'LE CID'	MASSENET, J.
ARAGONAISE	MASSENET, J.
ARAGONAISE	MASSENET, J.
ARAGONESA FROM PIECES ESPAGNOLES	FALLA, M. DE
ARAGONESA	LECUONA
ARAGON -- FROM SUITE ESPANOLA NO. 1	ALBENIZ, I.
ARAGON	LECUONA
ARAGON	LONGAS
ARAGON	LONGAS
ARAGON	LONGAS
ARBEITSBUCH FUR KLEINE KLAVIERSPIELER - 23	VOLKART-SCHLAGER
ARBUTUS -- INTERMEZZO	DAVIS, M.
ARBUTUS -- INTERMEZZO	DAVIS, M.
ARBUTUS	BLISS, P.
ARCADIA - HEFT 04, ZEHN KLEINE STUCKE	BADINGS
ARCADIA - HEFT 05, ZEHN KLEINE STUCKE	BADINGS
ARCA DI NOE, L' - 1. CAPRICCIO DEL CUCU	MONTANI
ARCA DI NOE, L' - 2. IN MORTE DI UNA CUCCIOLA	MONTANI
ARCA DI NOE, L' - 3. QUEL ROSIGNUOL CHE SI SOAVE	MONTANI
ARCHIPEL IV	BOUCOURECHLIEV
AREN'T YOU GLAD YOU'RE YOU	
ARENSKY WALTZ, THE	ARENSKY, A.
ARENSKY WALTZ, THE	ARENSKY, A.
ARE YOU LONESOME TONIGHT	BRADLEY
ARGENTINE NATIONAL AIRS, OP. 17 - BK. 1	AGUIRRE
ARGENTINE NATIONAL AIRS, OP. 17 - BK. 2	AGUIRRE
ARGONAISE	MASSENET, J.
ARGUMENT OF THE KATYDIDS	PHOENIX
ARIADNE MUSICA --PRELUDES AND FUGUES FOR PIANO OR	FISCHER, H.
ARIA AND TOCCATA	DELLO JOIO, N.
ARIA CON VARIAZIONE IN A MINOR	BACH, J.S.
ARIA CON VARIAZIONI--HARMONIOUS BLACKSMITH	HANDEL
ARIA CON VARIAZIONI	DE ANGELIS
ARIA FROM 'SONATA IN A MINOR'	BACH, J.S.
ARIA MIT VARIATIONEN --BRAHMS-VARIATIONEN--	HANDEL
ARIA VARIATA A LA MANIERA ITALIANA	BACH, J.S.
ARIA VARIATA IN A MINOR, ALLE MANIERA ITALIANA	BACH, J.S.
ARIA	BACH, W.F.
ARIA	PAPINEAU-COUTURE
ARIA	PEERSON, C.
ARIEL, OP. 151 -- SCHERZO VALSE	KERN, C. W.
ARIEL	GILLOCK
ARIEL	GILLOCK
ARIETTA CON VARIAZIONI -- HOBOKEN 17-2	HAYDN
ARIETTA DI BALLETTO--GLUCK	JOSEFFY, R.
ARIETTA IN C	BACH, J.S.
ARIETTA	ANDERSON, L.
ARIETTA	BACH, J.S.
ARIOSA	LEWIS, E.
ARIOSI FUR SOPRAN, VIOLINE UND GRISSES ORCHESTER,	HENZE, H.
ARIOSO --FROM THE CANTATA NO. 156--	BACH, J.S.
ARIOSO IN G	BACH, J.S.
ARIOSO	BACH, J.S.
ARIOSO	BACH, J.S.
ARIOSO	BACH, J.S.
ARIOSO	BACH, J.S.
ARIOSO	ROCHBERG, G.
ARIZONA SUITE	THOMPSON, J.
ARKANSAS FIDDLER	MOSSMAN, T.
ARKANSAS TRAVELER--OLD FIDDLER'S BREAKDOWN	GUION, D.
ARKANSAS TRAVELER, THE -- OLD FIDDLER'S TUNE, FREELY	PATTISON
ARKANSAS TRAVELER, THE	ZEPP--ED
ARKANSAS TRAVELER	DUNGAN
ARKANSAS TRAVELER	SCARMOLIN
ARLEQUIN ET PANTALON	DUBOIS, P. M.
ARLEQUIN	BERNHEIM

Title	Composer
ARLESIANA, L' - LAMENTO DI FEDERICO	CILEA
ARLESIENNE SUITE, INTERMEZZO	BIZET, G.
ARLESIENNE SUITE NOS. 1 AND 2	BIZET, G.
ARMEN'S VARIATION	KHATCHATURIAN
ARMENIA	MALIPIERO, G. F.
ARMENIA	MALIPIERO, G. F.
AROUND THE BEEHIVE	WERMEL
AROUND THE CAMPFIRE	ROBERTS
AROUND THE CLOCK	FULEIHAN, A.
AROUND THE KEYS AGAIN	COBB
AROUND THE KEYS	COBB
AROUND THE MAYPOLE	KOLINSKY
AROUND THE MULBERRY BUSH	WEYBRIGHT--ED.
AROUND THE MULBERRY BUSH	WEYBRIGHT
AROUND THE WORLD IN ALL KEYS	SCHAUM, J.
AROUND THE WORLD	BRIMHALL
ARPEGGIETTO	ECKSTEIN
ARPEGGIOS AND PIECES IN ALL KEYS, BK. 1	SCHAUM, J.--ED.
ARPEGGIOS AND PIECES IN ALL KEYS, BK. 1	SCHAUM, J.--ED.
ARPEGGIOS AND PIECES IN ALL KEYS, BK. 2	SCHAUM, J.--ED.
ARPEGGIOS AND PIECES IN ALL KEYS, BK. 2	SCHAUM, J.--ED.
ARPEGGIO ETUDES - D1	WARD, J.
ARPEGGIO ETUDES - D2	WARD, J.
ARPEGGIO ETUDES - D3	WARD, J.
ARPEGGIO ETUDES - D4	WARD, J.
ARPEGGIO PIANO SOLOS	SMALL, A.
ARPEGGIO WALTZ	ROLSETH, B.
ARPEGGI CONSONANTI E DISSONANTI	SCHININA, L.
ARRIVAL OF THE BROWNIES	ANTHONY, B. R.
ARRIVAL OF THE FRIENDS	LICHNER, P.
ARRIVAL OF THE QUEEN OF SHEBA, FROM 'SOLOMON'. CONCERT	HANDEL
ARRIVAL OF THE QUEEN OF SHEBA, FROM 'SOLOMON'	HANDEL
ARRIVAL OF THE QUEEN OF SHEBA	HANDEL
ARRIVAL OF THE QUEEN OF SHEBA	HANDEL
ARRIVEDERCI, ROMA	LANE, J.--ED.
ARRIVEDERCI, ROMA	WILLIAMS,
ARRORO	CASTRO, W.
ARRULLO	UGARTE
ARTE NATIVO ARGENTINO, BK. 01	CHAZARRETA, A.
ARTE NATIVO ARGENTINO, BK. 02	CHAZARRETA, A.
ARTE NATIVO ARGENTINO, BK. 03	CHAZARRETA, A.
ARTE NATIVO ARGENTINO, BK. 04	CHAZARRETA, A.
ARTE NATIVO ARGENTINO, BK. 09	CHAZARRETA, A.
ARTE NATIVO ARGENTINO, BK. 10	CHAZARRETA, A.
ARTE NATIVO ARGENTINO, BK. 11	HOVHANESS, A.
ARTINIS	STRAUSS, J.
ARTIST'S LIFE, OP. 316	STRAUSS, J.
ARTIST'S LIFE, OP. 316	STRAUSS, J.
ARTIST'S LIFE	STRAUSS, J.
ARTIST'S LIFE	STRAUSS, J.
ARTIST'S LIFE	STRAUSS, J.
ARTIST'S LIFE	STRAUSS, J.
ARTISTRY IN JAZZ --MODERN RHYTHMIC CLASSICS--	WHITFORD
ARTISTS'S LIFE	STRAUSS, J.
ARTISTS' LIFE--WALTZ, OP. 316	STRAUSS, J.
ART OF FINGERING IN PIANO PLAYING, THE	MUSAFIA
ART OF FINGER DEVELOPMENT, OP. 740 --COMPLETE	CZERNY
ART OF FINGER DEXTERITY, OP. 740. SELECTION OF 14	CZERNY
ART OF FINGER DEXTERITY, OP. 740--50 STUDIES IN	CZERNY
ART OF FINGER DEXTERITY, OP. 740--50 STUDIES IN	CZERNY
ART OF FINGER DEXTERITY, OP. 740--50 STUDIES IN	CZERNY
ART OF FINGER DEXTERITY, OP. 740--50 STUDIES IN	CZERNY
ART OF FINGER DEXTERITY, OP. 740--50 STUDIES IN	CZERNY
ART OF FINGER DEXTERITY, OP. 740--50 STUDIES IN	CZERNY
ART OF FINGER DEXTERITY, OP. 740	CZERNY
ART OF FINGER DEXTERITY --KUNST DER	CZERNY
ART OF FINGER DEXTERITY --KUNST DER	CZERNY
ART OF MODULATION, THE	SALZEDO, C. *
ART OF MUSIC FOR THE ADULT BEGINNER, THE	ROSEMOND, G.
ART OF PHRASING, THE--26 MELODIOUS STUDIES, OP.	HELLER, S.
ART OF PHRASING, THE--26 MELODIOUS STUDIES, OP.	HELLER, S.
ART OF PHRASING, THE, OP. 16	HELLER, S.
ART OF PHRASING	STEINER
ART OF PLAYING THE HARPSICHORD, THE -- L'ART DE	COUPERIN, F.
ART OF ROCK	GORDON
ART OF SCALES‡ TWENTY-FOUR PRELUDES	STRAVINSKY, S.
ART OF SCALES, 24 PRELUDES	STRAVINSKY, S.
ART OF THE FUGUE, THE	BACH, J.S.
ART OF THE FUGUE, THE	BACH, J.S.
ART OF THE FUGUE	BACH, J.
ART OF THE FUGUE	BACH, J.S.
ART OF THE SUITE	PESSI
ART TATUM IMPROVISATIONS, NO. 2	TATUM, A.
ASE'S DEATH, OP. 46 NO. 2	GRIEG
ASE'S DEATH --PEER GYNT SUITE NO.1--	GRIEG
ASE'S DEATH FROM THE PEER GYNT SUITE, OP. 46	GRIEG
ASH GROVE, THE	SHAW, C.
ASH GROVE, THE	WATSON
ASH GROVE	OLSON--ED.
ASK THE MOON, REVERIE	HOPKINS, H.
ASLEEP IN THE DEEP	PETRIE
ASOLO BELLS FOR 2 PIANOS	HIER, E.
ASOLO BELLS	HIER, E.
ASSEDIO DI CORINTO, L' - OVERTURE	ROSSINI, G.
ASSIM NINAVA MAMAN	VILLA-LOBOS, H.
ASSISE	GUILLOU, R.
ASTERS	PANELLA, L.
ASTER SCHOTTISCHE	STREABBOG
ASTRAZIONE	ANDRIESSEN, J.
ASTRONAUT, THE	LAST, J.
ASTRONAUTS SALUTE	BURCH, S.
ASTRONAUT ADVENTURE	SCHAUM, W.
ASTURIAS. LEYENDA -- NO. 5, FROM SUITE ESPANOLA NO. 1	ALBENIZ, I.
ASTURIAS -- FROM SUITE ESPANOLA NO. 1	ALBENIZ, I.
ASTURIAS -- NO. 2, ESPAGNE -- SOUVENIRS	ALBENIZ, I.
ASTURIAS FROM 'SUITE ESPANOLA'	ALBENIZ, I.
AS THE DANCE GOES ON	LICHNER, P.
AS THE GIRLS GO -- SELECTION	ADAMSON *
AS THE GIRLS GO	ADAMSON *
ATHALIA, PRIESTS' MARCH, EASY	MENDELSSOHN
ATRITONISCHE MUSIK III	STAEPS, H. U.
ATTACK OF THE UHLANS	BOHM
ATTAQUE DES UHLANS--GRAND MILITARY GALOP, OP. 213	BOHM
ATTAQUE DES UHLANS -- GALOP	BOHM
ATTIC PLAYROOM, THE	STILWELL
AT A CELLO RECITAL	WEISLEDER, A.
AT A DARKY CAMP MEETING	MILLS, K.
AT A FOOTBALL GAME	DUNGAN
AT A GEORGIA CAMP MEETING -- SIMP.	MOSSMAN, T.
AT A GEORGIA CAMP MEETING	MILLS, K.
AT CHRISTMAS TIDE	RODGERS, I.--ED
AT CHURCH	DVORINE
AT DAWNING	CADMAN, C.
AT EASE IN ALL KEYS, BK. 1	STEINER
AT EASE IN ALL KEYS, BK. 2	STEINER
AT EVENING	WRIGHT, L.

Title	Composer
AT FULL SPEED	WHEELER, V. B.
AT GRANDMA'S HOUSE - BIG CLOCK AND LITTLE CLOCK,	KOUNTZ, R.
AT HOME	LICHNER, H.
AT MY TEACHER'S STUDIO	SCHAUM, J.--ED.
AT PLAY	FREDERICKS
AT SUNDOWN, REVERIE	WILSON, G.
AT SUNDOWN	LANE, J.--ED.
AT SUNSET	CHRISTOPHER, G.
AT THE BALLET SCHOOL	WERMEL
AT THE BALLET	GARROW, L.
AT THE BALLET	GILLOCK
AT THE BALLET	GILLOCK
AT THE BALLET	HAYES
AT THE BALLET	PARK
AT THE BALL -- 8-HANDS, SET	ZILCHER
AT THE BALL GAME, MARCH	REED, H.
AT THE BALL GAME	HIGGINS
AT THE BARBER SHOP	RICHTER
AT THE BARBER SHOP	SCHER, W.
AT THE BAZAAR	SCHER, W.
AT THE CAMPFIRE, OP. 124	KRENTZLIN, R.
AT THE CARNIVAL	BRUSSELS, I.
AT THE CARNIVAL	BURNAM
AT THE CARNIVAL	HOWELL
AT THE CIRCUS, GALOP	REED, H.
AT THE CIRCUS	BILBRO, M.
AT THE CIRCUS	FRANCO, J.
AT THE CIRCUS	GRETCHANINOFF
AT THE CIRCUS	SCHER, W.
AT THE CONCERT HALL	RICKER
AT THE CONCERT	BOSTELMANN
AT THE COUNTY FAIR, MARCH	MARTIN, G.
AT THE COUNTY FAIR, MARCH	MARTIN, G.
AT THE COUNTY FAIR	DITTENHAVER
AT THE CRAFTMAN'S FAIR	DITTENHAVER
AT THE DANCE RECITAL	WEISLEDER, A.
AT THE DANCE	KETTERER, E.
AT THE DANCE	MARTIN, G.
AT THE DANCE	PANELLA, L.
AT THE DONNYBROOK FAIR	SCOTT, J.
AT THE FAIR	WERNER, J.
AT THE FLEA CIRCUS	WERMEL
AT THE FOUNTAIN	BRUSSELS, I.
AT THE FOUNTAIN	HOWELL
AT THE FRENCH COURT	LYON
AT THE ICE BALLET	RODGERS, I.
AT THE ICE PALACE	KEVAN
AT THE ICE SKATING RINK	SCHER, W.
AT THE JAZZ BAND BALL	LA ROCCA *
AT THE KEYBOARD, BK. 1	LAST, J.
AT THE KEYBOARD, BK. 2	LAST, J.
AT THE KEYBOARD, BK. 3	LAST, J.
AT THE KEYBOARD, BK. 4	LAST, J.
AT THE LAWN FETE	HOLT, EILSEL
AT THE MASQUERADE	JAHN, C.
AT THE MOVIES	WERMEL
AT THE OLD SWIMMIN HOLE	PERRY, P.
AT THE PARTY, WALTZ	HOPKINS, H.
AT THE PARTY	BILBRO, M.
AT THE PARTY	SMITH
AT THE PHOTOGRAPHERS, OP. 98 NO. 1 -- TWO PIANOS,	WILSON, M.
AT THE PIANO, BK. 1	GOULD, M.
AT THE PIANO, BK. 2	GOULD, M.
AT THE PIANO - BOOK 1	FROST
AT THE PIANO - BOOK 2	FROST
AT THE PIANO - BOOK 3	FROST
AT THE PIANO - BOOK 4	FROST
AT THE PLAYGROUND	SCHWAB
AT THE SEASHORE	CROCKER, D.
AT THE SEA - SHINING MORNING, THE ROCKEY BEACH, ROUGH	GUILLAUME
AT THE SEA SHORE--8 PIECES WITH WORDS	KORANIEVSKY, M.
AT THE SKATING CARNIVAL	AARON, M.
AT THE STROKE OF MIDNIGHT	MUNN, W.
AT THE TRADING POST	GARROW, L.
AT THE TULIP FESTIVAL	FREDERICKS
AT THE TYPEWRITER	BURNAM
AT VESPERS	ARMOUR
AUBADES	GOLDMAN, R.
AUBADE -- PIANO REDUCTION --	POULENC, F.
AUBADE - PIANO SOLO PART	POULENC, F.
AUBADE D'MOUR	MONTI, V.
AUBADE FLEURIE	GANNE
AUBADE	POULENC, F.
AUBREY	BRADLEY,
AUFFORDERUNG ZUM TANZ, OP. 65	WEBER, VON
AUFFORDERUNG ZUM TANZ -- C-DUR OP. 65	WEBER, VON
AUFFORDERUNG ZUM TANZ -- DES-DUR OP. 65	WEBER, VON
AUFSCHWUNG, OP. 12 NO. 2--FANTASIESTUCKE	SCHUMANN, R.
AUFSCHWUNG -- SOARING	SCHUMANN, R.
AUFSCHWUNG - SOARING	SCHUMANN, R.
AUF VERWACHSENEM PFADE. 15 KLAVIERSTUCKE	JANACEK
AUF WIEDERSEHN	LICHNER, H.
AUGENBLICKE IN DER NATUR. 10 LEICHTE BAGATELLEN, OP.	HANUS, J.
AUGUSTINA DE ARAGON. GRAN JOTA ARAGONESA	BLANCO
AULD LANG SYNE	STANLEY--ED
AUNT SUSANNAH, OP. 98 NO. 3 -- TWO PIANOS, EIGHT HANDS	WILSON, M.
AURA LEE	BURNAM--ED
AURA LEE	STEINER--ED.
AURA LEE	STEINER
AUSGEWAHLTE KLAVIERWERKE. 18 STUCKE AUS DEN SECHS	KRIEGER
AUSGEWAHLTE KLAVIERWERKE, BAND 1 - 25 SONATEN	SCARLATTI, A.
AUSGEWAHLTE KLAVIERWERKE, BAND 2 - 24 SONATEN UND	SCARLATTI, A.
AUSGEWAHLTE KLAVIERWERKE	FISCHER, J.
AUSGEWAHLTE KLAVIERWERKE	FROBERGER
AUSGEWAHLTE KLAVIERWERKE	HANDEL
AUSGEWAHLTE KLAVIERWERKE	PACHELBEL
AUSGEWAHLTE STUCKE, BK. 1	COUPERIN, F.
AUSTRALIAN SUITE	FIALA
AUSTRIAN DANCES	BITTNER, J.
AUSTRIAN SONG, OP. 69	PACHER, J. A.
AUSWAHL, 9 BEL. STUCKE	MOUSSORGSKY
AUSWAHL -- 12 AUSGEWAHLTE STUCKE	TSCHAIKOWSKY
AUSWAHL -- 12 LEICHTE STUCKE	GRETCHANINOFF
AUSWAHL -- 14 ORIGINAL-KLAVIER-STUCKE	MOZART, W. A.
AUSWAHL -- 15 AUSGEWAHLTE KOMPOSITIONEN	HAYDN
AUSWAHL -- 15 DER BEKANNTESTEN STUCKE	GRIEG
AUSWAHL -- 22 BEL. STUCKE	SCHUBERT
AUSWAHL -- 23 BEKANNTE STUCKE	MENDELSSOHN
AUSWAHL -- 28 BEK. STUCKE	SCHUMANN, R.
AUSWAHL -- 9 BEL. STUCKE	RACHMANINOFF, S.
AUSWAHL -- 9 BEL STUCKE	LISZT
AUSWAHL --25 AUSGEWAHLTE STUCKE--	BACH, J.S.
AUSWAHL - 14 AUSGEWAHLTE STUCKE	BRAHMS
AUSWAHL - 14 BEL. STUCKE	BEETHOVEN
AUSWAHL - 25 VIELGESPIELTE STUCKE	HANDEL
AUSWAHL - 38 BEL. STUCKE, BK. 1	CHOPIN
AUSWAHL - 38 BEL. STUCKE, BK. 2	CHOPIN

AUS DEM BOHMERWALDE, OP. 68	DVORAK
AUS DEM JUGENDLANDE	KRENTZLIN, R.
AUS DEM LEBEN, OP. 11	KREJCI, M.
AUS ITALIEN, OP. 16. SYMPHONIC POEM	STRAUSS, R.
AUS MEINEM TAGEBUCH, FROM MY DIARY, OP. 82, BK. 1--12	REGER
AUS MEINEM TAGEBUCH, FROM MY DIARY, OP. 82, BK. 2--10	REGER
AUS MEINEM TAGEBUCH, FROM MY DIARY, OP. 82, BKS. 3-4	REGER
AUS OSTERREICH -- AUSTRIAN FOLK DANCES	KORDA--ED
AUS SMETANAS OPERN	SMETANA
AUTHENTIC 'FIRST BACH'	BACH, J.S.
AUTHENTIC 'FIRST BEETHOVEN'	BEETHOVEN
AUTHENTIC 'FIRST HANDEL'	HANDEL
AUTOMNE, L'	MILHAUD, D.
AUTOMOBILE -- NO. 1, FROM FIVE EASY PIECES	DELUNE
AUTOUR	JOLAS, B.
AUTUMN, FROM 'THE SEASONS'	GLAZOUNOW, A.
AUTUMN, OP. 35 NO. 2	CHAMINADE
AUTUMN, OP. 35 NO. 2	CHAMINADE
AUTUMN BREEZES	SADLON
AUTUMN COLOR	LARSON
AUTUMN FANTASY	MARTIN, H.
AUTUMN FIELDS	STEVENS, E.
AUTUMN FLOWERS, WALTZ	STREABBOG
AUTUMN IN NEW YORK	DUKE
AUTUMN IS HERE	GILLOCK
AUTUMN IS HERE	GILLOCK
AUTUMN LEAVES	BRIMHALL,
AUTUMN LEAVES	BRUSSELS, I.
AUTUMN LEAVES	QUIXLEY, F.
AUTUMN LEAVES	WOOD, W.
AUTUMN NOCTURNE	MYROW
AUTUMN NYMPH	BERMONT, H.
AUTUMN REVERIE	CHOPIN
AUTUMN REVERIE	MUELLER, C.
AUTUMN SERENADE	DE ROSE, P.
AUTUMN SHADES	HAYES
AUTUMN SONG	WEYBRIGHT
AUTUMN SONG	WEYBRIGHT
AUTUMN SPLENDOR	ROLFE, W.
AUTUMN SPLENDOR	ROLFE, W.
AUTUMN THOUGHTS - FROM SEVEN FLOWERS FROM A PIANIST'S	GIASSON, P.
AUTUMN THOUGHTS	GIASSON, P.
AUTUMN TIME	ROBERTS
AUTUMN	RAYMOND, J.
AUTUMN	WHITFORD
AUX ETOILES	DUPARC, H.
AUX TUILERIES	ALLIER
AU BOIS FLEURI -- 1. CHANTOISEAU, 2. SYLPHIDES	FIEVET, P.
AU BORD D'UNE SOURCE--FROM PREMIERE ANNEE DE	LISZT
AU BORD D'UNE SOURCE	LISZT
AU BORD D'UNE SOURCE	LISZT
AU BORD D'UNE SOURCE	LISZT
AU CLAIR DE LA LUNE	BULL
AU CLAIR DE LA LUNE	LULLI, A. DE
AU COUVENT--FROM PETITE SUITE	BORODIN, A.
AU FOYER, OP. 183	GRETCHANINOFF
AU GRE DES ONDES, 6 PETITES PIECES	DUTILLEUX
AU JARDIN--IDYLLE ETUDE	BALAKIREV
AU JARDIN DES BETES SAUVAGES, VOL. 1 -- LA BETE A BON	VELLONES, P.
AU JARDIN DES BETES SAUVAGES, VOL. 1 -- LA MEDUSE	VELLONES, P.
AU JARDIN DES BETES SAUVAGES, VOL. 1 -- LES CROCODILES	VELLONES, P.
AU JARDIN DES BETES SAUVAGES, VOL. 1 -- LES DAUPHINS	VELLONES, P.
AU JARDIN DES BETES SAUVAGES, VOL. 1 -- LES TORTUES	VELLONES, P.
AU JARDIN DES BETES SAUVAGES, VOL. 1 -- LE CRABE DES	VELLONES, P.
AU JARDIN DES BETES SAUVAGES, VOL. 1 -- LE LEZARD VERT	VELLONES, P.
AU JARDIN DES BETES SAUVAGES, VOL. 1 -- LE POU DE MER	VELLONES, P.
AU JARDIN DES BETES SAUVAGES, VOL. 1	VELLONES, P.
AU JARDIN DES BETES SAUVAGES, VOL. 2 -- L'AUTRUCHE	VELLONES, P.
AU JARDIN DES BETES SAUVAGES, VOL. 2 -- L'HAMADRYAS	VELLONES, P.
AU JARDIN DES BETES SAUVAGES, VOL. 2 -- L'HIPPOPOTAME	VELLONES, P.
AU JARDIN DES BETES SAUVAGES, VOL. 2 -- L'OISEAU LYRE	VELLONES, P.
AU JARDIN DES BETES SAUVAGES, VOL. 2 -- LA BICHE	VELLONES, P.
AU JARDIN DES BETES SAUVAGES, VOL. 2 -- LES PINGOUINS	VELLONES, P.
AU JARDIN DES BETES SAUVAGES, VOL. 2 -- LES VERS	VELLONES, P.
AU JARDIN DES BETES SAUVAGES, VOL. 2 -- LE CACATOES A	VELLONES, P.
AU JARDIN DES BETES SAUVAGES, VOL. 2	VELLONES, P.
AU MATIN, OP. 83	GODARD, B.
AU MATIN -- AT MORN	GODARD, B.
AU MATIN SUR LES CIMES	GALOS
AU MATIN	GODARD, B.
AU PARC MONCEAU - CHAT JOUANT AVEC LES OISEAUX, SUR LE	FERROUD, P. O.
AU PARC MONCEAU - NONCHALANTE	FERROUD, P. O.
AU PAYS TOURANGEAU	DUBOIS
AU TEMPS DES CERISES	CARMAN
AU TOMBEAU DE RAVEL	GIAZOTTO
AVALANCHE, L', OP. 45 NO. 2	HELLER, S.
AVALANCHE, OP. 45, NO. 2	HELLER, S.
AVALANCHE, OP. 45 NO. 2	HELLER, S.
AVALANCHE IN A MINOR, OP. 45 NO. 2	HELLER, S.
AVALANCHE	HELLER, S.
AVANT DERNIERES PENSES	SATIE, E.
AVANT PRINTEMPS, OP. 99	GREGH
AVA	SALVADOR
AVENTURES DU ROI PAUSOLE, LES -- SUITE --	HONEGGER, A.
AVE MARIA, FANTASIE	SCHUBERT
AVE MARIA, OP. 52 NO. 6	SCHUBERT
AVE MARIA, OP. 52 NO. 6	SCHUBERT
AVE MARIA, WORDS	SCHUBERT
AVE MARIA	BACH, J.S. *
AVE MARIA	BACH, J.S. *
AVE MARIA	BACH, J.S. *
AVE MARIA	BACH, J.S. *
AVE MARIA	BACH, J.S.
AVE MARIA	BACH, J.S. *
AVE MARIA	BACH, J.S. *
AVE MARIA	BACH, J.S. *
AVE MARIA	GOUNOD, C.
AVE MARIA	GOUNOD, C. *
AVE MARIA	LISZT
AVE MARIA	SCHUBERT *
AVE MARIA	SCHUBERT
AVE MARIA	SCHUBERT
AVE MARIA	SCHUBERT
AVE MARIA	SCHUBERT *
AVE MARIA	SCHUBERT *
AVE MARIA	SCHUBERT
AVE MARIA	SCHUBERT
AVE MARIA	SCHUBERT
AVE MARIS STELLA	GANDINI
AVE VERUM -- MIT TEXT K.V. 618	MOZART, W. A.
AVIATION SUITE	GROFE, F.
AVIATORS ON PARADE	GIOVANNI
AVOWAL	RALSTON, F.
AWAKENING OF THE LION	DEKONTSKI
AWAY IN A MANGER	MUELLER, C.
AWAY IN A MANGER	MUELLER, C.
AWAY IN A MANGER	RICHTER, A.
AWAY TO THE WOODS	SOUERS
AY-AY-AY -- FAMOUS SERENADE --	FREIRE
AY, AY, AY, TRANS.	GROOMS--ED
AY, AY, AY	ROLFE, W.--ED
AY, AY, AY	SCARMOLIN
AYLESFORDER STUCKE	HANDEL
AZELEA	SEIDT, J.
AZURE	ELLINGTON
A B C PAPERS	CLARK, F.
A B C	SCARMOLIN
A CANZONE'E NAPULE	
A DOS D'ANE -- NO. 3, FROM FIVE EASY PIECES	DELUNE
A EDVARD GRIEG	COUTURE
A FRANGESA, MARCH	COSTA
A HISTORIA DA CAIPIRINHA	VILLA-LOBOS, H.
A L'APPROCHE DU SOIR	GALOS
A L'EXPOSITION .. MUSICAL ILLUSTRATIONS -- AURIC,	
A L'OMBRE DE ''TORRE BERMEJA''	RODRIGO, J.
A LAPIZ -TRES APUNTES PARA PIANO	ENRIQUEZ, M.
A LA BIEN-AIMEE. VALSE, OP. 59 NO. 2	SCHUETT
A LA BIEN-AIMEE	DESREZ
A LA BIEN AIMEE, C MAJOR	SCHUETT
A LA BIEN AIMEE -- LOVE WALTZ -- D MAJOR	SCHUETT
A LA BIEN AIMEE	SCHUETT
A LA BIEN AIMEE	WEYBRIGHT
A LA CAMPAGNE, BK. 1	DERE
A LA CAMPAGNE, BK. 2	DERE
A LA CAMPAGNE, BK. 3	DERE
A LA MANIERE DE ... BORODIN, D'INDY, CHABRIER, RAVEL	CASELLA, A. *
A LA MANIERE DE ... BORODIN, D'INDY, CHABRIER, RAVEL	RAVEL *
A LA MANIERE DE ... WAGNER, FAURE, BRAHMS, DEBUSSY,	CASELLA, A.
A LA MANIERE DE BORODINE	RAVEL
A LA MANIERE DE CHABRIER	RAVEL
A LA MEMOIRE DE LILY BOULANGER	BLANC DE
A LA MENUETTO, OP. 125 NO. 2	SINDING
A LA MODE	KAYE, E.
A LA PRADERA	GRANADOS
A LA VALSE, IMPROMPTU, G MAJOR	BOHM
A MANHA DA PIERRETTE	VILLA-LOBOS, H.
A MAO DIREITA TEM UMA ROSEIRA	VILLA-LOBOS, H.
A MODA DA CARRANQUINHA	VILLA-LOBOS, H.
A MON MOULIN, PIECE IMITATIVE	WACHS, P.
A NOTTE ALTA - MUSICAL POEM	CASELLA, A.
A POBRESINHA SERTANEJA	VILLA-LOBOS, H.
A SARAGOSSE	CARMAN
A TAZZA,' CAFE	
A TOI, OP. 150	WALDTEUFEL, E.
A TO G - A VERY FIRST MUSICAL ALPHABET BOK	HOFSTAD, M.
A TRAVERS BOIS -- REVERIE -- OP. 151	HITZ, F.
A TRAVERS BOIS	FISCHER
A TRAVERS BOIS	FISCHER
A UNA FARFALLA	COUTURE
A UNE MAIN--FOR THE LEFT HAND ALONE	LANGLOIS, T.
BA-BA- BLACK SHEEP	THOMPSON, J.
BAA, BAA, BLACK SHEEP	ROLFE, W.
BABAR COMES TO AMERICA	TROTTER *
BABBLING BROOK, A	JUDD, A.
BABETTE'S PIANO BOOK - EASY SUITE	KOCH, F.
BABETTES PIANO BOOK	KOCH, F.
BABETTE	ARMOUR
BABILLAGES	DIET
BABILLAGE	BACHMANN, G.
BABILLAGE	DEL CASTILLO
BABY-POLKA	PAUL
BABY, BABY ALL THE TIME	
BABY'S FAMILY--A PROLE DO BEBE, SERIES 2--NO. 1,	VILLA-LOBOS, H.
BABY'S FAMILY--A PROLE DO BEBE, SERIES 2--NO. 2,	VILLA-LOBOS, H.
BABY'S FAMILY--A PROLE DO BEBE, SERIES 2--NO. 3, THE	VILLA-LOBOS, H.
BABY'S FAMILY--A PROLE DO BEBE, SERIES 2--NO. 4, THE	VILLA-LOBOS, H.
BABY'S FAMILY--A PROLE DO BEBE, SERIES 2--NO. 5, THE	VILLA-LOBOS, H.
BABY'S FAMILY--A PROLE DO BEBE, SERIES 2--NO. 6, THE	VILLA-LOBOS, H.
BABY'S FAMILY--A PROLE DO BEBE, SERIES 2--NO. 7, THE	VILLA-LOBOS, H.
BABY'S FAMILY--A PROLE DO BEBE, SERIES 2--NO. 8, THE	VILLA-LOBOS, H.
BABY'S FAMILY--A PROLE DO BEBE, SERIES 2--NO. 9, THE	VILLA-LOBOS, H.
BABY'S FAMILY, THE -- A PROLE DO BEBE, BK. 1	VILLA-LOBOS, H.
BABY'S LULLABY	RENNARD
BABY BOOGIE	MORLEY *
BABY DANCING	HARSANYI
BABY DON'T GET HOOKED ON ME	BRADLEY,
BABY ELEPHANT WALK	BRIMHALL,
BABY GRAND, THE	STEINER
BABY GRAND, THE	STEINER
BABY I'M-A WANT YOU	BRADLEY,
BABY KANGAROO	TRUXELL, E.
BABY LOOK AT YOU	JOHNSON, S. *
BABY MOUSE	RICHTER, A.
BABY SCHOOL -- 40 SELECTIONS FOR BEGINNERS' BALLET	SKJERNE--ED.
BACAROLLE -- TALES OF HOFFMAN	OFFENBACH
BACH--AN INTRODUCTION TO HIS PIANO WORKS	BACH, J.S.
BACH-SCHAUM, BK. 1	BACH, J.S.
BACH-SCHAUM, BK. 1	BACH, J.S.
BACH-SCHAUM, BK. 2	BACH, J.S.
BACH-SCHAUM, BK. 2	BACH, J.S.
BACH, BEETHOVEN AND BRAHMS	BACH, J.S. *
BACH'S SONS	
BACH'S SONS	
BACHARACH AND DAVID'S TOP TEN	BRIMHALL,
BACHBUCHLEIN FUR CLAVIER	BACH, J.S.
BACHBUCHLEIN FUR CLAVIER	BACH, J.S.
BACHETTE	WIGHAM, M.
BACHIANAS BRASILEIRAS - SUITE NO. 4 , DANCE	VILLA-LOBOS, H.
BACHIANAS BRASILEIRAS - SUITE NO. 4 , PRELUDE	VILLA-LOBOS, H.
BACHIANAS BRASILEIRAS - SUITE NO. 4 , SONG OF THE	VILLA-LOBOS, H.
BACHIANAS BRASILEIRAS - SUITE NO. 4 , SONG	VILLA-LOBOS, H.
BACHIANAS BRASILEIRAS NO. 3	VILLA-LOBOS, H.
BACH ALBUM	BACH, J.S.
BACH FAMILY, THE. VOL. 1	BACH, J.S.
BACH FAMILY, THE. VOL. 2	BACH, J.S.
BACH FAMILY, THE -- 14 PIECES	GEIRINGER,
BACH FOR BEGINNERS, BK. 1	BACH, J.S.
BACH FOR BEGINNERS, BK. 2	BACH, J.S.
BACH FOR EARLY GRADES, BOOK 1	BACH, J.S.
BACH FOR EARLY GRADES, BOOK 2	BACH, J.S.
BACH FOR EARLY GRADES, BOOK 3	BACH, J.S.
BACH FOR PIANO ENSEMBLE	BACH, J.S. *
BACH IS FUN	BACH, J.S.
BACH ORGAN PRELUDES	BACH, J.S.
BACH	BACH, J.S.
BACKYARD BOOGIE	PETRIE-WINGATE
BACKYARD BOOGIE	STEINER
BACK COUNTRY BALLAD	STORR, S.
BACK HOME AGAIN IN INDIANA	HANLEY, J.
BACK TO CALIFORNIA	BRADLEY,
BACK TO SCHOOL--8 PIECES WITH WORDS	KORANIEVSKY, M.

BADINAGE	HERBERT
BADINAGE	HIER, E.
BADINAGE	PIERNE, P.
BADINAGE	POULENC, F.
BADINAGE	TCHEREPNIN
BADINAGE	WHITFORD--ED.
BADINERIE	BACH, J.S.
BADINERIE	BACH, J.S.
BADINERIE	RIBAULT, A.
BAD AND THE BEAUTIFUL, THE	RAKSIN, D.
BAGATELLE, OP. 11 NO. 1 BALLADE	KORN, P.
BAGATELLE, OP. 11 NO. 2 SCHERZO	KORN, P.
BAGATELLE, OP. 11 NO. 3 PRELUDE	KORN, P.
BAGATELLE, OP. 11 NO. 4 BURLESKE	KORN, P.
BAGATELLE, OP. 11 NO. 5 INTERMEZZO	KORN, P.
BAGATELLE, OP. 11 NO. 6 DANCE	KORN, P.
BAGATELLE, OP. 11 NO. 7 TORCH SONG	KORN, P.
BAGATELLE, OP. 11 NO. 8 PASSACAGLIA POLKA	KORN, P.
BAGATELLE, OP. 33 NO. 1	BEETHOVEN
BAGATELLE, OP. 4	BOZAY, A.
BAGATELLE, OP. 9	SCHROETER, I.
BAGATELLEN -- BERCEUSE, SCHERZANDO, MELODIE,	BARTOS, J. Z.
BAGATELLEN UND IMPROMPTUS	SMETANA
BAGATELLES, OP. 1	POSER
BAGATELLES, OP. 119 AND OP. 126	BEETHOVEN
BAGATELLES, OP. 119	BEETHOVEN
BAGATELLES, OP. 119	BEETHOVEN
BAGATELLES, OP. 126	BEETHOVEN
BAGATELLES, OP. 33	BEETHOVEN
BAGATELLES, OP. 5 - TEN PIECES FOR PIANO	TCHEREPNIN
BAGATELLES, OP. 5	TCHEREPNIN
BAGATELLES, OP. 5	TCHEREPNIN
BAGATELLES AND IMPROMPTUS	SMETANA
BAGATELLES OP. 5, 10 NOS.	TCHEREPNIN
BAGATELLES	BEETHOVEN
BAGATELLES	DAVID
BAGATELLES	KOSA, G.
BAGATELLES	RAWSTHORNE, A.
BAGATELLES	TREPANIER
BAGATELLE CUBANA	RAPHLING
BAGATELLE CUBANA	RAPHLING
BAGATELLE CUBANA	RAPHLING
BAGATELLE IN A MINOR	BEETHOVEN
BAGATELLE IN D, OP.33 NO.6	BEETHOVEN
BAGATELLE IN E FLAT, OP. 33 NO. 1	BEETHOVEN
BAGATELLE IN E FLAT, OP. 33 NO. 1	BEETHOVEN
BAGATELLE IN E FLAT, OP.33 NO. 1	RAPHLING
BAGATELLE ISRAELI	RAPHLING
BAGATELLE ISRAELI	BEETHOVEN
BAGATELLE NOUVELLE IN G MINOR, OP. 119 NO. 1	LISZT
BAGATELLE SANS TONALITE	FRANK
BAGATELLE	MARTINU, B.
BAGATELLE	MCGRAW
BAGATELLE	RODRIGO, J.
BAGATELLE	SAMPSON, G.
BAGATELLE	SCHAUM, J.--ED.
BAGDAD BOOGIE	GILLOCK
BAGDAD	GILLOCK
BAGDAD	APPLEBAUM
BAGHDAD SUITE	DE BELLIS
BAGLIORI	MILKEY, E.
BAGPIPES AND DRUMS	BANKS, M.
BAGPIPES	BURNAM
BAGPIPE AND KILT	DVORINE
BAGPIPE CAPERS	SEVERAC
BAIGNEUSES AU SOLEIL	GUASTAVINO
BAILECITO	GUASTAVINO
BAILECITO	IGLESIAS VILLOUD
BAILECITO	LOPEZ BUCHARDO
BAILECITO	LOPEZ BUCHARDO
BAILECITO	PERCUOCO
BAILETE - ENTRADA, TIRANA, BOLERO, DANZA DE CORTE,	TURINA, J.
BAION	KASNER
BAISERS D'OISEAUX	MICHEUZ, G.
BAISER D'UN ANGE -- NOCTURNE --	KINKEL, C.
BAISEZ, MIGNON, PETITE VALSE	MARCUS
BAJO UN ALERO	FOSSATI
BAKER'S DOZEN, A--13 PIECES TO READ AT SIGHT--	DILLER, A.
BAKER STREET SKETCHES	DURAND, A.
BAKING COOKIES	HOPKINS, H.
BALADINE, LA, CAPRICE	LYSBERG, C. B.
BALALAIKA	SCHER, W.
BALANCELLE, IN THE SWING	WACHS, P.
BALANESE DANCER	DUNGAN
BALI HA'I	HAMMERSTEIN *
BALKANTANZE	TAJCEVIC, M.
BALKAN IMPRESSIONS, IN 2 VOLS., VOL. 1, 10 PIECES FROM	BRESGEN
BALKAN IMPRESSIONS, IN 2 VOLS., VOL. 2, 10 PIECES FROM	BRESGEN
BALKY DONKEY, THE	WEBB
BALKY MULE	DUNGAN
BALL-VISION	SMETANA
BALLAD, FROM 'FIFTEEN HUNGARIAN PEASANT SONGS'	BARTOK
BALLADE, OP. 100 NO. 15	BURGMUELLER
BALLADE, OP. 100	BURGMUELLER
BALLADE, OP. 12	MAURAT, E.
BALLADE, OP. 19	FAURE, G.
BALLADE, OP. 21	LIADOW, A.
BALLADE, OP. 24	GRIEG
BALLADE, OP. 24	GRIEG
BALLADE, OP. 40--VARIATIONS ON A HURDY-GURDY THEME	RATHAUS, K.
BALLADE, OP. 57	BLANCHET
BALLADE, OP. 9	DOBROWEN, I.
BALLADEN OP. 10	BRAHMS
BALLADES, OP. 10	BRAHMS
BALLADES -- ENGLISH TEXT --	CHOPIN
BALLADES -- FR. TEXT --	CHOPIN
BALLADES --4-- AND IMPROMPTUS --3--	CHOPIN
BALLADES	CHOPIN
BALLADES	CHOPIN
BALLADES	CHOPIN
BALLADES	CHOPIN
BALLADES	CHOPIN
BALLADETTE	ANDERSON, L.
BALLADE CONCERTANTE, OP. 59	DELANNOY
BALLADE DANS LE COSMOS	LAPEYRE, T.
BALLADE DE LA GEOLE DE READING	IBERT
BALLADE DE LA NEIGE	SCHMITT
BALLADE DU LAC BLANC	PAITA, F.
BALLADE FOR PIANO AND ORCHESTRA, OP. 19	FAURE, G.
BALLADE G MOLL, OP. 118 NO. 3	BRAHMS
BALLADE IN A-FLAT, OP. 47	CHOPIN
BALLADE IN A FLAT, OP. 47	CHOPIN
BALLADE IN A FLAT MAJOR, OP. 47	CHOPIN
BALLADE IN A MINOR 'DAS GEISTERSCHIFF' OP. 1	TAUSIG
BALLADE IN B FLAT	SPILIOS
BALLADE IN D MINOR, OP. 10 NO. 1	BRAHMS
BALLADE IN F, OP. 38	CHOPIN
BALLADE IN F, OP. 38	CHOPIN
BALLADE IN F MAJOR, OP. 38	CHOPIN
BALLADE IN F MINOR, OP. 52	CHOPIN
BALLADE IN F SHARP MINOR, OP. 85 NO. 1	SCHARWENKA, X.
BALLADE IN G MINOR, OP. 118 NO. 3	BRAHMS
BALLADE IN G MINOR, OP. 118 NO. 3	BRAHMS
BALLADE IN G MINOR, OP. 118 NO. 3	BRAHMS
BALLADE IN G MINOR, OP. 23	CHOPIN
BALLADE IN G MINOR, OP. 23	CHOPIN
BALLADE IN G MINOR, OP. 23	CHOPIN
BALLADE IN THE FORM OF VARIATIONS	DE ANGELIS
BALLADE MAURESQUE	GUTIERREZ-PONCE
BALLADE NO. 2	LISZT
BALLADE OF LONDON NIGHTS	IRELAND, J.
BALLADE	BURGMUELLER
BALLADE	DEBUSSY
BALLADE	DEBUSSY
BALLADE	FARKAS, F.
BALLADE	LEFEBVRE
BALLADE	MARTIN, F.
BALLADE	MEYEROWITZ
BALLADE	POOT, M.
BALLADE	RAWSTHORNE, A.
BALLADE	WURMSER, L.
BALLADS	LISZT
BALLAD AND TRAINS	BARTLEY, E.
BALLAD NO. 1--1941	TANSMAN, A.
BALLAD NO. 2--1941	TANSMAN, A.
BALLAD NO. 3--1941	TANSMAN, A.
BALLAD NO. 3	TERNI
BALLAD OF THE BELLS	CHAGY
BALLAD OF THE GREEN BERETS	
BALLAD	FAURE, G.
BALLAD	KRAFT
BALLAD	SOULE
BALLAD	TEBOLDI
BALLERINA, THE	GOULD, M.
BALLERINA, THE	MARTIN, H.
BALLERINA IN WHITE	VOLZ, H.
BALLERINA IN WHITE	VOLZ, H.
BALLERINA OF THE ICE	WEB
BALLERINA WALTZ	GREEN, R.
BALLERINA	JESSE, M.
BALLERINA	KERR, R. N.
BALLERINA	LAKE, G.
BALLERINA	MELECCI, A.
BALLERINA	STEVENS
BALLERINA	ROLSETH, B.
BALLET-DANCER, THE	FUCIK
BALLETTOUVERTURE, OP. 319	DE ANGELIS
BALLETTO AD USUM INFANTIS	SCHUBERT
BALLETT MUSIK 2 G-DUR AUS ROSAMUNDE	TSCHAIKOWSKY
BALLET -- LE LAC DES CYGNES	BLISS, A.
BALLET "ADAM ZERO", PIANO SCORE	BLISS, A.
BALLET "CHECKMATE", PIANO SCORE	BIZET, G.
BALLET 'LES BOHEMIENNES' --JOLIE FILLE DE PERTH--	BLISS, A.
BALLET "MIRACLE IN THE GORBALS", PIANO SCORE	SCHAUM, J.--ED.
BALLET BOOK	PERRIN
BALLET DANCER	BERLIOZ
BALLET DES TROYENS A CARTHAGE	LUIGINI
BALLET EGYPTIEN -- SUITE 1 --	LUIGINI
BALLET EGYPTIEN	DEBUSSY
BALLET FROM PETITE SUITE	MAMORSKY, M.
BALLET IN BLUE	ROBYN
BALLET MINIATURE	SCHUBERT
BALLET MUSIC, ROSAMUND	SCHUBERT
BALLET MUSIC, ROSAMUND	SCHUBERT
BALLET MUSIC - ROSAMUNDE	HARTLEY, W.--ED
BALLET MUSIC FOR ORCHESTRA ARR. FOR TWO PIANO-FOUR	LADD, A.
BALLET MUSIC FOR THE DANCE STUDIO	GLUCK
BALLET MUSIC FROM ''ORPHEUS''	SCHUBERT
BALLET MUSIC FROM 'ROSAMUNDE', OP. 26	HARALDSTED--ED.
BALLET MUSIC OF THE ROYAL DANISH BALLET, BK.	HARALDSTED--ED.
BALLET MUSIC OF THE ROYAL DANISH BALLET, BK.	KODALY, Z.
BALLET MUSIC	
BALLET MUSIC	GOUNOD, C.
BALLET NO. 1, FAUST	SCHER, W.
BALLET OF THE DOLLS	BROWN, A.
BALLET ON SKATES, OP. 126	ECKSTEIN
BALLET PROFILE	WILSON, M.
BALLET SCENE, THE	SKJERNE--ED.
BALLET SCHOOL--WILHELM HANSEN EDITION	SKJERNE--ED.
BALLET SCHOOL -- 100 SELECTIONS FROM THE MASTERS FOR	AARON, M.
BALLET STACCATO	CARMAN
BALLET THEME -- WALTZ -- FROM ''CRUNCH, CRUNCH''	WRIGHT, N.
BALLET WALTZ, A	CZAJANEK
BALLET	DEBUSSY
BALLET	MORRIS, H.
BALLET	ARLEN, C.
BALLOONS	GAY, A.
BALLOONS	TALBOT
BALLOONS	SCHER, W.
BALLOON MAN	SCHER, W.
BALLOON MAN	THOMASON, E.
BALLOON WALTZ	VERDI
BALLO IN MASCHERA, UN - EASY FANTASIA	ARNOLD, H.
BALL GAME, A	MCCLUSKY
BALL THREE	JOUBERTI
BAL CHEZ LE MINISTRE, UN -- MAZURKA --	JOUBERTI
BAL CHEZ LE MINISTRE, UN -- MAZURKA --	GOUNOD, C.
BAL D'ENFANTS, LE, VALSE	MAY *
BAL MASQUE CHEZ LES OIES	SMETANA
BAL VISION	HAZELLE
BAMBA BOOGIE	GIOVANNI
BAMBOO GROVE	STERNKLAR, A.
BAMIDBAR -- IN THE DESERT	VOLKART, H.
BAND, THE -- MARCH	BRANT
BANDA, BANDURRIA	VOLPATTI
BANDERILLEROS, LES	DUNYON
BAND CONCERT, THE	DUNYON
BAND CONCERT, THE	WARD
BAND PLAYED ON, THE	WARD
BAND PLAYED ON, THE	WARE
BAND PLAYED ON	MACLACHIAN, T.
BANJO-BOUNCE	GOTTSCHALK
BANJO, THE -- SET	CHILDERS, L.
BANJO, THE	GARROW
BANJO BILL	GLOVER, D.
BANJO ON MY KNEE	JESSE, M.
BANJO PETE	WRIGHT, L.
BANJO PICKER, THE	WRIGHT, L.
BANJO PICKER	STILWELL
BANJO PLAYER, THE	BLAKE, D.
BANJO PLAYER	VANNORT, I.
BANJO SERENADER	AARON, M.
BANJO SERENADE	

BANJO SERENADE	GEORGE,
BANJO SONG	KETTERER, E.
BANJO SONG	WEYBRIGHT--ED.
BANJO SONG	WEYBRIGHT
BANNERS HIGH	COURSEY, R. DE
BANNER MELODIES	CRIST, D.
BAR-Z BARN DANCE	KIRKPATRICK
BARAZA	BLISS, A.
BARBARA, WALTZ -- ONE PIANO, SIX HANDS --	GREENWALD, M.
BARBARA, WALTZ	GREENWALD, M.
BARBARA	PERKINS, F.
BARBE-BLEUE	OFFENBACH
BARBERINI'S MINUET	HASSE, J.
BARBER OF SEVILLE, ABRIDGED	ROSSINI, G.
BARBER OF SEVILLE, TRANS.	ROSSINI, G.
BARBER SHOP RAG	KRENZ, B.
BARBIERE DI SIVIGLIA, IL -- COMPLETE OPERA --	ROSSINI, G.
BARBIERE DI SIVIGLIA, IL - CAVATINA - UNA VOCE POCO FA	ROSSINI, G.
BARBIERE DI SIVIGLIA, IL - OVERTURE	ROSSINI, G.
BARBIERE DI SIVIGLIA, IL - OVERTURE	ROSSINI, G.
BARCAROLA, OP. 202 -- FROM MALLORCA	ALBENIZ, I.
BARCAROLA, OP. 23	ALBENIZ, I.
BARCAROLA, OP. 92 NO. 3	ALBENIZ, I.
BARCAROLETTE	AGAY, D.
BARCAROLE	VAN DYKE
BARCAROLLE, BEAUTIFUL NIGHT	OFFENBACH
BARCAROLLE, CIEL SANS NUAGES, OP. 92, NO. 3 -- FROM 12	ALBENIZ, I.
BARCAROLLE, FROM THE BALLET 'SEBASTIAN'	MENOTTI
BARCAROLLE, JUNE	TSCHAIKOWSKY
BARCAROLLE, OBERON	WEBER, VON
BARCAROLLE, OBERON	WEBER, VON
BARCAROLLE, OP. 11 NO. 1	RACHMANINOFF, S.
BARCAROLLE, OP. 18 NO. 1	MACDOWELL
BARCAROLLE, OP. 38 NO. 1	ALKAN
BARCAROLLE, OP. 38 NO. 2	ALKAN
BARCAROLLE, OP. 44	LIADOW, A.
BARCAROLLE, OP. 45	GRANADOS
BARCAROLLE, OP. 60	CHOPIN
BARCAROLLE, OP. 60	CHOPIN
BARCAROLLE, OP. 62 NO. 4	SCHARWENKA, X.
BARCAROLLE, OP. 65 NO. 3	ALKAN
BARCAROLLE, OP. 67 NO. 4	ALKAN
BARCAROLLE, OP. 70 NO. 5	ALKAN
BARCAROLLE, TALES OF HOFFMANN	OFFENBACH
BARCAROLLES, IMPROMPTUS, NOCTURNES	FAURE, G.
BARCAROLLE AND POLKA	LAST, J.
BARCAROLLE FROM THE BALLET 'SEBASTIAN'	MENOTTI
BARCAROLLE FROM THE BALLET 'SEBASTIAN'	MENOTTI
BARCAROLLE IN F SHARP MAJOR, OP. 60	CHOPIN
BARCAROLLE IN F SHARP	CHOPIN
BARCAROLLE IN G MAJOR	EHRLICH, G.
BARCAROLLE NO. 01, OP. 20	MARTUCCI
BARCAROLLE NO. 01, 2, 3	ROGER-DUCASSE
BARCAROLLE NO. 02	FRONTINI
BARCAROLLE NO. 07, OP. 90	FAURE, G.
BARCAROLLE NO. 08, OP. 96	FAURE, G.
BARCAROLLE NO. 09, OP. 101	FAURE, G.
BARCAROLLE NO. 10	FAURE, G.
BARCAROLLE NO. 11	FAURE, G.
BARCAROLLE NO. 12	FAURE, G.
BARCAROLLE NO. 13	FAURE, G.
BARCAROLLE VENETIENNE	GODARD, B.
BARCAROLLE	BEHR, F.
BARCAROLLE	BUTLER, J.
BARCAROLLE	CASELLA, A.
BARCAROLLE	DEMARQUEZ
BARCAROLLE	FERTE
BARCAROLLE	GILLOCK
BARCAROLLE	GILLOCK
BARCAROLLE	KULLMANN
BARCAROLLE	MARET, L.
BARCAROLLE	OETTING, H.
BARCAROLLE	OFFENBACH
BARCAROLLE	OFFENBACH
BARCAROLLE	OFFENBACH
BARCAROLLE	OFFENBACH
BARCAROLLE	SCHWARTZ, H.
BARCAROLLE	SORET
BARCAROLLE	STEINERT, A.
BARCAROLLE	WATERMAN
BARCELONA BAZAAR	WERMEL
BARCHETTA	NEVIN
BARCHETTA	NEVIN
BARDE, DER, OP. 64--ORCH	SIBELIUS
BARDOLINO	HYMAN, D.
BARDO SONATA	HOVHANESS, A.
BARD OF LISGOLLE	TRIMBLE
BAREBACK RIDER, THE	DVORINE
BAREFOOT BOY	MOKREJS
BARE BACK RIDER, THE	KREVIT, W.
BARE NOVEMBER DAY, HARPSICHORD	HOVHANESS, A.
BARNARD WHITEFIELDS'SAMERICAN FOLK SONG ALBUM	WHITEFIELD--ED
BARNYARD FROLICS	BLACKFORD, V.
BARNYARD SAILORS	FARISS, M.
BARN DANCE, 'SIS HOPKINS'	MAYER
BARN DANCE TONIGHT	KOEHLER, C.
BARN DANCE TONIGHT	KOEHLER, C.
BARN DANCE	DE VITO, A.
BARN DANCE	DUNGAN
BARN DANCE	DUNGAN
BARN DANCE	GRAHAM
BARN DANCE	HOWELL, C. R.
BARN DANCE	JUDD, A.
BARN DANCE	TURNER, J.
BARN DANCE	PALMER, W. A.
BAROQUE FOLK	
BAROQUE PIANO MUSIC	
BAROQUE SUITE IN D MINOR	BUTLER, J.
BARREL ORGAN, OP. 107, NO. 9	NIEMANN
BARTERED BRIDE, POLKA	SMETANA
BARTERED BRIDE OVERTURE	SMETANA
BARTOKIANA	ROCHBERG, G.
BARTOK ALBUM	BARTOK
BARTOK FOR TWO	BARTOK
BARTOK IS EASY - 15 MELODIOUS PIECES FOR THE YOUNG	BARTOK
BARUFFE DI PIERROT E PIERETTE, LE	GUARINO, C.
BASEBALL GAME	CRERIE, E.
BASEBALL LEAGUE, THE	SCHAUM, J.--ED.
BASIC PIANO FOR THE MUSIC EDUCATOR AND CLASSROOM	CHEYETTE, I.
BASIC PIANO TECHNIQUE BOOK 1	VEON
BASIC PIANO TECHNIQUE BOOK 2	VEON
BASIC TECHNIQUE FOR JAZZ PIANO	CAHN
BASIC TECHNIQUE FOR POPULAR PIANO	CAHN
BASIC TIMING FOR PIANIST	SMALL, A.
BASKETBALL PEP SONG	SCHAUM, J.--ED.
BASKETBALL	SKAGGS
BASKET DANCE	CROSBY, M.
BASKET OF PRIZE KITTENS, A	WILSON, M.
BASKET OF ROSES	ALBERS
BASKET OF ROSES	ALBERS
BASLER MASSARBEIT	KRENEK, E.
BASLER MASSARBEIT	KRENEK, E.
BASSO OSTINATO	DOLGOW, R.
BASSO OSTINATO	GIACCHINO
BASSO OSTINATO	SOENSTEVOLD
BASS GONE CRAZY	AMMONS
BASS ON TOP	LEWIS
BASS SINGER, THE	BESTHOFF, M.
BAT, THE	STRAUSS, J.
BATMAN THEME	HEFTI, N.
BATMAN THEME	LANE, J.--ED.
BATON TWIRLER	TILLETT, J.
BATTER UP	BONNIE
BATTER UP	GARROW, L.
BATTLE CRY OF FREEDOM	ROOT
BATTLE HYMN OF THE REPUBLIC--TWO PIANOS-EIGHT HANDS--	SCHAUM, J.--ED.
BATTLE HYMN OF THE REPUBLIC, THE	HOWE
BATTLE HYMN OF THE REPUBLIC	BRIMHALL,
BATTLE HYMN OF THE REPUBLIC	HOWE
BATTLE HYMN OF THE REPUBLIC	HOWE
BATTLE HYMN OF THE REPUBLIC	HOWE
BATTLE HYMN OF THE REPUBLIC	SCHAUM, J.--ED.
BATTLE HYMN OF THE REPUBLIC	SHORES--ED.
BATTLE HYMN OF THE REPUBLIC	STEFFE --ED
BATTLE OF GETTYSBURG	PAULL
BATTLE OF GETTYSBURG	TCHEREPNIN
BATTLE OF MANASSAS	TOM, BLIND
BATTLE OF THE SEWING MACHINES, THE --1874--	HYDE, F.
BATTLE OF WATERLOO, THE	ANDERSON
BAUER-DILLER-QUAILE COURSE--PIANO METHOD FOR CLASS AND	BAUER, H. *
BAUER-DILLER-QUAILE COURSE--PIANO METHOD FOR CLASS AND	BAUER, H. *
BAVARIAN SUITE, OP. 21	DERKSEN
BAVARIAN YODELER	JESSE, M.
BAVARIAN YODELER	JESSE, M.
BAYRISCHE LANDLER, OP. 36	SCHMID
BAYRISCHE LANDLER, OP. 36	SCHMID ,
BA DOAN KHUC	TON-THAT, T.
BE-BOP BOOGIE	SCHAUM, J.--ED.
BEACHCOMBER	RICHARDSON, C.
BEACH BALL BOOGIE	SCHAUM, J.
BEADED MOCCASINS	FROST
BEAR, PLAYING SOLDIERS, THE	REBIKOV
BEAR, THE	TURNER, O.
BEARCAT CRAWL	LEWIS
BEAR AND THE BEEHIVES, THE	GRAHAM, R.
BEAR AND THE OPOSSUM, THE	DITTENHAVER
BEAR DANCE, FROM 'TEN EASY PIECES'	BARTOK
BEAR DANCE	BARTOK
BEAR DANCE	SCHER, W.
BEATNIK FLY	KING *
BEAT GOES ON, THE	BONO
BEAUTIFUL BLUE DANUBE IN C	STRAUSS, J.
BEAUTIFUL BLUE DANUBE	STRAUSS, J.
BEAUTIFUL BLUE DANUBE	STRAUSS, J.
BEAUTIFUL BLUE DANUBE	STRAUSS, J.
BEAUTIFUL CHIMES AT SUNSET	LANGE, A.
BEAUTIFUL CITY	BRADLEY,
BEAUTIFUL DREAMER	FOSTER
BEAUTIFUL DREAMER	FOSTER
BEAUTIFUL DREAMER	FOSTER
BEAUTIFUL HEAVEN	FERNANDEZ, O.
BEAUTIFUL ISLE OF SOMEWHERE	FEARIS, J. S.
BEAUTIFUL ISLE OF SOMEWHERE	STEINER--ED.
BEAUTIFUL MAY, OP. 375	STRAUSS, J.
BEAUTIFUL MOONLIGHT	MCADAMS, G.
BEAUTIFUL OHIO --FOX TROT	EARL *
BEAUTIFUL OHIO	EARL
BEAUTIFUL OHIO	SCHAUM, J.
BEAUTIFUL SAVIOUR	STEINER--ED.
BEAUTIFUL SAVIOUR	STEINER
BEAUTIFUL STAR OF HEAVEN	DRUMHELLER
BEAUTIFUL STAR OF HEAVEN	DRUMHELLER
BEAUTIFUL SUNDAY	BOONE, D.
BEAUTIFUL SUNDAY	LANE, J.--ED.
BEAUTIFUL THAILAND	KENT
BEAUTY AND GRACE	ROSZA
BEAUTY AND GRACE	
BEAUTY AND GRACE	
BEAUTY AND THE BEAST	FRANCE
BEAU JEUDI,UN	GARCIN, M.
BEBE DORME	MONTANARI
BEBE	PIRANI
BECAUSE, A FLAT MAJOR	D'HARDELOT
BECAUSE, B FLAT MAJOR	D'HARDELOT
BECAUSE, C MAJOR	D'HARDELOT
BECAUSE YOU'RE MINE	LANE, J.--ED.
BECAUSE YOU'RE YOU	HERBERT
BECAUSE	D'HARDELOT
BECAUSE	D'HARDELOT
BECAUSE	D'HARDELOT
BECKYS WALTZ	RAEZER, C.
BEDTIME STORY -- LULLABY	BACH, W.F.
BEDTIME STORY	BACH, W.F.
BEDTIME TUNE, A	FOSTER, I. R.
BEDTIME	FISHER, E.
BED TIME STORIES	AMES, J.
BEE, THE	SCHUBERT
BEEHIVE, THE	WATKINS
BEEN TO CANAAN	BRADLEY,
BEER BARREL POLKA	BROWN *
BEER BARREL POLKA	BROWN *
BEES A-BUZZIN'	SCHER, W.
BEETHOVEN'S 'ADELAIDE' OP. 176, FOUR HANDS	BEETHOVEN
BEETHOVEN'S BEST KNOWN PIANO SONATAS	BEETHOVEN
BEETHOVEN FOR EVERYBODY	BEETHOVEN
BEETHOVEN FOR THE YOUNG PIANIST	BEETHOVEN
BEETHOVEN FOR THE YOUNG	BEETHOVEN
BEETHOVEN IS FUN	BEETHOVEN
BEETHOVEN OVERTURES, THE -- EGMONT, CORIOLANUS,	BEETHOVEN
BEETHOVEN	BEETHOVEN
BEE AND THE BUTTERCUP, THE	ECKHARDT, F.
BEE AND THE BUTTERFLY, THE	SCHER, W.
BEE HAPPY	SCHER, W.
BEE HIVE, THE	ALT, H.
BEE HIVE, THE	ALT, H.
BEE IN THE CLOCK, THE	SCHER, W.
BEGGAR'S OPERA. ABRIDGED.	GAY *
BEGGAR'S OPERA. ABRIDGED	PEPUSCH
BEGGAR'S OPERA	WEILL, K.
BEGINNER'S BOOGIE WOOGIE	WHITEFIELD
BEGINNER'S GUIDE TO POPULAR PIANO PLAYING	KAHN, M.
BEGINNER'S OWN BOOK	NEWMAN
BEGINNER'S ROCK 'N' ROLL PIANO BOOK	SMALL, A.
BEGINNERS' SCALES AND ARPEGGIOS	LOVELOCK, W.
BEGINNERS PIECES, OP. 39	KABALEVSKY

Title	Composer/Editor
BEGINNERS PIECES, OP. 51	LOESCHORN, A.
BEGINNERS PLAY BOOGIE WOOGIE	SPIVAK, S.
BEGINNINGS	BRIMHALL,
BEGINNING AT THE PIANO	FROST
BEGINNING PIANO FOR ADULTS	BASTIEN
BEGINNING PIANO STUDY, PT. 1	ROCHNER
BEGINNING PIANO STUDY, PT. 2	ROCHNER
BEGINNING PIANO STUDY, PT. 3	ROCHNER
BEGINNING PIANO STUDY, PT. 4 BK. 1	ROCHNER
BEGINNING PIANO STUDY, PT. 4 BK. 2	ROCHNER
BEGINNING PIANO STUDY, PT. 5	ROCHNER
BEGIN THE BEGUINE	PORTER, C.
BEGIN THE BEGUINE	PORTER, C.
BEGIN THE BEGUINE	PORTER, C.
BEGIN THE BEGUINE	PORTER, C.
BEGIN THE BEGUINE	PORTER, C.
BEGLEITSATZE -- DAS CHORALWERK -- HEFT 1, 25 SATZE ZU	BORNEFELD
BEGLEITSATZE -- DAS CHORALWERK -- HEFT 2, 28 SATZE ZU	BORNEFELD
BEGLEITSATZE -- DAS CHORALWERK -- HEFT 3, 31 SATZE ZU	BORNEFELD
BEGLEITSATZE -- DAS CHORALWERK -- HEFT 4, 29 SATZE,	BORNEFELD
BEGLEITSATZE -- DAS CHORALWERK -- HEFT 5, 30 SATZE,	BORNEFELD
BEGLEITSATZE -- DAS CHORALWERK -- HEFT 6, 32 SATZE ZU	BORNEFELD
BEGLEITSATZE - DAS CHORALWERK, BK. 1	BORNEFELD
BEGLEITSATZE - DAS CHORALWERK, BK. 2	BORNEFELD
BEGLEITSATZE - DAS CHORALWERK, BK. 3	BORNEFELD
BEGLEITSATZE - DAS CHORALWERK, BK. 4	BORNEFELD
BEGLEITSATZE - DAS CHORALWERK, BK. 5	BORNEFELD
BEGLEITSATZE - DAS CHORALWERK, BK. 6	BORNEFELD
BEHIND THE DOOR	SCARMOLIN
BEHIND THE WINDOWS	WEYBRIGHT
BEHIND THE WINDOWS	WEYBRIGHT
BELAFONTE FOLK SONG BOOK, THE	
BELIEVE ME ENDEARING CHARMS	FREEMAN
BELIEVE ME IF ALL THOSE ENDEARING CHARMS	ARMOUR
BELINDA'S SUITE NO. 1	SYMONS
BELINDA'S SUITE NO. 2	SYMONS
BELL, THE	HANSON
BELLA ADDORMENTATA, LA	ZECCHI
BELLE INSOUCIANTE, LA -- LE CAHIER DE SYLVINE, NO. 3	DELANNOY
BELLE OF THE BALL, WALTZ	BRANNAN
BELLE OF THE BALL	ANDERSON, L.
BELLS, BELLS, BELLS	PELZ
BELLS, THE	BASSETT
BELLS -- 6-HANDS	ROWLEY
BELLS ACROSS THE VALLEY	WRIGHT, N.
BELLS ARE RINGING	
BELLS ARE RINGING	
BELLS AT EVENING	PERRIN
BELLS AT TWILIGHT	ROLFE, W.
BELLS OF ANDORRA	ECKSTEIN
BELLS OF AVALON, THE -- SIMP.	MOSSMAN, T.
BELLS OF BERGHALL CHURCH, THE, OP. 65B	SIBELIUS
BELLS OF MARIEMONT, THE	WEYBRIGHT
BELLS OF MARIEMONT, THE	WEYBRIGHT
BELLS OF MOSCOW, EASY	RACHMANINOFF, S.
BELLS OF MOSCOW	RACHMANINOFF, S.
BELLS OF NORMANDY	KING, S.
BELLS OF NOTRE DAME	LECOUPPEY, F. *
BELLS OF ST. MARY'S, WALTZ	LESTRANGE--ED
BELLS OF ST. MARY'S, WALTZ	SPAULDING, G.
BELLS OF ST. MARY'S, WALTZ	ST. QUENTIN--ED
BELLS OF ST. MARY'S	
BELLS OF TIBET	BARBELLE, P.
BELLS	KIRK
BELLS	MAMLOK, U. L.
BELLS	ROGERS, B.
BELL AND THE LITTLE BELL, THE	KETTERER, E.
BELL AT THE FOUNTAIN	FROST
BELL DOTH TOLL, THE	CLARK, M. E.--ED
BELL MAZURKA	LANGE, G.
BELL SONATINA	STEEL
BELL TONES, OP. 81	HEINS, C.
BELL TOWER, THE	ANSON, G.
BELWIN PIANO METHOD, BK. 1	WEYBRIGHT--ED.
BELWIN PIANO METHOD, BK. 1	WEYBRIGHT
BELWIN PIANO METHOD, BK. 2	WEYBRIGHT--ED.
BELWIN PIANO METHOD, BK. 2	WEYBRIGHT
BELWIN PIANO METHOD, BK. 3	WEYBRIGHT--ED.
BELWIN PIANO METHOD, BK. 3	WEYBRIGHT
BELWIN PIANO METHOD, BK. 4	WEYBRIGHT--ED.
BELWIN PIANO METHOD, BK. 4	WEYBRIGHT
BELWIN PIANO METHOD, BK. 5	WEYBRIGHT--ED.
BELWIN PIANO METHOD, BK. 5	WEYBRIGHT
BEL MELODIEN I. LEICHT. SATZ	TSCHAIKOWSKY
BEN-HUR	ROSZA
BENEDICTION DE DIEU DANS LA SOLITUDE	LISZT
BENEDICTION NUPTIALE, OP. 9	SAINT-SAENS
BENTLEY ALBUM, A	BENTLEY
BENTLEY SECOND ALBUM	BENTLEY
BEN HUR CHARIOT RACE MARCH	PAULL
BEN HUR CHARIOT RACE	PAULL
BEN HUR CHARIOT RACE	PAULL
BEN HUR CHARIOT RACE	PAULL
BEN HUR CHARIOT RACE	PAULL
BEN HUR CHARIOT RACE	PAULL
BEN	BRADLEY,
BERCELONNETTE	MAZELLIER, J.
BERCEMENT	ARBEAU, P.
BERCEUSE, JOCELYN	GODARD, B.
BERCEUSE, NO. 20	CILEA
BERCEUSE, OP. 13 NO. 7	ILJINSKY, A.
BERCEUSE, OP. 13 NO. 7	ILJINSKY, A.
BERCEUSE, OP. 57	CHOPIN
BERCEUSE, OP. 57	CHOPIN
BERCEUSE --CRADLE SONG--, OP. 41 NO. 1	GRIEG
BERCEUSE --LULLABY--, OP. 38 NO. 1	GRIEG
BERCEUSE -- CRADLE SONG	DELBRUCK
BERCEUSE -- CRADLE SONG	HAUSER
BERCEUSE AND CAPRICCIO	DVORAK
BERCEUSE AND DIALOGUE	FRACKENPOHL, A.
BERCEUSE AND FINALE --FIREBIRD	STRAVINSKY, I.
BERCEUSE CONTRE AVIONS -- LE CAHIER DE SYLVINE, NO. 4	DELANNOY
BERCEUSE D'AUTOMNE	RODRIGO, J.
BERCEUSE DANS UN HAMAC	JOLIVET, A.
BERCEUSE DE PRINTEMPS	RODRIGO, J.
BERCEUSE FROM 'JOCELYN'	GODARD, B.
BERCEUSE FROM 'JOCELYN'	GODARD, B.
BERCEUSE HEROIQUE	DEBUSSY
BERCEUSE IN D FLAT, OP. 57	CHOPIN
BERCEUSE IN D FLAT MAJOR, OP. 57	CHOPIN
BERCEUSE IN G FLAT MAJOR, OP. 13	ILJINSKY, A.
BERCEUSE IN G MAJOR, OP. 38 NO. 4	GRIEG
BERCEUSE IN G	SCHYTTE
BERCEUSE POUR LES ORPHELINS D'ESPAGNE--1938	NIN
BERCEUSE SUR LE NOM DE FAURE	RAVEL
BERCEUSE SUR LE NOM DE FAURE	RAVEL
BERCEUSE	BILOTTI
BERCEUSE	BUSONI

Title	Composer/Editor
BERCEUSE	DE CASTERA
BERCEUSE	DE FRANCMESNIL
BERCEUSE	FELINE
BERCEUSE	GALLON, J.
BERCEUSE	GETTY, G.
BERCEUSE	GODARD, B.
BERCEUSE	OLSEN, O.
BERCEUSE	POZZOLI
BERCEUSE	SPENDIAROW
BERCEUSE	TANTILLO
BERCEUSE	TOMASI, H.
BERCEUSE	VOORMOLEN
BERGERES DE TRIANON, GAVOTTE, OP. 209	LANDRY
BERGERETTE, OP. 23	GREGH
BERGERETTE	LANDRY
BERGERS A LA FONTAINE	LANERY *
BERGERS WATTEAU, LES OP. 5	GREGH
BERGERS WATTEAU, LES OP. 5	GREGH
BERGERS WATTEAU, LES OP. 5	GREGH
BERGLIOT, OP. 42	GRIEG
BERGSOMMER, ACHT KLEINE STUCKE	SUTERMEISTER, H.
BERNARD WHITEFELD'S AMERICAN FOLK SONG ALBUM	WHITEFIELD
BERNA	TREVARTHEN, R.
BERRICHONNE, LA, DANSE CARACTERISTIQUE	WACHS, P.
BERRY BASKET, THE, BK. 1	
BERRY BASKET, THE, BK. 2	
BERUHMTES LARGO -- ERLEICHTERT	HANDEL
BERUHMTES LARGO	HANDEL
BERUHMTES LARGO	HANDEL
BERUHMTES MENUETT AUS DEM D-DUR DIVERTIMENTO -- K.V.	MOZART, W. A.
BERUHMTE MELODIEN	DVORAK
BESS YOU IS MY WOMAN	RUBINSTEIN--ED
BEST OF ALL, THE	SCARMOLIN--ED
BEST OF BACH	BACH, J.S.
BEST OF BEETHOVEN	BEETHOVEN
BEST OF BRIMHALL, BK. 1	BRIMHALL,
BEST OF BRIMHALL, BK. 2	BRIMHALL,
BEST OF BRIMHALL, BK. 3	BRIMHALL,
BEST OF CHOPIN	CHOPIN
BEST OF GRIEG	GRIEG
BEST OF JOHN LANE, THE	LANE, J.--ED
BEST OF MOZART	MOZART, W. A.
BEST OF SACRED MUSIC	BRIMHALL,
BEST OF SCHUBERT	SCHUBERT
BEST OF TSCHAIKOWSKY	TSCHAIKOWSKY
BEST OF WEYBRIGHT, BK. 1	WEYBRIGHT
BEST OF WEYBRIGHT, BK. 2	WEYBRIGHT
BEST OF WEYBRIGHT, BK. 3	WEYBRIGHT
BEST OF YOUNG WORLD	ROGERS, E. T.
BETTINA'S POLKA	SMETANA
BETTINAS POLKA	SMETANA
BETTY'S FIRST WALTZ	LIGHT, F. M.
BETTY'S HIGH CHAIR	LIGHT, F. M.
BETTY'S WALTZ -- ONE PIANO, 6 HANDS --	MARTIN, G.
BETTY'S WALTZ	MARTIN, G.
BETTY'S WALTZ	MARTIN, G.
BETTY'S WOODEN SHOE DANCE	LIGHT, F. M.
BETTY'S WOODEN SHOE DANCE	LIGHT, F. M.
BETTY BLUE EYES	BONNER
BETTY JANE WALTZ	HELTMAN
BETTY LOU, MINUET	PROEHL, H.
BETWEEN 18TH AND 19TH ON CHESTNUT STREET	OSBORNE *
BEWITCHED	SINGER, L.--ED
BEWITCHED	
BEYER MODERNIZED	STEINER
BEYOND THE RIO GRANDE	LOWENSTEIN
BEYOND THE SEA	
BEYOND THE SUNSET	LANE, J.--ED.
BE HAPPY - BE LUCKY	REID
BE WISE	KERR, R. N.
BHARATE SANGITA--INDIAN MUSIC--	SCHRAMM
BI-CENTENNIAL MARCH	VOLZ, H.
BIALLO E ROSSO	BOCCOSI, BIO
BIBLE, THE	MAYUZUMI
BIBLE TELLS ME SO, THE	BRIMHALL,
BIBLICAL SONATAS# NO. 1--THE BATTLE BETWEEN DAVID AND	KUHNAU, J.
BIBLICAL SONATAS# NO. 1 -- THE BATTLE BETWEEN DAVID	KUHNAU, J.
BIBLICAL SONATAS# NO. 2 -- SAUL CURED BY DAVID WITH	KUHNAU, J.
BIBLICAL SONATAS# NO. 3 -- THE WEDDING OF JACOB--	KUHNAU, J.
BIBLICAL SONATAS# NO. 4 -- HEZEKIAH WHO, BEING SICK	KUHNAU, J.
BIBLICAL SONATAS# NO. 5 -- GIDEON, THE DELIVERER OF	KUHNAU, J.
BIBLICAL SONATAS# NO. 6 -- THE DEATH AND BURIAL OF	KUHNAU, J.
BIBLICAL SONATA NO. 5	KUHNAU, J.
BICHE DANS LA NEIGE	BARLOW
BICYCLE BUILT FOR TWO, A	DACRE
BICYCLE RACE, A	TRAVIS, B.
BICYCLE RIDE	ALT, H.
BICYCLE RIDE	CHAGY
BICYCLE RIDE	THOMAS, J. J.
BICYCLE STUNTS	PRIGGE, D.
BICYCLE TUNE	DITTENHAVER
BIEN AMADA, LA--VALENCIA	PADILLA, J.
BIEN GENTILLE	WACHS, P.
BIG-NOTE BOOK, THE -- MINIATURE MELODIES FOR LITTLE	WEYBRIGHT
BIG-NOTE BOOK	
BIG BAD WOLF	ANSON, G.
BIG BANDS, THE	LINDSAY, C.
BIG BASS DRUM	GODDARD, W.
BIG BASS FIDDLE, THE	HOPKINS, H.
BIG BASS FIDDLE HUMORESQUE -- ONE PIANO, 6 HANDS --	HOPKINS, H.
BIG BASS FIDDLE	DE VITO, A.
BIG BASS SINGER, THE	ROLFE
BIG BASS VIOL	HOLLANDER
BIG BEN BOUNCE	TEMPLETON
BIG BOY BOOGIE	STEINER
BIG BROWN BEAR	RAEZER, C.
BIG CHIEF HIC-CUP	NOONA, W.
BIG COWBOY AND THE LITTLE COWBOY, THE	ACKERMANN, D.
BIG DRUM MAJOR, THE, MARCH -- ONE PIANO, 6 HANDS --	HOPKINS, H.
BIG DRUM MAJOR	HOPKINS, H.
BIG FEET JOHNNIE	GANZ
BIG INDIAN CHIEF	ROVENGER
BIG NOTE CARNIVAL--100--	
BIG NOTE CHRISTMAS CAROLS	HUNEKE--ED
BIG NOTE CHRISTMAS FAVORITES	MOORE--ED
BIG NOTE PARADE--150--	
BIG RED FIRE ENGINE, THE	BASTIEN
BIG ROCK CANDY MOUNTAIN	MOSSMAN, T.
BIG SEVENTY-FIVE SONG BOOK, THE - EASY BIG NOTE PIANO	
BIG SOLDIER, THE, MARCH	HOPKINS, H.
BIG SPENDER	LANE, J.--ED.
BIG 3'S BEST IN POPS	
BIG 3'S 20 BIG HITS OF TODAY	
BIJOUX CHERIS, PETITE VALSE -- SIMPLIFIED VERSION	DESSAUX
BIJOUX CHERIS, PETITE VALSE	DESSAUX
BIKE HIKE	SCHAUM, J.
BIKE RIDE	BRIMHALL, J.

BILDER AUS DEM OSTEN OP. 66 — SCHUMANN, R.
BILDER EINER AUSSTELLUNG — MOUSSORGSKY
BILDER EINER AUSSTELLUNG — MOUSSORGSKY
BILLBOARD MARCH, THE — KLOHR, J. N.
BILLIE BEAVER — BALDWIN, E.
BILLY THE KID — COPLAND
BILLY THE KID — COPLAND
BILLY THE KID — WEYBRIGHT--ED.
BILLY THE KID — WEYBRIGHT
BILL BAILEY — SMALL, A.
BILL EVANS PIANO SOLOS — EVANS
BILL EVANS PLAYS — EVANS
BILL IRWIN'S MAGIC STUDY SERIES -CHORD CONSTRUCTION — IRWIN--ED.
BILL IRWIN'S MAGIC STUDY SERIES - DIMINISHED CHORD — IRWIN--ED.
BILL IRWIN'S MAGIC STUDY SERIES - MODERN FILL MAGIC — IRWIN--ED.
BILL IRWIN'S MAGIC STUDY SERIES - MODERN MELODY MAGIC — IRWIN--ED.
BILL IRWIN'S MAGIS STUDY SERIES - RHYTHM ACCOMPANIMENT — IRWIN--ED.
BILL
BIMBI SOLDATI — MONTANARI
BINIOU, LE — DURAND
BIONDA IN GONDOLETTA, LA — MAYR
BIRCH-BARK CANOE — TAYLOR
BIRDLING, OP. 43 NO. 4 — GRIEG
BIRDLING, OP. 43 NO. 4 — GRIEG
BIRDLING, OP. 43 NO. 4 — GRIEG
BIRDS IN OUR GARDEN — BILBRO, M.
BIRDS IN SPRINGTIME — KVELVE
BIRDS N'BEES — THIELMANS
BIRDS OF A FEATHER - 10 EASY PIECES — HARVEY, VIVIEN
BIRDS OF PARADISE--VALSE MIGNONNE, OP. 78 NO. 1 — STREABBOG
BIRDS OF PARADISE, WALTZ — STREABBOG
BIRDS OF PASSAGE — POLDINI, E.
BIRDS ON A BOUGH — ROESSING, H.
BIRDS — FISHER--ED
BIRD AS PROPHET, OP. 82 NO. 7 — SCHUMANN, R.
BIRD CALLS — HAYDN
BIRD CHATTER — STEVENS, E.
BIRD IN THE TREETOP — ERB
BIRD OF PARADISE — ELLINGTON
BIRD SONGS AT EVENTIDE
BIRD SONG AT MORNING — SYMONS
BIRTHDAY BELLS — BECK
BIRTHDAY BOUQUET -- THEME AND VARIATIONS
BIRTHDAY OF A KING, THE — NEIDLINGER, W.
BIRTHDAY PARTY — DUMM
BIRTHDAY PARTY — MACLACHLIN, T.
BIRTHDAY PARTY — PREVIN, A.
BIRTHDAY PARTY — RAPHLING
BIRTHDAY PARTY — RAPHLING
BIRTHDAY TO A KING — NEIDLINGER, W.
BIRTH OF THE BLUES, THE — HENDERSON
BIRTH OF THE BLUES, THE — HENDERSON
BISCAYNE BOOGIE --MODERN RHYTHMIC CLASSICS-- — WHITFORD
BIST DU BEI MIR -- FROM THE NOTENBUCHLEIN OF A. M. — BACH, J.S.
BIST DU BEI MIR — BACH, J.S.
BIST DU BEI MIR — BACH, J.S.
BIST DU BEI MIR — BACH, J.S.
BITS AND PIECES — FENNIMORE
BITTERER SPOTT, OP. 17 — PROKOFIEFF
BITTERSWEET — BRIDGE, F.
BIT MISCHIEVOUS, A — ELMER, C.
BIT OF BLUE, A — DUMM
BIT OF FOLKSY, A — ROZIN
BLACK-FOREST CLOCK, THE--SALON POLKA, OP. 224 — HEINS
BLACKBERRY JACK — GODDEN, R.
BLACKIE AND WHITEY — SCHAUM, J.--ED.
BLACKSMITH, THE — BRAHMS
BLACKSMITH, THE — HELLER, S.
BLACKSMITH IN THE WOODS — MICHAELIS, J.
BLACK AND TAN FANTASY — MILEY *
BLACK AND WHITE - AND - BRIAN'S SONG — BRADLEY,
BLACK AND WHITE RAG — BOTSFORD, G.
BLACK AND WHITE RAG — BOTSFORD, G.
BLACK AND WHITE — BRADLEY,
BLACK AND WHITE — BRIMHALL,
BLACK AND WHITE — LOSEY
BLACK AND WHITE — VOLPATTI
BLACK BEAUTY — SCHAUM, J.--ED.
BLACK BIRD, A TALE — SCHILLER, F.
BLACK BOOTS — BEISSERT
BLACK CAT, THE — GRAHAM, R.
BLACK CAT TANGO — BASTIEN
BLACK EBONY — SCARMOLIN
BLACK EYED SUSAN — KOHLER, F.
BLACK EYES — THOMPSON, J.
BLACK FOREST OWL, THE — POOLE, C.
BLACK HAWK WALTZ, THE — WALSH, M.
BLACK HAWK WALTZ — WALSH, M.
BLACK HAWK WALTZ — WALSH, M.
BLACK HAWK WALTZ — WALSH, M.
BLACK HAWK WALTZ — WALSH, M.
BLACK HAWK WALTZ — WALSH, M.
BLACK HAWK WALTZ — WALSH, M.
BLACK HAWK WALTZ — WALSH, M.
BLACK HAWK WALTZ — WALSH *
BLACK KEY ETUDE — CHOPIN
BLACK KEY WALTZ — BALOGH
BLACK LIGHTS, OP. 74 — HARTMANN
BLACK MAGIC — KAHL
BLACK MAGIC — WHITE, G.
BLACK NOTE POLKA — MCGRAW
BLACK PIRATES — SEUEL *
BLACK ROSES, OP. 36 NO. 1 — SIBELIUS
BLACK SAPPHIRE — GROFE, F.
BLACK STEPPING STONES — HAYES
BLANC ET NOIR, VALSE, OP. 314 NO. 2 — STREABBOG
BLANIK — SMETANA
BLATTER UND BLUTEN, LEAVES AND BLOSSOMS — REGER
BLAZE AWAY — HOLZMANN, A.
BLESS THE BEASTS AND CHILDREN — BRADLEY,
BLESS THIS HOUSE — BRAHE, M.
BLESS THIS HOUSE — BRAHE, M.
BLEST BE THE TIE THAT BINDS -- HYMN — FAWCETT
BLEST BE THE TIE THAT BINDS — FAWCETT
BLINKING OWLS — MOKREJS
BLITHE BELLS -- ARIA, "SHEEP MAY GRAZE IN SAFETY" — BACH, J.S.
BLITHE SPIRIT — AARON, M.
BLOC-NOTES, OP. 37 — BALLIF
BLOOD, SWEAT, AND TEARS
BLOOMER GIRL
BLOSSOMS IN A POOL — GRAHAM, R.
BLOSSOM TIME — ROMBERG, S.
BLOWIN' IN THE WIND — DYLAN
BLOWING BELL AND SNOW WHIRL — GOULD, E.
BLOW THAT BUGLE — GLOVER, D.
BLOW THE MAN DOWN — MOSSMAN, T.
BLUE-PINK — SCHIFRIN
BLUEBELLS IN SPRING — MARTIN, H.

BLUEBELLS OF SCOTLAND, THE — ANDERSON, L.
BLUEBIRDS — TROJE-MILLER
BLUEBIRD BOOGIE WOOGIE — AMMONS
BLUEBIRD BOOGIE WOOGIE — AMMONS
BLUES, FROM 'INTERPLAY' — GOULD, M.
BLUESETTE — GIMBEL *
BLUESETTE — GIMBEL *
BLUESMEN, THE — SMALL, A.
BLUES AND HOW — NELSON, O.
BLUES AND THE ABSTRACT TRUTH — ARLEN, H.
BLUES IN THE NIGHT — GROVE
BLUES MOTIF — DENNIS, M.
BLUES PIANO STYLES — SIGNORELLI *
BLUES SERENADE, A — DUNGAN
BLUES — DUNGAN
BLUES — DUVERNOY, J.
BLUETTE--WALTZ, OP. 272 NO. 1 — MACDOWELL
BLUETTE IN E FLAT, OP. 46 NO. 8 — DUVERNOY, J.
BLUETTE VALSE — GAUTIER, L.
BLUETTE — CHAGY
BLUE BALLAD — SCHER, W.
BLUE BALLET SHOES — ARCHER, I.
BLUE BALLET — REISER, V.
BLUE BALLET — SCHILLER, F.
BLUE BIRD, MELODIE — OLEMAN, L.
BLUE BIRD WALTZ -- HESITATION — SCHAUM, J.--ED.
BLUE BOOGIE — SCHAUM, J.--ED.
BLUE BOOGIE — DORE, L.
BLUE BUTTERFLIES — MAINVILLE
BLUE BUTTERFLIES — GILLOCK
BLUE BUTTERFLY — SCHER, W.
BLUE CANDLELIGHT
BLUE CHRISTMAS
BLUE CLARINET — LANGENFELD
BLUE CLASSIQUE — BALKE, C.
BLUE DAISIES OP. 140 — MANA-ZUCCA
BLUE DANUBE IN REVERSE — STRAUSS, J.
BLUE DANUBE OP. 314 — STRAUSS, J.
BLUE DANUBE WALTZ, D MAJOR — STRAUSS, J.
BLUE DANUBE WALTZ, EASY — STRAUSS, J.
BLUE DANUBE WALTZ, THE — STRAUSS, J.
BLUE DANUBE WALTZ --SIMPLIFIED-- — STRAUSS, J.
BLUE DANUBE WALTZ — STRAUSS, J.
BLUE DANUBE WALTZ — STRAUSS, J.
BLUE DANUBE WALTZ — STRAUSS, J.
BLUE DANUBE WALTZ — STRAUSS, J.
BLUE DANUBE WALTZ — STRAUSS, J.
BLUE DANUBE WALTZ — STRAUSS, J.
BLUE DANUBE WALTZ — STRAUSS, J.
BLUE DANUBE WALTZ — STRAUSS, J.
BLUE DANUBE WALTZ — STRAUSS, J.
BLUE DANUBE WALTZ — WEYBRIGHT
BLUE DANUBE — STRAUSS, J.
BLUE DANUBE — STRAUSS, J.
BLUE DANUBE — STRAUSS, J.
BLUE DANUBE — STRAUSS, J.
BLUE DANUBE — STRAUSS, J.
BLUE ETUDE -- IN POPULAR STYLE — WEYBRIGHT
BLUE ETUDE — WEYBRIGHT
BLUE FAIRY — FRIML, R.
BLUE FLAME, BLUES — STANLEY
BLUE FOUNTAIN — ECKSTEIN
BLUE GARDEN, THE — LORAINE, P.
BLUE GNU — DANFORD, A.
BLUE GRAPES — DUNGAN
BLUE HORIZON — WHITFORD
BLUE LAGOON — RUSSELL
BLUE MAX, THE — GOLDSMITH, J.
BLUE MIST — REEVES, R.
BLUE MONDAY — STEINER
BLUE MOOD — GILLOCK
BLUE MOON — HART *
BLUE MOON — LANE, J.--ED.
BLUE MOON
BLUE PAGODA, THE — DECOURSEY, R.
BLUE RHYTHM — WERMEL
BLUE RIBBON PIANO ALBUM — FLAMMER--ED.
BLUE RIDGE DIVISION — ROCERETO, M.
BLUE ROOM, THE — RODGERS
BLUE SCARECROW, THE — LUDWIG
BLUE STREAK — RAPHLING
BLUE TAIL FLY — SCHAUM, J.--ED.
BLUE TANGO -- SIMP. — KING, S.--ED.
BLUE TANGO — ANDERSON, L.
BLUE TANGO — ANDERSON, L.
BLUE UMBRELLA — EDELSON
BLUE VELVET
BLUE VELVET
BLUE VIOLINS — MARTIN
BLUE WINDMILLS — GLOVER, D.
BLUMENLIED, EASY — LANGE, G.
BLUMENSTUECK, OP. 19 — SCHUMANN, R.
BLUMENSTUECK, OP. 19 — SCHUMANN, R.
BLUMENSTUECK, OP. 19 — SCHUMANN, R.
BLUMLISALP -- RASPBERRY ROSE — TREVARTHEN, R.
BOASTFUL LITTLE MONKEY — SEINBERG
BOATING SONG — FINLAYSON, W.
BOATMAN'S SONG, THE — MOREY, F.
BOAT RACE, GALOP — HOPKINS, H.
BOAT RIDE AT SILVER SPRINGS — MITTLER
BOAT SONG AT DUSK — BINDER, A. W.
BOAT SONG — MENDELSSOHN
BOBOLINK, POLKA — SCHILLER, F.
BOBOLINK POLKA — WOLCOTT, J. T.
BOBOLINK — COKELY, C.
BOBOLINK — KETTERER, E.
BOBOLINK — NOFKA, R.
BOB WHITE — CRERIE, E.
BOCCACERIE - 5 PORTRAITS POUR LE DECAMERON — DELVINCOURT
BOCETOS. COLLECTION OF EASY PIECES — GRANADOS
BOCETOS PIANISTICOS — LERMA, P.
BODAS EN LA MONTANA — PAHISSA
BODY AND SOUL — GREEN
BODY AND SOUL — GREEN
BOEUF SUR LE TOIT, LE — MILHAUD, D.
BOGEY MAN, THE — LONG, L.
BOHEMA CZARDAS — MICHIELS
BOHEME, LA -- COMPLETE OPERA -- — PUCCINI
BOHEME, LA -- MUSETTA'S WALTZ — PUCCINI
BOHEME, LA - CHE GELIDA MANINA — PUCCINI
BOHEME, LA - CHE GELIDA MANINA — PUCCINI
BOHEME, LA - EASY FANTASIA — PUCCINI
BOHEME, LA - FANTASIA — PUCCINI
BOHEME, LA - FANTASIA — PUCCINI
BOHEME, LA - IO NON CHE UNA POVERA STANZETTA — LEONCAVALLO
BOHEME, LA - MUSETTA'S WALTZ SONG — PUCCINI
BOHEME, LA - MUSETTA'S WALTZ SONG — PUCCINI

BOHEME, LA - MUSETTA'S WALTZ SONG	PUCCINI
BOHEME, LA - MUSETTA'S WALTZ SONG	PUCCINI
BOHEME, LA - SELECTION	PUCCINI
BOHEME, LA - SI, MI CHIAMANO MIMI	PUCCINI
BOHEME, LA - SI, MI CHIAMANO MIMI	PUCCINI
BOHEMIAN DANCES	SMETANA
BOHEMIAN DANCE NO. 2‡ 'THE LITTLE PULLET'	SMETANA
BOHEMIAN FOLK SONG	PARSONS
BOHEMIAN GIRL, I DREAMT I DWELT, E FLAT MAJOR	BALFE
BOHEMIAN GIRL, I DREAMT I DWELT	BALFE
BOHEMIAN GIRL, THEN YOU'LL REMEMBER	BALFE
BOHEMIAN POLKA	SMETANA
BOHEMIENS, LES	DELIOUX
BOHMISCHE TANZE	SMETANA
BOHMISCHE VARIATIONEN DES 18. JAHRHUNDERTS	STEPHAN *
BOIS DE BOULOGNE	PETIT, P.
BOITE A MUSIQUE	BEAUCAMP
BOITE A MUSIQUE	SGAMBATI
BOITE DE COULEURS--NO. 01, CADMIUM ORANGE	LAVAGNE
BOITE DE COULEURS--NO. 09, MAUVE	LAVAGNE
BOITE DE COULEURS--NO. 11, INDIGO	LAVAGNE
BOITE DE COULEURS--NO. 12, ARC EN CIEL	LAVAGNE
BOITE DE PANDORE, LA	BARRAINE, E.
BOLANGO	DILSNER
BOLD ADVENTURER	CLAY, S.
BOLD KNIGHT, THE	HOPKINS, H.
BOLD PIRATE	HOWELL, I.
BOLERO, OP. 12 NO. 5	MOSZKOWSKI
BOLERO, OP. 12 NO. 5	MOSZKOWSKI
BOLERO, OP. 12 NO. 5	MOSZKOWSKI
BOLERO, OP. 19	CHOPIN
BOLERO, OP. 19	CHOPIN
BOLERO, OP. 76 NO. 2	BURGMUELLER
BOLERO -- BOUQUET DE PENSEES --	STREABBOG
BOLERO IN A MINOR, OP. 27	LACK, T.
BOLERO IN BLUE	MITTLER
BOLERO ON THE MOON	SLACK
BOLERO RITMICO	LONGAS
BOLERO	MOSZKOWSKI
BOLERO	RAVEL
BOLERO	RAVEL
BOLERO	RAVEL
BOLERO	THOMPSON, J.
BOLSHOI BAGATELLE	NEVIN
BOMBARDO-CARILLON	ALKAN
BOMBARDON CHIFONE	BRANT
BONJOUR, PRINTEMPS	WACHS, P.
BONJOUR COLOMBINE, OP. 86	CARMAN
BONNIE, BONNIE LASSIE	BURNAM
BONNIE BLUE BELL, THE	MERRICK, F.
BONNIE BOOGIE	STEINER
BONN SONATAS, THE	BEETHOVEN
BONN SONATAS, THE	BEETHOVEN
BONN SONATA NO. 1	BEETHOVEN
BONN SONATA NO. 2	BEETHOVEN
BONSOIR, MADAME LA LUNE	MARINIER
BON PETIT DIABLE, LE	BEAUCAMP
BOOGIE-BOO-YOU	HIBBS, C.
BOOGIE-WOOGIE IN THE KITCHEN	SINATRA, R.
BOOGIE-WOOGIE IN THE PARLOR	SINATRA, R.
BOOGIE AND BLUES	AGAY, D.--ED
BOOGIE AT THE FAIR	KLEINMAN, A.
BOOGIE BEET	ELAINE, M.
BOOGIE BOOK	SCHAUM, J.--ED.
BOOGIE BRIGADE	GROVE, R.
BOOGIE BUGLE	SPIVAK, S.
BOOGIE ETUDE	BINKLEY
BOOGIE ETUDE	BINKLEY
BOOGIE EXPRESS	SCHAUM, J.--ED.
BOOGIE FUN FOR THE PIANO	MARTIN, H.
BOOGIE FUN	WEYBRIGHT
BOOGIE FUN	WEYBRIGHT
BOOGIE HOP	WEYBRIGHT
BOOGIE HOP	WEYBRIGHT
BOOGIE IS MY BEAT	SCHAUM, J.
BOOGIE JUNIOR	WEYBRIGHT
BOOGIE JUNIOR	WEYBRIGHT
BOOGIE MAN, THE	SCHAUM, J.--ED.
BOOGIE ON THE BRIDGE	GARROW, L.
BOOGIE ON THE SHANNON RIVER	RUSSELL
BOOGIE THE WOOGIE	GOULD, M.
BOOGIE VARIATIONS -- MORE BOOGIE FUN	WEYBRIGHT
BOOGIE VARIATIONS	WEYBRIGHT
BOOGIE WOOGIE BARBECUE	SPIVAK, S.
BOOGIE WOOGIE CARNIVAL	SPIVAK, S.
BOOGIE WOOGIE COASTER	SPIVAK, S.
BOOGIE WOOGIE COCKTAIL	KERSEY
BOOGIE WOOGIE ETUDE	GOULD, M.
BOOGIE WOOGIE ETUDE	GOULD, M.
BOOGIE WOOGIE FOR ADULT STUDENTS	SPIVAK, S.
BOOGIE WOOGIE FOR ADVANCED BEGINNERS	WHITEFIELD
BOOGIE WOOGIE FOR FOUR HANDS	WHITEFIELD
BOOGIE WOOGIE FOR GOOD PLAYERS	WHITEFIELD
BOOGIE WOOGIE FOR THE YOUNG PIANIST	STEINER
BOOGIE WOOGIE FOR YOUNG STUDENTS	SPIVAK, S.
BOOGIE WOOGIE HOLIDAY	SPIVAK, S.
BOOGIE WOOGIE IN BLUE	MITTLER
BOOGIE WOOGIE IN C --MODERN RHYTHMIC CLASSICS--	WHITFORD
BOOGIE WOOGIE IN 15 LANGUAGES	SPIVAK, S.
BOOGIE WOOGIE MAYPOLE	SPIVAK, S.
BOOGIE WOOGIE NOCTURNE	SPIVAK, S.
BOOGIE WOOGIE NOCTURNE	SPIVAK, S.
BOOGIE WOOGIE PARADE	SPIVAK, S.
BOOGIE WOOGIE PIANO ARRANGEMENTS, BK. 1 - EASY	PAPARELLI
BOOGIE WOOGIE PIANO ARRANGEMENTS, BK. 3 - MEDIUM	PAPARELLI
BOOGIE WOOGIE PRAYER	LEWIS *
BOOGIE WOOGIE SCHOOL DAYS	GLOVER, D.
BOOGIE WOOGIE STOMP	AMMONS
BOOGIE	SIEGMEISTER
BOOGIE	SIEGMEISTER
BOOGIN' ON THE DOWNBEAT	JOHNSON, S.
BOOK FOR OLDER BEGINNERS -- OLD EDITION	WILLIAMS, J.
BOOK OF CHIMES	PALMER
BOOK OF EASY PIANO PIECES	STAIRS, L.
BOOK OF PIANO PIECES	KETTERER, E.
BOOK OF RHYTHM	BRADLEY
BOOK OF TRIOS, FOR ONE PIANO, SIX HANDS	WEYBRIGHT
BOOK OF TRIOS -- ONE PIANO, SIX HANDS	WEYBRIGHT
BOOK 01, PRE-A -- FOR THE EARLIEST BEGINNER	SCHAUM, J.
BOOK 02, A -- THE RED BOOK	SCHAUM, J.
BOOK 03, B -- THE BLUE BOOK	SCHAUM, J.
BOOK 04, C -- THE PURPLE BOOK	SCHAUM, J.
BOOK 05, D -- THE ORANGE BOOK	SCHAUM, J.
BOOK 06, E -- THE VIOLET BOOK	SCHAUM, J.
BOOK 07, F -- THE BROWN BOOK	SCHAUM, J.
BOOK 08, G -- THE AMBER BOOK	SCHAUM, J.
BOOK 09, H -- THE GREY BOOK	SCHAUM, J.
BOOK 10, AFTER H BOOK, BK. 1	SCHAUM, J.
BOOK 10, AFTER H BOOK, BK. 2	SCHAUM, J.
BOOM BOOM	SCARMOLIN
BORN FREE	BRADLEY,
BORN FREE	BRADLEY,
BORN FREE	BRADLEY,
BOROVA, 7 DANSES TCHEQUES	MARTINU, B.
BOSSA NOVA ROMA	DRAO
BOSSA NOVA TIME	DRAO
BOSTON 'PARTITA'	SCHULHOFF
BOSTON MUSIC CO.'S CHRISTMAS CAROL BOOK	WALLIS--ED
BOSUN, THE	LEE, E. M.
BOULANGER MARCH	DESORMES
BOULEVARDIER	CURZON, F.
BOUNCE DANCE	COWELL
BOUNCE THE BALL	RICHTER
BOUNCING ALONG	CATIZONE, J. M.
BOUNCING BALL	KEVAN
BOUNCING THE BALL	CARTER
BOUNCING THE BALL	KALMANOFF
BOUNCING THE BALL	KALMANOFF
BOUNCING THE BALL	QUIXLEY, F.
BOUND FOR BIRMINGHAM	EZELL, H.
BOUQUETIERE, LA	STREABBOG
BOUQUET	ROSETTA, G.
BOUQUET	WHITFORD
BOURDONNEMENT D'ABEILLES	MICHEUZ, G.
BOUREE A LA BAGATELLE	DILSNER
BOUREE FANTASQUE	CHABRIER
BOUREE IN C MAJOR AND BOURREE IN C MINOR--FROM CELLO	BACH, J.S.
BOUREE	MOZART, W. A.
BOUREE	MOZART, W. A.
BOURREE, FROM L'EVENTAIL DE JEANNE	DELANNOY
BOURREES D'AUVERGNE	CANTELOUBE
BOURREE FANTASTIQUE	CHABRIER
BOURREE FOR THE LEFT HAND, OP. 135, NO. 4	SAINT-SAENS
BOURREE IN B MINOR--FROM VIOLIN SONATA NO. 2	BACH, J.S.
BOURREE IN C AND BOURREE IN C MINOR	BACH, J.S.
BOURREE IN D FROM SUITE NO. 3 FOR ORCH -- TRANSCRIBED	BACH, J.S.
BOURREE IN G MAJOR--TRS. FROM CELLO SUITE NO. 3	BACH, J.S.
BOURREE	HANDEL
BOURREE	HANDEL
BOURREE	KUHNAU, J.
BOURREE	WEYBRIGHT
BOURREE	WEYBRIGHT
BOWL OF PANSIES	REYNARD
BOWL OF PANSIES	REYNARD
BOY'S FAVORITE SOLO ALBUM	ECKARD, W.
BOY'S MARCH	DUNHILL, T.
BOY'S MERRY-GO-ROUND	GADE, N.
BOY' ROUND DANCE	GADE, N.
BOYN-GURLITT --EIGHTY-FIVE ETUDES TO DEVELOP	ROBYN
BOYS' BOOK OF PIECES	
BOYS BOOK	SCHAUM, J.--ED.
BOY AND HIS PIANO	KING, S.
BOY AND THE ROSE, THE	SCHUBERT
BOY FRIEND, THE	
BOY MEETS HORN	ELLIS, N.
BOY SCOUTS, MARCH	HOPKINS, H.
BOY SCOUTS MARCH	KVELVE
BOY SCOUTS MARCH	SCHIEFELBEIN, F.
BOY SCOUT PARADE	ARNOLD, H.
BOY SOLDIER	GANZ
BOY WITH GUITAR	GARROW, L.
BOZZETTI SICILIANI	MARCHESE
BOZZETTI	PICCIOLI
BOZZETTI	RUDAN
BRADLEY'S BEST OF THE BEST - BREAD	BRADLEY,
BRADLEY'S BEST OF THE BEST - BROADWAY	BRADLEY,
BRADLEY'S BEST OF THE BEST - CAROLE KING	BRADLEY,
BRADLEY'S BEST OF THE BEST - CHRISTMAS CAROLS	BRADLEY,
BRADLEY'S BEST OF THE BEST - COUNTRY HITS	BRADLEY,
BRADLEY'S BEST OF THE BEST - MOTION PICTURE HITS	BRADLEY,
BRADLEY'S BEST OF THE BEST - POPULAR SACRED SONGS	BRADLEY,
BRADLEY'S BEST OF THE BEST - POP TEACHING PIECES	BRADLEY,
BRADLEY'S BIG NOTE BLOCKBUSTERS	BRADLEY,
BRADLEY'S CHRISTMAS JOY - ISSUE NO. 1	BRADLEY,
BRADLEY'S COUNTRY JOY - ISSUE NO. 1	BRADLEY,
BRADLEY'S DOUBLE JOY - PIANO DUETS	BRADLEY,
BRADLEY'S HYMN JOY - ISSUE NO. 1	BRADLEY,
BRADLEY'S JEROME KERN ALBUM	KERN, J.
BRADLEY'S POPULAR JOY - ISSUE NO. 1	BRADLEY,
BRADLEY'S POPULAR JOY - ISSUE NO. 2	BRADLEY,
BRADLEY'S POPULAR JOY - ISSUE NO. 3	BRADLEY,
BRADLEY'S POPULAR JOY - ISSUE NO. 4	BRADLEY,
BRADLEY'S SUPERSTARS	BRADLEY,
BRADLEY'S SUPER POPULAR MUSIC	BRADLEY,
BRADLEY'S TODAY'S SOUND PIANO SOLOS	BRADLEY,
BRADLEY - LIKE IT IS TODAY - EASY PIANO HIT PARADE NO.	BRADLEY,
BRADLEY - LIKE IT IS TODAY - EASY PIANO HIT PARADE NO.	BRADLEY,
BRADLEY - LIKE IT IS TODAY - EASY PIANO HIT PARADE NO.	BRADLEY,
BRADLEY - LIKE IT IS TODAY - EASY PIANO HIT PARADE NO.	BRADLEY,
BRADLEY CLASSICAL SERIES - ECCOSSAISES	BEETHOVEN
BRADLEY CLASSICAL SERIES - FUR ELISE	BEETHOVEN
BRADLEY CLASSICAL SERIES - HAPPY FARMER, THE	SCHUMANN, R.
BRADLEY CLASSICAL SERIES - HUNTING SONG	SCHUMANN, R.
BRADLEY CLASSICAL SERIES - MINUTE WALTZ, OP. 64 NO. 1	CHOPIN
BRADLEY CLASSICAL SERIES - MOONLIGHT SONATA	BEETHOVEN
BRADLEY CLASSICAL SERIES - NOCTURNE IN E FLAT, OP. 9	CHOPIN
BRADLEY CLASSICAL SERIES - PRELUDE IN A - AND -	CHOPIN
BRADLEY CLASSICAL SERIES - PRELUDE IN E MINOR, OP. 28	CHOPIN
BRADLEY CLASSICAL SERIES - PRELUDE NO. 1 IN C FROM THE	BACH, J.S.
BRADLEY CLASSICAL SERIES - SOLDIER'S MARCH	SCHUMANN, R.
BRADLEY CLASSICAL SERIES - SONATINA NO. 01 IN G	BEETHOVEN
BRADLEY CLASSICAL SERIES - TWO-PART INVENTION NO. 1 IN	BACH, J.S.
BRADLEY CLASSICAL SERIES - TWO-PART INVENTION NO. 8 IN	BACH, J.S.
BRADLEY CLASSICAL SERIES - TWO MINUETS IN G	BACH, J.S.
BRADLEY CLASSICAL SERIES - WILD HORSEMAN, THE	SCHUMANN, R.
BRADLEY PIANO DUETS - BLESS THE BEASTS AND CHILDREN	BRADLEY,
BRADLEY PIANO DUETS - BORN FREE	BRADLEY,
BRADLEY PIANO DUETS - BRIAN'S SONG	BRADLEY,
BRADLEY PIANO DUETS - CANDY MAN, THE	BRADLEY,
BRADLEY PIANO DUETS - IF	BRADLEY,
BRADLEY PIANO DUETS - JOY TO THE WORLD	BRADLEY,
BRADLEY PIANO DUETS - MISTY	BRADLEY,
BRADLEY PIANO DUETS - MORNING AFTER, THE	BRADLEY,
BRADLEY PIANO DUETS - WAY WE WERE, THE	BRADLEY,
BRAHMS AND DVORAK FOR TWO	BRAHMS *
BRAHMS AT THE PIANO	BRAHMS
BRAHMS AT THE PIANO	BRAHMS
BRAHMS DUETS SIMPLIFIED	BRAHMS
BRAHMS FOR THE YOUNG PIANIST	BRAHMS
BRAHMS LULLABY	BRAHMS
BRAHMS WALTZES SIMPLIFIED	BRAHMS
BRAHMS	BRAHMS
BRANDENBURG CONCERTOS, BK. 1	BACH, J.S.
BRANDENBURG CONCERTOS, BK. 1	BACH, J.S.

BRANDENBURG CONCERTOS, BK. 2	BACH, J.S.
BRANDENBURG CONCERTOS, BK. 2	BACH, J.S.
BRANDENBURG CONCERTOS, VOL. 1	BACH, J.S.
BRANDENBURG CONCERTOS, VOL. 2	BACH, J.S.
BRANDENBURG CONCERTO NO. 1 IN F	BACH, J.S.
BRANDENBURG CONCERTO NO. 1 IN F	BACH, J.S.
BRANDENBURG CONCERTO NO. 1	BACH, J.S.
BRANDENBURG CONCERTO NO. 2 IN F	BACH, J.S.
BRANDENBURG CONCERTO NO. 2 IN F	BACH, J.S.
BRANDENBURG CONCERTO NO. 3 IN G	BACH, J.S.
BRANDENBURG CONCERTO NO. 3 IN G	BACH, J.S.
BRANDENBURG CONCERTO NO. 3	BACH, J.S.
BRANDENBURG CONCERTO NO. 4 IN G	BACH, J.S.
BRANDENBURG CONCERTO NO. 4 IN G	BACH, J.S.
BRANDENBURG CONCERTO NO. 5 IN D	BACH, J.S.
BRANDENBURG CONCERTO NO. 5 IN D	BACH, J.S.
BRANDENBURG CONCERTO NO. 5 IN D	BACH, J.S.
BRANDENBURG CONCERTO NO. 6 IN B-FLAT	BACH, J.S.
BRANDENBURG CONCERTO NO. 6 IN B FLAT	BACH, J.S.
BRANLE	WEYBRIGHT
BRASILIAN SUITE 1 - OLD SONG	FERNANDEZ, O.
BRASILIAN SUITE 1 - SERENADE	FERNANDEZ, O.
BRASILIAN SUITE 1 - SWEET CRADLE	FERNANDEZ, O.
BRASILIAN SUITE 2 - DANCE	FERNANDEZ, O.
BRASILIAN SUITE 2 - PRELUDE	FERNANDEZ, O.
BRASILIAN SUITE 2 - SONG	FERNANDEZ, O.
BRASILIAN SUITE 3 - NEGRO DANCE	FERNANDEZ, O.
BRASILIAN SUITE 3 - SERENADE	FERNANDEZ, O.
BRASILIAN SUITE 3 - SONG	FERNANDEZ, O.
BRASS BAND OF PARADE	KLEINMAN, A.
BRAVADO	WEYBRIGHT
BRAVADO	WEYBRIGHT
BRAVE KNIGHT, THE	KETTERER, E.
BRAVOURA VARIATIONS --1810-1830--	PUCHLET--ED
BRAZILIANA	WEYBRIGHT
BRAZILIANA	WEYBRIGHT
BRAZILIANA	WEYBRIGHT
BRAZILIAN POLKA	ROBINSON, A. *
BRAZILIAN POLKA	ROBINSON, A. *
BRAZILIAN SAMBA	KASZNER
BRAZILIAN SLEIGH BELLS	COX
BRAZILIAN SONG	MOZART, W. A.
BREAD AND BUTTER WALTZ	
BREAD AND BUTTER	
BREAKERS	CRERIE, E.
BREAKING UP IS HARD TO DO	BRADLEY,
BREAKS, FILLER, ENDINGS AND INTRODUCTIONS FOR POPULAR	KAHN, M.
BREAK AWAY	FENTON, R.
BREATH OF A BREEZE	EMERY
BREVISSIME PRETEXTE, BAGATELLE ET ETUDE	ORLAND, H.
BRIAN'S SONG	BRADLEY,
BRIAN'S SONG	BRADLEY,
BRIAN BORU'S MARCH--AN IRISH PATROL	HUGHES, H.
BRIC-A-BRAC -- 1935 -- BALLET	TANSMAN, A.
BRICCIOLE	RIETI
BRIDAL CHORUS. WEDDING MARCH--FROM 'LOHENGRIN'	WAGNER
BRIDAL CHORUS, LOHENGRIN, E FLAT MAJOR	WAGNER
BRIDAL CHORUS, LOHENGRIN	WAGNER
BRIDAL CHORUS FROM 'LOHENGRIN'	WAGNER
BRIDAL CHORUS FROM LOHENGRIN	WAGNER
BRIDAL MARCH FROM 'LOHENGRIN'	WAGNER
BRIDAL SONG, FROM ''LOHENGRIN''	WAGNER
BRIDAL SONG FROM 'LOHENGRIN'	WAGNER
BRIDAL SUITE	PEACOCK, K.
BRIEF ENCOUNTER	OLSON
BRIEF STANZA	GRIFFIS, E.
BRIGADOON -- SELECTION	LERNER *
BRIGADOON	BRIMHALL,
BRIGADOON	LERNER *
BRIGHT BLUE SEA, THE	ERB
BRILLIANTE	WIGHAM, M.
BRILLIANT FANTASIA FROM 'IL TROVATORE'	VERDI
BRILLIANT PIANO SOLOS	
BRIMHALL'S ENCYCLOPEDIA OF SCALES AND ARPEGGIOS	BRIMHALL,
BRIMHALL'S LOVE THEMES FROM THE GODFATHER AND OTHER	BRIMHALL,
BRIMHALL'S POPULAR LATIN TEACHING PIECES, NO. 1	BRIMHALL,
BRIMHALL'S POPULAR LATIN TEACHING PIECES, NO. 2	BRIMHALL,
BRIMHALL'S POPULAR LATIN TEACHING PIECES, NO. 3	BRIMHALL,
BRIMHALL'S SACRED MUSIC OF TODAY	BRIMHALL,
BRIMHALL'S 62 EASY-TO-PLAY POP PIANO PIECES	BRIMHALL,
BRIMHALL'S 64 POPULAR PIANO TEACHING PIECES	BRIMHALL,
BRIMHALL ISSUE NO. 01	BRIMHALL,
BRIMHALL ISSUE NO. 02	BRIMHALL,
BRIMHALL ISSUE NO. 03	BRIMHALL,
BRIMHALL ISSUE NO. 04	BRIMHALL,
BRIMHALL ISSUE NO. 05	BRIMHALL,
BRIMHALL ISSUE NO. 06	BRIMHALL,
BRIMHALL ISSUE NO. 07	BRIMHALL,
BRIMHALL ISSUE NO. 08	BRIMHALL,
BRIMHALL ISSUE NO. 09	BRIMHALL,
BRIMHALL ISSUE NO. 10	BRIMHALL,
BRIMHALL ISSUE NO. 11	BRIMHALL,
BRIMHALL ISSUE NO. 12	BRIMHALL,
BRIMHALL ISSUE NO. 14	BRIMHALL,
BRIMHALL ISSUE NO. 15	BRIMHALL,
BRIMHALL ISSUE NO. 16	BRIMHALL,
BRIMHALL ISSUE NO. 17	BRIMHALL,
BRIMHALL ISSUE NO. 18 AN APPLE FOR THE TEACHER	BRIMHALL,
BRIMHALL ISSUE NO. 20	BRIMHALL,
BRISK MARCH, A	STERNKLAR, A.
BRISK WINDS	SCHAUM, J.--ED.
BRITISH BALLADS AND FOLK SONGS	BAEZ, J.
BRITISH FOLK SONG AND COUNTRY DANCE	FERGUSON, H.
BRITISH GRENADIERS, THE	WEYBRIGHT--ED.
BRITISH GRENADIERS, THE	WEYBRIGHT--ED.
BRITISH GRENADIERS AND HERE'S A HEALTH UNTO HIS	TWINNING, W. L.
BRITISH GRENADIERS	ROLFE, W.--ED
BROADWAY AND 52ND	THIRNE
BROADWAY AT NIGHT	GROFE, F.
BROADWAY CLASSICS FOR PIANO, BK. 1	AGAY, D.--ED
BROADWAY CLASSICS FOR PIANO, BK. 2	AGAY, D.--ED
BROADWAY CLASSICS FOR PIANO, BK. 3	AGAY, D.--ED
BROADWAY CLASSICS FOR PIANO DUETS, BK. 2	AGAY, D.--ED
BROADWAY CLASSICS FOR PIANO DUETS, BK. 2	AGAY, D.--ED
BROADWAY CLASSICS FOR PIANO DUETS, BK. 3	AGAY, D.--ED
BROADWAY SHOWCASE OF FAMOUS MELODIES, BK. 1	AGAY, D.--ED
BROADWAY SHOWCASE OF FAMOUS MELODIES, BK. 2	AGAY, D.--ED
BROADWAY SHOWCASE OF FAMOUS MELODIES, BK. 3	AGAY, D.--ED
BROCELIANDE AU MATIN	LADMIRAULT
BROKEN CHORD ETUDES - B1	WARD, J.
BROKEN CHORD ETUDES - B2	WARD, J.
BROKEN CHORD ETUDES - B3	WARD, J.
BROKEN CHORD ETUDES - B4	WARD, J.
BROKEN CLOCK, THE	BASTIEN
BROKEN INTERVAL ETUDES - E1	WARD, J.
BROKEN INTERVAL ETUDES - E2	WARD, J.
BROKEN INTERVAL ETUDES - E3	WARD, J.
BROKEN INTERVAL ETUDES - E4	WARD, J.
BROKEN LITTLE MUSIC BOX, THE	VILLA-LOBOS, H.
BROKEN MELODY, THE	VANBIENE, A.
BROKEN RING	SCHIEFELBEIN, F.
BROKEN ROCKING HORSE, THE	MACKOWN, M.
BRONCO PETE	DUNGAN
BRONZE STATUE	BARTH, H.
BROOKLET, THE, OP. 81, NO. 3	HELLER, S.
BROOKLET IS SINGING, THE	JEAN, E.
BROTHERS	TREVARTHEN, R.
BROTHER JAMES'S AIR	BAIN, J.
BROUILLARDS FROM PRELUDES, BK. 2	DEBUSSY
BROUILLARD MONTAIT DOUCEMENT DANS LA NUIT	BLANC DE
BROWN-EYED DOLLY	JOYNER, B.
BROWN-EYED SUZY	PELS, W.
BROWNIE'S COURTSHIP	HEAPS, S.
BROWNIES' CARNIVAL	THOMPSON, J.
BROWNIES	LEONI, F.
BROWN BEAR BOOGIE	KENT, A.
BROWN LEAVES OF FALL	COMSTOCK
BRUBECK, VOL. 1	BRUBECK
BRUBECK, VOL. 2	BRUBECK
BRUDER SINGER. 270 LIEDER UNSERES VOLKES IN LEICHTEN	BAUM--ED. *
BRUDER SINGER	BAUM--ED. *
BRUJO AYMARA	IGLESIAS VILLOUD
BRUNE ET BLONDE	FORBES
BRUYERES FROM PRELUDES, BK. 2	DEBUSSY
BUBBLE, THE--''HIGH JINKS''	FRIML, R.
BUBBLES	WERMEL
BUBBLE GUM	MCCULLEN, A.
BUBBLE GUM	RUSSELL
BUBBLE SONG	TROJE-MILLER
BUCCANEER, THE	KETTERER, E.
BUCCANEER	GROVE
BUCEPHALE, PREMIER GALOP -- SIMPLIFIED VERSION	DESSAUX
BUCEPHALE, PREMIER GALOP	DESSAUX
BUCKING BRONCO BOOGIE	SCHUMANN, R.
BUCKING BRONCO	KREVIT, W.
BUCK 'N' WING	STEVENS, E.
BUCOLICS FOR PIANO	LUTOSLAWSKI
BUDDING BLOSSOMS	MCADAMS, G.
BUDDY SQUIRREL	OLDENBURG, E.
BUDS AND BLOSSOMS, OP. 107--12 MELODIOUS STUDIES	GURLITT
BUDS AND BLOSSOMS	FEDERE
BUFFALO HUNT, THE	POOLE, C.
BUFFOON DANCE	GABRIEL, M.
BUFFOON	SCHER, W.
BUGGY RIDE, THE	COBB
BUGLE, DRUM AND FIFE	STARER
BUGLER'S HOLIDAY	ANDERSON, L.
BUGLER'S NIGHTMARE	MELVIN, B.
BUGLERS' HOLIDAY	KRAEHENBUEHL
BUGLERS MARCH	CROSBY, M.
BUGLES AND DRUMS	DVORINE
BUGLES ON PARADE	KARP
BUGLE CALL RAG -- SIMP.	MOSSMAN, T.
BUGLE CALL RAG	WALLER, F.
BUGLE CALL	MEUTTMAN, M.
BUG BASS TUBA, THE	DE VITO, A.
BUILDING A SNOW MAN	BURNAM
BUILDING	ALT
BULERIAS	ALBENIZ, A.
BULERIAS	LONGAS
BULGARIAN SONGS AND DANCES, BK. 1	BENUSSAN, M.
BULGARIAN SONGS AND DANCES, BK. 2	BENUSSAN, M.
BULL-FROG AND THE TOAD, THE.	COBB
BULLFIGHTER, THE	SCHER, W.
BULLITT, THEME FROM	SCHIFRIN
BULL DOG	BARTH, H.
BULL IN A CHINA SHOP	ANSON, G.
BUMBLE-BEE, THE	RIMSKY-KORSAKOFF
BUMPY JEEP, THE	SCHER, W.
BUNCH OF DAISIES, A, VALSE	MARTIN, G.
BUNCH OF DAISIES, A	MARTIN, G.
BUNNY LAKE IS MISSING, MAIN THEME	
BUNNY TRACKS	STAIRS, L.
BUNTE BLAETTER, OP. 99	SCHUMANN, R.
BUNTE BLATTER, OP. 36 - BK. 1	REGER
BUNTE BLATTER, OP. 36 - BK. 2	REGER
BUNTE BLUMEN OP. 111	LICHNER, H.
BUNTE GEDANKEN IM WALZERTAKT	FISCHER, E.
BUNTE RHYTHMEN	MYERS, F.
BUONA NOTTE, FROM 'DAY IN VENICE'	NEVIN
BUON PIERINO, IL	PIZZINI
BURATTINI IN MARCIA	TANTILLO
BUREAUCRATIC SONATINA	SATIE, E.
BURGER ALS EDELMANN, OP. 60 - COMPLETE BALLET	STRAUSS, R.
BURGMUELLER-SCHAUM, BK. 1	BURGMUELLER
BURGMUELLER-SCHAUM, BK. 1	BURGMUELLER
BURGMUELLER-SCHAUM, BK. 2	BURGMUELLER
BURGMUELLER SCHAUM, BK. 2	BURGMUELLER
BURLESCA, OP. 81 NO. 3	TARENGHI
BURLESCA	WEYBRIGHT
BURLESCA	WEYBRIGHT
BURLESKEN, OP. 31 NO. 3, DER JONGLEUR	TOCH, E.
BURLESKEN, OP. 31	TOCH, E.
BURLESKE	STRAUSS, R.
BURLESQUE AND PASTORALE	HAWES, J.
BURLESQUE	CROOT
BURLESQUE	STRAUSS, R.
BURLESQUE	STRAUSS, R.
BURLESQUE	ZUPKO
BURNAM BOOK, THE	BURNAM
BURNING OF ROME MARCH	PAULL
BURNING OF ROME	PAULL
BURNING OF ROME	PAULL
BURRO, THE	THOMPSON, J.
BURRO TRAIL	ROZIN
BURSTING BUBBLES	GIMBEL
BUSINESS IN E FLAT --MODERN RHYTHMIC CLASSICS--	WHITFORD
BUST BUTTERFLIES	SCHER, W.
BUSY BIRDFEEDER, THE	TAKACS, J.
BUSY BIRDS	FOSTER, I. R.
BUSY BUGLER, THE	FROST
BUSY BUNNY AND DADDY'S NEW CAR	SCHER, W.
BUSY CARPENTER, THE	TOWNSEND
BUSY DAYS, BK. 1	HEIDELBERGER, P.
BUSY DAYS, BK. 2	HEIDELBERGER, P.
BUSY DAYS, BK. 3	HEIDELBERGER, P.
BUSY DAY	ELWELL, H.
BUSY DRUMMER	LAWLOR, G.
BUSY FINGERS	QUINCKE, W.
BUSY LITTLE BEE	RICHTER
BUSY LITTLE CLOCK, THE -- WITH WORDS	VANNORT, I.
BUSY LITTLE CLOCK	ARNOLD, H.
BUSY LITTLE RICKSHAW BOY	SCHER, W.
BUSY LITTLE TRAIN, THE	KARP, D.

Title	Composer
BUSY MILL WHEEL, THE	JESSE, M.
BUSY SAW-MILL, THE	BILBRO, M.
BUSY TRACTOR MAN, THE	TOWNSEND
BUSY WOODPECKER, THE	BESTHOFF, M.
BUSY WORK FOR BEGINNERS	PERRY, J. H.
BUS RIDE	COURSEY, R. DE
BUS STOP	WHITE
BUTTERCUPS	PANELLA, L.
BUTTERFLIES, OP. 158 NO. 1	GURLITT
BUTTERFLIES, OP. 59 NO. 2	LEGE, W.
BUTTERFLIES, THE	COUPERIN, P.
BUTTERFLIES AND BEES	WERMEL
BUTTERFLIES	FRIML, R.
BUTTERFLIES	KRUL
BUTTERFLY, A	BEVERLY
BUTTERFLY, BUTTERFLY AND SHIP A-SAILING	ROLFE, W.
BUTTERFLY, BUTTERFLY	BERGENFELD, N.
BUTTERFLY, OP. 43 NO. 1	GRIEG
BUTTERFLY, OP. 43 NO. 1	GRIEG
BUTTERFLY, OP. 43 NO. 1	GRIEG
BUTTERFLY, OP. 43 NO. 1	GRIEG
BUTTERFLY, OP. 43 NO. 1	GRIEG
BUTTERFLY, OP. 43 NO. 1	GRIEG
BUTTERFLY, OP. 81 NO. 4--BAGATELLE	MERKEL, G.
BUTTERFLY, OP. 81 NO. 4	MERKEL, G.
BUTTERFLY, OP. 81 NO. 4	MERKEL, G.
BUTTERFLY, THE -- FROM ''IN SPRINGTIME,'' OP. 36 NO. 4	WRIGHT, N.
BUTTERFLY, THE	CARRER
BUTTERFLY, THE	LAVALLEE, C.
BUTTERFLY, THE	LEGE, W.
BUTTERFLY -- LE PAPILLON	LAVALLEE, C.
BUTTERFLY BALLET	CHAGY
BUTTERFLY CHASE	HELLER, P.
BUTTERFLY DANCE, OP. 69	GODARD, C.
BUTTERFLY DANCE	MILES
BUTTERFLY DANCE	MILES
BUTTERFLY ETUDE	CHOPIN
BUTTERFLY ETUDE	CHOPIN
BUTTERFLY LAGOON	DAY, R.
BUTTERFLY OP. 43 NO. 1 --PAPILLON--	GRIEG
BUTTERFLY PAPILLON	GRIEG
BUTTERFLY TIME	BURNAM
BUTTERFLY WALTZ, THE	BRETON
BUTTERFLY WALTZ, THE	MARTIN, H.
BUTTERFLY WALTZ	KAHL
BUTTERFLY WALTZ	LUDOVIC, G.
BUTTERFLY WINGS	DILLON, F.
BUTTERFLY WINGS	KING
BUTTERFLY	HOPKINS, H.
BUTTERFLY	LAVALLEE, C.
BUTTERFLY	MERKEL, G.
BUTTERSCOTCH HOP, THE	SUDDARDS
BUT BEAUTIFUL	
BUZZY BUZZY BEE	CACAVAS
BYE-LOW TUNE	WHITE, R.
BYE, BYE BABY	
BYWAYS	BACON, E.
BY A BLUE LAGOON	ECKSTEIN
BY A BLUE LAGOON	ECKSTEIN
BY A BLUE LAGOON	ECKSTEIN
BY A BLUE LAGOON	KING
BY A ROADSIDE FIRE	RODGERS, I.
BY A SYLVAN LAKE	GILLOCK
BY A SYLVAN LAKE	GILLOCK
BY CANDLELIGHT	STEINER
BY HECK	
BY MYSELF, BK. 1	FRISCH, F. T.
BY MYSELF, BK. 2	FRISCH, F. T.
BY SILENT HEARTH, FROM 'MEISTERSINGER'	WAGNER
BY THE BEAUTIFUL BLUE DANUBE--J. STRAUSS--CONCERT	SCHULZ-EVLER
BY THE BEAUTIFUL SEA	CARROLL
BY THE BEND OF THE RIVER--BARCAROLLE	EDWARDS, C.
BY THE BROOKLET	RUNGEE
BY THE BROOKSIDE	TOURS
BY THE BROOK	BRUSSELS, I.
BY THE CRADLE	DIETRICH
BY THE CRADLE	GRIEG
BY THE FIRESIDE	CONN, D.
BY THE FOUNTAIN	WILSON, M.
BY THE LAKE OF WALLENSTADT	LISZT
BY THE SEASHORE--CONCERT ETUDE	SMETANA
BY THE SEA	BENTLEY
BY THE SEA	MANN
BY THE SEA	POSCA
BY THE SEA	POSCA
BY THE SEA	POSCA
BY THE SEA	SCHUBERT
BY THE SLEEPY LAGOON	
BY THE SPRING	GURLITT
BY THE TIME I GET TO PHOENIX	BRADLEY,
BY THE TIME I GET TO PHOENIX	BRIMHALL,
BY WAYS IN ETUDE LAND	ROBYN
C'ERA UN RE	PIZZINI
CABALETTA, OP. 83	LACK, T.
CABALETTA, OP. 83	LACK, T.
CABALETTA, OP. 83	LACK, T.
CABALETTA	LACK, T.
CABALGATA	BONESATTI
CABBAGE WALTZ, THE	SCHAUM, J.
CABLE CAR CAPER	HANNA
CACHE-CACHE, OP. 3 NO. 12	PIERNE
CACTUS JACK	WILSON
CACTUS TOWN	MCKAY, G.
CADENCIA	NOEL
CADENZAS FOR CONCERTI BY MOZART AND BEETHOVEN	TAGLIAPIETRA, C.
CADENZAS FOR K365	MOZART, W. A.
CADENZAS FOR MOZART K365	REINECKE
CADENZAS FOR 3 CONCERTI -- BEETHOVEN, MOZART --	CASADESUS, R.
CADENZAS FROM MOZART'S PIANO CONCERTOS	KRAUS--ED
CADENZAS TO BEETHOVEN CONCERTOS NOS. 3, 4. TO MOZART	SCHUMANN, C.
CADENZAS TO BEETHOVEN CONCERTO IV	BUELOW
CADENZAS TO BEETHOVEN PIANO CONCERTI NOS. 1-4	KEMPFF
CADENZAS TO CONCERTI NOS. 1-4	BEETHOVEN
CADENZAS TO CONCERTOS 1, 3, 4	BEETHOVEN
CADENZAS TO EIGHT MOZART CONCERTI --K.456, K.459,	MUELLER, A. E.
CADENZAS TO HAYDN CONCERTO IN D	BADURA-SKODA
CADENZAS TO MOZART'S CONCERTO NO. 22 IN E FLAT	CASADESUS, R.
CADENZAS TO MOZART'S PIANO CONCERTI	BADURA-SKODA
CADENZAS TO MOZART CONCERTO IN C, K. 467	WUEHRER
CADENZAS TO MOZART CONCERTO IN C MINOR, K. 491	WUEHRER
CADENZAS TO MOZART CONCERTO IN D MINOR, K. 466	BADURA-SKODA
CADENZAS TO MOZART CONCERTO IN D MINOR, K. 466	BRENDEL
CADENZAS TO MOZART CONCERTO IN E FLAT, K. 482	BADURA-SKODA
CADENZAS TO PIANO CONCERTOS BY BEETHOVEN HIMSELF	BEETHOVEN
CADENZAS TO THE CONCERTO IN D	HAYDN
CADENZA - CONCERTO IN D, OP. 21	HAYDN
CADENZA - CONCERTO K271 IN E FLAT	MOZART, W. A.
CADENZA - CONCERTO K413 IN F	MOZART, W. A.
CADENZA - CONCERTO K414 IN A	MOZART, W. A.
CADENZA - CONCERTO K466 IN D MINOR	MOZART, W. A.
CADENZA - CONCERTO K482 IN E FLAT	MOZART, W. A.
CADENZA - CONCERTO K537 IN D	MOZART, W. A.
CADENZA - SONATA K333 IN B FLAT	MOZART, W. A.
CADENZA AND INTRODUCTIONS TO MOZART CONCERTO IN C	BADURA-SKODA
CADENZA TO BEETHOVEN CONCERTO III	DREYSCHOCK
CADENZA TO BEETHOVEN CONCERTO III	LISZT
CADENZA TO CONCERTO NO. 02 IN B FLAT, OP. 19	BEETHOVEN
CADENZA TO CONCERTO NO. 03 IN C MINOR, OP. 37	BEETHOVEN
CADENZA TO CONCERTO NO. 04 IN G, OP. 58	BEETHOVEN
CADENZA TO MOZART CONCERTO IN C, K. 503	BADURA-SKODA
CADENZA TO MOZART CONCERTO IN C, K. 503	GULDA
CADENZA TO MOZART CONCERTO IN D, K. 537 -- CORONATION	GULDA
CADENZA TO MOZART CONCERTO IN D MINOR, K. 466	BEETHOVEN
CADENZA TO MOZART CONCERTO K.467	HOFFMANN, PH. K.
CADENZA TO MOZART CONCERTO K.482	HOFFMANN, PH. K.
CADENZA TO MOZART CONCERTO K.488	HOFFMANN, PH. K.
CADENZA TO MOZART CONCERTO K.491	HOFFMANN, PH. K.
CADENZA TO MOZART CONCERTO K.503	HOFFMANN, PH. K.
CADENZA TO MOZART CONCERTO K.595	HOFFMANN, PH. K.
CADENZA TO THE BEETHOVEN CONCERTO IN CM, OP. 37, FIRST	REINECKE
CADENZA TO THE CONCERTO NO. 3 IN C MINOR, OP.	BEETHOVEN
CADENZA TO THE LISZT 2ND HUNGARIAN RHAPSODY	RACHMANINOFF, S.
CADET'S REVIEW, THE	REBE
CADETS ON PARADE	KETTERER, E.
CADIZ. CANCION -- NO. 4, FROM SUITE ESPANOLA NO. 1	ALBENIZ, I.
CADIZ -- FROM SUITE ESPANOLA NO. 1	ALBENIZ, I.
CADIZ	ALBENIZ, I.
CAESAR AND CLEOPATRA THEME	NORTH, A
CAFE MOZART WALTZ	
CAGED LION, THE	SUMMERS
CAGE DANCER	FULEIHAN, A.
CAGE SOCIETY RAG	LEWIS *
CAHIERS D'EPIGRAMMES	AMY, G.
CAHIER D'ELISABETH, LE	HAUDEBERT
CAHIER D'EVE, LE	HAUDEBERT
CAHIER ROMAND, LE	HONEGGER, A.
CAISSONS GO ROLLING ALONG, THE	GRUBER, E.
CAISSONS GO ROLLING ALONG	SCHAUM, J.--ED.
CAISSON SONG	ROYAL--ED
CAKE WALK	RAPHLING
CALEIDOSCOPE--AMERICAN RHYTHMS, BK. 1	SCHOLZ
CALEIDOSCOPE--AMERICAN RHYTHMS, BK. 2	SCHOLZ
CALENDAR SCENES	KRAEHENBUEHL
CALENDRIER DU PETIT BERGER, LE, BK. 1	MIGOT
CALENDRIER DU PETIT BERGER, LE, BK. 2	MIGOT
CALICO CLOWN, THE	MARTIN, H.
CALICO WALTZ	GARROW, L.
CALIFORNIA MONTAGE	GRUSIN
CALIFORNIA SONATA	OWENS
CALINDA, FROM 'KOANGA'	DELIUS, F.
CALINDA, FROM 'KOANGA'	DELIUS, F.
CALINERIE, MELODIE ENFANTINE, OP. 86	RAVINA, H.
CALLIOPE, THE	VOLKART, H.
CALLIOPE	GALLEZ
CALLIOPE	GARROW, L.
CALL ME	HATCH
CALL OF THE CANYON	MCKAY, G.
CALL OF THE RANGE	BRODSKY, M.
CALM AS THE NIGHT	BOHM
CALM IN THE FOREST	YOUNG
CALOP PARISIEN	CANNON, P.
CALVARY, TRANSCRIPTION	FREEMAN
CALYPSO BOY	MOSS, E.
CALYPSO DANCE	REEVES, R.
CALYPSO INTERLUDE	RUSSELL
CALYPSO PARTY	BRODSKY, M.
CAMBIATE PER PIANOFORTE	HUZELLA
CAMEL, THE	BLAKE, D.
CAMELLIA-MELODIE	YON, S. C.
CAMELOT SELECTION	
CAMELOT	
CAMELOT	
CAMEL RIDE, THE	KEVAN
CAMEL TRAIN -- DESCRIPTIVE	BAINES, W.
CAMEL TRAIN	BAINES, W.
CAMINITO DE BELEN	GIANNEO
CAMPANELLA, LA. ETUDE NO. 3-- PAGANINI-LISZT -- WITH	BUSONI
CAMPANELLA, LA	LISZT
CAMPANE A FESTA. EPITHALAMIUM, OP. 12 NO. 8	SGAMBATI
CAMPANE FAN DIN DON	FERRARI-TRECATE
CAMPANITAS DE FIESTA	CASTRO, W.
CAMPERS	LOPEZ BUCHARDO
CAMPFIRE SONGS	SCHAUM, J.
CAMPING AT NIGHT	SANDBOURNE
CAMPTOWN RACES	FOSTER
CAMP MEETING	BACON, E.
CAMP OF THE GYPSIES	BEHR, F.
CAMP OF THE GYPSIES	MARTIN, H.
CAN-CAN	
CAN-CAN	
CAN'T HELP LOVIN' DAT MAN -- SHOWCASE	
CANADIAN CAPERS	CHANDLER *
CANADIAN CAPERS	CHANDLER *
CANADIAN CAPERS	CHANDLER *
CANADIAN CHILDHOOD - SUITE	GIASSON, P.
CANADIAN CHILDHOOD - SUITE	GIASSON, P.
CANADIAN DANCE SUITE	KNAUER
CANADIAN FESTIVAL ALBUM -- FAVORITE WORKS FOR STUDENTS	
CANADIAN FESTIVAL ALBUM -- FAVORITE WORKS FOR STUDENTS	
CANADIAN SUNSET	
CANADIAN SUNSET	
CANADIAN SUNSET	
CANAL STREET BOOGIE	WESTERVELT, M.
CANARIE FROM L'EVENTAIL DE JEANNE	ROLAND
CANCAO DO TIO BARNABE	COSME, L.
CANCAO SERTANEJA	GUARNIERI
CANCAO TRISTE E DANCA BRASILEIRA	SANTORSOLA, G.
CANCIONERO, EL	GAILLARD
CANCION DEL AIRE	MURILLO, E.
CANCION DEL CARRETERO	LOPEZ BUCHARDO
CANCION DE CUNA PARA BIBI	SEBASTIANI, P.
CANCION MEXICANA	VASQUEZ, C.
CANCION NO. 3	AGUIRRE
CANCION POQUITA	VALENTI, M.
CANCION TRISTE	FICHER
CANCION Y DANZA, NO. 1--QUASI MODERATO	MOMPOU, F.
CANCION Y DANZA, NO. 2--LENTO	MOMPOU, F.
CANCION Y DANZA, NO. 3--MODERE	MOMPOU, F.
CANCION Y DANZA, NO. 4--MODERATO	MOMPOU, F.
CANCION Y DANZA, NO. 5	MOMPOU, F.
CANCION Y DANZA, NO. 7	MOMPOU, F.
CANCION Y DANZA, NO. 8	MOMPOU, F.
CANCION	IGLESIAS VILLOUD
CANCO I DANSA	MOMPOU, F.

CANCY CANE CAPERS	LAKE, G.
CANDIDATES COMPANION, ELEMENTARY	CHING
CANDIDATES COMPANION, PRIMARY	CHING
CANDIDA	LANE, J.--ED.
CANDIDE	CASTELNUOVO-TEDE
CANDID CAMERA - FOR THE YOUNGEST PIANISTS	RAPHLING
CANDID CAMERA - FOR YOUNGEST PIANISTS	RAPHLING
CANDLELIGHT AND CRINOLINE	MARTIN, H.
CANDLELIGHT CONCERTO	KASSCHAU, H.
CANDLELIGHT ENCORES	GLOVER, D.
CANDLELIGHT MOODS	HOWELL
CANDLELIGHT SERENADE	CHOPIN
CANDLELIGHT SUPPER CLUB	GLOVER, D.
CANDLELIGHT	ARMOUR
CANDLE IN THE WIND	ALTER, L.
CANDLE LIGHT WALTZ	BRAGDON
CANDY'S DANCE	FAHNESTOCK
CANDY BAND	PHIPPENY
CANDY CANE LANE	KASTLER, A.
CANDY CANE MARCH	DVORINE
CANDY DOLLY	GAYNOR
CANDY MAN, THE - AND - BORN FREE	BRADLEY,
CANDY MAN, THE	BRADLEY,
CANDY MAN, THE	BRADLEY,
CANDY MAN, THE	BRIMHALL,
CANDY MAN	BRICUSSE *
CANDY PARADE	LAKE, G.
CANDY STORE BLUES	JEFFRIES *
CANDY SUITE	SCHER, W.
CANDY TOWN	LAKE, G.
CANOE SONG	DITTENHAVER
CANON-VALSETTE - FROM FIVE PIECES FOR YOUNG PIANISTS	RIETI
CANON - VALSETTE	RIETI
CANON A LA SEPTIEME, PUBLISHED WITH AMY FAY DEPPE	MOSCHELES, I.
CANON HILL	KARP
CANON IN A MINOR	SHAW, M.
CANON	RESPIGHI
CANOPE FROM PRELUDES, BK. 2	DEBUSSY
CANTABILE	FRANCK, C.
CANTABILE	RACHMANINOFF, S.
CANTANDO VAN LOS PASTORES--VILLANCICO	ROMERO, M. *
CANTARES DE MI CANTAR	GILARDI
CANTAR	LASALA
CANTER	BUTLER, J.
CANTEYODJAYA	MESSIAEN, O.
CANTIQUE D'AMOUR--HARMONIES POETIQUES ET RELIGIEUSES,	LISZT
CANTIQUE DE NOEL -- O HOLY NIGHT	BURNAM
CANTIQUE DE NOEL	ADAM, A.
CANTIQUE DE NOEL	ADAM, A.
CANTI DELLA STAGIONE ALTA	PIZZETTI
CANTOS DE ESPANA, OP. 232 -- COMPLETE	ALBENIZ, I.
CANTOS DE ESPANA - AIRS OF SPAIN - OP. 232	ALBENIZ, I.
CANTO DEL GUAJIRO	LECUONA
CANTO DI PRIMAVERA	CIMATTI
CANTO NAPOLETANO	BELLINI
CANTS MAGICS, 1919	MOMPOU, F.
CANTUS FIRMUS	MIHALOVICI
CANZONA E SONATA, OP. 22	ZIPP
CANZONA	GIDEON, M.
CANZONE--FROM VENEZIA E NAPOLI	LISZT
CANZONE, VALZER, BUONA NOTTE	COUTURE
CANZONEN 1592	MERULO
CANZONETTA, HARPSICHORD	ANDRIESSEN, H.
CANZONETTA, OP. 62A--STR ORCH	SIBELIUS
CANZONETTA ABRUZZESE	DE NARDIS
CANZONETTA IN D, OP. 28 NO. 2	SCHUETT
CANZONETTA IN E, OP. 28 NO. 2	DALCROZE
CANZONETTA	FRANCHETTI
CANZONETTA	HOLLAENDER
CANZONETTA	NEVIN
CANZONETTA	RICCI, F. R.
CANZONETTA	ROWLEY
CANZONE BARBERA	GUARINO, C.
CANZONE MONTANARA	CAGNACCI
CANZONE MONTANARA	CAGNACCI
CAN CAN DANCE	OFFENBACH
CAN CAN	OFFENBACH
CAN CAN	OFFENBACH
CAN YOU	KERR, R. N.
CAPANNA, UNA BIMBA, UNA STELLA, UNA	MASETTI
CAPERS OF A CLOWN	HOWELL, I.
CAPRICANTE--MARCHE DU CONCERT	WACHS, P.
CAPRICANTE, MARCH DU CONCERT	WACHS, P.
CAPRICCETTI, OP. 36	TOCH, E.
CAPRICCETTO	BECK
CAPRICCIETTO	GILLOCK
CAPRICCIETTO	GILLOCK
CAPRICCIO-- B FLAT-- ON THE DEPARTURE OF HIS BELOVED	BACH, J.S.
CAPRICCIO, ARIA UND FINALE, 1963, FUR KLAVIER UND	REUTTER, H.
CAPRICCIO, FANTASY, SONATA, FUGUES, MINUETS	BACH, J.S.
CAPRICCIO, OP. 11	GOLDSCHMIDT
CAPRICCIO, OP. 23H	KADOSA
CAPRICCIO, OP. 28, NO. 6	DOHNANYI
CAPRICCIO, OP. 28	BACEVICIUS
CAPRICCIO, OP. 6	GOEHR, A.
CAPRICCIO, SCHERZO	MENDELSSOHN
CAPRICCIOS AND INTERMEZZOS, OP. 76	BRAHMS
CAPRICCIO -- SONATINA NO. 02	GENZMER
CAPRICCIO -- 1953 --	BAUR
CAPRICCIO - REVISED 1949 VERSION	STRAVINSKY, I.
CAPRICCIO ALLA SOLIDATESCA, OP. 50 NO. 1	ALKAN
CAPRICCIO AND FUGUE	FUX
CAPRICCIO B-DUR, BWV 992 --DIE ABREISE--	BACH, J.S.
CAPRICCIO B-DUR -- DIE ABREISE, BWV 992	BACH, J.S.
CAPRICCIO BRILLANTE, OP. 22	MENDELSSOHN
CAPRICCIO BRILLANTE, OP. 22	MENDELSSOHN
CAPRICCIO BRILLANTE	MENDELSSOHN
CAPRICCIO ESPAGNOL, OP. 34	RIMSKY-KORSAKOFF
CAPRICCIO ESPAGNOL, OP. 34	RIMSKY-KORSAKOFF
CAPRICCIO ESPAGNOL, OP. 34	RIMSKY-KORSAKOFF
CAPRICCIO ESPAGNOL, OP. 34	RIMSKY-KORSAKOFF
CAPRICCIO ESPAGNOL	RIMSKY-KORSAKOFF
CAPRICCIO FOR PIANO AND ORCHESTRA --SCORE AND PARTS ON	BEN-HAIM
CAPRICCIO FOR PIANO DUET	BENNETT, R.
CAPRICCIO FUR KLAVIER UND ORCHESTER, OP. 19	RIEDE
CAPRICCIO IN B FLAT, S. 992	BACH, J.S.
CAPRICCIO IN B MINOR, OP. 2, NO. 4 -- FROM FOUR PIECES	DOHNANYI
CAPRICCIO IN B MINOR, OP. 2 NO. 4	DOHNANYI
CAPRICCIO IN B MINOR, OP. 76 NO. 2	BRAHMS
CAPRICCIO IN B MINOR, OP. 76 NO. 2	BRAHMS
CAPRICCIO IN E, LONGO 10--TRANSCRIBED FOR CONCERT-USE	SCARLATTI, D.
CAPRICCIO IN E FLAT ON A POLISH FOLKSONG -- 1953	FINKE
CAPRICCIO IN F-SHARP MINOR, OP. 5	MENDELSSOHN
CAPRICCIO IN THE FORM OF A BOLERO	ALFONSO
CAPRICCIO IN 5 MOVEMENTS	BORDES
CAPRICCIO ITALIEN OP. 45	TSCHAIKOWSKY
CAPRICCIO ITALIEN	TSCHAIKOWSKY
CAPRICCIO ITALIEN	TSCHAIKOWSKY
CAPRICCIO NO. 2	SHEPHERD
CAPRICCIO ON FIVE NOTES, OP. 23	HOIBY, L.
CAPRICCIO ON THE DEPARTURE OF A BELOVED BROTHER	BACH, J.S.
CAPRICCIO ON THE DEPARTURE OF A BROTHER	BACH, J.S.
CAPRICCIO ON THE INTERVAL OF A SECOND	DELLO JOIO, N.
CAPRICCIO SOPRA LA LONTANANZA DEL SUO FRATELLO	BACH, J.S.
CAPRICCIO	BROWN, C.
CAPRICCIO	CAGGIANO
CAPRICCIO	CHAYNES
CAPRICCIO	DA-OZ, RAM
CAPRICCIO	EDEL, Y.
CAPRICCIO	FONTANA
CAPRICCIO	GRENZ
CAPRICCIO	GRUNEWALD
CAPRICCIO	HARVEY, VIVIEN
CAPRICCIO	HAUBIEL, C.
CAPRICCIO	HAYDN
CAPRICCIO	PETIT, P.
CAPRICCIO	POULENC, F.
CAPRICCIO	SCARMOLIN
CAPRICCIO	SCELSI
CAPRICCIO	STRAVINSKY, I.
CAPRICCI DI MASCHERE	GUARINO, C.
CAPRICCI RITMICI -- 1949/50	HEISS
CAPRICCI	STEFFAN, J. A.
CAPRICE-BURLESQUE OP. 3	GABRILOWITSCH,
CAPRICE-VALSE -- FROM "WEDDING CAKE", OP. 76	SAINT-SAENS
CAPRICE-VALSE FROM "WEDDING CAKE"	SAINT-SAENS
CAPRICE, OP. 12 NO. 5	PROKOFIEFF
CAPRICE, OP. 4	SAINT-SAENS
CAPRICES, VOL. 1	LUNDE, J.
CAPRICES, VOL. 2	LUNDE, J.
CAPRICES DE PIERRETTE, LES	PERROT
CAPRICE -- BASED ON FINALE OF 'BAL MASQUE' --	POULENC, F.
CAPRICE - ARABESQUE EN FORME D'UN ETUDE	LESCHETIZKY
CAPRICE ARABE	SAINT-SAENS
CAPRICE A LA SCARLATTI, OP. 14, NO. 3	PADEREWSKI, I.
CAPRICE BRILLANTE	LEYBACH, I.
CAPRICE BY SAINT-SAENS, ON AIRS FROM 'ALCESTE'	GLUCK
CAPRICE ESPAGNOL, OP. 37	MOSZKOWSKI
CAPRICE ESPAGNOL, OP. 37	MOSZKOWSKI
CAPRICE ESPAGNOL, OP. 37	MOSZKOWSKI
CAPRICE ESPAGNOL, OP. 37	MOSZKOWSKI
CAPRICE ESPAGNOL	MOSZKOWSKI
CAPRICE HEROIQUE, OP. 106	SAINT-SAENS
CAPRICE HIPPIQUE	STERNBERG
CAPRICE IN A MINOR	STEINER
CAPRICE IN C	GOODRICH
CAPRICE MODERNE	MELVIN, B.
CAPRICE NO. 1, OP. 2	MARTUCCI
CAPRICE NO. 2, OP. 3	MARTUCCI
CAPRICE ON THE AIRS DE BALLET FROM GLUCK'S 'ALCESTE'	SAINT-SAENS
CAPRICE RHYTHMIQUE -- ON A THEME BY PAGANINI --	KARTUN
CAPRICE ROMANTIQUE	SANCAN, P.
CAPRICE VIENNOIS --STUDENT EDITION--	KREISLER
CAPRICE VIENNOIS --STUDENT EDITION--	KREISLER
CAPRICE VIENNOIS	KREISLER
CAPRICE VIENNOIS	KREISLER
CAPRICE VIENNOIS	KREISLER
CAPRICE VIENNOIS	KREISLER
CAPRICE	BRUSSELS, I.
CAPRICE	ELIOT
CAPRICE	MAILLARD, P.
CAPRICE	NAGY, M.
CAPRICE	OGILVY, F.
CAPRICE	PIERNE, P.
CAPRICE	WEYBRIGHT
CAPRICE	WEYBRIGHT
CAPRICHOS - 1959	DI MAJO, G.
CAPRICHO ESPANOL, OP. 39	GRANADOS
CAPRICORN FLAKES, FOR PIANO, HARPSICHORD,	MELLNAES
CAPTAIN'S COMMAND	SCHIEFELBEIN, F.
CAPTAIN'S MARCH, THE	HOPKINS, H.
CAPTAINS AND THE KINGS, THE	ANDERSON, L.
CAPTAIN CANDY	GLOVER, D.
CAPTAIN GENERAL	LOUKA, M.
CAPTAIN HOOK OF THE PIRATE BAND	MILES
CAPTAIN JIM, MARCH	HOPKINS, H.
CAPTAIN JINKS	GUENTHER
CAPTAIN KIDD	BLAKE, D. G.
CAPTAIN KIDD	WALDO, J.
CAPTAIN WEATHERBRAVE OF THE SEA	JESSE, M.
CARACAS, CONGA	STANLEY
CARACTERES	POUSSEUR, H.
CARAMEL MOU--1921--JAZZ BAND	MILHAUD, D.
CARAVAN, OP. 30, NO. 1	GAITO
CARAVAN, THE	HOLLIDAY, J.
CARAVAN, THE	THOMPSON, J.
CARAVANES	FELINE
CARAVAN	KAHL
CARA NINA	WEYBRIGHT--ED.
CARA NINA	WEYBRIGHT--ED.
CARDINAL, THE -- MAIN THEME	
CARDINAL STAY WITH ME, THE	
CAREFREE BUTTERFLY	PELS, W.
CAREFREE	COBB
CAREFREE	HAEHNEL
CAREFREE	WIGHAM, M.
CARELESS MARY	HOPKINS, H.
CAREZZA. WALTZ, OP. 39	GRANADOS
CARIBBEAN BLUE	OLSON
CARIBBEAN CRUISE	BERGER
CARIBBEAN DANCE	BENJAMIN
CARIBBEAN LOVE SONG	RUSSELL
CARIBBEAN MOONLIGHT	GARROW, L.
CARILLON, THE	MILNES
CARILLONS, LES	LESUR, D.
CARILLON BELLS	KENT, A.
CARILLON DE CYNTHERE, LE	MONNIKENDAM
CARILLON DE CYNTHERE	COUPERIN, F.
CARILLON DE FLANDRE	FRANCAIX, J.
CARILLON MAGICO, IL -- BALLET --	PICK-MANGIAGALLI
CARILLON	HARTLEY, W.
CARILLON	HEINS, C.
CARILLON	TARENGHI
CARIOCA -- SHOWCASE	
CARIOCA	
CARLE BOOGIE	CARLE, F
CARL FISCHER NOTE SPELLER	HOLT, H.--ED
CARL RICHTER PIANO DUETS, BK. 02	RICHTER, C.--ED
CARMAN'S WHISTLE, THE	BYRD, W.
CARMELA -- FANTASIE --	CURTIS
CARMELA -- WALTZ --	CURTIS
CARMELA	WALTER
CARMEN. COMPLETE.	BIZET, G.
CARMEN. COMPLETE OPERA IN PIANO SOLO ARRANGEMENT	BIZET, G.

CARMEN. FANTASY. TWO PIANOS, EIGHT HANDS   BIZET, G.
CARMEN, EASY TRANS.   BIZET, G.
CARMEN, ENTR'ACTE   BIZET, G.
CARMEN, HABANERA   BIZET, G.
CARMEN, MARCH   BIZET, G.
CARMEN, TOREADOR SONG   BIZET, G.
CARMENA, VALSE   WILSON
CARMEN -- TOREADOR SONG, HABANEA   NEVIN--ED
CARMEN BALLET   BIZET, G.
CARMEN CAVALLARO'S PARADE OF HITS   CAVALLARO--ED.
CARMEN CAVALLARO -- MODERN INTERPRETATIONS FOR PIANO   CAVALLARO--ED.
CARMEN OVERTURE -- FOR ONE PIANO, SIX HANDS   BIZET, G.
CARMEN SYLVA   IVANOVICI, J.
CARNABAL DAS CRIANCAS BRASILEIRAS -- PEIRRETTE'S HANDS   VILLA-LOBOS, H.
CARNABAL DAS CRIANCAS BRASILEIRAS -THE DEVIL'S WHIP   VILLA-LOBOS, H.
CARNATIONS   CRERIE, E.
CARNAVAL, FOR 2 PIANOS 8 HANDS   GUIRAUD, E.
CARNAVAL, OP. 9   SCHUMANN, R.
CARNAVAL, OP. 9   SCHUMANN, R.
CARNAVAL, OP. 9   SCHUMANN, R.
CARNAVAL, OP. 9   SCHUMANN, R.
CARNAVAL, OP. 9   SCHUMANN, R.
CARNAVAL, OP. 9   SCHUMANN, R.
CARNAVAL, OP. 9   SCHUMANN, R.
CARNAVALITO   SICILIANI
CARNAVAL HEROIQUE -- RYTHMES DE GUERRE   LAZARUS, D.
CARNAVAL OP. 9   SCHUMANN, R.
CARNET DE DESSINS - 20 EASY PIECES   CHAILLEY
CARNIVAL, THE   RAEZER, C.
CARNIVAL --MODERN RHYTHMIC CLASSICS--   WHITFORD
CARNIVAL CAPERS   SCHER, W.
CARNIVAL CAPERS   SCHER, W.
CARNIVAL CHA CHA   BASTIEN
CARNIVAL D'AIX   MILHAUD, D.
CARNIVAL DANCERS   CHAUNCEY, R. G.
CARNIVAL DANCERS   CHAUNCEY, R. G.
CARNIVAL DANCER   WERMEL
CARNIVAL DAYS   ROZIN
CARNIVAL IN RIO   GILLOCK
CARNIVAL IN RIO   GILLOCK
CARNIVAL IN SPAIN   SCHER, W.
CARNIVAL OF ROSES   MARTIN, G.
CARNIVAL OF THE ANIMALS   SAINT-SAENS
CARNIVAL OF THE ANIMALS   SAINT-SAENS
CARNIVAL OF THE   SAINT-SAENS
CARNIVAL OF VENICE   BENEDICT
CARNIVAL OF VENICE   JORDA, L.
CARNIVAL OF VENICE   LISZT
CARNIVAL OF VENICE   LUDOVIC, G.
CARNIVAL OF VENICE   OESTEN
CARNIVAL OF VENICE   PAGANINI, N.
CARNIVAL OF VENICE   SCHAUM, J.--ED.
CARNIVAL PROCESSION   LAST, J.
CARNIVAL SCENE, MARCH OF FLOWER GIRLS   WACHS, P.
CARNIVAL   FREED
CARNIVAL   MERRILL, B.
CARNIVAL   OWENS
CARNIVAL   REISER, V.
CAROL, A   DREISBACH
CAROLE KING PIANO SOLOS   KING, C.
CAROLINA CAKEWALK   DITTENHAVER
CAROLINA ON MY MIND   KING
CAROLINA WALTZ   DUMM
CAROLING KEYS   GRAY, D.
CAROLLERS
CAROLLING OF THE BIRDS, OP. 156   MICHEUZ, G.
CAROLLING OF THE BIRDS, OP. 156   MICHEUZ, G.
CAROLS AND HYMNS FOR FOUR HANDS   BOUD, C.
CAROLS FOR CHRISTMAS   BRADY--ED
CAROLS FOR CHRISTMAS   DAVIES--ED.
CAROLS FOR CHRISTMAS   FREDRICH,
CAROLS FOR DECEMBER   ZEPP--ED
CAROLS FROM MANY NATIONS   KOCH, F.
CAROLS FROM MANY NATIONS   KOCH, F.
CAROLS OF MANY LANDS   PEERY, R. R.--ED
CAROLS YOU KNOW   PAYNE, W.
CAROL KAYE ORIGINAL SONGBOOK   KAYE, C.
CAROL OF THE BELLS   BRIMHALL,
CAROL OF THE DRUM   DAVIS, M.
CAROL TUNES   HELYER, M.
CAROUSEL, THE   TRAEGER
CAROUSEL AND FERRIS WHEEL --PIANO SOLO OR 2 PIANOS, 4   IRVING
CAROUSEL CALLIOPE   SHARPLES
CAROUSEL IN PARIS   KING
CAROUSEL RIDE   MILLIGAN
CAROUSEL WALTZ   ECKSTEIN
CAROUSEL WALTZ
CAROUSEL   BERMONT, G.
CAROUSEL   COBB
CAROUSEL   DAVIS, J.
CAROUSEL   HENDERSON
CAROUSEL   JESSE, M.
CAROUSEL   WHITFORD
CAROVANA   PRIANO
CARO MIO BEN   GIORDANI
CARPENTER'S SONG, THE   BURNAM
CARPENTERS   WEYBRIGHT
CARRIAGE TRADE, THE   GIASSON, P.
CARRIAGE TRADE, THE   GIASSON, P.
CARRIER PIGEON   RAVINA, H.
CARROT TALKS, THE   DUNGAN
CARRY ME BACK TO OLD VIRGINNY   BLAND
CARTAGENA   NOONA, W.
CARTAS DE AMOR -- VALSES INTIMOS -- OP. 44   GRANADOS
CARTELES   BERNAL, J.
CART WHEELS   FROST
CART WHEELS   FROST
CASCADE, LA OP. 37   PAUER
CASCADE, LA   PAUER
CASCADE, OP. 37   PAUER
CASCADE, THE, OP. 233   HEINS, C.
CASCADES, THE--WITH PRELIMINARY STUDIES--   MACLACHLIN, T.
CASCADING STARS   KAHN, M.
CASSE-NOISETTE, OP. 71   TSCHAIKOWSKY
CASSE NOISETTE   TSCHAIKOWSKY
CASTANETS AND TAMBOURINES   ROBINSON, A.
CASTANETS AND TAMBOURINES   THOMPSON, J.
CASTANETS   BRAGDON
CASTANETS   GILLOCK
CASTANETS   GILLOCK
CASTANETS   REBE
CASTANETTA   WEYBRIGHT
CASTANETTA   WEYBRIGHT
CASTELLANAS   PARRA, B. G. DE
CASTELLI DI GIULIETTA E ROMEO   PEDROLLO
CASTELNUOVO SUL CARSO 1915   SCUDERI

CASTILIAN AFTERNOON   HOLT, EILSEL
CASTILLA. SEGUIDILLAS -- NO. 7, FROM SUITE ESPANOLA   ALBENIZ, I.
CASTILLA -- FROM SUITE ESPANOLA NO. 1   ALBENIZ, I.
CASTILLA   ALBENIZ, I.
CASTLES AND KINGS   KOHN
CASTLE IN THE SAND   DITTENHAVER
CAT-FUGUE, LONGO 499   SCARLATTI, D.
CAT'S DELIGHT   EDGINTON
CAT'S FUGUE   SCARLATTI, D.
CATALOGUE D'OISEAUX, BK. 1   MESSIAEN, O.
CATALOGUE D'OISEAUX, BK. 2   MESSIAEN, O.
CATALOGUE D'OISEAUX, BK. 3   MESSIAEN, O.
CATALOGUE D'OISEAUX, BK. 4   MESSIAEN, O.
CATALOGUE D'OISEAUX, BK. 5   MESSIAEN, O.
CATALOGUE D'OISEAUX, BK. 6   MESSIAEN, O.
CATALOGUE D'OISEAUX, BK. 7   MESSIAEN, O.
CATALUNA -- FROM SUITE ESPANOLA NO. 1   ALBENIZ, I.
CATALUNA -- NO. 2, FROM SUITE ESPANOLA NO. 1   ALBENIZ, I.
CATA ARQUENA   IGLESIAS VILLOUD
CATCH-UP. TAPE RECORDER AND 2 PIANOS --OR 4 PIANOS--   HAMPTON
CATCHING THE SCHOOL BUS   HIBBS, C.
CATCHY TUNE, A.   LIPPMAN
CATCH ME IF YOU CAN   HIBBS, C.
CATCH ME   BRODSKY, M.
CATCH ME   GARROW
CATCH ME   GELBER
CATCH 1 -- CEMBALO SOLO   HAUBENSTOCK-RAMA
CATCH 2   HAUBENSTOCK-RAMA
CATCH 2   HAUBENSTOCK-RAMA
CATERPILLAR RIDE   RICHTER, A.
CATERPILLAR   COBB
CATHEDRAL AT TWILIGHT, THE   WAGNESS
CATHEDRAL BELLS   WIGGINS, M.
CATHEDRAL CHIMES   ARNOLD *
CATHEDRAL CHIMES   FRANK
CATHEDRAL CHIMES   REISER, V.
CATHEDRAL CHIMES   WINROTH, G.--ED
CATHEDRAL MEDITATION, EASY   LEMARE, E.
CATHEDRAL MEDITATION -- ANDANTINO   LEMARE, E.
CATHEDRAL OF LEARNING   ROCERETO, M.
CATHEDRAL REVERIE   GIOVANNI
CATHOLIC CHRISTMAS SONGS FOR THE YOUNG PIANIST   CURCIO
CATHOLIC HYMNS   SCHAUM, J.--ED.
CATHOLIC SONGS FOR THE YOUNG PIANIST   CURCIO
CATS   LAST, J.
CATTLE ROUNDUP   STEINER
CAT AND MOUSE   LAKE, G.
CAT AND THE MOUSE   COPLAND
CAT AND THE MUSIC BOX   ROSNER
CAT AND THE SQUIRREL, THE   ALT, H.
CAT AT NIGHT   BASTIEN
CAT CHARMS   MELLERS, W.
CAT ON A HOT TIN ROOF   WOLCOTT, C.
CAT SAT ON A CHAIR OF GOLD, THE -- FOR 1 OR MORE   ALT, H.
CAT TAILS   BAIRD *
CAT TAILS   KETTERER, E.
CAT TALE   GLOVER, D.
CAUCASIAN MARCH   SCHER, W.
CAUCASIAN SCENES, BK. 1   YGOUW
CAUCASIAN SCENES, BK. 2 -- NEW CAUCASIAN SCENES -- YGOUW
CAUCASIAN SHEPHERD   STEINER
CAUCASIAN SKETCHES, OP. 10--SUITE IN 4 PARTS   IPPOLITOV-IVANOV
CAUCASIAN SKETCHES, OP. 10   IPPOLITOV-IVANOV
CAUSERIE BADINE   FARJALL
CAUSE IT'S CHRISTMAS -- VOCAL EDITION   FICHTER
CAUSE IT'S CHRISTMAS   FICHTER
CAVALCATE   MALIPIERO, G. F.
CAVALLARO'S KEYBOARD CREATIONS   CAVALLARO
CAVALLERIA RUSTICANA--FANTASIA--   MASCAGNI, P.
CAVALLERIA RUSTICANA, INTERMEZZO, EASY   MASCAGNI, P.
CAVALLERIA RUSTICANA, INTERMEZZO   MASCAGNI, P.
CAVALLERIA RUSTICANA, INTERMEZZO   MASCAGNI, P.
CAVALLERIA RUSTICANA -- COMPLETE OPERA --   MASCAGNI, P.
CAVALLERIA RUSTICANA - GRAND FANTASY   MASCAGNI, P.
CAVALLERIA RUSTICANA - INTERMEZZO -- ORIGINAL -- MASCAGNI, P.
CAVALLERIA RUSTICANA - INTERMEZZO   MASCAGNI, P.
CAVALLERIA RUSTICANA - INTERMEZZO   MASCAGNI, P.
CAVALLERIA RUSTICANA - PRELUDE   MASCAGNI, P.
CAVALLERIA RUSTICANA - SELECTIONS   MASCAGNI, P.
CAVALLERIA RUSTICANA - SELECTIONS   MASCAGNI, P.
CAVALLERIA RUSTICANA 'INTERMEZZO'   MASCAGNI, P.
CAVALLERIA RUSTICANA   MASCAGNI, P.
CAVALRY TROT   RUBINSTEIN, B.
CAVATINA FROM THE THIRTEENTH QUARTET OP. 130   BEETHOVEN
CAVATINA   LOW, J.
CAVERN BY THE SEA, A   BURNAM
CECILE WALTZ   MCKEE
CECILE WALTZ   MCKEE
CEDAR BROOK WALTZ   PERRY, P.
CELEBRATED 'BATTLE OF PRAGUE, THE. ' --CA. 1788   KOCVARA
CELEBRATED MINUET, OP. 14 NO. 1   PADEREWSKI, I.
CELEBRATED SONATAS --24-- IN 4 VOLS., VOL. 1   CLEMENTI
CELEBRATED SONATAS --24-- IN 4 VOLS., VOL. 2   CLEMENTI
CELEBRATED SONATAS --24-- IN 4 VOLS., VOL. 3   CLEMENTI
CELEBRATED SONATAS --24-- IN 4 VOLS., VOL. 4   CLEMENTI
CELEBRATED WALTZ IL TROVATORE   VERDI
CELEBRATIONS AND EPILOGUE   KUBIK, G.
CELEBRATIONS IN THE SACRED FOREST   RIMSKY-KORSAKOFF
CELEBRATION   GROVE
CELEBRE MELODIE HONGROISE EN SI FLAT   LISZT
CELEBRE SERENADE, OP. 21   HEYKENS
CELEBRE SERENADE DE MANDOLINES   DESORMES
CELESTE PRIERE -- REVERIE --   GAUTIER, L.
CELLIST, THE   SCOVILL
CELLIST   WRIGHT, L.
CELLO PLAYER, OP. 12 NO. 5   MCINTYRE, E.
CELLO PLAYER   HAYES
CELLO REVERIE   ROZIN
CELLO SERENADE   STEVENS
CELLO SONG   MONTGOMERY, L.
CELLO WALTZES   TAYLOR
CEMBALO-KOMPOSITIONEN   POGLIETTI
CEMBALO WORKS --SONATA D'INTAVOLATURA, 1716--   ZIPOLI
CENA DELLE BEFFE, LA - GRAND FANTASY FROM ACTS 1 AND 2   GIORDANO
CENDRILLON, VALSE, OP. 279   STREABBOG
CENDRILLON -- CINDERELLA -- BALLET   DELANNOY
CENDRILLON - VALSE   DELANNOY
CENTRAL AVENUE DRAG   JOHNSON, S.
CENTRAL PARK ROMANCE   MOSSMAN, T.
CENTURY OVERTURE, OPERA GEMS   GREENWALD, M.
CERDANA - EN TARTANE   SEVERAC
CERDANA - LES FETES   SEVERAC
CERDANA - LES MULETIERS DEVANT LE CHRIST DE LLIVIA   SEVERAC
CERDANA - LE RETOUR DES MULETIERS   SEVERAC
CERDANA - MENETRIERS ET GLANEUSES   SEVERAC
CERDANA   SEVERAC
CEREMONIAL   OLSON

CERISETTE, POLKA-MAZURKA, OP. 280   STREABBOG
CERTAIN SMILE, A   LANE, J.--ED.
CE QU'A VU LE VENT D'OUEST FROM PRELUDES, BK. 1   DEBUSSY
CE QUE CHANTE L'EAU VIVE   GUENIFFEY
CE QUE DANSAIT GRAND'MERE   WALTER
CHA-CHA-LITA   BAUER
CHACARERA, OP. 8 NO. 1   NAPOLITANO
CHACARERA   GILARDI
CHACONNE, OP. 59   ROUBIER, H.
CHACONNE, OP. 62, FOR 2 PIANOS 8 HANDS   DURAND, A.
CHACONNE, S. 1004   BACH, J.S.
CHACONNE AND SCHERZO   SETER, M.
CHACONNE AND TOCCATA FOR TWO PIANOS   PHILLIPS, R.
CHACONNE F-DUR   HANDEL
CHACONNE G-DUR   HANDEL
CHACONNE IN A MINOR, OP. 62   DURAND, A.
CHACONNE IN D MINOR--FROM THE SONATA FOR VIOLIN SOLO,   BACH, J.S.
CHACONNE IN D MINOR-- LEFT HAND   BACH, J.S.
CHACONNE IN D MINOR, S. 1004E   BACH, J.S.
CHACONNE IN D MINOR BY BACH ARRANGED FOR THE LEFT HAND   BACH, J.S. *
CHACONNE IN G   HANDEL
CHACONNE IN G   HANDEL
CHACONNE NO. 2 -- FROM SUITE ANCIENNE NO. 2 --   ALBENIZ, I.
CHACONNE WITH 62 VARIATIONS IN G   HANDEL
CHACONNE   DURAND, A.
CHACONNE   DURAND, A.
CHACONNE   FINKBEINER
CHACONNE   HEISS
CHACONNE   JOHNSON, L.
CHACONNE   WOLPE
CHAIN OF WALTZES, 1927   NIN
CHAMBER CONCERTO NO. 1 IN C, OP. 153   NIEMANN
CHAMBER CONCERTO   SIEGL, O.
CHAMBER FANTASY ON THEMES FROM BIZET'S ''CARMEN''   BUSONI
CHAMBER MUSIC   CHOPIN
CHAMBER OF COMMERCE MARCH   NIRELLA, D.
CHAMPAGNE   BLEY
CHANG-CHUNG   BECK
CHANGE OF THE GUARDS -- ENGLISH FOLK MELODIES   STEINER
CHANGING OF THE GUARD   BURNAM
CHANGING PLACES   BURNAM
CHANGING SCENES   BRILLHART
CHANGING THE GUARD   DUMM
CHANSON, PASTORAL, DANSE   MIHALOVICI
CHANSONS NAIVES   JOLIVET, A.
CHANSON ARABE   LAMOTHE
CHANSON A MA POUPEE   SAMAZEUILH
CHANSON BOHEME DE CARMEN --BIZET   MOSZKOWSKI
CHANSON D'APPROCHE   JOLAS, B.
CHANSON D'AUTOMNE   BAZELAIRE
CHANSON DES FLEURS   LANGE, G.
CHANSON DE JANE-LA-GAILLARDE   PERILHOU
CHANSON DE LA FILEUSE   MARC, E.
CHANSON DE LA GRAND'MAMAN, OP. 3 NO. 2   PIERNE
CHANSON DE MAITRE WOLFF, OP. 97   CARMAN
CHANSON DE MATIN   ELGAR, E.
CHANSON DE NUIT   ELGAR, E.
CHANSON DE PRINTEMPS   HENSELT, A.
CHANSON DE TROUBADOUR   DESENCLOS, A.
CHANSON DU BON VIEUX TEMPS, OP. 28   BACHMANN, G.
CHANSON DU MULETIER, LA   PESSE
CHANSON DU VENT   GALLON, J.
CHANSON ET DANSE NO. 09   MOMPOU, F.
CHANSON ET DANSE NO. 10   MOMPOU, F.
CHANSON INDOUE, E FLAT MAJOR   RIMSKY-KORSAKOFF
CHANSON INDOUE, G MAJOR   RIMSKY-KORSAKOFF
CHANSON MILITAIRE   GRETCHANINOFF
CHANSON MILITAIRE   GRETCHANINOFF
CHANSON POUR BERCER   SAMUEL ROUSSEAU
CHANSON POUR UN AUTRE TEMPS   LECONTE, G. W.
CHANSON RUSSE, EASY   SMITH, SYDNEY
CHANSON RUSSE, OP. 31   SMITH, SYDNEY
CHANSON RUSSE, OP. 31   SMITH, SYDNEY
CHANSON TRISTE, OP. 40 NO. 2   TSCHAIKOWSKY
CHANSON TRISTE, OP. 40 NO. 2   TSCHAIKOWSKY
CHANSON TRISTE, OP. 40 NO. 2   TSCHAIKOWSKY
CHANSON TRISTE IN G MINOR, OP. 40 NO. 2   TSCHAIKOWSKY
CHANSON TRISTE OP. 40 NO. 2   TSCHAIKOWSKY
CHANSON   FRIML, R.
CHANSON   SMETANA
CHANTIS INTIMES - BK. 1   BLANCAFORT
CHANTIS INTOMES - BK. 2   BLANCAFORT
CHANTS D'ANTAN -- CHILDREN'S SUITE   ESPLA
CHANT D'ALLIANCE   BEETHOVEN *
CHANT D'AMOUR, OP. 10 NO. 2   PADEREWSKI, I.
CHANT D'AUTOMNE   PIERNE, P.
CHANT DES BATELIERS DE LA VOLGA, OP. 97   GLAZOUNOW, A.
CHANT DE BERGER   VIEU
CHANT DE GUERRE   HURE
CHANT DE JOIE   HONEGGER, A.
CHANT DE NIGAMON, LE   HONEGGER, A.
CHANT DU PAYSEN   RENDANO
CHANT DU PRINTEMPS   PIERNE, P.
CHANT DU ROSSIGNOL   STRAVINSKY, I.
CHANT ET REFRAIN   TCHEREPNIN
CHANT FUNEBRE, OP. 9   MAGNARD
CHANT INTIME   DUCHOW
CHANT OF THE BIRD WOMAN   STORR, S.
CHANT POLONAIS, OP. 74 NO. 5   CHOPIN *
CHANT POLONAIS, OP. 74 NO. 5   CHOPIN *
CHANT SANS PAROLES, OP. 2 NO. 3   TSCHAIKOWSKY
CHANT SANS PAROLES, OP. 2 NO. 3   TSCHAIKOWSKY
CHANT SANS PAROLES OP. 2 NO. 3   TSCHAIKOWSKY
CHANT SANS PAROLES   SAUVREZIS
CHANT SANS PAROLES   TSCHAIKOWSKY
CHANT TO AUTUMN MOON   VOLZ, H.
CHANT   FRANCHETTI
CHAPEAU BAS   ALKAN
CHAPEL BELLS   MASTERS
CHAPEL CHIMES   GREENWALD, M.
CHAPEL ECHOES   PEERY, R. R.--ED
CHAPEL IN THE FOREST   JUNGMAN, A.
CHAPEL IN THE MOUNTAINS   SMITH, L.
CHAPEL IN THE WOODS   LANGE, G.
CHAPEL MUSINGS   PEERY, R. R.
CHAPEL PIANIST NO. 1   PANKOW, E.
CHAPEL PIANIST NO. 2   PANKOW, E.
CHAPEL PIANIST NO. 3   PANKOW, E.
CHAPINIANA   MARROQUIN, J.
CHAPITRES TOURNES EN TOUS SENS   SATIE, E.
CHAPPEL'S EASYPLAY PIANO SERIES, BK. 1 -- FILM THEMES
CHAPPEL'S EASYPLAY PIANO SERIES, BK. 2 -- LOVE THEMES
CHAPPEL'S EASYPLAY PIANO SERIES, BK. 3 -- SHOWSTOPPERS
CHAPPEL'S EASYPLAY PIANO SERIES -- THE BEST OF COUNTRY
CHAPPELL'S FAMOUS MELODIES   CARVER--ED
CHAPPELL'S FAMOUS MELODIES   SINGER, L.--ED
CHAPPELL'S FAVORITES   STONE, E.--ED

CHAPPELL'S SACRED SONG FAVORITES
CHARACTERISTIC STUDIES - FANTASY   MONTANI
CHARACTERISTIC STUDIES - 3 AMERICAN STUDIES   MONTANI
CHARACTERISTIC STUDIES - 3 HUMOROUS STUDIES   MONTANI
CHARACTERISTIC STUDIES   MONTANI
CHARACTERISTIC SUITE   SMITH, J.
CHARADE
CHARGE DES AMAZONS   SPINDLER
CHARGE OF THE HUSSARS   SPINDLER
CHARGE OF THE UHLANS, OP. 213   BOHM
CHARGE OF THE UHLANS   BOHM
CHARLESTON PARISIEN   MOULIN
CHARLES THE CHESTY CHIPMUNK   MESEROLE, H. T.
CHARLOTTE IN APRIL
CHARMAINE   LANE, J.--ED.
CHARMANTE, OP. 67   GROTON, F.
CHARMANTE   GROTON, F.
CHARMANTE   ROGERS
CHARMES DE L'ETUDE, LES -- 12 LITTLE PIECES WITHOUT   GAUTIER, L.
CHARMES DE L'ETUDE, LES - COLIBRI   GAUTIER, L.
CHARMES DE L'ETUDE, LES - EN FORET   GAUTIER, L.
CHARMES DE L'ETUDE, LES - GIRALDA   GAUTIER, L.
CHARMES DE L'ETUDE, LES - JOUR DE FETE   GAUTIER, L.
CHARMES DE L'ETUDE, LES - LA BONNE FEE   GAUTIER, L.
CHARMES DE L'ETUDE, LES - LEGER PAPILLON   GAUTIER, L.
CHARMES DE L'ETUDE, LES - LE MASCARET   GAUTIER, L.
CHARMES DE L'ETUDE, LES - MISS ALICE   GAUTIER, L.
CHARMES DE L'ETUDE, LES - PENSEE FUGITIVE   GAUTIER, L.
CHARMES DE L'ETUDE, LES - PERLES DU MATIN   GAUTIER, L.
CHARMES DE L'ETUDE, LES - SOUS LES ORANGERS   GAUTIER, L.
CHARMES DE L'ETUDE, LES - VOL D'OISEAUX   GAUTIER, L.
CHARMES   MOMPOU, F.
CHARMEUSE DE PEINES   MOTTU
CHARME D'AMOUR   CREMIEUX
CHARMING PRINCESS   TRUXELL, E.
CHARMING WALTZES   WALDTEUFEL, E.
CHARMING   WILSON, M.
CHARM BRACELET, THE   WAXMAN
CHARM OF CHAMBER MUSIC   SCHUBERT
CHARTREUSE KITTEN   KING
CHASE AUX GAZELLES, LA, OP. 11   CALVINI, A.
CHASE ME   GARROW, L.
CHASIDIC TUNE   KARP
CHASING SQUIRRELS, SCHOTTISCHE   REED, H.
CHASSE, LA--NO. 5 OF THE ETUDES AFTER PAGANINI--   LISZT
CHASSE, LA -- 1ST AND 2ND VERSIONS --   LISZT
CHASSE, SCHERZO, OP. 103   BAZELAIRE
CHASSE INTERNALE   KOLLING, C.
CHATELAINE, LA   LE DUC
CHATTANOOGA CHOO CHOO   LANE, J.--ED.
CHATTE, LA -- BALLET -- .. HYMNE FINAL   SAUGUET
CHATTE, LA -- BALLET -- .. INVOCATION A APHRODITE   SAUGUET
CHATTE, LA -- BALLET --   SAUGUET
CHATTERBOX - FROM SEVEN FLOWERS FROM A PIANIST'S   GIASSON, P.
CHATTERBOX   FRIML, R.
CHATTERBOX   GIASSON, P.
CHATTERING BROOK   ERB
CHATTERING CHIPMUNKS   GILLEY, E.
CHA CHA --MODERN RHYTHMIC CLASSICS--   WHITFORD
CHA CHA DOLL   MARTIN, G.
CHA CHA DOLL   MARTIN, G.
CHA CHA ON THE BEACH   RUSSELL
CHEER-UP   RICHTER
CHEERFULNESS   ROWE, D.
CHEERFUL STORY, A   BRUSSELS, I.
CHEERFUL TUNE, THE   HEADINGTON
CHEERLEADER, THE   PLANK, E.
CHEERY CHIPMUNK   CHAGY
CHEER LEADER   ERB
CHERISH   BRADLEY,
CHERISH   BRIMHALL
CHEROKEE BRAVES   DITTENHAVER
CHEROKEE CLAM-BAKE   KIMES, K.
CHEROKEE   NOBLE
CHEROKEE   NOBLE *
CHERRIES RIPE   STEINER
CHERRY BLOSSOMS   TROJA
CHERRY BLOSSOM TIME   ERB
CHERRY BLOSSOM TIME   KING
CHERRY BLOSSOM   NICHOLLS, H.
CHERRY PINK AND APPLE BLOSSOM WHITE
CHERRY RED   JOHNSON, S.
CHERRY TREE, THE   HOPKINS, H.
CHERUBINISCHE SONATA   HERRMANN, H.
CHESHIRE ROUNDS   THIMAN
CHESS-SERENADE, 1945 -- SET   RIETI
CHEVRIER QUI PASSE, LE -- NO. 4, FROM FIVE EASY PIECES   DELUNE
CHEYENNE   VAN ALSTYNE, E.
CHEZ GRAND-PAPA   STREABBOG
CHEZ GRAND'MAMAN   STREABBOG
CHIAPANECAS -- MEXICAN HAT DANCE   BURNAM
CHIAPANECAS   BOSSI, F.
CHIAPANECAS   DE CAMPO--ED
CHIAPANECAS   SAVINO--ED.
CHIARINA, OP. 33 -- BALLET IN ONE ACT   BLACHER
CHICADEE FROM BEETHOVEN'S SYMPHONY NO. 8   ROLFE, W.
CHICAGO ON MY MIND   AMMONS
CHICK-A-DEE, THE   AARON, M.
CHICKADEE, THE   MATHESON
CHICKADEE   LAKE, G.
CHICKADEE   MATHESON
CHICKEN HOP   DVORINE
CHICKEN REEL
CHICKEN REEL   SCHAUM, J.--ED.
CHICO' BOOGIE WOOGIE   KENT, H.
CHIEF RED FEATHER   LIVELY, K.
CHIEF RED FEATHER   SCHER, W.
CHIEF SOARING EAGLE   DITTENHAVER
CHILD'S BOOK OF FOLK-TUNES, A--SUPPLEMENTARY READING   WESTERVELT, M.
CHILD'S BOOK OF HYMNS   PEERY, R. R.--ED
CHILD'S CHRISTMAS, A   JOYNER, B.--ED
CHILD'S CZERNY   ARNOLD, F.
CHILD'S DAY, A -- SUITE OF 14 PIECES   SARSON, M.
CHILD'S DAY -- 14 PIECES   SARSON, M.
CHILD'S DAY   GRETCHANINOFF
CHILD'S FIRST MUSIC BOOK   WILLIAMS, J.
CHILD'S PICTURE BOOK, A   LAMONTAINE, J.
CHILD'S PLAY - TWELVE PIECES FOR THE GROWING PIANIST   RAPHLING
CHILD'S PLAY   BEHR, F.
CHILD'S PLAY   RAPHLING
CHILD'S PRIMER, A   ROLFE, W.
CHILD'S WORLD IN MUSIC, A   PERL, H. F.
CHILD'S WORLD   DONALDSON
CHILDHOOD DAYS OF FAMOUS COMPOSERS -- CHILD BRAHMS   BRAHMS
CHILDHOOD DAYS OF FAMOUS COMPOSERS -- CHILD CHOPIN   CHOPIN
CHILDHOOD DAYS OF FAMOUS COMPOSERS -- CHILD HANDEL   HANDEL
CHILDHOOD MEMORIES, SERIES 1   FERRARI-TRECATE

CHILDHOOD MEMORIES, SERIES 2	FERRARI-TRECATE
CHILDHOOD SCENES, OP. 70	TARENGHI
CHILDREN'S ALBUM, OP. 210	KOEHLER
CHILDREN'S ALBUM, OP. 210	KOEHLER
CHILDREN'S ALBUM, OP. 98	GRETCHANINOFF
CHILDREN'S ALBUM, OP. 98	GRETCHANINOFF
CHILDREN'S ALBUM, VOL. 1	KHATCHATURIAN
CHILDREN'S ALBUM, VOL. 2	KHATCHATURIAN
CHILDREN'S BOOK, OP. 98	GRETCHANINOFF
CHILDREN'S BOOK	FREY--ED
CHILDREN'S BOOK	GRETCHANINOFF
CHILDREN'S BOOK	SHOSTAKOVITCH
CHILDREN'S CARNIVAL	STREABBOG
CHILDREN'S CHRISTMAS	NORMAN
CHILDREN'S CONCERTO--CURWEN EDITION	HAYDN
CHILDREN'S CONCERTO, OP. 68 -- 1 PIANO 6 HANDS --	BILLEMA
CHILDREN'S CORNER	DEBUSSY
CHILDREN'S DANCES	KODALY, Z.
CHILDREN'S DANCE FROM 'HANSEL AND GRETEL'	HUMPERDINCK, E.
CHILDREN'S DAY- SIX PIECES	SIEGMEISTER
CHILDREN'S DREAMS - 10 EASY PIECES	DE ANGELIS
CHILDREN'S EXERCISE, OP. 218	KOEHLER
CHILDREN'S FAVORITE CHRISTMAS CAROLS	WILLAN
CHILDREN'S FESTIVAL--LITTLE SUITE	PINTO, O.
CHILDREN'S FESTIVAL, THE--HUNGARIAN DANCE, OP. 31	ENGEL, S.
CHILDREN'S FRIEND, OP. 243, BK. 1	KOEHLER
CHILDREN'S FRIEND, OP. 243, BK. 2	KOEHLER
CHILDREN'S FRIEND, OP. 87. 50 EASY AND MELODIOUS	WOHLFAHRT
CHILDREN'S FRIEND, THE OP. 87	WOHLFAHRT
CHILDREN'S GAMES	BIZET, G.
CHILDREN'S JAZZ PIECES	ALFASSY, L.--ED
CHILDREN'S JEST, A	MOUSSORGSKY
CHILDREN'S MARCH- OVER THE HILLS AND FAR AWAY	GRAINGER, P.
CHILDREN'S MARCHING SONG	LANE, J.--ED.
CHILDREN'S MARCH	SCHUBERT
CHILDREN'S MINUET	BELL
CHILDREN'S PARADE, THE	DITTENHAVER
CHILDREN'S PARADISE - 6 EASY PIECES	BILLI
CHILDREN'S PIANO PIECES -- POPULAR EDITION	BRIMHALL,
CHILDREN'S PIANO PIECES BY SOVIET COMPOSERS	
CHILDREN'S PIANO PIECES THE WHOLE WORLD PLAYS	
CHILDREN'S PIANO PIECES	PANZERA, M.
CHILDREN'S PIANO RECITAL, BK. 1	MENDELSSOHN
CHILDREN'S PIECE, OP. 72 NO. 5 - FOR TWO PIANOS, EIGHT	MENDELSSOHN
CHILDREN'S PIECES, OP. 72	MENDELSSOHN
CHILDREN'S PIECES, OP. 72	KHATCHATURIAN
CHILDREN'S PIECES	PROKOFIEFF
CHILDREN'S PIECES	TREHARNE
CHILDREN'S PLAYTIME PIECES	HUMPERDINCK, E.
CHILDREN'S PRAYER, THE -- FROM HANSEL AND GRETEL	LOESCHHORN, A.
CHILDREN'S STUDIES, OP. 181, VOL. 1	LOESCHHORN, A.
CHILDREN'S STUDIES, OP. 181, VOL. 2	MAIER, G. *
CHILDREN'S TECHNIC BOOK	TSCHAIKOWSKY
CHILDREN'S TSCHAIKOWSKY	
CHILDREN'S TV WONDERLAND SONG BOOK	
CHILDREN'S VERY FIRST PIANO PIECES	FERNANDEZ, O.
CHILDREN'S VISIONS - LITTLE CORTEGE	FERNANDEZ, O.
CHILDREN'S VISIONS - MYSTERIOUS DANCE	FERNANDEZ, O.
CHILDREN'S VISIONS - NOCTURNAL ROUND	SMOLANOFF
CHILDRENS SUITE FOR PIANO	GREENWALD, M.
CHILDREN AT PLAY, CAPRICE	MORGEN, M.
CHILDREN AT PLAY	GRIFFIS, E.
CHILD ASLEEP, A	HOVHANESS, A.
CHILD IN THE GARDEN, OP. 168	CHANLER, T.
CHILD IN THE HOUSE, A	WEYBRIGHT--ED.
CHILEAN FOLK SONG, A	WEYBRIGHT--ED.
CHILEAN FOLK SONG	MARTINO
CHILI-BEAN	DUNGAN
CHIMES AT PARANA	WAGENSEIL, G. C.
CHIMES IN THE VATICAN IN ROME	PLANQUETTE
CHIMES OF NORMANDY, SEL. 1	PLANQUETTE
CHIMES OF NORMANDY, SEL. 2	PLANQUETTE
CHIMES OF NORMANDY, SEL. 3	FROST
CHIMES THROUGH THE MIST	ERB
CHIMING BELLS	STILWELL
CHIMING BELLS	WEBSTER, J.
CHIMING BELLS	BURNAM
CHIMNEY SMOKE FROM SNOW	BRIMHALL,
CHIM CHIM CHER-EE	BASTIEN
CHINATOWN	ROGERS
CHINATOWN	
CHINA BOY	
CHINA CLIPPER	SCHAUM, J.--ED.
CHINA DOLL PARADE	ZAMECNIK
CHINA DOLL PARADE	ZAMECNIK
CHINA DOLL PARADE	ZAMECNIK
CHINA DOLL PARADE	ZAMECNIK
CHINA DOLL	ANDERSON, L.
CHINA DOLL	ECKSTEIN
CHINA NIGHTS -- SHINA NO YORU	SEDORES
CHINESE BAGATELLES, OP. 51, NO. 3	TCHEREPNIN
CHINESE BOY, THE	STONE, C.
CHINESE CARNIVAL	WERMEL
CHINESE CHASE	ELISIA, SR.
CHINESE CHATTER	ANSON, G.
CHINESE CHATTER	ROSNER
CHINESE CHATTER	SCHER, W.
CHINESE CHECKERS	GLOVER, D.
CHINESE CHECKERS	GLOVER, D.
CHINESE DANCE 'NUTCRACKER SUITE'	TSCHAIKOWSKY
CHINESE DANCE IN B FLAT FROM NUTCRACKER SUITE	TSCHAIKOWSKY
CHINESE DANCE	KAPLAN
CHINESE DANCE	TSCHAIKOWSKY
CHINESE DREAM	LAWLOR, G.
CHINESE FAIRY TALE, A	SCHER, W.
CHINESE LANDSCAPE	BENTLEY
CHINESE LULLABY	BIRCSAK, T.
CHINESE LULLABY	ROBINSON, A.
CHINESE MAIDEN	WHITFORD
CHINESE MARKET PLACE, A	SCHER, W.
CHINESE SANDMAN	BESTHOFF, M.
CHINESE SERENADE	ANSON, G.
CHINESE SNOWMAN, THE	BASTIEN
CHINESE STORY	BRUSSELS, I.
CHINESE TEA PARTY	BASTIEN
CHINESE TEMPLE GONGS	HARVEY, VIVIEN
CHINESE TEMPLE GONGS	HARVEY, VIVIEN
CHINESE TEMPLE SCENE	DILLON, F.
CHING-CHEE	BRODSKY, M.
CHING CHONG ALLEY	DAVIS, J.
CHINOISE, A LA, OP. 39	ORNSTEIN, L.
CHINOISERIE	BENJAMIN
CHIN CHI CHA	SWAN *
CHIP'S BOOGIE-WOOGIE	HATRAK
CHIPPY CHIPMUNK	BEAUMONT
CHIPS FROM OTHER BLOCKS	THOMPSON, J.
CHIQUITO -- TANGO	BERNA

CHIRIBIRI-BINGO	NEVIN
CHIT-CHAT	REISER, V.
CHITARRATA ITALIENNE	SCHER, W.
CHITARRATA	LOTTINI
CHITTY CHITTY BANG BANG	LANE, J.--ED.
CHITTY CHITTY BANG BANG	
CHOCOLATE BUNNY'S LOVE SONG	CONFREY, E.
CHOCOLATE RIPPLE	THOMAS, F.
CHOCOLATE SOLDIER	COBB
CHOEUR-BARCAROLLE D'OBERON	WEBER, VON *
CHOEUR-BARCAROLLE FROM OBERON	WEBER, VON *
CHOEUR DES PRETRES DE DAGON, FROM SAMSON	HANDEL *
CHOEUR DES PRETRES DE DAGON	HANDEL *
CHOICE COLLECTION OF LESSONS	PURCELL, H.
CHOIR SINGER, THE	BESTHOFF, M.
CHOLA APASIONADA, LA	IGLESIAS VILLOUD
CHOO, CHOO, CHOO	ROGERS, E.
CHOO CHOO BOOGIE	SCHAUM, J.--ED.
CHOP-STIX UNLIMITED	HUMPHREYS
CHOPIN-SCHAUM, BK. 1	CHOPIN
CHOPIN-SCHAUM, BK. 1	CHOPIN
CHOPIN-SCHAUM, BK. 2	CHOPIN
CHOPIN-SCHAUM, BK. 2	CHOPIN
CHOPIN, MUSIC TO REMEMBER	CHOPIN
CHOPIN'S POLONAISE IN BOOGIE	CHOPIN
CHOPIN ALBUM	CHOPIN
CHOPIN FOR EVERYBODY	CHOPIN
CHOPIN FOR THE YOUNG PIANIST	CHOPIN
CHOPIN FOR THE YOUNG	CHOPIN
CHOPIN IN MINIATURE	CHOPIN
CHOPIN SAMPLER	CHOPIN
CHOPIN SELECTED WALTZES	CHOPIN
CHOPIN SIMPLIFIED	CHOPIN
CHOPIN	CHOPIN
CHOPSTICKS, WALTZ	DE LULLI, A.
CHOPSTICKS, WALTZ	DE LULLI, A.
CHOPSTICKS -- HUMORESQUE	SCARMOLIN
CHOPSTICKS DE LUXE	GARROW, L.
CHOPSTICKS FOR THREE -- FOR 1 PIANO 6 HANDS	STEINER
CHOPSTICKS	SCALINO
CHOP BOOGIE	SCHAUM, J.--ED.
CHOP STICKS	DE LULLI, A.
CHOP STICKS	SCHAUM, J.--ED.
CHOP STICKS	SCHAUM, J.--ED.
CHOP SUEY BOOGIE	ROZIN
CHORAL-SPIEL-BUCH. 30 CHORALSATZE	REDA
CHORAL-SPIEL-BUCH	REDA
CHORALBUCH	DOERFFEL--ED
CHORALE, PRELUDE, FUGUE	FRANCK, C.
CHORALE, VARIATIONS AND FINALE	RIETI
CHORALE, VARIATIONS AND FINALE	RIETI
CHORALE, VARIATIONS AND SONATINA	PETYREK, F.
CHORALES AND SACRED ARIAS--317--MEHRSTIMIGE CHORAELE.	BACH, J.S.
CHORALES AND SACRED ARIAS--317--MEHRSTIMIGE CHORAELE.	BACH, J.S.
CHORALE -- ''JESU, JOY OF MAN'S DESIRING'' -- FROM	BACH, J.S.
CHORALE -- JESUS BLEIBET MEINE FREUDE FROM CANTATA 147	BACH, J.S.
CHORALE AND FUGUE ON A THEME BY J. S. BACH	BERGGRUN, J.
CHORALE AND VARIATIONS	GIACCHINO
CHORALE BY BACH, A	BACH, J.S.
CHORALE FROM CANTATA 147	BACH, J.S.
CHORALE IN STYLE OF HANDEL	DAVID, A.
CHORALE PRELUDES -- A ROSE BREAKS INTO BLOOM, OP. 122	BRAHMS
CHORALE PRELUDES -- O GOD, THOU HOLY GOD, OP. 122 NO.	BRAHMS
CHORALE PRELUDE	WRIGHT
CHORALE PRELUDE	BACH, J.S.
CHORALE	PIERNE
CHORAL A L'EGLISE, OP. 3 NO. 8	DRISCHNER
CHORAL FANTASY ON 'LOBET DEN HERRN'	LECOUPPEY, F.
CHORAL PRELUDE	ROPARTZ
CHORAL VARIE	HOLT, H.
CHORD-A-TUNE	HARRISON
CHORDING THE KEYBOARD	PODOLSKY, L. *
CHORDS, CADENCES, TRANSPOSITION	STEVENS
CHORDS, CADENCES AND ARPEGGIOS	OREM, P. W.
CHORDS AND ARPEGGIOS	GLOVER, D. *
CHORDS AND KEYS	GLOVER, D. *
CHORDS AND KEYS	MCGINLEY
CHORDS AND MELODIES - CHRISTMAS SONGS TO ARRANGE	MCGINLEY
CHORDS AND MELODIES - TUNES YOU KNOW	MCGINLEY
CHORDS AND MELODIES - 20 TUNES TO ARRANGE, SET 1	MCGINLEY
CHORDS AND MELODIES - 20 TUNES TO ARRANGE, SET 2	MCGINLEY
CHORDS AND MELODIES - 20 TUNES TO ARRANGE, SET 3	MCGINLEY
CHORDS AND MELODIES - 20 TUNES TO ARRANGE, SET 4	MCGINLEY
CHORDS AND MELODIES SERIES - ADVANCED LEVEL 1	MCGINLEY
CHORDS AND MELODIES SERIES - BEGINNER'S LEVEL 1	HANDEL *
CHORDS AND MELODIES SERIES - BEGINNER'S LEVEL 2	MCGINLEY
CHORDS AND MELODIES SERIES - INTERMEDIATE LEVEL 1	MCGINLEY
CHORDS AND MELODIES SERIES - INTERMEDIATE LEVEL 2	STEINER
CHORDS FOR PLEASURE -- MARCHES, WALTZES AND DANCES	BISHOP
CHORDS IN ACTION	DE VITO, A.
CHORD APPROACH TO 'POP' PIANO PLAYING, BK. 1	DE VITO, A.
CHORD APPROACH TO 'POP' PIANO PLAYING, BK. 2	DE VITO, A.
CHORD APPROACH TO 'POP' PIANO PLAYING, BK. 3	DE VITO, A.
CHORD APPROACH TO 'POP' PIANO PLAYING, BK. 4	KAHN, M.
CHORD CONSTRUCTION AND HINTS FOR POPULAR PIANO PLAYING	STEINER
CHORD DUETS	WARD, J.
CHORD ETUDES - K1	WARD, J.
CHORD ETUDES - K2	WARD, J.
CHORD ETUDES - K3	WARD, J.
CHORD ETUDES - K4	JACOBUS, D.
CHORD FROLIC	DE VITO, A.
CHORD PIANIST --SUPPLEMENTARY BOOKS TO BE USED WITH	NEVIN
CHORD PRELUDE	NEVIN
CHORD PRELUDE	STEINER
CHORD STUDIES AND PIECES, BK. 1	STEINER
CHORD STUDIES AND PIECES, BK. 2	SILL, H.
CHORD SYSTEM PIANO COURSE - BK. 1	SILL, H.
CHORD SYSTEM PIANO COURSE - BK. 2	SILL, H.
CHORD SYSTEM PIANO COURSE - BK. 3	SILL, H.
CHORD SYSTEM PIANO COURSE - BK. 4	SILL, H.
CHORD SYSTEM PIANO COURSE - BK. 5	SILL, H.
CHORD SYSTEM PIANO COURSE - BK. 6	SILL, H.
CHORD SYSTEM PIANO COURSE - STARTER SET, BK. A	SILL, H.
CHORD SYSTEM PIANO COURSE - STARTER SET, BK. B	SILL, H.
CHOROS NO. 5--ALMA BRASILEIRA	VILLA-LOBOS, H.
CHORO TORTURADO	GUARNIERI
CHORO	SANTORSOLA, G.
CHOSE EN SOI 'A', OP. 45A	PROKOFIEFF
CHOSE EN SOI 'B', OP. 45B	PROKOFIEFF
CHRISTMAS ALBUM. VIOLIN AND V'CELLO AD LIB.	
CHRISTMAS ALBUM -- PIANO DUET	SCHAUM, J.--ED.
CHRISTMAS ALBUM -- 14 CHRISTMAS SONGS WITH GERMAN TEXT	DIEHL--ED
CHRISTMAS ALBUM	SCHAUM, J.--ED.
CHRISTMAS ALBUM	SCHAUM, J.--ED.
CHRISTMAS ALBUM	SCHAUM, J.--ED.
CHRISTMAS ALBUM	TRAVAGLIA
CHRISTMAS AT THE PIANO	GILLOCK
CHRISTMAS AT THE PIANO	ROGERS--ED.

Title	Composer/Editor
CHRISTMAS AT THE PIANO	STEINER
CHRISTMAS AT THE PIANO	TOLSON, P.
CHRISTMAS BELLS, OP. 129	NIEMANN
CHRISTMAS BELLS MARCH, OP. 17	WYMAN, A.
CHRISTMAS BELLS MARCH, OP. 17	WYMAN, A.
CHRISTMAS BELLS WALTZ	HILL
CHRISTMAS BELLS	GADE, N.
CHRISTMAS BOOK FOR PIANISTS	ANSON, G.
CHRISTMAS BOOK	THOMPSON, J.
CHRISTMAS CANZONA	KRAEHENBUEHL
CHRISTMAS CAROL, A	AUBERGE, A. D'
CHRISTMAS CAROLER	DALLIN--ED.
CHRISTMAS CAROLS --WITH WORDS--	WATSON--ED.
CHRISTMAS CAROLS -- FOR THE VERY YOUNG	STEINER
CHRISTMAS CAROLS - BOOK 1	KAHL--ED
CHRISTMAS CAROLS - BOOK 2	KAHL--ED
CHRISTMAS CAROLS - BOOK 3	KAHL--ED
CHRISTMAS CAROLS FOR BEGINNERS	BLAKE, J. *
CHRISTMAS CAROLS FOR CHILDREN	HUNTLEY, C.--ED
CHRISTMAS CAROLS FOR CHILDREN	HUNTLEY, C.--ED
CHRISTMAS CAROLS FOR EVERYONE	HARDING, R.--ED
CHRISTMAS CAROLS FOR LITTLE BOYS AND GIRLS	RODGERS, I.--ED
CHRISTMAS CAROLS FOR LITTLE PIANISTS	CURCIO--ED
CHRISTMAS CAROLS FOR MULTIPLE PIANOS	BASTIEN
CHRISTMAS CAROLS IN VERY EASY ARRANGEMENTS FOR PIANO	RICHTER, A.
CHRISTMAS CAROLS MADE EASY TO PLAY AND SING	MASON, M. B.
CHRISTMAS CAROLS ROCK	JONES *
CHRISTMAS CAROLS TO PLAY AND SING	WAGNESS--ED.
CHRISTMAS CAROLS	DEE, M.
CHRISTMAS CAROLS	FROST
CHRISTMAS CAROLS	ROLFE, W.--ED
CHRISTMAS CAROLS	WALLIS--ED
CHRISTMAS CAROL BOOK	PEERY, R. R.--ED
CHRISTMAS CAROL SONGBOOK, THE	SMALL, A.
CHRISTMAS CAROL	BENTLEY
CHRISTMAS CHIMES	BLAKE, D.
CHRISTMAS CHIMES	DARDENELLE, L.
CHRISTMAS CHIMES	GOERDELER, R.
CHRISTMAS CHIMES	KAHL
CHRISTMAS CHIMES	VANDERSLOOT, F.
CHRISTMAS CONCERTO IN G. SCORE/HARPSICHORD SOLO PART	PREDIERI, G.
CHRISTMAS DUETS	KAHL--ED
CHRISTMAS ECHOES	DASHER, J.
CHRISTMAS EVE, OP. 43	HEINS, C.
CHRISTMAS EVE, OP. 43	HEINS, C.
CHRISTMAS EVE	GROFE, F.
CHRISTMAS EVE	HEINS, C.
CHRISTMAS FANTASY	MOORE
CHRISTMAS FASTASIA	MUELLER, C.
CHRISTMAS FAVORITES	MOORE--ED
CHRISTMAS HOLIDAY	PALMER, W. A.
CHRISTMAS HYMNS	ROLFE, W.--ED
CHRISTMAS IN MEXICO -- WITH WORDS	WESTERVELT,
CHRISTMAS IN THE SOUTH -- WITH WORDS	WESTERVELT,
CHRISTMAS IS HERE	HOPKINS, H.
CHRISTMAS LULLABY, A	MCKINNEY
CHRISTMAS LULLABY	DASHER, J.
CHRISTMAS LULLABY	STEINER
CHRISTMAS MEDLEY -- 1. HARK, THE HERALD ANGELS SING,	STEINER
CHRISTMAS MEDLEY	DASHER, J.
CHRISTMAS MELODIES IN EASY ARRANGEMENTS	RICHTER, A.--ED.
CHRISTMAS MORNING	SCHAUM, J.--ED.
CHRISTMAS MUSIC, BK. 1 --SECULAR--	WEYBRIGHT--ED.
CHRISTMAS MUSIC, BK. 1 -- SECULAR	WEYBRIGHT
CHRISTMAS MUSIC, BK. 1	PACE, R.
CHRISTMAS MUSIC, BK. 2 --SACRED--	WEYBRIGHT--ED.
CHRISTMAS MUSIC, BK. 2 -- SACRED	WEYBRIGHT
CHRISTMAS MUSIC, SECOND COLLECTION	PACE, H.
CHRISTMAS MUSIC FOR DUET	DELLO JOIO, N.
CHRISTMAS MUSIC	GLOVER, D. *
CHRISTMAS MUSIC	GLOVER, D. *
CHRISTMAS MUSIC	
CHRISTMAS NIGHTINGALE	KOSCHINSKY
CHRISTMAS RECITAL	AGAY, D.--ED
CHRISTMAS RHAPSODY	SCHAUM, J.--ED.
CHRISTMAS SONG, THE	BRIMHALL
CHRISTMAS SONGS AND SOLOS	ZEPP--ED
CHRISTMAS SONGS	DE VITO, A.--ED.
CHRISTMAS SONG	KROGMANN, C. W.
CHRISTMAS SUITE, A	YOUNG, G.
CHRISTMAS TIDE	SHACKLEY--ED.
CHRISTMAS TRANSCRIPTIONS FOR PIANO	AULD, W. J.
CHRISTMAS TREE, THE	GREAN
CHRISTMAS TREE, VOL. 1	LISZT
CHRISTMAS TREE, VOL. 2	LISZT
CHRISTMAS TREE FAIRY	LAMONT
CHRISTMAS TREE	LISZT
CHRISTMAS TREE	RICHTER, A.
CHRISTOPHER COLUMBUS	STEINER
CHRISTOPHER COLUMBUS	DVORINE
CHROMAMORPHE 2	TAKAHASHI
CHROMAT. FANTASIE UND FUGE, BWV 903	BACH, J.S.
CHROMATIC FANTASIE UND FUGE, BWV 903	BACH, J.S.
CHROMATIC FANTASY AND FUGUE--VIENNA URTEXT EDITION	BACH, J.S.
CHROMATIC FANTASY AND FUGUE, CONCERTO IN THE ITALIAN	BACH, J.S.
CHROMATIC FANTASY AND FUGUE, URTEXT, WITH 2 VARIANTS	BACH, J.S.
CHROMATIC FANTASY AND FUGUE IN D MINOR, S. 903	BACH, J.S.
CHROMATIC FANTASY AND FUGUE	BACH, J.S.
CHROMATIC FANTASY AND FUGUE	BACH, J.S.
CHROMATIC FANTASY AND FUGUE	BACH, J.S.
CHROMATIC FANTASY AND FUGUE	BACH, J.S.
CHROMATIC FANTASY AND FUGUE	BACH, J.S.
CHROMATIC FANTASY AND FUGUE	BACH, J.S.
CHROMATIC HEY-DAY	NEVIN
CHROMATIC NOCTURNE	STEINER
CHROMATIC POLKA	SCHER, W.
CHROMATIC SONATA	YARDUMIAN, R.
CHROMATIC STUDY	MANNINO, V.
CHROMATIC WALTZ, EASY	GODARD, B.
CHROMATIC WALTZ	AGAY, D.
CHRYSANTHEMUMS	LEONI, F.
CHUGGING DOWN THE RIVER	ASHLEY, H.
CHURCH AND CHAPEL VOLUNTARIES	DREISBACH
CHURCH MOUSE, THE	OBENCHAIN, V.
CHURCH MUSICIAN, LEVEL 1	GLOVER, D. *
CHURCH MUSICIAN, LEVEL 2	GLOVER, D. *
CHURCH MUSICIAN, LEVEL 3	GLOVER, D. *
CHURCH MUSICIAN, LEVEL 4	GLOVER, D. *
CHURCH MUSICIAN, LEVEL 5	GLOVER, D. *
CHURCH MUSICIAN, LEVEL 6	GLOVER, D. *
CHURCH MUSICIAN, PRIMER LEVEL	GLOVER, D. *
CHURCH PIANIST, THE. NOS 1 AND 3	
CHURCH PIANIST'S HYMNAL, THE	
CHURCH PIANO MUSIC	SETCHELL
CIACCONA DEI TEMPI DI GUERRA--1943	KAHN, E.I.
CIACONA	BUXTEHUDE
CIBEL, MINUET, SARABAND	LOEILLET
CICLO BRASILEIRO - DANCE OF THE WHITE INDIAN	VILLA-LOBOS, H.
CICLO BRASILEIRO - JUNGLE FESTIVAL	VILLA-LOBOS, H.
CICLO BRASILEIRO - MINSTREL IMPRESSIONS	VILLA-LOBOS, H.
CICLO BRASILEIRO - NATIVE PLANTING SONG	VILLA-LOBOS, H.
CICLO PIANISTICO--CASTILLO DE ALMODOVAR, EL, OP. 88	TURINA, J.
CICLO PIANISTICO--CONCERTO WITHOUT ORCHESTRA, OP. 88	TURINA, J.
CICLO PIANISTICO--FIVE PRELUDES, OP. 80	TURINA, J.
CICLO PIANISTICO--PARTITA IN C, OP. 57	TURINA, J.
CICLO PIANISTICO--PIEZA ROMANTICA, OP. 64	TURINA, J.
CICLO PIANISTICO--RINCONES DE SANLUCAR, OP. 78	TURINA, J.
CICLO PIANISTICO--TOCCATA AND FUGUE, OP. 50	TURINA, J.
CICLO PLATERESCO--FANTASIA CINEMATOGRAFICA, OP. 103	TURINA, J.
CICLO PLATERESCO--LINTERNA MAGICA, OP. 101	TURINA, J.
CID, LE - ARAGONAISE	MASSENET, J.
CID, LE - ARAGONAISE	MASSENET, J.
CIELITO LINDO -- MEXICAN FOLK SONG	WEYBRIGHT
CIELITO LINDO	FERNANDEZ, O.
CIELITO LINDO	FERNANDEZ, O.
CIELITO LINDO	FERNANDEZ
CIELITO LINDO	THOMPSON, J.--ED
CIGALE JOYEUSE, LA	BALOGH
CIMAISE	TISNE, A.
CINCO PIEZAS BAILABLES	HERNANDEZ
CINCO PRELUDIOS	GALINDO, B.
CINDERELLA, OP. 97 --TEN PIECES FROM THE BALLET--	PROKOFIEFF
CINDERELLA, TEN PIECES FROM THE BALLET, OP. 97	PROKOFIEFF
CINDERELLA'S MINUET	FOSSEY, E.
CINDERELLA'S WALTZ, FROM 'CINDERELLA' BALLET	PROKOFIEFF
CINDERELLA AT THE BALL	VANNORT, I.
CINDERELLA DANCES	REBE
CINDERELLA MARCH	HAMMERSTEIN *
CINDERELLA SUITE	BARRETT
CINDERELLA WALTZ	HAMMERSTEIN *
CINDERELLA	BRIMHALL
CINDERELLA	HAMMERSTEIN *
CINDERELLA	HAMMERSTEIN *
CINDERELLA	RICHTER, A.
CINDERELLA	WILLIAMS
CINDERELLA	WILLIAMS
CINEMA	SATIE, E.
CINERAMA HOLIDAY	
CINESINA	MONTANARI
CINQUANTAINE, LA, EASY	GABRIEL, M.
CINQUANTAINE, LA	GABRIEL, M.
CINQUANTAINE, LA	GABRIEL, M. *
CINQUANTAINE, LA	MARIE
CINQUANTAINE, LA	MARIE
CINQUANTAINE, LA	MARIE
CINQUE BREVI IMPRESSIONI	VIRGILIO, N.
CINQUE STUDI PER DOMANI	MALIPIERO, G. F.
CINQ 'BIS' -- FUNF ZUGABEN, 1965	FRANCAIX, J.
CINQ CHANTS NEGRES	FAIRCHILD
CINQ ETUDES POUR LA MAIN DROIT, EN FORME DE SUITE	MIGOT
CINQ IMPRESSIONS ENFANTINES	WURMSER, L.
CINQ PIECES	DELVINCOURT
CINQ POSITIONS, LES -- 80 SELECTIONS FROM THE MASTERS	SKJERNE--ED.
CIPRESSI	CASTELNUOVO-TEDE
CIPRESSI	CINQUE
CIRBIRIBIN, WALTZ	PESTALOZZA
CIRCLE DANCE	KARP
CIRCLING 'ROUND	WRIGHT, N.
CIRCO--SUITE	MOLLEDA, J. M.
CIRCUS-POLKA F. ORCHESTER, KLAVIERAUSZUG	STRAVINSKY, I.
CIRCUS-POLKA	STRAVINSKY, I.
CIRCUS BAND, THE	STAIRS, L.
CIRCUS CLOWNS	AARON, M.
CIRCUS CLOWN	BENFORD
CIRCUS COMES TO TOWN, THE	CROSBY, M.
CIRCUS COMES TO TOWN, THE	HOFSTAD, M.
CIRCUS DAYS	BERMONT, H.
CIRCUS DAYS	SCHER, W.
CIRCUS DAY - TWO PIANOS, EIGHT HANDS	BENSON, E.
CIRCUS DAY	DITTENHAVER
CIRCUS DAY	MCINTYRE, E.
CIRCUS ELEPHANTS	KROEGER, E. R.
CIRCUS PARADE, THE -- WITH WORDS	ERB
CIRCUS PARTY	ANTHONY, G. W.
CIRCUS PONY	LIVELY, K.
CIRCUS RIDER, THE	REBE
CIRCUS SCENES	ROGERS, E.
CIRCUS SCRAP BOOK	BENUSSAN, M.
CIRCUS WALTZ	HENDERSON
CIRCUS WORLD	LANE, J.--ED.
CIRCUS	OLSON
CIRIBIRIBIN	PESTALOZZA
CITIZEN'S GALOP, THE	VOLTI
CITY BY THE BAY, THE	CORY, G.
CITY BY THE BAY - SHORT SUITE	CORY, G. *
CITY SET	VERNE
CIUDAD DE LAS PUERTAS DE ORO, LA -- BALLET, WITH	GAITO
CLAIR DE LUNE FROM SUITE BERGAMASQUE	DEBUSSY
CLAIR DE LUNE	DEBUSSY
CLAIR DE LUNE	DEBUSSY
CLAIR DE LUNE	DEBUSSY
CLAIR DE LUNE	DEBUSSY
CLAIR DE LUNE	DEBUSSY
CLAIR DE LUNE	DEBUSSY
CLAIR DE LUNE	DEBUSSY
CLAIR DE LUNE	DEBUSSY
CLAIR DE LUNE	DEBUSSY
CLAIR DE LUNE	DEBUSSY
CLAIR DE LUNE	DEBUSSY
CLAIR DE LUNE	DEBUSSY
CLAIR DE LUNE	DEBUSSY
CLAIR DE LUNE	DEBUSSY
CLAIR DE LUNE	DEBUSSY
CLAIR DE LUNE	DEBUSSY
CLAIR DE LUNE	DEBUSSY
CLAIR DE LUNE	DEBUSSY
CLAIR DE LUNE	DEBUSSY
CLAIR DE LUNE	DEBUSSY
CLAIR DE LUNE	DEBUSSY
CLAIR DE LUNE	DEBUSSY
CLAIR DE LUNE	DEBUSSY
CLAIR DE LUNE	IVANOVICI, J.
CLAIR DE LUNE	RITCHIE--ED
CLAP, COUNT, AND PLAY, BK. 1	VANDRE
CLAP, COUNT, AND PLAY, BK. 2	VANDRE
CLAPPING SONG	POOLE, C.
CLAP HANDS -- CHIAPANECAS	BURNAM--ED
CLAP HANDS DANCE -- CHIAPENECAS	BURNAM--ED
CLARINET, THE	GROOMS

Title	Composer
CLARINET CANDY	ANDERSON, L.
CLARINET MARMALADE	RAGAS *
CLASSICAL ALBUM--TWELVE ORIGINAL PIECES	
CLASSICAL ALBUM FOR THE YOUNG	LOESCHHORN,
CLASSICAL ALBUM OF ORIGINAL PIANO PIECES FOR EARLY	
CLASSICAL DUETS, BK. 1	GRAY, D.
CLASSICAL DUETS, BK. 2	GRAY, D.
CLASSICAL FAVORITES - BK. 8	DE VITO, A.--ED.
CLASSICAL GAS	BRIMHALL,
CLASSICAL MINIATURES	ROVENGER--ED.
CLASSICAL PIANO ALBUM -- 39 EASY ORIGINAL COMPOSITIONS	SCHOBERLECHNER,
CLASSICAL SYMPHONY, OP. 25	PROKOFIEFF
CLASSICAL SYMPHONY	PROKOFIEFF
CLASSICAL THEMES FOR PEOPLE WHO HATE CLASSICAL MUSIC	
CLASSICS, THE	SMALL, A.
CLASSICS ARE FUN, BK. 1	HIRSCHBERG,
CLASSICS AS DUETS, BK. 1	BAUER, M.--ED
CLASSICS AS DUETS, BK. 1	BAUER, M.--ED
CLASSICS AS DUETS, BK. 2	BAUER, M.--ED
CLASSICS AS DUETS, BK. 2	BAUER, M.--ED
CLASSICS FOR ADULTS, BK. 1	GUENTHER--ED
CLASSICS FOR LITTLE FOLK	LYON
CLASSICS FOR PIANO, BK. 1	FROST
CLASSICS FOR PIANO, BK. 2	FROST
CLASSICS FOR THE CHURCH PIANIST	EARHART, L.
CLASSICS FOR THE YOUNG PIANIST, BK. 1	LANKFORD--ED.
CLASSICS FOR THE YOUNG PIANIST, BK. 2	LANKFORD--ED.
CLASSICS GO BOOGIE, THE	NEVIN
CLASSICS MADE EASY, BK. 1	ETTS, M.--ED *
CLASSICS MADE EASY, ONE	WOLFE, W.
CLASSICS OF RENOWN, BK. 1	SCHAUM, J.--ED.
CLASSICS OF RENOWN, BK. 2	SCHAUM, J.--ED.
CLASSICS TO MODERNS IN THE INTERMEDIATE GRADES	
CLASSICS	
CLASSIC CARNIVAL -- 3 MOVEMENT	GILLOCK
CLASSIC CARNIVAL	GILLOCK
CLASSIC COLLECTION NO. 1	WHITFORD--ED.
CLASSIC DANCES OF MOZART AND BEETHOVEN	BEETHOVEN *
CLASSIC ERA PIANO MUSIC	
CLASSIC GEMS OF STEPHEN FOSTER	FOSTER
CLASSIC KEYBOARD MUSIC	SAUER--ED
CLASSIC MELODIES	CRIST, D.
CLASSIC PIANO RAGS	JOPLIN, S. *
CLASSIC SONATAS, VOL. 1 - INTERMEDIATE 'A'	PODOLSKY, L.--ED
CLASSIC SONATAS, VOL. 2 - INTERMEDIATE 'B'	PODOLSKY, L.--ED
CLASSIC SONATAS, VOL. 3 - ADVANCING	PODOLSKY, L.--ED
CLASSIC SONATAS, VOL. 4 - ADVANCING	PODOLSKY, L.--ED
CLASSIC TO CONTEMPORARY PIANO MUSIC	
CLASSIC VARIATIONS	BEETHOVEN *
CLAUDIA, WALTZ	GREENWALD, M.
CLAVECINISTES FRANCAIS -- COLLECTION OF PIECES BY	
CLAVECINISTES FRANCAIS -- COLLECTION OF PIECES BY	
CLAVECINISTES FRANCAIS -- COLLECTION OF PIECES BY	
CLAVECINISTES FRANCAIS -- COLLECTION OF PIECES BY	
CLAVECIN OBTEMPERANT SUITE, OP. 107	SCHMITT, F.
CLAVICEMBALISTI ITALIANI --16 PIECES--	MONTANI
CLAVICHORD PIECES 1 -- INCLUDING QUATRRE	COUPERIN, F.
CLAVIER-BUCHLEIN VOR W.F. BACH	BACH, J.S.
CLAVIER-BUCHLEIN VOR W. FR. BACH	BACH, J.S.
CLAVIER-SONATINEN DES 18 JAHRHUNDERTS	KREUTZ--ED.
CLAVIER-UEBUNG -- KEYBOARD PRACTICE -- PARTS 2-4	BACH, J.S.
CLAVIER-UEBUNG -- KEYBOARD PRACTICE -- PARTS 2-4	BACH, J.S.
CLAVIERBUCH EINER SCHWABISCHEN HERZOGIN	HERRMANN--ED
CLAVIERMUSIK	CABEZON, A.
CLAVIERSTUCKE FUR ANFANGER --18 JAHRHUNDERT	KREUTZ--ED.
CLAVIERSTUCK	BEETHOVEN
CLAVIERSTUECKE, OP. 76	BRAHMS
CLAVIERUEBUNG --1728--	LUEBECK
CLAYTON'S GRAND MARCH	BLAKE, C.
CLAYTON'S GRAND MARCH	BLAKE, C.
CLAYTON'S GRAND MARCH	BLAKE, C.
CLEAR THE TRACK POLKA	STRAUSS, J.
CLEAR TRACK AHEAD	MERKUR
CLEMENTINE CAPERS	ROSNER
CLIMBIN' AND SCREAMIN'	JOHNSON, S.
CLIMBING IN THE CHERRY TREE	BASTIEN
CLIMBING	MACLACHIAN, T.
CLIMBING	MACLACHIAN, T.
CLIMB EV'RY MOUNTAIN	HAMMERSTEIN *
CLIMB EV'RY MOUNTAIN	HAMMERSTEIN *
CLOCHES A TRAVERS LES FEUILLES FROM IMAGES, BK. 2	DEBUSSY
CLOCHES DANS LE SOIR	GALOS
CLOCHES DE PAQUES	SAUVREZIS
CLOCHETTE, LA, RONDINO, OP. 241	STREABBOG
CLOCHETTES, LES	DURAND DE CRAU
CLOCHETTES -- GALOP --	DURAND DE CRAU
CLOCHE DES MORTS	ROPARTZ
CLOCK, THE--WITH WORDS	RICHTER
CLOCK, THE	KULLAK, T.
CLOCKS -- WHAT TIME IS IT	NICHOL *
CLOCKWORK DOLL, THE	THOMAS, C. J.
CLOCK AND THE PIANO, THE	WHITFORD
CLOCK FROM OVER THERE	GANZ
CLOCK IN MY ROOM	PERRIN
CLOCK IN THE HALL	STAIRS, L.
CLOCK MAN	BLAKE, D.
CLOCK ON THE STAIRS	ANSON, G.
CLOCK SERENADE	GROVE
CLOCK SHOP, THE	EHRENBERG
CLOG DANCE FROM LA FILLE MAL GARDEE	HEROLD
CLOG DANCE	EDWARDS
CLOG DANCE	HANSON
CLOSE TO YOU	BRIMHALL,
CLOSE YOUR EYES	BRIMHALL,
CLOUDS FLOATING BY	HART, G. R.
CLOUDS ON A HILLTOP	WEYBRIGHT
CLOUDS ON A HILLTOP	WEYBRIGHT
CLOUDS	BRADLEY,
CLOUDS	GLOVER, D.
CLOUDS	KARP
CLOUDS	PARK, S.
CLOUDS	MANA-ZUCCA
CLOUDY DAY, A	ROZIN
CLOUDY SKIES	MILLIGAN
CLOUD PATTERNS	KOHLER, F.
CLOVER BLOSSOMS	KABALEVSKY
CLOWN, A COZY WALTZ, THE	BLOCH, E.
CLOWN, THE	HACKH, O.
CLOWN, THE	KERN, C. W.
CLOWN'S REVERIE AND DANCE	KOUTZEN, B.
CLOWNING	AARON, M.
CLOWNING	BECK
CLOWNING	RICHMAN, A.
CLOWNS, THE	KREVIT, W.
CLOWNS, THE	KREVIT, W.
CLOWNS DANCE, THE	BRUSSELS, I.
CLOWNS MARCH	ROTA
CLOWNS	COFFEY, J. R.
CLOWNS	GILLOCK
CLOWNS	GLOVER, D.
CLOWNS	KABALEVSKY
CLOWNS	LAKE, G.
CLOWN ANTICS	ROBINSON, A.
CLOWN CAPERS	ROZIN
CLOWN DANCE, THE	KOEHLER, C.
CLOWN DANCE, THE	KOEHLER, C.
CLOWN DANCE	BILBRO, M.
CLOWN DANCE	FISHER, G.
CLOWN PRANKS, CAPRICE	QUINN
CLOWN	NAT, Y.
CLUMPING ALONG	BALOGH
COASTER, THE	CALLAN, L.
COASTING OP. 9	BURLEIGH, C.
COAXING THE PIANO	CONFREY, Z.
COBBLER, COBBLER	REBE
COBBLESTONES	REISFELD
COCK-A-DOODLE DOO	TOWNSEND
COCKER SPANIEL	BARTH, H.
COCKLES AND MUSSELS	STEINER
COCKTAIL'S DANCE	CASELLA, A.
COCKTAIL PARTY FOR THE YOUNG	ALAIN, M.
COCK A DOODLE DO	THOMAS, C. J.
COCONUT TREES IN HAWAII	BURNAM
COCO	
COFFRE A JOUETS,LE	GARCIN, M.
COINS DE SEVILLE--SUITE NO. 1	TURINA, J.
COIN DE CLAUDINET, LE	TOMASI, H.
COLE PORTER, THE WONDERFUL WORLD OF	PORTER, C.
COLE PORTER ALBUM	PORTER, C.
COLLECCION DE BAILES ESPANOLAS--16 DANCES	NAVAS, G.
COLLECCION DE BAILES POPULARES ESPANOLES -- 26 POPULAR	ARISTA--ED
COLLECCION DE CANTOS E BAILES POPULARES ESPANOLES --	ROMERO--ED
COLLECCION DE VIHUELISTAS ESPANOLES DEL SIGLO XVI, BK.	NARVAEZ
COLLECTED KEYBOARD WORKS, VOL. 1	BOHM
COLLECTED KEYBOARD WORKS, VOL. 2	BOHM
COLLECTED KEYBOARD WORKS	JOPLIN, S.
COLLECTION MODERNE, BK. 2	
COLLECTION OF EARLY AMERICAN KEYBOARD MUSIC, A	MCCLENNY, A.--ED
COLLECTION OF EXERCISES AND SCALES	HERZ, H.
COLLECTION OF PIANO SOLOS	SMALL, A.
COLLEEN	CLAYTON, R.
COLLEGE LIFE, MARCH	FRANTZEN
COLLEGE LIFE MARCH	FRANTZEN
COLLEGE MARCH MEDLEY	HAWLEY
COLLODIANA OR PINOCCHIO AND CO.	FERRARI-TRECATE
COLOMBINELLA -- SERENADE --	DELABRE
COLONEL BOGEY MARCH ALBUM	ALFORD, K.
COLONEL BOGEY	ALFORD, K.
COLONEL BOGEY	ALFORD, K.
COLONEL BOGEY	ALFORD, K.
COLONEL BOGEY	ALFORD, K.
COLONIAL MANSION	GOODMAN, J.
COLONIAL PORTRAIT	GOULD, M.
COLORED LEAVES, OP. 99	SCHUMANN, R.
COLORED LEAVES, OP. 99	SCHUMANN, R.
COLORED LEAVES, OP. 99	SCHUMANN, R.
COLORED LEAVES	WEISLEDER, A.
COLORED WINDMILLS	DAY, R. E.
COLOR GUARDS	ROZIN
COLOUR MY WORLD	BRIMHALL,
COLUMBINE AND THE ANNOYED HARLEQUIN	ANDERSEN, K.
COMBINATION FLASH CARDS	KIRBY, M. B.
COME, FAIRIES, COME	BURNAM
COME, LET'S DANCE	HOPSON, E.
COME, LITTLE BLUEBIRD	KOUNTZ, R.
COME, SWEET DEATH--KOMM' SUSSER TOD	BACH, J.S.
COME, SWEET DEATH	BACH, J.S.
COMEDIAN'S GALLOP, OP. 26	KABALEVSKY
COMEDIANS, THE	ROSENTHAL, L.
COME AFTER ME	FICHANDLER, W.
COME ALL YE FAITHFUL AND FIRST NOEL	SPENCER, J.
COME ALL YE FAITHFUL AND SANTA CLAUS	SPENCER, J.
COME ALL YE FAITHFUL	FREEMAN
COME AND PLAY, WALTZ	HOPKINS, H.
COME AND PLAY WITH ME	GLOVER, D.
COME AND PLAY	FROST
COME AND PLAY	GRAY, D.
COME BACK TO ERIN, TRANSPOSED	MEACHAM, F.
COME BACK TO ERIN	CLARIBEL
COME BACK TO SORRENTO	DE CURTIS
COME BACK TO SORRENTO	DI CURTIS
COME BACK TO SORRENTO	STEVENS
COME DANCE THE POLKA	SCHER, W.
COME OUT, COME OUT	BRODSKY, M.
COME OUT KIDS	KRAFT, L.
COME PIOVEVA	
COME RAIN OR COME SHINE	SINGER, L.--ED
COME SATURDAY MORNING	BRIMHALL,
COME TO THE FAIR	MARTIN, E.
COME TO THE FAIR	MARTIN, E.
COME WHERE MY LOVE LIES DREAMING	FOSTER
COMICAL FINGERS	DEE, M.
COMIN' THRU THE RYE	STANLEY--ED
COMING OF SPRING, THE	BROUWERS, S. B.
COMMANCHE	STEVENS
COMMANDOS	GLOVER, D.
COMMAND OF THE KEYBOARD - BK. 1 THROUGH BK. 4	MIROVITCH, A.
COMMENCEMENT DAY, OP. 190 FOR ONE PIANO, SIX HANDS	CRAMMOND, C. C.
COMMENCEMENT DU PIANO, LE - BAL D'ENFANTS	GAUTIER, L.
COMMENCEMENT DU PIANO, LE - LA SAINTE CATHERINE	GAUTIER, L.
COMMENCEMENT DU PIANO, LE - LES PETITS BATEAUX	GAUTIER, L.
COMMENCEMENT DU PIANO, LE - LES PETITS TOURISTS	GAUTIER, L.
COMMENCEMENT DU PIANO, LE - LE SAINTE NICOLAS	GAUTIER, L.
COMMENCEMENT DU PIANO, LE - UNE SURPRISE A PETIT PERE	GAUTIER, L.
COMMENCEMENT GRAND MARCH	HUDSON
COMPANIONS AT THE KEYBOARD	BLAKE--ED
COMPANION SERIES - BOOK 1	FROST
COMPANION SERIES - BOOK 2	FROST
COMPANION SERIES - PREPARATORY	FROST
COMPARSA, LA	LECUONA
COMPARSA, LA	LECUONA
COMPARSA, LA	LECUONA
COMPARSA, LA	LECUONA
COMPENDIUM OF PIANO TECHNIQUE, BK. 1	
COMPLAINTE POUR L'ENFANT REVEUR	BONNAL, E.
COMPLETE COURSE OF POINTER SYSTEM FOR PIANO	
COMPLETE DANCES FOR PIANO, VOL. 1	SCHUBERT
COMPLETE DANCES FOR PIANO, VOL. 2	SCHUBERT
COMPLETE KEYBOARD WORKS	TALLIS
COMPLETE METHOD, BK. 1	DE ANGELIS
COMPLETE METHOD, BK. 2	DE ANGELIS
COMPLETE METHOD, BK. 3	DE ANGELIS
COMPLETE METHOD, BK. 4	DE ANGELIS
COMPLETE METHOD, BK. 5	DE ANGELIS

COMPLETE METHOD, BK. 6	DE ANGELIS
COMPLETE OVERTURES	SCHUMANN, R.
COMPLETE PEANUTS KEYBOARD FUN SERIES	GUARALDI
COMPLETE PIANO SONATAS, BK. 1	BACH, W.F.
COMPLETE PIANO SONATAS, BK. 2	BACH, W.F.
COMPLETE PIANO SONATAS, BK. 3	BACH, W.F.
COMPLETE PIANO SONATAS AND VARIATIONS FOR SOLO PIANO	BRAHMS
COMPLETE PIANO SONATAS	PROKOFIEFF
COMPLETE PIANO TRANSCRIPTIONS, CADENZAS, AND EXERCISES	BRAHMS
COMPLETE PIANO WORKS--VOL. 1	BRAHMS
COMPLETE PIANO WORKS--VOL. 2--	BRAHMS
COMPLETE PIANO WORKS--VOL. 3--	BRAHMS
COMPLETE PIANO WORKS, IN 5 VOLS. CLOTH-BOUND	SCHUMANN, R.
COMPLETE PIANO WORKS, VOL. 1# SONATAS	WEBER, VON
COMPLETE PIANO WORKS, VOL. 1# SONGS WITHOUT WORDS	MENDELSSOHN
COMPLETE PIANO WORKS, VOL. 1	CHOPIN
COMPLETE PIANO WORKS, VOL. 1 OP. 5, 7, 14, 16, 33,	GRIEG
COMPLETE PIANO WORKS, VOL. 2# OP. 5, 7, 14, 16, 33,	MENDELSSOHN
COMPLETE PIANO WORKS, VOL. 2# PIANO PIECES	WEBER, VON
COMPLETE PIANO WORKS, VOL. 2	CHOPIN
COMPLETE PIANO WORKS, VOL. 2	GRIEG
COMPLETE PIANO WORKS, VOL. 3# OP. 28, 35, 54, 82, 83,	MENDELSSOHN
COMPLETE PIANO WORKS, VOL. 3# VARIATIONS AND CONCERTOS	WEBER, VON
COMPLETE PIANO WORKS, VOL. 3	CHOPIN
COMPLETE PIANO WORKS, VOL. 3	GRIEG
COMPLETE PIANO WORKS, VOL. 4# CONCERTI--ARR. PF.	MENDELSSOHN
COMPLETE PIANO WORKS, VOL. 5# SUPPLEMENT	MENDELSSOHN
COMPLETE PIANO WORKS IN 3 VOLS. CLOTH-BOUND	CHOPIN
COMPLETE PIANO WORKS IN 3 VOLS. CLOTH-BOUND	GRIEG
COMPLETE PIANO WORKS IN 5 VOLS. VOL. 1	SCHUMANN, R.
COMPLETE PIANO WORKS IN 5 VOLS. VOL. 2	SCHUMANN, R.
COMPLETE PIANO WORKS IN 5 VOLS. VOL. 3	SCHUMANN, R.
COMPLETE PIANO WORKS IN 5 VOLS. VOL. 4	SCHUMANN, R.
COMPLETE PIANO WORKS IN 5 VOLS. VOL. 5	SCHUMANN, R.
COMPLETE ROCK PIANO METHOD	KONOWITZ, B.
COMPLETE SCHOOL OF TECHNIC	PHILIPP, I.
COMPLETE SERIES OF SIGHT READING AND EAR TESTS, BK. 1	BENNETT, E. *
COMPLETE SERIES OF SIGHT READING AND EAR TESTS, BK. 2	BENNETT, E. *
COMPLETE SERIES OF SIGHT READING AND EAR TESTS, BK. 3	BENNETT, E. *
COMPLETE SERIES OF SIGHT READING AND EAR TESTS, BK. 4	BENNETT, E. *
COMPLETE SERIES OF SIGHT READING AND EAR TESTS, BK. 5	BENNETT, E. *
COMPLETE SERIES OF SIGHT READING AND EAR TESTS, BK. 6	BENNETT, E. *
COMPLETE SERIES OF SIGHT READING AND EAR TESTS, BK. 7	BENNETT, E. *
COMPLETE SHORTER WORKS FOR PIANO	BRAHMS
COMPLETE SONATAS FOR PIANO, VOL. 1A --NOS. 1-18--	HAYDN
COMPLETE SONATAS FOR PIANO, VOL. 1B --NOS. 19-35--	HAYDN
COMPLETE SONATAS FOR PIANO, VOL. 2 --NOS. 36-52--	HAYDN
COMPLETE SONATAS FOR PIANO, VOL. 3 --NOS. 53-62--	HAYDN
COMPLETE SONATAS FOR PIANOFORTE SOLO	SCHUBERT
COMPLETE WORKS, BK. 1	BRAHMS
COMPLETE WORKS, BK. 1	MENDELSSOHN
COMPLETE WORKS, BK. 1	SCHUMANN, R.
COMPLETE WORKS, BK. 2	BRAHMS
COMPLETE WORKS, BK. 2	MENDELSSOHN
COMPLETE WORKS, BK. 2	SCHUMANN, R.
COMPLETE WORKS, BK. 3	MENDELSSOHN
COMPLETE WORKS, BK. 3	SCHUMANN, R.
COMPLETE WORKS, BK. 4	SCHUMANN, R.
COMPLETE WORKS, BK. 5	SCHUMANN, R.
COMPLETE WORKS, BK. 6	SCHUMANN, R.
COMPLETE WORKS, BK. 7	SCHUMANN, R.
COMPLETE WORKS FOR CLAVECIN	LEROUX, GASPARD
COMPLETE WORKS FOR CLAVICEMBALO, BK. 01 -- 1-50 --	SCARLATTI, D.
COMPLETE WORKS FOR CLAVICEMBALO, BK. 02 -- 51-100 --	SCARLATTI, D.
COMPLETE WORKS FOR CLAVICEMBALO, BK. 03 -- 101-150 --	SCARLATTI, D.
COMPLETE WORKS FOR CLAVICEMBALO, BK. 04 -- 151-200 --	SCARLATTI, D.
COMPLETE WORKS FOR CLAVICEMBALO, BK. 05 -- 201-250 --	SCARLATTI, D.
COMPLETE WORKS FOR CLAVICEMBALO, BK. 06 -- 251-300 --	SCARLATTI, D.
COMPLETE WORKS FOR CLAVICEMBALO, BK. 07 -- 301-350 --	SCARLATTI, D.
COMPLETE WORKS FOR CLAVICEMBALO, BK. 08 -- 351-400 --	SCARLATTI, D.
COMPLETE WORKS FOR CLAVICEMBALO, BK. 09 -- 401-450 --	SCARLATTI, D.
COMPLETE WORKS FOR CLAVICEMBALO, BK. 10 -- 451-500 --	SCARLATTI, D.
COMPLETE WORKS FOR CLAVICEMBALO, BK. 11 --	SCARLATTI, D.
COMPLETE WORKS FOR CLAVICEMBALO, BK. 11 - THEMATIC	SCARLATTI, D.
COMPLETE WORKS FOR CLAVICEMBALO - NO. 10 IN C MINOR	SCARLATTI, D.
COMPLETE WORKS FOR CLAVICEMBALO - NO. 108 IN D MINOR	SCARLATTI, D.
COMPLETE WORKS FOR CLAVICEMBALO - NO. 114 IN E-FLAT	SCARLATTI, D.
COMPLETE WORKS FOR CLAVICEMBALO - NO. 14 IN D	SCARLATTI, D.
COMPLETE WORKS FOR CLAVICEMBALO - NO. 142 IN E-FLAT	SCARLATTI, D.
COMPLETE WORKS FOR CLAVICEMBALO - NO. 23 IN E	SCARLATTI, D.
COMPLETE WORKS FOR CLAVICEMBALO - NO. 256 IN C-SHARP	SCARLATTI, D.
COMPLETE WORKS FOR CLAVICEMBALO - NO. 263 IN B MINOR	SCARLATTI, D.
COMPLETE WORKS FOR CLAVICEMBALO - NO. 265 IN D	SCARLATTI, D.
COMPLETE WORKS FOR CLAVICEMBALO - NO. 33 IN B MINOR	SCARLATTI, D.
COMPLETE WORKS FOR CLAVICEMBALO - NO. 345 IN A	SCARLATTI, D.
COMPLETE WORKS FOR CLAVICEMBALO - NO. 387 IN G	SCARLATTI, D.
COMPLETE WORKS FOR CLAVICEMBALO - NO. 413 IN D MINOR	SCARLATTI, D.
COMPLETE WORKS FOR CLAVICEMBALO - NO. 422 IN D MINOR	SCARLATTI, D.
COMPLETE WORKS FOR CLAVICEMBALO - NO. 433 IN F	SCARLATTI, D.
COMPLETE WORKS FOR CLAVICEMBALO - NO. 449 IN B MINOR	SCARLATTI, D.
COMPLETE WORKS FOR CLAVICEMBALO - NO. 46 IN B-FLAT	SCARLATTI, D.
COMPLETE WORKS FOR CLAVICEMBALO - NO. 463 IN D	SCARLATTI, D.
COMPLETE WORKS FOR CLAVICEMBALO - NO. 463 IN D	SCARLATTI, D.
COMPLETE WORKS FOR CLAVICEMBALO - NO. 49 IN G MINOR	SCARLATTI, D.
COMPLETE WORKS FOR CLAVICEMBALO - NO. 494 IN A	SCARLATTI, D.
COMPLETE WORKS FOR CLAVICEMBALO - NO. 499 IN G MINOR	SCARLATTI, D.
COMPLETE WORKS FOR PIANO SOLO, BK. 1	BRAHMS
COMPLETE WORKS FOR PIANO SOLO, BK. 2	BRAHMS
COMPLETE WORKS FOR PIANO SOLO, BK. 3	BRAHMS
COMPLETE WORKS FOR PIANO SOLO IN 3 VOLS. --THE SET,	BRAHMS
COMPLETE WORKS OF FRANZ LISZT -- VOL. 1 TRANSCENDENTAL	LISZT
COMPLETE WORKS OF FRANZ LISZT -- VOL. 1 TRANSCENDENTAL	LISZT
COMPLETE WORKS OF FRANZ LISZT -- VOL. 2 ETUDES, CLOTH	LISZT
COMPLETE WORKS OF FRANZ LISZT -- VOL. 2 ETUDES, PAPER	LISZT
COMPLETE WORKS OF FRANZ LISZT -- VOL. 3 HUNGARIAN	LISZT
COMPLETE WORKS OF FRANZ LISZT -- VOL. 3 HUNGARIAN	LISZT
COMPLIMENT D'ANNIVERSAIRE	DAMASE, J. M.
COMPONIMENTI MUSICALI	MUFFAT
COMPOSER-PIANISTS	SCHAUM, J.--ED.
COMPOSERS FOR THE KEYBOARD -- FROM BEETHOVEN TO	ANTHONY, G.
COMPOSERS FOR THE KEYBOARD -- FROM BYRD TO BEETHOVEN,	ANTHONY, G.
COMPOSERS FOR THE KEYBOARD -- FROM PURCELL TO MOZART,	ANTHONY, G.
COMPOSERS FOR THE KEYBOARD -- FROM SCHUBERT TO	ANTHONY, G.
COMPOSING A RONDO WITH BEETHOVEN -- SIMP.	MOSSMAN, T.
COMPOSITIONS. SUPPLEMENT	SCHUBERT
COMPOSITIONS, OP. 3, 10, 60	WEBER, VON
COMPOSITIONS -- ORGAN --	FRESCOBALDI
COMPOSITIONS BY CONTEMPORARY ITALIAN COMPOSERS, BK. 1	MONTANI
COMPOSITIONS BY CONTEMPORARY ITALIAN COMPOSERS, BK. 2	MONTANI
COMPOSITIONS BY CONTEMPORARY ITALIAN COMPOSERS, BK. 3	MONTANI
COMPOSITIONS FOR PIANO, OP. 52	DVORAK
COMPOSITIONS	BULL
COMPOSITIONS	BUXTEHUDE
COMPOSITIONS	BYRDE, W.
COMPOSIZIONI PER ORGANO E CEMBALO, HEFT 1 - 12	TRABACI
COMPOSIZIONI PER ORGANO E CEMBALO, HEFT 2 - 7 CANZONI	TRABACI
COMPOSIZIONI PER PIANO, BAND 1 -- 6 DIVERTIMENTI, OP.	STEPAN
COMPOSIZIONI PER PIANO, BAND 2	STEPAN
CONCEPTS	ECKSTEIN
CONCERT, POUR PIANO ET ORCHESTRE, OP. 2	DUPONT, J.
CONCERTANTE	PICCIOLI
CONCERTINA	THOMPSON, J.
CONCERTINA	THOMPSON, J.
CONCERTINO, OP. 21 FUR KLAVIER, 9 BLASER UND	ANTONIOU
CONCERTINO, OP. 43	GAL, H.
CONCERTINO, OP. 94, FUR 2 QUERFLOTEN, CEMBALO UND	BURKHARD, W.
CONCERTINO --DIVERTIMENTO-- IN C. WITH 2 VIOLINS,	HAYDN
CONCERTINO --DIVERTIMENTO IN C	HAYDN
CONCERTINO -- SET	FOSS, L.
CONCERTINO -- 1931	TANSMAN, A.
CONCERTINO -- 1937	PISTON, W.
CONCERTINO CLASSIQUE	LIPATTI, D.
CONCERTINO FOR OBOE, PIANO AND STRINGS	SYDEMAN, W.
CONCERTINO FOR PIANO AND ORCHESTRA	ANDERSON, G.
CONCERTINO FOR PIANO AND STRINGS	CANNON, P.
CONCERTINO FOR PIANO	LANCEN
CONCERTINO FOR SMALL HANDS	HATTORI, T.
CONCERTINO FOR 2 PIANOS AND ORCHESTRA	SKALKOTTAS, N.
CONCERTINO FOR 3 PIANOS -- WITHOUT ORCHESTRA --	PHILIPP, I.
CONCERTINO FUR EIN TASTENINSTRUMENT UND STREICHER, OP.	GRABNER
CONCERTINO FUR KLAVIER, SCHLAGZEUG UND	KELTERBORN
CONCERTINO FUR KLAVIER, 9 BLASER UND SCHLAGZEUG	VOGT
CONCERTINO FUR KLAVIERTRIO UND STREICHORCHESTER	MARTINU, B.
CONCERTINO FUR KLAVIER -- LINKE HAND -- UND ORCHESTER	MARTINU, B.
CONCERTINO FUR KLAVIER UND KAMMERORCHESTER	STAEMPFLI, E.
CONCERTINO FUR KLAVIER UND KLEINES ORCHESTER,	FRANCAIX, J.
CONCERTINO FUR KLAVIER UND ORCHESTER, KLAVIERAUSZUG	BECK, C.
CONCERTINO FUR KLAVIER UND ORCHESTER	MARTINU, B.
CONCERTINO FUR KLAVIER UND STREICHORCHESTER	ZIMMER
CONCERTINO IN B MINOR	CARPENTER, J.
CONCERTINO IN C, OP. 210, PIANO SCORE	CZERNY
CONCERTINO IN C, OP. 210, SET OF PARTS	CZERNY
CONCERTINO IN E FLAT. WITH TWO VIOLINS, V'CELLO	ABEL
CONCERTINO IN E	MONTANI
CONCERTINO IN G MINOR FOR PIANO AND ORCHESTRA, TWO	WAGNER, J.
CONCERTINO NO. 02 FUR KLAVIER UND KLEINES ORCHESTER	BUECHTGER
CONCERTINO NO. 2	GENZMER
CONCERTINO ON FAMILIAR TUNES	AVERY, R.
CONCERTINO POUR PIANO ET ORCHESTRE DE CHAMBRE	CASANOVA, A.
CONCERTINO	CARPENTER, J.
CONCERTINO	DONENFELD, J.
CONCERTINO	FARKAS, F.
CONCERTINO	GAERTNER
CONCERTINO	HONEGGER, A.
CONCERTINO	KADOSA
CONCERTINO	PERSICHETTI
CONCERTI AFTER OTHER COMPOSERS. 16 CONCERTI IN 3	BACH, J.S.
CONCERTI AFTER OTHER COMPOSERS. 16 CONCERTI IN 3	BACH, J.S.
CONCERTI AFTER OTHER COMPOSERS. 16 CONCERTI IN 3	BACH, J.S.
CONCERTI AND OTHER WORKS WITH ORCHESTRA	LISZT
CONCERTI IN G AND A MINOR	VIVALDI *
CONCERTI K.271, 450, 466, 467, 482, 488, 491, 537	MOZART, W. A.
CONCERTO, FIRST MOVEMENT--CONCERT TRANSCRIPTION OF	GRIEG
CONCERTO, FIRST MOVEMENT--CONCERT TRANSCRIPTION	SCHUMANN, R.
CONCERTO, OP. 13	BRITTEN, B.
CONCERTO, OP. 13	WOLF, W.
CONCERTO, OP. 20	EINEM, G.
CONCERTO, OP. 20	SCRIABINE, A.
CONCERTO, OP. 23	TSCHAIKOWSKY
CONCERTO, OP. 24	HOFFMEISTER
CONCERTO, OP. 28	BLACHER
CONCERTO, OP. 30	APOSTEL
CONCERTO, OP. 30	RIMSKY-KORSAKOFF
CONCERTO, OP. 31	ROZSA, M.
CONCERTO, OP. 35 FOR PIANO, TRUMPET, STRINGS	SHOSTAKOVITCH
CONCERTO, OP. 37	CASADESUS, R.
CONCERTO, OP. 39	SPITZMULLER, A.
CONCERTO, OP. 39	THARICHEN, W.
CONCERTO, OP. 42	SCHOENBERG
CONCERTO, OP. 42	SCHOENBERG
CONCERTO, OP. 42	SCHROEDER
CONCERTO, OP. 44. SCORE --DOUBLING AS PIANO PART--	VALEN
CONCERTO, OP. 56	MARTELLI, M.
CONCERTO, OP. 7, NO. 5	BACH, J.
CONCERTO, OP. 85	HUMMEL, J. N.
CONCERTO, THEME	GRIEG
CONCERTOS	CHOPIN
CONCERTO -- 1932	DANDELOT
CONCERTO -- 1936	KHATCHATURIAN
CONCERTO -- 1938, REV. 1942	MOHAUPT, R.
CONCERTO -- 1949 --	POULENC, F.
CONCERTO -- 1950	CILENSEK, J.
CONCERTO -- 1962	SCHULLER, G.
CONCERTO -- 1964-65	CARTER
CONCERTO -- 2 PNO/ORG/HPCHD	LUCCHINETTI, G.
CONCERTO AFTER VIVALDI -- OP. 3 NO. 9	BACH, J.S.
CONCERTO AMERICANA	THOMPSON, J.
CONCERTO A CINQUE, OP. 50	KLEBE, G.
CONCERTO BREVE FOR PIANO AND ORCHESTRA	MONTSALVATGE, X.
CONCERTO DE CAMERA, OP. 16	ZBINDEN, J. F.
CONCERTO DE MAI, OP. 50 -- 1949-50	DELANNOY
CONCERTO EN UT MINEUR	PIERNE
CONCERTO F-DUR FUR KLAVIER--CEMBALO UND ORCHESTER MIT	HAYDN
CONCERTO FOR A YOUNG PIANIST --SOLO AND 2ND PIANO--	TONSING
CONCERTO FOR HARPSICHORD. POCKET SCORE	EVETT
CONCERTO FOR HARPSICHORD -- 1954	MIEG, P.
CONCERTO FOR HARPSICHORD	FALLA, M. DE
CONCERTO FOR PIANO AND ORCH. -- PNO. SOLO	NAT, Y.
CONCERTO FOR PIANO AND ORCH. , PIANO RED.	ROUSSEL, A.
CONCERTO FOR PIANO AND ORCHESTRA, 1967	STEINER, G.
CONCERTO FOR PIANO AND ORCHESTRA ARR. FOR TWO PIANO	HARTLEY, W.
CONCERTO FOR PIANO AND ORCHESTRA	CAGE
CONCERTO FOR PIANO AND ORCHESTRA	CHAVEZ, C.
CONCERTO FOR PIANO AND ORCHESTRA	CHAVEZ, C.
CONCERTO FOR PIANO AND ORCHESTRA	MARTINO
CONCERTO FOR PIANO AND ORCHESTRA	SESSIONS, R.
CONCERTO FOR PIANO AND ORCHESTRA	SMITH, J.
CONCERTO FOR PIANO AND SMALL ORCHESTRA	SCHUMAN, W.
CONCERTO FOR PIANO AND SMALL ORCHESTRA	SCHUMAN, W.
CONCERTO FOR PIANO AND STRING ORCHESTRA	CASTEREDE, J.
CONCERTO FOR PIANO AND VIOLA OBBLIGATO -- 2-PNO RED.	BACH, J. C. F.
CONCERTO FOR PIANO AND WINDS	STRAVINSKY, I.
CONCERTO FOR PIANO AND WIND OCTET ACCOMPANIMENT -- SET	MCPHEE, C.
CONCERTO FOR PIANO	HOUDY
CONCERTO FOR PIANO 4-HANDS, STRINGS, PERCUSSIONS	SMOLANOFF
CONCERTO FOR PIANO 4-HANDS AND ORCHESTRA	PARCHMAN, G.
CONCERTO FOR THE LEFT HAND--SOLO PART	RAVEL
CONCERTO FOR THE LEFT HAND	RAVEL
CONCERTO FOR TWO PIANOS, BRASS AND PERCUSSION --IN	BROWN
CONCERTO FOR TWO PIANOS, WINDS AND PERCUSSION	BOWLES, P.
CONCERTO FOR TWO PIANOS AND ORCHESTRA, OP. 33 --	LOPATNIKOFF
CONCERTO FOR TWO PIANOS AND ORCHESTRA -- THREE PIANO	BLISS, A.
CONCERTO FOR TWO PIANOS	WIGHAM, M.
CONCERTO FOR VIOLIN, PIANO AND STRING QUARTET	CHAUSSON

CONCERTO FOR YOUNG AMERICANS	ECKSTEIN
CONCERTO FOR 2 PIANOS --WITH ORCH. ACC. IN PIANO	BACH, C.P.E.
CONCERTO FOR 2 PIANOS --WITH ORCH. ACC. IN PIANO 3--	BACH, C.P.E.
CONCERTO FOR 2 PIANOS -- 3 PIANOS, 6 HANDS --	BETTINELLI
CONCERTO FOR 2 PIANOS -- 3 PIANOS, 6 HANDS --	ZAFRED
CONCERTO FOR 2 PIANOS AND ORCHESTRA -- PIANO SCORE	MILHAUD, D.
CONCERTO FOR 2 PIANOS AND ORCHESTRA -- 3 PNO RED	PISTON, W.
CONCERTO FOR 2 PIANOS AND ORCHESTRA	TANSMAN, A.
CONCERTO FOR 2 PIANOS	MARTINU, B.
CONCERTO FOR 2 SOLO PIANOS	DIAMOND, D.
CONCERTO FUR QUERFLOTE, V, TROMP, KLAVIER, SCHLAGZEUG	SCHAEFER
CONCERTO GROSSO FOR ORGAN AND PIANO	GARLICK, A.
CONCERTO GROSSO FUR 2 VIOLINEN, VIOLONCELLO, ORCHESTER	BORKOVEC
CONCERTO IN A, SCH NO. 1055	BACH, J.S.
CONCERTO IN A --URTEXT--	BACH, J.S.
CONCERTO IN A FUR CEMBALO -- KLAVIER UND	BACH, J.
CONCERTO IN A MAJOR FOR PIANOFORTE AND ORCHESTRA IN	HANDEL
CONCERTO IN A MAJOR FOR PIANOFORTE AND ORCHESTRA IN	HANDEL
CONCERTO IN A MINOR, OP. 16. ABRIDGED PIANO SOLO	GRIEG
CONCERTO IN A MINOR, OP. 16	GRIEG
CONCERTO IN A MINOR, OP. 16	GRIEG
CONCERTO IN A MINOR, OP. 16	GRIEG
CONCERTO IN A MINOR, OP. 16	GRIEG
CONCERTO IN A MINOR, OP. 16	GRIEG
CONCERTO IN A MINOR, OP. 17	PADEREWSKI, I.
CONCERTO IN A MINOR, OP. 54. ABRIDGED	SCHUMANN, R.
CONCERTO IN A MINOR, OP. 54	SCHUMANN, R.
CONCERTO IN A MINOR, OP. 54	SCHUMANN, R.
CONCERTO IN A MINOR -- OPENING THEME	GRIEG
CONCERTO IN A MINOR -- WITH ACCOMPANIMENT ARRANGED FOR	SCHUMANN, R.
CONCERTO IN A MINOR FOR 4 PIANOS, SCH NO.1065	BACH, J.S.
CONCERTO IN A MINOR	GRIEG
CONCERTO IN A MINOR	GRIEG
CONCERTO IN A MINOR	GRIEG
CONCERTO IN A MINOR	SCHUMANN, R.
CONCERTO IN A MINOR	SCHUMANN, R.
CONCERTO IN B-FLAT, OP. 15 NO. 1	CAMBINI
CONCERTO IN B-FLAT	PUCCINI, D. V.
CONCERTO IN B FLAT, OP. 13, NO. 4	BACH, J.
CONCERTO IN B FLAT, OP. 4, NO. 6. SCORE/HARPSICHORD	HANDEL
CONCERTO IN B FLAT MAJOR, OP. 83	BRAHMS
CONCERTO IN B FLAT MINOR	TSCHAIKOWSKY
CONCERTO IN B MINOR -- FREE TRANSCRIPTION BY TAMBURINI	VIVALDI
CONCERTO IN C -- 6-HANDS	BACH, J.S.
CONCERTO IN C FOR 2 PIANOS --2 COPIES--	BACH, J.S.
CONCERTO IN C FOR 2 PIANOS	BACH, J.S.
CONCERTO IN C MAJOR, NO. 21 -- THEME FROM 'ELVIRA	MOZART, W. A.
CONCERTO IN C MINOR FOR 2 PIANOS --2 COPIES--	BACH, J.S.
CONCERTO IN C MINOR FOR 2 PIANOS	BACH, J.S.
CONCERTO IN C MINOR	BACH, J.S.
CONCERTO IN C MINOR	BACH, J.S.
CONCERTO IN C SHARP MINOR, OP. 30	RIMSKY-KORSAKOFF
CONCERTO IN C	CLEMENTI
CONCERTO IN C	DUKELSKY
CONCERTO IN C	HAYDN
CONCERTO IN C	HAYDN
CONCERTO IN D, OP. 49	ROWLEY
CONCERTO IN D, SCH NO. 1054	BACH, J.S.
CONCERTO IN D --WITH HAYDN CADENZAS--	HAYDN
CONCERTO IN D FLAT	KHATCHATURIAN
CONCERTO IN D MAJOR	HAYDN
CONCERTO IN D MINOR, AFTER MARCELLO OBOE CONCERTO	BACH, J.S.
CONCERTO IN D MINOR, OP. 15	BRAHMS
CONCERTO IN D MINOR, SCH NO. 1052	BACH, J.S.
CONCERTO IN D MINOR FOR PIANO, VIOLIN AND STRING	MENDELSSOHN
CONCERTO IN D MINOR FOR 2 PIANOS AND ORCHESTRA -- SOLO	POULENC, F.
CONCERTO IN D MINOR	BACH, C.P.E.
CONCERTO IN D MINOR	BACH, C.P.E.
CONCERTO IN D MINOR	BACH, J.S.
CONCERTO IN D MINOR	BACH, J.S.
CONCERTO IN D MINOR	BACH, J.S.
CONCERTO IN D MINOR	BACH, J.S.
CONCERTO IN D MINOR	MARCELLO *
CONCERTO IN D MINOR	THOMPSON, J.
CONCERTO IN D MINOR	WOOD, H.
CONCERTO IN D	BACH, C.P.E.
CONCERTO IN D	HAYDN
CONCERTO IN D	HAYDN
CONCERTO IN D	HAYDN
CONCERTO IN D	HAYDN
CONCERTO IN E, OP. 59	KOZELUCH, L.
CONCERTO IN E, SCH. NO. 1053	MOSZKOWSKI
CONCERTO IN ES, DUMBARTON OAKS FUR KAMMERORCHESTER	BACH, J.S.
CONCERTO IN E --URTEXT--	STRAVINSKY, I.
CONCERTO IN E FLAT. JUGENDKONZERT	BACH, J.S.
CONCERTO IN E FLAT, K365 FOR 2 PIANOS AND ORCHESTRA	BEETHOVEN
CONCERTO IN E FLAT, OP. 31	MOZART, W. A.
CONCERTO IN E FOR 2 PIANOS AND ORCHESTRA	PFITZNER, H.
CONCERTO IN E MINOR, OP. 5	MENDELSSOHN
CONCERTO IN E	DOHNANYI
CONCERTO IN F. SCORE, HARPSICHORD SOLO PART	FINNEY
CONCERTO IN F, SECOND MOVEMENT	GRAUN
CONCERTO IN F - CONCERT TRANSCRIPTION	GERSHWIN
CONCERTO IN F MINOR, OP. 114	GERSHWIN
CONCERTO IN F MINOR, SCH NO. 1056	REGER
CONCERTO IN F MINOR --URTEXT--	BACH, J.S.
CONCERTO IN F MINOR	BACH, J.S.
CONCERTO IN F MINOR	BACH, J.S.
CONCERTO IN F	GERSHWIN
CONCERTO IN F	HAYDN
CONCERTO IN F	LINEK
CONCERTO IN F	MENOTTI
CONCERTO IN F	PAISIELLO, G.
CONCERTO IN F	STAMITZ, K.
CONCERTO IN G, OP. 15 NO. 3	CAMBINI
CONCERTO IN G --WITH CADENZAS--	HAYDN
CONCERTO IN G FUR CEMBALO -- KLAVIER UND	BACH, J.
CONCERTO IN G MINOR, OP. 33	DVORAK
CONCERTO IN G MINOR, SCH NO. 1058	BACH, J.S.
CONCERTO IN G MINOR	BACH, J.S.
CONCERTO IN G MINOR	TELEMANN, G.P. *
CONCERTO IN G MINOR	VIOTTI
CONCERTO IN G MINOR	WAGNER
CONCERTO IN G	HAYDN
CONCERTO IN G	HAYDN
CONCERTO IN G	RAVEL
CONCERTO IN G	RAVEL
CONCERTO IN JAZZ -- THEMES	PHILLIPS, D.
CONCERTO IN JAZZ	PHILLIPS, D.
CONCERTO IN JAZZ	PHILLIPS, D.
CONCERTO IN JAZZ	PHILLIPS, D.
CONCERTO IN JAZZ	PHILLIPS, D.
CONCERTO IN RONDO -- 1957 --	BUCCHI
CONCERTO IN THE ITALIAN STYLE	BACH, J.S.
CONCERTO IN THE ITALIAN STYLE	BACH, J.S.

CONCERTO IN THE ITALIAN STYLE	BACH, J.S.
CONCERTO IN THE MIXOLYDIAN MODE	RESPIGHI
CONCERTO K037 IN F	MOZART, W. A.
CONCERTO K039 IN B FLAT	MOZART, W. A.
CONCERTO K041 IN G	MOZART, W. A.
CONCERTO K043 IN D	MOZART, W. A.
CONCERTO K175 IN D --ORCH RED--	MOZART, W. A.
CONCERTO K175 IN D --SOLO ONLY--	MOZART, W. A.
CONCERTO K175 IN D MAJOR --CADENZA BY S. STRAVINSKY--	MOZART, W. A.
CONCERTO K238 IN B FLAT --CADENZA BY S. STRAVINSKY--	MOZART, W. A.
CONCERTO K238 IN B FLAT --ORCH RED--	MOZART, W. A.
CONCERTO K238 IN B FLAT --SOLO ONLY--	MOZART, W. A.
CONCERTO K246 IN C --ORCH RED--	MOZART, W. A.
CONCERTO K246 IN C --SOLO ONLY--	MOZART, W. A.
CONCERTO K246 IN C	MOZART, W. A.
CONCERTO K271 IN E FLAT	MOZART, W. A.
CONCERTO K271 IN E FLAT	MOZART, W. A.
CONCERTO K271 IN E FLAT	MOZART, W. A.
CONCERTO K271 IN E FLAT	MOZART, W. A.
CONCERTO K271 IN E FLAT	MOZART, W. A.
CONCERTO K365 IN E FLAT, FOR TWO PIANOS	MOZART, W. A.
CONCERTO K365 IN E FLAT --TWO COPIES--	MOZART, W. A.
CONCERTO K382 IN D	MOZART, W. A.
CONCERTO K413 IN F --ORCH RED--	MOZART, W. A.
CONCERTO K413 IN F --SOLO ONLY--	MOZART, W. A.
CONCERTO K413 IN F	MOZART, W. A.
CONCERTO K413 IN F	MOZART, W. A.
CONCERTO K414 IN A	MOZART, W. A.
CONCERTO K414 IN A	MOZART, W. A.
CONCERTO K414 IN A	MOZART, W. A.
CONCERTO K414 IN A	MOZART, W. A.
CONCERTO K415 IN C --ORCH RED--	MOZART, W. A.
CONCERTO K415 IN C --SOLO ONLY--	MOZART, W. A.
CONCERTO K415 IN C	MOZART, W. A.
CONCERTO K415 IN G	MOZART, W. A.
CONCERTO K449 IN E FLAT	MOZART, W. A.
CONCERTO K449 IN E FLAT	MOZART, W. A.
CONCERTO K450 IN B FLAT --ORCH RED--	MOZART, W. A.
CONCERTO K450 IN B FLAT --SOLO ONLY--	MOZART, W. A.
CONCERTO K450 IN B FLAT	MOZART, W. A.
CONCERTO K450 IN B FLAT	MOZART, W. A.
CONCERTO K450 IN B FLAT	MOZART, W. A.
CONCERTO K450 IN B FLAT	MOZART, W. A.
CONCERTO K451 IN D --ORCH RED--	MOZART, W. A.
CONCERTO K451 IN D --SOLO ONLY--	MOZART, W. A.
CONCERTO K453 IN G --ORCH RED--	MOZART, W. A.
CONCERTO K453 IN G --SOLO ONLY--	MOZART, W. A.
CONCERTO K453 IN G	MOZART, W. A.
CONCERTO K453 IN G	MOZART, W. A.
CONCERTO K453 IN G	MOZART, W. A.
CONCERTO K456 IN B FLAT --CADENZAS BY MOZART AND	MOZART, W. A.
CONCERTO K456 IN B FLAT	MOZART, W. A.
CONCERTO K456 IN B FLAT	MOZART, W. A.
CONCERTO K459 IN F --ORCH RED--	MOZART, W. A.
CONCERTO K459 IN F --SET--	MOZART, W. A.
CONCERTO K459 IN F --SOLO ONLY--	MOZART, W. A.
CONCERTO K459 IN F	MOZART, W. A.
CONCERTO K459 IN F	MOZART, W. A.
CONCERTO K465 IN C	MOZART, W. A.
CONCERTO K466 IN A - PIANO REDUCTION	MOZART, W. A.
CONCERTO K466 IN D MINOR --ORCH RED--	MOZART, W. A.
CONCERTO K466 IN D MINOR --SOLO ONLY--	MOZART, W. A.
CONCERTO K466 IN D MINOR	MOZART, W. A.
CONCERTO K466 IN D MINOR	MOZART, W. A.
CONCERTO K466 IN D MINOR	MOZART, W. A.
CONCERTO K466 IN D MINOR	MOZART, W. A.
CONCERTO K466 IN D MINOR	MOZART, W. A.
CONCERTO K467 IN C --ORCH RED--	MOZART, W. A.
CONCERTO K467 IN C --SOLO ONLY--	MOZART, W. A.
CONCERTO K467 IN C	MOZART, W. A.
CONCERTO K467 IN C	MOZART, W. A.
CONCERTO K467 IN C	MOZART, W. A.
CONCERTO K467 IN C	MOZART, W. A.
CONCERTO K482 IN E FLAT --ORCH RED--	MOZART, W. A.
CONCERTO K482 IN E FLAT --SOLO ONLY--	MOZART, W. A.
CONCERTO K482 IN E FLAT --W. HUMMEL CADENZAS--	MOZART, W. A.
CONCERTO K482 IN E FLAT	MOZART, W. A.
CONCERTO K482 IN E FLAT	MOZART, W. A.
CONCERTO K488 IN A	MOZART, W. A.
CONCERTO K488 IN A	MOZART, W. A.
CONCERTO K488 IN A	MOZART, W. A.
CONCERTO K488 IN A	MOZART, W. A.
CONCERTO K488 IN A	MOZART, W. A.
CONCERTO K488 IN A	MOZART, W. A.
CONCERTO K491 IN C MINOR --ORCH RED--	MOZART, W. A.
CONCERTO K491 IN C MINOR --SOLO ONLY--	MOZART, W. A.
CONCERTO K491 IN C MINOR - PIANO REDUCTION	MOZART, W. A.
CONCERTO K491 IN C MINOR	MOZART, W. A.
CONCERTO K491 IN C MINOR	MOZART, W. A.
CONCERTO K491 IN C MINOR	MOZART, W. A.
CONCERTO K503 IN C --W. PH. K. HOFFMANN CADENZA--	MOZART, W. A.
CONCERTO K503 IN C - PIANO REDUCTION	MOZART, W. A.
CONCERTO K503 IN C	MOZART, W. A.
CONCERTO K503 IN C	MOZART, W. A.
CONCERTO K503 IN C	MOZART, W. A.
CONCERTO K537 IN D--'CORONATION'	MOZART, W. A.
CONCERTO K537 IN D -- ''CORONATION''	MOZART, W. A.
CONCERTO K537 IN D 'CORONATION' --ORCH RED--	MOZART, W. A.
CONCERTO K537 IN D 'CORONATION' --SOLO ONLY--	MOZART, W. A.
CONCERTO K537 IN D	MOZART, W. A.
CONCERTO K537 IN D	MOZART, W. A.
CONCERTO K595 IN B FLAT --ORCH RED--	MOZART, W. A.
CONCERTO K595 IN B FLAT --SOLO ONLY--	MOZART, W. A.
CONCERTO K595 IN B FLAT	MOZART, W. A.
CONCERTO K595 IN B FLAT	MOZART, W. A.
CONCERTO K595 IN B FLAT	MOZART, W. A.
CONCERTO LEGGIERO	DYSON, G.
CONCERTO NO. 01, OP. 1	RACHMANINOFF, S.
CONCERTO NO. 01, OP. 10	PROKOFIEFF
CONCERTO NO. 01, OP. 17	SAINT-SAENS
CONCERTO NO. 01, OP. 2	RACHMANINOFF, S.
CONCERTO NO. 01, OP. 25	MENDELSSOHN
CONCERTO NO. 01, OP. 92	GLAZOUNOW, A.
CONCERTO NO. 01 -- OPENING THEME	TSCHAIKOWSKY
CONCERTO NO. 01 IN A MINOR, OP. 15	MACDOWELL
CONCERTO NO. 01 IN A MINOR	SAUGUET

CONCERTO NO. 01 IN B FLAT MINOR, OP. 23	ABRIDGED	TSCHAIKOWSKY
CONCERTO NO. 01 IN B FLAT MINOR, OP. 23		TSCHAIKOWSKY
CONCERTO NO. 01 IN B FLAT MINOR, OP. 23		TSCHAIKOWSKY
CONCERTO NO. 01 IN B FLAT MINOR, OP. 23		TSCHAIKOWSKY
CONCERTO NO. 01 IN B FLAT MINOR, OP. 23		TSCHAIKOWSKY
CONCERTO NO. 01 IN B FLAT MINOR		TSCHAIKOWSKY
CONCERTO NO. 01 IN B FLAT MINOR		TSCHAIKOWSKY
CONCERTO NO. 01 IN C, OP. 15		BEETHOVEN
CONCERTO NO. 01 IN C, OP. 15		BEETHOVEN
CONCERTO NO. 01 IN C, OP. 15		BEETHOVEN
CONCERTO NO. 01 IN C, OP. 15		BEETHOVEN
CONCERTO NO. 01 IN C MAJOR, OP. 1		BEETHOVEN
CONCERTO NO. 01 IN C MINOR, OP. 35		SHOSTAKOVITCH
CONCERTO NO. 01 IN C MINOR FOR 2 PIANOS, SCH NO. 1060		BACH, J.S.
CONCERTO NO. 01 IN D FLAT, OP. 10		PROKOFIEFF
CONCERTO NO. 01 IN D MINOR, OP. 15		BRAHMS
CONCERTO NO. 01 IN D MINOR, OP. 15		BRAHMS
CONCERTO NO. 01 IN D MINOR, OP. 15		BRAHMS
CONCERTO NO. 01 IN D MINOR, OP. 15		BRAHMS
CONCERTO NO. 01 IN D MINOR FOR 3 PIANOS, SCH NO. 1063		BACH, J.S.
CONCERTO NO. 01 IN E FLAT		LISZT
CONCERTO NO. 01 IN E FLAT		LISZT
CONCERTO NO. 01 IN E FLAT		LISZT
CONCERTO NO. 01 IN E MINOR, OP. 11		CHOPIN
CONCERTO NO. 01 IN E MINOR, OP. 11		CHOPIN
CONCERTO NO. 01 IN E MINOR, OP. 11		CHOPIN
CONCERTO NO. 01 IN E MINOR, OP. 11		CHOPIN
CONCERTO NO. 01 IN E MINOR, OP. 11		CHOPIN
CONCERTO NO. 01 IN E MINOR, OP. 11		CHOPIN
CONCERTO NO. 01 IN F SHARP MINOR, OP. 1		RACHMANINOFF, S.
CONCERTO NO. 01 IN F SHARP MINOR, OP. 1		RACHMANINOFF, S.
CONCERTO NO. 01 IN F SHARP MINOR, OP. 1		RACHMANINOFF, S.
CONCERTO NO. 01 IN G MINOR, OP. 25		MENDELSSOHN
CONCERTO NO. 01 IN G MINOR, OP. 25		MENDELSSOHN
CONCERTO NO. 01		BARTOK
CONCERTO NO. 01		GINASTERA
CONCERTO NO. 01		JACOB, G.
CONCERTO NO. 01		RAWSTHORNE, A.
CONCERTO NO. 01		SANTORO, C.
CONCERTO NO. 01		TANSMAN, A.
CONCERTO NO. 02, OP. 100		GLAZOUNOW, A.
CONCERTO NO. 02, OP. 102		SHOSTAKOVITCH
CONCERTO NO. 02, OP. 102		SHOSTAKOVITCH
CONCERTO NO. 02, OP. 16		PROKOFIEFF
CONCERTO NO. 02, OP. 18		RACHMANINOFF, S.
CONCERTO NO. 02, OP. 18		RACHMANINOFF, S.
CONCERTO NO. 02, OP. 21		EGGE
CONCERTO NO. 02, OP. 22		SAINT-SAENS
CONCERTO NO. 02, OP. 23		MACDOWELL
CONCERTO NO. 02, OP. 50		MEDTNER, N.
CONCERTO NO. 02, THEMES FROM ALL 3 MVTS.		RACHMANINOFF, S.
CONCERTO NO. 02, THEME FROM 1ST MOVEMENT		RACHMANINOFF, S.
CONCERTO NO. 02 --THE STUDENT--		PITFIELD
CONCERTO NO. 02 -- PIANO SOLO, WITH ORCHESTRA REDUCED		HOSSEIN, A.
CONCERTO NO. 02 -- 1946		GUARNIERI
CONCERTO NO. 02 FOR PIANO AND ORCHESTRA -- OR WIND		STARER
CONCERTO NO. 02 FOR PIANO AND ORCHESTRA		FULEIHAN, A.
CONCERTO NO. 02 FOR TWO PIANOS		BABIN
CONCERTO NO. 02 FOR 2 PIANOS AND PERCUSSION -- PIANO		MILHAUD, D.
CONCERTO NO. 02 FOR 2 PIANOS AND PERCUSSION -- 4		MILHAUD, D.
CONCERTO NO. 02 IN A		LISZT
CONCERTO NO. 02 IN A		LISZT
CONCERTO NO. 02 IN A		LISZT
CONCERTO NO. 02 IN A		LISZT
CONCERTO NO. 02 IN B FLAT, OP. 19		BEETHOVEN
CONCERTO NO. 02 IN B FLAT, OP. 19		BEETHOVEN
CONCERTO NO. 02 IN B FLAT, OP. 19		BEETHOVEN
CONCERTO NO. 02 IN B FLAT, OP. 19		BEETHOVEN
CONCERTO NO. 02 IN B FLAT, OP. 83		BRAHMS
CONCERTO NO. 02 IN B FLAT, OP. 83		BRAHMS
CONCERTO NO. 02 IN B FLAT, OP. 83		BRAHMS
CONCERTO NO. 02 IN B FLAT, OP. 83		BRAHMS
CONCERTO NO. 02 IN B FLAT MAJOR, OP. 19		BEETHOVEN
CONCERTO NO. 02 IN C FOR 2 PIANOS, SCH NO. 1061		BACH, J.S.
CONCERTO NO. 02 IN C FOR 3 PIANOS, SCH NO. 1064		BACH, J.S.
CONCERTO NO. 02 IN C MINOR, OP. 18--THEMES FROM 1ST		RACHMANINOFF, S.
CONCERTO NO. 02 IN C MINOR, OP. 18--THEMES FROM 3RD		RACHMANINOFF, S.
CONCERTO NO. 02 IN C MINOR, OP. 18--THEMES FROM 3RD		RACHMANINOFF, S.
CONCERTO NO. 02 IN C MINOR, OP. 18		RACHMANINOFF, S.
CONCERTO NO. 02 IN C MINOR , OP. 18		RACHMANINOFF, S.
CONCERTO NO. 02 IN D MINOR, OP. 23		MACDOWELL
CONCERTO NO. 02 IN D MINOR, OP. 40		MENDELSSOHN
CONCERTO NO. 02 IN D MINOR, OP. 40		MENDELSSOHN
CONCERTO NO. 02 IN D MINOR, OP. 40		MENDELSSOHN
CONCERTO NO. 02 IN E, OP. 12		ALBERT, E. D'
CONCERTO NO. 02 IN F, OP. 102		SHOSTAKOVITCH
CONCERTO NO. 02 IN F MINOR, OP. 21		CHOPIN
CONCERTO NO. 02 IN F MINOR, OP. 21		CHOPIN
CONCERTO NO. 02 IN F MINOR, OP. 21		CHOPIN
CONCERTO NO. 02 IN F MINOR, OP. 21		CHOPIN
CONCERTO NO. 02 IN F MINOR, OP. 21		CHOPIN
CONCERTO NO. 02 IN F MINOR, OP. 21		CHOPIN
CONCERTO NO. 02 IN G, OP. 44		TSCHAIKOWSKY
CONCERTO NO. 02 IN G MINOR, OP. 16		PROKOFIEFF
CONCERTO NO. 02 IN G MINOR, OP. 22		SAINT-SAENS
CONCERTO NO. 02 IN G MINOR, OP. 22		SAINT-SAENS
CONCERTO NO. 02		BARTOK
CONCERTO NO. 02		BLOCH, W.
CONCERTO NO. 02		CASTELNUOVO-TEDE
CONCERTO NO. 02		DAMASE, J. M.
CONCERTO NO. 02		FULEIHAN, A.
CONCERTO NO. 02		HELM, E.
CONCERTO NO. 02		HODDINOTT, A.
CONCERTO NO. 02		HOSSEIN, A.
CONCERTO NO. 02		JACHINO
CONCERTO NO. 02		LANDOWSKI
CONCERTO NO. 02		MARTINU, B.
CONCERTO NO. 02		MATHIAS, W.
CONCERTO NO. 02		MYSLIVECEK
CONCERTO NO. 02		RACHMANINOFF, S.
CONCERTO NO. 02		RAWSTHORNE, A.
CONCERTO NO. 02		TANSMAN, A.
CONCERTO NO. 02		TCHEREPNIN
CONCERTO NO. 02		TSCHAIKOWSKY
CONCERTO NO. 03, OP. 26		PROKOFIEFF
CONCERTO NO. 03, OP. 30		RACHMANINOFF, S.
CONCERTO NO. 03, OP. 30		RACHMANINOFF, S.
CONCERTO NO. 03, OP. 33 'THE STORM'		STEIBELT
CONCERTO NO. 03, OP. 47		KADOSA
CONCERTO NO. 03, OP. 50		KABALEVSKY
CONCERTO NO. 03, OP. 60		MEDTNER, N.
CONCERTO NO. 03 IN C, OP. 26		PROKOFIEFF
CONCERTO NO. 03 IN C MINOR, OP. 37. ABRIDGED PIANO		BEETHOVEN
CONCERTO NO. 03 IN C MINOR, OP. 37 - CADENZA FOR THE		BEETHOVEN
CONCERTO NO. 03 IN C MINOR, OP. 37		BEETHOVEN
CONCERTO NO. 03 IN C MINOR, OP. 37		BEETHOVEN
CONCERTO NO. 03 IN C MINOR, OP. 37		BEETHOVEN
CONCERTO NO. 03 IN C MINOR, OP. 37		BEETHOVEN
CONCERTO NO. 03 IN C MINOR, OP. 37		BEETHOVEN
CONCERTO NO. 03 IN C MINOR FOR 2 PIANOS, SCH NO. 1062		BACH, J.S.
CONCERTO NO. 03 IN C SHARP MINOR, PIANO SOLO SCORE		RIES
CONCERTO NO. 03 IN C		GIORDANI
CONCERTO NO. 03 IN D MINOR, OP. 30		RACHMANINOFF, S.
CONCERTO NO. 03 IN D MINOR, OP. 30		RACHMANINOFF, S.
CONCERTO NO. 03 IN D MINOR, OP. 30		RACHMANINOFF, S.
CONCERTO NO. 03		BARTOK
CONCERTO NO. 03		HODDINOTT, A.
CONCERTO NO. 03		KABALEVSKY
CONCERTO NO. 03		MARTINU, B.
CONCERTO NO. 03		MILHAUD, D.
CONCERTO NO. 04, OP. 40		RACHMANINOFF, S.
CONCERTO NO. 04, OP. 44		SAINT-SAENS
CONCERTO NO. 04 FOR THE LEFT HAND, OP. 53		PROKOFIEFF
CONCERTO NO. 04 IN C. HARPSICHORD SOLO PART		WESLEY, C.
CONCERTO NO. 04 IN C MINOR, OP. 44		SAINT-SAENS
CONCERTO NO. 04 IN C MINOR, OP. 44		SAINT-SAENS
CONCERTO NO. 04 IN D MINOR, OP. 70		RUBINSTEIN
CONCERTO NO. 04 IN D MINOR, OP. 70		RUBINSTEIN
CONCERTO NO. 04 IN G, OP. 58. ABRIDGED PIANO SOLO		BEETHOVEN
CONCERTO NO. 04 IN G, OP. 58		BEETHOVEN
CONCERTO NO. 04 IN G, OP. 58		BEETHOVEN
CONCERTO NO. 04 IN G, OP. 58		BEETHOVEN
CONCERTO NO. 04 IN G, OP. 58		BEETHOVEN
CONCERTO NO. 04 IN G MAJOR, OP. 58		BEETHOVEN
CONCERTO NO. 04		MILHAUD, D.
CONCERTO NO. 05, OP. 103		SAINT-SAENS
CONCERTO NO. 05, OP. 103		SAINT-SAENS
CONCERTO NO. 05, OP. 55		PROKOFIEFF
CONCERTO NO. 05, OP. 96		TCHEREPNIN
CONCERTO NO. 05 IN D		GIORDANI
CONCERTO NO. 05 IN E FLAT,-OP. 73 --EMPEROR--.		BEETHOVEN
CONCERTO NO. 05 IN E FLAT, OP. 73 --EMPEROR--		BEETHOVEN
CONCERTO NO. 05 IN E FLAT, OP. 73 -- ''EMPEROR''		BEETHOVEN
CONCERTO NO. 05 IN E FLAT, OP. 73 -- ''EMPEROR''		BEETHOVEN
CONCERTO NO. 05 IN E FLAT, OP. 73 'EMPEROR'		BEETHOVEN
CONCERTO NO. 05 IN E FLAT, OP. 73		BEETHOVEN
CONCERTO NO. 05 IN E FLAT MAJOR--OP. 73-- 'EMPEROR'		BEETHOVEN
CONCERTO NO. 05 IN F, OP. 103		SAINT-SAENS
CONCERTO NO. 05 IN F, OP. 103		SAINT-SAENS
CONCERTO NO. 05 IN G, OP. 55		PROKOFIEFF
CONCERTO NO. 05		MILHAUD, D.
CONCERTO NO. 06, OP. 99		TCHEREPNIN
CONCERTO OP. 13, NO. 2 IN D, URTEXT		BACH, J.
CONCERTO PATHETIQUE IN E MINOR		LISZT
CONCERTO PATHETIQUE IN E MINOR		LISZT
CONCERTO PER DUE PIANO FORTI SOLI		STRAVINSKY, I.
CONCERTO PETITE		CACAVAS
CONCERTO POUR CLAVECIN ET ENSEMBLES INSTRUMENTALES		FRANCAIX, J.
CONCERTO POUR TROIS PIANOS ET ORCHESTRE A CORDES, FOR		CASADESUS, R.
CONCERTO POUR UN POEM INCONNU -- PIANO, STRING ORCH.		BRENET, T.
CONCERTO QUASI UNA FANTASIA		BENJAMIN
CONCERTO SEMISERIO FUR 2 KLAVIERE UND ORCHESTER		EDER
CONCERTO SENTIMENTO		NEWMAN, M.
CONCERTO SENZA ORCHESTRA		ANDRIESSEN, J.
CONCERTO SYMPHONIQUE NO. 3, OP. 45 AND SCHERZO FROM		LITOLFF
CONCERTO SYMPHONIQUE		BLOCH, E.
CONCERTO SYMPHONIQUE		LITOLFF
CONCERTO THEME FROM PIANO CONCERTO, OP. 92		GLAZOUNOW, A.
CONCERTO TRANSCRIPTIONS OF FAVORITE HYMNS		KOHLMANN, C.
CONCERTO WALTZ		WRIGHT, L.
CONCERTO		ANGERER
CONCERTO		ANSON, G.
CONCERTO		CAMMAROTA
CONCERTO		CASTERA
CONCERTO		COPLAND
CONCERTO		CRAS
CONCERTO		DAMASE, J. M.
CONCERTO		FERGUSON, H.
CONCERTO		GAGNEBIN
CONCERTO		GRUNENWALD
CONCERTO		HAIEFF, A.
CONCERTO		JOLIVET, A.
CONCERTO		JONGEN, J.
CONCERTO		MANNINO, V.
CONCERTO		MILHAUD, D.
CONCERTO		NAT, Y.
CONCERTO		NIN-CULMELL, J.
CONCERTO		PANUFNIK, A.
CONCERTO		PERAGALLO, M.
CONCERTO		PERSICHETTI
CONCERTO		PIJPER
CONCERTO		POOT, M.
CONCERTO		RIETI
CONCERTO		SANCAN, P.
CONCERTO		ZAFRED
CONCERTPIECE IN F MINOR OP. 79		WEBER, VON
CONCERTSTUCK, OP. 79		WEBER, VON
CONCERTSTUCK IN F MINOR, OP. 79		WEBER, VON
CONCERTSTUECK		HARSANYI
CONCERT ALLEGRO WITH INTRODUCTION, OP. 134,		SCHUMANN, R.
CONCERT ALLEGRO		CHOPIN
CONCERT CHAMPETRE		POULENC, F.
CONCERT D'ETE, FOR PIANO AND STRING ORCHESTRA		GRUNENWALD
CONCERT DES MONDES SOUTERRAINS -- NO. 3 --		SAUGUET
CONCERT ETUDES - FOREST MURMERS, GNOMENREIGEN		LISZT
CONCERT ETUDE NO. 2		ROWLEY
CONCERT ETUDE NO. 3 IN D FLAT		LISZT
CONCERT FOR CLAVECIN		MARTIN, F.
CONCERT HYMN TRANSCRIPTIONS		SMITH, T.
CONCERT INTERPRETATION OF OP. 11, NO. 2 BY SCHOENBERG		BUSONI
CONCERT IN THE PARK		BERMONT, H.
CONCERT LYRIQUE FOR HARPSICHORD		OERTZEN, R. VON
CONCERT OF THE BEES		VOLZ, H.
CONCERT PARAPHRASE ON 'RIGOLETTO'		VERDI *
CONCERT PARAPHRASE ON 'RIGOLETTO'		VERDI *
CONCERT PIECES, OP. 2, 13, 14, 22 --ARR. FOR PIANO		CHOPIN
CONCERT PIECE IN F MINOR, OP. 79		WEBER, VON
CONCERT PIECE IN F MINOR, OP. 79		WEBER, VON
CONCERT RETROSPECTIF		GIRNATIS
CONCERT RONDO, K382		MOZART, W. A.
CONCERT RONDO IN D, K382		MOZART, W. A.
CONCERT SET FOR PIANO		BINKERD
CONCERT STUDIES, IN C		WRIGHT, N.
CONCERT STUDY ON THE 'SAILORS HORNPIPE'		DICKS, E. A.
CONCERT TRANSCRIPTIONS FROM HER REPERTOIRE -- PRELUDE		HABERBIER, E.
CONCERT TRANSCRIPTION OF HUNGARIAN RHAPSODY NO. 19		RIVE-KING *
CONCERT TRANSCRIPTION OF HUNGARIAN RHAPSODY NO. 21		LISZT
CONCERT WALTZ--MEMORIES OF OLD VIENNA		CHENOWETH, W.

CONCERT WALTZ, FROM 'DER ROSENKAVALIER'	STRAUSS, R.
CONCERT WALTZ, FROM 'DER ROSENKAVALIER'	STRAUSS, R.
CONCERT WALTZ, FROM 'DER ROSENKAVALIER'	STRAUSS, R.
CONCERT WALTZ	ELLIOTT
CONCERT WALTZ	MONTGOMERY, B.
CONCHITA, POLKA, OP. 92, NO. 5 -- FROM 12 PIECES	ALBENIZ, I.
CONCIERTO DE DOS ORGANOS ODER FUR 2 HARFEN ODER 2	BLANCO
CONDOR PASA, EL	ROBLES
CONFETTI	KAPER, B.
CONFIDENCE, OP. 19 NO. 4	MENDELSSOHN
CONFIDENCES	WESLY
CONFIDENCE	STUBBLEFIELD
CONFIDENCE	VERRALL, J.
CONGA, LA	DVORINE
CONGA IN G	POOLE, C.
CONGRATULATIONS MINUET	BEETHOVEN
CONGRATULATION MINUET	BEETHOVEN
CONJUROS	GARCIA MORILLO
CONNECTICUT MARCH	NASSANN
CONQUERORS, ONE PIANO - SIX HANDS	BLISS, P.
CONSERVATORY SONATINA ALBUMS, BK. 1	WILKS, N.
CONSERVATORY SONATINA ALBUMS, BK. 2	WILKS, N.
CONSOLATION, OP. 30 NO. 3	MENDELSSOHN
CONSOLATIONS, NO. 1	LISZT
CONSOLATIONS, NO. 3	LISZT
CONSOLATIONS AND LIEBESTRAUME	LISZT
CONSOLATIONS NO. 3 IN D FLAT	LISZT
CONSOLATIONS NO. 5 IN E	LISZT
CONSOLATIONS	LISZT
CONSOLATIONS	LISZT
CONSOLATIONS	LISZT
CONSOLATION	ARMOUR
CONSOLATION	MENDELSSOHN
CONSTERNATION	SHEARING, G.
CONSTRUCTION HUMAINE, OP. 49 -- ABSTRACT BALLET	SPITZMULLER, A.
CONTEMPLACION, OP. 99	TURINA, J.
CONTEMPLATION, OP. 47, NO. 23	HELLER, S.
CONTEMPORAINS,LES BK.1	DESCAVES, L.
CONTEMPORAINS,LES BK.2	DESCAVES, L.
CONTEMPORAINS,LES BK.3	DESCAVES, L.
CONTEMPORAINS,LES BK.4	DESCAVES, L.
CONTEMPORARIES OF BACH	
CONTEMPORARIES OF PURCELL	
CONTEMPORARIES OF TELEMAN	FREY--ED
CONTEMPORARY BASS LINES FOR ALL KEYBOARD INSTRUMENTS	KAYE, CAROL
CONTEMPORARY BULGARIAN PIANO MUSIC, BK. 1	GERIG, HANS--ED.
CONTEMPORARY BULGARIAN PIANO MUSIC, BK. 2	GERIG, HANS--ED.
CONTEMPORARY COLLECTION, NO. 1	GOLDSTEIN *
CONTEMPORARY COMPOSERS	SCHAUM, J.--ED.
CONTEMPORARY CZECHOSLOVAKIAN PIANO MUSIC, BK. 1	GERIG, HANS--ED.
CONTEMPORARY CZECHOSLOVAKIAN PIANO MUSIC, BK. 2	GERIG, HANS--ED.
CONTEMPORARY GREEK PIANO MUSIC, BK. 1	GERIG, HANS--ED.
CONTEMPORARY GREEK PIANO MUSIC, BK. 2	GERIG, HANS--ED.
CONTEMPORARY PIANO LITERATURE, BK. 1	CLARK, F.--ED.
CONTEMPORARY PIANO LITERATURE, BK. 2	CLARK, F.--ED.
CONTEMPORARY PIANO LITERATURE, BK. 3	CLARK, F.--ED.
CONTEMPORARY PIANO LITERATURE, BK. 4	CLARK, F.--ED.
CONTEMPORARY PIANO LITERATURE, BK. 5	CLARK, F.--ED.
CONTEMPORARY PIANO LITERATURE, BK. 6	CLARK, F.--ED.
CONTEMPORARY PIANO REPERTOIRE	HINSON, M. *
CONTEMPORARY PIANO REPERTOIRE	HINSON, M. *
CONTEMPORARY PIANO TECHNIQUE	MORAWECK
CONTEMPORARY RUMANIAN MUSIC, BK. 1	GERIG, HANS--ED.
CONTEMPORARY RUMANIAN MUSIC, BK. 2	GERIG, HANS--ED.
CONTEMPORARY SOVIET PIANO MUSIC, BK. 1	GERIG, HANS--ED.
CONTEMPORARY SOVIET PIANO MUSIC, BK. 2	GERIG, HANS--ED.
CONTEMPORARY STYLES FOR THE JAZZ PIANIST -- BK. 1	MEHEGAN, J.
CONTEMPORARY STYLES FOR THE JAZZ PIANIST -- BK. 2	MEHEGAN, J.
CONTEMPORARY STYLES FOR THE JAZZ PIANIST -- BK. 3	MEHEGAN, J.
CONTEMPORARY YUGOSLAVIAN PIANO MUSIC, BK. 2	GERIG, HANS--ED.
CONTEMPORARY YUGOSLAVIAN PIANO MUSIC -- BK. 1	GERIG, HANS--ED.
CONTENTED CLOCK	GAY, G.
CONTENTED FAIRY, THE, FOR ONE PIANO SIX HANDS	SPAULDING, G. L.
CONTENTMENT WALTZ	MARTIN, G.
CONTENTMENT	FROST
CONTENTMENT	FROST
CONTES D'ESPAGNE, BK. 1 - DANS LES JARDINS DE MURCIA	TURINA, J.
CONTES D'ESPAGNE, BK. 1 - DEVANT LA TOUR DE CLAVERO	TURINA, J.
CONTES D'ESPAGNE, BK. 1 - LA CALETA	TURINA, J.
CONTES D'ESPAGNE, BK. 1 - MIRAMAR, LE CHEMIN DE LA	TURINA, J.
CONTES D'ESPAGNE, BK. 1 - ROMPEOLAS	TURINA, J.
CONTES D'ESPAGNE, BK. 1 - UNE VIEILLE EGLISE A LOGRONO	TURINA, J.
CONTES D'ESPAGNE, BK. 1	TURINA, J.
CONTES D'ESPAGNE, BK. 2 - BUVEURS DE MANZANILLA	TURINA, J.
CONTES D'ESPAGNE, BK. 2 - CHANSONS DE LA NUIT	TURINA, J.
CONTES D'ESPAGNE, BK. 2 - CHANSON MAURESQUE	TURINA, J.
CONTES D'ESPAGNE, BK. 2 - CORDOUE EN FETE	TURINA, J.
CONTES D'ESPAGNE, BK. 2 - LA MOSQUEE	TURINA, J.
CONTES D'ESPAGNE, BK. 2 - PROMENADE	TURINA, J.
CONTES D'ESPAGNE, BK. 2 - TOURNOI CHEVALERESQUE	TURINA, J.
CONTES D'ESPAGNE, BK. 2	TURINA, J.
CONTES DE MOURRICES	DUBOIS, P. M.
CONTES POUR LE PIANO	LAJTHA
CONTE D'AVRIL	WIDOR, CH.
CONTE DE NOEL	CARMAN
CONTE NO. 2	SAMINSKY
CONTINENTAL FAVORITES	SCHAUM, J.
CONTINENTAL POLKA	ROZIN
CONTINENTAL SERENADE	GOULD, M.
CONTINUALLY	CORGHI
CONTINUUM FUR CEMBALO	LIGETI, G.
CONTRA-DANCES	BEETHOVEN
CONTRAPUNCTUS INVERSUS DER FUGA XV FROM 'THE ART OF	BACH, J.S.
CONTRARY ME	ERB
CONTRASTS FOR PIANO	RIETI
CONTRASTS FOR TWO PIANOS	CHRISTIANSEN, L.
CONTRASTS	HELYER, M.
CONTRASTS	OSBORNE, W.
CONTRASTS	RIETI
CONTRASTS	SIMS
CONTRA DANCES	BEETHOVEN
CONTRA DANCE	BEETHOVEN
CONTRA DANCE	BEETHOVEN
CONTRA DANCE	BEETHOVEN
CONTRA DANCE	BEETHOVEN
CONTRE DANCES	BEETHOVEN
CONTRE DANCE NO. 1	BEETHOVEN
CONVENT BELLS	LUDOVIC, G.
CONVENT BELLS	LUDOVIC, G.
CONVERSATIONAL PIECES, THREE	DE VITO, A.
CONVERSATION PIECES	EARLE
CONVERSATION	BALOGH
CON AMORE	BEAUMONT, P.
CON AMORE	BEAUMONT, P.
CON AMORE	BEAUMONT, P.
CON AMORE	REID
CON FUOCO, OP. 125 NO. 1	SINDING
CON FUOCO, OP. 25 NO. 1	SINDING
COOLIE CART	GLOVER, D.
COOL BLUE	GARROW, L.
COOL MULE	KAHN, M.
COOL REVEILLE	TOWNSEND
COOL SCHOOL	SCHAUM, W.
COPLA INTRUSA, LA	RODRIGO, M.
COPPELIA, COMPLETE ILLUSTRATED	DELIBES, L.
COPPELIA, SELECTIONS FROM	DELIBES, L.
COPPELIA, VALSE LENTE	DELIBES, L.
COPPELIA -- TANZ-SUITE	DELIBES, L.
COPPELIA -- VALSE LENTE	DELIBES, L.
COPPELIA BALLET -- VALSE LENTE	DELIBES, L.
COPPELIA BALLET	DELIBES, L.
COPPELIA WALTZ	DELIBES, L.
COPPELIA	DELIBES, L.
COPPELIA	HOFSTAD, M.
COPY-CAT	LAMONTAINE, J.
COPYCATS	THOMAS, C. J.
COPY CAT	ROZIN
COPY ME	JUDD, A.
COQUETA, LA, FANDANGO	BOROWSKI, E.
COQUETTE, THE	GREGH
COQUETTERIE, OP. 30	GREY, F.
COQUETTERIE	GREEN *
COQUETTE	RIMSKY-KORSAKOFF
COQ D'OR, HYMN TO SUN	STREABBOG
CORA, WALTZ	CASTRO, J. M.
CORALES CRIOLLOS NO. 1	ALBENIZ, I.
CORDOBA--FROM ''SONGS OF SPAIN''	ALBENIZ, I.
CORDOBA, OP. 232, NO. 4 -- FROM CANTOS DE ESPANA	ALBENIZ, I.
CORDOBA, OP. 232, NO. 4 -- FROM CANTOS DE ESPANA	ALBENIZ, I.
CORDOBA	LECUONA
CORDOBA	LECUONA
CORDOBA	LECUONA
CORNFLOWER WALTZES	COOTE
CORNISH MAY DANCE --2 PIANOS, 8 HANDS--	ECKSTEIN
CORNISH RHAPSODY -- COMPLETE	BATH
CORNISH RHAPSODY -- THEME	BATH
CORNISH RHAPSODY	BATH
CORNISH RHAPSODY	BATH
CORNISH RHAPSODY	BATH
CORN FLAKES	KAHN, M.
CORN HUSKIN'	MCHALE, M.
CORN PONE SHUFFLE	KING, S.
CORONATION MARCH--'LE PROPHETE'	MEYERBEER, G.
CORONATION MARCH, A	DUDLEY, R.
CORONATION MARCH, PROPHET	MEYERBEER, G.
CORONATION MARCH, PROPHET	MEYERBEER, G.
CORONATION MARCH -- FROM ''LE PROPHETE'' -- 6-HANDS	MEYERBEER, G.
CORONATION MARCH -- FROM ''LE PROPHETE''	MEYERBEER, G.
CORONATION MARCH	MEYERBEER, G.
CORONATION SCENE -- FROM ''BORIS GODOUNOFF'' -- SET	MOUSSORGSKY
CORONATION WALTZ - TWO PIANOS, EIGHT HANDS	MEYERBEER, G.
CORPORAL TIM	BINKLEY
CORPORAL TIM	BINKLEY
CORPUS CHRISTI EN SEVILLA -- FROM IBERIA	ALBENIZ, I.
CORRENTE IN G	HANDEL
CORRESPONDENCES	FARKAS, F.
CORRICOLO, IL, GALOP, OP. 24	DE GRAU
CORRICOLO, IL -- GALOP --	DURAND DE CRAU
CORRICOLO, IL	DURAND DE CRAU
CORRIDA -- 10 OF SPAIN'S MOST POPULAR PASODOBLES IN	RETTENBERG--ED
COPROBOREE FOR 2 OR 3 PIANOS	BROWN, E.
CORRO DE LAS NINAS, EL -- 60 SPANISH FOLKSONGS FOR	MONTALBAN--ED
CORSAGE WALTZ	SCHAUM, J.
CORSAIRE,LE--PAS DE DEUX--	DRIGO, R. *
CORTEGE--PRELUDE	CHENOWETH, W.
CORTEGE -- DE PETITE SUITE	DEBUSSY
CORTEGE DES ADORATEURS DU FEU	SCHMITT
CORTEGE DU BERRY	DUCLOS, P.
CORTEGE DU SARDAR	IPPOLITOV-IVANOV
CORTEGE ORIENTAL	KOWALSKI, H.
CORTEGE	BAZELAIRE
CORTEGE	BOULANGER, L.
CORTEGE	DEBUSSY
COSMIC CLOUDS	FRANK
COSMIC CLOUDS	FRANK
COSMIC LIGHTS	FRANK
COSSACKS	REBE
COSSACKS	SCHER, W.
COSSACK DANCE, A FOLK SONG	WEYBRIGHT
COSSACK DANCE	AUBERT
COSSACK DANCE	GEIGER
COSSACK DANCE	WEYBRIGHT--ED.
COSTENA	HERNANDEZ
COTTONTAILS, OP. 10	BURLEIGH, C.
COTTONTAIL PARADE	KOCH, E.
COTTON BLOSSOM TIME	BLAKE, D.
COTTON FLUFF	SMITH
COTTON PICKERS	MARTIN
COTTON PICKER	MARTIN
COTTON PICKIN' BOOGIE	MYDDLETON
COTTON PICKIN' PETE	SCHER, W.
COTTON SHUFFLE	WILSON
COUCOU, LE --RONDEAU--	DAQUIN, C.
COUCOU, LE -- RONDO --	DAQUIN, C.
COUCOU, LE	DAQUIN, C.
COUCOU, LE	SAEGEL
COUCOU, LE	STREABBOG
COUCOU	ROUGNON
COULEURS DE LA CITE CELESTE	MESSIAEN, O.
COUNTRY COTTAGE	PERRY, N.
COUNTRY DANCE, A	SAMPSON, G.
COUNTRY DANCE	BEETHOVEN
COUNTRY DANCE	DE VITO, A.
COUNTRY DANCE	FICHANDLER, W.
COUNTRY DANCE	HAYDN
COUNTRY DANCE	HEINS, C.
COUNTRY DANCE	JESSE, M.
COUNTRY DANCE	JUDD, A.
COUNTRY DANCE	KEENAN
COUNTRY DANCE	MACFADYEN, A.
COUNTRY DANCE	NEVIN
COUNTRY DANCE	SLONIMSKY
COUNTRY FIDDLER, THE	TRAVIS, B.
COUNTRY GARDENS--EASY VERSION--	GRAINGER, P.
COUNTRY GARDENS--ENGLISH MORRIS-DANCE TUNE--	GRAINGER, P.
COUNTRY GARDENS--ESPECIALLY EASY VERSION--	GRAINGER, P.
COUNTRY GARDENS, ENGLISH DANCE	GROOMS
COUNTRY GARDENS -- EASY	FREDERICKS
COUNTRY GARDENS -- ENGLISH MORRIS-DANCE TUNE --	GRAINGER, P.--ED
COUNTRY GARDENS -- ENGLISH MORRIS-DANCE TUNE	GRAINGER, P.--ED
COUNTRY GARDENS	BAINES, W.
COUNTRY GARDENS	KING, S.--ED.
COUNTRY GARDENS	KING, S.--ED.

COUNTRY GARDENS	MENDEL, S.	CRAWDAD, THE	STEINER
COUNTRY GARDENS	MITTLER--ED	CRAZY COMPOSER	GYLDMARK, S.
COUNTRY GARDENS	SCHIEFELBEIN, F.	CRAZY HORSES	BRIMHALL,
COUNTRY GARDENS	SPENCER, J.	CRAZY ORGAN RAG	JOPLIN *
COUNTRY GARDENS	WALLIS	CRAZY RHYTHM	MEYER *
COUNTRY GARDENS	WILLIAMS--ED.	CRAZY VIOLINS	WILDMAN
COUNTRY GARDENS	WILLIAMS, J.	CREATING MUSIC AT THE PIANO, BK. 1	PALMER-LETHCO
COUNTRY GARDENS	WILLIAMS, J.	CREATING MUSIC AT THE PIANO, BK. 2	PALMER-LETHCO
COUNTRY GARLAND, A	THIMAN	CREATING MUSIC AT THE PIANO, BK. 3	PALMER-LETHCO
COUNTRY JIG IN C MAJOR	GUION, D.	CREATING MUSIC AT THE PIANO, BK. 4	PALMER-LETHCO
COUNTRY JIG IN D MAJOR	GUION, D.	CREATING MUSIC AT THE PIANO -- RECITAL BOOK 1	PALMER-LETHCO
COUNTRY LANE	MARSHALL, L.	CREATING MUSIC AT THE PIANO -- RECITAL BOOK 2	PALMER-LETHCO
COUNTRY LIFE	DUNHILL	CREATING MUSIC AT THE PIANO -- TEACHER'S MANUAL FOR	PALMER-LETHCO
COUNTRY OUTING	LAST, J.	CREATION DU MONDE,LA, NO.2 LA CREATION	DANDELOT
COUNTRY POPS	BRADLEY,	CREATION DU MONDE,LA, NO.4 LA NUIT	DANDELOT
COUNTRY ROAD		CREATION DU MONDE, LE -- BALLET	MILHAUD, D.
COUNTRY SCENE	GLOVER, D.	CREATIVE INTERVAL STUDIES	STEINER
COUNTRY SNAPSHOTS	GREENHILL, H.	CREATIVE KEYBOARD SOUNDS	BUTLER, A.
COUNTRY STYLE		CREATIVE PIANO SOLOS, BK. 1	LANE, J.
COUNTRY TOWN, A. SUITE	MACONCHY	CREATIVE TECHNIQUE FOR PIANO	DEE, M.
COUNTRY TUNES TO SING AND PLAY	DUNGAN	CREEL, THE	RAWSTHORNE, A.
COUNTRY WESTERN	DE VITO, A.--ED.	CREOLE LULLABY	EZELL, H.
COUNTY FAIR	HAYES	CREPESCULE	GRATTON
COUNT BASIE BOOGIE WOOGIE BLUES		CREPUSCOLI	OREFICE, G.
COUNT DOWN	BURNAM	CREPUSCULE, LE	MONIOT
COUPERIN PIANO COURSE, BK. 01	COUPERIN	CREPUSCULE OP. 36 NO. 2	FRIML, R.
COUPERIN PIANO COURSE, BK. 02	COUPERIN	CREPUSCULE	FOURDRAIN
COUPERIN PIANO COURSE, BK. 03	COUPERIN	CREPUSCULE	WURMSER, L.
COURANTE FROM 'IN CLASSIC STYLE'	LAST, J.	CRESCENDO	LASSON, P.
COURANTE IN E MINOR	LULLY, J.	CRESCENDO	LASSON, P.
COURANTE	BACH, J.S.	CRESCENDO	LASSON, P.
COURANTE	LULLY	CRESCENDO	LASSON, P.
COURANTS D'AIRS	CLAUDE, M.	CRICKET, THE	RICHMAN, A.
COURENTE	ZIPOLI	CRICKETS	ERB
COURSE FOR PIANISTS, BK. 1 --BEGINNER'S BOOK	WEYBRIGHT	CRICKET AND BUMBLE BEE	CHADWICK, G.
COURSE FOR PIANISTS, BK. 1 --BEGINNERS--	WEYBRIGHT	CRICKET AND BUMBLE BEE	SCHAUM, J.--ED.
COURSE FOR PIANISTS, BK. 2 --FOLLOW-UP--	WEYBRIGHT	CRICKET AND THE BUMBLE BEE, THE	CHADWICK, G.
COURSE FOR PIANISTS, BK. 2 -- FOLLOW-UP BOOK	WEYBRIGHT	CRICKET AND THE BUMBLE BEE	CHADWICK, G.
COURSE FOR PIANISTS, BK. 3 --KEY SIGNATURES--	WEYBRIGHT	CRICKET AND THE BUMBLE BEE	CHADWICK, G.
COURSE FOR PIANISTS, BK. 3 -- KEY AND SIGNATURE BOOK	WEYBRIGHT	CRIMSON BLUSHES	LESTER, I.
COURSE FOR PIANISTS, BK. 4 --SCALES AND CHORDS--	WEYBRIGHT	CRIMSON BLUSHES	LESTER, I.
COURSE FOR PIANISTS, BK. 4 -- SCALE AND CHORD BOOK	WEYBRIGHT	CRIMSON DAWN	CARRE
COURSE FOR PIANISTS, BK. 5 --DANCE FORMS--	WEYBRIGHT	CRIMSON SET	CLARK, M.--ED.
COURSE FOR PIANISTS, BK. 5 -- DANCE FORM BOOK	WEYBRIGHT	CRINOLINE AND LACE	GOULD, M.
COURSE FOR PIANISTS, BK. 6 --CLASSICS BOOK--	WEYBRIGHT	CRIPPLE CREEK	WEYBRIGHT--ED.
COURSE FOR PIANISTS, BK. 6	WEYBRIGHT	CRIPPLE CREEK	WEYBRIGHT
COURSE FOR PIANISTS, CHRISTMAS MUSIC-- SECULAR, BK. 1	WEYBRIGHT	CRISS CROSS	GEORGE
COURSE FOR PIANISTS, CHRISTMAS MUSIC -- SACRED, BK. 2	WEYBRIGHT	CRISS CROSS	SMITH
COURSE FOR PIANISTS, DOUBLE PLAY	WEYBRIGHT	CRISS CROSS	SMITH
COURSE FOR PIANISTS, ETUDES FOR PIANISTS OF JUNIOR	WEYBRIGHT	CRISTALLI	WISSE
COURSE FOR PIANISTS, ETUDES FOR PIANISTS OF JUNIOR	WEYBRIGHT	CRISTALLI	WISSE
COURSE FOR PIANISTS, TECHNIC FOR PIANISTS OF JUNIOR	WEYBRIGHT	CRISTO DE LA CALAVERA, EL, OP. 30	TURINA, J.
COURSE FOR PIANISTS, TECHNIC FOR PIANISTS OF JUNIOR	WEYBRIGHT	CROCODILE, THE	HELLER, E.
COURSE FOR PIANISTS WORKBOOK, BK. 1	WEYBRIGHT	CROCODILE TEARS	STEINER
COURSE FOR PIANISTS WORKBOOK, BK. 2	WEYBRIGHT	CROCODILE	TROWBRIDGE, L.
COURSE FOR PIANISTS WORKBOOK, BK. 3	WEYBRIGHT	CROOKED MARCH, A	KING
COURSE FOR PIANISTS WORKBOOK, BK. 4	WEYBRIGHT	CROQUEMBOUCHES	DELVINCOURT
COURSE OF PIANO STUDIES -- SELECTED AND GRADED BY	FRYER, H.--ED	CROQUIS D'AUTOMNE - DANSE AU VILLAGE	ROPARTZ
COURSE OF PIANO STUDIES -- SELECTED AND GRADED BY	FRYER, H.--ED	CROQUIS D'AUTOMNE - JOYEUSE AUBADE	ROPARTZ
COURSE OF PIANO STUDIES -- SELECTED AND GRADED BY	FRYER, H.--ED	CROQUIS D'AUTOMNE - SOIR DE TOUSSAINT	ROPARTZ
COURSE OF PIANO STUDIES -- SELECTED AND GRADED BY	FRYER, H.--ED	CROQUIS D'AUTOMNE - UNE ENFANT REVE	ROPARTZ
COURSE OF PIANO STUDIES -- SELECTED AND GRADED BY	FRYER, H.--ED	CROQUIS D'AUTOMNE - UN PATRE CHANTE	ROPARTZ
COURSE OF PIANO STUDIES -- SELECTED AND GRADED BY	FRYER, H.--ED	CROQUIS D'AUTOMNE	ROPARTZ
COURSE OF PIANO STUDIES -- SELECTED AND GRADED BY	FRYER, H.--ED	CROQUIS D'ENFANTS - A LA CAMPAGNE	SOUBEYRAN
COURS DE PIANO, NO.1 ABC	LECOUPPEY, F.	CROQUIS D'ENFANTS - A LA MAISON	SOUBEYRAN
COURS DE PIANO, NO.2 ALPHABET	LECOUPPEY, F.	CROQUIS D'ENFANTS - LA MAISON ENDORMIE	SOUBEYRAN
COURS DE PIANO, NO.3 LE PROGRES	LECOUPPEY, F.	CROQUIS D'ENFANTS - LA RETOUR DE L'ECOLE	SOUBEYRAN
COURS DE PIANO, NO.5 AGILITE	LECOUPPEY, F.	CROQUIS D'ENFANTS - PRIERE DU SOIR	SOUBEYRAN
COURS DE PIANO POUR ADULTES. PREMIER LIVRE	AARON, M.	CROQUIS D'ETE - PETITE RONDE FRANCAISE	ROPARTZ
COURT MINUET	CROCKER, D.	CROQUIS D'ETE	ROPARTZ
COVERED WAGON, THE	MANN, M.	CROQUIS DE ROUTE -- 12 PIECES --	WOOLLETT
COVERED WAGON SUITE, THE	THOMPSON, J.	CROQUIS DE ROUTE - EN CUEILLANT DES FLEURS	WOOLLETT
COW-COW BOOGIE	RAYE *	CROQUIS DE ROUTE - LE BUCHERON ET LE BERGER	WOOLLETT
COWBOY AND HIS BANJO, THE	HART, N.	CROQUIS DE ROUTE - LE JOUEUR DE VIELLE	WOOLLETT
COWBOY AND HIS BANJO, THE	SCHAUM, J.--ED.	CROQUIS DE ROUTE	PIERNE, P.
COWBOY BAND, THE	BOWN, P.	CROQUIS ET AGACERIES D'UN GROS BONHOMME EN BOIS	SATIE, E.
COWBOY BOOGIE	SCHAUM, J.--ED.	CROQUIS MARITIMES	ORBAN
COWBOY BOOK	SCHAUM, J.--ED.	CROQUIS POUR LA JEUNESSE	LEHMAN, E.
COWBOY CHARLEY	VANDEVERE, J. L.	CROQUIS	MARESCOTTI, A.
COWBOY DOE -- 14 PIECES FOR BEGINNERS	TAIT, G. *	CROSS HAND ETUDES - F1	WARD, J.
COWBOY LAMENT	DE VITO, A.	CROSS HAND ETUDES - F2	WARD, J.
COWBOY NOCTURNE	ROGERS, E.	CROSS HAND ETUDES - F3	WARD, J.
COWBOY ON THE TRAIL	RICHTER, A.	CROSS HAND ETUDES - F4	WARD, J.
COWBOY POKE	AARON, M.	CROSS OVER THE BRIDGE	KARP
COWBOY SONATINA	GREEN, R.	CROW'S FEET	ROGERS, E.
COWBOY SONGS	HUNTLEY--ED	CROWN IMPERIAL	WALTON, W.
COWBOY SONG	GEORGE	CROWN MELODIES	CRIST, D.
COWBOY TIME --BIG NOTE-- --175--		CROW AND THE SCARECROW, THE	TOWNSEND
COWBOY	COBB	CRUISE ON THE RIVER, A	VOLKART, H.
COWGIRL, THE	TOWNSEND	CRUSADE, PIANO STYLINGS	WEYBRIGHT
COWKEEPER'S TUNE AND COUNTRY DANCE, OP. 63 NO. 2	GRIEG	CRUSADER'S HYMN -- A SILESIAN FOLK MELODY	WEYBRIGHT--ED.
COWSLIP BELLS	STAIRS, L.	CRUSADERS' HYMN	ROLFE, W.
COYAS BAJANDO LA MONTANA	DE ROGATIS	CRUSADER MARCH	SMITH, T.
CRACKER JACK	KREVIT, W.	CRUSADE PIANIST NO. 1	SMITH, T.
CRACKLIN ROSIE	BRIMHALL,	CRUSADE PIANIST NO. 2	SMITH, T.
CRACOVIENNE FANTASTIQUE	PADEREWSKI, I.	CRUSADE PIANIST NO. 3	SMITH, T.
CRACOVIENNE FANTASTIQUE	PADEREWSKI, I.	CRUSADE PIANIST NO. 4	RIEGGER, W.
CRADLE-SONG, OP. 49 NO. 4	BRAHMS	CRY, THE	RIEGGER, W.
CRADLE-SONG, OP. 49 NO. 4	BRAHMS	CRY, THE	LANE, J.--ED.
CRADLED CLOUD	LINDFORS	CRYING IN THE CHAPEL	ECKSTEIN
CRADLE SONG, A	WEYBRIGHT	CRYPTIC	CRIST, D.
CRADLE SONG, OP. 124 NO. 6	SCHUMANN, R.	CRYSTAL MELODIES	CATIZONE, J. M.
CRADLE SONG, OP. 124 NO. 6	SCHUMANN, R.	CRYSTAL	MONTI, V. *
CRADLE SONG, OP. 27	KABALEVSKY	CSARDAS	MONTIEL OLVERA,
CRADLE SONG, OP. 49 NO. 4	BRAHMS	CUATRO DANZAS MEXICANAS	PONCE, M.
CRADLE SONG -- BERCEUSE, OP. 57	CHOPIN	CUATRO DANZAS MEXICANAS	RODRIGO, J.
CRADLE SONG -- BERCEUSE	DELBRUCK	CUATRO ESTAMPAS ANDALUZAS	SEBASTIANI, P.
CRADLE SONG -- BERCEUSE	HAUSER	CUATRO PRELUDIOS NO. 1	SEBASTIANI, P.
CRADLE SONG AND 'I LOVE THEE'	GRIEG	CUATRO PRELUDIOS NO. 2	SEBASTIANI, P.
CRADLE SONG AND SOLVEJG'S SONG	GRIEG	CUATRO PRELUDIOS NO. 3	SEBASTIANI, P.
CRADLE SONG	BRAHMS	CUATRO PRELUDIOS NO. 4	ALBENIZ, I.
CRADLE SONG	BRAHMS	CUBA. CAPRICE -- NO. 8, FROM SUITE ESPANOLA NO. 1	MILLER, C.
CRADLE SONG	BRAHMS	CUBANAISE	FALLA, M. DE
CRADLE SONG	BRAHMS	CUBANA FROM PIECES ESPAGNOLES	ACKERMANN, D.
CRADLE SONG	KJERULF	CUBANERA	WHITFORD
CRADLE SONG	MALDEN, G.	CUBAN CAPERS --MODERN RHYTHMIC CLASSICS--	SCHAUM, J.--ED.
CRADLE SONG	MOZART, W. A.	CUBAN MAMBO	HIBBS, C.
CRADLE SONG	PALMGREN, S.	CUBAN NIGHTS	GERSHWIN
CRADLE SONG	SCHUBERT	CUBAN OVERTURE	GERSHWIN
CRADLE SONG	SHULMAN	CUBAN OVERTURE	ALBENIZ, I.
CRADLE SONG	WHEELER, V. B.	CUBA -- FROM SUITE ESPANOLA NO. 1	STEINER
CRAGGY GARDENS IN THE SPRING	DITTENHAVER	CUBS AND BROWNIES AT THE PIANO	WEYBRIGHT
CRAPSHOOTERS, THE	LANE, E.	CUB IS THE YOUNGLING, THE	PRIGGE, O.
CRAVISTAS PORTUGUEZES, BK. 1	KASTNER--ED.	CUB SCOUT MARCH	PITTALUGA
CRAVISTAS PORTUGUEZES, BK. 2	KASTNER--ED.	CUCKOLD'S FAIR, THE -- LA ROMERIA DE LOS CORNUDOS --	OLDENBURG, E.
		CUCKOO, CUCKOO	

Title	Composer
CUCKOO, THE--RONDO	DAQUIN, C.
CUCKOO, THE	DAQUIN, C.
CUCKOO, THE	SWANSON
CUCKOO'S CALL, THE	BRAGDON
CUCKOO'S CALL	SOCHTING
CUCKOO AND NIGHTINGALE	HANDEL
CUCKOO BIRD, THE	GIASSON, P.
CUCKOO BIRD, THE	GIASSON, P.
CUCKOO BIRD, THE	ERB
CUCKOO CLOCK, THE	CRERIE, E.
CUCKOO CLOCK	SCHER, W.
CUCKOO IN THE CLOCK	MARTIN, G.
CUCKOO SONG -- ONE PIANO, SIX HANDS --	JONASSOHN
CUCKOO SONG	MARTIN, G.
CUCKOO SONG	JONNASSON
CUCKOO WALTZ	CORONARO
CUCULO E L'ALBA, IL	GRANADOS
CUENTOS DE LA JUVENTUD, OP. 1	SUFFERN, C.
CUENTOS DE NINOS	GARCIA MORILLO
CUENTOS PARA NINOS TRAVIESOS - SERIES 2	CHAVARRI
CUENTO DE LA PRINCESA DEL GUISANTE -- CUENTOS Y	ROSSINI, G.
CUJUS ANIMAM FROM STABAT MATER	VAUGHN
CUMBERLAND COUNTY FEUD	MATOS RODRIGUEZ
CUMPARSITA, LA	MATOS RODRIGUEZ
CUMPARSITA, LA	RODRIGUEZ, R.
CUNNING CUPID	HILSHER, F.
CURIOUS CAT, THE	STEADMAN, A.
CURIOUS STORY, OP. 138 NO. 9	HELLER, S.
CURIOUS STORY IN F MAJOR, OP. 138 NO. 9	HELLER, S.
CURIOUS STORY	HELLER, S.
CURIOUS STORY	HELLER, S.
CURIOUS STORY	HELLER, S.
CURTAIN TIME - MELODIES FROM THE MODERN THEATRE	AGAY, D.--ED
CUTE LITTLE FIGURE, THE	LIPPMAN
CUTE	RAEZER, C.
CUT THE PIGEON WING	SAINT-SAENS
CYGNE, LE	SAINT-SAENS
CYGNE, LE	SCHMOLL, A.
CYMBALS AND CASTANETS	SCHMOLL, A.
CYMBALS AND CASTANETS	KRAMER, A. W.
CYPRESSES	DUNCAN
CYPRESS SWAMP	STREABBOG
CYPRUS, WALTZ	MUNN, W.
CY AND CINDY	MOSKOWITZ
CZARA	MICHIELS
CZARDAS, DANSE STYRIENNE	MACDOWELL
CZARDAS, OP. 24 NO. 4	SCHER, W.
CZARDAS FANTASY	LISZT
CZARDAS MACABRE	MONRI, V.
CZARDAS NO. 1	MONTI, V.
CZARDAS NO. 1	SCHER, W.
CZARDAS RHAPSODY	SCHER, W.
CZARDAS RHAPSODY	MONTI, V.
CZARDAS	GANNE
CZARDAS	MONTI, V. *
CZARDAS	MONTI, V.
CZARINA, LA	GANNE
CZARINE, LA, MAZURKA RUSSE	GANNE
CZARINE, MAZURKA RUSSE	COLE--ED
CZECHOSLOVAKIAN FOLK SONGS	
CZECH FOLK DANCES AND SONGS	WEINBERGER, J.
CZECH RHAPSODY	TCHEREPNIN
CZECH SONG, OP. 27, NO. 5	CZERNY
CZERNY-SCHAUM, BK.1	CZERNY
CZERNY-SCHAUM, BK.2	BASTIEN--ED.
CZERNY AND HANON FOR THE INTERMEDIATE GRADES	CZERNY
CZERNY AT ITS BEST, OP. 299	CZERNY
CZERNY AT ITS BEST, OP. 740	CZERNY
CZERNY GERMER, BK. 1	CZERNY
CZERNY GERMER, BK. 2	CZERNY
CZERNY GERMER, BK. 3	SCHAUM, J.
CZERNY IN ALL KEYS, BK. 1	SCHAUM, J.
CZERNY IN ALL KEYS, BK. 2	PARAY, P.
D'UNE AME	DEBUSSY
D'UN CAHIER D'ESQUISSES	MOESCHINGER
D'UN CAHIER VALAISAN -- AUS EINEM WALLISER SKIZZENBUCH	BOULANGER, L.
D'UN JARDIN CLAIR	BOULANGER, L.
D'UN VIEUX JARDIN	ROLFE
DADDY'S WALTZ	TROWBRIDGE, L.
DADDY LONGLEGS	ERB
DAFFODILS ARE HERE	PANELLA, L.
DAFFODILS	PELS, W.
DAFFODILS	SIMON *
DAFFY DAFFODIL	HERBERT
DAGGER DANCE--FROM ''NATOMA''	GIORZA
DAGHELA AVANTI UN PASSO	KAPR
DAHEIM, HEFT 2	PANELLA, L.
DAHLIAS	STREABBOG
DAHLIA POLKA	STREABBOG
DAHLIA POLKA	JENKINS, M.
DAILY DOZEN, THE	LAKE
DAILY DOZEN - BOOK 1	LAKE
DAILY DOZEN - BOOK 2	SCHWALM, R.
DAILY EXERCISES	TAUSIG
DAILY EXERCISES	DOHNANYI
DAILY FINGER EXERCISES, BK. 1	DOHNANYI
DAILY FINGER EXERCISES, BK. 2	DOHNANYI
DAILY FINGER EXERCISES, BK. 3	BERINGER, O. *
DAILY PIANOFORTE EXERCISES	TAUSIG
DAILY STUDIES	KETTERER, E.
DAINTY BALLET DANCER	KOHLER, F.
DAINTY DAFFODILS	MILES
DAINTY DAFFODILS	MILES
DAINTY DAFFODILS	PANELLA, L.
DAINTY DAMOZEL	MOZART, W. A.
DAINTY DANCE	BARNES, B.
DAINTY DOLL	FOSTER
DAINTY LADY	RENNARD
DAINTY LITTLE MISS	POLDINI, E.
DAINTY MARCH, OP. 15 NO. 2	BARNES, B.
DAINTY MISS	
DAINTY MISS	BESTHOFF, M.
DAINTY TOES	LEONI, F.
DAISIES	RACHMANINOFF, S.
DAISIES	SMETANA
DALIBOR. POTPOURRI AUS DER OPER	BAUDRIER
DAME A LA LICORNE, LA	DOUGLAS
DAN, THE PICCOLO MAN	DAQUIN, C.
DANCE-CAPRICE, OP. 28 NO. 3	TSCHAIKOWSKY
DANCE, CANDY FAIRY	KARP
DANCE, DANCE THE HORA	SHOSTAKOVITCH
DANCE, FROM THE BALLET 'THE GOLDEN AGE,' OP. 22	BENTLEY
DANCE, GYPSY	GOEDICKE
DANCE, OP. 36 NO. 21	GOEDICKE
DANCE, REVERIE, MAZURKA, OP. 36	WHITFORD
DANCE, THE	LITTOFF
DANCER, THE	

Title	Composer
DANCERS, THE	GREENWALD, M.
DANCERS, THE	GREENWALD, M.
DANCERS OF DELPHES FROM PRELUDES, BK. 1	DEBUSSY
DANCES, BK. 1	SCHUBERT
DANCES, BK. 2	SCHUBERT
DANCES, VOL. 1	SCHUBERT
DANCES, VOL. 2	SCHUBERT
DANCES -- BAROQUE TO JAZZ NO. 13, BK. 1	AGAY, D.--ED
DANCES -- BAROQUE TO JAZZ NO. 13, BK. 2	AGAY, D.--ED
DANCES -- BAROQUE TO JAZZ NO. 13, BK. 3	AGAY, D.--ED
DANCES -- IN THE FORM OF VARIATIONS ON A RUSSIAN THEME	ILLIASHENKO
DANCES -- WALTZES, 'LAENDLER', GERMAN DANCES,	SCHUBERT
DANCES AND MARCHES	MOZART, W. A.
DANCES AND PIECES --14--	HAYDN
DANCES AND PIECES	BEETHOVEN
DANCES AND PIECES	LOEHLEIN
DANCES AND PIECES	SCHUBERT
DANCES AND WALTZES	SCHUBERT
DANCES FOR THE LITTLE PIANIST, BK. 1	CARABELLA
DANCES FOR THE LITTLE PIANIST, BK. 2	CARABELLA
DANCES FROM FAMOUS BALLETS	MAYER
DANCES FROM FAMOUS OPERAS	MAYER
DANCES FROM GALANTA	KODALY, Z.
DANCES IN MAJOR AND MINOR	PODOLSKY, L. *
DANCES IN THE CANEBRAKES -- THREE PIECES, 1. NIMBLE	PRICE, F.
DANCES OF MAROSSZEK	KODALY, Z.
DANCES OF THE BAROQUE ERA, BK. 1	NAGY, O. *
DANCES OF THE BAROQUE ERA, BK. 2	NAGY, O.--ED.
DANCES OF THE DOLLS. SEVEN PIECES FOR PIANO	SHOSTAKOVITCH
DANCES OF THE PEOPLE	BURCHENAL, E.
DANCES OF 7 CENTURIES	GRAETZER
DANCES	DVORAK
DANCES	LISZT
DANCES	SCHUBERT
DANCES	SCHUBERT
DANCES	SCHUBERT
DANCES	SEROUX
DANCE -- SONATA, OP. 23	JEMNITZ, A.
DANCE ALBUM	SCHUBERT
DANCE ALLEGRO	KARP
DANCE AND BE MERRY -- A LITTLE SUITE	WILKINSON, P.
DANCE AND QUIET TIME	BLYTH
DANCE CAPRICE, OP. 28 NO. 3	GRIEG
DANCE CAPRICE, OP. 28 NO. 3	GRIEG
DANCE CAPRICE	MELECCI, A.
DANCE CREOLE	BINKLEY
DANCE CREOLE	BINKLEY
DANCE DES FANTOMES	SMITH, SYDNEY
DANCE DIVERTISSEMENT	WAGNER
DANCE ETUDES	PORTNOFF, M.--ED
DANCE FLOOR WHISPERS	STEINER
DANCE FOR A HOLIDAY	MOORE
DANCE FOR HARPSICHORD	DELIUS, F.
DANCE FROM 'THE GOLDEN AGE' BALLET, OP. 22	SHOSTAKOVITCH
DANCE FROM BALLET-MUSIC FOR 'ROSAMUNDE'	JORDA, L.
DANCE FROM FAR AWAY, A	SILVERMAN
DANCE FROM RED POPPY	GLIERE
DANCE FROM THE RIO GRANDE VALLEY	PISK
DANCE IN F, OP. 2, NO. 2	TCHEREPNIN
DANCE IN THE BARN	SOULE
DANCE LIGHTLY	RAEZER, C.
DANCE MACABRE	SAINT-SAENS
DANCE MACABRE	SAINT-SAENS
DANCE MARDI GRAS	WHITFORD
DANCE MINIATURES, SET 1. MINUET AND HORNPIPE	FULTON, N.
DANCE MINIATURES, SET 2. TARANTELLA AND RHUMBA	FULTON, N.
DANCE MINIATURES, SET 3. POLONAISE AND TANGO	FULTON, N.
DANCE MINIATURES, SET 4. WALTZ AND HUNGARIAN DANCE	FULTON, N.
DANCE MINIATURES	GARRATT
DANCE MUSIC FROM THREE CENTURIES--CURWEN EDITION	LAMBERT--ED.
DANCE OF ANITRA, OP. 46 NO. 3	GRIEG
DANCE OF ANITRA, OP. 46 NO. 3	GRIEG
DANCE OF AN ANCIENT RITUAL	BOYDELL
DANCE OF AN OSTRACIZED IMP	CURZON, F.
DANCE OF AYSHE	KHATCHATURIAN
DANCE OF BEARS --BAERTANZ--	HEINS, C.
DANCE OF ELVES, OP. 12 NO. 4	GRIEG
DANCE OF HARRILD	GARCIA MORILLO
DANCE OF JULIE	TAYLOR, C.
DANCE OF PUCK FROM PRELUDES, BK. 1	DEBUSSY
DANCE OF SPAIN	IRVING, M.
DANCE OF THE ADOLESCENT	COPLAND
DANCE OF THE ATOMS	BENBOW
DANCE OF THE BRAVES	BEATON, C.
DANCE OF THE BROWNIES	KNIGHT
DANCE OF THE BUTTERFLIES	GREENWALD, M.
DANCE OF THE BUTTERFLIES	WISE
DANCE OF THE CANDY FAIRY--FROM NUTCRACKER SUITE	TSCHAIKOWSKY
DANCE OF THE CANDY FAIRY	TSCHAIKOWSKY
DANCE OF THE CANNIBALS	STEVENS, R.
DANCE OF THE CHINA DOLL	KING, S.
DANCE OF THE CHRISTMAS GOOSE	GIASSON, P.
DANCE OF THE CLOCKS	KING, S.
DANCE OF THE CLOWNS, OP. 26 NO. 1	EILENBERG
DANCE OF THE CLOWNS	ECKSTEIN
DANCE OF THE CRICKETS	ROLFE
DANCE OF THE DAFFOOILS	ADAIR, M.
DANCE OF THE DEBUTANTES, OP. 37 NO. 25	LEMOINE, H.
DANCE OF THE DEMON	HOLST
DANCE OF THE DEMON	ZUCCARO
DANCE OF THE DEWDROPS	LOUKA, M.
DANCE OF THE DEW DROPS	LOUKA, M.
DANCE OF THE DHASSIDIM	RAPHLING
DANCE OF THE DOLLS	REEG, G. A.
DANCE OF THE DOLLS	RICKER
DANCE OF THE DOLLS	SHOSTAKOVITCH
DANCE OF THE DORIAN YOUTH	HAUBIEL, C.
DANCE OF THE DUTCH DOLL	KING, S.
DANCE OF THE DWARFS	AARON, M.
DANCE OF THE DWARFS	AARON, M.
DANCE OF THE DWARFS	AARON, M.
DANCE OF THE ELVES, ONE PIANO - SIX HANDS	GRIEG
DANCE OF THE ELVES, OP. 3	SAPELLNIKOFF
DANCE OF THE FAIRIES	MEACHAM, C.
DANCE OF THE FAIRIES	TAKACS, J.
DANCE OF THE FAIRY QUEEN	BUGBEE, L. A.
DANCE OF THE FIREFLIES, OP. 21	PENNINGTON, S.
DANCE OF THE FLEAS	DUNGAN
DANCE OF THE FLOWERS	WHITFORD--ED.
DANCE OF THE GNOMES, OP. 95 NO. 3	WILLIAMS, F.
DANCE OF THE GNOMES	POLDINI, E.
DANCE OF THE GOBLINS	SMITH
DANCE OF THE GOLDENRODS	FITZPATRICK,
DANCE OF THE GYPSIES	CRERIE, E.
DANCE OF THE HOBGOBLINS	BENTLEY
DANCE OF THE HONEYBEES	RICHMOND
DANCE OF THE HONEYBEES	RICHMOND

DANCE OF THE HONEYBEES	RICHMOND
DANCE OF THE HOURS--BALLET FROM 'LA GIOCCONDA'	PONCHIELLI
DANCE OF THE HOURS, GIOCONDA	PONCHIELLI
DANCE OF THE HOURS - FROM THE OPERA 'LA GIOCANDA'	PONCHIELLI
DANCE OF THE HOURS	PONCHIELLI
DANCE OF THE KEWPIES	PANELLA, L.
DANCE OF THE LOCOMOTIVES, OP. 57	READ, G.
DANCE OF THE MARIONETTES	VOLKART, H.
DANCE OF THE MARTIANS	SKAGGS
DANCE OF THE MAYBELLS	SCHIEFELBEIN, F.
DANCE OF THE MEDICINE MAN	CHAGY
DANCE OF THE MIDGETS	GREENWALD, M.
DANCE OF THE MOON DWELLERS	ECKSTEIN
DANCE OF THE MOON FAIRIES	CROSBY, M.
DANCE OF THE MOON MEN	KOCH, F.
DANCE OF THE PANSIES	MARTIN, G.
DANCE OF THE PAPER DOLLS	MCSWEEN, F. W.
DANCE OF THE PINK PETALS	RICHARDSON, G.
DANCE OF THE PUPPETS	COOKE
DANCE OF THE PUPPETS	MARTIN
DANCE OF THE PUPPETS	MARTIN *
DANCE OF THE RADISHES	BURNAM
DANCE OF THE REED-FLUTES--FROM NUTCRACKER SUITE	TSCHAIKOWSKY
DANCE OF THE REED FLUTES IN D FROM NUTCRACKER SUITE	TSCHAIKOWSKY
DANCE OF THE ROBINS	DEPPEN
DANCE OF THE ROBINS	DEPPEN
DANCE OF THE ROSEBUDS	KEATS, F.
DANCE OF THE ROSEBUDS	KEATS, F.
DANCE OF THE ROSEBUDS	KEATS, F.
DANCE OF THE ROSE MAIDENS	KHATCHATURIAN
DANCE OF THE RUSSIAN SAILORS	GLIERE
DANCE OF THE RUSSIAN SAILORS	GLIERE
DANCE OF THE RUSSIAN SAILORS	GLIERE
DANCE OF THE SEA NYMPHS	PLATZMAN
DANCE OF THE SEVEN VEILS, FROM 'SALOME'	STRAUSS, R.
DANCE OF THE SEVEN VEILS, FROM 'SALOME'	STRAUSS, R.
DANCE OF THE SNOWFLAKES	LOUKA, M.
DANCE OF THE SNOWMAN	HART, G. R.
DANCE OF THE SPIRITS FROM 'ORPHEUS'	GLUCK
DANCE OF THE STARS	GODARD, C.
DANCE OF THE SUGAR PLUM FAIRY, E MINOR FROM NUTCRACKER	TSCHAIKOWSKY
DANCE OF THE SUGAR PLUM FAIRY -- FROM 'THE NUTCRACKER	TSCHAIKOWSKY
DANCE OF THE SUGAR PLUM FAIRY	TSCHAIKOWSKY
DANCE OF THE SUNBEAMS, OP. 34 NO. 8	CADMAN, C.
DANCE OF THE SWALLOWS	ADAMS, R. G.
DANCE OF THE TUMBLERS -- FROM ''THE SNOW MAIDEN'' --	RIMSKY-KORSAKOFF
DANCE OF THE WIND	CROCKER, D.
DANCE OF THE WOODEN SHOES	MACGREGOR
DANCE OF THE WOODEN SHOES	SCHULDT, M.
DANCE OF THE WOODSPRITES	SADLON
DANCE OF THE YOUNG KURDS	KHATCHATURIAN
DANCE ON THE GREEN	BOHM
DANCE ON THE LAWN	KULLAK, T.
DANCE ON THE LAWN	REED, H.
DANCE PANELS	COPLAND
DANCE PARTY FOR THE YOUNG	ALAIN, M.
DANCE PASTORALLE -- RONDINO	MCKAY, G.
DANCE PIECE FOR PIANO	LOPATNIKOFF
DANCE PRELUDES--NO. 1	HURST, G.
DANCE PRELUDES--NO. 2	HURST, G.
DANCE PRELUDES--NO. 3	HURST, G.
DANCE PRELUDES--NO. 4	HURST, G.
DANCE RHAPSODY, A	DELIUS, F.
DANCE RHYTHMS FOR PIANO	DEFILIPPI, A.
DANCE RHYTHMS	DE FILIPPI, A.
DANCE RUSSE --PETROUCHKA	STRAVINSKY, I.
DANCE RUSSE -- PETROUSHKA	STRAVINSKY, I.
DANCE RUSSE	STRAVINSKY, I.
DANCE SET NO. 1 AN AMERICAN BOURREE	GREEN, R.
DANCE SET NO. 2 AN AMERICAN PASTROAL	GREEN, R.
DANCE SET NO. 3 AN AMERICAN RIGAUDON	GREEN, R.
DANCE SKETCHES	HERRMANN
DANCE SOLILOQUY	KUBIK, G.
DANCE SONATA FOR TWO PIANOS	GREEN, R.
DANCE SONG	GRIFFES, C.
DANCE SUITE, OP. 23--1945	SCHISKE, K.
DANCE SUITE NO. 2	MCKAY, G.
DANCE SUITE OF SIX EASY PIECES	COCKSHOTT, G.
DANCE SUITE	BARTOK
DANCE SUITE	JOUBERT, J.
DANCE SUITE	KURKA, R.
DANCE THEME AND VARIATIONS	GREEN, R.
DANCE TOCCATA	AGAY, D.
DANCE TO THE CLASSICS	ROSMAN, M.
DANCE TUNE	POWERS, M.
DANCE VARIATIONS ON CHILDREN'S SONGS	POSER
DANCE POLONAISE	MARTIN, G.
DANCE	FIALA
DANCE	GODDEN, R.
DANCE	JAQUE, R.
DANCE	KABALEVSKY
DANCE	LORDANSKY
DANCE	TROIANI
DANCING -- 3 PIECES	BENNER, L.
DANCING ALONG	KARP
DANCING ANTIQUE	ENGLISH, G.
DANCING AT THE FAIR	KLEINMAN, A.
DANCING BEAR, THE	ERB
DANCING BELLS	DONENFELD, J.
DANCING BELLS	MARTIN
DANCING BONES	KOCH, E.
DANCING BURRO	GARROW, L.
DANCING BUTTERCUPS	HOPSON, B.
DANCING BUTTERFLY, A	BRUSSELS, I.
DANCING BY CANDLELIGHT	BENTLEY
DANCING CASTANETS	OGLE, L.
DANCING CHECKERS	LUDWIG
DANCING CHORDS	BURKE, F.
DANCING CLOCK	REEVES, R.
DANCING CRICKET	HOUSE, A.
DANCING DAFFODILS	REBE
DANCING DOLL, THE	POLDINI, E.
DANCING DOLL	POLDINI, E.
DANCING DOLL	POLDINI, E.
DANCING DOLL	POLDINI, E.
DANCING DOLL	STIEFEL, E.
DANCING DOLORES	BESTHOFF, M.
DANCING ELVES	MUNSON, C.
DANCING FAIRIES, ONE PIANO - SIX HANDS	MATTINGLY, J.
DANCING FINGERS	CERVENKA
DANCING GIRL, THE	HEINS, V.
DANCING GNOMES	WEISLEDER, A.
DANCING GRASSHOPPERS	SCHER, W.
DANCING IN A DREAM	MCKAY, G.
DANCING IN ISRAEL	BRODSKY, M.
DANCING IN THE MOONLIGHT	MANA-ZUCCA
DANCING IN THE WIND	DITTENHAVER
DANCING KEYBOARD, THE	AGAY, D.--ED
DANCING LEAVES	AGAY, D.
DANCING LEAVES	GOBBAERTS
DANCING LEAVES	PAYTON, P.
DANCING LEPRECHAUNS	STAIRS, L.
DANCING LESSON, THE	ROLSETH, B.
DANCING LESSON	LAMBERT, C.
DANCING LETTERS TO LEDA	VAN HULSE, C.
DANCING MAGPIE	ETTORE, E.
DANCING MOSQUITOES	SCHER, W.
DANCING NORTH WIND, THE	SCHER, W.
DANCING ON A CLOUD	MARTIN, H.
DANCING ON SKATES	DUNGAN
DANCING ON THE DYKE	ERB
DANCING ON THE TIGHTROPE	BECK
DANCING PUPPETS, FOR ONE PIANO, SIX HANDS	SCHER, W.
DANCING PUPPETS	SCHER, W.
DANCING PUPPETS	SCHER, W.
DANCING RAINDROPS	REBE
DANCING RAINDROPS	RODGERS, I.
DANCING SCARECROW	SCHER, W.
DANCING SENORITAS	SCHER, W.
DANCING SHADOWS	REISER, V.
DANCING SNOWFLAKES	REISER, V.
DANCING SNOWMAN	WERMEL
DANCING SPIDERS	SCHER, W.
DANCING SPIRITS	BOHM
DANCING STRINGS	WHITFORD
DANCING SUNBEAMS	CROCKER, D.
DANCING SUNBEAMS	FICHANDLER, W.
DANCING SUNBEAMS	HOLT, ERNEST
DANCING SUNBEAMS	JESTON, I. H.
DANCING THE MENUET FROM CHOPIN'S PRELUDE, OP. 28	ROLFE, W.
DANCING WATERS	TRUXELL, E.
DANCING WAVELETS	AARON
DANCING WITH THE BREEZE	OGLE, L.
DANCING	FULEIHAN, A.
DANDELION MARCH	CRERIE, E.
DANDY-LION, THE	BAUER
DANDY CANDY	PELZ
DANISH DANCER, THE	MARTIN, H.
DANISH PASTRY	STEINER
DANNY'S DOZEN--PIECES FOR YOUNG PEOPLE	ROTHCHILD, F.
DANNY BOY	BURNAM--ED
DANSAS BRASILEIRAS	SANTORO, C.
DANSA BRASILEIRA	GUARNIERI
DANSA BRASILEIRA	ROWLAND
DANSA BRASILIERA	GUARNIERI
DANSA NEGRA	GUARNIERI
DANSA NEGRA	GUARNIERI
DANSES, MARCHES ET CORTEGES POPULAIRES DU PAYS BASQUE	BORDES
DANSES ANCIENNES	LANJEAN, M.
DANSES ANDALOUSES - 1. RITMO	INFANTE
DANSES ANDALOUSES - 2. SENTIMIENTO	INFANTE
DANSES ANDALOUSES - 3. GRACIA	INFANTE
DANSES BRETONNES, BK. 1	CANTELOUBE
DANSES ET CONTREDANSES - BK. 1	MOTTU
DANSES ET CONTREDANSES - BK. 3	MOTTU
DANSES ET CONTREDANSES - BK. 4	MOTTU
DANSES ET CONTREDNASES - BK. 2	MOTTU
DANSES GITANES, BK. 1 - SACRO-MONTE	TURINA, J.
DANSES GITANES, BK. 1 - ZAMBRA, DANZA RITUAL,	TURINA, J.
DANSES GITANES, BK. 2 - FIESTA DE LA CALDERAS,	TURINA, J.
DANSES GOTHIQUES	SATIE, E.
DANSES GROTESQUES	MATICIC
DANSES POPULAIRES TURQUES	MANAS
DANSES ROUMAINES	LIPATTI, D.
DANSES	DEBUSSY
DANSES 1. DANSE SACREE, 2. DANSE PROFANE	DEBUSSY
DANSEUSES DE PELPHES	DEBUSSY
DANSEZ, FILLETTES	ROUGNON
DANSE - SACRE ET PROFANE	DEBUSSY
DANSE BIZARRE, OP. 107 NO. 2	FONTAINE, L. J.
DANSE BOHEMIENNE	DEBUSSY
DANSE DES AUTOMATES	KOSMA, J.
DANSE DES ELFES, OP. 18	REISSIGER
DANSE DES FEES, POLKA	JAELL
DANSE DES MILLIARDS	SCHMITT
DANSE DES TREILLES	SEVERAC
DANSE DE DIABLES	BEAUCAMP
DANSE DE LA POUPEE FROM LA BOITE A JOUJOUX	DEBUSSY
DANSE DE NEGRILLONS -- ''LA PANTOUFLE DE VAIR''	DELANNOY
DANSE DE TROIS ARLEQUINS	FRANCAIX, J.
DANSE ECOSSAISE	BAKER, F. T.
DANSE EN FAMILLE -- 20 SHORT AND VERY EASY DANCES --	POURNY
DANSE EN MI FLAT MINEUR	TCHEREPNIN
DANSE FLORENTINE	LACK, J.
DANSE HONGROISE	DUVAL, P.
DANSE HUMORISTIQUE	LEVY, E.
DANSE INFERNALE--FIREBIRD	STRAVINSKY, I.
DANSE KURDE, OP. 52	KOUGELL, A.
DANSE MACABRE, FOR 2 PIANOS 8 HANDS	SAINT-SAENS
DANSE MACABRE, OP. 40	SAINT-SAENS
DANSE MACABRE, OP. 40	SAINT-SAENS
DANSE MACABRE, OP. 40	SAINT-SAENS
DANSE MACABRE	SAINT-SAENS
DANSE MACABRE	SAINT-SAENS
DANSE MACABRE	SAINT-SAENS
DANSE MACABRE	SAINT-SAENS
DANSE MODERNE, OP. 9 NO. 1	DENNEE
DANSE NEGRE, OP. 58 NO. 5	SCOTT, C.
DANSE ORIENTALE, OP. 74 NO. 1	SCOTT, C.
DANSE POLONAISE, MAZURKA	MARTIN, G.
DANSE POUR PIERROT	MERIGOT, F.
DANSE RITUELLE DU SABBATH	SAMINSKY
DANSE RUSSE, OP. 40 NO. 10	TSCHAIKOWSKY
DANSE RUSSE TREPAK, OP. 71	TSCHAIKOWSKY
DANSE RUSSE	SCHER, W.
DANSE RUSSE	STRAVINSKY, I.
DANSE SACREE	BLOCH, E.
DANSE	DEBUSSY
DANSE	DEBUSSY
DANSE	DEBUSSY
DANSE	DEBUSSY
DANSE	MANEN, C.
DANS L'ILLE DE PINANG	DE BOURGUIGNON
DANS L'OMBRE DE LA MONTAGNE -- PAYSAGE	ROPARTZ
DANS L'OMBRE DE LA MONTAGNE -- QUAND LA LUMIERE S'EN	ROPARTZ
DANS L'OMBRE DE LA MONTAGNE -- RONDE	ROPARTZ
DANS L'OMBRE DE LA MONTAGNE -- SUR LA ROUTE	ROPARTZ
DANS L'OMBRE DE LA MONTAGNE -- VIEILLE EGLISE	ROPARTZ
DANS L'OMBRE DE LA MONTAGNE	ROPARTZ
DANS LA CLAIRE NUIT	NIVERD, L.
DANS LA FORET - L'ECHO	STRIMER
DANS LA FORET - LA ROSEE	STRIMER
DANS LA FORET - PETITE FLEUR SOLITAIRE	STRIMER

DANS LA FORET - RONDE NOCTURNE	STRIMER
DANS LA FORET - SOIR PAISIBLE	STRIMER
DANS LA FORET	STRIMER
DANS LA NUIT -- FROM SILLAGES	AUBERT
DANS LA RUE - AU MANEGE	STRIMER
DANS LA RUE - AU SON DU MOTEUR	STRIMER
DANS LA RUE - CATHERINETTE	STRIMER
DANS LA RUE - ORGUE DE BARBARIE	STRIMER
DANS LA RUE - SUR LE BANC D'UN PETIT SQUARE	STRIMER
DANS LA RUE	STRIMER
DANS LE BOIS	HITZ, F.
DANS LE SOMBRE NUIT	NIVERD, L.
DANS MON PAYS, OP. 16	MILOIEVITCH
DANUBE BOOGIE	STEINER
DANUBE WAVES, WALTZES	IVANOVICI, J.
DANZA, LA	ROSSINI, G.
DANZA, LA	ROSSINI, G.
DANZA, LA	ROSSINI, G.
DANZA, LA	ROSSINI, G.
DANZA, LA	ROSSINI, G. *
DANZA, LA	ROSSINI *
DANZAS AFRO CUBANAS	LECUONA
DANZAS ARGENTINAS	GINASTERA
DANZAS CASTELLANAS	COLLET
DANZAS CUBANAS	LECUONA
DANZAS DE LAS NUSTAS	MILICI
DANZAS ESPANOLAS, OP. 37	GRANADOS
DANZAS ESPANOLAS, VOL. 1	GRANADOS
DANZAS ESPANOLAS, VOL. 2	GRANADOS
DANZAS ESPANOLAS, VOL. 3	GRANADOS
DANZAS ESPANOLAS, VOL. 4	GRANADOS
DANZAS ET MELODIES ANCIENNES, BK. 1	
DANZAS ET MELODIES ANCIENNES, BK. 2	
DANZAS FANTASTICAS, OP. 22--NO. 1, EXALTACION	TURINA, J.
DANZAS FANTASTICAS, OP. 22--NO. 2, ENSUENO	TURINA, J.
DANZAS FANTASTICAS, OP. 22--NO. 3, ORGIA	TURINA, J.
DANZA CAPRICHO	LUZZATTI
DANZA CRIOLLA, OP. 1	TERZIAN, A.
DANZA CRIOLLA	SICILIANI
DANZA CRIOLLA	TOSAR, H.
DANZA DELLE BAMBOLE	PRIANO
DANZA DEL BURATINO E DELLA BAMBOLA, LA	RECLI
DANZA DEL COMBATE	VALCARCEL, T.
DANZA DEL CUERVO	GOMEZ CARRILLO
DANZA DEL DESTINO	GOMBAU
DANZA DEL GURI	SICILIANI
DANZA DE JALISCO	COPLAND
DANZA DE LAS BAILARINAS CORTESANAS - FROM 'APURIMAC',	NAPOLITANO
DANZA DE LA CAPA ROJA	GUARINO, C.
DANZA DE LA CHINA QUERENDONA	LASALA
DANZA DE LOS 'LAIKAS'	IGLESIAS VILLOUD
DANZA DE NEGROS	LIMA *
DANZA DI GALATEA	VENTICINQUE
DANZA ESOTICA	MASCAGNI, P.
DANZA ESPANA	NAGY, M.
DANZA EXOTICA	LEY, S.
DANZA E CANZONE A BALLO	DEL CORONA
DANZA FESTIVA, OP. 38, NO. 3	MEDTNER, N.
DANZA IRISTE	GRANADOS
DANZA LENTA	FRANCK, C.
DANZA LENTA	GRANADOS
DANZA LUCUMI	LECUONA
DANZA LUCUMI	LECUONA
DANZA LUCUMI	LECUONA
DANZA MATTUTINA	SALVATORI
DANZA NEGRA	LECUONA
DANZA NORVEGESE, OP. 35, NO. 2	GRIEG
DANZA SANTIAGUENA	GOMEZ CARRILLO
DANZA SLAVA, OP. 72, NO. 2	DVORAK
DANZA SPAGNOLA	PALOMBI
DANZA UNGHERESA NO. 5	BRAHMS
DANZA VOTIVA	CIMATTI
DANZA	CARPENTER, J.
DANZA	GARCIA ACEVEDO
DANZETTA	BRANT
DANZE DEL RE DAVID, LE	CASTELNUOVO-TEDE
DANZON CUBANO	COPLAND
DANZON CUBANO	COPLAND
DANZON	LOPEZ BUCHARDO
DANZON	RAPHLING
DAPHNIS AND CHLOE	RAVEL
DAPHNIS ET CHLOE	RAVEL
DAPHNIS ET CHLOE	RAVEL
DAPHNIS ET CHLOE	RAVEL
DAPPLE GRAY	REBE
DARDANUS -- AIRS DE BALLET, SUITE 1	RAMEAU
DARDANUS -- AIRS DE BALLET, SUITE 2	RAMEAU
DAREDEVIL	COULTHARD
DARING COSSACK	NOONA, W.
DARING PRINCE AND 9 OTHER PIECES, THE	DILLER, A.
DARKIE'S DREAM, THE	LANSING
DARKTOWN STRUTTERS' BALL	LANE, J.--ED.
DARK EYES	BENDA, R.
DARK EYES	GROOMS--ED
DARK EYES	KRENZ, B.
DARK EYES	MEDINA--ED.
DARK EYES	PEERY, R. R.
DARK NIGHT	LIND, L. S.
DARK RIDERS, THE	FAITH
DARK RIVER AND DISTANT BELL. HARPSICHORD	HOVHANESS, A.
DARN THAT DREAM	VAN HEUSEN, J.
DARTING IN AND OUT, POLKA	ARMOUR
DASHING ALONG	KARP
DAS AMRUMER TAGEBUCH, OP. 30	JARNACH, P.
DAS BUCH DER MOTIVE UND THEMEN AUS SAMTLICHEN OPERN	WAGNER
DAS BUCH DER MOTIVE UND THEMEN AUS SAMTLICHEN OPERN	WAGNER
DAS ERSTE KLAVIERBUCH, HEFT 1 - DER QUINTRAUM	ROEHR *
DAS ERSTE KLAVIERBUCH, HEFT 1 - DER QUINTRAUM	ROEHR *
DAS ERSTE KLAVIERBUCH, HEFT 2 - DER DUR-BEREICH	ROEHR *
DAS ERSTE KLAVIERBUCH, HEFT 2 - DER DUR-BEREICH	ROEHR *
DAS ERSTE KLAVIERBUCH, HEFT 3 - DER MOLL-BEREICH	ROEHR *
DAS ERSTE KLAVIERBUCH, HEFT 3 - DER MOLL-BEREICH	ROEHR
DAS ERSTE KLAVIERBUCH - METHODISCHER LEITFADEN	ROEHR *
DAS ERSTE WORT, OP. 11	BACEVICIUS
DAS FROHE RHEINLIEDER-BUCH, BAND 01	
DAS FROHE RHEINLIEDER-BUCH, BAND 02	
DAS GOLDENE MARSCH-BUCH, BAND 01	
DAS GOLDENE MARSCH-BUCH, BAND 02	
DAS GORLITZER TABULATURBUCH. 100 VIERSTIMMIGE CHORALE	SCHEIDT
DAS GROSSVATERBUCH OP. 119	GRETCHANINOFF
DAS KINDERBUCH OP. 98	GRETCHANINOFF
DAS KLASSIKER-BUCH, BAND 01	REHBERG--ED.
DAS KLASSIKER-BUCH, BAND 02	REHBERG--ED.
DAS KLASSIKERBUCH, KOMPLETT IN LEINEN GEBUNDEN	REHBERG--ED.
DAS KLINGENDE BUCH, BAND 1	
DAS KLINGENDE BUCH, BAND 2	
DAS KLINGENDE BUCH, BAND 3	
DAS LIEBSTE LIED, BAND 01	
DAS LIEBSTE LIED, BAND 02	
DAS NEUE KINDERLIEDERBUCH, AUSWAHL FUR KLAVIER ZU VIER	SCHUNGELER,
DAS NEUE KINDERLIEDERBUCH	SCHUNGELER,
DAS NEUE KINDERLIEDERBUCH	SCHUNGELER,
DAS NEUE KINDERLIEDERBUCH	SCHUNGELER, H.
DAS NEUE KLAVIERBUCH, BAND 1	
DAS NEUE KLAVIERBUCH, BAND 2	
DAS NEUE OPERETTEN-BUCH, BAND 01	
DAS NEUE OPERETTEN-BUCH, BAND 02	
DAS NEUE OPERETTEN-BUCH, BAND 03	
DAS NEUE OPERETTEN-BUCH, BAND 04	
DAS NEUE OPERETTEN-BUCH, BAND 05	
DAS NEUE VOLKSLIEDERBUCH	SCHUNGELER, H.
DAS NEUE VOLKSLIEDERBUCH	SCHUNGELER, H.
DAS NEUE WEG. AUSGEWAHLTE ETUDEN UND STUDIEN, HEFT 03	SCHUNGELER, H.
DAVENPORT BLUES	BEIDERBECKE, B.
DAVIDSBUENDLERTAENZE, OP. 6	SCHUMANN, R.
DAVIDSBUENDLERTAENZE, OP. 6	SCHUMANN, R.
DAVIDSBUENDLER DANCES, OP. 6	SCHUMANN, R.
DAVIDSBUNDLER, OP. 6	SCHUMANN, R.
DAVID -- BALLET --	SAUGUET
DAVID HIRSCHBERG PIANO COURSE	HIRSCHBERG,
DAWN IN NORMANDY	RIBERT, J.
DAWN MISTS	HAUBIEL, C.
DAWN OF A SPRING	KEAN, H.
DAWN ON LOTUS LAKE	KING, S.
DAY'S END	READ, G.
DAYBREAK	WHITFORD
DAYS OF WINE AND ROSES	MANCINI
DAYS OF WINE AND ROSES	MANCINI
DAYS OF WINE AND ROSES	MANCINI *
DAY AT THE BEACH, A	BENTLEY
DAY BY DAY	BRADLEY,
DAY BY DAY	SCHWARTZ, S.
DAY DREAMING	BRODSKY, M.
DAY DREAMS	CURCIO
DAY DREAMS	GILLOCK
DAY DREAMS	MILLER, S.
DAY DREAMS	PORTER
DAY DREAMS	RASBACH, O.
DAY DREAMS	RASBACH, O.
DAY DREAMS	ROBINSON, A.
DAY IN-DAY OUT	DUMM
DAY IN SPRING	EZELL, H.
DAY IN THE COUNTRY, A	RUBINSTEIN
DAY IN THE JUNGLE, A	GEORGE
DAY IN THE LIFE OF A FOOL, A	LANE, J.--ED.
DAY IN THE LIFE OF A FOOL, A	WILLIAMS,
DAY IN THE PETERBOROUGH WOODS, A--BOBOLINK	HIER, E.
DAY IN THE PETERBOROUGH WOODS, A--SUNSET AT HILLCREST	HIER, E.
DAY IN THE PETERBOROUGH WOODS, A--WHIPPOORWILL, THE	HIER, E.
DAY IN THE PETERBOROUGH WOODS, A--WOOD-THRUSH, THE	HIER, E.
DAY IN VENICE, A --VENEZIA--	NEVIN
DAY IN VENICE, A --VENEZIA--	NEVIN
DAY IN VENICE --SUITE--	NEVIN
DAY IS DONE	YARROW
DAY OF JUBILO	MOSSMAN, T.
DAY WITH GRANDMA, A	SCHER, W.
DAY WITH PETER AND PENNY	LAST, J.
DEARLY BELOVED -- SHOWCASE	
DEAR HEART	
DEAR HEART	
DEAR SANTA	JOYNER, B.
DEAR WORLD	BRIMHALL
DEATH AND TRANSFIGURATION, OP. 24. SYMPHONIC POEM	STRAUSS, R.
DEATH AND TRANSFIGURATION, OP. 24. TWO PIANOS, EIGHT	STRAUSS, R.
DEATH AND TRANSFIGURATION, OP. 24	STRAUSS, R.
DEATH OF ASE --PEER GYNT SUITE NO.1--	GRIEG
DEATH RAY BOOGIE	JOHNSON, S. *
DEATH RAY BOOGIE	JOHNSON, S. *
DEA MORTA DELL'ACROPOLI, UNA	PARMICIANO
DEBATE	BALOGH
DEBUSSY AND RAVEL	DEBUSSY *
DEBUSSY MASTERPIECES	DEBUSSY
DEBUSSY	DEBUSSY
DEBUTANTE	ECKSTEIN
DEBUTANTE	VAN HULSE, C.
DEBUT DU PIANO, LE	ZILCHER
DEBUT	THOMPSON, J.--ED
DEDICATIONS	MASETTI
DEDICATION	SCHUMANN, R. *
DEDICATION	SCHUMANN, R. *
DEEP BLUE --MODERN RHYTHMIC CLASSICS--	WHITFORD
DEEP GORGE, A	BURNAM
DEEP IN THE HEART OF TEXAS	SWANDER, D.
DEEP PURPLE SONG BOOK	
DEEP PURPLE	DE ROSE, P.
DEEP PURPLE	LANE, J.--ED.
DEEP PURPLE	WILLIAMS,
DEEP PURPLE	
DEEP PURPLE	
DEEP PURPLE	
DEEP RHYTHM, BOOGIE-WOOGIE	STANLEY
DEEP RIVER, TRANS.	GROOMS--ED
DEEP RIVER	KELBERENE--ED
DEEP RIVER	MOSSMAN, T.
DEEP RIVER	REISFELD--ED
DEEP RIVER	ROLFE, W.--ED
DEER IN THE CLEARING	RAGANINI, A.
DEFINITE PURPOSE STUDIES, BK. 1 - PRELIMINARY	BRADLEY
DEFINITE PURPOSE STUDIES, BK. 2 - PRIMARY	BRADLEY
DEFINITE PURPOSE STUDIES, BK. 3 - ELEMENTARY	BRADLEY
DELFT DANCES	KOREVAAR
DELICIAS DEL CAMPO--SUITE	SERRA, M.
DELILAH	LANE, J.--ED.
DELILAH	LANE, J.--ED.
DELILAH	FAHNESTOCK
DELTA, THE	BRIMHALL,
DELUXE WALT DISNEY SONGBOOK	BLACHER
DEMETER -- 1963 -- BALLET IN 4 SCENES	GREENWALD, M.
DEMETRIUS, MARCH	LANGE, G.
DEM EIGEN -- THINE OWN	NAZARETH, E.
DENGOZA--BRAZILIAN MAXIXE-TANGO	STREABBOG
DEPARTURE, OP. 100, NO. 7	SAINTON
DEPARTURE OF THE PEQUOD, THE	FAY, AMY
DEPPE FINGER EXERCISES FOR RAPIDLY DEVELOPING AN	CHARPENTIER, G.
DEPUIS LE JOUR	DESSAUX
DERBY, LE -- GALOP --	DESSAUX
DERBY, LE	VARGUES
DERNIERE GAVOTTE, LA	MASSENET, J.
DERNIER SOMMEIL DE LA VIERGE, LE	GURLITT
DER ANFANGER OP. 211	GURLITT
DER ERSTE VORTRAG OP. 210	STRAVINSKY, I.
DER ERSTE -- BERCEUSE	STRAVINSKY, I.
DER FEUERVOGEL -- BERCEUSE	STRAVINSKY, I.
DER FEUERVOGEL -- DANSE INFERNALE, BERCEUSE ET FINALE	STRAVINSKY, I.
DER FEUERVOGEL -- RONDE DES PRINCESSES	STRAVINSKY, I.
DER FREISCHUTZ, FANTASIE	WEBER, VON

DER FREIZCHUTZ, TRANS. WEBER, VON
DER GROSSE PISCHNA, 60 PROGRESSIVE TECHNISCHE UBUNGEN PISCHNA *
DER GUTE FREUND. LEICHTE VOLKS-TANZ- UND OPERNMELODIEN LUTTGERS--ED
DER JUNGE MOZART, 19 ORIGINAL-STUCKE DES 6- UND 8 MOZART, W. A.
DER LANGSAME WALZER
DER LINDENBAUM SCHUBERT
DER NEUE GRADUS AD PARNASSUM, BK. 1 CLEMENTI
DER NEUE GRADUS AD PARNASSUM, BK. 2 CLEMENTI
DER NEUE GRADUS AD PARNASSUM VON CLEMENTI NEBST SCHUNGELER, H.
DER NEUE GRADUS AD PARNASSUM VON CLEMENTI NEBST SCHUNGELER, H.
DER NEUE GURLITT, 64 LEICHTE STUCKE -- BK. 1 GURLITT
DER NEUE GURLITT, 64 LEICHTE STUCKE -- BK. 2 GURLITT
DER NEUE WEG. AUSGEWAHLTE ETUDEN UND STUDIEN, HEFT 01 SCHUNGELER, H.
DER NEUE WEG. AUSGEWAHLTE ETUDEN UND STUDIEN, HEFT 02 SCHUNGELER, H.
DER PRAKTISCHE CZERNY, STUDIEN UND ETUDEN AUS DEM GES. MAYER *
DER PRAKTISCHE CZERNY, STUDIEN UND ETUDEN AUS DEM GES. MAYER *
DER PRAKTISCHE CZERNY, STUDIEN UND ETUDEN AUS DEM GES. MAYER *
DER PRAKTISCHE CZERNY, STUDIEN UND ETUDEN AUS DEM GES. MAYER *
DER SPIELGARTEN VOLKART-SCHLAGER
DER TAG DES KINDES OP. 109 GRETCHANINOFF
DER TONKREIS - HEFT 01, RUNDHERUM VOLKART-SCHLAGER
DER TONKREIS - HEFT 02, EIN TAGESLAUF VOLKART-SCHLAGER
DER TONKREIS HASSLER, J.
DER WIMPEL, FAHRTENLIEDER LUTZ--ED
DER WUNDERGARTEN REIN--ED *
DER ZUPFGEIGENHANSL SALZMANN--ED
DESAFINADO HENDRICKS *
DESCANSADO CLARE, A.
DESCRIPTIONS AUTOMATIQUES--1913 SATIE, E.
DESDE LA REJA HUGUET Y TAGELL
DESDE MI TERRAZA, OP. 104 TURINA, J.
DESEO, OP. 40 -- CONCERT ETUDE ALBENIZ, I.
DESERTED BALLROOM GOULD, M.
DESERTED ISLE, A SCHER, W.
DESERT CARAVAN, THE BRUSSELS, I.
DESERT DANCE KLEMM, E.
DESERT DANCE SCHER, W.
DESERT DRUMS KELLEY, R.
DESERT SANDS FERRELL, B.
DESERT SAND GLOVER, D.
DESERT SCENE CHAGY
DESERT SONG, THE ROMBERG, S.
DESERT SONG ROMBERG, S.
DESERT SUNSET THOMPSON, J.
DESIDERIO, IL CRAMER, J.
DESIRE WHITFORD
DESSINS COMMENTES --7 PIECES-- KELEMEN
DESTRY RIDES AGAIN
DES ABENDS, OP. 12 NO. 1--FANTASIESTUCKE SCHUMANN, R.
DES PAS SUR LA NEIGE FROM PRELUDES, BK. 1 DEBUSSY
DEUTSCHE REIGEN UND ROMANZEN OP. 51 HAAS
DEUTSCHE TANZE OP. 10 NO. 7 UND 17, ST.-V.S. 14/17 REGER
DEUTSCHE TANZE OP. 33 SCHUBERT
DEUTSCHE TANZE OP. 4 WEBER, VON
DEUTSCHLAND-LIED HAYON--ED.
DEUTSCHLAND-LIED HAYON
DEUTSCHMEISTER REGIMENTS-MARSCH JUREK, W. A.
DEUXIEME CONCERTO, EDITION A SAINT-SAENS
DEUXIEME CONCERTO, EDITION B SAINT-SAENS
DEUXIEME CONCERTO DAMASE, J. M.
DEUXIEME MAZURKA IN B FLAT, OP. 54 GODARD, B.
DEUXIEME SONATE POUR PIANO JOLIVET, A.
DEUXIEME SONATE POUR PIANO MIHALOVICI
DEUXIEME SYMPHONIE INDY, V. D'
DEUXIEME VALSE BRILLANTE IN B FLAT, OP. 56 GODARD, B.
DEUX AIRS A DANSER, NO.1 WURMSER, L.
DEUX AIRS A DANSER, NO.2 WURMSER, L.
DEUX ALOUETTES - TWO LARKS LESCHETIZKY
DEUX ARABESQUES, NO.1 DEBUSSY
DEUX ARABESQUES, NO.2 DEBUSSY
DEUX ARABESQUES COMPLETE DEBUSSY
DEUX ARABESQUES DEBUSSY
DEUX CROQUIS - 1. POUR LA MAIN GAUCHE 2. TOCCATA STALLAERT, A.
DEUX ESQUISSES HONEGGER, A.
DEUX ETUDES,NO.1, BROUILLAGE PETIT, P.
DEUX ETUDES,NO.2 MOULIN A CAFE PETIT, P.
DEUX ETUDES DE CONCERT EN OCTAVES -- D'APRES LES AISBERG, D. S.
DEUX GROTESQUES, OP. 20 BACEVICIUS
DEUX HOMMAGES EN FORME D'ETUDE ORTHEL
DEUX IMAGES BARTOK
DEUX PIECES - AIR BRETON FAVRE
DEUX PIECES - VALSE MELANCOLIQUE FAVRE
DEUX PIECES FACILES BOZZA
DEUX PIECES HEBRAIQUES--1956 TANSMAN, A.
DEUX PIECES ORIGINALES -- 1. SOUS LE BRILLANT SOLEIL PESSE
DEUX PIECES ORIGINALES -- 2. MARCHE TRIOMPHALE, FOR 2 PESSE
DEUX PIECES POUR CLAVECIN--FACSIMILE-- SUTER
DEUX PIECES DIET
DEUX PIECES JONGEN, J.
DEUX PIECES LAPEYRE, T.
DEUX PIECES MAILLARD
DEUX PRELUDES MIRANDOLLE
DEVELOPING TECHNIC AND MUSICIANSHIP ZEPP
DEVELOPMENT OF VELOCITY, OP. 40, BK. 1--SCALES ROGERS, J.
DEVELOPMENT OF VELOCITY, OP. 40, BK. 2--ARPEGGIOS ROGERS, J.
DEVILISH INSPIRATION, OP. 4 NO. 4 PROKOFIEFF
DEVOTIONAL MUSIC STEINER
DEVOTION KETELBEY, A.
DEW DROPS FICHANDLER, W.
DEW DROP STONE, E.
DEW ON THE ROSE, THE EWING, M.
DEXTER BLUES MCSHANN
DE CAMPTOWN RACES FOSTER
DE MI TIERRA, SUITE NO. 1 UGARTE
DE MI TIERRA, SUITE NO. 2 UGARTE
DE ROMERIA. DANZA LEONESA FERNANDEZ, E. *
DE SANTIS ALBUMS - FOR LITTLE PIANISTS, BK. 1 DE SANTIS
DE SANTIS ALBUMS - FOR LITTLE PIANISTS, BK. 2 DE SANTIS
DE TOUTES PETITES PIECES HAZART
DE TULPENFEEST KARST
DIABELLI MARCH DIABELLI
DIABELLI SCHERZO DIABELLI
DIABELLI VARIATIONS, OP. 120 BEETHOVEN
DIABELLI VARIATIONS BEETHOVEN
DIABOLIQUE, LA, ETUDE LEYBACH, I.
DIALOGE LOPATNIKOFF
DIALOGHI NO. 1 - 'CON MANUEL DE FALLA' MALIPIERO, G. F.
DIALOGHI NO. 2 - 'BETWEEN TWO PIANOS' MALIPIERO, G. F.
DIALOGHI NO. 3 - 'CON JACOPONE DA TODI' -- FOR VOICE MALIPIERO, G. F.
DIALOGUES. 4 PIECES FERTE
DIALOGUES MOMPOU, F.
DIALOGUE -- 1965 URBANNER, E.
DIALOGUE AND DANCE OF THE HEAVYWEIGHT AND DWARF BLOCH, E.
DIALOGUE ET SERENITE NOEL, P. *
DIAMONDS ARE A GIRL'S BEST FRIEND
DIAMONDS ARE FOREVER LANE, J.--ED.

DIAMONDS SIMON
DIANA -- FOR TWO PIANOS, EIGHT HANDS HOLST
DIANA -- GRAND VALSE DE CONCERT HOLST
DIANA HOLST
DIANE LANE, J.--ED.
DIANE POLLACK *
DIARY OF A CHILD LECUONA
DIARY BRADLEY,
DICHTER UND BAUER, EASY SUPPE, F.
DICITENCELLO VUIE
DIDDLE OF DUM TOWNSEND
DIDN'T WE BRIMHALL,
DIECI BAGATELLE CORRADINI
DIES MELODIAS VASCAS GURIDI
DIEU VAINQUEUR -- FINAL FUGUE -- HAUDEBERT
DIE BOSNIAKEN KOMMEN -- MARCH WAGNES, F.
DIE ERSTEN SCHRITTE DES JUGEND KLAVIERSPIELERS OP. 82 GURLITT
DIE ERSTE ZEIT AM KLAVIER, OP. 50 ZILCHER
DIE FORELLE--THE TROUT SCHUBERT
DIE FORELLE SCHUBERT
DIE GROSSE OPER, BAND 01 LUTZ--ED
DIE GROSSE OPER, BAND 02 LUTZ--ED
DIE JAHRESZEITEN OP. 37 --DEZEMBER--WEIHNACHTEN TSCHAIKOWSKY
DIE JAHRESZEITEN OP. 37 -- APRIL--SCHNEEGLOCKCHEN TSCHAIKOWSKY
DIE JAHRESZEITEN OP. 37 -- JUNI--BARCAROLE TSCHAIKOWSKY
DIE JAHRESZEITEN OP. 37 -- NOVEMBER--TROIKA TSCHAIKOWSKY
DIE JAHRESZEITEN OP. 37 -- OKTOBER--HERBSTLIED TSCHAIKOWSKY
DIE JUGEND TANZT KRENTZLIN,
DIE JUGEND TANZT KRENTZLIN,
DIE KLASSIKER UND IHRE ZEITGENOSSEN BEETHOVEN *
DIE LEICHTESTEN GELAUFIGKEITSETUDEN OP. 83 - BK. 2 GURLITT
DIE LORELEI SCHUBERT ‹
DIE MOLDAU SMETANA
DIE MUHLE OP. 17 NO. 3 JENSEN, A.
DIE NACHT, ROMANZE OP. 44 NO. 1 RUBINSTEIN
DIE OPER IM HEIM, BAND 1
DIE OPER IM HEIM, BAND 2
DIE PASSION IN 9 INVENTIONEN, OP. 25 REUTTER, H.
DIE SECHS SAMMLUNGEN VON SONATEN, FREIEN FANTASIEN AND BACH, C.P.E.
DIE SECHS SAMMLUNGEN VON SONATEN, FREIEN FANTASIEN UND BACH, C.P.E.
DIE SECHS SAMMLUNGEN VON SONATEN, FREIEN FANTASIEN UND BACH, C.P.E.
DIE SECHS SAMMLUNGEN VON SONATEN, FREIEN FANTASIEN UND BACH, C.P.E.
DIE SECHS SAMMLUNGEN VON SONATEN, FREIEN FANTASIEN UND BACH, C.P.E.
DIE SECHS SAMMLUNGEN VON SONATEN, FREIEN FANTASIEN UND BACH, C.P.E.
DIE SOHNE BACH -- ORIGINAL-KLAVIER-WERKE DER 4 SOHNE REHBERG--ED.
DIE VERDI-OPER VERDI
DIE WIENER SONATINEN MOZART, W. A.
DIFFICULT DECISION CHENEY, T,
DIGEST OF PIANO PIECES FOR LEFT HAND ALONE FOX
DIGEST OF SHORT PIANO WORKS, A HAYDN
DIGGING IN YUCCA FLAT STORR, S.
DILL-PICKLES JOHNSON, C.
DILLER-PAGE CAROL BOOK, THE DILLER, A. *
DILLER-PAGE CAROL BOOK= 38E DILLER, A. *
DILLER-PAGE SONG-BOOKS, THE, VOL. 1 DILLER, A. *
DILLER-PAGE SONG-BOOKS, THE, VOL. 2 DILLER, A. *
DING DONG BELL STAIRS, L.
DINOSAURS ROGERS, E.
DINOSAUR DITTIES SCHAUM, J.
DIPTYQUE MEDITERRANEEN D'INDY, V.
DIP IN THE POOL, A MANA-ZUCCA
DIRGE, OP. 26 -- 12-HANDS, SET POWELL, B.
DIRGE PENTLAND, B.
DIRGE TOLLEFSEN, A.
DIS-CONCERTO PRESS
DISAPPOINTED SERENADER, THE BRAHMS
DISCOVERIES AT THE PIANO, BK. 1 PAPORISZ, Y.
DISCOVERIES AT THE PIANO, BK. 2 PAPORISZ, Y.
DISCOVERIES AT THE PIANO, BK. 3 PAPORISZ, Y.
DISNEY CLASSICS RICHTER--ED
DISNEY SHOWCASE KAHN, M.--ED *
DISTANT BELLS AT EVENING HOLT, EILSEL
DISTANT BELL AND DESERTED COTTAGE, A RICKER, E.
DISTANT CHIMES GEORGE
DISTANT HILLS, THE STEVENS
DISTANT PANORAMA REDDING, E.
DISTANT TIMES, DISTANT PLACES MAYER
DISTINCTIVE PROGRAM PIECES MCINTOSH
DITTER V. DITTERSDORF, 20 ENGLISCHE TANZE HERRMANN--ED
DITTO STROUSE
DIURNES GUILLOU, R.
DIVAGANDO PLATANIA, P.
DIVAGAZIONI COUTURE
DIVA DE L'EMPIRE, LA SATIE, E.
DIVERSIONS. FIVE PIECES, OP. 78A TOCH, E.
DIVERSIONS FOR PIANO -- LEFT HAND, OP. 21 BRITTEN, B.
DIVERSIONS FOR PIANO BENNETT, R.
DIVERSIONS CARPENTER, J.
DIVERSIONS MOPPER, I.
DIVERSION GREENHILL, H.
DIVERSION WHITFORD
DIVERSITIES CALABRO, L.
DIVERSITIES KENNINS
DIVERTIMENTI --SONATINAS-- 6. URTEXT HAYDN
DIVERTIMENTI PER DUE PIANOFORTE HENZE, H.
DIVERTIMENTO, OP. 11 MOYZES, A.
DIVERTIMENTO, OP. 32 FERNANDEZ GIL
DIVERTIMENTO, OP. 43 PROKOFIEFF
DIVERTIMENTO -- 5 PIECES JOUBERT, J.
DIVERTIMENTO CONTRAPPUNTISTICO GHEDINI
DIVERTIMENTO FOR PIANO AND STRINGS ARGENTO, D.
DIVERTIMENTO IN A MINOR ANDRE
DIVERTIMENTO IN C, OP. 47 BLANCHET
DIVERTIMENTO IN D MAJOR HAYDN
DIVERTIMENTO DUBOIS, P. M.
DIVERTIMENTO FUGA
DIVERTIMENTO RUDAN
DIVERTISSEMENT, OP. 43B PROKOFIEFF
DIVERTISSEMENTS -- SET MILHAUD, D.
DIVERTISSEMENT HONGROIS MICHIELS
DIVERTISSEMENT ON A PASTORAL THEME PIERNE
DIVERTISSEMENT IBERT
DIVERTISSEMENT KONT, P.
DIVERTISSEMENT SEROUX
DIVERTISSMENT, OP. 43B PROKOFIEFF
DIVINE STAR MASDEA, V.
DIVISIONS ON A GROUND BASS STUPP
DIXIELAND CHA CHA CHA SWAN *
DIXIELAND JAZZ FOR PIANO KING, S.
DIXIELAND STOMP --MODERN RHYTHMIC CLASSICS-- WHITFORD
DIXIE BOOGIE ZEPP--ED
DIXIE LAND, VARIATIONS GROBE
DIXIE WITH A BEAT TOWNSEND
DIXIE EMMETT
DIXIE EMMETT
DIXIE EMMETT
DIXIE WEYBRIGHT

Title	Composer/Editor
DIX ETUDES ATONALES, DONT 2 DE CONCERT --SELON LA	FALK
DIX ETUDES DE CONCERT, BK. 1	DUBOIS, P. M.
DIX ETUDES DE CONCERT, BK. 2	DUBOIS, P. M.
DIX ETUDES DE CONCERT	DUBOIS, P. M.
DIX ETUDES DE TECHNIQUE ET DE STYLE	DERE
DIX ETUDES FACILES	DERE
DIX PETITES ETUDES MODERNES	JACOB, C.
DIX PETITES ETUDES	WURMSER, L.
DIX PIECES IN ONE BOOK	ALBENIZ, I.
DIZZY BUTTERFLY, OP. 99	BALLATORE, P.
DIZZY FINGERS	CONFREY, Z.
DIZZY FINGERS	POTTER, H.
DIZZY PIANO	MARTIN, G.--ED
DIZZY	BRIMHALL,
DO-RE-MI	HAMMERSTEIN *
DO, RE, MI, FA WALTZ, OP. 138	STREABBOG
DOCE HABANERAS POPULARES	AGUILA--ED
DOCK-SIDE SUITE	ROWLEY
DOCTOR DOOLITTLE	
DOCTOR FAUSTUS	STEINER
DODECAPHONIC EPISODES	TAL, J.
DODGING A DIVORCEE	
DOES YOUR CHEWING GUM LOSE ITS FLAVOR ON THE BEDPOST	KAHN, M.--ED
DOG AND HIS TAIL	KOCH, F.
DOHNANYI MASTERPIECES	DOHNANYI
DOLCE APRILE	DE CRESCENZO
DOLENTE IMAGINE	BELLINI
DOLITA, SPANISH DANCE	WEISLEDER, A.
DOLL'S BALL, THE	MARTIN, G.
DOLL'S DANCES	SHOSTAKOVITCH
DOLL'S DANCE	MOREY, F.
DOLL'S DREAM, OP. 202 NO. 4	OESTEN
DOLL'S DREAM	OESTEN
DOLL'S DREAM	OESTEN
DOLL'S LAMENT, THE	FRANCK, C.
DOLL'S LAMENT, THE	FRANCK, C.
DOLLIE'S DREAM	OESTEN
DOLLIE'S MARCH	SEIDT, J.
DOLLIE'S POLKA	SEIDT, J.
DOLLIE'S SONG	SEIDT, J.
DOLLIE'S WALTZ	SEIDT, J.
DOLLS - CHOCOLATE CAKE GIRL VENDOR	FERNANDEZ, O.
DOLLS - ITALIAN PEASANT GIRL	FERNANDEZ, O.
DOLLS - PORTUGUESE SHEPHERDESS	FERNANDEZ, O.
DOLLS - RUSSIAN GIRL WOODCUTTER	FERNANDEZ, O.
DOLLS - SPANISH BALLERINA	FERNANDEZ, O.
DOLLS HAVE A PARTY, THE	LECUONA
DOLLY'S DREAM AND AWAKENING	OESTEN
DOLLY'S DREAM	LEWIS, M.
DOLLY'S LULLABY	PIETSCH, E.
DOLLY'S MINUET	WEISLEDER, A.
DOLLY - SET OF SIX ORIGINAL PIECES, OP. 56	FAURE, G.
DOLLY SUITE, OP. 56	FAURE, G.
DOLL DANCE	BROWN, N. H.
DOLL DANCE	LANE, J.--ED.
DOLL DANCE	
DOLL DANCE	
DOLL HOUSE, THE	TEBOLDI
DOLL THAT CRIED, THE	BURNAM
DOLORES, OP. 170	WALDTEUFEL, E.
DOLORES, SP. WALTZ	WALDTEUFEL, E.
DOLORES, WALTZ	WALDTEUFEL, E.
DOLORES -- THE DESERT FLOWER, OP. 86	BROWN, A.
DOLORES	WALDTEUFEL, E.
DOLOROSA	GALOS
DOLPHINS	HART, F.
DOMINO --SUITE FANTASTIQUE--	LANCEN
DON'T BLAME ME	LANE, J.--ED.
DON'T EVER LEAVE ME -- SHOWCASE	
DON'T IT MAKE YOU WANTA GO HOME	BRADLEY,
DON'T WANT TO PRACTICE BLUES	GLOVER, D.
DONALD THE DINOSAUR	SCHAUM, J.--ED.
DONKEY AND THE ZEBRA	SEIDER, S.
DONKEY RIDE, A	STROUSE
DONKEY RIDE	DUNGAN
DONKEY RIDE	FICHANDLER, W.
DONKEY RIDE	SCHER, W.
DONKEY SERENADE, THE--ARRANGED FOR EITHER HAND ALONE,	FRIML, R.
DONKEY SERENADE, THE--FROM 'THE FIREFLY'	FRIML, R. *
DONKEY SERENADE, THE -- SET	FRIML, R. *
DONKEY SERENADE, THE	FRIML, R.
DONKEY SERENADE, THE	FRIML, R.
DONKEY SERENADE, THE	FRIML, R.
DONKEY WALKS ALONG THE BEACH, THE --9 PIECES--	KELEMEN
DONKEY WITH A SOMBRERO	GLOVER, D.
DONNA DIANA, OVERTURE	REZNICEK
DONNA E MOBILE, RIGOLETTO	VERDI
DON GIOVANNI. OVERTURE. TWO PIANOS, EIGHT HANDS	MOZART, W. A.
DON GIOVANNI - DEH VIENI ALLA FINESTRA	MOZART, W. A.
DON GIOVANNI - EASY FANTASIA	MOZART, W. A.
DON GIOVANNI	MOZART, W. A.
DON JUAN, OP. 20. TWO PIANOS, EIGHT HANDS	STRAUSS, R.
DON JUAN, OP. 20	STRAUSS, R.
DON JUAN MINUET	MOZART, W. A.
DON PASQUALE, OVERTURE	DONIZETTI
DON QUICHOTTE--PAS DE DEUX--	MINKUS, L. *
DON QUIXOTE, OP. 35	STRAUSS, R.
DON QUIXOTE -- COMPLETE BALLET	NABOKOFF, N.
DOO-DAD BOOGIE	GLOVER, D.
DOODLIN' DRUMMER, THE.	LAMPERT *
DOODLING	BENFORD
DOODLING	CARRE
DOORS INTO MUSIC - BOOK 1	DAVIS *
DOORS INTO MUSIC - BOOK 2	DAVIS *
DOORS INTO MUSIC - BOOK 3	DAVIS *
DOORS INTO MUSIC - BOOK 4	DAVIS *
DOORS INTO MUSIC THEORY - BOOK 1	DAVIS *
DOORS INTO MUSIC THEORY - BOOK 2	DAVIS *
DOORS INTO TECHNIC - BOOK 1	DAVIS *
DOORS INTO TECHNIC - BOOK 2	DAVIS *
DOORS INTO TECHNIC - BOOK 3	DAVIS *
DOORS INTO TECHNIC - BOOK 4	DAVIS *
DOPO THE DONKEY	DVORINE
DOPPELKONZERT FUR KLAVIER UND QUERFLOTE, 2 OB UND	SCHULHOFF
DOPPELKONZERT IN E FLAT FUR KLAVIER, CEMBALO UND	BACH, C.P.E.
DORA POLKA	STREABBOG
DORFSERENADE	SUK
DORIAN DUDE, THE	OWEN
DORIAN GRAY -- BALLET IN 6 SCENES	FUERST, P. W.
DORIAN TUNE	FRACKENPOHL, A.
DORMIDITO LE VI YO	SANTONJA, O.
DORMI CARLA	MAGONE
DOROTHY--OLD ENGLISH DANCE	SMITH, S.
DOROTHY -- OLD ENGLISH DANCE	SMITH, S.
DOROTHY	SMITH, S.
DOS DANZAS CUBANAS	GRAMATGES
DOS SONATAS DE EL ESCORIAL -- 1928	HALFFTER, R.
DOUBLE-THREADS	CAPES, D.
DOUBLE CONCERTO IN E FLAT, K365	MOZART, W. A.
DOUBLE CONCERTO K365 IN E FLAT	MOZART, W. A.
DOUBLE DOZEN FOR SMALL FINGERS	TAKACS, J.
DOUBLE DUETS, EASY ARRANGEMENTS -- 8-HANDS, SET	HUBICKI, M.
DOUBLE EXPOSURE	NAGY, M.
DOUBLE FEATURE	PELZ, W.
DOUBLE MELODIES, ONE PIANO - SIX HANDS	MACGREGOR
DOUBLE NOTE ETUDES -- H1	WARD, J.
DOUBLE NOTE ETUDES -- H2	WARD, J.
DOUBLE NOTE ETUDES -- H3	WARD, J.
DOUBLE NOTE ETUDES -- H4	WARD, J.
DOUBLE PLAY	WEYBRIGHT
DOUBLE PLAY	WEYBRIGHT
DOUDOU CHIEN SAVANT	DESCHAMPS, J.
DOULCES NOSTALGIES -- 1935 --	GAILLARD
DOUTE	ROUSSEL, A.
DOUZE PRELUDES -- POEMES, OP. 58	TOURNEMIRE, C.
DOUZE PRELUDES	TREBINSKY, A.
DOUZE VARIATIONS ROMANTIQUES	ERMANN
DOVE, THE -- LA PALOMA, EASY	YRADIER
DOVE, THE -- LA PALOMA	TREHDE--ED
DOVE, THE -- LA PALOMA	TWITCHELL--ED
DOVE, THE -- LA PALOMA	YRADIER
DOWNBEAT'S 88 KEYS TO FAME	
DOWNLAND	LAST, J.
DOWNSTREAM, INTERRUPTED SERENADE	KENNAWAY
DOWNTOWN STREET MARCH	KARP
DOWNTOWN	BRIMHALL,
DOWNTOWN	HATCH
DOWN A COUNTRY LANE	COPLAND
DOWN A COUNTRY LANE	HELYER, M.
DOWN A COUNTRY LANE	VALENTI, M.
DOWN A CROOKED LANE	HOPKINS, H.
DOWN BY THE LAZY RIVER	BRIMHALL,
DOWN BY THE MERRY MATANZIE	PORTER, W.
DOWN BY THE STATION -- SIMP.	KING, S.--ED.
DOWN HOME MELODY	HYMAN, D.
DOWN HOME RAG	SWEATMAN, W.
DOWN IN THE VALLEY	BURNAM
DOWN IN THE VALLEY	ECKSTEIN--ARR.
DOWN IN THE VALLEY	PRIGGE, O.
DOWN IN THE VALLEY	SCHAUM, J.--ED.
DOWN MEMORY LANE	RICHTER
DOWN ON THE BAYOU	ARCHER, I.
DOWN SOUTH, MYDDLETON	GAMSE
DOWN SOUTH	BLAKE
DOWN SOUTH	MYDDLETON
DOWN THE RIVER	BLAKE, D.
DOWN THE ROAD A PIECE	RAYE
DOWN THE ROAD A PIECE	RAYE
DOWN THE SHADY PATH	JENKINS, C.
DOWN THE WAGON TRAIL	GARROW
DOWN THE WINDOW PANE	WEYBRIGHT
DOWN THE WINDOW PANE	WEYBRIGHT
DOWN THE WITCHES' LANE	WEYBRIGHT
DOWN THE WITCHES' LANE	WEYBRIGHT
DOWN TO THE SEA	LAST, J.
DOZEN A DAY PIANO BOOKS, BK. 1 -- ELEMENTARY	BURNAM
DOZEN A DAY PIANO BOOKS, BK. 2 -- TRANSITIONAL	BURNAM
DOZEN A DAY PIANO BOOKS, BK. 3 -- LOWER-HIGHER	BURNAM
DOZEN A DAY PIANO BOOKS, BK. 4 -- HIGHER	BURNAM
DOZEN A DAY PIANO BOOKS, PREPARATORY -- PRIMARY	BURNAM
DOZEN DUETS FOR PIANO, A	WEYBRIGHT--ED.
DOZEN DUETS FOR PIANO	WEYBRIGHT
DOZEN FOLK TUNES FROM VARIOUS LANDS, A	BURNAM
DOZEN PIANO DUETS, BK. 1	BURNAM
DOZEN PIANO DUETS, BK. 2	BURNAM
DOZEN PIANO DUETS, BK. 3	BURNAM
DOZEN PIANO PIECES IN VARIOUS STYLES, BK. 1	BURNAM
DOZEN PIANO PIECES IN VARIOUS STYLES, BK. 2	BURNAM
DOZEN PIANO PIECES IN VARIOUS STYLES, BK. 3	BURNAM
DOZEN PIANO PIECES IN VARIOUS STYLES, BK. 4	BURNAM
DOZEN WALTZES	BURNAM
DO IT NOW	ROBINSON, E.
DO IT YOURSELF ON THE NINE GOLDEN KEYS TO EASY READING	COBB
DO I LOVE YOU -- BECAUSE YOU'RE BEAUTIFUL	HAMMERSTEIN *
DO YOU KNOW THE WAY TO SAN JOSE	BRIMHALL,
DO YOU REMEMBER THE LAST SILENCE	HOVHANESS, A.
DR. GRADUS AD PARNASSUM FROM THE CHILDREN'S CORNER	DEBUSSY
DR. GRADUS AD PARNASSUM	DEBUSSY
DR. GRADUS AD PARNASSUM	DEBUSSY
DR. KILDARE THEME	LANE, J.--ED.
DRAGONETTE	OFFENBACH
DRAGONFLY, THE, OP. 11 NO. 4	SMITH, H.
DRAGON FLY, POLKA MAZURKA	STRAUSS, J.
DRAGON FLY, THE	STRAUSS, J.
DRAGO ROSSO, IL -- BALLET --	SAVAGNONE
DREAM, A - 10 FANTASIES -- ILLUSTRATED --	VERGANTI
DREAM, A	GUENTHER
DREAMER, THE	GRADI, R. G.
DREAMING, BARCAROLLE	HOPKINS, H.
DREAMING, REVERIE	STRAUSS, J.
DREAMING, WALTZ	AGUERO
DREAMING - TRAUMEREI, OP. 15 NO. 7	SCHUMANN, R.
DREAMING OF OLD VIENNA	SCHER, W.
DREAMING OF SANTA CLAUS	MARTIN, G.
DREAMING OF SANTA CLAUS	MARTIN, G.
DREAMING	HEISER-DAILY
DREAMING	KENINS
DREAMING	KRUL
DREAMING	LICHNER, P.
DREAMING	WEYBRIGHT
DREAMING	WEYBRIGHT
DREAMLAND	DVORINE
DREAMLAND	WHITFORD
DREAMS, ONE PIANO - SIX HANDS	BLISS, V.
DREAMS AND DRUMS	SLONIMSKY
DREAMS AT THE FIRESIDE --TRAEUME AM KAMIN--, OP. 143	REGER
DREAMS OF HAPPY HOURS	HOLT, EILSEL
DREAMS OF LOVE NO. 3 IN A FLAT --LIEBESTRAUME--	LISZT
DREAMS OF SPRING	CROCKER, V.
DREAMS OF THE PAST, WALTZ	STREABBOG
DREAMS OF YESTERDAY	ECKSTEIN
DREAMS OF YESTERDAY	ECKSTEIN
DREAMS ON THE BOSPHORUS, OP. 32	ESPEN, T.
DREAMS	WHITFORD
DREAMTIME	ENGLAND, G.
DREAMY-TIME SONG	MUNN, W.
DREAMY MELODY	KOCH, F.
DREAMY MOOD, A	BRUSSELS, I.
DREAM AT TWILIGHT	STRAUSS, R.
DREAM BALLAD	ECKSTEIN
DREAM BIRD	MCADAMS, G.
DREAM BOAT	GARROW, L.
DREAM CLOUDS	RAEZER, C.
DREAM DANCERS	ECKSTEIN

DREAM DANCE	RICKER
DREAM INTERLUDE	NEVIN
DREAM MELODY	PANELLA, L.
DREAM OF A DOLL	ALPERT, P.
DREAM OF A DOLL	MERKUR--ED
DREAM OF A WALTZ	JAHN, C.
DREAM OF CHRISTMAS, A	KETELBEY, A.
DREAM OF LITTLE BOY BLUE	RICHTER
DREAM OF LOVE, EASY	LISZT
DREAM OF LOVE -- LIEBESTRAUM NO. 3 IN A FLAT	LISZT
DREAM OF LOVE	LISZT
DREAM OF LOVE	LISZT
DREAM OF OLWEN, THE	WILLIAMS
DREAM OF OLWEN, THE	WILLIAMS
DREAM OF OLWEN, THE	WILLIAMS
DREAM OF THE SANDMAN	OSWALT, C.
DREAM OF THE SHEPHERDESS	LABITZKY, A.
DREAM OF THE TIN SOLDIER	SCHER, W.
DREAM SHIP	TSCHAIKOWSKY
DREAM STREET	MALNECK *
DREAM THOUGHTS	SCHIEFELBEIN, F.
DREAM TIME	FEDERER, R.
DREAM TIME	ROBINSON, W. E.
DREAM WALTZ	DITTENHAVER
DREAM WALTZ	WHITFORD
DREISTG. SINFONIEN --INVENTIONEN-- BWV 787-801	BACH, J.S.
DREISTG. SINFONIEN -- INVENTIONEN, BWV 787-801	BACH, J.S.
DREIZIG KONZERT-ETUDEN, BK. 1	DEGEN
DREIZIG KONZERT-ETUDEN, BK. 2	DEGEN
DREIZIG KONZERT-ETUDEN, BK. 3	DEGEN
DREI CAPRICCI	BROZ
DREI DUTZEND KLAVIERFANTASIEN	TELEMANN, G.P.
DREI ECOSSAISES, OP. 72 NO. 3	CHOPIN
DREI EPISODEN AUS DEM BALLETT 'MARSIA'	DALLAPICCOLA
DREI ETUDEN	SMETANA
DREI ETUDEN	SMETANA
DREI FUGEN FUR KLAVIER NACH J. A. REINKEN -- BWV 965,	BACH, J.S.
DREI FUGEN UBER B A C H	PEPPING, E.
DREI GRAZIOSE WALZER -- K.V. 536/586	MOZART, W. A.
DREI INTERMEZZI OP. 117	BRAHMS
DREI KLAVIER-SONATEN, 1936, NO. 01 IN A	HINDEMITH
DREI KLAVIER-SONATEN, 1936, NO. 02 IN G	HINDEMITH
DREI KLAVIER-SONATEN, 1936, NO. 03 IN B FLAT	HINDEMITH
DREI KLAVIERSTUCKE, OP. 12	SCHULTHESS, W.
DREI KLAVIERSTUCKE -- BURLESCA, INTERMEZZO, TOCCATA --	SLAVICKY, K.
DREI KLAVIERSTUCKE	BUECHTGER
DREI KLAVIERSTUCKE	CHOPIN
DREI KLAVIERSTUCKE	SUK
DREI KLEINE KLAVIERSTUCKE	MALER, W.
DREI KLEINE SONATINEN	NIEMANN
DREI KOMPOSITIONEN AUS DEM REVOLUTIONSJAHR 1848	SMETANA
DREI KOMPOSITIONEN	REINER
DREI LEICHTE KLAVIERSONATEN	BACH, C.P.E.
DREI LEICHTE KLAVIERSONATEN	BACH, C.P.E.
DREI PAVANEN UBER DAS GLEICHE THEMA VON BULL, CABEZON,	GOEBELS--ED
DREI POETISCHE POLKAS	DOBIAS
DREI POLKAS -- E, G MINOR, A --	SMETANA
DREI RONDOS UBER VOLKSWEISEN	BARTOK
DREI SALONPOLKAS, OP. 7 NO. 1 IN F SHARP	SMETANA
DREI SALONPOLKAS, OP. 7	SMETANA
DREI SINFONISCHE TANZE	SCOTT, C.
DREI SONATEN FUR CEMBALO -- 1751 --	RITTER, J. C.
DREI SONATINEN, OP. 29 NO. 2	DRIESSLER
DREI SONATINEN	DEGEN
DREI SPATE KLAVIERSTUCKE	LISZT
DREI STUCKE --1951--	BROWN, E.
DREI TOCCATEN, OP. 29 NO. 1	DRIESSLER
DREI TSCHECHISCHE TANZE	FLOSSMAN
DREI VARIATIONEN UBER EIN IRISCHES VOLKSLIED OP. 105-4	BEETHOVEN
DREI VORTRAGSSTUCKE	VITASEK
DREI ZAHME KLAVIERSTUCKCHEN	FINKBEINER
DRESSING FOR SCHOOL	ROGERS, E.
DRESS PARADE	RICKER
DRIFTING ALONG	HIBBS, C.
DRIFTING AND DREAMING	ROLFE, W.
DRIFTING CLOUDS	HOWELL
DRIFTING CLOUDS	RASBACH, O.
DRIFTING MOON	BENTLEY
DRIFTING ON, FOX TROT	SANTLY
DRIFTING ON	JOHNSON, S.
DRIFTING SANDS	BECK
DRIFTING	BRIED, F.
DRIFTING	GLOVER, D.
DRIFTING	JOYNER, B.
DRIFTWOOD	MILLER, L.
DRIGO SERENADE	DRIGO, R.
DRINKING SONG -- FROM 'DIE FLEDERMAUS'	STRAUSS, J.
DRINK TO ME ONLY WITH THINE EYES	JONSON
DRINK TO ME ONLY WITH THINE EYES	SCARMOLIN
DRINK TO ME ONLY WITH THINE EYES	SPENCER, J.
DROLLERIES, OP. 12 NO. 5	WILM, M. VON
DROWSY COWBOY	ROBINSON, A.
DROWSY COWBOY	ROBINSON, A.
DROWSY DILEMMA	STREET, A. A.
DROWSY JUNE	DANIEL, K.
DROWSY LAND	CRERIE, E.
DROWSY TIME	ROBINSON, A.
DRUID'S CIRCLE FROM 'DOWNLAND'	LAST, J.
DRUMMER BOY, THE	BRUSSELS, I.
DRUMMER BOY	ERB
DRUMSTICKS	STEINER
DRUMS FROM A DISTANCE	STEVENS, E.
DRUM BOOGIE	WEYBRIGHT
DRUM BOOGIE	WEYBRIGHT
DRUM CORPS	JESSE, M.
DRUM MAJOR, THE	SELBY, V.
DRUM MAJOR, THE	STEVENS, E.
DRUM MAJOR	ERB
DRUM WALTZ	
DRUNKEN SAILOR, THE -- ONE PIANO, EIGHT HANDS--	KRAEHENBUEHL
DRY BONES	SCHAUM, J.
DUBLIN IRISH JIG	BASTIEN
DUBLIN TOWN	THOMPSON, J.
DUCHIN'S, EDDY, PIANORAMA	DUCHIN
DUCKS ON THE POND	ARANT, B.
DUELING BANJO	BRIMHALL,
DUERMETE NINO	PERCUOCO
DUET, VIOLIN AND HARPSICHORD	HOVHANESS, A.
DUETS --4-- URTEXT. FOR PIANO SOLO	BACH, J.S.
DUETS ARE FUN, BK. 1	HIRSCHBERG, D.
DUETS ARE FUN, BK. 2	HIRSCHBERG, D.
DUETS FOR BEGINNERS, OP. 1 -- BK. 1	NEUMANN, F.
DUETS FOR CHILDREN, BK. 1	WALTON, W.
DUETS FOR CHILDREN, BK. 2	WALTON, W.
DUETS FOR CHRISTMAS	MARWICK, M. *
DUETS FOR EVERYBODY	MITTLER--ED
DUETS FOR EVERYONE, BK. 1	WILLFORT, E. S.

DUETS FOR EVERYONE, BK. 2	WILLFORT, E. S.
DUETS FOR FUN, BK. 1	BASTIEN
DUETS FOR FUN, BK. 2	BASTIEN
DUETS FOR PIANO, SET 1	PACE, R.--ED
DUETS FOR PIANO, SET 2	PACE, R.--ED
DUETS FOR YOUNG PIANISTS	
DUETS FROM THE HYMNAL	ROGERS, E. T.
DUETS IN 3/4 TIME	KAHL
DUETS IN 4/4 TIME	KAHL
DUETS OF EARLY AMERICAN MUSIC	MCCLENNY, A.--ED
DUETS OF WELL-KNOWN TUNES	EVERETT--ED
DUETS OF WELL-KNOWN TUNES	EVERETT--ED
DUETS ON FOUR BRAZILIAN SONGS	VERNE
DUETS	BRAHMS
DUETTO CONCERTANTE, AFTER MOZART -- SET	BUSONI
DUET ALBUM, BK. 1	SCHAUM, J.--ED.
DUET ALBUM, BK. 2	SCHAUM, J.--ED.
DUET ALBUM, BK. 3	SCHAUM, J.--ED.
DUET ALBUMS FOR 2 BEGINNERS, BK. 1--THE GREEN DUET	DILLER, A. *
DUET ALBUMS FOR 2 BEGINNERS, BK. 2--THE BROWN DUET	DILLER, A. *
DUET BOOK 1	GOLDBERGER,
DUET BOOK 2	GOLDBERGER,
DUET BOOK 3	GOLDBERGER,
DUET FUN WITH THREE CHORDS	ZEPP--ED
DUET MELODIES	CRIST, D.
DUET PLAYING, BK. 1	PODOLSKY, L.
DUET PLAYING, BK. 2	PODOLSKY, L.
DUET PLAYING, BK. 3	PODOLSKY, L.
DUET PLAYING, BK. 4	PODOLSKY, L.
DUET PLAYING, BK. 5	PODOLSKY, L.
DUET RECITAL BOOK, BK. 1	AGAY, D.--ED
DUET RECITAL BOOK, BK. 2	AGAY, D.--ED
DUET RECITAL BOOK, BK. 3	AGAY, D.--ED
DUE DANZA BARBARE	BOTTINO, G.
DUE SONATE	CLEMENTI
DUE VALZER	MOZART, W. A.
DUKE AND DUCHESS	BEETHOVEN
DUKE ELLINGTON'S BEST	ELLINGTON
DUKE ELLINGTON AT THE PIANO	ELLINGTON
DUMKA, OP. POSTH.	MARTINU, B.
DUMKA, OP. 35	DVORAK
DUMKA, OP. 35	DVORAK
DUMKA, OP. 59	ᵀ'HOWSKY
DUMKA AND FURIANT, OP. 12	J RAK
DUMKA UND FURIANT, OP. 12 NO. 2	DVORAK
DUMP TRUCKS ON PARADE	BASTIEN
DUO - 1954	CORDERO, R.
DUO PIANISM	CASTELNUOVO-TEDE
DURCH DUR UND MOLL, OP. 61, BK. 1	SCHUMANN, G.
DURCH DUR UND MOLL, OP. 61, BK. 2	SCHUMANN, G.
DURCH DUR UND MOLL, OP. 61, BK. 3	SCHUMANN, G.
DUSK	GIBBS
DUSTING THE PIANO	BOWN, P.
DUSTY ROADS, THE	WEYBRIGHT
DUTCH DANCERS AND IN THE CLOCK STORE	LINDFORS, E.
DUTCH DANCE	GREIM
DUTCH DANCE	MCHALE, M.
DUTCH DANCE	MELECCI, A.
DUTCH DANCE	RICKER, E.
DUTCH DANCE	THOMPSON, J.
DUTCH PIANO ALBUM NO. 2	
DUTCH PIANO ALBUM NO. 3	
DUTCH SPINNING SONG -- A FOLK SONG	WEYBRIGHT
DUTCH SPINNING SONG	WEYBRIGHT--ED.
DUTCH TWINS	WARD
DUTCH WALTZ	KAINE
DU BIST DIE RUH'	SCHUBERT *
DU BIST DIE RUH'	SCHUBERT *
DU RYTHME A L'EXPRESSION, BK. 1	ABSIL, J.
DU RYTHME A L'EXPRESSION, BK. 2	ABSIL, J.
DU UND DU -- FLEDERMAUS WALTZ	STRAUSS, J.
DVORAKANA, FOX TROT, FANTASIE	GROOMS
DYING POET, THE	GOTTSCHALK
DYING POET	GOTTSCHALK
DYING WAIF -- THE FANTASIA	SEIDT, J.
DYNAMIC MOTION	COWELL
E. T. PAULL'S MARCH FOLIO, NO. 1	PAULL
EAGLE, THE	MACDOWELL
EARLIEST PIANO COMPOSITIONS. HARD COVER	MOZART, W. A.
EARLY ADVANCED CLASSICS TO MODERNS	
EARLY AMERICAN MUSIC	MCCLENNY, A.--ED
EARLY AMERICAN SONGS	JOHNSON, M.--ED.
EARLY AND LATE WOEKS	LISZT
EARLY CALIFORNIA	RASBACH, O.
EARLY CLASSICS FOR THE PIANO	MIROVITCH,
EARLY ENGLISH SONATINAS	ROWLEY
EARLY EVERY MORNING	WEYBRIGHT
EARLY EVERY MORNING	WEYBRIGHT
EARLY FRENCH KEYBOARD MUSIC, BK. 1	FERGUSON,
EARLY FRENCH KEYBOARD MUSIC, BK. 2	FERGUSON,
EARLY GERMAN KEYBOARD MUSIC, BK. 1	FERGUSON,
EARLY GERMAN KEYBOARD MUSIC, BK. 2	FERGUSON,
EARLY IN THE MORNING	LEANDER *
EARLY ITALIAN KEYBOARD MUSIC, BK. 1	FERGUSON,
EARLY ITALIAN KEYBOARD MUSIC, BK. 2	FERGUSON,
EARLY ITALIAN PIANO MUSIC OF THE 17TH CENTURY	SHAW
EARLY ITALIAN PIANO MUSIC	ESPOSITO, M.--ED
EARLY KEYBOARD MUSIC, BK. 1--W. BYRDE TO A. SCARLATTI	OESTERLE--ED.
EARLY KEYBOARD MUSIC, BK. 2--F. COUPERIN TO J. RAMEAU	OESTERLE--ED.
EARLY KEYBOARD TECHNIC, BK. A	DRAW
EARLY KEYBOARD TECHNIC, BK. B	DRAW
EARLY KEYBOARD TECHNIC, BK. C	DRAW
EARLY KEYBOARD TECHNIC, BK. D	DRAW
EARLY KEYBOARD WORKS -- BK. 1	WECKMANN, M.
EARLY KEYBOARD WORKS -- BK. 2	WECKMANN, M. *
EARLY KEYBOARD WORKS -- BK. 3	WECKMANN, M. *
EARLY KEYBOARD WORKS -- BK. 4	REINKEN, J. A. *
EARLY KEYBOARD WORKS -- BK. 5	BOEHM, G. *
EARLY MORNING ROOSTER	ROGERS, E.
EARLY MORN	LANCIANNI
EARLY ONE MORNING -- 1962 VERSION	SCOTT, C.
EARLY ONE MORNING	
EARLY ORIGINAL CLASSICS	LANNING--ED
EARLY ROBIN	CRUICKSHANK
EARLY TECHNICAL STUDIES FROM SCHMITT-HANON--140--	SCHMITT, A. *
EARLY TO BED	WEYBRIGHT
EARLY TO BED	WEYBRIGHT
EASEMENTS FOR PIANO	WYMAN, D. C.
EASIER PIECES FOR PIANO	HANDEL
EASIER THAN EASY	RICHTER
EASIEST CHRISTMAS CAROLS	SMALL, A.
EASIEST ORIGINAL PIECES FOR PIANO	CHOPIN
EASIEST ORIGINAL PIECES FOR PIANO	HAYDN
EASIEST ORIGINAL PIECES FOR PIANO	MOZART, W. A.
EASIEST ORIGINAL PIECES FOR PIANO	SCHUBERT
EASIEST ORIGINAL PIECES	BEETHOVEN
EASIEST ORIGINAL PIECES	SCHUMANN, R.

EASIEST SONATINA ALBUM	HOFFMAN--ED
EASIEST STUDIES, OP. 151	KOEHLER
EASIEST STUDIES IN VELOCITY, OP. 83	GURLITT
EASIEST TUNE BOOK OF SACRED SONGS AND SOLOS, OP. 32	PIKE, E. F.
EASTERN DANCE	WORTZMAN, N.
EASTERTIME	KAHL
EASTER BUNNY, THE	OBENCHAIN, V.
EASTER HYMN, TRANS.	FREEMAN
EASTER LILLIES, REVERIE	MARTIN, G.
EASTER LILY	HOWELL, I.
EASTER MORNING	
EASTER SERENADE	MARTINO
EASTER SONG	HOPKINS, H.
EASTER TIME	CATIZONE, J. M.
EASTER	CARTER, B.
EAST EUROPEAN FOLKSONG SUITE	MAROS, R.
EAST INDIAN DANCER	MUNN, W.
EAST SIDE, WEST SIDE	LAWLOR, G.
EASY-BEAT BIG NOTE PIANO	
EASY-GOING WALTZ	GRIFFIN, A.
EASY-WAY PIANO -- BEGINNERS METHOD FOR CHILDREN	CURRY
EASY ALBUM, AN	SCHUBERT
EASY ALBUM FOR BOYS	ANTHONY, G.
EASY ALBUM FOR GIRLS	ANTHONY, G.
EASY AND PROGRESSIVE STUDIES, OP. 100	BURGMUELLER
EASY ANIMAL PIECES	KRAFT, L.
EASY ANIMAL PIECES	KRAFT, L.
EASY APPROACH TO THE PIANO, BK. 1	LANE, J.
EASY APPROACH TO THE PIANO, BK. 2	LANE, J.
EASY BOOGIE WOOGIE DUETS	WHITEFIELD
EASY BOOKS, BK. 1	MODONA
EASY BOOKS, BK. 2	MODONA
EASY BOOKS, BK. 3	MODONA
EASY CHORALE PRELUDES	TELEMANN, G.P.
EASY CHORDS FOR STANDARD HITS	KAHN, M.
EASY CLASSICS TO MODERNS	
EASY COMPOSITIONS -- WITH HAYDN-EASY COMPOSITIONS --	MOZART, W. A.
EASY COMPOSITIONS --WITH MOZART'S EASY COMPOSITIONS	HAYDN
EASY COMPOSITIONS --8--	BEETHOVEN
EASY COMPOSITIONS	BEETHOVEN
EASY COMPOSITIONS	BEETHOVEN
EASY COMPOSITIONS	BEETHOVEN
EASY COMPOSITIONS	BEETHOVEN
EASY COMPOSITIONS	MOZART, W. A.
EASY DANCES AND PIECES --23--	HANDEL
EASY DANCE PIECES	HILLER
EASY DANCE PIECES	KREBS
EASY DANCE PIECES	MUFFAT
EASY DOES IT FOR PIANO - NO. 1	
EASY DOES IT FOR PIANO - NO. 2	
EASY DOES IT FOR PIANO - NO. 3	
EASY DOES IT FOR PIANO - NO. 4	
EASY DOES IT	OLIVER *
EASY DUETS FOR PIANO	
EASY ELIZABETHANS	CRAXTON, H.--ED.
EASY FANTASIES FROM FAMOUS OPERAS, BK. 1	CHIESA *
EASY FANTASIES FROM FAMOUS OPERAS, BK. 2	CHIESA *
EASY FOR ME TO PLAY AND SING	WILSON
EASY FOUR HAND PIECES FOR CHILDREN, OP. 87	WOHLFAHRT
EASY FUGUES AND LITTLE PIECES	TELEMANN, G.P.
EASY FUGUES AND LITTLE PIECES	TELEMANN, G.P.
EASY FUGUES AND SHORT PEICES	TELEMANN, G.P.
EASY IMPROMPTUS--A MELODY AFTER MENDELSSOHN, OP. 34	WRIGHT, N.
EASY IMPROMPTUS--WALTZ IN B FLAT, OP. 32	WRIGHT, N.
EASY LISZT--12 FAMOUS CONCERT PIECES, ARRANGED FOR	LISZT
EASY MINIATURES -- 21 PIECES BY FRANCK, SCHUMANN,	FRICKERT--ED
EASY NOTEBOOK NO. 3	MODONA
EASY ORIGINAL PIANO DUETS	GOLDBERGER,
EASY PIANO CHRISTMAS CAROLS	SMALL, A.
EASY PIANO DUETS --ONE PIANO--	NEVIN
EASY PIANO DUETS ARRANGED FROM MUSIC OF THE 17TH AND	BEER, L. J.--ED
EASY PIANO DUETS IN FIVE FINGER POSITION	
EASY PIANO DUETS	BEER, L. J.--ED
EASY PIANO DUETS	FREY--ED
EASY PIANO HYMN PIECES	
EASY PIANO MUSIC OF OLD MASTERS	FISCHER, H.
EASY PIANO PIECES --12--	BEETHOVEN
EASY PIANO PIECES FOR CHILDREN, BK. 2	AGAY, D.
EASY PIANO PIECES	MOZART, W. A.
EASY PIANO PIECES	
EASY PIECES, OP. 27	KABALEVSKY
EASY PIECES, OP. 39	KABALEVSKY
EASY PIECES --12--	HANDEL
EASY PIECES FOR PIANO AND ORGAN	
EASY PIECES FOR PIANO	THIEFFRY
EASY PIECES	NIELAND, H.
EASY POLYPHONIC STUDIES	BRIMHALL,
EASY POPULAR PIANO TEACHING PIECES, ISSUE NO. 1	BRIMHALL,
EASY POPULAR PIANO TEACHING PIECES, ISSUE NO. 2	METIS
EASY POP ROCK SKETCHES	POZZOLI
EASY SIGHT-READING STUDIES -- IL SOLFEGGIO AL	LINDO, S.
EASY SOLOS FOR PIANO	BACH, C.P.E.
EASY SONATAS, WQ 22	LONGO, A.
EASY SONATA IN D	POZZOLI
EASY SONATINA IN THE CLASSIC STYLE	KUHNAU, J.
EASY SUITE MOVEMENTS	METIS
EASY TOGETHER	HENDERSON, R.
EASY TO LEARN POPULAR PIANO MUSIC	
EASY TO LOVE	
EASY TO PLAY HITS THROUGH THE YEARS - VOL. 1	
EASY TO PLAY HITS THROUGH THE YEARS - VOL. 2	
EASY TO PLAY PIANO DUETS	
EASY TO PLAY PIANO PIECES	
EASY TUNES FOR TWO	SCHMITT
EASY VARIATIONS, OP. 40/1	KABALEVSKY
EASY VELOCITY STUDIES FROM KOEHLER-DUVERNOY--65--	KOEHLER *
EASY WEDDING MUSIC NO. 1	
EAUX-FORTEX -- SUITE	HUGON, G.
EBBEN, N'ANDRO LONTANA	CATALANI
EBB TIDE	LANE, J.--ED.
EBB TIDE	MAXWELL
EBB TIDE	
EBB TIDE	
EBREZZA D'AMORE	WESLY
ECCENTRIC DANCE	OGLE, J.
ECCOSSAISES	SCHUBERT
ECCO WALTZ, THE	ORTOLANI
ECHO--FRENCH OVERTURE--	BACH, J.S.
ECHO, WALTZ	STREABBOG
ECHOES FROM AUSTRIA	KRENEK, E.
ECHOES FROM AUSTRIA	KRENEK, E.
ECHOES FROM SCOTIA	GODARD, C.
ECHOES FROM THE THEATER	SCHUMANN, R.
ECHOES OF BROADWAY -- WITH WORDS	MARTIN, G.--ED
ECHOES OF GYPSIES	BURNAM
ECHOES OF HOLLYWOOD -- WITH WORDS	MARTIN, G.--ED
ECHOES OF SCOTLAND	BURNAM

ECHOES OF SPRING	FRIML, R.
ECHOES OF THE BALL	GILLET, E.
ECHOES OF THE BALL	GILLET, E.
ECHOES OF THE BALL	GILLET, E.
ECHOES OF THE CHIMES	PANELLA, L.
ECHOES OF THE CIVIL WAR	BERMONT, G.
ECHOES OF VIENNA	REISER, V.
ECHOES OF VIENNA	WRIGHT, N.
ECHOING LAUGHTER	MCKAY, S.
ECHOS DU PASSE	LANGE, G.
ECHO IN THE CANYON	STORR, S.
ECHO SONG	GEORGE
ECHO SONG	HOPKINS, H.
ECHO TANGO	STEWART
ECHO WALTZ	KAHL
ECHO WALTZ	MALTZMAN
ECHO WALTZ	STREABBOG
ECHO	JOYNER, B.
ECKSTEIN PIANO COURSE, BK. 1 --175--	ECKSTEIN
ECKSTEIN PIANO COURSE, BK. 2 --175--	ECKSTEIN
ECKSTEIN PIANO COURSE, BK. 3 --140--	ECKSTEIN
ECKSTEIN PIANO COURSE, BK. 4 --150--	ECKSTEIN
ECKSTEIN PIANO COURSE, BK. 5 --65--	ECKSTEIN
ECKSTEIN PIANO COURSE, BK. 6 --100--	ECKSTEIN
ECKSTEIN PIANO COURSE - ADULT PIANO, BK. 1 --95--	ECKSTEIN
ECKSTEIN PIANO COURSE - ADULT PIANO, BK. 2 --65--	ECKSTEIN
ECLIPSE	WHITFORD
ECOLE DU JEU LIE, L'	KOECHLIN, C.
ECOLE DU MECANISME, OP. 120 --15 ETUDES--	DUVERNOY, J.
ECOLE PRIMAIRE, OP. 176--25 ELEMENTARY STUDIES	DUVERNOY, J.
ECOLE PRIMAIRE, OP. 176 --TWENTY-FIVE EASY AND	DUVERNOY, J.
ECOLE PROGRESSIVE FOR PIANO 4 HANDS, BK.1, PREFACE	COLOMER, B.
ECOLE PROGRESSIVE FOR PIANO 4 HANDS, BK.2,	COLOMER, B.
ECOLE PROGRESSIVE FOR PIANO 4 HANDS, BK.3, VIGNETTES	COLOMER, B.
ECOLE PROGRESSIVE FOR PIANO 4 HANDS, BK.4, DE DO A SI	COLOMER, B.
ECOLE PROGRESSIVE FOR PIANO 4 HANDS, DEBUT LE PETIT	COLOMER, B.
ECOSSAISE, OP. 72, NO. 3	CHOPIN
ECOSSAISE, OP. 72, NO. 3	CHOPIN
ECOSSAISES, OP. 41 --2 PIANOS, 8 HANDS--	DVORAK
ECOSSAISES --6-- AND GERMAN DANCES --12--	BEETHOVEN
ECOSSAISES IN E FLAT	BEETHOVEN
ECOSSAISES	BEETHOVEN *
ECOSSAISES	BEETHOVEN
ECOSSAISES	BEETHOVEN
ECOSSAISES	BEETHOVEN
ECOSSAISES	BEETHOVEN
ECOSSAISE AND RONDINO	BEETHOVEN
ECOSSAISE IN B FLAT	BEETHOVEN
ECOSSAISE IN E FLAT	BEETHOVEN
ECOS DE LA PARRANDA -- NO. 2, FROM SIX PIECES ON	GRANADOS
ECOUTEZ CETTE HISTOIRE	RAZIGADE
ECSTASY	WHITFORD
EDDY DUCHIN'S PIANO TECHNIQUE	DUCHIN
EDDY DUCHIN AT THE PIANO	DUCHIN
EDELVEILCHEN	HEINS, C.
EDELWEISS, EASY	LANGE, G.
EDELWEISS, PURE AS SNOW	LANGE, G.
EDELWEISS -- PURE AS SNOW	LANGE, A.
EDELWEISS - PURE AS SNOW	LANGE, G.
EDELWEISS GLIDE WALTZ	VANDERBECK, F.
EDELWEISS GLIDE WALTZ	VANDERBECK, F.
EDELWEISS GLIDE	VANDERBECK, F.
EDELWEISS GLIDE	VANDERBECK, F.
EDELWEISS GLIDE	VANDERBECK, F.
EDELWEISS GLIDE	VANDERBECK, F.
EDELWEISS	HAMMERSTEIN *
EDELWEISS	LANGE, G.
EDINBURGH CASTLE	BURNAM
EFFET DU SOLEIL	FOURDRAIN
EFFLUVES	KULLMANN
EGEGH	KONT, P.
EGGS PERT HEN, THE	SCHAUM, J.--ED.
EGMONT, OP. 84. COMPLETE	BEETHOVEN
EGMONT OUVERTURE OP. 84	BEETHOVEN
EGMONT OVERTURE, OP. 84. TWO PIANOS, EIGHT HANDS	BEETHOVEN
EGMONT OVERTURE	BEETHOVEN
EGYPTIAN BALLET	PACHETTI
EGYPTIAN DANCERS	VOLZ, H.
EGYPTIAN GIRL, THE	RAMEAU
EIDOLONS	KOUTZEN, B.
EIDOLONS	KOUTZEN, B.
EIDOLONS	KOUTZEN, B.
EIGHTEENTH CENTURY DANCES -- HOW TO ADD MELODIC	EARLE
EIGHTEENTH CENTURY ITALIAN KEYBOARD MUSIC	MALIPIERO, G.
EIGHTEENTH CENTURY MUSIC OF COLONIAL AMERICA	WRIGHT--ED
EIGHTEENTH VARIATION, FROM RAPSODIE ON A THEME OF	RACHMANINOFF, S.
EIGHTEENTH VARIATION, FROM RAPSODIE ON A THEME OF	RACHMANINOFF, S.
EIGHTEENTH VARIATION -- FROM RAPSODIE ON A THEME BY	RACHMANINOFF, S.
EIGHTEEN CHARACTERISTIC STUDIES, OP. 109	BURGMUELLER
EIGHTEEN CHARACTERISTIC STUDIES, OP. 109	BURGMUELLER
EIGHTEEN CHARACTERISTIC STUDIES, OP. 109	BURGMUELLER
EIGHTEEN EASY PIANO PIECES	PURCELL, H.
EIGHTEEN FAMOUS ARIAS -- TESORO DEL MELODRAMMA --	FANENGHI
EIGHTEEN GRANDES ETUDES POUR L'ENSEIGNEMENT SUPERIEUR	HUMMEL, J. N.
EIGHTEEN HYMN DUETS--11 HAVE DESCANTS FOR FLUTE,	LIPSCOMB--ED.
EIGHTEEN HYMN TRANSCRIPTIONS	KOHLMANN, C.
EIGHTEEN ITALIAN HARPSICHORD PIECES	SILVESTRI
EIGHTEEN LITTLE PRELUDES AND FUGUES	BACH, J.S.
EIGHTEEN LOVE SONG WALTZES, OP. 52 -- SATB AD LIB	BRAHMS
EIGHTEEN LOVE SONG WALTZES, OP. 52 -- SATB AD LIB	BRAHMS
EIGHTEEN LOVE SONG WALTZES, OP. 52 -- SATB AD LIB	BRAHMS
EIGHTEEN MARCHES	SCHUBERT
EIGHTEEN NOCTURNES	FIELD, J.
EIGHTEEN NOCTURNES	FIELD, J.
EIGHTEEN ORIGINAL CADENZAS AND FOUR FERMATAS TO MOZART	STRAVINSKY, S.
EIGHTEEN ORIGINAL CADENZAS AND 4 FERMATAS TO MOZART	STRAVINSKY, S.
EIGHTEEN ORIGINAL PIANO DUETS BY BIZET, DVORAK, FAURE,	BALOGH--ED
EIGHTEEN POPULAR SONGS	SCHULZ, J.
EIGHTEEN SELECTED PIECES, BK. 1	GODARD, B.
EIGHTEEN SELECTED PIECES, BK. 2	GODARD, B.
EIGHTEEN SELECTED PIECES, FOR STUDENTS	MAYKAPAR
EIGHTEEN SHORT PRELUDES	BACH, J.S.
EIGHTEEN SIXTY-FIVE A.D.	HAUBIEL, C.
EIGHTEEN STUDIES, OP. 109	BURGMUELLER
EIGHTEEN STUDIES, OP. 42	ROWLEY
EIGHTEEN STUDIES TO CHOPIN ETUDES, OP. 10 AND 25 --UN	WUEHRER
EIGHTEEN TWELVE OVERTURE, OP. 49	TSCHAIKOWSKY
EIGHTEEN TWELVE OVERTURE	TSCHAIKOWSKY
EIGHTEEN TWELVE OVERTURE	TSCHAIKOWSKY
EIGHTS SUITES OF LESSONS	ROSEINGRAVE, T.
EIGHTY-FOUR STUDIES, BK. 1	CRAMER, J.
EIGHTY-FOUR STUDIES, BK. 2	CRAMER, J.
EIGHTY-FOUR STUDIES, BK. 3	CRAMER, J.
EIGHTY-FOUR STUDIES, BK. 4	CRAMER, J.
EIGHTY-FOUR STUDIES, VOL. 1	CRAMER, J.
EIGHTY-FOUR STUDIES, VOL. 2	CRAMER, J.
EIGHTY-FOUR STUDIES, VOL. 3	CRAMER, J.

EIGHTY-FOUR STUDIES, VOL. 4	CRAMER, J.
EIGHTY CHORALE PRELUDES OF THE SEVENTEENTH AND	KELLER--ED.
EIGHTY SONATAS PARA INSTRUMENTOS DE TECLA, HEFT 1 --	SEIXAS
EIGHTY SONATAS PARA INSTRUMENTOS DE TECLA, HEFT 2 --	SEIXAS
EIGHTY SONATAS PARA INSTRUMENTOS DE TECLA, HEFT 3 --	SEIXAS
EIGHTY SONATAS PARA INSTRUMENTOS DE TECLA, HEFT 4 --	SEIXAS
EIGHT BAGATELLES	ROSENTHAL, M.
EIGHT BOZZETTI FACILI	GORINI FALCO
EIGHT CANTILENAS - HOMAGE TO BACH	TANSMAN, A.
EIGHT CHARACTER STORIES FOR YOUNG FOLKS -- WITH WORDS	DUNGAN
EIGHT CHARACTER STORIES FOR YOUNG FOLKS -- WITH WORDS	DUNGAN
EIGHT CHARACTER STORIES FOR YOUNG FOLKS -- WITH WORDS	DUNGAN
EIGHT CHARACTER STORIES FOR YOUNG FOLKS -- WITH WORDS	DUNGAN
EIGHT CHARACTER STORIES FOR YOUNG FOLKS -- WITH WORDS	DUNGAN
EIGHT CHARACTER STORIES FOR YOUNG FOLKS -- WITH WORDS	DUNGAN
EIGHT CHARACTER STORIES FOR YOUNG FOLKS -- WITH WORDS	DUNGAN
EIGHT CHARACTER STORIES FOR YOUNG FOLKS -- WITH WORDS	DUNGAN
EIGHT CHILDREN'S MINIATURES	SICILIANO
EIGHT CONCERT ETUDES, OP. 55	BLANCHET
EIGHT DUETS FOR BEGINNERS	BLAKE, J.
EIGHT EASY PIANO PIECES	BURKHARD, W.
EIGHT EASY PIECES	STREABBOG
EIGHT EPISODES, OP. 115, BK. 1	REGER
EIGHT EPISODES, OP. 115, BK. 2	REGER
EIGHT EPISODES, OP. 115	REGER
EIGHT ETUDES, OP. 42	SCRIABINE, A.
EIGHT ETUDES FOR THE PIANO	CASADESUS, R.
EIGHT FANTASIESTUECKE, OP. 12	SCHUMANN, R.
EIGHT FRENCH FOLK TUNES	HOLMAN, D.
EIGHT FUGUES FOR ORGAN OR CLAVIER, 3 THREE-PART FUGUES	BACH, W.F.
EIGHT HANDS AT TWO PIANOS, BK. 1	WATTS *
EIGHT HARMONIC IMPROVISATIONS	SHUKEN
EIGHT IMPROMPTUS, OP. 90 AND 142	SCHUBERT
EIGHT INTERVALS, THE	BLAKE
EIGHT INTROSPECTIONS	THORNE
EIGHT LARGE SUITES, THE	HANDEL
EIGHT LIGHT HEARTED VARIATIONS ON THE JOLLY MILLER--	HYSON
EIGHT LITTLE NIGHT FANCIES	EDGINTON
EIGHT LITTLE PIANO PIECES, OP. 54B--1956	SCHOLLUM, R.
EIGHT LITTLE PIECES	ROHOZINSKI
EIGHT LITTLE PRELUDES AND FUGUES FOR ORGAN	BACH, J.S.
EIGHT MELODIOUS PIECES, OP. 174 -- SET	GURLITT
EIGHT MINUETS WITH TRIOS, K315A	MOZART, W. A.
EIGHT MINUETS WITH TRIOS	MOZART, W. A.
EIGHT MINUETS	SCHUBERT
EIGHT MUSICAL SCENES	MICHELI AGOSTINI
EIGHT NOCTURNES	FAURE, G.
EIGHT NOCTURNES	FAURE, G.
EIGHT NOCTURNES	POULENC, F.
EIGHT NOVELETTES--NO. 1, CAPRICE	TANSMAN, A.
EIGHT NOVELETTES--NO. 2, ETUDE	TANSMAN, A.
EIGHT NOVELETTES--NO. 3, EXOTIQUE--DANSE JAVANAISE	TANSMAN, A.
EIGHT NOVELETTES--NO. 4, DANSE TZIGANE	TANSMAN, A.
EIGHT NOVELETTES--NO. 5, OBERTAS--DANSE POLONAISE	TANSMAN, A.
EIGHT NOVELETTES--NO. 6, BLUES	TANSMAN, A.
EIGHT NOVELETTES--NO. 7, PRELUDE AND FUGUE	TANSMAN, A.
EIGHT NOVELETTES--NO. 8, IMPROVISATION	TANSMAN, A.
EIGHT NOVELETTES	STANZANI, E.
EIGHT OCTAVE-STUDIES, OP. 25	DOERING, C. H.
EIGHT ORGAN CHORALE-PRELUDES	BACH, J.S.
EIGHT PARTITAS	GRAUPNER
EIGHT PIANO PIECES --1946--	KRENEK, E.
EIGHT PIANO PIECES	DIAMOND, D.
EIGHT PIANO PIECES	KRENEK, E.
EIGHT PIECES, OP. 76	BRAHMS
EIGHT PIECES, OP. 9	KREIN, J.
EIGHT PIECES, SERIES 1	LAUMES, D.
EIGHT PIECES, SERIES 2	LAUMES, D.
EIGHT PIECES --CAPRICCIOS AND INTERMEZZI-- OP. 76	BRAHMS
EIGHT PIECES --CAPRICCI AND INTERMEZZI-- OP. 76	BRAHMS
EIGHT PIECES BREVES, OP. 84	FAURE, G.
EIGHT PIECES FOR PIANO	TCHEREPNIN
EIGHT PIECES IN THE FORM OF ETUDES	KOUGELL, A.
EIGHT POETIC PIECES - JOYOUS DAY	PAHISSA
EIGHT POETIC PIECES	PAHISSA
EIGHT POPULAR RUSSIAN SONGS, OP. 58	LIADOW, A.
EIGHT POPULAR WALTZES	LANNER, J. F. C.
EIGHT PRELUDES, OP. 11	CAZDEN, N.
EIGHT PRELUDES -- WITH FIVE SKETCHES, PISK	LUENING, O.
EIGHT PRELUDES	MARTIN, F.
EIGHT PRELUDES	TCHEREPNIN
EIGHT RECITAL ENCORES	MIRANTE
EIGHT RECITAL PIECES FOR YOUNG PIANISTS, BK. 1-A	BETTS
EIGHT RECITAL PIECES FOR YOUNG PIANISTS, BK. 2 -	BETTS
EIGHT RECITAL PIECES FOR YOUNG PIANISTS, BK. 3 -	BETTS
EIGHT RECITAL PIECES FOR YOUNG PIANISTS, BK. 4 -	BETTS
EIGHT RECITAL SOLOS	MIRANTE--ED.
EIGHT SLAVONIC DANCES, OP. 46 -- VOL. 1	DVORAK
EIGHT SLAVONIC DANCES, OP. 46 -- VOL. 2	DVORAK
EIGHT SLAVONIC DANCES, OP. 72 -- VOL. 1	DVORAK
EIGHT SLAVONIC DANCES, OP. 72 -- VOL. 2	DVORAK
EIGHT SUITES AND EIGHT VARIOUS PIECES	PURCELL, H.
EIGHT VALSE SENTIMENTALES AND WALTZES	SCHUBERT
EIGHT VARIATIONS IN G, K. 24 AND SEVEN VARIATIONS IN	MOZART, W. A.
EIGHT VARIATIONS IN G KV 24 / SEVEN VARIATIONS IN D KV	MOZART, W. A.
EIGHT VARIOUS COMPOSITIONS	HAYDN
EIGHT WALTZES, OP. 54 -- VOL. 1	DVORAK
EIGHT WALTZES, OP. 54 -- VOL. 2	DVORAK
EINE KLEINE NACHTMUSIK--SERENADE--K525	MOZART, W. A.
EINE KLEINE NACHTMUSIK, A LITTLE NIGHT MUSIC	MOZART, W. A.
EINE KLEINE NACHTMUSIK, K525 -- SONDERAUSSTATTUNG	MOZART, W. A.
EINE KLEINE NACHTMUSIK, K525	MOZART, W. A.
EINE KLEINE NACHTMUSIK, K525	MOZART, W. A.
EINE KLEINE NACHTMUSIK, K525	MOZART, W. A.
EINE KLEINE NACHTMUSIK, K525	MOZART, W. A.
EINE KLEINE NACHTMUSIK, ROMANZE	MOZART, W. A.
EINE KLEINE NACHTSMUSIK, K525	MOZART, W. A.
EINE VERGNEUGTE KLAVIERMUSIK	BENDER
EINE VERGNUGTE KLAVIERMUSIK	BENDER
EINFACHE REDE	ABRAMSKY, A.
EIN SOMMERNACHTS TRAUM -- HOCHZEITSMARSCH OP. 61 NO. 9	MENDELSSOHN
EKLOGE NO. 1	SIBELIUS
EKSTATO, OP. 7 -- 1953 --	ERBSE
ELECTRIC CUCKOO AND OTHER PIECES	OFFUTT
ELECTRIC	PADWA, V.
ELECTRONIC COMPUTER, THE	GILLOCK
ELECTRONIC COMPUTER, THE	GILLOCK
ELEGIAC MELODIES, OP. 34	GRIEG
ELEGIAC NOCTURNE	HAUBIEL, C.
ELEGIAC SONATA	HELFER, W.
ELEGIA DE LA AUSENCIA	PONCE, M.
ELEGIE, MELODIE	MASSENET, J.
ELEGIE, OP. 3 NO. 1	RACHMANINOFF, S.
ELEGIE, OP. 3 NO. 1	RACHMANINOFF, S.
ELEGIE, 1959 -- SET	POULENC, F.
ELEGIES	BUSONI

ELEGIE IN C SHARP MINOR, OP. 88	NOLLET, E.
ELEGIE IN C SHARP MINOR, OP. 88	NOLLET, E.
ELEGIE IN E MINOR, OP. 10	MASSENET, J.
ELEGIE OP. 3 NO. 1	RACHMANINOFF, S.
ELEGIE	ETTORE, E.
ELEGIE	HURE
ELEGIE	HUSA, K.
ELEGIE	KALINNIKOFF
ELEGIE	VITTADINI
ELEGY, OP. 10	MASSENET, J.
ELEGY, OP. 88	NOLLET, E.
ELEGY FOR PIANO	COOPER, J.
ELEGY FOR TWO PIANOS, 1963	PARCHMAN, G.
ELEGY	HARTEVELD
ELEGY	KRAEHENBUEHL
ELEGY	LAMBERT, C.
ELEGY	MASSENET, J.
ELEGY	MASSENET, J.
ELEGY	MUSSO
ELEGY	RAMEAU
ELEMENTARY INSTRUCTION BOOK, OP. 101	BEYER, F.
ELEMENTARY INSTRUCTION BOOK	BEYER, F.
ELEMENTARY METHOD	BEYER, F.
ELEMENTARY PIANO PIECES	
ELEMENTARY PRACTICAL COURSE, BK. 1 - PRINCIPLES OF	LECARPENTIER, A.
ELEMENTARY PRACTICAL COURSE, BK. 2 - 25 STUDIES AND 12	LECARPENTIER, A.
ELEMENTARY PRINCIPLES OF PIANO TECHNIQUE	BLANCARD
ELEMENTARY STUDIES, OP. 176	DUVERNOY, J.
ELEMENTARY STUDIES, OP. 176	DUVERNOY, J.
ELEMENTARY STUDIES, OP. 176	DUVERNOY, J.
ELEMENTS DE TECHNIQUE --TEXT IN FRENCH-- FOR YOUNG	VINCK
ELEMENTS OF PIANO-PLAYING, OP. 30	BIEHL, A.
ELEMENTS OF PIANO TECHNIQUE, THE	HUTCHESON
ELEMENTS OF PIANO TECHNIQUE ARRANGED ON A RHYTHMIC	BELLAIRS
ELEPHANT'S JOKE, THE	BURNAM
ELEPHANT'S MEMORY	
ELEPHANT'S TRUNK, THE	RICHTER
ELEPHANTS, LES	VOORMOLEN
ELEPHANT SPEAKS, THE	WEYBRIGHT
ELEPHANT SPEAKS, THE	WEYBRIGHT
ELEPHANT WALK	ECKSTEIN
ELEVATION	FLORSHEIM
ELEVATOR OPERATOR	STEINER
ELEVENTH HOUR	SUKMAN, H.
ELEVEN APHORISMS	GASULEAS, S.
ELEVEN BAGATELLES, OP. 19	HALFFTER, R.
ELEVEN BAGATELLES	BEETHOVEN
ELEVEN BAGATELLES	URBANNER, E.
ELEVEN CHILDREN'S PIECES	CASELLA, A.
ELEVEN CHORALE PRELUDES, OP. 122	BRAHMS
ELEVEN CHORALE PRELUDES FROM THE LITTLE ORGAN BOOK --	BACH, J.S.
ELEVEN FRENCH FAVORITES	BUSH--ED.
ELEVEN INTERLUDES	TANSMAN, A.
ELEVEN LITTLE PIECES FOR PIANO, OP. 31	BURKHARD, W.
ELEVEN PIANO DUETS BY THE MASTERS -- INTERMEDIATE	ZEITLIN--ED *
ELEVEN PIANO DUETS BY THE MASTERS	ZEITLIN--ED *
ELEVEN PRELUDES, OP. 23 AND OP. 3, NO. 2	RACHMANINOFF, S.
ELEVEN PRELUDES	ALDERIGHI
ELEVEN PRELUDES	ARCHER, V.
ELEVEN SONATINAS, OP. 151, 168	DIABELLI
ELEVEN SONATINAS, OP. 151 AND OP. 168	DIABELLI
ELEVEN STUDIES IN MODERN TECHNIQUE	DE ANGELIS
ELEVEN VIENNESE DANCES	BEETHOVEN
ELFENTANZ, OP. 12 NO. 4	GRIEG
ELFENTANZ, OP. 12 NO. 4	GRIEG
ELFIN COBBLER, THE	FORBES, M.
ELFIN DANCE, OP. 12, NO. 4	GRIEG
ELFIN DANCE, OP. 12 NO. 4	GRIEG
ELFIN DANCE, OP. 12 NO. 4	GRIEG
ELFIN DANCE, OP. 33 NO. 5	JENSEN, A.
ELFIN DANCE, OP. 33 NO. 5	JENSEN, A.
ELFIN DANCE, OP. 46 NO. 5	MACDOWELL
ELFIN DANCE	HEINS, C.
ELFIN DANCE	JENSEN, A.
ELFIN FROLIC, OP. 59 NO. 6	LEMONT, C. W.
ELF AND THE FAIRY, THE	BENTLEY
ELF DANCES, THE	SMITH
ELF KLEINE KLAVIERSTUCKE FUR DIE JUGEND, OP. 158	DISTLER
ELF KLEINE STUCKE FUR KLAVIER, OP. 31	BURKHARD, W.
ELF MAN'S SERENADE, THE	GAYNOR
ELIS, DREI NACHTSTUCKE, 1961	HOLLIGER, H.
ELISENDA SUITE -- EL JARDI	GRANADOS
ELISIR D'AMORE, L', EASY FANTASIA	DONIZETTI
ELISIR D'AMORE, L' - FURTIVA LAGRIMA, UNA	DONIZETTI
ELISIR D'AMORE, L' - FURTIVA LAGRIMA, UNA	DONIZETTI
ELIZABETHAN SUITE	BARTLETT, E.
ELIZABETH WALTZ	MARTIN, G.
ELIZABETH WALTZ	MARTIN, G.
ELLA JENKINS SONG BOOK FOR CHILDREN	JENKINS, E.
ELMER'S TUNE	LANE, J.--ED.
ELOGE DE LA DANSE	FRANCAIX, J.
ELOISE	ORTOLANI
ELVES AND FAIRIES, OP. 38	ROWLEY
ELVES IN THE FOREST	BERKMAN, V.
ELVES SPINNING	HAUBIEL, C.
ELYSIAN SUITE	STORR, S.
EL BEJUCO	BOWLES, P.
EL BURRITO	RASBACH, O.
EL BURRO FLAUTISTA	FICHER
EL CAMINO REAL, SUITE	MCDONALD, H.
EL CAPITAN	SOUSA
EL CAPITAN	SOUSA
EL CHOCLO, TANGO ARGENTINE	VILLOLDO
EL CHOCLO	VILLOLDO
EL CID -- MUSICAL HIGHLIGHTS	
EL CONDOR PASA	ROBLES
EL CONDOR PASA	ROBLES
EL CORRO DE LAS NINAS	MONTALBAN, R.
EL COSACO ANSIOSO	SICCARDI, H.
EL CUBANA -- A BEGUINE	WEYBRIGHT
EL CUBANA	WEYBRIGHT
EL DACHTERAN. MARCHE ORIENTALE--FROM 'MINIATURES'	RUBINSTEIN
EL DIABLO COJUELO -- THE LIMPING DEVIL	NOONA, W.
EL INDIO	BOWLES, P.
EL JALEO DE XERES	BOSSI, F.
EL LEON Y EL RATON	FICHER
EL MEXICANITO	
EL MIRINAQUE	LECUONA
EL MUCHACHO	REED, H.
EL PELELE	GRANADOS
EL PRIMER LIBRO MUSICAL DEL NINO--SPANISH EDITION OF	WILLIAMS, J.
EL RELICARIO	PADILLA, J.
EL SALON MEXICO	COPLAND
EL SALON MEXICO	COPLAND
EL VIEJO CASTILLO MORO	CHAVARRI
EMBARQUEMENT POUR CYTHERE, L' -- VALSE-MUSETTE -- SET	POULENC, F.
EMBELLISHMENT ETUDES - G1	WARD, J.

EMBELLISHMENT ETUDES - G2	WARD, J.
EMBELLISHMENT ETUDES - G3	WARD, J.
EMBELLISHMENT ETUDES - G4	WARD, J.
EMBLEM OF PEACE -- MARCH	REEG, G. A.
EMBRACEABLE YOU	GERSHWIN
EMBRACEABLE YOU	GERSHWIN
EMBRACEABLE YOU	GERSHWIN
EMBRYONS DESSECHES	SATIE, E.
EMERALDS	SIMON
EMERALD DANCE	KARP
EMERALD TANGO	KARP
EMOTIONS	HUE, G.
EMOTION	KOLZ, E.
EMPEROR WALTZ, OP. 437	STRAUSS, J.
EMPEROR WALTZ, OP. 437	STRAUSS, J.
EMPEROR WALTZ, THE, OP. 437	STRAUSS, J.
EMPEROR WALTZ	STRAUSS, J.
EMPEROR WALTZ	STRAUSS, J.
EMPEROR WALTZ	STRAUSS, J.
EMPEROR WALTZ	STRAUSS, J.
EMPEROR WALTZ	STRAUSS, J.
EMULATION, OP. 314 - 20 LITTLE PIECES	DUVERNOY, J.
ENAMOURED WATCHMAKER, THE	MONFRED
ENCANTADA	JOHNSON
ENCHANTED BOATMAN	STRIMER, J.
ENCHANTED DANCER, THE	MARTIN, H.
ENCHANTED FOREST, THE	MARTIN, H.
ENCHANTED ISLAND	SCHAUM, J.--ED.
ENCHANTED LAKE -- BALLET --	ZANINELLI
ENCHANTED NIGHT	ECKSTEIN
ENCHANTED PLANET, THE	ROBERTS
ENCHANTED PRINCESS, THE	MARTIN, H.
ENCHANTED SEA	METIS, F.
ENCHANTED SEA	METIS, F.
ENCHANTED SLIPPER, THE	VANNORT, I.
ENCHANTMENT	HANSON *
ENCHANTMENT	REISER, V.
ENCHIRIDION, KLEINE STUCKE	ZIMMERMAN
ENCORE STUNTS	PELZ
ENCORE	SPEARE-LUTYENS,
END OF DAY	HALLBAUER, H.
ENFANTAISIES	BRUNET, J.
ENFANTILLAGES PITTORESQUES	SATIE, E.
ENFANTILLAGE	CANNONE
ENFANTINES, LES, OP. 73, BK. 1	PHILIPP, I.
ENFANTINES, LES, OP. 73, BK. 2	PHILIPP, I.
ENFANTINES	BLOCH, E.
ENFANTINES	MILHAUD, D.
ENFANT CHERI - LITTLE DEAREST	BOHM
ENFANT S'AMUSE, L'	FANO, G. A.
ENGINE ROOM	PISK
ENGLISCHE SUITEN	BACH, J.S.
ENGLISH COUNTRYSIDE, AN	WORTLEY
ENGLISH DANCES	DITTERSDORF,
ENGLISH FOLK SONG SUITE	VAUGHAN
ENGLISH SUITES--BK. 1, SUITES 1-3	BACH, J.S.
ENGLISH SUITES--BK. 2, SUITES 4-6	BACH, J.S.
ENGLISH SUITES--URTEXT--, VOL. 1	BACH, J.S.
ENGLISH SUITES--URTEXT--, VOL. 2	BACH, J.S.
ENGLISH SUITES,ORNAMENTATION, GERMAN TEXT	BACH, J.S.
ENGLISH SUITES, BK. 1	BACH, J.S.
ENGLISH SUITES, BK. 2	BACH, J.S.
ENGLISH SUITES, S. 806-811, VOL. 1	BACH, J.S.
ENGLISH SUITES, S. 806-811, VOL. 2	BACH, J.S.
ENGLISH SUITES --URTEXT--, COMPLETE IN 1 VOL.	BACH, J.S.
ENGLISH SUITES -- CLOTH	BACH, J.S.
ENGLISH SUITES -- URTEXT -- VOL. 1	BACH, J.S.
ENGLISH SUITES -- URTEXT -- VOL. 2	BACH, J.S.
ENGLISH SUITES	BACH, J.S.
ENGLISH SUITES	BACH, J.S.
ENGLISH SUITES	BACH, J.S.
ENGLISH SUITES 1-3	BACH, J.S.
ENGLISH SUITES 4-6	BACH, J.S.
ENGLISH SUITE -- PIANO OR HARPSICHORD	CASTELNUOVO-TEDE
ENGLISH TUNES AND DANCES	EDGINTON
ENGLISH VILLAGE SUITE	HOWELL--ED.
ENJOYING THE PIANO	DEBUSSY
ENJOY DEBUSSY	HOFSTAD, M.
ENJOY YOUR PIANO WITH CHORDS	SUNSHINE *
ENLLORO -- VOODOO- NOON	STRAUSS, R.
ENOCH ARDEN, OP. 38. MELODRAMA	SELVA
ENSEIGNEMENT MUSICAL DE LA TECHNIQUE DU PIANO, L'	SELVA
ENSEIGNEMENT MUSICAL DE LA TECHNIQUE DU PIANO, L'	SELVA
ENSEIGNEMENT MUSICAL DE LA TECHNIQUE DU PIANO, L'	SELVA
ENSEIGNEMENT MUSICAL DE LA TECHNIQUE DU PIANO, L'	SELVA
ENSEIGNEMENT MUSICAL DE LA TECHNIQUE DU PIANO, L'	SELVA
ENSEIGNEMENT MUSICAL DE LA TECHNIQUE DU PIANO, L'	SELVA
ENSEMBLE AT TWO PIANOS. COMPILATION	
ENSEMBLE BOOK -- EASY DUETS	RICHTER
ENSEMBLE MUSIC FOR GROUP PIANO	LYKE--ED.
ENSENADA	BRITAIN
ENTERTAINER, THE	JOPLIN, S.
ENTERTAINMENTS FOR PIANO	BINKERD
ENTRANCE OF THE GLADIATORS	FUCIK
ENTREE DES GLADIATEURS -- MARCH --	FUCIK
ENTRETIENS, OP. 46	TCHEREPNIN
ENTRY OF THE GLADIATORS	FUCIK
ENTRY OF THE ZANIES	MACDONALD
EN AUTOMNE - BROUILLARDS D'AURORE, CIEL GRIS, ELAN	SAUVREZIS
EN AUTOMNE, OP. 36 NO. 4	MOSZKOWSKI
EN BARQUE	WOOLLETT
EN BATEAU, FROM PETITE SUITE	DEBUSSY
EN BATEAU, FROM PETITE SUITE	DEBUSSY
EN BATEAU -- DE PETITE SUITE	DEBUSSY
EN BATEAU -- FROM THE 'PETITE SUITE'	DEBUSSY
EN BATEAU	DEBUSSY
EN BATEAU	DEBUSSY
EN BLANC ET NOIR	DEBUSSY
EN BRETAGNE, OP. 13 -- COMPLETE	RHENE-BATON
EN CARRIOLE	MARGAT, Y.
EN CHEMINANT, CHANSON, OP. 90	CARMAN
EN COURANT	SWINSTEAD, F.
EN EL ALHAMBRA -- NO. 4, FROM RECUERDOS DE VIAJE	ALBENIZ, I.
EN EL MAR -- NO. 1 FROM RECUERDOS DE VIAJE	ALBENIZ, I.
EN EL PLAYA -- NO. 7, FROM RECUERDOS DE VIAJE	ALBENIZ, I.
EN HABIT DE CHEVAL	SATIE, E.
EN IMAGES - BK. 1	BOUTRY
EN IMAGES - BK. 2	BOUTRY.
EN ITALIE	LELEU
EN LANGUEDOC - A CHEVAL DANS LA PRAIRIE	SEVERAC
EN LANGUEDOC - LE JOUR DE LA FOIRE AU MAS	SEVERAC
EN LANGUEDOC - SUR L'ETANG, LE SOIR	SEVERAC
EN LANGUEDOC - VERS LA MAS EN FETE	SEVERAC
EN LANGUEDOC	SEVERAC
EN LA ALHAMBRA -- FROM RECUERDOS DE VIAJE	ALBENIZ, I.

EN MI VIEJO SAN JUAN	ROUGNON
EN PROMENADE	GALOS
EN REGARDANT LE CIEL	DESORMES
EN REVANT DE LA REVEU	DESORMES
EN REVANT DE LA REVEU	DESORMES
EN REVENANT DE LA REVEU	LECUONA
EN TRES POR CUATRO	SEVERAC
EN VACANCES, BK. 1 - INVOCATION A SCHUMANN	SEVERAC
EN VACANCES, BK. 1 - LES CARESSES DE GRAND-MAMAN	SEVERAC
EN VACANCES, BK. 1 - LES PETITES VOISINES ENVISITE	SEVERAC
EN VACANCES, BK. 1 - OU L'ON ENTEND UNE VIEILLE BOITE	SEVERAC
EN VACANCES, BK. 1 - RONDE DANS LE PARC	SEVERAC
EN VACANCES, BK. 1 - TOTO DEGUISE EN SUISSE D'EGLISE	SEVERAC
EN VACANCES, BK. 1 - VALSE ROMANTIQUE	SEVERAC
EN VACANCES, BK. 1	SEVERAC
EN VACANCES, BK. 2 - LA VASQUE AUX COLOMBES	SEVERAC
EN VACANCES, BK. 2 - LES 2 MOUSQUETAIRES	SEVERAC
EN VACANCES, BK. 2	SEVERAC
EN VACANCES - INVOCATION A SCHUMANN	SEVERAC
EN VACANCES - LES CARESSES DE GRAND'MAMAN	SEVERAC
EN VACANCES - LES PETITES VOISINES EN VISITE	SEVERAC
EN VACANCES - RONDE DANS LE PARC	SEVERAC
EN VACANCES - TOTO DEGUISE EN SUISSE D'EGLISE AND MIMI	SEVERAC
EN VACANCES - VALSE ROMANTIQUE	SEVERAC
EN VACANCES - VIELLES BOITE A MUSIQUE	SEVERAC
EN VACANCES	SEVERAC
EN VOYAGE	FAIRCHILD
EPIGRAFE	CASTELNUOVO-TEDE
EPIGRAMMATA ALIA, OP. 21	SULPIZI, F.
EPIGRAMME, OP. 8	KADOSA
EPIGRAMME -- 5 PIECES, OP. 17	WELLESZ, E.
EPIGRAMME FUR KLAVIER - 1964	FORTNER, W.
EPIGRAMME POUR PIANO	AMY, G.
EPIGRAMS AND EVOLUTION	REYNOLDS
EPIGRAMS	RAMEY, P.
EPIGRAPHE POUR UNE STELE	TISNE, A.
EPILOGUE D'UN CONTE D'AMOUR--BERCEUSE--,OP.35 NO.1	MARTINON, J.
EPISODES, BK. 1	FLOYD, C.
EPISODES, BK. 2	FLOYD, C.
EPISODES, OP. 12	PROKOFIEFF
EPISODES, 12 PIECES	TCHEREPNIN
EPISODES	FLAGELLO, N.
EPISODES	FLAGELLO, N.
EPISODES	FLAGELLO, N.
EPISODES	LLOYD, N.
EPISODE OF THE TOAD	REISTRUP, J.
EPISODE	COWELL
EPITAFIO	KOPTAGEL, Y.
EPITAPH TO ALBAN BERG	VOGEL
EPITHALAMIUM -- VARIATIONS FOR PIANO AND STRING	FULEIHAN, A.
EPITHALAMIUM -- VARIATIONS FOR PIANO AND STRING	FULEIHAN, A.
EQUISSES - IMPROVISATION, DEDICACE, PRELUDE,	DEBREVILLE
ERA UN PAJARITO	CASTRO, W.
EREIGNISSE 4 AND 5, OP. 12	POLOWINKIN, L.
EREIGNIS 3, OP. 10	POLOWINKIN, L.
ERIC STEINER PIANO COURSE--JUNIOR APPROACH	STEINER
ERIC STEINER PIANO COURSE--SENIOR APPROACH	STEINER
ERIC STEINER PIANO COURSE, BK. 1	STEINER--ED.
ERIC STEINER PIANO COURSE, BK. 2	STEINER--ED.
ERIC STEINER PIANO COURSE, BK. 3	STEINER--ED.
ERIC STEINER PIANO COURSE, BK. 4	STEINER--ED.
ERIC STEINER PIANO COURSE, BK. 5	STEINER--ED.
ERIC STEINER PIANO COURSE, POST-GRADUATE COURSE, BK. 1	STEINER--ED.
ERIC STEINER PIANO COURSE, POST-GRADUATE COURSE, BK. 2	STEINER--ED.
ERIE CANAL, THE	WEYBRIGHT--ED.
ERINNERUNGEN AN PILSEN	SMETANA
ERINNERUNG	BRUCKNER
ERITANA -- FROM IBERIA	ALBENIZ, I.
ERLKING	SCHUBERT *
ERLKING	SCHUBERT *
ERL KING, THE	SCHUBERT *
ERL KING, THE	SCHUBERT *
ERL KING, THE	SCHUBERT
ERNANI - EASY FANTASIA	VERDI
ERNEUTE BILDER, OP. 28	VOMACKA
EROTIK, OP. 43 NO. 5	GRIEG
EROTIKON, OP. 43 NO. 5	GRIEG
ERREURS PHYSIOLOGIQUES ET LA TRANSFORMATION DE LA	STEINHAUSEN
ERSTER WALZER ES-DUR OP. 83 NO. 1	DURAND, A.
ERSTES KLAVIERKONZERT IN C, OP. 20 -	STERKEL, F. X.
ERSTES KLAVIERSPIEL. EIN LEHRGANG FUR DEN	EMONTS, F.
ERSTES KLAVIERSPIEL. EIN LEHRGANG FUR DEN	EMONTS, F.
ERSTES SPIEL ZU VIER HANDEN. 34 ALTE VOLKSLIEDER IN	WOLTERS
ERSTES SPIEL ZU VIER HANDEN. 34 ALTE VOLKSLIEDER IN	WOLTERS
ERSTE KLAVIERBUCH, DAS -- BK. 1, FIVE-FINGER POSITION	ROEHR--ED. *
ERSTE KLAVIERBUCH, DAS -- BK. 2, MAJOR KEYS	ROEHR--ED. *
ERSTE KLAVIERBUCH, DAS -- BK. 3, MINOR KEYS	ROEHR--ED. *
ERSTE SONATA FUR KLAVIER	SAPP, G.
ERWACHE, O HERZ. 2 VARIATIONSFANTASIEN UBER GEISTLICHE	VYCPALEK
ESCALES	IBERT
ESCAPADE, ETUDE	BEAUCAMP
ESCAPADES	BRUSSELS, I.
ESCAPADES	WIJDEVELD
ESCAPADE	BRODSKY, M.
ESCAPADE	WHITFORD
ESCAPE TO SHERWOOD	RICKER, E.
ESCARCEO CRIOLLO	MAIZTEGUI, I.
ESCENAS POETICAS Y LIBRA DE HORAS	GRANADOS
ESCENAS ROMANTICAS	GRANADOS
ESCENAS ROMANTICAS	GRANADOS
ESCENA Y DANZA CHARRA	GOMBAU
ESERCIZI DI OTTAVE IN TUTTE LE TONALITA, OP. 28	SCHININA, L.
ESKAPADEN EINES GASSENHAUERS--PARODY VARIATIONS	PILLNEY
ESPAGNOLA -- FROM TWO SPANISH FOLK SONGS	WEYBRIGHT
ESPANA, OP. 165 -- COMPLETE	ALBENIZ, I.
ESPANA, OP. 165 NO. 1	ALBENIZ, I.
ESPANA, OP. 165	ALBENIZ, I.
ESPANA, OP. 165	WALDTEUFEL, E.
ESPANA, OP. 236	WALDTEUFEL, E.
ESPANA, SP. WALTZ	ALBENIZ, I.
ESPANA - SIX ALBUM LEAVES - OP. 165	MARQUINA
ESPANA CANI	
ESPANA CANI	CHABRIER
ESPANA RHAPSODY	CHABRIER
ESPANA WALTZ	CHABRIER
ESPANA	CHABRIER
ESPANA	MADURO, C.
ESPANA	NEVIN
ESPANITA	GOETSCHY
ESPOIR DU RETOUR, L' -- CAPRICE --	GOETSCHY
ESPOIR DU RETOUR, L' -- CAPRICE --	GOETSCHY
ESPOIR DU RETOUR, L'	RANDS, B.
ESPRESSIONE IV	KADOSA
ESQUISSES, OP. 28B	JONGEN, L.
ESQUISSES - 1. RHAPSODIE	JONGEN, L.
ESQUISSES - 2. POLICHINELLE	JONGEN, L.
ESQUISSES - 3. BERCEUSE POUR UN COEUR LASSE	JONGEN, L.

Title	Composer
ESQUISSES - 4. POCHADE	JONGEN, L.
ESQUISSES - 5. RYTHMES DE DANSES	JONGEN, L.
ESQUISSES - 6. FANTASQUE	JONGEN, L.
ESQUISSES - 7. MASCARADE	JONGEN, L.
ESQUISSES DE DANSES	MARTINU, B.
ESQUISSES ENFANTINES, BK. 1	NERINI, E.
ESQUISSES ENFANTINES, BK. 2	NERINI, E.
ESQUISSES TECHNIQUES, OP. 97	MOSZKOWSKI
ESQUISSES	DELACROIX, R.
ESQUISSES	DUBOIS, P. M.
ESQUISSES	ROGER-DUCASSE
ESQUISSES	SAMAZEUILH
ESQUISSES 48 MOTIFS, OP. 63, BK. 1	ALKAN
ESQUISSES 48 MOTIFS, OP. 63, BK. 2	ALKAN
ESQUISSES 48 MOTIFS, OP. 63, BK. 3	ALKAN
ESQUISSES 48 MOTIFS, OP. 63, BK. 4	ALKAN
ESQUISSE	BERTHELEMY
ESSENTIAL FINGER EXERCISES	DOHNANYI
ESTAMPAS INFANTILES, 1930	NAVARRO, M.
ESTAMPES, COMPLETE	DEBUSSY
ESTAMPES - SUITE OF 3 PIECES-	DEBUSSY
ESTAMPES	DEBUSSY
ESTANCIA	GINASTERA
ESTELLE	CARLE, F.
ESTHONIAN FOLK SONG	ROSSI, G.
ESTILO	FERRERO
ESTILO	GUASTAVINO
ESTRANGEMENT	RALSTON, F.
ESTRELLITA	PONCE, M.
ESTRELLITA	PONCE, M.
ESTRELLITA	PONCE, M.
ESTRELLITA	PONCE, M.
ESTRELLITA	PONCE, M.
ESTRUCTURA IV, 1966	BENGUERREL, X.
ESTUDIANTINA, OP. 191	WALDTEUFEL, E.
ESTUDIANTINA, WALTZES	WALDTEUFEL, E.
ESTUDIANTINA	WALDTEUFEL, E.
ESTUDIOS O CAPRICHOS	ARRIAGA, J. C.
ESTUDIO HOMENAJE A CHOPIN	CHAVEZ, C.
ESURIENTES FROM THE MAGNIFICAT	BACH, J.S.
ES DESFILE	FICHER
ES SINGT DER RHEIN	HOSER *
ETENRAKU FOR PIANO OR CARILLON	DE JONG, C.
ETERNAL HYMNS	SMALL, A.
ETHELINDA, MAZURKA	GREENWALD, M.
ETINCELLES--MORCEAU CARACTERISTIQUE, OP. 36 NO. 6	MOSZKOWSKI
ETINCELLES	WALDTEUFEL, E.
ETOILE, POEME SYMPHONIQUE	DESREZ
ETTA WALTZ	KRAEMER, C.
ETUDE--A GLEE, OP. 85 BIS, NO. 5	FRIML, R.
ETUDE--1949	WILDGANS, F.
ETUDE--1951	POOT, M.
ETUDE, OP. 2 NO. 1	SCRIABINE, A.
ETUDE, OP. 22 NO. 1	WOLLENHAUPT
ETUDE, OP. 27	KABALEVSKY
ETUDE, OP. 37	LIADOW, A.
ETUDENSTUDIE, OP. 36--1951	SCHISKE, K.
ETUDEN FUR KLAVIER, 5 TIMES 10 - ZEHN ANFANGS-ETUDEN,	TOCH, E.
ETUDEN FUR KLAVIER, 5 TIMES 10 - ZEHN EINFACHE ETUDEN,	TOCH, E.
ETUDEN FUR KLAVIER, 5 TIMES 10 - ZEHN KONZERT-ETUDEN,	TOCH, E.
ETUDEN FUR KLAVIER, 5 TIMES 10 - ZEHN KONZERT-ETUDEN,	TOCH, E.
ETUDEN FUR KLAVIER, 5 TIMES 10 - ZEHN	TOCH, E.
ETUDEN FUR KLAVIER, 5 TIMES 10 - ZEHN VORTRAGS-ETUDEN,	TOCH, E.
ETUDEN FUR KLAVIER, 5 TIMES 10 - ZEHN VORTRAGS-ETUDEN,	TOCH, E.
ETUDES-TABLEAUX, OP. 33. COMPLETE	RACHMANINOFF, S.
ETUDES-TABLEAUX, OP. 33 , NOS. 3 AND 5	RACHMANINOFF, S.
ETUDES-TABLEAUX, OP. 33 AND 39	RACHMANINOFF, S.
ETUDES, ALBUM OF, VOL. 1	KOEHLER--ED
ETUDES, ALBUM OF, VOL. 2	KOEHLER--ED
ETUDES, BK. 1	ABSIL, J.
ETUDES, BK. 2	ABSIL, J.
ETUDES, BKS. 1 AND 2	LISZT
ETUDES, OP. 10 AND 25	CHOPIN
ETUDES, OP. 10	CHOPIN
ETUDES, OP. 10	CHOPIN
ETUDES, OP. 125 NO. 1 AND 21	HELLER, S.
ETUDES, OP. 25	CHOPIN
ETUDES, OP. 42	SCRIABINE, A.
ETUDES -- CLOTH	CHOPIN
ETUDES --27-- COMPLETE	CHOPIN
ETUDES ACROSTICHES EN FORME DE VARIATIONS	WEBER, A.
ETUDES AND POLKAS, BK. 1	MARTINU, B.
ETUDES AND POLKAS, BK. 2	MARTINU, B.
ETUDES AND POLKAS, BK. 3	MARTINU, B.
ETUDES BK. 1 - OP. 10 -- ENGLISH TEXT --	CHOPIN
ETUDES BK. 1 - OP. 10 -- FR. TEXT --	CHOPIN
ETUDES BK. 2 - OP. 25 -- ENGLISH TEXT --	CHOPIN
ETUDES BK. 2 - OP. 25 -- FR. TEXT --	CHOPIN
ETUDES BY GREAT MASTERS --DER GERADE WEG--, VOL. 1	HERRMANN, K.--ED
ETUDES BY GREAT MASTERS --DER GERADE WEG--, VOL. 2	HERRMANN, K.--ED
ETUDES BY GREAT MASTERS --DER GERADE WEG--, VOL. 3	HERRMANN, K.--ED
ETUDES CLASSIQUES TIREES DES GRANDS MAITRES, SERIES 1	PHILIPP, I.--ED.
ETUDES CLASSIQUES TIREES DES GRANDS MAITRES, SERIES 1	PHILIPP, I.--ED.
ETUDES CLASSIQUES TIREES DES GRANDS MAITRES, SERIES 2	PHILIPP, I.--ED.
ETUDES D'EXECUTION TRANSCENDANTE, BK. 1 -- NOS. 1-4 --	LISZT
ETUDES D'EXECUTION TRANSCENDANTE, BK. 2 -- NOS. 5-8 --	LISZT
ETUDES D'EXECUTION TRANSCENDANTE, BK. 3 -- NOS. 9-12	LISZT
ETUDES D'EXECUTION TRANSCENDANTE, OP. 11. VOL. 1	LIAPUNOFF
ETUDES D'EXECUTION TRANSCENDANTE, OP. 11. VOL. 2	LIAPUNOFF
ETUDES D'EXECUTION TRANSCENDANTE, OP. 11. VOL. 3	LIAPUNOFF
ETUDES D'EXECUTION TRANSCENDANTE, OP. 11. VOL. 4	LIAPUNOFF
ETUDES D'EXECUTION TRANSCENDANTE, VOL. 1	LISZT
ETUDES D'EXECUTION TRANSCENDANTE, VOL. 1	LISZT
ETUDES D'EXECUTION TRANSCENDANTE, VOL. 2	LISZT
ETUDES D'EXECUTION TRANSCENDANTE, VOL. 2	LISZT
ETUDES D'EXECUTION TRANSCENDANTE - EROICA	LISZT
ETUDES D'EXECUTION TRANSCENDANTE - MAZEPPA	LISZT
ETUDES D'EXECUTION TRANSCENDANTE	LISZT
ETUDES D'EXECUTION TRANSCENDANTE	LISZT
ETUDES ENFANTINES, OP. 37	LEMOINE, H.
ETUDES ENFANTINES, OP. 37	LEMOINE, H.
ETUDES ENFANTINES, OP. 37	LEMOINE, H.
ETUDES ENFANTINES, OP. 37	LEMOINE, H.
ETUDES ENFANTINES, OP. 37	LEMOINE, H.
ETUDES FOR PIANISTS, BK. 1	WEYBRIGHT
ETUDES FOR PIANISTS, BK. 2	WEYBRIGHT
ETUDES FOR PIANO BASED ON FOLKSONGS, BK. 1 -	VUATAZ
ETUDES FOR PIANO BASED ON FOLKSONGS, BK. 2 - ETUDES	VUATAZ
ETUDES FOR PIANO BASED ON FOLKSONGS, BK. 3 - ETUDES	VUATAZ
ETUDES FOR PIANO BASED ON FOLKSONGS, BK. 4 - ETUDES	VUATAZ
ETUDES FOR 2 PIANOS	MARTIN, F.
ETUDES IN F MINOR, A FLAT, D FLAT -- POST.	CHOPIN
ETUDES IN TONALITY, OP. 44	ROWLEY
ETUDES MIGNONNES, OP. 60	RAVINA, H.
ETUDES POUR AGRESSEURS, BK. 1	LOUVIER
ETUDES POUR AGRESSEURS, BK. 2	LOUVIER
ETUDES PROGRESSIVES, VOL.1	NOEL, P. *
ETUDES PROGRESSIVES, VOL.2	NOEL, P. *
ETUDES	CHOPIN
ETUDES	CHOPIN
ETUDES	CHOPIN
ETUDES	CHOPIN
ETUDES	CHOPIN
ETUDES	CHOPIN
ETUDE -- IF I WERE A BIRD	HENSELT, A.
ETUDE BOOK 1	GOLDBERGER,
ETUDE BOOK 2	GOLDBERGER,
ETUDE BOOK 3	GOLDBERGER,
ETUDE BRILLANTE	BECK
ETUDE DE CONCERT, OP. 36	MACDOWELL
ETUDE DE CONCERT, OP. 38 NO. 1	ALKAN
ETUDE DE CONCERT IN D FLAT --UN SOSPIRO--	LISZT
ETUDE DE CONCERT IN F MINOR	LISZT
ETUDE DE LEGATO OP. 81 NO. 3	MOSZKOWSKI
ETUDE DE STYLE	RAVINA, H.
ETUDE DU RYTHME, BK. 3 - RYTHMES SIMULTANES	DANDELOT
ETUDE EN MI FLAT	MAILLARD
ETUDE EN TIERCES MAJEURES CHROMATIQUES	SAINT-SAENS
ETUDE ET DANSE	DAVID
ETUDE FOR PIANO	FERTE
ETUDE FOR PIANO	HALL
ETUDE FOR THE LEFT HAND, OP. 36	BLUMENFELD
ETUDE FOR THE LEFT HAND	BARTOK
ETUDE IN A FLAT, OP. 25 NO. 1	CHOPIN
ETUDE IN A FLAT, OP. 5	LIADOW, A.
ETUDE IN A FLAT MAJOR, OP. 25 NO. 1	CHOPIN
ETUDE IN A MINOR, OP. 10 NO. 2	CHOPIN
ETUDE IN A MINOR, OP. 25 NO. 11	CHOPIN
ETUDE IN A MINOR, OP. 25 NO. 4	CHOPIN
ETUDE IN A MINOR	GAYRHOS, E.
ETUDE IN A	AARON, M.
ETUDE IN B FLAT, OP. 65 NO. 1	SCRIABINE, A.
ETUDE IN B FLAT MINOR, OP. 4 NO. 3	SZYMANOWSKI
ETUDE IN B MINOR, OP. 15 NO. 12--'GHOST'	SCHYTTE
ETUDE IN C MINOR, OP. 10 NO. 12 - REVOLUTIONARY	CHOPIN
ETUDE IN C MINOR, OP. 10 NO. 12 'REVOLUTION'	CHOPIN
ETUDE IN C MINOR, OP. 10 NO. 12	CHOPIN
ETUDE IN C MINOR, OP. 10 NO. 12	CHOPIN
ETUDE IN C MINOR, OP. 10 NO. 12	CHOPIN
ETUDE IN C MINOR, OP. 10 NO. 12	CHOPIN
ETUDE IN C SHARP, OP. 65 NO. 2	SCRIABINE, A.
ETUDE IN C SHARP MINOR, OP. 10 NO. 4	CHOPIN
ETUDE IN C SHARP MINOR, OP. 2 NO. 1	SCRIABINE, A.
ETUDE IN C SHARP MINOR, OP. 25 NO. 7	CHOPIN
ETUDE IN D, OP. 32 NO. 2	MOSZKOWSKI
ETUDE IN D FLAT--UN SOSPIRO	LISZT
ETUDE IN D SHARP MINOR, OP. 8 NO. 12	SCRIABINE, A.
ETUDE IN E, OP. 10 NO. 3	CHOPIN
ETUDE IN E, OP. 10 NO. 3	CHOPIN
ETUDE IN E, OP. 10 NO. 3	CHOPIN
ETUDE IN E FLAT MINOR, OP. 10 NO. 6	CHOPIN
ETUDE IN E MAJOR, OP. 10 NO. 3	CHOPIN
ETUDE IN E MAJOR -- TRISTESSE, OP. 10 NO. 3	CHOPIN
ETUDE IN E MAJOR	CHOPIN
ETUDE IN E MINOR	GILLOCK
ETUDE IN E	CHOPIN
ETUDE IN F, OP. 104 NO. 2	MENDELSSOHN
ETUDE IN F MINOR, OP. 10 NO. 9	CHOPIN
ETUDE IN F MINOR, OP. 25 NO. 2	CHOPIN
ETUDE IN F SHARP MAJOR, OP. 36 NO. 13	ARENSKY, A.
ETUDE IN G, OP. 18 NO. 3	MOSZKOWSKI
ETUDE IN G, OP. 25 NO. 9 - BUTTERFLY	CHOPIN
ETUDE IN G, OP. 65 NO. 3	SCRIABINE, A.
ETUDE IN G FLAT, OP. 10 NO. 5 - BLACK KEY	CHOPIN
ETUDE IN G FLAT, OP. 10 NO. 5	CHOPIN
ETUDE IN G FLAT, OP. 10 NO. 5	CHOPIN
ETUDE IN G FLAT, OP. 25 NO. 9	CHOPIN
ETUDE IN G FLAT, OP. 25 NO. 9	CHOPIN
ETUDE IN G FLAT MAJOR, OP. 10 NO. 5	CHOPIN
ETUDE IN G FLAT MAJOR, OP. 25 NO. 9	CHOPIN
ETUDE IN SI FLAT	PAPINEAU-COUTURE
ETUDE JOYEUSE	GOLZ
ETUDE MELODIC	HAYES
ETUDE MELODIQUE OP. 21 NO. 5	SGAMBATI
ETUDE MELODIQUE	ROGERS, J.
ETUDE MIGNONNE IN D, OP. 16 NO. 1	SCHUETT
ETUDE NO. 02 IN A MINOR	LISZT
ETUDE NO. 04 -- IN FIFTHS --	SZANTO
ETUDE NO. 1, ALLEGRO LEGGIERO	COULTHARD
ETUDE NO. 1 - TEMPO GIUSTO	BABIN
ETUDE NO. 12 IN B FLAT MINOR--'CHASSE NEIGE'	LISZT
ETUDE NO. 2, LENTO	COULTHARD
ETUDE NO. 2 - ADAGIETTO CANTABILE	BABIN
ETUDE NO. 3, TOCCATA	COULTHARD
ETUDE NO. 3 - VELOCE	BABIN
ETUDE NO. 4, CON FUOCO	COULTHARD
ETUDE NO. 4 - VIVACE	BABIN
ETUDE ON WHITE KEYS	GOLDMAN, R.
ETUDE OP. 2 NO. 1	PROKOFIEFF
ETUDE OP. 2 NO. 2	PROKOFIEFF
ETUDE OP. 2 NO. 3	PROKOFIEFF
ETUDE OP. 2 NO. 4	PROKOFIEFF
ETUDE ORIENTAL NO. 3 -- IN FOURTHS --	SZANTO
ETUDE POESIES, OP. 53 AND OP. 59	HABERBIER, E.
ETUDE ROMANTIQUE	FRAGGI
ETUDE SCHERZO	TANSMAN, A.
ETUDE SUR DES MODES ANTIQUES	JOLIVET, A.
ETUDE TABLEAU IN A MINOR, OP. 39 NO. 2	RACHMANINOFF, S.
ETUDE TABLEAU IN A MINOR, OP. 39 NO. 6	RACHMANINOFF, S.
ETUDE TABLEAU IN B MINOR, OP. 39 NO. 4	RACHMANINOFF, S.
ETUDE TABLEAU IN C MAJOR, OP. 33	RACHMANINOFF, S.
ETUDE TABLEAU IN C MINOR, OP. 39 NO. 1	RACHMANINOFF, S.
ETUDE TABLEAU IN C MINOR, OP. 39 NO. 7	RACHMANINOFF, S.
ETUDE TABLEAU IN D MAJOR, OP. 39 NO. 9	RACHMANINOFF, S.
ETUDE TABLEAU IN D MINOR, OP. 39 NO. 8	RACHMANINOFF, S.
ETUDE TABLEAU IN E FLAT MINOR, OP. 39 NO. 5	RACHMANINOFF, S.
ETUDE TABLEAU IN F SHARP MINOR, OP. 39 NO. 3	RACHMANINOFF, S.
ETUDE	DANFOLD
ETUDE	DESOLIS
ETUDE	GOLZ
ETUDE	GRETCHANINOFF
ETUDE	HAYES
ETUDE	REISTRUP, J.
ETUDE	RESPIGHI
ETUDE	TANSMAN, A.
ET LA LUNE DESCEND SUR LE TEMPLE FROM IMAGES, BK. 2	DEBUSSY
EUGEN ONEGIN--POLONAISE	TSCHAIKOWSKY *
EUGEN ONEGIN--POLONAISE	TSCHAIKOWSKY
EUNICE CAPRICE, THE	LEE, N.
EUROPEAN FOLK DANCES	HERRMANN--ED
EUROPEAN FOLK SONGS	THURM--ED.

EUROPEAN NATIONAL ANTHEMS	BARESEL, A.--ED.
EUSKAL HERRIA	BORDES
EVANGELION, PART 1	CASTELNUOVO-TEDE
EVANGELION, PART 2	CASTELNUOVO-TEDE
EVANGELION, PART 3	CASTELNUOVO-TEDE
EVANGELION, PART 4	CASTELNUOVO-TEDE
EVANGELISTIC PIANO PLAYING	SCHULER, G. S.
EVENING, OP. 65	PROKOFIEFF
EVENING AND MORNING--TWO LITTLE PASTORALES	AGAY, D.
EVENING BELLS	BILLI
EVENING CHIMES, OP. 201	HEINS, C.
EVENING CONCERTO, NO. 1	GLOVER, D.
EVENING HARMONIES	THOMPSON, J.
EVENING IN GRENADE FROM THE ESTAMPES	DEBUSSY
EVENING IN HAVANA	THOMPSON, J.
EVENING IN HAWAII	SCHER, W.
EVENING IN SEVILLE	REISER, V.
EVENING IN THE COUNTRY	BARTOK
EVENING IN THE COUNTRY	BARTOK
EVENING IN THE COUNTRY	BARTOK
EVENING MIST	RENNARD
EVENING MOODS	FELTON, W.
EVENING MUSIC	PALMER
EVENING OF GLAMOUR	STEINER
EVENING PRAYER, FROM 'HANSEL AND GRETEL'	HUMPERDINCK, E.
EVENING REVERIE	CRERIE, E.
EVENING SERENADE	STEVENS, E.
EVENING SHADOWS FROM CHOPIN'S NOCTURNE	ROLFE, W.
EVENING SHADOWS	ROBINSON, A.
EVENING SONG	KHATCHATURIAN
EVENING SONG	KHATCHATURIAN
EVENING SONG	SCHWAB
EVENING SONG	ZUPKO
EVENING STAR -- TANNHAUSER	WAGNER
EVENING STAR -- TANNHAUSER	WAGNER
EVENING STAR -- TANNHAUSER	WAGNER *
EVENING STAR 'TANNHAUSER'	WAGNER
EVENING STAR	VOLZ, H.
EVENING STAR	WAGNER *
EVENING STAR	WHITFORD--ED.
EVENSONG IN F	MARTIN, E.
EVENSONG	MARTIN, E.
EVENTIDE	HILL
EVERGLADES	HILL
EVERGREEN WALTZ	STODDARD
EVERLASTING HYMNS	ZEPP--ED
EVERYBODY'S FAVORITE PIANO PIECES	
EVERYBODY LIKES THE PIANO, BK. 1	ESTELLA
EVERYBODY LIKES THE PIANO, BK. 2	ESTELLA
EVERYBODY LIKES THE PIANO, BK. 3	ESTELLA
EVERYBODY LIKES THE PIANO, BK. 4	ESTELLA
EVERYBODY LIKES THE PIANO, BK. 5	ESTELLA
EVERYBODY LIKES THE PIANO, PREPARATORY BOOK	ESTELLA
EVERYTHING'S COMING UP ROSES	SINGER, L.--ED
EVERYTHING HAPPENS TO ME	
EVERYTHING IS BEAUTIFUL	BRIMHALL,
EVERYTHING I OWN	BRADLEY,
EVERY DAY IS SATURDAY	CACAVAS
EVERY DAY OF MY LIFE	LANE, J.--ED.
EVERY NIGHT WHEN THE SUN GOES DOWN	WEYBRIGHT--ED.
EVERY NIGHT WHEN THE SUN GOES IN	WEYBRIGHT
EVOCACIONES, OP. 46	TURINA, J.
EVOCACION -- FROM IBERIA	ALBENIZ, I.
EVOCACION DE ANDALUCIA	PALAU, M.
EVOCACION GOYESCA -- BALLET	SERRANO, G.
EVOCACION GOYESCA	SERRANO, G.
EVOCACION MALAGUENA	FRANCO, J.
EVOCACION	HAUBIEL, C.
EVOCATION, OP. 6	SCIORTINO, E.
EVOCATIONS -- FOUR CHANTS FOR PIANO, SPECIAL EDITION	RUGGLES, C.
EVOCATIONS -- FOUR CHANTS FOR PIANO	RUGGLES, C.
EVOCATIONS -- TRS. BY THE COMPOSER FROM THE SYMPHONIC	BLOCH, E.
EVOCATION VESPERALE -- PRELUDE	DAVID
EVOCATION	RIEGGER, W.
EVOCATION	RIEGGER, W.
EVOCATION	SAMAZEUILH
EVOCATION	SMITH, H.
EVOLUZIONI, OP. 19	KROL, B.
EX-VOTO	BLOCH, E.
EXACTLY LIKE YOU	BRYANT--ED.
EXACTLY LIKE YOU	MCHUGH
EXAMINATION BLUES	ROZIN
EXCELSIOR, SACRED SONG MED.	HAWLEY
EXCELSIOR - EASY FANTASY	MARENCO
EXCERPT FROM 'DANSE MACABRE'	SAINT-SAENS
EXCITING ADVENTURES - SEVEN DESCRIPTIVE PIANO SOLOS	RICHTER, A.
EXCITING ERA OF ZEZ CONFREY	CONFREY, Z.
EXCURSIONS--130--	
EXCURSIONS, OP. 20	BARBER, S.
EXCURSION	MCKAY, G.
EXERCICES DES CINQ DOIGTS, OP. 32	RIE, B.
EXERCICES DE TENUES	PHILIPP, I.
EXERCICES DE TENUES	PHILLIP, I.
EXERCICES ET ETUDES TECHNIQUES DE PIANO POUR LA MAIN	PHILIPP, I.
EXERCICES PRATIQUES POUR LE PIANO, OP. 9	PHILIPP, I.
EXERCICES PREPARATORIES DE AD. HENSELT	PHILIPP, I.--ED.
EXERCICES PROGRESSIFS DE J. PISCHNA	PHILIPP, I.--ED.
EXERCISES ANALYTIQUES POUR LES OEUVRES DE CHOPIN	PHILIPP, I.
EXERCISES AND MELODIES FOR CHILDREN, OP. 218	KOEHLER
EXERCISES AND PRELUDES, OP. 21	HERZ, H.
EXERCISES AND SCALES	HERZ, H.
EXERCISES AND STUDIES IN STACCATO OCTAVE-PLAYING, OP.	DOERING, C. H.
EXERCISES AND STUDIES IN THUMB PASSAGES	POZZOLI
EXERCISES DE VIRTUOSITE, BK. 1	ROGER-DUCASSE
EXERCISES DE VIRTUOSITE, BK. 2	ROGER-DUCASSE
EXERCISES ET ETUDES POUR LA MAIN GAUCHE SEULE, OP. 89	BERENS, H.
EXERCISES FOR INDEPENDENCE OF THE FINGERS, BK. 1	PHILIPP, I.
EXERCISES FOR INDEPENDENCE OF THE FINGERS, BK. 2	PHILIPP, I.
EXERCISES FOR PIANO	GANZ
EXERCISES FOR RHYTHMIC STUDY, BK. 1	ENGELS, M. W.
EXERCISES IN VELOCITY	PHILIPP, I.
EXERCISES ON THE BLACK KEYS	PHILIPP, I.
EXERCISE IN F MINOR	SALTYKOV
EXODUS, MAIN THEME	GOLD
EXODUS	
EXOTIC DANCE	SHEPHERD
EXPECTATION WALTZ	STEINER
EXPERIMENT IN TERROR	
EXPLORATIONS, BK. 1	MCKAY, G.
EXPLORER '88'	BENFORD
EXPLORING THE ATTIC	ROGERS, E.
EXPOSITIONS FOR PIANO	TAUTENHAHN, G.
EXPRESSIONS, OP.81- TEN PIECES FOR PIANO	TCHEREPNIN
EXPRESSION THROUGH MELODY	STEINER
EXPRESSIVE DYNAMICS	MIROVITCH, A.
EXPRESSIVE RHYTHMIC ACTIVITIES FOR CHILDREN	CLARK, R. *
EXTEMPORE, OP. 24	VACKAR
EXTENSION STUDIES FOR SMALL HANDS, OP. 166	ATHERTON, F. P.
E L'UCCELLINO - BERCEUSE	PUCCINI
F.B.I. MARCH	PROKOFIEFF
FABEL, OP. 12 NO. 6--FANTASIESTUCKE	SCHUMANN, R.
FABELN -- 1924 --	MARTINU, B.
FABLE, A	SCARMOLIN
FABLE, OP. 2 NO. 2	SMETANA
FABLES	MARTINU, B.
FABLIAU OP. 75 NO. 2	RAFF, J.
FABLIAU	NOEL, P. *
FABRIC	COWELL
FACADE EXCERPTS -- FOX TROT	WALTON, W.
FACADE EXCERPTS -- POPULAR SONG	WALTON, W.
FACADE EXCERPTS -- POPULAR SONG	WALTON, W.
FACADE EXCERPTS -- SWISS YODELLING SONG	WALTON, W.
FACADE EXCERPTS -- TANGO	WALTON, W.
FACADE EXCERPTS -- VALSE	WALTON, W.
FACES OF JAZZ	SMITH, H.
FACETIOUS	BRIGGS, R.
FACE THE MUSIC, BOOK 1	DEE, M.
FACE THE MUSIC, BOOK 2	DEE, M.
FACHCUX, LES -- BALLET -- .. LES JOUEURS DE BOULES	AURIC
FACHCUX, LES -- BALLET -- .. LE MAITRE A DANSER	AURIC
FACHCUX, LES -- BALLET -- .. NOCTURNE	AURIC
FACHCUX, LES -- BALLET --	AURIC
FACILITY STUDIES FROM CZERNY--90--	CZERNY
FADED LOVE LETTER	FEDERER, R.
FADED MEMORIES	OBERG, O. S.
FADETTE, IMPROMPTU	BOHM
FAIR, THE--OP. 101 NO. 8	GURLITT
FAIR, THE -- KERMESSE	GURLITT
FAIR, THE	MACLACHLAN, T.
FAIREST LORD JESUS	SCHAUM, J.--ED.
FAIRIES' FROLIC	THOMPSON, J.
FAIRIES' HARP, THE	THOMPSON, J.
FAIRIES' LULLABY	CROSBY, M.
FAIRIES' LULLABY	MARTIN, G.
FAIRY'S KISS -- REVISED 1950 VERSION	STRAVINSKY, I.
FAIRYLAND WALTZ	PARENTE, SR. E.
FAIRYLAND	WALLINGTON, G.
FAIRY BARQUE, THE	AARON, M.
FAIRY BARQUE	SMALLWOOD
FAIRY BELLS	DUNHILL, T.
FAIRY BELL	BRAGDON
FAIRY DANCE, OP. 12 NO. 4	GRIEG
FAIRY DANCE	EIOT, M.
FAIRY DOLL, THE	ROLSETH, B.
FAIRY FLUTE, THE	JAMES, W. G.
FAIRY FOOTSTEPS	FARRAR, F. E.
FAIRY LAKE, BARCAROLLE	HOPKINS, H.
FAIRY LAND MUSIC	PIAGET, A.
FAIRY LULLABY -- 6-HANDS	EMERY
FAIRY PIPERS	BREWER, A. H.
FAIRY POLKA, OP. 93 NO. 3	SPINDLER
FAIRY QUEEN, THE	TAKACS, J.
FAIRY QUEEN GAVOTTE	MONTE, M.
FAIRY QUEEN MARCH	MONTE, M.
FAIRY QUEEN MAZURKA	MONTE, M.
FAIRY QUEEN REVERIES	MONTE, M.
FAIRY QUEEN WALTZ	MONTE, M.
FAIRY QUEEN WALTZ	RAEZER, C.
FAIRY SNOWFLAKES	NAVARRO, L.
FAIRY SPINNING WHEEL	HAUBIEL, C.
FAIRY STORIES--DANCING UNDER THE MAY-APPLES	NEIDLINGER, W.
FAIRY STORIES--WATER-SPRITES' BARCAROLE, THE	NEIDLINGER, W.
FAIRY TALE, OP. 135 NO. 2	WEYBRIGHT
FAIRY TALE, OP. 20 NO. 1	MEDTNER, N.
FAIRY TALE, OP. 26 NO. 1	MEDTNER, N.
FAIRY TALE, OP. 26 NO. 1	MEDTNER, N.
FAIRY TALE, OP. 26 NO. 2	MEDTNER, N.
FAIRY TALE, OP. 26 NO. 4	MEDTNER, N.
FAIRY TALE, OP. 51, NO. 1	MEDTNER, N.
FAIRY TALE, OP. 51, NO. 2	MEDTNER, N.
FAIRY TALE, OP. 51, NO. 3	MEDTNER, N.
FAIRY TALE, OP. 51, NO. 4	MEDTNER, N.
FAIRY TALE, OP. 51, NO. 5	MEDTNER, N.
FAIRY TALE, OP. 51, NO. 6	MEDTNER, N.
FAIRY TALE, OP. 65, NO. 3	PROKOFIEFF
FAIRY TALES, OP. 26 --COMPLETE	MEDTNER, N.
FAIRY TALES, OP. 6	ISSERLIS, J.
FAIRY TALES	TALBOT
FAIRY TALE	GRATTON
FAIRY TALE	KOMZAK
FAIRY TALE	PELS, W.
FAIRY WEDDING WALTZ, OP. 120	TURNER, J.
FAIRY WEDDING WALTZ	TURNER, J.
FAIRY WEDDING WALTZ	TURNER, J.
FAIRY WEDDING	TURNER, J.
FAIRY WISH, THE	HOPKINS, H.
FAIR AND WARM	ROZIN
FAIR KIRMESS	GURLITT
FAISEZ RISETTE, VALSE MIGNONNE	FISCHER
FAITHFUL	WILSON, M.
FAITH OF OUR FATHERS, A HYMN	FABER
FAITH OF OUR FATHERS	FABER
FALBALAS	VOORMOLEN
FALENCES -- SYMPHONIC SUITE --	DUPERIER
FALLING IN LOVE WITH LOVE	SINGER, L.--ED
FALLING IN LOVE WITH LOVE	
FALLING LEAVES, REVERIE	MUELLER, C.
FALLING PETALS	WHITFORD
FALLING SNOW	SLATER, N.
FALLING WATERS, REVERIE	FITZPATRICK,
FALLING WATERS	TRAUX, J.
FALLING WATERS	TRAUX, J.
FALLING WATERS	TRUAX, J.
FALLING WATERS	TRUAX, J.
FALSE ALARM	BRODSKY, M.
FAMILIAR HYMNS FOR THE PIANO	WILSON, J. F.
FAMILIAR MELODIES IN SONATINA STYLE	SMALL, A.
FAMILIAR MELODIES	COBB
FAMILIAR TUNES FOR FOUR SMALL HANDS	
FAMILY ALBUM	DELLO JOIO, N.
FAMILY HYMN BOOK, THE	BURNAM
FAMILY MUSIC BOOK, THE	
FAMILY PETS	LAKE, G.
FAMOUS FRENCH COMPOSERS	BUSH--ED.
FAMOUS GAVOTTE	LULLY
FAMOUS MELODIES FOR THE YOUNG PIANIST	KIRBY, W.--ED.
FAMOUS MELODIES FOR THE YOUNG PIANIST	KIRBY, W.
FAMOUS MELODIES IN FIVE FINGER POSITION	ROZIN--ED
FAMOUS MELODY ALBUM FOR VERY EARLY GRADES	SCHER, W.--ED
FAMOUS MELODY ALBUM FOR VERY EARLY GRADES	SCHER, W.--ED
FAMOUS MINUET - FROM QUINTET, OP. 13 NO. 5	BOCCHERINI
FAMOUS MINUET - FROM QUINTET, OP. 13 NO. 5	BOCCHERINI
FAMOUS MOVEMENTS FROM GREAT SYMPHONIES	PELS, W.--ED.
FAMOUS PIANO PIECES	

FAMOUS PIANO SOLOS -- SCHAUM REPERTOIRE	SCHAUM, J.
FAMOUS PIECES -- WITH HARPSICHORD REGISTRATION -- BK.	PATORNI *
FAMOUS PIECES -- WITH HARPSICHORD REGISTRATION -- BK.	PATORNI *
FAMOUS PIECES -- WITH HARPSICHORD REGISTRATION -- BK.	PATORNI *
FAMOUS SACRED SONGS	PEERY, R. R.--ED
FAMOUS THEMES IN THE MODERN MANNER	LIEFELD--ED.
FAMOUS WALZES	STRAUSS, J.
FANCIES FREE. TONE-POEMS FOR YOUNG PIANISTS--SINGING	SEUEL-HOLST, M.
FANCIES FREE. TONE-POEMS FOR YOUNG PIANISTS--THREE AND	SEUEL-HOLST, M.
FANCIFUL	WILSON, M.
FANCIULLA DEL WEST, LA - 1ST EASY FANTASIA	PUCCINI
FANCIULLA DEL WEST, LA - 2ND EASY FANTASIA	PUCCINI
FANCIULLEZZA, BK. 1	FRANCESCHI
FANCIULLEZZA, BK. 2	FRANCESCHI
FANCIULLI ALLEGRI NO. 1	BECUCCI
FANCIULLI ALLEGRI NO. 2	BECUCCI
FANCIULLI ALLEGRI NO. 3	BECUCCI
FANCY, A	SOWERBY, L.
FANCY FREE	CANFIELD, J.
FANCY FREE	GROVE
FANCY FROLIC	REISER, V.
FANDANGO ON THE NAME OF AMPARO ITURBI	CASTELNUOVO-TEDE
FANDANGO	BROUTMAN, E.
FANDANGO	PERKINS, F.
FANDANGO	SOLER, A.
FANDANGO	SOLER, A.
FANFARE, FROM L'EVENTAIL DE JEANNE	RAVEL
FANFARE, SICK ON SATURDAY, JUGGLING -- TWELVE-TONE SET	UTZLER
FANFARE AND MARCH	NAGY, M.
FANFARE FROM 'WILLIAM TELL'	ROSSINI, G.
FANFARE POUR CHASSE--CURWEN EDITION	ROSSINI, G.
FANFARE TANGO	NORMAN *
FANFARE	GILLOCK
FANFARE	HANDEL
FANGT AN ZU MUSIZIEREN--LITTLE PIECES	SCHOLLUM, R.
FANGT AN ZU MUSIZIERIEN--90 LITTLE PIECES FOR THE	SCHOLLUM, R.
FANNY, MAIN THEME	
FANNY	
FANTAISIE, OP. 103	SCHUBERT
FANTAISIE, OP. 111	FAURE, G.
FANTAISIE, OP. 5	RACHMANINOFF, S.
FANTAISIE, OP. 8	AUBERT
FANTAISIE BRILLANTE	WEBER, VON
FANTAISIE DE CONCERT	DUBOIS, P. M.
FANTAISIE FACILE, OP. 39 NO. 3	VERDI
FANTAISIE FOR PIANO AND ORCHESTRA	TCHEREPNIN
FANTAISIE IN C MINOR	BACH, J.S.
FANTAISIE MILITAIRE OP. 121	PIXIS
FANTAISIE MILITAIRE SUR LES HUGUENOTS --MEYERBEER	RAFF, J.
FANTAISIE POUR PIANO ET ORCHESTRE	WIDOR, CH.
FANTAISIE SUR LES HUGUENOTS --MEYERBEER OP. 20	THALBERG
FANTAISIE SUR UN THEME ANCIEN	LANCEN
FANTAISIE	DEBUSSY
FANTAISIE	ERICOURT
FANTASIA, BERCEUSE, BARCAROLLE	CHOPIN
FANTASIA, IMPROMPTUS, MOMENTS MUSICAUX	SCHUBERT
FANTASIA, OP. 15	SCHUBERT *
FANTASIA, OP. 17	SCHUMANN, R.
FANTASIA, OP. 28	BUTTING, M.
FANTASIAS, IMPROMPTUS, MOMENTS MUSICAUX	SCHUBERT
FANTASIAS AND FUGUES, VOL. 1	BACH, J.S.
FANTASIAS AND FUGUES, VOL. 2	BACH, J.S.
FANTASIAS AND RONDOS	MOZART, W. A.
FANTASIA -- 1955 --	BETTINELLI
FANTASIA AND FUGUE--TOCCATA--, IN D	BACH, J.S.
FANTASIA AND FUGUE IN A MINOR	BACH, J.S.
FANTASIA AND FUGUE IN A MINOR	BACH, J.S.
FANTASIA AND FUGUE IN G MINOR FOR ORGAN	BACH, J.S.
FANTASIA AND FUGUE IN G MINOR FOR ORGAN	BACH, J.S. *
FANTASIA AND FUGUE IN G MINOR FOR ORGAN	BACH, J.S. *
FANTASIA CINESE	VIDUSSO
FANTASIA CONCERTANTE	STARER
FANTASIA CONTRAPPUNTISTICA -- COMPLETE ORIGINAL	BUSONI
FANTASIA CONTRAPPUNTISTICA	LEIGHTON
FANTASIA FOR MUSICAL CLOCKWORK	MOZART, W. A.
FANTASIA FROM 'IL TROVATORE'	VERDI
FANTASIA FROM 'RIGOLETTO'	VERDI
FANTASIA IN A MINOR, AFTER J.S. BACH	BUSONI
FANTASIA IN C, OP. 15--'WANDERER'	SCHUBERT
FANTASIA IN C, OP. 15	SCHUBERT
FANTASIA IN C, OP. 17	SCHUMANN, R.
FANTASIA IN C MAJOR	HAYDN
FANTASIA IN C MINOR,PRELUDIO CON FUGA IN A MINOR,	BACH, J.S.
FANTASIA IN C MINOR, K475	MOZART, W. A.
FANTASIA IN C MINOR AND PRELUDIO CON FUGA IN A MINOR	BACH, J.S.
FANTASIA IN C MINOR	BACH, J.S.
FANTASIA IN C MINOR	BACH, J.S.
FANTASIA IN C MINOR	BACH, J.S.
FANTASIA IN C MINOR	MOZART, W. A.
FANTASIA IN C	HAYDN
FANTASIA IN D MINOR, K397	MOZART, W. A.
FANTASIA IN D MINOR	LEE, N.
FANTASIA IN D MINOR	MOZART, W. A.
FANTASIA IN D MINOR	MOZART, W. A.
FANTASIA IN E FLAT	CANTU
FANTASIA IN F MINOR, OP. 103	SCHUBERT
FANTASIA IN F MINOR	MOZART, W. A.
FANTASIA IN F SHARP MINOR --1831	WAGNER
FANTASIA ITALIANA, OP. 75	TURINA, J.
FANTASIA K396 IN C MINOR	MOZART, W. A.
FANTASIA K397 IN D MINOR	MOZART, W. A.
FANTASIA K475, AND SONATA K457 IN C MINOR, SCH NO. 18	MOZART, W. A.
FANTASIA K475 IN C MINOR	MOZART, W. A.
FANTASIA MEXICANA	COPLAND
FANTASIA NO. 2	BARTOK
FANTASIA ON FIVE NOTES--''ARBOS''--OP. 83	TURINA, J.
FANTASIA OR SONATA IN G, OP. 78	SCHUBERT
FANTASIA SOPRA UN MOTIVO, 1951	MOEVS, R.
FANTASIA	DURAND, P.
FANTASIA	LEES, B.
FANTASIA	MORTARI
FANTASIA	OMIZZOLO
FANTASIA	PERAGALLO, M.
FANTASIA	STARER
FANTASIA	TELEMANN, G.P.
FANTASIA	WEBER, VON
FANTASIA	ZANINELLI
FANTASIE-IMPROMPTU, OP. 66	CHOPIN
FANTASIE-IMPROMPTU, OP. 66	CHOPIN
FANTASIE-IMPROMPTU IN C SHARP MINOR, OP. 66--FROM THE	CHOPIN
FANTASIE-IMPROMPTU IN C SHARP MINOR, OP. 66	CHOPIN
FANTASIE-IMPROMPTU IN C SHARP MINOR, OP. 66	CHOPIN
FANTASIE-POLONAISE, OP. 5	SUK
FANTASIE-TARENTELLE	BINET
FANTASIE, SPIN, SPIN	ROSSI, G.

FANTASIES, BK. 1	BENJAMIN
FANTASIES, BK. 2	BENJAMIN
FANTASIES, IMPROMPTUS, MOMENTS MUSICAUX	SCHUBERT
FANTASIES, OP. 116	BRAHMS
FANTASIES, OP. 116	BRAHMS
FANTASIES, OP. 116	BRAHMS
FANTASIES, PRELUDES AND FUGUES -- CLOTH	BACH, J.S.
FANTASIES, PRELUDES AND FUGUES	BACH, J.S.
FANTASIESTUCKE, OP. 12 NO. 9--CURWEN EDITION	SCHUMANN, R.
FANTASIESTUCKE, OP. 12	SCHUMANN, R.
FANTASIESTUCKE, OP. 12	SCHUMANN, R.
FANTASIESTUCKE -- FANTASY PIECES --, OP. 12 NO. 2 -	SCHUMANN, R.
FANTASIESTUCKE -- FANTASY PIECES --, OP. 12	SCHUMANN, R.
FANTASIESTUCKE OP. 12 NO. 2 AUFSCHWUNG	SCHUMANN, R.
FANTASIESTUCKE OP. 12 NO. 3 AND 4 WARUM UND GRILLEN	SCHUMANN, R.
FANTASIESTUECK, OP. 12	SCHUMANN, R.
FANTASIES AND FUGUES	BACH, J.S.
FANTASIES CHOISIES	TELEMANN, G.P.
FANTASIES POUR LE CLAVESSIN	TELEMANN, G.P.
FANTASIES	TELEMANN, G.P.
FANTASIE AND FUGUE IN G MINOR--FOR ORGAN	BACH, J.S.
FANTASIE BURLESQUE	MESSIAEN, O.
FANTASIE C-DUR -- HOBOKEN 17-4	HAYDN
FANTASIE C-MOLL -- K.V. 396	MOZART, W. A.
FANTASIE C-MOLL -- K.V. 475	MOZART, W. A.
FANTASIE D-MOLL -- K.V. 397	MOZART, W. A.
FANTASIE ESPAGNOLE	WACHS, P.
FANTASIE FOR CLAVECIN OR PIANO	BARRAINE, E.
FANTASIE FUR 2 KLAVIERE, OP. 19	HESSENBERG, K.
FANTASIE IMPROMPTU, OP. 66 NO. 4	CHOPIN
FANTASIE IMPROMPTU, OP. 66	CHOPIN
FANTASIE IMPROMPTU IN C SHARP MINOR, OP. 66	CHOPIN
FANTASIE IN C-MOLL, BWV 906	BACH, J.S.
FANTASIE IN C-MOLL -- BWV 906	BACH, J.S.
FANTASIE IN C -- 'GRAZER FANTASIE' --	SCHUBERT
FANTASIE IN C MAJOR, H. XVII-4	HAYDN
FANTASIE IN D MINOR, K397	MOZART, W. A.
FANTASIE IN D	CRIST, B.
FANTASIE IN F MINOR, OP. 103 -- D. 940	SCHUBERT
FANTASIE IN F MINOR, OP. 49	CHOPIN
FANTASIE IN F MINOR, OP. 49	CHOPIN
FANTASIE IN F MINOR, OP. 49	CHOPIN
FANTASIE PASTORALE	MILHAUD, D.
FANTASIE SUR LES VALSES DE JOHANN STRAUSS -- SET	TANSMAN, A.
FANTASIE SUR UN MOTIF DE SARABANDE	ELLIOTT, R.
FANTASIE SUR 2 AIRS ANGEVINS	LEKEU
FANTASIE UND FUGE C-DUR -- K.V. 394	MOZART, W. A.
FANTASIE	D'INDY, V.
FANTASIE	DEBREVILLE
FANTASIE	KAPRAL
FANTASIE	MILLER, J.
FANTASIE	SCHUBERT
FANTASMAGORIE, OP. 3 NO. 3	PIERNE
FANTASMAGORIE -- SCHERZO --	GRUNENWALD
FANTASQUE	MARESCOTTI, A.
FANTASTICKS, THE	
FANTASTICKS, THE	
FANTASTIC DANCES, OP. 18, NO. 1	GAITO
FANTASTIC DANCES, OP. 18, NO. 2	GAITO
FANTASTIC DANCES, OP. 18, NO. 3	GAITO
FANTASTIC DANCES	SHOSTAKOVITCH
FANTASTIC DANCE	DELIUS, F.
FANTASTIC HORSEMAN, THE	FERNANDEZ, O.
FANTASTIC SYMPHONY, OP. 14	BERLIOZ
FANTASY-IMPROMPTU, OP. 66	CHOPIN
FANTASY, OP. 17	SCHUMANN, R.
FANTASY, OP. 17	SCHUMANN, R.
FANTASY, OP. 17	SCHUMANN, R.
FANTASY, OP. 2	ORLAND, H.
FANTASY, OP. 28	MENDELSSOHN
FANTASY, OP. 51	MARTUCCI
FANTASY -- SET	MARTINU, B.
FANTASY -- 1937	TANSMAN, A.
FANTASY -SUITE NO. 1- ,OP. 5	RACHMANINOFF, S.
FANTASY - THE FAREWELL	SMIT, L.
FANTASY AND FUGUE K394, FANTASIES K396 AND 397, URTEXT	MOZART, W. A.
FANTASY AND FUGUE ON THE NAME B-A-C-H	LISZT
FANTASY C MAJOR --'WANDERER FANTASIE'--, D 760	SCHUBERT
FANTASY AND TOCCATA, 1940	MARTINU, B.
FANTASY ELEGY AND TOCCATA	MORAWETZ
FANTASY FOR A MUSICAL CLOCK, K608	MOZART, W. A.
FANTASY FOR PIANO, OP. 9	SPINNER
FANTASY FOR PIANO, 1972	ZUR, M.
FANTASY FOR PIANO --'GRAZER FANTASIE'	SCHUBERT
FANTASY FOR PIANO AND ORCHESTRA	DUPONT
FANTASY FOR PIANO	MOSS, L.
FANTASY FOR PIANO	WILSON, G.
FANTASY IN B MINOR, OP. 28	SCRIABINE, A.
FANTASY IN C, OP. 15	SCHUBERT
FANTASY IN C, OP. 17	SCHUMANN, R.
FANTASY IN C MAJOR - WANDERER FANTASIA	SCHUBERT
FANTASY IN C MAJOR	HAYDN
FANTASY IN C MINOR	BACH, J.S.
FANTASY IN D MAJOR	ROPARTZ
FANTASY IN D MAJOR	TELEMANN, G.P.
FANTASY IN D MINOR, K397	MOZART, W. A.
FANTASY IN D MINOR, K397	MOZART, W. A.
FANTASY IN E MAJOR	TELEMANN, G.P.
FANTASY IN G MINOR, OP. 77	BEETHOVEN
FANTASY IN SPRING RHYTHM, OP. 12C	EGGE
FANTASY LAND	
FANTASY NO. 1, FROM ''PEPITA-JIMINEZ''	ALBENIZ, I.
FANTASY NO. 2, FROM ''PEPITA-JIMINEZ''	ALBENIZ, I.
FANTASY ON 'IN DULCI JUBILO'	RUSSELL
FANTASY ON AN OSSETIN TUNE	HOVHANESS, A.
FANTASY ON A THEME OF LISZT 1967	MCCABE, J.
FANTASY ON MOZART'S 'DON GIOVANNI'	LISZT
FANTASY ON SOUSA'S STARS AND STRIPES	KAYLIN, S.
FANTASY ON THREE ENGLISH FOLKSONGS--PIANO QUARTETTE--	HYSON--ED.
FANTASY PIECES, OP. 12	SCHUMANN, R.
FANTASY PIECES, OP. 12	SCHUMANN, R.
FANTASY PIECES, OP. 26	REGER
FANTASY PIECES, OP. 6--BARCAROLLE--	GRIFFES, C.
FANTASY PIECES, OP. 6--NOTTURNO--	GRIFFES, C.
FANTASY PIECES, OP. 6--SCHERZO--	GRIFFES, C.
FANTASY PIECES	DEL TREDICI
FANTASY PIECE FOR PIANO, 1966	STEINER, G.
FANTASY RONDO	FOSS, L.
FANTASY WHIRLWIND	GILLOCK
FANTASY	BENNETT, R.
FANTASY	COPLAND
FANTASY	FINNEY
FANTASY	HOVHANESS, A.
FANTASY	KARP
FANTASY	LAZARUS
FANTASY	LESUR, D.

FANTASY	NOVIKOFF
FANTASY	PENTLAND, B.
FANTOCHES	DEBUSSY
FANTOCHES	TOMASI, H.
FAREWELL TO A HERO	TSCHAIKOWSKY
FAREWELL TO THE ALPS	BOHM
FAREWELL TO THE MOUNTAINS	HOVHANESS, A.
FAREWELL TO THE PIANO	BEETHOVEN
FAREWELL TO THE PIANO	BEETHOVEN
FAREWELL TO THE PIANO	BEETHOVEN
FAREWELL TO THE PIANO	BEETHOVEN
FAREWELL	BROWN
FARMERETTE	POTTER, H.
FARMER BOOGIE - BASED ON THE HAPPY FARMER OF SCHUMANN	ZEPP
FARMER COMES TO TOWN, A	WEYBRIGHT--ED.
FARMER COMES TO TOWN, THE	WEYBRIGHT
FARMER DANCE	OLDENBURG, E.
FARMER IN THE DELL, THE -- AN ENGLISH SINGING GAME	WEYBRIGHT
FARMER IN THE DELL, THE	WEYBRIGHT--ED.
FARMYARD CAT , FROM 'FARMYARD PARADE'	LAST, J.
FARMYARD PARADE	LAST, J.
FARM MEDLEY, A -- OLD MACDONALD AND ZIP COON	WEYBRIGHT
FARM MEDLEY, A	WEYBRIGHT--ED.
FAR AWAY, REMEMBER ME	BRINKMANN
FAR TO GO FROM "MONDAY'S CHILD"	LAST, J.
FASCHINGSSCHWANK, OP. 26	SCHUMANN, R.
FASCHINGSSCHWANK, OP. 26	SCHUMANN, R.
FASCHINGSSCHWANK AUS WIEN, OP. 26	SCHUMANN, R.
FASCHINGSSCHWANK AUS WIEN, OP. 26	SCHUMANN, R.
FASCHINGSSCHWANK AUS WIEN, OP. 26	SCHUMANN, R.
FASCHINGSSCHWANK AUS WIEN, OP. 26	SCHUMANN, R.
FASCHINGSSCHWANK AUS WIEN -- CARNAVAL OF VIENNA -- OP.	SCHUMANN, R.
FASCHINGSSCHWANK AUS WIEN -- CARNIVAL JEST FROM VIENNA	SCHUMANN, R.
FASCHINGSSCHWANK WIEN, OP. 26	SCHUMANN, R.
FASCINATING RHYTHM	GERSHWIN
FASCINATING RHYTHM	GERSHWIN
FASCINATION-GAMSE	MARCHETTI, F.
FASCINATION -- SIMP.	MARCHETTI, F.
FASCINATION -- VARIATIONS ON THE THEME FOR PIANO	SNYDER, W.
FASCINATION WALTZ	MARCHETTI, F.
FASCINATION	ADAMS, B.
FASCINATION	BRIMHALL,
FASCINATION	DE VITO, A.
FASCINATION	MARCHETTI, F.
FASCINATION	MARCHETTI, F.
FASCINATION	MARCHETTI, F.
FASCINATION	MARCHETTI, F.
FAST MAIL GALOP, FOR TWO PIANOS, EIGHT HANDS	STREABBOG
FATA MORGANA E L'ORCO, LA, OP. 27	BOSSI, R.
FATHER, IN THY MYSTERIOUS PRESENCE KNEELING	MASON, L.
FATHER CHRISTMAS	SCHAUM, J.--ED.
FATHER OF WATERS	GROFE, F.
FATHER VICTORY, FRENCH MARCH	GANNE
FAUNS, THE, OP. 60	CHAMINADE
FAUNS, THE - SYLVAINS	CHAMINADE
FAUST. SOLDIERS' CHORUS. TWO PIANOS, EIGHT HANDS	GOUNOD, C.
FAUST. VALSE. TWO PIANOS, EIGHT HANDS	GOUNOD, C.
FAUST, FLOWER SONG	GOUNOD, C.
FAUST, SOLDIERS' CHORUS	GOUNOD, C.
FAUST, VALSE	GOUNOD, C. *
FAUST -- DUO	GOUNOD, C.
FAUST - EASY FANTASIA	GOUNOD, C.
FAUST - WALTZES	GOUNOD, C.
FAUST - WALTZES	GOUNOD, C.
FAUST - WALTZES	GOUNOD, C.
FAUST - WALTZ	GOUNOD, C.
FAUST BALLET, NO. 1	GOUNOD, C.
FAUST BALLET, NO. 6	GOUNOD, C.
FAUST BALLET	GOUNOD, C.
FAUST UP TO DATE	LUTZ
FAUST WALTZ	GOUNOD, C.
FAUST	GOUNOD, C.
FAUST	GOUNOD, C.
FAUVETTE, LA -- CAPRICE --	FISCHER
FAVILLE CAPRICCIO	SILVESTRI
FAVOLE DI PERAULT	SOMMI
FAVORITA, LA - EASY FANTASIA	DONIZETTI
FAVORITES FOR THE PIANIST, HYMNS NO. 1	WHITFORD--ED.
FAVORITES FOR THE PIANIST, NO. 01	WHITFORD--ED.
FAVORITES FOR THE PIANIST, NO. 02	WHITFORD--ED.
FAVORITES FOR THE PIANIST, NO. 03	WHITFORD--ED.
FAVORITES FOR THE PIANIST, NO. 04	WHITFORD--ED.
FAVORITES FOR THE PIANIST, NO. 05	WHITFORD--ED.
FAVORITES FOR THE PIANIST, NO. 06	WHITFORD--ED.
FAVORITES FOR THE PIANIST, NO. 07	WHITFORD--ED.
FAVORITES FOR THE PIANIST, NO. 08	WHITFORD--ED.
FAVORITES FOR THE PIANIST, NO. 09	WHITFORD--ED.
FAVORITES FOR THE PIANIST, NO. 10	WHITFORD--ED.
FAVORITES FOR THE PIANIST, NO. 11	WHITFORD--ED.
FAVORITES FOR THE PIANIST, NO. 12	WHITFORD--ED.
FAVORITES FOR THE PIANIST, NO. 13	WHITFORD--ED.
FAVORITES FOR THE PIANIST, NO. 14	WHITFORD--ED.
FAVORITES FOR THE PIANIST, NO. 15	WHITFORD--ED.
FAVORITES FOR THE PIANIST, NO. 16	WHITFORD--ED.
FAVORITES FOR THE PIANIST, NO. 17	WHITFORD--ED.
FAVORITES FOR THE PIANIST, NO. 18	WHITFORD--ED.
FAVORITES FOR THE PIANIST, NO. 19	WHITFORD--ED.
FAVORITES FOR THE PIANIST, NO. 20	WHITFORD--ED.
FAVORITES FROM THE HYMNAL NO. 1	ROGERS, E. T.
FAVORITES FROM THE HYMNAL NO. 2	ROGERS, E. T.
FAVORITES FROM YOUNG WORLD	ROGERS, E. T.
FAVORITE BRAHMS HUNGARIAN DANCES	BRAHMS
FAVORITE CATHOLIC HYMNS	THOMPSON, J.--ED
FAVORITE CHRISTMAS MELODIES	SPENCER, J.
FAVORITE CHRISTMAS MELODIES	
FAVORITE COMPOSITIONS	MOZART, W. A.
FAVORITE FOLKSONGS	LIPSCOMB--ED.
FAVORITE FOLK SONGS	JOYNER, B.--ED
FAVORITE FOLK TUNES	HOWELL--ED.
FAVORITE HYMNS, EASY TO READ, PLAY, SING	WATSON--ED.
FAVORITE HYMNS FOR THE PIANO	LYALL, M.--ED
FAVORITE HYMNS IN EASY ARRANGEMENTS FOR PIANO DUET	RICHTER, A.
FAVORITE HYMNS MADE EASY --BIG NOTE-- --200--	
FAVORITE HYMNS TO PLAY AND SING IN EASY PIANO	WILLIAMS, L.
FAVORITE MELODIES FOR THE ADULT	WILLIAMS, J.
FAVORITE MELODIES MADE EASY	SPENCER, J.
FAVORITE PIECES	SCHUBERT
FAVORITE REELS AND JIGS	
FAVORITE SACRED CLASSICS	WILLIAMS--ED.
FAVORITE SONGS OF THE NINETIES	FREMONT, R.--ED.
FAVORITE THEME, A -- FROM FANTASIE IMPROMPTU	CHOPIN
FAVORITE TUNES FOR PIANO	GARSCIA
FAVORITE TUNES	PAIN, E.
FAVORITLANDLERWALZER	HUMMEL, J. N.
FAVOURITES -- 12 EASY PIECES	DUKE, H.
FAWN, THE	SCHILLER, W.
FAWN IN THE FOREST	ADLER, M.
FEAST IN THE EAST	STEINER
FEATHER DANCE--VALSE-CAPRICE	DUCELLE, P.
FEATHER IN MY CAP	BOSTELMANN
FEBRUARY PIECES FOR PIANO, AND OCTET '61 FOR JASPER	CARDEW
FEDORA - INTERLUDIO	GIORDANO
FEDORA - SELECTIONS, BK. 1	GIORDANO
FEDORA - SELECTIONS, BK. 2	GIORDANO
FEDORA - SELECTIONS	GIORDANO
FEEDING THE DOLPHINS	SCHAUM, J.--ED.
FEET IN THE JUNGLE	WEYBRIGHT
FELICIANA	PERKINS, F.
FELICIE NANTEUIL, VALSE	IBERT
FEMMES D'ESPAGNE, BK. 1 - LA MADRILENE CLASSIQUE,	TURINA, J.
FEMMES D'ESPAGNE, BK. 2 - LA GITANE AMOUREUSE, LA	TURINA, J.
FEMMES DE SEVILLE - LA POTIERE DE TRIANA, JOLIE FILLE,	TURINA, J.
FENETRE SUR LE JARDIN	MARTINU, B.
FERNANDE, VALSE LENTE	LORMER
FERNANDO, SCHOTT	GREENWALD, M.
FERRANTE AND TEICHER INTERPRETATIONS FOR SOLO PIANO	
FERRIQUE	IBERT
FERRIS WHEEL, THE	RICHTER
FERRIS WHEEL	RAPHLING
FESTA DELLA MAMMA, LA	BILLI
FESTIVAL AT BAGDAD, SCHEHEREZADE	RIMSKY-KORSAKOFF
FESTIVAL BELLS	BIZET, G.
FESTIVAL FUGUES	GREEN, R.
FESTIVAL FUGUE	BACH, J.S.
FESTIVAL GROUPS FOR PIANO SELECTED BY ARTHUR BENJAMIN,	HANDEL
FESTIVAL GROUPS FOR PIANO SELECTED BY ARTHUR BENJAMIN,	BENJAMIN
FESTIVAL GROUPS FOR PIANO SELECTED BY ARTHUR BENJAMIN,	DUNHILL
FESTIVAL GROUPS FOR PIANO SELECTED BY ARTHUR BENJAMIN,	DIBDIN
FESTIVAL GROUPS FOR PIANO SELECTED BY ARTHUR BENJAMIN,	HARRISON, L.
FESTIVAL GROUPS FOR PIANO SELECTED BY ARTHUR BENJAMIN,	FARJEON
FESTIVAL GROUPS FOR PIANO SELECTED BY ARTHUR BENJAMIN,	GLIERE
FESTIVAL GROUPS FOR PIANO SELECTED BY ARTHUR BENJAMIN,	HOOK
FESTIVAL GROUPS FOR PIANO SELECTED BY ARTHUR BENJAMIN,	FARJEON
FESTIVAL GROUPS FOR PIANO SELECTED BY ARTHUR BENJAMIN,	DUNCOMBE
FESTIVAL GROUPS FOR PIANO SELECTED BY ARTHUR BENJAMIN,	ROWLEY
FESTIVAL GROUPS FOR PIANO SELECTED BY ARTHUR BENJAMIN,	BENJAMIN
FESTIVAL GROUPS FOR PIANO SELECTED BY ARTHUR BENJAMIN,	DUNHILL
FESTIVAL GROUPS FOR PIANO SELECTED BY ARTHUR BENJAMIN,	FISCHER, H.
FESTIVAL GROUPS FOR PIANO SELECTED BY ARTHUR BENJAMIN,	JONES, S. T.
FESTIVAL GROUPS FOR PIANO SELECTED BY ARTHUR BENJAMIN,	HAYDN
FESTIVAL GROUPS FOR PIANO SELECTED BY ARTHUR BENJAMIN,	BACH, J.S.
FESTIVAL GROUPS FOR PIANO SELECTED BY ARTHUR BENJAMIN,	BEETHOVEN
FESTIVAL GROUPS FOR PIANO SELECTED BY ARTHUR BENJAMIN,	QUILTER
FESTIVAL GROUPS FOR PIANO SELECTED BY ARTHUR BENJAMIN,	MUNN, W.
FESTIVAL GROUPS FOR PIANO SELECTED BY ARTHUR BENJAMIN,	BROOM, P.
FESTIVAL GROUPS FOR PIANO SELECTED BY ARTHUR BENJAMIN,	MOY
FESTIVAL IN BRAZIL	RIMSKY-KORSAKOFF
FESTIVAL MARCH -- 6-HANDS	BEHR, F.
FESTIVAL OF SOLOS	SCHAUM, J.
FESTIVAL OF SOLOS	SCHAUM, J.
FESTIVAL OF THE DRAGON	HAUBIEL, C.
FESTIVAL OVERTURE	SHOSTAKOVITCH
FESTIVAL	GLOVER, D.
FESTIVAL	HAUBIEL, C.
FESTIVAL	MOWREY, D.
FESTIVAL	SCHER, W.
FESTIVAL	WHITFORD
FESTIVE DANCE	GURLITT
FESTIVE DANCE	GURLITT
FESTIVE PIECE	BAUERNFEIND
FESTIVE PIECE	GILLOCK
FESTIVIANA	GROFE, F.
FESTOUVERTURE, OP. 70	FOERSTER
FEST IM SUEDEN, OP. 6 -- DANCE-DRAMA IN ONE ACT	BLACHER
FETES, NOCTURNE	DEBUSSY
FETES DE L'ENFANCE, LES	WACHS, P.
FETES LOINTAINES	MOMPOU, F.
FETES	DEBUSSY
FETE DE LA BERGERE, LA	MIGOT
FETE FANTASQUE, UNE	FREED, I.
FEUILLES LIBRES	TCHEREPNIN
FEUILLES MORTES FROM PRELUDES, BK. 2	DEBUSSY
FEUILLETS D'ALBUM -- UNE VALSE	SAUGUET
FEUILLETS D'ALBUM -- UN NOCTURNE	SAUGUET
FEUILLETS D'ALBUM -- UN SCHERZO	SAUGUET
FEUILLETS D'ALBUM - ARIETTE, REVE, GIGUE	POULENC, F.
FEUILLETS DE VOYAGE, BK. 1	SCHMITT, F.
FEUILLETS DE VOYAGE, BK. 2	SCHMITT, F.
FEUX-FOLLETS, OP. 24 NO. 3	PHILIPP, I.
FEUX-FOLLETS -- JACK O'LANTERNS -- OP. 24 NO. 3 -- SET	PHILIPP, I.
FEUX FOLLETS--NO.5 OF THE TRANSCENDENTAL ETUDES--	LISZT
FEU ROLLANT	DUVERNOY, J.
FIABA ARMONIOSA - 7 PIECES	CAPUS
FIANCAILLES	WESLY
FICARAS SOSINHA	GUARNIERI
FICARAS SOSINHA	GUARNIERI
FICKLE COUNTRY MAID, THE	COUPERIN, P.
FIDDLE-FADDLE -- SIMP.	KING, S.
FIDDLE-FADDLE	ANDERSON, L.
FIDDLE-FADDLE	ANDERSON, L.
FIDDLERS BOOGIE, THE	LOCKYER
FIDDLER ON THE GREEN	HINSON, M.
FIDDLER ON THE ROOF	BOCK, J.
FIDDLE BOOGIE DEE	LYON
FIDDLE STICKS	TRUXELL, E.
FIDDLE TUNE	GLEDHILL, C.
FIDDLE TUNE	GRAHAM, R.
FIDDLIN' JOE	MOORE *
FIDELIO OVERTURE, OP. 72B. TWO PIANOS, EIGHT HANDS	BEETHOVEN
FIELD ARTILLERY SONG	ROYAL--ED
FIELD MOUSE	REISTRUP, J.
FIESTA GITANA, LA	HARPER, M.
FIESTA IN MEXICO	ARCHER, I.
FIESTA MEXICANA	DE SOLIS
FIESTA TIME	ECKSTEIN
FIESTA TIME	OLDENBURG, E.
FIESTA	AGAY, D.--ED
FIESTA	CANFIELD, J.
FIESTA	GILLOCK
FIESTA	GILLOCK
FIESTA	ROGERS
FIFERS, THE	DANDRIEU, P.
FIFERS, THE	DANDRIEU, P.
FIFE AND DRUM, THE	RUSSELL
FIFE AND DRUM CORPS	KELLEY, R.
FIFE AND DRUM DORPS	NEVIN
FIFE AND DRUM	RUSSELL
FIFTEEN CAROLS FOR TWO	JOHNSON
FIFTEEN CHILDREN'S PIECES, OP. 27, BK. 1	KABALEVSKY
FIFTEEN DESCRIPTIVE MINIATURES	SCHER, W.
FIFTEEN EASY PIECES	BEETHOVEN
FIFTEEN EASY STUDIES FOR THE SMALL HAND	POZZOLI
FIFTEEN ETUDES DE VIRTUOSITE, OP. 72	MOSZKOWSKI

FIFTEEN ETUDES DE VIRTUOSITE, OP. 72	MOSZKOWSKI
FIFTEEN ETUDES DE VIRTUOSITE, OP. 72	MOSZKOWSKI
FIFTEEN ETUDES MELODIQUES, OP. 43	NOLLET, E.
FIFTEEN ETUDES MELODIQUES	PHILIPP, I.
FIFTEEN EXERCICES	KARTUN
FIFTEEN EXERCISES AND STUDIES ON BROKEN CHORDS	ROGERS, J.
FIFTEEN FAVORITE WALTZES	WALDTEUFEL, E.
FIFTEEN FINGERS	TATE, P.
FIFTEEN HUMOROUS PIANO PIECES	STEINER
FIFTEEN HUNGARIAN PEASANT SONGS	BARTOK
FIFTEEN LITTLE COMPOSITIONS FOR LITTLE PIANISTS	DIONISI
FIFTEEN LITTLE DANCES OF THE 18TH CENTURY	SCHOCH
FIFTEEN LITTLE DANCES	BEETHOVEN
FIFTEEN LITTLE PICTURES	ROWLEY
FIFTEEN LITTLE PIECES ON FIVE-NOTE PATTERNS	AGAY, D.
FIFTEEN LITTLE VARIATIONS	SKALKOTTAS, N.
FIFTEEN MAHRISCHE VOLKSLIEDER	JANACEK
FIFTEEN MEDIUM GRADE PIANO SOLOS	
FIFTEEN MELODIOUS STUDIES, OP. 43	NOLLET, E.
FIFTEEN MEN IN A PIRATE BOAT	BURNAM
FIFTEEN MODERATELY EASY PIECES FOR THE YOUNG	TANSMAN, A.
FIFTEEN MODERATELY EASY PIECES FOR THE YOUNG	TANSMAN, A.
FIFTEEN MODERATELY EASY PIECES FOR THE YOUNG	TANSMAN, A.
FIFTEEN MODERATELY EASY PIECES FOR THE YOUNG	TANSMAN, A.
FIFTEEN MODERATELY EASY PIECES FOR THE YOUNG	TANSMAN, A.
FIFTEEN MODERATELY EASY PIECES FOR THE YOUNG	TANSMAN, A.
FIFTEEN MODERATELY EASY PIECES FOR THE YOUNG	TANSMAN, A.
FIFTEEN MODERATELY EASY PIECES FOR THE YOUNG	TANSMAN, A.
FIFTEEN MODERATELY EASY PIECES FOR THE YOUNG	TANSMAN, A.
FIFTEEN PREPARATORY STUDIES TO CZERNY'S "SCHOOL OF	LECOUPPEY, F.
FIFTEEN RECREATIVE ETUDES	SCHER, W.
FIFTEEN SELECTED STUDIES, OP. 20	KESSLER
FIFTEEN STUDIES, OP. 26	LECOUPPEY, F.
FIFTEEN STUDIES FOR THE LEFT HAND, OP. 92	MOSZKOWSKI
FIFTEEN STUDIES IN EXPRESSION, OP. 44	CONCONE, G.
FIFTEEN STUDIES IN STYLE, OP. 31	CONCONE, G.
FIFTEEN STUDIES IN STYLE AND EXPRESSION, OP. 25	CONCONE, G.
FIFTEEN THREE-PART INVENTIONS	BACH, J.S.
FIFTEEN TWO-PART INVENTIONS	BACH, J.S.
FIFTEEN VARIATIONS ON A 12 TONE SERIES	KOFFLER, J.
FIFTH AVENUE POODLE	BASTIEN
FIFTH AVENUE POODLE	GLOVER, D.
FIFTH GRADE PIANO BOOK	WILLIAMS, J.
FIFTH GRADE TECHNIC	THOMPSON, J.
FIFTH NOCTURNE, OP. 52	LEYBACH, I.
FIFTH NOCTURNE IN A FLAT, OP. 52	LEYBACH, I.
FIFTH NOCTURNE	FIELD, J.
FIFTH NOCTURNE	LEYBACH, I.
FIFTH NOCTURNE	LEYBACH, I.
FIFTH ROOT OF FIVE -- 2 PNO AND PERC, SET OF 4 SCORES	KASEMETS, U.
FIFTH SONATA, OP. 31	BARTH, H.
FIFTH SYMPHONY	BEETHOVEN
FIFTH WALTZ, EASY	GODARD, B.
FIFTY-EIGHT TUNEFUL TECHNICAL STUDIES, BK. 1	SPIVAK, S.
FIFTY-FIVE AND ONE-HALF PIANO SOLOS	
FIFTY-FIVE PIANO CLASSICS - PAST AND PRESENT	
FIFTY-FIVE PIANO CLASSICS	
FIFTY-FIVE POPULAR PIANO TEACHING PIECES	
FIFTY-FIVE SMALL PIANO PIECES, BK. 1	KADOSA
FIFTY-FIVE SMALL PIANO PIECES, BK. 2	KADOSA
FIFTY-FOUR FAMOUS MARCHES FOR PIANO	
FIFTY-NINE FAMOUS PIANO SOLOS	
FIFTY-NINE PIANO SOLOS YOU LIKE TO PLAY	
FIFTY-ONE ETUDES	BRAHMS
FIFTY-ONE EXERCISES, OP. POSTH. BK. 1	BRAHMS
FIFTY-ONE EXERCISES, OP. POSTH. BK. 2	BRAHMS
FIFTY-ONE EXERCISES	BRAHMS
FIFTY-ONE EXERCISES	BRAHMS
FIFTY-ONE MARZURKAS	CHOPIN
FIFTY-ONE PIANO PIECES FROM THE MODERN REPERTOIRE	
FIFTY-ONE STUDIES	BRAHMS
FIFTY-SEVEN PIANO PIECES CHILDREN LIKE TO PLAY	
FIFTY-SIX MAZURKAS	CHOPIN
FIFTY-SIX PIANO CLASSICS	
FIFTY-THREE PIANO SOLOS IN THE EARLY GRADES	
FIFTY-THREE STUDIES BASED ON 26 CHOPIN ETUDES, VOL. 1	GODOWSKY, L.
FIFTY-THREE STUDIES BASED ON 26 CHOPIN ETUDES, VOL. 2	GODOWSKY, L.
FIFTY-THREE STUDIES BASED ON 26 CHOPIN ETUDES, VOL. 3	GODOWSKY, L.
FIFTY-THREE STUDIES BASED ON 26 CHOPIN ETUDES, VOL. 4	GODOWSKY, L.
FIFTY-THREE STUDIES BASED ON 26 CHOPIN ETUDES, VOL. 5	GODOWSKY, L.
FIFTY-TWO GREAT ROCK AND ROLL HITS	
FIFTY BY JOHN LENNON AND PAUL MCCARTNEY, EASY BIG NOTE	LENNON *
FIFTY ETUDES MINIATURES DE METRIQUE ET DE RHYTHMIQUE,	DALCROZE
FIFTY ETUDES MINIATURES DE METRIQUE ET DE RHYTHMIQUE,	DALCROZE
FIFTY ETUDES MINIATURES DE METRIQUE ET DE RHYTHMIQUE,	DALCROZE
FIFTY ETUDES MINIATURES DE METRIQUE ET DE RHYTHMIQUE,	DALCROZE
FIFTY MEISTERCHORAELE	WOLFRAM
FIFTY MINI-ESERCIZI	BALLARO, E.
FIFTY PIANO COMPOSITIONS	SCHUMANN, R.
FIFTY PIECES WITHOUT OCTAVES FOR BEGINNERS, OP. 70	BERENS, H.
FIFTY POLYPHONIC PIECES	EBBENHORST
FIFTY POPULAR BIGNOTE PIANO TEACHING PIECES, BK. 1	BRIMHALL,
FIFTY POPULAR BIGNOTE PIANO TEACHING PIECES, BK. 2	BRIMHALL,
FIFTY POPULAR TEACHING PIECES FOR EASY PIANO	BRIMHALL,
FIFTY RUSSIAN FOLK SONGS	TSCHAIKOWSKY
FIFTY SECOND GRADE ETUDES	THOMPSON, J.
FIFTY SELECTED STUDIES--FROM OP. 45, 46, 47	HELLER, S.
FIFTY SELECTED STUDIES--IN SPANISH	CRAMER, J.
FIFTY SELECTED STUDIES, BK. 1	CRAMER, J.
FIFTY SELECTED STUDIES, BK. 2	CRAMER, J.
FIFTY SELECTED STUDIES, BK. 3	CRAMER, J.
FIFTY SELECTED STUDIES, BK. 4	CRAMER, J.
FIFTY SELECTED STUDIES, FROM OP. 29, 32, 100, 134	BERTINI
FIFTY SELECTED STUDIES, FROM OP. 29, 32, 100	BERTINI
FIFTY SELECTED STUDIES	CRAMER, J.
FIFTY SONGS -- FIFTY STATES	SCHAUM, J.
FIGARO'S WEDDING, OVERTURE	MOZART, W. A.
FIGURINE - 6 LITTLE PIECES ON 5 NOTES	SICILIANO
FILEUSE, LA, OP. 157 NO. 2	RAFF, J.
FILEUSES PRES DE CARANTEC, OP. 13 NO. 5	RHENE-BATON
FILIGREE	DOIGE
FILL-INS FOR THE PIANIST	WHITFORD
FILLE DU TAMBOUR-MAJOR. FANTASY. TWO PIANOS, EIGHT	OFFENBACH
FILLING STATION	THOMSON, V.
FILM IN MINIATURE	MARTINU, B.
FILS DES ETIOLES, LE	SATIE, E.
FINALE GAUDIOSO - NO. 3 FROM SUITE FOR PIANO	KOCH, J.
FINALE GRANDIOSO	KOCH, J.
FINALE IN A FLAT, FROM SONATA NO. 8	HAYDN
FINALE	ALKAN
FINAL EXAM BLUES	BASTIEN
FINEST MUSIC SERIES -- BEETHOVEN	BEETHOVEN
FINEST MUSIC SERIES -- GRIEG	GRIEG
FINEST MUSIC SERIES -- LISZT	LISZT
FINEST MUSIC SERIES -- STRAUSS	STRAUSS, J.
FINGAL'S CAVE -- THE HEBRIDES -- OVERTURE	MENDELSSOHN

FINGERPOWER, BK. 1	SCHAUM, J.
FINGERPOWER, BK. 2	SCHAUM, J.
FINGERPOWER, BK. 3	SCHAUM, J.
FINGERPOWER, BK. 4	SCHAUM, J.
FINGERPOWER, BK. 5	SCHAUM, J.
FINGERPOWER, BK. 6	SCHAUM, J.
FINGERPOWER, PREP BOOK	SCHAUM, J.
FINGERS IN FLIGHT	CORBMAN
FINGERS PLAY -- SONGS FOR LITTLE FINGERS	MILLER, M. *
FINGER FABLES	CORBMAN
FINGER FLIGHT	OLDENBURG, E.
FINGER FREEDOM	CORBMAN
FINGER FROLICS -- 1. CHASING RABBITS	BRODSKY, M.
FINGER FROLICS -- 2. CUCKOO ON A SPREE	BRODSKY, M.
FINGER FROLICS -- 4. CAMP SPIRIT	BRODSKY, M.
FINGER FUN	ADLER, M.
FINGER FUN	WEYBRIGHT
FINGER FUN	WEYBRIGHT
FINGER PAINTINGS	FAITH
FINGER PLAY	ZAJAN, P. *
FINGER PUPPETS	NAGY, M.
FINGER TALK	TEMPLETON, V.
FINGER TECHNIQUE STUDIES	PAUER
FINGER TRICKS	OLDENBURG, E.
FINIAN'S RAINBOW	
FINIAN'S RAINBOW	
FINLANDIA, OP. 26 NO. 7	SIBELIUS
FINLANDIA, OP. 26 NO. 7	SIBELIUS
FINLANDIA, OP. 26 NO. 7	SIBELIUS
FINLANDIA	SIBELIUS
FINLANDIA	SIBELIUS
FINLANDIA	SIBELIUS
FINNISH FOLK TUNES, OP. 27	BUSONI
FINSON ET FAUVETTE	BARBOT
FIORELLINO, OP. 43 NO. 5	MARTUCCI
FIREBIRD, RONDE DES PRINCESSES	STRAVINSKY, I.
FIRECRACKER, GALOP	MARTIN, G.
FIREFLIES FROLIC	SPENCER, R.
FIREFLIES IN THE GRASS	WADLEY
FIREFLIES ON PARADE	BENNETT, R.
FIREFLIES ON PARADE	BENNETT, R.
FIREFLIES	BAUER, M.
FIREFLIES	BURKE, T.
FIREFLIES	FERNANDEZ, O.
FIREFLIES	GEST, E.
FIREFLIES	KAHL
FIREFLY AND THE FROG, THE	WEISLEDER, A.
FIREFLY WALTZES, THE--"THE FIREFLY"	FRIML, R.
FIREFLY	BILOTTI
FIREFLY	TROWBRIDGE, L.
FIREWORKS--FEUX D'ARTIFICE--	DEBUSSY
FIRE AND FLAME	LOUKA, M.
FIRE AND RAIN	
FIRE DANCE	ECKSTEIN
FIRE DANCE	HUERTER, C.
FIRE DRILL	LINCOLN, H.
FIRE OF SPRING	IRELAND, J.
FIRMEZA, LA	GILARDI
FIRST ALBUM FOR CHILDREN, OP. 210	KOEHLER
FIRST AND SECOND GRADE STUDY PIECES	PARLOW, E.
FIRST ARABESQUE, FOR 2 PIANOS 8 HANDS	DEBUSSY
FIRST ARABESQUE	DEBUSSY
FIRST ARABESQUE	DEBUSSY
FIRST ARABESQUE	DEBUSSY
FIRST BEGINNING -- 100 EASY PIECES	CZERNY
FIRST BOOK, A	BEETHOVEN
FIRST BOOK, A	GURLITT
FIRST BOOK, A	HANDEL
FIRST BOOK FOR THE ADULT BEGINNER	WILLIAMS, J.
FIRST BOOK OF FAVORITE HYMNS	ROGERS, E. T.
FIRST BOOK OF HANON	HANON, C.
FIRST BOOK OF HYMNS AND CAROLS, A	FREDRICH, F.--ED
FIRST BOOK OF TECHNICAL EXERCISES--WITH SPECIAL	QUAILE, E.
FIRST BOOK OF TUNES TO PLAY	GOODRICH
FIRST BOOK	BACH, J.S.
FIRST BOOK	HAYDN
FIRST BOUQUET OF WALTZES, A	THORNTON
FIRST BUD, OP. 15 NO. 1	HURD, E.
FIRST CHOPIN	CHOPIN
FIRST CHRISTMAS - A STORY WITH MUSIC	RICHTER, A.
FIRST CLASSICS, BK. 1 - PRELIMINARY	BRADLEY
FIRST CLASSICS, BK. 2 - PRIMARY	BRADLEY
FIRST CLASSICS, BK. 3 - ELEMENTARY-TRANSITIONAL	BRADLEY
FIRST CLASSICS, THE	AGAY, D.--ED
FIRST CLASSIC COLLECTION	
FIRST COMPOSERS - BACH	BACH, J.S.
FIRST COMPOSERS - BEETHOVEN	BEETHOVEN
FIRST COMPOSERS - HANDEL	HANDEL
FIRST COMPOSERS - MOZART	MOZART, W. A.
FIRST COMPOSERS - SCHUBERT	SCHUBERT
FIRST CONCERTO DA CAMERA ADAGIO MOVEMENT	ALKAN
FIRST CONCEPTO DA CAMERA IN A MINOR, OP. 10 NO. 1	ALKAN
FIRST CONCERTO DA CAMERA IN A MINOR, OP. 10	ALKAN
FIRST CONCERTO IN C MAJOR	SOLER, A.
FIRST CONCERT	LAST, J.
FIRST COURSE, BK. 1 - PREPARATORY	BRADLEY
FIRST COURSE, BK. 2 - PRELIMINARY	BRADLEY
FIRST COURSE, BK. 3 - PRIMARY	BRADLEY
FIRST COURSE, BK. 4 - ELEMENTARY	BRADLEY
FIRST DANCING CLASS, THE	BASTIEN
FIRST DAY OF SPRING, THE	ANDERSON, L.
FIRST DUETS, THE	AGAY, D.--ED
FIRST DUET BOOK--GERMAN EDITION	DILLER, A. *
FIRST DUET BOOK--50 DUETS	DILLER, A. *
FIRST DUET BOOK FOR LITTLE JACKS AND JILLS, A	RODGERS, I.
FIRST DUET BOOK	ECKSTEIN
FIRST EASTER - A STORY WITH MUSIC	RICHTER, A.
FIRST EXERCISES IN POLYPHONIC STYLE - 50 SHORT CANONS	POZZOLI
FIRST FAVORITES	
FIRST FLIGHT OF A LITTLE BIRD, THE	BOSTELMANN
FIRST FLIGHT	GOULD, E.
FIRST FLOWER	STREABBOG
FIRST FUN AT THE PIANO	BRIMHALL,
FIRST GRADE ETUDES - SECOND PIANO ACCOMPANIMENTS	THOMPSON, J.
FIRST GRADE ETUDES	THOMPSON, J.
FIRST GRADE PEDAL BOOK	KASSCHAU, H.
FIRST GRADE PIANO BOOK	WILLIAMS, J.
FIRST GRADE PIANO PIECES	BLAKE, J. *
FIRST GRADE SUPPLEMENT	STEINER
FIRST HAYDN BOOK, A	HAYDN
FIRST HAYDN BOOK, THE, MEMORIES OF OLD VIENNA	HAYDN
FIRST HAYDN BOOK, THE	HAYDN
FIRST INSTRUCTION BOOK, BK. 1	WAGNER, E. D.
FIRST INSTRUCTION IN PIANO-PLAYING--100 RECREATIONS	CZERNY
FIRST INSTRUCTOR IN PIANO PLAYING	CZERNY
FIRST JAZZ	KING
FIRST LESSON, THE	KROGMANN, C. W.

FIRST LESSONS, BK. 1	BACH, J.S.
FIRST LESSONS, BK. 1	BACH, J.S.
FIRST LESSONS, BK. 2	BACH, J.S.
FIRST LESSONS, OP. 117	GURLITT
FIRST LESSONS, THE--TWENTY-FOUR LITTLE MELODIES, OP.	GURLITT
FIRST LESSONS FOR THE DANCE BAND PIANIST	GIRLAMO, F.
FIRST LESSONS IN BACH, BK. 1	BACH, J.S.
FIRST LESSONS IN BACH, BK. 2	BACH, J.S.
FIRST LIGHTS ON PIANO PLAYING	MATTHAY, T.
FIRST LITTLE TUNES	RICHTER
FIRST LOSS, OP. 68 NO. 16--ALBUM FOR THE YOUNG	SCHUMANN, R.
FIRST LOSS, OP. 68 NO. 16	SCHUMANN, R.
FIRST LOSS, OP. 68 NO. 16	SCHUMANN, R.
FIRST MARCH -- ALLA MARCIA MODERATO	DAHL
FIRST MARCH	ROBINSON, A.
FIRST MAZURKA, OP. 25	GODARD, B.
FIRST MELODY LESSONS	BILBRO, M.
FIRST MOMENTS AT THE PIANO, PART 1	THOMAS, H. T.
FIRST MOMENTS AT THE PIANO, PART 2	THOMAS, H. T.
FIRST NOCTURNE	RUSSELL
FIRST NOEL, THE	PIKLER
FIRST NOEL, THE	STEINER
FIRST NOEL, THE	WALLIS--ED
FIRST NOEL AND COME ALL YE FAITHFUL	SPENCER, J.
FIRST PEDAL-STUDIES--24 PROGRESSIVE EXERCISES AND	DILLER, A. *
FIRST PEDAL STUDIES	GAYNOR
FIRST PEER GYNT SUITE, OP. 46	GRIEG
FIRST PIANO BOOK, BK. 1	HILLEMANN *
FIRST PIANO BOOK, BK. 2	HILLEMANN *
FIRST PIANO BOOK, BK. 3	HILLEMANN *
FIRST PIANO BOOK FOR LITTLE JACKS AND JILLS, A--FOR	RODGERS, L.
FIRST PIANO DUETS--SEVEN EASY PIECES	KOLINSKI, M.
FIRST PIANO DUETS	CAMPBELL
FIRST PIANO LESSONS	SARSON, M.
FIRST PIANO LESSONS	SARSON, M.
FIRST PIECES FOR FOUR HANDS	SOLTERS
FIRST POPULAR PIANO PIECES, NO. 1	BRIMHALL,
FIRST POPULAR PIANO PIECES, NO. 2	BRIMHALL,
FIRST POPULAR PIANO PIECES, NO. 3	BRIMHALL,
FIRST PROM WALTZ	KLEINMAN, A.
FIRST READING EXPERIENCES	BASTIEN
FIRST RECITAL, THE	AGAY, D.
FIRST ROSE OF SPRING WALTZ	HOPKINS, H.
FIRST ROUNDS FOR PIANO -- FOR 2 PLAYERS	BURROWS
FIRST ROUNDS FOR PIANO -- FOR 3 AND 4 PLAYERS	BURROWS
FIRST ROUNDS FOR PIANO -- ONE PIANO, SIX HANDS --	BURROWS
FIRST ROUNDS	BURROWS
FIRST RUMANIAN RHAPSODY	ENESCO
FIRST SCARLATTI	SCARLATTI, D.
FIRST SCHOOL, OP. 599	CZERNY
FIRST SOLO BOOK	COBB
FIRST SONATA	MEYER
FIRST SONATA	OLSON
FIRST SONATINA, A	BASTIEN
FIRST SONATINAS -- AN INTRODUCTION TO THE CLASSICS	MATHEWS, W.--ED
FIRST SONATINA BOOK, THE	PALMER, W.
FIRST SONATINA IN F MAJOR -- IN FOUR MOVEMENTS	COBB
FIRST STEPHEN FOSTER	HOFSTAD, M.
FIRST STEPS -- EASY DUETS	MAYKAPAR
FIRST STEPS -- PRIMI PASSI -- 12 VERY EASY PIECES	MONTANARO
FIRST STEPS IN BACH	BACH, J.S.
FIRST STEPS OF THE YOUNG PIANIST, THE--100 NEW AND	GURLITT
FIRST STEPS OF THE YOUNG PIANIST, THE--100 NEW AND	GURLITT
FIRST STEP IN BALLET, THE -- 40 SELECTIONS FROM THE	SKJERNE--ED.
FIRST STUDENT, THE, VOL. 1	BACH, J.S.
FIRST STUDENT, THE, VOL. 2	BACH, J.S.
FIRST STUDIES, OP. 50	KOEHLER
FIRST STUDIES, OP. 50	KOEHLER
FIRST STUDIES, OP. 50	KOEHLER
FIRST STUDIES, VOL. 1	BACH, J.S.
FIRST STUDIES, VOL. 2	BACH, J.S.
FIRST STUDIES --14 PIECES IN PROGRESSIVE ORDER.	HANDEL
FIRST SUITE OF SIX EASY PIECES	DUKE, H.
FIRST TEN LESSONS, THE - A MANUAL FOR TEACHERS	GRINDEA, C.
FIRST TERM AT THE PIANO	BARTOK
FIRST TERM	BARTOK
FIRST THANKSGIVING, THE	
FIRST THEORY LESSONS FOR YOUNG PIANIST, BK. 1	KEIGHLEY, T.
FIRST THREE COMPOSITIONS, THE	
FIRST TIME AROUND	MOZART, W. A.
FIRST TIME EVER I SAW YOUR FACE, THE	BRADLEY,
FIRST VALSE-IMPROMPTU	NOEL, P. *
FIRST VALSE OP. 83	DURAND, A.
FIRST VELOCITY STUDIES	HORVATH, G.
FIRST VIOLET, THE	BEHR, F.
FIRST VIOLET	BEHR, F.
FIRST WALTZ	GODARD, B.
FIRST WORKBOOK OF SCALES AND CHORDS	FREDRICH, F.
FIRST YEAR -- COMPLETE, NEW EDITION	WILLIAMS, J.
FIRST YEAR -- PART 1	WILLIAMS, J.
FIRST YEAR BACH	BACH, J.S.
FIRST YEAR CLASSICS	THOMPSON, J.--ED
FIRST YEAR DUETS	TWINN, S.
FIRST YEAR DUETS	TWINN, S.
FIRST YEAR ESSENTIALS	FREED
FIRST YEAR IN MUSIC DUETS, BK. 1	SUGARMAN--ED
FIRST YEAR IN MUSIC DUETS, BK. 2	SUGARMAN--ED
FIRST YEAR IN MUSIC DUETS, BK. 3	SUGARMAN--ED
FIRST YEAR IN MUSIC DUETS, BK. 4	SUGARMAN--ED
FIRST YEAR PIANO LESSONS	WATERMAN *
FIRST YEAR PIANO LESSONS	WATERMAN *
FIR TREE	SCHIEFELBEIN, F.
FISCHER'S FIRST PIANO BOOK, PART 1	FISCHER, H.
FISCHER'S FIRST PIANO BOOK, PART 2	FISCHER, H.
FISHERMAIDEN'S SONG, THE	DUNHILL, T.
FISHIN'	CANFIELD, J.
FISHING BY MOONLIGHT	MILFORD
FISH SCALES	TOWNSEND
FISH STORIES -- 4 PIECES	BENNER, L.
FITZWILLIAM VIRGINAL BOOK, BK. 1	FULLER *
FITZWILLIAM VIRGINAL BOOK, BK. 2	FULLER *
FITZWILLIAM VIRGINAL BOOK, THE	FULLER-MAITLAND-
FITZWILLIAM VIRGINAL BOOK	MONTANI
FIVE ADVANCED TECHNICAL STUDIES	MURRAY, B.
FIVE AMUSEMENTS	KERN, F.
FIVE ANIMAL PICTURES, OP. 54	BERNSTEIN, L.
FIVE ANNIVERSARIES	BACH, J.S.
FIVE BACH DUETS	BACH, J.S.
FIVE BACH DUETS	ALBERT, E. D'
FIVE BAGATELLES, OP. 29	DVORAK
FIVE BAGATELLES, OP. 47	FERGUSON, H.
FIVE BAGATELLES	GRAITZER, G.
FIVE BAGATELLES	TARDOS, B.
FIVE BAGATELLES	WEBER, B.
FIVE BAGATELLES	LAKNER, Y.
FIVE BIRTHDAYS	AMMONS
FIVE BOOGIE WOOGIE PIANO SOLOS	

FIVE BRAHMS WALTZES - NO. 1 AND 2	BRAHMS
FIVE BRAHMS WALTZES - NO. 3	BRAHMS
FIVE BRAHMS WALTZES - NO. 4	BRAHMS
FIVE BRAHMS WALTZES - NO. 5	BRAHMS
FIVE BY TEN, WORKS BY CONTEMPORARY ENGLISH COMPOSERS	ROWLEY
FIVE BY TEN, WORKS BY CONTEMPORARY ENGLISH COMPOSERS	ROWLEY
FIVE BY TEN, WORKS BY CONTEMPORARY ENGLISH COMPOSERS	ROWLEY
FIVE BY TEN, WORKS BY CONTEMPORARY ENGLISH COMPOSERS	ROWLEY
FIVE BY TEN, WORKS BY CONTEMPORARY ENGLISH COMPOSERS	ROWLEY
FIVE CAPRICES	STARER
FIVE CHORALES -- 8-HANDS, SET	BACH, J.S.
FIVE CHRISTMAS SONGS	FORLIVESI
FIVE COMPOSITIONS	BROGI
FIVE CONCERTI AND CHORAL FANTASY, OP. 80	BEETHOVEN
FIVE COUNTRY DANCES	BEN-HAIM
FIVE COUNTRY DANCES	LAVRY
FIVE DANCES	CRESTON
FIVE DANCES	SEDLAK, A.
FIVE DANCE PIECES, OP. 42	WELLESZ, E.
FIVE DIVERSIONS	DICKINSON, P.
FIVE DUETS FOR TWENTY FINGERS	WILSON, S.
FIVE DUETS FOR YOUNG PIANISTS	STARER
FIVE DUETS	BACH, J.S.
FIVE EASY LITTLE PIECES	SIRIANNI
FIVE EASY PIANO PIECES	LEVY, M. D.
FIVE EASY PIECES, OP. 139, NO. 1 - PAGLIACCETTO	BOSSI, M. E.
FIVE EASY PIECES, OP. 139, NO. 2 - CAPITAN FRACASSA	BOSSI, M. E.
FIVE EASY PIECES, OP. 139, NO. 3 - PIERROT IN AMBASCIA	BOSSI, M. E.
FIVE EASY PIECES, OP. 139, NO. 4 - LIBELLULE	BOSSI, M. E.
FIVE EASY PIECES, OP. 139, NO. 5 - LA DANZATRICE	BOSSI, M. E.
FIVE EASY PIECES	MANZINO
FIVE EASY PIECES	STRAVINSKY, I.
FIVE EASY PIECES	STRAVINSKY, I.
FIVE EASY SOLOS	ROGERS
FIVE EPISODES FOR PIANO	LEMELAND, A.
FIVE EPISODES FOR PIANO	TRIMBLE
FIVE ESTUDIOS	GUARNIERI
FIVE ETUDES-CAPRICES	ORTHEL
FIVE ETUDES, OP. 23C	KADOSA
FIVE ETUDES	FRANCAIX, J.
FIVE ETUDES	TREBINSKY, A.
FIVE FINGERPRINTS	LEEDS, R.
FIVE FINGERS ON FIVE KEYS, BK. 01	RICHTER, C.--ED
FIVE FINGERS ON FIVE KEYS, BK. 02	RICHTER, C.--ED
FIVE FINGERS PIECES	SWINSTEAD, F.
FIVE FINGER BOOGIE	GLOVER, D.
FIVE FINGER EXERCISES, OP. 16	SCHMITT, A.
FIVE FINGER EXERCISES, PART 1	SCHMITT, A.
FIVE FINGER EXERCISES, PART 2	SCHMITT, A.
FIVE FINGER EXERCISES	SCHMITT, A.
FIVE FINGER FAVORITES	LEVINE
FIVE FINGER FUN	PECHMAN
FIVE FORECASTS FOR PIANO	RAPHLING
FIVE FORGERIES	DICKINSON, P.
FIVE FOR FOUR	THOMPSON, J.
FIVE FRENCH PIECES	WAGNER-REGENY,
FIVE FUNDAMENTAL STUDIES FOR DAILY EXERCISE, FROM	CLEMENTI
FIVE GAY FINGERS	KING, M.
FIVE GRIMACES, OP. POSTH.	SATIE, E.
FIVE HARPSICHORD PIECES FROM DR. JOHN BULL'S FLEMISH	BULL, J.
FIVE HUMORESQUES	REGER
FIVE IMAGES	DELLO JOIO, N.
FIVE IMPRESSIONS--1934	TANSMAN, A.
FIVE IMPROVISATIONS	BEACH, H. H. A.
FIVE INVENTIONS, OP. 38	OLSEN, P.
FIVE LISZT DISCOVERIES--CURWEN EDITION	LISZT
FIVE LITTLE CHICKENS	HOPKINS, H.
FIVE LITTLE DANCES, OP. 24	CRESTON
FIVE LITTLE PIECES -- 1938 --	GIANNEO
FIVE LITTLE PIECES	GOLIO
FIVE LITTLE PIECES	MAXWELL DAVIES,
FIVE LITTLE PIECES	TONON
FIVE LYRIC PIECES FROM OP. 12	GRIEG
FIVE LYRIC STUDIES	ROWLEY
FIVE MALTESE DANCES	CAMILLERI, C.
FIVE MARCHES	MENDELSSOHN
FIVE MINIATURES FOR PIANO	TREVARTHEN, R.
FIVE MINIATURES	GRETCHANINOFF
FIVE MINIATURES	WHITE, P.
FIVE MINUTES WITH MR. THORNHILL	
FIVE MORCEAUX CARACTERISTIQUE EN FORME D'ETUDES, OP.	WOLLENHAUPT
FIVE MOUVEMENTS BREFS	RIVIER, J.
FIVE MOVEMENTS FOR PIANO, 1960	LEWIS, R. H.
FIVE MOVEMENTS FOR PIANO	MILLER, J.
FIVE NIGHT PIECES	SCULTHORPE, P.
FIVE O'CLOCK FOX-TROT	RAVEL
FIVE O'CLOCK TRAFFIC	STEVENS, E.
FIVE OVER TWELVE - FIVE PRELUDES	ULEHLA, L.
FIVE OVER TWELVE	ULEHLA, L.
FIVE PAIRS OF SONATAS	SCARLATTI, D.
FIVE PECAS INFANTIS	GUARNIERI
FIVE PIANO PIECES, OP. 23	STOHR, R.
FIVE PIANO PIECES, OP. 39	KRENEK, E.
FIVE PIANO PIECES	BAZELON, I.
FIVE PIANO PIECES	DELIUS, F.
FIVE PIANO PIECES	KAROLYI
FIVE PIANO RHAPSODIES	SIMS
FIVE PICKANINNIES	MACGREGOR
FIVE PIECES--1958	YUN, I.
FIVE PIECES, OP. 12	SCHILLINGER, J.
FIVE PIECES, OP. 44	KORNAUTH, E.
FIVE PIECES -- SELECTED FOR UFAM CONTESTANTS	BOIZARD, G.
FIVE PIECES -- 1928-30 --	FREED, I.
FIVE PIECES FOR CHILDREN	KOCH, F.
FIVE PIECES FOR ORCHESTRA, OP. 16	SCHOENBERG
FIVE PIECES FOR PIANO, 1970	SARDA, A.
FIVE PIECES FOR YOUNG PIANISTS -- 1. PRELUDE	RIETI
FIVE PIECES FOR YOUNG PIANISTS -- 2. CANON	RIETI
FIVE PIECES FOR YOUNG PIANISTS -- 3. VALSETTE	RIETI
FIVE PIECES FOR YOUNG PIANISTS -- 4. TARANTELLA	RIETI
FIVE PIECES FOR YOUNG PIANISTS -- 5. SILLY POLKA	RIETI
FIVE PIECES FOR YOUNG PIANISTS	RIETI
FIVE PIECES FOR YOUNG PIANISTS	RIETI
FIVE PIECES FROM THE FIRST STUDY OF BACH	BACH, J.S.
FIVE PIECES	CINTOLESI
FIVE PIECES	GRAY, D.
FIVE PIECES	RENZI
FIVE PIECE SET	PISK
FIVE PLUS FIVE	FITCH, J.
FIVE PORTUGUESE FOLK SONGS	STEVENS, H.
FIVE PRELUDES, OP. 15	SCRIABINE, A.
FIVE PRELUDES, OP. 16	SCRIABINE, A.
FIVE PRELUDES, OP. 4	FICHER
FIVE PRELUDES, OP. 7	HOIBY, L.
FIVE PRELUDES, OP. 74	SCRIABINE, A.
FIVE PRELUDES, OP. 74	SCRIABINE, A.
FIVE PRELUDES AND A NOCTURNE	FAITH

FIVE PRELUDES FOR GUITAR--NO. 1	VILLA-LOBOS, H.
FIVE PRELUDES FOR GUITAR--NO. 2	VILLA-LOBOS, H.
FIVE PRELUDES FOR GUITAR--NO. 3	VILLA-LOBOS, H.
FIVE PRELUDES FOR GUITAR--NO. 5	VILLA-LOBOS, H.
FIVE PRELUDES FOR GUITAR	VILLA-LOBOS, H.
FIVE PRELUDES FOR PIANO	STARER
FIVE PRELUDES FOR PIANO	TRAVIS, B.
FIVE PRELUDES	HEDGES
FIVE PRELUDES	SHOSTAKOVITCH
FIVE PRELUDES	SZONYI, E.
FIVE PRELUDES	UGARTE
FIVE RICERCATE, FANTASIA --1575-- FOR HARPSICHORD OR	RODIO
FIVE SARCASMS, OP. 17	PROKOFIEFF
FIVE SECULAR SONG VARIATIONS AND DANCE MOVEMENTS	SCHEIDT
FIVE SELECTED PIECES	FROBERGER
FIVE SETS OF VARIATIONS, OP. 51, BK. 1 - FIVE HAPPY	KABALEVSKY
FIVE SETS OF VARIATIONS, OP. 51, BK. 2 - MERRY DANCE	KABALEVSKY
FIVE SETS OF VARIATIONS, OP. 51, BK. 3 - GRAY DAY	KABALEVSKY
FIVE SETS OF VARIATIONS, OP. 51, BK. 4 - SEVEN	KABALEVSKY
FIVE SETS OF VARIATIONS, OP. 51 - SIX VARIATIONS ON	KABALEVSKY
FIVE SETS OF VARIATIONS, OP. 51	KABALEVSKY
FIVE SHORT PIECES, OP. 33	BUTTING, M.
FIVE SHORT PIECES	CORRADINI
FIVE SHORT PIECES	NEUGEBOREN
FIVE SHORT PRELUDES	HARSANYI
FIVE SKETCHES -- WITH EIGHT PRELUDES	PISK *
FIVE SKETCHES IN SEPIA	BLOCH, E.
FIVE SONATINAS -- OP. 24 NOS. 1-2, OP. 54, 58, 60	DIABELLI
FIVE SONATINAS IN THE CLASSIC STYLE	POZZOLI
FIVE SONATINAS	DIABELLI
FIVE SPANISH DANCES, OP. 12 -- COMPLETE	MOSZKOWSKI
FIVE SPANISH DANCES, OP. 12 -- NO. 1 IN C	MOSZKOWSKI
FIVE SPANISH DANCES, OP. 12 -- NO. 5 IN D -- BOLERO	MOSZKOWSKI
FIVE SPANISH DANCES, OP. 12 -- SET	MOSZKOWSKI
FIVE SPANISH DANCES, OP. 12	MOSZKOWSKI
FIVE STUDIES, OP. 22	LEIGHTON
FIVE STUDIES, VOL. 1	BRAHMS
FIVE STUDIES, VOL. 2	BRAHMS
FIVE STUDIES FOR PIANO	BENNETT, R.
FIVE TALES FROM ANDERSEN	VICTORY, G.
FIVE THUMBNAIL SKETCHES	FICHANDLER, W.
FIVE TONES, FIVE FINGERS	FUSSL, K.
FIVE TRIBUTES	FULEIHAN, A.
FIVE TWO-PART INVENTIONS, OP. 14	CRESTON
FIVE TWO-PART INVENTIONS	CRESTON
FIVE VARIOUS AND SUNDRY	PHILLIPS, B.
FIVE VERY SHORT PIECES	FULEIHAN, A.
FIVE VISIONARY LANDSCAPES	HOVHANESS, A.
FIVE WALTZES, OP. 8 AND FROM FOREIGN PARTS, OP. 23	MOSZKOWSKI
FIVE WALTZES FROM OP. 39, TRANSCRIBED BY THE COMPOSER	BRAHMS
FIVE WALTZES	BRITTEN, B.
FLAGSHIP, THE	DVORINE
FLAGS ON PARADE	GLOVER, D.
FLAG DAY PARADE	BRODSKY, M.
FLAIR STYLINGS FOR PIANO OF DAYS OF WINE AND ROSES	
FLAMENCO -- THREE PIECES	ASINS ARBO
FLAMENCO	GILLOCK
FLAMENCO	GILLOCK
FLAMENCO	NEVIN
FLAMENCO	SCHER, W.
FLAMENQUERAS, 1952 -- SET	SURINACH, C.
FLAME VINE	BILBRO, M.
FLAMING TAMBOURINE	NOONA, W.
FLAMMES SOMBRES, OP. 73	SCRIABINE, A.
FLAPPERETTE -- SIMP.	MOSSMAN, T.
FLAPPERETTE	GREER, J.
FLAPPERETTE	POLLA, W.--ED
FLASHING PEARLS	SPIELER
FLASH CARDS, BK. 1	KIRBY, M. B.
FLASH CARDS, BK. 2	KIRBY, M. B.
FLASH CARDS, BK. 3	KIRBY, M. B.
FLASH CARDS, BK. 4	KIRBY, M. B.
FLASH CARDS	MASON, I.
FLATTERER, THE -- LA LISONJERA	CHAMINADE
FLATTERER, THE	CHAMINADE
FLATTERER, THE	CHAMINADE
FLATTERER	CHAMINADE
FLATTERY	RAVINA, H.
FLEDERMAUS, DIE, WALTZ	STRAUSS, R.
FLEDERMAUS, DIE	STRAUSS, J.
FLEDERMAUS, DIE	STRAUSS, J.
FLEDERMAUS - CONCERT PARAPHRASE	STRAUSS, J. *
FLEDERMAUS FANTASY	CHASINS, A.
FLEDERMAUS PARAPHRASE--ON AIRS FROM 'THE BAT' BY J.	KOVACS, S.
FLEDERMAUS PARAPHRASE--ON AIRS FROM 'THE BAT'	STRAUSS, J.
FLEDGLINGS, THE	KETTERER, E.
FLEETING FANCIES	SCHIEFELBEIN, F.
FLEETING HOURS, PASTORALE	BRINKMANN
FLEETING HOURS	LOUKA, M.
FLEURS DES CHAMPS	WARMS
FLEURS DE FRANCE	TAILLEFERRE, G.
FLEUR D'ETE -- POLKA --	DESSAUX
FLEUR D'ETE	DESSAUX
FLEUR DE LYS	LANSDELL, C.
FLICKERING CANDLE, THE	WAGENAAR, B.
FLICKERING SHADOWS	ALT, H.
FLICKERING SHADOWS	ELDON, M.
FLIGHTS OF FANCY	TEMPLETON
FLIGHT OF FANCY	FRANK
FLIGHT OF THE BUMBLE BEE, THE	RIMSKY-KORSAKOFF
FLIGHT OF THE BUMBLE BEE -- FROM ''TSAR SALTAN'' --	RIMSKY-KORSAKOFF
FLIGHT OF THE BUMBLE BEE	RIMSKY-KORSAKOFF
FLIGHT OF THE BUMBLE BEE	RIMSKY-KORSAKOFF
FLIGHT OF THE BUMBLE BEE	RIMSKY-KORSAKOFF
FLIGHT OF THE BUMBLE BEE	RIMSKY-KORSAKOFF
FLIGHT OF THE BUMBLE BEE	RIMSKY-KORSAKOFF
FLIGHT OF THE BUMBLE BEE	RIMSKY-KORSAKOFF
FLIGHT OF THE BUMBLE BEE	RIMSKY-KORSAKOFF
FLIGHT OF THE FIREFLY, THE	HOWELL, I.
FLIGHT	BACON
FLIGHT	BUTLER, J.
FLIGHT	MALTZMAN
FLIPPER	LANE, J.--ED.
FLITTINGS FROM THE PAST	KINKEL, C.
FLOATING ZEPHYRS	ENGELMANN, H. U.
FLOATING	REISTRUP, J.
FLOATING	STANTON, E.
FLOETENUHRSTUECKE	HAYDN
FLOODS OF SPRING	RACHMANINOFF, S.
FLORAL CLOCK, THE	BURNAM
FLORAL PARADE, THE, VALSE -- ONE PIANO, SIX HANDS --	MARTIN, G.
FLORAL PARADE, THE, VALSE	MARTIN, G.
FLORA WALTZ, OP. 294	SPINDLER
FLOREINE WALTZ	SCHUSTER
FLORENCE POLKA	STREABBOG
FLORES DE ESPANA -- 38 FOLK SONGS WITH SPANISH TEXT	HERNANDEZ--ED

FLORES DE MUSICA. WERKE FUR TASTENINSTRUMENTE ODER	COELHO, P.M.R.
FLORES DE MUSICA. WERKE FUR TASTENINSTRUMENTE ODER	COELHO, P.M.R.
FLORES DE NARANJO	LUDOVIC, G.
FLORYSE EN SA TOURELLE	GUENIFFEY
FLOTENUHRSTUCKE. 32 STUCKE FUR SPIELUHREN,	HAYDN
FLOTENUHRSTUCKE	HAYDN
FLOTSAM	AARON, M.
FLOTS ARGENTES	WACHS, P.
FLOWER-FRUIT-AND-THORN-PIECES, OP. 82--18	HELLER, S.
FLOWERS - FROM 'A CHILD LOVES'	MILHAUD, D.
FLOWERS AND FERNS, TONE POEM	KEISER
FLOWERS AND FERNS	KEISER
FLOWERS IN A TEMPLE GARDEN	BURNAM
FLOWERS IN THE FOREST	BURNS
FLOWERS I HAVE SEEN	HEGEDUS, A.
FLOWERS OF THE FOREST	BURNS
FLOWER DRUM SONG	HAMMERSTEIN *
FLOWER DRUM SONG	HAMMERSTEIN *
FLOWER DUETS, THE, BK. 1	SMITH, J.
FLOWER FAIRY, THE	VANNORT, I.
FLOWER IN THE CRANNIED WALL	HOLT, EILSEL
FLOWER IN THE WIND	BINDER, A. W.
FLOWER MARKET IN SPAIN, A	HARPER, M.
FLOWER QUIZ, A	HOWELL, I.
FLOWER SONG, OP. 39	LANGE, G.
FLOWER SONG, OP. 39	LANGE, G.
FLOWER SONG, OP. 39	LANGE, G.
FLOWER SONG, OP. 39	LANGE, G.
FLOWER SONG	LANGE, A.
FLOWER SONG	LANGE, G.
FLUCHTIGE ERSCHEINUNGEN, OP. 22	PROKOFIEFF
FLUCHTIGE GEDANKEN OP. 115	GRETCHANINOFF
FLUFFY AND DUFFY	ROBINSON, A.
FLUTE, THE	GROOMS
FLUTTERING BUTTERFLIES - TWO PIANOS, EIGHT HANDS	DAY, R.
FLUTTERING BUTTERFLIES	BOHM
FLUTTERING LEAVES IN A MINOR, OP. 147 NO. 2	KOELLING
FLUTTERING LEAVES IN D, OP. 147, NO. 3	KOELLING
FLUTTERING LEAVES	KOLLING, C.
FLY-AWAY	ROOT, F. W.
FLYING AN AIRPLANE	TRAVIS, B.
FLYING BIRDS	MELVIN, B.
FLYING G-MEN	SCHAUM, J.--ED.
FLYING LEAF, OP. 123 NO. 10	SPINDLER
FLYING LEAF, OP. 123	SPINDLER
FLYING LEAVES, OP. 147--ALLEGRO IN C	KOELLING
FLYING LEAVES, OP. 147--ALLEGRO MOLTO IN A MINOR	KOELLING
FLYING LEAVES, OP. 147--PRESTISSIMO IN D	KOELLING
FLYING LEAVES, OP. 16	HAAS
FLYING LEAVES	KOLLING, C.
FLYING SAUCERS	DEIS
FLYING SAUCER	BENFORD
FLYING SQUIRRELS' PLAYTIME	HOFSTAD, M.
FLYING	WEYBRIGHT
FLY AWAY KITE	HOFSTAD, M.
FLY ME TO THE MOON --BOSSA NOVA--	HOWARD
FOGBOUND	FIELDS, I.
FOGGY DAY, A	SINGER, L.--ED
FOGGY DEW, THE -- AN IRISH FOLK SONG	WEYBRIGHT--ED.
FOGGY DEW	WEYBRIGHT--ED.
FOGOTTEN DREAMS	ANDERSON, L.
FOG HORN WARNINGS	TUTTLE, T. K.
FOIRE AUX CROUTES, LA -- 12 LITTLE TABLEAUX	DESPORTES
FOLIES D'ESPAGNE, LES	BACH, C.P.E.
FOLIES D'ESPAGNE - VARIATIONEN U. D. FOLLIA	GOEBELS--ED
FOLIO -- 1952/53 -- AND FOUR SYSTEMS -- 1954 --	BROWN, E.
FOLIO	CASHMAN *
FOLK-DANCES AND SINGING GAMES	BURCHENAL, E.
FOLK-DANCES FROM OLD HOMELANDS	BURCHENAL, E.
FOLK-DANCE MUSIC --ADAPTED FOR USE IN PHYSICAL	BURCHENAL, E. *
FOLK-ROCK IMAGES	SMITH, T.
FOLKSONG, OP. 12 NO. 5	GRIEG
FOLKSONG PIANO RECITAL	RAPHLING
FOLK AND COUNTRY SONG	SCHAUM, J.--ED.
FOLK BLUES	
FOLK DANCE -- IN HUNGARIAN STYLE	RILEY, D.
FOLK DANCE	OSBORNE, W.
FOLK FESTIVAL	SCHAUM, J.
FOLK FROM THE VILLAGE, THE -- A GERMAN FOLK TUNE FOR	WEYBRIGHT--ED.
FOLK FROM THE VILLAGE, THE	WEYBRIGHT--ED.
FOLK HOLIDAY	BISHOP
FOLK MELODIES FOR PIANO	DEFILIPPI, A.
FOLK MELODIES FOR PIANO	LUTOSLAWSKI
FOLK ROCK	ADAMS
FOLK SONGS AND DANCES -- MUSIC FOR CHILDREN	SCHAUM, J.--ED.
FOLK SONGS AND FAMOUS PICTURES	MASON, I.
FOLK SONGS AND FOLK DANCES, BK. 1	AGAY, D.--ED
FOLK SONGS AND FOLK DANCES, BK. 2	AGAY, D.--ED
FOLK SONGS AND FOLK DANCES, BK. 3	AGAY, D.--ED
FOLK SONGS AND RHYTHMIC DANCES	GILLOCK
FOLK SONGS FOR PIANO, BK. 1	LINDO, S.
FOLK SONGS FOR PIANO, BK. 2	LINDO, S.
FOLK SONGS OF ISRAEL	SCHER, W.
FOLK SONGS OF THE NORTH	SCHAUM, J.
FOLK SONGS OF THE SOUTH	SCHAUM, J.
FOLK SONGS OF TODAY	RICHTER
FOLK SONG BOOK	SCHAUM, J.--ED.
FOLK SONG BOOK 1	GOLDBERGER,
FOLK SONG BOOK 2	GOLDBERGER,
FOLK SONG BOOK 3	GOLDBERGER,
FOLK SONG SETTINGS	PACE, R.
FOLK SONG STORIES	MCKAY, G.
FOLK SONG SUITE, OP. 21	KADOSA
FOLK TALES FOR TWO	NAGY, M.
FOLK TUNE--HOMAGE TO GRIEG	LAMARCHE, P.
FOLK TUNES FOR FUN	BASTIEN--ED.
FOLK TUNE BOOGIE	NEVIN
FOLK TUNE SONATA	THOMPSON, J.
FOLK TUNE TIME	KASSCHAU,
FOLK VARIATIONS	GLOVER, D.
FOLK WAYS, U. S. A., BK. 1	SIEGMEISTER
FOLK WAYS, U. S. A., BK. 2	SIEGMEISTER
FOLK WAYS, U. S. A., BK. 3	SIEGMEISTER
FOLLOW ME, ONE PIANO - SIX HANDS	MACGREGOR
FOLLOW ME	ANSON, G.
FOLLOW ME	DOUGLAS
FOLLOW ME	NEVIN
FOLLOW THE BAND	FLETCHER
FOLLOW THE LEADER	BLAKE, M. D.
FOLLOW THE LEADER	ERB
FOLLOW THE LEADER	HIBBS, C.
FOLLOW THE LEADER	RENNARD
FOLLOW WASHINGTON	STEINER
FOND HEARTS MUST PART	LANGE, G.
FOOTPRINTS ON THE MOON	HARRIS
FOOTSTEPS OF SPRING	BLACK, M.
FOOTSTEPS	RICHTER

FOOT IN THE DOOR, A	FULEIHAN, A.
FOOT IT FEATLY	GRANT, J.
FORAINS, LES -- BALLET --	SAUGUET
FOREIGN AGENT	KELLEY
FOREIGN INTRIGUE CONCERTO	NORMAN
FORELLE, DIE	SCHUBERT
FOREST BROOK	EMERY
FOREST DAWN	THOMPSON, J.
FOREST DAWN	THOMPSON, J.
FOREST ECHOES	FERRELL, B.
FOREST ELF, THE	KRAFT
FOREST FAIRYLAND	MARTIN, H.
FOREST LULLABY, OP. 1056	VOLZ, H.
FOREST NOCTURNE	ROBINSON, A.
FOREST NOCTURNE	ROBINSON, A.
FOREST OF JOSHUA TREES	BURNAM
FOREST PEACE	BENJAMIN
FOREST SCENES--WALDSZENEN, OP. 82	SCHUMANN, R.
FOREST SCENES, OP. 82	SCHUMANN, R.
FOREST SCENES, OP. 82	SCHUMANN, R.
FOREST SCENES, OP. 82	SCHUMANN, R.
FOREST SCENES, OP. 82	SCHUMANN, R.
FOREST SCENES, OP. 82	SCHUMANN, R.
FOREST VOICES	BLAKE, D.
FOREVER AND EVER	LANE, J.--ED.
FOREVER AND EVER	
FORGET-ME-NOT	RAEZER, C.
FORGET DOMANI	LANE, J.--ED.
FORGET ME NOT	MEISTER, W.
FORGE IN THE FOREST, THE	MICHAELIS, J.
FORGOTTEN DREAMS -- SIMP.	STEINER--ED.
FORGOTTEN WALTZ NO. 4 -- QUATRIEME VALSE OUBLIEE	LISZT
FORGOTTEN WALTZ	LISZT
FORLANA	COOK, P.
FORLANE	KOHS, E. B.
FORM UND AUSDRUCK, 15 POLYPHONIC PIECES, BK. 1	SIEGL, O.
FORM UND AUSDRUCK, 15 POLYPHONIC PIECES, BK. 2	SIEGL, O.
FORM 4# BROKEN SEQUENCES --IN PREPARATION--	WOLPE
FORTUNATE FELINE	DUMM
FORTY-EIGHT BRIMHALL WORLD FAMOUS 3-CHORD PIANO SONGS	BRIMHALL,
FORTY-EIGHT EASY PIANO DUETS	
FORTY-EIGHT STUDIES WITHOUT WORDS	MENDELSSOHN
FORTY-EIGHT STUDIES, OP. 29 - BK. 1	BERTINI
FORTY-EIGHT STUDIES, OP. 32 - BK. 2	BERTINI
FORTY-EIGHT STUDIES - 'THE LITTLE PISCHNA'	PISCHNA
FORTY-EIGHT TUNEFUL TECHNICAL STUDIES, BK. 2	SPIVAK, S.
FORTY-FIVE SELECTED COMPOSITIONS, BK. 1	GRIEG
FORTY-FIVE SELECTED COMPOSITIONS, BK. 2	GRIEG
FORTY-FIVE SELECTED PIECES	GRIEG
FORTY-FOUR NOW SOUNDS - JOHN BRIMHALL, EASY PIANO	BRIMHALL,
FORTY-FOUR ORIGINAL PIANO DUETS -- HAYDN TO STRAVINSKY	ECKARD, W.--ED
FORTY-FOUR SMALL PIANO PIECES BY NINE HUNGARIAN	RESCHOFSKY,
FORTY-FOUR SMALL PIANO PIECES BY NINE HUNGARIAN	RESCHOFSKY,
FORTY-NINERS' CAN-CAN	
FORTY-NINE PIECES FOR SMALL HANDS	TUERK
FORTY-ONE DELIGHTFUL LITTLE STUDIES	DE ANGELIS
FORTY-ONE ELEMENTARY LITTLE STUDIES	DE ANGELIS
FORTY-SEVEN FAMOUS PIANO PIECES	BRIMHALL,
FORTY-SIX CADENCES ORIGINALES	MOZART, W. A.
FORTY-SIX CONTEMPORARY PIANO SOLOS	
FORTY-SIX EASY ARRANGEMENTS OF SACRED MELODIES--WITH	LIPSCOMB--ED.
FORTY-SIX ORIGINAL PIANO CLASSICS	
FORTY-SIX SHORT PIECES FOR PIANO	FRANCK, C.
FORTY-THREE LITTLE PIECES AND STUDIES	BARTOK *
FORTY-THREE SONATAS --URTEXT--, COMPLETE IN 4 VOLS.#	HAYDN
FORTY-THREE SONATAS --URTEXT--, COMPLETE IN 4 VOLS.#	HAYDN
FORTY-TWO SONATAS, VOL. 1	HAYDN
FORTY-TWO SONATAS, VOL. 2	HAYDN
FORTY-TWO SONATAS, VOL. 3	HAYDN
FORTY-TWO SONATAS, VOL. 4	HAYDN
FORTY BARS FOR FORTY FINGERS, FOR 2 PIANOS AND 8 HANDS	ROY
FORTY CHILDREN'S EXERCISES AND MELODIES, OP. 218	KOEHLER
FORTY CHRISTMAS CAROLS FOR VOICE AND PIANO	HINKLE, N.--ED
FORTY DAILY EXERCISES, OP. 337	CZERNY
FORTY DAILY EXERCISES, OP. 337	CZERNY
FORTY DAILY EXERCISES, OP. 337	CZERNY
FORTY FATHOMS	ARMOUR
FORTY FAVORITE PIECES, SIMPLIFIED	STEINBRECHER--ED
FORTY HITS OF OUR TIMES-POPULAR SONGS IN BIG NOTES FOR	
FORTY MELODIOUS EXERCISES - TRANSCRIBED FROM WORKS BY	CZERNY *
FORTY MELODIOUS STUDIES FOR SMALL HANDS, OP. 43	LONGO, A.
FORTY PIANO COMPOSITIONS	CHOPIN
FORTY PIANO PARTNERS - ELEMENTARY DUETS	STRIMER, J.--ED
FORTY PIANO SELECTIONS BY MODERN COMPOSERS	
FORTY STUDIES FOR PERFECTION, BK. 1	TAGLIAPIETRA, G.
FORTY STUDIES FOR PERFECTION, BK. 2	TAGLIAPIETRA, G.
FORT TICONDEROGA	STEINER
FORWARD, MARCH -- 6-HANDS	BILBRO, M.
FORWARD MARCH -- 6-HANDS	OLDENBURG, E.
FORWARD MARCH	GLOVER
FORWARD STEPS	MARTIN
FORZA DEL DESTINO, LA - OVERTURE	VERDI
FORZA DEL DESTINO, LA - VERGINE DEGLI ANGELI, LA	VERDI
FOR A BROKEN DOLL	GRIFFIS, E.
FOR A LITTLE GIRL	RUSSELL
FOR A YOUNG PIANIST, BK. 1	KREUTZER
FOR A YOUNG PIANIST, BK. 2	KREUTZER
FOR A YOUNG PIANIST, BOOK 1	KREUTZER
FOR A YOUNG PIANIST, BOOK 2	KREUTZER
FOR CHILDREN--EIGHTY-FIVE PIECES WITHOUT OCTAVES FOR	BARTOK
FOR CHILDREN--EIGHTY-FIVE PIECES WITHOUT OCTAVES FOR	BARTOK
FOR CHILDREN, BK. 1	BARTOK
FOR CHILDREN, BK. 2	BARTOK
FOR CHILDREN, VOL. 1	BARTOK
FOR CHILDREN, VOL. 2	BARTOK
FOR CHILDREN	RICHARDSON
FOR ELISE --FUER ELISE--	BEETHOVEN
FOR ELISE	BEETHOVEN
FOR FOUR HANDS	SCHER, W.
FOR GIRLS WHO PLAY	THOMPSON, J.--ED
FOR LEFT HAND ALONE - BK. 1	THOMPSON, J.
FOR LEFT HAND ALONE - BK. 1	THOMPSON, J.
FOR ME--LITTLE RECITAL PIECES, OP. 76	TAKACS, J.
FOR ME AND MY GAL -- SIMP.	MOSSMAN, T.
FOR ME AND MY PIANO, BK. 1	
FOR ME AND MY PIANO, BK. 2	
FOR ME AND MY PIANO, BK. 3	
FOR ME AND MY TEACHER	WILSON
FOR MY DOLLY	GAIL
FOR MY DOLLY	GAIL
FOR NIMBLE FINGERS	BAUER, M.
FOR ONCE IN MY LIFE	BRADLEY,
FOR PIANO AND METRONOME	AGAY, D.
FOR PIANO 1	WOLFF, C.
FOR PREPARED PIANO	WOLFF, C.
FOR SIGHT READING, BK. 1	DEUTSCH, L.
FOR SIGHT READING, BK. 2	DEUTSCH, L.
FOR SIGHT READING, VOL. 1	DEUTSCH, L.
FOR SIGHT READING, VOL. 2	DEUTSCH, L.
FOR TALENTED BEGINNERS, BK. 1	HOPKINS, A.
FOR TALENTED BEGINNERS, BK. 2	HOPKINS, A.
FOR THE FIRST TIME	HANSON
FOR THE GOOD TIMES	BRIMHALL,
FOR THE HOME - BOOK 1	GANSCHALS
FOR THE HOME - BOOK 2	GANSCHALS
FOR THE LITTLEST	MORTARI
FOR THE PIANO	KURKA, R.
FOR THE YOUNG - 24 BAGATELLES	TAGLIAPIETRA, C.
FOR THE YOUNG - 3 CONCERT STUDIES	DE ANGELIS
FOR YOU ALONE	BURNAM
FOSSIL SUITE	KOPTAGEL, Y.
FOSTER MELODIES FOR YOUNG FOLKS	FOSTER
FOUNDATION, THE	ROSEMOND, G.
FOUNTAIN, OP. 6 NO. 1	REYNALD, G.
FOUNTAIN, THE, EASY	BOHM
FOUNTAIN, THE, OP. 221	BOHM
FOUNTAIN, THE	BOHM
FOUNTAIN, THE	DRIVER, P.
FOUNTAIN IN CENTRAL PARK	DE ROSE, P.
FOUNTAIN IN THE RAIN	GILLOCK
FOUNTAIN IN THE RAIN	GILLOCK
FOUR-HAND COLLECTION -- 42 MELODIOUS AND INSTRUCTIVE	OESTERLE
FOUR-HAND RECREATIONS	WILMANS--ED
FOUR-HAND SONATA FOR PIANO	RAPHLING
FOURTEEN BAGATELLES, OP. 6	BARTOK
FOURTEEN BAGATELLES, OP. 6	BARTOK
FOURTEEN CANONIC INVENTIONS FOR YOUNG COMPOSERS	KUPFERMAN, M.
FOURTEEN CANONIC INVENTIONS FOR YOUNG COMPOSERS	KUPFERMAN, M.
FOURTEEN CAPRICE-ETUDES IN OCTAVES	PHILIPP, I.
FOURTEEN KEYS	WARD
FOURTEEN LARGE-NOTE PIECES FOR THE PIANO	
FOURTEEN LITTLE PIANO PIECES FOR EARLY GRADES	THOMAS, C. J.
FOURTEEN NEW LOVE SONG WALTZES, OP. 65A -- SATB AD LIB	BRAHMS
FOURTEEN NEW LOVE SONG WALTZES, OP. 65A -- SATB AD LIB	BRAHMS
FOURTEEN PIANO DUETS FOR THE EARLY GRADES	SCHER, W.--ED
FOURTEEN PIANO PIECES BY CANADIAN COMPOSERS	
FOURTEEN PIECES FOR THE PIANO	LISZT
FOURTEEN SKETCHES IN STYLE FOR YOUNG ARTISTS	WAGNESS
FOURTEEN SONATAS, ACCORDING TO THE AUTOGRAPHS AND IN	SCHUBERT
FOURTEEN SONATAS, ACCORDING TO THE AUTOGRAPHS AND IN	SCHUBERT
FOURTEEN STUDIES, BK. 1	JOSEPHS, W.
FOURTEEN STUDIES, BK. 2	JOSEPHS, W.
FOURTEEN TRADITIONAL AIRS	JOHNSON
FOURTEEN WALTZES	CHOPIN
FOURTH BARCAROLLE	GODARD, B.
FOURTH DEUCE, THE	SHEARING, G.
FOURTH DIMENSION	CONFREY, Z.
FOURTH GAVOTTE, OP. 77	PROKOFIEFF
FOURTH GRADE ETUDES	THOMPSON, J.
FOURTH GRADE PIANO BOOK	WILLIAMS, J.
FOURTH OF JULY PARADE	ROGERS
FOURTH OF JULY	
FOURTH PIANO BOOK FOR JACKS AND JILLS, A--ILLUSTRATED	RODGERS, I.
FOURTH PIANO SONATA	ANTHEIL, G.
FOURTH ROMANESQUE, BKS. 1 AND 2	FAIRCHILD
FOURTH ROMANESQUE, BKS. 3 AND 4	FAIRCHILD
FOURTH SINGS, THE	NORDORFF, P.
FOURTH YEAR	WILLIAMS, J.
FOUR AMERICAN VARIATIONS ON A THEME BY PAGANINI	PERI
FOUR AND TWENTY MELODIES	BENTLEY
FOUR ANNIVERSARIES	BERNSTEIN, L.
FOUR BAGATELLES	SOPRONI, J.
FOUR BALLADES, OP. 10	BRAHMS
FOUR BALLADES, OP. 10	BRAHMS
FOUR BALLADES, OP. 10	BRAHMS
FOUR BALLADES AND FOUR IMPROMPTUS	CHOPIN
FOUR BALLADS, OP. 10	BRAHMS
FOUR BELLS AND ALL'S WELL--ONE PIANO-EIGHT HANDS--	SCHAUM, J.--ED.
FOUR BREVITIES	GUENTHER
FOUR BY EIGHT	PEDERSON-KRAG
FOUR CAMEOS	FAITH
FOUR CAPRICHOS, OP. 57	KADOSA
FOUR CENTURIES OF KEYBOARD MUSIC - BOOK 1	MCGRAW--ED
FOUR CENTURIES OF KEYBOARD MUSIC - BOOK 2	MCGRAW--ED
FOUR CENTURIES OF KEYBOARD MUSIC - BOOK 3	MCGRAW--ED
FOUR CENTURIES OF KEYBOARD MUSIC - BOOK 4	MCGRAW--ED
FOUR CHARACTERISTIC WALTZES	COLERIDGE-TAYLOR
FOUR CHARACTER STUDIES	TEMPLETON
FOUR CHORALE PRELUDES	BACH, J.S.
FOUR CIRCUS PIECES	CONFREY, E.
FOUR CLAVIER COMPOSITIONS	BACH, J.S.
FOUR CONCERT PIECES -- 2ND PIANO PART ONLY, TO BE USED	CHOPIN
FOUR CONCERT PIECES	CHOPIN
FOUR CONCERT PIECES	CHOPIN
FOUR COUNTRY DANCES--2 PIANOS, 8 HANDS--	SCHUBERT
FOUR COURTLY DANCES -- SET	BACH, J.S.
FOUR DANCES - DANZA MORBIDA, DANZA SCHERZOSA, DANZA	CRAS
FOUR DANCES FOR YOUNG PIANISTS	JAMES, W. G.
FOUR DANCE MEASURES	BACH, J.S.
FOUR DANCE MINIATURES	WILKINSON, P.
FOUR DANCE PIECES, OP. 96	SPRONGL, N.
FOUR DANSES MINIATURES	TANSMAN, A.
FOUR DIRGES	BARTOK
FOUR DIRGES	BARTOK
FOUR DUETS -- URTEXT --	BACH, J.S.
FOUR DUETS	BACH, J.S.
FOUR EASY LITTLE PIECES	SACCHI
FOUR EASY PIECES, OP. 105	ZILCHER
FOUR EASY PIECES, OP. 218	ZILCHER
FOUR EASY PIECES FOR TEACHER AND STUDENT - POUR	LABEY *
FOUR EASY PIECES	MONTANARI
FOUR EASY SONATAS	BACH, C.P.E.
FOUR EPITAPHS, OP. 79	TAKACS, J.
FOUR ETUDES, OP. 2	PROKOFIEFF
FOUR ETUDES, OP. 2	PROKOFIEFF
FOUR ETUDES, OP. 2	PROKOFIEFF
FOUR ETUDES, OP. 7--NO. 1 IN C MINOR	STRAVINSKY, I.
FOUR ETUDES, OP. 7--NO. 2 IN D	STRAVINSKY, I.
FOUR ETUDES, OP. 7--NO. 3 IN E MINOR	STRAVINSKY, I.
FOUR ETUDES, OP. 7--NO. 4 IN F-SHARP	STRAVINSKY, I.
FOUR ETUDES, OP. 7	STRAVINSKY, I.
FOUR ETUDES RYTHMIQUES	MOTTU
FOUR ETUDES TRANSCRIBED FOR THE LEFT HAND	CHOPIN *
FOUR ETUDES	SMITH, L.
FOUR FAIRY TALES, OP. 26	MEDTNER, N.
FOUR FANTASIES, OP. 6	FANO, G. A.
FOUR FANTASIES ON AMERICAN FOLK SONGS, OP. 4	TOWNSEND
FOUR FANTASMES	RIVIER, J.
FOUR FAVORITE PRELUDES- OP.28, NOS.4, 6, 7, 20	CHOPIN
FOUR FOR PIANO. A SHORT SUITE	BRIGHT
FOUR FRAGMENTS FROM THE CANTERBURY TALES. FOR	TRIMBLE
FOUR FREEDOMS SYMPHONY	BENNETT, R.
FOUR FUGUES, OP. 72, FOUR MARCHES, OP. 76, SEVEN	SCHUMANN, R.
FOUR FUGUES, OP. 72	SCHUMANN, R.

FOUR HANDS AT THE KEYBOARD
FOUR HAND FANCIES — MANA-ZUCCA
FOUR HAND MELODIES — CRIST, D.
FOUR HAND RECREATIONS, BK. 1
FOUR HAND RECREATIONS, BK. 2
FOUR IDEAS FOR PIANO — CUSTER, A.
FOUR IDEAS FOR PIANO — CUSTER, A.
FOUR IMPROMPTUS, OP. 142 — SCHUBERT
FOUR IMPROMPTUS, OP. 90 — SCHUBERT
FOUR IMPROMPTUS, OP. 90 — SCHUBERT
FOUR IMPROMPTUS — HARRIES, D.
FOUR INDIAN LOVE LYRICS — WOODFORD-FINDEN
FOUR INTERLUDES — BARNETT
FOUR INTERMEZZI — CASANOVA, A.
FOUR INVENTIONS, OP. 26 — KLEBE, G.
FOUR INVENTIONS FOR PIANO — KAY, U.
FOUR IN A ROWBOAT — STEINER
FOUR IN D — ARNELL
FOUR JUKE BOX PIECES — HAIEFF, A.
FOUR KEYBOARD SETTINGS OF FOLK TUNES — ROGERS, S. E.
FOUR LANDSCAPES — WAGNER, J.
FOUR LITTLE FUGUES, OP. 43--78 — MIASKOVSKY
FOUR LITTLE INVENTIONS — ROWLEY
FOUR LITTLE PIECES, OP. 14 — KABALEVSKY
FOUR LITTLE PIECES, OP. 31A, AND FANTASY, OP. 31B — APOSTEL
FOUR LITTLE PIECES, OP. 32 — MACDOWELL
FOUR LITTLE PIECES - BERCEUSE SOUVENIR — FRANCMESNIL
FOUR LITTLE PIECES - LE BON VIEUX TEMPS — FRANCMESNIL
FOUR LITTLE PIECES - PRELUDE — FRANCMESNIL
FOUR LITTLE POEMS, OP. 32--REV. 1906 — MACDOWELL
FOUR LITTLE POEMS, OP. 32, REV. 1906, NO. 1--THE EAGLE MACDOWELL
FOUR LITTLE POEMS, OP. 32, REV. 1906, NO. 2--THE BROOK MACDOWELL
FOUR LITTLE POEMS, OP. 32, REV. 1906, NO. 3--MOONSHINE MACDOWELL
FOUR LITTLE POEMS, OP. 32, REV. 1906, NO. 4--WINTER — MACDOWELL
FOUR LITTLE POEMS, OP. 32 — MACDOWELL
FOUR LITTLE TUNES — SANDBOURNE
FOUR MAGIC CHORDS FOR PIANO
FOUR MAINS DU PREMIER AGE, LE - BERCEUSE LOINTAIN — DE LA TOMBELLE
FOUR MAINS DU PREMIER AGE, LE - DEPART POUR LE CHAMPS — DE LA TOMBELLE
FOUR MAINS DU PREMIER AGE, LE — DE LA TOMBELLE
FOUR MERRY CLOWNS — ERB
FOUR MINIATURES FOR YOUNG PIANISTS — KINGMAN
FOUR MINIATURES — WAGNER, J.
FOUR MORCEAUX, OP. 23 — MILOIEVITCH
FOUR NENIES, OP. 8B — BARTOK
FOUR NOCTURNES — TANSMAN, A.
FOUR NOTES — BACON, E.
FOUR O'CLOCK — HOPKINS, H.
FOUR ORCHESTRAL SUITES — BACH, J.S.
FOUR PARTITAS AND OVERTURE — BACH, J.S.
FOUR PENNELATE IN WALTZ TEMPO — ZECCA, G.
FOUR PIANO BLUES — COPLAND
FOUR PIANO PIECES, OP. 119 — BRAHMS
FOUR PIANO PIECES, OP. 119 — BRAHMS
FOUR PIANO PIECES, OP. 119 — BRAHMS
FOUR PIANO PIECES, OP. 14 — KREIN, J.
FOUR PIANO PIECES, OP. 22 — VALEN
FOUR PIANO PIECES, OP. 3 — EISLER
FOUR PIANO PIECES FOR CHILDREN — KADOSA
FOUR PIANO PIECES — BAUER, M.
FOUR PIECES, OP. 119 — BRAHMS
FOUR PIECES, OP. 119 — BRAHMS
FOUR PIECES, OP. 119 — BRAHMS
FOUR PIECES, OP. 119 — BRAHMS
FOUR PIECES, OP. 2 — PROKOFIEFF
FOUR PIECES, OP. 32 — PROKOFIEFF
FOUR PIECES, OP. 35 — TRAPP, M.
FOUR PIECES, OP. 4 — PROKOFIEFF
FOUR PIECES, OP. 4 — PROKOFIEFF
FOUR PIECES, OP. 65 — BORTKIEWICZ
FOUR PIECES, OP. 79 — KAUFMANN, A.
FOUR PIECES -- SELECTED FOR UFAM CONTESTANTS — BOIZARD, G.
FOUR PIECES - AU CREPUSCULE — MARSICK
FOUR PIECES - LES ELFES — MARSICK
FOUR PIECES - LES PLAINTES D'ATYS — MARSICK
FOUR PIECES - PRELUDE, SERENADE, AIR, DANCE — HARSANYI
FOUR PIECES - SCHERZO — MARSICK
FOUR PIECES FOR ONE PIANO FOUR HANDS — AITKEN, H.
FOUR PIECES FOR PIANO — COHEN, A.
FOUR PIECES FOR PIANO — LEIBOWITZ, R.
FOUR PIECES FOR PIANO — LIEBERMAN, F.
FOUR PIECES FOR PIANO — NELHYBEL, V.
FOUR PIECES FOR PIANO — NELHYBEL, V.
FOUR PIECES FROM BEFORE — TCHEREPNIN, I.
FOUR PIECES FROM THE MULLINER BOOK — TALLIS
FOUR PIECES IN C — TCHEREPNIN, N.
FOUR PIECES POUR PIANO - COLOMBINE — CHAMINADE
FOUR PIECES POUR PIANO - LES NOCES D'OR — CHAMINADE
FOUR PIECES POUR PIANO - MARCHE IMPROMPTU — CHAMINADE
FOUR PIECES POUR PIANO - PAS DES SYLPHES — CHAMINADE
FOUR PIECES POUR PIANO - PAS DES SYLPHES — CHAMINADE
FOUR PIECES — COULTHARD
FOUR PIECES — FRIBOULET
FOUR POLISH DANCES--1931 — TANSMAN, A.
FOUR POLKAS — SMETANA
FOUR POPULAR CASTILIAN MELODIES — ASINS ARBO
FOUR PRELETUDES -- 1. WATERMEADOWS — TAYLOR, C.
FOUR PRELETUDES -- 2. DANCE, A — TAYLOR, C.
FOUR PRELETUDES -- 3. FAREWELL, A — TAYLOR, C.
FOUR PRELETUDES -- 4. PUNCH AND JUDY — TAYLOR, C.
FOUR PRELUDES, OP. 34, NOS. 13, 16, 17, 24 — SHOSTAKOVITCH
FOUR PRELUDES, OP. 48 — SCRIABINE, A.
FOUR PRELUDES, OP. 5 — KABALEVSKY
FOUR PRELUDES AND FUGUES IN OLDEN STYLE , OP. 7 — KATTNIGG, R.
FOUR PRELUDES FOR PIANO — ROBERTS
FOUR PRELUDES SYNCOPES — MONFRED
FOUR PRELUDES — GELBRUN, A.
FOUR PRELUDES — MOMPOU, F.
FOUR PRELUDES — SATIE, E.
FOUR PRELUDIOS UNITONALES — GILARDI
FOUR RHAPSODIES, NO. 1 — DOHNANYI
FOUR RHAPSODIES, NO. 2 — DOHNANYI
FOUR RHAPSODIES, NO. 3 — DOHNANYI
FOUR RHYTHMIC FANTASIES — BORDES
FOUR RIDDLES — RUSSELL
FOUR ROMANCES SANS PAROLES — MILHAUD, D.
FOUR ROMANTIC PIECES — RAWSTHORNE, A.
FOUR RONDOS, OP. 60 — KABALEVSKY
FOUR RONDOS, OP. 60 — KABALEVSKY
FOUR RUMANIAN DANCES - NO. 1 — ALFANO
FOUR RUMANIAN DANCES - NO. 2 — ALFANO
FOUR RUMANIAN DANCES - NO. 3 — ALFANO
FOUR RUMANIAN DANCES - NO. 4 — ALFANO
FOUR SCENES FOR PIANO, 1961 — MOSS, L.
FOUR SEASONAL PRELUDES — SMART, D.
FOUR SEASONS, THE — VIVALDI
FOUR SHORT NATURE PIECES — BRANT

FOUR SHORT PIECES — CARRA
FOUR SKETCHES -- ECLOGUE, MADRIGAL, ALAMEDA, SOBFE LA — MILHAUD, D.
FOUR SONATINAS, OP. 151 — DIABELLI
FOUR SONATINAS — ANDRIESSEN, J.
FOUR SONATINAS — FROST
FOUR SONATINAS — LUCIUK
FOUR SONATINAS — MARGOLA
FOUR SONATINES, OP. 214 — TAURIELLO, A.
FOUR SONATINES, OP. 214 — GURLITT
FOUR SQUARE MARCH FOR FOUR PIANOS -- COMPLETE — BRANT, A.
FOUR SQUARE MARCH FOR PIANOS -- EASY SOLO PART — BRANT, A.
FOUR STAR SIGHT READING, GRADE 1, REVISED EDITION — BERLIN, B.
FOUR STAR SIGHT READING, GRADE 2 — BERLIN, B. *
FOUR STAR SIGHT READING, GRADE 3 — BERLIN, B. *
FOUR STAR SIGHT READING, GRADE 4, REVISED EDITION — BERLIN, B.
FOUR STAR SIGHT READING, GRADE 5 — BERLIN, B.
FOUR STAR SIGHT READING, GRADE 6 — BERLIN, B.
FOUR STAR SIGHT READING, GRADE 7 — BERLIN, B.
FOUR STAR SIGHT READING, GRADE 8 — BERLIN, B.
FOUR STUDIES AFTER DOMENICO SCARLATTI, OP. 56 — RATHAUS, K.
FOUR STUDIES AFTER DOMENICO SCARLATTI — SCARLATTI, D.
FOUR STUDIES WITHOUT WORDS--INTRODUCING TWO AGAINST — DEIS
FOUR SUITES* 'FOR CLAVICHORDE OR LUTE' — BUXTEHUDE
FOUR SUITES, ARR. REGER. COMPLETE — BACH, J.S. *
FOUR SUITES, OP. 59 — BOISMORTIER, J.
FOUR SYMPHONIES — SCHUMANN, R.
FOUR TONE PICTURES, OP. 14 — RIEGGER, W.
FOUR TONE PICTURES FOR PIANO SOLO — RIEGGER, W.
FOUR TURKISH PIANO PIECES, OP. 9 — ERINC, C.
FOUR VARIATIONS ON A THEME BY PAGANINI — LABUNSKI, W.
FOUR VERY EASY MINUETS — HAYDN
FOX, THE, THEME FROM — SCHIFRIN
FOXY KITTEN — FRIML, R.
FOX AHEAD — HAUBIEL, C.
FOX AND GOOSE — MARTIN, G.
FOX AND HOUNDS — GARROW, L.
FOX CHASE, THE — ALLISON, I.
FOX FIRE — BECK
FOX POPULAR SONG FAVORITES — FLETCHER, L.--ED
FOX TROT — SERLY
FOX VARIATIONS, OP. 75 — ARNELL
FRAGMENTS — LANE, L.
FRAGMENTS — SCHER, W.
FRAIS VALLON — LANDRY
FRANCAISES, BK. 1 — SAUGUET
FRANCAISES, BK. 2 -- NOUVELLES FRANCAISES -- — SAUGUET
FRANCAISE — IBERT
FRANCETTE ET PIA--NO. 01, PIA EST VENU EN FRANCE — VILLA-LOBOS, H.
FRANCETTE ET PIA--NO. 02, PIA A VU FRANCETTE — VILLA-LOBOS, H.
FRANCETTE ET PIA--NO. 03, PIA A PARLE A FRANCETTE — VILLA-LOBOS, H.
FRANCETTE ET PIA--NO. 04, PIA ET FRANCETTE JOUENT — VILLA-LOBOS, H.
FRANCETTE ET PIA--NO. 05, FRANCETTE EST FACHEE — VILLA-LOBOS, H.
FRANCETTE ET PIA--NO. 06, PIA EST PARTI POUR LA GUERRE — VILLA-LOBOS, H.
FRANCETTE ET PIA--NO. 07, FRANCETTE EST TRISTE — VILLA-LOBOS, H.
FRANCETTE ET PIA--NO. 08, PIA REVIENT DE LA GUERRE — VILLA-LOBOS, H.
FRANCETTE ET PIA--NO. 09, FRANCETTE EST CONTENTE — VILLA-LOBOS, H.
FRANCETTE ET PIA--NO. 10, FRANCETTE ET PIA JOUENT POUR — VILLA-LOBOS, H.
FRANCINE DANCES — TAYLOR, EDNA
FRANCIS OF ASSISI - THEME — NASCIMBENE
FRANKIE AND JOHNNY BOOGIE — WHITFORD--ED.
FRANKIE AND JOHNNY — SCHAUM, J.--ED.
FRANKIE CARLE'S METHOD OF PIANO STYLING — CARLE, F.
FRANKIE CARLE'S PIANO CONCEPTIONS — CARLE, F.
FRANKIE CARLE'S PIANO STYLINGS — CARLE, F.
FRANK ZAPPA SONG BOOK, BK. 1
FRANTIC FINGERS — FIELDS, I.
FRANTIC FOR FIVE — DELUGG *
FRANZ, OUVERTURE C-MOLL, BWV 831 — BACH, J.S.
FRANZ, OUVERTURE C-MOLL — BACH, J.S.
FRANZOSISCHE SUITEN — BACH, J.S.
FRASQUITA, BOLERO, OP. 276 — STREABBOG
FRASQUITA SERENADE — LEHAR
FRASQUITA SERENADE — LEHAR
FRA DIAVOLO FANTASY -- EASY TRANSCRIPTION — AUBER
FREDERIKA -- A GERMAN FOLK SONG — WEYBRIGHT
FREDERIKA — WEYBRIGHT--ED.
FREEDOMS FOUNDATION MARCH — LOBODA, S.
FREE AIR — GROFE, F.
FREE AND EASY MARCH — ROLFE, W.
FREE SETTING OF BRAHMS' CRADLE SONG, OP. 49, NO. 4 — GRAINGER, P.
FREE — BRIMHALL,
FREISCHUTZ, FANTASIE — WEBER, VON
FREISCHUTZ, PRAYER — WEBER, VON
FRENCH AND BELGIAN MASTERS OF THE XVII AND XVIII — PHILIPP, I.--ED.
FRENCH BAROQUE MUSIC FOR THE YOUNG PIANIST — ZEITLIN--ED
FRENCH CHILD'S SONG — BEHR, F.
FRENCH CHILD'S SONG — BEHR, F.
FRENCH DOLL — GILLOCK
FRENCH DOLL — GILLOCK
FRENCH GAME SONGS -- CHANTS DE JEUX FRANCAIS — DE CESARE
FRENCH MUSICAL CLOCK, A — MERKUR
FRENCH OVERTURE AND ITALIAN CONCERTO,URTEXT — BACH, J.S.
FRENCH RIVER BOAT, ADAPTED FROM THE NOCTURNE OP. 37 — CHOPIN
FRENCH SERENADE, OP. 62 NO. 3 — GRIEG
FRENCH SUITES, URTEXT — BACH, J.S.
FRENCH SUITES --URTEXT--, COMPLETE IN 1 VOL. — BACH, J.S.
FRENCH SUITES -- CLOTH — BACH, J.S.
FRENCH SUITES -- URTEXT -- — BACH, J.S.
FRENCH SUITES — BACH, J.S.
FRENCH SUITES — BACH, J.S.
FRENCH SUITES — BACH, J.S.
FRENCH SUITES — BACH, J.S.
FRENCH SUITES — BACH, J.S.
FRENTE AL PESEBRE — CINQUE
FRERE JACQUES' CONCERT — GEST, E.
FRESCOBALDA, LA — FRESCOBALDI
FRESHMAN MARCH — PANELLA, L.
FRESQUE MARINE — SAUVREZIS
FRIEDE AUF ERDEN, OP. 174--A CHRISTMAS POTPOURRI — OSCHEIT, M.
FRIENDLY DEER — PECHMAN
FRIENDLY FROLICS -- FOR 2 PIANOS 8 HANDS — DAY, R. E.
FRIENDSHIP MARCH — LANE, J.--ED.
FRIENDSHIP SERENADE — HOWARD, M. B.
FRIENDSHIP — STEINER
FRIENDS — HEAPS, S.
FRIENDS — BACON, E.
FRIENDS — PECHMAN
FRILEUSE, LA, VALSE — THUILLIER
FRINGES OF A BALL -- WALTZ VARIATIONS ON A THEME BY W. — STARER
FRISKY FAWN — MELVIN, B.
FRISKY GALOP — STREABBOG
FRISKY LAMB, THE — BEAUMONT
FRISKY SQUIRRELS AND TO A LITTLE INDIAN — SCHER, W.
FROG, THE — VOLKART, H.
FROGGIE AND THE FISHES, THE — SCARMOLIN
FROGS, THE — JACOB, G.
FROG AND THE BUTTERFLY, THE — HIBBS, C.

FROG AND THE POLLIWOG, THE	FORREST, S.
FROG DANCE, OP. 1010 NO. 8	VOLZ, H.
FROG HE WOULD A-WOOING GO	WATSON
FROG POOL, THE	BASSET, R.
FROHER SINN -- MERRY MOOD	LICHNER, H.
FROHE WEIHNACHT	LUTZ--ED
FROHLICHE TANZE NACH ALTEN WEISEN	EMONTS, F.
FROHLICH LASST UNS MUSIZIEREN	
FROLICKING FAUNS	DE VITO, A.
FROLICKING WAVES	WIGGINS, M.
FROLICKY, ROLLICKY, WIND	COBURN
FROLICKY GRASSHOPPER, THE	ERB, M.
FROLICSOME FINGERS	KING
FROLIC OF THE FROGS, WALTZ	WATSON
FROLIC OUTDOORS, A	HOPKINS, H.
FROLIC	AGAY, D.
FROLIC	BUTLER, J.
FROLIC	OGILVY, F.
FROLIC	PARENTE, SR. E.
FROM 'WAY DOWN SOUTH--TURKEY IN DE STRAW	RASBACH, O.
FROM ANCIENT TO MODERN	ROWLEY
FROM ANDERSEN'S FAIRY TALES, OP. 30	BORTKIEWICZ
FROM AN ARTIST'S SKETCHBOOK	STOKER
FROM A COMPOSER'S NOTE BOOK	BAUER
FROM A LIGHTHOUSE WINDOW	BURNAM
FROM A STORY BOOK	FOLDES
FROM A WINDOW	RICHMAN, A.
FROM BACH TO BARTOK, BK. 1	AGAY, D.--ED
FROM BACH TO BARTOK, BK. 2	AGAY, D.--ED
FROM BACH TO BARTOK, BK. 3	AGAY, D.--ED
FROM BACH TO BROADWAY	
FROM BOHEMIA'S WOODS AND FIELDS	SMETANA
FROM COUNTY DERRY	ARMOUR
FROM DIXIELAND	RASBACH, O.
FROM FAMOUS NOTEBOOKS	KREUTZER--ED
FROM FAR AND WIDE, OP. 37 -- 20 EASY INSTRUCTIVE	TAKACS, J.
FROM FIVE WALTZES, OP. 8 NO. 01	MOSZKOWSKI
FROM FIVE WALTZES, OP. 8 NO. 02	MOSZKOWSKI
FROM FIVE WALTZES, OP. 8 NO. 03	MOSZKOWSKI
FROM FIVE WALTZES, OP. 8 NO. 04	MOSZKOWSKI
FROM FOREIGN PARTS, OP. 23--GERMANY	MOSZKOWSKI
FROM HERE TO THERE	BULL
FROM HOLBERG'S TIME, OP. 40	GRIEG
FROM MY DIARY	SESSIONS, R.
FROM MY GARDEN	FRIML, R.
FROM MY GARDEN	HEAPS, S.
FROM MY SKETCH BOOK, OP. 39	ROWLEY
FROM MY SKETCH BOOK, 5 PIECES	RAW, W. A.
FROM MY WINDOW	GRAY, D.
FROM MY WINDOW	SIEGMEISTER
FROM NEW ORLEANS	BRUSSELS, I.
FROM NOAH'S ARK	SCHER, W.
FROM RAGTIME TO ROCK AND ROLL	AGAY, D.--ED
FROM RAMEAU TO GRIEG	
FROM SAN DOMINGO	BENJAMIN
FROM THE AEGEAN	FULEIHAN, A.
FROM THE BALLET	GOLDSCHMIDT
FROM THE BEGINNING	LEE, E. M.
FROM THE BOHEMIAN FOREST, OP. 68	DVORAK
FROM THE COLOR WHEEL	NAGY, F.
FROM THE COUNTRY - PICTURES FOR THE YOUNG PIANIST	KOCH, J.
FROM THE COUNTRY	KOCH, J.
FROM THE DIARY OF A FLY	BARTOK
FROM THE HIGHLANDS	KOCH, F.
FROM THE MONADNOCK REGION	WAGNER, J.
FROM THE NORTH WOODS	MCKAY, G.
FROM THE ORGAN LOFT	WRIGHT, L.
FROM THE ORIENT	DOUGLAS
FROM THE RUSSIAN STEPPES	ECKHARDT, F.
FROM THE SEVEN DAYS	STOCKHAUSEN, K.
FROM THE TERRACE	BERNSTEIN, E.
FROM THIS MOMENT ON	SINGER, L.--ED
FROM YOUTHFUL DAYS - TEN PIECES FOR STUDENTS	RAKOV
FRONTIER DAY	KERR, H.
FRONTIER TOWN	GEORGE
FRONTIER	MORITZ, E.
FRONT ROW CENTER	REISMAN
FROSTY THE SNOWMAN	LANE, J.--ED.
FROSTY THE SNOW MAN AND OTHER CHRISTMAS SONGS	
FROST KING	SCHIEFELBEIN, F.
FROST ON THE PUMPKINS	JUDD, A.
FRUEHLINGSERWACHEN, EASY	BACH, J.S.
FRUEHLINGSERWACHEN	BACH, J.S.
FRUEHLINGSERWACHEN	ESPEN, T.
FRUEHLINGSLIED, EASY	MENDELSSOHN
FRUEHLINGSLIED, STUDY	HOLLAENDER
FRUEHLINGSRAUCHEN, EASY	SINDING
FRUEHLINGSRAUCHEN	SINDING
FRUHLING, OP. 22A	SUK
FRUHLING AN DER BERGSTRASSE, OP. 72	RICHARTZ
FRUHLING IM GARTEN. 4 KLAVIERSTUCKE FUR KINDER	MARTINU, B.
FRUSTRATED FLOORWALKER	PERKINS, F.
FUGAL CONCERTO IN G MINOR	YOUNG
FUGA IN DO MINORE, K426	MOZART, W. A.
FUGENBUCHLEIN. 17 KLEINE FUGEN	FISCHER, J. *
FUGENBUCHLEIN	DOFLEIN--ED.
FUGENSONATE NO. 1, OP. 11	LEUKAUF, R.
FUGHETTAS -- 18 LITTLE PRELUDES AND FUGUES FOR TWO	BACH, J.S.
FUGHETTA	BACH, J.S.
FUGHETTA	CHRUSZCH, R.
FUGHETTES --6--	HANDEL
FUGHETTES NOS. 5 AND 6	HANDEL
FUGUES --6-- AND FUGUETTES --6--. URTEXT.	HANDEL
FUGUES AND POLONAISES--12--	BACH, W.F.
FUGUES OF THE WELL-TEMPERED CLAVIER	BACH, J.S.
FUGUE -- 1913 -- LEFT HAND/TWO HANDS	DOHNANYI
FUGUE AND ROMANCE	WEISGALL, H.
FUGUE A LA GIGUE -- BWV577--	BACH, J.S.
FUGUE IN A MINOR, NO. 20 OF ''THE WELL-TEMPERED	BACH, J.S.
FUGUE IN C MINOR, K426 AND SONATA K448 IN D	MOZART, W. A.
FUGUE IN G MINOR, K401	MOZART, W. A.
FUGUE IN G MINOR 'THE LITTLE'	BACH, J.S.
FUGUE IN G MINOR	BACH, J.S.
FUGUE NO. 5, WELL TEMPERED CLAVICHORD	BACH, J.S.
FULL OF FUN	BECK
FUN-A-RAMA	SCHER, W.
FUNCTIONAL PIANO	RUMMO
FUNDAMENTALS OF PIANO TECHNIQUE, BK. 1# DAILY	CONUS, O.
FUNDAMENTALS OF PIANO TECHNIQUE, BK. 2# ADVANCED	CONUS, L.
FUNDAMENTAL PRINCIPLES OF POPULAR PIANO	KENTON, W.
FUNERAILLES	LISZT
FUNERAILLES	LISZT
FUNERAILLES	LISZT
FUNERAL MARCH, OP. 26	BEETHOVEN
FUNERAL MARCH -- SONATA NO. 2	CHOPIN
FUNERAL MARCH - FROM SONATA, OP. 35	CHOPIN
FUNERAL MARCH - FROM SONATA, OP. 35	CHOPIN

FUNERAL MARCH OF A MARIONETTE	GOUNOD, C.
FUNERAL MARCH OF A MARIONETTE	GOUNOD, C.
FUNERAL MARCH	CHOPIN
FUNFARE	SCHER, W.
FUNFTE NOCTURNE OP. 31	SGAMBATI
FUNFUNDZWANZIG AUSGEWAHLTE STUCKE	BACH, J.S.
FUNFZEHN UNGARISCHE BAUERNLIEDER	BARTOK
FUNFZEHN WALZER	BEETHOVEN
FUNFZEHN WALZER	MOZART, W. A.
FUNF BAGATELLEN -- 1953 --	DOUBRAVA
FUNF CAPRICCI	BARTOS, J.
FUNF DEUTSCHE WEIHNACHTSLIEDER	SCHROEDER, H.
FUNF ETUDEN, OP. 10	SCHROETER, H.
FUNF KONTRASTE, OP. 16	LOPATNIKOFF
FUNF KONZERT-ETUDEN OP. 52 -- DIE LAUTE	TCHEREPNIN
FUNF KONZERT-ETUDEN OP. 52 -- KASPERLSPIEL	TCHEREPNIN
FUNF KONZERT-ETUDEN OP. 52 -- LOBGES	TCHEREPNIN
FUNF KONZERT-ETUDEN OP. 52 -- SCHATTENSPIIEL	TCHEREPNIN
FUNF KONZERT-ETUDEN OP. 52 -- WIDMUNG AN CHINA	TCHEREPNIN
FUNF NOCTURNOS, OP. 36	CHLUBNA
FUNF PORTRAITS	FRANCAIX, J.
FUNF SONATEN	KOZELUCH, L.
FUNF TIENTOS - RICERCARE	COELHO, P.M.R.
FUNF UND ZWANZIG LEICHTE ETUDEN OP. 100	BURGMUELLER
FUNICULI-FUNICULA -- SIMP.	DENZA
FUNICULI-FUNICULA	DENZA
FUNICULI-FUNICULA	DENZA
FUNNY BUNNY	GLOVER, D.
FUNNY BUNNY	MILLER, L.
FUNNY ESKIMO	STEVENS
FUNNY FACE	BRADLEY,
FUNNY FACE	BRIMHALL,
FUNNY FOX	LAKE, G.
FUNNY FROG, THE	GLOVER, D.
FUNNY FROG	GODDARD, W.
FUNNY GIRL	
FUNNY GIRL	
FUNNY LITTLE MANNIKINS	WERMEL
FUNNY OLD CLOWN	CROSBY, M.
FUNNY PELICAN	ROBINSON, A.
FUNNY PELICAN	ROBINSON, A.
FUN ALL DAY -- INTRODUCTORY BOOK	FRISCH, F. T.
FUN AND FROLIC	THORNTON
FUN AT THE CIRCUS	CROCKER, D.
FUN AT THE CIRCUS	LIDDIARD, I.
FUN AT THE CIRCUS	LINDFORS, E.
FUN AT THE FAIR	DAVIS, J.
FUN AT THE FAIR	KLEINMAN, A.
FUN AT THE PIANO	
FUN FAIR	LAST, J.
FUN FOR FOUR HANDS	FICHANDLER, W.
FUN FOR TWO -- A BOOK OF PIANO DUETS	PROCTER, A.
FUN FOR TWO	KARP
FUN FOR TWO	KRAFT
FUN IN SCALE PLAYING	BILBRO, M.
FUN IN SONG	CERVENKA
FUN IN THE POOL	TILLETT, J.
FUN IN THE SNOW - OPTIONAL 2ND PIANO PART	RENNARD
FUN OF FUN	BRUSSELS, I.
FUN OF THE FAIR	GRAY, D.
FUN ON THE KEYS--47 EASY PIANO PIECES	FOUTS, M.
FUN ON THE 4TH	ROBINSON, A.
FUN TIME	ELAINE, M.
FUN TIME	STEINER--ED.
FUN TO PLAY	PROCTOR
FUN TUNE DUETS	WILSON
FUN WITH A FUGUE	NEVIN
FUN WITH FIVE FAVORITE SONGS	ZEPP--ED
FUN WITH FOLK TUNES	SASLAW, E.--ED
FUN WITH FOUR CHORDS	ZEPP
FUN WITH MY LOU	WEYBRIGHT--ED.
FUN WITH MY LOU	WEYBRIGHT--ED.
FUN WITH NEW STEPS AHEAD	MARTIN
FUN WITH PIANO	PRICE, T.
FUN WITH SIGHT READING, BK. 1	AGAY, D.--ED
FUN WITH SIGHT READING, BK. 2	AGAY, D.--ED
FUN WITH SIGHT READING, BK. 3	AGAY, D.--ED
FUN WITH THREE CHORDS - BOOK 1	ZEPP
FUN WITH THREE CHORDS - BOOK 2	ZEPP
FUN	ROGERS, E.
FURIANT IN D, OP. 42 NO. 1	DVORAK
FURIANT IN F, OP. 42 NO. 2	DVORAK
FURIANT	SMETANA
FURIANT	WARRACK, G.
FUR ELISE --ALBUMBLATT--	BEETHOVEN
FUR ELISE ALBUMBLATT	BEETHOVEN
FUR FLISE OP. 173	BEETHOVEN
FUR ELISE	BEETHOVEN
FUR ELISE	BEETHOVEN
FUR ELISE	BEETHOVEN
FUR ELISE	BEETHOVEN
FUR ELISE	BEETHOVEN
FUR ELISE	BEETHOVEN
FUR ELISE	BEETHOVEN
FUR ELISE	BEETHOVEN
FUR ELISE	BEETHOVEN
FUR ELISE	BEETHOVEN
FUR KLEINE HANDE, OP. 95	SCHMID
FUR KLEINE LEUTE. 30 LEICHTE KLAVIERSTUCKE FUR DEN	VOLKART-SCHLAGER
FUZZY BEAR	TREVARTHEN, R.
G'WON TRAIN	BOWN
GAIEMENT	STAUB, V.
GAIETY	HAUBIEL, C.
GAIETY	MIDDLEBROOK
GAIETY	TOLLEFSEN, A.
GAILLARDE D'UNE PESTE JOYEUSE -- OPERA-BALLET --	SAMINSKY
GAILY THEY DANCE	WEYBRIGHT--ED.
GAILY	HAUBIEL, C.
GAIOLA E MARECHIARO	LIUZZI
GAIS BATELIERS, CHANSON	HITZ, F.
GAITE DU COEUR	SMITH, SYDNEY
GAITE	BAZELAIRE
GAI LABOUREUR, LE	VOGEL
GALANTE GAVOTTE, OP. 43	RICHARTZ
GALANTE TIRATORE, IL -- BALLET --	VERETTI
GALAWAY FESTIVAL	COURSEY, R. DE
GALAXY OF GREAT HITS	MARTIN, G.--ED
GALLITO QUE CANTA, EL	ANDREWS
GALLOPING COMEDIANS	KABALEVSKY
GALLOPING PONY	CANFIELD, J.
GALLOPING	DITTENHAVER
GALLOPING	GEGENHEIMER, C. .
GALOP -- FROM 'MASQUERADE SUITE'	KHATCHATURIAN
GALOP DU DIABLE, OP. 42	LUDOVIC
GALOP FROM 'MASQUERADE' SUITE	KHATCHATURIAN

GALWAY PIPER, THE	RIEGGER, W.--ED.
GAMBIT	DIAMOND, D.
GAMBOLING	NOEL, H.
GAME OF DANCE	BERKOWITZ
GAMMES DIATONIQUES ET CHROMATIQUES	FERTE
GANG THAT SANG 'HEART OF MY HEART'	LANE, J.--ED.
GARCON MEUNIER, LE	ZILCHER
GARDENIAS	FEDERER, R.
GARDENS IN SPRING, OP. 112, NO. 6	NIEMANN
GARDENS IN THE RAIN FROM THE ESTAMPES	DEBUSSY
GARDENS IN THE RAIN	DEBUSSY
GARDEN AT EVENING, A	ECKSTEIN
GARDEN DANCE, A	VARGAS
GARDEN DANCE, A	VARGAS
GARDEN FLOWERS	RIEGGER, W.
GARDEN IN SPRING, A	COMSTOCK
GARDEN IN THE SEA	SCHER, W.
GARDEN MUSIC, OP. 117	NIEMANN
GARDEN OF DREAMS	LINCOLN, H.
GARDEN PARTY	REISER, V.
GARDEN PARTY	STEINER
GARDEN WALTZ, THE	HOPKINS, H.
GARGOYLES	KAHALI, V.
GARIBALDI FOI A MISSA	VILLA-LOBOS, H.
GARIBALDI HYMN -- WITH WORDS --	OLIVIERI
GARIBALDI HYMN -- WITH WORDS --	OLIVIERI
GARLAND FOR GRIEG, A, BK. 2	GRIEG
GARLAND OF ROSES	STREABBOG
GARY MCFARLAND TOUCH, THE	MCFARLAND, G.
GASLIGHT BLUES	KAHN, M.
GASLIGHT WALTZ	STEINER
GASPARD DE LA NUIT	RAVEL
GATHERING DAISIES	SCHIEFELBEIN, F.
GATO, OP. 8 NO. 3	NAPOLITANO
GATO, OP. 8 NO. 3	NAPOLITANO
GATO	AGUIRRE
GATO	GUASTAVINO
GATO	GUASTAVINO
GATO	NAPOLITANO
GATO	SAMMARTINO
GAUCHO	BOTELLI
GAUDIA RURIS	MONTANI
GAVOTA	PONCE, M.
GAVOTTA ALL'ANTICA	CARABELLA
GAVOTTE--BOURREE--IN B MINOR--FROM VIOLIN SONATA NO. 2	BACH, J.S.
GAVOTTE, ENGLISH SUITE NO. 3	BACH, J.S.
GAVOTTE, FRENCH SUITE NO. 4	BACH, J.S.
GAVOTTE, FROM ''MIGNON''	THOMAS, A.
GAVOTTE, FROM 'CLASSICAL SYMPHONY'	PROKOFIEFF
GAVOTTE, FROM CLASSICAL SYMPHONY	PROKOFIEFF
GAVOTTE, IPHIGENIA IN AULIS	GLUCK
GAVOTTE, LA BOURBONAISE U. RAMEAU, LE TAMBOURINU.	COUPERIN, F.
GAVOTTE, MIGNON	THOMAS, A.
GAVOTTE, OP. 12 NO. 2	PROKOFIEFF
GAVOTTE, OP. 12	PROKOFIEFF
GAVOTTE, OP. 32 NO. 3	PROKOFIEFF
GAVOTTE, OP. 32 NO. 3	PROKOFIEFF
GAVOTTE, OP. 77 NO. 4	PROKOFIEFF
GAVOTTE, OP. 92, NO. 1 -- FROM 12 PIECES	ALBENIZ, I.
GAVOTTE -- FROM SUITE, OP. 90	SAINT-SAENS
GAVOTTE 'MIGNON'	THOMAS, A.
GAVOTTE AND BOURREE	DAVENPORT, G.
GAVOTTE AND MINUETTINO	GALLON, J.
GAVOTTE AND MUSETTE--FROM SUITE OP. 200	RAFF, J.
GAVOTTE AND MUSETTE, OP. 24	VALEN
GAVOTTE AND MUSETTE -- FROM THE SUITE, OP. 200 -- SET	RAFF, J.
GAVOTTE AND MUSETTE FROM THE SUITE, OP. 200 -- SET	RAFF, J.
GAVOTTE AND MUSETTE	DE RUBERTIS
GAVOTTE AS-MOLL OP. 14	SGAMBATI
GAVOTTE D-DUR UND MARTINI, GAVOTTE	GOSSEC
GAVOTTE DANS LE STYLE DE JADIS	LEPITRE
GAVOTTE DEBUTANTES, SWEET 17	ABTLER
GAVOTTE DES BALLERINES	ARNAUD, A.
GAVOTTE DES MATHURINS	LEMAIRE
GAVOTTE DES MATHURINS	LEMAIRE
GAVOTTE DES PETITS	PESSE
GAVOTTE DES VERS LUISANTS	LINCKE, P.
GAVOTTE DE LA POUPEE, OP. 203	STREABBOG
GAVOTTE FAVORITE DE MARIE-ANTOINETTE	NEUSTEDT
GAVOTTE FAVORITE DE MARIE-ANTOINETTE	NEUSTEDT
GAVOTTE FOR TWO PIANOS	HAUBIEL, C.
GAVOTTE FROM 'CLASSICAL SYMPHONY'	PROKOFIEFF
GAVOTTE FROM 'MANON'	MASSENET, J.
GAVOTTE IN A FLAT	DE RUBERTIS
GAVOTTE IN A MAJOR--FROM 'IPHIGENIA IN AULIS'	GLUCK
GAVOTTE IN A MAJOR --FROM 'IPHIGENIA IN AULIS' BY	BRAHMS--ED.
GAVOTTE IN B FLAT	HANDEL
GAVOTTE IN B MINOR, SECOND VIOLIN SONATA	BACH, J.S.
GAVOTTE IN B MINOR FROM VIOLIN SONATA NO. 2--BACH	SAINT-SAENS
GAVOTTE IN B MINOR	BACH, J.S.
GAVOTTE IN B MINOR	MORENO GANS, J.
GAVOTTE IN D FROM THE 6TH 'CELLO-SONATA OF BACH	MASON, J.
GAVOTTE IN E FROM VIOLIN SONATA NO. 6--BACH	SAINT-SAENS
GAVOTTE IN E MAJOR--FROM VIOLIN SONATA NO. 6	BACH, J.S.
GAVOTTE IN F MAJOR	BEETHOVEN
GAVOTTE IN F SHARP	PROKOFIEFF
GAVOTTE IN G FROM 5TH FRENCH SUITE	BACH, J.S.
GAVOTTE IN G MAJOR	BACH, J.S.
GAVOTTE IN G MINOR--FROM ENGLISH SUITE NO. 3	BACH, J.S.
GAVOTTE IN G MINOR	BACH, J.S.
GAVOTTE IN G	WILLAUME
GAVOTTE LOUIS XV	GREGH
GAVOTTE MIGNONNE	TOURS
GAVOTTE MODERNE	LEMAIRE
GAVOTTE NO. 2	MARTINI, G.
GAVOTTE UND GOSSEC, GAVOTTE D-DUR	RAMEAU
GAVOTTE WITH VARIATIONS IN A MINOR	BARTH, H.
GAVOTTE	CASTILLO, D.
GAVOTTE	DIEMER
GAVOTTE	GLUCK
GAVOTTE	GOSSEC
GAVOTTE	GOSSEC
GAVOTTE	GOSSEC
GAVOTTE	HANDEL
GAVOTTE	LEONCAVALLO
GAVOTTE	MARTIN, G. B.
GAVOTTE	MARTINI, G.
GAVOTTE	PABST
GAVOTTE	RAMEAU
GAVOTTE	STRIMER, J.
GAVOTTE	SWINSTEAD, F.
GAYETY	SOSNIK, H.
GAYETY	
GAYETY	
GAYNOR-SCHAUM PEDAL STUDIES	SCHAUM, J.
GAY BUTTERFLIES - TWO PIANOS, EIGHT HANDS	BENSON, E.
GAY BUTTERFLIES IN SPRINGTIME	VANNORT, I.
GAY CAPRICE, A	DUPIN, M.
GAY CAPRICE	WIGHAM, M.
GAY CAVALIER, THE	KETTERER, E.
GAY DAFFODILS	STEVENS, M.
GAY DANCE, A	SWINSTEAD, F.
GAY DANCE	RENNARD
GAY GAVOTTE, A	ROCKWOOD, G.
GAY GAVOTTE, A	ROCKWOOD, G.
GAY GONDOLIERES -- BARCAROLE -- 6-HANDS	VANDEVERE, J. L.
GAY GOUCHO	BRODSKY, M.
GAY GRETCHEN	COPELAND, B.
GAY GYPSY	REISER, V.
GAY JIG, A	VERRALL, J.
GAY KANGAROO, THE	KAPLAN
GAY LARKS GO MODERN, THE	RAEZER, C.
GAY MARCH. TWO PIANOS, TWELVE HANDS	EDGINTON
GAY MARCH, A	KABALEVSKY
GAY MASQUERADE	KING, S.
GAY MELODY	RAMEAU
GAY MOOD	BRES, D. J.
GAY NINETIES BOOK	SCHAUM, J.--ED.
GAY PARADE, THE	HACKNEY, B. L.
GAY PICTURES	HELYER, M.
GAY PICTURE	LUENING, O.
GAY PROMENADE, A	FROST
GAY SENORITA	ELAINE, SR.
GAY SENORITA	HUNEKE
GAY TARANTELLA	ERB
GAY TUNES	BENTLEY
GAY VIENNA	REBE
GAY VIENNA	VOLZ, H.
GAZELLE, LA, POLKA	WOLLENHAUPT
GAZOUILLEMENT DES OISEAUX, LE	BILLEMA
GAZOUILLEMENT DES OISEAUX, LE	BILLEMA
GAZOUILLIS D'OISEAUX	WALTER
GAZZA LADRA, LA - OVERTURE	ROSSINI, G.
GAZZA LADRA, LA - OVERTURE	ROSSINI, G.
GEBURTSTAGSMARSCH OP. 85 NO. 1	SCHUMANN, R.
GEDICHTE NACH HEINRICH HEINE--OP. 31 NO. 2 IN F	MACDOWELL
GEISHA, THE	JONES, S.
GEMINI	KARP
GEMS OF STEPHEN FOSTER	ROLFE, W.--ED
GENERAL BOOM BOOM	POLDINI, E.
GENERAL BOULANGER'S MARCH	DESORMES
GENERAL BUM-BUM	POLDINI, E.
GENERAL GRANT'S GRAND MARCH	MACK, E.
GENERAL GRANT'S GRAND MARCH	MACK, E.
GENERAL GRANT'S GRAND MARCH	MACK, E.
GENERAL GRANT'S GRAND MARCH	MACK, E.
GENERAL GRANT'S MARCH	MACK, E.
GENERAL LAVINE - ECCENTRIC FROM PRELUDES, BK. 2	DEBUSSY
GENERAL PERSHING -- MARCH	VANDERSLOOT, F.
GENERAL WITH THE PAPER HAT, THE	PETRICH, F. C.
GENESIS	BARLOW, D.
GENIE OF THE WATER, THE	CORTES, R.
GENTILLESSE	BAZELAIRE
GENTILLE A CROQUER, PETITE POLKA	DESSAUX
GENTIL PRINTEMPS	PESSE
GENTLEMEN, START YOUR ENGINES	BURLEY
GENTLE ANNIE	FOSTER
GENTLE BREEZES	DIVERNOIS, J. P.
GENTLE BREEZE	DOUGLAS
GENTLE FLIGHT	DITTENHAVER
GENTLE IS THE BREEZE	ROLLINS, G.
GENTLE IS THE BREEZE	ROLLINS, G.
GENTLE ON MY MIND	BRIMHALL,
GENTLE ON MY MIND	LANE, J.--ED.
GENTLE ON MY MIND	WILLIAMS,
GENTLE WIND, THE	SZCZENIOWSKI, B.
GENTLY	HAUBIEL, C.
GEORGE FRIEDRICH HANDEL, BK. 1 -- ADVANCED	HANDEL
GEORGE FRIEDRICH HANDEL, BK. 2 -- EARLY ADVANCED	HANDEL
GEORGE GERSHWIN ALBUM	GERSHWIN
GEORGE M. COHAN CAVALCADE, BK. 1	STICKLES--ED
GEORGE M. COHAN CAVALCADE, BK. 2	STICKLES--ED
GEORGE M. PLAYER PIANO BOOK	COOK--ED
GEORGE M. SIMPLIFIED HITS	DAHLEN--ED
GEORGE THE GIANT	TOWNSEND
GEORGE WASHINGTON VARIATIONS	KRENEK, E.
GEORGE WASHINGTON	BASTIEN
GEORGIA MINSTREL BAND	ROSE, E.
GEORGINE'S POLKA	SMETANA
GEORGINEN-POLKA IN D	SMETANA
GEORGY GIRL	CRERIE, E.
GERANIUMS	WEYBRIGHT--ED.
GERMAN 'CLAP HANDS' DANCE	WEYBRIGHT--ED.
GERMAN CLAP DANCE	BEETHOVEN
GERMAN DANCES. ORIGINAL	BEETHOVEN
GERMAN DANCES --12-- AND ECOSSAISES --6--	BEETHOVEN *
GERMAN DANCES	MOZART, W. A.
GERMAN DANCES	SCHUBERT
GERMAN DANCE IN E MAJOR	SCHUBERT
GERMAN DANCE IN G MAJOR	MOZART, W. A.
GERMAN DANCE NO. 2	BEETHOVEN
GERMAN DANCE	BEETHOVEN
GERMAN DANCE	FISCHER--ED
GERMAN KEYBOARD MUSIC OF THE SEVENTEENTH AND	FISCHER--ED
GERMAN KEYBOARD MUSIC OF THE SEVENTEENTH AND	FISCHER--ED
GERMAN KEYBOARD MUSIC OF THE SEVENTEENTH AND	TELEMANN, G.P.
GERMAN KEYBOARD MUSIC OF THE SEVENTEENTH AND	TELEMANN, G.P.
GERMAN KEYBOARD MUSIC OF THE SEVENTEENTH AND	BENDA, R.
GERMAN KEYBOARD MUSIC OF THE SEVENTEENTH AND	BACH, C.P.E.
GERMAN KEYBOARD MUSIC OF THE SEVENTEENTH AND	FISCHER--ED
GERMAN MASTERS OF THE 17TH AND 18TH CENTURIES	
GERMAN NATIONAL SONG	WILHELM, C.
GERRY GIRAFFE	NEVIN
GERSHWIN, THE BEST OF HOLLYWOOD	GERSHWIN
GERSHWIN AT THE KEYBOARD	GERSHWIN
GERTRUDE'S DREAM WALTZ	BEETHOVEN
GERTRUDE'S DREAM WALTZ	BEETHOVEN
GERTRUDE'S DREAM WALTZ	BEETHOVEN
GERTRUDE'S DREAM WALTZ	BEETHOVEN
GESAMMELTE WERKE--PNO/ORG/HPCHD	ZACHOW, F. W.
GESANG VON DER KREUZSPINNE, DER, OP. 27 NO. 4	SIBELIUS
GESANG VON DER KREUZSPINNE, OP. 27 NO. 4--WITH	SIBELIUS
GESPENSTER OP. 34	HAAS
GESTES D'ENFANTS - A LA VOLEE	SAUVREZIS
GESTES D'ENFANTS	SAUVREZIS
GESTURES, I, II AND III FOR PREPARED PIANO	SMITH, STUART
GESU BAMBINO, GRADE 02	YON, P. A.
GESU BAMBINO, GRADE 03	YON, P. A.
GESU BAMBINO, GRADE 04	YON, P. A.
GESU BAMBINO	YON, P. A.
GETTING ACQUAINTED AT THE PIANO -- BK. 1 -- PRACTICE	COBB
GETTING THERE AND TRIAD STOMP	SKIPPER

GETTING TO KNOW YOU	HAMMERSTEIN *
GET ME TO THE CHURCH ON TIME	BRIMHALL,
GET MOVING BOOGIE	REID
GHOST HOUSE--WITH WORDS	WIGGINS, M.
GHOSTS ON THE STAIRS	RICKER, E.
GHOST HOUSE	EDELSON
GHOST IN THE CHIMNEY, THE--OP. 81 NO. 10	KULLAK, T.
GHOST IN THE CHIMNEY	ECKSTEIN
GHOST IN THE CHIMNEY	KULLAK, T.
GHOST MARCH	PECHMAN
GHOST ROAMS AT MIDNIGHT, THE	CURRIE, E.
GHOST STALKS AT MIDNIGHT, THE	BECK
GHOST STORY, A	MARTIN, G.
GHOST TOWN	DONENFELD, J.
GHOST WALKS, THE	CANFIELD, J.
GHOST WALKS, THE	MARTIN, H.
GHOST WALTZ	GETTY, G.
GIANNINA MIA--''THE FIREFLY''	FRIML, R.
GIANNINA MIA--''THE FIREFLY''	FRIML, R.
GIANNINA MIA--FROM 'THE FIREFLY'	FRIML, R.
GIANNI SCHICCHI - O MIO BABBINO CARO	PUCCINI
GIANTS OF RAGTIME	MORATH, M.
GIARDINI NOTTURNI	SANTOLIQUIDO
GIDDY GIRL, A	IBERT
GIFTS AND SEMBLANCES	HAIEFF, A.
GIGA -- HARMONIC STUDY EDITION	LEO, L.
GIGA CON VARIAZIONI FROM SUITE IN D MINOR, OP. 91	RAFF, J.
GIGA IN B FLAT	PARADIES, P. D.
GIGA	GETTY, G.
GIGI	SINGER, L.--ED
GIGI	
GIGUES -- IMAGES POUR ORCHESTRE, NO. 1	DEBUSSY
GIGUES -- IMAGES POUR ORCHESTRE, NO. 1	DEBUSSY
GIGUES	DEBUSSY
GIGUE ET AIR DE BALLET DANS LE STYLE ANCIEN, OP. 24	ALKAN
GIGUE IN A MINOR	SILAS, E.
GIGUE IN B FLAT, FROM FIRST PARTITA	BACH, J.S.
GIGUE IN B FLAT, FROM THE FIRST PARTITA	BACH, J.S.
GIGUE IN B FLAT MINOR	GRAUN
GIGUE IN B MINOR, FROM THE THIRD FRENCH SUITE	BACH, J.S.
GIGUE IN B MINOR	BACH, J.S.
GIGUE IN D FROM SUITE NO. 3 FOR ORCH -- TRANSCRIBED IN	BACH, J.S.
GIGUE K574 IN G, AND ADAGIO K540 IN B MINOR	MOZART, W. A.
GIGUE	BACH, J.S.
GIGUE	BARTH, H.
GIGUE	BASTIEN
GIGUE	DIEMER
GIGUE	LOURIE
GIGUE	WEYBRIGHT
GIGUE	WEYBRIGHT
GIG	ARNE
GILLOCK COLLECTION, THE	GILLOCK
GIMNASIA MUSICAL PARA LA ESCUELA -- MUSIC AND DIAGRAMS	RIVERA--ED.
GINEVRINA, LA	MARGOLA
GINGERBREAD HOUSE, THE	ROZIN
GINGERETTE	BUCHANAN, R.
GINGERSNAP BRIGADE, THE	ECKSTEIN
GINGER SNAP BRIGADE, THE	ECKSTEIN
GINNY'S DANCE	KNIGHT
GIOCONDA, LA - DANCE OF THE HOURS	PONCHIELLI
GIOCONDA, LA - DANCE OF THE HOURS	PONCHIELLI
GIOCONDA, LA - DANCE OF THE HOURS	PONCHIELLI
GIOCONDA, LA - DANCE OF THE HOURS	PONCHIELLI
GIOCONDA, LA - EASY FANTASIA	PONCHIELLI
GIOCONDA, LA - FANTASIA	PONCHIELLI
GIOCONDA BALLET	PONCHIELLI
GIOCO DEL CUCU, IL	MASETTI
GIORNO DI FESTA MARCIA, OP. 85, NO. 1, CANTO DELLA	SCHUMANN, R.
GIPSIES ARE COMING, THE	SCHER, W.
GIPSY AIRS, OP. 20	SARASATE
GIPSY DANCE--FROM SONATINA, OP. 149 NO. 6	LICHNER, H.
GIPSY MAZURKA, OP. 102	BOHM
GIPSY REVELS	REISER, V.
GIPSY RONDO	HAYDN
GIPSY RONDO	HAYDN
GIRASOLE BALDANZOSO, IL	BOCCI
GIRLS' BOOK	SCHAUM, J.--ED.
GIRLS' FAVORITE SOLO ALBUM	ECKARD, W.--ED
GIRL AND HER PIANO	KING, S.
GIRL AT THE PIANO	
GIRL FROM IPANEMA, THE	BRIMHALL,
GIRL FROM IPANEMA, THE	GIMBEL *
GIRL FROM PAPHOS, THE	FULEIHAN, A.
GIRL IN SATIN, THE	ANDERSON, L.
GIRL OF MY DREAMS-- SIMP.	MOSSMAN, T.
GIRL WITH THE FLAXEN HAIR FROM PRELUDES, BK.1	DEBUSSY
GISELLE -- BALLET-PANTOMINE IN 2 ACTS	ADAM, A.
GISELLE -- BALLET TOLD IN WORDS AND MUSIC	ADAM, A.
GITANA, LA, WALTZES	BUCALOSSI
GITANA, OP. 156	HEINS, C.
GITANA	MENDOZA-NAVA, J.
GITANE, LA -- SOUVENIR D'ESPAGNE --	STREABBOG
GITANERIAS	INFANTE
GITANERIAS	LAPARRA, R.
GITANERIAS	LECUONA
GITANERIAS	LECUONA
GITANERIAS	LECUONA
GITANERIAS	LECUONA
GIVE AND TAKE	KISH, A.
GIVE ME THAT OLD-TIME RELIGION -- SPIRITUAL	STEINER--ED.
GIVE MY REGARDS TO BROADWAY	COHAN, G. M.
GIVE MY REGARDS TO BROADWAY	COHAN
GIVE MY REGARDS TO BROADWAY	COHAN
GIVE MY REGARDS TO BROADWAY	COHAN
GIVE MY REGARDS TO BROADWAY	SMALL, A.
GLADIOLAS	PANELLA, L.
GLASPERLEM OP. 123	GRETCHANINOFF
GLASS BEADS, OP. 123	GRETCHANINOFF
GLASS BEADS	GRETCHANINOFF
GLASS SLIPPER, THE	GILLOCK
GLATTEIS, PERPETUUM MOBILE	FISCHER, E.
GLENDALE WALTZ	HARVEY
GLENDY BURKE, THE	FOSTER
GLENDY BURKE, THE	FOSTER
GLIDER, THE	WAGNESS
GLIDING ALONG	KARP
GLIDING	COVEY, E.
GLIDING	FRACKENPOHL, A.
GLIDING	JOYNER, B.
GLIMPSE OF CUBA	DUNGAN
GLINT FRA BARNAS VERDEN --FROM THE CHILDREN'S WORLD--	LUDT
GLISSANDO MAZURKA, OP. 259 NO. 2	BOHM
GLISSANDO MAZURKA, OP. 259 NO. 2	BOHM
GLISSANDO MAZURKA	BOHM
GLISTENING GLIDER	HOPSON, E.
GLOCK OU L'HISTOIRE D'UN CLOWN	NABERT, C.

GLORIA, MARCH	LOSEY
GLORIA MARCH	LOSEY
GLORY, GLORY HALLELUJAH	HOWE, J. W.
GLORY OF LOVE	HILL, B.
GLORY TO GOD	WRIGHT, N.
GLOVER'S BEST	GLOVER, D.
GLOW WORM-- ORIGINAL	LINCKE, P.
GLOW WORM, THE	LINCKE, P.
GLOW WORM, THE	LINCKE, P.
GLOW WORM, THE	LINCKE, P.
GLOW WORM -- EASY	LINCKE, P.
GLOW WORM -- SIMP.	LINCKE, P.
GLOW WORM	LINCKE, P.
GLOW WORM	LINCKE, P.
GLOW WORM	LINCKE, P.
GLOW WORM	LINCKE, P.
GLOW WORM	LINCKE, P.
GLOW WORM	LINCKE, P.
GLOW WORM	LINCKE, P.
GLOW WORM	LINCKE, P.
GLOW WORM	REISER, V.
GLUCK, MELODIE	SGAMBATI
GNOMENREIGEN--CONCERT ETUDE	LISZT
GNOMENREIGEN--CONCERT ETUDE	LISZT
GNOME IN THE METRONOME, THE	RICKMAN
GNOME PASSES BY, A	MELLICHAMP, N.
GNOSSIENNE NO. 1	SATIE, E.
GNOSSIENNE NO. 1	SATIE, E.
GNOSSIENNE NO. 2	SATIE, E.
GNOSSIENNE NO. 3	SATIE, E.
GOATHORN DANCE --GUKKOSLATTEN--	EGGE
GOAT AND THE TOM-CAT, THE	COBB
GOBLIN'S NIGHT OUT	MARTIN, H.
GOBLINS, THE	BELWOOD, E.
GOBLINS --PIANO, 6 HANDS--	GREIN
GOBLINS	CANFIELD, J.
GOBLINS	CURRIE, E.
GOBLIN GO-AROUND	COMMOSS
GODCHILD	WALLINGTON, G.
GODFATHER WALTZ	BRIMHALL,
GOD BE WITH YOU TILL WE MEET AGAIN	ROLFE, W.--ED
GOD OF OUR FATHERS	WARREN
GOD OF OUR FATHERS	WEYBRIGHT--ED.
GOD SAVE THE KING, AIR VARIE	HUMMEL, J. N.
GOD SAVE THE QUEEN --PARAPHRASE--	LISZT
GOERLITZ TABULATUR 1650 --100 CHORALES--	SCHEIDT
GOIN' HOME	DVORAK
GOIN' OUT OF MY HEAD	
GOIN' TO TOWN	
GOING AWAY BLUES	KAHN, M.
GOING FISHING	JOHNSON, S.
GOING LATIN --MODERN RHYTHMIC CLASSICS--	HOPKINS, H.
GOING MY WAY	WHITFORD
GOING OUT OF MY HEAD	BRADLEY,
GOING SWIMMING	HOPKINS, H.
GOING TO A PARTY	MAY
GOING TO MARKET	ROLFE, W.
GOING TO THE FAIR	WEYBRIGHT
GOING TO THE FAIR	WEYBRIGHT
GOING TO TOWN BOOGIE	SPIVAK, S.
GOLD, UPDATED	KING, C.
GOLDBERG VARIATIONS, S. 998	BACH, J.S.
GOLDBERG VARIATIONS, THE	BACH, J.S.
GOLDBERG VARIATIONS, URTEXT	BACH, J.S.
GOLDBERG VARIATIONS -- URTEXT --	BACH, J.S.
GOLDBERG VARIATIONS	BACH, J.S.
GOLDBERG VARIATIONS	BACH, J.S.
GOLDBERG VARIATIONS	BACH, J.S.
GOLDENROD	HARVEY
GOLDENROD	ROBINSON, A.
GOLDEN AUTUMN	REEG, G. A.
GOLDEN BUTTERFLY, MEDITATION	HOPKINS, H.
GOLDEN CHAIN	BOSCOVICH
GOLDEN COACH, THE	GIASSON, P.
GOLDEN COCKEREL, THE - HYMN TO THE SUN	RIMSKY-KORSAKOFF
GOLDEN DAWN	MCADAMS, G.
GOLDEN GLOW	RUNGEE
GOLDEN HARP, THE	SCHER, W.
GOLDEN LIBRARY, BK. 1 - VARIOUS COMPOSERS	LONGO--ED.
GOLDEN LIBRARY, BK. 2 - BEETHOVEN, HAYDN, MOZART	BEETHOVEN *
GOLDEN LIBRARY, BK. 3 - VARIOUS COMPOSERS	LONGO--ED.
GOLDEN LIBRARY, BK. 4 - MENDELSSOHN, SCHUBERT,	MENDELSSOHN *
GOLDEN LIBRARY, BK. 5 - BELLINI, DONIZETTI, ROSSINI,	BELLINI *
GOLDEN LIBRARY, BK. 6 - GLUCK, MEYERBEER, WAGNER,	GLUCK *
GOLDEN LIBRARY, BK. 7 - BACH, HANDE	BACH, J.S. *
GOLDEN ROD WALTZ -- ONE PIANO, SIX HANDS --	HOPKINS, H.
GOLDEN SHOWERS	PANELLA, L.
GOLDEN SONGS OF RODGERS AND HAMMERSTEIN	BRIMHALL,
GOLDEN STAR POLKA	STREABBOG
GOLDEN STAR WALTZ	STREABBOG
GOLDEN STAR WALTZ	STREABBOG
GOLDEN SUNSET WALTZ -- SOLO - DUET	RICHARDS, B.
GOLDEN SUNSET WALTZ	RICHARDS, B.
GOLDEN WEDDING, EASY	GABRIEL, M.
GOLDEN WEDDING, THE	GABRIEL, M.
GOLDEN YEARS, THE	ANDERSON, L.
GOLDFISH--POISSONS D'OR--	DEBUSSY
GOLDFISH, OP. 158	HEINS, C.
GOLDFISH IN THE BOWL	BERMONT, G.
GOLDFISH	GILLOCK
GOLDFISH	GILLOCK
GOLD AND SILVER WALTZ	LEHAR
GOLD AND SILVER WALTZ	LEHAR
GOLD AND SILVER WALTZ	LEHAR
GOLD AND SILVER WALTZ	LEHAR
GOLLIWOG'S DANCE	HOWELL
GOLLIWOG'S DANCE	KOCH, F.
GOLLIWOG'S PARADE	LINDFORS, E.
GOLLIWOGG'S CAKE-WALK FROM THE CHILDREN'S CORNER	DEBUSSY
GOLLIWOGG'S CAKE-WALK	DEBUSSY
GOLLIWOGG'S CAKE-WALK	DEBUSSY
GOLLIWOGS AT PLAY	ECKSTEIN
GOLLYWOG	BAUMER, C.
GOLONDRINA, LA	SERRADELL
GOLONDRINA, LA	SERRADELL
GONDOLIERA, OP. 41	MOSZKOWSKI
GONDOLIERA	MOSZKOWSKI
GONDOLIERA	NOVIKOFF
GONDOLIERI	NEVIN
GONDOLIERS, OP. 25, NO. 2 FROM 'A DAY IN VENICE SUITE'	NEVIN
GONDOLIERS	NEVIN
GONDOLIERS	NEVIN
GONDOLIER WALTZES	ROEDER
GONE HUNTING	KLEINMAN, A.
GONE IS SORROW, GONE IS SADNESS	BACH, J.S.

Title	Composer/Editor
GOOD, THE BAD, AND THE UGLY, THE	MORRICONE, E.
GOODBYE, OLD PAINT	WEYBRIGHT--ED.
GOODBYE OLD PAINT	WEYBRIGHT--ED.
GOODBY MY LADY LOVE	HOWARD, J.
GOODNIGHT LADIES	ARMOUR
GOODNIGHT LADIES	STANLEY--ED
GOOD 'N' GROOVY	METIS
GOOD EVENING SCHOTTISCHE	BASSLER
GOOD HUMOR, OP. 18. HUMORESQUES	HAAS
GOOD KING WENCESLAS	WALLIS
GOOD MORNIN' MRS. SIPPI	HUMPHREYS
GOOD MORNING, STARSHINE	LANE, J.--ED.
GOOD MORNING - 12 PIECES	BRADLEY
GOOD MORNING	LECUONA
GOOD MORROW, GOSSIP JOAN	WEYBRIGHT--ED.
GOOD MORROW, GOSSIP JOAN	WEYBRIGHT--ED.
GOOD NIGHT AND LULLABY	BEGNAC
GOOD NIGHT BOAT, THE	SCHAUM, J.--ED.
GOOD NIGHT SWEETHEART	LANE, J.--ED.
GOOD NIGHT SWEETHEART	
GOOD NIGHT	SEWELL
GOOD OLD DAYS, THE	COWELL
GOOD SHIP ROVER, THE	PETRICH, F. C.
GOOD TIMES SONGS	SCHAUM, J.
GOOD TIME TUNES	KING
GOOFY MONKEY	NEVIN
GOOSEY GOOSEY GANDER AND PRETTY MAID	ROLFE, W.
GOOSE CHASE -- THE GALOP	DIETS, J.
GOPAK FROM 'THE FAIR AT SOROCHINSK' -- SIMP.	MOUSSORGSKY
GOPAK	MOUSSORGSKY
GOPAK	MOUSSORGSKY
GOPHER HOLE DANCE	WESTON, P.
GORILLA, THE	GRAHAM, R.
GORLITZER TABLATURE BOOK, THE	SCHEIDT
GOSPEL CAMEOS	SCHAUM, J.--ED.
GOSPEL HYMNS	THOMPSON, J.--ED
GOSPEL HYMN PIANIST	
GOSPEL MEETING	MARTINO
GOSPEL PIANO PROFILES	SCHAUM, J.--ED.
GOSPEL PIANO PROFILES	SCHAUM, J.--ED.
GOSPEL SONG FAVORITES FOR THE PIANO	CHATHAM, B.
GOSPEL VIGNETTES	SCHAUM, J.--ED.
GOSSIPS, THE	REISER, V.
GOSSIP	FISHER, G.
GOTHIC DANCE	HAUBIEL, C.
GOTTERDAMMERUNG -- GER AND ENG SUPERLINEAR TEXT	WAGNER
GOTTSCHALK - A COMPENDIUM OF PIANO MUSIC	GOTTSCHALK
GOTTSCHALK PIANO ALBUM	GOTTSCHALK
GOUCHES - THREE LITTLE PIECES, OP. 189	GRETCHANINOFF
GOYESCAS, PART 1	GRANADOS
GOYESCAS, PART 2	GRANADOS
GOYESCAS - SUITE OF 6 PIECES-	GRANADOS
GO AWAY LITTLE GIRL	BRADLEY,
GO DOWN MOSES	ZEPP--ED
GO FOR BAROQUE	VAUGHN, J.
GO GO GO	GLOVER, D.
GO TELL AUNT RHODY	NEVIN
GO TIGER GO	GLOVER, D.
GRAB BAG	CARLETON, B.
GRACE, LA	BOHM
GRACE, LA	BOHM
GRACE, OP. 149 NO. 5	MAYER, C.
GRACE, OP. 302 NO. 5	BOHM
GRACEFUL BALLERINA	SCHER, W.
GRACEFUL BALLET DANCER, THE	BRUSSELS, I.
GRACEFUL BALLET DANCER, THE	BRUSSELS, I.
GRACEFUL GAZELLE, THE	SCHER, W.
GRACEFUL GHOST RAG, THE	BOLCOM, W.
GRACEFUL LADY, THE	LEMONT, C. W.
GRACEFUL MAIDS	LEVENSON, B.
GRACE AND FAVOR, ONE PIANO - SIX HANDS	MANGDON, C.
GRACE AND FAVOR - TWO PIANOS, EIGHT HANDS	LANGDON, C.
GRACE WALTZ, OP. 207	BOHM
GRACIEUSEMENT. WALTZ -- NO. 2, FROM FIVE EASY PIECES	DELUNE
GRACIOUS LADY	BALLATORE, P.
GRADED COUPERIN, THE	COUPERIN, F.
GRADED PIANO PIECES	
GRADED RAMEAU, THE	RAMEAU
GRADED SCARLATTI, THE	SCARLATTI, D.
GRADED SIGHT-READING - BOOK 1	
GRADED SIGHT-READING - BOOK 2	
GRADED SIGHT-READING - BOOK 3	
GRADED SIGHT-READING - BOOK 4	
GRADED SIGHT READING EXERCISES FOR PIANO, BK. 1	MACMILLAN, E. *
GRADED SIGHT READING EXERCISES FOR PIANO, BK. 2	MACMILLAN, E. *
GRADUATION BALL	STRAUSS, J.
GRADUATION DANCE	FICHANDLER, W.
GRADUATION WALTZ	AGAY, D.
GRADUATION WALTZ	AGAY, D.
GRADUS, BK. 1	ADLER, S.
GRADUS, BK. 2	ADLER, S.
GRADUS AD PARNASSUM. 29 SELECTED STUDIES	CLEMENTI
GRADUS AD PARNASSUM--100 EXERCISES, BK. 1	CLEMENTI
GRADUS AD PARNASSUM--100 EXERCISES, BK. 2	CLEMENTI
GRADUS AD PARNASSUM--29 SELECTED STUDIES, PLUS SCALES	CLEMENTI
GRADUS AD PARNASSUM--29 SELECTED STUDIES, PLUS SCALES	CLEMENTI
GRADUS AD PARNASSUM, BK. 1	CLEMENTI
GRADUS AD PARNASSUM, BK. 2	CLEMENTI
GRADUS AD PARNASSUM, BK. 3	CLEMENTI
GRADUS MODERNE, LE--NO. 1, MOUVEMENT	WURMSER, L.
GRADUS MODERNE, LE--NO. 2, MAIN GAUCHE SEULE	WURMSER, L.
GRADUS MODERNE, LE--NO. 3, PAPILLONS BLANCS	WURMSER, L.
GRADUS MODERNE, LE--NO. 4, PETITE TOCCATA	WURMSER, L.
GRADUS MODERNE, LE--NO. 5, L'ENJOUEE	WURMSER, L.
GRADUS MODERNE, LE--NO. 6, ARABESQUES	WURMSER, L.
GRANADA -- FROM SUITE ESPANOLA NO. 1	ALBENIZ, I.
GRANADA - SIMPLIFIED	LARA, A.
GRANADA - TEACHING EDITION	LARA, A.
GRANADA FROM 'SUITE ESPANOLA'	ALBENIZ, I.
GRANADA	LARA, A.
GRANADA	LARA, A.
GRANADA	LECUONA
GRANDEUR OF THE SEA	HIBBS, C.
GRANDE MARCH DE CONCERT	WOLLENHAUPT
GRANDE PIECE SYMPHONIQUE	FRANCK, C.
GRANDE POLKA DE CONCERT, OP. 1	BARTLETT, H.
GRANDE POLONAISE BRILLANTE, PRECEDED BY AN ANDANTE	CHOPIN
GRANDE POLONAISE ES-DUR	WEBER, VON
GRANDE SONATA -- AFTER THE STRING TRIO, OP. 3 --	BEETHOVEN
GRANDE SONATE, OP. 33	ALKAN
GRANDE SONATE C MINOR OP. 56 --1844	THALBERG
GRANDE VALSE BRILLANTE, OP. 37	HERZ, H.
GRANDE VILLE, LA -- 1935 -- BALLET IN 3 TABLEAUX	TANSMAN, A.
GRANDFATHER'S CLOCK, THE	MAXIM, F.
GRANDFATHER'S CLOCK	KARGANOFF
GRANDFATHER'S CLOCK	MAXIM, F.
GRANDFATHER'S THEME	NORTH, A.
GRANDFATHERS BOOK, OP. 119	GRETCHANINOFF
GRANDFATHERS BOOK	GRETCHANINOFF
GRANDMA'S MUSIC BOX	MARTIN, H.
GRANDMA'S ROCKING CHAIR	ARNOLD, H.
GRANDMA AND GRANDPA, OP. 98 NO. 2 -- ONE PIANO, EIGHT	WILSON, M.
GRANDMOTHER'S MINUET, OP. 68 NO. 2	GRIEG
GRANDPA'S CLOCK	HOPKINS, H.
GRANDPA'S DANCE ALBUM	
GRANDPA'S ROCKING CHAIR	KEVAN
GRANDPAPA PLAYS IN THE MONDAY NIGHT BAND	HOLLANDER
GRANDPERE'S CLOCK	MAINVILLE
GRANDS POUR LES PETITS,LES--NO.2 UN SOIR CHEZ ANNA	BEAUCAMP
GRANDS POUR LES PETITS,LES--NO.3 LE PETIT SECRET DE	BEAUCAMP
GRANDS POUR LES PETITS,LES--NO.4 DANS LES JARDINS DE	BEAUCAMP
GRANDS POUR LES PETITS,LES--NO.5 LE MIROIR DE CLAUDE	BEAUCAMP
GRANDS POUR LES PETITS,LES--NO.6 UN PETIT TOUR AVEC	BEAUCAMP
GRAND CANYON SUITE	GROFE, F.
GRAND CANYON	THOMPSON, J.
GRAND CANYON	THOMPSON, J.
GRAND CANYON	THOMPSON, J.
GRAND FANTASIA AND TOCCATA	FINZI, G.
GRAND GALOP CHROMATIQUE, OP. 12	LISZT
GRAND IMPERIAL MARCH	DRUMHELLER
GRAND MARCH	KRAEHENBUEHL
GRAND PAS CLASSIQUE--PAS DE DEUX--	ALKAN
GRAND POLKA DE CONCERT	BARTLETT, H.
GRAND POLONAISE, OP. 21	WEBER, VON
GRAND PRIX - THEME	JARRE, M.
GRAND SONATA IN G, OP. 37	TSCHAIKOWSKY
GRAND SONATA NO. 1, OP. 11	SCHUMANN, R.
GRAND SONATA NO. 1 IN F-SHARP MINOR, OP. 11	SCHUMANN, R.
GRAND TARANTELLE	GOTTSCHALK
GRAND TOUR	MCKUEN
GRAND VALSE BRILLANTE, OP. 18	CHOPIN
GRAND VALSE DE CONCERT, OP. 41	GLAZOUNOW, A.
GRAND VALSE DE CONCERT	MATTEL, T.
GRAND VENEUR	CROISEZ, A.
GRANITES	RUDHYAR, D.
GRANITES -- THREE PAEANS	RUDHYAR, D.
GRANNY SERVING TEA	GLOVER, D.
GRAN MARCHA DE LOS SUBSECRETARIOS	RODRIGO, J.
GRASSHOPPER, THE	JOYNER, B.
GRASSHOPPER'S PICNIC	CORBMAN
GRASSHOPPERS' DANCE	BUCALOSSI
GRASSHOPPERS' DANCE	MARTIN, E.
GRASSHOPPERS HOLIDAY	ECKHARDT, F.
GRASSHOPPERS	DUNGAN
GRASSHOPPERS	DUNGAN
GRASSHOPPERS	MCHALE, M.
GRASSHOPPERS	ROZIN
GRASSHOPPER REEL	GRAHAM, R.
GRASSHOPPER SERENADE	WERMEL
GRASSY DELLS	RUNGEE
GRAVE TOCCATA	GARTENLAUB, O.
GRAY BIRCH	CHAGY
GRAY MOONLIGHT	KING, S.
GRAY MULE, THE	HAYES
GRAY RABBIT	DUNGAN
GRAZIOSA --ROMANCE SANS PAROLES	THALBERG
GRAZIOSO FROM THE ST. ANTHONY CHORALE	HAYDN
GREAT ADVENTURE, THE	RODGERS
GREAT BALLETS -- CLASSIC MELODIES	SCHAUM, J.--ED.
GREAT BALLET MUSIC	MITTLER--ED
GREAT COMPOSERS -- CLASSIC MELODIES	SCHAUM, J.--ED.
GREAT CONCERTO MUSIC	MITTLER--ED
GREAT DANE	BARTH, H.
GREAT FRENCH SONGS FOR LITTLE HANDS	VOGEL--ED
GREAT HYMNS OF THE CHURCH	SMITH, T.
GREAT HYMNS	ENGEL, S.--ARR.
GREAT IMPOSTER, THE	
GREAT LITTLE ARMY	ALFORD, K.
GREAT MASTERS, THE	SAUER--ED
GREAT MASTERS	HIRSCHBERG,
GREAT MASTERS	HIRSCHBERG,
GREAT MUSIC OF DUKE ELLINGTON	ELLINGTON
GREAT MUSIC	MININBERG--ED *
GREAT MUSIC	MININBERG--ED *
GREAT OPERAS -- CLASSIC MELODIES	SCHAUM, J.--ED.
GREAT OPERA MUSIC	MITTLER--ED
GREAT PIANO MUSIC	
GREAT SMOKY MOUNTAINS	GLOVER, D.
GREAT SONGS FROM THOROUGHLY MODERN MILLIE	
GREAT SONGS FROM THOROUGHLY MODERN MILLIE	
GREAT SONGS OF THE YEAR - 1973 EDITION	
GREAT SYMPHONIES -- CLASSIC MELODIES	SCHAUM, J.--ED.
GREAT SYMPHONY MUSIC	MITTLER--ED
GREAT THEMES MADE EASY FOR PIANO	DAVIS, J. R.--ED
GREAT WALTZ MUSIC	MITTLER--ED
GRECIAN SUITE	STORR, S.
GRECO, EL	INGHELBRECHT, D.
GREEK DANCE	HRUBY, V.
GREEK MINIATURES, BK. 1	CONSTANTINIDIS,
GREEK MINIATURES, BK. 2	CONSTANTINIDIS,
GREEK MINIATURES, BK. 3	CONSTANTINIDIS,
GREEN,GREEN GRASS OF HOME	BRIMHALL,
GREENSLEEVES -- VARIATIONS ON THE THEME FOR PIANO	SNYDER, W.
GREENSLEEVES - WHAT CHILD IS THIS	ZEPP--ED
GREENSLEEVES	BRIMHALL,
GREENSLEEVES	BURNAM--ED
GREENSLEEVES	CAMEO--ED
GREENSLEEVES	HARVEY, VIVIEN
GREENSLEEVES	MENDEL, S.
GREENSLEEVES	REBE
GREENSLEEVES	SMALL, A.
GREENSLEEVES	VAUGHAN
GREENSLEEVES	VAUGHAN
GREENSLEEVES	VAUGHAN
GREENSLEEVES	WATSON
GREENWICH WITCH	CONFREY, Z.
GREENWILLOW	LOESSER, F.
GREEN CATHEDRAL, THE	HAHN, C.
GREEN EARTH	STOLZE, R.
GREEN GOBLINS, THE	SMOLIN, H.
GREEN GREEN GRASS OF HOME	BRADLEY,
GREEN LANTERNS	SCHER, W.
GREEN LEAVES OF SUMMER, THE	TIOMKIN, D.
GREEN LEAVES OF SUMMER	LANE, J.--ED.
GREEN LEAVES OF SUMMER	WILLIAMS,
GREEN LEAVES OF SUMMER	
GREEN REFLECTIONS	MILNES
GREEN WILLOW DANCE	WESTON, P.
GREETINGS OF SPRING, OP. 16	HERTRICH
GREETING CARDS - AMPARO ITURBI, OP. 170 NO. 6	CASTELNUOVO-TEDE
GREETING CARDS - ANDRE PREVIN, OP. 170 NO. 1	CASTELNUOVO-TEDE
GREETING CARDS - GIESEKING, OP. 170 NO. 5	CASTELNUOVO-TEDE
GREMLINS	MOORE

GREMLIN HOP — ROBERTS
GRENADA. SERENATA -- NO. 1, FROM SUITE ESPANOLA NO. 1 — ALBENIZ, I.
GRETEL AMD HANS — SCHER, W.
GREY DAY AND OUT IN THE SUN — SALTER, L.
GRIEG--SELECTED WORKS — GRIEG
GRIEG'S PIANO CONCERTO, FIRST MOVEMENT--CONCERT — GRAINGER, P.
GRIEGIOLA, FOX TROT FANTASIE — GROOMS
GRIEG CONCERTO — GRIEG
GRIEG FOR THE YOUNG — GRIEG
GRIEG — GRIEG
GRILLEN, OP. 12 NO. 4--FANTASIESTUCKE — SCHUMANN, R.
GRILLEN, OP. 12 NO. 4 — SCHUMANN, R.
GRIZZLY BEAR, THE — TONNER, P.
GROBSCHMIED-VARIATIONEN — HANDEL
GROTESQUE MARCH — SINDING
GROUNDWORK OF THE LESCHETIZKY METHOD, THE — BREE, M.
GROWING MELODY — BAISDEN
GROWING PEANUTS — DUNGAN
GROWN-UP BEGINNER'S BOOK — FELTON, W.
GRYPHON AND THE MOCK TURTLE — SIMMONS, H.
GUADALCANAL MARCH — RODGERS
GUADALQUIVIR — INFANTE
GUADALQUIVIR — LECUONA
GUAJIRA — ALFONSO
GUANTAMERA — SNYDER, W.
GUANTANAMERA — BRIMHALL,
GUANTANAMERA — BRIMHALL,
GUARACHA, THIRD MOV'T FROM LATIN-AMERICAN SYMPHONETTE — GOULD, M.
GUARACHA — AGAY, D.
GUARANY, IL - OVERTURE — GOMES
GUARDIAN ANGEL — SEIDT, J.
GUARDS' MARCH — STREABBOG
GUARDS' MARCH — STREABBOG
GUERRA, LA — PRATELLA
GUESS AGAIN - FOUR SOLOS — RUSSELL
GUESS WHO — RICHTER
GUGLIELMO RATCLIFF - DREAM OF RATCLIFF — MASCAGNI, P.
GUIA PRATICO--2ND ALBUM — VILLA-LOBOS, H.
GUIA PRATICO--3RD ALBUM — VILLA-LOBOS, H.
GUIA PRATICO - BK. 1 — VILLA-LOBOS, H.
GUIA PRATICO - BK. 8 — VILLA-LOBOS, H.
GUIA PRATICO - BK. 9 — VILLA-LOBOS, H.
GUIA PRATICO — VILLA-LOBOS, H.
GUIDELINES TO IMPROVISATION - BK. 1 — KAHN
GUIDELINES TO IMPROVISATION - BK. 2 — KAHN
GUIDELINES TO IMPROVISATION - BK. 3 — KAHN
GUIDE TO IMPROVISATION, A - FOR THE KEYBOARD — LAPORTE, J.
GUIGNOL ET PANDORE -- BALLET IN ONE ACT — JOLIVET, A.
GUILD MUSICIANSHIP BOOK, PART 1 — LINDFORS, E.
GUILD MUSICIANSHIP BOOK, PART 2 — LINDFORS, E.
GUILD REPERTOIRE - ELEMENTARY A — ALLISON *
GUILD REPERTOIRE - ELEMENTARY B — ALLISON *
GUILD REPERTOIRE - ELEMENTARY C — ALLISON *
GUILD REPERTOIRE - ELEMENTARY D — ALLISON *
GUILD REPERTOIRE - INTERMEDIATE A — ALLISON *
GUILD REPERTOIRE - INTERMEDIATE B — ALLISON *
GUILD REPERTOIRE - INTERMEDIATE C — ALLISON *
GUILD REPERTOIRE - INTERMEDIATE D — ALLISON *
GUILD REPERTOIRE - INTERMEDIATE E — ALLISON *
GUILD REPERTOIRE - INTERMEDIATE F — ALLISON *
GUILD REPERTOIRE - PREPARATORY A — ALLISON *
GUILD REPERTOIRE - PREPARATORY B — ALLISON *
GUILD REPERTOIRE - PREPARATORY C — ALLISON *
GUILD REPERTOIRE - PREPARATORY D — ALLISON *
GUILLAUME TELL - EASY FANTASIA — ROSSINI, G.
GUILLAUME TELL - OVERTURE — ROSSINI, G.
GUILLAUME TELL - PASTORALE FROM THE OVERTURE — ROSSINI, G.
GUIRLANDES AND FLAMMES SOMBRES, OP. 73 NOS. 1 AND 2 — SCRIABINE, A.
GUIRLANDES — NOEL, P. *
GUIRLANDE -- HARPSICHORD — DAMASE, J. M.
GUIRLANDE — JACOB, M.
GUITAR, OP. 45 NO. 2 — MOSZKOWSKI
GUITAR, OP. 45 NO. 2 — MOSZKOWSKI
GUITAR, OP. 45 NO. 2 — MOSZKOWSKI
GUITAR, THE — GAYNOR
GUITARE — MARTELLI, H.
GUITARRE, OP. 45 NO. 2 — MOSZKOWSKI
GUITARRERIAS — HUGUET Y TAGELL
GUITARS — GLOVER, D.
GUITAR BOOGIE SHUFFLE — SMITH *
GUITAR MAN, THE — BRADLEY,
GUITAR PLAYER, THE — BULL
GUITAR SERENADE, THE — GAYNOR
GUITAR SERENADE — GAYNOR
GUM DROP TREE — ARCHER, I.
GUNS OF NAVARONE, THE — TIOMKIN, D.
GUS THE GRASSHOPPER — TOWNSEND
GUY FROM CENTRAL HIGH, THE - 20 PIANO PIECES FOR THE — KING, S.
GYMNASTIK AUF TASTEN -- EXERCISES IN FINGER AND HAND — HEISS
GYMNOPEDIE NO. 1 — SATIE, E.
GYMNOPEDIE NO. 1 — SATIE, E.
GYMNOPEDIE NO. 2 — SATIE, E.
GYMNOPEDIE NO. 2 — SATIE, E.
GYMNOPEDIE NO. 3 — SATIE, E.
GYMNOPEDIE NO. 3 — SATIE, E.
GYMNOPEDIE NO. 3 — SATIE, E.
GYPSY, THE — REED, D.
GYPSY BARON OVERTURE, THE — STRAUSS, J.
GYPSY BARON POLKA — STRAUSS, J.
GYPSY BARON WALTZES — STRAUSS, J.
GYPSY CAMP, THE — ERB
GYPSY CAMP, THE — THOMPSON, J.
GYPSY CAMP FIRES — ECKSTEIN
GYPSY CAMP — CANFIELD, J.
GYPSY DANCERS — WARD
GYPSY DANCE FROM 'CARMEN' — BIZET, G.
GYPSY DANCE — LICHNER, H.
GYPSY DANCE — SARASATE
GYPSY DREAMS — GIASSON, P.
GYPSY EARRINGS — ADAMS, B.
GYPSY ECHOES — ROTHGEB, M.
GYPSY ENCAMPMENT, THE — BEHR, F.
GYPSY FANTASY — DUNYAN, J.
GYPSY LEGEND — MANTOVANI
GYPSY LIFE — DUPIN, M.
GYPSY LIFE — DUPIN, M.
GYPSY LIFE — WAGNESS
GYPSY LOVE SONG — HERBERT
GYPSY LOVE SONG — HERBERT
GYPSY RHAPSODY, OP. 20 — SARASATE
GYPSY RHAPSODY — ROSNER
GYPSY RONDO — HAYDN
GYPSY RONDO — HAYDN
GYPSY RONDO — HAYDN
GYPSY SONG, FROM 'IL TROVATORE' — VERDI
GYPSY SPRING DANCE — COLEMAN, C.
GYPSY STRINGS — SCHER, W.

GYPSY SWEETHEART — HERBERT
GYPSY TALES — ROZIN
GYPSY TANGO — MARTIN, G.
GYPSY WAGONS — ROBBINS
GYPSY —
GYPSY —
HABABERA, A — FLETCHER, G.
HABANERA, FROM 'CARMEN' — BIZET, G.
HABANERA, FROM 'CARMEN' — BIZET, G.
HABANERA, OP. 65, NO. 3 — MOSZKOWSKI
HABANERA - RAPSODIE ESPAGNOLE — RAVEL
HABANERA DE CINNA — HOWE
HABANERA FROM ''CARMEN'' -- 8-HANDS, SET — BIZET, G.
HABANERA — BIZET, G.
HABANERA — CHABRIER
HABANERA — CHABRIER
HABANERA — HALFFTER, E.
HABANERA — LONGAS
HABANERA — WEYBRIGHT
HABITANT SKETCHES — ARCHER, V.
HACIENDO NONITO — CASTRO, W.
HAD MY VERSES WINGS — HAHN, R.
HALF STEP WALTZ — HAYS
HALLELUJAH, FROM 'MESSIAH' — HANDEL
HALLELUJAH CHORUS, FROM MESSIAH — HANDEL
HALLELUJAH CHORUS -- FROM 'MESSIAH' — HANDEL
HALLELUJAH CHORUS — HANDEL
HALLELUJAH CHORUS — HANDEL
HALLOWE'EN NIGHT — DVORINE
HALLOWE'EN NIGHT — HOPKINS, H.
HALLOWE'EN PRANKS, CAPRICE — MARTIN, G.
HALLOWE'EN — BURTON
HALLOWE'EN — COBB
HALLOWEEN NIGHT — AARON, M.
HALLOWEEN NIGHT — BRUSSELS, I.
HALLOWEEN PRANKS — ROZIN
HALLOWEEN —
HALL OF MIRRORS, ONE PIANO - SIX HANDS — LANGDON, C.
HALL OF MIRRORS - TWO PIANOS, EIGHT HANDS — LANGDON, C.
HAMBURG, OP. 107 — NIEMANN
HAMLET, OP. 35 -- CHORAL BALLET IN ONE PROLOGUE AND 3 — BLACHER
HAMLET -- LA FETE DU PRINTEMPS — THOMAS, A.
HAMLET — THOMAS, A.
HAMPELMANN FANG AN. TWELVE MARCHES — DICHLER-SEDLACEK
HAMPS BOOGIE-WOOGIE — HAMPTON, L.
HANDBOOK FOR CHURCH PIANIST — AULD, W. J.
HANDEL-BUCHLEIN — HERRMANN--ED
HANDEL'S MESSIAH — HANDEL
HANDEL ALBUM, A - THE EASIEST PIECES — HANDEL
HANDEL PLAYS FOR THE KING -- SIMP. — MOSSMAN, T.
HANDFUL OF PLEASANT DELIGHTS, A — DRAKEFORD, R.
HANDKERCHIEF DANCE — STEINER
HANDSPRINGS — NEVIN
HANDS ACROSS THE TABLE, SIMPLIFIED — MOSSMAN, T.--ED
HANDS ACROSS THE TABLE -- SIMP. — MOSSMAN, T.
HANDS OF TIME, THE — BRADLEY,
HAND IN HAND — BRODSKY, M.
HAND ME DOWN MY WALKIN' CANE — STANLEY--ED
HAND ORGAN MAN, THE — TSCHAIKOWSKY
HANGING MOSS ON THE BAYOU TREES — BURNAM
HANG 'EM HIGH — FRONTIERE, D.
HANKY-PANKY — MARTINO
HANNIBAL'S MARCH — BRIMHALL, J.
HANON-CZERNY — CZERNY *
HANON-FROST - BOOK 1 — HANON, C.
HANON-FROST - BOOK 2 — HANON, C.
HANON-SCHAUM, BK.1 — HANON, C.
HANON-SCHAUM, BK.2 — HANON, C.
HANON, OGGI — SERAFINI, C.
HANON FOR TWO — RICHTER, A.--ED.
HANON IN ALL KEYS — HANON
HANON PREPARATORY BOOK — HANON, C.
HANON THROUGH THE KEYS — HANON, C.
HANON VIRTUOSO PIANIST, PART 1 — BURDICK--ED
HANON VIRTUOSO PIANIST, PART 2 — BURDICK--ED
HANON WITH A BEAT — TOWNSEND
HANSEL AND GRETEL--ADAPTED AS A CHILDREN'S OPERA-STORY — HUMPERDINCK, E.
HANSEL AND GRETEL--ADAPTED FROM HUMPERDINCK AS A — HAUPT, L. VON
HANSEL AND GRETEL, PRAYER — HUMPERDINCK, E.
HANSEL AND GRETEL, SUSY LITTLE SUSY — HUMPERDINCK, E.
HANSEL AND GRETEL, THE LITTLE MAN — HUMPERDINCK, E.
HANSEL AND GRETEL SUITE — SCHAUM, J.--ED.
HANSEL AND GRETEL — HUMPERDINCK, E.
HANSEL UND GRETEL -- ABENDSEGEN UND ENGELREIGEN — HUMPERDINCK, E.
HANSEL UND GRETEL -- KNUSPERWALZER — HUMPERDINCK, E.
HANSEL UND GRETEL -- VORSPIEL — HUMPERDINCK, E.
HANS BRINKER, OR THE SILVER SKATES — CLEMENTS--ED.
HANTS — GLOVER, D.
HAPPENINGS — ROWLEY
HAPPENING — RAPHLING
HAPPIEST GIRL IN THE WHOLE U.S.A., THE — BRADLEY,
HAPPINESS HILL--2, 3, OR 4 PIANOS — METIS, F.
HAPPINESS IS — PARNES *
HAPPINESS IS —
HAPPINESS — JEAN, E.
HAPPITAT — WIGHAM, M.
HAPPY-GO-LUCKY — BRUSSELS, I.
HAPPY-GO-LUCKY — LARSON
HAPPY AGE, THE - 1. THE LITTLE SHARPSHOOTER — BILLI
HAPPY AGE, THE - 2. WITH FULL SAILS — BILLI
HAPPY AGE, THE - 3. ON GREEN MEADOWS — BILLI
HAPPY AGE, THE - 4. VILLAGE BELLS — BILLI
HAPPY AGE, THE - 5. THE FIRST SORROW — BILLI
HAPPY AGE, THE - 6. THE LITTLE GEISHA — BILLI
HAPPY AND GAY — HOPKINS, H.
HAPPY AND GAY — KEYS
HAPPY BANJO — SCHULDT, M.
HAPPY BAREFOOT BOY —
HAPPY BEE, THE — KENT, A.
HAPPY BIRD DAY — SCHAUM, J.--ED.
HAPPY BIRTHDAY, DEAR LUDWIG -- VARIATIONS IN THE STYLE — HILL
HAPPY BIRTHDAY TO YOU --WITH WORDS-- — HILL--ARR.
HAPPY BIRTHDAY — STIEFEL, E.
HAPPY BLUEBIRD —
HAPPY BUGLER, THE — PAYMER, A.
HAPPY CHILDHOOD — MARTIN, G.
HAPPY CHILDREN — MARTIN, E.
HAPPY CHRISTMAS — MARLOWE
HAPPY COWBOY — RENNARD
HAPPY DANCERS - TWO PIANOS, EIGHT HANDS — DAY, R.
HAPPY DANCE — FICHANDLER, W.
HAPPY DAYS, BK. 1 — HEIDELBERGER, P.
HAPPY DAYS, BK. 2 — HEIDELBERGER, P.
HAPPY DAYS, BK. 3 — HEIDELBERGER, P.
HAPPY DAYS — EHMKE, R.
HAPPY DAYS — STUBBLEFIELD
HAPPY DREAM — TSCHAIKOWSKY

Title	Composer
HAPPY FAIRY TALE, A	SHOSTAKOVITCH
HAPPY FARMER, OP. 68 NO. 10	SCHUMANN, R.
HAPPY FARMER, OP. 68 NO. 10	SCHUMANN, R.
HAPPY FARMER, OP. 68 NO. 10	SCHUMANN, R.
HAPPY FARMER, THE	SCHUMANN, R.
HAPPY FARMER, THE	SCHUMANN, R.
HAPPY FARMER, TRANS.	SCHUMANN, R.
HAPPY FROGMEN	MELVIN, B.
HAPPY GO LUCKY	FAHNESTOCK
HAPPY GO LUCKY	HIBBS, C.
HAPPY GO LUCKY	NEVIN
HAPPY GO LUCKY	PROCTER, A.
HAPPY GO LUCKY	SCHER, W.
HAPPY GUY	PECHMAN
HAPPY HALF HOURS IN MELODYLAND	BILBRO, M.
HAPPY HAMSTERS	KREUTZER
HAPPY HARVEST	MOZART, W. A.
HAPPY HEART	LANE, J.--ED.
HAPPY HOBO	HAYES
HAPPY HOBO	HAZELLE
HAPPY HOLIDAY	ANSON, G.--ED
HAPPY HOLIDAY	GILLOCK
HAPPY HOLIDAY	GILLOCK
HAPPY HOLIDAY	GILLOCK
HAPPY HOLIDAY	GREEN, R.
HAPPY HOLIDAY	HIBBS, C.
HAPPY HOLLAND	GLOVER, D.
HAPPY HOP-A-LONG	MARTIN, H.
HAPPY HOP TOADS	BESTHOFF, M.
HAPPY HOURS	WENRICH, P.
HAPPY HOUR BOOK	WILLIAMS, J.
HAPPY HOUR WALTZ	MASOEA, V.
HAPPY HUFF, THE	SUDDARDS
HAPPY HUFF	SUDDARDS
HAPPY HUNTING	
HAPPY INTERVALS - CHILDREN'S STUDIES	VORLOVA, S.
HAPPY INTERVALS - CHILDREN'S STUDIES	VORLOVA, S.
HAPPY LIFE, A	GLIERE
HAPPY LITTLE FINGERS	METZGER
HAPPY LITTLE MEN	BRODSKY, M.
HAPPY NEW YEAR	ROZIN
HAPPY ORGAN	
HAPPY PIRATE	CROCKER, D.
HAPPY PLAYING, BK. 1	FRISCH, F. T.
HAPPY PUPPY, THE	SCHER, W.
HAPPY SAM THE BANJO MAN	GIOVANNI
HAPPY SILLY SONG	GLOVER, D.
HAPPY SKATERS, THE	HOLLANDER
HAPPY SONGS FOR CHILDREN	
HAPPY SONG	RICKER
HAPPY STORY, A	CANFIELD, J.
HAPPY THOUGHTS	CRERIE, E.
HAPPY TIME, BK. 1 - PRIMARY	TANSMAN, A.
HAPPY TIME, BK. 2 - ELEMENTARY	TANSMAN, A.
HAPPY TIME, BK. 3 - INTERMEDIATE	TANSMAN, A.
HAPPY TIMES --25 SHORT PIECES FOR DEVELOPING TECHNIC	BENTLEY
HAPPY TIMES	DE VITO, A.
HAPPY TIME	GROVE, R.
HAPPY WALTZ, A	DIEMENTE, E.
HAPPY WALTZ, THE	LOGIS *
HAPPY WANDERER, THE -- SIMP. VERSION	MOLLER *
HAPPY WANDERER, THE -- TRANSCRIPTION	MOLLER *
HAPPY WANDERER, THE	MOLLER *
HAPPY WANDERER, THE	MOLLER *
HAPPY WITCH, THE	BASTIEN
HAPPY YOUTH, POLKA	MARTIN, G.
HARBINGER OF SPRING	ROLFE, W.
HARBINGER OF SPRING	ROLFE, W.
HARBOR LIGHTS	SINGER, L.--ED
HARBOR LIGHTS	WEYBRIGHT
HARBOR LIGHTS	WEYBRIGHT
HARBOR LIGHTS	
HARBOR ROMANCE	STOLZ
HARD TIMES - PARAPHRASE ON A FOLK THEME	FREED
HARD TIMES COME AGAIN NO MORE	FOSTER
HARES ON THE MOUNTAINS	MERRICK, F.
HARE AND THE TORTOISE, THE	ALT, H.
HARE AND THE TORTOISE - A STORY WITH MUSIC	RICHTER, A.
HARE BELL	SMALLWOOD
HARK, HARK, THE LARK	SCHUBERT *
HARK, HARK, THE LARK	SCHUBERT *
HARK, HARK, THE LARK	SCHUBERT *
HARK, HARK, THE LARK	SCHUBERT *
HARK, HARK THE LARK	SCHUBERT *
HARK THE HERALD ANGELS SING	HARDING, R.
HARK THE HERALD ANGELS SING	MENDELSSOHN
HARLEM NOCTURNE	HAGEN *
HARLEQUIN SERENADE, EASY	DRIGO, R.
HARLEQUIN	GILLOCK
HARLEQUIN	GILLOCK
HARLEQUIN	RICHARDSON, W.
HARMONICA-PLAYER, THE--FROM ''ALLEY TUNES''	GUION, D.
HARMONICA-PLAYER, THE -- FROM ''ALLEY TUNES -- 3	GUION, D.
HARMONICA JOE	SCARMOLIN
HARMONICA WIZARD --MARCH--	SOUSA
HARMONICA WIZARD	SOUSA
HARMONIC EXERCISES FOR PIANO	FISCHER, C.
HARMONIES DELUXE -- 6 WORLD-FAMOUS MELODIES IN	KING, S.--ED.
HARMONIES ET LIGNES, 8 PETITES PIECES POUR PIANO, OP.	FALCINELLI
HARMONIES POETIQUES AND RELIGIEUSES	LISZT
HARMONIOUS BLACKSMITH, THE -- VARIATIONS	HANDEL
HARMONIOUS BLACKSMITH, THE	HANDEL
HARMONIOUS BLACKSMITH, THE	HANDEL
HARMONIOUS BLACKSMITH	HANDEL
HARMONIOUS BLACKSMITH	HANDEL
HARMONIOUS BLACKSMITH	HANDEL
HARMONIOUS ETUDES, OP. 50	RAVINA, H.
HARMONIZATION-TRANSPOSITION AT THE KEYBOARD	KERN
HARMONY FOR PIANO, BK. 1	STEINER
HARMONY FOR PIANO, BK. 2	STEINER
HARMS HITS THROUGH THE YEARS FOR PIANO	
HARMS HITS THROUGH THE YEARS MADE EASY	DAVIS, J. R.--ED
HARNASIE, OP. 55 -- BALLET IN 3 ACTS	SZYMANOWSKI
HAROLD FLAMMER DUET ALBUM	RIEGGER, W.--ED.
HARPE DES ANGES	VASSEUR
HARPE EOLIENNE	SMITH, SYDNEY
HARPSICHORD DIVISIONS --IN PREPARATION	WUORINEN
HARPSICHORD MUSIC OF THE SEVENTEENTH AND EIGHTEENTH	HERRMANN, K.--ED
HARPSICHORD MUSIC OF THE SEVENTEENTH AND EIGHTEENTH	HERRMANN, K.--ED
HARPSICHORD PIECES	COUPERIN, F.
HARPSICHORD PLAYER, THE --SONATA IN C--	MOZART, W. A.
HARPSICHORD TECHNIQUE	PATORNI *
HARP ETUDE	CHOPIN
HARP OF LIFE, THE	COWELL
HARP OF THE MERMAID, THE	
HARRIGAN	COHAN, G. M.
HARVEST CHANT	FULEIHAN, A.
HARVEST DANCE	EMERY
HARVEST DANCE	GLOVER, D.
HARVEST DANCE	MCHALE, M.
HARVEST DANCE	WHITE
HARVEST HYMN	STEINER
HARVEST IN BOHEMIA	CZERNY
HARVEST TIDE	LANGE, G.
HARVEST TIME	STONE, E.
HASSIDIC DANCES	STUTSCHEWSKY, J.
HAUNTED GARRET, THE	HOPKINS, H.
HAUNTED HOUSE, A	BURNAM
HAUNTED HOUSE, ON THE LAKE, DONKEY RIDE	OMALLEY
HAUNTED HOUSE, THE	GLOVER, D.
HAUNTED HOUSE	AARON, M.
HAUNTED HOUSE	BENJAMIN
HAUNTED TREE, THE	GILLOCK
HAUNTING HORN, THE	SLONIMSKY
HAUNTING	SCHIFRIN, L.
HAUSMARCHEN OP. 35, 43, 53 - BK. 1	HAAS
HAUSMARCHEN OP. 35, 43, 53 - BK. 2	HAAS
HAUSMARCHEN OP. 35, 43, 53 - BK. 3	HAAS
HAUSMUSIK. 7 STUCKE FUR DIE 7 TAGE DER WOCHE	KRENEK, E.
HAUSMUSIK -- SEVEN PIECES FOR THE SEVEN DAYS OF THE	KRENEK, E.
HAUSMUSIK FUR WEIHNACHTEN --ALTE UND NEUE	LECHNER--ED
HAUSMUSIK FUR WEIHNACHTEN -- ALTE UND NEUE	LECHNER--ED
HAVAH NAGILAH	KAHN, M.--ED
HAVAH NAGILAH	MERKUR--ED
HAVAH NAGILAH	MERKUR--ED
HAVANA HOLIDAY	COBB
HAVANA HOLIDAY	COBB
HAVANA NIGHTS	CHABRIER
HAVA NAGILA -- ISRAELI FOLK DANCE	
HAVA NAGILA	BRADLEY,
HAVA NAGILA	ZEPP--ED
HAVA NAGILA	ZEPP--ED
HAVE FUN PLAYING JAZZ	LINDSAY, C.
HAVE FUN PLAYING PIANO	ARANY--ED
HAVE YOURSELF A MERRY LITTLE CHRISTMAS	LANE, J.--ED.
HAVE YOU EVER BEEN LONELY	DE ROSE, P.
HAVE YOU EVER BEEN LONELY	SCHAUM, J.
HAVE YOU EVER SEEN THE RAIN	BRIMHALL,
HAVE YOU SEEN	BASTIEN
HAVING A BALL	AGAY, D.--ED *
HAVING FUN	EISBERG, B.
HAVING FUN	RAYMOND, J.
HAVING FUN	RAYMOND, J.
HAVING FUN	WIGHAM, M.
HAWAIIAN DELIGHT -- FOLK MELODIES	STEINER
HAWAIIAN FAREWELL	SUTHERLAND, J.
HAWAIIAN GUITARS	MCSWEEN, F. W.
HAWAIIAN MUSIC	SCHAUM, J.--ED.
HAWAIIAN NIGHTS	GREY, F.
HAWAIIAN NOCTURNE	SCHAUM, J.--ED.
HAWAIIAN NOCTURNE	WESTON, L.
HAWAIIAN TWILIGHT	TIEMAN, J.
HAWAIIAN WARRIOR'S DANCE	SCHAUM, J.--ED.
HAWAIIAN WEDDING SONG, THE	BRIMHALL,
HAWAIIAN WEDDING SONG	MARSHALL
HAWAII	BAETZ, C.
HAYDN-SCHAUM, BK. 1	HAYDN
HAYDN-SCHAUM, BK. 2	HAYDN
HAYDN GO-SEEK	HAYDN
HAYDN GOES HUNTING -- SIMP.	MOSSMAN, T.
HAYDN TO GRIEG, FROM	
HAYDN VARIATIONS, OP. 56B --ST. ANTHONY CHORALE AND 4	BRAHMS
HAYDN VARIATIONS, OP. 56B --2 COPIES--	BRAHMS
HAYDN VARIATIONS, OP. 56B	BRAHMS *
HAYDN VARIATIONS, OP. 56B	BRAHMS *
HAYDN	HAYDN
HAYSEED	DVORINE
HAZEL'S BOOGIE WOOGIE	SCOTT, H.
HAZEL SCOTT FIVE SOLOS -- BOOGIE WOOGIE TO THE	SCOTT, H.
HE, THE NOBLIEST OF ALL	SCHUMANN, R.
HE'S GOT THE WHOLE WORLD IN HIS HANDS	AGAY, D.--ED
HE'S GOT THE WHOLE WORLD IN HIS HANDS	BURNAM--ED
HE'S GOT THE WHOLE WORLD IN HIS HANDS	FRANGIPANE--ED
HE'S GOT THE WHOLE WORLD IN HIS HANDS	KASSCHAU,
HE'S GOT THE WHOLE WORLD IN HIS HANDS	SCHAUM, J.--ED.
HE'S GOT THE WHOLE WORLD IN HIS HANDS	SMALL, A.--ED
HE'S GOT THE WHOLE WORLD IN HIS HANDS	THOMPSON, J.--ED
HE'S GOT THE WHOLE WORLD IN HIS HANDS	ZEPP--ED
HE'S GOT THE WHOLE WORLD IN HIS HAND	KASSCHAU,
HEADIN' FOR THE CORRAL	AULBACH, F.
HEADIN' HOME	MARTINO
HEADS UP	LLOYD, L.
HEAD SHAKIN'	BOWN
HEAP BIG CHIEF	ANSON, G.
HEARTS AND FLOWERS	TOBANI
HEARTS AND FLOWERS	TOBANI
HEARTS AND FLOWERS	TOBANI
HEARTS AND FLOWERS	TOBANI
HEARTS AND FLOWERS	TOBANI
HEARTS AND FLOWERS	TOBANI
HEART OF THE OPERETTA, THE	
HEATHERED HILLS	REBE
HEATHER ROSE	LANGE, A.
HEATHER ROSE	LANGE, G.
HEATHER ROSE	LANGE, G.
HEAV'N, HEAV'N	ECKHARDT, F.--ED
HEAVENWARD, MARCH RELIGIOSO	VILBRE
HEAVENWARD MARCH	VILBRE
HEBE, ONE PIANO - SIX HANDS	BRATTON
HEBREW DANCE	KARP
HEBREW RHAPSODY	FENSTOCK, B.
HEBREW SONGS FOR THE YOUNG PIANIST, BK. 1	STEINER--ED.
HEBREW SONGS FOR THE YOUNG PIANIST, BK. 2	STEINER--ED.
HECTIC HIGHWAY	ROBINSON
HEDGE OF BRACKEN, A	ROWLEY
HEDGE ROSE	WERNER, F.
HEELIE JEEBIE	ATKINS
HEIDENROESLEIN, OP. 3 NO. 3	SCHUBERT
HEIDENROESLEIN	SCHUBERT
HEINZELMANNCHENS WACHTPARADE, OP. 5, ERLEICHTERT	NOACK, K.
HEINZELMANNCHENS WACHTPARADE, OP. 5	NOACK, K.
HEINZELMANNCHENS WACHTPARADE, OP. 5	NOACK, K.
HELDENLEBEN, EIN, OP. 40 -- ORCH	STRAUSS, R.
HELENA POLKA	SCHAUM, J.--ED.
HELICOPTER, THE	NEVIN
HELIOTROPE	LICHNER, H.
HELLO, DOLLY	BRIMHALL,
HELLO, DOLLY	BRIMHALL,
HELLO, YOUNG LOVERS	HAMMERSTEIN *
HELP COMPOSE FOR PIANO AND AUDIENCE	HAYS, D.
HELP YOURSELF TO HARMONY, BK. 1	BURNAM
HELP YOURSELF TO HARMONY, BK. 2	BURNAM
HELTER SKELTER	HIBBS, C.
HEN, THE -- LA POULE	RAMEAU

HENRY, THE CAT	GLOVER, D.
HEP KITTENS	GLOVER, D.
HERALDOS — THREE PIECES	BACARISSE
HERBARIUM	RUDAN
HERB ALPERT AND THE TIAJUANA BRASS	BRIMHALL,
HERDSMAN'S COTTAGE, THE	HEINS, C.
HERD GIRL'S DREAM, THE	LABITZKY, A.
HERE, THERE AND EVERYWHERE	BENTLEY
HERE'S BOOGIE WOOGIE	KING
HERE'S BOOGIE WOOGIE	
HERE'S MORE BOOGIE WOOGIE	KING
HERE'S THAT RAINY DAY	
HERE'S THE CHURCH	REBE
HERE COMES SANTA CLAUS	LANE, J.--ED.
HERE COMES THE BAND	CURCIO
HERE COMES THE BAND	GARROW, L.
HERE COMES THE CIRCUS	AGAY, D.
HERE COMES THE GENERAL	CURCIO
HERE COMES THE RODEO PARADE	ROBINSON, A.
HERE COMES THE TRAIN	KING
HERE COMES THE TUBA	PELS, W.
HERE SPOT	VANDEVERE, J. L.
HERE WE GO	HOPKINS, H.
HERE WE GO	PORTER, W.
HERITAGE HYMN BOOK	KREUTZER--ED
HERMA	XENAKIS, I.
HERO'S MARCH	RICKER, E.
HERODIADE -- BALLET EXTRACT	MASSENET, J.
HERODIADE -- 1944, ORCHESTER-REZITATION NACH STEPHANE	HINDEMITH
HERR JESU CHRIST, DICH ZU UNS WEND -- LORD CHRIST,	BACH, J.S.
HER KISS VALSE	HELTMAN
HER NAME IS SUZANNE	HAYMAN, R.
HESITATION -- WALTZ --	FAUCHEY
HEURES JUVENILES	DELVINCOURT
HEURES SECULAIRES ET INSTANTANEES	SATIE, E.
HEURE DU COUVRE-FEU, L' OP. 56	NOLLET, E.
HEURE DU REVE, L'	WESLY
HEXACHORDUM APOLLINIS, ARIETTE IN F, CIACONEN IN C UND	PACHELBEL
HEXAHEDRON	STARER
HEXENTANZ--FANTASIESTUCKE, OP. 17 NO. 2	MACDOWELL
HEXENTANZ, EASY	MACDOWELL
HEXENTANZ -- WITCHES DANCE	MACDOWELL
HEY, DIDDLE, DIDDLE AND POOR DOG	ROLFE, W.
HEY, GIRL	BRADLEY,
HEY, LOOK ME OVER	BRIMHALL,
HEY, MR. BANJO	STEINER--ED.
HEY JUDE	LENNON *
HEY PEDRO	NAGY, M.
HE AIN'T HEAVY...HE'S MY BROTHER	BRIMHALL,
HE DOES - SHE DOESN'T	THORNE
HE WHO LOVES AND RUNS AWAY--''THE FIREFLY''	FRIML, R.
HE	LANE, J.--ED.
HE	LANE, J.--ED.
HI-DE-HO —THAT OLD SWEET ROLL--	BRADLEY,
HI-LILI, HI-LO	DEUTSCH *
HI-LILI, HI-LO	LANE, J.--ED.
HI, SPRING	ERB
HIDALGO, DANSE ANDALOUSE, OP. 214	LANDRY
HIDDEN WATERFALL, THE	CHENOWETH, W.
HIDE AND SEEK	ALT
HIDE AND SEEK	JAMES, W. G.
HIDE AND SEEK	RAEZER, C.
HIDE THE THIMBLE	DITTENHAVER
HIDING IN THE GARDEN	SHARP
HIDING IN THE GARDEN	SHARP
HIGHLANDER SUITE	SUCHON, E.
HIGHLAND COUNTRY DANCE	BIRCSAK, T.
HIGHLAND CRADLE	WATSON, S.
HIGHLAND ECHO	WATSON, S.
HIGHLIGHTS OF FAMILIAR HYMNS IN TRANSCRIPTION	ANTHONY, G.
HIGHLIGHTS OF FAMILIAR MUSIC, BK. 1, INTERNATIONAL	ANTHONY, G.
HIGHLIGHTS OF FAMILIAR MUSIC, BK. 1	AGAY, D.--ED
HIGHLIGHTS OF FAMILIAR MUSIC, BK. 2, INTERNATIONAL	ANTHONY, G.
HIGHLIGHTS OF FAMILIAR MUSIC, BK. 2	AGAY, D.--ED
HIGHLIGHTS OF FAMILIAR MUSIC FOR PIANO DUET --39	AGAY, D.--ED
HIGHLIGHTS OF FAMILIAR REPERTOIRE	ANTHONY, G.
HIGHLIGHTS OF FAMILIAR SACRED MUSIC	ANTHONY, G.
HIGHWAYMAN, THE	FAITH
HIGHWAYS IN ETUDE LAND	ROBYN
HIGH AND THE MIGHTY, THE	TIOMKIN, D.
HIGH IN A TREE	BURNAM
HIGH JINKS	ERB, M.
HIGH ON A HILLTOP	BRADY, D.
HIGH SCHOOL HARMONIES	KING, S.
HIGH SPIRITS	GROVE
HIGH TIME	MANCINI
HIKERS SONG, THE	GODDEN, R.
HIKING	BEETZ
HIKING	RICHTER
HILARIOUS CURTAIN OPENER AND RITOURNELLE	COWELL
HILD LOVES, A	MILHAUD, D.
HILL-BILLY TUNE	WEAVER, P.
HILLS OF ANACAPRI, THE, FROM PRELUDES, BK. 1	DEBUSSY
HILLTOP DANCE	TAYLOR, EDNA
HILL SONG	NORDOFF, P.
HILL TOPS FAIRY	RUNGEE
HINDU-LIED AUS SADKO	RIMSKY-KORSAKOFF
HINDU DANCER	ELAINE, W.
HINDU DANCING GIRL	MCSWEEN, F. W.
HIPPITY-HOP	WARD
HIPPITY, HIPPITY, HOP	ERB
HIPPITY HOP	HOPKINS, H.
HIPPOPOTAMUS, THE	COBB
HIPPOPOTAMUS HORNPIPE	POOLE, C.
HIPPOPOTAMUS	WAXMAN
HIRONDELLE ET LE PRISONNIER, L'	CROISEZ, A.
HIRONDELLE ET LE PRISONNIER, L'	CROISEZ, A.
HISTOIRES	IBERT
HISTOIRE DE LA PETITE THERESE DE L'ENFANT-JESUS	TCHEREPNIN
HISTOIRE DE MES POUPEES, L' -- LITTLE SUITE	DIENY, A.
HISTORIETTES, OP. 118	GRETCHANINOFF
HISTORIETTES	DIET
HIS LIFE TOLD IN HIS MUSIC	MOZART, W. A.
HITS FROM 'DAMN YANKEES'	ADLER, R. *
HITS OF TODAY--EASY PIANO-- SERIES 1	FRANK--ED.
HITS OF TODAY--EASY PIANO-- SERIES 2	FRANK--ED.
HITS OF TODAY--EASY PIANO-- SERIES 3	FRANK--ED.
HIT FESTIVAL -- 41 FAMOUS MELODIES WITH WORDS	MARTIN, G.--ED
HI FI SUITE	FEATHER
HOBBY HORSES	RAEZER, C.
HOBBY HORSE	SCHER, W.
HOBBY ON THE GREEN -- SET	RUFTY, H.
HOBGOBLINS	BACKHELM, P.
HOBGOBLINS	JOSEPHUS, SR.
HOBGOBLIN	MILNER, A.
HOCHZEISTAG AUF TROLDHAUGEN OP. 65 NO. 6	GRIEG
HOCHZEITSSZENEN	SMETANA
HOCHZEITSTAG AUF TROLDHAGEN	GRIEG
HOCH HEIDECKSBURG, MARSCH - OP. 10, ERLEICHTERT	HERZER, R.
HOCH HEIDECKSBURG, MARSCH - OP. 10	HERZER, R.
HOCH HEIDECKSBURG, OP. 10, MARSCH	HERZER, R.
HOCUS POCUS	STEINER
HOCUS POCUS	
HOE DOWN AND SATURDAY NIGHT WALTZ, FROM "RODEO"	COPLAND
HOE DOWN	BISHOP
HOE DOWN	GLOVER, D.
HOE DOWN	HUNTLEY, H.
HOFISCHE TANZE	TAUBERT
HOLBERG SUITE, OP. 40	GRIEG
HOLIDAYS	CUMMINGS, R.
HOLIDAY BELLS	PROCTER, A.
HOLIDAY BOOK, THE	POST, R.--ED
HOLIDAY BOOK, THE	POST, R.--ED
HOLIDAY DIARY, OP. 5	BRITTEN, B.
HOLIDAY FOR THE HACKNEYED	DUMM
HOLIDAY HORA	BRODSKY, M.
HOLIDAY IN HAIFA	STECHER *
HOLIDAY IN HAITI	HAYMAN, R.
HOLIDAY IN LISBON, FOLK DANCE	STEINER
HOLIDAY IN MEXICO	BERMONT, H.
HOLIDAY IN MEXICO	MARTIN, H.
HOLIDAY IN NAPLES	DE RIENZO
HOLIDAY IN NAPLES	SCHER, W.
HOLIDAY IN SWITZERLAND	HOLLOWAY, J.
HOLIDAY IN TOWN	PARKER, B.
HOLIDAY MARCH	JOYNER, B.
HOLIDAY MOOD	DE VITO, A.
HOLIDAY PLAY	AARON, M.
HOLIDAY POLKA	KARP
HOLIDAY SERENADE	BASTIEN
HOLIDAY SKETCHES	HELYER, M.
HOLIDAY SONG, A	DE VITO, A.
HOLIDAY WALTZ	CHAGY
HOLIDAY	CARLEY, I. M.
HOLIDAY	PARK, S.
HOLIDAY	PONCE, E.
HOLIDAY	STEIN, L.
HOLIDAY	WHITFORD
HOLLAND FESTIVAL	AARON, M.
HOLLYHOCK AND HONEY BEE	BLAKE, D.
HOLLYWOOD BOOGIE	JOHNSON, S.
HOLLY JOLLY CHRISTMAS, A	BRADLEY,
HOLY, HOLY, HOLY	DYKES
HOLY, HOLY, HOLY	DYKES
HOLY BOY	IRELAND, J.
HOLY CITY, THE	ADAMS, S.
HOLY CITY, THE	ADAMS, S.
HOLY CITY, THE	ADAMS, S.
HOLY CITY	ADAMS, S.
HOLY CITY	ADAMS, S.
HOLY CITY	ADAMS, S.
HOLY NIGHT, SILENT NIGHT, EASY	GRUBER, F.
HOLY NIGHT, SILENT NIGHT	GRUBER, F.
HOLY NIGHT	GRUBER, F.
HOMAGE A MOZART	FINE, I.
HOMAGE TO BACH-BOOK 1	HAUBIEL, C.
HOMAGE TO BACH-BOOK 2	HAUBIEL, C.
HOMAGE TO HAYDN	DEBUSSY
HOMAGE TO HIERONYMOUS BOSCH	MEYEROWITZ
HOMAGE TO RAVEL	STEVENS
HOMAGE TO TCHAIKOVSKY	PITFIELD
HOMBRE	ROSE, D.
HOME, SWEET HOME, TRANS.	LANGE, G.
HOME, SWEET HOME, VAR.	BISHOP
HOME, SWEET HOME, VAR.	SLACK
HOMENAJE A ALBENIZ	MORENO GANS, J.
HOMENAJE A FALLA	SCIAMMARELLA
HOMESICK LILT	COWELL
HOMEWARD BOUND-MARCH	ANTHONY, B. R.
HOME -- SIMP.	MOSSMAN, T.
HOME AGAIN	BRADLEY,
HOME DREAMS	NOFKA, R.
HOME FOR CHRISTMAS	
HOME GUARD, THE -- ONE PIANO, SIX HANDS --	GREENWALD, M.
HOME GUARD, THE	GREENWALD, M.
HOME IN THE MEADOW	LANE, J.--ED.
HOME ON THE RANGE -- AMERICAN COWBOY	SPENCER, J.
HOME ON THE RANGE	ROLFE, W.--ED
HOME ON THE RANGE	THOMPSON, J.
HOME ON THE RANGE	WALLIS--ED
HOME STRETCH	ANDERSON, L.
HOME SWEET HOME, RONDO	BISHOP
HOME SWEET HOME OP. 72	THALBERG
HOME SWEET HOME	BISHOP, R.
HOME TO OUR MOUNTAINS	VERDI
HOMLIEST WOMAN, THE	BLOCH, E.
HOMMAGE A ALBAN BERG	WILSON
HOMMAGE A ALBERT ROUSSEL	HONEGGER, A.
HOMMAGE A ARTHUR HONEGGER - 1955	SUTERMEISTER, H.
HOMMAGE A CHOPIN--1949	VILLA-LOBOS, H.
HOMMAGE A CHOPIN -- 12 ETUDES -- BK. 1	GRADSTEIN
HOMMAGE A CHOPIN -- 12 ETUDES -- BK. 2	GRADSTEIN
HOMMAGE A CHOPIN -- 12 ETUDES -- BK. 3	GRADSTEIN
HOMMAGE A CLAUDE DEBUSSY	SEROUX
HOMMAGE A CZERNY -- 20 DIVERTISSEMENTS --	PLE
HOMMAGE A DOMENICO SCARLATTI	BITSCH
HOMMAGE A MA JEUNESSE	GIDEON, M.
HOMMAGE A MUSSET	BLANC
HOMMAGE A POULENC	DUBOIS, P. M.
HOMMAGE A PROKOFIEFF	MAILLARD VERGER
HOMMAGE A RAMEAU FROM IMAGES BK. 1	DEBUSSY
HOMMAGE A S. PICKWICK FROM PRELUDES, BK. 2	DEBUSSY
HOMMAGE	DELA
HONDO	MARKOWITZ, R.
HONEYSUCKLE, WALTZ	STREABBOG
HONEYSUCKLE	OHLSON, M.
HONEY BEE	FERRELL, B.
HONEY BELL, POLKA MAZ	STREABBOG
HONEY BELL POLKA	STREABBOG
HONEY	BRIMHALL,
HONEY	LANE, J.--ED.
HONG KONG BOOGIE	KENT, A.
HONG KONG HOLIDAY	NEVIN
HONG KONG NIGHTS	MACLACHLIN, T.
HONG KONG	NEWMAN, L.
HONKY-TONK RAGTIME PIANO	TERRY--ED
HONKY TONK BOOGIE	MARTIN, H.
HONKY TONK TRAIN	LEWIS *
HOOTIE'S IGNORANT OIL	ANDERSON *
HOOTIE BLUES	MCSHANN *
HOOTIE THE OWL	TROWBRIDGE, L.

HOOTY THE OWL	HOFSTAD, M.
HOP-ALONG POLKA	ROZIN
HOP-SKIP-AND-JUMP	ANSON, G.
HOP-SKIP-AND-JUMP	ANSON, G.
HOP-TOAD, THE	FROST
HOP, HOP, HOP	WEYBRIGHT--ED.
HOP, HOP, HOP	WEYBRIGHT
HOP, SKIP AND PLAY	WRIGHT, K.
HOPAK -- SECOND PIANO PART	NEVIN
HOPAK	MOUSSORGSKY
HOPAK	MOUSSORGSKY
HOPAK	MOUSSORGSKY
HOPAK	NEVIN
HOPAK	VOVK
HOPEFUL TRAVELLER, THE --22 PIECES FOR BOYS--	EDGINTON
HOPES ADRIFT	JARVIS
HOPI HOOP DANCE	SCHAUM, J.--ED.
HOPI SNAKE DANCE	JOLIVET, A.
HOPPING AND RUNNING	ANDERSON, M.
HOPPING SPARROW, THE	GODDEN, R.
HOPPING	KABALEVSKY
HOPSCOTCH	RICKER
HOP ALONG LITTLE FROGGIE	WIGHAM, M.
HOP HOP	FISCHER
HOP HOP	FISCHER
HOP O'MY THUMB	FOX
HOP SCOTCH POLKA	HATRAK
HOP SCOTCH	AVERY, R.
HOP SCOTCH	GLOVER, D.
HOP SCOTCH	ROTHGEB, M.
HOP SCOTCH	WEBB
HOP SCOTCH	WEDBERG, M.
HOP TOADS	MCHALE, M.
HOP TOAD	ROSSMAN, F. A.
HOP TOAD	STILWELL
HORACE VICTORIEUX	HONEGGER, A.
HORA STACCATO	DINICU *
HORA TIME	KARP
HORA	BINDER
HORNPIPE	CARRE
HORNPIPE	CARRE
HORNPIPE	DAVIS, K.
HORNPIPE	ROWLEY
HORN BOOGIE	SCHAUM, J.
HORSEBACK RIDE	GILLOCK
HORSEBACK RIDE	GILLOCK
HORSEMAN, OP. 27, THE.	KABALEVSKY
HORSEMAN, THE	SCHUMANN, R.
HORSE AND BUGGY	ANDERSON, L.
HORSE DRAWN CARRIAGE	BURNAM
HORTUS CONCLUSUS, BK. 1	MALIPIERO, G. F.
HOTEL CARIBBEAN	PECHMAN
HOT CANARY, THE	NERO
HOT DOGS AND CHILI	AUSTIN
HOT POTATOES	TOWNSEND
HOUR GLASS WALTZ	SCHAUM, J.
HOUR OF PARTING	MCADAMS, G.
HOUR OF PRAYER	LOUKA, M.
HOUR OF SONG, THE	LAIS
HOUSEHOLD MUSE, THE	MILHAUD, D.
HOUSE IN THE TREE, A	DOIGE
HOUSE OF FUNNY MIRRORS	SCHAUM, J.--ED.
HOUSE OF THE RISING SUN, THE	BRADLEY,
HOUSE OF THE RISING SUN, THE	BRIMHALL,
HOUSE PARTY TUNES	SCHAUM, J.
HOWELL'S CLAVICHORD, BK. 1	HOWELLS, H.
HOWELL'S CLAVICHORD, BK. 2	HOWELLS, H.
HOW ARE THINGS IN GLOCCA MORRA	SINGER, L.--ED
HOW ARE THINGS IN GLOCCA MORRA	
HOW ARE YOU THIS MORNING	CRERIE, E.
HOW D'YOU DO, MY PARTNER	BRODSKY, M.
HOW DO YOU DO	CRERIE, E.
HOW GREAT THOU ART	BOCK, F.--ED
HOW HIGH THE MOON	SINGER, L.--ED
HOW INSENSITIVE	BRIMHALL,
HOW INSENSITIVE	GIMBEL *
HOW LOVELY ARE THY DWELLINGS	BRAHMS
HOW THE WEST WAS WON	LANE, J.--ED.
HOW THE WEST WAS WON	
HOW TO PLAY CHORD PIANO IN 10 DAYS	SHINN, D.
HOW TO PLAY LIKE A PLAYER PIANO	WATSON
HOW TO PLAY LUSH, MODERN, 'MOOD' PIANO	SHINN, D.
HOW TO PLAY PIANO BY EAR	SHINN, D.
HOW TO PLAY POPULAR MUSIC	BRIMHALL,
HOW TO PLAY ROCK 'N' ROLL PIANO	PALMER, W. A.
HOW TO SUCCEED IN BUSINESS WITHOUT REALLY TRYING	LOESSER, F.
HOW TO TEACH RHYTHMS AND RHYTHM BANDS -- FIFTEEN	KRAWITZ, I. *
HOW TO TEACH RHYTHMS AND RHYTHM BANDS	KRAWITZ, I. *
HOW TO TEACH YOURSELF ALL ABOUT CHORDS	SHINN, D.
HOW TO TEACH YOURSELF HARMONY -- INSTANTLY	SHINN, D.
HPSCHD	CAGE
HUAHUA, LA	GOMEZ CARRILLO
HUAINO	IGLESIAS VILLOUD
HUELLA, OP. 49	AGUIRRE
HUELLA	AGUIRRE
HUELLA	NAPOLITANO
HUELLA	SAMMARTINO
HUES OF BLUES	SHULMAN
HUES OF BLUES	SHULMAN
HUGENOTS, FANTASIE	MEYERBEER, G.
HUGENOTS, THE, PAGE'S SONG	MEYERBEER, G.
HUIT DANSES EXOTIQUES	FRANCAIX, J.
HUIT ETUDES	CASADESUS, R.
HUIT PETITES PIECES ENFANTINES	COX, H.
HULA DANCER	GLOVER, D.
HULA GIRLS IN HAWAII	BURNAM
HULDIGUNGSMARSCH, OP. 56 NO. 3	GRIEG
HULDIGUNGSMARSCH AUS, SIGURD JORSALFAR	GRIEG
HUMMINGBIRD, THE	RENNARD
HUMMING BIRD, THE	BIRCSAK, T.
HUMMING BIRD, THE	GIARD, C.
HUMMING BIRD, WALTZ -- ONE PIANO, SIX HANDS --	SCHILLER, F.
HUMMING BIRD, WALTZ	SCHILLER, F.
HUMMING BIRD	WRIGHT, N.
HUMMING SONG	SCHUMANN, R.
HUMORESKE, OP. 10 NO. 5	RACHMANINOFF, S.
HUMORESKE, OP. 10 NO. 5	RACHMANINOFF, S.
HUMORESKE, OP. 101 NO. 7 -- ERLEICHTERT --	DVORAK
HUMORESKE, OP. 101 NO. 7 -- ONE PIANO, SIX HANDS --	DVORAK
HUMORESKE, OP. 101 NO. 7 -- ORIGINAL --	DVORAK
HUMORESKE, OP. 20	SCHUMANN, R.
HUMORESKE, TRANSPOSED	DVORAK
HUMORESKEN, OP. 101	DVORAK
HUMORESKEN, OP. 6	GRIEG
HUMORESKE IN G FLAT MAJOR, OP. 101 NO. 7	DVORAK
HUMORESKE IN G MAJOR, OP. 101 NO. 7--ORIGINAL IN G	DVORAK
HUMORESKE OP. 101 NO. 7	DVORAK

HUMORESKE OP. 101 NO. 7	DVORAK
HUMORESKE	DVORAK
HUMORESKE	DVORAK
HUMORESKE	DVORAK
HUMORESKE	LEVINE
HUMORESKE	NORDIO
HUMORESKE	POWERS, M.
HUMORESQUE, ONE PIANO - SIX HANDS	MACGREGOR
HUMORESQUE, OP. 10 NO. 2	TSCHAIKOWSKY
HUMORESQUE, OP. 10 NO. 2	TSCHAIKOWSKY
HUMORESQUE, OP. 101, NO. 7	DVORAK
HUMORESQUE, OP. 101, NO. 7	DVORAK
HUMORESQUE, OP. 101, NO. 7	DVORAK
HUMORESQUE, OP. 101, NO. 7	DVORAK
HUMORESQUE, OP. 125 NO. 3	SINDING
HUMORESQUE, OP. 20	SCHUMANN, R.
HUMORESQUE, OP. 20	SCHUMANN, R.
HUMORESQUE, OP. 20	SCHUMANN, R.
HUMORESQUE, OP. 79 NO. 2	REGER
HUMORESQUES, OP. 6	GRIEG
HUMORESQUES	ABSIL, J.
HUMORESQUE IN G, OP. 10 NO. 2	TSCHAIKOWSKY
HUMORESQUE IN G FLAT, OP. 101 NO. 7 - TRANSPOSED IN G	DVORAK
HUMORESQUE NEGRE	GRUNN, H.
HUMORESQUE	DVORAK
HUMORESQUE	DVORAK
HUMORESQUE	LARENNE, L.
HUMORESQUE	MELECCI, A.
HUMORESQUE	OGILVY, F.
HUMORESQUE	POULENC, F.
HUMORESQUE	RACHMANINOFF, S.
HUMORESQUE	TAKACS, J.
HUMOROUS SKETCH --2 PIANOS, 8 HANDS--	PROKOFIEFF
HUMPTY DUMPTY AND PETER, PETER	ROLFE, W.
HUMPTY DUMPTY	SHUMAKER, F. M.
HUMPTY DUMPTY	WARD
HUNDRED BEST SHORT CLASSICS, BK. 1	WHITEMORE--ED.
HUNDRED BEST SHORT CLASSICS, BK. 2	WHITEMORE--ED.
HUNDRED BEST SHORT CLASSICS, BK. 3	WHITEMORE--ED.
HUNDRED BEST SHORT CLASSICS, BK. 4	WHITEMORE--ED.
HUNDRED BEST SHORT CLASSICS, BK. 5	SAMUEL--ED.
HUNDRED BEST SHORT CLASSICS, BK. 6	SAMUEL--ED.
HUNDRED BEST SHORT CLASSICS, BK. 7	SAMUEL--ED.
HUNGARIAN, OP. 39 NO. 12	MACDOWELL
HUNGARIAN CAPRICE, OP. 7	KETTERER, E.
HUNGARIAN CONCERT POLKA	ALFOLDY, I.
HUNGARIAN DANCES, BK. 1--NOS. 01-10	BRAHMS
HUNGARIAN DANCES, BK. 1, NOS. 1-10	BRAHMS
HUNGARIAN DANCES, BK. 1 - 1-10	BRAHMS
HUNGARIAN DANCES, BK. 1	BRAHMS
HUNGARIAN DANCES, BK. 1	BRAHMS
HUNGARIAN DANCES, BK. 2--NOS. 11-21	BRAHMS
HUNGARIAN DANCES, BK. 2, NOS. 11-21	BRAHMS
HUNGARIAN DANCES, BK. 2 - 11-21	BRAHMS
HUNGARIAN DANCES, BK. 2	BRAHMS
HUNGARIAN DANCES, BK. 2	BRAHMS
HUNGARIAN DANCES, BK. 2	BRAHMS
HUNGARIAN DANCES, NOS. 1-21	BRAHMS
HUNGARIAN DANCES, VOL. 1	BRAHMS
HUNGARIAN DANCES, VOL. 2	BRAHMS
HUNGARIAN DANCES IN 2 VOLS., VOL.1	BRAHMS
HUNGARIAN DANCES IN 2 VOLS., VOL.2	BRAHMS
HUNGARIAN DANCES NOS. 5, 6, 7	BRAHMS
HUNGARIAN DANCES NOS. 5, 6 AND 7	BRAHMS
HUNGARIAN DANCES 1-10	BRAHMS
HUNGARIAN DANCE NO. 01	BRAHMS
HUNGARIAN DANCE NO. 03 IN F	BRAHMS
HUNGARIAN DANCE NO. 03	BRAHMS
HUNGARIAN DANCE NO. 05 IN F SHARP MINOR	BRAHMS
HUNGARIAN DANCE NO. 05	BRAHMS
HUNGARIAN DANCE NO. 05	BRAHMS
HUNGARIAN DANCE NO. 05	BRAHMS
HUNGARIAN DANCE NO. 05	BRAHMS
HUNGARIAN DANCE NO. 05	BRAHMS
HUNGARIAN DANCE NO. 05	BRAHMS
HUNGARIAN DANCE NO. 05	BRAHMS
HUNGARIAN DANCE NO. 05	BRAHMS
HUNGARIAN DANCE NO. 06 FOR TWO PIANOS, EIGHT HANDS	BRAHMS
HUNGARIAN DANCE NO. 06 IN D FLAT	BRAHMS
HUNGARIAN DANCE NO. 06 IN D FLAT	BRAHMS
HUNGARIAN DANCE NO. 06	BRAHMS
HUNGARIAN DANCE NO. 06	BRAHMS
HUNGARIAN DANCE NO. 07 IN F	BRAHMS
HUNGARIAN DANCE NO. 07	BRAHMS
HUNGARIAN DANCE NO. 07	BRAHMS
HUNGARIAN DANCE	ENGELMANN, H. U.
HUNGARIAN DANCE	MICHIELS
HUNGARIAN DANCE	REINHOLD, H.
HUNGARIAN DANCE	REINHOLD, H.
HUNGARIAN FANTASY	LISZT
HUNGARIAN FANTASY	LISZT
HUNGARIAN FANTASY	LISZT
HUNGARIAN FANTASY	LISZT
HUNGARIAN FANTASY	LISZT
HUNGARIAN FANTASY	SCHER, W.
HUNGARIAN FESTIVAL	WERMEL
HUNGARIAN FOLK SONGS	PETYREK, F.
HUNGARIAN MARCH, EASY	KOWALSKI, H.
HUNGARIAN MARCH, OP. 13	KOWALSKI, H.
HUNGARIAN MARCH	KOWALSKI, H.
HUNGARIAN MARCH	SCHUBERT
HUNGARIAN RHAPSODIES, VOL. 1	LISZT
HUNGARIAN RHAPSODIES, VOL. 2	LISZT
HUNGARIAN RHAPSODY NO. 01	LISZT
HUNGARIAN RHAPSODY NO. 02 -- SET	LISZT
HUNGARIAN RHAPSODY NO. 02 -- 8-HANDS, SET	LISZT
HUNGARIAN RHAPSODY NO. 02	LISZT
HUNGARIAN RHAPSODY NO. 02	LISZT
HUNGARIAN RHAPSODY NO. 02	LISZT
HUNGARIAN RHAPSODY NO. 02	LISZT
HUNGARIAN RHAPSODY NO. 02	LISZT
HUNGARIAN RHAPSODY NO. 02	LISZT
HUNGARIAN RHAPSODY NO. 02	LISZT
HUNGARIAN RHAPSODY NO. 02	LISZT
HUNGARIAN RHAPSODY NO. 02	LISZT
HUNGARIAN RHAPSODY NO. 02	LISZT
HUNGARIAN RHAPSODY NO. 06	LISZT
HUNGARIAN RHAPSODY NO. 06	LISZT
HUNGARIAN RHAPSODY NO. 06	LISZT
HUNGARIAN RHAPSODY NO. 09	LISZT
HUNGARIAN RHAPSODY NO. 10	LISZT

HUNGARIAN RHAPSODY NO. 11	LISZT
HUNGARIAN RHAPSODY NO. 12	LISZT
HUNGARIAN RHAPSODY NO. 13	LISZT
HUNGARIAN WEDDING SCENE	SCHER, W.
HUNGARIAN	HAUSER
HUNGARIAN	MACDOWELL
HUNGARIAN	MACDOWELL
HUNGARIAN	MACDOWELL
HUNGARY, RAPSODIE MIGNONNE, OP. 410	KOELLING
HUNGARY, RAPSODIE MIGNONNE	KOELLING
HUNGARY --RHAPSODIE MIGNONNE--	KOELLING
HUNGARY FOR TWO PIANOS, EIGHT HANDS	KOELLING
HUNGARY	KOELLING
HUNGRY PUSSY, THE	ERB
HUNTERS, THE	GLOVER, D.
HUNTERS AWAY	BLAKE, D.
HUNTERS AWAY	BLAKE, D.
HUNTERS JOY	SCHIEFELBEIN, F.
HUNTING SONG, OP. 101 NO. 19	GURLITT
HUNTING SONG, OP. 19 NO. 3	MENDELSSOHN
HUNTING SONG, OP. 68 NO. 7	SCHUMANN, R.
HUNTING SONG, OP. 68 NO. 7	SCHUMANN, R.
HUNTING SONG	HOPSON, E.
HUNTING SONG	SCHUMANN, R.
HUNTING SONG	SPINDLER
HUNTING SONG	SWINSTEAD, F.
HUNTING SON	GURLITT
HURDY-GURDY MAN, THE	LIPSCOMB
HURDY-GURDY	KUNC, B.
HURDY-GURDY	KUNC, B.
HURDY GURDY	ERB
HURDY GURDY	RICHTER
HURRICANE HILDA	ROZIN
HURRY, HURRY	BARTHELSON, J.
HURRYING HOME	HOPKINS, H.
HURRY UP, MOON DREAMING, MOTORCYCLES -- TWELVE-TONE	UTZLER
HURTING EACH OTHER	BRADLEY,
HUSH...HUSH, SWEET CHARLOTTE	LANE, J.--ED.
HUSH-A-BYE DOLLY	BASTIEN
HUSH, BE STILL AND MARY'S LAMB	ROLFE, W.
HUSHABY	KETTERER, E.
HUSH BABY, MY DARLING	REBE
HUSTLER, THE -THEME	HOPKINS, K.
HYDROFOIL RIDE	MELVIN, B.
HYMENEE	WESLY
HYMN-TUNE PRELUDE	VAUGHAN
HYMNE A DIE SONNE AUS DER GOLDENE HAHN	RIMSKY-KORSAKOFF
HYMNE A LA JUSTICE, OP. 14	MAGNARD
HYMNE A VENUS, OP. 17	MAGNARD
HYMNE DE GLORIFICATION--1954	MILHAUD, D.
HYMNS AND GOSPEL SONGS	SCHAUM, J.--ED.
HYMNS AT THE PIANO	GILLOCK
HYMNS FOR PIANO, BK. 1	BASTIEN--ED.
HYMNS FOR PIANO, BK. 2	BASTIEN--ED.
HYMNS FOR THE BEGINNING PIANIST	HOLCOMB, L.
HYMNS FOR THE YOUNG PIANIST	STEINER
HYMNS FOR TWO	ROGERS, E. T.
HYMNS FOR TWO	WARD--ED
HYMNS FOR TWO	WARD--ED
HYMNS FOR YOU TO PLAY AND SING	WARD--ED
HYMNS OF FAITH	SCHAUM, J.
HYMNS OF FAITH	THOMPSON, J.--ED
HYMNS OF NATIONS --15--	
HYMNS TO PLAY AND SING	ECKARD, W.
HYMNS TO PLAY AND SING	ROGERS--ED
HYMNS TO REMEMBER	LIPSCOMB--ED.
HYMNS WE LOVE	BERMONT, H.--ED
HYMNS WE LOVE	
HYMNS WITH EASY CHORDS	GRANT, L.--ED
HYMNS	SANFORD--ED
HYMN ALBUM	SCHAUM, J.--ED.
HYMN DUETS FOR CHILDREN	SCHAUM, J.--ED.
HYMN FAVORITES FOR PIANO	MCKINNEY
HYMN PRIMER	SCHAUM, J.--ED.
HYMN PRIMER	SCHAUM, J.
HYMN TO A CELESTIAL MUSICIAN	HOVHANESS, A.
HYMN TO THE SUN GOD --LE COQ D'OR--	RIMSKY-KORSAKOFF
HYMN TO THE SUN	MENDEL, S.
HYMN TO THE SUN	RIMSKY-KORSAKOFF
HYMN TUNES FOR BEGINNERS	RENNICK, E.
HYMN TUNES FOR PIANO--110--	
HYMN TUNE PRELUDES FOR THE PIANO, NO. 1	LYALL, M.--ED
HYMN TUNE PRELUDES FOR THE PIANO, NO. 2	LYALL, M.--ED
HYMN TUNE PRELUDES FOR THE PIANO, NO. 3	SHANKO, S.
HYMN TUNE SET	GREEN, R.
HYMN VARIATIONS FOR PIANO	
HYMN VERSES AND ANTIPHONS	TALLIS
I'D LIKE TO TEACH THE WORLD TO SING	LANE, J.--ED.
I'LL ALWAYS BE IN LOVE WITH YOU	BRYANT--ED.
I'LL BE HOME FOR CHRISTMAS	BRIMHALL,
I'LL BE SEEING YOU	KAHAL *
I'LL BE SEEING YOU	KAHAL *
I'LL BE SEEING YOU	KAHAL *
I'LL BE THERE	DAVIS, J.
I'LL FOLLOW MY SECRET HEART	SINGER, L.--ED
I'LL HOLD YOUR HAND IN MY HAND -- FROM 'LA BOHEME'	PUCCINI
I'LL NEVER FALL IN LOVE AGAIN	BRIMHALL,
I'LL NEVER SMILE AGAIN	LOWE
I'LL SEE YOU IN MY DREAMS	LANE, J.--ED.
I'LL TAKE YOU HOME AGAIN, KATHLEEN	WESTENDORFF
I'M ALWAYS CHASING RAINBOWS	CARROLL *
I'M ALWAYS CHASING RAINBOWS	LANE, J.--ED.
I'M AN EDUCATED DOG	DOIGE
I'M A LITTLE BLACK SHEEP	TRUXELL, E.
I'M HENRY THE EIGHTH, I AM	LANE, J.--ED.
I'M IN THE MOOD FOR LOVE	LANE, J.--ED.
I'M SITTING ON TOP OF THE WORLD	
I'VE GOT A LITTLE LIST	GILBERT *
I'VE GOT YOU UNDER MY SKIN	SINGER, L.--ED
I'VE GROWN ACCUSTOMED TO HER FACE	BRIMHALL,
I'VE GROWN ACCUSTOMED TO HER FACE	SINGER, L.--ED
I'VE TOLD EV'RY LITTLE STAR	
I'VE TOLD EV'RY LITTLE STAR	
IBERIA, BK. 1	ALBENIZ, I.
IBERIA, BK. 2	ALBENIZ, I.
IBERIA, BK. 3	ALBENIZ, I.
IBERIA, VOL. 1	ALBENIZ, I.
IBERIA, VOL. 1	ALBENIZ, I.
IBERIA, VOL. 2	ALBENIZ, I.
IBERIA, VOL. 2	ALBENIZ, I.
IBERIA, VOL. 3	ALBENIZ, I.
IBERIA, VOL. 3	ALBENIZ, I.
IBERIA, VOL. 4	ALBENIZ, I.
IBERIA, VOL. 4	ALBENIZ, I.
IBERIA -- IMAGES POUR ORCHESTRE, NO. 2	DEBUSSY
IBERIA SUITE, BK. 1	ALBENIZ, I.
IBERIA SUITE, BK. 2	ALBENIZ, I.

IBERIA SUITE, BK. 3	ALBENIZ, I.
IBERIA SUITE, BK. 4	ALBENIZ, I.
IBERIA	DEBUSSY
ICEBERG MEADOW	COPE, D.
ICEBERY BOOGIE	MELVIN, B.
ICE BALLET, THE	FLETCHER
ICE BALLET	AARON, M.
ICE CARNIVAL IN VIENNA	SCHER, W.
ICE CARNIVAL	AARON, M.
ICE CARNIVAL	KETTERER, E.
ICE CARNIVAL	SCHAUM, J.--ED.
ICE CREAM MAN	HOPKINS, H.
ICE GLIDING WALTZ	BURNAM
ICE SKATERS' FROLIC, THE	VANNORT, I.
ICE SKATERS	BURTON
ICE SKATING	DUNGAN
ICE SKATING	DUNGAN
ICE SKATING	GARROW, L.
ICH LIEBE DICH, OP. 41 NO. 3	GRIEG
ICH LIEBE DICH	GRIEG
ICH LIEBE DICH	GRIEG
ICICLES	MCHALE, M.
ICICLE WING-DING	CAROSONE
IDA, POLKA	STREABBOG
IDA, SWEET AS APPLE CIDER	STEINER
IDA --JAZZ ARR.--	WHITFORD--ED.
IDA POLKA MAZURKA	STREABBOG
IDEALE	TOSTI
IDEALE	TOSTI
IDEAL PIANO SERIES, BK. 1	REMARK, M.
IDEAL PIANO SERIES, BK. 2	REMARK, M.
IDEAL WRITING SERIES, BK. 1	REMARK, M.
IDEAL WRITING SERIES, BK. 2	REMARK, M.
IDEAS. FOUR PIECES, OP. 69	TOCH, E.
IDILIO, OP. 134	LACK, T.
IDILIO IN A FLAT, OP. 134	LACK, T.
IDILIO MEXICANO FOR 2 PIANOS	PONCE, M.
IDILIO	LACK, T.
IDILLIO	HAUBIEL, C.
IDLE MOMENTS, WALTZ -- ONE PIANO, SIX HANDS --	LICHNER, P.
IDYLL, OP. 24 NO. 6	SIBELIUS
IDYLLE, OP. 7 NO. 4	SUK
IDYLLE -- NACHGELASSENES TRIO ZUR SYMPHONIE NO. 09 --	BRUCKNER
IDYLLE D'ENFANTS	BEYER, F.
IDYLL	CHABRIER
IDYLS, OP. 34	GADE, N.
IDYLS, 5 PIANO PIECES, OP. 21	WELLESZ, E.
IF -- TWO PIANOS AND PRE-RECORDED TAPE	HAYS, D.
IF EVER I WOULD LEAVE YOU	SINGER, L.--ED
IF I COULD BE	BENSON
IF I COULD TELL YOU	FIRESTONE, I.
IF I GIVE MY HEART TO YOU	LANE, J.--ED.
IF I LOVED YOU	
IF I WERE A BIRD	HENSELT, A.
IF I WERE A RICH MAN	BOCK, J.
IF I WERE A SUNBEAM	WADLEY
IF MY FRIENDS COULD SEE ME NOW	LANE, J.--ED.
IF WE ONLY HAVE LOVE	LANE, J.--ED.
IF YOU COULD READ MY MIND	LIGHTFOOT
IF	BRADLEY,
IKE MILLER'S REEL	KILPATRICK
ILES DES PRINCES, LES	MANAS
ILE DE FEU NO. 1	MESSIAEN, O.
ILE DE FEU NO. 2	MESSIAEN, O.
ILLEGAL TENDER -- PREPARED PIANO AND BASSOON	MACBRIDE, D.
ILLUSION	WHITFORD
ILLUSTRATED ALPHABET - FOR PIANO AND CHILDREN	RAPHLING
ILLUSTRATED ALPHABET	RAPHLING
ILYLLE, OP. 62	LYSBERG, C. B.
IL BACIO -- EASY TRANSCRIPTION	ARDITI
IL BACIO -- THE KISS, WALTZ	ARDITI
IL BACIO	ARDITI
IL BACIO	ARDITI
IL BACIO	ARDITI
IL CAVALLINO DA CORSA - THE LITTLE RACEHORSE	MELVIN, B.
IL CIGNO	MARCHI, G.
IL CLAINETTO	LOSAVIO, G.
IL CORRICOLO, GALOP, OP. 24	DE GRAU
IL ETAIT UNE FOIS	MAURICE, P.
IL GUITARRISTA	MELVIN, B.
IL MAESTRO E SCOLARE --SONATA--	PFEIFFER, A.
IL PIANISTA VIRTUOSO, 60 ESERCIZI	HANON, C.
IL PRESEPE	FANCELLI, L.
IL ROSSIGNOLO. ARIA CON VARIAZIONI ED ARIA BIZARRA	POGLIETTI
IL SILENZIO	
IL TROVATORE, ANVIL CHORUS, EASY	VERDI
IL TROVATORE, ANVIL CHORUS	VERDI
IL TROVATORE, EASY TRANS.	VERDI
IL TROVATORE, FANTASIE	VERDI
IL TROVATORE, FANTASIE	VERDI
IL TROVATORE, FANTASIE	VERDI
IL TROVATORE, GYPSY SONG	VERDI
IL TROVATORE, HOME TO OUR MOUNTAINS	VERDI
IL TROVATORE, MISERERE, EASY	VERDI
IL TROVATORE, MISERERE	VERDI
IL TROVATORE, SELECTION	VERDI
IL TROVATORE WALTZ	VERDI
IMAGENES INFANTILES, BK. 1	SANTA CRUZ, D.
IMAGENES INFANTILES, BK. 2	SANTA CRUZ, D.
IMAGES--1ST SERIES	DEBUSSY
IMAGES--2ND SERIES	DEBUSSY
IMAGES, BK. 1	DEBUSSY
IMAGES, BK. 1	DEBUSSY
IMAGES D'ENFANTS	MAGIN, M.
IMAGES D'ENFANTS	MILOSZ *
IMAGES D'EPINAL -- SYMPHONIC SUITE --	DUPERIER
IMAGES D'EPINAL -- 1939	GAILLARD
IMAGES POUR LES CONTES DU TEMPS PASSEE	DELVINCOURT
IMAGES SONORES - ARIETTE AILEE	CHRETIEN
IMAGES SONORES - L'OISEAU-FEE	CHRETIEN
IMAGES SONORES - RONDE DES SCOUTS	CHRETIEN
IMAGES SONORES - YASMINA DANSE	CHRETIEN
IMAGES SONORES - YOLE FLEURIE	CHRETIEN
IMAGES SONORES	CHRETIEN
IMAGINATIONS	BRONS
IMAGINATION	
IMAGO DAL MONTE PELLEGRINO	FANO, G. A.
IMPATIENCE, OP. 45 NO. 18	HELLER, S.
IMPERIAL MELODIES	CRIST, D.
IMPETUOSO	HOWELL
IMPISH PRANKS	KOCH, E.
IMPLORANDO	BORGI
IMPORTANT EVENT, OP. 15 NO. 6--SCENES FROM CHILDHOOD	SCHUMANN, R.
IMPOSSIBLE DREAM, THE. --FROM 'MAN OF LA MANCHA'	DARION *
IMPOSSIBLE DREAM, THE. -- FROM 'MAN OF LA MANCHA'	DARION *
IMPOSSIBLE DREAM, THE -- FROM 'MAN OF LA MANCHA'	DARION *
IMPOSSIBLE DREAM, THE -- FROM 'MAN OF LA MANCHA'	DARION *

Title	Composer
IMPOSSIBLE DREAM, THE -- FROM 'MAN OF LA MANCHA'	DARION *
IMPOSSIBLE DREAM, THE	BRIMHALL,
IMPRESIONES DE MI TIERRA	LASALA
IMPRESIONES MUSICALES	ESPLA
IMPRESION ANDALUZA. THREE PIECES	GUTIERREZ-PONCE
IMPRESSIONES INTIMAS--1911-1914	MOMPOU, F.
IMPRESSIONE D'ORIENTE, OP. 66 NO. 1	SCHUMANN, R.
IMPRESSIONIST ERA PIANO MUSIC	
IMPRESSIONI DAL VERO NO. 1	MALIPIERO, G. F.
IMPRESSIONI	COUTURE
IMPRESSIONS, BK. 1	POZZOLI
IMPRESSIONS, BK. 2	POZZOLI
IMPRESSIONS, 3 PIECES	GRAENER, P.
IMPRESSIONS DE BRETAGNE - EN ALLANT AU PARDON, BINIOUS	DUHAMEL
IMPRESSIONS DE MER	MANZIARLY, M. DE
IMPRESSIONS DE MINORQUE	KOPTAGEL, Y.
IMPRESSIONS DE VOYAGE	WOOLLETT
IMPRESSIONS ET REFLETS	NIVERO, L.
IMPRESSIONS FROM AN ARTIST'S LIFE	SCHELLING, E.
IMPRESSIONS OF THE FAR EAST--IN THE CHINESE CITY	NIEMANN
IMPRESSIONS	FROST
IMPRESSIONS	GROVLEZ
IMPRESSIONS	WHITFORD
IMPRESSION OF THE ARGENTINE	DUNGAN
IMPROMPRU	ALOYSIUS, SR.
IMPROMPTU-CAPRICE, OP. 9	PIERNE
IMPROMPTU-ROCOCO, OP. 58 NO. 2 -- SET	SCHUETT
IMPROMPTU, OP. 14	DOBROWEN, I.
IMPROMPTU, OP. 17	MARTUCCI
IMPROMPTU, OP. 28 NO. 3	REINHOLD, H.
IMPROMPTUS, MOMENTS MUSICAUX. CLOTH-BOUND	SCHUBERT
IMPROMPTUS, MOMENTS MUSICAUX, 3 PIANO PIECES	SCHUBERT
IMPROMPTUS, 12 VARIATIONS, OP. 5	SCHUMANN, R.
IMPROMPTUS --4--	CHOPIN
IMPROMPTUS - MOMENTS MUSICAUS DREI KLAVIERSTUCKE	SCHUBERT
IMPROMPTUS AND MOMENTS MUSICAUX -- CLOTH	SCHUBERT
IMPROMPTUS AND MOMENTS MUSICAUX	SCHUBERT
IMPROMPTUS AND MOMENTS MUSICAUX	SCHUBERT
IMPROMPTUS AND MOMENTS MUSICAUX	SCHUBERT
IMPROMPTUS ON A ROMANCE BY CLARA WIECK, OP. 5	SCHUMANN, R.
IMPROMPTUS	CARRER
IMPROMPTUS	CHOPIN
IMPROMPTUS	CHOPIN
IMPROMPTUS	CHOPIN
IMPROMPTUS	CHOPIN
IMPROMPTUS	CHOPIN
IMPROMPTUS	CRAS
IMPROMPTUS	SCHUBERT
IMPROMPTU - NO. 1 FROM SUITE FOR PIANO	KOCH, J.
IMPROMPTU - SCHERZETTO	DALCROZE
IMPROMPTU AND TOCCATA, 1965	SUNY, S.
IMPROMPTU AS-DUR, OP. 142 NO. 2	SCHUBERT
IMPROMPTU AS-DUR, OP. 90 NO. 4	SCHUBERT
IMPROMPTU A LA MAZUR, OP. 2 NO. 3	SCRIABINE, A.
IMPROMPTU B-DUR, OP. 142 NO. 3	SCHUBERT
IMPROMPTU C-MOLL, OP. 90 NO. 1	SCHUBERT
IMPROMPTU ELEGIAQUE, OP. 90 NO. 3	SCHUBERT
IMPROMPTU ES-DUR, OP. 90 NO. 2	SCHUBERT
IMPROMPTU G-DUR, OP. 90	SCHUBERT
IMPROMPTU GES-DUR, OP. 90 NO. 3	SCHUBERT
IMPROMPTU IN A, OP. 66 -- SET	REINECKE
IMPROMPTU IN A FLAT, OP. 142 NO. 2	SCHUBERT
IMPROMPTU IN A FLAT, OP. 142 NO. 2	SCHUBERT
IMPROMPTU IN A FLAT, OP. 142 NO. 2	SCHUBERT
IMPROMPTU IN A FLAT, OP. 142 NO. 2	SCHUBERT
IMPROMPTU IN A FLAT, OP. 142 NO. 4	SCHUBERT
IMPROMPTU IN A FLAT, OP. 29	CHOPIN
IMPROMPTU IN A FLAT, OP. 90 NO. 4	CHOPIN
IMPROMPTU IN A FLAT, OP. 90 NO. 4	SCHUBERT
IMPROMPTU IN A FLAT, OP. 90 NO. 4	SCHUBERT
IMPROMPTU IN A FLAT, OP. 90 NO. 4	SCHUBERT
IMPROMPTU IN A FLAT, OP. 90 NO. 4	SCHUBERT
IMPROMPTU IN A FLAT MAJOR, OP. 29	CHOPIN
IMPROMPTU IN B FLAT, OP. 142 NO. 3	SCHUBERT
IMPROMPTU IN B FLAT, OP. 142 NO. 3	SCHUBERT
IMPROMPTU IN B FLAT, OP. 142 NO. 3	SCHUBERT
IMPROMPTU IN C MINOR, OP. 90 NO. 1	SCHUBERT
IMPROMPTU IN C SHARP MINOR, OP. 28 NO. 3	REINHOLD, H.
IMPROMPTU IN C SHARP MINOR, OP. 28 NO. 3	RHEINHOLD, H.
IMPROMPTU IN C SHARP MINOR, OP. 66	CHOPIN
IMPROMPTU IN C	SANTOLIQUIDO
IMPROMPTU IN D MINOR UND HUMORESKE IN F SHARP	DVORAK
IMPROMPTU IN E FLAT, OP. 90 NO. 2	SCHUBERT
IMPROMPTU IN E FLAT, OP. 90 NO. 2	SCHUBERT
IMPROMPTU IN E FLAT, OP. 90	SCHUBERT
IMPROMPTU IN E FLAT MINOR	MILLER
IMPROMPTU IN F, OP. 36	CHOPIN
IMPROMPTU IN F MINOR, OP. 142 NO. 1	SCHUBERT
IMPROMPTU IN F SHARP MAJOR, OP. 36	CHOPIN
IMPROMPTU IN F SHARP MINOR, OP. 31 NO. 2	FAURE, G.
IMPROMPTU IN G FLAT, OP. 90 NO. 3 -- TRANSPOSED IN G	SCHUBERT
IMPROMPTU IN G FLAT, OP. 90 NO. 3	SCHUBERT
IMPROMPTU IN G FLAT, OP. 90 NO. 3	SCHUBERT
IMPROMPTU NO. 1, OP. 32	MAURAT, E.
IMPROMPTU NO. 1 IN A-FLAT, OP. 29	CHOPIN
IMPROMPTU NO. 1	FAURE, G.
IMPROMPTU NO. 1	SINGERY
IMPROMPTU NO. 2, OP. 34	MAURAT, E.
IMPROMPTU NO. 2	FAURE, G.
IMPROMPTU NO. 3, OP. 36	MAURAT, E.
IMPROMPTU NO. 3	FAURE, G.
IMPROMPTU NO. 4, OP. 91	FAURE, G.
IMPROMPTU NO. 5, OP. 102	FAURE, G.
IMPROMPTU VALSE	MARGAT, Y.
IMPROMPTU	ALFONSO
IMPROMPTU	ARNELL
IMPROMPTU	BALBO
IMPROMPTU	CARPENTER, J.
IMPROMPTU	DE FRANCMESNIL
IMPROMPTU	DUMAS, L.
IMPROMPTU	KOCH, J.
IMPROMPTU	MACONCHY
IMPROMPTU	MILLER
IMPROMPTU	PILLOIS
IMPROMPTU	REISER, V.
IMPROMPTU	ROGER-DUCASSE
IMPROMPTU	SOUERS
IMPROMPTU	SPIES, C.
IMPROMPTU	STRICKLAND, L.
IMPROMPTU	TSCHAIKOWSKY
IMPROMPTU	WHITFORD
IMPROVISACION	TOSAR ERRECART,
IMPROVISATA --ON 2 NORWEGIAN FOLK SONGS--, OP. 29	GRIEG
IMPROVISATION, OP. 31 NO. 1	MEDTNER, N.
IMPROVISATIONEN OP. 18 -- BK. 1, ST.-V.S. 30	REGER
IMPROVISATIONEN OP. 18 -- BK. 2, ST.-V.S. 30	REGER
IMPROVISATIONS, NOS. 1-6	POULENC, F.
IMPROVISATIONS, NOS. 7-12	POULENC, F.
IMPROVISATIONS, OP. 20	BARTOK
IMPROVISATIONS --FACSIMILE--	TAMAS
IMPROVISATIONS FOR CHILDREN	LUCIUK
IMPROVISATIONS ON CHILDREN'S SONGS	WARD-STEINMAN,
IMPROVISATIONS	ARRIEU
IMPROVISATIONS	HARTLEY, W.
IMPROVISATIONS	SANDERS, J.
IMPROVISATION --MODERN RHYTHMIC CLASSICS--	WHITFORD
IMPROVISATION AND MELODY	BROWN, A.
IMPROVISATION NO. 01	POULENC, F.
IMPROVISATION NO. 02	CHAILLY, L.
IMPROVISATION NO. 02	POULENC, F.
IMPROVISATION NO. 03	POULENC, F.
IMPROVISATION NO. 04	POULENC, F.
IMPROVISATION NO. 05	POULENC, F.
IMPROVISATION NO. 06	POULENC, F.
IMPROVISATION NO. 07	POULENC, F.
IMPROVISATION NO. 08	POULENC, F.
IMPROVISATION NO. 09	POULENC, F.
IMPROVISATION NO. 10	POULENC, F.
IMPROVISATION NO. 13	POULENC, F.
IMPROVISATION NO. 14	POULENC, F.
IMPROVISATION NO. 15	POULENC, F.
IMPROVISATION ON A MORMON HYMN, 'COME, COME, YE	JOHANNESEN, G.
IMPROVISATION ON A NURSERY TUNE	RICHARDSON, A.
IMPROVISATION ON BLUE DANUBE	REGER
IMPROVISATION ON CHRISTMAS TUNES - SERIES 1	MEAD
IMPROVISATION ON CHRISTMAS TUNES - SERIES 2	MEAD
IMPROVISATION ON THE BACH CHORALE ''WIE WOHL IST MIR,	BUSONI
IMPROVISATION	FERTE
IMPROVISATION	GRIFFIS, E.
IMPROVISATION	MIGHAM, M.
IMPROVISO	GUARNIERI
IMPS AND FAIRIES	WOLPAW
IMP IN THE CLOCK	RICHTER
IM FLUG, BK. 1	FREY
IM FLUG, BK. 2	FREY
IM FREIEN -- 5 PIECES, BK. 1	BARTOK
IM FREIEN -- 5 PIECES, BK. 2	BARTOK
IM GRUNEN OP. 99	GRETCHANINOFF
IM GRUNEN OP. 99	GRETCHANINOFF
IM NEBEL	JANACEK
IM PARADIES-WIENER VOLKSLIED	KREISLER
IM SCHUSTERLADEN	TURINA, J.
IM VIOLINSCHLUSSEL -- FIFTEEN LEICHTE STUCKE	
IN-A-GADDA-DA-VIDA	INGLE
INCANTATIONS. KONZERT NO. 4 FUR KLAVIER UND ORCHESTER	MARTINU, B.
INCA WAR SONG	FREED, I.
INCH-ME PINCH-ME	SCHAUM, J.--ED.
INCI NIN KITABI	SAYGUN, A.
INCONTRO CON BEETHOVEN	BEETHOVEN
INCONTRO CON CLEMENTI--BK. 1, 6 PICCOLI PEZZI, OP. 42	CLEMENTI
INCONTRO CON CLEMENTI--BK. 2, 24 VALZER, OP. 38, 39	CLEMENTI
INCONTRO CON HAYDN	HAYDN
INCREDIBLE STRING BAND, THE	
INDIANA --BACK HOME AGAIN IN INDANA	BRYANT--ED.
INDIANA	MACDONALD *
INDIANISCHES TAGEBUCH, VOL. 1	BUSONI
INDIANS ON THE WARPATH	POOLE, C.
INDIAN BOY	RICHTER
INDIAN BRAVES	BLAKE, D.
INDIAN BRAVE	BRODSKY, M.
INDIAN CHIEF, THE	WEYBRIGHT
INDIAN DANCE IN THE FIRELIGHT	MCINTYRE, E.
INDIAN DANCE	LINDFORS, E.
INDIAN DRUM-BEATS	HOLLANDER
INDIAN DRUM	DAVIS, K.
INDIAN FEATHER	WEBB
INDIAN FUN	ADAMS, B.
INDIAN HUNTERS OF THE PLAINS	WEYBRIGHT
INDIAN HUNTERS OF THE PLAINS	WEYBRIGHT
INDIAN LAMENT	DVORAK *
INDIAN LOVE CALL	FRIML, R.
INDIAN LOVE CALL	FRIML, R.
INDIAN LOVE CALL	FRIML, R.
INDIAN LOVE CALL	FRIML, R.
INDIAN MEDICINE MAN	RICHTER, A.
INDIAN NURSERY	BHATIA, V.
INDIAN POW-WOW	BRUSSELS, I.
INDIAN PRINCESS	GLOVER, D.
INDIAN RAIN DANCE	STOCKBRIDGE, J.
INDIAN RAIN DANCE	WEBSTER, J.
INDIAN RITUAL DANCE	COX
INDIAN SMOKE SIGNALS	SCHAUM, J.--ED.
INDIAN SUMMER - SUITE	GIASSON, P.
INDIAN SUMMER - SUITE	GIASSON, P.
INDIAN SUMMER	ARMOUR
INDIAN SUMMER	COOK, P.
INDIAN SUMMER	GRAHAM, R.
INDIAN SUMMER	HERBERT
INDIAN SUMMER	MIDDLEBROOK
INDIAN SUNSET	KLEMM, G.
INDIAN SUN DANCE	MCCLUSKY
INDIAN TRIBESMEN	WEYBRIGHT
INDIAN TRIBESMEN	WEYBRIGHT
INDIAN WAR-CALL	WRIGHT, M.
INDIAN WAR-DANCE	ROLSETH, B.
INDIAN WARRIOR	AUSTIN
INDIAN WAR DANCE -- FROM THREE PIECES FOR THE PIANO	MERKUR
INDIAN WAR DANCE	KEVAN
INDIAN WAR DANCE	RIPPEL, M.
INDIA	AARON, M.
INDISCHE SUITE	SCOTT, C.
INDRODUKTION UND FUGE, OP. 22	JANACEK
INFATIGABLES, LES, GALOP, OP. 243	STREABBOG
INGRID'S LAMENT --PEER GYNT SUITE 2--	GRIEG
INN, THE, FROM 'FOREST SCENES'	SCHUMANN, R.
INNOCENTS ABROAD	ZACHARIAS
INNO DI MAMELI -- WITH WORDS --	NOVARO
INNO DI MAMELI -- WITH WORDS --	NOVARO
INNO PONTIFICIO	HALLMAYR
INPUT AND OUTPUT - FOR THE YOUNGEST PIANISTS	RAPHLING
INPUT AND OUTPUT - FOR THE YOUNGEST PIANIST	RAPHLING
INQUISITIVE WOMEN--PIANO SCORE WITH SUPERLINEAR TEXT	WOLF-FERRARI, E.
INSCRIPTIONS	SCHAT
INSECTES DANSENT,LES	LUCAS, M.
INSPIRATIONS FROM THE PIANO	WILLIAMS, D. M.
INSPIRATION	WHITFORD
INSTANT MODULATOR	
INSTANT PIANO PHASE 1	
INSTANT PIANO PHASE 2	
INSTANT PICTURE CHORD PIANO NO. 1	NEALE, J.--ED
INSTANT PICTURE CHORD PIANO NO. 2, BOB DYLAN	DYLAN
INSTRUCTIVE COURSE OF PIECES, BK. 1--ELEMENTARY AND	OESTERLE

INSTRUMENTAL GREATS	
INTERLUDE, FROM ''PEPITA-JIMINEZ''	ALBENIZ, I.
INTERLUDE FROM 'POEME DE L'AMOUR ET DE LA MER'	CHAUSSON
INTERLUDE	BRIMHALL, J.
INTERLUDE	SENTER, G.
INTERLUDE	SILVERS *
INTERLUDE	STEWART, H.
INTERMEDE IN D MINOR	POULENC, F.
INTERMEDIO -- NO. 4, FROM ''EL BAILE DE LUIS ALONSO''	GIMINEZ
INTERMEDIO -- NO. 4, FROM ''L'A BODA DE LUIS ALONSO''	GIMINEZ
INTERMEZZI--SERIES 1, NOS. 1-6	TANSMAN, A.
INTERMEZZI--SERIES 2, NOS. 7-12	TANSMAN, A.
INTERMEZZI--SERIES 3, NOS. 13-18	TANSMAN, A.
INTERMEZZI--SERIES 4, NOS. 19-24	TANSMAN, A.
INTERMEZZI, OP. 4	SCHUMANN, R.
INTERMEZZI, OP. 4	SCHUMANN, R.
INTERMEZZI	CASTRO, W.
INTERMEZZO, BIRTHDAY SUITE	BOHM
INTERMEZZO, CAV. RUSTICANA	MASCAGNI, P.
INTERMEZZO, CAV. RUSTICANA	MASCAGNI, P.
INTERMEZZO, OP. 36	VALEN
INTERMEZZO, OP. 40 NO. 1	KRAMER, A. W.
INTERMEZZO, OP. 6	VOMACKA
INTERMEZZO, PETITE SUITE	BORODIN, A.
INTERMEZZO AND BALLADE, OP. 16 NO. 3	ALBERT, E. D'
INTERMEZZO ET CAPRICCIO	NOEL, P. *
INTERMEZZO FROM 'GOYESCAS'	GRANADOS
INTERMEZZO FROM 'THE COMEDIANS'	KABALEVSKY
INTERMEZZO FROM PAGLIACCI	LEONCAVALLO
INTERMEZZO IN A, OP. 118 NO. 2	BRAHMS
INTERMEZZO IN A FLAT--1943	POULENC, F.
INTERMEZZO IN A FLAT, OP. 76 NO. 3	BRAHMS
INTERMEZZO IN A MINOR, OP. 118 NO. 1	BRAHMS
INTERMEZZO IN A MINOR, OP. 2, NO. 2 -- FROM FOUR	DOHNANYI
INTERMEZZO IN C, OP. 119 NO. 3	BRAHMS
INTERMEZZO IN C, OP. 119 NO. 3	BRAHMS
INTERMEZZO IN E, OP. 116 NO. 4	BRAHMS
INTERMEZZO IN E, OP. 116 NO. 6	BRAHMS
INTERMEZZO IN E FLAT, OP. 117 NO. 1	BRAHMS
INTERMEZZO IN E FLAT	BRAHMS
INTERMEZZO IN E MINOR, OP. 119 NO. 2	BRAHMS
INTERMEZZO IN F MINOR, OP. 2, NO. 3 -- FROM FOUR	DOHNANYI
INTERMEZZO IN OCTAVES, OP. 44 NO. 4	LESCHETIZKY
INTERMEZZO NO. 01	COUTURE
INTERMEZZO NO. 02	COUTURE
INTERMEZZO NO. 03	COUTURE
INTERMEZZO NO. 1 IN C	POULENC, F.
INTERMEZZO NO. 2 IN D-FLAT	POULENC, F.
INTERMEZZO NO. 2	PONCE, M.
INTERMEZZO ORIENTALE	ROGERS, J.
INTERMEZZO RUSSE, OP. 136	FRANKE, M.
INTERMEZZO SINFONICO--'CAVALLERIA RUSTICANA'	MASCAGNI, P.
INTERMEZZO VENETIEN	MOREL, G.
INTERMEZZO	BRAHMS
INTERMEZZO	CZAJANEK
INTERMEZZO	DAMASE, J. M.
INTERMEZZO	DRYE, S. L.
INTERMEZZO	ECKSTEIN
INTERMEZZO	GEORGE
INTERMEZZO	HOWELL
INTERMEZZO	HOWELL
INTERMEZZO	SCHMIDT, F.
INTERMEZZO	WHITFORD
INTERMITENCIAS	SANTORO, C.
INTERNATIONAL CHRISTMAS - 139 SONGS ANDCAROLS	RICHTER, A.
INTERNATIONAL LIBRARY OF PIANO MUSIC	GREISSLE,
INTERPLAY-- AMERICAN CONCERTETTE IN FOUR MOVEMENTS	GOULD, M.
INTERPRETATIONS FOR PIANO, NO. 1	SHEARING, G.
INTERPRETATIONS FOR PIANO, NO. 2	SHEARING, G.
INTERPRETATIONS FOR PIANO, NO. 3	SHEARING, G.
INTERPRETATIONS FOR PIANO, NO. 4	SHEARING, G.
INTERPRETATIONS FOR PIANO, NO. 5	SHEARING, G.
INTERPRETATIONS FOR PIANO, NO. 6	SHEARING, G.
INTERPRETATIONS FOR PIANO, NO. 7	SHEARING, G.
INTERRUPTED STORY	PERLE, G.
INTERVALS - SEVEN STUDIES FOR PIANO, OP. 37	NAKADA
INTERVAL PLAY	HEIDSIEK
INTERVAL STUDIES	BECKWITH
INTIMA, OP. 2 NO. 2	AGUIRRE
INTIMITE	ROPARTZ
INTRADA	WEYBRIGHT
INTRADA	WEYBRIGHT
INTRATA	BACH, J.S.
INTRATA	GRIFFIS, E.
INTRIGUE	WHITFORD
INTRODUCTION, ARIA, AND FINALE	ALDERIGHI
INTRODUCTION, FUGUE, AND FINALE, OP. 15 -- 1957 --	HALFFTER, C.
INTRODUCTION, PASSACAGLIA AND FUGUE, OP. 96	REGER
INTRODUCTIONS AND ENDINGS	HENDERSON, R.
INTRODUCTION AND ALLEGRO APPASSIONATA, OP. 92, CONCERT	SCHUMANN, R.
INTRODUCTION AND ALLEGRO APPASSIONATO, OP. 92 AND	SCHUMANN, R.
INTRODUCTION AND CAPRICCIO	CHANCE, J. B.
INTRODUCTION AND DANCE FOR TWO PIANOS	HEMMER, E.
INTRODUCTION AND FUGATO	HARRIS, C. K.
INTRODUCTION AND FUGUE	VAUGHAN
INTRODUCTION AND RAG	RAPHLING
INTRODUCTION AND RONDO ALLA BURLESCA, OP. 23 NO. 1	BRITTEN, B.
INTRODUCTION AND RONDO CAPRICCIOSO, OP. 28	SAINT-SAENS
INTRODUCTION AND SONATINA	WIGHAM, M.
INTRODUCTION ET ALLEGRO	RAVEL
INTRODUCTION ET ALLEGRO	RAVEL
INTRODUCTION ET ALLEGRO	RAVEL
INTRODUCTION ET TOCCATA	MARTINON, J.
INTRODUCTION TO BACH, AN	THOMPSON, J.--ED
INTRODUCTION TO BACH	BACH, J.S.
INTRODUCTION TO BEETHOVEN	BEETHOVEN
INTRODUCTION TO CHOPIN, VOL. 1--56 COMPOSITIONS	CHOPIN
INTRODUCTION TO CHOPIN, VOL. 2--56 COMPOSITIONS	CHOPIN
INTRODUCTION TO HANDEL	HANDEL
INTRODUCTION TO HANON	MELECCI, A.
INTRODUCTION TO HIS PIANO WORKS, AN	BEETHOVEN
INTRODUCTION TO HIS PIANO WORKS	CHOPIN
INTRODUCTION TO MOZART	MOZART, W. A.
INTRODUCTION TO PIANO CLASSICS, VOL. 1	MIROVITCH,
INTRODUCTION TO PIANO CLASSICS, VOL. 2	MIROVITCH,
INTRODUCTION TO PIANO CLASSICS, VOL. 3	MIROVITCH,
INTRODUCTION TO SCHUMANN	SCHUMANN, R.
INTRODUCTION TO THE ART OF ROCK	GORDON, L.
INTRODUCTION TO THE PERFORMANCE OF BACH, BK. 1	TURECK, R.
INTRODUCTION TO THE PERFORMANCE OF BACH, BK. 2	TURECK, R.
INTRODUCTION TO THE PERFORMANCE OF BACH, BK. 3	TURECK, R.
INTRODUCTION TO THE ROMANTICS	MIROVITCH,
INTRODUCTION TO THE STUDY OF BACH, VOL. 1	BACH, J.S.
INTRODUCTION TO THE STUDY OF BACH, VOL. 2	BACH, J.S.
INTRODUCTION UND PERPETUUM	GERSTER, O.
INTRODUCTION	SAMGIORGI
INTRODUCTORY PIANO EXERCISES FOR CONTEMPORARY MUSIC --	CAMILLERI, C.
INTROS, BREAKS, FILLERS AND FADEOUTS	BERGENFELD, N.
INVENCIONES	GONZALEZ AVILA,
INVENCION	CHAVEZ, C.
INVENTION, PREMIER DOUBLE	BARTHOLOMEE
INVENTION, 2 PART, NO. 8	BACH, J.S.
INVENTIONEN	TCHEREPNIN, S.
INVENTIONS. SUPPLEMENT 1* SINFONIAS 4, 5, 7, 9, 11	BACH, J.S.
INVENTIONS, FACSIMILE, WITH FOREWORD BY RALPH	BACH, J.S.
INVENTIONS, OP. 13	SPINNER
INVENTIONS, URTEXT. 15 2-PART INVENTIONS AND 15 3-PART	BACH, J.S.
INVENTIONS, 2 PART	BACH, J.S.
INVENTIONS, 3 PART	BACH, J.S.
INVENTIONS --URTEXT--, COMPLETE IN 1 VOL. CLOTH-BOUND	BACH, J.S.
INVENTIONS -- SINFONIAS -- IN THREE PARTS, S. 787-801	BACH, J.S.
INVENTIONS AND SINFONIAS -- CLOTH	BACH, J.S.
INVENTIONS AND SINFONIAS -- URTEXT --	BACH, J.S.
INVENTIONS AND SINFONIAS --2 AND 3 PART INVENTIONS,	BACH, J.S.
INVENTIONS AND SINFONIAS --2 AND 3 PART INVENTIONS,	BACH, J.S.
INVENTIONS AND SINFONIAS	BACH, J.S.
INVENTIONS AND SINFONIAS	BACH, J.S.
INVENTIONS IN TWO PARTS, S. 772-786	BACH, J.S.
INVENTIONS IN TWO PARTS, S. 772-786	BACH, J.S.
INVENTIONS	BACH, J.S.
INVENTION IN SYNCOPATION	HANNA
INVENTION	BARATI
INVENTION	DIEMER
INVENTION	FOLDES
INVENTIO THREE FOR HARPSICHORD	HEIDER
INVISIBLE PRINCE, THE	BARTH, H.
INVITATION A LA MUSIQUE	VELLONES, P.
INVITATION A LA VALSE, OP. 65	WEBER, VON
INVITATION TO MUSIC -- BEGINNING PIANO FOR TEEN-AGE	GEISSMAR, E.
INVITATION TO THE DANCE, OP. 65. TWO PIANOS, EIGHT	WEBER, VON
INVITATION TO THE DANCE, OP. 65	WEBER, VON
INVITATION TO THE DANCE, OP. 65	WEBER, VON
INVITATION TO THE DANCE, OP. 65	WEBER, VON
INVITATION TO THE DANCE, OP. 65	WEBER, VON
INVITATION TO THE DANCE, OP. 65	WEBER, VON
INVITATION TO THE DANCE, OP. 65	WEBER, VON *
INVITATION TO THE DANCE, OP. 65	WEBER, VON
INVITATION TO THE DANCE, OP. 65	WEBER, VON
INVITATION TO THE DANCE, OP. 65	WEBER, VON
INVITATION TO THE DANCE, OP. 65	WEBER, VON
INVITATION TO THE DANCE IN D FLAT, OP. 65	WEBER, VON
INVITATION TO THE DANCE	JAHN, C.
INVITATION TO THE DANCE	WEBER, VON
INVITATION TO THE DANCE	WEBER, VON
INVITATION TO THE DANCE	WEYBRIGHT
INVITATION	KAPER, B.
INVOCAZIONE	CILEA
IN ALL DIRECTIONS -- A COLLECTION OF PIECES FOR THE	POOT, M.
IN AN OLD CHALET	KING
IN AN OLD WORLD VILLAGE	HOPKINS, H.
IN AN ORIENTAL MARKET PLACE	WANSBOROUGH, H.
IN ARPEGGIO LAND	REEVES, R.
IN AUTUMN, CONCERT OVERTURE, OP. 11	GRIEG
IN AUTUMN, CONCERT OVERTURE, OP. 11	GRIEG
IN AUTUMN, OP. 36 NO. 4	MOSZKOWSKI
IN AUTUMN	STEVENS, E.
IN A CANOE	MARSHALL, L.
IN A CANOE	MCGRAW
IN A CONTRARY MOOD	ANSON, G.
IN A DONKEY CART	ROSNER
IN A FAIRY GARDEN	RAEZER, C.
IN A FIELD OF DAISIES	RICHTER
IN A GARDEN GAY	LAST, J.
IN A GONDOLA	HEINS, C.
IN A GYPSY TEA ROOM	REISER, V.
IN A GYPSY TEA ROOM	REISER, V.
IN A GYPSY TENT	RAEZER, C.
IN A HINDUSTANI MARKET	HARPER, M.
IN A LAZY SPRING	MOORE
IN A LITTLE OUTRIGGER CANOE -- WITH WORDS	BURNAM
IN A LITTLE SPANISH TOWN	LANE, J.--ED.
IN A LOG CABIN	DITTENHAVER
IN A MIST	BEIDERBECKE, B.
IN A MIST	
IN A MIST	
IN A MONASTERY GARDEN	KETELBEY, A.
IN A MONASTERY GARDEN	KETELBEY, A.
IN A PAGODA	HAUBIEL, C.
IN A PARADE	RICKER, E.
IN A PATIO--SPANISH SERENADE	CHENOWETH, W.
IN A PENSIVE MOOD --MODERN RHYTHMIC CLASSICS--	WHITFORD
IN A RED SPANISH SHAWL	ARCHER, I.
IN A SAIL-BOAT	ENDRES, O.
IN A SAILBOAT	RICHTER, A.
IN A SEA CRADLE	PHILLIPS
IN A SENTIMENTAL MOOD	ELLINGTON
IN A SPACE SHIP	FROST
IN A SPANISH GARDEN	HOLT, EILSEL
IN A SPANISH VILLAGE	REISER, V.
IN A SYRIAN BAZAAR	HARPER, M.
IN A TREETOP SO TALL	ERB
IN A TURKISH BAZAAR	HOPKINS, H.
IN A VANITY BOX	RODGERS, I.
IN A VIENNESE GARDEN	WANDERMAN
IN BALL COSTUME, VALSE	LANGE, G.
IN BLUE TONE	BRUSSELS, I.
IN BOHEMIA	SMETANA
IN CARACAS	PERRIN
IN CHILDREN'S LAND, OP. 46	NIEMANN
IN CHURCH	THOMAS, C. J.
IN CHURCH	WEYBRIGHT
IN CLASSIC STYLE	LAST, J.
IN COLONIAL DAYS	RASBACH, O.
IN COMMAND -- SIMPLIFIED	PANELLA, L.
IN CREOLE COMPANY	HOLT, EILSEL
IN DAYS OF OLD--AUGUSTIN	DILLER, A.
IN DAYS OF OLD--GOSSIP JOAN	DILLER, A.
IN DAYS OF OLD--REAP THE FLAX	DILLER, A.
IN DAYS OF OLD--THE JUDGE'S DANCE	DILLER, A.
IN DESPAIR, OP. 4	PROKOFIEFF
IN DULCI JUBILO	RUSSELL
IN ELFLAND	SEUEL-HOLST, M.
IN FLORIDA MOONLIGHT, OP. 11	CRAWFORD, C.
IN FOURTEEN HUNDRED NINETY-TWO	OLSON
IN GAY MADRID	REISER, V.
IN GOLDEN AUTUMN	SAROLA
IN GRANDMA'S CLOSET	BRODSKY, M.
IN HANGING GARDENS	DAVIES, E. J.
IN HANGING GARDENS	DAVIES, E. J.
IN HANGING GARDENS	DAVIES, E. J.

Title	Composer
IN HINDULAND	SCHER, W.
IN HONOLULU	BURNAM
IN LICORICE CANDY LAND	TRAVIS, B.
IN MAY, LITTLE FOLKSONG	MARTIN, G.
IN MAY, OP. 575 NO. 2	BEHR, F.
IN MAY, OP. 575 NO. 2	BEHR, F.
IN MERRY MOOD	CRERIE, E.
IN MERRY MOOD	KLEINMAN, A.
IN MEXICO	MUNN, W.
IN MODO DI TARANTELLA	SANGIORGI
IN MOMMY'S HIGH HEELS	DITTENHAVER
IN MY AIRPLANE	RICHTER, A.
IN MY CANOE, BOAT SONG	HOPKINS, H.
IN MY GARDEN	FIRESTONE, I.
IN MY GARDEN	QUINCKE, W.
IN MY MERRY OLDSMOBILE	EDWARDS, C.
IN MY MERRY OLDSMOBILE	EDWARDS, G.
IN MY NEIGHBOR'S GARDEN	NEVIN
IN MY NINE LIVES	SCHICKELE, P.
IN MY ROCKING CHAIR	RICHTER
IN MY WHITE BOAT	MUNN, W.
IN MY WHITE BOAT	MUNN, W.
IN NEUES LEBEN -- SOKOL-FEST-MARSCH --	SUK
IN OLD MADRID	IBBOTSON, E. M.
IN OLD NEW YORK, FROM 'THE RED MILL'	HERBERT
IN OLD VIENNA	GILLOCK
IN OLD VIENNA	GILLOCK
IN OUR CHERRY TREE	CHAUNCEY, R. G.
IN OUTER SPACE	AARON, M.
IN RANK AND FILE, OP. 249 NO. 1	LANGE, G.
IN RANK AND FILE MARCH	LANGE, A.
IN RANK AND FILE	LANGE, G.
IN ROSE TIME	ARMOUR
IN SCHUBERT'S DAY, OP. 109	KRENTZLIN, R.
IN SCHUBERT'S DAY, OP. 109	KRENTZLIN, R.
IN SEVILLE	BLAKE, D.
IN SHADOW TOWN	JEAN, E.
IN SHADY NOOK, REVERIE	DIETS, J.
IN SICILY -- TARANTELLA	AARON, M.
IN SILENT FORESTS, OP. 9 -- STIMMUNGSBILDER, BK. 1	STRAUSS, R.
IN SILENT FORESTS, OP. 9 -- STIMMUNGSBILDER, BK. 2	STRAUSS, R.
IN SILENT FORESTS, OP. 9 -- STIMMUNGSBILDER, BK. 3	STRAUSS, R.
IN SILENT FORESTS, OP. 9 -- STIMMUNGSBILDER, BK. 4	STRAUSS, R.
IN SILENT FORESTS, OP. 9 -- STIMMUNGSBILDER, BK. 5	STRAUSS, R.
IN SOGNO	CATALANI
IN SPANISH STYLE	BRUSSELS, I.
IN SPRINGTIME, OP. 36 NO. 3--THE BUTTERFLY	WRIGHT, N.
IN SPRINGTIME	MARTIN, G.
IN SPRING	CANFIELD, J.
IN SUNNY FIELDS	JOYNER, B.
IN SUNNY SOUTH AMERICAN -- SIMP.	MOSSMAN, T.
IN SUNNY SPAIN	REISER, V.
IN SUNNY SPAIN	SEWELL
IN TEMPO DI MINUETTO	ALALEONE
IN THE ALPINE HUT, OP. 240	LANGE, G.
IN THE AUTUMN	VERRALL, J.
IN THE BAZAAR	ECKSTEIN
IN THE BIRD SHOP	LONG, L.
IN THE CANOE	BARNES, G. M.
IN THE CANOE	CROCKER, D.
IN THE CASTLE GARDEN	DITTENHAVER
IN THE CASTLE	LONGMIRE
IN THE CLOCK STORE AND DUTCH DANCERS	LINDFORS, E.
IN THE COTTON-FIELDS	MACLACHLIN, T.
IN THE COUNTRY, WALTZ	HOPKINS, H.
IN THE COUNTRY	SCHIEFELBEIN, F.
IN THE DAYS OF CHOPIN	MCHALE, M.
IN THE FOOTHILLS	SEUEL-HOLST, M.
IN THE FOREST TALL	BURNAM
IN THE FOREST	HIBBS, C.
IN THE FORGE	JUNGMAN, A.
IN THE GARDEN, WALTZ	MAYKAPAR
IN THE GARDEN OF LOVE	HEINDOT
IN THE GARDEN	LANE, J.--ED.
IN THE GARDEN	MARTIN, G.
IN THE GARDEN	SCHIEFELBEIN, F.
IN THE GLOAMING, TRANS.	GROOMS--ED
IN THE GYPSY CAMP, OP. 424, NO. 3	BEHR, F.
IN THE HALL OF THE MOUNTAIN-KING, OP. 46 NO. 4	GRIEG
IN THE HALL OF THE MOUNTAIN KING, OP. 46 NO. 4	GRIEG
IN THE HALL OF THE MOUNTAIN KING --A STUDY IN	GRIEG
IN THE HALL OF THE MOUNTAIN KING --PEER GYNT SUITE	GRIEG
IN THE HALL OF THE MOUNTAIN KING FROM THE PEER GYNT	GRIEG
IN THE HALL	SMETANA
IN THE HAMMOCK -- SCENE SENTIMENTALE, OP. 19 --	POWELL, J.
IN THE HAMMOCK	ROBINSON, A.
IN THE HEATHER	YOUNG
IN THE HILLS OF PALESTINE	HARPER, M.
IN THE JUNGLE	WILSON, M.
IN THE LAND OF ISRAEL	BRODSKY, M.
IN THE LAND OF THE DWARFS	SCHER, W.
IN THE LAND OF THE EMIR	HERBERT
IN THE LITTLE RED SCHOOL HOUSE	WILSON *
IN THE LUXEMBOURG GARDENS--REVERIE	MANNING, K.
IN THE MEADOW, OP. 243	LANGE, G.
IN THE MEADOW, OP. 95 NO. 2	LICHNER, H.
IN THE MEADOW	LANGE, A.
IN THE MISTS	JANACEK
IN THE MONTH OF MAY	BEHR, F.
IN THE MONTH OF MAY	BEHR, F.
IN THE MONTH OF ROSES	JUDD, A.
IN THE MOOD	GARLAND
IN THE MOOD	GARLAND *
IN THE MOOD	GARLAND
IN THE MOOD	GARLAND
IN THE MOONLIGHT	REBE
IN THE MORNING EARLY	JENKINS, C.
IN THE NIGHT	BLOCH, E.
IN THE NORTHLAND	SEUEL-HOLST, M.
IN THE OLD CASTLE, OP. 85 NO. 3	DVORAK
IN THE ORIENT	NOVICH, C.
IN THE PARK	ROFF
IN THE PINEY WOODS	COBB
IN THE PIRATE'S CAVE	PANELLA, L.
IN THE PLAYROOM	KRUL
IN THE QUEEN'S COMPANY	HOLT, EILSEL
IN THE ROSE GARDEN	LANGE, P.
IN THE SADDLE	WEYBRIGHT
IN THE SHADE OF THE OLD APPLE TREE	VAN ALSTYNE, E.
IN THE SPIRIT OF '76	STECHER *
IN THE STEPPES OF CENTRAL ASIA	BORODIN, A.
IN THE STEPPES OF CENTRAL ASIA	BORODIN, A.
IN THE STILL OF THE NIGHT	SINGER, L.--ED
IN THE SULTAN'S PALACE	RIMSKY-KORSAKOFF
IN THE SWEET BYE AND BYE	WEBSTER, J.
IN THE SWING--MAZURKA DE SALON	WACHS, P.
IN THE SWING	WALDO, J.
IN THE SWISS ALPS	DITTENHAVER
IN THE TOY SHOP -- ONE PIANO, SIX HANDS	ANSON, G.
IN THE TREETOPS	COBB
IN THE TWILIGHT	GANSCHALS
IN THE TWILIGHT	WHEELER, V. B.
IN THE VILLAGE	MIRSALIS, W.
IN THE WOODS -- SUITE	WILLFORT, E. S.
IN THE WOODS -- 4 PIECES	BENNER, L.
IN THE WOODS	BRAGDON
IN THE WOODS	DUNGAN
IN THE WOOD	THOMAS, C. J.
IN TIME	WEYBRIGHT
IN TIME	WEYBRIGHT
IN TUNE WITH THE TIMES	BRADLEY,
IN TWILIGHT	GANSCHALS
IN VARIOUS MOODS	LISZT
IRENE	MCCARTHY *
IRISHMAN DANCES	COWELL
IRISH AIRS, MEDLEY MARCH	KEISER
IRISH AIRS	PAPE, W.
IRISH AIR -- ST. PATRICK WAS A GENTLEMAN	
IRISH DANCE	BLAKE, D.
IRISH FANCY	BECK
IRISH FAVORITES FOR PIANO	DAVIS, J. R.--ED
IRISH JIG	FITZGERALD
IRISH LAD	COBB
IRISH MEDLEY	FAIRCHILD
IRISH MEDLEY	FAIRCHILD
IRISH MOOD	DE VITO, A.
IRISH TUNE FROM COUNTY DERRY	GRAINGER, P.
IRISH WASHERWOMAN, THE	WEYBRIGHT--ED.
IRISH WASHERWOMAN	REEL
IRISH WASHERWOMAN	SOWERBY, L.
IRIS -- FROM THREE PIECES FOR THE PIANO	MERKUR
IRIS -- INTERMEZZO	RENARD, P.
IRIS - EASY FANTASIA	MASCAGNI, P.
IRIS - HYMN TO THE SUN	MASCAGNI, P.
IRIS	THORNTON
IRL ALLISON PIANO LIBRARY -- ELEMENTARY A, PRG 01	ALLISON, I.--ED
IRL ALLISON PIANO LIBRARY -- ELEMENTARY A, PRG 02	ALLISON, I.--ED
IRL ALLISON PIANO LIBRARY -- ELEMENTARY B	ALLISON, I.--ED
IRL ALLISON PIANO LIBRARY -- ELEMENTARY C	ALLISON, I.--ED
IRL ALLISON PIANO LIBRARY -- ELEMENTARY D	ALLISON, I.--ED
IRL ALLISON PIANO LIBRARY -- INTERMEDIATE A, PRG 01	ALLISON, I.--ED
IRL ALLISON PIANO LIBRARY -- INTERMEDIATE A, PRG 02	ALLISON, I.--ED
IRL ALLISON PIANO LIBRARY -- INTERMEDIATE B, PRG 01	ALLISON, I.--ED
IRL ALLISON PIANO LIBRARY -- INTERMEDIATE B, PRG 02	ALLISON, I.--ED
IRL ALLISON PIANO LIBRARY -- INTERMEDIATE C, PRG 01	ALLISON, I.--ED
IRL ALLISON PIANO LIBRARY -- INTERMEDIATE C, PRG 02	ALLISON, I.--ED
IRL ALLISON PIANO LIBRARY -- INTERMEDIATE D, PRG 01	ALLISON, I.--ED
IRL ALLISON PIANO LIBRARY -- INTERMEDIATE D, PRG 02	ALLISON, I.--ED
IRL ALLISON PIANO LIBRARY -- INTERMEDIATE E, PRG 01	ALLISON, I.--ED
IRL ALLISON PIANO LIBRARY -- INTERMEDIATE E, PRG 02	ALLISON, I.--ED
IRL ALLISON PIANO LIBRARY -- INTERMEDIATE F, PRG 01	ALLISON, I.--ED
IRL ALLISON PIANO LIBRARY -- INTERMEDIATE F, PRG 02	ALLISON, I.--ED
IRL ALLISON PIANO LIBRARY -- PREPARATORY A, PRG 01	ALLISON, I.--ED
IRL ALLISON PIANO LIBRARY -- PREPARATORY A, PRG 02	ALLISON, I.--ED
IRL ALLISON PIANO LIBRARY -- PREPARATORY B, PRG 01	ALLISON, I.--ED
IRL ALLISON PIANO LIBRARY -- PREPARATORY B, PRG 02	ALLISON, I.--ED
IRL ALLISON PIANO LIBRARY -- PREPARATORY C, PRG 01	ALLISON, I.--ED
IRL ALLISON PIANO LIBRARY -- PREPARATORY C, PRG 02	ALLISON, I.--ED
IRL ALLISON PIANO LIBRARY -- PREPARATORY D, PRG 01	ALLISON, I.--ED
IRL ALLISON PIANO LIBRARY -- PREPARATORY D, PRG 02	ALLISON, I.--ED
IRMELIN PRELUDE	DELIUS, F.
IRONSIDE	JONES
IRON LACE BALCONIES	BURNAM
IRON MASTER	GREENWALD, M.
ISABEAU -- COMPLETE OPERA --	MASCAGNI, P.
ISABELLA ORSINI - INTERMEZZO	BROGI
ISLAMEY. FANTAISIE ORIENTALE	BALAKIREV
ISLAMEY	BALAKIREV
ISLAND FLOWER, A HAWAIIAN SONG	WEYBRIGHT
ISLAND FLOWER	WEYBRIGHT--ED.
ISLAND SONG	RUSSELL
ISLE OF CAPRI	
ISLE OF THE DEAD, OP. 29	RACHMANINOFF, S.
ISN'T IT A PITY	BRIMHALL,
ISOLE	MAINI
ISRAELI CARNIVAL	PHILLIPS, D.
ISRAELI DANCE	KARP
ISRAELI DANCE	KARP
ISRAELI FAVORITES	SCHER, W.--ED
ISRAELI WALTZ	NEVIN
ISRAEL RHAPSODY	RAPHLING
ISTANTANEE DI ANNA MARIA	CHAILLY, L.
IT'S ALL RIGHT WITH ME	SINGER, L.--ED
IT'S A DATE	BRODSKY, M.
IT'S A GAME	GLOVER, D.
IT'S A GRAND NIGHT FOR SINGING	HAMMERSTEIN *
IT'S A GRAND NIGHT FOR SINGING	HAMMERSTEIN *
IT'S A GUMDROP TREE	LAKE
IT'S A LOW DOWN DIRTY SHAME	JOHNSON, S. *
IT'S A SMALL WORLD	BRIMHALL,
IT'S BEGINNING TO LOOK LIKE CHRISTMAS	WILSON, M.
IT'S CHRISTMAS TIME	AUBERGE, A. D'
IT'S DE-LOVELY	SINGER, L.--ED
IT'S DELIGHTFUL DOWN IN CHILE	
IT'S EASY TO PLAY PIANO THE THREE CHORD WAY	
IT'S GOING TO TAKE SOME TIME	BRADLEY,
IT'S IMPOSSIBLE	BRIMHALL,
IT'S IMPOSSIBLE	
IT'S LOVELY HERE	RACHMANINOFF, S.
IT'S NOT UNUSUAL	BRIMHALL,
IT'S NOT UNUSUAL	GRUSIN
IT'S NOT UNUSUAL	MILLS *
IT'S ONE OF THOSE NIGHTS --YES LOVE--	BRADLEY,
IT'S PLAYTIME	GLOVER, D.
IT'S RAINING OUT	BASTIEN
IT'S RAINING	FOLDES
IT'S RAINING	MILLS
IT'S RAINING	RICHTER
IT'S SNOWING	KARST
IT'S TOO LATE	BRADLEY,
ITALIANA IN ALGERI, L' - OVERTURE	ROSSINI, G.
ITALIANA IN ALGERI, L' - OVERTURE	ROSSINI, G.
ITALIAN CONCERTO--ARR. IN HARPSICHORD STYLE	BACH, J.S.
ITALIAN CONCERTO, ARR. IN HARPSICHORD STYLE -- SET	BACH, J.S.
ITALIAN CONCERTO, S. 971, AND PARTITA IN B MINOR, S.	BACH, J.S.
ITALIAN CONCERTO AND FRENCH OVERTURE--URTEXT--	BACH, J.S.
ITALIAN CONCERTO AND FRENCH OVERTURE -- URTEXT --	BACH, J.S.
ITALIAN CONCERTO	BACH, J.S.
ITALIAN CONCERTO	BACH, J.S.
ITALIAN CONCERTO	BACH, J.S.
ITALIAN CONCERTO	BACH, J.S.
ITALIAN CONCERTO	BACH, J.S.
ITALIAN DANCE -- 8-HANDS	MACGREGOR
ITALIAN FOLK SONG	

ITALIAN MARCH	CATON, F.
ITALIAN MASTERS, BK. 1	
ITALIAN MASTERS, BK. 2	
ITALIAN MASTERS OF THE XVII AND XVIII CENTURIES	PHILIPP, I.--ED.
ITALIAN POLKA	RACHMANINOFF, S.
ITALIAN POLKA	RACHMANINOFF, S.
ITALIAN POLKA	RACHMANINOFF, S.
ITALIAN POLKA	RACHMANINOFF, S.
ITALIAN ROYAL MARCH	GAMBETTI
ITALIAN STREET SONG	HERBERT
ITALIENISCHES KONZERT -- BWV 971	BACH, J.S.
ITALIEN IM LIED	LUTZ--ED
ITZY BITZY SPIDER	BERTRAND, C.
IT AIN'T GONNA RAIN	STEINER
IT AIN'T NECESSARILY SO	GERSHWIN
IT MIGHT AS WELL BE SPRING	HAMMERSTEIN *
IT MIGHT AS WELL BE SPRING	HAMMERSTEIN *
IT NEVER RAINS IN SOUTHERN CALIFORNIA	LANE, J.--ED.
IT REALLY CAN HAPPEN	LEONCAVALLO
IT STARTED ALL OVER AGAIN	
IT TAKES A THIEF	GRUSIN
IT TAKES TWO - SIX PIECES -	KOCH, F.
IT TAKES TWO - SIX PIECES FOR YOUNG PIANISTS	KOCH, F.
IT WAS A GOOD TIME	LANE, J.--ED.
IT WAS A VERY GOOD YEAR	BRIMHALL,
IT WON'T STOP RAINING	LAWNER, M.
IVAN SINGS	KHATCHATURIAN
IVAN SINGS	KHATCHATURIAN
IVORY TIPS	ALPERT, P.
IVRESSE	FRONTINI
I AIN'T DOWN YET	WILLSON, M.
I AM ... I SAID	BRIMHALL,
I AM A HAPPY CLOWN	HOUSE, A.
I AM FROM SIAM	STECHER *
I AM LITTLE	SUCHON, E.
I AM WOMAN	BRIMHALL,
I BELIEVE IN MUSIC	BRADLEY,
I BELIEVE	DRAKE *
I BELIEVE	SCHAUM, J.
I CAN'T GET STARTED	SINGER, L.--ED
I CAN'T GIVE YOU ANYTHING BUT LOVE -- SIMP.	MOSSMAN, T.
I CAN DREAM, CAN'T I	SINGER, L.--ED
I CAN PLAY WITH A METRONOME	BURNAM
I CAN SEE CLEARLY NOW	LANE, J.--ED.
I CAN SEE CLEARLY NOW	NASH, J.
I CLAVICEMBALISTI ITALIANI. 20 KOMPOSITIONEN	DELLA CIAIA *
I CONCENTRATE ON YOU	SINGER, L.--ED
I COULD HAVE DANCED ALL NIGHT	SINGER, L.--ED
I COULD WRITE A BOOK	
I DIDN'T KNOW WHAT TIME IT WAS	SINGER, L.--ED
I DO, I DO	GLOVER, D.
I DON'T CARE	RICE *
I DON'T KNOW HOW TO LOVE HIM	LANE, J.--ED.
I DON'T WANT TO SET THE WORLD ON FIRE	FOSTER
I DREAMED OF JEANIE	
I DREAM OF YOU	MUNGER, S.
I FEEL SAD	NOONA, W.
I FOUND A STAR	BRADLEY,
I GOT A NAME	RUBINSTEIN--ED
I GOT PLENTY O' NUTTIN'	STONE, E.--ED
I GOT PLENTY O' NUTTIN'	
I GOT PLENTY O' NUTTIN'	GERSHWIN
I GOT RHYTHM - IMPROMPTU VARIATIONS	GERSHWIN
I GOT RHYTHM - VARIATIONS	GERSHWIN
I GOT RHYTHM	MAINVILLE
I HAVE A LITTLE SHADOW	STAIRS, L.
I HEARD A BLUEBIRD	SINGER, L.--ED
I HEARD A FOREST PRAYING	BRADLEY,
I KNEW YOU WHEN	BURNAM
I KNOW A BANK	HUBICKI, M.
I KNOW THAT THEME, BK. 1	BURNAM
I KNOW THAT THEME, BK. 2	BRIMHALL,
I LEFT MY HEART IN SAN FRANCISCO	HIRSCHBERG,
I LIKE DUETS, BK. 1	LAKE
I LIKE FROGS	NEVIN
I LIKE MUSIC	HIRSCHBERG, D.
I LIKE PIECES, BK. 1	STEINER
I LIKE TO PLAY THE PIANO	LAUDER, H.
I LOVE A LASSIE	ARLEN, H.
I LOVE A PARADE	JESSE, M.
I LOVE A PARADE	JENSVOLD, J.--ED
I LOVE CHRISTMAS MUSIC	STAIRS, L.
I LOVE LITTLE PUSSY	SINGER, L.--ED
I LOVE PARIS	GRIEG
I LOVE THEE, OP. 41 NO. 3, AND CRADLE SONG	GRIEG
I LOVE THEE, OP. 41 NO. 3	GRIEG
I LOVE THEE, OP. 41 NO. 3	GRIEG
I LOVE THEE, OP. 41 NO. 3	GRIEG
I LOVE THEE	HOPKINS, H.
I LOVE THEE	BOND
I LOVE TO TELL THE STORY	JACOBS *
I LOVE YOU TRULY	SINGER, L.--ED
I LOVE YOU TRULY	HOPKINS, H.
I LOVE YOU	LANE, J.--ED.
I NEED THEE EVERY HOUR	BRADLEY,
I NEED YOU NOW	BRIMHALL,
I NEVER PROMISED YOU A ROSE GARDEN	PRIGGE, O.--ED
I NEVER PROMISED YOU A ROSE GARDEN	WAGNESS--ED.
I PLAY CAROLS AT CHRISTMAS TIME	BRODSKY, M.
I PLEDGE ALLEGIANCE -- A PATRIOTIC ALBUM FOR ALL	PORTER, A.
I SAW A HORSE	ROLFE, W.
I SAW A LITTLE BIRD	HARDING, R.
I SAW SHIP A'SAILING AND BUTTERFLY	SINGER, L.--ED
I SAW THREE SHIPS	
I SEE YOUR FACE BEFORE ME	ATKINS
I THINK OF YOU	
I WANT A BIG BUTTER AND EGG MAN	MASKELL, C. H.
I WANT A GIRL	SINGER, L.--ED
I WANT THE TWILIGHT AND YOU	KAHN, M.--ED
I WAS DOING ALL RIGHT	ALPERT, P.
I WAS KAISER BILL'S BATMAN -- SIMP.	GREENAWAY *
I WAS KAISER BILL'S BATMAN	HAMMERSTEIN *
I WHISTLE A HAPPY TUNE	HAMMERSTEIN *
I WHISTLE A HAPPY TUNE	LANE, J.--ED.
I WILL NEVER PASS THIS WAY AGAIN	BRADLEY,
I WILL WAIT FOR YOU	
I WILL WAIT FOR YOU	
I WILL WAIT FOR YOU	ERB
I WISH I WERE A DUCK	WEYBRIGHT--ED.
I WISH I WUZ A MOLE	BRADLEY,
I WOKE UP IN LOVE THIS MORNING	NILES, J.
I WONDER AS I WANDER--APPALACHIAN FOLK CAROL	WIGHAM, M.
I WONDER WHERE THE ROBINS GO	JELESNIK, E.
J. F. K. MARCH	HUBLER, E.
J'ACCOMPAGNE LA DANSE, VOL. 1	HUBLER, E.
J'ACCOMPAGNE LA DANSE, VOL. 2	

JACK-IN-THE-BOX	LEIGHTON
JACK-IN THE BOX	DUNGAN
JACK AND JILL AND POLLY FLINDERS	ROLFE, W.
JACK AND JILL IN HAPPYLAND	MOREY, F.
JACK AND JILL	KETTERER, E.
JACK AND THE BEANSTALK - A STORY WITH MUSIC	RICHTER, A.
JACK BE NIMBLE	CROSBY, M.
JACK FROST, ONE PIANO - SIX HANDS	MATTINGLY, J.
JACK IN THE BOX, OP. POSTH.	SATIE, E.
JACK IN THE BOX	CONFREY, Z.
JACK IN THE BOX	SEINBERG
JACK O'LANTERN PARTY	CROSBY, M.
JACK RABBIT	MCGRAW
JACK TAR	KELLEY
JACOBEAN SUITE	STEEL
JADE SET	CLARK, M.--ED.
JAGERLIEDCHEN, OP. 68 NO. 7	SCHUMANN, R.
JAHRESKREIS. KLAVIER INVENTIONEN UBER DEUTSCHE	MALER, W.
JAHRMARKT, DER	KOERPPEN, A.
JALOPY JUNCTION	TRUED
JALOUSIE	GADE, N.
JALOUSIE	GADE, N.
JALOUSIE	GADE, N.
JALOUSIE	GADE, N.
JAMAICALYPSO	BENJAMIN
JAMAICAN RUMBA	BENJAMIN
JAMAICAN RUMBA	BENJAMIN
JAMAICAN RUMBA	BENJAMIN
JAMAICAN TANGO	MARTIN, H.
JAMAICA --MODERN RHYTHMIC CLASSICS--	WHITFORD
JAMBOREE	PELS, W.
JAMBOREE	ROZIN
JAMES TAYLOR	TAYLOR, J.
JAMIE'S MUSIC BOX	KLEINMAN, A.
JANIE'S FIRST WALTZ	KLEINMAN, A.
JANIE IS HER NAME	HENDERSON
JANMAATEN --TWO HUMORESQUES FROM THE PORT OF HAMBURG--	NIEMANN
JAPANESE BALLADE	YAMADA, C.
JAPANESE DOLL DANCE	ROBYN
JAPANESE FESTIVAL - SEVENTEEN PIANO PIECES FOR	NAKADA
JAPANESE FIRE DANCE	LOUKA, M.
JAPANESE GARDEN	GLOVER, D.
JAPANESE JUGGLER	MERKUR
JAPANESE LANTERN, A	HOPKINS, H.
JAPANESE LANTERNS	SCHER, W.
JAPANESE RICKSHA	CHAGY
JAPANESE STUDY, OP. 27 NO. 2	POLDINI, E.
JAPANESE SUNSET, A	DEPPEN
JAPANESE SUNSET, A	DEPPEN
JAPANESE WALTZ	BECK
JARABE TAPATIO, HAT DANCE	BLOCK--ED
JARDINS D'ANDALOUSIE	TURINA, J.
JARDINS D'ENFANTS - MARCHE, L'ENFANT S'ENDORT, BOITE A	TURINA, J.
JARDINS SOUS LA PLUIE	DEBUSSY
JARDINS SOUS LA PLUIE	DEBUSSY
JARDINS SOUS LA PLUIE	DEBUSSY
JARDINS SOUS LA PLUIE	DEBUSSY
JARDINS SOUS LA PLUIE	DEBUSSY
JARDINS SOUS LA PLUIE	DEBUSSY
JARDIN DES AMOURS, LE	CASADESUS, H.
JARDIN DE CATHERINE, LE	DANDELOT
JARDIN DE CLAUDE, LE	DANDELOT
JARDIN DE MARIE, LE -- EIGHT EASY PIECES	DANDELOT
JARDIN DE SYLVIE, LE	DANDELOT
JARDIN DU PARADIS, LE -- LA DANSE DE LA SORCIERE	TANSMAN, A.
JAUNESSE	DE LA TOMBELLE
JAUNTY STROLL	RIGUETTE
JAUNT TO TOWN	PROCTER, A.
JAVALI	SCHRAMM
JAVOTTE	SAINT-SAENS
JAYBIRDS JIG	ROGERS, E.
JAY MCSHANN BOOGIE WOOGIE AND BLUES PIANO SOLOS	MCSHANN,
JAZZ-ROCK STUDIES -- THE BLOCK-CHORD STYLE	FORNUTO
JAZZ, ROCK, POP AND BLUES PIANO IMPROVISATION METHOD,	BURNS *
JAZZ, ROCK, POP AND BLUES PIANO IMPROVISATION METHOD,	BURNS *
JAZZ, ROCK, POP AND BLUES PIANO IMPROVISATION METHOD,	BURNS *
JAZZ, ROCK, POP AND BLUES PIANO IMPROVISATION METHOD,	BURNS *
JAZZ, ROCK, POP AND BLUES PIANO IMPROVISATION METHOD,	BURNS *
JAZZETTES	BERKOWITZ
JAZZETTE	JOYNER, B.
JAZZ ALLEGRETTO	NEVIN
JAZZ ANDANTINO	NEVIN
JAZZ AND BLUES, BK. 1	CLARK, F.--ED.
JAZZ AND BLUES, BK. 2	CLARK, F.--ED.
JAZZ AND BLUES, BK. 3	CLARK, F.--ED.
JAZZ AND BLUES, BK. 4	CLARK, F.--ED.
JAZZ AND BLUES, BK. 5	CLARK, F.--ED.
JAZZ AND BLUES, BK. 6	CLARK, F.--ED.
JAZZ AND BLUES - 12 INCH LP RECORD --BOOKS 1-6--	CLARK, F.--ED.
JAZZ A GOGO	STECHER *
JAZZ BOURREE	MEHEGAN, J.
JAZZ BOURREE	MEHEGAN, J.
JAZZ CAPER	MEHEGAN, J.
JAZZ CONCERTO NO. 2	ROGER-ROGER
JAZZ CZERNY	CZERNY *
JAZZ DUETS	AGAY, D.--ED
JAZZ FESTIVAL BOOGIE	KENT, A.
JAZZ FINGERS	NEVIN
JAZZ FOR JUNIOR	GORDON
JAZZ FOR PIANO, BK. 1	KONOWITZ, B.
JAZZ FOR PIANO, BK. 2	KONOWITZ, B.
JAZZ FOR THE YOUNG IN HEART	KAYE
JAZZ GALLERY	MARTIN, G.--ED
JAZZ HANON	HANON, C. *
JAZZ IMPRESSIONS OF JAPAN	BRUBECK
JAZZ IMPRESSIONS OF NEW YORK	BRUBECK
JAZZ IMPROVISATIONS, BK. 3 --SWING AND EARLY	MEHEGAN, J.
JAZZ IMPROVISATIONS --CONTEMPORARY PIANO STYLES	MEHEGAN, J.
JAZZ JAMBOREE	NEVIN
JAZZ LEGATO	ANDERSON, L.
JAZZ LEGATO	MERKUR--ED
JAZZ MAG RAG, THE.	ALBAM
JAZZ MASKS NO. 2, OP. 30A	GRUENBERG, L.
JAZZ ME BLUES	
JAZZ MINIATURE	NEVIN
JAZZ ORIGINALS	SANTISI, R.
JAZZ PIANIST, THE -- BK. 1	MEHEGAN, J.
JAZZ PIANIST, THE -- BK. 2	MEHEGAN, J.
JAZZ PIANIST, THE -- BK. 3	MEHEGAN, J.
JAZZ PIANIST, THE -- BOOK 1 WITH INSTRUCTION RECORD	MEHEGAN, J.
JAZZ PIANO STYLES	DENNIS, M.
JAZZ PIANO TECHNIQUE	LAURENT
JAZZ PIZZICATO	ANDERSON, L.
JAZZ PIZZICATO	MERKUR--ED
JAZZ PRELUDES	MEHEGAN, J.
JAZZ PRELUDE --MODERN RHYTHMIC CLASSICS--	WHITFORD

JAZZ PRELUDE	NEVIN
JAZZ SCENES -- BLUE NOTE BOOGIE, CHOO CHOO STOMP, LAZY	KONOWITZ, B.
JAZZ SERENADE --MODERN RHYTHMIC CLASSICS--	WHITFORD
JAZZ SOLOS	AGAY, D.--ED
JAZZ SONATINA, OP. 11	ZBINDEN, J. F.
JAZZ SPOOKS	KONOWITZ, B.
JAZZ STUDIES -- NO. 1 -- SET	HILL, E. B.
JAZZ SUITE	KAHN, M.
JAZZ TANGO	CHAGY
JAZZ TARANTELLA	CHAGY
JAZZ TOCCATA	RAPHLING
JAZZ WALTZ	KONOWITZ, B.
JEALOUS EYES	KING, S.
JEANIE WITH LIGHT BROWN HAIR	FOSTER
JEANNIE WITH THE LIGHT BROWN HAIR	FOSTER
JEANNIE WITH THE LIGHT BROWN HAIR	FOSTER
JEANNIE WITH THE LIGHT BROWN HAIR	FOSTER
JEANNIE WITH THE LIGHT BROWN HAIR	FOSTER
JEANNIE WITH THE LIGHT BROWN HAIR	FOSTER
JEANNINE	LANE, J.--ED.
JEAN AND BABETTE	ECKSTEIN
JEAN	BRADLEY,
JEAN	BRIMHALL,
JEEPERS CREEPERS	CANFIELD, J.
JEFFERSON AIRPLANE, THE	
JELLY JIG - WILSON CLOG	GUENTHER
JENNY'S GONE	TREVARTHEN, R.
JENNY LIND POLKA	WALLERSTEIN, A.
JENNY LIND WALTZ	MELECCI, A.
JEREZ -- FROM IBERIA	ALBENIZ, I.
JERICHO FOR TWO PIANOS OR ONE PIANO FOUR HANDS	BACON, E.
JERSEY BOUNCE	
JERUSALEM, THE GOLDEN	FREEMAN
JESTER, THE	KREBS
JESTER, THE	WIGGINS, M.
JESTERS, THE	WEYBRIGHT
JESTERS, THE	WEYBRIGHT
JESTING--BADINERIE	JAQUE, R.
JESTING	GOEB, H.
JESU, JOY OF MAN'S DESIRE --FROM CANTATA NO. 147--	BACH, J.S.
JESU, JOY OF MAN'S DESIRE --FROM CANTATA NO. 147--	BACH, J.S.
JESU, JOY OF MAN'S DESIRING --CHORALE FROM CANTATA NO.	BACH, J.S.
JESU, JOY OF MAN'S DESIRING -- CHORALE FROM CANTATA	BACH, J.S.
JESU, JOY OF MAN'S DESIRING	BACH, J.S.
JESU, JOY OF MAN'S DESIRING	BACH, J.S.
JESU, JOY OF MAN'S DESIRING	BACH, J.S.
JESU, JOY OF MAN'S DESIRING	BACH, J.S.
JESU, JOY OF MAN'S DESIRING	BACH, J.S.
JESU, JOY OF MAN'S DESIRING	BACH, J.S.
JESU, JOY OF MAN'S DESIRING	BACH, J.S.
JESU, JOY OF MAN'S DESIRING	BACH, J.S.
JESU, JOY OF MY LIFE	BACH, J.S.
JESU, MAN'S DESIRE	BACH, J.S.
JESUS, JOY OF MAN'S DESIRE--JESUS BLEIBET MEINE	BACH, J.S.
JESUS CHRISTUS UNSER HEILAND -- JESUS CHRIST, OUR	BACH, J.S.
JESUS CHRIST SUPERSTAR	RICE *
JESUS LOVES ME, THIS I KNOW	REID--ED
JESUS LOVES THE LITTLE CHILDREN	ROOT, G.
JESUS SONGS	
JESU JOY OF MAN'S DESIRING	BACH, J.S.
JETAWAY	NEVIN
JET BOMBER	SAVAGE
JET MARCH, THE	MARTIN, H.
JET PILOTS	WILSON
JEUNES AU PIANO, LES--BK. 1--MIREILLE ET LES	TANSMAN, A.
JEUNES AU PIANO, LES--BK. 2--MARIANNE DEVANT LE	TANSMAN, A.
JEUNES AU PIANO, LES--BK. 3--L'AUTOBUS	TANSMAN, A.
JEUNES AU PIANO, LES--BK. 4--AU TELESCOPE--RATHER	TANSMAN, A.
JEUNES AU PIANO, LES -- BK. 1, EN TOURNANT LA T.S.F.	TANSMAN, A.
JEUNES AU PIANO, LES -- BK. 2, PIECES DE FANTAISIE --	TANSMAN, A.
JEUNES AU PIANO, LES -- BK. 3, FEUILLETS ALBUM -- LESS	TANSMAN, A.
JEUNES AU PIANO, LES -- BK. 4, QUATRE PIECES FUGUEES	TANSMAN, A.
JEUNES FILLES	ROPARTZ
JEUNE FILLE FRANCAISE, UNE -- LITTLE SUITE --	MONFRED
JEUX D'EAUX A LA VILLA D'ESTE, LES	LISZT
JEUX D'EAUX A LA VILLA D'ESTE	LISZT
JEUX D'EAU DE LA VILLA D'ESTE	LISZT
JEUX D'EAU	RAVEL
JEUX D'EAU	RAVEL
JEUX D'EAU	RAVEL
JEUX D'EAU	RAVEL
JEUX D'EAU	RAVEL
JEUX D'EAU	RAVEL
JEUX D'ENFANTS, OP. 22	BIZET, G.
JEUX D'ENFANTS --CHILDREN AT PLAY--, OP. 22	BIZET, G.
JEUX D'ENFANTS -- CHILDREN AT PLAY--, OP. 22. 6 PIECES	BIZET, G.
JEUX D'ENFANTS	BIZET, G.
JEUX D'ENFANTS	BIZET, G.
JEUX D'ENFANTS	BIZET, G.
JEUX D'ENFANTS	PIRIOU
JEUX DE BARRES	PIERNE, P.
JEUX DE BEAUTE	FRAGGI
JEUX DE NUAGES	LEVY, E.
JEUX DE PLEIN AIR	TAILLEFERRE, G.
JEUX DE VAGUES	ZAGON
JEU DE LA CACHETTE	PIERNE, P.
JEWISH DANCE	KARP
JEWISH FOLK AND HOLIDAY SONGS	SCHAUM, J.--ED.
JEWISH FOLK SONGS	STEINER
JEWISH SONGS AND DANCES--PIANO SETTINGS WITH WORDS AND	SCHER, W.
JEWISH SONGS AND DANCES	SCHER, W.--ED
JE JOUE DU PIANO	PHILLIPS, R.
JE JOUE POUR MAMAN--NO. 01, PETIT AIR	TANSMAN, A.
JE JOUE POUR MAMAN--NO. 02, AIR BOHEMIEN	TANSMAN, A.
JE JOUE POUR MAMAN--NO. 03, JEU	TANSMAN, A.
JE JOUE POUR MAMAN--NO. 04, ORIENTALE	TANSMAN, A.
JE JOUE POUR MAMAN--NO. 05, VALSE	TANSMAN, A.
JE JOUE POUR MAMAN--NO. 06, MELODIE	TANSMAN, A.
JE JOUE POUR MAMAN--NO. 07, BOURREE	TANSMAN, A.
JE JOUE POUR MAMAN--NO. 08, FANFARE	TANSMAN, A.
JE JOUE POUR MAMAN--NO. 09, MELOPEE ARABE	TANSMAN, A.
JE JOUE POUR MAMAN--NO. 10, MENUET	TANSMAN, A.
JE JOUE POUR MAMAN--NO. 11, POLKA	TANSMAN, A.
JE JOUE POUR MAMAN--NO. 12, AIR HONGROIS	TANSMAN, A.
JE JOUE POUR PAPA--NO. 01, AUX CHAMPS	TANSMAN, A.
JE JOUE POUR PAPA--NO. 02, ORGUE DE BARBARIE	TANSMAN, A.
JE JOUE POUR PAPA--NO. 03, A LA PECHE	TANSMAN, A.
JE JOUE POUR PAPA--NO. 04, AIR FAMILIER DE PAPA	TANSMAN, A.
JE JOUE POUR PAPA--NO. 05, LES PETITS SOLDATS	TANSMAN, A.
JE JOUE POUR PAPA--NO. 06, BATEAUX A VOILE	TANSMAN, A.
JE JOUE POUR PAPA--NO. 07, L'OURSON	TANSMAN, A.
JE JOUE POUR PAPA--NO. 08, PETITE POLKA	TANSMAN, A.
JE JOUE POUR PAPA--NO. 09, VALSETTE	TANSMAN, A.
JE JOUE POUR PAPA--NO. 10, A TROIS TEMPS	TANSMAN, A.
JE JOUE POUR PAPA--NO. 11, PETIT PROBLEME	TANSMAN, A.

JE JOUE POUR PAPA--NO. 12, AIR SERIEUX	TANSMAN, A.
JE TE VEUX	SATIE, E.
JHALA	HOVHANESS, A.
JIBBIDY F AND A-C-E	WARD
JIGS AND REELS	GREGG
JIG FOR A CONCERT	GREEN, R.
JIG FROM "WEST SUITE", FOR 2 PIANOS 8 HANDS	PACE, R.
JIG WALTZ -- SET	KLEIN, J.
JIG	CATON, F.
JIG	FRANCE
JIMBO'S LULLABY FROM THE CHILDREN'S CORNER	DEBUSSY
JIMMIE CRACK CORN, BOOGIE	MARTIN, G.
JIMMY BUGS	CARRE
JIM CROCE SONG BOOK	CROCE, J.
JIM DOLAN, PRIVATE EYE	SCARMOLIN
JINGLE BELLS FROM THE THREE CHRISTMAS SONGS	RICHTER, A.
JINGLE BELLS JUBILEE	CAMEO--ED
JINGLE BELLS MARCH	HARVEY
JINGLE BELLS MARCH	HARVEY
JINGLE BELLS	ARMOUR
JINGLE BELLS	BRADLEY,
JINGLE BELLS	NICHOLAS
JINGLE BELLS	SCHIEFELBEIN, F.
JINGLE BELLS	SCHIEFELBEIN, F.
JINGLE BELL ROCK	
JINGLE JACK, CAPRICE	HOPKINS, H.
JINGLE JANGLE, CHRISTMAS SONG	HOPKINS, H.
JINGLE JANGLE, XMAS SONG	HOPKINS, H.
JITTERBUG WALTZ	WALLER, T.
JO-JO THE JUGGLER	STEVENS, E.
JO-JO THE JUGGLER	STEVENS, E.
JOAN BAEZ SONGBOOK, THE	BAEZ, J.
JOCELYN, BERCEUSE, EASY	GODARD, B.
JOCKO	ROZIN
JOEY'S SONG	REISMAN *
JOEY	
JOGGIN' ALONG	BRODSKY, M.
JOGGING	NEVIN
JOHANN SEBASTIAN BACH, BK. 1 -- EARLY INTERMEDIATE	BACH, J.S.
JOHANN SEBASTIAN BACH, BK. 2 -- ADVANCING INTERMEDIATE	BACH, J.S.
JOHANN SEBASTIAN BACH, BK. 3 -- EARLY ADVANCED	BACH, J.S.
JOHANN STRAUSS	STRAUSS, J.
JOHNNY-JUMP-UPS	MCSWEEN, F. W.
JOHNNY-JUMP-UP	HART, G. R.
JOHNNY APPLESEED	SCHAUM, J.
JOHNNY GET YOUR HAIR CUT	WEYBRIGHT--ED.
JOHNNY GET YOUR HAIR CUT	WEYBRIGHT
JOHNNY JUMPED THE OCEAN	SCHAUM, J.--ED.
JOHNNY JUMP UP	BEAUMONT, V.
JOHNNY JUMP UP	BEAUMONT, V.
JOHNSON RAG	HALL *
JOHN AND JULIE	GREEN
JOHN BRIMHALL'S APPLE FOR THE TEACHER NO. 2	BRIMHALL,
JOHN BRIMHALL'S BEST OF BLUES, BOOGIE AND JAZZ	BRIMHALL,
JOHN BRIMHALL'S BEST OF BROADWAY SHOW TUNES	BRIMHALL,
JOHN BRIMHALL'S BEST OF COUNTRY SONGS	BRIMHALL,
JOHN BRIMHALL'S BEST OF FOLK - POPS	BRIMHALL,
JOHN BRIMHALL'S BEST OF MOTION PICTURE THEMES	BRIMHALL,
JOHN BRIMHALL'S BEST OF POP WALTZES	BRIMHALL,
JOHN BRIMHALL'S COLOUR MY WORLD	BRIMHALL,
JOHN BRIMHALL'S ENO TEACHING PIECES, ISSUE NO. 3	BRIMHALL,
JOHN BRIMHALL'S ENO TEACHING PIECES, ISSUE NO. 4	BRIMHALL,
JOHN BRIMHALL'S EXERCISES IN RHYTHM	BRIMHALL,
JOHN BRIMHALL'S INTERMEDIATE CLASSICAL SOLOS	BRIMHALL,
JOHN BRIMHALL'S INTERMEDIATE PIANO SOLOS	BRIMHALL,
JOHN BRIMHALL'S LATEST GROOVY PIANO PIECES	BRIMHALL,
JOHN BRIMHALL'S PIANO POWER	BRIMHALL,
JOHN BRIMHALL'S POPULAR PIANO PIECES	BRIMHALL,
JOHN BRIMHALL'S THE ARISTOCATS	BRIMHALL,
JOHN BRIMHALL'S WORLD'S GREATEST HITS OF POPULAR PIANO	BRIMHALL,
JOHN BRIMHALL'S 101 EASY-TO-PLAY 'POPS'	BRIMHALL,
JOHN BRIMHALL'S 62 CHILDREN'S PIANO PIECES	BRIMHALL,
JOHN BRIMHALL GOLD	BRIMHALL,
JOHN BRIMHALL HAWAIIAN WEDDING SONG AMD OTHER HITS	BRIMHALL,
JOHN BRIMHALL OMNIBUS OF POPULAR PIANO TEACHING PIECES	BRIMHALL,
JOHN BRIMHALL PIANO METHOD, BK. 1	BRIMHALL,
JOHN BRIMHALL PIANO METHOD, BK. 2	BRIMHALL,
JOHN BRIMHALL PIANO METHOD, BK. 2	BRIMHALL,
JOHN BRIMHALL PIANO METHOD, BK. 3	BRIMHALL,
JOHN BRIMHALL PIANO METHOD, BK. 4	BRIMHALL,
JOHN BRIMHALL PIANO METHOD, BK. 5	BRIMHALL,
JOHN BRIMHALL PIANO METHOD, THE PRIMER	BRIMHALL,
JOHN BRIMHALL PIANO METHOD - IN FRENCH, PRIMER	BRIMHALL,
JOHN BRIMHALL PIANO METHOD - IN SPANISH, BK. 1	BRIMHALL,
JOHN JACOB NILES' SONG BOOK FOR PIANO	NILES, J.
JOHN LANE'S BEST OF COUNTRY MUSIC	LANE, J.--ED
JOHN LANE'S EASY PIANO DUETS, NO. 1	LANE, J.--ED
JOHN LANE'S EASY PIANO DUETS, NO. 2	LANE, J.--ED
JOHN LANE'S FAVORITE HYMNS	LANE, J.--ED
JOHN LANE'S HAVE FAITH	LANE, J.--ED
JOHN LANE'S INTERMEDIATE PIANO SOLOS, BK. 1	LANE, J.--ED
JOHN LANE'S INTERMEDIATE PIANO SOLOS, BK. 2	LANE, J.--ED
JOHN LANE GOES TO NASHVILLE	LANE, J.--ED
JOHN LANE PLAYS BACHARACH HITS	BACHARACH
JOHN LANE PLAYS BIG MOVIE HITS	LANE, J.
JOHN LANE PLAYS JOHNNY CASH HITS	CASH
JOHN LANE SALUTES THE SEVENTIES	LANE, J.--ED
JOHN LANE SAYS 'KIDS ARE PEOPLE TOO'	LANE, J.
JOHN THOMPSON'S CHRISTMAS CAROLS	THOMPSON, J.--ED
JOHN THOMPSON'S CHRISTMAS CAROL BOOK	THOMPSON, J.--ED
JOHN THOMPSON'S DELUXE BOOK OF CHRISTMAS CAROLS	THOMPSON, J.
JOHN W. SCHAUM ''POP'' COURSE--''POP'' BK. 1	SCHAUM, J.
JOHN W. SCHAUM ''POP'' COURSE--''POP'' BK. 2	SCHAUM, J.
JOHN W. SCHAUM ''POP'' COURSE--''POP'' BK. 3	SCHAUM, J.
JOHN W. SCHAUM ''POP'' COURSE--''POP'' BK. 4	SCHAUM, J.
JOHN W. SCHAUM ADULT COURSE--ADULT BOOK 1	SCHAUM, J.
JOHN W. SCHAUM ADULT COURSE--ADULT BOOK 2	SCHAUM, J.
JOHN W. SCHAUM ADULT COURSE--ADULT BOOK 3	SCHAUM, J.
JOHN W. SCHAUM PIANO COURSE--''AFTER THE H-BOOK, BK.	SCHAUM, J.
JOHN W. SCHAUM PIANO COURSE--''AFTER THE H-BOOK, BK.	SCHAUM, J.
JOHN W. SCHAUM PIANO COURSE--A, THE RED BOOK	SCHAUM, J.
JOHN W. SCHAUM PIANO COURSE--B, THE BLUE BOOK	SCHAUM, J.
JOHN W. SCHAUM PIANO COURSE--C, THE PURPLE BOOK	SCHAUM, J.
JOHN W. SCHAUM PIANO COURSE--D, THE ORANGE BOOK	SCHAUM, J.
JOHN W. SCHAUM PIANO COURSE--E, THE VIOLET BOOK	SCHAUM, J.
JOHN W. SCHAUM PIANO COURSE--F, THE BROWN BOOK	SCHAUM, J.
JOHN W. SCHAUM PIANO COURSE--G, THE AMBER BOOK	SCHAUM, J.
JOHN W. SCHAUM PIANO COURSE--H, THE GREY BOOK	SCHAUM, J.
JOHN W. SCHAUM PIANO COURSE--PRE-A, THE GREEN BOOK	SCHAUM, J.
JOIN THE PARADE	BRUSSELS, I.
JOIN TOGETHER	BRIMHALL,
JOKER, THE	SCHAUM, J.--ED.
JOKING	MANA-ZUCCA
JOLIES LEGENDES, LES	PERCHERON
JOLIES VIENNOISES, LES	ZIEHRER
JOLITY	WILSON, M.
JOLI GILLES, ENTR'ACTE	POISE

Title	Composer
JOLLY ASTRONAUT, THE	NEVIN
JOLLY BARBER, THE	BRODSKY, M.
JOLLY BOY, THE	RATHBONE, G.
JOLLY BOY	CRERIE, E.
JOLLY CAPTAIN, THE	DE VITO, A.
JOLLY CHRISTMAS MELODIES	RODGERS, I.--ED
JOLLY COPPERSMITH, THE	PETER, C.
JOLLY ELEPHANT, THE.	COBB
JOLLY FINGERS -- SECOND PIANO PART	NEVIN
JOLLY FINGERS	NEVIN
JOLLY JALOPY	GROVE
JOLLY JIM	RASCHIG
JOLLY JINGLES	DEE, M.
JOLLY JUGGLER, THE	REISER, V.
JOLLY JUGGLER	DAVIS, J.
JOLLY LITTLE CHINAMAN	SCHER, W.
JOLLY LITTLE MANNEQUIN	SCHER, W.
JOLLY LITTLE SAILOR	HOFSTAD, M.
JOLLY LITTLE SAMBO	CROSBY, M.
JOLLY MEN ARE WE	STILWELL
JOLLY MILLER	BERMONT, H.
JOLLY MINSTRELS	BECHTER, K.
JOLLY MINSTRELS	BECHTER, K.
JOLLY OLD SAINT NICHOLAS FROM THE THREE CHRISTMAS	RICHTER, A.
JOLLY POSTMAN, THE	MCHALE, M.
JOLLY RICKSHA BOY	SCHER, W.
JOLLY SAILOR LADS	BERMONT, H.
JOLLY SAILOR MARCH	BRONSON, M.
JOLLY SANTA CLAUS	RICHTER
JOLLY WALTZ, A	MANA-ZUCCA
JOLLY WALTZ	DUNYON
JONATHAN EDWARDS	EDWARDS, J.
JONQUILS	DAVIS, M.
JOSEPHINE	BIVENS *
JOSEPHINE	LANE, J.--ED.
JOSEPHINE	
JOSEPHSLEGENDE, OP. 63 -- COMPLETE BALLET	STRAUSS, R.
JOSE MELIS PIANO MOODS	MELIS, J.
JOSHUA BOOGIE, THE -- JOSHUA FIT DE BATTLE OF JERICHO	WEYBRIGHT
JOSHUA BOOGIE, THE	WEYBRIGHT
JOSHUA FIT DE BATTLE OB JERICHO	WEYBRIGHT--ED.
JOSHUA FIT DE BATTLE OF JERICHO	WEYBRIGHT--ED.
JOSHUA FIT DE BATTLE OF JERICHO	ZEPP--ED
JOSHUA FIT DE BATTLE OF JERICHO	ZEPP--ED
JOTA ARAGONESA IN A	SORIANO, A. P.
JOTA ARAGONESA UND TANGO, OP. 164	ALBENIZ, I.
JOTA ARAGONESA UND TANGO, OP. 164	ALBENIZ, I.
JOTA ARAGONESA	LONGAS
JOTA	HARTLEY, W.
JOTA	LARREGLA, J.
JOUEUSES D'OSSELETS	HENRY, C.
JOURNEE D'UN PETIT ENFANT BIEN SAGE, LA -- 6 LITTLE	FIEVET, P.
JOURNEY TO BETHLEHEM	WILLIAMS, C.
JOUR DE FETE AU PAYS BASQUE	CASTERA
JOYEUSE AUBADE, OP. 54	GREGH
JOYEUSE BANDE, MARCHE, OP. 277	STREABBOG
JOYEUSE ESPAGNE, VALSE BRILLANTE	ALLIER
JOYEUX MATIN	MERIGOT, F.
JOYEUX PAPILLONS, LES -- CAPRICE -- OP. 8	GREGH
JOYEUX PAPILLONS, LES OP. 8	GREGH
JOYEUX PRINTEMPS	ROUGNON
JOYFUL CANARY -- JOYEUX CANARI	DE PRINCE
JOYFUL DAYS	THORNTON
JOYFUL MESSAGE	SCHIEFELBEIN, F.
JOYFUL PEASANT	SCHUMANN, R.
JOYOUS BELLS	ROBINSON
JOYOUS DANCE	KARP
JOYOUS ETUDE	WIGHAM, M.
JOYOUS FARMER	SCHUMANN, R.
JOYOUS MOMENTS, VALSE, OP. 87 NO. 2	SMITH, W.
JOYOUS PEASANT, OP. 68 NO. 10	SCHUMANN, R.
JOYOUS WALTZ	MACLACHLIN, T.
JOYS OF YOUTH	KNIGHT
JOY DANCERS	RAEZER, C.
JOY OF BACH	AGAY, D.--ED
JOY OF BOOGIE AND BLUES, THE	AGAY, D.--ED
JOY OF CLASSICS, THE	AGAY, D.--ED
JOY OF FOLK SONGS, THE	AGAY, D.--ED
JOY OF JAZZ, THE	STEINER
JOY OF LIFE	AGAY, D.--ED
JOY OF PIANO DUETS, THE	AGAY, D.--ED
JOY OF PIANO	WAGNER, J.
JOY PEAL	WAGNER
JOY PEAL	RICHTER, A.
JOY TO THE WORLD FROM THE THREE YULETIDE MELODIES	BERMONT, H.
JOY TO THE WORLD	BRADLEY,
JOY TO THE WORLD	BRADLEY,
JOY TO THE WORLD	BRIMHALL,
JOY TO THE WORLD	WALLIS
JOY TO THE WORLD	THORNTON
JOY TUNES	BACH, J.S.
JOY	BRADLEY,
JOY	LANE, J.--ED.
JOY	PIERSON, A.
JOY	DETT, N.
JUBA	STEINER
JUBILATION, RECITAL ETUDE	WILLIAMS
JUBILEE MARCH	WEYBRIGHT
JUBILO -- OLD AMERICAN SONG	LOWENSTEIN
JUBILO	WEYBRIGHT--ED.
JUBILO	CROCKER, D.
JUDY'S BALL	COLLINS, J.
JUDY COLLINS SONGBOOK, THE	CASTRO, W.
JUEGOS	LAPARRA, R.
JUERGAS	NOVAK
JUGEND. 21 KLAVIERSTUCKE, OP. 55 - BK. 1	NOVAK
JUGEND. 21 KLAVIERSTUCKE, OP. 55 - BK. 2	BOSSI
JUGEND-ALBUM OP. 122, BK. 1	BOSSI
JUGEND-ALBUM OP. 122, BK. 2	VOGEL
JUGENDALBUM. 20 KLAVIERSTUCKE, OP. 25 IN	REGER
JUGENDALBUM OP. 17 -- BK. 1 ST.-V.S. 28	REGER
JUGENDALBUM OP. 17 -- BK. 2 ST.-V.S. 28	GURLITT
JUGENDALBUM OP. 62	DIABELLI
JUGENDFREUDEN, OP. 163	DOBROWEN, I.
JUGENDSONATA, OP. 5	KERN, C. W.
JUGGLER, THE OP. 192 NO. 6	BRUSSELS, I.
JUGGLER, THE	GILLOCK
JUGGLER, THE	REISER, V.
JUGGLERESS, OP. 52, NO. 4	MOSZKOWSKI
JUGGLERS, THE	HARMON, M. S.
JUGGLERY--ETUDE, OP. 107 NO. 3	GODARD, B.
JUGGLER CLOWN, THE	MCGRAW
JUGGLER	GILLOCK
JUGGLE BOOGIE - LITTLE BROWN JUG	ZEPP--ED
JUGUETES DE BAZAR -- BK. 1, SIX EASY PIECES	AGUILAR
JUGUETES DE BAZAR -- BK. 3, SIX EASY PIECES	AGUILAR
JUGUETES	SAENZ
JUKEBOX BOOGIE	KENT, A.
JULIANNE	GRIFFIS, E.
JULIET'S VALSE	GOUNOD, C.
JULY 4TH SQUARE DANCE	BASTIEN
JUMPIEST GRASSHOPPER, THE	GODDARD, W.
JUMPIN' AND COMIN' DOWN THE RIVER	KING
JUMPIN' JACK RABBIT	PINCKARD
JUMPIN' JALOPY	NEVIN
JUMPIN' JALOPY	ROBINSON, A.
JUMPIN' JALOPY	ROBINSON, A.
JUMPIN' JALOPY	KAHN, M.
JUMPIN' JUPITER	AARON, M.
JUMPING-JACKS	MCCLEARY
JUMPING BEANS	MCHALE, M.
JUMPING BEANS	TEMPLETON, V.
JUMPING BEANS	VALENTI, M.
JUMPING BEAN	BILBRO, M.
JUMPING BEAN	RIGUETTE
JUMPING BUNS	TOWNSEND
JUMPING DUCK	SCARLINO
JUMPING FROG	SHARP
JUMPING JACKS	SHARP
JUMPING JACKS	ARCHER
JUMPING JACK	FINLAYSON, W.
JUMPING JACK	HOPKINS, H.
JUMPING JACK	ROWLEY
JUMPING JACK	RICHTER
JUMPING ROPE	SCHAUM, J.
JUMPING ROPE	JOYNER, B.
JUMP JOHNNY JUMP	TSCHAIKOWSKY
JUNE. BARCAROLLE IN G MINOR, OP. 37 NO. 6	TSCHAIKOWSKY
JUNE, BARCAROLLE	BEAUMONT
JUNE JOY	LANE, J.--ED.
JUNE NIGHT	KOHLER, F.
JUNE ROSES	BRIMHALL,
JUNGLE BOOK, THE	MOORE
JUNGLE CARAVEN	LECUONA
JUNGLE DRUMS	MORALES
JUNGLE FANTASY	SIMMONS, T.
JUNGLE FLOWER, THE	BEAULIEU
JUNGLE RHUMBA	MILLIGAN
JUNIE THE JITTERBUG	MITTLER--ED
JUNIOR AMERICAN PIANO CONCEERTO	SCHAUM, J.
JUNIOR ANIMAL JINGLES	STEINER
JUNIOR CLASSICS, BK. 1	STEINER
JUNIOR CLASSICS, BK. 2	CZERNY
JUNIOR CZERNY	KARP
JUNIOR DUETS FOR YOUNG PIANISTS	HANON, C.
JUNIOR HANON	HANON, C.
JUNIOR HANON	BARRETT--ED
JUNIOR HYMNAL FOR PIANO	KAHL--ED
JUNIOR HYMNBOOK - BOOK 1	KAHL--ED
JUNIOR HYMNBOOK - BOOK 2	KAHL--ED
JUNIOR HYMNBOOK - BOOK 3	GORDON
JUNIOR JAZZ	PANELLA, L.
JUNIOR MARCH	KING, S.
JUNIOR MISS PLAYS PIANO	KING, S.
JUNIOR MISTER PLAYS PIANO	WALDTEUFEL, E.
JUNIOR PROM WALTZ	MUNN, W.--ED.
JUNIOR RECITAL--FOURTEEN PIANO SOLOS FOR THE YOUNG	
JUST AS THOUGH YOU WERE HERE	CATIZONE, J. M.
JUST A HUMMIN'	
JUST A KISS APART	KAHN, M.--ED
JUST BEGUINE-ING	ALFASSY, L.--ED
JUST BLUES	MANA-ZUCCA
JUST FOOLING	WEYBRIGHT
JUST FOR BOYS -- A COLLECTION OF FAVORITE PIANO PIECES	BELL, W.--ARR.
JUST FOR FUN - HIT TUNES EVERYBODY KNOWS	BELL, W.--ARR.
JUST FOR FUN - MELODIES EVERYBODY KNOWS	BELL, W.--ARR.
JUST FOR FUN - POPS EVERYBODY KNOWS	BELL, W.--ARR.
JUST FOR FUN - SHOW TUNES EVERYBODY KNOWS	WEYBRIGHT
JUST FOR GIRLS -- A COLLECTION OF FAVORITE PIANO	
JUST FOR GIRLS	RICHTER
JUST FOR ME	RICHTER
JUST FOR ME	SINGER, L.--ED
JUST IN TIME	SCHAUM, J.--ED.
JUST LIKE ME	ROBINSON, A.
JUST LOAFIN'	LAWLOR, G.
JUST POLIN' ALONG	BILBRO, M.
JUST STARTING	CADZOW
JUST SUPPOSE	MARTIN, H.
JUST TRAVELIN' ALONG	MALTZMAN
JUST WANDERING	SPAULDING, G. L.
JUST WE TWO	ZEPP
JUST WRITE	APREA
JUVENILIA -- THIRTY-FIVE LITTLE PIECES FOR THE	STORR, S.
KABUKI DANCE	RAVEL
KADDISCH -- MELODIE HEBRAIQUE	FOLDES
KADENZA ZU KLAVIERKONZERT IN C, K467 BY W. A. MOZART	FOLDES
KADENZA ZU KLAVIERKONZERT IN C, K503 BY W. A. MOZART	FOLDES
KADENZA ZU KLAVIERKONZERT IN E FLAT, K482 BY W. A.	FOLDES
KADENZA ZU KLAVIERKONZERT IN G, K453 BY W. A. MOZART	MOZART, W. A.
KADENZEN ZU DEN KLAVIERKONZERTEN -- K.V. 365, 453,	BEETHOVEN
KADENZEN ZU DEN KLAVIERKONZERTEN OP. 15 U. 58--1.	BADURA-SKODA
KADENZEN ZU MOZARTS KLAVIERKONZERTEN K175, 238, 415,	KADOSA
KALEIDOSCOPE, OP. 61	LEES, B.
KALEIDOSCOPES	GEORGE
KALEIDOSCOPE -- DUET BOOK 1	GEORGE
KALEIDOSCOPE -- DUET BOOK 2	GEORGE
KALEIDOSCOPE -- DUET BOOK 2	GEORGE
KALEIDOSCOPE -- DUET BOOK 3	GEORGE
KALEIDOSCOPE -- DUET BOOK 4	CORIGLIANO, J.
KALEIDOSCOPE -- SET	GEORGE
KALEIDOSCOPE -- SOLO BOOK 1	GEORGE
KALEIDOSCOPE -- SOLO BOOK 2	GEORGE
KALEIDOSCOPE -- SOLO BOOK 3	GEORGE
KALEIDOSCOPE -- SOLO BOOK 4	GEORGE
KALEIDOSCOPE -- SOLO BOOK 5	NELHYBEL, V.
KALEIDOSCOPE - FOR YOUNG PIANISTS, BK. 1	NELHYBEL, V.
KALEIDOSCOPE - FOR YOUNG PIANISTS, BK. 1	NELHYBEL, V.
KALEIDOSCOPE - FOR YOUNG PIANISTS, BK. 2	NELHYBEL, V.
KALEIDOSCOPE - FOR YOUNG PIANISTS, BK. 2	JENKINS, M.
KALEIDOSCOPE	ROZSA, M.
KALEIDOSCOPE	RUIZ-PIPO
KALEIDOSCOPE	STEINER
KALEIDOSCOPE	
KALISTOE	ZUCCA
KAMENNOI-OSTROW --REVE ANGELIQUE--, OP. 10 NO. 22	RUBINSTEIN
KAMENNOI-OSTROW	RUBINSTEIN
KAMENNOI-OSTROW	RUBINSTEIN
KAMENNOI-OSTROW	RUBINSTEIN
KAMENNOI-OSTROW	RUBINSTEIN
KAMENNOI-OSTROW	RUBINSTEIN
KAMMERKONZERT FUR KLAVIER UND KLEINES ORCHESTER	STUDER
KAMMERMUSIK NO. 02, KLAVIER-KONZERT, OP. 36 NO. 1 -	HINDEMITH

PIANO MUSIC IN PRINT

TITLE INDEX

Title	Composer/Editor
KAMMERMUSIK	FORTNER, W.
KANAWAHA RIVER	COOK, P.
KANGAROO, THE	MCGRAW
KANGAROO'S POCKET, THE	COBB
KANGAROOS	GEORGE
KANGAROO HOPS	FROST
KANGAROO HOP	NEVIN
KANSAS CITY FAREWELL	JOHNSON, S.
KARELIA SUITE, OP. 11	SIBELIUS
KARPATHIA CZARDAS	BERENY
KATE KEARNEY WALTZ	GUENTHER
KATHENKA'S MUSIC BOOK	ANDRIESSEN, J.
KATHLEEN MAVOURNEEN, TRANS.	FREEMAN
KATHY'S THEME	OSSER *
KATHY'S WALTZ	OBENCHAIN, V.
KATINKA--"KATINKA"	FRIML, R.
KATZENFUGE	SCARLATTI, D.
KAWANA -- 3 PIECES	PIER, G.
KAY LANDE'S ABC-123	LANDE
KEEP IN STEP	MILLIGAN
KEEP THE STAR-SPANGLED BANNER WAVING	BEAUMONT
KELLY GROUND	LUMSDAINE, D.
KENTUCKY BABE	GEIBEL
KENTUCKY BABE	GEIBEL *
KENTUCKY TROTTER	PERKINS, F.
KERMESSE -- THE FAIR	GURLITT
KERMESSE A CHARLEROI	FRID, G.
KERMESSE VALSE FROM L'EVENTAIL DE JEANNE	SCHMITT, F.
KERRY DANCE, THE	ROLFE, W.--ED
KERRY DANCE	MOLLOY, J. L.
KEYBOARD ARTS PIANO REPERTOIRE SERIES, BK. 1	
KEYBOARD ARTS PIANO REPERTOIRE SERIES, BK. 2	
KEYBOARD ARTS PIANO REPERTOIRE SERIES, BK. 3	
KEYBOARD ARTS PIANO REPERTOIRE SERIES, BK. 4	
KEYBOARD ARTS PIANO REPERTOIRE SERIES, BK. 5	
KEYBOARD ARTS PIANO REPERTOIRE SERIES, BK. 6	
KEYBOARD ATTACKS	THOMPSON, J.
KEYBOARD BALLET	WEYBRIGHT
KEYBOARD BALLET	WEYBRIGHT
KEYBOARD BELL	KING
KEYBOARD BUILDER -- BOOK 3	DUCKWORTH, G.
KEYBOARD CAMEOS--100--	
KEYBOARD CARICATURES	MORITZ, E.
KEYBOARD CAVALCADE--50--	
KEYBOARD CHORDS	MIROVITCH, A.
KEYBOARD CONCERTO IN B FLAT, OP.4 NO. 6 -- SECOND MVT	HANDEL
KEYBOARD DISCOVERER -- BOOK 2	DUCKWORTH, G.
KEYBOARD DUETS NO. 1	SMITH, T.
KEYBOARD DUETS NO. 2	SMITH, T.
KEYBOARD ESSAYS	LANNACCONE, A.
KEYBOARD EXPLORER -- BOOK 1	DUCKWORTH, G.
KEYBOARD FUNDAMENTALS - BOOK 1	FISK
KEYBOARD FUNDAMENTALS - BOOK 2	FISK
KEYBOARD FUNDAMENTALS - BOOK 3	FISK
KEYBOARD FUNDAMENTALS - TEACHER'S MANUAL	FISK
KEYBOARD GAMBOLS--A MERRY CHASE	DUNN, H.
KEYBOARD GAMES FOR THE VERY YOUNG PIANIST	LAST, J.
KEYBOARD GAMES	RICHTER
KEYBOARD HARMONY AND TRANSPOSITION	VEON
KEYBOARD HARMONY COURSE, BK. 1--FEATURING MELODY	DILLER, A.
KEYBOARD HARMONY COURSE, BK. 2--FEATURING HARMONIC	DILLER, A.
KEYBOARD HARMONY COURSE, BK. 3--FEATURING HARMONIZING	DILLER, A.
KEYBOARD HARMONY COURSE, BK. 4--FEATURING HARMONIZING	DILLER, A.
KEYBOARD HARMONY	CARTER
KEYBOARD HARMONY	GLOVER, D. *
KEYBOARD HARMONY	GLOVER, D. *
KEYBOARD HIT-KIT, THE	
KEYBOARD INTERPRETATION	KASSCHAU, H.
KEYBOARD KALEIDOSCOPE, BK. 1 --100--	
KEYBOARD KALEIDOSCOPE, BK. 2 --125--	
KEYBOARD MEDLEYS	HUGHES--ED.
KEYBOARD MODULATIONS	FULLER
KEYBOARD MUSICIANSHIP - GROUP PIANO FOR ADULTS, BK. 1	LYKE *
KEYBOARD MUSICIANSHIP - GROUP PIANO FOR ADULTS, BK. 2	LYKE *
KEYBOARD MUSICIAN -- BOOK 4	DUCKWORTH, G.
KEYBOARD MUSIC -- BACH GESELLSCHAFT EDITION	BACH, J.S.
KEYBOARD MUSIC OF THE BAROQUE AND ROCOCO, BK. 1	GERIG, HANS--ED.
KEYBOARD MUSIC OF THE BAROQUE AND ROCOCO, BK. 2	GERIG, HANS--ED.
KEYBOARD MUSIC OF THE BAROQUE AND ROCOCO, BK. 3	GERIG, HANS--ED.
KEYBOARD MUSIC OF THE SEVENTEENTH CENTURY	BARTH, H.
KEYBOARD PATTER	WEYBRIGHT
KEYBOARD PATTER	WEYBRIGHT
KEYBOARD PERFORMER	DUCKWORTH, G.
KEYBOARD PHRASING AND SHADING	MIROVITCH, A.
KEYBOARD PICTURES	HAUBIEL, C.
KEYBOARD SECRETS	BLAKE
KEYBOARD SONATAS, BK. 1	HURLEBUSCH
KEYBOARD SONATAS, BK. 2	HURLEBUSCH
KEYBOARD STACCATO	MIROVITCH, A.
KEYBOARD SUITES	PURCELL, H.
KEYBOARD TALENT HUNT	SCHAUM, J.
KEYBOARD TECHNIC, MORE, FOR THE OLDER STUDENT	RICHTER
KEYBOARD TECHNIC FOR THE OLDER STUDENT	RICHTER
KEYBOARD THEORY, BK. 1	CLARK, F.--ED.
KEYBOARD THEORY, BK. 2	CLARK, F.--ED.
KEYBOARD THEORY, BK. 3	CLARK, F.--ED.
KEYBOARD THEORY, BK. 4	CLARK, F.--ED.
KEYBOARD THEORY, BK. 5	CLARK, F.--ED.
KEYBOARD THEORY, BK. 6	CLARK, F.--ED.
KEYBOARD TOWN	ROBYN
KEYBOARD TRAINING IN HARMONY, BK. A	HEACOX
KEYBOARD TRAINING IN HARMONY, BK. B	HEACOX
KEYWAYS TO MUSIC, BK. 1 --IN PREP--	HOY *
KEY OF GLEE, THE	SCHAUM, J.--ED.
KEY RELATIVES	LINDFORS
KEY TO MUSIC TEACHING -- TEACHER'S MANUAL	KIRBY, M. B.
KHAMMA	DEBUSSY
KIDDIES ON THE KEYS	SLONIMSKY
KIDDY CAROL BOOK	RICHARDSON, A.
KIDS 'N' KEYBOARDS	METIS
KID CONCERTO	ANSON, G.
KID FROM RED BANK	
KID KONCERTO	ANSON, G.
KILLARNEY	GROFE, F.
KILTIES ARE COMING --PIANO, 6 HANDS--	KEENAN
KINDERGARTEN CLASS BOOK	RICHTER
KINDERGARTEN PIANO METHOD, BK. 1	KIRBY, M. B.
KINDERGARTEN PIANO METHOD, BK. 2	KIRBY, M. B.
KINDERGARTEN PIANO METHOD, BK. 3	KIRBY, M. B.
KINDERGARTEN PIANO METHOD, BK. 4	KIRBY, M. B.
KINDERHERZEN. 35 KLAVIERSTUCKE	RIHOVSKY
KINDERKONZERT	MARGOLA
KINDERLIEDERQUELL --39 CHILDREN'S SONGS--	KELLER, G.
KINDERLIEDER UND VOLKSLIEDER FUR DEN SYSTEMATISCHEN	GABSCHUSS--ED
KINDERSCENEN -- SCENES FROM CHILDHOOD --, OP. 15 NO. 7	SCHUMANN, R.
KINDERSCENEN -- SCENES FROM CHILDHOOD --, OP. 15 NO. 7	SCHUMANN, R.
KINDERSCENEN -- SCENES FROM CHILDHOOD --, OP. 15	SCHUMANN, R.
KINDERSZENEN -- 1950	DICHLER
KINDERSZENEN OP. 15 -- VIER STUCKE	SCHUMANN, R.
KINDERSZENEN OP. 15	SCHUMANN, R.
KINDERSZENEN	SCHUMANN, R.
KINDERSZENEN	SCHUMANN, R.
KINDERTRAUME, OP. 74--VOL. 1	JUON, P.
KINDERTRAUME, OP. 74--VOL. 2	JUON, P.
KINDER CONCERTO	HAYDN
KINDER CONCERTO	MOZART, W. A.
KINDER SPIELEN ZUR WEIHNACHT. 19 WEIHNACHTSLIEDER FUR	POHL, V.--ED *
KINDER SPIELEN ZUR WEIHNACHT -- 19 CHRISTMAS SONGS	
KINDER SPIELEN ZUR WEIHNACHT	BUSCHBAUM *
KINDER SPIELEN ZUR WEIHNACHT	BUSCHBAUM *
KINDER SPIELEN ZUR WEIHNACHT	POHL, V.--ED *
KING'S GUARD, THE	COBB
KING'S JESTER, THE	ROGERS, E.
KING'S REVIEW, THE, FOR ONE PIANO SIX HANDS	BAINES, W.
KING'S REVIEW, THE	BAINES, W.
KING'S REVIEW	BAINES, W.
KING AND I, THE	HAMMERSTEIN *
KING AND I, THE	HAMMERSTEIN *
KING ARTHUR, MARCH	HOPKINS, H.
KING CHRISTIAN SUITE--BALLADE	SIBELIUS
KING CHRISTIAN SUITE--NOCTURNE AND SERENADE	SIBELIUS
KING LION	BRODSKY, M.
KING MIDAS	STORR, S.
KING OF KINGS, THE	ROSZA
KING OF THE ROAD	BRIMHALL
KIRAVANI-RAMAPRIYA LOTUS DANCE	SCHRAMM
KISMET	WRIGHT, R. *
KISS AN ANGEL GOOD MORNING	LANE, J.--ED.
KISS ME AGAIN	HERBERT
KISS OF SPRING	ROLFE, W.
KISS WALTZ, OP. 411	STRAUSS, J.
KISS WALTZ, THE -- IL BACIO	ARDITI
KISS YOUR HAND, MAZURKA, OP. 127	HEINS, C.
KISS	HILSHER, F.
KITES IN THE WIND	MELECCI, A.
KITE AND THE PIGEONS, THE	GRAHAM, R.
KITE CAPERS	SHAW, E. B.
KITE STORY, A	DITTENHAVER
KITTEN AND THE MOUSE, THE	HART, G. R.
KITTEN GAMES	REISER, V.
KITTEN ON THE KEYS -- SIMP.	MOSSMAN, T.--ED
KITTEN ON THE KEYS	CONFREY, Z.
KITTEN ON THE KEYS	MERKUR--ED
KITTEN ON THE KEYS	MORGAN--ED. *
KITTEN ON THE KEYS	POLLA, W.--ED
KITTY CAT	BASTIEN
KLANGSPIELE OP. 99, BK. 1	HAAS
KLANGSPIELE OP. 99, BK. 2	HAAS
KLASSIKER UND ROMANTIKER -- SHORT WORKS BY BACH,	SCHOLZ--ED
KLASSISCHE KLAVIERMUSIK ALTER SPANISCHER MEISTER --	NIN--ED
KLASSISCHE KLAVIERMUSIK ALTER SPNISCHER MEISTER -- BK.	NIN--ED
KLASSISCHE LIEBLINGSSTUCKE	
KLAVIER-BUCHLEIN	TELEMANN, G.P.
KLAVIER-SUITE, OP. 2	JUROWSKY
KLAVIER-UBUNGEN DES FRANK. DORFSCHULMEISTERS GEORG AD.	KRESS--ED.
KLAVIERBUCHLEIN -- 10 KLEINE UBUNGEN FUR DEN ANFANG --	KAMINSKI
KLAVIERBUCHLEIN FUR ANNA MAGDALENA BACH, 1725 --	BACH, J.S.
KLAVIERBUCHLEIN FUR ANNA MAGDALENA BACH VON 1722 UND	BACH, J.S.
KLAVIERBUCHLEIN FUR PETER	MARX
KLAVIERBUCHLEIN FUR WILHELM FRIEDEMANN BACH -- NEUE	BACH, J.S.
KLAVIERBUCHLEIN	KAMINSKI
KLAVIERCHORALBUCH. 206 KLAVIERSATZE ZUM EVANGELISCHEN	BAUM--ED *
KLAVIERCHORALBUCH	BAUM--ED. *
KLAVIERKOMPOSITIONEN, HEFT 2	STEPAN--ED
KLAVIERKOMPOSITIONEN, HEFT 3	STEPAN--ED
KLAVIERKOMPOSITIONEN AUS DEM JAHR 1912	KVAPIL
KLAVIERKOMPOSITIONEN DES ALTEN SPANIEN UND PORTUGAL.	UNDARRA *
KLAVIERKOMPOSITIONEN	SMETANA
KLAVIERKONZERT, OP. 33	WEISMANN, J.
KLAVIERKONZERT, OP. 37	SCHAEFER
KLAVIERKONZERT IN A, K488, KLAVIERAUSZUG	MOZART, W. A.
KLAVIERKONZERT IN A, K488	MOZART, W. A.
KLAVIERKONZERT IN A, K488	MOZART, W. A.
KLAVIERKONZERT IN C, K503, KLAVIERAUSZUG	MOZART, W. A.
KLAVIERKONZERT IN C, K503	MOZART, W. A.
KLAVIERKONZERT IN C, K503	MOZART, W. A.
KLAVIERKONZERT IN C MINOR, K491, KLAVIERAUSZUG	MOZART, W. A.
KLAVIERKONZERT IN C MINOR, K491	MOZART, W. A.
KLAVIERKONZERT IN G FUR KLAVIER UND ORCHESTER,	HEIM, W.
KLAVIERKONZERT NO. 01	MARTINU, B.
KLAVIERKONZERT NO. 02 - KLAVIERAUSZUG	MARTINU, B.
KLAVIERKONZERT NO. 02 IN G	TSCHAIKOWSKY
KLAVIERKONZERT NO. 02	BORKOVEC
KLAVIERKONZERT NO. 02	MARTINU, B.
KLAVIERKONZERT NO. 03 - KLAVIERAUSZUG	MARTINU, B.
KLAVIERKONZERT NO. 03	MARTINU, B.
KLAVIERKONZERT NO. 03	MARTINU, B.
KLAVIERKONZERT NO. 04	KRENEK, E.
KLAVIERMUSIK, OP. 37 NO. 1, UBUNG IN DREI STUCKEN	HINDEMITH
KLAVIERMUSIK, OP. 37 NO. 2, REIHE KLEINE STUCKE	HINDEMITH
KLAVIERMUSIK AUS ALTER ZEIT	SWEELINCK *
KLAVIERMUSIK FUR KINDER	KONT, P.
KLAVIERMUSIK IN VIER TEILEN, TEIL 1 - 10 STUCKE	KNORR, E.L. VON
KLAVIERMUSIK IN VIER TEILEN, TEIL 1 - 10 STUCKE	KNORR, E.L. VON
KLAVIERMUSIK IN VIER TEILEN, TEIL 2 - 10 STUCKE	KNORR, E.L. VON
KLAVIERMUSIK IN VIER TEILEN, TEIL 2 - 10 STUCKE	KNORR, E.L. VON
KLAVIERMUSIK IN VIER TEILEN, TEIL 3 - 10 STUCKE	KNORR, E.L. VON
KLAVIERMUSIK IN VIER TEILEN, TEIL 3 - 10 STUCKE	KNORR, E.L. VON
KLAVIERMUSIK IN VIER TEILEN, TEIL 4 - 10 STUCKE	KNORR, E.L. VON
KLAVIERMUSIK IN VIER TEILEN, TEIL 4 - 10 STUCKE	KNORR, E.L. VON
KLAVIERMUSIK NACH VOLKSLIEDERN--16 PIECES BASED ON	WEISS, E.
KLAVIERMUSIK NACH VOLKSLIEDERN, BK. 1 - OP. 40	MARX
KLAVIERMUSIK NACH VOLKSLIEDERN, BK. 2 - OP. 59	MARX
KLAVIERMUSIK NACH VOLKSLIEDERN	REIN
KLAVIERSCHULE, BAND 01	SCHUNGELER, H.
KLAVIERSCHULE, BAND 02	SCHUNGELER, H.
KLAVIERSONATA NO. 02 - 1953	SCHROEDER, H.
KLAVIERSONATEN 1 -- 1-7 --	DUSSEK, J.
KLAVIERSONATEN 2 -- 8-16 --	DUSSEK, J.
KLAVIERSONATEN 3 -- 17-23 --	DUSSEK, J.
KLAVIERSONATEN 4 -- 24-29 --	DUSSEK, J.
KLAVIERSTUCK, OP. POSTH.	WEBERN, A.
KLAVIERSTUCKE OP. 118	BRAHMS
KLAVIERSTUCKE OP. 119	BRAHMS
KLAVIERSTUCKE	HAUBENSTOCK-RAMA
KLAVIERSTUCKE	VORISEK
KLAVIERSTUCKE 1, 6 STUCKE	BECK, C.
KLAVIERSTUCKE 2, 5 STUCKE	BECK, C.
KLAVIERSTUCKE IN QUARTEN, OP. 3	SALMHOFER, FR.
KLAVIERSTUDIE NO. 1--1968	SOEGIJO, P. G.
KLAVIERSTUECKE FUR CHARLOTTE	GEISSLER
KLAVIERSTUK NO. 1	DEBRAS, L.

KLAVIERSUITE AUS 'VIEL LARMEN UM NICHTS', OP. 11   KORNGOLD, E. W.
KLAVIERTANZE DER J. S. BACH-ZEITGENOSSEN. 29   PETZOLD *
KLAVIERTANZE   KREUTZ --ED.
KLAVIERUBUNG, TEIL 3   BACH, J.S.
KLAVIERUBUNG NACH VOLKSLIEDERN, HEFT 1 - 20 STUCKE MIT   MICHEELSEN
KLAVIERUBUNG NACH VOLKSLIEDERN, HEFT 1 - 32 STUCKE MIT   MICHEELSEN
KLAVIERUBUNG NACH VOLKSLIEDERN, HEFT 2 - 20 STUCKE MIT   MICHEELSEN
KLAVIERUBUNG NACH VOLKSLIEDERN, HEFT 3 - LEICHTE SUITE   MICHEELSEN
KLAVIERUBUNG NACH VOLKSLIEDERN, HEFT 3 - LEICHTE SUITE   MICHEELSEN
KLAVIERUEBUNG --URTEXT--. PART 1# PARTITAS, VOL. 1   BACH, J.S.
KLAVIERUEBUNG --URTEXT--. PART 1# PARTITAS, VOL. 2   BACH, J.S.
KLAVIERUEBUNG --URTEXT--. PART 2# ITALIAN CONCERTO AND   BACH, J.S.
KLAVIERUEBUNG --URTEXT--. PART 3# 4 DUETS --FOR PIANO   STUDER
KLAVIERUEBUNG --URTEXT--. PART 4# GOLDBERG VARIATIONS   BACH, J.S.
KLAVIERUEBUNG   KREBS
KLAVIERWERKE - 1, DIE ERSTEN ZYKLEN   SMETANA
KLAVIERWERKE - 2, STUDIENSTUCKE UND SONATEN AUS DEM   SMETANA
KLAVIERWERKE 1. DIE ACHT GROSSEN SUITEN -- HALLISCHE   HANDEL
KLAVIER GESCHICHTEN AM KLAVIER   FREY
KLEIN. KLAVIERBUCH, OP. 53   SCHMID
KLEINEN KLAVIERSTUCKE, DIE - 27 STUCKE, MEIST AUS DEN   BACH, J.S.
KLEINES KLAVIERBUCH   GENZMER
KLEINES KONZERT FUR KLAVIER, STREICHER UND SCHLAGZEUG   LEHNER
KLEINES KONZERT FUR STREICHER, KLAVIER ZU 4 HANDEN UND   STUDER
KLEINES KONZERT IN F FUR CEMBALO UND KLEINES ORCHESTER   HAYDN
KLEINES MENUETT   RICHARTZ
KLEINES SPIELBUCH   AHRENS
KLEINES SPIELBUCH   AHRENS
KLEINE BLUMEN, KLEINE BLATTER OP. 64   LICHNER, H.
KLEINE CHORALVORSPIELE, BK. 1   BENDER
KLEINE CHORALVORSPIELE, BK. 2   BENDER
KLEINE CHORALVORSPIELE, BK. 3   BENDER
KLEINE CHORALVORSPIELE ZUM GOTTESDIENSTLICHEN   BENDER
KLEINE CHORALVORSPIELE ZUM GOTTESDIENSTLICHEN   BENDER
KLEINE CHORALVORSPIELE ZUM GOTTESDIENSTLICHEN   BENDER
KLEINE FANTASIEN   TELEMANN, G.P.
KLEINE HANDSTUCKE FUR ANGEHENDE KLAVIERSPIELER. 50   TUERK
KLEINE HANDSTUCKE FUR ANGEHENDE KLAVIERSPIELER   TUERK
KLEINE HANDSTUCKE   TUERK
KLEINE HAUSMUSIK, OP. 24   HESSENBERG, K.
KLEINE KLAVIERMUSIK, OP. 45 NO. 4   HINDEMITH
KLEINE KLAVIERSTUCKE, HEFT 01   WILLERT-ORFF, G.
KLEINE KLAVIERSTUCKE, HEFT 02   WILLERT-ORFF, G.
KLEINE KLAVIERSTUCKE, HEFT 03   WILLERT-ORFF, G.
KLEINE KLAVIERSTUCKE, HEFT 04   WILLERT-ORFF, G.
KLEINE KLAVIERSTUCKE, OP. 28   REUTTER, H.
KLEINE KLAVIERSUITE, OP. 12   JIRAK
KLEINE LEICHTE KLAVIERSTUCKE -- 18 JAHRHUNDERT   KREUTZ--ED.
KLEINE MUSIKANTENSTUCKE   KUKUCK
KLEINE SALONMUSIK   KONT, P.
KLEINE SONATE IN D   KNORR, E.L. VON
KLEINE SONATE   RUYNEMAN
KLEINE SONATE   SCHELB
KLEINE SPIELMUSIK FUR KLAVIER   MICHEELSEN
KLEINE SPIELMUSIK   MICHEELSEN
KLEINE STUCKE FUR KLAVIER -- 10 STUCKE AUS   BACH, C.P.E.
KLEINE SUITE, OP. 42   KABELAC
KLEINE SUITE, OP. 9   BARTOS, J.
KLEINE SUITE   PONC
KLEINE WELT   VOLKART-SCHLAGER
KLEINMEISTER DER KLASSIK   DONATH--ED
KLEINSTADTBILDER, OP. 49   TOCH, E.
KLEIN JUTKA -- 12 PIECES   KOSA, G.
KLEIS   MARIE
KLINGENDE MELODIEN, BAND 01   KRENTZLIN,
KLINGENDE MELODIEN, BAND 02   KRENTZLIN,
KLINGENDE MELODIEN, BAND 03   KRENTZLIN,
KNECHT RUPRECHT   URBACH, E.
KNICK-KNACKS   STEINER
KNIGHT, THE   NOONA, W.
KNIGHTSBRIDGE MARCH
KNIGHTS AND LADIES   ARCHER
KNIGHT FORLORN AND OFF TO THE TOURNEY, THE   HOWELL, D.
KNIGHT IN ARMOR   ROGERS, E.
KNIGHT RUPERT, FOR TWO PIANOS, EIGHT HANDS   SCHUMANN, R.
KNIGHT RUPERT, OP. 68 NO. 12--ALBUM FOR THE YOUNG   SCHUMANN, R.
KNIGHT RUPERT   SCHUMANN, R.
KNIGHT WALTZ, A--PIANO QUARTETTE--   DE PUE
KNIVES AND FORKS   GLOVER
KNOCKIN' ON HEAVEN'S DOOR   BRADLEY,
KNOCKOUT   WALLINGTON, G.
KNOCK THREE TIMES
KNOW YOUR MUSIC, BK. 1   MALOOF
KNOW YOUR MUSIC, BK. 2   MALOOF
KNOW YOUR MUSIC, BK. 3   MALOOF
KNOW YOUR MUSIC, BK. 4   MALOOF
KNOW YOUR SCALES AND ARPEGGIOS   RICHTER
KNOW YOUR SCALES   LEVINE
KNUTE ROCKNE   GROFE, F.
KO-OLA-U   HOVHANESS, A.
KOBOLD, OP. 71 NO. 3   GRIEG
KOBOLDSTANZ, OP. 85 NO. 8
KOHLER'S SCALES AND CHORDS   KOHLER, F.
KOL NIDRE
KOMM SUESSER TOD   BACH, J.S.
KOMPOSITIONEN FUR CEMBALO. 9 STUCKE   BYRD, W. *
KOMPOSITIONEN FUR ORGEL UND CEMBALO   ROSEINGRAVE, T.
KONFIGURATIONEN   ZIMMERMAN
KONZERT-ETUDE -- COUPLET SANS PAROLES   SAUER
KONZERT-ETUDE -- NO. 26 PREGHIERA   SAUER
KONZERT-ETUDE -- NO. 6 FRISSON DE FEUILLES   SAUER
KONZERT-ETUDE - GNOMENREIGEN   LISZT
KONZERT-ETUDE - UN SOSPIRO   LISZT
KONZERT-ETUDE - WALDESRAUSCHEN   LISZT
KONZERT-ETUDE FIS-MOLL OP. 10 NO. 2   SGAMBATI
KONZERT-RONDO A-DUR, K.V. 386 FUR KLAVIER UND   MOZART, W. A.
KONZERT-RONDO A-DUR -- K.V. 386 FUR KLAVIER UND   MOZART, W. A.
KONZERTANTE MUSIK -- 1958   BAUR
KONZERTINO, OP. 168 FUR KLAVIER, STREICHER UND   ANTONIOU
KONZERTMUSIK FUR KLAVIER, BLECHBL. UND HARFEN, OP. 49   HINDEMITH
KONZERTSTUCKE--'*RUCKBLICKE'--OP. 61   SCHOLLUM, R.
KONZERTSTUCKE, OP. 21   MOHLER
KONZERTSTUCK FUR KLAVIER UND ORCHESTER -- OP. POSTH.   DISTLER
KONZERTSTUCK FUR KLAVIER UND ORCHESTER -- OP. POSTH.   DISTLER
KONZERTSTUCK IN F MINOR, OP. 79   WEBER, VON
KONZERTSTUCK
KONZERT F-DUR FUR KLAVIER -- CEMBALO UND ORCHESTER --   HAYDN
KONZERT FUR CEMBALO -- KLAVIER -- UND STREICHER   PFEIFFER, A.
KONZERT FUR CEMBALO -- KLAVIER -- UND STREICHER   ZACH
KONZERT FUR CEMBALO MIT STREICH-ORCHESTER -- K.V. 107   MOZART, W. A.
KONZERT FUR CEMBALO MIT STREICH-ORCHESTER ES-DUR   MOZART, W. A.
KONZERT FUR CEMBALO MIT STREICH-ORCHESTER G-DUR   MOZART, W. A.
KONZERT FUR CEMBALO UND STREICHORCHESTER, OP. 14   DISTLER
KONZERT FUR CEMBALO UND STREICHORCHESTER   FUCHS, R.
KONZERT FUR KAMMERORCHESTER MIT OBLIGATEM KLAVIER   GROSS
KONZERT FUR KLAVIER UND KLEINES ORCHESTER, OP. 15   KATTNIGG, R.

KONZERT FUR KLAVIER UND ORCHESTER, KLAVIERAUSZUG   FRANCAIX, J.
KONZERT FUR KLAVIER UND ORCHESTER, KLAVIERAUSZUG   GENZMER
KONZERT FUR KLAVIER UND ORCHESTER, KLAVIERAUSZUG   RIDKY
KONZERT FUR KLAVIER UND ORCHESTER, KLAVIERAUSZUG   SCHULLER, G.
KONZERT FUR KLAVIER UND ORCHESTER, KLAVIERAUSZUG   SUTERMEISTER, H.
KONZERT FUR KLAVIER UND ORCHESTER, OP. 15,   LOPATNIKOFF
KONZERT FUR KLAVIER UND ORCHESTER, OP. 19,   FRICKER, P.
KONZERT FUR KLAVIER UND ORCHESTER, OP. 26   DUSSEK, J.
KONZERT FUR KLAVIER UND ORCHESTER, OP. 27   DRIESSLER
KONZERT FUR KLAVIER UND ORCHESTER, OP. 38 -   TOCH, E.
KONZERT FUR KLAVIER UND ORCHESTER, OP. 46   RIDKY
KONZERT FUR KLAVIER UND ORCHESTER, OP. 46   RIDKY
KONZERT FUR KLAVIER UND ORCHESTER, 1945 --   HINDEMITH
KONZERT FUR KLAVIER UND ORCHESTER IN G MINOR, OP. 33,   DVORAK
KONZERT FUR KLAVIER UND ORCHESTER IN G MINOR, OP. 33   DVORAK
KONZERT FUR KLAVIER UND ORCHESTER   BARTA
KONZERT FUR KLAVIER UND ORCHESTER   EBEN
KONZERT FUR KLAVIER UND ORCHESTER   JIRKO
KONZERT FUR KLAVIER UND ORCHESTER   KALABIS
KONZERT FUR KLAVIER UND ORCHESTER   OBOUSSIER
KONZERT FUR KLAVIER UND ORCHESTER   PEPPING, E.
KONZERT FUR KLAVIER UND ORCHESTER   RIDKY
KONZERT FUR KLAVIER UND ORCHESTER   VOGT
KONZERT FUR ZWEI KLAVIERE   BRESGEN
KONZERT FUR 2 KLAVIERE F-DUR   BACH, W.F.
KONZERT FUR 2 KLAVIERE UND ORCHESTER   DUSSEK, J.
KONZERT FUR 2 KLAVIERE UND ORCHESTER   KRENEK, E.
KONZERT FUR 2 KLAVIERE UND ORCHESTER   NOVAK
KONZERT G-DUR FUR KLAVIER -- CEMBALO, 2 VIOL. UND   HAYDN
KONZERT G-DUR FUR KLAVIER -- CEMBALO UND   HANDEL
KONZERT IN A FUR CEMBALO -- KLAVIER -- UND STREICHER   DITTERSDORF,
KONZERT IN A FUR CEMBALO -- KLAVIER -- UND STREICHER   NICHELMANN
KONZERT IN A MINOR FUR ZWEI CEMBALI   KREBS
KONZERT IN B FLAT, OP. 4 NO. 6 FUR KLAVIER -- ORGEL,   HANDEL
KONZERT IN C FUR KLAVIER -- CEMBALO -- UND STREICHER   HAYDN
KONZERT IN C FUR KLAVIER UND STREICHER   GIORDANI
KONZERT IN C FUR KLAVIER UND STREICHORCHESTER,   SCHROTER, J. S.
KONZERT IN D MINOR FUR CEMBALO ODER ORGEL, QUERFLOTE   CORRETTE
KONZERT IN E FLAT -- 1784 -- FUR KLAVIER UND   BEETHOVEN
KONZERT IN F FUR CEMBALO -- ORGEL -- UND STREICHER --   GRAUN
KONZERT IN F FUR CEMBALO UND STREICHER   BACH, C.P.E.
KONZERT IN F FUR VIOLINE, CEMBALO UND STREICHER --   HAYDN
KONZERT IN F MINOR FUR CEMBALO -- KLAVIER -- UND   BACH, J.
KONZERT IN F SHARP MINOR FUR KLAVIER UND ORCHESTER   HILLER
KONZERT IN G FUR CEMBALO UND STREICHORCHESTER   BENDA, R.
KONZERT IN G FUR KLAVIER UND ORCHESTER, KLAVIERAUSZUG   HELM, E.
KONZERT IN G MINOR FUR CEMBALO UND STREICHER   BACH, C.P.E.
KONZERT IN G MINOR FUR CEMBALO UND STREICHORCHESTER   BENDA, R.
KONZERT IN G MINOR FUR KLAVIER UND ORCHESTER, OP. 33   DVORAK
KONZERT NO. 01 FUR KLAVIER UND ORCHESTER, 1950,   HENZE, H.
KONZERT NO. 02 FUR KLAVIER UND KAMMERORCHESTER, OP.   MOESCHINGER
KONZERT NO. 02 FUR KLAVIER UND ORCHESTER,   SUTERMEISTER, H.
KONZERT NO. 02 FUR KLAVIER UND ORCHESTER, OP. 27   SEARLE, H.
KONZERT NO. 02 FUR KLAVIER UND ORCHESTER IN EINEN   HENZE, H.
KONZERT NO. 02 IN G FUR CEMBALO -- KLAVIER -- UND   HAYDN
KONZERT NO. 02 NACH HINDUSTAN, KLAVIERAUSZUG   CHISHOLM, E.
KONZERT NO. 03 FUR KLAVIER UND ORCHESTER,   SUTERMEISTER, H.
KONZERT NO. 05 IN G MINOR   ARNE
KOOKABURRA -- AUSTRALIAN ROUND   CLARK, M. E.
KOPENICKER KLAVIERBUCH, BK. 1   SPIES, L.
KOPENICKER KLAVIERBUCH, BK. 2   SPIES, L.
KOREAN BLUEBIRD   BERNSTEIN, S.
KREISLERIANA, OP. 16   SCHUMANN, R.
KREISLERIANA, OP. 16   SCHUMANN, R.
KREISLERIANA, OP. 16   SCHUMANN, R.
KREISLERIANA, OP. 16   SCHUMANN, R.
KREISLERIANA, OP. 16   SCHUMANN, R.
KREISLERIANA, OP. 16   SCHUMANN, R.
KREISLERIANA, OP. 16   SCHUMANN, R.
KREISLERIANA, OP. 16   SCHUMANN, R.
KRISHNA   DERE
KRISS KROSS KAPERS -- SECOND PIANO PART   NEVIN
KRISS KROSS KAPERS   NEVIN
KUBINIANA OP. 13 --10 PIECES--   APOSTEL
KUCKUCK, KUCKUCK. VARIATIONEN UBER 5 BEKANNTE   TWITTENHOFF
KUM BAH YAH -- AFRICAN FOLK SONG   BROUTMAN--ED
KUNSTLERLEBEN   STRAUSS, J. *
KUNTERBUNT   HUMBERT, G.
KURZE UND LEICHTE STUCKE   WEILL, K.
KURZE UND LEICHTE STUCKE   BACH, C.P.E.
KUTTENBERGER MENUETTBUCHLEIN. 15 MENUETTE AUS DER   SNIZKOVA--ED
KUTZTOWN REEL -- A PA. DUTCH FOLK TUNE   NEARING, H.
KWAZY WABBIT   NEVIN
KWAZY WABBIT   SCHAUM, J.--ED.
KYRENIA   FULEIHAN, A.
L-O-V-E   BRADLEY,
L'AFFAIRE   MYROW, J.
L'AGILITE--25 PROGRESSIVE STUDIES FOR MECHANISM AND   LECOUPPEY, F.
L'ALBUM DE LISETTE ET POULOT   PASCAL, C.
L'ALLEGRO SCIATORE   GILIO, L.
L'ALOUETTE--GLINKA   BALAKIREV
L'ALOUETTE TRANSKRIPTION   GLINKA
L'ANGELUS, IMPROMPTU   GOUNOD, C.
L'APPEL DU PRINTEMPS, SYMPHONIE   DESREZ
L'APPRENTI SORCIER   DUKAS, P.
L'APPRENTI SORCIER   DUKAS, P. *
L'APRES-MIDI D'UN FAUNE   DEBUSSY
L'ARGENTINE -- SILVERY WHISTLE   KETTERER, E.
L'ARLESIENNE. FANTASY. TWO PIANOS, EIGHT HANDS   BIZET, G.
L'ARLESIENNE. FIRST MINUET. TWO PIANOS, EIGHT HANDS   BIZET, G.
L'ARLESIENNE--TWO CONCERT SUITES   BIZET, G.
L'ARLESIENNE-SUITE 1-2   BIZET, G.
L'ARLESIENNE, INTERMEZZO   BIZET, G.
L'ARLESIENNE, INTERMEZZO   BIZET, G.
L'ARLESIENNE, MINUETTO   BIZET, G.
L'ARLESIENNE, 2 CONCERT SUITES   BIZET, G.
L'ARLESIENNE SUITE NO.1   BIZET, G.
L'ARLESIENNE SUITE NO.2   BIZET, G.
L'ARLESIENNE   BIZET, G.
L'ARMONICO PRATICO AL CIMBALO   GASPARINI, F.
L'ARPISTA FANTASTIC, OP. 93 'P'   NEGLIA, F.
L'ART D'ETRE GRAND-PERE, BK. 1   NERINI, E.
L'ART D'ETRE GRAND-PERE, BK. 2   NERINI, E.
L'ART DE TOUCHER LE CLAVECIN   COUPERIN, F.
L'ART DE TOUCHER LE CLAVECIN   COUPERIN, F.
L'ART DE VARIER, OP. 57   REJCHA
L'ART DE VARIER, OP. 57   REJCHA
L'AUTOMNE-VALSE, OP. 170   ALBENIZ, I.
L'ECLOSION   JOACHIM, O.
L'ECRAN DES JEUNES FILLES   ROLAND *
L'ENFANT EN PRIERE   GALOS
L'ENFANT ET LES SORTILEGES -- FIVE O'CLOCK FOX-TROT   RAVEL
L'ENFANT ET LES SORTILEGES   RAVEL
L'ENFANT S'AMUSE -- SUITE OF 5 PIECES   CANNON, P.
L'HABITANT EN ROUTE   MELECCI, A.
L'HEURE ESPAGNOLE   RAVEL
L'HEURE EXQUISE   HAHN, R.

L'HIRONDELLE -- THE SWALLOW --	DAQUIN, C.
L'IL LIZA JANE	LANE, J.--ED.
L'INDISCRET	ROPARTZ
L'INGENUE--VALSE, OP. 81 NO. 1--FOR LEFT HAND ALONE--	KROGMANN, C. W.
L'INSECTARIUM FUR CEMBALO -- KLAVIER	FRANCAIX, J.
L'ISLE JOYEUSE	DEBUSSY
L'ISLE JOYEUSE	DEBUSSY
L'ISLE JOYEUSE	DEBUSSY
L'OEUVRE DE PIANO IN 3 VOLUMES, VOL. 1	ALAIN, J.
L'OEUVRE DE PIANO IN 3 VOLUMES, VOL. 2	ALAIN, J.
L'OEUVRE DE PIANO IN 3 VOLUMES, VOL. 3	ALAIN, J.
L'ORAGE DANS LES ALPES	GALOS
LABBRA CORALLINE	BECUCCI
LABYRINTH DANCE	HAUER, J.
LACES AND FRILLS FROM CHOPIN'S MAZURKA	ROLFE, W.
LACE MAKER LADY	BURNAM
LACHIAN DANCES	JANACEK
LAC DE COME, LE	GALOS
LAC DE GARDE, LE	GALOS
LADIES DRILL MARCH	BURNAM
LADS AND LASSIES GAY	HALL, F.
LADYBUG WALTZ	SPECTOR
LADY BUG	SCHUMANN, R.
LADY BUG	SCHUMANN, R.
LADY CAPRICE	HOLT, EILSEL
LADY FAN TAN	BRODSKY, M.
LADY GRACEFUL	HOLT, EILSEL
LADY IN VELVET	PECHMAN
LADY IN WAITING, THE	ANDERSON, L.
LADY L - THEME	FRANCAIX *
LADY MOON, REVERIE	HOPKINS, H.
LADY OF SHALOTT, THE -- EXCERP FROM THE BALLET	BLISS, A.
LADY OF SPAIN -- SIMPLIFIED	EVANS
LADY OF SPAIN	EVANS
LADY OF SPAIN	EVANS *
LADY OF SPAIN	EVANS
LADY OF SPAIN	EVANS
LADY POMPADOUR	MOREL, G.
LAGOON BOOGIE	LYON
LAGOON WALTZ, OP. 411	STRAUSS, J.
LAGOON	THOMPSON, J.
LAI	MANENTI
LAKE, THE	RATHBONE, G.
LAKE BY MOONLIGHT	GILLNESS
LAKE IN THE MOUNTAINS	VAUGHAN
LAKE MIRROR	MORITZ, E.
LAKE OF VAN SONATA	HOVHANESS, A.
LAMBERTS CLAVICHORD	HOWELLS, H.
LAMBS IN THE VALLEY	DITTENHAVER
LAMENTATIONS DE RACHEL	SAMINSKY
LAMENTATION OF A DOLL	FRANCK, C.
LAMENTATION	WARD
LAMENTO CAMPERO	UGARTE
LAMENTO IN E MINOR	BACH, W.F.
LAMENT	ALLEN
LAMENT	EDWARDS
LAME D'ARGENT	LATOUR
LAME DUCK, THE	HAYES
LANCER'S QUADRILLE	SCHAUM, J.--ED.
LANCERS, THE	LEDUC, A.
LANCIERS, LES	BEYER, F.
LANDLERISCHE TANZE -- SET	SCHUBERT
LANDLER AND OTHER DANCES	SCHUBERT
LANDLER UND KINDERMARSCH	SCHUBERT
LANDLER	MOZART, W. A.
LANDLER	SUK
LANDLICHE GARTEN	GRAINGER, P.
LANDMARKS OF EARLY AMERICAN MUSIC 1760-1800--32	GOLDMAN--ED. *
LANDSCAPES OF ISRAEL	STUTSCHEWSKY, J.
LAND OF DREAMS	
LAND OF HOPE AND GLORY--THEME FROM POMP AND	ELGAR, E.
LAND OF HOPE AND GLORY	ELGAR, E.
LAND OF HOPE AND GLORY	ELGAR, E.
LANGAGE DES FLEURS, LE	GALOS
LANGAGE DE MARGUERITES, LE	STREABBOG
LANGUAGE, THE	PRIESING *
LANGUAGE OF THE PIANO	BRAZELTON
LANTERNS	
LARA'S THEME - 'DOCTOR ZHIVAGO'	JARRE, M.
LARA'S THEME - DOCTOR ZHIVAGO	WILLIAMS,
LARA'S THEME - DOCTOR ZHIVAGO	
LARGER PIANO COMPOSITIONS, BK. 2	BACH, J.S.
LARGE NOTE PIANO PIECES	
LARGE NOTE PIANO SOLOS FOR READING AND RHYTHM	
LARGHETTO AND ALLEGRO IN E FLAT	MOZART, W. A.
LARGHETTO A CAPRICCIO	HUMMEL, J. N.
LARGHETTO UND ALLEGRO IN E FLAT FUR 2 KLAVIERE -- OHNE	MOZART, W. A.
LARGO -- NEVER MORE TO ROAM --	DVORAK
LARGO FROM 'SERSE'	HANDEL
LARGO FROM 'SERSE'	HANDEL
LARGO FROM 'XERXES'	HANDEL
LARGO FROM 'XERXES'	HANDEL
LARGO FROM THE ''NEW WORLD'' SYMPHONY	DVORAK
LARGO FROM THE 'NEW WORLD SYMPHONY'	DVORAK
LARGO FROM THE 'NEW WORLD SYMPHONY'	DVORAK
LARGO FROM THE 'NEW WORLD SYMPHONY'	DVORAK
LARGO FROM THE CLAVIER CONCERTO IN F MINOR	BACH, J.S.
LARGO FROM THE NEW WORLD SYMPHONY	DVORAK
LARGO IN E FLAT FROM 'L'INVERNO' -- CONCERTO	VIVALDI
LARGO	CALTABIANO
LARGO	DVORAK
LARGO	DVORAK
LARGO	HANDEL
LARGO	HANDEL
LARGO	HANDEL
LARGO	MULE
LARGO	MULE
LARGO	MULE
LARK, THE	GLINKA
LARK, THE	GLINKA
LARK, THE	GLINKA
LARK, THE	MOSHER
LARK'S MORNING SONG	KOLLING, C.
LARK'S SONG, ALBUM FOR THE YOUNG	TSCHAIKOWSKY
LARKSPURS	PANELLA, L.
LARKSPUR	ROLFE, W.
LAST DREAM OF THE VIRGIN	MASSENET, J.
LAST GOODBYE BLUES	JOHNSON, S. *
LAST HOPE, THE, OP. 16	GOTTSCHALK
LAST HOPE	GOTTSCHALK
LAST MAZURKA, THE --F MINOR	CHOPIN
LAST MUSICAL THOUGHTS	WEBER, VON
LAST PAVANE, THE	GRANADOS
LAST PIECES	FELDMAN
LAST RHAPSODY THEME, THE	
LAST ROSE OF SUMMER	GROOMS--ED
LAST ROSE OF SUMMER	HITZEL--ED
LAST SMILE, THE	WOLLENHAUPT
LAST SPRING, OP. 34 NO. 2	GRIEG
LAST SPRING	GILLOCK
LAST SPRING	GILLOCK
LAST SPRING	GILLOCK
LAST TIME I SAW HIM	BRADLEY,
LAST WALTZ	WEBER, VON
LAS FRIAS MONTANAS	RUIZ ARMENGOL,
LAS PALOMAS	FICHER
LATERNE, LATERNE, SONNE, MOND UND STERNE. 23	DIETRICH--ED.
LATERNE, LATERNE, SONNE, MOND UND STERNE	DIETRICH--ED.
LATE PIANO WORKS	LISZT
LATIN-AMERICAN ART MUSIC--SELECTED FROM THE WORKS OF	LANGE, F.--ED.
LATIN AMERICAN FAVORITES	TUCKMAN
LATIN AMERICAN GAME SONGS	DE CESARE
LATIN AMERICAN MINIATURES	PERRIN
LATIN AMERICAN MUSIC	SCHAUM, J.--ED.
LATIN AMERICAN RHYTHMS AND IMPROVISATIONS FOR PIANO	MORALES
LATIN HOLIDAY	BASTIEN
LATIN RHYTHMS	DRAO--ED
LATIN WITH BAGPIPE	OGLE, L.
LATTER-DAY LULLABIES	WARD-STEINMAN,
LATVIAN LULLABY	BENTLEY
LAUDA, FUGA, AND CAVATINA	LOMBARDO
LAUGHING CLOWN	SCHER, W.
LAUGHING GIANT	SCHER, W.
LAUGHING SONG -- FROM 'DIE FLEDERMAUS'	STRAUSS, J.
LAUGHING TROMBONE POLKA	SIMPSON
LAUGHING WATERS	BECK
LAUNCHING A ROCKET	BURNAM
LAUNE, OP. 11	KRICKA
LAURA LEE	TREVARTHEN, R.
LAURA	LANE, J.--ED.
LAURA	RASKIN, D.
LAUTERBACH	SCHIEFELBEIN, F.
LAVAPIES -- FROM IBERIA	ALBENIZ, I.
LAVENDEL-FUGE	DIETRICH
LAVENDER'S BLUE	SCHAUM, J.--ED.
LAVENDER LADY, THE	DUNHILL, T.
LAWRENCE WELK'S AROUND THE WORLD --NO. 3	WELK, L.
LAWRENCE WELK'S POLKA FOLIOS --NO. 1	WELK, L.
LAZY AFTERNOON	SINGER, L.--ED
LAZY ANDY ANT -- TWO PIANOS AND VOICE	WOLPE
LAZY DAZE	KAHN, M.
LAZY LIZ	ROBINSON, W. E.
LAZY MARY AND OH DEAR, ONE PIANO - SIX HANDS	MACGREGOR
LAZY MOON -- PIANO SOLO WITH WORDS	JOHNSON, R.
LAZY PICCANINNY	MOWREY, D.
LAZY RHAPSODY	
LAZY RHAPSODY	
LAZY RIVER	SCHIEFELBEIN, F.
LAZY STROLL, A	SLATES, P.
LAZY WIND	WADLEY
LA 'NIMURA', DANSE	MIGOT
LA BALADINE	LYSBERG, C. B.
LA BANDOLINE	COUPERIN, F.
LA BELLE HELENE	OFFENBACH
LA BOHEME, MUSETTA'S WALTZ	PUCCINI
LA BOHEME, SELECTION	PUCCINI
LA BOITE A JEUX -- PIECES ENFANTINES	WERNER, J.
LA BOITE A MUSIQUE, BK. 1	HENRY, C.
LA BOITE A MUSIQUE, BK. 2	HENRY, C.
LA BOITE A MUSIQUE, BK. 3	HENRY, C.
LA BONDOLINE, RONDEAU	COUPERIN, P.
LA BONNE JOURNEE - BAVARDAGE	FEVRIER
LA BONNE JOURNEE - JOYEUX REVEIL	FEVRIER
LA BONNE JOURNEE - SAUTE-MOUTON	FEVRIER
LA BOURREE DE VINCENT	RAMEAU
LA CAMPANELLA	LISZT *
LA CAMPANELLA	LISZT *
LA CAMPANELLA	LISZT
LA CAMPANELLA	LISZT
LA CAMPANELLA	LISZT
LA CARINA	MOSCHELES, I.
LA CAROLINE	BACH, C.P.E.
LA CASCADE, OP. 223	HEINS, C.
LA CASCADE, OP. 37	PAUER
LA CASCADE DES ROSES, OP. 80	ASCHER
LA CATHEDRALE ENGLOUTIE FROM PRELUDES, BK. 1	DEBUSSY
LA CATHEDRALE ENGLOUTIE	DEBUSSY
LA CHACE FUR CEMBALO SOLO	HUBER
LA CHAMADE	FRONTIERE, D.
LA CHANSON DE FORTUNIO	OFFENBACH
LA CHANSON DE FORTUNIO	OFFENBACH
LA CHASSE INFERNALE, GALOP	KOELLING
LA CHASSE	BURGMUELLER
LA CHATELAINE	LE DUC
LA CHUMPARSITA	RODRIGUEZ, R.
LA CHUPADERO, RHUMBA	REISFELD
LA CINQUANTAINE	GABRIEL, M.
LA CINQUANTAINE	MARIE
LA CLE DU PIANISTE	VERNY, F.
LA CONGA	DVORINE
LA CUCARACHA BAILARINA	MELVIN, B.
LA CUCARACHA BOOGIE	STEINER
LA CUCARACHA	GOULD--ED
LA CUCARACHA	MERKUR--ED
LA CUMPARSITA	RODRIGUEZ, R.
LA CZARINA -- MAZURKA	GANNE
LA CZARINE, MAZURKA, EASY	GANNE
LA CZARINE	GANNE
LA DAME DANS LA LUNE	FRANCAIX, J.
LA DAME DANS LA LUNE	FRANCAIX, J.
LA DANSE DES FEES, POLKA	JAELL
LA DANZARINA	REISER, V.
LA DANZA	ROSSINI, G.
LA DIABOLIQUE, ETUDE	LEYBACH, I.
LA DONNA E MOBILE	VERDI
LA FETE CHEZ THERESE	HANN, R.
LA FIESTA BOOGIE	KENT, A.
LA FILEUSE, OP. 157 NO. 2	RAFF, J.
LA FILEUSE F SHARP, OP. 157 NO. 2	RAFF, J.
LA FILEUSE OP. 157 NO. 2	RAFF, J.
LA FILLEUSE	RAFF
LA FILLE AUX CHEVEAUX DE LIN	DEBUSSY
LA FLEURIE	COUPERIN, F.
LA FONTAINE, ODYLLE, OP. 31	LYSBERG, C. B.
LA FONTAINE, OP. 221	BOHM
LA GIARA -- DER GROSSE KRUG	CASELLA, A.
LA GIARA	CASELLA, A.
LA GIOCONDA, DANCE OF HOURS	PONCHIELLI
LA GITANA, WALTZ	BUCALOSSI
LA GOLONDRINA -- THE SWALLOW, EASY	SERRADELL
LA GOLONDRINA -- THE SWALLOW	SERRADELL
LA GOLONDRINA	SERRADELL
LA GOLONDRINA	SERRADELL
LA GRACE	BOHM

Title	Composer
LA GRISI	TOMASI, H.
LA GROTTE DE CRISTAL, POLKA-MAZURKA	BARDIN-ROYER
LA HABANERA	LECUONA
LA HARPE -- HARP SOUNDS	JUNGMAN, A.
LA JEUNESS D'HERCULE, OP. 50	SAINT-SAENS
LA JOLIE HONGROISE, VALSE	FISCHER
LA KORRIGANE	WIDOR, CH.
LA LECTURE AU PIANO, VOL. 1 - 86 EXERCISES	BERIOT
LA LECTURE MUSICALE AU PIANO, PART 1	ROUGNON
LA LECTURE MUSICALE AU PIANO, PART 2	ROUGNON
LA LIEBRE Y LA TORTUGA	FICHER
LA LISONJERA, EASY	CHAMINADE
LA LISONJERA	CHAMINADE
LA MADONNA	SWEET, A.
LA MANOLA -- SERENADE ESPAGNOLE	EILENBERG
LA MANO ABAJO, CONGA	REISFELD
LA MARCHANDE D'EAU	ARROYO, R.
LA MARIAGE DE LA TROUHADEC	AURIC
LA MARIPOSA	SANDOVAL
LA MATTCHICHE--CELEBRATED SPANISH MARCH	BOREL-CLERC, C.
LA MATTINATA	LEONCAVALLO
LA MELODIEUSE	DAQUIN, C.
LA MEMOIRE	LEVENSON, B.
LA MER	DEBUSSY
LA MER	DEBUSSY
LA MER	DEBUSSY
LA MONA Y LOS MONOS	FICHER
LA NUIT	CACAVAS
LA PALOMA -- THE DOVE	YRADIER
LA PALOMA	YRADIER
LA PALOMA	YRADIER
LA PASTORALE	AURIC
LA PERI	DUKAS, P.
LA PETITE FILEUSE, OP. 114	BINET
LA PETITE POLKA CANADIENNE	MELECCI, A.
LA PLAINTE, AU LOIN, DU FAUNE	DUKAS, P.
LA PLAYA DE MALAGA	HARPER
LA PLUS QUE LENTE, VALSE	DEBUSSY
LA PLUS QUE LENTE, VALSE	DEBUSSY
LA PLUS QUE LENTE	DEBUSSY
LA POULE	RAMEAU
LA POULE	RAMEAU
LA POULE	RAMEAU
LA PRECIEUSE IM STILE VON COUPERIN	KREISLER
LA PRIMA DONNA, SCHOT.	KING
LA PUERTA DEL VINO FROM PRELUDES, BK. 2	DEBUSSY
LA REGATTA VENETIANA	LISZT
LA REGATTA VENITIANA	ROSSINI, G. *
LA ROSITA	DUPONT
LA SERENADE INTERROMPUE FROM PRELUDES, BK. 1	DEBUSSY
LA SERENADE	METRA, O.
LA SERENATA--TRANSCRIPTION AFTER MELODY BY BRAGA	HITZ, F.
LA SERENATA	BRAGA
LA SERENATA	BRAGA
LA SERENATA	BRAGA
LA SERENATTA -- ANGEL'S SERENADE	WEYBRIGHT
LA SORELLA, A SPANISH MARCH	ALBERT, C. D'
LA SORELLA	DELIBES, L.
LA SOURCE	VI CHIARI
LA SPAGNOLA -- SPAN. MAIDEN	CHIATRI
LA SPAGNOLA	DICHIARI
LA SPAGNOLA	DICHIARI
LA TERRASSE DES AUDIENCES FROM PRELUDES, BK. 2	DEBUSSY
LA TRAGEDIE DE SOLOME	SCHMITT, F.
LA TRAVIATA, FANTASIE	VERDI
LA TRAVIATA, PRELUDE	VERDI
LA TROMPETTE CLASSIQUE, VOL. B POUR LE PIANO	POLLIN, N.
LA TZIGANE	GANNE
LA VALSE	RAVEL
LA VALSE	RAVEL
LA VALSE	RAVEL
LA VALSE	RAVEL
LA VIERGE-DERNIER SOMMEIL	MASSENET, J.
LA VIRTUOSITE, VOL.1	KOEHLER
LA VIRTUOSITE, VOL.2,BK.1--EXERCISES--	KOEHLER
LA VIRTUOSITE, VOL.2,BK.2--OCTAVES--	KOEHLER
LA VIRTUOSITE, VOL.3,BK.1	KOEHLER
LA VIRTUOSITE, VOL.3,BK.2	KOEHLER
LA ZINGANA, MAZURKA	BOHM
LA ZINGNA MAZURKA	BOHM
LEAD, KINDLY LIGHT	DYKES
LEAD, KINDLY LIGHT	FREEMAN--ED.
LEAD KINDLY LIGHT, A HYMN	WEYBRIGHT
LEAPING SQUIRREL	TRUXELL, E.
LEAP FROG	BURTON
LEARNING TO DANCE	KAHL
LEARNING TO PLAY, BK. 1	STECHER *
LEARNING TO PLAY, BK. 2	STECHER *
LEARNING TO PLAY, BK. 3	STECHER *
LEARNING TO PLAY, BK. 4	STECHER *
LEARNING TO READ, LEARNING TO PLAY	STANISLAUS
LEARN TO FINGER WITHOUT NUMBERS	CURCIO
LEARN TO PLAY GOSPEL PIANO	HARTNESS, R.
LEAVES FROM MY NOTEBOOK	WILSON
LEAVES IN THE WIND	VALENTI, M.
LECONS, CHACONNE, PIECES, 6 GRAND FUGUES	HANDEL
LECONS, PIECES, GRAND FUGUES, FUGHETTES	HANDEL
LECONS DE CLAVECIN	BEMETZRIEDER, A.
LECUONAS BEST MADE EASIER FOR YOU	LECUONA
LEDGER LINES AND SPACES THRU CHORD PROGRESSION	CRERIE, E.
LEE RIGG, THE	GOLDMAN, R.
LEFT, RIGHT, MARCH ALONG	KETTERER, E.
LEFT, RIGHT MARCH	GARROW, L.
LEFT FOOT, RIGHT FOOT -- ORIGINAL	SCHIEFELBEIN, F.
LEFT FOOT, RIGHT FOOT -- SIMPLIFIED	SCHIEFELBEIN, F.
LEFT FOOT, RIGHT FOOT MARCH FOLIO	
LEFT FOOT, RIGHT FOOT MARCH	SCHIEFELBEIN, F.
LEFT HAND INVERSIONS OF FIVE CHOPIN ETUDES FOR PIANO	CHAVEZ, C.
LEFT HAND RHYTHMS	HENDERSON, R.
LEFT HAND STUDIES, BK. 1	SCHAUM, J.
LEFT HAND STUDIES, BK. 2	SCHAUM, J.
LEGATO AND NON LEGATO	MIROVITCH, A.
LEGEND, OP. 12 NO. 6	PROKOFIEFF
LEGENDEN, OP. 59	DVORAK
LEGENDES NO. 2--ST. FRANCOIS DE PAULE, MARCHANT SUR	LISZT
LEGENDE DE NUIT	MASON, I.
LEGENDE EPIQUE -- SET	POOT, M.
LEGENDE ET PASSEGGIATA	NOEL, P. *
LEGENDE HEROIQUE	BOSKOFF
LEGENDE VOM GLUCK, OP. 83	FOERSTER
LEGENDE	BECK
LEGENDE	DE FRANCMESNIL
LEGENDE	HAUSERMAN, J.
LEGENDS, OP. 59 -- BK. 1	DVORAK
LEGENDS, OP. 59 -- BK. 2	DVORAK
LEGENDS	BECK
LEGEND OF AN ANCIENT LAND	RICKER, E.
LEGEND OF SLEEPY HOLLOW, THE -- A PROGRAM CONCERTO --	KASSCHAU, H.
LEGEND OF THE GLASS MOUNTAIN, THE	ROTA
LEGEND OF THE GLASS MOUNTAIN, THE	ROTA
LEGEND OF THE WATERS	GREY, F.
LEGEND	FAITH
LEGER LINE CIRCUS	DUNYON
LEGER LINE DRILLS AND PIECES	STEINER
LEGINKA	KHATCHATURIAN
LEHRER UND SCHULER, HOBOKEN 17A	HAYDN
LEICHTES MARSCHBUCH -- ERFOLGREICHE MARSCHE	LECHNER--ED
LEICHTES TANZBUCH	KROME--ED
LEICHTE CLAVIER-SONATEN DES 18 JAHRHUNDERTS	KREUTZ--ED
LEICHTE FUGEN UND KLEINE STUCKE	TELEMANN, G.P.
LEICHTE KLAVIERMUSIK DER ROMANTIK UND NACHROMANTIK	EMONTS, F.--ED
LEICHTE KLAVIERMUSIK DES BAROK	EMONTS, F.--ED
LEICHTE KLAVIERSTUCKE. 12 STUCKE DES SECHS- UND	MOZART, W. A.
LEICHTE KLAVIERSTUCKE A. D., MUSIKALISCHEN	BACH, J.
LEICHTE KLAVIERSTUCKE VON BACHS SOHNEN BIS BEETHOVEN	EMONTS, F.--ED
LEICHTE SONATEN -- G, A MINOR, G MINOR, D, WQ 22, 33,	BACH, C.P.E.
LEICHTE SONATINEN. 16 KLEINE STUCK	VANHAL
LEICHTE STUCKE	TUERK
LEICHTE TANZE, HEFT 01	SEIBER, M.
LEICHTE TANZE, HEFT 02	SEIBER, M.
LEICHTE TANZE -- HOBOKEN 9-10, NO. 1-12 UND HOBOKEN	HAYDN
LEICHTE TENZE	SEIBER, M.
LEIPZIGER KLAVIERBUCH -- SMALL PIANO WORKS BY DEHNERT,	DEHNERT
LEIPZIG PIANO MUSIC - PAST AND PRESENT	
LEISE FLEHEN--SERENADE	SCHUBERT *
LEISE FLEHEN MEINE LIEDER -- 23 SCHUBERT MELODIES IN	SCHUBERT *
LEISE FLEHEN	LISZT *
LEMONADE FOR SALE	BRODSKY, M.
LEMONS AND LIMES -- A LA LIMA Y AL LIMON	DE LEON *
LEMON DROP	WALLINGTON, G.
LENORE -- SYMPHONIC POEM --	DUPARC, H.
LENORE -- SYMPHONIC POEM --	DUPARC, H.
LENTO, FROM 'TWO PIERROT PIECES'	SCOTT, C.
LENTO --2 PIERROT PIECES--	SCOTT, C.
LENTO	GEORGE
LENTO	SCOTT, C.
LENTO	SCOTT, C.
LENTO	SCOTT, C.
LENTO	SCOTT, C.
LENTO	SCOTT, C.
LENTO	SCOTT, C.
LEONOREN-OUV. OP. 72 NO. 3	BEETHOVEN
LEROY ANDERSON'S BEST	ANDERSON, L.
LESSONS IN MUSIC WRITING, PART 1	BERLIN, B.
LESSONS IN MUSIC WRITING, PART 2	BERLIN, B.
LESSONS IN MUSIC WRITING, PART 3	BERLIN, B.
LES ADIEUX	DUSSEK, J.
LES BARRICADES MYSTERIEUSES	COUPERIN, F.
LES BICHES -- ADAGIETTO NO. 2	POULENC, F.
LES BICHES -- ANDANTINO NO. 3	POULENC, F.
LES BICHES -- BALLET	POULENC, F.
LES BICHES -- COMPLETE	POULENC, F.
LES BICHES -- OVERTURE NO. 1	POULENC, F.
LES BOUQUINISTES DU QUAI MALAQUAIS	MARTINU, B.
LES CAPRICES DE MA POUPEE --PETITE SUITE--	DEFOSSEZ
LES CHAMEAUX	DAMASE, J. M.
LES CINQ ETAGES	SAUGUET
LES CINQ POSITIONS--WILHELM HANSEN EDITION	SKJERNE--ED.
LES CLASSIQUES FAVORIS DU PIANO	LACK, T.
LES CLOCHETTES	THOMPSON, J.
LES CONTES D'HOFFMANN--BARCAROLLE. INTERMEZZO	OFFENBACH
LES CONTES D'HOFFMANN--BARCAROLLE. O BELLE NUIT	OFFENBACH
LES CYCLOPS	RAMEAU
LES DANSES EXTRAVAGANTES DU GNOME FARCEUR	BOUTRY
LES DELICES DE VIENNE, VALSE	SAUER
LES EXERCISES ET LES JEUX -- 16 PROGRESSIVE PIECES FOR	MARCEL, L. A.
LES EXERCISES ET LES JEUX -- 16 PROGRESSIVE PIECES FOR	MARCEL, L. A.
LES FOUS DE BASSAN	DUBOIS, P. M.
LES HABITS NEUF DE ROI -- THE KING'S NEW CLOTHES	TANSMAN, A.
LES INDES GALANTES -- FIRST SUITE	RAMEAU
LES INSOLITES	BONDON, J.
LES JARDINS DANS LA PLUIE -- GARDENS IN THE RAIN	DEBUSSY
LES LILLIPUTIENNES, OP. 125	BINET
LES MILLIONS D'ARLEQUIN	DRIGO, R.
LES MOIS, OP. 74, BK. 1	ALKAN
LES MOIS, OP. 74, BK. 2	ALKAN
LES MOIS, OP. 74, BK. 3	ALKAN
LES MOIS, OP. 74, BK. 4	ALKAN
LES MYRTLES, VALSE DE SALON	WACHS, P.
LES OFFRANDES OUBLIEES	MESSIAEN, O.
LES PAGINETTES, OP. 133	BINET
LES PATINEURS, SKATERS	WALDTEUFEL, E.
LES PETITS ARTISTES	TREMER, J.
LES PETITS METIERS, BK. 1	ROSENTHAL, M.
LES PETITS METIERS, BK. 2	ROSENTHAL, M.
LES PETITS MOULINS A VENT	COUPERIN, F.
LES PETITS POLKEURS, POLKA MIGNONNE	DESSAUX
LES PIECES DE CLAVESSIN	CHAMBONNIERES,
LES PIERROTS, WALTZ	STREABBOG
LES PRELUDES--SYMPHONIC POEM NO. 3	LISZT
LES PRINCIPES DU CLAVECIN	DE
LES RENCONTRES	IBERT
LES REVERANCES NUPTIALES	BOISMORTIER, J.
LES RITOURNELLES	MARTINU, B.
LES SAUVAGES	RAMEAU
LES SOIREES DE NAZELLES	POULENC, F.
LES SONGES MERVEILLEUX	BITSCH
LES SONS ET LES PARFUMS FROM PRELUDES , BK. 1	DEBUSSY
LES SPIRALES, OP. 36	STEFFEN, W.
LES SYLPHES--IMPROMPTU-VALSE	BACHMANN, G.
LES SYLPHES, VALSE	BACHMANN, G.
LES SYLPHES, VALSE	BACHMANN, G.
LES SYLPHIDES	HEINS, C.
LES SYLVAINS -- THE FAUNS --	CHAMINADE
LES TOURBILLONS	DANDRIEU, J.
LES TRICOTEUSES	COUPERIN, F.
LET'ER GO	WOOD, W.
LET'S ARRANGE CHRISTMAS SONGS	ZEPP--ED
LET'S BE GAY -- POLISH FOLK SONG	WEYBRIGHT
LET'S BUY A CLOCK	SMITH, H.
LET'S CALYPSO	TOWNSEND
LET'S COMPOSE A SONG	ZEPP
LET'S DANCE AND SING	REBE
LET'S DANCE GAY	GRAINGER, P.
LET'S DISCOVER MUSIC - MY FIRST PIANO BOOK	CROCKER, D.
LET'S DISCOVER MUSIC - MY FIRST THEORY WORK BOOK	CROCKER, D.
LET'S DISCOVER MUSIC - MY FIRST WRITING BOOK	CROCKER, D.
LET'S DO DUETS	HOWELL, I.--ED
LET'S DO THE POLKA	KLEINMAN, H.
LET'S FLY TO THE MOON	CATIZONE, J. M.
LET'S GET AWAY FROM IT ALL	
LET'S GET TECHNICAL	ZEPP
LET'S GO BOOGIE WOOGIE	GIRLAMO, F.
LET'S GO BOOGIE	REID

LET'S GO HIKING	BENJAMIN
LET'S GO LATIN AMERICAN	GIRLAMO, F.
LET'S GO TO THE SYMPHONY	TROJE-MILLER--ED
LET'S HAVE FUN	OBENCHAIN, V.
LET'S HAVE FUN	STEVENS, E.
LET'S IMPROVISE - BOOK 1	ZEPP
LET'S IMPROVISE - BOOK 2	ZEPP
LET'S JOIN THE ARMY	THOMPSON, J.--ED
LET'S LEARN ALL THE NOTES AND READ BETTER	ALLISON, I.
LET'S LEARN CHORDS - BOOK 1	ZEPP
LET'S LEARN CHORDS - BOOK 2	ZEPP
LET'S LEARN MAJOR SCALES AND CHORDS	ZEPP
LET'S LEARN MINOR SCALES AND CHORDS	ZEPP
LET'S LEARN TO COUNT - BOOK 1	EMIG, L.
LET'S LEARN TO COUNT - BOOK 2	EMIG, L.
LET'S LOOK OUTDOORS	STEVENS, L.
LET'S MAKE MUSIC --50 PIECES FOR THE PIANO CLASS--	ENOCH
LET'S PLAY A JOKE	ROZIN
LET'S PLAY A LIMERICK	ROZIN
LET'S PLAY A RIDDLE	ROZIN
LET'S PLAY CHRISTMAS CAROLS	ZEPP--ED
LET'S PLAY CHRISTMAS DUETS	ZEPP--ED
LET'S PLAY CHRISTMAS FAVORITES	ZEPP--ED
LET'S PLAY DUETS, BK. 1	WILSON, S.
LET'S PLAY DUETS, BK. 2	WILSON, S.
LET'S PLAY DUETS	DITTENHAVER
LET'S PLAY FAVORITES	ZEPP--ED
LET'S PLAY HYMNS	KREUTZER--ED
LET'S PLAY HYMNS	KREUTZER
LET'S PLAY HYMNS	ZEPP--ED
LET'S PLAY MORE FAVORITES	ZEPP--ED
LET'S PLAY PLAYER-PIANO STYLE	WATSON--ED.
LET'S PLAY TAG	FOLDES
LET'S PLAY TAG	HARVEY, VIVIEN
LET'S PLAY TOGETHER, 3 VOLS. 18 SHORT, EASY AND	ANTIGA
LET'S PLAY TRIOS FOR ONE PIANO -- SIX HANDS	RENNICK, E.
LET'S PLAY TRIOS	RENNICK, E.
LET'S PLAY WITH TWO HANDS	BLAKE
LET'S PLAY	KETTERER, E.
LET'S TRANSPOSE	ZEPP
LET'S WALTZ	HIBBS, C.
LET'S WATCH THE CLOCK	ENDRES, O.
LET'S WRITE AND PLAY	BURROWS *
LETS GO TO THE THEATRE	LAST, J.
LETS PLAY A PIANO DUET, BK. 1	GARSCIA
LETS PLAY A PIANO DUET, BK. 2	GARSCIA
LETS PLAY CAROLS	BERMONT, H.--ED
LETS PLAY DUETS	TATE, P.
LETTERS AND NOTES--LAWSON-GOULD EDITION	PARKER, A.--ED.
LETTERS TO A FRIEND	GRETCHANINOFF
LETTER FROM AUNTIE	LICHNER, P.
LET IT BE ME	BRIMHALL,
LET IT BE ME	CURTIS *
LET IT BE	LENNON *
LET IT SNOW, LET IT SNOW	BRIMHALL,
LET ME CALL YOU SWEETHEART --BIG NOTES	BRYANT--ED.
LET ME CALL YOU SWEETHEART --LARGE NOTE--	WHITSON *
LET ME CALL YOU SWEETHEART	FRIEDMAN
LET ME CALL YOU SWEETHEART	SCHAUM, J.
LET ME CALL YOU SWEETHEART	WHITSON *
LET ME CALL YOU SWEETHEART	WHITSON *
LET THERE BE PEACE ON EARTH	BRIMHALL,
LET THE SUNSHINE IN	LANE, J.--ED.
LET US HAVE MUSIC SERIES - CHRISTMAS	
LET US HAVE MUSIC SERIES - MARCHING	
LET US HAVE MUSIC SERIES - PIANO, JUNIOR --125--	
LET US HAVE MUSIC SERIES - PIANO, VOL. 1 --86--	
LET US HAVE MUSIC SERIES - PIANO, VOL. 2 --48--	
LET US HAVE MUSIC SERIES - YOUNG PEOPLE --PIANO WITH	
LEVANTE. TEN MELODIES AND DANCE THEMES	ESPLA
LEVINE'S PIANO COURSE - BOOK 1	LEVINE
LEVINE'S PIANO COURSE - BOOK 2	LEVINE
LEXICON OF BEASTIES, A	ZANINELLI
LEYENDA, BARCAROLLE -- NO. 2, FROM RECUERDOS DE VIAJE	ALBENIZ, I.
LEYENDA - ASTURIAS -	ALBENIZ, I.
LEYENDA DEL VIEJO APARCERO	LASALA
LEYENDA DE LA GIRALDA, LA, OP. 40	TURINA, J.
LEYENDA	ALBENIZ, I.
LE BAISER DE L'ENFANT-JESUS	MESSIAEN, O.
LE BAL. SUITE	LESUR, D.
LE BEAU PAPILLON	GARROW, L.
LE BOBINO	GOLDMAN, R.
LE BON PASTEUR -- FROM LE MARTYR DE ST. SEBASTIEN	DEBUSSY
LE CAHIER DU LECTEUR OU LA RECREATION PIANISTIQUE, BK.	PASCAL, C.
LE CAHIER DU LECTEUR OU LA RECREATION PIANISTIQUE, BK.	PASCAL, C.
LE CANTIQUE DES CANTIQUES -- BALLET CHANTE	HONEGGER, A.
LE CARNAVAL DES ANIMAUX, NO. 01 -- INTRODUCTION ET	SAINT-SAENS
LE CARNAVAL DES ANIMAUX, NO. 02 -- POULES ET COQS	SAINT-SAENS
LE CARNAVAL DES ANIMAUX, NO. 03 -- HEMIONES	SAINT-SAENS
LE CARNAVAL DES ANIMAUX, NO. 04 -- TORTUES	SAINT-SAENS
LE CARNAVAL DES ANIMAUX, NO. 05 -- L'ELEPHANT	SAINT-SAENS
LE CARNAVAL DES ANIMAUX, NO. 06 -- KANGOUROUS	SAINT-SAENS
LE CARNAVAL DES ANIMAUX, NO. 07 -- AQUARIUM	SAINT-SAENS
LE CARNAVAL DES ANIMAUX, NO. 08 -- PERSONNAGES A	SAINT-SAENS
LE CARNAVAL DES ANIMAUX, NO. 09 -- LE COUCOU AU FOND	SAINT-SAENS
LE CARNAVAL DES ANIMAUX, NO. 10 -- VOLIERE	SAINT-SAENS
LE CARNAVAL DES ANIMAUX, NO. 11 -- PIANISTES	SAINT-SAENS
LE CARNAVAL DES ANIMAUX, NO. 12 -- FOSSILES	SAINT-SAENS
LE CARNAVAL DES ANIMAUX, NO. 13 -- LE CYGNE	SAINT-SAENS
LE CARNAVAL DES ANIMAUX, NO. 14 -- FINAL	SAINT-SAENS
LE CARNAVAL DES ANIMAUX -- COMPLETE	SAINT-SAENS
LE CAVALIER FANTASTIQUE--ETUDE ARTISTIQUE, OP. 42, NO.	GODARD, B.
LE CHANT DE LA MER	SAMAZEUILH
LE CHANT DU BATELIER	GALOS
LE CHANT DU BERGER	GALOS
LE CHEMIN DE FER, OP. 27	ALKAN
LE CHEVALIER ET LA DAMOISELLE	GAUBERT, P.
LE CID -- BALLET EXTRACT	MASSENET, J.
LE COIN DES ENFANTS	GARTENLAUB, O.
LE COUCOU	DAQUIN, C.
LE COUCOU	DAQUIN, C.
LE CYGNE -- THE SWAN	SAINT-SAENS
LE CYGNE -- THE SWAN	SAINT-SAENS
LE DESIR, OP. 14	CRAMER, H.
LE DESIR	CRAMER, H.
LE DIABLE DANS LE BEFROI	INGHELBRECHT, D.
LE DOUX SOMMEIL DES FEES -- FROM 'L'ALBUM DE LISETTE	PASCAL, C.
LE FESTIN D'ESOPE, OP. 39	ALKAN
LE FESTIN DE L'ARAIGNEE, OP. 17	ROUSSEL, A.
LE FOU DE LA DAME -- SARABANDE	DELANNOY
LE GIBET FROM GASPARD DE LA NUIT	RAVEL
LE GRILLON DU FOYER	MASSENET, J.
LE JARDINIER DE SAMOS	IBERT
LE LAC DE COME	GALOS
LE LIVRE D'ANNE-MARIE	MIGOT
LE LIVRE DE NOEMIE, 10 ETUDES FACILES	BITSCH
LE MARAIS ET SES MOULINS	DAVID
LE MARCHAND DE LUNETTES	DELANNOY
LE PAPILLON--ETUDE DE CONCERT	LAVALLEE, C.
LE PERE LA VICTOIRE, MARCH	GANNE
LE PETITS RIEN	MOZART, W. A.
LE PETIT BAISER, VALSE MIGNINNE	DESSAUX
LE PETIT BAISER, VALSE MIGNONNE -- SIMPLIFIED VERSION	DESSAUX
LE PETIT BOUQUET, POLKA-MAZURKA MIGNONNE	DESSAUX
LE PETIT CARNIVAL, SCHOTTISCHE	STREABBOG
LE PETIT CZERNY, 30 ETUDES	CZERNY
LE PETIT ELFE 'FERME-L'OEIL'	SCHMITT, F.
LE PETIT NEGRE	DEBUSSY
LE PETIT NEGRE	DEBUSSY
LE PETIT NEGRE	DEBUSSY
LE PETIT REIN -- THE TRIFLE	COUPERIN, F.
LE PETIT RIEN	CRAMER, J.
LE PETIT TRAIN DE PAIMPOL	MARGAT, Y.
LE PETIT VIRTUOSE	VAILLANT, H.
LE PIANO CLASSIQUE, VOL. A	CLASSENS
LE PIANO CLASSIQUE, VOL. B	CLASSENS
LE PIANO CLASSIQUE, VOL. C	CLASSENS
LE PIANO CLASSIQUE, VOL. D	CLASSENS
LE PIANO CLASSIQUE, VOL. E	CLASSENS
LE PIANO CLASSIQUE, VOL. F	CLASSENS
LE PIANO CLASSIQUE, VOL. G	CLASSENS
LE PIANO INSPIRE DU FOLKLORE	ARMA, P.
LE POLICHINELLE	VILLA-LOBOS, H.
LE RECONTRE	SAUGUET
LE RENDEZ-VOUS BALLET	DUCLOS, P.
LE RENDEZVOUS	DUCLOS, P.
LE ROUET D'OMPHALE, OP. 31, FOR 2 PIANOS 8 HANDS	SAINT-SAENS
LE ROUET D'OMPHALE, OP. 31	SAINT-SAENS
LE SECRET, INTERMEZZO-PIZZICATO	GAUTIER, L.
LE SECRET, INTERMEZZO PIZZICATO FOR ONE PIANO, SIX	GAUTIER, L.
LE SECRET	GAUTIER, L.
LE SECRET	GAUTIER, L.
LE SECRET	GAUTIER, L.
LE SECRET	GAUTIER, L.
LE SOMMEIL DE L'ENFANT JESUS. BERCEUSE FOR PIANO	BUESSER
LE TAMBORIN	RAMEAU
LE TAMBOURIN	RAMEAU
LE TAMBOUR BAT AUX CHAMPS, OP. 50 NO. 2	ALKAN
LE TEMPLE ABANDONNE	OLLONE, M. D'
LE TIC-TOC-CHOC -- OR LES MAILLOTINS	COUPERIN, F.
LE TOMBEAU DE CARRILLO	MARIE
LE TOMBEAU DE COUPERIN	RAVEL
LE TOMBEAU DE COUPERIN	RAVEL
LE TOURNOI SINGULIER	ROLAND *
LE TRAIN BLEU	MILHAUD, D.
LE TRESOR D'ORPHEE	FRANCISQUE, A.
LE TRILLE	PHILIPP, I.
LE TRIOMPHE DE BACCHUS	DEBUSSY
LE VENT --ETUDE DE CONCERT, OP. 10 NO. 1	STRELEZKI
LI'L DARLIN'	
LI'L RED CABBOSE	MELVIN, B.
LIBERTY BELL, THE, MARCH	SOUSA
LIBERTY FAIR MARCH	NIRELLA, D.
LIBRO PRELIMINAR DE PIANO PARA NINOS - SPANISH EDITION	WILLIAMS, J.
LICHTERTANZ DER BRAUTE	RUBINSTEIN
LICORICE STICKS	SCARMOLIN
LIEBESFREUD --STUDENT EDITION--	KREISLER
LIEBESFREUD --STUDENT EDITION--	KREISLER
LIEBESFREUD	KREISLER
LIEBESFREUD	KREISLER
LIEBESFREUD	KREISLER *
LIEBESFREUD	KREISLER
LIEBESFREUD	KREISLER
LIEBESLEID --STUDENT EDITION--	KREISLER
LIEBESLEID	KREISLER
LIEBESLIED, OP. 7 NO. 1	SUK
LIEBESLIEDER-WALZER OP. 52	BRAHMS
LIEBESLIEDER, OP. 52 -- CHORUS AD LIB	BRAHMS
LIEBESLIEDER WALTZES OP. 52 AND NEW LIEBESLIEDER	BRAHMS
LIEBESLIED --STUDENT EDITION--	KREISLER
LIEBESLIED	KREISLER
LIEBESLIED	KREISLER
LIEBESTRAUM, NO. 1	LISZT
LIEBESTRAUME -- NO. 1 AS-DUR	LISZT
LIEBESTRAUME -- NO. 2 E-DUR	LISZT
LIEBESTRAUME -- NO. 3 AS-DUR	LISZT
LIEBESTRAUME AND 3 NOCTURNES	LISZT
LIEBESTRAUME NO. 2 IN E	LISZT
LIEBESTRAUME NO. 3 IN A FLAT	LISZT
LIEBESTRAUME NO. 3 IN A FLAT	LISZT
LIEBESTRAUME NO. 3	LISZT
LIEBESTRAUME	LISZT
LIEBESTRAUME	LISZT
LIEBESTRAUM -- LOVE DREAMS --	LISZT
LIEBESTRAUM	LISZT
LIEBESTRAUM	LISZT
LIEBESTRAUM	LISZT
LIEBESTRAUM	LISZT
LIED- UND TANZVARIATIONEN DER SWEELINCK-SCHULE	BREIG--ED
LIEDERBEGLEITUNG	NOLL, G.
LIEDER IM VOLKSTON	SCHULZ
LIEDER OHNE WORTE -- OP. 19 NO. 3 A-DUR -- JAGERLIED	MENDELSSOHN
LIEDER OHNE WORTE -- OP. 19 NO. 6 G-MOLL UND OP. 30	MENDELSSOHN
LIEDER OHNE WORTE -- OP. 30 NO. 3 E-DUR UND OP. 67 NO.	MENDELSSOHN
LIEDER OHNE WORTE -- OP. 62 NO. 5 A-MOLL -- 3. VENET.	MENDELSSOHN
LIEDVARIATIONEN	SCHEIDT
LIEDVARIATIONEN	SWEELINCK
LIES	
LIFE OF LOVE, THE	ETTORE, E.
LIFE ON THE OCEAN WAVE, A -- SAILORS' MARCH	STEINER
LIFT EV'RY VOICE AND SING	JOHNSON, J. R.
LIFT UP YOUR HEADS	WILLIAMS, T.
LIGHTHOUSE, THE	HELLER, E.
LIGHT 'N BRIGHT	OLSON
LIGHT AND LIVELY	ECKSTEIN
LIGHT AND SHADOW	STONE, E.
LIGHT AS A FEATHER	MAGNEY, R.
LIGHT CAVALRY -- OVERTURE -- 8-HANDS, SET	SUPPE, F.
LIGHT CAVALRY OVERTURE	SUPPE, F.
LIGHT CLASSICS, BK. 1	BRADLEY
LIGHT CLASSICS, BK. 2	BRADLEY
LIGHT CLASSICS, BK. 3	BRADLEY
LIGHT CLASSICS	STEINER
LIGHT HEART	SWINSTEAD, F.
LIGHT MY FIRE	
LIKE BLUE	PREVIN, A.
LIKE SOMEONE IN LOVE	
LIKE YOUNG	PREVIN, A.
LILA'S THEME - THE STRIPPER	GOLDSMITH, J.
LILACS, OP. 21 NO. 5	RACHMANINOFF, S.
LILACS	CRERIE, E.
LILACS	RACHMANINOFF, S.
LILAC TIME	HOWELL

Title	Composer
LILLI MARLENE	SCHULTZE
LILLI MARLENE	SCHULTZE
LILT	CLARK, M. E.
LILY, POLKA	STREABBOG
LILY OF THE VALLEY, OP. 14	SMITH, SYDNEY
LILY PADS	LOCKE
LILY POLKA	STREABBOG
LILY POLKA	STREABBOG
LILY	LICHNER, H.
LIMEHOUSE BLUES	BRAHAM
LINCOLNSHIRE POACHER	SILVESTER, F. C.
LINDARAJA	DEBUSSY
LINDARAJA	DEBUSSY
LINDA DI CHAMONIX - EASY FANTASIA	DONIZETTI
LINDA ROSE	GODDEN, R.
LINDEGGER LANDLER	KNAB, A.
LINDEN LEA	VAUGHAN
LINDEN TREE, THE -- LINDENBAUM --	SCHUBERT
LINES FOR THE FALLEN, SOPRANO AND 2 PIANOS, 4 HANDS	LYBBERT
LINGERING MEMORIES	MOSS, E.
LINNET, THE	REA
LION, THE	GARROW
LION AND THE MOUSE, THE - A STORY WITH MUSIC	RICHTER, A.
LIRICA ESPANOLA, OP. 54 -- VOL. 1	ESPLA
LIRICA ESPANOLA, OP. 54 -- VOL. 2	ESPLA
LIRICA ESPANOLA, OP. 54 -- VOL. 3 --	ESPLA
LIRICA ESPANOLA, OP. 54 -- VOL. 4 --	ESPLA
LISONJERA, LA. OP. 50	CHAMINADE
LISTEN SOLDIERS, MARCH	HOPKINS, H.
LISTEN TO LEARN	QUIST
LISTEN TO THE MOCKING BIRD -- VARIATION	DRUMHELLER
LISTEN TO THE MOCKING BIRD	HOFFMAN
LISTEN TO THE MOCKING BIRD	MEACHAM, F.
LISTEN TO THE RAIN	JESSE, M.
LISTEN TO THE WOODPECKER	BRODSKY, V.
LISTEN TO YOURSELF -- BK. 2-UPPER ELEMENTARY GRADES	MIROVITCH, A.
LISZT ALBUM, BK. 1	LISZT
LISZT ALBUM, BK. 2	LISZT
LISZT	LISZT
LITANIES DU FEU ET DE LA MER NO. 1	NUNES, E.
LITTLEST BALLERINA	WIGHAM, M.
LITTLEST CLOWN, THE	CABLE *
LITTLEST REINDEER, THE	JOYNER, B.
LITTLE ADMIRAL	HELLARD, R. A.
LITTLE ALMOND EYES	SCHER, W.
LITTLE ALMOND EYES	SCHER, W.
LITTLE ANTELOPE	ANGELL
LITTLE ARGUMENT, A	MCGRAW
LITTLE ATTIC OF DREAMS	GREY, F.
LITTLE BALLADE	MILLER, H.
LITTLE BALLAD FROM CHOPIN'S OP. 47	ROLFE, W.
LITTLE BALLAD	MCDOUGLE, A.
LITTLE BALLERINA	GLADKOVSKY
LITTLE BALLERINA	TAYLOR
LITTLE BALLERINA	WRIGHT, N.
LITTLE BALLET	SCHER, W.
LITTLE BANDMASTER, THE	ERB
LITTLE BARN DANCE, A	HOFSTAD, M.
LITTLE BEAR CUB SEES THE WORLD ON HIS OWN	BECK
LITTLE BELLS OF KYOTE	CADZOW
LITTLE BEN	GRIEG
LITTLE BIRD, OP. 43 NO. 4	SINCIRT, H.
LITTLE BIRD, THE	GLOVER
LITTLE BIRD'S SONG, THE	COBB
LITTLE BIRDS	HOUSE, A.
LITTLE BIRD AT MY WINDOW	JESSE, M.
LITTLE BIRD IN SPRING, A	OLDENBURG, E.
LITTLE BIRD IN THE TREE	REBE
LITTLE BIRD	WEYBRIGHT
LITTLE BLACK TRAIN BOOGIE	GREENWALD, M.
LITTLE BLUE EYES	SKAAGS
LITTLE BLUE LADY	ROLFE, W.
LITTLE BO-PEEP	FOLDES
LITTLE BOATS ON THE POND	KETTERER, E.
LITTLE BOAT DANCE, A	THOMAS, J. J.
LITTLE BOBOLINK	RAVINA, H.
LITTLE BOLERO, OP. 62	LYON
LITTLE BOOGIE TUCKER	LYON
LITTLE BOOGIE WALL CLOCK	ROSNER
LITTLE BOOGIE WOOGIE	ANSON, G.
LITTLE BOY BLUES	ENGELMANN, H. U.
LITTLE BOY BLUE	HOPKINS, H.
LITTLE BOY BLUE	HOPKINS, H.
LITTLE BRAKEMAN	THOMAS, C. J.
LITTLE BROOK, THE	HOPKINS, H.
LITTLE BROWN BUNNY	GARROW
LITTLE BROWN HEN	STANLEY--ED
LITTLE BROWN JUG	HELLER, E.
LITTLE BROWN THRUSH, THE	EZELL, H.
LITTLE BUCKAROO	MACLACHLIN, T.
LITTLE BUGLER, THE	LAKE, G.
LITTLE BUNNY	STECHER *
LITTLE CABALLERO	ARRIEU
LITTLE CANARY, THE -- LE PETITE CANARD	STREABBOG
LITTLE CARNIVAL, GALOP	BURNAM
LITTLE CHAPEL IN THE MOONLIGHT	HOPSON, E.
LITTLE CHIEF RED FEATHER	HIRSCHBERG, D.
LITTLE CHINESE FISHERMAN	SCHULDT, M.
LITTLE CHIPPEWA INDIAN	ZIPP
LITTLE CHRISTMAS BOOK FOR ROSWITHA	
LITTLE CLASSICS. 67 EASY PIECES SELECTED FROM THE	
LITTLE CLASSICS. 67 EASY PIECES SELECTED FROM THE	ROVENGER--ED.
LITTLE CLASSICS	MORHANGE *
LITTLE CLAVIER, THE .... SUPPLEMENT 1 - 20 SHORT	MORHANGE *
LITTLE CLAVIER, THE .... SUPPLEMENT 2 - 14 PIECES FOR	MORHANGE *
LITTLE CLAVIER, THE - AN INTRODUCTION TO THE PIANO	BACH, J.S.
LITTLE CLAVIER BOOK	DARWEN, J.
LITTLE CLOCK, THE	ROBINSON, A.
LITTLE CLOG DANCE	HAYDN
LITTLE CONCERTO	ROZIN
LITTLE CONCERTO	LESSARD, J.
LITTLE CONCERT -- SUITE	SCHER, W.
LITTLE CONCERT POLKA	LESSARD, J.
LITTLE CONCERT SUITE	LESSARD, J.
LITTLE CONCERT SUITE	SCHER, W.
LITTLE COSSACKS	BROWN, L.
LITTLE COUNTRY DANCE	HOFSTAD, M.
LITTLE COWBOY RIDES AGAIN	ROSNER
LITTLE COWBOY	TOWNSEND
LITTLE CUBAN BOY	HENSEL, R.
LITTLE DANCE, A	HENSEL, R.
LITTLE DANCE, A	DITTENHAVER
LITTLE DANCER, THE	CARPENTER, J.
LITTLE DANCER	LARSON
LITTLE DANCER	STREABBOG
LITTLE DANCER	HAYDN
LITTLE DANCES FOR THE YOUNG	BACH, J.S.
LITTLE DANCES	
LITTLE DANCING MASTER	DIETS, J.
LITTLE DANDY	ERB
LITTLE DEAREST, GAVOTTE	BOHM
LITTLE DEAREST --GAVOTTE--	BOHM
LITTLE DEER, THE	MILLER *
LITTLE DOG, RUNNING	BASTIEN
LITTLE DOG BOOGIE	SCHAUM, W.
LITTLE DOG TALES	ADAIR, Y.
LITTLE DONKEY IN THE SNOW	BRANDT, D.
LITTLE DRUMMER BOY, THE -- SIMP.	DAVIS, K. *
LITTLE DRUMMER BOY	KAISER
LITTLE DRUM MAJOR, THE	WILLIAMS, J.
LITTLE DUCKY	HOPKINS, H.
LITTLE DUET FOR PIANO	HARTLEY, W.
LITTLE DUTCH DANCE, A	ARMOUR
LITTLE DUTCH DANCE	CRAMM, H.
LITTLE DUTCH DANCE	MORGEN, M.
LITTLE DUTCH DANCE	ROBINSON, W. E.
LITTLE ELF, THE	DITTENHAVER
LITTLE ETUDES FOR LITTLE FINGERS, BK. 1	BILBRO, M.
LITTLE ETUDES FOR LITTLE FINGERS, BK. 2	BILBRO, M.
LITTLE ETUDES	GARSCIA
LITTLE FAIRY MARCH	STREABBOG
LITTLE FAIRY MARCH	STREABBOG
LITTLE FAIRY MARCH	STREABBOG
LITTLE FAIRY MARCH	STREABBOG
LITTLE FAIRY POLKA	STREABBOG
LITTLE FAIRY POLKA	STREABBOG
LITTLE FAIRY SCHOTTISCHE	STREABBOG
LITTLE FAIRY SCHOTTISCHE	STREABBOG
LITTLE FAIRY SCHOTTISCHE	STREABBOG
LITTLE FAIRY WALTZ, OP. 105 NO. 1	STREABBOG
LITTLE FAIRY WALTZ	STREABBOG
LITTLE FAIRY WALTZ	STREABBOG
LITTLE FAIRY WALTZ	STREABBOG
LITTLE FAIRY WALTZ	STREABBOG
LITTLE FAIRY WALTZ	STREABBOG
LITTLE FANTASY	SYMONS
LITTLE FINGERS MAKE MUSIC	STUBBLEFIELD
LITTLE FLATTERER	MACK, F.
LITTLE FRENCH BOY	TOWNSEND
LITTLE FRENCH CAFE	WANDERMAN
LITTLE FRENCH DOLL -- ONE PIANO, SIX HANDS --	HOPKINS, H.
LITTLE FRENCH MUSIC BOX	DAY, R. E.
LITTLE FROG, A	MANN, M.
LITTLE FROG, THE	GARROW, L.
LITTLE GAVOTTE, A	FOSTER, I. R.
LITTLE GAVOTTE, A	GEIGER
LITTLE GAVOTTE	HAYES
LITTLE GHOSTS ARE MARCHING	STEINER
LITTLE GIRL, BIG GIRL	LOVEJOY
LITTLE GIRL'S WALTZ, A	FISHER, E.
LITTLE GIRL BLUE -- SHOWCASE	
LITTLE GIRL FROM LITTLE ROCK, A	
LITTLE GIRL FROM MARS	SKAGGS
LITTLE GIRL	HYDE *
LITTLE GOLDEN DAFFODIL	BEAUMONT, V.
LITTLE GOLDEN DAFFODIL	BEAUMONT, V.
LITTLE GOLDEN HARP, THE	STEPHENS, A.
LITTLE GOLDEN HARP, THE	STEPHENS, A.
LITTLE GOLDFISH	BALLATORE, P.
LITTLE GRAY SQUIRREL	WRIGHT, K.
LITTLE GREEN APPLES	BRIMHALL,
LITTLE GREY HOME IN THE WEST	
LITTLE GYPSY, THE, OP. 55 NO. 1	KUHLAU, F.
LITTLE GYPSY RHAPSODY	TAYLOR
LITTLE G MINOR ORGAN FUGUE	BACH, J.S.
LITTLE HANON, THE	HANON, C.
LITTLE HANS	GODDEN, R.
LITTLE HARPIST, THE	BENTLEY
LITTLE HARPIST	KERR
LITTLE HARPIST	ROBBINS
LITTLE HILDER	GEIGER
LITTLE HILLS, THE	WEYBRIGHT
LITTLE HORSE WITH THE BROKEN LEG, THE -- O CAVALINHO	GUARNIERI
LITTLE HUNGARIAN MELODY OP. 503 NO. 13	BEHR, F.
LITTLE HUNTING SONG	SCHUMANN, R.
LITTLE HYMNAL FOR PIANO, A	RICHTER
LITTLE IDA'S FLOWERS OVERTURE	KLENAU, P. V.
LITTLE IDA'S WALTZ	KLENAU, P. V.
LITTLE INDIAN BRAVE	MITCHELL, M. A.
LITTLE INDIAN CHIEF	STRICKLAND, L.
LITTLE INJUN BRAVE	HOPKINS, H.
LITTLE INSECTS	GILBOA
LITTLE INVENTION	SKAGGS
LITTLE IRISH DANCE, A	ERB
LITTLE ISRAELI BOY	TOWNSEND
LITTLE JAZZ WALTZ	VALENTI, M.
LITTLE JEWEL, A--OP. 87	BIEDERMANN, A.
LITTLE JOKE, A, OP. 27	KABALEVSKY *
LITTLE JOURNEY	DITTENHAVER
LITTLE JUMBO	TRUXELL, E.
LITTLE KEYBOARD PIECES, BWV 933-938	BACH, J.S.
LITTLE KEYBOARD PIECES	BACH, C.P.E.
LITTLE KNOWN PIANO PIECES	BEETHOVEN
LITTLE KNOWN PIECES	BACH, J.S.
LITTLE KNOWN PIECES	CHOPIN
LITTLE KNOWN PIECES	MOZART, W. A.
LITTLE LADY	ECKSTEIN
LITTLE LAMB	MOSS, E.
LITTLE LEAD GENERAL, THE	GLOVER
LITTLE LOST BEAR	KREVIT, W.
LITTLE LULLABY, A	CURRIE, R.
LITTLE LULLABY, A	VOLKART, H.
LITTLE LYKING, THE	NILES, J.
LITTLE LYRICAL SCENE, A	KABALEVSKY
LITTLE MAJORETTE	NEVIN
LITTLE MAJORETTE	NEVIN
LITTLE MAN, THE, HANSEL AND GRETEL	HUMPERDINCK, E.
LITTLE MARCH, A	WRIGHT, N.
LITTLE MARCH	FINLAYSON, W.
LITTLE MARCH	ROBINSON, A.
LITTLE MAZURKA -- A CZECHOSLAVAKIAN FOLK TUNE	WEYBRIGHT
LITTLE MEXICAN BURRO	KLEINMAN, A.
LITTLE MILL, THE	WIGHAM, M.
LITTLE MINUET	BOSTELMANN
LITTLE MISCHIEF	WIGHAM, M.
LITTLE MISCHIEVOUS	DRAYTON
LITTLE MISS BLUEBIRD	ERB
LITTLE MISS DANCER	SCHER, W.
LITTLE MISS MUFFET	VANNORT, I.
LITTLE MISS QUACK-QUACK	ERB
LITTLE MOUSE, A	WARD
LITTLE MUSICAL ZOO, THE	MARCHI
LITTLE MUSICIANS	FRONTINI
LITTLE MUSIC BOOK OF ANNA MAGDALENA - 12 SELECTED	BACH, J.S.
LITTLE MUSIC BOOK OF ANNA MAGDALENA BACH --20 PIECES--	BACH, J.S.

LITTLE NAVAJO	LITTOFF
LITTLE NEGRO, THE	DEBUSSY
LITTLE NEGRO	DEBUSSY
LITTLE NOCTURNE	SCHER, W.
LITTLE ORCHESTRA	BOSTELMANN
LITTLE ORPHAN WALTZ	KOUNTZ, R.
LITTLE PACKBURRO, THE	KOEHLER, C.
LITTLE PACKBURRO, THE	KOEHLER, C.
LITTLE PAPER DOLL, THE -- SET	VILLA-LOBOS, H.
LITTLE PASTORALE	LUBIN, E.
LITTLE PATRIOT, OP. 15 NO. 7	KROGMANN, C. W.
LITTLE PENGUIN	RICHTER
LITTLE PEOPLE AMERICA	BRADLEY,
LITTLE PET DUCK	RICHTER, A.
LITTLE PIANIST, THE--73 EASY PROGRESSIVE	CZERNY
LITTLE PIANIST, THE--73 EASY PROGRESSIVE	CZERNY
LITTLE PIANIST, THE--73 EASY PROGRESSIVE	CZERNY
LITTLE PIANISTS, OP. 189 - 40 RECREATIONS	KOEHLER
LITTLE PIANIST	HOFSTAD, M.
LITTLE PIANO BOOK. SELECTION OF EASIEST PIECES AND	HAYDN
LITTLE PIANO BOOKS, VOL. 1# PRE-BACH MASTERS	
LITTLE PIANO BOOKS, VOL. 2# CONTEMPORARIES OF BACH	
LITTLE PIANO BOOKS, VOL. 3# THE CLASSICAL PERIOD	
LITTLE PIANO BOOKS, VOL. 4# THE ROMANTIC PERIOD	
LITTLE PIANO BOOK --18 PIECES--	BACH, J.S.
LITTLE PIANO BOOK FOR PETER	MARX
LITTLE PIANO BOOK	HANDEL
LITTLE PIANO BOOK	KAMINSKI
LITTLE PIANO BOOK	PERSICHETTI
LITTLE PIANO BOOK	SCARLATTI, D.
LITTLE PIANO BOOK	WAGNER
LITTLE PIANO SCENES	ANTHONY, G. W.
LITTLE PIECE, A	SCHUMANN, R.
LITTLE PIECES - CHORAL	ROPARTZ
LITTLE PIECES - CLOCHES DU SOIR	ROPARTZ
LITTLE PIECES - L'ANGELUS	ROPARTZ
LITTLE PIECES - LE GLAS	ROPARTZ
LITTLE PIECES - PAR LES CHAMPS	ROPARTZ
LITTLE PIECES - POUR GAUD	ROPARTZ
LITTLE PIECES - TRISTESSE	ROPARTZ
LITTLE PIECES FOR LITTLE PEOPLE	KUNC, B.
LITTLE PIECE	KHATCHTURIAN
LITTLE PISCHNA, THE--48 PRACTICE-PIECES--INTRODUCTION	PISCHNA
LITTLE PISCHNA	WOLFF, B. C.
LITTLE PLAYERS GROWING UP	KERR, R. N.
LITTLE PLAYERS HAVE ARRIVED	KERR, R. N.
LITTLE PLAYERS	KERR, R. N.
LITTLE PLAYMATES	MALLARD, C. S.
LITTLE POLISH DANCE, A	HOUSE, A.
LITTLE POLLY FLINDERS	ROLFE, W.
LITTLE PRELUDES AND FUGUES -- CLOTH	BACH, J.S.
LITTLE PRELUDES AND FUGUES --24--	BACH, J.S.
LITTLE PRELUDES AND FUGUES	BACH, J.S.
LITTLE PRELUDES AND FUGUES	BACH, J.S.
LITTLE PRELUDES AND FUGUES	BACH, J.S.
LITTLE PRELUDES AND OTHER WORKS	BACH, J.S.
LITTLE PRELUDES	BACH, J.S.
LITTLE PRELUDE AND FUGUE, OP. 68 NO. 40--ALBUM FOR THE	SCHUMANN, R.
LITTLE PRELUDE	KRAFT
LITTLE PRELUDE	RICCARDI, J.
LITTLE PRELUDE	VANNORT, I.
LITTLE PRINCE, OP. 15 NO. 1	KROGMANN, C. W.
LITTLE PUPPETS ON PARADE	HAYES
LITTLE PUSSY-CAT	MANA-ZUCCA
LITTLE RACE HORSE, THE	TRAVIS, B.
LITTLE RANGE RIDER, THE	MARTIN, E.
LITTLE RANGE RIDER, THE	MARTIN, E.
LITTLE RECRUIT	SCHIEFELBEIN, F.
LITTLE REDSKIN	HOPKINS, H.
LITTLE RED HEN AND THE PEPPERMINT STICK, THE	SUDDARDS
LITTLE RED MONKEY	JORDAN, J.
LITTLE RED MONKEY	LANE, J.--ED.
LITTLE RED WAGON	HOPKINS, H.
LITTLE RHAPSODIES ON FOLK-THEMES	AGAY, D.
LITTLE RHYMES TO SING AND PLAY -- FIVE-FINGER	HOFSTAD, M.--ED
LITTLE ROCKING HORSE, THE	AMES, J.
LITTLE ROCK GETAWAY	SULLIVAN, J.
LITTLE ROGUISH CLOWN	RICKER, E.
LITTLE RONDEAU	KASZNER
LITTLE RONDO IN G	BEETHOVEN
LITTLE RONDO	MARTIN, G.
LITTLE SAGEBRUSH ALL AROUND	BURNAM
LITTLE SAILBOAT, THE	KALMANOFF
LITTLE SAILBOAT, THE	KALMANOFF
LITTLE SAILBOATS	DURNAM
LITTLE SAILBOAT	ROBINSON, W. E.
LITTLE SALLY WATERS	GREENWOOD
LITTLE SALZBURG DANCE BOOK	MOZART, W. A.
LITTLE SCHERZO, OP. 3, NO. 3	SELIVANOV
LITTLE SCOTCH BOY	TOWNSEND
LITTLE SERENADE	GRUENFELD
LITTLE SHADOW	ERB
LITTLE SHEPHERD, THE, FROM THE CHILDREN'S CORNER	DEBUSSY
LITTLE SHEPHERD, THE	KOUNTZ, R.
LITTLE SHEPHERDESS, THE	STEVENS, E.
LITTLE SHEPHERD	HAYES
LITTLE SHEPHERD	MAYKAPAR
LITTLE SKATING STAR	RAEZER, C.
LITTLE SLAVONIC RHAPSODY	THOMPSON, J.
LITTLE SLEEPY SONG -- RUN AND SKIP	HAYES
LITTLE SOLDIERS, THE	READ, G.
LITTLE SOLDIERS, THE	READ, G.
LITTLE SOLDIERS MARCHING	BARBERA
LITTLE SONATA, OP. 27 -- 1957	HARTIG
LITTLE SONATA, OP. 51	TAKACS, J.
LITTLE SONATA IN B MINOR, OP. 32 NO. 1	HOELLER
LITTLE SONATA IN G, OP. 32 NO. 2	HOELLER
LITTLE SONATA	KUPFERMAN, M.
LITTLE SONATA	KUPFERMAN, M.
LITTLE SONATA	KUPFERMAN, M.
LITTLE SONATA	KUPFERMAN, M.
LITTLE SONATA	WATSON
LITTLE SONATINA	REEVES, R.
LITTLE SONG, A	KABALEVSKY
LITTLE SONGS AND SOLOS	ZEPP
LITTLE SONGS THAT TEACH	
LITTLE SONGS TO PLAY AND SING	BENTLEY
LITTLE SONG	PHILLIPS, B.
LITTLE SONG	RICHTER
LITTLE SPANISH BOY	TOWNSEND
LITTLE SPARROW, THE	MANA-ZUCCA
LITTLE SPINNER, THE, OP. 114	ZILCHER
LITTLE SPORTSMAN, THE	MOREAU
LITTLE STUDIES, OP. 181 BK.1	LOESCHHORN
LITTLE STUDIES, OP. 181 BK.1	LOESCHHORN
LITTLE SUITE, OP. 1--1935	SCHISKE, K.

LITTLE SUITE, OP. 13 NO. 1	POSER
LITTLE SUITE -- 1959 --	BAUERNFEIND
LITTLE SUITE FOR PIANO	FONTRIERE, G.
LITTLE SUITE FOR PIANO	FONTRIERE, G.
LITTLE SUITE NO. 1	DOPPELBAUER
LITTLE SUITE OF ROUMANIAN FOLK DANCES	DRAGOI
LITTLE SUITE	BORODIN, A.
LITTLE SUITE	BOUSTEAD, A.
LITTLE SUITE	FONTRIERE, G.
LITTLE SUITE	HARRIS, R.
LITTLE SUITE	KADOSA
LITTLE SUITE	KIRCHNER, L.
LITTLE SUITE	SANGIORGI
LITTLE SUITE	TANSMAN, A.
LITTLE SUITE	WOOD, O.
LITTLE SWEETHEART WALTZ	ROLFE, W.
LITTLE SWISS BOY	TOWNSEND
LITTLE SWISS CLOCK, THE	ROSSMAN, F. A.
LITTLE SWISS MUSIC BOX	POTTER, E.
LITTLE TAMBOURINES	BRAVIS, B.
LITTLE TANGO	FICHANDLER, W.
LITTLE TARANTELLE	KLEINMAN, A.
LITTLE TARANTELLE	MACLACHLAN
LITTLE TECHNICS	BRADLEY
LITTLE TIN TRUMPET	ANSON, G.
LITTLE TOCCATA	DOLIN
LITTLE TOCCATA	STIEFEL, E.
LITTLE TRAIN OF CAIPIRA, THE - TOCCATA FROM "BACHIANAS	VILLA-LOBOS, H.
LITTLE TRAIN OF THE CAIPIRA, THE -- TOCCATA, FROM	VILLA-LOBOS, H.
LITTLE TRAIN OF THE CAIPIRA, THE - FROM BACHIANAS	VILLA-LOBOS, H.
LITTLE TRAPEZE GIRL	JONES, J.
LITTLE TREASURY SERIES -- CLASSICS, BK. 1	LAMBERT, C.--ED
LITTLE TREASURY SERIES -- CLASSICS, BK. 2	LAMBERT, C.--ED
LITTLE TREASURY SERIES -- CLASSICS, BK. 3	LAMBERT, C.--ED
LITTLE TREASURY SERIES -- CLASSICS, BK. 4	LAMBERT, C.--ED
LITTLE TREASURY SERIES -- ETUDES, BK. 1	LAMBERT, C.--ED
LITTLE TREASURY SERIES -- ETUDES, BK. 2	LAMBERT, C.--ED
LITTLE TREASURY SERIES -- FOLK SONGS AND DANCES, BK. 1	LAMBERT, C.--ED
LITTLE TREASURY SERIES -- FOLK SONGS AND DANCES, BK. 2	LAMBERT, C.--ED
LITTLE TREASURY SERIES -- PIECETIME	ETTS, M.--ED
LITTLE TREASURY SERIES -- PLAYTIME	ETTS, M.--ED
LITTLE TREASURY SERIES -- POLYPHONIC PIECES, BK. 1	LAMBERT, C.--ED
LITTLE TREASURY SERIES -- POLYPHONIC PIECES, BK. 2	LAMBERT, C.--ED
LITTLE TREASURY SERIES -- RECITAL CLASSICS, BK. 1	LAMBERT, C.--ED
LITTLE TREASURY SERIES -- RECITAL CLASSICS, BK. 2	LAMBERT, C.--ED
LITTLE TREASURY SERIES -- SONATINAS, BK. 1	LAMBERT, C.--ED
LITTLE TREASURY SERIES -- SONATINAS, BK. 2	LAMBERT, C.--ED
LITTLE TREASURY SERIES - CLASSICS, BK. 1	LAMBERT, C.--ED
LITTLE TREASURY SERIES - CLASSICS, BK. 2	LAMBERT, C.--ED
LITTLE TREASURY SERIES - CLASSICS, BK. 3	LAMBERT, C.--ED
LITTLE TREASURY SERIES - CLASSICS, BK. 4	LAMBERT, C.--ED
LITTLE TREASURY SERIES - FOLK SONGS AND DANCES, BK. 1	LAMBERT, C.--ED
LITTLE TREASURY SERIES - FOLK SONGS AND DANCES, BK. 2	LAMBERT, C.--ED
LITTLE TREASURY SERIES - PIECETIME	ETTS, M.
LITTLE TREASURY SERIES - PLAYTIME	ETTS, M.
LITTLE TREASURY SERIES - POLYPHONICS, BK. 1	LAMBERT, C.--ED
LITTLE TREASURY SERIES - POLYPHONICS, BK. 2	LAMBERT, C.--ED
LITTLE TREASURY SERIES - RECITAL CLASSICS, BK. 1	
LITTLE TREASURY SERIES - RECITAL CLASSICS, BK. 2	
LITTLE TREASURY SERIES - SONATINAS, BK. 1	LAMBERT, C.--ED
LITTLE TREASURY SERIES - SONATINAS, BK. 2	LAMBERT, C.--ED
LITTLE TRUMPETER, THE	KEVAN, G. A.
LITTLE TRUMPETER, THE	THOMAS, C. J.
LITTLE TUNES FOR LITTLE FOLK	LYON
LITTLE VALSE	FOLDES
LITTLE VIENNESE DANCE BOOK	SCHUBERT
LITTLE VIRTUOSO SUITE, A	THOMPSON, J.
LITTLE WAGON, THE	DRING
LITTLE WALTZ, A	RATHBONE, G.
LITTLE WALTZES FROM OP. 9A	SCHUBERT
LITTLE WALTZ	DURNAM
LITTLE WALTZ	SCHILINGER
LITTLE WANDERER	LANGE, G.
LITTLE WHITE BURRO	FINLAYSON, W.
LITTLE WHITE CHURCH	HOPKINS, H.
LITTLE WHITE DONKEY	IBERT
LITTLE WINDMILLS, THE -- SET	COUPERIN, F.
LITTLE WINDMILLS	COUPERIN, P.
LITTLE WOODEN SOLDIER	LANE, J.--ED.
LITTLE YELLOW DUCKLING	ERB
LIVELY DANCE, A	CLARK, H. A.
LIVELY DANCE, A	STEVENS, M.
LIVELY RABBIT, THE	HOUSE, A.
LIVE FOR LIFE	LAI, F.
LIVING PIANO TECHNIQUE, BK. 1	HERRMANN, K.
LIVING PIANO TECHNIQUE, BK. 2	HERRMANN, K.
LIVING PIANO TECHNIQUE, BK. 3	HERRMANN, K.
LIVING TOGETHER, GROWING TOGETHER - AND - QUESTION ME	BRADLEY,
LIVING TOGETHER, GROWING TOGETHER	BRADLEY,
LIVRE BLEU, LE	SOUBEYRAN
LIVRE D'HEURES	MOTTU
LIVRE DES ENFANTS, LE - BK. 1	VOORMOLEN
LIVRE DES ENFANTS, LE - BK. 2	VOORMOLEN
LIZA	GERSHWIN
LIZA	GERSHWIN
LLANURA	GUASTAVINO
LOCH LOMMOND	ROLFE, W.--ED
LOCH LOMOND	SCHAUM, J.--ED.
LODOLETTA -- COMPLETE OPERA --	MASCAGNI, P.
LODOLETTA - SERENATA	MASCAGNI, P.
LODRON CONCERTO K242 --SET--	MOZART, W. A.
LODRON CONCERTO K242	MOZART, W. A.
LOEWE AND LERNER	LOEWE, F. *
LOFTY PEAKS	THOMPSON, J.
LOG CABIN SQUARE DANCE	SCHAUM, J.--ED.
LOHENGRIN, BRIDAL CHORUS	WAGNER
LOHENGRIN, BRIDAL CHORUS	WAGNER
LOHENGRIN, BRIDAL CHORUS	WAGNER
LOHENGRIN, PRELUDE, ACT 3	WAGNER
LOHENGRIN - CHORUS AND WEDDING MARCH	WAGNER *
LOHENGRIN - EASY FANTASIA	WAGNER
LOHENGRIN - WEDDING MARCH	WAGNER
LOHENGRIN - WEDDING MARCH	WAGNER
LOIN DE BAL	GILLET, E.
LOISIRS DU JEUNE AGE, LES - ARLEQUIN ET COLOMBINE	WACHS, F.
LOISIRS DU JEUNE AGE, LES - A FONTAINEBLEAU	WACHS, F.
LOISIRS DU JEUNE AGE, LES - A LA FETE DE ST. CLOUD	WACHS, F.
LOISIRS DU JEUNE AGE, LES - CARMEN	WACHS, F.
LOISIRS DU JEUNE AGE, LES - COQUETTE	WACHS, F.
LOISIRS DU JEUNE AGE, LES - DOUX AVEU	WACHS, F.
LOISIRS DU JEUNE AGE, LES - FETE A SORRENTE	WACHS, F.
LOISIRS DU JEUNE AGE, LES - LE PREMIER BAL	WACHS, F.
LOISIRS DU JEUNE AGE, LES - MIREILLE	WACHS, F.
LOISIRS DU JEUNE AGE, LES - RETOUR DU PRINTEMPS	WACHS, F.
LOISIRS DU JEUNE AGE, LES - SOUS LES ETOILES	WACHS, F.
LOISIRS DU JEUNE AGE, LES - UN SOIR A SEVILLE	WACHS, F.
LOISIRS DU JEUNE AGE, LES	WACHS, F.

LOI KRATHONG	KENT, A.
LOLA DANCES	SCHER, W.
LOLA FLORES	TUCCI
LOLA WALTZ	EVANS
LOLLIPOPS --MODERN RHYTHMIC CLASSICS--	WHITFORD
LOLLIPOP BRIGADE, THE	BLACK, M.
LOLLIPOP WALTZ	SCHAUM, J.
LOMBARDI, I - O SIGNORE DAL TETTO NATIO	VERDI
LONDONDERRY AIR -- FREE TRANSCRIPTION	
LONDONDERRY AIR	GROOMS--ED
LONDONDERRY AIR	NIEL
LONDONDERRY AIR	ROLFE, W.--ED
LONDONDERRY AIR	SCHAUM, J.--ED.
LONDONDERRY AIR	THOMPSON, J.
LONDONDERRY AIR	WILLIAMS, J.
LONDONDERRY AIR	ZEPP--ED
LONDON AGAIN SUITE	
LONDON BRIDGE BOOGIE	SPIVAK, S.
LONDON BRIDGE IS FALLING, THE	STIEFEL, E.
LONDON BRIDGE IS FALLING DOWN	
LONDON BRIDGE	GARROW
LONDON CALLING	LONGMIRE
LONDON FANTASIA -- THEME	
LONDON FANTASIA	
LONDON MONOLOGUES	GARRATT
LONDON SUITE	
LONDON TODAY	LAST, J.
LONELINESS	VERRALL, J.
LONELY AS A STAR	BUTLER
LONELY BIRD, THE	BOSTELMANN
LONELY COWBOY, THE	ROBINSON, A.
LONELY DANCER	FEDERER, R.
LONELY DESERT	ROBINSON, A.
LONELY DESERT	ROBINSON, A.
LONELY DOLPHIN, THE	SCHER, W.
LONELY ELF	HAUBIEL, C.
LONELY FLOWERS, FROM 'FOREST SCENES'	SCHUMANN, R.
LONELY LULLABY	GAY
LONELY SHORE	DVORINE
LONELY SWAN	RICCARDI, J.
LONELY WALTZ	AGAY, D.
LONELY WALTZ	AGAY, D.
LONELY WHISTLER, THE	NORMAN *
LONESOME GOLDFISH	BENFORD
LONESOME KITTEN	WEIGL, V.
LONESOME PRAIRIE, THE	RICKER, E.
LONESOME PRAIRIE	ARMBRUSTER
LONESOME PUPPET	KARP
LONESOME SONG	SIEGMEISTER
LONG-HAIRED LOVER FROM LIVERPOOL	BRADLEY,
LONGING -- SEHNSUCHT --	SCHULZ-WELDA
LONGING FOR HOME	JUNGMAN, A.
LONGING	AMES, J.
LONGING	BEETHOVEN
LONG AGO -- AND FAR AWAY	SINGER, L.--ED
LONG AGO AND FAR AWAY -- SHOWCASE	
LONG AND WINDING ROAD, THE	LENNON *
LONG DAY'S JOURNEY INTO NIGHT, THEME FROM	PREVIN, A.
LONG DE LA ROUTE, LE OP. 89	GREGH
LONG ISLAND RHAPSODY	
LONG JOURNEY, A	KARP
LONG WAIT, A	KARP
LOOK, NO FINGER NUMBERS, BK. 1	NEVIN
LOOK, NO FINGER NUMBERS, BK. 2	NEVIN
LOOKING-GLASS RIVER	WEYBRIGHT
LOOKING GLASS LAKE	FROST
LOOK AND LEARN WORKBOOK, BK. 1	COBB
LOOK AND LEARN WORKBOOK, BK. 2	COBB
LOOK AND LEARN	COBB
LOOK AND LISTEN, PART A -- ELEMENTARY SERIES, BASIC --	CLARK, F.
LOOK AND LISTEN, PART B -- ELEMENTARY SERIES, BASIC --	CLARK, F.
LOOK AND LISTEN, PART C -- ELEMENTARY SERIES, BASIC --	CLARK, F.
LOOK AND LISTEN, PART D -- ELEMENTARY SERIES, BASIC --	CLARK, F.
LOOK AND PLAY PIANO COURSE	MCCONATHY
LOOK AT ME	BRODSKY, M.
LOOK AT THAT	ROZIN
LOOK BEFORE YOU LEAP	SCARMOLIN
LOOK FOR THE SILVER LINING -- SHOWCASE	
LOOK FOR THE SILVER LINING	
LOOK OF LOVE, THE	BRADLEY,
LOPE ALONG COWBOY	DEE, M.
LOPSIDED	SHULMAN
LORD'S PRAYER, THE -- SET	MALOTTE, A.
LORD'S PRAYER, THE	MALOTTE, A.
LORD'S PRAYER, THE	MALOTTE, A.
LORD'S PRAYER, THE	MALOTTE, A.
LORD'S PRAYER, THE	MALOTTE, A.
LORD'S PRAYER	LANE, J.--ED.
LORD MAYOR'S SHOW	GRAY, D.
LORELEI, THE	
LORELEI	SCHIEFELBEIN, F.
LORELEI	SCHMEID, A.
LORELEI	SINDING
LORELEY - DANZA DELLE ONDINE	CATALANI
LORENA	BURNAM
LOSE BLATTER OP. 13 -- BK. 1 ST.-V.S. 20	REGER
LOSE BLATTER OP. 13 -- BK. 2 ST.-V.S. 20	REGER
LOSS OF LOVE	
LOST CHORD, THE	SULLIVAN, A.
LOST CHORD	SULLIVAN, A.
LOST FLUTE, THE. WITH NARRATOR AND PERCUSSION OR	TCHEREPNIN
LOST HORIZON	BRADLEY,
LOST LOVE	
LOTS OF FUN	ROLFE, W.
LOTS OF LUCK BOOGIE	REID
LOTUS-LAND	SCOTT, C.
LOTUSLAND, OP. 47 NO. 1	SCOTT, C.
LOTUS DANCE, THE	KENT, A.
LOTUS FESTIVAL	KING, S.
LOTUS FLOWERS IN THE WIND	SCHER, W.
LOTUS LAND, OP. 47 NO. 1	SCOTT, C.
LOTUS LAND, OP. 47 NO. 1	SCOTT, C.
LOTUS LAND, OP. 47 NO. 1	SCOTT, C.
LOTUS LAND	SCOTT, C.
LOTUS LAND	SCOTT, C.
LOUISA'S POLKA	SMETANA
LOUISE	CHARPENTIER, G.
LOUISE	MCADAMS, G.
LOUISIANA HAYRIDE	DIETZ *
LOUISIANA HAYRIDE	TUCCI, SCHAUM, J.--ED.
LOUISIANA LOU	ELLIOTT
LOUP, LE -- BALLET --	DUTILLEUX
LOUSADZAK	HOVHANESS, A.
LOUSNAG KISHER -- MOONLIGHT NIGHT	HOVHANESS, A.
LOVE'S DEPARTURE	SEIDT, J.
LOVE'S DREAM, NO. 3	LISZT
LOVE'S DREAM AFTER THE BALL	CZIBULKA

LOVE'S GOLDEN MEMORIES	MASKELL, C. H.
LOVE'S GOLDEN STAR	DRUMHELLER
LOVE'S GREETING, OP. 12	ELGAR, E.
LOVE'S GREETING	ELGAR, E.
LOVE'S GREETING	ELGAR, E.
LOVE'S GREETING	SEIDT, J.
LOVE'S LAST GREETING	MCADAMS, G.
LOVE'S LULLABY	SCHIEFELBEIN, F.
LOVE'S MEDITATION	SEIDT, J.
LOVE'S OLD SWEET SONG	MOLLOY, J.
LOVE'S OLD SWEET SONG	MOLLOY, J.
LOVE'S ORACLE, MAZURKA	BOHM
LOVE'S OWN KISS--''HIGH JINKS''	FRIML, R.
LOVE'S PARADISE	MEARES, J. C.
LOVE'S QUARREL	SEIDT, J.
LOVE'S REPROACHES	SCHATZ
LOVE'S TRIUMPH	SEIDT, J.
LOVELIEST NIGHT OF THE YEAR	LANE, J.--ED.
LOVELY LADY MOON	WEYBRIGHT
LOVELY NIGHT, ROMANCE	HOPKINS, H.
LOVERS NO MORE	ELLSTEIN, A.
LOVE AND DEVOTION	DRUMHELLER
LOVE AND FLOWERS	ALDRICH
LOVE AND PASSION	MESSINA, J.
LOVE DREAMS, WALTZ	GREENWALD, M.
LOVE DREAMS OP. 4	BROWN, A.
LOVE EN MASQUE, WALTZ	CHEVALIER
LOVE FROM BROADWAYS	
LOVE HER MADLY	
LOVE IN ARMS, WALTZ	BOHM
LOVE IN IDLENESS	MACBETH
LOVE IS A MANY-SPLENDORED THING	FAIN *
LOVE IS A MANY-SPLENDORED THING	LANE, J.--ED.
LOVE IS A MANY-SPLENDORED THING	
LOVE IS BLUE	BRIMHALL,
LOVE IS LIKE A FIREFLY--''THE FIREFLY''	FRIML, R.
LOVE IS ONLY LOVE	BRIMHALL,
LOVE MAKES THE WORLD GO 'ROUND	BERRILL, R.
LOVE MAKES THE WORLD GO 'ROUND	LANE, J.--ED.
LOVE MAKES THE WORLD GO 'ROUND	WILLIAMS,
LOVE MEANS --YOU NEVER HAVE TO SAY YOU'RE SORRY--	BRADLEY,
LOVE OF THREE ORANGES, MARCH	PROKOFIEFF
LOVE SOMEBODY, YES I DO- WITH 'SOUND THE FLUTE' FOR	CHURCHILL--ED
LOVE SONG, OP. 40	CADMAN, C.
LOVE SONG, WALKUERE	WAGNER
LOVE SONG -- MINNELIED --	SCHULZ-WELDA
LOVE SPRING	BOHM, J.C.
LOVE THAT BOOGIE	STEINER
LOVE THEME, ROMEO AND JULIET	TSCHAIKOWSKY
LOVE THEME FROM 'LA STRADA'	GALDIERI *
LOVE THEME FROM 'MADAME X,' -- SWEDISH RHAPSODY	WILDMAN
LOVE THEME FROM 'MANHATTAN TOWER'	JENKINS, M.
LOVE THEME FROM 'MARY, QUEEN OF SCOTS'	BARRY
LOVE THEME FROM 'THE GLENN MILLER STORY'	MANCINI
LOVE THEME FROM ROMEO AMD JULIET	BRIMHALL,
LOVE THEME FROM THE GODFATHER	BRIMHALL,
LOVE THOUGHTS, WALTZES	GREENWALD, M.
LOVE TOKENS -- SIMPLIFIED	PANELLA, L.
LOVE WALKED IN	SINGER, L.--ED
LOVE WALKED IN	
LOVE WALTZ, OP. 57, NO. 5	MOSZKOWSKI
LOVE WALTZ, OP. 59 NO. 2 - EASY	SCHUETT
LOVE WALTZ, OP. 59 NO. 2	SCHUETT
LOVING HEARTS MUST PART	LANGE, G.
LOWLANDS	KRAEHENBUEHL
LOWLAND LULLABY	MCGRAW
LT. KIJE SUITE	PROKOFIEFF
LUCIA, SEXTETTE	DONIZETTI
LUCIA DI LAMMERMOOR, SEXTETTE	DONIZETTI *
LUCIA DI LAMMERMOOR - EASY FANTASIA	DONIZETTI
LUCIA DI LAMMERMOOR - VERRANNO A TE AND TU CHE A DIO	DONIZETTI
LUCIA DI LAMMERMOOR	DONIZETTI
LUCIA DI LAMMERMOOR	DONIZETTI
LUCKY FOUR-LEAF CLOVER	TROJE-MILLER
LUCY ESCOTT VARIATIONS FOR HARPSICHORD, 1963 -	HENZE, H.
LUDUS TONALIS, 1942	HINDEMITH
LUIGI'S TARANTELLA	SCHER, W.
LUISENS POLKA IN E FLAT	SMETANA
LULLABY, JOCELYN, EASY	GODARD, B.
LULLABY, JOCELYN	GODARD, B.
LULLABY, OP. 13 NO. 7	ILJINSKY, A.
LULLABY, OP. 38 NO. 1	GRIEG
LULLABY -- WIEGENLIED -- OP. 49 NO. 4	BRAHMS
LULLABY -- WIEGENLIED -- OP. 49 NO. 4	BRAHMS
LULLABY -- WITH DANCE BY GERCHIK	SALUTRINSKAYA
LULLABY AND A HAPPY TUNE	FRACKENPOHL, A.
LULLABY AND A HAPPY TUNE	FRACKENPOHL, A.
LULLABY AND FESTA	POSTON, E.
LULLABY AND WALTZ	DONENFELD, J.
LULLABY FOR A BABY PANDA	FINE, I.
LULLABY FOR A CHERUB	STORR, S.
LULLABY FOR A DOLL	ROBBINS
LULLABY FOR A LAMBKIN	ECKSTEIN
LULLABY FOR A PAPOOSE	ELAINE, M.
LULLABY FOR A SLEEPY DOLL	NOBLES, O.
LULLABY FOR EVELINE	VOVK
LULLABY IN DOLL LAND	SCHAUM, J.--ED.
LULLABY IN THE DARK WIND	CADZOW
LULLABY LAND	BURNAM
LULLABY LAND	LINDFORS
LULLABY OF BIRDLAND	LANE, J.--ED.
LULLABY OF MEMORIES	FERNANDEZ, O.
LULLABY TO A FRENCH DOLL	MUNGER, S.
LULLABY	ANDERSON, M.
LULLABY	BRAHMS
LULLABY	BRAHMS
LULLABY	BRAHMS
LULLABY	BRAHMS
LULLABY	BRAHMS
LULLABY	BUREN, N.
LULLABY	CACAVAS
LULLABY	FIALA
LULLABY	FICHANDLER, W.
LULLABY	FOSTER
LULLABY	HAUBIEL, C.
LULLABY	ILJYNSKY
LULLABY	JEAN, E.
LULLABY	MOZART, W. A.
LULLABY	PANELLA, L.
LULLABY	PROCTER, A.
LULLABY	PUI KAI
LULLABY	RICKER, E.
LULLABY	ROBINSON, A.
LULLABY	STEEL
LULLABY	TSCHAIKOWSKY
LULLABY	TSCHAIKOWSKY

LULLABY	TSCHAIKOWSKY *
LUMBERJACK SONG	SCHAUM, J.
LUNA RHAPSODY	CACAVAS
LUNDU	GUARNIERI
LUNE D'AUTOMNE A IDZUOMO -- NO. 1, FROM DEUX IMAGES DU	GIL-MARCHEX
LUNE QUI DANSE, LA	AUBRY
LUSTIGEN FISCHERJUNG'S, DIE -- OP. 23, NO. 2	DERKSEN
LUSTIGE MUSIK	POLIVKA
LUSTSPIEL, OVERTURE	KELER BELA
LUSTSPIEL OVERTURE	KELLER, B.
LUTE, THE	KIRNBERGER, J.
LYDIA	ROSZA
LYDIA	ROSZA
LYRICAL PIECES, OP. 12	GRIEG
LYRICAL PIECES, OP. 38	GRIEG
LYRICAL PIECES, OP. 43	GRIEG
LYRICAL PIECES, OP. 47	GRIEG
LYRICAL PIECES, OP. 54	GRIEG
LYRICAL PIECES, OP. 68	GRIEG
LYRICAL PRELUDE, A	BRUSSELS, I.
LYRICAL	WALTHEW, R.
LYRIC ARABESQUE	LOCKWOOD, N.
LYRIC DANCE	BAUER
LYRIC PIECES, BK. 01, OP. 12	GRIEG
LYRIC PIECES, BK. 02, OP. 38	GRIEG
LYRIC PIECES, BK. 03, OP. 43	GRIEG
LYRIC PIECES, BK. 04, OP. 47	GRIEG
LYRIC PIECES, BK. 05, OP. 54	GRIEG
LYRIC PIECES, BK. 06, OP. 57, VOL. 1	GRIEG
LYRIC PIECES, BK. 06, OP. 57, VOL. 2	GRIEG
LYRIC PIECES, BK. 07, OP. 62, VOL. 1	GRIEG
LYRIC PIECES, BK. 07, OP. 62, VOL. 2	GRIEG
LYRIC PIECES, BK. 08, OP. 65, VOL. 1	GRIEG
LYRIC PIECES, BK. 08, OP. 65, VOL. 2	GRIEG
LYRIC PIECES, BK. 09, OP. 68	GRIEG
LYRIC PIECES, BK. 10, OP. 71	GRIEG
LYRIC PIECES, COMPLETE	GRIEG
LYRIC PIECES, OP. 12	GRIEG
LYRIC PIECES, OP. 12	GRIEG
LYRIC PIECES, OP. 38	GRIEG
LYRIC PIECES, OP. 43	GRIEG
LYRIC PIECES, OP. 57	GRIEG
LYRIC PIECES FOR THE YOUNG. 7 FAVORITE PIECES	GRIEG
LYRIC PIECES FOR THE YOUNG	DELLO JOIO, N.
LYRIC PIECE	STEVENS, H.
LYRIC PRELUDES	GILLOCK
LYRIC SKETCHES	DE NITO
LYRIC TO THE MOON	DITTENHAVER
LYRISCHE STUCKE 1 OP. 12	GRIEG
LYRISCHE STUCKE 3 -- AN D. FRUHLING OP. 43 NO. 6	GRIEG
LYRISCHE STUCKE 3 OP. 43	GRIEG
LYSISTRATA, OP. 34 -- BALLET IN 3 TABLEAUX	BLACHER
L ISLE JOYEUSE	DEBUSSY
M-I-S-S-I-P-P-I	LANE, J.--ED.
M-O-T-H-E-R	LANE, J.--ED.
MACARENA	MONTERDE, B.
MACBETH, OP. 23. SYMPHONIC POEM	STRAUSS, R.
MACDOWELL MASTERPIECES	MACDOWELL
MACEDONIAN MOUNTAIN DANCE	HOVHANESS, A.
MACK THE KNIFE	WEILL, K.
MACK THE KNIFE	WEILL, K.
MADAMA BUTTERFLY -- COMPLETE OPERA --	PUCCINI
MADAMA BUTTERFLY - FANTASIA APPASSIONATA	PUCCINI
MADAMA BUTTERFLY - FANTASIA	PUCCINI
MADAMA BUTTERFLY - FINALE OF ACT II -- HUMMING CHORUS	PUCCINI
MADAMA BUTTERFLY - ONE FINE DAY	PUCCINI
MADAMA BUTTERFLY - SELECTION	PUCCINI
MADAMA BUTTERFLY - 1ST EASY FANTASIA	PUCCINI
MADAMA BUTTERFLY - 2ND EASY FANTASIA	PUCCINI
MADAMA BUTTERFLY - 3RD EASY FANTASIA	PUCCINI
MADAME POMPADOUR	JOHANNING
MADCHEN KAM VOM STELLDICHEIN, OP. 37 NO. 5	SIBELIUS
MADDALENA	WEYBRIGHT--ED.
MADE EASY FOR THE PIANO -- COLE PORTER	RICHTER--ED
MADE EASY FOR THE PIANO -- GEORGE GERSHWIN, BK. 1	RICHTER--ED
MADE EASY FOR THE PIANO -- GEORGE GERSHWIN, BK. 2	RICHTER--ED
MADE EASY FOR THE PIANO -- GEORGE GERSHWIN, BK. 3	RICHTER--ED
MADE EASY FOR THE PIANO -- SIGMUND ROMBERG, BK. 2	RICHTER--ED
MADE EASY FOR THE PIANO -- VICTOR HERBERT, BK. 1	RICHTER--ED
MADE EASY FOR THE PIANO -- VICTOR HERBERT, BK. 2	RICHTER--ED
MADE EASY FOR THE PIANO -- VICTOR HERBERT, BK. 3	RICHTER--ED
MADE EASY FOR THE PIANO -- VINCENT YOUMANS	RICHTER--ED
MADE EASY FOR THE PIANO -- 20TH CENTURY HITS, BK. 1	RICHTER--ED
MADE EASY FOR THE PIANO -- 20TH CENTURY HITS, BK. 2	RICHTER--ED
MADONNA, LA	SWEET, A.
MADONNA PURITA -- BALLET --	BIZZELLI
MADONNA	HAUBIEL, C.
MADRAS SONATA	HOVHANESS, A.
MADRID. 5 ESTAMPAS	FEMENIA
MADRID	STRAVINSKY, I.
MADRIGALE IN D	SIMONETTI
MADRIGAL DE FRANCOIS I	LAMOTHE
MADRIGAL DIVINE	DETT, R.
MADRIGAL FROM 'FOUR SKETCHES'	MILHAUD, D.
MADRIGAL	FRAZZI
MADRIGAL	MERIGOT, F.
MADRIGAL	RIETI
MADRIGAL	SIMONETTI
MADRIGAL	SIMONETTI
MADRILENA, FANTAISIE ESPAGNOLE	WACHS, P.
MADRILENA	WACHS, P.
MAD MARCH WINDS	LAMBERT, C.
MAE	ORTOLANI
MAGIC BOOK, THE, OP. 76--6 PHANTASMAGORIAS--NO. 1, THE	NIEMANN
MAGIC BOOK, THE, OP. 76--6 PHANTASMAGORIAS	NIEMANN
MAGIC BOOK, THE, OP. 92--6 PHANTASMAGORIAS--NO. 6,	NIEMANN
MAGIC CIRCLE, THE	CARLEY, I. M.
MAGIC CIRCLE	LAST, J.
MAGIC CLOCK, THE	BALLATORE, P.
MAGIC EYE, THE	RAPHLING
MAGIC FINGER TECHNIQUE, BK. 1	BASTIEN
MAGIC FINGER TECHNIQUE, BK. 2	BASTIEN
MAGIC FINGER TECHNIQUE, BK. 3	BASTIEN
MAGIC FLUTE. ABRIDGED	MOZART, W. A.
MAGIC FLUTE, PRIESTS' MARCH	MOZART, W. A.
MAGIC FLUTE, THE -- OVERTURE	MOZART, W. A.
MAGIC FOUNTAIN, THE	GLOVER, D.
MAGIC GARDEN	RAEZER, C.
MAGIC GATE, THE	RETI, R.
MAGIC HORN, THE	ROSS
MAGIC HOUR, THE	MARTIN, H.
MAGIC KEYS, BK. 1	CURCIO
MAGIC KEYS, BK. 2	CURCIO
MAGIC KEYS, BK. 3	CURCIO
MAGIC LAMP, THE	RICHMAN, A.
MAGIC LINES AND SPACES, AN INTRODUCTION	MAURY, L.
MAGIC LINES AND SPACES, INSTRUCTION BK. 1	MAURY, L.
MAGIC LINES AND SPACES, INSTRUCTION BK. 2	MAURY, L.
MAGIC LINES AND SPACES, REPERTOIRE BK. 1	MAURY, L.
MAGIC LINES AND SPACES, REPERTOIRE BK. 2	MAURY, L.
MAGIC MANDARINS	NAGY, M.
MAGIC MIRRORS	GROVE
MAGIC PIANO IN ORCHESTRA LAND, THE	MELECCI, A.
MAGIC RIVER	CANICE
MAGNIFICENT PROCESSION, THE	GOUNOD, C.
MAGNOLIA -- INTERMEZZO	DAVIS, M.
MAGNOLIA BLOSSOMS--WALTZES	DEKOVEN, R.
MAGNOLIA TIME	MARTIN, H.
MAGNOLIA	WRIGHT, N.
MAH-NA, MAH-NA	UMILIANI
MAIDEN'S PRAYER, THE	BADARZEWSKA, T.
MAIDEN'S PRAYER, THE	BADARZEWSKA, T.
MAIDEN'S PRAYER	BADARZEWSKA, T.
MAIDEN'S PRAYER	BADARZEWSKA, T.
MAIDEN'S WISH, THE	CHOPIN
MAIDEN'S WISH, THE	CHOPIN *
MAIDEN'S WISH	CHOPIN *
MAIDEN'S WISH	CHOPIN *
MAIDEN'S WISH	CHOPIN
MAIDEN'S WISH	CHOPIN
MAIDEN AND THE NIGHTINGALE, THE	GRANADOS
MAIDEN AND THE NIGHTINGALE	GRANADOS
MAIDS OF CADIZ	DELIBES, L.
MAIDS OF MADRID, THE.	HAMILTON *
MAID IN GREEN, THE	BLAKE, D.
MAID OF GANGES, THE	MENDELSSOHN *
MAID OF SORRENTO	STEINER
MAID OF THE DAWN	HOLT, EILSEL
MAID OF THE GANGES, THE	MENDELSSOHN *
MAILA WALTZ	DELIBES, L.
MAILMAN	BURNAM
MAJESTIC	WILSON, M.
MAJESTY OF THE DEEP	HAMER, G. F.
MAJOLICA, POLKA	REES
MAJORETTES, THE	HART
MAJORS AND THEIR RELATIVES, THE	LINDFORS, E.
MAJOR AND MINOR SCALES	NICOLOSI
MAJOR MINIATURES FOR PIANO	COBB
MAJOR SCALES - BOOK 1	
MAJOR SCALES - BOOK 2	
MAJOR SCALES AND PIECES	BASTIEN--ED.
MAK, THE SHEEP STEALER	CHAPPELL, H.
MAKE BELIEVE	SMITH, H.
MAKE BELIEVE	
MAKE BELIEVE	
MAKE BELIEVE	
MAKE IT SNAPPY	GLOVER, D.
MAKE IT SNAPPY	OLSON
MAKE SOMEONE HAPPY	SINGER, L.--ED
MAKE YOUR OWN SCALES AND ARPEGGIOS	BENNER, L.
MAKING ENDS MEET --IN PREPARATION--	WUORINEN
MAKING MUSIC AT THE PIANO, BK. 1	SCHAUM, J.
MAKING MUSIC AT THE PIANO, BK. 2	SCHAUM, J.
MAKING MUSIC AT THE PIANO, BK. 3	SCHAUM, J.
MAKING MUSIC AT THE PIANO, BK. 4	SCHAUM, J.
MAKING MUSIC AT THE PIANO, BK. -5	SCHAUM, J.
MAKING MUSIC AT THE PIANO, BK. 6	SCHAUM, J.
MAKING MUSIC AT THE PIANO, BK. 7	SCHAUM, J.
MAKING MUSIC AT THE PIANO, BK. 8	SCHAUM, J.
MAKING MUSIC AT THE PIANO - BOOK 1	FREDRICH, F.
MAKING MUSIC AT THE PIANO - BOOK 2	FREDRICH, F.
MAKING MUSIC	BLAKE, J. *
MAKING SURE OF PIANO PLAY	FREDRICH, F.
MALAGA -- FROM IBERIA	ALBENIZ, I.
MALAGUENA, OP. 165, NO. 3 FROM 'ESPANA'	ALBENIZ, I.
MALAGUENA, OP. 165 NO. 3	ALBENIZ, I.
MALAGUENA, OP. 60, NO. 03--FROM ESPANA	ALBENIZ, I.
MALAGUENA --FROM BOABDIL--	MOSZKOWSKI
MALAGUENA - FROM 'BOABDIL'	MOSZKOWSKI
MALAGUENA AND HABANERA, OP. 21 NOS. 1 AND 2	SARASTE
MALAGUENA NO. 3	ALBENIZ, I.
MALAGUENA	ALBENIZ, I.
MALAGUENA	ALBENIZ, I.
MALAGUENA	LECUONA
MALAGUENA	LECUONA
MALAGUENA	LECUONA
MALAGUENA	LECUONA
MALAGUENA	LECUONA
MALAGUENA	LECUONA
MALAMBO	GINASTERA
MALAMBO	MILICI
MALEDICTION FOR PIANO AND STRINGS --SEARLE 121--	LISZT
MALERSTUDIEN, OP. 56 -- WALDEINSAMKEIT, DISPUT VON	FIBICH, Z.
MALIA	TOSTI
MALIA	TOSTI
MALLORCA, OP. 202	ALBENIZ, I.
MALLORCA - NUIT SUR LA BAIE DE PALMA	TURINA, J.
MALLORCA	TURINA, J.
MALVINA, VALSE MIGNONNE	LEDUC, A.
MAM'S GONE, GOODBYE	BOCAGE *
MAMA, PAPA IS WOUNDED, FROM THE SUITE, 'SIX SURREALIST	TRIGGS
MAMBO BOOGIE	SCHAUM, J.--ED.
MAMBO JAMBO	BAUER
MAMBO MARITA	KASSCHAU, H.
MAMBO MARITA	KASSCHAU, H.
MAME	BRIMHALL,
MAMMA, CARISSIMA	DE CRESCENZO
MAMMA, QUANTO T'AMO	DE CRESCENZO
MAMMY'S LULLABY	MOREY, F.
MAMMY BLUE	BRIMHALL,
MAMSELLE	LANE, J.--ED.
MANCHAS DE COLOR	MELO GORIGOYTIA,
MANCINI GENERATION	
MANDARIN'S SONG, THE	CACAVAS *
MANDARIN AND THE MULE, THE	GRAHAM, F.
MANDOLINA, MEXICAN SERENADE	LANGEY
MANDOLINE, SERENADE ESPAGNE	THOME, F.
MANDOLIN AND GUITAR, THE	GROOMS
MANDOLIN SERENADE	EILENBERG
MANHATTAN BLUES	NEVIN
MANHATTAN INTERLUDE --MODERN RHYTHMIC CLASSICS--	WHITFORD
MANHATTAN MANNIKIN	GLOVER, D.
MANHATTAN MANNIKIN	GLOVER, D.
MANHATTAN NOONLIGHT	ALTER, L.
MANHATTAN RHYTHM --MODERN RHYTHMIC CLASSICS--	WHITFORD
MANHATTAN SERENADE	ALTER, L.
MANHATTAN SERENADE	
MANHATTAN	HART, F. *
MANHATTAN	HART, F. *
MANICHORD CAPRICE	VOLZ, H.
MANIKINS	DUNHILL, T.
MANOJICO	MINGOTE, A.
MANOLA, LA, SERENADE	EILENBERG

MANOLETTO'S DANCE	PERRIN
MANON LESCAUT - FANTASIA	PUCCINI
MANON LESCAUT - INTERMEZZO ACT III	PUCCINI
MANON LESCAUT - IN QUELLE TRINE MORBIDE	PUCCINI
MANON	MASSENET, J.
MANO SINISTRA --SIX PIECES FOR LEFT HAND ONLY BY DUTCH	
MANSION OVER THE HILLTOP	LANE, J.--ED.
MANTILLA	ECKSTEIN
MANTILLA	REBE
MANUSCRIPT BOOK OF ELEMENTARY HARMONY, BK. 1	MACMAHON, D.
MANUSCRIPT BOOK OF ELEMENTARY HARMONY, BK. 2	MACMAHON, D.
MANUSCRIPT BOOK OF RUDIMENTS OF MUSIC, BK. 1	MACMAHON, D.
MANUSCRIPT BOOK OF RUDIMENTS OF MUSIC, BK. 2	MACMAHON, D.
MANY-A-MILE AWAY	COBB
MANZANILLO	ROBYN, A.
MANZANILLO	
MAN ALONE, A	BARRY
MAN AND A WOMAN, A	BRIMHALL
MAN FROM MINTON'S , THE	SHEARING, G.
MAN FROM U.N.C.L.E. - THEME	GOLDSMITH, J.
MAN IN THE MOON, THE	DITTENHAVER
MAN IN THE MOON, THE	THORNTON
MAN IN THE MOON	ANSON, G.
MAN I LOVE, THE	GERSHWIN
MAN I LOVE, THE	GERSHWIN
MAN I LOVE, THE	GERSHWIN
MAN I LOVE, THE	GERSHWIN
MAN OF LA MANCHA	DARION *
MAN OF LA MANCHA	DARION *
MAN ON THE FLYING TRAPEZE	SCHAUM, J.--ED.
MAPLE HILL FARM	TREVARTHEN, R.
MAPLE LEAF RAG	JOPLIN, S.
MAPLE LEAF RAG	JOPLIN, S.
MAPLE LEAF RAG	JOPLIN, S.
MAPLE LEAF RAG	JOPLIN, S.
MAPLE LEAF RAG	JOPLIN, S.
MAPLE LEAF RAG	JOPLIN, S.
MAPLE SUGARING	BACON, E.
MARACAS	THOMPSON, J.
MARBLES	ALT, H.
MARBLES	KREUTZER
MARCH, AIDA	VERDI
MARCH, BIRTHDAY SUITE	BOHM
MARCH, CARMEN	BIZET, G.
MARCH, FAUST	GOUNOD, C.
MARCH, FROM 'LOVE OF THE THREE ORANGES'	PROKOFIEFF
MARCH, FROM A COLLECTION OF 'PIECES FOR KLAVIER'	BACH, J.S.
MARCH, FROM CAPRICCIO, OP. 22	MENDELSSOHN
MARCH, LOHENGRIN	WAGNER
MARCH, NORMA	BELLINI
MARCH, OP. 12 NO. 1	PROKOFIEFF
MARCH, OP. 12 NO. 1	PROKOFIEFF
MARCH, OP. 40 NO. 1	ALKAN
MARCH, OP. 40 NO. 2	ALKAN
MARCH, OP. 40 NO. 3	ALKAN
MARCH, OP. 65, NO. 10	PROKOFIEFF
MARCH, PROPHET	MEYERBEER, G.
MARCH, TANNHAUSER	WAGNER
MARCHAND DES OISEAUX	TAILLEFERRE, G.
MARCHA DE LOS SOLDADOS DE PLOMO -- CUENTOS Y	CHAVARRI
MARCHA DO PEQUENO POLEGAR	PINTO, O.
MARCHA ORIENTAL -- NO. 4, FROM SIX PIECES ON SPANISH	GRANADOS
MARCHE--LOVE OF THREE ORANGES	PROKOFIEFF
MARCHE-SCHERZO, OP. 2	SAINT-SAENS
MARCHENBILDER, OP. 3 NO. 2 'DIE PRINZESSIN AUF DER	KORNGOLD, E. W.
MARCHENBILDER, OP. 3 NO. 7 'DAS MARCHEN SPRICHT DEN	KORNGOLD, E. W.
MARCHES, FIVE	MENDELSSOHN
MARCHES --4--	GRIEG
MARCHES AND SONGS WE LOVE--WITH WORDS AND	RODGERS, I.
MARCHES FOR THE YOUNG PIANIST	STEINER
MARCHES	SANFORD
MARCHES	SCHUBERT
MARCHE AUX FLAMBEAUS, OP. 32 FOR ONE PIANO, SIX HANDS	CLARK, S.
MARCHE AUX FLAMBEAUX	CLARK, S.
MARCHE A LA TURQUE--FROM THE ''RUINS OF ATHENS''	BEETHOVEN
MARCHE A LA TURQUE-FROM 'THE RUINS OF ATHENS'	BEETHOVEN
MARCHE DES ECOSSAIS	FRANCAIX, J.
MARCHE DES HEROS HONGROIS	FUCIK
MARCHE DES PETITS SOLDATS DE PLOMB	PIERNE
MARCHE DES REJOUIS BON-TEMPS	WACHS, P.
MARCHE DES TROUBADOURS, OP. 32	ROUBIER, H.
MARCHE DE CONCERT, CAP.	WACHS, P.
MARCHE DE CONCERT	WOLLENHAUPT
MARCHE DU SACRE DU PROPHETE	DE GARAUDE
MARCHE ECOSSAISE	DEBUSSY
MARCHE ECOSSAISE	DEBUSSY
MARCHE FROM L'EVENTAIL DE JEANNE	FERROUD, P. O.
MARCHE FUNEBRE--FROM SONATA, OP. 26	BEETHOVEN
MARCHE FUNEBRE--FROM SONATA IN B FLAT MINOR, OP. 35	CHOPIN
MARCHE FUNEBRE D'UNE MARIONNETTE	GOUNOD, C.
MARCHE FUNEBRE D'UNE MOUSME	MARIE
MARCHE FUNEBRE D'UNE MOUSME	MARIE
MARCHE FUNEBRE	CHOPIN
MARCHE FUNEBRE	LAZARUS
MARCHE GROTESQUE, OP. 32 NO. 1	SINDING
MARCHE GROTESQUE, OP. 32 NO. 1	SINDING
MARCHE GROTESQUE	SINDING
MARCHE HEROIQUE, OP. 34	SAINT-SAENS
MARCHE HEROIQUE, OP. 34	SAINT-SAENS
MARCHE HEROQUE	SPAULDING, G. L.
MARCHE INDIENNE	SELLENICK
MARCHE INDIENNE	SELLENICK
MARCHE JOYEUSE	HALFFTER, E.
MARCHE MIGNONNE, OP. 15 NO. 2 -- SET	POLDINI, E.
MARCHE MILITAIRE, OP. 51 NO. 1 -- SET	SCHUBERT
MARCHE MILITAIRE, OP. 51 NO. 1 -- 6 HANDS	SCHUBERT
MARCHE MILITAIRE, OP. 51 NO. 1	SCHUBERT
MARCHE MILITAIRE, OP. 51 NO. 1	SCHUBERT
MARCHE MILITAIRE, OP. 51 NO. 1	SCHUBERT
MARCHE MILITAIRE, OP. 51 NO. 1	SCHUBERT
MARCHE MILITAIRE FRANCAISE DE LA SUITE ALGERIENNE, OP.	SAINT-SAENS
MARCHE MILITAIRE	BILBRO, M.
MARCHE MILITAIRE	STREABBOG
MARCHE PERSANE	LANDRY
MARCHE PERSANE	LANDRY
MARCHE PONTIFICALE	GOUNOD, C.
MARCHE PONTIFICALE	GOUNOD, C.
MARCHE SLAVE, OP. 31 -- 8-HANDS, SET	TSCHAIKOWSKY
MARCHE SLAVE, OP. 31	TSCHAIKOWSKY
MARCHE SLAV	TSCHAIKOWSKY
MARCHE SOLEMNELLE	WESLY
MARCHE	OHLSON, M.
MARCHING ALONG TOGETHER	LANE, J.--ED.
MARCHING ALONG	CLARK, M. E.
MARCHING ALONG	ROBINSON, A.
MARCHING ELEPHANTS	SCHER, W.
MARCHING FINGERS	JOYNER, B.
MARCHING HOME	FOLDES
MARCHING IN THE PARADE	HOUSE, A.
MARCHING MARIONETTES	EISBERG, B.
MARCHING MARIONETTES	SCHER, W.
MARCHING MUSIC FOR JOHNNY APPLESEED	FLETCHER, G.
MARCHING ON TIPTOES	KORTE, K.
MARCHING ON	MCINTYRE, E.
MARCHING PIXIE	BENFORD
MARCHING SONG	GRIFFES, C.
MARCHING THRU GEORGIA	MEACHAM, F.--ED
MARCHING TOWARDS MORNING	GRANT, J.
MARCHING TO SCHOOL	BASTIEN
MARCHING TO THE MUSIC	STILWELL
MARCHING WITH THE BAND	WRIGHT, L.
MARCH --LOVE OF THREE ORANGES	PROKOFIEFF
MARCH -- FROM CONCERTSTUCK IN F MINOR, OP. 79 -- SET	WEBER, VON
MARCH -- FROM KONZERTSTUCK IN F MINOR	WEBER, VON
MARCH -- WITH SILVERI - RELIGIOUS HARMONY --	LONGHI
MARCH -- 6-HANDS	NOEL, H.
MARCH ALBUM	SCHAUM, J.--ED.
MARCH ALLA TURCA	MOZART, W. A.
MARCH AND DANCE ALBUM	SOMERVELL, A.
MARCH AND DRIPPING FAUCET	SHULMAN
MARCH AND WALTZ FROM --THE COMEDIANS	KABALEVSKY
MARCH CARILLON	HANSON
MARCH DE AVIATEURS, ONE PIANO - SIX HANDS	LEPRE, P.
MARCH EROICA	OFFUTT
MARCH FOR AMERICANS	GROFE, F.
MARCH FOR NEW SHOES	CADZOW
MARCH FOR SAILORS	WADLEY
MARCH FROM 'PETER AND THE WOLF'	PROKOFIEFF
MARCH FROM 'RUINS OF ATHENS'	BEETHOVEN
MARCH FROM 'THE LOVE OF THREE ORANGES', OP. 33	PROKOFIEFF
MARCH FROM 'UKRANIAN MINIATURES'	BARWINSKY, W.
MARCH FROM L'ARLESIENNE	BIZET, G.
MARCH FROM THE LOVE OF THREE ORANGES	PROKOFIEFF
MARCH FUNEBRE	CHOPIN
MARCH HONGROISE OP. 14	DELIOUX
MARCH HUMORESQUE -- ON A GROUND BASS -- OP. 17, NO. 1	DOHNANYI
MARCH IN D, ANNA MAGDALENA	BACH, J.S.
MARCH IN D	BACH, J.S.
MARCH IN F	BESTHOFF, M.
MARCH IN G FROM NUTCRACKER SUITE	TSCHAIKOWSKY
MARCH KINGS ALBUM FOR PIANO	ROVENGER--ED.
MARCH LORRAINE	WEYBRIGHT
MARCH MILITAIRE, OP. 51 NO. 1	SCHUBERT
MARCH MILITAIRE, OP. 51	SCHUBERT
MARCH MILITAIRE	BILBRO, M.
MARCH MILITAIRE	GREENWALD, M.
MARCH MILITAIRE	GREENWALD, M.
MARCH MILITAIRE	SCHUBERT
MARCH MILITAIRE	STREABBOG
MARCH MILITAIRE	STREABBOG
MARCH MINIATURE, OP. 43	TSCHAIKOWSKY
MARCH OF DWARFS, OP. 54 NO. 3	GRIEG
MARCH OF PROGRESS	WILLIAMS, F.
MARCH OF RUBBER BOOTS	ROGERS, E.
MARCH OF THE AMERICANS	NOBLITT, K. M.
MARCH OF THE ANIMALS	GARROW, L.
MARCH OF THE ANIMALS	GARROW, L.
MARCH OF THE ASTRONAUTS	DITTENHAVER
MARCH OF THE ASTRONAUTS	MEUX
MARCH OF THE ATHLETES	RAPHLING
MARCH OF THE BAGPIPES	MCSWEEN, F. W.
MARCH OF THE BELGIAN PARATROOPS	LEEMANS
MARCH OF THE BLUES	MERKUR--ED
MARCH OF THE BOY SCOUTS	GRANT, G. A.
MARCH OF THE BOY SCOUTS	MARTIN, G.
MARCH OF THE BOY SCOUTS	MARTIN, G.
MARCH OF THE BOY SCOUTS	MOREY, F.
MARCH OF THE CADETS	RASBACH, O.
MARCH OF THE CANDY-STICK MEN	TRAVIS, B.
MARCH OF THE CANDY CANES	MARTIN, H.
MARCH OF THE CANDY DOLLS	RENTON, V.
MARCH OF THE CANDY SOLDIERS	HOPSON, E.
MARCH OF THE CANDY SOLDIERS	HOPSON, E.
MARCH OF THE CATTAILS	SCHULDT, M.
MARCH OF THE CHAMPIONS	WALDO, J.
MARCH OF THE CHAMPIONS	WALDO, J.
MARCH OF THE CHORDS	FRAZEE, G. F.
MARCH OF THE CLOWNS	BEETZ
MARCH OF THE CORNSTALKS	MCHALE, M.
MARCH OF THE CRUSADERS	RICHTER
MARCH OF THE CUB SCOUTS	REBE
MARCH OF THE DOMINOS	SEUEL-HOLST, M.
MARCH OF THE DWARFS, OP. 54 NO. 3	GRIEG
MARCH OF THE DWARFS, OP. 54 NO. 3	GRIEG
MARCH OF THE DWARFS, OP. 54 NO. 3	GRIEG
MARCH OF THE DWARFS	GRIEG
MARCH OF THE DWARFS	GRIEG
MARCH OF THE ELEPHANTS	LEE, E.
MARCH OF THE FINGER SNAPS	POOLE, C.
MARCH OF THE FLEAS	GLOVER, D.
MARCH OF THE FLOWER GIRLS	WACHS, P.
MARCH OF THE FLOWER GIRLS	WACHS, P.
MARCH OF THE FLOWER GIRLS	WACHS, P.
MARCH OF THE GINGERBREAD MAN	WADLEY
MARCH OF THE GINGERBREAD MEN, OP. 12 NO. 1	REED, D.
MARCH OF THE GNOMES	KETTERER, E.
MARCH OF THE GRAND ARMY OF THE POTOMAC --1863--	BECKEL
MARCH OF THE GREEN BERETS	SCHER, W.
MARCH OF THE GREEN BERETS	SCHER, W.
MARCH OF THE GUARDS	STREABBOG
MARCH OF THE IMPS	KRAMER, A. W.
MARCH OF THE INDIANS	ELAINE, SR.
MARCH OF THE JACK O'LANTERNS	KETTERER, E.
MARCH OF THE JUMPING JACKS -- FOR ONE PIANO, SIX HANDS	BILBRO, M.
MARCH OF THE LEAD SOLDIERS --PIANO, 6 HANDS--	GREIM
MARCH OF THE LEAD SOLDIERS	PIERNE
MARCH OF THE LILLIPUTIANS	HIBBS, C.
MARCH OF THE LITTLE LEAD SOLDIERS	PIERNE
MARCH OF THE LOLLIPOPS	DAVIS, J.
MARCH OF THE MAGI KINGS	EDWARDS, C.
MARCH OF THE MARTIANS	RICKER
MARCH OF THE MARTIANS	TROJE-MILLER
MARCH OF THE MIGHTY	COBB
MARCH OF THE MINI-MARTIANS	STECHER *
MARCH OF THE MINUTE MEN	PADWA, V.
MARCH OF THE MOON FOLK	WATSON
MARCH OF THE MOON MEN	BERMONT, G.
MARCH OF THE MOON MEN	PROCTER, A.
MARCH OF THE PENGUINS	MCGRAW
MARCH OF THE PENGUINS	TALBOT
MARCH OF THE PHANTOM BRIGADE	BRODSKY, M.
MARCH OF THE PLASTIC SOLDIERS	BURCH, S.
MARCH OF THE PRIESTS, ATHALIA	MENDELSSOHN
MARCH OF THE PRIESTS, EASY	MENDELSSOHN

MARCH OF THE PRIESTS, MAGIC FLUTE	MOZART, W. A.
MARCH OF THE PRIESTS	MENDELSSOHN
MARCH OF THE PUPPETS	HAZELLE
MARCH OF THE RECRUITS	SCHMOLL, A.
MARCH OF THE ROBOTS	ROBERTS
MARCH OF THE SARDAR, EASY	IVANOW
MARCH OF THE SARDAR	IPPOLITOV-IVANOW
MARCH OF THE SCOUTS	KETTERER, E.
MARCH OF THE SHADOW-MEN, FROM THE 'FIRST CONCERT'	LAST, J.
MARCH OF THE SIAMESE CHILDREN, THE	HAMMERSTEIN *
MARCH OF THE SIAMESE CHILDREN	HAMMERSTEIN *
MARCH OF THE SIAMESE CHILDREN	RODGERS *
MARCH OF THE SIAMESE CHILDREN	RODGERS *
MARCH OF THE SPACE CADETS	DVORINE
MARCH OF THE SPOOKS	PORTER, C.
MARCH OF THE TELEVISION PUPPETS	RICHTER, A.
MARCH OF THE THREE KINGS--AIRS AND DANCES OF THE 18TH	DILLER, A.
MARCH OF THE TINY SOLDIERS	MUNN, W.
MARCH OF THE TINY SOLDIERS	MUNN, W.
MARCH OF THE TIN SOLDIERS	GRETCHANINOFF
MARCH OF THE TIN SOLDIERS	READ, G.
MARCH OF THE TOREADORS	BIZET, G.
MARCH OF THE TOYS, SIMPLIFIED	HERBERT
MARCH OF THE TOYS --FROM BABES IN TOYLAND--	HERBERT
MARCH OF THE TOYS -- SIMP.	HERBERT
MARCH OF THE TOYS	HERBERT
MARCH OF THE TOYS	HERBERT
MARCH OF THE TOYS	HERBERT
MARCH OF THE TOYS	HERBERT
MARCH OF THE TOYS	HERBERT
MARCH OF THE TOY PICCOLOS	EISBERG, B.
MARCH OF THE TOY SOLDIERS	TSCHAIKOWSKY
MARCH OF THE TRIADS	NEVIN
MARCH OF THE TROLLS	KEYSER, I.
MARCH OF THE TROLL DOLLS	BASTIEN
MARCH OF THE TWIRLERS	RAPHLING
MARCH OF THE WEE FOLK	GAYNOR
MARCH OF THE WEE FOLK	GAYNOR
MARCH OF THE WEE FOLK	GAYNOR
MARCH OF THE WHITE KEYS	RAYMOND, J.
MARCH OF THE WILD GEESE	FROST
MARCH OF THE YOUNG CADETS	MATHEWS, B. D.
MARCH OF VICTORY	WAGNESS
MARCH ON, AND PARADE	FRACKENPOHL, A.
MARCH ON THE BLACK KEYS	STEINER
MARCH PARAPHRASE ON A THEME OF BACH	STRIMER
MARCH PAST	SWINSTEAD, F.
MARCH PONTIFICAL	GOUNOD, C.
MARCH RUSSE	GANNE
MARCH SLAVE, OP. 31	TSCHAIKOWSKY
MARCH SLAVE, OP. 31	TSCHAIKOWSKY
MARCH SLAVE	TSCHAIKOWSKY
MARCH SLAV BOOGIE	MERKEL, N.
MARCH SLAV	TSCHAIKOWSKY
MARCH SONATINA NO. 1	GREEN, R.
MARCH STACCATO	WARD
MARCH TRIUMPHAL	ARMOUR
MARCH	BACH, J.S.
MARCH	FITCH, J.
MARCH	GNESSINA
MARCH	GRIFFES, C.
MARCH	GROVE, R.
MARCH	KRAFT
MARCH	LOURIE
MARCH	WESLEY, S.
MARCH	ZUPKO
MARCIA DI FANCIULLI, 4 LANDLER, MARCIA MILITARE	SCHUBERT
MARCIA EROICA, OP. 27 NO. 3	SCHUBERT
MARCIA NUZIALE	GILIO, L.
MARCIA UND GAVOTTA	BEETHOVEN
MARDI GRAS -- WITH WORDS	WESTERVELT,
MARDI GRAS PARADE	SCHIEFELBEIN, F.
MARDI GRAS	BURNAM
MARDI GRAS	DITTENHAVER
MARDI GRAS	GROFE, F.
MARECHIARE	TOSTI
MARECHIARE	TOSTI
MARGARET POLKA	DIVERNOIS, J. P.
MARGIE -- SIMP.	MOSSMAN, T.
MARGUERITE AU ROUET	SCHUBERT *
MARGUERITE PIAZZA'S CHRISTMAS CAROL SING ALONG PARTY	PIAZZA, M.--ED
MARIA, FROM 'WEST SIDE STORY'	BERNSTEIN, L.
MARIAGE A LILLIPUT, UN	TRANSLETEUR
MARIANNA	SINGER
MARIANNA	SINGER
MARIA LUCIA	GUARNIERI
MARIEE DE VILLAGE, FETE PAYSANNE, OP. 216	LANDRY
MARIEE DU MOULIN, LA	CROISEZ, A.
MARIEE DU MOULIN, LA	CROISEZ, A.
MARIENWUERMCHEN	SCHUMANN, R.
MARIETTA	ARMOUR
MARIE ANTOINETTE'S MUSIC BOX	GIOVANNI
MARIE	ARMOUR
MARIGOLDS	PANELLA, L.
MARILYN K. DAVIS GROUP PIANO METHOD - GROUP ACTIVITIES	DAVIS, M.
MARILYN K. DAVIS GROUP PIANO METHOD - GROUP ACTIVITIES	DAVIS, M.
MARINES' HYMN, THE	SCHAUM, J.
MARINES' HYMN, THE	ZEPP--ED
MARINES' HYMN	CARLETON, B.
MARINES' HYMN	MITTLER--ED
MARINES' HYMN	SCHAUM, J.--ED.
MARINES' HYMN	SPENCER, J.
MARINES' HYMN	WHITFORD--ED.
MARINES ON PARADE	DITTENHAVER
MARINES	VANDELLE
MARINE	FOURDRAIN
MARINE	INGHELBRECHT, D.
MARIONETTE, THE	THOMPSON, J.
MARIONETTEN. KLEINE STUCKE FUR KLAVIER, BK. 1	MARTINU, B.
MARIONETTEN. KLEINE STUCKE FUR KLAVIER, BK. 2	MARTINU, B.
MARIONETTEN. KLEINE STUCKE FUR KLAVIER, BK. 3	MARTINU, B.
MARIONETTEN-MUSIKEN	FINKE
MARIONETTES, OP. 54 -- NINE EASY PIECES	BORTKIEWICZ
MARIONETTES	COBB
MARIONETTES	GARDNER
MARIONETTES	ROHDE, E.
MARIONETTES	ROWLEY
MARIONETTE BALLET	HIBBS, C.
MARIONETTE WALTZ	POWERS, M.
MARIONETTE	ARNDT
MARIONETTE	ARNDT
MARIONETTE	STILL
MARIONNETTES, OP. 29	LIADOW, A.
MARITANA, SCENES THAT ARE BRIGHTEST	WALLACE
MARKETING	BENSON
MARK NEVIN'S EASY PIANO DUETS	NEVIN
MARK NEVIN PIANO COURSE, BK. 1	NEVIN
MARK NEVIN PIANO COURSE, BK. 2	NEVIN
MARK NEVIN PIANO COURSE, BK. 3	NEVIN
MARK NEVIN PIANO COURSE, BK. 4	NEVIN
MARK NEVIN PIANO COURSE, BK. 5	NEVIN
MARK NEVIN PIANO COURSE, PREPARATORY BOOK	NEVIN
MARLBOROUGH'S RETURN	MORILLO, R.
MARLBOROUGH S'EN VA-T-EN GUERRE	AURIC
MARQUISE, LA	MERANG
MARRIAGE OF FIGARO. ABRIDGED	MOZART, W. A.
MARSCH AUS, JEUX D'ENFANTS	BIZET, G.
MARSEILLAISE, LA	ROUGET DE LISLE
MARSEILLAISE, THE	BEYER, F.--ED
MARSHMALLOW MINSTRELS	CONFREY, E.
MARTHA. FANTASY. TWO PIANOS, EIGHT HANDS	FLOTOW
MARTHA. OVERTURE. TWO PIANOS, EIGHT HANDS	FLOTOW
MARTHA, EASY TRANSCRIPTION	FLOTOW
MARTHA, FANTASIE, OP. 39	FLOTOW
MARTHA, FOR TWO PIANOS, EIGHT HANDS	FLOTOW
MARTHA, SELECTIONS	FLOTOW
MARTHA'S VINEYARD	MAILMAN, M.
MARTIN'S MAJOR AND MINOR SCALES AND PRINCIPAL CHORDS	MARTIN, G.
MARTIN'S MAJOR AND MINOR SCALES AND PRINCIPAL CHORDS	MARTIN
MARTITA	MONTANARI
MARVIN KAHN'S SONG SHOWCASE	KAHN, M.--ED
MARY'S A GRAND OLD NAME	COHAN, G. M.
MARY'S LITTLE LAMB	ROLFE, W.
MARY'S OTHER LAMBS, FOR 1 PIANO 6 HANDS	WEYBRIGHT
MARY'S PET WALTZ	MACK, E.
MARYELLEN	HAYMAN, R.
MARY HAD A LITTLE LAMB - VARIATIONS	THOMPSON, J.
MARY HAD A LITTLE LAMB	WILSON
MARY JANE WALTZ	HELTMAN
MARY LOU -- SIMP.	MOSSMAN, T.
MARY LOU WILLIAMS FIVE BARRELHOUSE BOOGIE WOOGIE AND	WILLIAMS, LOU.
MARY POPPINS	BRIMHALL
MASCHERATA PICCOLA. CONCERTINO GIOCOSO FUR KLAVIER UND	THIEME
MASCHERE, LE - OVERTURE	MASCAGNI, P.
MASCHERE, LE - PRELUDIETTO TO ACT II	MASCAGNI, P.
MASKED RIDER	COBB
MASK OF THE AFICAN KING	GALLUB, B.
MASK	LESSARD, J.
MASK	LESSARD, J.
MASONIC FUNERAL MUSIC, K477	MOZART, W. A.
MASQUERADE WALTZ	SEINBERG
MASQUERADE	GOODMAN, J.
MASQUERADE	HEDGES
MASQUERADE	WHITFORD
MASQUES ET BERGAMASQUES	FAURE, G.
MASQUES	DEBUSSY
MASQUES	DEBUSSY
MASQUE DANCE	SWINSTEAD, F.
MASQUE	HURST, G.
MASSA'S IN DE COLD, COLD GROUND	FOSTER
MASSA'S IN THE COLD, COLD GROUND	FOSTER
MASTERING THE SCALES AND ARPEGGIOS	COOKE, J. F.
MASTERPIECE, THE	BRIMHALL,
MASTERPIECES OF PIANO MUSIC --17--	
MASTERPIECES	RAVEL
MASTERPIECES	SCRIABINE, A.
MASTERPIECES	SHOSTAKOVITCH
MASTERPIECES	STRAVINSKY, I.
MASTERPIECE ALBUM	TSCHAIKOWSKY
MASTERS AND THEIR MELODIES	EMERSON--ED
MASTERS BETWEEN BAROQUE AND ROMANTIC PERIODS	ALBERT, D'--ED
MASTERS FOR THE YOUNG. VOL. 1	HAYDN *
MASTERS FOR THE YOUNG. VOL. 2	BEETHOVEN *
MASTERS FOR THE YOUNG. VOL. 3	MENDELSSOHN *
MASTERS FOR THE YOUNG. VOL. 4	CHOPIN
MASTERS FOR THE YOUNG. VOL. 5	WEBER, VON *
MASTERS FOR THE YOUNG, IN 3 VOLS‡ VOL. 1	HAYDN *
MASTERS FOR THE YOUNG, IN 3 VOLS‡ VOL. 2	BEETHOVEN *
MASTERS FOR THE YOUNG, IN 3 VOLS‡ VOL. 3	MENDELSSOHN *
MASTERS OF OUR DAY --70--	
MASTERS OF THE ROCOCO, BK. 1 -- WORKS BY COUPERIN,	FREY--ED
MASTERS OF THE ROCOCO, BK. 2 -- WORKS BY COUPERIN,	FREY--ED
MASTERS OF THE 17TH CENTURY	
MASTERS OF THE 17TH CENTURY	
MASTER MELODIES --100--	
MASTER MELODIES FROM THE GREAT SYMPHONIES	PERRY, P.
MASTER MELODIES IN MINIATURE	MALOOF
MASTER METHOD PIANO NORMAL AND TEACHERS' MANUAL	HEIDELBERGER, P.
MASTER SERIES FOR THE YOUNG--VOL. 01--BACH	BACH, J.S.
MASTER SERIES FOR THE YOUNG--VOL. 06--SCHUBERT	SCHUBERT
MASTER SERIES FOR THE YOUNG--VOL. 06--WEBER	WEBER, VON
MASTER SERIES FOR THE YOUNG--VOL. 09--SCHUMANN	SCHUMANN, R.
MASTER SERIES FOR THE YOUNG--VOL. 12	TSCHAIKOWSKY
MASTER SERIES FOR THE YOUNG, VOL. 02--HANDEL--	HANDEL
MASTER SERIES FOR THE YOUNG, VOL. 03--HAYDN	HAYDN
MASTER SERIES FOR THE YOUNG, VOL. 04--MOZART	MOZART, W. A.
MASTER SERIES FOR THE YOUNG, VOL. 05--BEETHOVEN	BEETHOVEN
MASTER SERIES FOR THE YOUNG, VOL. 08--MENDELSSOHN	MENDELSSOHN
MASTER SERIES FOR THE YOUNG, VOL. 10--CHOPIN	CHOPIN
MASTER SERIES FOR THE YOUNG, VOL. 11 --GRIEG--	GRIEG
MASTER STUDIES IN MODERN STYLE	KING, S.
MASTER TOUCH -- BEETHOVEN, THE	HARRISON, S.--ED
MASTER TOUCH -- CHOPIN, THE	HARRISON, S.--ED
MASTER TOUCH -- MOZART, THE	HARRISON, S.--ED
MATCHMAKER	BOCK, J.
MATILDE DI SHABRAN - OVERTURE	ROSSINI, G.
MATINEE, LA	DUSSEK, J.
MATINEE MELODIES	AGAY, D.--ED
MATINES, SARABANDES ET GAILLARDES	DUBOSQC
MATIN SUR L'EAU	IBERT
MATIN	CHAMINADE
MATRIMONIO SEGRETO, IL - OVERTURE	CIMAROSA
MATROSENLIEBCHEN, OP. 23, NO. 1 -- POLKA	DERKSEN
MATT DENNIS PLAYS SCOTT JOPLIN	JOPLIN, S.
MAVERICK TRAIL	GRAHAM, R.
MAX AND MORITZ -- A MUSICAL STORY	MOHAUPT, R.
MAX MORATH'S GUIDE TO RAGTIME	MORATH, M.--ED.
MAYA MALDITA, LA	GAILLARD
MAYA	ORTOLANI
MAYFLOWERS--25 EASY PIECES, OP. 61	OESTEN
MAYFLOWER	MCADAMS, G.
MAYTIME	GRAY, D.
MAY BELLS RINGING	SIEWART
MAY DAY ON THE GREEN	POWER, H. B.
MAY I HAVE THIS DANCE	HIBBS, C.
MAY I NEVER LOVE AGAIN	
MAY NIGHT, OP. 27 NO. 4	PALMGREN, S.
MAY NIGHT	PALMGREN, S.
MAY NIGHT	PALMGREN, S.
MAY NIGHT	PALMGREN, S.
MAY NIGHT	PALMGREN, S.

MAY NIGHT	WARD
MAY POLE DANCE	MARTIN, G.
MAY POLE DANCE	SMITH
MAY THE GOOD LORD BLESS AND KEEP YOU	BRIMHALL,
MAY TIME	QUINCKE, W.
MAY YOU ALWAYS	LANE, J.--ED.
MAY 24, 1915	MAGLIONI
MAZERT NMAN REHANI -- THY HAIR IS LIKE BASIL LEAF--	HOVHANESS, A.
MAZOVIAN WEDDING	MACDONALD
MAZURKA, OP. 12 NO. 4	PROKOFIEFF
MAZURKA, OP. 17 NO. 2	CHOPIN
MAZURKA, OP. 24 NO. 2	LESCHETIZKY
MAZURKA, OP. 33 NO. 1	CHOPIN
MAZURKA, OP. 55 NO. 4	KLEIN, B.
MAZURKA, OP. 67 NO. 4	CHOPIN
MAZURKA, OP. 68 NO. 2	CHOPIN
MAZURKA, OP. 68 NO. 2	CHOPIN
MAZURKA, OP. 7 NO. 1	CHOPIN
MAZURKA, OP. 7 NO. 1	CHOPIN
MAZURKA, OP. 7 NO. 2	CHOPIN
MAZURKA, OP. 80 -- FROM RECUERDOS	ALBENIZ, I.
MAZURKA, OP. 92 NO. 10--FROM 12 PIECES	ALBENIZ, I.
MAZURKAS, BK. 1 .. OP. 6, 7, 17, 24, 30	CHOPIN
MAZURKAS, BK. 1	TANSMAN, A.
MAZURKAS, BK. 2 .. OP. 33, 41, 50, 56	CHOPIN
MAZURKAS, BK. 2	TANSMAN, A.
MAZURKAS, BK. 3 .. OP. 59, 63, 67, 68	CHOPIN
MAZURKAS, OP. 4 AND OP. 11	DOBROWEN, I.
MAZURKAS, OP. 50, BK. 1	SZYMANOWSKI
MAZURKAS, OP. 50, BK. 2	SZYMANOWSKI
MAZURKAS, OP. 50, BK. 3	SZYMANOWSKI
MAZURKAS, OP. 50, BK. 4	SZYMANOWSKI
MAZURKAS, OP. 50, BK. 5	SZYMANOWSKI
MAZURKAS, OP. 56	DVORAK
MAZURKAS --51--	CHOPIN
MAZURKAS	CHOPIN
MAZURKAS	CHOPIN
MAZURKAS	CHOPIN
MAZURKAS	CHOPIN
MAZURKAS	CHOPIN
MAZURKA DE SALON, OP. 81	ALBENIZ, I.
MAZURKA DE SALON NO. 4	PFEIFFER, A.
MAZURKA DE SALON NO. 4	PFEIFFER, A.
MAZURKA ELEGIACA, OP. 23 NO. 2	BRITTEN, B.
MAZURKA GLISSANDO	LECUONA
MAZURKA IN A FLAT MAJOR, OP. 24 NO. 3	CHOPIN
MAZURKA IN A MINOR, OP. 17 NO. 4	CHOPIN
MAZURKA IN A MINOR, OP. 59 NO. 1	CHOPIN
MAZURKA IN A MINOR, OP. 67 NO. 4	CHOPIN
MAZURKA IN A MINOR, OP. 68 NO. 2	CHOPIN
MAZURKA IN A MINOR, OP. 68 NO. 2	CHOPIN
MAZURKA IN A MINOR, OP. 7 NO. 2	CHOPIN
MAZURKA IN A MINOR	LICHNER, H.
MAZURKA IN A MINOR	VERHEY, T.
MAZURKA IN B FLAT, OP. 7 NO. 1 AND MAZURKA IN A MINOR,	CHOPIN
MAZURKA IN B FLAT, OP. 7 NO. 1	CHOPIN
MAZURKA IN B FLAT, OP. 7 NO. 1	CHOPIN
MAZURKA IN B FLAT, OP. 7 NO. 1	CHOPIN
MAZURKA IN B FLAT MAJOR, OP. 17 NO. 1	CHOPIN
MAZURKA IN B FLAT MAJOR, OP. 7 NO. 1	CHOPIN
MAZURKA IN B FLAT	CHOPIN
MAZURKA IN B MAJOR, OP. 63 NO. 1	CHOPIN
MAZURKA IN B MINOR, OP. 33 NO. 4	CHOPIN
MAZURKA IN C MAJOR, OP. 67 NO. 3	CHOPIN
MAZURKA IN D AND CONTREDANSE--CURWEN EDITION	CHOPIN
MAZURKA IN E MINOR, OP. 41 NO. 2	CHOPIN
MAZURKA IN F, OP. 68 NO. 3	CHOPIN
MAZURKA IN F MAJOR, OP. 68 NO. 3	DEBUSSY
MAZURKA IN F MINOR	CHOPIN
MAZURKA IN F SHARP MINOR, OP. 6 NO. 1	DEBUSSY
MAZURKA IN F SHARP MINOR	CHOPIN
MAZURKA IN G MINOR, OP. 67 NO. 2	CHOPIN
MAZURKA IN G MINOR, OP. 67 NO. 2	CHOPIN
MAZURKA IN G SHARP MINOR, OP. 33 NO. 1	GODDARD, B.
MAZURKA NO. 01, OP. 25	GODARD, B.
MAZURKA NO. 01	LEMAIRE
MAZURKA NO. 02	GODARD, B.
MAZURKA NO. 1	GODARD, B.
MAZURKA NO. 1	WIENIAWSKI
MAZURKA NO. 2	WEISLEDER, A.
MAZURKA NO. 2	BECUCCI
MAZURKA TIME	DEBUSSY
MAZURKA	DONENFELD, J.
MAZURKA	MARTINU, B.
MAZURKA	MEYER-HELMUND
MAZURKA	NOEL, H.
MAZURKA	SANGIORGI
MAZURKA	TSCHAIKOWSKY
MAZURKA	WILM, N. VON
MA BELLE QUI DANSE	WESTERHOUT
MA BELLE QUI DANSE	WESTERHOUT
MA BERGERE --OU LE PATRE DES MONTAGNES--	NIVELET
MA BLONDE AIMEE	VOLPATTI
MA CHERE LIBERTE, OP. 60 NO. 1	ALKAN
MEADOWLAND	KNIPPER
MEADOW BROOK, THE, ETUDE	MARTIN, G.
MEADOW BROOK, THE	MARTIN, G.
MEADOW LARK, THE	MCINTYRE, E.
MEADOW LARK, THE	RICHMAN, A.
MEADOW LARK	MARTIN, E.
MEADOW PRINCESS, THE	HOPKINS, H.
MEAN MAN	GLOVER, D.
MECANISME ET VIRTUOSITE DU PIANISTE	HUGOUNENC
MECHANICAL DOLL, THE	SHOSTAKOVITCH
MEDARDUS --SUITE--	OLSEN, P.
MEDIA DIFFICOLTA - VIER STUCKE	CASTELNUOVO-TEDE
MEDICINE MAN	ARMOUR
MEDIC THEME	
MEDIEVAL BALLAD	DE LUCIA, N.
MEDIEVAL FANTASY	HANNA
MEDIEVAL VARIATIONS - SUITE	RIETI
MEDIEVAL VARIATIONS - SUITE	RIETI
MEDIEVAL VARIATIONS	RIETI
MEDITATION, OP. 84	MORRIS, C.
MEDITATION, OP. 90	MORRISON, C.
MEDITATION, THAIS	MASSENET, J.
MEDITATION, THE ANGELUS	GODARD, B.
MEDITATIONS FOR PIANO	LA ROWE, J.
MEDITATIONS	MORRISON, C.
MEDITATION --FROM THAIS	MASSENET, J.
MEDITATION -- A PEDAL STUDY	OETTING, H.
MEDITATION -- FROM 'THAIS'	MASSENET, J.
MEDITATION 'THAIS'	MASSENET, J.
MEDITATION FROM 'THAIS'	MASSENET, J.
MEDITATION FROM 'THAIS'	MASSENET, J.
MEDITATION FROM THAIS	MASSENET, J.
MEDITATION ON A MOTIF OF C. DEBUSSY	KODALY, Z.
MEDITATION ON THE FIRST PRELUDE BY J. S. BACH	GOUNOD, C.
MEDITATION ON THE FIRST PRELUDE BY J. S. BACH	GOUNOD, C.
MEDITATION	BRIMHALL,
MEDITATION	GREENWALD, M.
MEDITATION	MORRISON, C.
MEDITATION	MORRISON, C.
MEDITATION	MORRISON, C.
MEDITERRANEAN CONCERTO -- THEMES	
MEDITERRANEAN CONCERTO	
MEDUSA, OP. 24 -- BALLET IN 3 SCENES	EINEM, G.
MEET AND KNOW THE PIANO, BK. 1	PRIGGE, O.
MEET AND KNOW THE PIANO, BK. 2	PRIGGE, O.
MEET COLE PORTER AT THE PIANO	PORTER, C.
MEET FREDERICK LOEWE AT THE PIANO	LOEWE, F.
MEET GEORGE GERSHWIN AT THE PIANO	GERSHWIN
MEET KURT WEILL AT THE PIANO	WEILL, K.
MEET MISTER MAMBO	AGAY, D.
MEET MODERN MUSIC, BK. 1	
MEET MODERN MUSIC, BK. 2	
MEET RICHARD RODGERS AT THE PIANO	RODGERS
MEET ROGER WILLIAMS	WILLIAMS, R.
MEET THE KEYS --100--	
MEET THE MASTERS	BENFORD--ED
MEET THE MASTERS	HOFSTAD, M.
MEET THE PIANO -- TEENAGE AND ADULT BEGINNERS	PACE, R.
MEFISTOFELE - EASY FANTASIA	BOITO
MEFISTO VALSE	LISZT
MEGRA CONSENTIDA	PARDAVE
MEINE STRAUSS-WALZER, BAND 01	STRAUSS, J.
MEINE STRAUSS-WALZER, BAND 02	STRAUSS, J.
MEINE STRAUSS-WALZER	STRAUSS, J.
MEINE VATERLAND -- ORIGINAL-BEARBEITUNG DES	SMETANA
MEIN HEIMATLAND	
MEIN KINDERLIEDERBUCH - 60 KINDERLIEDER, AUSWAHL FUR	LUTZ--ED
MEIN KINDERLIEDERBUCH - 60 KINDERLIEDER	LUTZ--ED
MEIN KINDERLIEDERBUCH	LUTZ--ED
MEIN MAI. KLAVIERSTUCKE, OP. 20	NOVAK
MEIN NOTIZBUCH, HEFT 1 - 6 STUCKE	PAUER
MEIN NOTIZBUCH, HEFT 2 - 6 STUCKE	PAUER
MEIN VATERLAND, HEFT 1 - VYSEHRAD	SMETANA
MEIN VATERLAND, HEFT 2 - DIE MOLDAU	SMETANA
MEIN VATERLAND, HEFT 3 - SARKA	SMETANA
MEIN VATERLAND, HEFT 4 - AUS BOHMENS HAIN UND FLUR	SMETANA
MEIN VATERLAND, HEFT 5 - TABOR	SMETANA
MEIN VATERLAND, HEFT 6 - BLANIK	SMETANA
MEIN VATERLAND -- ORIGINAL-BEARBEITUNG DES KOMPONISTEN	SMETANA
MEIN VATERLAND -- ORIGINAL-BEARBEITUNG DES KOMPONISTEN	SMETANA
MEIN VATERLAND -- ORIGINAL-BEARBEITUNG DES KOMPONISTEN	SMETANA
MEIN VATERLAND -- ORIGINAL-BEARBEITUNG DES KOMPONISTEN	SMETANA
MEIN VATERLAND GESAMTAUSGABE	SMETANA
MEIN VOLKSLIEDERBUCH - AUSWAHL FUR KLAVIER ZU VIER	LUTZ--ED
MEIN VOLKSLIEDERBUCH	LUTZ--ED
MEIN VOLKSLIEDERBUCH	LUTZ--ED
MEIN WEIHNACHTSBUCH -- 33 DER SCHONSTEN	LECHNER--ED
MEISTERBUCH. A COLLECTION OF FIFTY-FIVE CELEBRATED	
MEISTERCHORAELE --50--	WOLFRAM--ED
MEISTERSINGER, DIE -- GER AND ENG SUPERLINEAR TEXT	WAGNER
MEISTERSINGER -- VORSPIEL	WAGNER
MEISTERWERKE DER KLAVIERMUSIK, BK. 1 - 27 STUCKE	HANDEL *
MEI HERZIGES DIRNOL--AUSTRIAN FOLK-SONG, OP. 69 NO. 1	PACHER, J. A.
MEJESKA DANCE, OP. 30 NO. 2	MASON, I.
MEKTA IN THE ART OF KITA. FOR CHILDREN AND ADULTS,	ELDABH
MEKTA IN THE ART OF KITA. FOR CHILDREN AND ADULTS,	ELDABH
MELANCHOLY MAZURKA	DONENFELD, J.
MELANCHOLY SERENADE	
MELANCOLIE--1940	POULENC, F.
MELLOW CELLO, THE	STEINER
MELLOW MOON	CARLETON, B.
MELLO CELLO	TAYLOR
MELODAYS	SCHER, W.
MELODIA Y AIRE VARIADO	SAS, A.
MELODIA	COUTURE
MELODIC EXERCISES, BK. 1	HENNES, A.
MELODIC MOOD	CANFIELD, J.
MELODIC STUDIES, OP. 38. VOL. 1	LOESCHHORN, A.
MELODIC STUDIES, OP. 38. VOL. 2	LOESCHHORN, A.
MELODIC STUDIES, OP. 38. VOL. 3	LOESCHHORN, A.
MELODIC STUDIES, OP. 52. VOL. 1	LOESCHHORN, A.
MELODIC STUDIES, OP. 52. VOL. 2	LOESCHHORN, A.
MELODIC STUDIES, OP. 52. VOL. 3	LOESCHHORN, A.
MELODIC THEME FROM POLOVETZIAN DANCE	BORODIN, A.
MELODIC WALTZ	DE VITO, A.
MELODIE--NO. 2--IN G MAJOR. OP. 10, NO. 1	AUS DER OHE, A.
MELODIE, ELEGIE, EASY	MASSENET, J.
MELODIE, ELEGIE	MASSENET, J.
MELODIE, OP. 3 NO. 3	RACHMANINOFF, S.
MELODIE, OP. 3 NO. 3	RACHMANINOFF, S.
MELODIE, OP. 68 NO. 01--ALBUM FOR THE YOUNG	SCHUMANN, R.
MELODIE, OP. 8 NO. 3	PADEREWSKI, I.
MELODIEN-SCHATZ, FUNF LEICHTE KLAVIERSTUCKE, HEFT 2	
MELODIES ET PROVERBES	MONTBRUN, G.
MELODIES FOR CHURCH AND HOME	SHELLEY--ED.
MELODIES FROM 'MESSIAH'	HANDEL
MELODIES FROM ALL OVER THE WORLD	PAHLEN
MELODIES IN MINIATURE, BK. 1	DUNHILL
MELODIES IN MINIATURE, BK. 2	DUNHILL
MELODIES IN MINOR	STEINER
MELODIES OF THE MASTERS	SCARMOLIN--ED
MELODIES POPULAIRES ESPAGNOLES	NOGUERA
MELODIE -- ELEGY, OP. 10	MASSENET, J.
MELODIE 'ELEGIE' OP. 10	MASSENET, J.
MELODIE CHARMANTE	HOLT, EILSEL
MELODIE F-DUR OP. 3 NO. 1	RUBINSTEIN
MELODIE FROM 'CHANTS DU VOYAGEUR', OP. 8 NO. 3	PADEREWSKI, I.
MELODIE INTERIEURE, LA	GRUNEWALD
MELODIE IN E MINOR, OP. 10 NO. 4	RACHMANINOFF, S.
MELODIE IN F, OP. 3 NO. 1	RUBINSTEIN
MELODIE IN F, OP. 3 NO. 1	RUBINSTEIN
MELODIE MEDITATIVE IN E FLAT OP. 15, NO. 1	GODOWSKY, L.
MELODIE	RACHMANINOFF, S.
MELODIE	THOME, F.
MELODIOUS EXERCISES, OP. 125 -- BK. 1	HELLER, S.
MELODIOUS EXERCISES, OP. 149	DIABELLI
MELODIOUS EXERCISES, OP. 149	DIABELLI
MELODIOUS EXERCISES, OP. 62	BERENS, H.
MELODIOUS EXERCISES, OP.62	BERENS, H.
MELODIOUS MOMENTS	EDOUARD
MELODIOUS PIECES, OP. 149	DIABELLI
MELODIOUS PIECES, OP. 149	DIABELLI
MELODIOUS SONNET	BACON, E.
MELODIOUS TECHNICAL STUDIES FROM	STREABBOG *
MELODISCH-HARMONISCHE STUDIE, EINE	URAY, E. L.
MELODRAMEN FUR SPRECHER UND KLAVIER	FIBICH, Z.
MELODY--FROM 'ORFEO' BY GLUCK	SGAMBATI

MELODY, A	WEYBRIGHT
MELODY AND PRELUDE	CHOPIN
MELODY AND STATELY DANCE	OGILVY, F.
MELODY AND VARIATIONS	BEN-HAIM
MELODY AND VARIATION	ELIOT
MELODY BOOK, BK. 1	BLAKE
MELODY BOOK, BK. 2	BLAKE
MELODY CORNER	ROZIN
MELODY FROM ''ORFEO''	GLUCK
MELODY IN C	STUBBLEFIELD
MELODY IN F, OP. 23 NO. 2	RUBINSTEIN
MELODY IN F, OP. 3 NO. 1	RUBINSTEIN
MELODY IN F, OP. 3 NO. 1	RUBINSTEIN
MELODY IN F, OP. 3 NO. 1	RUBINSTEIN
MELODY IN F, OP. 3	RUBINSTEIN
MELODY IN F -- SIMPLIFIED	RUBINSTEIN
MELODY IN F	RUBINSTEIN
MELODY IN F	RUBINSTEIN
MELODY IN F	RUBINSTEIN
MELODY JOYS FOR GIRLS AND BOYS	
MELODY MODES AND MOODS THROUGH ALL THE KEYS	SWENSON, L.
MELODY NO. 1 OP. 68	SCHUMANN, R.
MELODY OF LOVE, OP. 600	ENGELMANN, H. U.
MELODY OF LOVE - CARY	ENGELMANN, H. U.
MELODY OF LOVE - ORIGINAL	ENGELMANN, H. U.
MELODY OF LOVE	ENGELMANN, H. U.
MELODY OF LOVE	ENGELMANN, H. U.
MELODY OF LOVE	ENGELMANN, H. U.
MELODY OF LOVE	ENGELMANN, H. U.
MELODY OF LOVE	ENGELMANN, H. U.
MELODY OF LOVE	ENGELMANN, H. U.
MELODY OF LOVE	ENGELMANN, H. U.
MELODY OF LOVE	REISER, V.
MELODY OF THE FLOWERS	REEG, G. A.
MELODY PRELUDES THROUGH THE KEYS	SWENSON, L.
MELODY RHYMES THROUGH ALL THE KEYS	SWENSON, L.
MELODY TREASURE, BK. 1	STEINER
MELODY TREASURE, BK. 2	STEINER
MELODY WALTZ	JOYNER, B.
MELODY WORK BOOK -- SUPPLEMENT TO BOOK 1	PACE, R.
MELODY	DAWES
MELODY	GROVE, R.
MELODY	RILEY, D.
MELODY	SCHUMANN, R.
MELODY	STEIN, L.
MELODY	THOME, F.
MELTING POT	FELTON, W.--ED
MEMOIRES D'UN CHAT	MAURICE, P.
MEMORIES OF DAYS GONE BY	LANGE, P.
MEMORIES OF HUNGARY	SCHER, W.
MEMORIES OF JOHANN STRAUSS	STRAUSS, J.
MEMORIES OF MALAGA	HARPER, M.
MEMORIES OF SUMMER DAYS	HOLT, EILSEL
MEMORIES OF YOUTH, OP. 11	ISSERLIS, J.
MEMORIES OF YOU	BLAKE
MEMORIES OF YOU	CARDEW
MEMORIES OF YOU	SCHAUM, J.
MEMORIE	PETRALIA
MEMORY, A	LONG, L.
MEMORY, A	OPRESKA
MEMORY CHEST, A	HOLT, EILSEL
MEMORY OF MAYTIME	GREY, F.
MENAGERIE, OP. 31 -- BALLET IN 5 TABLEAUX	KLEBE, G.
MENAGERIE	OLSON
MENDELSSOHN'S SONGS WITHOUT WORDS	MENDELSSOHN
MENDELSSOHN MOWS 'EM DOWN	TEMPLETON, A.
MENDELSSOHN	MENDELSSOHN
MENUET--FROM QUARTET,OP.76--	HAYDN *
MENUET, FROM SONATA OP. 49 NO. 2	BEETHOVEN
MENUET, OP. 14 NO. 1	PADEREWSKI, I.
MENUET, OP. 14 NO. 1	PADEREWSKI, I.
MENUET, SIMPLIFIED	PADEREWSKI, I.
MENUETTE	STEPAN
MENUETTINO-- CUENTOS Y FANTASIAS, NO. 2	CHAVARRI
MENUETTO, OP. 78	SCHUBERT
MENUETTO, POLACCA, 2 TRIOS --FROM BRANDENBURG CONCERTO	BACH, J.S.
MENUETTO -- FROM SYMPHONY NO. 3 -- SET	SCHUBERT
MENUETTO AND AIR	MOZART, W. A.
MENUETTO E GAVOTTA FROM PAGLIACI	LEONCAVALLO
MENUETTO IN B MINOR, OP. 78	SCHUBERT
MENUETTO IN B MINOR	SCHUBERT
MENUETT AUS D. ES-DUR-SYMPHONIE -- K.V. 543	MOZART, W. A.
MENUETT AUS DER SUITE, OP. 21	SUK
MENUETT FAVORI -- SIEHE BENDEL MUSIKALIKALISCHES	MOZART, W. A.
MENUETT G-DUR	BEETHOVEN
MENUETT IN A FLAT, OP. 28 NO. 1	DVORAK
MENUETT IN F, OP. 28 NO. 2	DVORAK
MENUETT IN G	BACH, J.S.
MENUETT OP. 77 NO. 10	MOSZKOWSKI
MENUETT	BOCCHERINI, L.
MENUET -- DE LA SONATINE	RAVEL
MENUET -- DE PETITE SUITE	DEBUSSY
MENUET AND TRIO, SYMPHONY NO. 39 IN E FLAT	MOZART, W. A.
MENUET ANTIQUE	RAVEL
MENUET A L'ANTIQUE, OP. 14 NO. 1	PADEREWSKI, I.
MENUET A L'ANTIQUE, OP. 14 NO. 1	PADEREWSKI, I.
MENUET A L'ANTIQUE	PADEREWSKI, I.J.
MENUET BASQUE	DONOSTIA
MENUET DU BOURGEOIS GENTILHOMME	LULLY
MENUET DU SOIR	LINCOLN
MENUET ET GAVOTTE DU SEPTUOR, OP. 65	SAINT-SAENS
MENUET ET VALSE, OP. 56	SAINT-SAENS
MENUET FROM L'ARLESIENNE --BIZET	GODOWSKY, L.
MENUET FROM SYMPHONY IN E FLAT --PIANO, 6 HANDS--	MOZART, W. A.
MENUET FROM SYMPHONY IN E FLAT	MOZART, W. A.
MENUET IN G, EASY	BEETHOVEN
MENUET IN G, OP. 14 NO. 1	PADEREWSKI, I.
MENUET NO. 2 IN G	BEETHOVEN
MENUET NO. 2 IN G	BEETHOVEN
MENUET NO. 2 IN G	BEETHOVEN
MENUET ON NAME OF HAYDN	RAVEL
MENUET PASTORAL	BOULNOIS
MENUET RUSSE	AKIMENKO
MENUET SUR LE NOM D'HAYDN	RAVEL
MENUET VIF	SCHMITT
MENUET	BACH, J.S.
MENUET	BOCCHERINI, L.
MENUET	BOCCHERINI
MENUET	DEBUSSY
MENUET	JAHN, C.
MENUET	MARPURG, F. W.
MENUET	MOZART, W. A.
MENUET	RAVEL
MENUET	RAVEL
MENUS PROPOS ENFANTINS	SATIE, E.
MEN AT WORK	MCKAY, G.

MEPHISTO WALTZ--EPISODE FROM LENAU'S 'FAUST', DANCE IN	LISZT
MEPHISTO WALTZ NO. 1	LISZT
MEPHISTO WALTZ	LISZT
MERCEDES--VALSE ESPAGNOLE	MIRO, E.
MERIGGIO	COUTURE
MERMAID, THE	SCHAUM, J.--ED.
MERMAIDS	NOBLES, O.
MERMAID -- MELODY FROM THE SEA	PHILLIPS, D.
MERRIE MUSIC BOX	GIASSON, P.
MERRILY O'ER THE HILLS	WIGHAM, M.
MERRILY WE PLAY AND SING	RENNICK, E.
MERRILY WE PLAY AND SWAY	RENNICK, E.
MERRY-GO-RONDO	POTTERBAUM, W.
MERRY-GO-ROUND, THE	BERLIN, B.
MERRY-GO-ROUND, THE	BRIMHALL, J.
MERRY-GO-ROUND WHIRL	LECUONA
MERRY-GO-ROUND	CANFIELD, J.
MERRY, MERRY WASH DAY	ERB
MERRYMAKERS, THE	THOMAS, J. J.
MERRYMAKERS	REISER, V.
MERRY ALBUM FOR THE YOUNG, A, OP. 122	POLDINI, E.
MERRY BOBOLINK, OP. 15 NO. 10	KROGMANN, C. W.
MERRY CHASE, A	PETERS, F.
MERRY CHASE	HOPSON, E.
MERRY CHRISTMAS--13 CHRISTMAS CAROLS IN VERY EASY	KIRBY, W.
MERRY CHRISTMAS, BK.1	BASTIEN--ED.
MERRY CHRISTMAS, BK.2	BASTIEN--ED.
MERRY CHRISTMAS, BK.3	BASTIEN--ED.
MERRY CHRISTMAS - THE HILLSIDE SINGERS	
MERRY CHRISTMAS CAROLS TO SING AND PLAY	BESTHOFF, M.
MERRY CHRISTMAS FROM JOHN BRIMHALL	BRIMHALL,
MERRY CHRISTMAS MARCH	HELTMAN
MERRY CHRISTMAS MUSIC	RICHTER, C.--ED
MERRY CRICKET, THE	SKAAGS
MERRY DANCE, A	YOUNG
MERRY DANCE	MACGREGOR
MERRY ELF, THE	WARD
MERRY FARMER, THE, OP. 68 NO. 10--ALBUM FOR THE YOUNG	SCHUMANN, R.
MERRY FROLIC	ROFF
MERRY GO-ROUND	DE VITO, A.
MERRY GO ROUND, SCHERZO	HOPKINS, H.
MERRY GO ROUND RIDE	KARP
MERRY GO ROUND WALTZ	KARP
MERRY GO ROUND	FREDERICKS
MERRY GURLITT --30 EASY PIECES--	GURLITT
MERRY JUGGLER, THE	GROVE, R.
MERRY LITTLE CLOCK	SCHER, W.
MERRY LITTLE CLOCK	SCHER, W.
MERRY LITTLE MILLWHEEL	JOYNER, B.
MERRY LITTLE RAINDROPS	SCHER, W.
MERRY MAJORETTE	CARLETON, B.
MERRY MAKERS, ONE PIANO - SIX HANDS	MATTINGLY, J.
MERRY MEADOWLARK, THE	TOWNSEND
MERRY MELODIES FOR LITTLE JACKS AND JILLS--ILLUSTRATED	RODGERS, I.
MERRY MERRY DANCE	KARP
MERRY MOMENTS	CARROLL
MERRY MOMENTS	CARROLL
MERRY MOOD - FROHER SINN	LEYBACH, I.
MERRY MORN, XMAS WALTZ	HOPKINS, H.
MERRY MOTHER GOOSE SUITE	HANNA
MERRY MOUNTAINEERS, THE	SMOLIN, H.
MERRY OLD SALT	SCHER, W.
MERRY PEASANT, THE, AND HUNTING SONG	SCHUMANN, R.
MERRY PEASANT, THE	SCHUMANN, R.
MERRY PEASANT AND HUNTING SONG	SCHUMANN, R.
MERRY SCISSOR GRINDER	SCHER, W.
MERRY TUNE, A	MORGEN, M.
MERRY TUNES FOR PIANO	
MERRY VARIATIONS	KASSCHAU, H.
MERRY VARIATIONS	KASSCHAU, H.
MERRY WIDOW, SELECTION	LEHAR
MERRY WIDOW, THE	LEHAR
MERRY WIDOW, VILIA	LEHAR
MERRY WIDOW WALTZ, SIMPLIFIED	LEHAR
MERRY WIDOW WALTZES, THE	LEHAR
MERRY WIDOW WALTZ	LEHAR
MERRY WIDOW WALTZ	LEHAR
MERRY WIDOW WALTZ	LEHAR
MERRY WIDOW WALTZ	LEHAR
MERRY WIDOW WALTZ	LEHAR
MERRY WIDOW	LEHAR
MERRY WIVES OF WINDSOR. OVERTURE. TWO PIANOS, EIGHT	NICOLAI
MESSAGE--FROM ''FLOWER-FRUIT-AND-THORN-PIECES''	HELLER, S.
MESSAGE, OP. 39	TCHEREPNIN
MESSAGE A CLAUDE DEBUSSY, 1929	NIN
MESSAGE OF PEACE	ENGELMANN, H. U.
MESSE DES PAUVRES	SATIE, E.
MESSIAH, THE, HALLELUJAH CHORUS	HANDEL
MESSIAH	HANDEL
MES PETITS CONCERTS - APRES LE CONCERT	WACHS
MES PETITS CONCERTS - BERTRAND ET RATON	WACHS
MES PETITS CONCERTS - BLANCHE ET VERMEILLE	WACHS
MES PETITS CONCERTS - LE RENDEZ-VOUS DE CHASSE	WACHS
MES PETITS CONCERTS - MENUET DE LA POUPEE	WACHS
MES PETITS CONCERTS - PROMENADE EN BARQUE	WACHS
METAMORPHOSES	CRESTON
METAMORPHOSES	HAUBIEL, C.
METAMORPHOSE D'EVE -- BALLET --	INGHELBRECHT, D.
METAMORPHOSE D'EVE SUITE	INGHELBRECHT, D.
METAPIECE -- MIMETICS	KAGEL, M.
METATHESES	TAKAHASHI
METER AND TIME VALUES	MACCARTNEY *
METHODE DE PIANO POUR LES ENFANTS	LECARPENTIER, A.
METHODE DE PIANO	LINDO, S.
METHODE ELEMENTAIRE, OP. 130	LEDUC, A.
METHODE DU RECUEIL DE CONNOISANCES ELEMENTAIRES POUR	BACH, J.
METHODE THEORIQUE ET PRATIQUE DE PIANO, PART 1	WIERNSBERGER, J.
METHODE	LACK
METHOD FOR BEGINNERS, OP. 599	CZERNY
METHOD FOR THE PIANO FORTE	DAMM, G.
METHOD FOR THE PIANO	SEUTIN
METHOD OF PIANO STYLING FOR BEGINNERS OR ADVANCED	CARLE, F.
METODO PRACTICO, OP. 249, BK. 1--IN SPANISH AND	KOEHLER
METODO TEORICO-PRACTICO DE LECTURA MUSICAL--IN SPANISH	MENOZZI, J.
METODO TEORICO PRACTICO	GRANADOS
METRONOME, THE	AMOS, L.
METROPOLITAN NOCTURNE	ALTER, L.
MEXICALI PROMENADE	BAUER
MEXICANA, A LA, OP. 35	ORNSTEIN, L.
MEXICANA -- A MEXICAN FOLK SONG	WEYBRIGHT
MEXICANA	LESLIE
MEXICAN 'CLAP HANDS' DANCE--TWO PIANOS-EIGHT HANDS--	SCHAUM, J.--ED.
MEXICAN 'CLAP HANDS' DANCE	SCHAUM, J.--ED.
MEXICAN BURRO, THE	KLEINMAN, A.
MEXICAN DANCE	SCARMOLIN
MEXICAN FIESTA	BASTIEN

MEXICAN FIESTA	FENSTOCK, B.
MEXICAN FIRE DANCE	MARLAND, A.
MEXICAN HAT DANCE	PARTICHALA
MEXICAN HAT DANCE	SCHAUM, J.--ED.
MEXICAN HAT DANCE	
MEXICAN HOLIDAY	ARNOLD, M.
MEXICAN JUMPING BEANS	BIRCSAK, T.
MEXICAN JUMPING BEAN	SCHER, W.
MEXICAN MOUNTAIN CLIMB	SHULMAN
MEXICAN MOUNTAIN CLIMB	SHULMAN
MEXICAN SERENADE	GARROW, L.
MEXICAN SUNDAY	RAYMOND, J.
MEXICO	BURNAM
ME AND BOBBY MCGEE	BRIMHALL,
ME AND JULIET	HAMMERSTEIN *
MIA, 6 IMPRESSIONS, NO. 1--MIA PREGA	LLONGUERAS, J.
MIA, 6 IMPRESSIONS, NO. 2--MIA JUGA	LLONGUERAS, J.
MIA, 6 IMPRESSIONS, NO. 3--MIA DANCA	LLONGUERAS, J.
MIA, 6 IMPRESSIONS, NO. 4--MIA CANTA	LLONGUERAS, J.
MIA, 6 IMPRESSIONS, NO. 6--MIA DORM	LLONGUERAS, J.
MIAMI BEACH RUMBA	FIELDS, I.
MIAMI BEACH RUMBA	FIELDS, I.
MIAOVARIAITONEN	DALLA VECCHIA
MICE IN THREE BLIND KEYS	COOK
MICHAEL AARON DUET BOOK	AARON, M.
MICHAEL FINNIGAN -- FOLK TUNE	STEINER
MICHELLE	LENNON *
MICROBINHO	MIGNONE
MID-DAY SIESTA	SCARMOLIN
MID-SUMMER NIGHTS DREAM	MENDELSSOHN
MID-TERM READER	COBB
MIDARE	OTAKA, H.
MIDDLE C AND ITS NEAR NEIGHBORS	MARTIN
MIDGET MARCH	THARALDSEN
MIDNIGHT -- PRELUDE FOR LEFT HAND	WIGGINS, M.
MIDNIGHT BELLS --STUDENT EDITION--	KREISLER
MIDNIGHT BELLS --STUDENT EDITION--	KREISLER
MIDNIGHT BELLS	HEUBERGER *
MIDNIGHT BELLS	KREISLER
MIDNIGHT COWBOY	BRIMHALL,
MIDNIGHT FIRE ALARM, THE	LINCOLN, H.
MIDNIGHT FIRE ALARM	LINCOLN, H.
MIDNIGHT FIRE ALARM	LINCOLN, H.
MIDNIGHT FIRE ALARM	LINCOLN, H.
MIDNIGHT IN MOSCOW --YOU CAN'T KEEP ME FROM LOVING	BRAND *
MIDNIGHT IN NEW YORK --MODERN RHYTHMIC CLASSICS--	WHITFORD
MIDNIGHT PETE	MCKUEN
MIDNIGHT REVELS	LOYND, G. M.
MIDNIGHT RIDERS	SCHER, W.
MIDNIGHT SUN, OP. 33	SPRINGER, M.
MIDNIGHT WALTZ	TAYLOR
MIDNIGHT	BARLOW
MIDSUMMER DAY DREAM AND IN A CAVERN	KURKA, R.
MIDSUMMER NIGHT'S DREAM. COMPLETE. ENGLISH-FRENCH TEXT	MENDELSSOHN
MIDSUMMER NIGHT'S DREAM. COMPLETE. GERMAN TEXT	MENDELSSOHN
MIDSUMMER NIGHT'S DREAM, A -- OVERTURE	MENDELSSOHN
MIDSUMMER NIGHT'S DREAM, A -- WEDDING MARCH	MENDELSSOHN
MIDSUMMER NIGHT'S DREAM, A -- WEDDING MARCH	MENDELSSOHN
MIDSUMMER NIGHT'S DREAM, NOCTURNE	MENDELSSOHN
MIDSUMMER NIGHT'S DREAM, OP. 76 - PARAPHRASE DE	MENDELSSOHN
MIDSUMMER NIGHT'S DREAM, OP. 76	MENDELSSOHN
MIDSUMMER NIGHT'S DREAM	REEVES, R.
MIDWAY AT THE FAIR	MAYER
MIDWAY MARCH	NEVIN
MIGHTY LAK' A ROSE	NEVIN
MIGHTY LAK' A ROSE	NEVIN
MIGHTY LAK' A ROSE	NEVIN
MIGHTY LAK' A ROSE	PICK-MANGIAGALLI
MIGNARDISES	THOMAS, A.
MIGNON, GAVOTTE	STREABBOG
MIGNONETTE POLKA	THOMAS, A.
MIGNON OVERTURE	THOMAS, A.
MIGNON	SULLIVAN, A.
MIKADO, THE, TIT WILLOW	BARTOK
MIKROKOSMOS, BKS. 1 AND 2	BARTOK
MIKROKOSMOS, BKS. 3, 4, 5 AND 6	WEYBRIGHT
MILDLY CONTEMPORARY, BK. 1	WEYBRIGHT
MILDLY CONTEMPORARY, BK. 1	WEYBRIGHT
MILDLY CONTEMPORARY, BK. 2	WEYBRIGHT
MILDLY CONTEMPORARY, BK. 2	WEYBRIGHT
MILDLY CONTEMPORARY, BK. 3	WEYBRIGHT
MILDLY CONTEMPORARY, BK. 3	SCHUBERT
MILITARMARSCH D-DUR OP. 51 NO. 1	SCHUBERT
MILITARMARSCH D-DUR OP. 51 NO. 1	SCHUBERT
MILITARMARSCH D-DUR OP. 51 NO. 1	HOPKINS, H.
MILITARY BAND, THE	SCHUBERT
MILITARY MARCH, EASY	SCHUBERT
MILITARY MARCH, NO. 1	SCHUBERT
MILITARY MARCH, OP. 51 NO. 1 -- ARR FOR TWO PIANOS,	SCHUBERT
MILITARY MARCH, OP. 51 NO. 1 -- 8-HANDS, SET	SCHUBERT
MILITARY MARCH, OP. 51 NO. 1	SCHUBERT
MILITARY MARCH, OP. 51 NO. 1	SCHUBERT
MILITARY MARCH --MARCHE MILITAIRE--, OP. 51 NO. 1	SCHUBERT
MILITARY MARCH IN D, OP. 51 NO. 1	SCHUBERT *
MILITARY MARCH IN D FLAT, OP. 51 NO. 1	SCHUBERT
MILITARY MARCH IN D	WALTER
MILITARY MARCH	SCHWAB
MILITARY PARADE	CHOPIN
MILITARY POLONAISE, EASY	CHOPIN
MILITARY POLONAISE, OP. 40 NO. 1	CHOPIN
MILITARY POLONAISE	CHOPIN
MILITARY POLONAISE	DIABELLI
MILITARY RONDO	CATIZONE, J. M.
MILJO	JENSEN, A.
MILL, THE, OP. 17 NO. 3	JENSEN, A.
MILL, THE, OP. 17 NO. 3	JENSEN, A.
MILL, THE	HOPKINS, H.
MILLER'S SONG, THE, WALTZ	RUSSELL
MILLER BOY -- VARIATIONS ON AN AMERICAN FOLK SONG	MCKEE
MILLICENT WALTZ	DRIGO, R.
MILLIONS OF HARLEQUIN, EASY	DRIGO, R.
MILLIONS OF HARLEQUIN	NEVIN
MILLS PIANO HITS	MACLACHLIN, T.
MILL BY THE BROOK, THE	RAPHLING
MILL ON THE FLOSS	MACONCHY
MILL RACE	MACK, F.
MILL WHEEL, THE	SCHWAB
MILL WHEEL, THE	WEYBRIGHT
MILL WHEEL, THE	GINASTERA
MILONGA	SAMMARTINO
MILONGA	SCHIFRIN, L.
MIMA	BRIMHALL,
MIMI	DITTENHAVER
MIMOSA WALTZ	QUIST
MINDING YOUR P'S AND Q'S - OPUS 1	

MINDING YOUR P'S AND Q'S - OPUS 2	QUIST
MINDING YOUR P'S AND Q'S - OPUS 3	QUIST
MING LING LAUNDRYMAN	GIOVANNI
MING LING	CLARK, M. E.
MING TOY	COOK
MING TOY	OLDENBURG, E.
MINHA TERRA	BARROZO NETTO
MINI-SCHERZO	NEVIN
MINIATURA	LANARO, L.
MINIATUREN. 8 KLEINE STUCKE	SARAUER
MINIATUREN, ACHT KLEINE STUCKE	TURINA, J.
MINIATURES. PROGRESSIVE PIECES FOR SMALL HANDS. VOL. 1	LANCEN
MINIATURES. PROGRESSIVE PIECES FOR SMALL HANDS. VOL. 2	LANCEN
MINIATURES--THIRTY SHORT STUDIES	OLDENBURG, E.
MINIATURES--24 EASY PIECES FOR THE DEVELOPMENT OF	REINHOLD, H.
MINIATURES -- PIANO PIECES TO DAILY MORNING EXERCISES	DICHLER-SEDLACEK
MINIATURES FOR PIANO--EARLY FRENCH	IRMER, VON--ED.
MINIATURES FOR PIANO--MISIKVERLAG ZUM PELIKAN EDITION	MOZART, W. A.
MINIATURES FOR PIANO--MUSIKVERLAG ZUM PELIKAN EDITION	HAYDN
MINIATURES FOR PIANO--OLD MASTERS--MUSIKVERLAG ZUM	IRMER, VON--ED.
MINIATURES FOR PIANO, VOL. 1	SCHONTHAL
MINIATURES FOR PIANO, VOL. 2	SCHONTHAL
MINIATURES FOR PIANO	GARSCIA
MINIATURES FOR 2 PIANOS	HAUBIEL, C.
MINIATURES POUR PETIT ALEXANDRE	KELKEL
MINIATURES	DRAGOI
MINIATURES	ROGERS
MINIATURES	STOLZE, R.
MINIATURES	TARDOS, B.
MINIATURE CONCERTO	ANSON, G.
MINIATURE CONCERTO	ROWLEY
MINIATURE DANCE SUITE	LAST, J.
MINIATURE DUETS --FOR TEACHER AND PUPIL--	GAYNOR
MINIATURE ETUDES	STEINER
MINIATURE PASTORALS, BK. 1	BRIDGE, F.
MINIATURE PASTORALS, BK. 2	BRIDGE, F.
MINIATURE SUITE	FIALA
MINIATURE SUITE	HARTLEY, W.
MINIATURE SUITE	SYMONS
MINIATURE VIENNESE MARCH --STUDENT EDITION--	KREISLER
MINITUNES	SCHER, W.
MINI SUITE NO. 1	WUENSCH
MINNELIEDER	SCHER, W.--ED
MINNELIED IN B FLAT	SCHROEDER, H.
MINNIE MOORE	HORNSTEIN
MINOR AND MAJOR - ORIENTAL WALTZ	STREABBOG
MINOR MOODS FOR MODERNS	MCKEE
MINOR PRELUDE, A	DILSNER
MINOR SCALES AND PIECES	SENTER, G.
MINOR WORKS	BASTIEN--ED.
MINOTA	CHOPIN
MINSTRELS FROM PRELUDES, BK. 1	MCADAMS, G.
MINSTRELS	DEBUSSY
MINSTREL BOY, THE	SCHER, W.
MINSTREL MAN, THE	GROOMS--ED
MINTIKA	FROST
MINUET--FROM DIVERTIMENTO K334 IN D	VILLA-LOBOS, H.
MINUET--FROM SYMPHONY K543 IN E FLAT	MOZART, W. A.
MINUET, ARR. FOR 3 OR 4 PARTS -- OPTIONAL PART FOR	MOZART, W. A.
MINUET, FRENCH SUITE 6	SCHUBERT
MINUET, FROM SUITE FRANCAISE	BACH, J.S.
MINUET, OP. 111 -- FROM SONATA NO. 7	DANIEL-LESUR
MINUET, OP. 14, NO. 1	ALBENIZ, I.
MINUET, OP. 77 NO. 10	PADEREWSKI, I.
MINUETS IN G MAJOR AND G MINOR NO. 01	MOSZKOWSKI
MINUETS IN G MAJOR AND G MINOR NO. 02	BACH, J.S.
MINUETTO, L'ARLESIENNE	BACH, J.S.
MINUETTO --2 PIANOS, 8 HANDS--	BIZET, G.
MINUETTO 'DON GIOVANNI', SIMPLIFIED	HAYDN
MINUETTO AND TRIO	MOZART, W. A.
MINUETTO ANTICO	HAYDN
MINUETTO A SYLVIA, OP. 92, NO. 2 -- FROM 12 PIECES	MICUCCI
MINUETTO E INTERMEZZO	ALBENIZ, I.
MINUETTO GIOCOSO IN C MAJOR	MOSER, C.
MINUETTO GIOCOSO	HAYDN
MINUETTO	HAYDN
MINUETTO	BOLZONI
MINUETTO	BOLZONI
MINUETTO	BROWN, C.
MINUETTO	GLASER
MINUETTO	RESPIGHI
MINUETTO	SCHALE, C. F.
MINUET -- FROM SUITE ANCIENNE NO. 3	ALBENIZ, I.
MINUET -- FROM SYMPHONY NO. 5 IN B FLAT -- SET	SCHUBERT
MINUET AND BURLESQUE	MANNINO, V.
MINUET AND GAVOTTE, OP. 65	SAINT-SAENS
MINUET AND TRIO FROM SYMPHONY IN E FLAT	MOZART, W. A.
MINUET AND TRIO	HAYDN
MINUET AND TRIO	LAIRD
MINUET AND TRIO	PLEYEL
MINUET ANTIQUE	RAVEL
MINUET A L'ANTIQUE	PADEREWSKI, I.
MINUET A LA BACH	KREVIT, W.
MINUET BY HANDEL, A	HANDEL
MINUET BY MOZART, A	MOZART, W. A.
MINUET FROM 'ALCINA'	HANDEL
MINUET FROM 'DON GIOVANNI'	MOZART, W. A.
MINUET FROM 'DON GIOVANNI'	MOZART, W. A.
MINUET FROM 'DON GIOVANNI'	MOZART, W. A.
MINUET FROM DON GIOVANNI	MOZART, W. A.
MINUET FROM DON JUAN	MOZART, W. A.
MINUET FROM SERENADE IN G	MOZART, W. A.
MINUET FROM SONATA, OP. 49 NO. 2	BEETHOVEN
MINUET FROM SONATA, OP. 49 NO. 2	BEETHOVEN
MINUET FROM SYMPHONY NO. 39	MOZART, W. A.
MINUET FROM SYMPHONY NO. 39	MOZART, W. A.
MINUET IN A MAJOR	BOCCHERINI, L.
MINUET IN B FLAT	HAYDN
MINUET IN B MINOR, OP. 78	SCHUBERT
MINUET IN B MINOR	BACH, J.S.
MINUET IN C	BEETHOVEN
MINUET IN D FROM DIVERTIMENTO NO. 17	MOZART, W. A.
MINUET IN D FROM SUITE NO. 4 FOR ORCH -- TRANSCRIBED	BACH, J.S.
MINUET IN D MINOR	BACH, J.S.
MINUET IN D MINOR	BACH, J.S.
MINUET IN E FLAT, FOR ONE PIANO, SIX HANDS	MOZART, W. A.
MINUET IN E FLAT MAJOR	BEETHOVEN
MINUET IN E FLAT	BEETHOVEN
MINUET IN E MINOR	SCARLATTI, D.
MINUET IN E MINOR	BACH, J.S.
MINUET IN F	BYINGTON
MINUET IN F	PULFORD, W.
MINUET IN G--OLD EDITION--	BEETHOVEN
MINUET IN G -- ONE PIANO, SIX HANDS --	BEETHOVEN
MINUET IN G MAJOR	BEETHOVEN
MINUET IN G MINOR	HANDEL
MINUET IN G MINOR	HANDEL

MINUET IN G MINOR	STOLZEL
MINUET IN G	BACH, J.S.
MINUET IN G	BEETHOVEN
MINUET IN G	BEETHOVEN
MINUET IN G	BEETHOVEN
MINUET IN G	BEETHOVEN
MINUET IN G	BEETHOVEN
MINUET IN G	BEETHOVEN
MINUET IN G	BEETHOVEN
MINUET IN G	BEETHOVEN
MINUET IN G	BEETHOVEN
MINUET IN G	BEETHOVEN
MINUET IN G	PURCELL, H.
MINUET IN G	VANHALL, J. B.
MINUET IN SWING	SMITH
MINUET K001 IN G--WITH TRIO	MOZART, W. A.
MINUET K355 IN D	MOZART, W. A.
MINUET MEDLEY	BACH, J.S.
MINUET NO. 1, ANNA MAGDALENA	BACH, J.S.
MINUET NO. 1	SATIE, E.
MINUET NO. 2, ANNA MAGDALENA	BACH, J.S.
MINUET NO. 3	ALBENIZ, I.
MINUET	BACH, J.S.
MINUET	BACH, J.S.
MINUET	BACH, J.S.
MINUET	HARRIS, C.
MINUET	LAUDISA
MINUET	MACCHI
MINUET	MCGRAW
MINUET	MEHUL, E. H.
MINUET	MOZART, W. A.
MINUET	PADEREWSKI, I.
MINUET	PADEREWSKI, I.
MINUET	PADEREWSKI, I.
MINUET	PADEREWSKI, I.
MINUET	RAMEAU
MINUET	RAMEAU
MINUET	ROBINSON, A.
MINUTE MELODIES - BK. 1	BERMONT, H.--ED
MINUTE MELODIES - BK. 2	BERMONT, H.--ED
MINUTE MUSIC FOR SMALL HANDS	ARCHER, V.
MINUTE WALTZ, EASY	CHOPIN
MINUTE WALTZ, OP. 64 NO. 1 -- VALSE IN D FLAT	CHOPIN
MINUTE WALTZ, OP. 64 NO. 1	CHOPIN
MINUTE WALTZ, OP. 64 NO. 1	CHOPIN
MINUTE WALTZ, OP. 64 NO. 1	CHOPIN
MINUZZOLO E LA SUA GIORNATA	CINTOLESI
MIRACLE DE NOTRE-DAME -- INCIDENTAL MUSIS TO THE PLAY	HONEGGER, A.
MIRACULOUS MANDARIN	BARTOK
MIRAGES, LES -- BALLET --	SAUGUET
MIRAGES ON THE NAME OF GIESEKING	CASTELNUOVO-TEDE
MIRAGE	BUTLER, J.
MIRAGE	FERNANDEZ, O.
MIRAGE	WHITFORD
MIRAGGI	OREFICE, G.
MIREILLE, WALTZ SONG	GOUNOD, C.
MIROIRS, KOMPLETT	RAVEL
MIROIRS, NO. 5 LA VALLEE DES CLOCHES	RAVEL
MIROIRS, SUITE--COMPLETE	RAVEL
MIROIRS -- NO. 1, NOCTUELLES	RAVEL
MIROIRS -- NO. 2, OISEAUX TRISTES	RAVEL
MIROIRS -- NO. 4, ALBORADA DEL GRACIOSO	RAVEL
MIROIRS -- NO. 5, LA VALLEE DES CLOCHES	RAVEL
MIROIRS	RAVEL
MIROIR DE VOTRE FAUST	POUSSEUR, H.
MIRRORS AND ME	ROZIN
MIRROR LAKE, THE	NIEMANN
MISCELLANEOUS COMPOSITIONS	CHOPIN
MISCELLANEOUS COMPOSITIONS	CHOPIN
MISCELLANEOUS COMPOSITIONS	MENDELSSOHN
MISCELLANEOUS COMPOSITIONS	WEBER, VON
MISCHIEF MAKERS	POWERS, M.
MISCHIEF MAKER	ROLLINS
MISCHIEVOUS ELF	BENTLEY
MISCHIEVOUS ELF	BENTLEY
MISCHIEVOUS LEPRECHAUN	ARCHER, I.
MISCHIEVOUS PIXIE	BENFORD
MISERERE, IL TROVATORE, EASY	VERDI
MISSION‡ IMPOSSIBLE	BRIMHALL,
MISSION BELLS	GILLOCK
MISSION BELLS	GILLOCK
MISSION BELLS	THOMPSON, J.
MISSISSIPPI SUITE	GROFE, F.
MISSOURI WALTZ	EPPEL *
MISS HAUMON	MERANG
MISS MODERN	RICHARDSON, W.
MISTER BUFFALO	RICHTER
MISTER BUNNY	OBENCHAIN, V.
MISTER ECHO	ROGERS, E.
MISTER FIVE BY FIVE	RAYE *
MISTER HIPPO'S BIG MOUTH	RICHTER
MISTER HIPPO	NEVIN
MISTER HOP-TOAD	BEAUMONT
MISTER LITTLE TOAD	COKELY, C.
MISTER LITTLE TOAD	COKELY, C.
MISTER POSSUM	RICHMAN, A.
MISTER WOOF	SUDDARDS
MISTOLERO, EL	GOMEZ CARRILLO
MISTRESS MARY	STAIRS, L.
MISTY EVENING	SCARMOLIN
MISTY VALLEY	YORKE, P.
MISTY	BRADLEY,
MISTY	BRIMHALL,
MIST ON THE LAKE AND TO THE TOP OF THE MOUNTAIN	KURKA, R.
MIST	HIBBS, C.
MIST	MILLER
MIS AMIGOS	GUASTAVINO
MITZY'S RENDEZVOUS	PARENTE, SR. E.
MIT ZWEEN STIMMEN, BK. 1	HERRMANN, K.
MIT ZWEEN STIMMEN, BK. 2	HERRMANN, K.
MIX-A-MODE	MURRAY
MI ALBUM DE CUBA	BRIMHALL,
MI AMIGO PEPITO	BRODSKY, M.
MNEMONIC PROCESS --FOR THE STUDY OF SCALES AND	DINSART
MOBILES -- 10 GRAPHIC IMPRESSIONS	SHAW, A.
MOCCASIN DANCE	LONG, L.
MOCCASIN FLOWER	STEINER
MODAL MARCH	ELAINE, M.
MODAL VARIATIONS FOR PIANO	GIANNINI
MODERATO, OP. 10 NO. 1	WEBER, VON
MODERNE STUDIE, DIE -- BK. 1	SCHOLZ
MODERNE STUDIE, DIE -- BK. 2, PART 1	SCHOLZ
MODERNE STUDIE, DIE -- BK. 2, PART 2	SCHOLZ
MODERNE TANZRHYTHMEN	OWEN--ED
MODERNE	WHITFORD
MODERN APPROACH TO POPULAR PLAYING, VOL. 1	FIELDS, I.
MODERN APPROACH TO POPULAR PLAYING, VOL. 2	FIELDS, I.
MODERN ART OF PIANO PLAYING, THE, BK. 1	MASON, I.
MODERN COURSE FOR PIANO - SECOND PIANO ACCOMPANIMENTS	THOMPSON, J.
MODERN COURSE FOR THE PIANO - A TUNEFUL DUET ALBUM FOR	THOMPSON, J.
MODERN FINGER GYMNASTICS	HABERBIER, E.
MODERN JAZZ QUARTET, THE --MJQ RELEASE	
MODERN MASTERS	NEVIN
MODERN MELODIES FOR POPULAR PIANO PLAYING	KAHN, M.
MODERN METHOD FOR KEYBOARD STUDY, A - COMPLETE SET	PROGRIS, J.
MODERN METHOD FOR KEYBOARD STUDY, A - VOL. 1	PROGRIS, J.
MODERN METHOD FOR KEYBOARD STUDY, A - VOL. 2	PROGRIS, J.
MODERN METHOD FOR KEYBOARD STUDY, A - VOL. 3	PROGRIS, J.
MODERN METHOD FOR KEYBOARD STUDY, A - VOL. 4	PROGRIS, J.
MODERN MINIATURES	AGAY, D.--ED
MODERN MUSIC BOX	RENNARD
MODERN PIANIST DUO-PIANO SERIES	NORDMAN--ED.
MODERN PIANIST SERIES, BK. 1	
MODERN PIANIST SERIES, BK. 2	
MODERN PIANIST SERIES, BK. 3	
MODERN PIANIST SERIES, BK. 4	
MODERN PIANIST SERIES - CHRISTMAS DUETS	
MODERN PIANIST SERIES - CHRISTMAS SKETCHES	
MODERN PIANIST SERIES - CZERNY FOR THE MODERN PIANIST	
MODERN PIANIST SERIES - DUO-CLASSICS	
MODERN PIANIST SERIES - DUO-FAVORITES	
MODERN PIANIST SERIES - DUO-MODS	
MODERN PIANIST SERIES - DUO-POPS	
MODERN PIANIST SERIES - GUIDE TO THE MODERN PIANIST	
MODERN PIANIST SERIES - MINIATURE CLASSICS	
MODERN PIANIST SERIES - ONE PIANO, FOUR HANDS	
MODERN PIANIST SERIES - SONGS OF FAITH	
MODERN PIANIST SERIES - SUPPLEMENTARY SONGS, BK. 1	
MODERN PIANIST SERIES - SUPPLEMENTARY SONGS, BK. 2	
MODERN PIANIST SERIES - SUPPLEMENTARY SONGS, BK. 3	
MODERN PIANIST SERIES - SUPPLEMENTARY SONGS, BK. 4	
MODERN PIANOFORTE METHOD	PETERS, W.
MODERN PIANO METHOD FOR BEGINNERS, A, PART 1, LEARNING	ARMOUR
MODERN PIANO METHOD FOR BEGINNERS, A, PART 2, NOTES,	ARMOUR
MODERN PIANO METHOD FOR BEGINNERS, A, PART 3, WRITING	ARMOUR
MODERN PIANO METHOD FOR BEGINNERS, A, PART 4, THE 2/4	ARMOUR
MODERN PIANO METHOD FOR BEGINNERS, A, PART 5,	ARMOUR
MODERN PIANO METHOD	CARRIER *
MODERN PIANO PIECES	
MODERN PIANO TECHNIQUE -- FR.-E. --	BLANCHET
MODERN PIANO TRANSCRIPTIONS	HEYWOOD, E.
MODERN RUSSIAN PIANO MUSIC -- AKIMENKO TO	
MODERN SCHOOL, OP. 299	DUVERNOY, J.
MODERN SOUNDS, BK. 1	GRYCE
MODERN SOUNDS, BK. 2	GRYCE
MODERN STYLES AND HARMONIC CONSTRUCTION	KAHN, M.
MODERN SUITE NO. 1, OP. 10--INTERMEZZO	MACDOWELL
MODERN SUITE NO. 1, OP. 10--PRELUDE	MACDOWELL
MODERN SUITE	SYMONS
MODERN SWANEE RIVER, THE	NEVIN
MODERN TECHNIC	AIKEN
MODERN TECHNIQUE OF THE PEDAL	SCHNABEL, K.
MODERN TEMPER, THE. A DANCE	SHIFRIN
MODEST VIOLET	RIDLEY, S. C.
MODES ENFANTINES, SEPT PIECES FACILES	WEBER, A.
MODE DE VALEURS ET D'INTENSITES	MESSIAEN, O.
MOHEE	MOSSMAN, T.
MOHRENTANZ UND MUMMENSCHANZ	VOLKART-SCHLAGER
MOINS QUE RIEN	LANCEN
MOLDAU, THE -- THEME	SMETANA
MOLDAU, THE	SMETANA
MOLE, THE	REISTRUP, J.
MOLL	CASTALDI, P.
MOMENTO CAPRICCIOSO, OP. 12	WEBER, VON
MOMENTO DOLOROSO	PONCE, M.
MOMENTS AT THE PIANO	ANTHONY, G.
MOMENTS MUSICAUX, D 780 --OP. 94--	SCHUBERT
MOMENTS MUSICAUX, OP. 80	POLDINI, E.
MOMENTS MUSICAUX, OP. 94	SCHUBERT
MOMENTS MUSICAUX, OP. 94	SCHUBERT
MOMENTS MUSICAUX OP. 94 NO. 2 AS-DUR	SCHUBERT
MOMENTS MUSICAUX OP. 94 NO. 3 F-MOLL	SCHUBERT
MOMENTS MUSICAUX	SCHUBERT
MOMENTS TO REMEMBER	RAPHLING
MOMENTS TO REMEMBER	RAPHLING
MOMENTS WITH MENDELSSOHN	MENDELSSOHN
MOMENT MUSICAL, OP. 44 NO. 3	REGER
MOMENT MUSICAL, OP. 94 NO. 1	SCHUBERT
MOMENT MUSICAL, OP. 94 NO. 2	SCHUBERT
MOMENT MUSICAL, OP. 94 NO. 2	SCHUBERT
MOMENT MUSICAL, OP. 94 NO. 3	SCHUBERT
MOMENT MUSICAL, OP. 94 NO. 3	SCHUBERT
MOMENT MUSICAL, OP. 94 NO. 3	SCHUBERT
MOMENT MUSICAL, OP. 94 NO. 3	SCHUBERT
MOMENT MUSICAL, OP. 94 NO. 3	SCHUBERT
MOMENT MUSICAL, OP. 94 NO. 3	SCHUBERT
MOMENT MUSICAL, OP. 94 NO. 4	SCHUBERT
MOMENT MUSICAL, OP. 94 NO. 5	SCHUBERT
MOMENT MUSICAL, OP. 94 NO. 6	SCHUBERT
MOMENT MUSICAL, OP. 94 NO. 6	SCHUBERT
MOMENT MUSICAL, OP. 94 NO.3	SCHUBERT
MOMENT MUSICAL -- LE CAHIER DE SYLVINE, NO. 2	DELANNOY
MOMENT MUSICAL IN F MINOR	SCHUBERT
MOMENT MUSICAL NO. 3	SCHUBERT
MOMENT MUSICAL	LESUR, D.
MOMENT MUSICAL	RACHMANINOFF, S.
MOMENT MUSICAL	SCHUBERT
MOMENT MUSICAL	SCHUBERT
MOMENT MUSICAL	SCHUBERT
MOMENT ORIENTALE	REEVES, R.
MOMO PRECOCE -- 1929	VILLA-LOBOS, H.
MONARCH BUTTERFLY	GEORGE
MONASTERY BELLS	WELY, L.
MONDAY'S CHILD	LAST, J.
MONDO-TONDO -- BALLET --	PORRINO
MONDO CANE	OLIVIERI *
MONKEY'S MARCH, THE	MILLER, L.
MONKEY'S PACHANGA	KASZNER
MONKEY'S WEDDING, THE	WEYBRIGHT
MONKEYSHINES	DONENFELD, J.
MONKEY ANTICS	ROBINSON, A.
MONKEY CAPERS	KENT, A.
MONKEY CHATTER	RICHTER
MONKEY SHINES NO. 1	MCDONALD, H.
MONKEY SHINES	KELLEY, R.
MONKEY SHINES	TRUXELL, L.
MONKEY WEASEL BOOGIE WOOGIE	GLOVER, D.
MONODY	SMALLEY, R.
MONOLOGUE IV FOR THE RIGHT HAND	MIMAROGLU, I.
MONOLOGUE	OLDENBURG, E.
MONOSONATA	KELTERBORN

MONOSONATA	KELTERBORN
MONTANESA FROM PIECES ESPAGNOLES	FALLA, M. DE
MONTETURLI	COUTURE
MONTPARNASSE	DOUCET, C.
MONTREAL	KNAUER
MON LAC	WITKOWSKY
MON RECITAL - LE COUCOU AND EN BERCANT CLAUDE	FRANCAIX, J.
MON RECITAL	FRANCAIX, J.
MON REVE, OP. 151	WALDTEUFEL, E.
MOODS, 1973	TAUTENHAHN, G.
MOODS	LUBIN, E.
MOODS	TUTTLE, T. K.
MOOD INDIGO, SIMP.	ELLINGTON
MOOD INDIGO	ELLINGTON
MOOD MODERNE	MELVIN, B.
MOON-PICTURES, OP. 21 -- AFTER H. C. ANDERSON'S	MACDOWELL
MOON, THE	WEYBRIGHT
MOONBEAMS, REVERIE	HOPKINS, H.
MOONBEAMS ON THE LAKE	FITZPATRICK,
MOONBEAMS	MARTINO
MOONBEAMS	PANELLA, L.
MOONGLOW	HUDSON *
MOONLIGHT -- PEDAL STUDY	COBB
MOONLIGHT AND ROSES	LANE, J.--ED.
MOONLIGHT AND ROSES	WILLIAMS,
MOONLIGHT CRUISE	ROGERS, E.
MOONLIGHT DANCE WALTZ	DIETS, J.
MOONLIGHT IN GRANADA	HUARTE
MOONLIGHT IN SANTA MARIA	DITTENHAVER
MOONLIGHT MEDITATIONS	BARTH, H.
MOONLIGHT MELODY	HIRSCHBERG, D.
MOONLIGHT MOOD	DE ROSE, P.
MOONLIGHT MOOD	
MOONLIGHT MOOD	
MOONLIGHT ON THE HUDSON	WILSON, G.
MOONLIGHT ON THE LAGOON	FRIML, R.
MOONLIGHT ON THE RIVER WALTZ	SEIDT, J.
MOONLIGHT ON THE WATER	SEIDT, J.
MOONLIGHT ON VENUS	SMITH
MOONLIGHT POEM	FIBICH, Z.
MOONLIGHT REVELS	ANDRE
MOONLIGHT SERENADE	MILLER *
MOONLIGHT SONATA, FIRST MVT.	BEETHOVEN
MOONLIGHT SONATA, FIRST MVT.	BEETHOVEN
MOONLIGHT SONATA, OP. 27 NO. 2 -- FIRST MOVEMENT	BEETHOVEN
MOONLIGHT SONATA, OP. 27 NO. 2 - FIRST MOVEMENT	BEETHOVEN
MOONLIGHT SONATA, OP. 27 NO. 2	BEETHOVEN
MOONLIGHT SONATA - FIRST MOVEMENT	BEETHOVEN
MOONLIGHT SONATA THEME	BEETHOVEN
MOONLIGHT SONATA	BEETHOVEN
MOONLIGHT SONATA	BEETHOVEN
MOONLIGHT SONATA	BEETHOVEN
MOONLIGHT SONATA	BEETHOVEN
MOONLIGHT WALTZ	ARMOUR
MOONLIGNT MELODY	CANTORE
MOONLIT CASTLE	TAYLOR
MOONLIT GARDEN	EZELL, H.
MOONLIT GARDEN	EZELL, H.
MOONLIT MEADOWS, OP. 65	PROKOFIEFF
MOONLIT MORNING	REISER, V.
MOONOCTURNE	NEVIN
MOONSTONES	SIMON
MOON BOAT, THE	KETTERER, E.
MOON BUGGY	KARP
MOON CLOUD	AARON, M.
MOON CRATER ROCK	CATIZONE, J. M.
MOON DAWN	FRIML, R.
MOON DAWN	FRIML, R.
MOON JUMP	BENFORD
MOON LIGHTS UP, THE	LECUONA
MOON MINIATURES	GREAVES, T.
MOON MIST	RODGERS
MOON MUSIC	HOFSTAD, M.
MOON OVER MIAMI	BRIMHALL,
MOON PASSING BEHIND THE CLOUDS, THE	STUART, P.
MOON RIVER	BRIMHALL,
MOON ROCKET, THE	ROLFE, W.
MOON SHADOWS	LANE, J.
MOON SHADOWS	ROLFE, W.
MOON SHADOWS	ROLFE, W.
MOON SHOT	CHILDERS, L.
MOON SONG, MEDITATION	HOPKINS, H.
MORAVIAN FOLK SONGS	JANACEK
MORAVIAN NATIONAL DANCES	JANACEK
MORCEAUX A 4 OU A 3 MAINS	AUBEL, D'
MORCEAUX CARACTERISTIQUE EN FORME D'ETUDES, OP. 22 NO.	WOLLENHAUPT
MORE, MORE, AND MORE -- UN GRAND AMOUR	PIAF *
MORESQUE AND CHANSON ARABE	GRANADOS
MORETTI CHE DANZANO	COSTANTINI
MORE BUSY WORK FOR THE YOUNG PIANIST	PERRY, J. H.
MORE CONCERT TRANSCRIPTIONS OF FAVORITE HYMNS	KOHLMANN, C.
MORE EASY CLASSICS TO MODERNS	
MORE FOLK TUNES FOR FUN	BASTIEN--ED.
MORE FUN IN SONG	CERVENKA
MORE MELODY RHYMES THROUGH ALL THE KEYS	SWENSON, L.
MORE MODERN MELODIES FOR POPULAR PIANO PLAYING	KAHN, M.
MORE NEW ORLEANS JAZZ STYLES -- ADVANCING INTERMEDIATE	GILLOCK
MORE OF ALL NATIONS TUNES	NICHOLLS, H.
MORE ONCE UPON A TIME STORIES OF THE GREAT MUSIC	ROBINSON, G. E.
MORE ONE, FOUR, FIVE	STEINER
MORE PARALLEL BARS	DUMM
MORE REAL COOL PIANO	MARTIN, G.
MORE SELECT SONATINAS, BK. 1	PODOLSKY, L.--ED
MORE SELECT SONATINAS, BK. 2	PODOLSKY, L.--ED
MORE SELECT SONATINAS, BK. 3	PODOLSKY, L.--ED
MORE STUNTS	RICHTER, A.
MORE THAN A MIRACLE	WILLIAMS,
MORE THAN YOU KNOW	
MORE THEMES FROM THE GREAT CONCERTOS	LEVINE, H.--ED
MORE	OLIVIERO *
MORE	OLIVIERO *
MORE	OLIVIERO *
MORE	OLIVIERO *
MORE	OLIVIERO *
MORE	OLIVIERO *
MORE 24 CARAT GOLD	BRADLEY,
MORE 24 CARAT GOLD	BRADLEY,
MORGEN KOMMT DER WEIHNACHTSMANN	DRATHS--ED
MORNING-MOOD, OP. 46 NO. 1	GRIEG
MORNING AFTER, THE	BRADLEY,
MORNING BLORIES	HART, G. R.
MORNING CHIMES	KREVIT, W.
MORNING GLORY	KOHLER, F.
MORNING IN MADRID	SCHILLIO, E. J.
MORNING IN THE HILLS	DITTENHAVER
MORNING MIST	STEVENS, E.
MORNING MOOD --PEER GYNT SUITE NO. 1--	GRIEG
MORNING MOOD --PEER GYNT SUITE NO. 1--	GRIEG
MORNING MOOD	GRIEG
MORNING MOOD	WHITFORD
MORNING NOON AND NIGHT	CROCKER, V.
MORNING OP. 46 NO. 1	GRIEG
MORNING PAPERS, OP. 279	STRAUSS, J.
MORNING PAPERS, OP. 279	STRAUSS, J.
MORNING PRAYER, NO. 130	STREABBOG
MORNING PRAYER, OP. 130 NO. 1	STREABBOG
MORNING PRAYER	KULLAK, T.
MORNING PRAYER	LICHNER, H.
MORNING PRAYER	STAIRS, L.
MORNING PRAYER	STREABBOG
MORNING PRAYER	STREABBOG
MORNING SONG	BEAMAN, M. L.
MORNING SUNBEAMS	ANTHONY, B. R.
MORNING	GRIEG
MORNING	PROKOFIEFF
MORRISON HOTEL -- THE DOORS	
MORRIS DANCE FROM 'HENRY VIII'	GERMAN, E.
MORRIS DANCE	COBB
MORSELS --'KOUSOCHKI'	SPIEGLEMAN
MORSICATHY	BERBERIAN, C.
MORT DE ROLAND, OP. 18	FERNANDEZ GIL
MORT DE TINTAGILES, LA -- POEME DRAMATIQUE POUR GRAND	LOEFFLER, C. M.
MOSAIC--1967	REICH, J.
MOSAICO SEVILLANO	TORROBA, F. M.
MOSAICS -- SIX PIANO PIECES ON HEBREW FOLK THEMES--	AGAY, D.
MOSAIC NO. 1, PIANO AND PERCUSSION	ELDABH
MOSAIC	MARGOLA
MOSAIQUE	MONTBRUN, G.
MOSEYIN' ALONG	STILWELL
MOSE - DAL TUO STELLATO SOGLIO	ROSSINI, G.
MOSE - DAL TUO STELLATO SOGLIO	ROSSINI, G.
MOSE - PRAYER	ROSSINI, G.
MOSQUITO	MCSWEEN, F. W.
MOSS ROSES	LANE, J.
MOST BEAUTIFUL GIRL, THE	BRADLEY,
MOST BEAUTIFUL GIRL IN THE WORLD	
MOST BEAUTIFUL LOVE SONGS, THE	FANENGHI
MOST BEAUTIFUL PAGES OF HARPSICHORD MUSIC, THE - BACH	MONTANI--ED
MOST BEAUTIFUL PAGES OF HARPSICHORD MUSIC, THE - DUTCH	MONTANI--ED
MOST BEAUTIFUL PAGES OF HARPSICHORD MUSIC, THE -	MONTANI--ED
MOST BEAUTIFUL PAGES OF HARPSICHORD MUSIC, THE -	MONTANI--ED
MOST BEAUTIFUL PAGES OF HARPSICHORD MUSIC, THE -	MONTANI--ED *
MOST BEAUTIFUL PAGES OF HARPSOCHORD MUSIC, THE -	MONTANI--ED
MOST HAPPY FELLA, THE	LOESSER, F.
MOST IMPORTANT TRAIN, A	MAYER
MOST POPULAR SERIES - VOL. 1, PIANO PIECES	
MOST POPULAR SERIES - VOL. 2, PIANO PIECES IN	
MOST POPULAR SERIES - VOL. 3A, TUNES YOU LIKE TO PLAY	
MOST POPULAR SERIES - VOL. 3B, TUNES YOU LIKE TO PLAY	
MOST POPULAR SERIES - VOL. 4, EASY PIECES FOR PIANO	
MOST POPULAR SERIES - VOL. 5, MUSIC FROM THE MASTERS	
MOST POPULAR SERIES - VOL. 6, EASY DUETS FOR PIANO	
MOST POPULAR SERIES - VOL. 7, NINETY-THREE SHORT	
MOTHER, SHAKE THE CHERRY TREE	DITTENHAVER
MOTHER'S LOVE, MELODY	MAYOR
MOTHER'S LULLABY	OGLE, L.
MOTHER'S LULLABY	WEISLEDER, A.
MOTHER GOOSE AT THE PIANO, BK. 1	STEINER
MOTHER GOOSE AT THE PIANO, BK. 2	STEINER
MOTHER GOOSE IN NOTELAND	PERRY, J. H.
MOTHER GOOSE MELODIES FOR THE YOUNG PIANIST--40	JOBSON, V.
MOTHER GOOSE SUITE	RAVEL
MOTHER GOOSE SUITE	RAVEL
MOTHER GOOSE SUITE	RAVEL
MOTHER HUBBARD AND SONG OF SIXPENCE	ROLFE, W.--ED
MOTHS	THOMPSON, J.
MOTION	WHITFORD
MOTIVATION	REISER, V.
MOTORCYCLE RIDE	RICHTER
MOTO PERPETUO, OP. 11 -- TRANSCRIPTION --	PAGANINI, N. *
MOTO PERPETUO -- RONDO FROM SONATA, OP. 24 --	WEBER, VON
MOTO PERPETUO FROM SONATA, OP. 24	WEBER, VON
MOTO PERPETUO	LAST, J.
MOTO PERPETUO	WEBER, VON
MOUNTAINTOPS AND FIELDS IN THE MORNING	KURKA, R.
MOUNTAIN AIR	WATSON
MOUNTAIN BELLE, SCHOTTISCHE	KINKEL, C.
MOUNTAIN BELLE SCHOTTISCHE	KINKEL, C.
MOUNTAIN BELLE SCHOTTISCHE	KINKEL, C.
MOUNTAIN BELLE SCHOTTISCHE	KINKEL, C.
MOUNTAIN BELLE SCHOTTISCHE	KINKEL, C.
MOUNTAIN BELLE	KINKEL, C.
MOUNTAIN BOOK	SCHAUM, J.--ED.
MOUNTAIN CONCERTO	SCHAUM, J.
MOUNTAIN DANCE NO. 2	HOVHANESS, A.
MOUNTAIN IDYLLS	HOVHANESS, A.
MOUNTAIN LAUREL	ROGERS
MOUNTAIN MAIDEN'S DREAM	ADAMS, R. G.
MOUNTAIN SPPING	BOHM
MOUNTAIN STREAM, THE, OP. 13	SMITH, SYDNEY
MOUNTAIN SUNRISE	FROST
MOUNTAIN TUNE -- SET	KEENEY, W.
MOUSE AND THE CLOCK	ERB
MOUSE GOES TO CHURCH, A	OBENCHAIN, V.
MOUSTACHE POLKA	VARGUES
MOUVEMENTS FUR KLAVIER UND ORCHESTER, KLAVIERAUSZUG	FORTNER, W.
MOUVEMENT PERPETUEL	ARRIEU
MOUVEMENT PERPETUEL	DAMASE, J. M.
MOUVEMENT PERPETUEL	PAPINEAU-COUTURE
MOVEMENTS	STRAVINSKY, I.
MOVEMENT	LYBBERT
MOVIE MYSTERY, A	SCHER, W.
MOVIE POPS	BRADLEY,
MOVIMENTI	DIONISI
MOVIN' THE BOOGIE	AMMONS *
MOVING ALONG	LEE, E. M.
MOZART-SCHAUM, BK. 1	MOZART, W. A.
MOZART-SCHAUM, BK. 2	MOZART, W. A.
MOZART, SIX VIENNESE SONATINAS	MOZART, W. A.
MOZART'S BEST KNOWN PIANO SONATAS	MOZART, W. A.
MOZART'S FIRST FIVE COMPOSITIONS	MOZART, W. A.
MOZART'S FIRST FIVE COMPOSITIONS	MOZART, W. A.
MOZART AT 8 -- THE CHELSEA NOTEBOOK	MOZART, W. A.
MOZART CADENZAS, K. 482	BRITTEN, B.
MOZART FOR THE YOUNG PIANIST	MOZART, W. A.
MOZART MINUET	NEVIN
MOZART ON TIPTOE	GODDEN, R.
MOZART SONATAS AND FANTASIES -- REVISED EDITION	MOZART, W. A.
MOZART SYMPHONY NO. 40	BRIMHALL,
MOZART VARIATIONS AND FUGUE, OP. 132A	REGER
MOZART VARIATIONS AND FUGUE, OP. 132	REGER

Title	Composer
MOZART VARIATIONS AND FUGUE, OP. 132	REGER
MOZART	MOZART, W. A.
MR. AND MRS. CUCKOO	SCHULDT, M.
MR. AND MRS. PETER RABBIT	HOFSTAD, M.
MR. AND MRS. STACCATO	MERKUR
MR. AND MRS. WOODPECKER	HOWELL, I.
MR. AND MRS. WREN	ERB
MR. BOJANGLES	WALKER
MR. B FLAT, OP. 86 NO. 3	SCARMOLIN
MR. CZERNY	CAZDEN, N.
MR. FUNNY MAN	MANA-ZUCCA
MR. GHOST GOES TO TOWN	HUDSON *
MR. HOBBS THEME	MANCINI
MR. LION	ROBINSON, A.
MR. LION	ROBINSON, A.
MR. LOLLIPOP AND HIS FRIEND	BORASTON, M.
MR. LUCKY	
MR. PORCUPINE TAKES A WALK	DVORINE
MR. SCARLATTI	KARP
MR. SNOWMAN	ROBINSON, A.
MR. SNOWMAN	ROBINSON, A.
MR. THIRD TAKES A WALK	RICHTER
MR. TURKEY GOES TO TOWN	GIOVANNI
MRS. CACKLE-CACKLE	ERB
MRS. MOUSIE	COBB
MUCHACHACHA	SWAN *
MUD CAT RAG	KRENZ, B.
MUFFIN MAN, THE	WEYBRIGHT
MULATO	ROLCAN, A.
MULE, THE	RICHMAN, A.
MULE DRIVER, THE. --EL MULETERO	CAHAN
MULLERLIED-VARIATIONEN -- UBER 'IHR BLUMLEIN ALLE' --	SCHUBERT
MULTI-KEY READING	BASTIEN
MUNASTERIO'E SANTA CHIARA	
MUNECA BAILA, LA -- CUENTOS Y FANTASIAS, NO. 4	CHAVARRI
MURMELNDES LUFTCHEN, FANTASIE OP. 21 NO. 4	JENSEN, A.
MURMURE, PETITE VALSE, OP. 87	CARMAN
MURMURE DE LA SOURCE, LE, IDYLLE, OP. 241	LACK
MURMURING BROOK	BOHM
MURMURING SPRING	BOHM
MURMURING WAVES	KALBERT
MURMURING ZEPHYRS	JENSEN, A.
MUROS VERDES	MONCAYO, J.
MUSAS DE ANDALUCIA, LAS, OP. 93--NO. 1, CLIO	TURINA, J.
MUSAS DE ANDALUCIA, LAS, OP. 93--NO. 7, URANIA	TURINA, J.
MUSAS DE ANDALUCIA, LAS, OP. 93--NO. 8, TERPISCORE	TURINA, J.
MUSCADINS, MARCH	WACHS, P.
MUSETTA'S WALTZ, LA BOHEME	PUCCINI
MUSETTA'S WALTZ --LA BOHEME--	PUCCINI
MUSETTA'S WALTZ SONG -- LA BOHEME	PUCCINI
MUSETTA'S WALTZ	NEVIN
MUSETTA'S WALTZ	PUCCINI
MUSETTE --2 PIANOS, 8 HANDS--	BACH, J.S. *
MUSETTE IN D, ANNA MAGDALENA	BACH, J.S.
MUSETTE IN D MAJOR	BACH, J.S.
MUSETTE IN D	BACH, J.S.
MUSETTE	BACH, J.S.
MUSETTE	BOIZARD, G.
MUSETTE	COURSEY, R. DE
MUSETTE	PFEIFFER, A.
MUSIC-BOX, THE	HEINS, C.
MUSIC-BOX, THE	POLDINI, E.
MUSIC-HALL DES MARIONNETTES, LE	MAURICE, P.
MUSIC, OP. 4	BURT, F.
MUSICALLY SPEAKING	BOLDON
MUSICAL ADVENTURES FOR FOUR LITTLE HANDS	FRIML, R.
MUSICAL ADVENTURES IN MARKSLAND	
MUSICAL BOX, THE	THOMAS, C. J.
MUSICAL BOX	POUISHNOFF, L.
MUSICAL CHILDREN'S FRIEND, THE, OP. 87 -- 50 MELODIOUS	WOHLFAHRT
MUSICAL CHRISTMAS CARDS --SIX PIECES--	
MUSICAL CLOCK	HEINS
MUSICAL CROSSWORD, A	KAYE, E.
MUSICAL EXERCISES	CORTOT
MUSICAL FORMS FROM A TO Z -- CYCLOPEDIA OF MASTERWORKS	PORTNOFF, M.--ED
MUSICAL GATEWAY	GRAY, D.
MUSICAL IMPRESSIONS - 8 EASY PIECES	MICHELI AGOSTINI
MUSICAL JOKE, K522	MOZART, W. A.
MUSICAL JOURNEY, A	MIRANTE
MUSICAL JOURNEY THROUGH EUROPE, A	STEINER
MUSICAL MEMORIES, OP. 16--LITTLE GAZELLE, NO. 3	DUCELLE, P.
MUSICAL MEMORIES, OP. 16--QUEEN OF DROWSY-LAND, NO. 2	DUCELLE, P.
MUSICAL MEMORIES, OP. 16 -- NO. 01, DANCING STARS --	DUCELLE, P.
MUSICAL MEMORIES, OP. 16 -- NO. 02, LILLIPUTIAN PARADE	DUCELLE, P.
MUSICAL MEMORIES, OP. 16 -- NO. 04, DANCE OF THE	DUCELLE, P.
MUSICAL MEMORIES, OP. 16 -- NO. 07, NITA, SPANISH	DUCELLE, P.
MUSICAL MEMORIES, OP. 16 -- 11, ALPINE SONG --	DUCELLE, P.
MUSICAL MINIATURES	APPLEBAUM
MUSICAL MOMENTS, BK. 1	GEORGE
MUSICAL MOMENTS, BK. 2	GEORGE
MUSICAL MOMENTS FOR YOUNG PIANISTS	POLDINI, E.
MUSICAL OFFERING. COMPLETE SCORE IN ORIGINAL CLEFS,	BACH, J.S.
MUSICAL OFFERING--URTEXT--. COMPLETE SCORE IN ORIGINAL	BACH, J.S.
MUSICAL OFFERING	BACH, J.S.
MUSICAL PEARLS - EASY TRANSCRIPTION OF FAMOUS PIECES,	CHIESA *
MUSICAL PEARLS - EASY TRANSCRIPTION OF FAMOUS PIECES,	CHIESA *
MUSICAL PIANO TEACHING, BK. 1	MAYER--ED. *
MUSICAL PIANO TEACHING, BK. 2	MAYER--ED. *
MUSICAL PLAYMATES	WIGHAM, M.
MUSICAL POWDER BOX	HAYES
MUSICAL SELF-PORTRAITS --FOURTEEN PIECES BY DUTCH	
MUSICAL SNUFF-BOX, THE--VALSE-BADINAGE, OP. 32	LIADOW, A.
MUSICAL SNUFF BOX, OP. 32	LIADOW, A.
MUSICAL SNUFF BOX	LIADOW, A.
MUSICAL SNUFF BOX	LIADOW, A.
MUSICAL SPEED DRILLS, BK. 1	RABEN
MUSICAL SPEED DRILLS, BK. 2	RABEN
MUSICAL SPEED DRILLS, BK. 3	RABEN
MUSICAL SWITCH	ALFORD, K.
MUSICAL TALES - 7 PIECES	VERGANTI
MUSICAL TYPIST	MUNRO, R.
MUSICAL VISIT TO FOREIGN LANDS, A -- 13 RECITAL AND	ANTHONY, G.
MUSICAL VISIT TO OUTER SPACE, A -- 9 RECITAL AND	ANTHONY, G.
MUSICAL VISIT TO THE CITY, A -- 12 RECITAL AND	ANTHONY, G.
MUSICAL VISIT TO THE COUNTRY, A -- 14 RECITAL AND	ANTHONY, G.
MUSICAL VISIT TO THE PARK, A -- 15 RECITAL AND	ANTHONY, G.
MUSICAL VISIT WITH THE MASTERS, A -- 16 CLASSICAL	
MUSICA CALLADA -- 9 PIECES --	MOMPOU, F.
MUSICA EN CUARTO TIEMPOS - MUSIC IN FOUR TEMPOS	BALADA, L.
MUSICA EN CUATRO TIEMPOS - MUSIC IN FOUR TEMPOS	BALADA, L.
MUSICA PARA NINOS	GIANNEO
MUSICA PER TRE PIANOFORTI -- 1935 --	DALLAPICCOLA
MUSICA VARIATA	GRAY, D.
MUSICA 1941	KOELLREUTTER, J.
MUSICIANLY SCALE PRACTICE	PITFIELD
MUSICIANSHIP THROUGH IMPROVISATION AT THE KEYBOARD --	RABINOFF, S.
MUSICIANSHIP THROUGH IMPROVISATION AT THE KEYBOARD --	RABINOFF, S.
MUSICIANSHIP THROUGH IMPROVISATION AT THE KEYBOARD --	RABINOFF, S.
MUSICLAND	
MUSIC AMONG THE PINES	WYMAN, A.
MUSIC AMONG THE PINES	WYMAN, A.
MUSIC AND GUIDE BOOK	XAVERIA, S.
MUSIC APPRECIATION IS FUN, BK. 1	HIRSCHBERG, D.
MUSIC APPRECIATION SERIES, BK. 01	RICHTER, C.--ED
MUSIC APPRECIATION SERIES, BK. 02	RICHTER, C.--ED
MUSIC BOX, CAPRICE	LIEBICH
MUSIC BOX, THE	HEINS, C.
MUSIC BOX, THE	SAXTON
MUSIC BOX, THE	WOLPAW
MUSIC BOX CHANSONETTE	KLEINMAN, A.
MUSIC BOX CONCERTO, THE	GERARD, J.
MUSIC BOX DANCE	KLEINMAN, A.
MUSIC BOX IN BLUE	DE ROSE, P.
MUSIC BOX PIANO ALBUM, THE	KLEINMAN, A.
MUSIC BOX RAG	ROBERTS
MUSIC BOX SONATINA, THE	MELECCI, A.
MUSIC BOX	CARNEVALI
MUSIC BOX	HOWELL
MUSIC BOX	MORGEN, M.
MUSIC BOX	POLDINI, E.
MUSIC BOX	POOLE, C.
MUSIC BY THE MASTERS	LANNING--ED
MUSIC EDUCATION SUPPLEMENT - COMPLETE SET 8-17 THROUGH	
MUSIC EDUCATION SUPPLEMENT - VOL. 1	
MUSIC EDUCATION SUPPLEMENT - VOL. 2	
MUSIC EDUCATION SUPPLEMENT - VOL. 3	
MUSIC EDUCATION SUPPLEMENT - VOL. 4	
MUSIC FLASHCARDS	BASTIEN
MUSIC FOR CHILDREN--8 PIECES	LIST, G.
MUSIC FOR CHILDREN, BK. 1	WALTON, W.
MUSIC FOR CHILDREN, BK. 2	WALTON, W.
MUSIC FOR CHILDREN, OP. 65--12 EASY PIECES	PROKOFIEFF
MUSIC FOR CHILDREN, OP. 65	PROKOFIEFF
MUSIC FOR CHILDREN, OP. 65	PROKOFIEFF
MUSIC FOR CHILDREN, OP. 65	PROKOFIEFF
MUSIC FOR EVERYBODY	MITTLER--ED
MUSIC FOR GYMNASTICAL EXERCISES	JANACEK
MUSIC FOR HAIKU	BULL
MUSIC FOR HAPPINESS, BK. 1	HIRSCHBERG,
MUSIC FOR HAPPINESS, BK. 2	HIRSCHBERG,
MUSIC FOR HOLIDAYS	GIRLAMO, F.
MUSIC FOR MODERNS	GROFE, F.
MUSIC FOR MY LADY	PERKINS, F.
MUSIC FOR OLDER BEGINNERS, BK. 1	KIRBY, M. B.
MUSIC FOR OLDER BEGINNERS, BK. 2	KIRBY, M. B.
MUSIC FOR PERCUSSION AND PIANO, 1971	DE BERADINIS, J.
MUSIC FOR PIANO, BK. 1	KNORR, E.L. VON
MUSIC FOR PIANO, BK. 1	PACE, R.
MUSIC FOR PIANO, BK. 2	KNORR, E.L. VON
MUSIC FOR PIANO, BK. 2	PACE, R.
MUSIC FOR PIANO, BK. 3	KNORR, E.L. VON
MUSIC FOR PIANO, BK. 3	PACE, R.
MUSIC FOR PIANO, BK. 4	PACE, R.
MUSIC FOR PIANO, BK. 5	KNORR, E.L. VON
MUSIC FOR PIANO, BK. 5	PACE, R.
MUSIC FOR PIANO, BK. 6	PACE, R.
MUSIC FOR PIANO, OP. 2 NO. I	DRIESSLER
MUSIC FOR PIANO, OP. 24	POSER
MUSIC FOR PIANO - 1957	BEN-HAIM
MUSIC FOR PIANO - 1967	BEN-HAIM
MUSIC FOR PIANO FOR THE OLDER BEGINNER	PACE, R.
MUSIC FOR PIANO STUDENTS	BENNER, L.
MUSIC FOR PIANO	FINE, I.
MUSIC FOR PIANO	FINE, I.
MUSIC FOR PIANO	YANNAY, Y.
MUSIC FOR PIANO 1	LEEUW, R.
MUSIC FOR SPECIAL OCCASIONS	GIRLAMO, F.
MUSIC FOR THE WEDDING	
MUSIC FOR TWO DANCERS	HARVEY, PATRICK
MUSIC FOR YOUNG PEOPLE	PROKOFIEFF
MUSIC FOR YOUNG POEPLE	KLEINSINGER, G.
MUSIC FROM MAKE-BELIEVE LAND	STEINER
MUSIC FROM SEAS AND SHIPS -- SET	DOUGHERTY, C.
MUSIC FROM THE MASTERS TO THE MINORS	
MUSIC FUN BOOK	MONTGOMERY, V.
MUSIC HISTORY PIECES	SCHAUM, J.--ED.
MUSIC IN MY FINGERS	LAKE
MUSIC IS A WORLD OF JOY	
MUSIC IS MY HOBBY	MITTLER--ED
MUSIC LAND--A FIRST PIANO BOOK FOR INDIVIDUAL OR CLASS	VANNORT, I.
MUSIC LESSONS HAVE BEGUN	FLETCHER
MUSIC LOVER'S PIANO BOOK	MOZART, W. A.
MUSIC LOVERS' DUETS - BOOK 1	WALLIS
MUSIC LOVERS' DUETS - BOOK 2	WALLIS
MUSIC MADE EASY, BK. 1	VILLE, M.
MUSIC MADE EASY, BK. 2	VILLE, M.
MUSIC MAKER BOOK 1	VEON
MUSIC MAKER BOOK 2	VEON
MUSIC MAKER BOOK 3	VEON
MUSIC MAN, THE	WILLSON, M.
MUSIC NOTEBOOK	BASTIEN
MUSIC OF ANTONIO CARLOS JOBIM STYLED FOR PIANO BY JOE	JOBIM
MUSIC OF CHANGES, VOL. 1	CAGE
MUSIC OF CHANGES, VOL. 2	CAGE
MUSIC OF CHANGES, VOL. 3	CAGE
MUSIC OF CHANGES, VOL. 4	CAGE
MUSIC OF FAITH, BK. 1	PORTNOFF, M.
MUSIC OF FAITH, BK. 2	ECKARD, W.
MUSIC OF FAITH, BK. 3	PARSONS
MUSIC OF LEROY ANDERSON, THE -- BK. 1	ANDERSON, L.
MUSIC OF NATURE, THE	HANUS, J.
MUSIC OF NATURE, THE	HANUS, J.
MUSIC OF PERCY GRAINGER, THE	GRAINGER, P.
MUSIC OF THE AMERICAN INDIAN	SCHAUM, J.--ED.
MUSIC OF THE UNION	GROBE
MUSIC OUTDOORS	STEINER
MUSIC READER - BOOK 1	FREDRICH, F.
MUSIC READER - BOOK 2	FREDRICH, F.
MUSIC READING FOR BEGINNERS	BASESCU, B.
MUSIC STUDY FOR ADULTS	
MUSIC THE WHOLE WORLD LOVES	WALLIS
MUSIC WE WILL HAVE	BURNAM
MUSIC WORKBOOK - BK. 1A	CLARK, F.--ED.
MUSIC WORKBOOK - BK. 1B	CLARK, F.--ED.
MUSIC WORKBOOK - BK. 2	CLARK, F.--ED.
MUSIC WORKBOOK - BK. 3	CLARK, F.--ED.
MUSIC YOU LOVE BY LEROY ANDERSON -- IN PREP.	NEVIN
MUSIC	BRADLEY,
MUSIC	HEINS, C.
MUSIC	WALLIS--ED
MUSIC	WALLIS
MUSIDORA -- MAZURKA --	TALEXY
MUSIKALISCHER ZEITVERTREIB--19 PIECES	RATHGEBER, V.

Title	Composer
MUSIKALISCHER ZEITVERTREIB AUF DEM CLAVIER	RATHGEBER, V.
MUSIKALISCHER ZEITVERTREIB AUF DEM KLAVIER	RATHGEBER, V.
MUSIKALISCHES BILDERBUCH	SZELENYI
MUSIKALISCHES MANCHERLEI--6 PIECES PUBLISHED FOR THE	BACH, C.P.E.
MUSIKANTEN, DIE KOMMEN	KNAB, A.
MUSIKANTEN, DIE KOMMEN	PUDELKO, W.
MUSIK AUS FRUHER ZEIT -- 1350-1650, BAND 01 -	APEL, W.--ED
MUSIK AUS FRUHER ZEIT -- 1350-1650, BAND 02 - ENGLAND,	APEL, W.--ED
MUSIK FUR CEMBALO	COUPERIN, F.
MUSIK FUR KLAVIER, OP. 2 NO. 2	DRIESSLER
MUSIK ZUM KEULENSCHWINGEN. 5 KLAVIERSTUCKE	JANACEK
MUSINGS	LINDFORS, E.
MUSING	FRANK
MUSIQUES AU JARDIN	ROPARTZ
MUSIQUES D'ESPAGNE	INFANTE
MUSIQUES INTIMES, BK. 2 OP. 29	SCHMITT, F.
MUSIQUES POUR PIANO	RIVIER, J.
MUSIQUETTES--1962	SKORZENY, F.
MUSIQUE DE BALLET	KOFFLER, J.
MUSIQUE ET MUSICIENS D'AUJOURD'HUI, BK. 1	CLASSENS
MUSIQUE ET MUSICIENS D'AUJOURD'HUI, BK. 2	CLASSENS
MUSIQUE ET MUSICIENS D'AUJOURD'HUI, BK. 3	CLASSENS
MUSIQUE POUR DEUX PIANOS	MERLET
MUSIQUE POUR FAIRE DANSER - BK. 1 .. LE MIELLEUX	DALCROZE
MUSIQUE POUR FAIRE DANSER - BK. 2 .. LA CUISINIERE	DALCROZE
MUSIQUE POUR PIANO	ARRIEU
MUSIQUE POUR TITI - APRES LA VODKA, REVE DU CACATOES,	KARJINSKY
MUSIQUE PUOR PETITES MAINS	BARRAUD
MUSIQUE QUASI UNA SONATA	KOFFLER, J.
MUST I GO	SCHMEID, A.
MUTED HARP, THE	CHAGY
MUTINY ON THE BOUNTY-LOVE THEME	LANE, J.--ED.
MUTINY ON THE BOUNTY	KAPER, B.
MUTTER, OP. 28	SUK
MUZIEK. HARPSICHORD, STRING ORCHESTRA. POCKET SCORE	VERHAAR
MUZIEK FOR HARPSICHORD	VERHAAR
MUZIKALE DIAS --12 CANONS AND 12 FUGHETTAS IN ALL	ROENTGEN
MYRA HESS ALBUM	HESS--ED.
MYRIOLOGUE	DIAMOND, D.
MYRTLES, THE, VALSE DE SALON	WACHS, P.
MYRTLE GALOP	STREABBOG
MYSTERIOUSLY	HAUBIEL, C.
MYSTERIOUS TALE, A	SCHER, W.
MYSTERY, A	HAUBIEL, C.
MYSTERY MOVIE THEME	MANCINI
MYSTERY STORY, A	ANSON, G.
MYSTERY STORY	HOPKINS, H.
MYSTIC FLUTE	HOVHANESS, A.
MY ARPEGGIO BOOK	HIRSCHBERG, D.
MY BANJO	HOPKINS, H.
MY BEAUTIFUL LADY	
MY BLUE HEAVEN	LANE, J.--ED.
MY BLUE HEAVEN	
MY BONNIE LIES OVER THE OCEAN	ARMOUR
MY BUDGIE	MELVIN, B.
MY BUNNY	HOPKINS, H.
MY CLOCK	BLAKE, D.
MY COUNTRY 'TIS OF THEE	CAREY, H.
MY COWBOY BOOTS	STAIRS, L.
MY DARLING, WALTZ	GREENWALD, M.
MY DOG, PAL	ELLIOTT
MY DOGGIE	PORTER, W.
MY DOG RUSTY	DITTENHAVER
MY DOLL'S LULLABY	HOPKINS, H.
MY EASTER BONNET	STAIRS, L.
MY ENGINE	HOFSTAD, M.
MY EVERYDAY HYMN BOOK	RICHTER, A.--ED.
MY FAIR LADY SELECTION	LOEWE, F.
MY FAIR LADY	LOEWE, F.
MY FAIR LADY	LOEWE, F.
MY FAVORITE CHOPIN	CHOPIN
MY FAVORITE CHRISTMAS CAROLS	HOLLANDER
MY FAVORITE CLASSICS	BRIMHALL,
MY FAVORITE CLASSICS	BRIMHALL,
MY FAVORITE DUET ALBUM --28--	
MY FAVORITE DUET ALBUM	ECKSTEIN--ED.
MY FAVORITE PROGRAM ALBUM --54--	
MY FAVORITE REPERTOIRE ALBUM --25--	
MY FAVORITE SOLO ALBUM	
MY FAVORITE THINGS	HAMMERSTEIN *
MY FAVORITE THINGS	HAMMERSTEIN *
MY FAVORITE TUNE	COBB
MY FIRST BACH-12 PIECES	BACH, J.S.
MY FIRST BEETHOVEN	BEETHOVEN
MY FIRST BOOGIE BOOK	LYON
MY FIRST CHOPIN	CHOPIN
MY FIRST CHRISTMAS BOOK	WEYBRIGHT--ED.
MY FIRST CHRISTMAS BOOK	WEYBRIGHT
MY FIRST CLASSICS	HOLLANDER
MY FIRST CLEMENTI	CLEMENTI
MY FIRST DANCE	BERMONT, G.
MY FIRST DANCE	ENGELMANN, H. U.
MY FIRST DUETS, BK. 1	HOLLANDER
MY FIRST GRIEG	GRIEG
MY FIRST HANDEL	HANDEL
MY FIRST HARPSICHORD BOOK	MONTANI
MY FIRST HYMNAL --FAVORITE CATHOLIC AND OTHER HYMNS--	RICHTER--ED
MY FIRST MARCH	DE VITO, A.
MY FIRST MENDELSSOHN	MENDELSSOHN
MY FIRST MOZART	MOZART, W. A.
MY FIRST MUSIC BOOK	RUSSELL
MY FIRST MUSIC WORKBOOK	HOWELL, I.
MY FIRST NOTE BOOK, BK. 1	RICHTER
MY FIRST NOTE BOOK, BK. 2	RICHTER
MY FIRST PIECE, ETUDE	HOPKINS, H.
MY FIRST PIECE	KERR, R. N.
MY FIRST RECORD FOR STUDENT, TEACHER, AND PARENT	LINDFORS, E.
MY FIRST SCHUBERT	SCHUBERT
MY FIRST SCHUMANN	SCHUMANN, R.
MY FIRST SONATA	SCHULDT, A.
MY FIRST SONG BOOK	RICHTER, A.
MY FIRST TOYS -- ROY POLY, AIRPLANE, DRUM	RICHTER, A.
MY FIRST TRIP TO MUSIC LAND	HOWELL, I.
MY FIRST TSCHAIKOWSKY	TSCHAIKOWSKY
MY FIRST WALTZ	KASSCHAU, H.
MY FIRST WALTZ	KASSCHAU, H.
MY FIRST WALTZ	ROLSETH, B.
MY FUNNY VALENTINE	BRIMHALL,
MY FUNNY VALENTINE	SINGER, L.--ED
MY GALLOPING STEED	ERB
MY GAL SAL	SMALL, A.
MY GIFT	DITTENHAVER
MY GOD IS REAL	LANE, J.--ED.
MY GREEN UMBRELLA	BASTIEN
MY HAMSTER CRAWLS -- CASE BOUND	RAMSIER, P.
MY HAMSTER CRAWLS -- PAPER	RAMSIER, P.
MY HANUKKAH SONG BOOK	ENGEL--ED *
MY HEART AT THY SWEET VOICE	SAINT-SAENS
MY HEART AT THY SWEET VOICE	SAINT-SAENS
MY HEART AT THY SWEET VOICE	SAINT-SAENS
MY HYMNS	JENSVOLD, J.--ED
MY KITE	KARP
MY LADY'S HARPSICHORD	GILLOCK
MY LADYE NEVELLS BOOKE OF VIRGINAL MUSIC	BYRD, W.
MY LADYE NEVELLS BOOKE	BYRD, W.
MY LADY GREENSLEEVES	SILVESTER, F. C.
MY LITTLE BROTHER	BRUSSELS, I.
MY LITTLE DOG	KARST
MY LITTLE GOLDFISH	HOPKINS, H.
MY LITTLE MOHEE, A FAMILY FOLKSONG -- KENTUCKY -- SET	NILES, J.
MY LITTLE PET, WALTZ	HOPKINS, H.
MY LOVE FOR YOU	DICAPUA
MY MELANCHOLY BABY	BRYANT--ED.
MY MERRY DRUM	BARRETT
MY MERRY MUSIC BOOK -- A METHOD FOR BEGINNERS	HUMBER, L. M.
MY MOTHER BIDS ME BIND MY HAIR	HAYDN
MY MUSICAL DIARY	ALT, H.
MY MUSIC BOX	WHITFORD
MY MUSIC COLOR BOOK	XAVERIA, S.
MY MUSIC DIARY	HENKLE, M.
MY MUSIC LETTER BOOK	XAVERIA, S.
MY MUSIC NOTE BOOK	XAVERIA, S.
MY MUSIC PICTURE BOOK	XAVERIA, S.
MY MUSIC RECORD	LINDFORS, E.
MY NEW BIKE	BASTIEN
MY NEW CAR	ALT, H.
MY NEW HAT	PERRIN
MY NEW SAXOPHONE	HOPKINS, H.
MY NOAH'S ARK	MAXWELL, D.
MY OLD KENTUCKY HOME -- VARIATIONS	FOSTER
MY OLD KENTUCKY HOME	FOSTER
MY OLD KENTUCKY HOME	FOSTER
MY OLD KENTUCKY HOME	FREEMAN
MY OWN HYMN BOOK	RICHTER, A.--ED.
MY PAL--WITH WORDS	VANNORT, I.
MY PAL AND I	BRUSSELS, I.
MY PET	CONFREY, Z.
MY PIANO BOOK, BK. 1	RICHTER
MY PIANO BOOK, BK. 2	RICHTER
MY PIANO BOOK, BK. 3	RICHTER
MY PIANO PLAY BOOK	GIOVANNI
MY PIANO SKETCHBOOK, PART 1	DITTENHAVER
MY PIANO SKETCHBOOK, PART 2	DITTENHAVER
MY PIANO WORKSHOP SERIES, BOOK 1--GET ACQUAINTED BOOK	DEE, M.
MY PIANO WORKSHOP SERIES, BOOK 2--ON WE GO	DEE, M.
MY PIANO WORKSHOP SERIES, BOOK 3--MORE TO LEARN	DEE, M.
MY PIANO WORKSHOP SERIES, BOOK 4--READY TO PLAY	DEE, M.
MY PICCOLO	ROBINSON, A.
MY PIGGY BANK	KREUTZER
MY POEM	SCHOEN
MY POLLYWOG	STAIRS, L.
MY PONY MACARONI	SNYDER, W.
MY POODLE FIFI	WATSON
MY POPGUN	RICHTER, A.
MY PRANCING PONY	STIEFEL, E.
MY PRAYER	MOORE
MY PRETTY CELLO	HOPKINS, H.
MY PRETTY HAT	HOPKINS, H.
MY PRETTY LITTLE PINK -- A MERRY FUGUE ON A SOUTHERN	PISK
MY REPERTOIRE OF FAMOUS COMPOSERS	STRIMER, J.--ED
MY ROCKING CHAIR	NOONA, A.
MY ROCKING HORSE	ROBINSON, W. E.
MY ROMANCE	
MY SCALE BOOK	HIRSCHBERG, D.
MY SCOTTISH FRIEND	BRUSSELS, I.
MY SECOND MUSIC WORKBOOK	HOWELL, I.
MY SHADOW	FICHANDLER, W.
MY SHADOW	HUNKE
MY SHADOW	JAMES, E. L.
MY SHADOW	MCSWEEN, F. W.
MY SHIP	SINGER, L.--ED
MY SNOWMAN	TIBBITTS, A.
MY STAR	CHAPLIN
MY STEP BY STEP HYMN BOOK	GLOVER, D.
MY SWEETHEART'S THE MAN IN THE MOON	THORNTON
MY SWEET LORD	BRIMHALL,
MY TEDDY BEAR	ARNOLD, H.
MY TOY BALLOON	SLONIMSKY
MY TOY DUCK	GILLOCK
MY TOY SOLDIER	WEYBRIGHT
MY TOY TRUMPET	ROGERS, E.
MY TREASURE WALTZ	BECUCCI
MY VALENTINE -- SALUTE D'AMOUR	ELGAR, E.
MY VALENTINE	HOPKINS, H.
MY VERY FIRST PIANO PROGRAM	ALLISON, I.--ED
MY WALKING, TALKING DOLL	BRODSKY, M.
MY WAY	BRIMHALL,
MY WEDDING DAY	SCHAUM, J.--ED.
MY WILD IRISH ROSE	OLCOTT
MY WISHING STAR	ERB
MY WISH FOR YOUR HAPPINESS	MCKAY, G.
MY WOODEN SHOES	MUNN, W.
MY WORK IS OVER	NOEL, H.
MY WORLD	BACON
MY YIDDISCHE MOMMA	BRIMHALL,
NABUCCO - EASY FANTASIA	VERDI
NABUCCO - VA, PENSIERO	VERDI
NACHSPIEL IN DREI TEILEN	WYTTENBACH, J.
NACHTSTIMMUNG	VOMACKA
NACHTSTUCK, OP. 23 NO. 4	SCHUMANN, R.
NACHTSTUCK, OP. 23 NO. 4	SCHUMANN, R.
NACHTSTUCK, OP. 23 NO. 4	SCHUMANN, R.
NACHTSTUCKE, OP. 23, AND THREE FANTASIESTUCKE, OP. 111	SCHUMANN, R.
NACHTSTUCKE, OP. 23 NO. 4	SCHUMANN, R.
NACHTSTUCKE, OP. 23	SCHUMANN, R.
NACHTSTUCKE, OP. 23	SCHUMANN, R.
NACH BACH -- FANTASY FOR HARPSICHORD OR PIANO	ROCHBERG, G.
NAIADES ET LE FAUNE INDISCRET, LES	SEVERAC
NAILA, PAS DES FLEURS	DELIBES, L.
NAILA -- LE PAS DE FLEURS	DELIBES, L.
NAILA WALTZ, EASY	DELIBES, L.
NAIN JAUNE, LE -- GALOP BRILLANT --	CHELU
NAIN JAUNE, LE -- GALOP BRILLANT --	CHELU
NAIVE LITTLE TALE	FERNANDEZ, O.
NAME OF THE GAME, THE	GRUSIN
NAME THAT SWINGS, A	ETTORE, E.
NANCY'S LULLABY	KENSLER
NANNERL MOZART'S PIANO BOOK	MOZART, L.
NANNERL NOTENBUCH --1759--. HARD COVER	MOZART, L.
NANNETTE	ARMOUR
NAPOLEON'S LAST CHARGE	ELLIS, E.
NAPOLEON'S LAST CHARGE	PAULL
NAPOLEON SUITE	FRANCAIX, J.
NAPOLI - BARCAROLLE, NOCTURNE, CAPRICE ITALIEN	POULENC, F.

Title	Composer
NAPOLI - MEDLEY OF FUNICULI FUNICULA AND O SOLE MIO	DENZA *
NAPOLI FROM 'IMPRESSIONS OF ITALY'	CHARPENTIER, G.
NARCISSUS, OP. 13 NO. 4	NEVIN
NARCISSUS, OP. 13 NO. 4	NEVIN
NARCISSUS, OP. 13 NO. 4	NEVIN
NARCISSUS, OP. 13 NO. 4	NEVIN
NARCISSUS, OP. 13 NO. 4	NEVIN
NARCISSUS, THEME	NEVIN
NARCISSUS	NEVIN
NARCISSUS	NEVIN
NARCISSUS	NEVIN
NARCISSUS	NEVIN
NARCISSUS	NEVIN
NARCISSUS	NEVIN
NARCISSUS	NEVIN
NARCISSUS	NEVIN
NATIONAL AIRS, MEDLEY MARCH	KAISER
NATIONAL AIRS	RANSOME, F.
NATIONAL DANCES OF EUROPE	MAYER
NATIONAL EMBLEM MARCH	BAGLEY, E.
NATIONAL EMBLEM MARCH	BAGLEY, E.
NATIONAL EMBLEM MARCH	BAGLEY, E.
NATIONAL SONG	GRIEG
NATIONAL VELVET - THEME	ARMBRUSTER
NATIVITY, THE -- 5 PIECES	BAXTER
NATYAMALIKA - DANCE SUITE	SCHRAMM
NATYAMALIKA - DANCE SUITE	SCHRAMM
NAUGHTY ANNIE, RONDO	HOPKINS, H.
NAUGHTY LITTLE RAINDROPS	SCHER, W.
NAUGHTY WALTZ, THAT	LEVY, S.
NAVAJO LULLABY	MCKAY, G.
NAVAJO WAR DANCE NO. 2	FARWELL, A.
NAVARRA	ALBENIZ, I.
NAVARRA	ALBENIZ, I.
NAVARRA	ALBENIZ, I.
NAVIDAD -- MIRACLE PANTOMINE IN 2 ACTS	TURINA, J.
NAVIDAD FROM ''MILAGRO IN 2 CUADROS'', OP. 16	TURINA, J.
NAVIGANTI, I	CASTELNUOVO-TEDE
NAZARETH	GOUNOD, C.
NA SERA'E MAGGIO	
NEAPOLITAN DANCE	TAYLOR, EDNA
NEAPOLITAN NIGHTS -- SIMPLIFIED	ZAMECNIK
NEAPOLITAN NIGHTS	ZAMECNIK
NEAPOLITAN SERENADE	TOSELLI
NEARBY A CAROUSEL--AMUSEMENT	NOEL, H.
NEARBY A CAROUSEL--CONVERSATION	NOEL, H.
NEARBY A CAROUSEL--MARCH	NOEL, H.
NEARBY A CAROUSEL--WALTZ	NOEL, H.
NEARER, MY GOD, TO THEE	FREEMAN
NEARER, MY GOD, TO THEE	MASON, L.
NEARER MY GOD TO THEE	DRUMHELLER
NEAR THE BAYOU	BRUSSELS, I.
NEAR THE BEGINNING	OLSON
NECESSITY STUDIES, OP. 299, BOOKS 1 AND 2 COMBINED	CZERNY
NECESSITY STUDIES FROM OP. 299, IN PROGRESSIVE ORDER	CZERNY
NEGEV CONCERTO	ELLSTEIN, A.
NEGRO AIRS	RANSOME, F.
NEIGE SUR ROME, LA	HONEGGER, A.
NEIGE	DUMAS, L.
NEIGHBORHOOD CIRCUS	DITTENHAVER
NELLA BASILICA DI SAN MARCO	CANTU
NELLA NOTTE	COUTURE
NELLY WAS A LADY	FOSTER
NEL COR PIU NON MI SIENTO, SIX VARIATIONS	BEETHOVEN
NEL GIARDINO SETTECENTESCO	PIZZINI
NENIA OP. 18 NO. 3	SGAMBATI
NENUPHARS, LES	FOURDRAIN
NEPOUMUCENE A MEGEVE	CLASSENS
NEPTUNE'S CAVE	LONG, L.
NERANTZULA	CALLINICOS
NERO, PETER, AT THE PIANO	NERO
NERO, PETER, OFF RECORD	NERO
NERVOUS GHOST	ROBINSON, A.
NERVOUS GHOST	ROBINSON, A.
NEST OF BABY BUNNIES, A	STAIRS, L.
NEU-ENGLAND-IDYLL OP. 62	MACDOWELL
NEUER ETUDENGANG, BK. 1	REHBERG--ED.
NEUER ETUDENGANG, BK. 2	REHBERG--ED.
NEUER ETUDENGANG -- BK. 1	REHBERG
NEUER ETUDENGANG -- BK. 2	REHBERG
NEUES BACH-HEFT. 5 WENIG BEKANNTE STUCKE FUR CEMBALO	BACH, J.S.
NEUES BACH-HEFT. 5 WENIG BEKANNTE STUCKE FUR CEMBALO	BACH, J.S.
NEUES BACH-HEFT	BACH, J.S.
NEUES BACH BUCH	BACH, J.S.
NEUES SONATINBUCH -- VORSTUFE	FREY--ED
NEUES SONATINENBUCH -- BK. 1	FREY--ED
NEUES SONATINENBUCH -- BK. 2	FREY--ED
NEUES VORTRAGSBUCH, HEFT 01	SCHUNGELER, H.
NEUES VORTRAGSBUCH, HEFT 02	SCHUNGELER, H.
NEUE ANLEITUNG FUR DAS KLAVIERSPIEL, BAND 01	BURKARD, J. A.
NEUE ANLEITUNG FUR DAS KLAVIERSPIEL, BAND 02	BURKARD, J. A.
NEUE ANLEITUNG FUR DAS KLAVIERSPIEL, BEIHEFT 01,	BURKARD, J. A.
NEUE ANLEITUNG FUR DAS KLAVIERSPIEL, BEIHEFT 02,	BURKARD, J. A.
NEUE CEMBALOMUSIK, HEFT 1	BIALIS *
NEUE ODYSSEE -- BALLET IN 5 TABLEAUX	BRUNS, V.
NEUE SCHULE DES KLAVIERSPIELS	TOBLER--ED
NEUE VARIATIONEN A-DUR	BEETHOVEN
NEUE WEIHNACHTSLIEDER	
NEUE WEIHNACHTSMUSIK. 18 WEIHNACHTSLIEDER IN 24 SATZEN	BORNEFELD *
NEUF PRELUDES, OP. 66	ALKAN
NEUMES RYTHMIQUES	MESSIAEN, O.
NEUNE KLEINE KLAVIERSTUCKE, BK. 1	BARTOK
NEUNE KLEINE KLAVIERSTUCKE, BK. 1	BARTOK
NEUNE KLEINE KLAVIERSTUCKE, BK. 2	BARTOK
NEVADA	
NEVERTHELESS	SINGER, L.--ED
NEVER BEEN TO SPAIN	BRADLEY,
NEVER CAN SAY GOODBYE	BRADLEY,
NEVER MY LOVE	ADDRISI
NEVER ON SUNDAY	BRIMHALL,
NEWSREEL SUITE	MITTLER
NEWS BEAT	OAKLAND, B.
NEWTON'S BOOGIE WOOGIE	PAPARELLI
NEW ADVENTURE	WEBER
NEW AND OLD	RIEGGER, W.
NEW BOY, THE	BRODSKY, M.
NEW BUSONI. EXERCISES AND STUDIES FROM THE	BUSONI
NEW BUSONI, THE. EXERCISES AND STUDIES FROM THE	BUSONI
NEW BUSONI, THE--EXERCISES AND STUDIES FROM	BUSONI
NEW BUSONI, THE--EXERCISES AND STUDIES FROM	BUSONI
NEW CAROLS FOR CHRISTMAS	MCKUEN
NEW CEMBALO MUSIC	GOEBELS
NEW CHRISTMAS MUSIC	BAUM--ED.
NEW CZERNY, THE, BK. 1	CZERNY
NEW CZERNY, THE, BK. 2	CZERNY
NEW CZERNY, THE, BK. 3	CZERNY
NEW CZERNY, THE, BK. 4	CZERNY
NEW CZERNY, THE, BK. 5	CZERNY
NEW DANCE	RIEGGER, W.
NEW DANCE	RIEGGER, W.
NEW DAWN FANTASY	REISER, V.
NEW DIRECTIONS	ANSON, G.--ED
NEW EASY GRADED CLASSIC ALBUM - BACH	BACH, J.S.
NEW EASY GRADED CLASSIC ALBUM - BEETHOVEN	BEETHOVEN
NEW EASY GRADED CLASSIC ALBUM - CHOPIN	CHOPIN
NEW EASY GRADED CLASSIC ALBUM - HANDEL	HANDEL
NEW EASY GRADED CLASSIC ALBUM - HAYDN	HAYDN
NEW EASY GRADED CLASSIC ALBUM - MOZART	MOZART, W. A.
NEW EASY GRADED CLASSIC ALBUM - OLD ENGLISH MASTERS	CHING--ED.
NEW EASY GRADED CLASSIC ALBUM - OLD FRENCH AND FLEMISH	CHING--ED.
NEW EASY GRADED CLASSIC ALBUM - SCARLATTI	SCARLATTI, D.
NEW EASY GRADED CLASSIC ALBUM - SCHUBERT	SCHUBERT
NEW EASY GRADED CLASSIC ALBUM - SCHUMANN	SCHUMANN, R.
NEW EASY GRADED CLASSIC ALBUM - SONATINA MOVEMENTS	CHING--ED.
NEW ENGLAND CONSERVATORY PIANO COURSE - ALBUM OF	
NEW ENGLAND CONSERVATORY PIANO COURSE - FIRST GRADE	
NEW ENGLAND CONSERVATORY PIANO COURSE - SECOND GRADE	
NEW ENGLAND CONSERVATORY PIANO COURSE - SELECTED	
NEW ENGLAND CONSERVATORY PIANO COURSE - SELECTED	
NEW ENGLAND CONSERVATORY PIANO COURSE - THIRD GRADE	
NEW ENGLAND CONSERVATORY PIANO COURSE - THIRTY-FIVE	
NEW ENGLAND IDYLLS	MACDOWELL
NEW ENGLAND SEASCAPE - FROM SEVEN FLOWERS FROM A	GIASSON, P.
NEW ENGLAND SEASCAPE	GIASSON, P.
NEW FLOWER SONG	ALDRICH
NEW GRADED CLASSIC ALBUM - GRIEG	GRIEG
NEW GRADED PEDALLING, BK. 1	CHING
NEW GRADED PEDALLING, BK. 2	CHING
NEW GRADED PIECES, BK. 1	CHING
NEW GRADED PIECES, BK. 2	CHING
NEW GRADED PIECES, BK. 3	CHING
NEW GRADED PIECES, BK. 4	CHING
NEW GRADED PIECES, BK. 5	CHING
NEW GRADED SIGHT-READING, BK. 1	CHING
NEW GRADED SIGHT-READING, BK. 2	CHING
NEW GRADED STUDIES, BK. 1	CHING
NEW GRADED STUDIES, BK. 2	CHING
NEW GRADED STUDIES, BK. 3	CHING
NEW GRADED STUDIES, BK. 4	CHING
NEW GRADED STUDIES, BK. 5	CHING
NEW GRADED TIME EXERCISES	CHING
NEW GRADUS AD PARNASSUM, THE -- HANDS TOGETHER--	PHILIPP, I.
NEW HORIZONS--12 PIECES FOR PIANO--INTRODUCTION TO	HELM, E.
NEW HORIZONS FOR TWO PIANOS, EIGHT HANDS	MERKUR
NEW HORIZONS	GIASSON, P.
NEW HORIZONS	GIASSON, P.
NEW HORIZONS	MERKUR
NEW INSTRUCTIONS FOR PLAYING THE HARPSICHORD,	
NEW MODERN PIANO STUDENT, BK. 1	BERLIN, B.
NEW MUSIC FOR THE PIANO--LAWSON-GOULD EDITION	PROSTAKOFF--ED.
NEW MUSIC FOR THE PIANO, A COMPILATION OF 22	
NEW ORLEANS BLUES	GLOVER, D.
NEW ORLEANS BLUES	GLOVER, D.
NEW ORLEANS JAZZ STYLES -- ADVANCING INTERMEDIATE	GILLOCK
NEW PIANO METHOD, BK. 1	SCHMOLL, A.
NEW PIANO METHOD, BK. 2	SCHMOLL, A.
NEW PIECES FOR ME	GARROW
NEW RAG	JOPLIN, S.
NEW RECITAL REPERTOIRE BY MASTERS OF THE 17TH, 18TH,	MIROVITCH,
NEW SCHOOL OF VELOCITY, BK. 1 -- 1-14 --	BERENS, H.
NEW SCHOOL OF VELOCITY, BK. 2 -- 15-26 --	BERENS, H.
NEW SCHOOL OF VELOCITY, BK. 3 -- 27-33 --	BERENS, H.
NEW SCHOOL OF VELOCITY, OP. 128	KOEHLER
NEW SCHOOL OF VELOCITY, OP. 61 - 40 EXERCISES,	BERENS, H.
NEW SCHOOL OF VELOCITY, OP. 834. 2 VOLS	CZERNY
NEW SCHOOL OF VELOCITY, OP. 834	CZERNY
NEW SCRIBNER MUSIC LIBRARY, VOL. 01 'EASY PIANO MUSIC	HANSON, H.--ED
NEW SCRIBNER MUSIC LIBRARY, VOL. 02 'KEYBOARD	HANSON, H.--ED
NEW SCRIBNER MUSIC LIBRARY, VOL. 03 'PIANO CLASSICS'	HANSON, H.--ED
NEW SCRIBNER MUSIC LIBRARY, VOL. 04 'A CENTURY OF	HANSON, H.--ED
NEW SCRIBNER MUSIC LIBRARY, VOL. 05 'ALL-TIME PIANO	HANSON, H.--ED
NEW SCRIBNER MUSIC LIBRARY, VOL. 06 'PIANO MUSIC FOR	HANSON, H.--ED
NEW SCRIBNER MUSIC LIBRARY, VOL. 07 'AT THE OPERA'	HANSON, H.--ED
NEW SCRIBNER MUSIC LIBRARY, VOL. 08 'MUSIC FOR THE	HANSON, H.--ED
NEW SCRIBNER MUSIC LIBRARY, VOL. 09 'HOME FAVORITES'	HANSON, H.--ED
NEW SCRIBNER MUSIC LIBRARY, VOL. 10 'ART SONGS'	HANSON, H.--ED
NEW SCRIBNER MUSIC LIBRARY, VOL. 11 'REFERENCE VOLUME'	HANSON, H.--ED
NEW SONATAS BY HAYDN - SONATA NO. 01	HAYDN
NEW SONATAS BY HAYDN - SONATA NO. 02	HAYDN
NEW SONATAS BY HAYDN - SONATA NO. 03	HAYDN
NEW SONATAS BY HAYDN - SONATA NO. 04	HAYDN
NEW SONATAS BY HAYDN - SONATA NO. 05	HAYDN
NEW SONATAS BY HAYDN - SONATA NO. 06	HAYDN
NEW SONATAS BY HAYDN - SONATA NO. 07	HAYDN
NEW SONATAS BY HAYDN - SONATA NO. 08	HAYDN
NEW SONATAS BY HAYDN - SONATA NO. 09	HAYDN
NEW SONATAS BY HAYDN - SONATA NO. 10	HAYDN
NEW SONGS FROM THE MOTION PICTURE 'SONG OF NORWAY'	WRIGHT, R. *
NEW SPANISH DANCES, OP. 65	MOSZKOWSKI
NEW SPRING	LANGE, G.
NEW WALTZES, 1965/7	RIETI
NEW WORLDS FOR THE YOUNG PIANIST, BK. 1	LESSARD, J.
NEW WORLDS FOR THE YOUNG PIANIST, BK. 2	LESSARD, J.
NEW WORLDS FOR THE YOUNG PIANIST, VOL. 1	LESSARD, J.
NEW WORLDS FOR THE YOUNG PIANIST, VOL. 2	LESSARD, J.
NEW WORLD SYMPHONY, LARGO, EASY	DVORAK
NEW WORLD SYMPHONY, LARGO	DVORAK
NEW YEAR'S EVE, OP. 68 NO. 43--ALBUM FOR THE YOUNG	SCHUMANN, R.
NEW YEAR'S SONG	HOPKINS, H.
NEW YORK IMPRESSIONS - LIGHT SUITE	KALMAN, C.
NEW YORK IMPRESSIONS	KALMAN, C.
NEW YORK NOCTURNE	DUKE, V.
NEW YORK SKY LINE	VILLA-LOBOS, H.
NE CINIS ET PULVIS SUPERBE--MOTET--	MOZART, W. A. *
NIBBLE MOUSE	RICHTER, A.
NICE WORK IF YOU CAN GET IT	SINGER, L.--ED
NICKELODEON	BECK
NICOLAS AND PIMPRENELLE	MARI, P.
NID DANS LES ROSES	FONTENAILLES
NIEGE TOMBE, LA	DERE
NIGHTFALL	KARP, D.
NIGHTFALL	WRIGHT
NIGHTINGALE, THE, FROM LE ROSSIGNOL	ALABIEFF
NIGHTINGALE, THE -- EASY TRANSCRIPTION	ALABIEFF *
NIGHTINGALE, THE	ALABIEFF *
NIGHTINGALE, THE	ALABIEFF *
NIGHTINGALE, THE	ALABIEFF *
NIGHTINGALE, THE	ALABIEFF *
NIGHTINGALE, THE	LISZT *
NIGHTINGALE'S TRILL	FISHER, E.
NIGHTINGALE	POGLIETTI
NIGHTS IN THE GARDENS OF SPAIN -- SOLO AND PIANO, 4	FALLA, M. DE

NIGHTS IN THE GARDENS OF SPAIN   FALLA, M. DE
NIGHTY NIGHT
NIGHT AND DAY   PORTER, C.
NIGHT AND DAY   PORTER, C.
NIGHT AND DAY   PORTER, C.
NIGHT AND DAY   PORTER, C.
NIGHT BEFORE CHRISTMAS, THE   ENGELMANN, H. U.
NIGHT BELLS   WEYBRIGHT
NIGHT CLOUDS   OLSON
NIGHT FIREWORKS   TRUXELL, E.
NIGHT FLIGHT TO MADRID   LESLIE
NIGHT FLIGHT   FAHNESTOCK
NIGHT FLOWER   WILSON
NIGHT HORSES   GETTY, G.
NIGHT IN BAGDAD   BECK
NIGHT IN VENICE, WALTZES   STRAUSS, J.
NIGHT JASMINE   BILBRO, M.
NIGHT MUSIC   ANSON, G.--ED
NIGHT OF GLADNESS   ANCLIFFE
NIGHT ON THE RIVER   KABALEVSKY
NIGHT PIECE -- NOTTURNO   BRITTEN, B.
NIGHT PIECE   SCHUMANN, R.
NIGHT RIDE, THE   PHILLIPS, S.
NIGHT ROVER   ERB
NIGHT SHADOWS   BILOHRUD
NIGHT SONG, A   SCHUMANN, R.
NIGHT SONG   DUTTON, T.
NIGHT SONG   SOULE
NIGHT THEY DROVE OLD DIXIE DOWN, THE   BRIMHALL,
NIGHT THEY INVENTED CHAMPAGNE, THE
NIGHT WALTZ FOR TWO PIANOS   BOWLES, P.
NIGHT WAS MADE FOR LOVE -- SHOWCASE
NIGHT WATCH
NIGHT WE CALLED IT A DAY
NIGHT WHISPERS   SINGER
NIGHT WINDS   KING, S.
NIGHT WIND   BECK
NIGHT   WHITFORD
NIMBLE FINGERS -- 14 PIECES   HELYER, M.
NIMROD   ELGAR, E.
NINA MARCH   EVANS
NINERIAS, BK. 1 - A LA MEMOIRE D'UN BEBE   TURINA, J.
NINERIAS, BK. 1 - BERCEUSE   TURINA, J.
NINERIAS, BK. 1 - CE QU'ON VOIT SUR LA GIRALDA TURINA, J.
NINERIAS, BK. 1 - DANSE DES POUPEES   TURINA, J.
NINERIAS, BK. 1 - DEFILE DES SOLDATS DE PLOMB TURINA, J.
NINERIAS, BK. 1 - JEUX   TURINA, J.
NINERIAS, BK. 1 - PRELUDE AND FUGUE   TURINA, J.
NINERIAS, BK. 1   TURINA, J.
NINERIAS, BK. 2 - A L'ECOLE   TURINA, J.
NINERIAS, BK. 2 - CARNAVAL DES ENFANTS   TURINA, J.
NINERIAS, BK. 2 - CONCHITA PLEURE   TURINA, J.
NINERIAS, BK. 2 - CONCHITA REVE   TURINA, J.
NINERIAS, BK. 2 - COURSE FEERIQUE   TURINA, J.
NINERIAS, BK. 2 - DIVERTISSEMENT   TURINA, J.
NINERIAS, BK. 2 - ENTREE DE COCHITA   TURINA, J.
NINERIAS, BK. 2 - PARADE   TURINA, J.
NINERIAS, BK. 2   TURINA, J.
NINETEEN NOCTURNES   CHOPIN
NINETEEN PIANO PIECES   LISZT
NINETEEN SONATAS--SPANISH AND ENGLISH   MOZART, W. A.
NINETEEN SONATAS, BK. 1--1-10--   MOZART, W. A.
NINETEEN SONATAS, BK. 2--11-19--   MOZART, W. A.
NINETEEN SONATINAS, OP. 44 AND 66   KUHLAU, F.
NINETEEN STUDIES   GUERRINI, G.
NINETY-FIVE EASY PIANO CLASSICS
NINETY-FIVE FOLK SONGS AND DANCES FOR PIANO
NINETY-NINE POPULAR PIANO TEACHING PIECES   BRIMHALL,
NINETY-ONE EASY PIANO DUETS
NINETY-THREE SHORT CLASSICS
NINETY GAY NINETIES FAVORITES
NINETY TRI-CHORD TUNES
NINE BAGATELLES   CREED
NINE CHORALE PRELUDES, VOL. 1   BACH, J.S.
NINE CHORALE PRELUDES, VOL. 2   BACH, J.S.
NINE CHRISTMAS SONGS   MONTANI
NINE EASY MINIATURES   AGAY, D.
NINE EASY PIECES   BONIS
NINE ENCORE PIECES   RAPHLING
NINE ETUDES-TABLEAUX, OP. 39   RACHMANINOFF, S.
NINE ETUDES TABLEAUX, OP. 39   RACHMANINOFF, S.
NINE FIRST-GRADE PIANO PIECES TO LEARN BY ROTE -- EASY DILLER, A.--ED
NINE FIRST-GRADE PIANO SOLOS TO LEARN BY ROTE--EASY TO DILLER, A.
NINE FOLK SONG PRELUDES   BERKOWITZ
NINE GOLDEN KEYS TO EASY READING   COBB
NINE HARPSICHORD PIECES   MONTANI
NINE INVENTIONS, OP. 13   TCHEREPNIN
NINE LITTLE LYRIC PIECES   KREUTZER
NINE LITTLE PIECES, BKS. 1, 2 AND 3   BARTOK
NINE LITTLE PIECES FOR PIANO   BECKLER, S.
NINE LITTLE PLAYTIME DUETS   KEYS
NINE MAZURKAS, OP. 25   SCRIABINE, A.
NINE NOCTURNES   FIELD, J.
NINE PIANO PIECES, OP. 3 AND VALSETTE   KODALY, Z.
NINE PIANO PIECES, OP. 3   KODALY, Z.
NINE PIECES   FROBERGER
NINE PLAYFUL PLOYS FOR PIANO   THORNE
NINE PORTRAITS   THOMSON, V.
NINE RONDOS   HUENTEN
NINE SELECTED SONATAS   SCARLATTI, D.
NINE SHORT PIECES -- 1941 --   AURIC
NINE SHORT SOLOS   THOMAS, H. T.
NINE SONATAS   PROKOFIEFF
NINE SONATAS   PROKOFIEFF
NINE SONATAS   SCARLATTI, D.
NINE SONATINAS--OP. 4, 49, 66   LICHNER, H.
NINE UNCRITICAL PIECES -- 1968   HARTZELL
NINE VARIATIONS ON A MINUET BY DUPORT, K573   MOZART, W. A.
NINNA-NANNA A GIANNI   ROSSI, R.
NINNA-NANNA DELLA BAMBOLA   CADERARA
NINNA-NANNA DELLA GATTA MEA   COUTURE
NINNA-NANNA DEL DOPOGUERRA   CASTELNUOVO-TEDE
NINNA-NANNA DI NATALE   PIZZINI
NINNA-NANNA   MOLFETTA
NINNA-NANNA   SILVA
NINNOLI MUSICALI   FERRARI-TRECATE
NINTH SYMPHONY   BEETHOVEN
NIP AND TUCK   WRAY, J.
NISPANIA   CASSADO
NO. 2 PIANO PIECES 1-4   STOCKHAUSEN, K.
NO. 4 PIANO PIECES 10   STOCKHAUSEN, K.
NO. 4 PIANO PIECES 5   STOCKHAUSEN, K.
NO. 4 PIANO PIECES 6   STOCKHAUSEN, K.
NO. 4 PIANO PIECES 7   STOCKHAUSEN, K.
NO. 4 PIANO PIECES 8   STOCKHAUSEN, K.
NO. 4 PIANO PIECES 9   STOCKHAUSEN, K.
NO. 7 PIANO PIECES 11 -- IN ROLL WITHOUT STAND STOCKHAUSEN, K.

NO. 7 PIANO PIECES 11 -- IN ROLL WITH STAND   STOCKHAUSEN, K.
NOBILISSIMA VISIONE, 1938 - KLAVIERAUSZUG   HINDEMITH
NOBODY HOME   BRODSKY, M.
NOBODY KNOWS, 12 NEGRO SPIRITUALS   SCHIBLER--ED
NOBODY KNOWS DE TROUBLE I'VE SEEN   REISFELD
NOBODY KNOWS DE TROUBLE I SEE   GROOMS
NOBODY KNOWS THE TROUBLE I'VE SEEN   FLETCHER
NOBODY KNOWS THE TROUBLE I'VE SEEN   SCHAUM, J.--ED.
NOCES DE COLOMBINE, LES   WACHS, P.
NOCES FANTASTIQUES, LES -- BALLET IN 2 ACTS   DELANNOY
NOCES FLEURIES   WACHS, P.
NOCES   MARKEWITCH
NOCE BRETONNE, LA   WILLAUME
NOCHE DE NAVIDAD   PAHISSA
NOCHE EN ESPANA   HAUBIEL, C.
NOCHE SERRANA   SICILIANI
NOCHE SEVILLANAS   TORROBA, F.M.
NOCTUELLES, FROM MIROIRS   RAVEL
NOCTUELLES   RAVEL
NOCTURNAL DANCE, OP. 3   ORLAND, H.
NOCTURNAL MOOD   BRUSSELS, I.
NOCTURNAL PRELUDE   RAPHLING
NOCTURNAL RHAPSODY   DE ROSE *
NOCTURNAL TANGIER   GODOWSKY, L.
NOCTURNE--OP. 09 NO. 2   CHOPIN
NOCTURNE, FROM 'SECOND QUARTET'   BORODIN, A.
NOCTURNE, MIDSUMMER NIGHT'S DREAM   MENDELSSOHN
NOCTURNE, NO. 05, EASY   LEYBACH, I.
NOCTURNE, NO. 05   FIELD, J.
NOCTURNE, OP. POSTH. IN C-SHARP MINOR   CHOPIN
NOCTURNE, OP. 15 NO. 2 IN F-SHARP   CHOPIN
NOCTURNE, OP. 15 NO. 2   CHOPIN
NOCTURNE, OP. 15 NO. 3   CHOPIN
NOCTURNE, OP. 23 NO. 4   SCHUMANN, R.
NOCTURNE, OP. 27 NO. 1 IN C-SHARP MINOR   CHOPIN
NOCTURNE, OP. 27 NO. 2 IN D FLAT   CHOPIN
NOCTURNE, OP. 29 NO. 10   WOLLENHAUPT
NOCTURNE, OP. 33 NO. 1   FAURE, G.
NOCTURNE, OP. 37 NO. 2   CHOPIN
NOCTURNE, OP. 4 NO. 2   LEYBACH, I.
NOCTURNE, OP. 48 NO. 1   CHOPIN
NOCTURNE, OP. 52 NO. 5   LEYBACH, I.
NOCTURNE, OP. 54 NO. 4 --SUMMER NIGHT--   GRIEG
NOCTURNE, OP. 54 NO. 4   GRIEG
NOCTURNE, OP. 54 NO. 4   GRIEG
NOCTURNE, OP. 54 NO. 4   GRIEG
NOCTURNE, OP. 55 NO. 1   CHOPIN
NOCTURNE, OP. 6 NO. 1   SNYDER
NOCTURNE, OP. 72 NO. 1 IN E MINOR   CHOPIN
NOCTURNE, OP. 9 NO. 2   CHOPIN
NOCTURNE, OP. 9 NO. 2   CHOPIN
NOCTURNE, OP. 9 NO. 6   LEYBACH, I.
NOCTURNELLE   HOSKINS, W.
NOCTURNES--CRITICAL COMMENTARY   CHOPIN
NOCTURNES, COMPLETE   FIELD, J.
NOCTURNES -- CLOTH   CHOPIN
NOCTURNES -- FETES   DEBUSSY
NOCTURNES -- NAUGES   DEBUSSY
NOCTURNES -- SIRENES   DEBUSSY
NOCTURNES - 1. NUAGES, 2. FETES   DEBUSSY
NOCTURNES - BK. 1 .. OP. 9, 15, 27, 32   CHOPIN
NOCTURNES - BK. 2 .. OP. 37, 48, 55, 62   CHOPIN
NOCTURNES WITH CADENZAS   HAMILTON, I.
NOCTURNES   CHOPIN
NOCTURNES   CHOPIN
NOCTURNES   CHOPIN
NOCTURNES   CHOPIN
NOCTURNES   CHOPIN
NOCTURNES   CHOPIN
NOCTURNES   CHOPIN
NOCTURNES   CHOPIN
NOCTURNETTE   NEVIN
NOCTURNE -- NACHTSTUCK --   SCHUMANN, R.
NOCTURNE B-DUR   FIELD, J.
NOCTURNE B FLAT, OP. 368 NO. 8   CZERNY
NOCTURNE DE RUBINSTEIN   TCHEREPNIN
NOCTURNE FOR MODERNS   NEVIN
NOCTURNE FOR PIANO   FERTE
NOCTURNE FOR THE LEFT HAND ALONE, OP. 9 NO. 2 SCRIABINE, A.
NOCTURNE FROM 'SECOND STRING QUARTET'   FICHANDLER, W.
NOCTURNE IN A FLAT, OP. 17   RAFF, J.
NOCTURNE IN A FLAT MAJOR, OP. 32 NO. 2   CHOPIN
NOCTURNE IN B, OP. 32 NO. 1   CHOPIN
NOCTURNE IN B FLAT, OP. 16 NO. 4   PADEREWSKI, I.
NOCTURNE IN B FLAT MAJOR   FIELD, J.
NOCTURNE IN B FLAT MINOR, OP. 9 NO. 1   CHOPIN
NOCTURNE IN B FLAT   SZYMANOWSKI
NOCTURNE IN B MAJOR, OP. 32 NO. 1   CHOPIN
NOCTURNE IN B MINOR, OP. 9 NO. 1   CHOPIN
NOCTURNE IN C MINOR, OP. 48 NO. 1   CHOPIN
NOCTURNE IN C SHARP MINOR, AND IN C MINOR   CHOPIN
NOCTURNE IN C SHARP MINOR, OP. POSTH.   CHOPIN
NOCTURNE IN C SHARP MINOR, OP. POSTH.   CHOPIN
NOCTURNE IN C SHARP MINOR, OP. 27 NO. 1 AND NOCTURNE CHOPIN
NOCTURNE IN D FLAT, OP. 27 NO. 2   CHOPIN
NOCTURNE IN D FLAT MAJOR, OP. 27 NO. 2   CHOPIN
NOCTURNE IN D FLAT MINOR   DEBUSSY
NOCTURNE IN D FLAT   BLOSE, J.
NOCTURNE IN D FLAT   DEBUSSY
NOCTURNE IN D FLAT   SCRIABINE, A.
NOCTURNE IN E FLAT, OP. 9 NO. 2   CHOPIN
NOCTURNE IN E FLAT, OP. 9 NO. 2   CHOPIN
NOCTURNE IN E FLAT, OP. 9 NO. 2   CHOPIN
NOCTURNE IN E FLAT, OP. 9 NO. 2   CHOPIN
NOCTURNE IN E FLAT, OP. 9 NO. 2   CHOPIN
NOCTURNE IN E FLAT, OP. 9 NO. 2   CHOPIN
NOCTURNE IN E FLAT MAJOR, OP. 9 NO. 2   CHOPIN
NOCTURNE IN E FLAT MAJOR, OP. 9 NO. 2   CHOPIN
NOCTURNE IN E FLAT   CHOPIN
NOCTURNE IN E MAJOR, OP. 62 NO. 2   CHOPIN
NOCTURNE IN E MINOR, OP. 72 NO. 1 --POSTHUMOUS-- CHOPIN
NOCTURNE IN F MAJOR, OP. 15 NO. 1   CHOPIN
NOCTURNE IN F MINOR, OP. 10 NO. 1   TSCHAIKOWSKY
NOCTURNE IN F MINOR, OP. 55 NO. 1   CHOPIN
NOCTURNE IN F MINOR, OP. 55 NO. 1   CHOPIN
NOCTURNE IN F MINOR 'LA SEPARATION'   GLINKA
NOCTURNE IN F SHARP, OP. 13 NO. 2   CHOPIN
NOCTURNE IN F SHARP MAJOR, OP. 15 NO. 2   CHOPIN
NOCTURNE IN F SHARP MINOR, OP. 70 NO. 2   MARTUCCI
NOCTURNE IN F SHARP MINOR   LIPATTI, D.
NOCTURNE IN F SHARP   CHOPIN
NOCTURNE IN G, OP. 37 NO. 2   CHOPIN
NOCTURNE IN G FLAT, OP. 70 NO. 1   MARTUCCI
NOCTURNE IN G FLAT   MALOOF

NOCTURNE IN G MAJOR, OP. 37 NO. 2	CHOPIN
NOCTURNE IN G MINOR, OP. 15 NO. 3	CHOPIN
NOCTURNE IN G MINOR, OP. 37 NO. 1	CHOPIN
NOCTURNE IN G MINOR, OP. 37 NO. 1	CHOPIN
NOCTURNE IN G MINOR	CHASINS, A.
NOCTURNE IN G SHARP, OP. 2, NO. 1	TCHEREPNIN
NOCTURNE IN G	FIELD, J.
NOCTURNE IN MI MINEUR	TCHEREPNIN
NOCTURNE IN SPRINGTIME	TRUXELL, E.
NOCTURNE NO. 01, OP. 17	MAURAT, E.
NOCTURNE NO. 01 IN B MINOR	ROWLEY
NOCTURNE NO. 01 IN E FLAT	FIELD, J.
NOCTURNE NO. 01 IN E FLAT	FIELD, J.
NOCTURNE NO. 01	PALOMBI
NOCTURNE NO. 02 IN B MINOR	PAITA, F.
NOCTURNE NO. 02	PALOMBI
NOCTURNE NO. 04, OP. 38	MAURAT, E.
NOCTURNE NO. 04 IN E FLAT, OP. 36	FAURE, G.
NOCTURNE NO. 04 IN E	ROWLEY
NOCTURNE NO. 04	SATIE, E.
NOCTURNE NO. 05 IN B FLAT, OP. 37	FAURE, G.
NOCTURNE NO. 05 IN B FLAT	FIELD, J.
NOCTURNE NO. 05 IN F	ROWLEY
NOCTURNE NO. 05	POULENC, F.
NOCTURNE NO. 05	SATIE, E.
NOCTURNE NO. 08 IN G	POULENC, F.
NOCTURNE NO. 09, OP. 97	FAURE, G.
NOCTURNE NO. 10, OP. 99	FAURE, G.
NOCTURNE NO. 11	FAURE, G.
NOCTURNE NO. 12	FAURE, G.
NOCTURNE NO. 13	FAURE, G.
NOCTURNE ON THE PRAIRIE	REISFELD
NOCTURNE UND SCHERZO, OP. 23	FRICKER, P.
NOCTURNE	BARBER, S.
NOCTURNE	BLANC
NOCTURNE	BOSKOFF
NOCTURNE	BRUSSELS, I.
NOCTURNE	CACAVAS
NOCTURNE	CASTELLINI
NOCTURNE	CHOPIN
NOCTURNE	CHOPIN
NOCTURNE	COLTRO
NOCTURNE	DANIEL-LESUR
NOCTURNE	DEFOSSE
NOCTURNE	DEL CORONA
NOCTURNE	DE FRANCMESNIL
NOCTURNE	DUMAS, L.
NOCTURNE	ELLIOTT
NOCTURNE	FALLA, M. DE
NOCTURNE	FASULLO
NOCTURNE	FERNANDEZ, O.
NOCTURNE	GILLOCK
NOCTURNE	GIRALDI
NOCTURNE	HARTEVELD
NOCTURNE	LOPEZ BUCHARDO
NOCTURNE	LOPEZ BUCHARDO
NOCTURNE	MASETTI
NOCTURNE	MOISSE, S.
NOCTURNE	MORLEY, G.
NOCTURNE	PENAU
NOCTURNE	PICCIOLI
NOCTURNE	RESPIGHI
NOCTURNE	RIVIER, J.
NOCTURNE	ROPARTZ
NOCTURNE	SALTA
NOCTURNE	SAVASTA
NOCTURNE	SEROUX
NOCTURNE	SPURLING, C.
NOCTURNE	TUTTLE, T. K.
NOCTURNE	WEYBRIGHT
NOCTURNO ANDALUZ	ECHEVARRIA
NOCTURNO IN A FLAT	REINECKE
NODDING BUTTERCUPS, NO. 3	YUILL, M.
NODDING POPPIES	STEVENS, M.
NODDING TOY-CHINAMAN, THE	THOMAS, C. J.
NODDING TULIPS	VANNORT, I.
NOEL-NOEL—18 CHRISTMAS CAROLS, ARRANGED FOR PIANO AND	KIRBY, W.
NOELS, HEFT 1 -- 'L'ORGANISTE LITURGIQUE', 12 --	DANDRIEU, P.
NOELS, HEFT 2 -- 'L'ORGANISTE LITURGIQUE', 16 --	DANDRIEU, P.
NOELS, HEFT 3 -- 'L'ORGANISTE LITURGIQUE', 19-20 --	DANDRIEU, P.
NOELS, HEFT 4 -- 'L'ORGANISTE LITURGIQUE', 22	DANDRIEU, P.
NOELS VARIES -- VARIATIONEN UBER WEIHNACHTSSTUCKE --	LEBEGUE
NOEL NOEL - 6 PIECES FOR CHILDREN	GAGNEBIN
NOEL TRISTE--BERCEUSE	THOMAS, J. M.
NOEL	BAEZ, J.
MOISETTES, LES -- NO. 1, FROM ''ORLEANAISES'' SUITE	BRASSARD
NOISY WOODPECKER	GARROW, L.
NOLA -- EASY ARR.	ARNDT
NOLA -- ORIGINAL	ARNDT
NOLA -- SIMPLIFIED	ARNDT
NOLA	ARNDT
NOLA	ARNDT
NOLA	ARNDT
NOLA	ARNDT
NOLA	ARNDT
NOLA	BRIMHALL,
NONAME -- CHROMATIC WALTZ	HAYES
NONCHALANCE	GAYFER, J. M.
NONE BUT THE LONELY HEART, OP. 6 NO. 6	TSCHAIKOWSKY
NONE BUT THE LONELY HEART, OP. 6 NO. 6	TSCHAIKOWSKY
NONE BUT THE LONELY HEART, OP. 6 NO. 6	TSCHAIKOWSKY
NONE BUT THE LONELY HEART	TSCHAIKOWSKY
NONE BUT THE LONELY HEART	TSCHAIKOWSKY
NONSENSE SONG	WEYBRIGHT
NON T'AMO PIU	TOSTI
NOON SIESTA	COULTHARD
NORDIC CANZONAS, IN 2 VOLS., VOL. 1	DRISCHNER
NORDIC CANZONAS, IN 2 VOLS., VOL. 2	DRISCHNER
NORMA, EASY TRANSCRIPTION	BELLINI
NORMA -- COMPLETE OPERA --	BELLINI
NORMA - CASTA DIVA	BELLINI
NORMA - CASTA DIVA	BELLINI
NORMA - DELL'AURA TUA PROFETICA	BELLINI
NORMA - EASY FANTASIA	BELLINI
NORMA - OVERTURE	BELLINI
NORMA - OVERTURE	BELLINI
NORMA	SICILIANI
NORSEMAN'S SONG	PECK, L.
NORSE SONG, OP. 68 NO. 41--ALBUM FOR THE YOUNG	SCHUMANN, R.
NORTENAS	CASELLA, E. M.
NORTENA	SAENZ
NORTH, SOUTH, EAST AND WEST	NICHOLLS, H.
NORTHERN DANCES AND FOLK TUNES, OP. 17	GRIEG
NORTHERN DANCES AND FOLK TUNES, OP. 17	GRIEG
NORTHERN LIGHTS	CARREL, B.
NORTHERN LIGHTS	DONATO, A.
NORTHERN LIGHTS	STERNKLAR, A.
NORTHERN SONG	SCHUMANN, R.
NORTHLAND INTERMEZZO	WIGHAM, M.
NORWEGIAN BRAUTZUG OP. 19 NO. 2	GRIEG
NORWEGIAN BRIDAL PARTY, OP. 19 NO. 2	GRIEG
NORWEGIAN BRIDAL PROCESSION, OP. 19 NO. 2	GRIEG
NORWEGIAN BRIDAL PROCESSION, OP. 19 NO. 2	GRIEG
NORWEGIAN BRIDAL PROCESSION, OP. 19 NO. 2	GRIEG
NORWEGIAN BRIDAL PROCESSION FOR TWO PIANOS, EIGHT	GRIEG
NORWEGIAN BRIDAL PROCESSION OP. 19 NO. 2	GRIEG
NORWEGIAN CARNIVAL, OP. 14	SVENDSEN
NORWEGIAN CONCERTO	GRIEG
NORWEGIAN COUNTRY DANCE	ROLSETH, B.
NORWEGIAN CRADLE SONG	MOREL, G.
NORWEGIAN DANCE, OP. 35 NO. 2	GRIEG
NORWEGIAN DANCE, OP. 35 NO. 2	GRIEG
NORWEGIAN DANCE, OP. 35 NO. 2	GRIEG
NORWEGIAN DANCE, OP. 35 NO. 3	GRIEG
NORWEGIAN DANCE, OP. 35 NO. 4	GRIEG
NORWEGIAN DANCES, OP. 35 NOS. 1 TO 4	GRIEG
NORWEGIAN DANCES, OP. 35	GRIEG
NORWEGIAN DANCE IN A MAJOR, OP. 35 NO. 2	GRIEG
NORWEGIAN DANCE	TOLLEFSEN, A.
NORWEGIAN FOLK TUNES, OP. 66	GRIEG
NORWEGIAN FOLK TUNES --22 SIMPLIFIED PIECES FROM	GRIEG
NORWEGIAN LULLABY	KVELVE
NORWEGIAN MELODIES, OP. 63	GRIEG
NORWEGIAN NOTEBOOK. 16 PIECES FROM NORDIC DANCES AND	GRIEG
NORWEGIAN PEASANT DANCES --SLATTER--, OP. 72	GRIEG
NORWEGIAN SKETCHES, OP. 19	GRIEG
NORWEGIAN SKETCHES, OP. 19	GRIEG
NORWEGIAN TANZE OP. 35	GRIEG
NOSEGAY	DITTENHAVER
NOSTALGIA ALPINA	PIZZINI
NOSTALGIA	AMADEI
NOSTALGIA	HAUBIEL, C.
NOSTALGIA	NOVIKOFF
NOSTALGIC WALTZES	FINNEY
NOSTALGIES	KULLMANN
NOSTALGIE DI NOVIZZE	GUERRINI, G.
NOSTALGIQUE	COBB
NOS VIELLES CHANSONS	FRANCAIX, A.
NOTEBOOKS FOR ANNA MAGDALENA BACH, 1725	BACH, J.S.
NOTEBOOKS FOR ANNA MAGDALENA BACH OF 1722 AND 1725	BACH, J.S.
NOTEBOOK ASSIGNMENTS	DEE, M.
NOTEBOOK FOR ANNA MAGDALENA, 1725 -- 19 EASY PIECES	BACH, J.S.
NOTEBOOK FOR ANNA MAGDALENA, 1725 -- 19 EASY PIECES	BACH, J.S.
NOTEBOOK FOR ANNA MAGDALENA, 1725	BACH, J.S.
NOTEBOOK FOR ANNA MAGDALENA BACH	BACH, J.S.
NOTEBOOK FOR BETTY-SUE BACH	BACH, P.D.Q. *
NOTEBOOK FOR MARIA ANNA	MOZART, L.
NOTEBOOK FOR W.F. BACH	BACH, J.S.
NOTEBOOK FOR WILHELM FRIEDEMANN BACH	BACH, J.S.
NOTEBOOK OF ANNA MAGDALENA BACH	BACH, J.S.
NOTENBUCHLEIN FUR ANNA MAGDALENA BACH, BWV 933	BACH, J.S.
NOTENBUCHLEIN FUR ANNA MAGDALENA BACH -- BWV 933	BACH, J.S.
NOTENBUCHLEIN	FISCHER, J.
NOTENBUCH FUR NANNERL MOZART	MOZART, L.
NOTENBUCH FUR WOLFGANG	MOZART, L.
NOTENMAPPE DES KLAVIERSCHULERS, HEFT 01	
NOTENMAPPE DES KLAVIERSCHULERS - TEIL 01	
NOTENMAPPE DES KLAVIERSCHULERS - TEIL 02 HOHERE	
NOTENMAPPE DES KLAVIERSCHULERS - TEIL 03 UNTERE	
NOTENMAPPE DES KLAVIERSCHULERS - TEIL 03 UNTERE	
NOTENMAPPE DES KLAVIERSCHULERS - VORSTUFE, HEFT 01	
NOTENMAPPE DES KLAVIERSCHULERS - VORSTUFE, HEFT 02	
NOTES FROM OTHER PENS	THOMPSON, J.--ED
NOTE 'N SPELL, BK. 01	HENDERSON
NOTE 'N SPELL, BK. 02	HENDERSON
NOTE GAMES	RAMSEY, A.
NOTE READER	AARON, M.
NOTE SPELLER AND EAR TRAINING BOOK	KAHN, M.
NOTE SPELLER	KASSCHAU, H.
NOTE SPELLING BOOK	GRIMM, C. W.
NOTHING EASIER--ILLUSTRATED	WILLIAMS, J.
NOTITIEBOEK V. HARPSICHORD	WIJDEVELD
NOTRE DAME DES ERMITES	TROMPEO
NOTTI VENEZIANE	CARNEVALI
NOTTURNO, OP. 54 NO. 4	GRIEG
NOTTURNO, OP. 54 NO. 4	GRIEG
NOTTURNO	KRAEHENBUEHL
NOTTURNO	RESPIGHI
NOT FOR SQUARES	FULEIHAN, A.
NOUS JOUONS POUR MAMAN, NO. 01 -- NOEL	TANSMAN, A.
NOUS JOUONS POUR MAMAN, NO. 02 -- AIR SOLENNEL	TANSMAN, A.
NOUS JOUONS POUR MAMAN, NO. 03 -- REVERIE	TANSMAN, A.
NOUS JOUONS POUR MAMAN, NO. 04 -- AIR A BERCER	TANSMAN, A.
NOUS JOUONS POUR MAMAN, NO. 05 -- CHORAL	TANSMAN, A.
NOUS JOUONS POUR MAMAN, NO. 06 -- VALSE	TANSMAN, A.
NOUS JOUONS POUR MAMAN, NO. 07 -- CHANSON	TANSMAN, A.
NOUS JOUONS POUR MAMAN, NO. 08 -- ARIETTA	TANSMAN, A.
NOUS JOUONS POUR MAMAN, NO. 09 -- TEMPO DI MINUETTO	TANSMAN, A.
NOUS JOUONS POUR MAMAN, NO. 10 -- AIR POPULAIRE	TANSMAN, A.
NOUS JOUONS POUR MAMAN, NO. 11 -- FINAL	TANSMAN, A.
NOUS JOUONS POUR MAMAN, NO. 11 -- PETITE CONTE	TANSMAN, A.
NOUVEAU GRADUS AD PARNASSUM, BK. 1	PHILIPP, I.--ED.
NOUVEAU TRAITE DE L'ACCOMPAGNEMENT	DE
NOUVELLES CADENCES DU CONCERTO EN RE MINEUR DE W. A.	SANCAN, P.
NOUVELLES ETUDE IN A FLAT MAJOR, NO. 2	CHOPIN
NOUVELLES ETUDE IN F MINOR, NO. 1	CHOPIN
NOUVELLES SUITES	RAMEAU
NOUVELLE METHODE, LE COUPPEY	DESCAVES, L. *
NOUVELLE METHODE	PERCHERON
NOVELETTE, OP. 17 NO. 1	MEDTNER, N.
NOVELETTE, OP. 21 NO. 7	SCHUMANN, R.
NOVELETTE, OP. 21 NO. 7	SCHUMANN, R.
NOVELETTE, OP. 99 NO. 9	SCHUMANN, R.
NOVELETTE, OP. 99 NO. 9	SCHUMANN, R.
NOVELETTES, OP. 21	SCHUMANN, R.
NOVELETTES, SEVEN	DE VITO, A.
NOVELETTE PETITE	BOHM
NOVELETTE	BECKWITH
NOVELETTE	BENUSSAN, M.
NOVELETTE	BUTLER, J.
NOVELETTE	HARSANYI
NOVELETTE	MCCLUSKY
NOVELLETTE, OP. 20	LIADOW, A.
NOVELLETTEN, OP. 21	SCHUMANN, R.
NOVELLETTEN, OP. 21	SCHUMANN, R.
NOVELLETTEN, OP. 21	SCHUMANN, R.
NOVELLETTES, OP. 21	SCHUMANN, R.
NOVELLETTES, OP. 21	SCHUMANN, R.
NOVELLETTE IN B MINOR, OP. 99 NO. 3	SCHUMANN, R.
NOVELLETTE IN E, OP. 21 NO. 7	SCHUMANN, R.
NOVELLETTE IN F, OP. 21 NO. 1	SCHUMANN, R.
NOVELTY SUITE	RAPHLING
NOVEL INSTRUCTION BOOK, OP. 66 -- 10 MELODIOUS PIECES	WILLNER, A.
NOVEMBER, TROIKA RIDE	TSCHAIKOWSKY

NOVIANDO	GILARDI
NOW COMES THE GENTLE SAVIOR	BACH, J.S.
NOW HYMNS FOR YOUNG PEOPLE	DRAESEL
NOW IS THE HOUR	KAIHAN *
NOW IS THE HOUR	KAIHAN *
NOW I LAY ME TO SLEEP	HAUBIEL, C.
NOZZE DI FIGARO, LE - OVERTURE	MOZART, W. A.
NO MORE DARK CLOUDS	BRODSKY, M.
NO ONE TO PLAY WITH	BRODSKY, M.
NO OTHER LOVE	HAMMERSTEIN *
NO STRINGS	RODGERS
NO STRINGS	RODGERS
NUAGES, NOCTURNE	DEBUSSY
NUAGES	DEBUSSY
NUBANUSIT	SZANTO
NUIT, LA -- BALLET --	SAUGUET
NUITS ALGERIENNES, OP. 98 - AU CAFE MAURE, ECHOS DU	GREGH
NUMBER SONGS	RICHTER
NURSERY, LA - BK. 1	INGHELBRECHT, D.
NURSERY, LA - BK. 2	INGHELBRECHT, D.
NURSERY, LA - BK. 4	INGHELBRECHT, D.
NURSERY, LA - BK. 5	INGHELBRECHT, D.
NURSERY, LA - BK. 6	INGHELBRECHT, D.
NURSERY, LA BK. 1 - PETIT PAPA, UNE SOURIS VERTE,	INGHELBRECHT, D.
NURSERY, LA BK. 2 - OU VAS-TU P'TITE BOITEUSE, LE	INGHELBRECHT, D.
NURSERY, LA BK. 4 - LA BONNE AVENTURE, LA BOULANGERE,	INGHELBRECHT, D.
NURSERY, LA BK. 5 - BONJOUR MA TANTE, BIQUETTE,	INGHELBRECHT, D.
NURSERY, LA BK. 6 - LE PETIT CHRISTOPHE, QUAND J'ETAIS	INGHELBRECHT, D.
NURSERY, LA	INGHELBRECHT, D.
NURSERY, LE	INGHELBRECHT, D.
NURSERY RHYMES DUETS	BROWN, M.
NURSERY RHYMES FOR TOTS	HARDING, R.
NURSERY SUITE	ELGAR, E.
NUR WALZER VON STRAUSS	STRAUSS, J.
NUSSKNACKER-SUITE OP. 71A	TSCHAIKOWSKY
NUTCRACKER -- COMPLETE, ILLUSTRATED	TSCHAIKOWSKY
NUTCRACKER SUITE, OP. 71A--WALTZ OF THE FLOWERS	TSCHAIKOWSKY
NUTCRACKER SUITE, OP. 71A - ARAB DANCE	TSCHAIKOWSKY
NUTCRACKER SUITE, OP. 71A - CHINESE DANCE, EASY	TSCHAIKOWSKY
NUTCRACKER SUITE, OP. 71A - MARCH, EASY	TSCHAIKOWSKY
NUTCRACKER SUITE, OP. 71A - MARCH	TSCHAIKOWSKY
NUTCRACKER SUITE, OP. 71A - TREPAK, EASY	TSCHAIKOWSKY
NUTCRACKER SUITE, OP. 71A - WALTZ OF THE FLOWERS, EASY	TSCHAIKOWSKY
NUTCRACKER SUITE, OP. 71A - DANCE OF THE REED FLUTES	TSCHAIKOWSKY
NUTCRACKER SUITE, THE, OP. 71A	TSCHAIKOWSKY
NUTCRACKER SUITE, THE, OP. 71A	TSCHAIKOWSKY
NUTCRACKER SUITE, THE, OP. 71A	TSCHAIKOWSKY
NUTCRACKER SUITE -- A STORY WITH MUSIC	TSCHAIKOWSKY
NUTCRACKER SUITE DE BALLET, THE -- CASSE-NOISETTE --	TSCHAIKOWSKY
NUTCRACKER SUITE DE BALLET -- CASSE-NOISETTE --	TSCHAIKOWSKY
NUTCRACKER SUITE DE BALLET -- CASSE-NOISETTE -- DANCE	TSCHAIKOWSKY
NUTCRACKER SUITE DE BALLET -- CASSE-NOISETTE -- FLOWER	TSCHAIKOWSKY
NUTCRACKER SUITE DE BALLET -- CASSE-NOISETTE -- MARCH	TSCHAIKOWSKY
NUTCRACKER SUITE DE BALLET -- CASSE NOISETTE -- DANCE	TSCHAIKOWSKY
NUTCRACKER SUITE	TSCHAIKOWSKY
NUTCRACKER SUITE	TSCHAIKOWSKY
NUTCRACKER SUITE	TSCHAIKOWSKY
NUTCRACKER SUITE	TSCHAIKOWSKY
NUTTIN FOR CHRISTMAS	LANE, J.--ED.
NUT TREE, THE	SCHAUM, J.--ED.
NYMPHS	SCHER, W.
O.O.MCINTYRE SUITE	WILLSON, M.
O, SOLE MIO	DICAPUA
O, SOLE MIO	DICAPUA
O, SO HAPPY	WIGHAM, M.
O'ER THE MOONLIT WATER	LEVENSON, B.
OAK AND THE ASH, THE -- PIANO SOLO WITH WORDS	STEINER
OASIS, THE	OLSON
OATS, PEAS, BEANS -- AN ENGLISH SINGING GAME	WEYBRIGHT
OBERON, BARCAROLLE	WEBER, VON
OBERON, BARCAROLLE	WEBER, VON
OBLIO -- SLOW WALTZ --	BARBIROLLI
OCCASIONS	FREDRICH, F.
OCEAN, THE	ALT, H.
OCEAN BY MOONLIGHT, THE	HAVEN
OCEAN SPRAY	LOUKA, M.
OCHO APUNTES	GURIDI
OCHSEN-MENUETT -- HOBOKEN 9-27	HAYDN
OCTAGON	MAYER
OCTAVE-STUDIES, OP. 281	LOEW, J.
OCTAVES AND CHORDS	PHILIPP, I.
OCTAVES VELOCITY	ROGERS
OCTAVE BOOK	THOMPSON, J.
OCTAVE ETUDES - J1	WARD, J.
OCTAVE ETUDES - J2	WARD, J.
OCTAVE ETUDES - J3	WARD, J.
OCTAVE ETUDES - J4	WARD, J.
OCTAVE STUDIES, BK. 1	SCHAUM, J.
OCTAVE STUDIES, BK. 2	SCHAUM, J.
OCTAVE STUDIES --6-- OP. 553	CZERNY
OCTAVE STUDY, OP. 33	CONCONE, G.
OCTAVE STUDY IN C	RUBINSTEIN
OCTET FOR JASPER JOHNS	CARDEW
OCTET FOR WIND INSTRUMENTS	STRAVINSKY, I.
ODDS AND ENDS	BRUCE, M. C.
ODE TO GERSHWIN	MOSSMAN, T.
ODE TO JOY	BEETHOVEN
ODE TO JOY	BEETHOVEN
ODE TO JOY	BEETHOVEN
OEUVRES COMPLETES	CHAMBONNIERES,
OEUVRE COMPLETES POUR LE CLAVECIN OU LE PIANOFORTE. 8	ECKARD, W.
OFFBEAT POLKA	GREEN, R.
OFFICER OF THE DAY	HALL, F.
OFF FOR A TRIP	JAMES, M.
OFF TO BE A SOLDIER AND DANCE ROUND AND ROUND	WEYBRIGHT
OFF TO CAMP	ANTHONY, B. R.
OFF TO CAMP	ECKSTEIN
OFF TO CAMP	FREDERICKS
OFF TO DONEGAL AND BACK	KEENAN
OFF TO SCHOOL	COURSEY, R. DE
OFF TO SEA	BRODSKY, M.
OFF TO THE COUNTRY	GLOVER, D.
OFF TO THE PICNIC	SOUERS
OFF WE GO--BOOK OF POETRY PIECES	DILLER, A. *
OFF WE GO AGAIN--SECOND BOOK OF POETRY PIECES	DILLER, A. *
OF A TAILOR AND A BEAR	MACDOWELL
OF BYGONE DAYS	HAUBIEL, C.
OF HUMAN BONDAGE - THEME	GOODWIN, R.
OF LONG AGO	STEVENS, E.
OGIVES	SATIE, E.
OH, DEAR - WHAT CAN THE MATTER BE	ZEPP--ED
OH, HOW LOVELY IS THE EVENING	WEYBRIGHT
OH, LADY BE GOOD	GERSHWIN
OH, PROMISE ME	DEKOVEN, R.
OH, PROMISE ME	DEKOVEN, R.
OH, SUSANNA	RUSH, L.
OH, THE DAYS OF THE KERRY DANCING	MOLLOY, J. L.
OH, WHAT A BEAUTIFUL MORNIN'	HAMMERSTEIN *
OH, YOU CRAZY MOON	WALTER
OHE, MAMAN	BURHARD *
OH -- MY PA-PA	WILLIAMS, M.
OH DEAR, WHAT CAN THE MATTER BE, ONE PIANO - SIX HANDS	WILLIAMS
OH DEAR, WHAT CAN THE MATTER BE -- FOR ONE PIANO, SIX	FOUNTAIN *
OH DIDN'T HE RAMBLE	SUK
OH FREUNDSCHAFT, OP. 36	LANE, J.--ED.
OH HAPPY DAY	BRODSKY, M.
OH ME, OH MY	SCHIEFELBEIN, F.
OH MY DEAR AUGUSTIN	FOSTER
OH SUSANNA	FOSTER
OH SUSANNA	JOHNSON, S. *
OH WEE BABY BLUES	HAMMERSTEIN *
OH WHAT A BEAUTIFUL MORNIN'	BURGMUELLER
OISEAUX DE NOTRE-DAME, LES	STREABBOG
OISEAUX DE PARADIS, WALTZ	MESSIAEN, O.
OISEAUX EXOTIQUES -- PIANO SOLO PART	RAVEL
OISEAUX TRISTES, FROM MIROIRS	RAVEL
OISEAUX TRISTES	HAMMERSTEIN *
OKLAHOMA	HAMMERSTEIN *
OKLAHOMA	GOODMAN, J.
OL' MAN RIVER	WILLIAMS, J.
OL' MAN RIVER	RICHTER
OLD-WORLD DANCE, AN	RICHTER
OLDER BEGINNER'S PIANO BOOK -- NEW EDITION	RICHTER
OLDER STUDENT, BK. 1	WINDSOR, B.
OLDER STUDENT, BK. 2	STEINER
OLDER STUDENT, BK. 3	KLEIN, B.
OLDE LAVENDER	PURCELL, H.
OLD ABE LINCOLN	MURRAY
OLD ADVENT HYMN, OP. 55 NO. 3	MEACHAM, F.--ED
OLD BACHELOR, THE	FOSTER
OLD BEGGARS, THE	FOSTER
OLD BLACK JOE, VARIATIONS	FOSTER
OLD BLACK JOE -- VARIATIONS	FOSTER
OLD BLACK JOE	BULL
OLD BLACK JOE	HOPKINS, H.
OLD BLACK JOE	BECK
OLD BROWN CAYUSE	RICHTER, A.
OLD CATHEDRAL, THE	ARMOUR
OLD CHIEF POWHATAN	ROLSETH, B.
OLD CHRISTMAS TREE	TEIKE, C.
OLD CHURCH ORGAN, THE	TAUBERT--ED.
OLD CLOCK, THE	READ, G.
OLD COMRADES	WIGHAM, M.
OLD CONTRADANCES FROM ENGLAND	PERRIN
OLD COURT DANCE, AN	SINGER, L.--ED
OLD COWBOY TRAIL	FOSTER
OLD DESERTED HOUSE	JAHN, C.
OLD DEVIL MOON	HAYDN
OLD DOG TRAY	ROWLEY
OLD ENGLISH DANCE, MENUET	KEVAN
OLD ENGLISH SONG -- I HAD A LITTLE NUT TREE	HARVEY, VIVIEN
OLD ENGLISH WORTHIES	POSER
OLD FASHIONED BALLROOM, AN	MACGREGOR
OLD FASHIONED DANCE, AN	FOSTER
OLD FOLKSONGS IN NEW SETTINGS	FOSTER
OLD FOLKS AT HOME, ONE PIANO - SIX HANDS	FOSTER
OLD FOLKS AT HOME	FOSTER
OLD FOLKS AT HOME	FOSTER
OLD FOLKS AT HOME	FOSTER
OLD FOLKS AT HOME	BROWN, L.
OLD FOLKS AT HOME	CROSBY, M.
OLD FOLK SONG, AN	HIBBS, C.
OLD FRENCH DANCE, AN	HIBBS, C.
OLD FRENCH DANCE - GAVOTTE	TSCHAIKOWSKY
OLD FRENCH DANCE AND GOVOTTE	STEGLICH--ED
OLD FRENCH SONG, AN	PROKOFIEFF
OLD GERMAN CHRISTMAS MUSIC -- CHRISTMAS PIECES BY	STANLEY--ED
OLD GRANDMOTHER'S TALES, OP. 31	SULLIVAN, J.
OLD GRAY MARE, THE	LIND, L. S.
OLD HAT BOOGIE	WINDRUSH, P.
OLD INDIAN TRAIL	FREEMAN--ED.
OLD IRELAND	MARSDEN, E.
OLD KENTUCKY HOME	TOBIAS *
OLD KITCHEN CLOCK, THE	STANLEY--ED
OLD LAMP LIGHTER, THE	HOPKINS, H.
OLD MACDONALD HAD A FARM	PAUER--ED
OLD MAN WINTER	PAUER--ED
OLD MASTERS, BK. 1 -- A COLLECTION OF 17TH AND 18TH	PAUER--ED
OLD MASTERS, BK. 2 -- A COLLECTION OF 17TH AND 18TH	PAUER--ED
OLD MASTERS, BK. 3 -- A COLLECTION OF 17TH AND 18TH	PAUER--ED
OLD MASTERS, BK. 4 -- A COLLECTION OF 17TH AND 18TH	PAUER--ED
OLD MASTERS, BK. 5 -- A COLLECTION OF 17TH AND 18TH	STEINER
OLD MASTERS, BK. 6 -- A COLLECTION OF 17TH AND 18TH	
OLD MASTERS FOR YOUNG ARTISTS	
OLD MASTERS FROM THE SIXTEENTH TO EIGHTEENTH	
OLD MASTERS FROM THE SIXTEENTH TO EIGHTEENTH	KELLER--ED.
OLD MASTERS OF PIANO MUSIC, VOL. 1# GERMAN	HERRMANN--ED
OLD MASTERS OF PIANO MUSIC, VOL. 2# FRENCH	KELLER--ED.
OLD MASTERS OF PIANO MUSIC, VOL. 3# ITALIAN	KELLER--ED.
OLD MASTERS OF PIANO MUSIC, VOL. 4# ENGLISH	
OLD MASTERS OF THE PIANO	
OLD MASTERS OF THE SEVENTEENTH AND EIGHTEENTH	
OLD MASTERS OF THE SEVENTEENTH AND EIGHTEENTH	
OLD MASTERS OF THE 16TH - 18TH CENTURIES	HARVEY, VIVIEN
OLD MILL, THE	HOPKINS, H.
OLD MOSS-COVERED CHURCH, AN	HOPKINS, H.
OLD MOSS COVERED CHURCH	ROLFE, W.
OLD MOTHER HUBBARD	GRIEG
OLD NORWEGIAN ROMANCE WITH VARIATIONS, OP. 51	MEACHAM, F.--ED
OLD OAKEN BUCKET, THE	DRUMHELLER
OLD OAKEN BUCKET -- VARIATIONS	SUGARMAN
OLD ORGAN GRINDER	COBEN
OLD PIANO ROLL BLUES, THE	JEAN, E.
OLD PICTURE, AN	DUNGAN
OLD PLANTATION	DUNGAN
OLD PLANTATION	GILLOCK
OLD PLANTATION	GILLOCK
OLD PLANTATION	THOMPSON, J.
OLD PUEBLOS	KREISLER
OLD REFRAIN, THE --STUDENT EDITION--	KREISLER
OLD REFRAIN, THE	QUIST
OLD RIVER BOAT, THE	REISER, V.
OLD ROCKING CHAIR, THE	FEDERER, R.
OLD ROMANCE, AN	LANE, J.--ED.
OLD RUGGED CROSS, THE	HOPKINS, H.
OLD SKIN FLINT	PROEHL, H.
OLD TIME BARN DANCE	BLAKE, D.
OLD TIME FIDDLER, THE	JESSE, M.
OLD UNCLE JOE PLAYS A CAKE-WALK TUNE	RICKER, E.
OLD VALENTINE, AN	MIROVITCH,
OLD VIENNA DANCES	

OLD VIENNESE MASTERS	KANN, H.--ED
OLD VIENNESE MELODY	ROLFE, W.--ED
OLD WALES	WINDRUSH, P.
OLD WATER-WHEEL	KING
OLD WITCH, THE	GLOVER, D.
OLD WITCH	ANSON, G.
OLD WOMAN LIVED IN A SHOE	ROLFE, W.
OLD WORLD MELODY	DUBSKY
OLE, GYPSY	HARPER, M.
OLE	OLSON
OLIVER - EASY PIANO	BART
OLIVER - PIANO SELECTIONS	BART
OLYMPIC STAR	GREEN, R.
OLZEN'S SCANDINAVIAN DANCE ALBUMS, BK. 1 --ACCORDION	
OMAGGIO A SCARLATTI	NAPOLI
OMAGGIO	MOSS, L.
OMAR	PANELLA, L.
OMBRE SULLO SCHERMO	FERRARI-TRECATE
ONCE AND THEN AGAIN	HIGGINS
ONCE IN A WHILE	LANE, J.--ED.
ONCE UPON A TIME, SUITE	LEEDS, R.
ONCE UPON A TIME STORIES OF THE GREAT MUSIC MASTERS	ROBINSON, G. E.
ONCE UPON A TIME	BECK
ONCE UPON A TIME	BECK
ONCE UPON A TIME	HIBBS, C.
ONCE UPON A TIME	STEVENS
ONCE UPON A TIME	TRUXELL, E.
ONDE - 2 STUDIES	CASTELNUOVO-TEDE
ONDINE FROM GASPARD DE LA NUIT	RAVEL
ONDINE FROM PRELUDES, BK. 2	DEBUSSY
ONE-A-PENNY	LAST, J.
ONE-PAGE PIANO VOLUNTARIES	PEERY, R. R.
ONE-THREE QUARTERS. PICC, FL, VN, VC, TRB, TBA, 2	MACERO
ONE, FOUR, FIVE	STEINER
ONE, TWO THREE DANCE WITH ME	PELS, W.
ONE BAD APPLE	BRIMHALL,
ONE BY ONE, TWO BY TWO	NOEL, H.
ONE DAY -- UNE JOURNEE	MILHAUD, D.
ONE FINGER PIANO	HILGER
ONE FINGER POLKA	MITTLER
ONE HANDED SOLITAIRE, NO. 1, 2 AND 3	NAGY, M.
ONE HAND ONLY	STEINER
ONE HAND WALTZ	HAYES
ONE HEART, ONE SOUL	STRAUSS, J.
ONE HE LOVES AND PUSSY CAT	ROLFE, W.
ONE HUNDRED AND SEVENTY-NINE EXERCICES D'EXTENSION	PHILIPP, I.
ONE HUNDRED AND SEVEN EASY-TO-PLAY HYMNS	
ONE HUNDRED AND SIXTY-ONE DANCES	SCHUBERT
ONE HUNDRED AND SIX GREATEST PIANO STUDIES, BK. 1,	KASSCHAU,
ONE HUNDRED AND SIX GREATEST PIANO STUDIES, BK. 2,	KASSCHAU,
ONE HUNDRED AND TENTH ST. RHUMBA	SUESSE, D.
ONE HUNDRED AND TEN EASY AND PROGRESSIVE EXERCISES,	CZERNY
ONE HUNDRED EASY STUDIES, OP. 139	CZERNY
ONE HUNDRED FIVE EASY PIANO PIECES	
ONE HUNDRED NINETY CHILDREN'S SONGS	
ONE HUNDRED OF THE GREATEST ROCK AND ROLL HITS	
ONE HUNDRED ONE CHORALES	BACH, J.S.
ONE HUNDRED PEDAL EXERCISES WITH ELEMENTARY PEDAL	BARESEL, A.
ONE HUNDRED PRACTICAL EXERCISES, OP. 139	CZERNY
ONE HUNDRED PROGRESSIVE EXERCISES, OP. 139	CZERNY
ONE HUNDRED PROGRESSIVE STUDIES WITHOUT OCTAVES, OP.	CZERNY
ONE HUNDRED RECREATIONS	CZERNY
ONE HUNDRED RECREATIONS	CZERNY
ONE HUNDRED SEVENTH FIELD ARTILLERY	NIRELLA, D.
ONE HUNDRED SEVENTY CHRISTMAS SONGS AND CAROLS	
ONE HUNDRED SIXTY EIGHT-MEASURE EXERCISES, OP. 821	CZERNY
ONE HUNDRED SIXTY EIGHT-MEASURE EXERCISES, OP. 821	CZERNY
ONE HUNDRED TWENTY-FIVE EXERCISES FOR	CZERNY
ONE HUNDRED TWENTY-FIVE EXERCISES IN PASSAGE-PLAYING,	CZERNY
ONE HUNDRED TWENTY-FIVE SHORT EXERCISES AND	CZERNY
ONE HUNDRED TWENTY AMERICAN SONGS	
ONE LESS BELL TO ANSWER	BRIMHALL,
ONE LOVELY MORNING	BILBRO, M.
ONE MAN SHOW	SHULMAN
ONE MORNING IN MAY -- SIMP.	MOSSMAN, T.
ONE MORNING IN MAY	MERKUR
ONE NOTE SAMBA	BRIMHALL,
ONE O'CLOCK JUMP	BASIE
ONE OF THOSE SONGS	BRIMHALL,
ONE OF THOSE SONGS	HOLT *
ONE PIANO FOUR HANDS	
ONE PLUS ONE-- 20 STUDIES FOR BEGINNERS	KASEMETS, U.
ONE PLUS ONE--10 EASY PIECES ON WELL-KNOWN SONGS	KASEMETS, U.
ONE PLUS ONE	ROGERS, E.
ONE PLUS ONE	ROGERS, E.
ONE ROSE, THE.	BRYANT--ED.
ONE SUNNY DAY	JOYNER, B.
ONE THOUSAND EXERCISES	HERZ, H.
ONE TIN SOLDIER	BRADLEY,
ONE WAY SONGBOOK	
ONLY A DREAM, REVERIE	EDDY
ONLY YESTERDAY	FAYE
ONOMASTICO DEL BABBO, OP. 209	DE CRESCENZO
ONWARD, CHRISTIAN SOLDIERS	SULLIVAN, J.
ONWARD CHRISTIAN SOLDIERS	SULLIVAN, A.
ON AN OVERGROWN PATH	JANACEK
ON A BRIGHT BLUE SEA	STEVENS, M.
ON A BRIGHT DAY	OGLE, L.
ON A BRIGHT SPRING MORN	RENNARD
ON A CLEAR DAY YOU CAN SEE FOREVER	
ON A CLEAR DAY YOU CAN SEE FOREVER	
ON A DOUBLE-DECKER BUS	RICHTER, A.
ON A HAYRIDE	STEVENS, E.
ON A HOBBY HORSE	ROGERS, E.
ON A MAY MORNING	MCKAY, G.
ON A MOONLIT LAKE	PASQUET, J.
ON A NIGHT IN JUNE	KING
ON A PARIS BOULEVARD	GILLOCK
ON A PARIS BOULEVARD	GILLOCK
ON A QUIET SHORE	DITTENHAVER
ON A RIVER BOAT	WIGGINS, M.
ON A SLOW BOAT TO CHINA	LOESSER, F.
ON A SMALL SCALE -- 28 SHORT PIECES BASED ON THE MAJOR	BAKER
ON A SUMMER SEA	FINLAYSON, W.
ON A SUMMER SEA	KETTERER, E.
ON A SUMMER SEA	KETTERER, E.
ON A SUMMER SEA	KETTERER, E.
ON A TEXAS TRAIL	REEVES, R.
ON A TRAPEZE	RICHTER, A.
ON A TRAPEZE	RICHTER
ON A VICTORIAN VERANDA	STORR, S.
ON A VISIT, MARCH	MARTIN, G.
ON A VISIT, MARCH	MARTIN, G.
ON CHRISTMAS EVE	ARCHER, V.
ON GREEN MEADOWS	FREDERICKS
ON GUARD MARCH	ROME *
ON HORSEBACK, ON THE LAWN	GRETCHANINOFF
ON MY BIKE	GRANT, J.
ON MY COLOR T. V.	ZEPP
ON MY POGO STICK	GRANT, J.
ON MY POLO STICK	SCHER, W.
ON MY WAY TO CHURCH	KRAMER, A. W.
ON MY WOODEN HORSE	SCHER, W.
ON PARADE -- 8-HANDS, SET	ZILCHER
ON PARADE	LICHNER, H.
ON PARADE	MACGREGOR
ON PARADE	READ, G.
ON PARADE	ROLSETH, B.
ON PARADE	SMITH, H.
ON PARADE	TOCABEN, L.
ON SILVER SKATES	FEDERER, R.
ON SKATES	KETTERER, E.
ON SKATES	KING
ON SUNSET HILL	ECKSTEIN
ON SWAN LAKE	WIGHAM, M.
ON THE AVENIDA	MACDONALD
ON THE BANKS OF THE WABASH	DRESSER
ON THE BEAUTIFUL BLUE DANUBE--CONCERT ARABESQUE	STRAUSS, J.
ON THE BEAUTIFUL BLUE DANUBE, OP. 314	STRAUSS, J.
ON THE BEAUTIFUL BLUE DANUBE, OP. 314	STRAUSS, J.
ON THE BEAUTIFUL BLUE DANUBE, OP. 314	STRAUSS, J.
ON THE BEAUTIFUL BLUE DANUBE, OP. 314	STRAUSS, J.
ON THE BEAUTIFUL BLUE DANUBE	STRAUSS, J.
ON THE BEAUTIFUL BLUE DANUBE	STRAUSS, J.
ON THE BLACKS AND WHITES	SLAVICKY, K.
ON THE BLUE LAGOON	MATTINGLY, J.
ON THE FLOAT	KREVIT, W.
ON THE GRAND CANAL	DOUGLAS
ON THE HIGH SEA	OLSON
ON THE HILLSIDE	ROWLEY
ON THE HOLY MOUNT, OP. 85 NO. 13	DVORAK
ON THE ICE AT SWEET BRIAR -- ARPEGGIO WALTZ	CRAWFORD, C.
ON THE ICE AT SWEET BRIAR	CRAWFORD, C.
ON THE ICE AT SWEET BRIAR	CRAWFORD, C.
ON THE ICE	KERR, R. N.
ON THE ISLAND OF KOO-KOO	BREAU, L.
ON THE LAGOON	MCSWEEN, F. W.
ON THE LAKE, BOAT SONG	HOPKINS, H.
ON THE LAKE, OP. 48	WILLIAMS, F.
ON THE LAKE	BRUSSELS, I.
ON THE LAWN	FOSTER, I. R.
ON THE LEVEE	HOLT, EILSEL
ON THE MAGIC LAKE	CRAWFORD, C.
ON THE MARCH	STEVENS
ON THE MEADOW	LICHNER, H.
ON THE MERRY-GO-ROUND	BASTIEN
ON THE MERRY-GO-ROUND	GRANT, J.
ON THE MERRY-GO-ROUND	RICHTER
ON THE MERRY GO ROUND	MONTGOMERY, L.
ON THE MOUNTAIN	HOKANSON, M.
ON THE MOVE -- SEVEN EASY ACTIVITIES	ANTHONY, G.
ON THE OPEN ROAD	JAMES, M.
ON THE OTHER HAND	MARWICK, M. *
ON THE PONY EXPRESS	KAHN, M.
ON THE PRAIRIE, OP. 23	LIADOW, A.
ON THE PROPER PERFORMANCE OF ALL BEETHOVEN'S WORKS FOR	CZERNY
ON THE PROPER PERFORMANCE OF ALL BEETHOVEN'S WORKS FOR	CZERNY
ON THE RACE TRACK	WILSON, M.
ON THE RANCHO	HARPER, M.
ON THE RIVER BOAT	DITTENHAVER
ON THE ROAD TO MANDALAY	SPEAKS, O.
ON THE ROAD TO MANDALAY	SPEAKS, O.
ON THE ROAD	PROCTER, A.
ON THE SEA--BARCAROLLE	KUHE, W.
ON THE SEA, OP. 22 NO. 6	SCHYTTE
ON THE SEA SHORE	SMETANA
ON THE SEA	HACKH, O.
ON THE STREET WHERE YOU LIVE	BRIMHALL,
ON THE STREET WHERE YOU LIVE	SINGER, L.--ED
ON THE SUNNY SIDE OF THE STREET	BRYANT--ED.
ON THE SUNNY SIDE OF THE STREET	FIELDS *
ON THE SUNNY SIDE OF THE STREET	MCHUGH
ON THE SURFACE OF THE MOON, FAR AWAY	BURNAM
ON THE SWING	SCARMOLIN
ON THE TOP OF OLD SMOKY -- IMPROVISATIONS FOR PIANO	SNYDER, W.
ON THE TRAIL	GROFE, F.
ON THE TRAIL	HOLLANDER
ON THE TRAIL	WILLIAMS,
ON THE TRAIL	
ON THE TRAIL	
ON THE TRAPEZE	CRERIE, E.
ON THE WAY TO DREAMTOWN	BESTHOFF, M.
ON TIPTOES	SCHMEID, A.
ON TIPTOES	STONE, E.
ON TOP OF OLD SMOKY	LAMBERT--ED.
ON TOP OF OLD SMOKY	SCHAUM, J.--ED.
ON WINGS OF SONGS	MENDELSSOHN *
ON WINGS OF SONG	MENDELSSOHN
ON WINGS OF SONG	MENDELSSOHN *
ON WINGS OF SONG	MENDELSSOHN
ON WINGS OF SONG	MENDELSSOHN
ON WINGS OF SONG	MENDELSSOHN *
ON WINGS OF SONG	MENDELSSOHN
ON WINGS OF SONG	MENDELSSOHN *
OOM-PAH MARCH	REID
OOMPAH POLKA	ROBINSON, W. E.
OOM PAH-PAH WALTZ	DONENFELD, J.
OP. 83A, OP. 92	MENDELSSOHN
OPALS -- TANGO	MERKUR
OPENING THEME OF THE B FLAT MINOR PIANO CONCERTO	TSCHAIKOWSKY
OPENING THEME OF THE B FLAT MINOR PIANO CONCERTO	TSCHAIKOWSKY
OPERATIC GEMS OVERTURE	GREENWALD,
OPERA BOOK	SCHAUM, J.--ED.
OPERA FANTASIES, VOL. 1	LISZT
OPERA FANTASIES, VOL. 2	LISZT
OPERETTEN-RAUSCH, MELODIENFOLGE MIT TEXT	HRUBY, V.
OPERN UND OPERETTEN, BAND 01	KRENTZLIN,
OPERN UND OPERETTEN, BAND 01	KRENTZLIN,
OPERN UND OPERETTEN, BAND 02	KRENTZLIN,
OPERN UND OPERETTEN, BAND 02	KRENTZLIN,
OPUS ONE	
ORACION DEL TORERO, LA, OP. 34	TURINA, J.
ORANGE BLOSSOMS	GRANFIELD, A.
ORANGE BLOSSOMS	LUDOVIC, G.
ORANGE BLOSSOMS	LUDOVIC, G.
ORATOIRE A LA CROISEE DES CHEMINS -- NO. 2, FROM	BRASSARD
ORATORIO DE NOEL	SAINT-SAENS
ORBIT NO. 2	HOVHANESS, A.
ORB AND SCEPTRE	WALTON, W.
ORCHESTRAL SUITES	BACH, J.S.
ORCHIDS IN THE MOONLIGHT -- SHOWCASE	
ORCHIDS IN THE MOONLIGHT	
ORCHIDS	PANELLA, L.

ORCHID GARDEN, THE, OP. 76--10 IMPRESSIONS OF THE FAR   NIEMANN
ORCHID SET   CLARK, M.--ED.
ORFEO - CHE FARO SENZA EURIDICE   GLUCK
ORFF-SCHULWERK, JUGENDMUSIK, KLEINES SPIELBUCH   ORFF
ORGAN-GRINDER IN THE RAIN   KLAUS, N.
ORGANIST, THE   LEMONT, C. W. *
ORGANIST, THE   LEMONT, C. W.
ORGAN AND KEYBOARD WORKS, BK. 1   GABRIELI, A.
ORGAN AND KEYBOARD WORKS, BK. 2   GABRIELI, A.
ORGAN AND KEYBOARD WORKS, BK. 3   GABRIELI, A.
ORGAN AND KEYBOARD WORKS, BK. 4   GABRIELI, A.
ORGAN AND KEYBOARD WORKS, BK. 5   GABRIELI, A.
ORGAN AND KEYBOARD WORKS, COMPLETE , BK. 1   FRESCOBALDI
ORGAN AND KEYBOARD WORKS, COMPLETE , BK. 2   FRESCOBALDI
ORGAN AND KEYBOARD WORKS, COMPLETE , BK. 3   FRESCOBALDI
ORGAN AND KEYBOARD WORKS, COMPLETE , BK. 4   FRESCOBALDI
ORGAN AND KEYBOARD WORKS, COMPLETE , BK. 5   FRESCOBALDI
ORGAN CHORALE PRELUDES -- BK 1-4   BACH, J.S.
ORGAN CHORAL PRELUDES, BK. 1   BACH, J.S.
ORGAN CHORAL PRELUDES, BK. 2   BACH, J.S.
ORGAN COMPOSITIONS BY BACH TRANSCRIBED FOR PIANO BY   BACH, J.S. *
ORGAN COMPOSITIONS BY BACH TRANSCRIBED FOR PIANO BY   BACH, J.S. *
ORGAN COMPOSITIONS IN 2 VOLS., VOL. 1   BACH, J.S.
ORGAN COMPOSITIONS IN 2 VOLS., VOL. 2   BACH, J.S.
ORGAN COMPOSITIONS TRANSCRIBED FOR PIANO BY LISZT.   BACH, J.S. *
ORGAN COMPOSITIONS TRANSCRIBED FOR PIANO BY LISZT.   BACH, J.S. *
ORGAN CONCERTI, OP. 4 BK. 1   HANDEL
ORGAN CONCERTI, OP. 4 BK. 2   HANDEL
ORGAN CONCERTOS, BK. 1   HANDEL
ORGAN CONCERTOS, BK. 2   HANDEL
ORGAN CONCERTO IN D MINOR   VIVALDI *
ORGAN FANTASIA AND FUGUE IN G MINOR   BACH, J.S. *
ORGAN FANTASIE AND FUGUE IN G MINOR   BACH, J.S.
ORGAN FUGUE IN G MINOR--THE LITTLE   BACH, J.S.
ORGAN GRINDER, THE   FOLDES
ORGAN GRINDER'S SWING -- SIMP.   MOSSMAN, T.--ED
ORGAN GRINDER'S SWING   HUDSON *
ORGAN GRINDER'S TARANTELLA   SCHER, W.
ORGAN GRINDER MAN   RICHTER, A.
ORGAN GRINDER   SCARMOLIN
ORGAN MAN AND THE MONKEYS, THE   ELISIA, SR.
ORGAN MELODIES   CRIST, D.
ORGAN PRELUDE AND FUGUE IN A MINOR   BRAHMS
ORGAN PRELUDE AND FUGUE IN D MINOR   BUXTEHUDE
ORGAN PRELUDE AND FUGUE IN E MINOR   BACH, J.S.
ORGAN PRELUDE IN C MINOR   BACH, J.S.
ORGAN PRELUDE IN E MINOR   BACH, J.S.
ORGAN PRELUDE IN G MINOR --AFTER SZANTO--   BACH, J.S.
ORGAN SONATA NO. 03 -- FIRST MOVEMENT   MENDELSSOHN
ORGAN TOCCATA AND FUGUE IN D MINOR -- SET   BACH, J.S.
ORGAN WORKS, BK. 1   BACH, J.S.
ORGAN WORKS, BK. 2   BACH, J.S.
ORGEL-TOCCATA UND FUGE D-MOLL   BACH, J.S.
ORGEL-TOCCATA UND FUGE D-MOLL, BWV 565   BACH, J.S.
ORGEL- UND KLAVIER-WERKE. GESAMTAUSGABE NACH DEM   FRESCOBALDI
ORGEL- UND KLAVIER-WERKE. GESAMTAUSGABE NACH DEM   FRESCOBALDI
ORGEL- UND KLAVIER-WERKE. GESAMTAUSGABE NACH DEM   FRESCOBALDI
ORGEL- UND KLAVIER-WERKE. GESAMTAUSGABE NACH DEM   FRESCOBALDI
ORGEL- UND KLAVIER-WERKE. GESAMTAUSGABE NACH DEM   FRESCOBALDI
ORGEL- UND KLAVIER-WERKE, BAND 1 -- INTONATIONEN   GABRIELI, A.
ORGEL- UND KLAVIER-WERKE, BAND 2 - 9 RICERCARI   GABRIELI, A.
ORGEL- UND KLAVIER-WERKE, BAND 3 - RICERCARI 2   GABRIELI, A.
ORGEL- UND KLAVIER-WERKE, BAND 4 - CANZONEN UND   GABRIELI, A.
ORGEL- UND KLAVIER-WERKE, BAND 5 - CANZONI ALLA   GABRIELI, A.
ORGELKONZERTE, OP. 4 FUR KLAVIER ODER ORGEL   HANDEL
ORGELKONZERTE, OP. 4 FUR KLAVIER ODER ORGEL   HANDEL
ORGELKONZERTE, OP. 4 NO. 1 IN G MINOR -- 'HALLISCHE   HANDEL
ORGELKONZERTE, OP. 4 NO. 2 IN B FLAT -- 'HALLISCHE   HANDEL
ORGELKONZERTE, OP. 4 NO. 3 IN G MINOR -- 'HALLISCHE   HANDEL
ORGELKONZERTE, OP. 4 NO. 4 IN F -- 'HALLISCHE   HANDEL
ORGELKONZERTE, OP. 4 NO. 5 IN F -- 'HALLISCHE   HANDEL
ORGELKONZERTE, OP. 4 NO. 6 IN B FLAT -- 'HALLISCHE   HANDEL
ORIENTALE, OP. 232, NO. 2 --FROM CANTOS DE ESPANA   ALBENIZ, I.
ORIENTALE, OP. 232, NO. 2 -- FROM CANTOS DE ESPANA   ALBENIZ, I.
ORIENTALE, OP. 50, NO. 9   CUI, C.
ORIENTALE   CUI, C.
ORIENTALE   CUI, C.
ORIENTAL DANCE, AN   CRERIE, E.
ORIENTAL DANCE   CRERIE, E.
ORIENTAL DANCE   KARP
ORIENTAL DANCE   KHATCHATURIAN
ORIENTAL DANCE   KLEINMAN, A.
ORIENTAL FROM 'DANZAS ESPANOLAS'   GRANADOS
ORIENTAL JUGGLERS   KLEINMAN, A.
ORIENTAL MYSTERY   SCHER, W.
ORIENTAL NIGHTS   TEITELBAUM
ORIENTAL ROMANCE 'PRINCE IGOR'   BORODIN, A.
ORIENTAL SKETCH   RACHMANINOFF, S.
ORIENTAL SONG   DEWDNEY, J. H.
ORIENTAL SONG   GLIERE
ORIENTAL TEA GARDEN   MERKUR
ORIGINAL AIRS AND DANCES   KREUTZER
ORIGINAL CADENZAS TO THE PIANO CONCERTI   BEETHOVEN
ORIGINAL CLASSICS, VOL. 1   WAGNESS--ED.
ORIGINAL CLASSICS, VOL. 2   WAGNESS--ED.
ORIGINAL COMPOSITIONS, BK. 1   SCHUBERT
ORIGINAL COMPOSITIONS, BK. 1   SCHUBERT
ORIGINAL COMPOSITIONS, BK. 2   SCHUBERT
ORIGINAL COMPOSITIONS, BK. 3   SCHUBERT
ORIGINAL COMPOSITIONS, BK. 4   SCHUBERT
ORIGINAL COMPOSITIONS, BK. 5   SCHUBERT
ORIGINAL COMPOSITIONS, COMPLETE IN 4 VOLS* VOL. 1   SCHUBERT
ORIGINAL COMPOSITIONS, COMPLETE IN 4 VOLS* VOL. 2   SCHUBERT
ORIGINAL COMPOSITIONS, COMPLETE IN 4 VOLS* VOL. 3   SCHUBERT
ORIGINAL COMPOSITIONS, COMPLETE IN 4 VOLS* VOL. 4   SCHUBERT
ORIGINAL COMPOSITIONS, VOL. 1-- CLOTH   SCHUBERT
ORIGINAL COMPOSITIONS, VOL. 1   LISZT
ORIGINAL COMPOSITIONS, VOL. 1   SCHUBERT
ORIGINAL COMPOSITIONS, VOL. 2 -- CLOTH   SCHUBERT
ORIGINAL COMPOSITIONS, VOL. 2   LISZT
ORIGINAL COMPOSITIONS, VOL. 2   SCHUBERT
ORIGINAL COMPOSITIONS, VOL. 3 -- CLOTH   SCHUBERT
ORIGINAL COMPOSITIONS, VOL. 3   SCHUBERT
ORIGINAL COMPOSITIONS -- CLOTH   MOZART, W. A.
ORIGINAL COMPOSITIONS FOR ONE PIANO, 4-HANDS   MOZART, W. A.
ORIGINAL COMPOSITIONS FOR PIANO, 4-HANDS   MENDELSSOHN
ORIGINAL COMPOSITIONS FOR PIANO, 4 HANDS   BEETHOVEN
ORIGINAL COMPOSITIONS FOR TWO PIANOS, FOUR HANDS   BEETHOVEN
ORIGINAL COMPOSITIONS FOR TWO PIANOS, FOUR HANDS   MOZART, W. A.
ORIGINAL COMPOSITIONS FOR TWO PIANOS - FOUR HANDS ,   SCHUMANN, R.
ORIGINAL COMPOSITIONS FOR TWO PIANOS - FOUR HANDS ,   SCHUMANN, R.
ORIGINAL COMPOSITIONS IN 1 VOL.   BEETHOVEN
ORIGINAL COMPOSITIONS IN 2 VOLS., VOL. 1   BEETHOVEN
ORIGINAL COMPOSITIONS IN 2 VOLS., VOL. 2   BEETHOVEN
ORIGINAL COMPOSITIONS   HAYDN
ORIGINAL COMPOSITIONS   MENDELSSOHN
ORIGINAL COMPOSITIONS   MOZART, W. A.
ORIGINAL COMPOSITIONS   MOZART, W. A.
ORIGINAL COMPOSITIONS   SCHUBERT
ORIGINAL COMPOSITIONS   SCHUMANN, R.
ORIGINAL COMPOSITIONS   WEBER, VON
ORIGINAL PIANO DUETS BY AMERICAN COMPOSERS   SCHAUM, J.--ED.
ORIGINAL PIANO REDUCTIONS   BEETHOVEN
ORNAMENTE, OP. 37 -- 1950 --   BLACHER
ORPHEE AUX ENFERS   OFFENBACH
ORPHEUS--ADAPTED AS A CHILDREN'S OPERA-STORY TO BE   GLUCK
ORPHEUS --GLUCK-- ADAPTED AS A CHILDREN'S OPERA-STORY   DEAN, L. *
ORPHEUS IN THE UNDERWORLD -- QUADRILLE   OFFENBACH *
ORPHEUS IN THRAZIEN, SUITE   KOERPPEN, A.
ORPHEUS UND EURYDIKE -- REIGEN SELIGER GEISTER UND   GLUCK
ORPHEUS   STRAVINSKY, I.
OSMOSE   CHARLES-HENRY
OSTENTATIOUS OSTRICH, THE   TREVARTHEN, R.
OSTINATO   BARTOK
OSTINATO   HENGEVELD
OS TRES CAVALHEIROSINHOS   VILLA-LOBOS, H.
OTELLO - EASY FANTASIA   VERDI
OTHER MAN'S GRASS IS ALWAYS GREENER, THE   BRIMHALL
OTTO, THE CLOWN   DAVIS, J.
OUR BABY, MELODY   HOPKINS, H.
OUR DIRECTOR MARCH   BIGELOW, F.
OUR DIRECTOR MARCH   BIGELOW, F.
OUR DIRECTOR   BIGELOW, F.
OUR FEARLESS ASTRONAUTS   FARISS, M.
OUR FIGHTING MEN   ROCERETO, M.
OUR FIRST DUETS FOR THE PIANO   BERLIN, B.
OUR FIRST DUET BOOK   BILBRO, M.
OUR FLAG   ADLER, S.
OUR LAST DANCE   BRUSSELS, I.
OUR MAN FLINT   GOLDSMITH, J.
OUR MAPLE TREE   JOYNER, B.
OUR REPUBLIC   BLAKE, D.
OUR ROMANCE, WALTZ   STANLEY
OUR SCHOOL BAND   GLOVER, D.
OUR SCHOOL BAND   RICHTER
OUR SCHOOL BAND   SCHER, W.
OUR SERENADE --MODERN RHYTHMIC CLASSICS--   WHITFORD
OUR SMALL WORLD   OLSON
OUR SQUADRON MARCH   HILSHER, F.
OUR TOWN   COPLAND
OUR VILLAGE IN WINTER -- SUITE OF 6 PIECES   SPURLING, C.
OUR WALTZ   KAYE, L.
OUR ZOO   GALLINI
OUTDOOR MUSIC   CHENEY, T.
OUTDOOR SONG   KRAFT, L.
OUTER SPACE   BUSH
OUTER SPACE   FERRELL, B.
OUTRAGE, THE - THEME   NORTH, A.
OUTSIDE-INSIDE PIECES   FITCH, J.
OUTWARD BOUND   KAHN, M.
OUT AND ABOUT   WILKINSON, P.
OUT FOR A STROLL   ANSON, G.
OUT OF CHILDHOOD   POLIN, C.
OUT OF DOORS SUITE   BARTOK
OUT OF MY DREAMS   HAMMERSTEIN *

OUVERTUREN-ALBUM, BAND 01
OUVERTUREN-ALBUM, BAND 02
OUVERTUREN-ALBUM, BAND 03
OUVERTURES CELEBRES   SCHUBERT, C.--ED
OUVERTURE DE TANNHAUSER, FOR 2 PIANOS 8 HANDS   WAGNER
OUVERTURE SYMPHONIQUE--ORCH   TANSMAN, A.
OUVERTURE ZUR VERKAUFTEN BRAUT -- FAKSIMILE DER   SMETANA
OVERCAST   ROZIN
OVERTURE, 'THE MAGIC FLUTE'   MOZART, W. A.
OVERTURE, CANTATA NO. 29   BACH, J.S.
OVERTURE, LIGHT CAVALRY   SUPPE, F.
OVERTURE, LIGHT CAVALRY   SUPPE, F.
OVERTURE, LUSTSPIEL   KELER BELA
OVERTURE, OP. 10   MAGNARD
OVERTURE, POET AND PEASANT, EASY   SUPPE, F.
OVERTURE, POET AND PEASANT   SUPPE, F.
OVERTURE, RAYMOND, EASY   THOMAS, A.
OVERTURE, RAYMOND   THOMAS, A.
OVERTURE, SCHERZO, FINALE   SCHUMANN, R.
OVERTURE, VARIATIONS AND FINALE   ROPARTZ
OVERTURE, WILLIAM TELL, EASY   ROSSINI, G.
OVERTURE, WILLIAM TELL   ROSSINI, G.
OVERTURE, WILLIAM TELL   ROSSINI, G.
OVERTURE, ZAMPA, EASY   HEROLD
OVERTURES, --6--   SUPPE, F.
OVERTURES, IN 5 VOLS* VOL. 1   AUBER *
OVERTURES, IN 5 VOLS* VOL. 2   BEETHOVEN *
OVERTURES, IN 5 VOLS* VOL. 3   MOZART, W. A. *
OVERTURES, IN 5 VOLS* VOL. 4   BIZET, G. *
OVERTURES, IN 5 VOLS* VOL. 5   FLOTOW *
OVERTURES, VOL. 1
OVERTURES, VOL. 2
OVERTURES, VOL. 3
OVERTURES, VOL. 4
OVERTURES, VOL. 5
OVERTURES   BELLINI *
OVERTURES   MENDELSSOHN
OVERTURES   ROSSINI, G. *
OVERTURES   SCHUMANN, R.
OVERTURES   TELEMANN, G.P.
OVERTURE --F--, ARIA VARIATA --A MINOR--, FANTASIAS   BACH, J.S.
OVERTURE 'MESSIAH'   HANDEL
OVERTURE FROM 'POET AND PEASANT'   SUPPE, F.
OVERTURE FROM 'TOMY'   BRIMHALL
OVERTURE FROM 'WILLIAM TELL'   ROSSINI, G.
OVERTURE FROM THE FIVE BAGATELLES   AURIC
OVERTURE ON THEMES FROM 'ORPHEUS'   OFFENBACH
OVERTURE TO ''HANSEL AND GRETEL'' -- SET   HUMPERDINCK, E.
OVERTURE TO MARRIAGE OF FIGARO   MOZART, W. A.
OVERTURE TO THE CIVILIAN BARBER   SCHICKELE, P.
OVERTURE 1812, THEMES   TSCHAIKOWSKY
OVER AND UNDER   SCARMOLIN
OVER HILL AND DALE, OP. 270   ENGELMANN, H. U.
OVER HILL AND DALE   POWELL, A.
OVER THE BARS   JOHNSON, S.
OVER THE BRIDGE   BROOM, P.
OVER THE FENCE IS OUT   RICKER, E.
OVER THE HILLS IN A SLEIGH   JESSE, M.
OVER THE HILLS IN A SLEIGH   JESSE, M.
OVER THE HILLS   GRAY, D.
OVER THE HILLS   HELYER, M.
OVER THE RAINBOW   ARLEN *
OVER THE RAINBOW   LANE, J.--ED.
OVER THE RAINBOW   WILLIAMS,
OVER THE RAINBOW
OVER THE RAINBOW
OVER THE RIVER AND THROUGH THE WOODS - THANKSGIVING   ZEPP--ED
OVER THE RIVER AND THROUGH THE WOOD   SCHAUM, J.--ED.
OVER THE WAVES, MEXICAN WALTZES   ROSAS
OVER THE WAVES, WALTZES   ROSAS

OVER THE WAVES WALTZ	ROSAS
OVER THE WAVES	ROSAS
OVER THE WAVES	ROSAS
OVER THE WAVES	ROSAS
OVER THE WAVES	ROSAS
OWL IN THE BELFRY	GRAHAM, R.
OWL IN THE BELFRY	GRAHAM
OWL IN THE MOONLIGHT	ROBINSON
OWL	PANELLA, L.
OX-CART, THE --2 PIANOS, 8 HANDS--	MOUSSORGSKY
OXENMENUET AND GYPSY RONDO	HAYDN
OXEN MINUET	HAYDN
OXEN MINUET	HAYDN
OZARK DANCE	CANFIELD, J.
OZARK REEL	STEVENS
O BURY ME NOT ON THE LONE PRAIRIE	WEYBRIGHT
O CAVALINHO DE PERNA QUEBRADA	GUARNIERI
O COME ALL FAITHFUL -- FIRST NOEL	SPENCER, J.
O COME ALL FAITHFUL -- SANTA CLAUS	RICHARDS, B.
O HOLY NIGHT	ADAM, A.
O HOLY NIGHT	ADAM, A.
O HOLY NIGHT	ADAM, A.
O HOLY NIGHT	ADAM, A.
O HOLY NIGHT	ADAMS, R. G.
O HOLY NIGHT	BRIMHALL,
O LITTLE TOWN OF BETHLEHEM	HARDING, R.
O PAESE D'O SOLE	
O POLICHINELLO	VILLA-LOBOS, H.
O PRIMAVERA	TIRINDELLI
O SANCTISSIMA - SICILIAN MARINERS' HYMN	THOMAS, A.--ED.
O SOLE MIO, SIMPLIFIED	DICAPUA
O SOLE MIO	DICAPUA
O SOLO MIO	DICAPUA
O WORSHIP THE KING -- A HYMN	HAYDN
O WUNDER, WAS WILL DAS BEDEUTEN	DRATHS--ED
P.Q'S PENCIL QUICKIES	QUIST
P'S AND Q'S OF PIANO ARTISTRY - BK. 1	QUIST
P'S AND Q'S OF PIANO ARTISTRY - BK. 2	QUIST
P'S AND Q'S OF PIANO ARTISTRY - BK. 3	QUIST
PACIFIC GRAND MARCH	DAVIS
PACIFIC 231	HONEGGER, A.
PADDLE WHEEL, THE	COOK, P.
PADDY THE FIDDLER	KENNAN
PADISHA, THE	LORAINE, W.
PAGANINI-ETUDES--NO. 2 IN E FLAT	LISZT
PAGANINI-ETUDES--NO. 3 IN G-SHARP MINOR--CONCERT	LISZT
PAGANINI-ETUDES--NO. 3 IN G-SHARP MINOR-- LA	LISZT
PAGANINI-ETUDES--NO. 4 IN E	LISZT
PAGANINI-ETUDES	LISZT
PAGANINI ETUDES AND FIVE OTHER CONCERT ETUDES	LISZT
PAGANINI PAYS A VISIT TO BACH	DE SOLIS
PAGANINI STUDIES	LISZT
PAGANINI VARIATIONS, OP. 35 BK. 1	BRAHMS
PAGANINI VARIATIONS, OP. 35 BK. 2	BRAHMS
PAGANINI VARIATIONS, OP. 35 COMPLETE	BRAHMS
PAGANINI VARIATIONS	BRAHMS
PAGANINI VARIATIONS	BRAHMS
PAGANINI VARIATIONS	BRAHMS
PAGAN LOVE SONG	LANE, J.--ED.
PAGAN POEMS	ROSSELLINI
PAGES D'ALBUM - FEUX FOLLETS	NERINI, E.
PAGES D'ALBUM - LA FILEUSE	NERINI, E.
PAGES D'ALBUM - LA SOURCE	NERINI, E.
PAGES D'ALBUM - PRELUDE	NERINI, E.
PAGES D'ALBUM - REVERIE	NERINI, E.
PAGES D'ALBUM - ROMANCE SANS PAROLES	NERINI, E.
PAGES D'ANARCHIPEL * ARCHIPEL 5D	BOUCOURECHLIEV
PAGES ENFANTINES - CANTILENE AND PETIT FRERE S'ENDORT	DEMIERRE
PAGES ENFANTINES - PETIT CANON AND POUR NOEL	DEMIERRE
PAGES ENFANTINES	CANAL, M.
PAGES ENFANTINES	DEMIERRE
PAGES ENFANTINES	NOEL, P. *
PAGES FROM A SUMMER JOURNAL	SMOLANOFF
PAGES MYSTIQUES	SATIE, E.
PAGE D'ALBUM	DEBUSSY
PAGINE DI GUERRA	CASELLA, A.
PAGINE MINUSCOLE - 12 SKETCHES	POZZOLI
PAGLIACCI -- COMPLETE OPERA --	LEONCAVALLO
PAGLIACCI -- PROLOGUE, VESTI LA GUIBBA	NEVIN
PAGLIACCI - ARIOSO	LEONCAVALLO
PAGLIACCI - INTERMEZZO AND UN TAL GIOCO	LEONCAVALLO
PAGLIACCI - INTERMEZZO	LEONCAVALLO
PAGLIACCI - MINUET AND SERENATA	LEONCAVALLO
PAGLIACCI - PROLOGUE	LEONCAVALLO
PAGODA BELLS	FOX
PAGODA LAND	OLDENBURG, E.
PAGODA	OLSON
PAGODES, FROM ESTAMPES	DEBUSSY
PAGODES FROM THE ESTAMPES	DEBUSSY
PAINTED SOLDIER	KARP
PAINTER'S SONG	BURNAM
PAINT BOX, THE	DONATO, A.
PAINT YOUR WAGON	
PAINT YOUR WAGON	
PAIN QUOTIDIEN	VUATAZ
PAIR OF DANDY LIONS, A	SUDDARDS
PAISAJE, OP. 35	GRANADOS
PAJAMA GAME, THE	ADLER, R. *
PAJARA PINTA, LA	ESPLA
PAL'S BRIGADE, THE	VANNORT, I.
PALACE GUARDS	GLOVER, D.
PALACE OF THE GRAND PANJANDRUM, THE -- AN ORIENTAL	PERKINS, F.
PALMS, THE, TRANS.	FAURE, J.
PALMS, THE, VAR.	FAURE, J.
PALMS, THE	FAURE, G.
PALMS, THE	FAURE, J.
PALM CANYON	MYROW, F.
PALOMA, LA	YRADIER
PALOMA, LA	YRADIER
PALOMINO	WATSON
PAL JOEY	
PAMPEANA	LASALA
PAMPEANITA	GAITO
PAMPEANO	GUASTAVINO
PANAMA	TYERS, W.
PANATHENAENZUG, OP. 74 FOR LEFT HAND	STRAUSS, R.
PANCHO'S SERENADE	HARPER, M.
PANDA PARADES	DUNGAN
PANIS ANGELICUS	FRANCK, C.
PANIS ANGELICUS	FRANCK, C.
PANSIES	LEONI, F.
PANSY BLOSSOMS	PANELLA, L.
PANSY FACES	KOHLER, F.
PANTINS DANSENT, LES	SATIE, E.
PANTOMIME--FROM 'PIECES MIGNONNES', OP. 77	MOSZKOWSKI
PANTOMIME PICTURES	LAST, J.
PANTOMIME	NEVIN

PANTOMIME	SCOTT-BAKER
PANTOMINE	NOEL, H.
PAN AMERICANA	HERBERT
PAOLINO. TANGO FOR LEFT HAND ALONE	BOZI, H. DE
PAPER BOATS	KIRBY-MASON, B.
PAPER BOATS	SCARMOLIN
PAPER BOY	GARROW, L.
PAPER DOLL	BLACK, M.
PAPER ROSES	BRADLEY,
PAPER SOLDIERS, MARCH	HOPKINS, H.
PAPILLON, EASY	LAVALLEE, C.
PAPILLON, EASY	MERKEL, G.
PAPILLON, ETUDE DE CONCERT	LAVALLEE, C.
PAPILLONS, OP. 2 -- WITH VARIATIONS ON THE NAME	SCHUMANN, R.
PAPILLONS, OP. 2	SCHUMANN, R.
PAPILLONS, OP. 2	SCHUMANN, R.
PAPILLONS, OP. 2	SCHUMANN, R.
PAPILLONS, OP. 2	SCHUMANN, R.
PAPILLONS, OP. 2	SCHUMANN, R.
PAPILLONS, OP. 2	SCHUMANN, R.
PAPILLONS, OP. 2	SCHUMANN, R.
PAPILLONS, OP. 2	SCHUMANN, R.
PAPILLONS D'AMOUR, VALSE	SCHUETT
PAPILLONS ROSES--IMPROMPTU, OP. 59 NO. 2	THOME, F.
PAPILLONS	ROSENTHAL, M.
PAPILLONS	ROSENTHAL, M.
PAPILLON -- BUTTERFLY --	GRIEG
PAPILLON -- BUTTERFLY --	MERKEL, G.
PAQUERETTES ET PRIMEVERES	NOEL, P. *
PAQUITA MIA	RAMOS, E.
PARACHUTISTS, THE	STEINER
PARADE, THE	ALT, H.
PARADES, OP. 57	PERSICHETTI
PARADE -- BALLET --	SATIE, E.
PARADE BOOK	SCHAUM, J.--ED.
PARADE FANTASQUE	PRESLE
PARADE GOES MARCHING BY	BURNAM
PARADE OF MARCHES	SCHAUM, J.
PARADE OF THE CHINESE DOLLS	WALKER
PARADE OF THE CLOWNS	AGAY, D.
PARADE OF THE CLOWNS	AGAY, D.
PARADE OF THE GOBLINS	LEE, E.
PARADE OF THE GRASSHOPPERS, OP. 65	PROKOFIEFF
PARADE OF THE LOLLIPOPS	BERMONT, H.
PARADE OF THE MANNEQUINS	KOCH, E.
PARADE OF THE MIDGETS	HOPSON, E.
PARADE OF THE PANDAS	FRICK
PARADE OF THE PENGUINS	STEVENS, E.
PARADE OF THE PENGUINS	WADE, D.
PARADE OF THE PLANETS	WRIGHT, K.
PARADE OF THE POOKAS	PADWA, V.
PARADE OF THE TEMPLARS	ARBOGAST
PARADE OF THE TIN SOLDIERS	FORREST, S.
PARADE OF THE TIN SOLDIERS	NEVIN
PARADE OF THE TOY SOLDIERS	JESSEL
PARADE OF THE WOODEN SOLDIERS -- SIMP.	JESSEL
PARADE OF THE WOODEN SOLDIERS	JESSEL
PARADE OF THE WOODEN SOLDIERS	JESSEL
PARADE OF THE WOODEN SOLDIERS	JESSEL
PARADE OF THE WOODEN SOLDIERS	JESSEL
PARADE OF THE WOODEN SOLDIERS	JESSEL
PARADE OF THE WOODEN SOLDIERS	JESSEL
PARADE	HOLLANDER
PARADE	IVEY
PARADE	KEYS
PARADE	ROGERS
PARADISE	KRAUKAUER *
PARAIS A TA FENETRE, OP. 28	GREGH
PARAKEETS IN BIRDLAND	BASTIEN
PARAKEET POLKA	ROGERS, E.
PARAKEET	BURNAM
PARALLEL BARS	DUMM
PARAPHRASES ON 'CHOPSTICKS'	TCHEREPNIN
PARAPHRASES ON OLD HEBREW FOLK SONGS, BK. 1	WOLFSON, J.
PARAPHRASES ON OLD HEBREW FOLK SONGS, BK. 2	WOLFSON, J.
PARAPHRASE UBER TSCHAIKOWSKYS BLUMEN-WALZER	GRAINGER, P.
PARASOL PARADE	STEINER
PARA ALICIA MUSICA	ENRIQUEZ, M.
PARC D'ATTRACTIONS -- EXPO 1937 -- 14 WORKS BY	TCHEREPNIN
PARERGON ZUR SINFONIA DOMESTICA, OP. 73 FOR LEFT HAND	STRAUSS, R.
PARE -- STOP	NOEL, H.
PARFUM D'EVENTAIL	GHIKA
PARIS, SUITE FOR 4 PIANOS -- SET	MILHAUD, D.
PARISIAN POLKA--2, 3, OR 4 PIANOS	METIS, F.
PARISIAN PROMENADE	GIASSON, P.
PARISIAN SCENE FROM 'MANON'	STEINER--ED.
PARISIAN SUITE	DUKE, V.
PARISIENNE	NEVIN
PARK AVENUE FANTASY	MALNECK *
PARLOR MELODIES	CRIST, D.
PARODIETTE	DE SAXE
PARSIFAL, GOOD FRIDAY SPELL	WAGNER
PARTHENIA IN-VIOLATA --MAYDEN MUSICKE--. FACSIMILE	
PARTHENIA IN-VIOLATA --MAYDEN MUSICKE--	DART, T.--ED.
PARTHENIA	BYRD, W. *
PARTING -- FOND HEARTS MUST PART --	LANGE, E.
PARTING SONG	SCHIEFELBEIN, F.
PARTITA. HARPSICHORD	DIJK, VAN
PARTITA. HARPSICHORD	PINKHAM
PARTITA--1953	SIEGL, O.
PARTITA--1961	STEARNS, P. P.
PARTITA, FOR PIANO OR HARPSICHORD	KOLZ, E.
PARTITA, OP. 58	TAKACS, J.
PARTITA, 1958 -- HARPSICHORD OR PIANO --	BRANDSTETTER
PARTITAS--BK. 1--NOS. 1-3	BACH, J.S.
PARTITAS--BK. 2--NOS. 4-6	BACH, J.S.
PARTITAS, BK. 1	BACH, J.S.
PARTITAS, BK. 2	BACH, J.S.
PARTITAS, 1, 2	FRESCOBALDI
PARTITAS --URTEXT--, VOL. 1	BACH, J.S.
PARTITAS --URTEXT--, VOL. 2	BACH, J.S.
PARTITAS -- URTEXT -- VOL. 1	BACH, J.S.
PARTITAS -- URTEXT -- VOL. 2	BACH, J.S.
PARTITAS ON TWO CHRISTMAS SONGS	DRISCHNER
PARTITAS 1-3	BACH, J.S.
PARTITAS 4-6	BACH, J.S.
PARTITA -- HARPSICHORD/PIANO	DUBOIS, P. M.
PARTITA -- SET	AURIC
PARTITA FOR PIANO AND ORCHESTRA	BRUNNER
PARTITA FOR PIANO	KRAFT, L.
PARTITA FUR KLAVIER UND ORCHESTER	BRUNNER
PARTITA FUR KLAVIER UND ORCHESTER	BRUNNER
PARTITA IN B FLAT MAJOR	BACH, J.S.
PARTITA IN B MINOR, S. 831, AND ITALIAN CONCERTO, S.	BACH, J.S.

Title	Composer
PARTITA IN C MINOR--FRENCH OVERTURE-- AND FANTASY AND	BACH, J.S.
PARTITA IN D, S. 828	BACH, J.S.
PARTITA NO. 1 IN B FLAT MAJOR	BACH, J.S.
PARTITA NO. 1 IN B FLAT MAJOR	BACH, J.S.
PARTITA NO. 1	BACH, J.S.
PARTITA NO. 1	KRAFT, L.
PARTITA NO. 1	ORBON, J.
PARTITA NO. 2 IN C MINOR	BACH, J.S.
PARTITA NO. 5 IN G MAJOR	BACH, J.S.
PARTITA ON 'ES IST EIN ROS ENTSPRUNGEN'	WEISMANN, J.
PARTITA PRIMAVERILE, OP. 132	WEISMANN, J.
PARTITA	BEALL, J.
PARTITA	BOIZARD, G.
PARTITA	FARQUHAR
PARTITA	FERGUSON, H.
PARTITA	GRUNENWALD
PARTITA	KUPFERMAN, M.
PARTITA	STEVENS, H.
PARTITA	TAILLEFERRE, G.
PARTITEN UND SONATEN	KUHNAU, J.
PARTITEN UND STUCKE	MUFFAT
PARTNERS AT THE KEYBOARD	KETTERER, E.
PARTNER QUARTET -- 'CAPTAIN JINKS' WITH 'PUSH THE	CHURCHILL--ED
PARTNER QUARTET - 'THE GALWAY PIPER' WITH 'SKIP TO MY	CHURCHILL--ED
PARTRIDGE FAMILY, THE - AT HOME WITH THEIR GREATEST	BRADLEY,
PARTY'S OVER, THE	SINGER, L.--ED
PARTY CLOTHES	SCHWAB
PARTY PIECES FOR YOUNG PLAYERS, 2 PNO. SCORE	BENNETT, R.
PARTY PIECES	LAST, J.
PARTY PIECE FOR YOUNG PLAYERS, PARTS	BENNETT, R.
PARTY PIECE FOR YOUNG PLAYERS	BENNETT, R.
PARTY POLKA	NAGY, M.
PARTY POLKA	PELS, W.
PARTY TIME	VOLZ, H.
PAR LES RUES ECLATANTES	LELEU
PASEOS	LAPARRA, R.
PASO DOBLE NO. 1	GEERSH, E.
PASQUA DI RESURREZIONE	MALIPIERO, G. F.
PASSACAGLIA, OP. 6	DOHNANYI
PASSACAGLIA -- ORGAN --	FRESCOBALDI
PASSACAGLIA - FROM SUITE NO. 7	HANDEL
PASSACAGLIA EBRAICA	RAPHLING
PASSACAGLIA IN C MINOR, S. 582	BACH, J.S.
PASSACAGLIA IN C MINOR	BACH, J.S.
PASSACAGLIA IN C MINOR	BACH, J.S.
PASSACAGLIA IN C MINOR	BACH, J.S.
PASSACAGLIA IN E --SUN HYMN--	DRISCHNER
PASSACAGLIA ON D-S-C-H-	STEVENSON, R.
PASSACAGLIA	COPLAND
PASSACAGLIA	DUCHOW
PASSACAGLIA	PIERNE
PASSACAGLIA	PISTON, W.
PASSACAGLIA	SAUNDERS, N.
PASSACAGLIA	SKALKOTTAS, N.
PASSACAGLIA	SOUERS
PASSACAGLIA	DAMASE, J. M.
PASSACAILLE FOR CLAVECIN OR PIANO	LESUR, D.
PASSACAILLE	SATIE, E.
PASSACAILLE	CROISEZ, A.
PASSAGE DU REGIMENT, LE	WARD, J.
PASSAGE ETUDES - C1	WARD, J.
PASSAGE ETUDES - C2	WARD, J.
PASSAGE ETUDES - C3	WARD, J.
PASSAGE ETUDES - C4	CASTELNUOVO-TEDE
PASSATEMPI	GUERRINI, G.
PASSEGGIATA NE CHIOSTRO, LA	MOZART, L.
PASSEPIED -- FROM NOTEBOOK FOR WOLFGANG	PIERNE, P.
PASSEPIED AND GIGUE	DELIBES, L.
PASSEPIED FROM ''LE ROI S'AMUSE''	BACH, J.S.
PASSEPIED	COUPERIN, F.
PASSEPIED	PIERNE, P.
PASSEPIED	PIJPER
PASSEPIED	MAYKAPAR
PASSING FANCE, THE MOTH	HOPKINS, H.
PASSING THE CHURCH	WOHLFAHRT
PASSION DES PROMETHEUS, DIE -- MARCH	CHRETIEN
PASTELS, BK. 2	ZANDSTRA
PASTELS, VOL. 1	ZANDSTRA
PASTELS, VOL. 2	WOLFORD, D.
PASTELS	SHAW
PASTEL BLUES	BURNAM
PASTEL DESERT COLORS	WEYBRIGHT
PASTEL MINUET	BENJAMIN
PASTORALE, ARIOSO AND FINALE	SCARLATTI, D.
PASTORALE, LONGO 413--ARRANGED FOR CONCERT-USE	POULENC, F.
PASTORALE, NO. 1 OF TROIS PIECES	FREED, I.
PASTORALES. EIGHT PIECES	KOECHLIN, C.
PASTORALES	SCARLATTI, D.
PASTORALE --SONATA NO. 1--	SCARLATTI, D.
PASTORALE -- L.413 -- AND CAPRICCIO -- L. 375 --	LAIRD
PASTORALE AND DANCE	WAGNER, J.
PASTORALE AND TOCCATA	SCARLATTI, D.
PASTORALE D-MOLL	HONEGGER, A.
PASTORALE D'ETE	AUCLERT
PASTORALE ET GAVOTTE--ALSO FOR HARPSICHORD--	BACH, J.S.
PASTORALE FROM 'CHRISTMAS ORATORIO'	POULENC, F.
PASTORALE FROM THREE PIECES	TAILLEFERRE, G.
PASTORALE IN C	GREGH
PASTORALE LOUIS XV, OP. 12	MOZART, W. A.
PASTORALE VARIEE K209B--ATTRIBUTED TO MOZART	ALLISON, I.
PASTORALE	BACH, J.S.
PASTORALE	COOKE
PASTORALE	GUIDA
PASTORALE	HARVEY, VIVIEN
PASTORALE	HARVEY, VIVIEN
PASTORALE	KOUGUELL
PASTORALE	KOUGUELL
PASTORALE	LAVAGNINO
PASTORALE	LUBIN, E.
PASTORALE	PLATT, W.
PASTORALE	POULENC, F.
PASTORALE	RIETI
PASTORALE	ROGER-DUCASSE
PASTORALE	ROWLEY
PASTORALE	SCARLATTI, D.
PASTORALE	SHULMAN
PASTORALE	WEYBRIGHT
PASTORALI DEL NATALE	FARINA
PASTORAL AND CAPRICCIO	SCARLATTI, D.
PASTORAL FROM 'CONCERTO GROSSO NO. 8'	CORELLI
PASTORAL NO. 1	HOVHANESS, A.
PASTORAL SONATA	SCARLATTI, A.
PASTORAL SYMPHONY FROM THE CHRISTMAS ORATORIO -- SET	BACH, J.S.
PASTORAL	LINDFORS, E.
PASTORAL	MORENO GANS, J.
PASTORAL	RODRIGO, J.
PASTORELLA DELLE ALPI	LISZT
PASTORELLA IN D FUR ORGEL -- KLAVIER -- UND STREICHER	WERNER
PASTORELLA ZUR WEIHNACHT IN G FUR ORGEL -- KLAVIER --	WERNER
PASTORES CHIQUITOS. VILLANICO POPULAR	BORONAT
PASTOURELLE, FROM THE BALLET 'L'EVENTAIL DE JEANNE'	POULENC, F.
PASTOURELLES, BK. 1	BITSCH
PASTOURELLES, BK. 2	BITSCH
PASTOURELLE FROM L'EVENTAIL DE JEANNE	POULENC, F.
PAS DES AMPHORES--AIR DE BALLET, NO. 2	CHAMINADE
PAS DES AMPHORES	CHAMINADE
PAS DES FLEURS--WALTZ FROM ''NAILA''	DELIBES, L.
PAS DES FLEURS, NAILA	DELIBES, L.
PAS DE DEUX	L'HERVILLIERS
PAS DE QUATRE	MEYER-LUTZ
PAS DE QUATRE	MEYER *
PAS DE TROIS--DE PAQUITA--	MINKUS, L. *
PAS DE VENDANGES--PAS DE DEUX--FROM GISELLE	BURGMUELLER *
PATHETIQUE SYMPHONY, THEME	TSCHAIKOWSKY
PATINEURS, LES, EASY	WALDTEUFEL, E.
PATINEURS, LES --THE SKATES--, OP. 183	WALDTEUFEL, E.
PATINEURS, LES -- SKATERS --	WALDTEUFEL, E.
PATINEURS, LES	WALDTEUFEL, E.
PATIO PARTY	KING, S.
PATRIE. OUVERTURE DRAMATIQUE	BIZET, G.
PATRIOTIC AMERICAN MELODIES	BACON, E.--ED
PATRIOTIC PRIMER	SCHAUM, J.
PATRIOTIC PRIMER	SCHAUM, J.
PATRIOTIC SONG, OP. 12 NO. 8	GRIEG
PATRIOTIC SONGS	DE VITO, A.--ED.
PATRIOTIC SONG	GRIEG
PATTAGLIA GIAPPONESE	BILLI
PATTERNS, BK. 1	SCHER, W.
PATTERNS, 1970	KLEIMAN, S.
PATTERNS	POWERS, M.
PAUL CARTER POPULAR PIANO COURSE, BK. 1	CARTER, P.
PAUL CARTER POPULAR PIANO COURSE, BK. 2	CARTER, P.
PAUL CARTER POPULAR PIANO COURSE, BK. 3	CARTER, P.
PAUL REVERE'S RIDE	PAULL
PAUL THE POKEY PORCUPINE	MESEROLE, H. T.
PAUSE DEL SILENCIO	MALIPIERO, G. F.
PAUVRES FOUS	WALTER
PAVANA-CAPRICHO, OP. 12	ALBENIZ, I.
PAVANA-CAPRICHO, OP. 12	ALBENIZ, I.
PAVANA, OP. 83	ALBENIZ, I.
PAVANA, OP. 92, NO. 8 -- FROM 12 PIECES	ALBENIZ, I.
PAVANA E MINUETTO	PICCIOLI
PAVANE BIJOU	CANTU
PAVANE FOR MELISANDE	PIRIOU
PAVANE LOUIS XV	CHANAUD
PAVANE POUR UNE ENFANTE -- INCLUDES TWO PARTS	RAVEL
PAVANE POUR UNE INFANTE DEFUNTE	RAVEL
PAVANE POUR UNE INFANTE DEFUNTE	RAVEL
PAVANE POUR UNE INFANTE DEFUNTE	RAVEL
PAVANE POUR UNE INFANTE DEFUNTE	RAVEL
PAVANE POUR UNE INFANTE DEFUNTE	RAVEL
PAVANE	ANDRIESSEN, H.
PAVANE	BOULNOIS
PAVANE	FAURE, G.
PAVANE	HOUDRET
PAVANE	RAVEL
PAVANE	RAVEL
PAVANE	RAVEL
PAVANE	RAVEL
PAVANNE -- SIMP.	MOSSMAN, T.--ED
PAVANNE	GOULD, M.
PAVANNE	GOULD, M.
PAVANNE	GOULD, M.
PAVILIONS OF INDUSTRY - THEME	GROFE, F.
PAVILLION D'ARMIDE -- COMPLETE BALLET	TCHEREPNIN, N.
PAYADA	LASALA
PAYSAGE--ETUDE NO. 3	LISZT
PAYSAGE, OP. 59 NO. 2	PROKOFIEFF
PAYSAGES - LA FONTAINE ET LA CLOCHE, LE LAC	MOMPOU, F.
PAYSAGES ET MARINES - BK. 1	KOECHLIN, C.
PAYSAGES ET MARINES - BK. 2	KOECHLIN, C.
PAYSAGES	DE FRAGUIER
PAYSAGE	CHAUSSON
PAY OFF, THE	BECHET
PA JIGS THEM ALL DOWN	COWELL
PEACEFUL	BRIMHALL,
PEACEMAKER, THE, MARCH	STURTEVANT
PEACE IN THE VALLEY	LANE, J.--ED.
PEACH-PICKERS' FROLIC	ANDREWS
PEACOCK, SONG WITHOUT WORDS	SCHILLER, F.
PEACOCK, THE	DUNGAN
PEACOCK, THE	DUNGAN
PEACOCK WALK	LAKE, G.
PEANUTS KEYBOARD FUN SERIES - A BOY NAMED CHARLIE	GUARALDI
PEANUTS KEYBOARD FUN SERIES - A CHARLIE BROWN	GUARALDI
PEANUTS KEYBOARD FUN SERIES - CHARLIE BROWN ALL STARS	GUARALDI
PEANUTS KEYBOARD FUN SERIES - HE'S YOUR DOG, CHARLIE	GUARALDI
PEANUTS KEYBOARD FUN SERIES - IT'S THE GREAT PUMPKIN,	GUARALDI
PEANUTS KEYBOARD FUN SERIES - IT WAS A SHORT SUMMER,	GUARALDI
PEANUTS KEYBOARD FUN SERIES - PIANO FUN BOOK	GUARALDI
PEANUTS KEYBOARD FUN SERIES - SUPPLEMENTARY SONGS FOR	GUARALDI
PEANUTS KEYBOARD FUN SERIES - YOU'RE IN LOVE, CHARLIE	GUARALDI
PEANUT BRITTLE	SENTER, G.
PEANUT VENDOR, THE	SIMONS
PEANUT VENDOR, THE	SIMONS
PEARLS AND LACES	LUDOVIC, G.
PEARLS OF FOAM	LANGE, G.
PEARLS ON VELVET	YOUNG, V.
PEARLS ON VELVET	
PEARLY DEW, OP. 6 NO. 3	REYNALD, G.
PEARLY DEWDROP	BIRBECK
PEARLY DEW DROPS, MAZURKA	BIRBECK
PEASANT'S DANCE OP. 208	BAUMFELDER, F.
PEASANT'S SONG, THE	HARKER, F.
PEASANT'S SONG	RENDANO
PEASANT DANCE	KOCH, E.
PEASANT DANCE	MOJSISOVICS, R.
PEASANT DANCE	REEVES, R.
PEASANT DANCE	SCHER, W.
PEASANT DANCE	WEYBRIGHT
PECAN NUT	FILAS
PECCADILLES IMPORTUNES	SATIE, E.
PECOS BILL	SCHAUM, J.--ED.
PEDAL, THE	MIROVITCH, A.
PEDAL PATTERNS	ANSON, G.
PEDAL PUSHERS	ANSON, G.
PEDAL STUDIES--SPANISH AND ENGLISH	PFEIFFER, A.
PEDRO DANCES	DE VITO, A.
PEDRO DANCES	SCHER, W.
PEE-WEE THE PICCOLO--WITH NARRATOR	KLEINSINGER, G.
PEEK-A-BOO	ROZIN
PEEK A BOO, I SEE YOU	NEVIN
PEER-GYNT-SUITE 1, OP. 46	GRIEG
PEER-GYNT-SUITE 1 -- ANITRAS TANZ OP. 46 NO. 3	GRIEG

PEER-GYNT-SUITE 2, OP. 55 — GRIEG
PEER-GYNT-SUITE 2 -- SOLVEJGS LIED OP. 55 NO. 4, — GRIEG
PEERLESS MELODIES — CRIST, D.
PEER GYNT. — GRIEG
PEER GYNT, OP. 28. 11 EXCERPTS — SAEVERUD
PEER GYNT, SELECTIONS — GRIEG
PEER GYNT SUITES — GRIEG
PEER GYNT SUITE - A STORY WITH — GRIEG,
PEER GYNT SUITE NO. 1, OP. 46. VOL. 1# MORNING MOOD. — GRIEG
PEER GYNT SUITE NO. 1, OP. 46. VOL. 2# DEATH OF ASE, — GRIEG
PEER GYNT SUITE NO. 1, OP. 46. VOL. 3# IN THE HALL OF — GRIEG
PEER GYNT SUITE NO. 1, OP. 46--ARRANGED BY COMPOSER — GRIEG
PEER GYNT SUITE NO. 1, OP. 46 — GRIEG
PEER GYNT SUITE NO. 1, OP. 46 — GRIEG
PEER GYNT SUITE NO. 2, OP. 55 — GRIEG
PEER GYNT SUITE NO. 2, OP. 55 — GRIEG
PEER GYNT SUITE NO. 2, OP. 55 — GRIEG
PEER GYNT SUITE 1 — GRIEG
PEGGY O'NEIL — LANE, J.--ED.
PEGLEG DANCE — COWELL
PEG LEG PETE — KEVAN
PEG O' MY HEART — LANE, J.--ED.
PEINTRE ET SON MODELE, LE -- BALLET -- — AURIC
PELICANS ON PARADE — MILLER
PELLEAS UND MELISANDE, SYMPHONIC POEM FOR ORCHESTRA — SCHOENBERG
PENCIL PLAY, PART A — CLARK, F.
PENCIL PLAY, PART B — CLARK, F.
PENCIL PLAY, PART C — CLARK, F.
PENCIL PLAY, PART D — CLARK, F.
PENDANT LA VALSE--CAPRICE, OP. 73 — LACK, T.
PENDANT LE BAL -- INTERMEZZO -- — GILLET, E.
PENDULUM, THE — RICHARDSON
PENELOPE-PRELUDE — FAURE, G.
PENGUIN, THE — LANE, J.
PENGUINS AT PLAY — HEIM, J.
PENGUINS — SCHER, W.
PENGUIN PARADE, THE — REISER, V.
PENNSYLVANIA POLKA — LEE *
PENNSYLVANIA TURNPIKE — VALENTINE, J.
PENNY-WHISTLE SONG, THE — ANDERSON, L.
PENNY ARCADE — RAPHLING
PENNY SHOW — SCARMOLIN
PENNY WHISTLE BLUE -- MAGIC GARDENS, THE. — CELE
PENNY WHISTLE — GEIGER
PENNY WHISTLE — GWYNN, F. *
PENNY WHISTLE — GWYNN, F.
PENSEES, OP. 62 — PROKOFIEFF
PENSEE DE COEUR — CANTORE
PENSEE FUGITIVE — SMETANA
PENSEE FUGITIVE — SMETANA
PENSIVE FLOWERET — HOLT, EILSEL
PENSIVE NOCTURNE — DVORINE
PENSIVE PIANO MOODS — DENNIS, M.
PENTATONE — PROCTOR
PEOMA FIESOLANO — RIETI
PEOPLE WILL SAY WE'RE IN LOVE — HAMMERSTEIN *
PEOPLE — SINGER, L.--ED
PEPITA JIMENEZ -- INTERLUDE — ALBENIZ, I.
PEPITA — DONENFELD, J.
PEPPERMINT CANDY — OBENCHAIN, V.
PEPPERMINT GUARD, THE — OFFUTT
PEPPERMINT POLKA — MARTIN, H.
PEPPERMINT STICK — FILAS
PEPPERMINT STICK — RICHMAN, A.
PEPPERMIT POPCORN — LUNDIE, K.
PEQUENA DANZA, FROM 'ESTANCIA' — GINASTERA
PEQUENA DANZA ESPANOLA — ITURBI, J.
PEQUENA MARCHA — CASTRO, J. M.
PEQUENA SUITE — FLEITES, V.
PEQUENA SUITE — HOLZMANN, R.
PEQUENECES--CHILDREN'S ALBUM OF EASY DANCES — PACHECO, J. F.
PERCEPTION — KAHN, M.
PERCIA -- A CHILEAN FOLK SONG — WEYBRIGHT
PERFECTION IN STYLE, OP. 755--25 FINISHING STUDIES — CZERNY
PERFECT DAY, A — BOND
PERFECT DAY, A — BOND
PERFECT DAY, A — BOND
PERFECT DAY, A — BOND
PERICON — SAMMARTINO
PERI WALTZES — ALBERT, C. D'
PERKY PANDA — KARP
PERKY PETE — KRAFT, L.
PERPETUAL MOTION--RONDO FROM THE SONATA, OP. 24 — WEBER, VON
PERPETUAL MOTION, OP. 24 — WEBER, VON
PERPETUAL MOTION — HAUBIEL, C.
PERPETUAL MOTION — HAYES
PERPETUAL MOTION — LESSARD, J.
PERPETUAL MOTION — LESSARD, J.
PERPETUUM MOBILE--ORIGINAL AND ARRANGEMENTS BY BRAHMS — WEBER, VON
PERPETUUM MOBILE, OP. 64 NO. 5 -- PERPETUAL MOTION — HAYDN
PERPETUUM MOBILE OP. 24 — WEBER, VON
PERPETUUM MOBILE — ALKAN
PERPETUUM MOBILE — ALKAN
PERRY MASON THEME —
PERRY SQUARE BOOGIE --MODERN RHYTHMIC CLASSICS-- — WHITFORD
PERSIAN BAZAAR — SWIFT, N.
PERSIMMONS--A NEGRO REVEL — GWYNN, F.
PERSONALITY —
PERSPECTIVES — BROWN, E.
PESCA SUBACQUEA - 9 MELODIOUS PIECES ON 5 NOTES — CONSIGLIO
PESKY FLY — PORTER, C.
PETE'S MIXTURE — JOHNSON, S.
PETER, JUDY AND SQUEAKY, FIRST PIANO BOOK — BERLIN, B.
PETER, JUDY AND SQUEAKY, SECOND PIANO BOOK — BERLIN, B.
PETER, PAUL AND MARY, HITS OF, MADE EASY FOR PIANO — DAVIS, J. R.--ED
PETER, PAUL AND MARY, MORE MADE EASY FOR PIANO — NEALE, J.--ED
PETER, PAUL AND MOMMY, EASY BIG NOTE PIANO —
PETER, PETER AND HUMPTY DUMPTY — ROLFE, W.
PETER'S BOOK — WILLAN
PETER AND THE WOLF, OP. 67 — PROKOFIEFF
PETER AND THE WOLF, OP. 67 — PROKOFIEFF
PETER AND THE WOLF, TRIUMPHANT MARCH — PROKOFIEFF
PETER AND THE WOLF --TRIUMPHAL MARCH-- — PROKOFIEFF
PETER AND THE WOLF — PROKOFIEFF
PETER AND THE WOLF — PROKOFIEFF
PETER AND THE WOLF — PROKOFIEFF *
PETER DUCHIN PIANO SHOWCASE — DUCHIN
PETER GUNN —
PETER PAN — BRIMHALL,
PETER PENGUIN'S PIANOFORTE BOOK — SAVILLE, A.
PETER PIPER — GRAY, D.
PETER RABBIT - A STORY WITH MUSIC — RICHTER, A.
PETER RABBIT AND THE TALES OF BEATRIX PORTER — BRIMHALL,
PETER RABBIT — TROWBRIDGE, L.
PETER SCHLEMIHL — RONNEFELD, P.

PETITES AQUARELLES MUSICALES - CHANSON D'AUTREFOIS — CARMAN
PETITES AQUARELLES MUSICALES - DANSE DU 18E SIECLE — CARMAN
PETITES AQUARELLES MUSICALES - FETE BRETONNE — CARMAN
PETITES AQUARELLES MUSICALES - MARCHE DU REGIMENT — CARMAN
PETITES AQUARELLES MUSICALES - MINUETTO CAPRICCIOSO — CARMAN
PETITES AQUARELLES MUSICALES - SCHERZETTINO — CARMAN
PETITES FEUILLES — SAUVREZIS
PETITES HISTOIRES — PIRIOU
PETITES MAINS, LES - GENTIL SOURIRE — TROJELLI
PETITES MAINS, LES - LES MARIONNETTES — TROJELLI
PETITES MAINS, LES - PRES D'UNE MERE — TROJELLI
PETITES MAINS, LES - RETOUR DE CLASSE — TROJELLI
PETITES MAINS, LES - SIMPLETTE — TROJELLI
PETITES MAINS, LES - UN PETIT BAL — TROJELLI
PETITES MAINS, LES — TROJELLI
PETITES PIECES POMPADOUR - GAVOTTE — PIERNE, P.
PETITES PIECES POMPADOUR — PIERNE, P.
PETITES VIOLONS DU ROI LOUIS XV, LES — LANDRY
PETITE BALLERINA, THE - FROM DANCE OF THE DOLLS — SHOSTAKOVITCH
PETITE BALLERINA — SINGER
PETITE BALLERINA — SKAGGS
PETITE BALLERINA — SKAGGS
PETITE BALLET — CATRE, J. F.
PETITE BALLET — ENDRES, O.
PETITE BERCEUSE — PRESLE
PETITE BOLERO — KIRK
PETITE BOLERO — RAVINA, H.
PETITE ESQUISSE — LAZZARI
PETITE ETUDE POUR LES MAINS ALTERNEES — GARTENLAUB, O.
PETITE ETUDE POUR LES TIERCES — GARTENLAUB, O.
PETITE ETUDE — MALHERBE, C.
PETITE ETUDE — RIEGGER, W.
PETITE GAVOTTE, LA — HEYNE
PETITE GAVOTTE - MUSETTE — DILSNER
PETITE GAVOTTE — MARIE
PETITE GYPSY DANCE — RICKER
PETITE MARCHE FROM THE FIVE BAGATELLES — AURIC
PETITE MARCHE — BENBOW
PETITE MAZURKA — KETTERER, E.
PETITE MELODIE — BEYER, F.
PETITE MELODY — BUTLER, J.
PETITE MENUET — WATERMAN
PETITE PARTITA — MAILMAN, M.
PETITE PAVANE — ELMER, C.
PETITE PRINCESSE A REVE, UNE — BARLOW
PETITE RHAPSODY — SPENCER, J.
PETITE RONDE SUR UNE CHANSON — LABEY
PETITE RONDO — MILLER
PETITE RUSSIAN RHAPSODIE — THOMPSON, J.
PETITE SUITE, COMPLETE — DEBUSSY
PETITE SUITE, FOR 2 PIANOS 8 HANDS — DEBUSSY
PETITE SUITE, FROM 'FORTY-FOUR DUOS FOR TWO VIOLINS' — BARTOK
PETITE SUITE '1830' — AUBE
PETITE SUITE BRIOCHINE — DJEMIL, E.
PETITE SUITE DE CONCERT — COLERIDGE-TAYLOR
PETITE SUITE POUR ENFANTS — HARSANYI
PETITE SUITE POUR PIANO — MAILLARD, P.
PETITE SUITE — AURIC
PETITE SUITE — BARTOK
PETITE SUITE — BORODIN, A.
PETITE SUITE — BORODIN, A.
PETITE SUITE — BORODIN, A.
PETITE SUITE — DEBUSSY
PETITE SUITE — DEBUSSY
PETITE SUITE — DEBUSSY
PETITE SUITE — DEBUSSY
PETITE SUITE — DEBUSSY
PETITE SUITE — DEBUSSY
PETITE SUITE — DE MENASCE, J.
PETITE SUITE — MANNES, L. D.
PETITE SUITE — ROGER-DUCASSE
PETITE SUITE — TCHEREPNIN
PETITE TARANTELLE — HELLER, S.
PETITE TARENTELLE IN E MINOR, OP. 46 NO. 7 — HELLER, S.
PETITE TYROLIENNE, OP. 242 — STREABBOG
PETITE VALSE E STORIELLA — PICCIOLI
PETITE WALTZ, THE — HEYNE
PETITE WALTZ — DE VITO, A.
PETITE WALTZ — HENSELT, A.
PETITE WALTZ — HILL, M.
PETITS BRETONS, LES, QUADRILLE MIGNON — LEDUC, A.
PETITS CONSCRITS, LES, MARCHE MILITAIRE, OP. 202 — STREABBOG
PETITS CONTES — SHOSTAKOVITCH
PETITS JONGLEURS, LES, AIR DE BALLET, OP. 314 NO. 1 — STREABBOG
PETITS PASTELS - SEVEN DRAWINGS FOR THE YOUNG PIANIST — FLAGELLO, N.
PETITS PASTELS - SEVEN DRAWINGS FOR YOUNG PIANISTS — FLAGELLO, N.
PETITS PRELUDES RECREATIFS - PRES DU RUISSEAU, BEBE — CHRETIEN
PETITS TABLEAUX PITTORESQUES POUR LA JEUNESSE - — AKIMENKO
PETITS TABLEAUX PITTORESQUES POUR LA JEUNESSE - PETITE — AKIMENKO
PETITS TABLEAUX PITTORESQUES POUR LA JEUNESSE - VIENS — AKIMENKO
PETITS TABLEAUX PITTORESQUES POUR LA JEUNESSE — AKIMENKO
PETITS VIETUOSES, LES - SIXTY SHORT TRANSCRIPTIONS IN —
PETITS VIRTUOSES, LES - SIXTY SHORT TRANSCRIPTIONS IN —
PETITS VIRTUOSES, LES - SIXTY SHORT TRANSCRIPTIONS IN —
PETITS VIRTUOSES, LES - SIXTY SHORT TRANSCRIPTIONS IN —
PETIT ALBUM FACILE - MA POUPEE PLEURE AND MA POUPEE — GAGNEUR
PETIT ALBUM FACILE — GAGNEUR
PETIT ALBUM POUR LA JEUNESSE — ZILCHER
PETIT BAISER, LE, VALSE MIGNONNE — DESSAUX
PETIT CANON PERPETUAL — ROUSSEL, A.
PETIT CAPRICE IN THE STYLE OF OFFENBACH — ROSSINI, G.
PETIT CARILLON, ESQUISSE — THUILLIER
PETIT CARNAVAL — MERIGOT, F.
PETIT CARNAVAL, GALOP — STREABBOG
PETIT CARNIVAL, SCHOTTISCHE — STREABBOG
PETIT CLASSIQUE, LE — MORHANGE *
PETIT CONCERT. HARPSICHORD, MEDIUM VOICE, VIOLIN, OBOE — TRIMBLE
PETIT DEMON, LE — HERZ, H.
PETIT FABLIER, LE — MIGOT
PETIT GRADUS AD PARNASSUM, BK. 1 — PHILIPP, I.--ED.
PETIT GRADUS AD PARNASSUM, BK. 2 — PHILIPP, I.--ED.
PETIT GRADUS AD PARNASSUM, BK. 3 — PHILIPP, I.--ED.
PETIT GRADUS AD PARNASSUM, BK. 4 — PHILIPP, I.--ED.
PETIT GRADUS AD PARNASSUM, BK. 5 — PHILIPP, I.--ED.
PETIT LIVRE DES TENUES, LE — DARMES
PETIT MESSE SOLENNELLE - PRELUDIO RELIGIOSO — ROSSINI, G.
PETIT PIANIST - LE PETIT SCHUMANN — SCHUMANN, R.
PETIT PIANIST - LE PETIT WOHLFAHRT-CZERNY, BK. 1 — CZERNY
PETIT PIANIST - LE PETIT WOHLFAHRT-CZERNY, BK. 2 — CZERNY
PETIT PRINTEMPS ET LA CHANSON DE MARIE-LOUISE — NOEL, P. *
PETIT ROMANTIQUE, LE — MORHANGE *
PETIT TANGO — HOPKINS, H.
PETIT THEME VARIE — BEAUCAMP
PETIT TRAIN DE PLAISIR, UN — ROSSINI, G.
PETOFI CZARDAS — CHORIN
PETROUCHKA - REVISED 1947 VERSION — STRAVINSKY, I.

PETROUCHKA - 3 MOVEMENTS -	STRAVINSKY, I.
PETROUCHKA	STRAVINSKY, I.
PETRUSHKA, DANSE RUSSE	STRAVINSKY, I.
PETTEGOLEZZO IN REFETTORIO	GUERRINI, G.
PETTICOAT POLKA	LANE, J.--ED.
PET SILHOUETTES, BK. 1	MCGRAW
PET SILHOUETTES, BK. 2	MCGRAW
PHADRA -- OUVERTURE	MASSENET, J.
PHANTASIEN FUR KLAVIER	PEPPING, E.
PHANTASIEN	PEPPING, E.
PHANTASIESTUCK OP. 113	DREYSCHOCK
PHANTASIE IN F SHARP MINOR, OP. 28	MENDELSSOHN
PHANTOM FOUNTAIN, THE	WRAGG
PHANTOM OF THE SEA	VOLZ, H.
PHANTOM REGIMENT, THE	ANDERSON, L.
PHANTOM RIDER, THE	RICKER, E.
PHANTOM RIDER, THE	SCHAUM, J.--ED.
PHILEMON AND BAUCIS. FANTASY. TWO PIANOS, EIGHT HANDS	GOUNOD, C.
PHILOPENA MAZURKA	HEINS, C.
PHOENIX	MOEVS, R.
PHRYGIAN FABLE	MILLS
PHRYGIAN TOCCATA	VERNE
PIANINO COLLECTION	
PIANIST'S ANTHOLOGY, THE--28 FAVORITE PIECES	OESTERLE--ED.
PIANIST'S DIGEST OF BAROQUE MUSIC	STANDEL--ED
PIANIST'S DIGEST OF BAROQUE MUSIC	STANDEL--ED
PIANIST'S DIGEST OF MODERN MUSIC	STANDEL--ED
PIANIST'S DIGEST OF MODERN MUSIC	STANDEL--ED
PIANIST'S FIRST AND SECOND YEARS, THE--47 FAVORITE	OESTERLE--ED.
PIANIST'S SECOND AND THIRD YEARS, THE--41 FAVORITE	OESTERLE--ED.
PIANISTES DE L'AVENIR, LES - 36 SHORT TRANSCRIPTIONS	
PIANISTES DE L'AVENIR, LES - 36 SHORT TRANSCRIPTIONS	
PIANISTES DE L'AVENIR, LES - 36 SHORT TRANSCRIPTIONS	
PIANISTS' DAILY TECHNIQUE, THE - PARTS 1 AND 2	POZZOLI
PIANISTS' DAILY TECHNIQUE, THE - PART 3	POZZOLI
PIANISTS' GUIDE	SGAMBATI
PIANISTS BOOK OF BACH CHORALES	BACH, J.S.
PIANISTS CHORD GUIDE, THE	LUBIN, E.
PIANOAGOGO	ALBRIGHT, W.
PIANOFORTE ALBUM, IN 2 VOLS# VOL. 1. ORIGINAL WORKS	BEETHOVEN *
PIANOFORTE ALBUM, IN 2 VOLS# VOL. 1	CLEMENTI *
PIANOFORTE ALBUM, IN 2 VOLS# VOL. 2. ARRANGEMENTS	BEETHOVEN *
PIANOFORTE ALBUM, IN 2 VOLS# VOL. 2	BIZET, G. *
PIANOFORTE TECHNICS--DAILY EXERCISES	LOESCHHORN, A.
PIANOLAND	
PIANOLA RAG	KRENZ, B.
PIANOTIME FAVORITES --BIG NOTE-- --120--	
PIANOVATIONS OF JOSE MELIS	
PIANO ACCOMPANIMENTS TO THE 'A' BOOK	SCHAUM, J.--ED.
PIANO ACCOMPANIMENTS TO THE 'A' BOOK	SCHAUM, J.--ED.
PIANO ALBUM - ORIGINAL PIECES FOR READING, RECITAL AND	AARON, M.
PIANO ALBUM	ROSSINI, G. *
PIANO ALL THE WAY -- LEVEL 1A	GILLOCK
PIANO ALL THE WAY -- LEVEL 1B	GILLOCK
PIANO ALL THE WAY -- LEVEL 2	GILLOCK
PIANO ALL THE WAY -- LEVEL 3	GILLOCK
PIANO ALL THE WAY -- LEVEL 4	GILLOCK
PIANO AND ITS ANCESTORS, THE -- AN ANTHOLOGY OF EARLY	GUENTHER--ED
PIANO ANTHOLOGY FOR THE YOUNG, BK. 01 - 27 PIECES	CESI, S. *
PIANO ANTHOLOGY FOR THE YOUNG, BK. 02 - 10 PIECES	CESI, S. *
PIANO ANTHOLOGY FOR THE YOUNG, BK. 03 - 10 PIECES	CESI, S. *
PIANO ANTHOLOGY FOR THE YOUNG, BK. 04 - 23 PIECES	CESI, S. *
PIANO ANTHOLOGY FOR THE YOUNG, BK. 05 - 10 PIECES	CESI, S. *
PIANO ANTHOLOGY FOR THE YOUNG, BK. 06 - 10 PIECES	CESI, S. *
PIANO ANTHOLOGY FOR THE YOUNG, BK. 07 - 13 PIECES	CESI, S. *
PIANO ANTHOLOGY FOR THE YOUNG, BK. 08 - 15 PIECES	CESI, S. *
PIANO ANTHOLOGY FOR THE YOUNG, BK. 10 - 14 PIECES	CESI, S. *
PIANO ANTHOLOGY FOR THE YOUNG, BK. 11 - 13 PIECES	CESI, S. *
PIANO ANTHOLOGY FOR THE YOUNG, BK. 12 - 14 PIECES	CESI, S. *
PIANO ANTICS IN BOOGIE STYLE	MELVIN, B.
PIANO ARPEGGIOS	GLOVER, D. *
PIANO AS ORCHESTRA, THE -- STUDIES IN SONORITIES	WILLNER, A.
PIANO BAZAAR	JOLLES
PIANO BEYOND, THE	HAUBIEL, C.
PIANO BOOKS FOR YOUNG PIANISTS -- A-BOOK FOR THE	GREEN, R.
PIANO BOOKS FOR YOUNG PIANISTS -- B-BOOK FOR THE	GREEN, R.
PIANO BOOKS FOR YOUNG PIANISTS -- C-BOOK FOR THE YOUNG	GREEN, R.
PIANO BOOKS FOR YOUNG PIANISTS -- D-BOOK FOR YOUNG	GREEN, R.
PIANO BOOKS FOR YOUNG PIANISTS -- E-BOOK FOR YOUNG	GREEN, R.
PIANO BOOKS FOR YOUNG PIANISTS -- F-BOOK FOR YOUNG	GREEN, R.
PIANO BOOK FOR ADULTS, BK. 1	NEVIN
PIANO BOOK FOR ADULTS, BK. 2	NEVIN
PIANO BOOK OF THE YOUNG HANDEL --10 PIECES--	HANDEL
PIANO CAMEOS	SCHER, W.
PIANO CLASSICS OF FOUR CENTURIES	RICHTER--ED
PIANO CLASSICS SIMPLIFIED	LEVINE, H.--ED
PIANO CLASSIC COLLECTION OF PIECES FOR THE	
PIANO COMPOSITIONS, BK. 1	BACH, C.P.E.
PIANO COMPOSITIONS, BK. 1	BEETHOVEN
PIANO COMPOSITIONS, BK. 2	BACH, C.P.E.
PIANO COMPOSITIONS, BK. 2	BACH, J.S.
PIANO COMPOSITIONS, BK. 2	BEETHOVEN
PIANO CONCERTO, OP. 38	BARBER, S.
PIANO CONCERTO, OP. 38	BARBER, S.
PIANO CONCERTO, OP. 54	SCHUMANN, R.
PIANO CONCERTO, OP. 90	PERSICHETTI
PIANO CONCERTO, THEME FROM FIRST MOVEMENT	TSCHAIKOWSKY
PIANO CONCERTO, THEME	RACHMANINOFF, S.
PIANO CONCERTO -- WITH ACCOMPANIMENT ARRANGED FOR	BLISS, A.
PIANO CONCERTO FOR TWO PIANOS IN C MINOR	BACH, J.S.
PIANO CONCERTO FOR TWO PIANOS IN C	BACH, J.S.
PIANO CONCERTO IN A MINOR, OP. 16. ABRIDGED	GRIEG
PIANO CONCERTO IN A MINOR, OP. 16. TWO PIANOS, EIGHT	GRIEG
PIANO CONCERTO IN A MINOR, OP. 16	GRIEG
PIANO CONCERTO IN A MINOR, THEME	GRIEG
PIANO CONCERTO IN A MINOR -- FIRST MOVEMENT	GRIEG
PIANO CONCERTO IN A MINOR	BACH, W.F.
PIANO CONCERTO IN B FLAT -- THEME AND VARIATION	TSCHAIKOWSKY
PIANO CONCERTO IN B FLAT MINOR, OP. 23	TSCHAIKOWSKY
PIANO CONCERTO IN B FLAT MINOR, THEME	TSCHAIKOWSKY
PIANO CONCERTO IN D FROM THE VIOLIN CONCERTO IN D, OP.	BEETHOVEN
PIANO CONCERTO IN D MINOR	BACH, J.S.
PIANO CONCERTO IN E MINOR	BACH, W.F.
PIANO CONCERTO IN F MINOR, OP. 16	HENSELT, A.
PIANO CONCERTO IN F MINOR	BACH, J.S.
PIANO CONCERTO NO. 01, EASY	TSCHAIKOWSKY
PIANO CONCERTO NO. 01 IN B FLAT MINOR, OP. 32	SCHARWENKA, X.
PIANO CONCERTO NO. 01 IN E FLAT	LISZT
PIANO CONCERTO NO. 01	BEETHOVEN
PIANO CONCERTO NO. 01	MORAWETZ
PIANO CONCERTO NO. 02, OP. 102	SHOSTAKOVITCH
PIANO CONCERTO NO. 02, OP. 22	SAINT-SAENS
PIANO CONCERTO NO. 02, OP. 22	SAINT-SAENS
PIANO CONCERTO NO. 02 IN A	LISZT
PIANO CONCERTO NO. 02 IN C MINOR -- THIRD MOVEMENT	RACHMANINOFF, S.
PIANO CONCERTO NO. 02	BEETHOVEN
PIANO CONCERTO NO. 02	RACHMANINOFF, S.
PIANO CONCERTO NO. 03, OP. 50 --"YOUTH"	KABALEVSKY
PIANO CONCERTO NO. 03 IN G MINOR, OP. 58	MOSCHELES, I.
PIANO CONCERTO NO. 03	BEETHOVEN
PIANO CONCERTO NO. 03	PROKOFIEFF
PIANO CONCERTO NO. 04, OP. 44	SAINT-SAENS
PIANO CONCERTO NO. 04	BEETHOVEN
PIANO CONCERTO NO. 05, OP. 103	SAINT-SAENS
PIANO CONCERTO NO. 05	BEETHOVEN
PIANO CONCERTO	BENNETT, R.
PIANO CONCERTO	BENNETT, R.
PIANO CONCERTO	BLISS, A.
PIANO CONCERTO	GRIEG
PIANO CONCERTO	GRIEG
PIANO CONCERTO	GRIEG
PIANO CONCERTO	HELPS
PIANO CONCERTO	HENSELT, A.
PIANO CONCERTO	JOUBERT, J.
PIANO CONCERTO	JOUBERT, J.
PIANO CONCERTO	KHATCHATURIAN
PIANO CONCERTO	TAILLEFERRE, G.
PIANO COURSE--TEACH ME TO PLAY--BK. 1	KASSCHAU, H.
PIANO COURSE--TEACH ME TO PLAY--BK. 2	KASSCHAU, H.
PIANO COURSE--TEACH ME TO PLAY--BK. 3	KASSCHAU, H.
PIANO COURSE--TEACH ME TO PLAY--BK. 4	KASSCHAU, H.
PIANO COURSE--TEACH ME TO PLAY--BK. 5	KASSCHAU, H.
PIANO COURSE--TEACH ME TO PLAY--PRELIMINARY BK.	KASSCHAU, H.
PIANO COURSE, BK. 1	AUBERGE, A. D'
PIANO COURSE, BK. 1	STEINER
PIANO COURSE, BK. 1	WAGNESS
PIANO COURSE, BK. 2	AUBERGE, A. D'
PIANO COURSE, BK. 2	STEINER
PIANO COURSE, BK. 2	WAGNESS
PIANO COURSE, BK. 3	AUBERGE, A. D'
PIANO COURSE, BK. 3	STEINER
PIANO COURSE, BK. 3	WAGNESS
PIANO COURSE, BK. 4	AUBERGE, A. D'
PIANO COURSE, BK. 4	STEINER
PIANO COURSE, BK. 5	AUBERGE, A. D'
PIANO COURSE, BK. 6	AUBERGE, A. D'
PIANO COURSE, PREPARATORY BOOK	WAGNESS
PIANO COURSE -- JUNIOR APPROACH	STEINER
PIANO COURSE -- SENIOR APPROACH	STEINER
PIANO COURSE - GRADE ONE, FRENCH EDITION	AARON, M.
PIANO COURSE - GRADE 1	AARON, M.
PIANO COURSE - GRADE 2, FRENCH EDITION	AARON, M.
PIANO COURSE - GRADE 2	AARON, M.
PIANO COURSE - GRADE 3, FRENCH EDITION	AARON, M.
PIANO COURSE - GRADE 3	AARON, M.
PIANO COURSE - GRADE 4	AARON, M.
PIANO COURSE - GRADE 5	AARON, M.
PIANO COURSE FOR JUNIORS, BK. 1	HIRSCHBERG, D.
PIANO COURSE FOR JUNIORS - PREPARATORY BOOK	HIRSCHBERG, D.
PIANO DIVERSIONS, BK. 1	ANTHONY, G.
PIANO DIVERSIONS, BK. 2	ANTHONY, G.
PIANO DUETS FOR CHILDREN	
PIANO DUETS FOR TWO YOUNG PUPILS	BILBRO, M.
PIANO DUETS OF THE CLASSICAL PERIOD	TOWSEND, D.--ED
PIANO DUETS THE WHOLE WORLD LOVES	WALLIS--ED
PIANO DUETS	CHOPIN
PIANO DUETS	COBB
PIANO DUETS	GLOVER, D. *
PIANO DUETS	GLOVER, D. *
PIANO DUETS	GLOVER, D.
PIANO DUETS	GLOVER, D.
PIANO DUET ALBUM OF BALLET FROM THE 'MELODY-WAY'	DEXTER, H.
PIANO DUET BOOK	AARON, M.
PIANO ECHOES	FEYER, G.
PIANO FANTASIE	FRANCO, C.
PIANO FANTASY	AITKEN, H.
PIANO FANTASY	MARTINO
PIANO FOR PLEASURE, BK. 1	GIRLAMO, F.
PIANO FOR PLEASURE, BK. 2	GIRLAMO, F.
PIANO FOR PLEASURE, BK. 3	GIRLAMO, F.
PIANO FOR PLEASURE, BK. 4	GIRLAMO, F.
PIANO FOR PLEASURE, BK. 5	GIRLAMO, F.
PIANO FOR PLEASURE, PREP BOOK	GIRLAMO, F.
PIANO FUNDAMENTALS -- BOOK 1-A	NAHUM *
PIANO FUNDAMENTALS -- STUDENT'S ASSIGNMENT BOOK	NAHUM *
PIANO FUNDAMENTALS -- TEACHER'S MANUAL	NAHUM *
PIANO FUN FARE	SCHAUM, J.
PIANO FUN WITH THEORY	POWERS, M.
PIANO FUN	MCCLUSKY
PIANO GAMES	DECESARE
PIANO HOUR, BK. 1 --175--	WEBBER--ED.
PIANO HOUR, BK. 2 --25--	WEBBER--ED.
PIANO HYMNSCRIPTIONS NO. 1	AULD, W. J.
PIANO HYMNSCRIPTIONS NO. 2	AULD, W. J.
PIANO HYMNS FOR THE LITURGICAL YEAR	GOODE
PIANO HYMN CLASSICS NO. 1	FRANK, R.
PIANO HYMN CLASSICS NO. 2	FRANK, R.
PIANO HYMN VOLUNTARIES. NOS 1, 2, AND 3	
PIANO INTERPRETATIONS, NO. 1	WILLIAMS, R.
PIANO INTERPRETATIONS, NO. 2	WILLIAMS, R.
PIANO INTERPRETATIONS, NO. 3	WILLIAMS, R.
PIANO IN PROGRESS, BK. 1	TANSMAN, A.
PIANO IN PROGRESS, BK. 2	TANSMAN, A.
PIANO LESSONS ARE FUN, BK. 1	HIRSCHBERG, D.
PIANO LITERATURE, BK. 1	CLARK, F.--ED.
PIANO LITERATURE, BK. 2	CLARK, F.--ED.
PIANO LITERATURE, BK. 3	CLARK, F.--ED.
PIANO LITERATURE, BK. 4 A	CLARK, F.--ED.
PIANO LITERATURE, BK. 4 B	CLARK, F.--ED.
PIANO LITERATURE, BK. 5 A	CLARK, F.--ED.
PIANO LITERATURE, BK. 5 B	CLARK, F.--ED.
PIANO LITERATURE, BK. 6 A	CLARK, F.--ED.
PIANO LITERATURE, BK. 6 B	CLARK, F.--ED.
PIANO LITERATURE, BK.1	BASTIEN--ED.
PIANO LITERATURE FOR THE INTERMEDIATE GRADES, BK. 3	BASTIEN--ED.
PIANO LITERATURE	BASTIEN--ED.
PIANO LYRICS AND SHORTER COMPOSITIONS	RIEG
PIANO MASTERPIECES	
PIANO MEDITATIONS FOR CHURCH AND HOME	HEAPS, S.--ED
PIANO METHOD. FRENCH TEXT	FERTE
PIANO METHOD, BK. 1	KOHLER, F.
PIANO METHOD, BK. 2	KOHLER, F.
PIANO METHOD, BK. 3	KOHLER, F.
PIANO METHOD FOR BEGINNERS	LAMBERT, A.
PIANO METHOD FOR CHILDREN, A--SPANISH AND ENGLISH	LECARPENTIER, A.
PIANO METHOD	BARTOK *
PIANO METHOD	FERTE
PIANO MISCELLANY	BINKERD
PIANO MOODS -- ORIGINAL MODERN PIANO SOLOS	KAHN, M.
PIANO MUSIC FOR BEGINNERS	SZARAI--ED. *
PIANO MUSIC FOR CHILDREN, VOL. 1	STRAVINSKY, S.

Title	Author
PIANO MUSIC FOR CHILDREN, VOL. 2	STRAVINSKY, S.
PIANO MUSIC FOR FOUR HANDS, BK. 1 -- CHILDREN- AND	SEDLACK, A.--ED
PIANO MUSIC FOR FOUR HANDS, BK. 2 FOLKSONGS AND DANCES	SEDLACK, A.--ED
PIANO MUSIC FROM AUSTRIA	KANN, H.--ED
PIANO MUSIC FROM SPAIN -- 15 PIECES FOR PIANO SOLO	ALBENIZ, I. *
PIANO MUSIC IN THE HOME, BK. 1	WEYBRIGHT--ED.
PIANO MUSIC IN THE HOME, BK. 1	WEYBRIGHT
PIANO MUSIC IN THE HOME, BK. 2	WEYBRIGHT
PIANO MUSIC IN THE HOME, BK. 3	WEYBRIGHT--ED.
PIANO MUSIC OF ALKAN, THE	ALKAN
PIANO MUSIC OF ERIC SATIE--ALBUM OF SELECTED WORKS	SATIE, E.
PIANO MUSIC ON FOLKSONGS, BK. 1 --OP. 40 --	MARX
PIANO MUSIC ON FOLKSONGS, BK. 2 --OP. 59 --	MARX
PIANO MUSIC READER, BK. 1	BRUGMANN, A.
PIANO MUSIC READER, BK. 2	BRUGMANN, A.
PIANO PARTNERS -- THE YOUNG PIANIST OR ADULT BEGINNER	DONALDSON, M.
PIANO PASTELS	ANTHEIL, G.
PIANO PEDAL SOLOS	GRAHAM
PIANO PIANO DIVERTISSMENTS	WAGNER, J.
PIANO PICTURES	FINLAYSON, W.
PIANO PIECE, OP. 33A	SCHOENBERG
PIANO PIECE, OP. 33B	SCHOENBERG
PIANO PIECES. COMPLETE	MOZART, W. A.
PIANO PIECES. SELECTED	MOZART, W. A.
PIANO PIECES, OP. 10, NOS. 1-7	RACHMANINOFF
PIANO PIECES, OP. 118	BRAHMS
PIANO PIECES, OP. 119	BRAHMS
PIANO PIECES, OP. 3, 9, 10, 16	HAUER, J.
PIANO PIECES, OP. 76	BRAHMS
PIANO PIECES --CLOTH--	BRAHMS
PIANO PIECES --SELECTION--	MOZART, W. A.
PIANO PIECES -- CLOTH	BEETHOVEN
PIANO PIECES -- CLOTH	HAYDN
PIANO PIECES -- SIMP.	
PIANO PIECES --11--	CHOPIN
PIANO PIECES --8--	DUSSEK, J.
PIANO PIECES FOR ADVANCED CHILDREN OR RETARDED ADULTS	LIEBERSON, G.
PIANO PIECES FOR ADVANCED CHILDREN OR RETARDED ADULTS	LIEBERSON, G.
PIANO PIECES FOR CHILDREN	
PIANO PIECES FOR PLEASURE	WILLIAMS, J.
PIANO PIECES FOR THE ADULT STUDENT	
PIANO PIECES FOR THE YOUNG STUDENT	
PIANO PIECES IN ONE VOLUME -- CLOTH	MOZART, W. A.
PIANO PIECES IN ONE VOLUME	MOZART, W. A.
PIANO PIECES THE WHOLE WORLD PLAYS	
PIANO PIECES	BEETHOVEN
PIANO PIECES	BEETHOVEN
PIANO PIECES	BRAHMS
PIANO PIECES	EINEM, G.
PIANO PIECES	HAYDN
PIANO PIECES	
PIANO PIECES	
PIANO PIECES 1-4	SMALLEY, R.
PIANO PIECES 1	BEDFORD, D.
PIANO PIECE 2	BEDFORD, D.
PIANO PLAYTIME, BK A	
PIANO PLAYTIME, BK B	
PIANO PLAYTIME, BK C	
PIANO PLAYTIME, BK D	
PIANO PLAYTIME, BK E	
PIANO PLAYTIME FOR BOYS	KING, S.
PIANO PLAYTIME FOR GIRLS	KING, S.
PIANO PLAYTIME	
PIANO PLAYTIME	
PIANO PLAY	MANA-ZUCCA
PIANO PLEASURE	WARD
PIANO PORTRAITS -- BK. 1 -- LOWER INTERMEDIATE GRADES	TEMPLETON, A.
PIANO PORTRAITS -- BK. 2 -- UPPER INTERMEDIATE GRADES	TEMPLETON, A.
PIANO PORTRAITS - SACRED SOLOS	SMITH, T.--ED
PIANO PRANKS	PORTNOFF
PIANO PRELUDES ON HYMNS AND CHORALES	GERIG, R.--ED
PIANO PRIMER	AARON, M.
PIANO PRIMER	CHING
PIANO PROGRESS--BOOK 1-A--LARGE NOTE EDITION	SCHAUB *
PIANO PROGRESS--BOOK 1-B--LARGE NOTE EDITION	SCHAUB *
PIANO PROGRESS--BOOK 2-A--LARGE NOTE EDITION	SCHAUB *
PIANO PROGRESS--BOOK 2-B--LARGE NOTE EDITION	SCHAUB *
PIANO PROGRESS--BOOK 3-A--LARGE NOTE EDITION	SCHAUB *
PIANO PROGRESS--BOOK 3-B--LARGE NOTE EDITION	SCHAUB *
PIANO PROGRESS, BOOK 1	SCHAUB *
PIANO PROGRESS, BOOK 2	SCHAUB *
PIANO PROGRESS, BOOK 3	SCHAUB *
PIANO REPERTOIRE	FROST
PIANO REPERTOIRE	GLOVER, D. *
PIANO REPERTOIRE	GLOVER, D. *
PIANO REPERTOIRE	GLOVER, D. *
PIANO REPERTOIRE	GLOVER, D. *
PIANO REPERTOIRE	GLOVER, D. *
PIANO REPERTOIRE	GLOVER, D.
PIANO REPERTOIRE	LUCKTENBERG *
PIANO SAMPLER	SCHER, W.--ED
PIANO SCENES	STEVENS, E.
PIANO SESSIONS - KINDERGARTEN SERIES‡ DANCING IN THE	MCGINLEY
PIANO SESSIONS - KINDERGARTEN SERIES‡ EVERYDAY PIECES	MCGINLEY
PIANO SESSIONS - KINDERGARTEN SERIES‡ FIRST WALTZ	MCGINLEY
PIANO SESSIONS - KINDERGARTEN SERIES‡ FUN AT THE FAIR	MCGINLEY
PIANO SESSIONS - KINDERGARTEN SERIES‡ LITTLE NOCTURNE	MCGINLEY
PIANO SESSIONS - KINDERGARTEN SERIES‡ LONG, LONG AGO	MCGINLEY
PIANO SESSIONS - KINDERGARTEN SERIES‡ ON TOP OF OLD	MCGINLEY
PIANO SESSIONS - KINDERGARTEN SERIES‡ READY TO PLAY	MCGINLEY
PIANO SESSIONS - KINDERGARTEN SERIES‡ RED RIVER VALLEY	MCGINLEY
PIANO SESSIONS - KINDERGARTEN SERIES‡ SONGS FOR	MCGINLEY
PIANO SESSIONS - KINDERGARTEN SERIES‡ STEPPING AND	MCGINLEY
PIANO SESSIONS - KINDERGARTEN SERIES‡ TRUDY TREBLE AND	MCGINLEY
PIANO SESSIONS - KINDERGARTEN SERIES‡ TWINKLE, TWINKLE	MCGINLEY
PIANO SESSIONS - KINDERGARTEN SERIES ‡ WALK IN THE	MCGINLEY
PIANO SESSIONS - KINDERGARTEN SERIES -‡ MR. AND MRS.	MCGINLEY
PIANO SESSIONS BASIC COURSE, BK. 1‡ EXPLORING MUSIC AT	MCGINLEY
PIANO SESSIONS BASIC COURSE, BK. 2‡ ADVENTURES IN	MCGINLEY
PIANO SESSIONS BASIC COURSE, BK. 3‡ KEYS TO CHORDS	MCGINLEY
PIANO SESSIONS BASIC COURSE, SUPP. MATERIAL FOR BK. 2‡	MCGINLEY
PIANO SET	JOLLES
PIANO SKETCHES	MANA-ZUCCA
PIANO SOLOS, VOL. 1 -- CLOTH	SCHUMANN, R.
PIANO SOLOS, VOL. 1	SCHUMANN, R.
PIANO SOLOS, VOL. 2 -- CLOTH	SCHUMANN, R.
PIANO SOLOS, VOL. 2	SCHUMANN, R.
PIANO SOLOS FROM 'THE EDDY DUCHIN STORY' --TO LOVE	
PIANO SOLOS	
PIANO SONATA, OP. 6	KURKA, R.
PIANO SONATA, OP. 94 NO. 2	TCHEREPNIN
PIANO SONATA, 1964	STEINER, G.
PIANO SONATA, 1966	MIMAROGLU, I.
PIANO SONATAS, BK. 1	HAYDN
PIANO SONATAS, BK. 2	HAYDN
PIANO SONATAS, BK. 3	HAYDN
PIANO SONATAS, BKS. 1, 2 AND 3	BEETHOVEN
PIANO SONATA -- IN PREPARATION --	WUORINEN
PIANO SONATA IN D MINOR	FINNEY
PIANO SONATA NO. 01	COPE, D.
PIANO SONATA NO. 01	FISHER, T.
PIANO SONATA NO. 01	GIGGY, F.
PIANO SONATA NO. 01	HAMILTON, I.
PIANO SONATA NO. 01	JOHNSON, R.
PIANO SONATA NO. 01	LADERMAN, E.
PIANO SONATA NO. 01	WILLNER, A.
PIANO SONATA NO. 02, OP. 26	COPE, D.
PIANO SONATA NO. 02	JOHNSON, R.
PIANO SONATA NO. 02	LADERMAN, E.
PIANO SONATA NO. 02	POZDRO, J.
PIANO SONATA NO. 03	COPE, D.
PIANO SONATA NO. 03	PERSICHETTI
PIANO SONATA NO. 03	RAPHLING
PIANO SONATA NO. 04	COPE, D.
PIANO SONATA NO. 04	COPE, D.
PIANO SONATA NO. 04	LEES, B.
PIANO SONATA NO. 04	PERSICHETTI
PIANO SONATA NO. 05	PERSICHETTI
PIANO SONATA NO. 06	PERSICHETTI
PIANO SONATA NO. 07	PERSICHETTI
PIANO SONATA NO. 08	PERSICHETTI
PIANO SONATA NO. 09	PERSICHETTI
PIANO SONATA NO. 10	PERSICHETTI
PIANO SONATA NO. 11	FULEIHAN, A.
PIANO SONATA NO. 11	PERSICHETTI
PIANO SONATA NO. 12	FULEIHAN, A.
PIANO SONATA NO. 14	FULEIHAN, A.
PIANO SONATA	BEN-HAIM
PIANO SONATA	BLISS, A.
PIANO SONATA	CARTER, E.
PIANO SONATA	JOHNSON, H.
PIANO SONATA	MATHIAS, W.
PIANO SONATA	SEARLE, H.
PIANO SONATA	SWANSON
PIANO SONATINA FOR YOUNG PERSONS	KURKA, R.
PIANO SONATINA	BAZELON, I.
PIANO SOUNDINGS	DUMM
PIANO STUDENTS CHOICE	SMALL, A.
PIANO STUDENT	GLOVER, D. *
PIANO STUDENT	GLOVER, D. *
PIANO STUDENT	GLOVER, D. *
PIANO STUDENT	GLOVER, D. *
PIANO STUDENT	GLOVER, D.
PIANO STUDENT	GLOVER, D.
PIANO STUDIES ON FOLKSONGS, BK. 1	MICHEELSEN
PIANO STUDIES ON FOLKSONGS, BK. 2	MICHEELSEN
PIANO STUDIES ON FOLKSONGS, BK. 3	MICHEELSEN
PIANO STUDIES	WIECK
PIANO STUDY--APPLICATION AND TECHNIQUE	PHILLIP, I.
PIANO STUDY	CRAWFORD, R.
PIANO STYLEPRINTS	DUMM
PIANO SUITE OP. 63	MOESCHINGER
PIANO SUITE	CUNNINGHAM, M.
PIANO TALK	MCCLUSKY
PIANO TEACHER'S COMPANION, THE -- CLOTHBOUND EDITION	MAIER, G.
PIANO TECHNIC, BK. 1	AARON, M.
PIANO TECHNIC, BK. 1	CLARK, F.--ED.
PIANO TECHNIC, BK. 2	AARON, M.
PIANO TECHNIC, BK. 2	CLARK, F.--ED.
PIANO TECHNIC, BK. 3	CLARK, F.--ED.
PIANO TECHNIC, BK. 4	CLARK, F.--ED.
PIANO TECHNIC, BK. 5	CLARK, F.--ED.
PIANO TECHNIC, BK. 6	CLARK, F.--ED.
PIANO TECHNIC	GLOVER, D. *
PIANO TECHNIC	GLOVER, D. *
PIANO TECHNIC	GLOVER, D. *
PIANO TECHNIC	GLOVER, D.
PIANO TECHNIC	GLOVER, D.
PIANO TECHNIC	GLOVER, D.
PIANO TECHNIQUE, BK. 1	DREWS
PIANO TECHNIQUE, BK. 2	DREWS
PIANO TECHNIQUE -- 'LE PIANO' --	LONG
PIANO TECHNIQUE	HURE
PIANO TECHNIQUE	TEICHMUELLER
PIANO THEORY	GLOVER, D. *
PIANO THEORY	GLOVER, D. *
PIANO THEORY	GLOVER, D. *
PIANO THEORY	GLOVER, D. *
PIANO THEORY	GLOVER, D. *
PIANO THEORY	GLOVER, D. *
PIANO THEORY	GLOVER, D. *
PIANO TIME	BLAKE, J. *
PIANO TRANSCRIPTIONS OF YOUR FAVORITE CHRISTMAS CAROLS	PARSONS
PIANO TRANSCRIPTIONS OF YOUR FAVORITE HYMNS	PARSONS
PIANO TUNER	PELS, W.
PIANO VARIATIONS, VOL. 1	STRAVINSKY, S.
PIANO VARIATIONS, VOL. 2	STRAVINSKY, S.
PIANO VARIATIONS	KODALY, E.
PIANO VARIATIONS	KOHS, E. B.
PIANO VOLUNTARIES NO. 1	ASHFORD
PIANO VOLUNTARIES ON HYMN TUNES	GOODE
PIANO VOLUNTARIES	MCKINNEY
PIANO VOLUNTARIES	PEERY, R. R.--ED
PIANO WARM-UPS	RICHTER
PIANO WITH A LATIN BEAT	FRANK, M.
PIANO WORKS, BK. 1, --OP. 1 TO OP. 24--	BRAHMS
PIANO WORKS, BK. 1 -- 19 SONATAS--	SCARLATTI, D.
PIANO WORKS, BK. 1	BRAHMS
PIANO WORKS, BK. 1	SCHUMANN, R.
PIANO WORKS, BK. 2, OP. 2, 7, 9 AND 18	SCHUMANN, R.
PIANO WORKS, BK. 2 --INCLUDES OP. 119 AND 5 ETUDES--	BRAHMS
PIANO WORKS, BK. 2 -- 18 SONATAS--	SCARLATTI, D.
PIANO WORKS, BK. 2	BRAHMS
PIANO WORKS, BK. 2	SCHUMANN, R.
PIANO WORKS, BK. 3, DAVIDSBUNDLER DANCES, OP. 6	SCHUMANN, R.
PIANO WORKS, BK. 3 -- 2 PIANO CONCERTI, PAGANINI	BRAHMS
PIANO WORKS, BK. 3	BRAHMS
PIANO WORKS, BK. 3	SCHUMANN, R.
PIANO WORKS, BK. 4	SCHUMANN, R.
PIANO WORKS, BK. 5	SCHUMANN, R.
PIANO WORKS, BK. 6	SCHUMANN, R.
PIANO WORKS, BK. 7	SCHUMANN, R.
PIANO WORKS, VOL. 1	BRAHMS
PIANO WORKS, VOL. 1	BRAHMS
PIANO WORKS, VOL. 1	HANDEL
PIANO WORKS, VOL. 2	BRAHMS
PIANO WORKS, VOL. 2	BRAHMS
PIANO WORKS, VOL. 2	HANDEL
PIANO WORKS, VOL. 3	HANDEL
PIANO WORKS, VOL. 4	HANDEL
PIANO WORKSHOP FOR YOUNG PIANISTS, BK. 1	GREEN, R.
PIANO WORKSHOP FOR YOUNG PIANISTS, BK. 2	GREEN, R.

PIANO WORKSHOP FOR YOUNG PIANISTS, BK. 3   GREEN, R.
PIANO WORKS --URTEXT-- IN 5 VOLUMES‡ VOL.1‡ 8 SUITES   HANDEL
PIANO WORKS --URTEXT-- IN 5 VOLUMES‡ VOL.2‡ 6 SUITES,   HANDEL
PIANO WORKS --URTEXT-- IN 5 VOLUMES‡ VOL.3‡ 2 SUITES,   HANDEL
PIANO WORKS --URTEXT-- IN 5 VOLUMES‡ VOL.4‡ 6 FUGUES,   HANDEL
PIANO WORKS --URTEXT-- IN 5 VOLUMES‡ VOL.5‡ PIANO BOOK   HANDEL
PIANO WORKS --2 VOLS.--. CLOTH-BOUND   BRAHMS
PIANO WORKS - SUPPLEMENT --URTEXT--. CAPRICCIOS--B   BACH, J.S.
PIANO WORKS   REICHA, A.
PICCADILLY CIRCUS   BURNAM
PICCADILLY CIRCUS   ERB
PICCADILLY WILLY   PERKINS, F.
PICCINO PICCIO - EASY PIECES ON 5 NOTES, SERIES 1   FERRARI-TRECATE
PICCINO PICCIO - EASY PIECES ON 5 NOTES, SERIES 2   FERRARI-TRECATE
PICCIOLI-5 SHORT PIECES   BALBO
PICCOLA DANZA   TANTILLO
PICCOLA GIAPPONESE   MONTANARI
PICCOLA SUITE   SANGIORGI
PICCOLE SCINTILLE - 15 EASY PIECES   POZZOLI
PICCOLI MARAT, IL -- COMPLETE OPERA --   MASCAGNI, P.
PICCOLI PIANISTI   GRAZIANI
PICCOLO, THE   RICHMAN, A.
PICCOLO 'GRADUS AD PARNASSUM' - 15 STUDIES PREPARATORY   POZZOLI
PICCOLO BARCAROLA   BOCCOSI, BIO
PICCOLO CONCERTO PER MURIEL COUVREUX FUR KLAVIER UND   DALLAPICCOLA
PICCOLO CONCERTO PER MURIEL COUVREUX FUR KLAVIER UND   DALLAPICCOLA
PICCOLO VALZER -- OP. POSTH. --   CATALANI
PICCOLO VALZER PER ROSARIA   SARDI, S.
PICKANINNY SERENADE   ECKSTEIN
PICKIN' UP PAW-PAWS   WEYBRIGHT
PICKING HOLLY   BRAGDON
PICKING PLUMS   HOWELL, C. R.
PICKLE CREEK DANCE   WESTON, P.
PICK A TUNE, BK. 1   DITTENHAVER
PICK A TUNE, BK. 2   DITTENHAVER
PICNIC FOR PELICANS   JACKSON, H.
PICNIC IN THE PARK   GARROW, L.
PICNIC PARTY   KREVIT, W.
PICNIC   DURING *
PICTURES AND TALES, OP. 2 -- 6 PIECES   WEIGL, K.
PICTURES AT AN ART EXHIBITION   MOUSSORGSKY
PICTURES AT AN EXHIBITION   MOUSSORGSKY
PICTURES AT AN EXHIBITION   MOUSSORGSKY
PICTURES AT AN EXHIBITION   MOUSSORGSKY
PICTURES AT AN EXHIBITION   MOUSSORGSKY
PICTURES AT AN EXPOSITION   MOUSSORGSKY
PICTURES AT THE PIANO   SCHER, W.
PICTURES FOR CHILDREN, OP. 37   REBIKOV
PICTURES FROM AN EXHIBITION   MOUSSORGSKY
PICTURES FROM AN EXHIBITION   MOUSSORGSKY
PICTURES FROM THE EAST, OP. 66   SCHUMANN, R.
PICTURES FROM THE EAST   SCHUMANN, R.
PICTURES FROM THE EAST   SCHUMANN, R.
PICTURES   WEYBRIGHT
PICTURE OF A MAN AND WIFE CONVERSING   SANDOVAL
PICTURE POINTERS   ECKSTEIN
PIECE, OP. 8   APOSTEL
PIECES AND SUITES   BARTOK
PIECES AN TITRES   TCHEREPNIN
PIECES ARE FUN, BK. 1   HIRSCHBERG, D.
PIECES ARE FUN, BK. 2   HIRSCHBERG, D.
PIECES ARE FUN, BK. 3   HIRSCHBERG, D.
PIECES A MARYJANE   WERNER, J.
PIECES BREVES, OP. 84   FAURE, G.
PIECES BREVES   DAMASE, J. M.
PIECES CHOISIES   RAMEAU
PIECES DE CLAVECIN, BK. 1   COUPERIN, F.
PIECES DE CLAVECIN, BK. 1   COUPERIN, F.
PIECES DE CLAVECIN, BK. 2   COUPERIN, F.
PIECES DE CLAVECIN, BK. 3   COUPERIN, F.
PIECES DE CLAVECIN, BK. 4   COUPERIN, F.
PIECES DE CLAVECIN, VOL. 1   COUPERIN, L.
PIECES DE CLAVECIN, VOL. 2   COUPERIN, L.
PIECES DE CLAVECIN - 1731   RAMEAU
PIECES DE CLAVECIN EN CONCERTS   RAMEAU
PIECES DE CLAVECIN   COUPERIN, F.
PIECES DE CLAVECIN   D'ANGLEBERT, J.
PIECES DE CLAVECIN   MATTHESON, J.
PIECES DE CLAVECIN   RAMEAU
PIECES DE CLAVECIN   RAMEAU
PIECES DE CLAVECIN   RAMEAU
PIECES DE CLAVECIN   RAMEAU
PIECES DE CLAVECIN 1   COUPERIN, F.
PIECES ENFANTINES, 1ST DEGREE   SANCAN, P.
PIECES ENFANTINES, 2ND DEGREE   SANCAN, P.
PIECES ESPAGNOLES   FALLA, M. DE
PIECES FOR ANGELA, OP. 47   LEIGHTON
PIECES FOR BARBARA   ZEISL, E.
PIECES FOR CHILDREN AND FOR GROWNUPS TO MAKE A NOTE OF   GREEN, R.
PIECES FOR CHILDREN   BARTOK
PIECES FOR CHILDREN   SCHOLZ
PIECES FOR ENJOYMENT   HIRSCHBERG, D.
PIECES FOR HARPSICHORD   HANDEL
PIECES FOR PIANO --PRELUDE, CORTEGE, BERCEUSE, DANCE--   ELWELL, H.
PIECES FOR PREPARED PIANO AND STRINGS. PIANO SOLO   MAYUZUMI
PIECES FOR PREPARED PIANO AND STRINGS. SCORE ALONE.   MAYUZUMI
PIECES FOR PREPARED PIANO AND STRINGS. SCORE AND PARTS   MAYUZUMI
PIECES FOR THE DEVELOPMENT OF TECHNIC   WRIGHT, N.
PIECES FOR THE DEVELOPMENT OF TECHNIC   WRIGHT, N.
PIECES FOR THE MUSICAL CLOCK   BEETHOVEN
PIECES FOR YOUNG PIANISTS   WILDER, A.
PIECES FROIDES - AIR A FAIRE FUIR   SATIE, E.
PIECES FROIDES - DANSE DE TRAVERS   SATIE, E.
PIECES FROM THE ITALIAN ROMANTICISTS   MONTANARI--ED *
PIECES INTIMES, OP. 88   COOLS
PIECES MINUSCULES POUR LES ENFANTS, BK. 1   LAZAR, F.
PIECES MINUSCULES POUR LES ENFANTS, BK. 2   LAZAR, F.
PIECES OF DREAMS   LANE, J.--ED.
PIECES OF EIGHT   MACERO
PIECES PITTORESQUES   CHABRIER
PIECES POETIQUES, BK. 1   SAUGET
PIECES POETIQUES, BK. 2   SAUGET
PIECES TRISTES   ROHOZINSKI
PIECES   GUILLOU, R.
PIECES   ZIPOLI
PIECE BREVE SUR LE NOM D'ALBERT ROUSSEL   POULENC, F.
PIECE EN FORME DE HABANERA   RAVEL
PIECE FOR PIANO   PARTOS, O.
PIECE HEROIQUE   FRANCK, C.
PIECE IN THE DORIAN MODE   ELAINE, M.
PIECE IN THE OLDEN STYLE   ROBBINS
PIECE ROMANTIQUE   MERIGOT, F.
PIECE   HARSANYI
PIEDIGROTTA 1924   CASTELNUOVO-TEDE
PIED PIPERS MARCH   KREVIT, W.
PIED PIPER   RAMSIER, P.
PIEGE DE MEDUSE, LE -- 7 PIECES --   SATIE, E.

PIERINO SI DIVERTE   FUGAZZA
PIERRETTE, OP. 41   CHAMINADE
PIERROT'S SERENADE   DESOLIS
PIERROTS, LES, WALTZ   STREABBOG
PIFF-PAFF   ENGELMANN, H. U.
PIGGY BANK TUNE   ECKSTEIN
PIGMENT -- BALLET IN 5 TABLEAUX   GEISSLER
PIJE KUBA, BOHEMIAN DANCE -- 8-HANDS, SET   MACGREGOR
PILAR, WALTZ, OP. 92, NO. 6 -- FROM 12 PIECES   ALBENIZ, I.
PILARICA, LA -- JOTA   ARIAS
PILGRIM'S CHORUS, FROM 'TANNHAUSER'   WAGNER
PILGRIM'S CHORUS   WAGNER
PILGRIMS' CHORUS, TANNHAUSER   WAGNER
PILGRIMS' CHORUS, TANNHAUSER   WAGNER
PILGRIM SUITE, THE   THOMPSON, J.
PILKY   JANACEK
PILLARS OF PIANO TECHNIC -- THE FIXED HAND, BK. A   PODOLSKY, L. *
PILLARS OF PIANO TECHNIC -- THE FIXED HAND, BK. B   PODOLSKY, L. *
PILLARS OF PIANO TECHNIC -- THE FIXED HAND, BK. C,   PODOLSKY, L. *
PILLARS OF PIANO TECHNIC -- THE FIXED HAND, BK. C,   PODOLSKY, L. *
PILLARS OF PIANO TECHNIC -- THE MOVING HAND   PODOLSKY, L. *
PILLARS OF PIANO TECHNIC -- THE STATIONARY HAND, BK. A   PODOLSKY, L. *
PILLARS OF PIANO TECHNIC -- THE STATIONARY HAND, BK. B   PODOLSKY, L. *
PILLOW FIGHT   ECKHARDT, F.
PINAFORE BALLET   MARTIN, H.
PINAFORE POLKA, THE   MARTIN, H.
PINBALL WIZARD   BRIMHALL,
PINCH A PENNY BOOGIE   REID
PINEAPPLES AND PALM TREES   MILLER, L.
PINEAPPLE POLKA   MARTIN, H.
PINEAPPLE POLL BALLET
PINEAPPLE RAG   JOPLIN, S.
PINES, THE   MATTHEWS, H. A.
PINETOP'S BLUES   SMITH
PINE CREEK   AMMONS *
PING-PONG PLAYERS   WERMEL
PING-PONG   MCGRAW
PING-PONG   ROZIN
PING PONG   ALT, H.
PING PONG   MCGRAW
PING PONG   STEINER
PINK, WALTZ   STREABBOG
PINKS   LEONI, F.
PINK BALLET   DUNGAN
PINK CLOVER   PORTER, C.
PINK LADY   STILWELL
PINK LEMONADE   WILSON
PINK MUSIC BOX   STRIMER, J.
PINK PANTHER   MANCINI
PINK PANTHER   MANCINI
PINK PETAL   SCHER, W.
PINK POODLE POLKA   REID
PINK   LICHNER, H.
PINOCCHIO, OP. 29   BOSSI, R.
PINOCCHIO SUITE   POZZOLI
PINWHEELS   BENFORD
PINWHEELS   GILLOCK
PIN WHEELS   KLAUSS, N.
PIPER'S TUNE, A   HAYES
PIPER AT THE GATES OF DAWN, THE   PILLING
PIPER OF SPRING, THE   GREENHILL, H.
PIPER PLAYS A TUNE, THE   DITTENHAVER
PIPES OF PAN   DOUGLAS
PIPES OF PAN   FISHER, E.
PIPE DREAM   HAMMERSTEIN *
PIPPERMINT GET -- WALTZ --   SEVERAC
PIRATE'S SONG   CARRE
PIRATE'S TALE, A   BROWN, L.
PIRATES' SONG   CARRE
PIRATES BOLD   WATSON
PIRATES CAVE   KEVAN, G. A.
PIRATES HORNPIPE   MCGRAW
PIRATE BOLD, A   GIOVANNI
PIRATE KING, THE   GILBERT AND
PIROUETTES   FERTE
PIROUETTES   STEINER
PIROUETTE   BERNSTEIN, M.
PIROUETTE   FRANK
PISANELLA, LA - 1. LA QUAI DU PORT DU FAMAGOUSTE   PIZZETTI
PISANELLA, LA - 2. LA DANZA DELLO SPARVIERO   PIZZETTI
PISANELLA, LA - 3. L'ESTAMPIE ROYALE   PIZZETTI
PISANELLA, LA - 4. LA DANSE DE L'AMOUR ET DE LA MORT   PIZZETTI
PISCHNA--TECHNICAL STUDIES   PISCHNA
PITTER PATTER   MACKOWN
PITTER PATTER   MACKOWN
PITTORESKEN, 4 PIANO-SOLI   FISCHER, E.
PITUSINES -- 4 EASY PIECES   AGUILAR
PIXIES' DANCE   KEYS
PIXIES' GAVOTTE, OP. 32 NO. 9   BROWN, A.
PIXIES' GOOD-NIGHT SONG, OP. 32 NO. 10   BROWN, A.
PIXIES' MARCH, THE   TAKACS, J.
PIXIES   CROCKER, D.
PIXIE PIANO BOOK   NUNEZ
PIXIE PIANO PLAYBOOK, BK. 2   NUNEZ
PIXIE TUNE SHOP   NUNEZ
PIXY PRANKS   HAYES
PIZZICATI--BALLET SYLVIA   DELIBES, L.
PIZZICATI--FROM 'SYLVIA'   DELIBES, L.
PIZZICATI FROM ''SYLVIA''   DELIBES, L.
PIZZICATI   DELIBES, L.
PIZZICATO, FROM 'RAYMONDA'   GLAZOUNOW, A.
PIZZICATO, POLKA, MILLIONS OF HARLEQUIN   DRIGO, R.
PIZZICATO POLKA   DELIBES, L.
PIZZICATO POLKA   STRAUSS, J.
PIZZICATO POLKA   STRAUSS, J.
PIZZICATO POLKA   STRAUSS, J.
PKK -- IN 1 BOOK   PROKOFIEFF *
PLABILES -- 12 SONGS WITHOUT WORDS   SHAW, A.
PLACES - SUITE   RUSSELL
PLACE IN THE SUN, A   MILLER
PLACID LAKE   WRIGHT, N.
PLACID LAKE   WRIGHT, N.
PLAINTES D'UNE POUPEE   FRANCK, C.
PLAINTIVE AIR   KRAMER, A. W.
PLAINT AT SUNDOWN   COOK
PLAINT   ELWELL, H.
PLAIN AND FANCY
PLAISIR D'AMOUR   MARTINI, G.
PLAISIR D'AMOUR   MARTINI, G.
PLAISIR D'AMOUR   MARTINI, G.
PLANTATION ECHOES   ROZIN
PLANTATION MELODY, OP. 11 NO. 3   SMITH, H.
PLANTATION PICNIC   REISER, V.
PLATINUM PUP, THE   ANSON, G.
PLAY-PARTY MEDLEY, A -- TUNES FROM CHILDHOOD   WEYBRIGHT
PLAY-WAY TO MUSIC SERIES - BY MYSELF, BOOK 1   FRISCH, F. T.
PLAY-WAY TO MUSIC SERIES - BY MYSELF, BOOK 2   FRISCH, F. T.

PLAY-WAY TO MUSIC SERIES - FUN ALL DAY, INTRODUCTORY	FRISCH, F. T.
PLAY-WAY TO MUSIC SERIES - HAPPY PLAYING, BOOK 1	FRISCH, F. T.
PLAY-WAY TO MUSIC SERIES - PLAY ALONG, BOOK 3	FRISCH, F. T.
PLAY-WAY TO MUSIC SERIES - SEE AND PLAY, BOOK 4	FRISCH, F. T.
PLAY-WAY TO MUSIC SERIES - SKIP ALONG, BOOK 2	FRISCH, F. T.
PLAYERA, OP. 5 NO. 5	GRANADOS
PLAYERA --E MINOR--	GRANADOS
PLAYFUL ECHO, THE	RICHTER
PLAYFUL KITTEN	RICCARDI, J.
PLAYFUL LITTLE KITTEN	BRUSSELS, I.
PLAYFUL LITTLE KITTEN	BRUSSELS, I.
PLAYFUL MOUSE, THE	WANDERMAN
PLAYFUL NYMPHS	LEE, E.
PLAYFUL PIANO --8 EASY SOLOS--	ROZIN
PLAYFUL PONIES	MCCLUSKY
PLAYFUL POODLE	REICH, M.
PLAYFUL PORPOISE	CRUICKSHANK
PLAYFUL PRANKS	RAEZER, C.
PLAYFUL PUPPY	CRERIE, E.
PLAYFUL RONDO	GREENE
PLAYFUL WIND	ARNOLD, H.
PLAYGROUND MARCH	BORASTON, M.
PLAYGROUND PANORAMA	BURNAM
PLAYGROUND	HEDGES
PLAYING AND SINGING THROUGH THE YEAR	PRIGGE, D.
PLAYING A GAME	BRUSSELS, I.
PLAYING BALL, OP. 27	KABALEVSKY
PLAYING CHECKERS	WEISLEDER, A.
PLAYING CLASSICS FOR PLEASURE	SPIVAK, S.--ED
PLAYING COWBOY	ROBINSON, A.
PLAYING FOR PLEASURE	SCHER, W.
PLAYING HOPSCOTCH	HOWELL
PLAYING IN THE SUNLIGHT	MARTIN, G.
PLAYING JACKS	ANDRE
PLAYING JACKS	GEORGE
PLAYING OPERATIC DUETS FOR PLEASURE, BK. 1 -- SIMP.	SPIVAK, S.--ED
PLAYING OPERATIC DUETS FOR PLEASURE, BK. 2 -- SIMP.	SPIVAK, S.--ED
PLAYING PIANO FOR PLEASURE, BK. 1	SPIVAK, S.--ED
PLAYING PIANO FOR PLEASURE, BK. 2	SPIVAK, S.--ED
PLAYING PIANO FOR PLEASURE, BK. 3	SPIVAK, S.--ED
PLAYING PLEASURE	
PLAYING SOLDIERS, MARCH	HOPKINS, H.
PLAYING TAG	HART
PLAYING TAG	VANNORT, I.
PLAYING THE PIANO, PART 2, FINGERS	MUNN, S.
PLAYING THE PIANO	MAIER, G.
PLAYING THROUGH THE HISTORY OF THE PIANO	STEINER
PLAYING TOGETHER	
PLAYING TO LEARN, BK. 1	STECHER *
PLAYING TO LEARN, BK. 2	STECHER *
PLAYING TO LEARN, BK. 3	STECHER *
PLAYING TO LEARN, BK. 4	STECHER *
PLAYING WITH CHORDS	GORNSTON *
PLAYING WITH PHRASES	SANDBOURNE
PLAYING WITH PLEASURE, BK. 1 -- A FIRST YEAR BOOK FOR	WEYBRIGHT
PLAYLAND SKETCHES	ROGERS
PLAYMATES	HAINES, H.
PLAYMATES	HOWELL, C. R.
PLAYTHINGS FOR PIANO	ALEXANDER, J.
PLAYTIME AT THE PIANO, BK.1	BASTIEN
PLAYTIME AT THE PIANO, BK.2	BASTIEN
PLAYTIME	FICHANDLER, W.
PLAYTIME	MAY, M.
PLAYTIME	PANELLA, L.
PLAYTIME	STEVENS, E.
PLAYTIME	THOMAS, C. J.
PLAY ALL THE TIME SIGNATURES	BURNAM
PLAY ALONG, BK. 3	FRISCH, F. T.
PLAY AND LISTEN	STEINER
PLAY AND SING YOUR FAVORITE SONGS	BROWN--ED
PLAY AND SING	RICHTER, A.--ED.
PLAY AND THINK	STEINER
PLAY AWAY SUITE NO. 1	FLETCHER
PLAY AWAY SUITE NO. 2	FLETCHER
PLAY AWAY SUITE NO. 3	FLETCHER
PLAY AWAY SUITE NO. 4	FLETCHER
PLAY BY TWOS BK. 1	BRIMHALL,
PLAY BY TWOS BK. 2	BRIMHALL,
PLAY FIDDLE PLAY	ALTMAN *
PLAY FIDDLE PLAY	DEUTSCH
PLAY GYPSIES - DANCE GYPSIES	KALMAN
PLAY GYPSIES - DANCE GYPSIES	KALMAN
PLAY IT NOW --BIG NOTE-- --150--	
PLAY PEN BOOK, THE	THOMAS, A.
PLAY PIANO LIKE ANDRE PREVIN, NO. 1	PREVIN, A.
PLAY PIANO LIKE ANDRE PREVIN, NO. 2	PREVIN, A.
PLAY PIANO LIKE GEORGE SHEARING	SHEARING, G.
PLAY PIANO OR ORGAN BY EAR	HENDERSON, R.
PLAY POPULAR - BE POPULAR	BERMONT, H.
PLAY THAT TUNE, BK. 1	BERMONT, H.--ED
PLAY THAT TUNE, BK. 2	BERMONT, H.--ED
PLAY THAT TUNE, BK. 3	BERMONT, H.--ED
PLAY THAT TUNE, BK. 4	BERMONT, H.--ED
PLAY THEM RAGS	
PLAY THE PIANO	FROST
PLAY THE SCALE OF C	BRONSON, M.
PLAY THE THING	MORRIS, C.
PLAY TIME ONE	GEORGE
PLAY TIME TWO	GEORGE
PLAY TIME 1	GEORGE
PLAY TIME 2	GEORGE
PLAY WITH PLEASURE -- AN ALBUM FOR THE GROWN-UP PIANO	FELTON, W.--ED
PLAY	MONSOUR *
PLEASANT DAY, A	FROST
PLEASANT DAY	TRUXELL, E.
PLEASANT DREAMS	KARP
PLEASANT PEASANT	SCHUMANN, R.
PLEASE DO COME TO THE FAIR	KLEINMAN, A.
PLEASURES OF YOUTH, OP. 163	DIABELLI
PLEASURES OF YOUTH, OP. 163	DIABELLI
PLEASURES OF YOUTH -- 6 SONATINAS ON 5 NOTES, OP. 163	DIABELLI
PLEASURES OF YOUTH	DIABELLI
PLEASURE PIECES	THORNTON
PLECTROS II -- 1966-I, FOR PIANO AND ELECTRONIC SOUNDS	LANZA, A.
PLECTROS I -- 1962-II, FOR ONE OR TWO PIANOS	LANZA, A.
PLEIN AIR	GUILLOU, R.
PLEIN SOLEIL	DE LA TOMBELLE
PLINK, PLANK, PLUNK	ANDERSON, L.
PLUIE DE BRILLANTS	VOLPATTI
PLUIE DE CORAIL, CAPRICE BRILLANT	DURAND DE CRAU
PLUIE DE CORAIL	DURAND DE CRAU
PLUIE DE DIAMANTS --SPARKLING SHOWERS--, OP. 160	WALDTEUFEL, E.
PLUIE DE FEU	STEFFENS, W.
PLUIE DE PERLES, LA -- WALTZ --	OSBORNE
POCHADES ANDALOUSES	INFANTE
POCHADES	LELEU
POEM, OP. 41, NO. 14	FIBICH, Z.
POEM, ROMANCE	FIBICH, Z.
POEMA AUTUNNALE	DE ANGELIS
POEMA FANTASTICO, OP. 98	TURINA, J.
POEMA SINGELO	VILLA-LOBOS, H.
POEME, OP. 71 NO. 1	SCRIABINE, A.
POEMES, OP. 69 NOS. 1 AND 2	SCRIABINE, A.
POEMES VIRGILIENS	DUBOIS, T.
POEMETTI - 12 PIECES	MENOTTI
POEMETTI LUNARI	MALIPIERO, G. F.
POEMETTI PASTORALI	DAVICO
POEMETTI	MENOTTI
POEME "CONTEMPLATION", OP. 5	BACEVICIUS
POEME ASTRAL, OP. 7	BACEVICIUS
POEME CONCERTANT	KULLMANN
POEME COSMIQUE, OP. 65	BACEVICIUS
POEME DES RIVAGES	D'INDY, V.
POEME FOR LEFT HAND, OP. 17	POHL, V.
POEME IN FORME D'UNE SONATE, OP. POSTH.	SCRIABINE, A.
POEME IN F SHARP, OP. 32 NO. 1	SCRIABINE, A.
POEME MYSTIQUE, OP. 6	BACEVICIUS
POEME NO. 40, OP. 10	BACEVICIUS
POEME PASTORAL	CARON-LEGRIS
POEME SATANIQUE, OP. 36	SCRIABINE, A.
POEME TRAGIQUE, OP. 34	SCRIABINE, A.
POEME	BOUTNIKOFF
POEME	COPPOLA, P.
POEME	READ, G.
POEMI	SCELSI
POEMS FOR PIANO, BK. 1	PERSICHETTI
POEMS FOR PIANO, BK. 2	PERSICHETTI
POEMS OF THE SEA--CYCLE	BLOCH, E.
POEMS	SCOTT, C.
POEM --MY MOONLIGHT MADONNA--	FIBICH, Z. *
POEM -- DRIFTING DOWN THE LAGOON --	FIBICH, Z.
POEM -- ERLEICHTERT -- UND FRUHLING UND JUGEND	FIBICH, Z.
POEM -- ORIGINAL -- UND IMAGE	FIBICH, Z.
POEM	FIBICH, Z.
POEM	FIBICH, Z.
POEM	FIBICH, Z.
POEM	KHATCHATURIAN
POESIES, OP. 74--AU CHEMIN SEME DE ROSES	POLDINI, E.
POESIES, OP. 74--CONTE PLAISANT	POLDINI, E.
POET'S NOTEBOOK, A	STOKER
POET'S REVERIE	HEINS, P.
POETICAL IMPRESSIONS, OP. 85 -- VOL. 1	DVORAK
POETICAL IMPRESSIONS, OP. 85 -- VOL. 2	DVORAK
POETICAL IMPRESSIONS, OP. 85 -- VOL. 3	DVORAK
POETIC IMPRESSIONS, OP. 85 - NO. 8 DANCE OF THE	DVORAK
POETIC IMPRESSIONS, OP. 85	DVORAK
POETIC STUDIES, OP. 53 AND 59	HABERBIER, E.
POETIC TONE-PICTURES, OP. 3	GRIEG
POETIC TONE-PICTURES, OP. 85	DVORAK
POETIC TONE PICTURE	GRIEG
POETIQUE DU PIANO, VOL.1	BELAUBRE, L.
POETIQUE DU PIANO, VOL.2	BELAUBRE, L.
POET AND PEASANT, OVERTURE	SUPPE, F.
POET AND PEASANT OVERTURE	SUPPE, F.
POET AND PEASANT OVERTURE	SUPPE, F.
POET AND PEASANT OVERTURE	SUPPE, F.
POET AND PEASANT OVERTURE	SUPPE, F.
POET AND PEASANT OVERTURE	SUPPE, F.
POGO STICK, THE	KEVAN
POGO STICK PARADE	MCSWEEN, F. W.
POINCIANA	SIMON
POINTER LIBRARY - A TREASURY OF INSPIRATIONAL SONGS	FORD, T. E.
POINTER LIBRARY - CAVALCADE OF POPS	
POINTER LIBRARY - FAMOUS HYMNS	
POINTER LIBRARY - GOLDEN POPS	
POINTER LIBRARY - HITS, HITS, HITS, VOL. 1	
POINTER LIBRARY - HITS, HITS, HITS, VOL. 2	
POINTER LIBRARY - MEMORIES OF CHRISTMAS	
POINTER LIBRARY - PARADE OF POPS, VOL. 1	
POINTER LIBRARY - PARADE OF POPS, VOL. 2	
POINTER LIBRARY - POPS FOR PLEASURE	
POINTER LIBRARY - POPS OF THE 60'S	
POINTER LIBRARY - POPS OF YESTERYEAR	
POINTER LIBRARY - POP PROMENADE	
POINTER LIBRARY - ROMANTIC OPERETTA	
POINTER LIBRARY - THEMES FROM THE CLASSICS	
POINTER LIBRARY - THE BEST OF COLE PORTER	PORTER, C.
POINTER LIBRARY - THE BEST OF GEORGE GERSHWIN	GERSHWIN
POINTER LIBRARY - THE BEST OF JEROME KERN	KERN, J.
POINTER LIBRARY - THE BEST OF LENNON AND MCCARTNEY	LENNON *
POINTER LIBRARY - THE NEW POPS	
POINTER LIBRARY - WORDS AND MUSIC BY IRVING BERLIN,	BERLIN, I.
POINTER LIBRARY - WORDS AND MUSIC BY IRVING BERLIN,	BERLIN, I.
POINTER SYSTEM - CAROLS	
POINTER SYSTEM - CLASSICS	
POINTER SYSTEM - FAVORITE SONGS	
POINTER SYSTEM - FOLK SONGS	
POINTER SYSTEM - GAY NINETIES	
POINTER SYSTEM - HOLIDAYS IN SONG	
POINTER SYSTEM - HYMNS	
POINTER SYSTEM - LATIN MOODS	
POINTER SYSTEM - SONGS OF MANY LANDS	
POINTER SYSTEM - SONGS THAT LIVE FOREVER	
POINTER SYSTEM - SONG MEMORIES	
POINTER SYSTEM - WALTZES OF VIENNA	
POINTER SYSTEM - WALTZES	
POINTER SYSTEM FOR PIANO, BK. 1	
POINTER SYSTEM FOR PIANO, BK. 2	
POINTER SYSTEM FOR PIANO, BK. 3	
POINTER SYSTEM FOR PIANO, BK. 4	
POINTER SYSTEM FOR PIANO, BK. 5	
POINT PANIC	SURFARIS
POLACCA, OP. 61 NO. 1	SCHUBERT
POLACCA BRILLANTE OP. 72	WEBER, VON
POLACCA	HELLER
POLAR BEARS, OP. 22 NO. 1	VIOLLE, B.
POLAR BEAR POLKA	CATIZONE, J. M.
POLCHINELLE	MALEZIEUX
POLICHINELLE, LA	VILLA-LOBOS, H.
POLICHINELLE, OP. 3 NO. 4	RACHMANINOFF, S.
POLICHINELLE, OP. 3 NO. 4	RACHMANINOFF, S.
POLICHINELLE, OP. 3 NO. 4	RACHMANINOFF, S.
POLICHINELLE	RACHMANINOFF, S.
POLICHINELLE	RACHMANINOFF, S.
POLICHINELLE	RACHMANINOFF, S.
POLISH CONTEMPORARY PIANO MINIATURES	
POLISH DANCE, A	SCHARWENKA, X.
POLISH DANCE, NO. 01	SCHARWENKA, X.
POLISH DANCE, OP. 3 NO. 1	SCHARWENKA, X.
POLISH DANCE, OP. 3 NO. 1	SCHARWENKA, X.
POLISH DANCE, OP. 3 NO. 1	SCHARWENKA, X.
POLISH DANCE, OP. 52	THOMA
POLISH DANCE IN E FLAT MINOR, OP. 3 NO. 1	SCHARWENKA, X.
POLISH DANCE NO. 1	SCHARWENKA, X.

POLISH DANCE	KETTERER, E.
POLISH DANCE	SCHARWENKA, X.
POLISH DANCE	SCHARWENKA, X.
POLISH DANCE	SCHARWENKA, X.
POLISH FANTASY, OP. 19	PADEREWSKI, I.
POLISH FESTIVAL DAY	HOLT, EILSEL
POLISH FOLK DANCES, OP. 55	MOSZKOWSKI
POLISH NATIONAL DANCE, OP. 3 NO. 1	SCHARWENKA, X.
POLISH NATIONAL DANCE	WIENIAWSKI
POLISH PEASANTS	REBE
POLISH WEDDING DANCE	OBENCHAIN, V.
POLKA-BURLESQUE	ROWLEY
POLKA, AGE D'OR	SHOSTAKOVITCH
POLKA, BARTERED BRIDE	SMETANA
POLKA, FROM THE BALLET 'L'AGE D' OR', OP. 22	SHOSTAKOVITCH *
POLKA, FROM THE BALLET 'THE GOLDEN AGE, OP. 22	SHOSTAKOVITCH
POLKAS	SMETANA
POLKA -- FROM BALLET L'AGE D'OR	SHOSTAKOVITCH
POLKA -- L'EVENTAIL DE JEANNE	MILHAUD, D.
POLKA AUS DER OPER 'DIE VERKAUFTE BRAUT'	SMETANA
POLKA BAND, THE	TAKACS, J.
POLKA BOHEME, OP. 82 NO. 7	RUBINSTEIN
POLKA BOOK	SCHAUM, J.--ED.
POLKA DES SOURIS BLANCHES	ALLIER
POLKA DE L'EQUILIBRISTE	BLANCAFORT
POLKA DOTS AND MOONBEAMS	
POLKA DOTS	ANSON, G.
POLKA DOTS	HODGSON, H.
POLKA DOT POLKA	BEYER, F.
POLKA DOT POLKA	BRAGDON
POLKA DOT PONY, THE	SCHER, W.
POLKA DOT	ELLIOTT
POLKA FESTIVAL	ROLFE, W.
POLKA FESTIVAL	SCHAUM, J.--ED.
POLKA FROM THE 'GOLDEN AGE'	SCHAUM, J.
POLKA FROM THE BALLET 'L'AGE D'OR', OP. 22	SHOSTAKOVITCH
POLKA FUGATA	SHOSTAKOVITCH
POLKA IN A MINOR	WARRACK, G.
POLKA IN F SHARP MAJOR, OP. 7, NO. 1	SMETANA
POLKA LAND	SMETANA
POLKA MAZURKA	KLEINMAN, A.
POLKA PETITE	ROBINSON, A.
POLKA SONATINA NO. 1	GREEN, R.
POLKA SONATINA NO. 2	GREEN, R.
POLKA SONATINA NO. 3	GREEN, R.
POLKA	BECUCCI
POLKA	CZERNY
POLKA	FICHER
POLKA	GRETCHANINOFF
POLKA	HOWELLS, H.
POLKA	MAYKAPAR
POLKA	MAYKAPAR
POLKA	TCHEREPNIN
POLKA	TSCHAIKOWSKY
POLKA	WEYBRIGHT
POLLUTION SOLUTION	SCHAUM, J.
POLLY'S LULLABY	DAVIS
POLLY AND PEGGY	PROEHL, H.
POLLY PUT THE KETTLE ON	ROLFE, W.--ED
POLLY WANTS A CRACKER	SCHER, W.
POLLY WOLLY BOOGIE	GARROW, L.
POLLY WOLLY DOODLE	ARMOUR--ED
POLLY WOLLY SWINGS	KARP, D.
POLLY	ZAMECNIK
POLLY	ZAMECNIK
POLLY	ZAMECNIK
POLL PARROT	COBB
POLO, EL -- FROM IBERIA	ALBENIZ, I.
POLONAISE, OP. 21	SCRIABINE, A.
POLONAISE, OP. 22--GRANDE POLONAISE BRILLANTE	CHOPIN
POLONAISE, OP. 22, ANDANTE SPINATO AND GRAND POLONAISE	CHOPIN
POLONAISE, OP. 26 NO. 1	CHOPIN
POLONAISE, OP. 40 NO. 1 'MILITARY'	CHOPIN
POLONAISE, OP. 42	BEETHOVEN
POLONAISE, OP. 44	CHOPIN
POLONAISE, OP. 46 NO. 12 -- SET	MACDOWELL
POLONAISE, OP. 53 'HEROIC'	CHOPIN
POLONAISE, OP. 53 'HEROIC'	CHOPIN
POLONAISE, OP. 53	CHOPIN
POLONAISE, OP. 53	CHOPIN
POLONAISE, OP. 53	CHOPIN
POLONAISE, OP. 53	CHOPIN
POLONAISE, OP. 65 MO. 8	ARENSKY, A.
POLONAISE, OP. 7 --PIANO, 6 HANDS--	KRAMER
POLONAISE, OP. 72	WEBER, VON
POLONAISE, OP. 77	SAINT-SAENS
POLONAISES--CRITICAL COMMENTARY	CHOPIN
POLONAISES, NOS. 01 AND 02	BACH, W.F.
POLONAISES, NOS. 03 AND 04	BACH, C.P.E.
POLONAISES, NOS. 05 AND 06	BACH, W.F.
POLONAISES, NOS. 07 AND 08	BACH, W.F.
POLONAISES, NOS. 09 AND 10	BACH, W.F.
POLONAISES, NOS. 11 AND 12	BACH, W.F.
POLONAISES -- CLOTH	CHOPIN
POLONAISES --10--	CHOPIN
POLONAISES	CHOPIN
POLONAISES	CHOPIN
POLONAISES	CHOPIN
POLONAISES	CHOPIN
POLONAISES	CHOPIN
POLONAISES	CHOPIN
POLONAISES	CHOPIN
POLONAISES	CHOPIN
POLONAISES	CHOPIN
POLONAISE AMERICAINE	CARPENTER, J.
POLONAISE BRILLANTE, OP. 72	WEBER, VON *
POLONAISE BRILLANTE, OP. 72	WEBER, VON *
POLONAISE BRILLANTE IN E-FLAT, OP. 72	WEBER, VON
POLONAISE D'AMOUR	SCHWAB
POLONAISE E FLAT , FOUR HANDS	SUPPUS, P.A.
POLONAISE FOR TWO	BRYANT--ED.
POLONAISE FROM 'MIGNON'	STEINER--ED.
POLONAISE IN A, OP. 40 NO. 1 --MILITAIRE--	CHOPIN
POLONAISE IN A, OP. 40 NO. 1 'MILITAR'	CHOPIN
POLONAISE IN A, OP. 40 NO. 1	CHOPIN
POLONAISE IN A, OP. 40 NO. 1	CHOPIN
POLONAISE IN A, OP. 40 NO. 1 --MILITARY--	CHOPIN
POLONAISE IN A FLAT, OP. 53 'OCTAVEN'	CHOPIN
POLONAISE IN A FLAT, OP. 53	CHOPIN
POLONAISE IN A FLAT, OP. 53	CHOPIN
POLONAISE IN A FLAT, OP. 53	CHOPIN
POLONAISE IN A FLAT, OP. 53	CHOPIN
POLONAISE IN A FLAT MAJOR, OP. 53	CHOPIN
POLONAISE IN A FLAT MAJOR, OP. 53	CHOPIN
POLONAISE IN A FLAT	CHOPIN
POLONAISE IN B FLAT, OP. 71 NO. 2	CHOPIN
POLONAISE IN B FLAT MINOR, OP. 21	SCRIABINE, A.
POLONAISE IN C, OP. 89	BEETHOVEN
POLONAISE IN C, OP. 89	BEETHOVEN
POLONAISE IN C MINOR, OP. 40 NO. 2	CHOPIN
POLONAISE IN C MINOR, OP. 40 NO. 2	CHOPIN
POLONAISE IN C MINOR	CHOPIN
POLONAISE IN C SHARP MINOR, OP. 26 NO. 1 'DRAMATISCH'	CHOPIN
POLONAISE IN C SHARP MINOR, OP. 26 NO. 1	CHOPIN
POLONAISE IN C SHARP MINOR, OP. 26 NO. 1	CHOPIN
POLONAISE IN C SHARP MINOR, OP. 26 NO. 1	CHOPIN
POLONAISE IN C	MOZART, L.
POLONAISE IN D, OP. 17 NO. 1	MOSZKOWSKI
POLONAISE IN E FLAT MINOR, OP. 26 NO. 2	CHOPIN
POLONAISE IN E FLAT MINOR, OP. 26 NO. 2	CHOPIN
POLONAISE IN E FLAT	DVORAK
POLONAISE IN E FLAT	DVORAK
POLONAISE IN G MINOR	BACH, J.S.
POLONAISE MILITAIRE, EASY	CHOPIN
POLONAISE MILITAIRE, OP. 40 NO. 1	CHOPIN
POLONAISE MILITAIRE, OP. 40 NO. 1	CHOPIN
POLONAISE MILITAIRE IN A, OP. 40 NO. 1	CHOPIN
POLONAISE MILITAIRE	CHOPIN
POLONAISE MILITAIRE	CHOPIN
POLONAISE NO. 02 IN E	LISZT
POLONAISE NO. 2	LISZT
POLONAISE ROMANTIQUE	SCHER, W.
POLONAISE	CHOPIN
POLONAISE	DE LEONE, F. D.
POLONAISE	THOMAS, A.
POLONAISE	WAGNER
POLONESA, OP. 92, NO. 9 -- FROM 12 PIECES	ALBENIZ, I.
POLOVETSIAN DANCE, PRINCE IGOR	BORODIN, A.
POLOVETSIAN DANCES, FROM 'PRINCE IGOR'	BORODIN, A.
POLTERGEIST, THE	MELVIN, B.
POLYCHROMATICS, OP. 16	GRUENBERG, L.
POLYMELODIE PREPARATOIRE	FRANCAIX, J.
POLYNESIAN NOCTURNE	GILLOCK
POLYNESIAN SUNSET	GARROW, L.
POLYPHEME -- LE SOMMEIL DE GALATHEE --	CRAS
POLYPHONES KLAVIERSPIEL, HEFT 01	EMONTS, F.
POLYPHONES KLAVIERSPIEL, HEFT 02	EMONTS, F.
POLYPHONE STUDIEN FUR ORCHESTER UND OBLIGATES KLAVIER	KARKOSCHKA
POLYPHONIC STUDIES, VOL. 1	HENGEVELD
POLYPHONIC STUDIES, VOL. 2	HENGEVELD
POLYPHONIE II	GUYONNET, J.
POLYRHYTHMS, OP. 50	ROWLEY
POMPONNETTE--AIR A DANSER, OP. 80	DURAND, A.
POMPONNETTE, AIR DE LOUIS XIV	DURAND, A.
POMPONNETTE	DURAND, A.
POMP AND CIRCUMSTANCE --ORIG--	ELGAR, E.
POMP AND CIRCUMSTANCE --THEME--	ELGAR, E.
POMP AND CIRCUMSTANCE - FULL CHORD VERSION	ELGAR, E.
POMP AND CIRCUMSTANCE - SMALL CHORD VERSION	ELGAR, E.
POMP AND CIRCUMSTANCE MARCH --8 HANDS--	ELGAR, E.
POMP AND CIRCUMSTANCE MARCH NO. 1 IN D	ELGAR, E.
POMP AND CIRCUMSTANCE MARCH NO. 1 IN D	ELGAR, E.
POMP AND CIRCUMSTANCE MARCH NO. 1	ELGAR, E.
POMP AND CIRCUMSTANCE MARCH NO. 4 IN G	ELGAR, E.
POMP AND CIRCUMSTANCE MARCH NO . 1 IN D	ELGAR, E.
POMP AND CIRCUMSTANCE MARCH	ELGAR, E.
POMP AND CIRCUMSTANCE MARCH	ELGAR, E.
POMP AND CIRCUMSTANCE NO. 1 IN D, OP. 39	ELGAR, E.
POMP AND CIRCUMSTANCE	ELGAR, E.
POMP AND CIRCUMSTANCE	ELGAR, E.
POMP AND PAGEATRY	COBB
PONANT 19	CONSTANT
POND IN THE WOOD, THE	WEYBRIGHT
PONIES PARADE	RAEZER, C.
PONIES	REBE
PONTEIOS -- PRELUDES -- BK. 2 -- 1-10 --	GUARNIERI
PONTEIOS -- PRELUDES -- BK. 2 -- 11-20 --	GUARNIERI
PONTEIOS -- PRELUDES -- BK. 3 -- 21-30 --	GUARNIERI
PONTEIOS -- PRELUDES -- BK. 4 -- 31-40 --	GUARNIERI
PONTEIOS -- PRELUDES -- BK. 5 -- 41-50 --	GUARNIERI
PONY RACE, OP. 70	FRIML, R.
PONY RACE	FROST
PONY RIDE, A	CLARK, J.
PONY RIDE, A	ERB
PONY RIDE, A	STAIRS, L.
PONY RIDE, THE - WALTZ	REED, H.
PONY RIDE	MCCREARY, D.
PONY RIDE	RAPHLING
PONY RIDE	SCARMOLIN
PONY RONDO	CRESTON
PONY TAIL	HAZELLE
PONY TROT	GILLNESS
PONY TROT	KING, S.
POODLES PRANCING	BASTIEN
POODLE DANCE	MELECCI, A.
POOL OF WATER LILIES	WILSON
POOR BUTTERFLY	HUBBELL
POOR BUTTERMILK	CONFREY, Z.
POOR DOG BRIGHT AND HEY DIDDLE	ROLFE, W.
POOR FIDO	PORTER, W.
POOR PIGGY BANK	ROBINSON, A.
POOR WAYFARING STRANGER	ZEPP--ED
POP-CORN BALLS	ROESSING, H.
POP-CORN	HUNEKE
POP-CORN	RAEZER, C.
POP-ROCK SKETCHES FOR PIANO DUET	METIS
POP, GOES THE PIANO, BK. 1	HANKINSON, R.
POP, GOES THE PIANO, BK. 2	HANKINSON, R.
POP, GOES THE PIANO, BK. 3	HANKINSON, R.
POP, GOES THE PIANO, BK. 4	HANKINSON, R.
POP, ROCK 'N BLUES, BK. 1	BASTIEN--ED.
POP, ROCK 'N BLUES, BK. 2	BASTIEN--ED.
POP, ROCK 'N BLUES, BK. 3	BASTIEN--ED.
POP'S SERENADE	GOULD, M.
POPCORN POLKA	MARTIN, H.
POPCORN	BRADLEY,
POPCORN	DAVIS, J.
POPEYE'S HORNPIPE	SAXTON
POPPIES	PANELLA, L.
POPPING CORN	HAYES
POPPO THE PORPOISE	LITTLEWOOD, R.
POPPY FIELD, THE, IDYLLE	SCHWAB
POPSICLE FROLIC	QUIST
POPS MADE EASY FOR PIANO	BRADLEY,
POPS OF THE 70'S	BRIMHALL,
POPULAR ARGENTINE AIRS, BK. 1	BOERO
POPULAR ARGENTINE AIRS, BK. 2	BOERO
POPULAR ARGENTINE AIRS, BK. 3	BOERO
POPULAR BEGINNER FOR TEEN-AGERS AND ADULTS	KAHN, M.

POPULAR CHOICE -- PIANO TEACHING PIECES	AGAY, D.--ED
POPULAR CHORD INSTRUCTOR	BRIMHALL,
POPULAR CHORD METHOD FOR BEGINNERS	STRONG, J.
POPULAR CLASSICS FOR PIANO	
POPULAR CLASSICS FOR PIANO	
POPULAR CLASSICS IN BIG NOTES --100--	
POPULAR DUETS, BK. 1 -- 26 PIECES, GRADE 1-2	FRAEMCKE--ED
POPULAR MASTERPIECES	AGAY, D.--ED
POPULAR MUSIC OF TODAY, NO. 1	BRIMHALL,
POPULAR MUSIC OF TODAY, NO. 2	BRIMHALL,
POPULAR MUSIC PIANO PLAYING	HENDERSON, R.
POPULAR PIANO CHORD METHOD FOR BEGINNERS	STRONG *
POPULAR PIANO CLASSICS	DE VITO, A.--ED.
POPULAR PIANO COLLECTIONS -- ALL AMERICAN MARCH FOLIO	WEYBRIGHT
POPULAR PIANO COLLECTIONS -- DUKES OF DIXIELAND,	WEYBRIGHT
POPULAR PIANO COLLECTIONS -- EXCITING ERA OF ZEZ	WEYBRIGHT
POPULAR PIANO COLLECTIONS -- FOLK ROCK FOR STUDENT	WEYBRIGHT
POPULAR PIANO COLLECTIONS -- FRANKIE CARLE'S PIANO	WEYBRIGHT
POPULAR PIANO COLLECTIONS -- FRANKIE CARLE'S PIANO	WEYBRIGHT
POPULAR PIANO COLLECTIONS -- GEORGE WALLINGTON	WALLINGTON, G.
POPULAR PIANO COLLECTIONS -- HAPPINESS IS	WEYBRIGHT
POPULAR PIANO COLLECTIONS -- HOW TO PLAY LIKE A PLAYER	WEYBRIGHT
POPULAR PIANO COLLECTIONS -- LATIN-AMERICAN MELODIES	WEYBRIGHT
POPULAR PIANO COLLECTIONS -- MILLS SONG SHINDIG	WEYBRIGHT
POPULAR PIANO COLLECTIONS -- MILLS SUMMER SOUNDS AND	WEYBRIGHT
POPULAR PIANO COLLECTIONS -- PLAY THEM RAGS	WEYBRIGHT
POPULAR PIANO COLLECTIONS -- RAGTIME TREASURES, JOSEPH	WEYBRIGHT
POPULAR PIANO COLLECTIONS -- TED MOSSMAN'S SIMPLIFIED	WEYBRIGHT
POPULAR PIANO COLLECTION -- RAGTIME PIANO	WEYBRIGHT
POPULAR PIANO FOR PLEASURE, BK. 1	WUHRER *
POPULAR PIANO FOR PLEASURE, BK. 2	WUHRER *
POPULAR PIANO FOR PLEASURE, BK. 3	WUHRER *
POPULAR PIANO PLAYING SIMPLIFIED	SHINN, D.
POPULAR RECITAL PIECES FOR PIANO, BK. 1	AGAY, D.--ED
POPULAR RECITAL PIECES FOR PIANO, BK. 2	AGAY, D.--ED
POPULAR RECITAL PIECES FOR PIANO, BK. 3	AGAY, D.--ED
POPULAR SONG CLASSICS FOR PIANO	SAVINO--ED.
POPULAR TEACHER'S CHOICE	BRADLEY,
POPULAR THEMES BY GREAT MASTERS	SCHIRMER--ED
POPULAR WALTZ	BRAHMS
POPULAR YUGOSLAVIAN DANCES	DOBRONITCH
POP - GOES THE PIANO, VOL. 1	HANKINSON, R.
POP - GOES THE PIANO, VOL. 2	HANKINSON, R.
POP - GOES THE PIANO, VOL. 3	HANKINSON, R.
POP - GOES THE PIANO, VOL. 4	HANKINSON, R.
POP CONCERT	AGAY, D.--ED
POP CORN AND COVERED WAGON	POOLE, C.
POP GOES THE WEASEL -- AMERICAN GAME SONG	WEYBRIGHT
POP GOES THE WEASEL	POOLE, C.
POP GOES THE WEASEL	SCHAUM, J.--ED.
POP GOES THE WEASEL	TRUXELL, E.
POP GOES THE WEASEL	TRUXELL, E.
POP GO THE CLASSICS	ROGERS--ED *
POP GUN PATROL	PERKINS, F.
POP PIANO COURSE, BK. 1	SCHAUM, J.
POP PIANO COURSE, BK. 2	SCHAUM, J.
POP PIANO COURSE, BK. 3	SCHAUM, J.
POP PIANO COURSE, BK. 4	SCHAUM, J.
PORCELAIN DOLL, THE	WARD
PORGY AND BESS	GERSHWIN
PORGY AND BESS	GERSHWIN
PORPOISES ON PARADE	DILSNER
PORTRAITS D'ESPAGNE - 1. CADIZ	DESOLIS
PORTRAITS D'ESPAGNE - 2. MADRID	DESOLIS
PORTRAITS D'ESPAGNE - 3. SEVILLA	DESOLIS
PORTRAITS FOR MODERN DANCE	CUNNINGHAM, M.
PORTRAITS HONGROIS HISTORIQUES	LISZT
PORTRAIT IN A GARDEN	LUBIN, E.
PORTRAIT IN BLUE	GIASSON, P.
PORTRAIT IN BLUE	GIASSON, P.
PORTRAIT OF A CITY	GIASSON, P.
PORTRAIT OF A DANCER	SZANTO
PORTRAIT OF A LADY	MELACHRINO, G.
PORTRAIT OF PARIS -- SECOND PIANO PART AVAILABLE	GILLOCK
PORTRAIT OF PARIS	GILLOCK
PORTRAIT	HELPS
PORTUGUESE AND SPANISH MUSIC OF THE 18TH CENTURY	JONAS--ED.
PORTUGUESE WASHERWOMEN, THE	POPP *
POR LAS CALLES DE SEVILLA, OP. 96	TURINA, J.
POSEIDON SONATA	HOVHANESS, A.
POSTHUMOUS WORKS	CHOPIN
POSTKARTEN, FUNF STUCKE	TURINA, J.
POSTLUDE - WARRIOR'S SONG	HELLER, S.
POSTLUDE	BRODSKY, M.
POSTLUDIUM	DOHNANYI
POSTMAN, THE	JEAN, E.
POST GRADUATE COURSE, BK. 1	STEINER
POST GRADUATE COURSE, BK. 2	STEINER
POTTER'S WHEEL	HIBBS, C.
POULE, LA -- THE HEN --	RAMEAU
POUPEE VALSANTE--WALTZ	POLDINI, E.
POUPEE VALSANTE --WALTZING DOLL--	POLDINI, E.
POUPEE VALSANTE	POLDINI, E.
POUPEE VALSANTE	POLDINI, E.
POUPEE VALSANTE	POLDINI, E.
POUPEE VALSANTE	POLDINI, E.
POUPEE VALSANTE	POLDINI, E.
POUPEE VALSANTE	POLDINI, E.
POUR ANNE	DUBOIS
POUR BERCER	BLANC
POUR DES MAINS AMIES -- SONATA IN FIVE MOVEMENTS	RIVIER, J.
POUR DES MAINS AMIES -- SUITE OF 5 NUMBERS	RIVIER, J.
POUR DIX PETITS DOIGTS D'ENFANTS	MERIGOT, F.
POUR LES BELLES ECOUTEUSES, SERENADE	DUBOIS, P. M.
POUR LES ENFANTS, BK. 1	TANSMAN, A.
POUR LES ENFANTS, BK. 2	TANSMAN, A.
POUR LES ENFANTS, BK. 3	TANSMAN, A.
POUR LES ENFANTS, BK. 4	TANSMAN, A.
POUR LES PETITES MAINS	PASCAL, A.
POUR LES PETITS -- LE PETIT NEGRE EST TRISTE	FAIRCHILD
POUR LES PETITS -- 6 EASY PIECES --	ORBAN
POUR LES PETITS	PHILIPP, I.
POUR LES TOUTS PETITS	MERIGOT, F.
POUR LE JOUR DE LA PREMIERE NEIGE AU VIEUX JAPON	INGHELBRECHT, D.
POUR LE PIANO - PRELUDE, DIVERTISSEMENTS, NOCTURNE,	ORBAN
POUR LE PIANO	DEBUSSY
POUR LE PIANO	DEBUSSY
POUR LE PIANO	DEBUSSY
POUR LE PIANO	DEBUSSY
POUR LE PIANO	FERTE
POUR MA MIEUX AIMEE	DUBOIS, P. M.
POUR MA POUPEE	MERIGOT, F.
POUR MES PETITS AMIS	MADELINE
POUR NOS BABYS, OP. 236	LANDRY
POUR NOS PETITS -- 6 LITTLE PIECES WITH LARGE NOTES --	WACHS, P.
POUR PETITES GRANDS, BK. 1	TCHEREPNIN

POUR PETITES GRANDS, BK. 2	TCHEREPNIN
POUR UNE ARBRE DE NOEL - CHEVEUX D'ANGES	GALLON, J.
POUR UNE ARBRE DE NOEL - CLOCHES D'ALLEGRESSE	GALLON, J.
POUR UNE ARBRE DE NOEL - DIVINE CRECHE	GALLON, J.
POUR UNE ARBRE DE NOEL - MAISON DE NEIGE	GALLON, J.
POUR UNE ARBRE DE NOEL - MOULIN ENCHANTE	GALLON, J.
POUR UNE ARBRE DE NOEL - PETIT OISEAU	GALLON, J.
POUR UNE ARBRE DE NOEL - ROIS MAGES	GALLON, J.
POUR UNE ARBRE DE NOEL - TAMBOURS ET TROMPETTES	GALLON, J.
POUR UNE PETITE BIEN SAGE - ARIETTE AND PASTORALE	SINGERY
POUR UNE PETITE BIEN SAGE - VALSETTE AND PETITE MARCHE	SINGERY
POUR UNE PETITE BIEN SAGE	SINGERY
POUR UNE PETIT MOUJICK	NAT, Y.
POUR YVONNE, 3 EASY LITTLE PIECES	RHENE-BATON
POUR 2 PETITS AMIS	SOUBEYRAN
POWDERED WIG	
POW WOW	HILL, M.
POW WOW	ROGERS, E.
PRACTICAL FINGER EXERCISES, OP. 802	CZERNY
PRACTICAL HARMONY AT THE KEYBOARD	HOUGHTON, W. E.
PRACTICAL METHOD, OP. 249. BK. 1	KOEHLER
PRACTICAL METHOD, OP. 249. BK. 2	KOEHLER
PRACTICAL METHOD, OP. 249. BK. 3	KOEHLER
PRACTICAL METHOD, OP. 249, BK. 1--IN SPANISH, ENGLISH,	KOEHLER
PRACTICAL METHOD, OP. 249, BK. 2--IN SPANISH, ENGLISH,	KOEHLER
PRACTICAL METHOD, OP. 249, BK. 3--IN SPANISH, ENGLISH,	KOEHLER
PRACTICAL METHOD, OP. 249, BK. 4--IN SPANISH, ENGLISH,	KOEHLER
PRACTICAL METHOD, OP. 300, BK. 1	KOEHLER
PRACTICAL METHOD, OP. 300, BK. 2	KOEHLER
PRACTICAL METHOD FOR BEGINNERS, OP. 599	CZERNY
PRACTICAL METHOD FOR BEGINNERS --ERSTER LEHRMEISTER--,	CZERNY
PRACTICAL METHOD FOR PIANO, OP. 300, VOL. 1	KOEHLER
PRACTICAL METHOD FOR PIANO, OP. 300, VOL. 2	KOEHLER
PRACTICAL METHOD FOR PLAYING IN CORRECT TIME, OP. 824	CZERNY
PRACTICAL METHOD FOR THE PIANOFORTE, BK. 1	KOEHLER
PRACTICAL THEORETICAL METHOD, BK. 01. ELEMENTS AND 20	CESI, B.
PRACTICAL THEORETICAL METHOD, BK. 02. EXERCISES AND	CESI, B.
PRACTICAL THEORETICAL METHOD, BK. 03. ARPEGGIOS	CESI, B.
PRACTICAL THEORETICAL METHOD, BK. 04. EQUALIZATION OF	CESI, B.
PRACTICAL THEORETICAL METHOD, BK. 05. REPEATED NOTES	CESI, B.
PRACTICAL THEORETICAL METHOD, BK. 06. WRIST MOVEMENT	CESI, B.
PRACTICAL THEORETICAL METHOD, BK. 07. OCTAVE TECHNIQUE	CESI, B.
PRACTICAL THEORETICAL METHOD, BK. 08. LEGATO	CESI, B.
PRACTICAL THEORETICAL METHOD, BK. 09. THIRDS--LEGATO--	CESI, B.
PRACTICAL THEORETICAL METHOD, BK. 10. DOUBLE NOTES	CESI, B.
PRACTICAL THEORETICAL METHOD, BK. 11. SIXTHS	CESI, B.
PRACTICAL THEORETICAL METHOD, BK. 12. ADVANCED	CESI, B.
PRAELUDIEN-ALBUM, OP. 6	WOLFRAM
PRAELUDIUM, FROM 1ST MODERN SUITE, OP. 10, NO. 1	MACDOWELL
PRAELUDIUM AND FUGUE	SPITZMULLER, A.
PRAELUDIUM IN E MINOR	MENDELSSOHN
PRAELUDIUM UND TOCCATA	FELD, J.
PRAELUDIUM	BENTLEY
PRAGA. SYMPHONISCHE DICHTUNG, OP. 26 -- KLAVIERAUSZUG	SUK
PRAGER KARNEVAL	SMETANA *
PRAIRIE DUSK--NOCTURNE	GUION, D.
PRAIRIE LULLABY	CADZOW
PRAIRIE NIGHT	GLOVER, D.
PRAIRIE NIGHT	GLOVER, D.
PRAIRIE RIDER	AARON, M.
PRAIRIE SNOW AND SHOOTING THE RAPIDS	KURKA, R.
PRAIRIE SONG AND COVERED WAGON	LAIRD
PRAIRIE SONG	AARON, M.
PRAIRIE SUNSET	STEVENS
PRAIRIE VISTA	MCKAY, G.
PRAIRIE WAGON	WORTZMAN, N.
PRAISIAN PROMENADE	GIASSON, P.
PRALUDIUM, ARIE UND FINALE	FRANCK, C.
PRALUDIUM, CHORAL UND FUGE	FRANCK, C.
PRALUDIUM IN D FLAT, OP. 28 NO. 15 'REGENTROPFEN'	CHOPIN
PRALUDIUM UND PASSACAGLIA	VRANA
PRALUDIUM 1 UND FUGE 1 -- BWV 846	BACH, J.S.
PRALUDIUM 2 UND FUGE 2 -- BWV 847	BACH, J.S.
PRALUDIUM 21 UND FUGE 21 -- BWV 866	BACH, J.S.
PRAM FLEET	THOMPSON, A. A.
PRANCING CLOWN	HEAPS, S.
PRANCING PONY, THE	KEVAN, G. A.
PRANCING PONY	PICKENS, M.
PRANCING PONY	RICHTER
PRANKS	WIGGINS, M.
PRANKS	WILSON *
PRAYER, DER FREISCHUTZ	WEBER, VON
PRAYER, HANSEL AND GRETEL	HUMPERDINCK, E.
PRAYER FROM BEETHOVEN'S SYMPHONY NO. 2, A	ROLFE, W.
PRAYER	KULLAK, T.
PRAYER	STRADELLA
PRAYER	WEYBRIGHT
PRAYING	WILSON, H.
PRE-CZERNY BOOK, A--BK. 1--40 STUDIES	QUAILE, E.
PRE-CZERNY BOOK, A--BK. 2--32 STUDIES	QUAILE, E.
PRE-READING EXPERIENCES	BASTIEN
PRE-READING SOLOS	BASTIEN
PRE-SCALE BOOK	STEINER
PRE-SCHOOL AND KINDERGARTEN BOOK	RICHTER
PRE-SCHOOL MUSIC BOOK, A.	DILLER, A. *
PRE-SCHOOL MUSIC BOOK, A	DILLER, A. *
PRE-SONATINA ALBUM	SMALL, A.
PREAMBLE	ALDWINCKLE
PREAMBULES DANS TOUS LES TONS, OP. 67	HUMMEL, J. N.
PREAMBULES DANS TOUS LES TONS	HENSELT, A.
PRECEPTOR, THE	
PRECIEUSE, LA	KREISLER
PRECIS	BIRTWISTLE, H.
PREDECESSORS OF BACH	
PREGON. CUBA	HALFFTER, E.
PRELIMINARY SCALES AND ARPEGGIOS	GRAY, D.
PRELIMINARY SCHOOL OF FINGER DEXTERITY, OP. 626	CZERNY
PRELIMINARY SCHOOL OF FINGER DEXTERITY, OP. 636	CZERNY
PRELIMINARY SCHOOL OF FINGER DEXTERITY --VORSCHULE DER	CZERNY
PRELIMINARY STUDIES --25 ORIGINAL PIECES--	BACH, J.S.
PRELUDE-NOCTURNE	RIETI
PRELUDE-PRESTO IN A-FLAT MINOR	SCUDERI
PRELUDE, ACT 3, LOHENGRIN	WAGNER
PRELUDE, ADAGIO AND FINALE	BORLENGHI
PRELUDE, AIR AND FINALE	FRANCK, C.
PRELUDE, ARIA, AND FINALE	FRANCK, C.
PRELUDE, ARIA AND FINALE	FRANCK, C.
PRELUDE, ARIA AND FINALE	FRANCK, C.
PRELUDE, ARIOSO ET FUGHETTE SUR LE NOM DE BACH	HONEGGER, A.
PRELUDE, CHORALE AND FUGUE	FRANCK, C.
PRELUDE, CHORALE AND FUGUE	FRANCK, C.
PRELUDE, CHORALE AND FUGUE	FRANCK, C.
PRELUDE, FUGUE AND ALLEGRO IN E FLAT, S. 998	BACH, J.S.
PRELUDE, FUGUE AND FANTASY	STEVENSON, R.
PRELUDE, FUGUE AND POSTLUDE	DU PLESIS, H.
PRELUDE, FUGUE AND VARIATIONS	FRANCK, C.
PRELUDE, FUGUE AND VARIATIONS	FRANCK, C.

Title	Composer
PRELUDE, F MAJOR, OP. 32	RACHMANINOFF, S.
PRELUDE, F MINOR, OP. 32	RACHMANINOFF, S.
PRELUDE, NOCTURNE AND DANCE	KASTLE
PRELUDE, NOCTURNE AND DANCE	KASTLE
PRELUDE, OP. 1 NO. 1	SZYMANOWSKI
PRELUDE, OP. 17 NO. 7	PROKOFIEFF
PRELUDE, OP. 2 NO. 2	SCRIABINE, A.
PRELUDE, OP. 23 NO. 5	RACHMANINOFF, S.
PRELUDE, OP. 232 NO. 1--FROM CANTOS DE ESPANA	ALBENIZ, I.
PRELUDE, OP. 29 NO. 1	VALEN
PRELUDE, OP. 29 NO. 2	VALEN
PRELUDE, OP. 3 NO. 2	RACHMANINOFF, S.
PRELUDE, OP. 9 NO. 1	SCIRABINE, A.
PRELUDE, OSTINATO AND FUGUE	FLAGELLO, N.
PRELUDE, OSTINATO AND FUGUE	FLAGELLO, N.
PRELUDE, OSTINATO AND FUGUE	FLAGELLO, N.
PRELUDE, SALUT ET DANSE	MIGOT
PRELUDE, TRAVIATA	VERDI
PRELUDE, VALSES ET MARCHES	NIVERD, L.
PRELUDE, WALTZ AND MARCH	KASSLER, M.
PRELUDES--CRITICAL COMMENTARY	CHOPIN
PRELUDES--OP. 04 NO. 01--INTRODUCIMENTO	MAURAT, E.
PRELUDES--OP. 04 NO. 02--CON SCLANCIO	MAURAT, E.
PRELUDES--OP. 04 NO. 03--FRETTOLOSAMENTE	MAURAT, E.
PRELUDES--OP. 04 NO. 04--DOLCEMENTE FERVOROSO	MAURAT, E.
PRELUDES--OP. 04 NO. 05--ARDITAMENTE	MAURAT, E.
PRELUDES--OP. 04 NO. 08--SDRUCCIOLONE	MAURAT, E.
PRELUDES--OP. 04 NO. 09--PER LA SINISTRA--FOR THE LEFT	MAURAT, E.
PRELUDES--OP. 04 NO. 10--LANGUIDAMENTE	MAURAT, E.
PRELUDES--OP. 04 NO. 11--SERPEGGIANDO	MAURAT, E.
PRELUDES--OP. 04 NO. 12--QUASI IMPROVISATO	MAURAT, E.
PRELUDES--OP. 04 NOS. 06-07--PIEGHEVOLMENTE,	MAURAT, E.
PRELUDES--OP. 27 NO. 32	MAURAT, E.
PRELUDES--OP. 27 NO. 33	MAURAT, E.
PRELUDES--OP. 27 NO. 34	MAURAT, E.
PRELUDES--OP. 27 NO. 35	MAURAT, E.
PRELUDES--OP. 27 NO. 36	MAURAT, E.
PRELUDES, BK. 1	DEBUSSY
PRELUDES, BK. 1	MIGOT
PRELUDES, BK. 1	NOEL, P. *
PRELUDES, BK. 1	TANSMAN, A.
PRELUDES, BK. 2	DEBUSSY
PRELUDES, BK. 2	MIGOT
PRELUDES, BK. 2	NOEL, P. *
PRELUDES, BK. 2	TANSMAN, A.
PRELUDES, FUGHETTAS, AND FUGUES	BACH, J.S.
PRELUDES, FUGUES, SUITES	BACH, J.S.
PRELUDES, LES -- SYMPHONIC POEM -- ARR. BY THE	LISZT
PRELUDES, LES	LISZT
PRELUDES, LES	LISZT
PRELUDES, OFFERTORIES AND POSTLUDES FOR THE PIANO, BK.	
PRELUDES, OFFERTORIES AND POSTLUDES	SCHAUM, J.--ED.
PRELUDES, OP. 10 NOS. 17-19	MAURAT, E.
PRELUDES, OP. 10 NOS. 20-24	MAURAT, E.
PRELUDES, OP. 10 NOS. 25-26	MAURAT, E.
PRELUDES, OP. 10 NOS. 27-28	MAURAT, E.
PRELUDES, OP. 10 NOS. 29-31	MAURAT, E.
PRELUDES, OP. 103	FAURE, G.
PRELUDES, OP. 28, NOS. 6, 7, 9, 20	CHOPIN
PRELUDES, OP. 28 NOS. 3 AND 4	CHOPIN
PRELUDES, OP. 28 UND OP. 45	CHOPIN
PRELUDES, OP. 28	CHOPIN
PRELUDES, THREE FAVORITE -- IN B MINOR, OP. 28 NO. 6 -	CHOPIN
PRELUDES -- CLOTH	CHOPIN
PRELUDES -- ENGLISH TEXT --	CHOPIN
PRELUDES -- FR. TEXT --	CHOPIN
PRELUDES -- SERIES 1 --	SCELSI
PRELUDES --25-- AND RONDOS --3--	CHOPIN
PRELUDES --25--	CHOPIN
PRELUDES - OP. 28 NO. 1 IN C MAJOR AND NO. 2 IN A	CHOPIN
PRELUDES - OP. 28 NO. 20 IN C MINOR AND NO. 21 IN B	CHOPIN
PRELUDES - OP. 28 NO. 4 IN E MINOR AND NO. 5 IN D	CHOPIN
PRELUDES - OP. 28 NO. 6 IN B MINOR AND NO. 7 IN A	CHOPIN
PRELUDES - OP. 28 NO. 8 IN F SHARP MINOR AND NO. 9 IN	CHOPIN
PRELUDES AND EXERCISES IN ALL THE MAJOR AND MINOR	CLEMENTI
PRELUDES AND EXERCISES	CLEMENTI
PRELUDES AND FUGUES--NOS. 1 IN C MAJOR, 2 IN C MINOR,	BACH, J.S.
PRELUDES AND FUGUES, OP. 61	KABALEVSKY
PRELUDES AND FUGUES	BACH, J.S.
PRELUDES AND NOCTURNES	SWENSON, L.
PRELUDES AND WALTZES	WOOLLETT
PRELUDES FLASQUES--POUR UN CHIEN	SATIE, E.
PRELUDES FOR PIANO	SMOLANOFF
PRELUDES	CHOPIN
PRELUDES	CHOPIN
PRELUDES	CHOPIN
PRELUDES	CHOPIN
PRELUDES	CHOPIN
PRELUDES	CHOPIN
PRELUDES	CHOPIN
PRELUDES	GERSHWIN
PRELUDES	GERSHWIN
PRELUDES	GERSHWIN
PRELUDES	MARTINU, B.
PRELUDES	MESSIAEN, O.
PRELUDES	PALESTER, R.
PRELUDE -- ''HAPPY BIRTHDAY''	HELLER, A.
PRELUDE -- NO. 1, AZULEJOS	ALBENIZ, I.
PRELUDE -- RAINDROP, OP. 28 NO. 15	CHOPIN
PRELUDE - FROM FIVE PIECES FOR YOUNG PIANISTS	RIETI
PRELUDE - TO A YOUNG DANCER	DELLO JOIO, N.
PRELUDE - TO A YOUNG MUSICIAN	DELLO JOIO, N.
PRELUDE AND CHORALE	YARDUMIAN, R.
PRELUDE AND DANCE, OP. 29 NO. 2	CRESTON
PRELUDE AND DANCE NO. 1	CRESTON
PRELUDE AND DIVERTIMENTO	SANGIORGI
PRELUDE AND DOUBLE FUGUE, OP. 7	SPITZMULLER, A.
PRELUDE AND FANTASY	ZANOTTI *
PRELUDE AND FILIGRANE, OP. 4	CHAMPAGNE
PRELUDE AND FUGUE, OP. 28	VALEN
PRELUDE AND FUGUE, OP. 35 NO. 6	MENDELSSOHN
PRELUDE AND FUGUE, OP. 46	ROUSSEL, A.
PRELUDE AND FUGUE, OP. 62	GLAZOUNOW, A.
PRELUDE AND FUGUE -- 1932	HALFFTER, R.
PRELUDE AND FUGUE IN A MINOR FOR ORGAN	BACH, J.S. *
PRELUDE AND FUGUE IN A MINOR FOR ORGAN	BACH, J.S. *
PRELUDE AND FUGUE IN A MINOR	BACH, J.S.
PRELUDE AND FUGUE IN A MINOR	BACH, J.S.
PRELUDE AND FUGUE IN A MINOR	BACH, J.S. *
PRELUDE AND FUGUE IN B	MACCHI
PRELUDE AND FUGUE IN C MINOR	BACH, J.S.
PRELUDE AND FUGUE IN D, S. 532	BACH, J.S.
PRELUDE AND FUGUE IN D, TRANSCRIBED BY JULIE RIVE-KING	HABERBIER, E.
PRELUDE AND FUGUE IN D MINOR	BUXTEHUDE
PRELUDE AND FUGUE IN E FLAT, S. 552	BACH, J.S.
PRELUDE AND FUGUE IN E MINOR, OP. 35 NO. 1	MENDELSSOHN
PRELUDE AND FUGUE IN E MINOR, OP. 35 NO. 1	MENDELSSOHN
PRELUDE AND FUGUE IN E MINOR	BACH, J.S.
PRELUDE AND FUGUE IN G MINOR -- ORGAN --	FRESCOBALDI
PRELUDE AND FUGUE IN G MINOR	GIACCHINO
PRELUDE AND FUGUE IN G	BACH, J.S.
PRELUDE AND FUGUE ON A NAME	BRUSSELMANS
PRELUDE AND FUGUE ON THE NAME 'BACH'	DE ANGELIS
PRELUDE AND FUGUE	AUCLERT
PRELUDE AND FUGUE	BACH, J.S.
PRELUDE AND FUGUE	D'ESPOSITO
PRELUDE AND FUGUE	DEBREVILLE
PRELUDE AND FUGUE	ENESCO
PRELUDE AND FUGUE	FRID, G.
PRELUDE AND FUGUE	OREFICE, G.
PRELUDE AND FUGUE	ROSSI, R.
PRELUDE AND GIGUE	RACHMANINOFF, S.
PRELUDE AND NOCTURNE FOR LEFT HAND, OP. 9	SCRIABINE, A.
PRELUDE AND PANTOMINE FROM ''JARDIN DE ORIENTE''	TURINA, J.
PRELUDE AND PASSACAGLIA, OP. 43	KORNAUTH, E.
PRELUDE AND SARABANDE	DAVENPORT, G.
PRELUDE AND SCHERZO IMPETUOSO	WHETTAM
PRELUDE AND SICILIANA FROM CAVALLERIA RUSTICANA	MASCAGNI, P.
PRELUDE AND TOCCATA, OP. 27	PICK-MANGIAGALLI
PRELUDE AND TOCCATA	ALFONSO
PRELUDE AND TOCCATA	BEN-YOHANAN
PRELUDE AND TOCCATA	CORRADINI
PRELUDE AND TOCCATA	GOULD, M.
PRELUDE AND TOCCATA	LUCAS, G.
PRELUDE AND TOCCATA	MALSIO, J.
PRELUDE AU COQ MATINAL	RODRIGO, J.
PRELUDE A DANSER	LANTIER, P.
PRELUDE A L'APRES-MIDI D'UNE FAUNE	DEBUSSY
PRELUDE A UN	MIGOT
PRELUDE BLUES FOR PIANO SOLO -- TO GEORGE GERSHWIN	GREEN, R.
PRELUDE CIS-MOLL, ERLEICHTART, OP. 2/3	RACHMANINOFF, S.
PRELUDE CIS-MOLL, OP. 3 NO. 2	RACHMANINOFF, S.
PRELUDE DE 'CATHEDRALES'	PIERNE
PRELUDE DE LA PORTE HEROIQUE DU CIEL	SATIE, E.
PRELUDE ELEGIAQUE	DUKAS, P.
PRELUDE EN TAPISSERIE	SATIE, E.
PRELUDE ESPAGNOLE	LITER, M.
PRELUDE ET FUGUE POUR LA MAIN GAUCHE SEULE	PONCE, M.
PRELUDE ET LEGENDE PERSANE	HOSSEIN, A.
PRELUDE ET TOCCATA	RUEFF
PRELUDE ET TOCCATO	ANDERSON, G. L.
PRELUDE FOR PIANO	SEARLE, H.
PRELUDE FOR PIANO	TAUTENHAHN, G.
PRELUDE FROM THE LEFT HAND ALONE, OP. 9 NO. 1	SCRIABINE, A.
PRELUDE FROM 'POUR LE PIANO'	DEBUSSY
PRELUDE FROM CANTATA 'GOTTES ZEIT IST DIE ALLERBESTE	BACH, J.S.
PRELUDE INTERMEZZO AND FUGUE	MONFRED
PRELUDE IN A, OP. 32 NO. 9	RACHMANINOFF, S.
PRELUDE IN A FLAT, OP. 23 NO. 8	RACHMANINOFF, S.
PRELUDE IN A FLAT, OP. 28 NO. 17	CHOPIN
PRELUDE IN A FLAT, OP. 35 NO. 4	SCHUETT
PRELUDE IN A MINOR, OP. 32 NO. 8	RACHMANINOFF, S.
PRELUDE IN A MINOR	DEBUSSY
PRELUDE IN B, OP. 32 NO. 11	RACHMANINOFF, S.
PRELUDE IN BLUE	WEYBRIGHT
PRELUDE IN B FLAT MINOR, OP. 23 NO. 2	RACHMANINOFF, S.
PRELUDE IN B FLAT MINOR, OP. 32 NO. 2	RACHMANINOFF, S.
PRELUDE IN B FLAT MINOR	LIADOW, A.
PRELUDE IN B MINOR, OP. 13 NO. 5	CHASINS, A.
PRELUDE IN B MINOR, OP. 32 NO. 10	RACHMANINOFF, S.
PRELUDE IN B MINOR	BACH, J.S.
PRELUDE IN B MINOR	REBE
PRELUDE IN C, FROM WELL-TEMPERED CLAVICHORD NO. 1	BACH, J.S.
PRELUDE IN C, OP. 12 NO. 7	PROKOFIEFF
PRELUDE IN C, OP. 12 NO. 7	PROKOFIEFF
PRELUDE IN C, OP. 32 NO. 1	RACHMANINOFF, S.
PRELUDE IN C MAJOR--FROM WELL-TEMPERED CLAVICHORD	BACH, J.S.
PRELUDE IN C MINOR, OP. 23 NO. 7	RACHMANINOFF, S.
PRELUDE IN C MINOR, OP. 75	BAZELAIRE
PRELUDE IN C MINOR, WALTZ FROM SUITE, OP. 17, ROMANCE	RACHMANINOFF, S.
PRELUDE IN C MINOR	BACH, J.S.
PRELUDE IN C MINOR	CHOPIN
PRELUDE IN C MINOR	RACHMANINOFF, S.
PRELUDE IN C MINOR	ZONDADARI
PRELUDE IN C SHARP MINOR, OP. 3 NO. 2	RACHMANINOFF, S.
PRELUDE IN C SHARP MINOR, OP. 3 NO. 2	RACHMANINOFF, S.
PRELUDE IN C SHARP MINOR, OP. 3 NO. 2	RACHMANINOFF, S.
PRELUDE IN C SHARP MINOR, OP. 3 NO. 2	RACHMANINOFF, S.
PRELUDE IN C SHARP MINOR, OP. 3 NO. 2	RACHMANINOFF, S.
PRELUDE IN C SHARP MINOR, OP. 3 NO. 2	RACHMANINOFF, S.
PRELUDE IN C SHARP MINOR, OP. 45	CHOPIN
PRELUDE IN C SHARP MINOR	RACHMANINOFF, S.
PRELUDE IN C SHARP MINOR	RACHMANINOFF, S.
PRELUDE IN C	BACH, J.S.
PRELUDE IN C	TEMPLETON
PRELUDE IN D, OP. 10 NO. 5	CHASINS, A.
PRELUDE IN D, OP. 23 NO. 3	RACHMANINOFF, S.
PRELUDE IN D FLAT, OP. 28 NO. 15 'RAINDROP'	CHOPIN
PRELUDE IN D FLAT, OP. 28 NO. 15 'RAINDROP'	CHOPIN
PRELUDE IN D FLAT, OP. 28 NO. 15	CHOPIN
PRELUDE IN D FLAT, OP. 32 NO. 13	RACHMANINOFF, S.
PRELUDE IN D FLAT, OP. 43 NO. 1	GLIERE
PRELUDE IN D FLAT	WILSON, R. J.
PRELUDE IN D FLAT	WILSON, R. J.
PRELUDE IN D FLAT	WILSON, R. J.
PRELUDE IN D MINOR, OP. 23 NO. 4	RACHMANINOFF, S.
PRELUDE IN D MINOR, OP. 28 NO. 24	CHOPIN
PRELUDE IN D MINOR, OP. 28 NO. 24	CHOPIN
PRELUDE IN D MINOR	GLOVER, D.
PRELUDE IN D MINOR	PORTER
PRELUDE IN D MINOR	RHENE-BATON
PRELUDE IN E, OP. 32 NO. 3	RACHMANINOFF, S.
PRELUDE IN E -- VIOLIN PARTITA NO.3--	BACH, J.S.
PRELUDE IN E FLAT, OP. 23, NO. 6	RACHMANINOFF, S.
PRELUDE IN E FLAT, OP. 23 NO. 6	RACHMANINOFF, S.
PRELUDE IN E FLAT, OP. 25 NO. 3	WRIGHT, N.
PRELUDE IN E FLAT MINOR, OP. 23 NO. 9	RACHMANINOFF, S.
PRELUDE IN E FLAT	BENOIST, A.
PRELUDE IN E FLAT	WRIGHT, N.
PRELUDE IN E MAJOR, OP. 32	RACHMANINOFF, S.
PRELUDE IN E MINOR, OP. 32 NO. 4	RACHMANINOFF, S.
PRELUDE IN E MINOR	CHOPIN
PRELUDE IN E MINOR	JACOBI
PRELUDE IN E MINOR	SIROONI
PRELUDE IN F, OP. 32 NO. 7	RACHMANINOFF, S.
PRELUDE IN F MINOR, OP. 28 NO. 18	CHOPIN
PRELUDE IN F MINOR, OP. 32 NO. 6	RACHMANINOFF, S.
PRELUDE IN F MINOR	BEETHOVEN
PRELUDE IN F MINOR	RODRIGUEZ, C.
PRELUDE IN F SHARP MINOR, OP. 23 NO. 1	RACHMANINOFF, S.

PRELUDE IN G, OP. 28 NO. 3	CHOPIN
PRELUDE IN G, OP. 32 NO. 5	RACHMANINOFF, S.
PRELUDE IN G FLAT, OP. 23 NO. 10	RACHMANINOFF, S.
PRELUDE IN G MAJOR	BACH, J.S.
PRELUDE IN G MINOR, OP. 23 NO. 5 -- 8-HANDS, SET	RACHMANINOFF, S.
PRELUDE IN G MINOR, OP. 23 NO. 5	RACHMANINOFF, S.
PRELUDE IN G MINOR, OP. 23 NO. 5	RACHMANINOFF, S.
PRELUDE IN G MINOR, OP. 23 NO. 5	RACHMANINOFF, S.
PRELUDE IN G MINOR, OP. 23 NO. 5	RACHMANINOFF, S.
PRELUDE IN G MINOR	UGARTE
PRELUDE IN G MINOR	WEYBRIGHT
PRELUDE IN G SHARP MINOR, OP. 28 NO. 12	CHOPIN
PRELUDE IN G SHARP MINOR, OP. 32 NO. 12	RACHMANINOFF, S.
PRELUDE IN G SHARP MINOR, OP. 32 NO. 12	RACHMANINOFF, S.
PRELUDE IN G	PURCELL, H.
PRELUDE IN PASTEL	ECKSTEIN
PRELUDE LE DELUGE	SAINT-SAENS
PRELUDE NO. 01 -- LEGGIERO	COULTHARD
PRELUDE NO. 01	SAVAGNONE
PRELUDE NO. 02 -- TORMENT	COULTHARD
PRELUDE NO. 02	DE MARIA
PRELUDE NO. 03 -- QUEST	COULTHARD
PRELUDE NO. 03 FOR PIANO AND ELECTRONIC SOUNDS --1964	SUBOTNICK
PRELUDE NO. 04 FOR PIANO AND ELECTRONIC SOUNDS --1966	SUBOTNICK
PRELUDE NO. 1	DE MARIA
PRELUDE ON 'HAPPY BIRTHDAY'	ROCHBERG, G.
PRELUDE ON THE WHITE KEYS	MODONA
PRELUDE PATHETIQUE	SCHER, W.
PRELUDE POUR LA TEMPETE	HONEGGER, A.
PRELUDE POUR UN POETE	MIGOT
PRELUDE ROMANTIQUE	MUNN, W.
PRELUDE TO ''THE AFTERNOON OF A FAUN'' -- SET	DEBUSSY
PRELUDE TO THE AFTERNOON OF A FAUN	DEBUSSY
PRELUDE TO THE STARS	OLIVER
PRELUDE TO THE STARS	OLIVER
PRELUDE TO THE	DEBUSSY
PRELUDE	BERKMAN, V.
PRELUDE	BILOTTI
PRELUDE	COUTURE
PRELUDE	DEL CORONA
PRELUDE	FIALA
PRELUDE	GRUNEWALD
PRELUDE	GUARINO, C.
PRELUDE	GUNST
PRELUDE	HARTEVELD
PRELUDE	HIER, E.
PRELUDE	LAFORTUNE, L.
PRELUDE	MACCHI
PRELUDE	MELECCI, A.
PRELUDE	MONATH
PRELUDE	MONATH
PRELUDE	MOORE
PRELUDE	PALMA
PRELUDE	PARTOS, O.
PRELUDE	PATTISON, L.
PRELUDE	RAVEL
PRELUDE	RIETI
PRELUDE	SANGIORGI
PRELUDE	SICILIANI
PRELUDE	SIGTENHORST-MEYE
PRELUDE	SMITH, J.
PRELUDE	WARRACK, G.
PRELUDE	WILSON, M.
PRELUDE 1967	BLAIN
PRELUDIO, DIFFERENCIAS, AND TOCCATA ON A THEME BY	CASTILLO
PRELUDIOS ENCADENADOS	PONCE, M.
PRELUDIO CON FUGA -- A MINOR--, FANTASIA --C MINOR--	BACH, J.S.
PRELUDIO CUBANO	ROLCAN, A.
PRELUDIO E FUGA IN E MINOR	GLAZOUNOW, A.
PRELUDIO SULL'ANNUNCIAZIONE DI LEONARDO DA VINCI	AMFITEATROF
PRELUDIO TRAGICO	PONCE, M.
PRELUDIO Y CAPRICHO	EITLER, E.
PRELUDIO Y FUGA SOBRE UN TEMA DE HANDEL	PONCE, M.
PRELUDIO Y FUGA SOBRE UN TEMA DE J. S. BACH	PONCE, M.
PRELUDIO Y TOCCATA	SAS, A.
PRELUDIO	BACH, J.S.
PRELUDIO	BAL, R.
PRELUDIO	ELIOT
PRELUDIUM AND TOCCATA	FELD, J.
PRELUDI AUTUNNALI	MALIPIERO, G. F.
PRELUDI DEL MAR	OREFICE, G.
PREMIERE SONATE	WERNER, J.
PREMIERE VALSE OUBLIEE	LISZT
PREMIERS CONCERTS	DESSAUX
PREMIER CONCERTO POUR PIANO	SAINT-SAENS
PREMIER GRAND CAPRICE	FRANCK, C.
PREMIER LIVRE DE PIECES DE CLAVECIN	DAQUIN, C.
PREMIER MAI, OP. 45	SMITH, SYDNEY
PREMIER MAZURKA, OP. 21	SAINT-SAENS
PREMIER QUATUOR	DEBUSSY
PREMIER VALSE	DURAND, A.
PREPARATION AU DECHIFFRAGE PIANISTIQUE	GARTENLAUB, O.
PREPARATORY EXERCISES. 5-FINGER EXERCISES. OP. 16	SCHMITT, A.
PREPARATORY EXERCISES, OP. 16A	SCHMITT, A.
PREPARATORY EXERCISES, OP. 16	SCHMITT, A.
PREPARATORY EXERCISES, OP. 16	SCHMITT, A.
PREPARATORY EXERCISES, OP. 16	SCHMITT, A.
PREPARATORY EXERCISES FOR THE PIANO, OP. 16	SCHMITT, A.
PREPARATORY EXERCISES FOR THE PIANO	SCHMITT, F.
PREPARATORY EXERCISES FOR THE USE OF THE PEDAL	PICCIOLI
PREPARATORY EXERCISES	SCHMITT, A.
PREPARATORY PEDAL EXERCISES FOR YOUNG PIANISTS	MASON, I.
PREPARATORY SCHOOL, OP. 101 --GERMAN, ENGLISH,	BEYER, F.
PREPARATORY SCHOOL, OP. 276	DUVERNOY, J.
PREPARATORY SCHOOLS OF FINGER DEXTERITY, OP. 636	CZERNY
PREPARATORY SCHOOL FOR YOUNG STUDENTS, OP. 101	BEYER, F.
PREPARATORY SCHOOL OF VELOCITY, OP. 276	DUVERNOY, J.
PREPARATORY SCHOOL TO BACH	LIFTL, F. J.
PREPARATORY SCHOOL TO THE SONATINA	LIFTL, F. J.
PREPOSTEROUS RHINOCEROS	SCHAUM, J.
PRESENCIAS, LAS, NO. 1 LODUVINA	GUASTAVINO
PRESENCIAS, LAS, NO. 2 ORTEGA	GUASTAVINO
PRESENCIAS, LAS, NO. 3 FEDERICO IGNACIO CESPEDES	GUASTAVINO
PRESENCIAS, LAS, NO. 4 MARIANA	GUASTAVINO
PRESENCIAS, LAS, NO. 5 HORACIO LAVALLE	GUASTAVINO
PRESIDENT KENNEDY MARCH	
PRESSER PIANO 'POPS' -- FAVORITE HIT MELODIES OLD AND	AGAY, D.--ED
PRESSER PIANO 'POPS' -- FAVORITE HIT MELODIES OLD AND	AGAY, D.--ED
PRESSER PIANO 'POPS' -- FAVORITE HIT MELODIES OLD AND	AGAY, D.--ED
PRESSER PIANO 'POPS' -- FAVORITE HIT MELODIES OLD AND	AGAY, D.--ED
PRESSER PIANO 'POPS' -- FAVORITE HIT MELODIES OLD AND	AGAY, D.--ED
PRESTIGE PIANO SOLOS -- SCHAUM REPERTOIRE	SCHAUM, J.
PRESTO FROM THE FANTASY IN F-SHARP MINOR, OP. 28	MENDELSSOHN
PRESTO IN B-FLAT	POULENC, F.
PRESTO NACH J.S. BACH	BRAHMS
PRES DU BAL -- SUITE --	SAUGUET
PRES DU MOULIN	CARMAN
PRETTY BUTTERFLIES, RONDO	GREENWALD, M.
PRETTY CAT	TROJE-MILLER
PRETTY DEWDROPS, MAZURKA	GREENWALD, M.
PRETTY LILLIES MORCEAU	TIDES, A.
PRETTY LITTLE DAISY	LEWIS, M.
PRETTY LITTLE SONG BIRD	SPAULDING, G. L.
PRETTY MOONBEAMS, MARCH	GREENWALD, M.
PRETTY MORNING GLORIES	BILBRO, M.
PRETTY PONY	ZIEGLER
PRETTY RAINBOW, REVERIE	GREENWALD, M.
PRETTY STARLIGHT, GAVOTTE	GREENWALD, M.
PRETTY SUNSHINE, WALTZ	GREENWALD, M.
PRETTY SUNSHINE, WALTZ	GREENWALD, M.
PRETTY VISIONS	VALENTI, M.
PREUSSISCHEN SONATEN, DIE, WQ 48, HEFT 1 -- B, B FLAT,	BACH, C.P.E.
PREUSSISCHEN SONATEN, DIE, WQ 48, HEFT 2 -- C MINOR,	BACH, C.P.E.
PREUSSISCHEN SONATEN, VOL. 1	BACH, C.P.E.
PREUSSISCHEN SONATEN, VOL. 2	BACH, C.P.E.
PRE A EMSEMBLE BOOK	SCHAUM, J.
PRE A SOLO BOOK	SCHAUM, J.
PRIERE, OP. 92, NO. 4 -- FROM 12 PIECES	ALBENIZ, I.
PRIESTS' MARCH, ATHALIA	MENDELSSOHN
PRIESTS' MARCH, ATHALIA	MENDELSSOHN
PRIMAIRE - FRENCH EDITION	AARON, M.
PRIMARY BOOK	SCHAUB *
PRIMA CAREZZA	DE CRESCENZO
PRIMA DONNA, LA, SCHOTTISCHE	KING
PRIMA DONNA, THE	GOULD, M.
PRIMI TOCHI	FERRARIS
PRIMROSE, THE	RICHMAN, A.
PRIMROSE, THE	RICHMAN, A.
PRIMROSE POLKA, OP. 294	SPINDLER
PRINCESA, LA -- SPANISH DANCE, OP. 5 NO. 2	MERZ, O.
PRINCESS AND THE PIRATE	CAMPBELL
PRINCESS CHARMING	ECKSTEIN
PRINCESS WALTZ	EWING, M.
PRINCE CHARMANT, LE	GALOS
PRINCE CHARMING WALTZ	NOSSE
PRINCE IGOR, POLOVETSIAN DANCE	BORODIN, A.
PRINCE IGOR OVERTURE	BORODIN, A.
PRINCE IGOR OVERTURE	BORODIN, A.
PRINCE IMPERIAL GALOP	COOTE
PRINCE ORLOFSKY'S SONG -- FROM 'DIE FLEDERMAUS'	STRAUSS, J.
PRINCIPLES OF PEDALING	PODOLSKY, L. *
PRINTANIERES	WERNER, J.
PRINTEMPS, LE--1919-1920--BK. 1	MILHAUD, D.
PRINTEMPS, LE--1919-1920--BK. 2	MILHAUD, D.
PRINTEMPS, 1931	DUKELSKY
PRINTEMPS	DEBUSSY
PRINTEMPS	ROUSSEL, A.
PRINTING PRESS	WORTZMAN, N.
PRINZESSIN TURANDOT, OP. 1 -- BALLET IN 2 TABLEAUX	EINEM, G.
PRISCILLA'S WEEK -- SEVEN LITTLE CHARACTERISTIC PIECES	BILBRO, M.
PRISCILLA MINUET	CORBRIDGE
PRISM	RICHMAN, A.
PRIVATE PETE	MCHALE, M.
PRIVATE WORLD, A	DIAMOND, D.
PRIZE, THE	GOLDSMITH, J.
PROCESSIONAL--FROM POMP AND CIRCUMSTANCE, OP. 39 NO. 1	ELGAR, E.
PROCESSIONAL	KRAMER, A. W.
PROCESSIONAL	LAMBERT, C.
PROCESSION DU ROCIO, LA	TURINA, J.
PROCESSION DU ROSIO, LA	TURINA, J.
PROCESSION OF THE MAGYARS	MUNGER, S.
PROCESSION OF THE NIGHT	SCHER, W.
PROCESSION OF THE SARDAR, EASY	IVANOW
PROCESSION OF THE SARDAR -- FROM 'CAUCASIAN SKETCHES'	IPPOLITOV-IVANOV
PROCESSION OF THE SARDAR	IPPOLITOV-IVANOV
PROCESSION OF THE SARDAR	IVANOW
PROCESSION OF THE SEVEN DWARFS	LONG, L.
PROCESSION TRISTE	MCKAY, G.
PROCESSION	BREVILLE
PROCESSION	ELWELL, H.
PROCESSION	LEE, E.
PRODE ANSELMO, IL	FERRARI-TRECATE
PROFILES, OP. 68	TOCH, E.
PROFILES IN COURAGE --THEME	RIDDLE
PROGRAM OF CLASSICS, A	AGAY, D.--ED
PROGRAM PIECES FOR THE YOUNGER CHILD, BK. 1	
PROGRESSIVE JAZZ FOR JUNIORS	KING, S.
PROGRESSIVE JAZZ FOR JUNIORS	KING, S.
PROGRESSIVE PIANO PIECES	
PROGRESSIVE PIANO TECHNIC, BK. 1	SCHAUM, J.--ED.
PROGRESSIVE PIANO TECHNIC, BK. 2	SCHAUM, J.--ED.
PROGRESSIVE STUDIES, VOL. 1	FERTE--ED
PROGRESSIVE STUDIES, VOL. 2	FERTE--ED
PROGRESSIVE STUDIES, VOL. 3	FERTE--ED
PROGRESSIVE STUDIES, VOL. 4	FERTE--ED
PROGRESSIVE STUDIES, VOL. 5	FERTE--ED
PROGRESSIVE STUDIES, VOL. 6	FERTE--ED
PROGRESSIVE STUDIES, VOL. 7	FERTE--ED
PROGRESSIVE STUDIES, VOL. 8	FERTE--ED
PROGRESSIVE STUDIES AND PIECES - HIGHER	BRADLEY
PROGRESSIVE STUDIES AND PIECES - PRIMARY	BRADLEY
PROKOFIEFF IS EASY - 12 MELODIOUS PIECES FOR THE YOUNG	PROKOFIEFF
PROKOFIEFF MASTERPIECES	PROKOFIEFF
PROLE DO BEBE - LITTLE PAPER DOLL	VILLA-LOBOS, H.
PROLE DO BEBE - LITTLE RUBBER DOLL	VILLA-LOBOS, H.
PROLE DO BEBE - PUNCHINELLO	VILLA-LOBOS, H.
PROLE DO BEBE	VILLA-LOBOS, H.
PROLOGUE, VARIATIONS AND EPILOGUE	DA-OZ, RAM
PROLOGUE	
PROMENADE, AU BORD DE L'ETANG	HUGON, G.
PROMENADE, OP. 59 NO. 1	PROKOFIEFF
PROMENADE, OP. 65	PROKOFIEFF
PROMENADES ENFANTINES A PARIS, BK. A	COELHO, P.M.R.
PROMENADES ENFANTINES A PARIS, BK. B	COELHO, P.M.R.
PROMENADES ENFANTINES A PARIS, BK. C	COELHO, P.M.R.
PROMENADES	BERNARD, O.
PROMENADE -- SUITE	DUKE, H.
PROMENADE -- 1915 --	FOURDRAIN
PROMENADE AU BOIS, OP. 143	GRETCHANINOFF
PROMENADE AU ZOO	PHILIPP, I.
PROMENADE ET TOCCATINA	DOURY, P.
PROMENADE	ANDERSON, L.
PROMENADE	ANDERSON, L.
PROMENADE	BUTLER, J.
PROMENADE	DAMASE, J. M.
PROMENADE	FICHANDLER, W.
PROMENADE	GILLOCK
PROMENADE	GILLOCK
PROMENADE	LEVITON
PROMENADE	MCKAY, G.
PROMENADE	STOUGHTON, R. S.
PROMISES, PROMISES	BRIMHALL,

PROPHETE, CORONATION MARCH, EASY	MEYERBEER, G.
PROPHETE, CORONATION MARCH	MEYERBEER, G.
PROPHET BIRD, OP. 82 NO. 7	SCHUMANN, R.
PROPHET BIRD, OP. 82 NO. 7	SCHUMANN, R.
PROPHET BIRD, THE, OP. 82 NO. 7--FOREST SCENES	SCHUMANN, R.
PROSLAMBANOMENOS	ABBOTT, A.
PROUD MARY	BRIMHALL,
PROUD MR. GOBBLER	EZELL, H.
PROUD MRS. HEN	ARNOLD, H.
PROWLING PUSSYCAT, THE	GILLOCK
PROWLING PUSSYCAT, THE	GILLOCK
PRUDENT OP. 41 INTRODUCTION ET ETUDE BRILLANTE	SGAMBATI
PRUSSIAN SONATAS WQ 48, BK. 1	BACH, C.P.E.
PRUSSIAN SONATAS WQ 48, BK. 2	BACH, C.P.E.
PSICOGRAMMA	DURKO
PUCK, OP. 71 NO. 3	GRIEG
PUCK, OP. 71 NO. 3	GRIEG
PUCK, OP. 71 NO. 3	GRIEG
PUCK, OP. 71 NO. 3	GRIEG
PUCK'S PIECES	LAST, J.
PUCK	ROSNER
PUCK	TAYLOR, C.
PUDDLES	GEST, E.
PUEBLITO, MI PUEBLO	GUASTAVINO
PUERILIA - 4 PIECES ON 5 NOTES	GHEDINI
PUERTA DE TIERRA -- NO. 5, FROM RECUERDOS DE VIAJE	ALBENIZ, I.
PUERTO, EL -- FROM IBERIA	ALBENIZ, I.
PUERTO, EL	ALBENIZ, I.
PUFF, THE MAGIC DRAGON	YARROW *
PUFF, THE MAGIC DRAGON	YARROW *
PUG NOSE	ROLFE, W.
PULCINELLA, OP. 53	BOZZA
PUMPKIN FACES	OBENCHAIN, V.
PUMPKIN MAN, THE	HOUSE, L.
PUNCHINELLO, OP. 3 NO. 4, EASY	RACHMANINOFF, S.
PUNCHINELLO, OP. 3 NO. 4	RACHMANINOFF, S.
PUNCH AND JUDY	ROGERS, E.
PUPAZZETTI	CASELLA, A.
PUPAZZI	SCHMITT, F.
PUPPET-SHOW	PENTLAND, B.
PUPPET'S HOLIDAY	FIELDS, I.
PUPPET'S TALE	KARP
PUPPETS, BK. 1	MARTINU, B.
PUPPETS, BK. 2	MARTINU, B.
PUPPETS, BK. 3	MARTINU, B.
PUPPETS DANCE, THE	LECUONA
PUPPETS ON PARADE	CHENOWETH, W.
PUPPETS ON PARADE	SCHER, W.
PUPPETS ON PARADE	SCHER, W.
PUPPETS ON THE MARCH	SADLON
PUPPET CARNIVAL	TRAVIS, B.
PUPPET DANCE, THE	SCHAUM, J.--ED.
PUPPET DANCE	FICHANDLER, W.
PUPPET DANCE	OSBORNE, W.
PUPPET ON A STRING	KARP
PUPPET PARADE	BEISSERT
PUPPET POLKA	AGAY, D.
PUPPET POLKA	AGAY, D.
PUPPET POLKA	BERMONT, H.
PUPPET SHOW, THE	STEINER
PUPPET SHOW	NEVIN
PUPPET SONGS FROM ''CARNIVAL''	ROBERTS
PUPPET WALTZ, THE	WIGHAM, M.
PUPPY'S TALE	GEORGE
PUPPY DOG GALOP	BUCCI, M.
PUPPY IS LOST	LANGE, E.
PURE AS SNOW -- EDELWEISS --	LANGE, A.
PURE AS SNOW -- EDELWEISS --	LANGE, G.
PURE AS SNOW	BELLINI
PURITANI, I - EASY FANTASIA	MACK, E.
PURITY	WHITFORD
PURPLE DUST	CALWELL
PURPLE PEAKS	LANE, J.--ED.
PUSHBIKE SONG, THE	PORTER, W.
PUSSY'S LESSON	MANNING
PUSSY CAT SONG	MCHALE, M.
PUSSY WILLOWS	RICHTER
PUSSY WILLOW	THOMPSON, J. *
PUSS IN BOOKS -- PIANO FOLIO FOR CHILDREN	BRIMHALL,
PUT YOUR HAND IN THE HAND	WEDBERG, G.
PUZZLE PIECE NO. 1	ANDERSON, L.
PYRAMID DANCE	ELLINGTON
PYRAMID	OLDENBURG, E.
QUACK, QUACK	MELOCCHI, V.
QUADRETTI ARMONIOSI	PICCIOLI
QUADRETTI	CHAMPAGNE
QUADRILHA BRASILEIRA -- 1942 -- ON A MARAJO ISLAND	STRAUSS, J.
QUADRILLE ON OFFENBACH'S 'LA VIE PARISIENNE'	BRUCKNER
QUADRILLE	SCHAUM, J.--ED.
QUADRILLE	OREFICE, G.
QUADRI DI BOEKLIN	CELLA
QUADRO ANTICO	COUTURE
QUANDPO ERA PRIMAVERA	WALTER
QUAND L'OISEAU CHANTE	NILSSON, BO
QUANTITATEN -- FACSIMILE EDITION	BACH, J.
QUARTET, OP. 8 NO. 2 --2 HARPSICHORDS‡ 1 CONCERTANTE,	VERDI
QUARTET, RIGOLETTO	BACH, J.
QUARTETT IN E FLAT, OP. 8 NO. 2 'ACCOMODATO PER DUE	GREEN, R.
QUARTET -- FOUR PRELUDES FOR PIANO OOLO	BARATI
QUARTET FOR HARPSICHORD, FLUTE, OBOE, BASS	VERDI
QUARTET FROM RIGOLETTO	SMETANA
QUARTET IN E MINOR --FROM MY LIFE--	BORODIN, A.
QUARTET NO. 2	TURINA, J.
QUARTIER DE SANTA-CRUZ, LE	ALKAN
QUASI-CACCIA, OP. 53	CASTRO, J. M.
QUASI POLKA	COUTURE
QUASI UNA FANTASIA	AUCLERT
QUATRE AIRS A DANSER	ARRIEU
QUATRE ETUDES-CAPRICES	ROGER-DUCASSE
QUATRE ETUDES	STUTSCHEWSKY, J.
QUATRE INATTENDUS POUR PIANO	MIGOT
QUATRE NOCTURNES	DUPRE, M.
QUATRE PIECES, OP. 19	PHILIPP, I.--ED.
QUATRE PIECES DE CONCERT, NO. 1, TARTINI--DANCE	PHILIPP, I.--ED.
QUATRE PIECES DE CONCERT, NO. 2, TARTINI--BALLET	PHILIPP, I.--ED.
QUATRE PIECES DE CONCERT, NO. 3,	PHILIPP, I.--ED.
QUATRE PIECES DE CONCERT, NO. 4, VERACINI--DANSE	BOIZARD, G.
QUATRE PIECES	GUILLOU, R.
QUATRE PIECES	LOUVIER
QUATRE PRELUDES POUR CORDES	TCHEREPNIN
QUATRE PRELUDES	TCHEREPNIN
QUATRE ROMANCES OP. 31	DESREZ
QUATRE VARIATIONS SUR UN THEME DE 'PRINTEMPS'	SAINT-SAENS
QUATRIEME CONCERTO, OP. 44	GODARD, B.
QUATRIEME MAZURKA IN B FLAT, OP. 103 NO. 4	LISZT
QUATRIEME VALSE OUBLIEE -- FORGOTTEN WALTZ	POULENC, F.
QUATRIEMME NOCTURNE IN C MINOR	
QUATRO VEZZEGGIATIVI IN MI-DO-RE	SARDI, S.
QUATUOR	DEBUSSY
QUATUOR	RAVEL
QUATUOR	RAVEL
QUEEN OF SHEBA. FANTASY. TWO PIANOS, EIGHT HANDS	GOUNOD, C.
QUEEN OF SHEBA BALLET	GOUNOD, C.
QUEEN OF THE NIGHT, VALSE	BOHM
QUEEN OF THE NIGHT	ARMOUR
QUEEN OF THE RODEO	STEINER
QUEJAS, O LA MAJA Y EL RUISENOR, FROM 'GOYESCAS'	GRANADOS
QUEJAS O LA MAJA Y EL RUISENOR -- NO. 4, FROM GOYESCAS	GRANADOS
QUELQUES DANSES, OP. 26 - DEDICACE ET SARABANDE,	CHAUSSON
QUELQUES EXERCISES POUR LE PIANO	WURMSER, L.
QUEL DIABLE	MARTIN, R. C.
QUERELLE DE FAUVETTES -- CAPRICE --	GUIRAUD
QUESTE DE DIEU, LA	D'INDY, V.
QUESTIONING	LAMONTAINE, J.
QUESTIONS AND ANSWERS	GLOVER, D.
QUESTO FU IL CARRO DELLA MORTE	CASTELNUOVO-TEDE
QUICK STEP	BLAKE, N.
QUIET AFTERNOON, A	ROREM, N.
QUIET DANCE	SMITH-MASTERS
QUIET ECHOES	BRODSKY, M.
QUIET HOUR, THE	CANFIELD, J.
QUIET LAGOON	GEORGE
QUIET NIGHTS OF QUIET STARS	BRIMHALL,
QUIET NIGHTS OF QUIET STARS	LEES *
QUIET RAIN, THE	BRUSSELS, I.
QUIET SAILING	CROSBY, M.
QUIET STORY	WERMEL
QUIET TIME	KUBIK, G.
QUILTIN' BEE	MCHALE, M.
QUINTET, OP. 114 'TROUT'	SCHUBERT
QUINZE ETUDES DE VIRTUOSITE, OP. 72	MOSZKOWSKI
QUINZE ETUDES DE VIRTUOSITE, OP. 72	MOSZKOWSKI
QUITE CATCHY	FAHNESTOCK
QUITE CONTRARY	EZELL, H.
QUIZ GAME	KLEMM, G.
QUI VIVE, GRAND GALOP DE CON.	GANZ
QUI VIVE, OP. 12 -- GRAND GALOP DE CONCERT	GANZ
QUI VIVE	GANZ
QUODLIBET ON AMERICAN FOLK TUNES. TWO PIANOS, EIGHT	DAHL
QUODLIBET	SOUTHAM, A.
R. A. F. MARCH PAST	WALFORD DAVIES,
RACCONTI DI FRIDA, I - 5 LITTLE TYROLEAN PIECES	MILLAN
RACCONTO D'INVERNO -- WINTER TALE -- BALLET --	ROSSELLINI
RACE HORSE	MILLS, D.
RACHMANINOFF'S PIANO CONCERTO NO. 2 IN C MINOR, OP.	GRAINGER, P.
RACHMANINOFF CONCERTO	RACHMANINOFF, S.
RACING PONIES, CAPRICE	HOPKINS, H.
RACING SEA HORSES	GARROW, L.
RACING SLEIGHS, THE -- 6-HANDS	DALE, A.
RACKETY COO--''KATINKA''	FRIML, R.
RACOON, THE ROBBER	RAGANINI, A.
RADIO CITY ALBUM, BK. 1	CHOPIN
RADIO CITY ALBUM, BK. 2	CHOPIN
RADIO CITY ALBUM, BK. 2	GRIEG
RADIO CITY ALBUM	BEETHOVEN
RADIO CITY ALBUM	BRAHMS
RADIO CITY ALBUM	MOZART, W. A.
RADIO CITY ALBUM	OFFENBACH
RADIO CITY ALBUM	RACHMANINOFF, S.
RADIO CITY ALBUM	RIMSKY-KORSAKOFF
RADIO CITY ALBUM	RUBINSTEIN
RADIO CITY ALBUM	SCHUBERT
RADIO CITY ALBUM	TSCHAIKOWSKY
RADIO CITY SNAPSHOTS	WAGNER, J.
RADIO MADRID, SUITE	TURINA, J.
RAG-TIME PARADE	SATIE, E.
RAGAMUFFIN	RIXNER
RAGA ROCK	KONOWITZ, B.
RAGE OVER A LOST PENNY, OP. 129	BEETHOVEN
RAGE OVER THE LOST PENNY, OP. 129	BEETHOVEN
RAGGEDY ANN SONG BOOK, A	
RAGGIO VERDE, IL	CASTELNUOVO-TEDE
RAGTIME BOOK	SCHAUM, J.--ED.
RAGTIME PIANO STYLES	DENNIS, M.
RAGTIME PIANO	
RAGTIME TREASURES	LAMB
RAG DOLL WALTZ	GREEN, R.
RAG DOLL	BROWN, N. H.
RAG DOLL	
RAG MAN	WEYBRIGHT
RAILROAD BOOGIE, THE -- I BEEN WORKIN' ON DE RAILROAD	WEYBRIGHT
RAIN, RAIN GO AWAY	BRODSKY, M.
RAIN, RAIN GO AWAY	SUGARMAN
RAIN'S MONOTONE, THE	BRAGDON
RAINBOW DIVISION MARCH	NIRELLA, D.
RAINBOW FANTASY	CHOPIN
RAINBOW IN THE SKY	SCARMOLIN
RAINBOW SCHOTTISCHE	KLEBER
RAINBOW	TARDOS, B.
RAINDROP, THE, EASY	CHOPIN
RAINDROP, THE, PRELUDE	CHOPIN
RAINDROPS IN THE WIND	HUMES, D.
RAINDROPS KEEP FALLIN' ON MY HEAD	BRIMHALL,
RAINDROPS	BENFORD
RAINDROPS	GREEN, R.
RAINDROP TAG	KNOWLTON, D.
RAINY DAY, A	BAUER, M.
RAINY DAY, A	DAVIS
RAINY DAY	BENJAMIN
RAINY DAY	GREEN, R.
RAINY DAY	HEARN, E. F.
RAIN CLOUDS AND SUNSHINE	RENNARD
RAIN DANCE	KING, S.
RAIN DANCE	WATSON
RAIN DROPS ARE WALTZING	DITTENHAVER
RAIN DROPS	HOWELL
RAIN IN SPAIN, THE	BRIMHALL,
RAIN IN SPAIN, THE	LOEWE, F.
RAIN IN THE NIGHT	REID
RAIN ON A RICE PADDY	HELLER, E.
RAIN ON THE LEAVES	KEYSOR, E.
RAIN ON THE ROOF	ROGERS, E.
RAIN	GRAHAM, M.
RAJAH MARCH	LOUKA, M.
RAKASTAVA	SIBELIUS
RAKES OF MALLOW, THE -- AN IRISH COUNTRY DANCE	WEYBRIGHT
RAKOCZY MARCH	BERLIOZ *
RAKOCZY MARCH	LISZT
RAMA-JAZZ AND JAZZARAMA	FERRELL, B.
RAMAGE D'OISEAUX, OP. 80	MISSLER
RAMBLIN' RABBIT	TILLERY, H.
RAMBLIN' RAG	KRENZ, B.
RAMBLING RHYTHM	WORTZMAN, N.
RAMONA	LANE, J.--ED.

RAMPLESTILTSKIN   LEEDS, R.
RAMROD RAG --MODERN RHYTHMIC CLASSICS--   WHITFORD
RANDY LOU DANCE   WESTON, P.
RANGERS ON PATROL   TRUXELL, E.
RAPHAEL   RAPHAEL, G.
RAPID FIRE, ETUDE, OP. 256--FOR RIGHT HAND ALONE   DUVERNOY, J.
RAPID FIRE, OP. 256--ETUDE   DUVERNOY, J.
RAPPEL DES OISEAUX   RAMEAU
RAPPEL DES OIXEAUX   RAMEAU
RAPSODIA ARAGONESA   GRANADOS
RAPSODIA ARGENTINA   QUARATINO
RAPSODIA CUBANA, OP. 66   ALBENIZ, I.
RAPSODIA ESPANOLA, OP. 70   ALBENIZ, I.
RAPSODIA ESPANOLA   ALBENIZ, I.
RAPSODIA ESPANOLA   ALBENIZ, I.
RAPSODIA NEGRA   LECUONA
RAPSODIA PORTUGUESA   HALFFTER, E.
RAPSODIA SANTIAGUENA   GOMEZ CARRILLO
RAPSODIA SINFONICA   TURINA, J.
RAPSODIE, OP. 43 ON A THEME BY PAGANINI -- ABRIDGED   RACHMANINOFF, S.
RAPSODIE, OP. 43 ON A THEME BY PAGANINI   RACHMANINOFF, S.
RAPSODIE ARAGONAISE AND RAPSODIE CATALNE   SENTIS, J. *
RAPSODIE ESPAGNOLE   RAVEL
RAPSODIE ESPAGNOLE   RAVEL
RAPSODIE ESPAGNOLE   RAVEL
RAPSODIE HEBRAIQUE--1938   TANSMAN, A.
RAPSODIE HONGROISE NO.12   LISZT
RAPSODIE RUSSE   GRETCHANINOFF
RAPUNZEL   LEEDS, R.
RATHER BLUE   OLSON
RATIONAL PRINCIPLES OF PIANOFORTE TECHNIQUE -- E. --   CORTOT
RATIONAL PRINCIPLES OF PIANOFORTE TECHNIQUE -- FR. --   CORTOT
RATIONAL PRINCIPLES OF PIANOFORTE TECHNIQUE -- GER. --   CORTOT
RATS AND MICE   ROLFE, W.
RAVINI'S SERENADE   RAVINI, E.
RAYMONDA, OP. 57 --COMPLETE BALLET--   GLAZOUNOW, A.
RAYMOND FANTASIA   THOMAS, J. J.
RAYMOND OVERTURE   THOMAS, A.
RAY CHARLES INSTRUMENTAL FOLIO   CHARLES
RAZORBACK REEL   DAVIS, A.
REACH FOR THE SKY -- FROM 'REACH FOR THE SKY'   ADDISON, J.
READER, PART A   CLARK, F.
READER, PART B   CLARK, F.
READER, PART C   CLARK, F.
READER, PART D   CLARK, F.
READING, BK.1   BASTIEN
READING, BK.2   BASTIEN
READING, BK.3   BASTIEN
READING TECHNIQUE   CLARK, F.
READING TIME   MAIER, G. *
READING WITH ACES IS EASY   FRANKLIN, A.
READ AND PLAY BY PATTERNS   RICHTER
READ AND PLAY SERIES --PARTNERS--, IN 3 VOLS‡ VOL. 1.   JOHNSON--ED.
READ AND PLAY SERIES --PARTNERS--, IN 3 VOLS‡ VOL. 2.   JOHNSON--ED.
READ AND PLAY SERIES --PARTNERS--, IN 3 VOLS‡ VOL. 3.   JOHNSON--ED.
READ AND PLAY SERIES IN 9 VOLS., VOL. 1‡ BEGINNERS   JOHNSON--ED.
READ AND PLAY SERIES IN 9 VOLS., VOL. 2‡ HANDS   JOHNSON--ED.
READ AND PLAY SERIES IN 9 VOLS., VOL. 3‡ MOVING   JOHNSON--ED.
READ AND PLAY SERIES IN 9 VOLS., VOL. 4‡ MAKING   JOHNSON--ED.
READ AND PLAY SERIES IN 9 VOLS., VOL.5‡ MINIATURE   JOHNSON--ED.
READ AND PLAY SERIES IN 9 VOLS., VOL.6‡ GAINING GROUND   JOHNSON--ED.
READ AND PLAY SERIES IN 9 VOLS., VOL.7‡ PRESSING ON   JOHNSON--ED.
READ AND PLAY SERIES IN 9 VOLS., VOL.8‡ NEAR THE TOP   JOHNSON--ED.
READ AND PLAY SERIES IN 9 VOLS., VOL.9‡ AT THE TOP   JOHNSON--ED.
READ AND REMEMBER   TOBIN, R.
REAL COOL BOOGIE   GLOVER
REAL COOL PIANO   ANTHONY, G.
REAPER'S PARTING KISS   HEINS, C.
REAPERS, THE   COUPERIN, F.
REC' ROOM ROCK   SCHAUM, J.--ED.
RECESS BELL, THE   FLOOD
PECESS BELL, THE   FLOOD
RECESS TIME   RICCARDI, J.
RECHT DES HERRN, DAS -- BALLET IN 2 TABLEAUX   BRUNS, V.
RECIPE FOR A LITTLE GIRL   BENSON
RECITAL BOOKS, BK. 1   AUBERGE, A. D'
RECITAL BOOKS, BK. 2   AUBERGE, A. D'
RECITAL BOOKS, BK. 3   AUBERGE, A. D'
RECITAL BOOK   SCHAUM, J.--ED.
RECITAL DUOS. COMPILATION
RECITAL ETUDES FOR PIANO   LAWLOR, G.
RECITAL EXPRESS   GABAYE
RECITAL FOR CHILDREN, A   MONFRED
RECITAL MUSIC FOR THE YOUNG PIANIST   STEINER
RECITAL PIECES, BK. 1
RECITAL PIECES, BK. 2
RECITAL PIECES -- 15 ORIGINAL PIECES   OESTERLE--ED
RECITAL PIECES FOR THE YOUNG PIANIST, BK. 1   NELHYBEL, V.
RECITAL PIECES FOR THE YOUNG PIANIST, BK. 2   NELHYBEL, V.
RECITAL REFRESHER SERIES -- CLAVIERSTUECK   BEETHOVEN
RECITAL REFRESHER SERIES -- FABLE, OP. 2 NO. 2   SMETANA
RECITAL REFRESHER SERIES -- FANFARE   HANDEL
RECITAL REFRESHER SERIES -- FOLK SONG   GRIEG
RECITAL REFRESHER SERIES -- LAMENTO IN E MINOR   BACH, W. F.
RECITAL REFRESHER SERIES -- MINUET   RAMEAU
RECITAL REFRESHER SERIES -- ORIENTAL SONG   GLIERE
RECITAL REFRESHER SERIES -- THE DOLL'S COMPLAINT   FRANCK, C.
RECITAL REFRESHER SERIES -- TO A HUMMING BIRD   MACDOWELL
RECITAL REFRESHER SERIES -- TRUMPET TUNE IN C MAJOR   PURCELL, H.
RECITAL REFRESHER SERIES -- TRUMPET TUNE IN D MAJOR   PURCELL, H.
RECITAL RHYTHMS   SCHAUM, J.
RECITATIVE - 1951   KUPFERMAN, M.
RECITATIVE   KUPFERMAN, M.
RECOLLECTIONS, OP. 29   MIASKOVSKY
RECOLLECTIONS OF JOHANN STRAUSS   THOMPSON, J.--ED
RECOLLECTIONS OF SCOTLAND, OP. 80   MOSCHELES, I.
RECOLLECTIONS   HELPS
RECONCILIATION, OP. 42   ALKAN
RECONCILIATION   NORTH, A.
RECONCILIATION   RALSTON, F.
RECORDED FAVORITES OF NINA SIMONE
RECORDED PIANO INTERPRETATIONS   WILLIAMS, R.
RECREATION, OP. 37   ROWLEY
RECREATION, OP. 78   FREY
RECREATION, SUITE ENFANTINE   PACCAGNINI, A.
RECREATIONAL PIANO ALBUM, BK. 1   STEINER
RECREATIONAL PIANO ALBUM, BK. 2   STEINER
RECREATIONAL PIECES, BK. 2   GALLUZZI
RECREATIONAL PIECES, BK. 2   GALLUZZI
RECREATIONS A LA CAMPAGNE   CASADESUS, H.
RECREATIONS   DONATO, A.
RECREATIONS   RUSSELL
RECREATIONS   TANSMAN, A.
RECREATION --12 EASY PIECES--, OP. 77   FREY
RECREATION FOR PIANO   SCHECHTMAN
RECUERDOS DE VIAJE - TRAVEL IMPRESSIONS -   ALBENIZ, I.
RECUERDO   LONGAS

RED-NOSED CLOWN   DUNGAN
REDEMPTION - MORCEAU SYMPHONIQUE   FRANCK, C.
REDEMPTION POLKA   HOFER
REDISCOVERED CLASSICS, BK. 1   HENDERSON
REDISCOVERED CLASSICS, BK. 2   HENDERSON
REDISCOVERED CLASSICS, BK. 3   HENDERSON
REDISCOVERED CLASSICS, BK. 4   HENDERSON
REDISCOVERED MASTERWORKS, BK. 1   CLEMENTI
REDISCOVERED MASTERWORKS, BK. 2   CLEMENTI
REDISCOVERED MASTERWORKS, BK. 3   CLEMENTI
REDWOODS AT BOHEMIAN GROVE   TEMPLETON, A.
REDWOOD TRAIL   SCHAUM, J.--ED.
RED BALLOON, THE   LAMBERT, C.
RED BALLOONS   WRIGHT, G.
RED CROSS FOR A BLUE LADY   BENNETT
RED DANCING SHOES   ARCHER, I.
RED DRUM   NOONA, W.
RED LIGHT, GREEN LIGHT   BASTIEN
RED PEPPER POLKA   ROSNER
RED POPPY BALLET, DANCE   GLIERE
RED RIVER VALLEY   BURNAM
RED RIVER VALLEY   ROLFE, W.--ED
RED ROSES FOR A BLUE LADY --SIMP.   KING, S.--ED.
RED SAILS IN THE SUNSET   WILLIAMS, H.
RED SAILS IN THE SUNSET   WILLIAMS *
RED SANDS OF MARS   DVORINE
RED SHOES BALLET, THE
RED SKELTON -- HIS PIANO BOOK   FRANK, M.
RED SQUARE   MOORE
RED UMBRELLA   FROST
RED VELVET WALTZ   CURCIO
RED WING   MILLS, K.
REELS AND JIGS   GREGG
REEL   BALOGH
REFLECTIONS -- FIVE PIECES FOR PIANO, OP. 86   TOCH, E.
REFLECTIONS - FROM SEVEN FLOWERS FROM A PIANIST'S   GIASSON, P.
REFLECTIONS AT THE PIANO   TOLSON, P.
REFLECTIONS IN MODERN JAZZ   WALDRON
REFLECTIONS IN THE RAIN   NOONA, W.
REFLECTIONS IN THE WATER FROM IMAGES, BK. 1   DEBUSSY
REFLECTIONS IN THE WATER   DEBUSSY
REFLECTIONS OF THE MOON   DUNGAN
REFLECTIONS ON THE WATER, OP. 5   DUBENSKY
REFLECTIONS   DAVID, M.
REFLECTIONS   DUNGAN
REFLECTIONS   DUNGAN
REFLECTIONS   GELBER
REFLECTIONS   GIASSON, P.
REFLECTIONS   REEG, G. A.
REFLECTIONS   WHITFORD
REFLECTION   DOIGE
REFLETS -- BALLET -- BK. 1 .. HEIDELBERG, COBLENTZ,   SCHMITT
REFLETS -- BALLET -- BK. 2 .. VIENNA, DRESDEN,   SCHMITT
REFLETS D'ALLEMAGNE, BK. 1 - HEIDELBERG, COBLENTZ,   SCHMITT
REFLETS D'ALLEMAGNE, BK. 2 - VIENNA, DRESDEN,   SCHMITT
REFLETS DANS L'EAU --IMAGES--   DEBUSSY
REFLETS DANS L'EAU   DEBUSSY
REFLETS DANS L'EAU   DEBUSSY
REFLETS DANS L'EAU   DEBUSSY
REFLETS DU PASSE - AH, VOUS DIRAI-JE MAMAN   BULL
REFLETS DU PASSE - AU CLAIR DE LA LUNE   BULL
REFLETS DU PASSE - IL PLEUT BERGERE   BULL
REFLETS DU PASSE - LA MARSEILLAISE   BULL
REFLETS DU PASSE - LE ROI DAGOBERT   BULL
REFLETS DU PASSE - MALBOROUGH   BULL
REFLEXOES HARMONICAS NO. 4   SARNO
REFRAIN DES BAIGNEUSES   WACHS, P.
REG-WINGED BLACKBIRDS   STAIRS, L.
REGATA VENEZIANA, LA   LISZT *
REGATA VENEZIANA, LA   ROSSINI, G.
REGATA VENEZIANA, LA   ROSSINI *
REGATTA, THE   AARON, M.
REGATTA VENETIANA   LISZT *
REGENCY WALTZ   HAYMAN, R.
REGENTS MARCH, THE. --SALIANT YEARS, MAIN THEME, THE.   RODGERS
REGIMENTAL MARCH OF THE ROYAL CANADIAN MOUNTED POLICE   O'NEILL, C.
REGIMENTAL SONG   MERKUR
REGIMENT QUE PASSE, LE   EILENBERG
REGIMENT QUI PASSE, LE   EILENBERG
REGINA COELI -- QUEEN OF HEAVEN   DIEMENTE, E.
REGRET, UN -- REVERIE --   GAUTIER, L.
REIHENPROPORTIONEN, OP. 25   STEFFEN, W.
REIHE KL. KLAVIERSTUCKE   BADINGS
REINHILD - RHAPSODY   SERENDERO, D.
REITER-BURLESQUE, EINE   FINKE
REJOICE, BELOVED CHRISTIANS   BACH, J.S.
REJOICE, BELOVED CHRISTIANS   SCIONTI
RELACHE -- BALLET --   SATIE, E.
RELATIVE TALE OF TRIAD AND SCALE, THE, OP. 20   FLOOD
RELEASE ME   LANE, J.--ED.
RELIGIOUS HARMONY -- WITH LONGHI - MARCH --   SILVERI
PELIGIOUS MELODIES - 23 PIECES   VITTADINI
RELIGIOUS MUSIC OF THE MASTERS   STEINER
RELIGIOUS SONGS
RELUCTANT BALLERINA   RICHMAN, A.
REMBRANCE OF POLAND   LEVENSON, B.
REMEMBERED HAPPINESS, A   MCKAY, G.
REMEMBER ME -- FAR AWAY --   BRINKMANN
REMEMBER ME   MASDEA, V.
REMEMBER   TOBIN, R.
REMEMBRANCE, OP. 71 NO. 6   JADASSOHN, S.
REMEMBRANCES, OP. 4 NO. 1   PROKOFIEFF
REMEMBRANCES   HEDGE, E.
REMEMBRANCE   REBER
REMEMBRANCE   THOME, F.
REMINISCENCES DE DON JUAN-- CONCERT-FANTASY ON MOTIFS   LISZT
REMINISCENCES DE HALKA --MONIUSZKO   OP. 2   TAUSIG
RENDEVOUS -- INTERMEZZO ROCOCO   ALETTER, W.
RENDEZ-VOUS DE CHASSE, LE   GAUTIER, L.
RENDEZ-VOUS DE CHASSE   CARMAN
RENDEZVOUS -- INTERMEZZO ROCOCO   ALETTER, W.
RENDEZVOUS   HASKELL
RENDEZVOUS   WHITFORD
REPASZ BAND -- SIMP.   MOSSMAN, T.
REPASZ BAND MARCH   LINCOLN, H.
REPASZ BAND   LINCOLN, H.
REPASZ BAND   LINCOLN, H.
REPASZ BAND   LINCOLN, H.
REPAZ BAND   LINCOLN, H.
REPENTIR -- REVERIE --   GAUTIER, L.
REPERTOIRE ALBUM, BK. 1   STEINER
REPERTOIRE ALBUM, BK. 2   STEINER
REPERTOIRE ALBUM -- HIGHER INTERMEDIATE, BK. 1   PODOLSKY, L. *
REPERTOIRE ALBUM -- INTERMEDIATE   PODOLSKY, L. *
REPERTOIRE ALBUM -- LOWER ELEMENTARY, BK. 1   PODOLSKY, L. *
REPERTOIRE ALBUM -- LOWER ELEMENTARY, BK. 2   PODOLSKY, L. *
REPERTOIRE ALBUM -- LOWER INTERMEDIATE, BK. 1   PODOLSKY, L. *

Title	Composer
REPERTOIRE ALBUM -- LOWER INTERMEDIATE, BK. 2	PODOLSKY, L. *
REPERTOIRE ALBUM -- UPPER ELEMENTARY, BK. 1	PODOLSKY, L. *
REPERTOIRE ALBUM -- UPPER ELEMENTARY, BK. 2	PODOLSKY, L. *
REPERTOIRE FOR FIRST YEAR PIANISTS	WATERMAN *
REPERTOIRE FOR SECOND YEAR PIANISTS	WATERMAN *
REPERTOIRE	THOMPSON, J.--ED
REPONSE A MANON -- INTERMEZZO --	GILLET, E.
REQUIEBROS, LOS -- NO. 1, FROM GOYESCAS	GRANADOS
RESSURECTION -- BALLET	TANSMAN, A.
RESTLESS BROOK	EZELL, H.
RESTLESS MOTION	DIEMENTE, E.
RESTLESS SEA, THE	BENTLEY
RESTLESS WIND	WARD
RESURECTION	ROUSSEL, A.
RETOUR D'ULYSSE, LE	HUE, G.
RETOUR DES HIRONDELLES, LE	DE CRESCENZO
RETOUR DES MOISSINNEURS, LE OP. 13	GREGH
RETOUR DES MOISSONNEURS, LE OP. 13	GREGH
RETOUR DES MOISSONNEURS, LE OP. 13	GREGH
RETOUR DE FETE -- FROM RUSTIQUES, OP. 5	ROUSSEL, A.
RETOUR DE YOSHIWARA -- NO. 2, FROM DEUX IMAGES DU	GIL-MARCHEX
RETOUR DU BERGER, LE	SETACCIOLI
RETRAITE ESPAGNOLE	RUIZ DEL PORTAL
RETRAITE ESPAGNOL	RUIZ DEL PORTAL
RETRAITE FROM THE FIVE BAGATELLES	AURIC
RETRAITE SLAVE	LEMAIRE
RETRAIT AUX FLAMBEAUX	DE VILLEBICHOT
REVE, UN -- REVERIE NOCTURNE --	GAUTIER, L.
REVEILLE	WEYBRIGHT
REVEIL AU COUVENT	WALTER
REVEIL DES OISEAUX	MESSIAEN, O.
REVEIL DU PRINTEMPS	MARTY
REVELRY	OGILVY, F.
REVELRY	RICHTER, A.
REVELRY	THORNTON
REVEL OF THE ELVES -- MORCEAU	TIDES, A.
REVEL OF THE ELVES -- MORCEAU	TIDES, A.
REVERIE, OP. 58 NO. 1	SIBELIUS
REVERIES DE MARGUERITE, LES	YUNG
REVERIES DE MARGUERITE	YUNG
REVERIE -- SIMP.	DEBUSSY
REVERIE ALBUM	
REVERIE AT TWILIGHT	BROWN, L.
REVERIE D'AUTOMNE	WESLY
REVERIE DE L'ENFANCE DE PANTAGRUEL	SATIE, E.
REVERIE DU SOIR, OP. 19 NO. 1	TSCHAIKOWSKY
REVERIE DU SOIR DE LA SUITE ALGERIENNE, OP. 60	SAINT-SAENS
REVERIE FROM THE FIVE BAGATELLES	AURIC
REVERIE	DEBUSSY
REVERIE	DEBUSSY
REVERIE	DEBUSSY
REVERIE	DEBUSSY
REVERIE	DEBUSSY
REVERIE	DEBUSSY
REVERIE	ELIOT
REVERIE	FERNANDEZ, O.
REVERIE	GREENWALD, M.
REVERIE	NOEL, P. *
REVERIE	PIERNE, P.
REVERIE	WEYBRIGHT
REVERIE	WILSON
REVES. 6 CHARAKTERSTUCKE	SMETANA
REVES NOSTALGIQUES -- FANTASY IN THE FORM OF	STEPAN
REVES	SMETANA
REVE D'ARLEQUIN	PERROT
REVE D'UN ANGE, OP. 44	LUDOVIC
REVE DE PRINTEMPS, MAZURKA	DESSAUX
REVE DOULOUREUX	AKIMENKO
REVUE DE CUISINE, LE, SUITE	MARTINU, B.
REZA	LOBO *
RE ENZO - INTERMEZZO	RESPIGHI
RHAPSODALITY BROWN	CUSTER, A.
RHAPSODALITY BROWN	CUSTER, A.
RHAPSODIC INTERLUDE -- TO BELA BARTOK FROM	GREEN, R.
RHAPSODIC MELODY	MOORE
RHAPSODIE, OP. 28A	KADOSA
RHAPSODIES, OP. 79, NOS. 1 AND 2	BRAHMS
RHAPSODIES HONGROISES, BK. 1--NO. 1-8	LISZT
RHAPSODIES HONGROISES, BK. 2--NO. 9-15	LISZT
RHAPSODIES HONGROISES NO. 02	LISZT
RHAPSODIES HONGROISES NO. 02	LISZT
RHAPSODIES HONGROISES NO. 03	LISZT
RHAPSODIES HONGROISES NO. 05	LISZT
RHAPSODIES HONGROISES NO. 06	LISZT
RHAPSODIES HONGROISES NO. 09	LISZT
RHAPSODIES HONGROISES NO. 10	LISZT
RHAPSODIES HONGROISES NO. 11	LISZT
RHAPSODIES HONGROISES NO. 12	LISZT
RHAPSODIES HONGROISES NO. 13	LISZT
RHAPSODIES HONGROISES NO. 14	LISZT
RHAPSODIES HONGROISES NO. 15	LISZT
RHAPSODIE BASQUE	BORDES
RHAPSODIE D'AUVERGNE, OP. 73	SAINT-SAENS
RHAPSODIE D'AUVERGNE, OP. 73	SAINT-SAENS
RHAPSODIE DE PRINTEMPS -- PIANO SOLO, WITH ORCHESTRA	DAMASE, J. M.
RHAPSODIE DE PRINTEMPS	INGHELBRECHT, D.
RHAPSODIE ESPAGNOLE	LISZT
RHAPSODIE G-MOLL OP. 79 NO. 2	BRAHMS
RHAPSODIE GAELIQUE	LADMIRAULT
RHAPSODIE G MINOR OP. 46	DREYSCHOCK
RHAPSODIE H-MOLL OP. 79 NO. 1	BRAHMS
RHAPSODIE HONGROISE, NO. 2	LISZT
RHAPSODIE HONGROISE NO. 02 -- SIMP.	LISZT
RHAPSODIE HONGROISE NO. 02	LISZT
RHAPSODIE HONGROISE	THOMPSON, J.
RHAPSODIE IN B MINOR, OP. 79 NO. 1	BRAHMS
RHAPSODIE IN E FLAT, OP. 119 NO. 4	BRAHMS
RHAPSODIE IN G MINOR, OP. 79 NO. 2	BRAHMS
RHAPSODIE NEGRE	POWELL, J.
RHAPSODIE NO. 01	LISZT
RHAPSODIE NO. 02	LISZT
RHAPSODIE NO. 02	LISZT
RHAPSODIE NO. 02	LISZT
RHAPSODIE NO. 03	LISZT
RHAPSODIE NO. 05	LISZT
RHAPSODIE NO. 06	LISZT
RHAPSODIE NO. 11	LISZT
RHAPSODIE NO. 12	LISZT
RHAPSODIE NO. 14	LISZT
RHAPSODIE NO. 20 -- RHAPSODIE ESPAGNOLE --	LISZT
RHAPSODIE ZINGARESE	ECKSTEIN
RHAPSODIE	HARSANYI
RHAPSODY, OP. 1 --FIRST VERSION--	BARTOK
RHAPSODY, OP. 1	BARTOK
RHAPSODY, OP. 119 NO. 4	BRAHMS
RHAPSODY, OP. 17	KREIN, J.
RHAPSODY, OP. 20--1945	SCHISKE, K.
RHAPSODY, OP. 79 NO. 2	BRAHMS
RHAPSODY FOR TWO	SCHER, W.
RHAPSODY IN BLUE, 'LITTLE'	GERSHWIN
RHAPSODY IN BLUE, MODIFIED	GERSHWIN
RHAPSODY IN BLUE, THEME FROM	GERSHWIN
RHAPSODY IN BLUE, THEME FROM	GERSHWIN
RHAPSODY IN BLUE	GERSHWIN
RHAPSODY IN BLUE	GERSHWIN
RHAPSODY IN BLUE	GERSHWIN
RHAPSODY IN C, OP. 11 NO. 3	DOHNANYI
RHAPSODY IN D MINOR FOR SOLO PIANO AND ORCH.	FEDERER, R.
RHAPSODY IN D MINOR	FEDERER, R.
RHAPSODY IN E FLAT MINOR, OP. 11 NO. 4	DOHNANYI
RHAPSODY IN E FLAT	WHITFORD
RHAPSODY IN E MINOR, OP. 119 NO. 4	BRAHMS
RHAPSODY IN F SHARP MINOR, OP. 11 NO. 2	DOHNANYI
RHAPSODY IN F SHARP MINOR, OP. 11 NO. 2	DOHNANYI
RHAPSODY IN G MINOR, OP. 11 NO. 2	DOHNANYI
RHAPSODY IN G MINOR, OP. 11 NO. 1	DOHNANYI
RHAPSODY IN RHYTHM --MODERN RHYTHMIC CLASSICS--	WHITFORD
RHAPSODY IN SWING	LUTECE
RHAPSODY ON THE THEME OF THE SONG 'SCHOOL YEAR'	KABALEVSKY
RHAPSODY ON UKRAINIAN THEMES, OP. 28	LIAPUNOFF
RHAPSODY	BENBOW
RHAPSODY	CASATI
RHAPSODY	IRELAND, J.
RHAPSODY	WIGHAM, M.
RHEINGOLD, DAS -- GER AND ENG SUPERLINEAR TEXT	WAGNER
RHEINH. VOLKSTANZE, OP. 69	RICHARTZ
RHINO - THEME	SCHIFRIN, L.
RHUMBA, LA CHUPADERO	REISFELD
RHUMBATINA	ROGERS
RHUMBA --2 PIANOS, 8 HANDS--	PACE, R.
RHUMBA RIO	KASSCHAU, H.
RHUMBA RIO	KASSCHAU, H.
RHUMBA TOCCATA	HARVEY, PAUL R.
RHUMBOOGIE	RAYE *
RHYME AND REASON--MUSICAL TERMS EXPRESSED IN PIANO	QUAILE, E.
RHYTHMES ESPAGNOLS--7 SPANISH DANCES	LAPARRA, R.
RHYTHMICAL PROBLEMS	GERMER, H.
RHYTHMICON, BK. 1 - 29 ELEMENTARY STUDIES	CRESTON
RHYTHMICON, BK. 1	CRESTON
RHYTHMICON, BK. 2 - 15 ELEMENTARY STUDIES	CRESTON
RHYTHMICON, BK. 2	CRESTON
RHYTHMICON, BK. 3 - 18 EASY STUDIES	CRESTON
RHYTHMICON, BK. 3	CRESTON
RHYTHMICON, BK. 4 - 15 LOWER INTERMEDIATE STUDIES	CRESTON
RHYTHMICON, BK. 4	CRESTON
RHYTHMICON, BK. 5	CRESTON
RHYTHMIC FEET -- SOFT SHOE DANCE	TRUXELL, E.
RHYTHMIC MUSIC, 10 PIECES, BK. 1	MEDAU, H.
RHYTHMIC MUSIC, 10 PIECES, BK. 2	MEDAU, H.
RHYTHMIC PRELUDE	BRUSSELS, I.
RHYTHMIC TRAINING FOR THE FINGERS, OP. 3--IN SPANISH	STAMATY, C.
RHYTHMIC VARIATIONS ON HANON, BK. 1	HANON, C.
RHYTHMIC VARIATIONS ON HANON, BK. 2	HANON, C.
RHYTHMIC WAY, THE	PARSONS
RHYTHMISCH-STILISTISCHE STUDIEN, BK. 1 -- JAZZ STUDIES	PIEPER, M.
RHYTHMISCHE KLAVIERSTUECKE, OP. 18 -- 1955 --	EDER
RHYTHMISCHE STUDIEN	SEIBER, M.
RHYTHMS AND BLUES, BK. 1	SCHAUM, J.
RHYTHMS AND DANCES FOR PRE-SCHOOL AND KINDEGARTEN	HARVEY, A.
RHYTHMS AND DANCES FOR PRE-SCHOOL AND KINDERGARTEN	HARVEY, SR. A.
RHYTHMS AND THE I-V7 CHORDS	PODOLSKY, L. *
RHYTHM AND BLUES, BK. 1	SCHAUM, J.
RHYTHM AND BLUES, BK. 2	SCHAUM, J.
RHYTHM AND BLUES, BK. 3	SCHAUM, J.
RHYTHM FACTORY	METIS
RHYTHM INTERLUDE --MODERN RHYTHMIC CLASSICS--	WHITFORD
RHYTHM LULLABY --MODERN RHYTHMIC CLASSICS--	WHITFORD
RHYTHM SINGER, THE	SHLIMOVITZ
RHYTHM TO COUNT, SING AND PLAY	COBB
RHYTHM WITH RHYME AND REASON	COBB
RICERCAR, THREE PART, FROM ''THE MUSICAL OFFERING''	BACH, J.S.
RICERCARE, CANZONEN UND FUGEN DES 17. UND 18. JH. FUR	CORNET *
RICERCARE, CANZONEN UND FUGEN	HILLEMANN--ED
RICERCARE AND TOCCATA ON A THEME FROM 'THE OLD MAID	MENOTTI
RICERCARE AND TOCCATA	MENOTTI
RICERCARE ON THE NAME 'GUIDO M. GATTI'	CASELLA, A.
RICERCARE ON THE NAME 'LUIGI DALLAPICCOLA'	CASTELNUOVO-TEDE
RICERCARE	SARACENI
RICERCARI, CANZONE AND FUGUES -- WORKS BY GABRIELI,	HILLEMANN--ED
RICERCARI	MIHALOVICI
RICERCARI 3, 4 --DELL'INTABULATURA D'ORGANO, VENICE,	BUUS, J.
RICERCAR A 3--THREE-PART FUGUE--RICERCAR A 6--SIX-PART	BACH, J.S.
RICERCAR A 6 VOCI --MUSICAL OFFERING--	BACH, J.S.
RICHIAMI DEL MARE	RUDAN
RICHIE HAVENS - ANTHOLOGY	HAVENS, R.
RICKSHAW MAN	NEVIN
RICORDANZE D'UNA FESTA CAMPESTRE	CANTU
RICORDATE MARCELLINO	GIACOBETTI *
RICORDATTI, OP. 96 -- SALON MAZURKA	ALBENIZ, I.
RICORDI ALBUMS - ANTOLOGIA DE MUSICA ARGENTINA --	RICORDI
RICORDI ALBUMS - AUTORES PERUANOS - 6 SELECTIONS	RICORDI
RICORDI ALBUMS - NEW SONGS OF NAPLES	RICORDI
RICORDI ALBUMS - 30 CLASSICAL AND ROMANTIC PIECES	RICORDI
RIDDLE, A	RICHTER, A.
RIDDLE, A	RICHTER
RIDDLES IN SONG	SCHOENFELD *
RIDE-A-COCK HORSE	DITTENHAVER
RIDE A BOOGIE HORSE	LYON
RIDE IN A JEEP, A	STEINER
RIDE LITTLE COWBOY	FOSSEY, E.
RIDE OF PAUL REVERE, THE	BURNAM
RIDE OF THE AMAZONS, OP. 321	SPINDLER
RIDE OF THE ASTRONAUT	RAPHLING
RIDE RANGER RIDE	OFFENBACH
RIDE THROUGH THE NIGHT	HAUBIEL, C.
RIDIN' ALONG MANDEVILLE TRAIL	CATIZONE, J. M.
RIDIN' ALONG	VOLKART, H.
RIDIN' ALONG	VOLKART, H.
RIDIN' THE RANGE	DAVIS, J.
RIDING A WESTERN TRAIL	DUNGAN
RIDING A WESTERN TRAIL	DUNGAN
RIDING BOOTS	CHAGY
RIDING MY BIKE	ROGERS, E.
RIDING ON A BUFFALO	LAKE, G.
RIDING ON A CAMEL	HOPSON, E.
RIDING ON A CAMEL	JESSE, M.
RIDING ON A STAR	LINO, L. S.
RIDING THE CLOUDS	MACLACHLIN, T.
RIDING THE MOUNTAIN PONY	MEUTTMAN, M.

RIDING THE RANGE	DEE, M.
RIDING THE RANGE	MELVIN, B.
RIDING THE RAPIDS	SAVAGE, H. S.
RIDING THE SUNSET	TRUXELL, E.
RIDING THE WAVES	GROVE, R.
RIENZI -- GER AND ENG SUPERLINEAR TEXT	WAGNER
RIFLESSI DEL MARE - 3 CHARACTERISTIC PIECES	POZZOLI
RIFLESSI LAGUNARI	FERRARI-TRECATE
RIGAUDON, OP. 12 NO. 3	PROKOFIEFF
RIGAUDON, OP. 46 NO. 1	GOEDICKE
RIGAUDONS DES PETITS VIOLONS ET HARTBOIS DE LOUIS XIV	
RIGAUDONS	ALKAN
RIGAUDON --HOLBERG SUITE--, OP. 40 NO. 5	GRIEG
RIGAUDON CHAMPETRE	DE FRAGUIER
RIGAUDON DES DARDANUS	RAMEAU
RIGAUDON	DAQUIN, C.
RIGAUDON	RAMEAU
RIGAUDON	RAMEAU
RIGAUDON	RAVEL
RIGAUDON	WEYBRIGHT
RIGGADOON	SYMONS
RIGHT ABOUT MARCH	POWELL, W.
RIGHT HAND TREATMENTS	HENDERSON, R.
RIGOLETTO, ABRIDGED	VERDI
RIGOLETTO--PARAPHRASE	VERDI *
RIGOLETTO, DONNA E MOBILE, EASY	VERDI
RIGOLETTO, DONNA E MOBILE	VERDI
RIGOLETTO, PARAPHRASE	VERDI *
RIGOLETTO, PARAPHRASE	VERDI *
RIGOLETTO, QUARTETTE	VERDI
RIGOLETTO -- COMPLETE OPERA --	VERDI
RIGOLETTO - CONCERT PARAPHRASE	VERDI
RIGOLETTO - EASY FANTASIA	VERDI
RIGOLETTO - FANTASIA	VERDI
RIGOLLETTO -- LA DONNA E MOBILE, QUARTET	NEVIN
RIKA	RABINOFF, S.
RINCON MAGICO, OP. 97--DESFILE EN FORMA DE SONATA	TURINA, J.
RING-A-RING	DITTENHAVER
RING AROUND WALTZ	DIETS, J.
RING OUT BELLS	BRODSKY, M.
RIO RHYTHM	WERMEL
RIPE APPLES	HOLST
RIPPLES	GLOVER, D.
RIPPLES	LAWSON, P.
RIPPLING BOOKLET	HOWELL
RIPPLING STREAM	MCHALE, M.
RIPPLING WATER, THE, FROM 'NATURE PIECES'	MANA-ZUCCA
RIPPLING WATERS	PIERSON
RIPPLING WAVES	ANTHONY, B. R.
RISONANZE	MALIPIERO, G. F.
RITE OF SPRING	STRAVINSKY, I.
RITMICA	NEGRETE
RITMOS -- FANTASIA COREOGRAFICA	TURINA, J.
RITMOS ARGENTINOS	TROIANI
RITORNELLE UND FUGHETTEN, OP. 68	SCHOECK
RITOURNELLES -- OR FOR HARP	DAMASE, J. M.
RITOURNELLES	SCHMITT
RITOURNELLE	COWELL
RITRATTO DI DON CHISCIOTTE	PETRASSI
RITTRATO DI DON CHISCIOTTE	PETRASSI
RIVERBOAT CAPTAIN, THE	TOWNSEND
RIVERBOAT SONATA	SCHAUM, J.--ED.
RIVERSONG	DITTENHAVER
RIVER AND THE MOON	WEYBRIGHT
RIVER BOAT	EZELL, H.
RIVER KWAI MARCH, THE	ARNOLD *
RIVER QUEEN FOR TWO PIANOS OR ONE PIANO FOUR HANDS	BACON, E.
RIVIERA FESTIVAL -- LE FETE DES AS, VALSE BRILLIANTE	AZZOLA *
ROADRUNNER	TOWNSEND
ROAD RUNNER	SCHAUM, J.
ROAD TO PIANO ARTISTRY, VOL. 1	SCIONTI
ROAD TO PIANO ARTISTRY, VOL. 2	SCIONTI
ROAD TO PIANO ARTISTRY, VOL. 3	SCIONTI
ROAD TO PIANO ARTISTRY, VOL. 4	SCIONTI
ROAD TO PIANO ARTISTRY, VOL. 5	SCIONTI
ROAD TO PIANO ARTISTRY, VOL. 6	SCIONTI
ROAD TO PIANO ARTISTRY, VOL. 7	SCIONTI
ROAD TO PIANO ARTISTRY, VOL. 8	SCIONTI
ROAD TO PIANO ARTISTRY, VOL. 9	SCIONTI
ROBBINS FOLIO OF POPULAR MARCHES, THE	
ROBERT PACE PIANO SERIES, BK. 1	PACE, R.
ROBERT PACE PIANO SERIES, BK. 2	PACE, R.
ROBERT PACE PIANO SERIES, BK. 3	PACE, R.
ROBERT THE RAMBLIN' RABBIT	MESEROLE, H. T.
ROBERT WHITFORD BREAK SHEET BOOK FOR PIANO	WHITFORD
ROBERT WHITFORD CHORD CHART FOR THE MODERN PIANIST	WHITFORD
ROBERT WHITFORD CLASSIC PIANO METHOD, BK. 01	WHITFORD--ED.
ROBERT WHITFORD CLASSIC PIANO METHOD, BK. 02	WHITFORD--ED.
ROBERT WHITFORD CLASSIC PIANO METHOD, BK. 03	WHITFORD--ED.
ROBERT WHITFORD CLASSIC PIANO METHOD, BK. 04	WHITFORD--ED.
ROBERT WHITFORD CLASSIC PIANO METHOD, BK. 05	WHITFORD--ED.
ROBERT WHITFORD CLASSIC PIANO METHOD, BK. 06	WHITFORD--ED.
ROBERT WHITFORD CLASSIC PIANO METHOD, BK. 07	WHITFORD--ED.
ROBERT WHITFORD CLASSIC PIANO METHOD, BK. 08	WHITFORD--ED.
ROBERT WHITFORD CLASSIC PIANO METHOD, BK. 09	WHITFORD--ED.
ROBERT WHITFORD CLASSIC PIANO METHOD, BK. 10	WHITFORD--ED.
ROBERT WHITFORD MODERN PIANO EFFECTS	WHITFORD
ROBERT WHITFORD MODERN PIANO METHOD, BK. 1	WHITFORD--ED.
ROBERT WHITFORD MODERN PIANO METHOD, BK. 2	WHITFORD--ED.
ROBERT WHITFORD MODERN PIANO METHOD, BK. 3	WHITFORD--ED.
ROBERT WHITFORD MODERN PIANO METHOD, BK. 4	WHITFORD--ED.
ROBERT WHITFORD TECHNIC FOR PIANISTS, BK. 1	WHITFORD
ROBERT WHITFORD TECHNIC FOR PIANISTS, BK. 2	WHITFORD
ROBERT WHITFORD TECHNIC FOR PIANISTS, BK. 3	WHITFORD
ROBERT WHITFORD TECHNIC FOR PIANISTS, BK. 4	WHITFORD
ROBERT WHITFORD TECHNIC FOR PIANISTS, BK. 5	WHITFORD
ROBERT WHITFORD TECHNIC FOR PIANISTS, BK. 6	WHITFORD
ROBIN, ROBIN	OLDENBURG, E.
ROBIN'S DEPARTURE, THE	FISHER, L.
ROBIN'S LULLABY, OP. 15 NO. 12	KROGMANN, C. W.
ROBIN'S RETURN, THE	FISHER, L.
ROBIN'S RETURN, THE	FISHER, L.
ROBIN'S SONG, THE	RICHTER
ROBINS RETURN CAPRICE	FISHER, L.
ROBIN HOOD AND HIS MERRY MEN	SCHAUM, J.--ED.
ROBIN REDBREAST, WALTZ	HOPKINS, H.
ROBIN REDBREAST	SCHILLER, F.
ROBIN REDBREAST	TROWBRIDGE, L.
ROBIN SINGS A MERRY TUNE	BENSON
ROBOTS	GREEN
ROBYN-HANKS HARMONY, BK. 1	ROBYN *
ROBYN-HANKS HARMONY, BK. 2	ROBYN *
ROBYN-HANKS HARMONY, BK. 3	ROBYN *
ROBYN-HANON -- TWENTY-FIVE EXERCISES WITH SPECIAL	ROBYN
ROBYN ROTE-CARDS	ROBYN
ROCK-A-BOGGIE	ROGERS
ROCK-A-BYE BABY	ROLFE, W.--ED
ROCK'EM BOOGIE	SIMMS
ROCKETS AND SATELLITES	SCHAUM, J.--ED.
ROCKET RANGER	LANGE, G.
ROCKIN' AROUND THE CHRISTMAS TREE	BRADLEY,
ROCKIN' IN RHYTHM	ELLINGTON
ROCKIN' LITTLE TALE, A	LEWIS
ROCKIN' THE BLUES AWAY	AGAY, D.
ROCKIN' THE SCALES	RUSSELL
ROCKING CHAIR TRIP	BURNAM
ROCKING DOLLY TO SLEEP	POND, S.
ROCKING HORSE POLKA	SCHER, W.
ROCKING HORSE SWING	DECOLA, F.
ROCKING LULLABY	MANCUSO, S.
ROCKING	JOHNSTON, R.
ROCKIN ROBBIN	LANE, J.--ED.
ROCKY BROOKLET	WETTACH, T.
ROCKY MOUNTAIN DANCE	KARP
ROCKY MOUNTAIN SKETCHES	MELECCI, A.
ROCKY ROAD	GLOVER, D.
ROCK 'EM BOOGIE	SIMMS
ROCK 'N' ROLL BOOGIE	SCHAUM, J.--ED.
ROCK 'N' ROLL PIANIST, THE	SMALL, A.
ROCK 'N' ROLL PIANO	MARTIN, G.
ROCK 'N BLUES FOR FUN	BASTIEN--ED.
ROCK AND ROLL BLUES	MARTIN, G.
ROCK AND ROLL BLUES	MARTIN, G.
ROCK AND ROLL CHA CHA CHA	SWAN *
ROCK AND ROLL LULLABY	BRADLEY,
ROCK AND ROLL LULLABY	MARTIN, G.
ROCK AND ROLL MELODY	REEVES, R.
ROCK CONCERT	BASTIEN
ROCK CRUSHER	DONATO, A.
ROCK LIZA	LEWIS
ROCK ME BABY	CASSIDY, D.
ROCK ME EASY	OLSON
ROCK MODES AND MOODS	METIS
ROCK MODES AND MOODS	METIS
ROCK OF AGES, TRANSCRIPTION	MILLWARD
ROCK PIANO STYLES	DENNIS, M.
ROCK WITH JAZZ, BK. 1	STECHER *
ROCK WITH JAZZ, BK. 2	STECHER *
ROCK WITH JAZZ, BK. 3	STECHER *
ROCK WITH JAZZ, BK. 4	STECHER *
ROCK WITH JAZZ, BK. 5	STECHER *
ROCOCO-INTERMEZZO	ALETTER
ROCOCO RONDO	BARRETT
RODENA -- FROM IBERIA	ALBENIZ, I.
RODENT REEL	KRAEHENBUEHL
RODEO -- WITH WORDS	WESTERVELT,
RODEO RIDERS	ERB, M.
RODEO RIDER	DONENFELD, J.
RODEO ROUND UP	BURNAM
RODEO	CANFIELD, J.
RODEO	COPLAND
RODGERS AND HAMMERSTEIN ALBUM	RODGERS *
RODGERS AND HAMMERSTEIN PLAY AND SING--SIMPLIFIED	RODGERS *
ROGUISHNESS	ERB
ROLL, JORDAN, ROLL	REISFELD--ED
ROLL'EM BOOGIE	SIMMS
ROLL'EM PETE	JOHNSON, S.
ROLLER COASTER RIDE	HELLER, E.
ROLLER COASTER	WRIGHT, L.
ROLLER SKATING	HAYES
ROLLER SKATING	KREBS, S.
ROLLING HOOPS	STEVENS, M.
ROLLING STONES	MACFADYEN, A.
ROLLING STONE GATHERS NO MOSS	SCARMOLIN
ROLLING WAVES	MELVIN, B.
ROLLING WAVES	PANELLA, L.
ROLLING WAVES	WERMEL
ROLLING WHEELS	BARATI
ROLL 'EM BOOGIE	SIMMS
ROMAGNA - 1. CANZONI DI PRIMAVERA	PRATELLA
ROMAGNA - 2. NOTTI, EBBREZZE E SANGUE	PRATELLA
ROMAGNA - 3. VORTICI DI DANZE	PRATELLA
ROMAGNA - 4. BACCANALE D'AUTUNNO	PRATELLA
ROMAGNA - 5. LA NOTTE DI NATALE	PRATELLA
ROMANCE, A	STREET, A. A.
ROMANCE, OP. 11 NO. 5	RACHMANINOFF, S.
ROMANCE, OP. 15 NO. 7	SCHUMANN, R.
ROMANCE, OP. 24 NO. 4 AND WALTZ, OP. 24 NO. 5	SIBELIUS
ROMANCE, OP. 24 NO. 9	SIBELIUS
ROMANCE, OP. 24 NO. 9	SIBELIUS
ROMANCE, OP. 28 NO. 2	SCHUMANN, R.
ROMANCE, OP. 28 NO. 2	SCHUMANN, R.
ROMANCE, OP. 28 NO. 2	SCHUMANN, R.
ROMANCE, OP. 5	TSCHAIKOWSKY
ROMANCE, OP. 5	TSCHAIKOWSKY
ROMANCE, OP. 5	TSCHAIKOWSKY
ROMANCE, OP.44 NO. 1	RUBINSTEIN
ROMANCES NUEVOS, NO. 1 LA NINA DEL RIO DULCE	GUASTAVINO
ROMANCES NUEVOS, NO. 2 EL CHICO QUE VINO DEL SUR	GUASTAVINO
ROMANCES	DEBUSSY
ROMANCE --ONE PIANO-SIX HANDS	RACHMANINOFF, S.
ROMANCE -- LE CAHIER DE SYLVINE, NO. 1	DELANNOY
ROMANCE AND MUSIC	TRUXELL, E.
ROMANCE BOHEMIENNE	BOLDI
ROMANCE DE CUYO	GUASTAVINO
ROMANCE DE SANTA FE	GUASTAVINO
ROMANCE FROM 'A LITTLE NIGHT MUSIC'	MOZART, W. A.
ROMANCE IN A FLAT	RIMSKY-KORSAKOFF
ROMANCE IN C	SAUGUET
ROMANCE IN D FLAT, OP. 24 NO. 9	SIBELIUS
ROMANCE IN D FLAT, OP. 24 NO. 9	SIBELIUS
ROMANCE IN D FLAT	SIBELIUS
ROMANCE IN D MINOR, OP. 32 NO. 3	SCHUMANN, R.
ROMANCE IN E FLAT, OP. 44 NO. 1	RUBINSTEIN
ROMANCE IN E FLAT, OP. 44	RUBINSTEIN
ROMANCE IN E FLAT	RUBINSTEIN
ROMANCE IN F, OP. 50	BEETHOVEN
ROMANCE IN F MINOR, OP. 5 NO. 1	TSCHAIKOWSKY
ROMANCE IN F MINOR, OP. 5	TSCHAIKOWSKY
ROMANCE IN RIO	ROGERS, E.
ROMANCE OF THE SPACE AGE	STEINER
ROMANCE OUBLIEE - THREE VERSIONS --1848 TO 1880 SEARLE	LISZT
ROMANCE SANS PAROLES --SONG WITHOUT WORDS, OP. 97 NO.	STREABBOG
ROMANCE SANS PAROLES	FAURE, G.
ROMANCE SANS PAROLES	REBER
ROMANCE SANS PAROLES	SAINT-SAENS
ROMANCE SANS PAROLES	STREABBOG
ROMANCE TZIGANE	SCHER, W.
ROMANCE	AUBERT
ROMANCE	CLERGUE
ROMANCE	DEBUSSY
ROMANCE	DUMAS, L.
ROMANCE	EIGES
ROMANCE	FONTANA

ROMANCE	GRETCHANINOFF
ROMANCE	LAFORGE, F.
ROMANCE	PIERSON, A.
ROMANCE	RATHBONE, G.
ROMANCE	SIBELIUS
ROMANCE	STEWART, H.
ROMANCE	TOURS
ROMANCE	WHITFORD
ROMANCING KEYBOARD, THE	AGAY, D.--ED
ROMANOFF AND JULIET	NASCIMBENE
ROMANTICS, THE	BREWER
ROMANTIC ALBUM FOR THE YOUNG -- 34 ORIGINAL PIECES OF	SCHOBERLECHNER,
ROMANTIC CAMEOS	SCHAUM, J.--ED.
ROMANTIC ERA PIANO MUSIC	
ROMANTIC ETUDE, OP. 10 NO. 3	CHOPIN
ROMANTIC MASTERS	BRAHMS *
ROMANTIC MASTERS	
ROMANTIC MOMENTS	WAGNER, J.
ROMANTIC MOMENTS	WAGNER
ROMANTIC REVERIE	MOORE
ROMANTIC RHAPSODY, OP. 5	TSCHAIKOWSKY
ROMANTIC WALTZES OF FRANZ SCHUBERT	SCHUBERT
ROMANTIC WALTZES OF FRANZ SCHUBERT	SCHUBERT
ROMANTIKER-BUCH FUR DIE JUGEND	KRENTZLIN,
ROMANTISCHE KLAVIERMUSIK - HEFT 1, CLARA SCHUMANN --	SCHUMANN, C.
ROMANTISCHE STUDIE--''ERWARTUNG''	SCHOLZ
ROMANTISCHE SUITE	KAPRAL
ROMANY LIFE	HERBERT
ROMANZA K205 IN A FLAT--ATTRIBUTED TO MOZART	MOZART, W. A.
ROMANZA	BALEANI, V.
ROMANZA	COUTURE
ROMANZE, OP. 15 NO. 7	SCHUMANN, R.
ROMANZE, OP. 28 NO. 2	SCHUMANN, R.
ROMANZE AS-DUR -- K.V. 205	MOZART, W. A.
ROMANZE F-MOLL OP. 5	TSCHAIKOWSKY
ROMANZE FIS-DUR OP. 28 NO. 2	SCHUMANN, R.
ROMANZ	MACDOWELL
ROMAN SKETCHES, OP. 7--CLOUDS	GRIFFES, C.
ROMAN SKETCHES, OP. 7--FOUNTAIN OF ACQUA PAOLA, THE	GRIFFES, C.
ROMAN SKETCHES, OP. 7--NIGHTFALL	GRIFFES, C.
ROMAN SKETCHES, OP. 7--WHITE PEACOCK, THE	GRIFFES, C.
ROMAN SUITE	PADWA, V.
ROMEO AND JULIET--EXCERPTS--	TSCHAIKOWSKY
ROMEO AND JULIET, LOVE THEME	TSCHAIKOWSKY
ROMEO AND JULIET, OP. 64	PROKOFIEFF
ROMEO AND JULIET, OP. 75 --TEN EXCERPTS--	PROKOFIEFF
ROMEO AND JULIET, WALTZ	GOUNOD, C.
ROMEO AND JULIET BALLET	GOUNOD, C.
ROMEO AND JULIET OVERTURE	TSCHAIKOWSKY
ROMEO AND JULIET OVERTURE	TSCHAIKOWSKY
ROMEO AND JULIET SUITE	VLAD
ROMERIKS SUITE	BJERCKE
RONDA DE LOS ANIMALES	FICHER
RONDA DI STRUMENTI	ORLANDO, S.
RONDA	CASTRO, W.
RONDEAU, PARTITA NO. 2	BACH, J.S.
RONDEAU FOR TWO PIANOS	STEWART, R.
RONDEAU FROM 'ABDELAZER'	PURCELL, H.
RONDEAU MILITAIRE	DIABELLI
RONDEAU	MESSIAEN, O.
RONDEAU	MESSIAEN, O.
RONDES DE PRINTEMPS -- IMAGES POUR ORCHESTRE, NO. 3	DEBUSSY
RONDES DE PRINTEMPS	DEBUSSY
RONDE D'AMOUR	WESTERHOUT
RONDE D'AMOUR	WESTERHOUT
RONDE DES LUTINS	NERINI, E.
RONDE ENFANTINE	MOREL, F.
RONDE FRANCAISE	BOELLMANN, L.
RONDINI	MODONA
RONDINO, OP. 29, NO. 2	HOVLAND
RONDINO, OP. 68, NO. 1	SIBELIUS
RONDINO - FROM 7 CHILDREN'S PIECES	PAHISSA
RONDINO GALOP	HUMMEL, J. N.
RONDINO ON A THEME OF BEETHOVEN	KREISLER
RONDINO ON A THEME OF BEETHOVEN	KREISLER *
RONDINO VON BEETHOVEN	KREISLER
RONDINO	KOEHLER
RONDINO	LEMONT, C. W.
RONDO-BOLERO FUR KLAVIER UND ORCHESTER	GIRNATIS
RONDO, K. 485, D MAJOR	MOZART, W. A.
RONDO, K. 511, A MINOR	MOZART, W. A.
RONDO, OP. 11	HUMMEL, J. N.
RONDO, OP. 51 NO. 1	BEETHOVEN
RONDO, OP. 51 NO. 2	BEETHOVEN
RONDO, OP. 51 NO. 2	BEETHOVEN
RONDO, OP. 59	KABALEVSKY
RONDO, OP. 59	KABALEVSKY
RONDO, OP. 59	KABALEVSKY
RONDO, OP. 73	CHOPIN
RONDO, OP. 87A	TCHEREPNIN
RONDOLETTES	BENTLEY
RONDOLETTO IN C, OP. 76 NO. 1	BURGMUELLER
RONDOLETTO IN C MAJOR, OP. 15	HUENTEN
RONDOLETTO	SARIA, T.
RONDOS, FANTASIAS	MOZART, W. A.
RONDOS, FANTASY	CHOPIN
RONDOS --3--	CHOPIN
RONDOS	CHOPIN
RONDOS	CHOPIN
RONDOS	CHOPIN
RONDOS	CHOPIN
RONDOS	SEROUX
RONDO -- LES ADIEUX --	DUSSEK, J.
RONDO A-MOLL -- K.V. 511	MOZART, W. A.
RONDO ALBUM	RUTHARDT--ED
RONDO ALL' ONGARESE -- HOBOKEN 15-25	HAYDN
RONDO ALLA TURCA--FROM SONATA K331 IN A	MOZART, W. A.
RONDO ALLA TURCA, FROM A MAJOR SONATA	MOZART, W. A.
RONDO ALLA TURCA, OP. 68 NO. 3	BURGMUELLER
RONDO ALLA TURCA, OP. 68	BURGMUELLER
RONDO ALLA TURCA -- FROM SONATA K331 IN A	MOZART, W. A.
RONDO ALLA TURCA FROM SONATA NO. 11	MOZART, W. A.
RONDO ALLA TURCA FROM SONATA NO. 11	MOZART, W. A.
RONDO A CAPRICCIO, OP. 129 -- ''RAGE OVER THE LOST	BEETHOVEN
RONDO A CAPRICCIO, OP. 129 'RAGE OVER THE LOST PENNY'	BEETHOVEN
RONDO A CAPRICCIO, OP. 129	BEETHOVEN
RONDO A CAPRICCIO IN G MAJOR, OP. 129	BEETHOVEN
RONDO A CAPRICCIO OP. 129 -- WUT UBER DEN VERLORENEN	BEETHOVEN
RONDO A LA TURQUE	MOZART, W. A.
RONDO BRILL. ES-DUR OP. 62	WEBER, VON
RONDO BRILLANTE, OP. 29	MENDELSSOHN
RONDO BRILLANTE, OP. 29	MENDELSSOHN
RONDO BRILLANTE, OP. 62	WEBER, VON
RONDO BRILLANTE, OP. 84 NO. 2	SCHUBERT
RONDO BRILLANTE IN E-FLAT, OP. 62 'LAGAITE'	WEBER, VON
RONDO BRILLANT IN E FLAT, OP. 29	MENDELSSOHN
RONDO BRILLIANTE, OP. 62	WEBER, VON
RONDO BURLESCO	SANGIORGI
RONDO C-DUR, OP. 51 NO. 1	BEETHOVEN
RONDO CAPRICCIOSO, OP. 14	MENDELSSOHN
RONDO CAPRICCIOSO, OP. 14	MENDELSSOHN
RONDO CAPRICCIOSO, OP. 14	MENDELSSOHN
RONDO CAPRICCIOSO, OP. 14	MENDELSSOHN
RONDO CAPRICCIOSO -- SET	MENDELSSOHN
RONDO CAPRICCIOSO IN E, OP. 14	MENDELSSOHN
RONDO CAPRICCIOSO OP. 14	MENDELSSOHN
RONDO CLASSIQUE	NOEL, P. *
RONDO D-DUR -- K.V. 485	MOZART, W. A.
RONDO F-DUR	BACH, J.
RONDO FOR PIANO	ETTORE, E.
RONDO FOR PIANO	KABALEVSKY
RONDO FOR PIANO	PAPINEAU-COUTURE
RONDO FROM FIFTH CONCERTO	BEETHOVEN
RONDO G-DUR, OP. 51 NO. 2	BEETHOVEN
RONDO IN A, K386	MOZART, W. A.
RONDO IN A MAJOR	HAYDN
RONDO IN A	BEETHOVEN
RONDO IN A	ROBINSON, W. E.
RONDO IN B MINOR FROM SUITE NO. 2 FOR ORCH --	BACH, J.S.
RONDO IN C, TWO PIANOS, EIGHT HANDS	SMETANA
RONDO IN C, OP. 51 NO. 1	BEETHOVEN
RONDO IN C, OP. 51 NO. 1	BEETHOVEN
RONDO IN C, OP. 51 NO. 1	BEETHOVEN
RONDO IN C, OP. 73	CHOPIN
RONDO IN C FOR 2 PIANOS, 8 HANDS	SMETANA
RONDO IN C MAJOR, OP. 51 NO. 1	BEETHOVEN
RONDO IN C	DIABELLI
RONDO IN C	PLEYEL
RONDO IN D, OP. 175 NO. 1 -- SET	GURLITT
RONDO IN E FLAT, OP. 11	HUMMEL, J. N.
RONDO IN E FLAT, OP. 175 NO. 2 -- SET	GURLITT
RONDO IN E FLAT	SIROONI
RONDO IN E MINOR, OP. 175 NO. 3 -- SET	GURLITT
RONDO IN G, OP. 51 NO. 2	BEETHOVEN
RONDO IN G	PLEYEL
RONDO K485 IN D	MOZART, W. A.
RONDO K511 IN A MINOR	MOZART, W. A.
RONDO MILITAIRE	DIABELLI
RONDO NACH C.M. VON WEBER	BRAHMS
RONDO ON ARGENTINE CHILDREN'S FOLK TUNES	GINASTERA
RONDO VILLAGEOIS	RAVINA, H.
RONDO VOM GOLDENEN KALB, OP. 13 -- BALLET IN 3 SCENES	EINEM, G.
RONDO	BERGER
RONDO	CANTU
RONDO	GRAITZER, G.
RONDO	HUMMEL, J. N.
RONDO	ROBINSON, S.
RONDO	TUERK
RONDO	WOLFF, B.
RONRONCITOS	UGARTE
RON BOUD PIANO STYLINGS	BOUD, R.
ROOSTER, THE--FROM 'THE DANCING SCHOOL IN NOAH'S ARK	MAXIM, F.
ROPE TRICKS	RUSSELL
ROSACE 2	TAKAHASHI
ROSALIE	SINGER, L.--ED
ROSAMUND, BALLET MUSIC	SCHUBERT
ROSAMUND, BALLET MUSIC	SCHUBERT
ROSAMUNDE. ENTR'ACTES AND BALLET MUSIC	SCHUBERT
ROSAMUNDE 'BALLET MUSIC'	SCHUBERT
ROSARY, THE - FOR ONE PIANO, SIX HANDS	NEVIN
ROSARY, THE	NEVIN
ROSARY, THE	NEVIN
ROSARY, THE	NEVIN
ROSARY, THE	NEVIN
ROSARY, THE	NEVIN
ROSA -- A FLEMISH FOLK SONG	WEYBRIGHT
ROSE-FAY, THE--MAZURKA-CAPRICE, OP. 185	HEINS, C.
ROSEMARY	BRIDGE, F.
ROSEN AUS DEM SUDEN, KONZERTWALZER	STRAUSS, J. *
ROSES FROM THE SOUTH, OP. 388	STRAUSS, J.
ROSES FROM THE SOUTH, OP. 388	STRAUSS, J.
ROSES FROM THE SOUTH	STRAUSS, J.
ROSES FROM THE SOUTH	STRAUSS, J.
ROSES OF PICARDY	
ROSES	ROLFE, W.
ROSES	WHITFORD
ROSETTE, VALSE, OP. 275	STREABBOG
ROSE FAY, OP. 185	HEINS, C.
ROSE GARDEN	BILBRO, M.
ROSE LEAVES	MARCEL, G.
ROSE MARIE	FRIML, R.
ROSE OF TRALEE, THE	GLOVER
ROSE OF TRALEE, THE	STEINER
ROSE PETALS	LAWSON, P.
ROSE WALTZ	POWELL, J.
ROSSIGNOL, LE--AIR RUSSE AFTER ALABIEFF--	ALABIEFF *
ROTARY MARCH	NIRELLA, D.
ROUMANIAN CHRISTMAS CAROLS	BARTOK
ROUMANIAN DANCE NO. 6	BARTOK
ROUMANIAN FOLK DANCES	BARTOK
ROUMANIAN RHAPSODY, NO. 1	ENESCO
ROUMANIAN RHAPSODY	ENESCO
ROUNDELAY, A	BUSH
ROUNDELAY -- SET	NICHOLS, J. H.
ROUNDHOUSE CAPRICCIOSO	KRENZ, B.
ROUNDS FOR READING	BURNAM
ROUND AND ROUND AND ROUND IT GOES	PELS, W.
ROUND AND ROUND THE VILLAGE	WEYBRIGHT
ROUND AND ROUND	BEESON, J.
ROUND AND ROUND	HAYES
ROUND THE GIPSY CAMPFIRE	AARON, M.
ROUND THE VILLAGE GREEN	TOBIN, R.
ROUND UP	ROBERTS
ROUND WE GO	GARROW
ROUSSEAU VARIATIONS	GRIFFIS, E.
ROW, BROTHER, ROW	BLAKE, D.
ROW, ROW, ROW, ONE PIANO - SIX HANDS	MACGREGOR
ROW, ROW, ROW YOUR BOAT	WEYBRIGHT
ROW ABOUT	AHMAD, R.
ROYAL BALLET	LEHAR
ROYAL BLUE	
ROYAL CONSERVATORY OF MUSIC, UNIVERSITY OF TORONTO --	
ROYAL CONSERVATORY OF MUSIC, UNIVERSITY OF TORONTO --	
ROYAL CONSERVATORY OF MUSIC, UNIVERSITY OF TORONTO --	
ROYAL CONSERVATORY OF MUSIC, UNIVERSITY OF TORONTO --	
ROYAL CONSERVATORY OF MUSIC, UNIVERSITY OF TORONTO --	
ROYAL CONSERVATORY OF MUSIC, UNIVERSITY OF TORONTO --	
ROYAL CONSERVATORY OF MUSIC, UNIVERSITY OF TORONTO --	
ROYAL CONSERVATORY OF MUSIC, UNIVERSITY OF TORONTO --	
ROYAL CONSERVATORY OF MUSIC, UNIVERSITY OF TORONTO --	
ROYAL CONSERVATORY OF MUSIC, UNIVERSITY OF TORONTO --	
ROYAL CONSERVATORY OF MUSIC, UNIVERSITY OF TORONTO --	
ROYAL CONSERVATORY OF MUSIC, UNIVERSITY OF TORONTO --	

ROYAL CONSERVATORY OF MUSIC, UNIVERSITY OF TORONTO --	
ROYAL CONSERVATORY OF MUSIC, UNIVERSITY OF TORONTO --	
ROYAL MARCH OF ITALY	GAMBETTI
RRR -- IN 1 BOOK	RACHMANINOFF, S.
RUBBER DUCKIE	BRIMHALL,
RUBE BLOOM'S GUIDE TO MODERN PIANO PLAYING	BLOOM
RUBE BLOOM'S MODERN JAZZ PIANO COURSE	BLOOM
RUBIES	SIMON
RUBY-DUBY-DU	WOLCOTT, C.
RUBY	LANE, J.--ED.
RUBY	ROEMHELD, H.
RUBY	
RUDEPOEMA	VILLA-LOBOS, H.
RUDOLPH'S CHRISTMAS ALBUM	WEYBRIGHT--ED.
RUDOLPH'S CHRISTMAS ALBUM	WEYBRIGHT
RUDOLPH THE RED-NOSED REINDEER	BRADLEY,
RUFFLES AND LACE	HOLLANDER
RUFFY AND TUFFY	SCHAUM, J.--ED.
RUFF AND TUFF	STEINER
RUINS OF ATHENS, TURKISH MARCH	BEETHOVEN
RUMANISCHE VOLKSTANZE	BARTOK
RUMANISCHE WEIHACHTSLIEDER	BARTOK
RUMBALERO	CAMARATA
RUMBA RASCAL	DECOLA, F.
RUMBA ROMANCE	DECOLA, F.
RUMBA TARANTELLA	CRESTON
RUMBA	DUNGAN
RUMORES DE LA CALETA, MALAGUENA -- NO. 6, FROM	ALBENIZ, I.
RUMORES DE LA CALETA -- FROM RECUERDOS DE VIAJE	ALBENIZ, I.
RUMORES DE LA CALETA - MALAGUENAS -	ALBENIZ, I.
RUMORES DE LA CALETA	ALBENIZ, I.
RUMPELSTILTSKIN	SCHUYLER
RUMPUS ROOM RUMBA	DOIGE
RUMPUS ROOM	STEINER
RUN-AWAY BALLOON	BASTIEN
RUN, LITTLE SQUIRREL	JOYNER, B.
RUNAWAY COLT	RUSSELL
RUNAWAY ELEPHANT, THE	SCHAUM, S.
RUNNING, RUNNING	ROLLINS, G.
RUNNING ALONG	KARP
RUNNING OFF THE RAILS --A LOCO-MOTIF	RICHARDSON, A.
RUNNING ON TIPTOES	PERRIN
RUNNING SMOOTHLY -- 24 PIECES EMBRACING TECHNICAL	STEINER
RUNNYMEDE RHAPSODY --WHERE THE WATERLILIES DREAM	KING
RUN ALONG LITTLE BROOK	ARNOLD, H.
RUN AND SKIP -- LITTLE SLEEPY SONG	HAYES
RUN LITTLE INDIAN	HOFSTAD, M.
RUN LITTLE LAMB	WILSON, S.
RUN MOUSE, RUN	GARROW
RUN RUN RUN	BRADLEY,
RURALIA HUNGARICA, OP. 32A	DOHNANYI
RURAL SKETCHES	JOHNSON, T.
RUSH-HOUR IN HONG KONG	CHASINS, A.
RUSHIN' DANCE	HOSKINS, W.
RUSH HOUR IN HONG KONG	CHASINS, A.
RUSSIAN DANCE. TREPAK--FROM NUTCRACKER SUITE	TSCHAIKOWSKY
RUSSIAN DANCE--''KATINKA''	FRIML, R.
RUSSIAN DANCE, OP. 7	ISSERLIS, J.
RUSSIAN DANCE, TREPAK, FROM NUTCRACKER SUITE	TSCHAIKOWSKY
RUSSIAN DANCE OP. 753	ENGELMANN, H. U.
RUSSIAN DANCE	GRETCHANINOFF
RUSSIAN EASTER FESTIVAL, OP. 36	RIMSKY-KORSAKOFF
RUSSIAN EASTER FESTIVAL, OP. 36	RIMSKY-KORSAKOFF
RUSSIAN FAIRY TALES, OP. 58	HARTMANN
RUSSIAN FOLK SONGS, IN PROGRESSIVE ORDER. NOS. 1, 2, 9	TSCHAIKOWSKY
RUSSIAN FOLK SONGS -- EASY-	TSCHAIKOWSKY
RUSSIAN FOLK SONG --WITH WEDDING DANCE BY LUBARSKY	ALEXANDROV
RUSSIAN FOLK SONG	GREENWALD,
RUSSIAN FOLK SONG	KABALEVSKY
RUSSIAN INTERMEZZO, OP. 136	FRANKE, T.
RUSSIAN INTERMEZZO	FRANKE, T.
RUSSIAN MARCH	GANNE
RUSSIAN MASTERS -- 14 ORIGINAL COMPOSITIONS BY	BORODIN, A. *
RUSSIAN MELODIES AND DANCES, OP. 31	BORTKIEWICZ
RUSSIAN MUSIC FOR THE YOUNG PIANIST -- BOOK 1	ZEITLIN--ED
RUSSIAN MUSIC FOR THE YOUNG PIANIST -- BOOK 2	ZEITLIN--ED
RUSSIAN MUSIC FOR THE YOUNG PIANIST -- BOOK 3	ZEITLIN--ED
RUSSIAN MUSIC FOR THE YOUNG PIANIST -- BOOK 4	ZEITLIN--ED
RUSSIAN MUSIC FOR THE YOUNG PIANIST -- BOOK 5	ZEITLIN--ED
RUSSIAN MUSIC FOR THE YOUNG PIANIST -- BOOK 6	ZEITLIN--ED
RUSSIAN PEASANT DANCE	SCHIEFELBEIN, F.
RUSSIAN PIANO MUSIC	
RUSSIAN PICNIC -- SET	ENDERS, H.
RUSSIAN PRELUDE	SLONIMSKY
RUSSIAN ROMANCE, OP. 30	FRIML, R.
RUSSIAN SONG, OP. 27, NO. 2	TCHEREPNIN
RUSSIAN SONG, OP. 31	SMITH, SYDNEY
RUSSIAN SONG	SMITH, S.
RUSSIAN THEME, OP.11 NO. 3	RACHMANINOFF, S.
RUSSLAN AND LUDMILLA	GLINKA
RUSTICA	ORREGO SALAS, J.
RUSTIC CHAPEL	ROLFE, W.
RUSTIC DANCE	CHENOWETH, W.
RUSTIC DANCE	HOWELL, C. R.
RUSTIC DANCE	HOWELL, C. R.
RUSTIC DANCE	HOWELL, C. R.
RUSTIC DANCE	HOWELL, C. R.
RUSTIC DANCE	HOWELL, C. R.
RUSTIC DANCE	HOWELL, C. R.
RUSTIC DANCE	HOWELL, C. R.
RUSTIC DANCE	HOWELL, C. R.
RUSTIC DANCE	HOWELL, C. R.
RUSTIC DANCE	JAQUE, R.
RUSTIC DANCE	STAIRS, L.
RUSTIC POLKA	TSCHAIKOWSKY
RUSTIC SONG, OP. 68 NO. 20--ALBUM FOR THE YOUNG	SCHUMANN, R.
RUSTIQUES, OP. 5	ROUSSEL, A.
RUSTLERS, BEWARE	KILPATRICK
RUSTLES OF SPRING, OP. 32 NO. 3	SINDING
RUSTLE OF SPRING, OP. 32 NO. 3	SINDING
RUSTLE OF SPRING, OP. 32 NO. 3	SINDING
RUSTLE OF SPRING, OP. 32 NO. 3	SINDING
RUSTLE OF SPRING	SINDING
RUSTLE OF SPRING	SINDING
RUSTLE OF SPRING	SINDING
RUSTLE OF SPRING	SINDING
RUSTLING ASPEN LEAVES	BASTIEN
RUSTLING LEAVES	LANGE, G.
RUTH, OP. 16 -- BALLET IN 2 ACTS	ERBSE
RYTHMES ET JEUX	DEMIERRE
RYTHMES GRECS	PONIRIDY
RYTHMES	HARSANYI
RYTHME ET ARTICULATION DES DOIGTS, OP. 42	RIE, B.
SABBATH CHIMES	KLICKMANN
SABBATH DAY MUSIC	RANDOLPH, J.--ED
SABOTIERE	CARMAN
SABOTIERE	CARMAN

SABRES DE BOIS, LES, OP. 314 NO. 3	STREABBOG
SABRE DANCE, GAYNE BALLET	KHATCHATURIAN
SABRE DANCE --FROM GAYNE--	KHATCHATURIAN
SABRE DANCE --FROM GAYNE--	KHATCHATURIAN
SABRE DANCE -- SIMP.	KHATCHATURIAN
SABRE DANCE BOOGIE	KHATCHATURIAN
SABRE DANCE FROM 'GAYNE BALLET'	KHATCHATURIAN
SABRE DANCE	KHATCHATURIAN
SABRE DANCE	KHATCHATURIAN
SABRE DANCE	KHATCHATURIAN
SABRE DANCE	KHATCHATURIAN
SABRE DANCE	KHATCHATURIAN
SACCADE	HELPS
SACK WALTZ, THE	METCALF, J.
SACK WALTZ	METCALF, J.
SACK WALTZ	METCALF, J.
SACK WALTZ	METCALF, J.
SACRED AND SECULAR PIANO ALBUM, BK. 1	HEAPS, S.
SACRED AND SECULAR PIANO ALBUM, BK. 2	HEAPS, S.
SACRED BOOK	SCHAUM, J.--ED.
SACRED CHRISTMAS DUETS	IBBERSON--ED
SACRED CLASSICS FOR FOUR HANDS-ONE PIANO	SMITH, T.
SACRED HOUR AT THE PIANO	ARNO--ED.
SACRED MOODS	KAHL
SACRED MUSIC	GARROW, L.
SACRED PIANIST	
SACRED PIANO ALBUM	GAHM--ED.
SACRED PIANO DUETS	
SACRED REFLECTIONS FOR PIANO DUET	
SACRED REFLECTIONS FOR PIANO SOLO	
SACRED SONGS AND HYMNS	ZEPP--ED
SACRED SONGS AND SPIRITUALS	NEVIN
SACRED SONGS FOR THE PIANO	BOCK, F.
SACRED SONGS IN THE CATHOLIC HOME	ROFF
SACRED TRANSCRIPTIONS -- PIANO NO. 1	AULD, W. J.
SACRED TRANSCRIPTIONS -- PIANO NO. 2	AULD, W. J.
SACRED TRANSCRIPTIONS -- PIANO NO. 3	AULD, W. J.
SACRED TRANSCRIPTIONS FOR PIANO	
SACY	VILLA-LOBOS, H.
SADDLE BOY BOOGIE	LYON
SADDLE SONG	RICKER, E.
SADKO - SONG OF INDIA	RIMSKY-KORSAKOFF
SADNESS AND MADNESS -- PHRYGIAN AND LOCRIAN MODES	BRUGMANN, A.
SAD CLOWN	SCHER, W.
SAD LITTLE CAT	STERNKLAR, A.
SAD LITTLE CLOWN	HUNEKE
SAD LITTLE PUPPY	SCHER, W.
SAD LITTLE SPINNER	BARLOW
SAD LITTLE TUNE, A	GNESSINA
SAD PUPPET, THE	BERNSTEIN, S.
SAD SEA, THE	WARD
SAD STORY	FREDERICKS
SAD THING, A	KING
SAD THOUGHTS OF THEE	ALLOWAYS
SAD WALTZ	FRACKENPOHL, A.
SAEMTLICHE WERKE FUER KLAVIER UND ORGEL	FISCHER, J.
SAFARI --MODERN RHYTHMIC CLASSICS--	WHITFORD
SAGEBRUSH COUNTRY	MCKAY, G.
SAGEBRUSH SERENADE	BENTLEY
SAID THE WIND TO ME	BRODSKY, M.
SAILBOATS	STAIRS, L.
SAILING ALONG THE SHORE	HIBBS, C.
SAILING IN THE TUB	ROGERS, E.
SAILING	HRUBY, V.
SAILOR-BOY	MACLACHLIN, T.
SAILOR'S DELIGHT	LEWIS
SAILOR'S JIG	NEVIN
SAILOR'S SONG, OP. 45 NO. 14	HELLER, S.
SAILOR'S SONG, OP. 68 NO. 1	GRIEG
SAILOR'S SONG, OP. 68 NO. 1	GRIEG
SAILOR'S SONG AND HORNPIPE -- FROM THREE PIECES FOR	MERKUR
SAILORS' DANCE	RATHBONE, G.
SAILORS SHINDIG	WERMEL
SAILORS SONG	SCHUMANN, R.
SAILOR BOY	ROBINSON, A.
SAILOR DANCES	WERMEL
SAILOR TUNE, A	CATON, F.
SAILS AT SUNDOWN	GREEN
SAILS FROM 'SEA SKETCHES'	MASON, I.
SAIL AWAY	
SAIL BOATS ON PARADE	MELVIN, B.
SAIL BOAT	MACKOWN
SAIL ON LITTLE BOAT	RICHTER
SAINTS' WHEEL	
SAINT ANTHONY CHORALE AND FOUR VARIATIONS	BRAHMS
SAINT ANTHONY CHORALE FROM VARIATIONS ON A THEME BY	BRAHMS
SALADE -- BALLET CHANTE	MILHAUD, D.
SALLY TRIES THE BALLET -- A MUSICAL PICTURE	WILLIAMS
SALMON, THE	BERGENFELD, N.
SALTARELLE, OP. 49	GREGH
SALTARELLE, OP. 49	GREGH
SALTARELLO, OP. 49	GREGH
SALTARELLO ABRUZZESE	DE NARDIS
SALTARELLO ABRUZZESE	DE NARDIS
SALTARELLO	LACK, T.
SALTARELLO	WAGENAAR, B.
SALT WATER BOOGIE	SCHAUM, J.--ED.
SALUTE TO AMERICA	REBE
SALUTE TO SAMUEL PEPYS	HARVEY, PATRICK
SALUTE TO THE COLORS	ANTHONY, B. R.
SALUTE TO THE COLORS	ANTHONY, B. R.
SALUTE TO THE COLORS	ANTHONY, B. R.
SALUT A PESTH--MARCHE HONGROISE DE CONCERT	KOWALSKI, H.
SALUT A PESTH	KOWALSKI, H.
SALUT CENDRE DU PAUVRE, OP. 45	ALKAN
SALUT D'AMOUR, OP. 12	ELGAR, E.
SALUT D'AMOUR -- LOVE'S GREETING	ELGAR, E.
SALUT D'AMOUR OP. 12	ELGAR, E.
SALUT D'AMOUR	ELGAR, E.
SALUT DU PRINTEMPS, OP. 16	HERTRICH
SALVE REGINA -- HAIL, HOLY QUEEN	DIEMENTE, E.
SAMARAI SWORD DANCE	NOONA, W.
SAMBA, YERBA BUENA	GUENTHER
SAMBALINA	KREVIT, W.
SAMBA SENORITA	KASSCHAU, H.
SAMBA SENORITA	KASSCHAU, H.
SAMBA	AGAY, D.
SAMBO'S BANJO	TODD
SAMMULUNG LEICHTER KLAVIERSTUCKE	HAYDN
SAMMY THE SAILOR	DAVIS, J.
SAMSON AND DELILA, MY HEART	SAINT-SAENS
SAMSON ET DALILA	SAINT-SAENS
SAMTLICHE KLAVIERFANTASIEN	BACH, W.F.
SAMTLICHE KLAVIERSONATEN, HEFT 1 - SONATEN G, A, B	BACH, W.F.
SAMTLICHE KLAVIERSONATEN, HEFT 2 - SONATEN D, D, E	BACH, W.F.
SAMTLICHE KLAVIERSONATEN, HEFT 3 - SONATEN C, C, F	BACH, W.F.

SANCTISSIMA	SCHIEFELBEIN, F.
SANCTISSIMA	THOMAS, A.
SANCTUARY OF THE HEART	KETELBEY, A.
SANDMAN'S LULLABY, THE	CROSBY, M.
SANDMAN'S SONG	MUNN, W.
SANDPAPER BALLET	ANDERSON, L.
SAND CASTLES	BARNES, M.
SANS OCTAVES -- 12 LITTLE PIECES -- BK. 1	LAZARE-LEVY
SANS OCTAVES -- 12 LITTLE PIECES -- BK. 2	LAZARE-LEVY
SANS OCTAVES -- 12 LITTLE PIECES -- VALSE LENTE	LAZARE-LEVY
SANTA'S ON HIS WAY	SCHAUM, J.
SANTA AND HIS SLEIGH - FOR PIANO, SIX HANDS	SEBASTIAN
SANTA CLAUS, XMAS TALE	HOPKINS, H.
SANTA CLAUS IS COMIN' TO TOWN	
SANTA CLAUS IS COMING TO TOWN	LANE, J.--ED.
SANTA CLAUS IS IN TOWN	MUNN, W.
SANTA CLAUS MARCH AND O COME ALL	RICHARDS, B.
SANTA LUCIA	LICHNER, H.
SANTA LUCIA	SCHAUM, J.--ED.
SANTA LUCIA	WEYBRIGHT--ED.
SAN FRANCISCO EL GRANDE	LECUONA
SAN FRANCISCO EL GRANDE	LECUONA
SAO PAULO BOOGIE	REID
SAO PAULO	FIELDS, I.
SAPHO. FANTASY. TWO PIANOS, EIGHT HANDS	GOUNOD, C.
SAPPHIRES	SIMON
SAPPHIRE SET	CLARK, M.--ED.
SARABANDE, FRENCH SUITE NO. 1	BACH, J.S.
SARABANDE -- NO.1, FROM SUITE ANCIENNE NO. 2	ALBENIZ, I.
SARABANDE FROM L'EVENTAIL DE JEANNE	ROUSSEL, A.
SARABANDE IN C MINOR	BACH, J.S.
SARABANDE IN F	HANDEL
SARABANDE LOINTAINE	RODRIGO, J.
SARABANDE ON THE THEME BY NICOLAS SIRET	DE ANGELIS
SARABANDE WITH VARIATIONS, SUITE 11,WATER MUSIC	HANDEL
SARABANDE	ARRIEU
SARABANDE	BOYDELL
SARABANDE	CASELLA, A.
SARABANDE	CORELLI
SARABANDE	COUPERIN, F.
SARABANDE	GILLOCK
SARABANDE	GILLOCK
SARABANDE	GILLOCK
SARABANDE	KOECHLIN, C.
SARABANDE	MAGLIONI
SARABANDE	WEYBRIGHT
SARABAND	ANDERSON, L.
SARABAND	ANDERSON, L.
SARAH	TAYLOR
SARCASMS, OP. 17	PROKOFIEFF
SARI	KALMAN
SASSAFRAS--LAWSON-GOULD EDITION	BACON, E.
SASSY PIECE	BECK
SASSY SUE	GLOVER, D.
SATANIC POEM, OP. 36	SCRIABINE, A.
SATANIC POEM	SCRIABINE, A.
SATELLITE	WATSON
SATURDAY IN THE PARK	BRIMHALL,
SATURDAY NIGHT	CANFIELD, J.
SAUCER MAN	GLOVER, D.
SAUCY SAUNTER	COBB
SAUDADES DAS SELVAS BRASILERIAS	VILLA-LOBOS, H.
SAUDADES DO BRAZIL--SUITE--BK. 1	MILHAUD, D.
SAUDADES DO BRAZIL--SUITE--BK. 2	MILHAUD, D.
SAUDADES DO BRAZIL--SUITE--NO. 3, LEME	MILHAUD, D.
SAUDADES DO BRAZIL--SUITE--NO. 5, IPANEMA	MILHAUD, D.
SAUNTERING ALONG	ANSON, G.
SAUT A LA CORDE, LE	PIERNE, P.
SAVAGE DANCE, A	LEONI, F.
SAY 'SI SI'	LECUONA
SBALZI	FERRARI-TRECATE
SCALA DI SETA, LA - OVERTURE	ROSSINI, G.
SCALA PIANO DUET ALBUM	STEEL
SCALES, CHORDS, ARPEGGIOS AND OCTAVES FOR PIANO	
SCALES, CHORDS AND ARPEGGIOS	MILLIGAN
SCALES, THE - BK. 1 -- SIMPLE SCALES --	SILVESTRI
SCALES, THE - BK. 2 -- SCALES IN THIRDS AND SIXTHS --	SILVESTRI
SCALES - MAJOR, MINOR AND CHROMATIC	MONTANI
SCALES AND ARPEGGIOS AT PLAY	TERRY, F.
SCALES AND ARPEGGIOS	BERKOWITZ
SCALES AND CADENCES	PRESSER, T.
SCALES AND CHORDS -- ALL THE MAJOR AND MINOR KEYS	SCHULZ, F. A.
SCALES AND CHORDS ARE FUN - BOOK 1 -- MAJOR	HIRSCHBERG, D.
SCALES AND CHORDS ARE FUN - BOOK 2 -- MINOR	HIRSCHBERG, D.
SCALES AND CHORDS FOR THE PIANO	DICKS, E. A.
SCALES AND CHORDS IN ALL THE MAJOR AND MINOR KEYS	SCHULZ, F. A.
SCALES AND CHORDS	KOHLER, L.
SCALES AND CHORDS	SCHULZ, F. A.
SCALES AND EXERCISES	HERZ, H.
SCALES AND EXERCISES--IN SPANISH	HERZ, H.
SCALES AND EXERCISES	HERZ, H.
SCALES AND EXERCISES	HERZ, H.
SCALES AND PIECES IN ALL KEYS, BK. 1	SCHAUM, J.--ED.
SCALES AND PIECES IN ALL KEYS, BK. 2	SCHAUM, J.--ED.
SCALES FOR JUNIORS - PART 1 MAJOR	HIRSCHBERG, D.
SCALES FOR JUNIORS - PART 2 MINOR	HIRSCHBERG, D.
SCALES FOR THE STUDY OF PIANO	BACCIGALUPI
SCALES IN ALL THE KEYS	POLLINI
SCALES IN DOUBLE NOTES -- THIRDS --	ABRAMS
SCALES IN THIRDS AND SIXTHS	MONTANI
SCALES	HERZ, H.
SCALE AND ARPEGGIO BOOK	CHING
SCALE AND ARPEGGIO MANUAL	MACFARREN, W.
SCALE ETUDES - A1	WARD, J.
SCALE ETUDES - A2	WARD, J.
SCALE ETUDES - A3	WARD, J.
SCALE ETUDES - A4	WARD, J.
SCALE MELODIES, BK. 1	STEINER
SCALE PATTERNS FOR YOUNG PIANISTS	CAVALHO, R.
SCALE SONG	ROGERS, E.
SCALE WALTZ	CROCKER, V.
SCALINATELLA	
SCALING A FENCE	TRAVIS, B.
SCAMPERING CHIPMUNKS	STAIRS, L.
SCAMPERING WHOLE STEPS	WIGHAM, M.
SCANDINAVIAN BOOGIE	SPIVAK, S.
SCANDINAVIAN DANCE SONG	WEYBRIGHT
SCARAMOUCHE	MILHAUD, D.
SCARBOROUGH FAIR	BRIMHALL,
SCARBOROUGH FAIR	BRIMHALL,
SCARBOROUGH FAIR	METIS
SCARBOROUGH FAIR	ZEPP--ED
SCARBO FROM GASPARD DE LA NUIT	RAVEL
SCARECROW ON A HOLIDAY	KAHN, M.
SCARECROW ON A HOLIDAY	KAHN, M.
SCARECROW SHUFFLE	STORR, S.
SCARECROW WALTZ	CRAIG, P.
SCARED SPOOK, THE	MCHALE, M.
SCARF-DANCE--AIR DE BALLET, NO. 3	CHAMINADE
SCARF DANCE	CHAMINADE
SCARF DANCE	CHAMINADE
SCARLATTIANA	CASELLA, A.
SCAPLATTI TO ALBENIZ	
SCARLET CAPE, THE	FEDERER, R.
SCARLET RIBBONS	SEGAL, J.
SCATTERING LEAVES	BAETZ, C.
SCATTER SHIELD	FULLER
SCENAS INFANTIS--MARCH, LITTLE SOLDIER	PINTO, O.
SCENAS INFANTIS--RUN, RUN	PINTO, O.
SCENAS INFANTIS -- MEMORIES OF CHILDHOOD	PINTO, O.
SCENAS INFANTIS	PINTO, O.
SCENES D'ENFANTS	MOMPOU, F.
SCENES DU MOYEN-AGE.. RONDE DE NUIT, LA VEILLEE, LE	BOELLMANN, L.
SCENES FROM AN IMAGINARY BALLET	COLERIDGE-TAYLOR
SCENES FROM CHILDHOOD--24 CHARACTERISTIC PIECES, OP.	KULLAK, T.
SCENES FROM CHILDHOOD, OP. 15, AND ALBUM FOR THE	SCHUMANN, R.
SCENES FROM CHILDHOOD, OP. 15, AND ALBUM FOR THE	SCHUMANN, R.
SCENES FROM CHILDHOOD, OP. 15	SCHUMANN, R.
SCENES FROM CHILDHOOD, OP. 15	SCHUMANN, R.
SCENES FROM CHILDHOOD, OP. 15	SCHUMANN, R.
SCENES FROM CHILDHOOD, OP. 15	SCHUMANN, R.
SCENES FROM CHILDHOOD, OP. 15	SCHUMANN, R.
SCENES FROM CHILDHOOD, OP. 15	SCHUMANN, R.
SCENES FROM CHILDHOOD, OP. 15	SCHUMANN, R.
SCENES FROM CHILDHOOD, OP. 62 AND 81	KULLAK, T.
SCENES FROM CHILDHOOD -- COMPLETE	KULLAK, T.
SCENES FROM CHILDHOOD - 1. BAGATELLA	MONTANARO
SCENES FROM CHILDHOOD - 2. LA CANZONE DEL RUSCELLO	MONTANARO
SCENES FROM CHILDHOOD - 3. LA TROTTOLA	MONTANARO
SCENES FROM CHILDHOOD - 4. DAMINE	MONTANARO
SCENES FROM CHILDHOOD - 5. PICCOLO ARABO	MONTANARO
SCENES FROM CHILDHOOD - 6. PICCOLE PATTUGLIE	MONTANARO
SCENES FROM CHILDHOOD	SCHUMANN, R.
SCENES FROM CHILDHOOD	SCHUMANN, R.
SCENES FROM CHILDHOOD	SCHUMANN, R.
SCENES IBERIENNES--8 SPANISH SCENES	LAPARRA, R.
SCENES MUNICIPALES	TOMASI, H.
SCENES OF CHILDHOOD	JELOBINSKY
SCENES OF CHILDHOOD	NAPOLI
SCENES OF CHILDHOOD	PICCIOLI
SCENES OF TRAVEL, OP. 17	JENSEN, A.
SCENES OF TRAVEL, OP. 17	JENSEN, A.
SCENES PASTORALES -- CHOEUR DES MOISSONNEURS	RABEY, R.
SCENES PITTORESQUES -- 1. RECUEILLEMENT	WURMSER, L.
SCENES PITTORESQUES -- 2. SCHERZETTO	WURMSER, L.
SCENES PITTORESQUES -- 3. SPLEEN	WURMSER, L.
SCENES PITTORESQUES -- 4. SOUVENIR	WURMSER, L.
SCENES PITTORESQUES -- 5. PRIERE	WURMSER, L.
SCENES PITTORESQUES -- 6. JEUX	WURMSER, L.
SCENES THAT ARE BRIGHTEST	WALLACE
SCENE D'ALSACE	PIERNE, P.
SCENE DE BALLET	CZIBULKA
SCENE ET DANSE EROTIQUES	VOORMOLEN
SCENE NAPOLITANE	BRUGNOLI
SCENTED POSIES	POWELL, W.
SCHEHERAZADE, OP. 35	RIMSKY-KORSAKOFF
SCHEHERAZADE, OP. 35	RIMSKY-KORSAKOFF
SCHEHERAZADE, OP. 35	RIMSKY-KORSAKOFF
SCHEHERAZADE	RIMSKY-KORSAKOFF
SCHEHEREZADE, FESTIVAL AT BAGDAD	RIMSKY-KORSAKOFF
SCHERSO CONCERTO	LITOLFF
SCHERZANDO CAPRICCIOSO	SEIBER, M.
SCHERZETTO	GALLON, J.
SCHERZETTO	HEDGES
SCHERZETTO	IBERT
SCHERZETTO	KREUTZER
SCHERZI, FANTASY IN F MINOR	CHOPIN
SCHERZINO, OP. 15	KOSSENDO
SCHERZINO, OP. 5 NO. 2	ORNSTEIN, L.
SCHERZINO IN F, OP. 18 NO. 2	MOSZKOWSKI
SCHERZINO	AKIMENKO
SCHERZINO	BENJAMIN
SCHERZINO	CROOT
SCHERZINO	MOUSSORGSKY
SCHERZINO	SIMMONS, H.
SCHERZINO	WIGHAM, M.
SCHERZINO	WIGHAM, M.
SCHERZI --4-- AND FANTASY	CHOPIN
SCHERZI AND FANTASY IN F MINOR, OP. 49	CHOPIN
SCHERZI AND FANTASY IN F MINOR, OP. 49	CHOPIN
SCHERZI	CHOPIN
SCHEPZO-DANSE	PIRIOU
SCHERZO-IMPROMPTU, OP. 73 NO. 2	GRIEG
SCHERZO-VALSE, OP. 40	MOSZKOWSKI
SCHERZO-WALTZ	CHABRIER
SCHERZO, CAPRICCIO, OP. 16 NO. 2	MENDELSSOHN
SCHERZO, FROM A MIDSUMMER NIGHT'S DREAM	MENDELSSOHN
SCHEPZO, FROM SONATA IN F MINOR, OP. 5	BRAHMS
SCHERZO, FROM SONATA OP. 2, NO. 3	BEETHOVEN
SCHERZO, GIGUE, ROMANCE, AND FUGHETTA, OP. 32	SCHUMANN, R.
SCHERZO, GIGUE, ROMANCE, FUGHETTE, OP. 32. ALSO	SCHUMANN, R.
SCHERZO, OP. 11 NO. 2	RACHMANINOFF, S.
SCHERZO, OP. 12 NO. 10	PROKOFIEFF
SCHERZO, OP. 16 NO. 2	MENDELSSOHN
SCHERZO, OP. 29, NO. 1	HOVLAND
SCHERZO, OP. 4	SALMHOFER, FR.
SCHERZO, OP. 42	DUPONT, J.
SCHERZO, OP. 5	ESPLA
SCHERZO, OP. 53 NO. 2	MARTUCCI
SCHERZO, OP. 7	DOBROWEN, I.
SCHERZO, OP. 87	SAINT-SAENS
SCHERZO, OP. 87	SAINT-SAENS
SCHERZOS	CHOPIN
SCHERZOS	CHOPIN
SCHERZOS	CHOPIN
SCHERZO --FROM CONCERTO SYMPHONIQUE NO. 4--	LITOLFF
SCHERZO -- GMUNDEN, 1903 --	BARTOK
SCHERZO -- 6-HANDS	JOHNSON, T.
SCHERZO 'PIP' -- A YORKSHIRE TERRIER	COATES, D.
SCHERZO AND MENUET	BEETHOVEN
SCHERZO AND SONATA	STRAVINSKY, I.
SCHERZO AND WALTZ	ETTORE, E.
SCHERZO A CAPRICCIO IN F-SHARP MINOR	MENDELSSOHN
SCHERZO A LA RUSSE, OP. 1, NO. 1	TSCHAIKOWSKY
SCHERZO A LA RUSSE, 1944 -- ORCH -- SET	STRAVINSKY, I.
SCHERZO A LA RUSSE FUR ORCHESTER, KLAVIERAUSZUG	STRAVINSKY, I.
SCHERZO ESPAGNOL	MADURO, C.
SCHERZO FANTASIE	BOUTRY
SCHERZO FANTASTIQUE -- ORCH. PART ARR. FOR SECOND	BLOCH, E.
SCHERZO FANTASTIQUE	YSOT, D'
SCHERZO FOR PIANO	HILLER
SCHERZO FROM TRIO, OP. 63	WEBER, VON *

SCHERZO FROM TRIO OP. 63	WEBER, VON
SCHERZO FUR ORCHESTER UND KLAVIER, KLAVIERAUSZUG	BARTOK
SCHERZO HUMORESQUE	KING, S.
SCHERZO HUMORISTIQUE, OP. 12 NO. 9	PROKOFIEFF
SCHERZO IN A FLAT	BORODIN, A.
SCHERZO IN B FLAT--POSTHUMOUS	SCHUBERT
SCHERZO IN B FLAT--POSTHUMOUS	SCHUBERT
SCHERZO IN B FLAT--POSTHUMOUS	SCHUBERT
SCHERZO IN B FLAT - POSTH.	SCHUBERT
SCHERZO IN B FLAT MINOR, OP. 31	CHOPIN
SCHERZO IN B FLAT MINOR, OP. 31	CHOPIN
SCHERZO IN B FLAT MINOR, OP. 32	CHOPIN
SCHERZO IN B MINOR, OP. 20	CHOPIN
SCHERZO IN B MINOR, OP. 20	CHOPIN
SCHERZO IN B MINOR	BALAKIREV
SCHERZO IN B MINOR	KARAM, F.
SCHERZO IN C SHARP MINOR, OP. 2 NO. 1 -- FROM FOUR	DOHNANYI
SCHERZO IN C SHARP MINOR, OP. 39	CHOPIN
SCHERZO IN DOUBLE-NOTES	MOWREY, D.
SCHERZO IN E-MOLL OP. 16 NO. 2	MENDELSSOHN
SCHERZO IN E FLAT MINOR, OP. 4	BRAHMS
SCHERZO IN E FLAT MINOR, OP. 4	BRAHMS
SCHERZO IN E FLAT MINOR, OP. 4	BRAHMS
SCHERZO IN E MINOR, OP. 16 NO. 2	MENDELSSOHN
SCHERZO IN E MINOR, OP. 16 NO. 2	MENDELSSOHN
SCHERZO IN E MINOR, OP. 16 NO. 2	MENDELSSOHN
SCHERZO IN G FROM STRING QUARTET, OP. 18 NO. 2 --	BEETHOVEN
SCHERZO NO. 01 IN B FLAT	SCHUBERT
SCHERZO NO. 1 IN B MINOR, OP. 20	CHOPIN
SCHERZO NO. 2 IN B-FLAT MINOR, OP. 31	CHOPIN
SCHERZO NO. 2	CECCARELLI
SCHERZO PARISIEN	LAPEYRE, T.
SCHERZO PETITE	ROBINSON, W. E.
SCHERZO ROMANTIQUE	NERINI, E.
SCHERZO VALSE -- PIECES PITTORESQUES, NO. 10	CHABRIER
SCHERZO	BACH, W.F.
SCHERZO	BILOTTI
SCHERZO	BORODIN, A.
SCHERZO	COKELY, C.
SCHERZO	COOKE, A.
SCHERZO	DE LA SALLE, SR.
SCHERZO	FRANCAIX, J.
SCHERZO	GOLDSCHMIDT
SCHERZO	HAUBIEL, C.
SCHERZO	HUMMEL, J. N.
SCHERZO	KOHS, E. B.
SCHERZO	NOVIKOFF
SCHERZO	PICHA
SCHERZO	RIEGGER, W.
SCHERZO	RUDAN
SCHERZO	SAVASTA
SCHERZO	SCHUBERT
SCHERZO	SOULE
SCHERZO	WEINBERGER, J.
SCHERZO	YSOT, D'
SCHERZO	ZABRACK, H.
SCHILFROHR, SAUSLE, OP. 36 NO. 4	SIBELIUS
SCHIRMER'S FAVORITE SACRED SONGS	STICKLES--ED
SCHIRMER'S MUSIC SPELLING-BOOK	TERHUNE, A.
SCHIRMER'S SELECT PIANO MUSIC--FOR ADVANCED GRADES	KASSCHAU,
SCHIRMER'S SELECT PIANO MUSIC--FOR EARLY GRADES	KASSCHAU,
SCHIRMER'S SELECT PIANO MUSIC--FOR INTERMEDIATE GRADES	KASSCHAU,
SCHIZZI	PANZANI
SCHMITT'S FIVE FINGER EXERCISES, PART 1	SCHMITT, A.
SCHMITT'S FIVE FINGER EXERCISES, PART 2	SCHMITT, A.
SCHNEEFLOCKEN, OP. 8, 6 PIECES--BK. 1	WILM, N. VON
SCHNEEFLOCKEN, OP. 8, 6 PIECES--BK. 2	WILM, N. VON
SCHON ROSMARIN --STUDENT EDITION--	KREISLER
SCHON ROSMARIN	KREISLER
SCHON ROSMARIN	KREISLER
SCHON ROSMARIN	KREISLER
SCHON ROSMARIN	KREISLER
SCHOOLDAY SUITE	HENDERSON
SCHOOLS OUT	LAWNER, M.
SCHOOL AND FRATERNITY MARCH	MUNN, W.
SCHOOL AND GYMNASSIUM MARCHES	HOLBROOK, N.--ED
SCHOOL BAND, THE	GAIL
SCHOOL BAND, THE	GAIL
SCHOOL BAND	COBB
SCHOOL BELL, THE	ROBINSON, A.
SCHOOL BELL	RICHTER
SCHOOL BOY MARCH	CRIST, D. W.
SCHOOL BUS -- STOP	MCBRIDE, R.
SCHOOL CARNIVAL MARCH	ROLFE, W.
SCHOOL DAYS -- SIMP.	MOSSMAN, T.
SCHOOL DAYS	BRYANT--ED.
SCHOOL DAYS	EDWARDS, G.
SCHOOL DRILL	PORTER, W.
SCHOOL FOR THE LEFT HAND, BK. 1, EXERCIES	WITTGENSTEIN, P.
SCHOOL FOR THE LEFT HAND, BK. 2, STUDIES	WITTGENSTEIN, P.
SCHOOL FOR THE LEFT HAND, BK. 3, TRANSCRIPTIONS	WITTGENSTEIN, P.
SCHOOL FOR THE PIANO PIANOFORTE -- BEGINNER'S BOOK,	PRESSER, T.
SCHOOL FOR THE PIANO PIANOFORTE -- PLAYER'S BOOK,	PRESSER, T.
SCHOOL FOR THE PIANO PIANOFORTE -- STUDENT'S BOOK,	PRESSER, T.
SCHOOL GIRLS' MARCH	BASLER, H. R.
SCHOOL IS OUT, MARCH	MARTIN, W.
SCHOOL MARCHES, BK. 2	MARCEL, G.
SCHOOL OF ADVANCED PIANO PLAYING	JOSEFFY, R.
SCHOOL OF ARPEGGIOS -- GER AND FR NOTES	WIEHMAYER, T.
SCHOOL OF DOUBLE NOTES, OP. 64	MOSZKOWSKI
SCHOOL OF DOUBLE NOTES	ROSSI, N.
SCHOOL OF EMBELLISHMENTS, THE--18 ETUDES FROM PART 2	LEBERT, S. *
SCHOOL OF ETUDES, BK. 1	KUEHNER, C.
SCHOOL OF ETUDES, BK. 2	KUEHNER, C.
SCHOOL OF ETUDES, BK. 3	KUEHNER, C.
SCHOOL OF LEGATO AND STACCATO, OP. 335--50 EXERCISES	CZERNY
SCHOOL OF LEGATO AND STACCATO, OP. 335	CZERNY
SCHOOL OF MECHANISM, OP. 120	DUVERNOY, J.
SCHOOL OF MECHANISM, OP. 120	DUVERNOY, J.
SCHOOL OF MECHANISM, THE--OP. 120--15 STUDIES	DUVERNOY, J.
SCHOOL OF MECHANISM, THE--OP. 120--15 STUDIES	DUVERNOY, J.
SCHOOL OF MECHANISM OP. 120	DUVERNOY, J.
SCHOOL OF OCTAVE-PLAYING, THE--OP. 48--BK. 1,	KULLAK, T.
SCHOOL OF OCTAVE-PLAYING, THE--OP. 48--BK. 2, SEVEN	KULLAK, T.
SCHOOL OF OCTAVES, OP. 48. VOL. 1	KULLAK, T.
SCHOOL OF OCTAVES, OP. 48. VOL. 2	KULLAK, T.
SCHOOL OF OCTAVES, OP. 48. VOL. 3	KULLAK, T.
SCHOOL OF OCTAVE PLAYING, BK. 1--EXERCISES	PHILIPP, I.
SCHOOL OF OCTAVE PLAYING, BK. 1	KULLAK, T.
SCHOOL OF OCTAVE PLAYING, BK. 2--EXAMPLES FROM	PHILIPP, I.
SCHOOL OF OCTAVE PLAYING, BK. 2	KULLAK, T.
SCHOOL OF OCTAVE PLAYING, BK. 3	KULLAK, T.
SCHOOL OF SCALES, CHORDS AND EMBELLISHMENTS, THE--28	BERENS, H.
SCHOOL OF SCALES -- ENG AND GER NOTES	WIEHMAYER, T.
SCHOOL OF SCALES AND DOUBLE NOTES, BKS. 1- 4	MOSZKOWSKI
SCHOOL OF THE LEFT HAND, OP. 302	KOEHLER
SCHOOL OF THE LEFT HAND, OP. 399	CZERNY
SCHOOL OF THE VIRTUOSO, OP. 365	CZERNY
SCHOOL OF THE VIRTUOSO, THE--60 STUDIES IN BRAVURA AND	CZERNY
SCHOOL OF THE VIRTUOSO --STUDIES IN BRAVURA AND	CZERNY
SCHOOL OF VELOCITY--40 STUDIES, OP. 61--COMPLETE	BERENS, H.
SCHOOL OF VELOCITY, OP. 141--24 SHORT STUDIES FOR	GURLITT
SCHOOL OF VELOCITY, OP. 299. COMPLETE	CZERNY
SCHOOL OF VELOCITY, OP. 299, BK. 1	CZERNY
SCHOOL OF VELOCITY, OP. 299, BK. 1	CZERNY
SCHOOL OF VELOCITY, OP. 299, BK. 2	CZERNY
SCHOOL OF VELOCITY, OP. 299, BK. 2	CZERNY
SCHOOL OF VELOCITY, OP. 299, BK. 3	CZERNY
SCHOOL OF VELOCITY, OP. 299, BK. 3	CZERNY
SCHOOL OF VELOCITY, OP. 299, BK. 4 0	CZERNY
SCHOOL OF VELOCITY, OP. 299, BKS. 1 AND 2	CZERNY
SCHOOL OF VELOCITY, OP. 299	CZERNY
SCHOOL OF VELOCITY, OP. 299	CZERNY
SCHOOL OF VELOCITY, OP. 299	CZERNY
SCHOOL OF VELOCITY, OP. 299	CZERNY
SCHOOL OF VELOCITY, OP. 61, BK. 1	BERENS, H.
SCHOOL OF VELOCITY, OP. 61, BK. 2	BERENS, H.
SCHOOL OF VELOCITY, OP. 61, BK. 3	BERENS, H.
SCHOOL OF VELOCITY, PART 1	CZERNY
SCHOOL OF VELOCITY, PART 2	CZERNY
SCHOOL OF VELOCITY, THE--40 STUDIES, OP. 299, BK. 1	CZERNY
SCHOOL OF VELOCITY, THE--40 STUDIES, OP. 299, BK. 2	CZERNY
SCHOOL OF VELOCITY, THE--40 STUDIES, OP. 299, BK. 3	CZERNY
SCHOOL OF VELOCITY, THE--40 STUDIES, OP. 299, BK. 4	CZERNY
SCHOOL OF VELOCITY, THE--40 STUDIES, OP. 299	CZERNY
SCHOOL OF VELOCITY, VOL. 1# NOS. 1-14	BERENS, H.
SCHOOL OF VELOCITY, VOL. 2# NOS. 15-26	BERENS, H.
SCHOOL OF VELOCITY, VOL. 3# NOS. 27-33	BERENS, H.
SCHOOL OF VELOCITY, VOL. 4# NOS. 34-40	BERENS, H.
SCHOOL OF VELOCITY --COMPLETE--	CZERNY
SCHOOL OF VELOCITY --SCHULE DER GELAEUFIGKEIT--, OP.	CZERNY
SCHOOL PICTURES, WALTZ	HOPKINS, H.
SCHUBERT FESTIVAL, A MEDLEY -- 1. ROSAMUNDE'S LOVE	SCHUBERT
SCHUBERT FOR THE YOUNG PIANIST	SCHUBERT
SCHUBERT WALTZ SAMPLER	SCHUBERT
SCHUMANN-SCHAUM	SCHUMANN, R.
SCHUMANN'S PIANO CONCERTO, FIRST MOVEMENT--CONCERT	GRAINGER, P.
SCHUMANN FOR THE YOUNG PIANIST	SCHUMANN, R.
SCHUMANN FOR THE YOUNG PIANIST	SCHUMANN, R.
SCHUMANN	SCHUMANN, R.
SCHUMEN MINIATURE, OP. 29	WLADIGEROFF, P.
SCHWANKE UND IDYLLEN OP. 55	GURLITT
SCHWARZE SONNE, OP. 31 -- BALLET IN 9 TABLEAUX	HARTIG
SCHWARZWEISSE TOCCATA	SROM
SCHWARZ UND WEISS	KUESTER, H.
SCINTILLEMENT D'ETOILES	LEMAIRE
SCISSORS GRINDER	ERB
SCISSORS GRINDER	PERRIN
SCISSORS GRINDER	SAVAGE, H. S.
SCISSORS MAN, THE	DVORINE
SCOOTER RACE	SCHER, W.
SCOOTER	DITTENHAVER
SCORPIO	COFFEY, J. R.
SCOTCH, SONATINA	GREEN, R.
SCOTCH DANCE, OP. 151	CHAMINADE
SCOTCH MELODIES--YE BANKS AND BRAES, BONNIE	PAPE, W.
SCOTCH PLAID	SCARMOLIN
SCOTCH POEM, OP. 31 NO. 2	MACDOWELL
SCOTCH POEM, OP. 31 NO. 2	MACDOWELL
SCOTCH POEM, OP. 31 NO. 2	MACDOWELL
SCOTCH STRATHSPEY AND REEL	GRAINGER, P.
SCOTTIE	BARTH, H.
SCOTTISH BALLAD, OP. 25 FOR TWO PIANOS AND ORCHESTRA	BRITTEN, B.
SCOTTISH ECHOES	SHIFFERLY, R.
SCOTTISH POEM	COURSEY, R. DE
SCOTTISH STORY	AARON, M.
SCOTT JOPLIN RAGTIME RAGE, BK. 1	JOPLIN, S.
SCOTT JOPLIN RAGTIME RAGE, BK. 2	JOPLIN, S.
SCOUTS ON PARADE	CROSBY, M.
SCOUT CAMPOREE	STEINER
SCRIABIN -- SELECTED WORKS	SCRIABINE, A.
SCRUB ME MAMA --WITH A BOOGIE BEAT--	RAYE
SCUOLA PREPARATORIA, OP. 101	BEYER, F.
SCUPPERNONG	WORK
SCURRY UP	GOODMAN, J.
SEA-GOING TIME	SEIDER, S.
SEA-GOING TIME	SEIDER, S.
SEA, THE	PALMGREN, S.
SEA, THE	WHITFORD
SEABISCUITS	BOLCOM, W.
SEAGULL	NEWMAN, S.
SEAGULL	SCHAUM, J.
SEALED WITH A KISS	LANE, J.--ED.
SEAL IT WITH A KISS	SINGER, L.--ED
SEASCAPE	GETTY, G.
SEASCAPE	GRAHAM
SEASHORE GAME, A	PHILLIPS, B.
SEASONS, OP. 37A	TSCHAIKOWSKY
SEASONS, OP. 67 --COMPLETE BALLET--	GLAZOUNOW, A.
SEASONS, THE, OP. 37A--12 CHARACTERISTIC PIECES	TSCHAIKOWSKY
SEASONS, THE, OP. 37A	TSCHAIKOWSKY
SEASONS, THE, OP. 73B	TSCHAIKOWSKY
SEASONS, THE	CASTELNUOVO-TEDE
SEASONS, THE	JEAN, E.
SEASONS, THE	TSCHAIKOWSKY
SEATTLE	BRADLEY,
SEA AQUARIUM	AARON, M.
SEA CHANTEY, A	WAGNESS
SEA CHANTEY, A	WEYBRIGHT
SEA FANTASY	SCHER, W.
SEA FANTASY	SCHER, W.
SEA FLEA	SOUTHAM, A.
SEA GARDENS	COOKE
SEA GULLS IN FLIGHT	HOWELL
SEA GULLS	HRUBY, V.
SEA GULL	GRAHAM, R.
SEA MISTS FROM 'SEA SKETCHES'	MASON, I.
SEA PICTURE, A	FRANKELL
SEA PIECES, OP. 55 AND NEW ENGLAND IDYLS, OP. 62	MACDOWELL
SEA PIECES	MACDOWELL
SEA PRINCESS, THE	HOFSTAD, M.
SEA SHANTEY -- BLOW THE MAN DOWN	
SEA SHANTIES	RICHARDS, S.
SEA SHANTY 'A SENTIMENTAL SAILOR' FROM 'SEA SKETCHES'	MASON, I.
SEA SHELLS	RUSSELL
SEA SHELLS	SCARMOLIN
SEA SPRAY	ROLFE, W.
SEA WALTZ, THE	MELVIN, B.
SECHSTE NOCTURNE OP. 33	SGAMBATI
SECHS ALBUMBLATTER, OP. 2 - NO. 1, 'A ROBERT SCHUMANN'	SMETANA
SECHS ALBUMBLATTER, OP. 2	SMETANA
SECHS BAGATELLEN OP. 126	BEETHOVEN
SECHS CONTRETANZE	BEETHOVEN

SECHS DEUTSCHE TANZE -- K.V. 536 NO. 6, 600 NO. 1, 2,   MOZART, W. A.
SECHS DEUTSCHE TANZE -- K.V. 586 NO. 6, 567 NO. 4, 5,   MOZART, W. A.
SECHS ECOSSAISEN   BEETHOVEN
SECHS ESTERHAZY-SONATEN -- BK. 1, HOBOKEN 16, 21-23   HAYDN
SECHS ESTERHAZY-SONATEN -- BK. 2, HOBOKEN 16, 24-26   HAYDN
SECHS FUGHETTEN   HANDEL
SECHS KLEINE FANTASIESTUCKE   SCHULTHESS, W.
SECHS KLEINE PRALUDIEN FUR ANFANGER -- BWV 933-938   BACH, J.S.
SECHS KURZE STUECKE ZUR PFLEGE DES POLYPHONEN SPIELS   BUSONI
SECHS LANDLERISCHE TANZE, K606   MOZART, W. A.
SECHS LANDLER UND 11 V. BRAHMS VIERHANDIG GESTZTE   SCHUBERT
SECHS LEICHTE SONATEN -- AUCH CEMBALO   BACH, J.
SECHS LEICHTE STUCKE   VANHAL
SECHS LEICHTE VARIATIONEN -- SCHWEIZERLIED F-DUR   BEETHOVEN
SECHS LEICHTE VARIATIONEN G-DUR   BEETHOVEN
SECHS MENUETE   BEETHOVEN
SECHS OUVERTUREN FUR CEMBALO   TELEMANN, G.P.
SECHS SONATEN ZU DEM, VERSUCH UBER DIE WAHRE ART, DAS   BACH, C.P.E.
SECHS SONATEN ZU DEM, VERSUCH UBER DIE WAHRE ART, DAS   BACH, C.P.E.
SECHS SONATEN ZU DEM VERSUCH UBER DIE WAHRE ART, DAS   BACH, C.P.E.
SECHS SONATEN   PAISIELLO, G.
SECHS SONATINEN, OP. 36   CLEMENTI
SECHS SONATINEN, OP. 54 - HEFT 1, SONATINEN IN C UND A   NOVAK
SECHS SONATINEN, OP. 54 - HEFT 2, SONATINEN IN F AND E   NOVAK
SECHS SONATINEN, OP. 54 - HEFT 3, SONATINEN IN D MINOR   NOVAK
SECHS SONATINEN -- HOBOKEN 16-4, 7, 8, 9, 10, 11   HAYDN
SECHS SONATINEN   BEETHOVEN
SECHS SONATINEN   MOZART, W. A.
SECHS STUCKE FUR KLAVIER -- CEMBALO OP. 1   SCHULZ
SECHS TIMES SECHS VARIATIONEN UBER TANZLIEDER   TWITTENHOFF
SECHS TOCCATEN   LEO, L.
SECHS VARIATIONEN F-DUR, OP. 34   BEETHOVEN
SECHS VARIATIONEN UBER 'NEL COR PIU NON MI SENTO'   BEETHOVEN
SECHS VARIATIONEN UBER EIN RUS SSISCHES VOLKSLIED OP.   BEETHOVEN
SECHS VARIIERTE THEMEN, OP. 105 -- VOL. 1   BEETHOVEN
SECHS VARIIERTE THEMEN, OP. 105 -- VOL. 2   BEETHOVEN
SECHS VERMESSENE   KRENEK, E.
SECHS VERMESSENE   KRENEK, E.
SECOND-PIANO PART TO THE 15 TWO-PART INVENTIONS OF   SAAR
SECONDO SCALES   ALT, H.
SECOND ALBUM FOR CHILDREN, OP. 246   KOEHLER
SECOND ARABESQUE, FOR 2 PIANOS 8 HANDS   DEBUSSY
SECOND ARABESQUE   DEBUSSY
SECOND ARABESQUE   DEBUSSY
SECOND ARABESQUE   DEBUSSY
SECOND AVENUE WALTZES, 1942 -- SET   RIETI
SECOND BOOK OF TONES AND TUNES   GEST, E.
SECOND CONCERTO DA CAMERA, OP. 10 NO. 2 IN C SHARP   ALKAN
SECOND CONCERTO DA CAMERA IN C SHARP MINOR, OP. 10   ALKAN
SECOND CONCERTO FOR 2 PIANOS AND ORCHESTRA   PARCHMAN, G.
SECOND CONCERTO   GALINDO, B.
SECOND CONCORD DUET BOOK   OSBORNE, E.
SECOND DUET BOOK--33 DUETS   DILLER, A. *
SECOND DUET BOOK FOR LITTLE JACKS AND JILLS, A   RODGERS, I.
SECOND FAMOUS MINUET   BOCCHERINI
SECOND GRADE BOOK OF MELODIC STUDIES   BUGBEE, L. A.
SECOND GRADE PIANO BOOK   WILLIAMS, J.
SECOND GRADE PIANO PIECES   BLAKE, J. *
SECOND HAND ROSE   HANLEY, J.
SECOND HAND ROSE   SCHAUM, J.--ED.
SECOND HUNGARIAN RHAPSODY   LISZT
SECOND HUNGARIAN RHAPSODY   LISZT
SECOND IMPROMPTU   LABUNSKI, W.
SECOND INDIAN SUITE   MACDOWELL
SECOND MARCH -- ALLA MARCIA FUNEBRE.   DAHL
SECOND MAZURKA, OP. 54   GODARD, B.
SECOND MAZURKA   GODARD, B.
SECOND MAZURKA   GODARD, B.
SECOND MAZURKA   WIENIAWSKI
SECOND MELODY IN E FLAT   JOSEFFY, R.
SECOND MELODY LESSONS   BILBRO, M.
SECOND MINUET   BESLEY, M.
SECOND MUSIC FUN BOOK   MONTGOMERY, V.
SECOND NOCTURNE, OP. 16 NO. 1   HODDINOTT, A.
SECOND NOCTURNE, OP. 4   LEYBACH, I.
SECOND PETITE SUITE   MARTELLI, H.
SECOND PIANO ACCOMPANIMENTS TO FIVE TWO-PART BACH   THOMPSON, J.
SECOND PIANO ACCOMPANIMENT TO MOZART'S SONATA IN C   GRIEG
SECOND PIANO BOOK FOR LITTLE JACKS AND JILLS,   RODGERS, I.
SECOND PIANO BOOK   GOODRICH
SECOND PIANO CONCERTO - THEMES   RACHMANINOFF, S.
SECOND PIANO PARTS TO 1ST SOLO BOOK PIECES BY DILLER   DILLER, A.
SECOND PIANO PARTS TO 6 SONATINAS, OP. 36 BY CLEMENTI   TIMM, H. C.
SECOND PIANO PARTS TO 6 SONATINAS, OP. 36 BY CLEMENTI   TIMM, H. C.
SECOND RHAPSODY   GERSHWIN
SECOND SOLO BOOK   COBB
SECOND SONATA 'THE AIRPLANE'   ANTHEIL, G.
SECOND SONATA   SHEPHERD
SECOND SONATA   ROREM, N.
SECOND SONATINA IN F MAJOR -- IN THREE MOVEMENTS   COBB
SECOND SUITE EN UT   MARESCOTTI, A.
SECOND SUITE OF SIX EASY PIECES   DUKE, H.
SECOND SUPPLEMENT TO THE METHOD BY MARTHE MORHANGE   DEMARQUEZ
SECOND TIME AROUND   LANE, J.--ED.
SECOND VALSE-IMPROMPTU   NOEL, P. *
SECOND VALSE, OP. 56   GODARD, B.
SECOND VALSE, OP. 56   GODARD, B.
SECOND VALSE, OP. 86   DURAND, A.
SECOND VALSE OUBLIEE   LISZT
SECOND VALSE   GODARD, B.
SECOND WALTZ   GODARD, B.
SECOND YEAR PIANO CLASSICS   THOMPSON, J.--ED
SECOND YEAR PIANO LESSONS   WATERMAN *
SECOND YEAR PIANO LESSONS   WATERMAN *
SECOND YEAR   WILLIAMS, J.
SECRET, LE -- INTERMEZZO -- 6-HANDS   GAUTIER, L.
SECRET, THE, EASY   GAUTIER, L.
SECRET, THE, INTERMEZZO   GAUTIER, L.
SECRET, THE   ALT, H.
SECRET DE POLICHINELLE   CARMAN
SECRET LOVE   FAIN
SECRET LOVE   WEBSTER
SECRET MISSION   OLSON
SECRET WAYS, THE   WILLIAMS
SECRET WISHES   LANGE, G.
SECRET   GARROW, L.
SECULAR CHRISTMAS DUETS   IBBERSON--ED
SEDIA EPISCOPALE DELLA CHIESA DEI SS. NEREO E   CARABELLA
SEDLON PIANO METHOD, BK. 1   SEDLON
SEDLON PIANO METHOD, BK. 2   SEDLON
SEE-SAW MARGERY DAW   REBE
SEEREISE, SUITE   TURINA, J.
SEESAW UP -- SEESAW DOWN   WEDBERG, G.
SEE AND GEE   WIGHAM, M.
SEE AND PLAY, BK. 4   FRISCH, F. T.
SEE SAW   EZELL, H.

SEE SAW   RICHTER
SEE SAW   ROGERS, E.
SEE THE EMPEROR   GREEN
SEE YOU IN SEPTEMBER   BRADLEY,
SEGUE, LA, DANSE LENTE   MIGOT
SEGUIDILLA, SPANISH DANCE   BOHM
SEGUIDILLAS, OP. 232, NO. 5 -- FROM CANTOS DE ESPANA   ALBENIZ, I.
SEGUIDILLAS, OP. 232 NO. 5   ALBENIZ, I.
SEGUIDILLAS   ALBENIZ, I.
SEGUIDILLAS   TORRANDELL
SEGUIDILLAS   TURINA, J.
SEHNSUCHTS, SCHMERZENS- UND HOFFNUNGWALZER   BEETHOVEN
SEHNSUCHT -- LONGING --   SCHULZ-WELDA
SEIS DANZAS   LOMBATO, D.
SEIS HABANERAS TRADICIONALES   JUAN--ED
SEIS PIEZAS   ARDEVOL, J.
SEIS PIEZAS   MARTIN, E.
SEIS PRELUDIOS   DURANTE
SEI STUDII E SEI DIVERTIMENTI PER CEMBALO   DURANTE
SELDOM SEEN HOLLOW   BACON, E.
SELECTED CHILDREN'S PIECES   BARTOK
SELECTED CLASSICAL AND MODERN WORKS, BK. 1   SAMMARTINO
SELECTED CLASSICAL AND MODERN WORKS, BK. 2   SAMMARTINO
SELECTED COMPOSITIONS, BK. 1 - 48 SONGS WITHOUT WORDS   MENDELSSOHN
SELECTED COMPOSITIONS, BK. 1   CHAMINADE
SELECTED COMPOSITIONS, BK. 2 - MISCELLANEOUS WORKS   MENDELSSOHN
SELECTED COMPOSITIONS, BK. 2   CHAMINADE
SELECTED COMPOSITIONS, BK. 3 - CAPRICCIOS, FANTASY AND   MENDELSSOHN
SELECTED COMPOSITIONS   BEETHOVEN
SELECTED COMPOSITIONS   BEETHOVEN
SELECTED COMPOSITIONS   HANDEL
SELECTED COMPOSITIONS   MARTUCCI
SELECTED COMPOSITIONS   SCARLATTI, A.
SELECTED COMPOSITIONS   SCHUBERT
SELECTED COMPOSITIONS   TSCHAIKOWSKY
SELECTED COMPOSITIONS   WEBER, VON
SELECTED EASY PIECES   CHOPIN
SELECTED ETUDES - L1   WARD, J.
SELECTED ETUDES - L2   WARD, J.
SELECTED ETUDES - L3   WARD, J.
SELECTED ETUDES - L4   WARD, J.
SELECTED FAVORITES   CHOPIN
SELECTED KEYBOARD WORKS   COUPERIN, F.
SELECTED KEYBOARD WORKS   FROBERGER
SELECTED KEYBOARD WORKS   PACHELBEL
SELECTED MOVEMENTS FROM THE SYMPHONIES NOS. 1, 2, 3,   BRUCKNER
SELECTED ORIGINAL COMPOSITIONS FOR PIANO, FOUR HANDS   SCHUBERT
SELECTED ORIGINAL COMPOSITIONS FOR PIANO, FOUR HANDS   SCHUBERT
SELECTED ORIGINAL COMPOSITIONS   SCHUBERT
SELECTED OVERTURES -- WITH BELLINI-SELECTED OVERTURES   ROSSINI, G.
SELECTED OVERTURES -- WITH BELLINI .... SELECTED   ROSSINI, G.
SELECTED OVERTURES -- WITH ROSSINI - SELECTED   BELLINI
SELECTED OVERTURES   BELLINI *
SELECTED PIANO COMPOSITIONS   BRAHMS
SELECTED PIANO COMPOSITIONS   DOHNANYI
SELECTED PIANO COMPOSITIONS   SCHUBERT
SELECTED PIANO MUSIC
SELECTED PIANO PIECES --24--   DVORAK
SELECTED PIANO PIECES   BACH, C.P.E.
SELECTED PIANO SOLOS BY ROMANTIC COMPOSERS, BK.
SELECTED PIANO SOLOS BY ROMANTIC COMPOSERS, BK.
SELECTED PIANO SOLOS BY ROMANTIC COMPOSERS, BK.
SELECTED PIANO SONATAS, BKS. 1 AND 2   HAYDN
SELECTED PIANO STUDIES - BOOK 1   CZERNY *
SELECTED PIANO STUDIES - BOOK 2   CZERNY *
SELECTED PIANO WORKS, VOL. 1* ETUDES   SCRIABINE, A.
SELECTED PIANO WORKS, VOL. 1   TSCHAIKOWSKY
SELECTED PIANO WORKS, VOL. 2   SCRIABINE, A.
SELECTED PIANO WORKS, VOL. 2   TSCHAIKOWSKY
SELECTED PIANO WORKS, VOL. 3   SCRIABINE, A.
SELECTED PIANO WORKS, VOL. 3   TSCHAIKOWSKY
SELECTED PIANO WORKS --FROM SECHS MUSIKALISCHEN   KRIEGER
SELECTED PIECES --22--   GRIEG
SELECTED PIECES --7--   HANDEL
SELECTED PIECES FOR CHILDREN, OP. 27 --17--   KABALEVSKY
SELECTED PIECES FOR PIANO   RAMEAU
SELECTED PIECES   COUPERIN, F.
SELECTED PIECES   COUPERIN, F.
SELECTED PIECES   DVORAK
SELECTED PIECES   PURCELL, H.
SELECTED PIECES   SMETANA
SELECTED PIECES   TSCHAIKOWSKY
SELECTED SONATAS FOR PIANO
SELECTED SONATINAS, BK. 1--ELEMENTARY
SELECTED SONATINAS, BK. 2--INTERMEDIATE
SELECTED SONATINAS, BK. 3--LOWER ADVANCED
SELECTED SONATINAS, VOL. 1* 14 SONATINAS   FERTE--ED
SELECTED SONATINAS, VOL. 2* 10 SONATINAS   FERTE--ED
SELECTED SONATINAS, VOL. 3* 8 SONATINAS   FERTE--ED
SELECTED STUDIES, BK. 1--170 STUDIES IN THE UPPER   CZERNY
SELECTED STUDIES, BK. 1 -- 52 STUDIES --   CZERNY
SELECTED STUDIES, BK. 1 - WITHOUT THUMB PASSAGES   CZERNY
SELECTED STUDIES, BK. 1   CZERNY
SELECTED STUDIES, BK. 1   KING, S.
SELECTED STUDIES, BK. 2--92 STUDIES IN THE MIDDLE   CZERNY
SELECTED STUDIES, BK. 2 -- 44 STUDIES --   CZERNY
SELECTED STUDIES, BK. 2 - FOR THUMB PASSAGES   CZERNY
SELECTED STUDIES, BK. 2   CZERNY
SELECTED STUDIES, BK. 2   KING, S.
SELECTED STUDIES, BK. 3 -- 34 STUDIES --   CZERNY
SELECTED STUDIES, BK. 3 - FOR THUMB PASSAGES   CZERNY
SELECTED STUDIES, BK. 3   CZERNY
SELECTED STUDIES, BK. 4 -- 20 STUDIES --   CZERNY
SELECTED VARIATIONS FOR PIANOFORTE   BEETHOVEN
SELECTED WORKS, URTEXT -- FOR ORGAN, PIANO, OR   BUXTEHUDE
SELECTED WORKS, VOL. 1   SWEELINCK
SELECTED WORKS FOR THE PIANO   BARTOK
SELECTED WORKS FOR THE PIANO   MOZART, W. A.
SELECTED WORKS FOR THE PIANO   PROKOFIEFF
SELECTED WORKS   BRAHMS
SELECTED WORKS   DEBUSSY
SELECTED WORKS   LISZT
SELECTED WORKS   SWEELINCK
SELECTED WORKS   ZIPOLI
SELECTIONS FROM ''GLORIANNA''   FRIML, R.
SELECTIONS FROM ''KATINKA''   FRIML, R.
SELECTIONS FROM ''ROBIN HOOD''   DEKOVEN, R.
SELECTIONS FROM ''SWEETHEARTS''   HERBERT
SELECTIONS FROM ''THE FIREFLY''   FRIML, R.
SELECTIONS FROM 'HAIR'
SELECTIONS FROM 'MAYTIME'   ROMBERG, S.
SELECTIONS FROM ANNA MAGDALENA'S NOTEBOOK   BACH, J.S.
SELECTIONS FROM LOVE STORY   BRIMHALL,
SELECTIONS FROM MAN OF LA MANCHA   BRIMHALL,
SELECTIONS FROM SIX FAVORITE OPERAS
SELECTIONS FROM THE CLASSICS   TOURBIE--ED.
SELECT PIANO MUSIC FOR ADVANCED GRADES   KASSCHAU, H.
SELECT PIANO MUSIC FOR EARLY GRADES   KASSCHAU, H.

SELECT PIANO MUSIC FOR INTERMEDIATE GRADES	KASSCHAU, H.
SELECT SONATINAS FOR PIANO, BK. 1	PODOLSKY, L.--ED
SELECT SONATINAS FOR PIANO, BK. 2	PODOLSKY, L.--ED
SELECT SONATINAS FOR PIANO, BK. 3	PODOLSKY, L.--ED
SELECT SONATINAS FOR PIANO, BK. 4	PODOLSKY, L.--ED
SELECT SONATINAS FOR PIANO, BK. 5	PODOLSKY, L.--ED
SEMBLANZAS CHILENAS	RIESCO, C.
SEMEUR D'ILLUSIONS, LE	GUENIFFEY
SEMI-SIMPLE VARIATIONS	BABBITT
SEMIRAMIDE - OVERTURE	ROSSINI, G.
SEMPER FIDELIS	JAHN, C.
SEMPER FIDELIS	SOUSA
SEMPER FIDELIS	SOUSA
SEMPER FIDELIS	SOUSA
SEMPRE FIDELIS	SOUSA
SEND OUT THY LIGHT -- ANTHEM	GOUNOD, C.
SENIOR MARCH	PANELLA, L.
SENNERS TRAUM, EASY	HEINS, C.
SENNERS TRAUM, OP. 171	HEINS, C.
SENORITA CONCHITA, LA -- NO. 5, FROM FIVE PIECES	DELUNE
SENORITA	MUNN, W.
SENSATIONAL 70 FOR THE 70'S, THE	
SENSATIONAL 70 FOR THE 70'S	BRADLEY,
SENTIMENTAL PARTING	PORTNOFF
SENZA NISCIUNO	
SEPARATE WAYS	BRIMHALL,
SEPTEMBER SONG	LIBERACE--ED
SEPTEMBER SONG	SINGER, L.--ED
SEPTEMBER SONG	
SEPTEMBER SONG	
SEPTET, OP. 20	BEETHOVEN
SEPTET, OP. 20	BEETHOVEN
SEPTET IN E FLAT, OP. 20	BEETHOVEN
SEPTET	STRAVINSKY, I.
SEPT HAIKAI	MESSIAEN, O.
SEPT TRANSPARENCES	ARMA, P.
SERAFINO	PIZZINI
SERAIT-CE L'AMOUR	MONFRED
SERA A SORRETO, UNA	DE CRESCENZO
SERA D'ESTATE	COUTURE
SERBIAN DANCES	TAJCEVIC, M.
SERENADE--'DON GIOVANNI'	MOZART, W. A.
SERENADE--EINE KLEINE NACHTMUSIK--	MOZART, W. A. *
SERENADE, FROM 'DON GIOVANNI'	MOZART, W. A.
SERENADE, FROM 'HASSAN'	DELIUS, F.
SERENADE, MILLIONS OF HARLEQUIN	DRIGO, R.
SERENADE, OP. 17, NO. 2	STRAUSS, R.
SERENADE, OP. 17	STRAUSS, J.
SERENADE, OP. 19 NO. 2	OLSEN, O.
SERENADE, OP. 19	JONGEN, J.
SERENADE, OP. 33 NO. 4	SINDING
SERENADE, OP. 33 NO. 4	SINDING
SERENADE, OP. 5 NO. 1	ORNSTEIN, L.
SERENADE, OP. 7	PIERNE
SERENADE, OP. 85 NO. 9	DVORAK
SERENADE, OP. 90 NO. 11	SCHUBERT
SERENADE, VALSE ESPAGNOLE	METRA, O.
SERENADE -- DON GIOVANNI	MOZART, W. A.
SERENADE -- STAENDCHEN --	SCHUBERT
SERENADE - STAENDCHEN	SCHUBERT
SERENADE 'EINE KLEINE NACHT MUSIK'	MOZART, W. A.
SERENADE AUS DEM STREICHQUARTETT IN F -- HOBOKEN 3-17	HAYDN
SERENADE A MAGALI	WITTMAN
SERENADE BADINE	MARIE
SERENADE D'ENFANTS	VOLPATTI
SERENADE DES ANGES	KINKEL, C.
SERENADE ESPAGNOLE	STRELEZKI
SERENADE FOR A WEALTHY WIDOW	FORESYTHE, R.
SERENADE FOR A WEALTHY WIDOW	
SERENADE FOR A WEALTHY WIDOW	
SERENADE FOR PIANO	PHILLIPS, B.
SERENADE FOR STRING QUARTET	ROPARTZ
SERENADE FOR THE DOLL FROM THE CHILDREN'S CORNER	DEBUSSY
SERENADE FROM 'L MILIONI D'ARLECCHINO'	DRIGO, R.
SERENADE FROM STRING QUARTET, OP. 3 NO. 5	HAYDN
SERENADE HONGROISE	WESLY
SERENADE IN A	STRAVINSKY, I.
SERENADE IN BLUE	MITTLER
SERENADE IN B FLAT MINOR, OP. 3 NO. 5	RACHMANINOFF, S.
SERENADE IN E MINOR, OP. 20	ELGAR, E.
SERENADE IN G, K525 --KLEINE NACHTMUSIK--	MOZART, W. A.
SERENADE IN THE NIGHT -- SIMP.	MOSSMAN, T.--ED
SERENADE NO. 02	PERSICHETTI
SERENADE NO. 07	PERSICHETTI
SERENADE NO. 08, OP. 62	PERSICHETTI
SERENADE NO. 08	PERSICHETTI
SERENADE NO. 3	ZILLIG
SERENADE NO. 3	ZILLIG
SERENADE OF PRINCE CHARMING	FERNANDEZ, O.
SERENADE OF THE MANDOLINS	EILENBERG
SERENADE ROMANTIQUE	SCHER, W.
SERENADE SICILIETTA	VONBLON, F.
SERENADE SUR LES DERNIERES VALSES D'UN FOU	BEYER, F.
SERENADE TO AN EMPTY ROOM	PALMER *
SERENADE TO A BREEZE	PINCKARD
SERENADE TO A MANDARIN	SCHER, W.
SERENADE TO A SKYSCRAPER	SUESSE, D.
SERENADE	CHAGRIN
SERENADE	DIEMER
SERENADE	DRIGO, R.
SERENADE	DRIGO, R.
SERENADE	ELGAR, E.
SERENADE	ELGAR, E.
SERENADE	FERROUD, P. O.
SERENADE	FULEIHAN, A.
SERENADE	GOUNOD, C.
SERENADE	GROFE, F.
SERENADE	JENSEN, A.
SERENADE	JESSE, M.
SERENADE	KARGANOFF
SERENADE	LEONCAVALLO
SERENADE	MOWREY, D.
SERENADE	PIERNE
SERENADE	ROMBERG, S.
SERENADE	ROMBERG, S.
SERENADE	ROPARTZ
SERENADE	SAMAZEUILH
SERENADE	SCHUBERT
SERENADE	SCHUBERT
SERENADE	SCHUBERT
SERENADE	SCHUBERT
SERENADE	SCHUBERT
SERENADE	SCHUBERT
SERENADE	SCHUBERT
SERENADE	TITL
SERENADE	TOSELLI

SERENADE	TOSELLI
SERENADE	TOSELLI
SERENADE	TOSELLI
SERENADE	WEYBRIGHT
SERENADE	WHITFORD
SERENAMENTE	COUTURE
SERENATA, LOVE IN IDLENESS	MACBETH
SERENATA, OP. 15 NO. 1	MOSZKOWSKI
SERENATA, OP. 15 NO. 2	MOSZKOWSKI
SERENATA ANDALUZA	FALLA, M. DE
SERENATA ANDALUZA	FALLA, M. DE
SERENATA ARABE	ALBENIZ, I.
SERENATA A DISPETTO	CILEA
SERENATA BURLESCA	AGAY, D.
SERENATA D'AMORE	MANTOVANI
SERENATA ESPANOLA	ALBENIZ, I.
SERENATA ESPANOLA	MALATS
SERENATA IN D, OP. 15 NO. 1	MOSZKOWSKI
SERENATA	ANDERSON, L.
SERENATA	BRACCO
SERENATA	METRA
SERENATA	METRA
SERENATA	MOSZKOWSKI
SERENATA	RODRIGO, J.
SERENATA	SCHER, W.
SERENATA	TOSTI
SERGEANT MAJOR	BRODSKY, M.
SERIE ARGENTINA DE DANZAS	SICILIANI
SERIE	MANNINO, V.
SERRANA	LASALA
SERRANITA	SICILIANI
SERRE AUX NENUPHARS	INGHELBRECHT, D.
SERVICE INTERLUDES	FULLER
SET OF EIGHT	GRIFFIS, E.
SET OF THREE INFORMALITIES, A--BLUES, SCHERZO,	PHILLIPS, B.
SET OF THREE	STEVENS, E.
SEVEN-BRANCHED CANDELABRA, THE	MILHAUD, D.
SEVENTEENTH CENTURY MASTERS	HERRMANN,
SEVENTEEN CONTEMPORARY DANCES	RAPHLING
SEVENTEEN EASY PIANO PIECES, OP. 27	KABALEVSKY
SEVENTEEN FOLK TUNES FOR PIANO	GARROW
SEVENTEEN LITTLE PRELUDES AND FUGUES	BACH, J.S.
SEVENTEEN SMALL PIECES, OP. 23	SCHREIBER, FR.
SEVENTEEN SONATAS OF OLD SPANISH MASTERS -- SONATAS BY NIN--ED	
SEVENTH SYMPHONY	BEETHOVEN
SEVENTY-FIVE FAMOUS PIANO PIECES	
SEVENTY-ONE RECITAL PIECES FOR PIANO	GRAHAM
SEVENTY-TWO ETUDES KARNATIQUES	CHARPENTIER, J.
SEVENTY-TWO VERSETL UND 12 TOCCATEN	MUFFAT
SEVENTY-TWO VERSETS AND TWELVE TOCCATAS	MUFFAT
SEVENTY SELECTED AND PROGRESSIVE STUDIES	CZERNY
SEVENTY SIX TROMBONES	WILLSON, M.
SEVEN ALL TIME HITS	ZEPP--ED
SEVEN ANNIVERSARIES -- CYCLE	BERNSTEIN, L.
SEVEN BAGATELLES, OP. 33, BK. 1	BEETHOVEN
SEVEN BAGATELLES, OP. 33	BEETHOVEN
SEVEN BAGATELLES, OP. 33	BEETHOVEN
SEVEN CHANTS DE TERROIR	D'INDY, V.
SEVEN CHARACTERISTIC PIECES	SMIT, L.
SEVEN CHILDREN'S PIECES	PAHISSA
SEVEN CHORALE PARTITAS FOR HARPSICHORD --PIANO-- OR	PACHELBEL
SEVEN DANCES	FREY
SEVEN DAYS A WEEK	BENNETT, R.
SEVEN DWARVES, THE	GRETCHANINOFF
SEVEN EASY LITTLE PIECES	MASETTI
SEVEN EASY PIECES - ON A 12 TONE ROW-	DE FILIPPI, A.
SEVEN EASY PIECES	BEETHOVEN
SEVEN EASY PIECES	DEFILIPPI, A.
SEVEN ECOSSAISES--CURWEN EDITION	WEBER, VON
SEVEN ETUDES, OP. 56	TCHEREPNIN
SEVEN FANTASIES, OP. 116	BRAHMS
SEVEN FROGGIES, GAVOTTE	HOPKINS, H.
SEVEN FUGUES--1953	WAGNER-REGENY,
SEVEN IMPRESSIONS FOR PIANO	BENTLEY
SEVEN KEY-MEN	MORRIS, C.
SEVEN LITTLE PIECES WITH COMIC VERSES	PODESVA, J.
SEVEN LITTLE PIECES	PODESVA, J.
SEVEN LITTLE SKETCHES	POZZOLI
SEVEN LITTLE STUDIES	CAMBISSA, G.
SEVEN MAGIC STEPS TO SPEED SIGHT READING	SHINN, D.
SEVEN MARCHES, OP. 47	ROWLEY
SEVEN MOBILES	RAPHLING
SEVEN MOBILES	RAPHLING
SEVEN MUSICAL MOMENTS	REIF, P.
SEVEN MUSICAL MOMENTS	REIF, P.
SEVEN MUSICAL MOMENTS	REIF, P.
SEVEN MUSIGRAMS	EDMONDS
SEVEN MUSIGRAMS	EDMONDS
SEVEN OUTDOOR PIECES	MCKAY, G.
SEVEN OVERTURES	MOZART, W. A.
SEVEN PASTORALS	WATSON, G.
SEVEN PIANO PIECES--1954	STAEMPFLI, E.
SEVEN PIANO PIECES, OP. 11	KODALY, Z.
SEVEN PIANO PIECES FOR CHILDREN	MIGNONE
SEVEN PIANO PIECES	LEVY, E.
SEVEN PIANO PIECES	SOPRONI, J.
SEVEN PIECES, FROM 'MIKROKOSMOS'	BARTOK
SEVEN PIECES, NO. 5	HANDEL
SEVEN PIECES, OP. 13	DOBROWEN, I.
SEVEN PIECES FOR FOUR HANDS	WHITFORD
SEVEN PIECES FOR PIANO	CHAVEZ, C.
SEVEN PIECES WITHOUT	RAPHLING
SEVEN PIECES WITHOUT	RAPHLING
SEVEN PIECES	BATE, ST.
SEVEN PIECES	CHAVEZ, C.
SEVEN PIECES	LOCKE
SEVEN PIECES	NAGAN, Z.
SEVEN PRELUDES, OP. 17	SCRIABINE, A.
SEVEN PRELUDES	BRERO
SEVEN PRELUDES	LAVIOLETTE, W.
SEVEN SHAKESPEARE SKETCHES	LOVELL
SEVEN SHORT PIECES	HONEGGER, A.
SEVEN SKETCHES, OP. 9	BARTOK
SEVEN SONATAS, VOL. 1	CLEMENTI
SEVEN SONATINAS, OP. 60 AND OP. 88	KUHLAU, F.
SEVEN SONATINAS, OP. 60 AND 88	KUHLAU, F.
SEVEN STUDIES, OP. 65	ALBENIZ, I.
SEVEN SUPPLEMENTARY EXERCISES	FULEIHAN, A.
SEVEN THESES FOR PIANO	CRESTON
SEVEN TOCCATAS AND FUGUES --URTEXT--, COMPLETE IN 1	BACH, J.S.
SEVEN TOCCATAS AND FUGUES -- URTEXT --	BACH, J.S.
SEVEN TOCCATAS	BACH, J.S.
SEVEN TOCCATAS	SCARLATTI, A.
SEVEN TRADITIONAL FRENCH NOELS	FRANCK, C.
SEVEN UP--DUETS	DOIGE
SEVEN VALSES POETICOS WITH PRELUDE AND POSTLUDE	GRANADOS
SEVEN VARIATIONS ON A THEME BY HAYDN	WATSON, S.

SEVEN VIENNESE GERMAN DANCES	SCHUBERT
SEVEN VIGNETTES	STARER
SEVEN WALTZES, OP. 86	KIRCHNER, T.
SEVILLA, SUITE PITTORESQUE--COMPLETE	TURINA, J.
SEVILLA, SUITE PITTORESQUE--NO. 1, SOUS LES ORANGERS	TURINA, J.
SEVILLA, SUITE PITTORESQUE--NO. 2, LE JEUDI SAINT A	TURINA, J.
SEVILLA, SUITE PITTORESQUE--NO. 3, LA FERIA	TURINA, J.
SEVILLANAS	TORRANDELL
SEVILLANA	INFANTE
SEVILLA -- FROM SUITE ESPAÑOLA NO. 1	ALBENIZ, I.
SEVILLA -- NO. 2, FROM SUITE ESPAÑOLA NO. 2	ALBENIZ, I.
SEVILLA -- NO. 3, FROM SUITE ESPAÑOLA NO. 1	ALBENIZ, I.
SEVILLA	ALBENIZ, I.
SEVILLA	ALBENIZ, I.
SEXTET, LUCIA - FOR LEFT HAND	LESCHETIZKY
SEXTETTE, LUCIA, EASY	DONIZETTI
SEXTETTE, LUCIA	DONIZETTI
SEXTET -- LUCIA DI LAMMERMOOR	DONIZETTI
SEXTUOR -- 1923 -- BALLET-BOUFFE	TANSMAN, A.
SE EQUIVOCO LA PALOMA	GUASTAVINO
SE TU M'AMI	PERGOLESI
SE	DENZA
SHADES OF BLUE	NEVIN
SHADOWS -- CONCERT VERSION	HAUBIEL, C.
SHADOWS IN THE LAGOON	TUTTLE, T. K.
SHADOWS IN THE POOL	CANFIELD, J.
SHADOWS OF THE NIGHT	PODESKA, I.
SHADOWS OF TWILIGHT, THE	EWING, M.
SHADOWS ON THE LAKE	LOUMEY, A.
SHADOWS ON THE MOON	GARROW, L.
SHADOWS ON THE WALL	RENNARD
SHADOWS ON THE WATER	LOUMEY, A.
SHADOWS	HAUBIEL, C.
SHADOWS	PARK
SHADOWS	WHITFORD
SHADOW BALLET	GREEN
SHADOW DANCE, OP. 39 NO. 8	MACDOWELL
SHADOW DANCE, OP. 39 NO. 8	MACDOWELL
SHADOW DANCERS	JOYNER, B.
SHADOW DANCE OF A BALLERINA	HOLLOWAY, J.
SHADOW DANCE	MACDOWELL
SHADOW DANCE	MACDOWELL
SHADOW DANCE	MACDOWELL
SHADOW OF YOUR SMILE, THE	
SHADOW OF YOUR SMILE	LANE, J.--ED.
SHADOW OF YOUR SMILE	WILLIAMS,
SHADOW PLAY	MCCLUSKY
SHADOW WALTZ	CROSBY, M.
SHADOW WALTZ	
SHAKESPEARE-SUITE, OP. 76	FOERSTER
SHALIMAR. SUITE	HOVHANESS, A.
SHALL WE PLAY A TRIO -- 1 PIANO 6 HANDS --	CITATI-BRACCI
SHALOM, 72 TRADITIONAL HEBREW MELODIES	SMALL, A.
SHANGRI-LA	LANE, J.--ED.
SHANGRI-LA	MAXWELL *
SHAPE OF THINGS, THE	ANSON, G.
SHARE THE FUN	KETTERER, E.
SHARP FOUR	FRACKENPOHL, A.
SHE'LL BE COMIN' ROUND THE MOUNTAIN	STANLEY--ED
SHEEP AND GOAT WALKIN' TO THE PASTURE--COWBOYS' AND	GUION, D.
SHEEP AND GOAT WALKIN' TO THE PASTURE, COWBOYS' AND	GUION, D.
SHEEP MAY SAFELY GRAZE	BACH, J.S.
SHEEP MAY SAFELY GRAZE	BACH, J.S.
SHEEP MAY SAFELY GRAZE	BACH, J.S.
SHEEP MAY SAFELY GRAZE	BACH, J.S.
SHEEP MAY SAFELY GRAZE	BACH, J.S.
SHEEP MAY SAFELY GRAZE	BACH, J.S.
SHEEP MAY SAFELY GRAZE	BACH, J.S.
SHEEP MAY SAFELY GRAZE	BACH, J.S.
SHEEP MAY SAFELY GRAZE	KASSCHAU,
SHEEP MAY SAFELY GRAZE	KASSCHAU, H.
SHEEP THAT SAFELY GRAZE	BACH, J.S.
SHEHERAZADE--SYMPHONIC SUITE, OP. 35	RIMSKY-KORSAKOFF
SHEHERAZADE, OP. 35 -- SYMPHONIC SUITE, ARR. BY THE	RIMSKY-KORSAKOFF
SHEIK OF ARABY, THE -- SIMP.	MOSSMAN, T.--ED
SHENANDOAH	BUTLER, J.
SHENANDOAH	ZEPP--ED
SHEPHERD'S BAGPIPES, THE	TAKACS, J.
SHEPHERD'S BAGPIPES, THE	TAKACS, J.
SHEPHERD'S DANCE, OP. 5	GREGH
SHEPHERD'S DANCE, THE	BAMPTON, R.
SHEPHERD'S DREAM, OP. 171	HEINS, C.
SHEPHERD'S DREAM, OP.171	HEINS, C.
SHEPHERD'S EVENING SONG	BLAKE, C.
SHEPHERD'S FLUTE, A	RICKER, E.
SHEPHERD'S HEY--ENGLISH MORRIS-DANCE TUNE--ORIGINAL	GRAINGER, P.
SHEPHERD'S HEY	WEYBRIGHT
SHEPHERD'S LULLABY, THE	ARMOUR
SHEPHERD'S MADRIGAL	KREISLER
SHEPHERD'S MADRIGAL	KREISLER
SHEPHERD'S NIGHT SONG	AGAY, D.
SHEPHERD'S REST	SCHIEFELBEIN, F.
SHEPHERD'S SONG AND DANCE	SCHER, W.
SHEPHERD'S SUITE	GRAHAM, W.
SHEPHERDESS' DREAM, EASY	LABITZKY, A.
SHEPHERDESS' DREAM, THE	LABITZKY, A.
SHEPHERD BOY, THE	WILSON, G.
SHEPHERD BOY, THE	WILSON, M.
SHEPHERD BOY	CHAGY
SHEPHERD BOY	WILSON, G.
SHEPHERD CALL, THE	ARMOUR
SHE DIDN'T SAY YES -- SHOWCASE	
SHE DOESN'T - TWO PIECES FOR PIANO SOLO	THORNE
SHE IS LOVELY--VALSE-BOSTON, OP. 208	LAUNAY, E.
SHIMMERING IVORIES	MELVIN, B.
SHIMMERING SEA	MOKREJS
SHINE BOOGIE	ZEPP--ED
SHIPBUILDERS, THE	SHEFFER
SHIP AHOY	BENTLEY
SHIP AHOY	HELYER, M.
SHIP AHOY	LOWENSTEIN
SHIRLEY PINECONE	TREVARTHEN, R.
SHOEMAKER, THE	COBB
SHOEMAKER'S HOLIDAY, THE	MACKAY
SHOEMAKER'S SHOP	FLETCHER
SHOESTRING WALTZ	DOIGE
SHOES OF THE FISHERMAN, THE	NORTH, A.
SHOE SHINE BOY	ARCHER, I.
SHOE SHINE BOY	
SHOO-SHOO BABY	MOORE
SHOOGY-SHOO, LITTLE TALE	HOPKINS, H.
SHOOTING STARS	VOLZ, H.
SHOOTING STAR	
SHORT'NIN' BREAD	SCARMOLIN--ED
SHORT'NIN' BREAD	SCHAUM, J.--ED.
SHORT'NIN' BREAD	WOLFE, J.
SHORT'NIN' BREAD	WOLFE, J.
SHORT'NIN' BREAD	ZEPP--ED
SHORTER PIANO COMPOSITIONS, BK. 1	BACH, J.S.
SHORTER WORKS FOR PIANOFORTE SOLO	SCHUBERT
SHORTNIN' BREAD	ROLFE, W.--ED
SHORT AND SWEET -- THREE SOLOS	ROGERS
SHORT AND SWEET	VALENTI, M.
SHORT CLASSICS YOUNG PEOPLE LIKE	KETTERER,
SHORT ETUDES WITH ORNAMENTS FOR PIANO	ROBYN
SHORT ETUDE	WEYBRIGHT
SHORT ORGAN PRELUDES AND FUGUES	BACH, J.S.
SHORT PIANO METHOD	LONG
SHORT PIANO PIECES	RAN, S.
SHORT PIANO PIECE	KAHN, E.I.
SHORT PIECE, OP. 6 NO. 2	GOEDICKE
SHORT PIECES --12--. MOVEMENTS FROM STRING QUARTETS	HAYDN
SHORT PIECES --18--	FRANCK, C.
SHORT PRELUDES AND FUGUES --24--	BACH, J.S.
SHORT PRELUDES AND FUGUES	BACH, J.S.
SHORT PRELUDES AND FUGUES	BACH, J.S.
SHORT PRELUDES AND FUGUES	BACH, J.S.
SHORT PRELUDES AND FUGUES	BACH, J.S.
SHORT PRELUDES AND FUGUES	BACH, J.S.
SHORT PRELUDES AND FUGUES	BACH, J.S.
SHORT PRELUDES AND FUGUES	BACH, J.S.
SHORT ROTE SOLOS	OWENS
SHORT SCHOOL OF VELOCITY, OP. 242	KOEHLER
SHORT SCHOOL OF VELOCITY WITHOUT OCTAVES, OP. 242	KOEHLER
SHORT SCHOOL OF VELOCITY	KOHLER, F.
SHORT SONATA IN A -- NO. 10 IN A SERIES 12	GREEN, R.
SHORT SONATA IN C -- NO. 01 IN A SERIES OF 12	GREEN, R.
SHORT SONATA IN C -- SECOND EDITION	GREEN, R.
SHORT SONATA IN D -- NO. 11 IN A SERIES OF 12	GREEN, R.
SHORT SONATA IN F -- NO. 02 IN A SERIES OF 12	GREEN, R.
SHORT SONATA NO. 1	KRAFT, L.
SHORT SONATA	PERLE, G.
SHORT SONATINA	WEYBRIGHT
SHORT STORIES	NABOKOFF, N.
SHORT STUDY, A	SCHUMANN, R.
SHORT SUITE IN F	LOURIE
SHORT SUITE	KUPFERMAN, M.
SHORT SUITE	KUPFERMAN, M.
SHORT SUITE	STEELE, G.
SHORT TOCCATA, A	WEYBRIGHT
SHOT IN THE DARK	
SHOUT FREEDOM	STRINGFIELD, L.
SHOVEL THAT SNOW	BURNAM
SHOVEL THAT SNOW	BURNAM
SHOWBOAT RAG	FILAS *
SHOWCASE, OP. 75	TCHEREPNIN
SHOWERS OF STARS	WACHS, P.
SHOWER OF PEARLS, VALSE	OSBORNE
SHOWER OF ROSES, OP. 80	ASCHER
SHOWER OF ROSES, REVERIE	MAY
SHOWER OF ROSES, SCHOTTISCHE	STREABBOG
SHOWER OF ROSES, WALTZ	STREABBOG
SHOWER OF ROSES	STREABBOG
SHOWER OF STARS	WACHS, P.
SHOWING OFF	ROGERS, E.
SHOW TIME	RAEZER, C.
SHUFFLE BOOGIE	MERKEL, N.
SHUTTLE COCK	BECK
SHVANDA -- POLKA AND FUGUE -- SET	WEINBERGER, J.
SI, SENORA, SPANISH SERENADE	HOPKINS, H.
SI, SI, BOSSA NOVA	DRAO
SIANG-SIN	HUE, G.
SIBERIA - DANCE OF THE BALALAIKAS	GIORDANO
SIBONEY	LANE, J.--ED.
SIBONEY	LECUONA
SIBONEY	
SICILIANA AND FURIANTE	ARNELL
SICILIANA	BACH, J.S.
SICILIANA	BENJAMIN
SICILIANA	MCQUATTIE, S.
SICILIANO--FROM SONATA NO. 2 FOR FLUTE AND HARPSICHORD	BACH, J.S.
SICILIANO--FROM SONATA NO. 2 FOR FLUTE AND HARPSICHORD	BACH, J.S.
SICILIANO --FROM FLUTE SONATA NO.2--	BACH, J.S.
SICILIANO AND RIGADON	CRAXTON, H.
SICILIANO FROM E FLAT SONATA FOR FLUTE AND CEMBALO S.	BACH, J.S.
SICILIANO FROM SONATA NO. 2 FOR FLUTE -- S. 1031B	BACH, J.S.
SICILIAN SCHERZO	ROSSELLINI
SICILIAN TARANTELLA	SCHER, W.
SICILIENNA FROM 'FLUTE AND PIANO SONATA'	BACH, J.S.
SICILIENNE, OP. 68 NO. 11--ALBUM FOR THE YOUNG	SCHUMANN, R.
SICILIENNE, OP. 68 NO. 11	SCHUMANN, R.
SICILIENNE, OP. 68 NO. 11	SCHUMANN, R.
SICILIENNE, OP. 78	FAURE, G.
SICILIENNE FOR 2 PIANOS	ROREM, N.
SICILIENNE	BACH, J.S.
SICILIENNE	DAVIS, K.
SIDEWALKS OF NEW YORK, THE	LAWLOR, G. *
SIDEWALKS OF NEW YORK, THE	LAWLOR, G. *
SIDEWALKS OF NEW YORK	LAWLOR, G. *
SIDEWALKS OF NEW YORK	LAWLOR, G. *
SIDEWALK CRACKS	ROGERS, E.
SIDE BY SIDE AT THE PIANO	ROVENGER--ED.
SIDE BY SIDE	KETTERER, E.
SIDE BY SIDE	WOODS, H.
SIDE SHOW	LAMBERT
SIDE SHOW	RAPHLING
SIDE STREET IN GOTHAM	ALTER, L.
SIEBEN BAGATELLEN, OP. 33	BEETHOVEN
SIEBEN CHORALPARTITEN FUR CEMBALO -- KLAVIER -- ODER	PACHELBEL
SIEBEN ELEGIEN	FORTNER, W.
SIEBEN KLAVIERKOMPOSITIONEN	AXMANN
SIEBEN KLAVIERSTUCKE FUR KINDER	REINER
SIEBEN KLEINE KLAVIERSTUCKE, OP. 12	HESSENBERG, K.
SIEBEN MAZURKEN, OP. 56	DVORAK
SIEBEN STUCKE, OP. 14	KABELAC
SIEBEN STUCKE FUR KLAVIER	SROM
SIEBEN TOCCATEN	SCARLATTI, A.
SIEBEN WALZER OP. 11 -- BK. 1 ST.-V.S. 18	REGER
SIEBEN WALZER OP. 11 -- BK. 2 ST.-V.S. 18	REGER
SIEGFRIED -- GER AND ENG SUPERLINEAR TEXT	WAGNER
SIEGFRIED IDYLL	WAGNER
SIEGFRIED IDYLL	WAGNER
SIEHE, TANZE UND MARSCHE, SEITE 15	STRAUSS, J.
SIEMPRE FLOR	REYNA
SIERRA, LA. FOLKLORE SUITE	ESPLA
SIESTA, LA, 1920	MALIPIERO, G. F.
SIESTA, LA	GUASTAVINO
SIESTA AT THE FIESTA	ALLEN
SIESTA SERENADE	DAVIS
SIESTA TIME	ANSON, G.
SIES ESTUDIOS ESPRESIVOS	GRANADOS
SIETE CANCIONES POPULARES ESPANOLAS	FALLA, M. DE
SIETE DE ABRIL	GOMEZ CARRILLO

SIETE MAZURKAS DE SALON, OP. 81	ALBENIZ, I.
SIETE PIEZAS INGANTILES	GIANNEO
SIETE PIEZAS	GALINDO, B.
SIFFLEUR ET SON CHIEN, LE	PRYOR
SIGHT-READING TESTS, BK. 1	DUKE, H.
SIGHT-READING TESTS, BK. 2	DUKE, H.
SIGHT READING, BK. 1-2	KIRBY, M. B.
SIGHT READING AT THE PIANO	MERRILL, M.
SIGHT READING EXERCISES	CZERNY
SIGHT READING FOR PIANO, BK. 1	SCHAUM, J.
SIGHT READING FOR PIANO, BK. 2	SCHAUM, J.
SIGHT READING FOR THE VERY YOUNG PIANIST	LAST, J.
SIGMUND ROMBERG 'EASY TO PLAY' PIANO DUETS	ROMBERG, S.
SIGNAL FROM MARS, A	TAYLOR
SIGNS SHALL FOLLOW SONGBOOK	
SIGN OF THE TIMES, THE	HATCH
SIGURD JORSALFAR, OP. 56. THREE PIECES	GRIEG
SIGURD JORSALFAR, OP. 56	GRIEG
SIHOUETTES, OP. 53	REGER
SIKORSKI ALBUM - KLINGENDE HEIMAT - FOLKSONGS FROM	SIKORSKI
SIKORSKI ALBUM - KLINGENDE HEIMAT - FOLKSONGS FROM	SIKORSKI
SILENT LOVE	LANGE, G.
SILENT NIGHT, HOLY NIGHT	FREDERICKS
SILENT NIGHT, HOLY NIGHT	GRUBER, F.
SILENT NIGHT, HOLY NIGHT	GRUBER, F.
SILENT NIGHT, HOLY NIGHT	GRUBER, F.
SILENT NIGHT, HOLY NIGHT	GRUBER, F.
SILENT NIGHT, HOLY NIGHT	SCHIEFELBEIN, F.
SILENT NIGHT, HOLY NIGHT	SCHIEFELBEIN, F.
SILENT NIGHT -- CHRISTMAS MEDLEY	GRUBER, F.
SILENT NIGHT -- VARIATIONS	CRERIE, E. *
SILENT NIGHT VARIATIONS	CRERIE, E. *
SILENT NIGHT	BRADLEY,
SILENT NIGHT	BRIMHALL,
SILENT NIGHT	GRUBER, F.
SILENT NIGHT	GRUBER, F.
SILENT NIGHT	GRUBER, F.
SILENT NIGHT	GRUBER, F.
SILENT NIGHT	GRUBER, F.
SILENT NIGHT	RICHTER, A.
SILENT PIG, THE	DUNGAN
SILENT PRAYER	LOUKA, M.
SILENT THOUGHTS	LINCOLN, H.
SILENZIO CANTATORE	
SILHOUETTES, OP. 23	ARENSKY, A.
SILHOUETTES, OP. 31--9 CHILDHOOD PICTURES	REBIKOV
SILHOUETTES, OP. 31	REBIKOV
SILHOUETTES, OP. 31	REBIKOV
SILHOUETTES, OP. 8	DVORAK
SILHOUETTES -- A COLLECTION OF 40 DANCES FROM J.S.	BACH, J.S. *
SILHOUETTES - L'AQUEDUC	TURINA, J.
SILHOUETTES - LA PHARE DE CADIX	TURINA, J.
SILHOUETTES - LA PUERTA DEL SOL	TURINA, J.
SILHOUETTES - LA TOUR DE L'OR	TURINA, J.
SILHOUETTES - LA TOUR DE LA VELA	TURINA, J.
SILHOUETTES DE CARNEVAL - 1. MASQUERADES	PICK-MANGIAGALLI
SILHOUETTES DE CARNEVAL - 2. CHANSON-SERENADE A	PICK-MANGIAGALLI
SILHOUETTES DE CARNEVAL - 3. ET PIERRETTE DANSAIT	PICK-MANGIAGALLI
SILHOUETTES DE CARNEVAL - 4. LA RONDE DES ARLEQUINS	PICK-MANGIAGALLI
SILHOUETTES	TURINA, J.
SILHOUETTE	WHITFORD
SILK STOCKINGS	
SILLAGES	AUBERT
SILLY BILLY	SCHAUM, J.--ED.
SILLY POLKA - FROM FIVE PIECES FOR YOUNG PIANISTS	RIETI
SILLY POLKA	RIETI
SILLY SEA HORSE	PHILLIPS, B.
SILVANO - EASY FANTASY NO. 1	MASCAGNI, P.
SILVANO - EASY FANTASY NO. 2	MASCAGNI, P.
SILVANO - NOCTURNE	MASCAGNI, P.
SILVERY THISTLE -- L'ARGENTINE --	KETTERER, E.
SILVERY WAVES	WYMAN, A.
SILVERY WAVES	WYMAN, A.
SILVER ANNIVERSARY WALTZ	TRUXELL, E.
SILVER ANNIVERSARY WALTZ	TRUXELL, E.
SILVER BAND MARCH	KLARKE
SILVER BELLS	BRIMHALL,
SILVER BELLS	REBE
SILVER BELLS	STREABBOG
SILVER BLADES	KETTERER, E.
SILVER CHIMES, INTERMEZZO	LORAINE, P.
SILVER MELODIES	CRIST, D.
SILVER MOONBEAMS -- SOLO OR DUET	RICHARDS, B.
SILVER MOONBEAMS	CRUICKSHANK
SILVER MOONBEAMS	RICHARDS, B.
SILVER NYMPH, THE--MAZURKA BRILLANTE, OP. 164	HEINS, C.
SILVER NYMPH, THE	HEINS, C.
SILVER NYMPH	HEINS, C.
SILVER SHIP	DITTENHAVER
SILVER SLEIGH BELLS	PAULL
SILVER SLIPPERS	ECKSTEIN
SILVER SLIPPERS	STEADMAN, A.
SILVER SPRING	MASON, W.
SILVER STARS, MAZURKA	BOHM
SILVER STARS, MAZURKA	BOHM
SILVER STARS, REVERIE	HOPKINS, H.
SILVER STARS	BOHM
SILVER STREAMLETS	REISER, V.
SILVER THREADS AMONG THE GOLD	DANKS
SILVER TRAY, CAPRICE	DRUMHELLER
SILVER TRUMPETS	VIVIANI
SIMON AND GARFUNKEL'S GREATEST HITS	BRADLEY,
SIMPLES COLETANEA	VILLA-LOBOS, H.
SIMPLE AVEU--ROMANCE SANS PAROLES, OP. 25	THOME, F.
SIMPLE AVEU -- CONFESSION	THOME, F.
SIMPLE AVEU	THOME, F.
SIMPLE CONFESSION -- SIMPLE AVEU, OP. 25	THOME, F.
SIMPLE CONFESSION	THOME, F.
SIMPLE ETUDES FOR ADVANCED BEGINNERS	KAPP, R.
SIMPLE ETUDES FOR ADVANCED BEGINNERS	KAPP, R.
SIMPLE ETUDES FOR ADVANCED BEGINNERS	KAPP, R.
SIMPLICITY	CARREL, B.
SIMPLIFIED BOOGIE WOOGIE	MOSSMAN, T.
SIMPLIFIED PIANO ARRANGEMENTS	SMITH, T.
SIMPLIFIED PIANO PIECES	FREY--ED
SIMPLIFIED SONG GEMS FOR PIANO	KENDALL--ED
SIMPLY BRADLEY - CHRISTMAS CAROLS	BRADLEY,
SIMPLY BRADLEY - FOLK BOOK	BRADLEY,
SIMPLY BRADLEY - HYMN BOOK	BRADLEY,
SIMPLY BRADLEY - MOVIE BOOK	BRADLEY,
SIMPLY BRADLEY - POP BOOK	BRADLEY,
SIMPLY BRADLEY - RUDOLPH THE RED-NOSED REINDEER AND	BRADLEY,
SIMPLY BRADLEY - SECOND POP BOOK, THE	BRADLEY,
SIMPLY BRADLEY - THE PARTRIDGE FAMILY	BRADLEY,
SINE NOMINE -- GRAVEN IMAGES NO. 3	WEISGALL, H.
SINFONIA, ARIOSO UND TOCCATA, OP. 59	CASELLA, A.
SINFONIA --FROM CHRISTMAS ORATORIO, PART 2--	BACH, J.S.
SINFONIA CONCERTANTE	WALTON, W.
SINFONIA FROM CANTATA 75	BACH, J.S.
SINFONIA NO. 1 FROM CANTATA 35	BACH, J.S.
SINFONIETTA, OP. 5	PROKOFIEFF
SINFONIETTA GIOCOSA	MARTINU, B.
SINFONIE 'MATHIS DER MALER', 1934 - KLAVIERAUSZUG	HINDEMITH
SINFONIE H-MOLL -- UNVOLLENDETE KLAVIERAUSZUG	SCHUBERT
SINFONIE IN E FLAT, 1940 - KLAVIERAUSZUG	HINDEMITH
SINFONIE MUSICALI, OP. 18 NOS. 1-6	VIADANA, DA
SINFONIE NO. 02, OP. 29 IN F	FOERSTER
SINFONIE NO. 08 IN G, OP. 88	DVORAK
SINFONIE NO. 09 IN E MINOR, OP. 95, 'AUS DER NEUEN	DVORAK
SINFONIE NO. 09 IN E MINOR, OP. 95, 'AUS DER NEUEN	DVORAK
SINFONISCHES KONZERT, OP. 21	BRESGEN
SINFONISCHE METAMORPHOSEN UBER THEMEN VON C. M. VON	HINDEMITH
SINFONISCHE TANZE, 1937 - KLAVIERAUSZUG	HINDEMITH
SING-LEE, CHINA-BOY	LIVELY, K. *
SING, LITTLE PUSSY CAT	GILLOCK
SING, ROBIN SING	SPAULDING, G. L.
SING, ROBIN SING	SPAULDING, G. L.
SINGING AND SWINGING	QUINCKE, W.
SINGING BIRD, THE	PRIGGE, O.
SINGING BIRDS--WITH WORDS	VANNORT, I.
SINGING BIRDS, POLKA	VOYE
SINGING BIRDS	ENDRES, O.
SINGING CELLO, THE	DUNGAN
SINGING CELLO	DE VITO, A.
SINGING COWBOY	CANFIELD, J.
SINGING FINGERS	DANIEL, K.
SINGING FINGERS	DAVIS, M.--ED
SINGING FIVE FINGERS	JOYNER, B.
SINGING FOUNTAIN, THE OP. 30	NIEMANN
SINGING FOUNTAIN, THE	BURNAM
SINGING FOUNTAIN, THE	TAYLOR, EDNA
SINGING IN THE GLEN, WALTZ	ARMOUR
SINGING IN THE MOONLIGHT	MACGREGOR, H.
SINGING IN THE MOONLIGHT	MACGREGOR
SINGING IN THE RAIN	LANE, J.--ED.
SINGING IN THE SADDLE	BURNAM
SINGING IN THE SUN	WEYBRIGHT
SINGING KEYS, BK. 1	
SINGING KEYS, BK. 2	
SINGING KEYS, BK. 3	
SINGING KEYS, BK. 4	
SINGING MELODIES	
SINGING PINES	LAUFMAN
SINGING SURF	HOWELL
SINGING TEA KETTLE	RUSSELL
SINGING TOUCH AND TECHNIQUE--25 EASY STUDIES FOR SMALL	STAMATY, C.
SINGING TOWER, THE	MUNN, W.
SINGING WATER	RUSSELL
SINGING ZITHER, THE	FREUNDORFER
SINGING	DITTENHAVER
SING AND PLAY TOGETHER	DAWSON
SING A SONG OF SIXPENCE	ROLFE, W.
SING A SONG OF SIXPENCE	SWINSTEAD, F.
SING LOW, SING HIGH	BRODSKY, M.
SING TOGETHER AT CHRISTMAS	PITCHER, G.--ED
SING WE NOW OF CHRISTMAS	RICHARDSON, A.
SING WITH ME -- SONGS OLD AND NEW	RICHTER
SIREN, VALSE	THOME, F.
SIRENES, LES, OP. 154	WALDTEUFEL, E.
SIRENES, NOCTURNE	DEBUSSY
SIRENETTA E IL PESCE TURCHINO, LA	CASTELNUOVO-TEDE
SIS HOPKINS, BARN DANCE	MAYER
SIT DOWN, SISTER	PINCKARD
SIT DOWN SISTER	WEYBRIGHT
SIUTE PITTORESQUE - DANSE GUERRIERE	FOURDRAIN
SIXIEME MOT, OP. 72	BACEVICIUS
SIXIEME NOCTURNE	POULENC, F.
SIXTEEN AGILITY STUDIES FOR SMALL HANDS	POZZOLI
SIXTEEN ELEMENTARY STUDIES, OP. 163	KOEHLER
SIXTEEN ESERCIZI SULLA POLIFONIA	MUGNAINI, D.
SIXTEEN FAVORITE WALTZES, VOL. 1	STRAUSS, J.
SIXTEEN FAVORITE WALTZES, VOL. 2	STRAUSS, J.
SIXTEEN GERMAN DANCES AND TWO ECOSSAISES, OP. 33, D.	SCHUBERT
SIXTEEN LITTLE CONCERT PIECES, OP. 99	SPRONGL, N.
SIXTEEN LITTLE PIANO PIECES	HANDEL
SIXTEEN LITTLE PIECES	SCHUBERT
SIXTEEN LYRIC STUDIES	MONTANI
SIXTEEN MASTERWORKS FOR PIANO	BEER, L. J.--ED
SIXTEEN MASTERWORKS FOR THE PIANO	KURANDA, M.--ED
SIXTEEN MASTERWORKS	KURANDA, M.--ED
SIXTEEN MEASURES OF KEYBOARD PLEASURES	STEINER
SIXTEEN PAWNS--PIANO QUARTETTE--	DE PUE
SIXTEEN PIECES FOR CHILDREN	BARTOK
SIXTEEN POLKAS	HILMAR
SIXTEEN PRELUDES	SCRIABINE, A.
SIXTEEN SELECTED ETUDES -- BRAHMS, CRAMER, KULLAK,	LUCAS--ED.
SIXTEEN SELECTED PIECES	MACDOWELL
SIXTEEN SHORT CONTEMPORARY PIECES FOR BEGINNERS	PARCHMAN, G.
SIXTEEN SONATAS OF OLD SPANISH MASTERS -- SONATAS BY	NIN--ED
SIXTEEN SONATAS	SCARLATTI, D.
SIXTEEN SONATEN	BENDA, R.
SIXTEEN STREABBOG PIECES	STEINER
SIXTEEN STUDIES OF MODERATE DIFFICULTY, OP. 224	KOEHLER
SIXTEEN SUITES, BK. 1 -- 1-8 --	HANDEL
SIXTEEN SUITES, BK. 1	HANDEL
SIXTEEN SUITES, BK. 2 -- 9-16 --	HANDEL
SIXTEEN SUITES, BK. 2	HANDEL
SIXTEEN WALTZES, OP. 39	BRAHMS
SIXTEEN WALTZES, OP. 39	BRAHMS
SIXTEEN WALTZES, OP. 39	BRAHMS
SIXTH AVENUE EXPRESS	AMMONS *
SIXTH AVENUE EXPRESS	AMMONS *
SIXTH FINGER TUNE	STROUSE
SIXTH NOCTURNE, OP. 91	LEYBACH, I.
SIXTH SENSE	NEVIN
SIXTH SONATA, OP. 32	BARTH, H.
SIXTH SONATA FOR PIANO	CHAVEZ, C.
SIXTY-EIGHT GREATEST COUNTRY HITS, MAMMOTH COLLECTION	
SIXTY-FIVE WORLD FAMOUS WALTZES	
SIXTY-FOUR PRELUDES, OP. 41--VOL. 2--	BLANCHET
SIXTY-FOUR PRELUDES, OP. 41--VOL. 3--	BLANCHET
SIXTY-FOUR PRELUDES, OP. 64--VOL. 1--	BLANCHET
SIXTY-NINE CHORALES WITH FIGURED BASS	BACH, J.S.
SIXTY-NINE CHORALES WITH FIGURED BASS	BACH, J.S.
SIXTY-ONE EASY TO PLAY HYMNS FOR PIANO	
SIXTY-ONE GEMS FOR PIANO	
SIXTY-SEVEN BRADLEY POP TEACHING PIECES FOR PIANO	BRADLEY,
SIXTY-THREE BEST OF THE YEAR -- BRIMHALL EASY PIANO --	BRIMHALL,
SIXTY-TWO POPULAR TEACHING PIECES	BRIMHALL,
SIXTY CHILDREN'S EXERCISES	CZERNY
SIXTY DAILY EXERCISES	PISCHNA
SIXTY DAILY EXERCISES	PISCHNA
SIXTY DAILY STUDIES	PISCHNA

SIXTY ETUDEN	CRAMER, J. *
SIXTY ETUDES, BK. 1	STEINER
SIXTY ETUDES, BK. 2	STEINER
SIXTY NEW PREPARATORY EXERCISES	PHILIPP, I.
SIXTY PIANO DUETS --PROGRESSIVE GRADED	
SIXTY PROGRESSIVE PIANO PIECES YOU LIKE TO PLAY	
SIXTY PROGRESSIVE STUDIES	PISCHNA
SIXTY SELECTED STUDIES -- GERMAN TEXT	CRAMER, J.
SIXTY SELECTED STUDIES	CRAMER, J.
SIXTY SELECTED STUDIES	CRAMER, J. *
SIXTY SONATAS, BK. 1	SCARLATTI, D.
SIXTY SONATAS, BK. 2	SCARLATTI, D.
SIXTY STUDI	CRAMER, J.
SIXTY VERY EASY PIECES --IN PROGRESSIVE ORDER--	TUERK
SIXTY WRITING LESSONS IN MUSICAL THEORY -- PART 1	MOY, E.
SIXTY WRITING LESSONS IN MUSICAL THEORY -- PART 2	MOY, E.
SIX ABSENCES POUR LE CLAVECIN, 1961	HENZE, H.
SIX ALBUM LEAVES, OP. 2	SMETANA
SIX ALL TIME FAVORITES	THOMPSON, J.
SIX APHORISMS FOR THE PIANO	FISHER, A.
SIX ARABESQUES	TANSMAN, A.
SIX BAGATELLES, OP. 12--1932	ROZSA, M.
SIX BAGATELLES, OP. 3	SAINT-SAENS
SIX BAGATELLES, OP. 76--1964	SACHSE, H. W.
SIX BAGATELLES	KADOSA
SIX BAGATELLES	KOLZ, E.
SIX BAGATELLES	PAPP, L.
SIX BAGATELLES	PEZZE
SIX BARCAROLLES	FAURE, G.
SIX BARCAROLLES	FAURE, G.
SIX BIBLICAL SONATAS	KUHNAU, J.
SIX BLACK KEY DUETS	SHAW, G.
SIX BOHEMIAN DANCES	SMETANA
SIX BOHEMIAN DANCES	SMETANA
SIX BURLESQUES, OP. 58	REGER
SIX CANONIC ETUDES, OP. 56	SCHUMANN, R.
SIX CANONS, OP. 142	CASTELNUOVO-TEDE
SIX CELEBRATED COMPOSITIONS	CHOPIN
SIX CHANSONS	ZYKAN, O. M.
SIX CHANTS POPULAIRES BRETONS	DANDELOT
SIX CHARACTERISTIC PIECES, OP. 1	SMETANA
SIX CHARACTERISTIC STUDIES	PEDRON
SIX CHARACTERS FROM SHAKESPEARE	GIBBS
SIX CHARAKTERISTISCHE KOMPOSITIONEN, OP. 1	SMETANA
SIX CHILDREN'S PIECES, OP. 34	ARENSKY, A.
SIX CHILDREN'S PIECES	SHOSTAKOVITCH
SIX CHOPIN ETUDES	CHOPIN
SIX CHORALE PRELUDES FROM OP. 12	BRAHMS
SIX CHRISTMAS CAROLS	WALLIS--ED
SIX CONCERTI FOR 2 KEYBOARD INSTRUMENTS -- COMPLETE	SOLER, A.
SIX CONCERTI FOR 2 KEYBOARD INSTRUMENTS -- NO. 1 IN C	SOLER, A.
SIX CONCERTI FOR 2 KEYBOARD INSTRUMENTS -- NO. 2 IN A	SOLER, A.
SIX CONCERTI FOR 2 KEYBOARD INSTRUMENTS -- NO. 3 IN G	SOLER, A.
SIX CONCERTI FOR 2 KEYBOARD INSTRUMENTS -- NO. 4 IN F	SOLER, A.
SIX CONCERTI FOR 2 KEYBOARD INSTRUMENTS -- NO. 5 IN A	SOLER, A.
SIX CONCERTI FOR 2 KEYBOARD INSTRUMENTS -- NO. 6 IN D	SOLER, A.
SIX CONCERTOS AFTER VIVALDI -- OP. 3, NOS. 3, 9, 12.	BACH, J.S.
SIX CONCERTO ETUDES	PETYREK, F.
SIX CONCERT ETUDES, BK. 1 AND 2	DOHNANYI
SIX CONCERT STUDIES AFTER CAPRICES BY PAGANINI, OP. 10	SCHUMANN, R.
SIX CONCERT STUDIES ON CAPRICES OF PAGANINI, OP. 10	SCHUMANN, R.
SIX CONSOLATIONS, NO. 3	LISZT
SIX CONSOLATIONS, NOS. 1 AND 2	LISZT
SIX CONSOLATIONS AND THREE LIEBESTRAEUME	LISZT
SIX CONSOLATIONS	LISZT
SIX CONSOLATIONS	LISZT
SIX CONTEMPORARY ETCHINGS	NEWSOME
SIX CUBAN DANCES	CERVANTES, E.
SIX DANCES IN BULGARIAN RHYTHM	BARTOK
SIX DANCE PRELUDES, OP. 18	LAMONTAINE, J.
SIX DANSES SUEDOISES	INGHELBRECHT, D.
SIX DUETS	FICHANDLER, W.
SIX EASY PIECES, OP. 139	ZILCHER
SIX EASY PIECES ON 5 NOTES - 1. MEDITANDO	MONTANARO
SIX EASY PIECES ON 5 NOTES - 2. NOSTALGIA SLAVA	MONTANARO
SIX EASY PIECES ON 5 NOTES - 3. IL SUONATORE DI	MONTANARO
SIX EASY PIECES ON 5 NOTES - 4. IL CARILLON DI LOLETTE	MONTANARO
SIX EASY PIECES ON 5 NOTES - 5. IL COMPLEANNO	MONTANARO
SIX EASY PIECES ON 5 NOTES - 6. IN MORTE DEL	MONTANARO
SIX EASY PIECES	KAUER, F.
SIX EASY PIECES	PIERNE, P.
SIX EASY PIECES	POOT, M.
SIX EASY PIECES	VANHAL
SIX EASY SONATAS	HAESSLER
SIX EASY SONATINAS FOR YOUNG PIANISTS, VOL. 1	STRAVINSKY, S.
SIX EASY SONATINAS FOR YOUNG PIANISTS, VOL. 2	STRAVINSKY, S.
SIX ECOSSAISES	BEETHOVEN
SIX ECOSSAISES	BEETHOVEN
SIX EPIGRAPHES ANTIQUES	DEBUSSY
SIX EPIGRAPHES ANTIQUES	DEBUSSY
SIX ETUDES-EXERCICES	FALKENBERG
SIX ETUDES-TABLEAUX, OP. 33	RACHMANINOFF, S.
SIX ETUDES-TABLEAUX, OP.33	RACHMANINOFF, S.
SIX ETUDES, BK. 1, OP. 52	SAINT-SAENS
SIX ETUDES, OP. 23	RUBINSTEIN
SIX ETUDES, OP. 23	RUBINSTEIN
SIX ETUDES, OP. 56	SCHUMANN, R.
SIX ETUDES CARACTERISTIQUES DE HAUTE TECHNIQUE	FUMET
SIX ETUDES CONCERT - LEGGIEREZZA, LA	LISZT
SIX ETUDES DE CONCERT - GNOMENREIGNEN	LISZT
SIX ETUDES DE CONCERT - SOSPIRO, UN	LISZT
SIX ETUDES DE CONCERT - WALDESRAUSCHEN	LISZT
SIX ETUDES DE CONCERT	LISZT
SIX ETUDES DE TRAVAIL OP. 21	TCHEREPNIN
SIX ETUDES IN CANON FORM	SCHUMANN, R.
SIX ETUDES POUR LA MAIN GAUCHE SEULE, OP. 135 --	SAINT-SAENS
SIX ETUDES POUR LA MAIN GAUCHE SEULE, OP. 135 --	SAINT-SAENS
SIX ETUDES POUR LA MAIN GAUCHE SEULE, OP. 135 -- MOTO	SAINT-SAENS
SIX ETUDES POUR LA MAIN GAUCHE SEULE, OP. 135	SAINT-SAENS
SIX ETUDES POUR LE PIANO, BK. 1, NO. 01 -- PRELUDE	SAINT-SAENS
SIX ETUDES POUR LE PIANO, BK. 1, NO. 02 -- POUR	SAINT-SAENS
SIX ETUDES POUR LE PIANO, BK. 1, NO. 03 -- PRELUDE ET	SAINT-SAENS
SIX ETUDES POUR LE PIANO, BK. 1, NO. 04 -- ETUDE DE	SAINT-SAENS
SIX ETUDES POUR LE PIANO, BK. 1, NO. 05 -- PRELUDE ET	SAINT-SAENS
SIX ETUDES POUR LE PIANO, BK. 1, NO. 06 -- EN FORME DE	SAINT-SAENS
SIX ETUDES POUR LE PIANO, BK. 1	SAINT-SAENS
SIX ETUDES POUR LE PIANO, BK. 2, NO. 01 -- TIERCES	SAINT-SAENS
SIX ETUDES POUR LE PIANO, BK. 2, NO. 02 -- TRAITS	SAINT-SAENS
SIX ETUDES POUR LE PIANO, BK. 2, NO. 03 -- PRELUDE ET	SAINT-SAENS
SIX ETUDES POUR LE PIANO, BK. 2, NO. 04 -- LES CLOCHES	SAINT-SAENS
SIX ETUDES POUR LE PIANO, BK. 2, NO. 05 -- TIERCES	SAINT-SAENS
SIX ETUDES POUR LE PIANO, BK. 2, NO. 06 -- TOCCATA	SAINT-SAENS
SIX ETUDES	ALLENDE
SIX ETUDES	RIBARI, A.
SIX ETUDES	TALMA, L.
SIX EXERCISES AND PRELUDES	BUSONI
SIX FAMOUS WALTZES	CHOPIN
SIX FANTASIAS AND FUGUES,URTEXT	BACH, J.S.
SIX FANTASIES AND SIX FUGUES	TELEMANN, G.P.
SIX FAVORITE MINUETS	HAYDN
SIX FINNISH FOLKSONGS	SIBELIUS
SIX FOR EIGHT--PIANO QUARTETTE--	BALKIN
SIX FRENCH SUITES, S. 812-817	BACH, J.S.
SIX FUGHETTE	HANDEL
SIX FUGUES --VOLUNTARIES-- FOR HARPSICHORD OR ORGAN	HANDEL
SIX GERMAN DANCES, K. 509	MOZART, W. A.
SIX GERMAN DANCES, K. 509	MOZART, W. A.
SIX GERMAN DANCES OP. POSTH	SCHUBERT
SIX GERMAN DANCES	BEETHOVEN
SIX GRANDES ETUDES AFTER N. PAGANINI	LISZT
SIX GRANDES ETUDES D'APRES PAGANINI	LISZT
SIX GRAND ETUDES	LISZT *
SIX GRAND MARCHES IN THE STYLE OF THE FIRST EMPIRE	FRANCAIX, J.
SIX GREEK MINIATURES	ALLENDE
SIX IMPROMPTUS, OP. 7	VORISEK
SIX IMPROMPTUS	BARRAUD
SIX INCA MELODIES	MAGGIONI
SIX INDISCRETIONS	RAPHLING
SIX INDISCRETIONS	RAPHLING
SIX INVENTIONS	MONNIKENDAM
SIX IRISH PIECES -- WORKS FROM THE 17TH AND 18TH	BREEN--ED
SIX KEYBOARD SONATAS FROM THE CLASSIC ERA	NEWMAN--ED.
SIX KLAVIERSTUCKE, OP. 52	DVORAK
SIX LACHISCHE TANZE	JANACEK
SIX LANDLER DANCES, K606	MOZART, W. A.
SIX LITTLE CHARACTERISTIC PIECES	BELLETTI
SIX LITTLE DANCES	MONTANI
SIX LITTLE FUGUES	HANDEL
SIX LITTLE HANDS AT ONE KEYBOARD -- A PREPARATORY BOOK	RODGERS, I. *
SIX LITTLE PIANO PIECES, OP. 19	SCHOENBERG
SIX LITTLE PIECES, OP. 11	RATHAUS, K.
SIX LITTLE PIECES -- 1953 --	DICHLER
SIX LITTLE PIECES - IL PLEUT	SOHY
SIX LITTLE PIECES FOR CHILDREN	MARGOLA
SIX LITTLE PIECES	CINTOLESI
SIX LITTLE PIECES	RESPIGHI
SIX LITTLE PIECES	SOHY
SIX LITTLE PRELUDES--NO. 1, DIALOGUE	PADWA, V.
SIX LITTLE PRELUDES--NO. 2, INTERLUDE	PADWA, V.
SIX LITTLE PRELUDES--NO. 3, LITTLE MARCH	PADWA, V.
SIX LITTLE PRELUDES--NO. 5, SHADOWS	PADWA, V.
SIX LITTLE PRELUDES	BACH, J.S.
SIX LITTLE PRELUDES	BACH, J.S.
SIX LITTLE RECITAL PIECES	THOMPSON, J.--ED
SIX MINIATURES FOR PIANO	BENARY
SIX MINIATURES STUDIES, BK. 1	PANUFNIK, A.
SIX MINIATURES STUDIES, BK. 2	PANUFNIK, A.
SIX MINIATURES	KREMENLIEV
SIX MINUETS	HAYDN, M.
SIX MINUETS	MOZART, W. A.
SIX MINUETS	MOZART, W. A.
SIX MODAL MINIATURES	STEVENS, E.
SIX MOMENTS FOR PIANO	SUDERBURG, R.
SIX MOMENTS MUSICAUX, OP. 16	RACHMANINOFF, S.
SIX MOMENTS MUSICAUX, OP. 16	RACHMANINOFF, S.
SIX MORCEAUX, OP. 52 NO. 1 INTERMEZZO	PROKOFIEFF
SIX MORCEAUX, OP. 52 NO. 2 RONDO	PROKOFIEFF
SIX MORCEAUX, OP. 52 NO. 3 ETUDE	PROKOFIEFF
SIX MORCEAUX, OP. 52 NO. 4 SCHERZINO	PROKOFIEFF
SIX MORCEAUX, OP. 52 NO. 5 ANDANTE	PROKOFIEFF
SIX MORCEAUX, OP. 52 NO. 6 SCHERZO	PROKOFIEFF
SIX MORCEAUX FACILES	GOUNOD, C.
SIX MORE SWINGY SOLOS	ZEPP
SIX NOCTURNES	DAVICO
SIX OCTAVE-STUDIES IN PROGRESSIVE DIFFICULTY, OP. 553	CZERNY
SIX OCTAVE-STUDIES IN THE FORM OF LITTLE FUGUES, OP.	PHILIPP, I.
SIX OCTAVE STUDIES, OP. 48	LONGO, A.
SIX ORGAN CHORALES	BACH, J.S.
SIX ORIGINAL PIECES, OP. 11	RACHMANINOFF, S.
SIX ORIGINAL PIECES, OP. 41	GLIERE
SIX ORNAMENTAL ETUDES	LEES, B.
SIX PAGANINI ETUDES	LISZT
SIX PARTITAS, CLAVIER-UEBUNG, PART 1 -- CLOTH	BACH, J.S.
SIX PARTITAS, CLAVIER-UEBUNG, PART 1	BACH, J.S.
SIX PARTITAS, S. 825-830, VOL. 1	BACH, J.S.
SIX PARTITAS, S. 825-830, VOL. 2	BACH, J.S.
SIX PARTITAS AND FRENCH OVERTURE	BACH, J.S.
SIX PARTITAS	BACH, J.S.
SIX PARTY PIECES	THOMPSON, J.--ED
SIX PETITES PIECES FACILES	HERMANN, R.
SIX PETITES PIECES RECREATIVES	POOT, M.
SIX PETITE PRELUDES, OP. 35A	KADOSA
SIX PETITS CROQUIS	BONNEAU
SIX PETITS PIECES	PETIT, P.
SIX PIANO PICTURES	HAGEMAN
SIX PIANO PIECES, OP. 118	BRAHMS
SIX PIANO PIECES, OP. 118	BRAHMS
SIX PIANO PIECES, OP. 118	BRAHMS
SIX PIANO PIECES, OP. 24	REGER
SIX PIANO PIECES, OP. 37	TIESSEN, H.
SIX PIANO PIECES, OP. 41	DOHNANYI
SIX PIANO PIECES FOR CHILDREN	ALOTIN, Y.
SIX PIECES, OP. 118	BRAHMS
SIX PIECES, OP. 118	BRAHMS
SIX PIECES, OP. 118	BRAHMS
SIX PIECES, OP. 52--NO. 2, RONDO	PROKOFIEFF
SIX PIECES, OP. 52--NO. 6, SCHERZO	PROKOFIEFF
SIX PIECES, OP. 94	REGER
SIX PIECES, 1957	KITTLER, R.
SIX PIECES - DANS LE PRE FLEURI	LABEY
SIX PIECES - RONDE	LABEY
SIX PIECES , OP. 118	BRAHMS
SIX PIECES BREVES - LA BASSE-COUR, LE ROUET, LE DEPART	ORBAN
SIX PIECES CLAIRES ET BIEN AEREES - CLAIRIERE	NIVERD, L.
SIX PIECES CLAIRES ET BIEN AEREES - CRINCRINS ET	NIVERD, L.
SIX PIECES CLAIRES ET BIEN AEREES - HALTE SOUS	NIVERD, L.
SIX PIECES CLAIRES ET BIEN AEREES - LE BOURRIQUET	NIVERD, L.
SIX PIECES CLAIRES ET BIEN AEREES - LE MOULIN DU VAL	NIVERD, L.
SIX PIECES CLAIRES ET BIEN AEREES - SOIR DE FETE AUX	NIVERD, L.
SIX PIECES FOR CHILDREN, OP. 72	MENDELSSOHN
SIX PIECES FOR CHILDREN, OP. 72	MENDELSSOHN
SIX PIECES FOR CHILDREN - CHEZ GUIGNOL	LERMYTE
SIX PIECES FOR CHILDREN - LA PETITE FUTEE	LERMYTE
SIX PIECES FOR CHILDREN - LES CLOCHETTES	LERMYTE
SIX PIECES FOR CHILDREN - LE PETIT BALLON ROUGE	LERMYTE
SIX PIECES FOR CHILDREN - PETIT MENUET	LERMYTE
SIX PIECES FOR CHILDREN - REVERIE	LERMYTE
SIX PIECES FOR PIANO, 1964	STEINKE, G.
SIX PIECES FROM ''SILHOUETTES'', OP. 31 -- SET	REBIKOV
SIX PIECES IN FORM OF CANONS, OP. 156	CASTELNUOVO-TEDE
SIX PIECES MIGNONNES POUE LES PETITES MAINS - EN	TROJELLI
SIX PIECES MIGNONNES POUR LES PETITES MAINS -	TROJELLI
SIX PIECES MIGNONNES POUR LES PETITES MAINS - COUCOU	TROJELLI
SIX PIECES MIGNONNES POUR LES PETITES MAINS - LA	TROJELLI

SIX PIECES MIGNONNES POUR LES PETITES MAINS - PAPILLON	TROJELLI
SIX PIECES MIGNONNES POUR LES PETITES MAINS - PAUVRE	TROJELLI
SIX PIECES MIGNONNES POUR LES PETITES MAINS	TROJELLI
SIX PIECES ON SPANISH FOLK SONGS -- COMPLETE	GRANADOS
SIX PIECES UKRAINIENNES, OP. 71	AKIMENKO
SIX PIECES VILLAGEOISES	REVILLE, H.
SIX PIECES	CASADESUS, R.
SIX PIECES	LABEY
SIX PIECES	LAZARUS
SIX PIECES	VREDENBURG
SIX POETIC TONE-PICTURES, OP. 3	GRIEG
SIX POLISH CHRISTMAS CAROLS	REBE--ED.
SIX POLISH SONGS	CHOPIN
SIX POLISH SONGS	CHOPIN *
SIX POLISH SONGS	CHOPIN *
SIX PRELUDES--1925	RODRIGUEZ, R.
SIX PRELUDES, OP. 12	DUPRE, M.
SIX PRELUDES, OP. 13	SCRIABINE, A.
SIX PRELUDES, OP. 38	CRESTON
SIX PRELUDES, OP. 6, BK. 1	CAAMANO
SIX PRELUDES, OP. 6, BK. 2	CAAMANO
SIX PRELUDES, OP. 6	MUCZYNSKI, R.
SIX PRELUDES, OP. 99	BURKHARD, W.
SIX PRELUDES, OP. 99	BURKHARD, W.
SIX PRELUDES - B-FLAT	NAT, Y.
SIX PRELUDES - B MINOR	NAT, Y.
SIX PRELUDES - F-SHARP MAJOR	NAT, Y.
SIX PRELUDES - LE BUCHARON	NAT, Y.
SIX PRELUDES - LE TEMPETE	NAT, Y.
SIX PRELUDES - PRELUDES A L'AUTOMNE	NAT, Y.
SIX PRELUDES AND FUGUES, OP. 35	MENDELSSOHN
SIX PRELUDES AND FUGUES, OP. 61	KABALEVSKY
SIX PRELUDES AND FUGUES, OP. 99--BK. 1	REGER
SIX PRELUDES AND FUGUES, OP. 99--BK. 2	REGER
SIX PRELUDES AND FUGUES	KLENAU, P. V.
SIX PRELUDES FOR PIANO	PUTSCHE, T.
SIX PRELUDES	BOWLES, P.
SIX PRELUDES	MIGNONE
SIX PRELUDES	MOMPOU, F.
SIX PRELUDES	NEUGEBOREN
SIX PRELUDES	ROGER-DUCASSE
SIX PRELUDES	USMANBAS, I.
SIX PRELUDES	VAUGHAN
SIX PRUSSIAN SONATAS, BK. 1	BACH, C.P.E.
SIX PRUSSIAN SONATAS, BK. 2	BACH, C.P.E.
SIX RECITAL PIECES FOR PIANO DUET, OP. 34-- VOL. 3 OF	ARENSKY, A.
SIX RECREATIONAL PIECES - 1. MARIONETTE INNAMORATE	MONTANARO
SIX RECREATIONAL PIECES - 2. CANZONE DELLA LAGUNA	MONTANARO
SIX RECREATIONAL PIECES - 3. AMABILITA	MONTANARO
SIX RECREATIONAL PIECES - 4. PICCOLA ARABA	MONTANARO
SIX RECREATIONAL PIECES - 5. TARANTELLA	MONTANARO
SIX RECREATIONAL PIECES - 6. FIORE ANDALUSO	MONTANARO
SIX RECREATIONS	NOEL, P. *
SIX ROMANTIC PIECES, OP. 19	SCALERO, R.
SIX SELECTED SONATAS	SCARLATTI, D.
SIX SHORT DANCE IMPRESSIONS, OP. 41	ROWLEY
SIX SHORT DANCE VARIATIONS	OMALLEY
SIX SHORT PIECES FOR PIANO	RIETI
SIX SHORT PIECES FOR PIANO	RIETI
SIX SHORT PIECES	HERMANN, R.
SIX SHORT PIECES	RIETI
SIX SHORT PRELUDES ON A TONE ROW	ROGERS, W. K.
SIX SKETCHES	KIRBY-MASON, B.
SIX SONATAS--A, B FLAT, F, A MINOR, D, G MINOR--	BACH, C.P.E.
SIX SONATAS--F MINOR, A MINOR, A, G, D MINOR, A FLAT--	BACH, C.P.E.
SIX SONATAS, OP. 3	RUTINI
SIX SONATAS, OP. 5	RUTINI
SIX SONATAS, OP. 6	RUTINI
SIX SONATAS FOR HARPSICHORD	DURANTE
SIX SONATAS FOR HARPSICHORD	GALUPPI
SIX SONATAS FOR PIANOFORTE, BK. 1-- NOS. 1, 2 AND 3	SOLER, A.
SIX SONATAS FOR PIANOFORTE, BK. 2 -- NOS. 4, 5 AND 6	SOLER, A.
SIX SONATAS FOR PIANO	FROST
SIX SONATAS	BACH, C.P.E.
SIX SONATAS	BACH, C.P.E.
SIX SONATAS	BACH, C.P.E.
SIX SONATAS	BLASCO DE NEBRA
SIX SONATAS	CLEMENTI
SIX SONATAS	FROST
SIX SONATAS	MARTINI, G.
SIX SONATAS	MARTINI, G.
SIX SONATAS	PAISIELLO, G.
SIX SONATINAS, BK. 1, NOS. 1-3	PERSICHETTI
SIX SONATINAS, BK. 2, NOS. 4-6	PERSICHETTI
SIX SONATINAS, OP. 163	DIABELLI
SIX SONATINAS, OP. 20	DUSSEK, J.
SIX SONATINAS, OP. 20	DUSSEK
SIX SONATINAS, OP. 30	SAEVERUD
SIX SONATINAS, OP. 36	CLEMENTI
SIX SONATINAS, OP. 36	CLEMENTI
SIX SONATINAS, OP. 36	CLEMENTI
SIX SONATINAS, OP. 36	CLEMENTI
SIX SONATINAS, OP. 36	WILLIS *
SIX SONATINAS, OP. 49	STEIBELT
SIX SONATINAS, OP. 54	GURLITT
SIX SONATINAS FOR PIANO	GEST, E.
SIX SONATINAS	BEETHOVEN
SIX SONATINAS	CLEMENTI
SIX SONATINAS	FRANCESCHI
SIX SONATINAS	GURLITT
SIX SONATINAS	HAYDN
SIX SONATINAS	HAYDN
SIX SONATINAS	NIELAND, J.
SIX SONATINAS	SORESINA
SIX SONGS--COMPLETE	COWELL
SIX SONGS WITHOUT WORDS, NOS. 3, 6, 12, 29, 30, 34	MENDELSSOHN
SIX SPANISH DANCES	ALBENIZ, I.
SIX SPANISH DANCES	ALBENIZ, I.
SIX SPANISH DANCES	PORRAS MOYA, V.
SIX STUDIES, OP. 23	RUBINSTEIN
SIX STUDIES IN SIXTHS, OP. 42	LONGO, A.
SIX STUDIES	LUPI
SIX SUITES FOR HARPSICHORD	PURCELL, H.
SIX SUITES	BACH, J.S.
SIX SURREALIST AFTERLUDES	TRIGGS
SIX SWINGY SOLOS	ZEPP
SIX SYMPHONIES	MOZART, W. A.
SIX TINY SONATAS	RAPHLING
SIX TINY SONATAS	RAPHLING
SIX TRADITIONAL MELODIES	SHAW, G.
SIX TWO-PART INVENTIONS	BARTH, H.
SIX VARIATIONS IN F, K054	MOZART, W. A.
SIX VARIATIONS ON 'NEL COR PIU NON MI SENTO'	BEETHOVEN
SIX VARIATIONS ON 'NEL COR PIU NON MI SENTO'	BEETHOVEN
SIX VARIATIONS ON AN ORIGINAL THEME	BEETHOVEN
SIX VARIATIONS ON A SWISS SONG	BEETHOVEN
SIX VARIATIONS ON B-A-C-H, OP. 10	RIMSKY-KORSAKOFF
SIX VARIATIONS ON NEL COR PIU NON MI SENTO	BEETHOVEN
SIX VARIATIONS ON THE DUET ''NEL COR PIU NON MI	BEETHOVEN
SIX VARIATIONS	SCHUBERT
SIX VERY EASY PIECES	FUGAZZA
SIX VIENNESE DANCES	FRIEDMAN
SIX VIENNESE SONATINAS	MOZART, W. A.
SIX VIENNESE SONATINAS	MOZART, W. A.
SIX VIENNESE SONATINAS	MOZART, W. A.
SIX VIENNESE SONATINAS	MOZART, W. A.
SIX VIENNESE SONATINAS	MOZART, W. A.
SIX VIENNESE SONATINAS	MOZART, W. A.
SIX VIENNESE SONATINAS	MOZART, W. A.
SIX WALTZES, OP. 22	REGER
SIX WALTZES -- LIEBESLIEDER, SET 1	BRAHMS
SIX WALTZES	BEETHOVEN
SIX WEDDING MARCHES	THOMPSON, J.--ED
SIX WHEEL CHASER	LEWIS
SIX WURTTEMBERG SONATAS, BK. 1	BACH, C.P.E.
SIX WURTTEMBERG SONATAS, BK. 2	BACH, C.P.E.
SIX WURTTEMBERG SONATAS, VOL. 1	BACH, C.P.E.
SIX WURTTEMBERG SONATAS, VOL. 2	BACH, C.P.E.
SIZILIETTA SERENADE	VONBLON, F.
SI J'ETAIS ROI - BAGATELLE	ADAM, A.
SI J'ETAIS ROI - FANTAISIE	ADAM, A.
SI J'ETAIS ROI - FANTAISIE	ADAM, A.
SI J'ETAIS ROI - OUVERTURE	ADAM, A.
SI J'ETAIS ROI - OVERTURE	ADAM, A.
SI J'ETAIS ROI - J'IGNORE SON NOM	ADAM, A.
SI MES VERS AVAIENT DES AILES	HAHN, R.
SI OISEAU J'ETAIS, OP. 2 NO. 6	HENSELT, A.
SI VERSAILLES M'ETAIT CONTE	FRANCAIX, J.
SI VOUS L'AVIEZ COMPRIS	DENZA
SKATER'S WALTZ, THE	WALDTEUFEL, E.
SKATER'S WALTZ	WALDTEUFEL, E.
SKATERS, THE	WALDTEUFEL, E.
SKATERS, THE	WALDTEUFEL, E.
SKATERS' WALTZ	WALDTEUFEL, E.
SKATERS' WALTZ	WALDTEUFEL, E.
SKATERS WALTZ	WALDTEUFEL, E.
SKATERS WALTZ	WALDTEUFEL, E.
SKATES, THE -- LES PATINEURS	LORAINE, P.
SKATING CARNIVAL, THE	MARSDEN, E.
SKATING LADY	FROST
SKATING WALTZ	CROSBY, M.
SKETCHES, OP. 9	BARTOK
SKETCHES AT THE BALLET	RUGER, J.
SKETCHES FOR PIANO, BK. 1	LANG, C. S.
SKETCHES FOR PIANO, BK. 2	LANG, C. S.
SKETCHES FOR PIANO, BK. 3	LANG, C. S.
SKETCHES FOR PIANO	FINLAYSON, W.
SKETCHES FROM HANS ANDERSEN	ADAIR, Y.
SKETCHES IN A MINOR	DRYE, S. L.
SKETCHES IN COLOUR-SET 1	STARER
SKETCHES IN COLOUR-SET 2	STARER
SKETCHES	ROWLEY
SKETCHES	VOVK
SKETCH --2 PIANOS, 8 HANDS--	SCHUMANN, R.
SKETCH	GIARD, C.
SKI-HIGH --FROM THE ST. MORITZ SUITE	YVOIRE
SKIDMORE MODERN KEYBOARD SERIES --ADVANCED --BLUE	MATTOS, E.
SKIDMORE MODERN KEYBOARD SERIES --INTERMEDIATE --GREEN	MASON, I.
SKIDMORE MODERN KEYBOARD SERIES --INTERMEDIATE --GREEN	RUMSHINSKY
SKIDMORE MODERN KEYBOARD SERIES --INTERMEDIATE --GREEN	MASON, I.
SKIDMORE MODERN KEYBOARD SERIES --SECONDARY --CAMEO	MASON, I.
SKIDMORE MODERN KEYBOARD SERIES --SECONDARY	MATTOS, E.
SKIDMORE MODERN KEYBOARD SERIES --SECONDARY --HAUNTED	AGAY, D.
SKIDMORE MODERN KEYBOARD SERIES --SECONDARY	AGAY, D.
SKIDMORE MODERN KEYBOARD SERIES --SECONDARY --STREET	AGAY, D.
SKIDMORE MODERN KEYBOARD SERIES --MALEKULA MOON DANCE	MASON, I.
SKIDMORE MODERN KEYBOARD SERIES - ENCHANTED ISLE	MASON, I.
SKIDMORE MODERN KEYBOARD SERIES - PASTELS	MASON, I.
SKIING	ROESSING, H.
SKILLS AND DRILLS, BK. 1	PACE, R.
SKILLS AND DRILLS, BK. 2	PACE, R.
SKILLS AND DRILLS, BK. 3	PACE, R.
SKILLS AND DRILLS, BK. 4	PACE, R.
SKILLS AND DRILLS, BK. 5	PACE, R.
SKILLS IN PIANO TECHNIC, BK. 1	STEINER
SKILLS IN PIANO TECHNIC, BK. 2	STEINER
SKILLS IN SCALES, BK. 1	STEINER
SKILLS IN SCALES, BK. 2	STEINER
SKIMORE MODERN KEYBOARD SERIES --ADVANCED --BLUE	MASON, I.
SKIPPING ALONG	HAYES
SKIPPING ROPE, DANCE	HOPKINS, H.
SKIPPING ROPE	BRANNAN
SKIPPING SONG	LIPSCOMB
SKIPPING TO SCHOOL	CROSBY, M.
SKIPPING	CANFIELD, J.
SKIPPY	THOMAS, C. J.
SKIPS	ANDERSON, M.
SKIP ALONG, BK. 2	FRISCH, F. T.
SKIP AND DANCE, WALTZ	HOPKINS, H.
SKIP AROUND AND SING	RAEZER, C.
SKIP TAG	GRAHAM
SKIP TO MY LOU	BECK
SKIP TO MY LOU	BERTRAND, C.
SKIP TO MY LOU	PRIGGE, O.
SKIP TO MY LOU	RIEGGER, W.--ED.
SKIP TO MY LOU	WEYBRIGHT--ED.
SKIZZEN, OP. 4 UND 5	SMETANA
SKIZZENBUCH	PALENICEK
SKIZZEN -- PIANO PIECES TO DAILY MORNING EXERCISES	DICHLER-SEDLACEK
SKIZZEN FUR KLAVIER UND KAMMERORCHESTER, OP. 19	WALDENMAIER
SKI PARTY	HIER, N.
SKI SLOPE	WARFEL, P.
SKOKIAAN	MSARURGWA *
SKOOTING ALONG	CRUICKSHANK
SKYSCRAPERS--BALLET	CARPENTER, J.
SKYSCRAPERS AND HARPS	ZEPP
SKY AND FOREST	RUNGEE
SKY BOATS	LINDFORS, E.
SKY FAIRIES	NICHOL *
SKY LINE	GROFE, F.
SKY LINE	KELLEY, S.
SLAP HAPPY	ZACHARIAS
SLAUGHTER ON TENTH AVENUE -- THEMES	RODGERS
SLAUGHTER ON TENTH AVENUE	RODGERS
SLAUGHTER ON TENTH AVENUE	RODGERS
SLAVA, OP. 11 NO. 6	RACHMANINOFF, S.
SLAVIC DANCES, OP. 46 -- BK. 1, NOS. 1-8	DVORAK
SLAVIC DANCES, OP. 72 -- BK. 2, NOS. 9-16	DVORAK
SLAVIC DANCE IN E MINOR, OP. 72	DVORAK
SLAVIC PIANO MUSIC, VOL. 1	
SLAVIC PIANO MUSIC, VOL. 2	

SLAVISCHE TANZWEISEN MIT VARIATIONEN   WEBER, E.
SLAVONIC DANCES, OP. 46 -- BK. 1   DVORAK
SLAVONIC DANCES, OP. 46 -- BK. 1   DVORAK
SLAVONIC DANCES, OP. 46   DVORAK
SLAVONIC DANCES, OP. 46   DVORAK
SLAVONIC DANCES, OP. 72 -- BK. 1   DVORAK
SLAVONIC DANCES, OP. 72 -- BK. 1   DVORAK
SLAVONIC DANCES, OP. 72   DVORAK
SLAVONIC DANCES, OP. 72   DVORAK
SLAVONIC DANCE IN E MINOR   DVORAK
SLAVONIC DANCE NO. 2   DVORAK
SLAVONIC DANCE NO. 6, EASY   DVORAK
SLAVONIC DANCE NO. 9   DVORAK
SLAVONIC DANCE   SCHER, W.
SLAVONIC RHAPSODIE   VOLZ, H.
SLAWISCHE TANZE, OP. 46   DVORAK
SLAWISCHE TANZE, OP. 46   DVORAK
SLAWISCHE TANZE, OP. 72   DVORAK
SLAWISCHE TANZE AUS OP. 46 UND 72   DVORAK
SLAWISCHE TANZE OP. 46 -- BK. 2   DVORAK
SLAWISCHE TANZE OP. 72 -- BK. 1   DVORAK
SLAWISCHE TANZE OP. 72 -- BK. 2   DVORAK
SLEEP-A-LOT LAND   RICHTER, A.
SLEEP, PRETTY SUSAN   KARST
SLEEPERS, AWAKE   BACH, J.S.
SLEEPERS, WAKE   BACH, J.S.
SLEEPERS, WAKE   BACH, J.S.
SLEEPERS, WAKE   BACH, J.S.
SLEEPING BEAUTY--WALTZ   TSCHAIKOWSKY
SLEEPING BEAUTY, VALSE LENTE   TSCHAIKOWSKY
SLEEPING BEAUTY --EXCERPTS--   TSCHAIKOWSKY
SLEEPING BEAUTY -- BALLET TOLD IN WORDS AND MUSIC   TSCHAIKOWSKY
SLEEPING BEAUTY -- PRINCESS, EXCERPTS   TSCHAIKOWSKY
SLEEPING BEAUTY WALTZ, THE   TSCHAIKOWSKY
SLEEPING BEAUTY WALTZ, THE   TSCHAIKOWSKY
SLEEPING LEPRACHAUN   BOYDELL
SLEEPING TULIP   BILBRO, M.
SLEEPYHEAD   ELLSWORTH
SLEEPYTIME   TRAEGER
SLEEPY ALLIGATOR, THE   BASTIEN
SLEEPY BAYOU   WILSON
SLEEPY BIRDS   ERB
SLEEPY BIRD   THOMAS, J. J.
SLEEPY BUGLER, THE   TUTTLE, T. K.
SLEEPY CUCKOO   HELLER, E.
SLEEPY EYES   TRAVIS, B.
SLEEPY HEAD AND THE CLOCKS ON THE STAIRS   STEEL
SLEEPY HEAD   HAYES
SLEEPY LAGOON   COATES, E.
SLEEPY LAGOON
SLEEPY LAGOON
SLEEPY LAKE   ANDRE
SLEEPY TIME AND WATER WHEEL   IVEY
SLEEPY TOWN EXPRESS   LANE, J.--ED.
SLEEPY TOWN   MUNN, W.
SLEEPY TOWN   ROZIN
SLEEPY WIND   DITTENHAVER
SLEEP BABY SLEEP   VOLZ, H.
SLEIGH-BELL SERENADE, A   GIASSON, P.
SLEIGH, THE--A LA RUSSE   KOUNTZ, R.
SLEIGH, THE -- ARR. BY THE COMPOSER -- SET   KOUNTZ, R.
SLEIGHING   MIDDLEBROOK
SLEIGH BELLS IN THE SNOW   GILLOCK
SLEIGH BELLS IN THE SNOW   HOWELL, I.
SLEIGH BELLS   GLOVER, D.
SLEIGH BELL SERENADE   GIASSON, P.
SLEIGH RIDE -- CHILDREN'S EDITION   STEINER--ED.
SLEIGH RIDE -- SIMP.   CURRIER
SLEIGH RIDE -- SIMP.   KING, S.--ED.
SLEIGH RIDE   ANDERSON, L.
SLEIGH RIDE   ANDERSON, L.
SLEIGH RIDE   ANDERSON, L. *
SLEIGH RIDE   GILLOCK
SLEIGH RIDE   GRAHAM, R.
SLEIGH RIDE   HUNEKE
SLEIGH RIDE   TSCHAIKOWSKY
SLICK TRICKS   DAVIS, J.
SLIGHTLY SQUARE ROUND DANCE   DOLIN
SLOWAKISCHE SONATINE, OP. 75   SCHNEIDER-TRNAVS
SLOWAKISCHE SUITE, OP. 32   NOVAK
SLOWAKISCHE TANZE, BAND 01   FELBER, R.
SLOWAKISCHE TANZE   FELBER, R.--ED
SLOW DANCE   AVSHALOMOV, J.
SLOW MINUET   GOODMAN, J.
SLOW MOVEMENT, FROM 'MOONLIGHT SONATA OP. 27 NO. 2'   BEETHOVEN
SLUMBER-SONG, OP. 101 NO. 6   GURLITT
SLUMBER-SONG, OP. 124 NO. 16--ALBUM-LEAVES   SCHUMANN, R.
SLUMBER SERENADE   STRIMER, J.
SLUMBER SONG--BERCEUSE--   GRETCHANINOFF
SLUMBER SONG /SIRIS DANCE   HOVHANESS, A.
SLUMBER SONG   PALMGREN, S.
SLUMBER SONG   SCHUBERT
SLUMBER SONG   WRIGHT, L.
SLUMBER STORY   ANSON, G.
SLUMBER   GRAUPNER
SMALL CHAMBER MUSIC   SZONYI, E.
SMALL FRY   EZELL, H.
SMALL PIECES   CURCIO
SMALL WORLD   SINGER, L.--ED
SMILE - HAVE A HAPPY DAY   BRADLEY,
SMILING KEYBOARD, THE   AGAY, D.--ED
SMOKE GETS IN YOUR EYES -- SHOWCASE
SMOKE GETS IN YOUR EYES
SMOKE GETS IN YOUR EYES
SMOKE GETS IN YOUR EYES
SMOKE RINGS   GIFFORD
SMOKE RINGS
SMOOTH SAILING   BEAUMONT
SMUGGLER, THE   SCHUMANN, R. *
SMUGGLERS   TAYLOR
SMUGGLERS OF ROMNEY MARSH, THE   NEWTON, E.
SNAKE CHARMER, THE   MUNN, W.
SNAKE CHARMER, THE   THOMAS, C. J.
SNAKE CHARMER PASSES BY, A   ELAINE, M.
SNAKE CHARMER   ECKSTEIN
SNAKE CHARMER   KARP
SNAKE CHARMER   SCHER, W.
SNAPPY AND SMOOTH   SANDBOURNE
SNAPPY SAMBA   DECOLA, F.
SNAPSHOTS IN SOUND   MASSEY, G.
SNEAKY CREEPY THINGS   GLOVER, D.
SNIPS AND SNAILS - TWELVE PIANO SOLOS FOR BOYS AND   EZELL, H.
SNOOPY'S CHRISTMAS   BRADLEY,
SNOW-FLAKES   RAWICZ
SNOW-WHITE PONY   DITTENHAVER

SNOWBIRD   BRIMHALL,
SNOWFALL   SOUERS
SNOWFALL
SNOWFLAKE'S STORY, THE   RICHTER
SNOWFLAKES OF WINTER, THE   COMSTOCK
SNOWFLAKES   HAUBIEL, C.
SNOWFLAKES   JUNAYEVSKY *
SNOWFLAKE CHASE   LINDFORS
SNOWFLAKE WALTZ   GOLDFARB
SNOWFLOWER   VALSEN *
SNOWMEN ON PARADE   KOCH, E.
SNOWS OF FUJI-YAMA   COWELL
SNOW AT DUSK   GOODMAN, J.
SNOW BELLS   ADAMS, B.
SNOW BIRD   GEST, E.
SNOW BIRD   GEST, E.
SNOW COVERED TREES ON A MOUNTAIN WHITE   BURNAM
SNOW COVERED TREES ON A MOUNTAIN WHITE   BURNAM
SNOW DROPS -- EASY DANCE WITHIN THE COMPASS OF 5   BEHR, F.
SNOW FAIRY   CHRISTENSEN, A.
SNOW FLAKES   RAWICZ
SNOW FLURRIES   GREEN
SNOW IS DANCING, THE, FROM THE CHILDREN'S CORNER   DEBUSSY
SNOW IS FALLING   CHAGY
SNOW MOUNTAINS   BRODSKY, M.
SNOW ON THE EVERGREENS   EMERY
SNOW ON THE HILLSIDE   JOYNER, B.
SNOW PARTY, THE   MARTIN, H.
SNOW PLOW AND ROTARY   BURNAM
SNOW QUEEN   ROUSE, E.
SNOW SCRAMBLE   BERLA, F.
SNOW TIME   SCHER, W.
SNOW WHITE AND THE SEVEN DWARFS   RICHTER--ED
SNOW WHITE   FERNANDEZ, O.
SNOW   ALT, H.
SOARING, OP. 4 NO. 2   PROKOFIEFF
SOARING -- AUFSCHWUNG --   SCHUMANN, R.
SOARING DRAGONFLY   BITTNER, J.
SOARING GULLS   DUNGAN
SOARING HIGH   RAEZER, C.
SOARING IN THE SKY   FERRELL, B.
SOARING WITH SCHUMANN -- SIMP.   MOSSMAN, T.
SOARING   REISTRUP, J.
SOARING   ROLFE, W.
SOBRE LAS OLAS--WALTZ   ROSAS
SOBRE LAS OLAS, VALSE, EASY   ROSAS
SOBRE LAS OLAS, VALSE   ROSAS
SOCIABILITY SONGS   SCHAUM, J.
SOCO GAP SQUARE DANCE   DITTENHAVER
SOEUR MONIQUE--RONDO   COUPERIN, F.
SOFTLY SNOWING   BENTLEY
SOFT LITTLE BREEZE   EZELL, H.
SOFT MIST   DALAM, H.
SOFT RAIN   STEVENS, E.
SOFT SHADOWS   SOUERS
SOGNO, UN   LUZZI
SOGNO DI NICOLETTA   RECLI
SOIREES DE VIENNE--VALSES-CAPRICES AFTER SCHUBERT, BK.   LISZT
SOIREES DE VIENNE--VALSES-CAPRICES AFTER SCHUBERT, BK.   LISZT
SOIREES DE VIENNE, WIENER ABENDE NACH KOMP. VON F.   LISZT
SOIREES DE VIENNE NO. 6   LISZT
SOIREES DE VIENNE   LISZT
SOIREES DE VIENNE   LISZT
SOIREE DANS GRENADE   DEBUSSY
SOIREE DE VIENNE, OP. 56 -- CONCERT PARAPHRASE ON   GRUENFELD
SOIREE EN GRENADE, FROM ESTAMPES   DEBUSSY
SOIRS A JUAN-LES-PINS   DUPONT, J.
SOIRS   SCHMITT, F.
SOIR DE TOUSSAINT EN CAMBRESIS   FRANCAIX, J.
SOIXANTAINE, LA   WACHS, P.
SOLDADITOS DE CARTON-- SIX VERY EASY PIECES, PART 1   AGUILAR
SOLDADITOS DE CARTON -- SIX VERY EASY PIECES, PART 2   AGUILAR
SOLDADITOS DE PLOMO   PERCUOCO
SOLDAT DE PLOMB, LE   SEVERAC
SOLDIER, SOLDIER, SOLDIER -- A FRENCH FOLK SONG   WEYBRIGHT
SOLDIERS' CHORUS FROM 'FAUST'   GOUNOD, C.
SOLDIERS' MARCH, OP. 68 NO. 02--ALBUM FOR THE YOUNG   SCHUMANN, R.
SOLDIERS' MARCH, OP. 68 NO. 2   SCHUMANN, R.
SOLDIERS' MARCH, OP. 68 NO. 2   SCHUMANN, R.
SOLDIERS' MARCH AND THE WILD RIDER   SCHUMANN, R.
SOLDIERS' MARCH   SCHUMANN, R.
SOLDIERS ALL, MARCH   ARMOUR
SOLDIERS AT PLAY   STAIRS, L.
SOLDIERS HOE DOWN   AGAY, D.
SOLDIERS MARCH, OP. 68 NO. 2 ALSO MELODY NO. 1   SCHUMANN, R.
SOLDIERS MARCH -- ONE PIANO, EIGHT HANDS --   WILSON, M.
SOLDIERS MARCH   MELLICHAMP, N.
SOLDIERS MARCH   SCHUMANN, R.
SOLDIERS ON PARADE--WITH WORDS   VANNORT, I.
SOLDIERS ON PARADE   ECKSTEIN
SOLDIERS ON PARADE   STEIN, G. M.
SOLDIERS PASS, THE   DRING
SOLDIERS PASS, THE   REBIKOV
SOLDIER IN THE RAIN
SOLEMN MELODY   WALFORD DAVIES,
SOLEMN SONG, BUTTINSKI MARCH   SKELLY
SOLFEGGIETTO   BACH, J.S.
SOLFEGGIETTO --FOR LEFT HAND--   BACH, C.P.E.
SOLFEGGIETTO IN C MINOR---INCLUDES ARR. FOR LEFT HAND   BACH, C.P.E.
SOLFEGGIETTO IN C MINOR   BACH, C.P.E.
SOLFEGGIETTO IN C MINOR   BACH, C.P.E.
SOLFEGGIETTO   BACH, C.P.E.
SOLFEGGIETTO   BACH, C.P.E.
SOLFEGGIETTO   BACH, C.P.E.
SOLFEGGIETTO   BACH, C.P.E.
SOLFEGGIETTO   BACH, C.P.E.
SOLFEGGIETTO   BACH, C.P.E.
SOLFEGGIETTO   BACH, C.P.E.
SOLFEGGIO   BACH, J.S.
SOLFEGGIO   BACH, C.P.E.
                                                         LANE, J.--ED.
SOLFEGIETTO IN C MINOR   BACH, J.S.
SOLFEGIETTO   BACH, C.P.E.
SOLIELS NOIRS   TISNE, A.
SOLILOQUY AT MIDNIGHT
SOLILOQUY   BLOOM
SOLILOQUY   BLOOM
SOLILOQUY   BOYKIN, H.
SOLILOQUY   WHITFORD
SOLITARY WANDERER, OP. 43 NO. 2   GRIEG
SOLITUDE -- SIMP.   MOSSMAN, T.
SOLITUDE FOR PIANO SOLO   RAYMOND, J.
SOLITUDE   BLOWER, M. *
SOLITUDE   ELLINGTON
SOLITUDE   FANO, G. A.
SOLITUDE   MERKUR--ED

SOLI AUS "ESSERCIZII MUSICI"	TELEMANN, G.P.
SOLO AND DUET ALBUM	STEINER
SOLO BOOK--1ST--GERMAN EDITION	DILLER, A. *
SOLO BOOK--1ST	DILLER, A. *
SOLO BOOK--2ND	DILLER, A. *
SOLO BOOK--3RD	DILLER, A. *
SOLO BOOK--4TH	DILLER, A. *
SOLO BOOK 1	GOLDBERGER,
SOLO BOOK 2	GOLDBERGER,
SOLO BOOK 3	GOLDBERGER,
SOLO GALLERY	NEVIN
SOLO JAMBOREE	SCHAUM, J.
SOLO JAMBOREE	SCHAUM, J.
SOLO PIECES OF TODAY, BK. 1	AGAY, D.--ED
SOLO PIECES OF TODAY, BK. 2	AGAY, D.--ED
SOLO PIECES OF TODAY, BK. 3	AGAY, D.--ED
SOLO REPERTOIRE FOR THE YOUNG PIANIST, BK. 1 --	GILLOCK
SOLO REPERTOIRE FOR THE YOUNG PIANIST, BK. 1	GILLOCK--ED
SOLO REPERTOIRE FOR THE YOUNG PIANIST, BK. 2 --	GILLOCK
SOLO REPERTOIRE FOR THE YOUNG PIANIST, BK. 2	GILLOCK--ED
SOLO REPERTOIRE FOR THE YOUNG PIANIST, BK. 2	GILLOCK--ED
SOLO REPERTOIRE FOR THE YOUNG PIANIST, BK. 3 -- EARLY	GILLOCK
SOLO REPERTOIRE FOR THE YOUNG PIANIST, BK. 4 -- EARLY	GILLOCK
SOLO SNACKS FOR THE PIANIST	MERKUR
SOLO TECHNIC BOOK	FROST
SOLO TIME U. S. A. --100--	
SOLVEJG'S SONG, OP. 52 NO. 4	GRIEG
SOLVEJG'S SONG, OP. 52 NO. 4	GRIEG
SOLVEJG'S SONG AND CRADLE SONG	GRIEG
SOMBRERO DANCE	ROZIN
SOMBRERO	COOK
SOMBRERO	ECKSTEIN
SOMEBODY'S KNOCKIN' AT YOUR DOOR	
SOMEBODY'S KNOCKING AT YOUR DOOR	STEINER--ED.
SOMEDAY NEVER COMES	BRIMHALL,
SOMEONE TO WATCH OVER ME	GERSHWIN
SOMEONE TO WATCH OVER ME	GERSHWIN
SOMEONE TO WATCH OVER ME	GERSHWIN
SOMETHING IN YOUR SMILE	LANE, J.--ED.
SOMETHING SEEMS TINGLE-INGLE-ING--"HIGH JINKS"	FRIML, R.
SOMETHING STUPID	BRIMHALL,
SOMETHING	BRIMHALL,
SOMETIMES I FEEL LIKE A MOTHERLESS CHILD	
SOMEWHERE, MY LOVE	LANE, J.--ED.
SOME DAY	SCARMOLIN
SOME ENCHANTED EVENING	HAMMERSTEIN *
SOME ENCHANTED EVENING	HAMMERSTEIN *
SOME KIND OF WONDERFUL	BRADLEY,
SOME SOUTHPAW PITCHING	IVES, C.
SOMMEREINDRUCKE, OP. 22B	SUK
SONADA DE ADIOS	RODRIGO, J.
SONATA--1927	POOT, M.
SONATA--1948	ROZSA, M.
SONATA--1961	SHERIFF, N.
SONATA--1962	SKORZENY, F.
SONATA--1968	ROSENFELD, G.
SONATA--1968	SCHWARZ-SCHILLIN
SONATA-CONTE, OP. 25 NO. 1	MEDTNER, N.
SONATA-FANTASY NO. 2, OP. 19	SCRIABINE, A.
SONATA, DAVID AND GOLIATH	KUHNAU, J.
SONATA, OP. POST. 120, D. 664, A MAJOR	SCHUBERT
SONATA, OP. 1	BERG, A.
SONATA, OP. 1	EISLER
SONATA, OP. 10	HARRIS, R.
SONATA, OP. 10	DU PLESIS, H.
SONATA, OP. 10	GOLDSCHMIDT
SONATA, OP. 11	HUSA, K.
SONATA, OP. 11	VRANA
SONATA, OP. 118 NO. 1, ALLEGRO	SCHUMANN, R.
SONATA, OP. 118 NO. 1, ALLEGRO	SCHUMANN, R.
SONATA, OP. 12	SHOSTAKOVITCH
SONATA, OP. 120, ANDANTE	SCHUBERT
SONATA, OP. 14 NO. 3	CLEMENTI
SONATA, OP. 14	SCHUMANN, R.
SONATA, OP. 145	HOVHANESS, A.
SONATA, OP. 16	HALFFTER, R.
SONATA, OP. 17	POSER
SONATA, OP. 2	GOEHR, A.
SONATA, OP. 20	VORISEK
SONATA, OP. 21	STEFFEN, W.
SONATA, OP. 26 NO. 2	CLEMENTI
SONATA, OP. 26	BARBER, S.
SONATA, OP. 28	THARICHEN, W.
SONATA, OP. 3--1936	SCHISKE, K.
SONATA, OP. 3 -- 1951	ERBSE
SONATA, OP. 3	PABLO, L. DE
SONATA, OP. 3	SPINNER
SONATA, OP. 34 BIS --F MINOR--. AFTER THE PIANO	BRAHMS
SONATA, OP. 37 NO. 2	BACEVICIUS
SONATA, OP. 39--1953-4--	SCHAEUBLE, H.
SONATA, OP. 39	BLACHER
SONATA, OP. 42, D. 845, A MINOR	SCHUBERT
SONATA, OP. 47	SAS, A.
SONATA, OP. 47	TOCH, E.
SONATA, OP. 5 NO. 5	RUTINI
SONATA, OP. 5	MEDTNER, N.
SONATA, OP. 52 NO. 3	BACEVICIUS
SONATA, OP. 58 NO. 01	HOLLER, K.
SONATA, OP. 58 NO. 02	HOLLER, K.
SONATA, OP. 6 -- 1953 --	ERBSE
SONATA, OP. 6	BRAUTIGAM
SONATA, OP. 6	KABALEVSKY
SONATA, OP. 60	ORREGO SALAS, J.
SONATA, OP. 64	SHOSTAKOVITCH
SONATA, OP. 66	BURKHARD, W.
SONATA, OP. 7 NO. 3	CLEMENTI
SONATA, OP. 7	VOMACKA
SONATA, OP. 70	ZANELLA
SONATA, OP. 84	MIASKOVSKY
SONATA, OP. 85	KILPINEN, Y.
SONATA, OP. 87	TOCH, E.
SONATA, OP. 9	CRESTON
SONATA, 1938	HINDEMITH
SONATA, 1942	HINDEMITH
SONATA, 1944	PETYREK, R.
SONATA, 1948	KIRCHNER, L.
SONATA, 1950	MOEVS, R.
SONATA, 1953 -- SET	POULENC, F.
SONATA, 1958	MARTINU, B.
SONATAS, BK. 1--"URTEXT" EDITION	BEETHOVEN
SONATAS, BK. 1, 1-11	HAYDN
SONATAS, BK. 1 -- OP. 42, 53, 120, 122, 143, 147 --	SCHUBERT
SONATAS, BK. 1	BEETHOVEN
SONATAS, BK. 1	BEETHOVEN
SONATAS, BK. 1	SCHUBERT
SONATAS, BK. 1	SCHUBERT

SONATAS, BK. 1	SOLER, A.
SONATAS, BK. 2--"URTEXT" EDITION	BEETHOVEN
SONATAS, BK. 2, 12-23	HAYDN
SONATAS, BK. 2 -- OP. 164, OP. POSTH. IN C MINOR, A,	SCHUBERT
SONATAS, BK. 2	BEETHOVEN
SONATAS, BK. 2	BEETHOVEN
SONATAS, BK. 2	SCHUBERT
SONATAS, BK. 2	SCHUBERT
SONATAS, BK. 2	SOLER, A.
SONATAS, BK. 3, 24-33	HAYDN
SONATAS, BK. 3	BEETHOVEN
SONATAS, BK. 3	SCHUBERT
SONATAS, BK. 3	SOLER, A.
SONATAS, BK. 4, 34-43	HAYDN
SONATAS, BK. 4	SOLER, A.
SONATAS, BK. 5	SOLER, A.
SONATAS, BK. 6	SOLER, A.
SONATAS, BKS. 1 AND 2	MOZART, W. A.
SONATAS, COMPLETE IN 2 VOLS. CLOTH-BOUND	BEETHOVEN
SONATAS, COMPLETE IN 2 VOLS. CLOTH-BOUND	SCHUBERT
SONATAS, FANTASIES, AND RONDOS, BK. 1	BACH, C.P.E.
SONATAS, FANTASIES, AND RONDOS, BK. 2	BACH, C.P.E.
SONATAS, IN 2 VOLS. CLOTH-BOUND	MOZART, W. A.
SONATAS, OP. 1, 2, 5	BRAHMS
SONATAS, OP. 14, NO. 1, E MAJOR AND NO. 2, G MAJOR	BEETHOVEN
SONATAS, OP. 24, 39, 49, 70	WEBER, VON
SONATAS, OP. 32, 33, 37	DIABELLI
SONATAS, OP. 38, 73	DIABELLI
SONATAS, SCHERZO AND BALLADES --CLOTH--	BRAHMS
SONATAS, SCHERZO AND BALLADES	BRAHMS
SONATAS, VOL. 1--CLOTH--	BEETHOVEN
SONATAS, VOL. 1--PAPER--	BEETHOVEN
SONATAS, VOL. 1 -- CLOTH	BEETHOVEN
SONATAS, VOL. 1 -- CLOTH	SCHUBERT
SONATAS, VOL. 1 -- 1-12 --	BEETHOVEN
SONATAS, VOL. 1	BACH, J.
SONATAS, VOL. 1	BACH, W.F.
SONATAS, VOL. 1	BACH, W.F.
SONATAS, VOL. 1	BEETHOVEN
SONATAS, VOL. 1	BEETHOVEN
SONATAS, VOL. 1	BEETHOVEN
SONATAS, VOL. 1	HAYDN
SONATAS, VOL. 1	MOZART, W. A.
SONATAS, VOL. 1	MOZART, W. A.
SONATAS, VOL. 1	MOZART, W. A.
SONATAS, VOL. 1	SCHUBERT
SONATAS, VOL. 1	SCHUBERT
SONATAS, VOL. 2--CLOTH--	BEETHOVEN
SONATAS, VOL. 2--PAPER--	BEETHOVEN
SONATAS, VOL. 2 -- CLOTH	BEETHOVEN
SONATAS, VOL. 2 -- CLOTH	SCHUBERT
SONATAS, VOL. 2 -- 13-23 --	BEETHOVEN
SONATAS, VOL. 2	BACH, J.
SONATAS, VOL. 2	BACH, W.F.
SONATAS, VOL. 2	BACH, W.F.
SONATAS, VOL. 2	BEETHOVEN
SONATAS, VOL. 2	BEETHOVEN
SONATAS, VOL. 2	BEETHOVEN
SONATAS, VOL. 2	HAYDN
SONATAS, VOL. 2	MOZART, W. A.
SONATAS, VOL. 2	MOZART, W. A.
SONATAS, VOL. 2	SCHUBERT
SONATAS, VOL. 2	SCHUBERT
SONATAS, VOL. 3 -- 24-32 --	BEETHOVEN
SONATAS, VOL. 3	BACH, W.F.
SONATAS, VOL. 3	BACH, W.F.
SONATAS, VOLS. 1 AND 2 IN ONE VOLUME--CLOTH	HAYDN
SONATAS, VOLS. 5 AND 6 IN PREPARATION	SOLER, A.
SONATAS, VOLUMES 1-4	SOLER, A.
SONATAS, VOL 2	MOZART, W. A.
SONATAS --URTEXT--, COMPLETE IN 1 VOL. CLOTH-BOUND	MOZART, W. A.
SONATAS --URTEXT--, COMPLETE IN 2 VOLS. CLOTH-BOUND	BEETHOVEN
SONATAS -- A MINOR, C, D MINOR--	BACH, J.S.
SONATAS --150-- IN 3 VOLS. VOL. 1	SCARLATTI, D.
SONATAS --150-- IN 3 VOLS. VOL. 2	SCARLATTI, D.
SONATAS --150-- IN 3 VOLS. VOL. 3	SCARLATTI, D.
SONATAS --4--	CLEMENTI
SONATAS --49--, VOL.1* NOS. 1-11	HAYDN
SONATAS --49--, VOL.2* NOS. 12-23	HAYDN
SONATAS --49--, VOL.3* NOS. 24-33	HAYDN
SONATAS --49--, VOL.4* NOS. 34-43	HAYDN
SONATAS --49--, VOL.5* SONATINAS --DIVERTIMENTI-- 6	HAYDN
SONATAS AND FANTASIAS -- ENG.-FR.-IT. -- BK. 1	MOZART, W. A.
SONATAS AND FANTASIAS -- ENG.-FR.-IT. -- BK. 2	MOZART, W. A.
SONATAS AND FANTASIES, BK. 1	MOZART, W. A.
SONATAS AND FANTASIES, BK. 2	MOZART, W. A.
SONATAS AND FANTASIES, BK. 3	MOZART, W. A.
SONATAS AND FANTASIES, BK. 4	MOZART, W. A.
SONATAS AND INTERLUDES --PREPARED PIANO--	CAGE
SONATAS AND PIECES, URTEXT--4 SONATAS, 12 VARIATIONS	BACH, C.P.E.
SONATAS AND SONATA MOVEMENTS --URTEXT--	BACH, J.S.
SONATAS AND SUITES - NO. 3 FIRST SONATA IN G	PERGOLESI
SONATAS AND SUITES	PERGOLESI
SONATAS COMPLETE IN ONE VOLUME -- CLOTH	MOZART, W. A.
SONATAS DE CASTILLA CON TOCCATA A MODO DE PREGON	RODRIGO, J.
SONATAS FOR PIANO, BK. 1 NOS. 1-5	HAYDN
SONATAS FOR PIANO, BK. 1	SOLER, A.
SONATAS FOR PIANO, BK. 2 NO. 6-10	HAYDN
SONATAS FOR PIANO, BK. 3	SOLER, A.
SONATAS FOR PIANO, VOL. 1	MOZART, W. A.
SONATAS FOR PIANO, VOL. 2	MOZART, W. A.
SONATAS FOR THE ELECTOR, WO O 47	BEETHOVEN
SONATAS FOR 1 PIANO 4 HANDS	DUSSEK, J.
SONATAS OP. 38 AND 73	DIABELLI
SONATAS URTEXT, BK. 1A --1-10--	MOZART, W. A.
SONATAS URTEXT, BK. 1B --11-20--	MOZART, W. A.
SONATAS URTEXT COMPLETE, BK. 1A, 1-7	BEETHOVEN
SONATAS URTEXT COMPLETE, BK. 1B, 8-15	BEETHOVEN
SONATAS URTEXT COMPLETE, BK. 1	BEETHOVEN
SONATAS URTEXT COMPLETE, BK. 2	BEETHOVEN
SONATAS URTEXT COMPLETE	MOZART, W. A.
SONATAS	CHOPIN
SONATAS	CHOPIN
SONATAS	CHOPIN
SONATAS	CHOPIN
SONATAS	CLEMENTI
SONATA --IN PREP--	MICHALSKY
SONATA -- SET	BOWLES, P.
SONATA -- 1. 10. 1905	JANACEK
SONATA -- 1933 --	FREED, I.
SONATA -- 1946	HEIDEN
SONATA -- 1955 --	BLANCAFORT
SONATA -- 1957 --	FUGA
SONATA --1958--	HENKEMANS
SONATA - SOUVENIR DE VENISE	DUKE, V.
SONATA ALBUM--26 SONATAS BY HAYDN, MOZART, AND	BEETHOVEN *
SONATA ALBUM--26 SONATAS BY HAYDN, MOZART, AND	BEETHOVEN *

SONATA ALBUM, BK. 1	SMETANA
SONATA ALBUM, BK. 2	SMETANA
SONATA ALBUM, VOL. 1	BEETHOVEN *
SONATA ALBUM, VOL. 2	BEETHOVEN *
SONATA ALBUM --2 VOLS. BOUND TOGETHER--. CLOTH-BOUND	
SONATA ALBUM	
SONATA ALL' ANTICA	RIETI
SONATA ALLEGRO IN G MINOR	SCARLATTI, D.
SONATA AND FUGUE, K448 AND K426	MOZART, W. A.
SONATA AND FUGUE --K448, 426--, WITH ADAGIO --K546--	MOZART, W. A.
SONATA A DUE CEMBALI IN G MINOR	MATTHESON, J.
SONATA BALLATA, OP. 21	GOERNER
SONATA BAROCCA--JULY, 1949	ZEISL, E.
SONATA BREVE NO. 1 IN D	URAY, E. L.
SONATA BREVE NO. 2 IN E MINOR	URAY, E. L.
SONATA BREVE	ADLER, S.
SONATA BREVE	CHAILLEY
SONATA BREVE	CORDERO, R.
SONATA BREVE	FERNANDEZ, O.
SONATA BREVE	LEES, B.
SONATA BREVE	NIN-CULMELL, J.
SONATA BREVIS -- FORMERLY ENTITLED 'SONATINA FOR PIANO	GREEN, R.
SONATA BREVIS NO. 2	WERLE, F.
SONATA BREVIS	LYBBERT
SONATA DA BALLO	ARMA, P.
SONATA DA CEMBALO IN G MINOR	MARCELLO
SONATA DA CHIESA FOR PIANO	READ, G.
SONATA DA CHIESA FOR TWO PIANOS	READ, G.
SONATA DE PRIMAVERA	CASTRO, J. M.
SONATA EN COLORES	BOSMANS, A.
SONATA EROICA, OP. 24	NOVAK
SONATA EROICA, OP. 50	MACDOWELL
SONATA EROICA IN G MINOR, OP. 50	MACDOWELL
SONATA EROICA NO. 02 IN G MINOR, OP. 50	MACDOWELL
SONATA ESPANOLA, OP. 53 -- 1949 --	ESPLA
SONATA FACILE K545 IN C	MOZART, W. A.
SONATA FANTASIA, OP. 59	TURINA, J.
SONATA FANTASIA	GUARINO, C.
SONATA FANTASIA	ROCHBERG, G.
SONATA FOR A CARILLON OF FOUR OCTAVES	BADINGS
SONATA FOR HARPSICHORD	PERSICHETTI
SONATA FOR LEFT HAND ALONE, OP. 179	REINECKE
SONATA FOR LEFT HAND OP. 40	KALKBRENNER
SONATA FOR ONE PIANO FOUR HANDS, OP. 25	LAMONTAINE
SONATA FOR PIANO, OP. 20	ORLAND, H.
SONATA FOR PIANO, OP. 5	WEINER
SONATA FOR PIANO, OP. 5	WEINER
SONATA FOR PIANOFORTE	GIANNINI
SONATA FOR PIANO NO. 01	HENSEL, R.
SONATA FOR PIANO	JOLIVET, A.
SONATA FOR PIANO	JOSTEN, W.
SONATA FOR PIANO	LLOYD, N.
SONATA FOR PIANO	PALMER
SONATA FOR PIANO	SHCHDRIN
SONATA FOR PIANO	TAL, J.
SONATA FOR PIANO	WESTIN, P.
SONATA FOR PIANO 4 HANDS	WOOLEN, R.
SONATA FOR TWO PIANOS AND PERCUSSION --COMPLETE--	BARTOK
SONATA FOR TWO PIANOS AND PERCUSSION --PERCUSSION	BARTOK
SONATA FOR TWO PIANOS AND PERCUSSION --PIANO PART--	BARTOK
SONATA FOR TWO PIANOS	KADOSA
SONATA FOR TWO PIANOS	WALKER, G.
SONATA FOR 2 PIANOS	PALMER
SONATA FOR 2 PIANOS	WILLIAMSON, E.
SONATA FUR KLAVIER, 5 BLASER, PAUKEN UND STREICHER	DOBIAS
SONATA FUR KLAVIER	EGK, W.
SONATA FUR ZWEI KLAVIER	GENZMER
SONATA GIOCOSA, OP. 96	NIEMANN
SONATA II	BADINGS
SONATA IN A, LONGO 345	SCARLATTI, D.
SONATA IN A, OP. 120	SCHUBERT
SONATA IN A, OP. 18 NO. 5	BACH, J.
SONATA IN A, OP. 18 NO. 5	BACH, J.
SONATA IN A -- SET	SCARLATTI, D.
SONATA IN A -- 1805 --	HOFFMANN, E. T.
SONATA IN A FLAT, SHO 0502 1/2, H 46	HAYDN
SONATA IN A FLAT	RIETI
SONATA IN A FLAT	RIETI
SONATA IN A FLAT	RIETI
SONATA IN A MAJOR, NO. 345	SCARLATTI, D.
SONATA IN A MAJOR, NO. 494	SCARLATTI, D.
SONATA IN A MINOR, OP. 42	SCHUBERT
SONATA IN A MINOR, OP. 87	WEISMANN, J.
SONATA IN A MINOR	SCHROEDER, H.
SONATA IN A	BACH, J.
SONATA IN A	BACH, J.
SONATA IN A	HALFFTER, C.
SONATA IN A	HARTLEY, W.
SONATA IN A	HOFFMANN, E. T.
SONATA IN B FLAT--SCH NO. 18	HAYDN
SONATA IN B FLAT, OP. 127	WEISMANN, J.
SONATA IN B FLAT --1831	WAGNER
SONATA IN B FLAT MINOR, OP. 35	CHOPIN
SONATA IN B FLAT MINOR	BALAKIREV
SONATA IN B FLAT	DUSCHEK
SONATA IN B FLAT	MARCELLO
SONATA IN B FLAT, OP. 5	STRAUSS, R.
SONATA IN B MINOR, OP. 58	CHOPIN
SONATA IN B MINOR	ADAMS, G.
SONATA IN B MINOR	DE LA CASINIERE
SONATA IN B MINOR	LISZT
SONATA IN B MINOR	LISZT
SONATA IN B MINOR	LISZT
SONATA IN B MINOR	LISZT
SONATA IN B MINOR	LISZT
SONATA IN B MINOR	WAGNER, J.
SONATA IN C. 1825. COMPLETED BY A. KNAB	SCHUBERT *
SONATA IN C--SCH NO. 05	HAYDN
SONATA IN C, OP. 140	SCHUBERT
SONATA IN C, SHO 0485 1/2, H 35	HAYDN
SONATA IN C, SHO 09659 1/2, H 15	HAYDN
SONATA IN C MAJOR, H. XVI-35	HAYDN
SONATA IN C MAJOR	SALMHOFER, FR.
SONATA IN C MAJOR	SCARLATTI, D.
SONATA IN C MAJOR	SCARLATTI, D.
SONATA IN C MINOR, OP. 34 NO. 1	HESSENBERG, K.
SONATA IN C MINOR, OP. 4	CHOPIN
SONATA IN C MINOR, SHO 09660 1/2, H20	HAYDN
SONATA IN C MINOR	CANTALLOS
SONATA IN C MINOR	SIEFERT
SONATA IN C SHARP MINOR--SCH NO. 06	HAYDN
SONATA IN C SHARP MINOR, SHO 0492 1/2, H 36	HAYDN
SONATA IN C	BACH, J.
SONATA IN C	BACH, J.
SONATA IN C	BACH, J.
SONATA IN C	BACH, J.
SONATA IN C	BACH, J.
SONATA IN C	BACH, J.
SONATA IN C	FURGERI
SONATA IN C	MOZART, W. A.
SONATA IN D--SCH NO. 07	HAYDN
SONATA IN D--SCH NO. 09	HAYDN
SONATA IN D--SCH NO. 19	HAYDN
SONATA IN D, ALLEGRETTO	BACH, J.
SONATA IN D, NO. 07	HAYDN
SONATA IN D, OP. 53	SCHUBERT
SONATA IN D, SHO 0488 1/2, H 37	HAYDN
SONATA IN D, SHO 3497 1/2, H 19	HAYDN
SONATA IN D MAJOR, H. XVI-37	HAYDN
SONATA IN D MAJOR	SCARLATTI, A.
SONATA IN D MINOR FOR HARPSICHORD OR PIANO	HERTEL
SONATA IN D MINOR	KORNGOLD, E. W.
SONATA IN D MINOR	SCARLATTI, D.
SONATA IN D	ALBENIZ, M.
SONATA IN D	ALBENIZ, M.
SONATA IN D	FERRER
SONATA IN D	GENZMER
SONATA IN D	SAUGUET
SONATA IN E--SCH NO. 17	HAYDN
SONATA IN E, 1945	MARAVILLA, L.
SONATA IN E, 1945	MARCKHL, E.
SONATA IN E FLAT--SCH NO. 01	HAYDN
SONATA IN E FLAT--SCH NO. 03	HAYDN
SONATA IN E FLAT, NO. 03	HAYDN
SONATA IN E FLAT, OP. 122	SCHUBERT
SONATA IN E FLAT, SHO 0499 1/2, H 49	DUSSEK, J.
SONATA IN E FLAT, SHO 0503 1/2, H 52	HAYDN
SONATA IN E FLAT -- ''DUETTO''	MUTHEL, J. G.
SONATA IN E MAJOR	SCARLATTI, D.
SONATA IN E MINOR. TWO PIANOS, EIGHT HANDS	SMETANA
SONATA IN E MINOR--SCH NO. 02	HAYDN
SONATA IN E MINOR, COTTA NO. 7	HAYDN
SONATA IN E MINOR, OP. 3	ROSENSTOCK, J.
SONATA IN E MINOR, OP. 7	GRIEG
SONATA IN E MINOR, OP. 7	GRIEG
SONATA IN E MINOR, OP. 7	GRIEG
SONATA IN E MINOR, SHO 0491 1/2, H34	HAYDN
SONATA IN E MINOR AND SONATA IN F	ANGLES
SONATA IN E MINOR	SCHIFF, H.
SONATA IN E	KNAB, A.
SONATA IN F--SCH NO. 13	HAYDN
SONATA IN F--SCH NO. 20	HAYDN
SONATA IN F--1959	WEYRAUCH, J.
SONATA IN F, SHO 0486 1/2, H 23	HAYDN
SONATA IN F FOR 2 PIANOS--1 COPY--	BACH, W.F.
SONATA IN F MAJOR	GRIFFES, C.
SONATA IN F MINOR, OP. 34B	BRAHMS
SONATA IN F MINOR, OP. 34	BRAHMS
SONATA IN F MINOR, OP. 5	BRAHMS
SONATA IN F MINOR	SHAPERO, H.
SONATA IN F SHARP MINOR, OP. 61	DUSSEK, J.
SONATA IN F SHARP MINOR	SCHUBERT
SONATA IN F	AURIC
SONATA IN F	BACH, W.F.
SONATA IN F	BACH, W.F.
SONATA IN F	MUCZYNSKI, R.
SONATA IN F	PERGOLESI
SONATA IN G--SCH NO. 11	HAYDN
SONATA IN G, OP. 37	TSCHAIKOWSKY
SONATA IN G, SHO 0484 1/2, H 27	HAYDN
SONATA IN G MINOR--SCH NO. 04	HAYDN
SONATA IN G MINOR, OP. 50 NO. 3--DIDONE	CLEMENTI
SONATA IN G MINOR	PLEYEL
SONATA IN G	BACH, C.P.E.
SONATA IN G	BACH, J.
SONATA IN G	BACH, J.
SONATA IN G	CAMPOS-PARSI, H.
SONATA IN MODUS LACSIVUS	SERLY
SONATA IN ONE MOVEMENT FOR TWO PIANOS -- EIGHT HAND	SMETANA
SONATA IN ONE MOVEMENT	JOUBERT, J.
SONATA I	BADINGS
SONATA K019D IN C	MOZART, W. A.
SONATA K135ANH. IN F, SHO NO. 0611 1/2	MOZART, W. A.
SONATA K135 IN F, SCH NO. 13	MOZART, W. A.
SONATA K279 IN C, SCH NO. 8	MOZART, W. A.
SONATA K279 IN C, SHO NO. 0612 1/2	MOZART, W. A.
SONATA K280 IN F, SCH NO. 2	MOZART, W. A.
SONATA K280 IN F, SHO NO. 0613 1/2	MOZART, W. A.
SONATA K282 IN E FLAT, SCH NO. 17	MOZART, W. A.
SONATA K282 IN E FLAT, SHO NO. 0639 1/2	MOZART, W. A.
SONATA K282 IN E FLAT	MOZART, W. A.
SONATA K283 IN G, SCH NO. 5	MOZART, W. A.
SONATA K283 IN G, SHO NO. 0608 1/2	MOZART, W. A.
SONATA K284 IN D, SCH NO. 9	MOZART, W. A.
SONATA K309 IN C, SCH NO. 10	MOZART, W. A.
SONATA K309 IN C, SHO NO. 0622 1/2	MOZART, W. A.
SONATA K310 IN A MINOR, SCH NO. 14	MOZART, W. A.
SONATA K310 IN A MINOR, SHO NO. 0632 1/2	MOZART, W. A.
SONATA K311 IN D, SCH NO. 12	MOZART, W. A.
SONATA K311 IN D, SHO NO. 0626 1/2	MOZART, W. A.
SONATA K330 IN C, SCH NO. 11	MOZART, W. A.
SONATA K330 IN C, SHO NO. 0609 1/2	MOZART, W. A.
SONATA K331 IN A, FRA NO. 11	MOZART, W. A.
SONATA K331 IN A, SCH NO. 16	MOZART, W. A.
SONATA K331 IN A, SHO NO. 0618 1/2	MOZART, W. A.
SONATA K331 IN A	MOZART, W. A.
SONATA K331 IN A	MOZART, W. A.
SONATA K332 IN F, FRA NO. 12	MOZART, W. A.
SONATA K332 IN F, SCH NO. 6	MOZART, W. A.
SONATA K332 IN F, SHO NO. 0614 1/2	MOZART, W. A.
SONATA K332 IN F	MOZART, W. A.
SONATA K333 IN B FLAT, ALLEGRO	MOZART, W. A.
SONATA K333 IN B FLAT, SCH NO. 7	MOZART, W. A.
SONATA K358 IN B	MOZART, W. A.
SONATA K381 IN D	MOZART, W. A.
SONATA K448 IN D AND FUGUE IN C MINOR, K426 --SET--	MOZART, W. A.
SONATA K448 IN D AND FUGUE IN C MINOR, K426 --SET--	MOZART, W. A.
SONATA K457 IN C MINOR, SCH NO. 18, AND FANTASIA K475	MOZART, W. A.
SONATA K457 IN C MINOR, SHO NO. 0637 1/2	MOZART, W. A.
SONATA K457 IN C MINOR	MOZART, W. A.
SONATA K533 IN F, SCH NO. 4	MOZART, W. A.
SONATA K545 IN C, FRA NO. 15	MOZART, W. A.
SONATA K545 IN C, SHO NO. 0607 1/2	MOZART, W. A.
SONATA K545 IN C	MOZART, W. A. *
SONATA K545 IN C	MOZART, W. A.
SONATA K570 IN B FLAT, SHO NO. 0709 1/2	MOZART, W. A.
SONATA K570 IN B FLAT	MOZART, W. A.
SONATA K576 IN D, SCH NO. 15	MOZART, W. A.
SONATA LEVANTINA	CHAVARRI
SONATA NO. 01--1958	RIEMANN, A.
SONATA NO. 01, OP. 12	SHOSTAKOVITCH

Title	Composer	Title	Composer
SONATA NO. 01, OP. 17 FOR PIANO SOLO	DEBUSMAN, E.	SONATA NO. 02	RAN, S.
SONATA NO. 01, OP. 18	BALLIF	SONATA NO. 02	ROREM, N.
SONATA NO. 01, OP. 29	TOEBOSCH	SONATA NO. 02	RUST
SONATA NO. 01, OP. 38 NO. 1--1939	RAPHAEL, G.	SONATA NO. 02	SIEGMEISTER
SONATA NO. 01, OP. 6	SCRIABINE, A.	SONATA NO. 02	STARER
SONATA NO. 01, OP. 67	HARTMANN	SONATA NO. 03, OP. 13	KADOSA
SONATA NO. 01, OP. 7	KADOSA	SONATA NO. 03, OP. 14	GARCIA MORILLO
SONATA NO. 01, OP. 74	GLAZOUNOW, A.	SONATA NO. 03, OP. 14	SCHUMANN, R.
SONATA NO. 01 -- 1942-47 --	DEGEN	SONATA NO. 03, OP. 23	SCRIABINE, A.
SONATA NO. 01 -- 1950 --	EDER	SONATA NO. 03, OP. 26	JEMNITZ, A.
SONATA NO. 01 -- 1956 --	MARGOLA	SONATA NO. 03, OP. 28	PROKOFIEFF
SONATA NO. 01 AND SONATA NO. 02	ORTALI	SONATA NO. 03, OP. 28	PROKOFIEFF
SONATA NO. 01 FOR PIANO	WALKER, G.	SONATA NO. 03, OP. 36	SZYMANOWSKI
SONATA NO. 01 IN C, OP. 1, ANDANTE	BRAHMS	SONATA NO. 03, OP. 40	HODDINOTT, A.
SONATA NO. 01 IN C, OP. 1	BRAHMS	SONATA NO. 03, OP. 46	KABALEVSKY
SONATA NO. 01 IN C	HAYDN	SONATA NO. 03, OP. 46	KABALEVSKY
SONATA NO. 01 IN C	MOZART, W. A.	SONATA NO. 03, OP. 46	KABALEVSKY
SONATA NO. 01 IN C	MOZART, W. A.	SONATA NO. 03, OP. 52	SCHOLZ
SONATA NO. 01 IN C	MOZART, W. A.	SONATA NO. 03, OP. 57	MACDOWELL
SONATA NO. 01 IN D MINOR, OP. 28	RACHMANINOFF, S.	SONATA NO. 03, OP. 58	CHOPIN
SONATA NO. 01 IN D MINOR, OP. 28	RACHMANINOFF, S.	SONATA NO. 03, OP. 68	ALBENIZ, I.
SONATA NO. 01 IN E FLAT, OP. 2	KRENEK, E.	SONATA NO. 03, OP. 92 NO. 4 --1943--	KRENEK, E.
SONATA NO. 01 IN F MINOR, OP. 1	PROKOFIEFF	SONATA NO. 03, 2ND MVT.	BOULEZ
SONATA NO. 01 IN F MINOR, OP. 1	PROKOFIEFF	SONATA NO. 03, 3RD MVT.	BOULEZ
SONATA NO. 01 IN F MINOR, OP. 1	PROKOFIEFF	SONATA NO. 03 -- 1927 --	SCHULHOFF
SONATA NO. 01 IN F MINOR, OP. 2 NO. 1	BEETHOVEN	SONATA NO. 03 -- 1957 --	MARGOLA
SONATA NO. 01 IN F MINOR, OP. 2 NO. 1	BEETHOVEN	SONATA NO. 03 FOR PIANOFORTE	STEVENS, H.
SONATA NO. 01 IN F MINOR, OP. 2 NO. 1	BEETHOVEN	SONATA NO. 03 IN A MINOR, OP. 28	PROKOFIEFF
SONATA NO. 01 IN F MINOR, OP. 2 NO. 1	BEETHOVEN	SONATA NO. 03 IN A MINOR , OP. 28	PROKOFIEFF
SONATA NO. 01 IN F MINOR, OP. 2 NO. 1	BEETHOVEN	SONATA NO. 03 IN B FLAT, OP. POSTH.	SCHUBERT
SONATA NO. 01 IN F SHARP MINOR, OP. 11	SCHUMANN, R.	SONATA NO. 03 IN B FLAT, OP. POSTH.	SCHUBERT
SONATA NO. 01 IN F SHARP MINOR, OP. 11	SCHUMANN, R.	SONATA NO. 03 IN C, OP. 2 NO. 3	BEETHOVEN
SONATA NO. 01 IN F SHARP MINOR, OP. 11	SCHUMANN, R.	SONATA NO. 03 IN C, OP. 2 NO. 3	BEETHOVEN
SONATA NO. 01 ON C, OP. 1	BRAHMS	SONATA NO. 03 IN C, OP. 2 NO. 3	BEETHOVEN
SONATA NO. 01 URTEXT	BEETHOVEN	SONATA NO. 03 IN C	MOZART, W. A.
SONATA NO. 01	BABIN	SONATA NO. 03 IN D MAJOR	ENESCO
SONATA NO. 01	BOULEZ	SONATA NO. 03 IN D MINOR, OP. 49	WEBER, VON
SONATA NO. 01	CASADESUS, R.	SONATA NO. 03 IN F MINOR, OP. 14	SCHUMANN, R.
SONATA NO. 01	FAITH	SONATA NO. 03 IN F MINOR, OP. 5	BRAHMS
SONATA NO. 01	FITELBERG	SONATA NO. 03 IN F MINOR, OP. 5	BRAHMS
SONATA NO. 01	FULEIHAN, A.	SONATA NO. 03 IN F MINOR, OP. 5	BRAHMS
SONATA NO. 01	GENZMER	SONATA NO. 03 IN F SHARP MINOR, OP. 23	SCRIABINE, A.
SONATA NO. 01	HAYDN	SONATA NO. 03 IN G MINOR, AND PRESTO PASSIONATA, OP.	SCHUMANN, R.
SONATA NO. 01	HODDINOTT, A.	SONATA NO. 03	ARDEVOL, J.
SONATA NO. 01	HURE	SONATA NO. 03	FULEIHAN, A.
SONATA NO. 01	IVES, C.	SONATA NO. 03	JACOBI, W.
SONATA NO. 01	KABALEVSKY	SONATA NO. 03	KABALEVSKY
SONATA NO. 01	KAPR	SONATA NO. 03	ORTALI
SONATA NO. 01	KORN, P.	SONATA NO. 03	PEPPING, E.
SONATA NO. 01	LEE, N.	SONATA NO. 03	PROKOFIEFF
SONATA NO. 01	POSER	SONATA NO. 03	REINER
SONATA NO. 01	PROKOFIEFF	SONATA NO. 03	RUST
SONATA NO. 01	PROKOFIEFF	SONATA NO. 03	SESSIONS, R.
SONATA NO. 01	RAPHLING	SONATA NO. 03	ZAFRED
SONATA NO. 01	RUST	SONATA NO. 04--1941--	TANSMAN, A.
SONATA NO. 01	WALKER, G.	SONATA NO. 04, OP. 26	GARCIA MORILLO
SONATA NO. 01	WALKER, G.	SONATA NO. 04, OP. 30	BARTH, H.
SONATA NO. 01	WHITE, J.	SONATA NO. 04, OP. 30	SCRIABINE, A.
SONATA NO. 02, OP. 13	POLOWINKIN, L.	SONATA NO. 04, OP. 54	KADOSA
SONATA NO. 02, OP. 174	GRETCHANINOFF	SONATA NO. 04, OP. 72	ALBENIZ, I.
SONATA NO. 02, OP. 22	SCHUMANN, R.	SONATA NO. 04 -- 1948	KRENEK, E.
SONATA NO. 02, OP. 25	WESTERMAN, G.	SONATA NO. 04 IN C MINOR, OP. 29	PROKOFIEFF
SONATA NO. 02, OP. 27 --PATETICA--	EGGE	SONATA NO. 04 IN C MINOR, OP. 29	PROKOFIEFF
SONATA NO. 02, OP. 27	HODDINOTT, A.	SONATA NO. 04 IN E - CHRISTMAS 1945	FINNEY
SONATA NO. 02, OP. 35	CHOPIN	SONATA NO. 04 IN E FLAT, OP. 7	BEETHOVEN
SONATA NO. 02, OP. 35	CHOPIN	SONATA NO. 04 IN E FLAT, OP. 7	BEETHOVEN
SONATA NO. 02, OP. 38 NO. 2--1939	RAPHAEL, G.	SONATA NO. 04 IN F SHARP MINOR, OP. 23	SCRIABINE, A.
SONATA NO. 02, OP. 38	VALEN	SONATA NO. 04 IN F	MOZART, W. A.
SONATA NO. 02, OP. 45 --NEW VERSION--	KABALEVSKY	SONATA NO. 04	DEGEN
SONATA NO. 02, OP. 45	KABALEVSKY	SONATA NO. 04	FORSMAN
SONATA NO. 02, OP. 45	KABALEVSKY	SONATA NO. 04	FORSMAN
SONATA NO. 02, OP. 5	PROTOPOPOFF, S.	SONATA NO. 04	FULEIHAN, A.
SONATA NO. 02, OP. 59	KRENEK, E.	SONATA NO. 04	HODDINOTT, A.
SONATA NO. 02, OP. 64	SHOSTAKOVITCH	SONATA NO. 04	MACDOWELL
SONATA NO. 02, OP. 75	GLAZOUNOW, A.	SONATA NO. 04	MARGOLA
SONATA NO. 02, OP. 82	HARTMANN	SONATA NO. 04	MORRIS, H.
SONATA NO. 02, OP. 9	KADOSA	SONATA NO. 04	PEPPING, E.
SONATA NO. 02 --FOR CARILLON--	BADINGS	SONATA NO. 04	PEPPING, E.
SONATA NO. 02 -- 'CONCORD, MASS., 1843-60'	IVES, C.	SONATA NO. 04	PROKOFIEFF
SONATA NO. 02 -- 1945 --	DEGEN	SONATA NO. 04	RUST
SONATA NO. 02 -- 1952	HEIDEN	SONATA NO. 05, OP. 22	ALEXANDROW, A.
SONATA NO. 02 -- 1961 --	BARTA	SONATA NO. 05, OP. 53	SCRIABINE, A.
SONATA NO. 02 'A LA MEMOIRE D'UN GRAND HOMME'	AXMANN	SONATA NO. 05, OP. 82	ALBENIZ, I.
SONATA NO. 02 IN A, OP. 2 NO. 2	BEETHOVEN	SONATA NO. 05 IN C, OP. 36	PROKOFIEFF
SONATA NO. 02 IN A, OP. 2 NO. 2	BEETHOVEN	SONATA NO. 05 IN C, OP. 39	PROKOFIEFF
SONATA NO. 02 IN A FLAT MAJOR, OP. 39	WEBER, VON	SONATA NO. 05 IN C MINOR, OP. 10 NO. 1	BEETHOVEN
SONATA NO. 02 IN B FLAT MINOR, OP. 35	CHOPIN	SONATA NO. 05 IN C MINOR, OP. 10 NO. 1	BEETHOVEN
SONATA NO. 02 IN B FLAT MINOR, OP 36	RACHMANINOFF, S.	SONATA NO. 05 IN C MINOR, OP. 10 NO. 1	BEETHOVEN
SONATA NO. 02 IN D MINOR, OP. 14	PROKOFIEFF	SONATA NO. 05 IN C MINOR, OP. 10 NO. 1	BEETHOVEN
SONATA NO. 02 IN D MINOR, OP. 14	PROKOFIEFF	SONATA NO. 05 IN C MINOR, OP. 38	PROKOFIEFF
SONATA NO. 02 IN D MINOR, OP. 14	PROKOFIEFF	SONATA NO. 05 IN C	HAYDN
SONATA NO. 02 IN D MINOR, OP. 14	PROKOFIEFF	SONATA NO. 05 IN F SHARP MINOR, OP. 53	SCRIABINE, A.
SONATA NO. 02 IN EINEM SATZ	TIPPETT, M.	SONATA NO. 05 URTEXT	BEETHOVEN
SONATA NO. 02 IN E MINOR, 1946	LINK, J.D.	SONATA NO. 05	HODDINOTT, A.
SONATA NO. 02 IN F SHARP MINOR, OP. 2	BRAHMS	SONATA NO. 05	PROKOFIEFF
SONATA NO. 02 IN G MINOR, OP. 22	SCHUMANN, R.	SONATA NO. 05	RAPHLING
SONATA NO. 02 IN G MINOR, OP. 22	SCHUMANN, R.	SONATA NO. 05	RAPHLING
SONATA NO. 02 IN G MINOR, OP. 22	SCHUMANN, R.	SONATA NO. 05	RUST
SONATA NO. 02 IN G SHARP MINOR, OP.19	SCRIABINE, A.	SONATA NO. 05	TANSMAN, A.
SONATA NO. 02 OP. 6 -- IN FORM OF VARIATIONS --	EISLER	SONATA NO. 05	WHITE, J.
SONATA NO. 02	KABALEVSKY	SONATA NO. 06, OP. 13	FEINBERG, S.
SONATA NO. 02 OP. 45	BOULEZ	SONATA NO. 06, OP. 82	PROKOFIEFF
SONATA NO. 02	DELLO JOIO, N.	SONATA NO. 06 IN A MAJOR, OP. 82	PROKOFIEFF
SONATA NO. 02	EVETT	SONATA NO. 06 IN F, OP. 10 NO. 2	BEETHOVEN
SONATA NO. 02	FULEIHAN, A.	SONATA NO. 06 IN F, OP. 10 NO. 2	BEETHOVEN
SONATA NO. 02	GALUPPI	SONATA NO. 06 IN F	MOZART, W. A.
SONATA NO. 02	GARCIA MORILLO	SONATA NO. 06	BACH, J.S.
SONATA NO. 02	GENZMER	SONATA NO. 06	PROKOFIEFF
SONATA NO. 02	HALFFTER, R.	SONATA NO. 06	RUST
SONATA NO. 02	HARTLEY	SONATA NO. 07, FINALE	HAYDN
SONATA NO. 02	HURE	SONATA NO. 07, OP. 64	SCRIABINE, A.
SONATA NO. 02	JACOBI, W.	SONATA NO. 07, OP. 83	PROKOFIEFF
SONATA NO. 02	JARNACH, P.	SONATA NO. 07 IN B FLAT, OP. 83	PROKOFIEFF
SONATA NO. 02	KABALEVSKY	SONATA NO. 07 IN B FLAT MAJOR, OP. 83	PROKOFIEFF
SONATA NO. 02	KAHNAU	SONATA NO. 07 IN D, OP. 10 NO. 3	BEETHOVEN
SONATA NO. 02	KERR, H.	SONATA NO. 07 IN D, OP. 10 NO. 3	BEETHOVEN
SONATA NO. 02	KOX	SONATA NO. 07 IN D, OP. 10 NO. 3	BEETHOVEN
SONATA NO. 02	LEE, N.	SONATA NO. 07 IN D, OP. 10 NO. 3	BEETHOVEN
SONATA NO. 02	MAIXANDEAU, M.	SONATA NO. 07 IN D	HAYDN
SONATA NO. 02	MARGOLA	SONATA NO. 07	DIETHELM
SONATA NO. 02	MEYER	SONATA NO. 07	PROKOFIEFF
SONATA NO. 02	MILHAUD, D.	SONATA NO. 07	RUST
SONATA NO. 02	NABOKOFF, N.	SONATA NO. 08, OP. 66	SCRIABINE, A.
SONATA NO. 02	NIGG, S.	SONATA NO. 08, OP. 84	PROKOFIEFF
SONATA NO. 02	PONCE, M.	SONATA NO. 08 IN B FLAT MAJOR, OP. 84	PROKOFIEFF
SONATA NO. 02	PROKOFIEFF		

SONATA NO. 08 IN C MINOR, OP. 13, 'PATHETIQUE'	BEETHOVEN
SONATA NO. 08 IN C MINOR, OP. 13 - GRANDE SONATA	BEETHOVEN
SONATA NO. 08 IN C MINOR, OP. 13 - PATHETIQUE	BEETHOVEN
SONATA NO. 08 IN C MINOR, OP. 13 'PATHETIQUE'	BEETHOVEN
SONATA NO. 08 IN C MINOR, OP. 13 'PATHETIQUE'	BEETHOVEN
SONATA NO. 08 IN C MINOR, OP. 13 'PATHETIQUE'	BEETHOVEN
SONATA NO. 08 IN C MINOR, OP. 13	BEETHOVEN
SONATA NO. 08 IN C MINOR, OP. 13	BEETHOVEN
SONATA NO. 08 URTEXT	BEETHOVEN
SONATA NO. 08	PROKOFIEFF
SONATA NO. 08	RUST
SONATA NO. 09, OP. 103	PROKOFIEFF
SONATA NO. 09, OP. 103	PROKOFIEFF
SONATA NO. 09, OP. 68	SCRIABINE, A.
SONATA NO. 09 IN C MAJOR, OP. 103	PROKOFIEFF
SONATA NO. 09 IN E, OP. 14 NO. 1, ALLEGRETTO	BEETHOVEN
SONATA NO. 09 IN E, OP. 14 NO. 1	BEETHOVEN
SONATA NO. 09 IN E, OP. 14 NO. 1	BEETHOVEN
SONATA NO. 09 IN E, OP. 14 NO. 1	BEETHOVEN
SONATA NO. 09 IN F, OP. 68	SCRIABINE, A.
SONATA NO. 09 URTEXT	BEETHOVEN
SONATA NO. 09	DIETHELM
SONATA NO. 09	FULEIHAN, A.
SONATA NO. 09	RUST
SONATA NO. 10, OP. 70	SCRIABINE, A.
SONATA NO. 10 IN C, OP. 70	SCRIABINE, A.
SONATA NO. 10 IN E MINOR	PASQUINI
SONATA NO. 10 IN G, OP. 14 NO. 2	BEETHOVEN
SONATA NO. 10 IN G, OP. 14 NO. 2	BEETHOVEN
SONATA NO. 10 IN G, OP. 14 NO. 2	BEETHOVEN
SONATA NO. 10 IN G, OP. 14 NO. 2	BEETHOVEN
SONATA NO. 10 IN MI MINORE	PASQUINI
SONATA NO. 10 URTEXT	BEETHOVEN
SONATA NO. 10	RUST
SONATA NO. 11 IN B FLAT, OP. 22	BEETHOVEN
SONATA NO. 11 IN B FLAT, OP. 22	BEETHOVEN
SONATA NO. 11	RUST
SONATA NO. 12 IN A FLAT, OP. 26 'FUNERAL MARCH'	BEETHOVEN
SONATA NO. 12 IN A FLAT, OP. 26 'TRAUERMARSCH'	BEETHOVEN
SONATA NO. 12 IN A FLAT, OP. 26 WITH FUNERAL MARCH	BEETHOVEN
SONATA NO. 12 IN A FLAT, OP. 26	BEETHOVEN
SONATA NO. 12	RUST
SONATA NO. 13 IN E FLAT, OP. 27 NO. 1 'FANTASIE'	BEETHOVEN
SONATA NO. 13 IN E FLAT, OP. 27 NO. 1	BEETHOVEN
SONATA NO. 13 IN E FLAT, OP. 27 NO. 1	BEETHOVEN
SONATA NO. 14 IN C SHARP MINOR, OP. 27 NO. 2,	BEETHOVEN
SONATA NO. 14 IN C SHARP MINOR, OP. 27 NO. 2 --FIRST	BEETHOVEN
SONATA NO. 14 IN C SHARP MINOR, OP. 27 NO. 2	BEETHOVEN
SONATA NO. 14 IN C SHARP MINOR, OP. 27 NO. 2	BEETHOVEN
SONATA NO. 14 IN C SHARP MINOR, OP. 27 NO. 2	BEETHOVEN
SONATA NO. 14 IN C SHARP MINOR, OP. 27 NO. 2	BEETHOVEN
SONATA NO. 14 IN C SHARP MINOR, OP. 27 NO. 2	BEETHOVEN
SONATA NO. 14 IN C SHARP MINOR, OP. 27 NO. 2	BEETHOVEN
SONATA NO. 14 IN C SHARP MINOR 'MOONLIGHT'	BEETHOVEN
SONATA NO. 14 URTEXT	BEETHOVEN
SONATA NO. 15 IN D, OP. 28 'PASTORAL'	BEETHOVEN
SONATA NO. 15 IN D, OP. 28 'PASTORAL'	BEETHOVEN
SONATA NO. 15 IN D, OP. 28 'PASTORAL'	BEETHOVEN
SONATA NO. 15 IN D, OP. 28 'PASTORALE'	BEETHOVEN
SONATA NO. 15 IN D, OP. 28	BEETHOVEN
SONATA NO. 16 IN G, OP. 31 NO. 1	BEETHOVEN
SONATA NO. 16 IN G, OP. 31 NO. 1	BEETHOVEN
SONATA NO. 17 IN D MINOR, OP. 31 NO. 2 'TEMPEST'	BEETHOVEN
SONATA NO. 17 IN D MINOR, OP. 31 NO. 2	BEETHOVEN
SONATA NO. 17 IN D MINOR, OP. 31 NO. 2	BEETHOVEN
SONATA NO. 17 IN D MINOR, OP. 31 NO. 2	BEETHOVEN
SONATA NO. 18 IN E FLAT, OP. 31 NO. 3	BEETHOVEN
SONATA NO. 18 IN E FLAT, OP. 31 NO. 3	BEETHOVEN
SONATA NO. 19 IN F, K.ANH. 135 AND 138A	MOZART, W. A.
SONATA NO. 19 IN G MINOR, OP. 49 NO. 1 'SONATINE'	BEETHOVEN
SONATA NO. 19 IN G MINOR, OP. 49 NO. 1	BEETHOVEN
SONATA NO. 19 IN G MINOR, OP. 49 NO. 1	BEETHOVEN
SONATA NO. 19 IN G MINOR, OP. 49 NO. 1	BEETHOVEN
SONATA NO. 19 IN G MINOR, OP. 49 NO 1	BEETHOVEN
SONATA NO. 20 IN G, OP. 49 NO. 2 'SONATINE'	BEETHOVEN
SONATA NO. 20 IN G, OP. 49 NO. 2	BEETHOVEN
SONATA NO. 20 IN G, OP. 49 NO. 2	BEETHOVEN
SONATA NO. 20 IN G, OP. 49 NO. 2	BEETHOVEN
SONATA NO. 20 IN G, OP. 49 NO. 2	BEETHOVEN
SONATA NO. 20 IN G, OP. 49 NO. 2	BEETHOVEN
SONATA NO. 21 IN C, OP. 53, 'WALDSTEIN'	BEETHOVEN
SONATA NO. 21 IN C, OP. 53, 'WALDSTEIN'	BEETHOVEN
SONATA NO. 21 IN C, OP. 53 'WALDSTEIN'	BEETHOVEN
SONATA NO. 21 IN C, OP. 53 'WALDSTEIN'	BEETHOVEN
SONATA NO. 21 IN C, OP. 53	BEETHOVEN
SONATA NO. 22 IN F, OP. 54	BEETHOVEN
SONATA NO. 23 IN F MINOR, OP. 57, 'APPASSIONATA'	BEETHOVEN
SONATA NO. 23 IN F MINOR, OP. 57, 'APPASSIONATA'	BEETHOVEN
SONATA NO. 23 IN F MINOR, OP. 57 'APPASSIONATA'	BEETHOVEN
SONATA NO. 23 IN F MINOR, OP. 57 'APPASSIONATA'	BEETHOVEN
SONATA NO. 23 IN F MINOR, OP. 57	BEETHOVEN
SONATA NO. 24 IN F SHARP, OP. 78	BEETHOVEN
SONATA NO. 24 IN F SHARP MINOR, OP. 78	BEETHOVEN
SONATA NO. 24 IN G, OP. 79 - ANDANTE	BEETHOVEN
SONATA NO. 24 IN G, OP. 79	BEETHOVEN
SONATA NO. 24 UN G, OP. 79	BEETHOVEN
SONATA NO. 25 IN G, OP. 79 'SONATINE'	BEETHOVEN
SONATA NO. 25 IN G, OP. 79	BEETHOVEN
SONATA NO. 25 IN G, OP. 79	BEETHOVEN
SONATA NO. 26 IN D FLAT, OP. 81A 'LES ADIEUX'	BEETHOVEN
SONATA NO. 26 IN E FLAT, OP. 81A 'LES ADIEUX'	BEETHOVEN
SONATA NO. 26 IN E FLAT, OP. 81A 'LES ADIEUX'	BEETHOVEN
SONATA NO. 26 URTEXT	BEETHOVEN
SONATA NO. 27 IN E MINOR, OP. 90	BEETHOVEN
SONATA NO. 27 IN E MINOR, OP. 90	BEETHOVEN
SONATA NO. 27 IN G	HAYDN
SONATA NO. 27 URTEXT	BEETHOVEN
SONATA NO. 28 'PERFIDIA'	CIMAROSA
SONATA NO. 28 IN A, OP. 101	BEETHOVEN
SONATA NO. 28 IN A, OP.101	BEETHOVEN
SONATA NO. 28 URTEXT	BEETHOVEN
SONATA NO. 29 IN B FLAT, OP. 106 'HAMMERKLAVIER'	BEETHOVEN
SONATA NO. 29 IN B FLAT, OP. 106 'HAMMERKLAVIER'	BEETHOVEN
SONATA NO. 29 IN B FLAT, OP. 106 'HAMMERKLAVIER'	BEETHOVEN
SONATA NO. 29 URTEXT	BEETHOVEN
SONATA NO. 30 -- THE CAT'S FUGUE	SCARLATTI, D.
SONATA NO. 30 IN E, OP. 109	BEETHOVEN
SONATA NO. 30 IN E, OP. 109	BEETHOVEN
SONATA NO. 31 IN A FLAT, OP. 110	BEETHOVEN
SONATA NO. 31 IN A FLAT, OP. 110	BEETHOVEN
SONATA NO. 32 IN C MINOR, OP. 111 -- FACSIMILE	BEETHOVEN

SONATA NO. 32 IN C MINOR, OP. 111	BEETHOVEN
SONATA NO. 32 IN C MINOR, OP. 111	BEETHOVEN
SONATA NO. 32 IN C MINOR, OP. 111	BEETHOVEN
SONATA NO. 34 IN E MINOR	HAYDN
SONATA NO. 35 IN C	HAYDN
SONATA ON JAZZ ELEMENTS	KUPFERMAN, M.
SONATA ON JAZZ ELEMENTS	KUPFERMAN, M.
SONATA ON JAZZ ELEMENTS	KUPFERMAN, M.
SONATA OP. 26 NO. 2 IN F SHARP MINOR	CLEMENTI
SONATA OP. 26 NO. 3	CLEMENTI
SONATA OP. 50 NO. 2 'DIDONE ABBANDONATA'	CLEMENTI
SONATA OR FANTASIA IN G, OP. 78	SCHUBERT
SONATA PASTORALE	DAHL
SONATA PATHETIQUE, OP. 13	BEETHOVEN
SONATA PER AMEDEO MODIGLIANA	ZAMANA
SONATA PER CEMBALO, HARMONIC STUDY EDITION -- WITH	LEO, L.
SONATA PER IL CLAVICEMBALO	DUSSEK, F. X.
SONATA PER PIANOFORTE	BLOCH, E.
SONATA PIAN E FORTE, FOR DOUBLE BRASS CHOIR. REDUCTION	GABRIELI, G.
SONATA POUR PIANO NO. 2	JOLIVET, A.
SONATA QUASI FANTASIA, OP. 40	VOMACKA
SONATA RICERCARE	HOVHANESS, A.
SONATA RITMICA, OP. 5	APOSTEL
SONATA ROMANTIQUE ON A SPANISH THEME	TURINA, J.
SONATA RUSTICA	SUCHON, E.
SONATA SCHERZO	BOUTRY
SONATA SERIA	DAHL
SONATA TRAGICA IN G MINOR, OP. 45	MACDOWELL
SONATA VARIATO -- NO. 03 --	FORSMAN
SONATA VARIATO - NO. 3	FORSMAN
SONATA	AMRAM
SONATA	BARTOK
SONATA	BARTOK
SONATA	BENNETT, R.
SONATA	BINKERD
SONATA	BOZZA
SONATA	BRAUN, Y.
SONATA	BRUNNER
SONATA	BRUNNER
SONATA	CASTEREDE, J.
SONATA	COPLAND
SONATA	COULTHARD
SONATA	DAMASE, J. M.
SONATA	DEBREVILLE
SONATA	DELDEN, VAN
SONATA	DESDERI
SONATA	DIAMOND, D.
SONATA	DUKELSKY
SONATA	ELWELL, H.
SONATA	ENGEL, L.
SONATA	FERNEYHOUGH
SONATA	FINNEY
SONATA	FLAGELLO, N.
SONATA	FLAGELLO, N.
SONATA	FLANAGAN, W.
SONATA	FLOYD, C.
SONATA	FRANCAIX, J.
SONATA	FRANCHETTI
SONATA	GIANNINI
SONATA	GINASTERA
SONATA	GUASTAVINO
SONATA	HALFFTER, E.
SONATA	HARSANYI
SONATA	HAYASHI, H.
SONATA	HENKEMANS
SONATA	HENZE, H.
SONATA	JEANNERET
SONATA	KELEMEN
SONATA	KELTERBORN
SONATA	KHATCHATURIAN
SONATA	KHATCHATURIAN
SONATA	KHATCHATURIAN
SONATA	KOLZ, E.
SONATA	KUBIK, G.
SONATA	LEES, B.
SONATA	LEEUW
SONATA	LEKEU
SONATA	LENG, A.
SONATA	LIEBERMANN, R.
SONATA	MANICKE, D.
SONATA	MATA, E.
SONATA	MECHEM, K.
SONATA	MILHAUD, D.
SONATA	MUTHEL, J. G.
SONATA	NABOKOFF, N.
SONATA	NIELSEN, R.
SONATA	NOETEL
SONATA	PASQUINI
SONATA	PERLE, G.
SONATA	PIJPER
SONATA	PIJPER
SONATA	PORTER
SONATA	RAPHLING
SONATA	RIBARI, A.
SONATA	ROBERTS
SONATA	SALZAR, A.
SONATA	SCELSI
SONATA	SEREBRIER, J.
SONATA	SESSIONS, R.
SONATA	SMETANA
SONATA	SMETANA
SONATA	SMIT, L.
SONATA	STARER
SONATA	STEINERT, A.
SONATA	STRAVINSKY, I.
SONATA	STRAVINSKY, I.
SONATA	SWAN
SONATA	SYDEMAN
SONATA	TERNI
SONATA	TIPPETT, M.
SONATA	WILLIAMSON, M.
SONATA 1962	FLAGELLO, N.
SONATA 1965	ARETZ, I.
SONATE, SECOND MOVEMENT--HARPSCHORD AND FLUTE--	BACH, J.S.
SONATEENERS	KING
SONATEN-TRIADE, OP. 11 NO. 3	MEDTNER, N.
SONATENBUCH -- 10 KLASSISCHE SONATEN VON BEETHOVEN,	HERRMANN--ED
SONATENBUCH DER VORKLASSIK	FREY--ED
SONATEN FUR LIEBHABER	FRICKERT--ED
SONATES MIGNONNES, OP. 150 AND RONDEAU MILITAIRE, OP.	DIABELLI
SONATES PRECLASSIQUES CHOISIES	
SONATE -- DUETTO --	MUTHEL, J. G.
SONATE A-MOLL OP. 61 NO. 2	HAAS
SONATE D-DUR OP. 61 NO. 1	HAAS
SONATE D'INTAVOLATURA - L'ORGANO E 'L CEMBALO	MARTINI, G.
SONATE DER STRASSE -- 1. 10. 1905 --	JANACEK
SONATE E-MOLL OP. 7	GRIEG

SONATE EN MI	INDY, V. D'
SONATE EN RE	GALUPPI
SONATE F-DUR OP. 26	DUSSEK, J.
SONATE FACILE D-DUR OP. 6	BEETHOVEN
SONATE G-DUR	BACH, J.
SONATE G-DUR	BACH, J.
SONATE G-DUR	BACH, J.
SONATE G-MOLL OP. 129	GRETCHANINOFF
SONATE IN A-DUR OP. 120	SCHUBERT
SONATE IN A-MOLL OP. 42	SCHUBERT
SONATE IN D MINOR FOR CEMBALO ODER KLAVIER	HERTEL
SONATE IN E FLAT	BOCCHERINI
SONATE IN E MINOR FOR 2 PIANOS, 8 HANDS	SMETANA
SONATE IN G-DUR OP. 78 DARAUS -- MENUETT	SCHUBERT
SONATE IN G-DUR OP. 78 FANTASIE	SCHUBERT
SONATE NO. 02 IN D MINOR, OP. 10	JEREMIAS
SONATE PASTORALE, OP. 253	LACK
SONATE PER CEMBALO	CIAJA, A.
SONATE POUR PIANO EN CINQ MOUVEMENTS	RIVIER, J.
SONATE	DUKAS, P.
SONATE	DUTILLEUX
SONATE	JIRKO
SONATE	KELTERBORN
SONATE	KORTE
SONATE	LAZAR, F.
SONATE	MIGOT
SONATE	MIHALOVICI
SONATE	NOETEL
SONATE	POLIVKA
SONATE	TISNE, A.
SONATE	WISSMER, P.
SONATINA. HARPSICHORD	KOX
SONATINA--1954	KANN, H.
SONATINA--1958	SPIES, L.
SONATINA, HIDE THE STICK, CHRISTMAS TREE	SALUTRINSKAYA
SONATINA, OP. 1	FIALA
SONATINA, OP. 11B	KADOSA
SONATINA, OP. 12 NO. 1	CIKKER
SONATINA, OP. 12	KOFFLER, J.
SONATINA, OP. 13, NO. 1	KABALEVSKY
SONATINA, OP. 13 NO. 1 IN C MAJOR	KABALEVSKY
SONATINA, OP. 13 NO. 1	KABALEVSKY
SONATINA, OP. 13 NO. 1	KABALEVSKY
SONATINA, OP. 13 NO. 2 IN G MAJOR	KABALEVSKY
SONATINA, OP. 13 NO. 2	KABALEVSKY
SONATINA, OP. 16	LARSSON, L. E.
SONATINA, OP. 25	TRAPP, M.
SONATINA, OP. 36 NO. 1	CLEMENTI
SONATINA, OP. 36 NO. 2	CLEMENTI
SONATINA, OP. 36 NO. 3	CLEMENTI
SONATINA, OP. 38	BEN-HAIM
SONATINA, OP. 42--1954	SCHISKE, K.
SONATINA, OP. 5	FANO, G. A.
SONATINA, OP. 55 NO. 1	KUHLAU, F.
SONATINA, OP. 55 NO. 2	KUHLAU, F.
SONATINA, OP. 55 NO. 3	KUHLAU, F.
SONATINA, OP. 55 NO. 6	KUHLAU, F.
SONATINA, OP. 7	LOPATNIKOFF
SONATINA, OP. 8	SCHROETER, H.
SONATINA, OP. 88 NO. 2--OLD EDITION--	KUHLAU, F.
SONATINA, OP. 9 NO. 4	JELINEK, H.
SONATINA, SECOND MOVEMENT	HASLINGER, T.
SONATINA, THIRD MOVEMENT	BERENS, H.
SONATINA, 1950	KOCH, F.
SONATINAS, BK. 1--OP. 20, 55, 59	KUHLAU, F.
SONATINAS, BK. 2--OP. 60, 88	KUHLAU, F.
SONATINAS, OP. 150 AND 152	DIABELLI
SONATINAS, OP. 151 AND 168	DIABELLI
SONATINAS, OP. 20	DUSSEK, J.
SONATINAS, OP. 24, 54, 58, 60	DIABELLI
SONATINAS, OP. 24 NOS. 54, 58, 60	DIABELLI
SONATINAS, OP. 36, 37, 38	CLEMENTI
SONATINAS, OP. 36	CLEMENTI
SONATINAS, OP. 36	CLEMENTI
SONATINAS, OP. 44, 66	KUHLAU, F.
SONATINAS, RONDOS AND PIECES, VOL. 1	KLEINMICHEL--ED
SONATINAS, RONDOS AND PIECES, VOL. 2	KLEINMICHEL--ED
SONATINAS, VOL. 1	KUHLAU, F.
SONATINAS, VOL. 2	KUHLAU, F.
SONATINAS, WITH 2ND PIANO ACC. BY RIEDEL, IN 2 VOLS*	KUHLAU, F. *
SONATINAS, WITH 2ND PIANO ACC. BY RIEDEL, IN 2 VOLS*	KUHLAU, F. *
SONATINAS --AFTER K213, 240--	MOZART, W. A.
SONATINAS -- PREPARATORY TO CLEMENTI, KUHLAU	PRISCHING,
SONATINAS --6--, OP. 20	DUSSEK, J.
SONATINAS --6-- COMPLETE	BEETHOVEN
SONATINAS AND RONDOS--32 SONATINAS AND RONDOS	KLEINMICHEL--ED
SONATINAS BY CLEMENTI AND OTHER COMPOSERS, BK. 1	CLEMENTI
SONATINAS BY CLEMENTI AND OTHER COMPOSERS, BK. 2	CLEMENTI
SONATINAS COMPLETE	BEETHOVEN
SONATINAS FOR PIANO, BK. 1	AGAY, D.--ED
SONATINAS FOR PIANO, BK. 2	AGAY, D.--ED
SONATINAS FOR PIANO, BK. 3	AGAY, D.--ED
SONATINAS OP. 36 NO. 3 AND 5	CLEMENTI
SONATINAS SERIES I, NO. 1	KOECHLIN, C.
SONATINAS SERIES I, NO. 2	KOECHLIN, C.
SONATINAS SERIES I, NO. 3	KOECHLIN, C.
SONATINAS SERIES I, NO. 4	KOECHLIN, C.
SONATINAS SERIES I, NO. 5	KOECHLIN, C.
SONATINAS SERIES II -- NEW -- NO. 1	KOECHLIN, C.
SONATINAS SERIES II -- NEW -- NO. 2	KOECHLIN, C.
SONATINAS SERIES II -- NEW -- NO. 3	KOECHLIN, C.
SONATINAS SERIES II -- NEW -- NO. 4	KOECHLIN, C.
SONATINAS	BEETHOVEN
SONATINAS	DIABELLI
SONATINAS	HAYDN
SONATINAS	KUHLAU, F.
SONATINAS	KUHLAU, F.
SONATINA -- ''IN DIEM NATIVITATIS CHRISTI, 1917'' --	BUSONI
SONATINA -- BALLET IN ONE ACT	HALFFTER, E.
SONATINA -- G	BEETHOVEN
SONATINA -- IN THREE MOVEMENTS	LEE, DAI-KEONG
SONATINA -- PRELUDE TO THE CANTATA ''GOD'S TIME IS THE BACH, J.S.	
SONATINA -- VIENNESE -- NO. 01, RONDO	MOZART, W. A.
SONATINA -- 1910 --	BUSONI
SONATINA -- 1954 --	DALLINGER
SONATINA -- 1955 --	DESSAU
SONATINA --1959	KHATCHATURIAN
SONATINA - DEATH VALLEY	PISK
SONATINA AD USUM INFANTIS	BUSONI
SONATINA ALBUM--ABRIDGED--15 FAVORITE SONATINAS	
SONATINA ALBUM--30 FAVORITE SONATINAS, RONDOS, AND	KOEHLER--ED
SONATINA ALBUM, VOL. 1	
SONATINA ALBUM, VOL. 2	
SONATINA ALBUM - FOUR SONATINAS FOR THE YOUNG PIANIST	COBB
SONATINA ALBUM	KOEHLER, L.
SONATINA ALBUM	KOEHLER
SONATINA AND SALON ALBUM--15 SONATINAS AND 15	

SONATINA BALLET, DANCE OF THE GYPSY	HALFFTER, E.
SONATINA BALLET, DANCE OF THE SHEPHERDESS	HALFFTER, E.
SONATINA BOOK, VOL. 1	VOLGER--ED
SONATINA BOOK, VOL. 2	VOLGER--ED
SONATINA BOOK 1	GOLDBERGER,
SONATINA BOOK 2	GOLDBERGER,
SONATINA BOOK 3	GOLDBERGER,
SONATINA BREVIS, AFTER BACH	BUSONI
SONATINA BUCOLICA	KAPRAL
SONATINA DA 6 PEZZI, OP. 3	WEBER, VON
SONATINA ESPANOLA	CASTRO, J. J.
SONATINA FOR HARPSICHORD	JACOBI, W.
SONATINA FOR HARPSICHORD	ROESGEN-CHAMPION
SONATINA FOR PIANO OR HARPSICHORD	ZIPP
SONATINA FOR PIANO	AHNELL, E.
SONATINA FOR PIANO	CALABRO, L.
SONATINA FOR PIANO	GIANNINI
SONATINA FOR PIANO	GOULD, M.
SONATINA FOR PIANO	RAWSTHORNE, A.
SONATINA FOR THE LEFT HAND	LIPATTI, D.
SONATINA FOR TWO PIANOS	PHILLIPS, R.
SONATINA FUR ZWEI KLAVIER	BECK
SONATINA GRAZIOSA, OP. 21 NO 1	WALZEL, L. M.
SONATINA HUNGARICA	AGAY, D.
SONATINA IN A, OP. 59 NO. 1	KUHLAU, F.
SONATINA IN A, OP. 60 NO. 2	KUHLAU, F.
SONATINA IN A, 1947	KNORR, E.L. VON
SONATINA IN A MINOR, OP. 27	KABALEVSKY
SONATINA IN A MINOR, OP. 88 NO. 3	KUHLAU, F.
SONATINA IN A MINOR, OP. 89 NO. 4	REGER
SONATINA IN A MINOR -- IN THREE MOVEMENTS	COBB
SONATINA IN B-FLAT	REIN
SONATINA IN C--FOR MANDOLIN AND CEMBALO, TRANSCRIBED	BEETHOVEN
SONATINA IN C, OP. 20 NO. 1	KUHLAU, F.
SONATINA IN C, OP. 4 NO. 1	LICHNER, H.
SONATINA IN C, OP. 55 NO. 1	KUHLAU, F.
SONATINA IN C, OP. 55 NO. 3	KUHLAU, F.
SONATINA IN C, OP. 66 NO. 1	LICHNER, H.
SONATINA IN C, 1947	PETYREK, R.
SONATINA IN CLASSIC STYLE	GILLOCK
SONATINA IN CLASSIC STYLE	GILLOCK
SONATINA IN CLASSIC STYLE	GILLOCK
SONATINA IN C MAJOR, OP. 36	CLEMENTI
SONATINA IN C MAJOR, OP. 36	CLEMENTI
SONATINA IN C MAJOR -- IN THREE MOVEMENTS	COBB
SONATINA IN C	STEIBELT
SONATINA IN C	WEBER, VON
SONATINA IN D, OP. 8 NO. 1	SEISS
SONATINA IN D, OP. 89 NO. 2	REGER
SONATINA IN D MAJOR, OP. 36	CLEMENTI
SONATINA IN D MAJOR	BENTLEY
SONATINA IN D	CALTABIANO
SONATINA IN E, OP. 48 NO. 5	MARX
SONATINA IN E FLAT	SUTERMEISTER, H.
SONATINA IN E MINOR, OP. 54 NO. 1	PROKOFIEFF
SONATINA IN E MINOR, OP. 89 NO. 1	REGER
SONATINA IN F, OP. 20 NO. 3	KUHLAU, F.
SONATINA IN F, OP. 89 NO. 3	REGER
SONATINA IN F MAJOR, OP. 36	CLEMENTI
SONATINA IN F MAJOR	BEETHOVEN
SONATINA IN F MAJOR	GEORGE
SONATINA IN F	BEETHOVEN
SONATINA IN G, OP. 20 NO. 1	DUSSEK, J.
SONATINA IN G, OP. 20 NO. 2	KUHLAU, F.
SONATINA IN G, OP. 249 NO. 2	SCHMITT, J.
SONATINA IN G, OP. 54 NO. 2	PROKOFIEFF
SONATINA IN G, OP. 55 NO. 2	KUHLAU, F.
SONATINA IN G MAJOR, OP. 36	CLEMENTI
SONATINA IN G MAJOR, OP. 36	CLEMENTI
SONATINA IN G MAJOR -- IN THREE MOVEMENTS	COBB
SONATINA IN G MAJOR	BEETHOVEN
SONATINA IN G MAJOR	BEETHOVEN
SONATINA IN G MAJOR	FROST
SONATINA IN G MAJOR	GEORGE
SONATINA IN G MINOR, NO. 2	CHILDERS, L.
SONATINA IN G	ATTWOOD
SONATINA IN G	BACH, C.P.E.
SONATINA IN G	BASTIEN
SONATINA IN G	BAUER
SONATINA IN G	BEETHOVEN
SONATINA IN G	BEETHOVEN
SONATINA IN G	BEETHOVEN
SONATINA IN G	THOMPSON, J.
SONATINA IN G	URBANCIC, V.
SONATINA IN SIGNO MAGNI ARNOLD	NIELSEN, R.
SONATINA IN THE STYLE OF MOZART	MELECCI, A.
SONATINA IN TRE DIVERTIMENTI	RENZI
SONATINA IN UN TEMPO, OP. 15 'P'	NEGLIA, F.
SONATINA IN 2 MOVEMENTS	ZANOTTI *
SONATINA LUSITANA	BOSMANS, A.
SONATINA NO. 01, OP. 12 NO. 1	POSER
SONATINA NO. 01, OP. 36	CLEMENTI
SONATINA NO. 01, OP. 7--1961	TJEKNAVORIAN, L.
SONATINA NO. 01 IN C, OP. 13 NO. 1	KABALEVSKY
SONATINA NO. 01 IN C, OP. 13	KABALEVSKY
SONATINA NO. 01 IN C MAJOR	TILLETT, J.
SONATINA NO. 01 IN G	BEETHOVEN
SONATINA NO. 01 IN G	BEETHOVEN
SONATINA NO. 01	BEETHOVEN
SONATINA NO. 01	FREED, I.
SONATINA NO. 01	HELLER, S.
SONATINA NO. 01	KUHLAU, F.
SONATINA NO. 01	PIJPER
SONATINA NO. 01	POLDINI, E.
SONATINA NO. 01	RAPHLING
SONATINA NO. 01	SIFLER, P.
SONATINA NO. 01	STEEL
SONATINA NO. 02--FUR DIE JUGEND	SCHIFF, A.
SONATINA NO. 02, OP. 10--1962	TJEKNAVORIAN, L.
SONATINA NO. 02, OP. 11	FUSSAN
SONATINA NO. 02, OP. 12 NO. 2	POSER
SONATINA NO. 02, OP. 36	CLEMENTI
SONATINA NO. 02 IN F	BEETHOVEN
SONATINA NO. 02 IN F	BEETHOVEN
SONATINA NO. 02 IN F	BEETHOVEN
SONATINA NO. 02 IN G	HUMBERT, G.
SONATINA NO. 02	ARCHER, V.
SONATINA NO. 02	BABIN
SONATINA NO. 02	BEETHOVEN
SONATINA NO. 02	BUSONI
SONATINA NO. 02	DEMENASCE, J.
SONATINA NO. 02	ESCOBAR, L.
SONATINA NO. 02	KUHLAU, F.
SONATINA NO. 02	LIER
SONATINA NO. 02	MOPPER, I.
SONATINA NO. 02	POLDINI, E.
SONATINA NO. 02	RAPHLING

Title	Composer
SONATINA NO. 02	RAPHLING
SONATINA NO. 02	STEEL
SONATINA NO. 02	TOSAR
SONATINA NO. 03--1933--	TANSMAN, A.
SONATINA NO. 03, OP. 28	ORTHEL
SONATINA NO. 03, OP. 44 NO. 1	POSER
SONATINA NO. 03, 1959	GENZMER
SONATINA NO. 03 IN THE TREBLE CLEF	GUARNIERI
SONATINA NO. 03	AGAY, D.
SONATINA NO. 03	AGAY, D.
SONATINA NO. 03	BEETHOVEN
SONATINA NO. 03	DEMENASCE, J.
SONATINA NO. 03	LAZARE-LEVY
SONATINA NO. 03	POLDINI, E.
SONATINA NO. 04, OP. 44 NO. 2	POSER
SONATINA NO. 04	BEETHOVEN
SONATINA NO. 05	BEETHOVEN
SONATINA NO. 06	BEETHOVEN
SONATINA NO. 2	KOCH, F.
SONATINA ON HUNGARIAN FOLKSONGS, OP. 23D	KADOSA
SONATINA OP. 20 NO. 1	KUHLAU, F.
SONATINA OP. 36 NO. 1	CLEMENTI
SONATINA OP. 48 NO. 3 -- SPRINGTIME	HOLST
SONATINA OP. 55 NO. 1	KUHLAU, F.
SONATINA PATETICA, OP. 39	THILMAN
SONATINA PERBREVIS AD USUM PETRI ET KAROLI MARIAE	NIELSEN, R.
SONATINA RITMICA	CORDERO, R.
SONATINA SCHOOL, BK. 1	KEIGHLEY, T.
SONATINA SCHOOL, BK. 2	KEIGHLEY, T.
SONATINA SCHOOL, BK. 3	KEIGHLEY, T.
SONATINA SERIA, OP. 51 NO. 1	RAPHAEL, G.
SONATINA TOCCATA	AGAY, D.
SONATINA ZOOLOGICA	CASTELNUOVO-TEDE
SONATINA	ABRIL
SONATINA	AMENGUAL, R.
SONATINA	AURIC
SONATINA	BARTOK
SONATINA	BARTOK
SONATINA	BARTOK
SONATINA	BAUERNFEIND
SONATINA	BERGER
SONATINA	BERLIN, J. D.
SONATINA	CASELLA, A.
SONATINA	CHAVEZ, C.
SONATINA	DEMARQUEZ
SONATINA	DIAMOND, D.
SONATINA	DOLIN
SONATINA	ETLER
SONATINA	ETTI
SONATINA	FORTNER, W.
SONATINA	FUGA
SONATINA	GIANNEO
SONATINA	GIURANNA
SONATINA	GOLDMAN, R.
SONATINA	GRISOLIA
SONATINA	GUASTAVINO
SONATINA	HAJDU, M.
SONATINA	HANDEL
SONATINA	HOVHANESS, A.
SONATINA	IRELAND, J.
SONATINA	KADOSA
SONATINA	KASZYCKI
SONATINA	KHATCHATURIAN
SONATINA	KHATCHATURIAN
SONATINA	KOUTZEN, B.
SONATINA	KUBIK, G.
SONATINA	LAKS
SONATINA	LANDOWSKI
SONATINA	LANGSTROTH, I.
SONATINA	LEOZ, J.G.
SONATINA	LIEBERMAN, F.
SONATINA	LOPEZ BUCHARDO
SONATINA	MASCAGNI, A.
SONATINA	MELECCI, A.
SONATINA	MOY, E.
SONATINA	OSBORNE, W.
SONATINA	PEPPING, E.
SONATINA	POWELL, MEL
SONATINA	REITER, A.
SONATINA	RIETI
SONATINA	ROBERTS
SONATINA	RODRIGUEZ, C.
SONATINA	RODRIGUEZ, R.
SONATINA	RUIZ ARMENGOL,
SONATINA	RUYNEMAN
SONATINA	SARAI, T.
SONATINA	SAYGUN, A.
SONATINA	SCHWARZ-SCHILLIN
SONATINA	STRATEGIER
SONATINA	SURINACH, C.
SONATINA	TANSMAN, A.
SONATINA	TARDOS, B.
SONATINA	THIRIET
SONATINA	THOMPSON, J.
SONATINA	TRIMBLE
SONATINA	VERETTI
SONATINA	WAGNER, J.
SONATINA	WAGNER, W.
SONATINA	WISOFF, G.
SONATINA	ZULAWSKI
SONATINA 1931	KOUTZEN, B.
SONATINE, OP. 110 NO. 1 G-DUR	GRETCHANINOFF
SONATINE, OP. 110 NO. 2 F-DUR	GRETCHANINOFF
SONATINE, OP. 16	ROUSSEL, A.
SONATINE, OP. 17	HESSENBERG, K.
SONATINE, OP. 49 NO. 1	LICHNER, H.
SONATINE, OP. 49 NO. 2	LICHNER, H.
SONATINEN ALTER TSCHECHISCHER MEISTER, 22 STUCKE	BENDA, R. *
SONATINEN UND 36	CLEMENTI
SONATINEN UND RONDI, HEFT 1	CLEMENTI *
SONATINEN UND RONDI, HEFT 2	HAYDN *
SONATINEN UND STUCKE FUR DEN KLAVIERUNTERRICHT, HEFT	ZUSCHNEID,
SONATINEN UND STUCKE FUR DEN KLAVIERUNTERRICHT, HEFT	ZUSCHNEID,
SONATINEN UND STUCKE FUR DEN KLAVIERUNTERRICHT, HEFT	ZUSCHNEID,
SONATINEN UND STUCKE FUR DEN KLAVIERUNTERRICHT, HEFT	ZUSCHNEID,
SONATINEN VORSTUFE --PREPARATORY SONATINA ALBUM--,	
SONATINEN VORSTUFE --PREPARATORY SONATINA ALBUM--,	
SONATINETTA, OP. 78B	TSCHAIKOWSKY
SONATINE -- 1930 --	KAPRAL
SONATINE -- 1944 --	KAPRAL
SONATINE ALLA SUITE -- FOUR MOVEMENTS	COBB
SONATINE BRILLANTE	CZERNY
SONATINE CLASSIQUE -- IN THREE MOVEMENTS	COBB
SONATINE CLAVECIN	BOUTRY
SONATINE HELLENIQUE	DESSAGNES
SONATINE IN A, OP. 48 NO. 1	MARX
SONATINE IN A MINOR, OP. 61	ALKAN

Title	Composer
SONATINE IN A MINOR	KABALEVSKY
SONATINE IN A MINOR	THOMPSON, J.
SONATINE IN D MINOR FUR CEMBALO, 2 QUERFLOTEN UND	BACH, C.P.E.
SONATINE IN D MINOR	FIBICH, Z.
SONATINE IN E, OP. 48 NO. 5	MARX
SONATINE IN E FLAT FUR CEMBALO, 2 QUERFLOTEN UND	BACH, C.P.E.
SONATINE IN F SHARP	RAVEL
SONATINE IN HARPSICHORD STYLE	THOMPSON, J.
SONATINE MONODIQUE	OHANA, M.
SONATINE NO. 03	MARTINON, J.
SONATINE NO. 04 SUR LES MODES HINDOUS	EMMANUEL, M.
SONATINE NUOVE, NO. 6	BACH, C.P.E.
SONATINE PASTORALLE, OP. 59 NO. 3	PROKOFIEFF
SONATINE ROMANTIQUE	TCHEREPNIN
SONATINE TRANSATLANTIQUE	TANSMAN, A.
SONATINE TRANSATLANTIQUE	TANSMAN, A.
SONATINE	BADINGS
SONATINE	BECK, C.
SONATINE	BITSCH
SONATINE	COELHO, P.M.R.
SONATINE	GERSTER, O.
SONATINE	GILLOCK
SONATINE	GILLOCK
SONATINE	KLOTZMAN, D. H.
SONATINE	KVAPIL
SONATINE	MERLET
SONATINE	MIGOT
SONATINE	MILHAUD, D.
SONATINE	MIRANDOLLE
SONATINE	MOYZES, M.
SONATINE	RAVEL
SONATINE	RAVEL
SONATINE	RAVEL
SONATINE	RAVEL
SONATINE	SCHMITT
SONATINE	SCHWARZ-SCHILLIN
SONATINE	STORR, S.
SONATINE 2	BECK, C.
SONETTE	LUCAS, T.
SONETTO 104 DEL PETRARCA--FROM DEUXIEME ANNEE DE	LISZT
SONETTO 123 DEL PETRARCA--FROM DEUXIEME ANNEE DE	LISZT
SONG, A	BACH, J.S.
SONGES, LES -- BALLET --	MILHAUD, D.
SONGES ROSES	WESLY
SONGMAN	
SONGS AND DANCES FOR LITTLE PIANISTS	CURCIO
SONGS AND RHYMES FOR HAPPY TIMES	SASLAW, E.
SONGS AND RIMES OF LATIN AMERICA	SASLAW, E.--ED
SONGS EN FRANCAIS	MALTZMAN--ED
SONGS FOR ALL YEAR LONG AND GOSH, WHAT A WONDERFUL	SLOTE, G. --ED
SONGS FOR BEGINNERS TO PLAY	KAHL
SONGS FOR CHRISTMAS-TIME	KASSCHAU, H.
SONGS FOR OUR TIMES	BAEZ, J.
SONGS FOR THE FRENCH CLASS -- LES CHANSONS POUR LA	DE CESARE
SONGS FOR THE GERMAN CLASS -- LIEDER FUR DIE DEUTSHE	DE CESARE
SONGS FOR THE ITALIAN CLASS -- CANZONI PER LA CLASSE	DE CESARE
SONGS FOR THE LITTLEST	PETRALIA
SONGS FOR THE SPANISH CLASS -- CANCIONES PARA LA CLASE	DE CESARE
SONGS FROM 'GREENWILLOW'	LOESSER, F.
SONGS FROM 'HANS CHRISTIAN ANDERSEN'	LOESSER, F.
SONGS FROM 'HOW TO SUCCEED IN BUSINESS WITHOUT REALLY	LOESSER, F.
SONGS FROM 'KISMET'	WRIGHT, R. *
SONGS FROM 'THE MUSIC MAN'	WILLSON, M.
SONGS FROM 'THE PAJAMA GAME'	ADLER, R. *
SONGS FROM 'THE UNSINKABLE MOLLY BROWN'	WILLSON, M.
SONGS FROM 'THE WORLD IS A GHETTO'	
SONGS FROM MUR ISLAND --SMALL PIANO SOLOS--	TAJCEVIC, M.
SONGS FROM THE OPERA SCHWARZER PETER	SCHULTZE
SONGS I CAN PLAY -- FOR THE EARLY BEGINNER	RICHTER
SONGS I SING IN SUNDAY SCHOOL	BOCK, F.--ED
SONGS MY MOTHER TAUGHT ME	DVORAK
SONGS MY MOTHER TAUGHT ME	DVORAK
SONGS MY MOTHER TAUGHT ME	DVORAK
SONGS OF AMERICANS	RICHTER
SONGS OF AMERICA	ECKHARDT, F.
SONGS OF A SWISS SUMMER	ALT, H.--ED
SONGS OF DON MCLEAN, THE	MCLEAN, D.
SONGS OF FAITH	FREEMAN--ED.
SONGS OF FAITH	STICKLES--ED
SONGS OF FRANCE	ECKHARDT, F.
SONGS OF FREDDIE HART, THE	HART, F.
SONGS OF HOPE AND INSPIRATION	
SONGS OF ITALY	ECKHARDT, F.
SONGS OF MY COUNTRY	RICHTER, A.--ED.
SONGS OF SCOTLAND	ECKHARDT, F.
SONGS OF SONNY JAMES	JAMES, S.
SONGS OF STEPHEN FOSTER	RICHTER, A.--ED.
SONGS OF THE GULF OF NAPLES	ROSSELLINI
SONGS OF THE SPIRIT - EASY HYMN ARRANGEMENTS FOR PIANO	SCARMOLIN--ED
SONGS WE LOVE TO PLAY	MENDELSSOHN
SONGS WITHOUR WORDS, NOS. 25-48	MENDELSSOHN
SONGS WITHOUT WORDS, NO. 01--SWEET REMEMBRANCE, OP. 19	MENDELSSOHN
SONGS WITHOUT WORDS, NO. 03--HUNTING-SONG, OP. 19 NO.	MENDELSSOHN
SONGS WITHOUT WORDS, NO. 04--CONFIDENCE, OP. 19 NO. 4	MENDELSSOHN
SONGS WITHOUT WORDS, NO. 06--VENETIAN BOAT-SONG NO. 1,	MENDELSSOHN
SONGS WITHOUT WORDS, NO. 09--CONSOLATION, OP. 30 NO. 3	MENDELSSOHN
SONGS WITHOUT WORDS, NO. 11--THE BROOK, OP. 30 NO. 5	MENDELSSOHN
SONGS WITHOUT WORDS, NO. 12--VENETIAN BOAT-SONG NO. 2,	MENDELSSOHN
SONGS WITHOUT WORDS, NO. 18--DUET, OP. 38 NO. 6	MENDELSSOHN
SONGS WITHOUT WORDS, NO. 29--VENETIAN BOAT-SONG NO. 3,	MENDELSSOHN
SONGS WITHOUT WORDS, NO. 30--SPRING-SONG, OP. 62 NO. 6	MENDELSSOHN
SONGS WITHOUT WORDS, NO. 34--SPINNING-SONG, OP. 67 NO.	MENDELSSOHN
SONGS WITHOUT WORDS, NO. 45--TARANTELLA, OP. 102 NO. 3	MENDELSSOHN
SONGS WITHOUT WORDS, NOS. 1-24	MENDELSSOHN
SONGS WITHOUT WORDS, OP. 17	FAURE, G.
SONGS WITHOUT WORDS, OP. 19 NO. 3	MENDELSSOHN
SONGS WITHOUT WORDS, OP. 19 NO. 4	MENDELSSOHN
SONGS WITHOUT WORDS, OP. 19 NO. 6	MENDELSSOHN
SONGS WITHOUT WORDS, OP. 30 NO. 3	MENDELSSOHN
SONGS WITHOUT WORDS, OP. 30 NO. 34	MENDELSSOHN
SONGS WITHOUT WORDS, OP. 82	TCHEREPNIN
SONGS WITHOUT WORDS, 11 SELECTED PIECES	MENDELSSOHN
SONGS WITHOUT WORDS -- SELECTIONS --	MENDELSSOHN
SONGS WITHOUT WORDS AND CHILDREN'S PIECES	MENDELSSOHN
SONGS WITHOUT WORDS	MENDELSSOHN
SONGS WITHOUT WORDS	MENDELSSOHN
SONGS WITH HAPPY THOUGHTS	BURNAM
SONGS	CHOPIN
SONG AND SOLO HIGHLIGHTS	ZEPP--ED
SONG AT TWILIGHT	TAYLOR, EDNA
SONG CARGO	MAIER, A.
SONG FOR ANNIE LOU	HOPKINS, H.
SONG FROM 'HARY JANOS'	KODALY, Z.
SONG FROM MASH	BRIMHALL,
SONG FROM OLD CHINATOWN	STEINER
SONG FROM THE EAST, A, OP. 54 NO. 2	SCOTT, C.

Title	Composer
SONG FROM THE HILLS	STEVENS, E.
SONG GEMS FROM CHOPIN	CHOPIN
SONG IN THE WOODS, A	HUNTEN, F.
SONG IS YOU	
SONG OF 'THE BIBLE'	LANE, J.--ED.
SONG OF EVENING -- RIGHT HAND ALONE	WEYBRIGHT
SONG OF HEAVEN	SWEET, A.
SONG OF INDIA--FROM 'SADKO'	RIMSKY-KORSAKOFF
SONG OF INDIA, A FROM 'SADKO'	RIMSKY-KORSAKOFF
SONG OF INDIA -- SIMP.	RIMSKY-KORSAKOFF
SONG OF INDIA	RIMSKY-KORSAKOFF
SONG OF INDIA	RIMSKY-KORSAKOFF
SONG OF INDIA	RIMSKY-KORSAKOFF
SONG OF INDIA	RIMSKY-KORSAKOFF
SONG OF JOY, A	LANE, J.--ED.
SONG OF JOY, THE	LANE, J.--ED.
SONG OF JOY	BEETHOVEN
SONG OF LONG AGO	BRADLEY,
SONG OF LOVE -- ROMANCE OP. 44, NO. 1	RUBINSTEIN
SONG OF LOVE	LANE, J.--ED.
SONG OF LOVE	
SONG OF LOVE	
SONG OF NORWAY	
SONG OF RUSSIA	TSCHAIKOWSKY
SONG OF SICILY	CRESTON
SONG OF SONGS	
SONG OF SPRING, A	STUBBLEFIELD
SONG OF THE ALPS, OP. 51	RYDER
SONG OF THE BAMBOO TREE	BENTLEY
SONG OF THE BAYOU	BLOOM, R.
SONG OF THE BAYOU	
SONG OF THE BAYOU	
SONG OF THE BELLS AND HORNPIPE	DRING
SONG OF THE BELLS	ANDERSON, L.
SONG OF THE BELLS	FINLAYSON, W.
SONG OF THE BELLS	TILLETT, J.
SONG OF THE BELL	ECKSTEIN
SONG OF THE BROOK, OP. 92	LACK, T.
SONG OF THE BROOK	LACK, T.
SONG OF THE BROOK	LACK, T.
SONG OF THE BROOK	SCHIEFELBEIN, F.
SONG OF THE CELLO	ROBINSON, W. E.
SONG OF THE CLOCK	IBBOTSON, E. M.
SONG OF THE DRUM	RISHER, A. P.
SONG OF THE FATHERLAND, OP. 12 NO. 8	GRIEG
SONG OF THE FLOWER	DRIVER, P.
SONG OF THE ISLANDS	KING
SONG OF THE ISLANDS	KING
SONG OF THE ISLANDS	KING
SONG OF THE ISLANDS	KING
SONG OF THE LARK, OP. 39 NO. 22	TSCHAIKOWSKY
SONG OF THE LARK, OP. 39 NO. 22	TSCHAIKOWSKY
SONG OF THE LARK, THE	TSCHAIKOWSKY
SONG OF THE MARINER	STEINER
SONG OF THE MOCKING BIRD	HART, G. R.
SONG OF THE MOUNTAINS	GERSCHEFSKI, E.
SONG OF THE MOUNTAIN BROOK	KUNKILL
SONG OF THE NIGHT	CHOPIN
SONG OF THE ORCHID	MELACHRINO, G.
SONG OF THE PINES	ADAIR, M.
SONG OF THE PRAIRIE	DVORINE
SONG OF THE RAILS	PLACE
SONG OF THE RAIN	BLAKE, D.
SONG OF THE RANGE	GREEN
SONG OF THE ROBIN	WARREN
SONG OF THE SAGEBRUSH	MCGRAW
SONG OF THE SEESAW	RISHER, A. P.
SONG OF THE SWALLOW	BOHM
SONG OF THE TREES	SURREY, C.
SONG OF THE VALLEY	HAUFRECHT
SONG OF THE VOLGA BOATMAN	GREENWALD,
SONG OF THE VOLGA BOATMAN	ROLFE, W.--ED
SONG OF THE WANDERER	MCCLUSKY
SONG OF THE WILD BEE	BENTLEY
SONG OF THE WILLOW	COPELAND, B.
SONG SHINDIG	KAHN, M. *
SONG SONATINA	GREEN, R.
SONG SUNG BLUE	BRIMHALL,
SONG TRANSCRIPTIONS	LISZT
SONG TUNE, THEATRE TUNE	BLOW
SONG WITHOUT WORDS, OP. 2 NO. 3	TSCHAIKOWSKY
SONG WITHOUT WORDS, OP. 2 NO. 3	TSCHAIKOWSKY
SONG WITHOUT WORDS, OP. 97 NO. 3 --ROMANCE SANS	STREABBOG
SONG WITHOUT WORDS, OP. 97 NO. 3	STREABBOG
SONG WITHOUT WORDS, OP. 97	STREABBOG
SONG WITHOUT WORDS	HANSEN
SONG WITHOUT WORDS	HOELZEL
SONG WITHOUT WORDS	SHAPERO, H.
SONG WITHOUT WORDS	TSCHAIKOWSKY
SONG WITHOUT WORDS	TSCHAIKOWSKY
SONG WITHOUT WORDS	TSCHAIKOWSKY
SONG WITHOUT WORDS	WRIGHT, N.
SONG WITHOUT WORDS	WRIGHT, N.
SONLUCAR DE BARRAMEDA--PROGRAM SONATA, OP. 24	TURINA, J.
SONNAMBULA, LA - EASY FANTASIA	BELLINI
SONNERIES DE LA ROSE-CROIX	SATIE, E.
SONNET POUR DALLAPICCOLA	WORONOFF, W.
SONNET	VOORMOLEN
SONORITES RYTHMIQUES	FREED, I.
SONS OF BACH -- THREE SONATAS FOR KEYBOARD	BACH, J.
SOONER AND LATER	WHITHORNE
SOPHIE UND SONATINE FUR SCHULE UND HAUS, AN	KONT, P.
SOPHISTICATED LADY -- SIMP.	MOSSMAN, T.
SOPHISTICATED LADY	ELLINGTON
SOPHISTICATED LADY	GOULD, M.
SOPHISTICATED LADY	MERKUR--ED
SOPHISTICATED SWING	MERKUR--ED
SOPHOMORE MARCH	PANELLA, L.
SORCERER'S APPRENTICE, THE	DUKAS, P.
SORCERER'S APPRENTICE	DUKAS, P.
SORCERER'S APPRENTICE	DUKAS, P.
SORRENTINA	VOLPATTI
SORRETO -- 1 PIANO 6 HANDS --	BILLI
SORRISI DI BIMBA, BK. 1	RINALDI
SORRISI INFANTILI - 25 LITTLE PIECES ON 5 NOTES	POZZOLI
SORRISI	BECUCCI
SORROW FOR A QUEEN	CHISOLM
SORROW OF A LONELY HEART	SALTA
SOUBENIRS DE MUNICH -- FANTASY IN FOR OF QUADRILLES,	CHABRIER
SOULAR BEAR	GLOVER, D.
SOUL MAKOSSA	
SOUNDFIGURES	ALEXANDER, H.
SOUNDS AND SILENCES, OP. 78	TAKACS, J.
SOUNDS FROM THE RINGING ROCKS	WALTERS
SOUNDS OF AUTUMN, REVERIE	OMER, BRO.
SOUNDS OF HOLLYWOOD	METIS--ED.

Title	Composer
SOUNDS OF HOLLYWOOD	METIS--ED.
SOUNDS OF THE SEVENTIES	BRIMHALL.
SOUND OF MUSIC, THE.	HAMMERSTEIN *
SOUND OF MUSIC, THE.	HAMMERSTEIN *
SOUND OF MUSIC, THE.	HAMMERSTEIN *
SOUND OF MUSIC, THE -- BEGINNERS PIANO BOOK	HAMMERSTEIN *
SOUND OF MUSIC, THE	BRIMHALL,
SOUND OF MUSIC, THE.	HAMMERSTEIN *
SOUND OF MUSIC SELECTIONS	RODGERS *
SOUND OF THE DRUMS	BRODSKY, M.
SOUND PIECE NO. 5 'SONATA FOR PIANO'	BECKER
SOUND TRACKS - SEVEN LITTLE PIECES	RAPHLING
SOUND TRACKS - 7 LITTLE PIECES	RAPHLING
SOURCE DE MON PAYS, LA	GALLON, J.
SOUSA'S FAMOUS MARCHES FOR PIANO SOLO	SOUSA
SOUSAPHONE SERENADE	OLSON
SOUSA ALBUM FOR PIANO SOLO	SOUSA
SOUSA ALBUM	SOUSA
SOUSA ALBUM	SOUSA
SOUS BOIS, OP. 6	STAUB, V.
SOUS BOIS, OP. 6	STAUB, V.
SOUS BOIS, OP. 6	STAUB, V.
SOUS L'OMBRAGE -- WALTZ --	GAUTIER, L.
SOUS L'OMBRAGE	GAUTIER, L.
SOUS LES CHENES, VALSE	THUILLIER
SOUS LES LAURIERS ROSES	SEVERAC
SOUS LE PALMIER, OP. 232, NO. 3 --FROM CANTOS DE	ALBENIZ, I.
SOUS LE PALMIER, OP. 232, NO. 3 -- FROM CANTOS DE	ALBENIZ, I.
SOUS UN BALCON	DE WAILLY
SOUTHERN ACCENT	SCHAUM, J.--ED.
SOUTHERN SONATINA	STONE, E.
SOUTHWARD FLOWS THE RIVER	COOK, P.
SOUTH AMERICAN PIANO MUSIC	LEVINE
SOUTH OF THE BORDER	BRYANT--ED.
SOUTH OF THE BORDER	KENNEDY *
SOUTH OF THE BORDER	MELECCI, A.
SOUTH OF THE RIO GRANDE	MILLER, J.
SOUTH PACIFIC	HAMMERSTEIN *
SOUTH PACIFIC	HAMMERSTEIN *
SOUTH RAMPART STREET PARADE	BAUDUC *
SOUVENIRS--BALLET SUITE, OP. 28	BARBER, S.
SOUVENIRS, OP. 28	BARBER, S.
SOUVENIRS -- SET	BARBER, S.
SOUVENIRS DE L'ANCIENNE ESPAGNE - DON JUAN	TURINA, J.
SOUVENIRS DE L'ANCIENNE ESPAGNE - ESTUDIANTINA	TURINA, J.
SOUVENIRS DE L'ANCIENNE ESPAGNE - HABANERA	TURINA, J.
SOUVENIRS DE L'ANCIENNE ESPAGNE - L'ETERNELLE CARMEN	TURINA, J.
SOUVENIRS DE L'ANCIENNE ESPAGNE	TURINA, J.
SOUVENIRS DE TAVERNY -- 7 PIECES --	GODARD
SOUVENIRS FOR PIANO	BRISMAN, H.
SOUVENIR DES CHAMPS	GALOS
SOUVENIR DE CHOPIN	HONEGGER, A.
SOUVENIR DE PORTO RICO	GOTTSCHALK
SOUVENIR DU BRESIL, OP. 10	POLONIO
SOUVENIR DU BRESIL	POLONIO
SOUVENIR DU TYROL - WALTZ NO. 1	LANDRY
SOUVENIR DU TYROL	LANDRY
SOUVENIR DU TYROL	LANDRY
SOUVENIR RUSSE, OP. 9	ISSERLIS, J.
SOUVENIR	DRDLA, F.
SOUVENIR	DRDLA, F.
SOUVENIR	DRDLA, F.
SOUVENIR	DRDLA, F.
SOUVENIR	DRDLA, F.
SOUVENIR	KARGANOFF
SO EASY	WILSON, S.
SO EASY	WILSON, S.
SO FAR AWAY	BRADLEY,
SO IN LOVE	PORTER, C.
SO LONG MARY	COHAN
SO MERRILY DANCING AND POOR LITTLE AUGUSTINE, ONE	MACGREGOR
SO NICE	BRIMHALL,
SO RARE	LANE, J.--ED.
SO SINGT MAN IN WIEN -- 32 FAMOUS VIENNESE SONGS IN	STEINBRECHER--ED
SO SLEEPY	WIGHAM, M.
SO YOU WON'T JUMP	RAMEY *
SPACE BOOGIE	ZEPP--ED
SPACE EXPLORERS	BASTIEN
SPACE EXPLORERS	BROWN, A.
SPACE EXPLORER	SCHAUM, J.--ED.
SPACE FLIGHT	ANSON, G.
SPACE FLIGHT	ANSON, G.
SPACE FLIGHT	LEE, E.
SPACE FLIGHT	NEVIN
SPACE PATROL	DAVIS, J.
SPACE TRAVELOGUE	BURNAM
SPACE WALK	SCHAUM, W.
SPAGHETTI RAG	LYONS *
SPAIN ON PARADE	
SPAIN	POOLE, C.
SPANISCHER MARSCH	RIXNER, J.
SPANISH AND LATIN AMERICAN SONGS AND DANCES	
SPANISH BLUES	KAHN, M.
SPANISH CAPRICE	MOSZKOWSKI
SPANISH CARNIVAL	HATCH
SPANISH COMPOSERS ALBUM	ALBENIZ, M. *
SPANISH DANCE, A	BUSSEY, M.
SPANISH DANCE, OP. 12, NO. 1. TWO PIANOS, EIGHT HANDS	MOSZKOWSKI
SPANISH DANCE, OP. 12 NO. 1 FLAMENCA --GYPSY DANCE--	MOSZKOWSKI
SPANISH DANCE, OP. 12 NO. 1	MOSZKOWSKI
SPANISH DANCE, OP. 12 NO. 1	MOSZKOWSKI
SPANISH DANCE, OP. 12 NO. 1	WEYBRIGHT
SPANISH DANCE, OP. 12 NO. 2 ROMANCE IN CORDOVA	MOSZKOWSKI
SPANISH DANCE, OP. 12 NO. 3 JUANA --ANDALUSIAN VITO--	MOSZKOWSKI
SPANISH DANCE, OP. 12 NO. 5 BOLERO --SIMPLIFIED--	MOSZKOWSKI
SPANISH DANCE, OP. 12 NO. 5 BOLERO	MOSZKOWSKI
SPANISH DANCE, OP. 12 NO. 5	MOSZKOWSKI
SPANISH DANCE, OP. 24	ASCHER
SPANISH DANCER, OP. 14 NO. 6	COPELAND, C.
SPANISH DANCERS	WATSON
SPANISH DANCES, OP. 12. NOS. 1, 2, 4	MOSZKOWSKI
SPANISH DANCES, OP. 12, NOS. 3, 5	LOSZKOWSKI
SPANISH DANCES, OP. 12 NO. 1	MOSZKOWSKI
SPANISH DANCES, OP. 12 NO. 5--BOLERO	MOSZKOWSKI
SPANISH DANCES, OP. 12	MOSZKOWSKI
SPANISH DANCES, OP. 12	MOSZKOWSKI
SPANISH DANCES, OP. 12	MOSZKOWSKI
SPANISH DANCES, OP. 22 NOS. 1 AND 2	SARASTE
SPANISH DANCE NO. 02	MOSZKOWSKI
SPANISH DANCE NO. 1 -- FROM ''LA VIE BREVE''	FALLA, M. DE
SPANISH DANCE NO. 1 -- FROM ''LA VIE BREVE''	FALLA, M. DE
SPANISH DANCE NO. 1	MOSZKOWSKI
SPANISH DANCE NO. 2 -- FROM ''LA VIE BREVE''	FALLA, M. DE
SPANISH DANCE NO. 2	MOSZKOWSKI
SPANISH DANCE NO. 4	MOSZKOWSKI
SPANISH DANCE NO. 5	MOSZKOWSKI

SPANISH DANCE OP. 12 NO. 1	MOSZKOWSKI
SPANISH DANCE	ELAINE, SR.
SPANISH DANCE	GRANADOS
SPANISH DANCE	GREENWALD, M.
SPANISH DANCE	KETTERER, E.
SPANISH DANCE	PFITZER, H.
SPANISH DANCE	ROGERS, F.
SPANISH DANCE	SHOSTAKOVITCH
SPANISH EYES	BRADLEY,
SPANISH FIESTA, A	THOMPSON, J.
SPANISH FLEA	BRIMHALL,
SPANISH GUITARS	SCHER, W.
SPANISH GYPSY DANCE	MOWREY, D.
SPANISH GYPSY	SCHER, W.
SPANISH LULLABY	ROBINSON, A.
SPANISH MAIDEN -- LA SPAGNOLA --	VI CHIARI
SPANISH MARIONETTES	CUI, C.
SPANISH MUSIC OF THE 15TH AND 16TH CENTURIES FOR THE	REE-BERNARD
SPANISH RHAPSODY--ARRANGED FOR PIANO AND ORCHESTRA	LISZT
SPANISH RHAPSODY	LISZT
SPANISH ROSES	ECKSTEIN
SPANISH SERENADE	OLSON
SPANISH SERENADE	REISER, V.
SPANISH SERENADE	STRELEZKI
SPANISH STUDENTS, WALTZES, EASY	WALDTEUFEL, E.
SPANISH STUDENTS, WALTZES	WALDTEUFEL, E.
SPANISH SURF	MEUX
SPANISH WALTZ	KRAEHENBUEHL
SPARKLERS	MCGRAW *
SPARKLES	KETTERER, E.
SPARKLETS	MILES
SPARKLETS	MILES
SPARKLETS	MILES
SPARKLING EYES	ANTHONY, B. R.
SPARKLING FINGERS	MILLER
SPARKLING FIREFLIES	MATTINGLY, J.
SPARKLING STARS	WHEELER, V. B.
SPARKS FROM OTHER ANVILS	THOMPSON, J.--ED
SPARKS	MOSZKOWSKI
SPARKS	THOMPSON, J.
SPATIALS - VARIATIONS FOR PIANO	WALKER, G.
SPATIALS - VARIATIONS FOR PIANO	WALKER, G.
SPAZZACAMINO, LO	VERDI
SPEAK LOW	SINGER, L.--ED
SPEAK SOFTLY LOVE--THE GODFATHER--	BRIMHALL,
SPECIAL STUDIES, VOL. 1* 20 STUDIES FOR THE LEFT HAND	FERTE--ED
SPECIAL STUDIES, VOL. 2* 20 STUDIES FOR BOTH HANDS	FERTE--ED
SPECIAL STUDIES, VOL. 3* 20 OCTAVE STUDIES	FERTE--ED
SPECTRA	MATSUSHITA, S.
SPECTRUM	KAHN, M.
SPECTRUM	WUENSCH
SPEEDING SATELLITE	HOPSON, E.
SPEKTRA	WALKER, G.
SPEKTRA	WALKER, G.
SPEKTREN FUR KLAVIER	RIEMANN, A.
SPELLBOUND CONCERTO -- THEME	ROSZA
SPELLBOUND CONCERTO	ROSZA
SPELLING FUN	ROGERS, E.
SPELLING LESSONS IN TIME AND NOTATION	BILBRO, M.
SPICECAKE WALK	PRESS
SPIDERS, FOR HARPSICHORD	ROREM, N.
SPIDER DANCE	NOONA, W.
SPIELBUCH, HEFT 01	GENZMER
SPIELBUCH, HEFT 02	GENZMER
SPIELBUCHLEIN FUR DEN ERSTEN ANFANG	
SPIELBUCHLEIN FUR DEN ERSTEN ANFANG	
SPIELBUCH FUR UTE. 50 KINDERLIEDER FUR DEN ERSTEN	BUECHTGER
SPIELDOSE, DIE--1951	STROHBACH, S.
SPIELDOSE -- ORIGINAL	SAUER
SPIELMUSIK. EINE REIHE 15 KLEINER STUCKE FUR KLAVIER	DEGEN
SPIELSTUCKE FUR KLAVIER. 36 STUCKE AUS DEM 'GETREUEN	TELEMANN, G.P.
SPIELSTUCKE FUR KLAVIER	TELEMANN, G.P.
SPIELZEUGKISTE, DIE--1952	STROHBACH, S.
SPIEL MIT FUNF TONEN. LIEDER UND STUCKE FUR DEN ERSTEN	EMONTS, F.--ED
SPIGOLATRICI, LE	ZANUTTA
SPIN, SPIN, ESTHONIAN FOLK SONG	ROSSI
SPIN, SPIN, SPIN	ROZIN
SPINGTIME SONATINA OP. 48 NO. 3 -- AWAY WITH THE	HOLST
SPINNER, THE	BAMPTON, R.
SPINNING-WHEEL, OP. 35 NO. 3	CHAMINADE
SPINNING AROUND	ARNOLD, H.
SPINNING SONG, A	ELLMENREICH, A.
SPINNING SONG, OP. 14 NO. 4	ELLMENREICH, A.
SPINNING SONG, OP. 14 NO. 4	ELLMENREICH, A.
SPINNING SONG, OP. 14 NO. 4	ELLMENREICH, A.
SPINNING SONG, S.W.W., 34	MENDELSSOHN
SPINNING SONG -- DUTCH BRIDE'S DANCE -- 12-HANDS, SET	MACGREGOR
SPINNING SONG	ELLMENREICH, A.
SPINNING SONG	ELLMENREICH, A.
SPINNING SONG	ELLMENREICH, A.
SPINNING TOP, THE	ANSON, G.
SPINNING TOP, THE	KETTERER, E.
SPINNING TO THE TOP	CROSBY, M.
SPINNING WHEEL, ETUDE	RAFF, J.
SPINNING WHEEL OF OMPHALE	SAINT-SAENS
SPINNING WHEEL	RAWICZ
SPIRITUALS AT THE PIANO	TOLSON, P.
SPIRIT FILLED SONGS	
SPIRIT OF AMERICA	PANELLA, L.
SPIRIT OF LIBERTY	KING
SPIRIT OF OUR BOYS	DENARD
SPIRIT OF THE U. S. A.	COBB
SPIRIT WALTZ	BEETHOVEN
SPOOKS ON HALLOWEEN	BASTIEN
SPOOKS ON PARADE	KEVAN
SPOOKS	ALT, H.
SPOOKS	DUNGAN
SPOOKS	ECKSTEIN
SPOOKS	POOLE, C.
SPOOKS	SALTER, L.
SPOOKY FAIRY TALE, A	SCHER, W.
SPOOKY GAMES	GLOVER, D.
SPOOKY HALLOWE'EN	ROBINSON, A.
SPOOKY HOLLOW	BROWN, A.
SPOOKY NIGHTMARE	ROLSETH, B.
SPOOKY NIGHTS	BEISSERT
SPOOK ON THE STAIRS	ANSON, G.
SPOON BREAD	BLACK, M.
SPOON RIVER, AMERICAN FOLKDANCE -- SET	GRAINGER, P.
SPORTS-A-RAMA	SCHER, W.
SPORTS ET DIVERTISSEMENTS	SATIE, E.
SPOSALIZIO--FROM DEUXIEME ANNEE DE PELERINAGE	LISZT
SPOTTED GIRAFFE, THE.	COBB
SPRAY PERFUME	BURNAM
SPRING, SWEET SPRING	LINCKE, P.
SPRING'S AWAKENING, OP. 3 NO. 1	ESPEN, T.
SPRING'S AWAKENING	BACH, C.P.E.
SPRING'S GREETING	MENDELSSOHN
SPRINGTANZ	SMETANA
SPRINGTIME DANCE	LOTH, L.
SPRINGTIME IN SORRENTO	KING, S.
SPRINGTIME IN THE AIR	TRUXELL, E.
SPRINGTIME IN THE AIR	TRUXELL, E.
SPRINGTIME IN THE FOREST	GREENHILL, H.
SPRINGTIME IN THE HILLS	ANDRE
SPRINGTIME PIECES	GRAVES, J.
SPRINGTIME SERENADE	HOWELL
SPRINGTIME SONATINA	SEUEL *
SPRINGTIME WALTZ	TAYLOR, EDNA
SPRINGTIME	STREABBOG
SPRINGTIME	TOCABEN, L.
SPRING BEAUTIFUL SPRING	LINCKE, P.
SPRING BLOSSOMS	STAIRS, L.
SPRING BOUQUET	ROGERS
SPRING BREEZES, ONE PIANO - SIX HANDS	BENSON, E.
SPRING BREEZES	BRUSSELS, I.
SPRING BREEZES	DITTENHAVER
SPRING DANCE	BLAKE, D.
SPRING DANCE	TAYLOR
SPRING DAWN	MASON, W.
SPRING DAY	BAUER, M.
SPRING DAY	CANFIELD, J.
SPRING FEVER	BEAUMONT
SPRING FEVER	BLOOM
SPRING FEVER	ROLFE, W.
SPRING FLOWERS	BERNA
SPRING FLOWERS	ROLFE, W.
SPRING FLOWERS	ROLFE, W.
SPRING GAMES AND DANCES	KABALEVSKY
SPRING GAMES AND DANCE	KABALEVSKY
SPRING IN THE GARDEN	MARTINU, B.
SPRING IS DANCING	ROWLEY
SPRING IS HERE	HART *
SPRING IS HERE	LAWTON
SPRING MOOD	REISER, V.
SPRING MORNING AND LITTLE MINUET	DRING
SPRING MORNING IN THE WOODS	BOSTELMANN
SPRING NIGHT	LISZT *
SPRING NIGHT	SCHUMANN, R. *
SPRING NIGHT	SCHUMANN, R. *
SPRING PLANTING AND SPARKLING WATER	KURKA, R.
SPRING RECITAL	AGAY, D.--ED
SPRING SERENADE	LAST, J.
SPRING SHOWERS, OP. 174	FINK, W.
SPRING SHOWERS	FINK, W.
SPRING SONG, A	BIALOSKY, M.
SPRING SONG, OP. 15	HENSELT, A.
SPRING SONG, OP. 18 NO. 1	MERKEL, G.
SPRING SONG, OP. 62 NO. 6	MENDELSSOHN
SPRING SONG, OP. 62 NO. 6	MENDELSSOHN
SPRING SONG, OP. 62 NO. 6	MENDELSSOHN
SPRING SONG, OP. 85 NO. 4	DVORAK
SPRING SONG, S.W.W., 39	MENDELSSOHN
SPRING SONG	HOLLINS, A.
SPRING SONG	MENDELSSOHN
SPRING SONG	MENDELSSOHN
SPRING SONG	MENDELSSOHN
SPRING SONG	MENDELSSOHN
SPRING SUITE	SYMONS
SPRING TULIPS	KOHLER, F.
SPRING VIOLETS -- 6-HANDS	BILBRO, M.
SPRING VIOLETS	RAEZER, C.
SPRING	BEHR, F.
SPRING	NOVIKOFF
SPRITE IN THE GRASS	FARJEON
SPY WITH A COLD NOSE	
SQUARES TONIGHT	PROCTER, A.
SQUARE DANCE, THE	WEYBRIGHT
SQUARE DANCES	SANFORD
SQUARE DANCE CALLER	RAPHLING
SQUARE DANCE FROM 'AMERICAN ALBUM'	RAPHLING
SQUARE DANCE SONATINA	GREEN, R.
SQUARE DANCE TUNE	ROGERS, E.
SQUARE DANCE	LAWNER, M.
SQUARE DANCING DOLLS	CANFIELD, J.
SQUARE DANCING	CURZON, F.
SQUIRREL, THE	DUBSKY
SQUIRREL'S FROLIC	SOUERS
SQUIRREL'S PARADE	BENJAMIN
SQUIRRELS' PICNIC, THE	ECKHARDT, F.
SQUIRRELS AT PLAY	BERLIN, B.
SQUIRRELS AT PLAY	CROCKER, D.
SQUIRRELS IN THE NUT TREE	RAGANINI, A.
SQUIRRELS	MELLICHAMP, N.
SQUIRREL CHASE	SUDDARDS
SQUIRREL CHASE	SUDDARDS
SQUIRREL	JEAN, E.
SRING-ATHRE, OP. 9--1962	TJEKNAVORIAN, L.
ST. CRISPIN'S DAY	HUBICKI, M.
ST. FRANCIS BIRD SERMON	LISZT
ST. FRANCIS WALKING OVER THE WAVES	LISZT
ST. LOUIS IMPROVISATIONS	STEINER
ST. MORITZ	FIELDS, I.
ST. PATRICK'S DAY PARADE	MARTIN, G.
STABAT MATER, CUJUS ANIMAM	ROSSINI, G.
STABILES -- 12 IMAGES	SHAW, A.
STACCATO, A TECHNICAL DISCUSSION	ABRAMS
STACCATO, CAPRICE, OP. 92, NO. 11 -- FROM 12 PIECES	ALBENIZ, I.
STACCATO BRETON--1948	THOMAS, A.
STACCATO DANCE	SHAPERO, H.
STACCATO ETUDE IN C	RUBINSTEIN
STADIUM MARCH	COBB
STAGECOACH ADVENTURE	MELVIN, B.
STAGECOACH TRAIL	BROUTMAN, E.
STAIRWAY TO THE SEA --SCALINATELLA	CIOFFI
STAIRWAY TO THE STARS	LANE, J.--ED.
STALACTITE	BLANC
STAMBOUL - STAMBOUL, LE PHANAR, EYOUB, GALATA	DEBREVILLE
STAMPEDE	MARSDEN, E.
STAMPEDE	RUSSELL
STAMP ON IT	NOONA, W.
STANCES DE MADAME DE POMPADOUR	SEVERAC
STANDARD FAVORITES - BK. A	DE VITO, A.--ED.
STANDARD GRADED COURSE OF STUDIES, GRADE 01	MATHEWS, W.
STANDARD GRADED COURSE OF STUDIES, GRADE 02	MATHEWS, W.
STANDARD GRADED COURSE OF STUDIES, GRADE 03	MATHEWS, W.
STANDARD GRADED COURSE OF STUDIES, GRADE 04	MATHEWS, W.
STANDARD GRADED COURSE OF STUDIES, GRADE 05	MATHEWS, W.
STANDARD GRADED COURSE OF STUDIES, GRADE 06	MATHEWS, W.
STANDARD GRADED COURSE OF STUDIES, GRADE 07	MATHEWS, W.
STANDARD GRADED COURSE OF STUDIES, GRADE 09	MATHEWS, W.
STANDARD GRADED COURSE OF STUDIES, GRADE 10	MATHEWS, W.
STANDARD MUSIC OF TODAY	BRIMHALL,
STANDCHEN, LEISE FLEHEN, FANTASIE	SCHUBERT

STANDIN' IN THE NEED OF PRAYER	REISFELD--ED
STAN KENTON ORIGINALS FOR PIANO	KENTON, S.
STAR-SPANGLED BANNER, THE----ARRANGED IN TWO KEYS,	SMITH, J.
STAR-SPANGLED BANNER, THE--ARR. IN A FLAT AND B FLAT	DILLER, A.
STAR-SPANGLED BANNER, THE--ARR. IN G	DILLER, A.
STAR-SPANGLED BANNER, THE -- SET	SMITH, J.
STAR-SPANGLED BANNER, THE	SMITH, J.
STAR-SPANGLED BANNER, THE	THOMPSON, J.--ED
STAR-SPANGLED BANNER, THE	WALLIS
STARLIGHT, FROM 'LIGHT PIECES'	MANA-ZUCCA
STARLIGHT FANTASIE -- IN POPULAR STYLE	WEYBRIGHT
STARLIGHT LULLABY	DITTENHAVER
STARLIGHT REVERIE	SEIDT, J.
STARLIGHT SERENADE	WHITFORD
STARLIGHT WALTZ	BRAINARD, C. S.
STARLIGHT WALTZ	BRAINARD, C. S.
STARLIGHT	MARSCHALL
STARLIT HOUR	DE ROSE, P.
STARRY WAY	HOPKINS, H.
STARRY WAY	ROLFE, W.
STARR SONG -- SOMEBODY LOVES ME	STARR
STARS, THE	SCHUBERT
STARS AND STRIPES FOREVER, THE -- ONE PIANO, SIX HANDS--	SOUSA
STARS AND STRIPES FOREVER --TRIO THEME--	SOUSA
STARS AND STRIPES FOREVER -- FINALE THEME	SOUSA
STARS AND STRIPES FOREVER -- 9 OTHER WELL-KNOWN	SOUSA
STARS AND STRIPES FOREVER	SOUSA
STARS AND STRIPES FOREVER	SOUSA
STARS AND STRIPES FOREVER	SOUSA
STARS AND STRIPES FOREVER	SOUSA
STARS AND STRIPES FOREVER	SOUSA
STARS AND STRIPES FOREVER	SOUSA
STARS AND STRIPES FOREVER	SOUSA
STARS AND STRIPES FOREVER	SOUSA
STARS AND STRIPES FOREVER	SOUSA
STARS IN THE LAKE -- ETUDE, OP. 10 NO. 3	CHOPIN
STARS OF GLORY	KENNEDY, A.
STARS OF THE SEA	KENNEDY, A.
STARS	FINLAYSON, W.
STARTIME	ROGERS
STARTING TOGETHER	STEINER
START AT THE PIANO, A	LUBIN, E.
STAR - EASY PIANO	
STAR DREAMS	KING, S.
STAR DUST -- SIMP.	CARMICHAEL
STAR DUST MAMBO	CARMICHAEL
STAR DUST	CARMICHAEL
STAR DUST	CARMICHAEL
STAR DUST	CARMICHAEL
STAR DUST	CARMICHAEL
STAR DUST	GOULD, M.--ED.
STAR DUST	MERKUR--ED
STAR FLOWER	BUTLER, J.
STAR GAZERS, THE	ROLFE, W.
STAR OF BETHLEHEM	ADAMS, G.
STAR OF HOPE, REVERIE	KENNEDY, A.
STAR OF HOPE -- ONE PIANO, SIX HANDS --	KENNEDY, A.
STAR OF HOPE	BATISTE, E.
STAR OF HOPE	KENNEDY, A.
STAR OF THE SEA	KENNEDY, A.
STAR OF THE SEA	KENNEDY, A.
STAR OF THE SEA	KENNEDY, A.
STAR OF THE SEA	KENNEDY, A.
STAR SAPPHIRES	RENTON, V.
STAR SPANGLED BANNER, THE FOR TWO PIANOS, EIGHT HANDS	SMITH--ED
STAR SPANGLED BANNER, THE	SMITH--ED
STAR SPANGLED BANNER 'AMERICA' 'AMERICA THE	SCHAUM, J.--ED.
STAR SPANGLED BANNER	ARMOUR--ED
STAR SPANGLED BANNER	SMITH--ED
STAR SPANGLED BANNER	SMITH--ED
STAR SPANGLED BANNER	SPENCER, J.
STAR SPANGLED BANNER	TRUXELL, E.
STATELY DANCE	RICHMAN, A.
STATELY PINE TREE, THE	FOSTER, I. R.
STATELY PRELUDE	WIGHAM, M.
STATE FAIR POLKA	BOLLINGTON, H.
STATE FAIR	HAMMERSTEIN *
STATE FAIR	HAMMERSTEIN *
STATUETTES	ACHRON, J.
STEAMBOAT'S A COMIN'	COURSEY, R. DE
STEAMBOAT RAG	BURNETT
STEEPLECHASE	ECKSTEIN
STENOGRAMS	HLAVAC, M.
STEP-BY-STEP PIANO COURSE, BK. 1	BURNAM
STEP-BY-STEP PIANO COURSE, BK. 2	BURNAM
STEP-BY-STEP PIANO COURSE, BK. 3	BURNAM
STEP-BY-STEP PIANO COURSE, BK. 4	BURNAM
STEP-BY-STEP PIANO COURSE, BK. 5	BURNAM
STEP-BY-STEP PIANO COURSE, BK. 6	BURNAM
STEPHANIE GAVOTTE	CZIBULKA
STEPHEN FOSTER FAVORITES	FOSTER
STEPHEN FOSTER FAVORITES	FOSTER
STEPHEN HELLER ALBUM	HELLER, S.
STEPPING HIGH	ANSON, G.
STEPPING HIGH	SMITH
STEPPING HIGH	VANNORT, I.
STEPPING OUT	COBB
STEPPING OUT	THOMAS, A.
STEPPING STONES TO THE PIANO	RICHTER
STEPPING STONES	KING, M.
STEPS FOR THE YOUNG PIANIST--A COURSE OF	KINSCELLA, H.
STEPS FOR THE YOUNG PIANIST--A COURSE OF	KINSCELLA, H.
STEPS FOR THE YOUNG PIANIST--A COURSE OF	KINSCELLA, H.
STEPS FOR THE YOUNG PIANIST--A COURSE OF	KINSCELLA, H.
STEPS TO THE MASTERS	BACH, J.S.
STEPS TO THE MASTERS	BEETHOVEN
STEPS TO THE MASTERS	CHOPIN
STEPS TO THE MASTERS	HAYDN
STEPS TO THE MASTERS	MOZART, W. A.
STEPS TO THE MASTERS	SCHUBERT
STEPS TO THE MASTERS	SCHUMANN, R.
STEP BY STEP SIGHT READING, BK. 1	SWINSTEAD, F.
STEP BY STEP SIGHT READING, BK. 2	SWINSTEAD, F.
STEP BY STEP STUDIES, BK. 1	SWINSTEAD, F.
STEP BY STEP STUDIES, BK. 2	SWINSTEAD, F.
STEP BY STEP STUDIES, BK. 3	SWINSTEAD, F.
STEP BY STEP STUDIES, BK. 4	SWINSTEAD, F.
STEP BY STEP STUDIES, BK. 5	SWINSTEAD, F.
STEP BY STEP STUDIES, BK. 6	SWINSTEAD, F.
STEP BY STEP TO THE CLASSICS, BK. 1	SWINSTEAD, F.
STEP BY STEP TO THE CLASSICS, BK. 2	SWINSTEAD, F.
STEP BY STEP TO THE CLASSICS, BK. 3	SWINSTEAD, F.
STEP BY STEP TO THE CLASSICS, BK. 4	SWINSTEAD, F.
STEP BY STEP TO THE CLASSICS, BK. 5	SWINSTEAD, F.
STEP BY STEP TO THE CLASSICS, BK. 6	SWINSTEAD, F.
STEP CAREFULLY	RICHTER, A.
STEP TO THE REAR	LANE, J.--ED.
STEVIE WINWOOD AND FRIENDS	WINWOOD, S.
STILLE, NACHT, HEILIGE NACHT	VOGEL
STILL WATERS	BURNAM
STIMME DER RUHE, OP. 14	JANECEK
STIMMUNGEN, EINDRUCKE UND ERINNERUNGEN, OP. 41, HEFT 1	FIBICH, Z.
STIMMUNGEN, EINDRUCKE UND ERINNERUNGEN, OP. 41, HEFT 2	FIBICH, Z.
STIMMUNGEN, EINDRUCKE UND ERINNERUNGEN, OP. 41, HEFT 3	FIBICH, Z.
STIMMUNGEN, EINDRUCKE UND ERINNERUNGEN, OP. 41, HEFT 4	FIBICH, Z.
STIMMUNGEN -- 1955 --	ANGERER
STIMMUNGSBILDER, OP. 9	STRAUSS, J.
STITCH IN TIME SAVES NINE	SCARMOLIN
STOCKHOLM CONCERTO	WILDMAN
STODOLA PUMPA	WEYBRIGHT
STOFFRESTE -- BALLET IN ONE ACT	RIEMANN, A.
STOMPING AT THE SAVOY	GOODMAN *
STOMPING AT THE SAVOY	
STONY HOLLOW	CAZDEN, N.
STOOP DANCE -- SET	KLEIN, J.
STOP, STOP, PRETTY WATER FROM BEETHOVEN'S SONATA, OP.	ROLFE, W.
STOP THE WORLD - I WANT TO GET OFF --EASY PIANO--	BRICUSSE *
STORM, THE	WEBER, H.
STORMY WEATHER	PASQUET, J.
STORY-BOOK WALTZ	AARON, M.
STORY BY THE MOUSE, THE	LYNES
STORY OF SIEGFRIED, THE	DILLER, A.
STORY OF THE OLD HOUSE IN THE WOODS	GAYNOR
STOUTHEARTED MEN	ROMBERG, S.
STRANGENESS OF HEART	SOMERS, H.
STRANGERS IN THE NIGHT	BRIMHALL,
STRANGERS IN THE NIGHT	SINGLETON *
STRANGE MUSIC	HAMMERSTEIN *
STRANGE MUSIC	SINGER, L.--ED
STRANGE MUSIC	
STRANGE PARTY, A	DITTENHAVER
STRANGE STORY, A	OLDENBURG, E.
STRATHSPEY AND AIR	HARVEY, VIVIEN
STRATHSPEY AND AIR	HARVEY, VIVIEN
STRAUSS FUR ALLE	STRAUSS, J.
STRAUSS SLOWAKISCHER LIEDER. 12 VOLKSLIEDER	STRAUSS, J. *
STRAUSS WALTZES	STRAUSS, J.
STRAUSS WALTZES	STRAUSS, J.
STRAUSS WALTZ ALBUM	STRAUSS, J.
STRAWBERRY HILL	ARCHER
STRAWBERRY TALKS, THE	DUNGAN
STRAW HAT AND CANE	MUNN, W.
STREABBOG--12 MELODIOUS PIECES, BK. 1	STREABBOG
STREABBOG--12 MELODIOUS PIECES, BK. 2	STREABBOG
STREABBOG ALBUM	STREABBOG
STREABBOG ALBUM	STREABBOG
STREAMLINER	WILSON
STREET ACROBATS, THE	HIGGINS
STREET FAIR	DITTENHAVER
STREET GAME AND WALTZ IN 5/4	DUBSKY
STREET OF A THOUSAND MEMORIES	PHILLIPS, D.
STREET PARADE	KLEINMAN, A.
STREET SCENES	FLETCHER
STREET SCENE	NEWMAN, A.
STREET SCENE	
STREPITOSO	NIGG, S.
STRICTLY POPULAR	KAHN, M.
STRICTLY SOLID	KAHN, M.
STRIDENCES	RIVIER, J.
STRIKE UP THE BAND	GERSHWIN
STRIKE UP THE BAND	WARD
STRING OF PEARLS, A	SINGER, L.--ED
STRING QUARTET, ANDANTE CANTABILE	TSCHAIKOWSKY
STRING QUARTET, OP. 30	CHAUSSON
STRING QUARTETS, BK. 1	BEETHOVEN
STRING QUARTET IN A MAJOR	CHAUSSON
STRING QUARTET IN A MINOR, OP. 17	LAZZARI
STRING QUARTET IN G MINOR, OP. 27	GRIEG
STRING QUARTET NO. 1	CRAS
STRING QUARTET NO. 2 IN D MINOR	SMETANA
STRING QUARTET NO. 4	MILHAUD, D.
STRING QUARTET NO. 5	MILHAUD, D.
STRIPPER, THE	
STROLLING ALONG	KARP
STROLLING ALONG	MCGRAW
STROLLING HARP PLAYER, THE	HARDING, M.
STROLLING PLAYERS, THE	JENKINS, C.
STROLLING RIP	BAMPTON, R.
STROLLING WITH MY DOG	POWERS, M.
STROLLING	GLOVER, D.
STROLLING	MERKUR--ED
STROLLING	ROLSETH, B.
STRUCTURES	BOULEZ
STRUCTURE FOR PIANO	STRAIGHT, W.
STRUTTERS FROLIC	RAEZER, C.
STRUTTERS FROLIC	RAEZER, C.
STRUTTIN' WITH SOME BARBECUE	RAYE *
STRUTTING	STANTON, E.
STUBBORN DONKEY	DIETRICH
STUBBORN PRINCESS	SZONYI, E.
STUCKE FUR DIE JUGEND OP. 69 -- DREI KLEINE SUITEN	HAAS
STUCKE FUR DIE JUGEND OP. 69 -- 7 KLAVIER VOR	HAAS
STUCKE FUR DIE SPIELUHR	BEETHOVEN
STUCKE FUR KLAVIER ODER CEMBALO	PURCELL, H.
STUDENT'S TREASURY OF MENDELSSOHN, A	MENDELSSOHN
STUDENT'S TREASURY OF MENDELSSOHN, A	MENDELSSOHN
STUDENTS' CHOICE, SET 1 --5 PIECES--	GEORGE
STUDENTS' CHOICE, SET 2 --5 PIECES--	GEORGE
STUDENTS' CHOICE, SET 3 --4 PIECES--	GEORGE
STUDENTS' CHOICE, SET 4 --4 PIECES--	GEORGE
STUDENTS ON PARADE	LARSON
STUDENT CLASSICS - BOOK 1	WARD--ED
STUDENT CLASSICS - BOOK 2	WARD--ED
STUDENT MEETS THE COMPOSER, A	RAPHLING--ED.
STUDENT PIANIST, THE	PELLEGRINI
STUDENT PIECE, DEWDROPS	MAYKAPAR
STUDENT PRINCE, THE, SELECTIONS FROM	KLARMAN--ED
STUDIEN IN GRAU, OP. 106	WELLESZ, E.
STUDIES, OP. 22, BK. 1	HAUER, J.
STUDIES, OP. 22, BK. 2	HAUER, J.
STUDIES, OP. 32. VOL. 1, NOS. 1-8	JENSEN, A.
STUDIES, OP. 32. VOL. 1, NOS. 9-18	JENSEN, A.
STUDIES, OP. 32. VOL. 3, NOS. 19-25	JENSEN, A.
STUDIES, VOL. 1. ELEVEN PIECES	GENZMER
STUDIES, VOL. 2. TEN PIECES	GENZMER
STUDIES AFTER BACH CHOPIN AND WEBER	BRAHMS
STUDIES AFTER CAPRICES BY PAGANINI, OP. 3	SCHUMANN, R.

STUDIES AFTER PAGANINI'S 'CAPRICES', OP. 3, AND	SCHUMANN, R.
STUDIES FOR THE BEGINNER	BUOGO
STUDIES FOR THE DEVELOPMENT OF TECHNIQUE AND	LOESCHHORN, A.
STUDIES FOR THE DEVELOPMENT OF TECHNIQUE AND	LOESCHHORN, A.
STUDIES FOR THE DEVELOPMENT OF TECHNIQUE AND	LOESCHHORN, A.
STUDIES FOR THE DEVELOPMENT OF TECHNIQUE AND	LOESCHHORN, A.
STUDIES FOR THE DEVELOPMENT OF TECHNIQUE AND	LOESCHHORN, A.
STUDIES FOR THE DEVELOPMENT OF TECHNIQUE AND	LOESCHHORN, A.
STUDIES FOR THE DEVELOPMENT OF TECHNIQUE AND	LOESCHHORN, A.
STUDIES FOR THE DEVELOPMENT OF TECHNIQUE AND	LOESCHHORN, A.
STUDIES FOR THE DEVELOPMENT OF TECHNIQUE AND	LOESCHHORN
STUDIES FOR THE LEFT HAND, OP. 399	CZERNY
STUDIES IN BLACK AND WHITE	SLONIMSKY, N.
STUDIES IN JAZZ HARMONY	MEHEGAN, J.
STUDIES IN LINE, 1941	PENTLAND, B.
STUDIES IN MECHANISM, OP. 849	CZERNY
STUDIES IN STYLE - SECOND PIANO ACCOMPANIMENTS FOR	THOMPSON, J.
STUDIES IN STYLE	THOMPSON, J.--ED
STUDIES IN VELOCITY	POZZOLI
STUDIES OF MEDIUM DIFFICULTY	POZZOLI
STUDIES ON CAPRICES OF PAGANINI, OP. 3	SCHUMANN, R.
STUDIES ON FAMOUS TUNES	KING, S.
STUDIES ON REPEATED NOTES	POZZOLI
STUDIES	WIECK
STUDIES 1. EASY STUDIES FOR CHILDREN	BRESGEN
STUDIO, OP. 47	MARTUCCI
STUDIO CANONICO IN OTTAVE	GIACCHINO
STUDIO DI CONCERTO, OP. 9	MARTUCCI
STUDIO ESATONICO	GIACCHINO
STUDIO IN RITMO	MUSEMECI, D.
STUDIO MONORITIMICO	CARABELLA
STUDIO ONE CONCERTO	OLIVER
STUDIO ONE CONCERTO	OLIVER *
STUDI -- BK. 1, 45 BREVI STUDI FACILI	CZERNY
STUDI -- BK. 2, 35 STUDI FACILI E PROGRESSIVI	CZERNY
STUDI -- BK. 3, 25 STUDI	CZERNY
STUDI GALANTI	MORTARI
STUDY, OP. 6 NO. 1	KREIDER, N.
STUDY FOR LEFT HAND, LUCIA	LESCHETIZKY
STUDY FOR THE LEFT HAND	BARTOK
STUDY IN BLUE	SAVINO
STUDY IN BROWN	
STUDY IN IRREGULAR RHYTHM	REIZENSTEIN, F.
STUDY IN JAZZ	KREUTZ
STUDY IN OCTAVES	CONCONE, G.
STUDY NO. 22	IVES, C.
STUDY OF THE PIANO, THE, BK. 1 - THE TECHNIQUE OF THE	FANO, G. A.
STUDY OF THE PIANO, THE, BK. 2 - CHORDS, ARPEGGIOS AND	FANO, G. A.
STUDY OF THE PIANO, THE, BK. 3 - POLYPHONIC STYLE,	FANO, G. A.
STUMBLING	CONFREY, Z.
STUMBLING	LANE, J.--ED.
STUNTS FOR PIANO	RICHTER, A.
STYLES AND TOUCHES	KREVIT, W.
STYLES FOR THE JAZZ PIANIST, BK. 1	MEHEGAN, J.
STYLES FOR THE JAZZ PIANIST, BK. 2	MEHEGAN, J.
STYLES FOR THE JAZZ PIANIST, BK. 3	MEHEGAN, J.
STYLE AND INTERPRETATION, BK. 1	FERGUSON, H.
STYLE AND INTERPRETATION, BK. 2	FERGUSON, H.
STYLE AND INTERPRETATION, BK. 3	FERGUSON, H.
STYLE AND INTERPRETATION, BK. 4	FERGUSON, H.
STYLISH FLAMINGO, THE.	COBB
STYRIAN COMPOSERS, WORKS FOR PIANO -- BK. 1	BLOCH, W. *
STYRIAN COMPOSERS, WORKS FOR PIANO -- BK. 2	HAIDMEYER *
STYRIAN COMPOSERS, WORKS FOR PIANO -- BK. 3	MIXA *
SUAVE SCHERZO	OLSON
SUBSTANCES CONVERGENTES	CHAYNES
SUBURBIS	MOMPOU, F.
SUBWAY IN THE SUNLIGHT	MAYER
SUBWAY RUSH	ROZIN
SUCCESSFUL PIANO SOLOS--SUITABLE FOR TEACHING, RECITAL	
SUCH A FUNNY BUNNY	BRODSKY, M.
SUCH LOVELY THINGS	NORTH, M.
SUENOS	LAPARRA, R.
SUGARLOAF MOUNTAIN	STEVENS, E.
SUGARLOAF	OLSON
SUGAR AND SPICE	KETTERING, K.
SUGAR BLUES	FLETCHER *
SUGAR COOKIES	GLOVER, D.
SUITE. HOMENAJE A ALBENIZ	ALFONSO
SUITE--ARIA AND BAGATELLE NO. 2	PAPINEAU-COUTURE
SUITE--PRELUDE AND BAGATELLE NO. 1	PAPINEAU-COUTURE
SUITE--RONDO	PAPINEAU-COUTURE
SUITE--1943--. FOR CARILLON	BADINGS
SUITE, OP. 1--ALLEMANDE, GAVOTTE, MUSETTE	ALBERT, E. D'
SUITE, OP. 100. HARPSICHORD	TCHEREPNIN
SUITE, OP. 11	JAQUE, R.
SUITE, OP. 13	MUCZYNSKI, R.
SUITE, OP. 14	BARTOK
SUITE, OP. 14	BARTOK
SUITE, OP. 15 -- SET	ARENSKY, A.
SUITE, OP. 15	ARENSKY, A.
SUITE, OP. 15	ARENSKY, A.
SUITE, OP. 18	JANECEK
SUITE, OP. 18	WEINER
SUITE, OP. 2	HOELLER
SUITE, OP. 21	SUK
SUITE, OP. 25	SCHOENBERG
SUITE, OP. 4B	BARTOK
SUITE, OP. 41	GEISER
SUITE, OP. 41	GEISER
SUITE, OP. 42 'VECCHIO STILE'	CILEA
SUITE, OP. 90	SAINT-SAENS
SUITE, OP. 95	WEISMANN, J.
SUITE, OP. 98	DVORAK
SUITE, OP. 98	DVORAK
SUITEN FUR TASTENINSTRUMENTE AUS 'MELOTHESIA', ACHT	PRESTON *
SUITES, VOL. 1 NOS. 1-8	HANDEL
SUITES, VOL. 2 NOS. 9-16	HANDEL
SUITES --6-- AND SUITE MOVEMENTS --2--. URTEXT.	BACH, J.S.
SUITES AND SONATAS	BACH, J.S.
SUITES	BACH, J.S.
SUITE -- 1933 --	DANDELOT
SUITE -- 1945 --	COLLUM
SUITE -- 1956 --	BAUR
SUITE - PRELUDE, ROMANCE, INTERMEZZO, NOCTURNE	HARSANYI
SUITE 'CONCISE'--7 PIECES--	APOSTEL
SUITE '1922', OP. 26	HINDEMITH
SUITE ALGERIENNE, OP. 60, FOR 2 PIANOS 8 HANDS	SAINT-SAENS
SUITE ALGERIENNE, OP. 60	SAINT-SAENS
SUITE ANDINE	LAVIN, C.
SUITE ANGLAISE -- 1930 --	GAILLARD
SUITE ARGENTINA	GUASTAVINO
SUITE A DEUX CLAVECINS	HANDEL
SUITE BERGAMASQUE -- 1. PRELUDE	DEBUSSY
SUITE BERGAMASQUE -- 2. MENUET	DEBUSSY
SUITE BERGAMASQUE -- 3. CLAIR DE LUNE	DEBUSSY

SUITE BERGAMASQUE	DEBUSSY
SUITE BERGAMASQUE	DEBUSSY
SUITE BERGAMASQUE	DEBUSSY
SUITE BERGAMASQUE	DEBUSSY
SUITE BERGAMASQUE	DEBUSSY
SUITE BERGAMASQUE	DEBUSSY
SUITE BRETONNE - CHANSON POPULAIRE	LADMIRAULT
SUITE BRETONNE - CHANT DES BUGALE-NOZ	LADMIRAULT
SUITE BRETONNE - DANSE DE 1 EPEE	LADMIRAULT
SUITE BRETONNE - RONDO	LADMIRAULT
SUITE BRETONNE - SCHERZO	LADMIRAULT
SUITE BREVE -- 5 PIECES --	HARSANYI
SUITE BREVE FOR YOUNG PIANISTS	DESENCLOS, A.
SUITE BREVE	AUBERT
SUITE BUCOLICA	KAPRAL
SUITE BUFFA -- OPERA FOR MALE PIANIST, SOPRANO AND	MESTRES-QUADRENY
SUITE CHAMPETRE, 1948 -- SET	RIETI
SUITE CONCERTANTE -- SET	MILHAUD, D.
SUITE CONCERTANTE	GOUNOD, C.
SUITE CUBANA PARA NINOS	GRAMATGES
SUITE DANS LE STYLE ANCIEN	MIROUZE
SUITE DANS LE STYLE ANCIEN	TANSMAN, A.
SUITE DE DANSES	GRUNENWALD
SUITE DE DANZAS CRIOLLAS	GINASTERA
SUITE DE FLANDES--GUITAR	PASTOR, S.
SUITE DE VALSES NO. 1	SANCHEZ GAVITO,
SUITE DE VALSES NO. 2	SANCHEZ GAVITO,
SUITE DE VALSES NO. 3	SANCHEZ GAVITO,
SUITE ENFANTINE, NO.1 GRAND-PERE BACH	BEAUCAMP
SUITE ENFANTINE, NO.2 LE PASSEUR D'EAU	BEAUCAMP
SUITE ENFANTINE, NO.3 MARCHANDE DE FLEURS	BEAUCAMP
SUITE ENFANTINE, NO.5 HISTOIRE SANS HISTOIRES	BEAUCAMP
SUITE ENFANTINE, NO.6 RONDE DES PUCES	BEAUCAMP
SUITE ENFANTINE	MALEINGRAU
SUITE EN SI	DOYEN, J.
SUITE EN SOL	MARESCOTTI, A.
SUITE EN 3 PARTIES	MIGOT
SUITE ESPAGNOLE	ALBENIZ, I.
SUITE ESPAGNOLE	ALBENIZ, I.
SUITE ESPAGNOLE	ALBENIZ, I.
SUITE ESPANOLA NO. 1 -- COMPLETE	ALBENIZ, I.
SUITE ESPANOLA NO. 1	ALBENIZ, I.
SUITE ESPANOLA	ALBENIZ, I.
SUITE FLORAL, OP. 97	VILLA-LOBOS, H.
SUITE FOR PIANO -- 'IN RITMO ANTICO'	ADAMIS, M.
SUITE FOR PIANO -- NOSTALGIE, RONDINO, ETE, DANSEUSE,	TARCAN, B.
SUITE FOR PIANO NO. 2, OP. 1 NO. 2	KADOSA
SUITE FOR PIANO	CORTES, R.
SUITE FOR PIANO	DELLO JOIO, N.
SUITE FOR PIANO	DICK, M.
SUITE FOR PIANO	HARRISON, L.
SUITE FOR PIANO	MORAWETZ
SUITE FOR PIANO	PASCAL, C.
SUITE FOR PIANO	RUSSELL
SUITE FOR PREPARED PIANO	WOLFF, C.
SUITE FOR THE PIANO, OP. 45	NIELSEN, C.
SUITE FOR THE PIANO	MILHAUD, D.
SUITE FOR THE VIRGINAL	JACOB, G.
SUITE FOR THE YOUNG	DELLO JOIO, N.
SUITE FOR YOUNG PEOPLE, BK. 1	BAZELON, I.
SUITE FOR YOUNG PEOPLE, BK. 2	BAZELON, I.
SUITE FOR 2 CEMBALI IN G MINOR	MATTHESON, J.
SUITE FOR 2 PIANOS	HENGEVELD
SUITE FRANCAISE POUR PIANO	TREBINSKY, A.
SUITE FRANCAISE	DANIEL-LESUR
SUITE FRANCAISE	POULENC, F.
SUITE FROM ''DER BURGER ALS EDELMANN''--ORCH	STRAUSS, R.
SUITE FROM BALLET ''ON STAGE'' -- SET	DELLO JOIO, N.
SUITE FROM THE BALLET 'ON STAGE'	DELLO JOIO, N.
SUITE FROM THE MONADNOCK REGION	WAGNER
SUITE FROM THE PARTITA IN E MAJOR FOR VIOLIN --	BACH, J.S.
SUITE FROM THE WATER MUSIC	HANDEL
SUITE FROM THE WATER MUSIC	HANDEL
SUITE FUR KLAVIER, OP. 22	PETRZELKA
SUITE FUR KLAVIER UND ORCHESTER, OP. 97	WEISMANN, J.
SUITE FUR KLAVIER	DEGEN
SUITE GEORGIENNE, OP. 57	TCHEREPNIN
SUITE GOTHIQUE	BOELLMANN, L.
SUITE GOTHIQUE	BOELLMANN, L.
SUITE GOTHIQUE	BOELLMANN, L.
SUITE GRECQUE POUR PIANO	MICHAELIDES
SUITE IM ALTEN STIL, OP. 21	JIRAK
SUITE INCAICA	CASELLA, E. M.
SUITE INFANTIL	BOERO
SUITE IN A, OP. 98	DVORAK
SUITE IN B MINOR	ZIPOLI
SUITE IN CANON-FORM, OP. 65 -- SET	ARENSKY, A.
SUITE IN C MAJOR, OP. 51, NO. 1	TCHEREPNIN
SUITE IN C MAJOR, OP. 51, NO. 2	TCHEREPNIN
SUITE IN C	COOKE, A.
SUITE IN C	GENZMER
SUITE IN D MINOR, OP. 1	ALBERT, E. D'
SUITE IN D	CASTILLO
SUITE IN FORMA DI VARIAZIONI	BOCCOSI, B.
SUITE IN G, FOR HARPSICHORD OR PIANO	EDMUNDS
SUITE IN 3/4 TIME	MITTLER
SUITE LANGUEDOCIENNE	KOSMA, J.
SUITE LIBURNICA	RUDAN
SUITE LOUIS XVI	MONTPELLIER, P.
SUITE MINIATURE, OP. 145	GRETCHANINOFF
SUITE MINIATURE	MARC, E.
SUITE MIRIM	GUARNIERI
SUITE NO. 1, OP. 14	ORREGO SALAS, J.
SUITE NO. 1	ALDERIGHI
SUITE NO. 1	DIERCKS
SUITE NO. 1	JOHNSTON, R.
SUITE NO. 1	LAZAR, F.
SUITE NO. 1	VOORMOLEN
SUITE NO. 2, OP. 17	RACHMANINOFF, S.
SUITE NO. 2, OP. 32	ORREGO SALAS, J.
SUITE NO. 2	AURIZIO, D'
SUITE NO. 2	JOHNSTON, R.
SUITE NO. 2	LAZAR, F.
SUITE NO. 3	SKALKOTTAS, N.
SUITE NO. 4, ON NETHERLANDS FOLK DANCES --FOR	BADINGS
SUITE NO. 4	SKALKOTTAS, N.
SUITE OF COUNTRY DANCES	BRYDSON, J.
SUITE OF LITTLE PIECES	ESPLA
SUITE OF SEVEN	CALABRO, L.
SUITE ON FIVE NOTES	FERNANDEZ, O.
SUITE ON GREEK THEMES	SALMON, K.
SUITE ON OLD TUNES	BECKWITH
SUITE PASSACAILLE FOR 2 PIANOS	HAUBIEL, C.
SUITE PERSANE	HENRY, C.
SUITE PER GIOCONDA	FURGERI
SUITE PITTORESQUE - DIMANCHE SOIR	FOURDRAIN
SUITE PITTORESQUE - DIVERTISSEMENT ORIENTAL	FOURDRAIN

Title	Composer
SUITE PITTORESQUE - FANTASIE BALLET	FOURDRAIN
SUITE PITTORESQUE - FETE JAPONAISE	FOURDRAIN
SUITE PITTORESQUE - VIEUX SOUVENIR	FOURDRAIN
SUITE POUR LE PIANO	DEBUSSY
SUITE POUR MELODYNE	ARRIEU
SUITE POUR PIANO - PRELUDE, SICILIENNE, BOURREE,	RODRIGO, J.
SUITE POUR PIANO	KAYSER, P. *
SUITE POUR PIANO	ROUSSEL, A.
SUITE PRINTANIERE - AUBADE	WESLY
SUITE PRINTANIERE - FLEURS ET PAPILLONS	WESLY
SUITE PRINTANIERE - IMPROMPTU	WESLY
SUITE PRINTANIERE - NOCTURNE	WESLY
SUITE PRINTANIERE - RONDE VILLAGEOISE	WESLY
SUITE ROMANTIQUE	CANTU
SUITE SUDISTE - COLIBRIS	POWELL
SUITE SUDISTE - ELEGIE NEGRE	POWELL
SUITE SUDISTE - POEME EROTIQUE	POWELL
SUITE SUDISTE	POWELL
SUITE SUR DES MOTIFS DE TERROIR	GUILLOU, R.
SUITE SYMPHONIQUE NO. 1 -- ORCH	MILHAUD, D.
SUITE SYMPHONIQUE	LELEU
SUITE VARIEE	TANSMAN, A.
SUITE WALLONNE - PROMENADE A LA CAMPAGNE, AU CABARET,	GUILLAUME
SUITE	ARNE
SUITE	BORLENGHI
SUITE	CARPIO VALDES,
SUITE	CORRADINI
SUITE	DEFAY
SUITE	FENNER
SUITE	GUARINO, C.
SUITE	HOVHANESS, A.
SUITE	LIEBERMAN, F.
SUITE	MANENTI
SUITE	MECHEM, K.
SUITE	NOVIKOFF
SUITE	POOT, M.
SUITE	PURCELL, H.
SUITE	REIZENSTEIN, F.
SUITE	ROWLEY
SUITE	SCALFATI
SUITE	SCARLATTI, D.
SUITE	STRATEGIER
SUITE	TARDOS, B.
SUITE	VADON
SULL'ALTALENA	MONTANARI
SULLA LAGUNA	CIMATTI
SULTAN'S BAND, MARCH	BROWN
SULTRY DAY IN NEW YORK	TEMPLETON, A.
SUL PRATO GIUCCANO I FIGLI DELLA GATTA MEA	COUTURE
SUMAJ	GOMEZ CARRILLO
SUMMER'S WONDERLAND	WOOD, L.
SUMMERTIME, RUBENSTEIN CONCERT ARR.	RUBINSTEIN--ED
SUMMERTIME, STONE CONCERT ARR.	STONE, E.--ED
SUMMERTIME IN VENICE	ICINI
SUMMERTIME PRELUDE	WIGHAM, M.
SUMMERTIME SUITE -- EIGHT PIECES FOR STUDENTS	BAUER, M.
SUMMERTIME	GERSHWIN
SUMMERTIME	GRAHAM, R.
SUMMERTIME	STONE, E.--ED
SUMMER AND WINTER, OP. C NO. 1	GROTON, F.
SUMMER AND WINTER	JEAN, E.
SUMMER CHURCHYARD	HAUBIEL, C.
SUMMER CLOUDS	TAYLOR
SUMMER DAYS	HOPKINS, H.
SUMMER EVENING	DUNGAN
SUMMER EVENING	DUNGAN
SUMMER EVENING	GARROW, L.
SUMMER EVENING	KEYSOR, C.
SUMMER GLORY	THORNTON
SUMMER HOLIDAY, A	MARCEL, G.
SUMMER HOLIDAYS	MCINTYRE, E.
SUMMER IN SICILY	REISER, V.
SUMMER JOURNAL, A, OP. 19	MUCZYNSKI, R.
SUMMER KNOWS, THE	LEGRAND *
SUMMER NIGHT	MARTIN, H.
SUMMER NIGHT	TILLERY, H.
SUMMER NIGHT	TRUXELL, E.
SUMMER NOCTURNE	WHITFORD
SUMMER PLACE, A, THEME FROM	STEINER *
SUMMER ROMANCE	RENNARD
SUMMER SAND	LANE, J.--ED.
SUMMER SHOWERS	ROZIN
SUMMER SKIES	ANDERSON, L.
SUMMER SMOKE	GREEN, R.
SUMMER SNOW FLOWERS	REID
SUMMER SOLILOQUY	GIASSON, P.
SUMMER SONG	ADAIR, M.
SUMMER SOUNDS AND OTHER BIG SONG HITS	DAHLEN
SUMMER STARLIGHT	MARTIN, H.
SUMMER STROLL, A	COMSTOCK
SUMMER SUNSET -- TO EDWARD MACDOWELL FROM	GREEN, R.
SUMMER WIND	MAYER
SUMMER	HOPKINS, H.
SUMMER	LICHNER, H.
SUMMER	RAYMOND, J.
SUMP'N SWEET	MARWICK, M. *
SUNBEAMS AND ROBINS	HIRSCHBERG, D.
SUNBEAM FROLIC	FLORENTINE, S.
SUNDAY, MONDAY OR ALWAYS	
SUNDAY IN THE PARK	KERR, R. N.
SUNDAY IN VERMONT	BRUSSELS, I.
SUNDAY MORNING, AND WHISTLING TUNE	LEFLEMING, C.
SUNDAY MORNING STROLL	KLEINMAN, A.
SUNDAY MORNING	BOHM
SUNDAY MORNING	ETHRIDGE
SUNDAY MORNING	GLOVER
SUNDAY MORNING	REISTRUP, J.
SUNDAY MORNING	SHIFFERLY, R.
SUNDAY PIANO MUSIC	
SUNDAY RIDE	ROGERS, E.
SUNDAY SCHOOL HYMNS -- MUSIC FOR CHILDREN	SCHAUM, J.--ED.
SUNDAY TRAFFIC	KAHN, M.
SUNLIGHT, FROM 'LIGHT PIECES'	MANA-ZUCCA
SUNLIT VALLEY	ROWLEY
SUNNYSIDE -- SCHOTTISCHE DE CONCERT	SPENCER, E. B.
SUNNY DAY, A	PECHMAN
SUNNY MORNING	ALDRED, H.
SUNNY SKIES	MELECCI, A.
SUNNY SONATINA, A	ANSON, G.
SUNNY	LANE, J.--ED.
SUNNY	WILLIAMS, M.
SUNRISE, SUNSET	BOCK, J.
SUNRISE AT SEA	FRANCO, J.
SUNRISE BOOGIE	CARLE, F. *
SUNRISE CANTER	DITTENHAVER
SUNRISE IN NAPOLI	CARLE, F. *
SUNRISE IN THE VALLEY	RODGERS
SUNRISE SERENADE -- PIANO SOLO	
SUNRISE SERENADE	
SUNRISE TRAIL	BLAKE, D.
SUNSET HOUR	FREDERICKS
SUNSET HOUR	QUINCKE, W.
SUNSET IN THE HILLS	WEYBRIGHT
SUNSET IN THE MOUNTAINS	WILSON
SUNSET ON THE SOUND	SAVAGE
SUNSET ON THE WATER	CRERIE, E.
SUNSET TRAIL, THE	WEYBRIGHT
SUNSET	GILLOCK
SUNSET	GILLOCK
SUNSET	MATTHEWS, H. A.
SUNSET	RODGERS
SUNSET	TALBOT
SUNSHINE SET	CLARK, M.--ED.
SUNSHINE WALTZ -- ONE PIANO, SIX HANDS --	HOPKINS, H.
SUNSHINY SHOWER, A	HOFSTAD, M.
SUNSHOWER	GEST, E.
SUNT LACRIMAE RERUM	LISZT
SUN DANCE	FRIEDMAN
SUN DOWN	GEST, E.
SUN ON THE SAND	BURNAM
SUONO IL PIANOFORTE - 19 LITTLE PIECES	POZZOLI
SUPER FLUMINA BABYLONIS, OP. 52	ALKAN
SUPER POPULAR MUSIC	BRADLEY,
SUPER 77, THE	BRADLEY,
SUPPLEMENT* TWO ORIGINAL WORKS, SIX TRANSCRIPTIONS	LISZT
SUPPLEMENTARY PIANO MATERIAL--ENSEMBLE BOOK FOR 'TEACH	KASSCHAU, H.
SUPPLEMENTARY PIANO STUDIES	VEON
SUPPOSE	SUDDARDS
SURF AND THE SANDPIPERS	DUNNAGAN, F.
SURF BOARD RIDER	BURNAM
SURF RIDERS, THE	AARON, M.
SURF SWING	KONOWITZ, B.
SURGING SEA, THE	BURNAM
SURGING SEA, THE	BURNAM
SURLES BORES DU DOURO, 1922	PEDRELL, C.
SURPRISE PARTY FOR THE YOUNG	ALAIN, M.
SURPRISE SYMPHONY, THE	HAYDN
SURREY WITH THE FRINGE ON TOP	HAMMERSTEIN *
SURREY WITH THE FRINGE ON TOP	HAMMERSTEIN *
SURREY WITH THE FRINGE ON TOP	RODGERS *
SURVEY OF PIANO LITERATURE -- LEVEL 1, BK. 1 -- EARLY	ANSON, G.--ED
SURVEY OF PIANO LITERATURE -- LEVEL 1, BK.2 -- THE	ANSON, G.--ED
SURVEY OF PIANO LITERATURE -- LEVEL 1, BK.3 -- THE	ANSON, G.--ED
SUR LA MER LOINTAINE	MOREAU
SUR LA PLAGE - BLONDINETTE	GAEL
SUR LA PLAGE - L'HORLOGE A MUSIQUE	GAEL
SUR LA PLAGE - MUSETTA	GAEL
SUR LA PLAGE - VALSE DES VAGUES	GAEL
SUR LES AILES DE LA CHANSON	KAEMPER
SUR LES MONTS BAIGNES D'AZUR	GUENIFFEY
SUR LE BORYSTHENE, OP. 51 - COMPLETE BALLET	PROKOFIEFF
SUR LE LAC MAJEUR	GALOS
SUR TROIS MARCHES DE MARBRE ROSE	BONHEUR
SUSANI, ALTE WEIHNACHTSLIEDER	SCHROEDER, H.
SUSAN BLUE	DITTENHAVER
SUSPENDED SENTENCE	PECK, R.
SUSPENSION	WHITFORD
SUSY, LITTLE SUSY -- GERMAN FOLK SONG, USED IN THE	HUMPERDINCK, E.
SUSY LITTLE SUSY, HANSEL AND GRETEL	HUMPERDINCK, E.
SUZANNE'S SECRET--PIANO SCORE WITH SUPERLINEAR GERMAN	WOLF-FERRARI, E.
SUZETTE	MOSSMAN, T.
SUZUKI PIANO SCHOOL, VOL. 1	SUZUKI, S.
SUZUKI PIANO SCHOOL, VOL. 2	SUZUKI, S.
SUZUKI PIANO SCHOOL, VOL. 3	SUZUKI, S.
SUZUKI PIANO SCHOOL, VOL. 4	SUZUKI, S.
SUZUKI PIANO SCHOOL, 12 INCH LP RECORD ALBUM FOR VOLS.	SUZUKI, S.
SUZUKI PIANO SCHOOL, 12 INCH LP RECORD ALBUM FOR VOLS.	SUZUKI, S.
SWALLOW, THE -- LA GOLONDRINA --	SERRADELL
SWALLOW, THE -- LA GOLONDRINA --	SERRADELL
SWALLOW, THE	BURGMUELLER
SWALLOW, THE	DAQUIN, C.
SWALLOW, VALSETTE	SCHILLER, F.
SWALLOW'S RETURN, THE	MARCEL, G.
SWAMP-FIRE	MOONEY
SWAN, THE--FROM 'CARNAVAL DES ANIMAUX'	SAINT-SAENS
SWAN, THE--FROM 'CARNAVAL DES ANIMAUX'	SAINT-SAENS
SWAN, THE--MELODY FROM THE 'CARNAVAL DES ANIMAUX'	SAINT-SAENS
SWAN, THE	ADLER, M.
SWAN, THE	MILLER, L.
SWAN, THE	PALMGREN, S.
SWAN, THE	SAINT-SAENS
SWAN, THE	SAINT-SAENS
SWAN, THE	SAINT-SAENS
SWAN'S FLIGHT	TSCHAIKOWSKY
SWANEE MOOD	FOSTER
SWANEE RIVER -- THEME, VARIATIONS AND FINALE	DESOLIS
SWANEE RIVER BOOGIE	WHITFORD--ED.
SWANS	GARROW, L.
SWAN LAKE, SEVEN EXCERPTS	TSCHAIKOWSKY
SWAN LAKE, TWELVE EXCERPTS, ILLUSTRATED	TSCHAIKOWSKY
SWAN LAKE -- BALLET TOLD IN WORDS AND MUSIC	TSCHAIKOWSKY
SWAN LAKE BALLET	TSCHAIKOWSKY
SWAN LAKE BALLET	TSCHAIKOWSKY
SWAN LAKE SUITE	TSCHAIKOWSKY
SWAN LAKE	TSCHAIKOWSKY
SWAN OF TUONELA, OP. 22 NO. 3--ORCH	SIBELIUS
SWAN OF TUONELA, THE, OP. 22 NO. 3 -- ORCH	SIBELIUS
SWAN ON THE MOONLIT LAKE	REBE
SWAN	SAINT-SAENS
SWARM OF BEES	BENFORD
SWAYING DAFFODILS	MCSWEEN, F. W.
SWAYING DAFFODILS	OVERLADE, A. R.
SWAYING DAFFODILS	OVERLADE, A. R.
SWAYING PALMS	REISER, V.
SWAYING PALMS	STOWE, F.
SWAYING TREETOPS	DANIEL, K.
SWAY DANCE	COWELL
SWAY GENTLY	CECERE, C.
SWAY GENTLY	CECERE, C.
SWEDISH DANCE	CHRISTENSEN, A.
SWEDISH POLKA	ALFVEN, H.
SWEDISH RHAPSODY --THEME	WILDMAN
SWEDISH RHAPSODY -- THEME	WILDMAN
SWEDISH RHAPSODY	FAITH *
SWEDISH RHAPSODY	WILDMAN
SWEDISH RHAPSODY	WILDMAN
SWEETEN CREEK	TREVARTHEN, R.
SWEETEST SOUNDS, THE	RODGERS
SWEETEST STORY EVER TOLD, THE	STULTS
SWEETEST STORY EVER TOLD, THE	STULTS
SWEETHEARTS--WALTZ	HERBERT
SWEETHEART TREE	
SWEETHEART WALTZES, GYPSY BARON	STRAUSS, J.
SWEETHEART WALTZ	STRAUSS, J.

Title	Name
SWEETLY SINGS THE BROOKLET	KETTERER, E.
SWEETS FOR PIANO	LEWIS, P. T.
SWEET AND LOVELY	LANE, J.--ED.
SWEET BABY JAMES	
SWEET BYE AND BYE, THE	WEBSTER
SWEET BYE AND BYE VARIATIONS	DRUMHELLER
SWEET BY AND BY, THE	WEBSTER
SWEET CARNATIONS, WALTZ	SRS. OF ST.
SWEET CAROLINE	BRIMHALL,
SWEET CHARITY	
SWEET COLLEEN, A	BURNAM
SWEET DREAMS, OP. 39 NO. 21	TSCHAIKOWSKY
SWEET DREAMS IN C, OP. 39 NO. 21	TSCHAIKOWSKY
SWEET DREAMS	LANGE, G.
SWEET DREAMS	OLSON
SWEET DREAMS	PORTER, W.
SWEET GENEVIEVE, TRANSCRIPTION	TUCKER *
SWEET HITCH-HIKER	BRIMHALL,
SWEET KISS, POLKA	KINKEL, C.
SWEET LORRAINE -- SIMP.	MOSSMAN, T.--ED
SWEET MEDITATIONS	KAY
SWEET MEMORIES	MCADAMS, G.
SWEET MOMENTS, REVERIE -- ONE PIANO, SIX HANDS	HOPKINS, H.
SWEET RECOLLECTIONS	BOHN, J.C.
SWEET RECOLLECTIONS	MCADAMS, G.
SWEET ROSIE O'GRADY NUGENT	FRANGIPANE--ED
SWEET ROSIE O'GRADY SIMP.	MOSSMAN, T.--ED
SWEET SEASONS	BRADLEY,
SWEET SEVENTEEN, GAVOTTE	ABTLER
SWEET SIXTEEN WALTZ	SCHER, W.
SWEET SIXTEEN	NEVIN
SWEET SIXTEEN	STEINER
SWEET STORY	LIBBY, R.
SWEET SUE - JUST YOU	YOUNG, V.
SWEET SURRENDER	BRADLEY,
SWEET SUSPENSE	DRUMHELLER
SWEET THOUGHTS OF YESTERDAY	MCADAMS, G.
SWEET VIOLETS	KOHLER, F.
SWEET VIOLET	HEINS, C.
SWEET VIOLET	SMALLWOOD
SWEET WILLIAM	RIDLEY, S. C.
SWIMMING-POOL, THE	ADLER, M.
SWING, THE	THOMAS, C. J.
SWINGIN' 'N SWAYIN'	ROBINSON, A.
SWINGIN' SHEPHERD BLUES	LANE, J.--ED.
SWINGIN' TECHNIC	SHORES
SWINGING ALONG	PARENTE, SR. E.
SWINGING HIGH AND LOW	COBB
SWINGING HIGH AND LOW	COBB
SWINGING IN A HAMMOCK	STEINER
SWINGING IN FAIRYLAND	HARKER, F.
SWINGING IN THE GARDEN	STILWELL
SWINGING IN THE PARK	KARP
SWINGING LANTERNS --CHINESE DANCE--	ECKSTEIN
SWINGING ON A STAR	
SWINGING SLEIGH BELLS	PHILLIPS, D.
SWINGING	WARD
SWINGING	WILSON, M.
SWINGMATISH	MCSHANN *
SWINGUET IN G	SCHAUM, J.--ED.
SWING ALONG	BURCH, S.
SWING AND SWAY	SHOEMAKER
SWING HIGH, SWING LOW	ROGERS
SWING IN OUR YARD, THE	KERR, R. N.
SWING LOW, SWING HIGH	REBE
SWING LOW, 21 SONGS UND EVERGREENS FUR KLAVIER UND	
SWING ME	GAIL
SWING ME	GAIL
SWING SONG, NOVELLETE	HOPKINS, H.
SWING SONG	ERB
SWING SONG	FONTAINE
SWING SONG	HAYES
SWING SONG	JEAN, E.
SWING THE BLUES	GARROW, L.
SWING THE SCALE	MELVIN, B.
SWING TUNE	PROCTER, A.
SWING YOUR PARTNER	GUENTHER--ED
SWING	HOLLANDER
SWING	VANNORT, I.
SWIRLING WATERS	MARRYOTT, R. E.
SWISS HOP	VELUCCI
SWISS MOUNTAIN SONG -- SWISS FOLK SONG	WEYBRIGHT
SWISS MUSIC BOX, THE	BURTON, L.
SWISS SONG	BANKS, M.
SWISS VALSE	VOLZ, H.
SWISS VILLAGE	BRIED, F.
SWISS VILLAGE	TODD
SWISS VILLAGE	TODD
SWISS WALTZ	KING, S.
SWISS WALTZ	KING, S.
SWISS YODEL SONG	VAN DYKE
SWORD DANCE, THE	STONE, E.
SWORD DANCE -- FROM BALLET 'GAYNE'	KHATCHATURIAN
SWORD DANCE	KHATCHATURIAN
SYLPHES, LES, EASY	BACHMANN, G.
SYLPHIDES, LES, CAPRICE	HEINS, C.
SYLPHIDES, LES -- BALLET --	CHOPIN
SYLPHIDES	CHOPIN
SYLVAINS, LES -- THE FAUNS --	CHAMINADE
SYLVIA, PIZZICATI	DELIBES, L.
SYLVIA, PIZZICATO, EASY	DELIBES, L.
SYLVIA -- PIZZICATI	DELIBES, L.
SYLVIA BALLET	DELIBES, L.
SYLVIA	SPEAKS, O.
SYMPATHY--FROM 'THE FIREFLY'	FRIML, R.
SYMPATHY WALTZ--''THE FIREFLY''	FRIML, R.
SYMPATHY WALTZ--''THE FIREFLY''	FRIML, R.
SYMPATHY WALTZ--''THE FIREFLY''	FRIML, R.
SYMPHONETTE	WHITFORD
SYMPHONIC DANCES, OP. 45	RACHMANINOFF, S.
SYMPHONIC DANCES, OP. 64 --ARR. BY COMPOSER--	GRIEG
SYMPHONIC ETUDES, OP. 13	SCHUMANN, R.
SYMPHONIC ETUDES, OP. 13	SCHUMANN, R.
SYMPHONIC ETUDES, OP. 13	SCHUMANN, R.
SYMPHONIC ETUDES, OP. 13	SCHUMANN, R.
SYMPHONIC PIECES, OP. 14	GRIEG
SYMPHONIC RHAPSODY	FRANCK, C.
SYMPHONIC VARIATIONS --2 COPIES--	FRANCK, C.
SYMPHONIC VARIATIONS ON AN ORIGINAL THEME, OP. 9	GROSZ, W.
SYMPHONIC VARIATIONS	FRANCK, C.
SYMPHONIC VARIATIONS	FRANCK, C.
SYMPHONIC VARIATIONS	FRANCK, C.
SYMPHONIC VARIATIONS	FRANCK, C.
SYMPHONIES, BK. 1--NOS. 1-5	BEETHOVEN
SYMPHONIES, BK. 1--NOS. 1-5	BEETHOVEN
SYMPHONIES, BK. 1 -- 1-3 --	BEETHOVEN
SYMPHONIES, BK. 2--NOS. 6-9	BEETHOVEN
SYMPHONIES, BK. 2--NOS. 6-9	BEETHOVEN
SYMPHONIES, BK. 2 -- 4-6 --	BEETHOVEN
SYMPHONIES, BK. 3 -- 7-9 --	BEETHOVEN
SYMPHONIES, COMPLETE IN 2 VOLS., VOL. 1	BRAHMS
SYMPHONIES, COMPLETE IN 2 VOLS., VOL. 2	BRAHMS
SYMPHONIES, COMPLETE IN 3 VOLS., VOL. 1	BRUCKNER
SYMPHONIES, COMPLETE IN 3 VOLS., VOL. 2	BRUCKNER
SYMPHONIES, COMPLETE IN 3 VOLS., VOL. 3	BRUCKNER
SYMPHONIES, OP. 38, 61, 97, 120. COMPLETE	SCHUMANN, R.
SYMPHONIES, VOL. 1	BEETHOVEN
SYMPHONIES, VOL. 2	BEETHOVEN
SYMPHONIES -- SELECTED -- BK. 1	HAYDN
SYMPHONIES -- SELECTED -- BK. 1	MOZART, W. A.
SYMPHONIES -- SELECTED -- BK. 2	HAYDN
SYMPHONIES -- SELECTED -- BK. 2	MOZART, W. A.
SYMPHONIES --12--	HAYDN
SYMPHONIES --4--	BRAHMS
SYMPHONIES --4--	SCHUBERT
SYMPHONIES AND SERENADES --12--, IN 2 VOLS* VOL. 1	MOZART, W. A.
SYMPHONIES AND SERENADES --12--, IN 2 VOLS* VOL. 2	MOZART, W. A.
SYMPHONIES BK. 1 -- 1-5 --	BEETHOVEN
SYMPHONIES BK. 2 -- 6-9 --	BEETHOVEN
SYMPHONIES FOR PIANO	RIOS, DE
SYMPHONIES FUR SOLOKLAVIER, BLASER, HARFE, UND	LUTYENS, E.
SYMPHONIES IN 2 VOLS., VOL. 1	BEETHOVEN
SYMPHONIES IN 2 VOLS., VOL. 2	BEETHOVEN
SYMPHONIES	BRAHMS
SYMPHONIE CONCERTANTE, OP. 60	SZYMANOWSKI
SYMPHONIE ESPAGNOLE, OP. 21	LALO, E.
SYMPHONIE FUR KLAVIER UND ORCHESTER, OP. 61 -	TOCH, E.
SYMPHONIE H-MOLL -- UNVOLL.	SCHUBERT
SYMPHONIE NO. 01 EN MI FLAT	BORODIN, A.
SYMPHONIE NO. 02 EN SI MINEUR	BORODIN, A.
SYMPHONIE NO. 1 FUR KONZERTANTES KLAVIER UND	JUROWSKY
SYMPHONISCHES KONZERT FUR KLAVIER UND ORCHESTER	FURTWANGLER
SYMPHONY, UNFINISHED, THEME	SCHUBERT
SYMPHONY "ROMEO AND JULIET", OP. 17	BERLIOZ
SYMPHONY IN B-FLAT MAJOR	CHAUSSON
SYMPHONY IN B MINOR, NO. 8--'UNFINISHED'	SCHUBERT
SYMPHONY IN B MINOR 'UNFINISHED' -- THEMES IN EASY	SCHUBERT
SYMPHONY IN B MINOR 'UNFINISHED'	SCHUBERT
SYMPHONY IN C MAJOR	DUKAS, P.
SYMPHONY IN D MINOR--MUSIC LOVER'S SYMPHONY SERIES,	FRANCK, C.
SYMPHONY IN D MINOR -- POEME DE LA FORET --	ROUSSEL, A.
SYMPHONY IN D MINOR	FRANCK, C.
SYMPHONY IN E FLAT, MINUET	MOZART, W. A.
SYMPHONY IN E FLAT, MINUET	MOZART, W. A.
SYMPHONY IN STEEL	GROFE, F.
SYMPHONY NO. 01, OP. 10	SHOSTAKOVITCH
SYMPHONY NO. 01 IN C, OP. 21	BEETHOVEN
SYMPHONY NO. 01 IN C MINOR, OP. 68	BRAHMS
SYMPHONY NO. 01	CHAUSSON
SYMPHONY NO. 01	DUKAS, P.
SYMPHONY NO. 01	MAGNARD
SYMPHONY NO. 01	MAHLER
SYMPHONY NO. 01	ROPARTZ
SYMPHONY NO. 02 IN D, OP. 36	BEETHOVEN
SYMPHONY NO. 02 IN D, OP. 73	BRAHMS
SYMPHONY NO. 02 IN F MINOR	ROPARTZ
SYMPHONY NO. 02	MAGNARD
SYMPHONY NO. 02	MAHLER
SYMPHONY NO. 03 IN E FLAT, OP. 55, 'EROICA'	BEETHOVEN
SYMPHONY NO. 03 IN E FLAT, OP. 55 'EROICA'	BEETHOVEN
SYMPHONY NO. 03 IN F, OP. 90	BRAHMS
SYMPHONY NO. 03	D'INDY, V.
SYMPHONY NO. 03	MAGNARD
SYMPHONY NO. 03	MAHLER
SYMPHONY NO. 03	MAHLER
SYMPHONY NO. 04 IN A MAJOR	MENDELSSOHN
SYMPHONY NO. 04 IN D MINOR, OP. 120 -- HORN -- 8	SCHUMANN, R.
SYMPHONY NO. 04 IN F MINOR, OP. 36	TSCHAIKOWSKY
SYMPHONY NO. 04	BRUCKNER
SYMPHONY NO. 04	BRUCKNER
SYMPHONY NO. 04	MAGNARD
SYMPHONY NO. 04	MAHLER
SYMPHONY NO. 05, ALLEGRO CON BRIO	BEETHOVEN
SYMPHONY NO. 05, ANDANTE CANTABILE	TSCHAIKOWSKY
SYMPHONY NO. 05, ANDANTE CON MOTO	BEETHOVEN
SYMPHONY NO. 05, THEME EASY	TSCHAIKOWSKY
SYMPHONY NO. 05, VICTORY THEME	BEETHOVEN
SYMPHONY NO. 05 IN B FLAT	BRUCKNER
SYMPHONY NO. 05 IN C MINOR, OP. 67	BEETHOVEN
SYMPHONY NO. 05 IN C MINOR, OP. 67	BEETHOVEN
SYMPHONY NO. 05 IN C MINOR	BEETHOVEN
SYMPHONY NO. 05 IN D MINOR, OP. 67	BEETHOVEN
SYMPHONY NO. 05 IN E MINOR, OP. 64	TSCHAIKOWSKY
SYMPHONY NO. 05 IN E MINOR, OP. 64	TSCHAIKOWSKY
SYMPHONY NO. 05 IN E MINOR 'FROM THE NEW WORLD'	DVORAK
SYMPHONY NO. 05	MAHLER
SYMPHONY NO. 05	MAHLER
SYMPHONY NO. 05	MAHLER
SYMPHONY NO. 05	MAHLER
SYMPHONY NO. 05	TSCHAIKOWSKY
SYMPHONY NO. 06, OP. 74 'PATHETIQUE'	TSCHAIKOWSKY
SYMPHONY NO. 06 IN B MINOR, OP. 74 --'PATHETIQUE'--	TSCHAIKOWSKY
SYMPHONY NO. 06 IN B MINOR, OP. 74 -- ''PATHETIQUE''	TSCHAIKOWSKY
SYMPHONY NO. 06 IN B MINOR, OP. 74	TSCHAIKOWSKY
SYMPHONY NO. 06 IN F, OP. 68 'PASTORAL'	BEETHOVEN
SYMPHONY NO. 07, ALLEGRETTO	BEETHOVEN
SYMPHONY NO. 07 IN A, OP. 92	BEETHOVEN
SYMPHONY NO. 08, ALLEGRETTO SCHERZANDO	BEETHOVEN
SYMPHONY NO. 08 IN B MINOR, ''UNFINISHED''	SCHUBERT
SYMPHONY NO. 08 IN B MINOR --'UNFINISHED'--	SCHUBERT
SYMPHONY NO. 08	SCHUBERT
SYMPHONY NO. 09, CHORAL THEME	BEETHOVEN
SYMPHONY NO. 09 IN C	SCHUBERT
SYMPHONY NO. 09 IN D MINOR, OP. 125 'CHORAL'	BEETHOVEN
SYMPHONY NO. 09 IN D MINOR, OP. 125	BEETHOVEN
SYMPHONY NO. 09 IN E MINOR, OP. 95 FROM 'THE NEW	DVORAK
SYMPHONY NO. 09	MAHLER
SYMPHONY NO. 10 IN C MAJOR	SCHUBERT
SYMPHONY NO. 16 IN G MAJOR	HAYDN
SYMPHONY NO. 38 IN D -- WITHOUT MINUET	MOZART, W. A.
SYMPHONY NO. 40 -- FIRST THEME	MOZART, W. A.
SYMPHONY NO. 40 -- THEMES	MOZART, W. A.
SYMPHONY NO. 41 IN C, K551	MOZART, W. A.
SYMPHONY ON A FRENCH MOUNTAIN AIR, OP.25	D'INDY, V.
SYMPHONY PATHETIQUE, THEME	TSCHAIKOWSKY
SYNCHRONISMS NO. 6	DAVIDOVSKY
SYNCOPATED CLOCK, THE, SIMP.	ANDERSON, L.
SYNCOPATED CLOCK, THE -- CHILDREN'S EDITION	STEINER--ED.
SYNCOPATED CLOCK, THE -- SIMP.	ANDERSON, L.
SYNCOPATED CLOCK, THE	ANDERSON, L.
SYNCOPATED CLOCK, THE	ANDERSON, L.
SYNCOPATED CLOCK	PARISH, M. *

Title	Composer
SYNCOPATED DOLL, THE	CARLE, F. *
SYNCOPATED SERENADE	STARER
SYNCOPATION MADE EASY - BOOK 1	THOMPSON, J.
SYNCOPATION MADE EASY - BOOK 2	THOMPSON, J.
SYNCO POPS	KING
SYNKOPEN, 4 PIANO-SOLI	FISCHER, E.
SYNTHETIC STUDY OF DAILY PIANO TECHNIQUE - 142	KARTUN
SYNTHETIC WALTZES -- SET OF 2 COPIES	THOMSON, V.
SYNTHETIC WALTZES -- SET OF 2 COPIES	THOMSON, V.
SYRTOS	FULEIHAN, A.
S KOMMT EIN VOGEL GEFLOGEN. IM STILE ALTERER UND	OCHS
S KOMMT EIN VOGEL GEFLOGEN. IM STILE ALTERER UND	OCHS
TA-RA-RA-BOUM DER-E	WALTER
TA'IAMIM	ROGERS
TABATIERE A MUSIQUE	BOUTRY
TABLA DANCE. PIANO, PERCUSSION ENSEMBLE	ELDABH
TABLEAUX D'UNE EXPOSITION	MOUSSORGSKY
TABLEAUX D'UNE EXPOSITION	MOUSSORGSKY
TABLEAUX DES PAYS-BAS. BK. 1	VOORMOLEN
TABLEAUX DES PAYS-BAS. BK. 2	VOORMOLEN
TABLEAUX DE VOYAGE, OP. 33	D'INDY, V.
TABLEAUX VIVANTS - FROM 'LA PASSION SELON SADE'	BUSSOTTI
TABLOID	GROFE, F.
TAG WALTZ	SWIFT, F.
TAG	BUTLER, J.
TAG	ROGERS, E.
TAHITI --MODERN RHYTHMIC CLASSICS--	WHITFORD
TAKES TWO TO DUET	SUGARMAN
TAKE HER TO JAMAICA	
TAKE ME IN YOUR ARMS -- SIMP.	MOSSMAN, T.--ED
TAKE OFF	GARROW, L.
TAKIN' IT SLOW	COVINGTON, W.
TAKING A WALK	FOLDES
TAKING IT EASY	MANA-ZUCCA
TALE, A	JADASSOHN, S.
TALES AND TUNES FROM GRAND OPERA	BLAKE--ED
TALES FROM THE FLAMENCO KINGDOM--1955	SURINACH, C.
TALES FROM THE VIENNA WOODS--WALTZ, OP. 325	STRAUSS, J.
TALES FROM THE VIENNA WOODS--WALTZ	STRAUSS, J.
TALES FROM THE VIENNA WOODS, OP. 325	STRAUSS, J.
TALES FROM THE VIENNA WOODS, OP. 325	STRAUSS, J.
TALES FROM THE VIENNA WOODS --WALTZ--, OP. 325	STRAUSS, J.
TALES FROM THE VIENNA WOODS WALTZ	STRAUSS, J.
TALES FROM THE VIENNA WOODS WALTZ	STRAUSS, J.
TALES FROM THE VIENNA WOODS WALTZ	STRAUSS, J.
TALES FROM THE VIENNA WOODS	STRAUSS, J.
TALES FROM THE VIENNA WOODS	STRAUSS, J.
TALES FROM THE VIENNA WOODS	STRAUSS, J.
TALES FROM THE VIENNA WOODS	STRAUSS, J.
TALES FROM THE VIENNA WOODS	STRAUSS, J.
TALES FROM THE VIENNA WOODS	STRAUSS, J.
TALES FROM THE VIENNA WOODS	STRAUSS, J.
TALES FROM VIENNA WOODS	STRAUSS, J.
TALES FROM VIENNA WOODS	STRAUSS, J.
TALES OF HOFFMAN, BARCAROLLE	OFFENBACH
TALES OF HOFFMAN, BARCAROLLE	OFFENBACH
TALES OF HOFFMANN. FANTASY. TWO PIANOS, EIGHT HANDS	OFFENBACH
TALES OF HOFFMANN - BARCAROLLE, SIMP.	OFFENBACH
TALES OF HOFFMANN - BARCAROLLE	OFFENBACH
TALES OF HOFFMANN - BARCAROLLE	OFFENBACH
TALES OF SCALES	SEIDER
TALES OF THE OLD GRANDMOTHER, OP. 31--4 PIECES	PROKOFIEFF
TALES OF THE OLD GRANDMOTHER, OP. 31	PROKOFIEFF
TALES OF THE VIENNA WOODS	STRAUSS, J.
TALE OF HALLOWEEN	JOYNER, B.
TALE OF LONG AGO, A	BENTLEY
TALKING CLOCK, THE	KAHL
TALKING GRACE NOTES	CATIZONE, J. M.
TALK TO THE ANIMALS	LANE, J.--ED.
TALL, TALL BUILDINGS	BURNAM
TALLY-HO RIDE, THE	DUTTON, T.
TALLY-HO	READ, G.
TALLY HO	HIER, E.
TALL IN THE SADDLE	MCBRIDE, R.
TALL TALE	KNIGHTON
TALL TREES	ARCHER, I.
TALL TREES	CANFIELD, J.
TAMARIU--SARDANA	TOLDRA, E. E.
TAMBOO	CAVEZ, F.
TAMBOURINE DANCE	DONENFELD, J.
TAMBOURINE	BLAKE, D. G.
TAMBOURINE	ROZIN
TAMBOURIN -- 6-HANDS	ROWLEY
TAMBOURIN CHINOIS --STUDENT EDITION--	KREISLER
TAMBOURIN CHINOIS	CHEDEVILLE, E.
TAMBOURIN CHINOIS	KREISLER
TAMBOURIN CHINOIS	KREISLER
TAMBOURIN	BENJAMIN
TAMBOURIN	BROWN, C.
TAMBOURIN	RAMEAU
TAMBOURIN	RAMEAU
TAMBOURIN	RAMEAU
TAMMY	BRIMHALL,
TAMZARA--TURKISH DANCE	KOPTAGEL, Y.
TAM O'SHANTER	WARREN
TAM O'SHANTER	WARREN
TAM O'SHANTER	WARREN
TANCREDI - OVERTURE	ROSSINI, G.
TANDELEI, OP. 575 NO. 3	BEHR, F.
TANGANA	LEWIS
TANGLEFOOT'S MAD CHASE	MOREY, F.
TANGLEWOOD AND TALES	HARVEY, VIVIEN
TANGLEWOOD TALES	HARVEY, VIVIEN
TANGO, OP. 165, NO. I -- FROM ESPANA	ALBENIZ, I.
TANGO, OP. 165 NO. 2	ALBENIZ, I.
TANGO, OP. 165 NO. 2	ALBENIZ, I.
TANGO, OP. 165	ALBENIZ, I.
TANGO, OP. 60, NO. 2 -- FROM ESPANA	ALBENIZ, I.
TANGOLETTA	ROBINSON, A.
TANGOS	CASTRO, J. M.
TANGO AMERICAINE	CARPENTER, J.
TANGO AMERICANO	MANCINI
TANGO BALLAD -- DREIGROSCHENOPER	WEILL, K.
TANGO BONGO	NEVIN
TANGO CARIOCA	THOMPSON, J.
TANGO D'AMOUR	WEINER
TANGO DES FRATELLINI FROM 'BOEUF SUR LE TOIT'	MILHAUD, D.
TANGO DE LA ROSA	DURAND, P.
TANGO ESPANOL FOR 2 PIANOS	GRIFFIS, E.
TANGO ESPANOL	GRIFFIS, E.
TANGO IN D	ALBENIZ, I.
TANGO IN D	ALBENIZ, I.
TANGO MODERNE	MARTIN, H.
TANGO MODERNE	MARTIN, H.
TANGO NO. 2. KONZERTTRANSKRIPTION	ALBENIZ, I.
TANGO NO. 2. TRANSCRIPTION	ALBENIZ, I.
TANGO NO. 2	ALBENIZ, I.
TANGO ON THE NAME OF ANDRE PREVIN	CASTELNUOVO-TEDE
TANGO PICASSO	WILDMAN *
TANGO ROMANCE	AGAY, D.
TANGO TIME IN RIO	MARTIN, H.
TANGO TIME	BURNAM
TANGO	ALBENIZ, I.
TANGO	BLAKE, D.
TANGO	FLETCHER
TANGO	GILARDI
TANGO	GUERRERO, A.
TANGO	MOWREY, D.
TANGO	STRAVINSKY, I.
TANGO	STRAVINSKY, I.
TANGO	STRAVINSKY, I.
TANGO	STRAVINSKY, I.
TANGO	TRUXELL, E.
TANGO	TRUXELL, E.
TANNHAEUSER - MARCH	WAGNER
TANNHAEUSER - MARCH	WAGNER
TANNHAEUSER - OVERTURE	WAGNER
TANNHAEUSER - PILGRIMS' CHORUS	WAGNER *
TANNHAEUSER - PILGRIMS' CHORUS	WAGNER
TANNHAEUSER OVERTURE -- FREE TRANSCRIPTION --	WAGNER *
TANNHAUSER--MARCH. ENTRANCE OF THE GUESTS INTO THE	WAGNER *
TANNHAUSER--MARCH. ENTRANCE OF THE GUESTS INTO THE	WAGNER *
TANNHAUSER, FANTASIE	WAGNER
TANNHAUSER, MARCH AND CHORUS	WAGNER
TANNHAUSER, PILGRIMS' CHORUS	WAGNER
TANNHAUSER, PILGRIMS' CHORUS	WAGNER
TANNHAUSER MARCH AND CHORUS	WAGNER
TANTALIZING --MODERN RHYTHMIC CLASSICS--	WHITFORD
TANTSTUCK	KONT, P.
TANZ-TYPEN, BAND 01	MERATH, S.
TANZ-TYPEN, BAND 02	MERATH, S.
TANZ, TANZ, GRETELEIN	LANG--ED
TANZBUCHLEIN, LES PETITS RIENS	MOZART, W. A.
TANZBUCHLEIN FUR KLAVIER	WEBER, VON
TANZENDES ROKOKO UND DIE ZEIT DER ROMANTIK, BAND 01	KRENTZLIN,
TANZENDES ROKOKO UND DIE ZEIT DER ROMANTIK, BAND 02	KRENTZLIN,
TANZENDE MASKEN, MARABU	FISCHER, E.
TANZE -- POLKA IN E, 10 MENUETTE, SCHOTTISCHE TANZE --	DVORAK
TANZE AUS EINEM ALTEN KLAVIERBUCH - 1800'S	OBERDORFFER--ED
TANZE F. D. JUGEND	SCHUBERT
TANZST, OP. 19	HINDEMITH
TANZSTUCKE. 14 TANZSATZE FUR KLAVIER	KINDERMANN
TANZSTUCKE	KINDERMANN
TANZSTUCKE	KIRNBERGER, J.
TANZSUITE	BARTOK
TANZVARIATIONEN	HOFFER, P.
TANZWEISEN, OP. 25, BK. 1	WILLNER, A.
TANZWEISEN, OP. 25, BK. 2	WILLNER, A.
TANZWEISEN UND RUNDGESANG	PEPPING, E.
TANZ	KARP
TAPESTRY	BRADLEY,
TAPESTRY	KING, C.
TAP DANCER, THE	SCHAUM, J.
TAP DANCE CONCERTO	
TAP DANCE	LINDFORS, E.
TAP DANCE	NEVIN
TARANTELLA--FROM VENEZIA E NAPOLI	LISZT
TARANTELLA, OP. 43	CHOPIN
TARANTELLA, OP. 44 NO. 6	MARTUCCI
TARANTELLA, OP. 65	PROKOFIEFF
TARANTELLA, OP. 85 NO. 2	HELLER, S.
TARANTELLA, S.W.W., 45	MENDELSSOHN
TARANTELLA - FROM FIVE PIECES FOR YOUNG PIANISTS	RIETI
TARANTELLA IN A FLAT, OP. 43	CHOPIN
TARANTELLA IN A FLAT, OP. 85 NO. 2	HELLER, S.
TARANTELLA IN A MINOR	DENNEE
TARANTELLA IN A MINOR	PIECZONKA, A.
TARANTELLA IN A MINOR	PIECZONKA, A.
TARANTELLA IN E MINOR	LOMAS, W.
TARANTELLA VICO	GIOVANNI
TARANTELLA	BOCCOSI, BIO
TARANTELLA	BOCCOSI, BIO
TARANTELLA	BRUSSELS, I.
TARANTELLA	COBB
TARANTELLA	GILLOCK
TARANTELLA	GILLOCK
TARANTELLA	LAWNER, M.
TARANTELLA	PIECZONKA, A.
TARANTELLA	PIECZONKA, A.
TARANTELLA	PIECZONKA, A.
TARANTELLA	POZZOLI
TARANTELLA	PROKOFIEFF
TARANTELLA	RIETI
TARANTELLA	ROGERS
TARANTELLA	THOMPSON, J.
TARANTELLA	TILLETT, J.
TARANTELLA	ZEPP--ED
TARANTELLE, OP. 13 NO. 1	MILLS
TARANTELLE, OP. 85 NO. 2	HELLER, S.
TARANTELLE, OP. 85	HELLER, S.
TARANTELLE BRILLANTE	SCARMOLIN
TARANTELLE IN E MINOR	PERIN, H.
TARANTELLE	DENNEE
TARANTELLE	HOUSE, A.
TARANTELLE	LUDOVIC, G.
TARANTELLE	MARSDEN, E.
TARANTELLE	MARTIN, G.
TARANTELL	STILWELL
TARA THEME -- MY OWN TRUE LOVE	STEINER
TARA THEME	STEINER
TARDE EN RINCON, LA	GUASTAVINO
TARENTELLE, OP. 3 NO. 15	PIERNE
TARENTELLE DE CESAR CUI	LISZT
TARENTELLE IN A FLAT MAJOR, OP. 43	CHOPIN
TARENTELLE IN A FLAT MAJOR, OP. 85 NO. 2	HELLER, S.
TARENTELLE IN D, OP. 77	NOLLET, E.
TARENTELLE	BEAUMONT, P.
TARENTELLE	FERTE
TARENTELLE	THUILLIER
TARENTELLE	TOMASI, H.
TARIK LAN LA	ARNOUX, G.
TARLO, IL	COLTRO
TARLO, IL	MALIPIERO, G. F.
TARTINA DI BURRO, LA	MOZART, W. A.
TASTE OF HONEY, A	BRIMHALL
TATTLETALE -- WITH WORDS	AARON, M.
TAUTROPFEN OP. 127A	GRETCHANINOFF
TCHAIKOWSKY	TSCHAIKOWSKY
TEACHER'S CHOICE, BK. 1	
TEACHER'S CHOICE, BK. 2	
TEACHER'S CHOICE, BK. 3	
TEACHER'S CHOICE FOR THE YOUNG PIANIST	SMALL, A.
TEACHER'S PET, BK. 01	LANE--ED.

TEACHER'S PET, BK. 02	LANE--ED.
TEACHER'S PET, BK. 03	LANE--ED.
TEACHER'S PET, BK. 04	LANE--ED.
TEACHER'S PET, BK. 05	LANE--ED.
TEACHER'S PET, BK. 06	LANE--ED.
TEACHER'S PET, BK. 07	LANE--ED.
TEACHER'S PET, BK. 08	LANE--ED.
TEACHER'S PET, BK. 09	LANE--ED.
TEACHER'S PET, BK. 10	LANE--ED.
TEACHER'S PET, BK. 11	LANE--ED.
TEACHER'S PET NO. 12-16 BIG HITS	LANE, J.
TEACHER'S PET NO. 13	LANE, J.
TEACHERS AND PUPILS OF J. S. BACH, VOL. 1	HERRMANN, K.--ED
TEACHERS AND PUPILS OF J. S. BACH, VOL. 2	HERRMANN, K.--ED
TEACHER AND PUPIL, A PRACTICAL COURSE OF 4-HAND PIANO	LOEW, J.
TEACHER AND PUPIL, A PRACTICAL COURSE OF 4-HAND PIANO	LOEW, J.
TEACHER AND PUPIL, BK. 1	LOEW, J.
TEACHER AND PUPIL, BK. 2	LOEW, J.
TEACHER AND PUPIL --40 PIECES--	RUTHARDT
TEACHER AND PUPIL	RUTHARDT
TEACHING FINGERS HOW TO PLAY POPS, ISSUE 1	BRIMHALL,
TEACHING FINGERS HOW TO PLAY POPS, ISSUE 2	BRIMHALL,
TEACHING FINGERS HOW TO PLAY POPS, ISSUE 3	BRIMHALL,
TEACHING FINGERS HOW TO PLAY POPS, ISSUE 4	BRIMHALL,
TEACHING FINGERS HOW TO PLAY SONGS FOR LITTLE	BRIMHALL,
TEARS	RACHMANINOFF, S.
TEASIN' THE IVORIES --MODERN RHYTHMIC CLASSICS--	WHITFORD
TEASING	GALLEZ
TEATRINO IN MUSICA	FERRARI-TRECATE
TEA FOR TWO	YOUMANS
TEA FOR TWO	YOUMANS
TEA FOR TWO	YOUMANS
TEA FOR TWO	YOUMANS
TEA FOR TWO	YOUMANS
TEA WITH A STRANGER - TABLEAU FOR PIANO	CORY, G.
TEA WITH A TOTAL STRANGER	CORY, G.
TECHNIC, BK. 1	BARTH, H.
TECHNIC, BK. 2	BARTH, H.
TECHNIC, BK. 3	BARTH, H.
TECHNICAL AIDS TO THE PLAYING OF SCALES, BROKEN	CHILDE, M.
TECHNICAL AIDS TO THE PLAYING OF SCALES, BROKEN	CHILDE, M.
TECHNICAL AIDS TO THE PLAYING OF SCALES, BROKEN	CHILDE, M.
TECHNICAL EXERCISES, BK. 01	LISZT
TECHNICAL EXERCISES, BK. 02	LISZT
TECHNICAL EXERCISES, BK. 03	LISZT
TECHNICAL EXERCISES, BK. 04	LISZT
TECHNICAL EXERCISES, BK. 05	LISZT
TECHNICAL EXERCISES, BK. 06	LISZT
TECHNICAL EXERCISES, BK. 07	LISZT
TECHNICAL EXERCISES, BK. 08	LISZT
TECHNICAL EXERCISES, BK. 09	LISZT
TECHNICAL EXERCISES, BK. 10	LISZT
TECHNICAL EXERCISES, BK. 11	LISZT
TECHNICAL EXERCISES, BK. 12	LISZT
TECHNICAL EXERCISES --COMPLETE--	LISZT
TECHNICAL EXERCISES FOR THE INDEPENDENCE OF TOUCH IN	TEBOLDI
TECHNICAL EXERCISES	PHILIPP, I.
TECHNICAL STUDIES--60 PROGRESSIVE EXERCISES, REVISED	PISCHNA
TECHNICAL STUDIES, BK. 1--SECTIONS 1-4	PLAIDY, L.
TECHNICAL STUDIES ON THE PENTATONIC SCALE	TCHEREPNIN
TECHNICAL STUDIES	PLAIDY, L.
TECHNICAL STUDIES	PLAIDY, L.
TECHNICAL VARIANTS	HANON, C.
TECHNIC BOOK	SEDERBERG
TECHNIC FOR ADULTS, BK. 1	HIRSCHBERG, D.
TECHNIC FOR BEGINNERS	RISHER, A. P.
TECHNIC FOR PIANISTS, BK. 1	WEYBRIGHT
TECHNIC FOR PIANISTS, BK. 2	WEYBRIGHT
TECHNIC FOR THE FIRST YEAR	THOMPSON, J.
TECHNIC FOR THIRDS, SIXTHS AND OCTAVES	PODOLSKY, L. *
TECHNIC FROM THE MASTERS	STEINER
TECHNIC INDISPENSABLES	ZEPP
TECHNIC IS FUN, BK. 1	HIRSCHBERG, D.
TECHNIC IS FUN, BK. 2	HIRSCHBERG, D.
TECHNIC IS FUN, BK. 3	HIRSCHBERG, D.
TECHNIC IS FUN, BK. 4	HIRSCHBERG, D.
TECHNIC IS FUN, BK. 5	HIRSCHBERG, D.
TECHNIC IS FUN - PREPARATORY BOOK	FLETCHER, S.
TECHNIC KNACKS	BUOGO
TECHNIC OF THE ARPEGGIO, BK. 1	ZEPP
TECHNIC PATTERNS - BOOK 1	ZEPP
TECHNIC PATTERNS - BOOK 2	ZEPP
TECHNIC PATTERNS - BOOK 3	ROBYN
TECHNIC TALES, BK. 1	ROBYN
TECHNIC TALES, BK. 2	ROBYN
TECHNIC TALES, BK. 3	SCHAUM, J.--ED.
TECHNIC THROUGH MELODY, BK. 1	SCHAUM, J.--ED.
TECHNIC THROUGH MELODY, BK. 2	CLARK, F.--ED.
TECHNIC TIME - PART A	CLARK, F.--ED.
TECHNIC TIME - PART B	AGAY, D.--ED
TECHNIC TREASURY, BK. 1	AGAY, D.--ED
TECHNIC TREASURY, BK. 2	AGAY, D.--ED
TECHNIC TREASURY, BK. 3	SCHAUM, J.--ED.
TECHNIC TRICKS, BK.1	SCHAUM, J.--ED.
TECHNIC TRICKS, BK.2	REBE
TECHNIC TUNES	ANSON, G.
TECHNIC TWISTERS	BARTH, H.
TECHNIC	DESCAVES, L.
TECHNIQUE, VOL.1	DESCAVES, L.
TECHNIQUE, VOL.2	KAEMPER
TECHNIQUES PIANISTIQUES	SMALL, A.
TECHNIQUE AND MELODY IN ALL KEYS	COBB
TECHNIQUE BUILDERS	COBB
TECHNIQUE BUILDERS	HOWELL, I.
TECHNIQUE BUILDER	PANELLA, L.
TECH TARTAN	BURNAM
TEDDY BEAR'S GOODNIGHT	BRATTON
TEDDY BEARS' PICNIC, THE	BRATTON
TEDDY BEARS' PICNIC, THE	MELECCI, A.
TEDDY BEARS ON PARADE	BENFORD
TEDDY BEAR WALTZ	WILSON, T.
TEDDY WILSON, PIANO PATTERNS	KASSERN, T. Z.
TEEN-AGE CONCERTO	KING, S.
TEEN-AGE TECHNIC	ANSON, G.
TEEN-TUNE	WHITE
TEETER TOTTER	STARER
TELEGRAPH, THE	REGER
TELEMANN VARIATIONS AND FUGUE, OP. 134	HOPKINS, H.
TELL ME, PUSSY	SCHER, W.
TELL ME PRETTY DAISY	MEEK
TELSTAR	HAYDN
TEMA CON VARIAZIONI IN C MAJOR	HANDEL
TEMA CON VARIAZIONI	VOTACEK
TEMA CON VARIAZIONI	PONCE, M.
TEMA MEXICANO VARIADO	APONTE-LEDEE, R.
TEMA Y SEIS DIFFERENCIAS	GUERRINI, G.
TEMPI DI CONCERTO	
TEMPLE CHIMES	OLSON
TEMPLE PRICESSIONAL AND DANCE	SLATES, P.
TEMPO AMERICANO FROM ''SYMPHONIE CONCERTANTE''	TANSMAN, A.
TEMPO DI GAVOTTA	BOYCE, W.
TEMPO DI GAVOTTA	MARCHI, G.
TEMPO DI MAZURKA, OP. 11	MARTUCCI
TEMPO DI MINUETTO IN D	SCHARWENKA, P.
TEMPO DI MINUETTO	ALLENDE
TEMPO DI MINUETTO	CARRER
TEMPO DI MINUETTO	MOZART, W. A.
TEMPO DI SAMBA	VIOZZI, G.
TEMPO DI VALZER	COUTURE
TEMPTATION RAG	LODGE, H.
TEMPTATION	BROWN *
TEMPTATION	
TEMPUS FUGIT	DAVIES, E. J.
TENCAO. AUSGEWAHLTE KONTRAPUNKTSTUCKE	DA COSTA DE
TENDERLY	BRIMHALL,
TENDERNESS, OP. 149 -- VALSE TENDRE	CHAMINADE
TENDER FLOWER, OP. 299 NO. 1	EGGHARD
TENDRE FANCHON	COUPERIN, F.
TEN BAGATELLES, OP. 51	KADOSA
TEN BAGATELLES, OP. 88	PEETERS
TEN BIG HITS, EASY TO PLAY, NO. 1	LANE, J.--ED
TEN BIG HITS, EASY TO PLAY, NO. 2	LANE, J.--ED
TEN BIG HITS, EASY TO PLAY, NO. 2	LANE, J.--ED
TEN BIG HITS, EASY TO PLAY, NO. 3	LANE, J.--ED
TEN CANTILENAS ARGENTINAS	GUASTAVINO
TEN CANTI PAESANI DEL MOLISE	DE RUBERTIS
TEN CELEBRATED OVERTURES	MOZART, W. A.
TEN CHARACTERISTIC DANCES	SCHER, W.
TEN CHILDREN'S PIECES, OP. 27, BK. 2	KABALEVSKY
TEN CHILDREN'S PIECES	SHULGIN
TEN CHRISTMAS CAROLS	WILLIAMS,
TEN CONCERT VARIATIONS	NEVIN
TEN CONCERT VARIATIONS	NEVIN
TEN DANCES IN LABANOTATION	CHILKOVSKY, N.
TEN DANCING FINGERS	FIELDS, I.
TEN DESCRIPTIVE SKETCHES	MCINTOSH
TEN DIVERSIONS FOR THE YOUNG PIANIST--COMPLETE	TANSMAN, A.
TEN DIVERSIONS FOR THE YOUNG PIANIST--TOCCATA	TANSMAN, A.
TEN DUETS FOR PIANO ON RHYMES FROM MOTHER GOOSE	POOL, K.
TEN EASY PIANO PIECES	SCARMOLIN
TEN EASY PIECES - LA JOLIE FLEUR DU JARDIN	KOECHLIN, C.
TEN EASY PIECES AND A CODA	THOMSON, V.
TEN EASY PIECES FOR PIANO	BARTOK
TEN EASY PIECES	BADEN
TEN EASY PIECES	BARTOK
TEN EASY PIECES	BARTOK
TEN EASY PIECES	FLOTHIUS
TEN EASY PIECES	KOECHLIN, C.
TEN ETUDES, OP. 15	BORTKIEWICZ
TEN ETUDES ON AKSAK RHYTHMS	SAYGUN, A.
TEN FAMOUS WALTZES	WALDTEUFEL, E.
TEN FANTASIEN AM KLAVIER --1968 --	DELAMOTTE
TEN FINGERS IN A FIVE FINGER POSITION	PORTNOFF, M.--ED
TEN FINGER ORCHESTRA	BOLDON
TEN FOLK AND RHYTHMICAL DANCES	HENGEVELD
TEN FOLK SONGS FOR FOUR HANDS, BK. 1 -- MELODIES	ARCHER--ED
TEN FOLK SONGS FOR FOUR HANDS, BK. 2 -- MELODIES	ARCHER--ED
TEN FOR DEBORAH	GOULD, M.
TEN FOR PLEASURE	HAUBIEL, C.
TEN GERMAN DANCES	HAYDN
TEN HUNGARIAN DANCES	BRAHMS
TEN IMPROVISATIONS FOR PIANO	RAMIREZ, L. A.
TEN LITTLE CHARACTERISTIC PIECES	POZZOLI
TEN LITTLE FINGERS	NEVIN
TEN LITTLE INDIANS -- ONE PIANO, EIGHT HANDS --	KRAEHENBUEHL
TEN LITTLE INDIANS --1 PIANO, 8 HANDS--	KRAEHENBUEHL--AR
TEN LITTLE PENGUINS	COBB
TEN LITTLE PIANO PIECES, OP. 12	PROKOFIEFF
TEN LITTLE PIECES	FINKE
TEN LITTLE WALTZES, OP. 59	WEISMANN, J.
TEN MUSICAL SKETCHES	SCHER, W.
TEN PETITES PIECES ENFANTINES POUR LES JEUNES	ORBAN
TEN PIANO PIECES FROM '32 PIANO PIECES'	SKALKOTTAS, N.
TEN PIANO PIECES FROM CINDERELLA, OP. 97	PROKOFIEFF
TEN PIECES, OP. 12	PROKOFIEFF
TEN PIECES, OP. 12	PROKOFIEFF
TEN PIECES, OP. 79A	REGER
TEN PIECES FOR PIANO AND ORGAN	BACH, J.S. *
TEN PIECES FOR TEACHERS AND STUDENTS	FINKE
TEN PIECES FROM 'THE SINGING NUN'	SOEUR SOURIRE
TEN PIECES IN MODERN DANCE RHYTHMS	DECOLA, F.
TEN PIECES	KODALY
TEN PIECES	SZEKERES
TEN POLONAISES	SCHUBERT
TENCAO POLYTONAL COMPOSITIONS FOR PIANO SOLO	FICHANDLER, W.
TEN POPULAR SONGS	FOSTER
TEN PRELUDES, OP. 23 --COMPLETE--	RACHMANINOFF, S.
TEN PRELUDES, OP. 23	RACHMANINOFF, S.
TEN PRELUDES, OP. 23	RACHMANINOFF, S.
TEN PRELUDES, OP. 23	RACHMANINOFF, S.
TEN PRELUDES	CHAVEZ, C.
TEN PRELUDES	GENZMER
TEN PRELUDES	GUASTAVINO
TEN PRELUDES	PLE
TEN RHYTHMICAL DANCES	HENGEVELD
TEN SELECTED PIECES -- EASY TRANSCRIPTION	ALBENIZ, I.
TEN SHORT COMPOSITIONS, OP. 44	REGER
TEN SHORT ESSAYS	KAY, U.
TEN SHORT PIECES	CASTRO, J. M.
TEN SHORT PIECES	SCIAMMARELLA
TEN SIMPLE PIECES, OP. 31, BK. 1	ORREGO SALAS, J.
TEN SIMPLE PIECES, OP. 31, BK. 2	ORREGO SALAS, J.
TEN SONATAS	SCHUBERT
TEN SONATAS	SCRIABINE, A.
TEN TECHNIC TUNES	ZEPP
TEN TRICKS FOR TEN FINGERS	MCHALE, M.
TEN TRILL STUDIES, OP. 2	KRAUSE, A.
TEN TUNES FOR TEN FINGERS	ANSON, G.
TEN VALSES CELEBRES, BK. 1	WALDTEUFEL, E.
TEN VALSES CELEBRES, BK. 2	WALDTEUFEL, E.
TEN VARIATIONS IN G, K. 45--'UNSER DUMMER POBEL MEINT'	MOZART, W. A.
TEN VARIATIONS IN G, K455	MOZART, W. A.
TEN VARIATIONS ON ''UNSER DUMMER POBEL MEINT'',	MOZART, W. A.
TEN VARIATIONS	SCHUBERT, T.
TEN WEST	FIEDEL
TEORICA Y PRACTICA ESCUELA DE PIANO, PARTE 1--ESCUELA	LEBERT, S. *
TEORICA Y PRACTICA ESCUELA DE PIANO, PARTE	LEBERT, S. *
TEPEES AND TOTEM POLES	WILSON, M.
TERCERA SONATA	CHAVEZ, C.
TERCERA SONATA	HALFFTER, R.
TERCERA SONATINA	PAZ, J.
TERESITA	COBB
TERRAIN OF SPAIN, THE	STECHER *

TERRIBLE TEMPERED CLAVICHORD, THE	LEWINE, R.
TESORO MIO, WALTZ	BECUCCI
TESORO MIO	BECUCCI
TESORO MIO	BECUCCI
TESORO MIO	BECUCCI
TESSINER KLAVIERBUCH, OP. 57	HOLLER, K.
TES YEUX -- I TUOI OCCHI --	BONINCONTRO
TES YEUX NOIRS	FERRARIS
TEUFELSTANZ AUS 'KANTINKA UND DER TEUFEL'	DVORAK
TEXAS COWBOY'S SONG	WEYBRIGHT
TEXAS GALOP	DRUMHELLER
THAIS, MEDITATION	MASSENET, J.
THAIS - MEDITATION	MASSENET, J.
THAIS - MEDITATION	MASSENET, J.
THAIS 'MEDITATION'	MASSENET, J.
THAIS	MASSENET, J.
THANKSGIVING HYMN	POST--ED
THANKSGIVING SCENE	CRAIG, P.--ED
THANKSGIVING SONG	GAYNOR
THANK HEAVEN FOR LITTLE GIRLS	
THAR SHE BLOWS	GREEN, H.
THAT'S FOR ME	BRODSKY, M.
THAT'S MY DESIRE -- SIMP.	KING, S.--ED.
THAT HAPPY FEELING	WARREN
THAT OLD TIME BEAT	KING, S.--ED.
THAT PROMISED LAND -- SPIRITUAL	COBB
THAT THIHG	NELSON
THEMATIC OCTAVE STUDIES -- IN THE FORM OF VARIATIONS	SMITH, W. G.
THEMA MIT VARIATIONEN, OP. 36	DVORAK
THEMA MIT VARIATIONEN -- DIE VIER TEMPERAMENTE -- FUR	HINDEMITH
THEMA MIT VARIATIONEN	JANACEK
THEME, FROM 'CONCERTO NO. 02'	RACHMANINOFF, S.
THEME, FROM PIANO CONCERTO IN A MINOR	GRIEG
THEME, FROM PIANO CONCERTO IN C MINOR	RACHMANINOFF, S.
THEME, VARIATIONS AND FUGUE	CALTABIANO
THEME, VARIATIONS AND FUGUE	URAY, E. L.
THEME, 8 VARIATIONS, AND DOUBLE FUGUE, OP. 2--1936	SCHISKE, K.
THEMELODIES FOR PIANO --70--	
THEMES FOR PIANO	WATSON
THEMES FOR THE SABBATH DAY--FOR THE PIANO, REED-ORGAN	
THEMES FROM 'J.B.'	AMRAM
THEMES FROM EURASIA	BRUBECK
THEMES FROM FAMOUS OVERTURES --100--	
THEMES FROM GREAT CHAMBER MUSIC	LEVINE, H.--ED
THEMES FROM MASTERWORKS, BK. 1	CLARK, F.--ED.
THEMES FROM MASTERWORKS, BK. 2	CLARK, F.--ED.
THEMES FROM MASTERWORKS, BK. 3	CLARK, F.--ED.
THEMES FROM PIANO CONCERTOS	THOMPSON, J.--ED
THEMES FROM PIANO CONCERTO	GRIEG
THEMES FROM PIANO CONCERTO	RACHMANINOFF, S.
THEMES FROM RONDO A CAPRICCIO, OP. 129 -- 8-HANDS, SET	BEETHOVEN
THEMES FROM THE GREAT BALLETS	LEVINE, H.--ED
THEMES FROM THE GREAT ORATORIOS	LEVINE, H.--ED
THEMES FROM THE GREAT PIANO CONCERTOS	LEVINE, H.--ED
THEMES FROM THE GREAT SYMPHONIES	LEVINE, H.--ED
THEMES FROM THE ORCHESTRAL REPERTOIRE	LEVINE, H.--ED
THEMES I'LL REMEMBER	BEETHOVEN
THEMES WITHOUT VARIATIONS	LEVINE, H.
THEMES WITH VARIATIONS	AGAY, D.--ED
THEME -- FIRST MOVEMENT -- FROM 'MOONLIGHT SONATA'	BEETHOVEN
THEME AND VARIATIONS, OP. 19 NO. 6	TSCHAIKOWSKY
THEME AND VARIATIONS, OP. 36	DVORAK
THEME AND VARIATIONS, OP. 40, NO. 2	KABALEVSKY
THEME AND VARIATIONS, OP. 58	MARTUCCI
THEME AND VARIATIONS, OP. 72	GLAZOUNOW, A.
THEME AND VARIATIONS, OP. 72	GLAZOUNOW, A.
THEME AND VARIATIONS, OP. 73	FAURE, G.
THEME AND VARIATIONS, OP. 73	FAURE, G.
THEME AND VARIATIONS, OP. 73	FAURE, G.
THEME AND VARIATIONS -- ZDENKA'S VARIATIONS	JANACEK
THEME AND VARIATIONS IN A MINOR, OP. 66	BACARISSE
THEME AND VARIATIONS IN F, K613 --SET--	MOZART, W. A.
THEME AND VARIATIONS IN ROCOCO STYLE	BENOIST, A.
THEME AND VARIATIONS ON A GERMAN FOLK TUNE	JONES, S. T.
THEME AND VARIATIONS	DIERCKS
THEME AND VARIATIONS	ETTORE, E.
THEME AND VARIATIONS	GUERRINI, G.
THEME AND VARIATIONS	HANDEL
THEME AND VARIATIONS	KASILAG, L.
THEME AND VARIATIONS	MURRAY
THEME AND VARIATIONS	MYROW, F.
THEME AND VARIATIONS	PANIZZA
THEME AND VARIATIONS	YOUNG
THEME ET VARIATIONS, OP. 19 NO. 6	TSCHAIKOWSKY
THEME ET VARIATIONS	BEAUCAMP
THEME ET VARIATIONS	DAMASE, J. M.
THEME ET VARIATIONS	DUMAS, L.
THEME ET VARIATIONS	GRUNEWALD
THEME ET VARIATIONS	LACROIX, N.
THEME ET VARIATIONS	PARAY, P.
THEME ET VARIATIONS	PRESLE
THEME FROM 'DON JUAN'	MOZART, W. A.
THEME FROM 'IL TROVATORE'	VERDI
THEME FROM 'LION IN WINTER'	
THEME FROM 'MOLDAU'	SMETANA
THEME FROM 'THE APARTMENT' -- SIMP.	WILLIAMS, C.
THEME FROM 'THE APARTMENT'	WILLIAMS, C.
THEME FROM 'THE APARTMENT'	WILLIAMS, C.
THEME FROM 'THE APARTMENT'	WILLIAMS, C.
THEME FROM 'THE APARTMENT	WILLIAMS, C.
THEME FROM 'THE DEADLY TRAP'	
THEME FROM 'THE UNTOUCHABLES'	RIDDLE, N.
THEME FROM 'UNFINISHED SYMPHONY'	SCHUBERT
THEME FROM 'Z'	
THEME FROM ANDANTINO	LEMARE, E.
THEME FROM A SUMMER PLACE	STEINER
THEME FROM A SUMMER PLACE	STEINER
THEME FROM ETUDE IN E	CHOPIN
THEME FROM FIFTH SYMPHONY --FIRST MVT.--	BEETHOVEN
THEME FROM FIFTH SYMPHONY	BEETHOVEN
THEME FROM FINLANDIA	SIBELIUS
THEME FROM FINLANDIA	SIBELIUS
THEME FROM FINLANDIA	SIBELIUS
THEME FROM FOREIGN INTRIGUE CONCERTO -- SIMPLIFIED	NORMAN
THEME FROM HUNGARIAN RHAPSODY NO. 2	LISZT
THEME FROM LIEBESTRAUME	LISZT
THEME FROM LIEBESTRAUME	LISZT
THEME FROM LOVE STORY	BRIMHALL
THEME FROM MELODY IN E FLAT	TSCHAIKOWSKY
THEME FROM NICHOLAS AND ALEXANDRA	BRADLEY,
THEME FROM PIANO CONCERTO, OP. 16	GRIEG
THEME FROM PIANO CONCERTO NO. 1 IN B FLAT	TSCHAIKOWSKY
THEME FROM PIANO CONCERTO NO. 1 IN B FLAT	TSCHAIKOWSKY
THEME FROM ROMEO AND JULIET	TSCHAIKOWSKY
THEME FROM RONDO IN D, OP. 53 NO. 2	SCHUBERT
THEME FROM SECOND PIANO CONCERTO, OP. 18	RACHMANINOFF, S.
THEME FROM SHAFT	BRADLEY,
THEME FROM SONATA IN C, FIRST MVT.	MOZART, W. A.
THEME FROM SONATA IN E FLAT, OP. 27 NO. 1	BEETHOVEN
THEME FROM SUMMER OF '42	LEGRAND
THEME FROM SURPRISE SYMPHONY	HAYDN
THEME FROM SYMPHONY IN D MINOR	FRANCK, C.
THEME FROM SYMPHONY NO. 15	MOZART, W. A.
THEME FROM SYMPHONY NO. 5 --2ND MVT. - ANDANTE CANT.--	TSCHAIKOWSKY
THEME FROM SYMPHONY NO. 6 --PATHETIQUE--	TSCHAIKOWSKY
THEME FROM THE FIRST MOVEMENT OF PIANO CONCERTO IN A	GRIEG
THEME FROM THE FIRST MOVEMENT OF PIANO CONCERTO IN A	GRIEG
THEME FROM THE FIRST MOVEMENT OF PIANO CONCERTO IN A	GRIEG
THEME FROM THE FIRST MOVEMENT OF PIANO CONCERTO NO. 1	TSCHAIKOWSKY
THEME FROM THE FIRST MOVEMENT OF THE 'MOONLIGHT'	BEETHOVEN
THEME FROM THE PERSUADERS	BARRY
THEME FROM THE SECOND MOVEMENT OF THE 'FIFTH SYMPHONY'	TSCHAIKOWSKY
THEME RUSSE, OP. 11 NO. 3	RACHMANINOFF, S.
THEME VARIE--1951	
THEME VARIE, FUGUE ET CHANSON, OP. 85	D'INDY, V.
THEME VARIE, OP. 16 NO. 3	PADEREWSKI, I.
THEME VARIE	GALLON, J.
THEME VARIE	MAURAT, E.
THEME WITH SIX VARIATIONS	HAYDN
THEME WITH VARIATIONS FROM OP. 26	BEETHOVEN
THEME WITH VARIATIONS	PADEREWSKI, I.
THEN AND NOW	DIAMOND, D.
THEORETICAL AND PRACTICAL METHOD, BK. 1	LEBERT, S.
THEORETICAL AND PRACTICAL METHOD, BK. 2	LEBERT, S.
THEORETICAL AND PRACTICAL METHOD, BK. 3	LEBERT, S.
THEORETICAL AND PRACTICAL METHOD - ABRIDGED EDITION IN	LEBERT, S.
THEORETICAL AND PRACTICAL PIANO-SCHOOL, PART	LEBERT, S. *
THEORETICAL AND PRACTICAL PIANO-SCHOOL, PART	LEBERT, S. *
THEORETICAL AND PRACTICAL PIANO-SCHOOL, PART	LEBERT, S. *
THEORETISCH-PRAKT. KLAVIERSCHULE, TEIL 01	ZUSCHNEID, K.
THEORETISCH-PRAKT. KLAVIERSCHULE, TEIL 02	ZUSCHNEID, K.
THEORY AND WORK BOOK, BK. 1	KIRBY, M. B.
THEORY AND WORK BOOK, BK. 2	KIRBY, M. B.
THEORY AND WORK BOOK, BK. 3	KIRBY, M. B.
THEORY AND WORK BOOK, BK. 4	KIRBY, M. B.
THEORY AND WORK BOOK, BK. 5	KIRBY, M. B.
THEORY AND WORK BOOK, BK. 6	KIRBY, M. B.
THEORY FOR PIANO STUDENTS, BK. 1	BENNER, L.
THEORY FOR PIANO STUDENTS, BK. 2	BENNER, L.
THEORY FOR PIANO STUDENTS, BK. 3	BENNER, L.
THEORY FOR PIANO STUDENTS, BK. 4	BENNER, L.
THEORY FOR THE PIANO -- A WORKBOOK, BK. 1	STEINER
THEORY FOR THE PIANO -- A WORKBOOK, BK. 2	STEINER
THEORY GUIDE BOOK, BK. 1	AGAY, D.--ED
THEORY GUIDE BOOK, BK. 2	AGAY, D.--ED
THEORY GUIDE BOOK, BK. 3	AGAY, D.--ED
THEORY IS FUN, BK. 1	HIRSCHBERG, D.
THEORY IS FUN, BK. 2	HIRSCHBERG, D.
THEORY IS FUN - SET 1	CASTELLI
THEORY IS FUN - SET 2	CASTELLI
THEORY PAPERS - VOLUME 1	FLETCHER
THEORY PAPERS - VOLUME 2	FLETCHER
THEORY PAPERS - VOLUME 3	FLETCHER
THERE'LL BE SOME CHANGES MADE	OVERSTREET
THERE'S A CRICKET IN THE HOUSE	COOK
THERE'S A HOLE IN MY BUCKET	STEINER
THERE'S A KIND OF HUSH	LANE, J.--ED.
THERE'S A SMALL HOTEL	SINGER, L.--ED
THERE AND BACK --A STRANGE PROCESSION-- 2 PIANOS, 8	KRAEHENBUEHL
THERE ARE SUCH THINGS	
THERE STANDS A LITTLE MAN	HUMPERDINCK, E.
THERE WAS A LITTLE GIRL	ROLFE, W.
THEY'RE OFF	QUINCKE, W.
THEY ALL PLAYED RAGTIME	
THEY CALL THE WIND MARIA	
THEY CAN'T TAKE THAT AWAY FROM ME	SINGER, L.--ED
THEY DIDN'T BELIEVE ME	
THIEF OF BAGDAD	CABLE *
THIEF OF BAGDAD	CABLE *
THINE OWN - DEIN ELGEN	LANGE, G.
THINGS I REMEMBER	FURZE
THINGS WE DO, THE	WEYBRIGHT
THINKING FINGERS, BK. 1	MAIER, G.
THINKING FINGERS, BK. 2	MAIER, G.
THINK OF ME	PIERSON, A.
THIRDS	TREVARTHEN, R.
THIRD DUET BOOK--23 DUETS	DILLER, A. *
THIRD GRADE PIANO BOOK	WILLIAMS, J.
THIRD GRADE PIECES	KOZAKIEWICZ
THIRD GRADE VELOCITY STUDIES	THOMPSON, J.
THIRD MAN THEME	
THIRD MARCH -- ALLA MARCIA ALLEGRO	DAHL
THIRD PIANO BOOK FOR LITTLE JACKS AND JILLS,	RODGERS, I.
THIRD STREET RHUMBA	SHAW, C.
THIRD STREET RHUMBA	SHAW, C.
THIRD SYMPHONY- THEME	BRAHMS
THIRD YEAR PIANO LESSONS	WATERMAN *
THIRD YEAR	WILLIAMS, J.
THIRTEEN DANCES -- WORKS BY DELANNOY, HARSANYI,	DELANNOY
THIRTEEN EASY IMPROVISATIONS	HENGEVELD
THIRTEEN EASY SHORT PIANO PIECES, FROM 'NOTEBOOK FOR	BACH, J.S.
THIRTEEN POETISCHE STIMMUNGBILDER, OP. 85	DVORAK
THIRTEEN POLONAISES	CHOPIN
THIRTEEN PRELUDES, OP. 32 - COMPLETE	RACHMANINOFF, S.
THIRTEEN PRELUDES, OP. 32	RACHMANINOFF, S.
THIRTEEN PRELUDES, OP. 32	RACHMANINOFF, S.
THIRTEEN PRELUDES, OP. 32	RACHMANINOFF, S.
THIRTEEN SERVICE PIECES FOR THE CHURCH PIANIST	BENDER
THIRTEEN STUDIES FOR THE LEFT HAND ALONE, OP. 53	BLANCHET
THIRTEEN TRANSCRIPTIONS FOR PIANO SOLO OF CHOPIN'S	GARVELMANN,
THIRTEEN VOLUNTARIES FOR THE CHURCH PIANIST	BENDER
THIRTY-FIVE EASY STUDIES WITHOUT OCTAVES, OP. 130	GURLITT
THIRTY-FIVE SONATAS, VOL. 1	SCARLATTI, D.
THIRTY-FIVE SONATAS, VOL. 2	SCARLATTI, D.
THIRTY-FOUR SONATAS, BK. 1	HAYDN
THIRTY-FOUR SONATAS, BK. 2	HAYDN
THIRTY-FOUR SONATAS, BK. 4	HAYDN
THIRTY-FOUR SONATINEN	BENDA, R.
THIRTY-ONE FAVORITE CHILDREN'S HYMNS	KEVAN
THIRTY-ONE HUNGARIAN PEASANT SONGS, BK. 1	WEINER
THIRTY-ONE HUNGARIAN PEASANT SONGS, BK. 2	WEINER
THIRTY-ONE HUNGARIAN PEASANT SONGS, VOL. 1	WEINER
THIRTY-ONE HUNGARIAN PEASANT SONGS, VOL. 2	WEINER
THIRTY-SEVEN UBUNGEN UND ETUDEN -- 2-3 --	FIBICH, Z.
THIRTY-SIX CADENZAS, K. 624	MOZART, W. A.
THIRTY-SIX CADENZAS TO PIANO CONCERTOS	MOZART, W. A.
THIRTY-SIX ETUDES DE DIFFICULTE TRANSCENDANTE	BERIOT
THIRTY-SIX FAVORITE FOLK SONGS FOR THE PIANO	YOUNG, I.--ED.
THIRTY-SIX FAVORITE FOLK SONGS FOR THE PIANO	YOUNG, I.--ED.
THIRTY-SIX FAVORITE MELODIES FOR THE PIANO	YOUNG, I.--ED.
THIRTY-SIX FAVORITE MELODIES FOR THE PIANO	YOUNG, I.--ED.
THIRTY-SIX RUSSIAN FOLK SONGS, IN PROGRESSIVE ORDER	TSCHAIKOWSKY
THIRTY-SIX VERY EASY ALL-TIME FAVORITES	SMALL, A.
THIRTY-THREE HITS FROM BROADWAY	AGAY, D.--ED

THIRTY-THREE TRADITIONAL AMERICAN SONGS — YOUNG, I.--ED.
THIRTY-TWO FEET AND EIGHT LITTLE TAILS — LANE, J.--ED.
THIRTY-TWO MORE HITS FROM BROADWAY — AGAY, D.--ED
THIRTY-TWO PIANO GAMES — FINNEY
THIRTY-TWO PIANO PARTNERS - GRADE 3 - DUETS — STRIMER, J.--ED
THIRTY-TWO PIECES FROM 'FOR CHILDREN' — BARTOK
THIRTY-TWO PRELUDES, OP. 119 — HELLER, S.
THIRTY-TWO PRELUDES, OP. 25 — MERK, G.
THIRTY-TWO SONATAS, VOL. 1 — CIMAROSA
THIRTY-TWO SONATAS, VOL. 2 — CIMAROSA
THIRTY-TWO SONATAS, VOL. 3 — CIMAROSA
THIRTY-TWO SONATAS FOR THE PIANOFORTE --IN TWO — BEETHOVEN
THIRTY-TWO VARIATIONS IN C MINOR, WO O 80 — BEETHOVEN
THIRTY-TWO VARIATIONS IN C MINOR — BEETHOVEN
THIRTY-TWO VARIATIONS ON AN ORIGINAL THEME IN C MINOR — BEETHOVEN
THIRTY-TWO VARIATIONS — BEETHOVEN
THIRTY BRILLIANT PRELUDES OP. 37 — CONCONE, G.
THIRTY CHANTS, 2ND SUITE, SIX CHANTS, OP. 38 — ALKAN
THIRTY CHANTS, 3RD SUITE, SIX CHANTS, OP. 65 — ALKAN
THIRTY CHANTS, 4TH SUITE, SIX CHANTS, OP. 67 — ALKAN
THIRTY CHANTS, 5TH SUITE, SIX CHANTS, OP. 70 — ALKAN
THIRTY ELEMENTARY STUDIES — POZZOLI
THIRTY LITTLE ETUDES — PARLOW, E.
THIRTY MINUETS OF PAST TIMES — SCHOCH
THIRTY NEW STUDIES IN TECHNICS, OP. 849--PREPARATORY — CZERNY
THIRTY NEW STUDIES IN TECHNIQUE--ETUDES DE — CZERNY
THIRTY PIANO COMPOSITIONS — MENDELSSOHN
THIRTY PIECES FOR BEGINNERS — TUERK
THIRTY PIECES IN THIRTY KEYS, BK. 1 — ANSON, G.--ED
THIRTY PIECES IN THIRTY KEYS, BK. 2 — ANSON, G.--ED
THIRTY PROGRESSIVE STUDIES, OP. 46--BK. 1 — HELLER, S.
THIRTY PROGRESSIVE STUDIES, OP. 46 — HELLER, S.
THIRTY PROGRESSIVE STUDIES, OP. 46 — HELLER, S.
THIRTY PROGRESSIVE STUDIES, OP. 46 — HELLER, S.
THIRTY PROGRESSIVE STUDIES, OP. 46 — HELLER, S.
THIRTY RHYTHMIC PANTOMIMES — GAYNOR
THIRTY SELECTED STUDIES — CONCONE, G.
THIRTY STUDIES IN MECHANISM, OP. 849 — CZERNY
THIRTY STUDIES IN MECHANISM, OP. 849 — CZERNY
THIRTY TECHNICAL STUDIES, OP. 10 — COHEN, M. J.
THIS 'N THAT — TOWNSEND
THIS CAN'T BE LOVE — SINGER, L.--ED
THIS GUY'S IN LOVE WITH YOU — BRIMHALL,
THIS IS MY COUNTRY — BRIMHALL,
THIS IS MY SONG — BRIMHALL,
THIS IS MY SONG — CHAPLIN
THIS IS OUR COUNTRY — BRIMHALL,
THIS IS ROGER WILLIAMS — WILLIAMS, R.
THIS IS THE NIGHT OF HALLOWEEN — JOYNER, B.
THIS LAND IS YOUR LAND — GUTHRIE
THIS LOVE OF MINE — JAY
THIS OLD MAN — SCHAUM, J.--ED.
THIS OLD MAN — SINTON, J.
THIS OLD MAN — WEYBRIGHT
THIS WAY TO MUSIC — COBB
THOMPSON-HANON, BOOK 1 — HANON, C.
THOMPSON-HANON, BOOK 2 — HANON, C.
THOMPSON ADULT PREPARATORY BOOK — THOMPSON, J.
THOMPSON EASIEST PIANO COURSE - PART 1 — THOMPSON, J.
THOMPSON EASIEST PIANO COURSE - PART 2 — THOMPSON, J.
THOMPSON EASIEST PIANO COURSE - PART 3 — THOMPSON, J.
THOMPSON EASIEST PIANO COURSE - PART 4 — THOMPSON, J.
THOMPSON EASIEST PIANO COURSE - PART 5 — THOMPSON, J.
THOMPSON EASIEST PIANO COURSE - PART 6 — THOMPSON, J.
THOMPSON EASIEST PIANO COURSE - PART 7 — THOMPSON, J.
THOMPSON EASIEST PIANO COURSE - PART 8 — THOMPSON, J.
THOMPSON MELODY ALL THE WAY - ACCOMPANIMENTS TO THE — THOMPSON, J.
THOMPSON MELODY ALL THE WAY - BOOK 1-A — THOMPSON, J.
THOMPSON MELODY ALL THE WAY - BOOK 1-B — THOMPSON, J.
THOMPSON MELODY ALL THE WAY - BOOK 2-A — THOMPSON, J.
THOMPSON MELODY ALL THE WAY - BOOK 2-B — THOMPSON, J.
THOMPSON MELODY ALL THE WAY - BOOK 3-A — THOMPSON, J.
THOMPSON MELODY ALL THE WAY - BOOK 3-B — THOMPSON, J.
THOMPSON MELODY ALL THE WAY - PREPARATORY BOOK — THOMPSON, J.
THOMPSON MODERN COURSE FOR THE PIANO - FIFTH GRADE — THOMPSON, J.
THOMPSON MODERN COURSE FOR THE PIANO - FIRST GRADE — THOMPSON, J.
THOMPSON MODERN COURSE FOR THE PIANO - FOURTH GRADE — THOMPSON, J.
THOMPSON MODERN COURSE FOR THE PIANO - SECOND GRADE — THOMPSON, J.
THOMPSON MODERN COURSE FOR THE PIANO - TEACHING LITTLE — THOMPSON, J.
THOMPSON MODERN COURSE FOR THE PIANO - TEACHING LITTLE — THOMPSON, J.
THOMPSON MODERN COURSE FOR THE PIANO - THIRD GRADE — THOMPSON, J.
THOROUGHBREDS — STEINER
THOROUGHLY MODERN MILLIE — BRIMHALL,
THOSE MAGNIFICENT MEN IN THEIR FLYING MACHINES — LANE, J.--ED.
THOSE WONDERFUL YEARS 1900-1920 —
THOUGHTS AT TWILIGHT REVERIE — SEIDT, J.
THOUGHTS OF LOVE --LIEBESLIED-- — GRIEG
THOUGHTS OF SPRING — JOYNER, B.
THOUSANDS OF MILLIONS OF STARS — WEYBRIGHT
THOUSAND AND ONE NIGHTS, OP. 346 — STRAUSS, J.
THOUSAND AND ONE NIGHTS — STRAUSS, J.
THOU FILLEST MY — SCHIEFELBEIN, F.
THREE-FOURS - NO. 06 — TAYLOR, S. C.
THREE-PART INVENTIONS — BACH, J.S.
THREE-PART INVENTIONS — BACH, J.S.
THREE-PART INVENTIONS — BACH, J.S.
THREE-PART INVENTIONS — BACH, J.S.
THREE-SCORE SET — SCHUMAN, W.
THREE AIRS A DANSER - GAVOTTE ET MUSETTE — LACK, T.
THREE AIRS A DANSER - GIGUE ECOSSAISE — LACK, T.
THREE AIRS A DANSER - MENUET ALSACIEN — LACK, T.
THREE ALL AMERICAN SONGS — COHAN
THREE AMERICAN TUNES--COTTON-EYE JO, THE BLUE BIRD, — WATSON, S.
THREE ANALYTICAL SONATINAS — LYNES
THREE ANCIENT DANCES — SYMONS
THREE ARGENTINIAN DANCES — GINASTERA
THREE ARMENIAN DANCES, OP. 2--1958 — TJEKNAVORIAN, L.
THREE BAGATELLES, OP. 13 — COOPER, J.
THREE BAGATELLES — ANDRIESSEN, J.
THREE BAGATELLES — BACH, JAN
THREE BAGATELLES — HAIEFF, A.
THREE BARCAROLLES — ROREM, N.
THREE BLIND MICE--ONE PIANO-SIX HANDS-- — SCHAUM, J.--ED.
THREE BLIND MICE, ONE PIANO - SIX HANDS — MACGREGOR
THREE BLIND MICE - 3 INTERPRETATIONS — ITURBI, J.
THREE BLIND MICE — RICHTER
THREE BUGS FOR PIANO — PUTSCHE, T.
THREE BURLESQUES, OP. 8C — BARTOK
THREE BURLESQUES, OP. 8C — BARTOK
THREE CADENZAS TO DITTERSDORF CONCERTO IN A — DOEBEREINER
THREE CADENZAS TO THE CONCERTO IN A — DITTERSDORF,
THREE CANONS IN HOMAGE TO GALILEO FOR PIANO AND THREE — MESTRES-QUADRENY
THREE CANONS IN HOMAGE TO GALILEO FOR PIANO AND THREE — MESTRES-QUADRENY
THREE CANONS — KORNAUTH, E.
THREE CAPRICES — OHANA, M.

THREE CHARACTER SKETCHES OF OLD LONDON — WILLAN
THREE CHEERS FOR THE SAILOR'S BRIDE — GILBERT AND
THREE CHEERS FOR THE TEAM — STEINER
THREE CHILDREN'S PROFILES — WOLFE
THREE CHILDREN AT ONE KEYBOARD -- 1 PIANO 6 HANDS -- — CITATI-BRACCI
THREE CHORDS IN THREE KEYS — STEINER
THREE CHRISTMAS SONGS -- JINGLE BELLS, JOLLY OLD SAINT — RICHTER, A.
THREE CLOCKS -- ONE PIANO, SIX HANDS -- — MELLICHAMP, N.
THREE CLOCKS — MELLICHAMP, N.
THREE COINS IN A FOUNTAIN — CAHN *
THREE COINS IN THE FOUNTAIN — LANE, J.--ED.
THREE COMPOSITIONS — BABBITT
THREE COMPOSITIONS — CAPPETTI
THREE COMPOSITIONS — GIACHETTI
THREE CONCERT STUDIES, OP. 24 — MOSZKOWSKI
THREE CONCERT STUDIES, OP. 51 — MOSCHELES, I.
THREE CONCERT STUDIES — TOSATTI
THREE CONNECTED PIECES — AITKEN, H.
THREE CONTRADANCES — BEETHOVEN
THREE COUNTRY DANCES — BEETHOVEN
THREE CREOLE DANCES — GAITO
THREE CZECH DANCES, 1926 — MARTINU, B.
THREE CZECH DANCES -- SET — MARTINU, B.
THREE DANCES FROM ''HENRY THE EIGHTH'' — GERMAN, E.
THREE DANCES FROM 'HENRY VIII' — GERMAN, E.
THREE DANCES FROM 'HENRY VIII' — GERMAN, E.
THREE DANCES FROM MASKERADE — KHATCHATURIAN
THREE DANCES IN MINIATURE — PICCIOLI
THREE DANCES — ANDRIESSEN, J.
THREE DANCES — FLAGELLO, N.
THREE DANCES — HERRARTE, M.
THREE DANCES — PLATAMONE
THREE DANCE PIECES, 1959 — KOLZ, E.
THREE DANCE POEMS NO. 1 REVE — INGHELBRECHT, D.
THREE DANCE POEMS NO. 2 LA DANSE POUR LES OISEAUX — INGHELBRECHT, D.
THREE DANCE POEMS NO. 3 L'ALBUM AUX PORTRAITS — INGHELBRECHT, D.
THREE DANSES ANDALOUSES - PETENERA, TANGO, ZAPATEADO — TURINA, J.
THREE DANZAS AMERICANAS — SICILIANI
THREE DAYS SONATINA — FRANKELL
THREE DOZEN FANTASIAS — TELEMANN, G.P.
THREE DREAM DANCES - NO. 02 — TAYLOR, S. C.
THREE EASY LITTLE PIECES — GUERRINI, G.
THREE EASY PIECES IN BLACK AND WHITE — NOEL, H.
THREE EASY PIECES — STRAVINSKY, I.
THREE EASY PIECES — STRAVINSKY, I.
THREE EASY SONATINAS — JOOSEN
THREE ECHOES — HOLCMAN, J.
THREE ECOSSAISES, OP. 72 — CHOPIN
THREE EPIGRAMS — PALMER
THREE ESQUISSES — BISQUERTT
THREE ETUDES, OP. 104B — MENDELSSOHN
THREE ETUDES, OP. 31 NO. 1 IN C — GLAZOUNOW, A.
THREE ETUDES, OP. 31 NO. 2 IN E — GLAZOUNOW, A.
THREE ETUDES, OP. 31 NO. 3 'LA NUIT' — GLAZOUNOW, A.
THREE ETUDES DE BRAVOURE, OP. 16--SCHERZI-- — ALKAN
THREE ETUDES DE BRAVOURE, OP.12--IMPROVISATIONS— — ALKAN
THREE ETUDES FROM OP. 104 AND SCHERZO A CAPRICCIO — MENDELSSOHN
THREE ETUDES TRANSCENDANTES — TANSMAN, A.
THREE ETUDES — CHAVEZ, C.
THREE ETUDES — CHOPIN
THREE ETUDES — FEJARD
THREE ETUDES — HELPS
THREE ETUDES — MATHE, E.
THREE ETUDES — PILATI
THREE ETUDES — SMETANA
THREE ETUDES — STALLAERT, A.
THREE ETUDES — WISSMER, P.
THREE FAMOUS BEARS — DUNGAN
THREE FANTASIAS — CARREIRA
THREE FANTASIESTUCKE, OP. 111, AND FOUR NACHTSTUCKE, — SCHUMANN, R.
THREE FANTASIESTUCKE, OP. 111 — SCHUMANN, R.
THREE FANTASIESTUCKE, OP. 111 — SCHUMANN, R.
THREE FANTASTIC DANCES, OP. 1 — SHOSTAKOVITCH
THREE FANTASTIC DANCES, OP. 5 — SHOSTAKOVITCH
THREE FANTASTIC DANCES — SHOSTAKOVITCH
THREE FANTASTIC DANCES — SHOSTAKOVITCH
THREE FAVOLETTE — TOCCHI
THREE FEULLETS D'ALBUM, OP. 47 - CONTE — PFEIFFER, A.
THREE FEULLETS D'ALBUM, OP. 47 - MENUET — PFEIFFER, A.
THREE FEULLETS D'ALBUM, OP. 47 - MUSETTE — PFEIFFER, A.
THREE FLORAL SCENES — THORNTON
THREE FOLK SETTINGS — SCHICKELE, P.
THREE FOR TWO — DRING
THREE FUGUES FOR PIANO ON THEMES BY J.A. REINKEN BWV — BACH, J.S.
THREE FUGUES — KREBS
THREE GERMAN DANCES — BEETHOVEN
THREE GRANDES ETUDES, OP. 76, NO. 1, FANTAISIE IN A — ALKAN
THREE GRANDES ETUDES, OP. 76, NO. 2, INTRODUCTION, — ALKAN
THREE GRANDES ETUDES, OP. 76, NO. 3, MOUVEMENT — ALKAN
THREE G MAJORS, THE--CURWEN EDITION — EELE, M.
THREE HAIKUS — HOVHANESS, A.
THREE HANDS AT THE PIANO — PELS, W.
THREE HUNDRED AND SEVENTY ONE HARMONIZED CHORALES AND — BACH, J.S.
THREE HUNDRED SEVENTY-ONE CHORALES, VOL. 1 — BACH, J.S.
THREE HUNDRED SEVENTY-ONE CHORALES, VOL. 2 — BACH, J.S.
THREE HUNDRED SEVENTY-ONE CHORALES — BACH, J.S.
THREE HUNGARIAN FOLKSONGS — BARTOK
THREE HUNGARIAN FOLK TUNES — BARTOK
THREE IMMAGINI — BORLENGHI
THREE IMPRESSIONES - HABANERA, LAS MOZAS DEL CANTARO, — NIN-CULMELL, J.
THREE IMPRESSIONS FOR PIANO — CUNNINGHAM, M.
THREE IMPROMPTUS, COMPLETE — TAYLOR, C.
THREE IMPROMPTUS, OP. 25, 31, 34 — FAURE, G.
THREE IMPROMPTUS, OP. 25, 31, 34 — FAURE, G.
THREE IMPROMPTUS -- 1940 -- — AURIC
THREE IMPROMPTUS — LANCEN
THREE IMPROMPTUS — MCCABE, J.
THREE IMPROVISATIONS ON A THEME OF DARIUS MILHAUD — WARD-STEINMAN,
THREE INTERLUDES FOR PIANO — IDYL *
THREE INTERLUDES FOR PIANO — TOKUNAGA, H.
THREE INTERLUDES — BARNETT
THREE INTERMEZZI, OP. 117 — BRAHMS
THREE INTERMEZZI, OP. 117 — BRAHMS
THREE INTERMEZZI, OP. 117 — BRAHMS
THREE INTERMEZZI, OP. 117 — BRAHMS
THREE INTERMEZZI, OP. 117 — BRAHMS
THREE INTERMEZZI, OP. 117 — BRAHMS
THREE INTERMEZZI, OP. 117 — BRAHMS
THREE INTERMEZZI, OP. 117 — BRAHMS
THREE INTERMEZZI — SPIES, C.
THREE INTERMEZZOS, OP. 117 — BRAHMS
THREE INVENTIONS — FRANCHETTI
THREE INVENTIONS — STRAVINSKY, S.
THREE IN BLUE — SOUTHAM, A.
THREE ISRAELI SKETCHES — STARER
THREE JAZZ DUETS — NEVIN
THREE JAZZ PRELUDES — GILLOCK

THREE KITTENS--ONE PIANO-SIX HANDS--	SCHAUM, J.--ED.
THREE LATE PIANO PIECES	LISZT
THREE LIEBESTRAEUME - NO. 3	LISZT
THREE LIEBESTRAEUME - NO. 3	LISZT
THREE LIEBESTRAEUME	LISZT
THREE LIEBESTRAEUME	LISZT
THREE LITTLE DANCES FOR PIANO, OP. 85	TOCH, E.
THREE LITTLE DUCKS	GARROW
THREE LITTLE DUCKS	MANA-ZUCCA
THREE LITTLE PIANO PIECES, OP. 6	SZELL, G.
THREE LITTLE PIECES - BARCAROLLE, SERENADE, PASTORALE	DAVICO
THREE LITTLE PIECES	BENJAMIN
THREE LITTLE PIECES	BRUCKNER
THREE LITTLE PIECES	SANGIORGI
THREE LITTLE PIECES	SAUVREZIS, A.
THREE LITTLE PIGS - A STORY WITH MUSIC	RICHTER, A.
THREE LITTLE PRELUDES	DEDIEU-PETERS
THREE LULLABIES	GIGGY, F.
THREE LYRIC PIECES	ELLIOTT, R.
THREE LYRIC PIECES	FINK, M.
THREE MACEDONIAN MINIATURES	BENSON
THREE MALTESE MINIATURES	CAMILLERI, C.
THREE MARCHES--QUASI DA CAVALLERIA--, OP. 37	ALKAN
THREE MARCHES FOR ANIMALS	RIETI
THREE MARCHES FROM 'SONATINA ALLA MARCIA'	DAHL
THREE MARCH RHYTHMS	BABIN
THREE MARIES	VILLA-LOBOS, H.
THREE MAZURKAS, OP. 24	RATHAUS, K.
THREE MAZURKAS	FITELBERG
THREE MELODIES	JEANNERET
THREE MENUETS, OP. 51	ALKAN
THREE MINIATURES FOR CHILDREN	SANTOLIQUIDO
THREE MINIATURES	FRACKENPOHL, A.
THREE MINIATURES	GOLD
THREE MINIATURES	HANSON
THREE MINIATURES	WARD-STEINMAN,
THREE MINUETS	EYBLER
THREE MONOGRAMS	FARKAS, F.
THREE MORCEAUX EN FORME DE POIRE	SATIE, E.
THREE MOVEMENTS, FROM 'PETROUCHKA' -- NO. 1 RUSSIAN	STRAVINSKY, I.
THREE MOVEMENTS, FROM 'PETROUCHKA' -- NO. 2 CHEZ	STRAVINSKY, I.
THREE MOVEMENTS, FROM 'PETROUCHKA' -- NO. 3 SHROVE -	STRAVINSKY, I.
THREE MOVEMENTS, FROM 'PETROUCHKA'	STRAVINSKY, I.
THREE MOVEMENTS	ESPLA
THREE MUSKETEERS, THE--PIANO TRIO--	SCHAUM, J.--ED.
THREE NATIONALITIES	REED, H. O.
THREE NEW FANTASIES	BENJAMIN
THREE NOCTURNES--1963--HPCHD	ZENDER, H.
THREE NOCTURNES -- 1957	HAUFRECHT
THREE NOCTURNES - NO. 1	SATIE, E.
THREE NOCTURNES - NO. 2	SATIE, E.
THREE NOCTURNES - NO. 3	SATIE, E.
THREE NOCTURNES	ALKAN
THREE NOCTURNES	MIHALOVICI
THREE NOCTURNES	VIERNE
THREE NOELS	DANIEL-LESUR
THREE NOVELETTES	ROWLEY
THREE NOVELTY RAGS	ALBRIGHT, W.
THREE O'CLOCK IN THE MORNING	LANE, J.--ED.
THREE O'CLOCK IN THE MORNING	
THREE OLE'UNS -- CINDY-SHENANDOAH-JOSHUA	EICHHORN, H. W.
THREE ON ONE -- PIANO TRIO	WEYBRIGHT
THREE OPEN-AIR WALTZES	HORDER
THREE OPERATIC FANTASIES FOR PIANO SOLO	THALBERG
THREE ORGAN CHORALE PRELUDES	BACH, J.S.
THREE PAGE SONATA	IVES, C.
THREE PALS - FOR ONE PIANO, SIX HANDS	REID
THREE PATRIOTIC SONGS	ZEPP--ED
THREE PETITES ESQUISSES - CAUSERIE MATINALE, PETITE	LE GRAND
THREE PETITES PIECES ESPAGNOLES - SIESTE ANDALOUSE	LONGAS
THREE PETITES PIECES ESPAGNOLES	LONGAS
THREE PEZZETINI, OP. 42	ORTHEL
THREE PIANO MOODS. NO. 1, LYRICAL	SCHUMAN, W.
THREE PIANO MOODS. NO. 2, PENSIVE	SCHUMAN, W.
THREE PIANO MOODS. NO. 3, DYNAMIC	SCHUMAN, W.
THREE PIANO MOODS	SCHUMAN, W.
THREE PIANO PIECES, OP. POSTH.	SCHUBERT
THREE PIANO PIECES, OP. 1	KATTNIGG, R.
THREE PIANO PIECES, OP. 11	SCHOENBERG
THREE PIANO PIECES, OP. 34	SPRINGER, M.
THREE PIANO PIECES, OP. 59	NIELSEN, C.
THREE PIANO PIECES -- POSTHUMOUS IMPROMPTUS	SCHUBERT
THREE PIANO PIECES	BABIN
THREE PIANO PIECES	BLACHER
THREE PIANO PIECES	HARTLEY, W.
THREE PIANO PIECES	WOOD, H.
THREE PIANO SKETCHES	FRANCO, J.
THREE PIANO SONATAS	LATROBE, C. I.
THREE PIECES, FROM 'TWELVE PRELUDES'	KARDOS
THREE PIECES, OP. 18	GOEHR, A.
THREE PIECES, OP. 2	GARCIA MORILLO
THREE PIECES, OP. 23	WEBER, B.
THREE PIECES, OP. 32, RIGHT HAND ALONE	ABRIL
THREE PIECES, OP. 49	ROUSSEL, A.
THREE PIECES, OP. 84	ANDERGASSEN
THREE PIECES, OP. 96	PROKOFIEFF
THREE PIECES, POSTHUMOUS	MENDELSSOHN
THREE PIECES - PRELUDE, HOMMAGE A RAVEL, DANCE	HONEGGER, A.
THREE PIECES AND A FINALE FOR PIANO AND TAPE	SYDEMAN, W.
THREE PIECES BREVES	FRIBOULET
THREE PIECES BY J. S. BACH	BACH, J.S. *
THREE PIECES ENFANTINES - MAMAN EST TRISTE, TOUTE	DALCROZE
THREE PIECES FOR CHILDREN - BERCEUSE	MATHIEU
THREE PIECES FOR CHILDREN - HOMMAGE A MOZART	MATHIEU
THREE PIECES FOR CHILDREN - TRISTESSE	MATHIEU
THREE PIECES FOR CHILDREN	MORTARI
THREE PIECES FOR CHILDREN	TEBOLDI
THREE PIECES FOR ONE PIANO FOUR HANDS	JAMBOR, A.
THREE PIECES FOR PIANO, 1961	STEINER, G.
THREE PIECES FOR PIANO	BEUCHTGER
THREE PIECES FOR PIANO	GARLICK, A.
THREE PIECES FOR PIANO	SLAVICKY, A.
THREE PIECES FOR TWO LEFT HANDS	PHILLIPS, R.
THREE PIECES MAROCAINES	WOLFF, B.
THREE PIECES MIGNONNES - PETITE GAVOTTE, PETIT MENUET,	DALCROZE
THREE PIECES ON FOLKTUNES, OP. 35--1951	SCHISKE, K.
THREE PIECES PITTORESQUES - DANSE SAUVAGE	MATHIEU
THREE PIECES PITTORESQUES - LES MOUETTES	MATHIEU
THREE PIECES PITTORESQUES - PROCESSION D'ELEPHANTS	MATHIEU
THREE PIECES	BARBERA
THREE PIECES	BENUSSAN, M.
THREE PIECES	CHITI, G.
THREE PIECES	DE FRAGUIER
THREE PIECES	DE SABATA
THREE PIECES	FUX
THREE PIECES	GIACCHINO
THREE PIECES	GINASTERA

THREE PIECES	JONES, C.
THREE PIECES	KHATCHATURIAN
THREE PIECES	KHATCHATURIAN
THREE PIECES	KOPTAGEL, V.
THREE PIECES	MALIPIERO, G. F.
THREE PIECES	MARGOLA
THREE PIECES	REIZENSTEIN, F.
THREE PIECES	REMACHA, F.
THREE PIECES	TAGLIAPIETRA, C.
THREE PIECES	THIELE, S.
THREE PLAY-FULL DUETS	GIASSON, P.
THREE PLAY-FULL DUETS	GIASSON, P.
THREE POEMA CAMPESTRI	CASTELNUOVO-TEDE
THREE POEMS, OP. 34	HARTMANN
THREE POEMS	MOURAVIEFF, L.
THREE POLKAS	SMETANA
THREE POLYPHONIC PIECES	SIEGL, O.
THREE POPULAR HUNGARIAN SONGS	BARTOK
THREE POSITIONS OF HARMONIZED SCALES	DE SOLIS
THREE PRELUDES, OP. 104A	MENDELSSOHN
THREE PRELUDES, OP. 104	MENDELSSOHN
THREE PRELUDES, OP. 15	FEINBERG, S.
THREE PRELUDES - PRELUDE TRISTE, OBSESSION, CHANT DE	SCHMITT, F.
THREE PRELUDES AND FUGUES	HOVHANESS, A.
THREE PRELUDES FOR PIANO	ANDERSON, G.
THREE PRELUDES	ALOTIN, Y.
THREE PRELUDES	DELIUS, F.
THREE PRELUDES	ELWELL, H.
THREE PRELUDES	GLOVER, D.
THREE PRELUDES	GRAMATGES
THREE PRELUDES	GRIFFES, C.
THREE PRELUDES	KENNAN, K.
THREE PRELUDES	LAVAGNE
THREE PRELUDES	LEE, DAI-KEONG
THREE PRELUDES	LEES, B.
THREE PRELUDES	PALMER
THREE PRELUDES	RIETI
THREE PRELUDES	WURMSER, L.
THREE PRELUDES	YARDUMIAN, R.
THREE QUARTER-TONE PIECES --PAPPASTAVROU--	IVES, C.
THREE RAG-CAPRICES	MILHAUD, D.
THREE RECITAL DANCES -- PARADE POLKA, WALTZ SERENADE,	AGAY, D.
THREE RHAPSODIES ON FOUR NOTES	TREVARTHEN, R.
THREE ROMANCES, OP. 28	SCHUMANN, R.
THREE ROMANCES, OP. 28	SCHUMANN, R.
THREE ROMANCES, OP. 28	SCHUMANN, R.
THREE ROMANCES, OP. 28	SCHUMANN, R.
THREE ROMANCES, OP. 28	SCHUMANN, R.
THREE ROMANCES, OP. 43	KLEBE, G.
THREE ROMAN CLOISTERS	CARABELLA
THREE RONDOS ON FOLK TUNES	BARTOK
THREE RONDOS	PAPP, L.
THREE SARABANDES - NO. 1	SATIE, E.
THREE SARABANDES - NO. 2	SATIE, E.
THREE SARABANDES - NO. 3	SATIE, E.
THREE SATIRICAL SARCASMS	READ, G.
THREE SEASCAPES	LAST, J.
THREE SHORT FANTASIES FOR PIANO, OP. 16	BLACKWOOD, E.
THREE SHORT PIANO PIECES	HAYWARD, L.
THREE SHORT PIECES	AUCLERT
THREE SHORT PIECES	CHANLER, T.
THREE SHORT PIECES	DELL'ANNO
THREE SHORT PIECES	DELL'ANNO
THREE SHORT PIECES	ORTHEL
THREE SHORT STORIES	REIZENSTEIN, F.
THREE SINGULAR PIECES, OP. 44 -- 1951 --	DOHNANYI
THREE SKETCHES, OP. 6	WELLESZ, E.
THREE SKETCHES, OP. 7	GAL, H.
THREE SKETCHES	BRIDGE, F.
THREE SMALL PIECES	KADOSA
THREE SONATAS--1751--HARPSICHORD	RITTER, J. C.
THREE SONATAS, CONCERTO IN C MINOR, AND MISCELLANEOUS	BACH, J.S.
THREE SONATAS, OP. 118	SCHUMANN, R.
THREE SONATAS, OP. 32, 33, 37	DIABELLI
THREE SONATAS, OP. 32, 33 AND 37	DIABELLI
THREE SONATAS FOR THE YOUNG, OP. 118	SCHUMANN, R.
THREE SONATAS FOR YOUNG PEOPLE, OP. 118	SCHUMANN, R.
THREE SONATAS	BRAHMS
THREE SONATAS	CHOPIN
THREE SONATAS	DIABELLI
THREE SONATAS	MUTHEL, J. G.
THREE SONATINAS, OP. 12	SHEBALIN
THREE SONATINAS, OP. 29 NO. 2	DRIESSLER
THREE SONATINAS	GUASTAVINO
THREE SONGS WITHOUT WORDS	BEN-HAIM
THREE SONNETS	SOMERS, H.
THREE SOUTH AMERICAN SKETCHES	PREVIN, A.
THREE SPANISH DANCES--1938--NO. 1, DANSE MURCIENNE	NIN
THREE SPANISH DANCES--1938--NO. 2, DANSE ANDALOUSE	NIN
THREE SPANISH DANCES--1938--NO. 3, DANSE IBERIENNE NO. 2	NIN
THREE SPANISH PIECES	DOTRAS-VILA
THREE SPECIAL STUDIES FOR THE CROSSING OF THE HANDS	TAGLIAPIETRA, C.
THREE STUDIES, OP. 18	BARTOK
THREE STUDIES FOR PIANO, OP. 5	LAYTON, B.
THREE STUDIES FOR PIANO	ROVICS, H.
THREE SUITES FROM THE NOTEBOOK FOR WOLFGANG	MOZART, L.
THREE SWINGY BOATMEN	NEVIN
THREE TEMPS NO. 1	JOLIVET, A.
THREE TOCCATAS, OP. 29 NO. 1	DRIESSLER
THREE TONE PICTURES, OP. 5--LAKE AT EVENING, THE	GRIFFES, C.
THREE TONE PICTURES, OP. 5--NIGHT WINDS, THE	GRIFFES, C.
THREE TONE PICTURES, OP. 5--VALE OF DREAMS, THE	GRIFFES, C.
THREE TRANSCRIPTIONS ON MOTIFS BY JOHANN STRAUSS, OP.	SCHULHOF, O.
THREE TRANSCRIPTIONS ON MOTIFS BY JOHANN STRAUSS, OP.	SCHULHOF, O.
THREE TRANSCRIPTIONS ON MOTIFS BY JOHANN STRAUSS, OP.	SCHULHOF, O.
THREE TRIFLES	TAYLOR, C.
THREE TRISTIA, OP. 38B	KADOSA
THREE TROLLS, THE--WITH WORDS	ECKSTEIN
THREE TWO PART INVENTIONS	COPE, D.
THREE VALSES DU PRECIEUX DEGOUTE	SATIE, E.
THREE VALSE NOCTURNES	SCHMITT, F.
THREE VARIATIONS ON 'CADET ROUSSELLE'	VACHEY
THREE VARIATIONS	MOMPOU, F.
THREE VAUDEVILLE MARCHES	RIETI
THREE VAUDEVILLE MARCHES	RIETI
THREE VERY EASY LITTLE PIECES - LA ROSE, LA VIOLETTE,	MALEZIEUX
THREE VERY EASY LITTLE PIECES	LEPITRE
THREE VERY EASY SONATINAS, OP. 18A	KADOSA
THREE VICTORIAN PORTRAITS	LEGINSKA, E.
THREE WALTZES, OP. 122	PROKOFIEFF
THREE WALTZES, OP. 98	SCHUBERT
THREE WALTZES -- 1 PIANO 6 HANDS --	MONTANI
THREE WALTZES	LAPARRA, R.
THREE WALTZES	MAGONE
THREE WALTZES	MILHAUD, D.
THREE WALTZES	SCHUBERT
THREE WAY DUETS	ROGERS--ED *

THREE WINTER POTATOES	CARDEW
THREE WITCHES, FROM "MACBETH"	VERDI
THREE YULETIDE MELODIES -- JOY TO THE WORLD, AWAY IN A	RICHTER, A.
THRENODY	VIOZZI, G.
THROUGH THE ASTEROIDS	SAEGER
THROUGH THE KALEIDOSCOPE	PERRY, N.
THROUGH THE KEYS	PACE, R.
THROUGH THE LOOKING GLASS	TAYLOR, DEEMS
THROUGH THE WOODS	PECHMAN
THROUGH WOOD AND DALE	FREDERICKS
THROWING KISSES, MAZURKA	BOHM
THROWING KISSES	HEINS, C.
THROWING KISSES	HINES, C.
THRU' THE CASTLE GATE	BLAKE
THRUMMING AND HUMMING	KEENAN
THUMBNAIL SKETCHES	BISHOP
THUMERS NEUE ETUDEN-SCHULE - VORBEREITUNGSSCHULE, HEFT	THUMER
THUMERS NEUE ETUDEN-SCHULE - VORBEREITUNGSSCHULE, HEFT	THUMER
THUMERS NEUE ETUDEN-SCHULE - 01 VORST., ELEMENTARSTUFE	THUMER
THUMERS NEUE ETUDEN-SCHULE - 02 VORST., ELEMENTARSTUFE	THUMER
THUMERS NEUE ETUDEN-SCHULE - 03, HOHERE ELEMENTARSTUFE	THUMER
THUMERS NEUE ETUDEN-SCHULE - 04, HOHERE ELEMENTARSTUFE	THUMER
THUMERS NEUE ETUDEN-SCHULE - 05A, UNTER MITTELSTUFE	THUMER
THUMERS NEUE ETUDEN-SCHULE - 05B, UNTER MITTELSTUFE	THUMER
THUNDERER	SOUSA
THUNDER ROAD CHASE	MARSHALL
THUS SPAKE ZARATHUSTRA, OP. 30. SYMPHONIC POEM	STRAUSS, R.
THUS SPAKE ZARATHUSTRA, OP. 30. TWO PIANOS, EIGHT	STRAUSS, R.
THUS SPAKE ZARATHUSTRA, OP. 30	STRAUSS, R.
TIABEOC FOR PIANO	WASHBURN, G.
TIAJUANA TAXI	BRIMHALL,
TIA JUANA TANGO	NEVIN
TIC-TAC-TOE	KRAFT, L.
TIC-TAC-TOE	SINGER
TIC-TOC-CHOC, LE	COUPERIN, F.
TICK-TOC, LITTLE CLOCK	BRUSSELS, I.
TICK-TOCK TOCCATA -- A 'TIMEPIECE'	HAUFRECHT
TICK-TOCK	MATTINGLY, J.
TICKLIN' TOES	PRICE, F.
TICKLING THOUGHT, A	VALENTI, M.
TICK TOCK, SONG OF THE CLOCK	JESSE, M.
TICK TOCK	KETTERER, E.
TICK TOCK	KVELVE
TICK TOCK	LAIS
TIC TAC	SUPINO
TIC TOCCATINA	LEACOCK, L.
TIDBITS	HELLARD, R. A.
TIDDLYWINKS	ROGERS, E.
TIDDLY WINKS	ROGERS
TIDINGS OF CHRISTMAS	ZEPP--ED
TIENTOS UND FUGEN A. D. 'OBRAS DE MUSICA'	CABEZON, A.
TIERRA LINDA	GUASTAVINO
TIE ME KANGAROO DOWN	BRIMHALL,
TIGER RAG	
TIGER RAG	ANDREWS
TIGHT-ROPE DANCER, THE	MILICI
TILCARENO, EL	
TILL EULENSPIEGEL'S MERRY PRANKS, OP. 28. ABRIDGED	STRAUSS, R.
TILL EULENSPIEGEL'S MERRY PRANKS, OP. 28. TWO PIANOS,	STRAUSS, R.
TILL EULENSPIEGEL'S MERRY PRANKS, OP. 28	STRAUSS, R.
TILL EULENSPIEGEL'S MERRY PRANKS	STRAUSS, R.
TILL THERE WAS YOU	WILLSON, M.
TILL WE MEET AGAIN	LICHNER, P.
TILL	SINGER, L.--ED
TILL	WILLIAMS, R.--ED
TILT TOP	ROGERS, E.
TIMBER AUCTION POLKA	STRAUSS, J.
TIME-EXCHANGE, THE - FOR THE YOUNGEST PIANIST	RAPHLING
TIME CHANGES	BRUBECK
TIME CHANGES	KONOWITZ, B.
TIME EXCHANGE - FOR THE YOUNGEST PIANISTS	RAPHLING
TIME FOR BED	EDELSON, E.
TIME FOR US, A --ROMEO AND JULIET --	BRIMHALL,
TIME MACHINE, THE	RUSSELL
TIME MARCHES ON	BELTON, J.
TIME MARCHES ON	DUMM
TIME ON MY HANDS	LANE, J.--ED.
TIME ON MY HANDS	
TIME TO BEGIN -- ELEMENTARY SERIES, BASIC --	CLARK, F.
TIME TO PLAY FOLKSONGS	PETERS--ED
TIME TO PLAY MARCHES	ROBBINS--ED
TIME TO PLAY POLKAS	JAY--ED
TIME TO PLAY WALTZES	ANDREWS--ED
TIME TO PLAY	WARD
TIMID LITTLE BEE, THE	SCHER, W.
TIMOTHY MIXOLYDIAN	KRAFT, L.
TINGLE-TANGLE	REISINGER, O.
TINIEST ANGEL, THE	HALLSTROM *
TINKER, TAILOR	SWINSTEAD, F.
TINKER BELL AND THE PIRATE	SEIDER, S.
TINKLING BELLS	KEVAN
TINSEL TOES	REISER, V.
TINTENKLECKSE, 4 PIANO-SOLI	FISCHER, E.
TINY TECHNIC	THOMPSON, J.
TIN SOLDIER, THE	HACKH, O.
TIN SOLDIER'S WEDDING MARCH	KOLINSKI
TIN SOLDIERS MARCH, OP. 39 NO. 5	TSCHAIKOWSKY
TIP-TOE THRU' THE TULIPS WITH ME	BURKE *
TIPS FOR JUNIOR PIANISTS	DEE, M.
TIPS PIANISTS	DEE, M. *
TIP MY DOG	NICHOL *
TIP TOP TUNES, BK. 1	GLOVER, D.
TIP TOP TUNES, BK. 2	GLOVER, D.
TIP TOP TUNES, BK. 3	GLOVER, D.
TIP TOP TUNES	PEERY, R. R.
TIRA O SEU PESINHO	VILLA-LOBOS, H.
TIRED CUCKOO, THE	ANSON, G.
TIRED HIKERS	BESTHOFF, M.
TIRELESS TRAVELER, THE	GROVE
TIRESOME RAINDROPS	EZELL, H.
TIRESOME WOODPECKER, THE	THOMPSON, J.
TISHOMINGO BLUES	WILLIAMS
TIS RAINING	GRUNN, H.
TIT WILLOW, THE MIKADO	SULLIVAN, A.
TI JACQUES SUITE	PRICHARD
TI JACQUES SUITE	PRITCHARD
TOAD GOES FOR A RIDE, FROM 'LET'S GO TO THE THEATRE'	LAST, J.
TOBOGGAN RIDE	ARNOLD, H.
TOBOGGAN RIDE	MELECCI, A.
TOBOGGAN RIDE	PARK, S.
TOCATTA	DESCARRIES
TOCCATA. HARPSICHORD	SMIT SIBINGA
TOCCATA--1956	SHERMAN, N.
TOCCATA--1959	SCHOLZ
TOCCATA-ZAPATEO	RIZO, M.
TOCCATA, ADAGIO AND FUGA	BACH, J.S.
TOCCATA, FROM 'NEW AND OLD'	RIEGGER, W.

TOCCATA, FROM POUR LE PIANO	DEBUSSY
TOCCATA, OP. 090	CZERNY
TOCCATA, OP. 11	PROKOFIEFF
TOCCATA, OP. 11	PROKOFIEFF
TOCCATA, OP. 11	PROKOFIEFF
TOCCATA, OP. 111, NO. 6	SAINT-SAENS
TOCCATA, OP. 40	CASADESUS, R.
TOCCATA, OP. 51A	PEETERS
TOCCATA, OP. 54--1946	TAKACS, J.
TOCCATA, OP. 7	ROMANETTE, J.
TOCCATA, OP. 7	SCHUMANN, R.
TOCCATA, OP. 7	SCHUMANN, R.
TOCCATA, OP. 7	SCHUMANN, R.
TOCCATA, OP. 7	SCHUMANN, R.
TOCCATA, OP. 7	SCHUMANN, R.
TOCCATA, OP. 7	SCHUMANN, R.
TOCCATA, OP. 92	CZERNY
TOCCATA, 1965	BAVICCHI, J.
TOCCATA, AND FANTASY AND FUGUE IN A MINOR	BACH, J.S.
TOCCATAS, BK. 1	FRESCOBALDI
TOCCATAS, BK. 2	FRESCOBALDI
TOCCATAS, S. 910-13	BACH, J.S.
TOCCATAS -- CLOTH	BACH, J.S.
TOCCATAS AND FUGUES --4--	BACH, J.S.
TOCCATAS AND FUGUES --7-- COMPLETE	BACH, J.S.
TOCCATAS AND SONATAS	BACH, J.S.
TOCCATAS BY OLD ITALIAN MASTERS	BOGHEN
TOCCATAS	BACH, J.S.
TOCCATAS	BACH, J.S.
TOCCATAS	FRESCOBALDI
TOCCATA --FANTASIA AND FUGUE--	BACH, J.S.
TOCCATA -- ETUDE	DICHLER
TOCCATA -- HARMONIC STUDY EDITION WITH OPTIONAL SECOND	GALUPPI
TOCCATA -- IMPROVISANO-PERCOSSO	MARCEL, L. A.
TOCCATA -- THE MACHINE	HOFER, M.
TOCCATA -- 1935 --	GUARNIERI
TOCCATA -- 1956 --	FROSCHAUER
TOCCATA - ETUDE NO. 6 -,OP. 222	SAINT-SAENS
TOCCATA ALBUM	BALOGH--ED
TOCCATA ALLA DANZA	MATHIAS
TOCCATA AND AIR VARIE--HPCHD	STAEMPFLI, E.
TOCCATA AND CANZONE -- VCL AD LIB	FRESCOBALDI
TOCCATA AND CHACONNE, OP. 13	KRENEK, E.
TOCCATA AND FUGUE, OP. 56--LEFT HAND	TAKACS, J.
TOCCATA AND FUGUE --G MINOR--, PRELUDE AND FUGUE --A	BACH, J.S.
TOCCATA AND FUGUE FOR ORGAN IN D MINOR	BACH, J.S.
TOCCATA AND FUGUE IN A MINOR -- ORGAN --	FRESCOBALDI
TOCCATA AND FUGUE IN A MINOR -- ORGAN --	FRESCOBALDI
TOCCATA AND FUGUE IN D MINOR--THE DORIAN	BACH, J.S.
TOCCATA AND FUGUE IN D MINOR FOR ORGAN	BACH, J.S.
TOCCATA AND FUGUE IN D MINOR	BACH, J.S.
TOCCATA AND FUGUE IN D MINOR	BACH, J.S.
TOCCATA AND FUGUE IN D MINOR	BACH, J.S.
TOCCATA AND FUGUE NO. 5	HOVHANESS, A.
TOCCATA AND FUGUE	GUARINO, C.
TOCCATA AND FUGUE	PETYREK, F.
TOCCATA AND SOUTH AMERICAN DANCE -- FROM CHILDREN AT	TANSMAN, A.
TOCCATA AND VARIATIONS	HONEGGER, A.
TOCCATA BREVE	SOUERS
TOCCATA BRILLANTE	CLARK, J.
TOCCATA DI BRAVURA	SCARLATTI, D.
TOCCATA FOR HARPSICHORD	FAGO
TOCCATA FOR HARPSICHORD	FAGO
TOCCATA FOR PIANO	BARTOW, N.
TOCCATA FOR 2 PIANOS	FULEIHAN, A.
TOCCATA FROM THE FIFTH SYMPHONY FOR ORGAN	WIDOR, CH.
TOCCATA FURIOSA	KAROLYI
TOCCATA FUR KLAVIER UND ORCHESTER, OP. 33,	FRICKER, P.
TOCCATA FUR 2 KLAVIERE	RAPHAEL, G.
TOCCATA IN A MINOR	SCARLATTI, A.
TOCCATA IN A	PARADIES, P. D.
TOCCATA IN A	PARADIES, P. D.
TOCCATA IN C, OP. 7	SCHUMANN, R.
TOCCATA IN C, OP. 92	CZERNY
TOCCATA IN C, S. 564	BACH, J.S.
TOCCATA IN C MAJOR, OP. 92	CZERNY
TOCCATA IN C MAJOR, OP. 92	CZERNY
TOCCATA IN C MAJOR	BACH, J.S.
TOCCATA IN D MAJOR	BACH, J.S.
TOCCATA IN D MINOR, OP. 1	TCHEREPNIN
TOCCATA IN D MINOR, S. 565	BACH, J.S.
TOCCATA IN D MINOR	DITTENHAVER
TOCCATA IN D	VERETTI
TOCCATA IN E MINOR	BACH, J.S.
TOCCATA IN E MINOR	PALAU, M.
TOCCATA IN E	KREBS
TOCCATA IN FOUR MOVEMENTS FOR HARPSICHORD OR PIANO	LESSARD, J.
TOCCATA IN FOUR MOVEMENTS	LESSARD, J.
TOCCATA IN G FLAT 'MOTO PERPETUO' OP. 13	GODOWSKY, L.
TOCCATA IN THE DORIAN MODE	BACH, J.S.
TOCCATA NO. 1, OP. 30A	MOESCHINGER
TOCCATA NO. 1, OP. 30A	MOESCHINGER
TOCCATA NO. 2, OP. 30B	MOESCHINGER
TOCCATA NO. 2, OP. 30B	MOESCHINGER
TOCCATA NO. 2 OF TROIS PIECES	POULENC, F.
TOCCATA NO. 2	ANTHEIL, G.
TOCCATA NO. 3, OP. 72	MOESCHINGER
TOCCATA NO. 3, OP. 72	MOESCHINGER
TOCCATA ON THE CUCKOO'S SONG	PASQUINI
TOCCATA OSTINATO	PALMER
TOCCATA SUR LE NOM D'ALBERT ROUSSEL	IBERT
TOCCATA UND FUGE IN D-DUR -- BWV 912	BACH, J.S.
TOCCATA	APREA
TOCCATA	ARIZAGA, R.
TOCCATA	ARRIEU
TOCCATA	ARRIEU
TOCCATA	BALES
TOCCATA	BLYTH
TOCCATA	BOZZA
TOCCATA	BRERO
TOCCATA	BRUSSELS, I.
TOCCATA	BUSONI
TOCCATA	CAMPOLIETI
TOCCATA	CARABELLA
TOCCATA	CASELLA, A.
TOCCATA	CASTRO, J. J.
TOCCATA	CASTRO, J. M.
TOCCATA	CHANLER, T.
TOCCATA	CHARPENTIER, J.
TOCCATA	CONTILLI
TOCCATA	DAUTREMER, M.
TOCCATA	DESSAGNES
TOCCATA	DI MARTINO
TOCCATA	ORYE, S. L.
TOCCATA	DUBOIS, P. M.

TOCCATA	ENGELMANN, H. U.
TOCCATA	FERTE
TOCCATA	FRANCO, J.
TOCCATA	FRAZZI
TOCCATA	FUGA
TOCCATA	FUGA
TOCCATA	GIURANNA
TOCCATA	GUARNIERI
TOCCATA	GUILLOU, J.
TOCCATA	HAUBIEL, C.
TOCCATA	HEILLER, A.
TOCCATA	HURST, G.
TOCCATA	JURAFSKY
TOCCATA	KELKEL
TOCCATA	KHATCHATURIAN
TOCCATA	KHATCHATURIAN
TOCCATA	KHATCHATURIAN
TOCCATA	KHATCHATURIAN
TOCCATA	KHATCHATURIAN
TOCCATA	KOHS, E. B.
TOCCATA	KOPTAGEL, Y.
TOCCATA	LAMONTAINE, J.
TOCCATA	LAVAGNINO
TOCCATA	LESSARD, J.
TOCCATA	LOURIE
TOCCATA	MAGONE
TOCCATA	MANENTI
TOCCATA	MILANO, R.
TOCCATA	NOEL, P. *
TOCCATA	ORBON, J.
TOCCATA	PARADIES, P. D.
TOCCATA	PARADIES, P. D.
TOCCATA	PARADIES, P. D.
TOCCATA	PARADIES, P. D.
TOCCATA	PASCAL, C.
TOCCATA	PENTLAND, B.
TOCCATA	PETRASSI
TOCCATA	PURCELL, H.
TOCCATA	RAVEL
TOCCATA	RESPIGHI
TOCCATA	ROREM, N.
TOCCATA	SALVATORI
TOCCATA	SANCAN, P.
TOCCATA	SANGIORGI
TOCCATA	SANJUAN, P.
TOCCATA	SCHMIDT, F.
TOCCATA	STEINER
TOCCATA	STEINER
TOCCATA	TAMBURINI
TOCCATA	TAURIELLO, A.
TOCCATA	VIOZZI, G.
TOCCATA	WERLE, F.
TOCCATINA, OP. 27	KABALEVSKY
TOCCATINA, OP. 75	ALKAN
TOCCATINA - THE WIND	FREED, I.
TOCCATINA	CHAGY
TOCCATINA	KABALEVSKY
TOCCATINA	LONGMIRE
TOCCATINA	ROZIN
TOCCATINA	SHCHDRIN
TOCCATINA	SZONYI, E.
TOCO, MY SHETLAND PONY	MANN, M.
TODAY'S BIG COUNTRY HITS, BK. 5	
TODAY'S POP SCENE, BK. 1	
TODAY	LANE, J.--ED.
TOE DANCER	CROCKER, D.
TOGETHER WITH THE YOUNG MOZART --15 PIECES--	MOZART, W. A.
TOKYO TOCCATINA	NEVIN
TOLD AT TWIGHLIGHT	HALL, E.
TOMAHAWK DANCE	CARLETON, B.
TOMAHAWK TRAIL	TILLERY, H.
TOMBEAU DE DU FAULT, LE	MIGOT
TOMBEAU ROMANTIQUE	GAILLARD
TOMBOYS	STEINER
TOMMELISE'S SONG	REISTRUP, J.
TOMMELISE -- COMPLETE	REISTRUP, J.
TOMMY'S MARCH	HOPKINS, H.
TOMMY'S NEW DRUM	PRESTON, M. L.
TOMMY'S NEW DRUM	PRESTON, M. L.
TOMMY CAT --MODERN RHYTHMIC CLASSICS--	WHITFORD
TOMPALL AND THE GLAZER BROTHERS	
TOM FOOLERY	BRODSKY, M.
TOM TOM PARADE	TRACY, G.
TONADAS, BK. 1	NIN-CULMELL, J.
TONADAS, BK. 2	NIN-CULMELL, J.
TONADAS, BK. 3	NIN-CULMELL, J.
TONADAS, BK. 4	NIN-CULMELL, J.
TONAL MOODS FOR KEYBOARD MUSICIANS	LINDFORS, E.
TONE COLORS	MIROVITCH, A.
TONE PICTURES, OP. 35	SPRINGER, M.
TONE PICTURES, OP. 51. TWELVE PIECES FOR BEGINNERS	LOESCHHORN, A.
TONE PICTURES, OP. 88	HOFMANN
TONE POEM	BUTLER, J.
TONE POEM	YOUNG
TONE PORTRAIT, A	MCDONALD, H.
TONE SKETCHES AT THE PIANO	PHIPPEN
TONE STORIES	ROWE, D.
TONI'S TUNE	PHILLIPS, D.
TONIGHT--FROM 'WEST SIDE STORY'	BERNSTEIN, L.
TONIGHT, FROM 'WEST SIDE STORY'	BERNSTEIN, L.
TONLEITERN UND AKKORDE DURCH ALLE DUR-UND	LECHNER--ED
TONLEITERN UND AKKORDE	SCHUNGELER, H.
TONSTUCKE FUR VIER HANDE, HEFT 01	TUERK
TONSTUCKE FUR VIER HANDE, HEFT 02	TUERK
TONY'S TARANTELLE	STORR, S.
TOO YOUNG	SCHER, W.
TOPICS OF THE TROPICS	BRADLEY,
TOPOLINO VA SOLDATO	HAZELLE
TOPOLINO	PIZZINI
TOPSY-TURVY-TOY	AMADEI
TOPSY-TURVY	ROGERS, E.
TOPSY TURVY	HIBBS, C.
TOP HITS OF 1972	STEINER
TOP POP TUNES	NEVIN
TOP TEN BRIMHALL KIDDIE SHEETS ARRANGEMENTS	BRIMHALL,
TOP TEN CLASSICAL PIANO SOLOS, BK. 1	BRIMHALL,
TOP TUNES IN BIG NOTES --150--	
TORCHLIGHT DANCE	SARTORIO
TORCHLIGHT PROCESSION	CLARK, S.
TORCH DANCE --FACKELTANZ--, OP. 51	MOSZKOWSKI
TOREADOR'S SONG FROM ''CARMEN'' -- 8-HANDS, SET	BIZET, G.
TOREADOR SONG, CARMEN	BIZET, G.
TOREROS, LOS -- BALLET PANTOMIME --	COLLET
TOREROS DE CARTON -- CUENTOS Y FANTASIAS, NO. 3	CHAVARRI
TOREROS	BACARISSE

TORNADES	RIVIER, J.
TORNADO	DRAKE *
TORRENTS	RIVIER, J.
TORRE BERMEJA, OP. 92 NO. 12	ALBENIZ, I.
TORRE BERMEJA, SERENADE, OP. 92, NO. 12 -- FROM 12	ALBENIZ, I.
TORTILLAS FOR SALE	GARROW, L.
TOSCA, CONCERT MEDLEY	PUCCINI
TOSCA -- COMPLETE OPERA --	PUCCINI
TOSCA - CAPRICCIO-FANTASIA	PUCCINI
TOSCA - E LUCEVAN LE STELLE	PUCCINI
TOSCA - FANTASIA	PUCCINI
TOSCA - FANTASIA	PUCCINI
TOSCA - O DOLCI BACI	PUCCINI
TOSCA - POT-POURRI	PUCCINI
TOSCA - VISSI D'ARTE, VISSI D'AMORE	PUCCINI
TOSCA - 1ST EASY FANTASIA	PUCCINI
TOSCA - 2ND EASY FANTASIA	PUCCINI
TOTENTANZ. TOCCATA NACH HOLBEIN FUR KLAVIER UND	BRESGEN
TOUCH, TONE, TECHNIC	ECKSTEIN
TOUCH - EXERCISES ON 5 NOTES, BK. 1	FRUGATTA
TOUCH - EXERCISES ON 5 NOTES, BK. 2	FRUGATTA
TOUCH AND GO, BK. 1	KASSCHAU, H.
TOUCH AND GO, BK. 2	KASSCHAU, H.
TOUCH AND GO, BK. 3	KASSCHAU, H.
TOUCH AND RHYTHM TECHNIQUES FOR THE JAZZ PIANIST	MEHEGAN, J.
TOUCH AND TECHNIC	SHERWOOD
TOUCH ME IN THE MORNING	BRADLEY,
TOUCH OF YOUR HAND	
TOUCH PIECE FOR PIANO	READ, G.
TOUCH TECHNIQUE FOR EVERY PIANIST	DEE, M.
TOUGH GUY	GLOVER, D.
TOURBILLON, LE, FIRST GRANDE VALSE, OP. 15	MATTEI
TOURBILLON, VALSE DE CONCERT, EASY	MATTEI
TOURBILLON, VALSE DE CONCERT	MATTEI
TOUR DE FRANCE	BLAKE
TOUR DU MONDE EN MINIATURE, LE	TANSMAN, A.
TOUR OF THE WORLD IN TWENTY MINUTES --18 EASY PIECES--	ARMA, P.
TOUTE SIMPLEMENT ET PETITE ETUDE MELODIQUE	NIVERD, L.
TOWN AND COUNTRY	FURZE
TOWN HOUSE MAXIXE -- FROM 'GOLDILOCKS'	ANDERSON, L.
TOYLAND	HERBERT
TOYLAND	HERBERT
TOYLAND	HERBERT
TOYLAND	HERBERT
TOYLAND	NEVIN
TOYMAKER'S SHOP	GREEN, R.
TOYMAKERS DREAM	FOLDEN
TOYMAKERS DREAM	GOLDEN
TOYSHOP PARADE	HOWELL, C. R.
TOYS ON PARADE	MELECCI, A.
TOYS	DE VITO, A.
TOYTOWN BRIGADE	BEISSERT
TOY BALLOON	KARP
TOY BAND, THE	KEVAN
TOY BOAT, THE	AARON, M.
TOY BOX, THE	GLOVER, D.
TOY BUGLE	TEMPLETON, V.
TOY CAROUSEL	REBE
TOY DRUM	ROBINSON, A.
TOY MAKER, THE, AND HOP, SKIP, AND JUMP	HARMER
TOY MARCH	RICHARDSON, A.
TOY PARADE, THE	READ, G.
TOY PARADE	READ, G.
TOY PARADE	REEVES, R.
TOY PARADE	VOVK
TOY POODLE	NEVIN
TOY RONDO	PHILLIPS, B.
TOY SHOP BAND -- FOR ONE PIANO, SIX HANDS	EZELL, H.
TOY SHOP FROLICS	SCHER, W.
TOY SHOP RAG	VUIK, J.
TOY SOLDIERS MARCH --STUDENT EDITION--	KREISLER
TOY SOLDIERS MARCH	TSCHAIKOWSKY
TOY SOLDIERS ON PARADE	GIOVANNI
TOY SOLDIERS ON PARADE	MACLACHLAN
TOY SOLDIERS ON PARADE	REISER, V.
TOY SOLDIERS	FERRELL, B.
TOY SOLDIER	MELECCI, A.
TOY SYMPHONY	HAYDN
TOY TIGER	MANCINI *
TOY TOWN BRIGADE	BEISSERT
TOY TRAIN CHOO-CHOO--WITH WORDS	WAXMAN
TOY TRUMPET	SCOTT, C.
TOY WALTZ	STEVENS, E.
TO AND FRO - AND TO AGAIN	REISER, V.
TO AN ICE SKATER -- LEFT HAND ALONE	WEYBRIGHT
TO A BUTTERFLY	LINDFORS
TO A CYPRESS TREE	FROST
TO A DAISY	SCHER, W.
TO A HUMMING BIRD	MACDOWELL
TO A LONELY SWAYING PINE	BASTIEN
TO A LOST PET	LINDFORS, E.
TO A PARADE	FROST
TO A REDWOOD TREE	BERNA
TO A ROSEBUD	ALLISON, I.
TO A SOUTHERN PINE	COOK, P.
TO A VIOLET	SCHIEFELBEIN, F.
TO A VIOLET	SCHIEFELBEIN, F.
TO A WATER LILY	MACDOWELL
TO A WATER LILY	MACDOWELL
TO A WATER LILY	MACDOWELL
TO A WILD ROSE, OP. 51	MACDOWELL
TO A WILD ROSE	MACDOWELL
TO A WILD ROSE	MACDOWELL
TO A WILD ROSE	MACDOWELL
TO A WILD ROSE	MACDOWELL
TO A WILD ROSE	MACDOWELL
TO A WILD ROSE	MACDOWELL
TO A WILD ROSE	MACDOWELL
TO A WILD ROSE	MACDOWELL
TO A WILD ROSE	MACDOWELL
TO A WILD ROSE	MACDOWELL
TO A WILD ROSE	MACDOWELL
TO HORSE AND AWAY	REBE
TO MARKET, TO MARKET	REBE
TO MY FRENCH DOLL	SCHER, W.
TO MY LITTLE WHITE KITTEN	SCHER, W.
TO OUR GIRLS	SMETANA
TO ROBERT SCHUMANN	SMETANA
TO SPRING, OP. 43 NO. 6	GRIEG
TO SPRING, OP. 43 NO. 6	GRIEG
TO SPRING, OP. 43 NO. 6	GRIEG
TO SPRING, OP. 43 NO. 6	GRIEG
TO SPRING, OP. 43 NO. 6	GRIEG
TO SPRING	GRIEG

TO SPRING	GRIEG
TO THE EVENING STAR--FROM 'TANNHAUSER'	WAGNER
TO THE MOON AND BEYOND	WEYBRIGHT
TO THE MOON AND BEYOND	WEYBRIGHT
TO THE MOON	SWINSTEAD, F.
TO THE RISING SUN	TORJUSSEN
TO THE SETTING SUN	MELECCI, A.
TO THE SPRING, OP. 43 NO. 6	GRIEG
TO THE SUNRISE	RUNGEE
TO THE SWALLOW	REISTRUP, J.
TO THE WALTZ, IMPROMPTU	BOHM
TRACES	BRADLEY,
TRACY'S THEME	FONRAT
TRADITIONAL DANCES OF SPAIN	FONRAT
TRADITIONAL HEBREW SONGS	ROZIN--ED
TRADITIONAL MUSIC OF ISRAEL	TUCKMAN
TRAEUERMUSIK	SHIFRIN
TRAFFIC COP, THE	RICHTER
TRAFFIC DANCE	STOLZE, R.
TRAGIC POEM, OP. 34	SCRIABINE, A.
TRAGIC POEM, OP. 34	SCRIABINE, A.
TRAILING ARBUTUS	PRUTTING
TRAILING THE LONESOME ROAD	STEINER
TRAIL OF THE COVERED WAGON	STEVENS
TRAIL RIDGE	BRES, D. J.
TRAIL TO MEXICO, THE	WEYBRIGHT
TRAIN, THE	PERRIN
TRAINING IN MUSIC, BK. 1	BRADLEY
TRAINING IN MUSIC, BK. 2	BRADLEY
TRAINING IN MUSIC, BK. 3	BRADLEY
TRAINING IN MUSIC, BK. 4	BRADLEY
TRAINING OF THE LEFT HAND--46 EXERCISES AND 25 STUDIES	BERENS, H.
TRAINING OF THE LEFT HAND, OP. 89	BERENS, H.
TRAINS A COMIN'	KEVAN
TRAINS	ECKSTEIN
TRAIN TRACKS	MCKAY, G.
TRAMP, THE	SWINSTEAD, F.
TRAMP, TRAMP, TRAMP	CRERIE, E.
TRAMPOLINE TRICKS	CHAGY
TRAMP AWAY	CAZDEN, N.
TRANQUIL MOOD	PECHMAN
TRANSCRIPTIONS	LISZT
TRANSCRIPTION OF HENSELT'S 'SI OISEAU J'ETAIS' OP. 2	GODOWSKY, L.
TRANSCRIPTION OF RAFF'S 'LA FILEUSE' OP. 157, NO. 02	RAFF, J. *
TRANSFORMATIONS FOR PIANO, 1963	BLUMENFELD
TRANSPARENCES, NO. 2, MIROUR D'EAU	LELEU
TRANSPARENCE	ARMA, P.
TRANSPOSITION CHART - MAJOR KEYS	HENDERSON, R.
TRANSPOSITION CHART - MINOR KEYS	HENDERSON, R.
TRANSPOSITION FOR PIANO	STEINER
TRAPEZE ACT	STRUM, E.
TRAPEZE ACT	STRUM, E.
TRAPEZE PERFORMERS, THE	MOWREY, D.
TRAPEZE WALTZ	KREVIT, W.
TRASNE	BOUTRY
TRAUERMARSCH, OP. 72 NO. 2	CHOPIN
TRAUERMARSCH A. D. SONATA, OP. 35	CHOPIN
TRAUERMARSCH AUS DER SONATE OP. 26 AS-DUR	BEETHOVEN
TRAUME, LIEBE, TANZE, OP. 4	RETI, R.
TRAUMEREI, AND ROMANZE	SCHUMANN, R.
TRAUMEREI, OP. 15 NO. 7--SCENES FROM CHILDHOOD	SCHUMANN, R.
TRAUMEREI, OP. 9, NO. 4	STRAUSS, R.
TRAUMEREI AND ROMANCE, OP. 15, NO. 7	SCHUMANN, R.
TRAUMEREI AND ROMANCE, OP. 15 NO. 7	SCHUMANN, R.
TRAUMEREI AND ROMANCE	SCHUMANN, R.
TRAUMGEBILE E	EHLERT, LOUIS
TRAVELER'S SONG - TWO PIANOS, EIGHT HANDS	SCHUMANN, R.
TRAVELERS OF THE AIR	ERB
TRAVELIN' WEST	EZELL, H.
TRAVELING ALONG	KARP
TRAVELING TUNE, A	VALENTI, M.
TRAVELOGUE, SUITE --7 PIECES--	HORDER
TRAVELOGUES OF MELODY--13 MELODIES FROM 13	SCHER, W.
TRAVELOGUES OF MELODY -- 13 MELODIES FROM 13 COUNTRIES	SCHER, W.--ED
TRAVELOGUE 2, ANOTHER SUITE --7 PIECES--	HORDER
TRAVELS OF A FOLK TUNE	BRODSKY, M.
TRAVELS OF MR. THUMB	BOSTELMANN
TRAVELS	FAITH
TRAVEL PIECES, OP. 21	BORTKIEWICZ
TRAVEL SCENES	KING, S.
TRAVIATA, ABRIDGED	VERDI
TRAVIATA, EASY TRANSCRIPTION	VERDI
TRAVIATA, FANTASIE	VERDI
TRAVIATA, LA, PRELUDE	VERDI
TRAVIATA, LA -- COMPLETE OPERA --	VERDI
TRAVIATA, LA - BRINDISI	VERDI
TRAVIATA, LA - EASY FANTASIA	VERDI
TRAVIATA, LA - FANTASIA	VERDI
TRAVIATA, LA - PRELUDE TO ACT III AND ADDIO, DEL	VERDI
TRAVIATA, LA - PRELUDE TO ACT I	VERDI
TRAVIATA, LA - PRELUDE TO ACT I	GAY
TREASURE CHEST	STRAUSS, J.
TREASURE WALTZ, OP. 418	STRAUSS, J.
TREASURE WALTZ, OP. 418	
TREASURY OF EASY CLASSICS, A	
TREASURY OF EASY CLASSICS, A	
TREASURY OF INSPIRATIONAL SONGS	FORD, T. E.
TREASURY OF POPULAR CLASSICS	
TREASURY OF THE PIANO SONATA, A	
TREES	PARK, S.
TREES	RASBACH, O.
TREES	RASBACH, O.
TREES	RASBACH, O.
TREES	RASBACH, O.
TREE PICTURES	LAST, J.
TREE SQUIRREL, THE	LAKE, G.
TREE TOP SERENADE	ROBISION
TREIZE ETUDES CONTRAPUNTIQUES, OP. 43	BLANCHET
TREMOLO, REVERIE	ROSELLEN
TREPAK, NUTCRACKER SUITE	TSCHAIKOWSKY
TRES AIRES CRIOLLOS	AGUIRRE
TRES AIRES POPULARES ARGENTINOS	AGUIRRE
TRES DANZAS ARGENTINAS	GIANNEO
TRES DANZAS BOLIVIANAS	MENDOZA-NAVA, J.
TRES DANZAS EN ESTILO POPULAR ARGENTINO	FICHER
TRES DANZAS HEBRAICAS	FICHER
TRES DIVERTIMENTOS	MONTSALVATGE, X.
TRES HOJAS DE ALBUM, OP. 22	HALFFTER, E.
TRES JOLIE --CHARMING--, OP. 159	WALDTEUFEL, E.
TRES JOLIE	WALDTEUFEL, E.
TRES JOLIE	WALDTEUFEL, E.
TRES MINIATURAS	LECUONA
TRES PECES PER A PIANO	SOLER, J.
TRES PIEZAS	MONCAYO, J.
TRES TOCATAS	GRAITZER, G.
TRES Y CINCO	MURRAY
TRE DITIRAMBI, OP. 65	TOMASEK
TRE ESPRESSIONI	RANDS, R.
TRE GIORNI, AIR DE PERGOLESE	THALBERG
TRE IMPROVVISAZIONI - 1957	DONATONI, F.
TRE PERSONAGGI IN CERCA DI REQUIEM	BOTTINO, G.
TRE PEZZI -- DAI 'DUETTINI'	CLEMENTI
TRE PICCOLI PEZZO	BELLISARIO, A.
TRE SCHERZINI	KREJCI, I.
TRIADS ON PARADE	BECK, F.
TRIADS ON PARADE	ELAINE, SR.
TRIAD TUNE	SMITH
TRIANA -- FROM IBERIA	ALBENIZ, I.
TRIANA -- SET	ALBENIZ, I.
TRIANA	ALBENIZ, I.
TRIANA	ALBENIZ, I.
TRICKS AND TREATS	DAVIS
TRICKS FOR TWO -- EASY DUETS	RICHTER
TRICKS WITH TRIADS, SET 1	FORNUTO
TRICKS WITH TRIADS, SET 2	FORNUTO
TRICKS WITH TRIADS, SET 3 -- A LA MODE	FORNUTO
TRICKY TRAFFIC	GARROW, L.
TRICK OR TREAT	SCHER, W.
TRICK OR TREAT	SCHER, W.
TRICK OR TREAT	TILLERY, H.
TRILBY -- GALOP BRILLIANT --	THUILLIER
TRILL, THE	PHILIPP, I.
TRILL WALTZ	WRAY, J.
TRILOGIA--EL POEMA INFINITO, OP. 77	TURINA, J.
TRILOGIA--HIPOCRATES, OP. 86	TURINA, J.
TRILOGIA--OFRENDA, OP. 85	TURINA, J.
TRIO, 1969 -- PIANO AND TWO PERCUSSIONISTS	STEINER, G.
TRIOMPHE DE BACCHUS --ARR. BY COMPOSER--	DEBUSSY
TRIO NO. 3 -- PIANO AND TWO PERCUSSIONISTS	BAVICCHI, J.
TRIPLETTA	WEYBRIGHT
TRIPLE CONCERTO, OP. 89	D'INDY, V.
TRIPLE PLAY. ONDES MARTENOT AND 2 PIANOS, 4 HANDS	HAMPTON
TRIPPING ALONG	THOMPSON, A. A.
TRIPPING LIGHTLY	KIRBY, M. B.
TRIPPING THROUGH THE WOODS	DORN
TRIPTYCHON, OP. 98	WELLESZ, E.
TRIPTYCH INTERLOCHEN -- A SUITE FOR PIANO	BRANT, A.
TRIPTYQUE MONTAGNARO	MALAWSKI
TRIPTYQUE	EDEL, Y.
TRIP THROUGH YELLOWSTONE PARK, A	CHRISTIANSEN
TRIP TO MARS	MELVIN, B.
TRIP TO NIAGARA, A	CORNISH, W.
TRIP TO THE MOON, A	RAPHLING
TRIP TO THE WONDERLAND OF MUSIC -- A PIANO SCHOOL FOR	SCHOBERLECHNER,
TRIP TO THE WONDERLAND OF MUSIC -- A PIANO SCHOOL FOR	SCHOBERLECHNER,
TRIP TO VENICE, A--THE BELL	WRIGHT, N.
TRISTAN -- 1965 -- BALLET IN 7 SCENES	BLACHER
TRISTAN AND ISOLDE--ISOLDE'S LOVE-DEATH	WAGNER *
TRISTAN AND ISOLE -- PRELUDE	WAGNER
TRISTAN UND ISOLDE--ISOLDE'S LOVE-DEATH	WAGNER *
TRISTAN UND ISOLDE -- GER SUPERLINEAR TEXT	WAGNER
TRISTAN UND ISOLDE - LIEBESTOD	WAGNER *
TRISTE, OP. 8 NO. 2	NAPOLITANO
TRISTESSE	PIERNE, P.
TRITSCH TRATSCH POLKA, OP. 214	STRAUSS, J.
TRITSCH TRATSCH POLKA	STRAUSS, J.
TRITTICO LIRICO - 1. LA RONDA NOTTURNA	PRATELLA
TRITTICO LIRICO - 2. LA CONZONE DI LUISA	PRATELLA
TRITTICO LIRICO - 3. PIFFERATA INVERNALE	PRATELLA
TRIUMPHAL MARCH--PETER AND THE WOLF	PROKOFIEFF
TRIUMPHAL MARCH, OP. 56 NO. 3	GRIEG
TRIUMPHAL MARCH --SIGURD JORSALFAR--, OP. 56, NO. 3	GRIEG
TRIUMPHAL MARCH --SIGURD JORSALFAR--, OP. 56 NO. 3	GRIEG
TRIUMPHAL MARCH FROM 'AIDA'	VERDI
TRIUMPHAL MARCH FROM 'AIDA'	VERDI
TRIUMPHAL MARCH FROM 'AIDA'	VERDI
TRIUMPHANT MARCH, PETER AND THE WOLF	PROKOFIEFF
TRIUNFO, EL	SAMMARTINO
TROIKA EN TRAINEAUX IN E, OP. 37 NO. 11	TSCHAIKOWSKY
TROIKA RIDE, NOVEMBER, OP. 37 NO. 11	TSCHAIKOWSKY
TROIKA RIDE	TSCHAIKOWSKY
TROISIEME CONCERTO, OP. 29	SAINT-SAENS
TROISIEME MAZURKA, OP. 66	SAINT-SAENS
TROIS ANDANTES ROMANTIQUES, OP. 13	ALKAN
TROIS CHANSONS ET DANSES ESPAGNOLES	SURINACH, C.
TROIS CHORALS NO. 01	FRANCK, C.
TROIS CHORALS NO. 02	FRANCK, C.
TROIS CHORALS NO. 03	FRANCK, C.
TROIS ECOSSAISES	CHOPIN
TROIS ENFANTINES	BEAUCAMP
TROIS EPIGRAMMES	MIGOT
TROIS EPITAPHES	ARMA, P.
TROIS ESQUISSES - CLIGNE-MUSETTE	FEVRIER
TROIS ESQUISSES - SOIR	FEVRIER
TROIS ESQUISSES - VALSE	FEVRIER
TROIS ESQUISSES	MARTINU, B.
TROIS ETUDES DE CONCERT -- LAMENTO, LEGIERO, SOSPIRO	LISZT
TROIS ETUDES DE JAZZ, OP. 2	STRAUSS, E.
TROIS INSTANTS MUSICAUX -- 1927 --	CAPDEVIELLE
TROIS MORCEAUX DANS LE GENRE PATHETIQUE, OP. 15	ALKAN
TROIS MORCEAUX	NIVERD, L.
TROIS NOCTURNES DANTESQUES	MIGOT
TROIS PENSEES MUSICALES, OP. 75	BACEVICIUS
TROIS PETITES FANTAISIES, OP. 41	ALKAN
TROIS PETITES PIECES MONTEES	SATIE, E.
TROIS PETITS PIANOS	LAUSNAY, G.
TROIS PIECES, OP. 8	DUPONT, J.
TROIS PIECES -- NO. 1 ELEGIE	WURMSER, L.
TROIS PIECES -- NO. 2 INTERLUDE	WURMSER, L.
TROIS PIECES -- NO. 3 AIR DE BALLET	WURMSER, L.
TROIS PIECES BREVES	MARC, E.
TROIS PIECES EN DO POUR LES JEUNES	HUGON, G.
TROIS PIECES EN FORME DE	BUNDERVOET
TROIS PIECES NEGRES	LAMBERT, C.
TROIS PIECES POUR UNE ESPAGNOLADE	PITTALUGA
TROIS PIECES	DUBOIS, P. M.
TROIS PIECES	MIRANDOLLE
TROIS PIECES	MONTBRUN, G.
TROIS POINTES SECHES	RIVIER, J.
TROIS POLKAS DE SALON, OP. 7	SMETANA
TROIS PRELUDES EN FORME DE BLUES	TANSMAN, A.
TROIS PRELUDES	MAILLARD
TROIS PRELUDES	PETRONIO
TROIS RHAPSODIES -- 1. FRANCAISE, 2. POLONAISE, 3.	SCHMITT, F.
TROIS SONATINES, OP. 257	LACK
TROJANS AT CARTHAGE. FANTASY ON THEMES FROM THE OPERA.	BERLIOZ
TROLDTOG, EASY	GRIEG
TROLDTOG, OP. 54 NO. 3	GRIEG
TROMPEUR DE SEVILLE, LE -- BALLET IN ONE ACT	NIN-CULMELL, J.
TROPICAL NIGHT	AARON, M.
TROPICAL	GOULD, M.
TROPICANA	WEYBRIGHT
TROPIC CARNIVAL	WEYBRIGHT
TROPIC ISLAND, A	GILLOCK

TROPIC NIGHTS --MODERN RHYTHMIC CLASSICS--	WHITFORD
TROPIC NIGHT	WILLIAMS, L. A.
TROPISMEN	OTTE, H.
TROT, PONY TROT	JOYNER, B.
TROTTING PONY	CANFIELD, J.
TROTTING	RICHTER
TROUBADOUR, THE	ROGERS, E.
TROUBLED WATERS	BONDS
TROUBLED WATERS	BONDS
TROUT, THE	SCHUBERT
TROUT, THE	SCHUBERT
TROVATORE. ABRIDGED	VERDI
TROVATORE, IL, ANVIL CHORUS, EASY	VERDI
TROVATORE, IL, ANVIL CHORUS	VERDI
TROVATORE, IL, EASY TRANSCRIPTION	VERDI
TROVATORE, IL, FANTASIE	VERDI
TROVATORE, IL, FANTASIE	VERDI
TROVATORE, IL, GYPSY SONG	VERDI
TROVATORE, IL, HOME TO OUR MOUNTAINS	VERDI
TROVATORE, IL, MISERERE	VERDI
TROVATORE, IL -- COMPLETE OPERA --	VERDI
TROVATORE, IL - EASY FANTASIA	VERDI
TROVATORE, IL - FANTASIA	VERDI
TROVATORE, IL - MISERERE	VERDI
TRUE BLUE LADY	SCHAUM, J.--ED.
TRUE LOVE	SCHIEFELBEIN, F.
TRUE LOVE	SINGER, L.--ED
TRUMPETER'S LULLABY, A	ANDERSON, L.
TRUMPETER'S SERENADE	SPINDLER
TRUMPETS	GLOVER, D.
TRUMPET MARCH	HEIMLER
TRUMPET MARCH	WRIGHT, K.
TRUMPET PARADE	KARP
TRUMPET PIECE AND AIR IN D	PURCELL, H.
TRUMPET TUNE IN D MAJOR	PURCELL, H.
TRUMPET TUNE	PURCELL, H.
TRUMPET VOLUNTARY AND TRUMPET TUNE	PURCELL, H.
TRUMPET VOLUNTARY	PROKOFIEFF
TRUMPET VOLUNTARY	PURCELL, H.
TRUMPET VOLUNTARY	PURCELL, H.
TRY AND CATCH ME	ROBBINS
TRY TO REMEMBER	SINGER, L.--ED
TSCHAIKOWSKY'S PIANO CONCERT IN B FLAT	GRAINGER, P.
TSCHAIKOWSKY CONCERTO	TSCHAIKOWSKY
TSCHAIKOWSKY FOR THE YOUNG PIANIST	TSCHAIKOWSKY
TSCHAIKOWSKY FOR THE YOUNG	TSCHAIKOWSKY
TSCHAIKOWSKY GEMS	STEINER
TSCHAIKOWSKY MADE EASY FOR EVERYONE	TSCHAIKOWSKY
TSCHECHISCHE BALLADE, OP. 9	OSTRCIL
TSCHECHISCHE KLASSIKER, BAND 1 - 16 STUCKE	BECVAROVSKY *
TSCHECHISCHE KLASSIKER, BAND 2 - 9 STUCKE	DUSSEK, J. *
TSCHECHISCHE MUSIK IN DOMALICE	KUBA
TSCHECHISCHE TANZE 1 AND 2	SMETANA
TU, CA NUN CHIAGNE	ERB
TUG OF WAR	LICHNER, H.
TULIP, OP. 111 NO. 4	SCHER, W.
TULIP TIME IN HOLLAND	ERB
TULIP TIME	REBE
TULIP TIME	THOMPSON, J.
TULIP	LICHNER, H.
TUMBLE-TOWN CAKEWALK	WEYBRIGHT
TUMBLE-TOWN WATERFALL	WEYBRIGHT
TUMBLE-WEED	BLISS, P.
TUMBLERS, THE	THOMASON, E.
TUMBLEWEED TRAIL	FRANTZ, C.
TUMBLEWEED	DILSNER
TUMBLEWEED	SAXMAN
TUMBLING CLOWNS	FROST
TUMBLING JACK	CROSBY, M.
TUMBLING STREAM	ROBERTS
TUMBLING	BASTIEN
TUMBLING	CRERIE, E.
TUMBLING	KING, S.
TUMBLING	WEYBRIGHT
TUNANTE CATAMARQUENO, EL	GOMEZ CARRILLO
TUNE-A-RAMA	SCHER, W.
TUNEFUL RHYTHM PATTERNS	STEINER
TUNEFUL TASKS FOR PIANO STUDENTS OF THE SECOND GRADE	TERRY, F.
TUNEFUL TASKS	THOMPSON, J.
TUNEFUL TECHNIC - BK. 1	THOMPSON, J.
TUNEFUL TECHNIC - BK. 2	THOMPSON, J.
TUNEFUL TECHNIC	KING--ED *
TUNEFUL TECHNIC	KING *
TUNEFUL TEN	SOULE
TUNEFUL VARIETIES, BK. 1	BERMONT, H.--ED
TUNEFUL VARIETIES, BK. 2	BERMONT, H.--ED
TUNELETS	SCHER, W.
TUNERAMA	PORTNOFF, M.--ED
TUNES AND DANCES FROM SILJUSTOL. VOL. 1. OP. 21	SAEVERUD
TUNES AND DANCES FROM SILJUSTOL. VOL. 2. OP. 22	SAEVERUD
TUNES AND DANCES FROM SILJUSTOL. VOL. 3. OP. 24	SAEVERUD
TUNES AND DANCES FROM SILJUSTOL. VOL. 4. OP. 25	SAEVERUD
TUNES AROUND THE CLOCK	MCGRAW
TUNES AT THE KEYBOARD	LAST, J.
TUNES FOR EVERYBODY -- 65 FAMOUS PIECES IN EASY	HARVEY, VIVIEN
TUNES FOR FOUR HANDS -- ORIGINAL COMPOSITIONS FROM	BEER, L. J.--ED
TUNES FOR FOUR HANDS -- ORIGINAL COMPOSITIONS FROM	BEER, L. J.--ED
TUNES FOR LITTLE PLAYERS	KERR, R. N.
TUNES FOR TECHNIC	HOWELL, I.
TUNES FOR THE PIANIST, NO. 1	WHITFORD--ED.
TUNES FOR THE PIANIST, NO. 2	WHITFORD--ED.
TUNES FOR THE PIANIST, NO. 3	WHITFORD--ED.
TUNES FOR THE PIANIST, NO. 4	WHITFORD--ED.
TUNES FOR TWO, BK. 1	SCHAUM, J.
TUNES FOR TWO, BK. 1	SCHAUM, J.
TUNES FOR TWO, BK. 2	SCHAUM, J.
TUNES FOR TWO, BK. 2	SCHAUM, J.
TUNES FROM FAR AND NEAR	REBE
TUNES FROM FAR AWAY -- 50 EASY ARRANGEMENTS OF	HERRMANN--ED
TUNES FROM MANY LANDS	DILLER, A.--ED *
TUNES FROM THE 18TH CENTURY, NO. 4--FLOURISH	BAUER, H.
TUNES IN FOLK STYLE	STEVENS, E.
TUNES OF ALL NATIONS	NICHOLLS, H.
TUNES OF ALL TIME	GRAY, D.
TUNES OF THE U. S. A., ONE PIANO SIX HANDS	MACGREGOR
TUNES TWO CAN PLAY	PELS, W.
TUNES WITH THE TEEN-AGE TOUCH	KING, S.
TUNES YOU LIKE TO PLAY	
TUNES YOU LIKE TO PLAY	
TUNE FOR A BOY GOING TO SCHOOL AND TUNE FOR A BOY	BOWLES, P.
TUNE FOR A MUSICAL TOY, A	BAYLEY
TUNE FOR TWO HANDS	CATIZONE, J. M.
TUNE TIME - PART B	CLARK, F.--ED.
TUNE TIME - PART B	CLARK, F.--ED.
TUNE TIME FOR TWO	MARTIN, H.
TUNE TIME FOR TWO	MARTIN, H.
TUNE TIME	RICHTER
TURANDOT - 1ST EASY FANTASIA	PUCCINI
TURANDOT - 2ND EASY FANTASIA	PUCCINI
TURKEY, TURKEY	LAKE, G.
TURKEY GOBBLER, THE	OBENCHAIN, V.
TURKEY IN THE STRAW--COWBOYS' AND OLD FIDDLERS'	GUION, D.
TURKEY IN THE STRAW--TWO PIANOS-EIGHT HANDS--	SCHAUM, J.--ED.
TURKEY IN THE STRAW	BONNEL *
TURKEY IN THE STRAW	GROOMS--ED
TURKEY IN THE STRAW	LAIS--ED
TURKEY IN THE STRAW	SCHAUM, J.--ED.
TURKEY IN THE STRAW	THOMPSON, J.
TURKEY IN THE STRAW	WEYBRIGHT
TURKEY KNOB	TREVARTHEN, R.
TURKISCHER MARSCH -- K.V. 331	MOZART, W. A.
TURKISCHER MARSCH AUS, DIE RUINEN VON ATHEN	BEETHOVEN
TURKISH DANCE SUITE	ALNAR, F.
TURKISH DANCE	SCHER, W.
TURKISH MARCH--RUINS OF ATHENS	BEETHOVEN *
TURKISH MARCH, EASY	MOZART, W. A.
TURKISH MARCH, RUINS OF ATHENS	BEETHOVEN
TURKISH MARCH FROM ''THE RUINS OF ATHENS'' -- SET	BEETHOVEN
TURKISH MARCH FROM 'RUINS OF ATHENS'	BEETHOVEN
TURKISH MARCH FROM 'THE RUINS OF ATHENS'--BEETHOVEN	RUBINSTEIN
TURKISH MARCH FROM SONATA IN A	MOZART, W. A.
TURKISH MARCH	MOZART, W. A.
TURKISH REVELS	LEE, E.
TURKISH RONDO	KRENTZLIN, R.
TURNABOUT DUETS	RUSSELL
TURNING HAND SPRINGS	THOMPSON, A. A.
TURNING WHEELS	TIBBITTS, A.
TURN YE TO ME	ANDERSON, L.
TURTLE AT THE ZOO	BASTIEN
TURTLE TALK	GEORGE
TUSSEDANS --GNOME DANCE--	TANGEN
TUSSLE	CHAGRIN
TUTTIFANTCHEN - TANZ DER HOLZPUPPEN	HINDEMITH
TUTTI DE CONCERTO, DANS LE GENRE ANCIEN OP. 63, NO. 15	ALKAN
TUTTI LE SCALE PER PIANOFORTE, BK. 1	SCHININA, L.
TUTTI LE SCALE PER PIANOFORTE, BK. 2	SCHININA, L.
TUXEDO JUNCTION	DVORINE
TV CIRCUS	GARROW
TV COWBOY	HOLT, EILSEL
TWAS NIGHT IN VENICE	BOWMAN *
TWELFH STREET RAG	BOWMAN *
TWELFTH STREET RAG	BOWMAN *
TWELFTH STREET RAG	BOWMAN *
TWELFTH STREET RAG	JELINEK, H.
TWELVE-TONE MUSIC, OP. 15 BK. 1, FOUR 2-PART	JELINEK, H.
TWELVE-TONE MUSIC, OP. 15 BK. 2, SIX LITTLE	JELINEK, H.
TWELVE-TONE MUSIC, OP. 15 BK. 3, THREE DANCE PIECES	JELINEK, H.
TWELVE-TONE MUSIC, OP. 15 BK. 4, FOUR TOCCATAS	JELINEK, H.
TWELVE-TONE MUSIC, OP. 15 BK. 5, SUITE IN E	SCHLOSS, J.
TWELVE-TONE SUITE	HILLER
TWELVE-TONE VARIATIONS FOR PIANO	GINASTERA
TWELVE AMERICAN PRELUDES, BK. 1	GINASTERA
TWELVE AMERICAN PRELUDES, BK. 2	HOVHANESS, A.
TWELVE ARMENIAN FOLK SONGS	ALEXANDER, J.
TWELVE BAGATELLES	ALEXANDER, J.
TWELVE BAGATELLES	ALEXANDER, J.
TWELVE BAGATELLES	ROCHBERG, G.
TWELVE BAGATELLES	BURGMUELLER
TWELVE BRILLIANT AND MELODIOUS STUDIES, OP. 105	BURGMUELLER
TWELVE BRILLIANT STUDIES, OP. 105	HENSELT, A.
TWELVE CHARACTERISTIC CONCERT STUDIES, OP. 2	FARINA
TWELVE CHARACTERISTIC PIECES, BK. 1 - EASY	FARINA
TWELVE CHARACTERISTIC PIECES, BK. 2 - MEDIUM-DIFFICULT	MOSCHELES, I.
TWELVE CHARACTERISTIC STUDIES, OP. 95	GLIERE
TWELVE CHILDREN'S PIECES, OP. 31	SWIFT, N.
TWELVE CHILDREN'S PIECES	PEETERS
TWELVE CHORALE PRELUDES, OP. 114. VOL. 1	PEETERS
TWELVE CHORALE PRELUDES, OP. 114. VOL. 2	LAMBARDO
TWELVE CONTEMPORARY PIECES FOR CHILDREN	NORTH, A.
TWELVE DANCE PRELUDES	GRADY, J.
TWELVE DAYS OF CHRISTMAS, THE	BRIMHALL
TWELVE DAYS OF CHRISTMAS	SCHAUM, J.--ED.
TWELVE DAYS OF CHRISTMAS	SCHAUM, W.--ED
TWELVE DAYS OF CHRISTMAS	PASCAL, C.
TWELVE DECHIFFRAGES	KOEHLER
TWELVE EASIEST STUDIES, OP. 151	STREABBOG
TWELVE EASY AND MELODIOUS STUDIES, OP. 64--SECOND	KABALEVSKY
TWELVE EASY PIANO PIECES	WEBER, VON
TWELVE EASY PIECES, OP. 3 AND OP. 10	BERTINI
TWELVE EASY PIECES, OP. 84	HANDEL
TWELVE EASY PIECES	HANDEL
TWELVE EASY PIECES	HARSANYI
TWELVE EASY PIECES	HAYDN
TWELVE EASY PIECES	HAYDN
TWELVE EASY PIECES	HAYDN
TWELVE EASY RECREATIONS	SCARLATTI, D.
TWELVE EASY SCARLATTI SONATAS	KOEHLER
TWELVE EASY STUDIES, OP. 157	KOEHLER
TWELVE EASY STUDIES OP. 157	KOHLER, F.
TWELVE EASY STUDIES	ROBOTTI
TWELVE ESERCIZI	KOECHLIN, C.
TWELVE ESQUISSES - BK. 1	KOECHLIN, C.
TWELVE ESQUISSES - BK. 2	DEBUSSY
TWELVE ETUDES, BK. 1	DEBUSSY
TWELVE ETUDES, BK. 2	LISZT
TWELVE ETUDES, OP. 1	MACDOWELL
TWELVE ETUDES, OP. 39	MACDOWELL
TWELVE ETUDES, OP. 39	SCRIABINE, A.
TWELVE ETUDES, OP. 8	SCRIABINE, A.
TWELVE ETUDES, OP. 8	SCRIABINE, A.
TWELVE ETUDES, OP. 8	LISZT
TWELVE ETUDES, VOL. 1	LISZT
TWELVE ETUDES, VOL. 2	LISZT
TWELVE ETUDES D'EXECUTION TRANSCENDANTE	BOLCOM, W.
TWELVE ETUDES FOR PIANO	MOSZKOWSKI
TWELVE ETUDES FOR THE LEFT HAND ALONE, OP. 92	ALKAN
TWELVE ETUDES IN MINOR KEYS, BK. 1	ALKAN
TWELVE ETUDES IN MINOR KEYS, BK. 2	ALKAN
TWELVE ETUDES IN MINOR KEYS, NO. 01, COMME LE VENT--A	ALKAN
TWELVE ETUDES IN MINOR KEYS, NO. 02, RYTHME	ALKAN
TWELVE ETUDES IN MINOR KEYS, NO. 03, SCHERZO	ALKAN
TWELVE ETUDES IN MINOR KEYS, NO. 04, ALLEGRO	ALKAN
TWELVE ETUDES IN MINOR KEYS, NO. 05, MARCHE FUNEBRE--F	ALKAN
TWELVE ETUDES IN MINOR KEYS, NO. 06, MENUET--B FLAT	ALKAN
TWELVE ETUDES IN MINOR KEYS, NO. 07, FINALE--E FLAT	ALKAN
TWELVE ETUDES IN MINOR KEYS, NO. 08, CONCERTO-ALLEGRO	ALKAN
TWELVE ETUDES IN MINOR KEYS, NO. 09,	ALKAN
TWELVE ETUDES IN MINOR KEYS, NO. 10, ALLEGRO ALA	ALKAN
TWELVE ETUDES IN MINOR KEYS, NO. 11, OUVERTURE--B	ALKAN
TWELVE ETUDES PIANISTIQUES POUR LA MAIN GAUCHE, OP.	HERARD
TWELVE EXCURSIONS FOR THE YOUNG PIANIST	SARAKATSANNIS

TWELVE FAMOUS PIECES	ALBENIZ, I.
TWELVE FANTASIAS AND 4 PIECES	HANDEL
TWELVE FAVORITES	STRIMER, J.--ED
TWELVE FOUR-HAND PIANO PIECES, OP. 85	SCHUMANN, R.
TWELVE GERMAN DANCES	BEETHOVEN
TWELVE GERMAN DANCES	MOZART, W. A.
TWELVE GLIMPSES INTO 20TH CENTURY IDIOMS	WUENSCH
TWELVE HYMN TUNES	PAYNE, W.
TWELVE IMAGES EN COURTS PRELUDES	DIEUDONNE
TWELVE IMPRESSIONS, NOS. 1-6	STONE, D.
TWELVE IMPRESSIONS, NOS. 7-12	STONE, D.
TWELVE INVENTIONS FOR PIANO SOLO	GREEN, R.
TWELVE KOCHELER LAENDLER, OP. 135	NIEMANN
TWELVE KOCHELER LAENDLER, OP. 136	NIEMANN
TWELVE LAENDLER, OP. 171	SCHUBERT
TWELVE LAENDLER	SCHUBERT
TWELVE LITTLE FANTASY STUDIES, OP. 13	ROWLEY
TWELVE LITTLE PIECES - LA BALLE	KOECHLIN, C.
TWELVE LITTLE PIECES AND PRELUDES	BERTINI
TWELVE LITTLE PIECES FOR BEGINNERS	CESI, B.
TWELVE LITTLE PIECES	HESS
TWELVE LITTLE PIECES	KOECHLIN, C.
TWELVE LITTLE PRELUDES	BACH, J.S.
TWELVE LITTLE PRELUDES	BACH, J.S.
TWELVE LITTLE RECITAL PIECES	ABENDROTH
TWELVE LITTLE SKETCHES FOR CHILDREN, OP. 182	GRETCHANINOFF
TWELVE LITTLE STEMLESS COMPOSITIONS	CRERIE, E.
TWELVE LITTLE STUDIES, OP. 157	KOEHLER
TWELVE LITTLE STUDIES FOR DEVELOPMENT OF VELOCITY, OP.	KOEHLER
TWELVE MELODIES FROM THE MOUNTAINS AND THE PLAINS	TROIANI
TWELVE MELODIOUS AND CHARACTERISTIC PIECES, OP. 51	LOESCHHORN, A.
TWELVE MELODIOUS PIECES, OP. 6 AND 8	ENKE
TWELVE MELODIOUS STUDIES, OP. 63	STREABBOG
TWELVE MELODIOUS STUDIES, OP. 63	STREABBOG
TWELVE MELODIOUS STUDIES	LEMONT, C. W.
TWELVE MENUETTOS, VOL. 1	MOZART, W. A.
TWELVE MENUETTOS, VOL. 2	MOZART, W. A.
TWELVE MINNELIEDER -- 2 AND 4 HANDS	REDA
TWELVE MINUETS	FUX
TWELVE MINUETS	HAYDN
TWELVE MINUETS	MUTHEL, J. G.
TWELVE MOSAICS	WILDER, A.
TWELVE O'CLOCK HIGH - THEME	FRONTIERE, D.
TWELVE ORGAN CONCERTI IN 2 VOLS‡ VOL. 1	HANDEL
TWELVE ORGAN CONCERTI IN 2 VOLS‡ VOL. 2	HANDEL
TWELVE PETITES PIECES, BK. 1	DEBRIE
TWELVE PETITES PIECES, BK. 2	DEBRIE
TWELVE PETITES PIECES FACILES	KOECHLIN, C.
TWELVE PIANO IMPRESSIONS	ROZIN
TWELVE PIANO PIECES	MOZART, W. A.
TWELVE PIANO SKETCHES	BRUSSELS, I.
TWELVE PIANO SKETCHES	BRUSSELS, I.
TWELVE PIECES ENFANTINES	DE FRANCMESNIL
TWELVE PIECES FOR TEN FINGERS	STARER
TWELVE PIECES IN RELATED KEYS, BK. 1	CURRIE, E.
TWELVE PIECES IN RELATED KEYS, BK. 2	CURRIE, E.
TWELVE PIECES IN THE FORM OF STUDIES	DRING
TWELVE PIECES	TUERK
TWELVE PLAYTIME PIECES	OLDENBURG, E.
TWELVE POLONAISIES	BACH, W.F.
TWELVE PRELUDES, OP. 25	WRIGHT, N.
TWELVE PRELUDES ON AKSAK RHYTHMS	SAYGUN, A.
TWELVE PRELUDES	KOECHLIN, C.
TWELVE PRELUDES	MIGOT
TWELVE PRELUDES	TREBINSKY, A.
TWELVE SELECTED SONATAS FOR PIANO, BK. 01	FRISKIN--ED
TWELVE SELECTED SONATAS FOR PIANO, BK. 02	FRISKIN--ED
TWELVE SHORT CHILDREN'S PIECES, OP. 35B	KADOSA
TWELVE SHORT OCTAVE-STUDIES, OP. 118	WOLFF, B.
TWELVE SHORT PIANO PIECES, WRITTEN IN THE 12-TONE	KRENEK, E.
TWELVE SHORT PIANO PIECES	HAYDN
TWELVE SHORT PIECES AND PRELUDES FOR BEGINNERS	BERTINI
TWELVE SHORT PIECES	DEFILIPPI, A.
TWELVE SHORT PIECES	DELACHI
TWELVE SHORT PIECES	DE FILIPPI, A.
TWELVE SILHOUETTEN, OP. 8	DVORAK
TWELVE SKETCHES --DOUZE DESSINS	TUREL
TWELVE SMALL STUDIES	SLAVICKY, K.
TWELVE SONATAS, BK. 1--NOS. 1-7	CLEMENTI
TWELVE SONATAS, BK. 1	CLEMENTI
TWELVE SONATAS, BK. 1	PLATTI, G. B.
TWELVE SONATAS, BK. 2--NOS. 8-12	CLEMENTI
TWELVE SONATAS, BK. 2	CLEMENTI
TWELVE SONATAS, BK. 2	PLATTI, G. B.
TWELVE SONATAS	GALUPPI
TWELVE SONATAS	RUST
TWELVE SONATINAS‡ OP. 20, OP. 55, OP. 59	KUHLAU, F.
TWELVE SONATINAS--OP. 36, 37, 38	CLEMENTI
TWELVE SONATINAS, BK. 1 -- OP. 36 --	CLEMENTI
TWELVE SONATINAS, BK. 1 -- OP. 36 --	CLEMENTI
TWELVE SONATINAS, BK. 2 -- OP. 37 AND 38 --	CLEMENTI
TWELVE SONATINAS, OP. 20, 55, 59	KUHLAU, F.
TWELVE SONATINAS, OP. 20, 55 AND 59	KUHLAU, F.
TWELVE SONATINAS, OP. 36-37-38	CLEMENTI
TWELVE SONATINAS, OP. 36, 37, 38 COMPLETE	CLEMENTI
TWELVE SONATINAS, OP. 36, 37, 38 COMPLETE	CLEMENTI
TWELVE SONATINAS, OP. 36, 37, 38	CLEMENTI
TWELVE SPANISH DANCES, BK. 1	GRANADOS
TWELVE SPANISH DANCES, BK. 2	GRANADOS
TWELVE SPANISH DANCES	GRANADOS
TWELVE STUDIES, OP. 105	BURGMUELLER
TWELVE STUDIES, OP. 26	THALBERG
TWELVE STUDIES, OP. 43	ROWLEY
TWELVE STUDIES FOR DEVELOPMENT OF VELOCITY, OP. 15	BRAUER, F.
TWELVE STUDIES FOR PIANO	PUTSCHE, T.
TWELVE STUDIES IN THIRDS, OP. 35	LONGO, A.
TWELVE STUDIES	NEUPERT, E.
TWELVE STUDI DA CONCERTO	CAMMAROTA
TWELVE SYMPHONIC ETUDES, OP. 13	SCHUMANN, R.
TWELVE SYMPHONIC STUDIES, OP. 13	SCHUMANN, R.
TWELVE SYMPHONIES, BK. 1	HAYDN
TWELVE SYMPHONIES, BK. 1	MOZART, W. A.
TWELVE SYMPHONIES, BK. 2	HAYDN
TWELVE SYMPHONIES, BK. 2	MOZART, W. A.
TWELVE TELL-A-TALE TUNES	MASON, I.
TWELVE TIME TWELVE--FUGUES FOR PIANO	SOMERS, H.
TWELVE TONADAS IN POPULAR CHILEAN STYLE	ALLENDE
TWELVE TRAVEL TUNES	ROSNER
TWELVE TWELVE-TONE PIECES FOR CHILDREN	JOACHIM, O.
TWELVE TWO-PART FUGUES	LANZA
TWELVE VARIATIONS IN C, K265	MOZART, W. A.
TWELVE VARIATIONS IN C ON 'AH VOUS DIRAI-JE MAMAN,'	MOZART, W. A.
TWELVE VARIATIONS IN C ON 'AH VOUS DIRAIJE, MAMAN,' K.	MOZART, W. A.
TWELVE VARIATIONS ON AN ORIGINAL THEME FOR TWO PIANOS	PARCHMAN, G.
TWELVE VERY EASY AND MELODIOUS STUDIES, OP. 63--FIRST	STREABBOG
TWELVE VERY EASY AND MELODIOUS STUDIES, OP. 63	STREABBOG
TWELVE VIRTUOSO STUDIES, OP. 46--NO. 1, NOVELETTE	MACDOWELL
TWELVE VIRTUOSO STUDIES, OP. 46--NO. 10, MARCH WIND	MACDOWELL
TWELVE VIRTUOSO STUDIES, OP. 46--NO. 11, IMPROMPTU	MACDOWELL
TWELVE VIRTUOSO STUDIES, OP. 46--NO. 12, POLONAISE	MACDOWELL
TWELVE VIRTUOSO STUDIES, OP. 46--NO. 2, MOTO	MACDOWELL
TWELVE VIRTUOSO STUDIES, OP. 46--NO. 4,	MACDOWELL
TWELVE VIRTUOSO STUDIES, OP. 46--NO. 7, BURLESQUE	MACDOWELL
TWELVE VIRTUOSO STUDIES, OP. 46	MACDOWELL
TWELVE WALTZES FOR THE YOUNG	MOZART, W. A.
TWELVE WALTZES	STRAUSS, J.
TWENTIETH CENTURY ERA PIANO MUSIC	
TWENTIETH CENTURY PIANO MUSIC, BK. 1A	FROST--ED
TWENTIETH CENTURY PIANO MUSIC, BK. 1B	FROST--ED
TWENTIETH CENTURY PIANO MUSIC, BK. 2A	FROST--ED
TWENTIETH CENTURY PIANO MUSIC, BK. 2B	FROST--ED
TWENTIETH CENTURY PIANO MUSIC, BK. 3A	FROST--ED
TWENTIETH CENTURY PIANO MUSIC, BK. 3B	FROST--ED
TWENTY-EIGHT MELODIOUS PIECES ON 5 NOTES, OP. 149	DIABELLI
TWENTY-EIGHT MINIATURE ETUDES	KETTERER, E.
TWENTY-EIGHT PIECES ON 5 NOTES, OP. 149	DIABELLI
TWENTY-EIGHT PLEASING STUDIES FOR EQUALIZATION OF THE	KETTERER, E.
TWENTY-EIGHT STAR MELODIES, BK. 1	BERMONT, H.--ED
TWENTY-EIGHT VARIATIONS, OP. 15	WEIGL, K.
TWENTY-FIVE COUPERIN PIECES	COUPERIN, F.
TWENTY-FIVE EASY AND PROGRESSIVE STUDIES, OP. 100--BK.	BURGMUELLER
TWENTY-FIVE EASY AND PROGRESSIVE STUDIES, OP. 100--BK.	BURGMUELLER
TWENTY-FIVE EASY AND PROGRESSIVE STUDIES, OP. 100	BURGMUELLER
TWENTY-FIVE EASY AND PROGRESSIVE STUDIES, OP. 100	BURGMUELLER
TWENTY-FIVE EASY AND PROGRESSIVE STUDIES WITH SPECIAL	BIEHL, A.
TWENTY-FIVE EASY AND PROGRESSIVE STUDIES WITH SPECIAL	BIEHL, A.
TWENTY-FIVE EASY AND PROGRESSIVE STUDIES WITH SPECIAL	BIEHL, A.
TWENTY-FIVE EASY ETUDES, OP. 100	BURGMUELLER
TWENTY-FIVE EASY STUDIES, OP. 100	BURGMUELLER
TWENTY-FIVE EASY STUDIES, OP. 100	BURGMUELLER
TWENTY-FIVE EASY STUDIES, OP. 100	BURGMUELLER
TWENTY-FIVE EASY STUDIES WITHOUT OCTAVES, OP. 100	BERTINI
TWENTY-FIVE EASY STUDIES WITHOUT OCTAVES, OP.100	BERTINI
TWENTY-FIVE ELEMENTARY STUDIES, OP. 137	BERTINI
TWENTY-FIVE ELEMENTARY STUDIES, OP. 176	DUVERNOY, J.
TWENTY-FIVE ELEMENTARY STUDIES	DUVERNOY, J.
TWENTY-FIVE ETUDES, OP. 32--PRELIMINARY STUDIES TO THE	JENSEN, A.
TWENTY-FIVE ETUDES, OP. 32--PRELIMINARY STUDIES TO THE	JENSEN, A.
TWENTY-FIVE ETUDES	CHOPIN
TWENTY-FIVE FANTASIES FROM ''ARTE DE TANER	SANTA MARIA, T.
TWENTY-FIVE FIRST-GRADE PIANO PIECES--COMPANION PIECES	DILLER, A. *
TWENTY-FIVE KLEINE KLAVIERSTUCKE FUR KINDER	DEGEN
TWENTY-FIVE MELODIC STUDIES, OP. 24	CONCONE, G.
TWENTY-FIVE MELODIC STUDIES	CONCONE, G.
TWENTY-FIVE MELODIOUS ETUDES, OP. 100	CROISEZ, A.
TWENTY-FIVE MELODIOUS STUDIES, OP. 45--BK. 1, NOS. 1-9	HELLER, S.
TWENTY-FIVE MELODIOUS STUDIES, OP. 45	HELLER, S.
TWENTY-FIVE MELODIOUS STUDIES, OP. 45	HELLER, S.
TWENTY-FIVE MELODIOUS STUDIES, OP. 45	HELLER, S.
TWENTY-FIVE MELODIOUS STUDIES, OP. 45	HELLER, S.
TWENTY-FIVE PETITS ETUDES TRES FACILES, OP. 156	LEDUC, A.
TWENTY-FIVE POETIC ETUDES, OP. 96	POLDINI, E.
TWENTY-FIVE PRELUDES, OP. 31	ALKAN
TWENTY-FIVE PRELUDES	CHOPIN
TWENTY-FIVE PRELUDES	PERRACHIO
TWENTY-FIVE PRIMARY ETUDES, OP. 166	BERTINI
TWENTY-FIVE PROGRESSIVE PIECES	BURGMUELLER
TWENTY-FIVE SHORT AND MELODIOUS STUDIES, OP. 108	SCHYTTE
TWENTY-FIVE SOLFEGGI, BK. 1	DEL VALLE
TWENTY-FIVE SOLFEGGI, BK. 2	DEL VALLE
TWENTY-FIVE SONATAS -- NOS. 58, 104, 187, 263, 324,	SCARLATTI, D.
TWENTY-FIVE STUDIES, OP. 100	BURGMUELLER
TWENTY-FIVE STUDIES, OP. 100	BURGMUELLER
TWENTY-FIVE STUDIES, OP. 114	HUENTEN
TWENTY-FIVE STUDIES, OP. 32, BK. 1 -- 1-8 --	JENSEN, A.
TWENTY-FIVE STUDIES, OP. 32, BK. 2 -- 9-18 --	JENSEN, A.
TWENTY-FIVE STUDIES, OP. 32, BK. 3 -- 19-25 --	JENSEN, A.
TWENTY-FIVE STUDIES, OP. 47	HELLER, S.
TWENTY-FIVE STUDIES, OP. 47	HELLER, S.
TWENTY-FIVE STUDIES, OP. 78	STEIBELT
TWENTY-FIVE STUDIES FOR DEVELOPMENT OF RHYTHM AND	HELLER, S.
TWENTY-FIVE STUDIES FOR RHYTHM, OP. 47	HELLER, S.
TWENTY-FIVE STUDIES FOR RHYTHM AND EXPRESSION, OP.	HELLER, S.
TWENTY-FIVE STUDIES FOR RHYTHM AND EXPRESSION, OP. 47	HELLER, S.
TWENTY-FIVE STUDIES FOR RHYTHM AND EXPRESSION, OP. 47	HELLER, S.
TWENTY-FIVE STUDIES FOR RHYTHM AND EXPRESSION, OP. 47	HELLER, S
TWENTY-FIVE STUDIES FOR SMALL HANDS, OP. 100	BERTINI
TWENTY-FIVE STUDIES FOR THE 1ST GRADE, OP. 100	BERTINI
TWENTY-FIVE STUDIES FOR THE 2ND GRADE, OP. 29	BERTINI
TWENTY-FIVE STUDIES FOR THE 3RD GRADE, OP. 32	BERTINI
TWENTY-FIVE STUDIES FOR THE 4TH GRADE, OP. 134	BERTINI
TWENTY-FIVE STUDIES FROM OP. 46	HELLER, S.
TWENTY-FIVE STUDIES FROM OP. 46	HELLER, S.
TWENTY-FIVE STUDIES OF RHYTHM AND EXPRESSION, OP. 47	HELLER, S.
TWENTY-FOUR BRILLIANT PRELUDES IN ALL THE MAJOR AND	CONCONE, G.
TWENTY-FOUR BRILLIANT PRELUDES	CONCONE, G.
TWENTY-FOUR CARAT GOLD	BRADLEY, W.
TWENTY-FOUR CARAT GOLD	ENGEL, S.--ARR.
TWENTY-FOUR EASY AND PROGRESSIVE STUDIES	POZZOLI
TWENTY-FOUR EASY MELODIOUS FIVE-FINGER EXERCISES, OP.	CZERNY
TWENTY-FOUR EASY MELODIOUS STUDIES, OP. 50	GURLITT
TWENTY-FOUR EASY PIECES, OP. 81 VOL. 1	WILM, N. VON
TWENTY-FOUR EASY PIECES, OP. 81 VOL. 2	WILM, N. VON
TWENTY-FOUR EASY STUDIES IN MECHANISM	POZZOLI
TWENTY-FOUR EASY TECHNICAL STUDIES	KADOSA
TWENTY-FOUR ETUDES FOR PIANO, BK. 1	RAPHLING
TWENTY-FOUR ETUDES FOR PIANO, BK. 2	RAPHLING
TWENTY-FOUR ETUDES FOR PIANO, VOL. 1	RAPHLING
TWENTY-FOUR ETUDES FOR PIANO, VOL. 2	RAPHLING
TWENTY-FOUR FAVORITE CAROLS, MADE EASY TO PLAY AND	SUDDARDS
TWENTY-FOUR KLEINE ETUDEN IN WALZFORM	HASSLER, J.
TWENTY-FOUR LITTLE CANONS ON THE BLACK KEYS	KODALY, Z.
TWENTY-FOUR LITTLE PIECES, OP. 24	LONGO, A.
TWENTY-FOUR LITTLE PIECES, OP. 39	KABALEVSKY
TWENTY-FOUR LITTLE PIECES FOR CHILDREN OP. 39	KABALEVSKY
TWENTY-FOUR LITTLE PIECES	BACH, C.P.E.
TWENTY-FOUR LITTLE STUDIES ON ARPEGGIOS IN ALL THE	LONGO, A.
TWENTY-FOUR MEASURES OF KEYBOARD PLEASURES	STEINER
TWENTY-FOUR MELODIOUS AND PROGRESSIVE STUDIES, OP. 131	GURLITT
TWENTY-FOUR MELODIOUS PIECES, OP. 101	BERTINI
TWENTY-FOUR MELODIOUS STUDIES, OP. 125	HELLER, S.
TWENTY-FOUR MELODIOUS STUDIES OF MEDIUM DIFFICULTY,	GURLITT
TWENTY-FOUR MINIATURES IN PRELUDE FORM, OP. 34	THOMPSON, J.
TWENTY-FOUR MINIATURES IN PRELUDE FORM FOR STUDY --	THOMPSON, J.
TWENTY-FOUR NEGRO MELODIES	COLERIDGE-TAYLOR
TWENTY-FOUR OCTAVE-STUDIES, OP. 100	GURLITT
TWENTY-FOUR OCTAVE STUDIES OF MEDIUM DIFFICULTY, OP.	VOGT, J.
TWENTY-FOUR PEZZI DAL LIBRO DI ANNA MAGDALENA	BACH, J.S.
TWENTY-FOUR PIECES, BK. 1	SCARLATTI, D.
TWENTY-FOUR PIECES, BK. 2	SCARLATTI, D.
TWENTY-FOUR PIECES FOR CHILDREN, OP. 39	KABALEVSKY
TWENTY-FOUR PIECES FOR CHILDREN	KABALEVSKY

TWENTY-FOUR PIECES IN 2 VOLUMES - VOL. 1	CORELLI
TWENTY-FOUR PIECES IN 2 VOLUMES - VOL. 2	CORELLI
TWENTY-FOUR PIECES	BACH, C.P.E.
TWENTY-FOUR PRELUDES, BK. 1, NOS. 1-12	GAL, H.
TWENTY-FOUR PRELUDES, BK. 2, NOS. 13-24	GAL, H.
TWENTY-FOUR PRELUDES, COMPLETE	RACHMANINOFF, S.
TWENTY-FOUR PRELUDES, OP. 11	SCRIABINE, A.
TWENTY-FOUR PRELUDES, OP. 11	SCRIABINE, A.
TWENTY-FOUR PRELUDES, OP. 28	CHOPIN
TWENTY-FOUR PRELUDES, OP. 34. VOL. 1	SHOSTAKOVITCH
TWENTY-FOUR PRELUDES, OP. 34. VOL. 2	SHOSTAKOVITCH
TWENTY-FOUR PRELUDES, OP. 34	BACARISSE
TWENTY-FOUR PRELUDES, OP. 34	SHOSTAKOVITCH
TWENTY-FOUR PRELUDES, OP. 34	SHOSTAKOVITCH
TWENTY-FOUR PRELUDES, OP. 37 BK. 1	BUSONI
TWENTY-FOUR PRELUDES, OP. 37 BK. 2	BUSONI
TWENTY-FOUR PRELUDES, OP. 38	KABALEVSKY
TWENTY-FOUR PRELUDES, OP. 38	KABALEVSKY
TWENTY-FOUR PRELUDES, OP. 38	KABALEVSKY
TWENTY-FOUR PRELUDES, OP. 38	KABALEVSKY
TWENTY-FOUR PRELUDES, OP. 81	HELLER, S.
TWENTY-FOUR PRELUDES, OP. 81	HELLER, S.
TWENTY-FOUR PRELUDES, OP.11	SCRIABINE, A.
TWENTY-FOUR PRELUDES -- 1924 -- VOL. 1	CASADESUS, R.
TWENTY-FOUR PRELUDES -- 1924 -- VOL. 2	CASADESUS, R.
TWENTY-FOUR PRELUDES -- 1924 -- VOL. 3	CASADESUS, R.
TWENTY-FOUR PRELUDES -- 1924 -- VOL. 4	CASADESUS, R.
TWENTY-FOUR PRELUDES AND FUGUES, OP. 87. VOL. 1	SHOSTAKOVITCH
TWENTY-FOUR PRELUDES AND FUGUES, OP. 87. VOL. 2	SHOSTAKOVITCH
TWENTY-FOUR PRELUDES AND FUGUES, OP.87--BK. 1	SHOSTAKOVITCH
TWENTY-FOUR PRELUDES AND FUGUES, OP.87--BK. 2	SHOSTAKOVITCH
TWENTY-FOUR PRELUDES AND FUGUES, OP.87--BK. 3	SHOSTAKOVITCH
TWENTY-FOUR PRELUDES AND FUGUES, OP.87--BK. 4	SHOSTAKOVITCH
TWENTY-FOUR PRELUDES AND FUGURES, OP. 87	SHOSTAKOVITCH
TWENTY-FOUR PRELUDES IN ALL KEYS - BK. 1	LUTECE
TWENTY-FOUR PRELUDES IN ALL KEYS - BK. 2	LUTECE
TWENTY-FOUR PRELUDES IN ALL THE MAJOR AND MINOR KEYS	DEMIERRE
TWENTY-FOUR PRELUDES IN ALL THE MAJOR AND MINOR KEYS	DEMIERRE
TWENTY-FOUR PRELUDES IN ALL THE MAJOR AND MINOR KEYS	DEMIERRE
TWENTY-FOUR PRELUDES	MONTANI
TWENTY-FOUR PRELUDES	SHOSTAKOVITCH
TWENTY-FOUR PROGRESSIVE PIANO DUETS YOU LIKE TO PLAY	
TWENTY-FOUR SHORT PRELUDES AND FUGUES --URTEXT--,	BACH, J.S.
TWENTY-FOUR SONATAS, VOL. 1	CIMAROSA
TWENTY-FOUR SONATAS, VOL. 2	CIMAROSA
TWENTY-FOUR SONATAS, VOL. 3	CIMAROSA
TWENTY-FOUR SONATAS	SCARLATTI, D.
TWENTY-FOUR SONG TRANSCRIPTIONS, BK. 1	LISZT *
TWENTY-FOUR SONG TRANSCRIPTIONS, BK. 1	SCHUBERT *
TWENTY-FOUR SONG TRANSCRIPTIONS, BK. 2	LISZT *
TWENTY-FOUR SONG TRANSCRIPTIONS, BK. 2	SCHUBERT *
TWENTY-FOUR STUDIES--FINISHING-LESSONS FOR ADVANCED	MOSCHELES, I.
TWENTY-FOUR STUDIES--FINISHING-LESSONS FOR ADVANCED	MOSCHELES, I.
TWENTY-FOUR STUDIES, OP. 20	KESSLER
TWENTY-FOUR STUDIES, OP. 29 --PREPARATORY SONATINAS TO	BERTINI
TWENTY-FOUR STUDIES, OP. 29 --PREPARATORY SONATINAS TO	BERTINI
TWENTY-FOUR STUDIES, OP. 29 --PREPARATORY TO THE	BERTINI
TWENTY-FOUR STUDIES, OP. 32 --SEQUEL TO OP. 29--	BERTINI
TWENTY-FOUR STUDIES FOR EXPRESSION AND RHYTHM, OP. 125	HELLER, S.
TWENTY-FOUR STUDIES FOR PERFECTION, OP. 70 BK. 1 --	MOSCHELES, I.
TWENTY-FOUR STUDIES FOR PERFECTION, OP. 70	MOSCHELES, I.
TWENTY-FOUR STUDIES FOR RHYTHM AND EXPRESSION, OP. 125	HELLER, S.
TWENTY-FOUR STUDIES FOR RHYTHM AND EXPRESSION, OP. 125	HELLER, S.
TWENTY-FOUR STUDIES FOR THE LEFT HAND, OP. 718	CZERNY
TWENTY-FOUR STUDIES FOR THE LEFT HAND, OP. 718	CZERNY
TWENTY-FOUR STUDIES ON SCALES AND ARPEGGIOS, OP. 85	GURLITT
TWENTY-FOUR SYMPHONIES, IN 4 VOLS* VOL. 1	HAYDN
TWENTY-FOUR SYMPHONIES, IN 4 VOLS* VOL. 2	HAYDN
TWENTY-FOUR SYMPHONIES, IN 4 VOLS* VOL. 3	HAYDN
TWENTY-FOUR SYMPHONIES, IN 4 VOLS* VOL. 4	HAYDN
TWENTY-FOUR WALTZ ETUDES	HAESSLER
TWENTY-NINE VERY EASY FOLK SONGS	SMITH--ED
TWENTY-ONE BIGGEST HITS OF TODAY	
TWENTY-ONE PIECES	CHOPIN
TWENTY-SEVEN SELECTED SONATAS	SCARLATTI, D.
TWENTY-SIX CLASSIC DANCES	RAPHLING
TWENTY-SIX SONATAS, BK. 1	SCARLATTI, D.
TWENTY-SIX SONATAS, BK. 2	SCARLATTI, D.
TWENTY-THREE DANCES	BEETHOVEN
TWENTY-THREE EASY PIECES	BACH, J.S.
TWENTY-THREE PIECES FOR CHILDREN	SCHLOSS, J.
TWENTY-THREE STUDIES FOR CHILDREN	SCHLOSS, J.
TWENTY-THREE STUDIES FROM 'GRADUS AD PARNASSUM'	CLEMENTI
TWENTY-THREE STUDIES FROM 'GRADUS AD PARNASSUM'	CLEMENTI
TWENTY-THREE VOLKSTANZE AUS MAHREN	JANACEK
TWENTY-TWO PIECES FOR CHILDREN, OP. 27	KABALEVSKY
TWENTY-TWO PIECES	SCARLATTI, D.
TWENTY-TWO ROMANTIC DANCES	RAPHLING
TWENTY-TWO VARIATIONS ON A WELL-KNOWN THEME	ARNELL
TWENTY CHILDREN-STUDIES WITHOUT OCTAVES, OP. 79	BERENS, H.
TWENTY EASY DANCES	WEBER, VON
TWENTY EASY PIECES BASED ON POPULAR POLISH SONGS	TANSMAN, A.
TWENTY EASY PIECES FROM NOTEBOOK FOR ANNA MAGDALENA	BACH, J.S.
TWENTY EASY RECREATIONS	
TWENTY EASY STUDIES, OP. 159	KOEHLER
TWENTY FAVORITES FOR TWO PIANISTS	SMALL, A.
TWENTY FINGERS --LITTLE MOSAIC--	HARTECK
TWENTY FINGERS - BOOK 1	WARD
TWENTY FINGERS - BOOK 2	WARD
TWENTY FINGERS - DUETS	BEEBE
TWENTY FOUR PRELUDES	SHOSTAKOVITCH
TWENTY LESSON COURSE IN EVANGELISTIC PIANO PLAYING	SHINN, D.
TWENTY LITTLE FUGUES FOR ORGAN OR PIANO	TELEMANN, G.P.
TWENTY LITTLE FUGUES	TELEMANN, G.P.
TWENTY LITTLE INSTRUCTIVE PIECES	DIABELLI *
TWENTY LITTLE PIECES -- SUPPLEMENT NO. 1 TO 'LE PETIT	DEMARQUEZ
TWENTY LITTLE PIECES	MARTUCCI
TWENTY MELODIOUS STUDIES, OP. 52	LOESCHHORN, A.
TWENTY ONE EVOLUTIONS, OP. 4	CAZDEN, N.
TWENTY PIANO COMPOSITIONS	MOZART, W. A.
TWENTY PIANO DUETS -- FOR THE INTERMEDIATE GRADES	SCHER, W.--ED
TWENTY PIANO DUET TRANSCRIPTIONS OF FAVORITE HYMNS	KOHLMANN, C.
TWENTY PIANO STUDIES FOR BEGINNERS, BK. 1	KASEMETS, U.
TWENTY PIANO TRANSCRIPTIONS	LISZT
TWENTY PIECES COMPOSED WHEN 4 TO 6 YEARS OLD	MOZART, W. A.
TWENTY PIECES FROM BACH'S BOOK FOR HIS SON FRIEDMANN	BACH, J.S.
TWENTY PRELUDES IN THE FORM OF CANONS	DELACHI
TWENTY REGARDS SUR L'ENFANT JESUS	MESSIAEN, O.
TWENTY RHAPSODIES -- 19 HUNGARIAN AND RHAPSODIE	LISZT
TWENTY RHAPSODIES -- 19 HUNGARIAN AND RHAPSODIE	LISZT
TWENTY SCALE STUDIES	POZZOLI
TWENTY SELECTED SONATAS	SCARLATTI, D.
TWENTY SELECTED STUDIES FROM OP. 100	BURGMUELLER
TWENTY SKETCHES, OP. 22	PROKOFIEFF
TWENTY SONATAS, BK. 1 -- 1-10 --	HAYDN
TWENTY SONATAS, BK. 1	HAYDN
TWENTY SONATAS, BK. 2 -- 11-20 --	HAYDN
TWENTY SONATAS, BK. 2	HAYDN
TWENTY SONATAS	MOZART, W. A.
TWENTY STUDIES IN CONTINUOUS SCALE AND CHORD PASSAGES,	KOEHLER
TWENTY STUDIES IN VELOCITY	BARROZO
TWENTY STUDIES ON THE SINGING TOUCH, OP. 30	CONCONE, G.
TWENTY THOUSAND LEAGUES UNDER THE SEA	SCHAUM, J.--ED.
TWICE FIVE PIECES -- EASY	VILLA-LOBOS, H.
TWICE TOLD TALE	PELS, W.
TWICE TOLD THEMES, BK. 1 --COMPILATION--	
TWICE TOLD THEMES, BK. 2 --COMPILATION--	
TWIDDLE DEE DEE	SCHER, W.
TWILIGHT BELL	CHAGY
TWILIGHT DREAMS	PROEHL, H.
TWILIGHT HOUR	SAVINO
TWILIGHT INTERLUDE	STEINER
TWILIGHT IN SLEEPY HOLLOW	LANE, J.
TWILIGHT LULLABY	HAINES, E.
TWILIGHT MOOD	FULEIHAN, A.
TWILIGHT NOCTURNE	YOUNG, V.
TWILIGHT REVERIE	AULBACH, F.
TWILIGHT REVERIE	GUY
TWILIGHT SERENADE	ANTONINI
TWILIGHT SERENADE	ANTONINI
TWILIGHT SERENADE	MASKELL, C. H.
TWILIGHT SERENADE	WHITFORD
TWILIGHT WALTZ	CHAGY
TWILIGHT WALTZ	STEVENS
TWILIGHT	BRUSSELS, I.
TWILIGHT	CATON, F.
TWILIGHT	GREIM
TWINKLE, TWINKLE, LITTLE STAR -- FOR ONE PIANO, SIX	WILLIAMS
TWINKLE, TWINKLE, LITTLE STAR -- ONE PIANO, SIX HANDS	GEORGE
TWINKLETOES	ECKSTEIN
TWINKLE TOES, DANCE	HOPKINS, H.
TWINKLE TOES	MILLER
TWINKLING STAR	KAHL
TWIN TUNES	PELZ, W.
TWIRLING BATONS	COBB
TWIRLING BATON	HOUSE, A.
TWISTING THE TWIST	ESTELLA
TWITTERING OF THE BIRDS	BILLEMA
TWO-PART AURAL PRACTICE BOOK	BRADLEY
TWO-PART FANCIES	CAPES, D.
TWO-PART INVENTIONS	BACH, J.S.
TWO-PART INVENTIONS	BACH, J.S.
TWO-PART INVENTIONS	BACH, J.S.
TWO-PART INVENTIONS	BACH, J.S.
TWO-PART INVENTIONS	BACH, J.S.
TWO-PART INVENTIONS	BACH, J.S.
TWO-PART INVENTIONS	BACH, J.S.
TWO-PART INVENTIONS	BACH, J.S.
TWO-PART INVENTIONS	BACH, J.S.
TWO-PART INVENTION IN F	BACH, J.S.
TWO-PART INVENTION NO. 04 IN D MINOR	BACH, J.S.
TWO-PART INVENTION NO. 08 IN F MAJOR	BACH, J.S.
TWO-PART INVENTION NO. 13 IN A MINOR	BACH, J.S.
TWO-PART INVENTION NO. 14 IN B FLAT MAJOR	BACH, J.S.
TWO-PIANO ALBUM FOR THE FIRST YEAR	THOMPSON, J.
TWO'S COMPANY -- A FIRST 2-PIANO BOOK	ANSON, G.
TWO'S COMPANY	HELYER, M.
TWO 'BURLINGHAM' BROTHERS, THE	BLOCH, E.
TWO ACQUEFORTI TUNISINE - LA DANZARTRICE ARABA	SANTOLIQUIDO
TWO ACQUEFORTI TUNISINE - 1. LA NOTTE SAHARIANA	SANTOLIQUIDO
TWO ALBUM LEAVES, OP. 5 NO. 7 AND OP. 5 NO. 22--CURWEN	SMETANA
TWO ALBUM LEAVES	GRAY, D.
TWO ALPINE SINGERS	WORTZMAN, N.
TWO AMERICAN CHRISTMAS CAROLS	CAROL--ED.
TWO AMERICAN SKETCHES	GRISELLE, T.
TWO AND A PIANO, BK. 1	LAST, J.
TWO AND A PIANO, BK. 2	LAST, J.
TWO AND A PIANO, BK. 3	LAST, J.
TWO AND A PIANO, BK. 4	LAST, J.
TWO AND A PIANO, BK. 5	LAST, J.
TWO AND THREE PART INVENTIONS -- FACSIMILE	BACH, J.S.
TWO AND THREE PART INVENTIONS	BACH, J.S.
TWO AND THREE PART INVENTIONS	BACH, J.S.
TWO AND THREE PART INVENTIONS	BACH, J.S.
TWO AND THREE PART INVENTIONS	BACH, J.S.
TWO AND THREE PART INVENTIONS	BACH, J.S.
TWO AND THREE PART INVENTIONS	BACH, J.S.
TWO AND TWENTY CHRISTMAS CAROLS	COBB
TWO ANGELS, THE	BLUMENTHAL
TWO ARABESQUES	DEBUSSY
TWO ARABESQUES	DEBUSSY
TWO ARABESQUES	DEBUSSY
TWO ARIOSI WITH TWELVE VARIATIONS	MUTHEL, J. G.
TWO AT ONE PIANO, BK. 2	GEORGE
TWO AT ONE PIANO	GEORGE
TWO AT ONE PIANO	GEORGE
TWO BAGATELLES	AGAY, D.
TWO BAGATELLES	LAST, J.
TWO BITS O'SCOTCH	NAGY, M.
TWO BLUES	RAPHLING
TWO BOOKS OF STUDY FOR PIANISTS. COMPLETE	CARDEW
TWO BOP IMPRESSIONS	LITER, M.
TWO BOURREES -- SET	PURCELL, H.
TWO BUTTERFLIES	ADLER, M.
TWO BY TWO	RODGERS *
TWO CAPRICES POETIQUES - IL LAMENTO, LA LEGGIEREZZA	LISZT
TWO CAPRICES	BRAHMS *
TWO CHARACTERISTIC PIECES	KHATCHATURIAN
TWO CHORALES	ROBERTS
TWO CHRISTMAS SONGS -- JINGLE BELLS, JOLLY OLD ST.	RICHTER
TWO CONCERT ETUDES AND TWO LEGENDS	LISZT
TWO CONCERT ETUDES	LISZT
TWO CONCERT TRANSCRIPTIONS	TAUSIG
TWO COUNTRYSIDE SKETCHES	ROZIN
TWO COUNTRYSIDE SKETCHES	ROZIN
TWO COUNTRY SKETCHES--FROLIC	AGAY, D.
TWO COUNTRY SKETCHES--SHEPHERD'S NIGHT SONG	AGAY, D.
TWO COUNTRY SKETCHES	WILKINSON, P.
TWO CUCKOO CLOCKS, THE	SCARMOLIN
TWO DANCES -- PALUCCA	WAGNER
TWO DANCES	BARTLEY
TWO DANCES	KLEPPER
TWO DANCES	MARTINU, B.
TWO DANSES - DANSE ALLEGRE	DE CASTERA
TWO DANSES - PETITE VALSE	DE CASTERA
TWO DANSES CARACTERISTIQUES .. DANZA GITANA, DANZA	GRANADOS
TWO DANZAS CATALANAS	PAHISSA
TWO DESERT SKETCHES -- PAPAGO FLUTE AND DESERT	GRAHAM, R.
TWO DOZEN DANCES	SCHUBERT
TWO EASY LITTLE PIECES	BIZZELLI

TWO EASY SONATAS, OP. 49 NO. 1 IN G MINOR AND NO. 2 IN	BEETHOVEN
TWO EASY TWIN PIECES WHICH CAN BE PLAYED SEPARATELY AS	WOZENCRAFT, M.
TWO ECOSSAISES	BEETHOVEN
TWO ELEGIAC MELODIES, OP. 34	GRIEG
TWO ELEGIES, OP. 59	MEDTNER, N.
TWO ELEGIES, OP. 8B	BARTOK
TWO ELEGIES, OP. 8B	BARTOK
TWO ESSAYS FOR PIANO	RAPHLING
TWO ESSAYS FOR PIANO	RAPHLING
TWO ETUDES, OP. 10	LAZARE-LEVY
TWO ETUDES -- C MAJOR AND A MINOR --	GALLON, J.
TWO ETUDES IN G FLAT	CHOPIN
TWO ETUDES	ANDRIESSEN, J.
TWO ETUDES	SLONIMSKY
TWO FAMILIAR HYMNS -- 1. THE DOXOLOGY, 2. NOW THANK WE	WEYBRIGHT
TWO FAMILIAR THEMES	WEYBRIGHT
TWO FANTASIES -- GMUNDEN, 1903 --	BARTOK
TWO FEUILLETS D'ALBUM	DALCROZE
TWO FILM STUDIES	CASTELNUOVO-TEDE
TWO FLOWERS --ZWEI BLUMEN OP. 364--	KOELLING
TWO FOLK SONGS -- DANCING AND BAGPIPES PLAYING	WEYBRIGHT
TWO FOLK TUNES FOR 8 HANDS AT 2 PIANOS	BARRETT--ED.
TWO FORGOTTEN PIECES	CHOPIN
TWO FOR THE SHOW	KAHN, M.
TWO FRENCH SONGS AND I SAW THREE SHIPS	FERGUSON, H.
TWO FRENCH TUNES. PIANO, SIX HANDS	BUTCHER--ARR.
TWO FROGS	ROBBINS
TWO GAVOTTES BRETONNES - NO. 1	BOURGAULT-DUCOUD
TWO GAVOTTES BRETONNES - NO. 2	BOURGAULT-DUCOUD
TWO GHAZALS	HOVHANESS, A.
TWO GRAND WALTZES, OP. 27, 129	KALLIWODA
TWO GUITARS	GROOMS--ED
TWO GUITARS	JAMES, M.--ED
TWO GUITARS	MEDINA--ED.
TWO GUITARS	MITTLER--ED
TWO GUITARS	POLLA, W.--ED
TWO GUITARS	THOMPSON, J.
TWO HAPPY FARMERS	SCHUMANN, R.
TWO HUNDRED JIGS, REELS AND COUNTRY DANCES	
TWO HUNDRED SHORT TWO-PART CANONS, OP. 14	KUNZ
TWO HUNDRED SHORT 2-PART CANONS FOR THE BEGINNER, OP.	KUNZ
TWO IMAGES, OP. 10	BARTOK
TWO IMPRESSIONS FOR TWO PIANOS	KOCH, F.
TWO IMPROMPTUS, OP. 12	SCRIABINE, A.
TWO IMPROMPTUS, OP. 14	SCRIABINE, A.
TWO IMPROMPTUS, OP. 142 NOS. 2 AND 3	SCHUBERT
TWO IMPROMPTUS, OP. 90 NOS. 2 AND 4	SCHUBERT
TWO IMPROMPTUS	DELA
TWO IMPROMPTUS	GRANADOS
TWO IMPROVISATIONS -- GRAVEN IMAGES NO. 6	WEISGALL, H.
TWO IMPROVISATIONS ON HUNGARIAN FOLK SONGS	AGAY, D.
TWO INTERMEZZI, OP. 28	ZIPP
TWO INVENTIONS	LUENING, O.
TWO ISTANTANEE	CHAILLY, L.
TWO JAMAICAN STREET SONGS	BENJAMIN
TWO JAPANESE FOLK SONGS	OLSEN, A. L.
TWO JAPANESE MELODIES	SZANTO
TWO LARKS, THE--IMPROMPTU, OP. 2 NO. 1	LESCHETIZKY
TWO LARKS	LESCHETIZKY
TWO LEGENDES - 1. ST. FRANCOIS D'ASSISE - LA	LISZT
TWO LEGENDES - 2. ST. FRANCOIS DE PAULE MARCHANT SUR	LISZT
TWO LEGENDS	LISZT
TWO LITTLE FROGGIES, OP. 7 NO. 10	CRAMM, H.
TWO LITTLE PIECES	DUBSKY
TWO LITTLE PIECES	RICHARTZ
TWO LITTLE PLAYERS - FORTY-EIGHT SELECTIONS	
TWO LITTLE SHOES -- FROM THE CHARM BRACELET	WAXMAN
TWO LITTLE WOODPECKERS	SCHER, W.
TWO LOVES - THEME	KAPER, B.
TWO LUNAIRES, OP. 33 - 1. COLLOQUE AU CLAIR DE LUNE	PICK-MANGIAGALLI
TWO LUNAIRES, OP. 33 - 2. LA DANSE D'OLAF	PICK-MANGIAGALLI
TWO MELODIES, OP. 53	GRIEG
TWO MENUETS -- G MAJOR NO. 1, G MINOR NO. 2	BACH, J.S.
TWO MENUETS	HAYDN
TWO MINIATURES - DUETTINO, VALSE MELANCOLIQUE	LAZZARI
TWO MINIATURES	FERNANDEZ, O.
TWO MINUETS -- FROM ''MUSIC FOR THE ROYAL FIREWORKS''	HANDEL
TWO MINUETS	BACH, J.S.
TWO MINUETS	BACH, J.S.
TWO MINUS ONE - THE 'DO-IT-YOURSELF' COMPOSING BOOK	KOCH, F.
TWO MINUS ONE - THE 'DO-IT-YOURSELF' COMPOSING BOOK	KOCH, F.
TWO MIRROR FUGUES --CONTRAPUNCTUS 13--. ART OF THE	BACH, J.S.
TWO MODERN BAROQUE DANCES	SIMMONS, H.
TWO MOODS	GARROW
TWO MOUVEMENTS	ROBBONE
TWO NOCTURNES, OP. 15	MOSSOLOW, A.
TWO NOCTURNES, OP. 84	HARTMANN
TWO OF A KIND	DEE, M.
TWO OF US	MAIER, G. *
TWO OLD DANCES	LUBIN, E.
TWO OLD ITALIAN AIRS	PHILIPP, I.
TWO OPERA FANTASIES* PARAPHRASES ON RIGOLETTO AND	VERDI *
TWO PAIRS OF SHOES	DVORKIN, J.
TWO PARROTS, THE	KIRNBERGER, J.
TWO PARTITAS	GRUENEWALD
TWO PART 'INTENTION'	NEVIN
TWO PART INVENTIONS--NOS. 01, 03, 04--	BACH, J.S.
TWO PART INVENTIONS	BACH, J.S.
TWO PART INVENTION NO. 11	BACH, J.S.
TWO PART INVENTION NO. 12	BACH, J.S.
TWO PART INVENTION NO. 8	BACH, J.S.
TWO PIANISTS AT ONE PIANO, BK. 1	STEINER
TWO PIANISTS AT ONE PIANO, BK. 2	STEINER
TWO PIANOS ARE FUN, BK. 1	HIRSCHBERG,
TWO PIANO PIECES. KINDERSCHERZ, INTERMEZZO	MOUSSORGSKY
TWO PIANO PIECES	ASCHER, L.
TWO PIANO PIECES	KHATCHATURIAN
TWO PIANO PIECES	SCOTT, C.
TWO PIANO PORTRAITS	TAYLOR, E.
TWO PIANO PORTRAITS	TAYLOR, E.
TWO PIECCES	GWILT, D.
TWO PIECES, OP. 22	GLAZOUNOW, A.
TWO PIECES, OP. 3	PROKOFIEFF
TWO PIECES, OP. 44	BLANCHET
TWO PIECES, OP. 57	SCRIABINE, A.
TWO PIECES -- WALSE CAPRICE, DANSE	KHATCHATURIAN
TWO PIECES - ARLEQUIN	ALFANO
TWO PIECES - VALSE COQUETTE	ALFANO
TWO PIECES - 1. RISONANZE NOSTALGICHE	CILEA
TWO PIECES - 2. FESTA SILANA	CILEA
TWO PIECES A LA MANIERE DE	PILLOIS
TWO PIECES CARACTERISTIQUES - DANSE ORGIAQUE	BERVILLY
TWO PIECES CARACTERISTIQUES - FESTA NAPOLITANA	WESLY
TWO PIECES CARACTERISTIQUES - HUERE TRISTE	BERVILLY
TWO PIECES CARACTERISYIQUES - TORMENTO DE AMORE	WESLY
TWO PIECES FOR CLAVECIN	MARTINU, B.
TWO PIECES FOR PIANO DUET	MCGRAW
TWO PIECES FOR PIANO	HARTLEY, W.
TWO PIECES FOR PIANO	HOLST
TWO PIECES FOR PIANO	LEFEVRE, A.
TWO PIECES FOR SMALL ORCHESTRA	DELIUS, F.
TWO PIECES FOR SOLO PIANO -- THE TIME FOR FUN AND WHEN	WEYBRIGHT
TWO PIECES HUMORISTIQUE	LEVY, E.
TWO PIECES IN ANTIQUE STYLE	MIHALY, A.
TWO PIECES IN ANTIQUE STYLE	MIHALY, A.
TWO PIECES	ATKINS
TWO PIECES	DUKELSKY
TWO PIECES	KHATCHATURIAN
TWO PIECES	KONSTANTINOFF
TWO PIECES	TOTZAUER, H.
TWO PLAYERS AT THE PIANO - BOOK 1	FROST
TWO PLAYERS AT THE PIANO - PREPARATORY BOOK	FROST
TWO PLUS TWO - TWELVE LITTLE PIECES	RAPHLING
TWO PLUS TWO - TWELVE LITTLE PIECES	RAPHLING
TWO POEMES	GAGNEUR
TWO POEMS, OP. 32	SCRIABINE, A.
TWO POEMS, OP. 32	SCRIABINE, A.
TWO POEMS, OP. 71	SCRIABINE, A.
TWO POLONAISES	LISZT
TWO POLYTONAL STUDIES - NO. 1	BLANC DE
TWO POLYTONAL STUDIES - NO. 2	BLANC DE
TWO PRELUDES, OP. 28 NOS. 20 AND 21	CHOPIN
TWO PRELUDES, OP. 34 NOS. 14 AND 34	SHOSTAKOVITCH
TWO PRELUDES, OP. 67	SCRIABINE, A.
TWO PRELUDES - OP. 28 NOS. 7 AND 20	CHOPIN
TWO PRELUDES - OP. 28 NOS. 7 AND 20	CHOPIN
TWO PRELUDES AND FUGUES, OP. 87	SHOSTAKOVITCH
TWO PRELUDES FOR PIANO	BRUSSELS, I.
TWO PRELUDES IN ALL MAJOR KEYS, OP. 39	BEETHOVEN
TWO PRELUDES IN IMPRESSIONISTIC MOOD	ORGAD, B. Z.
TWO PRELUDES	ALLENDE
TWO PRELUDES	BOUTNIKOFF
TWO PRELUDES	MONFRED
TWO PRELUDES	PONIRIDY
TWO PRELUDES	SOENSTEVOLD
TWO QUIET SONGS	OSBORNE, W.
TWO RHAPSODIES, OP. 79	BRAHMS
TWO RHAPSODIES, OP. 79	BRAHMS
TWO RHAPSODIES, OP. 79	BRAHMS
TWO RHAPSODIES, OP. 79	BRAHMS
TWO RHAPSODIES, OP. 79	BRAHMS
TWO RHAPSODIES, OP. 79	BRAHMS
TWO RHAPSODIES, OP. 79	BRAHMS
TWO RICERCARE ON THE NAME "BACH"	CASELLA, A.
TWO ROUMANIAN DANCES, OP. 8A	BARTOK
TWO ROUMANIAN DANCES, OP. 8A	BARTOK
TWO SARABANDES, OP. POSTH.	BRAHMS
TWO SARABANDES AND GIGUES	BRAHMS
TWO SCHERZOS, OP. POSTH.	SCHUBERT
TWO SHEPHERDS	LAWLOR, G.
TWO SHORT ETUDES -- F MAJOR AND G MAJOR --	GALLON, J.
TWO SHORT PIECES	KAY, U.
TWO SHORT PIECES	LE GUILLARD
TWO SHORT SUITES FOR YOUNG PIANISTS	RICHTER
TWO SIMPLE PIANO DUETS	ARNELL
TWO SONATAS, OP. 11, 22	SCHUMANN, R.
TWO SONATAS, OP. 38 AND 73	DIABELLI
TWO SONATAS AND LITTLE ROMANCE	ALLISON, I.
TWO SONATAS IN B FLAT	CLEMENTI
TWO SONATAS	CLEMENTI
TWO SONATAS	HASSE
TWO SONATAS	WAGNER
TWO SONATINAS, OP. 14	BLACHER
TWO SONATINAS, OP. 152	NIEMANN
TWO SONATINAS, OP. 40 --AUTUMN - WINTER--	ROWLEY
TWO SONATINAS, OP. 40 --SPRING - SUMMER--	ROWLEY
TWO SONATINAS, OP. 49	JOHNSON, L.
TWO SONATINAS IN G AND F	BEETHOVEN
TWO SONATINAS	DEHNERT
TWO SONATINAS	EINEM, G.
TWO SONATINAS	LAZARE-LEVY
TWO SONATINAS	REITER, A.
TWO SONATINAS	SCHROEDER, H.
TWO SONGS FOR CHRISTMAS --SILENT NIGHT AND ADESTE	
TWO SPANISH DANCES	ALBENIZ, I.
TWO SPANISH DANCES	MEDIA VILLA
TWO STEPHEN FOSTER SONGS -- NELLY BLY AND BEAUTIFUL	WEYBRIGHT--ED.
TWO STRAUSS WALTZES	WEYBRIGHT
TWO STUDIES, OP. 29	WELLESZ, E.
TWO STUDIES --PERPETUUM MOBILE-- IN D.	BRAHMS *
TWO STUDIES --PERPETUUM MOBILE--	WEBER, VON *
TWO STUDIES FOR PIANO	LUTOSLAWSKI
TWO STUDIES FOR REPEATED NOTES	CINTOLESI
TWO STUDIES	CRAXTON, H.
TWO STUDI DA CONCERTO	OREFICE, G.
TWO SUITES, OP. 26	KRENEK, E.
TWO SYMPHONIES, NO. 3 AND NO. 4	MENDELSSOHN
TWO TWO-PART INVENTIONS	JAQUE, R.
TWO TWO-PART SONATAS K046--CURWEN EDITION	MOZART, W. A.
TWO UKRANIAN FOLK SONGS	LEONTOVICH
TWO VALSES	TAILLEFERRE, G.
TWO VERY EASY SONATAS	HAYDN
TWO VERY FIRST PIECES -- CHURCH BELLS AND LITTLE BROWN	KETTERER, E.
TWO WALTZES, OP. 6	DOBROWEN, I.
TWO WALTZES IN C	GERSHWIN
TWO WALTZES	BRAHMS
TWO WALTZ TRANSCRIPTIONS	STRAUSS, J.
TWO WINTER PIECES	ROGERS, E.
TWO WOODEN PUPPETS ON A STRING	SCHER, W.
TWO 18TH CENTURY DANCES	PENNY, M.--ED.
TYPES - VIEUX BEAU, BOURGEOISE DE QUALITE, BUSINESSMAN	FERROUD, P. O.
TYPEWRITER, THE	ANDERSON, L.
TYROLESE AND HIS CHILD	LICHNER, H.
TYROLESE WALTZ	VOLZ, H.
TZIGANE, LA, MAZURKA	GANNE
TZIGANE	WILSON
U.S.A. VOL. 1	
U. S. AIR FORCE	CRAWFORD
U. S. AIR FORCE	CRAWFORD
U. S. MARSHALL	TOWNSEND
UBUNGEN UND ETUDEN	FIBICH, Z.
UCCELLI, GLI -- THE BIRDS --	RESPIGHI
UGLY DUCKLING, THE	SIFLER, P.
UMA, DUAS ANGOLINHAS	VILLA-LOBOS, H.
UMBRELLAS	MIDDLEBROOK
UMBRELLA IN THE WIND	TUTTLE, T. K.
UMBRELLA TIME	BURNAM
UMBRELLA IN THE WIND	TUTTLE, T. K.
UNCHAINED MELODY	SINGER
UNCLE NED	FOSTER
UNCLE REMUS--OP. 51, OP. 7--	MACDOWELL
UNCLE ZEB WITH HIS FIDDLE	ANTHONY, B. R.
UNDECIDED	ROBIN *
UNDECIDED	ROBIN *

Title	Composer
UNDER MY LOVED ONE'S WINDOW	LANGE, G.
UNDER MY WINDOW	STAIRS, L.
UNDER PARIS SKIES	BRIMHALL,
UNDER PARIS SKIES	GIRAUD
UNDER THE BIG TOP SERIES -BALLOONS FOR SALE	BOGIN
UNDER THE BIG TOP SERIES -BIG TOP PARADE	BOGIN
UNDER THE BIG TOP SERIES -MARCH OF THE ELEPHANTS	BOGIN
UNDER THE BIG TOP SERIES -PONY WALTZ	BOGIN
UNDER THE BIG TOP SERIES -PUPS ON A SEESAW	BOGIN
UNDER THE BIG TOP SERIES -SAD CLOWN, THE.	BOGIN
UNDER THE BIG TOP	STECHER *
UNDER THE CATHEDRAL TOWER	HOLT, EILSEL
UNDER THE CRESCENT MOON	HARPER, M.
UNDER THE DOUBLE EAGLE, OP. 159	WAGNER, J.
UNDER THE DOUBLE EAGLE --MARCH--	WAGNER, J.
UNDER THE DOUBLE EAGLE -- MARCH	WAGNER, J.
UNDER THE DOUBLE EAGLE MARCH	WAGNER, J.
UNDER THE DOUBLE EAGLE	WAGNER, J.
UNDER THE DOUBLE EAGLE	WAGNER, J.
UNDER THE DOUBLE EAGLE	WAGNER, J.
UNDER THE DOUBLE EAGLE	WAGNER, J.
UNDER THE HAWAIIAN MOON	GREY, F.
UNDER THE LEAVES, OP. 29	THOME, F.
UNDER THE LEAVES	SCHWAB
UNDER THE LEAVES	THOME, F.
UNDER THE LEAVES	THOME, F.
UNDER THE LINDENS, MAZURKA	SARTORIO
UNDER THE LINDEN TREE	NIEDT *
UNDER THE MISTLETOE	ENGELMANN, H. U.
UNDER THE ROSE-ARBOR	DUTTON, T.
UNDER THE STARS AND STRIPES	ROOSEVELT
UNDER THE TENT OF THE SKY	DITTENHAVER
UNDER THE TOP SERIES -JUGGLER, THE.	BOGIN
UNDER THE WILLOW TREE--FROM 'VANESSA'	BARBER, S.
UNE AVENTURE DE BABAR	VELLONES, P.
UNE BARQUE SUR L'OCEAN, FROM MIROIRS	RAVEL
UNE BARQUE SUR L'OCEAN	RAVEL
UNE FETE A TRIANON, OP. 52	ROUBIER, H.
UNE FETE A TRIANON, OP. 52	ROUBIER, H.
UNE FETE MADRID	THOME, F.
UNE FUSEE, OP. 55--INTRODUCTION ET IMPROMPTU--	ALKAN
UNE JOURNEE	MILHAUD, D.
UNE PETITE BARCAROLLE	CAPLET, D.
UNE PETITE BERCEUSE	CAPLET, D.
UNE PETITE DANSE SLOVAQUE	CAPLET, D.
UNE PETITE MARCHE BIEN FRANCAISE	CAPLET, D.
UNE REJOUISSANCE	ROSSINI, G.
UNE SEMAINE DU PETIT ELFE FERME-L'OEIL -- OR LES	SCHMITT, F.
UNE TOUTE PETITE MATINEE	BEYER, F.
UNE TOUTE PETITE MATINEE	BEYER, F.
UNE TOUTE PETITE SOIREE	BEYER, F.
UNE TOUTE PETITE SOUREE	BEYER, F.
UNE VALSE POUR PIANO	MARGAT, Y.
UNFINISHED SYMPHONY, 2 THEMES	SCHUBERT
UNGARISCHER TANZE NO. 11-21	BRAHMS
UNGARISCHER TANZ NO. 05	BRAHMS
UNGARISCHER TANZ NO. 05	BRAHMS
UNGARISCHER TANZ NO. 05	BRAHMS
UNGARISCHER TANZ NO. 06	BRAHMS
UNGARISCHER TANZ NO. 06	BRAHMS
UNGARISCHER TANZ	BRAHMS
UNGARISCHE RHAPSODIEN NO. 01	LISZT
UNGARISCHE RHAPSODIEN NO. 02, M. D. BER. KADENZ	LISZT
UNGARISCHE RHAPSODIEN NO. 05, HEROIDE-ELEGIAQUE	LISZT
UNGARISCHE RHAPSODIEN NO. 06	LISZT
UNGARISCHE RHAPSODIEN NO. 14	LISZT
UNGARISCHE RHAPSODIEN NO. 15, RACOCZY-MARSCH	LISZT
UNGARISCHE RHAPSODIE NO. 02, M. D. BER. KADENZ	LISZT
UNGARISCHE RHAPSODIE NO. 02	LISZT
UNGARISCHE ZIGEUNERWEISEN	TAUSIG
UNITED STATES VICTORY MARCH	SCHIRMER, R.
UNITED WE STAND	HILLER
UNIVERSAL PIANO STUDIES--OP. 169, 170	LOESCHHORN, A.
UNIVERSITY PIANO SERIES -- A COURSE OF STUDY FOR THE	PYLE, H.
UNKNOWN CLASSICS FOR THE PIANO--CURWEN EDITION	WERNER--ED.
UNSEREN MADCHEN	SMETANA
UNSER LIEDERBUCH	
UNSINKABLE MOLLY BROWN, THE	WILLSON, M.
UNSTERBLICHER SCHUBERT, 20 BEKANNTE MELODIEN	SCHUBERT
UNSTERBLICHE OPERETTEN	
UNSTERBLICHE WALZER, BAND 01	
UNSTERBLICHE WALZER, BAND 02	
UNSTERBLICHE WALZER, BAND 03	
UNTERHALTSAME KLAVIERLEHSTUCKE	SIEGL, O.
UNTERWEGS. KLAVIERSTUCKE, OP. 9	VYCPALEK
UN NID D'AIGLE, POLKA	BRACY
UN PEASANT FARDEAU, MON PHARMACIEN	DELACROIX, R.
UN PETIT RIEN	SCHELLING, E.
UN PETIT TRUC EMBETANT	CAPLET, D.
UN PETIT TRUC EMBETANT	CAPLET, D.
UN PEU DE TOUT	LELEU
UN PRELUDE DOMINICAL ET SIX PIECES A DANSER	ROPARTZ
UN SOIR A NAPLES	GALOS
UP, UP AND AWAY	BRADLEY,
UP, UP AND AWAY	BRIMHALL,
UPSIDE DOWN CAKE	ZEPP--ED
UPSY-DAISY	GARROW
UPS AND DOWNS	SLATES, P.
UPWARD WAY, THE	LEE, E. M.
UP AND AWAY	DRING, M.
UP AND DOWN THE MOUNTAINSIDE	GWYNN, F.
UP AROUND THE BEND	BRIMHALL,
UP HILL AND DOWN DALE	BAYNON, A.
UP IN A SWING	KLEINMAN, A.
UP IN A SWING	LITTOFF
UP IN A SWING	MONTAINE
UP IN CENTRAL PARK	ROMBERG, S. *
UP IN THE CLOUDS	CURCIO
UP IN THE CLOUDS	PETERS, F.
UP IN THE SWING	STEVENS, E.
UP ON A PLAYGROUND SWING	KALMANOFF
UP ON A PLAYGROUND SWING	KALMANOFF
UP ON THE HOUSE TOP	SCHAUM, J.--ED.
VACANCES POUR PIANO, ALBUM 1	RUEFF
VACANCES POUR PIANO, ALBUM 2	RUEFF
VACATION BOOGIE	GLOVER, D.
VACATION SCENES	RODGERS, I.
VACATION TIME	LICHNER, R.
VAGUE MEMORIES	TOLLEFSEN, A.
VALCIK IN D FLAT	MOKREJS
VALCIK IN D FLAT	MOKREJS
VALCIK IN D FLAT	MOKRJES
VALENTINE PARTY, WALTZ	MARTIN, G.
VALE OF SONG	ROLFE
VALIANT YEARS, THE. --REGENT MARCH	RODGERS
VALLEE DES CLOCHES, FROM MIROIRS	RAVEL
VALLEE DES CLOCHES	RAVEL
VALLEY OF FRANCE, MEDITATION	GIRARD
VALLEY OF ROSES WALTZ	MESSINA, J.
VALS-CAPRICHO	FALLA, M. DE
VALSA NO. 6	GUARNIERI
VALSA NO. 7	GUARNIERI
VALSA NO. 8	GUARNIERI
VALSA NO. 9	GUARNIERI
VALSE--"FAUST"	GOUNOD, C. *
VALSE--FROM SUITE FOR 2 PIANOS, OP. 15	ARENSKY, A.
VALSE-ARABESQUE IN E FLAT, OP. 82	LACK, T.
VALSE-ARABESQUE	FREY
VALSE-BLUETTE	DRIGO, R.
VALSE-CAPRICE IN E FLAT	RUBINSTEIN
VALSE-CAPRICE	GROVLEZ
VALSE-CAPRICE	ROGERS, J.
VALSE-IMPROMPTU IN A FLAT	LISZT
VALSE-IMPROMPTU	UPCRAFT, M.
VALSE, NO. 02, EASY	DURAND, A.
VALSE, OP. 100 NO. 2, FOR ONE PIANO, SIX HANDS	STREABBOG
VALSE, OP. 11 NO. 4	RACHMANINOFF, S.
VALSE, OP. 12 NO. 2 -- DANSE HUMORESQUE	STOJOWSKI, S.
VALSE, OP. 18	CHOPIN
VALSE, OP. 2	LEVITZKI, M.
VALSE, OP. 2	LEVITZKI, M.
VALSE, OP. 2	LEVITZKI, M.
VALSE, OP. 3 NO. 13	PIERNE
VALSE, OP. 32 NO. 4	PROKOFIEFF
VALSE, OP. 36 NO. 7	ARENSKY, A.
VALSE, OP. 64 NO. 1, EASY	CHOPIN
VALSE, OP. 64 NO. 2	CHOPIN
VALSE, OP. 64 NO. 3	CHOPIN
VALSE, OP. 83	DURAND, A.
VALSE, OP. 88 NO. 5, EASY	GODARD, B.
VALSES, BK. 1	STRAUSS, J.
VALSES, BK. 2	STRAUSS, J.
VALSES -- DANSE DES RAINETTE	RAVEL
VALSES NOBLES, OP. 52	FLOTHIUS
VALSES NOBLES ET SENTIMENTALES	RAVEL
VALSES NOBLES ET SENTIMENTALES	RAVEL
VALSES VIENNOISES	KODALY, E.
VALSES VIENNOISES	LANNER, J. F. C.
VALSETTE IN E MINOR, OP. 40 NO. 1	SIBELIUS
VALSETTE	BOROWSKI, F.
VALSETTE	COBB
VALSETTE	CURRIE, E.
VALSETTE	KODALY, Z.
VALSETTE	SIBELIUS
VALSE -- ''LA PANTOUFLE DE VAIR''	DELANNOY
VALSE -- POSTHUMOUS, OP. 70 NO. 2	CHOPIN
VALSE -- SET	LEVITZKI, M.
VALSE A-DUR OP. 10 NO. 2	RACHMANINOFF, S.
VALSE ALSACIENNE	FOURDRAIN
VALSE ARABESQUE, OP. 82	LACK, T.
VALSE ARABESQUE, OP. 82	LACK, T.
VALSE BERCEUSE	NOVIKOFF
VALSE BLANCHE	MARGIS, A.
VALSE BLANCHE	MARGIS, A.
VALSE BLEUE IN E FLAT	MARGIS, A.
VALSE BLEUE	MARGIS, A.
VALSE BLEUE	MARGIS, A.
VALSE BLEUE	MARGIS, A.
VALSE BLUETTE, AIR DE BALLET	DRIGO, R.
VALSE BLUETTE	DRIGO, R.
VALSE BLUETTE	REISER, V.
VALSE BLUE	MARGIS, A.
VALSE BOHEMIENE	TAYLOR, S. C.
VALSE BREVE, 1949 -- SET	SAUGUET
VALSE BRILLANTE -- SET	MANA-ZUCCA
VALSE BRILLANTE AS-DUR	MOSZKOWSKI
VALSE BRILLANTE IN A FLAT, OP. 34 NO. 1	CHOPIN
VALSE BRILLANTE IN A FLAT -- 8-HANDS, SET	MOSZKOWSKI
VALSE BRILLANTE IN A FLAT	MOSZKOWSKI
VALSE BRILLANTE IN OCTAVES, OP. 33	CONCONE, G.
VALSE BRILLANTE NO. 2 IN D-FLAT MAJOR, OP. 20	SCHULHOFF
VALSE BRILLANTE OP. 34 NO. 2	CHOPIN
VALSE BRILLANTE	CONCONE, G.
VALSE BRILLANTE	MANA-ZUCCA
VALSE BRILLIANTE, OP. 148	SPINDLER
VALSE BRILLIANTE	MOSZKOWSKI
VALSE BURLESQUE	THOMPSON, J.
VALSE BURLESQUE	THOMPSON, J.
VALSE CAPRICE IN E FLAT	RUBINSTEIN
VALSE CAPRICE	NEWLAND, R.
VALSE CAPRICE	NEWLAND, R.
VALSE CAPRICE	SAVAGE, H. S.
VALSE CAPRICE	SEIDT, J.
VALSE CAPRICIEUSE	BRIDGE, F.
VALSE CARESSANTE	RESPIGHI
VALSE CHALOUPEE --APACHE DANCE--	OFFENBACH
VALSE CHANSON	LAST, J.
VALSE CHANTEE	TRUXELL, E.
VALSE CHANTEE	TRUXELL, E.
VALSE CHARMANTE	MAINVILLE
VALSE CHRISTINE	FRIML, R.
VALSE CHROMATIQUE, OP. 88	GODARD, B.
VALSE CHROMATIQUE --5TH WALTZ-- IN G, OP. 88	GODARD, B.
VALSE CHROMATIQUE	GODARD, B.
VALSE CHROMATIQUE	GODARD, B.
VALSE CHROMATIQUE	THOMPSON, J.
VALSE D'AMOUR, OP. 130 NO. 5	REGER
VALSE D'AMOUR	BRAUNON
VALSE D'AMOUR	FRONTINI
VALSE D'AMOUR	HOPKINS, H.
VALSE D'MOUR, OP. 57 NO. 5	MOSZKOWSKY
VALSE DES FLEURS	TSCHAIKOWSKY
VALSE DES FLEURS	TSCHAIKOWSKY
VALSE DES PAPILLONS, OP. 108	LUDOVIC, G.
VALSE DE BALLET	LAST, J.
VALSE DE LA REINE	TAYLOR, S. C.
VALSE ELAINE	RASBACH, O.
VALSE ELEGANTE	REISER, V.
VALSE ELEGANTE	REISER, V.
VALSE ESPAGNOLE	LANG
VALSE ETUDE	GILLOCK
VALSE FAVORITE	MOZART, W. A.
VALSE FOR PIANO	ETTORE, E.
VALSE FROM L'EVENTAIL DE JEANNE	IBERT
VALSE FROM SERENADE OP.48	TSCHAIKOWSKY
VALSE FROM SLEEPING BEAUTY,OP.66	TSCHAIKOWSKY
VALSE FROM SWAN LAKE,OP.20	TSCHAIKOWSKY
VALSE FROM THE FIVE BAGATELLES	AURIC
VALSE FROM THE SUITE, OP. 15 -- SET	ARENSKY, A.
VALSE FUGITIVE	RIETI
VALSE FUGITIVE	RIETI
VALSE GAIE	LAST, J.

VALSE GENTILE	PIERSON, A.
VALSE GRACIEUSE	SCARMOLIN
VALSE GRACILE	BODYCOMBE, A.
VALSE HONGROISE	HARRIS, C.
VALSE IMPROMPTU, OP. 19 NO. 1 FOR LEFT HAND	POHL, V.
VALSE IMPROMPTU	LISZT
VALSE IN A, OP. 10 NO. 2	RACHMANINOFF, S.
VALSE IN A FLAT MAJOR, OP. 62 NO. 11	GURLITT
VALSE IN A FLAT MAJOR, OP. 86	DURAND, A.
VALSE IN A MINOR--CURWEN EDITION	CHOPIN
VALSE IN A MINOR	GRIEG
VALSE IN C MAJOR	DENEE
VALSE IN C SHARP MINOR, OP. 64 NO. 2	CHOPIN
VALSE IN C SHARP MINOR, OP. 64 NO. 2	CHOPIN
VALSE IN D FLAT, OP. 64 NO. 1	CHOPIN
VALSE IN D FLAT -- MINUTE WALTZ, OP. 64 NO. 1	CHOPIN
VALSE IN D FLAT	CHOPIN
VALSE IN D FLAT	CHOPIN
VALSE IN E, OP. 34 NO. 1	MOSZKOWSKI
VALSE IN E, OP. 34 NO. 1	MOSZKOWSKI
VALSE IN E FLAT, OP. 39 NO. 8	TSCHAIKOWSKY
VALSE IN E FLAT, OP. 83	DURAND, A.
VALSE IN E FLAT MAJOR, OP. 83	DURAND, A.
VALSE IN E FLAT	DURAND, A.
VALSE JESSICA	ROLFE, W.
VALSE JOLIE, LA. --PRETTY WALTZ, THE.	THIELMANS
VALSE LENTE, COPPELIA	DELIBES, L.
VALSE LENTE, NAILA, EASY	DELIBES, L.
VALSE LENTE, OP. 17 NO. 2	SCHUETT
VALSE LENTE FROM ''COPPELIA''	DELIBES, L.
VALSE LENTE FROM ''SYLVIA''	DELIBES, L.
VALSE LENTE FROM ''SYLVIA''	DELIBES, L.
VALSE LENTE FROM ''COPPELIA'	DELIBES, L.
VALSE LENTE FROM THE SLEEPING BEAUTY BALLET	TSCHAIKOWSKY
VALSE LENTE NO. 02	DOLMETCH
VALSE LENTE	GODDEN, R.
VALSE LENTE	HAYES
VALSE LENTE	YSOT, D'
VALSE LENT D'AMOUR INQUIET	SAUGUET
VALSE LUCILLE, OP. 85 BIS, NO. 1	FRIML, R.
VALSE LUCILLE, OP. 85 BIS, NO. 1	FRIML, R.
VALSE MAURESQUE	TAYLOR, S. C.
VALSE MELANCOLIQUE	LITER, M.
VALSE MELODIE	RODGERS, I.
VALSE MELODIQUE	KETTERER, E.
VALSE MIGNON	HOWELL
VALSE MINIATURE	KARGANOFF
VALSE MODERATO, OP. 124 NO. 10	SCHUMANN, R.
VALSE MODERNE	OAKLAND, B.
VALSE NO. 02, EASY	GODARD, B.
VALSE NO. 2 EN SOL, OP. 15	PIERNE
VALSE NOBLE, OP. 77 NO. 9	SCHUBERT
VALSE NOCTURNE	SCHER, W.
VALSE NONCHALANTE, OP. 110	SAINT-SAENS
VALSE NOVELETTE	JUDD, A.
VALSE OUBLIEE	LISZT
VALSE OUBLIEE	LISZT
VALSE PAPILLON	BRETON
VALSE PARISIENNE	FRIML, R.
VALSE PETITE	CRERIE, E.
VALSE PETITE	KETTERER, E.
VALSE PETITE	SEWELL
VALSE POUDREE	POPY
VALSE ROMANTIQUE, OP. 19 NO. 2 FOR LEFT HAND	POHL, V.
VALSE ROMANTIQUE, OP. 62B--SM ORCH	SIBELIUS
VALSE ROMANTIQUE NO. 2	CHABRIER
VALSE ROMANTIQUE	BOSKOFF
VALSE ROMANTIQUE	DEBUSSY
VALSE ROMANTIQUE	DEBUSSY
VALSE ROMANTIQUE	SZYMANOWSKI
VALSE RUBATO	COBB
VALSE RUSTIQUE	TAYLOR, S. C.
VALSE SENTIMENTALE IN F MINOR, OP. 51 NO. 6	TSCHAIKOWSKY
VALSE SENTIMENTALE IN F MINOR, OP. 51 NO. 6	TSCHAIKOWSKY
VALSE SENTIMENTALE	TSCHAIKOWSKY
VALSE SERENADE, EASY	METRA
VALSE SERENADE	METRA
VALSE SERENADE	POLDINI, E.
VALSE SIMPLE	SAVINO
VALSE TRISTE, OP. 44 -- ORCH	SIBELIUS
VALSE TRISTE, OP. 44	SIBELIUS
VALSE TRISTE, OP. 44	SIBELIUS
VALSE TRISTE, OP. 44	SIBELIUS
VALSE TRISTE, OP. 44	SIBELIUS
VALSE TRISTE FROM CHOPIN'S OP. 34 NO. 2	ROLFE, W.
VALSE TRISTE	GILLOCK
VALSE TRISTE	GILLOCK
VALSE TRISTE	SIBELIUS
VALSE TRISTE	SIBELIUS
VALSE TRISTE	SIBELIUS
VALSE TRISTE	SIBELIUS
VALSE VIENNOISE	WRIGHT, N.
VALSE VOLUPTUEUX	FRONTINI
VALSE	BILOTTI
VALSE	DURAND, A.
VALSE	LANCEN
VALSE 1900	CASTRO, J. M.
VALS MINIATURA	LECUONA
VALS ROMANTICO	GREVI
VALZER ALL'ANTICA	SANGIORGI
VALZER AND IN MODO DI RUMBA	MARINUZZI
VALZER CAMPESTRE	MOZART, W. A.
VALZER FAVORITO	ROGERS, J.
VALZER GLISSANDO	FRONTINI
VALZER IDEAL	CHOPIN
VALZER IN LA MIN.	VILLA-LOBOS, H.
VAMOS TODOS CIRANDAR	HOVHANESS, A.
VANADOUR	
VANESSA	
VARCA NAPULITANA	
VARIACIONES APOLINEAS, OP. 25	GARCIA MORILLO
VARIACIONES GREGORIANAS, OP. 15	CAAMANO
VARIACIONES	GARCIA MORILLO
VARIACIONES 1942, OP. 10	GARCIA MORILLO
VARIANTI VIRTUOSO 1965	KOCH, E.
VARIATIONEN, OP. 13	HENZE, H.
VARIATIONEN, OP. 31	FRICKER, P.
VARIATION 'ICH GIENG EINMAL SPATIEREN' FUR CEMBALO	HASSLER, H.
VARIATIONEN F-MOLL -- HOBOKEN 17-6	HAYDN
VARIATIONEN FUR KLAVIER, K24, 25, 179, 180, 264, 352,	MOZART, W. A.
VARIATIONEN FUR KLAVIER UBER 'GIB MIR DIE BLUMEN'	SILCHER
VARIATIONEN UBER, AH, VOUS DIRAI-JE-MAMAN -- K.V. 265	MOZART, W. A.
VARIATIONEN UBER DEN BELIEBTEN WIENER TRAUER-WALZER --	CZERNY
VARIATIONEN UBER EIN ALTES BAUERNLIED	SCHWARZ
VARIATIONEN UBER EIN THEMA VON ROBERT SCHUMANN, OP. 68	NOVAK
VARIATIONEN UND CAPRICCIO UBER 'MARLBROUGH S'EN	VOGLER, G. J.
VARIATIONEN	NOETEL
VARIATIONEN 1	PEPPING, E.
VARIATIONEN 2	PEPPING, E.
VARIATIONS, COMPLETE	MOZART, W. A.
VARIATIONS--OP. 54, 82, 83	MENDELSSOHN
VARIATIONS, 'LA RICORDANZA' , OP. 33	CZERNY
VARIATIONS, BK. 1	BEETHOVEN
VARIATIONS, BK. 2	BEETHOVEN
VARIATIONS, NEL COR	BEETHOVEN
VARIATIONS, OP. 21, NOS. 1 AND 2	BRAHMS
VARIATIONS, OP. 21	BRAHMS
VARIATIONS, OP. 22	MCCABE, J.
VARIATIONS, OP. 26	VAN HULSE, C.
VARIATIONS, OP. 27	WEBERN, A.
VARIATIONS, OP. 32	MENDELSSOHN
VARIATIONS, OP. 36, 'ENIGMA'	ELGAR, E.
VARIATIONS, OP. 36, 'ENIGMA'	ELGAR, E.
VARIATIONS, OP. 36, 'ENIGMA'	ELGAR, E.
VARIATIONS, OP. 40	KABALEVSKY
VARIATIONS, OP. 40	SYDERMAN
VARIATIONS, OP. 43	KABALEVSKY
VARIATIONS, OP. 54A -- 1954	RIEGGER, W.
VARIATIONS, OP. 64 -- SET	WILM, N. VON
VARIATIONS, VOL. 1	BEETHOVEN
VARIATIONS, VOL. 2	BEETHOVEN
VARIATIONS, VOL.1	BEETHOVEN
VARIATIONS, VOL.2	BEETHOVEN
VARIATIONS --EASY ON 'LA CI DAREM' FROM DON GIOVANNI	CZERNY
VARIATIONS --IN PREP--	BROWN
VARIATIONS -- CLOTH	MOZART, W. A.
VARIATIONS -- COMPLETE	MOZART, W. A.
VARIATIONS -- 1940 --	EISLER
VARIATIONS - COMPLETE-	MOZART, W. A.
VARIATIONS - SUITE	KUPFERMAN, M.
VARIATIONS - SUITE	KUPFERMAN, M.
VARIATIONS ACADEMIQUES - SUITE	RIETI
VARIATIONS ACADEMIQUES	RIETI
VARIATIONS ACADEMIQUES	RIETI
VARIATIONS AND FANTASIA ON A THEME OF SCHOENBERG, OP.	FRAENKEL
VARIATIONS AND FINALE IN D	SZANTO
VARIATIONS AND FUGUE IN C MAJOR	PETYREK, F.
VARIATIONS AND FUGUE ON A THEME BY BACH, OP. 81	REGER
VARIATIONS AND FUGUE ON A THEME BY HANDEL, OP. 24	BRAHMS
VARIATIONS AND FUGUE ON A THEME BY HANDEL, OP. 24	BRAHMS
VARIATIONS AND FUGUE ON A THEME OF BEETHOVEN, OP. 86	REGER
VARIATIONS AND FUGUE ON A THEME OF HANDEL, OP. 24	BRAHMS
VARIATIONS AND FUGUE	BARTOW, N.
VARIATIONS AND FUGUE	ORREGO SALAS, J.
VARIATIONS AND FUGUE	SCELSI
VARIATIONS AND PAPILLONS, OP. 1/2	SCHUMANN, R.
VARIATIONS A DANSER	MOREAU
VARIATIONS A LOISIR, OP. 25	MAURAT, E.
VARIATIONS BRILLIANTES SUR ' THE LAST ROSE OF SUMMER	HERZ, H.
VARIATIONS BY BEETHOVEN	BEETHOVEN
VARIATIONS CHROMATIQUES, OP. 3 --CONCERT EDITION--	BIZET, G.
VARIATIONS COMPLETE	MOZART, W. A.
VARIATIONS EN FA	LETELIER, A.
VARIATIONS EN FORME DE PETITES ETUDES	HERARD
VARIATIONS EN METRES VARIABLES, OP. 12	HARTIG
VARIATIONS EN UT DIESE MINEUR, OP. 22	DUPRE, M.
VARIATIONS FOR AN ALBUM	PERSICHETTI
VARIATIONS FOR PIANO, BK. 1	BEETHOVEN
VARIATIONS FOR PIANO, BK. 2	BEETHOVEN
VARIATIONS FOR PIANO, OP. 23	VALEN
VARIATIONS FOR PIANO, VOL. 1	BEETHOVEN
VARIATIONS FOR PIANO, VOL. 1	MOZART, W. A.
VARIATIONS FOR PIANO, VOL. 2	BEETHOVEN
VARIATIONS FOR PIANO, VOL. 2	MOZART, W. A.
VARIATIONS FOR PIANOFORTE, COMPLETE, VOL. 1 -- CLOTH	BEETHOVEN
VARIATIONS FOR PIANOFORTE, COMPLETE, VOL. 1	BEETHOVEN
VARIATIONS FOR PIANOFORTE, COMPLETE, VOL. 2--CLOTH	BEETHOVEN
VARIATIONS FOR PIANOFORTE, COMPLETE, VOL. 2	BEETHOVEN
VARIATIONS FOR PIANO ON 'GIB MIR DIE BLUMEN'	SILCHER
VARIATIONS FOR PIANO ON 'MARY HAD A LITTLE LAMB' -	BALLANTINE
VARIATIONS FOR PIANO ON 'MARY HAD A LITTLE LAMB' -	BALLANTINE
VARIATIONS FOR PIANO	MOZART, W. A.
VARIATIONS FOR PIANO	SMOLANOFF
VARIATIONS INTERLUDE ET FINALE	DUKAS, P.
VARIATIONS IN A MINOR ON A THEME BY PAGANNINI, OP. 35	BRAHMS
VARIATIONS IN C MINOR	SHAPERO, H.
VARIATIONS IN C	AARON, M.
VARIATIONS IN D, OP. 40, NO. 1	KABALEVSKY
VARIATIONS IN D, OP. 40 NO. 1. 12 EASY VARIATIONS ON A	KABALEVSKY
VARIATIONS IN D --ON A THEME BY THOMAS MORE	CHOPIN
VARIATIONS IN E FLAT ON AN ORIGINAL THEME	SCHUMANN, R.
VARIATIONS IN F, H. XVII-6	HAYDN
VARIATIONS IN F MINOR	HAYDN
VARIATIONS IN GREENSLEEVES	HARVEY, VIVIEN
VARIATIONS IN G	SMIT, L.
VARIATIONS IN SEARCH OF A THEME	REISFELD
VARIATIONS NO. 1	PEPPING, E.
VARIATIONS NO. 2	PEPPING, E.
VARIATIONS ON 'AH, VOUS DIRAI-JE, MAMAN, K.265	MOZART, W. A.
VARIATIONS ON 'AH, VOUS DIRAI-JE, MAMAN' OP. 39 NO. 1	LONGO, A.
VARIATIONS ON 'AH, VOUS DIRAI-JE, MAMAN'	BACH, J. C. F.
VARIATIONS ON 'AH, VOUS DIRAI-JE, MAMAN'	MOZART, W. A.
VARIATIONS ON 'AH, VOUS DIRAI-JE, MAMAN'	MOZART, W. A.
VARIATIONS ON 'AH, VOUS DIRAI-JE MAMAN' K265	MOZART, W. A.
VARIATIONS ON 'FOLLIA DI SPAGNA'	SCARLATTI, A.
VARIATIONS ON 'HOMAGE TO DEBUSSY' BY DE FALLA	CASADESUS, R.
VARIATIONS ON 'LONDON BRIDGE IS FALLING DOWN'	ROBERTSON
VARIATIONS ON 'MY YOUNG LIFE HATH AN END'	SWEELINCK
VARIATIONS ON 'OH SUSANNA'	NEVIN
VARIATIONS ON 'O DEAR WHAT CAN THE MATTER BE'	POOLE, C.
VARIATIONS ON 'RULE BRITANICA' FROM ALFRED --DR. ARNE	KALKBRENNER
VARIATIONS ON 'SKIP TO MY LOU'	ROGERS
VARIATIONS ON 'THE LAST ROSE OF SUMMER'	GLINKA
VARIATIONS ON 'VERA LANGUORES'	GANDINI
VARIATIONS ON 'YANKEE DOODLE' --IN THE MANNER OF	BRAGGIOTTI, M.
VARIATIONS ON AN AMERICAN FOLK SONG	KABALEVSKY
VARIATIONS ON AN EGYPTIAN FOLKSONG	RAHIM, G. A.
VARIATIONS ON AN OLD PEASANT SONG	SCHWARZ
VARIATIONS ON AN ORIGINAL THEME, OP. 3	SPITZMULLER, A.
VARIATIONS ON AN ORIGINAL THEME	ROBERTS
VARIATIONS ON A CHILDREN'S THEME	DESDERI
VARIATIONS ON A FLOWER DRUM SONG -- TWO PREPARED	DIERCKS
VARIATIONS ON A FRENCH FOLKSONG. PIANO --HARPSICHORD--	LEEUW, T.
VARIATIONS ON A GREEK FOLK SONG, OP. 6	SPINKS
VARIATIONS ON A KINDERGARTEN TUNE --MY TOY BALLOON--	SLONIMSKY
VARIATIONS ON A MINOR THEME	GLOVER, D.
VARIATIONS ON A MINUET BY FISCHER, K.179	MOZART, W. A.
VARIATIONS ON A NURSERY RHYME, OP. 25	DOHNANYI
VARIATIONS ON A NURSERY TUNE, 'THREE BLIND MICE' IN	EVANS
VARIATIONS ON A PLAY TUNE	BOEHMER, A.
VARIATIONS ON A POLISH FOLK SONG, OP. 10	SZYMANOWSKI
VARIATIONS ON A POPULAR POLISH THEME, OP. 51	LIADOW, A.
VARIATIONS ON A POPULAR SONG -- L'AVOCAT --	SOULAGE
VARIATIONS ON A RECITATIVE	SCHOENBERG

Title	Composer
VARIATIONS ON A RUSSIAN SONG	GLINKA
VARIATIONS ON A THEME BY BEETHOVEN, OP. 35	SAINT-SAENS
VARIATIONS ON A THEME BY BEETHOVEN, OP. 35	SAINT-SAENS
VARIATIONS ON A THEME BY CHOPIN, OP. 22	RACHMANINOFF, S.
VARIATIONS ON A THEME BY CHOPIN	MOMPOU, F.
VARIATIONS ON A THEME BY CLEMENTI, OP. 61	BLACHER
VARIATIONS ON A THEME BY HAYDN, OP. 56A	BRAHMS
VARIATIONS ON A THEME BY HAYDN, OP. 56B	BRAHMS
VARIATIONS ON A THEME BY HAYDN, OP. 56B	BRAHMS
VARIATIONS ON A THEME BY HAYDN, OP. 56B	BRAHMS
VARIATIONS ON A THEME BY HAYDN	BRAHMS
VARIATIONS ON A THEME BY HAYDN	BRAHMS
VARIATIONS ON A THEME BY PAGANINI, OP. 35, BK. 1	BRAHMS
VARIATIONS ON A THEME BY PAGANINI, OP. 35, BK. 2	BRAHMS
VARIATIONS ON A THEME BY PAGANINI	BRAHMS
VARIATIONS ON A THEME BY PAGANINI	LUTOSLAWSKI
VARIATIONS ON A THEME BY RAMEAU FOR CLAVECIN AND	DAMASE, J. M.
VARIATIONS ON A THEME BY ROBERT SCHUMANN, OP. 23	BRAHMS
VARIATIONS ON A THEME BY SCHUMANN, OP. 23	BRAHMS
VARIATIONS ON A THEME BY SCHUMANN, OP. 9	BRAHMS
VARIATIONS ON A THEME OF BEETHOVEN, OP. 35	SAINT-SAENS
VARIATIONS ON A THEME OF CORELLI	RACHMANINOFF, S.
VARIATIONS ON A THEME OF GLINKA, OP. 35	LIADOW, A.
VARIATIONS ON A THEME OF PAGANINI, OP. 35	BRAHMS
VARIATIONS ON A THEME OF PAGANINI, OP. 35	BRAHMS
VARIATIONS ON A THEME OF SCHUMANN, OP. 9	BRAHMS
VARIATIONS ON A TRADITIONAL MELODY --DRINK TO ME ONLY	KENNAWAY
VARIATIONS ON A WALTZ BY JOHANN STRAUSS	KOFFLER, J.
VARIATIONS ON A YEMENITE THEME	BINDER
VARIATIONS ON BACH'S 'WEININ, KLAGEN'	LISZT
VARIATIONS ON HYMN TUNES	CURRIE, E.--ED
VARIATIONS ON L'HOMME ARME	KOHS, E. B.
VARIATIONS ON LA CENERENTOLA	HERZ, H.
VARIATIONS ON NON PIU MESTA FROM ROSSINI'S LA	HERZ, H.
VARIATIONS ON THE BASE OF HUNGARIAN FOLK SONG, OP. 32	WEINER
VARIATIONS ON THE MANE 'ABEGG', OP. 1	SCHUMANN, R.
VARIATIONS ON THE NAME ''ABEGG'', OP. 1	SCHUMANN, R.
VARIATIONS ON THE NAME 'ABEGG', OP. 1 -- WITH	SCHUMANN, R.
VARIATIONS ON THE NAME 'ABEGG', OP. 1	SCHUMANN, R.
VARIATIONS ON THE THEME, LITTLE SUZI	STONE, M.
VARIATIONS ON YANKEE DOODLE IN THE MANNER OF BACH,	BRAGGIOTTI, M.
VARIATIONS SERIEUSES, OP. 54	MENDELSSOHN
VARIATIONS SERIEUSES, OP. 54	MENDELSSOHN
VARIATIONS SERIEUSES, OP. 54	MENDELSSOHN
VARIATIONS SERIEUSES, OP. 54	MENDELSSOHN
VARIATIONS SERIEUSES	MENDELSSOHN
VARIATIONS SUR UNE CHACONNE	CASELLA, A.
VARIATIONS SUR UN THEME DE RAMEAU	DAMASE, J. M.
VARIATIONS SUR UN THEME FRIVOLE--'1830'--1934	NIN
VARIATIONS SUR UN THEME HURON	MOISSE, S.
VARIATIONS SUR UN THEME RUSSE, OP. 49	LIAPUNOFF
VARIATIONS SYMPHONIQUES	FRANCK, C.
VARIATIONS SYMPHONIQUES	FRANCK, C.
VARIATIONS VOL. 1	BEETHOVEN
VARIATIONS VOL. 2	BEETHOVEN
VARIATIONS	BACH, J.S.
VARIATIONS	BLAKE, D.
VARIATIONS	CAZDEN, N.
VARIATIONS	COPLAND
VARIATIONS	KUPFERMAN, M.
VARIATIONS	LEE, N.
VARIATIONS	LEIGHTON
VARIATIONS	MOZART, W. A.
VARIATIONS	NOETEL
VARIATIONS	PAPP, L.
VARIATIONS	POOT, M.
VARIATIONS	ROSZA
VARIATIONS	SAENZ
VARIATIONS	WALLINGTON, G.
VARIATION ON A WALTZ BY DIABELLI --1822 SEARLE 147	LISZT
VARIAZIONI CONCERTANTI	ZAFRED
VARIAZIONI GIOCONDE -- 1957 --	FUGA
VARIED AIR AND VARIATIONS	IVES, C.
VARIETES PIANISTIQUES, BK. 1	DE VILLERMONT,
VARIETES PIANISTIQUES, BK. 2	DE VILLERMONT,
VARIETES PIANISTIQUES, BK. 3	DE VILLERMONT,
VARIETES PIANISTIQUES, BK. 4	DE VILLERMONT,
VARIETIE OF LUTE LESSONS - 1610. LAUTENTABULATUR FUR	DOWLAND, R.
VARIETY IN TIME SIGNATURES	STEINER
VARIOUS PIANO PIECES	SCHUMANN, C.
VARIOUS PIECES --URTEXT-- IN 2 VOLUMES, VOL.1	BEETHOVEN
VARIOUS PIECES --URTEXT-- IN 2 VOLUMES, VOL.2	BEETHOVEN
VARIOUS PIECES - BK. 1	CHOPIN
VARIOUS PIECES - BK. 2	CHOPIN
VARIOUS PIECES INCLUDING COMPLETE BAGATELLES	BEETHOVEN
VARIOUS PIECES	MOZART, W. A.
VARIOUS PIECES	SCHUBERT
VARIOUS WORKS, VOL. 1	BACH, J.S.
VARIOUS WORKS, VOL. 2	BACH, J.S.
VARITY AND SPICE FOR PIANO	COBB
VARSOVIANA	STRAUSS, J.
VASCONGADA -- NO. 3, FROM SIX PIECES ON SPANISH FOLK	GRANADOS
VASCONIA -- THREE PIECES ON POPULAR BASQUE THEMES	GURIDI
VAUDEVILLE A DANSER	MOFFAT--ED
VECCHIO MINUETTO OP. 18 NO. 2	SGAMBATI
VECINOS BUENOS, TANGO	STANLEY
VEDRAI CARINO -- FROM ''DON GIOVANNI'' -- 8-HANDS, SET	MOZART, W. A.
VEGA, LA -- NO. 1, ALHAMBRA SUITE	ALBENIZ, I.
VEIL DANCE	SCHER, W.
VEIL DANCE	WRIGHT, N.
VEINTE PIEZAS FACILES	PONCE, M.
VELOCITY STUDIES, BK. 3 --21-30--, OP. 173	KOEHLER
VELVET NOCTURNE - FROM SEVEN FLOWERS FROM A PIANIST'S	GIASSON, P.
VELVET NOCTURNE	GIASSON, P.
VENDEMMIA	PETRALIA
VENETIAN BOAT SONG, OP. 19 NO. 6 -- SONG WITHOUT WORDS	MENDELSSOHN
VENETIAN BOAT SONG, OP. 19 NO. 6	MENDELSSOHN
VENETIAN BOAT SONG, OP. 19 NO. 6	MENDELSSOHN
VENETIAN BOAT SONG, OP. 30 NO. 6	MENDELSSOHN
VENETIAN BOAT SONG, OP. 30 NO. 6	MENDELSSOHN
VENETIAN BOAT SONG, S.W.W., 6	MENDELSSOHN
VENETIAN HOLIDAY -- TARANTELLA	SCHER, W.
VENETIAN LOVE SONG	NEVIN
VENETIAN REVERIE, A	HALL, F.
VENEZIANISCHER KARNEVAL, OP. 21 -- BALLET IN 7 PARTS	ROTSCHER, K.
VENEZIA E NAPOLI--SUPPLEMENT TO DEUXIEME ANNEE DE	LISZT
VENEZIA E NAPOLI -- GONDOLIERA	LISZT
VENEZIA E NAPOLI -- TARANTELLA	LISZT
VENEZIA E NAPOLI	LISZT
VENEZUELA VALSE	MILLER, L.
VENITIENNE--FOURTH BARCAROLLE, OP. 110 NO. 2	GODARD, B.
VENITIENNE, 4TH, BARCAROLLE	GODARD, B.
VENTA DE LOS GATOS, LA, OP. 32	TURINA, J.
VENT DANS LES RUINES, LE --EN CHAMPAGNE, 1915--	IBERT
VENT LEGER COURBE LES BRANCHES, UN	BLANC DE
VERADERO	
VERDUGO VIEW WALTZ	CARREL, B.
VERITABLES PRELUDES FLASQUES--POUR UN CHIEN	SATIE, E.
VERLIEBTE TASTEN	FISCHER, E.
VERMISCHTE HANDSTUCKE -- 18 JH.	KREUTZ
VERSCHIEDENE WERKE -- CAMPANELLA, N. PAGANINI	LISZT
VERSCHIEDENE WERKE -- CONSOLATIONS	LISZT
VERSCHIEDENE WERKE -- FUNERAILLES	LISZT
VERSCHIEDENE WERKE -- LA REGATA VENEZIANA	LISZT
VERSCHIEDENE WERKE -- LEGENDE NO. 1	LISZT
VERSCHIEDENE WERKE -- LEGENDE NO. 2	LISZT
VERSCHIEDENE WERKE -- MEPHISTO-WALZER	LISZT
VERSCHIEDENE WERKE -- POLONAISE NO. 2 E-DUR	LISZT
VERSCHIEDENE WERKE -- RIGOLETTO-PARAPHRASE	LISZT
VERS LA FLAMME, OP. 72	SCRIABINE, A.
VERS LA FLAMME, OP. 72	SCRIABINE, A.
VERS LA FLAMME	SCRIABINE, A.
VERS LES ETOILES	GAILLARD
VERTICAL CONSTRUCTION	SCHRAMM
VERTICAL CONSTRUCTION	SCHRAMM
VERTIGE, LE -- GALOP --	GAUTIER, L.
VERY EASIEST EXERCISES, OP. 190	KOEHLER
VERY EASIEST FAVORITE SONGS	ERB
VERY EASIEST STUDIES, THE, OP. 190	KOEHLER
VERY EASIEST STUDIES, THE, OP. 190	KOEHLER
VERY EASY PIANO PIECES, VOL. 1	AGAY, D.--ED
VERY EASY PIANO PIECES, VOL. 2	AGAY, D.--ED
VERY EASY PIANO PIECES FOR CHILDREN, BK. 1	AGAY, D.
VERY EASY PIECES FOR CHILDREN	GARSCIA
VERY FIRST CLASSICS, BK. 1	GRAY, D.
VERY FIRST CLASSICS, BK. 3	GRAY, D.
VERY FIRST CLASSICS	HOFSTAD, M.--ED
VERY FIRST DUETS	HAUPT, L. VON
VERY FIRST DUET BOOK	SMALL, A.
VERY FIRST DUET BOOK	
VERY FIRST FAVORITES--ARRANGED FOR PIANO IN	HOFSTAD, M.--ED
VERY FIRST HYMNS	HOFSTAD, M.--ED
VERY FIRST PIANO BOOK, A--THE STORY OF TONY IN WORDS	QUAILE, E.
VERY FIRST PIANO BOOK	WILLIAMS, J.
VERY FIRST PIANO SOLOS - BOOK 1	CURCIO
VERY FIRST PIANO SOLOS - BOOK 2	CURCIO
VERY FIRST PIANO SOLO BOOK	SMALL, A.
VERY FIRST SONATA, A	ANSON, G.
VERY FIRST STUDIES, OP. 190	KOEHLER
VERY IMPORTANT PERSON	HARRIS
VERY YOUNG PIANIST, WORKBOOK A	BASTIEN
VERY YOUNG PIANIST, WORKBOOK B	BASTIEN
VERY YOUNG PIANIST	BASTIEN
VERY YOUNG PIANIST	BASTIEN
VERY YOUNG PIANIST	BASTIEN
VESPERS IN SILVARA	COOK, P.
VESPERS	GODDEN, R.
VESPER BELLS ARE RINGING	PORTER, W.
VESPER MELODIES	CRIST, D.
VESPRI SICILIANI, I - OVERTURE	VERDI
VESTIDINHO BRANCO	VILLA-LOBOS, H.
VEXATIONS	SATIE, E.
VICAR OF BRAY, THE	KASSCHAU, H.
VICAR OF BRAY, THE	KASSCHAU, H.
VICTORIA, MARCH	GREENWALD, M.
VICTORY AT SEA --THEME	RODGERS
VICTORY AT SEA	RODGERS
VICTORY MARCH OF THE ELEPHANTS	FINE, I.
VICTORY PRELUDE	WARE, H.
VICTOR HERBERT FAVORITES	HERBERT
VIDALA	LOPEZ BUCHARDO
VIDALA	PALMA
VIDALA	UGARTE
VIDALITAY, OP. 8 NO. 4	NAPOLITANO
VIDALITA -- 1 PIANO 6 HANDS --	TORRA
VIEJO CASTILLO MORO, IL -- CUENTOS Y FANTASIAS NO. 5	CHAVARRI
VIELLE CAPITALE, LA	DELA
VIENNA-ON-THE-HUDSON	GIASSON, P.
VIENNA BEAUTIES, WALTZES	ZIEHRER
VIENNA BLOOD, OP. 354	STRAUSS, J.
VIENNA BLOOD, OP. 354	STRAUSS, J.
VIENNA ECHOES	
VIENNA LIFE	STRAUSS, J.
VIENNA LIFE	STRAUSS, J.
VIENNA ROSES	KOUNTZ, R.
VIENNA VALSE	VOLZ, H.
VIENNA WOODSHED -- JAZZ WALTZ	MEHEGAN, J.
VIENNESE CLOCK FROM 'HARY JANOS'	KODALY, Z.
VIENNESE DANCE, NO. 4	FRIEDMAN
VIENNESE DANCE, NO. 5	FRIEDMAN
VIENNESE DANCE, NO. 6	FRIEDMAN
VIENNESE LANTERN WALTZ	JAY *
VIENNESE MASTERS -- 14 PIECES FROM THE BAROQUE,	KANN, H.--ED
VIENNESE MELODY	ROBINSON, A.
VIENNESE MELODY	THOMPSON, J.
VIENNESE MINUET	MOZART, W. A.
VIENNESE POPULAR SONG -- THE OLD REFRAIN	MANNEY, C.
VIENNESE SKETCHES	NICHOLLS, H.
VIENNESE WALTZ, A	WEYBRIGHT
VIENNESE WALTZES, OP. 42 -- BK. 1	FUCHS, R.
VIENNESE WALTZES, OP. 42 -- BK. 2	FUCHS, R.
VIENNESE WALTZ	MACLACHIAN, T.
VIENNESE WALTZ	MACLACHIAN, T.
VIENNESE WHISPERS	WRIGHT, N.
VIENNOISE -- SUITE --	PIERNE
VIERHANDIGES KLASSIKERBUCH -- LEICHTE BIS	REHBERG--ED.
VIERHANDIGES KLAVIERBUCH -- LEICHTE BIS MITTELSCHWERE	HERRMANN--ED *
VIERHANDIGES SPIELBUCH FUR DEN ERSTEN ANFANG	EMONTS, F.
VIERHANDIGES SPIELBUCH	EMONTS, F.--ED
VIERHANDIGES TANZBUCHLEIN	KAESTNER--ED *
VIERHANDIGES VORTRAGSBUCH, BAND 01	SCHUNGELER,
VIERHANDIGES VORTRAGSBUCH, BAND 02	SCHUNGELER,
VIERSTIMMIGE RICERCARE IN DEN ACHT KIRCHENTONARTEN	PALESTRINA, G.
VIER FUGHETTEN, OP. 2	FRICKER, P.
VIER IMPROMPTUS, OP. 17	FRICKER, P.
VIER KOMPOSITIONEN AUS DER JUGEND	SUK
VIER POLKAS	SMETANA
VIER SONATINEN OP. 94, BK. 1	HAAS
VIER SONATINEN OP. 94, BK. 2	HAAS
VIER STUCKE	KAPR
VIER SUSANAS UBER 'SUZANNE UN JOUR'	COELHO, P.M.R.
VIER UND FUNFZIG KLAVIER MEL. ETUDEN OP. 187	GURLITT
VIER ZWEISTIMMIGE INVENTIONEN, OP. 5	BARTOS, J. Z.
VIEUX SEQUINS ET VIEILLES CUIRASSES	SATIE, E.
VIEWED FROM A STARPOINT	CHISOLM
VIE BREVE, LA -- SPANISH DANCE NO. 1 -- SET	FALLA, M. DE
VIE BREVE, LA -- SPANISH DANCE NO. 1	FALLA, M. DE
VIE BREVE, LA -- SPANISH DANCE NO. 2	FALLA, M. DE
VIGNETTE	STEINER
VIJAG	HOVHANESS, A.

VIKING	GLOVER, D.
VILIA	LEHAR
VILLAGEOISES -- EASY PIECES --	POULENC, F.
VILLAGEOISES - POLKA AND LITTLE RONDO	POULENC, F.
VILLAGEOISES - VALSE TYROLIENNE	POULENC, F.
VILLAGE BELLS	SCHIEFELBEIN, F.
VILLAGE BLACKSMITH, THE	HEINS, P.
VILLAGE CHOIR, THE	HOLLANDER
VILLAGE DANCE -- DANCE VILLAGEOISE, OP. 10 NO. 1	PENNINGTON, S.
VILLAGE DANCE	PROCTER, A.
VILLAGE FAIR	GROVE, R.
VILLAGE NIGHTFALL	WILSON, S.
VILLAGE ON THE GREEN	BROWN, A.
VILLAGE PARADE	KITTREDGE, M.
VILLAGE SQUARE DANCE	CHAGY
VILLAGE WEDDING	COURSEY, R. DE
VILLANCICOS DE ESPANA -- 15 VILLANCICOS WITH SPANISH	AGUILA--ED
VILLANCICO	GIANNEO
VILLANELLE	LEFEVRE, A.
VILLA DI QUERCETO, LA	COUTURE
VINCENT	LANE, J.--ED.
VINDOBONA, INTRODUCTION AND WALTZES -- SET	LANNER, J. F. C.
VINE STREET BOOGIE	MCSHANN
VINGT PETITES ETUDES, OP. 91 - BK. 1	MOSZKOWSKI
VINGT PETITES ETUDES, OP. 91 - BK. 2	MOSZKOWSKI
VINTNERS DAUGHTER, THE	ROSZA
VIOLETS AND ROSES	CROCKER, V.
VIOLETS AND ROSES	MARTIN, G.
VIOLETS FOR YOUR FURS	
VIOLETTES, OP. 148	WALDTEUFEL, E.
VIOLET FROM MOZART'S SONATA NO. 12, THE	ROLFE, W.
VIOLET WALTZ	STREABBOG
VIOLET WALTZ	STREABBOG
VIOLIN CONCERTO, OP. 61. ABRIDGED PIANO SOLO	BEETHOVEN
VIOLIN CONCERTO, OP. 64. ABRIDGED PIANO SOLO ARR.	MENDELSSOHN
VIOLIN CONCERTO, THEME	TSCHAIKOWSKY
VIRDORA	MCADAMS, G.
VIRGIN'S SLUMBER SONG, THE, MARIA WIEGENLIED, OP. 76	REGER
VIRGINALISTS, THE	SCHAUM, J.--ED.
VIRGINIA REEL	MOSZKOWSKI
VIRTUOSITY STUDIES 'AD ASPERA', OP. 72	HANON, C.
VIRTUOSO PIANIST. COMPLETE	HANON, C.
VIRTUOSO PIANIST, BK. 1	HANON, C.
VIRTUOSO PIANIST, BK. 2	HANON, C.
VIRTUOSO PIANIST, BK. 3	HANON, C.
VIRTUOSO PIANIST, IN 60 EXERCISES. COMPLETE	HANON, C.
VIRTUOSO PIANIST, IN 60 EXERCISES. COMPLETE	HANON, C.
VIRTUOSO PIANIST, THE, BK. 1	HANON, C.
VIRTUOSO PIANIST, THE, BK. 2	HANON, C.
VIRTUOSO PIANIST, THE, BK. 1	HANON, C.
VIRTUOSO PIANIST, THE, BK. 1	HANON, C.
VIRTUOSO PIANIST, THE, BK. 1	HANON, C.
VIRTUOSO PIANIST, THE, BK. 2	HANON, C.
VIRTUOSO PIANIST, THE, BK. 3	HANON, C.
VIRTUOSO PIANIST, THE, BK. 3	HANON, C.
VIRTUOSO PIANIST, THE, COMPLETE	HANON, C.
VIRTUOSO PIANIST, THE --COMPLETE--	HANON, C.
VIRTUOSO PIANISTS, THE	HANON, C.
VIRTUOSO PIANIST IN SEVENTEEN EXERCISES, BK. 3	HANON, C.
VIRTUOSO PIANIST IN SIXTY EXERCISES, COMPLETE	HANON, C.
VIRTUOSO PIANIST IN TWENTY-TWO EXERCISES, BK. 2	HANON, C.
VIRTUOSO PIANIST IN TWENTY EXERCICES, BK. 1	HANON, C.
VIRTUOSO PIANIST IN 60 EXERCISES, THE	HANON, C.
VIRTUOSO PIANIST IN 60 EXERSICES, THE--IN SPANISH	HANON, C.
VIRTUOSO TECHNIQUE	CRESTON
VIRTUOUS WIFE, THE	PURCELL, H.
VISIONS D'UN ANGELO	DE CRESCENZO
VISIONS ET PROPHETIES	BLOCH, E.
VISIONS FUGITIVES, OP. 22	PROKOFIEFF
VISIONS FUGITIVES, OP. 22	PROKOFIEFF
VISIONS FUGITIVES, OP. 22	PROKOFIEFF
VISIONS FUGITIVES	PROKOFIEFF
VISIONS	WHITFORD
VISION OF GOLDEN SUNSET	MCADAMS, G.
VISION	SAMINSKY
VISITING GREEK, A	CARREL, B.
VISIT TO ARGENTINA, A	HARPER, M.
VISIT TO ISRAEL	TANSMAN, A.
VISIT TO MEXICO	HARPER, M.
VISIT TO PUERTO RICO, A	HARPER, M.
VISIT TO SPAIN	HARPER, M.
VISTAS	MCKAY, G.
VITALBA E BIANCOSPINO	CASTELNUOVO-TEDE
VITAMINS PLUS	DUNGAN
VITA DELL'UOMO -- BALLET --	SAVINIO
VITO, EL -- EDITION A - ORIGINAL --	INFANTE
VITO, EL -- EDITION B - SIMPLIFIED --	INFANTE
VIVACE NON TANTO, OP. 19 NO. 3	KLEIN, B.
VIVA EL TORERO -- SPANISH MARCH --	POPY
VIVA MARIA	LEVY, E.
VIVA NAVARRA--JOTA DE CONCIERTO	LARREGLA, J.
VIVE LA COMPAGNIE	STEINER
VOCALISE, OP. 34 NO. 14	RACHMANINOFF, S.
VOCALISE	RACHMANINOFF, S.
VOEUX	TCHEREPNIN
VOGELS ALS PROPHET, OP. 82 NO. 7	SCHUMANN, R.
VOICES IN THE WOODS	HART, G. R.
VOICES OF SPRING--WALTZ, OP. 410	STRAUSS, J.
VOICES OF SPRING, OP. 410	STRAUSS, J.
VOICES OF SPRING, OP. 410	STRAUSS, J.
VOICES OF SPRING, OP. 57 -- CONCERT PARAPHRASE ON	GRUENFELD
VOICES OF SPRING	BOHM
VOICES OF SPRING	NEVIN--ED.
VOICES OF SPRING	SCHER, W.
VOICES OF SPRING	STRAUSS, J.
VOICES OF SPRING	STRAUSS, J.
VOICES OF SPRING	STRAUSS, J.
VOICE OF THE GUNS	ALFORD, K.
VOICE OF THE HEART, THE	VAN GAEL, H.
VOILES FROM PRELUDES, BK. 1	DEBUSSY
VOLARE	LANE, J.--ED.
VOLARE	MELIS, J.
VOLEUR D'ETINCELLES, LE	BOUTRY
VOLGA BOAT SONG	GREENWALD,
VOLKS-UND KINDERLIEDER	SCHAEFER, R.
VOLKSLIEDBUCHLEIN	DIETRICH--ED.
VOLKSLIEDBUCHLEIN	DIETRICH--ED.
VOLKSTANZBUCHLEIN	TWITTENHOFF--ED
VON BACH BIS BEETHOVEN -- 41 LEICHTE ORIG.-STUCKE, BK.	REHBERG--ED.
VON BACH BIS BEETHOVEN -- 41 LEICHTE ORIG.-STUCKE, BK.	REHBERG--ED.
VON BARTOK BIS STRAVINSKY	EMONTS, F.--ED
VON DEN MADCHEN, OP. 64 -- 12 PIECES	STOHR, R.
VON EWIGER SEHNSUCHT, OP. 33	NOVAK
VON RYAN MARCH	GOLDSMITH, J.
VOODOO	HAUBIEL, C.
VORREI	TOSTI
VOUAGE D'UNE HIRONDELLE	CROISEZ, A.
VOX CATHEDRALIS FOR 2 PIANOS	HAUBIEL, C.
VOYAGER'S FAREWELL	BERLIN, B.
VOYAGE - A CYCLE OF FIVE PIECES FOR PIANO	SCHUMAN, W.
VOYAGE D'UNE HIRONDELLE	CROISEZ, A.
VOYAGE D'UNE HIRONDELLE	CROISEZ, A.
VOYAGE D'UNE HIRONDELLE	CROISEZ, A.
VOYAGE TO THE BOTTOM OF THE SEA	SAWTELL, P.
VRAIS DEBUTS DU PIANO, LES	MANGEOT, A.
VURRIA	
VYSHERAD	SMETANA
WABASH CANNON BALL	SCHAUM, J.--ED.
WACHTERLIED, OP. 12 NO. 3	GRIEG
WAGGIN' TRAIN	STECHER *
WAGNER-LISZT ALBUM--9 TRANSCRIPTIONS FROM WAGNER'S	WAGNER *
WAGNERIANA	GROOMS
WAGNER FOR THE YOUNG PIANIST	WAGNER
WAGNESS ADULT PIANO COURSE, VOL. 1	WAGNESS
WAGNESS ADULT PIANO COURSE, VOL. 2	WAGNESS
WAGNESS PIANO COURSE, BK. 4	WAGNESS--ED.
WAGON TRAILS	MILLIGAN
WAGON TRAIN, THE	DVORINE
WAGON TRAIN, THE	DVORINE
WAHOO, INDIAN DANCE	MOHO-NALI
WAIKIKI RUN	FULLER
WAITING FOR THE MAIL	LICHNER, P.
WAITING ON THE CORNER	SANDBOURNE
WAKE UP	ERB
WAKE UP	RICHTER, A.
WALDESRAUSCHEN--CONCERT ETUDE	LISZT
WALDESRAUSCHEN -- FOREST MURMURS--	LISZT
WALDMEISTER--OVERTURE	STRAUSS, J.
WALDSCENEN -- FOREST SCENES --, OP. 82	SCHUMANN, R.
WALKIN' THE BOOGIE	AMMONS *
WALKING ALONG	KARP
WALKING AND WHISTLING	DAVIS, J.
WALKING HOME	ROLLINS, G.
WALKING IN THE WOODS	MEUTTMAN, M.
WALKING SONG -- SET	THOMSON, V.
WALKING THE DOG	ALT, V.
WALKING THE DOG	GARROW, L.
WALKING TO SCHOOL	WEYBRIGHT
WALKING TUNE, A	FRACKENPOHL, A.
WALKS WITH ISOLDE--SPAZIERGANGE MIT ISOOLDE, OP. 70,	SCHOLLUM, R.
WALKUERE, DIE - RIDE OF THE VALKYRIES	WAGNER
WALKUERE, DIE - SIEGMUND'S SPRING SONG	WAGNER
WALK A MILE IN MY SHOES	BRADLEY, W.
WALK THROUGH THE PARK, A	STEINER
WALK TO THE PARADISE GARDEN, FROM 'A VILLAGE ROMEO AND	DELIUS, F.
WALLACE THE WADDING WOODCHUCK	MESEROLE, H. T.
WALLY, LA - 1ST EASY FANTASIA	CATALANI
WALLY, LA - 2ND EASY FANTASIA	CATALANI
WALLY, LA - 3RD EASY FANTASIA	CATALANI
WALLY, LA A SERA - PRELUDE TO ACT III	CATALANI
WALLY, LA A SERA - PRELUDE TO ACT III	CATALANI
WALL CLOCK, THE	HAYES
WALTZ--FROM ''FAUST''	GOUNOD, C.
WALTZ--1919	POULENC, F.
WALTZ-CAPRICES, OP. 37	GRIEG
WALTZ-CAPRICES, OP. 37	GRIEG
WALTZ-LULLABY, OP. 89	VAN GAEL, H.
WALTZ, A -- 1949 -- SET	AURIC
WALTZ, FROM 'SLEEPING BEAUTY'	TSCHAIKOWSKY
WALTZ, FROM SERENADE FOR STRINGS	TSCHAIKOWSKY
WALTZ, OP. 100 NO. 2 -- 6-HANDS	STREABBOG
WALTZ, OP. 101 NO. 11	GURLITT
WALTZ, OP. 101 NO. 11	GURLITT
WALTZ, OP. 18 IN E FLAT	CHOPIN
WALTZ, OP. 18 IN E FLAT	CHOPIN
WALTZ, OP. 23	GLAZOUNOW, A.
WALTZ, OP. 30 FROM 'GOLDEN MOUNTAIN'	SHOSTAKOVITCH
WALTZ, OP. 34 NO. 1 IN A FLAT	CHOPIN
WALTZ, OP. 34 NO. 1 IN A FLAT	CHOPIN
WALTZ, OP. 34 NO. 2 IN A MINOR	CHOPIN
WALTZ, OP. 34 NO. 2 IN A MINOR	CHOPIN
WALTZ, OP. 34 NO. 3 IN F	CHOPIN
WALTZ, OP. 34 NO. 3	CHOPIN
WALTZ, OP. 38	SCRIABINE, A.
WALTZ, OP. 39 NO. 1	BRAHMS
WALTZ, OP. 39 NO. 15	BRAHMS
WALTZ, OP. 39 NO. 15	BRAHMS
WALTZ, OP. 39 NO. 15	BRAHMS
WALTZ, OP. 39 NO. 3	BRAHMS
WALTZ, OP. 42 IN A FLAT	CHOPIN
WALTZ, OP. 44 NO. 3	GLAZOUNOW, A.
WALTZ, OP. 64 NO. 1 IN D FLAT 'MINUTE'	CHOPIN
WALTZ, OP. 64 NO. 1 IN D FLAT	CHOPIN
WALTZ, OP. 64 NO. 1	CHOPIN
WALTZ, OP. 64 NO. 2 IN C SHARP	CHOPIN
WALTZ, OP. 64 NO. 2 IN C SHARP	CHOPIN
WALTZ, OP. 64 NO. 2	CHOPIN
WALTZ, OP. 64 NO. 3 IN A FLAT	CHOPIN
WALTZ, OP. 65	PROKOFIEFF
WALTZ, OP. 69 NO. 1 IN A FLAT	CHOPIN
WALTZ, OP. 69 NO. 1 IN A FLAT	CHOPIN
WALTZ, OP. 69 NO. 1	CHOPIN
WALTZ, OP. 69 NC. 2 IN B MINOR	CHOPIN
WALTZ, OP. 70 NO. 2 IN F MINOR	CHOPIN
WALTZ, OP. 70 NO. 3 IN D FLAT	CHOPIN
WALTZ, THE --70--	
WALTZER IN E FLAT--CURWEN EDITION	WEBER, VON
WALTZES, CHIMES OF NORMANDY	PLANQUETTE
WALTZES, EIGHT	CHOPIN
WALTZES, MERRY WIDOW	LEHAR
WALTZES, OP. 39. SIMPLIFIED	BRAHMS
WALTZES, OP. 39	BRAHMS
WALTZES, OP. 39	BRAHMS
WALTZES, OP. 39	BRAHMS
WALTZES, OP. 39	BRAHMS
WALTZES, OP. 39	BRAHMS
WALTZES, OP. 39	BRAHMS
WALTZES, OP. 39	BRAHMS
WALTZES, OP. 39	BRAHMS
WALTZES, OP. 39	BRAHMS
WALTZES, OP. 39	BRAHMS
WALTZES, OP. 54	DVORAK
WALTZES, OP. 8	MOSZKOWSKI
WALTZES, SET 1	SCHUBERT
WALTZES, SET 2	SCHUBERT
WALTZES, SET 3	SCHUBERT
WALTZES, SET 4	SCHUBERT
WALTZES, SET 5	SCHUBERT
WALTZES, THREE	CHOPIN
WALTZES, VOL. 1	WALDTEUFEL, E.
WALTZES, VOL. 2	WALDTEUFEL, E.
WALTZES, 1,2,8,15, OP. 39	BRAHMS
WALTZES -- CLOTH	CHOPIN

WALTZES -- EUGENE ONEGIN, SERENADE FOR STRINGS, SWAN	TSCHAIKOWSKY
WALTZES --14--	CHOPIN
WALTZES AND DANCES --7--	GRIEG
WALTZES FOR PIANO SOLO 1. ADAPTED BY THE COMPOSER	BRAHMS
WALTZES FOR THE YOUNG PIANIST	STEINER
WALTZES FROM "LA REGINETTA DELLE ROSE"	LEONCAVALLO
WALTZES FROM OP. 9A	SCHUBERT
WALTZES ON A MUSIC BOX	KLEINMAN, A.
WALTZES	BRAHMS
WALTZES	BRAHMS
WALTZES	CHOPIN
WALTZES	CHOPIN
WALTZES	CHOPIN
WALTZES	CHOPIN
WALTZES	CHOPIN
WALTZES	CHOPIN
WALTZES	CHOPIN
WALTZES	CHOPIN
WALTZES	GIORDANO
WALTZES	LAZARE-LEVY
WALTZES	MOORE
WALTZES	SCHUBERT
WALTZES	SMETANA
WALTZE FROM SUITE, OP. 15	ARENSKY, A.
WALTZING AT SUNDOWN	DITTENHAVER
WALTZING BALLERINA	JOYNER, B.
WALTZING BALLERINA	NEVIN
WALTZING BEAR, THE	RICHTER, A.
WALTZING BEAR	SCHER, W.
WALTZING BIRD, THE	FROST
WALTZING BUGLE BOY	
WALTZING BY CANDLELIGHT	SCHER, W.
WALTZING CAT, THE	ANDERSON, L.
WALTZING CAT, THE	STEINER--ED.
WALTZING CHIMPANZEE, THE	OLSON, R.
WALTZING DAFFODILS/LET'S DANCE GRANDMA	SCHER, W.
WALTZING DOLL, EASY	POLDINI, E.
WALTZING DOLL -- POUPEE VALSANTE	POLDINI, E.
WALTZING DOLL	POLDINI, E.
WALTZING FLAMINGO, THE	DONENFELD, J.
WALTZING FLAMINGOES	ARCHER, I.
WALTZING GIRAFFE, THE	DONENFELD, J.
WALTZING GYPSIES	SCHER, W.
WALTZING IN THE GARDEN	BECK, M.
WALTZING IN THE NIGHT -- FROM NOCTURNE IN E FLAT OP. 9	CHOPIN
WALTZING JUGGLER	SCHER, W.
WALTZING KEYS	ROZIN
WALTZING MATILDA	COSAN, M.
WALTZING MATILDA	COWAN *
WALTZING ON ICE	PHILLIPS, D.
WALTZING PARAKEET, THE	SCHAUM, J.--ED.
WALTZING PEACOCK	SCHER, W.
WALTZING POODLE	GARROW, L.
WALTZING PUPPET	SCHER, W.
WALTZING PUSSYCATS	MCHALE, M.
WALTZING SNOW MAN	WEISLEDER, A.
WALTZING SUNBEAMS	BRUSSELS, I.
WALTZING THIRDS	SCHUNKE
WALTZING WILLOWS	REISER, V.
WALTZING WITH STRAUSS	MOSSMAN, T.
WALTZING	ROBINSON, A.
WALTZ -- FROM 'THE COMEDIANS'	KABALEVSKY
WALTZ -- SET	WILM, N. VON
WALTZ -- THEN MARCH	CAMPBELL
WALTZ -- 6-HANDS	NOEL, H.
WALTZ 'JOY'	SADLON
WALTZ AND CHORUS FROM ''FAUST'' -- 8-HANDS, SET	GOUNOD, C.
WALTZ AT MAXIM'S	
WALTZ BOOK	SCHAUM, J.--ED.
WALTZ CAPRICE	STRAUSS, J.
WALTZ DREAM, A	STRAUS, O.
WALTZ DREAM	STRAUS, O.
WALTZ FANTASIE	BICHEL, M.
WALTZ FOR A BALLERINA	RICHTER, A.
WALTZ FOR A BALL	HAMMERSTEIN *
WALTZ FOR A LITTLE DOLL	STEVENS, E.
WALTZ FOR A PENNY, A	WATSON
WALTZ FOR CINDERELLA, A	GIASSON, P.
WALTZ FOR CINDERELLA, A	GIASSON, P.
WALTZ FOR JUDY	JOYNER, B.
WALTZ FOR MILADY	PERKINS, F.
WALTZ FOR ONE HAND--FOR EITHER HAND ALONE	PIETSCH, E.
WALTZ FOR TWO PIANOS	COURSEY, R. DE
WALTZ FOR TWO PIANOS	COURSEY, R. DE
WALTZ FROM -- MASQUERADE SUITE	KHATCHATURIAN
WALTZ FROM -- THE BRONZE HORSEMAN	GLIERE
WALTZ FROM 'FAUST', OP. 196 NO. 1	GOUNOD, C.
WALTZ FROM 'THE BIRDCATCHER'	ZELLER
WALTZ FROM CINDERELLA BALLET	PROKOFIEFF
WALTZ FROM CINDERELLA	PROKOFIEFF
WALTZ FROM FLEDERMAUS	STRAUSS, J.
WALTZ FROM SERENADE, OP. 48	TSCHAIKOWSKY
WALTZ FROM SERENADE FOR STRINGS, OP. 48	TSCHAIKOWSKY
WALTZ FROM SERENADE FOR STRINGS	TSCHAIKOWSKY
WALTZ FROM SERENADE FOR STRINGS	TSCHAIKOWSKY
WALTZ FROM THE BALLET 'THE SLEEPING BEAUTY'	TSCHAIKOWSKY
WALTZ FROM THE SLEEPING BEAUTY	TSCHAIKOWSKY
WALTZ IMPROVISATION	RASBACH, O.
WALTZ INTERLUDE, 'LET MY SONG FILL YOUR HEART'	CHARLES
WALTZ INTERLUDE	RAYMOND, J.
WALTZ IN A, OP. 54, NO. 1	DVORAK
WALTZ IN A FLAT, OP. 34 NO. 1 'VALSE BRILLANTE'	CHOPIN
WALTZ IN A FLAT, OP. 34 NO. 1	CHOPIN
WALTZ IN A FLAT, OP. 34 NO. 1	CHOPIN
WALTZ IN A FLAT, OP. 39 NO. 15	BRAHMS
WALTZ IN A FLAT, OP. 39 NO. 15	BRAHMS
WALTZ IN A FLAT, OP. 39 NO. 15	BRAHMS
WALTZ IN A FLAT, OP. 39 NO. 15	BRAHMS
WALTZ IN A FLAT, OP. 42	CHOPIN
WALTZ IN A FLAT, OP. 64 NO. 3	CHOPIN
WALTZ IN A FLAT, OP. 64 NO. 3	CHOPIN
WALTZ IN A FLAT, OP. 69 NO. 1 AND WALTZ IN B MINOR,	CHOPIN
WALTZ IN A FLAT, OP. 69 NO. 1	CHOPIN
WALTZ IN A FLAT MAJOR, OP. 42	CHOPIN
WALTZ IN A FLAT MAJOR, OP. 64, NO. 3	CHOPIN
WALTZ IN A FLAT MAJOR, OP. 69, NO. 1	CHOPIN
WALTZ IN A FLAT MAJOR	BRAHMS
WALTZ IN A MAJOR, OP. 16	PLANTE
WALTZ IN A MAJOR, OP. 54 NO. 1	DVORAK
WALTZ IN A MINOR, OP. 12 NO. 2	GRIEG
WALTZ IN A MINOR, OP. 12 NO. 2	GRIEG
WALTZ IN A MINOR, OP. 34, NO. 2	CHOPIN
WALTZ IN A MINOR, OP. 34 NO. 2	CHOPIN
WALTZ IN A MINOR, OP. 34 NO. 2	CHOPIN
WALTZ IN A MINOR	GRIEG
WALTZ IN BLUE	MITTLER
WALTZ IN B MINOR, OP. 69, NO. 2	CHOPIN
WALTZ IN B MINOR, OP. 69 NO. 2	CHOPIN
WALTZ IN C SHARP MINOR, OP. 64, NO. 2	CHOPIN
WALTZ IN C SHARP MINOR, OP. 64 NO. 2	CHOPIN
WALTZ IN C SHARP MINOR, OP. 64 NO. 2	CHOPIN
WALTZ IN D FLAT, OP. 64 -- MINUTE WALTZ	CHOPIN
WALTZ IN D FLAT, OP. 64 NO. 1 - MINUTE	CHOPIN
WALTZ IN D FLAT, OP. 64 NO. 1 'MINUTEN'	CHOPIN
WALTZ IN D FLAT, OP. 64 NO. 2 --MINUTE--	CHOPIN
WALTZ IN D FLAT, OP. 70 NO. 3	CHOPIN
WALTZ IN D FLAT MAJOR, OP. 64, NO. 1--MINUTE	CHOPIN
WALTZ IN D FLAT MAJOR, OP. 70, NO. 3	CHOPIN
WALTZ IN D	MOZART, W. A.
WALTZ IN D	OGILVY, F.
WALTZ IN E FLAT, OP. 18	CHOPIN
WALTZ IN E FLAT, OP. 18	CHOPIN
WALTZ IN E FLAT, OP. 70 NO. 2	CHOPIN
WALTZ IN E FLAT MAJOR, OP. 18--GRANDE VALSE BRILLIANTE	CHOPIN
WALTZ IN E FLAT MAJOR, OP. 18--GRANDE VALSE BRILLIANTE	CHOPIN
WALTZ IN E MAJOR	CHOPIN
WALTZ IN E MINOR--POSTH.--	CHOPIN
WALTZ IN E MINOR, OP. POSTHUMOUS	CHOPIN
WALTZ IN E MINOR, OP. 38, NO. 7	GRIEG
WALTZ IN E MINOR, OP. 38 NO. 7	GRIEG
WALTZ IN E MINOR , NO. 14	CHOPIN
WALTZ IN E MINOR	CHOPIN
WALTZ IN F, OP. 34 NO. 3	CHOPIN
WALTZ IN F MINOR, OP. 70, NO. 2	CHOPIN
WALTZ IN F	WARD
WALTZ IN G FLAT, OP. 70 NO. 1 - WALTZ IN A FLAT, OP.	CHOPIN
WALTZ IN G FLAT, OP. 70 NO. 1	CHOPIN
WALTZ IN G FLAT MAJOR, OP. 70, NO. 1	CHOPIN
WALTZ IN G FLAT MAJOR	LORA
WALTZ IN G	BEETHOVEN
WALTZ IN G	BRAHMS
WALTZ IN JAZZ TIME	GIASSON, P.
WALTZ IN JAZZ TIME	GIASSON, P.
WALTZ KING, THE--16 FAVORITE WALTZES	STRAUSS, J.
WALTZ K600 NO. 1	MOZART, W. A.
WALTZ ME AROUND, TOO	WOZENCRAFT, M.
WALTZ ME AROUND	WOZENCRAFT, M.
WALTZ MODERNE	HIBBS, C.
WALTZ MOOD	NOBLITT, K.
WALTZ NO. 01, OP. 26	GODDARD, B.
WALTZ NO. 01	GODARD, B.
WALTZ NO. 01	GODARD, B.
WALTZ NO. 01	NERINI, E.
WALTZ NO. 02	GODARD, B.
WALTZ NO. 02	LANDRY
WALTZ OF THE BELLS	SCHER, W.
WALTZ OF THE BLUE FAIRY	CLARK, T.
WALTZ OF THE BLUE FAIRY	MILLIGAN
WALTZ OF THE DOLLS	CROCKER, D.
WALTZ OF THE DREAM FAIRY	DITTENHAVER
WALTZ OF THE FLOWERS--FROM NUTCRACKER SUITE	TSCHAIKOWSKY
WALTZ OF THE FLOWERS FROM "NUTCRACKER"	TSCHAIKOWSKY
WALTZ OF THE FLOWERS FROM "NUTCRACKER"	TSCHAIKOWSKY
WALTZ OF THE FLOWERS FROM THE "NUTCRACKER SUITE"	TSCHAIKOWSKY
WALTZ OF THE FLOWERS IN D FROM NUTCRACKER SUITE	TSCHAIKOWSKY
WALTZ OF THE FLOWERS	TSCHAIKOWSKY
WALTZ OF THE FLOWERS	TSCHAIKOWSKY
WALTZ OF THE FLOWERS	TSCHAIKOWSKY
WALTZ OF THE FLOWERS	TSCHAIKOWSKY
WALTZ OF THE FLOWERS	TSCHAIKOWSKY
WALTZ OF THE FLOWERS	TSCHAIKOWSKY
WALTZ OF THE FLOWER FAIRIES	CROSBY, M.
WALTZ OF THE FLOWER FAIRIES	CROSBY, M.
WALTZ OF THE GHOSTS	CHAGY
WALTZ OF THE PEACOCKS	BERMONT, H.
WALTZ OF THE PEPPERMINT STICKS	TRAVIS, B.
WALTZ OF THE ROSES	RODGERS, I.
WALTZ OF THE SHADOWS	MELECCI, A.
WALTZ OF THE TOREADORS, THE	HOTCHKISS, J.
WALTZ OF THE TOYS	BERMONT, G.
WALTZ OF THE TOYS	BERMONT, G.
WALTZ OF THE WEE FINGERS	VANNORT, I.
WALTZ OF THE WINDS	ROZIN
WALTZ ON THE GREEN	BEATON, C.
WALTZ ON WHITE KEYS	FREED, I.
WALTZ ON 2 NOTES	MODONA
WALTZ REFLECTIONS	FROST
WALTZ REVERIE, A	ECKSTEIN
WALTZ REVERIE	ROBBINS, L.
WALTZ SIMPLICE	NOONA, W.
WALTZ SONG, MIREILLE	GOUNOD, C.
WALTZ THEME	ADDINSELL
WALTZ THEME	ADDINSELL
WALTZ TIME	HIER, E.
WALTZ TIME	WEYBRIGHT
WALTZ WITH ME	PARENTE, SR. E.
WALTZ YOU SAVED FOR ME	LANE, J.--ED.
WALTZ YOU SAVED FOR ME	SAVINO--ED.
WALTZ YOU SAVED FOR ME	
WALTZ	BECUCCI
WALTZ	BRAHMS
WALTZ	GLOVER, D.
WALTZ	GRETCHANINOFF
WALTZ	KRAFT
WALTZ	LAMARCHE, P.
WALTZ	LAWNER, M.
WALTZ	LOURIE
WALTZ	NAGY, M.
WALTZ	POOLE, C.
WALTZ	THOMAS, C. J.
WALT DISNEY'S BAMBI	BRIMHALL,
WALT DISNEY'S MARY POPPINS	BRIMHALL,
WALT DISNEY'S PIANO CLASSICS, NO. 1 MICKEY MOUSE	BRIMHALL,
WALT DISNEY'S PIANO CLASSICS, NO. 2 PETER PAN	BRIMHALL,
WALT DISNEY'S PIANO CLASSICS, NO. 3 ALICE IN	BRIMHALL,
WALT DISNEY'S PIANO CLASSICS, NO. 4 BABES IN TOYLAND	BRIMHALL,
WALT DISNEY'S PIANO CLASSICS, NO. 5 CINDERELLA	BRIMHALL,
WALT DISNEY'S PIANO CLASSICS, NO. 6 LADY AND THE TRAMP	BRIMHALL,
WALT DISNEY FAVORITES	BASTIEN--ED.
WALT DISNEY 50 HAPPY YEARS, 50 HAPPY HITS	BRIMHALL,
WALZER, OP. 14	AUS DER OHE, A.
WALZER, OP. 54	DVORAK
WALZER AUS DER SERENADE FUR STREICHORCHESTER OP. 48	TSCHAIKOWSKY
WALZER IN A AND D FLAT, OP. 54 NO. 1	DVORAK
WALZER OP. 39	BRAHMS
WALZER OP. 39	BRAHMS
WALZER	CHOPIN
WALZER	SCHUBERT
WALZER	SMETANA
WALZES, OP. 39	BRAHMS
WANDA, THE WALTZING WALRUS	GARROW, L.

Title	Composer
WANDERER-FANTASIE OP. 15	SCHUBERT
WANDERER FANTASIE, OP. 15	SCHUBERT
WANDERING BROOK, THE	SOUERS
WANDERING CARAVAN	SCHER, W.
WANDERING COWBOY, THE	BRIMHALL, J.
WANDERING MINISTREL	DITTENHAVER
WANDERING MINISTREL, THE	ARMOUR
WANDERING	MENDELSSOHN
WAND OF YOUTH, SUITE 1	ELGAR, E.
WAND OF YOUTH, SUITE 2	ELGAR, E.
WAR- - ALL DAY MUSIC	
WARBLINGS AT EVE	RICHARDS, B.
WARRIOR'S SONG, OP. 45 NO. 15	HELLER, S.
WARRIOR'S SONG, OP. 45 NO. 15	HELLER, S.
WARRIOR'S SONG, OP. 45 NO. 15	HELLER, S.
WARRIOR'S SONG, OP. 45 NO. 15	HELLER, S.
WARRIOR'S SONG	HELLER, S.
WARSAW CONCERTO -- THEME EASY	ADDINSELL
WARSAW CONCERTO -- THEME	ADDINSELL
WARSAW CONCERTO	ADDINSELL
WARSAW CONCERTO	ADDINSELL
WARUM, OP. 12 NO. 3--FANTASIESTUCKE	SCHUMANN, R.
WAR CHIEF BOOGIE	HAZELLE
WAR DANCE AND THE SAD INDIAN BOY	POOLE, C.
WAR MARCH OF THE PRIESTS, EASY	MENDELSSOHN
WAR MARCH OF THE PRIESTS, FROM 'ATHALIA'	MENDELSSOHN
WAR MARCH OF THE PRIESTS, OP. 74	MENDELSSOHN
WAR MARCH OF THE PRIESTS -- ATHALIE	MENDELSSOHN
WAR MARCH OF THE PRIESTS -- FROM ''ATHALIA''	MENDELSSOHN
WAR MARCH OF THE PRIESTS FROM 'ATHALIA', OP. 74	MENDELSSOHN
WAR MARCH OF THE PRIESTS	MENDELSSOHN
WAR MARCH OF THE PRIETS 'ATHALIA'	MENDELSSOHN
WASHINGTON POST, THE	SOUSA
WASHINGTON POST MARCH, THE	SOUSA
WASHINGTON POST MARCH	SOUSA
WASHINGTON POST MARCH	SOUSA
WASHINGTON POST MARCH	SOUSA
WAS DIE HIRTEN ALLES ERLEBTEN -- WEIHNACHTSMUSIK FUR	BURKHARD, W.
WAS DIE HIRTEN ALLES ERLEBTEN	BURKHARD, W.
WAS UNSRE KINDER SINGEN	LANG--ED *
WATCHING BREAKERS AND CONVERSATIONS AT SUNDOWN	KURKA, R.
WATCHING MY SAIL BOAT	BRUSSELS, I.
WATCHING THE SOLDIERS	HOPKINS, H.
WATCHMAN'S SONG, OP. 12 NO. 3	GRIEG
WATCHMAN'S SONG, OP. 12 NO. 3	GRIEG
WATCH WHAT HAPPENS	
WATCH WHAT HAPPENS	
WATCH YOUR STEP	KERR
WATER-WHEEL, THE	KEYSOR, C.
WATER, WATER, WILDFLOWER	GREENWOOD
WATERFALL, THE--ARPEGGIO WALTZ	HOBSON, M.
WATERFALL, THE --LA CASCADE--	HEINS, C.
WATERFALL	DUNGAN
WATERFALL	RODGERS
WATERS OF YOSEMITE	TRUAX, J.
WATER BUG, THE	MILES
WATER BUG, THE	MILES
WATER BUG, THE	MILES
WATER LILIES, GAVOTTE	REES
WATER LILIES	KOHLER, F.
WATER LILIES	MIDDLEBROOK
WATER LILIES	WILSON, S.
WATER MUSIC, ADAGIO-BOURREE	HANDEL
WATER MUSIC, ANDANTE-HORNPIPE	HANDEL
WATER MUSIC SUITE	HANDEL
WATER MUSIC	HANDEL
WATER NYMPHS	BRIDGE, F.
WATER SPRITES AT PLAY	HOWELL
WATER SPRITES	FLETCHER, L.
WATER SPRITES	FLETCHER, L.
WATER SPRITE	GOODRICH
WATER SPRITE	TOLLEFSEN, A.
WATER WHEEL, THE.	BAUER, M.
WATER WHEEL, THE	WIGGINS, M.
WATER WHEELS	WILSON
WATER WHEEL	COBB
WATUSI TRUMPETS	
WAVELETS	CANFIELD, J.
WAVES OF THE DANUBE--WALTZ	IVANOVICI, J.
WAVES OF THE DANUBE -- BOOGIE WOOGIE	IVANOVICI, J.
WAVES OF THE DANUBE WALTZ	IVANOVICI, J.
WAVES OF THE DANUBE	IVANOVICI, J.
WAVES OF THE DANUBE	IVANOVICI, J. *
WAVES OF THE DANUBE	IVANOVICI, J.
WAVES OF THE DANUBE	IVANOVICI, J.
WAVES OF THE DANUBE	IVANOVICI, J.
WAVES OF THE DANUBE	IVANOVICI, J.
WAVES OF THE OCEAN, GALOP	BLAKE, C.
WAYFARING STRANGER, THE -- ONE PIANO, SIX HANDS --	KRAEHENBUEHL
WAYFARING STRANGER	STEINER
WAYSIDE CHAPEL, THE	WILSON, G.
WAYSIDE CHAPEL, THE	WILSON, G.
WAYSIDE CHAPEL, THE	WILSON, G.
WAYSIDE CHAPEL	WILSON, G.
WAYSIDE ROSE, THE, OP. 177	FISCHER
WAYWARD WIND	
WAY DOWN UPON THE SWANEE RIVER	FOSTER
WAY UP NORTH	SHEPHERD
WAY WE WERE, THE	BRADLEY,
WAY WE WERE, THE	BRADLEY,
WAY WE WERE, THE	BRADLEY,
WE'LL GO FISHIN' IN A CRAWDAD HOLE	WEYBRIGHT--ED.
WE'RE IN THE NAVY NOW	THOMPSON, J.--ED
WEARING OF THE GREEN	EMMET *
WEARY PLOWMAN, THE	BUTLER
WEATHER CONVERSATION	WEYBRIGHT
WEB OF LOVELINESS	MEUX
WEDDING-DAY AT TROLDHAUGEN	GRIEG
WEDDING-WALTZ FROM ''DER SCHLEIER DER PIERETTE'' --	DOHNANYI
WEDDING CAKE	STRAUSS, J.
WEDDING DANCE --WITH RUSSIAN FOLK SONG BY ALEXANDROV	LUBARSKY
WEDDING DANCE	PRESS
WEDDING DANCE	PRESS
WEDDING DAY AT TROLDHAUGEN, OP. 65 NO. 6	GRIEG
WEDDING DAY AT TROLDHAUGEN, OP. 65 NO. 6	GRIEG
WEDDING DAY AT TROLDHAUGEN, OP. 65 NO. 6	GRIEG
WEDDING DAY AT TROLDHAUGEN, OP. 65 NO. 6	GRIEG
WEDDING DAY AT TROLDHAUGEN	GRIEG
WEDDING MARCH, FROM 'MID-SUMMER NIGHT'S DREAM'	MENDELSSOHN
WEDDING MARCH FROM 'LOHENGRIN'	WAGNER
WEDDING MARCH FROM 'LOHENGRIN'	WAGNER
WEDDING MARCH FROM 'MIDSUMMER NIGHT'S DREAM'	MENDELSSOHN
WEDDING MARCH	MENDELSSOHN
WEDDING MARCH	MENDELSSOHN
WEDDING MARCH	MENDELSSOHN
WEDDING MARCH	MENDELSSOHN
WEDDING MARCH	MENDELSSOHN
WEDDING MUSIC FOR PIANO SOLO	
WEDDING MUSIC	SCHAUM, J.--ED.
WEDDING OF JACK AND JILL	LANE, J.--ED.
WEDDING OF THE DOLLS	BURNAM
WEDDING OF THE PAINTED DOLL	BROWN *
WEDDING OF THE PAINTED DOLL	LANE, J.--ED.
WEDDING OF THE WINDS	HALL, F.
WEDDING OF THE WINDS	HALL, F.
WEDDING OF THE WINDS	HALL, F.
WEDDING OF THE WINDS	HALL, F.
WEDDING OF THE WINDS	HALL, F.
WEDDING PRAYER	DUNLAP, F.
WEDDING RING WALTZ	HAUBIEL, C.
WEDDING SCENES	SMETANA
WEDDING SONGS --225--	
WEDDING SONG	BRIMHALL,
WEDDING TIME	KENDALL
WEEK OF BIRTHDAYS	BENNETT, R.
WEEPING WILLOW, THE	SCHER, W.
WEEPING WILLOW	JOPLIN, S.
WEE BOBBY ROBIN	ERB
WEE FOLKS' MARCH	RAEZER, C.
WEE 3 MARTIANS	GARROW
WEIGHTLESS, AND MECHANICAL MAN	ALT, H.
WEIHNACHTEN - 6 LEICHTE KLAVIERSTUCKE, OP. 20	BARTOS, J.
WEIHNACHTLICHE HAUSMUSIK -- ELABORATIONS OF 5	PILLNEY--ED
WEIHNACHTS-ALBUM	ZILCHER
WEIHNACHTSABEND, DER, OP. 137	NIEMANN
WEIHNACHTSBUCH. MUSIK AUS 36 ALTEN WEIHNACHTSLIEDERN	DEGEN
WEIHNACHTSBUCH. MUSIK AUS 36 ALTEN WEIHNACHTSLIEDERN	DEGEN
WEIHNACHTSBUCH. MUSIK AUS 36 ALTEN WEIHNACHTSLIEDERN	DEGEN
WEIHNACHTSBUCHLEIN FUR ROSWITHA	ZIPP
WEIHNACHTSLIEDER. KLAVIERAUSGABE ZUM QUEMPAS-BUCH. DIE	
WEIHNACHTSLIEDER FUR KLAVIER. DIE 40 WEIHNACHTSLIEDER	
WEIHNACHTSMUSIK FUR KLAVIER	BOHME--ED
WEIHNACHTSSONATINE, OP. 71 NO. 1	BURKHARD, W.
WEIHNACHTSSONATINE, OP. 71	BURKHARD, W.
WEIHNACHTSTRAUM, FANTASIE UBER, STILLE NACHT OP. 17	REGER
WEIHNACHTSTRAUM OP. 17 NO. 9 ST.-V.S. 29	REGER
WEIHNACHTS LIEDERBUCH, DAS -- 40 CHRISTMAS SONGS WITH	STROHBACH,
WEIRD STORY, A	OGILVY, F.
WEIRD TALE	SCHIEFELBEIN, F.
WELK, LAWRENCE, FAVORITES FOR HONKY TONK PIANO	LITTLE--ED
WELL-PAMPERED PIANIST, THE	AGAY, D.--ED
WELL-TEMPERED CLAVICHORD, BK. 1	BACH, J.S.
WELL-TEMPERED CLAVICHORD, BK. 1	BACH, J.S.
WELL-TEMPERED CLAVICHORD, BK. 2	BACH, J.S.
WELL-TEMPERED CLAVICHORD, BK. 2	BACH, J.S.
WELL-TEMPERED CLAVICHORD, THE--BK. 1	BACH, J.S.
WELL-TEMPERED CLAVICHORD, THE--BK. 1	BACH, J.S.
WELL-TEMPERED CLAVICHORD, THE--BK. 2	BACH, J.S.
WELL-TEMPERED CLAVICHORD, THE--BK. 2	BACH, J.S.
WELL-TEMPERED CLAVICHORD, THE--FIRST 24 PRELUDES AND	BACH, J.S.
WELL-TEMPERED CLAVICHORD, THE--FIRST 24 PRELUDES AND	BACH, J.S.
WELL-TEMPERED CLAVICHORD, THE--FIRST 24 PRELUDES AND	BACH, J.S.
WELL-TEMPERED CLAVICHORD, THE, BK. 1	BACH, J.S.
WELL-TEMPERED CLAVIER, THE--VOL. 1	BACH, J.S.
WELL-TEMPERED CLAVIER, THE--VOL. 1	BACH, J.S.
WELL-TEMPERED CLAVIER, THE--VOL. 2	BACH, J.S.
WELL-TEMPERED CLAVIER, THE--VOL. 2	BACH, J.S.
WELL-TEMPERED CLAVIER, THE--VOL. 3	BACH, J.S.
WELL-TEMPERED CLAVIER, THE--VOL. 4	BACH, J.S.
WELL-TEMPERED CLAVIER, THE--VOL. 5	BACH, J.S.
WELL-TEMPERED CLAVIER, THE--VOL. 6	BACH, J.S.
WELL-TEMPERED CLAVIER, THE--VOL. 7	BACH, J.S.
WELL-TEMPERED CLAVIER, THE--VOL. 8	BACH, J.S.
WELL-TEMPERED CLAVIER, THE, BK. 1	BACH, J.S.
WELL-TEMPERED CLAVIER, THE, BK. 1	BACH, J.S.
WELL-TEMPERED CLAVIER, THE, BK. 2	BACH, J.S.
WELL-TEMPERED CLAVIER, THE, BK. 2	BACH, J.S.
WELL-TEMPERED CLAVIER, THE, VOL. 1 --URTEXT--	BACH, J.S.
WELL-TEMPERED CLAVIER, THE, VOL. 1	BACH, J.S.
WELL-TEMPERED CLAVIER, THE, VOL. 1	BACH, J.S.
WELL-TEMPERED CLAVIER, THE, VOL. 1	BACH, J.S.
WELL-TEMPERED CLAVIER, THE, VOL. 1	BACH, J.S.
WELL-TEMPERED CLAVIER, THE, VOL. 1	BACH, J.S.
WELL-TEMPERED CLAVIER, THE, VOL. 2 --URTEXT--	BACH, J.S.
WELL-TEMPERED CLAVIER, THE, VOL. 2	BACH, J.S.
WELL-TEMPERED CLAVIER, THE, VOL. 2	BACH, J.S.
WELL-TEMPERED CLAVIER, THE, VOL. 2	BACH, J.S.
WELL-TEMPERED CLAVIER, THE, VOL. 2	BACH, J.S.
WELL-TEMPERED CLAVIER, THE, VOL. 2	BACH, J.S.
WELL-TEMPERED CLAVIER, THE -- PART 1 -- CLOTH	BACH, J.S.
WELL-TEMPERED CLAVIER, THE -- PART 1 -- WITHOUT	BACH, J.S.
WELL-TEMPERED CLAVIER, THE -- PART 1 -- WITHOUT	BACH, J.S.
WELL-TEMPERED CLAVIER, THE -- PART 1	BACH, J.S.
WELL-TEMPERED CLAVIER, THE -- PART 2 -- CLOTH	BACH, J.S.
WELL-TEMPERED CLAVIER, THE -- PART 2 -- WITHOUT	BACH, J.S.
WELL-TEMPERED CLAVIER, THE -- PART 2 -- WITHOUT	BACH, J.S.
WELL-TEMPERED CLAVIER, THE -- PART 2	BACH, J.S.
WELL-TEMPERED CLAVIER --URTEXT--, COMPLETE IN 2 VOLS.	BACH, J.S.
WELL-TEMPERED CLAVIER --URTEXT--, COMPLETE IN 2 VOLS.	BACH, J.S.
WERE I A BIRD, OP. 2 NO. 6	HENSELT, A.
WERKEN VOOR CLAVECIMBEL	FIOCCO, J.
WERKEN VOOR CLAVECIMBEL	LOEILLET
WERKE FUR CEMBALO. SUITEN NO. 1, 4 UND 6 IN H, C UND D	DANDRIEU, P.
WERKE FUR KLAVIER ZU VIER HANDEN, K19D, 381, 358, 497,	MOZART, W. A.
WERKE FUR ORGEL UND CEMBALO, BK. 2 -- CEMBALO	ZIPOLI
WERKE FUR ORGEL UND CLAVIER -- GESAMTAUSGABE DER	PACHELBEL
WERKE FUR TASTENINSTRUMENTE -- PARTHIEN IN A MINOR, F,	FUX
WERKE FUR 2 KLAVIERE, K488 UND 426 -- NEUE	MOZART, W. A.
WERTHER	MASSENET, J.
WESTERN LULLABY	ROBINSON, A.
WESTERN NOCTURNE	HIBBS, C.
WESTERN ONTARIO CONSERVATORY OF MUSIC -- GRADED	
WESTERN ONTARIO CONSERVATORY OF MUSIC -- GRADED	
WESTERN ONTARIO CONSERVATORY OF MUSIC -- GRADED	
WESTERN ONTARIO CONSERVATORY OF MUSIC -- GRADED	
WESTERN ONTARIO CONSERVATORY OF MUSIC -- GRADED	
WESTERN ONTARIO CONSERVATORY OF MUSIC -- GRADED	
WESTERN ONTARIO CONSERVATORY OF MUSIC -- GRADED	
WESTERN ONTARIO CONSERVATORY OF MUSIC -- GRADED	
WESTERN ONTARIO CONSERVATORY OF MUSIC -- GRADED	
WESTERN ONTARIO CONSERVATORY OF MUSIC -- TECHNICAL	
WESTERN ONTARIO CONSERVATORY OF MUSIC -- TECHNICAL	
WESTERN SERENADE	VALENTI, M.
WESTERN SKY	GREEN, R.

Title	Composer
WESTERN SONG	BAUER
WESTERN STORY, A	ROGERS, E.
WESTERN WALTZ	DONENFELD, J.
WESTMORELAND-KAHN PIANO COURSE, BK. 1, STUDENT'S	WESTMORELAND-KAH
WESTMORELAND-KAHN PIANO COURSE, BK. 1, TEACHER'S	WESTMORELAND-KAH
WESTMORELAND-KAHN PIANO COURSE, BK. 2, STUDENT'S	WESTMORELAND-KAH
WESTMORELAND-KAHN PIANO COURSE, BK. 2, TEACHER'S	WESTMORELAND-KAH
WESTMORELAND-KAHN PIANO COURSE, BK. 3, STUDENT'S	WESTMORELAND-KAH
WESTMORELAND-KAHN PIANO COURSE, BK. 3, TEACHER'S	WESTMORELAND-KAH
WESTWARD HO	MCHALE, M.
WEST COUNTRY SUITE	LEE
WEST SIDE STORY, SELECTIONS FROM	BERNSTEIN, L.
WEST SIDE STORY, SELECTIONS FROM	BERNSTEIN, L.
WEYBRIGHT DUET BOOK	WEYBRIGHT
WEYBRIGHT DUET BOOK	WEYBRIGHT
WEYBRIGHT SOLO PIANO ALBUM, BK. 1	WEYBRIGHT
WEYBRIGHT SOLO PIANO ALBUM, BK. 1	WEYBRIGHT
WEYBRIGHT SOLO PIANO ALBUM, BK. 2	WEYBRIGHT
WEYBRIGHT SOLO PIANO ALBUM, BK. 3	WEYBRIGHT
WE ARE TOGETHER	LANE, J.--ED.
WE COWBOYS	WEYBRIGHT
WE COWBOYS	WEYBRIGHT
WE FOLLOW THE BAND - FOR ONE PIANO, SIX HANDS	VANDEVERE
WE GATHER TOGETHER	POST--ED
WE GO HIKING - FOR ONE PIANO, SIX HANDS	VANDEVERE
WE GO MARCHING	WRIGHT, N.
WE GO SAILING - FOR ONE PIANO, SIX HANDS	VANDEVERE
WE KISS IN A SHADOW	HAMMERSTEIN *
WE NEED A LITTLE CHRISTMAS	BRIMHALL,
WE SING-WE PLAY --HAPPY SONGS FOR LITTLE VOICES	KNIPPEL--ED.
WE TWO	EZELL, H.
WE WALTZ - FOR ONE PIANO, SIX HANDS	VANDEVERE
WE WISH YOU A MERRY CHRISTMAS, BK. 1	STECHER *
WE WISH YOU A MERRY CHRISTMAS, BK. 2	STECHER *
WE WISH YOU A MERRY CHRISTMAS	NEVIN
WHAT'S THIS	COWELL
WHAT ARE YOU DOING THE REST OF YOUR LIFE	LANE, J.--ED.
WHAT A DIFFERENCE A DAY MADE	GREVER *
WHAT A LONG FREIGHT TRAIN	ALT
WHAT CHILD IS THIS	SCHAUM, W.--ED
WHAT COLOR IS THE TREE TOAD	HOFSTAD, M.
WHAT IS A YOUTH --ROMEO AND JULIET --	BRIMHALL,
WHAT NOW MY LOVE	BECAUD
WHAT NOW MY LOVE	BECAUD *
WHAT SHALL WE DO WHEN WE ALL GO OUT	WEYBRIGHT
WHAT THE WORLD NEEDS NOW IS LOVE	BRIMHALL,
WHEELS	ALT, H.
WHEELS	GROFE, F.
WHEELS	OLSON
WHEN A MAID COMES KNOCKING AT YOUR HEART--''THE	FRIML, R.
WHEN DAY IS DONE	KATCHER
WHEN IT'S SLEEPY TIME DOWN SOUTH -- SIMP.	MOSSMAN, T.--ED
WHEN IT'S SPRINGTIME IN THE ROCKIES	LANE, J.--ED.
WHEN IT'S SPRINGTIME IN THE ROCKIES	
WHEN I GO WALKING	DITTENHAVER
WHEN I GROW TOO OLD TO DREAM	LANE, J.--ED.
WHEN I GROW TOO OLD TO DREAM	
WHEN I RIDE A BUCKING BRONCO -- WITH WORDS	BURNAM
WHEN JOHNNY COMES MARCHING HOME --CONCERT VARIATIONS--	WATSON
WHEN JOHNNY COMES MARCHING HOME	KRAEHENBUEHL--AR
WHEN JOHNNY COMES MARCHING HOME	LAMBERT
WHEN MARIA SINGS AND PLAYS HER GUITAR	JESSE, M.
WHEN MY BIRTHDAY COMES	RICHTER
WHEN NIGHT BEGINS	BRODSKY, M.
WHEN NOTES GO SKIPPING	BLAKE
WHEN NOTES GO WALKING	BLAKE
WHEN TEACHER'S AWAY	GLOVER, D.
WHEN THE HEART IS YOUNG	LANG, V.
WHEN THE MOON COMES OVER THE MOUNTAIN	LANE, J.--ED.
WHEN THE SAINTS GO MARCHING IN	FRANGIPANE--ED
WHEN THE SAINTS GO MARCHING IN	SCHAUM, J.--ED.
WHEN THE SAINTS GO MARCHING	FRANGIPANE--ED
WHEN THE SUN GOES DOWN	ANSON, G.
WHEN WOLVES MET	SUCHON, E.
WHEN YOU AND I WERE YOUNG 'MAGGIE BOOGIE'	SCHAUM, J.--ED.
WHEN YOU AND I WERE YOUNG MAGGIE -- VARIATIONS	DRUMHELLER
WHEN YOU AND I WERE YOUNG MAGGIE	BUTTERFIELD
WHEN YOU SAY LOVE	BRADLEY,
WHEN YOU WORE A TULIP	LANE, J.--ED.
WHEN YOU WORE A TULIP	
WHERE'ER YOU WALK	HANDEL
WHERE ARE THOSE PIRATES BOLD	ZEPP--ED
WHERE ARE YOU GOING PRETTY MAID	ROLFE, W.
WHERE BUFFALO ROAM	SCHAUM, J.--ED.
WHERE DO I BEGIN --LOVE STORY --	BRIMHALL,
WHERE GO THE CLOUDS	DITTENHAVER
WHERE IS CINDERELLA	HAMMERSTEIN *
WHERE IS THE LOVE	BRADLEY,
WHERE MEMORY DWELLS	DRUMHELLER
WHERE OR WHEN	
WHERE PLAYING FINGERS BEGIN	FROST
WHERE THE CITRONS BLOOM	STRAUSS, J.
WHERE THE RIVER SHANNON FLOWS	RUSSELL
WHERE THE SHADOW LIES	HAUBIEL, C.
WHILE STROLLING THROUGH THE PARK ONE DAY	SCHAUM, J.--ED.
WHILE WALTZING, OP. 73	LACK, T.
WHIMSEYS	ROSCO
WHIMSIES	TAYLOR, C.
WHIMS -- GRILLEN, OP. 12 NO. 4	SCHUMANN, R.
WHIMS - GRILLEN, OP. 12 NO. 4	SCHUMANN, R.
WHIMS	SMITH
WHIP-POOR-WILL	ARNOLD, H.
WHIRLIGIGS	ERB
WHIRLIGIG	RUBINSTEIN, B.
WHIRLIGIG	WEYBRIGHT
WHIRLING ALONG	MCGRAW
WHIRLING AND TWIRLING	VANNORT, I.
WHIRLING DANCERS	DITTENHAVER
WHIRLING DANCERS	WATSON
WHIRLING DERVISHES CHORUS	BEETHOVEN *
WHIRLING DERVISH	ANSON, G.
WHIRLING DERVISH	HAUBIEL, C.
WHIRLING LEAVES	BURNAM
WHIRLPOOL	REISER, V.
WHIRLWIND POLKA	HOLST
WHIRLWIND	CROCKER, D.
WHIRLWIND	GILLOCK
WHIRLWIND	HOWELL
WHIRLY-BIRD	CHAGY
WHIRLYBIRD	COBB
WHIRLY BIRD	GARROW, L.
WHISPERINGS OF LOVE, VALSE	KINKEL, C.
WHISPERING HOPE	HAWTHORNE, A.
WHISPERING HOPE	HAWTHORNE, A.
WHISPERING HOPE	HAWTHORNE, A.
WHISPERING HOPE	HAWTHORNE, A.
WHISPERING RAIN	KRENZ, B.
WHISPERING WIND, THE	MALTZMAN
WHISPERING WINDS	KING, S.
WHISPERING	COBURN *
WHISPERING	LANE, J.--ED.
WHISTLER AND HIS DOG	PRYOR
WHISTLER AND HIS DOG	PRYOR
WHISTLIN' TUNE	DONENFELD, J.
WHISTLING BOY	JOYNER, B.
WHISTLING BOY	MCSWEEN, F. W.
WHISTLING COWBOY	GARROW
WHISTLING DOWN THE ROAD I GO	MUNN, W.
WHISTLING FARMER BOY, THE	VANNORT, I.
WHISTLING FARM BOY	MILLIGAN
WHISTLING GONDOLIER, THE	MARTIN, E.
WHISTLING GONDOLIER, THE	MARTIN
WHISTLING PARAKEET, THE	PARKER, J.
WHISTLING TUNE -- OSTINATO	KUBIK, G.
WHISTLING TUNE	ROGERS, E.
WHITECAPS	CARRE
WHITECAPS	CARRE
WHITE AND BLACK IVORIES	STEINER
WHITE BUTTERFLY	CANICE
WHITE CAPS. RONDO FROM SONATINA	COULTHARD
WHITE CLIFFS OF DOVER, THE.	BRYANT--ED.
WHITE CLIFFS OF DOVER, THE	BURNAM
WHITE CLOUDS	STEVENS
WHITE HERON	DUNGAN
WHITE MICE	HIBBS, C.
WHITE NOTES, THE	GREENE, H.
WHITE ORCHIDS	COOKE
WHITE ORCHIDS	DE ROSE, P.
WHITE ROSES - 15 VERY EASY PIECES	DE ANGELIS
WHITE SAILS IN THE MOONLIGHT	ARCHER, I.
WHITE SAILS	LANE, J.
WHITE SWAN	FROST
WHITE TULIPS	LANE, J.
WHITE VIOLETS	WHITFORD
WHITHER THOU GOEST	LANE, J.--ED.
WHIZ, GOES THE TRAIN	ERB, M.
WHO'S THAT KNOCKING	CLARK, M. E.
WHO'S THAT TAPPING AT MY WINDOW	WEYBRIGHT
WHODUNIT	KELLEY, R.
WHOO'S WHOO	SCARMOLIN
WHOOP 'ER UP	WOOD, W.
WHO IS SYLVIA	SCHUBERT
WHO SAID DREAMS DON'T COME TRUE	AKST *
WHO	
WHYDAH VARIATIONS	BUSH
WHY DAISIES DANCE	RICHTER, A.
WHY DON'T DUCKS GET WET	ELLIOTT
WHY DO I LOVE YOU	
WHY TRY TO CHANGE ME NOW	
WHY WAS I BORN	
WHY	BRIMHALL,
WHY	SCHUMANN, R.
WICHTELMANNCHEN OP. 27	HAAS
WICKED WORLD WALTZ--2, 3, OR 4 PIANOS	METIS, F.
WIDE MISSOURI, THE	SCHAUM, J.--ED.
WIDMUNG -- DEDICATION --, OP. 25 NO. 1	SCHUMANN, R.
WIDMUNG	SCHUMANN, R. *
WIDMUNG	SCHUMANN, R. *
WIEGENLIED, OP. 41 NO. 1, AND 'ICH LIEBE DICH' OP. 41	GRIEG
WIEGENLIED -- CRADLE SONG --	HAUSER
WIEGENLIED -- MIT TEXT	MOZART, W. A.
WIEGENLIED OP. 49 NO. 4	BRAHMS
WIEGENLIED UND CAPRICCIO	DVORAK
WIEGENLIED	SCHUBERT
WIEN, WEIB UND GESANG	STRAUSS, J. *
WIEN, WIEN NUR DU ALLEIN	
WIENER BLUT	STRAUSS, J.
WIENER HOFBALL MINUETS	HAYDN
WIENER LUFT	DOUCET, C.
WIENER TANZE UND STUCKE	SCHUBERT
WIGWAM DANCE	HOPKINS, H.
WIGWAM LULLABY	JESSE, M.
WILD BLOSSOMS	QUINCKE, W.
WILD DAISIES	BASTIEN
WILD HORSEMAN, THE, OP. 68 NO. 08--ALBUM FOR THE YOUNG	SCHUMANN, R.
WILD HORSEMAN, THE, OP. 68 NO. 8	SCHUMANN, R.
WILD HORSEMAN, THE, OP. 68 NO. 8	SCHUMANN, R.
WILD HORSES	FREED, S.
WILD RIDER, THE	SCHUMANN, R.
WILD RIDER, THE	SCHUMANN, R.
WILD RIDERS	ERB
WILD ROSES	LEONI, F.
WILD ROSE WALTZ	READ, E.
WILL-O'-THE-WISP--CAPRICCIETTO	JUNGMANN, A.
WILLIAM TELL -- FANFARE	ROSSINI, G.
WILLIAM TELL OVERTURE, EASY	ROSSINI, G.
WILLIAM TELL OVERTURE	ROSSINI, G.
WILLIAM TELL	ROSSINI, G.
WILLIE THE WAFFLE	SUDDARDS
WILLIE WE HAVE MISSED YOU	FOSTER
WILLIS ROADWAY BIG NOTE PIECES	
WILLIS ROADWAY PIANO BOOK FOR CHILDREN	
WILLIS ROADWAY TO CLASSICS	
WILLIS ROADWAY TO PIANO DUETS	
WILLOWS, THE	MELECCI, A.
WILLOWS ARE NEW, THE --AFTER WANG WEI'S YANG KUANG--	CHOU WEN-CHUNG
WILLOWS ARE WALTZING	LUBIN, E.
WILLY-NILLY WALTZ	MARTINA
WILL O' THE WISP	JUNGMAN, A.
WILL O' THE WISP	TROWBRIDGE, L.
WILL YOU REMEMBER--FROM 'MAYTIME'	ROMBERG, S.
WILL YOU REMEMBER--FROM 'MAYTIME'	ROMBERG, S.
WILL YOU REMEMBER--FROM 'MAYTIME'	ROMBERG, S.
WILL YOU REMEMBER--FROM 'MAYTIME'	ROMBERG, S.
WILL YOU STILL BE MINE	
WILSON CLOG AND JELLY JIG	GUENTHER
WIND-UP SOLDIER	GLOVER, D.
WIND, THE--ETUDE, OP. 15, NO. 2	ALKAN
WINDING RIVER	GARROW, L.
WINDING ROAD, THE	COBB
WINDJAMMER	
WINDMILL, THE	DAGINCOURT, P.
WINDMILLS AND TULIPS	MUNN, W.
WINDMILLS OF YOUR MIND, THE	LANE, J.--ED.
WINDMILLS OF YOUR MIND	LANE, J.--ED.
WINDMILLS	MARTINO
WINDMILL LAND	FURZE
WINDOW WASHER, THE	HELLER, E.
WINDSHIELD WIPER ROCK	NOBLITT, K. M.
WINDSOR DANCES, THE	HARRIS, W. H.
WINDSOR MELODY, THE	GAY
WINDY DAY, A, CAPRICE	HOPKINS, H.

Title	Composer
WINDY WEATHER	WRIGHT, L.
WINDY	BRIMHALL,
WIND AND SAIL	LAKE, G.
WIND CRADLE	DANIEL, K.
WIND DOTH BLOW, THE	MYERS, T.
WIND IN THE PINES	HOWELL
WIND IN THE PLAIN, THE, FROM PRELUDES, BK. 1	DEBUSSY
WIND IN THE TREES	BARTHELSON, J.
WIND IS WILD, THE	MCCLUSKY
WIND OVER THE PINES	WRIGHT, N.
WINE, WOMEN AND SONG, OP. 333	STRAUSS, J.
WINE, WOMEN AND SONG, OP. 333	STRAUSS, J.
WING FOO OP. 1 NO. 1	BURLEIGH, C.
WINNING DANCE TEAM	STEINER
WINSOME	WEYBRIGHT
WINTERREIGEN, OP. 13 -- TEN BAGATELLES	DOHNANYI
WINTER FROLIC	IBBOTSON, E. M.
WINTER FROST	WEYBRIGHT
WINTER LANDSCAPE	TAYLOR, C.
WINTER MOONLIGHT	DILLON, F.
WINTER SUNSET	STRUM, E.
WINTER WINDS	ROBINSON, A.
WINTER WIND	ANSON, G.
WINTER WIND	EISLER
WINTER WIND	GLOVER, D.
WINTER WONDERLAND	BRADLEY,
WINTER WONDERLAND	BRADLEY,
WINTER WONDERLAND	BRIMHALL,
WINTER	RAYMOND
WIRE-HAIRED FOX-TERRIER	BARTH, H.
WIR BAUEN EINE STADT, KLAVIERSTUCKE FUR KINDER, 1931	HINDEMITH
WIR MUSIZIEREN AN ZWEI KLAVIEREN. 12 KLEINE STUCKE	BACH, J.S. *
WIR SINGEN ALLE MIT	PIECHLER--ED
WIR SPIELEN VIERHANDIG, 12 LEICHTE VORTRAGSSTUCKE	HUMMEL, J. N. *
WIR SPIELEN ZUR WEIHNACHT, OP. 43. SOPRANO RECORDER	WERNER, F.--ED.
WIR SPIELEN ZUR WEIHNACHT, OP. 43. 26 OLD CHRISTMAS	WERNER, F.--ED.
WISE OLD-OWL, THE	STAIRS, L.
WISE OLD OWL	BASTIEN
WISHBONE WALTZ	ECKSTEIN
WISHING STAR, THE	VANNORT, I.
WISHING STAR WALTZ	SCHAUM, J.--ED.
WISHING WALTZ	GLOVER, D.
WISH FROM BEETHOVEN'S SYMPHONY NO. 3, A	ROLFE, W.
WISH YOU WERE HERE	SINGER, L.--ED
WISH YOU WERE HERE	
WISTFUL LITTLE GIRL	GANZ
WISTFUL LITTLE PRINCESS, THE	DONATO, A.
WISTFUL MAZURKA	GRETCHANINOFF
WISTFUL TUNE	JUDD, A.
WISTFUL WALTZ	MCGRAW
WITCH, THE	MURRAY, B.
WITCHCRAFT	BRIMHALL,
WITCHCRAFT	ROGERS
WITCHCRAFT	STEINER
WITCHES' DANCE, OP. 17, NO. 2	MACDOWELL
WITCHES' DANCE, OP. 17 NO. 2	MACDOWELL
WITCHES' DANCE, OP. 17	MACDOWELL
WITCHES' DANCE, OP. 74	SCHYTTE
WITCHES' DANCE --HEXENTANZ--, OP. 17, NO. 2	MACDOWELL
WITCHES' DANCE	LEMONT, C. W.
WITCHES' DANCE	MACDOWELL
WITCHES' REVELS, OP. 66 NO. 24	SCHYTTE
WITCHES' REVELS	SCHYTTE
WITCHES AT MIDNIGHT	MCGRATH
WITCHES FLIGHT, B FLAT	RUSSELL
WITCHES IN THE SKY	OBENCHAIN, V.
WITCHES IN THE WIND	ADAMS
WITCHES PARTY, ON THE BROOMSTICK	EZELL, H.
WITCHES REVEL	SCHYTTE
WITCH SONG, THE. MELODRAMA	SCHILLINGS
WITHIN A JEWEL BOX	BURNAM
WITHOUT A SONG	ELISCU *
WITHOUT YOU	BRIMHALL,
WITH A NOTE OF SADNESS	WILSON, M.
WITH A SONG IN MY HEART	RODGERS
WITH A SONG IN MY HEART	RODGERS
WITH CHARMING GRACE	ROLFE, W.
WITH FRILLS AND BOWS--WITH WORDS	VANNORT, I.
WITH HOUND AND HORN	BILBRO, M.
WITH MY LOVE, EASY	BEAUMONT, P.
WITH THE BEETLES	REISTRUP, J.
WITH TWENTY FINGERS, VOL. 1	VAN SLYCK, N.
WITH TWENTY FINGERS, VOL. 2	VAN SLYCK, N.
WITH TWENTY FINGERS, VOL. 3	VAN SLYCK, N.
WITH YOU, MY OWN	FLYNN *
WIZARD OF OZ, THE	HERBERT
WIZARD OF THE NILE, THE	
WOHIN OP. 25 NO. 2	SCHUBERT
WOHLKLINGENDE FINGERSPRACHE, DIE--FUGUES AND PIECES	MATTHESON, J.
WOMAN'S KISS, A--"THE FIREFLY"	FRIML, R.
WOMEN COMPOSERS OF THE UNITED STATES	SCHAUM, J.--ED.
WON'T YOU COME HOME, BILL BAILEY	STEINER
WON'T YOU COME OVER TO MY HOUSE	VAN ALSTYNE, E.
WONDERFUL GUY, A	RODGERS *
WONDERFUL GUY, THE	HAMMERSTEIN *
WONDERFUL MUSIC OF CHRISTMAS	NEVIN
WONDERFUL ONE	LANE, J.--ED.
WONDERFUL ONE	SAVINO--ED.
WONDERFUL TOWN	LEWIS *
WONDERFUL WORLD OF BROADWAY, BK. 1	
WONDERFUL WORLD OF BROADWAY, BK. 2	
WONDERFUL WORLD OF BROADWAY, BK. 3	
WONDERFUL WORLD OF BROADWAY, BK. 4	
WONDERFUL WORLD OF BROADWAY, BK. 5	
WONDERFUL WORLD OF RICHARD RODGERS, THE. -- EASYPLAY	RODGERS
WONDERFUL WORLD	ERB
WONDER OF YOU, THE	KNIGHT
WOOD-NYMPH'S FROLIC	AARON, M.
WOODBINE	SMALLWOOD
WOODCHOPPER'S BALL	BISHOP *
WOODCHOPPER AND THE LINNET	GODARD, B.
WOODEN PRINCE --COMPLETE BALLET--	BARTOK
WOODEN SHOES	AARON, M.
WOODEN SHOES	KEENAN
WOODEN SHOE DANCE	BISHOP
WOODEN SHOE DANCE	BLAKE, D.
WOODEN SHOE DANCE	KOUNTZ, R.
WOODEN SHOE DANCE	WRAY, J.
WOODEN SHOE DANCE	WRIGHT
WOODEN SHOE POLKA	REEVES, R.
WOODEN SOLDIERS ON PARADE	JESSEL
WOODLANDS	COLOMBATTI, H.
WOODLAND CASCADE	AARON, M.
WOODLAND DREAMS, OP. 65	WYMAN, A.
WOODLAND ECHOES, NO. 1	YUILL, M.
WOODLAND ECHOES, OP. 34	WYMAN, A.
WOODLAND ECHOES, OP. 34	WYMAN, A.
WOODLAND ECHOES REVERIES	SEIDT, J.
WOODLAND ECHOES	WYMAN, A.
WOODLAND FAIRY	FERNANDEZ, O.
WOODLAND FROLIC	OLDENBURG, E.
WOODLAND LEGEND, A	GILLOCK
WOODLAND ORCHESTRA	JEAN, E.
WOODLAND PINES	RUNGEE
WOODLAND SKETCHES, OP. 51	MACDOWELL
WOODLAND SKETCHES, OP. 51	MACDOWELL
WOODLAND SKETCHES	MACDOWELL
WOODLAND SKETCHES	MACDOWELL
WOODLAND SKETCHES	MACDOWELL
WOODLAND VOICE	MARTIN, G.
WOODLAND WALTZ	CRERIE, E.
WOODLAND WALTZ	GWYNN, F.
WOODLAND WATERFALL	FRAZEE, G. F.
WOODPECKER, THE	DITTENHAVER
WOODPECKER, THE	RICHTER
WOODPECKER	CALWELL
WOODPECKER	PANELLA, L.
WOODS AT DAWN	KERR, R. N.
WOODS AT NIGHT	RASBACH, O.
WOODY HERMAN FIVE BOOGIE WOOGIE AND BLUES SOLOS	HERMAN
WOOD BIRD'S CAROL, OP. 16 NO. 7	BARTH, O.
WOOD CUTTER	HAZELL
WOOD LAND LEGEND, A	GILLOCK
WOOD MAGIC	COUGILL, B.
WOOD NYMPH'S HARP, THE	REA
WOOD NYMPH'S SERENADE, NO. 2	YUILL, M.
WOOD SPRITE, THE	SCHUMANN, J.
WORKBOOK IN MUSICAL NOTATION, BK. 1	STEINER
WORKBOOK IN MUSICAL NOTATION, BK. 2	STEINER
WORKS FOR KEYBOARD INSTRUMENTS	BACH, J.S.
WORKS FOR ORGAN AND KEYBOARD	PACHELBEL
WORKS FOR PIANO, 4 HANDS --VIENNA URTEXT 'ED.--	MOZART, W. A.
WORKS FOR PIANO AND ORCHESTRA	CHOPIN
WORKS FOR PIANO AND ORCHESTRA	CHOPIN
WORKS FOR PIANO FOUR HANDS	MOZART, W. A.
WORKS FOR PIANO OR ORGAN	PACHELBEL
WORKS FOR 2 PIANOS KV 448 AND 426	MOZART, W. A.
WORK AND PLAY, BK. 1	ROBINSON, E. *
WORK AND PLAY, BK. 1	VOSS, L.
WORK AND PLAY, BK. 2	ROBINSON, E. *
WORK AND PLAY, BK. 2	VOSS, L.
WORK AND PLAY, BK. 3	VOSS, L.
WORLD'S FAIR SUITE	GROFE, F.
WORLD'S GREATEST MELODIES	POLLA, W.--ED.
WORLDS GREATEST BOOK OF CLASSIC THEMES	BRIMHALL,
WORLDS GREATEST BOOK OF WEDDING SONGS	BRIMHALL,
WORLDS GREATEST DIXIELAND PIANO SOLOS	BRIMHALL,
WORLDS GREATEST HITS FOR CHORD PLAYING	BRIMHALL,
WORLDS GREATEST HITS FROM 1900-1919	BRIMHALL,
WORLDS GREATEST HITS OF COUNTRY MUSIC	BRIMHALL,
WORLDS GREATEST HITS OF POPULAR CHORALS	BRIMHALL,
WORLDS GREATEST HITS OF THE WONDERFUL CHILD	BRIMHALL,
WORLDS GREATEST JAZZ PIANO SOLOS AND SONGS	BRIMHALL,
WORLDS GREATEST NATIONAL ANTHEMS	BRIMHALL,
WORLD AROUND	SCHER, W.
WORLD FAMOUS CHRISTMAS CAROLS	BERLIN, B.
WORLD FAMOUS MARCH ALBUM	
WORLD FAMOUS MELODIES	THOMPSON, J.--ED
WORLD FAMOUS PIANO CLASSICS	FREY--ED
WORLD FAMOUS PIANO PIECES	FREY--ED
WORLD FAMOUS PIANO PIECES	
WORLD FAMOUS SONGS	
WORLD FAMOUS WALTZ ALBUM	
WORLD IS A CIRCLE, THE - AND - REFLECTIONS	BRADLEY,
WORLD IS A CIRCLE, THE	BRADLEY,
WORLD IS WAITING FOR THE SUNRISE, THE	SINGER, L.--ED
WORLD IS WAITING FOR THE SUNRISE, THE	
WORLD KNOWN MELODIES	THOMPSON, J.--ED
WORLD OF MODERN PIANO MUSIC, THE.	
WORLD OF OPERA, THE	
WORRIED MAN BLUES, THE -- AN EARLY AMERICAN TUNE	WEYBRIGHT
WORSHIP HYMNS FOR PIANO	WINANS, W. L.
WOULDN'T BE LOVERLY	SINGER, L.--ED
WOW, NEW SHOES	GLOVER, D.
WRIST AND ARM TECHNIC	THOMPSON, J. *
WRITE AND PLAY MAJOR SCALES	GLOVER, D. *
WRITE AND PLAY MINOR SCALES	GLOVER, D. *
WRITE AND PLAY THE SCALES AND CHORDS	ECKSTEIN
WRITE AND PLAY TIME - PART A	CLARK, F.--ED.
WRITE AND PLAY TIME - PART B	CLARK, F.--ED.
WUNDERBAR -- SHOWCASE	
WURTEMBERG SONATAS WQ 49, BK. 1	BACH, C.P.E.
WURTEMBERG SONATAS WQ 49, BK. 2	BACH, C.P.E.
WURTTEMBERGISCHEN SONATEN, DIE, WQ 49, HEFT 1 -- A	BACH, C.P.E.
WURTTEMBERGISCHEN SONATEN, DIE, WQ 49, HEFT 2 -- B	BACH, C.P.E.
WYNKEN, BLYNKEN AND NOD	FIELD, E. *
WYNKUM AND BLYNKUM	HOPKINS, H.
XENIEN, OP. 27	KLUSSMANN
XENOPHONE ET LA SYBILLE	BACH, C.P.E.
XERXES, LARGO, EASY	HANDEL
YAFFLE, THE	MACONCHY
YAN, 6 IMPRESSIONS, NO. 1--YAN PREGA	LLONGUERAS, J.
YAN, 6 IMPRESSIONS, NO. 2--YAN JUGA	LLONGUERAS, J.
YAN, 6 IMPRESSIONS, NO. 3--YAN DANCA	LLONGUERAS, J.
YAN, 6 IMPRESSIONS, NO. 4--YAN CANTA	LLONGUERAS, J.
YAN, 6 IMPRESSIONS, NO. 5--YAN PLORA	LLONGUERAS, J.
YAN, 6 IMPRESSIONS, NO. 6--YAN DORM	LLONGUERAS, J.
YANCEY SPECIAL	LEWIS *
YANINA	BERLIN, B.
YANKEES IN FRANCE	NIRELLA, D.
YANKEE DOODLE -- PIANO TRIO	WEYBRIGHT--ED.
YANKEE DOODLE BOY	COHAN
YANKEE DOODLE DANDIED	ROGERS
YANKEE DOODLE DANDY	COHAN
YANKEE DOODLE DOODLES -- A THEME AND TWELVE VARIATIONS	DAVIS, J.
YANKEE DOODLE	BISHOP
YANKEE DOODLE	STIEFEL, E.
YANKEE DOODLE	WALLIS
YARAVI - FROM 'APURIMAC', OP. 5	NAPOLITANO
YAYA, THE DOLL	FERNANDEZ, O.
YELLOW BIRD	LUBOFF, N.
YELLOW BIRD	LUBOFF, N.
YELLOW BUTTERFLIES	EVANS, M. L.
YELLOW BUTTERFLIES	STEVENS, E.
YELLOW BUTTERFLY	DVORINE
YELLOW BUTTERFLY	MACLACHLAN
YELLOW CHICK	COBB
YELLOW JACKET	CHAGY
YELLOW JONQUILS	JOHANNING
YELLOW JONQUILS	JOHANNING
YELLOW ROLLS-ROYCE - THEME	ORTOLANI
YELLOW ROSE OF TEXAS	SCHAUM, J.--ED.
YERBA BUENA, SAMBA	GUENTHER
YES, I WILL	KREVIT, W.
YES, THEY LOVE ME	TAYLOR
YESTERDAY'S PIANO SOLOS - BOOK 1	CURCIO--ED
YESTERDAY'S PIANO SOLOS - BOOK 2	CURCIO--ED
YESTERDAY'S PIANO SOLOS	CURCIO--ED

Title	Composer/Editor
YESTERDAYS	RITTMAN--ED
YESTERDAYS	STONE, E.--ED
YESTERDAY	LENNON *
YES INDEED	
YE MERRIE WINTER	BLAKE, D.
YO-YO, THE	WILLIAMS, M.
YOLANDA	RAMOS, E.
YOU'D BE SO NICE TO COME HOME TO	SINGER, L.--ED
YOU'LL NEVER WALK ALONE -- SHOWCASE	
YOU'LL NEVER WALK ALONE	
YOU'LL NEVER WALK ALONE	
YOU'LL NEVER WALK ALONE	
YOU'RE A GRAND OLD FLAG	COHAN
YOU'RE A GRAND OLD FLAG	COHAN
YOU'RE A GRAND OLD FLAG	COHAN
YOU'RE A GRAND OLD FLAG	COHAN
YOU'RE THE COMPOSER	STEINER
YOU'VE GOT A FRIEND	BRADLEY,
YOU'VE GOT A FRIEND	BRADLEY,
YOUNGER THAN SPRINGTIME	HAMMERSTEIN *
YOUNGER THAN SPRINGTIME	
YOUNG AMERICANS	DONENFELD, J.
YOUNG AMERICA AT THE PIANO, BK. 1	AHEARN *
YOUNG AND WARM AND WONDERFUL	SINGER
YOUNG ARTIST, THE	THOMPSON, J.--ED
YOUNG DAYS	KIMES, K.
YOUNG EXPLORER AT THE PIANO, THE	BURROWS *
YOUNG LOVE	BRADLEY,
YOUNG MACDONALD HAD A FARM	ZEPP--ED
YOUNG MOZART FOR THE YOUNG PIANIST, BK. 1	MOZART, W. A.
YOUNG MOZART FOR THE YOUNG PIANIST, BK. 2	MOZART, W. A.
YOUNG MUSICIANS, THE VERY EASIEST OF PIECES	SCHWALM, R.
YOUNG MUSICIANS -- THE VERY EASIEST CHILDREN'S PIECES	SCHWALM, R.
YOUNG OFFICER, THE--OP. 270, NO. 5	BAUMFELDER, F.
YOUNG PEOPLE'S SONATINE	CALABRO, L.
YOUNG PEOPLE AT THE PIANO, BKS. 1 AND 2	BARTOK
YOUNG PIANIST, BK. 1 - ELEMENTARY	KREUTZER
YOUNG PIANIST, BK. 2 - ELEMENTARY	KREUTZER
YOUNG PIANIST, BK. 3 - ELEMENTARY	KREUTZER
YOUNG PIANIST, BK. 4	KREUTZER
YOUNG PIANIST, BK. 5	KREUTZER
YOUNG PIANIST, BK. 6	KREUTZER
YOUNG PIANIST, THE - BOOK 4	KREUTZER
YOUNG PIANIST, THE - BOOK 5	KREUTZER
YOUNG PIANIST, THE - BOOK 6	KREUTZER
YOUNG PIANIST, THE - ELEMENTARY BOOK 1	KREUTZER
YOUNG PIANIST, THE - ELEMENTARY BOOK 2	KREUTZER
YOUNG PIANIST, THE - ELEMENTARY BOOK 3	KREUTZER
YOUNG PIANIST'S BACH, THE	BACH, J.S.
YOUNG PIANIST'S FIRST BIG NOTE SOLOS	GILLOCK
YOUNG PIANIST'S FIRST BOOK	AGAY, D.--ED
YOUNG PIANIST'S FIRST CHRISTMAS	GILLOCK
YOUNG PIANIST'S FIRST CHRISTMAS	GILLOCK
YOUNG PIANIST'S FIRST CHRISTMAS	GILLOCK
YOUNG PIANIST'S HANDEL, THE, BK. 1	HANDEL
YOUNG PIANIST'S HANDEL, THE, BK. 2	HANDEL
YOUNG PIANIST'S REPERTOIRE, BK. 1	WATERMAN *
YOUNG PIANIST'S REPERTOIRE, BK. 2	WATERMAN *
YOUNG PIANISTS' JOYFUL HOUR, BK. 1	BERLIN, B. *
YOUNG PIANISTS' JOYFUL HOUR, BK. 2	BERLIN, B. *
YOUNG PIANIST	BINKERD
YOUNG PIANO PRODIGY, THE	BESTHOFF, M.
YOUNG PRINCE AND PRINCESS, THE	RIMSKY-KORSAKOFF
YOUNG RECITALIST, THE--15 PIANO SOLOS FOR THE	MUNN--ED.
YOUNG RECITALIST, THE	THOMPSON, J.--ED
YOUNG SOLOIST AT THE PIANO, THE, BK. 01	STEINER
YOUNG SOLOIST AT THE PIANO, THE, BK. 02	STEINER
YOUNG VIRTUOSO, THE -- FOR THE EARLY GRADES	AGAY, D.
YOUNG VIRTUOSO PIANIST, IN 40 EXERCISES	HANON, C.
YOUNG WORLD PIANIST	BOCK, F.
YOURE SO VAIN	BRIMHALL,
YOURS--QUIEREME MUCHO	ROIG
YOURS --QUIEREME MUCHO	ROIG
YOUR BACH BOOK	BACH, J.S.
YOUR CHOPIN BOOK	CHOPIN
YOUR FAVORITE DUETS	ANTHONY, G.
YOUR FAVORITE NEGRO SPIRITUALS	
YOUR FAVORITE NEGRO SPIRITUALS	ANTHONY, G.
YOUR FAVORITE SOLOS FOR ADVANCED PIANISTS	ANTHONY, G.
YOUR FAVORITE SOLOS	RICHTER, A.--ED.
YOUR FAVORITE SONGS	AGAY, D.
YOUR FIRST SOLO BOOK -- ELEMENTARY	BERMONT, H.--ED
YOUR HIT TUNES - GREEN BOOK	BERMONT, H.--ED
YOUR HIT TUNES - RED BOOK	LISZT
YOUR LISZT BOOK	MOZART, W. A.
YOUR MOZART BOOK	STEINER
YOUR OWN HARMONIES	AGAY, D.
YOUR PIANO PIECES GRADED FOR YOU	ANTHONY, G.
YOUR SECOND SOLO BOOK	SCRIABINE, A. *
YOUR VERY FIRST FAVORITE SOLOS	PORTER, W.
YOUTHFUL AND EARLY WORKS OF ALEXANDER AND JULIAN	SHLONSKY, V.
YOUTH AND BEAUTY--BOOK 4	KAHN, M.
YOUTH AND BEAUTY DANCE	RICHTER
YOUTH SUITE FOR PIANO	LYON
YOUVE GOT RHYTHM	CLARABELL
YOU ADD THE CHORDS - HOW TO HARMONIZE AT THE PIANO	CLARIBEL
YOU AND I IN MUSIC LAND	SPAULDING, G. L.
YOU AND I WALTZ	STRAUSS, J.
YOU AND I WALTZ	STRAUSS, J.
YOU AND I	HAMMERSTEIN *
YOU AND YOU--WALTZES FROM 'THE BAT'	HAMMERSTEIN *
YOU AND YOU FROM 'FLEDERMAUS'	HOLLANDER
YOU ARE BEAUTIFUL	HOLLANDER
YOU ARE BEAUTIFUL	HOLLANDER
YOU CAN PLAY PIANO SERIES, LEVEL 1 -- YOU CAN PLAY	HOLLANDER
YOU CAN PLAY PIANO SERIES, LEVEL 1 -- YOU CAN PLAY	HOLLANDER
YOU CAN PLAY PIANO SERIES, LEVEL 2 -- YOU CAN PLAY	HOLLANDER
YOU CAN PLAY PIANO SERIES, LEVEL 2 -- YOU CAN PLAY	HOLLANDER
YOU CAN PLAY PIANO SERIES, LEVEL 2 -- YOU CAN PLAY	HOLLANDER
YOU CAN PLAY PIANO SERIES, LEVEL 2 -- YOU CAN PLAY	HOLLANDER
YOU CAN PLAY PIANO SERIES, LEVEL 3 -- YOU CAN PLAY	HOLLANDER
YOU CAN PLAY PIANO SERIES, LEVEL 3 -- YOU CAN PLAY	HOLLANDER
YOU CAN PLAY PIANO SERIES, LEVEL 3 -- YOU CAN PLAY	RICHTER
YOU CAN PLAY THE PIANO, BK. 1	RICHTER
YOU CAN PLAY THE PIANO, BK. 2	RICHTER
YOU CAN PLAY THE PIANO, BK. 3	HAVILL, L.
YOU CAN SIGHT READ -- THE PLEASURES OF PIANO SIGHT	HAVILL, L.
YOU CAN SIGHT READ -- THE PLEASURES OF PIANO SIGHT	
YOU DON'T HAVE TO KNOW	LANE, J.--ED.
YOU DON'T MESS AROUND WITH JIM	BROWN *
YOU TELL ME YOUR DREAMS	STEINER
YOU TELL ME YOUR DREAMS	LANE, J.--ED.
YOU WERE MEANT FOR ME	JESSE, M.
YO HO, FOR THE SAILOR BOY	GLOVER, D.
YO HO, THE SAILOR'S SONG	LECUONA
YO TE QUIERO SIEMPRE	BRADLEY,
YO YO	JAMES, M.
YO YO	
YULETIDE BELLS	GOERDELER, R.
YULETIDE BELLS	GOERDELER, R.
YULETIDE MEDLEY	DASHER, J.
YULE SLUMBER LILT, OP. 143. SIX EASY CHRISTMAS PIECES	NIEMANN
YVONNE EN VISITE	ALBENIZ, I.
Y LA MEGRA BAILABA	LECUONA
ZADOK THE PRIEST‡ THREE PIECES	HANDEL
ZADOK THE PRIEST, 3 PIECES	HANDEL
ZAMBA, OP. 40	AGUIRRE
ZAMBA DE VARGAS	SAMMARTINO
ZAMBRA, OP. 92, NO. 7 -- FROM 12 PIECES	ALBENIZ, I.
ZAMBRA -- NO. 5, FROM SIX PIECES ON SPANISH FOLK SONGS	GRANADOS
ZAMBRA GITANA	LECUONA
ZAMBRA GRANADINA. ORIENTAL DANCE	ALBENIZ, I.
ZAMPA, OVERTURE	HEROLD
ZAMPANO	ROTA *
ZAMPA OVERTURE	HEROLD
ZAMPA OVERTURE	HEROLD
ZANZIBAR	
ZAPATEADO, OP. 23 NO. 2	SARASATE
ZAPATEADO -- NO. 6, FROM SIX PIECES ON SPANISH FOLK	GRANADOS
ZARAGOZA -- NO. 1, FROM SUITE ESPANOLA NO. 2	ALBENIZ, I.
ZAR SULTAN - FLIGHT OF THE BUMBLE BEE	RIMSKY-KORSAKOFF
ZAUBERLEHRING, DIE -- BALLET --	GRENZ
ZAUBERSTUNDEN	HUMBERT, G.
ZEHN FANTASIEN AM KLAVIER -- 1968 --	DELAMOTTE
ZEHN FUGEN	REJCHA
ZEHN FUNFTONSTUCKE AUF ZEHN TASTEN, HEFT 2	BADINGS
ZEHN FUNFTONSTUCKE AUF ZEHN WEISSEN TASTEN, HEFT 1	BADINGS
ZEHN KLEINE PRALUDIEN, OP. 35	HESSENBERG, K.
ZEHN KLEINE STUCKE OHNE DAUMENUNTERSATZ, HEFT 3	BADINGS
ZEHN KURZE VORTRAGSSTUCKE FUR DIE JUGEND	KOPELENT
ZEHN VARIIERTE THEMEN, OP. 107 -- VOL. 1	BEETHOVEN
ZEHN VARIIERTE THEMEN, OP. 107 -- VOL. 2	BEETHOVEN
ZEHN VARIIERTE THEMEN, OP. 107 -- VOL. 3	BEETHOVEN
ZEHN WEIHNACHTSLIEDER, AM KLAVIER ZU SINGEN UND ZU	REDA
ZEHN WEIHNACHTSLIEDER	REDA
ZEHPYRS FROM MELODYLAND, OP. 15--MERRY BOBOLINK	KROGMANN, C. W.
ZEPHIRE ET FLORE	DUKELSKY
ZEPHRS	PANELLA, L.
ZEPHYRS FROM MELODYLAND, OP. 15--LITTLE PRINCE	KROGMANN, C. W.
ZEPHYRS FROM MELODYLAND, OP. 15--ROBIN'S LULLABY	KROGMANN, C. W.
ZEPHYRS FROM MELODYLAND, OP. 15--SANTA CLAUS GUARDS	KROGMANN, C. W.
ZEPHYRS FROM MELODYLAND, OP. 15 -- NO. 01, LITTLE	KROGMANN, C. W.
ZEPHYRS FROM MELODYLAND, OP. 15 -- NO. 07, LITTLE	KROGMANN, C. W.
ZEPHYRS FROM MELODYLAND, OP. 15 -- NO. 12, ROBIN'S	KROGMANN, C. W.
ZEPHYRS FROM MELODYLAND, OP. 15	KROGMANN, C. W.
ZEPHYRS FROM MELODYLAND, OP. 15	KROGMANN, C. W.
ZEPP PIANO COURSE - BOOK 1	ZEPP
ZEPP PIANO COURSE - BOOK 2	ZEPP
ZEPP PIANO COURSE - BOOK 3	ZEPP
ZEPP PIANO COURSE - BOOK 4	ZEPP
ZEPP PIANO COURSE - BOOK 5	ZEPP
ZEPP PIANO COURSE - PREPARATORY BOOK	ZEPP
ZIGEUNER	COWARD
ZINGANA, LA, EASY	BOHM
ZINGANA, LA -- MAZURKA	BOHM
ZINGARI	LEONCAVALLO
ZIPPY	CATIZONE, J. M.
ZIP A DEE DO DAH	LANE, J.--ED.
ZIRKUS, SUITE	TURINA, J.
ZODIAN	REIZENSTEIN, F.
ZODIAQUE, LE, 12 ETUDES	MIGOT
ZOETTE	VOLPATTI
ZOO, THE	MELECCI, A.
ZOO, TIERE FUR KLAVIER	SCOTT, C.
ZOOLOGICAL COMICALITIES	TURNER, O.
ZOOLOGICAL IMPRESSIONS	MASSEUS
ZOO PARADE, THE	MCHALE, M.
ZOO PARADE, THE	SCHAUM, J.--ED.
ZORBA THE GREEK - THEME	LANE, J.--ED.
ZORBA THE GREEK - THEME	THEODORAKIS, M.
ZORTZICO, OP. 165, NO. 6 -- FROM ESPANA	ALBENIZ, I.
ZUHAUSE -- VARIATIONS IN 4 MOVEMENTS	PEPPING, E.
ZUHAUSE -- 4 VARIATIONSSATZE --	PEPPING, E.
ZU ZWEIEN	HUMBERT, G.
ZU ZWEIT MEHR FREUD. KLEINE STUCKE ZUM ANFANG, ERSTE	VOLKART-SCHLAGER
ZU ZWEIT MEHR FREUD. KLEINE STUCKE ZUM ANFANG, ZWEITE	VOLKART-SCHLAGER
ZWANZIG DEUTSCHE TANZE OP. 10 -- BK. 1 ST.-V.S. 14	REGER
ZWANZIG DEUTSCHE VOLKSTANZE	DOFLEIN--ED.
ZWANZIG DEUTSCHE VOLKSTANZE	DOFLEIN--ED.
ZWANZIG KLEINE FUGEN FUR ORGEL ODER KLAVIER	TELEMANN, G.P.
ZWANZIG KLEINE TANZE	BEETHOVEN
ZWANZIG KLEINE TANZE	HANDEL
ZWANZIG SONATE BRILLANTI	SCARLATTI, D.
ZWEIHUNDDREISSIG SONATINEN UND RONDO, HEFT 1 -	CLEMENTI *
ZWEISTG. INVENTIONEN -- BWV 772-786	BACH, J.S.
ZWEIZEHN TOCCATEN UND 72 VERSETL	MUFFAT
ZWEI APHORISMEN UM EIN NACHTSTUCK, OP. 52	EDER
ZWEI BRASILIANISCHE RHAPSODIEN, OP. 110	NIEMANN
ZWEI FURIANTE, OP. 42	DVORAK
ZWEI KLAVIERKOMPOSITIONEN -- LES ADIEUX UND LA	DUSSEK, J.
ZWEI KLAVIERKOMPOSITIONEN	BORKOVEC
ZWEI KLAVIERSTUCKE --FANTASIE FIS-MOLL, RONDO E-MOLL	BACH, C.P.E. *
ZWEI KLAVIERSTUCKE -- FANTASIEFIS-MOLL-RONDO E-MOLL	BACH, C.P.E.
ZWEI KLEINE PERLEN	DVORAK
ZWEI KLEINE SONATEN	JUST, J. A.
ZWEI LEICHTE SONATEN IN G AND F	BEETHOVEN
ZWEI LEICHTE SONATEN	BEETHOVEN
ZWEI MARSCHE	KRICKA
ZWEI ROMANZEN	PEPPING, E.
ZWEI SCHERZI B UND DES	SCHUBERT
ZWEI SCHERZI	FIBICH, Z.
ZWEI SONATEN, NO. 01	PEPPING, E.
ZWEI SONATEN, NO. 02	PEPPING, E.
ZWEI SONATEN -- F-ES --	BACH, C.P.E.
ZWEI SONATEN	BACH, C.P.E.
ZWEI SONATINEN, OP. 44A, B IN G UND E MINOR	GEBHARD
ZWEI STUCKE FUR VIER HANDE -- E. W. WOLF -- SONATE, W.	KREUTZ--ED.
ZWEI TANZE -- VALSE UND POLKA -- AUS 'SPALICEK'	MARTINU, B.
ZWEI TANZE AUS DER OPER 'EVA' -- SOUSEDSKA/POLKA --	FOERSTER
ZWEI TOCCATEN	ROSSI
ZWEI UND DREISSIG VARIATIONEN C-MOLL	BEETHOVEN
ZWIEFACHE --A LA MEMOIRE DE FRANZ SCHUBERT--	LANCEN
ZWOLFTONSPIEL -- APRIL, 1956	HAUER, J. M.
ZWOLF DEUTSCHE TANZE	BEETHOVEN
ZWOLF ETUDEN OP. 105	BURGMUELLER
ZWOLF KLEINE ETUDEN	SLAVICKY, K.
ZWOLF KLEINE PRALUDIEN -- BWV 924-930, 939-942, 999	BACH, J.S.
ZWOLF MELODISCHE ETUDEN, OP. 16	DUSSEK, J.
ZWOLF MELODISCHE ETUDEN, OP. 16	DUSSEK, J.
ZWOLF MINIATUREN	BLOCH, W.
ZWOLF MINNELIEDER	REDA
ZWOLF MINNELIEDER	REDA
ZWOLF PRALUDIEN -- 1954 --	SOKOLA
ZWOLF SONATINEN, OP. 20 NOS. 1-3, OP. 55 NOS. 1-6,	KUHLAU, F.
ZWOLF STUDIEN, OP. 38	FRICKER, P.
12 MENUETTE	MUTHEL, J. G.

ABBOTT, A. T.

    METHOD FOR GAINING A PERFECT KNOWLEDGE OF THE NOTES, ETC., FOR
    BEGINNERS ON THE PIANOFORTE, A

        PHILADELPHIA   1893   11P   BMFGAP
          PRESSER, THEODORE, COMPANY
  LC * NP

  INT * MEX
  PL4 * AT4

ABRAHAM, GERALD

  CHOPIN'S MUSICAL STYLE---1939

        LONDON   1960   116P   BCMSNT
          OXFORD UNIVERSITY PRESS
  AS * BP * BR * CP * ES * IU * LC * NP * TO * UA * UC * UI * UK * UM
  UO * US * UT * UU * YU
  IND * INT * MEX
  PM3 * PM6 * PM8 * PM9 * PM14

ADAMS, JAMES B.

  FAMILIAR INTRODUCTION TO THE FIRST PRINCIPLES OF MUSIC, A ...FOR
  THE USE OF BEGINNERS ON THE HARPSICHORD, PIANO FORTE OR ORGAN

        LONDON   1780+   42P   BFITTF
          ADAMS, JAMES B.
  LC

  GLO * INT * MEX
  PL4 * PL12 * AT4

ADAMS, JOHN S.

  FIVE THOUSAND MUSICAL TERMS..A COMPLETE DICTIONARY WITH A TREATISE
  ON PLAYING THE ORGAN OR PIANO BY FIGURES, ETC.

        BOSTON   1851   167P   BFTMTA
          DITSON, OLIVER, COMPANY
  BP * BR * LC * NP * TO * UC * UI * UO * UW

  MEX
  PL12 * KS10 * GI12

ADAMS, JULIETTE

  CHAPTERS FROM A MUSICAL LIFE

        CHICAGO   1903   139P   BCFAML
          ADAMS, C.
  ES * LC

  NP6

ADAMS, JULIETTE

  RECENT DEVELOPMENTS IN TEACHING CHILDREN TO PLAY THE PIANO

        CHICAGO   1923   23P   BRDITC
          SUMMY, CLAYTON F.
  BP * NP

  MEX
  AT5

ADAMS, JULIETTE

  WHAT THE PIANO WRITING OF EDWARD MACDOWELL MEANS TO THE PIANO
  STUDENT

        MONTREAT, N. C.   1913   23P   BWTPWO
          LINDEN PRESS
  ES * LC * NP

  PM1 * PM3

ADLER, KURT

  ART OF ACCOMPANYING AND COACHING, THE ---1965

        NEW YORK   1971   260P   BAOAAC
          DA CAPO PRESS
  BP * BR * CP * ES * IU * LC * SA * TO * UA * UI * UK * UM * UO * US
  UT * UW * YU
  BIB * CHR * ILL * INT * LDR * MEX * MSF * PHO
  KI3 * KI5 * KI6 * PL9 * PL12 * KS7 * AP4 * AP6 * AP7 * EP2 * EP6

AEBERSOLD, JAMEY

  NEW APPROACH TO JAZZ IMPROVISATION, A --VOL. 1

        NEW ALBANY, IND.   1967   33P   BNATJI
          AEBERSOLD, JAMEY
  IU

  MEX
  KS6

AEOLIAN COMPANY, THE

  AEOLIAN PIANOS, THE ---WEBER, STECK, STROUD

        NEW YORK   1917   16P   BAPWSS
          AEOLIAN COMPANY, THE
  LC

  ILL
  KI6 * KI7 * KI9 * KI12

AEOLIAN COMPANY, THE

  AUDIOGRAPHIC MUSIC

        NEW YORK   1928   70P   BAM
          AEOLIAN COMPANY, THE
  UM

  ILL * INT * PHO
  NP6 * KI9 * KI10 * KI12 * KI13 * KI15

AEOLIAN COMPANY, THE

  CATALOG OF AEOLIAN MUSIC ARRANGED FOR 46-NOTE INSTRUMENTS

        NEW YORK   1904+ 320P   BCOAMA
          AEOLIAN COMPANY, THE
  LC

  KI10 * PM6 * PM12

AEOLIAN COMPANY, THE

  CATALOG OF METROSTYLE AND THEMODIST MUSIC FOR THE PIANOLA AND
  PIANOLA PIANO...ISSUED TO JULY, 1906--VOL. 1

        NEW YORK   1906+ 327P   BCOMAT
          AEOLIAN COMPANY, THE
  LC * NP

  INT
  KI10 * PM6 * PM12

AEOLIAN COMPANY, THE

  CATALOG OF MUSIC-ROLLS FOR THE DUO-ART REPRODUCING PIANO

        NEW YORK   1924   254P   BCOMRF
          AEOLIAN COMPANY, THE
  NP

  INT * PHO
  KI10 * PM6 * PM12

AEOLIAN COMPANY, THE

  CATALOG OF MUSIC AND MUSICAL LITERATURE---PIANOLA RECORDS

        NEW YORK   1902+ 303P   BCOMAM
          AEOLIAN COMPANY, THE
  LC

  KI10 * KI15 * PM12

AEOLIAN COMPANY, THE

  CATALOG OF MUSIC FOR THE PIANOLA, PIANOLA PIANO AND
  AERIOLA--CONTAINING A COMPLETE LIST OF MUSIC PUBLISHED TO JULY 1,
  1905--VOL. 1
        NEW YORK   1905   598P   BCOMFT
          AEOLIAN COMPANY, THE
  LC * NP

  INT
  KI10 * PM6 * PM12

AEOLIAN COMPANY, THE

  CATALOG OF THE AEOLIAN

        NEW YORK   1898   78P   BCOTA
          AEOLIAN COMPANY, THE
  LC

  ILL * PHO
  KI4 * KI5 * KI6 * KI9 * KI10 * KI12 * KI13 * KI15 * GI5

AEOLIAN COMPANY, THE

  COMPLETE CATALOG OF MUSIC ROLLS FOR THE DUO-ART REPRODUCING PIANO

        NEW YORK   1924   192P   BCCOMR
          AEOLIAN COMPANY, THE
  BP * NP

  INT * PHO
  KI10 * PM6

AEOLIAN COMPANY, THE

  CONFIDENTIAL MANUAL FOR SALESMEN OF THE DUO-ART REPRODUCING
  PIANO---8 FOLDOUTS--1 OF FACSIMILES
        NEW YORK   1923+   BCMFSO
          AEOLIAN COMPANY, THE
  LC

  GI5

AEOLIAN COMPANY, THE

  DUO-ART BOOK OF MUSIC, THE

        NEW YORK   1924   63P   BDABOM
          AEOLIAN COMPANY, THE
  NP

  INT
  KI10 * PL8 * AT10 * EP3 * EP6

AEOLIAN COMPANY, THE

    DUO-ART PIANO MUSIC...RECORDED BY MORE THAN 250 PIANISTS

| | NEW YORK | 1927 | 480P | BDAPMR |
| | AEOLIAN COMPANY, THE | | | |

    BP * ES * LC * NP * UC * UW

    APP * PHO
    NP5 * KI10 * PM5 * PM12

AEOLIAN COMPANY, THE

    DUO-ART PIANO MUSIC

| | NEW YORK | 1917 | 148P | BDAPM |
| | AEOLIAN COMPANY, THE | | | |

    LC * NP

    INT
    KI10 * PM12 * GI13

AEOLIAN COMPANY, THE

    DUO-ART REPRODUCING PIANO, THE ..THE DUO-ART REPRODUCING PIANO
    SERVICE MANUAL

| | NEW YORK | 1927+ | 46P | BDARPT |
| | AEOLIAN COMPANY, THE | | | |

    LC

    KI8 * KI10

AEOLIAN COMPANY, THE

    LIBRARY OF DUO-ART MUSIC ROLLS

| | NEW YORK | 1924 | 246P | BLODAM |
| | AEOLIAN COMPANY, THE | | | |

    LC

    INT * PHO
    KI10 * PM6 * PM12 * GI4 * GI13

AEOLIAN COMPANY, THE

    METROSTYLE-THEMODIST AND METRO-ART MUSIC ROLLS FOR THE PIANOLA AND
    PIANOLA PIANO--6 VOLS., 1910-1917

| | NEW YORK | 1910 | | BMTAMA |
| | AEOLIAN COMPANY, THE | | | |

    LC

    KI10 * PM6 * PM12

AEOLIAN COMPANY, THE

    METROSTYLE, THE

| | NEW YORK | 1903 | 89P | BM |
| | AEOLIAN COMPANY, THE | | | |

    LC * NP

    ILL
    KI10 * PM6 * PM12

AEOLIAN COMPANY, THE

    METROSTYLE AND THEMODIST MUSIC CATALOG FOR THE PIANOLA AND PIANOLA
    PIANO, JULY, 1910

| | NEW YORK | 1910 | 225P | BMATMC |
| | AEOLIAN COMPANY, THE | | | |

    LC

    KI10 * PM6 * PM12

AEOLIAN COMPANY, THE

    MUSIC FOR THE AEOLIAN GRAND--SUPPLEMENT

| | NEW YORK | 1901+ | 200P | BMFTAG |
| | AEOLIAN COMPANY, THE | | | |

    LC

    KI10 * PM6 * PM12

AEOLIAN COMPANY, THE

    MUSIC FOR THE AEOLIAN GRAND

| | NEW YORK | 1901 | 679P | BMFTAG |
| | AEOLIAN COMPANY, THE | | | |

    LC

    KI10 * PM6 * PM12 * GI4

AEOLIAN COMPANY, THE

    MUSIC FOR THE ORCHESTRELLE AND AEOLIAN GRAND

| | NEW YORK | 1901 | 679P | BMFTOA |
| | AEOLIAN COMPANY, THE | | | |

    LC * NP

    KI10 * PM6 * PM12

AEOLIAN COMPANY, THE

    MUSIC FOR THE PIANOLA AND THE AERIAL PIANO--4 VOLS.

| | NEW YORK | 1901 | 227P | BMFTPA |
| | AEOLIAN COMPANY, THE | | | |

    LC

    KI10 * PM6 * PM12

AEOLIAN COMPANY, THE

    NEW MUSIC FOR THE AEOLIAN GRAND, THE PIANOLA, AND THE AERIOL PIANO

| | NEW YORK | 1901 | 45P | BNMFTA |
| | AEOLIAN COMPANY, THE | | | |

    KI10 * PM6 * PM12

AEOLIAN COMPANY, THE

    PIANISTS WHO HAVE MADE RECORDS FOR THE DUO-ART PIANO

| | NEW YORK | 1917 | 51P | BPWHMR |
| | AEOLIAN COMPANY, THE | | | |

    NP

    INT * PHO
    NP5 * KI10 * GI13

AEOLIAN COMPANY, THE

    PIANOLA AND PIANOLA PIANO MUSIC CATALOG, THE ..SIXTY-FIVE NOTE
    MUSIC

| | NEW YORK | 1910 | 482P | BPAPPM |
| | AEOLIAN COMPANY, THE | | | |

    LC * NP

    KI10 * PM6 * PM12

AEOLIAN COMPANY, THE

    PIANOLA PIANO, THE

| | NEW YORK | 1905 | 8P | BPP |
| | AEOLIAN COMPANY, THE | | | |

    LC

    ILL * PHO
    KI3 * KI4 * KI5 * KI6 * KI9 * KI10 * KI12 * KI13 * KI15

AEOLIAN COMPANY, THE

    SPECIAL SURVEY CONDUCTED--IN 1889--FOR LYON AND HEALY, INC.,
    STEINWAY AND CO., AND THE AEOLIAN CO., BY ROBERT RAWLS UPDEGRAFF, A

| | NEW YORK | 1930 | 374P | BSSCIE |
| | AEOLIAN COMPANY, THE | | | |

    LC * NP

    INT
    KI1 * KI12 * GI1 * GI2 * GI3 * GI5 * GI6

AEOLIAN COMPANY, THE

    SUPPLEMENTARY CATALOG OF MUSIC FOR THE AEOLIAN GRAND AND
    ORCHESTRELLE...FOR FIFTY-EIGHT NOTE INSTRUMENTS, PUBLISHED FROM
    JULY 1901 TO JULY 1906

| | NEW YORK | 1906 | 300P | BSCOMF |
| | AEOLIAN COMPANY, THE | | | |

    LC * NP

    KI10 * PM6 * PM12

AEOLIAN COMPANY, THE

    WEIGHT OF EVIDENCE ON THE TRUE MUSICAL WORTH OF THE PIANOLA AND ITS
    ABSOLUTE SUPREMACY IN ITS FIELD, THE

| | NEW YORK | 1914 | 33P | BWOEOT |
| | AEOLIAN COMPANY, THE | | | |

    NP

    INT
    NP6 * KI5 * KI10 * KI12 * AP8 * GI13

AGUILAR, EMANUEL

    HOW TO LEARN THE PIANOFORTE

| | LONDON | 1883 | 58P | BHTLTP |
| | GROOMBRIDGE | | | |

    BR

    MEX
    PL4 * AT4

AGUILAR, EMANUEL

    LITTLE BOOK ABOUT LEARNING THE PIANOFORTE, A

| | LONDON | 1866 | 71P | BLBALT |
| | GROOMBRIDGE AND SONS | | | |

    BP * BR * LC * NP

    INT * MEX
    NP6 * PL1 * PL7 * AT7 * PT10

AHEARN, ELLA MASON *
BLAKE, DOROTHY GAYNOR *
    ADULT EXPLORER AT THE PIANO, THE

            CINCINNATI   1937   60P   BAEATP
                WILLIS MUSIC COMPANY
    IU * OC * SA

    ILL * INT * LDR * MEX
    PL4 * PL10 * AT4 * AT6 * AT7

AHRENS, CORA B. *
ATKINSON, G. D.
    FOR ALL PIANO TEACHERS

            OAKVILLE, ONTARIO   1955   131P   BFAPT
                HARRIS, FREDERICK, MUSIC COMPANY
    BR * CU * ES * IU * LC * MI * NP * SA * TO * UI

    APP * BIB * IND * MEX
    KI1 * PL7 * PL8 * PL10 * PL12 * AT3 * AT5 * AT6 * PT1 * PT6 * PT8 *
    PT9 * PT10 * KS3 * AP1 * AP6 * AP8 * GI2 * GI9

ALBARDA, JAN H.

    WOOD, WIRE AND QUILL..AN INTRODUCTION TO THE HARPSICHORD

            TORONTO   1968   93P   BWWAQA
                COACH HOUSE PRESS
    AS * BR * IU * LC * TO * UA

    CHR * GLO * ILL * IND * PHO
    KI3 * KI5 * KI6 * KI9 * KI12 * KI13 * KI14

ALBIG, GEORGE L.

    HOW TO PLAY THE PLAYER

            RIDGEFIELD PARK, N.J.   1921   16P   BHTPTP
                ALBIG, GEORGE L.
    LC * NP

    INT
    KI10 * AT4 * AP3

ALBRECHTSBERGER, JOHANN GEORG

    ALBRECHTSBERGER'S COLLECTED WRITINGS ON THOROUGH-BASS, HARMONY AND
    COMPOSITION, FOR SELF-INSTRUCTION--3 VOLS. IN 1---1792

            LONDON   1855   256P   BACWOT
                NOVELLO, EWER AND COMPANY
    IU * LC * NP

    INT * MEX
    PL11 * KS4 * KS10 * PM3

ALBRECHTSBERGER, JOHANN GEORG

    ALBRECHTSBERGER'S ELEMENTARY WORK ON THE SCIENCE OF
    MUSIC..INCLUDING THOROUGH BASS, HARMONY AND COMPOSITION--12 PTS.

            PHILADELPHIA   1842   72P   BAEWOT
                OSBOURNE, JAMES G.
    NP

    INT * MEX
    PL12 * KS4 * KS10

ALBRECHTSBERGER, JOHANN GEORG

    METHODS OF HARMONY, FIGURED BASE, AND COMPOSITION...ADAPTED FOR
    SELF-INSTRUCTION--2 VOLS., 1835-1844

            LONDON   1835   BMOHFB
                COCKS, R., AND COMPANY
    BR * LC * NP

    APP * IND * INT
    NP4 * KS10 * PM3 * PM6

ALBRECHTSBERGER, JOHANN GEORG

    PRINCIPLES OF ACCOMPANIMENT OR THOROUGH BASS

            LONDON   1822+   35P   BPOAOT
                CHAPPELL AND COMPANY
    BR * NP

    KS10 * KS11 * EP6

ALCHIN, CARRIE A.

    APPLIED HARMONY--REVISED AND WITH ADDITIONAL CHAPTERS BY VINCENT
    JONES--2 VOLS.

            HOLLYWOOD, CAL.   1958   287P   BAHRAW
                HIGHLAND MUSIC COMPANY
    IU * LC * NP

    APP * INT * MEX
    PL4 * PL13 * KS4 * KS8

ALCHIN, CARRIE A.

    KEYBOARD HARMONY--3 VOLS. IN 1, 1923-1926

            LOS ANGELES   1923   173P   BKHTVI
                ALCHIN, C. A.
    LC * NP

    IND * INT * MEX
    PL4 * KS4

ALDRICH, PUTNAM

    PRINCIPAL AGREMENTS OF THE SEVENTEENTH AND EIGHTEENTH CENTURIES,
    THE ..A STUDY IN MUSICAL ORNAMENTATION---UNPUBLISHED THESIS

            CAMBRIDGE, MASS.   1942   568P   BPAOTS
                HARVARD UNIVERSITY
    IU * LC * TO * UA

    INT * MEX
    AP7

ALLEN, MARGARET *
NILES, ANNE
    CREATIVE MOTION

            ANDERSON, S. C.   1971   157P   BCM
                DROKE HOUSE PUBLISHERS
    IU * LC

    ILL * MEX * PHO
    PL3 * PL4 * PL12 * PL13 * AT3 * PT3 * PT4 * PM9 * AP4

ALLEY, MARGUERITE *
ALLEY, JEAN
    PASSIONATE FRIENDSHIP, A ..CLARA SCHUMANN AND BRAHMS---LETTERS TO
    EACH OTHER
            LONDON   1956   214P   BPFCSA
                STAPLES PRESS
    BR * LC * NP * UI

    NP6

ALLISON, IRL

    LET'S LEARN ALL THE NOTES AND READ BETTER..FOR ALL PIANO PUPILS,
    5-50
            AUSTIN, TEX.   1967   28P   BLLATN
                ALLISON, I., PUBLISHER
    LC

    PL4 * AT4 * KS3

ALTMAN, FRANCES

    GEORGE GERSHWIN, MASTER COMPOSER

            MINNEAPOLIS   1968   235P   BGGMC
                DENISON, T. S.
    LC

    BIB * INT
    NP4 * PM3

AMERICAN NEWS COMPANY

    ROMANCE OF A PIANO, THE

            NEW YORK   1870   49P   BROAP
                AMERICAN NEWS COMPANY
    BP

    KI1 * KI2

AMERICAN PHOTO PLAYER COMPANY

    INSTALLATION, CARE AND OPERATION OF THE PHOTOPLAYER---1920+

            VESTAL, N. Y.   1967   16P   BICAOO
                VESTAL PRESS
    NP

    ILL * INT * LDR * PHO
    KI3 * KI5 * KI6 * KI8 * KI10 * KI12

AMERICAN PIANO CORPORATION

    AMPICO, THE ..A DESCRIPTION OF ITS PERFORMANCE...

            NEW YORK   1922+   28P   BAADOI
                AMERICAN PIANO CORPORATION
    LC * NP

    KI5 * KI6 * KI8 * KI10 * KI11

AMERICAN PIANO CORPORATION

    AMPICO, THE ..SERVICE MANUAL 1929

            NEW YORK   1929   57P   BASMNT
                AMERICAN PIANO CORPORATION
    LC * NP

    KI5 * KI6 * KI8 * KI10 * KI11

AMERICAN PIANO CORPORATION

    AMPICO REPRODUCING PIANO, INSPECTOR'S REFERENCE BOOK, THE ---1923

            CLIFTON, N. J.   1960+   18P   BARPIR
                AMERICAN PIANO SUPPLY COMPANY
    LC * NP

    CHR * ILL * INT
    KI3 * KI5 * KI6 * KI8 * KI10

AMERICAN PIANO CORPORATION

AMPICO REPRODUCING PIANO, THE ..INSPECTOR'S INSTRUCTION BOOK, 1919,
WITH 1920 SUPPLEMENT

VESTAL, N. Y.   1967+   71P   BARPII
VESTAL PRESS
NP

CHR * ILL * INT * LDR
KI3 * KI5 * KI6 * KI8 * KI10

AMERICAN PIANO CORPORATION

CATALOGUE OF MUSIC FOR THE AMPICO, A ..A LIST OF THE RECORDINGS OF
PIANISTS WHOSE ART IS THUS PRESERVED FOR PRESENT DAY MUSIC LOVERS
AND FOR POSTERITY
NEW YORK   1925   351P   BCOMFT
AMPICO CORPORATION
ES * LC * UT * UU

KI10 * PM2 * PM6 * PM12 * GI13

AMERICAN PIANO CORPORATION

CATALOGUE OF MUSIC FOR THE AMPICO, A --A LIST OF THE RECORDINGS OF
PIANISTS...TOGETHER WITH SHORT BIOGRAPHIES OF MANY OF THE COMPOSERS
AND ARTISTS AND NOTES ON THE MUSIC
NEW YORK   1923   300P   BCOMFT
AMERICAN PIANO CORPORATION
LC

NP5 * KI10 * PM6 * PM12 * GI13

AMERICAN SCHOOL OF PIANO TUNING

TRAINING AS A PIANO TECHNICIAN--8 VOLS. IN 1

NEW YORK   1966   107P   BTAAPT
AMERICAN SCHOOL OF PIANO TUNING
LC

ILL * IND * INT * LDR * PHO
AT4 * KI8 * GI5

AMERICAN STEEL AND WIRE COMPANY

NERVES OF STEEL..THE STORY OF AMERICAN PIANO WIRE AND ITS
DEVELOPMENT BY THE AMERICAN STEEL AND WIRE CO.

NEW YORK   1936   12P   BNOSTS
AMERICAN STEEL AND WIRE COMPANY

KI3 * KI6 * KI12 * GI5

AMEY, ELLEN

CONSCIOUS CONTROL IN PIANO STUDY

NEW YORK   1921   99P   BCCIPS
FLAMMER, HAROLD
BP * BR * CU * LC * NP * UK

INT * MEX
PL3 * PL4 * PL5 * PL7 * PL8 * PL13 * PL14 * PT6 * PT8 * PT9 * PT10
KS1 * AP7

AMPICO CORPORATION

AMPICO REPRODUCING PIANO..A SUPPLEMENT TO 'PIANO MUSIC, ITS
COMPOSERS AND CHARACTERISTICS AND MUSIC APPRECIATION', BY CLARENCE
G. HAMILTON...
NEW YORK   1925   24P   BARPAS
AMPICO CORPORATION
LC

KI10 * PM3 * PM6 * PM12 * GI2

AMPICO CORPORATION

SUPREMACY OF AMPICO MUSIC..UNIT TWO OF A COURSE IN AMPICO
SALESMANSHIP

NEW YORK   1924   48P   BSOAMU
BUSINESS TRAINING CORPORATION
LC

KI10 * PM12 * GI5

ANDERSON-MULDER COMPANY

DEALER'S HANDBOOK OF PIANOS AND THEIR MAKERS

CHICAGO   1950   35P   BDHOPA
ANDERSON-MULDER COMPANY
LC

INT
KI12 * GI5

ANDERSON, ARVID C.

MASTERS OF MUSIC---CHOPIN AND LISZT

WASHINGTON, D. C.   1948   102P   BMOMCA
REVIEW AND HERALD
IU * LC

ILL
NP5

ANDERSON, J. CLARK

GOOD MUSIC EXPLAINED..WHAT ALL GOOD PIANISTS SHOULD KNOW

FRESNO, CAL.   1916   BGMEWA
PACIFIC SCHOOL OF MUSIC
LC

INT
PL4 * PL8 * PL12 * PL15 * PT1 * KS4 * AP4 * AP6 * AP8

ANDERSON, WILLIAM P.

MUSIC AS A CAREER

NEW YORK   1939   271P   BMAAC
OXFORD UNIVERSITY PRESS
BR * IU * NP

NP6 * NP7 * AT1 * AT10 * AP1 * AP9 * GI5 * GI6 * GI9

ANDERSON, WILLIAM R.

RACHMANINOV AND HIS PIANO CONCERTOS

LONDON   1947   24P   BRAHPC
HINRICHSEN EDITION, LTD.
BR * CU * ES * NP * TO

APP * DIS * MEX
NP4 * PM8 * PM9 * PM12

ANON

ADVICE TO A NOBLEMAN...ON THE MANNER IN WHICH HIS CHILDREN SHOULD
BE INSTRUCTED ON THE PIANOFORTE--2ND. ED.
LONDON   1819   72P   BATANO
HUNTER, R.
BR * YU

PL2 * PL4 * AT4 * AT5 * AT13

ANON

CHILD'S INTRODUCTION TO THOROUGH BASS, THE ..IN CONVERSATIONS OF A
FORTNIGHT, BETWEEN A MOTHER, AND HER DAUGHTER OF TEN YEARS OLD
LONDON   1819   96P   BCITTB
BALDWIN, CRADOCK AND JOY
LC

CHR * INT * MEX
AT5 * KS10

ANON

COMPLEAT TUTOR FOR THE HARPSICHORD OR SPINNET, WHEREIN IS SHEWN THE
ITALIAN MANNER OF FINGERING, THE ...WITH RULES FOR A THOROUGH
BASS, AND TUNING
LONDON   1760+   36P   BCTFTH
THOMPSON, C. AND S.
LC

ILL * MEX
KI8 * PL4 * PL12 * AT4 * PT6 * KS10 * AP7

ANON

DIGITORIUM, THE --MINIATURE DUMB PIANO

LONDON   1800+   12P   BDMDP
CHAPPELL AND COMPANY
NP

CHR * LDR * MEX
KI2 * KI10 * KI14 * AT4

ANON

ESSAY ON THE CHIROGYMNAST..OR, FINGER EXERCISES APPLIED TO...ALL
SORTS OF MUSICAL INSTRUMENTS
LONDON   1843+   31P   BEOTCO
MARTIN, M.
NP

ILL * INT * MEX
NP6 * PT5 * PT14

ANON

FASHIONABLE PRECEPTOR, FOR THE PIANO-FORTE AND HARPSICHORD, WHEREIN
THE ART OF PLAYING ON THESE INSTRUMENTS IS FULLY EXPLAIN'D, THE
LONDON   1800+   38P   BFPFTP
HODSOLL, W., AND RILEY, E.
LC

MEX
PL4 * PL12 * AT4 * PT6 * PT9 * AP7

ANON

FIRST STEPS TO THOROUGH BASE, IN 12 FAMILIAR LESSONS BETWEEN A
TEACHER AND PUPIL
BOSTON   1833   110P   BFSTTB
LORING, J.
LC

AT4 * KS10

ANON

GENERAL OBSERVATIONS ON MUSIC AND REMARKS ON MR. LOGIER'S SYSTEM OF
MUSICAL EDUCATION..WITH AN APPENDIX

      EDINBURGH   1817   115P   BGOOMA
      STEVENSON, DUNCAN, AND COMPANY
LC

INT * MEX
NP6 * NP7 * AT4 * PT10 * PT14

ANON

GUIDE TO THE MUSICAL TUITION OF VERY YOUNG CHILDREN, BY AN OLD LADY

      LONDON   1868   16P   BGTTMT
      AUGENER AND COMPANY
BR * NP

MEX
PL7 * PL12 * PT4 * PT9 * PT10

ANON

GUIDE TO THE PROPER USE OF THE PIANOFORTE PEDALS, WITH EXAMPLES OUT
OF THE HISTORICAL CONCERTS OF ANTON RUBINSTEIN

      LONDON   1897   44P   BGTTPU
      BOSWORTH AND COMPANY
BR * LC * OC

INT * MEX
PM7 * AP1 * AP8

ANON

HOW TO LEARN TO PLAY THE PIANO WELL, BY ONE WHO HAS TAUGHT HIMSELF

      LONDON   1880   14P   BHTLTP
      NOVELLO, EWER AND COMPANY
BR

PL11 * AT2 * AT4

ANON

HOW TO TUNE YOUR OWN PIANOFORTE..OR, THE WAY TO KEEP YOUR
PIANOFORTE IN ORDER, ETC.

      MANCHESTER   1885   14P   BHTTYO
      HEYWOOD AND SON
BR

KI3 * KI8

ANON

HUMANISTIC STUDIES IN HONOR OF JOHN CALVIN METCALF---INCLUDES
'THOMAS JEFFERSON VISITS ENGLAND AND BUYS A HARPSICHORD', BY A. B.
SHEPPERSON--UNIV. OF VIRGINIA STUDIES, VOL. 1
      CHARLOTTESVILLE, VA.   1941   338P   BHSIHO
      UNIVERSITY OF VIRGINIA
LC

NP6 * KI4 * KI14

ANON

LIFE AND WORKS OF GUSTAVE SATTER, THE ..A BIOGRAPHICAL SKETCH IN
MEMORIAM OF THE GREAT PIANIST AND COMPOSER

      MACON, GA.   1879   23P   BLAWOG
      SEIFERT AND SMITH, PRINTERS
LC

NP4 * PM3

ANON

LIFE AND WORKS OF STEPHEN HELLER, THE PIANOFORTE COMPOSER, THE ..A
BIOGRAPHICAL SKETCH, WITH ESSAYS UPON HELLER'S ETUDES

      PHILADELPHIA   1884+   BLAWOS
      PRESSER, THEODORE, COMPANY

NP4 * NP6 * PM3 * PM6

ANON

MASTER RULES FOR SUCCESSFUL PIANO PRACTICE..A COLLECTION OF
EIGHTEEN SETS...

      PHILADELPHIA   1910   49P   BMRFSP
      PRESSER, THEODORE, COMPANY
NP

PL7

ANON

NEW AND COMPLETE INSTRUCTIONS FOR THE HARPSICHORD, PIANO FORTE OR
ORGAN...TO WHICH IS ADDED...THE RULES OF THOROUGH BASS

      LONDON   1700+   32P   BNACIF
      ASTOR, G.
LC

MEX
PL4 * PL12 * AT4 * PT6 * KS10 * AP7

ANON

NEW INSTRUCTIONS FOR PLAYING THE HARPSICHORD, PIANOFORTE OR
SPINET--FACSIMILE---1789

      NEW YORK   1967   36P   BNIFPT
      BROUDE BROTHERS
IU * LC * NP * YU

CHR * GLO * ILL * MEX
KI8 * KI14 * PL4 * PL12 * AT4 * PT6 * PT9 * KS4 * KS10 * AP7

ANON

NEW PIANOFORTE KEYBOARD, THE ..CARD AND GAME, THE A.B.C. OF MUSIC

      LONDON   1903   BNPKCA
      MILES, H.
BR

KI5 * PL2 * PL4

ANON

OLD PIANO, THE ..A FANTASIA, WITH VARIATIONS HIGH FANTASTICAL,
ETC...IN VERSE

      MANCHESTER   1872   63P   BOPAFW
      O'CONNOR, B.
BR

KI2

ANON

PIANOFORTE POCKET COMPANION, THE ..OR, A POPULAR VIEW OF THE
SCIENCE AND PRACTICE OF MUSIC

      LONDON   1815   227P   BPPCOA
BR

INT * TAB
KI5 * KI8 * PL4 * KS4 * KS8

ANON

PIANO IN TWELVE LESSONS

      LONDON   1902   16P   BPITL
      RITCHIE-LISCARD, W.
BR

MEX
PL4 * AT4

ANON

PIANO LOVER, THE ..BY VARIOUS AUTHORS

      LONDON   1935   15P   BPLBVA
BR

KI2 * KI9

ANON

PLAYING THE HARPSICHORD, SPINET OR PIANO FORTE MADE EASY BY NEW
INSTRUCTIONS

      LONDON   1775+   37P   BPTHSO
      LONGMAN, LUKEY AND COMPANY
NP * YU

GLO * ILL * MEX * TAB
KI8 * PL4 * PT6 * KS10 * AP7

ANON

PRECEPTOR, FOR THE PIANOFORTE, THE ORGAN OR HARPSICHORD, THE
--FACSIMILE---1795+

      NEW YORK   1967   32P   BPFTPT
      BROUDE BROTHERS
IU * NP

CHR * GLO * ILL * MEX
KI8 * KI14 * PL4 * PL12 * AT4 * PT6 * PT9 * KS4 * KS10 * AP7

ANON

QUESTIONS AND ANSWERS ON THE SCIENCE AND ART OF PIANOFORTE
CONSTRUCTION

      LONDON   1925+   32P   BQAAOT
      MUSICAL OPINION

KI5

ANON

REPAIRING THE PIANOFORTE, WITH CHAPTERS ON REGULATING, TONING,
POLISHING, CASE REPAIRING, ETC.

      LONDON   1917   77P   BRTPWC
      MUSICAL OPINION, AND MUSIC TRADE REVIEW
BR * NP

ILL * INT * LDR
KI6 * KI8

ANON

RULES..OR A SHORT AND COMPLEAT METHOD FOR ATTAINING TO PLAY A
THOROUGH BASS UPON THE HARPSICHORD OR ORGAN

    LONDON   1730+   42P   BROASA
        WALSH, I.
LC

AT4 * KS10

ANON

SHORT INSTRUCTIONS FOR TUNING A PIANO-FORTE..WRITTEN BY 'MUSICUS
IGNORAMUS', FOR THE USE OF AMATEURS MORE IGNORANT THAN HIMSELF

    LONDON   1809   44P   BSIFTA
        BECKET, I., AND PORTER, J.
LC

TAB
KI8

ANON

THOROUGH BASS AT ONE VIEW, WITH DIRECTIONS FOR ACCOMPANIMENT AND
PROPER EXAMPLES

    LONDON   1700+   4P   BTBAOV
        THOMPSON'S WAREHOUSE
LC

AT4 * KS10

ANSON, GEORGE

CONTEMPORARY PIANO MUSIC OF THE AMERICAS, COMPILED BY GEORGE ANSON
FOR THE 1959 BIENNIAL CONVENTION OF THE M.T.N.A. IN KANSAS CITY,
MO., FEB. 24-28

    FT. WORTH, TEX.   1959   39P   BCPMOT
        MUSIC TEACHERS' NATIONAL ASSOCIATION
LC

INT
PM6

ANTCLIFFE, HERBERT

SUCCESSFUL MUSIC TEACHER, THE ..WORDS OF ADVICE

    LONDON   1914+   36P   BSMTWO
        AUGENER, LTD.

AT1 * AT3 * AT11 * AT13 * GI5

ANTRIM, DORAN K.

TEACHING MUSIC AND MAKING IT PAY

    PHILADELPHIA   1927   113P   BTMAMI
        PRESSER, THEODORE, COMPANY
IU * LC * NP

ILL * PHO
AT1 * AT3 * AT8 * AT9 * AT11 * AT13 * AT14 * GI5

APEL, WILLI

HISTORY OF KEYBOARD MUSIC TO 1700, THE --TRANSLATED AND REVISED BY
HANS TISCHLER---1967, IN GERMAN

    BLOOMINGTON, IND.   1972   878P   BHOKMT
        INDIANA UNIVERSITY PRESS
BR * IU * LC * NP * SA

APP * BIB * IND * INT * MEX
NP1 * KI1 * KI3 * KI5 * KI6 * KI9 * KI14 * PM1 * PM3 * PM4 * PM5 *
PM7 * PM8 * PM9 * PM14

APEL, WILLI

MASTERS OF THE KEYBOARD

    CAMBRIDGE, MASS.   1947   323P   BMOTK
        HARVARD UNIVERSITY PRESS
BP * BR * CP * CU * ES * IU * LC * MI * NP * OC * TO * UA * UC * UI
UK * UM * UO * US * UT * UU * UW * YU
BIB * ILL * IND * INT * LDR * MEX * MSF * PHO
KI1 * KI2 * KI5 * KI6 * KI7 * KI9 * KI13 * KI14 * PM3 * PM7 * PM8 *
PM13 * PM14 * PM15 * AP3 * AP4 * AP5

APPEL, PEARL *
ALEXANDER, RUTH
HARMONY AT THE PIANO LESSON, A COMPANION TO PIANO STUDY

    CHICAGO   1940   48P   BHATPL
        APPEL-ALEXANDER
LC

INT * MEX
AT4 * KS4

ARIZONA STATE MUSIC TEACHERS ASSOCIATION

GUIDE TO TEACHING PIANO--REV. ED.---1958

    PHOENIX, ARIZ.   1967   16P   BGTTPR
        ARIZONA STATE MUSIC TEACHERS ASSOCIATION
AS * UT

AT1

ARNIM, ANNA L.

COMPLETE COURSE OF WRIST AND FINGER GYMNASTICS, A --3RD. ED.---1880

    LONDON   1894   98P   BCCOWA
        HUTCHINGS AND CROWSLEY
BR * NP

INT
PT5

ARNOLD, FRANCK THOMAS

ART OF ACCOMPANIMENT FROM A THOROUGH-BASS, AS PRACTICED IN THE
17TH. AND 18TH. CENTURIES, THE --2 VOLS.---1931

    NEW YORK   1961   918P   BAOAFA
        DOVER PUBLICATIONS, INC.
IU * LC * NP

MEX
PL4 * AT4 * KS4 * KS10 * KS11 * EP6

ARONSON, MAURICE

KEY TO THE MINIATURES OF LEOPOLD GODOWSKY, A ..ANALYTICAL ESSAYS ON
THE FORTY-SIX 'MINIATURES FOR PIANO-FOUR HANDS'--6 VOLS.

    NEW YORK   1935   21P   BKTTMO
        FISCHER, CARL, INC.
BR * LC

INT
NP6 * PM3 * PM8 * PM9

ARPIN, PAUL

LIFE OF LOUIS MOREAU GOTTSCHALK

    NEW YORK   1852+   14P   BLOLMG
MI * NP

ILL
NP4 * PM3 * GI13

ASHBURNHAM, GEORGE

STORY OF UNIQUE PIANO TUITION, THE

    WOKING, SURREY, ENGLAND   1964   51P   BSOUPT
        ASHBURNHAM SCHOOL OF MUSIC
BR * LC * MI

AT1 * AT2 * AT4

ASSOCIATION FOR RECORDED SOUND COLLECTIONS

PRELIMINARY DIRECTORY OF SOUND RECORDING COLLECTIONS IN THE UNITED
STATES AND CANADA, A

    NEW YORK   1967   157P   BPDOSR
        NEW YORK PUBLIC LIBRARY
IU * LC * MI * TO * UM

DIS * INT
KI10 * KI15 * PM12 * GI4 * GI12

AULD, WILDA J.

HANDBOOK FOR THE CHURCH PIANIST, A

    KANSAS CITY   1964   96P   BHFTCP
        LILLENAS PUBLISHING COMPANY
BP * CP * IU * LC

INT * CHR * MEX
PL4 * PL12 * PT1 * KS4 * KS7 * KS8 * PM14 * PM15 * AP8

AUTOPIANO COMPANY

PLAYER PIANO POINTERS

    VESTAL, N. Y.   1967   31P   BPPP
        VESTAL PRESS
NP

ILL * IND * LDR
KI5 * KI6 * KI8 * KI10 * KI12

AUTO PNEUMATIC ACTION COMPANY

HOW TO TEST AND REGULATE THE WELTE-MIGNON REPRODUCING PIANO

    NEW YORK   1924   23P   BHTTAR
        AUTO PNEUMATIC ACTION COMPANY
NP

INT * LDR * PHO
KI5 * KI6 * KI8 * KI10

AUTO PNEUMATIC ACTION COMPANY

WELTE-MIGNON BOOK...OF FAMOUS ARTISTS, THE

    NEW YORK   1927   72P   BWMBOF
        AUTO PNEUMATIC ACTION COMPANY
LC * NP

INT * LDR * PHO
NP5 * KI10 * GI13

AXTENS, FLORENCE

FIRST SIX MONTHS IN THE PIANO CLASS, THE ..A MANUAL FOR TEACHERS

       LONDON   1932   24P   BFSMIT
           HAWKES AND SON
BR

PL4 * AT4 * AT7

AXTENS, FLORENCE

PIANO CLASS INSTRUCTION FOR CHILDREN AND ADULT CLASSES..A MANUAL
FOR TEACHERS

       LONDON   1939   62P   BPCIFC
           HAWKES AND SON
BR * IU * LC * NP

LDR * MEX
AT7

AXTENS, FLORENCE

PIANO CLASS METHOD..THE FIRST TWELVE MONTHS IN THE PIANO CLASS

       LONDON   1933   36P   BPCMTF
           BOOSEY AND HAWKES
CU * LC * NP * SA

CHR * INT * MEX * PHO
PL4 * PL12 * AT4 * AT5 * AT7 * PT9

AZULAY, GERTRUDE

CHOPIN..THE STORY OF THE BOY WHO MADE BEAUTIFUL MELODIES

       NEW YORK   1932   16P   BCTSOT
           BOOSEY AND COMPANY, LTD.
LC

ILL
NP4 * PM3 * GI10

BABBINGTON, CHARLES

TUNING AND REPAIRING PIANOFORTES..THE AMATEURS GUIDE--2ND. ED.

       LONDON   1902   72P   BTARPT
           GILL, L. U.
BR * IU * LC

IND * INT * MEX
KI4 * KI8 * KI12

BABBITT, WILLIAM

PHYSIOLOGICAL METHOD FOR PLAYING THE PIANO-FORTE, DESIGNED AS A
MANUAL OF TECHNIQUE, AND TO SUPERCEDE THE EXCESSIVE PRACTICE OF
'STUDIES' AND 'FIVE-FINGER' EXERCISES, A
       NEW YORK   1880   12P   BPMFPT
           WEBB, F. H.
LC

INT * MEX
AT4 * PT1 * PT3 * PT6 * PT8 * AP7

BABITZ, SOL

ON USING EARLY KEYBOARD FINGERING--REPRINT OF 3 ARTICLES FROM THE
'DIAPASON' IN 1969

       LOS ANGELES   1969   23P   BOUEKF
           EARLY MUSIC LABORATORY
IU

KI14 * PT6

BACH, CARL PHILIPP EMANUEL

CARL PHILIPP EMANUEL BACH'S AUTOBIOGRAPHY..FACSIMILE OF ORIGINAL
EDITION OF 1773 WITH CRITICAL ANNOTATIONS BY WILLIAM S. NEWMAN

       HILVERSUM   1967   20P   BCPEBA
           KNUF, FRITS A. M.
IU * LC

NP6

BACH, CARL PHILIPP EMANUEL

ESSAY ON THE TRUE ART OF PLAYING KEYBOARD INSTRUMENTS---TWO PTS.,
1753-1762, IN GERMAN

       NEW YORK   1948   449P   BEOTTA
           NORTON, W. W., AND COMPANY, INC.
AS * BP * BR * CP * CU * ES * IU * LC * MI * NP * OC * TO * UA * UC
UI * UK * UM * UO * US * UT * UU * UW * YU
BIB * ILL * INT * MEX
PT6 * KS5 * KS10 * AP7 * EP6

BACHE, CONSTANCE

BROTHER MUSICIANS..REMINISCENCES OF EDWARD AND WALTER BACHE

       LONDON   1901   330P   BBMROE
           METHUEN AND COMPANY, LTD.
BP * BR * ES * NP * UA

APP * ILL * IND * INT * MEX * PHO * TAB
NP3 * NP6 * PM6

BACON, ERNST

NOTES ON THE PIANO

       SYRACUSE, N. Y.   1963   167P   BNOTP
           SYRACUSE UNIVERSITY PRESS
AS * BP * BR * CP * CU * ES * IU * LC * MI * NP * OC * SA * TO * UA
UI * UM * UO * US * UT * UU * UW * YU
INT
PL7 * AT1 * PT3 * PT8 * PT9 * PM4 * AP7 * AP8 * EP1 * GI2

BADURA-SKODA, EVA *
BADURA-SKODA, PAUL
INTERPRETING MOZART ON THE KEYBOARD---1957, IN GERMAN

       LONDON   1962   319P   BIMOTK
           BARRIE AND ROCKLIFF
AS * BP * BR * CP * ES * IU * LC * MI * NP * OC * SA * TO * UA * UC
UI * UK * UM * UO * US * UW * YU
BIB * ILL * IND * MEX
KI3 * KI9 * PL12 * PM4 * PM8 * PM9 * PM11 * PM15 * AP7 * AP8

BAGBY, ALBERT MORRIS

LISZT'S WEIMAR

       NEW YORK   1961   125P   BLW
           YOSELOFF, THOMAS
BP * IU * LC * MI * NP * SA * TO * UA

INT * PHO
NP4

BAGGER, EUGENE S.

EMINENT EUROPEANS..STUDIES IN CONTINENTAL REALITY---PADEREWSKI

       NEW YORK   1922   283P   BEESIC
           PUTNAM'S, G. P., SONS
BR * LC * NP

ILL * INT
NP4 * PM3 * GI13

BAILLIE, ALEXANDER--SUPPOSED AUTHOR

INTRODUCTION TO THE KNOWLEDGE AND PRACTICE OF THE THORO' BASS, AN

       EDINBURGH   1717   11P   BITTKA
           BAILLIE, ALEXANDER
LC

MEX * TAB
PL4 * AT4 * KS8 * KS10

BAINES, ANTHONY

EUROPEAN AND AMERICAN MUSICAL INSTRUMENTS

       LONDON   1966   174P   BEAAMI
           BATSFORD, B. T.
BR * IU * LC

KI3 * KI5 * KI6 * KI9 * KI12 * KI13

BAINES, ANTHONY

MUSICAL INSTRUMENTS THROUGH THE AGES--REV. ED.---1961

       LONDON   1966   344P   BMITTA
           FABER AND FABER
BR * IU * LC * NP

BIB * GLO * ILL * IND * LDR * MEX * PHO
KI3 * KI5 * KI6 * KI12 * KI13 * KI14

BAINTON, HERBERT G.

PIANO, ITS CONSTRUCTION AND CARE, THE

       PROVIDENCE, R. I.   1915   38P   BPICAC
           EVANS PRINTING COMPANY
LC

INT
KI5 * KI6 * KI8

BAKER, DAVID

JAZZ IMPROVISATION..A COMPREHENSIVE METHOD OF STUDY FOR ALL PLAYERS

       CHICAGO   1969   183P   BJIACM
           MAHER, J.
IU

BIB * CHR * DIS * ILL * MEX * PHO * TAB
PL10 * PT9 * KS4 * KS6

BAKER, HENRIETTE

PRACTICAL METHOD FOR THE PIANOFORTE FOR PRIVATE CLASS LESSONS--2
BKS.

                       1894+   51P   BPMFTP
           BONER, W. H., AND COMPANY
LC

INT * MEX
AT4 * AT7

BAKER, PERCY

STUDIES IN MODULATION FOR PRACTICAL AND THEORETICAL PURPOSES

       LONDON   1923   56P   BSIMFP
       REEVES, WILLIAM
BR * LC * NP

MEX
KS8

BALDWIN PIANO COMPANY

MANUALO, THE PLAYER PIANO THAT IS ALL BUT HUMAN, THE ..CARE,
REGULATION, REPAIR

       CINCINNATI   1916   54P   BMTPPT
       BALDWIN PIANO COMPANY, THE
LC

KI8 * KI10 * KI12

BALLANTINE, BILL

PIANO, THE ..AN INTRODUCTION TO THE INSTRUMENT

       NEW YORK   1971   128P   BPAITT
       WATTS, F.
LC

BIB * DIS * GLO * ILL * IND * INT * LDR * PHO
NP5 * KI3 * KI5 * KI6 * KI8 * KI9 * KI12 * KI13 * AP3 * GI10

BALTIMORE--MUSEUM OF ART

MUSICAL INSTRUMENTS AND THEIR PORTRAYAL IN ART---EXHIBIT--BALTIMORE
MUSEUM OF ART, APRIL 26 TO JUNE 2, 1946

       BALTIMORE   1946   48P   BMIATP
       BALTIMORE MUSEUM OF ART
IU * LC

GLO * ILL * INT
KI9 * KI12 * KI13 * KI14 * KI15 * GI15

BAMBERGER, LOUIS

MEMORIES OF SIXTY YEARS IN THE TIMBER AND PIANOFORTE TRADES

       LONDON   1930   270P   BMOSYI
       LOW, S., MARSTON AND COMPANY, LTD.
BR * LC * NP

ILL * INT
NP6 * KI1 * KI5 * KI10 * KI12 * GI5

BANISTER, HENRY C.

ART OF MODULATING, THE --A SERIES OF PAPERS ON MODULATION AT THE
PIANOFORTE---62 MUSICAL EXAMPLES

       NEW YORK   1901   87P   BAOMAS
       CROWN PUBLISHERS
BR

MEX
KS8

BANISTER, HENRY C.

HARMONIZING OF MELODIES, THE ..A TEXT-BOOK FOR STUDENTS AND
TEACHERS

       LONDON   1905+   67P   BHOMAT
       REEVES, WILLIAM
LC * NP

INT * MEX
PL12 * KS4 * KS8

BANTLY, BENEDICT

SIMPLE TREATISE ON SCALES AND ARPEGGIOS FOR PIANO, A --3 VOLS.

       NEW YORK   1920   59P   BSTOSA
       LUCKHARDT AND BELDER
LC

INT * MEX
PT9

BARBEDETTE, HIPPOLYTE

STEPHEN HELLER..HIS LIFE AND WORKS

       LONDON   1877   89P   BSHHLA
       ASHDOWN AND PARRY
BR * IU * LC

APP * INT * MSF
NP4 * PM3 * PM6

BARBOUR, JAMES MURRAY

TUNING AND TEMPERAMENT---1951

       NEW YORK   1972   228P   BTATNF
       DA CAPO PRESS
AS * BP * BR * ES * IU * LC * MI * NP * OC * TO * UA * UI * UM * UT

BIB * CHR * GLO * ILL * IND * INT * TAB
KI8

BARFORD, PHILIP

KEYBOARD MUSIC OF C. P. E. BACH, THE ..CONSIDERED IN RELATION TO
HIS MUSICAL AESTHETIC AND THE RISE OF THE SONATA PRINCIPLE

       LONDON   1965   186P   BKMOCP
       BARRIE AND ROCKLIFF
AS * BP * BR * CP * ES * IU * LC * MI * NP * OC * TO * UA * UI * UM
UO * US * UT * UU * UW
APP * BIB * DIS * IND * INT * MEX * MSF
NP3 * PM3 * PM4 * PM8 * PM9 * PM14 * AP3 * AP4

BARNETT, DAVID

PERFORMANCE OF MUSIC, THE ..A STUDY IN TERMS OF THE PIANOFORTE

       NEW YORK   1972   232P   BPOMAS
       UNIVERSE BOOKS
IU * LC

APP * GLO * MEX
PL4 * PL5 * PL7 * PL12 * PL15 * PT3 * AP3 * AP4

BARNETT, JOHN FRANCIS

MUSICAL REMINISCENCES AND IMPRESSIONS---TEACHER, PIANIST, CONDUCTOR

       LONDON   1906   341P   BMRAIT
       HODDEN AND STOUGHTON
LC * NP

ILL * IND * INT * MEX * PHO
NP6

BARNWELL, V. T.

BARNWELL'S NORMAL KEYBOARD AND STAFF STUDIES--THE MENTAL
PRE-PERCEPTION METHOD...FOR SCHOOLS AND CLASSES

       ATLANTA   1912   96P   BBNKAS
       BARNWELL, V. T.
LC

ILL * INT * MEX * TAB
PL4 * AT4 * AT7 * PT9 * KS3 * KS4 * KS7

BARRY, KEITH LEWIS

CHOPIN AND HIS FOURTEEN DOCTORS

       SYDNEY   1934   BCAHFD

NP4 * GI12 * GI15

BARTELS, LEO F. *
DOLGE, R.

PERFORATING OF MUSIC ROLLS WITH THE LEABARJAN PERFORATOR, THE

       HAMILTON, OHIO   1919   31P   BPOMRW
       LEABARJAN MANUFACTURING COMPANY, THE
LC * NP

GLO * ILL * INT * LDR * MEX * PHO * TAB
KI10 * PM12 * GI4

BARTH, HANS

TECHNIC..FOR DEVELOPING AN EARLY FOUNDATION IN PIANO PLAYING

       NEW YORK   1935   51P   BTFDAE
       FISCHER, J., AND BRO.
LC * NP * US

INT * MEX
PT4 * PT9 * PT10

BARTH, HANS

TECHNIC..THE ENTIRE 25 BRANCHES FOR DEVELOPING TECHNIC NECESSARY TO
GOOD PIANO PLAYING, INCLUDING RHYTHMIC AND DYNAMIC VARIATIONS--2
VOLS.---1935

       NEW YORK   1949+   102P   BTTETF
       FISCHER, J., AND BRO.
LC * NP

INT * MEX
PL12 * PL15 * PT1 * PT11

BARTHELEMON, FRANCOIS H.

NEW TUTOR FOR THE HARPSICHORD OR PIANO FORTE, WHEREIN THE FIRST
PRINCIPLES OF MUSIC ARE FULLY EXPLAINED, A

       LONDON   1795+   36P   BNTFTH
       BARTHELEMON, FRANCOIS H.
LC

MEX
PL4 * PL12 * AT4 * PT6

BARTHOLOMEW, RALPH I.

MAKING OF A STEINWAY, THE

       NEW YORK   1929   18P   BMOAS
       STEINWAY AND SONS
UT

ILL
KI3 * KI5 * KI6 * KI12

BARTOK, BELA *
RESCHOVSKY, SANDOR
BARTOK-RESCHOVSKY PIANO METHOD---1913

       BUDAPEST   1967   79P   BBRPMN
          EDITIO MUSICA
  CU

  CHR * LDR * MEX * PHO
  AT4

BASTIEN, JAMES W. *
BASTIEN, JANE SMISOR
BEGINNING PIANO FOR ADULTS

       PARK RIDGE, ILL.   1968   212P   BBPFA
          GENERAL WORDS AND MUSIC COMPANY
  IU * SA

  APP * CHR * GLO * ILL * IND * INT * MEX * PHO * TAB
  PL4 * PL5 * PL7 * PL10 * PL11 * PL12 * PL13 * PL14 * PL15 * AT4 *
  AT6 * AT7 * PT9 * PT10 * KS3 * KS4 * KS5 * KS7 * EP4

BASTIEN, JAMES W.

HOW TO TEACH PIANO SUCCESSFULLY

       PARK RIDGE, ILL.   1973   496P   BHTTPS
          KJOS, NEIL A.
  IU * SA

  APP * BIB * IND * INT * LDR * MEX * PHO
  NP8 * PL4 * PL8 * AT1 * AT2 * AT3 * AT5 * AT6 * AT7 * AT8 * AT9 *
  AT13 * AT14 * PM4 * AP7 * GI5 * GI8 * GI9 * GI13

BAUER, HAROLD

HAROLD BAUER, HIS BOOK---1948

       NEW YORK   1969   306P   BHBHBN
          GREENWOOD PRESS
  AS * BP * BR * CP * IU * LC * NP * OC * SA * UA * UC * UI * UK * UO
  US * UT * YU
  ILL * IND * MEX * PHO
  NP6

BAUER, HAROLD

PIANIST'S WARMING-UP EXERCISES FOR THE MAINTENANCE AND IMPROVEMENT
OF TECHNICAL FLUENCY, THE

       NEW YORK   1950   12P   BPWUEF
          SCHIRMER, G., INC.
  UT

  PT5 * PT10

BAUER, HAROLD *
DILLER, ANGELA
PIANO METHOD FOR CLASS AND INDIVIDUAL INSTRUCTION--2 VOLS.

       NEW YORK   1931+   108P   BPMFCA
          SCHIRMER, G., INC.
  LC

  ILL * INT * MEX * PHO
  AT4 * AT5 * AT7

BAUER, HAROLD

PRIMER FOR PRACTICAL KEYBOARD MODULATION, A

       NEW YORK   1949   15P   BPFPKM
          SCHIRMER, G., INC.
  ES * IU * LC * NP * UI * UT * UW

  APP * INT * MEX
  KS8

BAUGHAN, EDWARD ALGERNON

IGNACE JAN PADEREWSKI

       LONDON   1908   92P   BIJP
          LANE, JOHN, LTD.
  BP * BR * ES * LC * MI * NP * OC * UA * LC * UT * UW * YU

  ILL * PHO
  NP4 * AT3 * PM3 * GI13

BAVIN, JOHN T.

PIANO CLASS INSTRUCTOR

       LONDON   1930+   BPCI
          HAWKES AND SON

  PL4 * AT4 * AT7

BAXTER, JAMES

INDUCTIVE GRAMMAR OF MUSIC, FOR CLASS, PRIVATE LESSON, OR SELF
STUDY, CONTAINING ELEMENTS OF MUSIC, NOTATION, THOROUGH BASE, AND
MUSICAL RENDITION
       FRIENDSHIP, N. Y.   1874   80P   BIGOMF
          CRANDALL, J. C.
  LC

  PL4 * PL11 * AT4 * AT7 * KS10

BAXTER, JAMES

NEW SCHOOL OF MUSIC, THE ..PRACTICAL THOROUGH BASE CULTURE, FOR
SELF-STUDY, PRIVATE LESSON AND CLASS TEACHING

       NEW YORK   1878   88P   BNSOMP
          CADY, C. M.
  LC

  PL4 * PL11 * AT4 * AT7 * KS10

BEAUFORT, RAPHAEL

FRANZ LISZT, THE STORY OF HIS LIFE--TO WHICH IS ADDED..'LISZT AS A
LITTERATEUR', ESSAY BY T. C. MARTIN

       BOSTON   1887   233P   BFLTSO
          DITSON, OLIVER, COMPANY
  BR * IU * LC * NP

  APP * ILL
  NP3 * PM9

BECKER, JULIUS

CONCISE TREATISE ON HARMONY, ACCOMPANIMENT, AND COMPOSITION, FOR
THE USE OF MUSICAL AMATEURS, A --IN 10 LECTURES

       LONDON   1845   31P   BCTOHA
          EWER AND COMPANY
  BR * LC * NP

  INT * MEX
  PL4 * KS4 * KS8 * KS11 * EP6 * GI11

BECKERMAN, H. J.

AMERICAN SCHOOL OF RAGTIME PIANO PLAYING, THE

       CHICAGO   1913+   46P   BASORP
          AMERICAN MUSICAL COLLEGE
  NP

  INT * MEX
  PL4 * AT4 * PT10 * KS6

BECKETT, WALTER

LISZT

       NEW YORK   1956   185P   BL
          FARRAR, STRAUSS AND CUDAHY
  IU * LC * NP

  APP * BIB * ILL * IND * INT * LDR * MEX
  NP3 * PM8 * PM9 * PM13

BEDBROOK, GERALD STARES

KEYBOARD MUSIC FROM THE MIDDLE AGES TO THE BEGINNINGS OF THE
BAROQUE---1949

       NEW YORK   1970   186P   BKMFTM
          DA CAPO PRESS
  BP * BR * CP * CU * IU * LC * MI * NP * OC * UA * UC * UI * UK * UM
  UO * US * UT * UW

  KI14 * PM3 * PM7 * PM14 * PM15

BEHREND, WILLIAM

LUDWIG VAN BEETHOVEN'S PIANOFORTE SONATAS

       NEW YORK   1927   199P   BLVBPS
          DUTTON, E. P., AND COMPANY
  BP * BR * CU * ES * LC * MI * NP * UA * UC * UK * UO * YU

  BIB * ILL * IND * INT
  PM3 * PM9 * PM14

BEMETZRIEDER, ANTON

ABSTRACT OF A NEW METHOD OF TEACHING THE PRINCIPLES OF MUSIC,
RESPECTING THE ART OF MODULATION, ACCOMPANYMENT, AND COMPOSITION

       LONDON   1782   55P   BAOANM
          BEMETZRIEDER, ANTON
  LC

  PL4 * AT4 * KS8 * KS11 * EP6

BEMETZRIEDER, ANTON

ACCOUNT OF A NEW WAY OF CONSIDERING MUSICK, AND TEACHING
IT--INTENDED TO SERVE AS AN EXPLANATION OF AND COMPANION TO HIS NEW
LESSONS FOR THE HARPSICHORD
       LONDON   1783   62P   BAOANW
          BEMETZRIEDER, ANTON
  LC * NP

  INT * MEX
  KI14 * PT1 * KS3 * KS4 * KS11 * EP6

BEMETZRIEDER, ANTON

ART OF MODULATING, ILLUSTRATED, THE

       LONDON   1792   39P   BAOMI
          SKILLERN, T.
  IU * LC * NP

  MEX
  KS8

BEMETZRIEDER, ANTON

    ART OF TUNING OUR INSTRUMENTS MADE INTERESTING AND EASY TO ALL
    STUDENTS IN MUSIC, THE

          LONDON   1808+   11P   BAOTOI
            GOULDING, PHIPPS, D'ALMAINE AND COMPANY
  LC

  INT * MEX
  KI8

BEMETZRIEDER, ANTON

    COMPENDIUM OF A NEW METHOD OF MUSIC...WITH THE AUTHOR'S PRINCIPLES
    AND METHOD OF TEACHING

          LONDON   1783+   62P   BCOANM
            BEMETZRIEDER, ANTON
  LC * NP

  INT * MEX
  PL4 * AT3 * AT4 * AT5 * AT6 * KS3 * KS4 * KS10 * AP7 * EP6

BEMETZRIEDER, ANTON

    GAMUT AND COMMON CHORD IN ALL KEYS, FINGERED FOR THE HARPSICHORD,
    THE ..WITH VARIOUS LESSONS FROM DIFFERENT AUTHORS FOR YOUNG
    SCHOLARS
          LONDON   1785+   33P   BGACCI
            BEMETZRIEDER, ANTON
  LC

  MEX
  PL4 * AT4 * PT6 * AP7

BEMETZRIEDER, ANTON

    MUSIC MADE EASY TO EVERY CAPACITY, IN A SERIES OF DIALOGUES..BEING
    PRACTICAL LESSONS FOR THE HARPSICHORD

          LONDON   1778   249P   BMMETE
            RANDALL, W.
  BR * ES * IU * LC * NP * TO * UA

  INT * MEX
  PL4 * PL7 * PL12 * AT4 * KS4

BEMETZRIEDER, ANTON

    NEW GUIDE TO MUSIC, IN FRENCH AND ENGLISH, A

          LONDON   1780+   22P   BNGTMI
            GOULDING, G.
  NP

  MEX * TAB
  PL4 * PL12 * PT6 * KS4 * KS7 * AP7

BEMETZRIEDER, ANTON

    NEW LESSONS FOR THE HARPSICHORD

          LONDON   1783   120P   BNLFTH
            BEMETZRIEDER, ANTON
  BR * ES * LC * TO * UA

  KI14 * PL2 * PL4 * KS4

BENDER, GEORGE CHARLES

    BUSINESS MANUAL FOR PIANO TEACHERS

          PHILADELPHIA   1910   109P   BBMFPT
            PRESSER, THEODORE, COMPANY
  BP * IU * LC * UT

  ILL * INT * LDR * TAB
  AT9 * GI5

BENEDICT, LADY *
GODDARD, ARABELLA *
    HOW TO PLAY THE PIANOFORTE

          LONDON   1884   140P   BHTPTP
            REL. TR. SOC.
  BP * BR

  PL2 * PL11 * AT4

BENEDICT, MILO ELLSWORTH

    THIRTY-THREE SUGGESTIONS IN ONE LESSON..FOR THE GUIDANCE AND
    ENCOURAGEMENT OF THOSE WHO PLAY THE PIANO

          BOSTON   1915   40P   BTTSIO
            THOMPSON, C. W.
  BP

  PL2 * AT2

BENNER, LORA

    BENNER BLUE BOOK, THE ..PRACTICAL MANUAL OF PIANO TEACHING--4TH.
    ED.

          SCHENECTADY, N. Y.   1965   45P   BBBBPM
            BENNER PUBLISHERS
  IU * SA * UI

  BIB * CHR * INT * TAB
  PL4 * PL7 * PL10 * AT4 * AT5 * AT8 * AT9 * PM4 * PM6 * GI5 * GI6

BENNER, LORA

    BENNER GOLD BOOK, THE ..PIANO MATERIAL AND TEACHING METHODS--3RD.
    ED.

          SCHENECTADY, N. Y.   1966   39P   BBGBPM
            BENNER PUBLISHERS
  IU * SA * UI

  BIB * CHR * INT * MEX
  PL4 * AT3 * AT5 * PT1 * PT9 * PT10 * PT11 * PM3 * PM5 * PM6 * EP4 *
  EP5

BENNER, LORA

    THEORY FOR PIANO STUDENTS--1ST. YEAR, PRIVATE OR CLASS--5 VOLS.,
    1963-1968

          NEW YORK   1963   264P   BTFPSF
            SCHIRMER, G., INC.
  IU * LC

  IND * INT * MEX
  PL4 * AT4 * KS4

BENNETT, BEULAH VARNER

    PIANO CLASSES FOR EVERYONE..A PRACTICAL GUIDE FOR PIANO TEACHERS

          NEW YORK   1969   75P   BPCFEA
            PHILOSOPHICAL LIBRARY
  LC * SA * UI

  AT1 * AT7

BENNETT, JOSEPH

    FREDERIC CHOPIN--NOVELLO'S BIOGRAPHY PRIMERS

          NEW YORK   1884+   85P   BFCNBP
            NOVELLO, EWER AND COMPANY
  BR * LC * NP

  IND * INT
  NP4 * PM3

BEREGSZASZY, LAJOS

    OBSERVATIONS CONCERNING IMPROVEMENTS IN THE CONSTRUCTION OF THE
    SOUNDING BOARD OF PIANO-FORTES---IN ENGLISH, FRENCH, GERMAN AND
    HUNGARIAN
          BUDAPEST   1862   31P   BOCIIT
            HERZ, J.
  LC

  NP6 * KI5

BERGER, FRANCESCO

    FIRST STEPS AT THE PIANOFORTE

          LONDON   1894   160P   BFSATP
            NOVELLO, EWER AND COMPANY
  BR * LC * NP * UM

  INT * MEX
  PL4 * PL12 * PL15 * AT4 * PT4 * PT8 * PT9 * PT10

BERINGER, OSCAR

    FIFTY YEARS EXPERIENCE OF PIANOFORTE TEACHING AND PLAYING

          LONDON   1907   72P   BFYEOP
            BOSWORTH AND COMPANY, LTD.
  BR * LC

  NP6

BERKOWITZ, FREDA

    ON LUTES, RECORDERS AND HARPSICHORDS..MEN AND MUSIC OF THE BAROQUE

          NEW YORK   1967   168P   BOLRAH
            ATHENEUM PUBLISHERS
  LC * NP

  GLO * ILL
  KI14

BERLIN, BORIS *
BOYLE, MURIEL *
    BORIS BERLIN MUSICAL KINDERGARTEN PIANO METHOD, THE.. GUIDE FOR
    TEACHERS

          TORONTO   1940   80P   BBBMKP
            HEINTZMAN
  LC * TO

  ILL * INT * LDR * MEX
  AT4 * AT5

BERNER, ALFRED *
VANDER MEER, J. H.
    PRESERVATION AND RESTORATION OF MUSICAL INSTRUMENTS..PROVISIONAL
    RECOMMENDATIONS

          LONDON   1967   77P   BPAROM
            EVELYN, ADAMS AND MACKAY
  BR * LC

  KI8

BERNING, ALICE B. *
BERNHART, G. FRED
    KEYBOARD EXPERIENCES FOR CLASSROOM TEACHERS

            DUBUQUE, IOWA   1968   237P   BKEFCT
                BROWN, WILLIAM C., COMPANY
    LC

    ILL * MEX
    PL4 * AT4 * AT7 * KS5

BERNSTEIN, MARTIN--COMPILER

    SCORE READING..A SERIES OF GRADED EXCERPTS

            NEW YORK   1947   106P   BSRASO
                WITMARK, M., AND SONS
    IU * LC * NP

    IND * INT * MEX * TAB
    KS9

BERTENSSON, SERGEI *
LEYDA, JAY
    SERGEI RACHMANINOFF, A LIFETIME IN MUSIC

            NEW YORK   1956   464P   BSRALI
                NEW YORK UNIVERSITY PRESS
    AS * BP * BR * ES * IU * LC * MI * NP * OC * TO * UA * UM

    APP * DIS * ILL * IND * INT * MEX * PHO
    NP3

BERTINI, HENRI

    BERTINI'S SELF-TEACHING CATECHISM OF MUSIC FOR THE PIANOFORTE

            LONDON   1880+   40P   BBSTCO
                MUSICAL BOUQUET OFFICE
    NP

    APP * CHR * MEX
    PL4 * PL11 * PT4 * PT9

BESSARABOFF, NICHOLAS

    ANCIENT EUROPEAN MUSICAL INSTRUMENTS...IN THE LESLIE LINDSAY MASON
    COLLECTION AT THE MUSEUM OF FINE ARTS
            BOSTON   1941   503P   BAEMII
                HARVARD UNIVERSITY PRESS
    BR * IU * LC * NP

    APP * BIB * ILL * IND * INT * LDR * MEX * PHO * TAB
    KI3 * KI5 * KI6 * KI12 * KI14

BEVITT, ZAY RECTOR

    CLASS PROCEDURE FOR 40 LESSONS IN PIANO PLAYING BY HARMONY DIAGRAMS

            SAN FRANCISCO   1929   75P   BCPFFL
                SHERMAN CLAY AND COMPANY
    BR * LC

    INT
    AT4 * AT7 * KS4

BEVITT, ZAY RECTOR

    PIANO PLAYING BY HARMONY DIAGRAMS..STUDENT'S BOOK

            SAN FRANCISCO   1925   48P   BPPBHD
                SHERMAN CLAY AND COMPANY
    BR * ES

    PL2 * AT4

BEVITT, ZAY RECTOR

    PIANO PLAYING BY HARMONY DIAGRAMS..TEACHER'S MANUAL

            SAN FRANCISCO   1925+   63P   BPPBHD
                SHERMAN CLAY AND COMPANY
    BR * ES * LC * MI

    PL2 * AT4

BIART, VICTOR

    PIANIST'S GUIDE, THE ..A SERIES OF PAMPHLETS ON THE TEACHING AND
    RENDERING OF STANDARD PIANO PIECES
            NORWALK, CONN.   1934+   66P   BPGASO
                GORHAM PRESS, THE
    LC

    MEX
    AT4 * AT10 * AT14 * PM3 * PM8 * PM14

BIDOU, HENRI

    CHOPIN

            NEW YORK   1927   267P   BC
                KNOPF, ALFRED A., INC.
    BR * LC * NP

    ILL * MEX * MSF
    NP4 * PM3

BIE, OSKAR

    HISTORY OF THE PIANOFORTE AND PIANOFORTE PLAYERS, A ---1899

            NEW YORK   1966   336P   BHOTPA
                DA CAPO PRESS
    AS * BP * BR * CP * CU * ES * IU * LC * MI * NP * SA * TO * UA * UC
    UI * UK * UM * UO * US * UT * UU * UW * YU
    ILL * IND * INT * LDR * MSF * PHO
    NP3 * NP4 * KI3 * PM3 * PM7

BILL, EDWARD LYMAN

    PIANO SAVING AND HOW TO ACCOMPLISH IT

            NEW YORK   1909   32P   BPSAHT
                BILL, E. L.
    LC * NP

    KI8

BISHOP, DOROTHY

    CHORDS IN ACTION

            NEW YORK   1956   63P   BCIA
                FISCHER, CARL, INC.
    ES * IU * OC * SA * US * UT * UW

    INT * MEX
    KS1 * KS2 * KS4 * KS5 * KS7

BLAKE, DOROTHY

    FIRST STEPS IN CHORD PLAYING

            CINCINNATI   1930   BFSICP
                WILLIS MUSIC COMPANY

    PL4 * AT4 * KS4

BLAKE, DOROTHY

    FIRST STEPS IN THE USE OF THE PEDAL FOR PIANO

            CINCINNATI   1925   25P   BFSITU
                WILLIS MUSIC COMPANY
    LC

    INT * MEX
    AT4 * AP8

BLOCKLEY, JOHN

    PIANIST'S CATECHISM, THE ---1880

            LONDON   1955   78P   BPCEE
                ASCHERBERG, HOPWOOD AND CREW
    BP * BR * LC * SA

    APP * CHR * MEX
    PL4 * PL7 * PT4 * PT8

BLOM, ERIC

    BEETHOVEN'S PIANOFORTE SONATAS DISCUSSED---1938

            NEW YORK   1968   251P   BBPSDN
                DA CAPO PRESS
    BP * BR * CP * CU * ES * IU * LC * MI * NP * TO * UA * UC * UK * UM
    UO * UT * UW
    BIB * IND * MEX
    PM3 * PM7 * PM8 * PM9 * PM10 * PM11 * PM15 * AP3 * AP4

BLOM, ERIC

    ROMANCE OF THE PIANO, THE ---1928

            NEW YORK   1969   241P   BROTPN
                DA CAPO PRESS
    AS * BP * BR * CU * ES * IU * LC * SA * TO * UA * UC * UM * US * UT
    YU
    BIB * ILL * IND * LDR * MEX * PHO
    KI3 * KI5 * KI6 * KI9 * KI12 * KI13 * KI14 * PM7

BLYTHER, JAMES H.

    HOW TO TUNE YOUR OWN PIANO

            CAMDEN, N. J.   1961   49P   BHTTYO
                BLYTHER'S PIANO COMPANY
    LC

    KI8

BOAL, DEAN *
BOAL, ELLEN
    CONCEPTS AND SKILLS FOR THE PIANO..TEACHER'S MANUAL 1---CLASS
    INSTRUCTION
            NEW YORK   1969   BCASFT
                CANYON PRESS

    AT3 * AT4 * AT7

BOALCH, DONALD HOWARD

MAKERS OF THE HARPSICHORD AND CLAVICHORD, 1440 TO 1840

      LONDON   1956   169P   BMOTHA
        RONALD, G.
AS * BP * BR * CP * CU * ES * IU * LC * MI * NP * OC * TO * UA * UC
UI * UK * UM * UO * US * UT * UU * UW * YU
BIB * GLO * ILL * IND * PHO
KI3 * KI5 * KI14

BODDINGTON, HENRY

CATALOGUE OF MUSICAL INSTRUMENTS, PRINCIPALLY ILLUSTRATIVE OF THE
HISTORY OF THE PIANOFORTE

      MANCHESTER   1888   BCOMIP
        FALKNER, G., AND SONS
BR * TO

ILL
KI3 * KI13 * KI15

BODKY, ERWIN

INTERPRETATION OF BACH'S KEYBOARD WORKS, THE

      CAMBRIDGE, MASS.   1960   421P   BIOBKW
        HARVARD UNIVERSITY PRESS
AS * BP * BR * CP * CU * ES * IU * LC * MI * OC * TO * UA * UC * UI
UK * UM * UO * UT * UU * UW * YU
APP * BIB * CHR * ILL * IND * INT * LDR * MEX * MSF * PHO * TAB
KI3 * KI14 * PL12 * PM3 * PM4 * PM7 * PM8 * PM9 * PM14 * AP3 * AP4
AP6 * AP7 * AP8

BOGIANCKINO, MASSIMO

HARPSICHORD MUSIC OF DOMENICO SCARLATTI, THE

      ROME   1967   138P   BHMODS
        DESANTIS
IU * UA

BIB * INT * MEX
NP3 * KI14 * PM3

BOLTON, HETTY

HOW TO PRACTICE

      LONDON   1937   36P   BHTP
        ELKIN AND COMPANY, LTD.
BR * ES * IU * LC * SA * UI * UW

APP * INT * MEX
PL5 * PL6 * PL7 * PL8 * PL12 * PL14 * PT1 * PT2 * PT6 * PT8 * AP4

BOLTON, HETTY

ON TEACHING THE PIANO

      LONDON   1954   93P   BOTTP
        NOVELLO AND COMPANY, LTD.
AS * BR * CP * CU * IU * LC * MI * SA * UI * UM * UT * UW

APP * CHR * INT * MEX
PL3 * PL4 * PL6 * PL7 * PL8 * PL10 * PL14 * AT3 * AT4 * AT11 * PT1
PT4 * PT7 * PT9 * PT11 * KS3 * AP4 * AP6

BONE, AUDREY E.

JANE WILHELMINA STIRLING, 1804-1859..THE FIRST STUDY OF THE LIFE OF
CHOPIN'S PUPIL AND FRIEND

      GERRADS CROSS, BUCKS, ENGLAND 1960   107P   BJWSEH
        BONE, AUDREY
BR * LC * NP

APP * ILL * INT * PHO
NP3

BONPENSIERE, LUIGI

NEW PATHWAYS TO PIANO TECHNIQUE..A STUDY OF THE RELATIONS BETWEEN
MIND AND BODY

      NEW YORK   1953   128P   BNPTPT
        PHILOSOPHICAL LIBRARY
BR * CP * CU * ES * IU * LC * MI * NP * SA * TO * UA * UI * UK * UO
US * UT * UW * YU
CHR * IND * INT * LDR * MEX
PL1 * PL2 * PL3 * PL5 * PL7 * PL11 * PT3 * PT4 * PT6 * KS3 * KS5

BOOTH, VICTOR

WE PIANO TEACHERS--REVISED BY ADELE FRANKLIN---1946

      LONDON   1971   135P   BWPTRB
        SKEFFINGTON AND SONS, LTD.
BR * CP * CU * ES * IU * LC * NP * SA * UA * US

APP * BIB * IND * INT * MEX * PHO
PL1 * PL2 * PL4 * PL5 * PL7 * PL9 * PL12 * AT1 * AT2 * AT3 * PT4 *
PT6 * PT7 * PT8 * PT10 * KS3 * AP4 * AP8

BORREN, CHARLES VAN DEN

SOURCES OF KEYBOARD MUSIC IN ENGLAND, THE ---1913

      WESTPORT, CONN.   1970   378P   BSOKMI
        GREENWOOD PRESS
AS * BP * BR * CP * ES * IU * LC * MI * NP * OC * SA * TO * UA * UC
UI * UK * UM * UO * US * UT * UU * UW * YU
APP * CHR * IND * INT * MEX
KI3 * KI6 * KI9 * KI14 * PM3 * PM7 * PM13 * PM14 * PM15 * AP3 *
AP4

BORST, ALBERT W.

ADVICE TO YOUNG STUDENTS OF THE PIANOFORTE

      PHILADELPHIA   1881   8P   BATYSO
        PRESSER, THEODORE, COMPANY
BR * LC

AT1

BOS, COENRAAD V.

WELL-TEMPERED ACCOMPANIST, THE

      PHILADELPHIA   1949   162P   BWTA
        PRESSER, THEODORE, COMPANY
AS * BP * BR * CP * IU * LC * MI * NP * OC * SA * UA * UI * UO * US
UT * UW
DIS * MEX * PHO
NP6 * AP3 * AP4 * AP5 * EP6

BOSWORTH, HARRIETTE DEXTER

IDEAS FOR YOUNG PIANO TEACHERS

      BOSTON   1931   67P   BIFYPT
        DITSON, OLIVER, COMPANY
CU * ES * LC * US

MEX
PL12 * AT3 * AT5

BOTTOMLEY, JOSEPH

NEW SYSTEM OF PRACTICING AND TEACHING THE PIANOFORTE, A

      SHEFFIELD   1847   135P   BNSOPA
        SAXTON AND CHALONER
BR * YU

PL2 * PL7 * AT2 * AT4

BOUCOURECHLIEV, ANDRE

CHOPIN..A PICTORIAL BIOGRAPHY---137 ILLUSTRATIONS

      NEW YORK   1963   144P   BCAPBO
        VIKING PRESS, THE
BR * LC * NP

APP * ILL * IND * LDR * MSF * PHO
NP9

BOWEN, CAROLYN

OUTLINES FOR TRAINING PIANO TEACHERS

      MINNEAPOLIS   1924   89P   BOFTPT
        SCHMITT, P. A.
LC * MI * NP

BIB * CHR * INT * MEX * TAB
PL3 * PL4 * PL10 * PL12 * AT7 * AT9 * PT4 * KS3 * KS4 * KS7

BOWEN, CATHERINE DRINKER

FREE ARTIST..THE STORY OF ANTON AND NICHOLAS RUBINSTEIN

      NEW YORK   1939   412P   BFATSO
        RANDOM HOUSE
AS * BP * BR * ES * IU * MI * NP * OC * TO * UA * UI * UM * UT

APP * ILL * IND * PHO
NP3 * PM3 * PM6

BOWEN, YORK

PEDALLING THE MODERN PIANOFORTE---1936

      LONDON   1964   28P   BPTMPN
        OXFORD UNIVERSITY PRESS
BP * BR * CU * ES * IU * LC * SA * YU

CHR * MEX
KI5 * KI6 * PT8 * PM4 * AP8

BOWEN, YORK

SIMPLICITY OF PIANO TECHNIQUE, THE

      LONDON   1961   36P   BSOPT
        GALAXY MUSIC COMPANY
BR * IU * LC * MI * NP * SA * TO

IND
KI6 * PT1 * PT3 * PT4 * PT8 * PT9

BOWERS, Q. DAVID

ENCYCLOPEDIA OF AUTOMATIC MUSICAL INSTRUMENTS---INCLUDES A
DICTIONARY OF AUTOMATIC MUSICAL INSTRUMENT TERMS

      VESTAL, N. Y.   1972   1008P   BEOAMI
        VESTAL PRESS
IU * LC

BIB * IND * INT * PHO
KI10 * KI12 * KI13 * KI15 * GI5

BOWERS, Q. DAVID

GUIDEBOOK OF AUTOMATIC MUSICAL INSTRUMENTS, A. --2 VOLS.

      VESTAL, N. Y.   1967   697P   BGOAMI
         VESTAL PRESS
IU * LC * NP

ILL * IND * PHO
KI10 * KI13

BOWERS, Q. DAVID

PUT ANOTHER NICKEL IN..A HISTORY OF COIN-OPERATED PIANOS

      VESTAL, N. Y.   1966   243P   BPANIA
         VESTAL PRESS
LC * NP

ILL * PHO
KI10 * KI13

BOWMAN, EDWARD M.

MASTER LESSONS IN PIANOFORTE PLAYING, 'LETTERS FROM A MUSICIAN TO
HIS NEPHEW'

      PHILADELPHIA   1911   151P   BMLIPP
         PRESSER, THEODORE, COMPANY
BR * LC

NP6 * PM11

BOYD, MALCOLM

BACH'S INSTRUMENTAL COUNTERPOINT

      LONDON   1967   39P   BBIC
         BARRIE AND ROCKLIFF
IU * LC * NP

INT * MEX
KS4 * PM8 * PM14

BOYD, MALCOLM

HARMONIZING 'BACH' CHORALES

      LONDON   1967   40P   BHBC
         BARRIE AND ROCKLIFF
LC * NP

APP * IND * MEX * TAB
KS4 * PM3 * PM14

BRADLEY, VAN ALLEN

MUSIC FOR THE MILLIONS..THE KIMBALL PIANO AND ORGAN STORY

      CHICAGO   1957   334P   BMFTMT
         REGNERY, H., COMPANY
AS * BP * CP * IU * LC * MI * NP * OC * SA * TO * UI * UO * UT * UW

ILL * IND * LDR * PHO

BRAGARD, ROGER

MUSICAL INSTRUMENTS IN ART AND HISTORY

      NEW YORK   1967   281P   BMIIAA
         VIKING PRESS, THE
BR * IU * LC * NP

APP * BIB * GLO * ILL * IND * LDR * PHO
KI1 * KI2 * KI3 * KI5 * KI6 * KI9 * KI13 * KI14

BRANDT, LEONIE

SCIENCE IN MODERN PIANOFORTE PLAYING

      PHILADELPHIA   1922   46P   BSIMPP
         PRESSER, THEODORE, COMPANY
BR * LC * NP * UC

CHR * INT * MEX * PHO
PL7 * PL12 * PT1 * PT2 * PT3 * PT4 * PT6 * PT8 * PT9 * PT10

BRANSON, DAVID

JOHN FIELD AND CHOPIN

      NEW YORK   1972   216P   BJFAC
         ST. MARTIN'S PRESS
IU * LC

BIB * IND * INT * MEX
NP3 * PM3 * PM8 * PM9 * PM14 * AP4

BRECKENRIDGE, WILLIAM KILGORE

HINTS FOR PIANO NORMAL STUDIES

      NEW YORK   1955   177P   BHFPNS
         VANTAGE PRESS, INC.
BP * CP * CU * IU * LC * NP * OC * TO * UT

APP * BIB
PL7 * PL8 * PL12 * AT3 * PT5 * PT8 * PT9 * PT10 * KS3 * AP4 * AP8 *
AP9 * GI1

BREE, MADAME MALWINE

GROUNDWORK OF THE LESCHETIZKY METHOD, THE ---1902

      NEW YORK   1969   121P   BGOTLM
         HASKELL HOUSE PUBLISHERS
BP * CP * ES * IU * LC * NP * OC * SA * UA * UC * UI * UK * UM * UO
US * UT
APP * INT * MEX * PHO
PL7 * PT3 * PT4 * PT6 * PT8 * PT9 * PT10 * AP4 * AP8

BREITHAUPT, RUDOLPH MARIA

NATURAL PIANO-TECHNIC..SCHOOL OF WEIGHT TOUCH--2 VOLS.

      LEIPZIG   1909   100P   BNPTSO
         KAHNT, C. F., NACHFOLGER
BP * BR * CU * LC * NP * OC * US * YU

ILL * MEX * PHO
PL7 * PT3 * PT4 * PT7 * PT8 * PT9 * PT10

BREMNER, ROBERT

HARPSICHORD OR SPINNET MISCELLANY, THE --KEYBOARD TUTOR---FACSIMILE
EDITION OF PUBLICATION, CIRCA 1765

      WILLIAMSBURG, VA.   1972   26P   BHOSMK
         COLONIAL WILLIAMSBURG FOUNDATION, THE

MEX
PL4 * AT4 * PM4

BREMONT, ANNA

WORLD OF MUSIC, THE --THE GREAT COMPOSERS

      NEW YORK   1892   253P   BWOMTG
         BRENTANO
BR * LC * NP

INT
NP4

BREMONT, ANNA

WORLD OF MUSIC, THE --THE GREAT VIRTUOSI

      LONDON   1892   257P   BWOMTG
         GIBBINGS, W. W.
BP * BR * CP * ES * LC * MI * NP * UA * UC * UM * YU

NP5

BRESLIN, HOWARD

CONCERT GRAND---GOTTSCHALK

      NEW YORK   1963   307P   BCGG
         DODD, MEAD AND COMPANY
LC

INT
NP4 * PM3

BRIDGER, JOHN HENRY

HOW TO HARMONIZE MELODIES, WITH HINTS ON WRITING FOR STRINGS AND
PIANOFORTE ACCOMPANIMENTS

      LONDON   1909   104P   BHTHMW
         REEVES, WILLIAM
BR * LC * NP * SA

APP * BIB * INT * MEX
KS4 * KS8 * KS11 * PM5 * EP6

BRIED, FREDERICK

STIMULATION IN PIANO STUDY..HOW PARENTS CAN STIMULATE AND MAINTAIN
THEIR CHILD'S INTEREST IN PIANO PLAYING

      BROOKLYN, N. Y.   1945   24P   BSIPSH
         STUDIO TREND PUBLISHERS
LC

INT
KI4 * PL3 * AT5 * AT13 * GI11

BRIGGS, GILBERT A.

MUSICAL INSTRUMENTS AND AUDIO

      BRADFORD, SOMERSET, ENGLAND   1965   238P   BMIAA
         WHARFEDALE WIRELESS WORKS
BR * IU * LC

APP * BIB * ILL * IND * INT * LDR * MEX * PHO * TAB
KI3 * KI5 * KI6 * KI7 * KI8 * KI10 * KI11 * GI4

BRIGGS, GILBERT A.

PIANOS, PIANISTS AND SONICS

      BRADFORD, SOMERSET, ENGLAND   1951   192P   BPPAS
         WHARFEDALE WIRELESS WORKS
BP * BR * CP * CU * IU * LC * MI * NP * OC * SA * UI * UO * UT

CHR * GLO * ILL * INT * LDR * MEX * PHO * TAB
NP8 * KI3 * KI4 * KI5 * KI6 * KI7 * KI8 * KI9 * KI13 * KI14 * PL7 *
PL8 * PT8 * AP8 * GI4

BRIGHAM, ELEANOR

    SCALES..THEIR HISTORY, THEORY, FINGERING AND TECHNICAL USE ON THE
    PIANOFORTE

        NEW YORK   1918   29P   BSTHTF
           SCHIRMER, G., LTD.
    IU * LC

    LDR * MEX
    PT6 * PT9

BRINKMAN, JOSEPH *
BRINKMAN, DEXTER
    PIANO MUSIC..AVAILABLE EDITIONS RECOMMENDED---ADDENDA, 1959

        ANN ARBOR, MICH.   1956   BPMAER
           UNIVERSITY OF MICHIGAN
    LC * MI

    PM6 * PM15

BRINSMEAD, E.

    HISTORY OF THE PIANOFORTE, THE ..WITH AN AN ACCOUNT OF THE THEORY
    OF SOUND AND ALSO OF THE MUSIC AND MUSICAL INSTRUMENTS OF THE
    ANCIENTS---1879
        DETROIT   1969   201P   BHOTPW
           GALE RESEARCH COMPANY
    BP * BR * CP * CU * ES * IU * LC * MI * NP * SA * UI * UM * YU

    APP * LDR * MEX
    KI1 * KI2 * KI3 * KI5 * KI6 * KI7 * KI14

BRISKIER, ARTHUR

    NEW APPROACH TO PIANO TRANSCRIPTIONS AND INTERPRETATION OF JOHANN
    SEBASTIAN BACH'S MUSIC

        NEW YORK   1958   48P   BNATPT
           FISCHER, CARL, INC.
    AS * BP * ES * IU * LC * NP * SA * UA * UT

    BIB * INT * MEX
    KI9 * PM2 * PM3 * AP3 * AP4 * AP5

BRITISH BROADCASTING CORPORATION--CENTRAL MUSIC LIBRARY

    CHAMBER MUSIC CATALOGUE

        LONDON   1965   610P   BCMC
           BRITISH BROADCASTING CORPORATION
    BR * IU * LC * TO

    PM6 * EP1

BRITISH BROADCASTING CORPORATION--CENTRAL MUSIC LIBRARY

    PIANO AND ORGAN CATALOGUE--2 VOLS.

        LONDON   1965   1274P   BPAOCT
           BRITISH BROADCASTING CORPORATION
    BR * IU * LC * TO * UA

    PM6

BRITISH COLUMBIA--DEPT. OF EDUCATION

    PIANOFORTE AND VIOLIN FOR HIGH SCHOOL STUDENTS

        VICTORIA, B. C.   1945   29P   BPAVFH
           BANFIELD, C. F.
    LC

    INT * MEX * TAB
    PM6

BROADWOOD, JAMES SHUDI

    SOME NOTES--ON THE HARPSICHORD AND PIANOFORTE--MADE BY J. S.
    BROADWOOD, 1838, WITH OBSERVATIONS AND ELUCIDATIONS BY H. F.
    BROADWOOD
    LONDON   1862   14P   BSNOTH
           JOHNSON, W. S., AND COMPANY
    BR * YU

    KI2 * KI3 * KI12 * KI14

BROADWOOD, JOHN AND SONS

    BROADWOOD COLLECTION OF ANTIQUE INSTRUMENTS, THE ..FORERUNNERS OF
    THE MODERN PIANOFORTE, ON VIEW AT THE BROADWOOD GALLERIES

        LONDON   1910+   16P   BBCOAI
           BROADWOOD AND SONS
    BR

    KI13 * KI14 * KI15

BROADWOOD, JOHN AND SONS

    BROADWOOD CONCERTS--HISTORICAL NOTES BY ROBIN H.
    LEGGES..PROGRAMMES, 6 NOV. 1902--28 MARCH 1912--125 PTS.

        LONDON   1912   BBCHNB
           BROADWOOD AND SONS
    BR

    PM7 * PM13

BROADWOOD, JOHN AND SONS

    CATALOGUE OF BOOKS IN THE LIBRARY OF JOHN BROADWOOD AND SONS'
    MANUFACTORY

        LONDON   1874   116P   BCOBIT
           WITHERBY AND COMPANY
    BR

    KI12 * KI15

BROADWOOD, JOHN AND SONS

    CATALOGUE OF JOHN BROADWOOD AND SONS, LTD. LATEST MODELS, INCLUDING
    BROADWOOD PLAYER PIANOS

        LONDON   1900+   BCOJBA
           BROADWOOD AND SONS
    YU

    KI2 * KI3 * KI10 * KI12 * KI13 * KI15

BROADWOOD, JOHN AND SONS

    INFORMATION CONCERNING PIANOFORTES OF USE AND OF INTEREST..A VADE
    MECUM FOR ALL WHO POSSESS, OR CONTEMPLATE PURCHASING, EITHER A
    GRAND OR AN UPRIGHT INSTRUMENT
        LONDON   1895   173P   BICPOU
           BROADWOOD AND SONS
    BR

    KI4 * KI5 * KI6 * KI12

BROADWOOD, JOHN AND SONS

    INTERNATIONAL EXHIBITION, 1862..LIST OF PIANOFORTES AND
    OF...SAMPLES AND MODELS

        LONDON   1862   55P   BIEEST
           INTERNATIONAL EXHIBITION OF 1862
    BR

    KI12 * KI15

BROADWOOD, JOHN AND SONS

    PIANOFORTES..WITH USEFUL AND INTERESTING INFORMATION CONCERNING
    THEM

        LONDON   1890   92P   BPWUAI
           BROADWOOD AND SONS
    BR * LC

    KI1 * KI2 * KI3

BROCKWAY, WALLACE *
WEINSTOCK, HERBERT
    MEN OF MUSIC..THEIR LIVES, TIMES, AND ACHIEVEMENTS--REV.
    ED.---CHOPIN AND LISZT--1939

        NEW YORK   1958   649P   BMOMTL
           SIMON AND SCHUSTER, INC.
    BR * IU * LC * NP

    DIS * ILL * IND * INT * PHO
    NP4 * PM3

BROOK, DONALD

    MASTERS OF THE KEYBOARD

        LONDON   1946   183P   BMOTK
           ROCKLIFF PUBLISHING CORPORATION
    BP * BR * CP * CU * ES * IU * LC * MI * NP * SA * TO * UA * UC * UI
    UM * UO * US * UT
    ILL * INT * PHO
    NP3 * NP4 * NP5

BROOKSHAW, SUSANNA

    CONCERNING CHOPIN IN MANCHESTER--ON A CONCERT, AT WHICH CHOPIN
    PLAYED, HELD IN MANCHESTER, AUG. 28, 1848

        MANCHESTER   1937   27P   BCCIMO
           BATES, RICHARD
    BR

    NP4

BROTHERHOOD, JAMES

    BROTHERHOOD 'TECHNICON' AND HOW TO USE IT, THE

        BRATTLEBORO, VT.   1885+   16P   BBTAHT
           CARPENTER, E. P., COMPANY
    BP * UC

    LDR
    PL7 * PT5 * PT14

BROTHERHOOD, JAMES

    DEVELOPMENT OF THE HAND FOR PIANO-FORTE PLAYING BY MEANS OF A
    SCIENTIFIC APPARATUS, THE ...PAPER READ BEFORE THE M.T.N.A. IN NEW
    YORK IN 1885
    NEW YORK   1885   10P   BDOTHF
           MUSIC TEACHERS' NATIONAL ASSOCIATION
    NP

    NP6 * PT3 * PT5 * PT14

BROTHERHOOD, JAMES

    IMPROVED METHOD IN PIANO TEACHING, AND RECENT IDEAS OF LEADING
    AMERICAN TEACHERS, AN ---ESSAY READ BEFORE THE M.T.N.A. IN NEW
    YORK IN 1889
          NEW YORK   1889   15P   BIMIPT
            FOOTE, J. H.
    IU * LC

    NP6 * AT3 * AT4

BROTHERHOOD, JAMES

    KNOWLEDGE OF THE RELATION OF PHYSIOLOGY AND ANATOMY TO PIANO
    PLAYING, A
          NEW YORK   1888   16P   BKOTRO
            FOOTE, J. H.
    LC * NP

    PT3

BROTHERHOOD, JAMES

    MUSCLES USED IN PIANO-PLAYING..WITH EXPLANATORY NOTES AND DIAGRAMS

          NEW YORK   1887   15P   BMUIPP
            SCHIRMER, G., INC.
    LC

    INT * LDR
    PT3

BROTHERHOOD, JAMES

    SCIENCE AND ART AS TWIN SISTERS..BEING A SECOND TREATISE UPON THE
    TECHNICON---EXTRACTS FROM LETTERS
          STRATFORD, ONTARIO   1884   29P   BSAAAT
    NP * UC

    LDR * CHR
    PT5 * PT14 * AT4

BROTHERHOOD, JAMES

    SENSITIVE PIANO TOUCH AND WAYS AND MEANS TO ITS ACQUIREMENT---A
    LECTURE AT CHAUTAUQUA
          NEW YORK   1890+   16P   BSPTAW
            FOOTE, J. H.
    LC

    NP6 * PT3 * PT8

BROTHERHOOD, JAMES

    TECHNICON, THE..A TREATISE UPON THE DEVELOPMENT OF PIANOFORTE
    TECHNIQUE...MECHANICAL APPARATUS FOR DEVELOPING MUSCLE---FROM A
    LETTER TO DR. HANS VON BUELOW
          STRATFORD, ONTARIO   1884   29P   BTATUT
    NP

    APP
    AT4 * PT2 * PT3 * PT14

BROUGHTON, JULIA *
DODD, LILLIE-MAYES
    SIXTEEN LESSON PLANS..A MANUAL FOR PROGRESSIVE SERIES
    TEACHERS--PIANO LESSONS
          ST. LOUIS   1950   80P   BSLPAM
            ART PUBLICATION SOCIETY
    BR * LC

    AT4 * AT14

BROUGHTON, JULIA

    SUCCESS IN PIANO TEACHING

          NEW YORK   1956   123P   BSIPT
            VANTAGE PRESS, INC.
    CP * CU * IU * LC * MI * NP * SA

    INT * APP
    PL8 * PL12 * AT2 * AT3 * AT6 * AT7 * KS3 * EP1 * GI5

BROWER, HARRIETTE

    ART OF THE PIANIST, THE

          NEW YORK   1911   209P   BAOTP
            FISCHER, CARL, INC.
    BP * BR * ES * LC * MI * NP * OC * US

    PL6 * PL7 * PL8 * AT3 * AT4 * AT5 * PT1 * PT2 * PT4 * PT8 * PT9 *
    PT10 * AP4 * AP8

BROWER, HARRIETTE

    HOME HELP IN MUSIC STUDY

          NEW YORK   1918   211P   BHHIMS
            STOKES, FREDERICK A., COMPANY
    BP * ES * LC * NP

    ILL * INT
    PL4 * PL6 * PL7 * PL10 * PL12 * PL13 * AT7

BROWER, HARRIETTE

    HOW A DEPENDABLE PIANO TECHNIQUE WAS WON

          BOSTON   1929   71P   BHADPT
            DITSON, OLIVER, COMPANY
    LC * NP * US

    INT * LDR * MEX
    PL4 * PL6 * PL7 * PT4 * PT5 * PT6 * PT7 * PT8 * PT9 * PT10

BROWER, HARRIETTE

    MODERN MASTERS OF THE KEYBOARD

          NEW YORK   1926   303P   BMMOTK
            STOKES, FREDERICK A., COMPANY
    BP * ES * IU * LC * MI * NP * SA * UA * UO * US * UU * UW * YU
    PHO
    NP4 * NP5 * NP8 * PL7 * PL8 * AT1 * PT1 * PT7 * PM3 * AP4

BROWER, HARRIETTE

    PIANO MASTERY..TALKS WITH MASTER PIANISTS AND TEACHERS...

          NEW YORK   1915   299P   BPMTWM
            STOKES, FREDERICK A., COMPANY
    BP * CP * ES * LC * NP * OC * SA * TO * UC * UI * UK * UO * US
    PHO
    NP8 * PL7 * AT1 * AT5 * PT1 * PT3 * PT7 * PT8 * AP4

BROWER, HARRIETTE

    PIANO MASTERY, SECOND SERIES

          NEW YORK   1917   273P   BPMSS
            STOKES, FREDERICK A., COMPANY
    AS * CU * ES * LC * MI * NP * OC * SA * UA * UC * UI * UK * UM * UO
    US * UT
    PHO
    NP8 * PL7 * AT1 * AT5 * PT1 * PT3 * PT7 * PT8 * AP4

BROWER, HARRIETTE

    SELF-HELP IN PIANO STUDY

          NEW YORK   1920   229P   BSHIPS
            STOKES, FREDERICK A., COMPANY
    BP * ES * LC * NP * OC * UK

    INT * LDR * MEX * PHO
    PL4 * PL5 * PL7 * PL8 * PL11 * PL12 * AT3 * AT4 * AT10 * AT11 *
    AT13 * PT4 * PT5 * PT6 * PT7 * PT8 * PT9 * PT10

BROWER, HARRIETTE

    STORY-LIVES OF MASTER MUSICIANS

          NEW YORK   1922   371P   BSLOMM
            STOKES, FREDERICK A., COMPANY
    BR * CP * LC * NP * TO * UA * UC * UO * UU

    ILL * INT
    PM3

BROWER, HARRIETTE

    WHAT TO PLAY--WHAT TO TEACH

          PHILADELPHIA   1925   281P   BWTPWT
            PRESSER, THEODORE, COMPANY
    CP * ES * LC * MI * NP * SA * UA * UM * US

    INT
    NP7 * PM3 * PM4 * PM5 * PM6 * PM9 * PM11 * PM13 * PM15

BROWN, JEAN PARKMAN

    INTERVALS, CHORDS AND EAR TRAINING FOR YOUNG PIANOFORTE STUDENTS

          BOSTON   1897   110P   BICAET
            DITSON, OLIVER, COMPANY
    LC * NP

    APP * INT * MEX * TAB
    PL4 * PL10 * PT9 * KS8

BROWN, MAURICE J. E.

    CHOPIN..AN INDEX OF HIS WORKS IN CHRONOLOGICAL ORDER--2ND. REV.
    ED.---1960
          LONDON   1972   214P   BCAIOH
            MACMILLAN COMPANY, THE
    AS * BP * BR * CP * CU * ES * IU * LC * MI * NP * OC * TO * UA * UC
    UI * UM * UO * US * UT * UW * YU
    APP * IND * INT * MEX
    PM6 * PM15

BROWN, MAURICE J. E.

    SCHUBERT'S VARIATIONS

          LONDON   1954   104P   BSV
            MACMILLAN COMPANY, THE
    AS * BP * BP * CP * CU * ES * IU * LC * MI * NP * TO * UC * UI * UK
    UM * UO * US * UT * UW * YU
    APP * INT * MEX
    PM3 * PM8 * PM9 * PM14 * PM15 * AP4

BRUXNER, MERVYN

MASTERING THE PIANO

        NEW YORK   1973   139P   BMTP
            ST. MARTIN'S PRESS
LC * NP

IND * INT * MEX
PL7 * PT4 * PT9 * PM8 * EP1 * GI11

BUCHAROFF, SIMON

MODERN PIANIST'S TEXT BOOK, THE

        NEW YORK   1931   110P   BMPTB
            ALLEGRO MUSICAL ART LEAGUE OF AMERICA, INC.
BP * LC

CHR * GLO * INT * MEX * PHO
PL12 * KS8 * PT6 * PT9 * PT10 * AP7

BUCHNER, ALEXANDER

MECHANICAL MUSICAL INSTRUMENTS---174 NUMBERED PLATES

        LONDON   1959   110P   BMMIOH
            BATCHWORTH PRESS
BP * BR * CP * ES * IU * LC * NP * OC * UA * UK * UT * YU

CHR * ILL * INT * LDR * MEX * MSF * PHO
KI10 * KI13 * KI14

BUCHNER, ALEXANDER

MUSICAL INSTRUMENTS THROUGH THE AGES

        LONDON   1950+   38P   BMITTA
            SPRING BOOKS
LC * NP

ILL * IND * INT
KI3 * KI13 * KI14

BUCK, PERCY

PSYCHOLOGY FOR MUSICIANS

        LONDON   1944   115P   BPFM
            OXFORD UNIVERSITY PRESS
BP * BR * CP * ES * IU * LC * NP * OC * TO * UA * UC * UI * UK * UM
UO * UT * UU * YU
BIB * IND * INT * LDR * MEX
PL3 * PL8 * AT3 * PT2 * GI2

BUCK, PERCY

UNFIGURED HARMONY--2ND. ED.---1911

        OXFORD   1920   174P   BUHSEN
            CLARENDON PRESS
BP * BR * CP * ES * IU * LC * MI * NP * OC * TO * UC * UK * UM * UT
UW * YU
INT * MEX
KS4 * KS8 * KS10

BUCKLEY, OLIVIA DUSSEK

MUSICAL TRUTHS..OR, AN ANALYSIS OF MUSIC AND AN ESSAY ON THE PAST
AND PRESENT MODE OF PIANOFORTE INSTRUCTION

        LONDON   1843   51P   BMTOAA
            BUCKLEY, OLIVIA DUSSEK
BP * BR * NP

INT * MEX
NP5 * PL12 * PL15 * PT6 * AP6 * AP9

BUECKELMANN, BERNARDUS

EIGHT FUGUES FROM J. S. BACH'S 'W.T.C.', WITH ANALYTICAL NOTES IN
COLOR AND APPENDED HARMONIC SCHEME

        BOSTON   1891+   BEFFJS
            SCHMIDT, A. P.

PM8 * PM14

BUELOW, GEORGE J.

THOROUGH-BASS ACCOMPANIMENT ACCORDING TO JOHANN DAVID HEINICHEN

        BERKELEY, CAL.   1966   316P   BTBAAT
            UNIVERSITY OF CALIFORNIA PRESS
IU * LC * NP

APP * BIB * CHR * ILL * IND * INT * MEX * TAB
KS10 * KS11 * EP6

BUELOW, HANS GUIDO VON

APPLIED PIANO TECHNIC..300 EXTRACTS FOR DAILY PRACTICE FROM
STANDARD WORKS OF PIANO LITERATURE..SELECTED ON THE PRINCIPLES
RECOMMENDED BY HANS VON BUELOW
        LEIPZIG   1890+   63P   BAPTTH
            BOSWORTH AND COMPANY
NP

INT * MEX
PT10 * PT13

BUELOW, HANS GUIDO VON

CORRESPONDENCE OF HANS VON BUELOW AND RICHARD STRAUSS

        NEW YORK   1935   104P   BCOHVB
            BOOSEY AND HAWKES
BR * IU * LC * NP

NP6

BUELOW, HANS GUIDO VON

EARLY CORRESPONDENCE OF HANS VON BUELOW, THE ---EDITED BY HIS
WIDOW---1896
        NEW YORK   1972   266P   BECOHV
            VIENNA HOUSE
BR * IU * LC * NP

ILL * IND
NP6

BUELOW, HANS GUIDO VON

HANS VON BUELOW..A BIOGRAPHICAL SKETCH..HIS VISIT TO AMERICA

        NEW YORK   1875   10P   BHVBAB
            NESBITT, G. F., AND COMPANY
NP

NP4

BUELOW, HANS GUIDO VON

LETTERS OF HANS VON BUELOW---INCLUDES CORRESPONDENCE TO KARL
KLINDWORTH AND CARL BECHSTEIN
        NEW YORK   1931   434P   BLOHVB
            KNOPF, ALFRED A., INC.
BR * IU * LC * NP

IND * INT * MEX
NP6

BULL, STORM

INDEX TO BIOGRAPHIES OF CONTEMPORARY COMPOSERS

        NEW YORK   1964   405P   BITBOC
            SCARECROW PRESS, THE
BR * IU * LC * NP

PM3

BUNGER, RICHARD

WELL-PREPARED PIANO, THE

        COLORADO SPRINGS   1973   45P   BWPP
            COLORADO COLLEGE MUSIC PRESS, THE

KI1 * KI6 * KI7

BUONAMICI, CARLO

PRACTICAL POINTS ON PIANO PLAYING

        BOSTON   1921   47P   BPPOPP
            DITSON, OLIVER, COMPANY
TO

PL1 * AP1

BUONAMICI, GIUSEPPE

ART OF SCALE STUDY FOR THE PIANOFORTE, THE ...AS TAUGHT TO HIS
PUPILS
        LONDON   1903   68P   BAOSSF
            AUGENER AND COMPANY
LC

AT4 * PT9

BURCH, GLADYS

FAMOUS PIANISTS FOR BOYS AND GIRLS

        NEW YORK   1943   156P   BFPFBA
            BARNES, A. S., AND COMPANY
LC * MI * UA * UK * UU

IND * ILL * PHO
NP3 * NP4 * NP5 * GI10

BURCH, GLADYS

MODERN COMPOSERS FOR YOUNG PEOPLE---FIRST PUBLISHED AS 'A CHILD'S
BOOK OF FAMOUS COMPOSERS'--1939
        NEW YORK   1941   207P   BMCFYP
            DODD, MEAD AND COMPANY
BR * IU * LC * NP

IND * PHO
NP5 * GI10

BURK, JOHN N.

CLARA SCHUMANN..A ROMANTIC BIOGRAPHY

      NEW YORK   1940   438P   BCSARB
         RANDOM HOUSE
AS * BR * ES * LC * NP * OC * TO * UA * UM * UT

IND * PHO
NP4

BURROWES, JOHN FRECKLETON

GUIDE TO PRACTICE ON THE PIANOFORTE

      NEW YORK   1841   36P   BGTPOT
         RILEY, F.
BR * LC * NP

APP * INT
PL7 * PT8 * PT9 * PT10 * KS7

BURROWES, JOHN FRECKLETON

PIANOFORTE PRIMER, THE ..CONTAINING THE RUDIMENTS OF MUSIC
CALCULATED EITHER FOR PRIVATE TUITION OR TEACHING IN
CLASSES---1830+
      NEW YORK   1909   86P   BPPCTR
         SCHIRMER, G., INC.
BP * BR * CP * ES * IU * LC * NP * OC * SA * UC * UM * US * UT * UW
YU
APP * INT * MEX
PL4 * AT4 * AT7

BURROWES, JOHN FRECKLETON

THOROUGH-BASS PRIMER, THE ..CONTAINING EXPLANATIONS AND EXAMPLES OF
THE RUDIMENTS OF HARMONY, WITH 50 EXERCISES

      LONDON   1819   107P   BTBPCE
         CLEMENTI AND COMPANY
BR * IU * LC * NP

MEX
AT4 * KS4 * KS10

BURROWS, RAYMOND

ADVANCED PIANO CLASS, THE --REPRINT..PROCEEDINGS OF THE M.E.N.C.,
1947

      CHICAGO   1947   9P   BAPCRP
         MUSIC EDUCATORS NATIONAL CONFERENCE
IU * UI

AT7

BURROWS, RAYMOND

ELEMENTARY PIANO INSTRUCTION IN COLLEGE

      NEW YORK   1944   54P   BEPIIC
         TEACHERS COLLEGE, COLUMBIA UNIVERSITY
BP * IU * LC * SA * UI

APP * BIB * INT
PL4 * PL8 * PL10 * AT4 * AT5 * AT6 * AT7 * KS3 * KS5 * KS7 * PM5 *
PM6 * EP6 * GI2 * GI8

BURROWS, RAYMOND

HANDBOOK FOR TEACHING PIANO CLASSES

      CHICAGO   1952   87P   BHFTPC
         MUSIC EDUCATORS NATIONAL CONFERENCE
CP

AT7

BURROWS, RAYMOND

PIANO IN SCHOOL, A MEMORANDUM FOR SCHOOL ADMINISTRATORS

      CHICAGO   1949   14P   BPISAM
         MUSIC EDUCATORS NATIONAL CONFERENCE
IU * LC * NP * UI * UK * UM

AT7 * GI8

BUSONI, FERRUCCIO

FERRUCCIO BUSONI--LETTERS TO HIS WIFE---1895

      LONDON   1938   319P   BFBLTH
         ARNOLD, EDWARD
BR * LC * NP

IND * ILL * PHO
NP6

BUSSLER, LUDWIG

HARMONIC EXERCISES AT THE PIANOFORTE FOR BEGINNERS AND ADVANCED
PUPILS

      NEW YORK   1890   56P   BHEATP
         SCHIRMER, G., INC.
LC * NP

INT * MEX
KS4 * KS8

BUTLER, STANLEY

GUIDE TO THE BEST IN CONTEMPORARY PIANO MUSIC..AN ANNOTATED LIST OF
GRADED SOLO PIANO MUSIC PUBLISHED SINCE 1950--VOL. 1, LEVELS
1-5--VOL. 2, LEVELS 6-8
      METUCHEN, N. J.   1973   368P   BGTTBI
         SCARECROW PRESS, THE, INC.
IU * LC

INT
PM6

BYERLY, DOROTHEA J.

ADVENTURES OF PETER THE PIANO, THE ..AN ILLUSTRATED STORY FOR
CHILDREN

      PHILADELPHIA   1947   52P   BAOPTP
         DITSON, OLIVER, COMPANY
IU * LC

ILL
KI1 * GI10

BYRON, MAY CLARISSA

DAY WITH FREDERIC CHOPIN, A

      LONDON   1911   48P   BDWFC
         HODDER AND STOUGHTON
BR * LC * NP

ILL
NP4 * PM3 * GI10

CALAND, ELIZABETH

ARTISTIC PIANO PLAYING, AS TAUGHT BY LUDWIG DEPPE

      NASHVILLE, TENN.   1903   109P   BAPPAT
         OLYMPIAN PUBLISHING COMPANY
ES * IU * LC * NP * SA

INT * LDR * MEX * PHO
PL7 * PL8 * PT2 * PT3 * PT4 * PT5 * PT8 * PT9 * PT10 * AP4 * AP8

CALDWELL, JOHN

ENGLISH KEYBOARD MUSIC BEFORE THE NINETEENTH CENTURY---EXTENSIVE
BIBLIOGRAPHY

      NEW YORK   1973   328P   BEKMBT
         PRAEGER, FREDERICK A.
IU

APP * BIB * IND * INT * MEX * MSF * TAB
PM3 * PM5 * PM6 * PM7 * PM8 * PM14

CALLAGHAN, JAMES

ZIP CHORDMASTER..BEGINNERS HOME COURSE FOR PIANO AND ORGAN

      UNIVERSITY CITY, CAL. 1965   11P   BZCBHC
         CALLAGHAN, JAMES
LC

CHR * INT * MEX
PL11 * AT4 * KS4

CALLENDER, ROMAINE

TEACHER'S MANUAL, A WORK DESIGNED TO SUPPLEMENT...'THE FIRST TEN
WEEKS AT THE PIANO'
      NEW YORK   1913   51P   BTMAWD
         FISCHER, CARL, INC.
BR * LC

MEX * PHO
PL4 * PL12 * AT3 * AT4 * AT5 * PT4 * PT5 * PT9 * PM6

CAMPBELL, LE ROY B.

TRUE FUNCTION OF RELAXATION IN PIANO PLAYING, THE

      ST. LOUIS   1922   97P   BTFORI
         ART PUBLICATIONS SOCIETY
BP * CU * ES * LC * NP * OC * UA

IND * LDR * MEX * PHO
PT1 * PT2 * PT3 * PT4 * PT5 * PT7 * PT8 * PT10

CAMPBELL, LE ROY B.

VELOCITY PLUS

      NEW YORK   1940   60P   BVP
         CREATIVE MUSIC PUBLISHERS
AS * ES * UI * UT

LDR * MEX
PL7 * PT1 * PT2 * PT4 * PT7 * PT8 * PT9 * PT10

CANAVE, PAZ CORAZON G.

RE-EVALUATION OF THE ROLE PLAYED BY C. P. E. BACH IN THE
DEVELOPMENT OF THE CLAVIER SONATA---PUBLISHED DISSERTATION
      WASHINGTON, D. C.   1956   186P   BRDTRP
         CATHOLIC UNIVERSITY PRESS
BP * BR * ES * IU * NP * TO * UC * UI * UM * UO

APP * BIB * INT * MEX * TAB
NP3 * PM3 * PM5 * PM7 * PM8 * PM9 * PM14 * AP7

CAPEN, C. L.

MUSIC TEACHER'S VADE-MECUM, THE ..A GUIDE IN THE CHOICE OF MUSIC
FOR THE USE OF TEACHERS AND STUDENTS

    BOSTON   1888   22P   BMTVMA
        BOSTON MUSIC COMPANY
LC

INT
AT14 * PM6

CAPPS, STANLEY M.

CAPPS SYSTEM OF IMPROVISING FOR PIANO, THE --A MODERN COURSE OF
KEYBOARD HARMONY

                    1924   32P   BCSOIF
    CAPPS, STANLEY M.
LC

KS4 * KS5

CARL, SYLVESTER

CARL'S DICTIONARY OF CHORDS...REFERENCE BOOK FOR CUED-IN HARMONY OF
POPULAR MUSIC..MODULATIONS, RESOLUTIONS, TRANSPOSITIONS

    BROOKLYN, N. Y.   1940   28P   BCDOCR
    CARL, SYLVESTER, PUBLISHERS
LC

GLO * INT * TAB
KS4 * KS7 * KS8

CARLSON, EFFIE B.

BIO-BIBLIOGRAPHICAL DICTIONARY OF TWELVE-TONE AND SERIAL COMPOSERS,
A ---EXTRACTED FROM PIANO LITERATURE

    METUCHEN, N. J.   1970   233P   BBBDOT
    SCARECROW PRESS, THE, INC.
IU * LC * NP

BIB * INT
NP5 * PM3 * PM14

CARMI, AVNER *
CARMI, HANNAH
IMMORTAL PIANO, THE

    NEW YORK   1960   286P   BIP
    CROWN PUBLISHERS
BP * BR * CP * IU * LC * NP * UA * UC * UT

ILL * INT * MEX * PHO
KI12 * KI13 * GI13

CARMIENCKE, ALBERT G.

MECHANICS OF PIANO PLAYING, THE

    CHICAGO   1905   39P   BMOPP
    SUMMY, CLAYTON F., COMPANY
LC

INT * MEX * TAB
PL12 * PT5 * PT9 * PT10

CARPE, ADOLPH

GROUPING, ARTICULATING AND PHRASING IN MUSICAL INTERPRETATION..A
SYSTEMATIC EXPOSITION FOR PLAYERS, TEACHERS AND ADVANCED STUDENTS

    LONDON   1898   108P   BGAAPI
    BOSWORTH AND COMPANY, LTD.
BR * ES * LC * NP

INT * MEX
PL12 * AP6

CARPE, ADOLPH

PIANIST AND THE ART OF MUSIC, THE ..A TREATISE ON PIANO PLAYING FOR
TEACHERS AND STUDENTS

    CHICAGO   1893   160P   BPATAO
    LYON AND HEALY
LC * NP

INT * MEX
PL4 * PL7 * PL9 * AT1 * PT1 * PT4 * PT6 * PT8 * PT9 * PT10 * PM5 *
AP4 * AP6

CARR, BENJAMIN

ANALYTICAL INSTRUCTOR FOR THE PIANO FORTE, OP. 15, THE --IN 3 PTS.

    PHILADELPHIA   1826   108P   BAIFTP
    CARR, BENJAMIN
LC

APP * GLO * ILL * MEX
PL4 * PL5 * PL12 * PL15 * PT6 * AP7

CARPE, JOHN

PSYCHOLOGY OF PIANO TEACHING, THE ..A TEXTBOOK FOR TEACHERS,
STUDENTS AND PARENTS

    RACINE, WIS.   1933   95P   BPOPTA
    CONSERVATORY PUBLISHING COMPANY
BP * CP * CU * LC * NP * SA * UM * UT

APP * BIB * CHR * INT * MEX * TAB
PL4 * PL8 * AT2 * AT3 * AT7 * AT9 * PT4 * PT6 * PT10 * AP7 * AP8 *
GI5 * GI9

CARRENO, TERESA

POSSIBILITIES OF TONE COLOR BY ARTISTIC USE OF PEDALS

    CINCINNATI   1919   33P   BPOTCB
    CHURCH, THE JOHN, COMPANY
BP * BR * CU * ES * NP * TO

MEX * PHO
KI5 * PT4 * PT9 * AP6 * AP8

CARTER, BUENTA

ADVANCED KEYBOARD HARMONY WITH ILLUSTRATIVE PIANO PIECES

    NEW YORK   1937+   43P   BAKHWI
    SUMMY, CLAYTON F., COMPANY
LC

ILL * MEX
KS4

CARTER, BUENTA

BEGINNER'S PIANO BOOK FOR OLDER STUDENTS...DESIGNED FOR THE OLDER
CHILD, THE ADULT AND FOR CLASSES

    CHICAGO   1932+   61P   BBPBFO
    SUMMY, CLAYTON F., COMPANY
LC

ILL * INT * MEX
PL4 * AT4 * AT7 * PT8 * PT9 * PT10 * AP8

CARTER, BUENTA

KEYBOARD HARMONY WITH ILLUSTRATIVE PIANO PIECES

    NEW YORK   1935   47P   BKHWIP
    SUMMY, CLAYTON F., COMPANY

KS4

CARTER, BUENTA

TRANSPOSITION PATTERNS, FOR THE PIANO...APPROACHED THROUGH HARMONIC
AND MELODIC ANALYSIS

    CHICAGO   1938+   23P   BTPFTP
    SUMMY, CLAYTON F., COMPANY
LC

INT * MEX
KS7

CARUTHERS, JULIA LOIS

PIANO TECHNIC FOR CHILDREN

    CHICAGO   1903   142P   BPTFC
    SUMMY, CLAYTON F., COMPANY
LC * UM

INT * MEX * PHO
PL7 * PL12 * PT4 * PT6 * PT9 * PT10

CARY, MRS. C. S. P.

PIANO-FORTE CLASS BOOK, CONTAINING PRACTICAL RUDIMENTAL LESSONS FOR
STUDENTS OF MUSIC

    ROCHESTER, N. Y.   1873   189P   BPCBCP
    SHAW, J. P.
ES * LC

ILL * INT * MEX
KI4 * PL4 * PL7 * PL12 * AT11 * AT13 * PT4 * PT8 * KS7

CASTELLINI, JOHN EDWARD

RUDIMENTS OF MUSIC..A NEW APPROACH WITH APPLICATION TO THE KEYBOARD

    NEW YORK   1962   239P   BROMAN
    NORTON, W. W., AND COMPANY, INC.
ES * IU * LC * MI

APP * GLO * IND * INT * LDR * MEX
KI3 * PL4 * PL7 * PL12 * PT9 * KS4 * KS5 * KS7 * AP8 * EP6

CAUCHI, PAUL

CHOPIN..CENTENNIAL MEMORY 1849-1949..A LECTURE

    GZIRA, EAST MALTA   1949   11P   BCCMEH
    ROBERTS PRESS
BR

NP4 * NP6 * PM3

CAVALLARO, CARMEN

KEYBOARD HARMONY..A NEW MODERN PIANO METHOD---POPULAR IDIOM

    NEW YORK   1949   59P   BKHANM
    CAVALLARO PUBLICATIONS
IU * LC

MEX * PHO
AT4 * KS4 * KS6 * EP6

CHAPIN, VICTOR

GIANTS OF THE KEYBOARD

        PHILADELPHIA   1967   189P   BGOTK
           LIPPINCOTT, J. B., COMPANY
BP * CP * ES * IU * LC * MI * NP * SA * UA * UI * UM * UO

DIS * ILL * IND * PHO
NP3 * NP4 * NP5 * KI3

CHAPPLE, STANLEY

CLASS WAY TO THE KEYBOARD, THE

        LONDON   1937   94P   BCWTTK
           BOSWORTH AND COMPANY, LTD.
BP * CP * CU * ES * IU * LC * MI * OC * UT * UW

INT * MEX
PL4 * PL6 * PL10 * PL12 * PL13 * AT5 * AT7 * KS3 * KS4 * KS5 * KS7
KS8 * AP6 * AP7 * EP6

CHAROL, SIMON

NEW APPROACH TO THE STUDY OF THE PIANOFORTE, A ---IN ITALIAN AND
ENGLISH

        ROME   1956   40P   BNATTS
           CHAROL, SIMON
LC

APP * INT * MEX * PHO
AT4 * PT3 * PT4 * PT6 * PT9 * PT10

CHASE, MARY WOOD

NATURAL LAWS IN PIANO TECHNIC

        BOSTON   1910   128P   BNLIPT
           DITSON, OLIVER, COMPANY
AS * BP * BR * ES * IU * LC * NP * SA * UK * US * UW

CHR * IND * INT * MEX * PHO
PL7 * PL8 * PL12 * PT3 * PT4 * PT8 * PT9 * PT10 * PT11 * AP4 * AP8
AP9

CHASINS, ABRAM

SPEAKING OF PIANISTS

        NEW YORK   1957   283P   BSOP
           KNOPF, ALFRED A., INC.
AS * BP * BR * CP * ES * IU * LC * MI * NP * OC * SA * TO * UA * UC
UI * UK * UM * UO * US * UT * UU * YU
IND * INT
NP3 * NP4 * NP5 * NP8 * PM3 * AP4 * GI4 * GI5

CHASINS, ABRAM *
STILES, VILLA
VAN CLIBURN LEGEND, THE

        NEW YORK   1959   238P   BVCL
           DOUBLEDAY AND COMPANY
AS * BR * CP * ES * IU * LC * NP * OC * UC * UI

IND * PHO
NP3 * NP4

CHASTEK, WINIFRED

KEYBOARD SKILLS..SIGHT READING, TRANSPOSITION, HARMONIZATION,
IMPROVISATION

        BELMONT, CAL.   1967   215P   BKSSRT
           WADSWORTH PUBLISHING COMPANY
ES * LC * UI * UO * UT * UW

APP * IND * MEX
PL4 * AT4 * AT6 * AT7 * KS3 * KS4 * KS5 * KS7

CHEYETTE, IRVING

BASIC PIANO FOR THE MUSIC EDUCATOR AND CLASSROOM TEACHER

        BRYN MAWR, PA.   1954   90P   BBPFTM
           PRESSER, THEODORE, COMPANY
IU * LC

INT * MEX
PL4 * PL10 * AT4 * AT7 * PT10 * KS4 * EP6

CHICKERING AND SONS

ACHIEVEMENT..AN ASCENDING SCALE, BEING A SHORT HISTORY OF THE HOUSE
OF CHICKERING AND SONS

        BOSTON   1920+   31P   BAAASB
LC

KI3 * KI12

CHICKERING AND SONS

CHICKERING AND SONS, MANUFACTURER OF GRAND, SQUARE AND UPRIGHT
PIANO-FORTES..ILLUSTRATED CATALOGUE

        NEW YORK   1875+   47P   BCASMO
           DENISON AND SMITH, PRINTER
LC

KI12 * KI15

CHICKERING AND SONS

CHICKERING AND SONS PIANOFORTES AT THE CENTENNIAL EXHIBITION,
PHILADELPHIA, 1876

                          1876   BCASPA
LC

KI12 * KI15

CHICKERING AND SONS

CHICKERING CENTENNIAL CELEBRATION, APRIL 1823-1923

        NEW YORK   1923   6P   BCCCAE
           WANAMAKER, JOHN
NP

KI3 * KI12

CHICKERING AND SONS

COMMEMORATION OF THE FOUNDING OF THE HOUSE OF CHICKERING AND SONS,
1823-1903, THE

        BOSTON   1904   93P   BCOTFO
           UNIVERSITY PRESS, THE
BP * CP * ES * LC * NP * UK * UM * UO

ILL * PHO
KI12 * GI5

CHICKERING AND SONS

HISTORICAL MUSICAL EXHIBITION..CATALOGUE OF THE EXHIBITION,
HORTICULTURAL HALL, BOSTON, JAN. 11-26, 1902

        BOSTON   1902   78P   BHMECO
           BARTA PRINTERS
LC * NP

KI4 * KI9 * KI12 * KI15 * GI5

CHICKERING AND SONS

ILLUSTRATED CATALOGUE OF PIANO FORTES

        NEW YORK   1871   23P   BICOPF
           CHICKERING AND SONS
NP

ILL
KI4 * KI9 * KI12 * KI13 * KI15

CHICKERING AND SONS

JONAS CHICKERING CENTENNIAL CELEBRATION, THE ..A TRIBUTE TO THE
LIFE AND WORK OF JONAS CHICKERING

        NEW YORK   1924   55P   BJCCCA
           CHICKERING AND SONS
LC

NP6 * KI12

CHICKERING AND SONS

JONAS CHICKERING CENTENNIAL CELEBRATION, 1823-1923..IN
COMMEMORATION OF THE ONE HUNDREDTH ANNIVERSARY OF THE FOUNDING OF
THE HOUSE OF CHICKERING
        CHELTENHAM, N. Y.   1923   20P   BJCCCE
LC * NP

KI3 * KI12

CHICKERING AND SONS

NEW ILLUSTRATED CATALOGUE OF PIANOFORTES, A

        NEW YORK   1874   38P   BNICOP
           CHICKERING AND SONS
NP

ILL * INT
KI5 * KI12 * KI13 * KI15

CHICKERING AND SONS

PIANO-FORTES AT THE EXHIBITION OF 1856

        BOSTON   1857   30P   BPATEO
           BALCH, E. L., PRESS OF
LC

KI12 * KI15

CHICKERING BROTHERS, CHICAGO

PIANO-FORTES AND THEIR MANUFACTURE, WITH ILLUSTRATED CATALOGUE
SHOWING THEIR VARIOUS STYLES

        CHICAGO   1893   26P   BPATMW
           CHICKERING BROTHERS
LC

KI5 * KI12 * KI15

CHILDERS, LEMUEL

CHORD DICTIONARY..DESIGNED FOR TEACHERS, STUDENTS AND SELF-TAUGHT
PLAYERS OF POPULAR MUSIC

      TULSA, OKLA.   1953   BCDDFT
        CHILDERS, LEMUEL
LC

PL11 * AT4 * KS4 * KS6

CHILDERS, LEMUEL

PLAYING THE PIANO BY EAR

      TULSA, OKLA.   1943   33P   BPTPBE
        CHILDERS, LEMUEL
LC

INT
PL12 * KS4 * KS8 * KS12 * AP8

CHILTON, CARROLL B.

DE-ASSIFICATION OF MUSIC, THE ..A PROPAGANDIST MAGAZINE, OF ONE
NUMBER, CONTAINING NEWS OF IMPORTANCE TO ALL MUSIC LOVERS,
ESPECIALLY TO ALL OWNERS OF PLAYER PIANOS
      NEW YORK   1922   39P   BDOMAP
        CHILTON, C. B.
BR * LC * NP

CHR * ILL * LDR * MEX
KI10 * GI12

CHING, JAMES

AMATEUR PIANIST'S COMPANION, THE

      LONDON   1956   112P   BAPC
        PROWSE, KEITH, MUSIC PUBLISHING COMPANY, LTD.
BP * BR * CP * IU * LC * MI * NP * SA * UI

APP * INT * MEX * PHO * TAB
PL7 * PL12 * PT1 * PT2 * PT3 * PT4 * GI11

CHING, JAMES

BETTER BEGINNINGS..A FIRST BOOK FOR EVERYONE WHO WANTS TO BECOME A
REALLY GOOD PIANIST AND MUSICIAN

      LONDON   1949+   BBBAFB
        BOSWORTH AND COMPANY, LTD.
LC

MEX
PL4 * AT4

CHING, JAMES

CANDIDATE'S COMPANION TO THE EXERCISES, SCALES, BROKEN CHORDS,
SIGHT READING AND AURAL TESTS OF THE ASSOCIATED BOARD PIANO
EXAMINATIONS, THE --GRADES 1 AND 2 --2 VOLS.
      LONDON   1956   56P   BCCTTE
        PROWSE, KEITH, MUSIC PUBLISHING COMPANY, LTD.
LC

INT * MEX
PL10 * AT10 * PT6 * PT8 * PT9 * PT10 * KS3

CHING, JAMES

ENTIRELY NEW SOLUTION TO THE PROBLEMS OF PIANO STUDY AT HOME, AN
--A PROSPECTUS

      LONDON   1960   BENSTT
        PIANOPHONE TUITION, LTD.
BR

PL2 * PL11 * AT4

CHING, JAMES

FOREARM ROTATION---A SEQUEL TO 'THE ROTARY ROAD'--15 PHOTOS AND 115
EXERCISES

      LONDON   1926   17P   BFRAST
        FORSYTH BROTHERS
LC

APP * INT * MEX * PHO
PL7 * PT3 * PT4 * PT5 * PT10

CHING, JAMES

LET'S PLAY THE PIANO..THE FIRST MUSIC BOOK FOR CHILDREN OF ALL
AGES---EXTENSIVE STORY TEXT

      LONDON   1936   31P   BLPTPT
        MITRE PRESS, THE
LC

ILL * MEX
PL4 * AT4 * AT5

CHING, JAMES

MUSCULAR RELAXATION, A SIMPLE EXPLANATION

      LONDON   1927   11P   BMRASE
        FORSYTH BROTHERS
BR

PT3 * PT7

CHING, JAMES

NEW GRADED PEDALLING FOR PIANO, THE --BKS. 1 AND 2

      LONDON   1956   55P   BNGPFP
        PROWSE, KEITH, MUSIC PUBLISHING COMPANY, LTD.
LC

INT * MEX
AP8

CHING, JAMES

NEW GRADED SIGHT READING FOR PIANO, THE --BKS. 1 AND
2---ONE-MEASURE EXCERPTS

      LONDON   1955   48P   BNGSRF
        PROWSE, KEITH, MUSIC PUBLISHING COMPANY, LTD.
LC

INT * MEX
KS3

CHING, JAMES

NEW GRADED TIME EXERCISES, FOR PIANO, THE

      LONDON   1960   36P   BNGTEF
        PROWSE, KEITH, MUSIC PUBLISHING COMPANY, LTD.
LC

INT * MEX
PL12

CHING, JAMES

ON TEACHING PIANO TECHNIQUE TO CHILDREN

      LONDON   1962   65P   BOTPTT
        PROWSE, KEITH, MUSIC PUBLISHING COMPANY, LTD.
BR * CP * ES * IU * LC * MI * SA * UI

APP * LDR * MEX
AT4 * AT5 * AT7 * PT3 * PT4 * PT8 * PT10

CHING, JAMES

PERFORMER AND AUDIENCE..AN INVESTIGATION INTO THE PSYCHOLOGICAL
CAUSES OF ANXIETY AND NERVOUSNESS IN PLAYING, SINGING OR SPEAKING
BEFORE AN AUDIENCE
      OXFORD   1947   96P   BPAAAI
        HALL, LTD.
BR * CP * IU * LC * TO * UC * UI * UT

PL3 * PL7 * AT3 * AP3 * AP9 * GI3 * GI13

CHING, JAMES

PIANIST'S HOME STUDY COURSES, THE

      LONDON   1960   BPHSC
        PIANOPHONE TUITION LIMITED
BR

PL2 * PL11 * AT4

CHING, JAMES

PIANO PLAYING, A PRACTICAL METHOD--A NEW EDITION OF 'PIANO
TECHNIQUE..THE MODERN SYNTHESIS'--25 LECTURES GIVEN IN LONDON IN
1944-1945
      LONDON   1946   365P   BPPAPM
        BOSWORTH AND COMPANY
BR * CP * CU * IU * LC * MI * NP * SA * TO * UC * UI * UM * UO * US
UT
CHR * INT * LDR * MEX
PL3 * PL7 * AT3 * PT1 * PT2 * PT3 * PT4 * PT7 * PT8 * PT10 * AP4

CHING, JAMES

PIANO TECHNIQUE..FOUNDATION PRINCIPLES

      LONDON   1934   117P   BPTFP
        MURDOCH, WILLIAM, COMPANY
BP * BR * CU * UA

PT1

CHING, JAMES

PLAYING AND TEACHING OF BACH, THE ..A GUIDE FOR TEACHERS, STUDENTS
AND EXAMINATION CANDIDATES
      LONDON   1931   59P   BPATOB
        FORSYTH BROTHERS, LTD.
ES

PL1 * AT1 * GI9

CHING, JAMES

POINTS ON PEDALLING

      LONDON   1930   39P   BPOP
        FORSYTH BROTHERS LTD.
CP * CU * LC * MI * SA

APP * INT * MEX
PT8 * AP6 * AP8

CHING, JAMES

ROTARY ROAD, AN EASY PILGRIMAGE BY EIGHT SHORT STEPS, THE --FOREARM
ROTATION---FOUR-PAGE FOREWORD AND 8 PIECES

    LONDON   1929+   BRRAEP
    FORSYTH BROTHERS, LTD.

PT10

CHING, JAMES

SIDELIGHTS ON TOUCH..TOGETHER WITH 101 QUESTIONS, SUITABLE FOR
CANDIDATES STUDY FOR THE PIANOFORTE TEACHING DIPLOMAS--PT.
1..ANSWERS TO THE 101 QUESTIONS--PT. 2
    LONDON   1929   70P   BSOTTW
    FORSYTH BROTHERS, LTD.
BR * ES * LC * MI * NP

APP * ILL * LDR * MEX * PHO * TAB
PT4 * PT7 * PT8 * PT10

CHING, JAMES

STUDIES FOR BASIC PIANO TECHNIQUE..WRITTEN AND SELECTED WITH
TECHNICAL COMMENTARY--3 VOLS.

    CHICAGO   1957   96P   BSFBPT
    SUMMY, CLAYTON F., COMPANY
IU * LC

INT * MEX
PL4 * PL12 * PL15 * PT1 * PT8 * PT11 * AP6 * AP9

CHING, JAMES

TEACHING OF TECHNIQUE TO CHILDREN, THE --4 PTS.

    SEDLESCOMBE, SUSSEX, ENGLAND 1932   BTOTTC
    CHING, JAMES
BR

AT5 * PT1

CHING, JOAN ELIZABETH

APPROACH TO PIANO TEACHING---ALSO CATALOGUED UNDER
AUTHORSHIP..BETTY REEVES
    LONDON   1955   94P   BATPTA
    BOSWORTH AND COMPANY, LTD.
BR * CU * LC * NP

APP * LDR * MEX
PL4 * PL10 * PL14 * PT1 * PT8 * PT9 * PT10 * KS3 * AP4 * AP8

CHING, JOAN ELIZABETH

OURSELVES AND OUR PUPILS---ALSO CATALOGUED UNDER AUTHORSHIP..BETTY
REEVES
    LONDON   1951   42P   BOAOPA
    WALSH, HOLMES AND COMPANY
BR * LC

INT
AT3 * AT5 * AT9 * AT10 * AT13

CHISSELL, JOAN

CHOPIN--'GREAT COMPOSERS' SERIES

    NEW YORK   1965   94P   BCGCS
    CROWELL, T. Y., COMPANY
BR * LC

ILL * IND * INT * MEX * MSF * PHO
NP4 * PM3

CHISSELL, JOAN

SCHUMANN PIANO MUSIC--B.B.C. MUSIC GUIDE, NO. 25

    SEATTLE   1972   72P   BSPMBB
    UNIVERSITY OF WASHINGTON PRESS
LC

PM3 * PM6

CHITTENDEN, KATE S.

SYNTHETIC CATECHISM, THE ..538 QUESTIONS AND ANSWERS FOR USE IN
CONNECTION WITH THE SYNTHETIC METHOD FOR THE PIANOFORTE--PT. 1

    NEW YORK   1895   56P   BSCFTE
    SILVER BURDETT
ES * NP * OC

INT
PL4 * AT4 * AT10

CHITY, R.

NEW SCHOOL OF SCALE PLAYING--COLOR PATTERNS

                       1960+   BNSOSP
    WEINGARTEN

PT9

CHOPIN, FREDERIC

CHOPIN'S LETTERS--COLLECTED BY HENRY OPIENSKI..TRANSLATED BY E. L.
VOYNICH---1931

    NEW YORK   1971 420P   BCLCBH
    VIENNA HOUSE
BR * IU * NP

IND
NP6

CHOPIN, FREDERIC

SELECTED CORRESPONDENCE OF FREDERYK F. CHOPIN--COLLECTED BY
BRONISLAW E. SYDOW..TRANSLATED BY ARTHUR HEDLEY---1953, IN FRENCH

    NEW YORK   1963 400P   BSCOFF
    MCGRAW-HILL BOOK COMPANY
BR * LC * NP

ILL * INT * MEX * TAB
NP6

CHRISTENSEN, INGA

INGA - PLAY--MEMOIRS

    NEW YORK   1952 202P   BIPM
    EXPOSITION PRESS
BP * CP * LC * NP * SA * TO * US * UT

INT * PHO
NP6 * GI13

CHRISTIANI, ADOLPH FRIEDRICH

PRINCIPLES OF EXPRESSION IN PIANOFORTE PLAYING, THE

    NEW YORK   1886 303P   BPOEIP
    HARPER AND BROTHERS
BP * BR * CU * ES * IU * LC * MI * NP * OC * TO * UA * UC * UI * UK
UM * UO * US * UT * UW * YU
CHR * INT * MEX * TAB
PL1 * PL2 * PL4 * PL5 * PT1 * AP3 * AP4 * AP5 * AP6

CHRISTIANSEN, FREDERICK M.

PRACTICAL MODULATION FOR ADVANCED STUDENTS---43 LESSONS

    MINNEAPOLIS   1916   43P   BPMFAS
    AUGSBURG PUBLISHING HOUSE
LC

INT * MEX
KS8

CHURCHILL, VIRGINIA PEAKES

MODERN TEACHER'S GUIDE TO PIANO AND PIANO CLASS TEACHING

    BOSTON   1956 155P   BMTGTP
    HOMEYER, C. W.
CU * ES * LC * MI * UI * UK * UT

BIB * CHR * DIS * INT * MEX * PHO
PL4 * PL7 * PL10 * AT4 * AT7 * PT1 * KS3 * PM5 * PM6

CHURCHILL, VIRGINIA PEAKES

NINETEEN FIFTY-SIX SUPPLEMENT TO THE MODERN TEACHER'S GUIDE TO
PIANO AND PIANO-CLASS TEACHING
    BOSTON   1956+ 56P   BNFSST
    HOMEYER, C. W.
LC

APP * INT * PHO
KI15 * PL10 * PL12 * PL14 * AT4 * AT5 * AT7 * PT1 * KS3 * PM5 *
PM6

CHURCHILL, WILLIAM--SUPPOSED AUTHOR

MARVELLOUS YEAR, THE ...CRITICAL SKETCHES OF CELEBRATED MEN, THE
CENTENNIAL OF WHOSE BIRTH WAS, FOR THE MOST PART, IN 1809---CHOPIN

    NEW YORK   1909 104P   BMYCSO
    HUEBSCH, B. W.
NP

ILL * INT
NP5 * GI12 * GI15

CLAPE, EDWARD

ANALYSIS OF PRACTICAL THOROUGH BASS

    LONDON   1835+ 29P   BAOPTB
    PURDAY, Z. T.
LC

MEX
KS10 * PM8

CLARE, EDWARD

NEW TREATISE OF PRACTICAL THOROUGH BASS, A

    LONDON   1841   31P   BNTOPT
    COCKS, R., AND COMPANY
NP

MEX
KS10

CLARK, MADAM STEINEGER

RELIGION AND ROMANCE OF A PIANIST'S LIFE---AUTOBIOGRAPHY

LONDON   1896+   BRAROA
PURE MUSIC SOCIETY

NP6 * GI13

CLARKE, HUGH ARCHIBALD

ART OF PIANOFORTE PLAYING, THE --TEXT BOOK FOR BEGINNERS

PHILADELPHIA   1889+   BAOPPT
PRESSER, THEODORE, COMPANY

PL4 * AT4 * AP1 * AP2 * AP3 * AP4 * AP5 * AP6

CLARKE, HUGH ARCHIBALD

THEORY EXPLAINED TO PIANO STUDENTS..OR PRACTICAL LESSONS IN HARMONY

PHILADELPHIA   1892   29P   BTETPS
PRESSER, THEODORE, COMPANY
LC * NP

APP * INT * MEX
KS4

CLEMENCIC, RENE

OLD MUSICAL INSTRUMENTS

NEW YORK   1968   120P   BOMI
PUTNAM'S, G. P., SONS
LC

CHR * ILL * INT * PHO * TAB
KI3 * KI5 * KI6 * KI7 * KI9 * KI12 * KI13 * KI14 * KI15

CLEMENS, CLARA

MY HUSBAND GABRILOWITSCH

NEW YORK   1938   351P   BMHG
HARPER AND BROTHERS
AS * BP * BR * CP * ES * LC * NP * OC * SA * TO * UA * UC * UI * UK
UM * UO * UT * YU
APP * IND * PHO
NP4

CLEMENTI, MUZIO

CLEMENTI'S SELECTION OF PRACTICAL HARMONY FOR THE ORGAN OR
PIANOFORTE--4 VOLS., 1803-1815

LONDON   1803   567P   BCSOPH
BATES, W. C.
LC * NP

MEX
KS4

CLEMENTI, MUZIO

INTRODUCTION TO THE ART OF PLAYING ON THE PIANOFORTE---1801+

NEW YORK   1973   66P   BITTAO
DA CAPO PRESS
ES * NP * YU

GLO * MEX
PL4 * PL12 * PT6 * PT9 * AP7

CLIFFORD, S. M.

ADVENTURES IN PIANOLAND..TWELVE LESSONS FOR TEACHERS OF PIANO
CLASSES

NEW YORK   1929   BAIPTL
FISCHER, J., AND BRO.
US

AT4 * AT7

CLOSSON, ERNEST

HISTORY OF THE PIANO

LONDON   1947   168P   BHOTP
ELEK, P., LTD.
BP * BR * CP * CU * ES * IU * LC * MI * NP * OC * UC * UI * UM * UO
US * UT * UW * YU
BIB * IND * PHO
KI3 * KI5 * KI6 * KI9

COATES, HENRY

CHOPIN--NOVELLO'S BIOGRAPHIES OF GREAT MUSICIANS

LONDON   1939   16P   BCNBOG
NOVELLO AND COMPANY, LTD.
BR

NP4

COCHRAN, MARY

ULTIMATE PRINCIPLES OF PIANOFORTE TEACHING AND PLAYING

SYDNEY   1938   273P   BUPOPT
PALING, W. H., AND COMPANY
BR * US

PL1 * AT1 * AP1

COCKSHOOT, JOHN V.

FUGUE IN BEETHOVEN'S PIANO MUSIC, THE

LONDON   1959   212P   BFIBPM
ROUTLEDGE AND KEGAN PAUL
AS * BP * BR * CP * CU * ES * IU * LC * MI * NP * OC * UA * UC * UI
UM * UO * UT * UW * YU
APP * BIB * IND * INT * MEX * MSF
PM3 * PM8 * PM14

COGGINS, JOSEPH

COMPANION TO THE MUSICAL ASSISTANT, A ..CONTAINING ALL THAT IS
TRULY USEFUL TO THE THEORY AND PRACTICE OF THE PIANOFORTE...
LONDON   1824   115P   BCTTMA
POWER, J.
BR * LC * MI

PL3 * PL7

COGGINS, JOSEPH

GOVERNESS'S MUSICAL ASSISTANT, CONTAINING ALL THAT IS TRULY USEFUL
TO THE THEORY AND PRACTICE OF THE PIANO FORTE, THE
LONDON   1815   33P   BGMACA
COGGINS, JOSEPH
BR

PL4 * PL7 * AT4

COHEN, HARRIET

BUNDLE OF TIME, A ..THE MEMOIRS OF HARRIET COHEN

LONDON   1969   330P   BBOTTM
FABER AND FABER
BR * ES * LC * UA

NP6

COHEN, HARRIET

MUSIC'S HANDMAID

LONDON   1936   160P   BMH
FABER AND FABER
BP * BR * CP * CU * ES * IU * LC * MI * NP * OC * SA * UA * US * UT

IND * MEX
NP7 * PL8 * PL12 * PT8 * PM3 * PM11 * AP4

COIT, LOTTIE ELLSWORTH

CHILD CHOPIN, THE ...WITH DIRECTIONS FOR PRESENTATION WITH A
MINIATURE STAGE SETTING OR AS A MUSICAL PLAYLET
PHILADELPHIA   1946   20P   BCCWDF
PRESSER, THEODORE, COMPANY
LC

NP2 * GI10 * GI12

COKER, JERRY

IMPROVISING JAZZ

ENGLEWOOD CLIFFS, N. J.   1964   115P   BIJ
PRENTICE-HALL, INC.
BP * BR * ES * IU * LC * NP * SA * UA * UM * UT

APP * CHR * INT * MEX * TAB
PL4 * KS6

COLEMAN, H. P.

PIANO CLASS, THE

LONDON   1972   BPC
BOSWORTH AND COMPANY, LTD.

MEX
AT4 * AT7

COLOMBATTI, HAROLD

PRACTICAL COURSE IN TRANSPOSITION, A

NEW YORK   BPCIT
BELWIN, INC.

KS7

COLOMBATTI, HAROLD

 PROGRESSIVE SIGHT READING EXERCISES---FOR PIANO

    MELBOURNE   1967 19P BPSREF
     ALLAN'S MUSIC, PTY. LTD.
 LC

 MEX
 KS3

CONKLIN-HAPP, SUZANNE

 APPLIED KEYBOARD HARMONY

    DUBUQUE, IOWA   1968 121P BAKH
     BROWN, WILLIAM C., COMPANY
 LC

 LDR * MEX
 PL4 * PL12 * PL14 * KS4

COOK, J. LAWRENCE

 PIANO HANDBOOK ON BOOGIE WOOGIE, BLUES, AND BARRELHOUSE..3 EASY TO
 PLAY PIANO METHODS IN ONE BOOK

    NEW YORK   1944 28P BPHOBW
     CAPITOL SONGS
 LC

 MEX
 AT4 * KS6 * AP4

COOKE, CHARLES

 PLAYING THE PIANO FOR PLEASURE--REV. ED.---1941

    NEW YORK   1960 186P BPTPFP
     SIMON AND SCHUSTER, INC.
 AS * BP * BR * CP * CU * ES * IU * LC * MI * NP * SA * TO * UI * UM
 UO * US * UW
 APP * BIB * LDR * MEX
 PL4 * PL7 * PL8 * PL9 * PL12 * PT1 * KS3 * GI11

COOKE, JAMES FRANCIS

 EVERY MAN HIS OWN TUNER..AN EASY AND CERTAIN GUIDE TO TUNING THE
 GRAND, UPRIGHT AND SQUARE PIANO

    PATERSON, N. J.   1908 77P BEMHOT
     HEUSSER, A. H.
 LC

 KI8

COOKE, JAMES FRANCIS

 GREAT MEN AND FAMOUS MUSICIANS ON THE ART OF MUSIC

    PHILADELPHIA   1925 446P BGMAFM
     PRESSER, THEODORE, COMPANY
 ES * IU * LC * NP * OC * SA * UA * UO * UW

 MEX * PHO
 NP8 * AT1 * AT6 * PT3 * PT8 * KS6

COOKE, JAMES FRANCIS

 GREAT PIANISTS ON PIANO PLAYING..STUDY TALKS WITH FOREMOST
 VIRTUOSI--2ND. ED.---1913

    PHILADELPHIA   1917 418P BGPOPP
     PRESSER, THEODORE, COMPANY
 BR * CP * CU * ES * LC * MI * NP * OC * SA * UA * UC * UI * UK * UM
 UO * US
 CHR * ILL * MEX * PHO
 NP8 * PL1 * PL2 * PL7 * PT8 * AP9 * GI3

COOKE, JAMES FRANCIS

 HOW TO MEMORIZE MUSIC

    PHILADELPHIA   1948 138P BHTMM
     PRESSER, THEODORE, COMPANY
 BP * CP * CU * ES * IU * LC * MI * NP * UA * UI * UM * UO

 ILL * MEX
 NP6 * PL8

COOKE, JAMES FRANCIS

 IGNACE JAN PADEREWSKI

    PHILADELPHIA   1928 18P BIJP
     PRESSER, THEODORE, COMPANY
 LC

 NP4

COOKE, JAMES FRANCIS

 LOUIS MOREAU GOTTSCHALK..A SHORT BIOGRAPHY

    PHILADELPHIA   1928 18P BLMGAS
     PRESSER, THEODORE, COMPANY
 LC

 PHO
 NP4 * PM3

COOKE, JAMES FRANCIS

 MUSIC MASTERS OLD AND NEW..A SERIES OF EDUCATIONAL BIOGRAPHIES...

    PHILADELPHIA   1919 82 BMMOAN
     PRESSER, THEODORE, COMPANY
 BR * LC * NP

 NP5

COOKE, MAX

 HOW TO PREPARE FOR PIANOFORTE...SUGGESTIONS FOR A.M.E.B.
 EXAMINATIONS--5 VOLS.

    MELBOURNE   1961   BHTPFP
     ALLAN'S MUSIC, PTY. LTD.
 LC

 INT
 AT10

COPP, EVELYN A.

 WHAT IS THE FLETCHER MUSIC METHOD

    BROOKLINE, MASS 1915 98P BWITFM
     COPP, EVELYN A.
 LC * NP

 PHO
 AT3 * AT4 * PT1 * PT6 * PT9 * KS4

COPP, LAURA R.

 SOME SECRETS OF SUCCESS IN PLAYING IN PUBLIC

    PHILADELPHIA   1929 19P BSSOSI
     PRESSER, THEODORE, COMPANY
 LC

 AP1 * AP2 * AP3 * AP4 * AP6 * AP9

COPPAGE, HOWARD W.

 PIANO, CHORDS AND HARMONY---REPRODUCED FROM MANUSCRIPT

    PHOENIX, ARIZ.   1954 32P BPCAHR
     COPPAGE ENTERPRISES
 LC

 GLO * INT * MEX * TAB
 KS4

CORDER, FREDERICK

 FERENCZ LISZT--HALF-TITLE..MASTERS OF MUSIC

    NEW YORK   1925 178P BFLHTM
     HARPER AND BROTHERS
 BR * LC * NP

 APP * IND * INT
 NP3 * PM3 * PM6

CORFE, JOSEPH

 THOROUGH BASS SIMPLIFIED

    LONDON   1820+ 56P BTBS
     PRESTON
 LC

 MEX
 KS10

CORTOT, ALFRED

 ALFRED CORTOT'S STUDIES IN MUSICAL INTERPRETATION, SET DOWN BY
 JEANNE THIEFFRY

    LONDON   1937 278P BACSIM
     HARRAP, GEORGE G., AND COMPANY, LTD.
 BP * BR * CU * ES * IU * LC * MI * NP * OC * TO * UC * UW * YU

 APP * IND * INT * MEX * PHO
 PM3 * PM9 * PM14

CORTOT, ALFRED

 FRENCH PIANO MUSIC

    LONDON   1932 208P BFPM
     OXFORD UNIVERSITY PRESS
 AS * BP * BR * CP * IU * LC * MI * NP * OC * UA * UC * UI * UK * UM
 US * UT * UU * UW * YU

 PM3 * PM8 * PM9 * PM11 * PM15

CORTOT, ALFRED

 IN SEARCH OF CHOPIN

    NEW YORK   1952 268P BISOC
     ABELARD-SCHUMANN
 AS * BP * BR * CP * CU * IU * LC * MI * NP * UC * UK * YU

 BIB * DIS * ILL
 NP3 * NP4 * NP7 * PM5 * PM12

CORTOT, ALFRED

PIANO MUSIC OF CLAUDE DEBUSSY, THE

       LONDON   1922   24P   BPMOCD
        CHESTER, J. AND W., LTD.
AS * BP * BR * ES * IU * LC * MI * NP * UM * UU

PM3 * PM9 * PM15

CORTOT, ALFRED

RATIONAL PRINCIPLES OF PIANOFORTE TECHNIQUE

       PARIS   1928   102P   BRPOPT
        EDITIONS M. SENART
CP * CU * ES * LC * NP * OC * UO * UT * UW

PT1 * PT2

COUPERIN, FRANCOIS

ART DE TOUCHER LE CLAVECIN, L' ---IN FRENCH, GERMAN AND ENGLISH

       LEIPZIG   1933   39P   BADTLC
        BREITKOPF AND HAERTEL
AS * BP * BR * ES * IU * LC * MI * NP * OC * TO * UA * UC * UI * UK
UM * US * UT * UU * UW * YU
MEX
PL4 * PL7 * PL12 * PT6 * PM7 * PM11 * AP3 * AP4 * AP7 * AP9

COVIELLO, AMBROSE

CHOICE OF A BEETHOVEN SONATA FOR DIPLOMA EXAMINATIONS, THE --NOTES
ON 17 SONATAS

       LONDON   1934   51P   BCOABS
        OXFORD UNIVERSITY PRESS
BR * NP * TO

INT * LDR
PM3 * PM8 * PM14

COVIELLO, AMBROSE

DIFFICULTIES OF BEETHOVEN PIANOFORTE SONATAS, AN ANALYSIS OF COMMON
FAULTS IN PERFORMANCE, WITH SUGGESTIONS FOR THEIR CURE--ANALYSIS
OF 8 SONATAS--4 VOLS.
       LONDON   1933   150P   BDOBPS
        OXFORD UNIVERSITY PRESS
BP * BR * ES * IU * LC * MI * NP * UM

CHR * INT * MEX
PM8 * PM14 * PM15 * AP4

COVIELLO, AMBROSE

FOUNDATIONS OF PIANOFORTE TECHNIC

       LONDON   1934   99P   BFOPT
        OXFORD UNIVERSITY PRESS
BP * CP * CU * ES * IU * SA * UT

CHR * IND * INT * LDR * MEX * TAB
PT3 * PT4 * PT6 * PT7 * PT8 * PT9 * PT10 * AP8

COVIELLO, AMBROSE

WHAT MATTHAY MEANT

       LONDON   1948   72P   BWMM
        BOSWORTH AND COMPANY, LTD.
CP * IU * LC * MI * NP * YU

BIB * CHR
KI6 * PL7 * PL8 * PL10 * PL12 * PL14 * PL15 * PT3 * PT4 * PT6 *
PT7 * PT8 * AP8

CRAMER, JOHN BAPTIST

INSTRUCTIONS FOR THE PIANOFORTE---CONTAINS ALSO A SET OF 28
SONATINAS

       LONDON   1822   142P   BIFTPC
        CHAPPELL AND COMPANY
IU * LC

APP * GLO * ILL * INT * MEX
PL4 * PL12 * PL15 * AT4 * PT6 * PT9 * KS7 * AP8

CRANMER, PHILIP

TECHNIQUE OF ACCOMPANIMENT, THE --THE STUDENT'S MUSIC LIBRARY

       LONDON   1970   108P   BTOATS
        DOBSON, DENNIS, LTD.
IU * LC * NP

APP * IND * MEX
KS11 * EP6

CRAWFORD, THOMAS J.

CRAWFORD SYSTEM OF KEYBOARD HARMONY AND TRANSPOSITION, THE

       TORONTO   1953   64P   BCSOKH
        CANADIAN MUSIC SALES CORPORATION
LC

INT * MEX
KS4 * KS7 * KS8

CRONK, CUTHBERT H.

WORKS OF ANTON RUBINSTEIN, NOV. 1829-NOV. 1894, THE ..A STUDY

       LONDON   1900   24P   BWOARN
        NOVELLO AND COMPANY
BR

PM3

CROTCH, WILLIAM

ELEMENTS OF MUSICAL COMPOSITION..COMPREHENDING THE RULES OF
THOROUGH BASS, AND THE THEORY OF TUNING

       LONDON   1812   136P   BEOMCC
        LONGMAN, HURST, REES, ORME AND BROWN
BR * LC * NP

MEX
KS10

CROTCH, WILLIAM

PRACTICAL THOROUGH BASS, OR, THE ART OF PLAYING FROM A FIGURED BASS
ON THE ORGAN OR PIANO FORTE

       LONDON   1820+   18P   BPTBOT
        WELSH AND HAWES
LC

MEX
KS10

CROTCH, WILLIAM

PRELUDES FOR THE PIANO FORTE, COMPOSED IN VARIOUS STYLES..TO WHICH
ARE PREFIXED THE RUDIMENTS OF PLAYING THAT INSTRUMENT

       LONDON   1823   48P   BPFTPF
        ROYAL HARMONIC INSTITUTION
LC

MEX
PL4 * AT4

CROUCH, M. S.

SYSTEMATIC FINGERING OF THE ARPEGGIOS OF COMMON CHORDS, ETC., THE

       LONDON   1928   BSFOTA
        PHILLIPS AND PAGE
BR

PT6 * PT9

CULSHAW, JOHN

CONCERTO, THE

       LONDON   1949   72P   BC
        PARRISH, MAX, AND COMPANY, LTD.
AS * BR * IU * LC * MI * NP * UM

ILL * IND * LDR * MEX * MSF
PM3 * PM7 * PM8 * PM9 * PM14 * PM15 * AP3 * AP4

CULSHAW, JOHN

SERGEI RACHMANINOFF..THE MAN AND HIS MUSIC

       LONDON   1949   174P   BSRTMA
        DOBSON, DENNIS, LTD.
BP * BR * ES * IU * LC * MI * NP * OC * TO * UA * UT

APP * BIB * INT * MEX * PHO
NP3 * PM3 * PM6 * PM8 * PM9 * PM14 * EP7

CURCIO, LOUISE

MUSICIAN'S HANDBOOK FOR THE DEVELOPMENT OF MANUAL SUPPLENESS AND
STRENGTH, THE

       NEW YORK   1968   24P   BMHFTD
        PATELSON, THE JOSEPH, MUSIC HOUSE
SA

INT * PHO
PT2 * PT3 * PT5 * PT10

CURCIO, LOUISE

SINGLE NOTE, THE

       NEWARK, N. J.   1965   196P   BSN
        ROSE EDUCATION PUBLISHERS
LC

PHO
PL10 * KI3 * PT3 * PT6 * PT8

CURTIS, ALAN

SWEELINCK'S KEYBOARD MUSIC..A STUDY OF ENGLISH ELEMENTS IN
SEVENTEENTH-CENTURY DUTCH COMPOSITION

       LONDON   1972   243P   BSKMAS
        BROWN, SIR THOMAS, INSTITUTE
LC

APP * BIB * ILL * IND * INT * MEX * MSF * PHO
PM3 * PM7 * PM8 * PM9 * PM14

CURWEN, ANNIE JESSY

CHILD PIANIST, THE

    LONDON   1888+   BCP
        CURWEN, J., AND SONS, LTD.

    MEX
    PL4 * AT4 * EP4

CURWEN, ANNIE JESSY

PSYCHOLOGY APPLIED TO MUSIC TEACHING

    LONDON   1920   304P   BPATMT
        CURWEN, J., AND SONS, LTD.
    BP * BR * ES * LC * NP * OC * TO * UA * UK * UO

    APP * ILL * IND * INT * MEX
    PL3 * PL7 * PL8 * AT3 * AT4 * PT6 * PT9

CURWEN, ANNIE JESSY

TEACHER'S GUIDE...TO MRS. CURWEN'S PIANOFORTE METHOD, 'THE CHILD
PIANIST', THE --16TH. ED.---1890+

    LONDON   1913   398P   BTGTMC
        CURWEN, J., AND SONS, LTD.
    BR * IU * LC * SA * TO * US

    APP * CHR * IND * INT * MEX * TAB
    PL4 * PL10 * PL12 * AT3 * AT4 * AT5 * AT6 * AT11 * PT9 * PT10 *
    KS7

CZERNY, CARL

COMPLETE THEORETICAL AND PRACTICAL PIANO FORTE SCHOOL, FROM THE
FIRST RUDIMENTS OF PLAYING, TO THE HIGHEST AND MOST REFINED STATE
OF CULTIVATION, OP. 500---SUPPLEMENT IN 1845
    LONDON   1839   219P   BCTAPP
        COCKS, R., AND COMPANY
    BR * LC * NP

    INT * MEX * MSF * TAB
    PL4 * PL5 * PL8 * PL12 * PL15 * PT4 * PT8 * PT9 * PT10 * PT11 *
    KS3 * KS5 * KS7 * KS9 * PM14 * AP4 * AP7 * AP8

CZERNY, CARL

LETTERS ON THOROUGH-BASS...FORMING THE SECOND PART OF THE LETTERS
ON TEACHING THE PIANOFORTE

    LONDON   1840+   105P   BLOTBF
        COCKS, R., AND COMPANY
    BR * LC * NP

    APP * INT
    NP6 * AT4 * KS8 * KS10

CZERNY, CARL

LETTERS TO A YOUNG LADY ON THE ART OF PLAYING THE PIANOFORTE

    LONDON   1838   82P   BLTAYL
        COCKS, L.
    BP * BR * ES * LC * NP * OC * UC * US * YU

    INT * MEX
    PL4 * PL12 * PT6 * PT8 * KS4 * KS5 * KS10 * PM10 * AP7

CZERNY, CARL

NEW EXERCISES ON HARMONY AND THOROUGH BASS...FORMING A PRACTICAL
APPENDIX TO HIS CELEBRATED LETTERS ON THOSE SUBJECTS
    LONDON   1846   32P   BNEOHA
        COCKS, R., AND COMPANY
    LC

    INT * MEX
    KS4 * KS10

CZERNY, CARL

ON THE PROPER PERFORMANCE OF ALL BEETHOVEN'S WORKS FOR THE PIANO

    BRYN MAWR, PA.   1970   109P   BOTPPO
        PRESSER, THEODORE, COMPANY
    IU

    APP * INT * MEX
    PM3 * AP3 * AP4

D'ABREU, GERALD

PLAYING THE PIANO WITH CONFIDENCE---1964

    NEW YORK   1971   126P   BPTPWC
        ST. MARTIN'S PRESS
    BP * BR * CP * ES * IU * LC * SA * TO * UA * UI * UO

    PL7 * PL8 * PL12 * PT1 * PT7 * PT10 * AP1 * AP4 * AP9 * GI3

DAHL, ANTON

SOUL OF GENIUS, THE ..ITS MUSICAL DEVELOPMENT AND HOW THE WORLD AT
LARGE ACCEPTS IT..WHAT EVERY MUSICIAN SHOULD KNOW..PIANO, GREATEST
INSTRUMENT IN THE WORLD, AND WHY
    LOS ANGELES   1918   62P   BSOGIM
        STANDARD PRINTING COMPANY
    LC

    KI6 * PL3 * PL7 * AT4 * PT8 * AP8 * GI3 * GI13

DALE, BENJAMIN J.

HARMONY, COUNTERPOINT AND IMPROVISATION

    LONDON   1940   106P   BHCAI
        NOVELLO AND COMPANY, LTD.
    BR * LC

    INT
    KS4 * KS7 * AP6 * AP7

DALE, KATHLEEN

NINETEENTH CENTURY PIANO MUSIC, A HANDBOOK FOR PIANISTS

    LONDON   1954   320P   BNCPMA
        OXFORD UNIVERSITY PRESS
    AS * BP * BR * CP * CU * ES * IU * LC * MI * NP * OC * TO * UA * UC
    UI * UM * UO * US * UT * UW * YU
    APP * BIB * IND * INT * MEX * TAB
    KI3 * KI6 * PT11 * PM3 * PM9 * PM14 * PM15 * EP4

DALE, WILLIAM

TSCHUDI THE HARPSICHORD MAKER

    LONDON   1913   81P   BTTHM
        CONSTABLE AND COMPANY, LTD.
    BP * BR * ES * LC * MI * NP * OC * UM * UT * UW

    ILL * INT * PHO
    KI12 * KI14

DANIELL, CHARLES A.

TRUE PIANO-TUNER, THE ..CONTAINING SIMPLE DIRECTIONS FOR TUNING,
REGULATING AND REMEDYING DEFECTS OF THE PIANOFORTE

    CINCINNATI   1881   56P   BTPTCS
        CHURCH, THE JOHN, COMPANY
    LC

    ILL * MEX
    KI8

DANIELS, BESS

PIANO COURSE..TEACHER'S BOOK, FOR CLASS OR INDIVIDUAL INSTRUCTION

    BOSTON   1936   71P   BPCTBF
        GINN AND COMPANY
    LC

    MEX
    AT4 * AT7

DANIELS, BESS *
LEAVITT, HELEN S.
PIANO COURSE EITHER FOR CLASS OR FOR INDIVIDUAL INSTRUCTION

    BOSTON   1936   88P   BPCEFC
        GINN AND COMPANY
    LC * MI

    AT4 * AT7

DANIELS, BESS

PLAYING PIANO AT SIGHT--MECHANICS FOR THE ADULT BEGINNER

    NEW YORK   1949   48P   BPPASM
        OMEGA MUSIC EDITION
    LC * NP

    MEX
    KS3

DANIELS, BESS *
LEAVITT, HELEN S.
WORLD OF MUSIC, THE ..PIANO COURSE..TEACHERS' BOOK, FOR CLASS OR
INDIVIDUAL INSTRUCTION
    NEW YORK   1936   71P   BWOMPC
        GINN AND COMPANY
    LC

    MEX
    PL4 * PL7 * PL12 * PL13 * AT4 * AT7 * AT8 * PT4 * PT8 * KS4 * AP6 *
    AP8

DANNREUTHER, EDWARD

MUSICAL ORNAMENTATION--IN TWO PARTS

    LONDON   1893   395P   BMOITP
        NOVELLO AND COMPANY, LTD.
    BP * BR * CP * ES * IU * LC * MI * NP * OC * SA * TO * UA * UC * UI
    UK * UM * UO * US * UT * UW * YU
    IND * INT * MEX
    AP7

DARBYSHIRE, JOHN H.

CONSTANT K--18600, THE ..ITS USE IN THEORY AND PRACTICE

    LONDON   1963   7P   BCKETS
        INSTITUTE OF MUSICAL INSTRUMENT TECHNOLOGY
    BR * TO

    LDR
    KI2

DARDENELLE, LOUISE

HARMONY-FIRST METHOD FOR THE PIANO...FOR CHILD AND ADULT BEGINNERS, WITH 'COLOR SYSTEM' OF CHORD ANALYSIS...FOR CLASS AND INDIVIDUAL INSTRUCTION

NEW YORK   1936   96P   BHFMFT
PAULL-PIONEER MUSIC CORPORATION
LC * NP

ILL * INT * LDR * MEX
AT4 * AT5 * AT6 * AT7 * KS4 * KS7

DARLOW, DENYS

MUSICAL INSTRUMENTS--JUNIOR REFERENCE BOOKS, NO. 12--2ND. ED.

LONDON   1962   80P   BMIJRB
BLACK, A. AND C.
LC

INT * LDR * PHO
KI3 * KI5 * KI6 * KI7 * KI9 * KI12 * KI13 * KI14 * GI10

DARRELL, ROBERT D.--COMPILER

SCHIRMER'S GUIDE TO BOOKS ON MUSIC AND MUSICIANS--A PRACTICAL BIBLIOGRAPHY

NEW YORK   1951   400P   BSGTBO
SCHIRMER, G., INC.
BR * IU * LC * NP

APP * IND * INT
PM5 * PM15

DART, THURSTON

INTERPRETATION OF MUSIC, THE --4TH. ED.---1954

NEW YORK   1967   192P   BIOMFE
HARPER AND ROW PUBLISHERS, INC.
AS * BP * BR * CP * CU * ES * IU * LC * MI * NP * OC * SA * TO * UA
UC * UI * UK * UM * UO * US * UT * UU * UW * YU
BIB * GLO * IND * INT * MEX * TAB
KI3 * KI9 * PM3 * AP3 * AP4 * AP7

DAVID, ELIZABETH HARBISON

I PLAYED THEIR ACCOMPANIMENTS

NEW YORK   1940   246P   BIPTA
APPLETON-CENTURY, D., COMPANY, INC.
BP * BR * ES * IU * LC * NP * UA

IND * PHO
NP6 * EP6

DAVIS, HARRY

INSTANT PIANO..A UNIQUE METHOD OF READING AND CHORDING FROM THE VERY BEGINNING

WESTBURY, LONG ISLAND, N. Y. 1970   76P   BIPAUM
DAVIS, H., INSTANT MUSIC
LC

MEX
PL5 * PL11 * AT4 * KS4

DAVIS, LIONEL

KEYBOARD INSTRUMENTS..THE STORY OF THE PIANO---YOUNGER READERS

MINNEAPOLIS   1963   41P   BKITSO
LERNER PUBLICATIONS, INC.
ES * IU * LC * MI * OC * UI * UT

ILL * LDR * MEX
KI3 * KI5 * PL4 * GI10

DAVIS, LUCILE

READ AND PLAY..RAPID CHORD CONSTRUCTION--REV. ED.---1943

SPOKANE, WASH.   1947   7P   BRAPRC
DAVIS, LUCILE
LC

AT4 * KS3 * KS4

DAVIS, MARILYN K.

GROUP ACTIVITIES AT THE KEYBOARD

NEW YORK   1958   28P   BGAATK
BOURNE
LC

INT
AT4 * AT5 * AT7

DAVISON, JAMES W.

FREDERICK CHOPIN...A MEMOIR

LONDON   1845+   BFCAM
BOOSEY, T., AND COMPANY

NP4 * PM3

DAVISON, JAMES W.

FREDERIC FRANCOIS CHOPIN..CRITICAL AND APPRECIATIVE ESSAY---1843

LONDON   1927+   29P   BFFCCA
REEVES, WILLIAM
BR * LC * NP

ILL
NP4 * NP6 * PM3 * PM6 * PM8 * PM9 * PM14

DAVISON, JUNE *
SCHAUB, ARDELLA
PIANO PROGRESS..AN APPROACH TO MUSIC FOR THE PARTIALLY SIGHTED--2 VOLS.

PITTSBURGH   1972   64P   BPPAAT
VOLKWEIN BROTHERS, INC.

AT3 * AT4

DAWES, FRANCIS E.

DEBUSSY PIANO MUSIC--B.B.C. MUSIC GUIDE---COMPOSITIONAL ASPECT

LONDON   1969   64P   BDPMBB
BRITISH BROADCASTING CORPORATION
BR * LC

INT * MEX
PM3 * PM8 * PM9 * PM14

DAWSON, FREDERICK

PIANOFORTE, THE

GLASGOW   1922   16P   BP
PATERSON SONS AND COMPANY
BR * ES * LC

KS1 * KS2

DECKER, TOM W.

CONSOLE SYSTEM, THE ..A TEXT FOR MODERN PIANO AND ORGAN TO BE USED IN CONJUNCTION WITH THE CONSOLE SYSTEM ELECTRONIC TEACHING MACHINE

MOBILE, ALA.   1965   BCSATF
DECKER CONSOLE SYSTEM
LC

KI11 * AT4 * AT7 * AT8

DELUXE REPRODUCING ROLL CORPORATION

LIBRARY OF DELUXE--REPRODUCING--MUSIC RECORDS

NEW YORK   1927+   323P   BLODRM
DELUXE REPRODUCING ROLL CORPORATION
LC * NP

ILL * INT * PHO
PM12

DELUXE ROLL CORPORATION

LIBRARY OF DELUXE WELTE-MIGNON MUSIC RECORDS FOR REPRODUCING PIANOS EQUIPPED WITH THE WELTE-MIGNON

CHICAGO   1924   BLODWM
DELUXE ROLL CORPORATION
BP * MI

KI10 * PM12

DEMUTH, NORMAN

FRENCH PIANO MUSIC...A SURVEY WITH NOTES ON ITS PERFORMANCE

LONDON   1959   179P   BFPMAS
MUSEUM PRESS
AS * BP * BR * CP * ES * IU * LC * MI * NP * SA * UA * UC * UM * UO
US * UT * YU
APP * IND * INT * MEX * PHO
PM3 * PM7 * PM8 * PM9 * PM15

DENHAM, GEORGE

MASTERY OF THE KEYBOARD

LONDON   1923   59P   BMOTK
PALMER, C.
BR * NP

IND * INT * MEX
PT4 * PT8 * PT9

DENSMORE, FRANCES

HANDBOOK OF THE COLLECTION OF MUSICAL INSTRUMENTS IN THE UNITED STATES NATIONAL MUSEUM

WASHINGTON, D. C.   1927   164P   BHOTCO
GOVERNMENT PRINTING OFFICE
BR * IU * LC * NP

BIB
KI3 * KI14 * KI15

DENT, EDWARD J.

FERRUCCIO BUSONI, A BIOGRAPHY

       LONDON   1933   368P   BFBAB
          OXFORD UNIVERSITY PRESS
BP * BR * ES * IU * LC * MI * NP * OC * TO * UA * UC * UI * UK * UM
UT * UU * UW
APP * ILL * IND * INT * LDR * PHO
NP3 * AT12 * PM3 * PM6

DENVER--PUBLIC SCHOOLS

CLASS-PIANO TEACHERS HANDBOOK

       DENVER   1965   54P   BCPTH
          DENVER PUBLIC SCHOOLS--DIV. OF INSTRUCTIONAL SERVICES
IU * SA

BIB * CHR * TAB
PL4 * AT4 * AT5 * AT7 * AT8 * AT9 * PM6 * EP1 * GI6 * GI9

DEUTSCH, LEONHARD

PIANO..GUIDED SIGHT-READING

       CHICAGO   1950   107P   BPGSR
          NELSON-HALL COMPANY
AS * BP * BR * CP * CU * ES * LC * MI * NP * OC * SA * TO * UI * UT
UW
BIB * CHR * INT
PL8 * PL9 * PL10 * PL11 * PL12 * AT3 * PT2 * PT6 * PT7 * PT8 * KS3

DE BOER, JOSEPHINE

MALLORCAN MOODS IN CONTEMPORARY ART AND LITERATURE--CONTAINS
'GEORGE SAND AND CHOPIN IN MALLORCA'

       WILLIAMSPORT, PA.   1938   72P   BMMICA
          BAYARD PRESS, THE
LC

NP4 * GI15

DE LARA, ADELINA

FINALE---MEMOIRS OF LAST SURVIVING PUPIL OF CLARA SCHUMANN

       LONDON   1955   222P   BFMOLS
          BURKE PUBLISHING COMPANY, LTD.
BP * BR * LC * NP * UA * UI * UM

DIS * INT * PHO
NP6

DE SOLIS, SOLITO

THREE POSITIONS OF HARMONIZED SCALES, THE --SHOWN IN ALL KEYS

       NEW YORK   1956   15P   BTPOHS
          MILLS MUSIC, INC.
LC

INT * MEX
PT9 * KS4

DE WITT, EDYTHE

EDYTHE DE WITT'S METHOD FOR CLASS PIANO...WRITTEN TO GIVE CORRECT
NOTE READING, CORRECT FINGERING AND TO CULTIVATE PERFECT RHYTHM

       CINCINNATI   1939   38P   BEDMFC
          ZIMMERMAN PRINTERS
LC

INT * PHO
PL4 * PL12 * AT4 * AT7 * AT10 * PT6 * KS3

DICKERSON, RUTH A.

NEW APPROACH TO PIANO TECHNIQUE, A

       NEW YORK   1962   44P   BNATPT
          PAGEANT PRESS, INC.
CP * IU * LC * MI * NP * SA * UI

INT
PT1 * PT3 * PT4 * PT8 * PT9

DICKEY, ALBERT W.

PRACTICAL PIANO TUNING..A METHOD WITH A DO-IT-YOURSELF OUTLOOK

       MADISON, N. J.   1959   19P   BPPTAM
LC * NP

BIB * CHR * GLO * LDR
KI8

DICKINSON, ALLAN E.

BACH'S FUGAL WORKS

       LONDON   1956   280P   BBFW
          PITMAN, I., AND SONS, LTD.
BP * BR * CP * CU * IU * LC * MI * NP * OC * TO * UA * UC * UI * UM
UO * UU * UW * YU
APP * BIB * CHR * GLO * IND * INT * MEX
PM3 * PM8 * PM14 * PM15

DIDIMUS, HENRY

BIOGRAPHY OF LEOPOLD DE MEYER...ROYAL COURT PIANIST...TO THEIR
MAJESTIES, THE EMPERORS OF AUSTRIA AND RUSSIA

       LONDON   1845   32P   BBOLDM
          PALMER AND CLAYTON
LC

APP * ILL
NP4 * NP7

DIDIMUS, HENRY

BIOGRAPHY OF LOUIS MOREAU GOTTSCHALK, THE AMERICAN PIANIST AND
COMPOSER--REPRINT FROM 'GRAHAM'S MAGAZINE', JANUARY, 1853

       PHILADELPHIA   1853   22P   BBOLMG
          DEACON AND PETERSON, PRINTERS
LC

NP4 * PM3

DIEHL, ALICE M.

MUSICAL MEMORIES--SOME LESSONS WITH HENSELT

       LONDON   1897   319P   BMMSLW
          BENTLEY, R., AND SON
BP * BR * LC * NP * UA * YU

IND
NP4 * AT12 * AT13

DIEHL, ALICE M.

TRUE STORY OF MY LIFE, THE

       LONDON   1908   347P   BTSOML
          LANE, J., LTD.
BP * BR * LC * UA * UO * YU

NP6

DIETZ, FRANZ RUDOLF

INTONIEREN VON FLUEGELN, DAS --GRAND VOICING---IN GERMAN, ENGLISH,
FRENCH, SWEDISH AND ITALIAN

       FRANKFURT AM MAIN   1968   55P   BIVFGV
          VERLAG DAS MUSIKINSTRUMENT
LC

INT * PHO
KI8

DIETZ, FRANZ RUDOLF

REGULIEREN VON FLUEGELN BEI STEINWAY, DAS --REGULATION OF THE
STEINWAY GRAND ACTION, THE ---IN GERMAN, ENGLISH, FRENCH, ITALIAN
AND DUTCH

       FRANKFURT AM MAIN   1963   82P   BRVFBS
          VERLAG DAS MUSIKINSTRUMENT
BR * IU * LC * NP

BIB * INT * PHO
KI5 * KI6 * KI8 * KI12

DILLER, ANGELA

FIRST PEDAL-STUDIES FOR THE PIANO, 24 PROGRESSIVE EXERCISES AND
PIECES

       NEW YORK   1942   23P   BFPFTP
          SCHIRMER, G., INC.
LC

INT * MEX
AT4 * AP8

DILLER, ANGELA

KEYBOARD HARMONY COURSE..A CREATIVE METHOD BASED ON EAR-TRAINING--4
VOLS., 1936-1949

       NEW YORK   1936   344P   BKHCAC
          SCHIRMER, G., INC.
BR * IU * LC * NP

INT * MEX
PL10 * KS4

DILLER, ANGELA

KEYBOARD MUSIC STUDY..A CREATIVE METHOD BASED ON EAR-TRAINING--IN
TWO BOOKS, 1936-1937

       NEW YORK   1936   65P   BKMSAC
          SCHIRMER, G., INC.
BP * LC * NP * UU

PL10 * AT4

DILLER, ANGELA

SPLENDOR OF MUSIC, THE

       NEW YORK   1957   214P   BSOM
          SCHIRMER, G., INC.
BP * BR * CP * CU * ES * IU * LC * NP * OC * SA * TO * UI * UK * UM
UO * US * UT * UU * UW

PL4 * PL7 * PL8 * PL10 * PL12 * AT1 * AT5 * AT6 * AT7 * AT8 * AT9 *
PT1 * PT3 * PT6 * PT8 * KS4 * AP6 * AP9

DITSON COMPANY

TEACHING PIECES AND HOW TO TEACH THEM

BOSTON   1901   288P   BTPAHT
            DITSON, OLIVER, COMPANY
    NP

    INT * MEX
    AT1 * AT4 * PM6 * PM9 * PM15

DOBBIE, E. A.

AUSTRALIAN PIANOFORTE TUTOR

SYDNEY   1922   71P   BAPT
            PALING, W. H., AND COMPANY, LTD.
    LC

    INT * MEX
    PL4 * PL12 * AT4 * PT6 * PT8 * PT9 * KS4 * KS8

DODD, FLORENCE

BERLIN TEST CLASS, THE ..OR, FORTY-EIGHT PROGRESSIVE LESSONS IN THE
ART OF PIANO PLAYING--BY THE METHOD OF A. K. VIRGIL

LONDON   1899   166P   BBTCOF
            VIRGIL PRACTICE CLAVIER COMPANY
    BR * ES

    PL1 * PL2

DOLE, NATHAN H.

FAMOUS COMPOSERS--2 VOLS.---CHOPIN AND LISZT--1891+

LONDON   1936   866P   BFCTVC
            METHUEN AND COMPANY
    BR * IU * LC * NP

    ILL
    NP5

DOLE, NATHAN H.

LIVES OF THE MUSICIANS, THE ...WITH PORTRAITS

LONDON   1904   456P   BLOTMW
            SIMPKIN, MARSHALL AND COMPANY
    BR

    NP5

DOLGE, ALFRED

PIANOS AND THEIR MAKERS..A COMPREHENSIVE HISTORY OF THE
PIANO---1911

NEW YORK   1972   478P   BPATMA
            DOVER PUBLICATIONS, INC.
    BP * CP * ES * IU * LC * MI * NP * UA * UC * UI * UM * UO * US * YU

    APP * ILL * IND * LDR * PHO
    KI2 * KI3 * KI4 * KI5 * KI6 * KI7 * KI8 * KI9 * KI10

DOLMETSCH, ARNOLD

INTERPRETATION OF MUSIC OF THE SEVENTEENTH AND EIGHTEENTH
CENTURIES, THE ---1915

SEATTLE   1969   493P   BIOMOT
            UNIVERSITY OF WASHINGTON PRESS
    AS * BP * BR * CP * ES * IU * LC * MI * NP * OC * TO * UA * UC * UI
    UK * UM * UO * US * UT * UU * UW * YU
    BIB * GLO * IND * INT * MEX
    KI3 * KI9 * KI14 * PL12 * PT6 * KS10 * AP7

DONALDSON, GEORGE

CATALOGUE OF THE MUSICAL INSTRUMENTS AND OBJECTS FORMING THE
DONALDSON MUSEUM--IN THE ROYAL COLLEGE OF MUSIC

LONDON   1899   BCOTMI

    KI1 * KI9 * KI15

DONINGTON, ROBERT

INSTRUMENTS OF MUSIC, THE --3RD. REV. ED.---1949

LONDON   1970   262P   BIOMTR
            METHUEN AND COMPANY, LTD.
    BR * IU * LC * NP

    APP * CHR * GLO * ILL * IND * LDR * MEX * PHO
    KI3 * KI5 * KI6 * KI7 * KI9 * KI13 * KI14 * EP3

DONINGTON, ROBERT

INTERPRETATION OF EARLY MUSIC, THE

LONDON   1963   605P   BIOEM
            FABER AND FABER
    AS * BP * BR * CP * CU * ES * IU * LC * MI * NP * OC * TO * UA * UC
    UI * UK * UM * US * UT * UU * UW * YU
    APP * BIB * IND * MEX * MSF * TAB
    KI14 * PL12 * PL15 * KS4 * KS5 * KS10 * AP3 * AP4 * AP7 * EP6

DONINGTON, ROBERT

PERFORMER'S GUIDE TO BAROQUE MUSIC, A

LONDON   1973   320P   BPGTBM
            FABER AND FABER
    IU

    BIB * IND * MEX * MSF
    KI14 * PL12 * PL14 * PL15 * KS5 * KS10 * PM3 * PM7 * PM8 * PM9 *
    PM14 * AP3 * AP4 * AP6 * AP7 * EP6

DORIAN, FREDERICK

HISTORY OF MUSIC IN PERFORMANCE, THE ---1942

NEW YORK   1966   387P   BHOMIP
            NORTON, W. W., AND COMPANY
    AS * BP * BR * CP * ES * IU * LC * MI * NP * OC * TO * UA * UC * UI
    UK * UM * UO * US * UT * UU * UW * YU
    BIB * ILL * IND * MEX * MSF * PHO * TAB
    PM3 * PM7 * AP3 * AP4 * AP5

DRAKE, HARRY

FROM PIANO TUNER TO PLAYER EXPERT

LONDON   1924   105P   BFPTTP
            MUSICAL OPINION
    LC * NP

    ILL * INT * LDR
    KI8 * KI10

DRAKE, HARRY

PLAYER-PIANO EXPLAINED, THE --PAMPHLET

LONDON   1922+   40P   BPEP
            MUSICAL OPINION
    BR * LC * NP

    ILL * LDR
    KI5 * KI6 * KI10

DRAKE, HARRY

PNEUMATIC PLAYER, THE ..THE REGULATION AND REPAIR OF SOME MODERN
TYPES

LONDON   1921   78P   BPPTRA
            MUSICAL OPINION
    NP

    ILL * INT * LDR
    KI8 * KI10

DRAKE, HARRY

REPAIRING THE PLAYER PIANO

LONDON   1927+   32P   BRTPP
            MUSICAL OPINION

    KI8 * KI10

DRAKE, KENNETH

SONATAS OF BEETHOVEN AS HE PLAYED AND TAUGHT THEM, THE

CINCINNATI   1972   209P   BSOBAH
            MUSIC TEACHERS' NATIONAL ASSOCIATION
    IU * LC

    BIB * IND * INT * MEX * TAB
    PL12 * PL15 * PT8 * PM3 * PM7 * PM8 * PM9 * PM14 * AP3 * AP4 * AP6
    AP7 * AP8

DRY, WAKELING

CHOPIN--'MUSIC OF THE MASTERS' SERIES

LONDON   1926   118P   BCMOTM
            LANE, JOHN, LTD.
    BR * LC

    BIB * INT * MEX
    NP3 * PM3 * PM4 * PM9 * PM14

DUCAT, EVA

ANOTHER WAY OF MUSIC---AUTOBIOGRAPHY

LONDON   1928   202P   BAWOMA
            CHAPMAN AND HALL
    BR * LC

    PHO
    NP6

DUCKWORTH, GUY

KEYBOARD MUSICIANSHIP

NEW YORK   1970   261P   BKM
            FREE PRESS, THE
    BR * IU * LC * NP * SA

    INT * MEX
    PL3 * PL4 * PL5 * PL6 * PL7 * PL9 * PL10 * PL12 * PL13 * AT4 * AT6
    AT7 * PT6 * PT9 * KS3 * KS4 * KS5

DUFFEE, GERTRUDE BANKS

PIANO STUDY..A GUIDE TO TEACHER AND STUDENT

        PHILADELPHIA   1895   118P   BPSAGT
        NATIONAL BUREAU OF ENGRAVING
LC

ILL * INT * MEX
KI3 * PL1 * PL5 * PL9 * PL12 * AT3 * PT4 * PT6 * PT9 * PT10

DUMESNIL, MAURICE

HOW TO PLAY AND TEACH DEBUSSY

        NEW YORK   1932   23P   BHTPAT
        SCHROEDER AND GUNTHER
AS * CP * ES * LC * NP * UC * US * UT * UW * YU

ILL * MEX
PT6 * PT8 * PM3 * PM9 * AP3 * AP4 * AP8

DUMM, ROBERT W.

IN BLACK AND WHITE

        BOSTON   1962   44P   BIBAW
        BOSTON MUSIC COMPANY
IU * SA

INT * LDR * PHO
PL6 * PL8 * PL12 * AT1 * AT2 * AT3 * AT5 * PT4 * AP4 * AP5 * AP6 * AP8 * AP9

DUNHAM, ROWLAND W.

PRACTICAL TRANSPOSITION, FOR PIANISTS AND ORGANISTS

        NEW YORK   1952   60P   BPTFPA
        FISCHER, J., AND BRO.
LC

INT * MEX
KS7

DUNLOP, AGNES MARY

DUET---STORY OF CLARA AND ROBERT SCHUMANN

        LONDON   1968   213P   BDSOCA
        EVANS BROTHERS, LTD.
LC

NP4 * PM3 * GI10

DUNN, JOHN PETRIE

BASIS OF PIANOFORTE PLAYING, THE

        LONDON   1933   99P   BBOPP
        OXFORD UNIVERSITY PRESS
BP * BR * CU * ES * IU * LC * NP * SA * UT * YU

APP * INT * MEX
KI5 * KI6 * KI7 * PT3 * PT4 * PT8 * PT9 * PT10

DUNN, JOHN PETRIE

ORNAMENTATION IN THE WORKS OF FREDERIC CHOPIN---1921

        NEW YORK   1971   75P   BOITWO
        DA CAPO PRESS
BR * CU * ES * IU * LC * NP * UT

IND * MEX
PM3 * PM9 * AP7

DUNWELL, WILFRID

PIANOFORTE ACCOMPANIMENT WRITING

        LONDON   1950   55P   BPAW
        HAMMOND, A., AND COMPANY
BR * IU * LC * NP * SA

APP * INT * MEX
KS4 * KS11

DUSSEK, JOHANN L.

DUSSEK'S INSTRUCTIONS ON THE ART OF PLAYING THE PIANOFORTE OR
HARPSICHORD, BEING A COMPLEAT TREATISE OF THE FIRST RUDIMENTS OF
MUSIC
        LONDON   1797   47P   BDIOTA
        CORRI, DUSSEK AND COMPANY
LC * NP

APP * CHR * MEX
PL3 * PL4 * PL7 * PL11 * PL12 * PT4 * PT6 * PT9

DUTTON, CHUCK *
CONNOR, JOSEPH
    MUSIC FOR FUN..PROFESSIONAL COURSE USING THE CHUCK DUTTON
    STREAMLINED CHORD SYSTEM

        BERKELEY, CAL.   1942   18P   BMFFPC
        DUTTON, CHUCK
LC

ILL * MEX
AT4 * KS4 * KS6

EARL, S. G.

REPAIRING THE PLAYER PIANO..INFORMATION USEFUL TO PIANOFORTE TUNERS
AND REPAIRERS

        LONDON   1920+   31P   BRTPPI
        MUSICAL OPINION AND MUSIC TRADE REVIEW
LC * NP

ILL * LDR
KI5 * KI6 * KI8

EARLES, ADELAIDE L. S. T.

PIANO PLAYING OF THE FUTURE, FOR EVERY GOOD PIANIST, THE

        HADLEIGH, SUFFOLK, ENGLAND   1937   75P   BPPOTF
        EPOCH DELIVERY COMPANY
BR

PL1 * PL2

EARLES, ADELAIDE L. S. T.

SHORT ESSAY ON THE GENERAL NEED FOR SCIENTIFIC PIANOFORTE PLAYING,
A

        HADLEIGH, SUFFOLK, ENGLAND   1929   14P   BSEOTG
        EPOCH DELIVERY COMPANY
BP * BR

PL1 * PL2

EBERHARDT, GOBY

MY SYSTEM FOR PRACTICING THE VIOLIN AND PIANO, BASED UPON
PSYCHO-PHYSIOLOGICAL PRINCIPLES

        NEW YORK   1908   51P   BMSFPT
        FISCHER, CARL, INC.
BP * NP

INT * MEX * PHO
PL3 * PT3 * PT4 * PT6 * PT7 * PT9 * PT10

EDINBURGH UNIVERSITY--DEPT. OF EARLY KEYBOARD INSTRUMENTS

RUSSELL COLLECTION AND OTHER EARLY KEYBOARD INSTRUMENTS IN ST.
CECILIA'S HALL, THE --COMPILED BY SIDNEY NEWMAN AND PETER WILLIAMS

        EDINBURGH   1968   79P   BRCAOE
        EDINBURGH UNIVERSITY PRESS
BR * IU * LC

CHR * ILL * IND * INT * LDR * PHO
KI3 * KI5 * KI6 * KI9 * KI12 * KI13 * KI14 * KI15

EDWARDS, RUTH

COMPLEAT MUSIC TEACHER FOR TEACHERS, PARENTS AND STUDENTS

        LOS ALTOS, CAL.   1970   150P   BCMTFT
        GERON-X, INC.
IU * LC

APP * INT * MEX
PL7 * PL13 * AT1 * AT3 * AT4 * AT5 * AT6 * AT7 * AT9 * AT11 * PM1 *
AP4 * GI7

EGBERT, MARION S.

KEYBOARD EXPERIENCE IN THE CLASSROOM MUSIC PROGRAM..HANDBOOK FOR
CLASSROOM TEACHERS

        NEW YORK   1959   49P   BKEITC
        BOURNE
LC * OC

INT * LDR * MEX * PHO
PL4 * KS7 * EP6

EGBERT, MARION S.

SEEING WHAT WE SING, AN AID THROUGH KEYBOARD EXPERIENCE TO THE
UNDERSTANDING OF THE MUSIC FUNDAMENTALS ENCOUNTERED IN THE
CLASSROOM
        BOSTON   1955   31P   BSWWSA
        BIRCHARD, C. C., AND COMPANY
LC

INT * MEX
PL4 * AT7 * KS4

EHLERT, LOUIS

FROM THE TONE WORLD--ESSAYS---TAUSIG, CHOPIN AND LISZT--2ND.
ED.---1884

        NEW YORK   1893+   397P   BFTTWE
        TRETBAR, C. F.
LC * NP

INT
NP6

EHLERT, LOUIS

LETTERS ON MUSIC, TO A LADY

        BOSTON   1870   216P   BLOMTA
        DITSON, OLIVER, COMPANY
BP * BR * ES * IU * LC * NP * OC * UM

INT
NP6

EHRENFECTER, C. A.

DELIVERY IN THE ART OF PIANOFORTE PLAYING

    LONDON   1891   64P   BDITAO
    REEVES, WILLIAM, LTD.
BP * BR * ES * NP * SA * UA * US

IND * INT * MEX
PL12 * AP4 * AP6

EHRENFECTER, C. A.

TECHNICAL STUDY IN THE ART OF PIANOFORTE PLAYING--DEPPE'S
PRINCIPLES---ORIGINALLY A SERIES OF LETTERS IN THE 'MUSICAL
STANDARD'
    LONDON   1891   114P   BTSITA
    REEVES, WILLIAM, LTD.
BR * ES * NP * OC * SA * UA * YU

INT * MEX
NP7 * PT4 * PT6 * PT8 * PT9 * PT10 * AP8

EHRLICH, ALFRED HEINRICH

CELEBRATED PIANISTS OF THE PAST AND PRESENT--139 BIOGRAPHIES, WITH
PORTRAITS

    PHILADELPHIA   1894   423P   BCPOTP
    PRESSER, THEODORE, COMPANY
AS * BP * BR * CP * ES * IU * LC * MI * NP * SA * UI * US * UT * UU
YU
ILL * INT
NP3 * NP4 * NP5

EHRLICH, ALFRED HEINRICH

HOW TO PRACTICE ON THE PIANO..REFLECTIONS AND SUGGESTIONS

    NEW YORK   1901   60P   BHTPOT
    SCHIRMER, G., INC.
BP * CP * ES * IU * LC * NP * OC * SA

INT * MEX
PL7 * PT4 * PT9 * PT10 * PT11

EHRLICH, ALFRED HEINRICH

HOW TO PRACTICE THE PIANOFORTE..SPECULATIONS AND ADVICE

    NEW YORK   1879   40P   BHTPTP
    SCHUBERTH, E.
IU * LC * NP

MEX
PL7

EHRLICH, ALFRED HEINRICH

ORNAMENTATION IN BEETHOVEN'S PIANOFORTE-WORKS, THE

    NEW YORK   1898   12P   BOIBPW
    SCHUBERTH, E.
IU * LC * NP

MEX
PM3 * PM14 * AP7

EHRLICH, ALFRED HEINRICH

ORNAMENTATION IN JOH. SEB. BACH'S PIANOFORTE-WORKS, THE

    NEW YORK   1898   20P   BOIJSB
    SCHUBERTH, E.
LC * TO

INT * MEX
AP7

EICHBERG, OSCAR

ANALYTICAL AND HISTORICAL REMARKS ON ANTON RUBINSTEIN'S CYCLE OF
SEVEN PIANOFORTE RECITALS...

    LONDON   1888   44P   BAAHRO

BR

NP7 * PM7 * PM13

EICHMANN, A. H. *
HAUERT, ROBERT
WILHELM BACKHAUS

    GENEVA   1958   31P   BWB
    KISTER, RENE
BR * LC * NP * SA

DIS * PHO
NP3 * NP4

EISENBERG, JACOB

ARTISTIC PIANIST, THE ..NATURAL TECHNICS IN PIANO MASTERY..FROM
STUDENT TO ARTIST--THE AUTHOR'S 'WEIGHT AND RELAXATION METHOD FOR
THE PIANOFORTE', REWRITTEN AND ENLARGED
    LONDON   1929+   236P   BAPNTI
    REEVES, WILLIAM
BR * CU * ES * LC * NP * SA * TO

APP * CHR * IND * INT * LDR * MEX * PHO
KI6 * PL2 * AT3 * AT4 * PT3 * PT4 * PT6 * PT7 * PT8 * PT9 * PT10 *
AP4 * AP8 * AP9 * GI2 * GI13

EISENBERG, JACOB

LET ME HELP YOU, MY ANCESTORS AND I..A COMPREHENSIVE JUVENILE
HISTORY OF THE PIANO

    NORTH BERGEN, N. J.   1964   64P   BLMHYM
    JAY-ROGER MUSIC COMPANY
LC

ILL * PHO
KI3 * KI5 * KI6 * KI7 * KI9 * KI10 * KI12 * KI13 * KI14 * GI10

EISENBERG, JACOB

ROMANCE OF KEYS AND TONES..THE PIANO, ITS ORIGIN AND DEVELOPMENT,
AND THE FORCES WHICH ENCOURAGED ITS GROWTH

    NORTH BERGEN, N. J.   1956   66P   BROKAT
    JAY-ROGER MUSIC COMPANY
LC

INT * TAB
KI3 * KI12

EISENBERG, JACOB

WEIGHT AND RELAXATION METHOD FOR THE PIANOFORTE

    NEW YORK   1922   126P   BWARMF
    EISENBERG, JACOB, PUBLISHING COMPANY
CU * IU * LC * NP

IND * INT * LDR * PHO
PL7 * PL12 * AT11 * PT3 * PT4 * PT6 * PT7 * PT8 * PT9 * PT10 * AP4
GI2

ELKAN, IDA

PIANO SIGHTREADING CAN BE TAUGHT

    NEW YORK   1948   63P   BPSCBT
    MUSIC SIGHTREADING PUBLICATIONS
BP * CP * ES * IU * LC * NP * SA * UM

INT * LDR * PHO
KS3

ELKAN, IDA

PRACTICAL PIANO PLAYING MANUAL AND THEORY WRITING BOOK

    NEW YORK   1939   52P   BPPPMA
    FISCHER, CARL, INC.
LC

CHR
PL4 * PL10 * PL12 * KS3 * KS4 * KS7

ELKAN, IDA

TECHNICAL WORK IN EAR-TRAINING FOR THE PIANO..A METHOD FOR PRIVATE
AND CLASS INSTRUCTION--2 VOLS. IN 1, 1933-1943---COPYRIGHT IN 1926
    NEW YORK   1933   BTWIET
    FISCHER, CARL, INC.
LC * NP

MEX
PL10 * AT4 * AT7 * KS3

ELLINGHAM, HARRY

HOW TO USE A PLAYER-PIANO

    LONDON   1922   208P   BHTUAP
    RICHARDS, G., LTD.
BR * LC * NP

GLO * CHR * GLO * ILL * INT
KI3 * KI4 * KI5 * KI6 * KI8 * AP3 * EP6 * GI14

ELLIS, HAVELOCK

AFFIRMATIONS--LITERARY ESSAYS---CHOPIN

    LONDON   1898   248P   BALES
    SCOTT, WALTER, PUBLISHING COMPANY
BR * LC

NP6

ELLIS, HAVELOCK

NEW SPIRIT, THE --ESSAYS---CHOPIN--1891

    NEW YORK   1930   292P   BNSECE
    MODERN LIBRARY, THE
BR * LC

NP6

EMERICH, PAUL

ROAD TO MODERN MUSIC, THE

    NEW YORK   1960   33P   BRTMM
    SOUTHERN MUSIC PUBLISHING COMPANY
BP * CP * ES * IU * LC * MI * NP * UC * UI * UM * UO * UT * YU

IND * INT * MEX
PM6 * PM7 * PM8 * AP4

EMERY, WALTER

    BACH'S ORNAMENTS

            LONDON   1953   164P   BBO
            NOVELLO AND COMPANY, LTD.
    BP * BR * CP * CU * ES * IU * LC * MI * NP * OC * SA * TO * UA * UC
    UI * UM * UO * US * UT * UU * UW * YU
    APP * IND * INT * MEX * MSF * TAB
    PM3 * AP7

EMERY, WALTER

    EDITIONS AND MUSICIANS

            LONDON   1957   54P   BEAM
            NOVELLO AND COMPANY, LTD.
    BP * BR * CP * CU * ES * IU * LC * NP * SA * TO * UC * UI * UK * UM
    UO * UT * UW * YU
    CHR * INT * MEX
    PM4

ENGEL, CARL

    MUSICAL INSTRUMENTS---78 WOODCUT ILLUSTRATIONS

            NEW YORK   1876   128P   BMISEW
            CHAPMAN AND HALL
    BR * IU * LC * NP

    ILL * IND * LDR
    KI6 * KI7 * KI13 * KI14

ENGEL, CARL

    MUSICAL INSTRUMENTS--REV. ED.---1876

            LONDON   1908   146P   BMIREE
            HER MAJESTY'S STATIONERY OFFICE
    BR * LC

    ILL * IND * INT * MEX * PHO
    KI3 * KI5 * KI6 * KI7 * KI9 * KI13 * KI14

ENGEL, CARL

    PIANIST'S HANDBOOK, THE ..A GUIDE FOR THE RIGHT COMPREHENSION AND
    PERFORMANCE OF OUR BEST PIANOFORTE MUSIC

            LONDON   1853   217P   BPHAGF
            HOPE AND COMPANY
    BR * ES * NP

    GLO * IND * INT * MEX
    KI3 * KI5 * PL7 * PT8 * KS3 * PM8 * PM10 * AP8

ENGELBRECHT, J. G.

    MATERIA MUSICA, OR MATERIALS FOR THE PIANIST..A CLASS BOOK

            NEW YORK   1868   144P   BMMOMF
            DITSON, C. H., AND COMPANY
    LC

    GLO * IND * INT * MEX
    PL4 * PL12 * AT7 * PT8 * PT9 * AP7 * AP8

EPWORTH PIANOS

    BOOK ABOUT PIANOS IN GENERAL AND THE EPWORTH IN PARTICULAR, A

            CHICAGO   1906   39P   BBAPIG
            WILLIAMS ORGAN AND PIANO COMPANY
    NP

    ILL * PHO
    KI4 * KI5 * KI6 * KI9 * KI12 * KI13

ERWIN, GARNET PARKER

    KEYBOARD STORIES FOR CLASS AND INDIVIDUAL INSTRUCTION---1939

            NEW YORK   1942   56P   BKSFCA
            SUMMY, CLAYTON F., COMPANY
    LC

    MEX
    AT4 * AT7

ETHIER, JOSEPH A.

    ETHIER'S GREAT NON-SUCH SELF-INSTRUCTOR IN THE ART OF ACCOMPANYING
    BY EAR

            BUFFALO, N. Y.   1901   84P   BEGNSS
            ETHIER, J. A.

    PL11 * KS12 * EP6

EVANS, EDWIN

    HANDBOOK TO THE PIANOFORTE WORKS OF JOHANNES BRAHMS---1936

            NEW YORK   1970   327P   BHTTPW
            FRANKLIN, B.
    AS * BR * CP * CU * ES * IU * LC * MI * NP * OC * SA * TO * UA * UC
    UI * UM * UO * US * UT * UW
    BIB * CHR * IND * MEX * TAB
    PM3 * PM5 * PM7 * PM8 * PM9 * PM10 * PM15 * AP3 * AP4

EVANS, EDWIN

    HOW TO ACCOMPANY AT THE PIANO

            LONDON   1917   231P   BHTAAT
            REEVES, WILLIAM
    BP * BR * CP * ES * IU * LC * NP * SA * YU

    IND * MEX * TAB
    KS4 * KS5 * EP6

EVANS, EVERETT J.

    SELF-TEACHING CHORD BOOK FOR THE PIANO OR ORGAN..SHOWS HOW TO PLAY
    THE ACCOMPANIMENT TO ANY MELODY

            EAST ORANGE, N. J.   1923   32P   BSTCBF
            EVANS, EVERETT J.
    LC

    PL11 * KS4 * EP6

EVANS MUSIC COMPANY

    EVANS' GRADED STUDY GUIDE FOR THE PIANOFORTE AND DICTIONARY OF
    MUSICAL TERMS

            BOSTON   1912   77P   BEGSGF
            EVANS MUSIC COMPANY
    LC

    GLO * INT
    KI15 * PM6

EVERHART, POWELL

    PIANIST'S ART, THE ..A COMPREHENSIVE MANUAL ON PIANO PLAYING FOR
    THE STUDENT AND TEACHER

            ATLANTA   1958   396P   BPAACM
            EVERHART, POWELL
    BP * CP * CU * ES * IU * LC * MI * NP * OC * TO * UI * YU

    PL1 * PL3 * PL4 * PL8 * PL12 * AT4 * PT1 * PT2 * PT3 * PT4 * PT9 *
    KS3 * AP6 * AP7 * AP8

EWEN, DAVID

    COMPOSERS OF YESTERDAY..A BIOGRAPHICAL AND CRITICAL GUIDE TO THE
    MOST IMPORTANT COMPOSERS OF THE PAST

            NEW YORK   1937   488P   BCOYAB
            WILSON, H. W., COMPANY
    IU * LC * NP

    APP * BIB * ILL * IND * INT * PHO
    NP5

EWEN, DAVID

    COMPOSERS SINCE 1900..A BIOGRAPHICAL AND CRITICAL GUIDE

            NEW YORK   1969   639P   BCSNHA
            WILSON, H. W., COMPANY
    IU * LC

    APP * BIB * INT * PHO
    NP5 * PM3

EWEN, DAVID

    GREAT COMPOSERS, 1300-1900..A BIOGRAPHICAL AND CRITICAL GUIDE

            NEW YORK   1966   429P   BGCTHN
            WILSON, H. W., COMPANY
    BR * LC

    NP5 * PM3

EWEN, DAVID

    MEN AND WOMEN WHO MAKE MUSIC

            NEW YORK   1939   274P   BMAWWM
            CROWELL, THOMAS Y., COMPANY
    BR * LC * NP

    IND * INT * PHO
    NP5

EWEN, DAVID

    MEN AND WOMEN WHO MAKE MUSIC

            NEW YORK   1945   244P   BMAWWM
            READERS PRESS, THE
    LC * NP

    INT * PHO
    NP5

EWEN, DAVID

    MEN AND WOMEN WHO MAKE MUSIC

            NEW YORK   1949   233P   BMAWWM
            MERLIN PRESS, INC.
    IU * LC

    INT * PHO
    NP5

EWEN, DAVID

    WORLD OF GREAT COMPOSERS, THE

           ENGLEWOOD CLIFFS, N. J.   1962   576P   BWOGC
           PRENTICE-HALL, INC.
    IU * LC

    APP * IND * INT
    NP5 * PM3 * PM6

EXECUTIVE COMMITTEE OF CHOPIN YEAR 1949

    CHOPIN YEAR 1949 IN POLAND, THE

           WARSAW   1949   52P   BCYNFN
           EXECUTIVE COMMITTEE OF CHOPIN YEAR 1949
    IU

    ILL * LDR * PHO
    NP3 * PM3 * GI6

EYE GATE HOUSE

    COMPOSERS OF MANY LANDS AND MANY TIMES..A PICTURE STORY IN
    COLOR--FILMSTRIP..234 FRAMES---FOR YOUNG VIEWERS--CHOPIN

           JAMAICA, N. Y.   1954   BCOMLA
           EYE GATE HOUSE, INC.
    IU

    ILL
    NP9

FAELTEN, CARL

    PEDAL EXERCISES FOR PIANOFORTE

           BOSTON   1900   12P   BPEFP
           SCHMIDT, A. P.
    LC * NP

    INT * MEX
    AP8

FAELTEN, CARL

    TEACHER'S MANUAL FOR PIANOFORTE COURSE, THE

           BOSTON   1889   57P   BTMFPC
           NEW ENGLAND CONSERVATORY OF MUSIC
    LC * NP

    APP * INT * MEX
    AT4 * AT7 * PM6

FAELTEN, CARL *
FAELTEN, REINHOLD
TRANSPOSITION READER--FUNDAMENTAL TRAINING COURSE FOR PIANOFORTE

           BOSTON   1895   58P   BTRFTC
           SCHMIDT, A. P.
    LC * NP

    APP * INT * CHR * MEX
    PL4 * AT4 * KS7

FAELTEN, REINHOLD

    CATECHISM OF THE FAELTEN SYSTEM, A

           BOSTON   1908   24P   BCOTFS
           SCHMIDT, A. P.
    LC * UI

    MEX
    AT4

FAIRLIE, GERARD

    PIANIST SHOOTS FIRST, THE ---PSYCHOLOGICAL STORY

           LONDON   1938   288P   BPSFPS
           HODDER AND STOUGHTON, LTD.
    BR * LC

    GI12 * GI15

FALKENER, ROBERT

    INSTRUCTIONS FOR PLAYING THE HARPSICHORD..WHEREIN IS FULLY
    EXPLAINED THE MYSTERY OF THOROUGH BASS...TO WHICH IS ADDED, EXACT
    RULES FOR TUNING THE HARPSICHORD--2ND. ED.
           LONDON   1774   44P   BIFPTH
           FALKENER, ROBERT
    LC

    INT * MEX
    KI8 * PL4 * PL12 * AT4 * PT6 * KS7 * KS10 * EP6

FARJEON, HARRY

    ART OF PIANO PEDALLING, THE ..TWO VOLUMES IN ONE

           LONDON   1923   35P   BAOPPT
           WILLIAMS, JOSEPH, LTD.
    ES * IU * NP * UT

    INT * MEX
    AP8

FARJEON, HARRY

    ART OF PIANO PHRASING, THE

           LONDON   1931   17P   BAOPP
           WILLIAMS, JOSEPH, LTD.
    ES * IU * SA

    INT * MEX
    AP6

FARNSWORTH, EDWARD C.

    THREE GREAT EPOCH-MAKERS IN MUSIC---CHOPIN

           PORTLAND   1912   106P   BTGEMI
           SMITH AND SALE, PRINTERS
    IU * LC * NP

    INT
    NP5

FAUST, OLIVER C.

    PIANOFORTE TUNER'S POCKET COMPANION, THE ..COMPILED FROM THE NOTES
    OF MR. O. C. FAUST

           NORWICH, CONN.   1899   25P   BPTPCC
           POTTER, C. P.
    LC

    KI8

FAY, AMY

    DEPPE FINGER EXERCISES FOR RAPIDLY DEVELOPING AN ARTISTIC TOUCH IN
    PIANOFORTE PLAYING, CAREFULLY ARRANGED, CLASSIFIED AND EXPLAINED,
    THE
           CHICAGO   1890   11P   BDFEFR
           STRAUB, S. W., AND COMPANY

    PT8 * PT10

FAY, AMY

    MUSIC STUDY IN GERMANY---1880

           NEW YORK   1966   352P   BMSIGE
           DOVER PUBLICATIONS, INC.
    AS * BP * BR * CP * CU * ES * IU * LC * MI * NP * OC * SA * TO * UA
    UC * UI * UK * UM * UO * US * UT * UU * YU
    INT
    NP1 * NP2 * NP4 * NP5 * AT1 * AT4

FERAND, ERNEST T.

    IMPROVISATION IN NINE CENTURIES OF WESTERN MUSIC

           COLOGNE   1961   163P   BIINCO
           VOLK, A., VERLAG
    IU * LC * NP

    BIB * INT * MEX
    KS5

FERGUSON, DONALD NIVISON

    PIANO INTERPRETATION

           LONDON   1950   348P   BPI
           WILLIAMS AND NORGATE
    BR * LC * NP

    IND * INT * LDR * MEX
    PM3 * PM9 * PM14 * AP4

FERGUSON, DONALD NIVISON

    PIANO MUSIC OF SIX GREAT COMPOSERS---1947

           FREEPORT, N. Y.   1970   370P   BPMOSG
           BOOKS FOR LIBRARIES PRESS
    AS * BP * BR * CP * CU * ES * IU * LC * MI * NP * OC * SA * UA * UC
    UI * UM * UO * US * UT * UU * YU
    CHR * IND * INT * LDR * MEX
    KI5 * KI6 * KI9 * PT1 * PT4 * PT6 * PT8 * PT9 * PT10 * PM3 * PM6 *
    PM7 * PM8 * PM9 * PM15

FERRA I PERELLO, BARTOLOME

    CHOPIN AND GEORGE SAND IN THE CARTUJA DE VALLDEMOSA...

           PALMA DE MALLORCA..., SPAIN   1932   39P   BCAGSI

    BR * LC

    ILL
    NP4 * GI15

FERRIS, GEORGE TITUS

    GREAT MUSICAL COMPOSERS..GERMAN, FRENCH, AND ITALIAN

           LONDON   1889   334P   BGMCGF
           SCOTT, W.
    BR * NP

    NP5 * PM3

FERRIS, GEORGE TITUS

    GREAT VIOLINISTS AND PIANISTS, THE ---1881

        NEW YORK　　　　　　　　1892　　326P　　BGVAPE
         APPLETON, D., AND COMPANY
  BP * ES * IU * LC * NP * OC * UC * UM * US * UT * UU * YU

  NP4 * NP5

FERRIS, GEORGE TITUS

    SKETCHES OF GREAT PIANISTS AND GREAT VIOLINISTS, BIOGRAPHICAL AND
    ANECDOTAL--3RD. ED.

        LONDON　　　　　　　　　1900　　265P　　BSOGPA
         REEVES, WILLIAM
  LC

  INT
  NP5

FETIS, FRANCOIS JOSEPH

    HOW TO PLAY FROM SCORE...ON THE ORGAN OR PIANOFORTE

        LONDON　　　　　　　　　1888　　40P　　BHTPFS
         REEVES, WILLIAM
  BP * BR * ES * IU * NP * TO * UC * YU

  BIB * INT * MEX
  KS9 * EP6

FIELDEN, THOMAS

    MARKS AND REMARKS..MUSICAL EXAMINATIONS AND THEIR PROBLEMS

        LONDON　　　　　　　　　1957　　90P　　BMARME
         WILLIAMS, JOSEPH, LTD.
  BR * LC * OC

  INT * MEX
  PL10 * PL12 * PL14 * PT6 * PT8 * PT9 * KS3 * KS7 * AP9 * GI9

FIELDEN, THOMAS

    NEW APPROACH TO SCALES AND ARPEGGIOS, A

        LONDON　　　　　　　　　1949　　20P　　BNATSA
         WILLIAMS, JOSEPH, LTD.
  BR * LC * MI * NP * UT

  INT * MEX
  PL4 * PT9 * PT10

FIELDEN, THOMAS

    SCIENCE OF PIANOFORTE TECHNIC, THE --2ND. REV. ED.---1927

        LONDON　　　　　　　　　1934　　193P　　BSOPTS
         MACMILLAN COMPANY, THE
  BP * BR * CP * CU * ES * IU * LC * MI * NP * SA * UA * UC * UI * UK
  UO * UT * UU

  AT4 * PT1 * PT2 * PT3 * PT5 * PT6 * PT7 * PT8 * PT9

FILLINGHAM, ARTHUR H.

    GUIDE TO THE A.R.C.M. AND OTHER EXAMINATIONS IN THE ART OF
    PIANOFORTE TEACHING--2ND. ED.---1915+

        LEEDS, ENGLAND　　　　　1929　　56P　　BGTTAR
         FILLINGHAM, ARTHUR H.
  BR

  AT1 * GI9

FILLINGHAM, ARTHUR H.

    PIANOFORTE TEACHERS' EXAMINATION FOR THE A.R.C.M. DIPLOMA..A GUIDE
    TO CANDIDATES

        LONDON　　　　　　　　　1915　　31P　　BPTEFT
         NOVELLO AND COMPANY
  BR

  GI9

FILLMORE, JOHN C.

    PIANOFORTE MUSIC..ITS HISTORY, WITH BIOGRAPHICAL SKETCHES AND
    CRITICAL ESTIMATES OF ITS GREATEST MASTERS

        CHICAGO　　　　　　　　1883　　245P　　BPMIHW
         MACCOUN, T.
  BP * BR * CP * CU * ES * IU * LC * MI * NP * OC * SA * TO * UA * UC
  UI * UK * US * UT * YU
  IND * INT
  PT1 * PT2 * PM1 * PM3 * PM7

FILLMORE, THOMAS H.

    FILLMORE'S LIST OF CAREFULLY SELECTED AND GRADED WORKS FOR THE
    PIANOFORTE, TAKEN FROM THE LEADING PUBLISHERS OF EUROPE AND
    AMERICA
        PASADENA, CAL.　　　　　1904　　79P　　BFLOCS
         FILLMORE, T. H.
  LC

  INT
  PM6 * EP1 * EP4

FINCK, EDWARD J.

    AMERICAN PRIZE METHOD FOR PIANOFORTE

        PHILADELPHIA　　　　　　1889+　　　　　BAPMFP
         PRESSER, THEODORE, COMPANY

  AT4

FINCK, HENRY T.

    AEOLIAN, THE ..ITS ARTISTIC MERITS, DISTINCTION FROM MECHANICAL
    INSTRUMENTS, DOMESTIC, SOCIAL AND EDUCATIONAL VALUE, AND ITS
    INFLUENCE ON THE FUTURE OF MUSICAL CULTURE IN AMERICA
        NEW YORK　　　　　　　　1896　　24P　　BAIAMD
         AEOLIAN COMPANY, THE
  LC

  PHO
  KI9 * KI10 * KI12 * KI13

FINCK, HENRY T.

    CHOPIN AND OTHER MUSICAL ESSAYS---1889

        NEW YORK　　　　　　　　1910　　273P　　BCAOME
         SCRIBNERS, C., SONS
  BR * IU * LC * NP

  NP6 * PM3

FINCK, HENRY T.

    MASTERS OF THE PIANO

        NEW YORK　　　　　　　　1915　　11P　　BMOTP
         MENTOR ASSOCIATES
  NP

  NP1 * NP2

FINCK, HENRY T.

    PADEREWSKI AND HIS ART

        NEW YORK　　　　　　　　1896　　48P　　BPAHA
         LOOKER-ON PUBLISHING COMPANY
  BP * LC * NP * OC * UM * YU

  ILL * MSF
  NP4 * PM3 * AP4 * GI13

FINCK, HENRY T.

    SUCCESS IN MUSIC, AND HOW IT IS WON

        NEW YORK　　　　　　　　1909　　471P　　BSIMAH
         SCRIBNER'S, C., SONS
  BP * BR * ES * LC * MI * NP * OC * UC * UM * UO * US * UT * UU

  IND
  NP3 * NP4 * NP5

FINCK, HENRY T.

    TWENTY MUSICAL EVENINGS---PIANOLA PROGRAMS WITH NOTES AND COMMENTS

        NEW YORK　　　　　　　　1910　　　　　　BTMEPP
         AEOLIAN COMPANY, THE

  KI10 * PM13

FINNEGAN, BILL

    PIANO FACTS

        　　　　　　　　　　　　1954　　22P　　BPF

  LC * US

  INT
  KI4 * GI5

FISCHER, EDWIN

    BEETHOVEN'S PIANOFORTE SONATAS, A GUIDE FOR STUDENTS AND
    AMATEURS---1956, IN GERMAN

        LONDON　　　　　　　　　1959　　118P　　BBPSAG
         FABER AND FABER
  AS * BP * CP * CU * ES * IU * MI * NP * SA * TO * UA * UM * UO * US
  UT * UU * UW
  ILL * INT * MEX * MSF
  PM3 * PM8 * PM13 * PM14 * PM15 * AP3 * AP4

FISCHER, EDWIN

    REFLECTIONS ON MUSIC

        LONDON　　　　　　　　　1951　　47P　　BROM
         WILLIAMS AND NORGATE
  BR * LC * NP

  NP4 * NP6 * PM3 * PM9 * AP3

FISCHER, JERRY CREE

    PIANO TUNING, REGULATING AND REPAIRING...SELF INSTRUCTION...FOR THE
    PROFESSIONAL OR AMATEUR

        PHILADELPHIA   1907   219P   BPTRAR
           PRESSER, THEODORE, COMPANY
    BP * BR * LC * MI * NP * UK * US * UW

    CHR * ILL * IND * INT * LDR * PHO * TAB
    KI3 * KI5 * KI6 * KI8 * PL11

FISHER, HENRY

    PIANIST'S MENTOR..A TEXT BOOK FOR STUDENTS OF ALL GRADES--2ND. ED.

        LONDON   1899   168P   BPMATB
           CURWEN, J., AND SONS, LTD.

    AT4

FISHER, HENRY

    PSYCHOLOGY FOR MUSIC TEACHERS..THE LAWS OF THOUGHT APPLIED TO
    SOUNDS AND THEIR SYMBOLS, WITH OTHER RELEVANT MATTER

        LONDON   1905   181P   BPFMTT
           CURWEN, J., AND SONS, LTD.
    BR * LC

    AT3

FISK, BEATRICE H.

    KEYBOARD FUNDAMENTALS

        BOSTON   1947   BKF
           BOSTON MUSIC COMPANY
    LC

    PL1 * PL4

FISKE, ROGER

    BEETHOVEN CONCERTOS AND OVERTURES

        LONDON   1970   64P   BBCAO
           BRITISH BROADCASTING CORPORATION
    LC

    MEX
    PM3 * PM8 * PM14

FISKE, ROGER

    SCORE READING--BK. 3..CONCERTOS

        NEW YORK   1960   103P   BSRBTC
           OXFORD UNIVERSITY PRESS
    BR * IU * NP

    GLO * INT * MEX
    KS9 * KS10

FISKE, ROGER

    SCORE READING--BK. 4..ORATORIOS

        NEW YORK   1965   112P   BSRBFO
           OXFORD UNIVERSITY PRESS
    BR * IU * NP

    GLO * INT * MEX
    KS9

FLOOD, WILLIAM HENRY GRATTAN

    JOHN FIELD OF DUBLIN, THE INVENTOR OF THE NOCTURNE---1920

        NEW YORK   1972   28P   BJFODT
           MUSICAL SCOPE PUBLISHERS
    LC * NP

    ILL * INT
    NP4 * PM14

FOLDES, ANDOR

    KEYS TO THE KEYBOARD, A BOOK FOR PIANISTS

        LONDON   1950   117P   BKTTKA
           OXFORD UNIVERSITY PRESS
    AS * BP * BR * CP * CU * ES * IU * LC * MI * NP * OC * SA * UA * UC
    UI * UK * UO * US * UT * UU * UW
    CHR * INT * MEX
    PL6 * PL7 * PL8 * PT9 * PT10 * PM6 * AP1 * AP9

FOLDES, LILI

    TWO ON A CONTINENT

        NEW YORK   1947   254P   BTOAC
           DUTTON, E. P., AND COMPANY, INC.
    IU * LC * NP

    NP6 * GI13

FOOTE, ARTHUR W.

    MODULATION AND RELATED HARMONIC QUESTIONS

        NEW YORK   1919   99P   BMARHQ
           SCHMIDT, A. P., COMPANY
    BR * IU * LC * NP

    IND * INT * MEX
    KS4 * KS8

FOOTE, ARTHUR W.

    SOME PRACTICAL THINGS IN PIANO PLAYING

        BOSTON   1909   34P   BSPTIP
           SCHMIDT, A. P.
    BP * BR * ES * LC * NP * YU

    MEX
    KI6 * PL12 * PT6 * PT7 * PT8 * PT9 * AP6 * AP8

FORD, DONALD

    SINGING CLASS PIANIST AND ON PIANOFORTE ACCOMPANYING IN GENERAL,
    THE

        LONDON   1953   12P   BSCPAO
           WILLIAMS, JOSEPH, LTD.
    BR * CU * LC * NP

    ILL * MEX
    PT2 * KS3 * KS7 * KS9 * AP8 * EP6

FORMAN, DENIS

    MOZART'S CONCERTO FORM..THE FIRST MOVEMENTS OF THE PIANO CONCERTOS

        LONDON   1971   303P   BMCFTF
           HART-DAVIS
    IU * LC

    CHR * IND * MEX * TAB
    PL5 * PM3 * PM8 * PM9 * PM14

FORSEE, AYLESA

    ARTUR RUBINSTEIN, KING OF THE KEYBOARD

        NEW YORK   1969   178P   BARKOT
           CROWELL, THOMAS Y., COMPANY
    AS * IU * LC * NP

    IND * MEX
    NP4

FORTE, ALLEN

    COMPOSITIONAL MATRIX, THE ..MONOGRAPHS IN THEORY AND COMPOSITION

        BALDWIN, N. Y.   1961   95P   BCMMIT
           MUSIC TEACHERS' NATIONAL ASSOCIATION
    IU * LC * SA

    APP * INT * MEX * MSF
    KS10 * PM3 * PM8

FOSS, HUBERT J.--EDITOR

    HERITAGE OF MUSIC, THE --SECOND SERIES OF ESSAYS---CHOPIN AND LISZT

        LONDON   1934   263P   BHOMSS
           OXFORD UNIVERSITY PRESS
    BR * IU * LC * NP

    NP6

FOWLES, ERNEST

    HARMONY IN PIANOFORTE-STUDY..FOR THE INDIVIDUAL STUDENT--2 VOLS.,
    1918-1920

        LONDON   1918   201P   BHIPSF
           CURWEN, J., AND SONS, LTD.
    BR * LC * NP

    INT * MEX
    KS4 * KS8 * AP8

FOX, LILLA M.

    INSTRUMENTS OF POPULAR MUSIC..A HISTORY OF MUSICAL
    INSTRUMENTS---1966

        NEW YORK   1968   112P   BIOPMA
           ROY PUBLISHERS
    LC

    APP * BIB * GLO * ILL * IND * INT * LDR
    KI1 * KI3 * KI5 * KI13 * GI6

FRACKENPOHL, ARTHUR

    HARMONIZATION AT THE PIANO--2ND. ED.---1962

        DUBUQUE, IOWA   1970   230P   BHATPS
           BROWN, WILLIAM C., COMPANY
    CP * CU * ES * IU * LC * SA * UI * UO * UT

    APP * CHP * IND * INT * MEX
    PL4 * KS4

FRANZ, FREDERICK

    METRONOME TECHNIQUES

            NEW HAVEN, CONN.   1947   49P   BMT
            YALE UNIVERSITY PRESS
    BP * CP * ES * IU * LC * SA * UI * YU

    BIB * IND
    PL7 * PL8 * PL12

FRAY, JACQUES *
SAPERTON, DAVID A.
    HOW TO PLAY BY THE JACQUES FRAY SPEED METHOD

            NEW YORK   1949   121P   BHTPBP
            DOUBLEDAY AND COMPANY
    CP * IU * LC * NP

    CHR * GLO * INT * LDR * MEX
    PL4 * PL7 * PL11 * AT4

FREDERIC CHOPIN INTERNATIONAL COMPETITION--FIFTH

    FREDERIC CHOPIN INTERNATIONAL COMPETITIONS IN POLAND

            WARSAW   1954   38P   BFCICI
            SECRETARIAT--5TH. F. CHOPIN INTERNATIONAL COMPETITION
    IU * LC * NP

    ILL * PHO
    GI9

FREDRICH, FRANK

    KEY TO PIANO PLEASURE

            CHICAGO   1948   62P   BKTPP
            SUMMY, CLAYTON F.
    UI

    GI2

FREDRICH, FRANK

    PLAYING BY SEEING..A STUDY IN TRAINING AND PERCEPTION FOR BETTER
    READING AT THE PIANO
            MEDINA, OHIO   1950   22P   BPBSAS
            LYNNE PUBLICATIONS
    CU * ES * IU * OC * SA * UI * UU * UW

    BIB * CHR * INT * MEX
    PL3 * PL4 * PL5 * PL10 * AT3 * AT4 * AT7 * AT8 * KS3 * KS4

FRICK, PHILIPP J.

    ART OF MUSICAL MODULATION RENDERED EASY AND FAMILIAR, THE

            LONDON   1780+   7P   BAOMMR
            NAPIER, W.
    LC * NP

    INT * MEX
    KS8

FRICK, PHILIPP J.

    TREATISE ON THOROUGH BASS, A

            LONDON   1786   109P   BTOTT
            FRICK, PHILIIP J.
    LC * NP

    MEX
    KS10

FRIEDHEIM, ARTHUR

    LIFE AND LISZT..THE RECOLLECTIONS OF A CONCERT PIANIST

            NEW YORK   1961   335P   BLALTR
            TAPLINGER PUBLISHING COMPANY
    CP * ES * IU * LC * MI * NP * OC * SA * TO * UA * UC * UI * UM * US

    APP * ILL * IND * INT * MSF * PHO
    NP3 * NP4 * NP5

FRISCH, FAY TEMPLETON

    STEPS TO MUSICIANSHIP THROUGH GROUP PIANO--TEACHER'S MANUAL

            DEKALB, ILL.   1967   72P   BSTMTG
            WURLITZER COMPANY, THE
    LC * UI

    INT * MEX

FRISKIN, JAMES *
FREUNDLICH, IRWIN
    MUSIC FOR THE PIANO..A HANDBOOK OF CONCERT AND TEACHING MATERIAL
    FROM 1580-1952---1954
            NEW YORK   1973   432P   BMFTPA
            DOVER PUBLICATIONS, INC.
    BP * CP * CU * ES * IU * LC * MI * NP * OC * SA * TO * UA * UC * UI
    UK * UM * UO * US * UT * UW * YU
    APP * BIB * IND * INT
    PM4 * PM5 * PM9 * PM13 * PM14 * PM15

FRISKIN, JAMES

    PRINCIPLES OF PIANOFORTE PRACTICE, THE

            NEW YORK   1921   36P   BPOPP
            GRAY, H. W., COMPANY
    BR * IU * LC * NP * OC * SA * TO * UK * UM * UW * YU

    INT
    PL2 * PL7 * PL10 * PT8 * PT10 * KS3

FROST, EDWARD

    THALBEGARIAN (SIC) EXERCISES..OR, THE PIANIST'S DESIDERATA

            BOSTON   1860+   13P   BTEOTP
            DITSON, OLIVER, COMPANY
    LC

    MEX
    PL7 * PT4 * PT9

FRYER, HERBERT

    HINTS FOR PIANOFORTE PRACTICE--A SUGGESTED PLAN FOR DAILY
    STUDY---1916
            LONDON   1948   19P   BHFPPA
            CHAPPELL AND COMPANY
    BR * TO

    PL7 * AT4

FULLER-MAITLAND, J. A.

    FORTY-EIGHT, THE ..BACH'S WOHLTEMPERIRTES CLAVIER, FROM 'THE
    MUSICAL PILGRIM' SERIES--2 VOLS.
            FREEPORT, N. Y.   1970   76P   BFEBWC
            BOOKS FOR LIBRARIES PRESS
    AS * BR * CU * ES * IU * NP * OC * TO * UA * UC * UI * UK * UM * US
    UT * UW * YU
    INT * MEX
    PM8 * PM14 * PM15

FULLER-MAITLAND, J. A.

    KEYBOARD SUITES OF J. S. BACH, THE

            LONDON   1925   74P   BKSOJS
            OXFORD UNIVERSITY PRESS
    AS * BR * ES * IU * LC * NP * OC * UA * UI * UK * US * UW

    MEX
    PM3 * PM8 * PM14

FULLER-MAITLAND, J. A.

    MASTERS OF GERMAN MUSIC---CLARA SCHUMANN

            LONDON   1894   288P   BMOGMC
            OSGOOD, MCILVAINE AND COMPANY
    BP * NP

    NP5

FULLER-MAITLAND, J. A.

    MUSICIAN'S PILGRIMAGE, THE ..A STUDY IN ARTISTIC DEVELOPMENT

            LONDON   1899   152P   BMPASI
            SMITH, ELDER AND COMPANY
    BR * LC * NP

    AP1 * GI13

FULLER-MAITLAND, J. A.

    ROBERT SCHUMANN--'THE GREAT MUSICIANS' SERIES

            LONDON   1884   150P   BRSTGM
            SAMPSON, LOW, MARSTON, SEARLE AND RIVINGTON
    BR * LC * NP

    INT
    PM3 * PM6 * PM9

FULLER-MAITLAND, J. A.

    SCHUMANN'S PIANOFORTE WORKS

            LONDON   1927   59P   BSPW
            OXFORD UNIVERSITY PRESS
    AS * BR * ES * IU * LC * NP * OC * SA * TO * UA * UC * UK * UM * UT
    UW * YU
    MEX
    PM3 * PM8 * PM9 * PM13 * PM14 * PM15

FULLER, ESTHER MARY

    KEYBOARD MODULATIONS FOR ALL KEYBOARD INSTRUMENTS..552 TWO-MEASURE
    MODULATIONS
            WESTBURY, N. Y.   1964   48P   BKMFAK
            PRO ART PUBLISHERS
    LC

    INT * MEX
    KS8

FULLER, JANET E.

COMPLETE KNOWLEDGE OF PIANO TECHNIQUE, A

      LONDON   1930+   BCKOPT
       ORTMAN, HART AND COMPANY

PT1 * PT2

FULLER, JANET E.

COMPLETE KNOWLEDGE OF THE ESSENTIALS OF PIANOFORTE PLAYING, A

      LONDON   1930   38P   BCKOTE
       PITMAN, HART AND COMPANY, LTD.

PL4 * AT4

FUNKE, OTTO

PIANO AND HOW TO CARE FOR IT, THE ..PIANO TUNING IN THEORY AND
PRACTICE
      FRANKFURT AM MAIN   1961   65P   BPAHTC
       VERLAG DAS MUSIKINSTRUMENT
BP * BR * IU * LC * NP * TO * UI

INT * MEX
KI4 * KI5 * KI6 * KI8

FUREY, J.

BUILDING OF THE PIANO, THE

      LONDON   1929   78P   BBOTP
       MUSICAL OPINION
ES * LC * YU

CHR * ILL * INT * LDR * PHO
KI5 * KI6

GABRIEL, GILBERT W.

GREAT PIANISTS AND COMPOSERS

      NEW YORK   1927   104P   BGPAC
       CAXTON INSTITUTE, INC., THE
AS * BP * ES * LC * NP * OC * UA * UC * UO

BIB
NP5 * KI14 * PM3 * PM6 * PM14 * AP1

GABRY, GYORGY

OLD MUSICAL INSTRUMENTS

      BUDAPEST   1969   90P   BOMI
       CORVINA PRESS
LC

INT * PHO
KI3 * KI5 * KI6 * KI9 * KI12 * KI13 * KI14 * KI15

GALLICO, PAOLO

NEW METHOD FOR SYNCHRONIZED SCALE FINGERINGS, A

      NEW YORK   1930   33P   BNMFSS
       SCHIRMER, G., INC.
NP

INT * MEX
AT4 * PT9

GALPIN, FRANCIS W.

OLD ENGLISH INSTRUMENTS OF MUSIC--4TH. ED.---1910

      LONDON   1965   254P   BOEIOM
       METHUEN AND COMPANY, LTD.
BR * IU * LC * NP

APP * ILL * IND * INT * LDR * PHO
KI1 * KI3 * KI5 * KI9 * KI13 * KI14

GALPIN, FRANCIS W.

TEXTBOOK OF EUROPEAN MUSICAL INSTRUMENTS, A ---1937

      LONDON   1956   256P   BTOEMI
       BENN, ERNEST, LTD.
BR * IU * LC * NP

APP * BIB * ILL * IND * INT * LDR * PHO * TAB
KI1 * KI3 * KI5 * KI6 * KI9 * KI13 * KI14

GANZ, RUDOLPH

RUDOLPH GANZ EVALUATES MODERN PIANO MUSIC

      EVANSTON, ILL.   1968   54P   BRGEMP
       INSTRUMENTALIST COMPANY, THE
AS * BP * ES * LC * UA

INT
PM6 * PM15

GARRATT, PERCIVAL

ART OF PIANOFORTE PLAYING, THE

      LONDON   1927   93P   BAOPP
       FOULSHAM, W., AND COMPANY, LTD.
BR * ES * LC

APP * BIB * LDR * MEX
KI3 * PL7 * PL8 * PL9 * PL12 * PT5 * PT6 * PT8 * KS3 * KS7 * AP4 *
EP6

GARROWAY, WILL

PIANISM

      NEW YORK   1939   204P   BP
       FISCHER, CARL, INC.
BP * ES * LC * NP * UA

INT * LDR * MEX * PHO
PL7 * PL8 * PL10 * PL15 * AT10 * PT1 * PT4 * PT6 * PT8 * PT9 * KS3
KS4 * KS9 * AP5 * AP7 * AP9 * EP6

GARVIN, FLORENCE HOLLISTER

BEGINNINGS OF THE ROMANTIC PIANO CONCERTO, THE

      NEW YORK   1952   68P   BBOTRP
       VANTAGE PRESS, INC.
CP * CU * IU * LC * NP * SA * UC * UI * YU

BIB * MEX
PM3 * PM7 * PM8 * PM9 * PM15

GASPARINI, FRANCESCO

PRACTICAL HARMONIST AT THE HARPSICHORD, THE ---1708

      NEW HAVEN, CONN.   1963   102P   BPHATH
       YALE UNIVERSITY PRESS
BP * BR * CU * ES * IU * LC * MI * NP * OC * TO * UA * UI * UO * US
UT * UW * YU
INT * MEX
PL4 * KS4 * KS7 * KS8 * KS10 * AP7

GAT, JOZSEF

TECHNIQUE OF PIANO PLAYING, THE, --2ND. ED.---1958

      BUDAPEST   1965   276P   BTOPPS
       CORVINA PRESS
BP * BR * CP * CU * ES * IU * LC * MI * NP * SA * TO * UA * UK * UM
UO * UT * YU
APP * CHR * ILL * IND * LDR * MEX * PHO
PL4 * PL7 * PT1 * PT2 * PT3 * PT4 * PT5 * PT6 * PT7 * PT8 * PT9 *
PT10 * PT11 * KS5 * AP8

GATES, WILLEY F.

PIPE AND STRINGS..THREE HISTORIC AND DESCRIPTIVE SKETCHES...THE
EVOLUTION OF THE PIANOFORTE...
      CINCINNATI   1895   107P   BPASTH
       CHURCH, THE JOHN, COMPANY
LC * NP

ILL * IND * INT
KI3 * KI5 * KI6 * KI12 * KI14

GAVOTY, BERNARD *
HAUERT, ROGER
ALFRED CORTOT

      GENEVA   1955   32P   BAC
       KISTER, RENE
BP * BR * CP * ES * IU * LC * NP * SA * UU * UW

PHO
NP3 * NP4 * NP8

GAVOTY, BERNARD *
HAUERT, ROGER
ARTHUR RUBINSTEIN

      GENEVA   1956   32P   BAR
       KISTER, RENE
BP * IU * LC * NP * SA * UU

DIS * PHO
NP3 * NP4 * NP8

GAVOTY, BERNARD *
HAUERT, ROGER
CLAUDIO ARRAU

      GENEVA   1962   27P   BCA
       KISTER, RENE
BR * IU * LC * MI * NP

DIS * PHO
NP4

GAVOTY, BERNARD *
HAUERT, ROGER
SAMSON FRANCOIS

      GENEVA   1956   30P   BSF
       KISTER, RENE
AS * IU * LC * NP

DIS * PHO
NP4

GAVOTY, BERNARD *
HAUERT, ROGER
  WALTER GIESEKING

          GENEVA   1955   32P   BWG
            KISTER, RENE
  BP * BR * CP * IU * LC * SA * UI * UU * UW

  DIS * PHO
  NP3 * NP4

GAVOTY, BERNARD *
HAUERT, ROGER
  WANDA LANDOWSKA

          GENEVA   1957   32P   BWL
            KISTER, RENE
  AS * CP * ES * IU * LC * NP * SA * UU

  DIS * PHO
  NP3 * NP4

GAVOTY, BERNARD *
HAUERT, ROGER
  WITOLD MALCUZYNSKI

          GENEVA   1957   31P   BWM
            KISTER, RENE
  BP * BR * CP * IU * LC * NP

  DIS * PHO
  NP4

GEARY, ELEANOR MARGARET

  MUSICAL EDUCATION, WITH PRACTICAL OBSERVATIONS ON THE ART OF
  PIANOFORTE PLAYING

          LONDON   1851   96P   BMEWPO
            D'ALMAINE AND COMPANY
  BR * NP * YU

  INT
  PL4 * PL7 * PL12 * AT8 * PT4 * PT6 * PT8 * PT11 * PT14 * PM6 * AP8
  AP9

GEBHARD, HEINRICH

  ART OF PEDALLING, THE

          NEW YORK   1963   50P   BAOP
            COLOMBO, FRANCO, INC.
  AS * BP * CP * CU * ES * IU * LC * OC * SA * TO * UA * UI * UT * YU

  PL12 * PT8 * AP6 * AP8 * EP3

GEIB, WILLIAM

  GEIB'S PIANO-FORTE PRECEPTOR, AND MUSICAL GRAMMAR...A TREATISE ON
  TUNING THE PIANO-FORTE AND DIRECTIONS FOR ITS CARE AND REGULATION

          PHILADELPHIA   1850   104P   BGPPAM
            GEIB, WILLIAM
  LC * NP

  INT * MEX
  KI8 * PL4 * PT4 * PT6 * KS4

GEIB, WILLIAM

  TREATISE ON PRACTICAL HARMONIC INTONATION, A ..ALSO, A SYNOPSIS OF
  POPULAR HARMONY...

          PHILADELPHIA   1859   34P   BTOPHI
            ASHMEAD, H. B.
  LC

  INT
  KI8 * KS4

GEIB, WILLIAM

  TUNING THE PIANOFORTE..A NEW AND EASY METHOD OF HARMONIZING THE
  PIANO-FORTE BY A CIRCLE OF PERFECTLY CONSONANT FIFTHS...

          BOSTON   1869   30P   BTTPAN
            DITSON, OLIVER, COMPANY
  LC * NP

  MEX
  KI8

GEIRINGER, KARL

  MUSICAL INSTRUMENTS, THEIR HISTORY IN WESTERN CULTURE FROM THE
  STONE AGE TO THE PRESENT---1943

          NEW YORK   1965   340P   BMITHI
            OXFORD UNIVERSITY PRESS
  BR * IU * LC * NP

  BIB * ILL * IND * INT * LDR * PHO
  KI3 * KI5 * KI9 * KI12 * KI13 * KI14

GELATT, ROLAND

  MUSIC MAKERS..SOME OUTSTANDING MUSICAL PERFORMERS OF OUR DAY

          NEW YORK   1953   286P   BMMSOM
            KNOPF, ALFRED A., INC.
  AS * BP * ES * IU * LC * MI * NP * OC * UC * UM * UO * US * UT * UU

  IND * INT * PHO
  NP5

GEMINIANI, FRANCESCO

  ART OF ACCOMPANIMENT, OR A NEW AND WELL DIGESTED METHOD TO LEARN TO
  PERFORM THE THOROUGH BASS ON THE HARPSICHORD, WITH PROPRIETY AND
  ELEGANCE, THE --2 VOLS. IN 1
          LONDON   1775   76P   BAOAOA
            JOHNSON, J.
  IU * LC * NP

  INT * MEX
  KS4 * KS10 * EP6

GEMINIANI, FRANCESCO

  GUIDA ARMONICA, A DIZIONARIO ARMONICO..BEING A SURE GUIDE TO
  HARMONY AND MODULATION--SUPPLEMENT..1745+

          LONDON   1742   34P   BGAADA
            JOHNSON, J.
  BR * IU * LC * NP

  ILL * INT * MEX
  KS4 * KS8 * KS10

GEMINIANI, FRANCESCO

  RULES FOR PLAYING IN A TRUE TASTE ON THE VIOLIN, GERMAN FLUTE,
  VIOLONCELLO AND HARPSICHORD, PARTICULARLY THE THOROUGH BASS

          LONDON   1745+   19P   BRFPIA
            GEMINIANI, FRANCESCO
  BR * IU * LC * NP

  MEX
  AT4 * KS10

GEPPERT, WILLIAM

  OFFICIAL GUIDE TO PIANO QUALITY, THE ---4TH. ED.

          NEW YORK   1916   151P   BOGTPQ
            GEPPERT, WILLIAM, INC.
  LC

  INT
  KI4 * KI9 * KI10 * KI12 * GI5

GERMER, HEINRICH

  HOW OUGHT ONE TO STUDY PIANO-TECHNIC---1881, IN GERMAN

          LEIPZIG   1902   76P   BHOOTS
            HUG, GEBRUDER, AND COMPANY
  BR

  AT4 * PT1

GERMER, HEINRICH

  MANUAL OF TONE-PRODUCTION IN PIANOFORTE PLAYING, FROM 'TECHNICS OF
  PIANOFORTE PLAYING', OP. 30, PT. 1

          LEIPZIG   1897   65P   BMOTPI
            BREITKOPF AND HAERTEL

  PT1 * PT8

GERMER, HEINRICH

  MUSICAL ORNAMENTATION..DIDACTICO-CRITICAL TREATISE ON ALL OF THE
  ANCIENT AND MODERN EMBELLISHMENTS, WITH SPECIAL REFERENCE TO
  PIANOFORTE PLAYING..APPENDIX TO OP. 28--3RD. REV. ED.
          LEIPZIG   1890+   24P   BMODCT
            HUG, GEBRUDER, AND COMPANY
  BR

  AP7

GERMER, HEINRICH

  RHYTHMICAL PROBLEMS..SPECIAL STUDIES FOR MASTERING RHYTHMS
  DIFFERING BY NUMBER OF PARTS, WHETHER IN COMBINATION OR IN
  ALTERNATION
          NEW YORK   1882+   40P   BRPSSF
            SCHIRMER, G., INC.

  PL12

GERMER, HEINRICH

  TECHNICS OF PIANOFORTE PLAYING, THE ..MUSICAL ORNAMENTATION,
  APPENDIX TO OP. 28..MANUAL OF TONE-PRODUCTION IN PIANOFORTE PLAYING
  FROM 'HOW TO PLAY THE PIANOFORTE', OP. 30, PT. 1--3 VOLS. IN 1
          NEW YORK   1886   171P   BTOPPM
            SCHUBERTH, EDWARD, AND COMPANY
  BP * ES * LC * NP * UC * UM * UT * YU

  INT * MEX
  PT8 * PT9 * PT10 * AP7

GERMER, HEINRICH

  TECHNICS OF PIANOFORTE PLAYING REARRANGED AS A METHODICAL PLAN OF
  INSTRUCTION IN FOUR COURSES...OF STUDY, OP. 28, THE --10TH. ED.,
  ENLARGED AND IMPROVED--4 VOLS. IN 1
          LEIPZIG   1896+   BTOPPR
            HUG, G.

  AT4 * PT1

GERMER, HEINRICH

THEORETICO-PRACTICAL ELEMENTARY PIANO-FORTE SCHOOL FOR STUDENTS OF
THE LOWER, MIDDLE AND UPPER GRADES, OP. 32

    NEW YORK   1887+   162P   BTPEPS
        SCHUBERTH, EDWARD, AND COMPANY
LC * NP

INT * MEX
PL4 * PL15 * PT4 * PT8 * PT10 * PM14 * AP6

GEST, ELIZABETH

KEYBOARD HARMONY FOR JUNIORS

    BOSTON   1931   59P   BKHFJ
        DITSON, OLIVER, COMPANY
ES * IU * LC * SA * UI

CHR * INT * MEX
PL4 * AT5 * KS4 * GI10

GIBBS, GEORGE A., JR.

FIRST STEPS IN HARMONIZING MELODIES

    NEW YORK   1949   24P   BFSIHM
        KING MUSIC PUBLISHING CORPORATION
IU

IND * INT * MEX
KS4

GIBBS, GEORGE A., JR.

HARMONIZING MELODIES AT SIGHT

    NEW YORK   1949   26P   BHMAS
        KING MUSIC PUBLISHING CORPORATION
LC

CHR * INT * MEX
KS4 * KS5

GIBBS, GEORGE A., JR.

MODERN CHORD CONSTRUCTION AND ANALYSIS, FOR ALL INSTRUMENTS...AN
AID TO THE ART OF IMPROVISING

    NEW YORK   1938   36P   BMCCAA
        MILLS MUSIC, INC.
LC

INT * MEX
PL5 * KS4 * KS6

GIBBS, GEORGE A., JR.

SELF INSTRUCTION IN THE PIANO

    NEW YORK   1937+   60P   BSIITP
        NATIONAL LIBRARY PRESS
LC

ILL * INT * MEX
PL11 * AT4

GIBBS, POLLY

LISTS AND SUGGESTIONS FOR PIANO TEACHING

    BATON ROUGE, LA.   1961   98P   BLASFP
        LOUISIANA STATE UNIVERSITY
ES * UI

AT1 * PM6

GIDDINGS, THADDEUS P.

GIDDING'S PUBLIC SCHOOL CLASS METHOD FOR THE PIANO

    BOSTON   1919   75P   BGPSCM
        DITSON, OLIVER, COMPANY
CU * IU * LC * NP * UK * UM

ILL * PHO
AT7 * AT9 * PT2 * KS3 * GI5 * GI8

GIDE, ANDRE

NOTES ON CHOPIN

    NEW YORK   1949   126P   BNOC
        PHILOSOPHICAL LIBRARY
AS * IU * NP

INT * MEX
PM3

GIESEKING, WALTER *
LEIMER, KARL
PIANO TECHNIQUE---COMBINED REPUBLICATION OF.."THE SHORTEST WAY TO
PIANISTIC PERFECTION", AND, "RHYTHMICS, DYNAMICS, PEDAL AND OTHER
PROBLEMS OF PIANO PLAYING"
    NEW YORK   1972   140P   BPTCRO
        DOVER PUBLICATIONS, INC.

MEX
PL12 * PL15 * PT1 * PT3 * PT4 * PT6 * PT7 * PT8 * PT9 * AP4 * AP6 *
AP8

GIESKE, GEORGE

CARE OF THE PIANO AND PLAYER PIANO IN THE HOME, THE

    BLOOMINGTON, ILL.   1916   12P   BCOTPA
        CENTRAL PRINTING COMPANY
LC

KI8 * KI10

GIFFORD, ALEXANDER M.

PIANOFORTE AND HOW TO STUDY IT, THE

    LONDON   1928   63P   BPAHTS
        HENDERSON AND SPALDING
BR

PL1 * PL2 * PL3 * PL4 * PL7 * AT6 * GI11

GILBERT, RUSSELL S.

EMBRYO MUSICIAN, THE ..A METHOD OF INTRODUCING MUSIC TO LITTLE
CHILDREN THROUGH THE MEDIUM OF THE PIANO

    ORANGE, N. J.   1923   23P   BEMAMO
        GILBERT, RUSSELL S.
BP * NP

MEX
PL4 * PL12 * PL13 * PT8 * KS7

GILBERT, RUSSELL S.

SUGGESTED PIANO STUDY FOR THE VOCAL STUDENT

    PHILADELPHIA   1921   45P   BSPSFT
        HEIDELBERG PRESS, THE
LC * NP

APP * INT * MEX
PL4 * PL12 * KS4 * KS7 * KS8

GILBERTSON, ARNOLD B.

TEACHERS MANUAL FOR POPULAR PIANO PLAYING, DESIGNED FOR ALL
TEACHERS OF PIANO PLAYING, REGARDLESS OF THEIR PREVIOUS EXPERIENCE
WITH POPULAR MUSIC
    MINNEAPOLIS   1945   228P   BTMFPP
        GILBERTSON, ARNOLD B.
LC

ILL * INT * LDR * MEX
PL4 * PL5 * PL12 * KS4 * KS6 * KS7 * KS8 * AP7 * AP8

GILLESPIE, JOHN

FIVE CENTURIES OF KEYBOARD MUSIC..AN HISTORIC SURVEY FOR
HARPSICHORD AND PIANO

    BELMONT, CAL.   1965   463P   BFCOKM
        WADSWORTH PUBLISHING COMPANY, INC.
AS * BP * BR * ES * IU * LC * MI * NP * OC * SA * UA * UI * UK * UM
UO * US * UT * UW * YU
BIB * GLO * INT * LDR * MEX * PHO
KI13 * KI5 * KI6 * KI13 * KI14 * PT11 * PM3 * PM7 * PM8 * PM10 *
PM13 * PM14 * PM15

GIRDLESTONE, CUTHBERT

MOZART AND HIS PIANO CONCERTOS---FIRST PUBLISHED IN 1948 AS
'MOZART'S PIANO CONCERTOS'

    NEW YORK   1964   509P   BMAHPC
        DOVER PUBLICATIONS, INC.
AS * BP * BR * CP * CU * ES * IU * LC * MI * NP * OC * SA * TO * UA
UC * UI * UK * UM * US * UT * UW * YU
APP * INT * MEX
PM3 * PM8 * PM9 * PM13 * PM14 * PM15 * AP3 * AP4 * AP5

GIVENS, LARRY

RE-ENACTING THE ARTIST..A STORY OF THE AMPICO REPRODUCING PIANO

    VESTAL, N. Y.   1970   136P   BRTAAS
        VESTAL PRESS
IU * LC

ILL * INT * LDR * PHO
KI10 * AP3

GIVENS, LARRY

REBUILDING THE PLAYER PIANO

    NEW YORK   1963   164P   BRTPP
        VESTAL PRESS
CP * IU * LC * NP

APP * ILL * INT * LDR * TAB
KI8 * KI10

GLASFORD, IRENE A.

RHYTHM, REASON AND RESPONSE FOR THE MUSICIAN, PIANIST AND TEACHER

    NEW YORK   1970   154P   BRRARF
        EXPOSITION PRESS
LC * NP * UI

BIB * GLO * LDR * MEX * PHO
PL3 * PL5 * PL7 * PL12 * AT4 * PT3 * PT4 * PT5

GLEN, ANNIE

    HOW TO ACCOMPANY..A GUIDE TO THE ARTISTIC ACCOMPANIMENT OF ANY
    MUSICAL COMPOSITION, ETC.

           LONDON   1893   173P   BHTAAG
             COCKS, R., AND COMPANY
    BP * BR * NP

    INT * MEX
    KS3 * EP6

GLENNON, JAMES

    AUSTRALIAN MUSIC AND MUSICIANS

           SYDNEY   1968   291P   BAMAM
             RIGBY, LTD.
    IU * LC

    IND * INT * MEX * PHO
    NP5 * GI13

GLENNON, JAMES

    MAKING FRIENDS WITH PIANO MUSIC..THE HISTORY AND ANALYTICAL NOTES
    ON OVER 100 PIANO COMPOSITIONS WITH SHORT NOTES ON THE COMPOSERS

           ADELAIDE   1967   68P   BMFWPM
             RIGBY
    LC * UI

    GLO
    PM3 * PM5 * PM9

GLENNON, JAMES

    MAKING FRIENDS WITH PIANO MUSIC--SUPPLEMENT

           NEW YORK   1971   20P   BMFWPM
             CRESCENDO PUBLISHERS

    PM7 * PM9

GLENNON, JAMES

    MAKING FRIENDS WITH THE CONCERTO..HISTORICAL AND ANALYTICAL NOTES
    ON 70 CONCERTOS...VIVALDI, BACH, AND HANDEL TO THE PRESENT DAY,
    WITH SHORT NOTES ON THE COMPOSERS
           ADELAIDE   1964   80P   BMFWTC
             RIGBY
    LC

    GLO * ILL * INT
    PM8 * PM9 * PM14

GLINSKI, MATEUSZ

    CHOPIN'S LETTERS TO DELFINA

           WINDSOR, CANADA   1961   34P   BCLTD
             ASSUMPTION UNIVERSITY OF WINDSOR PRESS
    BR * LC * NP

    NP6

GLINSKI, MATEUSZ

    CHOPIN THE UNKNOWN

           WINDSOR, CANADA   1964   84P   BCTU
             ASSUMPTION UNIVERSITY OF WINDSOR PRESS
    BR * IU * LC

    BIB * ILL * IND * INT * MEX * PHO
    NP3 * PM3

GLOVER, ELLYE HOWELL

    HOW THE PIANO CAME TO BE

           CHICAGO   1913   60P   BHTPCT
             BROWNE AND HOWELL COMPANY
    BP * ES * LC * MI * NP * UM

    ILL * PHO
    KI3 * KI5 * KI9 * KI12 * KI13 * KI14

GLOYNE, HOWARD F.--M.D.

    CARL A. PREYER, THE LIFE OF A KANSAS MUSICIAN

           LAWRENCE, KAN.   1949   99P   BCAPTL
             UNIVERSITY OF KANSAS
    IU * LC * SA * UK

    APP * BIB * IND * INT * PHO
    NP3 * PM3 * PM7

GLYN, MARGARET H.

    ABOUT ELIZABETHAN VIRGINAL MUSIC AND ITS COMPOSERS..NEW ISSUE,
    EMBODYING RECENT DISCOVERIES---1924

           LONDON   1935   158P   BAEVMA
             REEVES, WILLIAM
    AS * BP * BR * ES * IU * LC * MI * NP * OC * TO * UA * UC * UI * UM
    US * UT * UW
    APP * BIB * INT * IND * MEX * MSF
    NP5 * PM7

GLYN, MARGARET H.

    NATIONAL SCHOOL OF VIRGINAL MUSIC IN ELIZABETHAN TIMES, THE

           LONDON   1917   BNSOVM

    YU

    KI2 * PM7

GOLDTHWAITE, SCOTT

    ORNAMENTATION IN MUSIC FOR THE KEYBOARD

           CHICAGO   1954   10P   BOIMFT
             SUMMY, CLAYTON F., COMPANY
    LC

    MEX
    AP7

GOODRICH, ALFRED JOHN

    GUIDE TO MEMORIZING MUSIC, A

           CINCINNATI   1906   111P   BGTMM
             CHURCH, THE JOHN, COMPANY
    ES * IU * LC * NP * TO * US

    INT * MEX
    PL8 * PM6

GOODRICH, ALFRED JOHN

    GUIDE TO PRACTICAL MUSICIANSHIP--INTENDED TO SUPERCEDE ROTE
    LEARNING..FOR STUDENTS OF PIANO, ORGAN OR VIOLIN

           PHILADELPHIA   1900   112P   BGTPMI
             HATCH MUSIC COMPANY

    PL14 * AT4

GOODRICH, ALFRED JOHN

    THEORY OF INTERPRETATION, APPLIED TO ARTISTIC MUSICAL PERFORMANCE

           PHILADELPHIA   1889   293P   BTOIAT
             PRESSER, THEODORE, COMPANY
    BP * ES * LC * MI * NP * UA * UC * UI * UM * US * UT * YU

    APP * IND * INT * MEX
    PL12 * PM7 * PM14 * AP3 * AP4 * AP6 * AP7 * EP6

GORDON, PHILIP

    SYLLABUS FOR PIANO AUDITIONS

           NEWARK, N. J.   1943   26P   BSFPA
             GRIFFITH MUSIC FOUNDATION

    PM6 * GI9

GORDON, STEPHEN T.

    GORDON'S NEW SCHOOL FOR THE PIANO-FORTE

           NEW YORK   1883   288P   BGNSFT
             GORDON, S. T., AND SON
    LC * NP

    CHR * GLO * ILL * INT * LDR * MEX * TAB
    PL4 * PL7 * PL12 * PT8 * PT9 * PT10 * KS4 * KS8 * KS10 * PM10 *
    AP6 * AP7 * AP9

GOSS, JOHN

    INTRODUCTION TO HARMONY AND THOROUGH-BASS WITH NUMEROUS EXAMPLES
    AND EXERCISES, AN

           LONDON   1833   98P   BITHAT
             CRAMER, ADDISON AND BEALE
    BR * LC

    MEX * TAB
    PL12 * KS4 * KS8 * KS10 * AP7

GOTTSCHALD, ERNEST

    BEETHOVEN'S PIANOFORTE SONATAS EXPLAINED FOR THE LOVERS OF THE
    MUSICAL ART, BY ERNST VON ELTERLEIN, PSEUD.

           LONDON   1875   120P   BBPSEF
             REEVES, WILLIAM
    BP * BR * ES * LC * TO * UC * UK * UO * US * UT

    PM3 * PM7 * PM9 * PM14

GOTTSCHALK, LOUIS MOREAU

    NOTES OF A PIANIST--EDITED BY JEANNE BEHREND---1881

           NEW YORK   1964   420P   BNOAPE
             KNOPF, ALFRED A., INC.
    AS * BP * BR * CP * ES * IU * LC * MI * NP * OC * TO * UA * UI * UK
    UM * UO * US * UT * YU
    BIB * ILL * IND * INT
    NP6

GOULD, BRIAN M.

BUYING A SQUARE PIANO

    BIRMINGHAM   1968   8P   BBASP
        NAPLES PRESS
BR * LC

KI4 * KI8

GOW, GEORGE C.

PROS AND CONS OF THE MECHANICAL PLAYER, THE --REPRINT..M.T.N.A.
PROCEEDINGS, SERIES 5

    HARTFORD, CONN.   1910   11P   BPACOT
        MUSIC TEACHERS' NATIONAL ASSOCIATION
LC * NP

KI10

GRABILL, ETHELBERT WARREN

MECHANICS OF PIANO TECHNIC, THE

    CHICAGO   1909   92P   BMOPT
        DONNELLEY, R. R., AND SONS
BP * IU * LC * MI * NP * OC * UK * UM * UO * US * UW * YU

INT
PL7 * PT3 * PT6 * PT8 * PT9 * PT10

GRAF, HENRY C.

SIMPLIFIED KEYBOARD HARMONY

    CHICAGO   1912   24P   BSKH
        LATONA SCHOOL OF POPULAR MUSIC
LC

GLO * ILL * MEX * TAB
KS4

GRAHAM, GEORGE FARQUHAR

GENERAL OBSERVATIONS UPON MUSIC AND REMARKS ON MR. LOGIER'S SYSTEM
OF MUSICAL EDUCATION..WITH AN APPENDIX...LETTERS RELATIVE TO THE
SYSTEM
    EDINBURGH   1817   49P   BGOUMA
        PURDIE, R.
NP

APP * INT * MEX
NP6 * NP7 * PL4 * AT4

GRAHAM, JAMES L.

MUSIC MADE EASY, PIANOFORTE TUTOR ON A NEW PLAN

    NEW YORK   1894   21P   BMMEPT
        NOVELLO, EWER AND COMPANY
LC

GLO * MEX
PL4 * PL12 * AT4 * PT9

GRAHAM, L. SIBLEY

TALES OF THE OLD VIRTUOSO..THE SPANISH COURT PIANIST--MARQUIS DON
ANTOINE--BY HIS FAVORITE PUPIL, L. SIBLEY GRAHAM
    BOSTON   1929   130P   BTOTOV
        CHRISTOPHER PUBLISHING HOUSE, THE
LC * NP

INT
NP4 * GI13

GRAHAM, MARY JANE

LETTER TO A YOUNG PIANOFORTE PLAYER, A

    LONDON   1840+   68P   BLTAYP
        WARD AND COMPANY
BP

PL2 * AT2

GRANTHAM, BILLY

HELLO TO THE BLUES..FUN WITH CHORDS..FUN AND INFORMATION ON PLAYING
THE BLUES--FOR GRADES 2 AND 3
    GREENSBORO, N. C.   1967   18P   BHTTBF
        GRANTHAM, BILLY
LC

INT * MEX
KS6 * AP4

GRAUPNER, GOTTLIEB

RUDIMENTS OF THE ART OF PLAYING ON THE PIANOFORTE...A PLAIN
DIRECTION FOR TUNING
    BOSTON   1819   51P   BROTAO
        GRAUPNER, G.
BP * LC * NP * US * YU

CHR * GLO * INT * MEX * TAB
PL4 * PL12 * PT9 * AP7 * AP8

GRAY, CECIL

BACH AND DAS WOHLTEMPERIRTE KLAVIER..ANALYTICAL NOTES, WITH AN
INTRODUCTION--VOL. 1
    LONDON   1934   BRADWK
        BACH SOCIETY PUBLICATIONS
BR

PM3 * PM8 * PM9 * PM15 * AP4 * AP7

GRAY, CECIL

CONTINGENCIES AND OTHER ESSAYS---LISZT

    NEW YORK   1947   199P   BCAOEL
        OXFORD UNIVERSITY PRESS
BR * IU * LC * NP

IND * INT * MEX
NP6 * PM9 * AP9 * EP7

GRAY, CECIL

FORTY-EIGHT PRELUDES AND FUGUES OF J. S. BACH, THE

    LONDON   1938   148P   BFEPAF
        OXFORD UNIVERSITY PRESS
BR * CP * CU * ES * IU * LC * OC * SA * TO * UA * UC * UI * UK * UT
UW * YU
INT * MEX
PM3 * PM8 * PM9 * PM15 * AP3 * AP4 * AP7

GRAY, CECIL

MUSICAL CHAIRS..OR, BETWEEN TWO STOOLS, BEING THE LIFE AND MEMOIRS
OF CECIL GRAY
    LONDON   1948   324P   BMCOBT
        HOME AND VAN THAL
BR * LC * NP * TO * UA

IND * INT
NP6

GRAY, WILLIAM L.

SELECTED AND GRADED LIST OF STUDIES AND PIECES FOR TEACHERS OF
PIANOFORTE, A
    MINNEAPOLIS   1916   18P   BSAGLO
        SCHMITT, P. A.
LC

INT * MEX
AT14 * PM6

GRAYDON, NELL *
SIZEMORE, MARGARET
AMAZING MARRIAGE OF MARIE EUSTIS AND JOSEF HOFMANN, THE

    COLUMBIA, S. C.   1965   216P   BAMOME
        SOUTH CAROLINA, THE UNIVERSITY OF, PRESS
AS * BR * ES * IU * LC * SA * UA * UI * UO * UT

BIB * IND * INT * PHO
NP4

GREW, SIDNEY

ART OF THE PLAYER-PIANO, THE ..A TEXTBOOK FOR STUDENT AND TEACHER

    LONDON   1922   333P   BAOTPP
        PAUL, KEGAN, TRENCH, TRUBNER AND COMPANY, LTD.
BR * LC * NP * OC * YU

IND * INT
KI10 * PL12 * AT11 * PM14 * AP6 * AP8

GREW, SIDNEY

FIRST BOOK OF THE PLAYER-PIANIST, THE

    LONDON   1925   136P   BFBOTP
        MUSICAL OPINION
BR * NP

IND * MEX * TAB
KI10 * PL12 * KS4 * PM6 * AP6 * AP8

GREW, SIDNEY

MAKERS OF MUSIC..THE STORY OF SINGERS AND INSTRUMENTALISTS

    LONDON   1925   365P   BMOMTS
        FOULIS, G. T., AND COMPANY
BP * ES * LC * NP * YU

ILL * IND * INT
NP5

GRIFFIN, RUSSELL B.

PIANOFORTE TELEGRAPHY, THE --THE MORSE TELEGRAPH CODE--INSTRUCTOR
ARRANGED FOR THE PIANOFORTE KEYS IN MUSICAL NOTATION
    QUINCY, ILL.   1906   3P   BPTTMT
        MORSE ART COMPANY, THE
LC

AT4 * GI12 * GI15

GRIFFIN, SISTER MARY ANNAROSE

    PIANO MATERIALS..GRADED AND COMPILED AS AN AID TO INSTRUCTORS

          MILWAUKEE   1953   59P   BMMGAC
              CARDINAL STRICH COLLEGE
    LC

    INT
    AT14 * PT13 * PM6

GRIMALDI, MARIA LOUISA

    ART OF PIANOFORTE PLAYING AND TEACHING, THE

          LONDON   1890+   41P   BAOPPA
              REEVES, WILLIAM
    BP

    PL1 * AT1

GRIMM, CARL W.

    HARMONY STUDY AT THE PIANO

          CINCINNATI   1913   138P   BHSATP
              WILLIS MUSIC COMPANY
    LC * NP

    INT * LDR * MEX * PHO * TAB
    KI8 * PL4 * PL5 * KS4 * KS7 * KS8

GRINDEA, CAROLA

    FIRST TEN LESSONS, THE ..A NEW APPROACH TO PIANO TEACHING

          LONDON   1964   22P   BFTLAN
              OXFORD UNIVERSITY PRESS
    IU * LC

    INT
    PL4 * PL6 * PL7 * PL12 * PL13 * PL15 * AT4 * AT5 * KS4 * KS5

GRONOWICZ, ANTONI

    CHOPIN---YOUNGER READERS

          NEW YORK   1943   202P   BCYR
              NELSON, T., AND SONS
    LC * NP * UM

    BIB * IND * LDR
    NP4 * GI10

GRONOWICZ, ANTONI

    PADEREWSKI, PIANIST AND PATRIOT

          NEW YORK   1943   216P   BPPAP
              NELSON, T., AND SONS
    AS * BP * ES * LC * MI * NP * UA * UC * UO * UW * YU

    ILL * IND * PHO
    NP4 * GI10 * GI13

GRONOWICZ, ANTONI

    SERGEI RACHMANINOFF

          NEW YORK   1946   153P   BSR
              DUTTON, E. P., AND COMPANY, INC.
    IU * LC * NP * UM

    APP * ILL * IND
    NP4 * GI10

GRUNDY, ENID

    HAPPY PIANIST, THE

          LONDON   1927   80P   BHP
              OXFORD UNIVERSITY PRESS
    BR * CU * IU * LC * NP

    MEX
    PL1 * PL2 * PL4 * PL7 * PL11 * PT6 * PT9 * PT11 * KS3 * AP8 * GI11

GUENTHER, FELIX

    PIANO AND ITS ANCESTORS, THE

          NEW YORK   1951   56P   BPAIA
              ASSOCIATED MUSIC PUBLISHERS
    BP * ES

    KI3 * KI14

GULBRANSEN-DICKINSON COMPANY

    GULBRANSEN SERVICE MANUAL---PLAYER PIANO

          CHICAGO   1922   91P   BGSMPP
              GULBRANSEN-DICKINSON COMPANY
    LC

    KI8 * KI10

GUTMANN, EMMA WILKINS

    TALKS WITH PIANO TEACHERS

          CHICAGO   1897   88P   BTWPT
              SUMMY, CLAYTON F., COMPANY
    BR * LC

    GLO * ILL * INT * MEX
    PL8 * PL10 * PL12 * KS3 * PM6 * AP6 * AP8

HAAKE, CHARLES JOHN *
MARTIN, GAIL H. *
TEACHING MUSIC READING IN THE OXFORD PIANO COURSE

          NEW YORK   1941   43P   BTMRIT
              FISCHER, CARL, INC.
    LC

    MEX
    PL4

HABETS, ALFRED

    BORODIN AND LISZT--VOL. 2--LISZT, AS SKETCHED IN THE LETTERS OF
    BORODIN

          LONDON   1896   199P   BBALVT
              DIGBY, LONG AND COMPANY
    BR * LC * NP

    INT
    NP6

HADDEN, JAMES CUTHBERT

    CHOPIN--'MASTER MUSICIANS' SERIES

          NEW YORK   1906   248P   BCMMS
              DUTTON, E. P., AND COMPANY
    BR * LC * NP

    APP * BIB * ILL * IND * INT * PHO
    NP4 * PM3

HADDEN, JAMES CUTHBERT

    MASTER MUSICIANS..A BOOK FOR PLAYERS, SINGERS AND LISTENERS

          CHICAGO   1911   254P   BMMABF
              MCCLURG, A. C.
    BP * BR * ES * LC * NP * OC * TO * UO

    ILL * INT
    NP5

HADDEN, JAMES CUTHBERT

    MODERN MUSICIANS..A BOOK FOR PLAYERS, SINGERS AND LISTENERS

          LONDON   1913   266P   BMMABF
              FOULIS, T. N.
    BP * BR * ES * LC * NP * OC * TO * UA * UC * UK * UO * US

    INT * PHO
    NP5

HADOW, SIR WILLIAM HENRY

    SONATA FORM---1896

          NEW YORK   1934+   184P   BSFENS
              GRAY, H. W., COMPANY
    BR * LC * NP

    INT * MEX
    PM3 * PM8 * PM14

HADOW, SIR WILLIAM HENRY

    STUDIES IN MODERN MUSIC--2ND. SERIES--9TH. ED.---CHOPIN

          LONDON   1913   312P   BSIMMS
              SEELEY, SERVICE AND COMPANY, LTD.
    BR * IU * LC * NP

    ILL * IND * PHO
    NP3 * PM3 * PM9

HAFER, HOWARD W.

    STUDY IN EQUAL TEMPERAMENT, A

          BAY CITY, TEX.   1940   12P   BSIET
              TRIBUNE PRINTING COMPANY
    ES * LC * NP

    INT
    KI8

HALDANE, CHARLOTTE

    GALLEY SLAVES OF LOVE, THE ..THE STORY OF MARIE D'AGOULT AND FRANZ
    LISZT

          LONDON   1957   243P   BGSOLT
              HARVILL PRESS
    LC * NP

    BIB * ILL * IND * INT
    NP4

HALL, CONSTANCE HUNTINGTON

    HELEN HOPEKIRK, 1856-1945

            CAMBRIDGE, MASS.   1954   41P   BHHEFS
            HALL, CONSTANCE HUNTINGTON
BP * ES * LC

INT * PHO
NP6 * PM6

HALLE, SIR CHARLES

    AUTOBIOGRAPHY OF CHARLES HALLE, WITH CORRESPONDENCE AND DIARIES,
THE ---1896

            NEW YORK   1973   215P   BAOCHW
            BARNES AND NOBLE
BR * IU * LC * NP

APP * PHO
NP6 * PM6

HALLE, SIR CHARLES

    CHARLES HALLE'S PRACTICAL PIANOFORTE SCHOOL--9 VOLS.

            LONDON   1873   BCHPPS
            FORSYTH BROTHERS
LC

AT4

HALLE, SIR CHARLES

    SIR C. HALLE..A SKETCH OF HIS CAREER AS A
MUSICIAN--REPRINT..'MANCHESTER WEEKLY TIMES'

            MANCHESTER   1890   77P   BSCHAS
            HEYWOOD, J.
NP

INT
NP4

HALLE, SIR CHARLES

    ST. JAMES HALL...C. HALLE'S PIANOFORTE RECITALS..MAY 5-JUNE 29,
1865..MAY 5-JUNE 22, 1871..MAY 2-JUNE 20, 1873--3 VOLS.

            LONDON   1873   BSJHCH
NP

NP7 * PM3 * PM8 * PM14 * GI13

HALLE, SIR CHARLES

    ST. JAMES HALL...MR. HALLE'S BEETHOVEN RECITALS, MAY 23-JULY 11,
1861, WITH ANALYSIS OF THE SONATAS

            LONDON   1862   353P   BSJHMH
            CHAPPEL AND COMPANY
BR * NP

MEX
NP7 * PM3 * PM8 * PM14 * GI13

HAMBOURG, MARK

    EIGHTH OCTAVE, THE ---CONTINUES THE RECORD, BEGUN IN 'FROM PIANO TO
FORTE'

            LONDON   1951   164P   BEOCTR
            WILLIAMS AND NORGATE
BP * LC * NP * UC

ILL * IND * PHO
NP6 * PM13 * GI13

HAMBOURG, MARK

    FROM PIANO TO FORTE..A THOUSAND AND ONE NOTES---AUTOBIOGRAPHY

            LONDON   1931   310P   BFPTFA
            CASSELL AND COMPANY
BR * ES * LC * NP * TO * UA * UC * UO

ILL * IND * PHO
NP6

HAMBOURG, MARK

    HOW TO PLAY THE PIANO--NEW AND ENLARGED EDITION OF 'HOW TO BECOME A
PIANIST'---1922

            LONDON   1923   122P   BHTPTP
            PEARSON, C. A.
BR * ES * LC * OC * TO * UA * UI * UT

INT * LDR * MEX * MSF
KI8 * PL7 * PL8 * PL14 * PT1 * PT6 * PT9 * PT10 * AP9

HAMBOURG, MARK

    HOW TO PREPARE FOR PLAYING IN CONCERT

            PHILADELPHIA   1929   19P   BHTPFP
            PRESSER, THEODORE, COMPANY
LC

PHO
AT9 * PT6 * KS4 * AP9

HAMILTON, ANNA H.

    KEYBOARD HARMONY AND TRANSPOSITION..A PRACTICAL COURSE OF KEYBOARD
WORK FOR EVERY PIANO AND ORGAN STUDENT--3 VOLS. IN 1

            CHICAGO   1916   80P   BKHATA
            SUMMY, CLAYTON F.
IU * LC * NP * TO

INT * MEX
KS4 * KS7

HAMILTON, CLARENCE G.

    FUTURE OF PIANO STUDY, THE ---FROM 'M.T.N.A. PROCEEDINGS', SERIES
26

            OBERLIN, OHIO   1931   6P   BFOPSF
            MUSIC TEACHERS' NATIONAL ASSOCIATION
LC

AT3

HAMILTON, CLARENCE G.

    MUSIC THEORY FOR PIANO STUDENTS

            BOSTON   1924   BMTFPS
            DITSON, OLIVER, COMPANY
BP * ES

KS4

HAMILTON, CLARENCE G.

    ORNAMENTS IN CLASSICAL AND MODERN MUSIC

            NEW YORK   1929   76P   BOICAM
            DITSON, OLIVER, COMPANY
IU * LC * NP

MEX
AP7

HAMILTON, CLARENCE G.

    PIANO MUSIC, ITS COMPOSERS AND CHARACTERISTICS

            BOSTON   1925   235P   BPMICA
            DITSON, OLIVER, COMPANY
BP * CP * ES * IU * LC * MI * NP * OC * SA * TO * UO * US * UT * UW
YU
BIB * ILL * IND * INT * LDR * MEX * PHO
KI3 * KI5 * KI6 * KI14 * PM3 * PM5 * PM7 * PM8 * PM9 * PM14 * PM15

HAMILTON, CLARENCE G.

    PIANO TEACHING..ITS PRINCIPLES AND PROBLEMS

            BOSTON   1910   171P   BPTIPA
            DITSON, OLIVER, COMPANY
BP * BR * CP * ES * LC * MI * NP * UA * UK * UO * US * UT * YU

CHR * ILL * IND * INT * PHO
PL12 * AT3 * AT4 * PT1 * KS1 * PM6 * PM10 * AP4 * AP9

HAMILTON, CLARENCE G.

    SUPPLEMENT TO PIANO MUSIC, ITS COMPOSERS AND CHARACTERISTICS, A
..AND MUSIC APPRECIATION...GIVING A LIST OF AMPICO RECORDINGS FOR
PRACTICAL USE IN ILLUSTRATING THE TEXT
            NEW YORK   1925   24P   BSTPMI
            AMPICO CORPORATION
LC

KI10 * PM12

HAMILTON, CLARENCE G.

    TOUCH AND EXPRESSION IN PIANO PLAYING

            BOSTON   1927   72P   BTAEIP
            DITSON, OLIVER, COMPANY
AS * BP * IU * LC * NP * OC * SA * UC * US * YU

IND * INT * MEX * PHO
PL12 * PT4 * PT7 * PT8 * AP4 * AP6 * AP8

HAMILTON, CLARENCE G.

    WHAT EVERY PIANO PUPIL SHOULD KNOW

            PHILADELPHIA   1928   160P   BWEPPS
            PRESSER, THEODORE, COMPANY
IU * LC * MI * NP * SA

CHR * ILL * INT * LDR * MEX * PHO * TAB
PL2 * PL4 * PL7 * PL8 * PL9 * PT2 * AP2 * AP9

HAMILTON, JAMES ALEXANDER

    CATECHISM OF THE RUDIMENTS OF HARMONY AND THOROUGHBASS, A ---1833

            LONDON   1842   102P   BCOTRD
            COCKS, R., AND COMPANY
BR * LC

APP * INT * MEX
KS4 * KS10

HAMILTON, JAMES ALEXANDER

HAMILTON'S PRACTICAL INTRODUCTION TO THE ART OF TUNING THE
PIANOFORTE

    LONDON   1858   84P   BHPITT
         COCKS, R., AND COMPANY
BR * LC * NP

BIB * INT * MEX * TAB
KI8

HANSING, SIEGFRIED

PIANOFORTE AND ITS ACOUSTIC PROPERTIES, THE --2ND. REV. ED.---1888,
IN GERMAN

    SCHWERIN, GERMANY   1904   223P   BPAIAP
         HANSING, SIEGFRIED
LC

ILL * INT * LDR * PHO * TAB
KI5 * KI6 * KI7

HANSMANN, RICHARD

THEORETICAL AND PRACTICAL PIANO-FORTE SCHOOL FOR THE JANKO
KEYBOARD---IN GERMAN AND ENGLISH

    VIENNA   1889   29P   BTAPPS
         REBAY AND ROBITSCHEK
LC * NP

ILL * INT
KI10 * AT4 * PT4 * PT6 * PT9 * AP8 * GI12

HANSON, JOHN R.

FORM IN SELECTED TWENTIETH-CENTURY PIANO CONCERTOS

    WASHINGTON, D. C.   1968   57P   BFISTC
         HEALTH, EDUCATION, AND WELFARE, DEPARTMENT OF
LC

INT * TAB
PM8 * PM14

HARDING, BERTITA

CONCERTO, THE STORY OF CLARA SCHUMANN

    LONDON   1962   288P   BCTSOC
         HARRAP AND COMPANY, LTD.
ES * NP * OC * TO * UK

APP * BIB * ILL * IND * PHO
NP3 * PM6 * GI13

HARDING, HENRY ALFRED

ANALYSIS OF FORM AS DISPLAYED IN BEETHOVEN'S 32 PIANOFORTE
SONATAS---1890

    LONDON   1923   67P   BAOFAD

BP * BR * IU * LC * MI * NP * OC * TO * UI * UK * UM * UW

INT
PM3 * PM8 * PM15

HARDING, HENRY ALFRED

MUSICAL ORNAMENTS SIMPLY EXPLAINED...NUMEROUS EXAMPLES...WITH 100
QUESTIONS AND EXERCISES

    CHICAGO   1910+   57P   BMOSEN
         SUMMY, CLAYTON F.
BR

AP7

HARDING, HENRY ALFRED

THREE HUNDRED AND FIFTY QUESTIONS ON THE FORM AND TONALITY OF
BEETHOVEN'S PIANOFORTE SONATAS, FORMING AN APPENDIX TO 'ANALYSIS OF
FORM'
    LONDON   1899   22P   BTHAFQ
         NOVELLO AND COMPANY, LTD.
BR * NP

PM8 * PM15

HARDING, ROSAMUND

PIANOFORTE, THE ..ITS HISTORY TRACED TO THE GREAT EXHIBITION OF
1851---1933

    NEW YORK   1973   528P   BPIHTT
         DA CAPO PRESS
BR * IU * LC * NP

APP * ILL * IND * LDR * MEX * PHO * TAB
KI3 * KI4 * KI5 * KI6 * KI7 * KI8 * KI9 * KI12 * KI13 * KI14

HARGISS, GENEVIEVE

MUSIC FOR ELEMENTARY TEACHERS..A PROGRAMMED COURSE IN BASIC THEORY
AND KEYBOARD CHORDING

    NEW YORK   1968   274P   BMFETA
         APPLETON-CENTURY-CROFTS
IU * LC

ILL * INT * MEX
PL4 * PL11 * AT4 * AT7 * KS4 * KS7

HARICH-SCHNEIDER, ETA

HARPSICHORD, THE ..AN INTRODUCTION TO TECHNIQUE, STYLE AND THE
HISTORICAL SOURCES---1954

    ST. LOUIS   1960   70P   BHAITT
         CONCORDIA PUBLISHING COMPANY
AS * BP * CP * CU * ES * IU * LC * MI * NP * OC * TO * UA * UC * UI
UK * US * UT * UU * UW * YU
BIB * PHO
KI1 * KI2 * KI5 * KI9 * KI14 * PT6 * PT8 * KS2 * AP6 * AP7

HARKNESS, ROBERT

BEGINNERS PIANO COURSE IN HYMN PLAYING BY CORRESPONDENCE

    SOUTH PASADENA, CAL. 1945   BBPCIH
         HARKNESS, ROBERT
BR * LC

ILL
PL11 * AT4 * PT4 * KS4

HARKNESS, ROBERT

GOSPEL SONG ACCOMPANIMENT..THE ROBERT HARKNESS METHOD FOR PIANO AND
ORGAN..HOME STUDY CORRESPONDENCE COURSE--REV. ED.

    SOUTH PASADENA, CAL. 1938   BGSATR
         HARKNESS, ROBERT
BR

MEX
PL11 * AT4 * EP6

HARKNESS, ROBERT

GOSPEL SONG PIANO ACCOMPANIMENT..THE ROBERT HARKNESS
METHOD..INTERNATIONAL CORRESPONDENCE COURSE

    SOUTH PASADENA, CAL. 1921   BGSPAT
         HARKNESS, ROBERT
BR

MEX
PL11 * AT4 * EP6

HARKNESS, ROBERT

HARKNESS PIANO METHOD OF EVANGELISTIC HYMN PLAYING, THE ..A
HOME-STUDY COURSE

    KANSAS CITY   1962   207P   BHPMOE
         LILLENAS PUBLISHING COMPANY
LC

INT * MEX
PL5 * PL8 * PL14 * PT1 * KS3 * KS5 * KS7 * KS8 * AP4 * AP6 * AP8 *
EP6

HARKNESS, ROBERT

HOME STUDY CORRESPONDENCE COURSE IN EVANGELISTIC HYMN PLAYING, FOR
PIANO AND ORGAN--ENL. REV. ED.

    SOUTH PASADENA, CAL   1942   BHSCCI
         HARKNESS, ROBERT
BR * LC

MEX
PL11 * AT4 * EP6

HARRIS, BEATRIX O.

YOUR PIANO AND HOW TO CARE FOR IT

    NUTLEY, N. J.   1916   7P   BYPAHT
         HARRIS, BEATRIX O.
LC

INT
KI8

HARRIS, CUTHBERT

FIRST STEPS IN EAR-TRAINING--FOR THE PIANO STUDENT

    BOSTON   1928   23P   BFSIET
         SCHMIDT, A. P., COMPANY
BR * LC * NP

INT * MEX
PL10 * PL12

HARRIS, REGINALD

HOW TO CHOOSE AN INSTRUMENT..PIANO AND STRINGS

    LONDON   1953   147P   BHTCAI
         FOUNTAIN PRESS
BP * BR * ES * LC * NP * SA

BIB * LDR * PHO
KI4 * KI5 * KI8 * KI9

HARRISON, SIDNEY

BEGINNING TO PLAY THE PIANO--A TEACHER'S HANDBOOK, INCLUDING THE
FIRST TELEVISION MUSIC LESSONS

    LONDON   1950   51P   BBTPTP
         OXFORD UNIVERSITY PRESS
BR * ES * SA

CHR * INT * LDR * MEX
PL4 * AT1 * AT2 * AT4 * AT5 * PT9 * PM11

HARRISON, SIDNEY

PIANO TECHNIQUE

LONDON   1953   77P   BPT
PITMAN, I., AND SONS, LTD.
BP * BR * CP * CU * ES * IU * LC * MI * NP * UA * UT * UW * YU

MEX
PL7 * PT1 * PT4 * PT7 * PT8 * AP6 * AP8 * AP9

HARRISON, SIDNEY

TEACHER NEVER TOLD ME--TIPS FOR STUDENTS

LONDON   1961   200P   BTNTMT
ELEK BOOKS, LTD.
BR * ES * LC * SA

NP7 * PL7 * PL8 * PM7 * AP4 * AP9 * GI2 * GI3 * GI5 * GI9

HARRISON, SIDNEY

YOUNG PERSON'S GUIDE TO PLAYING THE PIANO, THE

LONDON   1966   72P   BYPGTP
FABER AND FABER
ES * IU * LC * MI * SA * UW

IND * LDR * MEX
KI4 * KI6 * PL7 * PL8 * PL10 * PT3 * PT7 * PT8 * AP6 * AP8 * EP6

HARRISON, W. WELLS

SCHUBERT'S COMPOSITIONS FOR PIANO AND STRINGS--STRAD HANDBOOK NO. 2

NEW YORK   1916+   BSCFPA
SCRIBNER'S, CHARLES, SONS

PM3 * PM8 * PM14

HARSANYI, ZSOLT

IMMORTAL FRANZ..THE LIFE AND LOVES OF A GENIUS---FRANZ LISZT

NEW YORK   1937   486P   BIFTLA
STOKES, FREDERICK A., COMPANY
BR * IU * LC * NP

NP4 * PM3

HARTLINE, ELIZABETH DILL *
LYKE, JAMES B.
KEYBOARD MUSICIANSHIP, GROUP PIANO FOR ADULTS

CHAMPAIGN, ILL.   1969   200P   BKMGPF
STIPES PUBLISHING COMPANY
SA * UI

APP * MEX
PL4 * AT4 * AT6 * AT7 * KS3 * KS4 * KS5

HARTSHORN, WILLIAM C.

CONCERTO, THE --ANALYTICAL GUIDES---FIVE FOLDOUTS--EIGHT PAGES EACH

BOSTON   1965   40P   BCAGFF
GINN AND COMPANY
LC

INT * MEX
PM8 * PM14

HARVEY, ROBERT

MAGIC KEY TO KEYBOARD SUCCESS, THE

HOLLYWOOD, CAL.   1966   72P   BMKTKS
DELLAMO PRODUCTIONS
LC

ILL * INT * LDR * MEX
PL4 * PL7 * PL9 * AT4 * AT11 * PT1 * KS3

HASLUCK, PAUL N.

PIANOS..THEIR CONSTRUCTION, TUNING AND REPAIR

LONDON   1905   160P   BPTCTA
CASSELL AND COMPANY, LTD.
BP * ES * LC * UM

ILL * IND * LDR * MEX
KI4 * KI5 * KI6 * KI8

HAVILL, LORINA

YOU CAN SIGHT READ..THE PLEASURES OF PIANO SIGHT READING THROUGH
KEYBOARD HARMONY AND TECHNIQUE--2 VOLS.

BRYN MAWR, PA.   1967   214P   BYCSRT
PRESSER, THEODORE, COMPANY
LC

MEX
KS3 * KS4 * KS7 * EP6

HAWEIS, HUGH R.

MUSIC AND MORALS---CHOPIN

LONDON   1871   576P   BMAMC
STRAHAN AND COMPANY, PUBLISHERS
BR * IU * LC * NP

APP * ILL * MSF
NP4 * GI15

HAWKINS, JOHN SIDNEY

INQUIRY INTO THE NATURE AND PRINCIPLES OF THROUGH BASS, ON A NEW
PLAN, AN

LONDON   1817   87P   BIITNA
GOSNELL, S.
BR * LC * NP

MEX
KS10

HEACOX, ARTHUR EDWARD

HARMONY FOR EAR, EYE, AND KEYBOARD--1ST. YEAR

BOSTON   1922   184P   BHFEEA
DITSON, OLIVER, COMPANY
IU * LC * NP

IND * INT * MEX
KS4

HEACOX, ARTHUR EDWARD

KEYBOARD TRAINING IN HARMONY--PTS. 1 AND 2—725 GRADED
EXERCISES---1917

EVANSTON, ILL.   1961   122P   BKTIHP
SUMMY-BIRCHARD COMPANY
LC

INT * MEX
KS4

HECK, JOHANN CASPAR

ART OF FINGERING, THE ..OR, THE EASIEST AND SUREST METHOD HOW TO
LEARN TO PLAY ON THE HARPSICHORD

LONDON   1770+   35P   BAOFOT
RANDALL, W., AND I. ABELL
ES * IU * NP * TO

MEX
AT4 * PT6

HECK, JOHANN CASPAR

ART OF PLAYING THE HARPSICHORD, ILLUSTRATED BY A VARIETY OF
EXAMPLES, THE

LONDON   1775+   59P   BAOPTH
WELCKER
LC

MEX
KI14 * AT4 * AP3

HECK, JOHANN CASPAR

ART OF PLAYING THOROUGH BASS WITH CORRECTNESS ACCORDING TO THE TRUE
PRINCIPLES OF COMPOSITION, THE ---1768+

LONDON   1793   99P   BAOPTB
PRESTON, J.
BR * IU * LC * NP

CHR * MEX * MSF
KS10

HECK, JOHANN CASPAR

COMPLETE SYSTEM OF HARMONY..OR A REGULAR AND EASY METHOD TO ATTAIN
A FUNDAMENTAL KNOWLEDGE AND PRACTICE OF THOROUGH BASS, A

LONDON   1768   45P   BCSOHO
HECK, JOHANN CASPAR
BR * IU * LC * NP

INT * MEX
KS4 * KS10 * EP6

HECK, JOHANN CASPAR

SHORT AND FUNDAMENTAL INSTRUCTIONS FOR LEARNING THOROUGH BASS

LONDON   1770+   22P   BSAFIF
STATIONER'S HALL
BR * IU * LC * NP

MEX * MSF
KS10

HEDLEY, ARTHUR

CHOPIN--'MASTER MUSICIAN' SERIES--INCLUDES CATALOGUE OF WORKS--REV.
ED.---1947

LONDON   1963   214P   BCMMSI
DENT, J. M., AND SONS, LTD.
BR * IU * LC * NP

APP * BIB * ILL * IND * LDR * MEX * MSF * PHO
NP4 * PM3 * PM6

HEERINGEN, ERNEST VON

CELEBRATED INSTRUCTION BOOK FOR THE PIANOFORTE, CONTAINING THE PRINCIPLES OF HIS NEWLY INVENTED NOTATION

  NEW YORK   1850+ 118P BCIBFT
   HUNTINGTON AND SAVAGE
BP * LC * NP

ILL * IND * INT * MEX
PL4 * PL12 * PT4

HEIDELBERGER, PAULINE

MASTER METHOD..PIANO NORMAL AND TEACHER'S MANUAL

  CINCINNATI   1947 55P BMMPNA
   WILLIS MUSIC COMPANY
IU * LC

INT
PL4 * PL7 * PL8 * PL10 * PL12 * PL14 * AT3 * AT4 * AT7 * AT8 * AT9
AT13 * PT4 * PT5 * PT6 * PT9 * PT10 * KS3 * KS4 * KS7 * EP1

HEINE, HEINRICH

HEINE IN ART AND LETTERS---CHOPIN AND LISZT--1837

  LONDON   1895 250P BHIAAL
   SCOTT, WALTER, LTD.
BR * LC * NP

INT
NP6 * GI15

HELD, ERNST

RULES AND REASONS FOR CORRECT SCALE-FINGERING

  NEW YORK   1896 16P BRARFC
   CHURCH, THE JOHN, COMPANY
LC

INT * TAB
PT6 * PT9

HELMANN, JACOB N.

CONSCIOUSLY CONTROLLED PIANO TONE, THE --REV. ED.---1950

  NEW YORK   1969 197P BCCPTR
IU * LC * NP * UT

LDR * MEX * PHO
PT1 * PT4 * PT7 * PT8

HENDERSON, ARCHIBALD

CONTEMPORARY IMMORTALS---PADEREWSKI

  NEW YORK   1930 208P BCIP
   APPLETON, D., AND COMPANY
BR * LC * NP

ILL * INT * PHO
NP4 * GI15

HENDERSON, ARCHIBALD

MUSICAL MEMORIES---CONCERNS SEVERAL PIANISTS

  LONDON   1938 143P BMMCSP
   GRANT EDUCATIONAL COMPANY, LTD.
LC

ILL * IND * PHO
NP6 * AT12

HENDERSON, WILLIAM JAMES

EVOLUTION OF THE PIANO, THE

      1905+ BEOPT
LC

KI3 * KI14

HENDERSON, WILLIAM JAMES

PRELUDES AND STUDIES..MUSICAL THEMES OF THE DAY--SECTION 3..THE EVOLUTION OF PIANO MUSIC

  NEW YORK   1891 245P BPASMT
   LONGMANS, GREEN AND COMPANY
BP * BR * ES * IU * LC * NP * OC * TO * UA * UM * UT * UW

MEX
NP5 * KI3 * KI5 * KI6 * KI9 * PT6 * PT9 * PT12 * PM3 * PM7 * PM9 * PM14

HEPLER, EFFIE A.

EXERCISES IN TIME AND RHYTHM..A CONTRIBUTION TO MODERN PIANO TEACHING AND STUDY

  PHILADELPHIA   1901 35P BEITAR
   PRESSER, THEODORE, COMPANY
LC

INT * MEX
PL12 * AP6

HERBERT, JOHN BUNYAN

HOW TO WRITE AN ACCOMPANIMENT..HELPS AND HINTS FOR STUDENTS AND YOUNG COMPOSERS

  CINCINNATI   1903 107P BHTWAA
   FILLMORE BROTHERS COMPANY, THE
LC * UA

EP6

HERVEY, ARTHUR

FRANZ LISZT AND HIS MUSIC

  LONDON   1911 176P BFLAHM
   LANE, J.
BR * IU * LC * NP

APP * BIB * ILL * INT * MEX * TAB
NP3 * PM3

HERVEY, ARTHUR

FRENCH MUSIC IN THE NINETEENTH CENTURY---CHOPIN

  LONDON   1903 270P BFMITN
   RICHARDS, GRANT
BR * IU * LC * NP

IND * INT
NP4 * PM3

HERVEY, ARTHUR

RUBINSTEIN--'MAYFAIR BIOGRAPHIES', NO. 11

  LONDON   1922 28P BRMBNE
   MURDOCH
BR * LC * NP

NP4 * PM3

HERVEY, ARTHUR

SAINT-SAENS---1921

  FREEPORT, N. Y.   1969 159P BSSNTO
   BOOKS FOR LIBRARIES PRESS
BR * IU * LC * NP

APP * BIB * INT * MSF * PHO
NP3 * PM3 * PM6 * PM9 * PM14

HERZ, HENRI

MEISSNER'S MODERN, PRACTICAL SYSTEM OF TUNING THE PIANOFORTE..WITH A DESCRIPTION OF HERZ'S DACTYLION, OR FINGER-GUIDE

     1840+ BMMPSO
BR

KI8 * PT14

HERZ, HENRI

MY TRAVELS IN AMERICA---1840+

  MADISON, WIS.   1963 102P BMTIAE
   STATE HISTORICAL SOCIETY OF WISCONSIN
LC * NP * UA * UT

NP6

HERZ, HENRI

NEW AND COMPLETE PIANOFORTE SCHOOL

  NEW YORK   1844 133P BNACPS
   NUNNS, J. F.
BP * LC

INT * MEX
PL4 * PL9 * PL13 * PL14 * PL15 * PT6 * PT9 * PT10 * KS5 * AP8

HERZOG, SIGMUND *
DOENHOFF, ALBERT VON
PIANO TEACHER'S MANUAL, THE

  NEW YORK   1928 BPTM
   SCHIRMER, G., INC.
CP * YU

AT1 * AT2

HEUSCHNEIDER, KARIN

PIANO SONATA OF THE EIGHTEENTH CENTURY IN GERMANY, THE --CONTRIBUTIONS TO THE DEVELOPMENT OF THE PIANO SONATA--VOL. 2

  CAPE TOWN   1970 193P BPSOTE
   BALKEMA
IU * LC

BIB * IND * INT * MEX
PM3 * PM4 * PM7 * PM8 * PM14

HEUSCHNEIDER, KARIN

    PIANO SONATA OF THE EIGHTEENTH CENTURY IN ITALY, THE
    --CONTRIBUTIONS TO THE DEVELOPMENT OF THE PIANO SONATA--VOL. 1

            CAPE TOWN   1967   78P   BPSOTE
              BALKEMA
    AS * IU * LC * SA * UA * UT

    APP * BIB * IND * INT * MEX * TAB
    PM3 * PM7 * PM8 * PM15 * AP3 * AP4

HICKIN, WELTON

    PIANOFORTE ACCOMPANIMENT--'NOVELLO'S MUSIC PRIMERS', NO. 99

            LONDON   1923   77P   BPANMP
              NOVELLO AND COMPANY, LTD.
    BP * BR

    EP6

HIGGS, JAMES

    MODULATION--'NOVELLO'S MUSIC PRIMERS', NO. 31

            NEW YORK   1890   64P   BMNMPN
              NOVELLO, EWER AND COMPANY
    BR * IU * LC * NP

    INT * MEX
    KS8

HILES, JOHN

    CATECHISM FOR THE PIANOFORTE STUDENT, A ..CONTAINING A FULL
    EXPLANATION OF THE RUDIMENTS OF MUSIC
            LONDON   1871   BCFTPS
              BREWER, S., AND COMPANY
    BR

    MEX
    PL4 * AT4

HILES, JOHN

    CATECHISM OF HARMONY, THOROUGH-BASS, AND MODULATION, A ..WITH
    NUMEROUS EXAMPLES AND EXERCISES SELECTED FROM THE COMPOSITIONS OF
    ALBRECHTSBERGER, J. S. BACH, DR. CROTCH, ETC.
            LONDON   1877   170P   BCOHTB
              BREWER, S., AND COMPANY
    BR * NP

    MEX
    KS8 * KS10

HILES, JOHN

    KEY TO THE EXERCISES IN THE CATECHISM OF HARMONY, THOROUGH-BASS AND
    MODULATION
            LONDON   1882   133P   BKTTEI
              BREWER, S., AND COMPANY
    BR

    MEX
    AT4 * KS4 * KS8 * KS10

HILL, FRANK W.

    HARMONY AT THE KEYBOARD

            DUBUQUE, IOWA   1943   41P   BHATK
              BROWN, WILLIAM C., COMPANY
    LC

    CHR * INT
    KS4

HILL, GEORGE R.

    PRELIMINARY CHECKLIST OF RESEARCH ON THE CLASSIC SYMPHONY AND
    CONCERTO TO THE TIME OF BEETHOVEN, A --EXCLUDING HAYDN AND MOZART

            HACKENSACK, N. J.   1970   58P   BPCORO
              BOONIN, J.
    LC

    PM7 * PM14 * PM15 * GI14

HILL, JIM

    ART OF IMPROVISING, THE ..HOW TO PLAY POPULAR SONGS IN A MODERN
    SWING STYLE--2 VOLS.
            CHICAGO   1937   128P   BAOIHT
              COLE, M. M.
    LC

    MEX
    KS6

HILL, JIM

    ART OF TRANSPOSING FOR THE PIANO AT SIGHT, THE

            CHICAGO   1936   64P   BAOTFT
              COLE, M. M.
    ES * LC

    KS7

HILL, JIM

    CREATIVE IMPROVISING FOR THE RIGHT HAND..CREATIVE STUDIES IN
    IMPROVISING RIGHT HAND HARMONY...FOR THE PIANO OR ORGAN STUDENT
            WINONA, MINN.   1968   36P   BCIFTR
              POINTER PUBLICATIONS
    LC

    INT * MEX
    KS5 * KS6

HILL, JIM

    CREATIVE WORLD OF SCALES AND CHORDS, THE ..CREATIVE STUDIES IN
    KEYBOARD HARMONY
            WINONA, MINN.   1968   32P   BCWOSA
              POINTER PUBLICATIONS
    LC

    INT * MEX * PHO * TAB
    PL13 * KS4 * KS6

HILL, PAUL

    PIANO-MASTER CHORD CHART--CONSTRUCTION, ACCOMPANIMENT, AND SWING
    BASS
            NEW YORK   1953   23P   BPMCCC
              ROBBINS MUSIC CORPORATION
    LC * NP

    CHR * ILL * INT * MEX
    KS4 * KS6

HILL, RALPH--EDITOR

    CONCERTO, THE

            BALTIMORE   1952   448P   BC
              PENGUIN BOOKS
    AS * IU * LC * NP

    MEX
    PM8 * PM9

HILL, RALPH

    LISZT

            NEW YORK   1949   144P   BL
              WYN, A. A., INC.
    BR * IU * LC * NP

    BIB * ILL * TAB
    NP3 * PM3

HILL, SUMNER *
BROWN, O. B.
    TUNER'S MANUAL, THE

            BOSTON   1859   88P   BTM
              RUSSELL AND TOLMAN
    UM

    KI8

HINDLEY, GEOFFREY

    MUSICAL INSTRUMENTS

            LONDON   1971   159P   BMI
              HAMLYN
    IU * LC

    BIB * GLO * ILL * IND * INT * PHO
    KI3 * KI5 * KI6 * KI9 * KI12 * KI13 * KI14

HINSON, MAURICE

    GUIDE TO THE PIANIST'S REPERTOIRE

            BLOOMINGTON, IND.   1973   831P   BGTTPR
              INDIANA UNIVERSITY PRESS
    IU * LC * SA

    APP * BIB * IND * INT
    PM15

HINSON, MAURICE

    KEYBOARD BIBLIOGRAPHY--'NEW RESOURCES' SERIES

            CINCINNATI   1968   17P   BKBNRS
              MUSIC TEACHERS' NATIONAL ASSOCIATION
    SA

    GI1

HINSON, MAURICE

    PIANO TEACHER'S SOURCE BOOK--BIBLIOGRAPHY OF BOOKS ABOUT PIANOS AND
    PIANO MUSIC
            NEW YORK   1974   96P   BPTSBB
              BELWIN-MILLS PUBLISHING CORPORATION

    KI15 * PM5

HIPKINS, ALFRED JAMES

    DESCRIPTION AND HISTORY OF THE PIANOFORTE AND OLDER KEYBOARD
    STRINGED INSTRUMENTS, A

        LONDON   1896   130P   BDAHOT
           NOVELLO AND COMPANY, LTD.
  BR * CP * CU * ES * LC * MI * NP * TO * UA * UC * UI * UM * US * YU

  GLO * IND * ILL
  KI1 * KI2 * KI3 * KI5 * KI6 * KI14

HIPKINS, ALFRED JAMES

    GUIDE TO THE LOAN COLLECTION--OF THE INTERNATIONAL INVENTIONS
    EXHIBITION, LONDON--AND LIST OF MUSICAL INSTRUMENTS

        LONDON   1885   BGTTLC
           CLOWES, WILLIAM

  KI15

HIPKINS, ALFRED JAMES

    HISTORY OF THE PIANOFORTE, THE --REPRINT

        LONDON   1883   14P   BHOTPR
           JOURNAL OF THE SOCIETY OF ARTS
  BR * ES

  KI3

HIPKINS, ALFRED JAMES

    HOW CHOPIN PLAYED...FROM CONTEMPORARY IMPRESSIONS COLLECTED FROM
    THE DIARIES AND NOTE-BOOKS OF THE LATE A. J. HIPKINS

        LONDON   1932   39P   BHCPFC
           DENT, J. M.
  BP * BR * ES * LC * MI * NP * UC * UI * UW * YU

  APP * INT * PHO
  NP4 * PT8 * AP3 * GI13

HIPKINS, ALFRED JAMES

    MUSICAL INSTRUMENTS, HISTORIC, RARE AND UNIQUE---1888

        LONDON   1921   123P   BMIHRA
           BLACK, A. AND C., LTD.
  BR * IU * LC * NP

  ILL * IND * INT * MEX
  KI3 * KI5 * KI6 * KI9 * KI13 * KI14 * KI15

HIRT, FRANZ JOSEF

    STRINGED KEYBOARD INSTRUMENTS 1440-1880---1955, IN GERMAN

        BOSTON   1968   465P   BSKIFF
           BOSTON BOOK AND ART SHOP
  BP * ES * IU

  PHO
  KI1 * KI2 * KI3 * KI5 * KI6 * KI13 * KI14

HOBBS, HENRY

    PIANO IN INDIA, THE ..HOW TO KEEP IT IN ORDER, PRACTICAL
    INFORMATION ON REPAIRING, REGULATING, TUNING, PACKING, AND
    TREATMENT OF PIANOFORTES IN TROPICAL CLIMATES---1899
        CALCUTTA   1914   201P   BPIIHT
           THACKER, SPINK AND COMPANY
  BR * NP

  INT * LDR * MEX * PHO
  KI4 * KI5 * KI6 * KI8 * KI10 * KI12

HODGES, SISTER MABELLE L.

    CATALOGUE OF REPRESENTATIVE TEACHING MATERIALS FOR PIANO SINCE
    1900, A

        CHICAGO   1970   108P   BCORTM
           DE PAUL UNIVERSITY PRESS
  IU * LC

  INT
  AT14 * PM6

HOFFMAN, CARL

    HABIT IN PIANOFORTE PLAYING--ANALYTICAL STUDY OF CONTROL OF
    MOVEMENT AND HABIT FORMING

        PHILADELPHIA   1894+   29P   BHIPPA
           PRESSER, THEODORE, COMPANY

  PL3 * PT3 * PT4

HOFFMAN, RICHARD

    SOME MUSICAL RECOLLECTIONS OF FIFTY YEARS---INCLUDES LEOPOLD DE
    MEYER, LISZT, THALBERG, GOTTSCHALK, HALLE, AND VON BUELOW

        NEW YORK   1910   168P   BSMROF
           SCRIBNER'S, CHARLES, SONS
  IU * LC * NP

  MEX * MSF * PHO
  NP6

HOFFZIMMER, ERNST

    MUSICAL MEMORY, THE --INDIANA UNIVERSITY STUDIES, NO. 92

        BLOOMINGTON, IND.   1931   18P   BMMIUS
           INDIANA UNIVERSITY BOOKSTORE
  BR * IU * LC * OC * UA * UC * UO

  PL8

HOFHEIMER, GRACE

    TEACHING TECHNIQUES FOR THE PIANO

        NEW YORK   1954   78P   BTTFTP
           BELWIN, INC.
  CP * CU * ES * NP * UM * UT * UU * UW

  MEX
  PL7 * PL8 * PL12 * AT1 * PT4 * PT8 * PT9 * AP4 * AP8

HOFMANN, JOSEF

    PIANO PLAYING..A LITTLE BOOK OF SIMPLE SUGGESTIONS--REPRINTED FROM
    'THE LADIES' HOME JOURNAL'

        NEW YORK   1908   56P   BPPALB
           MCCLURE COMPANY, THE
  BR * LC * NP

  INT * PHO
  KI15 * PT4 * PT8 * AP4 * AP8

HOFMANN, JOSEF

    PIANO PLAYING, WITH PIANO QUESTIONS ANSWERED---PUBLISHED EARLIER AS
    TWO BOOKS IN 1908 AND 1909

        PHILADELPHIA   1920   272P   BPPWPQ
           PRESSER, THEODORE, COMPANY
  BP * BR * CP * CU * ES * IU * LC * MI * NP * OC * SA * UA * UI * UK
  UO * UT * UW * YU
  CHR * PHO
  NP3 * PL1 * PL3 * PL5 * PL7 * PT1 * PT8 * AP1 * AP4 * AP6

HOFMANN, JOSEF

    PIANO QUESTIONS ANSWERED..A LITTLE BOOK OF DIRECT ANSWERS TO TWO
    HUNDRED AND FIFTY QUESTIONS ASKED BY PIANO STUDENTS

        NEW YORK   1909   183P   BPQAAL
           DOUBLEDAY, PAGE AND COMPANY
  BR * LC * NP

  NP6

HOLCMAN, JAN

    LEGACY OF CHOPIN, THE

        NEW YORK   1954   113P   BLOC
           PHILOSOPHICAL LIBRARY
  AS * BP * ES * IU * LC * NP * UA * UI

  BIB * ILL * IND * INT * MSF
  NP3 * PL8 * PL9 * PL12 * PL15 * PM3 * PM10 * AP4 * AP6 * AP8

HOLDER, WILLIAM

    TREATISE ON THE NATURAL GROUNDS AND PRINCIPLES OF HARMONY, A ..TO
    WHICH IS ADDED,...RULES FOR PLAYING A THORROW-BASS...ALSO
    DIRECTIONS FOR TUNING AN HARPSICHORD OR SPINNET, BY G. KELLER
        LONDON   1731   206P   BTOTNG
           WILCOX, J.
  BR * IU * LC * NP

  APP * INT * MEX
  KI8 * PL8 * KS4 * KS7 * KS10

HOLLIDAY, MARGARET M.

    KEYBOARD MUSICIANSHIP--BKS. 1 AND 2

        BRIGHTON, ENGLAND   1961   46P   BKMBOA
           FREEMAN, H., AND COMPANY
  LC

  INT * MEX
  KS4 * KS7 * KS8

HOLMES, EDWARD

    ANALYTICAL AND THEMATIC INDEX OF MOZART'S PIANO WORKS

        LONDON   1852   84P   BAATIO
           NOVELLO, J. A.
  BR * NP

  INT * MEX
  PM3 * PM6 * PM8 * PM9 * PM14

HOLMES, GEORGE AUGUSTUS *
KARN, FREDERICK J.
    ANALYSIS OF PIANOFORTE COMPOSITIONS FROM THE CLASSICAL AND ROMANTIC
    SCHOOLS--4 VOLS.

        LONDON   1905   222P   BAOPCF
           WEEKES, A., AND COMPANY, LTD.
  BR * UI

  PM8 * PM9 * PM15

HOLT, HILDA

HARMONY AT YOUR KEYBOARD

NEW YORK   1950   108P   BHAYK
FISCHER, CARL, INC.
IU * LC

CHR * INT * MEX
KS4

HOLTZ, GUY

PIANO PROJECTS...A NEW APPROACH TO THE STUDY OF MODERN POPULAR
PIANO

CHICAGO   1942   12P   BPPANA
BERNING PUBLISHING COMPANY
LC

INT * MEX
KS6 * KS7

HOME, ETHEL

FIRST STEPS IN HARMONIZING MELODIES

LONDON   1931   33P   BFSIHM
OXFORD UNIVERSITY PRESS
BP

MEX
KS4

HOME, ETHEL

IMPROVISING..A SIMPLE METHOD OF TEACHING THE SUBJECT TO CHILDREN OF
AVERAGE ABILITY

LONDON   1925   23P   BIASMO
PAUL, KEGAN, TRENCH, TRUBNER AND COMPANY
BR * LC * NP

INT * MEX
PL13 * KS5 * EP6

HOOK, JAMES

GUIDA DI MUSICA..BEING A COMPLETE BOOK OF INSTRUCTIONS FOR
BEGINNERS ON THE HARPSICHORD OR PIANO FORTE

LONDON   1788+   25P   BGDMBA
PRESTON, J.
LC * NP * UC * UW * YU

INT * MEX
PL4 * PL12 * PM6 * AP7

HOOK, JAMES

GUIDA DI MUSICA..SECOND PART, CONSISTING OF SEVERAL HUNDRED
EXAMPLES...FROM TWO TO EIGHT NOTES...TO WHICH IS ADDED, A SHORT AND
CONCISE METHOD OF LEARNING, THORO' BASS
LONDON   1794   118P   BGDMSP
PRESTON AND SON
NP

IND * MEX
PT10 * PT11

HOOVER, CYNTHIA A.

HARPSICHORDS AND CLAVICHORDS

WASHINGTON, D. C.   1969   43P   BHAC
SMITHSONIAN INSTITUTION PRESS
IU * LC

BIB * ILL * PHO
KI3 * KI5 * KI14

HOOVER, CYNTHIA A.

MUSIC MACHINES--AMERICAN STYLE..A CATALOG OF THE EXHIBITION

WASHINGTON, D. C.   1971   139P   BMMASA
NATIONAL MUSEUM OF HISTORY AND TECHNOLOGY
IU * LC

BIB * ILL * INT * LDR * MEX * PHO * TAB
KI10 * KI13

HOPE, ERIC

AIDS TO TECHNIQUE

LONDON   1962   24P   BATT
ASHDOWN, EDWIN, LTD.
BR * SA

INT
PL7 * PT5 * PT10

HOPE, ERIC

HANDBOOK OF PIANO PLAYING, A

LONDON   1955   72P   BHOPP
DOBSON BOOKS, LTD.
BR * CP * CU * IU * LC * UT

MEX
PT1 * PT4 * PT8 * AP4 * AP8

HOPKINS, ANTHONY

TALKING ABOUT CONCERTOS..AN ANALYTICAL STUDY OF A NUMBER OF
WELL-KNOWN CONCERTOS, FROM MOZART TO THE PRESENT DAY

LONDON   1964   148P   BTACAA
HEINEMANN EDUCATIONAL BOOKS, LTD.
BR * ES * IU * LC * MI * NP * OC * SA * TO * UA

CHR * IND * MEX
PM3 * PM8 * PM14 * PM15

HOPKINS, ANTHONY

TALKING ABOUT SONATAS..A BOOK OF ANALYTICAL STUDIES, BASED ON A
PERSONAL VIEW

LONDON   1971   184P   BTASAB
HEINEMANN EDUCATIONAL BOOKS, LTD.
IU * LC * NP

CHR * IND * MEX
PM9 * AP4

HOPKINS, GEORGE P.

PIANO PLAYING FOR FUN--4 VOLS.

EUGENE, ORE.   1941   169P   BPPFFF
MUSIQUEST PUBLISHING COMPANY
LC

ILL * INT * LDR * TAB
AT4

HOPKINSON, CECIL

BIBLIOGRAPHICAL THEMATIC CATALOGUE OF THE WORKS OF JOHN FIELD,
1782-1837, A

LONDON   1961   175P   BBTCOT
HOPKINSON, CECIL
BR * IU * LC * NP

APP * BIB * ILL * IND * INT * MEX * MSF
NP4 * PM3 * PM5 * PM6

HORNIMAN MUSEUM AND LIBRARY, LONDON

HANDBOOK TO THE MUSEUM'S COLLECTION, BY JEAN L. JENKINS--2ND.
ED.---1958

LONDON   1970   104P   BHTTMC
INNER LONDON EDUCATIONAL AUTHORITY
LC

BIB * ILL * INT * PHO
KI3 * KI5 * KI6 * KI9 * KI13 * KI14 * KI15

HORNIMAN MUSEUM AND LIBRARY, LONDON

MUSICAL INSTRUMENTS

LONDON   1958   109P   BMI
LONDON COUNTY COUNCIL
BR * IU * LC * NP

ILL * INT * PHO
KI3 * KI5 * KI6 * KI9 * KI13 * KI14 * KI15

HORROCKS, CYRIL R. H.

STUDENT'S GUIDE TO THE ART OF TEACHING THE PIANOFORTE, THE --2ND.
REV. ED.---1915

LONDON   1930+   245P   BSGTTA
REEVES, WILLIAM
BP * IU * NP

APP * CHR * INT * MEX * TAB
PL4 * PL7 * PL8 * PL10 * PL12 * AT3 * AT4 * AT5 * PT1 * PT4 * PT8 *
PT9 * PT10 * PT11 * KS3 * PM4 * PM5 * PM6 * PM15 * AP4 * AP6 * AP8

HOUGHTON, WINIFRED E.

TEXTBOOK OF PRACTICAL HARMONY AT THE KEYBOARD

LONDON   1938   BTOPHA
HARRIS, FREDERICK, MUSIC COMPANY

KS4

HOWARD, GEORGE HENRY

OUTLINE OF TECHNIQUE..A GUIDE IN THE THEORY AND PRACTICE OF
MECHANISM IN PIANOFORTE PLAYING---REPRODUCED FROM HAND WRITTEN COPY

BATTLE CREEK, MICH.   1878   100P   BOOTAG
BATTLE CREEK REVIEW AND HERALD
BP * ES * LC * OC

INT
PT1

HOWE, ALFRED H.

SCIENTIFIC PIANO TUNING AND SERVICING--REV. ED.---1941

NEW YORK   1947   267P   BSPTAS
HOWE, A. J.
BP * BR * CP * ES * IU * LC * MI * NP * OC * UI * US * UT

BIB * CHR * GLO * ILL * IND * INT * LDR
KI4 * KI5 * KI6 * KI7 * KI8

HOWE, JAMES H.

PIANO-FORTE INSTRUCTOR, A ..OR, PREPARATORY SYSTEM OF PIANOFORTE
TECHNIQUE

       PHILADELPHIA   1887   69P   BPIOPS
          PRESSER, THEODORE, COMPANY
LC

AT4 * PT1

HOWELL, DOROTHY

KEYBOARD WORK FOR HARMONY STUDENTS

       LONDON   1963   14P   BKWFHS
          WEINBERGER
LC

INT * MEX
KS4 * KS8 * AP6

HOWELL, W. DEAN

PROFESSIONAL PIANO TUNING

       DEEP RIVER, CONN.   1966   130P   BPPT
          NEW ERA PRINTING COMPANY
NP * UI

APP * INT * LDR * MEX * PHO * TAB

HUBBARD, ELBERT

LITTLE JOURNEYS TO THE HOMES OF GREAT MUSICIANS--VOL. 8, NO.
3---CHOPIN

       EAST AURORA, N. Y.   1901   30P   BLJTTH
          ROYCROFTERS, THE
BR * IU * LC * NP

LDR
NP4 * PM3 * GI10

HUBBARD, ELBERT

LITTLE JOURNEYS TO THE HOMES OF GREAT MUSICIANS--VOL. 9, NO.
1---LISZT

       EAST AURORA, N. Y.   1901   32P   BLJTTH
          ROYCROFTERS, THE
BR * IU * LC * NP

NP4 * PM3 * GI10

HUBBARD, ELBERT

STORY OF THE STEINWAYS, THE --REPRINT FROM 'FRA' MAGAZINE

       EAST AURORA, N. Y.   1911   32P   BSOTSR
          ROYCROFTERS, THE
BP * LC * NP * UT

KI3 * KI12

HUBBARD, FRANK

HARPSICHORD REGULATING AND REPAIRING

       BOSTON   1963   48P   BHRAR
          TUNER'S SUPPLY, INC.
BP * CP * LC * OC * TO * UA * UI * UK * UM * UO * UT

GLO * IND * LDR
KI1 * KI3 * KI5 * KI6 * KI8 * KI14

HUBBARD, FRANK

THREE CENTURIES OF HARPSICHORD MAKING

       CAMBRIDGE, MASS.   1965   369P   BTCOHM
          HARVARD UNIVERSITY PRESS
AS * BP * CP * ES * IU * LC * MI * NP * OC * TO * UA * UI * UK * UM
UO * US * UT * UU * UW * YU
APP * BIB * GLO * ILL * IND * LDR
KI1 * KI3 * KI5 * KI6 * KI8 * KI9 * KI14

HUEFFER, FRANCIS

HALF A CENTURY OF MUSIC IN ENGLAND, 1837-1887..LISZT IN ENGLAND

       LONDON   1889   240P   BHACOM
          CHAPMAN AND HALL, LTD.
BR * LC * NP

INT
NP6 * PM3

HUEFFER, FRANCIS

MUSICAL STUDIES..A SERIES OF CONTRIBUTIONS BY FRANCIS HUEFFER,
REPUBLISHED FROM NEWSPAPERS AND MAGAZINES---CHOPIN

       EDINBURGH   1880   258P   BMSASO
          BLACK, A. AND C.
BR * LC * NP

INT
NP4 * PM3

HUENTEN, FRANZ

ABRIDGED EDITION OF F. HUENTEN'S CELEBRATED INSTRUCTIONS FOR THE
PIANO-FORTE---IN ENGLISH AND FRENCH

       NEW YORK   1830+   67P   BAEOFH
          FIRTH AND HALL
LC

INT * MEX
PL4 * PL7 * PL12 * AT4 * PT4 * PT6 * AP6 * AP7

HUENTEN, FRANZ

FRANZ HUENTEN'S CELEBRATED INSTRUCTIONS FOR THE PIANOFORTE--2ND.
ED.---FRENCH AND ENGLISH TEXT

       NEW YORK   1833+   105P   BFHCIF
          HALL, W., AND SON
BP * ES * LC * NP * TO * UM * UT * YU

GLO * ILL * MEX * TAB
PL4 * PL12 * PL15 * AT4 * AP7

HULL, ANNE

MAESTRO SPINETTI'S MUSIC SHOP--HARPSICHORD, CLAVICHORD,
PIANO--'YOUNG READERS' SERIES

       NEW YORK   1971   40P   BMSMSH
          DOUBLEDAY AND COMPANY
LC

ILL
KI5 * KI6 * KI9 * KI14 * GI10

HULL, ARTHUR EAGLEFIELD

THREE HUNDRED QUESTIONS ON PIANOFORTE TEACHING IN 30 GRADUATED
PAPERS..WITH APPENDIX OF 250 FURTHER REVISION QUESTIONS

       BOSTON   1917   40P   BTHQOP
          BOSTON MUSIC COMPANY
BR * NP

INT
PL5 * AT4 * AT11 * PT6 * PT8 * PT9 * PT10 * PT11 * KS3 * KS7 * PM8
PM10 * PM14 * AP6 * EP6

HULLAH, ANNA

THEODORE LESCHETIZKY

       NEW YORK   1906   85P   BTL
          LANE, J.
BP * BR * CP * ES * LC * NP * OC * UA * UK * UO * US

ILL * PHO
NP3

HULLAH, M. E.

FEW WORDS ABOUT MUSIC, CONTAINING HINTS TO AMATEUR PIANISTS, A

       LONDON   1851   BFWAMC

BR * YU

PL1 * GI11

HUME, RUTH *
HUME, PAUL

LION OF POLAND, THE ..THE STORY OF PADEREWSKI--JUNIOR BIOGRAPHIES

       NEW YORK   1962   188P   BLOPTS
          HAWTHORN BOOKS
LC * SA * UT

IND * INT * LDR
NP4 * GI10

HUMISTON, WILLIAM H.

ANTON RUBINSTEIN--'LITTLE BIOGRAPHIES'

       NEW YORK   1921   28P   BARLB
          BREITKOPF PUBLISHERS, INC.
LC * NP

NP4 * PM3

HUMISTON, WILLIAM H.

CHOPIN--'LITTLE BIOGRAPHIES'

       NEW YORK   1921   29P   BCLB
          BREITKOPF PUBLISHERS, INC.
LC * NP

GLO * INT * MSF
NP4 * PM3

HUMISTON, WILLIAM H.

FRIEDMAN--'LITTLE BIOGRAPHIES'

       NEW YORK   1921   24P   BFLB
          BREITKOPF PUBLISHERS, INC.
LC * NP

GLO * INT * MSF
NP4

HUMISTON, WILLIAM H.

    LISZT--'LITTLE BIOGRAPHIES'

                NEW YORK   1921   30P   BLLB
                   BREITKOPF PUBLISHERS, INC.
    LC * NP

    ILL * INT * MSF
    NP4 * PM3

HUMISTON, WILLIAM H.

    PADEREWSKI--'LITTLE BIOGRAPHIES'

                NEW YORK   1921   24P   BPLB
                   BREITKOPF PUBLISHERS, INC.
    LC * NP

    INT * PHO
    NP4 * PM3

HUMISTON, WILLIAM H.

    RACHMANINOFF--'LITTLE BIOGRAPHIES'

                NEW YORK   1921   25P   BRLB
                   BREITKOPF PUBLISHERS, INC.
    LC * NP

    GLO * INT * MSF * PHO
    NP4 * PM3

HUMMEL, JOHANN NEPOMUK

    COMPLETE THEORETICAL AND PRACTICAL COURSE OF INSTRUCTIONS ON THE
    ART OF PLAYING THE PIANOFORTE, A --2200 MUSICAL EXAMPLES---1828, IN
    GERMAN
                LONDON   1850   499P   BCTAPC
                   BOOSEY, T., AND COMPANY
    LC * NP

    INT * MEX * TAB
    NP3 * KI5 * KI6 * KI8 * PL4 * PL5 * PL12 * PL14 * PT4 * PT8 * KS5 *
    AP3 * AP7 * AP8

HUNEKER, JAMES GIBBONS

    CHOPIN..THE MAN AND HIS MUSIC---1901

                NEW YORK   1966   415P   BCTMAH
                   DOVER PUBLICATIONS
    AS * BP * BR * ES * IU * LC * MI * NP * OC * TO * UA * UC * UI * UM
    UO * US * UT * UU * UW * YU
    BIB * IND
    NP3 * PM3 * PM14 * PM15

HUNEKER, JAMES GIBBONS

    DEVELOPMENT OF PIANO MUSIC FROM THE DAYS OF THE CLAVICHORD AND
    HARPSICHORD TO THE PRESENT TIME, THE --REPRESENTED IN SIX PROGRAMS
    BY OSSIP GABRILOWITSCH
                NEW YORK   1915   16P   BDOPMF

    BP * LC * NP

    KI3 * KI14 * PM7 * AP3 * AP4

HUNEKER, JAMES GIBBONS

    FRANZ LISZT

                NEW YORK   1911   458P   BFL
                   SCRIBNER'S, CHARLES, SONS
    AS * BP * BR * CP * ES * IU * LC * MI * NP * OC * TO * UA * UC * UI
    UM * US * UT * UU * UW * YU
    ILL * IND * PHO
    NP3 * NP5 * AT12 * AT13 * PM3 * PM9

HUNEKER, JAMES GIBBONS

    INTIMATE LETTERS OF JAMES GIBBONS HUNEKER, COLLECTED AND EDITED BY
    JOSEPHINE HUNEKER
                NEW YORK   1936   322P   BILOJG
                   LIVERIGHT PUBLISHING CORPORATION
    BR * IU * LC * NP

    IND
    NP6

HUNEKER, JAMES GIBBONS

    MELOMANIACS..ESSAYS---CHOPIN AND LISZT

                NEW YORK   1917   350P   BMECAL
                   SCRIBNER'S, CHARLES, SONS
    BR * IU * LC * NP

    NP6 * PM3

HUNEKER, JAMES GIBBONS

    MEZZOTINTS IN MODERN MUSIC--6TH. ED.---CHOPIN AND LISZT--1901

                NEW YORK   1927   318P   BMIMMS
                   SCRIBNER'S, CHARLES, SONS
    IU * LC * NP

    IND
    NP5 * PM3

HUNEKER, JAMES GIBBONS

    OLD FOGY, HIS MUSICAL OPINIONS AND GROTESQUES---D'ALBERT,
    PADEREWSKI, JOSEFFY, PACHMANN

                PHILADELPHIA   1913   195P   BOFHMO
                   PRESSER, THEODORE, COMPANY
    AS * BR * CP * ES * LC * MI * NP * OC * TO * UA * UK * UM * UO * US
    UT * YU
    INT
    NP6 * PM10

HUNEKER, JAMES GIBBONS

    UNICORNS---CHOPIN

                NEW YORK   1917   361P   BUC
                   SCRIBNER'S, CHARLES, SONS
    BR * LC * NP

    NP6 * PM3

HUNEKER, JAMES GIBBONS

    VARIATIONS---CHOPIN, LISZT, AND PACHMANN

                NEW YORK   1921   279P   BVCLAP
                   SCRIBNER'S, CHARLES, SONS
    BR * IU * LC * NP

    INT
    NP6 * PM3

HUNT, REGINALD H.

    EXTEMPORIZATION FOR MUSIC STUDENTS

                LONDON   1968   62P   BEFMS
                   OXFORD UNIVERSITY PRESS
    LC

    APP * INT * MEX
    KS5 * KS8

HUNT, REGINALD H.

    HARMONY AT THE KEYBOARD

                LONDON   1970   96P   BHATK
                   OXFORD UNIVERSITY PRESS

    MEX
    KS4

HUNT, REGINALD H.

    TRANSPOSITION FOR MUSIC STUDENTS

                LONDON   1969   48P   BTFMS
                   OXFORD UNIVERSITY PRESS
    LC * NP

    INT * MEX
    KS7

HUNTEN, WILLIAM

    HUNTEN'S CELEBRATED PIANOFORTE SCHOOL

                CINCINNATI   1856   BHCPS
                   PETERS, W. C., AND SONS
    LC

    AT4

HUTCHESON, ERNEST

    ELEMENTS OF PIANO TECHNIQUE, THE

                BALTIMORE   1907   36P   BEOPT
                   KRANZ MUSIC COMPANY
    NP * TO

    MEX
    PT1 * PT9 * PT10

HUTCHESON, ERNEST

    GREAT MASTERS OF PIANO MUSIC, THE ..BACH, BEETHOVEN, SCHUMANN,
    CHOPIN, LISZT..A SERIES OF FIVE PROGRAMS--CRITICISMS

                NEW YORK   1922   16P   BGMOPM

    PM3 * PM13

HUTCHESON, ERNEST *
GANZ, RUDOLPH
    LITERATURE OF THE PIANO, THE ..A GUIDE FOR AMATEUR AND
    STUDENT--3RD. REV. ED.---1948
                NEW YORK   1964   429P   BLOTPA
                   KNOPF, ALFRED A., INC.
    AS * BP * BR * CP * CU * ES * IU * LC * MI * NP * OC * SA * TO * UA
    UC * UI * UK * UM * UO * US * UT * UU * UW * YU
    BIB * IND * INT * MEX * TAB
    KI6 * KI9 * KI14 * PT1 * PT6 * PM3 * PM5 * PM7 * PM8 * PM9 * PM11 *
    PM13 * PM15 * AP3 * AP4

HUTCHESON, ERNEST

    LITERATURE OF THE PIANO, THE --FROM THE 16TH. CENTURY TO THE
PRESENT TIME--A SURVEY IN SEVEN PROGRAMS

        LONDON   1924   20P   BLOTPF
            CHARLTON
BR * LC

INT
PL9 * PM6 * PM7 * PM8 * PM13

HUTCHINGS, ARTHUR

    BAROQUE CONCERTO, THE

        NEW YORK   1961   363P   BBC
            NORTON, W. W., AND COMPANY
BR * LC * NP

ILL * IND * MEX * MSF * PHO
PM7 * PM8 * PM9

HUTCHINGS, ARTHUR

    COMPANION TO MOZART'S PIANO CONCERTOS, A

        LONDON   1948   207P   BCTMPC
            OXFORD UNIVERSITY PRESS
AS * BP * BR * CP * CU * ES * IU * LC * MI * NP * OC * TO * UA * UC
UI * UM * UO * US * UT * UU * UW * YU
APP * BIB * MEX
PM3 * PM6 * PM7 * PM8 * PM9 * PM15 * AP3 * AP4

HUTT, DOREEN

    PIANO CLASS METHOD--BKS. 1 AND 2

        WATERLOO, ONTARIO   1966+   98P   BPCMBO
            WATERLOO MUSIC COMPANY
LC

ILL * INT * MEX
AT4 * AT7

ILIFFE, FREDERICK

    FORTY-EIGHT PRELUDES AND FUGUES OF JOHANN SEBASTIAN BACH ANALYZED
FOR THE USE OF STUDENTS, THE

        LONDON   1897   194P   BFEPAF
            NOVELLO AND COMPANY, LTD.
BR * IU * LC * NP * OC * SA * TO * UI * US * UT * UW

CHR * INT * MEX * TAB
PM3 * PM8 * PM15 * AP3 * AP4

INTERNATIONAL MUSICOLOGICAL CONGRESS..FIRST--1960--WORKS OF FREDERICK
CHOPIN
    BOOK OF THE FIRST INTERNATIONAL MUSICOLOGICAL CONGRESS DEVOTED TO
THE WORKS OF FREDERICK CHOPIN, THE ---IN POLISH, FRENCH, RUSSIAN,
ENGLISH, AND GERMAN
        WARSAW   1963   755P   BBOTFI
            POLISH SCIENTIFIC PUBLISHERS
BR * IU * LC

APP * BIB * ILL * INT * LDR * MEX * MSF * PHO * TAB
PM3 * PM8 * PM9 * PM14 * AP3 * AP4 * GI6

INTERNATIONAL MUSIC INSTITUTE FOR FREE IMPROVISATION

    METHODICAL WAY TO FREE IMPROVISATION, THE --AVANT-GARDE

        LAUSANNE   1960   24P   BMWTFI
            HIMA EDITION
LC

MEX
KS5

IRWIN, WILLIAM

    RHYTHM ACCOMPANIMENT MAGIC, FOR THE POPULAR PIANIST

        WINONA, MINN.   1968   28P   BRAMFT
            POINTER SYSTEM
LC

INT * MEX
PL12 * KS6 * EP6

ISAACS, EDWARD

    BLIND PIANO TEACHER, THE

        GLASGOW   1948   48P   BBPT
            MACLELLAN, WILLIAM
BR * ES * LC * MI * NP

INT
PL4 * PL9 * AT3 * AT11 * PT1 * PT6 * AP1

ISAACSON, CHARLES D.

    FACE TO FACE WITH GREAT MUSICIANS---CHOPIN AND LISZT

        NEW YORK   1918   247P   BFTFWG
            BONI AND LIVERIGHT
IU * LC * NP

INT * LDR
NP4 * PM3

IVES, WILLIAM

    SURE TEACHER..OR, CHILD'S FIRST COURSE FOR THE PIANOFORTE, THE
..COMPOSED AND ARRANGED UPON A NEW, SAFE AND EASY PLAN OF TEACHING

        NEW YORK   1900   16P   BSTOCF
            POND, W. A., AND COMPANY
LC

AT4 * AT5

IWASZKIEWICZ, JAROSLAW

    SUMMER AT NOHANT..A PLAY IN THREE ACTS---CHOPIN

        LONDON   1942   72P   BSANAP
            MINERVA PUBLISHING COMPANY
NP

PM3 * GI12 * GI15

JACKSON, EDWIN WARD

    GYMNASTICS FOR THE FINGERS AND WRIST

        LONDON   1865   72P   BGFTFA
            TRUEBNER, N., AND COMPANY
BR * CU * LC * MI * NP * OC * TO * UA * YU

LDR
PT3 * PT5

JACOB, GORDON P.

    HOW TO READ A SCORE

        NEW YORK   1944   67P   BHTRAS
            BOOSEY AND HAWKES
BR * LC * NP

INT * MEX
KS9

JAMES, BURNETT

    BRAHMS..A CRITICAL STUDY

        NEW YORK   1972   202P   BBACS
            PRAEGER
IU * LC

APP * BIB * ILL * IND * INT * MEX * PHO
NP3 * PM3

JAMES, PHILIP BRUTTON

    EARLY KEYBOARD INSTRUMENTS, FROM THEIR BEGINNINGS TO THE YEAR
1820---1930

        LONDON   1967   153P   BEKIFT
            HOLLAND PRESS, THE
BP * BR * CP * CU * ES * IU * LC * MI * NP * OC * TO * UC * UI * UK
UM * UO * US * UT * UW * YU
APP * ILL * IND * INT * PHO * TAB
KI3 * KI5 * KI6 * KI9 * KI13 * KII14 * KII15

JEANS, SIR JAMES HOPWOOD

    SCIENCE AND MUSIC

        NEW YORK   1937   258P   BSAM
            MACMILLAN COMPANY, THE
BP * BR * CP * ES * IU * LC * MI * NP * OC * TO * UA * UC * UI * UK
UM * UO * US * UT * UU * UW * YU
CHR * IND * LDR * MEX * PHO * TAB
KI6 * KI7 * KI9 * PT8

JEWETT, ALBERT DEWEY

    IDIOMATIC COURSE OF PIANO INSTRUCTION FOR CLASS WORK

        BOSTON   1940   43P   BICOPI
            BIRCHARD, C. C., AND COMPANY
ES * LC

INT * MEX * PHO * TAB
PL4 * PL6 * PL10 * PL12 * AT7 * PT1 * PT8 * PT9 * AP6

JOHNS, CLAYTON

    ESSENTIALS OF PIANOFORTE PLAYING, THE

        BOSTON   1909   84P   BEOPP
            DITSON, OLIVER, COMPANY
BP * CP * LC * NP * UC * UI * US

MEX * PHO
PL4 * PL5 * PL7 * PT4 * PT9 * PM8 * PM9 * AP6 * AP8

JOHNS, CLAYTON

    REMINISCENCES OF A MUSICIAN---LISZT AND PADEREWSKI

        CAMBRIDGE, MASS.   1929   132P   BROAML
            WASHBURN AND THOMAS
ES * LC * NP * UC * UO

INT * PHO
NP4 * NP6

JOHNSON, ARTEMAS N.

INSTRUCTIONS IN THE ART OF PLAYING CHURCH MUSIC UPON THE MELODEON, PIANOFORTE, OR ORGAN..A NEW SYSTEM OF THOROUGH BASE

FRIENDSHIP, N. Y.   1866   128P   BIITAO
BAXTER, J., AND COMPANY
LC

MEX
AT4 * KS10

JOHNSON, ARTEMAS N.

INSTRUCTIONS IN THOROUGH BASE..BEING A NEW AND EASY METHOD FOR LEARNING TO PLAY CHURCH MUSIC UPON THE PIANO FORTE OR ORGAN

BOSTON   1844+   120P   BIITBB
REED, G. P.
LC * NP

MEX
AT4 * KS10

JOHNSON, ARTEMAS N.

JOHNSON'S NEW METHOD FOR THOROUGH BASE..AN INSTRUCTION BOOK IN THE ART OF PLAYING CHURCH OR GLEE MUSIC

BOSTON   1906   128P   BJNMFT
DITSON, OLIVER, COMPANY
LC

MEX
KS10

JOHNSON, ARTEMAS N.

THOROUGH BASE, MELODEON, ORGAN AND HARMONY INSTRUCTION BOOK, WITH A NEW SYSTEM OF THOROUGH-BASE

NEW YORK   1892   276P   BTBMOA
GORDON, S. T., AND SON
LC

MEX
KS10

JOHNSON, HARRIETT

YOUR CAREER IN MUSIC

NEW YORK   1944   319P   BYCIM
DUTTON, E. P., AND COMPANY
BP * CP * CU * ES * IU * LC * MI * NP * OC * TO * UA * UC * UI * UK
UM * UO * US * UT * UW
APP * BIB * CHR * IND * INT
GI13

JOHNSON, JOHN BARHAM

KEYBOARD HARMONY FOR BEGINNERS

LONDON   1947   59P   BKHFB
OXFORD UNIVERSITY PRESS
BR * CP * ES * MI * NP

INT * MEX
PL4 * KS4

JOHNSON, REGINALD

COMMONSENSE IN SCALE AND ARPEGGIO PLAYING

LONDON   1947   17P   BCISAA
AUGENER, LTD.
BR * SA

CHR * INT * MEX * TAB
PL4 * PT9

JOHNSON, SARAH S.

HELPS TO TEACHER AND STUDENT ON THE FAELTEN SYSTEM

ATLANTA   1915   23P   BHTTAS
LESTER BOOK AND STATIONERY COMPANY
LC

AT4 * AT11

JOHNSON, THOMAS A.

PRINCIPLES OF PIANOFORTE PEDALLING, THE

LONDON   1953   12P   BPOPP
WEEKES, A., AND COMPANY, LTD.
BR * CU * IU * SA

CHR * INT * MEX
AP8

JOHNSON, VERA A.

SCIENTIFIC SIDE OF MUSIC IN SIMPLE, PRACTICAL FORM FOR TEACHERS AND STUDENTS

FITCHBURG, MASS.   1919   18P   BSSOMI
SENTINEL PRINTING COMPANY
LC

INT * LDR * MEX
PL5 * PL14 * PT9 * KS4

JOHNSTONE, J. ALFRED

ART OF EXPRESSION IN PIANOFORTE PLAYING, THE

LONDON   1902   79P   BAOEIP
WEEKES AND COMPANY
BR

AP4 * AP5 * AP6

JOHNSTONE, J. ALFRED

ART OF TEACHING PIANOFORTE PLAYING, THE --2ND. REV. ED.---1910

LONDON   1917   256P   BAOTPP
REEVES, WILLIAM
BP * BR * CU * ES * IU * NP * SA

MEX
PL7 * PL12 * AT1 * AT2 * PT1 * PT2 * PT4 * PT6 * PT9 * PT10 * PT11
PM6 * AP4 * AP8

JOHNSTONE, J. ALFRED

ESSENTIALS IN PIANOFORTE PLAYING, AND OTHER MUSICAL STUDIES...

LONDON   1913   243P   BEIPPA
REEVES, WILLIAM
BR * LC * OC * TO * UO

PHO
PL14 * AT3 * PT3 * PT7

JOHNSTONE, J. ALFRED

HOW TO USE THE PEDAL IN PIANO PLAYING

LONDON   1920+   15P   BHTUTP
ASHDOWN, E.

AP8

JOHNSTONE, J. ALFRED

METRONOMIC INDICATIONS FOR BACH'S PRELUDES AND FUGUES AND THE INVENTIONS, WITH HINTS ON THEIR INTERPRETATION

LONDON   1920   79P   BMIFBP
WILLIAMS, J., LTD.
BR * ES * LC

PL12

JOHNSTONE, J. ALFRED

MODERN TENDENCIES AND OLD STANDARDS IN MUSICAL ART

LONDON   1911   244P   BMTAOS
REEVES, WILLIAM
BR * LC * NP

APP
NP6

JOHNSTONE, J. ALFRED

NOTES ON THE INTERPRETATION OF 24 FAMOUS PIANO SONATAS OF BEETHOVEN

LONDON   1927   205P   BNOTIO
REEVES, WILLIAM
BR * CP * ES * LC * NP * UC * UT * YU

ILL * INT
PM3 * PM8 * PM14

JOHNSTONE, J. ALFRED

PHRASING IN PIANO PLAYING..AN ELEMENTARY GUIDE WITH EXAMPLES

NEW YORK   1913   23P   BPIPPA
WITMARK

MEX
AP6

JOHNSTONE, J. ALFRED

RUBATO, OR THE SECRET OF EXPRESSION IN PIANOFORTE PLAYING

LONDON   1925   56P   BROTSO
WILLIAMS, J., LTD.
BR * ES

AP4 * AP5 * AP6

JOHNSTONE, J. ALFRED

TOUCH, PHRASING AND INTERPRETATION

LONDON   1911   147P   BTPAI
REEVES, WILLIAM
BR * CP * ES * LC * NP * OC * SA * TO * UC

APP
PT8 * PM3 * PM4 * PM9 * AP3 * AP4 * AP6 * AP7

JONAS, ALBERTO

MASTER SCHOOL OF MODERN PIANO PLAYING AND VIRTUOSITY--3 PARTS IN 7
VOLS., 1922-1929---IN ENGLISH, GERMAN, FRENCH, AND SPANISH

         NEW YORK   1922   2027P   BMSOMP
         FISCHER, CARL, INC.
BP * IU * LC * NP * UC * UO * US * UT * YU

INT * MEX * PHO
PT6 * PT8 * PT9 * PT11 * PT13

JONAS, ALBERTO

PIANOSCRIPT BOOK..AN INVALUABLE AID TO TEACHER AND STUDENT IN
PRESERVING IMPORTANT ADVICE AND LESSON NOTES IN PERMANENT FORM

         PHILADELPHIA   1918   70P   BPBAIA
         PRESSER, THEODORE, COMPANY
LC * NP

INT * MEX
PL7 * PL9 * PL11 * PT4 * PT8 * PT9 * PT10 * PT11 * AP8

JONES, GRIFFITH

COMPLEAT INSTRUCTOR FOR THE HARPSICHORD OR PIANOFORTE, THE

         LONDON   1787   32P   BCIFTH
         GOLDING, GEORGE
LC * YU

ILL * MEX
PL4 * PL12 * PT6 * AP7

JONES, JOHN H.

PRACTICAL GUIDE TO THOROUGH BASS, A ..OR, HARMONY ILLUSTRATED AND
TAUGHT WITHOUT THE AID OF A MASTER

         NEW YORK   1853   110P   BPGTTB
         NEWMAN AND IVISON
LC * NP

MEX
PL11 * KS10

JONSON, GEORGE CHARLES

HANDBOOK TO CHOPIN'S WORKS, A

         LONDON   1905   287P   BHTCW
         HEINEMANN, W.
AS * BP * BR * CP * ES * IU * LC * MI * NP * OC * UA * UC * UK * UM
US * UW * YU
APP * BIB * INT * TAB
NP3 * PM3 * PM6 * PM9 * PM15

JOUSSE, JOHN

GUIDA ARMONICA, IN WHICH...CHORDS, ARE CLEARLY EXPLAINED AND
ILLUSTRATED...TO WHICH ARE ADDED CONCISE RULES, AND DIRECTIONS FOR
ACCOMPANYING
         LONDON   1808   91P   BGAIWC
         GOULDING, PHIPPS, D'ALMAINE AND COMPANY
LC

INT
PL4 * KS4 * KS8 * KS10 * EP6

JOUSSE, JOHN

JOUSSE'S CATECHISM OF MUSIC, AND BURROWES' PIANOFORTE PRIMER AND
GUIDE TO PRACTICE, COMBINED...

         BOSTON   1869   80P   BJCOMA
         BROWN, O. B.
LC * UA

AT4

KACZMAREK, REGINA A.

CATALOG OF SELECTED PIANO ROLLS FROM THE LIBRARY OF CONGRESS
COLLECTION, A

         WASHINGTON, D. C.   1960   322P   BCOSPR
         LIBRARY OF CONGRESS
LC

KI10 * PM12

KAISER, JOACHIM

GREAT PIANISTS OF OUR TIME

         LONDON   1971   230P   BGPOOT
         ALLEN AND UNWIN, LTD.
IU * LC

DIS * INT * MEX * PHO
NP4 * GI4 * GI13

KANZELL, MAXWELL

HOW TO READ MUSIC..A COMPLETELY NEW AND SIMPLIFIED APPROACH TO
READING MUSIC AT SIGHT--3RD. REV. ED.

         NEW YORK   1953   79P   BHTRMA
         FISCHER, CARL, INC.
LC * NP

ILL * INT * MEX
PL4 * KS3 * KS8

KARASOWSKI, MORITZ

FREDERIC CHOPIN..HIS LIFE, LETTERS AND WORKS--3RD. REV. ED.---1879

         LONDON   1938   479P   BFCHLL
         REEVES, WILLIAM
BR * IU * LC * NP

ILL * LDR * MSF * PHO
NP6 * PM3 * PM5 * PM14

KARLIN, AARON

KARLIN'S HARMONIC COURSE FOR PIANO IMPROVISING--4
VOLS.---REPRODUCED FROM MANUSCRIPT

         BROOKLYN, N. Y.   1943   316P   BKHCFP
         KARLIN, AARON
LC

INT * MEX
AT4 * KS3 * KS5

KASTNER, RUDOLPH

BEETHOVEN'S PIANO SONATAS AND ARTUR SCHNABEL

         LONDON   1935   55P   BBPSAA
         REEVES, WILLIAM
BP * BR * CU * ES * IU * LC * NP * OC * UC * UI * UT * YU

INT
NP3 * PM3 * PM7 * PM8 * PM9 * PM14

KASTNER, SANTIAGO

PARALLELS AND DISCREPANCIES BETWEEN ENGLISH AND SPANISH KEYBOARD
MUSIC OF THE 16TH. AND 17TH. CENTURIES--REPRINT FROM 'ANNURIO
MUSICAL', VOL. 7
         BARCELONA   1952   39P   BPADBE
         INSTITUTO ESPANOL DE MUSICOLOGIA DEL C.S.I.C.
IU * NP

PM7 * PM9 * AP3 * AP7

KATOWICE, POLAND--BIBLIOTECA PANSTWOWEJ

CHOPINIANA IN THE HIGH MUSIC SCHOOL LIBRARY IN
KATOWICE---BIBLIOGRAPHY OF MONOGRAPHS AND PERIODICAL
ARTICLES--TITLES IN SEVERAL LANGUAGES
         KATOWICE, POLAND   1961   33P   BCITHM
         BIBLIOTECA PANSTWOWEJ
IU

PHO
PM5

KAUFMANN, HELEN LOEB

ARTISTS IN MUSIC OF TODAY

         NEW YORK   1933   111P   BAIMOT
         GROSSET AND DUNLAP
BR * LC * NP

ILL * INT
NP5 * GI13

KEDDINGTON, J. BLAINE

CHORD-O-GRAPH METHOD OF KEYBOARD HARMONY---PRINTED FROM TYPED COPY

         SALT LAKE CITY   1942   37P   BCMOKH
         KEDDINGTON, J. B.
LC

INT * MEX
KS4

KEEFER, LUBOV

INFLUENCE OF ADAM MICKIEWICZ ON THE BALLADES OF CHOPIN, THE
--OFFPRINT FROM 'AMERICAN SLAVIC AND EAST EUROPEAN REVIEW'--VOL. 5

         BALTIMORE   1946   14P   BIOAMO
         KEEFER, LUBOV
LC * NP

PM3 * GI12 * GI15

KEELER, WALTER B.

THEORY OF THE NEW KEYBOARD, ARRANGED BY W. B. KEELER AND E. K.
WINKLER

         NEW YORK   1892   7P   BTOTNK
         JANKO CONSERVATORY OF MUSIC
LC

INT
KI5 * KI6 * GI12

KEILMAN, WILHELM

INTRODUCTION TO SIGHT READING

         NEW YORK   1972   58P   BITSR
         PETERS, C. F.

PL4 * KS3

KELBERINE, ALEXANDER

    FOUR FAMOUS PIANOFORTE SONATAS OF BEETHOVEN, THE --OP. 13, OP. 27,
    NO. 2, OP. 53, OP. 57

        GLEN ROCK, N. J.   1939   59P   BFFPSO
          FISCHER, J., AND BRO
    BP * LC * OC * SA

    INT * MEX
    PM3 * PM8 * PM11 * PM13 * PM15

KELLER, GOTTFRIED

    COMPLEAT METHOD, FOR ATTAINING TO PLAY A THOROUGH BASS UPON EITHER
    ORGAN, HARPSICHORD OR THEORBO LUTE, A

        LONDON   1707   15P   BCMFAT
          CULLEN, JOHN
    BR * LC * NP

    ILL * MEX
    KS10

KELLER, HERMANN

    PHRASING AND ARTICULATION---152 MUSICAL EXAMPLES

        NEW YORK   1965   117P   BPAAOH
          NORTON, W. W., AND COMPANY
    BP * BR * CP * ES * IU * LC * MI * OC * TO * UA * UI * UK * UM * UO
    UT * UU * UW
    BIB * IND * MEX
    AP6

KELLER, HERMANN

    THOROUGHBASS METHOD--NUMEROUS EXAMPLES FROM THE LITERATURE OF THE
    17TH. AND 18TH. CENTURIES

        NEW YORK   1965   97P   BTMNEF
          NORTON, W. W., AND COMPANY
    BR * IU * LC * NP

    INT * MEX
    KS4 * KS10

KELLEY, EDGAR STILLMAN

    CHOPIN THE COMPOSER---1913

        NEW YORK   1969   190P   BCTCNT
          COOPER SQUARE PUBLISHERS
    AS * BP * BR * CP * ES * IU * LC * MI * NP * OC * UA * UC * UK * UM
    UO * UW * YU
    INT * IND * MEX
    NP3 * PM3 * PM14 * AP3 * AP7

KELLEY, EDGAR STILLMAN

    MUSICAL INSTRUMENTS--3RD. YEAR OF A STUDY COURSE IN MUSIC
    UNDERSTANDING, ADOPTED BY THE NATIONAL FEDERATION OF MUSIC CLUBS

        BOSTON   1925   243P   BMITYO
          DITSON, OLIVER, COMPANY
    IU * LC * NP

    APP * ILL * IND * INT * LDR * MEX
    KI3 * KI5 * KI9 * KI13 * KI14 * GI6

KELLOGG, CHARLOTTE

    PADEREWSKI

        NEW YORK   1956   224P   BP
          VIKING PRESS, INC.
    BP * BR * CP * LC * NP * UC * UI

    IND
    NP4

KENDALL, ALAN

    WORLD OF MUSICAL INSTRUMENTS, THE ---CHIEFLY ILLUSTRATIONS

        NEW YORK   1972   128P   BWOMIC
          HAMLYN PUBLISHING GROUP, LTD.
    IU * LC

    CHR * ILL * IND * INT * LDR * MEX * PHO
    KI3 * KI5 * KI6 * KI7 * KI9 * KI13 * KI14

KENYON, CHARLES FREDERICK

    HOW TO MEMORIZE MUSIC

        LONDON   1904   56P   BHTMM
          REEVES, WILLIAM
    BP * BR * ES * IU * LC * NP * OC * TO * UC * YU

    MEX
    PL5 * PL6 * PL8 * PL9 * AT4 * PT8 * KS3

KENYON, CHARLES FREDERICK

    IMAGINARY INTERVIEWS WITH GREAT COMPOSERS..A SERIES OF VIVID PEN
    SKETCHES IN WHICH THE SALIENT CHARACTERISTICS AND THE OFTEN
    EXTRAVAGANT INDIVIDUALITY OF EACH COMPOSER ARE TRUTHFULLY PORTRAYED
        LONDON   1909   232P   BIIWGC
          REEVES, WILLIAM
    LC

    NP5 * NP8

KENYON, CHARLES FREDERICK

    MEMORIZING MUSIC

        LONDON   1927   127P   BMM
          RICHARDS PRESS, THE, LTD.
    LC * NP

    PL8

KENYON, MAX

    HARPSICHORD MUSIC..THE INSTRUMENTS, THE COMPOSERS, THE PLAYERS

        LONDON   1949   256P   BHMTIT
          CASSELL AND COMPANY, LTD.
    AS * BP * BR * CP * CU * ES * IU * LC * MI * NP * OC * TO * UC * UI
    UK * UM * UO * US * UT * UU * YU
    ILL * IND * MEX * PHO
    KI3 * KI5 * KI6 * KI9 * PM3 * PM7

KERN, ALICE M.

    HARMONIZATION-TRANSPOSITION AT THE KEYBOARD

        EVANSTON, ILL.   1963   182P   BHTATK
          SUMMY-BIRCHARD COMPANY
    CP * CU * ES * MI * OC * SA * UI * UM * UO

    INT * MEX
    PL4 * KS4 * KS8

KERN, ALICE M. *
TITUS, HELEN M.
    TEACHER'S GUIDEBOOK TO PIANO LITERATURE, THE --REV. ED.---1954+

        ANN ARBOR, MICH.   1964   185P   BTGTPL
          EDWARDS, J. W.
    BP * CP * ES * IU * LC * MI * NP * UA * UI * UM * UT * UW * YU

    IND * INT
    PM4 * PM6 * PM7 * PM15

KING, AUDREY

    PIANO CLASSES IN ELEMENTARY SCHOOLS

        LONDON   1938   12P   BPCIES
          REEVES, WILLIAM
    BR * LC

    CHR * MEX
    PL4 * AT4 * AT5 * AT7

KINSKY, GEORG--EDITOR

    HISTORY OF MUSIC IN PICTURES, A

        NEW YORK   1937   363P   BHOMIP
          DUTTON, E. P., AND COMPANY
    BR * IU * LC * NP

    ILL * IND * INT * LDR * MSF * PHO
    KI3 * KI13 * KI14

KIRBY, FRANK EUGENE

    SHORT HISTORY OF KEYBOARD MUSIC, A

        NEW YORK   1966   534P   BSHOKM
          FREE PRESS, THE
    AS * BP * BR * CP * ES * IU * LC * MI * OC * SA * TO * UA * UI * UK
    UM * UO * US * UT * UU * UW * YU
    APP * BIB * ILL * IND * LDR * MEX
    KI3 * KI5 * KI6 * KI12 * KI14 * PM3 * PM7 * PM8 * PM9 * PM14 * PM15

KIRBY, MAY B. KELLY

    KELLY KIRBY KINDERGARTEN PIANO METHOD, TEACHERS' COURSE, THE --BKS.
    1-4

        TORONTO   1948   280P   BKKKPM
          HARRIS, FREDERICK, MUSIC COMPANY
    LC

    PL3 * PL4 * PL12 * AT3 * AT4 * AT8 * PT1 * KS3

KIRKPATRICK, JOHN

    OBSERVATIONS ON FOUR VOLUMES AND SUPPLEMENT OF THE WORKS OF L. M.
    GOTTSCHALK IN THE NEW YORK PUBLIC LIBRARY
        NEW YORK   1931+   11P   BOOFVA
          NEW YORK PUBLIC LIBRARY
    NP * UM

    PM9

KIRKPATRICK, RALPH

    DOMENICO SCARLATTI---1953

        NEW YORK   1968   485P   BDSNFT
          CROWELL, T. Y., COMPANY
    BP * BR * CP * CU * ES * IU * LC * MI * NP * OC * TO * UA * UC * UI
    UK * UM * US * UT * UW * YU
    BIB * CHR * ILL * IND * INT * LDR * MEX * MSF * TAB
    NP3 * KI9 * KI14 * PM3 * PM6 * PM14 * PM15 * AP3 * AP4 * AP6 * AP7

KIRKWOOD, KENNETH P.

GARDEN IN POLAND, A ...ON CHOPIN'S BIRTHPLACE AND BURIAL

            KARACHI   1953   34P   BGIPOC
            KIRKWOOD, KENNETH P.
    BR * LC * NP

    PHO
    NP4

KLAUWELL, OTTO

ON MUSICAL EXECUTION...PRIMARILY WITH REFERENCE TO PIANO-PLAYING

            NEW YORK   1890   135P   BOMEPW
            SCHIRMER, G., INC.
    LC * UC

    AP1

KLAVARSKRIBO, SLEKKERVIER, HOLLAND

PRACTICAL CORRESPONDENCE COURSE FOR PIANOFORTE

            SLEKKERVIER, HOLLAND   1930+   49P   BPCCFP
            KLAVARSKRIBO
    BP

    PL2 * PL4 * PL11 * AT4

KLECZYNSKI, JAN

CHOPIN'S GREATER WORKS...HOW THEY SHOULD BE UNDERSTOOD...INCLUDING
CHOPIN'S NOTES FOR A "METHOD OF METHODS"--THREE LECTURES

            LONDON   1882+   115P   BCGWHT
            REEVES, WILLIAM
    BP * BR * CP * CU * ES * IU * LC * MI * NP * OC * TO * UA * UI * UK
    UM * UT * YU
    ILL * INT * MEX * MSF
    PM3 * PM9 * PM13 * PM14 * PM15

KLECZYNSKI, JAN

HOW TO PLAY CHOPIN--THREE LECTURES

            LONDON   1882   76P   BHTPCT
            REEVES, WILLIAM
    CP * LC * NP * SA * UO * US * UT * YU

    IND * INT * LDR * MEX
    NP4 * NP7 * PT4 * PT6 * PT9 * PT10 * PM3 * PM9 * PM14 * PM15 * AP3
    AP4 * AP5 * AP8

KLECZYNSKI, JAN

WORKS OF FREDERIC CHOPIN, THE ..THEIR PROPER INTERPRETATION--6TH.
ED.--THREE LECTURES AT VARSOVIA---1882

            LONDON   1935+   76P   BWOFCT
            REEVES, WILLIAM
    BP * BR * ES * IU * LC * NP * OC * UA * UI * UK * UM

    IND * ILL * MEX
    PM3 * PM9 * PM14 * AP3 * AP4

KLING, HENRI

TRANSPOSITION...A PRACTICAL AND AUTHORITATIVE GUIDE FOR ALL
INSTRUMENTS

            NEW YORK   1910   44P   BTAPAU
            FISCHER, CARL, INC.
    IU * LC

    INT * MEX
    KS7

KLOSE, F. J.

PRACTICAL HINTS FOR ACQUIRING THOROUGH BASS

            LONDON   1822   68P   BPHFAT
            OLLIER, C. AND J.
    LC

    KS10

KNOLLER, JACOB

FREE WILL OR DESTINY..ONE ACT PLAY AROUND CHOPIN---EARLY SUMMER,
1836

            NEW YORK   1950   13P   BFWODO
            KNOLLER, J.
    NP

    PM3 * GI12 * GI15

KNORR, JULIUS

KNORR'S METHODICAL GUIDE FOR TEACHERS OF MUSIC ON THE PIANOFORTE

            BOSTON   1854   64P   BKMGFT
            DITSON, OLIVER, COMPANY
    BP

    AT1 * AT2

KNOTT, THOMAS B.

PIANOFORTE FINGERING, ITS PRINCIPLES AND APPLICATIONS

            LONDON   1928   23P   BPFIPA
            OXFORD UNIVERSITY PRESS
    BR * CP * CU * ES * IU * NP * SA * YU

    APP * INT * MEX
    PT6

KOBBE, GUSTAV

PIANOLIST, THE ..A GUIDE FOR PIANOLA PLAYERS

            NEW YORK   1907   164P   BPAGFP
            MOFFAT, YARD AND COMPANY
    BP * BR * ES * LC * NP * UM * UO * UT * YU

    KI10 * PL11 * PM13 * GI11

KOBBE, GUSTAV

STRAIGHT TO THE HEART OF MUSIC---PLAYER-PIANO

            NEW YORK   1912   14P   BSTTHO
            AEOLIAN COMPANY, THE
    NP

    ILL * LDR * PHO
    KI10 * AP1

KOBYLANSKA, KRYSTYNA--EDITOR

CHOPIN IN HIS OWN LAND..DOCUMENTS AND SOUVENIRS

            NEW YORK   1956   306P   BCIHOL
            HEINMAN, W. S.
    BR * IU * LC

    BIB * ILL * IND * INT * MSF
    NP3 * NP9 * PM3

KOCH, CASPAR

PIANO STUDENT'S GRADUS AD PARNASSUM, THE ..PRESENTING THE
INTERPRETATION AND ORNAMENTATION OF SIXTEENTH AND SEVENTEENTH
CENTURY MUSIC
            GLEN ROCK, N. J.   1945   41P   BPSGAP
            FISCHER, J., AND BRO.
    BP * SA * TO

    BIB * INT * MEX * MSF
    PL12 * PM3 * PM7 * AP3 * AP4 * AP7

KOCHEVITSKY, GEORGE

ART OF PIANO PLAYING, THE ..A SCIENTIFIC APPROACH

            EVANSTON, ILL.   1967   68P   BAOPPA
            SUMMY-BIRCHARD COMPANY
    AS * BP * ES * IU * LC * SA * UI * UM * UO

    BIB * CHR * IND * INT * MEX * PHO
    NP2 * KI3 * PL7 * PT3 * PT4 * PT6 * PT7 * PT8 * PT12 * PT14 * AP5 *
    AP9

KOLANDER, MAX

KOLANDER'S ACCOMPANIMENT INSTRUCTOR FOR THE PIANO OR ORGAN

            SAN FRANCISCO   1904+   36P   BKAIFT
            MAX KOLANDER MUSIC HOUSE
    LC

    CHR * IND * INT
    KS5 * EP6

KOLLMANN, AUGUST F.

INTRODUCTION TO THE ART OF PRELUDING AND EXTEMPORISING IN SIX
LESSONS, FOR THE HARPSICHORD OR HARP, AN
            LONDON   1798   20P   BITTAO
            WORNUM, R.
    LC

    INT * MEX
    PL4 * KS4 * KS5

KOLLMANN, AUGUST F.

PRACTICAL GUIDE TO THOROUGH-BASS, A

            LONDON   1801   68P   BPGTTB
            KOLLMANN, AUGUST F.
    LC * NP

    MEX
    KS10

KOLLMANN, AUGUST F.

SECOND PRACTICAL GUIDE TO THOROUGH BASS, A

            LONDON   1807   46P   BSPGTT
            KOLLMANN, AUGUST F.
    BR * LC * NP

    MEX
    KS10

KORSTEN, BJARNE

RECENT NORWEGIAN PIANO MUSIC

```
        OSLO                    1965    23P       BRNPM
          NORSK KOMPONISTFORENING
LC * MI * UI * UT

DIS * MEX
PM3 * PM5 * PM8 * PM12 * PM15
```

KOSCIUSZKO FOUNDATION

TO IGNACE JAN PADEREWSKI, ARTIST, PATRIOT, HUMANITARIAN, 1918-1928

```
        NEW YORK                1928    206P      BTIJPA
          KOSCIUSZKO FOUNDATION
LC * NP * UT


NP4
```

KOTZSCHMAR, MARY ANN

HALF-HOUR LESSONS IN MUSIC..CLASS WORK FOR BEGINNERS AT THE PIANO

```
        BOSTON                  1907    122P      BHHLIM
          DITSON, OLIVER, COMPANY
BP * LC * NP * US

BIB * CHR * ILL * INT * LDR * MEX
PL4 * AT3 * AT4 * AT5 * AT7 * PM6
```

KRAEHENBUEHL, DAVID

KEYBOARD THEORY--6 VOLS.

```
        EVANSTON, ILL.          1965    288P      BKTSV
          SUMMY-BIRCHARD COMPANY
IU * LC * NP

APP * INT * MEX
KS4
```

KRAUS, ALESSANDRO B.

ONE-KEYBOARDED CLAVICYTHERIUM OF THE KRAUS COLLECTION IN FLORENCE, THE

```
        FLORENCE                1910    3P        BOKCOT
          LANDI, S.
NP


KI5 * KI6 * GI12
```

KRAUSE, E. W.

STUDIES IN MEASURE AND RHYTHM...FOR TEACHERS AND PUPILS, ALSO FOR SELF-INSTRUCTION

```
        PHILADELPHIA            1888    57P       BSIMAR
          PRESSER, THEODORE, COMPANY
LC

INT * MEX
PL11 * PL12
```

KRAUSE, E. W.

STUDIES IN MEASURE AND RHYTHM, FOR THE PIANOFORTE, TO DEVELOP AN EXACT PERCEPTION OF TONE DURATION AND RHYTHM IN MUSIC

```
        PHILADELPHIA            1901    11P       BSIMAR
          PRESSER, THEODORE, COMPANY
LC

MEX
PL11 * PL12
```

KRAUSE, E. W.

STUDY OF TIME AND MEASURE, THE --FOR PIANO STUDENTS

```
        PHILADELPHIA            1888              BSOTAM
          PRESSER, THEODORE, COMPANY


MEX
PL12
```

KREBS, T. L.

MANUAL OF MODULATION...FOR THE USE OF PIANISTS AND ORGANISTS

```
        CINCINNATI              1885    24P       BMOMFT
          CHURCH, THE JOHN, COMPANY
LC

INT * MEX
KS8
```

KREHBIEL, HENRY

PIANOFORTE AND ITS MUSIC, THE ---1911

```
        NEW YORK                1971    314P      BPAIMN
          COOPER SQUARE PUBLISHERS
AS * BP * BR * CP * CU * ES * IU * LC * MI * NP * OC * TO * UC * UI
UK * UM * US * UT * YU
ILL * IND * LDR * MEX * PHO
NP5 * KI3
```

KRUSZYNSKI, MICHAL

APPROACH TO THE PSYCHOLOGY OF PIANO TEACHING, AN

```
        HUDDERSFIELD, YORKS, ENGLAND 1960   55P    BATTPO
          WHITE, B. B.
BR * LC * SA

CHR * INT * LDR * MEX
KI4 * PL3 * PL4 * PL7 * AT3 * AT4 * AT5 * AT11 * PT4 * PT5 * PT9 *
PT10 * KS3 * AP4 * AP8
```

KUERSTEINER, JEAN PAUL

EXPERT AID TO ARTISTIC PIANO PLAYING

```
        NEW YORK                1910+   16P       BEATAP
          UNZ AND COMPANY
NP

PT6 * PT8 * PT10
```

KUHE, WILHELM

MY MUSICAL RECOLLECTIONS---CHOPIN

```
        LONDON                  1896    394P      BMMRC
          BENTLEY, R., AND SON
BP * BR * ES * LC * MI * NP

IND * INT * MSF * PHO
NP6
```

KULLAK, ADOLPH

AESTHETICS OF PIANOFORTE PLAYING, THE ---1861 IN GERMAN--1ST. ENGLISH ED. IN 1916

```
        NEW YORK                1972    327P      BAOPPE
          DA CAPO PRESS
BP * CU * ES * LC * NP * OC * UA * UC * UI * UO * US * UT * YU

INT * MEX
NP2 * NP3 * NP5 * AT4 * PT12 * AP4 * AP5
```

KULLAK, ADOLPH

ART OF THE TOUCH, THE ..A WORK FOR THE USE OF ADVANCED PLAYERS AND A GUIDE FOR TEACHING THE PIANOFORTE

```
        LEIPZIG                 1882              BAOTTA
          HOFMEISTER
ES * UM


AT1 * AT2 * PT8
```

KULLAK, FRANZ

BEETHOVEN'S PIANO PLAYING, WITH AN ESSAY ON THE EXECUTION OF THE TRILL---1901+

```
        NEW YORK                1973    101P      BBPPWA
          DA CAPO PRESS
BR * ES * IU * LC * NP * UC * UT * YU


NP3 * PL12 * PM14 * AP3 * AP4 * AP6 * AP7
```

LAHEE, HENRY C.

FAMOUS PIANISTS OF TODAY AND YESTERDAY

```
        BOSTON                  1900    345P      BFPOTA
          PAGE, C. L., AND COMPANY
BP * BR * CP * ES * IU * LC * MI * NP * OC * UC * UO * US

ILL * IND * INT * PHO * TAB
NP3 * NP4 * NP5
```

LAMAR, RICHARD

COLLEGE PIANO PEDAGOGY

```
        FREEMAN, S. D.          1968    109P      BCPP
          PINE HILL PRESS
IU * LC * UI

MEX
PL7 * PL8 * PL12 * AT1 * PT6 * PT7 * PT8 * PT9 * PT10 * PT11 * KS1
KS3 * PM3 * PM9 * AP4 * AP6 * AP7 * AP8 * EP4 * EP5
```

LAMOND, FREDERICK ARCHIBALD

BEETHOVEN..NOTES ON THE SONATAS...

```
        GLASGOW                 1944    14P       BBNOTS
          MACLEHOSE, ROBERT, AND COMPANY
BP * BR * NP


PM13 * PM14
```

LAMOND, FREDERICK ARCHIBALD

MEMOIRS OF FREDERICK LAMOND, THE

```
        GLASGOW                 1949    130P      BMOFL
          MACLELLAN, WILLIAM
BR * LC * NP * TO

ILL * INT * PHO
NP6
```

LAMOTTE, J.

    PIANO AND MUSICAL MATTERS

            BOSTON   1870   104P   BPAMM
                WHITE, SMITH AND PERRY
        BP

        PL2

LAMPE, JOHN F.

    PLAIN AND COMPENDIOUS METHOD OF TEACHING THOROUGH BASS, A ..WITH
    PROPER RULES FOR PRACTICE

            LONDON   1737   147P   BPACMO
                WILCOX, J.
        BR * IU * LC * NP

        MEX
        PL7 * AT4 * KS10

LANDAU, ROM

    IGNACE PADEREWSKI, MUSICIAN AND STATESMAN

            NEW YORK   1934   314P   BIPMAS
                CROWELL, THOMAS Y., COMPANY
        AS * BP * BR * CP * ES * LC * MI * NP * OC * UA * UC * UI * UM * US
        UT * YU
        BIB * IND * PHO
        NP4

LANDOWSKA, WANDA

    LANDOWSKA ON MUSIC--EDITED BY DENISE RESTOUT

            NEW YORK   1964   434P   BLOMEB
                STEIN AND DAY, INC.
        AS * BP * BR * CP * ES * IU * LC * MI * OC * SA * TO * UA * UI * UK
        UM * US * UU * UW * YU
        DIS * ILL * IND * MEX * MSF * PHO
        NP3 * NP4 * NP6 * KI3 * KI5 * KI6 * KI9 * KI14 * PL7 * PL12 * AT1 *
        PT6 * PT8 * PM3 * PM7 * PM8 * PM9 * PM11 * PM12 * PM14 * PM15 *
        AP3 * AP4 * AP5 * AP6 * AP7

LANDOWSKA, WANDA

    MUSIC OF THE PAST

            NEW YORK   1924   185P   BMOTP
                KNOPF, ALFRED A., INC.
        BR * ES * IU * LC * NP * OC * TO * UC * UK * UM * US * UT * UW * YU

        PM3 * PM7 * PM12 * PM13 * PM14 * PM15

LANDOWSKI, ALICE-WANDA

    DOMENICO SCARLATTI--NOTES TO ACCOMPANY GRAMOPHONE RECORDINGS

            LONDON   1935   7P   BDSNTA

        BR

        PL5 * GI2 * PM9 * PM13

LANG, CRAIG SELLAR

    HARMONY AT THE KEYBOARD

            LONDON   1959   28P   BHATK
                NOVELLO AND COMPANY, LTD.
        LC * UT

        KS4

LANG, EDITH *
WEST, GEORGE
    MUSICAL ACCOMPANIMENT OF MOVING PICTURES..A PRACTICAL MANUAL FOR
    PIANISTS AND ORGANISTS
            BOSTON   1920   64P   BMAOMP
                BOSTON MUSIC COMPANY
        BR * LC * NP

        ILL * IND * INT * MEX * PHO * TAB
        PT4 * PT8 * KS5 * KS7 * KS8 * AP8 * EP6 * GI12 * GI15

LANNING, RUSSELL

    BACH ORNAMENTATION

            ANN ARBOR, MICH.   1952+   61P   BBO
                EDWARDS, J. W.
        IU * LC * NP

        INT
        PL12 * PM3 * AP7

LASSIMONNE, DENISE *
FERGUSON, HOWARD
    MYRA HESS, BY HER FRIENDS

            LONDON   1966   119P   BMHBHF
                HAMILTON, H.
        BR * LC * MI * UA * UM * UT

        DIS * INT * PHO
        NP3

LASSIMONNE, DENISE

    OPENING THE SHUTTERS..A SHORT EXPOSITION ON THE TEACHINGS AND
    PERSONALITY OF TOBIAS MATTHAY

            LONDON   1961   10P   BOTSAS
                CLOWES, W.
        LC

        PHO
        NP4 * AT3

LAST, JOAN

    INTERPRETATION FOR THE PIANO STUDENT

            LONDON   1960   141P   BIFTPS
                OXFORD UNIVERSITY PRESS
        AS * BP * BR * CP * CU * IU * LC * NP * OC * SA * UI * UM * UO * UT
        UW
        IND * INT * MEX
        PL4 * PL5 * PL6 * PL7 * PL12 * PL14 * PT8 * AP4 * AP6 * AP7 * AP8 *
        AP9

LAST, JOAN

    INTRODUCTION TO PEDALLING

            LONDON   1963   16P   BITP
                GALAXY MUSIC CORPORATION
        BP * SA

        INT * MEX
        AP8

LAST, JOAN

    YOUNG PIANIST, THE ..A NEW APPROACH FOR TEACHERS AND STUDENTS--2ND.
    ED.---1954

            LONDON   1972   155P   BYPANA
                OXFORD UNIVERSITY PRESS
        AS * BP * BR * CP * CU * ES * IU * LC * MI * OC * SA * UA * UI * UO
        UT * UU * UW
        ILL * MEX
        PL4 * PL7 * PL10 * PL12 * PT4 * PT6 * PT8 * PT9 * KS3 * AP2 * AP4 *
        AP8

LASZLO, SZIGMOND *
MATEKA, BELA
    FRANZ LISZT..A BIOGRAPHY IN PICTURES---240 PICTORIAL ENTRIES

            BUDAPEST   1968   247P   BFLABI
                CORVINA PRESS
        BR

        ILL * IND * INT * LDR * MSF * PHO
        NP4 * NP9

LATOUR, T.

    LATOUR'S NEW AND IMPROVED METHOD OF INSTRUCTION FOR THE PIANO FORTE

            BOSTON   1830+   54P   BLNAIM
                BRADLEE, C.
        LC * NP

        MEX
        AT4

LAVIGNAC, ALBERT

    MUSIC AND MUSICIANS---1895, IN FRENCH

            NEW YORK   1899   518P   BMAMEN
                HOLT, HENRY, AND COMPANY
        AS * BP * BR * CP * ES * IU * LC * NP * TO * UA * UC * UK * UM * UO
        US * UT * UU * YU
        APP * ILL * IND * INT * MEX * TAB
        NP5 * KI3 * KI6 * KI9 * KI13 * KS4 * KS5

LAWRENCE, FREDERIC LOCKE

    MUSICIANS OF SORROW AND ROMANCE---CHOPIN

            LONDON   1913   144P   BMOSAR
                KELLY, C. H.
        BR * LC * NP

        ILL * INT
        NP4

LAWRENCE, FREDERIC LOCKE

    RATIONALE OF PIANO TECHNIQUE, THE

            CINCINNATI   1906   22P   BROPT
                JENNINGS, THE GEORGE B., COMPANY
        LC * NP * YU

        APP * INT * MEX
        PT3 * PT4 * PT9 * PT10 * AP8

LAWRENCE, LUCILE

    ART OF MODULATING, THE ..FOR HARPISTS, PIANISTS, ORGANISTS

            NEW YORK   1950   61P   BAOMFH
                SCHIRMER, G., INC.
        IU * LC

        INT * MEX
        KS8

LAWRENCE, SIDNEY

GUIDE TO REMEDIAL SIGHT READING FOR THE PIANO STUDENT, A

HEWLITT, N. Y.   1964   112P   BGTRSR
WORKSHOP MUSIC TEACHING PUBLICATIONS, INC.
ES * LC * NP * SA * UI * UM * UT

APP * BIB * CHR * LDR * MEX * PHO
KS3

LEACH, JOHN R.

FUNCTIONAL PIANO FOR THE TEACHER

ENGLEWOOD CLIFFS, N. J.   1968   163P   BFPFTT
PRENTICE-HALL, INC.
ES * IU * UI

APP * CHR * ILL * IND * INT * LDR * MEX
PL4 * PL11 * PL12 * AT4 * AT6 * AT7 * KS4

LEAVEY, LILIAN

JUNIOR SCHOOL PIANIST, THE --ADDRESSED TO THE NEW MUSIC TEACHER

LONDON   1933   53P   BJSPAT
OXFORD UNIVERSITY PRESS
BR

AT11 * EP1 * EP6

LEE, JENNETTE B.

UNFINISHED PORTRAITS..STORIES OF MUSICIANS AND ARTISTS---CHOPIN

NEW YORK   1916   255P   BUPSOM
SCRIBNER'S, CHARLES, SONS
LC * NP

ILL
NP4

LEFRANK, E.

HUMAN HAND, THE ..ITS CONSTRUCTION, MUSCLES, NERVES AND TENDONS IN
REFERENCE TO PIANOFORTE TECHNICS

NEW YORK   1886   23P   BHHICM
GRAND CONSERVATORY PUBLISHING COMPANY
LC * NP

ILL * INT
PT3 * PT4

LEHMER, ISABEL

KEYBOARD HARMONY..A COMPREHENSIVE APPROACH TO MUSICIANSHIP

BELMONT, CAL.   1967   232P   BKHACA
WADSWORTH PUBLISHING COMPANY, INC.
LC * UI * UM * UO

INT * MEX
KS4 * KS8

LEICHTENTRITT, HUGO

COMPLETE PIANOFORTE SONATAS OF BEETHOVEN, THE ---ANALYTICAL NOTES

NEW YORK   1936   16P   BCPSOB
ARTCRAFT LITHOGRAPH PRINTING COMPANY, INC.
LC

ILL * INT * PHO
PM8 * PM14

LEIGHTON, GEORGE A.

HARMONY, ANALYTICAL AND APPLIED

BOSTON   1927   208P   BHAAA
BOSTON MUSIC COMPANY
BR * IU * LC * NP

INT * MEX
KS4 * KS8

LEIMER, KARL *
GIESEKING, WALTER
RHYTHMICS, DYNAMICS, PEDAL, AND OTHER PROBLEMS OF PIANO
PLAYING---1938

NEW YORK   1972   64P   BRDPAO
DOVER PUBLICATIONS, INC.
BP * CP * CU * ES * IU * LC * NP * SA * TO * UI * UM * UO * UT * UW

INT * MEX
PL7 * PL12 * PT2 * PT4 * PT8 * PT9 * PT10 * PT11 * AP4 * AP6 * AP8

LEIMER, KARL *
GIESEKING, WALTER
SHORTEST WAY TO PIANISTIC PERFECTION, THE

PHILADELPHIA   1932   75P   BSWTPP
PRESSER, THEODORE, COMPANY
AS * BP * BR * CP * ES * IU * LC * NP * SA * UC * UI * UM * UO * YU

IND * INT * MEX * PHO
PL7 * PL10 * PT4 * PT7 * PT8 * PT9 * PT10 * PT11 * PM3 * PM8 * PM9
PM11 * AP4

LENHART, A.

ELEMENTS OF MUSIC..A CLEAR AND SYSTEMATIC ARRANGEMENT OF RULES FOR
THE PIANOFORTE..TO WHICH ARE ADDED BURROWE'S GUIDE TO PRACTICE AND
CZERNY'S CELEBRATED LETTERS ON THE ART OF PLAYING THE PIANO---1864
BOSTON   1892   60P   BEOMAC
DITSON, C. H., AND COMPANY
LC * OC

PL1 * PL2 * PL4

LENZ, WILHELM VON

GREAT PIANO VIRTUOSOS OF OUR TIME, FROM PERSONAL ACQUAINTANCE, THE
..LISZT, CHOPIN, TAUSIG, HENSELT---1899

NEW YORK   1973   169P   BGPVOO
DA CAPO PRESS
BP * IU * LC * MI * NP * SA * UA * UI * UM * UT

APP
NP3 * NP4 * NP5

LEONHARDT, GUSTAV M.

ART OF FUGUE, BACH'S LAST HARPSICHORD WORK, THE ..AN ARGUMENT

HAGUE, THE   1952   59P   BAOFBL
NIJHOFF, MARTINUS
BR * IU * NP

APP * BIB * INT * MEX
PM9 * AP3 * AP4

LESLIE, DORIS

POLONAISE---NOVELIZED BIOGRAPHY OF CHOPIN

LONDON   1943   272P   BPNBOC
HUTCHINSON AND COMPANY, LTD.
LC

NP4

LESSMANN, W. J. OTTO

FRANZ LISZT..EINE HULDIGUNG--FRANZ LISZT..A TRIBUTE

NEW YORK   1883   49P   BFLEHF
SCHIRMER, G., INC.
BR * LC * NP

NP4 * PM3 * GI13

LEVANT, OSCAR

MEMOIRS OF AN AMNESIAC

NEW YORK   1965   320P   BMOAA
PUTNAM'S, G. P., SONS
AS * BP * CP * IU * LC * MI * SA * UA * UK * UO * UT

NP6

LEVANT, OSCAR

SMATTERING OF IGNORANCE, A

NEW YORK   1940   267P   BSOI
DOUBLEDAY, DORAN
AS * BP * CP * ES * IU * LC * MI * NP * SA * TO * UA * UC * UI * UK
UM * UO * US * UT * UU * UW
INT
NP4 * NP6

LEVANT, OSCAR

UNIMPORTANCE OF BEING OSCAR, THE

NEW YORK   1968   255P   BUOBO
PUTNAM'S, G. P., SONS
CP * ES * LC * MI * OC * TO * UA * UC * UO

NP6

LEVINE, HENRY

KNOW YOUR SCALES..FOR PIANO STUDENTS OF ALL GRADES

BOSTON   1958   32P   BKYSFP
BOSTON MUSIC COMPANY
IU

CHR * ILL * INT * LDR * MEX
PL7 * PT6

LEVINE, JACK *
IAJIMA, TAKERU
UNDERSTANDING MUSICAL INSTRUMENTS..HOW TO SELECT YOUR
INSTRUMENT--REV. ED.
NEW YORK   1971   124P   BUMIHT
WARNE, F.

KI4 * GI10

LEVINE, JACK

WHAT MUSICAL INSTRUMENT FOR ME

| | NEW YORK | 1959 | 125P | BWMIFM |
| | STERLING PUBLISHING COMPANY |

BR * LC

ILL * IND * LDR * MEX * PHO
KI4 * PL14 * AT11

LEVINSKAYA, MARIA

LEVINSKAYA SYSTEM OF PIANOFORTE TECHNIC AND TONE COLOR, THE

| | LONDON | 1930 | 256P | BLSOPT |
| | DENT, J. M., AND SONS, LTD. |

BR * CU * LC * NP * SA * UA * UT * UW

APP * CHR * ILL * IND * INT * LDR * MEX
NP3 * NP7 * AT4 * PT2 * PT3 * PT4 * PT7 * PT8 * AP5

LEWIS, THOMAS C.

PROTEST AGAINST THE MODERN DEVELOPMENT OF UNMUSICAL TONE, A
--ORGANS, CHURCH BELLS, PIANOFORTES

| | LONDON | 1897 | 45P | BPATMD |
| | CHISWICK PRESS |

BR * NP

KI5 * KI6 * PT8

LE COUPPEY, FELIX

PIANO TEACHING..ADVICE TO PUPILS AND YOUNG TEACHERS---1868 IN
FRENCH

| | PHILADELPHIA | 1888 | 70P | BPTATP |
| | PRESSER, THEODORE, COMPANY |

BP * BR * IU * LC * SA * TO * US

TAB
PL3 * PL7 * PL8 * PL14 * AT3 * AT4 * AT5 * AT9 * AT10 * AT11 * PT1
PT11

LE MASSENA, CLARENCE E.

PADEREWSKI, 'THE MASTER OF MASTERS' ---REPRODUCED FROM TYPEWRITTEN
COPY

| | NEW YORK | 1925 | 42P | BPTMOM |
| | LE MASSENA, CLARENCE E. |

NP

NP4 * GI13

LE MASSENA, CLARENCE E.

SONGS OF SCHUBERT, A GUIDE FOR SINGERS, TEACHERS AND ACCOMPANISTS,
THE ---INTERPRETATIVE SUGGESTIONS BY HANS MERX

| | NEW YORK | 1929 | 184P | BSOSAG |
| | SCHIRMER, G., INC. |

BR * LC * NP

APP * INT * MEX
EP6

LE ROY, PERRY J.

HOW TO PLAY THE PIANO BY EAR..THE QUICK, EASY, SIMPLE WAY

| | NEW YORK | 1941 | 71P | BHTPTP |
| | SUNDIAL PRESS, THE |

LC

ILL * INT
AT4 * KS12

LHEVINNE, JOSEF

BASIC PRINCIPLES IN PIANOFORTE PLAYING---1924

| | NEW YORK | 1972 | 48P | BBPIPP |
| | DOVER PUBLICATIONS, INC. |

CP * CU * ES * LC * OC * US

ILL * CHR * LDR * MEX * PHO
PL4 * PL7 * PL8 * PL10 * PL12 * PL14 * PT1 * PT2 * PT4 * PT8 * AP8

LIEBERMAN, MAURICE

ELEMENTARY KEYBOARD HARMONY

| | NEW YORK | 1964 | 223P | BEKH |
| | NORTON, W. W., AND COMPANY, INC. |

BP * CP * ES * IU * LC * MI * NP * SA * UI * UK * UM

APP * CHR * INT * MEX * TAB
KS4 * KS8

LIEBERMAN, MAURICE

KEYBOARD HARMONY AND IMPROVISATION--2 VOLS.

| | NEW YORK | 1957 | 381P | BKHAIT |
| | NORTON, W. W., AND COMPANY, INC. |

AS * BP * CP * CU * ES * IU * LC * MI * NP * OC * SA * TO * UC * UI
UT * YU
APP * CHR * INT * MEX * CHR
KS4 * KS5 * KS7 * KS8 * AP7

LINDO, ALGERNON H.

APT OF ACCOMPANYING, THE

| | LONDON | 1916 | 109P | BAOA |
| | SCHIRMER, G., LTD. |

BP * BR * CP * CU * ES * IU * LC * MI * NP * SA * UC * UI * UK * UO
US * UW * YU
BIB * MEX * INT
KS3 * KS7 * KS10 * KS11 * EP3 * EP6

LINDO, ALGERNON H.

AURAL TESTS FOR EXAMINATIONS--SPECIALLY WRITTEN FOR TEACHERS AND
STUDENTS PREPARING FOR EXAMINATIONS

| | BOSTON | 1923 | 32P | BATFES |
| | BOSTON MUSIC COMPANY |

BR * LC

INT * MEX
PL4 * PL10 * PL12 * AT10 * KS4

LINDO, ALGERNON H. *
JOHNSTONE, J. ALFRED
INDIVIDUALITY IN PIANO TOUCH

| | LONDON | 1920+ | 55P | BIIPT |
| | REEVES, WILLIAM |

SA

APP * INT
PT8 * AP8

LINDO, ALGERNON H.

PEDALLING IN PIANOFORTE MUSIC

| | NEW YORK | 1922 | 185P | BPIPM |
| | DUTTON, E. P., AND COMPANY |

BR * CU * ES * IU * LC * NP * OC * SA * TO * UK * UM * UT

INT * MEX
KI6 * AP8

LINDO, ALGERNON H.

PIANOFORTE STUDY..HINTS FOR TEACHERS AND STUDENTS

| | LONDON | 1912 | 79P | BPSHFT |
| | AUGENER, LTD. |

BR * ES

PL1 * AT1

LINDO, ALGERNON H.

TREATISE ON MODULATION WITH TYPICAL EXAMPLES FROM WELL-KNOWN WORKS,
A

| | LONDON | 1913 | 75P | BTOMWT |
| | BOSWORTH AND COMPANY |

LC * NP

APP * MEX
KS8

LINGG, ANN M.

MEPHISTO WALTZ, THE STORY OF FRANZ LISZT

| | NEW YORK | 1951 | 307P | BMWTSO |
| | HOLT, HENRY, AND COMPANY |

BR * IU * LC * NP

DIS * IND
NP4 * PM3 * PM9

LINLEY, FRANCIS

NEW ASSISTANT TO THE PIANO-FORTE OR HARPSICHORD, A ...RULES FOR
THOROUGH BASS

| | NEW YORK | 1790+ | 32P | BNATTP |
| | CARR, B. |

LC * NP

AT4 * KS10

LISZT, FRANZ

FREDERIC CHOPIN--A BIOGRAPHICAL AND CRITICAL NOTICE---1852

| | NEW YORK | 1973 | 184P | BFCABA |
| | VIENNA HOUSE |

AS * BR * CP * ES * IU * LC * MI * NP * SA * TO * UA * UI * UK * UM
US * UT * UU * UW
INT
NP3 * NP4 * PM14

LISZT, FRANZ

LETTERS OF FRANZ LISZT--COLLECTED AND EDITED BY LA MARA..TRANSLATED
BY CONSTANCE BACHE--2 VOLS.

| | LONDON | 1894 | 1008P | BLOFLC |
| | GREVEL, H., AND COMPANY |

BP * BR * ES * IU * LC * NP * OC * UA * UK * UM * UO * UT

INT * MEX
NP6

LISZT, FRANZ

    LETTERS OF FRANZ LISZT TO MARIE ZU SAYN-WITTGENSTEIN, THE
    --TRANSLATED AND EDITED BY HOWARD E. HUGO

        CAMBRIDGE, MASS.   1953   376P   BLOFLT
        HARVARD UNIVERSITY PRESS
    AS * BP * BR * ES * IU * LC * NP * OC * TO * UA * UI * UM * UO * US
    UT * UU * UW

    NP6

LISZT, FRANZ

    LIFE OF CHOPIN--TRANSLATED BY JOHN BROADHOUSE

        LONDON   1899+   240P   BLOCTB
        REEVES, WILLIAM
    BP * BR * ES * LC * MI * NP * OC * UC * UT

    ILL * INT
    NP3

LISZT, FRANZ

    LIFE OF CHOPIN--TRANSLATED ONLY IN PART BY MARTHA WALKER COOK

        BOSTON   1863   202P   BLOCTO
        DITSON, OLIVER, COMPANY
    BP * BR * ES * IU * LC * MI * NP * OC * UM

    INT
    NP3 * PM3 * PM14

LITTLE, FRED W.

    LITTLE SYSTEM OF PLAYING THE PIANO BY EAR, THE

        PITTSBURGH   1909   12P   BLSOPT
        STANDARD PRINTING COMPANY
    LC

    ILL
    AT4 * KS12

LITZMANN, BERTHOLD

    CLARA SCHUMANN..AN ARTIST'S LIFE BASED ON MATERIAL FOUND IN DIARIES
    AND LETTERS--2 VOLS.---1913

        NEW YORK   1972   944P   BCSAAL
        VIENNA HOUSE
    BR * IU * LC * NP * UT

    ILL * IND * INT * MEX
    NP3 * NP6 * PM6

LIVERPOOL—PUBLIC LIBRARIES, MUSEUMS AND ART GALLERY

    PIANO, ITS MUSIC AND LITERATURE, THE ..CATALOGUE OF THE MUSIC
    LIBRARY--COMPILED BY K. H. ANDERSON

        LIVERPOOL   1949   102P   BPIMAL
        LIVERPOOL PUBLIC LIBRARIES
    BR * LC * MI

    PM6

LOCKE, MATTHEW

    MELOTHESIA..OR, CERTAIN GENERAL RULES FOR PLAYING UPON A
    CONTINUED-BASS

        LONDON   1673   93P   BMOCGR
        CARR, J.
    BR * IU * LC

    MEX
    PL4 * KS10

LOCKE, ROBINSON

    BLOOMFIELD-ZEISLER--ROBINSON LOCKE SCRAP BOOKS

        TOLEDO, OHIO   1920+   BBZRLS
        LOCKE, ROBINSON
    NP

    PHO
    NP4 * NP6 * NP9

LOCKE, ROBINSON

    BUSONI--ROBINSON LOCKE SCRAP BOOKS

        TOLEDO, OHIO   1920+   BBRLSB
        LOCKE, ROBINSON
    NP

    PHO
    NP4 * NP6 * NP9

LOCKE, ROBINSON

    GABRILOWITSCH--ROBINSON LOCKE SCRAP BOOKS--2 VOLS.

        TOLEDO, OHIO   1920+   BGRLSB
        LOCKE, ROBINSON
    NP

    PHO
    NP4 * NP6 * NP9

LOCKE, ROBINSON

    HOFMANN--ROBINSON LOCKE SCRAP BOOKS

        TOLEDO, OHIO   1920+   BHRLSB
        LOCKE, ROBINSON
    NP

    PHO
    NP4 * NP6 * NP9

LOCKE, ROBINSON

    PADEREWSKI--ROBINSON LOCKE SCRAP BOOKS--2 VOLS.

        TOLEDO, OHIO   1920+   BPRLSB
        LOCKE, ROBINSON
    NP

    PHO
    NP4 * NP6 * NP9

LOCKWOOD, ALBERT

    NOTES ON THE LITERATURE OF THE PIANO--RE-EDITED BY BROTHER, SAMUEL
    LOCKWOOD, FROM NOTES---1940

        NEW YORK   1968   235P   BNOTLO
        DA CAPO PRESS
    BP * BR * CP * CU * ES * IU * LC * MI * NP * OC * TO * UA * UC * UI
    UK * UM * UO * UT * UW * YU

    PM3 * PM6 * PM10 * PM15

LOEHR, JOHANN JOSEPH

    ESSAY ON THE THEORY AND PRACTICE OF TUNING, AN ...PIANOFORTES AND
    ORGANS

        LONDON   1853   64P   BEOTTA
        COCKS, R., AND COMPANY
    LC * NP

    INT
    NP6 * KI8

LOESCHMANN, DAVID

    DESCRIPTION AND USE OF THE PATENT ENHARMONIC PIANOFORTE

        LONDON   1812   21P   BDAUOT
        PHILLIPS, C. U.
    BP * BR

    KI3 * KI5

LOESSER, ARTHUR

    MEN, WOMEN AND PIANOS..A SOCIAL HISTORY

        NEW YORK   1954   654P   BMWAPA
        SIMON AND SCHUSTER, INC.
    AS * BP * BR * CP * CU * ES * IU * LC * MI * NP * OC * SA * TO * UA
    UC * UI * UK * UM * UO * US * UT * UU * UW * YU
    BIB * IND * INT
    NP1 * NP2 * NP5 * KI1 * KI2 * KI3 * KI5 * KI6 * KI9 * KI10 * KI12 *
    GI1 * GI2 * GI3 * GI5 * GI12

LOGGINS, VERNON

    WHERE THE WORD ENDS..THE LIFE OF LOUIS MOREAU GOTTSCHALK

        BATON ROUGE, LA.   1958   273P   BWTWET
        LOUISIANA STATE UNIVERSITY PRESS
    AS * BP * ES * IU * LC * MI * NP * OC * SA * UA * UM * UT

    BIB * ILL * IND * INT * MSF * PHO
    NP4

LOGIER, JOHANN BERNHARD

    AUTHENTIC ACCOUNT OF THE EXAMINATION OF PUPILS, INSTRUCTED IN THE
    NEW SYSTEM OF MUSICAL EDUCATION, BEFORE CERTAIN MEMBERS OF THE
    PHILHARMONIC SOCIETY AND OTHERS, AN
        LONDON   1818   41P   BAAOTE
        HUNTER, R.
    BR * LC * NP

    APP
    NP6 * PL4 * AT4 * AT10 * PT14

LOGIER, JOHANN BERNHARD

    COMPANION TO THE ROYAL PATENT CHIROPLAST, OR HAND-DIRECTOR, A ..A
    NEW INVENTED APPARATUS FOR FACILITATING THE ATTAINMENT OF A PROPER
    EXECUTION ON THE PIANO FORTE
        LONDON   1810+   42P   BCTTRP
        GREENE, J.
    NP

    ILL * INT * MEX
    PL4 * PT14 * AT5

LOGIER, JOHANN BERNHARD

    EXPLANATION AND DESCRIPTION OF THE ROYAL PATENT CHIROPLAST, OR
    HAND-DIRECTOR, AN ..A NEWLY INVENTED APPARATUS FOR FACILITATING
    THE ACQUIREMENT OF A PROPER EXECUTION ON THE PIANO FORTE
        LONDON   1814+   24P   BEADOT
        CLEMENTI AND COMPANY
    LC

    INT * MEX
    PL4 * AT4 * AT5 * PT14

LOGIER, JOHANN BERNHARD

FIRST COMPANION TO THE ROYAL PATENT CHIROPLAST OR HAND-DIRECTOR, THE --9TH. ED.

      LONDON   1818+   38P   BFCTTR
         GREEN, I.
BP * NP * YU

GLO * INT * MEX
PL4 * PL12 * AT4 * PT6

LOGIER, JOHANN BERNHARD

LOGIER'S SYSTEM OF THE SCIENCE OF MUSIC, HARMONY, AND PRACTICAL COMPOSITION..INCIDENTALLY COMPRISING THOROUGH BASS, WITH CONSIDERABLE ADDITIONS, ADAPTED FOR THE USE OF SCHOOLS
      LONDON   1843+   238P   BLSOTS
         BOOSEY, T., AND COMPANY
BR * LC * NP

MEX
AT4 * KS4 * KS10

LOGIER, JOHANN BERNHARD

LOGIER'S THEORETICAL AND PRACTICAL STUDY FOR THE PIANO FORTE, COMPRISING A SERIES OF COMPOSITIONS SELECTED FROM THE MOST CLASSICAL WORKS, ANCIENT AND MODERN--14 PTS. IN 1 VOL.
      LONDON   1832+   BLTAPS
         GREEN, J.
NP

MEX
AT4

LOGIER, JOHANN BERNHARD

REFUTATION OF THE FALLACIES AND MISREPRESENTATIONS CONTAINED IN A PAMPHLET ENTITLED 'AN EXPOSITION OF THE NEW SYSTEM OF MUSICAL EDUCATION'
      LONDON   1818   55P   BROTFA
         HUNTER, R.
BR * LC * NP

INT * MEX
NP6 * PL4 * AT4 * PT14

LOGIER, JOHANN BERNHARD

SEQUEL TO THE FIRST COMPANION TO THE CHIROPLAST

      CAMBRIDGE   1833+   27P   BSTTFC
         MUNROE, H. P.
BP * NP * YU

MEX
AT4 * PT9 * PT10 * KS4

LOGIER, JOHANN BERNHARD

SHORT ACCOUNT OF THE PROGRESS OF J. B. LOGIER'S SYSTEM OF MUSICAL EDUCATION IN BERLIN, A

      LONDON   1824   40P   BSAOTP
         HUNTER, R.
BR * LC

INT
AT4 * PT14

LOGIER, JOHANN BERNHARD

SYLLABUS OF THE SECOND EXAMINATION OF MR. LOGIER'S PUPILS, ON HIS NEW SYSTEM OF MUSICAL EDUCATION, A ...APPENDIX..DESCRIPTION OF THE ROYAL CHIROPLAST...ITS USE...IN TEACHING THE PIANO FORTE
      DUBLIN   1816   28P   BSOTSE
         CARRICK, J.
LC

INT * MEX
PL4 * PL7 * AT4 * AT9 * PT14 * AP9

LOGIER, JOHANN BERNHARD

SYSTEM OF THE SCIENCE OF MUSIC AND PRACTICAL COMPOSITION..INCIDENTALLY COMPRISING WHAT IS USUALLY UNDERSTOOD BY THE TERM THOROUGH BASS
      LONDON   1827   323P   BSOTSO
         GREEN, J.
BR * LC

ILL * INT
KS10

LOMAS, LULU GRAHAM

FIRST TEN PIANO LESSONS, LAID OUT FOR YOUNG TEACHERS, WITH CONSTRUCTIVE THINKING AND PSYCHOLOGICAL NOTES IN MASTER MUSICIAN BUILDING, THE
      OAK PARK, ILL.   1915   47P   BFTPLL
         LOMAS, LULU G.
LC

INT
AT3 * AT4 * AT5 * AT11 * PT4 * PT9 * KS3

LONDON--A COMMITTEE OF PROFESSORS

EXPOSITION OF THE MUSICAL SYSTEM OF MR. LOGIER..WITH STRICTURES ON HIS CHIROPLAST, AN

      LONDON   1818   83P   BEOTMS
         BUDD AND CALKIN
BR * LC * NP * UC

APP * INT * MEX
NP6 * NP7 * PL4 * AT4 * AT7 * PT14 * KS4

LONG, ESMOND R.--PATHOLOGIST

HISTORY OF THE THERAPY OF TUBERCULOSIS, AND THE CASE OF FREDERIC CHOPIN, A

      LAWRENCE, KAN.   1956   71P   BHOTTO
         UNIVERSITY OF KANSAS PRESS
BR * LC * NP

BIB * IND * INT
NP4 * GI12 * GI15

LONG, MARGUERITE

AT THE PIANO WITH DEBUSSY---1960, IN FRENCH

      LONDON   1972   112P   BATPWD
         DENT, J. M., AND SONS, LTD.
IU * LC

IND * MEX * PHO
PM3 * PM9

LONG, NOEL

HARMONY AND STYLE--3 VOLS.

      LONDON   1968   246P   BHASTV
         FABER AND FABER
BP * IU * LC

INT * MEX
KS8

LONGSTREET, H. P.

PRACTICAL FINGER CONTROL--10TH. ED.

      NEW YORK   1944   BPFCTE
         UNITED STATES SCHOOL OF MUSIC
LC

PT6 * PT10

LOVELOCK, WILLIAM

COMMON SENSE IN MUSIC TEACHING

      LONDON   1965   124P   BCSIMT
         BELL, G.
LC

AT1 * AT3

LOVELOCK, WILLIAM

ELEMENTARY ACCOMPANIMENT WRITING--CHIEFLY MUSIC, FOR EXAM CANDIDATE EXPECTED TO PROVIDE A PIANO ACCOMPANIMENT

      LONDON   1971   152P   BEAWCM
         BELL AND SONS
LC

INT * MEX
KS11

LOVELOCK, WILLIAM

FORMAL ANALYSIS OF THE SENIOR AND ADVANCED SENIOR PIANOFORTE PIECES OF TRINITY COLLEGE OF MUSIC

      LONDON   1937   19P   BFAOTS
         HAMMOND, A., AND COMPANY
BR

PM8

LOVELOCK, WILLIAM

ORNAMENTS AND ABBREVIATIONS FOR EXAMINATION CANDIDATES

      LONDON   1933   14P   BOAAFE
         HAMMOND, A., AND COMPANY

AT10 * AP7

LOVELOCK, WILLIAM

TESTS IN SIGHT READING, FOR PIANO..FROM FIRST GRADE TO DIPLOMA--3 VOLS.

      MELBOURNE   1962   108P   BTISRF
         ALLAN'S MUSIC, PTY. LTD.
LC

MEX
AT10 * KS3

LOVELOCK, WILLIAM

TRANSPOSITION AT THE KEYBOARD..PIANO..26 PAGES OF GRADED EXERCISES

      MELBOURNE   1967+   32P   BTATKP
         ALLAN'S MUSIC, PTY. LTD.
LC

KS7

LOWE, CLAUDE EDGERTON

ART OF PIANOFORTE PRACTICING, THE

          LONDON   1927   61P   BAOPP
            NOVELLO AND COMPANY, LTD.
BR * ES * OC * UC

PL7

LOWE, CLAUDE EDGERTON

BEETHOVEN'S PIANOFORTE SONATAS..HINTS ON THEIR RENDERING, FORM...

          LONDON   1921   205P   BBPSHO
            NOVELLO AND COMPANY, LTD.
BP * BR * ES * NP * YU

PM8 * PM9 * PM14

LOWE, CLAUDE EDGERTON

CANDIDATES GUIDE TO QUESTIONS AND ANSWERS AT PRACTICAL LOCAL
EXAMINATIONS, THE --IN PIANOFORTE PLAYING
          LONDON   1932   24P   BCGTQA
            HAMMOND, A., AND COMPANY
BR

AT10

LOWE, CLAUDE EDGERTON

FORM IN PIANOFORTE MUSIC--FOR THEORETICAL AND PRACTICAL EXAMS

          LONDON   1932   32P   BFIPMF
            HAMMOND, A., AND COMPANY
BP

PM14

LOWE, CLAUDE EDGERTON

PIANOFORTE TEACHER'S VADE MECUM, THE ..A CYCLOPEDIA FOR THE
PREPARATION OF CANDIDATES FOR ALL PIANOFORTE EXAMINATIONS
          LONDON   1937   23P   BPTVMA
            HAMMOND, A., AND COMPANY
BR

AT1 * AT2 * GI9

LOWE, CLAUDE EDGERTON

SUGGESTIONS FOR THE APPRECIATION AND INTERPRETATION OF PIANOFORTE
MUSIC
          LONDON   1915   BSFTAA
            WEEKES AND COMPANY
BR

PL1 * AP4 * GI2

LOWE, CLAUDE EDGERTON

VIVA VOCE..250 QUESTIONS AND ANSWERS FOR PIANOFORTE DIPLOMA
CANDIDATES
          LONDON   1931   24P   BVVTHF
            HAMMOND, A., AND COMPANY
BR

PL1 * AP1 * GI2

LOWE, CLAUDE EDGERTON

WORD-PHRASES TO BACH'S 48 FUGUES, WITH HINTS ON THE RENDERINGS OF
THE PRELUDES AND FUGUES
          LONDON   1924   47P   BWPTBF
            WEEKES, A., AND COMPANY
BP * BR

PM2 * PM9 * PM14

LOWERY, HARRY

GUIDE TO MUSICAL ACOUSTICS, A ---1956

          NEW YORK   1966   94P   BGTMAN
            DOVER PUBLICATIONS, INC.
AS * BP * BR * ES * IU * LC * MI * NP * OC * TO * UI * UM

BIB * CHR * INT * LDR * MEX * TAB
KI7 * AT10

LOWRY, MARGARET

KEYBOARD APPROACH TO HARMONY

          PHILADELPHIA   1949+   87P   BKATH
            PRESSER, THEODORE, COMPANY
IU * NP * UI

INT * MEX
KS4

LOYNES, W. H.

HOW TO PLAY THE PIANO IN ONE HOUR WITHOUT A TEACHER

          LONDON   1922   24P   BHTPTP
            DALLAS, J. E., AND SONS, LTD.
BR * LC

MEX
PL11 * AT4

LUBIN, ERNEST

PIANISTS CHORD MANUAL, THE

          NEW YORK   1972   48P   BPCM
            AMSCO MUSIC PUBLISHING COMPANY
LC

KS4

LUBIN, ERNEST

PIANO DUET, THE ...A GUIDE FOR PIANISTS

          NEW YORK   1970   221P   BPDAGF
            GROSSMAN PUBLISHERS
LC * SA

APP * ILL * IND * INT * MEX * PHO
PM3 * PM6 * PM8 * PM9 * PM14 * EP5

LUBIT, JULIA

PIANOFORTE THEORY COURSE FOR BEGINNERS' PIANO CLASS

            LUBIT, JULIA   1956   72P   BPTCFB
LC

AT7 * KS4

LUCKE, KATHARINE E.

PRACTICAL DRILL IN KEYBOARD HARMONY--2 VOLS., 1932-1940

          BALTIMORE   1932   48P   BPDIKH
            KRANZ MUSIC COMPANY
LC

CHR * INT * MEX
KS4

LUDDEN, WILLIAM

THOROUGH BASS SCHOOL, THE ..AN EASY AND PROGRESSIVE COURSE FOR
ACQUIRING A PRACTICAL KNOWLEDGE OF RUDIMENTAL HARMONY
          CINCINNATI   1896   112P   BTBSAE
            CHURCH, THE JOHN, COMPANY
LC

IND * INT * MEX
PL4 * KS10 * AP7

LUND, VICTOR E.

EVALUATION OF ELECTRONIC SELF-INSTRUCTION ON PIANO KEYBOARD, THE

          MONMOUTH, ORE.   1966   47P   BEOESI
            OREGON STATE SYSTEM OF HIGHER EDUCATION
AS * UA

KI11 * PL11

LYKE, JAMES

SELECTED LIST OF PIANO TEACHING MATERIALS PUBLISHED SINCE 1960, A
--PREPARED FOR THE 1963 PIANO CLINIC, UNIVERSITY OF ILLINOIS, OCT.
17-18
          URBANA, ILL.   1963   10P   BSLOPT
            UNIVERSITY OF ILLINOIS
UI

PM6

LYLE, WATSON

CAMILLE SAINT-SAENS, HIS LIFE AND ART---DISCUSSES CONCERTI AND
VARIAZONI
          NEW YORK   1923   210P   BCSHLA
            DUTTON, E. P., AND COMPANY
BR * IU * LC * NP

APP * BIB * INT * MEX
NP3 * PM3 * PM6 * PM9 * PM14

LYLE, WATSON

RACHMANINOFF, A BIOGRAPHY

          LONDON   1939   247P   BRAB
            REEVES, WILLIAM
BP * BR * IU * LC * NP * OC * TO * UT

IND * INT * PHO
NP3

LYONS, SISTER MARIE STEPHEN

    REAWAKENING OF INTEREST IN THE HARPSICHORD IN THE 20TH. CENTURY,
THE ---PUBLISHED THESIS

        NEW HAVEN, CONN.   1966   181P   BROIIT
            SISTERS OF MERCY CONVENT
    IU * YU

    KI3 * KI9 * KI14

MACDOWELL, MARIAN GRISWOLD

    RANDOM NOTES ON EDWARD MACDOWELL AND HIS MUSIC

        BOSTON   1950   36P   BRNOEM
            SCHMIDT, A. P., COMPANY
    BP * BR * ES * IU * LC * MI * NP * UI * UT

    INT * PHO
    NP6

MACEWAN, DESIREE

    FIRST TWO YEARS OF PIANOFORTE STUDY, THE

        LONDON   1930   46P   BFTYOP
            OXFORD UNIVERSITY PRESS
    BR * CU

    APP * IND * MEX
    PL4 * PL10 * PL12 * AT4 * KS3

MACEWEN, JOHN B.

    INTRODUCTION TO AN UNPUBLISHED EDITION OF THE PIANOFORTE SONATAS OF
BEETHOVEN, AN

        LONDON   1932   58P   BITAUE
            OXFORD UNIVERSITY PRESS
    BR * LC * NP

    INT * MEX
    PL4 * PL12

MACK, GLEN

    ADVENTURES IN IMPROVISATION AT THE KEYBOARD

        EVANSTON, ILL.   1970   54P   BAIIAT
            SUMMY-BIRCHARD COMPANY
    LC

    GLO * INT * MEX
    KS5

MACKENZIE, SIR ALEXANDER

    LISZT--'THE MAYFAIR BIOGRAPHIES', NO. 3

        LONDON   1922+   28P   BLTMBN
            MURDOCH, WILLIAM, COMPANY
    BR * NP

    ILL * MSF * PHO
    NP4 * PM3

MACKENZIE, SIR ALEXANDER

    LISZT--MASTERPIECES OF MUSIC

        NEW YORK   1913   63P   BLMOM
            STOKES, FREDERICK A., COMPANY
    BR * LC * NP

    ILL * LDR * MSF * PHO
    NP4 * PM3

MACKENZIE, SIR ALEXANDER

    MUSICIAN'S NARRATIVE, A ---CLARA SCHUMANN, VON BUELOW AND LISZT

        LONDON   1927   269P   BMNCSV
            CASSELL AND COMPANY, LTD.
    BR * LC * NP

    ILL * IND * INT
    NP4 * NP6 * KI8

MACKINNON, LILIAS

    MUSICAL SECRETS ON THE TECHNIQUE OF PIANO PLAYING

        LONDON   1946   95P   BMSOTT
            OXFORD UNIVERSITY PRESS
    BP * BR * IU * LC * NP * US

    PT1 * PT2

MACKINNON, LILIAS

    MUSIC BY HEART

        CAMBRIDGE   1938   141P   BMBH
            UNIVERSITY PRESS, THE
    BR * CP * CU * ES * IU * LC * NP * OC * TO * UC * UI * UO * UT * YU

    BIB
    PL8

MACKLIN, CHARLES B.

    ELEMENTARY PIANO PEDAGOGY, A GUIDE BOOK FOR YOUNG PIANO TEACHERS

        PHILADELPHIA   1925   165P   BEPPAG
            PRESSER, THEODORE, COMPANY
    UT

    AT1 * AT2

MACLEAN, CHARLES D.

    PRINCIPLES OF PIANOFORTE PRACTICE, THE

                        1880+   77P   BPOPP
    LC
    APP
    PL5 * PL7 * PL8 * AT4 * AT5 * PT5 * PT6 * PT9 * PT10 * KS3 * EP1

MACPHERSON, D.

    CATECHISM OF MUSIC, CHIEFLY ADAPTED FOR LEARNERS ON THE PIANOFORTE,
IN WHICH THE SIMPLE RUDIMENTS OF THE SCIENCE AND THE ART OF
PLAYING IN TIME ARE CLEARLY EXPLAINED
        EDINBURGH   1800+   124P   BCOMCA
            SUTHERLAND, J.
    MI

    PL4 * PL12

MACPHERSON, STEWART

    COMMENTARY ON BKS. 1 AND 2 OF THE FORTY-EIGHT PRELUDES AND FUGUES
OF JOHANN SEBASTIAN BACH, 1934-1937

        LONDON   1934   186P   BCOTFP
            NOVELLO AND COMPANY, LTD.
    BP * BR * CP * CU * ES * IU * LC * MI * NP * OC * SA * TO * UI

    MEX
    PM8 * PM9 * PM15

MACPHERSON, STEWART

    STUDIES IN PHRASING AND FORM

        LONDON   1932   167P   BSIPAF
            WILLIAMS, JOSEPH, LTD.
    BP * BR * CP * CU * ES * LC * OC * UA * UC * UI * UK * UM * US * UT

    INT * MEX * TAB
    PL5 * AP6

MACQUOID, PERCY *
EDWARDS, RALPH
    DICTIONARY OF ENGLISH FURNITURE, THE --VOL. 3---16 ILLUSTRATIONS OF
OLD KEYBOARD INSTRUMENTS

        NEW YORK   1927   385P   BDOEFV
            SCRIBNER'S, CHARLES, SONS
    BR * IU * LC

    ILL * IND * INT * PHO * TAB
    KI3 * KI12 * KI13 * KI14 * KI15 * GI15

MAHONY, CORNELIUS

    SELF-INSTRUCTOR FOR THE PIANOFORTE, CONTAINING C. MAHONY'S NEW
SYSTEM OF MUSICAL NOTATION FOR THE USE OF THE BLIND

        PHILADELPHIA   1853   45P   BSIFTP
            INSTITUTION FOR THE BLIND
    LC * NP

    PL11 * AT4

MAIER, GUY

    PIANO TEACHER'S COMPANION, THE

        NEW YORK   1963   110P   BPTC
            MILLS MUSIC, INC.
    BP * BR * CP * CU * ES * IU * LC * MI * OC * SA * UA * UI * UK * UM
    UO * US * UT * YU
    CHR * LDR * MEX * PHO
    PL7 * PL12 * AT2 * AT3 * AT5 * AT9 * PT3 * PT4 * PT6 * PT7 * PT8 *
    PT9 * PT10 * KS3 * PM11 * AP4 * AP8 * AP9 * EP5

MAIER, GUY *
CORZILIUS, HELENE
    PLAYING THE PIANO..A COURSE OF ROTE TRAINING FOR BEGINNERS--CLASS
OR PRIVATE INSTRUCTION..STUDENT'S BOOK

        NEW YORK   1929   56P   BPTPAC
            FISCHER, J., AND BRO.
    NP * UI

    INT * MEX
    PL4 * PL7 * PL12 * AT5 * AT7 * KS4

MAIER, GUY *
CORZILIUS, HELENE
    PLAYING THE PIANO--TEACHER'S MANUAL

        NEW YORK   1929   95P   BPTPTM
            FISCHER, J., AND BRO.
    BP * NP * US

    BIB * INT * MEX
    PL4 * PL7 * PL12 * AT3 * AT7 * AT13 * PT8 * KS4

MAINE, BASIL

    CHOPIN--'GREAT LIVES' SERIES

        NEW YORK   1933   128P   BCGLS
          WYN, A. A., INC.
    BR * IU * LC * NP

    APP * BIB * LDR
    NP4 * PM3

MAITLAND, GEORGE L.

    HOW TO CHANGE PITCH OF PIANOS, IN FOUR LESSONS

        PHILADELPHIA   1915   29P   BHTCPO
          MAITLAND, G. L.
    LC

    INT
    KI8

MANHIRE, WILSON

    CANDIDATE'S SCALE AND ARPEGGIO TESTS FOR THE PIANOFORTE, ETC., THE

        LONDON   1923   21P   BCSAAT
          REEVES, WILLIAM
    BR

    AT10 * PT9

MANHIRE, WILSON

    EXAMINATION CANDIDATE'S GUIDE TO SCALE AND ARPEGGIO PLAYING, ETC.,
    THE
        LONDON   1923   66P   BECGTS
          REEVES, WILLIAM
    BR

    MEX
    PT9 * GI9

MANHIRE, WILSON

    GUIDE TO THE A.R.C.M. AND OTHER EXAMINATIONS IN PIANOFORTE-TEACHING

        LONDON   1909   72P   BGTTAR
          LARWAY, J. H.
    BR

    MEX
    AT11 * GI9

MANHIRE, WILSON

    HINTS TO CANDIDATES FOR THE L.R.A.M. ASSOCIATED BOARD AND OTHER
    EXAMINATIONS IN PIANOFORTE PLAYING..BEING NOTES ON PREPARATION FOR
    BOTH BRANCHES OF THE EXAMINATIONS
        LONDON   1908   63P   BHTCFT
          LARWAY, J. H.
    BR

    MEX
    GI9

MANHIRE, WILSON

    MODEL ANSWERS TO QUESTIONS ON 'TOUCH' FOR CANDIDATES PREPARING FOR
    EXAMINATIONS IN PIANOFORTE PLAYING...FOUNDED ON THE TEACHING AND
    WRITINGS OF TOBIAS MATTHAY
        LONDON   1908   29P   BMATQO
          LARWAY, J. H.
    BR

    AT4 * PT8 * GI2

MANITOBA--DEPARTMENT OF EDUCATION

    PLAN FOR CREDITING OUTSIDE STUDY IN MUSIC UNDER PRIVATE INSTRUCTION
    FOR STUDENTS OF PIANO AND VIOLIN

        WINNIPEG   1925   31P   BPFCOS
          MANITOBA DEPARTMENT OF EDUCATION
    TO

    GI8

MANSFELDT, HUGO L.

    TECHNIC..A SYSTEM OF THE MOST NECESSARY DAILY EXERCISES TO PRODUCE
    A PERFECT PIANO TECHNIC IN THE SHORTEST POSSIBLE TIME--3
    VOLS.---1886
        NEW YORK   1906   116P   BTASOT
          FEIST, L.
    LC * NP

    INT
    PL12 * PT9 * PT10

MANUEL, ROLAND

    FREDERIC CHOPIN--'GREAT ANNIVERSARIES' SERIES

        PARIS   1949   19P   BFCGAS
          U.N.E.S.C.O.--DISTR. BY COLUMBIA UNIVERSITY PRESS
    BR * LC * NP

    BIB
    NP4

MARCUSE, SIBYL

    MUSICAL INSTRUMENTS..A COMPREHENSIVE DICTIONARY

        GARDEN CITY, N. Y.   1964   608P   BMIACD
          DOUBLEDAY AND COMPANY
    BR * IU * LC * NP

    INT * PHO
    KI13 * KI15

MARIAL, R.

    METHODS APPLICABLE TO GROUP TEACHING OR PRIVATE PIANO INSTRUCTION

        CHICAGO   1929   44P   BMATGT
          SUMMY, CLAYTON F., COMPANY
    BR * ES * LC * US

    INT * MEX
    PL5 * AT4 * AT7 * PT9 * KS3 * KS4

MARKS, ADOLF B.

    INTRODUCTION TO THE INTERPRETATION OF BEETHOVEN'S PIANO-FORTE WORKS

        CHICAGO   1914+   BITTIO
          SUMMY, CLAYTON F., COMPANY

    KI3 * PL12 * PT1 * PT6 * PM9 * AP4

MARKS, F. HELENA

    QUESTIONS ON MOZART'S PIANO SONATAS, DESIGNED AS A COMPANION VOLUME
    TO THE AUTHOR'S 'THE SONATA, ITS FORM AND MEANING'
        LONDON   1929   60P   BQOMPS
          REEVES, WILLIAM
    BR * ES

    PM3 * PM8 * PM9 * PM13

MARKS, F. HELENA

    SONATA, ITS FORM AND MEANING AS EXEMPLIFIED IN THE PIANO SONATAS BY
    MOZART, THE ..A DESCRIPTIVE ANALYSIS
        LONDON   1921   167P   BSIFAM
          REEVES, WILLIAM
    BP * BR * ES * IU * LC * NP * OC * TO * UI * UM * UW * YU

    PM3 * PM8 * PM9 * PM13

MARSDEN AND COMPANY

    HOW TO EXTEMPORIZE PIANO ACCOMPANIMENTS...RAPID AND SIMPLE METHOD
    OF ACQUIRING THE PROFICIENCY WITHOUT PREVIOUS KNOWLEDGE OF MUSIC
        NEW YORK   1886   8P   BHTEPA
          MARSDEN AND COMPANY
    LC

    KS5 * EP6

MARSH, JOHN

    RUDIMENTS OF THOROUGH BASS, THE

        LONDON   1810+   28P   BROTB
          GOULDING, D'ALMAINE, POTTER AND COMPANY
    LC

    MEX
    KS10

MARTENS, FREDERICK HERMAN

    PADEREWSKI--'LITTLE BIOGRAPHIES', VOL. 2

        NEW YORK   1922   28P   BPLBVT
          BREITKOPF AND HAERTEL
    NP * UK

    INT * PHO
    NP4 * PM3 * GI13

MARTENS, FREDERICK HERMAN

    RACHMANINOFF--'LITTLE BIOGRAPHIES', VOL. 2

        NEW YORK   1922   25P   BRLBVT
          BREITKOPF AND HAERTEL
    LC * OC

    NP4

MARTIN, H. T.

    EVERY WOMAN HER OWN PIANO TUNER..OR, HINTS AND AIDS TO PIANO TUNING

        BEAVER FALLS, PA.   1881   48P   BEWHOP
          MARTIN, H. T.
    LC

    KI8

MARTIN, THOMAS CARLAW

FRANZ LISZT..A SKETCH OF HIS LIFE AND PERSONALITY

LONDON   1886   104P   BFLASO
REEVES, WILLIAM
BR * NP

NP4

MARX, ADOLF BERNHARD

INTRODUCTION TO THE INTERPRETATION OF BEETHOVEN'S PIANO
WORKS---1863, IN GERMAN
CHICAGO   1895   151P   BITTIO
SUMMY, CLAYTON F., COMPANY
CP * CU * ES * LC * NP * UA * UI * UT * UW

INT * MEX
KI3 * PL12 * AT4 * PT6 * PM3 * PM8 * PM9 * PM14

MASON, DANIEL GREGORY

NEGLECTED SENSE IN PIANO PLAYING, A

NEW YORK   1912   53P   BNSIPP
SCHIRMER, G., INC.
BP * BR * CU * ES * LC * NP * UM * US * UT * YU

PL2 * PT2

MASON, DANIEL GREGORY

ROMANTIC COMPOSERS, THE ---CHOPIN AND LISZT

NEW YORK   1906   353P   BRCCAL
MACMILLAN COMPANY, THE
BR * IU * LC * NP

ILL * INT * MEX * PHO
NP4 * PM3

MASON, ELLA H. *
BURROWS, RAYMOND
ANSWERS TO CRITICISMS OF PIANO CLASS INSTRUCTION

NEW YORK   1930+   26P   BATCOP
NATIONAL BUREAU FOR THE ADVANCEMENT OF MUSIC
SA * UO * UW

INT
AT7

MASON, HENRY LOWELL

HOW HAS THE PIANOFORTE AS AN INSTRUMENT DEVELOPED SINCE
1876--REPRINT..M.T.N.A. PROCEEDINGS, 1928
HARTFORD, CONN.   1928   15P   BHHTPA
MUSIC TEACHERS' NATIONAL ASSOCIATION
BP * IU * LC * YU

KI3

MASON, HENRY LOWELL

MODERN ARTISTIC PIANOFORTE, THE ..ITS CONSTRUCTION

CAMBRIDGEPORT, MASS.   1903+   9P   BMAPIC
MASON, HENRY LOWELL
BP * BR * LC * NP

ILL * PHO
KI5

MASON, MARY B.

BOY MUSIC, A FIRST PIANO METHOD FOR BOYS BETWEEN 8 AND 16

PHILADELPHIA   1944   50P   BBMAFP
PRESSER, THEODORE, COMPANY
LC

ILL * INT * MEX
PL4 * AT4 * AT5

MASON, WILLIAM G.

ACCENTUAL TREATMENT OF EXERCISES AS APPLIED TO PIANOFORTE
PRACTICE--ESSAY FOR 9TH. ANNUAL M.T.N.A. CONVENTION, IN NEW YORK
NEW YORK   1885   14P   BATOEA
SCHUBERTH, E., AND COMPANY
LC * NP

PL7 * PT10

MASON, WILLIAM G.

MEMORIES OF A MUSICAL LIFE

NEW YORK   1901   306P   BMOAML
CENTURY COMPANY, THE
BP * CP * ES * IU * LC * MI * NP * OC * TO * UA * UK * UO * UT

APP * ILL * IND * MEX * MSF * PHO
NP3 * NP4 * NP5 * NP6

MASON, WILLIAM G. *
HOADLY, E. S.
METHOD FOR THE PIANO-FORTE, A

NEW YORK   1867   238P   BMFTP
MASON BROTHERS
NP

MEX
PL4 * AT4

MASON, WILLIAM G.

PADEREWSKI..A CRITICAL STUDY--'CENTURY LIBRARY OF MUSIC', VOL. 18

NEW YORK   1902   8P   BPACST
CENTURY COMPANY, THE
NP

ILL * PHO
NP4

MASON, WILLIAM G. *
MATHEWS, WILLIAM S. B.
PRIMER OF MUSIC, A ..BEING THE FIRST STEPS IN MUSICIANSHIP..FOR
STUDENTS OF THE PIANOFORTE
NEW YORK   1894   192P   BPOMBT
CHURCH, THE JOHN, COMPANY
LC * NP

GLO * IND * INT * MEX
PL4 * PL7 * PL12 * AT3 * AT4 * PT1 * PT6 * PT8 * PT9 * KS4 * KS7 *
AP8

MASON, WILLIAM G. *
HOADLY, E. S.
SYSTEM FOR BEGINNERS IN THE ART OF PLAYING UPON THE PIANOFORTE, A

BOSTON   1871   165P   BSFBIT
DITSON, OLIVER, AND COMPANY
LC * NP

ILL * MEX
PL4 * PL12 * PL15 * PT4 * PT6 * PT8 * PT9 * PT10

MASON, WILLIAM G.

SYSTEM OF TECHNICAL EXERCISES FOR THE PIANO-FORTE, A

BOSTON   1878   117P   BSOTEF
DITSON, OLIVER, AND COMPANY
LC * NP

ILL * INT * MEX * TA8
PL3 * PL7 * PL12 * PT3 * PT8 * PT9 * PT10 * AP8

MASON, WILLIAM G.

TOUCH, AS APPLIED TO PIANOFORTE PRACTICE--ESSAY FOR THE 10TH.
ANNUAL M.T.N.A. CONVENTION, IN BOSTON
ORANGE, N. J.   1886   18P   BTAATP
ORANGE CHRONICLE PRESS
LC * NP

PL7 * PT8

MASON, WILLIAM G.

TOUCH AND TECHNIC..FOR ARTISTIC PIANO PLAYING, OP. 44--4 VOLS. IN 1

PHILADELPHIA   1889   BTATFA
PRESSER, THEODORE, COMPANY
AS * LC * NP * UI

INT
PL4 * PL7 * PL12 * PT8 * AP6 * AP7

MASON AND HAMLIN ORGAN AND PIANO COMPANY

CATALOGUE OF PIANOFORTES EMBODYING LATEST IMPROVEMENTS

NEW YORK   1891   32P   BCOPEL
MASON AND HAMLIN ORGAN AND PIANO COMPANY
NP

KI12 * KI15

MATHEWS, WILLIAM S. B.

GREAT IN MUSIC, THE ..A SYSTEMATIC COURSE OF STUDY IN THE MUSIC OF
CLASSICAL AND MODERN COMPOSERS--ESSAYS--VOL. 2---INCLUDES SEVERAL
PIANISTS
CHICAGO   1902   424P   BGIMAS
MUSIC MAGAZINE PUBLISHING COMPANY
LC * NP

INT * PHO
NP4 * NP6 * PM3 * GI6

MATHEWS, WILLIAM S. B.

MASON'S PRINCIPLES OF VELOCITY AND ARM TOUCHES

PHILADELPHIA   1892+   BMPOVA
PRESSER, THEODORE, COMPANY

PL12 * PT8

MATHEWS, WILLIAM S. B.

SCHOOL OF THE PIANO PEDAL

       BOSTON   1906   83P   BSOTPP
          DITSON, OLIVER, COMPANY
LC

INT * MEX
PL6 * AP8

MATHEWS, WILLIAM S. B.

STUDIES IN PHRASING, MEMORIZING AND INTERPRETATION

       PHILADELPHIA   1882   30P   BSIPMA
          PRESSER, THEODORE, COMPANY
LC

MEX
PL8 * AP4 * AP6

MATHEWS, WILLIAM S. B.

STUDIES IN PHRASING SELECTED FROM THE WORKS OF THE BEST CLASSIC AND
ROMANTIC MASTERS--2 VOLS. IN 1

       PHILADELPHIA   1889   96P   BSIPSF
          PRESSER, THEODORE, COMPANY
LC * NP

INT * MEX
PL8 * AP4 * AP6

MATHEWS, WILLIAM S. B.

TEACHER'S MANUAL OF MASON'S PIANOFORTE TECHNICS

       CHICAGO   1901   118P   BTMOMP
          MUSICAL MAGAZINE PUBLISHING COMPANY
LC * NP

APP * INT * MEX
PL7 * AT4 * PT4 * PT7 * PT8 * PT9 * PT10 * AP8

MATHIS, WILLIAM STEPHAN

PIANIST AND CHURCH MUSIC, THE

       NEW YORK   1962   109P   BPACM
          ABINGTON PRESS
CP * ES * IU * LC * NP * OC * UM

APP * BIB * IND * INT * MEX
EP2 * EP6 * GI1 * GI13

MATTHAY, JESSIE H.

LIFE AND WORKS OF TOBIAS MATTHAY, THE

       LONDON   1945   114P   BLAWOT
          BOOSEY AND HAWKES
BP * BR * CP * ES * IU * LC * NP * SA * UI

APP * BIB * IND * PHO
NP3 * NP4

MATTHAY, TOBIAS A.

ACT OF MUSICAL CONCENTRATION, THE

       LONDON   1934   35P   BAOMC
          OXFORD UNIVERSITY PRESS
BR * CU * ES * LC * NP

APP * INT * MEX
PL3 * PL5 * PL6

MATTHAY, TOBIAS A.

ACT OF TOUCH IN ALL ITS DIVERSITY, THE ..AN ANALYSIS AND SYNTHESIS
OF PIANOFORTE TONE PRODUCTION

       LONDON   1903   328P   BAOTIA
          BOSWORTH AND COMPANY, LTD.
AS * BP * BR * CP * CU * ES * IU * LC * MI * NP * OC * SA * TO * UA
UI * UK * UM * US * UT * UW * YU
APP * CHR * IND * INT * LOR * TAB
KI4 * KI5 * KI6 * KI7 * KI9 * PL6 * PL7 * AT4 * PT3 * PT4 * PT7 *
PT8 * AP8

MATTHAY, TOBIAS A.

CHILD'S FIRST STEPS IN PIANOFORTE PLAYING, THE

       NEW YORK   1912   21P   BCFSIP
          SCHIRMER, G., INC.
BP * BR * CU * ES * LC * NP * YU

LOR * MEX
PL3 * PL4 * PL7 * PL11 * AT5 * PT4

MATTHAY, TOBIAS A.

EPITOME OF THE LAWS OF PIANOFORTE TECHNIQUE, AN

       NEW YORK   1931   60P   BEOTLO
          FISCHER, CARL, INC.
BP * BR * CP * ES * IU * LC * NP * TO

INT * MEX * PHO
PL3 * PL6 * PL7 * PL14 * PT3 * PT4 * PT6 * PT7 * PT8

MATTHAY, TOBIAS A.

FIRST LIGHTS ON PIANO-PLAYING

       LONDON   1942   39P   BFLOPP
          BOOSEY AND HAWKES
LC * NP * YU

INT * MEX * PHO
PL4 * PL12 * PT1 * PT4 * PT10

MATTHAY, TOBIAS A.

FIRST PRINCIPLES OF PIANOFORTE PLAYING--EXTRACT FROM 'THE ACT OF
TOUCH', DIRECTIONS FOR LEARNERS AND ADVICE TO TEACHERS

       LONDON   1905   128P   BFPOPP
          LONGMANS, GREEN, AND COMPANY
BR * CP * CU * ES * IU * LC * MI * NP * OC * TO * UK * US * UW * YU

GLO * ILL * INT * LOR * MEX * TAB
PL6 * PL12 * PL14 * KI6 * PT3 * PT6 * PT8 * AP8 * AP9

MATTHAY, TOBIAS A.

FOREARM ROTATION PRINCIPLE IN PIANOFORTE PLAYING, THE ..ITS
APPLICATION AND MASTERY

       LONDON   1912   12P   BFRPIP
          WILLIAMS, JOSEPH, LTD.
BR * CU * ES * NP * US * YU

MEX * PHO
AT4 * PT2 * PT4

MATTHAY, TOBIAS A.

INTRODUCTION TO PSYCHOLOGY FOR MUSIC TEACHERS, AN --THREE LECTURES

       LONDON   1939   66P   BITPFM
          OXFORD UNIVERSITY PRESS
BR * ES * LC * OC * UT

INT * MEX
PL3 * PL5 * PL8 * AT4

MATTHAY, TOBIAS A.

MUSICAL INTERPRETATION..ITS LAWS AND PRINCIPLES---1913

       FREEPORT, N. Y.   1970   168P   BMIILA
          BOOKS FOR LIBRARIES PRESS
BP * BR * CP * CU * ES * IU * LC * MI * NP * OC * TO * UA * UI * UK
UO * US * UT * UW
INT * MEX
PL4 * PL5 * PL6 * PL7 * PL8 * PL10 * PL12 * AT3 * AT11 * PT2 * PT6
PT8 * AP4 * AP8

MATTHAY, TOBIAS A.

NINE STEPS TOWARDS 'FINGER INDIVIDUALIZATION' THROUGH FOREARM
ROTATION, THE ..A SUPPLEMENT TO THE FIRST BOOK OF 'PIANIST'S FIRST
MUSIC MAKING' AND 'CHILD'S FIRST STEPS'
       LONDON   1924   BNSTFI
          ANGLO-FRENCH MUSIC COMPANY, THE
LC

INT * MEX
PT5 * PT10

MATTHAY, TOBIAS A.

ON COLORING AS DISTINCT FROM TONE-INFLECTION--A LECTURE

       LONDON   1937   25P   BOCADF
          OXFORD UNIVERSITY PRESS
BR * CU * ES * LC * NP * TO * UK * YU

MEX
PT8 * AP4

MATTHAY, TOBIAS A.

ON MEMORIZING AND PLAYING FROM MEMORY

       LONDON   1926   19P   BOMAPF
          OXFORD UNIVERSITY PRESS
BP * BR * CP * CU * ES * IU * NP * OC * SA * TO * UA * UI * UM * UT

MEX
PL5 * PL8

MATTHAY, TOBIAS A.

ON METHOD IN TEACHING

       LONDON   1921   35P   BOMIT
          OXFORD UNIVERSITY PRESS
BR * LC * NP * UM * US

INT * MEX
AT3 * AT4 * PT4

MATTHAY, TOBIAS A. *
SWINSTEAD, FELIX
PIANIST'S FIRST MUSIC MAKING, THE --3 VOLS.

       LONDON   1919   69P   BPFMMT
          ANGLO-FRENCH MUSIC COMPANY, THE
LC

INT * MEX * PHO
AT4 * AT5 * PT7 * PT8 * PT9

MATTHAY, TOBIAS A.

    PIANOFORTE TONE-PRODUCTION---SAME AS 'THE ACT OF TOUCH IN ALL ITS
    DIVERSITY'

            LONDON   1903   328P   BPTPSA
                LONGMANS, GREEN AND COMPANY, LTD.
    NP

    APP * CHR * IND * INT * LDR * TAB
    KI4 * KI5 * KI6 * KI7 * KI9 * PL6 * PL7 * AT4 * PT3 * PT4 * PT7 *
    PT8 * AP8

MATTHAY, TOBIAS A.

    PIANO FALLACIES OF TODAY

            LONDON   1939   45P   BPFOT
                OXFORD UNIVERSITY PRESS
    BP * BR * CU * LC * UT * YU

    NP2 * PT3 * PT4 * PT7 * PT8 * PT9

MATTHAY, TOBIAS A.

    PRACTICE TRIANGLE, THE ..EXERCISES FOR FOREARM ROTATION

            BOSTON   1915   2P   BPTEFF
                BOSTON MUSIC COMPANY
    LC

    PT10

MATTHAY, TOBIAS A.

    PRINCIPLES OF FINGERING AND LAWS OF PEDALLING

            LONDON   1911+   20P   BPOFAL
                BOSWORTH AND COMPANY, LTD.
    ES * NP

    MEX
    PT6 * PT8 * AP8

MATTHAY, TOBIAS A.

    PROBLEMS OF AGILITY, THE

            LONDON   1918   8P   BPOA
                ANGLO-FRENCH MUSIC COMPANY, THE
    BR * LC * NP

    PT4 * PT7 * PT8

MATTHAY, TOBIAS A.

    RELAXATION STUDIES IN THE MUSCULAR DISCRIMINATION REQUIRED FOR
    TOUCH, AGILITY AND EXPRESSION IN PIANO PLAYING

            LONDON   1908   142P   BRSITM
                BOSWORTH AND COMPANY, LTD.
    BP * BR * CP * CU * NP * OC * TO * UC * US * YU

    MEX * PHO
    PT2 * PT4 * PT7 * PT8 * PT9 * PT10

MATTHAY, TOBIAS A.

    SLUR OR COUPLET OF NOTES IN ALL ITS VARIETY, THE ..ITS
    INTERPRETATION AND EXECUTION--A LECTURE

            LONDON   1927   49P   BSOCON
                OXFORD UNIVERSITY PRESS
    BP * BR * ES * LC * NP * OC * US

    AP6

MATTHAY, TOBIAS A.

    SOME COMMENTARIES ON THE TEACHING OF PIANOFORTE TECHNIC..A
    SUPPLEMENT TO 'THE ACT OF TOUCH' AND 'FIRST PRINCIPLES'

            LONDON   1911   55P   BSCOTT
                BOSWORTH AND COMPANY, LTD.
    BP * BR * CP * CU * ES * LC * NP * OC * TO * UA * UC * UK * UM

    INT
    PL10 * PT4 * PT7 * PT8

MATTHAY, TOBIAS A.

    TEACHING OF PIANOFORTE TECHNIQUE, THE ..A SUPPLEMENT TO THE ACT OF
    TOUCH

            LONDON   1912   BTOPTA
                LONGMANS, GREEN AND COMPANY, LTD.
    CP * CU * LC * NP

    PT1 * PT2

MATTHAY, TOBIAS A.

    VISIBLE AND INVISIBLE IN PIANOFORTE TECHNIC, THE ..BEING A DIGEST
    OF THE AUTHOR'S TECHNICAL TEACHINGS UP TO DATE---1932

            LONDON   1960+   235P   BVAIIP
                OXFORD UNIVERSITY PRESS
    AS * BP * BR * CP * CU * ES * IU * LC * MI * NP * OC * SA * TO * UA
    UI * UK * UM * US * UT * UW * YU
    CHR * INT * MEX * LDR * PHO
    PT1 * PT2 * PT3 * PT4 * PT6 * PT7 * PT8

MATTHESON, JOHANN

    COMPLETE TREATISE OF THOROUGH BASS, A

            LONDON   1730+   32P   BCTOTB
                HODGSON, P.
    IU * LC

    MEX
    KS10

MATTHEWS, DENIS--EDITOR

    KEYBOARD MUSIC--ESSAYS ON KEYBOARD LITERATURE, EXCLUDING ORGAN

            NEW YORK   1972   386P   BKMEOK
                PRAEGER PUBLISHERS, INC.
    IU * LC

    IND * INT * MEX
    NP6 * PM3 * PM7 * PM8 * PM9 * PM14 * AP3 * AP4

MATTHEWS, DENIS

    BEETHOVEN PIANO SONATAS--B.B.C. MUSIC GUIDE, NO. 1

            LONDON   1967   56P   BBPSBB
                BRITISH BROADCASTING CORPORATION
    AS * BR * IU * LC * NP * UA

    INT * MEX
    PM3 * PM7 * PM8 * PM9 * PM11

MATTHEWS, DENIS

    IN PURSUIT OF MUSIC

            LONDON   1966   189P   BIPOM
                GOLLANCZ
    BR * ES * LC * MI * TO

    IND * MEX
    NP6 * GI4

MAUROIS, ANDRE

    FREDERIC CHOPIN---FOR YOUNGER READERS

            NEW YORK   1942   91P   BFCFYR
                HARPER AND BROS.
    IU * LC * NP

    ILL
    NP4 * PM3 * GI10

MAY, FLORENCE

    GIRLHOOD OF CLARA SCHUMANN, THE ..CLARA WIECK AND HER TIME

            LONDON   1912+   340P   BGOCSC
                LONGMANS, GREEN AND COMPANY
    BP * BR * ES * MI * NP * OC * TO

    APP * IND * MEX
    NP3 * PM6

MAYBERRY, JOHN HENRY

    PRACTICAL COURSE IN PIANO TUNING

            CHICAGO   1950   34P   BPCIPT
                NELSON-HALL
    BP * LC

    CHR * ILL * INT * PHO * TAB
    KI8

MAYO, WALDO

    CHOPIN---FOR YOUNGER READERS

            WESTPORT, CONN.   1945   40P   BCFYR
                HYPERION PRESS

    NP4 * GI10

MCALL, REGINALD L.

    PRACTICAL CHURCH SCHOOL MUSIC..METHODS AND TRAINING FOR SUCCESSFUL
    PIANO, VOCAL, AND PLATFORM LEADERSHIP

            NEW YORK   1932 *   237P   BPCSMM
                ABINGDON PRESS
    LC * NP

    APP * INT * LDR * MEX
    PL12 * PT8 * KS4

MCARTHUR, ALEXANDER

    ANTON RUBINSTEIN, A BIOGRAPHICAL SKETCH

            EDINBURGH   1889   154P   BARABS
                BLACK, A. AND C.
    BP * BR * ES * LC * MI * NP * OC

    INT
    NP3 * PM3 * PM6

MCARTHUR, ALEXANDER

    PIANOFORTE STUDY..HINTS ON PIANO PLAYING

        PHILADELPHIA   1897   141P   BPSHOP
          PRESSER, THEODORE, COMPANY
    LC * NP * OC * UK * US

    IND
    NP2 * NP3 * PL2 * PL7 * PT4 * PT8 * PM4 * AP4 * AP8 * GI2 * GI11 *
    GI13

MCCARTHY, ALBERT J.--EDITOR

    PIANO JAZZ..ESSAYS--2 VOLS., 1945-1946

        LONDON   1945   BPJETV
          JAZZ MUSIC BOOKS
    LC * NP

    NP6 * KS6 * GI13

MCCLANAHAN, RICHARD

    CADENCE, KEY TO MUSICAL CLARITY, THE ..A SIMPLE AND PRACTICAL
    APPROACH TO CLEAR PHRASING

        CLEVELAND   1970   101P   BCKTMC
          MCCLANAHAN, RICHARD
    IU * LC

    APP * BIB * IND * MEX
    PL5 * PL6 * PM8 * PM9 * AP3 * AP4

MCCLINTOCK, LORENE

    TEACH YOURSELF TO PLAY THE PIANO..BASED ON THE INTERVAL METHOD

        NEW YORK   1947   115P   BTYTPT
          CROWELL, T. Y., COMPANY
    CP * IU * LC * MI

    APP * IND * INT * MEX
    PL4 * PL11 * PL12 * AT4 * KS3 * KS4 * GI11

MCDOWELL, LOUISE

    PAST AND PRESENT--A CANADIAN MUSICIAN'S REMINISCENSES

        WINNIPEG   1958   211P   BPAPAC
          BULMAN BROTHERS, LTD.
    LC * TO

    NP6

MCEWEN, JOHN B.

    INTRODUCTION TO AN UNPUBLISHED EDITION OF THE PIANOFORTE SONATAS OF
    BEETHOVEN, AN

        LONDON   1932   58P   BITAUE
          OXFORD UNIVERSITY PRESS
    BR * ES * LC * NP * OC * YU

    INT * MEX
    PL4 * PL12 * PM4 * AP4

MCEWEN, JOHN B.

    PRINCIPLES OF PHRASING AND ARTICULATION IN MUSIC, THE

        LONDON   1916   75P   BPOPAA
          AUGENER, LTD.
    BR * NP

    AP6

MCEWEN, JOHN B.

    TEMPO RUBATO, OR TIME VARIATION IN MUSICAL PERFORMANCE

        LONDON   1928   47P   BTROTV
          OXFORD UNIVERSITY PRESS
    BP * BR * ES * LC * NP * TO

    CHR * INT * MEX * TAB
    PL12

MCFERRIN, CHARLES BETTEYS

    MOTHER'S PART IN HER CHILD'S MUSICAL EDUCATION, A ..OR, THE THINGS
    A PARENT MAY DO TO ENSURE INEVITABLE SUCCESS IN PIANO PLAYING

        CHICAGO   1910   291P   BMPIHC
          ALERT PUBLISHING COMPANY
    ES * LC

    CHR * ILL * INT * LDR * PHO
    KI4 * PL7 * AT11 * AT13 * PT4

MCHOSE, ALLEN IRVINE *
WHITE, DONALD F.
    KEYBOARD AND DICTATION MANUAL

        NEW YORK   1949   169P   BKADM
          APPLETON-CENTURY-CROFTS
    BR * IU * LC

    APP * INT * MEX
    AT7 * PL10 * PL12 * KS4 * KS5 * KS8 * KS10

MCHOSE, ALLEN IRVINE

    TEACHERS DICTATION MANUAL

        NEW YORK   1948   183P   BTDM
          CROFTS, F. S., AND COMPANY
    IU * LC * NP

    INT
    PL10 * PL12 * AT4 * AT7 * KS4 * KS8 * KS10

MCLAIN, MARGARET STARR

    CLASS PIANO

        BOSTON   1969   284P   BCP
          ALLYN AND BACON, INC.
    BP * ES * IU * LC * OC * SA * UT

    APP * CHR * IND * INT * LDR * MEX * TAB
    PL4 * PL6 * PL7 * PL8 * PL10 * PL11 * PL12 * PL13 * PL14 * PL15 *
    AT4 * AT6 * AT7 * KS3 * KS4 * KS5 * KS7 * KS8 * PM6

MCMILLAN, FIONA

    FINGERING OF SCALES AND ARPEGGIOS, THE

        LONDON   1934   8P   BFOSAA
          OXFORD UNIVERSITY PRESS
    BP * BR

    PT9

MCMILLAN, MARY LEE *
JONES, RUTH DORVAL
    MY HELENKA---IGNACE PADEREWSKI

        DURHAM, N. C.   1972   207P   BMHIP
          MOORE PUBLISHING COMPANY
    IU

    NP4 * PM3

MCNABB, GEORGE

    SELECTED LIST OF GRADED TEACHING MATERIAL FOR THE PIANO, A --3RD.
    ED.---REPUBLISHED IN 1972
        ROCHESTER, N. Y.   1959   37P   BSLOGT
          EASTMAN SCHOOL OF MUSIC, E. H. EASLEY
    BP * ES * LC * MI * NP * UA * UI * UT

    INT * MEX
    PM4 * PM6 * PM10 * PM15

MCTAMMANY, JOHN

    EVOLUTION OF THE PLAYER-PIANO MECHANISM---EXCERPT FROM 'PRESTO',
    VOL. 29, JAN. 4, 1912

        CHICAGO   1912   BEOTPP
          PRESTO PUBLISHING COMPANY
    NP

    KI3 * KI6 * KI10

MCTAMMANY, JOHN

    HISTORY OF THE PLAYER-PIANO, THE

        NEW YORK   1913   82P   BHOTPP
          MCTAMMANY, JOHN
    NP * YU

    INT * PHO
    KI3 * KI10

MCTAMMANY, JOHN

    TECHNICAL HISTORY OF THE PLAYER

        CHICAGO   1915   BTHOTP
          PRESTO PUBLISHING COMPANY

    KI3 * KI10

MEHEGAN, JOHN F.

    JAZZ IMPROVISATION..TONAL AND RHYTHMIC PRINCIPLES--4 VOLS.

        NEW YORK   1959   288P   BJITAR
          WATSON-GUPTILL PUBLICATIONS
    BP * ES * IU * LC * NP * UA * UM * UT

    INT * MEX
    KS6

MEHEGAN, JOHN F.

    JAZZ PIANIST, THE ..STUDIES IN THE ART AND PRACTICE OF JAZZ
    IMPROVISATION--3 VOLS. IN 1
        NEW YORK   1961   BJPSIT
          FOX, SAM, PUBLISHING COMPANY
    BP * LC * TO * UM

    INT * MEX
    KS6

MEHEGAN, JOHN F.

STUDIES IN JAZZ HARMONY

        NEW YORK   1962   43P   BSIJH
            FOX, SAM, PUBLISHING COMPANY
LC

CHR * INT * MEX
KS6

MEHEGAN, JOHN F.

STYLES FOR THE JAZZ PIANIST--BK. 1..THE RHYTHMIC SCHOOL

        NEW YORK   1962   43P   BSFTJP
            FOX, SAM, PUBLISHING COMPANY
LC * TO

INT * MEX
KS6 * AP4

MEHEGAN, JOHN F.

TOUCH AND RHYTHM TECHNIQUES FOR THE JAZZ PIANIST

        NEW YORK   1962   33P   BTARTF
            FOX, SAM, PUBLISHING COMPANY
LC * TO * UA

INT * MEX
PT8 * PT10 * KS6

MEHER, DONOVAN

HOW TO VAMP AT SIGHT..THE EASIEST AND CLEAREST METHOD OF
ACCOMPANYING MELODIES EVER PLACED BEFORE THE PUBLIC

        LONDON   1935+   16P   BHTVAS
            BROADHURST, A. V.
LC

INT
KS6 * EP6

MEHR, NORMAN

GROUP PIANO TEACHING

        EVANSTON, ILL.   1965   40P   BGPT
            SUMMY-BIRCHARD COMPANY
LC * OC * SA * UI * UO * UT * UW

INT * MEX
PL3 * PL4 * PL6 * PL12 * PL13 * PL14 * AT3 * AT4 * AT5 * AT7 * KS4

MEIER, NELLIE SIMMONS

LIONS' PAWS..THE STORY OF FAMOUS HANDS--INCLUDES MUSICIANS..JOSE
ITURBI, ERNEST SCHELLING, GEORGE GERSHWIN

        NEW YORK   1937   160P   BLPTSO
            MUSSEY, BARROWS
BR * LC

ILL * INT * LDR
PT3 * GI12

MEKOTA, BETH ANNA

TEACHING APPLIED MUSIC BY CLASS METHOD

        SEWARD, NEB.   1954   41P   BTAMBC
            CONCORDIA TEACHERS COLLEGE
UT

AT7

MEL-O-DEE MUSIC COMPANY

MELODEE MUSIC ROLLS..SEPTEMBER, 1920

        NEW YORK   1920   89P   BMMRSN
            MEL-O-DEE MUSIC COMPANY
NP

INT * PHO
KI10 * PM12

MELCHER, ROBERT A. *
WARCH, WILLARD F.
MUSIC FOR ADVANCED STUDY..A SOURCE BOOK OF EXCERPTS

        ENGLEWOOD CLIFFS, N. J.   1965   182P   BMFASA
            PRENTICE-HALL, INC.
BR * IU * LC

APP * INT * MEX
PL10 * KS3 * KS4

MELCHER, ROBERT A. *
WARCH, WILLARD F.
MUSIC FOR KEYBOARD HARMONY

        ENGLEWOOD CLIFFS, N. J.   1966   190P   BMFKH
            PRENTICE-HALL, INC.
BR * IU * LC * NP

INT * MEX
KS4

MELCHER, ROBERT A. *
WARCH, WILLARD F.
MUSIC FOR SCORE READING

        ENGLEWOOD CLIFFS, N. J.   1971   181P   BMFSR
            PRENTICE-HALL, INC.
LC * NP

INT * MEX
KS9

MELLERS, WILFRED

FRANCOIS COUPERIN AND THE FRENCH CLASSICAL TRADITION

        LONDON   1950   412P   BFCATF
            DOBSON, DENNIS, LTD.
AS * BP * BR * CP * ES * IU * LC * MI * NP * OC * TO * UA * UC * UI
UK * UM * UO * US * UT * UU * UW * YU
APP * BIB * DIS * ILL * IND * INT * MEX * PHO * TAB
PL12 * KS4 * PM3 * PM4 * PM6 * PM14 * AP3 * AP6 * AP7

MELLERS, WILFRED

SONATA PRINCIPLE, THE --CIRCA 1750

        LONDON   1957   237P   BSPCSF
            ROCKLIFF PUBLISHING CORPORATION
AS * BP * BR * CP * ES * IU * LC * MI * NP * OC * TO * UA * UC * UI
UK * UM * UO * US * UT * UU * UW * YU
ILL * INT * MEX * MSF
PM3 * PM14 * PM15

MELLING, E. H.

EXTEMPORIZING AT THE PIANO MADE EASY

        LONDON   1931   15P   BEATPM
            REEVES, WILLIAM
BR * CU

MEX
KS5

MERGES, P.

PRACTICAL RULES FOR PIANOFORTE PLAYING..TEXT BOOK FOR TEACHERS AND
PUPILS

        PHILADELPHIA   1881   78P   BPRFPP
            LEE AND WALKER
LC * OC

GLO * INT * MEX
PL7 * PT4 * PT6 * PT9 * PT10 * AP8 * EP6

MERRICK, FRANK

PRACTICING THE PIANO

        LONDON   1958   116P   BPTP
            BARRIE AND ROCKLIFF
AS * BP * BR * CP * ES * IU * LC * MI * SA * UI * UT * UW

IND * INT * MEX
PL7 * PL8 * PL12 * PT4 * PT6 * PT8 * PT9 * KS3 * KS7 * AP8

MERRILL, MYRTLE

SIGHT-READING AT THE PIANO

        NEW YORK   1953   45P   BSRATP
            MILLS MUSIC, INC.
CU * IU * SA

BIB * INT * MEX
PL4 * AT7 * PT8 * KS3

METROPOLITAN MUSEUM OF ART, NEW YORK

CATALOGUE OF THE CROSBY BROWN COLLECTION OF MUSICAL INSTRUMENTS OF
ALL NATIONS--3 VOLS.

        NEW YORK   1903   313P   BCOTCB
            METROPOLITAN MUSEUM OF ART
BR * CU * NP

IND * INT
KI3 * KI5 * KI6 * KI15

METROPOLITAN MUSEUM OF ART, NEW YORK

KEYBOARD INSTRUMENTS IN THE METROPOLITAN MUSEUM OF ART..A PICTURE
BOOK BY EMMANUEL WINTERNITZ

        NEW YORK   1961   48P   BKIITM
            METROPOLITAN MUSEUM OF ART
CU * IU * LC * MI * NP * OC * TO * UC * UI * UK * UW * YU

ILL * INT * LDR * PHO
KI3 * KI5 * KI6 * KI9 * KI13 * KI14 * KI15

MICHEL, NORMAN ELWOOD

HISTORICAL PIANOS, HARPSICHORDS AND CLAVICHORDS---1963

        PICO RIVERA, CAL.   1970   236P   BHPHAC
            MICHEL, N. E.
BP * CU * ES * IU * LC * MI * NP * TO * UA * UI * UK * UO

IND * PHO
KI3 * KI13 * KI14

MICHEL, NORMAN ELWOOD

MICHEL'S PIANO ATLAS---REPUBLISHED IN 1965 UNDER AUTHORSHIP..B.
PIERCE

        PICO RIVERA, CAL.   1947   243P   BMPARI
        MICHEL, N. E.
AS * BR * CP * CU * ES * IU * LC * MI * NP * OC * UA * UC * UI * UK
UM * US * UT * UW * YU
INT
KI3 * KI12

MICHEL, NORMAN ELWOOD

OLD PIANOS

        PICO RIVERA, CAL.   1954   181P   BOP
        MICHEL, N. E.
AS * CP * IU * LC * MI * NP * OC * UI * UK * UT * YU

IND * PHO
KI3 * KI5 * KI6

MICHIGAN MUSIC TEACHERS ASSOCIATION

PIANO TEACHER'S GUIDE

        ANN ARBOR, MICH.   1961   62P   BPTG
        MICHIGAN, UNIVERSITY OF, SCHOOL OF MUSIC
ES * IU * UI

BIB * INT
PM6 * PM15

MIDDLEMISS, CHARLES S.

NEW GRAPHIC NOTATION FOR KEYBOARD MUSIC, A

        CROWBOROUGH, SUSSEX, ENGLAND 1935   44P   BNGNFK
        MIDDLEMISS, CHARLES S.
BR * NP

INT * LDR * MEX
PL4

MIDKIFF, HELEN T.

CHURCH PIANIST, THE

        NASHVILLE, TENN.   1957   106P   BCP
        CONVENTION PRESS
LC

CHR * INT * LDR * MEX
PL5 * PT1 * EP6

MIESSNER, WILLIAM OTTO

MELODY WAY COURSE FOR CLASS OR PRIVATE PIANO INSTRUCTION, THE
..TEACHER'S MANUAL---REPRODUCED FROM TYPEWRITTEN COPY

        CHICAGO   1934   93P   BMWCFC
        FITZSIMMONS, H. T., COMPANY
UW

AT7

MILINOWSKI, MARTA

TERESA CARRENO, 'BY THE GRACE OF GOD'

        NEW HAVEN, CONN.   1940   410P   BTCBTG
        YALE UNIVERSITY PRESS
BP * BR * ES * IU * LC * MI * NP * OC * UA * UC * UO * US * YU

IND * INT * PHO
NP3

MILLER, ALLAN

BEGINNING PIANO FOR ADULTS

        NEW YORK   1970   127P   BBPFA
        MACMILLAN
IU * LC

APP * BIB * GLO * INT * MEX * PHO
PL4 * PL11 * AT6 * AT7 * PT1 * AP9

MILLER, EDWARD

ELEMENTS OF THOROUGH BASS AND COMPOSITION

        LONDON   1787   88P   BEOTBA
        LONGMAN AND BRODERIP
LC * NP

MEX
KS10

MILLER, EDWARD

INSTITUTES OF MUSIC, OR, EASY INSTRUCTIONS FOR THE HARPSICHORD

        LONDON   1780+   69P   BIOMOE
        LONGMAN AND BRODERIP
LC * NP

INT * MEX
PL4 * PL12 * AT4 * PT6 * KS7 * AP7

MILLER, JEWELL

POLONAISE MILITAIRE..THE LIFE AND WORK OF FREDERIC CHOPIN..A
DRAMATIC POEM IN THREE PARTS

        NEW YORK   1936   128P   BPMTLA
        PUTNAM'S, G. P., SONS
LC * NP

ILL * INT
NP4 * PM3 * GI15

MILNE, ALFRED FORBES

BEETHOVEN..THE PIANOFORTE SONATAS--2 VOLS.

        LONDON   1925   132P   BBTPST
        OXFORD UNIVERSITY PRESS
BR * CP * CU * ES * IU * OC * SA * UC * UI * UK * UW * YU

MEX * INT
PM3 * PM4 * PM5 * PM7 * PM8 * PM9 * PM15 * AP3 * AP4

MININBERG, IAN

VISUAL APPROACH TO PIANO TECHNIQUE, A

        NEW YORK   1937   36P   BVATPT
        SCHIRMER, G., INC.
BP * BR * ES * LC * NP

APP * INT * LDR * PHO
KI6 * PT3 * PT4 * PT8

MINNESOTA MUSIC TEACHERS ASSOCIATION

PIANO-THEORY EXAMINATION SYLLABUS

        MINNEAPOLIS   1970   100P   BPTES
        MINNESOTA MUSIC TEACHERS ASSOCIATION
SA

INT * LDR * MEX
PL4 * PL12 * AT10 * PT1 * PT9 * KS3 * KS4 * PM6 * GI9

MIZWA, STEPHEN P.--EDITOR

FREDERIC CHOPIN, 1810-1849

        NEW YORK   1949   108P   BFCETE
        MACMILLAN COMPANY, THE
IU * NP

ILL * LDR * MSF * PHO * TAB
NP3 * PM3

MOISEIVITCH, MAURICE

MOISEIVITCH--BENNO--, BIOGRAPHY OF A CONCERT PIANIST

        LONDON   1965   199P   BMBBOA
        MULLER, FREDERICK, LTD.
BP * BR * ES * IU * LC * MI * SA * TO * UO

IND * PHO
NP4

MOKREJS, JOHN

GREAT HARMONIC LAW OF CHORD PROGRESSION AND IMPROVISING, THE

        CEDAR RAPIDS, IOWA   1966   8P   BGHLOC
        ODOWAN PUBLISHING COMPANY
LC

KS4 * KS5

MOKREJS, JOHN

LESSONS IN SIGHT READING AT THE PIANO

        CHICAGO   1909   38P   BLISRA
        SUMMY, CLAYTON F., COMPANY
LC * NP * UT

KS3

MOKREJS, JOHN

SCIENCE OF FINGERING, THE ---FOR PIANO

        CHICAGO   1940   BSOFFP
        SUMMY, CLAYTON F., COMPANY
LC

MEX
PL15 * PT6 * PT8 * PT9

MOKREJS, JOHN

STORY OF NANYNKA, THE ..FIRST PIANO LESSONS FOR CHILDREN, PRIVATE
OR CLASS

        PHILADELPHIA   1932   40P   BSONFP
        PRESSER, THEODORE, COMPANY
LC

MEX
PL4 * AT4 * AT5 * AT7

MOLDENHAUER, HANS

   DUO-PIANISM---PUBLISHED DISSERTATION

       NEW YORK   1950   384P   BDPPD
         COLEMAN-ROSS COMPANY
  AS * BP * CP * CU * ES * IU * LC * MI * NP * OC * SA * TO * UA * UC
  UI * UM * UO * US * UT * UW * YU
  APP * BIB * DIS * IND * MEX
  PL7 * PL9 * PM3 * PM6 * PM7 * PM12 * PM15 * EP5

MOLLER, JOHN CHRISTOPHER

   SETT OF PROGRESSIVE LESSONS FOR THE HARPSICHORD OR PIANO FORTE, A

       LONDON   1795+   39P   BSOPLF
         LONGMAN AND BRODERIP
  LC * NP

  GLO * INT * MEX
  AT4 * AP7

MONTAGU-NATHAN, M.

   CONTEMPORARY RUSSIAN COMPOSERS---RACHMANINOFF

       LONDON   1917   329P   BCRCR
         PALMER AND HAYWARD
  IU * LC * NP

  ILL * IND * INT * PHO
  NP4 * PM3 * PM9

MONTAGU-NATHAN, M.

   HANDBOOK TO THE PIANO WORKS OF SCRIABIN

       LONDON   1922   16P   BHTTPW
         CHESTER, J. AND W., LTD.
  BP * BR * ES * LC * NP * OC * UI * UO * UT * YU

  ILL * MSF
  PM3 * PM5 * PM9 * PM15

MONTI, H. DE

   STRICTURES ON MR. LOGIER'S SYSTEM OF MUSICAL EDUCATION

       GLASGOW   1817   80P   BSOMLS
         TURNBULL, W.
  BR * NP

  INT * MEX
  NP7 * PL4 * AT4 * PT14

MOOR, WINIFRED

   TECHNICAL EXERCISES FOR THE EMANUEL MOOR DOUBLE KEYBOARD PIANO---IN
   ENGLISH, GERMAN AND FRENCH

       VIENNA   1922+   17P   BTEFTE
         UNIVERSAL-EDITION
  NP

  INT * MEX
  KI1 * PT11 * GI12

MOORE, GERALD

   AM I TOO LOUD..MEMOIRS OF AN ACCOMPANIST

       LONDON   1962   288P   BAITLM
         MACMILLAN COMPANY, THE
  BP * BR * CP * ES * IU * LC * NP * OC * SA * TO * UC * UM * UO * US
  UT
  PHO
  NP4 * NP6 * PL7 * EP6 * GI3 * GI4

MOORE, GERALD

   SINGER AND ACCOMPANIST..THE PERFORMANCE OF FIFTY SONGS

       LONDON   1953   232P   BSAATP
         MACMILLAN COMPANY, THE
  BP * BR * CP * CU * IU * LC * MI * NP * OC * TO * UA * UC * UI * UK
  UM * US * UT * UW
  IND * INT * MEX
  EP6

MOORE, GERALD

   UNASHAMED ACCOMPANIST, THE

       LONDON   1943   84P   BUA
         METHUEN AND COMPANY
  BP * BR * CP * ES * IU * LC * MI * NP * OC * SA * TO * UA * UC * UI
  UK * UM * UO * US * UT * UW * YU
  INT
  KS3 * KS7 * EP6

MOORE, HENRY K.

   CHILD'S PIANOFORTE BOOK, THE ..BEING A FIRST YEAR'S COURSE AT THE
   PIANOFORTE

       LONDON   1882   177P   BCPBBA
         SONNENSCHEIN, W. S., AND COMPANY
  BR * LC

  MEX
  AT4 * AT5

MOORE, HENRY K.

   MANUAL OF PIANOFORTE TUNING, A

       LONDON   1919   58P   BMOPT
         MUSICAL OPINION
  BR

  KI8

MOORE, MARY BURNHAM

   LURE OF THE PIANO THROUGH COORDINATION AND CONCENTRATION, THE

       LOS ANGELES   1940   35P   BLOTPT
         MOORE, M. B.
  LC * NP

  INT * MEX
  PL4 * PL10 * PT10 * KS4 * AP8

MORDEN, HARRY

   PLAYING THE PIANO BY EAR--3 PTS.

       LONDON   1927   BPTPBE
         MORDEN SCHOOL OF MUSIC
  BR

  KS12

MORGAN. ORLANDO

   J. S. BACH..48 PRELUDES AND FUGUES..ANALYSIS OF THE FUGUES

       LONDON   1931   16P   BJSBFP
         ASHDOWN, EDWIN, LTD.
  BP * LC

  PM3 * PM8

MORRILL, HENRY H.

   MANUAL OF PIANO FOR PUPILS AND TEACHERS

       TOPEKA, KAN.   1887   16P   BMOPFP
         HAMILTON, C. B., AND COMPANY
  LC

  GLO * MEX
  PL12 * PT1 * PT8 * PM6 * AP8

MORRIS, REGINALD OWEN

   FIGURED HARMONY AT THE KEYBOARD---PRINCIPALLY EXERCISES

       LONDON   1932   95P   BFHATK
         OXFORD UNIVERSITY PRESS
  IU * LC * NP

  INT * MEX
  KS4 * KS10

MOSCHELES, CHARLOTTE

   RECENT MUSIC AND MUSICIANS, AS DESCRIBED IN THE DIARIES AND
   CORRESPONDENCE OF IGNAZ MOSCHELES

       NEW YORK   1875   434P   BRMAMA
         HOLT, HENRY, AND COMPANY
  BR * IU * LC * NP * UA * UT

  APP * IND * INT * LDR * MEX
  NP3 * NP6 * PM6

MOSCOW, CHARLES E.

   PRACTICAL PIANO TUNER, THE ..A COMPREHENSIVE SIMPLE SET OF RULES
   AND EXPLANATIONS FOR SELF INSTRUCTION OF PIANO TUNING AND REPAIRING

       NEW YORK   1895   22P   BPPTAC
         FISCHER, C.
  LC

  ILL * INT * PHO
  KI8 * PL11

MOTT, ISAAC H. R.

   ADVICE AND INSTRUCTIONS FOR PLAYING THE PIANOFORTE WITH EXPRESSION
   AND BRILLIANT EXECUTION

       LONDON   1842+   108P   BAAIFP
         MOTT, ISAAC H. R.
  NP

  INT * MEX * TAB
  PL4 * PL7 * PL11 * PL12 * PL14 * PT4 * PT9 * AP4 * AP7

MUFFAT, GEORG

   ESSAY ON THOROUGHBASS, AN --MUSICOLOGICAL STUDIES AND DOCUMENTS,
   NO. 4---1699

       ROME   1961   128P   BEOTMS
         AMERICAN INSTITUTE OF MUSICOLOGY
  IU * LC * NP

  INT * MEX
  KS10

MURATA, KOH

    SECTIONAL TUNING OF THE PIANO

               TOKYO   1966   6P   BSTOTP
               GAKUSHOBO
IU

KI8

MURDOCH, WILLIAM

    BRAHMS..WITH AN ANALYTICAL STUDY OF THE COMPLETE PIANOFORTE WORKS

               LONDON   1933   394P   BBWAAS
               RICH AND COWAN
BR * ES * IU * LC * NP * OC * UA * UC * UI * UO * UT * YU

BIB * ILL * IND * PHO
NP3 * PM3 * PM6 * PM8 * PM9 * PM15 * EP3 * EP7

MURDOCH, WILLIAM

    CHOPIN..HIS LIFE---1935

               WESTPORT, CONN.   1971   410P   BCHLNT
               GREENWOOD PRESS
BR * IU * LC * NP

BIB * ILL * IND * INT * PHO
NP3 * PM3 * PM6

MURGIA, ADELAIDE

    LIFE AND TIMES OF CHOPIN, THE

               LONDON   1967   75P   BLATOC
               HAMLYN
LC

ILL * PHO
NP3 * NP9 * PM3

MURPHY, HOWARD A. *
MELCHER, ROBERT A.
    MUSIC FOR STUDY..A SOURCE BOOK OF EXCERPTS

               ENGLEWOOD CLIFFS, N. J.   1960   182P   BMFSAS
               PRENTICE-HALL, INC.
IU * LC

INT * MEX * TAB
PL5 * PL10 * KS3 * KS4 * KS9

MUSAFIA, JULIEN

    ART OF FINGERING IN PIANO PLAYING, THE

               NEW YORK   1971   90   BAOFIP
               MUSIC CORPORATION OF AMERICA, INC.

MEX
PT6

MUSICAL OPINION AND MUSIC TRADE REVIEW

    REPAIRING THE REED ORGAN AND HARMONIUM..INFORMATION USEFUL TO
    PIANOFORTE TUNERS AND REPAIRERS

               LONDON   1917   30P   BRTROA
               MUSICAL OPINION AND MUSIC TRADE REVIEW

KI8

MUSICIANS ADVISORY SERVICE

    MUSICIANS ADVISORY SERVICE FIRST MUSIC READER FOR PIANO..TEACHERS
    COPY

               NEW YORK   1941   45P   BMASFM
               MUSICIANS ADVISORY SERVICE, INC.
LC

INT * LDR * MEX
PL12 * AT4

MUSIC EDUCATION LEAGUE, INC.

    PIANO AUDITIONS SYLLABUS AND COMPREHENSIVE GUIDE FOR PIANO
    TEACHERS---1923

               NEW YORK   1952   102P   BPASAC
               MUSIC EDUCATION LEAGUE, INC.
IU

PM4 * PM6 * GI9

MUSIC EDUCATION LEAGUE

    COMPREHENSIVE GUIDE FOR PIANO TEACHERS AND PIANO AUDITION SYLLABUS

               NEW YORK   1963   181P   BCGFPT
               MUSIC EDUCATION LEAGUE, INC.
CP * CU * ES * IU * LC * OC * SA * UI * UT

APP * INT
PL9 * AT1 * PM4 * PM6 * EP1 * EP2 * EP4 * EP5 * GI9

MUSIC EDUCATORS NATIONAL CONFERENCE

    HANDBOOK FOR TEACHING PIANO CLASSES

               WASHINGTON, D. C.   1952   87P   BHFTPC
               MUSIC EDUCATORS NATIONAL CONFERENCE
AS * CP * CU * ES * IU * LC * MI * NP * OC * SA * UA * UC * UI * UM
UO * UT * UW * YU
BIB * CHR * INT * MEX * PHO * TAB
KI8 * AT4 * AT5 * AT6 * AT7 * AT8 * AT11 * AT14 * GI8

MUSIC EDUCATORS NATIONAL CONFERENCE

    KEYBOARD EXPERIENCE AND CLASS PIANO INSTRUCTION

               WASHINGTON, D. C.   1957   48P   BKEACP
               MUSIC EDUCATORS NATIONAL CONFERENCE
IU * LC

MEX * PHO
PL3 * AT5 * AT7

MUSIC EDUCATORS NATIONAL CONFERENCE

    MUSIC BEGINS WITH THE PIANO

               WASHINGTON, D. C.   1958   8P   BMBWTP
               MUSIC EDUCATORS NATIONAL CONFERENCE
SA * UI

INT * PHO
AT7 * GI2 * GI8

MUSIC EDUCATORS NATIONAL CONFERENCE

    TEACHING PIANO IN CLASSROOM AND STUDIO

               WASHINGTON, D. C.   1967   176P   BTPICA
               MUSIC EDUCATORS NATIONAL CONFERENCE
AS * BP * LC * SA * UA * UI * UM * UO

APP * BIB * CHR * INT * MEX
PL4 * PL8 * PL13 * AT1 * AT3 * AT4 * AT5 * AT6 * AT8 * AT11 * AT14
PT1 * KS3 * PM4 * PM6 * AP4

MUSIC EDUCATORS NATIONAL CONFERENCE

    TRAVELING THE CIRCUIT WITH PIANO CLASSES

               WASHINGTON, D. C.   1951   31P   BTTCWP
               MUSIC EDUCATORS NATIONAL CONFERENCE
ES * MI * SA * UC * UI * UM * UO * UT * UW

PHO
AT4 * AT5 * AT6 * AT7 * AT8

MUSIC INDUSTRY COUNCIL

    MUSIC EDUCATOR'S BUSINESS HANDBOOK, THE ---PUBLISHED OCCASIONALLY
    SINCE 1956--INCLUDES PIANO PURCHASE GUIDES

               WASHINGTON, D. C.   1970   47P   BMEBHP
               MUSIC EDUCATORS NATIONAL CONFERENCE
IU * LC

GI5

MUSIC PROJECT--NEW YORK CITY

    TEACHER'S GUIDE..A CREATIVE APPROACH TO PIANO CLASS TEACHING, BY
    JULES ORLIK

               NEW YORK   1941+   87P   BTGACA
               WORKS PROGRESS ADMINISTRATION--MUSIC ED. DIV.
LC

INT
PL10 * AT4 * AT7 * PT9 * KS4 * KS7 * PM6 * AP4 * EP1

NALDER, LAWRENCE MARCUS

    ESSAYS IN PIANOFORTE TECHNOLOGY

               LONDON   1923   62P   BEIPT
               MUSICAL OPINION
NP

ILL * TAB
NP6 * KI4 * KI8

NALDER, LAWRENCE MARCUS

    FIRST STEPS IN PIANO TUNING AND OTHER ESSAYS IN PIANOFORTE
    TECHNOLOGY

               LONDON   1947   80P   BFSIPT
               MUSICAL OPINION
BR * LC * NP * UC * UI * UW

CHR * MEX
KI2 * KI5 * KI6 * KI8

NALDER, LAWRENCE MARCUS

    MODERN PIANO, THE

               LONDON   1927   192P   BMP
               MUSICAL OPINION
BR * LC * NP * YU

CHR * INT * LDR * PHO * TAB
KI5 * KI6 * KI7 * KI8 * KI9 * PT8 * AP8

NALDER, LAWRENCE MARCUS

   PIANOFORTE CONSTRUCTION

LONDON	1927+	32P	BPC
MUSICAL OPINION			

   KI5 * KI6

NALDER, LAWRENCE MARCUS

   REPAIRING THE PIANOFORTE

LONDON	1927+	80P	BRTP
MUSICAL OPINION			

   KI5 * KI6 * KI8

NATIONAL BUREAU FOR THE ADVANCEMENT OF MUSIC

   GIVING OF HIGH SCHOOL CREDITS FOR PRIVATE MUSIC STUDY, THE ..A
   SURVEY--STATE BY STATE REVIEW

NEW YORK	1924	105P	BGOHSC
NATIONAL BUREAU FOR THE ADVANCEMENT OF MUSIC			

IU * LC * NP

APP * INT * TAB
PM6 * GI1 * GI2

NATIONAL BUREAU FOR THE ADVANCEMENT OF MUSIC

   GUIDE FOR CONDUCTING PIANO CLASSES IN THE SCHOOLS, A

NEW YORK	1928	31P	BGFCPC
NATIONAL BUREAU FOR THE ADVANCEMENT OF MUSIC			

UW

   AT7 * GI8

NATIONAL BUREAU FOR THE ADVANCEMENT OF MUSIC

   NATIONAL SURVEY OF PIANO CLASSES IN OPERATION

NEW YORK	1929	95P	BNSOPC
NATIONAL BUREAU FOR THE ADVANCEMENT OF MUSIC			

ES * LC * NP * SA * UA * UC * UW * YU

ILL * INT
AT7 * AT8 * GI5 * GI8

NATIONAL BUREAU FOR THE ADVANCEMENT OF MUSIC

   PIANO CLASSES AND THE PRIVATE TEACHER

NEW YORK	1930	44P	BPCATP
NATIONAL BUREAU FOR THE ADVANCEMENT OF MUSIC			

CU * ES * NP * SA

INT * PHO * TAB
AT3 * AT4 * AT7 * AT8 * GI8

NATIONAL BUREAU FOR THE ADVANCEMENT OF MUSIC

   PIANO CLASSES IN THE SCHOOLS..EDUCATIONAL VALUE OF IMPORTANT NEW
   MOVEMENT

NEW YORK	1926	31P	BPCITS
NATIONAL BUREAU FOR THE ADVANCEMENT OF MUSIC			

BP * CU * ES * LC * NP * SA

BIB * PHO
AT7 * AT8 * GI5 * GI8

NATIONAL BUREAU FOR THE ADVANCEMENT OF MUSIC

   PIANO CLASS INSTRUCTION

NEW YORK	1930+	6P	BPCI
NATIONAL BUREAU FOR THE ADVANCEMENT OF MUSIC			

UW

   AT7

NATIONAL GUILD OF PIANO TEACHERS

   GUILD SYLLABUS, THE ..STREAMLINED EDITION

AUSTIN, TEX.	1944	19P	BGSSE
NATIONAL GUILD OF PIANO TEACHERS			

LC

   GI5 * GI6

NATIONAL GUILD OF PIANO TEACHERS

   NATIONAL AUDITIONS FOR AMERICAN PIANO PUPILS

NEW YORK	1939	28P	BNAFAP
NATIONAL GUILD OF PIANO TEACHERS			

   GI6 * GI9

NATIONAL GUILD OF PIANO TEACHERS

   STUDENT'S HANDBOOK FOR ENTRANTS IN THE NATIONAL PIANO PLAYING
   AUDITIONS

NEW YORK	1945	24P	BSHFEI
NATIONAL GUILD OF PIANO TEACHERS			

LC

INT
GI6 * GI9

NATIONAL PIANO FOUNDATION

   GREATER REWARDS THROUGH CREATIVE PIANO TEACHING

CHICAGO	1960+	16P	BGRTCP
NATIONAL PIANO FOUNDATION			

SA

APP * CHR * LDR * PHO
AT4 * AT5 * AT7 * AT8 * AT13 * GI5

NATIONAL PIANO FOUNDATION

   KEYS TO SUCCESSFUL PIANO STUDIO ORGANIZATION

CHICAGO	1960+	20P	BKTSPS
NATIONAL PIANO FOUNDATION			

SA

CHR * ILL * LDR
AT7 * AT8 * GI5

NATIONAL PIANO MANUFACTURERS ASSOCIATION OF AMERICA

   STENCILLING OF PIANOS, THE

NEW YORK	1899	32P	BSOP
NATIONAL PIANO MANUFACTURERS ASSOCIATION OF AMERICA			

NP

INT
KI5 * KI12 * GI5

NATIONAL PIANO MANUFACTURERS ASSOCIATION

   CONSUMER INVESTIGATION FOR NATIONAL PIANO MANUFACTURERS
   ASSOCIATION, 1938..CONDUCTED BY LAWRENCE H. SELZ

NEW YORK	1938+	60P	BCIFNP
NATIONAL PIANO MANUFACTURERS ASSOCIATION			

NP

APP * CHR * INT
KI12 * GI5

NATIONAL PIANO TRAVELERS ASSOCIATION

   PIANO TRAVELERS ASSOCIATION BOOK, THE ..A REFERENCE BOOK CONTAINING
   OFFICERS, COMMITTEES AND MEMBERS OF THE ASSOCIATION

NEW YORK	1916	258P	BPTABA
RAND MCNALLY AND COMPANY			

LC * NP

INT
KI12 * GI5 * GI6

NAYLOR, EDWARD W.

   ELIZABETHAN VIRGINAL BOOK, AN ..A CRITICAL ESSAY ON THE CONTENTS OF
   A MANUSCRIPT IN THE FITZWILLIAM MUSEUM AT CAMBRIDGE---1905

NEW YORK	1970	220P	BEVBAC
DA CAPO PRESS			

BP * BR * CU * ES * IU * LC * MI * NP * TO * UC * UI * UM * UT * UW
YU

ILL * IND * MEX
PM3 * PM7 * PM8 * PM9 * PM11 * AP3 * AP4

NEAL, HARRY LEE

   WAVE AS YOU PASS

PHILADELPHIA	1958	212P	BWAYP
LIPPINCOTT, J. B., COMPANY			

ES * IU * LC * NP * UA * UO

NP3 * NP4 * NP6 * PL8 * EP5

NEBLING, ALBERT N. *
SLOTNICK, ALFRED M.
MUSIC INSTRUMENT CHECKLIST

MUSKOGEE, OKLA.	1967+	24P	BMIC
FINE ART, PHILATELIST			

LC

   KI15

NEILL, JACK

   NEILL IMPROVISING SYSTEM

CHICAGO	1925		BNIS
NEILL COMPANY, THE			

   KS5

NELSON, WENDELL

CONCERTO, THE --BROWN 'MUSIC HORIZON' SERIES

DUBUQUE, IOWA   1969   109P   BC8MHS
BROWN, WILLIAM C., COMPANY
LC

BIB * ILL * IND * INT * MEX
PM8 * PM14

NETZORG, BENDETSON

KEY-BOTTOM TONE

DETROIT   1950   44P   BKBT
NETZORG, B.
CP * CU * IU * UM

INT * MEX
PT6 * PT7 * PT8 * PT10

NEUHAUS, HEINRICH

ART OF PIANO PLAYING, THE

NEW YORK   1973   240P   BAOPP
PRAEGER PUBLISHERS
IU * LC

IND * INT * MEX * PHO
PL12 * AT9 * AT13 * PT1 * PT6 * PT7 * AP1 * AP8

NEUPERT, HANNS

CLAVICHORD, THE ---1956, IN GERMAN

KASSEL   1965   83P   BCNFSI
BAERENREITER
AS * BR * LC * MI * NP * OC * UA * UI * UM

ILL * MEX * PHO
KI3 * KI5 * KI6 * KI8 * KI9 * KI14

NEUPERT, HANNS

HARPSICHORD MANUAL..A HISTORY AND TECHNICAL DEVELOPMENT--2ND.
ED.---1960

KASSEL   1968   119P   BHMAHA
BAERENREITER
AS * BP * BR * CP * CU * ES * IU * LC * MI * NP * OC * TO * UA * UC
UI * UM * UO * UW * YU
ILL * PHO
KI3 * KI5 * KI6 * KI8 * KI14

NEVINS, WILLARD I. *
LAND, VIOLA
HARMONY AT THE KEYBOARD

NEW YORK   1946   48P   BHATK
GRAY, H. W., COMPANY
LC * NP

INT * MEX
KS4 * KS8

NEWCOMB, ETHEL

LESCHETIZKY AS I KNEW HIM---1923

NEW YORK   1967   320P   BLAIKH
DA CAPO PRESS
AS * BP * BR * CP * ES * IU * LC * MI * NP * OC * SA * TO * UA * UC
UI * UK * UM * UO * US * UU
BIB * CNG * IND * INT * PHO
NP3 * NP4 * AT4

NEWMAN, ELIZABETH

HOW TO TEACH MUSIC TO BEGINNERS

NEW YORK   1957   152P   BHTTMT
FISCHER, CARL, INC.
IU * LC * NP * UT

BIB * CHR * INT * MEX * TAB
PL4 * PL8 * PL10 * PL12 * PL13 * AT1 * AT2 * AT5 * PT1 * PT9 * KS4
KS7 * AP6 * GI2

NEWMAN, ELIZABETH

TEACHING MATERIAL GRADED ACCORDING TO HARMONIC STRUCTURE, CAREFULLY
SELECTED FOR PIANO INSTRUCTION IN THE EARLY GRADES

NEW YORK   1942   20P   BTMGAT
NEWMAN, ELIZABETH
LC

AT14 * PM5 * PM6

NEWMAN, ERNEST

MAN LISZT, THE ..A STUDY OF THE TRAGI-COMEDY OF A SOUL DIVIDED
AGAINST ITSELF

LONDON   1969   313P   BMLASO
GOLLANCZ, VICTOR, LTD.
BR * IU * LC * NP

BIB * ILL * IND * INT
NP3 * PM3

NEWMAN, ERNEST

PIANO-PLAYER AND ITS MUSIC, THE

LONDON   1920   187P   BPPAIM
RICHARDS, G., LTD.
BP * ES * LC * NP * OC * UO

MEX
KI10 * AP3

NEWMAN, WILLIAM S.

PERFORMANCE PRACTICES IN BEETHOVEN'S PIANO SONATAS..AN INTRODUCTION

NEW YORK   1971   100P   BPPIBP
NORTON, W. W., AND CO.
LC

BIB * IND * MEX * MSF * PHO
NP3 * KI5 * KI6 * PL12 * PT1 * PM3 * PM4 * PM6 * PM13 * AP3 * AP4 *
AP6 * AP7

NEWMAN, WILLIAM S.

PIANIST'S PROBLEMS, THE ..A MODERN APPROACH TO EFFICIENT PRACTICE
AND MUSICIANLY PERFORMANCE--REV. ED.---1950

NEW YORK   1956   168P   BPPAMA
HARPER AND ROW PUBLISHERS, INC.
AS * BP * BR * CP * CU * ES * IU * LC * MI * NP * OC * SA * TO * UA
UC * UI * UK * UM * UO * US * UT * UW * YU
BIB * CHR * ILL * IND * INT * LDR * MEX
PL5 * PL7 * PL8 * PL9 * PL10 * PL12 * PT3 * PT6 * PT8 * PT9 * PT10
KS3 * KS4 * AP2 * AP4 * AP6 * AP7 * AP8 * AP9

NEWMAN, WILLIAM S.

SELECTED LIST OF MUSIC RECOMMENDED FOR PIANO STUDENTS, A --4TH.
REV. ED.---1953

CHAPEL HILL, N. C.   1965   30P   BSLOMR
NORTH CAROLINA, UNIVERSITY OF, EXTENSION DIVISION
BP * IU * LC * OC * SA * UI * UM

PM6 * PM15

NEWMAN, WILLIAM S.

SONATA IN THE BAROQUE ERA, THE --A HISTORY OF THE SONATA IDEA, VOL.
1

CHAPEL HILL, N. C.   1959   447P   BSITBE
NORTH CAROLINA, UNIVERSITY OF, PRESS
AS * BP * BR * CP * ES * IU * LC * MI * NP * OC * TO * UA * UC * UI
UK * UM * UO * US * UT * UU * UW * YU
BIB * CHR * IND * INT * MEX * MSF
KI3 * KI9 * KI14 * PM3 * PM4 * PM5 * PM7 * PM8 * PM9 * PM14 * PM15
AP3 * AP4 * AP5 * AP7 * EP3 * EP4 * EP6

NEWMAN, WILLIAM S.

SONATA IN THE CLASSIC ERA, THE --A HISTORY OF THE SONATA IDEA, VOL.
2

CHAPEL HILL, N. C.   1963   897P   BSITCE
NORTH CAROLINA, UNIVERSITY OF, PRESS
AS * BP * BR * CP * ES * IU * LC * MI * NP * OC * TO * UA * UC * UI
UK * UM * UO * US * UT * UU * UW * YU
BIB * IND * INT * MEX * MSF * TAB
KI3 * KI9 * KI14 * PM3 * PM4 * PM5 * PM7 * PM8 * PM9 * PM14 * PM15
AP3 * AP4 * AP5 * AP7 * EP3 * EP4 * EP5 * EP6

NEWMAN, WILLIAM S.

SONATA SINCE BEETHOVEN, THE --A HISTORY OF THE SONATA IDEA, VOL. 3

CHAPEL HILL, N. C.   1969   854P   BSSBAH
NORTH CAROLINA, UNIVERSITY OF, PRESS
BR * IU * LC * NP * UA * UT

APP * BIB * CHR * IND * INT * MEX * MSF * TAB
PM3 * PM5 * PM7 * PM8 * PM9 * PM14

NEWMAN, WILLIAM S.

THIRTEEN KEYBOARD SONATAS OF THE EIGHTEENTH AND NINETEENTH
CENTURIES, WITH CRITICAL COMMENTARIES

CHAPEL HILL, N. C.   1947   175P   BTKSOT
NORTH CAROLINA, UNIVERSITY OF, PRESS
IU * LC * NP * UA * UM * UT

INT * MEX
PM3 * PM7 * PM8 * PM9 * PM14 * PM15

NEWTON, ERNEST

ELEMENTARY STUDIES IN TRANSPOSITION--BKS. 1 AND 2

LONDON   1916   94P   BESITB
WILLIAMS, JOSEPH, LTD.
IU

INT * MEX
KS7 * EP6

NEWTON, IVOR

AT THE PIANO--IVOR NEWTON..THE WORLD OF AN ACCOMPANIST

LONDON   1966   309P   BATPIN
HAMILTON, HAMISH, LTD.
BP * ES * IU * LC * MI * NP * OC * SA * UI * UK

IND * PHO
NP6 * AP4 * AP5 * AP9 * EP6

NEW ENGLAND CONSERVATORY

   NEW ENGLAND CONSERVATORY METHOD FOR THE PIANO-FORTE, THE
   ..COMPRISING THE FIRST THREE GRADES OF INSTRUCTION

        BOSTON   1898   270P   BNECMF
        DITSON, OLIVER, COMPANY
  LC

  MEX
  PL4 * AT4

NEW ENGLAND CONSERVATORY

   TEACHERS' GRADED LIST FOR THE PIANOFORTE

        BOSTON   1899   33P   BTGLFT
        NEW ENGLAND CONSERVATORY MUSIC STORE
  LC

  INT
  PM6 * EP1

NEW SCHOOL FOR MUSIC STUDY

   STUDY GUIDE FOR PIANO TEACHERS

        PRINCETON, N. J.   1967   136P   BSGFPT
        NEW SCHOOL FOR MUSIC STUDY
  LC

  AT1 * AT2

NEW YORK--PUBLIC LIBRARY

   LIST OF PIANO MUSIC IN THE CIRCULATION DEPARTMENT OF THE NEW YORK
   PUBLIC LIBRARY

        NEW YORK   1917   48P   BLOPMI
        NEW YORK PUBLIC LIBRARY
  LC * NP

  INT
  PM5 * PM6

NEW YORK STATE MUSIC TEACHERS' ASSOCIATION

   SYLLABUS FOR PIANO, 1970

        HOUGHTON, N. Y.   1970   25P   BSFPNS
        ANDREWS, JOHN M., TREASURER, N.Y.S.M.T.A.

  PM5 * PM6 * GI6

NICCHIA, LILLIAN

   PIANOFORTE STUDY..HINTS ON PIANO PLAYING

        PHILADELPHIA   1897   141P   BPSHOP
        PRESSER, THEODORE, COMPANY
  NP * OC * UK * US

  IND
  NP5 * KI10 * PL7 * PL14 * PT4 * PT8 * KS4 * PM3 * PM4 * PM8 * AP4

NICHOL, HENRY E.

   TRANSPOSITION AT SIGHT..FOR STUDENTS OF THE ORGAN AND
   PIANOFORTE--4TH. ED.

        LONDON   1917+   30P   BTASFS
        REEVES, WILLIAM
  BP * BR * SA

  MEX * TAB
  KS7

NICHOLLS, FREDERICK *
TOBIN, J. RAYMOND
   ADVENTURES IN IMPROVISATION

        LONDON   1937   22P   BAII
        WILLIAMS, JOSEPH, LTD.
  BP

  INT * MEX
  KS5

NICHOLS, JULIA E.

   COMMON SENSE CATECHISM..OR, PIANO AND ORGAN PUPIL'S COMPANION

        CINCINNATI   1882   64P   BCSCOP
        HELMICK, F. W.
  UM

  PL1 * PL2 * PL11

NICHOLSON, JAMES

   CONCISE TREATISE ON THOROUGHBASS, A

        LONDON   1796+   61P   BCTOT
        BLAND AND WELLER'S MUSIC WAREHOUSE
  LC

  MEX
  KS10

NIECKS, FREDERICK

   FREDERICK CHOPIN AS A MAN AND MUSICIAN--2 VOLS.---1888

        LONDON   1927   720P   BFCAAM
        NOVELLO AND COMPANY
  BR * IU * LC * NP

  APP * ILL * IND * INT * MSF
  NP3 * PM3 * PM6

NILES BRYANT SCHOOL OF PIANO TUNING

   CORRESPONDENCE COURSE IN 12 LESSONS, A

        WASHINGTON, D. C.   1947   110P   BCCITL
        NILES BRYANT SCHOOL OF PIANO TUNING
  LC

  INT * PHO
  KI8 * PL4 * PL11 * AT4

NIMITZ, DANIEL

   KEYBOARD MASTERS..STUDY GUIDE

        ALBANY, N. Y.   1968   168P   BKMSG
        STATE UNIVERSITY OF NEW YORK--OFFICE FOR CONTINUING ED.
  LC

  PL6 * AT4 * PM5 * PM7 * PM9 * PM12 * GI2 * GI8

NIXON, W.

   GUIDE TO INSTRUCTION ON THE PIANOFORTE, A --IN A SERIES OF SHORT
   ESSAYS

        CINCINNATI   1834   96P   BGTIOT
        DRAKE, J.
  ES * LC * NP * YU

  INT
  PL7 * PL12 * AT4 * PT4 * PT6

NOHL, LUDWIG

   LIFE OF LISZT--'BIOGRAPHIES OF MUSICIANS', VOL. 5

        CHICAGO   1884   198P   BLOLBO
        JANSEN, MCCLURG AND COMPANY
  BP * BR * ES * IU * LC * MI * NP * OC * SA * UA * UM * UT

  APP * INT
  NP4

NORTON, EDWARD Q.

   CONSTRUCTION, TUNING AND CARE OF THE PIANOFORTE--EDITED AND LARGELY
   RE-WRITTEN BY HENRY FISHER---1893

        BOSTON   1915   96P   BCTACO
        DITSON, OLIVER, COMPANY
  BP * BR * CP * ES * LC * NP * UK * UW

  APP * IND * INT * LOR
  KI5 * KI8

NOSSIG, ALFRED

   METHODS OF THE MASTERS OF PIANO TEACHING IN EUROPE, THE ..THE
   SECRET OF PADEREWSKI'S PLAYING--'CENTURY LIBRARY OF MUSIC', VOL. 18

        NEW YORK   1902   3P   BMOTMO
        CENTURY LIBRARY OF MUSIC, THE
  LC * NP

  ILL * PHO
  NP3 * GI13

O'NEILL, J. A.

   DESCRIPTION AND HISTORY OF THE PIANOFORTE, A

        LONDON   1896   BDAHOT
        NOVELLO, EWER AND COMPANY
  MI

  KI3 * KI5 * KI6

O'REAR, MRS. ASBURY S.

   SELF READING NOTES

        LOUISVILLE   1898   48P   BSRN
        MOYER AND SCHLICH
  LC

  CHR * INT * MEX
  PL7 * PL15 * PT5 * PT9 * KS3 * AP7

O'TOOLE, WILLIAM

   CREATIVE PIANO TECHNIC

        NEW YORK   1937   56P   BCPT
        CREATIVE MUSIC PUBLISHERS
  BP * IU * SA * UI

  MEX
  AT1 * AT4 * PT1 * PT2

O'TOOLE, WILLIAM

    FIVE YEAR GUIDE TO PIANO TEACHING, A

        NEW YORK   1949   BFYGTP
           CREATIVE MUSIC PUBLISHERS
    BP * CP * LC * UI * UT * UW

    ILL
    PM6 * PM15

O'TOOLE, WILLIAM

    KEYBOARD HARMONY---DUPLICATED FROM MANUSCRIPT

        NEW YORK   1961   24P   BKHDFM
           O'TOOLE, WILLIAM
    LC

    PL10 * KS4

OFFERGELD, ROBERT

    CENTENNIAL CATALOGUE OF THE PUBLISHED AND UNPUBLISHED COMPOSITIONS
    OF LOUIS MOREAU GOTTSCHALK, THE

        NEW YORK   1970   34P   BCCOTP
           STEREO REVIEW
    IU * LC

    ILL * INT * PHO
    NP4 * PM3 * PM6

OLIVER, EDWARD B.

    PRACTICAL TEXT-BOOK OF MUSIC, AS CONNECTED WITH THE ART OF PLAYING
    THE PIANOFORTE, A

        BOSTON   1853   59P   BPTBOM
           DITSON, OLIVER, COMPANY
    BP * LC * NP * UM

    APP * CHR * IND * INT * MEX
    PL4 * PL12 * PT4 * PT6 * PT8 * AP4

ORD-HUME, ARTHUR W. J. G.

    CLOCKWORK MUSIC..AN ILLUSTRATED HISTORY OF MECHANICAL MUSICAL
    INSTRUMENTS FROM THE MUSICAL BOX TO THE PIANOLA, FROM AUTOMATON
    LADY VIRGINAL PLAYERS TO ORCHESTRION
        NEW YORK   1973   334P   BCMAIH
           CROWN PUBLISHERS

    KI3 * KI5 * KI6 * KI9 * KI10 * KI13

ORD-HUME, ARTHUR W. J. G.

    PLAYER PIANO, THE HISTORY OF THE MECHANICAL PIANO AND HOW TO REPAIR
    IT

        NEW YORK   1970   296P   BPPTHO
           BARNES, A. S., AND COMPANY
    CU * LC * NP

    APP * BIB * ILL * IND * LDR * PHO
    KI2 * KI3 * KI5 * KI6 * KI8 * KI10

OREGON MUSIC TEACHERS ASSOCIATION

    PIANO MATERIALS

        PORTLAND   1952   21P   BPM
           OREGON MUSIC TEACHERS ASSOCIATION
    UA

    AT2 * PM6

OREM, PRESTON WARE

    MANUAL OF MODULATION

        PHILADELPHIA   1930   44P   BMOM
           PRESSER, THEODORE, COMPANY
    IU * NP * SA * TO

    APP * MEX * INT
    PL4 * KS8

ORLIK, JULES

    CREATIVE APPROACH TO PIANO CLASS TEACHING, A ---REPRODUCED FROM
    TYPEWRITTEN COPY

        NEW YORK   1941   87P   BCATPC
           WORK PROJECTS ADMINISTRATION--MUS. DIV.
    NP

    APP * INT * MEX
    PL4 * PL10 * AT5 * AT6 * AT7 * PT9 * PM6 * EP2

ORREY, LESLIE

    MUSIC AT THE KEYBOARD

        LONDON   1965   82P   BMATK
           BELL AND SONS
    BP * BR * CP * ES * IU * LC * SA * TO * UK * UO * YU

    APP * CHR * MEX * INT
    PL4 * PL12 * KS3 * KS4 * KS5 * KS7 * KS10 * KS12

ORTMANN, OTTO

    PHYSICAL BASIS OF PIANO TOUCH AND TONE, THE

        LONDON   1925   189P   BPBOPT
           PAUL, KEGAN, TRENCH, TRUBNER AND COMPANY
    BP * BR * CU * ES * IU * LC * MI * NP * TO * UI * UK * UO * US * UT * UU
    YU
    BIB * IND
    KI5 * KI6 * KI7 * KI9 * PT8

ORTMANN, OTTO

    PHYSIOLOGICAL MECHANICS OF PIANO TECHNIQUE, THE ---1929

        NEW YORK   1962   395P   BPMOPT
           DUTTON, E. P., AND COMPANY
    AS * BP * BR * CP * CU * ES * IU * LC * MI * NP * OC * SA * TO * UA
    UC * UI * UK * UM * UO * US * UT * UU * UW * YU
    BIB * IND * INT * LDR * MEX * PHO * TAB
    PT1 * PT2 * PT3 * PT4 * PT6 * PT7 * PT8 * PT9

OSBORNE, GEORGE A.

    REMINISCENSES OF FREDERIC CHOPIN

        LONDON   1880   BROFC

    NP6

OSTROVSKY, HENRY

    LESSON COURSE...THE COMPLETE OSTROVSKY FINGER EXERCISE, FOR
    PIANISTS, VIOLINISTS, 'CELLISTS

        LONDON   1914   22P   BLCTCO
           OSTROVSKY MUSICIANS' HAND DEVELOPMENT COMPANY
    BR

    PT10

OSTROVSKY, HENRY

    TECHNIQUE AND HAND DEVELOPMENT---USE OF A MACHINE

        LONDON   1914+   20P   BTAHDU
           OSTROVSKY, HENRY
    BR

    PT1 * PT3 * PT14

OTTERSTROEN, THORVALD

    THEORY OF MODULATION, A ---DUAL TEXT..ENGLISH AND GERMAN

        CHICAGO   1935   161P   BTOMDT
           UNIVERSITY OF CHICAGO PRESS
    BR * IU * LC * NP

    APP * INT * MEX * TAB
    KS8

PACE, ROBERT

    MUSIC ESSENTIALS FOR CLASSROOM TEACHERS--2ND. ED.---1961

        BELMONT, CAL.   1971   123P   BMEFCT
           WADSWORTH PUBLISHING COMPANY, INC.
    AS * CP * ES * IU * LC * MI * OC * SA * TO * UI * UT * UW

    APP * CHR * IND * INT * MEX
    PL4 * PL6 * PL7 * PL10 * PL12 * PL13 * PL14 * AT4 * AT6 * AT7 *
    KS4 * KS5 * KS7 * KS11

PACE, ROBERT

    PIANO FOR CLASSROOM MUSIC--2ND. ED.---1956

        ENGLEWOOD CLIFFS, N. J.   1970   140P   BPFCMS
           PRENTICE-HALL, INC.
    AS * BP * CP * CU * IU * LC * MI * NP * OC * SA * TO * UA * UI * UM
    UO * US * UT * UW * YU
    CHR * GLO * INT * LDR * MEX
    PL4 * PL13 * PL14 * AT6 * AT7 * AT8 * KS4 * KS5 * KS7

PADEREWSKI, IGNACE JAN

    CHOPIN..A DISCOURSE

        NEW YORK   1911   30P   BCAD
           SCHAAD, H. B.
    BP * LC * US * YU

    INT
    NP6

PADEREWSKI, IGNACE JAN *
LAWTON, MARY
    PADEREWSKI MEMOIRS, THE ---1938

        NEW YORK   1973   404P   BPMNTE
           VIENNA HOUSE
    AS * BP * BR * CP * IU * LC * MI * NP * OC * SA * UA * UC * UK * UM
    UO * UT * UW * YU
    IND * PHO
    NP6

PADEREWSKI FOUNDATION

    IGNACY JAN PADEREWSKI, 1860-1941..MEMORIAL ALBUM---IN ENGLISH AND
    POLISH

          NEW YORK   1953   56P   BIJPES
             PADEREWSKI FOUNDATION
    NP

    INT * PHO
    NP4

PAETKAU, DAVID H.

    GROWTH OF INSTRUMENTS AND INSTRUMENTAL MUSIC, THE

          NEW YORK   1962   393P   BGOIAI
             VANTAGE PRESS, INC.
    IU * LC * NP

    BIB * ILL * IND * INT * LDR * MEX * PHO
    KI4 * KI5 * KI6 * KI7 * KI9 * KI14

PAGE, C. E.

    MUSICAL INSTRUMENTS--MECHANICAL AGE LIBRARY

          LONDON   1960   144P   BMIMAL
             MULLER, FREDERICK, LTD.
    LC * NP

    APP * ILL * IND * INT * LDR * PHO
    KI3 * KI5 * KI6

PAIN, EVA

    BEGINNING TO PLAY THE PIANO..A MANUAL FOR TEACHERS

          LONDON   1966   45P   BBTPTP
             OXFORD UNIVERSITY PRESS
    BR * LC * SA * UI

    CHR * MEX * INT
    PL4 * PL13 * AT4 * AT5

PALME, RUDOLPH

    FIRST MONTHS IN PIANOFORTE INSTRUCTION, THE ---1870, IN GERMAN

          PHILADELPHIA   1911   85P   BFMIPI
             PRESSER, THEODORE, COMPANY
    ES * LC

    ILL * INT * MEX
    KI6 * PL10 * PL12 * PT4 * PT6 * PT8 * PT10

PALMER, ANNIE L.

    MUSIC TEACHERS' GUIDE TO THE GOLDBECK PIANO METHOD

          ST. LOUIS   1891   66P   BMTGTT
             CLAUS AND BARCLAY, PRINTERS
    LC

    ILL * INT * LDR
    PL8 * PL15 * AT4 * PT11 * PM6 * AP4 * AP6

PALMER, HORATIO R.

    PALMER'S PIANO PRIMER

          NEW YORK   1885   192P   BPPP
             PALMER, H. R.
    ES * LC * NP * UC

    CHR * GLO * ILL * INT * LDR * MEX * TAB
    PL4 * AT7 * PT6 * PT8 * PT9 * PT11 * PM10 * AP3 * AP7

PALMER, KING

    TEACH YOURSELF MUSIC

          LONDON   1944   183P   BTYM
             ENGLISH UNIVERSITIES PRESS
    BR * LC * NP

    MEX
    PL11 * AT4

PALMER, KING

    TEACH YOURSELF TO PLAY THE PIANO

          LONDON   1957   144P   BTYTPT
             ENGLISH UNIVERSITIES PRESS, THE
    CP * ES * IU * LC * NP * SA

    BIB * IND * LDR * MEX
    KI4 * KI8 * PL4 * PL7 * PL9 * PT1 * PT6 * AP4 * EP1 * GI11

PALMER, WILLARD A.--EDITOR

    CHOPIN..AN INTRODUCTION TO HIS PIANO WORKS

          PORT WASHINGTON, N. Y.   1972   BCAITH
             ALFRED MUSIC

    PM3 * PM8 * PM14 * AP4 * AP7 * AP8

PARKER, DOUGLAS C.

    PERCY ALDRIDGE GRAINGER, A STUDY

          NEW YORK   1918   36P   BPAGAS
             SCHIRMER, G., INC.
    BP * BR * LC * NP * OC

    MEX * MSF * PHO
    NP4 * PM6

PARKER, HENRY T.

    EIGHTH NOTES, VOICES AND FIGURES OF MUSIC AND THE DANCE---CHAPTER
    ON PIANISTS

          NEW YORK   1922   238P   BENVAF
             DODD, MEAD AND COMPANY
    LC * NP * SA

    APP
    NP6

PARKER, RICHARD G.

    TRIBUTE TO THE LIFE AND CHARACTER OF JONAS CHICKERING, 1798-1853, A
    --'BY ONE WHO KNEW HIM WELL'

          BOSTON   1854   162P   BTTTLA
             TEWKSBURY, W. P.
    LC * NP

    APP * ILL * INT
    NP6 * KI12

PARKINSON, HANS B.

    PIANO, THE ..ITS CARE

          LOS ANGELES   1922   18P   BPIC
             PARKINSON, HANS B.
    LC

    KI8

PARRISH, CARL

    EARLY PIANO AND ITS INFLUENCE ON KEYBOARD TECHNIQUE AND COMPOSITION
    IN THE EIGHTEENTH CENTURY

          SUPERIOR, WIS.   1953   438P   BEPAII
             RESEARCH MICROFILM PUBLISHERS
    IU * LC * UM * UT

    APP * ILL * INT * MEX
    KI3 * KI5 * KI6 * KI12 * KI14 * PM3 * PM6 * PM7 * PM14

PARSONS, ALBERT R.

    SCIENCE OF PIANO PRACTICE, THE

          NEW YORK   1886   70P   BSOPP
             SCHIRMER, G., INC.
    BP * LC * NP * UC * UK * UM * YU

    APP * CHR * INT * MEX
    PL7 * PT5 * PT11 * PT14 * PM10

PARSONS, ALBERT R.

    SYNTHETIC METHOD FOR THE PIANOFORTE, THE

          NEW YORK   1906   72P   BSMFTP
             SILVER BURDETT COMPANY
    NP * OC * UO * YU

    APP * INT * MEX
    PL4 * PL12 * PL15 * PT5 * PT9 * AP6

PARSONS, MARY H.

    RHYTHMIC WAY, THE

          BOSTON   1930   89P   BRW
             DITSON, OLIVER, COMPANY
    IU * NP * UW

    CHR * INT * MEX
    PL5 * PL12 * PT9

PASFIELD, WILLIAM R.

    MELODY MAKING, KEYBOARD HARMONY AND EXTEMPORISATION

          LONDON   1959   36P   BMMKHA
             WILLIAMS, JOSEPH
    LC * UT

    INT * MEX
    KS5

PASQUALI, NICOLO

    ART OF FINGERING THE HARPSICHORD, THE

          EDINBURGH   1760+   43P   BAOFTH
             BREMNER, R.
    IU * LC * TO * UM

    MEX
    AT5 * AT6 * PL4 * PT6 * PT9 * PT11 * AP7

PASQUALI, NICOLO

THOROUGH-BASS MADE EASY..OR, PRACTICAL RULES FOR FINDING AND
APPLYING ITS VARIOUS CHORDS WITH LITTLE TROUBLE, ETC.

        EDINBURGH   1757   48P   BTBMEO
            BREMNER, R.
BR * LC * NP

KS10

PATTERSON, ANNIE WILSON

PROFESSION OF MUSIC AND HOW TO PREPARE FOR IT, THE

        LONDON   1926   235P   BPOMAH
            GARDNER, W., DARTON AND COMPANY, LTD.
BR * LC * NP

APP * IND * INT
EP6 * GI5 * GI13

PATTON, VICTOR S.

LEARN TO PLAY POPULAR PIANO BY NOTE IN 20 EASY LESSONS...HOME STUDY
METHOD
        CINCINNATI   1939   37P   BLTPPP
            ZIMMERMAN PRINTERS
LC

INT * MEX
PL7 * PL11 * AT4 * KS3 * KS4 * KS5 * KS6

PAUER, ERNST

ART OF PIANOFORTE PLAYING, THE

        LONDON   1877+   88P   BAOPP
            NOVELLO AND COMPANY
BP * BR * TO * UC * YU

AP1 * AP2

PAUER, ERNST

DICTIONARY OF PIANISTS AND COMPOSERS FOR THE PIANOFORTE..WITH AN
APPENDIX OF MANUFACTURERS FOR THE INSTRUMENT
        LONDON   1896+   156P   BDOPAC
            NOVELLO, EWER AND COMPANY
BP * BR * LC * NP * OC * TO * UM

INT
NP3 * KI12 * KI15 * PM3

PAUER, ERNST

ERNST PAUER'S SIX HISTORICAL PERFORMANCES OF PIANOFORTE MUSIC

        LONDON   1863   173P   BEPSHP
            GOLBOURN, W. J.
NP

APP * INT
PM3 * PM7 * PM9

PAULSON, JOSEPH

MODERN KEYBOARD HARMONY AND IMPROVISATION

        NEW YORK   1946   BMKHAI
            KING MUSIC PUBLISHING CORPORATION
LC * NP

CHR * INT * MEX
KS4 * KS5

PAYNE, ALBERT

CELEBRATED PIANISTS OF THE PAST AND PRESENT--139 BIOGRAPHIES, WITH
PORTRAITS---ALSO CATALOGUED UNDER THE AUTHORSHIP..ALFRED HEINRICH
EHRLICH
        PHILADELPHIA   1894   423P   BCPOTP
            PRESSER, THEODORE, COMPANY
AS * BP * BR * CP * ES * IU * LC * MI * NP * SA * UI * US * UT * UU
YU
ILL * INT
NP3 * NP4 * NP5

PEABODY INSTITUTE, BALTIMORE

GRADED LIST OF SOME USEFUL WORKS FOR PIANO STUDY---REVISED BY
CARLOTTA HELLER
        BALTIMORE   1942   35P   BGLOSU
            PEABODY CONSERVATORY PREPARATORY DEPARTMENT
LC

PM6 * PM14 * EP1

PEARCE, CHARLES WILLIAM

ART OF THE PIANO TEACHER, THE

        LONDON   1916   352P   BAOTPT
            BOOSEY AND HAWKES
BP * BR * CU * LC * NP * TO * UK * UO

APP * ILL * INT * MEX
PL7 * PL8 * PL12 * PL15 * AT4 * AT8 * AT11 * PT3 * PT6 * PT8 * PT9
PT10 * KS4 * KS8 * PM14 * AP7 * AP8 * EP6 * GI5

PEDERSON, GALE

KEY TO THE KEYS..A SELF-TAUGHT PIANO METHOD FOR ADULTS AND TEEN
AGERS--PHONODISC..INSTRUCTION BOOK
        WILMINGTON, DEL.   1967   18P   BKTTKA
            PIANO PLAYHOUSE
LC

ILL * INT * MEX
PL11 * AT4 * PM12

PEDERSON, OLAF

MEMORY TESTS FOR PIANOFORTE PLAYING ---7 PIECES WITH INSTRUCTIONS

        LONDON   1934   18P   BMTFPP
            WARREN AND PHILLIPS
LC

INT
PL8

PEERY, ROB ROY

PRACTICAL KEYBOARD MODULATION

        PHILADELPHIA   1944+   68P   BPKM
            PRESSER, THEODORE, COMPANY
CP * IU * NP * SA

INT * MEX
KS8

PELTIER, LOUIS O.

PIANO TUNER'S GUIDE, THE

        SOMERVILLE, MASS.   1877   24P   BPTG
            PELTIER, L. O.
LC

INT * MEX
KI8

PELZ, EDWARD

ON PIANOFORTE MANUFACTURE, ESPECIALLY IN AMERICA

        LEIPZIG   1865   13P   BOPMEI
            SCHUBERTH, J., AND COMPANY
NP

ILL * LDR
KI3

PELZ, WILLIAM

BASIC KEYBOARD SKILLS--2ND. ED.---1963

        BOSTON   1968   184P   BBKSSE
            ALLYN AND BACON, INC.
BP * CP * CU * ES * IU * LC * MI * OC * SA * TO * UA * UI * UM * UT
UU * UW * YU
APP * CHR * IND * INT * MEX * TAB
KS3 * KS5 * KS7 * PM6

PENGELLY, J. BRADFORD

PENGELLY BLUE BOOK OF STYLE, THE ...A STUDY OF THE ART OF STYLING
AS APPLIED TO MUSICAL INSTRUMENTS
        CHICAGO   1942   253P   BPBBOS
            MUSIC TIMES COMPANY
LC

INT
KI3 * KI5 * KI9 * KI12 * KI13 * GI5 * GI15

PERRY, ADELAIDE TROWBRIDGE

COMPENDIUM OF PIANO MATERIAL--2ND. ED.---1929

        LOS ANGELES   1939   151P   BCOPMS
            SOUTHERN CALIFORNIA, UNIVERSITY OF, PRESS
BP * CP * ES * LC * MI * NP * UK * US * UT * YU

INT
PM6 * PM15

PERRY, ADELAIDE TROWBRIDGE *
AID, HAZEL YOKO
GUIDE TO PIANO STUDY FOR CLASS OR INDIVIDUAL INSTRUCTION, A

        NEW YORK   1954   BGTPSF
            KALMUS, EDWIN F.
BP * LC

ILL * INT * MEX
PL5 * PL9 * PL13 * AT7 * AT8 * PT1 * KS3

PERRY, EDWARD B.

DESCRIPTIVE ANALYSES OF PIANO WORKS, FOR THE USE OF TEACHERS,
PLAYERS, AND MUSIC CLUBS
        PHILADELPHIA   1902   290P   BDAOPW
            PRESSER, THEODORE, COMPANY
AS * BP * BR * CP * ES * LC * MI * NP * OC * SA * TO * UA * UM * UO
US * UT * UW
INT
PM3 * PM13 * PM14 * PM15 * AP4 * AP5

PERRY, EDWARD B.

    STORIES OF STANDARD TEACHING PIECES FOR THE PIANOFORTE

                PHILADELPHIA   1910   236P   BSOSTP
                PRESSER, THEODORE, COMPANY
    BP * BR * CP * ES * IU * LC * MI * NP * SA * TO * UA * UO * US

    IND * INT
    PM3 * PM6 * PM9 * PM15 * AP5

PETERS, WILLIAM C.

    ECLECTIC PIANOFORTE SCHOOL, THE ..ARRANGED FROM THE WORKS OF THE
    BEST EUROPEAN COMPOSERS WITH SELECTIONS FROM EMINENT AMERICAN
    AUTHORS
                NEW YORK   1855   224P   BEPSAF
                HALL, W., AND SON
    BP * CU * LC * UM

    INT
    PL4 * PT9 * KS10

PETERS, WILLIAM C.

    ELEMENTS OF THOROUGH BASE, ADAPTED TO THE WANTS OF YOUNG PUPILS

                NEW YORK   1856   68P   BEOTBA
                PETERS, W. M.
    LC

    INT * MEX
    KS8 * KS10

PETERSILEA, CARLYLE

    PIANO PLAYING..GENERAL MUSICAL INSTRUCTION FROM BEGINNING TO END

                BOSTON   1891   120P   BPPGMI
                CROKE PRINTING COMPANY
    BP

    PL1 * PL2 * AP1 * AP2

PETERSILIA, FRANZ

    STUDY WITH AMUSEMENT, A SERIES OF PROGRESSIVE LESSONS FOR THE
    PIANOFORTE...INCLUDING THE FIRST PRINCIPLES OF HARMONY--2 PTS.
                BOSTON   1847   63P   BSWAAS
                REED, G. P.
    BP * NP

    INT * MEX
    AT4 * KS4

PETERSON, FRANKLIN

    HANDBOOK OF MUSICAL FORM--PART 2 OF THE PIANIST'S HANDBOOK

                LONDON   1898   182P   BHOMFP
                AUGENER, LTD.
    BR * SA

    IND * LDR * MEX * TAB
    PM3 * PM7 * PM14

PETERSON, FRANKLIN

    THEORETIC COMPANION TO PRACTICE--PART I OF THE PIANIST'S HANDBOOK

                LONDON   1898   70P   BTCTPP
                AUGENER, LTD.
    BR * NP * SA

    CHR * INT * LDR * MEX
    KI3 * KI5 * KI6 * PL4 * PL7 * PL8 * PL12 * PT6 * PT10 * KS3 * PM9 *
    AP4 * AP7 * EP6

PETERSON, HOUSTON--EDITOR

    GREAT TEACHERS, PORTRAYED BY THOSE WHO STUDIED UNDER THEM--INCLUDES
    'A TYPICAL LESSON..LESCHETIZKY', BY ETHEL NEWCOMB
                NEW YORK   1946   351P   BGTPBT
                RANDON HOUSE
    BR * IU * LC

    IND * INT
    NP6 * AT3 * AT12

PETRI, LILLIAN JEFFREY

    MIND OVER MUSCLE..A TECHNICAL ECONOMY FOR PIANISTS

                CHICAGO   1924   140P   BMOMAT
                GAMBLE HINGED MUSIC COMPANY
    BR * LC * MI

    INT * MEX * PHO
    PL7 * AT4 * PT7 * PT8 * PT9 * PT10

PFEFFERKORN, OTTO W.

    PIANISTIC HINTS

                GAINESVILLE, GA.   1911   34P   BPH
                BRENAN PUBLISHING COMPANY, THE
    LC

    CHR * INT
    PL9 * PL12 * PL15 * PT7 * KS4 * AP7

PFEIFFER, WALTER

    PIANO KEY AND WHIPPEN, THE ..AN ANALYSIS OF THEIR RELATIONSHIPS IN
    DIRECT BLOW ACTIONS---1948, IN GERMAN

                FRANKFURT AM MAIN   1967   73P   BPKAWA
                VERLAG DAS MUSIKINSTRUMENT
    BR * ES * IU * LC

    ILL
    KI5 * KI6 * KI8

PHILIPP, ISIDOR

    SOME REFLECTIONS ON PIANO PLAYING

                PHILADELPHIA   1928   23P   BSROPP
                ELKAN-VOGEL COMPANY
    UK * US

    NP6 * AP1

PHILIPP, ISIDOR

    TRILL IN THE WORKS OF BEETHOVEN, THE

                BOSTON   1910   19P   BTITWO
                DITSON, OLIVER, COMPANY
    BP

    PT2

PHILIPP, LILLIE H.

    PIANO STUDY..APPLICATION AND TECHNIQUE

                NEW YORK   1969   91P   BPSAAT
                MUSIC CORPORATION OF AMERICA
    LC * NP

    INT * MEX * PHO
    PL6 * PL7 * PL8 * PL15 * AT4 * AT6 * PT4 * PT5 * PT6 * PT8 * PT9 *
    PT10 * PT11 * KS3 * AP6 * AP7 * AP8

PHILLIPS, CHARLES

    PADEREWSKI..THE STORY OF A MODERN IMMORTAL

                LONDON   1933   563P   BPTSOA
                MACMILLAN AND COMPANY
    BP * BR * ES * IU * LC * MI * NP * OC * UA * UK * UM * UO * UW

    APP * IND * INT * PHO
    NP3 * PM3 * PM6

PHILLIPSON, WENTWORTH

    GUIDE TO YOUNG PIANOFORTE TEACHERS AND STUDENTS

                LONDON   1872   62P   BGTYPT
                PHILLIPSON, WENTWORTH
    BR * NP

    APP * INT * MEX
    KI4 * PL7 * PL9 * PL12 * PL15 * AT4 * AT11 * PT6 * PT8 * PT10 *
    AP7 * AP8

PIANO, ORGAN AND MUSICAL INSTRUMENT WORKERS INTERNATIONAL UNION OF
AMERICA
    CONSTITUTION OF THE PIANO, ORGAN AND MUSICAL INSTRUMENT WORKERS'
    INTERNATIONAL UNION OF AMERICA

                CHICAGO   1898   4P   BCOTPO
                MUSICAL INSTRUMENT WORKERS INTERNATIONAL UNION OF AMERICA
    LC

    KI12 * GI15

PICHIER, PAUL

    PIANIST'S TOUCH, THE ..METHOD AND THEORY OF PAUL PICHIER

                MARSHALL, CAL.   1972   260P   BPTMAT
                PERELIN PUBLISHERS
    LC

    AT4 * PT8

PIERCE, B.

    PIERCE PIANO ATLAS--6TH. ED.---ORIGINALLY PUBLISHED AS 'MICHEL'S
    PIANO ATLAS' IN 1947

                LONG BEACH, CAL.   1965   243P   BPPASE
                PIERCE B.
    CP * IU * LC * NP * TO * UO * UW

    INT
    KI12 * KI13 * KI15

PIERCE, DORA *
LEAVEY, LILLIAN
    INTRODUCTION TO SIGHT READING, AN

                LONDON   1947   BITSR
                OXFORD UNIVERSITY PRESS
    LC

    KS3

PIERCE, DORA *
LEAVEY, LILLIAN
 READ AND ENJOY--2 VOLS.

    LONDON   1935 28P   BRAETV
     OXFORD UNIVERSITY PRESS
 LC

 INT * MEX
 KS3

PIERCE, DORA *
LEAVEY, LILLIAN
 SIGHT READING TESTS FOR BEGINNERS--2 VOLS., 1930-1933

    LONDON   1930   BSRTFB
     OXFORD UNIVERSITY PRESS
 LC

 INT * MEX
 KS3

PIGGOTT, PATRICK

 LIFE AND MUSIC OF JOHN FIELD, 1782-1837, THE

    BERKELEY, CAL.   1974 303P BLAMOJ
     UNIVERSITY OF CALIFORNIA PRESS
 IU

 APP * BIB * ILL * IND * INT * MEX * MSF * PHO
 NP3 * PM3 * PM14 * GI13

PILLING, DOROTHY

 HARMONIZATION OF MELODIES AT THE KEYBOARD--BKS. 1 AND 2

    LONDON   1952+ 48P   BHOMAT
     FORSYTH BROTHERS
 BR * LC * NP

 INT
 KS4 * KS8 * KS10

PILLING, DOROTHY

 KEY TO THE HARMONIZATION OF MELODIES AT THE KEYBOARD--BK. 1

    LONDON   1960   BKTTHO
     FORSYTH BROTHERS
 BR

 KS4

PINCHERLE, MARC

 WORLD OF THE VIRTUOSO, THE

    NEW YORK   1963 192P BWOTV
     NORTON, W. W., AND COMPANY
 BP * BP * ES * IU * LC * MI * NP * OC * TO * UI * UK * UM * UO * UT

 ILL * INT * MSF
 KI3 * KI5 * KI14 * AP3 * AP4

PIRANI, EUGENIO DI

 SECRETS OF THE SUCCESS OF GREAT MUSICIANS

    PHILADELPHIA   1922 321P BSOTSO
     PRESSER, THEODORE, COMPANY
 BP * ES * LC * NP * UA

 ILL * INT * PHO
 NP5 * PM3

PLAIDY, LOUIS

 PIANOFORTE TEACHER'S GUIDE, THE

    NEW YORK   1876 36P   BPTG
     SCHUBERTH, E.
 BP * BR * ES * LC * NP * OC * YU

 APP * CHR * IND * MEX
 PL4 * AT1 * PT4 * PT9 * PT10

PLAIDY, LOUIS

 PIANO TEACHER, THE

    BOSTON   1875 41P   BPT
     DITSON, OLIVER, COMPANY
 BP * LC

 MEX
 PL6 * AT3 * PM10 * PT1 * PT8 * PT9

PLANTIGA, LEON B.

 SCHUMANN AS CRITIC

    NEW HAVEN, CONN. 1967 354P BSAC
     YALE UNIVERSITY PRESS
 IU * LC

 APP * BIB * IND * INT
 NP7 * PM10 * GI15

PLATT, CAROLYN

 CAROLYN PLATT METHOD FOR PIANO, THE --GROUP INSTRUCTION--TEACHER'S
 MANUAL---TYPEWRITTEN COPY

    PORTLAND, ORE. 1940 28P   BCPMFP
     EMPIRE SERVICE CORPORATION
 LC

 PL7 * PL8 * PL10 * PL14 * AT3 * AT7 * AT9 * PT1 * PT9 * KS7 * AP6 *
 AP8

PLAYER-PIANO, THE

 FOUR HUNDRED OF THE BEST ADS OF 1911 DEVOTED TO PIANOS AND
 PLAYER-PIANOS

    NEW YORK   1912 84P   BFHOTB
     PLAYER-PIANO, THE
 LC

 ILL * INT * PHO
 KI4 * KI9 * KI12 * KI13

PLAYFORD, JOHN

 MUSICKS HAND-MAID..NEW LESSONS AND INSTRUCTIONS FOR THE VIRGINALS
 OR HARPSYCHORD

    LONDON   1678 72P   BMHMNL
     PLAYFORD, J.
 IU * LC

 ILL * MEX
 KI14 * PL4 * AT4

POINTER SYSTEM, INC.

 GUIDE TO THE MODERN PIANIST, A

    WINONA, MINN. 1963 18P   BGTTMP
     POINTER SYSTEM, INC.
 LC

 INT
 PL15 * AT10 * PT8 * PT10 * KS3 * KS4 * AP4 * AP6 * AP8

POLISH RESEARCH AND INFORMATION SERVICE

 FREDERIC CHOPIN--CENTENNIAL 1849-1949, BACKGROUND MATERIAL---ELEVEN
 ARTICLES

    NEW YORK   1949 28P   BFCCEF
     POLISH RESEARCH AND INFORMATION SERVICE
 IU * LC

 NP4 * NP6 * PM3

POLISH RESEARCH AND INFORMATION SERVICE

 FREDERIC CHOPIN CENTENNIAL--1949---EIGHT ARTICLES

    NEW YORK   1949 47P   BFCCNF
     POLISH RESEARCH AND INFORMATION SERVICE
 IU * LC

 ILL * LDR * MSF * PHO
 NP4 * NP6 * PM3

PORTE, JOHN F.

 CHOPIN, THE COMPOSER AND HIS MUSIC

    NEW YORK   1935 193P BCTCAH
     SCRIBNER'S, CHARLES, SONS
 BP * LC * NP * OC * UA * UO * YU

 BIB * DIS * ILL
 NP3 * PM3 * PM14 * AP3

PORTE, JOHN F.

 EDWARD MACDOWELL, A GREAT AMERICAN TONE POET..HIS LIFE AND MUSIC

    LONDON   1922 180P BEMDAG
     PAUL, KEGAN, TRENCH, TRUBNER AND COMPANY
 BP * BR * ES * IU * LC * MI * NP * OC * TO * UA * UM * UO * UT * UW

 IND * INT * MEX
 NP4 * NP6 * PM3 * PM6 * PM9

PORTER, FRANK A. *
PORTER, LAURA H.
 TEACHERS' MANUAL FOR THE PORTER PIANOFORTE COURSE

    BOSTON   1933 34P   BTMFTP
     WOOD, B. F., MUSIC COMPANY, THE
 LC

 INT * MEX * PHO
 AT3 * AT4

POTAMKIN, FRANK

 MODERN PIANO PEDAGOGY

    PHILADELPHIA   1936 221P BMPP
     ELKAN-VOGEL COMPANY
 BP * BP * CP * CU * ES * IU * LC * MI * NP * SA * US * YU

 APP * BIB * MEX
 PL4 * PL7 * PL8 * PL10 * PL12 * AT3 * AT9 * PT4 * PT8 * PT9 * KS3 *
 PM2 * AP6 * AP8

POTOCKA, COMTESSE ANGELE

    THEODOR LESCHETIZKY

            NEW YORK   1903   307P   BTL
               CENTURY COMPANY, THE
    BP * BR * CP * ES * IU * LC * MI * NP * SA * TO * UA * UC * UK * UM
    UO * US * UT
    INT * PHO
    NP3 * NP4

POURTALES, GUY DE

    FRANZ LISZT, THE MAN OF LOVE

            NEW YORK   1926   299P   BFLTMO
               HOLT, HENRY, AND COMPANY
    BR * IU * LC * NP

    NP4 * PM3

POURTALES, GUY DE

    POLONAISE, THE LIFE OF CHOPIN---ENGLISH EDITION, 'FREDERICK CHOPIN,
    A MAN OF SOLITUDE'

            NEW YORK   1927   349P   BPTLOC
               HOLT, HENRY, AND COMPANY
    BR * IU * LC * NP

    BIB * ILL * IND
    NP3 * PM3

POWERS-WADSWORTH, L.

    PIANIST'S GUIDE TO TECHNICAL FREEDOM, THE ..2 VOLS. IN 1

            WHEATON, ILL.   1961   88P   BPGTTF
               WHEATON COLLEGE
    UI

    LDR * MEX
    PL1 * PL2 * AT1 * AT2 * AT5 * AT6 * PT1 * PT2 * PT5

POWERS, J. HAROLD

    MUSIC'S GLAMOROUS HALL OF FAME..SHORT ARTICLES ABOUT FAMOUS NAMES,
    COMPOSERS, VIRTUOSOS AND SINGERS---DESCRIPTIVE AND ANECDOTAL

            NEW YORK   1972   104P   BMGHOF
               CARLTON PRESS

    NP5 * GI13

PRATT, SILAS G.

    PIANIST'S MENTAL VELOCITY, THE ..A SYSTEMATIC PREPARATION OF THE
    MIND OF PIANO PLAYERS TO THINK MUSIC IN GROUPS

            NEW YORK   1905   68P   BPMVAS
               BRAINARD'S, S., SONS COMPANY, THE
    LC

    APP * INT * MEX
    PL4 * PL5 * AT4 * PT9 * KS4

PRELLEUR, PETER

    HARPSICHORD ILLUSTRATED AND IMPROV'D, WHEREIN IS SHEWN THE ITALIAN
    MANNER OF FINGERING, THE

            LONDON   1740+   48P   BHIAIW
               DICEY, W.
    LC

    GLO * IND * INT * MEX
    KI8 * PL4 * PT6 * KS7 * KS10 * AP7

PRENTICE, THOMAS RIDLEY

    MUSICIAN, THE ..A GUIDE FOR PIANOFORTE STUDENTS--6 VOLS.

            PHILADELPHIA   1886   541P   BMAGFP
               PRESSER, THEODORE, COMPANY
    BP * BR * ES * NP * OC * SA * TO

    CHR * IND * INT * MEX * TAB
    PL9 * PL11 * PM3 * PM6 * PM8 * PM9 * PM13 * PM14 * PM15 * AP4

PRENTICE THOMAS RIDLEY

    HAND GYMNASTICS, FOR THE SCIENTIFIC DEVELOPMENT OF THE MUSCLES USED
    IN PLAYING THE PIANOFORTE

            LONDON   1893   40P   BHGFTS
               NOVELLO AND COMPANY, LTD.
    BR * IU * LC * NP * SA * UW

    LDR
    PT2 * PT3 * PT5 * PT14

PRENTNER, MARIE

    MODERN PIANIST..BEING MY EXPERIENCES IN THE TECHNIQUE AND EXECUTION
    OF PIANOFORTE PLAYING ACCORDING TO THE PRINCIPLES OF PROFESSOR
    LESCHETIZKY
            PHILADELPHIA   1903+   87P   BMPBME
               PRESSER, THEODORE, COMPANY
    BP * LC * NP * OC * UC * UI * UT * UU

    ILL * INT * MEX
    PL7 * PL12 * AT4 * PT4 * PT8 * PT9 * PT10 * AP8

PRESTO--EDITORIAL STAFF

    MUSICAL INSTRUMENTS AT THE WORLD'S COLUMBIAN EXPOSITION, CHICAGO,
    1893

            CHICAGO   1895   328P   BMIATW
               PRESTO COMPANY, THE
    LC * NP

    ILL * IND * LDR * PHO
    KI4 * KI5 * KI7 * KI9 * KI12 * KI13 * KI15

PRESTO PUBLISHING COMPANY

    PRESTO BUYERS' GUIDE TO PLAYER-PIANOS AND PIANOS

            CHICAGO   1907   184P   BPBGTP
               PRESTO PUBLISHING COMPANY
    LC * NP

    INT
    KI1 * KI4 * KI5 * KI12

PRIESING, DOROTHY *
TECKLIN, LIBBIE
    LANGUAGE OF THE PIANO..A WORKBOOK IN THEORY AND KEYBOARD HARMONY

            NEW YORK   1959   88P   BLOTPA
               FISCHER, CARL, INC.
    CU * ES * IU * LC * NP * UT

    BIB * MEX
    PL4 * PT9 * KS4 * KS5

PROCTOR, CHARLES

    HARMONIZATION AT THE KEYBOARD

            LONDON   1961   160P   BHATK
               JENKINS, LTD.
    BR * CU * ES * IU * LC * NP * SA * UC * UT

    BIB * IND * INT * MEX
    PL4 * PL14 * KS4 * KS5 * KS8

PROSNAK, JAN

    FREDERIC CHOPIN INTERNATIONAL PIANO COMPETITIONS, THE

            WARSAW   1970   134P   BFCIPC
               FREDERIC CHOPIN SOCIETY
    IU * LC

    APP * ILL * LDR * PHO
    PM3 * AP4 * GI9

PSTROKONSKY, JULES DE

    NEW METHOD OF TEACHING THE PIANOFORTE

            NEW YORK   1879   47P   BNMOTT
               KNOWLES, W.
    LC * NP

    PL7 * AT4 * PT10 * PT11

PUGNO, RAOUL

    LESSONS OF RAOUL PUGNO, THE ..WITH A BIOGRAPHY OF CHOPIN BY M.
    MICHEL DELINES

            LONDON   1911   71P   BLORPW
               BOOSEY, T., AND COMPANY
    BR

    NP6 * AT12 * PM3 * PM11 * GI13

PULVER, JEFFREY

    DICTIONARY OF OLD ENGLISH MUSIC AND MUSICAL INSTRUMENTS, A

            NEW YORK   1923   247P   BDOOEM
               DUTTON, E. P., AND COMPANY
    BR * IU * LC * NP

    CHR * ILL * INT * LDR * MEX * PHO
    KI3 * KI5 * KI6 * KI14 * KI15

PUPIN, ANNIE

    HOW TO PRACTICE..OR HINTS TO PIANO-FORTE STUDENTS ON THE METHOD OF
    PRACTISING FINGER-EXERCISES, ETUDES AND PIECES

            BOSTON   1882   66P   BHTPOH
               DITSON, OLIVER, AND COMPANY
    LC

    ILL * INT * MEX * TAB
    PL5 * PL7 * PL8 * PT9 * PT10

PUPIN, ANNIE

    SCALES, THE ..THEIR FORMATION, FINGERING, AND HOW TO PRACTICE
    THEM..TO WHICH IS ADDED A SYSTEM OF FINGERING THE ARPEGGIOS OF THE
    COMMON CHORD
            NEW YORK   1879   32P   BSTFFA
               POND, W. A.
    NP

    MEX
    PL7 * PT6 * PT9

PYLE, HOWARD WILLETT

    PRACTICAL TREATISE ON TUNING AND REPAIRING THE PIANOFORTE, A

              PHILADELPHIA   1906   58P   BPTOTA
              PEPPER
    BP * LC

    ILL * IND * INT * LDR * PHO
    KI8

QUINN, MARCUS LUCIUS

    HOW TO STUDY MUSIC AND LEARN TO PLAY PIANO OR ORGAN

              CHICAGO   1915   64P   BHTSMA
              MARCUS LUCIUS QUINN CONSERVATORY OF MUSIC
    LC * NP

    INT * MEX * PHO
    PL11 * AT3 * AT4 * AT11

QUINTE, MICHAEL S.

    MODULATIONARY HARMONY BOOK

              WEST HOLLYWOOD, CAL.   1963   32P   BMHB
              QUINTE RECORDING COMPANY
    LC

    INT * MEX
    KS4 * KS7 * KS8 * AP8

QUIST, BOBBIE LEE *
PERDEW, RUTH
    LISTEN TO LEARN--KEYBOARD HARMONY

              NEW YORK   1969   23P   BLTLKH
              FISCHER, G.
    LC

    INT * MEX * PHO
    KS4

RABINOF, SYLVIA

    MUSICIANSHIP THROUGH IMPROVISATION AT THE KEYBOARD--BK.
    1---DUPLICATED FROM TYPEWRITTEN MANUSCRIPT, WITH MUSICAL EXAMPLES

              BRYN MAWR, PA.   1969   31P   BMTIAT
              PRESSER, THEODORE, COMPANY
    LC

    MEX
    KS5

RABSON, GRACE RUBIN

    INFLUENCE OF ANALYTICAL PRESTUDY IN MEMORIZING PIANO MUSIC, THE
    ---THESIS

              NEW YORK   1937   53P   BIOAPI
              ARCHIVES OF PSYCHOLOGY
    BR * ES * IU * LC * NP * UA * UO * US

    APP * BIB * MEX * TAB
    PL8

RACHMANINOFF, SERGEI

    RACHMANINOFF'S RECOLLECTIONS, TOLD TO OSKAR VON RIESEMANN---1934

              FREEPORT, N. Y.   1970   272P   BRRTTO
              BOOKS FOR LIBRARIES PRESS
    BP * BR * ES * IU * LC * MI * NP * OC * UA * UC * UI * UK * UM * UO
    UT * UU * UW
    APP * ILL * IND * INT * MEX * MSF * PHO
    NP6 * PM6

RADCLIFFE, PHILIP

    SCHUBERT PIANO SONATAS--B.B.C. MUSIC GUIDE, NO. 17

              LONDON   1967   56P   BSPSBB
              BRITISH BROADCASTING COMPANY
    IU * LC * NP * UI

    MEX
    PM5 * PM7 * PM8 * PM9

RAINBOW, BERNARR J. G.--EDITOR

    HANDBOOK FOR MUSIC TEACHERS--2 VOLS.

              LONDON   1964   BHFMTT
              NOVELLO AND COMPANY, LTD.

    AT1 * AT14

RAMANN, LINA

    FRANZ LISZT, ARTIST AND MAN--2 VOLS.---ONLY VOL. 1, 1811-1840,
    TRANSLATED

              LONDON   1882   413P   BFLAAM
              ALLEN AND COMPANY
    BR * LC * NP

    INT
    NP4

RAMUL, PETER

    PSYCHO-PHYSICAL FOUNDATIONS OF MODERN PIANO TECHNIQUE, THE

              LEIPZIG   1931   127P   BPPFOM
              KAHNT, C. F., NACHFOLGER
    ES * LC

    INT * MEX * PHO
    PL7 * PL8 * PL12 * PT3 * PT7 * PT8 * AP8

RAPEE, ERNO--ARRANGER

    ERNO RAPEE'S ENCYCLOPEDIA OF MUSIC FOR PICTURES---LISTED BOTH BY
    MOOD AND COUNTRY

              NEW YORK   1925   510P   BEREOM
              BELWIN, INC.
    BR * LC * NP

    INT
    PM13 * EP6 * GI12

RAPEE, ERNO--ARRANGER

    MOTION PICTURE MOODS FOR PIANISTS AND ORGANISTS

              NEW YORK   1924+   678P   BMPMFP
              SCHIRMER, G., INC.
    LC * NP

    IND * INT * MEX
    PM13 * EP6 * GI12

RAST, LAURENCE R.

    LET'S FIND OUT ABOUT MUSIC..WURLITZER ELEMENTARY PIANO WORKBOOKS,
    FOR USE WITH MULTIPLE PIANO--2 VOLS.

              DEKALB, ILL.   1970   112P   BLFOAM
              WURLITZER COMPANY, THE
    LC

    MEX
    PL4 * PL13 * KS4

RAYSON, ETHEL

    POLISH MUSIC AND CHOPIN ITS LAUREATE, ETC.

              LONDON   1916   64P   BPMACI
              REEVES, WILLIAM
    BR * LC * NP

    ILL * IND * INT * PHO
    NP4 * PM3

REDDIE, CHARLES FREDERICK

    PIANOFORTE PLAYING ON ITS TECHNICAL AND AESTHETIC SIDES

              BOSTON   1911   120P   BPPOIT
              BOSTON MUSIC COMPANY
    BR * CU * ES * LC * NP

    IND * MEX
    PL12 * PT8 * KS3 * AP4 * AP6 * AP8

REED, CLARE OSBORNE

    CONSTRUCTIVE HARMONY AND IMPROVISATION

              CHICAGO   1927   159P   BCHAI
              SUMMY, CLAYTON F., COMPANY
    BR * IU * LC * NP

    IND * INT * MEX
    KS4 * KS6 * KS8

REED, MARY G.

    KEYBOARD ROAD IN MUSIC LAND, AND OTHER STORIES---FOR CHILDREN

              BOSTON   1939   64P   BKRIML
              HUMPHRIES, B., INC.
    LC

    ILL * IND
    KI1 * GI10

REEDER, BETAH

    SINGING TOUCH, THE

              NEW YORK   1943   64P   BST
              GALAXY MUSIC CORPORATION
    BP * CP * CU * ES * IU * LC * NP * SA * TO * UI * UM * YU

    LDR * MEX * TAB
    KI3 * KI6 * KI7 * KI9 * PT3 * PT4 * PT7 * PT8 * PT12 * AP6 * AP8

REES-DAVIES, IVAN

    TRANSPOSITION AT THE KEYBOARD

              LONDON   1930+   67P   BTATK
              CURWEN, J., AND SONS, LTD.
    LC

    INT * MEX
    KS3 * KS7 * EP6

REESER, EDUARD

    SONS OF BACH, THE

        STOCKHOLM   1949   63P   BSOB
           CONTINENTAL BOOK COMPANY
    BR * IU * LC * NP

    BIB * ILL * INT * MEX * MSF
    NP5

REEVES, BETTY

    APPROACH TO PIANO TEACHING---ALSO CATALOGUED UNDER AUTHORSHIP..JOAN
    ELIZABETH CHING

        LONDON   1955   94P   BATPTA
           BOSWORTH AND COMPANY, LTD.
    BR * CU * LC * NP

    APP * LDR * MEX
    PL4 * PL10 * PL14 * PT1 * PT8 * PT9 * PT10 * KS3 * AP4 * AP8

REEVES, BETTY

    AURAL TRAINING--MONOGRAPH ON THE ART OF PIANO TEACHING, NO. 2

        LONDON   1951   38P   BATMOT
           WALSH, HOLMES AND COMPANY
    BR * LC

    PL10

REEVES, BETTY

    OURSELVES AND OUR PUPILS--MONOGRAPH ON THE ART OF PIANO TEACHING,
    NO. 1---ALSO CATALOGUED UNDER AUTHORSHIP..JOAN ELIZABETH CHING

        LONDON   1951   42P   BOAOPM
           WALSH, HOLMES AND COMPANY
    BR * LC

    INT
    AT3 * AT5 * AT9 * AT10 * AT13

REEVES, WILLIAM

    REEVES' POPULAR PIANOFORTE TUTOR..RUDIMENTS OF MUSIC, EXERCISES
    WITH POPULAR AIRS, MAJOR AND MINOR SCALES

        LONDON   1882+   BRPPTR
           REEVES, WILLIAM

    MEX
    PL4 * AT4 * PT9

REGER, MAX

    ON THE THEORY OF MODULATION

        NEW YORK   1903   50P   BOTTOM
           KALMUS, EDWIN F.
    AS * CP * ES * IU * NP * SA * UI * UO * US * UT * UU

    KS8

REGER, MAX

    SUPPLEMENT TO THE THEORY OF MODULATION

        LEIPZIG   1904   50P   BSTTTO
           KAHNT, C. F., NACHFOLGER
    LC * NP * UC * UI * UK * UM

    INT * MEX
    KS8

REINAGLE, CAROLINE

    FEW WORDS ON PIANOFORTE PLAYING, A

        LONDON   1854   32P   BFWOPP
           NOVELLO AND COMPANY, LTD.
    BR * NP

    MEX
    PL12 * PT6 * PT8 * KS3 * KS4 * AP6 * AP7

REINECKE, KARL H.

    BEETHOVEN PIANOFORTE SONATAS, THE ..LETTERS TO A LADY

        LONDON   1898   142P   BBPSLT
           AUGENER, LTD.
    BR * IU * LC * NP * UI * YU

    MEX
    PM8 * PM9 * PM11 * PM15

REINECKE, KARL H.

    WHAT SHALL WE PLAY--NOT UNLIKE CZERNY'S 'LETTERS TO A YOUNG
    LADY'---PAMPHLET

        PHILADELPHIA   1886+   BWSWPN
           PRESSER, THEODORE, COMPANY

    AT3 * AT14 * PM6

RELFE, JOHN

    REMARKS ON THE PRESENT STATE OF MUSICAL INSTRUCTION...THOROUGH BASS

        LONDON   1819   44P   BROTPS
           HATCHARD, J., ET AL
    BR * LC

    KS10

REMBUSCH, JOSEPH ADAM

    PIANOS AND MUSICAL INSTRUMENTS DISCUSSED FROM AN UNSANITARY
    STANDPOINT

        SANTA MARIA, CAL.   1912   16P   BPAMID
           SANTA MARIA TIMES
    LC

    PHO
    KI1 * GI15

RENAUD, EMILIANO

    RENAUD-PHONE PIANO METHOD..A PIANO COURSE THROUGH THE MEDIUM OF
    GRAMOPHONE RECORDS TOGETHER WITH A GUIDE BOOK OF DUPLICATE
    INSTRUCTIONS
        NEW YORK   1920   BRPPMA
           RENAUD-PHONE PIANO METHOD, INC.
    BR * LC

    PL11 * AT4 * PM12

RENNIE, BLANCHE H.

    HAND CULTURE FOR PIANISTS, VIOLINISTS AND 'CELLISTS--FINGER, HAND
    AND ARM GYMNASTICS AT THE PIANO GIVING STRENGTH, FREEDOM AND
    INDEPENDENCE
        LONDON   1923   69P   BHCFPV
           BOSWORTH AND COMPANY, LTD.
    LC

    INT * PHO
    PT5 * PT6 * PT10

RETI, RUDOLPH

    THEMATIC PATTERNS IN SONATAS OF BEETHOVEN

        LONDON   1966   204P   BTPISO
           FABER AND FABER
    AS * BP * ES * IU * LC * MI * OC * UA * UI * UK * UM * UO * US * UT
    UU * UW
    MEX
    PM8

REVESZ, GEZA

    PSYCHOLOGY OF A MUSICAL PRODIGY, THE ---1925

        FREEPORT, N. Y.   1970   180P   BPOAMP
           BOOKS FOR LIBRARIES PRESS
    BP * BR * ES * IU * LC * NP * OC * SA * UA * UM * UT

    IND * INT * LDR * MEX * PHO
    NP2 * NP3 * NP4

REZITS, JOSEPH

    SOURCE MATERIALS FOR PIANO TECHNIQUES

        BLOOMINGTON, IND.   1965   82P   BSMFPT
           INDIANA UNIVERSITY SCHOOL OF MUSIC
    IU * OC * SA * UI

    INT * MEX
    PL2 * PL5 * PL7 * PL10 * PL11 * PL13 * PL14 * AT6 * AT7 * PT6 *
    PT9 * KS2 * KS3 * KS4 * KS5 * KS7 * KS8 * EP6

REZITS, JOSEPH

    TEACHER'S GUIDE TO THE NEW SCRIBNER MUSIC LIBRARY

        NEW YORK   1973   42P   BTGTTN
           SCRIBNER'S, CHARLES, SONS
    IU * SA

    INT * MEX
    PL5 * PL6 * PL7 * PL11 * PL12 * PT2 * PT6 * PM6 * PM9 * PM13 * PM15
    AP4 * EP4 * EP6 * GI2

RHODES, ALFRED

    CURIOSITIES OF THE KEY-BOARD AND THE STAFF...SHOWN TO BE UPON A
    SCIENTIFIC BASIS ACCORDING TO THE LAW OF RADIATION FROM FIXED
    CENTRES, WHICH UNDERLIE THE CONSTRUCTION OF THE KEYBOARD
        LONDON   1896   250P   BCOTKA
           AUGENER AND COMPANY
    BP * LC

    CHR * INT * MEX
    KI3 * PL4 * PT4 * KS3 * KS8

RICHARDSON, ALFRED M.

    EXTEMPORE PLAYING..FORTY LESSONS IN THE ART OF KEYBOARD
    COMPOSING--ORGAN AND PIANO

        NEW YORK   1922   137P   BEPFLI
           SCHIRMER, G., INC.
    BR * IU * LC * NP

    INT * MEX
    KS5 * KS8

RICHARDSON, NATHAN

    INKLINGS FOR THE LOVERS OF MUSIC, PART 1..CULTIVATION OF THE ART OF
    TEACHING AND PLAYING THE PIANOFORTE

           BOSTON   1853   23P   BIFTLO
           RICHARDSON, NATHAN
  BP * NP

  NP4 * PL4 * AT4

RICHARDSON, NATHAN

    NEW METHOD FOR THE PIANOFORTE..ADDED, RUDIMENTS OF HARMONY AND
    THOROUGH-BASS

           BOSTON   1859   238P   BNMFTP
           DITSON, OLIVER, COMPANY
  NP * TO * UM * UO * UW

  GLO * ILL * INT * LDR
  PL4 * PL12 * PM10 * AT4 * PT4 * PT8 * PT9 * PT10

RICHNER, THOMAS

    ORIENTATION FOR INTERPRETING MOZART'S PIANO SONATAS

           NEW YORK   1963   96P   BOFIMP
           TEACHERS COLLEGE, COLUMBIA UNIVERSITY
  BP * CP * CU * ES * IU * MI * NP * OC * SA * UC * UI * UK * UO * US
  UT * UU * UW * YU
  BIB * INT * MEX
  KI3 * PM3 * PM7 * PM8 * PM9 * PM11 * PM15 * AP7

RICHTER, ADA

    TEACHING HINTS

           NEW YORK   1960+   31P   BTH
           MUSIC PUBLISHERS HOLDING CORPORATION
  SA

  BIB * LDR * MEX
  PL4 * PL7 * PL8 * AT4 * AT5 * PT1 * PT8 * KS3 * AP2 * AP8

RICKER, EARL

    MUSIC LESSONS FOR YOUR CHILD

           STERLING, ILL.   1963   32P   BMLFYC
           DARWIN PUBLICATIONS
  SA

  INT
  KI4 * PL7 * PL8 * PL12 * PL14 * AT5 * AT9 * AT11 * AT13 * PT4 *
  PT6 * PT8 * KS3 * KS4

RIEFLING, REIMAR

    PIANO PEDALLING---1957, IN NORWEGIAN

           LONDON   1962   68P   BPPNFS
           OXFORD UNIVERSITY PRESS
  AS * BP * BR * CP * CU * ES * IU * LC * MI * NP * OC * SA * TO * UI
  UO * UT * UW
  BIB * CHR * IND * MEX
  KI3 * AP4 * AP7 * AP8

RIEMANN, HUGO

    ANALYSIS OF J. S. BACH'S WOHLTEMPIERTES KLAVIER--2 PTS.

           LONDON   1890   210P   BAOJSB
           AUGENER AND COMPANY
  BP * BR * CU * ES * LC * NP * OC * TO * UA * UC * UI * UK * UM * UO
  US * UT * UU * YU
  MEX
  PM3 * PM8 * PM9 * PM15

RIEMANN, HUGO

    CATECHISM OF PIANOFORTE PLAYING---1888, IN GERMAN

           LONDON   1892   92P   BCOPPE
           AUGENER, LTD.
  BP * BR * ES * LC * NP * OC * TO * UC * UI * UT * YU

  IND * LDR * MEX
  KI1 * PL1 * PT1 * AP1 * AP4 * AP6

RIEMANN, HUGO

    COMPARATIVE PIANOFORTE SCHOOL--4 BKS.---BK. 3 TRANSLATED BY J. C.
    FILLMORE

           MILWAUKEE   1887+   BCPSFB
           KOHLING, WILLIAM, AND COMPANY

  AT4

RIEMANN, HUGO

    INTRODUCTION TO PLAYING FROM SCORE

    *   LONDON   1904   120P   BITPFS
           AUGENER AND COMPANY
  BR * LC * NP

  INT * MEX
  KS9

RIEMANN, HUGO

    PRACTICAL GUIDE TO THE ART OF PHRASING...ANALYSIS OF CLASSIC AND
    ROMANTIC COMPOSERS

           NEW YORK   1890   147P   BPGTTA
           SCHIRMER, G., INC.
  LC * NP

  INT * MEX
  PM8 * AP6

RIGBY, CHARLES

    SIR CHARLES HALLE..A PORTRAIT FOR TODAY

           MANCHESTER   1952   180P   BSCHAP
           DOLPHIN PRESS, THE
  BR * LC * NP

  ILL * IND * INT * PHO
  NP3 * GI13

RIMBAULT, EDWARD FRANCIS

    CHAPPELL AND CO.'S PRACTICAL DIRECTIONS UPON THE ART OF TUNING THE
    PIANOFORTE

           LONDON   1865+   54P   BCACPD
           CHAPPELL AND COMPANY
  BR * NP

  ILL * INT * MEX
  KI6 * KI8 * KI13

RIMBAULT, EDWARD FRANCIS

    PIANOFORTE, THE ..ITS ORIGIN, PROCESS AND CONSTRUCTION

           LONDON   1860   420P   BPIOPA
           COCKS, R., AND COMPANY
  BP * BR * CP * ES * IU * LC * MI * NP * OC * TO * UC * UM * UO * US
  UT * YU
  APP * IND * INT * LDR * MEX * TAB
  KI3 * KI5 * KI6 * KI8 * KI10 * KI12 * KI13 * KI14

RIPIN, EDWIN M.--EDITOR

    KEYBOARD INSTRUMENTS..STUDIES IN KEYBOARD ORGANOLOGY---10 ESSAYS

           EDINBURGH   1972   146P   BKISIK
           EDINBURGH UNIVERSITY PRESS
  IU * LC * NP

  BIB * ILL * INT * LDR * PHO * TAB
  KI3 * KI5 * KI6 * KI7 * KI9 * KI12 * KI13 * KI14 * KI15

RIPIN, EDWIN M.

    COUPLET HARPSICHORD IN THE CROSBY BROWN COLLECTION, THE --FROM 'THE
    METROPOLITAN MUSEUM JOURNAL', VOL. 2

           NEW YORK   1969   10P   BCHITC
           METROPOLITAN MUSEUM OF ART

  KI14

ROBBINS, EDGAR A.

    AMERICAN METHOD FOR THE PIANOFORTE

           BOSTON   1877   74P   BAMFTP
           ROBBINS, E. A.
  NP

  CHR * MEX
  PL4 * AT4 * PT10 * KS4 * KS8 * AP6

ROBERT, WALTER

    PIANO STUDY IN SOVIET-RUSSIAN SCHOOLS OF MUSIC--REPRINT..'JOURNAL
    OF RESEARCH IN MUSIC EDUCATION', FALL, 1964

           WASHINGTON, D. C.   1964   12P   BPSISR
           MUSIC EDUCATORS NATIONAL CONFERENCE
  IU * SA

  AT3 * PL9 * PM6

ROBILLIARD, EILEEN D.

    PERSISTENT PIANIST, THE ..A BOOK FOR THE LATE BEGINNER AND THE
    ADULT RE-STARTER

           LONDON   1967   92P   BPPABF
           OXFORD UNIVERSITY PRESS
  AS * BP * BR * CP * CU * LC * MI * OC * UA * UI * UO * UT

  APP
  PL4 * PL7 * AT3 * PT3 * GI11

ROBINSON, HELENE

    BASIC PIANO FOR ADULTS

           BELMONT, CAL.   1964   108P   BBPFA
           WADSWORTH PUBLISHING COMPANY
  AS * BP * IU * OC * UI * UT

  CHR * GLO * IND * INT * LDR * MEX
  PL4 * PL7 * PL8 * PL10 * PL11 * PL12 * PL13 * PL14 * PL15 * AT4 *
  AT6 * AT7 * KS3 * KS4 * KS5 * KS7 * KS8

ROBYN, LOUISE

    FIRST YEAR ESSENTIALS IN KEYBOARD HARMONY

        CHICAGO   1943   16P   BFYEIK
          ROBYN TEACHING SERVICE
LC

MEX
KS4

ROBYN, LOUISE

    HAND BUILDING AND HAND STRETCHING EXERCISES

        CHICAGO   1942+   8P   BHBAHS
          ROBYN TEACHING SERVICE
LC

PT5 * PT10

ROBYN, LOUISE

    HOW TO TEACH PIANO TO THE CHILD BEGINNER..A TEXT BOOK FOR TEACHERS
    AND MOTHERS
        CHICAGO   1922   62P   BHTTPT
          SUMMY, CLAYTON F., COMPANY
BP * BR * LC * NP * UK * UO * US * UW

INT * LDR * MEX
PL4 * PL8 * PL10 * PL12 * AT5 * AT13 * PT5 * PT9 * KS7 * AP8

ROBYN, LOUISE

    ROBYN-HANKS HARMONY, THE ..A JUNIOR COURSE--BKS. 1-3, 1936-1938

        PHILADELPHIA   1936   155P   BRHHAJ
          DITSON, OLIVER, COMPANY
IU

ILL * INT * LDR * MEX
PL10 * KS4

ROBYN, LOUISE

    TECHNIC TALES FOR THE CHILD AT THE PIANO--BKS. 1-3..TEACHER'S
    MANUAL
        BOSTON   1927   99P   BTTFTC
          DITSON, OLIVER, COMPANY
IU * SA

INT * LDR * MEX * PHO
PT1 * PT2 * PT4 * PT6 * PT7 * PT10

RODMAN, MOLLY C.

    LET'S TRY SOMETHING NEW..A BOOK OF RECITAL AND TEACHING IDEAS FOR
    PIANO TEACHERS
        LOS ANGELES   1946   14P   BLTSNA
          CLARK MIMEOGRAPH-BOOK PUBLISHING COMPANY
LC

INT
AT9

ROEDER, CARL M.

    LIBERATION AND DELIBERATION IN PIANO TECHNIC

        NEW YORK   1941   51P   BLADIP
          SCHROEDER AND GUNTHER, INC.
AS * LC * NP * UO

INT * MEX
PT1 * PT5 * AP8

ROEDER, CARL M.

    PRACTICAL KEYBOARD HARMONY, A

        NEW YORK   1939   32P   BPKH
          SCHROEDER AND GUNTHER, INC.
IU * LC * NP

IND * INT * MEX
KS4

ROEDER, ELWOOD S.

    TIME-SPACE CONCEPTION OF THE GEOMETRY AND SPEED OF MOTION AT THE
    PIANO KEYBOARD, A ---MIMEOGRAPHED COPY
        ALLENTOWN, PA.   1935   10P   BTSCOT
          ROEDER, E. S.
LC

PL12 * PT4

ROEHL, HARVEY

    KEYS TO A MUSICAL PAST...ILLUSTRATED TREATISE ON THE VARIOUS TYPES
    OF MECHANICAL MUSICAL INSTRUMENTS
        NEW YORK   1968   48P   BKTAMP
          VESTAL PRESS
LC * NP

PHO
KS3 * KI4 * KI5 * KI6 * KI7 * KI9 * KII10 * KII12 * KII13

ROEHL, HARVEY

    PLAYER PIANO, AN HISTORICAL SCRAPBOOK, THE

        WATKINS GLEN, N. Y.   1958   251P   BPPAHS
          CENTURY HOUSE
BP * CP * LC

BIB * ILL * IND * INT * PHO
KI3 * KI4 * KI5 * KI6 * KI9 * KII10 * KII12 * KII13 * KII15

ROEHL, HARVEY

    PLAYER PIANO TREASURY..THE SCRAPBOOK HISTORY OF THE MECHANICAL
    PIANO IN AMERICA--2ND. ED.---1961
        NEW YORK   1973   316P   BPPTTS
          VESTAL PRESS
BP * CP * LC * NP * OC * UI * UO * UT

ILL * INT * PHO
KI3 * KI5 * KI6 * KI9 * KII10 * KII12 * KII13 * KII15 * PM12

ROLLAND, ROMAIN

    BEETHOVEN..WITH A BRIEF ANALYSIS OF THE SONATAS...BY A. EAGLEFIELD
    HULL--3RD. REV. ED.---1919
        FREEPORT, N. Y.   1969   244P   BBWABA
          BOOKS FOR LIBRARIES PRESS
BR * IU * LC * NP

ILL * IND * INT * MEX * MSF
NP3 * PM3 * PM6 * PM8 * PM9 * PM14

ROOT, CATHERINE ADAMS *
BOSTWICK, IRENE
    LISTEN, SING AND PLAY..CLASS LESSONS FOR PIANO AND VOICE

        DUBUQUE, IOWA   1953   132P   BLSAPC
          BROWN, WILLIAM C., COMPANY
LC

INT * MEX * PHO
PL4 * PL7 * AT7 * PT4 * KS3 * EP6

ROSE, ALGERNON SIDNEY

    A439, BEING THE AUTOBIOGRAPHY OF A PIANO BY 25 MUSICAL
    SCRIBES---COLLECTION OF ESSAYS
        LONDON   1900   255P   BAFHTN
          SANDS AND COMPANY
BR * ES * NP

INT
NP6

ROSE, ALGERNON SIDNEY

    ON CHOOSING A PIANO

        LONDON   1903   144P   BOCAP
          SCOTT, WALTER, PUBLISHING COMPANY
BR * LC

KI4

ROSENCRANTZ, ISIDOR B.

    PIANO, ITS CONSTRUCTION AND RELATION TO TONE, PITCH AND
    TEMPERAMENT, THE ..WITH DIRECTIONS HOW...TO LEARN THE ART OF PIANO
    TUNING
        CHICAGO   1902   32P   BPICAR
          TUNELLA COMPANY, THE
LC

ILL * MEX * PHO
KI5 * KI6 * KI8

ROSENTHAL, MORIZ

    OLD AND THE NEW SCHOOL OF PIANO PLAYING, THE --TYPEWRITTEN COPY

        ST. LOUIS   1924   4P   BOATNS
          ROSENTHAL, MORIZ
LC

NP4 * PL15 * PT8 * AP8

ROSS, CHARLES

    RIGHT FOOT FORWARD..A FIRST BOOK ON PEDALLING FOR ADULT STUDENTS

        LONDON   1938   BRFFAF
          ELKIN AND COMPANY, LTD.
LC

INT * MEX
AP8

ROSTAND, CLAUDE

    LISZT

        NEW YORK   1972   192P   BL
          GROSSMAN PUBLISHERS
LC

APP * BIB * ILL * IND * MEX * MSF * PHO
NP3 * NP8 * PT1 * PT11 * PM3 * PM9 * PM13 * PM14 * AP3 * AP4

ROTHSCHILD, FRITZ

HANDBOOK TO THE PERFORMANCE OF THE 48 PRELUDES AND FUGUES OF J. S.
BACH ACCORDING TO THE RULES OF THE OLD TRADITION, A

        LONDON   1955   78P   BHTTPO
        BLACK, ADAM AND CHARLES
BP * BR * CU * ES * LC * NP * OC * TO * UA * UC * UI * UM * UT * YU

MEX
PM8 * PM9 * PM15

ROTHSCHILD, FRITZ

LOST TRADITION IN MUSIC, THE --PT. 1..RHYTHM AND TEMPO IN J. S.
BACH'S TIME

        LONDON   1953   325P   BLTIMP
        BLACK, ADAM AND CHARLES
AS * BP * BR * CP * CU * ES * IU * LC * MI * NP * OC * UA * UC * UI
UK * UM * UO * US * UT * UU * UW * YU
APP * BIB * CHR * IND * INT * MEX * MSF
PL12 * PT8 * PM3 * PM4 * PM8 * PM9 * PM13 * PM14 * AP3 * AP4 * AP5
AP6

ROTHSCHILD, FRITZ

LOST TRADITION IN MUSIC, THE --PT. 2..MUSICAL PERFORMANCE IN THE
TIMES OF MOZART AND BEETHOVEN

        LONDON   1961   122P   BLTIMP
        BLACK, ADAM AND CHARLES
AS * BP * BR * CP * CU * ES * IU * LC * MI * NP * OC * UA * UC * UI
UK * UM * UO * US * UT * UU * UW * YU
APP * BIB * CHR * IND * INT * MEX * MSF
PL12 * PT8 * PM3 * PM4 * PM8 * PM9 * PM13 * PM14 * AP3 * AP4 * AP5
AP6

ROUSSELOT, JEAN

FRANZ LISZT

        LONDON   1960   248P   BFL
        CAPE, JONATHON
BR * ES * IU * LC * NP * SA * TO * UC

ILL * PHO
NP4

ROWBOTHAM, JOHN F.

HOW TO VAMP..A PRACTICAL GUIDE TO THE ACCOMPANIMENT OF SONGS BY THE
UNSKILLED MUSICIAN

        LONDON   1895   24P   BHTVAP
        GILL, L. UPCOTT
BR * NP

MEX
KS6 * EP6

ROWBOTHAM, JOHN F.

PRIVATE LIFE OF THE GREAT COMPOSERS, THE ---CHOPIN AND LISZT

        LONDON   1892   340P   BPLOTG
        ISBISTER AND COMPANY, LTD.
BR * LC * NP

ILL
NP4 * PM3

ROWLEY, ALEC

DO'S AND DONT'S FOR MUSICIANS..A HANDBOOK FOR TEACHERS AND
PERFORMERS

        LONDON   1951   67P   BDADFM
        ASHDOWN, LTD.
BR * CU * IU * LC * NP * SA * UA * UT

APP
PL4 * PL6 * PL10 * AT3 * AT5 * PT8 * KS3 * AP4 * AP8 * AP9 * GI2 *
GI9

ROWLEY, ALEC

FOUR HANDS--ONE PIANO..A LIST OF WORKS FOR DUET PLAYERS--A GUIDE TO
ORIGINAL LITERATURE

        LONDON   1940   38P   BFHOPA
        OXFORD UNIVERSITY PRESS
BP * BR * IU * LC * NP * UT * UW

IND * INT
PM6 * PM7 * PM15 * EP4

ROWLEY, ALEC *
TOBIN, J. RAYMOND
GRADED TESTS IN PRACTICAL MUSICIANSHIP AND MUSICAL INITIATIVE--IN
THREE BOOKS

        LONDON   1930+   BGTIPM
        WILLIAMS, JOSEPH, LTD.

PL4 * PL12 * PL14 * KS7 * KS8 * AP6

ROWLEY, ALEC *
TOBIN, J. RAYMOND
HARMONIZATION AT THE PIANO--IN THREE STAGES

        LONDON   1937   70P   BHATPI
        WILLIAMS, JOSEPH, LTD.
IU * SA

INT * MEX
KS4

ROWLEY, ALEC *
TOBIN, J. RAYMOND
MELODY MAKING AT THE PIANO--IN THREE STAGES

        LONDON   1937   62P   BMMATP
        WILLIAMS, JOSEPH, LTD.
BP * IU * SA

INT * MEX
PL13 * KS2 * KS11

ROWLEY, ALEC *
TOBIN, J. RAYMOND
MUSICAL FORM AT THE PIANO

        LONDON   1942   16P   BMFATP
        WILLIAMS, JOSEPH, LTD.
BP * IU * LC

INT * MEX
PM14

ROWLEY, ALEC

PRACTICAL MUSICIANSHIP, A HANDBOOK FOR TEACHERS AND STUDENTS

        LONDON   1941   26P   BPMAHF
        WILLIAMS, JOSEPH, LTD.
BR * IU

MEX
PL4 * PL6 * PL7 * PL14 * AT3 * AT10 * PT9 * KS3 * KS4 * KS8 * KS12
AP6 * GI2

ROWLEY, ALEC *
TOBIN, J. RAYMOND
SIGHT READING AT THE PIANO--IN THREE STAGES

        LONDON   1936   51P   BSRATP
        WILLIAMS, JOSEPH, LTD.
IU * SA

INT * MEX
KS3

ROWLEY, DAISY WOODRUFF

NINE HUNDRED MODEL LESSONS FOR PIANO TEACHERS

        BIRMINGHAM, ALA.   1911   316P   BNHMLF
        DISPATCH PRINTING COMPANY
LC

INT
AT4 * AT11

RUBINSTEIN, ANTON

AUTOBIOGRAPHY OF ANTON RUBINSTEIN, 1829-1889, THE ---1890

        NEW YORK   1969   171P   BAOARE
        HASKELL HOUSE PUBLISHERS
AS * BP * BR * ES * IU * LC * NP * OC * TO * UA * UC * UI * UM * UT
UW * YU
INT
NP6

RUBINSTEIN, ANTON

CONVERSATION ON MUSIC, A

        NEW YORK   1892   146P   BCOM
        TRETBAR, CHARLES F.
AS * BP * BR * CP * ES * IU * LC * NP * OC * SA * UC * UT * YU

NP6 * KI3 * PM3 * PM7 * PM9

RUBINSTEIN, ARTUR

MY YOUNG YEARS

        NEW YORK   1973   478P   BMYY
        KNOPF, ALFRED A., INC.
IU * LC

IND * INT * PHO
NP6 * GI13

RUBINSTEIN, BERYL

OUTLINE OF PIANO PEDAGOGY--REV. ED.---1929

        NEW YORK   1947   70P   BOOPPR
        FISCHER, CARL, INC.
BP * CP * CU * ES * IU * LC * NP * OC * SA * UA * UI * UM * UO * US
UT
INT
PL7 * PL12 * AT3 * AT4 * AT11 * PT1 * PT3 * PT4 * PT7 * PT8 * PT9 *
PT10 * PM1 * PM3 * PM4 * AP4 * AP5 * AP6 * AP8

RUBINSTEIN, BERYL

PIANIST'S APPROACH TO SIGHT READING AND MEMORIZING, THE

        NEW YORK   1950   67P   BPATSR
        FISCHER, CARL, INC.
AS * CP * CU * ES * IU * LC * MI * NP * OC * UA * UI * UM * US * UT

INT * MEX
PL8 * KS3 * PM6

RUSSELL, LOUIS ARTHUR

DEVELOPMENT OF ARTISTIC PIANOFORTE TOUCH

                                    1895+   BDOAPT

PT8

RUSSELL, LOUIS ARTHUR

EMBELLISHMENTS OF MUSIC, THE ..A STUDY OF THE ENTIRE RANGE OF
MUSICAL ORNAMENTS FROM THE TIME OF JOHANN SEBASTIAN BACH

        PHILADELPHIA   1894   66P   BEOMAS
           PRESSER, THEODORE, COMPANY
BP * BR * ES * LC * NP * OC * UC * UI * UK * US * UW * YU

INT
AP7

RUSSELL, RAYMOND

CATALOGUE OF THE BENTON FLETCHER COLLECTION OF EARLY KEYBOARD
INSTRUMENTS AT FENTON HOUSE, HAMPSTEAD

        LONDON   1957   26P   BCOTBF
           COUNTRY LIFE LIMITED FOR THE NATIONAL TRUST
LC * TO

INT * PHO
KI5 * KI6 * KI9 * KI12 * KI14 * KI15

RUSSELL, RAYMOND

EARLY KEYBOARD INSTRUMENTS--VICTORIA AND ALBERT MUSEUM..'SMALL
PICTURE BOOKS', NO. 48

        LONDON   1959   31P   BEKIVA
           HER MAJESTY'S STATIONERY OFFICE
BR * OC * UI * UW * YU

PHO
KI3 * KI14 * KI15

RUSSELL, RAYMOND

HARPSICHORD AND THE CLAVICHORD, THE --2ND. ED., REVISED BY HOWARD
SCHOTT---1959

        LONDON   1973   208P   BHATCS
           FABER AND FABER
AS * BP * BR * CP * CU * ES * IU * LC * MI * NP * OC * TO * UA * UC
UI * UK * UM * UO * US * UT * UU * UW * YU
APP * BIB * ILL * IND * INT * LDR * PHO
KI3 * KI5 * KI6 * KI8 * KI9 * KI12 * KI13 * KI14 * KI15

RUTTKAY, GEORGE

CHOPIN, HIS LIFE TOLD IN ANECDOTAL FORM---FOR YOUNGER READERS

        NEW YORK   1945   40P   BCHLTI
           DUELL, SLOAN AND PEARCE, INC.
LC * NP

ILL
NP4 * PM3 * GI10

RYAN, THOMAS

RECOLLECTIONS OF AN OLD MUSICIAN---GOTTSCHALK, JONAS CHICKERING,
AND ANTON RUBINSTEIN

        NEW YORK   1899   274P   BRDAOM
           DUTTON, E. P., AND COMPANY
LC * NP

ILL * INT * PHO
NP6 * PM3

SACHS, CURT

EVOLUTION OF PIANO MUSIC, 1350-1700, THE

        NEW YORK   1944   39P   BEOPMT
           MARKS, EDWARD B., MUSIC CORPORATION
BP * LC * NP * SA * UA * UI * US * UT

ILL * INT * MEX
NP5 * KI3 * KI14 * PM7 * PM13 * PM15

SACHS, CURT

HISTORY OF MUSICAL INSTRUMENTS, THE

        NEW YORK   1940   505P   BHOMI
           NORTON, W. W., AND COMPANY
BR * IU * LC * NP

GLO * ILL * IND * LDR * PHO
KI3 * KI5 * KI6 * KI9 * KI14

SACKETT, SHELTON

NOCTURNE..A CHOPIN-PLAY IN ONE ACT

        NEW YORK   1927   37P   BNACPI
           FRENCH, S.
LC * NP

INT
NP4 * GI12 * GI15

SAERCHINGER, CESAR

ARTUR SCHNABEL, A BIOGRAPHY

        LONDON   1957   354P   BASAB
           CASSELL AND COMPANY, LTD.
AS * BP * BR * CP * ES * IU * LC * MI * NP * OC * SA * TO * UA * UC
UI * UK * UM * UO * US * UT * UU * UW * YU
APP * BIB * DIS * IND * INT * PHO
NP3 * NP4

SAFONOFF, WASSILI

NEW FORMULA FOR THE PIANO TEACHER AND PIANO STUDENT

        BOSTON   1915   30P   BNFFTP
           DITSON, OLIVER, COMPANY
BP * NP * OC * YU

INT * MEX
PL12 * PT1 * PT8 * PT9 * PT10 * PT11

SAINT-SAENS, CAMILLE

MUSICAL MEMORIES---LISZT

        BOSTON   1919   282P   BMML
           SMALL, MAYNARD AND COMPANY
IU * LC

PHO
NP6

SALAMAN, CHARLES

PIANISTS OF THE PAST..PERSONAL RECOLLECTIONS BY THE LATE CHARLES
SALAMAN--REPRINT FROM 'BLACKWOODS EDINBURGH MAGAZINE', SEPT., 1901

        NEW YORK   1970   24P   BPOTPP
           MUSICAL SCOPE PUBLISHERS
LC * NP * SA

NP5

SALESKI, GDAL

FAMOUS MUSICIANS OF A WANDERING RACE

        NEW YORK   1927   463P   BFMOAW
           BLOCH PUBLISHING COMPANY
BR * IU * LC * NP

NP5

SALESKI, GDAL

FAMOUS MUSICIANS OF JEWISH ORIGIN

        NEW YORK   1949   716P   BFMOJO
           BLOCH PUBLISHING COMPANY
BP * ES * LC * NP * SA * TO * UA * UT

PHO
NP3 * NP4 * NP5 * NP8

SALSBURY, JANET

CONCISE ANALYSIS OF BEETHOVEN'S 32 PIANOFORTE SONATAS, A

        LONDON   1931   30P   BCAOBT
           WEEKES, A., AND COMPANY, LTD.
BR * LC * NP

INT * TAB
PM8 * PM14

SALSBURY, JANET

SHORT AND CONCISE ANALYSIS OF MOZART'S 22 PIANOFORTE SONATAS, A

        CHICAGO   1914   51P   BSACAO
           SUMMY, CLAYTON F., COMPANY
BR * LC * NP

INT * MEX * TAB
PM8 * PM14

SAMAROFF, OLGA

AMERICAN MUSICIAN'S STORY, AN

        NEW YORK   1939   326P   BAMS
           NORTON, W. W., AND COMPANY
ES * LC * NP * OC * UA * UI * UO * UT

PHO
NP6

SAMPSON, BROOK

DIGEST OF THE ANALYSES OF THE 48 FUGUES IN THE WELL-TEMPERED
CLAVIER

        LONDON   1907   403P   BDOTAO

UI

IND * MEX * TAB
PM8 * PM15

SAMPSON, BROOK

OUTLINE ANALYSIS OF EACH OF BACH'S FORTY-EIGHT FUGUES--IN THE 'DAS WOHLTEMPERIRTE CLAVIER'

    LONDON   1905+   36P   BOAOEO
        VINCENT MUSIC COMPANY
IU

MEX
PM8

SAULS, RANDY

HOW TO READ KEYBOARD MUSIC

    VAN NUYS, CAL.   1966   20P   BHTRKM
        INSTRUCTORS' PUBLICATIONS
LC

MEX
KS3

SAULS, RANDY

THINKING MUSICIANS' APPLICATION OF MODERN HARMONY, THE ..HOW TO FIND HARMONIES FOR MELODIES

    VAN NUYS, CAL.   1966   52P   BTMAOM
        INSTRUCTORS' PUBLICATIONS
LC

CHR * INT * MEX
PL10 * KS4 * KS7

SAVLER, ROBERTA--EDITOR

SELECTIONS FROM THE PIANO TEACHER, 1958-1963

    EVANSTON, ILL.   1963   134P   BSFTPT
        SUMMY-BIRCHARD COMPANY
CP * LC * OC * TO * US

ILL * MEX * PHO
PL2 * AT2 * PT2 * PM2 * AP2

SAWYER, FRANK J.

EXTEMPORIZATION

    LONDON   1890+   64P   BE
        NOVELLO, EWER AND COMPANY
BR * IU * LC * NP

MEX
KS5

SCHAAF, EDWARD O.

ART OF PIANO PLAYER TRANSCRIPTION, THE ..MAKING OF PERFORATED ROLLS

    NEWARK, N. J.   1915   20P   BAOPPT
        BAKER PRINTING COMPANY
LC * NP

INT * LDR * MEX
KI10 * PL12 * PL15 * PT8 * PM14 * AP6 * AP7 * GI14

SCHAAF, EDWARD O.

ESSAYS AND ARTICLES ON MUSICAL SUBJECTS, PARTICULARLY PLAYER-PIANO---TYPESCRIPTS AND CLIPPINGS FROM PERIODICALS..'MUSICAL ADVANCE', 'BRITISH MUSICIAN', AND 'MUSICAL NEWS', 1928-1931
    NEW YORK   1931+   BEAAOM
        SCHAAF, E. O.
NP

NP6 * KI10

SCHAAF, EDWARD O.

FUNDAMENTAL PRINCIPLES INVOLVED IN THE COMPOSING AND ARRANGING OF MUSIC FOR THE PLAYER-PIANO, THE --EXCERPTS..'THE MUSIC TRADE REVIEW', 1919-1920
    NEW YORK   1919   22P   BFPIIT
        MUSIC TRADE REVIEW, THE
NP

INT * MSF
KI10 * PL15 * PT8 * KS8 * PM3 * AP4 * AP6 * AP7

SCHAAF, EDWARD O.

MUSICAL INDIVIDUALITY OF THE PLAYER PIANO, THE ---EXCERPTS..'THE MUSIC TRADE REVIEW', 1922-1923
    NEW YORK   1922   BMIOTP
        MUSIC TRADE REVIEW
NP

MSF
KI10 * PL12 * PL15 * PT8 * PT9 * AP4 * AP7 * AP8

SCHALLENBERG, EVERT W.

FREDERIC CHOPIN--SYMPHONIA BOOKS..'HISTORY OF MUSIC' SERIES

    STOCKHOLM   1949   57P   BFCSBH
        CONTINENTAL BOOK COMPANY
BR * IU * LC * NP

BIB * ILL * LDR * MSF * PHO
NP4 * PM3

SCHAUFFLER, LAWRENCE

PIANO TECHNIC..MYTH OR SCIENCE

    CHICAGO   1937   123P   BPTMOS
        GAMBLE HINGED MUSIC COMPANY
BP * CP * CU * ES * IU * LC * OC * SA * UA * UI * UW

BIB * CHR * ILL * INT * LDR * MEX * PHO
PT1 * PT2 * PT3 * PT4 * PT6 * PT7 * PT8 * PT9 * PT10

SCHAUFFLER, ROBERT HAVEN

FLORESTAN..THE LIFE AND WORK OF ROBERT SCHUMANN---1945

    NEW YORK   1963   574P   BFLAWO
        DOVER PUBLICATIONS, INC.
AS * BP * BR * CP * IU * LC * MI * NP * OC * TO * UA * UC * UI * UM
UO * US * UT * UU * UW * YU
BIB * CHR * DIS * GLO * ILL * IND * INT * MEX
NP3 * PM3 * PM5 * PM6 * PM8 * PM9 * PM12 * PM14 * PM15 * EP3 * EP4
EP5

SCHAUFFLER, ROBERT HAVEN

MUSICAL AMATEUR, THE

    BOSTON   1911   262P   BMA
        HOUGHTON MIFFLIN COMPANY
BR * IU * LC * NP

INT
PL6 * GI11

SCHAUFFLER, ROBERT HAVEN

SCIENCE OF PRACTICE, THE

    NEW YORK   BSOP
        CAXTON INSTITUTE, THE

PL7

SCHELLING, ERNEST *
HAAKE, CHARLES *
OXFORD PIANO COURSE, TEACHER'S FIRST MANUAL

    LONDON   1929   187P   BOPCTF
        OXFORD UNIVERSITY PRESS
BR * ES * IU * LC * MI * NP * OC * SA * TO * UA * UI * UK * US * UW

CHR * IND * INT * MEX
PL4 * PL7 * PL9 * PL10 * PL12 * PL13 * PL14 * AT1 * AT2 * AT3 *
AT4 * AT5 * AT7 * AT8 * AT11 * PT1 * PT2 * PT4 * PT8 * KS1 * KS3 *
AP4 * GI2 * GI5 * GI8 * GI9
SCHELLING, ERNEST *
HAAKE, CHARLES *
OXFORD PIANO COURSE, TEACHER'S SECOND MANUAL

    LONDON   1932   239P   BOPCTS
        OXFORD UNIVERSITY PRESS
IU * LC * MI * NP * OC * SA * UI * US

APP * IND * INT * LDR
PL5 * PL12 * PL13 * AT1 * AT3 * AT4 * AT5 * AT7 * AT8 * PT1 * PT8 *
PT10 * PT11 * KS3 * KS4 * KS7 * KS8 * PM6 * PM8 * PM9 * AP4 * AP5 *
AP6 * AP8 * GI2

SCHENKER, HEINRICH

FIVE GRAPHIC MUSIC ANALYSES---INCLUDES TWO CHOPIN ETUDES..OP. 10, NO. 8 AND NO. 12

    NEW YORK   1969   61P   BFGMAI
        DOVER PUBLICATIONS, INC.
LC

PM8

SCHERER, HERBERT

PIANO PRACTICING

    NEW YORK   1958   87P   BPP
        MILLS MUSIC, INC.
NP

INT * MEX
PL7 * PL12 * PT6 * PT7 * PT8 * PT9 * PT10 * AP4 * AP8

SCHIRMER, G.

NEW PIANO-TEACHER'S GUIDE..A GRADED AND CLASSIFIED LIST OF PIANO MUSIC SELECTED FROM THE PUBLICATIONS OF G. SCHIRMER, INC., NEW YORK

    NEW YORK   1923   197P   BNPTGA
        SCHIRMER, G., INC.
LC

INT
AT14 * PM6

SCHLIEDER, FREDERICK W.

LYRIC COMPOSITION THROUGH IMPROVISATION--2 VOLS., 1927-1946

    NEW YORK   1927   262P   BLCTIT
        BIRCHARD, C. C., AND COMPANY
BR * IU * LC * NP

CHR * IND * MEX
PL4 * AT10 * KS4 * KS8 * AP6

SCHMECKEL, CARL D.

  PIANO OWNER'S GUIDE, THE

              SHEBOYGAN, WIS.   1971   114P   BPOG
                APEX PIANO PUBLISHERS
        LC

        ILL * INT
        KI4 * KI5 * KI6 * KI8

SCHMITT, HANS

  NATURAL LAWS OF MUSICAL EXPRESSION, THE

              CHICAGO   1894   47P   BNLOME
                SUMMY, CLAYTON F.
        LC * NP * TO

        AP4 * AP5

SCHMITT, HANS

  PEDALS OF THE PIANOFORTE, THE --FOUR LECTURES

              PHILADELPHIA   1893   99P   BPOTPF
                PRESSER, THEODORE, COMPANY
        AS * BP * BR * CP * CU * ES * IU * LC * NP * UA * UC * UM * UO

        MEX
        AP8

SCHMITZ, ELIE ROBERT

  CAPTURE OF INSPIRATION, THE

              NEW YORK   1944   111P   BCOI
                FISCHER, CARL, INC.
        BP * CP * CU * NP * UA * UC * US * UT * YU

        BIB * GLO * LDR * MEX
        PL3 * PL5 * PL7 * PT3 * PT6 * PT9 * PT10 * AP4 * AP8 * AP9

SCHMITZ, ELIE ROBERT

  PIANO WORKS OF CLAUDE DEBUSSY, THE

              NEW YORK   1950   234P   BPWOCD
                DUELL, SLOAN AND PEARCE
        AS * BP * CP * CU * ES * IU * LC * MI * NP * OC * UA * UC * UI * UK
        UM * UO * UT * UW * YU
        APP * BIB * ILL * INT * LDR * MEX * PHO * TAB
        NP3 * PM3 * PM6 * PM7 * PM8 * PM9 * PM14 * PM15 * AP3 * AP4 * AP5 *
        AP6 * AP8

SCHNABEL, ARTUR

  MUSIC AND THE LINE OF MOST RESISTANCE---1942

              NEW YORK   1969   91P   BMATLO
                DA CAPO PRESS
        BP * BR * CP * CU * ES * IU * LC * MI * NP * OC * TO * UA * UC * UK
        UM * UO * US * UT * UW * YU
        INT
        NP6 * GI1

SCHNABEL, ARTUR

  MY LIFE AND MUSIC

              NEW YORK   1963   224P   BMLAM
                ST. MARTIN'S PRESS
        AS * BP * BR * CP * ES * IU * LC * MI * NP * OC * SA * TO * UC * UI
        UK * UM * UO * US * UT * UU * UW * YU
        APP * INT * PHO
        NP6 * GI1

SCHNABEL, ARTUR

  REFLECTIONS ON MUSIC..A LECTURE---IN ENGLISH AND GERMAN

              NEW YORK   1933   32P   BROMAL
                SIMON AND SCHUSTER
        BP * BR * ES * NP * OC * TO * UC * UM * UT

        NP6

SCHNABEL, KARL ULRICH

  MODERN TECHNIQUE OF THE PEDAL

              NEW YORK   1954   39P   BMTOTP
                MILLS MUSIC, INC.
        CU * IU * NP * SA * UI * UM * UW

        CHR * MEX
        AP4 * AP8

SCHNEIDER, FRIEDRICH

  SCHNEIDER'S TREATISE ON THOROUGH BASS AND HARMONY

              BOSTON   1851   28P   BSTOTB
                DITSON, OLIVER, COMPANY
        LC

        MEX
        KS10

SCHNEIDER, HANS

  WORKING OF THE MIND IN PIANO TEACHING AND PLAYING, THE

              NEW YORK   1923   80P   BWOTMI
                SCHROEDER AND GUNTHER
        ES * LC * MI * NP * US

        BIB * INT * LDR
        PL3 * PL6 * PL7 * PL8 * PL12 * AT3 * PT3 * PT8 * AP3

SCHNITTKIND, HENRY T. *
THOMAS, DANA LEE
  FORTY FAMOUS COMPOSERS---CHOPIN AND LISZT

              GARDEN CITY, N. Y.   1948   437P   BFFCCA
                HALCYON HOUSE
        BR * IU * LC * NP

        ILL * INT
        NP5

SCHNITTKIND, HENRY T.

  LIVING BIOGRAPHIES OF GREAT COMPOSERS---CHOPIN AND LISZT

              NEW YORK   1940+   326P   BLBOGC
                GARDEN CITY PUBLISHING COMPANY, INC.
        BR * LC * NP

        ILL * INT
        PM3

SCHOLES, PERCY

  APPRECIATION OF MUSIC BY MEANS OF THE PIANOLA AND DUO-ART, THE

              LONDON   1925   155P   BAOMBM
                OXFORD UNIVERSITY PRESS
        BP * BR * CP * LC * NP * OC * UW

        APP * ILL * INT * MEX
        KI10 * KI14 * PM3 * PM8 * PM9 * PM14

SCHONBERG, HAROLD

  COLLECTOR'S CHOPIN AND SCHUMANN, THE --KEYSTONE BOOKS

              PHILADELPHIA   1959   256P   BCCASK
                LIPPINCOTT, J. B., COMPANY
        NP

        INT
        NP4 * PM3 * PM6 * PM8 * PM9 * PM12 * PM14

SCHONBERG, HAROLD

  GREAT PIANISTS, THE

              NEW YORK   1963   448P   BGP
                SIMON AND SCHUSTER, INC.
        AS * BP * BR * CU * ES * IU * LC * MI * NP * OC * SA * TO * UA * UI
        UK * UM * UO * US * UT * UU * UW * YU
        ILL * IND * INT * LDR * MEX * PHO
        NP1 * NP2 * NP4 * NP5

SCHONBERG, HAROLD

  LIVES OF THE GREAT COMPOSERS, THE ---CHOPIN AND LISZT

              NEW YORK   1970   599P   BLOTGC
                NORTON, W. W., AND COMPANY, INC.
        IU * LC * NP

        BIB * ILL * IND * INT * PHO
        NP5 * PM3 * PM8 * PM9 * PM14

SCHOTT, HOWARD

  PLAYING THE HARPSICHORD

              LONDON   1971   223P   BPTH
                FABER AND FABER
        IU * LC

        APP * ILL * IND * INT * MEX * PHO
        KI3 * KI4 * KI8 * PL5 * PL12 * PT6 * PT8 * PM4 * AP6 * AP7 * EP1

SCHULER, GEORGE S.

  ACCOMPANIST'S MANUAL, THE

              CHICAGO   1925   25P   BAM
                BIBLE INSTITUTE COLPORTAGE ASSOCIATION, THE
        LC

        KS11 * EP6

SCHULER, GEORGE S.

  EVANGELISTIC PIANO PLAYING

              PHILADELPHIA   1922   39P   BEPP
                PRESSER, THEODORE, COMPANY
        BP * LC

        INT * MEX
        KS4 * KS5 * KS7 * EP6

SCHULTZ, ARNOLD

    RIDDLE OF THE PIANIST'S FINGER, THE

          NEW YORK   1936   317P   BROTPF
            FISCHER, CARL, INC.
BP * BR * CP * CU * ES * IU * LC * MI * NP * OC * SA * UA * UI * UK
UT * UW * YU
IND * LDR * MEX
NP7 * AT4 * PT3 * PT4 * PT5 * PT6 * PT7 * PT8

SCHULZE, RICHARD ALLEN

    HOW TO BUILD A BAROQUE CONCERT HARPSICHORD

          NEW YORK   1954   42P   BHTBAB
            PAGEANT PRESS
BP * ES * IU * LC * MI * NP * OC * UA * UT

APP * BIB * INT * LDR
KI3 * KI5 * KI6 * KI9 * KI14

SCHUMANN, CLARA

    LETTERS OF CLARA SCHUMANN AND JOHANNES BRAHMS, 1853-1896--2
    VOLS.--EDITED BY DR. BERTHOLD LITZMANN---1927

          NEW YORK   1972   609P   BLOCSA
            VIENNA HOUSE, INC.
BR * IU * LC * MI * NP * TO * UA * UM

IND * INT * LDR * MEX
NP6

SCHUMANN, EUGENIE

    MEMOIRS OF EUGENIE SCHUMANN---1927

          NEW YORK   1970   217P   BMOESN
            BOOKS FOR LIBRARIES PRESS
BR * IU * LC * NP * UA * UT

ILL * IND * MEX * MSF * PHO
NP6

SCHUMANN, FERDINAND

    REMINISCENCES OF CLARA SCHUMANN AS FOUND IN THE DIARY OF HER
    GRANDSON FERDINAND SCHUMANN OF DRESDEN

          ROCHESTER, N. Y.   1949   41P   BROCSA
            SCHUMANN MEMORIAL FOUNDATION
IU * LC * NP * UM

INT * PHO
NP6

SCHUMANN, ROBERT

    ADVICE TO YOUNG MUSICIANS--FROM 'MUSIC AND MUSICIANS'---1876

          WINONA, MINN.   1910   15P   BATYMF
            MAR DE MAR MUSIC COMPANY
BR * LC

NP6 * PL14 * AT3

SCHUMANN, ROBERT

    EARLY LETTERS OF ROBERT SCHUMANN, ORIGINALLY PUBLISHED BY HIS
    WIFE---1888

          ST. CLAIR SHORES, MICH.   1970   307P   BELORS
            SCHOLARLY PRESS
BR

NP6

SCHUMANN, ROBERT

    LETTERS OF ROBERT SCHUMANN, THE --SELECTED AND EDITED BY KARL
    STORCK

          NEW YORK   1971   299P   BLORSS
            BLOM, B.
BR * LC

ILL * IND * INT
NP6

SCHUMANN, ROBERT

    LIFE OF ROBERT SCHUMANN TOLD IN HIS LETTERS, THE --2 VOLS.

          LONDON   1890   BLORST
            BENTLEY, R., AND SON
BR

NP6

SCHUMANN, ROBERT

    ON MUSIC AND MUSICIANS---1854, IN GERMAN--FIRST ENGLISH EDITION IN
    1877

          NEW YORK   1970   274P   BOMAME
            PANTHEON BOOKS, INC.
AS * BP * BR * CP * ES * IU * LC * MI * NP * OC * SA * TO * UA * UC
UI * UK * UO * US * UT * UU * UW * YU
ILL * MEX
NP3 * NP4 * NP7 * PM3 * PM9 * AP4 * AP5

SCHUMANN, ROBERT

    RULES AND MAXIMS FOR YOUNG MUSICIANS--FROM 'MUSIC AND MUSICIANS'

          LONDON   1878   10P   BRAMFY
            REEVES, WILLIAM
BR * IU

PL14 * AT3

SCHUYLER, PHILLIPA DUKE

    ADVENTURES IN BLACK AND WHITE--AUTOBIOGRAPHY

          NEW YORK   1960   302P   BAIBAW
            SPELLER, R. AND SONS, PUBLISHERS, INC.
BR * IU * LC * NP * UT

IND * INT * PHO
NP6

SCHWIMMER, FRANCISKA

    GREAT MUSICIANS AS CHILDREN

          GARDEN CITY, N. Y.   1929   238P   BGMAC
            DOUBLEDAY, DORAN
BR * IU * LC * NP

NP5 * PM3 * GI10

SCIONTI, SILVIO

    L'ARTE PIANISTICA..SYSTEM OF PIANO ARTISTRY--- IN ITALIAN AND
    ENGLISH

          MILAN   1961+   59P   BLPSOP
            EDIZIONI CURCI
CU * LC

APP * INT * MEX * PHO
PL12 * PT1 * PT8 * PT9 * PT10

SCONCIA, JOHN A.

    ANALYTICAL INSTRUCTOR FOR THE PIANO FORTE, CONTAINING THE
    PRINCIPLES OF MUSIC, DESIGNED FOR SCHOOLS, CLASSES, AND SELF
    INSTRUCTION...
          NEW YORK   1843   96P   BAIFTP
            CHRISTMAN, C. G.
NP

MEX
PL4 * PL11 * AT4 * AT7

SCONCIA, JOHN A.

    SCONCIA'S NEW SYSTEM OF INSTRUCTION IN MUSIC AS A SCIENCE..OR, A
    TRUE BASIS TO THE SELF INSTRUCTOR, FOR THE PIANO FORTE

          BALTIMORE   1826   43P   BSNSOI
            SCONCIA, JOHN A.
   LC

CHR * INT * MEX * TAB
PL4 * PL11 * PT6 * PT10 * KS4

SCOTT, MARY M.

    WHAT CAN I PLAY..A BOOK ABOUT MUSICAL INSTRUMENTS

          LONDON   1945   95P   BWCIPA
            QUALITY PRESS, LTD.
BR * IU * LC * NP

APP * INT * PHO
KI4 * PL1

SCOTT, WAYNE

    HANDBOOK OF CHORD PROGRESSIONS

          BOULDER, COLO.   1968   125P   BHOCP
            PRUETT PRESS, INC.
CU * LC

INT * MEX
KS4

SCOVILL, MODENA

    KEYBOARD HARMONY--REV. ED.---1939

          NEW YORK   1971   54P   BKHREN
            FISCHER, CARL, INC.
IU * LC * NP

INT * MEX
KS4

SEARLE, HUMPHREY

    MUSIC OF LISZT, THE --2ND. REV. ED.---1954

          MAGNOLIA, MASS.   1968   207P   BMOLSR
            SMITH, P.
AS * BP * BR * CP * CU * ES * IU * LC * MI * NP * OC * TO * UA * UC
UI * UK * UM * UO * US * UT * UU * UW * YU
APP * BIB * IND * INT * MEX
NP3 * PM3 * PM4 * PM6 * PM8 * PM9 * PM15 * EP7

SEGUEL, MANIA

    CHOPIN'S TEMPO RUBATO

          ALTHAM, LANCASHIRE, ENGLAND   1928   26P   BCTR
          OLD PARSONAGE PRESS
    BR

    NP4 * PL12 * AP3 * AP4

SEROFF, VICTOR

    COMMON SENSE IN PIANO STUDY

          NEW YORK   1970   64P   BCSIPS
          FUNK AND WAGNALLS
    IU * LC * UA

    INT * MEX
    KI4 * KI6 * KI7 * PL7 * AT9 * PT1 * PT6

SEROFF, VICTOR

    DEBUSSY, MUSICIAN OF FRANCE

          NEW YORK   1956   367P   BDMOF
          PUTNAM'S, G. P., SONS
    AS * BP * BR * ES * IU * LC * MI * NP * UA * UI * UM * UT

    NP4

SEROFF, VICTOR

    FRANZ LISZT

          NEW YORK   1966   152P   BFL
          MACMILLAN COMPANY, THE
    ES * IU * LC * MI * NP * OC * UA * UI

    DIS * ILL * LDR * PHO
    NP4

SEROFF, VICTOR

    FREDERIC CHOPIN

          NEW YORK   1964   118P   BFC
          MACMILLAN COMPANY, THE
    ES * IU * LC * MI * NP * OC

    APP * DIS * ILL * IND * INT * LDR
    NP4

SEROFF, VICTOR

    MAURICE RAVEL

          NEW YORK   1953   310P   BMR
          HOLT, HENRY, AND COMPANY
    IU * LC * MI * NP

    APP * BIB * DIS * ILL * IND * LDR * MSF * PHO
    NP4

SEROFF, VICTOR

    RACHMANINOFF

          NEW YORK   1950   269P   BR
          SIMON AND SCHUSTER, INC.
    AS * BR * CP * ES * IU * LC * MI * NP * OC * SA * UA * UI * UK * US
    UT * UW * YU
    BIB * IND * INT * PHO
    NP3 * NP4

SEROFF, VICTOR

    WOLFGANG AMADEUS MOZART

          NEW YORK   1965   124P   BWAM
          MACMILLAN COMPANY, THE
    ES * IU * LC * NP * UI

    CHR * DIS * ILL * IND
    NP4

SEYMOUR, HARRIET AYER

    HOME MUSIC LESSONS..HOW TO FIND YOUR MUSICAL SELF

          NEW YORK   1930   48P   BHMLHT
          FISCHER, CARL, INC.
    LC * NP

    INT * PHO
    PL6 * PL11 * PL13 * AT13 * KS4 * GI11

SEYMOUR, HARRIET AYER

    HOW TO THINK MUSIC

          NEW YORK   1910   59P   BHTTM
          SCHIRMER, G., INC.
    BP * BR * ES * IU * NP * OC * UM * UT * UW

    CHR * INT * MEX
    PL4 * PL6 * PL12 * AT3 * AT4 * AT5 * KS4 * PM6

SEYMOUR, HARRIET AYER

    PHILOSOPHY OF MUSIC, THE ..WHAT MUSIC CAN DO FOR YOU

          NEW YORK   1920   197P   BPOMWM
          HARPER AND BROS.
    AS * BP * ES * IU * NP * UA * UT

    BIB * DIS * MEX
    PL4 * AT3 * AT5 * GI2

SEYMOUR, MARY ALICE IVES

    LIFE AND LETTERS OF LOUIS MOREAU GOTTSCHALK

          BOSTON   1870   213P   BLALOL
          DITSON, OLIVER, COMPANY
    BR * LC * MI * NP * UM

    NP4 * NP6

SHATTUCK, ARTHUR

    MEMOIRS OF ARTHUR SHATTUCK, THE ..WITH AN ACCOUNT OF HIS CAREER BY
    WILLARD LUEDTKE

          NEENAH, WIS.   1961   247P   BMOASW
          SHATTUCK, ARTHUR
    CP * LC * NP

    ILL * INT * PHO
    NP6 * PM13 * GI13

SHEDLOCK, JOHN S.

    BEETHOVEN'S PIANOFORTE SONATAS..THE ORIGIN AND RESPECTIVE VALUES OF
    VARIOUS READINGS

          LONDON   1918   51P   BBPSTO
          AUGENER, LTD.
    BR * CP * ES * IU * LC * NP * OC * SA * US * UT * UU * YU

    IND * INT * MEX
    PM3 * PM4 * PM5 * PM8 * PM9 * PM15 * AP3 * AP4

SHEDLOCK, JOHN S.

    PIANOFORTE SONATA, THE ..ITS ORIGIN AND DEVELOPMENT---1895

          NEW YORK   1964   245P   BPSIOA
          DA CAPO PRESS
    AS * BP * BR * CP * CU * ES * IU * LC * MI * NP * OC * SA * TO * UA
    UI * UK * UM * UO * UT * UU * UW * YU
    ILL * IND * INT * MEX
    PM3 * PM7 * PM8 * PM14 * PM15

SHEEHY, EMMA DICKSON

    THERE'S MUSIC IN CHILDREN--REV. ED.---1946

          NEW YORK   1952   152P   BTMICR
          HOLT, RINEHART AND WINSTON, INC.
    AS * BP * BR * CP * ES * IU * LC * MI * NP * OC * TO * UA * UC * UI
    UK * UM * US * UT * UU * UW
    BIB * DIS * INT * PHO
    PL6 * PL13

SHEFTE, ARTHUR G.

    KEYBOARD HARMONY SIMPLIFIED

          CHICAGO   1925   43P   BKHS
          FORSTER MUSIC PUBLISHERS
    NP

    CHR * INT * MEX * TAB
    KS4

SHEFTE, ARTHUR G.

    PIANO IMPROVISING--2 VOLS., 1936-1938

          CHICAGO   1936   128P   BPITVN
          FORSTER MUSIC PUBLISHERS
    LC * NP

    INT * MEX
    KS4 * KS5

SHEFTEL, PAUL

    EXPLORING KEYBOARD FUNDAMENTALS

          NEW YORK   1970   226P   BEKF
          HOLT, RINEHART AND WINSTON
    LC * SA

    APP * BIB * GLO * IND * INT * MEX
    PL4 * PL7 * PT6 * PT10 * KS3 * KS4 * KS5

SHELDON, JAY

    ALL ABOUT MUSIC..A COMPLETE BOOK OF MUSICAL THEORY FOR PIANISTS AND
    OTHER STUDENTS

          BOSTON   1955   75P   BAAMAC
          BOSTON MUSIC COMPANY
    LC

    INT * MEX
    PL4 * KS4

SHELDON, ROBERT--COMPILER

   EGON PETRI-ALEXANDER LIBERMANN NOTES ON THE ART AND TECHNIQUE OF
   PIANOFORTE PLAYING

       COLUMBIA, MO.   1957   BEPALN
       MISSOURI, UNIVERSITY OF
   AS

   PL1 * PL2 * PT1 * PT2 * AP1 * AP2

SHEPARD, FRANK H.

   HOW TO MODULATE..MODULATING FROM ANY KEY TO ANY OTHER

       BETHEL, CONN.   1890   66P   BHTMMF
       SHEPARD, FRANK H.
   LC * NP

   INT * MEX
   KS3 * KS8

SHEPARD, FRANK H.

   PIANO TOUCH AND SCALES..AN ANALYSIS OF THE FUNDAMENTAL PRINCIPLES
   OF TOUCH AND THEIR PROPER DEVELOPMENT

       BETHEL, CONN.   1890   46P   BPTASA
       SHEPARD, FRANK H.
   LC

   INT * MEX
   PL5 * PL12 * PT7 * PT8 * PT9 * PT10

SHEPARD, ROBERT

   COMPLETE SCALE AND ARPEGGIO MANUAL

       EVANSTON, ILL.   1956   24P   BCSAAM
       SUMMY, CLAYTON F., COMPANY
   IU * LC

   INT * MEX
   PL7 * PT6 * PT9

SHEPARD, ROBERT

   HARMONIZING..HOW TO PLAY SIMPLE ACCOMPANIMENTS TO A MELODY AT THE
   KEYBOARD

       CHICAGO   1956   24P   BHHTPS
       SUMMY, CLAYTON F., COMPANY
   LC * NP

   MEX
   KS4 * KS5 * EP6

SHERWOOD MUSIC SCHOOL

   PIANO LESSONS AND TESTS--4TH. REV. ED.---1945+

       CHICAGO   1959   BPLATF
       SHERWOOD MUSIC SCHOOL
   LC

   INT * MEX
   PL4 * PL6 * PL7 * PL8 * PL9 * PL11 * PL12 * PL14 * AT4 * AT5 * AT6
   AT10 * PT1 * PM8 * PM9 * AP3 * AP4 * AP6 * AP7

SHINN, DUANE

   HOW PEOPLE MAKE MONEY IN MUSIC

       MEDFORD, ORE.   1971   38P   BHPMMI
       SHINN MUSIC AIDS
   IU

   PHO
   G15

SHINN, FREDERICK G.

   MUSICAL MEMORY AND ITS CULTIVATION

       LONDON   1898   73P   BMMAIC
       VINCENT MUSIC COMPANY, THE
   BP * BR * CP * IU * LC * NP * OC * UA * UI * UK * UO * YU

   IND * INT
   PL8

SHORTRIDGE, JOHN D.

   ITALIAN HARPSICHORD BUILDING IN THE 16TH. AND 17TH.
   CENTURIES--REPRINT..'MUSEUM OF HISTORY AND TECHNOLOGY', PAPER 15

       WASHINGTON, D. C.   1960   14P   BIHBIT
       SMITHSONIAN INSTITUTION, THE
   IU * LC * TO * UO * UW

   ILL * LDR * MEX * PHO * TAB
   KI5 * KI14

SHUMWAY, STANLEY

   HARMONY AND EAR TRAINING AT THE KEYBOARD

       DUBUQUE, IOWA   1970   187P   BHAETA
       BROWN, WILLIAM C., COMPANY
   LC

   INT * MEX
   PL10 * KS4 * KS8

SHUTER, ROSAMUND

   PSYCHOLOGY OF MUSICAL ABILITY, THE

       LONDON   1968   347P   BPOMA
       BUTLER AND TANNER, LTD.
   BR * IU * LC * NP

   APP * BIB * CHR * IND * INT * TAB
   PL1 * AT3 * AT10

SILOTI, ALEXANDER

   MY MEMORIES OF LISZT

       EDINBURGH   1913   76P   BMMOL
       METHUEN-SIMPSON, LTD.
   LC * NP * OC

   MSF * PHO
   NP4

SIMPSON, ELIZABETH

   BASIC PIANOFORTE TECHNIQUE...BASED ON THE SCIENCE OF PIANOFORTE
   TECHNIQUE BY THOMAS FIELDEN

       LONDON   1933   72P   BBPTBO
       MACMILLAN COMPANY, THE
   BR * CP * CU * ES * LC * NP * US * UW

   BIB * INT * MEX
   PT4 * PT6 * PT7 * PT8 * PT9 * KS3

SIMPSON, KENNETH

   KEYBOARD HARMONY AND IMPROVISATION

       LONDON   1963   89P   BKHAI
       LENGNICK, A., AND COMPANY, LTD.
   BR * LC * NP

   APP * INT * MEX
   PT1 * PT10 * KS4 * KS5

SITWELL, SACHEVERELL

   BACKGROUND FOR DOMENICO SCARLATTI..1685-1757, WRITTEN FOR HIS
   250TH. ANNIVERSARY

       LONDON   1935+   168P   BBFDSS
       FABER AND FABER, LTD.
   BR * IU * LC * NP

   INT
   NP3 * PM3

SITWELL, SACHEVERELL

   LISZT---1934

       NEW YORK   1967   400P   BLNTF
       DOVER PUBLICATIONS, INC.
   AS * BP * BR * CP * ES * IU * LC * MI * NP * OC * TO * UA * UC * UI
   UM * UO * US * UT * UU * UW * YU
   BIB * ILL * IND * INT
   NP3 * PM3 * PM6

SKINNER, BELLE

   BELLE SKINNER COLLECTION OF OLD MUSICAL INSTRUMENTS, HOLYOKE,
   MASSACHUSETTS, THE ..A DESCRIPTIVE CATALOGUE COMPILED UNDER THE
   DIRECTION OF WILLIAM SKINNER
       PHILADELPHIA   1933   210P   BBSCOO
       BECK ENGRAVING COMPANY
   BR * IU * LC * NP

   APP * BIB * ILL * IND * INT * MSF * PHO
   KI3 * KI5 * KI6 * KI7 * KI9 * KI14

SKUTLEY, MILDRED A.

   MUSIC FOR YOU..A SUPPLEMENTAL WORK BOOK FOR INDIVIDUAL OR CLASS
   INSTRUCTION..THE KEYBOARD APPROACH TO FUNDAMENTALS OF MUSIC

       PHOENIX, ARIZ.   1957   57P   BMFYAS
       SKUTLEY, M. A.
   LC

   GLO * ILL * LDR
   PL4 * AT4 * AT5 * AT7 * AT10

SLENCZYNSKA, RUTH *
BIANCOLLI, LOUIS LEOPOLD
   FORBIDDEN CHILDHOOD

       GARDEN CITY, N. Y. 1957   263P   BFC
       DOUBLEDAY AND COMPANY
   AS * BP * BR * CP * ES * IU * LC * NP * UA * UC * UI * UK * UO * US

   INT * LDR
   NP6

SLENCZYNSKA, RUTH *
LINGG, ANN M.
   MUSIC AT YOUR FINGERTIPS

       NEW YORK   1961   160P   BMAYF
       DOUBLEDAY AND COMPANY
   BP * BR * CP * ES * IU * LC * MI * NP * OC * SA * TO * UI * UM * UO
   UU * UW * YU

   PL6 * PL7 * PL9 * PL12 * AT5 * PT6 * PT9 * AP7 * AP9

SMELTZER, JEANNIE R.--COMPILER

OUTLINES AND GRADES FOR THE USE OF PIANO TEACHERS

CHICAGO 1909 2P BOAGFT
LIBBY AND SHERWOOD PRINTING COMPANY
LC

INT
PL4 * PL7 * PL8 * PL12 * AT7 * PT1 * PT8 * PT9 * KS3 * KS5 * KS7 *
AP4 * AP6 * AP8

SMITH, A. G. WARREN

BEGINNER'S GUIDE, THE ..FOR ALL COMMENCING THE STUDY OF THE
PIANOFORTE

LONDON 1935 28P BBGFAC
WARREN AND PHILLIPS
BR * LC

GLO * INT * MEX
PL4 * PL7 * PL12 * PL15 * PT9 * AT10

SMITH, BILLYE MULLINS

PIANO REPERTOIRE GUIDE

WINTER HAVEN, FLA. BPRG

PM6 * PM15

SMITH, CYRIL

DUET FOR THREE HANDS...AS TOLD TO JOYCE EGGINTON

LONDON 1958 224P BDFTHA
ANGUS AND ROBERTSON
BR * LC * MI * NP

INT * PHO
NP6 * GI13

SMITH, EDWIN S.

PIANO BY EAR

WAYNE, MICH. 1943 55P BPBE
MAIN STREET PUBLISHING COMPANY, THE
LC

CHR * ILL * INT
PL4 * PL12 * AT4 * KS12

SMITH, FANNY MORRIS

NOBLE ART, A ..THREE LECTURES ON THE EVOLUTION AND CONSTRUCTION OF
THE PIANO

NEW YORK 1892 160P BNATLO
DE VINNE PRESS, THE
BP * ES * LC * NP * UM * YU

ILL * INT * LDR * MEX * PHO
KI3 * KI4 * KI5 * KI6 * KI7 * KI9 * KI13 * KI15

SMITH, HERMANN

ART OF TUNING THE PIANOFORTE, THE ...ON THE THEORY OF EQUAL
TEMPERAMENT

LONDON 1902 90P BAOTTP
REEVES, WILLIAM
BR * IU * LC * NP * SA

CHR * INT * MEX * TAB
KI5 * KI6 * KI8

SMITH, HOWARD G.

ANYONE CAN PLAY THE PIANO BY EAR IN FIVE EASY LESSONS..A-B-C PIANO
METHOD

1942 14P BACPTP
SMITH, HOWARD G.
LC

INT
AT4 * KS6 * KS12

SMITH, JULIA

MASTER PIANIST..THE CAREER AND TEACHING OF CARL FRIEDBERG

NEW YORK 1963 183P BMPTCA
PHILOSOPHICAL LIBRARY
BP * ES * LC * NP * TO * UI * UO

APP * IND * PHO
NP3 * NP4 * NP7 * PM11

SMITH, MACDONALD

FROM BRAIN TO KEYBOARD..A SYSTEM OF HAND AND FINGER CONTROL FOR
PIANISTS AND STUDENTS

BOSTON 1917 63P BFBTKA
DITSON, OLIVER, COMPANY
BR * CP * ES * LC * UI * UK * UO * UT * UW

MEX * PHO
PT1 * PT3 * PT5 * PT9 * PT10

SMITH, THOMAS

ART OF PLAYING AT SIGHT, THE

LONDON 1890+ BAOPAT
ASHDOWN, EDWIN, LTD.

KS3

SMITH, THOMAS

CONCISE AND PRACTICAL EXPLANATION OF THE RULES OF SIMPLE HARMONY
AND THOROUGH-BASS, A

LONDON 1873 BCAPEO

BR

KS4 * KS10

SMITH, THOMAS

HOW TO LEARN TO PLAY THE PIANO WELL

LONDON 1890+ BHTLTP
ASHDOWN, EDWIN, LTD.

AT4

SMITH, THOMAS

HOW TO TUNE YOUR OWN PIANO

LONDON 1890+ BHTTYO
ASHDOWN, EDWIN, LTD.

KI8

SMITH, THOMAS

LITTLE DIFFICULTIES WHICH OCCUR IN PIANOFORTE PLAYING

LONDON 1890+ 32P BLDWOI
ASHDOWN, EDWIN, LTD.
NP

MEX
PL4 * PL12 * PL15 * AP6 * AP7 * AP8

SMITH, USELMA CLARK

KEYBOARD HARMONY..LEARNING BY HEARING

BOSTON 1916 87P BKHLBH
BOSTON MUSIC COMPANY
BR * LC * NP

CHR * INT * MEX
PL4 * KS4 * KS8

SMITH, VERA K.

YOUNG PIANO TEACHER, WITH 75 HELPFUL TEACHING QUESTIONS, THE

LONDON 1956 32P BYPTWS
HAMMOND, A., AND COMPANY
BR * LC

AT3 * AT11

SMITHERS, WELSFORD

PIANO TEACHER'S GUIDE, THE ..A HUNDRED QUESTIONS FOR YOUNG TEACHERS

MELBOURNE 1937 44P BPTGAH
ALLAN'S MUSIC, PTY. LTD.
LC

INT * MEX
PM6 * AT10 * AT11

SORABJI, KAIKHOSRU

AROUND MUSIC---PACHMAN, CHOPIN AND LISZT

LONDON 1932 250P BAMPCA
UNICORN PRESS, THE
BR * LC * NP

IND * INT
NP5 * AT4 * PT8 * PM3 * PM10 * PM14 * GI3

SOREL, CLAUDETTE

COMPENDIUM OF PIANO TECHNIQUE--39 ETUDES SELECTED FROM OVER 4000,
BY 75 COMPOSERS, DURING THREE CENTURIES

NEW YORK 1970 128P BCOPTT
MARKS, EDWARD B., MUSIC CORPORATION
IU * LC * NP

INT * MEX
PT6 * PT9 * PT12 * PT13 * PL7 * PM3

SOREL, CLAUDETTE *
DIAMOND, ROBERT M.
    INDEPENDENT LEARNING APPROACH TO PIANO SIGHT READING, AN

              FREDONIA, N. Y.   1968   18P   BILATP
                 STATE UNIVERSITY COLLEGE
    IU

    LDR * PHO * TAB
    AT10 * KS3 * PM6

SOREL, CLAUDETTE

    MIND YOUR MUSICAL MANNERS, OFF AND ON STAGE..A HANDBOOK OF STAGE
    ETIQUETTE

              NEW YORK   1972   72P   BMYMMO
                 MARKS, EDWARD B., MUSIC CORPORATION
    LC * SA

    APP * ILL * TAB
    AP9 * GI5 * GI6 * GI9 * GI13

SOUTH KENSINGTON MUSEUM, LONDON

    CATALOGUE OF THE SPECIAL EXHIBITION OF ANCIENT MUSICAL INSTRUMENTS

              LONDON   1872   48P   BCOTSE
                 STRANGEWAYS, J.
    BR * LC

    INT
    KI5 * KI6 * KI9 * KII12 * KII13 * KII14 * KII15

SOUTH KENSINGTON MUSEUM, LONDON

    DESCRIPTIVE CATALOGUE OF THE MUSICAL INSTRUMENTS IN THE SOUTH
    KENSINGTON MUSEUM, A ...BY CARL ENGEL

              LONDON   1870   82P   BDCOTM
                 CHAPMAN AND HALL
    BR * LC

    ILL * IND * MEX
    KI3 * KI5 * KI6 * KI9 * KII12 * KII13 * KII14 * KII15

SOUTH KENSINGTON MUSEUM, LONDON

    DESCRIPTIVE CATALOGUE OF THE MUSICAL INSTRUMENTS IN THE SOUTH
    KENSINGTON MUSEUM, A --2ND. ED.--PRECEDED BY AN ESSAY ON THE
    HISTORY OF MUSICAL INSTRUMENTS---1874
              NEW YORK   1971   402P   BDCOTM
                 BLOM, B.
    BR * LC * NP

    APP * ILL * IND * INT * MEX
    KI3 * KI5 * KI6 * KI7 * KI9 * KII14

SPAETH, SIGMUND *
HOWARD, JOHN TASKER
    AMPICO IN MUSIC STUDY, THE

              NEW YORK   1925   125P   BAIMS
                 AMPICO CORPORATION
    BP * LC * MI * NP * YU

    DIS * INT
    KII10 * PM3 * PM6 * GI4

SPAETH, SIGMUND

    DEDICATION, THE LOVE STORY OF CLARA AND ROBERT SCHUMANN

              NEW YORK   1950   180P   BDTLSO
                 HOLT, HENRY, AND COMPANY
    AS * BR * LC * NP * UA

    BIB * DIS * IND * INT
    NP4

SPAETH, SIGMUND

    MAXIMS TO MUSIC..TRADITIONAL PROVERBS, MOTTOES AND MAXIMS OF THE
    WORLD FITTED TO MUSIC FOR THE WELL-TEMPERED PIANO-CHILD

              NEW YORK   1939   64P   BMTMTP
                 MCBRIDE, ROBERT M., AND COMPANY
    LC * NP

    INT
    GI10 * GI12 * GI15

SPENCER, ALLEN

    FOUNDATION OF PIANO TECHNIC, THE

              CHICAGO   1932   23P   BFOPT
                 FITZSIMMONS, H. T., COMPANY
    LC

    INT * MEX
    PL3 * PT4 * PT6 * PT9

SPENCER, BERNARD

    POPULAR PIANO...A CORRESPONDENCE COURSE OF THE EASTERN SCHOOLS OF
    MUSIC--10 VOLS.---TYPEWRITTEN COPY

              NEW YORK   1943   BPPACC
                 SPENCER, BERNARD
    LC

    INT * MEX * TAB
    PL4 * PL11 * PL12 * KS4 * KS6 * PT9 * EP6

SPENCER, CHARLES C.

    RUDIMENTS OF THE ART OF PLAYING THE PIANOFORTE, THE ...WITH
    NUMEROUS EXERCISES AND LESSONS

              LONDON   1851   136P   BROTAO
                 WEALE
    BR * OC

    PL2 * PL4

SPILLANE, DANIEL

    HISTORY OF THE AMERICAN PIANOFORTE..ITS TECHNICAL DEVELOPMENT, AND
    THE TRADE---1890
              NEW YORK   1969   383P   BHOTAP
                 DA CAPO PRESS
    AS * BP * ES * IU * LC * NP * OC * UI * UM

    APP * ILL * IND * INT * LDR
    KI3 * KI5 * KI6 * KI8 * KI9 * KII12 * KII13 * KII14

SPILLANE, DANIEL

    PIANO, THE ..SCIENTIFIC, TECHNICAL, AND PRACTICAL INSTRUCTIONS
    RELATING TO TUNING, REGULATING AND TONING
              NEW YORK   1893   108P   BPSTAP
                 BILL, E. L.
    BR * LC * MI * NP * UA * UM

    ILL * INT * LDR * MEX
    KI8

SQUIRE, RUSSEL N. *
MOUNTNEY, VIRGINIA R.
    CLASS PIANO FOR ADULT BEGINNERS--2ND. ED.---1964

              ENGLEWOOD CLIFFS, N. J.   1971   173P   BCPFAB
                 PRENTICE-HALL, INC.
    IU * LC * SA * UI * UT

    APP * ILL * INT * LDR * MEX
    KI1 * PL4 * PL6 * PL7 * PL9 * PL10 * PL12 * AT6 * AT7 * PT6 * PT9 *
    PT10 * PT11 * KS4 * AP7 * AP8 * EP1 * EP4 * EP6

STAINKAMPH, EILEEN

    FORM AND ANALYSES OF MOZART'S PIANOFORTE SONATAS, THE

              MELBOURNE   1967   35P   BFAAOM
                 ALLAN'S MUSIC, PTY. LTD.
    LC

    INT * MEX
    PM8 * PM14

STAINKAMPH, EILEEN

    FORM AND ANALYSIS OF THE COMPLETE BEETHOVEN'S PIANOFORTE SONATAS

              MELBOURNE   1968   61P   BFAAOT
                 ALLAN'S MUSIC, PTY. LTD.
    LC * UI

    INT
    PM8 * PM14

STANDARD PLAYER ACTION COMPANY

    PRINCIPLES OF PLAYER ACTION OPERATION--3RD. ED.

              NEW YORK   1925   47P   BPOPAO
                 STANDARD PLAYER ACTION COMPANY
    NP

    ILL * INT * LDR * PHO
    KI5 * KI6 * KI8 * KII10

STANDARD PNEUMATIC ACTION COMPANY

    DESCRIPTION OF STANDARD PNEUMATIC PLAYER ACTION, WITH SUGGESTIONS
    FOR REGULATING AND REPAIRING

              NEW YORK   1918   28P   BDOSPP
                 STANDARD PNEUMATIC ACTION COMPANY
    NP

    ILL * LDR * PHO
    KI5 * KI6 * KI8 * KII10 * KII12 * KII13

STANLEY, ALBERT A.

    CATALOGUE OF THE STEARNS COLLECTION OF MUSICAL INSTRUMENTS

              ANN ARBOR, MICH.   1918   260P   BCOTSC
                 UNIVERSITY OF MICHIGAN
    BR * IU * LC * NP

    APP * BIB * IND * INT * MEX * PHO
    KI1 * KI3 * KII14 * KII15

STANLEY, JANE

    BASIC ROUTINES IN ELEMENTARY PIANO TEACHING THROUGH THE FIRST THREE
    YEARS..A PRACTICAL REFERENCE FOR STUDIO TEACHERS, SCHOOLS, PARENTS
    AND STUDENTS
              LONG BEACH, CAL.   1953   52P   BBRIEP
                 STANLEY, JANE
    LC

    INT
    PL4 * PL7 * PL8 * PL9 * PL12 * AT11 * PT1 * PT8 * PT9 * KS4 * GI5

STARKEY, EVELYN

PIANO CLASS WORKBOOK FOR FIRST YEAR STUDENTS

BLOOMINGTON, IND.   1965   57P   BPCWFF
INDIANA UNIVERSITY SCHOOL OF MUSIC
IU * SA

CHR * INT * LDR * MEX * TAB
PL4 * PL10 * PL11 * PL12 * PL13 * PL14 * PL15 * AT4 * AT6 * AT7 *
PT9 * KS3 * KS4 * KS5 * KS7 * AP8

STARR, WILLIAM J. *
STARR, CONSTANCE
BASIC PIANO TECHNIQUE FOR THE CLASSROOM TEACHER

DUBUQUE, IOWA   1971   122P   BBPTFT
BROWN, WILLIAM C., COMPANY
IU * LC

APP * IND * INT * MEX * PHO
AT4 * AT5 * AT7

STATHAM, HENRY H.

MY THOUGHTS ON MUSIC AND MUSICIANS---CHOPIN AND LISZT

LONDON   1892   475P   BMTOMA
CHAPMAN AND HALL, LTD.
BR * LC * NP

IND * INT * MEX
NP5 * PM3

STECK AND COMPANY

ILLUSTRATED CATALOG...GRAND AND UPRIGHT PIANOS

NEW YORK   1907   23P   BICGAU
STECK, GEORGE, AND COMPANY
NP

ILL * PHO
KI4 * KI9 * KII12 * KII13 * KII15 * GI12

STEGLICH, RUDOLF

MOZARTS FLUEGEL KLINGT WIEDER--MOZART'S PIANO SOUNDS AGAIN---WITH
FRENCH AND ENGLISH TRANSLATIONS
NUERNBERG   1937   15P   BMFKWM
PIANOHAUS WILHELM RUECH
BR * LC

ILL * PHO
KI3 * KI6 * KI7 * KI9 * KII12 * KII14

STEIN, ERWIN

FORM AND PERFORMANCE

LONDON   1962   183P   BFAP
FABER AND FABER
BP * BR * CP * CU * ES * IU * LC * MI * NP * OC * SA * TO * UA * UC
UI * UM * UO * US * UT * UU * UW * YU
IND * INT * MEX
PL12 * PM3 * PM8 * PM9 * PM14 * AP3 * AP4 * AP5 * AP6

STEINER, ERIC

MASTER TUNES AND MUSIC TESTS FOR THE PIANO STUDENT

NEW YORK   1948   33P   BMTAMT
SCHIRMER, G., INC.
IU * LC * NP

MEX
AT10

STEINERT, MORRIS

CATALOGUE OF THE M. STEINERT COLLECTION OF KEYED AND STRING
INSTRUMENTS...AT THE WORLD'S COLUMBIAN EXPOSITION...INTERNATIONAL
EXPOSITION FOR MUSIC AND THEATER, VIENNA, 1892
NEW HAVEN, CONN.   1893   30P   BCOTMS
TUTTLE, MOREHOUSE AND TAYLOR
BR * LC

KII14 * KII15

STEINERT, MORRIS

MORRIS STEINERT COLLECTION OF KEYED AND STRINGED INSTRUMENTS, THE
..WITH VARIOUS TREATISES ON THE HISTORY OF THESE INSTRUMENTS

NEW YORK   1893   170P   BMSCOK
TRETBAR, C. F.
BP * BR * LC * MI * NP * TO * UA * UC * UI * UM * UT * YU

INT * PHO
KI3 * KI5 * KI6 * KI7 * KI9 * KII12 * KII13 * KII14 * AP3

STEINERT, MORRIS

REMINISCENCES OF MORRIS STEINERT, COMPILED AND ARRANGED BY JANE
MARLIN

NEW YORK   1900   267P   BROMSC
PUTNAM'S, G. P., SONS
BP * BR * CP * ES * LC * MI * NP * UA * UC * UI * UM * US * UT * UW

IND * PHO
NP6

STEINWAY, THEODORE E.

PEOPLE AND PIANOS..A CENTURY OF SERVICE TO MUSIC---1853-1953

NEW YORK   1953   122P   BPAPAC
STEINWAY AND SONS
AS * BP * CP * CU * ES * IU * LC * MI * NP * OC * SA * UC * UI * US
UT * UW * YU
ILL * INT * LDR * MSF * PHO
NP2 * KI3 * KI5 * KI6 * KI9 * KII12 * KII13 * GI5

STEINWAY AND SONS

BOOK OF ART PIANO CASES

NEW YORK   1901   29P   BBOAPC
STEINWAY AND SONS
LC * NP

ILL * PHO
KI4 * KI5 * KI9 * KII12 * KII13 * KII15 * GI5

STEINWAY AND SONS

ILLUSTRATED CATALOGUE OF--STEINWAY AND SONS...PIANOFORTES

NEW YORK   1888   14P   BICOSA
STEINWAY AND SONS
NP

ILL * INT * LDR * PHO
KI4 * KI5 * KI6 * KI8 * GI5

STEINWAY AND SONS

ILLUSTRATED CATALOGUE OF PIANOS

NEW YORK   1875   38P   BICOP
GREEN, S. W.
NP

ILL * INT
KI4 * KI5 * KI8 * KI9 * KII13 * KII15 * GI5

STEINWAY AND SONS

ILLUSTRATED CATALOGUE OF STEINWAY AND SONS' PIANOS

NEW YORK   1882   24P   BICOSA
STEINWAY AND SONS
NP

ILL * INT * LDR
KI4 * KI5 * KI6 * KI9 * KII12 * KII15 * GI5

STEINWAY AND SONS

ILLUSTRATED CIRCULAR AND CATALOGUE OF PIANOFORTES--MANUFACTURERS OF
GRAND, SQUARE AND UPRIGHT PIANOFORTES
NEW YORK   1876   36P   BICACO
STEINWAY AND SONS
NP

ILL * INT * LDR
KI3 * KI4 * KI5 * KI6 * KI7 * KI9 * KII12 * KII13 * KII15 * GI5

STEINWAY AND SONS

INIMITABLE TONE..'PRICE LIST OF PIANOS MADE BY STEINWAY AND SONS,
HAMBURG'
NEW YORK   1960   24P   BITPLO
STEINWAY AND SONS
NP

PHO * TAB
KI4 * KI9 * KII12 * KII13 * KII15 * GI5

STEINWAY AND SONS

PIANOFORTES

NEW YORK   1921   28P   BP
STEINWAY AND SONS
LC

PHO
KI3 * KI4 * KI9 * KII12 * KII13 * GI5

STEINWAY AND SONS

PORTRAITS OF MUSICAL CELEBRITIES

NEW YORK   1894   73   BPOMC
STEINWAY AND SONS
IU * LC

INT * PHO
NP6 * KI7 * KI9 * KII12 * GI13

STEINWAY AND SONS

PORTRAITS OF MUSICAL CELEBRITIES

NEW YORK   1906   147P   BPOMC
STEINWAY AND SONS
LC * NP

PHO
NP6 * KII12 * GI13

STEINWAY AND SONS

    PORTRAITS OF MUSICAL CELEBRITIES

          NEW YORK   1913   84P   BPOMC
             STEINWAY AND SONS
    LC

    INT * PHO
    KI4 * KI9 * KI12 * GI13

STEINWAY AND SONS

    PORTRAITS OF MUSICAL CELEBRITIES

          NEW YORK   1922   97P   BPOMC
             STEINWAY AND SONS
    NP

    PHO
    KI4 * KI9 * KI12 * GI13

STEINWAY AND SONS

    PORTRAITS OF MUSICAL CELEBRITIES

          NEW YORK   1926   111P   BPOMC
             STEINWAY AND SONS
    IU

    APP * PHO
    KI4 * KI9 * KI12 * GI13

STEINWAY AND SONS

    PORTRAITS OF MUSICAL CELEBRITIES

          NEW YORK   1929   107P   BPOMC
             STEINWAY AND SONS
    NP

    PHO
    KI4 * KI9 * KI12 * GI13

STEINWAY AND SONS

    PORTRAITS OF MUSICAL CELEBRITIES

          NEW YORK   1904   97P   BPOMC
             ROST, H. A.
    BP * BR * ES * NP * SA * UC * UT

    APP * ILL * MSF * PHO
    NP2

STEINWAY AND SONS

    STEINWAY..YESTERDAY, TODAY, TOMORROW

          NEW YORK   1948   29P   BSYTT
             STEINWAY AND SONS
    LC * NP

    ILL
    KI3 * KI5 * KI9 * KI12 * GI5

STEINWAY AND SONS

    STEINWAY AND SONS' PIANO-FORTE MANUFACTORY AT 'STEINWAY', LONG
    ISLAND CITY

          NEW YORK   1881   8P   BSASPM
             STEINWAY AND SONS
    NP

    ILL
    KI5 * KI12 * KI13 * GI5

STEINWAY AND SONS

    STEINWAY OF TODAY, THE ..A FAMILY OF PIANO MANUFACTURERS THROUGH
    FOUR GENERATIONS

          NEW YORK   14P   BSOTAF
             BRADFORD, WILLIAM, PRESS
    UT

    KI3 * KI12

STEINWAY AND SONS

    STEINWAY PROGRESS..AN APPRECIATION BY I. J. PADEREWSKI

          NEW YORK   1916   5P   BSPAAB
             STEINWAY AND SONS
    NP

    PHO
    NP6 * KI9 * KI12 * GI13

STEPHENSON, LILIAN E.

    BEGONE, DULL PRACTICE..SUGGESTIONS FOR STUDENTS AND
    TEACHERS--LISTENING, MUSICAL SHAPES

          LONDON   1967   BBDPSF
             HAMMOND, A., AND COMPANY

    PL6 * PL7 * AP6

STERNBERG, CONSTANTIN I. VON

    ETHICS AND ESTHETICS OF PIANO PLAYING

          NEW YORK   1917   103P   BEAEOP
             SCHIRMER, G., INC.
    BP * BR * CU * LC * NP * OC

    LDR * MEX
    PL3 * PL6 * PL12 * PL15 * PM7 * AP4 * AP6 * GI3

STERNBERG, CONSTANTIN I. VON

    TEMPO RUBATO AND OTHER ESSAYS

          NEW YORK   1920   150P   BTRAOE
             SCHIRMER, G., INC.
    BR * LC * NP * OC * UA * UC * UM * UT

    MEX
    NP6 * PL12 * PL14 * AP3

STEVENS, A. M.

    HOW TO PLAY THE PIANO AND ORGAN..OR, KEY TO THE SCIENCE AND THEORY
    OF MUSIC

          FARGO, N. D.   1889   34P   BHTPTP
             STEVENS, A. M.
    LC

    AT4 * KS4

STEVENS, EVERETT

    CHORDS, CADENCES, AND ARPEGGIOS

          GLEN ROCK, N. J.   1956   35P   BCCAA
             FISCHER, J., AND BRO.
    LC

    INT * MEX
    PT9 * KS4

STEVENS, FLOYD A.

    COMPLETE COURSE IN PROFESSIONAL PIANO TUNING, REPAIR, AND
    REBUILDING

          CHICAGO   1972   216P   BCCIPP
             NELSON-HALL COMPANY
    IU * LC

    CHR * ILL * IND * INT * LDR * PHO
    KI3 * KI4 * KI5 * KI6 * KI7 * KI8 * KI11 * GI5

STEVENS, PARAN

    REPORT UPON MUSICAL INSTRUMENTS..PARIS UNIVERSAL EXPOSITION, 1867

          WASHINGTON, D. C.   1869   18P   BRUMIP
             GOVERNMENT PRINTING OFFICE
    BR * LC

    KI3 * KI5 * KI12

STEVENS, WILLIAM S.

    TREATISE ON PIANO-FORTE, CONTAINING THE PRINCIPLES OF FINE PLAYING
    ON THAT INSTRUMENT, A

          LONDON   1811   17P   BTOPCT
             JONES, M.
    LC

    APP * GLO * INT * MEX
    PL14 * PT8 * GI2

STEWART, REID

    HOW TO PASS MUSIC EXAMINATIONS--PIANO--A GUIDE FOR TEACHERS AND
    STUDENTS

          LONDON   1933   125P   BHTPME
             PITMAN, I., AND SONS, LTD.
    BR * LC

    APP * BIB * INT
    PL7 * PL8 * PL10 * PL12 * AT1 * AT10 * PT8 * PT9 * KS3 * AP8 * EP6

STODDARD, HOPE

    FROM THESE COMES MUSIC

          NEW YORK   1952   256P   BFTCM
             CROWELL, THOMAS Y., COMPANY
    IU * LC

    IND * LDR * MEX
    KI3 * KI5 * KI6 * KI7 * KI14

STOOKES, SACHA

    ART OF ROBERT CASADESUS, THE

          LONDON   1960   71P   BAORC
             FORTUNE PRESS
    BR * CU * IU * LC * MI * NP * SA

    APP * DIS
    NP4 * NP7 * PM3 * PM9

STORMEN, WIN

    FIFTY YEARS OF POPULAR PIANO TECHNIQUES IN THE U.S.A.

        NEW YORK   1962   242P   BFYOPP
          ARCO PUBLISHING COMPANY
    LC * NP

    INT * MEX * TAB
    PL12 * PT12 * KS4 * KS6

STORMEN, WIN

    JAZZ PIANO..DIXIELAND TO MODERN JAZZ, BLUES, BOOGIE, RAGTIME,
    SWING, BOP, LOCKED HAND

        NEW YORK   1958+   40P   BJPDTM
          ARCO PUBLISHING COMPANY
    LC

    INT * MEX
    KS6 * AP4

STORMEN, WIN

    JAZZ PIANO..EARLY BLUES TO CONTEMPORARY MODERN JAZZ, HOW TO PLAY
    GREAT JAZZ STYLES

        NEW YORK   1967   48P   BJPEBT
          PROGRESS MUSIC
    LC

    DIS * MEX
    KS6 * AP4

STORMEN, WIN

    LINK TO MODERN MUSIC INSTRUCTION, THE

        NEW YORK   1954   200P   BLTMMI
          PROGRESS MUSIC COMPANY
    IU * LC * NP

    ILL * IND * MEX * TAB
    KS4 * KS5 * KS7 * KS8

STORMEN, WIN

    MODERN PIANO IMPROVISATION..BASIC PRINCIPLES ADAPTED FROM THE 'LINK
    TO MODERN MUSIC INSTRUCTION', INTERMEDIATE, ADVANCED

        NEW YORK   1955   32P   BMPIBP
          PROGRESS MUSIC COMPANY
    LC

    INT * MEX * TAB
    KS4 * KS6

STORMEN, WIN

    POPULAR ACCOMPANYING

        NEW YORK   1955   32P   BPA
          PROGRESS MUSIC COMPANY
    LC

    ILL * INT * MEX * TAB
    KS6 * EP6

STORMEN, WIN

    POPULAR KEYBOARD HARMONY

        NEW YORK   1955   32P   BPKH
          PROGRESS MUSIC COMPANY
    LC

    CHR * INT * MEX
    KS4 * KS6

STORMEN, WIN

    POPULAR PIANO SELF-TAUGHT---1956

        NEW YORK   1966   103P   BPPSTN
          ARCO PUBLISHING COMPANY
    LC

    ILL * INT * MEX
    PL11 * AT4 * KS6

STORMEN, WIN

    YOUR GUIDE TO PLAYING AND WRITING POPULAR MUSIC--REV. ED.

        NEW YORK   1958   64P   BYGTPA
          ARCO PUBLISHING COMPANY
    LC * NP

    INT * MEX * TAB
    KS4 * KS6 * KS7 * EP6

STRACHEY, MARJORIE C.

    NIGHTINGALE, THE ..A LIFE OF CHOPIN--IN THE FORM OF FICTION

        LONDON   1925   305P   BNALOC
          LONGMANS, GREEN AND COMPANY, LTD.
    BR * LC * NP

    ILL
    NP4 * PM3

STRAKACZ, ANIELA

    PADEREWSKI AS I KNEW HIM

        NEW BRUNSWICK, N. J.   1949   338P   BPAIKH
          RUTGERS UNIVERSITY PRESS
    AS * BP * CP * IU * LC * MI * NP * OC * UA * UC * UI * YU

    IND * PHO
    NP4

STRAUCH BROTHERS

    MANUFACTURE OF PIANOFORTE ACTION, THE ..ITS RISE AND DEVELOPMENT

        NEW YORK   1891   68P   BMOPAI
          GILES COMPANY
    IU * LC * NP * YU

    ILL * LDR * PHO
    KI3 * KI5 * KI6 * KI12 * KI13 * KI14 * GI5

STRELEZKI, ANTON

    PERSONAL RECOLLECTIONS OF CHATS WITH LISZT, IN 1869---1893

        NEW YORK   1970   23P   BPROCW
          MUSICAL SCOPE PUBLISHERS
    BR * SA

    NP8

STROHBER PIANO COMPANY

    PNEUMATIC PLAYER MECHANISM AND DESCRIPTIVE CATALOG OF STROHBER AND
    HOFFMANN PLAYER PIANOS

        CHICAGO   1916   40P   BPPMAD
          STROHBER PIANO COMPANY
    LC

    ILL * INT * PHO
    KI5 * KI6 * KI8 * KI10 * KI12 * KI13 * KI15

STUCKENSCHMIDT, HANS H.

    FERRUCCIO BUSONI..CHRONICLE OF A EUROPEAN---1967, IN GERMAN

        NEW YORK   1972   224P   BFBCOA
          ST. MARTIN'S PRESS
    IU * LC * NP

    ILL * IND * INT * PHO
    NP3 * AT12 * PM3 * GI13

STUCKENSCHMIDT, HANS H.

    MAURICE RAVEL..VARIATIONS ON HIS LIFE AND WORK

        PHILADELPHIA   1968   271P   BMRVOH
          CHILTON BOOK COMPANY
    BR * IU * LC

    APP * IND * INT
    NP3 * PM3 * PM8 * PM9 * PM14

SUCHOFF, B.

    GUIDE TO THE MIKROKOSMOS OF BELA BARTOK, A --PUBLISHED
    THESIS---1956

        LONDON   1971   152P   BGTTMO
          BOOSEY AND HAWKES
    BP * CP * CU * ES * IU * LC * NP * OC * TO * UA * UI * UM * UT * YU

    IND * MEX
    PM8 * PM9 * PM11 * PM15

SUDDS, WILLIAM F.

    NATIONAL SCHOOL FOR PIANOFORTE, THE

        MILWAUKEE   1881   BNSFP
          ROLFING, W.
    CU

    AT4

SUMMY-BIRCHARD COMPANY

    HANDBOOK FOR PIANO TEACHERS..COLLECTED ARTICLES ON SUBJECTS RELATED
    TO PIANO TEACHING

        EVANSTON, ILL.   1958   112P   BHFPTC
          SUMMY-BIRCHARD COMPANY
    ES * IU * LC * NP * OC * SA * UI * UM * UO * UT

    BIB * CHR * ILL * INT * LDR * MEX
    PL12 * AT1 * AT3 * AT5 * PT3 * PT4 * PT8 * PM3 * PM11 * AP3 * AP4 *
    AP7 * AP8 * AP9

SUMNER, WILLIAM L.

    PIANOFORTE, THE --3RD. ED.---1966

        LONDON   1971   223P   BPTENS
          MACDONALD AND COMPANY, LTD.
    AS * BP * ES * IU * LC * MI * NP * OC * SA * TO * UI * UM * UO * US
    UT
    APP * BIB * CHR * IND * INT * LDR * MEX * PHO * TAB
    KI3 * KI5 * KI6 * KI8 * KI9 * KI12 * KS7 * PM3

SUR, WILLIAM R.--EDITOR

KEYBOARD EXPERIENCE AND PIANO CLASS INSTRUCTION

```
            WASHINGTON, D. C.          1957      48P       BKEAPC
                MUSIC EDUCATORS NATIONAL CONFERENCE
CP * ES * IU * NP * UC * UI * UT

MEX * PHO * TAB
AT4 * AT7 * GI8
```

SUR, WILLIAM R.--EDITOR

PIANO INSTRUCTION IN THE SCHOOLS

```
            WASHINGTON, D. C.          1949      63P       BPIITS
                MUSIC EDUCATORS NATIONAL CONFERENCE
CP * ES * IU * LC * MI * NP * OC * SA * TO * UC * UI * UK * UM * UO
US * UT * UW
APP * BIB * IND * INT * PHO * TAB
AT2 * AT5 * AT7 * AT8 * AT11 * GI5 * GI8
```

SUTHERLAND, ADELAIDE K.--COMPILER

WHAT SHALL I PLAY..PREFERENCES FOR PIANO AND ORGAN..GUIDE TO CHOICE
MUSICAL COMPOSITIONS...BY DISTINGUISHED PIANISTS, TEACHERS, AND
MUSICAL CONNOISSEURS
```
            CHICAGO                    1895     109P       BWSIPP
                GLADSTONE PUBLISHING COMPANY, THE
LC

INT
AT14 * PM6 * PM10
```

SUZUKI, SHIN'ICHI

SUZUKI PIANO SCHOOL---4 VOLS.

```
            EVANSTON, ILL.             1970     124P       BSPSFV
                SUMMY-BIRCHARD COMPANY
IU * LC

MEX
PL6 * PL7 * PL8 * PL14
```

SWENSON, LUCILE B.

DISCOVERING THE PIANO..THE MULTIPLE KEY APPROACH..STUDY GUIDE AND
GOALS FOR TEACHER AND STUDENT--NEW REV. ED.---KEYBOARD HARMONY
```
            SALT LAKE CITY             1969      80P       BDTPTM
                SWENSON, LUCILE B.
LC

CHR * INT * MEX
PL5 * PL8 * AT4 * AT10 * PT6 * PT9 * KS3 * KS4 * KS7 * KS8
```

SWISHER, WALTER SAMUEL

PSYCHOLOGY FOR THE MUSIC TEACHER

```
            BOSTON                     1927      78P       BPFTMT
                DITSON, OLIVER, COMPANY
AS * LC * NP

AT3
```

SZABOLCSI, BENCE

TWILIGHT OF F. LISZT, THE

```
            BUDAPEST                   1959     134P       BTOFL
                COVINA PRESS
BR * ES * IU * LC * MI * NP * SA * TO * UA * UC * UI * US * UT * UW

APP * INT * MEX
NP3 * NP4 * NP7
```

SZIGETI, JOSEPH

TEN BEETHOVEN SONATAS FOR PIANO AND VIOLIN, THE

```
            URBANA, ILL.               1965      57P       BTBSFP
                AMERICAN STRING TEACHERS ASSOCIATION
IU * LC * NP

ILL * IND * INT * MEX * PHO
PM3 * PM8 * PM9 * PM14
```

TANKARD, GEOFFREY

FOUNDATIONS OF PIANOFORTE TECHNIQUE

```
            NEW YORK                   1960      32P       BFOPT
                GALAXY MUSIC CORPORATION
LC

INT * MEX
PL12 * PT8 * PT10 * AP6 * AP8
```

TANKARD, GEOFFREY

PIANOFORTE DIPLOMAS

```
            LONDON                     1958     140P       BPD
                ELKIN AND COMPANY
BR * LC * SA * TO

INT
KI3 * KI6 * KI7 * PL6 * PL7 * PL8 * PL9 * PT8 * PT9 * PT10 * KS3 *
PM3 * PM5 * PM6 * AP4 * AP9 * GI5 * GI9
```

TANKARD, GEOFFREY

SPECIMEN ANSWERS TO THE QUESTIONS IN PIANOFORTE DIPLOMAS

```
            LONDON                     1961      39P       BSATTQ
                ELKIN AND COMPANY
BR * LC

INT
PL9 * PL12 * PL14 * AT10 * PT8 * PT9 * AP8
```

TAPPER, THOMAS

ABC OF KEYBOARD HARMONY, THE

```
            BOSTON                     1943      27P       BABCOK
                SCHMIDT, A. P., COMPANY
LC * NP

INT * MEX
PL4 * KS4 * AP6
```

TAPPER, THOMAS

EDUCATION OF THE MUSIC TEACHER, THE

```
            PHILADELPHIA               1914     223P       BEOTMT
                PRESSER, THEODORE, COMPANY
BP * BR * CP * ES * IU * LC * NP * OC * TO * UC * UI * UO * UT

APP * CHR * INT * MEX
KI10 * PL3 * AT1 * AT2 * AT3 * AT10 * GI2 * GI6 * GI8 * GI9 * GI13
```

TARCZYNSKI-ALF, TADEUSZ

HOMAGE TO CHOPIN---TEXT IN POLISH AND ENGLISH

```
            GLASGOW                    1942      31P       BHTCTI
                POLISH LIBRARY
BR * LC * NP

PHO
NP4 * PM3
```

TARNOWSKI, STANISLAS

CHOPIN..AS REVEALED BY EXTRACTS FROM HIS DIARY--2ND. ED.---1905

```
            NEW YORK                   1972      55P       BCARBE
                MUSICAL SCOPE PUBLISHERS
BP * BR * ES * LC * NP * OC * UC * UI

ILL * PHO
NP4 * NP6
```

TAWASTSTJERNA, ERIK

PIANOFORTE COMPOSITIONS OF SIBELIUS, THE

```
            HELSINKI                   1957     104P       BPCOS
                KUSTANNUSOSAKEY-HTIO OTAVA
BR * LC * NP

INT * MEX * MSF * PHO
PM3 * PM9
```

TAYLER, E. DOUGLAS

MIND-POWER IN MUSIC FOR STUDENTS, TEACHERS AND PERFORMERS

```
            LONDON                     1924      30P       BMPIMF
                BOSWORTH AND COMPANY
BR * LC

INT
PL3 * AT3 * AP9 * GI3 * GI13
```

TAYLER, E. DOUGLAS

MODULATION MADE EASY

```
            LONDON                     1922      37P       BMME
                BOSWORTH AND COMPANY
BR

KS8
```

TAYLER, E. DOUGLAS

SECRET OF MUSICAL EXPRESSION, WITH SPECIAL REFERENCE TO PIANOFORTE
PLAYING, THE
```
            LONDON                     1920      28P       BSOMEW
                BOSWORTH AND COMPANY
BR * UC

AP4 * AP5
```

TAYLER, E. DOUGLAS

SECRET OF SUCCESSFUL PRACTICE, THE

```
            LONDON                     1919      30P       BSOSP
                BOSWORTH AND COMPANY
BR * UC

MEX
PL7 * PT3 * PT5 * PT6 * AP9
```

TAYLOR, ERIC R.

    INTRODUCTION TO SCORE PLAYING, AN

        NEW YORK   1970   77P   BITSP
           OXFORD UNIVERSITY PRESS
    IU * LC

    APP * INT * MEX * TAB
    KS9 * PM6

TAYLOR, ERIC R.

    PLAYING FROM AN ORCHESTRAL SCORE

        NEW YORK   1967   104P   BPFAOS
           OXFORD UNIVERSITY PRESS
    IU * LC

    IND * INT * MEX * TAB
    KS9

TAYLOR, FRANCIS

    REEVES' VAMPING TUTOR FOR PLAYING BY EAR

        LONDON   1880+   19P   BRVTFP
           REEVES, WILLIAM
    BP * NP

    KS12

TAYLOR, FRANKLIN

    PRIMER OF PIANOFORTE PLAYING

        NEW YORK   1878   126P   BPOPP
           APPLETON, D., AND COMPANY
    BP * BR * ES * NP * OC * UO * UU

    MEX * TAB
    PL12 * PT6 * PT8 * PT10 * KS4 * AP6 * AP7 * AP8

TAYLOR, FRANKLIN

    TECHNIQUE AND EXPRESSION IN PIANOFORTE PLAYING

        LONDON   1897+   126P   BTAEIP
           NOVELLO AND COMPANY, LTD.
    BP * BR * ES * IU * NP * TO * UC * YU

    IND * INT * MEX
    PL5 * PL7 * PL12 * PT6 * PT8 * PT9 * AP4 * AP6 * AP7 * AP8

TAYLOR, GEORGE C.

    FIRST STEPS TO THE PIANOFORTE

        NEW YORK   1854   BFSTTP
           HUNTINGTON, F. J.
    YU

    PL2 * PL4 * AT4

TAYLOR, H.

    ORNAMENTS IN MUSIC

        LONDON   1900+   15P   BOIM
           WEEKES AND COMPANY
    LC

    INT * MEX
    AP7

TAYLOR, ROBERT L.

    RUNNING PIANIST, THE ---PERCY GRAINGER

        NEW YORK   1950   340P   BRPPG
           DOUBLEDAY AND COMPANY
    LC * NP

    NP3 * PM4 * GI13

TEMPLIER, PIERRE D.

    ERIK SATIE---1932, IN FRENCH

        CAMBRIDGE, MASS.   1969   127P   BESNTT
           MASSACHUSETTS INSTITUTE OF TECHNOLOGY PRESS
    IU * LC

    DIS * ILL * LDR * MEX * MSF * PHO
    PM3 * PM9

TERWILLIGER, GORDON B.

    PIANO TEACHERS PROFESSIONAL HANDBOOK

        ENGLEWOOD CLIFFS, N. J.   1965   254P   BPTPH
           PRENTICE-HALL, INC.
    BP * CP * ES * IU * LC * MI * OC * SA * UI * UK * UM * UO * UT * UW
    YU
    APP * BIB * CHR * IND * INT * LDR * TAB
    KI8 * PL7 * AT1 * AT2 * AT3 * AT5 * AT6 * AT8 * AT9 * AT12 * EP4 *
    EP5 * EP6 * GI5 * GI6 * GI8 * GI9 * GI13

THACKRAY, RUPERT M.

    PLAYING FOR DANCE..THE PLACE OF THE PIANIST IN THE TEACHING OF
    DANCE

        LONDON   1963   84P   BPFDTP
           NOVELLO AND COMPANY
    BR * LC

    APP * INT * MEX
    PL13 * KS4 * KS5 * EP6 * GI15

THAYER, E. D.

    SHORT CUTS TO PIANO TECHNIQUE

        NEW YORK   BSCTPT
           BELWIN, INC.
    BP * BR * CP * CU * ES * NP * OC * SA * TO * UC * UI * UK * UM * UO
    US * UW * YU

    PT1 * PT2

THIMAN, ERIC H.

    PIANOFORTE TESTS IN INITIATIVE AND INTELLIGENCE AS SET IN DIPLOMA
    EXAMINATIONS

        LONDON   1939   8P   BPTIIA
           AUGENER, LTD.
    LC * NP

    INT * MEX
    AT10

THOMPSON, JOHN

    TEACHING PIANO IN CLASSES

        PHILADELPHIA   1932   78P   BTPIC
           PRESSER, THEODORE, COMPANY
    LC * OC * US

    ILL * INT * LDR * MEX
    PL4 * AT3 * AT4 * AT7 * AT8 * AT11

THOMPSON, KENNETH

    DICTIONARY OF TWENTIETY-CENTURY COMPOSERS, A --1911-1971

        NEW YORK   1973   666P   BDOTCC
           ST. MARTIN'S PRESS
    IU

    APP * INT
    NP5 * PM3 * PM6

THOMPSON, OSCAR

    DEBUSSY, MAN AND ARTIST---1937

        NEW YORK   1967   395P   BDMAAN
           DOVER PUBLICATIONS, INC.
    AS * BP * BR * CP * ES * IU * LC * MI * NP * OC * SA * TO * UA * UC
    UI * UK * UM * UO * US * UT * UW * YU
    BIB * IND * PHO
    NP3 * NP4 * PM13 * PM15

THRELFALL, ROBERT

    SERGEI RACHMANINOFF

        LONDON   1974   75P   BSR
           BOOSEY AND HAWKES

    NP3

TISCHLER, HANS

    PRACTICAL HARMONY, AN INTEGRATED COURSE IN THE PRINCIPLES OF
    HARMONIC-MELODIC WRITING, KEYBOARD IMPROVISATION AND MODULATION

        BOSTON   1964   302P   BPHAIC
           ALLYN AND BACON, INC.
    IU * LC * NP

    APP * IND * INT * MEX
    KS4 * KS5 * KS8

TISCHLER, HANS

    STRUCTURAL ANALYSIS OF MOZART'S PIANO CONCERTOS, A --MUSICOLOGICAL
    STUDIES, NO. 10---PARALLEL TEXTS..IN ENGLISH, GERMAN AND FRENCH

        BROOKLYN, N. Y.   1966   140P   BSAOMP
           INSTITUTE OF MEDIAEVAL MUSIC, LTD., THE
    BP * BR * CP * ES * IU * LC * MI * NP * OC * TO * UA * UI * UK * UM
    UO * US * UT * UW * YU
    INT * MEX
    PM3 * PM8 * PM14

TOBIN, JOSEPH RAYMOND

    ADVENTURES IN MUSICIANSHIP

        LONDON   1941   16P   BAIM
           WILLIAMS, JOSEPH, LTD.
    LC * SA

    INT * MEX
    PL2 * PL4 * PL6 * PL10 * PL11 * KS7 * KS8

TOBIN, JOSEPH RAYMOND

COMMON SENSE IN SIGHT READING..A GUIDE FOR PIANO TEACHERS

    LONDON   1957   38P   BCSISR
        WILLIAMS, JOSEPH, LTD.
BP * BR * NP * UM

INT * MEX
PL8 * PL12 * PT6 * PT8 * KS3 * AP6

TOBIN, JOSEPH RAYMOND

FUN WITH FINGERING, A FIRST-OF-ALL BOOK ON EASY FINGERING AND
CORRECT HANDSHAPE FOR PIANO BEGINNERS

    LONDON   1939   15P   BFWFAF
        WILLIAMS, J., LTD.
LC

AT4 * PT4 * PT6

TOBIN, JOSEPH RAYMOND

HOW TO IMPROVISE PIANO ACCOMPANIMENTS

    LONDON   1956   47P   BHTIPA
        OXFORD UNIVERSITY PRESS
BR * CP * ES * IU * LC * MI * NP * SA * TO * UI * UO

INT * MEX
PL4 * PL8 * KS5 * KS8 * EP6

TOBIN, JOSEPH RAYMOND

MEMORY PLAYING AT THE PIANO

    LONDON   1944   15P   BMPATP
        WILLIAMS, JOSEPH, LTD.
SA

MEX
PL8

TOBIN, JOSEPH RAYMOND

MODULATION AT THE PIANO--IN THREE STAGES

    LONDON   1937   62P   BMATPI
        WILLIAMS, JOSEPH, LTD.
IU * SA

CHR * INT * MEX
KS8

TOBIN, JOSEPH RAYMOND

MOZART AND THE SONATA FORM..A COMPANION BOOK TO ANY EDITION OF
MOZART'S PIANO SONATAS---1916

    NEW YORK   1971   156P   BMATSF
        DA CAPO PRESS
BP * BR * ES * IU * LC * NP * SA * UA * UI * UM * UT * UW

IND
PM8 * PM15

TOBIN, JOSEPH RAYMOND

PREPARING FOR KEYBOARD TESTS IN MUSICIANSHIP EXAMINATIONS, JUNIOR
GRADE

    LONDON   1957   31P   BPFKTI
        HAWKES AND SON
BR

PL14 * AT4

TOBIN, JOSEPH RAYMOND

READ AND REMEMBER..TWELVE STUDY PIECES TO FACILITATE PLAYING FROM
MEMORY

    LONDON   1934+   12P   BRARTS
        OXFORD UNIVERSITY PRESS
LC

MEX
PL8 * KS3

TOBIN, JOSEPH RAYMOND

TRANSPOSING AT THE PIANO--IN THREE STAGES

    LONDON   1937   66P   BTATPI
        WILLIAMS, JOSEPH, LTD.
IU * NP * SA

INT * MEX
KS7

TOMLINSON, ANNA M.

ANNA M. TOMLINSON'S FORTY LESSONS ON HOW TO DEVELOP A PIANO HAND

    BERWYN, ILL.   1915   8P   BAMTFL
        TOMLINSON, ANNA M.
LC

PT4 * PT10

TONK, WILLIAM

MEMOIRS OF A--PIANO--MANUFACTURER

    NEW YORK   1926   311P   BMOAPM
        PRESTO PUBLISHING COMPANY
NP

IND * INT * PHO
NP6 * KI10 * KI12

TOVEY, DONALD FRANCIS

COMPANION TO BEETHOVEN'S PIANO SONATAS, A ..COMPLETE
ANALYSES--BAR-TO-BAR

    LONDON   1947   301P   BCTBPS
        OXFORD UNIVERSITY PRESS
BP * BR * CP * ES * IU * LC * MI * NP * OC * TO * UA * UC * UI * UK
UM * UO * US * UT * UU * UW * YU
INT * MEX
PM8 * PM14 * PM15

TOWNSEND, WILLIAM

BALANCE OF ARM IN PIANO TECHNIQUE--4TH. REV. ED.---1903

    LONDON   1932   77P   BBOAIP
        BOSWORTH AND COMPANY, LTD.
BR * NP

INT * MEX * PHO
PL3 * PL7 * PT5 * PT6 * PT8

TOWNSEND, WILLIAM

MODERN PIANO TEACHING

    LONDON   1911   208P   BMPT
        BOSWORTH AND COMPANY, LTD.
BR

AT1 * AT2

TRACY, GEORGE L.

PRACTICAL GUIDE TO THE STUDY OF TRANSPOSITION, A

    NEW YORK   1915   19P   BPGTTS
        EVANS MUSIC COMPANY
LC

MEX
KS7

TRAVIS, JOHN W.

GUIDE TO RESTRINGING, A

    MIDDLEBURG, VA.   1961   272P   BGTR
        MIDDLEBURG PRESS
BP * IU * LC * NP * OC * UI

CHR * INT * ILL * LDR * TAB
KI8 * GI5

TRAVIS, JOHN W.

LET'S TUNE UP

    TACOMA PARK, MD.   1968   375P   BLTU
        TRAVIS, JOHN W.
BP * CP * LC * NP

BIB * GLO * IND * LDR * MEX * PHO
KI1 * KI3 * KI5 * KI6 * KI7 * KI8

TRUE, LYLE C.

HOW AND WHAT TO PLAY FOR MOVING PICTURES..A MANUAL AND GUIDE FOR
PIANISTS

    SAN FRANCISCO   1914   24P   BHAWTP
        MUSIC SUPPLY COMPANY
BR * CP * LC

KS2 * AP2

TUFTS, JOHN W.

TECHNIC AND NOTATION AS APPLIED TO THE PIANOFORTE

    CHICAGO   1898+   136P   BTANAA
        SUMMY, CLAYTON F.
LC

ILL * INT * LDR * MEX * TAB
PT4 * PT6 * PT8 * PT9

TURECK, ROSALYN

INTRODUCTION TO THE PERFORMANCE OF BACH, AN--3 VOLS.

    LONDON   1960   86P   BITTPO
        OXFORD UNIVERSITY PRESS
AS * BP * IU * NP * SA * UC * UM * UT * YU

GLO * INT * MEX
PL5 * PT6 * PM3 * PM4 * PM8 * PM9 * AP3 * AP4 * AP7 * AP8

TYSON, ALAN

    AUTHENTIC ENGLISH EDITIONS OF BEETHOVEN, THE --'ALL SOULS STUDIES',
    NO. 1

        LONDON   1963   152P   BAEEOB
          FABER AND FABER
    BR * IU * LC * NP

    APP * BIB * ILL * IND * INT * MEX * MSF
    PM3 * PM4

TYSON, ALAN

    THEMATIC CATALOG OF THE WORKS OF MUZIO CLEMENTI

        TUTZING, GERMANY   1967   136P   BTCOTW
          SCHNEIDER, HANS
    IU * LC

    APP * INT * MEX
    PM6

UMINSKA, ZOFIA *
KENNEDY, H. E.
    CHOPIN, THE CHILD AND THE LAD

        LONDON   1925   91P   BCTCAT
          METHUEN AND COMPANY
    LC * NP

    ILL * MEX
    NP4 * GI10

UNDERWOOD, REX

    GHOST NOTE PATTERN BUILDERS FOR VISUALIZING THE STRUCTURE OF
    SCALES, INTERVALS AND TRIADS..FOR GENERAL USE IN TEACHING PIANO,
    VOICE, STRING AND WIND INSTRUMENTS
        EUGENE, ORE.   1941   19P   BGNPBF
          UNDERWOOD, REX

    PL4 * PT9

UNITED STATES--LIBRARY OF CONGRESS..DIVISION OF BIBLIOGRAPHY

    BRIEF LIST OF REFERENCES ON THE PIANO AND THE PIANO PLAYER
    INDUSTRY..DECEMBER 20, 1921---TYPEWRITTEN COPY

        WASHINGTON, D. C.   1921   8P   BBLORO
          LIBRARY OF CONGRESS
    NP

    KI10 * KI12

UNITED STATES--NATIONAL RECOVERY ADMINISTRATION

    CODE OF FAIR COMPETITION FOR THE PIANO MANUFACTURING INDUSTRY AS
    APPROVED ON NOV. 4, 1933 BY PRESIDENT ROOSEVELT

        WASHINGTON, D. C.   1933   5P   BCOFCF
          GOVERNMENT PRINTING OFFICE
    LC

    KI12 * GI5

UNITED STATES MUSEUM OF HISTORY AND TECHNOLOGY

    CHECKLIST OF KEYBOARD INSTRUMENTS AT THE SMITHSONIAN INSTITUTION, A

        WASHINGTON, D. C.   1967   79P   BCOKIA
          SMITHSONIAN INSTITUTION..DIVISION OF MUSICAL INSTRUMENTS
    IU * LC

    GLO * INT * MEX * PHO
    KI14 * KI15

UNITED STATES PATENT OFFICE

    COLLECTION OF LETTERS PATENT RELATING TO THE CONSTRUCTION OF
    PIANOS, 1877-1901

        WASHINGTON, D. C.   1901   BCOLPR
          UNITED STATES PATENT OFFICE
    LC

    KI5 * KI12 * GI5

UNITED STATES TRAINING SERVICE

    COURSES OF INSTRUCTION IN PIANO MAKING, TOGETHER WITH A SECTION ON
    PLAYER PIANOS, PNEUMATIC ACTIONS, PIANO ACTIONS, AND KEYS

        WASHINGTON, D. C.   1919   67P   BCOIIP
          GOVERNMENT PRINTING OFFICE
    LC

    TAB
    KS5 * KS6 * KS10

UNSCHULD, MARIE VON

    PIANIST'S HAND, THE ..A SYSTEMATIC METHOD...ACCORDING TO THE
    PRINCIPLES OF PROF. TH. LESCHETITZKY

        NEW YORK   1909   88P   BPHASM
          FISCHER, CARL, INC.
    ES * LC * NP * UC * UK * UT * YU

    APP * INT * MEX * PHO
    PL7 * PL8 * PL14 * PT4 * PT8 * PT9 * PT10 * AP8

UPTON, GEORGE P.

    MUSICAL MEMORIES..MY RECOLLECTIONS OF CELEBRITIES OF THE HALF
    CENTURY, 1850-1900---GOTTSCHALK

        CHICAGO   1908   345P   BMMMRO
          MCCLURG AND COMPANY
    BR * IU * LC * NP

    NP6

VALLAS, LEON

    THEORIES OF CLAUDE DEBUSSY, MUSICIEN FRANCAIS, THE ---1929

        NEW YORK   1967   189P   BTOCDM
          DOVER PUBLICATIONS, INC.
    IU * LC

    PM3

VANT, ALBERT B.

    PIANO SCALE MAKING

        NEW YORK   1927   95P   BPSM
          VANT, ALBERT B.
    BP * LC

    ILL * INT * LDR * TAB
    KI6 * KI7

VANTYN, SIDNEY

    MODERN PIANOFORTE TECHNIQUE

        NEW YORK   1919   166P   BMPT
          DUTTON, E. P., AND COMPANY
    BP * BR * LC * NP * UC

    MEX
    KI4 * PL7 * PL12 * PT3 * PT4 * PT6 * PT8 * PT9 * PT10 * AP5 * AP6 *
    AP8

VAN APPLEDORN, MARY J.

    KEYBOARD, SINGING AND DICTATION MANUAL

        DUBUQUE, IOWA   1968   182P   BKSADM
          BROWN, WILLIAM C., COMPANY
    LC

    ILL * INT * MEX
    PL4 * PL10 * PL12

VAN ATTA, HARRISON LOUIS--EDITOR

    TREATISE ON THE PIANO AND PLAYER PIANO, A

        DAYTON, OHIO   1914   151P   BTOTPA
          OHIO PRINTING COMPANY
    BP * LC * NP

    ILL * INT * LDR * PHO
    KI5 * KI6 * KI8 * KI10 * KI13

VAN DER VELPEN, JEAN

    HARMONY AND THOROUGH BASS--2 VOLS., 1909-1910

        CHICAGO   1909   351P   BHATBT
          SUMMY, CLAYTON F., COMPANY
    LC * NP

    INT * MEX
    PL4 * KS4 * KS10

VAN DER WEYDE, PETER H.

    INSTRUCTIONS IN PLAYING THE PIANO-FORTE WITH AEOLIAN ATTACHMENT

        NEW YORK   1910+   10P   BIIPTP
          VAN DER WEYDE, PETER H.
    NP

    KI10 * AT4 * AP3

VAN NOORDEN, C.

    FREAK PIANOS---SCRAPBOOK

        LONDON   1900+   80P   BFPS
          VAN NOORDEN, C.
    NP

    ILL * LDR
    KI2 * KI3 * KI5 * KI9

VEINUS, ABRAHAM

    CONCERTO, THE ---1944

        NEW YORK   1964   317P   BCNFF
          DOVER PUBLICATIONS, INC.
    BR * IU * LC * NP * SA

    BIB * IND
    PM3 * PM7 * PM8 * PM9 * PM14 * AP3 * AP4

VEINUS, ABRAHAM

    VICTOR BOOK OF CONCERTOS

          NEW YORK   1948   450P   BVBOC
            SIMON AND SCHUSTER, INC.
    IU * LC * NP

    DIS * GLO * INT * MEX
    PM4 * PM8 * PM9 * PM14

VENABLE, MARY

    INTERPRETATION OF PIANO MUSIC, THE

          BOSTON   1913   252P   BIOPM
            DITSON, OLIVER, COMPANY
    BR * CP * CU * ES * IU * LC * MI * NP * OC * TO * UA * UC * UI * UO
    US * UT * UW
    CHR * IND * INT * MEX
    KI6 * PL4 * PT3 * PT4 * PT6 * PT8 * PT10 * PM3 * PM8 * PM9 * PM11 *
    PM15 * AP3 * AP4 * AP6 * AP7 * AP8

VENDEN, LEONARD

    MUSICIAN'S LIGHTNING MODULATION GUIDE..INFORMATION, EXAMPLES, CHORD
     FORMULAS
          COLLEGE PLACE, WASH.   1959   2P   BMLMGI
            VENDEN, LEONARD
    LC

    KS8

VENINO, ALBERT F.

    PEDAL METHOD FOR THE PIANO, A

          NEW YORK   1893   52P   BPMFTP
            SCHUBERTH, E., AND COMPANY
    NP * OC * TO * UC

    APP * INT * MEX
    PL12 * AP8

VERNAZZA, MARCELLE

    BASIC MATERIALS FOR THE PIANO STUDENT

          DUBUQUE, IOWA   1963   151P   BBMFTP
            BROWN, WILLIAM C., COMPANY
    CP * ES * IU * LC * SA * UI * UO * UW

    DIS * INT * MEX
    PT9 * PT10 * KS4 * KS5 * KS8 * AP8 * PM6 * PM12

VERNE, MATHILDE

    CHORDS OF REMEMBRANCE---BY A PUPIL OF CLARA SCHUMANN

          LONDON   1936   288P   BCORBA
            HUTCHINSON AND COMPANY
    BR * LC * NP * UC

    ILL * IND * INT * PHO
    NP6 * GI13

VIARD-LOUIS, JENNY

    MUSIC AND THE PIANO

          LONDON   1884   239P   BMATP
            GRIFFITH AND FARRAN
    BP * BR * LC * NP

    IND * INT * MEX
    NP5 * PM3 * PM7 * AP4 * PT7

VICTORIA AND ALBERT MUSEUM, SOUTH KENSINGTON

    CATALOGUE OF MUSICAL INSTRUMENTS..VOL. 1, KEYBOARD
    INSTRUMENTS--EDITED BY RAYMOND RUSSELL

          LONDON   1968   140P   BCOMIV
            HER MAJESTY'S STATIONERY OFFICE
    BP * BR * IU * LC * MI * NP * TO * UA

    APP * BIB * ILL * IND * INT * PHO
    KI5 * KI6 * KI7 * KI9 * KI12 * KI13 * KI14 * KI15

VICTORIA AND ALBERT MUSEUM, SOUTH KENSINGTON

    EXAMPLES OF ART WORKMANSHIP OF VARIOUS AGES AND COUNTRIES..MUSICAL
    INSTRUMENTS IN THE SOUTH KENSINGTON MUSEUM..WITH DESCRIPTIONS BY
    CARL ENGEL, ETC.
          LONDON   1869   BEOAWO
            VICTORIA AND ALBERT MUSEUM
    BR

    KI3 * KI5 * KI9 * KI13 * KI14

VICTORIA AND ALBERT MUSEUM, SOUTH KENSINGTON

    LIST OF PHOTOGRAPHS OF OBJECTS IN THE VICTORIA AND ALBERT
    MUSEUM--PART 8..DEPARTMENT OF WOODWORK--SECTION G..MUSICAL
    INSTRUMENTS
          LONDON   1928   11P   BLOPOO
            VICTORIA AND ALBERT MUSEUM
    LC

    KI13 * KI15

VICTORIA AND ALBERT MUSEUM, SOUTH KENSINGTON

    MUSICAL INSTRUMENTS AS WORKS OF ART..VOL. 1, KEYBOARD
    INSTRUMENTS--EDITED BY JOHN POPE-HENNESSY

          LONDON   1968   101P   BMIAWO
            HER MAJESTY'S STATIONERY OFFICE
    BR * IU * LC

    ILL * INT * PHO
    KI3 * KI9 * KI13 * KI14

VICTORIA AND ALBERT MUSEUM, SOUTH KENSINGTON

    PICTURE BOOK OF KEYBOARD MUSICAL INSTRUMENTS, A

          LONDON   1929   20P   BPBOKM
            LONDON BOARD OF EDUCATION
    LC

    KI13 * KI14 * KI15

VILLOING, ALEXANDER

    RUBINSTEIN'S FINGER EXERCISES..TECHNICAL STUDIES FROM THE
    THEORETICAL AND TECHNICAL PIANOFORTE METHOD BY A. VILLOING

          CINCINNATI   1901   57P   BRFETS
            WILLIS, W. H., AND COMPANY
    LC

    MEX
    AT4 * PT10

VINING, HARRISON S.

    SIMPLE AND COMPLETE PRIMER FOR THE PIANOFORTE, THE

          NEW YORK   1885   68P   BSACPF
            SCHIRMER, G., INC.
    LC * UK * YU

    APP * GLO * ILL * INT * MEX * TAB
    PL4 * PL12 * AT4 * PT6 * PT9 * KS4 * KS7 * KS8 * AP7

VINING, HARRISON S.

    WHYS AND WHEREFORES..QUESTIONS AND ANSWERS FOR PIANO STUDENTS

          PHILADELPHIA   1888+   BWAWQA
            PRESSER, THEODORE, COMPANY

    PL4 * PL14

VINQUIST, MARY *
ZASLAW, NEAL
    PERFORMANCE PRACTICE..A BIBLIOGRAPHY

          NEW YORK   1971   114P   BPPAB
            NORTON, W. W., AND COMPANY, INC.
    IU * LC

    BIB * IND * INT
    AP3

VIRGIL, ALMON K.

    EDUCATION IN MUSIC..LESSONS TO TEACHERS IN THE INSTRUCTION OF
    PARENTS
          NEW YORK   1907   70P   BEIMLT
            VIRGIL, A. K.
    BR * LC * NP * UC

    CHR
    PL4 * PL7 * AT3 * AT4 * AT5 * AT10 * AT11 * AT13 * PT4 * PT5 * PT6
    PT10 * GI1

VIRGIL, ALMON K.

    FOUNDATION EXERCISES IN PIANO PLAYING FROM FIRST RUDIMENTS TO
    HIGHEST ARTISTIC FINISH..THE VIRGIL CLAVIER METHOD ENLARGED--2
    VOLS.---1889
          NEW YORK   1906   498P   BFEIPP
            VIRGIL, A. K.
    LC * NP

    APP * CHR * INT * MEX * PHO
    PL7 * PL10 * PL12 * AT4 * PT4 * PT5 * PT6 * PT8 * PT9 * PT10 * PT11
    KS3

VIRGIL, ALMON K.

    PUPIL'S RECORD BOOK, THE ..SHOWING HOW TO SUCCEED AND HOW TO FAIL

          NEW YORK   1912   48P   BPRBSH
            VIRGIL, A. K.
    BR

    AT4 * PL2

VIRGIL, ALMON K.

    SPECIAL TECHNIC COURSE IN THE VIRGIL CLAVIER METHOD--6 PTS.

          NEW YORK   1900   BSTCIT
            VIRGIL, A. K.
    BR

    AT4 * PT2

VIRGIL, ALMON K.

STEP BY STEP..TEXTBOOK IN PIANO PLAYING..HANDBOOK FOR TEACHERS

NEW YORK   1904   BSBSTI
VIRGIL, A. K.
BR * LC * US

APP * INT * TAB
PL7 * PL8 * PL12 * AT8 * PT4 * PT5 * PT6 * PT8 * PT10 * AP6

VIRGIL, ALMON K.

TECHNIPHONE MANUAL..INSTRUCTIONS AND EXERCISES IN THE USE OF THE
TECHNIPHONE IN THE TEACHING AND PRACTICE ON THE PIANO

NEW YORK   1886   38P   BTMIAE
TECHNIPHONE COMPANY, THE
NP

ILL * INT * MEX
KI10 * PT5 * PT8 * PT10

VIRGIL, ALMON K.

VIRGIL CLAVIER METHOD, THE --2 VOLS.

NEW YORK   1904   BVCMTV
FRIEDMAN, IRA J.
UT

AT4

VIRGIL, ANTHA MINERVA

ELEMENTARY EXERCISES IN SIGHT READING...FROM THE VIRGIL METHOD

NEW YORK   1902   15P   BEEISR
VIRGIL, MRS. A. M.
LC

INT * MEX
PL4 * PT8 * KS3

VIRGIL, ANTHA MINERVA

INSTRUCTIVE TALKS TO PIANO STUDENTS

NEW YORK   1900   57P   BITTPS
VIRGIL, MRS. A. M.
LC

PL7 * PL12 * PT1 * PT5

VIRGIL, ANTHA MINERVA

PIANO PEDALS, THE

NEW YORK   1912   34P   BPP
VIRGIL PIANO SCHOOL COMPANY, THE
NP

MEX
AP8

VIRGIL, ANTHA MINERVA

PRACTICAL EXERCISES IN THEORY AND HARMONY PLAYING...LEADING TO
IMPROVISATION AND COMPOSITION

NEW YORK   1928   39P   BPEITA
VIRGIL PIANO SCHOOL COMPANY
LC

INT * MEX
KS4 * KS5 * KS8

VIRGIL, ANTHA MINERVA

VIRGIL METHOD OF PIANOFORTE TECHNIC, THE --2 VOLS.

NEW YORK   1902   396P BVMOPT
VIRGIL PIANO CONSERVATORY, PUBLICATION DEPT.
LC * NP

INT * MEX * PHO
PL10 * PL12 * PT5 * PT9 * PT10 * PT14 * KS3

VISUOLA CORPORATION

BLAZING A NEW TRAIL IN PIANO PLAYING

NEW YORK   1927   34P   BBANTI
VISUOLA CORPORATION
BP

AT4

VUILLERMOZ, EMILE

GABRIEL FAURE

PHILADELPHIA   1969   265P BGF
CHILTON BOOK COMPANY
IU * LC

DIS * IND * LDR
PM3 * PM6 * PM8 * PM9 * PM12 * PM14

WAGNER, CHARLES A.

HOW TO SELECT A GOOD PIANO

BELDING, MICH.   1915   36P   BHTSAG
WAGNER, CHARLES A.
LC

ILL
KI4 * KI5 * KI6 * GI5

WAGNER, JOHN J.

NUMERICAL METHOD OF PIANO ACCOMPANIMENTS, A --WITH CHARTS

1920   15P   BNMOPA
WAGNER, JOHN J.
LC

KS11 * EP6

WAIT, WILLIAM B.

NORMAL COURSE OF PIANO TECHNIC, THE

PHILADELPHIA   1890+   175P BNCOPT
PRESSER, THEODORE, COMPANY

AT4 * PT10

WALKER, ADAM

PHILOSOPHY OF THE HARPSICHORD, EXPLAINING HOW THAT INSTRUMENT IS
KEPT MOST CONSTANTLY IN TUNE WITHOUT ASSISTANCE

1775   BPOTHE
ES

KI3 * KI8 * KI14

WALKER, ALAN--EDITOR

CHOPIN COMPANION, THE ..PROFILES OF THE MAN AND THE MUSICIAN---1966

NEW YORK   1973   312P BCCPOT
NORTON, W. W., AND COMPANY
AS * BP * CP * ES * IU * LC * MI * NP * OC * TO * UI * UK * UM * UO
US * UT * UU * UW * YU
APP * BIB * DIS * ILL * IND * INT * MEX * MSF * PHO * TAB
NP3 * NP6 * PM3 * PM6 * PM8 * PM9 * PM14

WALKER, ALAN--EDITOR

FRANZ LISZT, THE MAN AND HIS MUSIC---ESSAYS BY SACHEVERALL SITWELL
AND OTHERS

LONDON   1970   471P BFLTMA
BARRIE AND JENKINS
LC * NP

APP * BIB * ILL * IND * INT * MEX * MSF * PHO
NP3 * NP6 * AT12 * PM3 * PM6 * PM9

WALKER, ALAN--EDITOR

ROBERT SCHUMANN..THE MAN AND HIS MUSIC---SYMPOSIUM--13 AUTHORS

LONDON   1972   489P BRSTMA
BARRIE AND JENKINS
LC

APP * BIB * ILL * IND * INT * MEX * MSF
NP3 * PM3 * PM6 * PM8 * PM9 * PM14 * EP1 * EP7

WALKER, ALAN

LISZT

LONDON   1971   108P BL
FABER AND FABER
IU * LC * NP

DIS * ILL * IND * MEX * PHO
NP3 * PM3 * GI10

WALKER, BETTINA

MY MUSICAL EXPERIENCES

LONDON   1892   324P BMME
BENTLEY, R., AND SON
AS * BP * BR * ES * LC * NP * UA

INT * MSF
NP3 * NP6 * GI13

WALLACE, WILLIAM

LISZT, WAGNER, AND THE PRINCESS

LONDON   1927   196P BLWATP
PAUL, KEGAN, TRENCH, TRUBNER AND COMPANY, LTD.
BR * LC * NP

BIB * IND * INT * PHO
NP5 * PM3

WARRACK, JOHN H.

 SIX GREAT COMPOSERS---CHOPIN

    LONDON   1958 176P BSGCC
    HAMILTON, HAMISH, LTD.
 BR * LC

 ILL * PHO
 NP5 * PM3

WARRACK JOHN H.

 CHAIKOVSKY SYMPHONIES AND CONCERTOS--B.B.C. MUSIC GUIDES, NO. 16

    LONDON   1969 56P BCSACB
    BRITISH BROADCASTING CORPORATION
 IU * LC * NP

 IND * MEX
 PM3 * PM8 * PM9 * PM14

WARREN, CLARENCE H.--EDITOR

 MEN BEHIND THE MUSIC, THE ---CHOPIN AND LISZT

    LONDON   1931 156P BMBTMC
    ROUTLEDGE, G., AND SONS, LTD.
 BR * LC * NP

 NP4 * PM3

WARRINER, JOHN

 HANDBOOK ON THE ART OF TEACHING AS APPLIED TO MUSIC..FOR THE USE OF
 STUDENTS

    LONDON   1916 196P BHOTAO
    TRINITY COLLEGE
 BR

 AT3

WARRINER, JOHN

 TRANSPOSITION, KEYBOARD AND ORCHESTRAL--2 PTS., 1893-1908

    NEW YORK   1893 56P BTKAOT
    NOVELLO, EWER AND COMPANY
 BR * LC * NP

 INT * MEX
 KS3 * KS7 * KS8 * AP7 * EP6

WASHINGTON STATE MUSIC TEACHERS ASSOCIATION

 PIANO TEACHING GUIDE--GRADES 1-8

    SEATTLE   1961   BPTGGO
    WASHINGTON STATE MUSIC TEACHERS ASSOCIATION
 UW

 AT1 * AT2 * PM6

WEATHERLY, FREDERICK EDWARD

 PIANO AND GOWN--REMINISCENCES

    LONDON   1926 311P BPAGR
    PUTNAM'S, G. P., SONS
 LC * NP * UT

 NP6

WEBBE, SAMUEL

 HARMONY EPITOMIZED, BEING A SHORT EXPLANATION OF FIGURED BASSES,
 TOGETHER WITH THE MOST NECESSARY RULES FOR ACCOMPANIMENT

    LONDON   1810+ 31P BHEBAS
    HODSELL, W.
 LC

 MEX
 PL4 * KS8 * KS10 * EP6

WEBBE, WILLIAM H.

 PIANISTS' 'ABC' PRIMER AND GUIDE--WITH AN APPENDIX

    LONDON   1900 207P BPABCP
    FORSYTH BROTHERS, LTD.
 BR

 PL4 * AT4

WEBBE, WILLIAM H.

 PIANOFORTE PLAYING..JOTTINGS BY W. H. WEBBE--2ND. ED.

    LONDON   1893   BPPJBW
    WEEKES AND COMPANY
 BR

 NP6

WEBER PIANO COMPANY

 WEBER GRAND, SQUARE AND UPRIGHT PIANO-FORTES, THE

    EAST ROCHESTER, N. Y. 1886+ 32P BWGSAU
    WEBER PIANO COMPANY
 LC

 ILL * INT
 KI4 * KI5 * KI8 * KI9 * KI12 * KI13 * GI5

WEDGE, GEORGE ANSON

 KEYBOARD HARMONY

    NEW YORK   1924 194P BKH
    SCHIRMER, G., INC.
 IU * LC * NP

 INT * MEX * TAB
 KS4

WEINSTOCK, HERBERT

 CHOPIN, THE MAN AND HIS MUSIC

    NEW YORK   1949 336P BCTMAH
    KNOPF, ALFRED A.
 AS * IU * LC * NP

 APP * BIB * ILL * IND * INT * MEX * MSF * PHO
 NP3 * PM3

WEISER, ADOLPH

 TWO RIGHT HANDS..A GUIDE FOR THE DEVELOPMENT OF PIANO TECHNIQUE

    NEW YORK   1952 71P BTRHAG
    FISCHER, CARL, INC.
 CU * ES * IU * SA * UW

 LOR * MEX * PHO * TAB
 PL7 * PT2 * PT3 * PT4 * PT6 * PT8 * PT9 * PT10 * PT13

WEISER, BERNHARD D.

 KEYBOARD MUSIC--16TH.-20TH. CENTURIES

    DUBUQUE, IOWA   1971 151P BKMSTC
    BROWN, WILLIAM C., COMPANY
 IU * LC * UI

 BIB * DIS * IND * INT * LOR * PHO
 KI1 * PM3 * PM5 * PM7 * PM12

WEISSBUCH, ANTONIA

 KEYBOARD HARMONY MADE SIMPLE..THE NATURAL ROAD TO MUSICIANSHIP

    FAIR LAWN, N. J.   1957 124P BKHMST
    KIMBALL PRESS
 IU * LC * NP

 APP * INT * MEX
 KS4

WEITZMANN, CARL F.

 HISTORY OF PIANOFORTE-PLAYING AND PIANOFORTE-LITERATURE, A ---1879,
 IN GERMAN

    NEW YORK   1969 379P BHOPPA
    DA CAPO PRESS
 AS * BP * CU * ES * IU * LC * MI * NP * OC * SA * UI * UK * US * YU

 IND * INT * LOR * MEX
 NP3 * NP4 * NP5 * KI3 * KI5 * KI6 * KI7 * KI12 * KI14 * PM3 * PM5 *
 PM7 * PM14 * PM15

WELBOURNE, EVE V.

 WELBOURNE WAY TO HOBBY PIANO PLAYING FOR ADULTS, THE --9 LESSONS

    DENVER   1955 12P BWWTHP
    MUSIC CENTER FOR THE HAND INCAPACITATED
 CP * LC * NP

 INT * MEX * PHO
 AT4 * GI11

WELLS, HOWARD

 EARS, BRAIN AND FINGERS..A TEXT BOOK FOR PIANO TEACHERS AND PUPILS

    BOSTON   1914 97P BEBAFA
    DITSON, OLIVER, COMPANY
 AS * BP * BR * CP * CU * ES * IU * LC * NP * SA * UC * UK * US * UT

 INT * MEX * PHO
 PL4 * PL8 * PL10 * PL12 * AT1 * AT2 * AT4 * AT5 * PT4 * PT9 * KS4 *
 AP6 * AP8

WELLS, HOWARD

 PIANIST'S THUMB, THE

    BOSTON   1926+ 72P BPT
    DITSON, OLIVER, COMPANY
 CP * ES * IU * NP * SA * TO * UK * US

 APP * INT * MEX * PHO
 PL7 * PT2 * PT3 * PT4 * PT9 * PT10 * PT13

WELSH, J. ROBERT

MAKING MUSIC AT THE KEYBOARD..BEGINNING PIANO...CLASS...AND EAR
TRAINING METHOD---BASED ON ORFF AND KODALY MUSIC EDUCATION SYSTEMS

    CHICAGO   1970   BMMATK
      LUDWIG INDUSTRIES

PL4 * PL10 * AT4 * AT7

WELTE-MIGNON CORPORATION

HOW TO TEST AND REGULATE THE AUTO DE LUXE WELTE-MIGNON REPRODUCING
PIANO

    CLIFTON, N. J.   1960+   48P   BHTTAR
      AMERICAN PIANO SUPPLY COMPANY
NP

ILL * INT * LDR
KI8 * KI10

WELTE-MIGNON CORPORATION

LIBRARY OF DELUXE WELTE-MIGNON MUSIC RECORDS FOR REPRODUCING PIANOS
EQUIPPED WITH THE WELTE-MIGNON

    NEW YORK   1924   436P   BLODWM
      DELUXE REPRODUCING ROLL CORPORATION
LC * NP

APP * PHO
NP4 * NP5 * KI10 * PM12 * PM13 * EP6

WELTE-MIGNON CORPORATION

LIBRARY OF WELTE-MIGNON MUSIC RECORDS

    NEW YORK   1927   323P   BLOWMM
      DELUXE REPRODUCING ROLL CORPORATION
BP * LC * MI * NP

APP * PHO
NP4 * NP5 * KI10 * PM12 * PM13 * EP6

WELTE ARTISTIC PLAYER-PIANO COMPANY

LIST OF MUSIC FOR THE WELTE-MIGNON PIANO--WITH SUPPLEMENT

    NEW YORK   1908   94P   BLOMFT
      WELTE ARTISTIC PLAYER-PIANO COMPANY
NP

KI10 * PM6

WEST, GEORGE FREDERICK

HINTS TO YOUNG TEACHERS OF THE PIANOFORTE

    LONDON   1881   19P   BHTYTO
      COCKS, R., AND COMPANY
BP * BR * LC * NP

APP
PL4 * AT1

WESTBROOK, BENJAMIN V.

SYSTEM OF STUDY OF SCALES AND CHORDS, A ..BEING CHAPTERS ON THE
ELEMENTS OF PIANOFORTE TECHNIQUE

    LONDON   1913   54P   BSOSOS
      REEVES, WILLIAM
BR * NP

INT * MEX
PL7 * PL12 * PT4 * PT6 * PT9

WESTERBY, HERBERT

APPROACH TO LISZT, THE ..A COURSE OF MODERN TONAL TECHNIQUE FOR THE
PIANO

    LONDON   1940+   46P   BATLAC
      REEVES, WILLIAM
BP

PT2 * PT8 * PM3

WESTERBY, HERBERT

BEETHOVEN AND HIS PIANO WORKS

    LONDON   1931   114P   BBAHPW
      REEVES, WILLIAM
BP * BR * ES * IU * LC * NP * SA * TO * UM

APP * CNG * ILL * MEX * MSF
PM3 * PM4 * PM8 * PM9 * PM15

WESTERBY, HERBERT

HISTORY OF PIANOFORTE MUSIC, THE ---1924

    NEW YORK   1971   407P   BHOPMN
      DA CAPO PRESS
AS * BP * BR * CP * CU * ES * IU * LC * MI * NP * UI * UK * UM * US
UT * UW * YU
APP * IND * MEX
PM3 * PM7 * PM15

WESTERBY, HERBERT

HISTORY OF THE PIANOFORTE

    PHILADELPHIA   1926+   BHOTP
      PRESSER, THEODORE, COMPANY

KI3

WESTERBY, HERBERT

HOW TO STUDY THE PIANOFORTE WORKS OF THE GREAT COMPOSERS

    LONDON   1914+   302P   BHTSTP
      REEVES, WILLIAM
BP * BR * CP * ES * IU * LC * NP * SA * UI * US * UW

BIB * ILL * IND * MEX
PM3 * PM4 * PM5 * PM7 * PM8 * PM13 * PM14 * PM15 * AP4

WESTERBY, HERBERT

INTRODUCTION TO RUSSIAN PIANO MUSIC--REPRINT.."MUSICAL OPINION"

    LONDON   1945   16P   BITRPM
      REEVES, WILLIAM
BR * LC * SA

BIB
PM13 * PM15

WESTERBY, HERBERT

LISZT, COMPOSER, AND HIS PIANO WORKS..DESCRIPTIVE GUIDE AND
CRITICAL ANALYSIS---1936

    WESTPORT, CONN.   1970   336P   BLCAHP
      GREENWOOD PRESS
BR * ES * IU * LC * MI * NP

BIB * DIS * ILL * IND * INT * MEX * TAB
NP3 * NP6 * AT12 * PT1 * PM3 * PM6 * PM8 * PM9 * PM14 * PM15 * AP9
EP7

WESTRUP, SIR JACK ALLAN

LISZT--NOVELLO'S BIOGRAPHIES OF GREAT MUSICIANS

    LONDON   1940   16P   BLNBOG
      NOVELLO AND COMPANY
BR * LC

NP4 * PM3

WESTRUP, SIR JACK ALLAN

MUSICAL INTERPRETATION---THIS BOOK ACCOMPANIED A SERIES OF B.B.C.
RADIO PROGRAMMES, WEEKLY, FROM APRIL 1 TO JUNE 3, 1971

    LONDON   1971   72P   BMITBA
      BRITISH BROADCASTING CORPORATION
IU * LC

BIB * ILL * MEX * MSF
PL4 * PL12 * PL14 * KS5 * KS10 * AP3 * AP4 * AP7 * AP9

WEYLAND, RUDOLPH H.

LEARNING TO READ MUSIC

    DUBUQUE, IOWA   1961   232P   BLTRM
      BROWN, WILLIAM C., COMPANY
CP * CU * ES * IU * LC * NP * UM * UW

PL4

WHEELER, BERTHA H.

MIND AND MECHANISM..THOUGHTS ON TEACHING AND THE PIANISTIC ART

    BOSTON   1909   54P   BMAMTO
      THOMPSON, C. W., AND COMPANY
NP

PL4 * AT1 * AT2 * AT3 * PT9

WHEELER, OPAL

FREDERIC CHOPIN, SON OF POLAND, EARLY YEARS--2 VOLS.---YOUNGER
READERS

    NEW YORK   1948   156P   BFCSOP
      DUTTON, E. P., AND COMPANY
BR * IU * LC * NP

ILL * LDR * MEX
NP4 * PM3 * GI10

WHITE, WILLIAM BRAID

PIANO PLAYING MECHANISMS

    NEW YORK   1925   240P   BPPM
      BILL, E. L.
LC * NP * UC

IND * LDR
KI3 * KI5 * KI6 * KI8 * KI10

WHITE, WILLIAM BRAID

PIANO TUNING AND ALLIED ARTS--5TH. ED.---1917

      NEW YORK   1948   290J   BPTAAA
      TUNERS SUPPLY COMPANY, INC.
BP * CP * ES * IU * LC * MI * NP * OC * SA * UI * UM * UT * YU

CHR * GLO * IND * INT * LDR * MEX * TAB
KI5 * KI6 * KI7 * KI8 * PT8

WHITE, WILLIAM BRAID

PLAYER-PIANIST, THE ..A GUIDE TO THE APPRECIATION AND
INTERPRETATION OF MUSIC THROUGH THE MEDIUM OF THE PLAYER-PIANO

      NEW YORK   1910   142P   BPPAGT
      BILL, E. L.
BR * LC * NP

INT
KI10 * PL12 * PT1 * PM7 * PM10 * AP4 * AP6 * GI2

WHITE, WILLIAM BRAID

PLAYER-PIANO UP TO DATE, THE

      NEW YORK   1914   204P   BPPUTD
      BILL, E. L.
BP * BR * LC * NP

LDR
KI3 * KI5 * KI6 * KI8 * KI10

WHITE, WILLIAM BRAID

REGULATION AND REPAIR OF PIANO AND PLAYER PIANO MECHANISM

      NEW YORK   1909   163P   BRAROP
      BILL, E. L.
BR * LC * NP * UC

ILL * INT * LDR
KI5 * KI6 * KI8 * KI10

WHITE, WILLIAM BRAID

TECHNICAL TREATISE ON PLAYER PIANO MECHANISM, A

      NEW YORK   1908   165P   BTTOPP
      BILL, E. L.
BR * CP * MI * NP * UI * UO

ILL * INT * LDR
KI5 * KI6 * KI8 * KI10

WHITE, WILLIAM BRAID

THEORY AND PRACTICE OF PIANOFORTE BUILDING

      NEW YORK   1906   160P   BTAPOP
      BILL, E. L.
BP * BP * ES * LC * SA * UM * UW

APP * LDR * TAB
KI3 * KI5 * KI6 * KI7 * KI8 * KI9 * KI10

WHITEMORE, CUTHBERT

COMMONSENSE IN PIANOFORTE PLAYING

      LONDON   1926   47P   BCIPP
      AUGENER, LTD.
BR * ES * IU * SA * UO

MEX
PL6 * PL7 * PL12 * PT3 * PT4 * PT8 * AP4 * AP8

WHITESIDE, ABBY

INDISPENSABLES OF PIANO PLAYING--2ND. ED.---1955

      NEW YORK   1961   155P   BIOPPS
      COLEMAN-ROSS COMPANY
AS * BP * BR * CP * CU * ES * IU * LC * MI * NP * OC * SA * UA * UC
UI * UM * UO * US * UT * UW * YU
IND * INT * MEX
PL8 * PL12 * AT1 * PT3 * PT4 * PT9 * PT10 * AP5 * AP8

WHITESIDE, ABBY

MASTERING THE CHOPIN ETUDES AND OTHER ESSAYS

      NEW YORK   1968   200P   BMTCEA
      COLEMAN-ROSS COMPANY
IU * LC * NP * UA

GLO * MEX
AT1 * AT2 * PT1 * PT2 * PT3 * PT4 * PM11 * AP1 * AP2 * AP9

WHITESIDE, ABBY

PIANIST'S MECHANISM, THE

      NEW YORK   1929   57P   BPM
      SCHIRMER, G., INC.
BR * CP * CU * ES * IU * LC * OC * US

ILL
AT4 * PT3 * PT4

WHITFORD, ROBERT

PIANO AND ITS MUSIC, THE --FROM 'MODERN PIANO COURSE'

      BUFFALO, N. Y.   1941   19P   BPAIMF
      WHITFORD, ROBERT, PUBLISHERS
  LC

INT
AT4 * AT11 * AT13 * AP4

WHITING, ARTHUR B.

LESSON OF THE CLAVICHORD, THE --REPRINT..'NEW MUSIC REVIEW'

      BOSTON   1909   27P   BLOTCR
      NEW MUSIC REVIEW
  LC

KI14 * AT4

WHITMER, THOMAS C.

ART OF IMPROVISATION, THE ..A HANDBOOK OF PRINCIPLES AND METHODS
FOR ORGANISTS, PIANISTS, TEACHERS...

      NEW YORK   1934   72P   BAOIAH
      WITMARK, M., AND SONS
  LC * NP

BIB * ILL * MEX
KS5 * KS7 * KS8

WIECK, FRIEDRICH

PIANO AND SONG..HOW TO TEACH, HOW TO LEARN, AND HOW TO FORM A
JUDGEMENT OF MUSICAL PERFORMANCES---2ND. ED. ENTITLED..PIANO AND
SINGING, DIDACTICAL AND POLEMICAL
      BOSTON   1875   189P   BPASHT
      DITSON, OLIVER, COMPANY
BR * IU * LC * MI * NP * US

PL1 * AT1 * AP1 * AP4

WIENER, HILDA

PENCIL PORTRAITS OF CONCERT CELEBRITIES---INCLUDES 24 PIANISTS

      LONDON   1937   199P   BPPOCC
      PITMAN, I., AND SONS, LTD.
BR * LC * NP

INT
NP5 * NP9 * GI13

WIER, ALBERT

PIANO, THE ..ITS HISTORY, MAKERS, PLAYERS AND MUSIC

      NEW YORK   1940   467P   BPIHMP
      LONGMANS, GREEN AND COMPANY
AS * BP * BR * CP * CU * ES * IU * LC * MI * NP * OC * SA * UA * UC
UI * UK * UM * US * UW
APP * BIB * DIS * GLO * IND * INT
NP1 * NP2 * NP5 * KI3 * KI5 * KI6 * KI8 * KI10 * KI12 * KI14 * PL8
AT1 * AT2 * AT7 * AT8 * AT11 * PT1 * PT3 * PT8 * PT9 * PT10 * PT12
PT14 * KS3 * PM3 * PM5 * PM7 * PM15 * AP4 * AP6 * AP8 * EP3 * EP5 *

WIERZYNSKI, CASIMIR

LIFE AND DEATH OF CHOPIN, THE

      NEW YORK   1949   434P   BLADOC
      SIMON AND SCHUSTER, INC.
BR * IU * LC * NP

BIB * ILL * IND * INT * LDR * MSF * PHO
NP3 * PM3

WILKINS-GUTMANN, EMMA

TALKS WITH PIANO TEACHERS

      CHICAGO   1897   88P   BTWPT
      SUMMY, CLAYTON F., COMPANY
CU * ES * LC * NP

APP * MEX
PL8 * PL10 * PL12 * AT1 * PT4 * AP6

WILKINSON, CHARLES W.

HOW TO INTERPRET MENDELSSOHN'S SONGS WITHOUT WORDS

      LONDON   1930   96P   BHTIMS
      REEVES, WILLIAM
BR * SA

MSF * ILL
PM8 * PM9 * PM14 * PM15

WILKINSON, CHARLES W.

HOW TO PLAY BACH'S 48 PRELUDES AND FUGUES

      LONDON   1939   135P   BHTPBF
      REEVES, WILLIAM
BP * BR * CP * ES * IU * LC * MI * NP * OC * UA * UO * UT

INT
PM8 * PM14 * PM15

WILKINSON, CHARLES W.

    HOW TO PLAY 110 FAVOURITE PIANO SOLOS

            LONDON   1935+   284P   BHTPOH
            REEVES, WILLIAM
    SA

    ILL * IND
    PM3 * PM8 * PM9 * PM11 * PM15 * AP4

WILKINSON, CHARLES W.

    WELL-KNOWN PIANO SOLOS..HOW TO PLAY THEM WITH UNDERSTANDING,
    EXPRESSION AND EFFECT
            PHILADELPHIA   1915   288P   BWKPSH
            PRESSER, THEODORE, COMPANY
    BR * CP * CU * ES * IU * LC * MI * NP * SA * TO * UA * UI * UK

    IND * INT
    PM3 * PM9 * PM11 * PM15 * AP4

WILLEBY, CHARLES

    FREDERIC FRANCOIS CHOPIN

            LONDON   1892   316P   BFFC
            LOW, SAMPSON, AND COMPANY
    BR * LC * NP

    APP * IND * INT
    NP3 * PM3 * PM6 * PM9

WILLIAMS, GUY BEVIER

    PIANISM..A COURSE IN NORMAL TRAINING

            LONDON   1930   25P   BPACIN
            WILLIAMS, A.
    BP

    AT1 * AT2

WILLIAMS, JEAN E. *
THOLEN, NELLIE
    MIND IN MUSIC, THE

            ST. LOUIS   1962   82P   BMIM
            WILLIAMS, JEAN E.
    LC

    APP * ILL * MEX * TAB
    PL4 * PL7 * PL12 * PT1 * PT9 * KS8

WILLIAMS, JEAN E.

    MODERN METHOD OF PIANO INSTRUCTION, A ..TEACHERS MANUAL

            ST. LOUIS   1932   112P   BMMOPI
            WILLIAMS, JEAN E.
    LC

    ILL * INT * LDR * MEX * TAB
    PL4 * PL8 * PL10 * PL12 * AT9 * PT4 * PT7 * PT8 * PT9 * PT10 * KS3
    KS4 * KS7 * AP4

WILLIAMS, JOHN M.

    WHAT TO TEACH AT THE VERY FIRST LESSON

            PHILADELPHIA   1925   63P   BWTTAT
            PRESSER, THEODORE, COMPANY
    LC * SA

    ILL * INT * LDR * MEX
    PL4 * PL7 * AT9 * PT1 * PT8 * PT9 * PT10 * AP6 * KS7 * EP6

WILLIAMS, PETER F.

    FIGURED BASS ACCOMPANIMENT--2 VOLS.

            EDINBURGH   1970   248P   BFBATV
            EDINBURGH UNIVERSITY PRESS
    LC

    ILL * INT * MEX * MSF
    KS10

WILLIS, AUBREY

    AUBREY WILLIS HOME STUDY COURSE IN PIANO TUNING AND REPAIRING

            ORLANDO, FLA.   1968   118P   BAWHSC
            AUBREY WILLIS SCHOOL OF PIANO TUNING AND REPAIRING
    LC

    INT
    KI15 * KI6 * KI8 * PL11 * AT4

WILLS, VERA G. *
MANNERS, ANDE
    PARENT'S GUIDE TO MUSIC LESSONS, A

            NEW YORK   1967   274P   BPGTML
            HARPER AND ROW PUBLISHERS, INC.
    BP * CP * ES * LC * OC * UT

    APP * BIB * DIS
    KI11 * PL7 * PL14 * AT13 * PM5 * GI6

WILSON, CHARLES J.

    SCALES TAUGHT IN ONE EASY LESSON, THE

            NEW YORK   1899   36P   BSTIOE
            PAULL, E. T., MUSIC COMPANY
    LC

    MEX
    PT9

WILSON, DAVID M.

    INSTRUCTION BOOK ON THE PIANO-PLAYER AND PLAYER-PIANO, AN
    ..CONTAINING A SHORT ACCOUNT OF THE ORIGIN AND DEVELOPMENT OF THESE
    INSTRUMENTS...
            LONDON   1911   126P   BIBOTP
            KRONHEIM, J. M., AND COMPANY
    BR * NP

    GLO * ILL * INT * PHO * TAB
    KI3 * KI5 * KI6 * KI8 * KI10 * PM10 * PM12 * AP3

WILSON, DAVID M.

    PLAYER-PIANO, THE ..ITS CONSTRUCTION..HOW TO PLAY, WHAT TO PLAY AND
    HOW TO PRESERVE IT AND MAKE ADJUSTMENTS WHEN NECESSARY
            LONDON   1923   104P   BPPICH
            PITMAN, I., AND SONS, LTD.
    BR * LC * NP

    GLO * IND * INT
    KI3 * KI4 * KI5 * KI6 * KI7 * KI8 * KI10 * KI12 * PT1

WILSON, MORRIS E.

    HOW TO HELP YOUR CHILD WITH MUSIC--2ND. ED.---1951

            NEW YORK   1962   170P   BHTHYC
            SCHUMANN, HENRY
    AS * BR * CP * CU * ES * IU * LC * NP * OC * UC * UI * UM * UU * UW

    IND * INT * TAB
    KI4 * KI8 * PL4 * PL7 * PL8 * AT5 * AT7 * AT9 * AT11 * KS12 * GI2 *
    GI9 * GI11

WILSON, MORRIS E.

    HOW TO PLAY BY EAR

            NEW YORK   1955   190P   BHTPBE
            ABELARD-SCHUMANN
    LC * NP * UA

    APP * INT * LDR * MEX
    PL4 * PL8 * PL12 * AT11 * PT9 * KS3 * KS4 * KS12 * AP4 * AP8 * EP6

WILSON, ROBINA BECKLES

    MUSICAL INSTRUMENTS--THE 'BYWAYS LIBRARY'

            NEW YORK   1966+   64P   BMITBL
            WALCK, H. Z.

    KI1 * GI10

WILSON, WILLIAM

    NEW FINGERING NOTATION FOR KEYBOARD MUSIC---REPRODUCED FROM
    TYPEWRITTEN COPY
            EDINBURGH   1933   8P   BNFNFK
            WILSON, WILLIAM
    BR

    PL4 * PT6

WING AND SONS

    BOOK OF COMPLETE INFORMATION ABOUT PIANOS, THE ...1868-1918, A FULL
    HALF CENTURY OF SUCCESS, 50TH. ANNIVERSARY
            NEW YORK   1918   139P   BBOCIA
            WING AND SONS, INC.
    AS * LC * NP * UI

    LDR * PHO
    KI2 * KI3 * KI4 * KI5 * KI6

WINN, CYRIL

    DO YOU ACCOMPANY

            LONDON   1938   31P   BDYA
            CURWEN, J., AND SONS, LTD.
    IU * LC * TO

    INT * MEX
    AP8 * EP6

WINNER, SEPTIMUS

    WINNER'S NEW SCHOOL FOR THE PIANO, IN WHICH THE INSTRUCTIONS ARE SO
    CLEARLY AND SIMPLY TREATED, AS TO MAKE IT UNNECESSARY TO REQUIRE A
    TEACHER
            BOSTON   1898   80P   BWNSFT
            DITSON, OLIVER, COMPANY
    LC

    GLO * MEX
    PL4 * PL11 * PT4 * PT6 * AP7

WINTERNITZ, EMANUEL

MUSICAL INSTRUMENTS AND THEIR SYMBOLISM IN WESTERN ART

NEW YORK   1967   240P   BMIATS
NORTON, W. W., AND COMPANY
BR * IU * LC

ILL * IND * INT * PHO
KI3 * KI9 * KI13 * KI14 * KI15

WINTERNITZ, EMANUEL

MUSICAL INSTRUMENTS OF THE WESTERN WORLD

NEW YORK   1967   259P   BMIOTW
MCGRAW-HILL
LC

BIB * ILL * IND * INT * PHO
KI3 * KI5 * KI6 * KI9 * KI12 * KI13 * KI14 * KI15

WOHL, JANKA

FRANCOIS LISZT..RECOLLECTIONS OF A COMPATRIOT

LONDON   1887   246P   BFLROA
WARD AND DOWNEY
BR * LC * NP

INT
NP6

WOLFENDEN, S.

TREATISE ON THE ART OF PIANOFORTE CONSTRUCTION, A --SUPPLEMENT

LONDON   1927   102P   BTOTAO
KING AND JARRETT, LTD.
NP

KI5

WOLFENDEN, S.

TREATISE ON THE ART OF PIANOFORTE CONSTRUCTION, A

LONDON   1916   172P   BTOTAO
UNWIN BROS., LTD.
BR * LC * NP * UC * YU

APP * ILL * IND * INT * LDR * PHO * TAB
KI5 * KI8

WOLFF, ERNST VICTOR

WITH REASON AND RHYME

NEW HAVEN, CONN.   1957   75P   BWRAR
WINTER, S.
ES * LC * NP * OC

NP6 * PL9 * AT9 * AT13 * PT9 * PM9 * AP4 * EP6 * GI3 * GI13

WOLFF, KONRAD

TEACHING OF ARTUR SCHNABEL, THE ..A GUIDE TO INTERPRETATION

LONDON   1972   189P   BTOASA
FABER AND FABER
IU * LC

APP * BIB * IND * INT * MEX * PHO
NP3 * PT1 * KS9 * PM9 * AP3 * AP4

WOLFRAM, THEODOR

PRACTICAL MODULATOR, OR, HOW TO LEARN TO MODULATE FROM ANY ONE KEY
TO ANY OTHER IN A SHORT TIME..FOR PIANO AND ORGAN PLAYERS
NEW YORK   1880   24P   BPMOHT
FISCHER, J., AND BRO.
LC

INT * MEX
KS8

WOLFRAM, VICTOR

SOSTENUTO PEDAL, THE

STILLWATER, OKLA.   1965   45P   BSP
OKLAHOMA STATE UNIVERSITY

BIB * INT * MEX * MSF
KI3 * KI5 * KI6 * KI9 * KI10 * KI12 * PM3 * AP3 * AP8 * GI5

WOLLENHAUPT, HEINRICH

METHOD FOR THE PIANOFORTE AND METHODICAL GUIDE FOR THE PIANO FORTE
TEACHER
NEW YORK   1861   73P   BMFTPA
HAGEN, THEODORE
LC * NP

CHR * MEX
PL4 * PL7 * AT4 * PM6 * EP4 * EP5

WOLLNER, GERTRUDE PRICE

IMPROVISATION IN MUSIC..WAYS TOWARDS CAPTURING MUSICAL IDEAS AND
DEVELOPING THEM
GARDEN CITY, N. Y.   1963   191P   BIIMWT
DOUBLEDAY AND COMPANY
BP * BR * CP * CU * ES * LC * MI * NP * OC * TO * UM * UO

BIB * CHR * INT * MEX
PL6 * PL12 * AT7 * KS5 * PT9 * EP6

WOOD, ALEXANDER

PHYSICS OF MUSIC, THE --4TH. ED.---1944

NEW YORK   1947   255P   BPOMFE
DOVER PUBLISHERS, INC.
AS * BP * BR * CP * ES * IU * LC * MI * NP * OC * SA * TO * UA * UC
UI * UK * UM * UO * US * UT * UU * UW * YU
CHR * ILL * IND * LDR * MEX * PHO * TAB
KI7

WOOD, CHARLES W.

FINGER AND WRIST GYMNASTICS--WITHOUT USE OF PIANO--FOR PIANO
STUDENTS AND TEACHERS--2ND. ED.---ORIGINAL TITLE..MUSCULAR TECHNICS
FOR PIANISTS--MANUAL OF FREE GYMNASTICS
TROY, N. Y.   1886   BFAWGW
MOORE, A. K.
LC

PT5

WOOD, CHARLES W.

LETTERS FROM MAJORCA---CHOPIN--NUMEROUS ILLUSTRATIONS

LONDON   1888   410P   BLFMCN
BENTLEY, R., AND SON
BR * LC

ILL
NP6

WOODHOUSE, GEORGE

ARTIST AT THE PIANO, THE ..THE ART OF MUSICAL INTERPRETATION

LONDON   1910   51P   BAATPT
NOVELLO AND COMPANY
BR * ES * IU * LC * NP * SA * TO

ILL * INT * MEX
PL3 * PL6 * PL12 * PT8 * AP4 * AP5

WOODHOUSE, GEORGE

CREATIVE TECHNIQUE, FOR ARTISTS IN GENERAL AND PIANISTS IN
PARTICULAR
LONDON   1921   54P   BCTFAI
AUGENER, LTD.
BR * ES * LC * NP * SA * UI * UK

INT
PT2 * PT3 * PT8 * PT12 * AP4

WOODHOUSE, GEORGE

FINGER EXERCISES FOR THE POCKET MUTANO

LONDON   1935+   12P   BFEFTP
AUGENER, LTD.
LC

INT * MEX
PT10 * PT14

WOODHOUSE, GEORGE

FROM KEYBOARD TO MUSIC

LONDON   1949   54P   BFKTM
AUGENER, LTD.
BR * LC * NP

CHR * INT * MEX
NP3 * PL8 * PT1 * PT2 * PT4 * PT6 * PT8 * PT10 * AP2 * AP9

WOODHOUSE, GEORGE

GUIDE TO THE NEW WAY TO PIANO TECHNIQUE, A

BOSTON   1949   28P   BGTTNW
SCHMIDT, P. A.
UT

WOODHOUSE, GEORGE

NEW PATH FOR PIANISTS, A ..THE MUTANO--MUTE PIANO--SYSTEM, ETC.

LONDON   1930   16P   BNPFPT
AUGENER, LTD.
BR * LC

PL6 * PL7 * PL11 * AT7 * PT8 * PM12 * EP6 * EP7

WOODHOUSE, GEORGE

NEW WAY TO PIANO TECHNIQUE, THE --8 VOLS.

            LONDON   1935   BNWTPT
            AUGENER, LTD.
    LC

    ILL * MEX
    PT9 * PT10

WOODHOUSE, GEORGE

REALISTIC APPROACH TO PIANO PLAYING, A

            LONDON   1953   56P   BRATPP
            AUGENER, LTD.
    BR * CP * CU * ES * IU * LC * NP * SA * UT

    CHR * INT
    KI6 * PL13 * PT4 * PT8 * PT9 * PT10 * AP4 * AP5 * AP8 * AP9

WOODMAN, HENRY STAUNTON

HOW TO TUNE A PIANO..HOW TO BUY A USED PIANO..HOW TO KEEP YOUR
PIANO IN GOOD CONDITION--2ND. ED.---1960

            HUNTINGTON, N. Y.   1963   65P   BHTTAP
            CORWOOD PUBLISHERS
    CP * ES * IU * LC * NP * SA

    BIB * CHR * ILL * INT * LDR * MEX * PHO * TAB
    KI4 * KI5 * KI6 * KI7 * KI8

WORCH, HUGO

PIANO MAKERS OF THE EVOLUTIONARY PERIOD..RARE ENGLISH AND AMERICAN
SQUARE PIANOS...FROM COLLECTION OF HUGO WORCH

            WASHINGTON, D. C.   1907   25P   BPMOTE
            HOWARD, G. E.
    LC

    ILL * PHO
    KI3 * KI5 * KI6 * KI9 * KI12 * KI13

WORCH, HUGO

WORCH PIANOS, AND A BRIEF SKETCH OF THE PIANOFORTE

            WASHINGTON, D. C.   1901   58P   BWPAAB
            WORCH, H.
    LC

    ILL * INT * PHO
    KI3 * KI4 * KI5 * KI6 * KI12 * KI13

WRIGHT, WILLIAM C.

GOLDEN MONITOR, FOR THE PIANOFORTE AND CABINET ORGAN, DESIGNED AS A
THOROUGH, PRACTICAL TEXTBOOK, THE

            AUGUSTA, GA.   1890   152P   BGMFTP
            WRIGHT, W. C.
    LC * MI * NP

    GLO * IND * INT * MEX
    KI8 * PL4 * PL12 * AT4 * KS4 * KS5 * KS7 * PT6 * PT8 * PT9 * PT10 *
    AP4 * AP7 * AP8

WRIGHT, WILLIAM C.

PIANOFORTE MANUAL, THE ..DESIGNED AS A COMPLETE PIANOFORTE PRIMER

            NEW YORK   1854   84P   BPMDAA
            MASON BROTHERS
    BP * ES * LC * NP * YU

    GLO * INT * MEX
    KI1 * PL4 * PL12 * PL15 * PT4 * PT8 * KS4 * KS7

WULSIN, LUCIEN

DWIGHT HAMILTON BALDWIN AND THE BALDWIN PIANO

            NEW YORK   1953   32P   BDHBAT
            NEWCOMER SOCIETY IN NORTH AMERICA
    BP * CP * LC * NP * UC * UO

    ILL
    NP6

WYMAN, ADDISON P.

WYMAN'S PIANO TEXTBOOK..CONTAINING A COMPLETE SYSTEM OF MUSICAL
NOTATION...TOGETHER WITH RULES FOR FINGERING THE SCALES, PRACTICAL
HINTS TO THE PUPIL...
            NEW YORK   1871   83P   BWPTCA
            POND, W. A., AND COMPANY
    LC * NP

    ILL * INT * MEX
    KI4 * PL4 * PL12 * PL15 * PT9

YALE UNIVERSITY--ART GALLERY

MUSICAL INSTRUMENTS AT YALE..A SELECTION OF WESTERN INSTRUMENTS
FROM THE 15TH. TO 20TH. CENTURIES..CATALOGUE BY SIBYL MARCUSE

            NEW HAVEN, CONN.   1960   47P   BMIAYA
            YALE UNIVERSITY
    LC * NP

    ILL * INT * PHO
    KI5 * KI6 * KI9 * KI12 * KI13

YALE UNIVERSITY--ART GALLERY

YALE COLLECTION OF MUSICAL INSTRUMENTS..CHECKLIST

            NEW HAVEN, CONN.   1968   43P   BYCOMI
            YALE UNIVERSITY
    IU

    IND * INT
    KI12 * KI14 * KI15

YALE UNIVERSITY SCHOOL OF MUSIC

CHECK-LIST OF WESTERN INSTRUMENTS IN THE COLLECTION OF MUSICAL
INSTRUMENTS--PART 1..KEYBOARD INSTRUMENTS--COMPILED BY SIBYL
MARCUSE
            NEW HAVEN, CONN.   1958   30P   BCLOWI
            YALE UNIVERSITY
    NP * UI

    INT
    KI15

YATES, PETER

AMATEUR AT THE KEYBOARD, AN

            NEW YORK   1964   300P   BAATK
            PANTHEON BOOKS
    AS * BP * BR * CP * ES * LC * MI * SA * TO * UI * UO * US * UT * UU
    UW * YU
    APP * IND * INT
    KI3 * KI5 * KI6 * KI7 * KII14 * PL4 * PL6 * PL9 * PL12 * PM1 * PM2 *
    PM3 * PM7 * EP3 * EP4 * EP6 * GI11

YOUFF, ULV

ULVEN, WRITTEN DURING RETIREMENT IN SWITZERLAND--AUTOBIOGRAPHY OF
PART OF HIS LIFE

            LONDON   1923   163P   BUWDRI
            CHAPMAN AND DODD, LTD.
    BR * LC * NP

    INT * PHO
    NP6 * GI13

YOUNG, PERCY M.

CONCERTO--'PHOENIX MUSIC GUIDES', NO. 1

            LONDON   1957   168P   BCPMGN
            PHOENIX HOUSE, LTD.
    BR * IU * LC * NP

    APP * DIS * IND * INT * LDR
    PM3 * PM7 * PM9 * PM14 * AP3 * AP4

YOUNG, PERCY M.

KEYBOARD MUSICIANS OF THE WORLD

            NEW YORK   1967   184P   BKMOTW
            ABELARD-SCHUMANN
    BP * CP * LC * SA * TO

    APP * DIS * ILL * IND * INT * LDR * MEX * MSF * PHO
    NP3 * NP4 * NP5 * KI3 * KII14 * PT12 * PM3 * PM7 * AP4

YOUNG, PERCY M.

MASTERS OF MUSIC

            LONDON   1965   BMOM
            BENN, ERNEST
    BR

    NP5

YOUNG, THOMAS C.

MAKING OF MUSICAL INSTRUMENTS, THE ---1939

            FREEPORT, N. Y.   1969   190P   BMOMIN
            BOOKS FOR LIBRARIES PRESS
    BR * IU * LC * NP

    ILL * INT * LDR * PHO
    KI4 * KI5 * KI6 * KI7 * KI12

ZEITLIN, POLDI *
GOLDBERGER, DAVID
THEORY PAPERS, THE --C.M.P. PIANO LIBRARY--2 VOLS., 1961-1963

            NEW YORK   1961   64P   BTPCMP
            CONSOLIDATED MUSIC PUBLISHERS
    LC * NP

    INT * MEX
    PL4 * PL12 * KS4

ZEPER, M. E. P.

READING OF MUSIC, THE ..A RATIONAL METHOD--NO. 1 OF A SERIES ON
PIANOFORTE PLAYING

            LONDON   1899   48P   BRDMAR
            VINCENT MUSIC COMPANY, LTD., THE
    BP * BR

    PL4

ZEPP, ARTHUR

    LET'S IMPROVISE--2 VOLS.

          NEW YORK   1957   67P   BLITV
             PRO-ART PUBLISHERS
    LC

    INT * MEX
    KS5

ZIMMERMAN, ALEX H. *
HAYTON, RUSSELL
    BASIC PIANO FOR THE COLLEGE STUDENT

          DUBUQUE, IOWA   1969   146P   BBPFTC
             BROWN, WILLIAM C., COMPANY
    LC

    APP * INT * MEX
    AT4 * AT7 * PT1 * PT6 * PT9

ZOFF, OTTO--EDITOR

    GREAT COMPOSERS THROUGH THE EYES OF THEIR CONTEMPORARIES---CHOPIN
    AND LISZT

          NEW YORK   1951   510P   BGCTTE
             DUTTON, E. P., AND COMPANY, INC.
    IU * LC * NP

    IND * INT
    NP5

ZUCH, ANNETT V. *
LEWIS, FREDERICK L.
    PIANO TEACHER, THE ..A BOOK OF SELF-INSTRUCTION

          NEW YORK   1940   31P   BPTABO
             DELPHI MUSIC PUBLISHERS
    LC

    ILL * INT * LDR * MEX
    PL11 * AT4

ZUCKERMANN, WOLFGANG JOACHIM

    MODERN HARPSICHORD, THE ..TWENTIETH CENTURY INSTRUMENTS AND THEIR
    MAKERS

          NEW YORK   1969   255P   BMHTCI
             OCTOBER HOUSE, INC.
    AS * IU * LC * UA

    APP * BIB * GLO * ILL * PHO
    KI3 * KI5 * KI6 * KI8 * KI9

ZUR HEIDE, KARL GERT

    DEEP SOUTH PIANO..THE STORY OF LITTLE BROTHER MONTGOMERY

          LONDON   1970   112P   BDSPTS
             STUDIO VISTA

    NP4 * KS6

ABC OF KEYBOARD HARMONY, THE
  TAPPER, THOMAS
ABOUT ELIZABETHAN VIRGINAL MUSIC AND ITS COMPOSERS..NEW ISSUE,
  GLYN, MARGARET H.
ABRIDGED EDITION OF F. HUENTEN'S CELEBRATED INSTRUCTIONS FOR THE
  HUENTEN, FRANZ
ABSTRACT OF A NEW METHOD OF TEACHING THE PRINCIPLES OF MUSIC,
  BEMETZRIEDER, ANTON
ACCENTUAL TREATMENT OF EXERCISES AS APPLIED TO PIANOFORTE
  MASON, WILLIAM G.
ACCOMPANIST'S MANUAL, THE
  SCHULER, GEORGE S.
ACCOUNT OF A NEW WAY OF CONSIDERING MUSICK, AND TEACHING IT--INTENDED
  BEMETZRIEDER, ANTON
ACHIEVEMENT..AN ASCENDING SCALE, BEING A SHORT HISTORY OF THE HOUSE OF
  CHICKERING AND SONS
ACT OF MUSICAL CONCENTRATION, THE
  MATTHAY, TOBIAS A.
ACT OF TOUCH IN ALL ITS DIVERSITY, THE ..AN ANALYSIS AND SYNTHESIS OF
  MATTHAY, TOBIAS A.
ADULT EXPLORER AT THE PIANO, THE
  AHEARN, ELLA MASON *
ADVANCED KEYBOARD HARMONY WITH ILLUSTRATIVE PIANO PIECES
  CARTER, BUENTA
ADVANCED PIANO CLASS, THE --REPRINT..PROCEEDINGS OF THE M.E.N.C., 1947
  BURROWS, RAYMOND
ADVENTURES IN BLACK AND WHITE--AUTOBIOGRAPHY
  SCHUYLER, PHILLIPA DUKE
ADVENTURES IN IMPROVISATION AT THE KEYBOARD
  MACK, GLEN
ADVENTURES IN IMPROVISATION
  NICHOLLS, FREDERICK *
ADVENTURES IN MUSICIANSHIP
  TOBIN, JOSEPH RAYMOND
ADVENTURES IN PIANOLAND..TWELVE LESSONS FOR TEACHERS OF PIANO CLASSES
  CLIFFORD, S. M.
ADVENTURES OF PETER THE PIANO, THE ..AN ILLUSTRATED STORY FOR CHILDREN
  BYERLY, DOROTHEA J.
ADVICE AND INSTRUCTIONS FOR PLAYING THE PIANOFORTE WITH EXPRESSION AND
  MOTT, ISAAC H. R.
ADVICE TO A NOBLEMAN...ON THE MANNER IN WHICH HIS CHILDREN SHOULD BE
  ANON
ADVICE TO YOUNG MUSICIANS--FROM 'MUSIC AND MUSICIANS'---1876
  SCHUMANN, ROBERT
ADVICE TO YOUNG STUDENTS OF THE PIANOFORTE
  BORST, ALBERT W.
AEOLIAN, THE ..ITS ARTISTIC MERITS, DISTINCTION FROM MECHANICAL
  FINCK, HENRY T.
AEOLIAN PIANOS, THE ---WEBER, STECK, STROUD
  AEOLIAN COMPANY, THE
AESTHETICS OF PIANOFORTE PLAYING, THE ---1861 IN GERMAN--1ST. ENGLISH
  KULLAK, ADOLPH
AFFIRMATIONS--LITERARY ESSAYS---CHOPIN
  ELLIS, HAVELOCK
AIDS TO TECHNIQUE
  HOPE, ERIC
ALBRECHTSBERGER'S COLLECTED WRITINGS ON THOROUGH-BASS, HARMONY AND
  ALBRECHTSBERGER, JOHANN GEORG
ALBRECHTSBERGER'S ELEMENTARY WORK ON THE SCIENCE OF MUSIC..INCLUDING
  ALBRECHTSBERGER, JOHANN GEORG
ALFRED CORTOT'S STUDIES IN MUSICAL INTERPRETATION, SET DOWN BY JEANNE
  CORTOT, ALFRED
ALFRED CORTOT
  GAVOTY, BERNARD *
ALL ABOUT MUSIC..A COMPLETE BOOK OF MUSICAL THEORY FOR PIANISTS AND
  SHELDON, JAY
AMATEUR AT THE KEYBOARD, AN
  YATES, PETER
AMATEUR PIANIST'S COMPANION, THE
  CHING, JAMES
AMAZING MARRIAGE OF MARIE EUSTIS AND JOSEF HOFMANN, THE
  GRAYDON, NELL *
AMERICAN METHOD FOR THE PIANOFORTE
  ROBBINS, EDGAR A.
AMERICAN MUSICIAN'S STORY, AN
  SAMAROFF, OLGA
AMERICAN PRIZE METHOD FOR PIANOFORTE
  FINCK, EDWARD J.
AMERICAN SCHOOL OF RAGTIME PIANO PLAYING, THE
  BECKERMAN, H. J.
AMPICO, THE ..A DESCRIPTION OF ITS PERFORMANCE...
  AMERICAN PIANO CORPORATION
AMPICO, THE ..SERVICE MANUAL 1929
  AMERICAN PIANO CORPORATION
AMPICO IN MUSIC STUDY, THE
  SPAETH, SIGMUND *
AMPICO REPRODUCING PIANO..A SUPPLEMENT TO 'PIANO MUSIC, ITS COMPOSERS
  AMPICO CORPORATION
AMPICO REPRODUCING PIANO, INSPECTOR'S REFERENCE BOOK, THE ---1923
  AMERICAN PIANO CORPORATION
AMPICO REPRODUCING PIANO, THE ..INSPECTOR'S INSTRUCTION BOOK, 1919,
  AMERICAN PIANO CORPORATION
AM I TOO LOUD..MEMOIRS OF AN ACCOMPANIST
  MOORE, GERALD
ANALYSIS OF FORM AS DISPLAYED IN BEETHOVEN'S 32 PIANOFORTE
  HARDING, HENRY ALFRED
ANALYSIS OF J. S. BACH'S WOHLTEMPIERTES KLAVIER--2 PTS.
  RIEMANN, HUGO
ANALYSIS OF PIANOFORTE COMPOSITIONS FROM THE CLASSICAL AND ROMANTIC
  HOLMES, GEORGE AUGUSTUS *
ANALYSIS OF PRACTICAL THOROUGH BASS
  CLARE, EDWARD
ANALYTICAL AND HISTORICAL REMARKS ON ANTON RUBINSTEIN'S CYCLE OF SEVEN
  EICHBERG, OSCAR
ANALYTICAL AND THEMATIC INDEX OF MOZART'S PIANO WORKS
  HOLMES, EDWARD
ANALYTICAL INSTRUCTOR FOR THE PIANO FORTE, CONTAINING THE PRINCIPLES OF
  SCONCIA, JOHN A.
ANALYTICAL INSTRUCTOR FOR THE PIANO FORTE, OP. 15, THE --IN 3 PTS.
  CARR, BENJAMIN
ANCIENT EUROPEAN MUSICAL INSTRUMENTS...IN THE LESLIE LINDSAY MASON
  BESSARABOFF, NICHOLAS
ANNA M. TOMLINSON'S FORTY LESSONS ON HOW TO DEVELOP A PIANO HAND
  TOMLINSON, ANNA M.
ANOTHER WAY OF MUSIC---AUTOBIOGRAPHY
  DUCAT, EVA
ANSWERS TO CRITICISMS OF PIANO CLASS INSTRUCTION
  MASON, ELLA H. *
ANTON RUBINSTEIN--'LITTLE BIOGRAPHIES'
  HUMISTON, WILLIAM H.
ANTON RUBINSTEIN, A BIOGRAPHICAL SKETCH
  MCARTHUR, ALEXANDER
ANYONE CAN PLAY THE PIANO BY EAR IN FIVE EASY LESSONS..A-B-C PIANO
  SMITH, HOWARD G.
APPLIED HARMONY--REVISED AND WITH ADDITIONAL CHAPTERS BY VINCENT
  ALCHIN, CARRIE A.

APPLIED KEYBOARD HARMONY
  CONKLIN-HAPP, SUZANNE
APPLIED PIANO TECHNIC..300 EXTRACTS FOR DAILY PRACTICE FROM STANDARD
  BUELOW, HANS GUIDO VON
APPRECIATION OF MUSIC BY MEANS OF THE PIANOLA AND DUO-ART, THE
  SCHOLES, PERCY
APPROACH TO LISZT, THE ..A COURSE OF MODERN TONAL TECHNIQUE FOR THE
  WESTERBY, HERBERT
APPROACH TO PIANO TEACHING---ALSO CATALOGUED UNDER AUTHORSHIP..BETTY
  CHING, JOAN ELIZABETH
APPROACH TO PIANO TEACHING---ALSO CATALOGUED UNDER AUTHORSHIP..JOAN
  REEVES, BETTY
APPROACH TO THE PSYCHOLOGY OF PIANO TEACHING, AN
  KRUSZYNSKI, MICHAL
AROUND MUSIC---PACHMAN, CHOPIN AND LISZT
  SORABJI, KAIKHOSRU
ARTHUR RUBINSTEIN
  GAVOTY, BERNARD *
ARTISTIC PIANIST, THE ..NATURAL TECHNICS IN PIANO MASTERY..FROM STUDENT
  EISENBERG, JACOB
ARTISTIC PIANO PLAYING, AS TAUGHT BY LUDWIG DEPPE
  CALAND, ELIZABETH
ARTISTS IN MUSIC OF TODAY
  KAUFMANN, HELEN LOEB
ARTIST AT THE PIANO, THE ..THE ART OF MUSICAL INTERPRETATION
  WOODHOUSE, GEORGE
ARTUR RUBINSTEIN, KING OF THE KEYBOARD
  FORSEE, AYLESA
ARTUR SCHNABEL, A BIOGRAPHY
  SAERCHINGER, CESAR
ART DE TOUCHER LE CLAVECIN, L' ---IN FRENCH, GERMAN AND ENGLISH
  COUPERIN, FRANCOIS
ART OF ACCOMPANIMENT, OR A NEW AND WELL DIGESTED METHOD TO LEARN TO
  GEMINIANI, FRANCESCO
ART OF ACCOMPANIMENT FROM A THOROUGH-BASS, AS PRACTICED IN THE 17TH.
  ARNOLD, FRANCK THOMAS
ART OF ACCOMPANYING, THE
  LINDO, ALGERNON H.
ART OF ACCOMPANYING AND COACHING, THE ---1965
  ADLER, KURT
ART OF EXPRESSION IN PIANOFORTE PLAYING, THE
  JOHNSTONE, J. ALFRED
ART OF FINGERING, THE ..OR, THE EASIEST AND SUREST METHOD HOW TO LEARN
  HECK, JOHANN CASPAR
ART OF FINGERING IN PIANO PLAYING, THE
  MUSAFIA, JULIEN
ART OF FINGERING THE HARPSICHORD, THE
  PASQUALI, NICOLO
ART OF FUGUE, BACH'S LAST HARPSICHORD WORK, THE ..AN ARGUMENT
  LEONHARDT, GUSTAV M.
ART OF IMPROVISATION, THE ..A HANDBOOK OF PRINCIPLES AND METHODS FOR
  WHITMER, THOMAS C.
ART OF IMPROVISING, THE ..HOW TO PLAY POPULAR SONGS IN A MODERN SWING
  HILL, JIM
ART OF MODULATING, ILLUSTRATED, THE
  BEMETZRIEDER, ANTON
ART OF MODULATING, THE ..FOR HARPISTS, PIANISTS, ORGANISTS
  LAWRENCE, LUCILE
ART OF MODULATING, THE --A SERIES OF PAPERS ON MODULATION AT THE
  BANISTER, HENRY C.
ART OF MUSICAL MODULATION RENDERED EASY AND FAMILIAR, THE
  FRICK, PHILIPP J.
ART OF PEDALLING, THE
  GEBHARD, HEINRICH
ART OF PIANOFORTE PLAYING, THE --TEXT BOOK FOR BEGINNERS
  CLARKE, HUGH ARCHIBALD
ART OF PIANOFORTE PLAYING, THE
  GARRATT, PERCIVAL
ART OF PIANOFORTE PLAYING, THE
  PAUER, ERNST
ART OF PIANOFORTE PLAYING AND TEACHING, THE
  GRIMALDI, MARIA LOUISA
ART OF PIANOFORTE PRACTICING, THE
  LOWE, CLAUDE EDGERTON
ART OF PIANO PEDALLING, THE ..TWO VOLUMES IN ONE
  FARJEON, HARRY
ART OF PIANO PHRASING, THE
  FARJEON, HARRY
ART OF PIANO PLAYER TRANSCRIPTION, THE ..MAKING OF PERFORATED ROLLS
  SCHAAF, EDWARD O.
ART OF PIANO PLAYING, THE ..A SCIENTIFIC APPROACH
  KOCHEVITSKY, GEORGE
ART OF PIANO PLAYING, THE
  NEUHAUS, HEINRICH
ART OF PLAYING AT SIGHT, THE
  SMITH, THOMAS
ART OF PLAYING THE HARPSICHORD, ILLUSTRATED BY A VARIETY OF EXAMPLES,
  HECK, JOHANN CASPAR
ART OF PLAYING THOROUGH BASS WITH CORRECTNESS ACCORDING TO THE TRUE
  HECK, JOHANN CASPAR
ART OF ROBERT CASADESUS, THE
  STOOKES, SACHA
ART OF SCALE STUDY FOR THE PIANOFORTE, THE ...AS TAUGHT TO HIS PUPILS
  BUONAMICI, GIUSEPPE
ART OF TEACHING PIANOFORTE PLAYING, THE --2ND. REV. ED.---1910
  JOHNSTONE, J. ALFRED
ART OF THE PIANIST, THE
  BROWER, HARRIETTE
ART OF THE PIANO TEACHER, THE
  PEARCE, CHARLES WILLIAM
ART OF THE PLAYER-PIANO, THE ..A TEXTBOOK FOR STUDENT AND TEACHER
  GREW, SIDNEY
ART OF THE TOUCH, THE ..A WORK FOR THE USE OF ADVANCED PLAYERS AND A
  KULLAK, ADOLPH
ART OF TRANSPOSING FOR THE PIANO AT SIGHT, THE
  HILL, JIM
ART OF TUNING OUR INSTRUMENTS MADE INTERESTING AND EASY TO ALL STUDENTS
  BEMETZRIEDER, ANTON
ART OF TUNING THE PIANOFORTE, THE ...ON THE THEORY OF EQUAL TEMPERAMENT
  SMITH, HERMANN
AT THE PIANO--IVOR NEWTON..THE WORLD OF AN ACCOMPANIST
  NEWTON, IVOR
AT THE PIANO WITH DEBUSSY---1960, IN FRENCH
  LONG, MARGUERITE
AUBREY WILLIS HOME STUDY COURSE IN PIANO TUNING AND REPAIRING
  WILLIS, AUBREY
AUDIOGRAPHIC MUSIC
  AEOLIAN COMPANY, THE
AURAL TESTS FOR EXAMINATIONS--SPECIALLY WRITTEN FOR TEACHERS AND
  LINDO, ALGERNON H.
AURAL TRAINING--MONOGRAPH ON THE ART OF PIANO TEACHING, NO. 2
  REEVES, BETTY
AUSTRALIAN MUSIC AND MUSICIANS
  GLENNON, JAMES
AUSTRALIAN PIANOFORTE TUTOR
  DOBBIE, E. A.

AUTHENTIC ACCOUNT OF THE EXAMINATION OF PUPILS, INSTRUCTED IN THE NEW
    LOGIER, JOHANN BERNHARD
AUTHENTIC ENGLISH EDITIONS OF BEETHOVEN, THE --'ALL SOULS STUDIES', NO.
    TYSON, ALAN
AUTOBIOGRAPHY OF ANTON RUBINSTEIN, 1829-1889, THE ---1890
    RUBINSTEIN, ANTON
AUTOBIOGRAPHY OF CHARLES HALLE, WITH CORRESPONDENCE AND DIARIES, THE
    HALLE, SIR CHARLES
A439, BEING THE AUTOBIOGRAPHY OF A PIANO BY 25 MUSICAL
    ROSE, ALGERNON SIDNEY
BACH'S FUGAL WORKS
    DICKINSON, ALLAN E.
BACH'S INSTRUMENTAL COUNTERPOINT
    BOYD, MALCOLM
BACH'S ORNAMENTS
    EMERY, WALTER
BACH AND DAS WOHLTEMPERIRTE KLAVIER..ANALYTICAL NOTES, WITH AN
    GRAY, CECIL
BACH ORNAMENTATION
    LANNING, RUSSELL
BACKGROUND FOR DOMENICO SCARLATTI..1685-1757, WRITTEN FOR HIS 250TH.
    SITWELL, SACHEVERELL
BALANCE OF ARM IN PIANO TECHNIQUE--4TH. REV. ED.---1903
    TOWNSEND, WILLIAM
BARNWELL'S NORMAL KEYBOARD AND STAFF STUDIES--THE MENTAL PRE-PERCEPTION
    BARNWELL, V. T.
BAROQUE CONCERTO, THE
    HUTCHINGS, ARTHUR
BARTOK-RESCHOVSKY PIANO METHOD---1913
    BARTOK, BELA *
BASIC KEYBOARD SKILLS--2ND. ED.---1963
    PELZ, WILLIAM
BASIC MATERIALS FOR THE PIANO STUDENT
    VEPNAZZA, MARCELLE
BASIC PIANOFORTE TECHNIQUE...BASED ON THE SCIENCE OF PIANOFORTE
    SIMPSON, ELIZABETH
BASIC PIANO FOR ADULTS
    ROBINSON, HELENE
BASIC PIANO FOR THE COLLEGE STUDENT
    ZIMMERMAN, ALEX H. *
BASIC PIANO FOR THE MUSIC EDUCATOR AND CLASSROOM TEACHER
    CHEYETTE, IRVING
BASIC PIANO TECHNIQUE FOR THE CLASSROOM TEACHER
    STARR, WILLIAM J. *
BASIC PRINCIPLES IN PIANOFORTE PLAYING---1924
    LHEVINNE, JOSEF
BASIC ROUTINES IN ELEMENTARY PIANO TEACHING THROUGH THE FIRST THREE
    STANLEY, JANE
BASIS OF PIANOFORTE PLAYING, THE
    DUNN, JOHN PETRIE
BEETHOVEN..NOTES ON THE SONATAS...
    LAMOND, FREDERICK ARCHIBALD
BEETHOVEN..THE PIANOFORTE SONATAS--2 VOLS.
    MILNE, ALFRED FORBES
BEETHOVEN..WITH A BRIEF ANALYSIS OF THE SONATAS...BY A. EAGLEFIELD
    ROLLAND, ROMAIN
BEETHOVEN'S PIANOFORTE SONATAS..HINTS ON THEIR RENDERING, FORM...
    LOWE, CLAUDE EDGERTON
BEETHOVEN'S PIANOFORTE SONATAS..THE ORIGIN AND RESPECTIVE VALUES OF
    SHEDLOCK, JOHN S.
BEETHOVEN'S PIANOFORTE SONATAS, A GUIDE FOR STUDENTS AND
    FISCHER, EDWIN
BEETHOVEN'S PIANOFORTE SONATAS DISCUSSED---1938
    BLOM, ERIC
BEETHOVEN'S PIANOFORTE SONATAS EXPLAINED FOR THE LOVERS OF THE MUSICAL
    GOTTSCHALD, ERNEST
BEETHOVEN'S PIANO PLAYING, WITH AN ESSAY ON THE EXECUTION OF THE
    KULLAK, FRANZ
BEETHOVEN'S PIANO SONATAS AND ARTUR SCHNABEL
    KASTNER, RUDOLPH
BEETHOVEN AND HIS PIANO WORKS
    WESTERBY, HERBERT
BEETHOVEN CONCERTOS AND OVERTURES
    FISKE, ROGER
BEETHOVEN PIANOFORTE SONATAS, THE ..LETTERS TO A LADY
    REINECKE, KARL H.
BEETHOVEN PIANO SONATAS--B.B.C. MUSIC GUIDE, NO. 1
    MATTHEWS, DENIS
BEGINNER'S GUIDE, THE ..FOR ALL COMMENCING THE STUDY OF THE PIANOFORTE
    SMITH, A. G. WARREN
BEGINNER'S PIANO BOOK FOR OLDER STUDENTS...DESIGNED FOR THE OLDER
    CARTER, BUENTA
BEGINNERS PIANO COURSE IN HYMN PLAYING BY CORRESPONDENCE
    HARKNESS, ROBERT
BEGINNINGS OF THE ROMANTIC PIANO CONCERTO, THE
    GARVIN, FLORENCE HOLLISTER
BEGINNING PIANO FOR ADULTS
    BASTIEN, JAMES W. *
BEGINNING PIANO FOR ADULTS
    MILLER, ALLAN
BEGINNING TO PLAY THE PIANO..A MANUAL FOR TEACHERS
    PAIN, EVA
BEGINNING TO PLAY THE PIANO--A TEACHER'S HANDBOOK, INCLUDING THE FIRST
    HARRISON, SIDNEY
BEGONE, DULL PRACTICE..SUGGESTIONS FOR STUDENTS AND
    STEPHENSON, LILIAN E.
BELLE SKINNER COLLECTION OF OLD MUSICAL INSTRUMENTS, HOLYOKE,
    SKINNER, BELLE
BENNER BLUE BOOK, THE ..PRACTICAL MANUAL OF PIANO TEACHING--4TH. ED.
    BENNER, LORA
BENNER GOLD BOOK, THE ..PIANO MATERIAL AND TEACHING METHODS--3RD. ED.
    BENNER, LORA
BERLIN TEST CLASS, THE ..OR, FORTY-EIGHT PROGRESSIVE LESSONS IN THE ART
    DODD, FLORENCE
BERTINI'S SELF-TEACHING CATECHISM OF MUSIC FOR THE PIANOFORTE
    BERTINI, HENRI
BETTER BEGINNINGS..A FIRST BOOK FOR EVERYONE WHO WANTS TO BECOME A
    CHING, JAMES
BIBLIOGRAPHICAL THEMATIC CATALOGUE OF THE WORKS OF JOHN FIELD,
    HOPKINSON, CECIL
BIO-BIBLIOGRAPHICAL DICTIONARY OF TWELVE-TONE AND SERIAL COMPOSERS, A
    CARLSON, EFFIE B.
BIOGRAPHY OF LEOPOLD DE MEYER...ROYAL COURT PIANIST...TO THEIR
    DIDIMUS, HENRY
BIOGRAPHY OF LOUIS MOREAU GOTTSCHALK, THE AMERICAN PIANIST AND
    DIDIMUS, HENRY
BLAZING A NEW TRAIL IN PIANO PLAYING
    VISUOLA CORPORATION
BLIND PIANO TEACHER, THE
    ISAACS, EDWARD
BLOOMFIELD-ZEISLER--ROBINSON LOCKE SCRAP BOOKS
    LOCKE, ROBINSON
BOOK ABOUT PIANOS IN GENERAL AND THE EPWORTH IN PARTICULAR, A
    EPWORTH PIANOS
BOOK OF ART PIANO CASES
    STEINWAY AND SONS

BOOK OF COMPLETE INFORMATION ABOUT PIANOS, THE ...1868-1918, A FULL
    WING AND SONS
BOOK OF THE FIRST INTERNATIONAL MUSICOLOGICAL CONGRESS DEVOTED TO THE
    INTERNATIONAL MUSICOLOGICAL CONGRESS..FIRST--1960--WORKS OF
BORIS BERLIN MUSICAL KINDERGARTEN PIANO METHOD, THE.. GUIDE FOR
    BERLIN, BORIS *
BORODIN AND LISZT--VOL. 2--LISZT, AS SKETCHED IN THE LETTERS OF BORODIN
    HABETS, ALFRED
BOY MUSIC, A FIRST PIANO METHOD FOR BOYS BETWEEN 8 AND 16
    MASON, MARY B.
BRAHMS..A CRITICAL STUDY
    JAMES, BURNETT
BRAHMS..WITH AN ANALYTICAL STUDY OF THE COMPLETE PIANOFORTE WORKS
    MURDOCH, WILLIAM
BRIEF LIST OF REFERENCES ON THE PIANO AND THE PIANO PLAYER
    UNITED STATES--LIBRARY OF CONGRESS--DIVISION OF BIBLIOGRAPHY
BROADWOOD COLLECTION OF ANTIQUE INSTRUMENTS, THE ..FORERUNNERS OF THE
    BROADWOOD, JOHN AND SONS
BROADWOOD CONCERTS--HISTORICAL NOTES BY ROBIN H. LEGGES..PROGRAMMES, 6
    BROADWOOD, JOHN AND SONS
BROTHERHOOD 'TECHNICON' AND HOW TO USE IT, THE
    BROTHERHOOD, JAMES
BROTHER MUSICIANS..REMINISCENCES OF EDWARD AND WALTER BACHE
    BACHE, CONSTANCE
BUILDING OF THE PIANO, THE
    FUREY, J.
BUNDLE OF TIME, A ..THE MEMOIRS OF HARRIET COHEN
    COHEN, HARRIET
BUSINESS MANUAL FOR PIANO TEACHERS
    BENDER, GEORGE CHARLES
BUSONI--ROBINSON LOCKE SCRAP BOOKS
    LOCKE, ROBINSON
BUYING A SQUARE PIANO
    GOULD, BRIAN M.
CADENCE, KEY TO MUSICAL CLARITY, THE ..A SIMPLE AND PRACTICAL APPROACH
    MCCLANAHAN, RICHARD
CAMILLE SAINT-SAENS, HIS LIFE AND ART---DISCUSSES CONCERTI AND
    LYLE, WATSON
CANDIDATE'S COMPANION TO THE EXERCISES, SCALES, BROKEN CHORDS, SIGHT
    CHING, JAMES
CANDIDATE'S SCALE AND ARPEGGIO TESTS FOR THE PIANOFORTE, ETC., THE
    MANHIRE, WILSON
CANDIDATES GUIDE TO QUESTIONS AND ANSWERS AT PRACTICAL LOCAL
    LOWE, CLAUDE EDGERTON
CAPPS SYSTEM OF IMPROVISING FOR PIANO, THE --A MODERN COURSE OF
    CAPPS, STANLEY M.
CAPTURE OF INSPIRATION, THE
    SCHMITZ, ELIE ROBERT
CARE OF THE PIANO AND PLAYER PIANO IN THE HOME, THE
    GIESKE, GEORGE
CARL'S DICTIONARY OF CHORDS...REFERENCE BOOK FOR CUED-IN HARMONY OF
    CARL, SYLVESTER
CARL A. PREYER, THE LIFE OF A KANSAS MUSICIAN
    GLOYNE, HOWARD F.--M.D.
CARL PHILIPP EMANUEL BACH'S AUTOBIOGRAPHY..FACSIMILE OF ORIGINAL
    BACH, CARL PHILIPP EMANUEL
CAROLYN PLATT METHOD FOR PIANO, THE --GROUP INSTRUCTION--TEACHER'S
    PLATT, CAROLYN
CATALOGUE OF BOOKS IN THE LIBRARY OF JOHN BROADWOOD AND SONS'
    BROADWOOD, JOHN AND SONS
CATALOGUE OF JOHN BROADWOOD AND SONS, LTD. LATEST MODELS, INCLUDING
    BROADWOOD, JOHN AND SONS
CATALOGUE OF MUSICAL INSTRUMENTS..VOL. 1, KEYBOARD INSTRUMENTS--EDITED
    VICTORIA AND ALBERT MUSEUM, SOUTH KENSINGTON
CATALOGUE OF MUSICAL INSTRUMENTS, PRINCIPALLY ILLUSTRATIVE OF THE
    BODDINGTON, HENRY
CATALOGUE OF MUSIC FOR THE AMPICO, A ..A LIST OF THE RECORDINGS OF
    AMERICAN PIANO CORPORATION
CATALOGUE OF MUSIC FOR THE AMPICO, A --A LIST OF THE RECORDINGS OF
    AMERICAN PIANO CORPORATION
CATALOGUE OF PIANOFORTES EMBODYING LATEST IMPROVEMENTS
    MASON AND HAMLIN ORGAN AND PIANO COMPANY
CATALOGUE OF REPRESENTATIVE TEACHING MATERIALS FOR PIANO SINCE 1900, A
    HODGES, SISTER MABELLE L.
CATALOGUE OF THE BENTON FLETCHER COLLECTION OF EARLY KEYBOARD
    RUSSELL, RAYMOND
CATALOGUE OF THE CROSBY BROWN COLLECTION OF MUSICAL INSTRUMENTS OF ALL
    METROPOLITAN MUSEUM OF ART, NEW YORK
CATALOGUE OF THE M. STEINERT COLLECTION OF KEYED AND STRING
    STEINERT, MORRIS
CATALOGUE OF THE MUSICAL INSTRUMENTS AND OBJECTS FORMING THE DONALDSON
    DONALDSON, GEORGE
CATALOGUE OF THE SPECIAL EXHIBITION OF ANCIENT MUSICAL INSTRUMENTS
    SOUTH KENSINGTON MUSEUM, LONDON
CATALOGUE OF THE STEARNS COLLECTION OF MUSICAL INSTRUMENTS
    STANLEY, ALBERT A.
CATALOG OF AEOLIAN MUSIC ARRANGED FOR 46-NOTE INSTRUMENTS
    AEOLIAN COMPANY, THE
CATALOG OF METROSTYLE AND THEMODIST MUSIC FOR THE PIANOLA AND PIANOLA
    AEOLIAN COMPANY, THE
CATALOG OF MUSIC-ROLLS FOR THE DUO-ART REPRODUCING PIANO
    AEOLIAN COMPANY, THE
CATALOG OF MUSIC AND MUSICAL LITERATURE---PIANOLA RECORDS
    AEOLIAN COMPANY, THE
CATALOG OF MUSIC FOR THE PIANOLA, PIANOLA PIANO AND AERIOLA--CONTAINING
    AEOLIAN COMPANY, THE
CATALOG OF SELECTED PIANO ROLLS FROM THE LIBRARY OF CONGRESS
    KACZMAREK, REGINA A.
CATALOG OF THE AEOLIAN
    AEOLIAN COMPANY, THE
CATECHISM FOR THE PIANOFORTE STUDENT, A ..CONTAINING A FULL EXPLANATION
    HILES, JOHN
CATECHISM OF HARMONY, THOROUGH-BASS, AND MODULATION, A ..WITH NUMEROUS
    HILES, JOHN
CATECHISM OF MUSIC, CHIEFLY ADAPTED FOR LEARNERS ON THE PIANOFORTE, IN
    MACPHERSON, D.
CATECHISM OF PIANOFORTE PLAYING---1888, IN GERMAN
    RIEMANN, HUGO
CATECHISM OF THE FAELTEN SYSTEM, A
    FAELTEN, REINHOLD
CATECHISM OF THE RUDIMENTS OF HARMONY AND THOROUGHBASS, A ---1833
    HAMILTON, JAMES ALEXANDER
CELEBRATED INSTRUCTION BOOK FOR THE PIANOFORTE, CONTAINING THE
    HEERINGEN, ERNEST VON
CELEBRATED PIANISTS OF THE PAST AND PRESENT--139 BIOGRAPHIES, WITH
    PAYNE, ALBERT
CELEBRATED PIANISTS OF THE PAST AND PRESENT--139 BIOGRAPHIES, WITH
    EHRLICH, ALFRED HEINRICH
CENTENNIAL CATALOGUE OF THE PUBLISHED AND UNPUBLISHED COMPOSITIONS OF
    OFFERGELD, ROBERT
CHAIKOVSKY SYMPHONIES AND CONCERTOS--B.B.C. MUSIC GUIDES, NO. 16
    WARRACK JOHN H.
CHAMBER MUSIC CATALOGUE
    BRITISH BROADCASTING CORPORATION--CENTRAL MUSIC LIBRARY
CHAPPELL AND CO.'S PRACTICAL DIRECTIONS UPON THE ART OF TUNING THE
    RIMBAULT, EDWARD FRANCIS

CHAPTERS FROM A MUSICAL LIFE
    ADAMS, JULIETTE
CHARLES HALLE'S PRACTICAL PIANOFORTE SCHOOL--9 VOLS.
    HALLE, SIR CHARLES
CHECK-LIST OF WESTERN INSTRUMENTS IN THE COLLECTION OF MUSICAL
    YALE UNIVERSITY SCHOOL OF MUSIC
CHECKLIST OF KEYBOARD INSTRUMENTS AT THE SMITHSONIAN INSTITUTION, A
    UNITED STATES MUSEUM OF HISTORY AND TECHNOLOGY
CHICKERING AND SONS, MANUFACTURER OF GRAND, SQUARE AND UPRIGHT
    CHICKERING AND SONS
CHICKERING AND SONS PIANOFORTES AT THE CENTENNIAL EXHIBITION,
    CHICKERING AND SONS
CHICKERING CENTENNIAL CELEBRATION, APRIL 1823-1923
    CHICKERING AND SONS
CHILD'S FIRST STEPS IN PIANOFORTE PLAYING, THE
    MATTHAY, TOBIAS A.
CHILD'S INTRODUCTION TO THOROUGH BASS, THE ..IN CONVERSATIONS OF A
    ANON
CHILD'S PIANOFORTE BOOK, THE ..BEING A FIRST YEAR'S COURSE AT THE
    MOORE, HENRY K.
CHILD CHOPIN, THE ...WITH DIRECTIONS FOR PRESENTATION WITH A MINIATURE
    COIT, LOTTIE ELLSWORTH
CHILD PIANIST, THE
    CURWEN, ANNIE JESSY
CHOICE OF A BEETHOVEN SONATA FOR DIPLOMA EXAMINATIONS, THE --NOTES ON
    COVIELLO, AMBROSE
CHOPIN..AN INDEX OF HIS WORKS IN CHRONOLOGICAL ORDER--2ND. REV.
    BROWN, MAURICE J. E.
CHOPIN..AN INTRODUCTION TO HIS PIANO WORKS
    PALMER, WILLARD A.--EDITOR
CHOPIN..AS REVEALED BY EXTRACTS FROM HIS DIARY--2ND. ED.---1905
    TARNOWSKI, STANISLAS
CHOPIN..A DISCOURSE
    PADEREWSKI, IGNACE JAN
CHOPIN..A PICTORIAL BIOGRAPHY---137 ILLUSTRATIONS
    BOUCOURECHLIEV, ANDRE
CHOPIN..CENTENNIAL MEMORY 1849-1949..A LECTURE
    CAUCHI, PAUL
CHOPIN..HIS LIFE---1935
    MURDOCH, WILLIAM
CHOPIN..THE MAN AND HIS MUSIC---1901
    HUNEKER, JAMES GIBBONS
CHOPIN..THE STORY OF THE BOY WHO MADE BEAUTIFUL MELODIES
    AZULAY, GERTRUDE
CHOPIN---FOR YOUNGER READERS
    MAYO, WALDO
CHOPIN---YOUNGER READERS
    GRONOWICZ, ANTONI
CHOPIN--'GREAT COMPOSERS' SERIES
    CHISSELL, JOAN
CHOPIN--'GREAT LIVES' SERIES
    MAINE, BASIL
CHOPIN--'LITTLE BIOGRAPHIES'
    HUMISTON, WILLIAM H.
CHOPIN--'MASTER MUSICIAN' SERIES--INCLUDES CATALOGUE OF WORKS--REV.
    HEDLEY, ARTHUR
CHOPIN--'MASTER MUSICIANS' SERIES
    HADDEN, JAMES CUTHBERT
CHOPIN--'MUSIC OF THE MASTERS' SERIES
    DRY, WAKELING
CHOPIN--NOVELLO'S BIOGRAPHIES OF GREAT MUSICIANS
    COATES, HENRY
CHOPIN, HIS LIFE TOLD IN ANECDOTAL FORM---FOR YOUNGER READERS
    RUTTKAY, GEORGE
CHOPIN, THE CHILD AND THE LAD
    UMINSKA, ZOFIA *
CHOPIN, THE COMPOSER AND HIS MUSIC
    PORTE, JOHN F.
CHOPIN, THE MAN AND HIS MUSIC
    WEINSTOCK, HERBERT
CHOPIN'S GREATER WORKS...HOW THEY SHOULD BE UNDERSTOOD...INCLUDING
    KLECZYNSKI, JAN
CHOPIN'S LETTERS--COLLECTED BY HENRY OPIENSKI..TRANSLATED BY E. L.
    CHOPIN, FREDERIC
CHOPIN'S LETTERS TO DELFINA
    GLINSKI, MATEUSZ
CHOPIN'S MUSICAL STYLE---1939
    ABRAHAM, GERALD
CHOPIN'S TEMPO RUBATO
    SEGUEL, MANIA
CHOPINIANA IN THE HIGH MUSIC SCHOOL LIBRARY IN KATOWICE---BIBLIOGRAPHY
    KATOWICE, POLAND--BIBLIOTECA PANSTWOWEJ
CHOPIN AND GEORGE SAND IN THE CARTUJA DE VALLDEMOSA...
    FERRA I PERELLO, BARTOLOME
CHOPIN AND HIS FOURTEEN DOCTORS
    BARRY, KEITH LEWIS
CHOPIN AND OTHER MUSICAL ESSAYS---1889
    FINCK, HENRY T.
CHOPIN COMPANION, THE ..PROFILES OF THE MAN AND THE MUSICIAN---1966
    WALKER, ALAN--EDITOR
CHOPIN IN HIS OWN LAND..DOCUMENTS AND SOUVENIRS
    KOBYLANSKA, KRYSTYNA--EDITOR
CHOPIN THE COMPOSER---1913
    KELLEY, EDGAR STILLMAN
CHOPIN THE UNKNOWN
    GLINSKI, MATEUSZ
CHOPIN YEAR 1949 IN POLAND, THE
    EXECUTIVE COMMITTEE OF CHOPIN YEAR 1949
CHOPIN
    BIDOU, HENRI
CHORD-O-GRAPH METHOD OF KEYBOARD HARMONY---PRINTED FROM TYPED COPY
    KEDDINGTON, J. BLAINE
CHORDS, CADENCES, AND ARPEGGIOS
    STEVENS, EVERETT
CHORDS IN ACTION
    BISHOP, DOROTHY
CHORDS OF REMEMBRANCE---BY A PUPIL OF CLARA SCHUMANN
    VERNE, MATHILDE
CHORD DICTIONARY..DESIGNED FOR TEACHERS, STUDENTS AND SELF-TAUGHT
    CHILDERS, LEMUEL
CHURCH PIANIST, THE
    MIDKIFF, HELEN T.
CLARA SCHUMANN..AN ARTIST'S LIFE BASED ON MATERIAL FOUND IN DIARIES AND
    LITZMANN, BERTHOLD
CLARA SCHUMANN..A ROMANTIC BIOGRAPHY
    BURK, JOHN N.
CLASS-PIANO TEACHERS HANDBOOK
    DENVER--PUBLIC SCHOOLS
CLASS PIANO FOR ADULT BEGINNERS--2ND. ED.---1964
    SQUIRE, RUSSEL N. *
CLASS PIANO
    MCLAIN, MARGARET STARR
CLASS PROCEDURE FOR 40 LESSONS IN PIANO PLAYING BY HARMONY DIAGRAMS
    BEVITT, ZAY RECTOR
CLASS WAY TO THE KEYBOARD, THE
    CHAPPLE, STANLEY

CLAUDIO ARRAU
    GAVOTY, BERNARD *
CLAVICHORD, THE ---1956, IN GERMAN
    NEUPERT, HANNS
CLEMENTI'S SELECTION OF PRACTICAL HARMONY FOR THE ORGAN OR
    CLEMENTI, MUZIO
CLOCKWORK MUSIC..AN ILLUSTRATED HISTORY OF MECHANICAL MUSICAL
    ORD-HUME, ARTHUR W. J. G.
CODE OF FAIR COMPETITION FOR THE PIANO MANUFACTURING INDUSTRY AS
    UNITED STATES--NATIONAL RECOVERY ADMINISTRATION
COLLECTION OF LETTERS PATENT RELATING TO THE CONSTRUCTION OF PIANOS,
    UNITED STATES PATENT OFFICE
COLLECTOR'S CHOPIN AND SCHUMANN, THE --KEYSTONE BOOKS
    SCHONBERG, HAROLD
COLLEGE PIANO PEDAGOGY
    LAMAR, RICHARD
COMMEMORATION OF THE FOUNDING OF THE HOUSE OF CHICKERING AND SONS,
    CHICKERING AND SONS
COMMENTARY ON BKS. 1 AND 2 OF THE FORTY-EIGHT PRELUDES AND FUGUES OF
    MACPHERSON, STEWART
COMMONSENSE IN PIANOFORTE PLAYING
    WHITEMORE, CUTHBERT
COMMONSENSE IN SCALE AND ARPEGGIO PLAYING
    JOHNSON, REGINALD
COMMON SENSE CATECHISM..OR, PIANO AND ORGAN PUPIL'S COMPANION
    NICHOLS, JULIA E.
COMMON SENSE IN MUSIC TEACHING
    LOVELOCK, WILLIAM
COMMON SENSE IN PIANO STUDY
    SEROFF, VICTOR
COMMON SENSE IN SIGHT READING..A GUIDE FOR PIANO TEACHERS
    TOBIN, JOSEPH RAYMOND
COMPANION TO BEETHOVEN'S PIANO SONATAS, A ..COMPLETE
    TOVEY, DONALD FRANCIS
COMPANION TO MOZART'S PIANO CONCERTOS, A
    HUTCHINGS, ARTHUR
COMPANION TO THE MUSICAL ASSISTANT, A ..CONTAINING ALL THAT IS TRULY
    COGGINS, JOSEPH
COMPANION TO THE ROYAL PATENT CHIROPLAST, OR HAND-DIRECTOR, A ..A NEW
    LOGIER, JOHANN BERNHARD
COMPARATIVE PIANOFORTE SCHOOL--4 BKS.---BK. 3 TRANSLATED BY J. C.
    RIEMANN, HUGO
COMPENDIUM OF A NEW METHOD OF MUSIC...WITH THE AUTHOR'S PRINCIPLES AND
    BEMETZRIEDER, ANTON
COMPENDIUM OF PIANO MATERIAL--2ND. ED.---1929
    PERRY, ADELAIDE TROWBRIDGE
COMPENDIUM OF PIANO TECHNIQUE--39 ETUDES SELECTED FROM OVER 4000, BY 75
    SOREL, CLAUDETTE
COMPLEAT INSTRUCTOR FOR THE HARPSICHORD OR PIANOFORTE, THE
    JONES, GRIFFITH
COMPLEAT METHOD, FOR ATTAINING TO PLAY A THOROUGH BASS UPON EITHER
    KELLER, GOTTFRIED
COMPLEAT MUSIC TEACHER FOR TEACHERS, PARENTS AND STUDENTS
    EDWARDS, RUTH
COMPLEAT TUTOR FOR THE HARPSICHORD OR SPINNET, WHEREIN IS SHEWN THE
    ANON
COMPLETE CATALOG OF MUSIC ROLLS FOR THE DUO-ART REPRODUCING PIANO
    AEOLIAN COMPANY, THE
COMPLETE COURSE IN PROFESSIONAL PIANO TUNING, REPAIR, AND REBUILDING
    STEVENS, FLOYD A.
COMPLETE COURSE OF WRIST AND FINGER GYMNASTICS, A --3RD. ED.---1880
    ARNIM, ANNA L.
COMPLETE KNOWLEDGE OF PIANO TECHNIQUE, A
    FULLER, JANET E.
COMPLETE KNOWLEDGE OF THE ESSENTIALS OF PIANOFORTE PLAYING, A
    FULLER, JANET E.
COMPLETE PIANOFORTE SONATAS OF BEETHOVEN, THE ---ANALYTICAL NOTES
    LEICHTENTRITT, HUGO
COMPLETE SCALE AND ARPEGGIO MANUAL
    SHEPARD, ROBERT
COMPLETE SYSTEM OF HARMONY..OR A REGULAR AND EASY METHOD TO ATTAIN A
    HECK, JOHANN CASPAR
COMPLETE THEORETICAL AND PRACTICAL COURSE OF INSTRUCTIONS ON THE ART OF
    HUMMEL, JOHANN NEPOMUK
COMPLETE THEORETICAL AND PRACTICAL PIANO FORTE SCHOOL, FROM THE FIRST
    CZERNY, CARL
COMPLETE TREATISE OF THOROUGH BASS, A
    MATTHESON, JOHANN
COMPOSERS OF MANY LANDS AND MANY TIMES..A PICTURE STORY IN
    EYE GATE HOUSE
COMPOSERS OF YESTERDAY..A BIOGRAPHICAL AND CRITICAL GUIDE TO THE MOST
    EWEN, DAVID
COMPOSERS SINCE 1900..A BIOGRAPHICAL AND CRITICAL GUIDE
    EWEN, DAVID
COMPOSITIONAL MATRIX, THE ..MONOGRAPHS IN THEORY AND COMPOSITION
    FORTE, ALLEN
COMPREHENSIVE GUIDE FOR PIANO TEACHERS AND PIANO AUDITION SYLLABUS
    MUSIC EDUCATION LEAGUE
CONCEPTS AND SKILLS FOR THE PIANO..TEACHER'S MANUAL 1---CLASS
    BOAL, DEAN *
CONCERNING CHOPIN IN MANCHESTER--ON A CONCERT, AT WHICH CHOPIN PLAYED,
    BROOKSHAW, SUSANNA
CONCERTO--'PHOENIX MUSIC GUIDES', NO. 1
    YOUNG, PERCY M.
CONCERTO, THE ---1944
    VEINUS, ABRAHAM
CONCERTO, THE --ANALYTICAL GUIDES---FIVE FOLDOUTS--EIGHT PAGES EACH
    HARTSHORN, WILLIAM C.
CONCERTO, THE --BROWN 'MUSIC HORIZON' SERIES
    NELSON, WENDELL
CONCERTO, THE STORY OF CLARA SCHUMANN
    HARDING, BERTITA
CONCERTO, THE
    CULSHAW, JOHN
CONCERTO, THE
    HILL, RALPH--EDITOR
CONCERT GRAND---GOTTSCHALK
    BRESLIN, HOWARD
CONCISE ANALYSIS OF BEETHOVEN'S 32 PIANOFORTE SONATAS, A
    SALSBUPY, JANET
CONCISE AND PRACTICAL EXPLANATION OF THE RULES OF SIMPLE HARMONY AND
    SMITH, THOMAS
CONCISE TREATISE ON HARMONY, ACCOMPANIMENT, AND COMPOSITION, FOR THE
    BECKER, JULIUS
CONCISE TREATISE ON THOROUGHBASS, A
    NICHOLSON, JAMES
CONFIDENTIAL MANUAL FOR SALESMEN OF THE DUO-ART REPRODUCING PIANO---8
    AEOLIAN COMPANY, THE
CONSCIOUSLY CONTROLLED PIANO TONE, THE --REV. ED.---1950
    HELMANN, JACOB N.
CONSCIOUS CONTROL IN PIANO STUDY
    AMEY, ELLEN
CONSOLE SYSTEM, THE ..A TEXT FOR MODERN PIANO AND ORGAN TO BE USED IN
    DECKER, TOM W.
CONSTANT K--18600, THE ..ITS USE IN THEORY AND PRACTICE
    DARBYSHIRE, JOHN H.

CONSTITUTION OF THE PIANO, ORGAN AND MUSICAL INSTRUMENT WORKERS'
   PIANO, ORGAN AND MUSICAL INSTRUMENT WORKERS INTERNATIONAL UNION OF
CONSTRUCTION, TUNING AND CARE OF THE PIANOFORTE--EDITED AND LARGELY
   NORTON, EDWARD Q.
CONSTRUCTIVE HARMONY AND IMPROVISATION
   REED, CLARE OSBORNE
CONSUMER INVESTIGATION FOR NATIONAL PIANO MANUFACTURERS ASSOCIATION,
   NATIONAL PIANO MANUFACTURERS ASSOCIATION
CONTEMPORAPY IMMORTALS---PADEREWSKI
   HENDERSON, ARCHIBALD
CONTEMPORARY PIANO MUSIC OF THE AMERICAS, COMPILED BY GEORGE ANSON FOR
   ANSON, GEORGE
CONTEMPORARY RUSSIAN COMPOSERS---RACHMANINOFF
   MONTAGU-NATHAN, M.
CONTINGENCIES AND OTHER ESSAYS---LISZT
   GRAY, CECIL
CONVERSATION ON MUSIC, A
   RUBINSTEIN, ANTON
CORRESPONDENCE COURSE IN 12 LESSONS, A
   NILES BRYANT SCHOOL OF PIANO TUNING
CORRESPONDENCE OF HANS VON BUELOW AND RICHARD STRAUSS
   BUELOW, HANS GUIDO VON
COUPLET HARPSICHORD IN THE CROSBY BROWN COLLECTION, THE --FROM 'THE
   RIPIN, EDWIN M.
COURSES OF INSTRUCTION IN PIANO MAKING, TOGETHER WITH A SECTION ON
   UNITED STATES TRAINING SERVICE
CRAWFORD SYSTEM OF KEYBOARD HARMONY AND TRANSPOSITION, THE
   CRAWFORD, THOMAS J.
CREATIVE APPROACH TO PIANO CLASS TEACHING, A ---REPRODUCED FROM
   ORLIK, JULES
CREATIVE IMPROVISING FOR THE RIGHT HAND..CREATIVE STUDIES IN
   HILL, JIM
CREATIVE MOTION
   ALLEN, MARGARET *
CREATIVE PIANO TECHNIC
   O'TOOLE, WILLIAM
CREATIVE TECHNIQUE, FOR ARTISTS IN GENERAL AND PIANISTS IN PARTICULAR
   WOODHOUSE, GEORGE
CREATIVE WORLD OF SCALES AND CHORDS, THE ..CREATIVE STUDIES IN KEYBOARD
   HILL, JIM
CURIOSITIES OF THE KEY-BOARD AND THE STAFF...SHOWN TO BE UPON A
   RHODES, ALFRED
DAY WITH FREDERIC CHOPIN, A
   BYRON, MAY CLARISSA
DE-ASSIFICATION OF MUSIC, THE ..A PROPAGANDIST MAGAZINE, OF ONE NUMBER,
   CHILTON, CARROLL B.
DEALER'S HANDBOOK OF PIANOS AND THEIR MAKERS
   ANDERSON-MULDER COMPANY
DEBUSSY, MAN AND ARTIST---1937
   THOMPSON, OSCAR
DEBUSSY, MUSICIAN OF FRANCE
   SEROFF, VICTOR
DEBUSSY PIANO MUSIC--B.B.C. MUSIC GUIDE---COMPOSITIONAL ASPECT
   DAWES, FRANCIS E.
DEDICATION, THE LOVE STORY OF CLARA AND ROBERT SCHUMANN
   SPAETH, SIGMUND
DEEP SOUTH PIANO..THE STORY OF LITTLE BROTHER MONTGOMERY
   ZUR HEIDE, KARL GERT
DELIVERY IN THE ART OF PIANOFORTE PLAYING
   EHRENFECTER, C. A.
DEPPE FINGER EXERCISES FOR RAPIDLY DEVELOPING AN ARTISTIC TOUCH IN
   FAY, AMY
DESCRIPTION AND HISTORY OF THE PIANOFORTE, A
   O'NEILL, J. A.
DESCRIPTION AND HISTORY OF THE PIANOFORTE AND OLDER KEYBOARD STRINGED
   HIPKINS, ALFRED JAMES
DESCRIPTION AND USE OF THE PATENT ENHARMONIC PIANOFORTE
   LOESCHMANN, DAVID
DESCRIPTION OF STANDARD PNEUMATIC PLAYER ACTION, WITH SUGGESTIONS FOR
   STANDARD PNEUMATIC ACTION COMPANY
DESCRIPTIVE ANALYSES OF PIANO WORKS, FOR THE USE OF TEACHERS, PLAYERS,
   PERRY, EDWARD B.
DESCRIPTIVE CATALOGUE OF THE MUSICAL INSTRUMENTS IN THE SOUTH
   SOUTH KENSINGTON MUSEUM, LONDON
DESCRIPTIVE CATALOGUE OF THE MUSICAL INSTRUMENTS IN THE SOUTH
   SOUTH KENSINGTON MUSEUM, LONDON
DEVELOPMENT OF ARTISTIC PIANOFORTE TOUCH
   RUSSELL, LOUIS ARTHUR
DEVELOPMENT OF PIANO MUSIC FROM THE DAYS OF THE CLAVICHORD AND
   HUNEKER, JAMES GIBBONS
DEVELOPMENT OF THE HAND FOR PIANO-FORTE PLAYING BY MEANS OF A
   BROTHERHOOD, JAMES
DICTIONARY OF ENGLISH FURNITURE, THE --VOL. 3---16 ILLUSTRATIONS OF OLD
   MACQUOID, PERCY *
DICTIONARY OF OLD ENGLISH MUSIC AND MUSICAL INSTRUMENTS, A
   PULVER, JEFFREY
DICTIONARY OF PIANISTS AND COMPOSERS FOR THE PIANOFORTE..WITH AN
   PAUER, ERNST
DICTIONARY OF TWENTIETY-CENTURY COMPOSERS, A --1911-1971
   THOMPSON, KENNETH
DIFFICULTIES OF BEETHOVEN PIANOFORTE SONATAS, AN ANALYSIS OF COMMON
   COVIELLO, AMBROSE
DIGEST OF THE ANALYSES OF THE 48 FUGUES IN THE WELL-TEMPERED CLAVIER
   SAMPSON, BROOK
DIGITORIUM, THE --MINIATURE DUMB PIANO
   ANON
DISCOVERING THE PIANO..THE MULTIPLE KEY APPROACH..STUDY GUIDE AND GOALS
   SWENSON, LUCILE B.
DO'S AND DONT'S FOR MUSICIANS..A HANDBOOK FOR TEACHERS AND PERFORMERS
   ROWLEY, ALEC
DOMENICO SCARLATTI---1953
   KIRKPATRICK, RALPH
DOMENICO SCARLATTI--NOTES TO ACCOMPANY GRAMOPHONE RECORDINGS
   LANDOWSKI, ALICE-WANDA
DO YOU ACCOMPANY
   WINN, CYRIL
DUET---STORY OF CLARA AND ROBERT SCHUMANN
   DUNLOP, AGNES MARY
DUET FOR THREE HANDS...AS TOLD TO JOYCE EGGINTON
   SMITH, CYRIL
DUO-ART BOOK OF MUSIC, THE
   AEOLIAN COMPANY, THE
DUO-ART PIANO MUSIC...RECORDED BY MORE THAN 250 PIANISTS
   AEOLIAN COMPANY, THE
DUO-ART PIANO MUSIC
   AEOLIAN COMPANY, THE
DUO-ART REPRODUCING PIANO, THE ..THE DUO-ART REPRODUCING PIANO SERVICE
   AEOLIAN COMPANY, THE
DUO-PIANISM---PUBLISHED DISSERTATION
   MOLDENHAUER, HANS
DUSSEK'S INSTRUCTIONS ON THE ART OF PLAYING THE PIANOFORTE OR
   DUSSEK, JOHANN L.
DWIGHT HAMILTON BALDWIN AND THE BALDWIN PIANO
   WULSIN, LUCIEN
EARLY CORRESPONDENCE OF HANS VON BUELOW, THE ---EDITED BY HIS
   BUELOW, HANS GUIDO VON

EARLY KEYBOARD INSTRUMENTS--VICTORIA AND ALBERT MUSEUM..'SMALL PICTURE
   RUSSELL, RAYMOND
EARLY KEYBOARD INSTRUMENTS, FROM THEIR BEGINNINGS TO THE YEAR
   JAMES, PHILIP BRUTTON
EARLY LETTERS OF ROBERT SCHUMANN, ORIGINALLY PUBLISHED BY HIS
   SCHUMANN, ROBERT
EARLY PIANO AND ITS INFLUENCE ON KEYBOARD TECHNIQUE AND COMPOSITION IN
   PARRISH, CARL
EARS, BRAIN AND FINGERS..A TEXT BOOK FOR PIANO TEACHERS AND PUPILS
   WELLS, HOWARD
ECLECTIC PIANOFORTE SCHOOL, THE ..ARRANGED FROM THE WORKS OF THE BEST
   PETERS, WILLIAM C.
EDITIONS AND MUSICIANS
   EMERY, WALTER
EDUCATION IN MUSIC..LESSONS TO TEACHERS IN THE INSTRUCTION OF PARENTS
   VIRGIL, ALMON K.
EDUCATION OF THE MUSIC TEACHER, THE
   TAPPER, THOMAS
EDWARD MACDOWELL, A GREAT AMERICAN TONE POET..HIS LIFE AND MUSIC
   PORTE, JOHN F.
EDYTHE DE WITT'S METHOD FOR CLASS PIANO...WRITTEN TO GIVE CORRECT NOTE
   DE WITT, EDYTHE
EGON PETRI-ALEXANDER LIBERMANN NOTES ON THE ART AND TECHNIQUE OF
   SHELDON, ROBERT--COMPILER
EIGHTH NOTES, VOICES AND FIGURES OF MUSIC AND THE DANCE---CHAPTER ON
   PARKER, HENRY T.
EIGHTH OCTAVE, THE ---CONTINUES THE RECORD, BEGUN IN 'FROM PIANO TO
   HAMBOURG, MARK
EIGHT FUGUES FROM J. S. BACH'S 'W.T.C.', WITH ANALYTICAL NOTES IN COLOR
   BUECKELMANN, BERNARDUS
ELEMENTARY ACCOMPANIMENT WRITING--CHIEFLY MUSIC, FOR EXAM CANDIDATE
   LOVELOCK, WILLIAM
ELEMENTARY EXERCISES IN SIGHT READING...FROM THE VIRGIL METHOD
   VIRGIL, ANTHA MINERVA
ELEMENTARY KEYBOARD HARMONY
   LIEBERMAN, MAURICE
ELEMENTARY PIANO INSTRUCTION IN COLLEGE
   BURROWS, RAYMOND
ELEMENTARY PIANO PEDAGOGY, A GUIDE BOOK FOR YOUNG PIANO TEACHERS
   MACKLIN, CHARLES B.
ELEMENTARY STUDIES IN TRANSPOSITION--BKS. 1 AND 2
   NEWTON, ERNEST
ELEMENTS OF MUSIC..A CLEAR AND SYSTEMATIC ARRANGEMENT OF RULES FOR THE
   LENHART, A.
ELEMENTS OF MUSICAL COMPOSITION..COMPREHENDING THE RULES OF THOROUGH
   CROTCH, WILLIAM
ELEMENTS OF PIANO TECHNIQUE, THE
   HUTCHESON, ERNEST
ELEMENTS OF THOROUGH BASE, ADAPTED TO THE WANTS OF YOUNG PUPILS
   PETERS, WILLIAM C.
ELEMENTS OF THOROUGH BASS AND COMPOSITION
   MILLER, EDWARD
ELIZABETHAN VIRGINAL BOOK, AN ..A CRITICAL ESSAY ON THE CONTENTS OF A
   NAYLOR, EDWARD W.
EMBELLISHMENTS OF MUSIC, THE ..A STUDY OF THE ENTIRE RANGE OF MUSICAL
   RUSSELL, LOUIS ARTHUR
EMBRYO MUSICIAN, THE ..A METHOD OF INTRODUCING MUSIC TO LITTLE CHILDREN
   GILBERT, RUSSELL S.
EMINENT EUROPEANS..STUDIES IN CONTINENTAL REALITY---PADEREWSKI
   BAGGER, EUGENE S.
ENCYCLOPEDIA OF AUTOMATIC MUSICAL INSTRUMENTS---INCLUDES A DICTIONARY
   BOWERS, Q. DAVID
ENGLISH KEYBOARD MUSIC BEFORE THE NINETEENTH CENTURY---EXTENSIVE
   CALDWELL, JOHN
ENTIRELY NEW SOLUTION TO THE PROBLEMS OF PIANO STUDY AT HOME, AN --A
   CHING, JAMES
EPITOME OF THE LAWS OF PIANOFORTE TECHNIQUE, AN
   MATTHAY, TOBIAS A.
ERIK SATIE---1932, IN FRENCH
   TEMPLIER, PIERRE D.
ERNO RAPEE'S ENCYCLOPEDIA OF MUSIC FOR PICTURES---LISTED BOTH BY MOOD
   RAPEE, ERNO--ARRANGER
ERNST PAUER'S SIX HISTORICAL PERFORMANCES OF PIANOFORTE MUSIC
   PAUER, ERNST
ESSAYS AND ARTICLES ON MUSICAL SUBJECTS, PARTICULARLY
   SCHAAF, EDWARD O.
ESSAYS IN PIANOFORTE TECHNOLOGY
   NALDER, LAWRENCE MARCUS
ESSAY ON THE CHIROGYMNAST..OR, FINGER EXERCISES APPLIED TO...ALL SORTS
   ANON
ESSAY ON THE THEORY AND PRACTICE OF TUNING, AN ...PIANOFORTES AND
   LOEHR, JOHANN JOSEPH
ESSAY ON THE TRUE ART OF PLAYING KEYBOARD INSTRUMENTS---TWO PTS.,
   BACH, CARL PHILIPP EMANUEL
ESSAY ON THOROUGHBASS, AN --MUSICOLOGICAL STUDIES AND DOCUMENTS, NO.
   MUFFAT, GEORG
ESSENTIALS IN PIANOFORTE PLAYING, AND OTHER MUSICAL STUDIES...
   JOHNSTONE, J. ALFRED
ESSENTIALS OF PIANOFORTE PLAYING, THE
   JOHNS, CLAYTON
ETHICS AND ESTHETICS OF PIANO PLAYING
   STERNBERG, CONSTANTIN I. VON
ETHIER'S GREAT NON-SUCH SELF-INSTRUCTOR IN THE ART OF ACCOMPANYING BY
   ETHIER, JOSEPH A.
EUROPEAN AND AMERICAN MUSICAL INSTRUMENTS
   BAINES, ANTHONY
EVALUATION OF ELECTRONIC SELF-INSTRUCTION ON PIANO KEYBOARD, THE
   LUND, VICTOR E.
EVANGELISTIC PIANO PLAYING
   SCHULER, GEORGE S.
EVANS' GRADED STUDY GUIDE FOR THE PIANOFORTE AND DICTIONARY OF MUSICAL
   EVANS MUSIC COMPANY
EVERY MAN HIS OWN TUNER..AN EASY AND CERTAIN GUIDE TO TUNING THE GRAND,
   COOKE, JAMES FRANCIS
EVERY WOMAN HER OWN PIANO TUNER..OR, HINTS AND AIDS TO PIANO TUNING
   MARTIN, H. T.
EVOLUTION OF PIANO MUSIC, 1350-1700, THE
   SACHS, CURT
EVOLUTION OF THE PIANO, THE
   HENDERSON, WILLIAM JAMES
EVOLUTION OF THE PLAYER-PIANO MECHANISM---EXCERPT FROM 'PRESTO', VOL.
   MCTAMMANY, JOHN
EXAMINATION CANDIDATE'S GUIDE TO SCALE AND ARPEGGIO PLAYING, ETC., THE
   MANHIRE, WILSON
EXAMPLES OF ART WORKMANSHIP OF VARIOUS AGES AND COUNTRIES..MUSICAL
   VICTORIA AND ALBERT MUSEUM, SOUTH KENSINGTON
EXERCISES IN TIME AND RHYTHM..A CONTRIBUTION TO MODERN PIANO TEACHING
   HEPLER, EFFIE A.
EXPERT AID TO ARTISTIC PIANO PLAYING
   KUERSTEINER, JEAN PAUL
EXPLANATION AND DESCRIPTION OF THE ROYAL PATENT CHIROPLAST, OR
   LOGIER, JOHANN BERNHARD
EXPLORING KEYBOARD FUNDAMENTALS
   SHEFTEL, PAUL
EXPOSITION OF THE MUSICAL SYSTEM OF MR. LOGIER..WITH STRICTURES ON HIS
   LONDON--A COMMITTEE OF PROFESSORS

EXTEMPORE PLAYING..FORTY LESSONS IN THE ART OF KEYBOARD
    RICHARDSON, ALFRED M.
EXTEMPORIZATION FOR MUSIC STUDENTS
    HUNT, REGINALD H.
EXTEMPORIZATION
    SAWYER, FRANK J.
EXTEMPORIZING AT THE PIANO MADE EASY
    MELLING, E. H.
FACE TO FACE WITH GREAT MUSICIANS---CHOPIN AND LISZT
    ISAACSON, CHARLES D.
FAMILIAR INTRODUCTION TO THE FIRST PRINCIPLES OF MUSIC, A ...FOR THE
    ADAMS, JAMES B.
FAMOUS COMPOSERS--2 VOLS.---CHOPIN AND LISZT--1891+
    DOLE, NATHAN H.
FAMOUS MUSICIANS OF A WANDERING RACE
    SALESKI, GDAL
FAMOUS MUSICIANS OF JEWISH ORIGIN
    SALESKI, GDAL
FAMOUS PIANISTS FOR BOYS AND GIRLS
    BURCH, GLADYS
FAMOUS PIANISTS OF TODAY AND YESTERDAY
    LAHEE, HENRY C.
FASHIONABLE PRECEPTOR, FOR THE PIANO-FORTE AND HARPSICHORD, WHEREIN THE
    ANON
FERENCZ LISZT--HALF-TITLE..MASTERS OF MUSIC
    CORDER, FREDERICK
FERRUCCIO BUSONI..CHRONICLE OF A EUROPEAN---1967, IN GERMAN
    STUCKENSCHMIDT, HANS H.
FERRUCCIO BUSONI--LETTERS TO HIS WIFE---1895
    BUSONI, FERRUCCIO
FERRUCCIO BUSONI, A BIOGRAPHY
    DENT, EDWARD J.
FEW WORDS ABOUT MUSIC, CONTAINING HINTS TO AMATEUR PIANISTS, A
    HULLAH, M. E.
FEW WORDS ON PIANOFORTE PLAYING, A
    REINAGLE, CAROLINE
FIFTY YEARS EXPERIENCE OF PIANOFORTE TEACHING AND PLAYING
    BERINGER, OSCAR
FIFTY YEARS OF POPULAR PIANO TECHNIQUES IN THE U.S.A.
    STORMEN, WIN
FIGURED BASS ACCOMPANIMENT--2 VOLS.
    WILLIAMS, PETER F.
FIGURED HARMONY AT THE KEYBOARD---PRINCIPALLY EXERCISES
    MORRIS, REGINALD OWEN
FILLMORE'S LIST OF CAREFULLY SELECTED AND GRADED WORKS FOR THE
    FILLMORE, THOMAS H.
FINALE---MEMOIRS OF LAST SURVIVING PUPIL OF CLARA SCHUMANN
    DE LARA, ADELINA
FINGERING OF SCALES AND ARPEGGIOS, THE
    MCMILLAN, FIONA
FINGER AND WRIST GYMNASTICS--WITHOUT USE OF PIANO--FOR PIANO STUDENTS
    WOOD, CHARLES W.
FINGER EXERCISES FOR THE POCKET MUTANO
    WOODHOUSE, GEORGE
FIRST BOOK OF THE PLAYER-PIANIST, THE
    GREW, SIDNEY
FIRST COMPANION TO THE ROYAL PATENT CHIROPLAST OR HAND-DIRECTOR, THE
    LOGIER, JOHANN BERNHARD
FIRST LIGHTS ON PIANO-PLAYING
    MATTHAY, TOBIAS A.
FIRST MONTHS IN PIANOFORTE INSTRUCTION, THE ---1870, IN GERMAN
    PALME, RUDOLPH
FIRST PEDAL-STUDIES FOR THE PIANO, 24 PROGRESSIVE EXERCISES AND PIECES
    DILLER, ANGELA
FIRST PRINCIPLES OF PIANOFORTE PLAYING--EXTRACT FROM 'THE ACT OF
    MATTHAY, TOBIAS A.
FIRST SIX MONTHS IN THE PIANO CLASS, THE ..A MANUAL FOR TEACHERS
    AXTENS, FLORENCE
FIRST STEPS AT THE PIANOFORTE
    BERGER, FRANCESCO
FIRST STEPS IN CHORD PLAYING
    BLAKE, DOROTHY
FIRST STEPS IN EAR-TRAINING--FOR THE PIANO STUDENT
    HARRIS, CUTHBERT
FIRST STEPS IN HARMONIZING MELODIES
    GIBBS, GEORGE A., JR.
FIRST STEPS IN HARMONIZING MELODIES
    HOME, ETHEL
FIRST STEPS IN PIANO TUNING AND OTHER ESSAYS IN PIANOFORTE TECHNOLOGY
    NALDER, LAWRENCE MARCUS
FIRST STEPS IN THE USE OF THE PEDAL FOR PIANO
    BLAKE, DOROTHY
FIRST STEPS TO THE PIANOFORTE
    TAYLOR, GEORGE C.
FIRST STEPS TO THOROUGH BASE, IN 12 FAMILIAR LESSONS BETWEEN A TEACHER
    ANON
FIRST TEN LESSONS, THE ..A NEW APPROACH TO PIANO TEACHING
    GRINDEA, CAROLA
FIRST TEN PIANO LESSONS, LAID OUT FOR YOUNG TEACHERS, WITH CONSTRUCTIVE
    LOMAS, LULU GRAHAM
FIRST TWO YEARS OF PIANOFORTE STUDY, THE
    MACEWAN, DESIREE
FIRST YEAR ESSENTIALS IN KEYBOARD HARMONY
    ROBYN, LOUISE
FIVE CENTURIES OF KEYBOARD MUSIC..AN HISTORIC SURVEY FOR HARPSICHORD
    GILLESPIE, JOHN
FIVE GRAPHIC MUSIC ANALYSES---INCLUDES TWO CHOPIN ETUDES..OP. 10, NO. 8
    SCHENKER, HEINRICH
FIVE THOUSAND MUSICAL TERMS..A COMPLETE DICTIONARY WITH A TREATISE ON
    ADAMS, JOHN S.
FIVE YEAR GUIDE TO PIANO TEACHING, A
    O'TOOLE, WILLIAM
FLORESTAN..THE LIFE AND WORK OF ROBERT SCHUMANN---1945
    SCHAUFFLER, ROBERT HAVEN
FORBIDDEN CHILDHOOD
    SLENCZYNSKA, RUTH *
FOREARM ROTATION---A SEQUEL TO 'THE ROTARY ROAD'--15 PHOTOS AND 115
    CHING, JAMES
FOREARM ROTATION PRINCIPLE IN PIANOFORTE PLAYING, THE ..ITS APPLICATION
    MATTHAY, TOBIAS A.
FORMAL ANALYSIS OF THE SENIOR AND ADVANCED SENIOR PIANOFORTE PIECES OF
    LOVELOCK, WILLIAM
FORM AND ANALYSES OF MOZART'S PIANOFORTE SONATAS, THE
    STAINKAMPH, EILEEN
FORM AND ANALYSIS OF THE COMPLETE BEETHOVEN'S PIANOFORTE SONATAS
    STAINKAMPH, EILEEN
FORM AND PERFORMANCE
    STEIN, ERWIN
FORM IN PIANOFORTE MUSIC--FOR THEORETICAL AND PRACTICAL EXAMS
    LOWE, CLAUDE EDGERTON
FORM IN SELECTED TWENTIETH-CENTURY PIANO CONCERTOS
    HANSON, JOHN R.
FORTY-EIGHT, THE ..BACH'S WOHLTEMPERIRTES CLAVIER, FROM 'THE MUSICAL
    FULLER-MAITLAND, J. A.
FORTY-EIGHT PRELUDES AND FUGUES OF J. S. BACH, THE
    GRAY, CECIL

FORTY-EIGHT PRELUDES AND FUGUES OF JOHANN SEBASTIAN BACH ANALYZED FOR
    ILIFFE, FREDERICK
FORTY FAMOUS COMPOSERS---CHOPIN AND LISZT
    SCHNITTKIND, HENRY T. *
FOR ALL PIANO TEACHERS
    AHRENS, CORA B. *
FOUNDATIONS OF PIANOFORTE TECHNIC
    COVIELLO, AMBROSE
FOUNDATIONS OF PIANOFORTE TECHNIQUE
    TANKARD, GEOFFREY
FOUNDATION EXERCISES IN PIANO PLAYING FROM FIRST RUDIMENTS TO HIGHEST
    VIRGIL, ALMON K.
FOUNDATION OF PIANO TECHNIC, THE
    SPENCER, ALLEN
FOUR FAMOUS PIANOFORTE SONATAS OF BEETHOVEN, THE --OP. 13, OP. 27, NO.
    KELBERINE, ALEXANDER
FOUR HANDS--ONE PIANO..A LIST OF WORKS FOR DUET PLAYERS--A GUIDE TO
    ROWLEY, ALEC
FOUR HUNDRED OF THE BEST ADS OF 1911 DEVOTED TO PIANOS AND
    PLAYER-PIANO, THE
FRANCOIS COUPERIN AND THE FRENCH CLASSICAL TRADITION
    MELLERS, WILFRED
FRANCOIS LISZT..RECOLLECTIONS OF A COMPATRIOT
    WOHL, JANKA
FRANZ HUENTEN'S CELEBRATED INSTRUCTIONS FOR THE PIANOFORTE--2ND.
    HUENTEN, FRANZ
FRANZ LISZT..A BIOGRAPHY IN PICTURES---240 PICTORIAL ENTRIES
    LASZLO, SZIGMOND *
FRANZ LISZT..A SKETCH OF HIS LIFE AND PERSONALITY
    MARTIN, THOMAS CARLAW
FRANZ LISZT..EINE HULDIGUNG--FRANZ LISZT..A TRIBUTE
    LESSMANN, W. J. OTTO
FRANZ LISZT, ARTIST AND MAN--2 VOLS.---ONLY VOL. 1, 1811-1840,
    RAMANN, LINA
FRANZ LISZT, THE MAN AND HIS MUSIC---ESSAYS BY SACHEVERALL SITWELL AND
    WALKER, ALAN--EDITOR
FRANZ LISZT, THE MAN OF LOVE
    POURTALES, GUY DE
FRANZ LISZT, THE STORY OF HIS LIFE--TO WHICH IS ADDED..'LISZT AS A
    BEAUFORT, RAPHAEL
FRANZ LISZT AND HIS MUSIC
    HERVEY, ARTHUR
FRANZ LISZT
    HUNEKER, JAMES GIBBONS
FRANZ LISZT
    ROUSSELOT, JEAN
FRANZ LISZT
    SEROFF, VICTOR
FREAK PIANOS---SCRAPBOOK
    VAN NOORDEN, C.
FREDERICK CHOPIN..A MEMOIR
    DAVISON, JAMES W.
FREDERICK CHOPIN AS A MAN AND MUSICIAN--2 VOLS.---1888
    NIECKS, FREDERICK
FREDERIC CHOPIN..HIS LIFE, LETTERS AND WORKS--3RD. REV. ED.---1879
    KARASOWSKI, MORITZ
FREDERIC CHOPIN---FOR YOUNGER READERS
    MAUROIS, ANDRE
FREDERIC CHOPIN--'GREAT ANNIVERSARIES' SERIES
    MANUEL, ROLAND
FREDERIC CHOPIN--A BIOGRAPHICAL AND CRITICAL NOTICE---1852
    LISZT, FRANZ
FREDERIC CHOPIN--CENTENNIAL 1849-1949, BACKGROUND MATERIAL---ELEVEN
    POLISH RESEARCH AND INFORMATION SERVICE
FREDERIC CHOPIN--NOVELLO'S BIOGRAPHY PRIMERS
    BENNETT, JOSEPH
FREDERIC CHOPIN--SYMPHONIA BOOKS..'HISTORY OF MUSIC' SERIES
    SCHALLENBERG, EVERT W.
FREDERIC CHOPIN, SON OF POLAND, EARLY YEARS--2 VOLS.---YOUNGER READERS
    WHEELER, OPAL
FREDERIC CHOPIN, 1810-1849
    MIZWA, STEPHEN P.--EDITOR
FREDERIC CHOPIN CENTENNIAL--1949---EIGHT ARTICLES
    POLISH RESEARCH AND INFORMATION SERVICE
FREDERIC CHOPIN INTERNATIONAL COMPETITIONS IN POLAND
    FREDERIC CHOPIN INTERNATIONAL COMPETITION--FIFTH
FREDERIC CHOPIN INTERNATIONAL PIANO COMPETITIONS, THE
    PROSNAK, JAN
FREDERIC CHOPIN
    SEROFF, VICTOR
FREDERIC FRANCOIS CHOPIN..CRITICAL AND APPRECIATIVE ESSAY---1843
    DAVISON, JAMES W.
FREDERIC FRANCOIS CHOPIN
    WILLEBY, CHARLES
FREE ARTIST..THE STORY OF ANTON AND NICHOLAS RUBINSTEIN
    BOWEN, CATHERINE DRINKER
FREE WILL OR DESTINY..ONE ACT PLAY AROUND CHOPIN---EARLY SUMMER, 1836
    KNOLLER, JACOB
FRENCH MUSIC IN THE NINETEENTH CENTURY---CHOPIN
    HERVEY, ARTHUR
FRENCH PIANO MUSIC..A SURVEY WITH NOTES ON ITS PERFORMANCE
    DEMUTH, NORMAN
FRENCH PIANO MUSIC
    CORTOT, ALFRED
FRIEDMAN--'LITTLE BIOGRAPHIES'
    HUMISTON, WILLIAM H.
FROM BRAIN TO KEYBOARD..A SYSTEM OF HAND AND FINGER CONTROL FOR
    SMITH, MACDONALD
FROM KEYBOARD TO MUSIC
    WOODHOUSE, GEORGE
FROM PIANO TO FORTE..A THOUSAND AND ONE NOTES---AUTOBIOGRAPHY
    HAMBOURG, MARK
FROM PIANO TUNER TO PLAYER EXPERT
    DRAKE, HARRY
FROM THESE COMES MUSIC
    STODDARD, HOPE
FROM THE TONE WORLD--ESSAYS---TAUSIG, CHOPIN AND LISZT--2ND. ED.---1884
    EHLERT, LOUIS
FUGUE IN BEETHOVEN'S PIANO MUSIC, THE
    COCKSHOOT, JOHN V.
FUNCTIONAL PIANO FOR THE TEACHER
    LEACH, JOHN R.
FUNDAMENTAL PRINCIPLES INVOLVED IN THE COMPOSING AND ARRANGING OF MUSIC
    SCHAAF, EDWARD O.
FUN WITH FINGERING, A FIRST-OF-ALL BOOK ON EASY FINGERING AND CORRECT
    TOBIN, JOSEPH RAYMOND
FUTURE OF PIANO STUDY, THE ---FROM 'M.T.N.A. PROCEEDINGS', SERIES 26
    HAMILTON, CLARENCE G.
GABRIEL FAURE
    VUILLERMOZ, EMILE
GABRILOWITSCH--ROBINSON LOCKE SCRAP BOOKS--2 VOLS.
    LOCKE, ROBINSON
GALLEY SLAVES OF LOVE, THE ..THE STORY OF MARIE D'AGOULT AND FRANZ
    HALDANE, CHARLOTTE
GAMUT AND COMMON CHORD IN ALL KEYS, FINGERED FOR THE HARPSICHORD, THE
    BEMETZRIEDER, ANTON

GARDEN IN POLAND, A ...ON CHOPIN'S BIRTHPLACE AND BURIAL
    KIRKWOOD, KENNETH P.
GEIB'S PIANO-FORTE PRECEPTOR, AND MUSICAL GRAMMAR...A TREATISE ON
    GEIB, WILLIAM
GENERAL OBSERVATIONS ON MUSIC AND REMARKS ON MR. LOGIER'S SYSTEM OF
    ANON
GENERAL OBSERVATIONS UPON MUSIC AND REMARKS ON MR. LOGIER'S SYSTEM OF
    GRAHAM, GEORGE FARQUHAR
GEORGE GERSHWIN, MASTER COMPOSER·
    ALTMAN, FRANCES
GHOST NOTE PATTERN BUILDERS FOR VISUALIZING THE STRUCTURE OF SCALES,
    UNDERWOOD, REX
GIANTS OF THE KEYBOARD
    CHAPIN, VICTOR
GIDDING'S PUBLIC SCHOOL CLASS METHOD FOR THE PIANO
    GIDDINGS, THADDEUS P.
GIRLHOOD OF CLARA SCHUMANN, THE ..CLARA WIECK AND HER TIME
    MAY, FLORENCE
GIVING OF HIGH SCHOOL CREDITS FOR PRIVATE MUSIC STUDY, THE ..A
    NATIONAL BUREAU FOR THE ADVANCEMENT OF MUSIC
GOLDEN MONITOR, FOR THE PIANOFORTE AND CABINET ORGAN, DESIGNED AS A
    WRIGHT, WILLIAM C.
GOOD MUSIC EXPLAINED..WHAT ALL GOOD PIANISTS SHOULD KNOW
    ANDERSON, J. CLARK
GORDON'S NEW SCHOOL FOR THE PIANO-FORTE
    GORDON, STEPHEN T.
GOSPEL SONG ACCOMPANIMENT..THE ROBERT HARKNESS METHOD FOR PIANO AND
    HARKNESS, ROBERT
GOSPEL SONG PIANO ACCOMPANIMENT..THE ROBERT HARKNESS
    HARKNESS, ROBERT
GOVERNESS'S MUSICAL ASSISTANT, CONTAINING ALL THAT IS TRULY USEFUL TO
    COGGINS, JOSEPH
GRADED LIST OF SOME USEFUL WORKS FOR PIANO STUDY---REVISED BY CARLOTTA
    PEABODY INSTITUTE, BALTIMORE
GRADED TESTS IN PRACTICAL MUSICIANSHIP AND MUSICAL INITIATIVE--IN THREE
    ROWLEY, ALEC *
GREATER REWARDS THROUGH CREATIVE PIANO TEACHING
    NATIONAL PIANO FOUNDATION
GREAT COMPOSERS, 1300-1900..A BIOGRAPHICAL AND CRITICAL GUIDE
    EWEN, DAVID
GREAT COMPOSERS THROUGH THE EYES OF THEIR CONTEMPORARIES---CHOPIN AND
    ZOFF, OTTO--EDITOR
GREAT HARMONIC LAW OF CHORD PROGRESSION AND IMPROVISING, THE
    MOKREJS, JOHN
GREAT IN MUSIC, THE ..A SYSTEMATIC COURSE OF STUDY IN THE MUSIC OF
    MATHEWS, WILLIAM S. B.
GREAT MASTERS OF PIANO MUSIC, THE ..BACH, BEETHOVEN, SCHUMANN, CHOPIN,
    HUTCHESON, ERNEST
GREAT MEN AND FAMOUS MUSICIANS ON THE ART OF MUSIC
    COOKE, JAMES FRANCIS
GREAT MUSICAL COMPOSERS..GERMAN, FRENCH, AND ITALIAN
    FERRIS, GEORGE TITUS
GREAT MUSICIANS AS CHILDREN
    SCHWIMMER, FRANCISKA
GREAT PIANISTS, THE
    SCHONBERG, HAROLD
GREAT PIANISTS AND COMPOSERS
    GABRIEL, GILBERT W.
GREAT PIANISTS OF OUR TIME
    KAISER, JOACHIM
GREAT PIANISTS ON PIANO PLAYING..STUDY TALKS WITH FOREMOST
    COOKE, JAMES FRANCIS
GREAT PIANO VIRTUOSOS OF OUR TIME, FROM PERSONAL ACQUAINTANCE, THE
    LENZ, WILHELM VON
GREAT TEACHERS, PORTRAYED BY THOSE WHO STUDIED UNDER THEM--INCLUDES 'A
    PETERSON, HOUSTON--EDITOR
GREAT VIOLINISTS AND PIANISTS, THE ---1881
    FERRIS, GEORGE TITUS
GROUNDWORK OF THE LESCHETIZKY METHOD, THE ---1902
    BREE, MADAME MALWINE
GROUPING, ARTICULATING AND PHRASING IN MUSICAL INTERPRETATION..A
    CARPE, ADOLPH
GROUP ACTIVITIES AT THE KEYBOARD
    DAVIS, MARILYN K.
GROUP PIANO TEACHING
    MEHR, NORMAN
GROWTH OF INSTRUMENTS AND INSTRUMENTAL MUSIC, THE
    PAETKAU, DAVID H.
GUIDA ARMONICA, A DIZIONARIO ARMONICO..BEING A SURE GUIDE TO HARMONY
    GEMINIANI, FRANCESCO
GUIDA ARMONICA, IN WHICH...CHORDS, ARE CLEARLY EXPLAINED AND
    JOUSSE, JOHN
GUIDA DI MUSICA..BEING A COMPLETE BOOK OF INSTRUCTIONS FOR BEGINNERS ON
    HOOK, JAMES
GUIDA DI MUSICA..SECOND PART, CONSISTING OF SEVERAL HUNDRED
    HOOK, JAMES
GUIDEBOOK OF AUTOMATIC MUSICAL INSTRUMENTS, A. --2 VOLS.
    BOWERS, Q. DAVID
GUIDE FOR CONDUCTING PIANO CLASSES IN THE SCHOOLS, A
    NATIONAL BUREAU FOR THE ADVANCEMENT OF MUSIC
GUIDE TO INSTRUCTION ON THE PIANOFORTE, A --IN A SERIES OF SHORT ESSAYS
    NIXON, W.
GUIDE TO MEMORIZING MUSIC, A
    GOODRICH, ALFRED JOHN
GUIDE TO MUSICAL ACOUSTICS, A ---1956
    LOWERY, HARRY
GUIDE TO PIANO STUDY FOR CLASS OR INDIVIDUAL INSTRUCTION, A
    PERRY, ADELAIDE TROWBRIDGE *
GUIDE TO PRACTICAL MUSICIANSHIP--INTENDED TO SUPERCEDE ROTE
    GOODRICH, ALFRED JOHN
GUIDE TO PRACTICE ON THE PIANOFORTE
    BURROWES, JOHN FRECKLETON
GUIDE TO REMEDIAL SIGHT READING FOR THE PIANO STUDENT, A
    LAWRENCE, SIDNEY
GUIDE TO RESTRINGING, A
    TRAVIS, JOHN W.
GUIDE TO TEACHING PIANO--REV. ED.---1958
    ARIZONA STATE MUSIC TEACHERS ASSOCIATION
GUIDE TO THE A.R.C.M. AND OTHER EXAMINATIONS IN PIANOFORTE-TEACHING
    MANHIRE, WILSON
GUIDE TO THE A.R.C.M. AND OTHER EXAMINATIONS IN THE ART OF PIANOFORTE
    FILLINGHAM, ARTHUR H.
GUIDE TO THE BEST IN CONTEMPORARY PIANO MUSIC..AN ANNOTATED LIST OF
    BUTLER, STANLEY
GUIDE TO THE LOAN COLLECTION--OF THE INTERNATIONAL INVENTIONS
    HIPKINS, ALFRED JAMES
GUIDE TO THE MIKROKOSMOS OF BELA BARTOK, A --PUBLISHED THESIS---1956
    SUCHOFF, B.
GUIDE TO THE MODERN PIANIST, A
    POINTER SYSTEM, INC.
GUIDE TO THE MUSICAL TUITION OF VERY YOUNG CHILDREN, BY AN OLD LADY
    ANON
GUIDE TO THE NEW WAY TO PIANO TECHNIQUE, A
    WOODHOUSE, GEORGE
GUIDE TO THE PIANIST'S REPERTOIRE
    HINSON, MAURICE

GUIDE TO THE PROPER USE OF THE PIANOFORTE PEDALS, WITH EXAMPLES OUT OF
    ANON
GUIDE TO YOUNG PIANOFORTE TEACHERS AND STUDENTS
    PHILLIPSON, WENTWORTH
GUILD SYLLABUS, THE ..STREAMLINED EDITION
    NATIONAL GUILD OF PIANO TEACHERS
GULBRANSEN SERVICE MANUAL---PLAYER PIANO
    GULBRANSEN-DICKINSON COMPANY
GYMNASTICS FOR THE FINGERS AND WRIST
    JACKSON, EDWIN WARD
HABIT IN PIANOFORTE PLAYING--ANALYTICAL STUDY OF CONTROL OF MOVEMENT
    HOFFMAN, CARL
HALF-HOUR LESSONS IN MUSIC..CLASS WORK FOR BEGINNERS AT THE PIANO
    KOTZSCHMAR, MARY ANN
HALF A CENTURY OF MUSIC IN ENGLAND, 1837-1887..LISZT IN ENGLAND
    HUEFFER, FRANCIS
HAMILTON'S PRACTICAL INTRODUCTION TO THE ART OF TUNING THE PIANOFORTE
    HAMILTON, JAMES ALEXANDER
HANDBOOK FOR MUSIC TEACHERS--2 VOLS.
    RAINBOW, BERNARR J. G.--EDITOR
HANDBOOK FOR PIANO TEACHERS..COLLECTED ARTICLES ON SUBJECTS RELATED TO
    SUMMY-BIRCHARD COMPANY
HANDBOOK FOR TEACHING PIANO CLASSES
    BURROWS, RAYMOND
HANDBOOK FOR TEACHING PIANO CLASSES
    MUSIC EDUCATORS NATIONAL CONFERENCE
HANDBOOK FOR THE CHURCH PIANIST, A
    AULD, WILDA J.
HANDBOOK OF CHORD PROGRESSIONS
    SCOTT, WAYNE
HANDBOOK OF MUSICAL FORM--PART 2 OF THE PIANIST'S HANDBOOK
    PETERSON, FRANKLIN
HANDBOOK OF PIANO PLAYING, A
    HOPE, ERIC
HANDBOOK OF THE COLLECTION OF MUSICAL INSTRUMENTS IN THE UNITED STATES
    DENSMORE, FRANCES
HANDBOOK ON THE ART OF TEACHING AS APPLIED TO MUSIC..FOR THE USE OF
    WARRINER, JOHN
HANDBOOK TO CHOPIN'S WORKS, A
    JONSON, GEORGE CHARLES
HANDBOOK TO THE MUSEUM'S COLLECTION, BY JEAN L. JENKINS--2ND.
    HORNIMAN MUSEUM AND LIBRARY, LONDON
HANDBOOK TO THE PERFORMANCE OF THE 48 PRELUDES AND FUGUES OF J. S. BACH
    ROTHSCHILD, FRITZ
HANDBOOK TO THE PIANOFORTE WORKS OF JOHANNES BRAHMS---1936
    EVANS, EDWIN
HANDBOOK TO THE PIANO WORKS OF SCRIABIN
    MONTAGU-NATHAN, M.
HAND BUILDING AND HAND STRETCHING EXERCISES
    ROBYN, LOUISE
HAND CULTURE FOR PIANISTS, VIOLINISTS AND 'CELLISTS--FINGER, HAND AND
    RENNIE, BLANCHE H.
HAND GYMNASTICS, FOR THE SCIENTIFIC DEVELOPMENT OF THE MUSCLES USED IN
    PRENTICE THOMAS RIDLEY
HANS VON BUELOW..A BIOGRAPHICAL SKETCH..HIS VISIT TO AMERICA
    BUELOW, HANS GUIDO VON
HAPPY PIANIST, THE
    GRUNDY, ENID
HARKNESS PIANO METHOD OF EVANGELISTIC HYMN PLAYING, THE ..A HOME-STUDY
    HARKNESS, ROBERT
HARMONIC EXERCISES AT THE PIANOFORTE FOR BEGINNERS AND ADVANCED PUPILS
    BUSSLER, LUDWIG
HARMONIZATION-TRANSPOSITION AT THE KEYBOARD
    KERN, ALICE M.
HARMONIZATION AT THE KEYBOARD
    PROCTOR, CHARLES
HARMONIZATION AT THE PIANO--IN THREE STAGES
    ROWLEY, ALEC *
HARMONIZATION AT THE PIANO--2ND. ED.---1962
    FRACKENPOHL, ARTHUR
HARMONIZATION OF MELODIES AT THE KEYBOARD--BKS. 1 AND 2
    PILLING, DOROTHY
HARMONIZING..HOW TO PLAY SIMPLE ACCOMPANIMENTS TO A MELODY AT THE
    SHEPARD, ROBERT
HARMONIZING 'BACH' CHORALES
    BOYD, MALCOLM
HARMONIZING MELODIES AT SIGHT
    GIBBS, GEORGE A., JR.
HARMONIZING OF MELODIES, THE ..A TEXT-BOOK FOR STUDENTS AND TEACHERS
    BANISTER, HENRY C.
HARMONY--FIRST METHOD FOR THE PIANO...FOR CHILD AND ADULT BEGINNERS,
    DARDENELLE, LOUISE
HARMONY, ANALYTICAL AND APPLIED
    LEIGHTON, GEORGE A.
HARMONY, COUNTERPOINT AND IMPROVISATION
    DALE, BENJAMIN J.
HARMONY AND EAR TRAINING AT THE KEYBOARD
    SHUMWAY, STANLEY
HARMONY AND STYLE--3 VOLS.
    LONG, NOEL
HARMONY AND THOROUGH BASS--2 VOLS., 1909-1910
    VAN DER VELPEN, JEAN
HARMONY AT THE KEYBOARD
    HILL, FRANK W.
HARMONY AT THE KEYBOARD
    HUNT, REGINALD H.
HARMONY AT THE KEYBOARD
    LANG, CRAIG SELLAR
HARMONY AT THE KEYBOARD
    NEVINS, WILLARD I. *
HARMONY AT THE PIANO LESSON, A COMPANION TO PIANO STUDY
    APPEL, PEARL *
HARMONY AT YOUR KEYBOARD
    HOLT, HILDA
HARMONY EPITOMIZED, BEING A SHORT EXPLANATION OF FIGURED BASSES,
    WEBBE, SAMUEL
HARMONY FOR EAR, EYE, AND KEYBOARD--1ST. YEAR
    HEACOX, ARTHUR EDWARD
HARMONY IN PIANOFORTE-STUDY..FOR THE INDIVIDUAL STUDENT--2 VOLS.,
    FOWLES, ERNEST
HARMONY STUDY AT THE PIANO
    GRIMM, CARL W.
HAROLD BAUER, HIS BOOK---1948
    BAUER, HAROLD
HARPSICHORD, THE ..AN INTRODUCTION TO TECHNIQUE, STYLE AND THE
    HARICH-SCHNEIDER, ETA
HARPSICHORDS AND CLAVICHORDS
    HOOVER, CYNTHIA A.
HARPSICHORD AND THE CLAVICHORD, THE --2ND. ED., REVISED BY HOWARD
    RUSSELL, RAYMOND
HARPSICHORD ILLUSTRATED AND IMPROV'D, WHEREIN IS SHEWN THE ITALIAN
    PRELLEUR, PETER
HARPSICHORD MANUAL..A HISTORY AND TECHNICAL DEVELOPMENT--2ND.
    NEUPERT, HANNS
HARPSICHORD MUSIC..THE INSTRUMENTS, THE COMPOSERS, THE PLAYERS
    KENYON, MAX

HARPSICHORD MUSIC OF DOMENICO SCARLATTI, THE
　BOGIANCKINO, MASSIMO
HARPSICHORD OR SPINNET MISCELLANY, THE --KEYBOARD TUTOR---FACSIMILE
　BREMNER, ROBERT
HARPSICHORD REGULATING AND REPAIRING
　HUBBARD, FRANK
HEINE IN ART AND LETTERS---CHOPIN AND LISZT--1837
　HEINE, HEINRICH
HELEN HOPEKIRK, 1856-1945
　HALL, CONSTANCE HUNTINGTON
HELLO TO THE BLUES..FUN WITH CHORDS..FUN AND INFORMATION ON PLAYING THE
　GRANTHAM, BILLY
HELPS TO TEACHER AND STUDENT ON THE FAELTEN SYSTEM
　JOHNSON, SARAH S.
HERITAGE OF MUSIC, THE --SECOND SERIES OF ESSAYS---CHOPIN AND LISZT
　FOSS, HUBERT J.--EDITOR
HINTS FOR PIANOFORTE PRACTICE--A SUGGESTED PLAN FOR DAILY STUDY---1916
　FRYER, HERBERT
HINTS FOR PIANO NORMAL STUDIES
　BRECKENRIDGE, WILLIAM KILGORE
HINTS TO CANDIDATES FOR THE L.R.A.M. ASSOCIATED BOARD AND OTHER
　MANHIRE, WILSON
HINTS TO YOUNG TEACHERS OF THE PIANOFORTE
　WEST, GEORGE FREDERICK
HISTORICAL MUSICAL EXHIBITION..CATALOGUE OF THE EXHIBITION,
　CHICKERING AND SONS
HISTORICAL PIANOS, HARPSICHORDS AND CLAVICHORDS---1963
　MICHEL, NORMAN ELWOOD
HISTORY OF KEYBOARD MUSIC TO 1700, THE --TRANSLATED AND REVISED BY HANS
　APEL, WILLI
HISTORY OF MUSICAL INSTRUMENTS, THE
　SACHS, CURT
HISTORY OF MUSIC IN PERFORMANCE, THE ---1942
　DORIAN, FREDERICK
HISTORY OF MUSIC IN PICTURES, A
　KINSKY, GEORG--EDITOR
HISTORY OF PIANOFORTE-PLAYING AND PIANOFORTE-LITERATURE, A ---1879, IN
　WEITZMANN, CARL F.
HISTORY OF PIANOFORTE MUSIC, THE ---1924
　WESTERBY, HERBERT
HISTORY OF THE AMERICAN PIANOFORTE..ITS TECHNICAL DEVELOPMENT, AND THE
　SPILLANE, DANIEL
HISTORY OF THE PIANOFORTE, THE ..WITH AN AN ACCOUNT OF THE THEORY OF
　BRINSMEAD, E.
HISTORY OF THE PIANOFORTE, THE --REPRINT
　HIPKINS, ALFRED JAMES
HISTORY OF THE PIANOFORTE AND PIANOFORTE PLAYERS, A ---1899
　BIE, OSKAR
HISTORY OF THE PIANOFORTE
　WESTERBY, HERBERT
HISTORY OF THE PIANO
　CLOSSON, ERNEST
HISTORY OF THE PLAYER-PIANO, THE
　MCTAMMANY, JOHN
HISTORY OF THE THERAPY OF TUBERCULOSIS, AND THE CASE OF FREDERIC
　LONG, ESMOND R.--PATHOLOGIST
HOFMANN--ROBINSON LOCKE SCRAP BOOKS
　LOCKE, ROBINSON
HOMAGE TO CHOPIN---TEXT IN POLISH AND ENGLISH
　TARCZYNSKI-ALF, TADEUSZ
HOME HELP IN MUSIC STUDY
　BROWER, HARRIETTE
HOME MUSIC LESSONS..HOW TO FIND YOUR MUSICAL SELF
　SEYMOUR, HARRIET AYER
HOME STUDY CORRESPONDENCE COURSE IN EVANGELISTIC HYMN PLAYING, FOR
　HARKNESS, ROBERT
HOW AND WHAT TO PLAY FOR MOVING PICTURES..A MANUAL AND GUIDE FOR
　TRUE, LYLE C.
HOW A DEPENDABLE PIANO TECHNIQUE WAS WON
　BROWER, HARRIETTE
HOW CHOPIN PLAYED..FROM CONTEMPORARY IMPRESSIONS COLLECTED FROM THE
　HIPKINS, ALFRED JAMES
HOW HAS THE PIANOFORTE AS AN INSTRUMENT DEVELOPED SINCE
　MASON, HENRY LOWELL
HOW OUGHT ONE TO STUDY PIANO-TECHNIC---1881, IN GERMAN
　GERMER, HEINRICH
HOW PEOPLE MAKE MONEY IN MUSIC
　SHINN, DUANE
HOW THE PIANO CAME TO BE
　GLOVER, ELLYE HOWELL
HOW TO ACCOMPANY..A GUIDE TO THE ARTISTIC ACCOMPANIMENT OF ANY MUSICAL
　GLEN, ANNIE
HOW TO ACCOMPANY AT THE PIANO
　EVANS, EDWIN
HOW TO BUILD A BAROQUE CONCERT HARPSICHORD
　SCHULZE, RICHARD ALLEN
HOW TO CHANGE PITCH OF PIANOS, IN FOUR LESSONS
　MAITLAND, GEORGE L.
HOW TO CHOOSE AN INSTRUMENT..PIANO AND STRINGS
　HARRIS, REGINALD
HOW TO EXTEMPORIZE PIANO ACCOMPANIMENTS...RAPID AND SIMPLE METHOD OF
　MARSDEN AND COMPANY
HOW TO HARMONIZE MELODIES, WITH HINTS ON WRITING FOR STRINGS AND
　BRIDGER, JOHN HENRY
HOW TO HELP YOUR CHILD WITH MUSIC--2ND. ED.---1951
　WILSON, MORRIS E.
HOW TO IMPROVISE PIANO ACCOMPANIMENTS
　TOBIN, JOSEPH RAYMOND
HOW TO INTERPRET MENDELSSOHN'S SONGS WITHOUT WORDS
　WILKINSON, CHARLES W.
HOW TO LEARN THE PIANOFORTE
　AGUILAR, EMANUEL
HOW TO LEARN TO PLAY THE PIANO WELL, BY ONE WHO HAS TAUGHT HIMSELF
　ANON
HOW TO LEARN TO PLAY THE PIANO WELL
　SMITH, THOMAS
HOW TO MEMORIZE MUSIC
　COOKE, JAMES FRANCIS
HOW TO MEMORIZE MUSIC
　KENYON, CHARLES FREDERICK
HOW TO MODULATE..MODULATING FROM ANY KEY TO ANY OTHER
　SHEPARD, FRANK H.
HOW TO PASS MUSIC EXAMINATIONS--PIANO--A GUIDE FOR TEACHERS AND
　STEWART, REID
HOW TO PLAY AND TEACH DEBUSSY
　DUMESNIL, MAURICE
HOW TO PLAY BACH'S 48 PRELUDES AND FUGUES
　WILKINSON, CHARLES W.
HOW TO PLAY BY EAR
　WILSON, MORRIS E.
HOW TO PLAY BY THE JACQUES FRAY SPEED METHOD
　FRAY, JACQUES *
HOW TO PLAY CHOPIN--THREE LECTURES
　KLECZYNSKI, JAN
HOW TO PLAY FROM SCORE...ON THE ORGAN OR PIANOFORTE
　FETIS, FRANCOIS JOSEPH

HOW TO PLAY THE PIANO--NEW AND ENLARGED EDITION OF 'HOW TO BECOME A
　HAMBOURG, MARK
HOW TO PLAY THE PIANOFORTE
　BENEDICT, LADY *
HOW TO PLAY THE PIANO AND ORGAN..OR, KEY TO THE SCIENCE AND THEORY OF
　STEVENS, A. M.
HOW TO PLAY THE PIANO BY EAR..THE QUICK, EASY, SIMPLE WAY
　LE ROY, PERRY J.
HOW TO PLAY THE PIANO IN ONE HOUR WITHOUT A TEACHER
　LOYNES, W. H.
HOW TO PLAY THE PLAYER
　ALBIG, GEORGE L.
HOW TO PLAY 110 FAVOURITE PIANO SOLOS
　WILKINSON, CHARLES W.
HOW TO PRACTICE..OR HINTS TO PIANO-FORTE STUDENTS ON THE METHOD OF
　PUPIN, ANNIE
HOW TO PRACTICE ON THE PIANO..REFLECTIONS AND SUGGESTIONS
　EHRLICH, ALFRED HEINRICH
HOW TO PRACTICE THE PIANOFORTE..SPECULATIONS AND ADVICE
　EHRLICH, ALFRED HEINRICH
HOW TO PRACTICE
　BOLTON, HETTY
HOW TO PREPARE FOR PIANOFORTE...SUGGESTIONS FOR A.M.E.B.
　COOKE, MAX
HOW TO PREPARE FOR PLAYING IN CONCERT
　HAMBOURG, MARK
HOW TO READ A SCORE
　JACOB, GORDON P.
HOW TO READ KEYBOARD MUSIC
　SAULS, RANDY
HOW TO READ MUSIC..A COMPLETELY NEW AND SIMPLIFIED APPROACH TO READING
　KANZELL, MAXWELL
HOW TO SELECT A GOOD PIANO
　WAGNER, CHARLES A.
HOW TO STUDY MUSIC AND LEARN TO PLAY PIANO OR ORGAN
　QUINN, MARCUS LUCIUS
HOW TO STUDY THE PIANOFORTE WORKS OF THE GREAT COMPOSERS
　WESTERBY, HERBERT
HOW TO TEACH MUSIC TO BEGINNERS
　NEWMAN, ELIZABETH
HOW TO TEACH PIANO SUCCESSFULLY
　BASTIEN, JAMES W.
HOW TO TEACH PIANO TO THE CHILD BEGINNER..A TEXT BOOK FOR TEACHERS AND
　ROBYN, LOUISE
HOW TO TEST AND REGULATE THE AUTO DE LUXE WELTE-MIGNON REPRODUCING
　WELTE-MIGNON CORPORATION
HOW TO TEST AND REGULATE THE WELTE-MIGNON REPRODUCING PIANO
　AUTO PNEUMATIC ACTION COMPANY
HOW TO THINK MUSIC
　SEYMOUR, HARRIET AYER
HOW TO TUNE A PIANO..HOW TO BUY A USED PIANO..HOW TO KEEP YOUR PIANO IN
　WOODMAN, HENRY STAUNTON
HOW TO TUNE YOUR OWN PIANOFORTE..OR, THE WAY TO KEEP YOUR PIANOFORTE IN
　ANON
HOW TO TUNE YOUR OWN PIANO
　BLYTHER, JAMES H.
HOW TO TUNE YOUR OWN PIANO
　SMITH, THOMAS
HOW TO USE A PLAYER-PIANO
　ELLINGHAM, HARRY
HOW TO USE THE PEDAL IN PIANO PLAYING
　JOHNSTONE, J. ALFRED
HOW TO VAMP..A PRACTICAL GUIDE TO THE ACCOMPANIMENT OF SONGS BY THE
　ROWBOTHAM, JOHN F.
HOW TO VAMP AT SIGHT..THE EASIEST AND CLEAREST METHOD OF ACCOMPANYING
　MEHER, DONOVAN
HOW TO WRITE AN ACCOMPANIMENT..HELPS AND HINTS FOR STUDENTS AND YOUNG
　HERBERT, JOHN BUNYAN
HUMANISTIC STUDIES IN HONOR OF JOHN CALVIN METCALF---INCLUDES 'THOMAS
　ANON
HUMAN HAND, THE ..ITS CONSTRUCTION, MUSCLES, NERVES AND TENDONS IN
　LEFRANK, E.
HUNTEN'S CELEBRATED PIANOFORTE SCHOOL
　HUNTEN, WILLIAM
IDEAS FOR YOUNG PIANO TEACHERS
　BOSWORTH, HARRIETTE DEXTER
IDIOMATIC COURSE OF PIANO INSTRUCTION FOR CLASS WORK
　JEWETT, ALBERT DEWEY
IGNACE JAN PADEREWSKI
　BAUGHAN, EDWARD ALGERNON
IGNACE JAN PADEREWSKI
　COOKE, JAMES FRANCIS
IGNACE PADEREWSKI, MUSICIAN AND STATESMAN
　LANDAU, ROM
IGNACY JAN PADEREWSKI, 1860-1941..MEMORIAL ALBUM---IN ENGLISH AND
　PADEREWSKI FOUNDATION
ILLUSTRATED CATALOG...GRAND AND UPRIGHT PIANOS
　STECK AND COMPANY
ILLUSTRATED CATALOGUE OF--STEINWAY AND SONS...PIANOFORTES
　STEINWAY AND SONS
ILLUSTRATED CATALOGUE OF PIANOS
　STEINWAY AND SONS
ILLUSTRATED CATALOGUE OF PIANO FORTES
　CHICKERING AND SONS
ILLUSTRATED CATALOGUE OF STEINWAY AND SONS' PIANOS
　STEINWAY AND SONS
ILLUSTRATED CIRCULAR AND CATALOGUE OF PIANOFORTES--MANUFACTURERS OF
　STEINWAY AND SONS
IMAGINARY INTERVIEWS WITH GREAT COMPOSERS..A SERIES OF VIVID PEN
　KENYON, CHARLES FREDERICK
IMMORTAL FRANZ..THE LIFE AND LOVES OF A GENIUS---FRANZ LISZT
　HARSANYI, ZSOLT
IMMORTAL PIANO, THE
　CARMI, AVNER *
IMPROVED METHOD IN PIANO TEACHING, AND RECENT IDEAS OF LEADING AMERICAN
　BROTHERHOOD, JAMES
IMPROVISATION IN MUSIC..WAYS TOWARDS CAPTURING MUSICAL IDEAS AND
　WOLLNER, GERTRUDE PRICE
IMPROVISATION IN NINE CENTURIES OF WESTERN MUSIC
　FERAND, ERNEST T.
IMPROVISING..A SIMPLE METHOD OF TEACHING THE SUBJECT TO CHILDREN OF
　HOME, ETHEL
IMPROVISING JAZZ
　COKER, JERRY
INDEPENDENT LEARNING APPROACH TO PIANO SIGHT READING, AN
　SOREL, CLAUDETTE *
INDEX TO BIOGRAPHIES OF CONTEMPORARY COMPOSERS
　BULL, STORM
INDISPENSABLES OF PIANO PLAYING--2ND. ED.---1955
　WHITESIDE, ABBY
INDIVIDUALITY IN PIANO TOUCH
　LINDO, ALGERNON H. *
INDUCTIVE GRAMMAR OF MUSIC, FOR CLASS, PRIVATE LESSON, OR SELF STUDY,
　BAXTER, JAMES
INFLUENCE OF ADAM MICKIEWICZ ON THE BALLADES OF CHOPIN, THE --OFFPRINT
　KEEFER, LUBOV

INFLUENCE OF ANALYTICAL PRESTUDY IN MEMORIZING PIANO MUSIC, THE
  RABSON, GRACE RUBIN
INFORMATION CONCERNING PIANOFORTES OF USE AND OF INTEREST..A VADE MECUM
  BROADWOOD, JOHN AND SONS
INGA - PLAY--MEMOIRS
  CHRISTENSEN, INGA
INIMITABLE TONE..'PRICE LIST OF PIANOS MADE BY STEINWAY AND SONS,
  STEINWAY AND SONS
INKLINGS FOR THE LOVERS OF MUSIC, PART 1..CULTIVATION OF THE ART OF
  RICHARDSON, NATHAN
INQUIRY INTO THE NATURE AND PRINCIPLES OF THROUGH BASS, ON A NEW PLAN,
  HAWKINS, JOHN SIDNEY
INSTALLATION, CARE AND OPERATION OF THE PHOTOPLAYER---1920+
  AMERICAN PHOTO PLAYER COMPANY
INSTANT PIANO..A UNIQUE METHOD OF READING AND CHORDING FROM THE VERY
  DAVIS, HARRY
INSTITUTES OF MUSIC, OR, EASY INSTRUCTIONS FOR THE HARPSICHORD
  MILLER, EDWARD
INSTRUCTIONS FOR PLAYING THE HARPSICHORD..WHEREIN IS FULLY EXPLAINED
  FALKENER, ROBERT
INSTRUCTIONS FOR THE PIANOFORTE---CONTAINS ALSO A SET OF 28 SONATINAS
  CRAMER, JOHN BAPTIST
INSTRUCTIONS IN PLAYING THE PIANO-FORTE WITH AEOLIAN ATTACHMENT
  VAN DER WEYDE, PETER H.
INSTRUCTIONS IN THE ART OF PLAYING CHURCH MUSIC UPON THE MELODEON,
  JOHNSON, ARTEMAS N.
INSTRUCTIONS IN THOROUGH BASE..BEING A NEW AND EASY METHOD FOR LEARNING
  JOHNSON, ARTEMAS N.
INSTRUCTION BOOK ON THE PIANO-PLAYER AND PLAYER-PIANO, AN ..CONTAINING
  WILSON, DAVID M.
INSTRUCTIVE TALKS TO PIANO STUDENTS
  VIRGIL, ANTHA MINERVA
INSTRUMENTS OF MUSIC, THE --3RD. REV. ED.---1949
  DONINGTON, ROBERT
INSTRUMENTS OF POPULAR MUSIC..A HISTORY OF MUSICAL INSTRUMENTS---1966
  FOX, LILLA M.
INTERNATIONAL EXHIBITION, 1862..LIST OF PIANOFORTES AND OF...SAMPLES
  BROADWOOD, JOHN AND SONS
INTERPRETATION FOR THE PIANO STUDENT
  LAST, JOAN
INTERPRETATION OF BACH'S KEYBOARD WORKS, THE
  BODKY, ERWIN
INTERPRETATION OF EARLY MUSIC, THE
  DONINGTON, ROBERT
INTERPRETATION OF MUSIC, THE --4TH. ED.---1954
  DART, THURSTON
INTERPRETATION OF MUSIC OF THE SEVENTEENTH AND EIGHTEENTH CENTURIES,
  DOLMETSCH, ARNOLD
INTERPRETATION OF PIANO MUSIC, THE
  VENABLE, MARY
INTERPRETING MOZART ON THE KEYBOARD---1957, IN GERMAN
  BADURA-SKODA, EVA *
INTERVALS, CHORDS AND EAR TRAINING FOR YOUNG PIANOFORTE STUDENTS
  BROWN, JEAN PARKMAN
INTIMATE LETTERS OF JAMES GIBBONS HUNEKER, COLLECTED AND EDITED BY
  HUNEKER, JAMES GIBBONS
INTONIEREN VON FLUEGELN, DAS --GRAND VOICING---IN GERMAN, ENGLISH,
  DIETZ, FRANZ RUDOLF
INTRODUCTION TO AN UNPUBLISHED EDITION OF THE PIANOFORTE SONATAS OF
  MACEWEN, JOHN B.
INTRODUCTION TO AN UNPUBLISHED EDITION OF THE PIANOFORTE SONATAS OF
  MCEWEN, JOHN B.
INTRODUCTION TO HARMONY AND THOROUGH-BASS WITH NUMEROUS EXAMPLES AND
  GOSS, JOHN
INTRODUCTION TO PEDALLING
  LAST, JOAN
INTRODUCTION TO PLAYING FROM SCORE
  RIEMANN, HUGO
INTRODUCTION TO PSYCHOLOGY FOR MUSIC TEACHERS, AN --THREE LECTURES
  MATTHAY, TOBIAS A.
INTRODUCTION TO RUSSIAN PIANO MUSIC--REPRINT..'MUSICAL OPINION'
  WESTERBY, HERBERT
INTRODUCTION TO SCORE PLAYING, AN
  TAYLOR, ERIC R.
INTRODUCTION TO SIGHT READING, AN
  PIERCE, DORA *
INTRODUCTION TO SIGHT READING
  KEILMAN, WILHELM
INTRODUCTION TO THE ART OF PLAYING ON THE PIANOFORTE---1801+
  CLEMENTI, MUZIO
INTRODUCTION TO THE ART OF PRELUDING AND EXTEMPORISING IN SIX LESSONS,
  KOLLMANN, AUGUST F.
INTRODUCTION TO THE INTERPRETATION OF BEETHOVEN'S PIANO-FORTE WORKS
  MARKS, ADOLF B.
INTRODUCTION TO THE INTERPRETATION OF BEETHOVEN'S PIANO WORKS---1863,
  MARX, ADOLF BERNHARD
INTRODUCTION TO THE KNOWLEDGE AND PRACTICE OF THE THORO' BASS, AN
  BAILLIE, ALEXANDER--SUPPOSED AUTHOR
INTRODUCTION TO THE PERFORMANCE OF BACH, AN--3 VOLS.
  TURECK, ROSALYN
IN BLACK AND WHITE
  DUMM, ROBERT W.
IN PURSUIT OF MUSIC
  MATTHEWS, DENIS
IN SEARCH OF CHOPIN
  CORTOT, ALFRED
ITALIAN HARPSICHORD BUILDING IN THE 16TH. AND 17TH.
  SHORTRIDGE, JOHN D.
I PLAYED THEIR ACCOMPANIMENTS
  DAVID, ELIZABETH HARBISON
J. S. BACH..48 PRELUDES AND FUGUES..ANALYSIS OF THE FUGUES
  MORGAN, ORLANDO
JANE WILHELMINA STIRLING, 1804-1859..THE FIRST STUDY OF THE LIFE OF
  BONE, AUDREY E.
JAZZ IMPROVISATION..A COMPREHENSIVE METHOD OF STUDY FOR ALL PLAYERS
  BAKER, DAVID
JAZZ IMPROVISATION..TONAL AND RHYTHMIC PRINCIPLES--4 VOLS.
  MEHEGAN, JOHN F.
JAZZ PIANIST, THE ..STUDIES IN THE ART AND PRACTICE OF JAZZ
  MEHEGAN, JOHN F.
JAZZ PIANO..DIXIELAND TO MODERN JAZZ, BLUES, BOOGIE, RAGTIME, SWING,
  STORMEN, WIN
JAZZ PIANO..EARLY BLUES TO CONTEMPORARY MODERN JAZZ, HOW TO PLAY GREAT
  STORMEN, WIN
JOHNSON'S NEW METHOD FOR THOROUGH BASE..AN INSTRUCTION BOOK IN THE ART
  JOHNSON, ARTEMAS N.
JOHN FIELD AND CHOPIN
  BRANSON, DAVID
JOHN FIELD OF DUBLIN, THE INVENTOR OF THE NOCTURNE---1920
  FLOOD, WILLIAM HENRY GRATTAN
JONAS CHICKERING CENTENNIAL CELEBRATION, THE ..A TRIBUTE TO THE LIFE
  CHICKERING AND SONS
JONAS CHICKERING CENTENNIAL CELEBRATION, 1823-1923..IN COMMEMORATION OF
  CHICKERING AND SONS
JOUSSE'S CATECHISM OF MUSIC, AND BURROWES' PIANOFORTE PRIMER AND GUIDE
  JOUSSE, JOHN

JUNIOR SCHOOL PIANIST, THE --ADDRESSED TO THE NEW MUSIC TEACHER
  LEAVEY, LILIAN
KARLIN'S HARMONIC COURSE FOR PIANO IMPROVISING--4 VOLS.---REPRODUCED
  KARLIN, AARON
KELLY KIRBY KINDERGARTEN PIANO METHOD, TEACHERS' COURSE, THE --BKS. 1-4
  KIRBY, MAY B. KELLY
KEY-BOTTOM TONE
  NETZORG, BENDETSON
KEYBOARD, SINGING AND DICTATION MANUAL
  VAN APPLEDORN, MARY J.
KEYBOARD AND DICTATION MANUAL
  MCHOSE, ALLEN IRVINE *
KEYBOARD APPROACH TO HARMONY
  LOWRY, MARGARET
KEYBOARD BIBLIOGRAPHY--'NEW RESOURCES' SERIES
  HINSON, MAURICE
KEYBOARD EXPERIENCES FOR CLASSROOM TEACHERS
  BERNING, ALICE B. *
KEYBOARD EXPERIENCE AND CLASS PIANO INSTRUCTION
  MUSIC EDUCATORS NATIONAL CONFERENCE
KEYBOARD EXPERIENCE AND PIANO CLASS INSTRUCTION
  SUP, WILLIAM R.--EDITOR
KEYBOARD EXPERIENCE IN THE CLASSROOM MUSIC PROGRAM..HANDBOOK FOR
  EGBERT, MARION S.
KEYBOARD FUNDAMENTALS
  FISK, BEATRICE H.
KEYBOARD HARMONY..A COMPREHENSIVE APPROACH TO MUSICIANSHIP
  LEHMER, ISABEL
KEYBOARD HARMONY..A NEW MODERN PIANO METHOD---POPULAR IDIOM
  CAVALLARO, CARMEN
KEYBOARD HARMONY..LEARNING BY HEARING
  SMITH, USELMA CLARK
KEYBOARD HARMONY---DUPLICATED FROM MANUSCRIPT
  O'TOOLE, WILLIAM
KEYBOARD HARMONY--REV. ED.---1939
  SCOVILL, MODENA
KEYBOARD HARMONY--3 VOLS. IN 1, 1923-1926
  ALCHIN, CARRIE A.
KEYBOARD HARMONY AND IMPROVISATION--2 VOLS.
  LIEBERMAN, MAURICE
KEYBOARD HARMONY AND IMPROVISATION
  SIMPSON, KENNETH
KEYBOARD HARMONY AND TRANSPOSITION..A PRACTICAL COURSE OF KEYBOARD WORK
  HAMILTON, ANNA H.
KEYBOARD HARMONY COURSE..A CREATIVE METHOD BASED ON EAR-TRAINING--4
  DILLER, ANGELA
KEYBOARD HARMONY FOR BEGINNERS
  JOHNSON, JOHN BARHAM
KEYBOARD HARMONY FOR JUNIORS
  GEST, ELIZABETH
KEYBOARD HARMONY MADE SIMPLE..THE NATURAL ROAD TO MUSICIANSHIP
  WEISSBUCH, ANTONIA
KEYBOARD HARMONY SIMPLIFIED
  SHEFTE, ARTHUR G.
KEYBOARD HARMONY WITH ILLUSTRATIVE PIANO PIECES
  CARTER, BUENTA
KEYBOARD HARMONY
  WEDGE, GEORGE ANSON
KEYBOARD INSTRUMENTS..STUDIES IN KEYBOARD ORGANOLOGY---10 ESSAYS
  RIPIN, EDWIN M.--EDITOR
KEYBOARD INSTRUMENTS..THE STORY OF THE PIANO---YOUNGER READERS
  DAVIS, LIONEL
KEYBOARD INSTRUMENTS IN THE METROPOLITAN MUSEUM OF ART..A PICTURE BOOK
  METROPOLITAN MUSEUM OF ART, NEW YORK
KEYBOARD MASTERS..STUDY GUIDE
  NIMITZ, DANIEL
KEYBOARD MODULATIONS FOR ALL KEYBOARD INSTRUMENTS..552 TWO-MEASURE
  FULLER, ESTHER MARY
KEYBOARD MUSIC--ESSAYS ON KEYBOARD LITERATURE, EXCLUDING ORGAN
  MATTHEWS, DENIS--EDITOR
KEYBOARD MUSIC--16TH.-20TH. CENTURIES
  WEISER, BERNHARD D.
KEYBOARD MUSICIANSHIP--BKS. 1 AND 2
  HOLLIDAY, MARGARET M.
KEYBOARD MUSICIANSHIP, GROUP PIANO FOR ADULTS
  HARTLINE, ELIZABETH DILL *
KEYBOARD MUSICIANSHIP
  DUCKWORTH, GUY
KEYBOARD MUSICIANS OF THE WORLD
  YOUNG, PERCY M.
KEYBOARD MUSIC FROM THE MIDDLE AGES TO THE BEGINNINGS OF THE
  BEDBROOK, GERALD STARES
KEYBOARD MUSIC OF C. P. E. BACH, THE ..CONSIDERED IN RELATION TO HIS
  BARFORD, PHILIP
KEYBOARD MUSIC STUDY..A CREATIVE METHOD BASED ON EAR-TRAINING--IN TWO
  DILLER, ANGELA
KEYBOARD ROAD IN MUSIC LAND, AND OTHER STORIES---FOR CHILDREN
  REED, MARY G.
KEYBOARD SKILLS..SIGHT READING, TRANSPOSITION, HARMONIZATION,
  CHASTEK, WINIFRED
KEYBOARD STORIES FOR CLASS AND INDIVIDUAL INSTRUCTION---1939
  ERWIN, GARNET PARKER
KEYBOARD SUITES OF J. S. BACH, THE
  FULLER-MAITLAND, J. A.
KEYBOARD THEORY--6 VOLS.
  KRAEHENBUEHL, DAVID
KEYBOARD TRAINING IN HARMONY--PTS. 1 AND 2--725 GRADED EXERCISES---1917
  HEACOX, ARTHUR EDWARD
KEYBOARD WORK FOR HARMONY STUDENTS
  HOWELL, DOROTHY
KEYS TO A MUSICAL PAST...ILLUSTRATED TREATISE ON THE VARIOUS TYPES OF
  ROEHL, HARVEY
KEYS TO SUCCESSFUL PIANO STUDIO ORGANIZATION
  NATIONAL PIANO FOUNDATION
KEYS TO THE KEYBOARD, A BOOK FOR PIANISTS
  FOLDES, ANDOR
KEY TO PIANO PLEASURE
  FREDRICH, JOHN FRANK
KEY TO THE EXERCISES IN THE CATECHISM OF HARMONY, THOROUGH-BASS AND
  HILES, JOHN
KEY TO THE HARMONIZATION OF MELODIES AT THE KEYBOARD--BK. 1
  PILLING, DOROTHY
KEY TO THE KEYS..A SELF-TAUGHT PIANO METHOD FOR ADULTS AND TEEN
  PEDERSON, GALE
KEY TO THE MINIATURES OF LEOPOLD GODOWSKY, A ..ANALYTICAL ESSAYS ON THE
  ARONSON, MAURICE
KNORR'S METHODICAL GUIDE FOR TEACHERS OF MUSIC ON THE PIANOFORTE
  KNORR, JULIUS
KNOWLEDGE OF THE RELATION OF PHYSIOLOGY AND ANATOMY TO PIANO PLAYING, A
  BROTHERHOOD, JAMES
KNOW YOUR SCALES..FOR PIANO STUDENTS OF ALL GRADES
  LEVINE, HENRY
KOLANDER'S ACCOMPANIMENT INSTRUCTOR FOR THE PIANO OR ORGAN
  KOLANDER, MAX
L'ARTE PIANISTICA..SYSTEM OF PIANO ARTISTRY---IN ITALIAN AND ENGLISH
  SCIONTI, SILVIO

LANDOWSKA ON MUSIC--EDITED BY DENISE RESTOUT
    LANDOWSKA, WANDA
LANGUAGE OF THE PIANO..A WORKBOOK IN THEORY AND KEYBOARD HARMONY
    PRIESING, DOROTHY *
LATOUR'S NEW AND IMPROVED METHOD OF INSTRUCTION FOR THE PIANO FORTE
    LATOUR, T.
LEARNING TO READ MUSIC
    WEYLAND, RUDOLPH H.
LEARN TO PLAY POPULAR PIANO BY NOTE IN 20 EASY LESSONS...HOME STUDY
    PATTON, VICTOR S.
LEGACY OF CHOPIN, THE
    HOLCMAN, JAN
LESCHETIZKY AS I KNEW HIM---1923
    NEWCOMB, ETHEL
LESSONS IN SIGHT READING AT THE PIANO
    MOKREJS, JOHN
LESSONS OF RAOUL PUGNO, THE ..WITH A BIOGRAPHY OF CHOPIN BY M. MICHEL
    PUGNO, RAOUL
LESSON COURSE...THE COMPLETE OSTROVSKY FINGER EXERCISE, FOR PIANISTS,
    OSTROVSKY, HENRY
LESSON OF THE CLAVICHORD, THE --REPRINT..'NEW MUSIC REVIEW'
    WHITING, ARTHUR B.
LET'S FIND OUT ABOUT MUSIC...WURLITZER ELEMENTARY PIANO WORKBOOKS, FOR
    RAST, LAURENCE R.
LET'S IMPROVISE--2 VOLS.
    ZEPP, ARTHUR
LET'S LEARN ALL THE NOTES AND READ BETTER..FOR ALL PIANO PUPILS, 5-50
    ALLISON, IRL
LET'S PLAY THE PIANO..THE FIRST MUSIC BOOK FOR CHILDREN OF ALL
    CHING, JAMES
LET'S TRY SOMETHING NEW..A BOOK OF RECITAL AND TEACHING IDEAS FOR PIANO
    RODMAN, MOLLY C.
LET'S TUNE UP
    TRAVIS, JOHN W.
LETTERS FROM MAJORCA---CHOPIN--NUMEROUS ILLUSTRATIONS
    WOOD, CHARLES W.
LETTERS OF CLARA SCHUMANN AND JOHANNES BRAHMS, 1853-1896--2
    SCHUMANN, CLARA
LETTERS OF FRANZ LISZT--COLLECTED AND EDITED BY LA MARA..TRANSLATED BY
    LISZT, FRANZ
LETTERS OF FRANZ LISZT TO MARIE ZU SAYN-WITTGENSTEIN, THE --TRANSLATED
    LISZT, FRANZ
LETTERS OF HANS VON BUELOW---INCLUDES CORRESPONDENCE TO KARL KLINDWORTH
    BUELOW, HANS GUIDO VON
LETTERS OF ROBERT SCHUMANN, THE --SELECTED AND EDITED BY KARL STORCK
    SCHUMANN, ROBERT
LETTERS ON MUSIC, TO A LADY
    EHLERT, LOUIS
LETTERS ON THOROUGH-BASS...FORMING THE SECOND PART OF THE LETTERS ON
    CZERNY, CARL
LETTERS TO A YOUNG LADY ON THE ART OF PLAYING THE PIANOFORTE
    CZERNY, CARL
LETTER TO A YOUNG PIANOFORTE PLAYER, A
    GRAHAM, MARY JANE
LET ME HELP YOU, MY ANCESTORS AND I..A COMPREHENSIVE JUVENILE HISTORY
    EISENBERG, JACOB
LEVINSKAYA SYSTEM OF PIANOFORTE TECHNIC AND TONE COLOR, THE
    LEVINSKAYA, MARIA
LIBERATION AND DELIBERATION IN PIANO TECHNIC
    ROEDER, CARL M.
LIBRARY OF DELUXE--REPRODUCING--MUSIC RECORDS
    DELUXE REPRODUCING ROLL CORPORATION
LIBRARY OF DELUXE WELTE-MIGNON MUSIC RECORDS FOR REPRODUCING PIANOS
    DELUXE ROLL CORPORATION
LIBRARY OF DELUXE WELTE-MIGNON MUSIC RECORDS FOR REPRODUCING PIANOS
    WELTE-MIGNON CORPORATION
LIBRARY OF DUO-ART MUSIC ROLLS
    AEOLIAN COMPANY, THE
LIBRARY OF WELTE-MIGNON MUSIC RECORDS
    WELTE-MIGNON CORPORATION
LIFE AND DEATH OF CHOPIN, THE
    WIERZYNSKI, CASIMIR
LIFE AND LETTERS OF LOUIS MOREAU GOTTSCHALK
    SEYMOUR, MARY ALICE IVES
LIFE AND LISZT..THE RECOLLECTIONS OF A CONCERT PIANIST
    FRIEDHEIM, ARTHUR
LIFE AND MUSIC OF JOHN FIELD, 1782-1837, THE
    PIGGOTT, PATRICK
LIFE AND TIMES OF CHOPIN, THE
    MURGIA, ADELAIDE
LIFE AND WORKS OF GUSTAVE SATTER, THE ..A BIOGRAPHICAL SKETCH IN
    ANON
LIFE AND WORKS OF STEPHEN HELLER, THE PIANOFORTE COMPOSER, THE ..A
    ANON
LIFE AND WORKS OF TOBIAS MATTHAY, THE
    MATTHAY, JESSIE H.
LIFE OF CHOPIN--TRANSLATED BY JOHN BROADHOUSE
    LISZT, FRANZ
LIFE OF CHOPIN--TRANSLATED ONLY IN PART BY MARTHA WALKER COOK
    LISZT, FRANZ
LIFE OF LISZT--'BIOGRAPHIES OF MUSICIANS', VOL. 5
    NOHL, LUDWIG
LIFE OF LOUIS MOREAU GOTTSCHALK
    ARPIN, PAUL
LIFE OF ROBERT SCHUMANN TOLD IN HIS LETTERS, THE --2 VOLS.
    SCHUMANN, ROBERT
LINK TO MODERN MUSIC INSTRUCTION, THE
    STORMEN, WIN
LIONS' PAWS..THE STORY OF FAMOUS HANDS--INCLUDES MUSICIANS...JOSE
    METER, NELLIE SIMMONS
LION OF POLAND, THE ..THE STORY OF PADEREWSKI--JUNIOR BIOGRAPHIES
    HUME, RUTH *
LISTEN, SING AND PLAY..CLASS LESSONS FOR PIANO AND VOICE
    ROOT, CATHERINE ADAMS *
LISTEN TO LEARN--KEYBOARD HARMONY
    QUIST, BOBBIE LEE *
LISTS AND SUGGESTIONS FOR PIANO TEACHING
    GIBBS, POLLY
LIST OF MUSIC FOR THE WELTE-MIGNON PIANO--WITH SUPPLEMENT
    WELTE ARTISTIC PLAYER-PIANO COMPANY
LIST OF PHOTOGRAPHS OF OBJECTS IN THE VICTORIA AND ALBERT MUSEUM--PART
    VICTORIA AND ALBERT MUSEUM, SOUTH KENSINGTON
LIST OF PIANO MUSIC IN THE CIRCULATION DEPARTMENT OF THE NEW YORK
    NEW YORK--PUBLIC LIBRARY
LISZT---1934
    SITWELL, SACHEVERELL
LISZT--'LITTLE BIOGRAPHIES'
    HUMISTON, WILLIAM H.
LISZT--'THE MAYFAIR BIOGRAPHIES', NO. 3
    MACKENZIE, SIR ALEXANDER
LISZT--MASTERPIECES OF MUSIC
    MACKENZIE, SIR ALEXANDER
LISZT--NOVELLO'S BIOGRAPHIES OF GREAT MUSICIANS
    WESTRUP, SIR JACK ALLAN
LISZT, COMPOSER, AND HIS PIANO WORKS..DESCRIPTIVE GUIDE AND CRITICAL
    WESTERBY, HERBERT

LISZT, WAGNER, AND THE PRINCESS
    WALLACE, WILLIAM
LISZT'S WEIMAR
    BAGBY, ALBERT MORRIS
LISZT
    BECKETT, WALTER
LISZT
    HILL, RALPH
LISZT
    ROSTAND, CLAUDE
LISZT
    WALKER, ALAN
LITERATURE OF THE PIANO, THE ..A GUIDE FOR AMATEUR AND STUDENT--3RD.
    HUTCHESON, ERNEST *
LITERATURE OF THE PIANO, THE --FROM THE 16TH. CENTURY TO THE PRESENT
    HUTCHESON, ERNEST
LITTLE BOOK ABOUT LEARNING THE PIANOFORTE, A
    AGUILAR, EMANUEL
LITTLE DIFFICULTIES WHICH OCCUR IN PIANOFORTE PLAYING
    SMITH, THOMAS
LITTLE JOURNEYS TO THE HOMES OF GREAT MUSICIANS--VOL. 8, NO. 3---CHOPIN
    HUBBARD, ELBERT
LITTLE JOURNEYS TO THE HOMES OF GREAT MUSICIANS--VOL. 9, NO. 1---LISZT
    HUBBARD, ELBERT
LITTLE SYSTEM OF PLAYING THE PIANO BY EAR, THE
    LITTLE, FRED W.
LIVES OF THE GREAT COMPOSERS, THE ---CHOPIN AND LISZT
    SCHONBERG, HAROLD
LIVES OF THE MUSICIANS, THE ...WITH PORTRAITS
    DOLE, NATHAN H.
LIVING BIOGRAPHIES OF GREAT COMPOSERS---CHOPIN AND LISZT
    SCHNITTKIND, HENRY T.
LOGIER'S SYSTEM OF THE SCIENCE OF MUSIC, HARMONY, AND PRACTICAL
    LOGIER, JOHANN BERNHARD
LOGIER'S THEORETICAL AND PRACTICAL STUDY FOR THE PIANO FORTE,
    LOGIER, JOHANN BERNHARD
LOST TRADITION IN MUSIC, THE --PT. 1..RHYTHM AND TEMPO IN J. S. BACH'S
    ROTHSCHILD, FRITZ
LOST TRADITION IN MUSIC, THE --PT. 2..MUSICAL PERFORMANCE IN THE TIMES
    ROTHSCHILD, FRITZ
LOUIS MOREAU GOTTSCHALK..A SHORT BIOGRAPHY
    COOKE, JAMES FRANCIS
LUDWIG VAN BEETHOVEN'S PIANOFORTE SONATAS
    BEHREND, WILLIAM
LURE OF THE PIANO THROUGH COORDINATION AND CONCENTRATION, THE
    MOORE, MARY BURNHAM
LYRIC COMPOSITION THROUGH IMPROVISATION--2 VOLS., 1927-1946
    SCHLIEDER, FREDERICK W.
MAESTRO SPINETTI'S MUSIC SHOP--HARPSICHORD, CLAVICHORD, PIANO--'YOUNG
    HULL, ANNE
MAGIC KEY TO KEYBOARD SUCCESS, THE
    HARVEY, ROBERT
MAKERS OF MUSIC..THE STORY OF SINGERS AND INSTRUMENTALISTS
    GREW, SIDNEY
MAKERS OF THE HARPSICHORD AND CLAVICHORD, 1440 TO 1840
    BOALCH, DONALD HOWARD
MAKING FRIENDS WITH PIANO MUSIC..THE HISTORY AND ANALYTICAL NOTES ON
    GLENNON, JAMES
MAKING FRIENDS WITH PIANO MUSIC--SUPPLEMENT
    GLENNON, JAMES
MAKING FRIENDS WITH THE CONCERTO..HISTORICAL AND ANALYTICAL NOTES ON 70
    GLENNON, JAMES
MAKING MUSIC AT THE KEYBOARD..BEGINNING PIANO...CLASS...AND EAR
    WELSH, J. ROBERT
MAKING OF A STEINWAY, THE
    BARTHOLOMEW, RALPH I.
MAKING OF MUSICAL INSTRUMENTS, THE ---1939
    YOUNG, THOMAS C.
MALLORCAN MOODS IN CONTEMPORARY ART AND LITERATURE--CONTAINS 'GEORGE
    DE BOER, JOSEPHINE
MANUALO, THE PLAYER PIANO THAT IS ALL BUT HUMAN, THE ..CARE,
    BALDWIN PIANO COMPANY
MANUAL OF MODULATION...FOR THE USE OF PIANISTS AND ORGANISTS
    KREBS, T. L.
MANUAL OF MODULATION
    OREM, PRESTON WARE
MANUAL OF PIANOFORTE TUNING, A
    MOORE, HENRY K.
MANUAL OF PIANO FOR PUPILS AND TEACHERS
    MORRILL, HENRY H.
MANUAL OF TONE-PRODUCTION IN PIANOFORTE PLAYING, FROM 'TECHNICS OF
    GERMER, HEINRICH
MANUFACTURE OF PIANOFORTE ACTION, THE ..ITS RISE AND DEVELOPMENT
    STRAUCH BROTHERS
MAN LISZT, THE ..A STUDY OF THE TRAGI-COMEDY OF A SOUL DIVIDED AGAINST
    NEWMAN, ERNEST
MARKS AND REMARKS..MUSICAL EXAMINATIONS AND THEIR PROBLEMS
    FIELDEN, THOMAS
MARVELLOUS YEAR, THE ...CRITICAL SKETCHES OF CELEBRATED MEN, THE
    CHURCHILL, WILLIAM--SUPPOSED AUTHOR
MASON'S PRINCIPLES OF VELOCITY AND ARM TOUCHES
    MATHEWS, WILLIAM S. B.
MASTERING THE CHOPIN ETUDES AND OTHER ESSAYS
    WHITESIDE, ABBY
MASTERING THE PIANO
    BRUXNER, MERVYN
MASTERS OF GERMAN MUSIC---CLARA SCHUMANN
    FULLER-MAITLAND, J. A.
MASTERS OF MUSIC---CHOPIN AND LISZT
    ANDERSON, ARVID C.
MASTERS OF MUSIC
    YOUNG, PERCY M.
MASTERS OF THE KEYBOARD
    APEL, WILLI
MASTERS OF THE KEYBOARD
    BROOK, DONALD
MASTERS OF THE PIANO
    FINCK, HENRY T.
MASTERY OF THE KEYBOARD
    DENHAM, GEORGE
MASTER LESSONS IN PIANOFORTE PLAYING, 'LETTERS FROM A MUSICIAN TO HIS
    BOWMAN, EDWARD M.
MASTER METHOD..PIANO NORMAL AND TEACHER'S MANUAL
    HEIDELBERGER, PAULINE
MASTER MUSICIANS..A BOOK FOR PLAYERS, SINGERS AND LISTENERS
    HADDEN, JAMES CUTHBERT
MASTER PIANIST..THE CAREER AND TEACHING OF CARL FRIEDBERG
    SMITH, JULIA
MASTER RULES FOR SUCCESSFUL PIANO PRACTICE..A COLLECTION OF EIGHTEEN
    ANON
MASTER SCHOOL OF MODERN PIANO PLAYING AND VIRTUOSITY--3 PARTS IN 7
    JONAS, ALBERTO
MASTER TUNES AND MUSIC TESTS FOR THE PIANO STUDENT
    STEINER, ERIC
MATERIA MUSICA, OR MATERIALS FOR THE PIANIST..A CLASS BOOK
    ENGELBRECHT, J. G.

MAURICE RAVEL..VARIATIONS ON HIS LIFE AND WORK
    STUCKENSCHMIDT, HANS H.
MAURICE RAVEL
    SEROFF, VICTOR
MAXIMS TO MUSIC..TRADITIONAL PROVERBS, MOTTOES AND MAXIMS OF THE WORLD
    SPAETH, SIGMUND
MECHANICAL MUSICAL INSTRUMENTS---174 NUMBERED PLATES
    BUCHNER, ALEXANDER
MECHANICS OF PIANO PLAYING, THE
    CARMIENCKE, ALBERT G.
MECHANICS OF PIANO TECHNIC, THE
    GRABILL, ETHELBERT WARREN
MEISSNER'S MODERN, PRACTICAL SYSTEM OF TUNING THE PIANOFORTE..WITH A
    HERZ, HENRI
MELODEE MUSIC ROLLS..SEPTEMBER, 1920
    MEL-O-DEE MUSIC COMPANY
MELODY MAKING, KEYBOARD HARMONY AND EXTEMPORISATION
    PASFIELD, WILLIAM R.
MELODY MAKING AT THE PIANO--IN THREE STAGES
    ROWLEY, ALEC *
MELODY WAY COURSE FOR CLASS OR PRIVATE PIANO INSTRUCTION, THE
    MIESSNER, WILLIAM OTTO
MELOMANIACS..ESSAYS---CHOPIN AND LISZT
    HUNEKER, JAMES GIBBONS
MELOTHESIA..OR, CERTAIN GENERAL RULES FOR PLAYING UPON A CONTINUED-BASS
    LOCKE, MATTHEW
MEMOIRS OF A--PIANO--MANUFACTURER
    TONK, WILLIAM
MEMOIRS OF AN AMNESIAC
    LEVANT, OSCAR
MEMOIRS OF ARTHUR SHATTUCK, THE ..WITH AN ACCOUNT OF HIS CAREER BY
    SHATTUCK, ARTHUR
MEMOIRS OF EUGENIE SCHUMANN---1927
    SCHUMANN, EUGENIE
MEMOIRS OF FREDERICK LAMOND, THE
    LAMOND, FREDERICK ARCHIBALD
MEMORIES OF A MUSICAL LIFE
    MASON, WILLIAM G.
MEMORIES OF SIXTY YEARS IN THE TIMBER AND PIANOFORTE TRADES
    BAMBERGER, LOUIS
MEMORIZING MUSIC
    KENYON, CHARLES FREDERICK
MEMORY PLAYING AT THE PIANO
    TOBIN, JOSEPH RAYMOND
MEMORY TESTS FOR PIANOFORTE PLAYING ---7 PIECES WITH INSTRUCTIONS
    PEDERSON, OLAF
MEN, WOMEN AND PIANOS..A SOCIAL HISTORY
    LOESSER, ARTHUR
MEN AND WOMEN WHO MAKE MUSIC
    EWEN, DAVID
MEN AND WOMEN WHO MAKE MUSIC
    EWEN, DAVID
MEN AND WOMEN WHO MAKE MUSIC
    EWEN, DAVID
MEN BEHIND THE MUSIC, THE ---CHOPIN AND LISZT
    WARREN, CLARENCE H.--EDITOR
MEN OF MUSIC..THEIR LIVES, TIMES, AND ACHIEVEMENTS--REV. ED.---CHOPIN
    BROCKWAY, WALLACE *
MEPHISTO WALTZ, THE STORY OF FRANZ LISZT
    LINGG, ANN M.
METHODICAL WAY TO FREE IMPROVISATION, THE --AVANT-GARDE
    INTERNATIONAL MUSIC INSTITUTE FOR FREE IMPROVISATION
METHODS APPLICABLE TO GROUP TEACHING OR PRIVATE PIANO INSTRUCTION
    MARIAL, R.
METHODS OF HARMONY, FIGURED BASE, AND COMPOSITION...ADAPTED FOR
    ALBRECHTSBERGER, JOHANN GEORG
METHODS OF THE MASTERS OF PIANO TEACHING IN EUROPE, THE ..THE SECRET OF
    NOSSIG, ALFRED
METHOD FOR GAINING A PERFECT KNOWLEDGE OF THE NOTES, ETC., FOR
    ABBOTT, A. T.
METHOD FOR THE PIANO-FORTE, A
    MASON, WILLIAM G. *
METHOD FOR THE PIANOFORTE AND METHODICAL GUIDE FOR THE PIANO FORTE
    WOLLENHAUPT, HEINRICH
METRONOME TECHNIQUES
    FRANZ, FREDERICK
METRONOMIC INDICATIONS FOR BACH'S PRELUDES AND FUGUES AND THE
    JOHNSTONE, J. ALFRED
METROSTYLE-THEMODIST AND METRO-ART MUSIC ROLLS FOR THE PIANOLA AND
    AEOLIAN COMPANY, THE
METROSTYLE, THE
    AEOLIAN COMPANY, THE
METROSTYLE AND THEMODIST MUSIC CATALOG FOR THE PIANOLA AND PIANOLA
    AEOLIAN COMPANY, THE
MEZZOTINTS IN MODERN MUSIC--6TH. ED.---CHOPIN AND LISZT--1901
    HUNEKER, JAMES GIBBONS
MICHEL'S PIANO ATLAS---REPUBLISHED IN 1965 UNDER AUTHORSHIP..B. PIERCE
    MICHEL, NORMAN ELWOOD
MIND-POWER IN MUSIC FOR STUDENTS, TEACHERS AND PERFORMERS
    TAYLER, E. DOUGLAS
MIND AND MECHANISM..THOUGHTS ON TEACHING AND THE PIANISTIC ART
    WHEELER, BERTHA H.
MIND IN MUSIC, THE
    WILLIAMS, JEAN E. *
MIND OVER MUSCLE..A TECHNICAL ECONOMY FOR PIANISTS
    PETRI, LILLIAN JEFFREY
MIND YOUR MUSICAL MANNERS, OFF AND ON STAGE..A HANDBOOK OF STAGE
    SOREL, CLAUDETTE
MODEL ANSWERS TO QUESTIONS ON 'TOUCH' FOR CANDIDATES PREPARING FOR
    MANHIRE, WILSON
MODERN ARTISTIC PIANOFORTE, THE ..ITS CONSTRUCTION
    MASON, HENRY LOWELL
MODERN CHORD CONSTRUCTION AND ANALYSIS, FOR ALL INSTRUMENTS...AN AID TO
    GIBBS, GEORGE A., JR.
MODERN COMPOSERS FOR YOUNG PEOPLE---FIRST PUBLISHED AS 'A CHILD'S BOOK
    BURCH, GLADYS
MODERN HARPSICHORD, THE ..TWENTIETH CENTURY INSTRUMENTS AND THEIR
    ZUCKERMANN, WOLFGANG JOACHIM
MODERN KEYBOARD HARMONY AND IMPROVISATION
    PAULSON, JOSEPH
MODERN MASTERS OF THE KEYBOARD
    BROWER, HARRIETTE
MODERN METHOD OF PIANO INSTRUCTION, A ..TEACHERS MANUAL
    WILLIAMS, JEAN E.
MODERN MUSICIANS..A BOOK FOR PLAYERS, SINGERS AND LISTENERS
    HADDEN, JAMES CUTHBERT
MODERN PIANIST..BEING MY EXPERIENCES IN THE TECHNIQUE AND EXECUTION OF
    PRENTNER, MARIE
MODERN PIANIST'S TEXT BOOK, THE
    BUCHAROFF, SIMON
MODERN PIANO, THE
    NALDER, LAWRENCE MARCUS
MODERN PIANOFORTE TECHNIQUE
    VANTYN, SIDNEY
MODERN PIANO IMPROVISATION..BASIC PRINCIPLES ADAPTED FROM THE 'LINK TO
    STORMEN, WIN

MODERN PIANO PEDAGOGY
    POTAMKIN, FRANK
MODERN PIANO TEACHING
    TOWNSEND, WILLIAM
MODERN TEACHER'S GUIDE TO PIANO AND PIANO CLASS TEACHING
    CHURCHILL, VIRGINIA PEAKES
MODERN TECHNIQUE OF THE PEDAL
    SCHNABEL, KARL ULRICH
MODERN TENDENCIES AND OLD STANDARDS IN MUSICAL ART
    JOHNSTONE, J. ALFRED
MODULATION--'NOVELLO'S MUSIC PRIMERS', NO. 31
    HIGGS, JAMES
MODULATIONARY HARMONY BOOK
    QUINTE, MICHAEL S.
MODULATION AND RELATED HARMONIC QUESTIONS
    FOOTE, ARTHUR W.
MODULATION AT THE PIANO--IN THREE STAGES
    TOBIN, JOSEPH RAYMOND
MODULATION MADE EASY
    TAYLER, E. DOUGLAS
MOISEIVITCH--BENNO--, BIOGRAPHY OF A CONCERT PIANIST
    MOISEIVITCH, MAURICE
MORRIS STEINERT COLLECTION OF KEYED AND STRINGED INSTRUMENTS, THE
    STEINERT, MORRIS
MOTHER'S PART IN HER CHILD'S MUSICAL EDUCATION, A ..OR, THE THINGS A
    MCFERRIN, CHARLES BETTEYS
MOTION PICTURE MOODS FOR PIANISTS AND ORGANISTS
    RAPEE, ERNO--ARRANGER
MOZART'S CONCERTO FORM..THE FIRST MOVEMENTS OF THE PIANO CONCERTOS
    FORMAN, DENIS
MOZARTS FLUEGEL KLINGT WIEDER--MOZART'S PIANO SOUNDS AGAIN---WITH
    STEGLICH, RUDOLF
MOZART AND HIS PIANO CONCERTOS---FIRST PUBLISHED IN 1948 AS 'MOZART'S
    GIRDLESTONE, CUTHBERT
MOZART AND THE SONATA FORM..A COMPANION BOOK TO ANY EDITION OF MOZART'S
    TOBIN, JOSEPH RAYMOND
MUSCLES USED IN PIANO-PLAYING..WITH EXPLANATORY NOTES AND DIAGRAMS
    BROTHERHOOD, JAMES
MUSCULAR RELAXATION, A SIMPLE EXPLANATION
    CHING, JAMES
MUSIC'S GLAMOROUS HALL OF FAME..SHORT ARTICLES ABOUT FAMOUS NAMES,
    POWERS, J. HAROLD
MUSIC'S HANDMAID
    COHEN, HARRIET
MUSICAL ACCOMPANIMENT OF MOVING PICTURES..A PRACTICAL MANUAL FOR
    LANG, EDITH *
MUSICAL AMATEUR, THE
    SCHAUFFLER, ROBERT HAVEN
MUSICAL CHAIRS..OR, BETWEEN TWO STOOLS, BEING THE LIFE AND MEMOIRS OF
    GRAY, CECIL
MUSICAL EDUCATION, WITH PRACTICAL OBSERVATIONS ON THE ART OF PIANOFORTE
    GEARY, ELEANOR MARGARET
MUSICAL FORM AT THE PIANO
    ROWLEY, ALEC *
MUSICAL INDIVIDUALITY OF THE PLAYER PIANO, THE ---EXCERPTS..'THE MUSIC
    SCHAAF, EDWARD O.
MUSICAL INSTRUMENTS..A COMPREHENSIVE DICTIONARY
    MARCUSE, SIBYL
MUSICAL INSTRUMENTS---78 WOODCUT ILLUSTRATIONS
    ENGEL, CARL
MUSICAL INSTRUMENTS--JUNIOR REFERENCE BOOKS, NO. 12--2ND. ED.
    DARLOW, DENYS
MUSICAL INSTRUMENTS--MECHANICAL AGE LIBRARY
    PAGE, C. E.
MUSICAL INSTRUMENTS--REV. ED.---1876
    ENGEL, CARL
MUSICAL INSTRUMENTS--THE 'BYWAYS LIBRARY'
    WILSON, ROBINA BECKLES
MUSICAL INSTRUMENTS--3RD. YEAR OF A STUDY COURSE IN MUSIC
    KELLEY, EDGAR STILLMAN
MUSICAL INSTRUMENTS, HISTORIC, RARE AND UNIQUE---1888
    HIPKINS, ALFRED JAMES
MUSICAL INSTRUMENTS, THEIR HISTORY IN WESTERN CULTURE FROM THE STONE
    GEIRINGER, KARL
MUSICAL INSTRUMENTS AND AUDIO
    BRIGGS, GILBERT A.
MUSICAL INSTRUMENTS AND THEIR PORTRAYAL IN ART---EXHIBIT--BALTIMORE
    BALTIMORE--MUSEUM OF ART
MUSICAL INSTRUMENTS AND THEIR SYMBOLISM IN WESTERN ART
    WINTERNITZ, EMANUEL
MUSICAL INSTRUMENTS AS WORKS OF ART..VOL. 1, KEYBOARD
    VICTORIA AND ALBERT MUSEUM, SOUTH KENSINGTON
MUSICAL INSTRUMENTS AT THE WORLD'S COLUMBIAN EXPOSITION, CHICAGO, 1893
    PRESTO--EDITORIAL STAFF
MUSICAL INSTRUMENTS AT YALE..A SELECTION OF WESTERN INSTRUMENTS FROM
    YALE UNIVERSITY--ART GALLERY
MUSICAL INSTRUMENTS IN ART AND HISTORY
    BRAGARD, ROGER
MUSICAL INSTRUMENTS OF THE WESTERN WORLD
    WINTERNITZ, EMANUEL
MUSICAL INSTRUMENTS THROUGH THE AGES--REV. ED.---1961
    BAINES, ANTHONY
MUSICAL INSTRUMENTS THROUGH THE AGES
    BUCHNER, ALEXANDER
MUSICAL INSTRUMENTS
    HINDLEY, GEOFFREY
MUSICAL INSTRUMENTS
    HORNIMAN MUSEUM AND LIBRARY, LONDON
MUSICAL INTERPRETATION..ITS LAWS AND PRINCIPLES---1913
    MATTHAY, TOBIAS A.
MUSICAL INTERPRETATION--THIS BOOK ACCOMPANIED A SERIES OF B.B.C. RADIO
    WESTRUP, SIR JACK ALLAN
MUSICAL MEMORIES..MY RECOLLECTIONS OF CELEBRITIES OF THE HALF CENTURY,
    UPTON, GEORGE P.
MUSICAL MEMORIES---CONCERNS SEVERAL PIANISTS
    HENDERSON, ARCHIBALD
MUSICAL MEMORIES---LISZT
    SAINT-SAENS, CAMILLE
MUSICAL MEMORIES--SOME LESSONS WITH HENSELT
    DIEHL, ALICE M.
MUSICAL MEMORY, THE --INDIANA UNIVERSITY STUDIES, NO. 92
    HOFFZIMMER, ERNST
MUSICAL MEMORY AND ITS CULTIVATION
    SHINN, FREDERICK G.
MUSICAL ORNAMENTATION..DIDACTICO-CRITICAL TREATISE ON ALL OF THE
    GERMER, HEINRICH
MUSICAL ORNAMENTATION--IN TWO PARTS
    DANNREUTHER, EDWARD
MUSICAL ORNAMENTS SIMPLY EXPLAINED...NUMEROUS EXAMPLES...WITH 100
    HARDING, HENRY ALFRED
MUSICAL REMINISCENCES AND IMPRESSIONS---TEACHER, PIANIST, CONDUCTOR
    BARNETT, JOHN FRANCIS
MUSICAL SECRETS ON THE TECHNIQUE OF PIANO PLAYING
    MACKINNON, LILIAS
MUSICAL STUDIES..A SERIES OF CONTRIBUTIONS BY FRANCIS HUEFFER,
    HUEFFER, FRANCIS

MUSICAL TRUTHS..OR, AN ANALYSIS OF MUSIC AND AN ESSAY ON THE PAST AND
  BUCKLEY, OLIVIA DUSSEK
MUSICIAN, THE ..A GUIDE FOR PIANOFORTE STUDENTS--6 VOLS.
  PRENTICE, THOMAS RIDLEY
MUSICIAN'S HANDBOOK FOR THE DEVELOPMENT OF MANUAL SUPPLENESS AND
  CURCIO, LOUISE
MUSICIAN'S LIGHTNING MODULATION GUIDE..INFORMATION, EXAMPLES, CHORD
  VENDEN, LEONARD
MUSICIAN'S NARRATIVE, A ---CLARA SCHUMANN, VON BUELOW AND LISZT
  MACKENZIE, SIR ALEXANDER
MUSICIAN'S PILGRIMAGE, THE ..A STUDY IN ARTISTIC DEVELOPMENT
  FULLER-MAITLAND, J. A.
MUSICIANSHIP THROUGH IMPROVISATION AT THE KEYBOARD--BK. 1---DUPLICATED
  RABINOF, SYLVIA
MUSICIANS ADVISORY SERVICE FIRST MUSIC READER FOR PIANO..TEACHERS COPY
  MUSICIANS ADVISORY SERVICE
MUSICIANS OF SORROW AND ROMANCE---CHOPIN
  LAWRENCE, FREDERIC LOCKE
MUSICKS HAND-MAID..NEW LESSONS AND INSTRUCTIONS FOR THE VIRGINALS OR
  PLAYFORD, JOHN
MUSIC AND MORALS---CHOPIN
  HAWEIS, HUGH R.
MUSIC AND MUSICIANS---1895, IN FRENCH
  LAVIGNAC, ALBERT
MUSIC AND THE LINE OF MOST RESISTANCE---1942
  SCHNABEL, ARTUR
MUSIC AND THE PIANO
  VIARD-LOUIS, JENNY
MUSIC AS A CAREER
  ANDERSON, WILLIAM P.
MUSIC AT THE KEYBOARD
  ORREY, LESLIE
MUSIC AT YOUR FINGERTIPS
  SLENCZYNSKA, RUTH *
MUSIC BEGINS WITH THE PIANO
  MUSIC EDUCATORS NATIONAL CONFERENCE
MUSIC BY HEART
  MACKINNON, LILIAS
MUSIC EDUCATOR'S BUSINESS HANDBOOK, THE ---PUBLISHED OCCASIONALLY SINCE
  MUSIC INDUSTRY COUNCIL
MUSIC ESSENTIALS FOR CLASSROOM TEACHERS--2ND. ED.---1961
  PACE, ROBERT
MUSIC FOR ADVANCED STUDY..A SOURCE BOOK OF EXCERPTS
  MELCHER, ROBERT A. *
MUSIC FOR ELEMENTARY TEACHERS..A PROGRAMMED COURSE IN BASIC THEORY AND
  HARGISS, GENEVIEVE
MUSIC FOR FUN..PROFESSIONAL COURSE USING THE CHUCK DUTTON STREAMLINED
  DUTTON, CHUCK *
MUSIC FOR KEYBOARD HARMONY
  MELCHER, ROBERT A. *
MUSIC FOR SCORE READING
  MELCHER, ROBERT A. *
MUSIC FOR STUDY..A SOURCE BOOK OF EXCERPTS
  MURPHY, HOWARD A. *
MUSIC FOR THE AEOLIAN GRAND--SUPPLEMENT
  AEOLIAN COMPANY, THE
MUSIC FOR THE AEOLIAN GRAND
  AEOLIAN COMPANY, THE
MUSIC FOR THE MILLIONS..THE KIMBALL PIANO AND ORGAN STORY
  BRADLEY, VAN ALLEN
MUSIC FOR THE ORCHESTRELLE AND AEOLIAN GRAND
  AEOLIAN COMPANY, THE
MUSIC FOR THE PIANO..A HANDBOOK OF CONCERT AND TEACHING MATERIAL FROM
  FRISKIN, JAMES *
MUSIC FOR THE PIANOLA AND THE AERIAL PIANO--4 VOLS.
  AEOLIAN COMPANY, THE
MUSIC FOR YOU..A SUPPLEMENTAL WORK BOOK FOR INDIVIDUAL OR CLASS
  SKUTLEY, MILDRED A.
MUSIC INSTRUMENT CHECKLIST
  NEBLING, ALBERT N. *
MUSIC LESSONS FOR YOUR CHILD
  RICKER, EARL
MUSIC MACHINES--AMERICAN STYLE..A CATALOG OF THE EXHIBITION
  HOOVER, CYNTHIA A.
MUSIC MADE EASY, PIANOFORTE TUTOR ON A NEW PLAN
  GRAHAM, JAMES L.
MUSIC MADE EASY TO EVERY CAPACITY, IN A SERIES OF DIALOGUES..BEING
  BEMETZRIEDER, ANTON
MUSIC MAKERS..SOME OUTSTANDING MUSICAL PERFORMERS OF OUR DAY
  GELATT, ROLAND
MUSIC MASTERS OLD AND NEW..A SERIES OF EDUCATIONAL BIOGRAPHIES...
  COOKE, JAMES FRANCIS
MUSIC OF LISZT, THE --2ND. REV. ED.---1954
  SEARLE, HUMPHREY
MUSIC OF THE PAST
  LANDOWSKA, WANDA
MUSIC STUDY IN GERMANY---1880
  FAY, AMY
MUSIC TEACHER'S VADE-MECUM, THE ..A GUIDE IN THE CHOICE OF MUSIC FOR
  CAPEN, C. L.
MUSIC TEACHERS' GUIDE TO THE GOLDBECK PIANO METHOD
  PALMER, ANNIE L.
MUSIC THEORY FOR PIANO STUDENTS
  HAMILTON, CLARENCE G.
MYRA HESS, BY HER FRIENDS
  LASSIMONNE, DENISE *
MY HELENKA---IGNACE PADEREWSKI
  MCMILLAN, MARY LEE *
MY HUSBAND GABRILOWITSCH
  CLEMENS, CLARA
MY LIFE AND MUSIC
  SCHNABEL, ARTUR
MY MEMORIES OF LISZT
  SILOTI, ALEXANDER
MY MUSICAL EXPERIENCES
  WALKER, BETTINA
MY MUSICAL RECOLLECTIONS---CHOPIN
  KUHE, WILHELM
MY SYSTEM FOR PRACTICING THE VIOLIN AND PIANO, BASED UPON
  EBERHARDT, GOBY
MY THOUGHTS ON MUSIC AND MUSICIANS---CHOPIN AND LISZT
  STATHAM, HENRY H.
MY TRAVELS IN AMERICA---1840+
  HERZ, HENRI
MY YOUNG YEARS
  RUBINSTEIN, ARTUR
NATIONAL AUDITIONS FOR AMERICAN PIANO PUPILS
  NATIONAL GUILD OF PIANO TEACHERS
NATIONAL SCHOOL FOR PIANOFORTE, THE
  SUDDS, WILLIAM F.
NATIONAL SCHOOL OF VIRGINAL MUSIC IN ELIZABETHAN TIMES, THE
  GLYN, MARGARET H.
NATIONAL SURVEY OF PIANO CLASSES IN OPERATION
  NATIONAL BUREAU FOR THE ADVANCEMENT OF MUSIC
NATURAL LAWS IN PIANO TECHNIC
  CHASE, MARY WOOD

NATURAL LAWS OF MUSICAL EXPRESSION, THE
  SCHMITT, HANS
NATURAL PIANO-TECHNIC..SCHOOL OF WEIGHT TOUCH--2 VOLS.
  BREITHAUPT, RUDOLPH MARIA
NEGLECTED SENSE IN PIANO PLAYING, A
  MASON, DANIEL GREGORY
NEILL IMPROVISING SYSTEM
  NEILL, JACK
NERVES OF STEEL..THE STORY OF AMERICAN PIANO WIRE AND ITS DEVELOPMENT
  AMERICAN STEEL AND WIRE COMPANY
NEW AND COMPLETE INSTRUCTIONS FOR THE HARPSICHORD, PIANO FORTE OR
  ANON
NEW AND COMPLETE PIANOFORTE SCHOOL
  HERZ, HENRI
NEW APPROACH TO JAZZ IMPROVISATION, A --VOL. 1
  AEBERSOLD, JAMEY
NEW APPROACH TO PIANO TECHNIQUE, A
  DICKERSON, RUTH A.
NEW APPROACH TO PIANO TRANSCRIPTIONS AND INTERPRETATION OF JOHANN
  BRISKIER, ARTHUR
NEW APPROACH TO SCALES AND ARPEGGIOS, A
  FIELDEN, THOMAS
NEW APPROACH TO THE STUDY OF THE PIANOFORTE, A ---IN ITALIAN AND
  CHAROL, SIMON
NEW ASSISTANT TO THE PIANO-FORTE OR HARPSICHORD, A ...RULES FOR
  LINLEY, FRANCIS
NEW ENGLAND CONSERVATORY METHOD FOR THE PIANO-FORTE, THE ..COMPRISING
  NEW ENGLAND CONSERVATORY
NEW EXERCISES ON HARMONY AND THOROUGH BASS...FORMING A PRACTICAL
  CZERNY, CARL
NEW FINGERING NOTATION FOR KEYBOARD MUSIC---REPRODUCED FROM TYPEWRITTEN
  WILSON, WILLIAM
NEW FORMULA FOR THE PIANO TEACHER AND PIANO STUDENT
  SAFONOFF, WASSILI
NEW GRADED PEDALLING FOR PIANO, THE --BKS. 1 AND 2
  CHING, JAMES
NEW GRADED SIGHT READING FOR PIANO, THE --BKS. 1 AND 2---ONE-MEASURE
  CHING, JAMES
NEW GRADED TIME EXERCISES, FOR PIANO, THE
  CHING, JAMES
NEW GRAPHIC NOTATION FOR KEYBOARD MUSIC, A
  MIDDLEMISS, CHARLES S.
NEW GUIDE TO MUSIC, IN FRENCH AND ENGLISH, A
  BEMETZRIEDER, ANTON
NEW ILLUSTRATED CATALOGUE OF PIANOFORTES, A
  CHICKERING AND SONS
NEW INSTRUCTIONS FOR PLAYING THE HARPSICHORD, PIANOFORTE OR
  ANON
NEW LESSONS FOR THE HARPSICHORD
  BEMETZRIEDER, ANTON
NEW METHOD FOR SYNCHRONIZED SCALE FINGERINGS, A
  GALLICO, PAOLO
NEW METHOD FOR THE PIANOFORTE..ADDED, RUDIMENTS OF HARMONY AND
  RICHARDSON, NATHAN
NEW METHOD OF TEACHING THE PIANOFORTE
  PSTROKONSKY, JULES DE
NEW MUSIC FOR THE AEOLIAN GRAND, THE PIANOLA, AND THE AERIOL PIANO
  AEOLIAN COMPANY, THE
NEW PATHWAYS TO PIANO TECHNIQUE..A STUDY OF THE RELATIONS BETWEEN MIND
  BONPENSIERE, LUIGI
NEW PATH FOR PIANISTS, A ..THE MUTANO--MUTE PIANO--SYSTEM, ETC.
  WOODHOUSE, GEORGE
NEW PIANO-TEACHER'S GUIDE..A GRADED AND CLASSIFIED LIST OF PIANO MUSIC
  SCHIRMER, G.
NEW PIANOFORTE KEYBOARD, THE ..CARD AND GAME, THE A.B.C. OF MUSIC
  ANON
NEW SCHOOL OF MUSIC, THE ..PRACTICAL THOROUGH BASE CULTURE, FOR
  BAXTER, JAMES
NEW SCHOOL OF SCALE PLAYING--COLOR PATTERNS
  CHITY, R.
NEW SPIRIT, THE --ESSAYS---CHOPIN--1891
  ELLIS, HAVELOCK
NEW SYSTEM OF PRACTICING AND TEACHING THE PIANOFORTE, A
  BOTTOMLEY, JOSEPH
NEW TREATISE OF PRACTICAL THOROUGH BASS, A
  CLARE, EDWARD
NEW TUTOR FOR THE HARPSICHORD OR PIANO FORTE, WHEREIN THE FIRST
  BARTHELEMON, FRANCOIS H.
NEW WAY TO PIANO TECHNIQUE, THE --8 VOLS.
  WOODHOUSE, GEORGE
NIGHTINGALE, THE ..A LIFE OF CHOPIN--IN THE FORM OF FICTION
  STRACHEY, MARJORIE C.
NINETEENTH CENTURY PIANO MUSIC, A HANDBOOK FOR PIANISTS
  DALE, KATHLEEN
NINETEEN FIFTY-SIX SUPPLEMENT TO THE MODERN TEACHER'S GUIDE TO PIANO
  CHURCHILL, VIRGINIA PEAKES
NINE HUNDRED MODEL LESSONS FOR PIANO TEACHERS
  ROWLEY, DAISY WOODRUFF
NINE STEPS TOWARDS 'FINGER INDIVIDUALIZATION' THROUGH FOREARM ROTATION,
  MATTHAY, TOBIAS A.
NOBLE ART, A ..THREE LECTURES ON THE EVOLUTION AND CONSTRUCTION OF THE
  SMITH, FANNY MORRIS
NOCTURNE..A CHOPIN-PLAY IN ONE ACT
  SACKETT, SHELTON
NORMAL COURSE OF PIANO TECHNIC, THE
  WAIT, WILLIAM B.
NOTES OF A PIANIST--EDITED BY JEANNE BEHREND---1881
  GOTTSCHALK, LOUIS MOREAU
NOTES ON CHOPIN
  GIDE, ANDRE
NOTES ON THE INTERPRETATION OF 24 FAMOUS PIANO SONATAS OF BEETHOVEN
  JOHNSTONE, J. ALFRED
NOTES ON THE LITERATURE OF THE PIANO--RE-EDITED BY BROTHER, SAMUEL
  LOCKWOOD, ALBERT
NOTES ON THE PIANO
  BACON, ERNST
NUMERICAL METHOD OF PIANO ACCOMPANIMENTS, A --WITH CHARTS
  WAGNER, JOHN J.
OBSERVATIONS CONCERNING IMPROVEMENTS IN THE CONSTRUCTION OF THE
  BEREGSZASZY, LAJOS
OBSERVATIONS ON FOUR VOLUMES AND SUPPLEMENT OF THE WORKS OF L. M.
  KIRKPATRICK, JOHN
OFFICIAL GUIDE TO PIANO QUALITY, THE ---4TH. ED.
  GEPPERT, WILLIAM
OLD AND THE NEW SCHOOL OF PIANO PLAYING, THE --TYPEWRITTEN COPY
  ROSENTHAL, MORIZ
OLD ENGLISH INSTRUMENTS OF MUSIC--4TH. ED.---1910
  GALPIN, FRANCIS W.
OLD FOGY, HIS MUSICAL OPINIONS AND GROTESQUES---D'ALBERT, PADEREWSKI,
  HUNEKER, JAMES GIBBONS
OLD MUSICAL INSTRUMENTS
  CLEMENCIC, RENE
OLD MUSICAL INSTRUMENTS
  GABRY, GYORGY
OLD PIANO, THE ..A FANTASIA, WITH VARIATIONS HIGH FANTASTICAL, ETC...IN
  ANON

OLD PIANOS
MICHEL, NORMAN ELWOOD
ONE-KEYBOARDED CLAVICYTHERIUM OF THE KRAUS COLLECTION IN FLORENCE, THE
KRAUS, ALESSANDRO B.
ON CHOOSING A PIANO
ROSE, ALGERNON SIDNEY
ON COLORING AS DISTINCT FROM TONE-INFLECTION--A LECTURE
MATTHAY, TOBIAS A.
ON LUTES, RECORDERS AND HARPSICHORDS..MEN AND MUSIC OF THE BAROQUE
BERKOWITZ, FREDA
ON MEMORIZING AND PLAYING FROM MEMORY
MATTHAY, TOBIAS A.
ON METHOD IN TEACHING
MATTHAY, TOBIAS A.
ON MUSICAL EXECUTION...PRIMARILY WITH REFERENCE TO PIANO-PLAYING
KLAUWELL, OTTO
ON MUSIC AND MUSICIANS---1854, IN GERMAN--FIRST ENGLISH EDITION IN 1877
SCHUMANN, ROBERT
ON PIANOFORTE MANUFACTURE, ESPECIALLY IN AMERICA
PELZ, EDWARD
ON TEACHING PIANO TECHNIQUE TO CHILDREN
CHING, JAMES
ON TEACHING THE PIANO
BOLTON, HETTY
ON THE PROPER PERFORMANCE OF ALL BEETHOVEN'S WORKS FOR THE PIANO
CZERNY, CARL
ON THE THEORY OF MODULATION
REGER, MAX
ON USING EARLY KEYBOARD FINGERING--REPRINT OF 3 ARTICLES FROM THE
BABITZ, SOL
OPENING THE SHUTTERS..A SHORT EXPOSITION ON THE TEACHINGS AND
LASSIMONNE, DENISE
ORIENTATION FOR INTERPRETING MOZART'S PIANO SONATAS
RICHNER, THOMAS
ORNAMENTATION IN BEETHOVEN'S PIANOFORTE-WORKS, THE
EHRLICH, ALFRED HEINRICH
ORNAMENTATION IN JOH. SEB. BACH'S PIANOFORTE-WORKS, THE
EHRLICH, ALFRED HEINRICH
ORNAMENTATION IN MUSIC FOR THE KEYBOARD
GOLDTHWAITE, SCOTT
ORNAMENTATION IN THE WORKS OF FREDERIC CHOPIN---1921
DUNN, JOHN PETRIE
ORNAMENTS AND ABBREVIATIONS FOR EXAMINATION CANDIDATES
LOVELOCK, WILLIAM
ORNAMENTS IN CLASSICAL AND MODERN MUSIC
HAMILTON, CLARENCE G.
ORNAMENTS IN MUSIC
TAYLOR, H.
OURSELVES AND OUR PUPILS---ALSO CATALOGUED UNDER AUTHORSHIP..BETTY
CHING, JOAN ELIZABETH
OURSELVES AND OUR PUPILS--MONOGRAPH ON THE ART OF PIANO TEACHING, NO.
REEVES, BETTY
OUTLINES AND GRADES FOR THE USE OF PIANO TEACHERS
SMELTZER, JEANNIE R.--COMPILER
OUTLINES FOR TRAINING PIANO TEACHERS
BOWEN, CAROLYN
OUTLINE ANALYSIS OF EACH OF BACH'S FORTY-EIGHT FUGUES--IN THE 'DAS
SAMPSON, BROOK
OUTLINE OF PIANO PEDAGOGY--REV. ED.---1929
RUBINSTEIN, BERYL
OUTLINE OF TECHNIQUE..A GUIDE IN THE THEORY AND PRACTICE OF MECHANISM
HOWARD, GEORGE HENRY
OXFORD PIANO COURSE, TEACHER'S FIRST MANUAL
SCHELLING, ERNEST *
OXFORD PIANO COURSE, TEACHER'S SECOND MANUAL
SCHELLING, ERNEST *
PADEREWSKI..A CRITICAL STUDY--'CENTURY LIBRARY OF MUSIC', VOL. 18
MASON, WILLIAM G.
PADEREWSKI..THE STORY OF A MODERN IMMORTAL
PHILLIPS, CHARLES
PADEREWSKI--'LITTLE BIOGRAPHIES', VOL. 2
MARTENS, FREDERICK HERMAN
PADEREWSKI--'LITTLE BIOGRAPHIES'
HUMISTON, WILLIAM H.
PADEREWSKI--ROBINSON LOCKE SCRAP BOOKS--2 VOLS.
LOCKE, ROBINSON
PADEREWSKI, 'THE MASTER OF MASTERS' ---REPRODUCED FROM TYPEWRITTEN COPY
LE MASSENA, CLARENCE E.
PADEREWSKI, PIANIST AND PATRIOT
GRONOWICZ, ANTONI
PADEREWSKI AND HIS ART
FINCK, HENRY T.
PADEREWSKI AS I KNEW HIM
STRAKACZ, ANIELA
PADEREWSKI MEMOIRS, THE ---1938
PADEREWSKI, IGNACE JAN *
PADEREWSKI
KELLOGG, CHARLOTTE
PALMER'S PIANO PRIMER
PALMER, HORATIO R.
PARALLELS AND DISCREPANCIES BETWEEN ENGLISH AND SPANISH KEYBOARD MUSIC
KASTNER, SANTIAGO
PARENT'S GUIDE TO MUSIC LESSONS, A
WILLS, VERA G. *
PASSIONATE FRIENDSHIP, A ..CLARA SCHUMANN AND BRAHMS---LETTERS TO EACH
ALLEY, MARGUERITE
PAST AND PRESENT--A CANADIAN MUSICIAN'S REMINISCENSES
MCDOWELL, LOUISE
PEDALING IN PIANOFORTE MUSIC
LINDO, ALGERNON H.
PEDALLING THE MODERN PIANOFORTE---1936
BOWEN, YORK
PEDALS OF THE PIANOFORTE, THE --FOUR LECTURES
SCHMITT, HANS
PEDAL EXERCISES FOR PIANOFORTE
FAELTEN, CARL
PEDAL METHOD FOR THE PIANO, A
VENINO, ALBERT F.
PENCIL PORTRAITS OF CONCERT CELEBRITIES---INCLUDES 24 PIANISTS
WIENER, HILDA
PENGELLY BLUE BOOK OF STYLE, THE ...A STUDY OF THE ART OF STYLING AS
PENGELLY, J. BRADFORD
PEOPLE AND PIANOS..A CENTURY OF SERVICE TO MUSIC---1853-1953
STEINWAY, THEODORE E.
PERCY ALDRIDGE GRAINGER, A STUDY
PARKER, DOUGLAS C.
PERFORATING OF MUSIC ROLLS WITH THE LEABARJAN PERFORATOR, THE
BARTELS, LEO F. *
PERFORMANCE OF MUSIC, THE ..A STUDY IN TERMS OF THE PIANOFORTE
BARNETT, DAVID
PERFORMANCE PRACTICE..A BIBLIOGRAPHY
VINQUIST, MARY *
PERFORMANCE PRACTICES IN BEETHOVEN'S PIANO SONATAS..AN INTRODUCTION
NEWMAN, WILLIAM S.
PERFORMER'S GUIDE TO BAROQUE MUSIC, A
DONINGTON, ROBERT
PERFORMER AND AUDIENCE..AN INVESTIGATION INTO THE PSYCHOLOGICAL CAUSES
CHING, JAMES
PERSISTENT PIANIST, THE ..A BOOK FOR THE LATE BEGINNER AND THE ADULT
ROBILLIARD, EILEEN D.
PERSONAL RECOLLECTIONS OF CHATS WITH LISZT, IN 1869---1893
STRELEZKI, ANTON
PHILOSOPHY OF MUSIC, THE ..WHAT MUSIC CAN DO FOR YOU
SEYMOUR, HARRIET AYER
PHILOSOPHY OF THE HARPSICHORD, EXPLAINING HOW THAT INSTRUMENT IS KEPT
WALKER, ADAM
PHRASING AND ARTICULATION---152 MUSICAL EXAMPLES
KELLER, HERMANN
PHRASING IN PIANO PLAYING..AN ELEMENTARY GUIDE WITH EXAMPLES
JOHNSTONE, J. ALFRED
PHYSICAL BASIS OF PIANO TOUCH AND TONE, THE
ORTMANN, OTTO
PHYSICS OF MUSIC, THE --4TH. ED.---1944
WOOD, ALEXANDER
PHYSIOLOGICAL MECHANICS OF PIANO TECHNIQUE, THE ---1929
ORTMANN, OTTO
PHYSIOLOGICAL METHOD FOR PLAYING THE PIANO-FORTE, DESIGNED AS A MANUAL
BABBITT, WILLIAM
PIANISM..A COURSE IN NORMAL TRAINING
WILLIAMS, GUY BEVIER
PIANISM
GARROWAY, WILL
PIANIST'S APPROACH TO SIGHT READING AND MEMORIZING, THE
RUBINSTEIN, BERYL
PIANIST'S ART, THE ..A COMPREHENSIVE MANUAL ON PIANO PLAYING FOR THE
EVERHART, POWELL
PIANIST'S CATECHISM, THE ---1880
BLOCKLEY, JOHN
PIANIST'S FIRST MUSIC MAKING, THE --3 VOLS.
MATTHAY, TOBIAS A. *
PIANIST'S GUIDE, THE ..A SERIES OF PAMPHLETS ON THE TEACHING AND
BIART, VICTOR
PIANIST'S GUIDE TO TECHNICAL FREEDOM, THE ..2 VOLS. IN 1
POWERS-WADSWORTH, L.
PIANIST'S HAND, THE ..A SYSTEMATIC METHOD...ACCORDING TO THE PRINCIPLES
UNSCHULD, MARIE VON
PIANIST'S HANDBOOK, THE ..A GUIDE FOR THE RIGHT COMPREHENSION AND
ENGEL, CARL
PIANIST'S HOME STUDY COURSES, THE
CHING, JAMES
PIANIST'S MECHANISM, THE
WHITESIDE, ABBY
PIANIST'S MENTAL VELOCITY, THE ..A SYSTEMATIC PREPARATION OF THE MIND
PRATT, SILAS G.
PIANIST'S MENTOR..A TEXT BOOK FOR STUDENTS OF ALL GRADES--2ND. ED.
FISHER, HENRY
PIANIST'S PROBLEMS, THE ..A MODERN APPROACH TO EFFICIENT PRACTICE AND
NEWMAN, WILLIAM S.
PIANIST'S THUMB, THE
WELLS, HOWARD
PIANIST'S TOUCH, THE ..METHOD AND THEORY OF PAUL PICHIER
PICHIER, PAUL
PIANIST'S WARMING-UP EXERCISES FOR THE MAINTENANCE AND IMPROVEMENT OF
BAUER, HAROLD
PIANISTIC HINTS
PFEFFERKORN, OTTO W.
PIANISTS' 'ABC' PRIMER AND GUIDE--WITH AN APPENDIX
WEBBE, WILLIAM H.
PIANISTS CHORD MANUAL, THE
LUBIN, ALEX
PIANISTS OF THE PAST..PERSONAL RECOLLECTIONS BY THE LATE CHARLES
SALAMAN, CHARLES
PIANISTS WHO HAVE MADE RECORDS FOR THE DUO-ART PIANO
AEOLIAN COMPANY, THE
PIANIST AND CHURCH MUSIC, THE
MATHIS, WILLIAM STEPHAN
PIANIST AND THE ART OF MUSIC, THE ..A TREATISE ON PIANO PLAYING FOR
CARPE, ADOLPH
PIANIST SHOOTS FIRST, THE ---PSYCHOLOGICAL STORY
FAIRLIE, GERARD
PIANO..GUIDED SIGHT-READING
DEUTSCH, LEONHARD
PIANO-FORTES AND THEIR MANUFACTURE, WITH ILLUSTRATED CATALOGUE SHOWING
CHICKERING BROTHERS, CHICAGO
PIANO-FORTES AT THE EXHIBITION OF 1856
CHICKERING AND SONS
PIANO-FORTE CLASS BOOK, CONTAINING PRACTICAL RUDIMENTAL LESSONS FOR
CARY, MRS. C. S. P.
PIANO-FORTE INSTRUCTOR, A ..OR, PREPARATORY SYSTEM OF PIANOFORTE
HOWE, JAMES H.
PIANO-MASTER CHORD CHART--CONSTRUCTION, ACCOMPANIMENT, AND SWING BASS
HILL, PAUL
PIANO-PLAYER AND ITS MUSIC, THE
NEWMAN, ERNEST
PIANO-THEORY EXAMINATION SYLLABUS
MINNESOTA MUSIC TEACHERS ASSOCIATION
PIANO, CHORDS AND HARMONY---REPRODUCED FROM MANUSCRIPT
COPPAGE, HOWARD W.
PIANO, ITS CONSTRUCTION AND CARE, THE
BAINTON, HERBERT G.
PIANO, ITS CONSTRUCTION AND RELATION TO TONE, PITCH AND TEMPERAMENT,
ROSENCRANTZ, ISIDOR B.
PIANO, ITS MUSIC AND LITERATURE, THE ..CATALOGUE OF THE MUSIC
LIVERPOOL--PUBLIC LIBRARIES, MUSEUMS AND ART GALLERY
PIANO, THE ..AN INTRODUCTION TO THE INSTRUMENT
BALLANTINE, BILL
PIANO, THE ..ITS CARE
PARKINSON, HANS B.
PIANO, THE ..ITS HISTORY, MAKERS, PLAYERS AND MUSIC
WIER, ALBERT
PIANO, THE ..SCIENTIFIC, TECHNICAL, AND PRACTICAL INSTRUCTIONS RELATING
SPILLANE, DANIEL
PIANOFORTE, THE ..ITS HISTORY TRACED TO THE GREAT EXHIBITION OF
HARDING, ROSAMUND
PIANOFORTE, THE ..ITS ORIGIN, PROCESS AND CONSTRUCTION
RIMBAULT, EDWARD FRANCIS
PIANOFORTE, THE --3RD. ED.---1966
SUMNER, WILLIAM L.
PIANOFORTE, THE
DAWSON, FREDERICK
PIANOFORTES..WITH USEFUL AND INTERESTING INFORMATION CONCERNING THEM
BROADWOOD, JOHN AND SONS
PIANOFORTES
STEINWAY AND SONS
PIANOFORTE ACCOMPANIMENT--'NOVELLO'S MUSIC PRIMERS', NO. 99
HICKIN, WELTON
PIANOFORTE ACCOMPANIMENT WRITING
DUNWELL, WILFRID
PIANOFORTE AND HOW TO STUDY IT, THE
GIFFORD, ALEXANDER M.
PIANOFORTE AND ITS ACOUSTIC PROPERTIES, THE --2ND. REV. ED.---1888, IN
HANSING, SIEGFRIED

PIANOFORTE AND ITS MUSIC, THE ---1911
    KREHBIEL, HENRY
PIANOFORTE AND VIOLIN FOR HIGH SCHOOL STUDENTS
    BRITISH COLUMBIA--DEPT. OF EDUCATION
PIANOFORTE COMPOSITIONS OF SIBELIUS, THE
    TAWASTSTJERNA, ERIK
PIANOFORTE CONSTRUCTION
    NALDER, LAWRENCE MARCUS
PIANOFORTE DIPLOMAS
    TANKARD, GEOFFREY
PIANOFORTE FINGERING, ITS PRINCIPLES AND APPLICATIONS
    KNOTT, THOMAS B.
PIANOFORTE MANUAL, THE ..DESIGNED AS A COMPLETE PIANOFORTE PRIMER
    WRIGHT, WILLIAM C.
PIANOFORTE MUSIC..ITS HISTORY, WITH BIOGRAPHICAL SKETCHES AND CRITICAL
    FILLMORE, JOHN C.
PIANOFORTE PLAYING..JOTTINGS BY W. H. WEBBE--2ND. ED.
    WEBBE, WILLIAM H.
PIANOFORTE PLAYING ON ITS TECHNICAL AND AESTHETIC SIDES
    REDDIE, CHARLES FREDERICK
PIANOFORTE POCKET COMPANION, THE ..OR, A POPULAR VIEW OF THE SCIENCE
    ANON
PIANOFORTE PRIMER, THE ..CONTAINING THE RUDIMENTS OF MUSIC CALCULATED
    BURROWES, JOHN FRECKLETON
PIANOFORTE SONATA, THE ..ITS ORIGIN AND DEVELOPMENT---1895
    SHEDLOCK, JOHN S.
PIANOFORTE STUDY..HINTS FOR TEACHERS AND STUDENTS
    LINDO, ALGERNON H.
PIANOFORTE STUDY..HINTS ON PIANO PLAYING
    MCARTHUR, ALEXANDER
PIANOFORTE STUDY..HINTS ON PIANO PLAYING
    NICCHIA, LILLIAN
PIANOFORTE TEACHER'S GUIDE, THE
    PLAIDY, LOUIS
PIANOFORTE TEACHER'S VADE MECUM, THE ..A CYCLOPEDIA FOR THE PREPARATION
    LOWE, CLAUDE EDGERTON
PIANOFORTE TEACHERS' EXAMINATION FOR THE A.R.C.M. DIPLOMA..A GUIDE TO
    FILLINGHAM, ARTHUR H.
PIANOFORTE TELEGRAPHY, THE --THE MORSE TELEGRAPH CODE--INSTRUCTOR
    GRIFFIN, RUSSELL B.
PIANOFORTE TESTS IN INITIATIVE AND INTELLIGENCE AS SET IN DIPLOMA
    THIMAN, ERIC H.
PIANOFORTE THEORY COURSE FOR BEGINNERS' PIANO CLASS
    LUBIT, JULIA
PIANOFORTE TONE-PRODUCTION---SAME AS 'THE ACT OF TOUCH IN ALL ITS
    MATTHAY, TOBIAS A.
PIANOFORTE TUNER'S POCKET COMPANION, THE ..COMPILED FROM THE NOTES OF
    FAUST, OLIVER C.
PIANOLA AND PIANOLA PIANO MUSIC CATALOG, THE ..SIXTY-FIVE NOTE MUSIC
    AEOLIAN COMPANY, THE
PIANOLA PIANO, THE
    AEOLIAN COMPANY, THE
PIANOLIST, THE ..A GUIDE FOR PIANOLA PLAYERS
    KOBBE, GUSTAV
PIANOS..THEIR CONSTRUCTION, TUNING AND REPAIR
    HASLUCK, PAUL N.
PIANOS, PIANISTS AND SONICS
    BRIGGS, A.
PIANOSCRIPT BOOK..AN INVALUABLE AID TO TEACHER AND STUDENT IN
    JONAS, ALBERTO
PIANOS AND MUSICAL INSTRUMENTS DISCUSSED FROM AN UNSANITARY STANDPOINT
    REMBUSCH, JOSEPH ADAM
PIANOS AND THEIR MAKERS..A COMPREHENSIVE HISTORY OF THE PIANO---1911
    DOLGE, ALFRED
PIANO AND GOWN--REMINISCENCES
    WEATHERLY, FREDERICK EDWARD
PIANO AND HOW TO CARE FOR IT, THE ..PIANO TUNING IN THEORY AND PRACTICE
    FUNKE, OTTO
PIANO AND ITS ANCESTORS, THE
    GUENTHER, FELIX
PIANO AND ITS MUSIC, THE --FROM 'MODERN PIANO COURSE'
    WHITFORD, ROBERT
PIANO AND MUSICAL MATTERS
    LAMOTTE, J.
PIANO AND ORGAN CATALOGUE--2 VOLS.
    BRITISH BROADCASTING CORPORATION--CENTRAL MUSIC LIBRARY
PIANO AND SONG..HOW TO TEACH, HOW TO LEARN, AND HOW TO FORM A JUDGEMENT
    WIECK, FRIEDRICH
PIANO AUDITIONS SYLLABUS AND COMPREHENSIVE GUIDE FOR PIANO
    MUSIC EDUCATION LEAGUE, INC.
PIANO BY EAR
    SMITH, EDWIN S.
PIANO CLASS, THE
    COLEMAN, H. P.
PIANO CLASSES AND THE PRIVATE TEACHER
    NATIONAL BUREAU FOR THE ADVANCEMENT OF MUSIC
PIANO CLASSES FOR EVERYONE..A PRACTICAL GUIDE FOR PIANO TEACHERS
    BENNETT, BEULAH VARNER
PIANO CLASSES IN ELEMENTARY SCHOOLS
    KING, AUDREY
PIANO CLASSES IN THE SCHOOLS..EDUCATIONAL VALUE OF IMPORTANT NEW
    NATIONAL BUREAU FOR THE ADVANCEMENT OF MUSIC
PIANO CLASS INSTRUCTION FOR CHILDREN AND ADULT CLASSES..A MANUAL FOR
    AXTENS, FLORENCE
PIANO CLASS INSTRUCTION
    NATIONAL BUREAU FOR THE ADVANCEMENT OF MUSIC
PIANO CLASS INSTRUCTOR
    BAVIN, JOHN T.
PIANO CLASS METHOD..THE FIRST TWELVE MONTHS IN THE PIANO CLASS
    AXTENS, FLORENCE
PIANO CLASS METHOD--BKS. 1 AND 2
    HUTT, DOREEN
PIANO CLASS WORKBOOK FOR FIRST YEAR STUDENTS
    STARKEY, EVELYN
PIANO COURSE..TEACHER'S BOOK, FOR CLASS OR INDIVIDUAL INSTRUCTION
    DANIELS, BESS
PIANO COURSE EITHER FOR CLASS OR FOR INDIVIDUAL INSTRUCTION
    DANIELS, BESS *
PIANO DUET, THE ...A GUIDE FOR PIANISTS
    LUBIN, ERNEST
PIANO FACTS
    FINNEGAN, BILL
PIANO FALLACIES OF TODAY
    MATTHAY, TOBIAS A.
PIANO FOR CLASSROOM MUSIC--2ND. ED.---1956
    PACE, ROBERT
PIANO HANDBOOK ON BOOGIE WOOGIE, BLUES, AND BARRELHOUSE..3 EASY TO PLAY
    COOK, J. LAWRENCE
PIANO IMPROVISING--2 VOLS., 1936-1938
    SHEFTE, ARTHUR G.
PIANO INSTRUCTION IN THE SCHOOLS
    SUR, WILLIAM R.--EDITOR
PIANO INTERPRETATION
    FERGUSON, DONALD NIVISON
PIANO IN INDIA, THE ..HOW TO KEEP IT IN ORDER, PRACTICAL INFORMATION ON
    HOBBS, HENRY

PIANO IN SCHOOL, A MEMORANDUM FOR SCHOOL ADMINISTRATORS
    BURROWS, RAYMOND
PIANO IN TWELVE LESSONS
    ANON
PIANO JAZZ..ESSAYS--2 VOLS., 1945-1946
    MCCARTHY, ALBERT J.--EDITOR
PIANO KEY AND WHIPPEN, THE ..AN ANALYSIS OF THEIR RELATIONSHIPS IN
    PFEIFFER, WALTER
PIANO LESSONS AND TESTS--4TH. REV. ED.---1945+
    SHERWOOD MUSIC SCHOOL
PIANO LOVER, THE ..BY VARIOUS AUTHORS
    ANON
PIANO MAKERS OF THE EVOLUTIONARY PERIOD..RARE ENGLISH AND AMERICAN
    WORCH, HUGO
PIANO MASTERY..TALKS WITH MASTER PIANISTS AND TEACHERS...
    BROWER, HARRIETTE
PIANO MASTERY, SECOND SERIES
    BROWER, HARRIETTE
PIANO MATERIALS..GRADED AND COMPILED AS AN AID TO INSTRUCTORS
    GRIFFIN, SISTER MARY ANNAROSE
PIANO MATERIALS
    OREGON MUSIC TEACHERS ASSOCIATION
PIANO METHOD FOR CLASS AND INDIVIDUAL INSTRUCTION--2 VOLS.
    BAUER, HAROLD *
PIANO MUSIC..AVAILABLE EDITIONS RECOMMENDED---ADDENDA, 1959
    BRINKMAN, JOSEPH *
PIANO MUSIC, ITS COMPOSERS AND CHARACTERISTICS
    HAMILTON, CLARENCE G.
PIANO MUSIC OF CLAUDE DEBUSSY, THE
    CORTOT, ALFRED
PIANO MUSIC OF SIX GREAT COMPOSERS---1947
    FERGUSON, DONALD NIVISON
PIANO OWNER'S GUIDE, THE
    SCHMECKEL, CARL D.
PIANO PEDALLING---1957, IN NORWEGIAN
    RIEFLING, REIMAR
PIANO PEDALS, THE
    VIRGIL, ANTHA MINERVA
PIANO PLAYING..A LITTLE BOOK OF SIMPLE SUGGESTIONS--REPRINTED FROM 'THE
    HOFMANN, JOSEF
PIANO PLAYING..GENERAL MUSICAL INSTRUCTION FROM BEGINNING TO END
    PETERSILEA, CARLYLE
PIANO PLAYING, A PRACTICAL METHOD--A NEW EDITION OF 'PIANO
    CHING, JAMES
PIANO PLAYING, WITH PIANO QUESTIONS ANSWERED---PUBLISHED EARLIER AS TWO
    HOFMANN, JOSEF
PIANO PLAYING BY HARMONY DIAGRAMS..STUDENT'S BOOK
    BEVITT, ZAY RECTOR
PIANO PLAYING BY HARMONY DIAGRAMS..TEACHER'S MANUAL
    BEVITT, ZAY RECTOR
PIANO PLAYING FOR FUN--4 VOLS.
    HOPKINS, GEORGE P.
PIANO PLAYING MECHANISMS
    WHITE, WILLIAM BRAID
PIANO PLAYING OF THE FUTURE, FOR EVERY GOOD PIANIST, THE
    EARLES, ADELAIDE L. S. T.
PIANO PRACTICING
    SCHEPER, HERBERT
PIANO PROGRESS..AN APPROACH TO MUSIC FOR THE PARTIALLY SIGHTED--2 VOLS.
    DAVISON, JUNE *
PIANO PROJECTS...A NEW APPROACH TO THE STUDY OF MODERN POPULAR PIANO
    HOLTZ, GUY
PIANO QUESTIONS ANSWERED..A LITTLE BOOK OF DIRECT ANSWERS TO TWO
    HOFMANN, JOSEF
PIANO REPERTOIRE GUIDE
    SMITH, BILLYE MULLINS
PIANO SAVING AND HOW TO ACCOMPLISH IT
    BILL, EDWARD LYMAN
PIANO SCALE MAKING
    VANT, ALBERT B.
PIANO SIGHTREADING CAN BE TAUGHT
    ELKAN, IDA
PIANO SONATA OF THE EIGHTEENTH CENTURY IN GERMANY, THE --CONTRIBUTIONS
    HEUSCHNEIDER, KARIN
PIANO SONATA OF THE EIGHTEENTH CENTURY IN ITALY, THE --CONTRIBUTIONS TO
    HEUSCHNEIDER, KARIN
PIANO STUDENT'S GRADUS AD PARNASSUM, THE ..PRESENTING THE
    KOCH, CASPAR
PIANO STUDY..APPLICATION AND TECHNIQUE
    PHILIPP, LILLIE H.
PIANO STUDY..A GUIDE TO TEACHER AND STUDENT
    DUFFEE, GERTRUDE BANKS
PIANO STUDY IN SOVIET-RUSSIAN SCHOOLS OF MUSIC--REPRINT..'JOURNAL OF
    ROBERT, WALTER
PIANO TEACHER, THE ..A BOOK OF SELF-INSTRUCTION
    ZUCH, ANNETT V. *
PIANO TEACHER, THE
    PLAIDY, LOUIS
PIANO TEACHER'S COMPANION, THE
    MAIER, GUY
PIANO TEACHER'S GUIDE, THE ..A HUNDRED QUESTIONS FOR YOUNG TEACHERS
    SMITHERS, WELSFORD
PIANO TEACHER'S GUIDE
    MICHIGAN MUSIC TEACHERS ASSOCIATION
PIANO TEACHER'S MANUAL, THE
    HERZOG, SIGMUND *
PIANO TEACHER'S SOURCE BOOK--BIBLIOGRAPHY OF BOOKS ABOUT PIANOS AND
    HINSON, MAURICE
PIANO TEACHERS PROFESSIONAL HANDBOOK
    TERWILLIGER, GORDON B.
PIANO TEACHING..ADVICE TO PUPILS AND YOUNG TEACHERS---1868 IN FRENCH
    LE COUPPEY, FELIX
PIANO TEACHING..ITS PRINCIPLES AND PROBLEMS
    HAMILTON, CLARENCE G.
PIANO TEACHING GUIDE--GRADES 1-8
    WASHINGTON STATE MUSIC TEACHERS ASSOCIATION
PIANO TECHNIC..MYTH OR SCIENCE
    SCHAUFFLER, LAWRENCE
PIANO TECHNIC FOR CHILDREN
    CARUTHERS, JULIA LOIS
PIANO TECHNIQUE..FOUNDATION PRINCIPLES
    CHING, JAMES
PIANO TECHNIQUE---COMBINED REPUBLICATION OF..'THE SHORTEST WAY TO
    GIESEKING, WALTER *
PIANO TECHNIQUE
    HARRISON, SIDNEY
PIANO TOUCH AND SCALES..AN ANALYSIS OF THE FUNDAMENTAL PRINCIPLES OF
    SHEPARD, FRANK H.
PIANO TRAVELERS ASSOCIATION BOOK, THE ..A REFERENCE BOOK CONTAINING
    NATIONAL PIANO TRAVELERS ASSOCIATION
PIANO TUNER'S GUIDE, THE
    PELTIER, LOUIS O.
PIANO TUNING, REGULATING AND REPAIRING...SELF INSTRUCTION...FOR THE
    FISCHER, JERRY CREE
PIANO TUNING AND ALLIED ARTS--5TH. ED.---1917
    WHITE, WILLIAM BRAID

PIANO WORKS OF CLAUDE DEBUSSY, THE
    SCHMITZ, ELIE ROBERT
PICTURE BOOK OF KEYBOARD MUSICAL INSTRUMENTS, A
    VICTORIA AND ALBERT MUSEUM, SOUTH KENSINGTON
PIERCE PIANO ATLAS--6TH. ED.---ORIGINALLY PUBLISHED AS 'MICHEL'S PIANO
    PIERCE, B.
PIPE AND STRINGS..THREE HISTORIC AND DESCRIPTIVE SKETCHES...THE
    GATES, WILLEY F.
PLAIN AND COMPENDIOUS METHOD OF TEACHING THOROUGH BASS, A ..WITH PROPER
    LAMPE, JOHN F.
PLAN FOR CREDITING OUTSIDE STUDY IN MUSIC UNDER PRIVATE INSTRUCTION FOR
    MANITOBA--DEPARTMENT OF EDUCATION
PLAYER-PIANIST, THE ..A GUIDE TO THE APPRECIATION AND INTERPRETATION OF
    WHITE, WILLIAM BRAID
PLAYER-PIANO, THE ..ITS CONSTRUCTION..HOW TO PLAY, WHAT TO PLAY AND HOW
    WILSON, DAVID M.
PLAYER-PIANO EXPLAINED, THE --PAMPHLET
    DRAKE, HARRY
PLAYER-PIANO UP TO DATE, THE
    WHITE, WILLIAM BRAID
PLAYER PIANO, AN HISTORICAL SCRAPBOOK, THE
    ROEHL, HARVEY
PLAYER PIANO, THE HISTORY OF THE MECHANICAL PIANO AND HOW TO REPAIR IT
    ORD-HUME, ARTHUR W. J. G.
PLAYER PIANO POINTERS
    AUTOPIANO COMPANY
PLAYER PIANO TREASURY..THE SCRAPBOOK HISTORY OF THE MECHANICAL PIANO IN
    ROEHL, HARVEY
PLAYING AND TEACHING OF BACH, THE ..A GUIDE FOR TEACHERS, STUDENTS AND
    CHING, JAMES
PLAYING BY SEEING..A STUDY IN TRAINING AND PERCEPTION FOR BETTER
    FREDRICH, FRANK
PLAYING FOR DANCE..THE PLACE OF THE PIANIST IN THE TEACHING OF DANCE
    THACKRAY, RUPERT M.
PLAYING FROM AN ORCHESTRAL SCORE
    TAYLOR, ERIC R.
PLAYING PIANO AT SIGHT--MECHANICS FOR THE ADULT BEGINNER
    DANIELS, BESS
PLAYING THE HARPSICHORD, SPINET OR PIANO FORTE MADE EASY BY NEW
    ANON
PLAYING THE HARPSICHORD
    SCHOTT, HOWARD
PLAYING THE PIANO..A COURSE OF ROTE TRAINING FOR BEGINNERS--CLASS OR
    MAIER, GUY *
PLAYING THE PIANO--TEACHER'S MANUAL
    MAIER, GUY *
PLAYING THE PIANO BY EAR--3 PTS.
    MORDEN, HARRY
PLAYING THE PIANO BY EAR
    CHILDERS, LEMUEL
PLAYING THE PIANO FOR PLEASURE--REV. ED.---1941
    COOKE, CHARLES
PLAYING THE PIANO WITH CONFIDENCE---1964
    D'ABREU, GERALD
PNEUMATIC PLAYER, THE ..THE REGULATION AND REPAIR OF SOME MODERN TYPES
    DRAKE, HARRY
PNEUMATIC PLAYER MECHANISM AND DESCRIPTIVE CATALOG OF STROHBER AND
    STROHBER PIANO COMPANY
POINTS ON PEDALLING
    CHING, JAMES
POLISH MUSIC AND CHOPIN ITS LAUREATE, ETC.
    RAYSON, ETHEL
POLONAISE---NOVELIZED BIOGRAPHY OF CHOPIN
    LESLIE, DORIS
POLONAISE, THE LIFE OF CHOPIN---ENGLISH EDITION, 'FREDERICK CHOPIN, A
    POURTALES, GUY DE
POLONAISE MILITAIRE..THE LIFE AND WORK OF FREDERIC CHOPIN..A DRAMATIC
    MILLER, JEWELL
POPULAR ACCOMPANYING
    STORMEN, WIN
POPULAR KEYBOARD HARMONY
    STORMEN, WIN
POPULAR PIANO...A CORRESPONDENCE COURSE OF THE EASTERN SCHOOLS OF
    SPENCER, BERNARD
POPULAR PIANO SELF-TAUGHT---1956
    STORMEN, WIN
PORTRAITS OF MUSICAL CELEBRITIES
    STEINWAY AND SONS
PORTRAITS OF MUSICAL CELEBRITIES
    STEINWAY AND SONS
PORTRAITS OF MUSICAL CELEBRITIES
    STEINWAY AND SONS
PORTRAITS OF MUSICAL CELEBRITIES
    STEINWAY AND SONS
PORTRAITS OF MUSICAL CELEBRITIES
    STEINWAY AND SONS
PORTRAITS OF MUSICAL CELEBRITIES
    STEINWAY AND SONS
PORTRAITS OF MUSICAL CELEBRITIES
    STEINWAY AND SONS
POSSIBILITIES OF TONE COLOR BY ARTISTIC USE OF PEDALS
    CARRENO, TERESA
PRACTICAL CHURCH SCHOOL MUSIC..METHODS AND TRAINING FOR SUCCESSFUL
    MCALL, REGINALD L.
PRACTICAL CORRESPONDENCE COURSE FOR PIANOFORTE
    KLAVARSKRIBO, SLEKKERVIER, HOLLAND
PRACTICAL COURSE IN PIANO TUNING
    MAYBERRY, JOHN HENRY
PRACTICAL COURSE IN TRANSPOSITION, A
    COLOMBATTI, HAROLD
PRACTICAL DRILL IN KEYBOARD HARMONY--2 VOLS., 1932-1940
    LUCKE, KATHARINE E.
PRACTICAL EXERCISES IN THEORY AND HARMONY PLAYING...LEADING TO
    VIRGIL, ANTHA MINERVA
PRACTICAL FINGER CONTROL--10TH. ED.
    LONGSTREET, H. P.
PRACTICAL GUIDE TO THE ART OF PHRASING...ANALYSIS OF CLASSIC AND
    RIEMANN, HUGO
PRACTICAL GUIDE TO THE STUDY OF TRANSPOSITION, A
    TRACY, GEORGE L.
PRACTICAL GUIDE TO THOROUGH-BASS, A
    KOLLMANN, AUGUST F.
PRACTICAL GUIDE TO THOROUGH BASS, A ..OR, HARMONY ILLUSTRATED AND
    JONES, JOHN H.
PRACTICAL HARMONIST AT THE HARPSICHORD, THE ---1708
    GASPARINI, FRANCESCO
PRACTICAL HARMONY, AN INTEGRATED COURSE IN THE PRINCIPLES OF
    TISCHLER, HANS
PRACTICAL HINTS FOR ACQUIRING THOROUGH BASS
    KLOSE, F. J.
PRACTICAL KEYBOARD HARMONY, A
    ROEDER, CARL M.
PRACTICAL KEYBOARD MODULATION
    PEERY, ROB ROY
PRACTICAL METHOD FOR THE PIANOFORTE FOR PRIVATE CLASS LESSONS--2 BKS.
    BAKER, HENRIETTE

PRACTICAL MODULATION FOR ADVANCED STUDENTS---43 LESSONS
    CHRISTIANSEN, FREDERICK M.
PRACTICAL MODULATOR, OR, HOW TO LEARN TO MODULATE FROM ANY ONE KEY TO
    WOLFRAM, THEODOR
PRACTICAL MUSICIANSHIP, A HANDBOOK FOR TEACHERS AND STUDENTS
    POWLEY, ALEC
PRACTICAL PIANO PLAYING MANUAL AND THEORY WRITING BOOK
    ELKAN, IDA
PRACTICAL PIANO TUNER, THE ..A COMPREHENSIVE SIMPLE SET OF RULES AND
    MOSCOW, CHARLES E.
PRACTICAL PIANO TUNING..A METHOD WITH A DO-IT-YOURSELF OUTLOOK
    DICKEY, ALBERT W.
PRACTICAL POINTS ON PIANO PLAYING
    BUONAMICI, CARLO
PRACTICAL RULES FOR PIANOFORTE PLAYING..TEXT BOOK FOR TEACHERS AND
    MERGES, P.
PRACTICAL TEXT-BOOK OF MUSIC, AS CONNECTED WITH THE ART OF PLAYING THE
    OLIVER, EDWARD B.
PRACTICAL THOROUGH BASS, OR, THE ART OF PLAYING FROM A FIGURED BASS ON
    CROTCH, WILLIAM
PRACTICAL TRANSPOSITION, FOR PIANISTS AND ORGANISTS
    DUNHAM, ROWLAND W.
PRACTICAL TREATISE ON TUNING AND REPAIRING THE PIANOFORTE, A
    PYLE, HOWARD WILLETT
PRACTICE TRIANGLE, THE ..EXERCISES FOR FOREARM ROTATION
    MATTHAY, TOBIAS A.
PRACTICING THE PIANO
    MERRICK, FRANK
PRECEPTOR, FOR THE PIANOFORTE, THE ORGAN OR HARPSICHORD, THE
    ANON
PRELIMINARY CHECKLIST OF RESEARCH ON THE CLASSIC SYMPHONY AND CONCERTO
    HILL, GEORGE R.
PRELIMINARY DIRECTORY OF SOUND RECORDING COLLECTIONS IN THE UNITED
    ASSOCIATION FOR RECORDED SOUND COLLECTIONS
PRELUDES AND STUDIES..MUSICAL THEMES OF THE DAY--SECTION 3..THE
    HENDERSON, WILLIAM JAMES
PRELUDES FOR THE PIANO FORTE, COMPOSED IN VARIOUS STYLES..TO WHICH ARE
    CROTCH, WILLIAM
PREPARING FOR KEYBOARD TESTS IN MUSICIANSHIP EXAMINATIONS, JUNIOR GRADE
    TOBIN, JOSEPH RAYMOND
PRESERVATION AND RESTORATION OF MUSICAL INSTRUMENTS..PROVISIONAL
    BERNER, ALFRED *
PRESTO BUYERS' GUIDE TO PLAYER-PIANOS AND PIANOS
    PRESTO PUBLISHING COMPANY
PRIMER FOR PRACTICAL KEYBOARD MODULATION, A
    BAUER, HAROLD
PRIMER OF MUSIC, A ..BEING THE FIRST STEPS IN MUSICIANSHIP..FOR
    MASON, WILLIAM G. *
PRIMER OF PIANOFORTE PLAYING
    TAYLOR, FRANKLIN
PRINCIPAL AGREMENTS OF THE SEVENTEENTH AND EIGHTEENTH CENTURIES, THE
    ALDRICH, PUTNAM
PRINCIPLES OF ACCOMPANIMENT OR THOROUGH BASS
    ALBRECHTSBERGER, JOHANN GEORG
PRINCIPLES OF EXPRESSION IN PIANOFORTE PLAYING, THE
    CHRISTIANI, ADOLPH FRIEDRICH
PRINCIPLES OF FINGERING AND LAWS OF PEDALLING
    MATTHAY, TOBIAS A.
PRINCIPLES OF PHRASING AND ARTICULATION IN MUSIC, THE
    MCEWEN, JOHN B.
PRINCIPLES OF PIANOFORTE PEDALLING, THE
    JOHNSON, THOMAS A.
PRINCIPLES OF PIANOFORTE PRACTICE, THE
    FRISKIN, JAMES
PRINCIPLES OF PIANOFORTE PRACTICE, THE
    MACLEAN, CHARLES D.
PRINCIPLES OF PLAYER ACTION OPERATION--3RD. ED.
    STANDARD PLAYER ACTION COMPANY
PRIVATE LIFE OF THE GREAT COMPOSERS, THE ---CHOPIN AND LISZT
    ROWBOTHAM, JOHN F.
PROBLEMS OF AGILITY, THE
    MATTHAY, TOBIAS A.
PROFESSIONAL PIANO TUNING
    HOWELL, W. DEAN
PROFESSION OF MUSIC AND HOW TO PREPARE FOR IT, THE
    PATTERSON, ANNIE WILSON
PROGRESSIVE SIGHT READING EXERCISES---FOR PIANO
    COLOMBATTI, HAROLD
PROS AND CONS OF THE MECHANICAL PLAYER, THE --REPRINT..M.T.N.A.
    GOW, GEORGE C.
PROTEST AGAINST THE MODERN DEVELOPMENT OF UNMUSICAL TONE, A --ORGANS,
    LEWIS, THOMAS C.
PSYCHO-PHYSICAL FOUNDATIONS OF MODERN PIANO TECHNIQUE, THE
    RAMUL, PETER
PSYCHOLOGY APPLIED TO MUSIC TEACHING
    CURWEN, ANNIE JESSY
PSYCHOLOGY FOR MUSICIANS
    BUCK, PERCY
PSYCHOLOGY FOR MUSIC TEACHERS..THE LAWS OF THOUGHT APPLIED TO SOUNDS
    FISHER, HENRY
PSYCHOLOGY FOR THE MUSIC TEACHER
    SWISHER, WALTER SAMUEL
PSYCHOLOGY OF A MUSICAL PRODIGY, THE ---1925
    REVESZ, GEZA
PSYCHOLOGY OF MUSICAL ABILITY, THE
    SHUTER, ROSAMUND
PSYCHOLOGY OF PIANO TEACHING, THE ..A TEXTBOOK FOR TEACHERS, STUDENTS
    CARRE, JOHN
PUPIL'S RECORD BOOK, THE ..SHOWING HOW TO SUCCEED AND HOW TO FAIL
    VIRGIL, ALMON K.
PUT ANOTHER NICKEL IN..A HISTORY OF COIN-OPERATED PIANOS
    BOWERS, Q. DAVID
QUESTIONS AND ANSWERS ON THE SCIENCE AND ART OF PIANOFORTE CONSTRUCTION
    ANON
QUESTIONS ON MOZART'S PIANO SONATAS, DESIGNED AS A COMPANION VOLUME TO
    MARKS, F. HELENA
RACHMANINOFF--'LITTLE BIOGRAPHIES', VOL. 2
    MARTENS, FREDERICK HERMAN
RACHMANINOFF--'LITTLE BIOGRAPHIES'
    HUMISTON, WILLIAM H.
RACHMANINOFF, A BIOGRAPHY
    LYLE, WATSON
RACHMANINOFF'S RECOLLECTIONS, TOLD TO OSKAR VON RIESEMANN---1934
    RACHMANINOFF, SERGEI
RACHMANINOFF
    SEROFF, VICTOR
RACHMANINOV AND HIS PIANO CONCERTOS
    ANDERSON, WILLIAM R.
RANDOM NOTES ON EDWARD MACDOWELL AND HIS MUSIC
    MACDOWELL, MARIAN GRISWOLD
RATIONALE OF PIANO TECHNIQUE, THE
    LAWRENCE, FREDERIC LOCKE
RATIONAL PRINCIPLES OF PIANOFORTE TECHNIQUE
    CORTOT, ALFRED
RE-ENACTING THE ARTIST..A STORY OF THE AMPICO REPRODUCING PIANO
    GIVENS, LARRY

RE-EVALUATION OF THE ROLE PLAYED BY C. P. E. BACH IN THE DEVELOPMENT OF
   CANAVE, PAZ CORAZON G.
READING OF MUSIC, THE ..A RATIONAL METHOD--NO. 1 OF A SERIES ON
   ZEPER, M. E. P.
READ AND ENJOY--2 VOLS.
   PIERCE, DORA *
READ AND PLAY..RAPID CHORD CONSTRUCTION--REV. ED.---1943
   DAVIS, LUCILE
READ AND REMEMBER..TWELVE STUDY PIECES TO FACILITATE PLAYING FROM
   TOBIN, JOSEPH RAYMOND
REALISTIC APPROACH TO PIANO PLAYING, A
   WOODHOUSE, GEORGE
REAWAKENING OF INTEREST IN THE HARPSICHORD IN THE 20TH. CENTURY, THE
   LYONS, SISTER MARIE STEPHEN
REBUILDING THE PLAYER PIANO
   GIVENS, LARRY
RECENT DEVELOPMENTS IN TEACHING CHILDREN TO PLAY THE PIANO
   ADAMS, JULIETTE
RECENT MUSIC AND MUSICIANS, AS DESCRIBED IN THE DIARIES AND
   MOSCHELES, CHARLOTTE
RECENT NORWEGIAN PIANO MUSIC
   KORSTEN, BJARNE
RECOLLECTIONS OF AN OLD MUSICIAN---GOTTSCHALK, JONAS CHICKERING, AND
   RYAN, THOMAS
REEVES' POPULAR PIANOFORTE TUTOR..RUDIMENTS OF MUSIC, EXERCISES WITH
   REEVES, WILLIAM
REEVES' VAMPING TUTOR FOR PLAYING BY EAR
   TAYLOR, FRANCIS
REFLECTIONS ON MUSIC..A LECTURE---IN ENGLISH AND GERMAN
   SCHNABEL, ARTUR
REFLECTIONS ON MUSIC
   FISCHER, EDWIN
REFUTATION OF THE FALLACIES AND MISREPRESENTATIONS CONTAINED IN A
   LOGIER, JOHANN BERNHARD
REGULATION AND REPAIR OF PIANO AND PLAYER PIANO MECHANISM
   WHITE, WILLIAM BRAID
REGULIEREN VON FLUEGELN BEI STEINWAY, DAS --REGULATION OF THE STEINWAY
   DIETZ, FRANZ RUDOLF
RELAXATION STUDIES IN THE MUSCULAR DISCRIMINATION REQUIRED FOR TOUCH,
   MATTHAY, TOBIAS A.
RELIGION AND ROMANCE OF A PIANIST'S LIFE---AUTOBIOGRAPHY
   CLARK, MADAM STEINEGER
REMARKS ON THE PRESENT STATE OF MUSICAL INSTRUCTION...THOROUGH BASS
   RELFE, JOHN
REMINISCENCES OF A MUSICIAN---LISZT AND PADEREWSKI
   JOHNS, CLAYTON
REMINISCENCES OF CLARA SCHUMANN AS FOUND IN THE DIARY OF HER GRANDSON
   SCHUMANN, FERDINAND
REMINISCENCES OF MORRIS STEINERT, COMPILED AND ARRANGED BY JANE MARLIN
   STEINERT, MORRIS
REMINISCENSES OF FREDERIC CHOPIN
   OSBORNE, GEORGE A.
RENAUD-PHONE PIANO METHOD..A PIANO COURSE THROUGH THE MEDIUM OF
   RENAUD, EMILIANO
REPAIRING THE PIANOFORTE, WITH CHAPTERS ON REGULATING, TONING,
   ANON
REPAIRING THE PIANOFORTE
   NALDER, LAWRENCE MARCUS
REPAIRING THE PLAYER PIANO..INFORMATION USEFUL TO PIANOFORTE TUNERS AND
   EARL, S. G.
REPAIRING THE PLAYER PIANO
   DRAKE, HARRY
REPAIRING THE REED ORGAN AND HARMONIUM..INFORMATION USEFUL TO
   MUSICAL OPINION AND MUSIC TRADE REVIEW
REPORT UPON MUSICAL INSTRUMENTS...PARIS UNIVERSAL EXPOSITION, 1867
   STEVENS, PARAN
RHYTHM, REASON AND RESPONSE FOR THE MUSICIAN, PIANIST AND TEACHER
   GLASFORD, IRENE A.
RHYTHMICAL PROBLEMS..SPECIAL STUDIES FOR MASTERING RHYTHMS DIFFERING BY
   GERMER, HEINRICH
RHYTHMICS, DYNAMICS, PEDAL, AND OTHER PROBLEMS OF PIANO PLAYING---1938
   LEIMER, KARL *
RHYTHMIC WAY, THE
   PARSONS, MARY H.
RHYTHM ACCOMPANIMENT MAGIC, FOR THE POPULAR PIANIST
   IRWIN, WILLIAM
RIDDLE OF THE PIANIST'S FINGER, THE
   SCHULTZ, ARNOLD
RIGHT FOOT FORWARD..A FIRST BOOK ON PEDALLING FOR ADULT STUDENTS
   ROSS, CHARLES
ROAD TO MODERN MUSIC, THE
   EMERICH, PAUL
ROBERT SCHUMANN..THE MAN AND HIS MUSIC---SYMPOSIUM--13 AUTHORS
   WALKER, ALAN--EDITOR
ROBERT SCHUMANN--'THE GREAT MUSICIANS' SERIES
   FULLER-MAITLAND, J. A.
ROBYN-HANKS HARMONY, THE ..A JUNIOR COURSE--BKS. 1-3, 1936-1938
   ROBYN, LOUISE
ROMANCE OF A PIANO, THE
   AMERICAN NEWS COMPANY
ROMANCE OF KEYS AND TONES..THE PIANO, ITS ORIGIN AND DEVELOPMENT, AND
   EISENBERG, JACOB
ROMANCE OF THE PIANO, THE ---1928
   BLOM, ERIC
ROMANTIC COMPOSERS, THE ---CHOPIN AND LISZT
   MASON, DANIEL GREGORY
ROTARY ROAD, AN EASY PILGRIMAGE BY EIGHT SHORT STEPS, THE --FOREARM
   CHING, JAMES
RUBATO, OR THE SECRET OF EXPRESSION IN PIANOFORTE PLAYING
   JOHNSTONE, J. ALFRED
RUBINSTEIN--'MAYFAIR BIOGRAPHIES', NO. 11
   HERVEY, ARTHUR
RUBINSTEIN'S FINGER EXERCISES..TECHNICAL STUDIES FROM THE THEORETICAL
   VILLOING, ALEXANDER
RUDIMENTS OF MUSIC..A NEW APPROACH WITH APPLICATION TO THE KEYBOARD
   CASTELLINI, JOHN EDWARD
RUDIMENTS OF THE ART OF PLAYING ON THE PIANOFORTE...A PLAIN DIRECTION
   GRAUPNER, GOTTLIEB
RUDIMENTS OF THE ART OF PLAYING THE PIANOFORTE, THE ...WITH NUMEROUS
   SPENCER, CHARLES L.
RUDIMENTS OF THOROUGH BASS, THE
   MARSH, JOHN
RUDOLPH GANZ EVALUATES MODERN PIANO MUSIC
   GANZ, RUDOLPH
RULES..OR A SHORT AND COMPLEAT METHOD FOR ATTAINING TO PLAY A THOROUGH
   ANON
RULES AND MAXIMS FOR YOUNG MUSICIANS--FROM 'MUSIC AND MUSICIANS'
   SCHUMANN, ROBERT
RULES AND REASONS FOR CORRECT SCALE-FINGERING
   HELD, ERNST
RULES FOR PLAYING IN A TRUE TASTE ON THE VIOLIN, GERMAN FLUTE,
   GEMINIANI, FRANCESCO
RUNNING PIANIST, THE ---PERCY GRAINGER
   TAYLOR, ROBERT L.
RUSSELL COLLECTION AND OTHER EARLY KEYBOARD INSTRUMENTS IN ST.
   EDINBURGH UNIVERSITY--DEPT. OF EARLY KEYBOARD INSTRUMENTS

SAINT-SAENS---1921
   HERVEY, ARTHUR
SAMSON FRANCOIS
   GAVOTY, BERNARD *
SCALES...THEIR HISTORY, THEORY, FINGERING AND TECHNICAL USE ON THE
   BRIGHAM, ELEANOR
SCALES, THE ..THEIR FORMATION, FINGERING, AND HOW TO PRACTICE THEM..TO
   PUPIN, ANNIE
SCALES TAUGHT IN ONE EASY LESSON, THE
   WILSON, CHARLES J.
SCHIRMER'S GUIDE TO BOOKS ON MUSIC AND MUSICIANS--A PRACTICAL
   DARRELL, ROBERT D.--COMPILER
SCHNEIDER'S TREATISE ON THOROUGH BASS AND HARMONY
   SCHNEIDER, FRIEDRICH
SCHOOL OF THE PIANO PEDAL
   MATHEWS, WILLIAM S. B.
SCHUBERT'S COMPOSITIONS FOR PIANO AND STRINGS--STRAD HANDBOOK NO. 2
   HARRISON, W. WELLS
SCHUBERT'S VARIATIONS
   BROWN, MAURICE J. E.
SCHUBERT PIANO SONATAS--B.B.C. MUSIC GUIDE, NO. 17
   RADCLIFFE, PHILIP
SCHUMANN'S PIANOFORTE WORKS
   FULLER-MAITLAND, J. A.
SCHUMANN AS CRITIC
   PLANTIGA, LEON B.
SCHUMANN PIANO MUSIC--B.B.C. MUSIC GUIDE, NO. 25
   CHISSELL, JOAN
SCIENCE AND ART AS TWIN SISTERS..BEING A SECOND TREATISE UPON THE
   BROTHERHOOD, JAMES
SCIENCE AND MUSIC
   JEANS, SIR JAMES HOPWOOD
SCIENCE IN MODERN PIANOFORTE PLAYING
   BRANDT, LEONIE
SCIENCE OF FINGERING, THE ---FOR PIANO
   MOKREJS, JOHN
SCIENCE OF PIANOFORTE TECHNIC, THE --2ND. REV. ED.---1927
   FIELDEN, THOMAS
SCIENCE OF PIANO PRACTICE, THE
   PARSONS, ALBERT R.
SCIENCE OF PRACTICE, THE
   SCHAUFFLER, ROBERT HAVEN
SCIENTIFIC PIANO TUNING AND SERVICING--REV. ED.---1941
   HOWE, ALFRED H.
SCIENTIFIC SIDE OF MUSIC IN SIMPLE, PRACTICAL FORM FOR TEACHERS AND
   JOHNSON, VERA A.
SCONCIA'S NEW SYSTEM OF INSTRUCTION IN MUSIC AS A SCIENCE..OR, A TRUE
   SCONCIA, JOHN A.
SCORE READING..A SERIES OF GRADED EXCERPTS
   BERNSTEIN, MARTIN--COMPILER
SCORE READING--BK. 3..CONCERTOS
   FISKE, ROGER
SCORE READING--BK. 4..ORATORIOS
   FISKE, ROGER
SECOND PRACTICAL GUIDE TO THOROUGH BASS, A
   KOLLMANN, AUGUST F.
SECRETS OF THE SUCCESS OF GREAT MUSICIANS
   PIRANI, EUGENIO DI
SECRET OF MUSICAL EXPRESSION, WITH SPECIAL REFERENCE TO PIANOFORTE
   TAYLER, E. DOUGLAS
SECRET OF SUCCESSFUL PRACTICE, THE
   TAYLER, E. DOUGLAS
SECTIONAL TUNING OF THE PIANO
   MURATA, KOH
SEEING WHAT WE SING, AN AID THROUGH KEYBOARD EXPERIENCE TO THE
   EGBERT, MARION S.
SELECTED AND GRADED LIST OF STUDIES AND PIECES FOR TEACHERS OF
   GRAY, WILLIAM L.
SELECTED CORRESPONDENCE OF FREDERYK F. CHOPIN--COLLECTED BY BRONISLAW
   CHOPIN, FREDERIC
SELECTED LIST OF GRADED TEACHING MATERIAL FOR THE PIANO, A --3RD.
   MCNABB, GEORGE
SELECTED LIST OF MUSIC RECOMMENDED FOR PIANO STUDENTS, A --4TH. REV.
   NEWMAN, WILLIAM S.
SELECTED LIST OF PIANO TEACHING MATERIALS PUBLISHED SINCE 1960, A
   LYKE, JAMES
SELECTIONS FROM THE PIANO TEACHER, 1958-1963
   SAVLER, ROBERTA--EDITOR
SELF-HELP IN PIANO STUDY
   BROWER, HARRIETTE
SELF-INSTRUCTOR FOR THE PIANOFORTE, CONTAINING C. MAHONY'S NEW SYSTEM
   MAHONY, CORNELIUS
SELF-TEACHING CHORD BOOK FOR THE PIANO OR ORGAN..SHOWS HOW TO PLAY THE
   EVANS, EVERETT J.
SELF INSTRUCTION IN THE PIANO
   GIBBS, GEORGE A., JR.
SELF READING NOTES
   O'REAR, MRS. ASBURY S.
SENSITIVE PIANO TOUCH AND WAYS AND MEANS TO ITS ACQUIREMENT---A LECTURE
   BROTHERHOOD, JAMES
SEQUEL TO THE FIRST COMPANION TO THE CHIROPLAST
   LOGIER, JOHANN BERNHARD
SERGEI RACHMANINOFF..THE MAN AND HIS MUSIC
   CULSHAW, JOHN
SERGEI RACHMANINOFF, A LIFETIME IN MUSIC
   BERTENSSON, SERGEI *
SERGEI RACHMANINOFF
   GRONOWICZ, ANTONI
SERGEI RACHMANINOFF
   THRELFALL, ROBERT
SETT OF PROGRESSIVE LESSONS FOR THE HARPSICHORD OR PIANO FORTE, A
   MOLLER, JOHN CHRISTOPHER
SHORTEST WAY TO PIANISTIC PERFECTION, THE
   LEIMER, KARL *
SHORT ACCOUNT OF THE PROGRESS OF J. B. LOGIER'S SYSTEM OF MUSICAL
   LOGIER, JOHANN BERNHARD
SHORT AND CONCISE ANALYSIS OF MOZART'S 22 PIANOFORTE SONATAS, A
   SALSBURY, JANET
SHORT AND FUNDAMENTAL INSTRUCTIONS FOR LEARNING THOROUGH BASS
   HECK, JOHANN CASPAR
SHORT CUTS TO PIANO TECHNIQUE
   THAYER, E. D.
SHORT ESSAY ON THE GENERAL NEED FOR SCIENTIFIC PIANOFORTE PLAYING, A
   EARLES, ADELAIDE L. S. T.
SHORT HISTORY OF KEYBOARD MUSIC, A
   KIRBY, FRANK EUGENE
SHORT INSTRUCTIONS FOR TUNING A PIANO-FORTE..WRITTEN BY 'MUSICUS
   ANON
SIDELIGHTS ON TOUCH..TOGETHER WITH 101 QUESTIONS, SUITABLE FOR
   CHING, JAMES
SIGHT-READING AT THE PIANO
   MERRILL, MYRTLE
SIGHT READING AT THE PIANO--IN THREE STAGES
   ROWLEY, ALEC *
SIGHT READING TESTS FOR BEGINNERS--2 VOLS., 1930-1933
   PIERCE, DORA *

SIMPLE AND COMPLETE PRIMER FOR THE PIANOFORTE, THE
 VINING, HARRISON S.
SIMPLE TREATISE ON SCALES AND ARPEGGIOS FOR PIANO, A --3 VOLS.
 BANTLY, BENEDICT
SIMPLICITY OF PIANO TECHNIQUE, THE
 BOWEN, YORK
SIMPLIFIED KEYBOARD HARMONY
 GRAF, HENRY C.
SINGER AND ACCOMPANIST..THE PERFORMANCE OF FIFTY SONGS
 MOORE, GERALD
SINGING CLASS PIANIST AND ON PIANOFORTE ACCOMPANYING IN GENERAL, THE
 FORD, DONALD
SINGING TOUCH, THE
 REEDER, BETAH
SINGLE NOTE, THE
 CURCIO, LOUISE
SIR C. HALLE..A SKETCH OF HIS CAREER AS A
 HALLE, SIR CHARLES
SIR CHARLES HALLE..A PORTRAIT FOR TODAY
 RIGBY, CHARLES
SIXTEEN LESSON PLANS..A MANUAL FOR PROGRESSIVE SERIES TEACHERS--PIANO
 BROUGHTON, JULIA *
SIX GREAT COMPOSERS---CHOPIN
 WARRACK, JOHN H.
SKETCHES OF GREAT PIANISTS AND GREAT VIOLINISTS, BIOGRAPHICAL AND
 FERRIS, GEORGE TITUS
SLUR OR COUPLET OF NOTES IN ALL ITS VARIETY, THE ..ITS INTERPRETATION
 MATTHAY, TOBIAS A.
SMATTERING OF IGNORANCE, A
 LEVANT, OSCAR
SOME COMMENTARIES ON THE TEACHING OF PIANOFORTE TECHNIC..A SUPPLEMENT
 MATTHAY, TOBIAS A.
SOME MUSICAL RECOLLECTIONS OF FIFTY YEARS---INCLUDES LEOPOLD DE MEYER,
 HOFFMAN, RICHARD
SOME NOTES--ON THE HARPSICHORD AND PIANOFORTE--MADE BY J. S. BROADWOOD,
 BROADWOOD, JAMES SHUDI
SOME PRACTICAL THINGS IN PIANO PLAYING
 FOOTE, ARTHUR W.
SOME REFLECTIONS ON PIANO PLAYING
 PHILIPP, ISIDOR
SOME SECRETS OF SUCCESS IN PLAYING IN PUBLIC
 COPP, LAURA R.
SONATA, ITS FORM AND MEANING AS EXEMPLIFIED IN THE PIANO SONATAS BY
 MARKS, F. HELENA
SONATAS OF BEETHOVEN AS HE PLAYED AND TAUGHT THEM, THE
 DRAKE, KENNETH
SONATA FORM---1896
 HADOW, SIR WILLIAM HENRY
SONATA IN THE BAROQUE ERA, THE --A HISTORY OF THE SONATA IDEA, VOL. 1
 NEWMAN, WILLIAM S.
SONATA IN THE CLASSIC ERA, THE --A HISTORY OF THE SONATA IDEA, VOL. 2
 NEWMAN, WILLIAM S.
SONATA PRINCIPLE, THE --CIRCA 1750
 MELLERS, WILFRED
SONATA SINCE BEETHOVEN, THE --A HISTORY OF THE SONATA IDEA, VOL. 3
 NEWMAN, WILLIAM S.
SONGS OF SCHUBERT, A GUIDE FOR SINGERS, TEACHERS AND ACCOMPANISTS, THE
 LE MASSENA, CLARENCE E.
SONS OF BACH, THE
 REESER, EDUARD
SOSTENUTO PEDAL, THE
 WOLFRAM, VICTOR
SOUL OF GENIUS, THE ..ITS MUSICAL DEVELOPMENT AND HOW THE WORLD AT
 DAHL, ANTON
SOURCES OF KEYBOARD MUSIC IN ENGLAND, THE ---1913
 BORREN, CHARLES VAN DEN
SOURCE MATERIALS FOR PIANO TECHNIQUES
 REZITS, JOSEPH
SPEAKING OF PIANISTS
 CHASINS, ABRAM
SPECIAL SURVEY CONDUCTED--IN 1889--FOR LYON AND HEALY, INC., STEINWAY
 AEOLIAN COMPANY, THE
SPECIAL TECHNIC COURSE IN THE VIRGIL CLAVIER METHOD--6 PTS.
 VIRGIL, ALMON K.
SPECIMEN ANSWERS TO THE QUESTIONS IN PIANOFORTE DIPLOMAS
 TANKARD, GEOFFREY
SPLENDOR OF MUSIC, THE
 DILLER, ANGELA
ST. JAMES HALL...C. HALLE'S PIANOFORTE RECITALS..MAY 5-JUNE 29,
 HALLE, SIR CHARLES
ST. JAMES HALL...MR. HALLE'S BEETHOVEN RECITALS, MAY 23-JULY 11, 1861,
 HALLE, SIR CHARLES
STEINWAY..YESTERDAY, TODAY, TOMORROW
 STEINWAY AND SONS
STEINWAY AND SONS' PIANO-FORTE MANUFACTORY AT 'STEINWAY', LONG ISLAND
 STEINWAY AND SONS
STEINWAY OF TODAY, THE ..A FAMILY OF PIANO MANUFACTURERS THROUGH FOUR
 STEINWAY AND SONS
STEINWAY PROGRESS..AN APPRECIATION BY I. J. PADEREWSKI
 STEINWAY AND SONS
STENCILLING OF PIANOS, THE
 NATIONAL PIANO MANUFACTURERS ASSOCIATION OF AMERICA
STEPHEN HELLER..HIS LIFE AND WORKS
 BARBEDETTE, HIPPOLYTE
STEPS TO MUSICIANSHIP THROUGH GROUP PIANO--TEACHER'S MANUAL
 FRISCH, FAY TEMPLETON
STEP BY STEP..TEXTBOOK IN PIANO PLAYING..HANDBOOK FOR TEACHERS
 VIRGIL, ALMON K.
STIMULATION IN PIANO STUDY..HOW PARENTS CAN STIMULATE AND MAINTAIN
 BRIED, FREDERICK
STORIES OF STANDARD TEACHING PIECES FOR THE PIANOFORTE
 PERRY, EDWARD B.
STORY-LIVES OF MASTER MUSICIANS
 BROWER, HARRIETTE
STORY OF NANYNKA, THE ..FIRST PIANO LESSONS FOR CHILDREN, PRIVATE OR
 MOKREJS, JOHN
STORY OF THE STEINWAYS, THE --REPRINT FROM 'FRA' MAGAZINE
 HUBBARD, ELBERT
STORY OF UNIQUE PIANO TUITION, THE
 ASHBURNHAM, GEORGE
STRAIGHT TO THE HEART OF MUSIC---PLAYER-PIANO
 KOBBE, GUSTAV
STRICTURES ON MR. LOGIER'S SYSTEM OF MUSICAL EDUCATION
 MONTI, H. DE
STRINGED KEYBOARD INSTRUMENTS 1440-1880---1955, IN GERMAN
 HIRT, FRANZ JOSEF
STRUCTURAL ANALYSIS OF MOZART'S PIANO CONCERTOS, A --MUSICOLOGICAL
 TISCHLER, HANS
STUDENT'S GUIDE TO THE ART OF TEACHING THE PIANOFORTE, THE --2ND. REV.
 HORROCKS, CYRIL R. H.
STUDENT'S HANDBOOK FOR ENTRANTS IN THE NATIONAL PIANO PLAYING AUDITIONS
 NATIONAL GUILD OF PIANO TEACHERS
STUDIES FOR BASIC PIANO TECHNIQUE..WRITTEN AND SELECTED WITH TECHNICAL
 CHING, JAMES
STUDIES IN JAZZ HARMONY
 MEHEGAN, JOHN F.

STUDIES IN MEASURE AND RHYTHM...FOR TEACHERS AND PUPILS, ALSO FOR
 KRAUSE, E. W.
STUDIES IN MEASURE AND RHYTHM, FOR THE PIANOFORTE, TO DEVELOP AN EXACT
 KRAUSE, E. W.
STUDIES IN MODERN MUSIC--2ND. SERIES--9TH. ED.---CHOPIN
 HADOW, SIR WILLIAM HENRY
STUDIES IN MODULATION FOR PRACTICAL AND THEORETICAL PURPOSES
 BAKER, PERCY
STUDIES IN PHRASING, MEMORIZING AND INTERPRETATION
 MATHEWS, WILLIAM S. B.
STUDIES IN PHRASING AND FORM
 MACPHERSON, STEWART
STUDIES IN PHRASING SELECTED FROM THE WORKS OF THE BEST CLASSIC AND
 MATHEWS, WILLIAM S. B.
STUDY GUIDE FOR PIANO TEACHERS
 NEW SCHOOL FOR MUSIC STUDY
STUDY IN EQUAL TEMPERAMENT, A
 HAFER, HOWARD W.
STUDY OF TIME AND MEASURE, THE --FOR PIANO STUDENTS
 KRAUSE, E. W.
STUDY WITH AMUSEMENT, A SERIES OF PROGRESSIVE LESSONS FOR THE
 PETERSILIA, FRANZ
STYLES FOR THE JAZZ PIANIST--BK. 1..THE RHYTHMIC SCHOOL
 MEHEGAN, JOHN F.
SUCCESSFUL MUSIC TEACHER, THE ..WORDS OF ADVICE
 ANTCLIFFE, HERBERT
SUCCESS IN MUSIC, AND HOW IT IS WON
 FINCK, HENRY T.
SUCCESS IN PIANO TEACHING
 BROUGHTON, JULIA
SUGGESTED PIANO STUDY FOR THE VOCAL STUDENT
 GILBERT, RUSSELL S.
SUGGESTIONS FOR THE APPRECIATION AND INTERPRETATION OF PIANOFORTE MUSIC
 LOWE, CLAUDE EDGERTON
SUMMER AT NOHANT..A PLAY IN THREE ACTS---CHOPIN
 IWASZKIEWICZ, JAROSLAW
SUPPLEMENTARY CATALOG OF MUSIC FOR THE AEOLIAN GRAND AND
 AEOLIAN COMPANY, THE
SUPPLEMENT TO PIANO MUSIC, ITS COMPOSERS AND CHARACTERISTICS, A ..AND
 HAMILTON, CLARENCE G.
SUPPLEMENT TO THE THEORY OF MODULATION
 REGER, MAX
SUPREMACY OF AMPICO MUSIC..UNIT TWO OF A COURSE IN AMPICO SALESMANSHIP
 AMPICO CORPORATION
SURE TEACHER..OR, CHILD'S FIRST COURSE FOR THE PIANOFORTE, THE
 IVES, WILLIAM
SUZUKI PIANO SCHOOL--4 VOLS.
 SUZUKI, SHIN'ICHI
SWEELINCK'S KEYBOARD MUSIC..A STUDY OF ENGLISH ELEMENTS IN
 CURTIS, ALAN
SYLLABUS FOR PIANO, 1970
 NEW YORK STATE MUSIC TEACHERS' ASSOCIATION
SYLLABUS FOR PIANO AUDITIONS
 GORDON, PHILIP
SYLLABUS OF THE SECOND EXAMINATION OF MR. LOGIER'S PUPILS, ON HIS NEW
 LOGIER, JOHANN BERNHARD
SYNTHETIC CATECHISM, THE ..538 QUESTIONS AND ANSWERS FOR USE IN
 CHITTENDEN, KATE S.
SYNTHETIC METHOD FOR THE PIANOFORTE, THE
 PARSONS, ALBERT R.
SYSTEMATIC FINGERING OF THE ARPEGGIOS OF COMMON CHORDS, ETC., THE
 CROUCH, M. S.
SYSTEM FOR BEGINNERS IN THE ART OF PLAYING UPON THE PIANOFORTE, A
 MASON, WILLIAM G. *
SYSTEM OF STUDY OF SCALES AND CHORDS, A ..BEING CHAPTERS ON THE
 WESTBROOK, BENJAMIN V.
SYSTEM OF TECHNICAL EXERCISES FOR THE PIANO-FORTE, A
 MASON, WILLIAM G.
SYSTEM OF THE SCIENCE OF MUSIC AND PRACTICAL COMPOSITION..INCIDENTALLY
 LOGIER, JOHANN BERNHARD
TALES OF THE OLD VIRTUOSO..THE SPANISH COURT PIANIST--MARQUIS DON
 GRAHAM, L. SIBLEY
TALKING ABOUT CONCERTOS..AN ANALYTICAL STUDY OF A NUMBER OF WELL-KNOWN
 HOPKINS, ANTHONY
TALKING ABOUT SONATAS..A BOOK OF ANALYTICAL STUDIES, BASED ON A
 HOPKINS, ANTHONY
TALKS WITH PIANO TEACHERS
 GUTMANN, EMMA WILKINS
TALKS WITH PIANO TEACHERS
 WILKINS-GUTMANN, EMMA
TEACHER'S GUIDE...TO MRS. CURWEN'S PIANOFORTE METHOD, 'THE CHILD
 CURWEN, ANNIE JESSY
TEACHER'S GUIDE..A CREATIVE APPROACH TO PIANO CLASS TEACHING, BY JULES
 MUSIC PROJECT--NEW YORK CITY
TEACHER'S GUIDEBOOK TO PIANO LITERATURE, THE --REV. ED.---1954+
 KERN, ALICE M. *
TEACHER'S GUIDE TO THE NEW SCRIBNER MUSIC LIBRARY
 REZITS, JOSEPH
TEACHER'S MANUAL, A WORK DESIGNED TO SUPPLEMENT...'THE FIRST TEN WEEKS
 CALLENDER, ROMAINE
TEACHER'S MANUAL FOR PIANOFORTE COURSE, THE
 FAELTEN, CARL
TEACHER'S MANUAL OF MASON'S PIANOFORTE TECHNICS
 MATHEWS, WILLIAM S. B.
TEACHERS' GRADED LIST FOR THE PIANOFORTE
 NEW ENGLAND CONSERVATORY
TEACHERS' MANUAL FOR THE PORTER PIANOFORTE COURSE
 PORTER, FRANK A. *
TEACHERS DICTATION MANUAL
 MCHOSE, ALLEN IRVINE
TEACHERS MANUAL FOR POPULAR PIANO PLAYING, DESIGNED FOR ALL TEACHERS OF
 GILBERTSON, ARNOLD B.
TEACHER NEVER TOLD ME---TIPS FOR STUDENTS
 HARRISON, SIDNEY
TEACHING APPLIED MUSIC BY CLASS METHOD
 MEKOTA, BETH ANNA
TEACHING HINTS
 RICHTER, ADA
TEACHING MATERIAL GRADED ACCORDING TO HARMONIC STRUCTURE, CAREFULLY
 NEWMAN, ELIZABETH
TEACHING MUSIC AND MAKING IT PAY
 ANTRIM, DORAN K.
TEACHING MUSIC READING IN THE OXFORD PIANO COURSE
 HAAKE, CHARLES JOHN *
TEACHING OF ARTUR SCHNABEL, THE ..A GUIDE TO INTERPRETATION
 WOLFF, KONRAD
TEACHING OF PIANOFORTE TECHNIQUE, THE ..A SUPPLEMENT TO THE ACT OF
 MATTHAY, TOBIAS A.
TEACHING OF TECHNIQUE TO CHILDREN, THE --4 PTS.
 CHING, JAMES
TEACHING PIANO IN CLASSES
 THOMPSON, JOHN
TEACHING PIANO IN CLASSROOM AND STUDIO
 MUSIC EDUCATORS NATIONAL CONFERENCE
TEACHING PIECES AND HOW TO TEACH THEM
 DITSON COMPANY

TEACHING TECHNIQUES FOR THE PIANO
    HOFHEIMER, GRACE
TEACH YOURSELF MUSIC
    PALMER, KING
TEACH YOURSELF TO PLAY THE PIANO..BASED ON THE INTERVAL METHOD
    MCCLINTOCK, LORENE
TEACH YOURSELF TO PLAY THE PIANO
    PALMER, KING
TECHNIC..A SYSTEM OF THE MOST NECESSARY DAILY EXERCISES TO PRODUCE A
    MANSFELDT, HUGO L.
TECHNIC..FOR DEVELOPING AN EARLY FOUNDATION IN PIANO PLAYING
    BARTH, HANS
TECHNIC..THE ENTIRE 25 BRANCHES FOR DEVELOPING TECHNIC NECESSARY TO
    BARTH, HANS
TECHNICAL EXERCISES FOR THE EMANUEL MOOR DOUBLE KEYBOARD PIANO---IN
    MOOR, WINIFRED
TECHNICAL HISTORY OF THE PLAYER
    MCTAMMANY, JOHN
TECHNICAL STUDY IN THE ART OF PIANOFORTE PLAYING--DEPPE'S
    EHRENFECTER, C. A.
TECHNICAL TREATISE ON PLAYER PIANO MECHANISM, A
    WHITE, WILLIAM BRAID
TECHNICAL WORK IN EAR-TRAINING FOR THE PIANO..A METHOD FOR PRIVATE AND
    ELKAN, IDA
TECHNICON, THE..A TREATISE UPON THE DEVELOPMENT OF PIANOFORTE
    BROTHERHOOD, JAMES
TECHNICS OF PIANOFORTE PLAYING, THE ..MUSICAL ORNAMENTATION, APPENDIX
    GERMER, HEINRICH
TECHNICS OF PIANOFORTE PLAYING REARRANGED AS A METHODICAL PLAN OF
    GERMER, HEINRICH
TECHNIC AND NOTATION AS APPLIED TO THE PIANOFORTE
    TUFTS, JOHN W.
TECHNIC TALES FOR THE CHILD AT THE PIANO--BKS. 1-3..TEACHER'S MANUAL
    ROBYN, LOUISE
TECHNIPHONE MANUAL..INSTRUCTIONS AND EXERCISES IN THE USE OF THE
    VIRGIL, ALMON K.
TECHNIQUE AND EXPRESSION IN PIANOFORTE PLAYING
    TAYLOR, FRANKLIN
TECHNIQUE AND HAND DEVELOPMENT---USE OF A MACHINE
    OSTROVSKY, HENRY
TECHNIQUE OF ACCOMPANIMENT, THE --THE STUDENT'S MUSIC LIBRARY
    CRANMER, PHILIP
TECHNIQUE OF PIANO PLAYING, THE, --2ND. ED.---1958
    GAT, JOZSEF
TEMPO RUBATO, OR TIME VARIATION IN MUSICAL PERFORMANCE
    MCEWEN, JOHN B.
TEMPO RUBATO AND OTHER ESSAYS
    STERNBERG, CONSTANTIN I. VON
TEN BEETHOVEN SONATAS FOR PIANO AND VIOLIN, THE
    SZIGETI, JOSEPH
TERESA CARRENO, 'BY THE GRACE OF GOD'
    MILINOWSKI, MARTA
TESTS IN SIGHT READING, FOR PIANO..FROM FIRST GRADE TO DIPLOMA--3 VOLS.
    LOVELOCK, WILLIAM
TEXTBOOK OF EUROPEAN MUSICAL INSTRUMENTS, A ---1937
    GALPIN, FRANCIS W.
TEXTBOOK OF PRACTICAL HARMONY AT THE KEYBOARD
    HOUGHTON, WINIFRED E.
THALBEGARIAN (SIC) EXERCISES..OR, THE PIANIST'S DESIDERATA
    FROST, EDWARD
THEMATIC CATALOG OF THE WORKS OF MUZIO CLEMENTI
    TYSON, ALAN
THEMATIC PATTERNS IN SONATAS OF BEETHOVEN
    RETI, RUDOLPH
THEODORE LESCHETIZKY
    HULLAH, ANNA
THEODOR LESCHETIZKY
    POTOCKA, COMTESSE ANGELE
THEORETICAL AND PRACTICAL PIANO-FORTE SCHOOL FOR THE JANKO
    HANSMANN, RICHARD
THEORETICO-PRACTICAL ELEMENTARY PIANO-FORTE SCHOOL FOR STUDENTS OF THE
    GERMER, HEINRICH
THEORETIC COMPANION TO PRACTICE--PART I OF THE PIANIST'S HANDBOOK
    PETERSON, FRANKLIN
THEORIES OF CLAUDE DEBUSSY, MUSICIEN FRANCAIS, THE ---1929
    VALLAS, LEON
THEORY AND PRACTICE OF PIANOFORTE BUILDING
    WHITE, WILLIAM BRAID
THEORY EXPLAINED TO PIANO STUDENTS..OR PRACTICAL LESSONS IN HARMONY
    CLARKE, HUGH ARCHIBALD
THEORY FOR PIANO STUDENTS--1ST. YEAR, PRIVATE OR CLASS--5 VOLS.,
    BENNER, LORA
THEORY OF INTERPRETATION, APPLIED TO ARTISTIC MUSICAL PERFORMANCE
    GOODRICH, ALFRED JOHN
THEORY OF MODULATION, A ---DUAL TEXT..ENGLISH AND GERMAN
    OTTERSTROEN, THORVALD
THEORY OF THE NEW KEYBOARD, ARRANGED BY W. B. KEELER AND E. K. WINKLER
    KEELER, WALTER B.
THEORY PAPERS, THE --C.M.P. PIANO LIBRARY--2 VOLS., 1961-1963
    ZEITLIN, POLDI *
THERE'S MUSIC IN CHILDREN--REV. ED.---1946
    SHEEHY, EMMA DICKSON
THINKING MUSICIANS' APPLICATION OF MODERN HARMONY, THE ..HOW TO FIND
    SAULS, RANDY
THIRTEEN KEYBOARD SONATAS OF THE EIGHTEENTH AND NINETEENTH CENTURIES,
    NEWMAN, WILLIAM S.
THIRTY-THREE SUGGESTIONS IN ONE LESSON..FOR THE GUIDANCE AND
    BENEDICT, MILO ELLSWORTH
THOROUGH-BASS ACCOMPANIMENT ACCORDING TO JOHANN DAVID HEINICHEN
    BUELOW, GEORGE J.
THOROUGH-BASS MADE EASY..OR, PRACTICAL RULES FOR FINDING AND APPLYING
    PASQUALI, NICOLO
THOROUGH-BASS PRIMER, THE ..CONTAINING EXPLANATIONS AND EXAMPLES OF THE
    BURROWES, JAMES FRECKLETON
THOROUGHBASS METHOD--NUMEROUS EXAMPLES FROM THE LITERATURE OF THE 17TH.
    KELLER, HERMANN
THOROUGH BASE, MELODEON, ORGAN AND HARMONY INSTRUCTION BOOK, WITH A NEW
    JOHNSON, ARTEMAS N.
THOROUGH BASS AT ONE VIEW, WITH DIRECTIONS FOR ACCOMPANIMENT AND PROPER
    ANON
THOROUGH BASS SCHOOL, THE ..AN EASY AND PROGRESSIVE COURSE FOR
    LUDDEN, WILLIAM
THOROUGH BASS SIMPLIFIED
    CORFE, JOSEPH
THREE CENTURIES OF HARPSICHORD MAKING
    HUBBARD, FRANK
THREE GREAT EPOCH-MAKERS IN MUSIC---CHOPIN
    FARNSWORTH, EDWARD C.
THREE HUNDRED AND FIFTY QUESTIONS ON THE FORM AND TONALITY OF
    HARDING, HENRY ALFRED
THREE HUNDRED QUESTIONS ON PIANOFORTE TEACHING IN 30 GRADUATED
    HULL, ARTHUR EAGLEFIELD
THREE POSITIONS OF HARMONIZED SCALES, THE --SHOWN IN ALL KEYS
    DE SOLIS, SOLITO
TIME-SPACE CONCEPTION OF THE GEOMETRY AND SPEED OF MOTION AT THE PIANO
    ROEDER, ELWOOD S.

TOUCH, AS APPLIED TO PIANOFORTE PRACTICE--ESSAY FOR THE 10TH. ANNUAL
    MASON, WILLIAM G.
TOUCH, PHRASING AND INTERPRETATION
    JOHNSTONE, J. ALFRED
TOUCH AND EXPRESSION IN PIANO PLAYING
    HAMILTON, CLARENCE G.
TOUCH AND RHYTHM TECHNIQUES FOR THE JAZZ PIANIST
    MEHEGAN, JOHN F.
TOUCH AND TECHNIC..FOR ARTISTIC PIANO PLAYING, OP. 44--4 VOLS. IN 1
    MASON, WILLIAM G.
TO IGNACE JAN PADEREWSKI, ARTIST, PATRIOT, HUMANITARIAN, 1918-1928
    KOSCIUSZKO FOUNDATION
TRAINING AS A PIANO TECHNICIAN--8 VOLS. IN 1
    AMERICAN SCHOOL OF PIANO TUNING
TRANSPOSING AT THE PIANO--IN THREE STAGES
    TOBIN, JOSEPH RAYMOND
TRANSPOSITION...A PRACTICAL AND AUTHORITATIVE GUIDE FOR ALL INSTRUMENTS
    KLING, HENRI
TRANSPOSITION, KEYBOARD AND ORCHESTRAL--2 PTS., 1893-1908
    WARRINER, JOHN
TRANSPOSITION AT SIGHT..FOR STUDENTS OF THE ORGAN AND PIANOFORTE--4TH.
    NICHOL, HENRY E.
TRANSPOSITION AT THE KEYBOARD..PIANO..26 PAGES OF GRADED EXERCISES
    LOVELOCK, WILLIAM
TRANSPOSITION AT THE KEYBOARD
    REES-DAVIES, IVAN
TRANSPOSITION FOR MUSIC STUDENTS
    HUNT, REGINALD H.
TRANSPOSITION PATTERNS, FOR THE PIANO...APPROACHED THROUGH HARMONIC AND
    CARTER, BUENTA
TRANSPOSITION READER--FUNDAMENTAL TRAINING COURSE FOR PIANOFORTE
    FAELTEN, CARL *
TRAVELING THE CIRCUIT WITH PIANO CLASSES
    MUSIC EDUCATORS NATIONAL CONFERENCE
TREATISE ON MODULATION WITH TYPICAL EXAMPLES FROM WELL-KNOWN WORKS, A
    LINDO, ALGERNON H.
TREATISE ON PIANO-FORTE, CONTAINING THE PRINCIPLES OF FINE PLAYING ON
    STEVENS, WILLIAM S.
TREATISE ON PRACTICAL HARMONIC INTONATION, A ..ALSO, A SYNOPSIS OF
    GEIB, WILLIAM
TREATISE ON THE ART OF PIANOFORTE CONSTRUCTION, A --SUPPLEMENT
    WOLFENDEN, S.
TREATISE ON THE ART OF PIANOFORTE CONSTRUCTION, A
    WOLFENDEN, S.
TREATISE ON THE NATURAL GROUNDS AND PRINCIPLES OF HARMONY, A ..TO WHICH
    HOLDER, WILLIAM
TREATISE ON THE PIANO AND PLAYER PIANO, A
    VAN ATTA, HARRISON LOUIS--EDITOR
TREATISE ON THOROUGH BASS, A
    FRICK, PHILIPP J.
TRIBUTE TO THE LIFE AND CHARACTER OF JONAS CHICKERING, 1798-1853, A
    PARKER, RICHARD G.
TRILL IN THE WORKS OF BEETHOVEN, THE
    PHILIPP, ISIDOR
TRUE FUNCTION OF RELAXATION IN PIANO PLAYING, THE
    CAMPBELL, LE ROY B.
TRUE PIANO-TUNER, THE ..CONTAINING SIMPLE DIRECTIONS FOR TUNING,
    DANIELL, CHARLES A.
TRUE STORY OF MY LIFE, THE
    DIEHL, ALICE M.
TSCHUDI THE HARPSICHORD MAKER
    DALE, WILLIAM
TUNER'S MANUAL, THE
    HILL, SUMNER *
TUNING AND REPAIRING PIANOFORTES..THE AMATEURS GUIDE--2ND. ED.
    BABBINGTON, CHARLES
TUNING AND TEMPERAMENT---1951
    BARBOUR, JAMES MURRAY
TUNING THE PIANOFORTE..A NEW AND EASY METHOD OF HARMONIZING THE
    GEIB, WILLIAM
TWENTY MUSICAL EVENINGS---PIANOLA PROGRAMS WITH NOTES AND COMMENTS
    FINCK, HENRY T.
TWILIGHT OF F. LISZT, THE
    SZABOLCSI, BENCE
TWO ON A CONTINENT
    FOLDES, LILI
TWO RIGHT HANDS..A GUIDE FOR THE DEVELOPMENT OF PIANO TECHNIQUE
    WEISER, ADOLPH
ULTIMATE PRINCIPLES OF PIANOFORTE TEACHING AND PLAYING
    COCHRAN, MARY
ULVEN, WRITTEN DURING RETIREMENT IN SWITZERLAND--AUTOBIOGRAPHY OF PART
    YOUFF, ULV
UNASHAMED ACCOMPANIST, THE
    MOORE, GERALD
UNDERSTANDING MUSICAL INSTRUMENTS..HOW TO SELECT YOUR INSTRUMENT--REV.
    LEVINE, JACK *
UNFIGURED HARMONY--2ND. ED.---1911
    BUCK, PERCY
UNFINISHED PORTRAITS..STORIES OF MUSICIANS AND ARTISTS---CHOPIN
    LEE, JENNETTE B.
UNICORNS---CHOPIN
    HUNEKER, JAMES GIBBONS
UNIMPORTANCE OF BEING OSCAR, THE
    LEVANT, OSCAR
VAN CLIBURN LEGEND, THE
    CHASINS, ABRAM *
VARIATIONS---CHOPIN, LISZT, AND PACHMANN
    HUNEKER, JAMES GIBBONS
VELOCITY PLUS
    CAMPBELL, LE ROY B.
VICTOR BOOK OF CONCERTOS
    VEINUS, ABRAHAM
VIRGIL CLAVIER METHOD, THE --2 VOLS.
    VIRGIL, ALMON K.
VIRGIL METHOD OF PIANOFORTE TECHNIC, THE --2 VOLS.
    VIRGIL, ANTHA MINERVA
VISIBLE AND INVISIBLE IN PIANOFORTE TECHNIC, THE ..BEING A DIGEST OF
    MATTHAY, TOBIAS A.
VISUAL APPROACH TO PIANO TECHNIQUE, A
    MININBERG, IAN
VIVA VOCE..250 QUESTIONS AND ANSWERS FOR PIANOFORTE DIPLOMA CANDIDATES
    LOWE, CLAUDE EDGERTON
WALTER GIESEKING
    GAVOTY, BERNARD *
WANDA LANDOWSKA
    GAVOTY, BERNARD *
WAVE AS YOU PASS
    NEAL, HARRY LEE
WEBER GRAND, SQUARE AND UPRIGHT PIANO-FORTES, THE
    WEBER PIANO COMPANY
WEIGHT AND RELAXATION METHOD FOR THE PIANOFORTE
    EISENBERG, JACOB
WEIGHT OF EVIDENCE ON THE TRUE MUSICAL WORTH OF THE PIANOLA AND ITS
    AEOLIAN COMPANY, THE
WELBOURNE WAY TO HOBBY PIANO PLAYING FOR ADULTS, THE --9 LESSONS
    WELBOURNE, EVE V.

WELL-KNOWN PIANO SOLOS..HOW TO PLAY THEM WITH UNDERSTANDING, EXPRESSION
     WILKINSON, CHARLES W.
WELL-PREPARED PIANO, THE
     BUNGER, RICHARD
WELL-TEMPERED ACCOMPANIST, THE
     BOS, COENRAAD V.
WELTE-MIGNON BOOK...OF FAMOUS ARTISTS, THE
     AUTO PNEUMATIC ACTION COMPANY
WE PIANO TEACHERS--REVISED BY ADELE FRANKLIN---1946
     BOOTH, VICTOR
WHAT CAN I PLAY..A BOOK ABOUT MUSICAL INSTRUMENTS
     SCOTT, MARY M.
WHAT EVERY PIANO PUPIL SHOULD KNOW
     HAMILTON, CLARENCE G.
WHAT IS THE FLETCHER MUSIC METHOD
     COPP, EVELYN A.
WHAT MATTHAY MEANT
     COVIELLO, AMBROSE
WHAT MUSICAL INSTRUMENT FOR ME
     LEVINE, JACK
WHAT SHALL I PLAY..PREFERENCES FOR PIANO AND ORGAN..GUIDE TO CHOICE
     SUTHERLAND, ADELAIDE K.--COMPILER
WHAT SHALL WE PLAY--NOT UNLIKE CZERNY'S 'LETTERS TO A YOUNG
     REINECKE, KARL H.
WHAT THE PIANO WRITING OF EDWARD MACDOWELL MEANS TO THE PIANO STUDENT
     ADAMS, JULIETTE
WHAT TO PLAY--WHAT TO TEACH
     BROWER, HARRIETTE
WHAT TO TEACH AT THE VERY FIRST LESSON
     WILLIAMS, JOHN M.
WHERE THE WORD ENDS..THE LIFE OF LOUIS MOREAU GOTTSCHALK
     LOGGINS, VERNON
WHYS AND WHEREFORES..QUESTIONS AND ANSWERS FOR PIANO STUDENTS
     VINING, HARRISON S.
WILHELM BACKHAUS
     EICHMANN, A. H. *
WINNER'S NEW SCHOOL FOR THE PIANO, IN WHICH THE INSTRUCTIONS ARE SO
     WINNER, SEPTIMUS
WITH REASON AND RHYME
     WOLFF, ERNST VICTOR
WITOLD MALCUZYNSKI
     GAVOTY, BERNARD *
WOLFGANG AMADEUS MOZART
     SEROFF, VICTOR

WOOD, WIRE AND QUILL--AN INTRODUCTION TO THE HARPSICHORD
     ALBARDA, JAN H.
WORCH PIANOS, AND A BRIEF SKETCH OF THE PIANOFORTE
     WORCH, HUGO
WORD-PHRASES TO BACH'S 48 FUGUES, WITH HINTS ON THE RENDERINGS OF THE
     LOWE, CLAUDE EDGERTON
WORKING OF THE MIND IN PIANO TEACHING AND PLAYING, THE
     SCHNEIDER, HANS
WORKS OF ANTON RUBINSTEIN, NOV. 1829-NOV. 1894, THE ..A STUDY
     CRONK, CUTHBERT H.
WORKS OF FREDERIC CHOPIN, THE ..THEIR PROPER INTERPRETATION--6TH.
     KLECZYNSKI, JAN
WORLD OF GREAT COMPOSERS, THE
     EWEN, DAVID
WORLD OF MUSIC, THE ..PIANO COURSE..TEACHERS' BOOK, FOR CLASS OR
     DANIELS, BESS *
WORLD OF MUSIC, THE --THE GREAT COMPOSERS
     BREMONT, ANNA
WORLD OF MUSIC, THE --THE GREAT VIRTUOSI
     BREMONT, ANNA
WORLD OF MUSICAL INSTRUMENTS, THE ---CHIEFLY ILLUSTRATIONS
     KENDALL, ALAN
WORLD OF THE VIRTUOSO, THE
     PINCHERLE, MARC
WYMAN'S PIANO TEXTBOOK..CONTAINING A COMPLETE SYSTEM OF MUSICAL
     WYMAN, ADDISON P.
YALE COLLECTION OF MUSICAL INSTRUMENTS..CHECKLIST
     YALE UNIVERSITY--ART GALLERY
YOUNG PERSON'S GUIDE TO PLAYING THE PIANO, THE
     HARRISON, SIDNEY
YOUNG PIANIST, THE ..A NEW APPROACH FOR TEACHERS AND STUDENTS--2ND.
     LAST, JOAN
YOUNG PIANO TEACHER, WITH 75 HELPFUL TEACHING QUESTIONS, THE
     SMITH, VERA K.
YOUR CAREER IN MUSIC
     JOHNSON, HARRIETT
YOUR GUIDE TO PLAYING AND WRITING POPULAR MUSIC--REV. ED.
     STORMEN, WIN
YOUR PIANO AND HOW TO CARE FOR IT
     HARRIS, BEATRIX O.
YOU CAN SIGHT READ..THE PLEASURES OF PIANO SIGHT READING THROUGH
     HAVILL, LORINA
ZIP CHORDMASTER..BEGINNERS HOME COURSE FOR PIANO AND ORGAN
     CALLAGHAN, JAMES

Notable Pianists and Piano Teachers

ADAMS, JULIETTE
    CHAPTERS FROM A MUSICAL LIFE
AEOLIAN COMPANY, THE
    AUDIOGRAPHIC MUSIC
AEOLIAN COMPANY, THE
    DUO-ART PIANO MUSIC...RECORDED BY MORE THAN 250 PIANISTS
AEOLIAN COMPANY, THE
    PIANISTS WHO HAVE MADE RECORDS FOR THE DUO-ART PIANO
AEOLIAN COMPANY, THE
    WEIGHT OF EVIDENCE ON THE TRUE MUSICAL WORTH OF THE PIANOLA AND
AGUILAR, EMANUEL
    LITTLE BOOK ABOUT LEARNING THE PIANOFORTE, A
ALBRECHTSBERGER, JOHANN GEORG
    METHODS OF HARMONY, FIGURED BASE, AND COMPOSITION...ADAPTED FOR
ALLEY, MARGUERITE *
    PASSIONATE FRIENDSHIP, A ..CLARA SCHUMANN AND BRAHMS---LETTERS TO
ALTMAN, FRANCES
    GEORGE GERSHWIN, MASTER COMPOSER
AMERICAN PIANO CORPORATION
    CATALOGUE OF MUSIC FOR THE AMPICO, A --A LIST OF THE RECORDINGS OF
ANDERSON, ARVID C.
    MASTERS OF MUSIC---CHOPIN AND LISZT
ANDERSON, WILLIAM P.
    MUSIC AS A CAREER
ANDERSON, WILLIAM R.
    RACHMANINOV AND HIS PIANO CONCERTOS
ANON
    ESSAY ON THE CHIROGYMNAST..OR, FINGER EXERCISES APPLIED TO...ALL
ANON
    GENERAL OBSERVATIONS ON MUSIC AND REMARKS ON MR. LOGIER'S SYSTEM
ANON
    HUMANISTIC STUDIES IN HONOR OF JOHN CALVIN METCALF---INCLUDES
ANON
    LIFE AND WORKS OF GUSTAVE SATTER, THE ..A BIOGRAPHICAL SKETCH IN
ANON
    LIFE AND WORKS OF STEPHEN HELLER, THE PIANOFORTE COMPOSER, THE ..A
APEL, WILLI
    HISTORY OF KEYBOARD MUSIC TO 1700, THE --TRANSLATED AND REVISED BY
APEL, WILLI
    MASTERS OF THE KEYBOARD
ARONSON, MAURICE
    KEY TO THE MINIATURES OF LEOPOLD GODOWSKY, A ..ANALYTICAL ESSAYS
ARPIN, PAUL
    LIFE OF LOUIS MOREAU GOTTSCHALK
AUTO PNEUMATIC ACTION COMPANY
    WELTE-MIGNON BOOK...OF FAMOUS ARTISTS, THE
AZULAY, GERTRUDE
    CHOPIN..THE STORY OF THE BOY WHO MADE BEAUTIFUL MELODIES
BACH, CARL PHILIPP EMANUEL
    CARL PHILIPP EMANUEL BACH'S AUTOBIOGRAPHY..FACSIMILE OF ORIGINAL
BACHE, CONSTANCE
    BROTHER MUSICIANS..REMINISCENCES OF EDWARD AND WALTER BACHE
BAGBY, ALBERT MORRIS
    LISZT'S WEIMAR
BAGGER, EUGENE S.
    EMINENT EUROPEANS..STUDIES IN CONTINENTAL REALITY---PADEREWSKI
BALLANTINE, BILL
    PIANO, THE ..AN INTRODUCTION TO THE INSTRUMENT
BAMBERGER, LOUIS
    MEMORIES OF SIXTY YEARS IN THE TIMBER AND PIANOFORTE TRADES
BARBEDETTE, HIPPOLYTE
    STEPHEN HELLER..HIS LIFE AND WORKS
BARFORD, PHILIP
    KEYBOARD MUSIC OF C. P. E. BACH, THE ..CONSIDERED IN RELATION TO
BARNETT, JOHN FRANCIS
    MUSICAL REMINISCENCES AND IMPRESSIONS---TEACHER, PIANIST,
BARRY, KEITH LEWIS
    CHOPIN AND HIS FOURTEEN DOCTORS
BASTIEN, JAMES W.
    HOW TO TEACH PIANO SUCCESSFULLY
BAUER, HAROLD
    HAROLD BAUER, HIS BOOK---1948
BAUGHAN, EDWARD ALGERNON
    IGNACE JAN PADEREWSKI
BEAUFORT, RAPHAEL
    FRANZ LISZT, THE STORY OF HIS LIFE--TO WHICH IS ADDED..'LISZT AS A
BECKETT, WALTER
    LISZT
BENNETT, JOSEPH
    FREDERIC CHOPIN--NOVELLO'S BIOGRAPHY PRIMERS
BEREGSZASZY, LAJOS
    OBSERVATIONS CONCERNING IMPROVEMENTS IN THE CONSTRUCTION OF THE
BERINGER, OSCAR
    FIFTY YEARS EXPERIENCE OF PIANOFORTE TEACHING AND PLAYING
BERTENSSON, SERGEI *
    SERGEI RACHMANINOFF, A LIFETIME IN MUSIC
BIDOU, HENRI
    CHOPIN
BIE, OSKAR
    HISTORY OF THE PIANOFORTE AND PIANOFORTE PLAYERS, A ---1899
BOGIANCKINO, MASSIMO
    HARPSICHORD MUSIC OF DOMENICO SCARLATTI, THE
BONE, AUDREY E.
    JANE WILHELMINA STIRLING, 1804-1859..THE FIRST STUDY OF THE LIFE
BOS, COENRAAD V.
    WELL-TEMPERED ACCOMPANIST, THE
BOUCOURECHLIEV, ANDRE
    CHOPIN..A PICTORIAL BIOGRAPHY---137 ILLUSTRATIONS
BOWEN, CATHERINE DRINKER
    FREE ARTIST..THE STORY OF ANTON AND NICHOLAS RUBINSTEIN
BOWMAN, EDWARD M.
    MASTER LESSONS IN PIANOFORTE PLAYING, 'LETTERS FROM A MUSICIAN TO
BRANSON, DAVID
    JOHN FIELD AND CHOPIN
BREMONT, ANNA
    WORLD OF MUSIC, THE --THE GREAT COMPOSERS
BREMONT, ANNA
    WORLD OF MUSIC, THE --THE GREAT VIRTUOSI
BRESLIN, HOWARD
    CONCERT GRAND---GOTTSCHALK
BRIGGS, GILBERT A.
    PIANOS, PIANISTS AND SONICS
BROCKWAY, WALLACE *
    MEN OF MUSIC..THEIR LIVES, TIMES, AND ACHIEVEMENTS---REV.
BROOK, DONALD
    MASTERS OF THE KEYBOARD
BROOKSHAW, SUSANNA
    CONCERNING CHOPIN IN MANCHESTER--ON A CONCERT, AT WHICH CHOPIN
BROTHERHOOD, JAMES
    DEVELOPMENT OF THE HAND FOR PIANO-FORTE PLAYING BY MEANS OF A
BROTHERHOOD, JAMES
    IMPROVED METHOD IN PIANO TEACHING, AND RECENT IDEAS OF LEADING
BROTHERHOOD, JAMES
    SENSITIVE PIANO TOUCH AND WAYS AND MEANS TO ITS ACQUIREMENT---A

BROWER, HARRIETTE
    MODERN MASTERS OF THE KEYBOARD
BROWER, HARRIETTE
    PIANO MASTERY..TALKS WITH MASTER PIANISTS AND TEACHERS...
BROWER, HARRIETTE
    PIANO MASTERY, SECOND SERIES
BROWER, HARRIETTE
    WHAT TO PLAY--WHAT TO TEACH
BUCKLEY, OLIVIA DUSSEK
    MUSICAL TRUTHS..OR, AN ANALYSIS OF MUSIC AND AN ESSAY ON THE PAST
BUELOW, HANS GUIDO VON
    CORRESPONDENCE OF HANS VON BUELOW AND RICHARD STRAUSS
BUELOW, HANS GUIDO VON
    EARLY CORRESPONDENCE OF HANS VON BUELOW, THE ---EDITED BY HIS
BUELOW, HANS GUIDO VON
    HANS VON BUELOW..A BIOGRAPHICAL SKETCH..HIS VISIT TO AMERICA
BUELOW, HANS GUIDO VON
    LETTERS OF HANS VON BUELOW---INCLUDES CORRESPONDENCE TO KARL
BURCH, GLADYS
    FAMOUS PIANISTS FOR BOYS AND GIRLS
BURCH, GLADYS
    MODERN COMPOSERS FOR YOUNG PEOPLE---FIRST PUBLISHED AS 'A CHILD'S
BURK, JOHN N.
    CLARA SCHUMANN..A ROMANTIC BIOGRAPHY
BUSONI, FERRUCCIO
    FERRUCCIO BUSONI--LETTERS TO HIS WIFE---1895
BYRON, MAY CLARISSA
    DAY WITH FREDERIC CHOPIN, A
CANAVE, PAZ CORAZON G.
    RE-EVALUATION OF THE ROLE PLAYED BY C. P. E. BACH IN THE
CARLSON, EFFIE B.
    BIO-BIBLIOGRAPHICAL DICTIONARY OF TWELVE-TONE AND SERIAL
CAUCHI, PAUL
    CHOPIN..CENTENNIAL MEMORY 1849-1949..A LECTURE
CHAPIN, VICTOR
    GIANTS OF THE KEYBOARD
CHASINS, ABRAM
    SPEAKING OF PIANISTS
CHASINS, ABRAM *
    VAN CLIBURN LEGEND, THE
CHICKERING AND SONS
    JONAS CHICKERING CENTENNIAL CELEBRATION, THE ..A TRIBUTE TO THE
CHISSELL, JOAN
    CHOPIN--'GREAT COMPOSERS' SERIES
CHOPIN, FREDERIC
    CHOPIN'S LETTERS--COLLECTED BY HENRY OPIENSKI..TRANSLATED BY E. L.
CHOPIN, FREDERIC
    SELECTED CORRESPONDENCE OF FREDERYK F. CHOPIN---COLLECTED BY
CHRISTENSEN, INGA
    INGA - PLAY--MEMOIRS
CHURCHILL, WILLIAM--SUPPOSED AUTHOR
    MARVELLOUS YEAR, THE ...CRITICAL SKETCHES OF CELEBRATED MEN, THE
CLARK, MADAM STEINEGER
    RELIGION AND ROMANCE OF A PIANIST'S LIFE---AUTOBIOGRAPHY
CLEMENS, CLARA
    MY HUSBAND GABRILOWITSCH
COATES, HENRY
    CHOPIN--NOVELLO'S BIOGRAPHIES OF GREAT MUSICIANS
COHEN, HARRIET
    BUNDLE OF TIME, A ..THE MEMOIRS OF HARRIET COHEN
COHEN, HARRIET
    MUSIC'S HANDMAID
COIT, LOTTIE ELLSWORTH
    CHILD CHOPIN, THE ...WITH DIRECTIONS FOR PRESENTATION WITH A
COOKE, JAMES FRANCIS
    GREAT MEN AND FAMOUS MUSICIANS ON THE ART OF MUSIC
COOKE, JAMES FRANCIS
    GREAT PIANISTS ON PIANO PLAYING..STUDY TALKS WITH FOREMOST
COOKE, JAMES FRANCIS
    HOW TO MEMORIZE MUSIC
COOKE, JAMES FRANCIS
    IGNACE JAN PADEREWSKI
COOKE, JAMES FRANCIS
    LOUIS MOREAU GOTTSCHALK..A SHORT BIOGRAPHY
COOKE, JAMES FRANCIS
    MUSIC MASTERS OLD AND NEW..A SERIES OF EDUCATIONAL BIOGRAPHIES...
CORDER, FREDERICK
    FERENCZ LISZT--HALF-TITLE..MASTERS OF MUSIC
CORTOT, ALFRED
    IN SEARCH OF CHOPIN
CULSHAW, JOHN
    SERGEI RACHMANINOFF..THE MAN AND HIS MUSIC
CZERNY, CARL
    LETTERS ON THOROUGH-BASS...FORMING THE SECOND PART OF THE LETTERS
DAVID, ELIZABETH HARBISON
    I PLAYED THEIR ACCOMPANIMENTS
DAVISON, JAMES W.
    FREDERICK CHOPIN..A MEMOIR
DAVISON, JAMES W.
    FREDERIC FRANCOIS CHOPIN..CRITICAL AND APPRECIATIVE ESSAY---1843
DENT, EDWARD J.
    FERRUCCIO BUSONI, A BIOGRAPHY
DE BOER, JOSEPHINE
    MALLORCAN MOODS IN CONTEMPORARY ART AND LITERATURE--CONTAINS
DE LARA, ADELINA
    FINALE---MEMOIRS OF LAST SURVIVING PUPIL OF CLARA SCHUMANN
DIDIMUS, HENRY
    BIOGRAPHY OF LEOPOLD DE MEYER...ROYAL COURT PIANIST...TO THEIR
DIDIMUS, HENRY
    BIOGRAPHY OF LOUIS MOREAU GOTTSCHALK, THE AMERICAN PIANIST AND
DIEHL, ALICE M.
    MUSICAL MEMORIES--SOME LESSONS WITH HENSELT
DIEHL, ALICE M.
    TRUE STORY OF MY LIFE, THE
DOLE, NATHAN H.
    FAMOUS COMPOSERS--2 VOLS.---CHOPIN AND LISZT--1891+
DOLE, NATHAN H.
    LIVES OF THE MUSICIANS, THE ...WITH PORTRAITS
DRY, WAKELING
    CHOPIN--'MUSIC OF THE MASTERS' SERIES
DUCAT, EVA
    ANOTHER WAY OF MUSIC---AUTOBIOGRAPHY
DUNLOP, AGNES MARY
    DUET---STORY OF CLARA AND ROBERT SCHUMANN
EHLERT, LOUIS
    FROM THE TONE WORLD--ESSAYS---TAUSIG, CHOPIN AND LISZT--2ND.
EHLERT, LOUIS
    LETTERS ON MUSIC, TO A LADY
EHRENFECTER, C. A.
    TECHNICAL STUDY IN THE ART OF PIANOFORTE PLAYING--DEPPE'S
EHRLICH, ALFRED HEINRICH
    CELEBRATED PIANISTS OF THE PAST AND PRESENT---139 BIOGRAPHIES, WITH
EICHBERG, OSCAR
    ANALYTICAL AND HISTORICAL REMARKS ON ANTON RUBINSTEIN'S CYCLE OF
EICHMANN, A. H. *
    WILHELM BACKHAUS

ELLIS, HAVELOCK
　　AFFIRMATIONS--LITERARY ESSAYS---CHOPIN
ELLIS, HAVELOCK
　　NEW SPIRIT, THE --ESSAYS---CHOPIN--1891
EWEN, DAVID
　　COMPOSERS OF YESTERDAY..A BIOGRAPHICAL AND CRITICAL GUIDE TO THE
EWEN, DAVID
　　COMPOSERS SINCE 1900..A BIOGRAPHICAL AND CRITICAL GUIDE
EWEN, DAVID
　　GREAT COMPOSERS, 1300-1900..A BIOGRAPHICAL AND CRITICAL GUIDE
EWEN, DAVID
　　MEN AND WOMEN WHO MAKE MUSIC
EWEN, DAVID
　　MEN AND WOMEN WHO MAKE MUSIC
EWEN, DAVID
　　MEN AND WOMEN WHO MAKE MUSIC
EWEN, DAVID
　　WORLD OF GREAT COMPOSERS, THE
EXECUTIVE COMMITTEE OF CHOPIN YEAR 1949
　　CHOPIN YEAR 1949 IN POLAND, THE
EYE GATE HOUSE
　　COMPOSERS OF MANY LANDS AND MANY TIMES..A PICTURE STORY IN
FARNSWORTH, EDWARD C.
　　THREE GREAT EPOCH-MAKERS IN MUSIC---CHOPIN
FAY, AMY
　　MUSIC STUDY IN GERMANY---1880
FERRA I PERELLO, BARTOLOME
　　CHOPIN AND GEORGE SAND IN THE CARTUJA DE VALLDEMOSA...
FERRIS, GEORGE TITUS
　　GREAT MUSICAL COMPOSERS..GERMAN, FRENCH, AND ITALIAN
FERRIS, GEORGE TITUS
　　GREAT VIOLINISTS AND PIANISTS, THE ---1881
FERRIS, GEORGE TITUS
　　SKETCHES OF GREAT PIANISTS AND GREAT VIOLINISTS, BIOGRAPHICAL AND
FINCK, HENRY T.
　　CHOPIN AND OTHER MUSICAL ESSAYS---1889
FINCK, HENRY T.
　　MASTERS OF THE PIANO
FINCK, HENRY T.
　　PADEREWSKI AND HIS ART
FINCK, HENRY T.
　　SUCCESS IN MUSIC, AND HOW IT IS WON
FISCHER, EDWIN
　　REFLECTIONS ON MUSIC
FLOOD, WILLIAM HENRY GRATTAN
　　JOHN FIELD OF DUBLIN, THE INVENTOR OF THE NOCTURNE---1920
FOLDES, LILI
　　TWO ON A CONTINENT
FORSEE, AYLESA
　　ARTUR RUBINSTEIN, KING OF THE KEYBOARD
FOSS, HUBERT J.--EDITOR
　　HERITAGE OF MUSIC, THE --SECOND SERIES OF ESSAYS---CHOPIN AND
FRIEDHEIM, ARTHUR
　　LIFE AND LISZT..THE RECOLLECTIONS OF A CONCERT PIANIST
FULLER-MAITLAND, J. A.
　　MASTERS OF GERMAN MUSIC---CLARA SCHUMANN
GABRIEL, GILBERT W.
　　GREAT PIANISTS AND COMPOSERS
GAVOTY, BERNARD *
　　ALFRED CORTOT
GAVOTY, BERNARD *
　　ARTHUR RUBINSTEIN
GAVOTY, BERNARD *
　　CLAUDIO ARRAU
GAVOTY, BERNARD *
　　SAMSON FRANCOIS
GAVOTY, BERNARD *
　　WALTER GIESEKING
GAVOTY, BERNARD *
　　WANDA LANDOWSKA
GAVOTY, BERNARD *
　　WITOLD MALCUZYNSKI
GELATT, ROLAND
　　MUSIC MAKERS..SOME OUTSTANDING MUSICAL PERFORMERS OF OUR DAY
GLENNON, JAMES
　　AUSTRALIAN MUSIC AND MUSICIANS
GLINSKI, MATEUSZ
　　CHOPIN'S LETTERS TO DELFINA
GLINSKI, MATEUSZ
　　CHOPIN THE UNKNOWN
GLOYNE, HOWARD F.--M.D.
　　CARL A. PREYER, THE LIFE OF A KANSAS MUSICIAN
GLYN, MARGARET H.
　　ABOUT ELIZABETHAN VIRGINAL MUSIC AND ITS COMPOSERS..NEW ISSUE,
GOTTSCHALK, LOUIS MOREAU
　　NOTES OF A PIANIST--EDITED BY JEANNE BEHREND---1881
GRAHAM, GEORGE FARQUHAR
　　GENERAL OBSERVATIONS UPON MUSIC AND REMARKS ON MR. LOGIER'S SYSTEM
GRAHAM, L. SIBLEY
　　TALES OF THE OLD VIRTUOSO..THE SPANISH COURT PIANIST--MARQUIS DON
GRAY, CECIL
　　CONTINGENCIES AND OTHER ESSAYS---LISZT
GRAY, CECIL
　　MUSICAL CHAIRS..OR, BETWEEN TWO STOOLS, BEING THE LIFE AND MEMOIRS
GRAYDON, NELL *
　　AMAZING MARRIAGE OF MARIE EUSTIS AND JOSEF HOFMANN, THE
GREW, SIDNEY
　　MAKERS OF MUSIC..THE STORY OF SINGERS AND INSTRUMENTALISTS
GRONOWICZ, ANTONI
　　CHOPIN---YOUNGER READERS
GRONOWICZ, ANTONI
　　PADEREWSKI, PIANIST AND PATRIOT
GRONOWICZ, ANTONI
　　SERGEI RACHMANINOFF
HABETS, ALFRED
　　BORODIN AND LISZT--VOL. 2--LISZT, AS SKETCHED IN THE LETTERS OF
HADDEN, JAMES CUTHBERT
　　CHOPIN--'MASTER MUSICIANS' SERIES
HADDEN, JAMES CUTHBERT
　　MASTER MUSICIANS..A BOOK FOR PLAYERS, SINGERS AND LISTENERS
HADDEN, JAMES CUTHBERT
　　MODERN MUSICIANS..A BOOK FOR PLAYERS, SINGERS AND LISTENERS
HADOW, SIR WILLIAM HENRY
　　STUDIES IN MODERN MUSIC--2ND. SERIES--9TH. ED.---CHOPIN
HALDANE, CHARLOTTE
　　GALLEY SLAVES OF LOVE, THE ..THE STORY OF MARIE D'AGOULT AND FRANZ
HALL, CONSTANCE HUNTINGTON
　　HELEN HOPEKIRK, 1856-1945
HALLE, SIR CHARLES
　　AUTOBIOGRAPHY OF CHARLES HALLE, WITH CORRESPONDENCE AND DIARIES,
HALLE, SIR CHARLES
　　SIR C. HALLE..A SKETCH OF HIS CAREER AS A
HALLE, SIR CHARLES
　　ST. JAMES HALL...C. HALLE'S PIANOFORTE RECITALS..MAY 5-JUNE 29,
HALLE, SIR CHARLES
　　ST. JAMES HALL...MR. HALLE'S BEETHOVEN RECITALS, MAY 23-JULY 11,

HAMBOURG, MARK
　　EIGHTH OCTAVE, THE ---CONTINUES THE RECORD, BEGUN IN 'FROM PIANO
HAMBOURG, MARK
　　FROM PIANO TO FORTE..A THOUSAND AND ONE NOTES---AUTOBIOGRAPHY
HARDING, BERTITA
　　CONCERTO, THE STORY OF CLARA SCHUMANN
HARRISON, SIDNEY
　　TEACHER NEVER TOLD ME--TIPS FOR STUDENTS
HARSANYI, ZSOLT
　　IMMORTAL FRANZ..THE LIFE AND LOVES OF A GENIUS---FRANZ LISZT
HAWEIS, HUGH R.
　　MUSIC AND MORALS---CHOPIN
HEDLEY, ARTHUR
　　CHOPIN--'MASTER MUSICIAN' SERIES--INCLUDES CATALOGUE OF
HEINE, HEINRICH
　　HEINE IN ART AND LETTERS---CHOPIN AND LISZT--1837
HENDERSON, ARCHIBALD
　　CONTEMPORARY IMMORTALS---PADEREWSKI
HENDERSON, ARCHIBALD
　　MUSICAL MEMORIES---CONCERNS SEVERAL PIANISTS
HENDERSON, WILLIAM JAMES
　　PRELUDES AND STUDIES..MUSICAL THEMES OF THE DAY--SECTION 3..THE
HERVEY, ARTHUR
　　FRANZ LISZT AND HIS MUSIC
HERVEY, ARTHUR
　　FRENCH MUSIC IN THE NINETEENTH CENTURY---CHOPIN
HERVEY, ARTHUR
　　RUBINSTEIN--'MAYFAIR BIOGRAPHIES', NO. 11
HERVEY, ARTHUR
　　SAINT-SAENS---1921
HERZ, HENRI
　　MY TRAVELS IN AMERICA---1840+
HILL, RALPH
　　LISZT
HIPKINS, ALFRED JAMES
　　HOW CHOPIN PLAYED...FROM CONTEMPORARY IMPRESSIONS COLLECTED FROM
HOFFMAN, RICHARD
　　SOME MUSICAL RECOLLECTIONS OF FIFTY YEARS---INCLUDES LEOPOLD DE
HOFMANN, JOSEF
　　PIANO PLAYING, WITH PIANO QUESTIONS ANSWERED---PUBLISHED EARLIER
HOFMANN, JOSEF
　　PIANO QUESTIONS ANSWERED..A LITTLE BOOK OF DIRECT ANSWERS TO TWO
HOLCMAN, JAN
　　LEGACY OF CHOPIN, THE
HOPKINSON, CECIL
　　BIBLIOGRAPHICAL THEMATIC CATALOGUE OF THE WORKS OF JOHN FIELD,
HUBBARD, ELBERT
　　LITTLE JOURNEYS TO THE HOMES OF GREAT MUSICIANS--VOL. 8, NO.
HUBBARD, ELBERT
　　LITTLE JOURNEYS TO THE HOMES OF GREAT MUSICIANS--VOL. 9, NO.
HUEFFER, FRANCIS
　　HALF A CENTURY OF MUSIC IN ENGLAND, 1837-1887..LISZT IN ENGLAND
HUEFFER, FRANCIS
　　MUSICAL STUDIES..A SERIES OF CONTRIBUTIONS BY FRANCIS HUEFFER,
HULLAH, ANNA
　　THEODORE LESCHETIZKY
HUME, RUTH *
　　LION OF POLAND, THE ..THE STORY OF PADEREWSKI--JUNIOR BIOGRAPHIES
HUMISTON, WILLIAM H.
　　ANTON RUBINSTEIN--'LITTLE BIOGRAPHIES'
HUMISTON, WILLIAM H.
　　CHOPIN--'LITTLE BIOGRAPHIES'
HUMISTON, WILLIAM H.
　　FRIEDMAN--'LITTLE BIOGRAPHIES'
HUMISTON, WILLIAM H.
　　LISZT--'LITTLE BIOGRAPHIES'
HUMISTON, WILLIAM H.
　　PADEREWSKI--'LITTLE BIOGRAPHIES'
HUMISTON, WILLIAM H.
　　RACHMANINOFF--'LITTLE BIOGRAPHIES'
HUMMEL, JOHANN NEPOMUK
　　COMPLETE THEORETICAL AND PRACTICAL COURSE OF INSTRUCTIONS ON THE
HUNEKER, JAMES GIBBONS
　　CHOPIN..THE MAN AND HIS MUSIC---1901
HUNEKER, JAMES GIBBONS
　　FRANZ LISZT
HUNEKER, JAMES GIBBONS
　　INTIMATE LETTERS OF JAMES GIBBONS HUNEKER, COLLECTED AND EDITED BY
HUNEKER, JAMES GIBBONS
　　MELOMANIACS..ESSAYS---CHOPIN AND LISZT
HUNEKER, JAMES GIBBONS
　　MEZZOTINTS IN MODERN MUSIC--6TH. ED.---CHOPIN AND LISZT--1901
HUNEKER, JAMES GIBBONS
　　OLD FOGY, HIS MUSICAL OPINIONS AND GROTESQUES---D'ALBERT,
HUNEKER, JAMES GIBBONS
　　UNICORNS---CHOPIN
HUNEKER, JAMES GIBBONS
　　VARIATIONS---CHOPIN, LISZT, AND PACHMANN
ISAACSON, CHARLES D.
　　FACE TO FACE WITH GREAT MUSICIANS---CHOPIN AND LISZT
JAMES, BURNETT
　　BRAHMS..A CRITICAL STUDY
JOHNS, CLAYTON
　　REMINISCENCES OF A MUSICIAN---LISZT AND PADEREWSKI
JOHNSTONE, J. ALFRED
　　MODERN TENDENCIES AND OLD STANDARDS IN MUSICAL ART
JONSON, GEORGE CHARLES
　　HANDBOOK TO CHOPIN'S WORKS, A
KAISER, JOACHIM
　　GREAT PIANISTS OF OUR TIME
KARASOWSKI, MORITZ
　　FREDERIC CHOPIN..HIS LIFE, LETTERS AND WORKS--3RD. REV. ED.---1879
KASTNER, RUDOLPH
　　BEETHOVEN'S PIANO SONATAS AND ARTUR SCHNABEL
KAUFMANN, HELEN LOEB
　　ARTISTS IN MUSIC OF TODAY
KELLEY, EDGAR STILLMAN
　　CHOPIN THE COMPOSER---1913
KELLOGG, CHARLOTTE
　　PADEREWSKI
KENYON, CHARLES FREDERICK
　　IMAGINARY INTERVIEWS WITH GREAT COMPOSERS..A SERIES OF VIVID PEN
KIRKPATRICK, RALPH
　　DOMENICO SCARLATTI---1953
KIRKWOOD, KENNETH P.
　　GARDEN IN POLAND, A ...ON CHOPIN'S BIRTHPLACE AND BURIAL
KLECZYNSKI, JAN
　　HOW TO PLAY CHOPIN--THREE LECTURES
KOBYLANSKA, KRYSTYNA--EDITOR
　　CHOPIN IN HIS OWN LAND..DOCUMENTS AND SOUVENIRS
KOCHEVITSKY, GEORGE
　　ART OF PIANO PLAYING, THE ..A SCIENTIFIC APPROACH
KOSCIUSZKO FOUNDATION
　　TO IGNACE JAN PADEREWSKI, ARTIST, PATRIOT, HUMANITARIAN, 1918-1928
KREHBIEL, HENRY
　　PIANOFORTE AND ITS MUSIC, THE ---1911

KUHE, WILHELM
    MY MUSICAL RECOLLECTIONS---CHOPIN
KULLAK, ADOLPH
    AESTHETICS OF PIANOFORTE PLAYING, THE ---1861 IN GERMAN--1ST.
KULLAK, FRANZ
    BEETHOVEN'S PIANO PLAYING, WITH AN ESSAY ON THE EXECUTION OF THE
LAHEE, HENRY C.
    FAMOUS PIANISTS OF TODAY AND YESTERDAY
LAMOND, FREDERICK ARCHIBALD
    MEMOIRS OF FREDERICK LAMOND, THE
LANDAU, ROM
    IGNACE PADEREWSKI, MUSICIAN AND STATESMAN
LANDOWSKA, WANDA
    LANDOWSKA ON MUSIC--EDITED BY DENISE RESTOUT
LASSIMONNE, DENISE *
    MYRA HESS, BY HER FRIENDS
LASSIMONNE, DENISE
    OPENING THE SHUTTERS..A SHORT EXPOSITION ON THE TEACHINGS AND
LASZLO, SZIGMOND *
    FRANZ LISZT..A BIOGRAPHY IN PICTURES---240 PICTORIAL ENTRIES
LAVIGNAC, ALBERT
    MUSIC AND MUSICIANS---1895, IN FRENCH
LAWRENCE, FREDERIC LOCKE
    MUSICIANS OF SORROW AND ROMANCE---CHOPIN
LEE, JENNETTE B.
    UNFINISHED PORTRAITS..STORIES OF MUSICIANS AND ARTISTS---CHOPIN
LENZ, WILHELM VON
    GREAT PIANO VIRTUOSOS OF OUR TIME, FROM PERSONAL ACQUAINTANCE, THE
LESLIE, DORIS
    POLONAISE---NOVELIZED BIOGRAPHY OF CHOPIN
LESSMANN, W. J. OTTO
    FRANZ LISZT..EINE HULDIGUNG--FRANZ LISZT..A TRIBUTE
LEVANT, OSCAR
    MEMOIRS OF AN AMNESIAC
LEVANT, OSCAR
    SMATTERING OF IGNORANCE, A
LEVANT, OSCAR
    UNIMPORTANCE OF BEING OSCAR, THE
LEVINSKAYA, MARIA
    LEVINSKAYA SYSTEM OF PIANOFORTE TECHNIC AND TONE COLOR, THE
LE MASSENA, CLARENCE E.
    PADEREWSKI, 'THE MASTER OF MASTERS' ---REPRODUCED FROM TYPEWRITTEN
LINGG, ANN M.
    MEPHISTO WALTZ, THE STORY OF FRANZ LISZT
LISZT, FRANZ
    FREDERIC CHOPIN--A BIOGRAPHICAL AND CRITICAL NOTICE---1852
LISZT, FRANZ
    LETTERS OF FRANZ LISZT--COLLECTED AND EDITED BY LA
LISZT, FRANZ
    LETTERS OF FRANZ LISZT TO MARIE ZU SAYN-WITTGENSTEIN, THE
LISZT, FRANZ
    LIFE OF CHOPIN--TRANSLATED BY JOHN BROADHOUSE
LISZT, FRANZ
    LIFE OF CHOPIN--TRANSLATED ONLY IN PART BY MARTHA WALKER COOK
LITZMANN, BERTHOLD
    CLARA SCHUMANN..AN ARTIST'S LIFE BASED ON MATERIAL FOUND IN
LOCKE, ROBINSON
    BLOOMFIELD-ZEISLER--ROBINSON LOCKE SCRAP BOOKS
LOCKE, ROBINSON
    BUSONI--ROBINSON LOCKE SCRAP BOOKS
LOCKE, ROBINSON
    GABRILOWITSCH--ROBINSON LOCKE SCRAP BOOKS--2 VOLS.
LOCKE, ROBINSON
    HOFMANN--ROBINSON LOCKE SCRAP BOOKS
LOCKE, ROBINSON
    PADEREWSKI--ROBINSON LOCKE SCRAP BOOKS--2 VOLS.
LOEHR, JOHANN JOSEPH
    ESSAY ON THE THEORY AND PRACTICE OF TUNING, AN ...PIANOFORTES AND
LOESSER, ARTHUR
    MEN, WOMEN AND PIANOS..A SOCIAL HISTORY
LOGGINS, VERNON
    WHERE THE WORD ENDS..THE LIFE OF LOUIS MOREAU GOTTSCHALK
LOGIER, JOHANN BERNHARD
    AUTHENTIC ACCOUNT OF THE EXAMINATION OF PUPILS, INSTRUCTED IN THE
LOGIER, JOHANN BERNHARD
    REFUTATION OF THE FALLACIES AND MISREPRESENTATIONS CONTAINED IN A
LONDON--A COMMITTEE OF PROFESSORS
    EXPOSITION OF THE MUSICAL SYSTEM OF MR. LOGIER..WITH STRICTURES ON
LONG, ESMOND R.--PATHOLOGIST
    HISTORY OF THE THERAPY OF TUBERCULOSIS, AND THE CASE OF FREDERIC
LYLE, WATSON
    CAMILLE SAINT-SAENS, HIS LIFE AND ART---DISCUSSES CONCERTI AND
LYLE, WATSON
    RACHMANINOFF, A BIOGRAPHY
MACDOWELL, MARIAN GRISWOLD
    RANDOM NOTES ON EDWARD MACDOWELL AND HIS MUSIC
MACKENZIE, SIR ALEXANDER
    LISZT--'THE MAYFAIR BIOGRAPHIES', NO. 3
MACKENZIE, SIR ALEXANDER
    LISZT--MASTERPIECES OF MUSIC
MACKENZIE, SIR ALEXANDER
    MUSICIAN'S NARRATIVE, A ---CLARA SCHUMANN, VON BUELOW AND LISZT
MAINE, BASIL
    CHOPIN--'GREAT LIVES' SERIES
MANUEL, ROLAND
    FREDERIC CHOPIN--'GREAT ANNIVERSARIES' SERIES
MARTENS, FREDERICK HERMAN
    PADEREWSKI--'LITTLE BIOGRAPHIES', VOL. 2
MARTENS, FREDERICK HERMAN
    RACHMANINOFF--'LITTLE BIOGRAPHIES', VOL. 2
MARTIN, THOMAS CARLAW
    FRANZ LISZT..A SKETCH OF HIS LIFE AND PERSONALITY
MASON, DANIEL GREGORY
    ROMANTIC COMPOSERS, THE ---CHOPIN AND LISZT
MASON, WILLIAM G.
    MEMORIES OF A MUSICAL LIFE
MASON, WILLIAM G.
    PADEREWSKI..A CRITICAL STUDY--'CENTURY LIBRARY OF MUSIC', VOL. 18
MATHEWS, WILLIAM S. B.
    GREAT IN MUSIC, THE ..A SYSTEMATIC COURSE OF STUDY IN THE MUSIC OF
MATTHAY, JESSIE H.
    LIFE AND WORKS OF TOBIAS MATTHAY, THE
MATTHAY, TOBIAS A.
    PIANO FALLACIES OF TODAY
MATTHEWS, DENIS--EDITOR
    KEYBOARD MUSIC--ESSAYS ON KEYBOARD LITERATURE, EXCLUDING ORGAN
MATTHEWS, DENIS
    IN PURSUIT OF MUSIC
MAUROIS, ANDRE
    FREDERIC CHOPIN---FOR YOUNGER READERS
MAY, FLORENCE
    GIRLHOOD OF CLARA SCHUMANN, THE ..CLARA WIECK AND HER TIME
MAYO, WALDO
    CHOPIN---FOR YOUNGER READERS
MCARTHUR, ALEXANDER
    ANTON RUBINSTEIN, A BIOGRAPHICAL SKETCH

MCARTHUR, ALEXANDER
    PIANOFORTE STUDY..HINTS ON PIANO PLAYING
MCCARTHY, ALBERT J.--EDITOR
    PIANO JAZZ..ESSAYS--2 VOLS., 1945-1946
MCDOWELL, LOUISE
    PAST AND PRESENT--A CANADIAN MUSICIAN'S REMINISCENSES
MCMILLAN, MARY LEE *
    MY HELENKA---IGNACE PADEREWSKI
MILINOWSKI, MARTA
    TERESA CARRENO, 'BY THE GRACE OF GOD'
MILLER, JEWELL
    POLONAISE MILITAIRE..THE LIFE AND WORK OF FREDERIC CHOPIN..A
MIZWA, STEPHEN P.--EDITOR
    FREDERIC CHOPIN, 1810-1849
MOISEIVITCH, MAURICE
    MOISEIVITCH--BENNO--, BIOGRAPHY OF A CONCERT PIANIST
MONTAGU-NATHAN, M.
    CONTEMPORARY RUSSIAN COMPOSERS---RACHMANINOFF
MONTI, H. DE
    STRICTURES ON MR. LOGIER'S SYSTEM OF MUSICAL EDUCATION
MOORE, GERALD
    AM I TOO LOUD..MEMOIRS OF AN ACCOMPANIST
MOSCHELES, CHARLOTTE
    RECENT MUSIC AND MUSICIANS, AS DESCRIBED IN THE DIARIES AND
MURDOCH, WILLIAM
    BRAHMS..WITH AN ANALYTICAL STUDY OF THE COMPLETE PIANOFORTE WORKS
MURDOCH, WILLIAM
    CHOPIN..HIS LIFE---1935
MURGIA, ADELAIDE
    LIFE AND TIMES OF CHOPIN, THE
NALDER, LAWRENCE MARCUS
    ESSAYS IN PIANOFORTE TECHNOLOGY
NEAL, HARRY LEE
    WAVE AS YOU PASS
NEWCOMB, ETHEL
    LESCHETIZKY AS I KNEW HIM---1923
NEWMAN, ERNEST
    MAN LISZT, THE ..A STUDY OF THE TRAGI-COMEDY OF A SOUL DIVIDED
NEWMAN, WILLIAM S.
    PERFORMANCE PRACTICES IN BEETHOVEN'S PIANO SONATAS..AN
NEWTON, IVOR
    AT THE PIANO--IVOR NEWTON..THE WORLD OF AN ACCOMPANIST
NICCHIA, LILLIAN
    PIANOFORTE STUDY..HINTS ON PIANO PLAYING
NIECKS, FREDERICK
    FREDERICK CHOPIN AS A MAN AND MUSICIAN--2 VOLS.---1888
NOHL, LUDWIG
    LIFE OF LISZT--'BIOGRAPHIES OF MUSICIANS', VOL. 5
NOSSIG, ALFRED
    METHODS OF THE MASTERS OF PIANO TEACHING IN EUROPE, THE ..THE
OFFERGELD, ROBERT
    CENTENNIAL CATALOGUE OF THE PUBLISHED AND UNPUBLISHED COMPOSITIONS
OSBORNE, GEORGE A.
    REMINISCENSES OF FREDERIC CHOPIN
PADEREWSKI, IGNACE JAN
    CHOPIN..A DISCOURSE
PADEREWSKI, IGNACE JAN *
    PADEREWSKI MEMOIRS, THE ---1938
PADEREWSKI FOUNDATION
    IGNACY JAN PADEREWSKI, 1860-1941..MEMORIAL ALBUM---IN ENGLISH AND
PARKER, DOUGLAS C.
    PERCY ALDRIDGE GRAINGER, A STUDY
PARKER, HENRY T.
    EIGHTH NOTES, VOICES AND FIGURES OF MUSIC AND THE DANCE---CHAPTER
PARKER, RICHARD G.
    TRIBUTE TO THE LIFE AND CHARACTER OF JONAS CHICKERING, 1798-1853,
PAUER, ERNST
    DICTIONARY OF PIANISTS AND COMPOSERS FOR THE PIANOFORTE..WITH AN
PAYNE, ALBERT
    CELEBRATED PIANISTS OF THE PAST AND PRESENT--139 BIOGRAPHIES, WITH
PETERSON, HOUSTON--EDITOR
    GREAT TEACHERS, PORTRAYED BY THOSE WHO STUDIED UNDER
PHILIPP, ISIDOR
    SOME REFLECTIONS ON PIANO PLAYING
PHILLIPS, CHARLES
    PADEREWSKI..THE STORY OF A MODERN IMMORTAL
PIGGOTT, PATRICK
    LIFE AND MUSIC OF JOHN FIELD, 1782-1837, THE
PIRANI, EUGENIO DI
    SECRETS OF THE SUCCESS OF GREAT MUSICIANS
PLANTIGA, LEON B.
    SCHUMANN AS CRITIC
POLISH RESEARCH AND INFORMATION SERVICE
    FREDERIC CHOPIN--CENTENNIAL 1849-1949, BACKGROUND
POLISH RESEARCH AND INFORMATION SERVICE
    FREDERIC CHOPIN CENTENNIAL--1949---EIGHT ARTICLES
PORTE, JOHN F.
    CHOPIN, THE COMPOSER AND HIS MUSIC
PORTE, JOHN F.
    EDWARD MACDOWELL, A GREAT AMERICAN TONE POET..HIS LIFE AND MUSIC
POTOCKA, COMTESSE ANGELE
    THEODOR LESCHETIZKY
POURTALES, GUY DE
    FRANZ LISZT, THE MAN OF LOVE
POURTALES, GUY DE
    POLONAISE, THE LIFE OF CHOPIN---ENGLISH EDITION, 'FREDERICK
POWERS, J. HAROLD
    MUSIC'S GLAMOROUS HALL OF FAME..SHORT ARTICLES ABOUT FAMOUS NAMES,
PUGNO, RAOUL
    LESSONS OF RAOUL PUGNO, THE ..WITH A BIOGRAPHY OF CHOPIN BY M.
RACHMANINOFF, SERGEI
    RACHMANINOFF'S RECOLLECTIONS, TOLD TO OSKAR VON RIESEMANN---1934
RAMANN, LINA
    FRANZ LISZT, ARTIST AND MAN--2 VOLS.---ONLY VOL. 1, 1811-1840,
RAYSON, ETHEL
    POLISH MUSIC AND CHOPIN ITS LAUREATE, ETC.
REESER, EDUARD
    SONS OF BACH, THE
REVESZ, GEZA
    PSYCHOLOGY OF A MUSICAL PRODIGY, THE ---1925
RICHARDSON, NATHAN
    INKLINGS FOR THE LOVERS OF MUSIC, PART 1..CULTIVATION OF THE ART
RIGBY, CHARLES
    SIR CHARLES HALLE..A PORTRAIT FOR TODAY
ROLLAND, ROMAIN
    BEETHOVEN..WITH A BRIEF ANALYSIS OF THE SONATAS...BY A. EAGLEFIELD
ROSE, ALGERNON SIDNEY
    A439, BEING THE AUTOBIOGRAPHY OF A PIANO BY 25 MUSICAL
ROSENTHAL, MORIZ
    OLD AND THE NEW SCHOOL OF PIANO PLAYING, THE --TYPEWRITTEN COPY
ROSTAND, CLAUDE
    LISZT
ROUSSELOT, JEAN
    FRANZ LISZT
ROWBOTHAM, JOHN F.
    PRIVATE LIFE OF THE GREAT COMPOSERS, THE ---CHOPIN AND LISZT

RUBINSTEIN, ANTON
    AUTOBIOGRAPHY OF ANTON RUBINSTEIN, 1829-1889, THE ---1890
RUBINSTEIN, ANTON
    CONVERSATION ON MUSIC, A
RUBINSTEIN, ARTUR
    MY YOUNG YEARS
RUTTKAY, GEORGE
    CHOPIN, HIS LIFE TOLD IN ANECDOTAL FORM---FOR YOUNGER READERS
RYAN, THOMAS
    RECOLLECTIONS OF AN OLD MUSICIAN---GOTTSCHALK, JONAS CHICKERING,
SACHS, CURT
    EVOLUTION OF PIANO MUSIC, 1350-1700, THE
SACKETT, SHELTON
    NOCTURNE..A CHOPIN-PLAY IN ONE ACT
SAERCHINGER, CESAR
    ARTUR SCHNABEL, A BIOGRAPHY
SAINT-SAENS, CAMILLE
    MUSICAL MEMORIES---LISZT
SALAMAN, CHARLES
    PIANISTS OF THE PAST..PERSONAL RECOLLECTIONS BY THE LATE CHARLES
SALESKI, GDAL
    FAMOUS MUSICIANS OF A WANDERING RACE
SALESKI, GDAL
    FAMOUS MUSICIANS OF JEWISH ORIGIN
SAMAROFF, OLGA
    AMERICAN MUSICIAN'S STORY, AN
SCHAAF, EDWARD O.
    ESSAYS AND ARTICLES ON MUSICAL SUBJECTS, PARTICULARLY
SCHALLENBERG, EVERT W.
    FREDERIC CHOPIN--SYMPHONIA BOOKS..'HISTORY OF MUSIC' SERIES
SCHAUFFLER, ROBERT HAVEN
    FLORESTAN..THE LIFE AND WORK OF ROBERT SCHUMANN---1945
SCHMITZ, ELIE ROBERT
    PIANO WORKS OF CLAUDE DEBUSSY, THE
SCHNABEL, ARTUR
    MUSIC AND THE LINE OF MOST RESISTANCE---1942
SCHNABEL, ARTUR
    MY LIFE AND MUSIC
SCHNABEL, ARTUR
    REFLECTIONS ON MUSIC..A LECTURE---IN ENGLISH AND GERMAN
SCHNITTKIND, HENRY T. *
    FORTY FAMOUS COMPOSERS---CHOPIN AND LISZT
SCHONBERG, HAROLD
    COLLECTOR'S CHOPIN AND SCHUMANN, THE --KEYSTONE BOOKS
SCHONBERG, HAROLD
    GREAT PIANISTS, THE
SCHONBERG, HAROLD
    LIVES OF THE GREAT COMPOSERS, THE ---CHOPIN AND LISZT
SCHULTZ, ARNOLD
    RIDDLE OF THE PIANIST'S FINGER, THE
SCHUMANN, CLARA
    LETTERS OF CLARA SCHUMANN AND JOHANNES BRAHMS, 1853-1896--2
SCHUMANN, EUGENIE
    MEMOIRS OF EUGENIE SCHUMANN---1927
SCHUMANN, FERDINAND
    REMINISCENCES OF CLARA SCHUMANN AS FOUND IN THE DIARY OF HER
SCHUMANN, ROBERT
    ADVICE TO YOUNG MUSICIANS--FROM 'MUSIC AND MUSICIANS'---1876
SCHUMANN, ROBERT
    EARLY LETTERS OF ROBERT SCHUMANN, ORIGINALLY PUBLISHED BY HIS
SCHUMANN, ROBERT
    LETTERS OF ROBERT SCHUMANN, THE --SELECTED AND EDITED BY KARL
SCHUMANN, ROBERT
    LIFE OF ROBERT SCHUMANN TOLD IN HIS LETTERS, THE --2 VOLS.
SCHUMANN, ROBERT
    ON MUSIC AND MUSICIANS---1854, IN GERMAN--FIRST ENGLISH EDITION IN
SCHUYLER, PHILLIPA DUKE
    ADVENTURES IN BLACK AND WHITE--AUTOBIOGRAPHY
SCHWIMMER, FRANCISKA
    GREAT MUSICIANS AS CHILDREN
SEARLE, HUMPHREY
    MUSIC OF LISZT, THE --2ND. REV. ED.----1954
SEGUEL, MANIA
    CHOPIN'S TEMPO RUBATO
SEROFF, VICTOR
    DEBUSSY, MUSICIAN OF FRANCE
SEROFF, VICTOR
    FRANZ LISZT
SEROFF, VICTOR
    FREDERIC CHOPIN
SEROFF, VICTOR
    MAURICE RAVEL
SEROFF, VICTOR
    RACHMANINOFF
SEROFF, VICTOR
    WOLFGANG AMADEUS MOZART
SEYMOUR, MARY ALICE IVES
    LIFE AND LETTERS OF LOUIS MOREAU GOTTSCHALK
SHATTUCK, ARTHUR
    MEMOIRS OF ARTHUR SHATTUCK, THE ..WITH AN ACCOUNT OF HIS CAREER BY
SILOTI, ALEXANDER
    MY MEMORIES OF LISZT
SITWELL, SACHEVERELL
    BACKGROUND FOR DOMENICO SCARLATTI..1685-1757, WRITTEN FOR HIS
SITWELL, SACHEVERELL
    LISZT---1934
SLENCZYNSKA, RUTH *
    FORBIDDEN CHILDHOOD
SMITH, CYRIL
    DUET FOR THREE HANDS...AS TOLD TO JOYCE EGGINTON
SMITH, JULIA
    MASTER PIANIST..THE CAREER AND TEACHING OF CARL FRIEDBERG
SORABJI, KAIKHOSRU
    AROUND MUSIC---PACHMAN, CHOPIN AND LISZT
SPAETH, SIGMUND
    DEDICATION, THE LOVE STORY OF CLARA AND ROBERT SCHUMANN
STATHAM, HENRY H.
    MY THOUGHTS ON MUSIC AND MUSICIANS---CHOPIN AND LISZT
STEINERT, MORRIS
    REMINISCENCES OF MORRIS STEINERT, COMPILED AND ARRANGED BY JANE
STEINWAY, THEODORE F.
    PEOPLE AND PIANOS..A CENTURY OF SERVICE TO MUSIC---1853-1953
STEINWAY AND SONS
    PORTRAITS OF MUSICAL CELEBRITIES
STEINWAY AND SONS
    PORTRAITS OF MUSICAL CELEBRITIES
STEINWAY AND SONS
    PORTRAITS OF MUSICAL CELEBRITIES
STEINWAY AND SONS
    STEINWAY PROGRESS..AN APPRECIATION BY I. J. PADEREWSKI
STERNBERG, CONSTANTIN I. VON
    TEMPO RUBATO AND OTHER ESSAYS
STOOKES, SACHA
    ART OF ROBERT CASADESUS, THE
STRACHEY, MARJORIE C.
    NIGHTINGALE, THE ..A LIFE OF CHOPIN--IN THE FORM OF FICTION

STRAKACZ, ANIELA
    PADEREWSKI AS I KNEW HIM
STRELEZKI, ANTON
    PERSONAL RECOLLECTIONS OF CHATS WITH LISZT, IN 1869---1893
STUCKENSCHMIDT, HANS H.
    FERRUCCIO BUSONI..CHRONICLE OF A EUROPEAN---1967, IN GERMAN
STUCKENSCHMIDT, HANS H.
    MAURICE RAVEL..VARIATIONS ON HIS LIFE AND WORK
SZABOLCSI, BENCE
    TWILIGHT OF F. LISZT, THE
TARCZYNSKI-ALF, TADEUSZ
    HOMAGE TO CHOPIN---TEXT IN POLISH AND ENGLISH
TARNOWSKI, STANISLAS
    CHOPIN..AS REVEALED BY EXTRACTS FROM HIS DIARY--2ND. ED.---1905
TAYLOR, ROBERT L.
    RUNNING PIANIST, THE ---PERCY GRAINGER
THOMPSON, KENNETH
    DICTIONARY OF TWENTIETY-CENTURY COMPOSERS, A --1911-1971
THOMPSON, OSCAR
    DEBUSSY, MAN AND ARTIST---1937
THRELFALL, ROBERT
    SERGEI RACHMANINOFF
TONK, WILLIAM
    MEMOIRS OF A--PIANO--MANUFACTURER
UMINSKA, ZOFIA *
    CHOPIN, THE CHILD AND THE LAD
UPTON, GEORGE P.
    MUSICAL MEMORIES..MY RECOLLECTIONS OF CELEBRITIES OF THE HALF
VERNE, MATHILDE
    CHORDS OF REMEMBRANCE---BY A PUPIL OF CLARA SCHUMANN
VIARD-LOUIS, JENNY
    MUSIC AND THE PIANO
WALKER, ALAN--EDITOR
    CHOPIN COMPANION, THE ..PROFILES OF THE MAN AND THE
WALKER, ALAN--EDITOR
    FRANZ LISZT, THE MAN AND HIS MUSIC---ESSAYS BY SACHEVERALL SITWELL
WALKER, ALAN--EDITOR
    ROBERT SCHUMANN..THE MAN AND HIS MUSIC---SYMPOSIUM--13 AUTHORS
WALKER, ALAN
    LISZT
WALKER, BETTINA
    MY MUSICAL EXPERIENCES
WALLACE, WILLIAM
    LISZT, WAGNER, AND THE PRINCESS
WARRACK, JOHN H.
    SIX GREAT COMPOSERS---CHOPIN
WARREN, CLARENCE H.--EDITOR
    MEN BEHIND THE MUSIC, THE ---CHOPIN AND LISZT
WEATHERLY, FREDERICK EDWARD
    PIANO AND GOWN--REMINISCENCES
WEBBE, WILLIAM H.
    PIANOFORTE PLAYING..JOTTINGS BY W. H. WEBBE--2ND. ED.
WEINSTOCK, HERBERT
    CHOPIN, THE MAN AND HIS MUSIC
WEITZMANN, CARL F.
    HISTORY OF PIANOFORTE-PLAYING AND PIANOFORTE-LITERATURE, A
WELTE-MIGNON CORPORATION
    LIBRARY OF DELUXE WELTE-MIGNON MUSIC RECORDS FOR REPRODUCING
WELTE-MIGNON CORPORATION
    LIBRARY OF WELTE-MIGNON MUSIC RECORDS
WESTERBY, HERBERT
    LISZT, COMPOSER, AND HIS PIANO WORKS..DESCRIPTIVE GUIDE AND
WESTRUP, SIR JACK ALLAN
    LISZT--NOVELLO'S BIOGRAPHIES OF GREAT MUSICIANS
WHEELER, OPAL
    FREDERIC CHOPIN, SON OF POLAND, EARLY YEARS--2 VOLS.---YOUNGER
WIENER, HILDA
    PENCIL PORTRAITS OF CONCERT CELEBRITIES---INCLUDES 24 PIANISTS
WIER, ALBERT
    PIANO, THE ..ITS HISTORY, MAKERS, PLAYERS AND MUSIC
WIERZYNSKI, CASIMIR
    LIFE AND DEATH OF CHOPIN, THE
WILLEBY, CHARLES
    FREDERIC FRANCOIS CHOPIN
WOHL, JANKA
    FRANCOIS LISZT..RECOLLECTIONS OF A COMPATRIOT
WOLFF, ERNST VICTOR
    WITH REASON AND RHYME
WOLFF, KONRAD
    TEACHING OF ARTUR SCHNABEL, THE ..A GUIDE TO INTERPRETATION
WOOD, CHARLES W.
    LETTERS FROM MAJORCA---CHOPIN--NUMEROUS ILLUSTRATIONS
WOODHOUSE, GEORGE
    FROM KEYBOARD TO MUSIC
WULSIN, LUCIEN
    DWIGHT HAMILTON BALDWIN AND THE BALDWIN PIANO
YOUFF, ULV
    ULVEN, WRITTEN DURING RETIREMENT IN SWITZERLAND--AUTOBIOGRAPHY OF
YOUNG, PERCY M.
    KEYBOARD MUSICIANS OF THE WORLD
YOUNG, PERCY M.
    MASTERS OF MUSIC
ZOFF, OTTO--EDITOR
    GREAT COMPOSERS THROUGH THE EYES OF THEIR CONTEMPORARIES---CHOPIN
ZUR HEIDE, KARL GERT
    DEEP SOUTH PIANO..THE STORY OF LITTLE BROTHER MONTGOMERY

Keyboard Instruments

ADLER, KURT
    ART OF ACCOMPANYING AND COACHING, THE ---1965
AEOLIAN COMPANY, THE
    AEOLIAN PIANOS, THE ---WEBER, STECK, STROUD
AEOLIAN COMPANY, THE
    AUDIOGRAPHIC MUSIC
AEOLIAN COMPANY, THE
    CATALOG OF AEOLIAN MUSIC ARRANGED FOR 46-NOTE INSTRUMENTS
AEOLIAN COMPANY, THE
    CATALOG OF METROSTYLE AND THEMODIST MUSIC FOR THE PIANOLA AND
AEOLIAN COMPANY, THE
    CATALOG OF MUSIC-ROLLS FOR THE DUO-ART REPRODUCING PIANO
AEOLIAN COMPANY, THE
    CATALOG OF MUSIC AND MUSICAL LITERATURE---PIANOLA RECORDS
AEOLIAN COMPANY, THE
    CATALOG OF MUSIC FOR THE PIANOLA, PIANOLA PIANO AND
AEOLIAN COMPANY, THE
    CATALOG OF THE AEOLIAN
AEOLIAN COMPANY, THE
    COMPLÉTE CATALOG OF MUSIC ROLLS FOR THE DUO-ART REPRODUCING PIANO
AEOLIAN COMPANY, THE
    DUO-ART BOOK OF MUSIC, THE
AEOLIAN COMPANY, THE
    DUO-ART PIANO MUSIC...RECORDED BY MORE THAN 250 PIANISTS

AEOLIAN COMPANY, THE
    DUO-ART PIANO MUSIC
AEOLIAN COMPANY, THE
    DUO-ART REPRODUCING PIANO, THE ..THE DUO-ART REPRODUCING PIANO
AEOLIAN COMPANY, THE
    LIBRARY OF DUO-ART MUSIC ROLLS
AEOLIAN COMPANY, THE
    METROSTYLE-THEMODIST AND METRO-ART MUSIC ROLLS FOR THE PIANOLA AND
AEOLIAN COMPANY, THE
    METROSTYLE, THE
AEOLIAN COMPANY, THE
    METROSTYLE AND THEMODIST MUSIC CATALOG FOR THE PIANOLA AND PIANOLA
AEOLIAN COMPANY, THE
    MUSIC FOR THE AEOLIAN GRAND--SUPPLEMENT
AEOLIAN COMPANY, THE
    MUSIC FOR THE AEOLIAN GRAND
AEOLIAN COMPANY, THE
    MUSIC FOR THE ORCHESTRELLE AND AEOLIAN GRAND
AEOLIAN COMPANY, THE
    MUSIC FOR THE PIANOLA AND THE AERIAL PIANO--4 VOLS.
AEOLIAN COMPANY, THE
    NEW MUSIC FOR THE AEOLIAN GRAND, THE PIANOLA, AND THE AERIOL PIANO
AEOLIAN COMPANY, THE
    PIANISTS WHO HAVE MADE RECORDS FOR THE DUO-ART PIANO
AEOLIAN COMPANY, THE
    PIANOLA AND PIANOLA PIANO MUSIC CATALOG, THE ..SIXTY-FIVE NOTE
AEOLIAN COMPANY, THE
    PIANOLA PIANO, THE
AEOLIAN COMPANY, THE
    SPECIAL SURVEY CONDUCTED--IN 1889--FOR LYON AND HEALY, INC.,
AEOLIAN COMPANY, THE
    SUPPLEMENTARY CATALOG OF MUSIC FOR THE AEOLIAN GRAND AND
AEOLIAN COMPANY, THE
    WEIGHT OF EVIDENCE ON THE TRUE MUSICAL WORTH OF THE PIANOLA AND
AHRENS, CORA B. *
    FOR ALL PIANO TEACHERS
ALBARDA, JAN H.
    WOOD, WIRE AND QUILL..AN INTRODUCTION TO THE HARPSICHORD
ALBIG, GEORGE L.
    HOW TO PLAY THE PLAYER
AMERICAN NEWS COMPANY
    ROMANCE OF A PIANO, THE
AMERICAN PHOTO PLAYER COMPANY
    INSTALLATION, CARE AND OPERATION OF THE PHOTOPLAYER---1920+
AMERICAN PIANO CORPORATION
    AMPICO, THE ..A DESCRIPTION OF ITS PERFORMANCE...
AMERICAN PIANO CORPORATION
    AMPICO, THE ..SERVICE MANUAL 1929
AMERICAN PIANO CORPORATION
    AMPICO REPRODUCING PIANO, INSPECTOR'S REFERENCE BOOK, THE ---1923
AMERICAN PIANO CORPORATION
    AMPICO REPRODUCING PIANO, THE ..INSPECTOR'S INSTRUCTION BOOK,
AMERICAN PIANO CORPORATION
    CATALOGUE OF MUSIC FOR THE AMPICO, A ..A LIST OF THE RECORDINGS OF
AMERICAN PIANO CORPORATION
    CATALOGUE OF MUSIC FOR THE AMPICO, A --A LIST OF THE RECORDINGS OF
AMERICAN SCHOOL OF PIANO TUNING
    TRAINING AS A PIANO TECHNICIAN--8 VOLS. IN 1
AMERICAN STEEL AND WIRE COMPANY
    NERVES OF STEEL..THE STORY OF AMERICAN PIANO WIRE AND ITS
AMPICO CORPORATION
    AMPICO REPRODUCING PIANO..A SUPPLEMENT TO 'PIANO MUSIC, ITS
AMPICO CORPORATION
    SUPREMACY OF AMPICO MUSIC..UNIT TWO OF A COURSE IN AMPICO
ANDERSON-MULDER COMPANY
    DEALER'S HANDBOOK OF PIANOS AND THEIR MAKERS
ANON
    COMPLEAT TUTOR FOR THE HARPSICHORD OR SPINNET, WHEREIN IS SHEWN
ANON
    DIGITORIUM, THE --MINIATURE DUMB PIANO
ANON
    HOW TO TUNE YOUR OWN PIANOFORTE..OR, THE WAY TO KEEP YOUR
ANON
    HUMANISTIC STUDIES IN HONOR OF JOHN CALVIN METCALF---INCLUDES
ANON
    NEW INSTRUCTIONS FOR PLAYING THE HARPSICHORD, PIANOFORTE OR
ANON
    NEW PIANOFORTE KEYBOARD, THE ..CARD AND GAME, THE A.B.C. OF MUSIC
ANON
    OLD PIANO, THE ..A FANTASIA, WITH VARIATIONS HIGH FANTASTICAL,
ANON
    PIANOFORTE POCKET COMPANION, THE ..OR, A POPULAR VIEW OF THE
ANON
    PIANO LOVER, THE ..BY VARIOUS AUTHORS
ANON
    PLAYING THE HARPSICHORD, SPINET OR PIANO FORTE MADE EASY BY NEW
ANON
    PRECEPTOR, FOR THE PIANOFORTE, THE ORGAN OR HARPSICHORD, THE
ANON
    QUESTIONS AND ANSWERS ON THE SCIENCE AND ART OF PIANOFORTE
ANON
    REPAIRING THE PIANOFORTE, WITH CHAPTERS ON REGULATING, TONING,
ANON
    SHORT INSTRUCTIONS FOR TUNING A PIANO-FORTE..WRITTEN BY 'MUSICUS
APEL, WILLI
    HISTORY OF KEYBOARD MUSIC TO 1700, THE --TRANSLATED AND REVISED BY
APEL, WILLI
    MASTERS OF THE KEYBOARD
ASSOCIATION FOR RECORDED SOUND COLLECTIONS
    PRELIMINARY DIRECTORY OF SOUND RECORDING COLLECTIONS IN THE UNITED
AUTOPIANO COMPANY
    PLAYER PIANO POINTERS
AUTO PNEUMATIC ACTION COMPANY
    HOW TO TEST AND REGULATE THE WELTE-MIGNON REPRODUCING PIANO
AUTO PNEUMATIC ACTION COMPANY
    WELTE-MIGNON BOOK...OF FAMOUS ARTISTS, THE
BABBINGTON, CHARLES
    TUNING AND REPAIRING PIANOFORTES..THE AMATEURS GUIDE--2ND. ED.
BABITZ, SOL
    ON USING EARLY KEYBOARD FINGERING--REPRINT OF 3 ARTICLES FROM THE
BADURA-SKODA, EVA *
    INTERPRETING MOZART ON THE KEYBOARD---1957, IN GERMAN
BAINES, ANTHONY
    EUROPEAN AND AMERICAN MUSICAL INSTRUMENTS
BAINES, ANTHONY
    MUSICAL INSTRUMENTS THROUGH THE AGES--REV. ED.---1961
BAINTON, HERBERT G.
    PIANO, ITS CONSTRUCTION AND CARE, THE
BALDWIN PIANO COMPANY
    MANUALO, THE PLAYER PIANO THAT IS ALL BUT HUMAN, THE ..CARE,
BALLANTINE, BILL
    PIANO, THE ..AN INTRODUCTION TO THE INSTRUMENT
BALTIMORE--MUSEUM OF ART
    MUSICAL INSTRUMENTS AND THEIR PORTRAYAL IN
BAMBERGER, LOUIS
    MEMORIES OF SIXTY YEARS IN THE TIMBER AND PIANOFORTE TRADES

BARBOUR, JAMES MURRAY
    TUNING AND TEMPERAMENT---1951
BARTELS, LEO F. *
    PERFORATING OF MUSIC ROLLS WITH THE LEABARJAN PERFORATOR, THE
BARTHOLOMEW, RALPH I.
    MAKING OF A STEINWAY, THE
BEDBROOK, GERALD STARES
    KEYBOARD MUSIC FROM THE MIDDLE AGES TO THE BEGINNINGS OF THE
BEMETZRIEDER, ANTON
    ACCOUNT OF A NEW WAY OF CONSIDERING MUSICK, AND TEACHING
BEMETZRIEDER, ANTON
    ART OF TUNING OUR INSTRUMENTS MADE INTERESTING AND EASY TO ALL
BEMETZRIEDER, ANTON
    NEW LESSONS FOR THE HARPSICHORD
BEREGSZASZY, LAJOS
    OBSERVATIONS CONCERNING IMPROVEMENTS IN THE CONSTRUCTION OF THE
BERKOWITZ, FREDA
    ON LUTES, RECORDERS AND HARPSICHORDS..MEN AND MUSIC OF THE BAROQUE
BERNER, ALFRED *
    PRESERVATION AND RESTORATION OF MUSICAL INSTRUMENTS..PROVISIONAL
BESSARABOFF, NICHOLAS
    ANCIENT EUROPEAN MUSICAL INSTRUMENTS...IN THE LESLIE LINDSAY MASON
BIE, OSKAR
    HISTORY OF THE PIANOFORTE AND PIANOFORTE PLAYERS, A ---1899
BILL, EDWARD LYMAN
    PIANO SAVING AND HOW TO ACCOMPLISH IT
BLOM, ERIC
    ROMANCE OF THE PIANO, THE ---1928
BLYTHER, JAMES H.
    HOW TO TUNE YOUR OWN PIANO
BOALCH, DONALD HOWARD
    MAKERS OF THE HARPSICHORD AND CLAVICHORD, 1440 TO 1840
BODDINGTON, HENRY
    CATALOGUE OF MUSICAL INSTRUMENTS, PRINCIPALLY ILLUSTRATIVE OF THE
BODKY, ERWIN
    INTERPRETATION OF BACH'S KEYBOARD WORKS, THE
BOGIANCKINO, MASSIMO
    HARPSICHORD MUSIC OF DOMENICO SCARLATTI, THE
BORREN, CHARLES VAN DEN
    SOURCES OF KEYBOARD MUSIC IN ENGLAND, THE ---1913
BOWEN, YORK
    PEDALLING THE MODERN PIANOFORTE---1936
BOWEN, YORK
    SIMPLICITY OF PIANO TECHNIQUE, THE
BOWERS, Q. DAVID
    ENCYCLOPEDIA OF AUTOMATIC MUSICAL INSTRUMENTS---INCLUDES A
BOWERS, Q. DAVID
    GUIDEBOOK OF AUTOMATIC MUSICAL INSTRUMENTS, A. --2 VOLS.
BOWERS, Q. DAVID
    PUT ANOTHER NICKEL IN..A HISTORY OF COIN-OPERATED PIANOS
BRAGARD, ROGER
    MUSICAL INSTRUMENTS IN ART AND HISTORY
BRIED, FREDERICK
    STIMULATION IN PIANO STUDY..HOW PARENTS CAN STIMULATE AND MAINTAIN
BRIGGS, GILBERT A.
    MUSICAL INSTRUMENTS AND AUDIO
BRIGGS, GILBERT A.
    PIANOS, PIANISTS AND SONICS
BRINSMEAD, E.
    HISTORY OF THE PIANOFORTE, THE ..WITH AN AN ACCOUNT OF THE THEORY
BRISKIER, ARTHUR
    NEW APPROACH TO PIANO TRANSCRIPTIONS AND INTERPRETATION OF JOHANN
BROADWOOD, JAMES SHUDI
    SOME NOTES--ON THE HARPSICHORD AND PIANOFORTE--MADE BY J. S.
BROADWOOD, JOHN AND SONS
    BROADWOOD COLLECTION OF ANTIQUE INSTRUMENTS, THE ..FORERUNNERS OF
BROADWOOD, JOHN AND SONS
    CATALOGUE OF BOOKS IN THE LIBRARY OF JOHN BROADWOOD AND SONS'
BROADWOOD, JOHN AND SONS
    CATALOGUE OF JOHN BROADWOOD AND SONS, LTD. LATEST MODELS,
BROADWOOD, JOHN AND SONS
    INFORMATION CONCERNING PIANOFORTES OF USE AND OF INTEREST..A VADE
BROADWOOD, JOHN AND SONS
    INTERNATIONAL EXHIBITION, 1862..LIST OF PIANOFORTES AND
BROADWOOD, JOHN AND SONS
    PIANOFORTES..WITH USEFUL AND INTERESTING INFORMATION CONCERNING
BUCHNER, ALEXANDER
    MECHANICAL MUSICAL INSTRUMENTS---174 NUMBERED PLATES
BUCHNER, ALEXANDER
    MUSICAL INSTRUMENTS THROUGH THE AGES
BUNGER, RICHARD
    WELL-PREPARED PIANO, THE
BYERLY, DOROTHEA J.
    ADVENTURES OF PETER THE PIANO, THE ..AN ILLUSTRATED STORY FOR
CARMI, AVNER *
    IMMORTAL PIANO, THE
CARPENO, TERESA
    POSSIBILITIES OF TONE COLOR BY ARTISTIC USE OF PEDALS
CARY, MRS. C. S. P.
    PIANO-FORTE CLASS BOOK, CONTAINING PRACTICAL RUDIMENTAL LESSONS
CASTELLINI, JOHN EDWARD
    RUDIMENTS OF MUSIC..A NEW APPROACH WITH APPLICATION TO THE
CHAPIN, VICTOR
    GIANTS OF THE KEYBOARD
CHICKERING AND SONS
    ACHIEVEMENT..AN ASCENDING SCALE, BEING A SHORT HISTORY OF THE
CHICKERING AND SONS
    CHICKERING AND SONS, MANUFACTURER OF GRAND, SQUARE AND UPRIGHT
CHICKERING AND SONS
    CHICKERING AND SONS PIANOFORTES AT THE CENTENNIAL EXHIBITION,
CHICKERING AND SONS
    CHICKERING CENTENNIAL CELEBRATION, APRIL 1823-1923
CHICKERING AND SONS
    COMMEMORATION OF THE FOUNDING OF THE HOUSE OF CHICKERING AND SONS,
CHICKERING AND SONS
    HISTORICAL MUSICAL EXHIBITION..CATALOGUE OF THE EXHIBITION,
CHICKERING AND SONS
    ILLUSTRATED CATALOGUE OF PIANO FORTES
CHICKERING AND SONS
    JONAS CHICKERING CENTENNIAL CELEBRATION, THE ..A TRIBUTE TO THE
CHICKERING AND SONS
    JONAS CHICKERING CENTENNIAL CELEBRATION, 1823-1923..IN
CHICKERING AND SONS
    NEW ILLUSTRATED CATALOGUE OF PIANOFORTES, A
CHICKERING AND SONS
    PIANO-FORTES AT THE EXHIBITION OF 1856
CHICKERING BROTHERS, CHICAGO
    PIANO-FORTES AND THEIR MANUFACTURE, WITH ILLUSTRATED CATALOGUE
CHILTON, CARROLL B.
    DE-ASSIFICATION OF MUSIC, THE ..A PROPAGANDIST MAGAZINE, OF ONE
CHURCHILL, VIRGINIA PEAKES
    NINETEEN FIFTY-SIX SUPPLEMENT TO THE MODERN TEACHER'S GUIDE TO
CLEMENCIC, RENE
    OLD MUSICAL INSTRUMENTS
CLOSSON, ERNEST
    HISTORY OF THE PIANO

COOKE, JAMES FRANCIS
EVERY MAN HIS OWN TUNER..AN EASY AND CERTAIN GUIDE TO TUNING THE
COVIELLO, AMBROSE
WHAT MATTHAY MEANT
CURCIO, LOUISE
SINGLE NOTE, THE
DAHL, ANTON
SOUL OF GENIUS, THE ..ITS MUSICAL DEVELOPMENT AND HOW THE WORLD AT
DALE, KATHLEEN
NINETEENTH CENTURY PIANO MUSIC, A HANDBOOK FOR PIANISTS
DALE, WILLIAM
TSCHUDI THE HARPSICHORD MAKER
DANIELL, CHARLES A.
TRUE PIANO-TUNER, THE ..CONTAINING SIMPLE DIRECTIONS FOR TUNING,
DARBYSHIRE, JOHN H.
CONSTANT K--18600, THE ..ITS USE IN THEORY AND PRACTICE
DARLOW, DENYS
MUSICAL INSTRUMENTS--JUNIOR REFERENCE BOOKS, NO. 12--2ND. ED.
DART, THURSTON
INTERPRETATION OF MUSIC, THE --4TH. ED.---1954
DAVIS, LIONEL
KEYBOARD INSTRUMENTS..THE STORY OF THE PIANO---YOUNGER READERS
DECKER, TOM W.
CONSOLE SYSTEM, THE ..A TEXT FOR MODERN PIANO AND ORGAN TO BE USED
DELUXE ROLL CORPORATION
LIBRARY OF DELUXE WELTE-MIGNON MUSIC RECORDS FOR REPRODUCING
DENSMORE, FRANCES
HANDBOOK OF THE COLLECTION OF MUSICAL INSTRUMENTS IN THE UNITED
DICKEY, ALBERT W.
PRACTICAL PIANO TUNING..A METHOD WITH A DO-IT-YOURSELF OUTLOOK
DIETZ, FRANZ RUDOLF
INTONIEREN VON FLUEGELN, DAS --GRAND VOICING---IN GERMAN, ENGLISH,
DIETZ, FRANZ RUDOLF
REGULIEREN VON FLUFGELN BEI STEINWAY, DAS --REGULATION OF THE
DOLGE, ALFRED
PIANOS AND THEIR MAKERS..A COMPREHENSIVE HISTORY OF THE
DOLMETSCH, ARNOLD
INTERPRETATION OF MUSIC OF THE SEVENTEENTH AND EIGHTEENTH
DONALDSON, GEORGE
CATALOGUE OF THE MUSICAL INSTRUMENTS AND OBJECTS FORMING THE
DONINGTON, ROBERT
INSTRUMENTS OF MUSIC, THE --3RD. REV. ED.---1949
DONINGTON, ROBERT
INTERPRETATION OF EARLY MUSIC, THE
DONINGTON, ROBERT
PERFORMER'S GUIDE TO BAROQUE MUSIC, A
DRAKE, HARRY
FROM PIANO TUNER TO PLAYER EXPERT
DRAKE, HARRY
PLAYER-PIANO EXPLAINED, THE --PAMPHLET
DRAKE, HARRY
PNEUMATIC PLAYER, THE ..THE REGULATION AND REPAIR OF SOME MODERN
DRAKE, HARRY
REPAIRING THE PLAYER PIANO
DUFFEE, GERTRUDE BANKS
PIANO STUDY..A GUIDE TO TEACHER AND STUDENT
DUNN, JOHN PETRIE
BASIS OF PIANOFORTE PLAYING, THE
EARL, S. G.
REPAIRING THE PLAYER PIANO..INFORMATION USEFUL TO PIANOFORTE
EDINBURGH UNIVERSITY--DEPT. OF EARLY KEYBOARD INSTRUMENTS
RUSSELL COLLECTION AND OTHER EARLY KEYBOARD INSTRUMENTS IN ST.
EISENBERG, JACOB
ARTISTIC PIANIST, THE ..NATURAL TECHNICS IN PIANO MASTERY..FROM
EISENBERG, JACOB
LET ME HELP YOU, MY ANCESTORS AND I..A COMPREHENSIVE JUVENILE
EISENBERG, JACOB
ROMANCE OF KEYS AND TONES..THE PIANO, ITS ORIGIN AND DEVELOPMENT,
ELLINGHAM, HARRY
HOW TO USE A PLAYER-PIANO
ENGEL, CARL
MUSICAL INSTRUMENTS---78 WOODCUT ILLUSTRATIONS
ENGEL, CARL
MUSICAL INSTRUMENTS--REV. ED.---1876
ENGEL, CARL
PIANIST'S HANDBOOK, THE ..A GUIDE FOR THE RIGHT COMPREHENSION AND
EPWORTH PIANOS
BOOK ABOUT PIANOS IN GENERAL AND THE EPWORTH IN PARTICULAR, A
EVANS MUSIC COMPANY
EVANS' GRADED STUDY GUIDE FOR THE PIANOFORTE AND DICTIONARY OF
FALKENER, ROBERT
INSTRUCTIONS FOR PLAYING THE HARPSICHORD..WHEREIN IS FULLY
FAUST, OLIVER C.
PIANOFORTE TUNER'S POCKET COMPANION, THE ..COMPILED FROM THE NOTES
FERGUSON, DONALD NIVISON
PIANO MUSIC OF SIX GREAT COMPOSERS---1947
FINCK, HENRY T.
AEOLIAN, THE ..ITS ARTISTIC MERITS, DISTINCTION FROM MECHANICAL
FINCK, HENRY T.
TWENTY MUSICAL EVENINGS---PIANOLA PROGRAMS WITH NOTES AND COMMENTS
FINNEGAN, BILL
PIANO FACTS
FISCHER, JERRY CREE
PIANO TUNING, REGULATING AND REPAIRING...SELF INSTRUCTION...FOR
FOOTE, ARTHUR W.
SOME PRACTICAL THINGS IN PIANO PLAYING
FOX, LILLA M.
INSTRUMENTS OF POPULAR MUSIC..A HISTORY OF MUSICAL
FUNKE, OTTO
PIANO AND HOW TO CARE FOR IT, THE ..PIANO TUNING IN THEORY AND
FUREY, J.
BUILDING OF THE PIANO, THE
GABRIEL, GILBERT W.
GREAT PIANISTS AND COMPOSERS
GABRY, GYORGY
OLD MUSICAL INSTRUMENTS
GALPIN, FRANCIS W.
OLD ENGLISH INSTRUMENTS OF MUSIC--4TH. ED.---1910
GALPIN, FRANCIS W.
TEXTBOOK OF EUROPEAN MUSICAL INSTRUMENTS, A ---1937
GARRATT, PERCIVAL
ART OF PIANOFORTE PLAYING, THE
GATES, WILLEY F.
PIPE AND STRINGS..THREE HISTORIC AND DESCRIPTIVE SKETCHES...THE
GEIB, WILLIAM
GEIB'S PIANO-FORTE PRECEPTOR, AND MUSICAL GRAMMAR...A TREATISE ON
GEIB, WILLIAM
TREATISE ON PRACTICAL HARMONIC INTONATION, A ..ALSO, A SYNOPSIS OF
GEIB, WILLIAM
TUNING THE PIANOFORTE..A NEW AND EASY METHOD OF HARMONIZING THE
GEIRINGER, KARL
MUSICAL INSTRUMENTS, THEIR HISTORY IN WESTERN CULTURE FROM THE
GEPPERT, WILLIAM
OFFICIAL GUIDE TO PIANO QUALITY, THE ---4TH. ED.
GIESKE, GEORGE
CARE OF THE PIANO AND PLAYER PIANO IN THE HOME, THE

GILLESPIE, JOHN
FIVE CENTURIES OF KEYBOARD MUSIC..AN HISTORIC SURVEY FOR
GIVENS, LARRY
RE-ENACTING THE ARTIST..A STORY OF THE AMPICO REPRODUCING PIANO
GIVENS, LARRY
REBUILDING THE PLAYER PIANO
GLOVER, ELLYE HOWELL
HOW THE PIANO CAME TO BE
GLYN, MARGARET H.
NATIONAL SCHOOL OF VIRGINAL MUSIC IN ELIZABETHAN TIMES, THE
GOULD, BRIAN M.
BUYING A SQUARE PIANO
GOW, GEORGE C.
PROS AND CONS OF THE MECHANICAL PLAYER, THE --REPRINT..M.T.N.A.
GREW, SIDNEY
ART OF THE PLAYER-PIANO, THE ..A TEXTBOOK FOR STUDENT AND TEACHER
GREW, SIDNEY
FIRST BOOK OF THE PLAYER-PIANIST, THE
GRIMM, CARL W.
HARMONY STUDY AT THE PIANO
GUENTHER, FELIX
PIANO AND ITS ANCESTORS, THE
GULBRANSEN-DICKINSON COMPANY
GULBRANSEN SERVICE MANUAL---PLAYER PIANO
HAFER, HOWARD W.
STUDY IN EQUAL TEMPERAMENT, A
HAMBOURG, MARK
HOW TO PLAY THE PIANO--NEW AND ENLARGED EDITION OF 'HOW TO BECOME
HAMILTON, CLARENCE G.
PIANO MUSIC, ITS COMPOSERS AND CHARACTERISTICS
HAMILTON, CLARENCE G.
SUPPLEMENT TO PIANO MUSIC, ITS COMPOSERS AND CHARACTERISTICS, A
HAMILTON, JAMES ALEXANDER
HAMILTON'S PRACTICAL INTRODUCTION TO THE ART OF TUNING THE
HANSING, SIEGFRIED
PIANOFORTE AND ITS ACOUSTIC PROPERTIES, THE --2ND. REV.
HANSMANN, RICHARD
THEORETICAL AND PRACTICAL PIANO-FORTE SCHOOL FOR THE JANKO
HARDING, ROSAMUND
PIANOFORTE, THE ..ITS HISTORY TRACED TO THE GREAT EXHIBITION OF
HARICH-SCHNEIDER, ETA
HARPSICHORD, THE ..AN INTRODUCTION TO TECHNIQUE, STYLE AND THE
HARRIS, BEATRIX O.
YOUR PIANO AND HOW TO CARE FOR IT
HARRIS, REGINALD
HOW TO CHOOSE AN INSTRUMENT..PIANO AND STRINGS
HARRISON, SIDNEY
YOUNG PERSON'S GUIDE TO PLAYING THE PIANO, THE
HASLUCK, PAUL N.
PIANOS..THEIR CONSTRUCTION, TUNING AND REPAIR
HECK, JOHANN CASPAR
ART OF PLAYING THE HARPSICHORD, ILLUSTRATED BY A VARIETY OF
HENDERSON, WILLIAM JAMES
EVOLUTION OF THE PIANO, THE
HENDERSON, WILLIAM JAMES
PRELUDES AND STUDIES..MUSICAL THEMES OF THE DAY--SECTION 3..THE
HERZ, HENRI
MEISSNER'S MODERN, PRACTICAL SYSTEM OF TUNING THE PIANOFORTE..WITH
HILL, SUMNER *
TUNER'S MANUAL, THE
HINDLEY, GEOFFREY
MUSICAL INSTRUMENTS
HINSON, MAURICE
PIANO TEACHER'S SOURCE BOOK--BIBLIOGRAPHY OF BOOKS ABOUT PIANOS
HIPKINS, ALFRED JAMES
DESCRIPTION AND HISTORY OF THE PIANOFORTE AND OLDER KEYBOARD
HIPKINS, ALFRED JAMES
GUIDE TO THE LOAN COLLECTION--OF THE INTERNATIONAL INVENTIONS
HIPKINS, ALFRED JAMES
HISTORY OF THE PIANOFORTE, THE --REPRINT
HIPKINS, ALFRED JAMES
MUSICAL INSTRUMENTS, HISTORIC, RARE AND UNIQUE---1888
HIRT, FRANZ JOSEF
STRINGED KEYBOARD INSTRUMENTS 1440-1880---1955, IN GERMAN
HOBBS, HENRY
PIANO IN INDIA, THE ..HOW TO KEEP IT IN ORDER, PRACTICAL
HOFMANN, JOSEF
PIANO PLAYING..A LITTLE BOOK OF SIMPLE SUGGESTIONS--REPRINTED FROM
HOLDER, WILLIAM
TREATISE ON THE NATURAL GROUNDS AND PRINCIPLES OF HARMONY, A ..TO
HOOVER, CYNTHIA A.
HARPSICHORDS AND CLAVICHORDS
HOOVER, CYNTHIA A.
MUSIC MACHINES--AMERICAN STYLE..A CATALOG OF THE EXHIBITION
HORNIMAN MUSEUM AND LIBRARY, LONDON
HANDBOOK TO THE MUSEUM'S COLLECTION, BY JEAN L. JENKINS--2ND.
HORNIMAN MUSEUM AND LIBRARY, LONDON
MUSICAL INSTRUMENTS
HOWE, ALFRED H.
SCIENTIFIC PIANO TUNING AND SERVICING--REV. ED.---1941
HUBBARD, ELBERT
STORY OF THE STEINWAYS, THE --REPRINT FROM 'FRA' MAGAZINE
HUBBARD, FRANK
HARPSICHORD REGULATING AND REPAIRING
HUBBARD, FRANK
THREE CENTURIES OF HARPSICHORD MAKING
HULL, ANNE
MAESTRO SPINETTI'S MUSIC SHOP--HARPSICHORD, CLAVICHORD,
HUMMEL, JOHANN NEPOMUK
COMPLETE THEORETICAL AND PRACTICAL COURSE OF INSTRUCTIONS ON THE
HUNEKER, JAMES GIBBONS
DEVELOPMENT OF PIANO MUSIC FROM THE DAYS OF THE CLAVICHORD AND
HUTCHESON, ERNEST *
LITERATURE OF THE PIANO, THE ..A GUIDE FOR AMATEUR AND
JAMES, PHILIP BRUTTON
EARLY KEYBOARD INSTRUMENTS, FROM THEIR BEGINNINGS TO THE YEAR
JEANS, SIR JAMES HOPWOOD
SCIENCE AND MUSIC
KACZMAREK, REGINA A.
CATALOG OF SELECTED PIANO ROLLS FROM THE LIBRARY OF CONGRESS
KEELER, WALTER B.
THEORY OF THE NEW KEYBOARD, ARRANGED BY W. B. KEELER AND E. K.
KELLEY, EDGAR STILLMAN
MUSICAL INSTRUMENTS--3RD. YEAR OF A STUDY COURSE IN MUSIC
KENDALL, ALAN
WORLD OF MUSICAL INSTRUMENTS, THE ---CHIEFLY ILLUSTRATIONS
KENYON, MAX
HARPSICHORD MUSIC..THE INSTRUMENTS, THE COMPOSERS, THE PLAYERS
KINSKY, GEORG--EDITOR
HISTORY OF MUSIC IN PICTURES, A
KIRBY, FRANK EUGENE
SHORT HISTORY OF KEYBOARD MUSIC, A
KIRKPATRICK, RALPH
DOMENICO SCARLATTI---1953
KOBBE, GUSTAV
PIANOLIST, THE ..A GUIDE FOR PIANOLA PLAYERS

KOBBE, GUSTAV
    STRAIGHT TO THE HEART OF MUSIC---PLAYER-PIANO
KOCHEVITSKY, GEORGE
    ART OF PIANO PLAYING, THE ..A SCIENTIFIC APPROACH
KRAUS, ALESSANDRO B.
    ONE-KEYBOARDED CLAVICYTHERIUM OF THE KRAUS COLLECTION IN FLORENCE,
KREHBIEL, HENRY
    PIANOFORTE AND ITS MUSIC, THE ---1911
KRUSZYNSKI, MICHAL
    APPROACH TO THE PSYCHOLOGY OF PIANO TEACHING, AN
LANDOWSKA, WANDA
    LANDOWSKA ON MUSIC--EDITED BY DENISE RESTOUT
LAVIGNAC, ALBERT
    MUSIC AND MUSICIANS---1895, IN FRENCH
LEVINE, JACK *
    UNDERSTANDING MUSICAL INSTRUMENTS..HOW TO SELECT YOUR
LEVINE, JACK
    WHAT MUSICAL INSTRUMENT FOR ME
LEWIS, THOMAS C.
    PROTEST AGAINST THE MODERN DEVELOPMENT OF UNMUSICAL TONE, A
LINDO, ALGERNON H.
    PEDALLING IN PIANOFORTE MUSIC
LOEHR, JOHANN JOSEPH
    ESSAY ON THE THEORY AND PRACTICE OF TUNING, AN ...PIANOFORTES AND
LOESCHMANN, DAVID
    DESCRIPTION AND USE OF THE PATENT ENHARMONIC PIANOFORTE
LOESSER, ARTHUR
    MEN, WOMEN AND PIANOS..A SOCIAL HISTORY
LOWERY, HARRY
    GUIDE TO MUSICAL ACOUSTICS, A ---1956
LUND, VICTOR E.
    EVALUATION OF ELECTRONIC SELF-INSTRUCTION ON PIANO KEYBOARD, THE
LYONS, SISTER MARIE STEPHEN
    REAWAKENING OF INTEREST IN THE HARPSICHORD IN THE 20TH. CENTURY,
MACKENZIE, SIR ALEXANDER
    MUSICIAN'S NARRATIVE, A ---CLARA SCHUMANN, VON BUELOW AND LISZT
MACQUOID, PERCY *
    DICTIONARY OF ENGLISH FURNITURE, THE --VOL. 3---16 ILLUSTRATIONS
MAITLAND, GEORGE L.
    HOW TO CHANGE PITCH OF PIANOS, IN FOUR LESSONS
MARCUSE, SIBYL
    MUSICAL INSTRUMENTS..A COMPREHENSIVE DICTIONARY
MARKS, ADOLF B.
    INTRODUCTION TO THE INTERPRETATION OF BEETHOVEN'S PIANO-FORTE
MARTIN, H. T.
    EVERY WOMAN HER OWN PIANO TUNER..OR, HINTS AND AIDS TO PIANO
MARX, ADOLF BERNHARD
    INTRODUCTION TO THE INTERPRETATION OF BEETHOVEN'S PIANO
MASON, HENRY LOWELL
    HOW HAS THE PIANOFORTE AS AN INSTRUMENT DEVELOPED SINCE
MASON, HENRY LOWELL
    MODERN ARTISTIC PIANOFORTE, THE ..ITS CONSTRUCTION
MASON AND HAMLIN ORGAN AND PIANO COMPANY
    CATALOGUE OF PIANOFORTES EMBODYING LATEST IMPROVEMENTS
MATTHAY, TOBIAS A.
    ACT OF TOUCH IN ALL ITS DIVERSITY, THE ..AN ANALYSIS AND SYNTHESIS
MATTHAY, TOBIAS A.
    FIRST PRINCIPLES OF PIANOFORTE PLAYING--EXTRACT FROM 'THE ACT OF
MATTHAY, TOBIAS A.
    PIANOFORTE TONE-PRODUCTION---SAME AS 'THE ACT OF TOUCH IN ALL ITS
MAYBERRY, JOHN HENRY
    PRACTICAL COURSE IN PIANO TUNING
MCFERRIN, CHARLES BETTEYS
    MOTHER'S PART IN HER CHILD'S MUSICAL EDUCATION, A ..OR, THE THINGS
MCTAMMANY, JOHN
    EVOLUTION OF THE PLAYER-PIANO MECHANISM---EXCERPT FROM 'PRESTO',
MCTAMMANY, JOHN
    HISTORY OF THE PLAYER-PIANO, THE
MCTAMMANY, JOHN
    TECHNICAL HISTORY OF THE PLAYER
MEL-O-DEE MUSIC COMPANY
    MELODEE MUSIC ROLLS..SEPTEMBER, 1920
METROPOLITAN MUSEUM OF ART, NEW YORK
    CATALOGUE OF THE CROSBY BROWN COLLECTION OF MUSICAL INSTRUMENTS OF
METROPOLITAN MUSEUM OF ART, NEW YORK
    KEYBOARD INSTRUMENTS IN THE METROPOLITAN MUSEUM OF ART..A PICTURE
MICHEL, NORMAN ELWOOD
    HISTORICAL PIANOS, HARPSICHORDS AND CLAVICHORDS---1963
MICHEL, NORMAN ELWOOD
    MICHEL'S PIANO ATLAS---REPUBLISHED IN 1965 UNDER AUTHORSHIP..B.
MICHEL, NORMAN ELWOOD
    OLD PIANOS
MININBERG, IAN
    VISUAL APPROACH TO PIANO TECHNIQUE, A
MOOR, WINIFRED
    TECHNICAL EXERCISES FOR THE EMANUEL MOOR DOUBLE KEYBOARD
MOORE, HENRY K.
    MANUAL OF PIANOFORTE TUNING, A
MOSCOW, CHARLES E.
    PRACTICAL PIANO TUNER, THE ..A COMPREHENSIVE SIMPLE SET OF RULES
MURATA, KOH
    SECTIONAL TUNING OF THE PIANO
MUSICAL OPINION AND MUSIC TRADE REVIEW
    REPAIRING THE REED ORGAN AND HARMONIUM..INFORMATION USEFUL TO
MUSIC EDUCATORS NATIONAL CONFERENCE
    HANDBOOK FOR TEACHING PIANO CLASSES
NALDER, LAWRENCE MARCUS
    ESSAYS IN PIANOFORTE TECHNOLOGY
NALDER, LAWRENCE MARCUS
    FIRST STEPS IN PIANO TUNING AND OTHER ESSAYS IN PIANOFORTE
NALDER, LAWRENCE MARCUS
    MODERN PIANO, THE
NALDER, LAWRENCE MARCUS
    PIANOFORTE CONSTRUCTION
NALDER, LAWRENCE MARCUS
    REPAIRING THE PIANOFORTE
NATIONAL PIANO MANUFACTURERS ASSOCIATION OF AMERICA
    STENCILLING OF PIANOS, THE
NATIONAL PIANO MANUFACTURERS ASSOCIATION
    CONSUMER INVESTIGATION FOR NATIONAL PIANO MANUFACTURERS
NATIONAL PIANO TRAVELERS ASSOCIATION
    PIANO TRAVELERS ASSOCIATION BOOK, THE ..A REFERENCE BOOK
NEBLING, ALBERT N. *
    MUSIC INSTRUMENT CHECKLIST
NEUPERT, HANNS
    CLAVICHORD, THE ---1956, IN GERMAN
NEUPERT, HANNS
    HARPSICHORD MANUAL..A HISTORY AND TECHNICAL DEVELOPMENT--2ND.
NEWMAN, ERNEST
    PIANO-PLAYER AND ITS MUSIC, THE
NEWMAN, WILLIAM S.
    PERFORMANCE PRACTICES IN BEETHOVEN'S PIANO SONATAS..AN
NEWMAN, WILLIAM S.
    SONATA IN THE BAROQUE ERA, THE --A HISTORY OF THE SONATA IDEA,
NEWMAN, WILLIAM S.
    SONATA IN THE CLASSIC ERA, THE --A HISTORY OF THE SONATA IDEA,

NICCHIA, LILLIAN
    PIANOFORTE STUDY..HINTS ON PIANO PLAYING
NILES BRYANT SCHOOL OF PIANO TUNING
    CORRESPONDENCE COURSE IN 12 LESSONS, A
NORTON, ANDREW J. O.
    CONSTRUCTION, TUNING AND CARE OF THE PIANOFORTE--EDITED AND
O'NEILL, J. A.
    DESCRIPTION AND HISTORY OF THE PIANOFORTE, A
ORD-HUME, ARTHUR W. J. G.
    CLOCKWORK MUSIC..AN ILLUSTRATED HISTORY OF MECHANICAL MUSICAL
ORD-HUME, ARTHUR W. J. G.
    PLAYER PIANO, THE HISTORY OF THE MECHANICAL PIANO AND HOW TO
ORTMANN, OTTO
    PHYSICAL BASIS OF PIANO TOUCH AND TONE, THE
PAETKAU, DAVID H.
    GROWTH OF INSTRUMENTS AND INSTRUMENTAL MUSIC, THE
PAGE, C. E.
    MUSICAL INSTRUMENTS--MECHANICAL AGE LIBRARY
PALME, RUDOLPH
    FIRST MONTHS IN PIANOFORTE INSTRUCTION, THE ---1870, IN GERMAN
PALMER, KING
    TEACH YOURSELF TO PLAY THE PIANO
PARKER, RICHARD G.
    TRIBUTE TO THE LIFE AND CHARACTER OF JONAS CHICKERING, 1798-1853,
PARKINSON, HANS B.
    PIANO, THE ..ITS CARE
PARRISH, CARL
    EARLY PIANO AND ITS INFLUENCE ON KEYBOARD TECHNIQUE AND
PAUER, ERNST
    DICTIONARY OF PIANISTS AND COMPOSERS FOR THE PIANOFORTE..WITH AN
PELTIER, LOUIS O.
    PIANO TUNER'S GUIDE, THE
PELZ, EDWARD
    ON PIANOFORTE MANUFACTURE, ESPECIALLY IN AMERICA
PENGELLY, J. BRADFORD
    PENGELLY BLUE BOOK OF STYLE, THE ...A STUDY OF THE ART OF STYLING
PETERSON, FRANKLIN
    THEORETIC COMPANION TO PRACTICE--PART I OF THE PIANIST'S HANDBOOK
PFEIFFER, WALTER
    PIANO KEY AND WHIPPEN, THE ..AN ANALYSIS OF THEIR RELATIONSHIPS IN
PHILLIPSON, WENTWORTH
    GUIDE TO YOUNG PIANOFORTE TEACHERS AND STUDENTS
PIANO, ORGAN AND MUSICAL INSTRUMENT WORKERS INTERNATIONAL UNION OF
    CONSTITUTION OF THE PIANO, ORGAN AND MUSICAL INSTRUMENT WORKERS'
PIERCE, B.
    PIERCE PIANO ATLAS--6TH. ED.---ORIGINALLY PUBLISHED AS 'MICHEL'S
PINCHERLE, MARC
    WORLD OF THE VIRTUOSO, THE
PLAYER-PIANO, THE
    FOUR HUNDRED OF THE BEST ADS OF 1911 DEVOTED TO PIANOS AND
PLAYFORD, JOHN
    MUSICKS HAND-MAID..NEW LESSONS AND INSTRUCTIONS FOR THE VIRGINALS
PRELLEUR, PETER
    HARPSICHORD ILLUSTRATED AND IMPROV'D, WHEREIN IS SHEWN THE ITALIAN
PRESTO--EDITORIAL STAFF
    MUSICAL INSTRUMENTS AT THE WORLD'S COLUMBIAN EXPOSITION, CHICAGO,
PRESTO PUBLISHING COMPANY
    PRESTO BUYERS' GUIDE TO PLAYER-PIANOS AND PIANOS
PULVER, JEFFREY
    DICTIONARY OF OLD ENGLISH MUSIC AND MUSICAL INSTRUMENTS, A
PYLE, HOWARD WILLETT
    PRACTICAL TREATISE ON TUNING AND REPAIRING THE PIANOFORTE, A
REED, MARY G.
    KEYBOARD ROAD IN MUSIC LAND, AND OTHER STORIES---FOR CHILDREN
REEDER, BETAH
    SINGING TOUCH, THE
REMBUSCH, JOSEPH ADAM
    PIANOS AND MUSICAL INSTRUMENTS DISCUSSED FROM AN UNSANITARY
RHODES, ALFRED
    CURIOSITIES OF THE KEY-BOARD AND THE STAFF...SHOWN TO BE UPON A
RICHNER, THOMAS
    ORIENTATION FOR INTERPRETING MOZART'S PIANO SONATAS
RICKER, EARL
    MUSIC LESSONS FOR YOUR CHILD
RIEFLING, REIMAR
    PIANO PEDALLING---1957, IN NORWEGIAN
RIEMANN, HUGO
    CATECHISM OF PIANOFORTE PLAYING---1888, IN GERMAN
RIMBAULT, EDWARD FRANCIS
    CHAPPELL AND CO.'S PRACTICAL DIRECTIONS UPON THE ART OF TUNING THE
RIMBAULT, EDWARD FRANCIS
    PIANOFORTE, THE ..ITS ORIGIN, PROCESS AND CONSTRUCTION
RIPIN, EDWIN M.--EDITOR
    KEYBOARD INSTRUMENTS..STUDIES IN KEYBOARD ORGANOLOGY---10 ESSAYS
RIPIN, EDWIN M.
    COUPLET HARPSICHORD IN THE CROSBY BROWN COLLECTION, THE --FROM
ROEHL, HARVEY
    KEYS TO A MUSICAL PAST...ILLUSTRATED TREATISE ON THE VARIOUS TYPES
ROEHL, HARVEY
    PLAYER PIANO, AN HISTORICAL SCRAPBOOK, THE
ROEHL, HARVEY
    PLAYER PIANO TREASURY..THE SCRAPBOOK HISTORY OF THE MECHANICAL
ROSE, ALGERNON SIDNEY
    ON CHOOSING A PIANO
ROSENCRANTZ, ISIDOR B.
    PIANO, ITS CONSTRUCTION AND RELATION TO TONE, PITCH AND
RUBINSTEIN, ANTON
    CONVERSATION ON MUSIC, A
RUSSELL, RAYMOND
    CATALOGUE OF THE BENTON FLETCHER COLLECTION OF EARLY KEYBOARD
RUSSELL, RAYMOND
    EARLY KEYBOARD INSTRUMENTS--VICTORIA AND ALBERT MUSEUM..'SMALL
RUSSELL, RAYMOND
    HARPSICHORD AND THE CLAVICHORD, THE --2ND. ED., REVISED BY HOWARD
SACHS, CURT
    EVOLUTION OF PIANO MUSIC, 1350-1700, THE
SACHS, CURT
    HISTORY OF MUSICAL INSTRUMENTS, THE
SCHAAF, EDWARD O.
    ART OF PIANO PLAYER TRANSCRIPTION, THE ..MAKING OF PERFORATED
SCHAAF, EDWARD O.
    ESSAYS AND ARTICLES ON MUSICAL SUBJECTS, PARTICULARLY
SCHAAF, EDWARD O.
    FUNDAMENTAL PRINCIPLES INVOLVED IN THE COMPOSING AND ARRANGING OF
SCHAAF, EDWARD O.
    MUSICAL INDIVIDUALITY OF THE PLAYER PIANO, THE ---EXCERPTS..'THE
SCHMECKEL, CARL D.
    PIANO OWNER'S GUIDE, THE
SCHOLES, PERCY
    APPRECIATION OF MUSIC BY MEANS OF THE PIANOLA AND DUO-ART, THE
SCHOTT, HOWARD
    PLAYING THE HARPSICHORD
SCHULZE, RICHARD ALLEN
    HOW TO BUILD A BAROQUE CONCERT HARPSICHORD
SCOTT, MARY M.
    WHAT CAN I PLAY..A BOOK ABOUT MUSICAL INSTRUMENTS

SEROFF, VICTOR
    COMMON SENSE IN PIANO STUDY
SHORTRIDGE, JOHN D.
    ITALIAN HARPSICHORD BUILDING IN THE 16TH. AND 17TH.
SKINNER, BELLE
    BELLE SKINNER COLLECTION OF OLD MUSICAL INSTRUMENTS, HOLYOKE,
SMITH, FANNY MORRIS
    NOBLE ART, A ..THREE LECTURES ON THE EVOLUTION AND CONSTRUCTION OF
SMITH, HERMANN
    ART OF TUNING THE PIANOFORTE, THE ..ON THE THEORY OF EQUAL
SMITH, THOMAS
    HOW TO TUNE YOUR OWN PIANO
SOUTH KENSINGTON MUSEUM, LONDON
    CATALOGUE OF THE SPECIAL EXHIBITION OF ANCIENT MUSICAL INSTRUMENTS
SOUTH KENSINGTON MUSEUM, LONDON
    DESCRIPTIVE CATALOGUE OF THE MUSICAL INSTRUMENTS IN THE SOUTH
SOUTH KENSINGTON MUSEUM, LONDON
    DESCRIPTIVE CATALOGUE OF THE MUSICAL INSTRUMENTS IN THE SOUTH
SPAETH, SIGMUND *
    AMPICO IN MUSIC STUDY, THE
SPILLANE, DANIEL
    HISTORY OF THE AMERICAN PIANOFORTE..ITS TECHNICAL DEVELOPMENT, AND
SPILLANE, DANIEL
    PIANO, THE ..SCIENTIFIC, TECHNICAL, AND PRACTICAL INSTRUCTIONS
SQUIRE, RUSSEL N. *
    CLASS PIANO FOR ADULT BEGINNERS--2ND. ED.---1964
STANDARD PLAYER ACTION COMPANY
    PRINCIPLES OF PLAYER ACTION OPERATION--3RD. ED.
STANDARD PNEUMATIC ACTION COMPANY
    DESCRIPTION OF STANDARD PNEUMATIC PLAYER ACTION, WITH SUGGESTIONS
STANLEY, ALBERT A.
    CATALOGUE OF THE STEARNS COLLECTION OF MUSICAL INSTRUMENTS
STECK AND COMPANY
    ILLUSTRATED CATALOG...GRAND AND UPRIGHT PIANOS
STEGLICH, RUDOLF
    MOZARTS FLUGEL KLINGT WIEDER--MOZART'S PIANO SOUNDS AGAIN---WITH
STEINERT, MORRIS
    CATALOGUE OF THE M. STEINERT COLLECTION OF KEYED AND STRING
STEINERT, MORRIS
    MORRIS STEINERT COLLECTION OF KEYED AND STRINGED INSTRUMENTS, THE
STEINWAY, THEODORE E.
    PEOPLE AND PIANOS..A CENTURY OF SERVICE TO MUSIC---1853-1953
STEINWAY AND SONS
    BOOK OF ART PIANO CASES
STEINWAY AND SONS
    ILLUSTRATED CATALOGUE OF--STEINWAY AND SONS...PIANOFORTES
STEINWAY AND SONS
    ILLUSTRATED CATALOGUE OF PIANOS
STEINWAY AND SONS
    ILLUSTRATED CATALOGUE OF STEINWAY AND SONS' PIANOS
STEINWAY AND SONS
    ILLUSTRATED CIRCULAR AND CATALOGUE OF PIANOFORTES--MANUFACTURERS
STEINWAY AND SONS
    INIMITABLE TONE..'PRICE LIST OF PIANOS MADE BY STEINWAY AND SONS,
STEINWAY AND SONS
    PIANOFORTES
STEINWAY AND SONS
    PORTRAITS OF MUSICAL CELEBRITIES
STEINWAY AND SONS
    PORTRAITS OF MUSICAL CELEBRITIES
STEINWAY AND SONS
    PORTRAITS OF MUSICAL CELEBRITIES
STEINWAY AND SONS
    PORTRAITS OF MUSICAL CELEBRITIES
STEINWAY AND SONS
    PORTRAITS OF MUSICAL CELEBRITIES
STEINWAY AND SONS
    PORTRAITS OF MUSICAL CELEBRITIES
STEINWAY AND SONS
    STEINWAY..YESTERDAY, TODAY, TOMORROW
STEINWAY AND SONS
    STEINWAY AND SONS' PIANO-FORTE MANUFACTORY AT 'STEINWAY', LONG
STEINWAY AND SONS
    STEINWAY OF TODAY, THE ..A FAMILY OF PIANO MANUFACTURERS THROUGH
STEINWAY AND SONS
    STEINWAY PROGRESS..AN APPRECIATION BY I. J. PADEREWSKI
STEVENS, FLOYD A.
    COMPLETE COURSE IN PROFESSIONAL PIANO TUNING, REPAIR, AND
STEVENS, PARAN
    REPORT UPON MUSICAL INSTRUMENTS..PARIS UNIVERSAL EXPOSITION, 1867
STODDARD, HOPE
    FROM THESE COMES MUSIC
STRAUCH BROTHERS
    MANUFACTURE OF PIANOFORTE ACTION, THE ..ITS RISE AND DEVELOPMENT
STROHBER PIANO COMPANY
    PNEUMATIC PLAYER MECHANISM AND DESCRIPTIVE CATALOG OF STROHBER AND
SUMNER, WILLIAM L.
    PIANOFORTE, THE --3RD. ED.---1966
TANKARD, GEOFFREY
    PIANOFORTE DIPLOMAS
TAPPER, THOMAS
    EDUCATION OF THE MUSIC TEACHER, THE
TERWILLIGER, GORDON B.
    PIANO TEACHERS PROFESSIONAL HANDBOOK
TONK, WILLIAM
    MEMOIRS OF A--PIANO--MANUFACTURER
TRAVIS, JOHN W.
    GUIDE TO RESTRINGING, A
TRAVIS, JOHN W.
    LET'S TUNE UP
UNITED STATES--LIBRARY OF CONGRESS..DIVISION OF BIBLIOGRAPHY
    BRIEF LIST OF REFERENCES ON THE PIANO AND THE PIANO PLAYER
UNITED STATES--NATIONAL RECOVERY ADMINISTRATION
    CODE OF FAIR COMPETITION FOR THE PIANO MANUFACTURING INDUSTRY AS
UNITED STATES MUSEUM OF HISTORY AND TECHNOLOGY
    CHECKLIST OF KEYBOARD INSTRUMENTS AT THE SMITHSONIAN INSTITUTION,
UNITED STATES PATENT OFFICE
    COLLECTION OF LETTERS PATENT RELATING TO THE CONSTRUCTION OF
VANT, ALBERT B.
    PIANO SCALE MAKING
VANTYN, SIDNEY
    MODERN PIANOFORTE TECHNIQUE
VAN ATTA, HARRISON LOUIS--EDITOR
    TREATISE ON THE PIANO AND PLAYER PIANO, A
VAN DER WEYDE, PETER H.
    INSTRUCTIONS IN PLAYING THE PIANO-FORTE WITH AEOLIAN ATTACHMENT
VAN NOORDEN, C.
    FREAK PIANOS---SCRAPBOOK
VENABLE, MARY
    INTERPRETATION OF PIANO MUSIC, THE
VICTORIA AND ALBERT MUSEUM, SOUTH KENSINGTON
    CATALOGUE OF MUSICAL INSTRUMENTS..VOL. 1, KEYBOARD
VICTORIA AND ALBERT MUSEUM, SOUTH KENSINGTON
    EXAMPLES OF ART WORKMANSHIP OF VARIOUS AGES AND COUNTRIES..MUSICAL
VICTORIA AND ALBERT MUSEUM, SOUTH KENSINGTON
    LIST OF PHOTOGRAPHS OF OBJECTS IN THE VICTORIA AND ALBERT

VICTORIA AND ALBERT MUSEUM, SOUTH KENSINGTON
    MUSICAL INSTRUMENTS AS WORKS OF ART..VOL. 1, KEYBOARD
VICTORIA AND ALBERT MUSEUM, SOUTH KENSINGTON
    PICTURE BOOK OF KEYBOARD MUSICAL INSTRUMENTS, A
VIRGIL, ALMON K.
    TECHNIPHONE MANUAL..INSTRUCTIONS AND EXERCISES IN THE USE OF THE
WAGNER, CHARLES A.
    HOW TO SELECT A GOOD PIANO
WALKER, ADAM
    PHILOSOPHY OF THE HARPSICHORD, EXPLAINING HOW THAT INSTRUMENT IS
WEBER PIANO COMPANY
    WEBER GRAND, SQUARE AND UPRIGHT PIANO-FORTES, THE
WEISER, BERNHARD D.
    KEYBOARD MUSIC--16TH.-20TH. CENTURIES
WEITZMANN, CARL F.
    HISTORY OF PIANOFORTE-PLAYING AND PIANOFORTE-LITERATURE, A
WELTE-MIGNON CORPORATION
    HOW TO TEST AND REGULATE THE AUTO DE LUXE WELTE-MIGNON REPRODUCING
WELTE-MIGNON CORPORATION
    LIBRARY OF DELUXE WELTE-MIGNON MUSIC RECORDS FOR REPRODUCING
WELTE-MIGNON CORPORATION
    LIBRARY OF WELTE-MIGNON MUSIC RECORDS
WELTE ARTISTIC PLAYER-PIANO COMPANY
    LIST OF MUSIC FOR THE WELTE-MIGNON PIANO--WITH SUPPLEMENT
WESTERBY, HERBERT
    HISTORY OF THE PIANOFORTE
WHITE, WILLIAM BRAID
    PIANO PLAYING MECHANISMS
WHITE, WILLIAM BRAID
    PIANO TUNING AND ALLIED ARTS--5TH. ED.---1917
WHITE, WILLIAM BRAID
    PLAYER-PIANIST, THE ..A GUIDE TO THE APPRECIATION AND
WHITE, WILLIAM BRAID
    PLAYER-PIANO UP TO DATE, THE
WHITE, WILLIAM BRAID
    REGULATION AND REPAIR OF PIANO AND PLAYER PIANO MECHANISM
WHITE, WILLIAM BRAID
    TECHNICAL TREATISE ON PLAYER PIANO MECHANISM, A
WHITE, WILLIAM BRAID
    THEORY AND PRACTICE OF PIANOFORTE BUILDING
WHITING, ARTHUR B.
    LESSON OF THE CLAVICHORD, THE --REPRINT..'NEW MUSIC REVIEW'
WIER, ALBERT
    PIANO, THE ..ITS HISTORY, MAKERS, PLAYERS AND MUSIC
WILLIS, AUBREY
    AUBREY WILLIS HOME STUDY COURSE IN PIANO TUNING AND REPAIRING
WILLS, VERA G. *
    PARENT'S GUIDE TO MUSIC LESSONS, A
WILSON, DAVID M.
    INSTRUCTION BOOK ON THE PIANO-PLAYER AND PLAYER-PIANO, AN
WILSON, DAVID M.
    PLAYER-PIANO, THE ..ITS CONSTRUCTION..HOW TO PLAY, WHAT TO PLAY
WILSON, MORRIS E.
    HOW TO HELP YOUR CHILD WITH MUSIC--2ND. ED.---1951
WING AND SONS
    BOOK OF COMPLETE INFORMATION ABOUT PIANOS, THE ...1868-1918, A
WINTERNITZ, EMANUEL
    MUSICAL INSTRUMENTS AND THEIR SYMBOLISM IN WESTERN ART
WINTERNITZ, EMANUEL
    MUSICAL INSTRUMENTS OF THE WESTERN WORLD
WOLFENDEN, S.
    TREATISE ON THE ART OF PIANOFORTE CONSTRUCTION, A --SUPPLEMENT
WOLFENDEN, S.
    TREATISE ON THE ART OF PIANOFORTE CONSTRUCTION, A
WOLFRAM, VICTOR
    SOSTENUTO PEDAL, THE
WOOD, ALEXANDER
    PHYSICS OF MUSIC, THE --4TH. ED.---1944
WOODHOUSE, GEORGE
    REALISTIC APPROACH TO PIANO PLAYING, A
WOODMAN, HENRY STAUNTON
    HOW TO TUNE A PIANO..HOW TO BUY A USED PIANO..HOW TO KEEP YOUR
WORCH, HUGO
    PIANO MAKERS OF THE EVOLUTIONARY PERIOD..RARE ENGLISH AND AMERICAN
WORCH, HUGO
    WORCH PIANOS, AND A BRIEF SKETCH OF THE PIANOFORTE
WRIGHT, WILLIAM C.
    GOLDEN MONITOR, FOR THE PIANOFORTE AND CABINET ORGAN, DESIGNED AS
WRIGHT, WILLIAM C.
    PIANOFORTE MANUAL, THE ..DESIGNED AS A COMPLETE PIANOFORTE PRIMER
WYMAN, ADDISON P.
    WYMAN'S PIANO TEXTBOOK..CONTAINING A COMPLETE SYSTEM OF MUSICAL
YALE UNIVERSITY--ART GALLERY
    MUSICAL INSTRUMENTS AT YALE..A SELECTION OF WESTERN INSTRUMENTS
YALE UNIVERSITY--ART GALLERY
    YALE COLLECTION OF MUSICAL INSTRUMENTS..CHECKLIST
YALE UNIVERSITY SCHOOL OF MUSIC
    CHECK-LIST OF WESTERN INSTRUMENTS IN THE COLLECTION OF MUSICAL
YATES, PETER
    AMATEUR AT THE KEYBOARD, AN
YOUNG, PERCY M.
    KEYBOARD MUSICIANS OF THE WORLD
YOUNG, THOMAS C.
    MAKING OF MUSICAL INSTRUMENTS, THE ---1939
ZUCKERMANN, WOLFGANG JOACHIM
    MODERN HARPSICHORD, THE ..TWENTIETH CENTURY INSTRUMENTS AND THEIR

Processes of Learning

ABBOTT, A. T.
    METHOD FOR GAINING A PERFECT KNOWLEDGE OF THE NOTES, ETC., FOR
ADAMS, JAMES B.
    FAMILIAR INTRODUCTION TO THE FIRST PRINCIPLES OF MUSIC, A ...FOR
ADAMS, JOHN S.
    FIVE THOUSAND MUSICAL TERMS..A COMPLETE DICTIONARY WITH A TREATISE
ADLER, KURT
    ART OF ACCOMPANYING AND COACHING, THE ---1965
AEOLIAN COMPANY, THE
    DUO-ART BOOK OF MUSIC, THE
AGUILAR, EMANUEL
    HOW TO LEARN THE PIANOFORTE
AGUILAR, EMANUEL
    LITTLE BOOK ABOUT LEARNING THE PIANOFORTE, A
AHEARN, ELLA MASON *
    ADULT EXPLORER AT THE PIANO, THE
AHRENS, CORA B. *
    FOR ALL PIANO TEACHERS
ALBRECHTSBERGER, JOHANN GEORG
    ALBRECHTSBERGER'S COLLECTED WRITINGS ON THOROUGH-BASS, HARMONY AND
ALBRECHTSBERGER, JOHANN GEORG
    ALBRECHTSBERGER'S ELEMENTARY WORK ON THE SCIENCE OF
ALCHIN, CARRIE A.
    APPLIED HARMONY--REVISED AND WITH ADDITIONAL CHAPTERS BY VINCENT

ALCHIN, CARRIE A.
    KEYBOARD HARMONY--3 VOLS. IN 1, 1923-1926
ALLEN, MARGARET *
    CREATIVE MOTION
ALLISON, IRL
    LET'S LEARN ALL THE NOTES AND READ BETTER..FOR ALL PIANO PUPILS,
AMEY, ELLEN
    CONSCIOUS CONTROL IN PIANO STUDY
ANDERSON, J. CLARK
    GOOD MUSIC EXPLAINED..WHAT ALL GOOD PIANISTS SHOULD KNOW
ANON
    ADVICE TO A NOBLEMAN...ON THE MANNER IN WHICH HIS CHILDREN SHOULD
ANON
    COMPLEAT TUTOR FOR THE HARPSICHORD OR SPINNET, WHEREIN IS SHEWN
ANON
    FASHIONABLE PRECEPTOR, FOR THE PIANO-FORTE AND HARPSICHORD,
ANON
    GUIDE TO THE MUSICAL TUITION OF VERY YOUNG CHILDREN, BY AN OLD
ANON
    HOW TO LEARN TO PLAY THE PIANO WELL, BY ONE WHO HAS TAUGHT HIMSELF
ANON
    MASTER RULES FOR SUCCESSFUL PIANO PRACTICE..A COLLECTION OF
ANON
    NEW AND COMPLETE INSTRUCTIONS FOR THE HARPSICHORD, PIANO FORTE OR
ANON
    NEW INSTRUCTIONS FOR PLAYING THE HARPSICHORD, PIANOFORTE OR
ANON
    NEW PIANOFORTE KEYBOARD, THE ..CARD AND GAME, THE A.B.C. OF MUSIC
ANON
    PIANOFORTE POCKET COMPANION, THE ..OR, A POPULAR VIEW OF THE
ANON
    PIANO IN TWELVE LESSONS
ANON
    PLAYING THE HARPSICHORD, SPINET OR PIANO FORTE MADE EASY BY NEW
ANON
    PRECEPTOR, FOR THE PIANOFORTE, THE ORGAN OR HARPSICHORD, THE
ARNOLD, FRANCK THOMAS
    ART OF ACCOMPANIMENT FROM A THOROUGH-BASS, AS PRACTICED IN THE
AULD, WILDA J.
    HANDBOOK FOR THE CHURCH PIANIST, A
AXTENS, FLORENCE
    FIRST SIX MONTHS IN THE PIANO CLASS, THE ..A MANUAL FOR TEACHERS
AXTENS, FLORENCE
    PIANO CLASS METHOD..THE FIRST TWELVE MONTHS IN THE PIANO CLASS
BACON, ERNST
    NOTES ON THE PIANO
BADURA-SKODA, EVA *
    INTERPRETING MOZART ON THE KEYBOARD---1957, IN GERMAN
BAILLIE, ALEXANDER--SUPPOSED AUTHOR
    INTRODUCTION TO THE KNOWLEDGE AND PRACTICE OF THE THORO' BASS, AN
BAKER, DAVID
    JAZZ IMPROVISATION..A COMPREHENSIVE METHOD OF STUDY FOR ALL
BANISTER, HENRY C.
    HARMONIZING OF MELODIES, THE ..A TEXT-BOOK FOR STUDENTS AND
BARNETT, DAVID
    PERFORMANCE OF MUSIC, THE ..A STUDY IN TERMS OF THE PIANOFORTE
BARNWELL, V. T.
    BARNWELL'S NORMAL KEYBOARD AND STAFF STUDIES--THE MENTAL
BARTH, HANS
    TECHNIC..THE ENTIRE 25 BRANCHES FOR DEVELOPING TECHNIC NECESSARY
BARTHELEMON, FRANCOIS H.
    NEW TUTOR FOR THE HARPSICHORD OR PIANO FORTE, WHEREIN THE FIRST
BASTIEN, JAMES W. *
    BEGINNING PIANO FOR ADULTS
BASTIEN, JAMES W.
    HOW TO TEACH PIANO SUCCESSFULLY
BAVIN, JOHN T.
    PIANO CLASS INSTRUCTOR
BAXTER, JAMES
    INDUCTIVE GRAMMAR OF MUSIC, FOR CLASS, PRIVATE LESSON, OR SELF
BAXTER, JAMES
    NEW SCHOOL OF MUSIC, THE ..PRACTICAL THOROUGH BASE CULTURE, FOR
BECKER, JULIUS
    CONCISE TREATISE ON HARMONY, ACCOMPANIMENT, AND COMPOSITION, FOR
BECKERMAN, H. J.
    AMERICAN SCHOOL OF RAGTIME PIANO PLAYING, THE
BEMETZRIEDER, ANTON
    ABSTRACT OF A NEW METHOD OF TEACHING THE PRINCIPLES OF MUSIC,
BEMETZRIEDER, ANTON
    COMPENDIUM OF A NEW METHOD OF MUSIC...WITH THE AUTHOR'S PRINCIPLES
BEMETZRIEDER, ANTON
    GAMUT AND COMMON CHORD IN ALL KEYS, FINGERED FOR THE HARPSICHORD,
BEMETZRIEDER, ANTON
    MUSIC MADE EASY TO EVERY CAPACITY, IN A SERIES OF DIALOGUES..BEING
BEMETZRIEDER, ANTON
    NEW GUIDE TO MUSIC, IN FRENCH AND ENGLISH, A
BEMETZRIEDER, ANTON
    NEW LESSONS FOR THE HARPSICHORD
BENEDICT, LADY *
    HOW TO PLAY THE PIANOFORTE
BENEDICT, MILO ELLSWORTH
    THIRTY-THREE SUGGESTIONS IN ONE LESSON..FOR THE GUIDANCE AND
BENNER, LORA
    BENNER BLUE BOOK, THE ..PRACTICAL MANUAL OF PIANO TEACHING--4TH.
BENNER, LORA
    BENNER GOLD BOOK, THE ..PIANO MATERIAL AND TEACHING METHODS--3RD.
BENNER, LORA
    THEORY FOR PIANO STUDENTS--1ST. YEAR, PRIVATE OR CLASS--5 VOLS.,
BERGER, FRANCESCO
    FIRST STEPS AT THE PIANOFORTE
BERNING, ALICE B. *
    KEYBOARD EXPERIENCES FOR CLASSROOM TEACHERS
BERTINI, HENRI
    BERTINI'S SELF-TEACHING CATECHISM OF MUSIC FOR THE PIANOFORTE
BEVITT, ZAY RECTOR
    PIANO PLAYING BY HARMONY DIAGRAMS..STUDENT'S BOOK
BEVITT, ZAY RECTOR
    PIANO PLAYING BY HARMONY DIAGRAMS..TEACHER'S MANUAL
BLAKE, DOROTHY
    FIRST STEPS IN CHORD PLAYING
BLOCKLEY, JOHN
    PIANIST'S CATECHISM, THE ---1880
BODKY, ERWIN
    INTERPRETATION OF BACH'S KEYBOARD WORKS, THE
BOLTON, HETTY
    HOW TO PRACTICE
BOLTON, HETTY
    ON TEACHING THE PIANO
BONPENSIERE, LUIGI
    NEW PATHWAYS TO PIANO TECHNIQUE..A STUDY OF THE RELATIONS BETWEEN
BOOTH, VICTOR
    WE PIANO TEACHERS--REVISED BY ADELE FRANKLIN---1946
BOSWORTH, HARRIETTE DEXTER
    IDEAS FOR YOUNG PIANO TEACHERS
BOTTOMLEY, JOSEPH
    NEW SYSTEM OF PRACTICING AND TEACHING THE PIANOFORTE, A

BOWEN, CAROLYN
    OUTLINES FOR TRAINING PIANO TEACHERS
BRANDT, LEONIE
    SCIENCE IN MODERN PIANOFORTE PLAYING
BRECKENRIDGE, WILLIAM KILGORE
    HINTS FOR PIANO NORMAL STUDIES
BREE, MADAME MALWINE
    GROUNDWORK OF THE LESCHETIZKY METHOD, THE ---1902
BREITHAUPT, RUDOLPH MARIA
    NATURAL PIANO-TECHNIC..SCHOOL OF WEIGHT TOUCH--2 VOLS.
BREMNER, ROBERT
    HARPSICHORD OR SPINNET MISCELLANY, THE --KEYBOARD
BRIED, FREDERICK
    STIMULATION IN PIANO STUDY..HOW PARENTS CAN STIMULATE AND MAINTAIN
BRIGGS, GILBERT A.
    PIANOS, PIANISTS AND SONICS
BROTHERHOOD, JAMES
    BROTHERHOOD 'TECHNICON' AND HOW TO USE IT, THE
BROUGHTON, JULIA
    SUCCESS IN PIANO TEACHING
BROWER, HARRIETTE
    ART OF THE PIANIST, THE
BROWER, HARRIETTE
    HOME HELP IN MUSIC STUDY
BROWER, HARRIETTE
    HOW A DEPENDABLE PIANO TECHNIQUE WAS WON
BROWER, HARRIETTE
    MODERN MASTERS OF THE KEYBOARD
BROWER, HARRIETTE
    PIANO MASTERY..TALKS WITH MASTER PIANISTS AND TEACHERS...
BROWER, HARRIETTE
    PIANO MASTERY, SECOND SERIES
BROWER, HARRIETTE
    SELF-HELP IN PIANO STUDY
BROWN, JEAN PARKMAN
    INTERVALS, CHORDS AND EAR TRAINING FOR YOUNG PIANOFORTE STUDENTS
BRUXNER, MERVYN
    MASTERING THE PIANO
BUCHAROFF, SIMON
    MODERN PIANIST'S TEXT BOOK, THE
BUCK, PERCY
    PSYCHOLOGY FOR MUSICIANS
BUCKLEY, OLIVIA DUSSEK
    MUSICAL TRUTHS..OR, AN ANALYSIS OF MUSIC AND AN ESSAY ON THE PAST
BUONAMICI, CARLO
    PRACTICAL POINTS ON PIANO PLAYING
BURROWES, JOHN FRECKLETON
    GUIDE TO PRACTICE ON THE PIANOFORTE
BURROWES, JOHN FRECKLETON
    PIANOFORTE PRIMER, THE ..CONTAINING THE RUDIMENTS OF MUSIC
BURROWS, RAYMOND
    ELEMENTARY PIANO INSTRUCTION IN COLLEGE
CALAND, ELIZABETH
    ARTISTIC PIANO PLAYING, AS TAUGHT BY LUDWIG DEPPE
CALLAGHAN, JAMES
    ZIP CHORDMASTER..BEGINNERS HOME COURSE FOR PIANO AND ORGAN
CALLENDER, ROMAINE
    TEACHER'S MANUAL, A WORK DESIGNED TO SUPPLEMENT...'THE FIRST TEN
CAMPBELL, LE ROY B.
    VELOCITY PLUS
CARMIENCKE, ALBERT G.
    MECHANICS OF PIANO PLAYING, THE
CARPE, ADOLPH
    GROUPING, ARTICULATING AND PHRASING IN MUSICAL INTERPRETATION..A
CARPE, ADOLPH
    PIANIST AND THE ART OF MUSIC, THE ..A TREATISE ON PIANO PLAYING
CARR, BENJAMIN
    ANALYTICAL INSTRUCTOR FOR THE PIANO FORTE, OP. 15, THE --IN 3 PTS.
CARRE, JOHN
    PSYCHOLOGY OF PIANO TEACHING, THE ..A TEXTBOOK FOR TEACHERS,
CARTER, BUENTA
    BEGINNER'S PIANO BOOK FOR OLDER STUDENTS...DESIGNED FOR THE OLDER
CARUTHERS, JULIA LOIS
    PIANO TECHNIC FOR CHILDREN
CARY, MRS. C. S. P.
    PIANO-FORTE CLASS BOOK, CONTAINING PRACTICAL RUDIMENTAL LESSONS
CASTELLINI, JOHN EDWARD
    RUDIMENTS OF MUSIC..A NEW APPROACH WITH APPLICATION TO THE
CHAPPLE, STANLEY
    CLASS WAY TO THE KEYBOARD, THE
CHASE, MARY WOOD
    NATURAL LAWS IN PIANO TECHNIC
CHASTEK, WINIFRED
    KEYBOARD SKILLS..SIGHT READING, TRANSPOSITION, HARMONIZATION,
CHEYETTE, IRVING
    BASIC PIANO FOR THE MUSIC EDUCATOR AND CLASSROOM TEACHER
CHILDERS, LEMUEL
    CHORD DICTIONARY..DESIGNED FOR TEACHERS, STUDENTS AND SELF-TAUGHT
CHILDERS, LEMUEL
    PLAYING THE PIANO BY EAR
CHING, JAMES
    AMATEUR PIANIST'S COMPANION, THE
CHING, JAMES
    BETTER BEGINNINGS..A FIRST BOOK FOR EVERYONE WHO WANTS TO BECOME A
CHING, JAMES
    CANDIDATE'S COMPANION TO THE EXERCISES, SCALES, BROKEN CHORDS,
CHING, JAMES
    ENTIRELY NEW SOLUTION TO THE PROBLEMS OF PIANO STUDY AT HOME, AN
CHING, JAMES
    FOREARM ROTATION---A SEQUEL TO 'THE ROTARY ROAD'--15 PHOTOS AND
CHING, JAMES
    LET'S PLAY THE PIANO..THE FIRST MUSIC BOOK FOR CHILDREN OF ALL
CHING, JAMES
    NEW GRADED TIME EXERCISES, FOR PIANO, THE
CHING, JAMES
    PERFORMER AND AUDIENCE..AN INVESTIGATION INTO THE PSYCHOLOGICAL
CHING, JAMES
    PIANIST'S HOME STUDY COURSES, THE
CHING, JAMES
    PIANO PLAYING, A PRACTICAL METHOD--A NEW EDITION OF 'PIANO
CHING, JAMES
    PLAYING AND TEACHING OF BACH, THE ..A GUIDE FOR TEACHERS, STUDENTS
CHING, JAMES
    STUDIES FOR BASIC PIANO TECHNIQUE..WRITTEN AND SELECTED WITH
CHING, JOAN ELIZABETH
    APPROACH TO PIANO TEACHING---ALSO CATALOGUED UNDER
CHITTENDEN, KATE S.
    SYNTHETIC CATECHISM, THE ..538 QUESTIONS AND ANSWERS FOR USE IN
CHRISTIANI, ADOLPH FRIEDRICH
    PRINCIPLES OF EXPRESSION IN PIANOFORTE PLAYING, THE
CHURCHILL, VIRGINIA PEAKES
    MODERN TEACHER'S GUIDE TO PIANO AND PIANO CLASS TEACHING
CHURCHILL, VIRGINIA PEAKES
    NINETEEN FIFTY-SIX SUPPLEMENT TO THE MODERN TEACHER'S GUIDE TO
CLARKE, HUGH ARCHIBALD
    ART OF PIANOFORTE PLAYING, THE --TEXT BOOK FOR BEGINNERS

CLEMENTI, MUZIO
   INTRODUCTION TO THE ART OF PLAYING ON THE PIANOFORTE---1801+
COCHRAN, MARY
   ULTIMATE PRINCIPLES OF PIANOFORTE TEACHING AND PLAYING
COGGINS, JOSEPH
   COMPANION TO THE MUSICAL ASSISTANT, A ..CONTAINING ALL THAT IS
COGGINS, JOSEPH
   GOVERNESS'S MUSICAL ASSISTANT, CONTAINING ALL THAT IS TRULY USEFUL
COHEN, HARRIET
   MUSIC'S HANDMAID
COKER, JERRY
   IMPROVISING JAZZ
CONKLIN-HAPP, SUZANNE
   APPLIED KEYBOARD HARMONY
COOKE, CHARLES
   PLAYING THE PIANO FOR PLEASURE--REV. ED.---1941
COOKE, JAMES FRANCIS
   GREAT PIANISTS ON PIANO PLAYING..STUDY TALKS WITH FOREMOST
COOKE, JAMES FRANCIS
   HOW TO MEMORIZE MUSIC
COUPERIN, FRANCOIS
   ART DE TOUCHER LE CLAVECIN, L' ---IN FRENCH, GERMAN AND ENGLISH
COVIELLO, AMBROSE
   WHAT MATTHAY MEANT
CRAMER, JOHN BAPTIST
   INSTRUCTIONS FOR THE PIANOFORTE---CONTAINS ALSO A SET OF 28
CROTCH, WILLIAM
   PRELUDES FOR THE PIANO FORTE, COMPOSED IN VARIOUS STYLES..TO WHICH
CURCIO, LOUISE
   SINGLE NOTE, THE
CURWEN, ANNIE JESSY
   CHILD PIANIST, THE
CURWEN, ANNIE JESSY
   PSYCHOLOGY APPLIED TO MUSIC TEACHING
CURWEN, ANNIE JESSY
   TEACHER'S GUIDE...TO MRS. CURWEN'S PIANOFORTE METHOD, 'THE CHILD
CZERNY, CARL
   COMPLETE THEORETICAL AND PRACTICAL PIANO FORTE SCHOOL, FROM THE
CZERNY, CARL
   LETTERS TO A YOUNG LADY ON THE ART OF PLAYING THE PIANOFORTE
D'ABREU, GERALD
   PLAYING THE PIANO WITH CONFIDENCE---1964
DAHL, ANTON
   SOUL OF GENIUS, THE ..ITS MUSICAL DEVELOPMENT AND HOW THE WORLD AT
DANIELS, BESS *
   WORLD OF MUSIC, THE ..PIANO COURSE..TEACHERS' BOOK, FOR CLASS OR
DAVIS, HARRY
   INSTANT PIANO..A UNIQUE METHOD OF READING AND CHORDING FROM THE
DAVIS, LIONEL
   KEYBOARD INSTRUMENTS..THE STORY OF THE PIANO---YOUNGER READERS
DENVER--PUBLIC SCHOOLS
   CLASS-PIANO TEACHERS HANDBOOK
DEUTSCH, LEONHARD
   PIANO..GUIDED SIGHT-READING
DE WITT, EDYTHE
   EDYTHE DE WITT'S METHOD FOR CLASS PIANO...WRITTEN TO GIVE CORRECT
DILLER, ANGELA
   KEYBOARD HARMONY COURSE..A CREATIVE METHOD BASED ON
DILLER, ANGELA
   KEYBOARD MUSIC STUDY..A CREATIVE METHOD BASED ON EAR-TRAINING--IN
DILLER, ANGELA
   SPLENDOR OF MUSIC, THE
DOBBIE, E. A.
   AUSTRALIAN PIANOFORTE TUTOR
DODD, FLORENCE
   BERLIN TEST CLASS, THE ..OR, FORTY-EIGHT PROGRESSIVE LESSONS IN
DOLMETSCH, ARNOLD
   INTERPRETATION OF MUSIC OF THE SEVENTEENTH AND EIGHTEENTH
DONINGTON, ROBERT
   INTERPRETATION OF EARLY MUSIC, THE
DONINGTON, ROBERT
   PERFORMER'S GUIDE TO BAROQUE MUSIC, A
DRAKE, KENNETH
   SONATAS OF BEETHOVEN AS HE PLAYED AND TAUGHT THEM, THE
DUCKWORTH, GUY
   KEYBOARD MUSICIANSHIP
DUFFEE, GERTRUDE BANKS
   PIANO STUDY..A GUIDE TO TEACHER AND STUDENT
DUMM, ROBERT W.
   IN BLACK AND WHITE
DUSSEK, JOHANN L.
   DUSSEK'S INSTRUCTIONS ON THE ART OF PLAYING THE PIANOFORTE OR
EARLES, ADELAIDE L. S. T.
   PIANO PLAYING OF THE FUTURE, FOR EVERY GOOD PIANIST, THE
EARLES, ADELAIDE L. S. T.
   SHORT ESSAY ON THE GENERAL NEED FOR SCIENTIFIC PIANOFORTE PLAYING,
EBERHARDT, GOBY
   MY SYSTEM FOR PRACTICING THE VIOLIN AND PIANO, BASED UPON
EDWARDS, RUTH
   COMPLEAT MUSIC TEACHER FOR TEACHERS, PARENTS AND STUDENTS
EGBERT, MARION S.
   KEYBOARD EXPERIENCE IN THE CLASSROOM MUSIC PROGRAM..HANDBOOK FOR
EGBERT, MARION S.
   SEEING WHAT WE SING, AN AID THROUGH KEYBOARD EXPERIENCE TO THE
EHRENFECTER, C. A.
   DELIVERY IN THE ART OF PIANOFORTE PLAYING
EHRLICH, ALFRED HEINRICH
   HOW TO PRACTICE ON THE PIANO..REFLECTIONS AND SUGGESTIONS
EHRLICH, ALFRED HEINRICH
   HOW TO PRACTICE THE PIANOFORTE..SPECULATIONS AND ADVICE
EISENBERG, JACOB
   ARTISTIC PIANIST, THE ..NATURAL TECHNICS IN PIANO MASTERY..FROM
EISENBERG, JACOB
   WEIGHT AND RELAXATION METHOD FOR THE PIANOFORTE
ELKAN, IDA
   PRACTICAL PIANO PLAYING MANUAL AND THEORY WRITING BOOK
ELKAN, IDA
   TECHNICAL WORK IN EAR-TRAINING FOR THE PIANO..A METHOD FOR PRIVATE
ENGEL, CARL
   PIANIST'S HANDBOOK, THE ..A GUIDE FOR THE RIGHT COMPREHENSION AND
ENGELBRECHT, J. G.
   MATERIA MUSICA, OR MATERIALS FOR THE PIANIST..A CLASS BOOK
ETHIER, JOSEPH A.
   ETHIER'S GREAT NON-SUCH SELF-INSTRUCTOR IN THE ART OF ACCOMPANYING
EVANS, EVERETT J.
   SELF-TEACHING CHORD BOOK FOR THE PIANO OR ORGAN..SHOWS HOW TO PLAY
EVERHART, POWELL
   PIANIST'S ART, THE ..A COMPREHENSIVE MANUAL ON PIANO PLAYING FOR
FAELTEN, CARL *
   TRANSPOSITION READER--FUNDAMENTAL TRAINING COURSE FOR PIANOFORTE
FALKENER, ROBERT
   INSTRUCTIONS FOR PLAYING THE HARPSICHORD..WHEREIN IS FULLY
FIELDEN, THOMAS
   MARKS AND REMARKS..MUSICAL EXAMINATIONS AND THEIR PROBLEMS
FIELDEN, THOMAS
   NEW APPROACH TO SCALES AND ARPEGGIOS, A

FISCHER, JERRY CREE
   PIANO TUNING, REGULATING AND REPAIRING...SELF INSTRUCTION...FOR
FISK, BEATRICE H.
   KEYBOARD FUNDAMENTALS
FOLDES, ANDOR
   KEYS TO THE KEYBOARD, A BOOK FOR PIANISTS
FOOTE, ARTHUR W.
   SOME PRACTICAL THINGS IN PIANO PLAYING
FORMAN, DENIS
   MOZART'S CONCERTO FORM..THE FIRST MOVEMENTS OF THE PIANO CONCERTOS
FRACKENPOHL, ARTHUR
   HARMONIZATION AT THE PIANO--2ND. ED.---1962
FRANZ, FREDERICK
   METRONOME TECHNIQUES
FRAY, JACQUES *
   HOW TO PLAY BY THE JACQUES FRAY SPEED METHOD
FREDRICH, FRANK
   PLAYING BY SEEING..A STUDY IN TRAINING AND PERCEPTION FOR BETTER
FRISKIN, JAMES
   PRINCIPLES OF PIANOFORTE PRACTICE, THE
FROST, EDWARD
   THALBEGARIAN (SIC) EXERCISES..OR, THE PIANIST'S DESIDERATA
FRYER, HERBERT
   HINTS FOR PIANOFORTE PRACTICE--A SUGGESTED PLAN FOR DAILY
FULLER, JANET E.
   COMPLETE KNOWLEDGE OF THE ESSENTIALS OF PIANOFORTE PLAYING, A
GARRATT, PERCIVAL
   ART OF PIANOFORTE PLAYING, THE
GARROWAY, WILL
   PIANISM
GASPARINI, FRANCESCO
   PRACTICAL HARMONIST AT THE HARPSICHORD, THE ---1708
GAT, JOZSEF
   TECHNIQUE OF PIANO PLAYING, THE, --2ND. ED.---1958
GEARY, ELEANOR MARGARET
   MUSICAL EDUCATION, WITH PRACTICAL OBSERVATIONS ON THE ART OF
GEBHARD, HEINRICH
   ART OF PEDALLING, THE
GEIB, WILLIAM
   GEIB'S PIANO-FORTE PRECEPTOR, AND MUSICAL GRAMMAR...A TREATISE ON
GERMER, HEINRICH
   RHYTHMICAL PROBLEMS..SPECIAL STUDIES FOR MASTERING RHYTHMS
GERMER, HEINRICH
   THEORETICO-PRACTICAL ELEMENTARY PIANO-FORTE SCHOOL FOR STUDENTS OF
GEST, ELIZABETH
   KEYBOARD HARMONY FOR JUNIORS
GIBBS, GEORGE A., JR.
   MODERN CHORD CONSTRUCTION AND ANALYSIS, FOR ALL INSTRUMENTS...AN
GIBBS, GEORGE A., JR.
   SELF INSTRUCTION IN THE PIANO
GIESEKING, WALTER *
   PIANO TECHNIQUE---COMBINED REPUBLICATION OF..'THE SHORTEST WAY TO
GIFFORD, ALEXANDER M.
   PIANOFORTE AND HOW TO STUDY IT, THE
GILBERT, RUSSELL S.
   EMBRYO MUSICIAN, THE ..A METHOD OF INTRODUCING MUSIC TO LITTLE
GILBERT, RUSSELL S.
   SUGGESTED PIANO STUDY FOR THE VOCAL STUDENT
GILBERTSON, ARNOLD B.
   TEACHERS MANUAL FOR POPULAR PIANO PLAYING, DESIGNED FOR ALL
GLASFORD, IRENE A.
   RHYTHM, REASON AND RESPONSE FOR THE MUSICIAN, PIANIST AND TEACHER
GOODRICH, ALFRED JOHN
   GUIDE TO MEMORIZING MUSIC, A
GOODRICH, ALFRED JOHN
   GUIDE TO PRACTICAL MUSICIANSHIP--INTENDED TO SUPERCEDE ROTE
GOODRICH, ALFRED JOHN
   THEORY OF INTERPRETATION, APPLIED TO ARTISTIC MUSICAL PERFORMANCE
GORDON, STEPHEN T.
   GORDON'S NEW SCHOOL FOR THE PIANO-FORTE
GOSS, JOHN
   INTRODUCTION TO HARMONY AND THOROUGH-BASS WITH NUMEROUS EXAMPLES
GRABILL, ETHELBERT WARREN
   MECHANICS OF PIANO TECHNIC, THE
GRAHAM, GEORGE FARQUHAR
   GENERAL OBSERVATIONS UPON MUSIC AND REMARKS ON MR. LOGIER'S SYSTEM
GRAHAM, JAMES L.
   MUSIC MADE EASY, PIANOFORTE TUTOR ON A NEW PLAN
GRAHAM, MARY JANE
   LETTER TO A YOUNG PIANOFORTE PLAYER, A
GRAUPNER, GOTTLIEB
   RUDIMENTS OF THE ART OF PLAYING ON THE PIANOFORTE...A PLAIN
GREW, SIDNEY
   ART OF THE PLAYER-PIANO, THE ..A TEXTBOOK FOR STUDENT AND TEACHER
GREW, SIDNEY
   FIRST BOOK OF THE PLAYER-PIANIST, THE
GRIMALDI, MARIA LOUISA
   ART OF PIANOFORTE PLAYING AND TEACHING, THE
GRIMM, CARL W.
   HARMONY STUDY AT THE PIANO
GRINDEA, CAROLA
   FIRST TEN LESSONS, THE ..A NEW APPROACH TO PIANO TEACHING
GRUNDY, ENID
   HAPPY PIANIST, THE
GUTMANN, EMMA WILKINS
   TALKS WITH PIANO TEACHERS
HAAKE, CHARLES JOHN *
   TEACHING MUSIC READING IN THE OXFORD PIANO COURSE
HAMBOURG, MARK
   HOW TO PLAY THE PIANO--NEW AND ENLARGED EDITION OF 'HOW TO BECOME
HAMILTON, CLARENCE G.
   PIANO TEACHING...ITS PRINCIPLES AND PROBLEMS
HAMILTON, CLARENCE G.
   TOUCH AND EXPRESSION IN PIANO PLAYING
HAMILTON, CLARENCE G.
   WHAT EVERY PIANO PUPIL SHOULD KNOW
HARGISS, GENEVIEVE
   MUSIC FOR ELEMENTARY TEACHERS..A PROGRAMMED COURSE IN BASIC THEORY
HARKNESS, ROBERT
   BEGINNERS PIANO COURSE IN HYMN PLAYING BY CORRESPONDENCE
HARKNESS, ROBERT
   GOSPEL SONG ACCOMPANIMENT..THE ROBERT HARKNESS METHOD FOR PIANO
HARKNESS, ROBERT
   GOSPEL SONG PIANO ACCOMPANIMENT..THE ROBERT HARKNESS
HARKNESS, ROBERT
   HARKNESS PIANO METHOD OF EVANGELISTIC HYMN PLAYING, THE ..A
HARKNESS, ROBERT
   HOME STUDY CORRESPONDENCE COURSE IN EVANGELISTIC HYMN PLAYING, FOR
HARRIS, CUTHBERT
   FIRST STEPS IN EAR-TRAINING--FOR THE PIANO STUDENT
HARRISON, SIDNEY
   BEGINNING TO PLAY THE PIANO--A TEACHER'S HANDBOOK, INCLUDING THE
HARRISON, SIDNEY
   PIANO TECHNIQUE
HARRISON, SIDNEY
   TEACHER NEVER TOLD ME--TIPS FOR STUDENTS

HARRISON, SIDNEY
  YOUNG PERSON'S GUIDE TO PLAYING THE PIANO, THE
HARTLINE, ELIZABETH DILL *
  KEYBOARD MUSICIANSHIP, GROUP PIANO FOR ADULTS
HARVEY, ROBERT
  MAGIC KEY TO KEYBOARD SUCCESS, THE
HEERINGEN, ERNEST VON
  CELEBRATED INSTRUCTION BOOK FOR THE PIANOFORTE, CONTAINING THE
HEIDELBERGER, PAULINE
  MASTER METHOD..PIANO NORMAL AND TEACHER'S MANUAL
HEPLER, EFFIE A.
  EXERCISES IN TIME AND RHYTHM..A CONTRIBUTION TO MODERN PIANO
HERZ, HENRI
  NEW AND COMPLETE PIANOFORTE SCHOOL
HILES, JOHN
  CATECHISM FOR THE PIANOFORTE STUDENT, A ..CONTAINING A FULL
HILL, JIM
  CREATIVE WORLD OF SCALES AND CHORDS, THE ..CREATIVE STUDIES IN
HOFFMAN, CARL
  HABIT IN PIANOFORTE PLAYING--ANALYTICAL STUDY OF CONTROL OF
HOFFZIMMER, ERNST
  MUSICAL MEMORY, THE --INDIANA UNIVERSITY STUDIES, NO. 92
HOFHEIMER, GRACE
  TEACHING TECHNIQUES FOR THE PIANO
HOFMANN, JOSEF
  PIANO PLAYING, WITH PIANO QUESTIONS ANSWERED---PUBLISHED EARLIER
HOLCMAN, JAN
  LEGACY OF CHOPIN, THE
HOLDER, WILLIAM
  TREATISE ON THE NATURAL GROUNDS AND PRINCIPLES OF HARMONY, A ..TO
HOME, ETHEL
  IMPROVISING..A SIMPLE METHOD OF TEACHING THE SUBJECT TO CHILDREN
HOOK, JAMES
  GUIDA DI MUSICA..BEING A COMPLETE BOOK OF INSTRUCTIONS FOR
HOPE, ERIC
  AIDS TO TECHNIQUE
HORROCKS, CYRIL R. H.
  STUDENT'S GUIDE TO THE ART OF TEACHING THE PIANOFORTE, THE --2ND.
HUENTEN, FRANZ
  ABRIDGED EDITION OF F. HUENTEN'S CELEBRATED INSTRUCTIONS FOR THE
HUENTEN, FRANZ
  FRANZ HUENTEN'S CELEBRATED INSTRUCTIONS FOR THE PIANOFORTE--2ND.
HULL, ARTHUR EAGLEFIELD
  THREE HUNDRED QUESTIONS ON PIANOFORTE TEACHING IN 30 GRADUATED
HULLAH, M. E.
  FEW WORDS ABOUT MUSIC, CONTAINING HINTS TO AMATEUR PIANISTS, A
HUMMEL, JOHANN NEPOMUK
  COMPLETE THEORETICAL AND PRACTICAL COURSE OF INSTRUCTIONS ON THE
HUTCHESON, ERNEST
  LITERATURE OF THE PIANO, THE --FROM THE 16TH. CENTURY TO THE
IRWIN, WILLIAM
  RHYTHM ACCOMPANIMENT MAGIC, FOR THE POPULAR PIANIST
ISAACS, EDWARD
  BLIND PIANO TEACHER, THE
JEWETT, ALBERT DEWEY
  IDIOMATIC COURSE OF PIANO INSTRUCTION FOR CLASS WORK
JOHNS, CLAYTON
  ESSENTIALS OF PIANOFORTE PLAYING, THE
JOHNSON, JOHN BARHAM
  KEYBOARD HARMONY FOR BEGINNERS
JOHNSON, REGINALD
  COMMONSENSE IN SCALE AND ARPEGGIO PLAYING
JOHNSON, VERA A.
  SCIENTIFIC SIDE OF MUSIC IN SIMPLE, PRACTICAL FORM FOR TEACHERS
JOHNSTONE, J. ALFRED
  ART OF TEACHING PIANOFORTE PLAYING, THE --2ND. REV. ED.---1910
JOHNSTONE, J. ALFRED
  ESSENTIALS IN PIANOFORTE PLAYING, AND OTHER MUSICAL STUDIES...
JOHNSTONE, J. ALFRED
  METRONOMIC INDICATIONS FOR BACH'S PRELUDES AND FUGUES AND THE
JONAS, ALBERTO
  PIANOSCRIPT BOOK..AN INVALUABLE AID TO TEACHER AND STUDENT IN
JONES, GRIFFITH
  COMPLEAT INSTRUCTOR FOR THE HARPSICHORD OR PIANOFORTE, THE
JONES, JOHN H.
  PRACTICAL GUIDE TO THOROUGH BASS, A ..OR, HARMONY ILLUSTRATED AND
JOUSSE, JOHN
  GUIDA ARMONICA, IN WHICH...CHORDS, ARE CLEARLY EXPLAINED AND
KANZELL, MAXWELL
  HOW TO READ MUSIC..A COMPLETELY NEW AND SIMPLIFIED APPROACH TO
KEILMAN, WILHELM
  INTRODUCTION TO SIGHT READING
KENYON, CHARLES FREDERICK
  HOW TO MEMORIZE MUSIC
KENYON, CHARLES FREDERICK
  MEMORIZING MUSIC
KERN, ALICE M.
  HARMONIZATION-TRANSPOSITION AT THE KEYBOARD
KING, AUDREY
  PIANO CLASSES IN ELEMENTARY SCHOOLS
KIRBY, MAY B. KELLY
  KELLY KIRBY KINDERGARTEN PIANO METHOD, TEACHERS' COURSE, THE
KLAVARSKRIBO, SLEKKERVIER, HOLLAND
  PRACTICAL CORRESPONDENCE COURSE FOR PIANOFORTE
KOBBE, GUSTAV
  PIANOLIST, THE ..A GUIDE FOR PIANOLA PLAYERS
KOCH, CASPAR
  PIANO STUDENT'S GRADUS AD PARNASSUM, THE ..PRESENTING THE
KOCHEVITSKY, GEORGE
  ART OF PIANO PLAYING, THE ..A SCIENTIFIC APPROACH
KOLLMANN, AUGUST F.
  INTRODUCTION TO THE ART OF PRELUDING AND EXTEMPORISING IN SIX
KOTZSCHMAR, MARY ANN
  HALF-HOUR LESSONS IN MUSIC..CLASS WORK FOR BEGINNERS AT THE PIANO
KRAUSE, E. W.
  STUDIES IN MEASURE AND RHYTHM...FOR TEACHERS AND PUPILS, ALSO FOR
KRAUSE, E. W.
  STUDIES IN MEASURE AND RHYTHM, FOR THE PIANOFORTE, TO DEVELOP AN
KRAUSE, E. W.
  STUDY OF TIME AND MEASURE, THE --FOR PIANO STUDENTS
KRUSZYNSKI, MICHAL
  APPROACH TO THE PSYCHOLOGY OF PIANO TEACHING, AN
KULLAK, FRANZ
  BEETHOVEN'S PIANO PLAYING, WITH AN ESSAY ON THE EXECUTION OF THE
LAMAR, RICHARD
  COLLEGE PIANO PEDAGOGY
LAMOTTE, J.
  PIANO AND MUSICAL MATTERS
LAMPE, JOHN F.
  PLAIN AND COMPENDIOUS METHOD OF TEACHING THOROUGH BASS, A ..WITH
LANDOWSKA, WANDA
  LANDOWSKA ON MUSIC--EDITED BY DENISE RESTOUT
LANDOWSKI, ALICE-WANDA
  DOMENICO SCARLATTI--NOTES TO ACCOMPANY GRAMOPHONE RECORDINGS
LANNING, RUSSELL
  BACH ORNAMENTATION

LAST, JOAN
  INTERPRETATION FOR THE PIANO STUDENT
LAST, JOAN
  YOUNG PIANIST, THE ..A NEW APPROACH FOR TEACHERS AND
LEACH, JOHN R.
  FUNCTIONAL PIANO FOR THE TEACHER
LEIMER, KARL *
  RHYTHMICS, DYNAMICS, PEDAL, AND OTHER PROBLEMS OF PIANO
LEIMER, KARL *
  SHORTEST WAY TO PIANISTIC PERFECTION, THE
LENHART, A.
  ELEMENTS OF MUSIC..A CLEAR AND SYSTEMATIC ARRANGEMENT OF RULES FOR
LEVINE, HENRY
  KNOW YOUR SCALES..FOR PIANO STUDENTS OF ALL GRADES
LEVINE, JACK
  WHAT MUSICAL INSTRUMENT FOR ME
LE COUPPEY, FELIX
  PIANO TEACHING..ADVICE TO PUPILS AND YOUNG TEACHERS---1868 IN
LHEVINNE, JOSEF
  BASIC PRINCIPLES IN PIANOFORTE PLAYING---1924
LINDO, ALGERNON H.
  AURAL TESTS FOR EXAMINATIONS--SPECIALLY WRITTEN FOR TEACHERS AND
LINDO, ALGERNON H.
  PIANOFORTE STUDY..HINTS FOR TEACHERS AND STUDENTS
LOCKE, MATTHEW
  MELOTHESIA..OR, CERTAIN GENERAL RULES FOR PLAYING UPON A
LOGIER, JOHANN BERNHARD
  AUTHENTIC ACCOUNT OF THE EXAMINATION OF PUPILS, INSTRUCTED IN THE
LOGIER, JOHANN BERNHARD
  COMPANION TO THE ROYAL PATENT CHIROPLAST, OR HAND-DIRECTOR, A ..A
LOGIER, JOHANN BERNHARD
  EXPLANATION AND DESCRIPTION OF THE ROYAL PATENT CHIROPLAST, OR
LOGIER, JOHANN BERNHARD
  FIRST COMPANION TO THE ROYAL PATENT CHIROPLAST OR HAND-DIRECTOR,
LOGIER, JOHANN BERNHARD
  REFUTATION OF THE FALLACIES AND MISREPRESENTATIONS CONTAINED IN A
LOGIER, JOHANN BERNHARD
  SYLLABUS OF THE SECOND EXAMINATION OF MR. LOGIER'S PUPILS, ON HIS
LONDON--A COMMITTEE OF PROFESSORS
  EXPOSITION OF THE MUSICAL SYSTEM OF MR. LOGIER..WITH STRICTURES ON
LOWE, CLAUDE EDGERTON
  ART OF PIANOFORTE PRACTICING, THE
LOWE, CLAUDE EDGERTON
  SUGGESTIONS FOR THE APPRECIATION AND INTERPRETATION OF PIANOFORTE
LOWE, CLAUDE EDGERTON
  VIVA VOCE..250 QUESTIONS AND ANSWERS FOR PIANOFORTE DIPLOMA
LOYNES, W. H.
  HOW TO PLAY THE PIANO IN ONE HOUR WITHOUT A TEACHER
LUDDEN, WILLIAM
  THOROUGH BASS SCHOOL, THE ..AN EASY AND PROGRESSIVE COURSE FOR
LUND, VICTOR E.
  EVALUATION OF ELECTRONIC SELF-INSTRUCTION ON PIANO KEYBOARD, THE
MACEWAN, DESIREE
  FIRST TWO YEARS OF PIANOFORTE STUDY, THE
MACEWEN, JOHN B.
  INTRODUCTION TO AN UNPUBLISHED EDITION OF THE PIANOFORTE SONATAS
MACKINNON, LILIAS
  MUSIC BY HEART
MACLEAN, CHARLES D.
  PRINCIPLES OF PIANOFORTE PRACTICE, THE
MACPHERSON, D.
  CATECHISM OF MUSIC, CHIEFLY ADAPTED FOR LEARNERS ON THE
MACPHERSON, STEWART
  STUDIES IN PHRASING AND FORM
MAHONY, CORNELIUS
  SELF-INSTRUCTOR FOR THE PIANOFORTE, CONTAINING C. MAHONY'S NEW
MAIER, GUY
  PIANO TEACHER'S COMPANION, THE
MAIER, GUY *
  PLAYING THE PIANO..A COURSE OF ROTE TRAINING FOR BEGINNERS--CLASS
MAIER, GUY *
  PLAYING THE PIANO--TEACHER'S MANUAL
MANSFELDT, HUGO L.
  TECHNIC..A SYSTEM OF THE MOST NECESSARY DAILY EXERCISES TO PRODUCE
MARIAL, P.
  METHODS APPLICABLE TO GROUP TEACHING OR PRIVATE PIANO INSTRUCTION
MARKS, ADOLF B.
  INTRODUCTION TO THE INTERPRETATION OF BEETHOVEN'S PIANO-FORTE
MARX, ADOLF BERNHARD
  INTRODUCTION TO THE INTERPRETATION OF BEETHOVEN'S PIANO
MASON, DANIEL GREGORY
  NEGLECTED SENSE IN PIANO PLAYING, A
MASON, MARY B.
  BOY MUSIC, A FIRST PIANO METHOD FOR BOYS BETWEEN 8 AND 16
MASON, WILLIAM G.
  ACCENTUAL TREATMENT OF EXERCISES AS APPLIED TO PIANOFORTE
MASON, WILLIAM G. *
  METHOD FOR THE PIANO-FORTE, A
MASON, WILLIAM G. *
  PRIMER OF MUSIC, A ..BEING THE FIRST STEPS IN MUSICIANSHIP..FOR
MASON, WILLIAM G. *
  SYSTEM FOR BEGINNERS IN THE ART OF PLAYING UPON THE PIANOFORTE, A
MASON, WILLIAM G.
  SYSTEM OF TECHNICAL EXERCISES FOR THE PIANO-FORTE, A
MASON, WILLIAM G.
  TOUCH, AS APPLIED TO PIANOFORTE PRACTICE--ESSAY FOR THE 10TH.
MASON, WILLIAM G.
  TOUCH AND TECHNIC..FOR ARTISTIC PIANO PLAYING, OP. 44--4 VOLS. IN
MATHEWS, WILLIAM S. B.
  MASON'S PRINCIPLES OF VELOCITY AND ARM TOUCHES
MATHEWS, WILLIAM S. B.
  SCHOOL OF THE PIANO PEDAL
MATHEWS, WILLIAM S. B.
  STUDIES IN PHRASING, MEMORIZING AND INTERPRETATION
MATHEWS, WILLIAM S. B.
  STUDIES IN PHRASING SELECTED FROM THE WORKS OF THE BEST CLASSIC
MATHEWS, WILLIAM S. B.
  TEACHER'S MANUAL OF MASON'S PIANOFORTE TECHNICS
MATTHAY, TOBIAS A.
  ACT OF MUSICAL CONCENTRATION, THE
MATTHAY, TOBIAS A.
  ACT OF TOUCH IN ALL ITS DIVERSITY, THE ..AN ANALYSIS AND SYNTHESIS
MATTHAY, TOBIAS A.
  CHILD'S FIRST STEPS IN PIANOFORTE PLAYING, THE
MATTHAY, TOBIAS A.
  EPITOME OF THE LAWS OF PIANOFORTE TECHNIQUE, AN
MATTHAY, TOBIAS A.
  FIRST LIGHTS ON PIANO-PLAYING
MATTHAY, TOBIAS A.
  FIRST PRINCIPLES OF PIANOFORTE PLAYING--EXTRACT FROM 'THE ACT OF
MATTHAY, TOBIAS A.
  INTRODUCTION TO PSYCHOLOGY FOR MUSIC TEACHERS, AN --THREE LECTURES
MATTHAY, TOBIAS A.
  MUSICAL INTERPRETATION..ITS LAWS AND PRINCIPLES---1913
MATTHAY, TOBIAS A.
  ON MEMORIZING AND PLAYING FROM MEMORY

MATTHAY, TOBIAS A.
     PIANOFORTE TONE-PRODUCTION---SAME AS 'THE ACT OF TOUCH IN ALL ITS
MATTHAY, TOBIAS A.
     SOME COMMENTARIES ON THE TEACHING OF PIANOFORTE TECHNIC..A
MCALL, REGINALD L.
     PRACTICAL CHURCH SCHOOL MUSIC..METHODS AND TRAINING FOR SUCCESSFUL
MCARTHUR, ALEXANDER
     PIANOFORTE STUDY..HINTS ON PIANO PLAYING
MCCLANAHAN, RICHARD
     CADENCE, KEY TO MUSICAL CLARITY, THE ..A SIMPLE AND PRACTICAL
MCCLINTOCK, LORENE
     TEACH YOURSELF TO PLAY THE PIANO..BASED ON THE INTERVAL METHOD
MCEWEN, JOHN B.
     INTRODUCTION TO AN UNPUBLISHED EDITION OF THE PIANOFORTE SONATAS
MCEWEN, JOHN B.
     TEMPO RUBATO, OR TIME VARIATION IN MUSICAL PERFORMANCE
MCFERRIN, CHARLES BETTEYS
     MOTHER'S PART IN HER CHILD'S MUSICAL EDUCATION, A ..OR, THE THINGS
MCHOSE, ALLEN IRVINE *
     KEYBOARD AND DICTATION MANUAL
MCHOSE, ALLEN IRVINE
     TEACHERS DICTATION MANUAL
MCLAIN, MARGARET STARR
     CLASS PIANO
MEHR, NORMAN
     GROUP PIANO TEACHING
MELCHER, ROBERT A. *
     MUSIC FOR ADVANCED STUDY..A SOURCE BOOK OF EXCERPTS
MELLERS, WILFRED
     FRANCOIS COUPERIN AND THE FRENCH CLASSICAL TRADITION
MERGES, P.
     PRACTICAL RULES FOR PIANOFORTE PLAYING..TEXT BOOK FOR TEACHERS AND
MERRICK, FRANK
     PRACTICING THE PIANO
MERRILL, MYRTLE
     SIGHT-READING AT THE PIANO
MIDDLEMISS, CHARLES S.
     NEW GRAPHIC NOTATION FOR KEYBOARD MUSIC, A
MIDKIFF, HELEN T.
     CHURCH PIANIST, THE
MILLER, ALLAN
     BEGINNING PIANO FOR ADULTS
MILLER, EDWARD
     INSTITUTES OF MUSIC, OR, EASY INSTRUCTIONS FOR THE HARPSICHORD
MINNESOTA MUSIC TEACHERS ASSOCIATION
     PIANO-THEORY EXAMINATION SYLLABUS
MOKREJS, JOHN
     SCIENCE OF FINGERING, THE ---FOR PIANO
MOKREJS, JOHN
     STORY OF NANYNKA, THE ..FIRST PIANO LESSONS FOR CHILDREN, PRIVATE
MOLDENHAUER, HANS
     DUO-PIANISM---PUBLISHED DISSERTATION
MONTI, H. DE
     STRICTURES ON MR. LOGIER'S SYSTEM OF MUSICAL EDUCATION
MOORE, GERALD
     AM I TOO LOUD..MEMOIRS OF AN ACCOMPANIST
MOORE, MARY BURNHAM
     LURE OF THE PIANO THROUGH COORDINATION AND CONCENTRATION, THE
MORRILL, HENRY H.
     MANUAL OF PIANO FOR PUPILS AND TEACHERS
MOSCOW, CHARLES E.
     PRACTICAL PIANO TUNER, THE ..A COMPREHENSIVE SIMPLE SET OF RULES
MOTT, ISAAC H. R.
     ADVICE AND INSTRUCTIONS FOR PLAYING THE PIANOFORTE WITH EXPRESSION
MURPHY, HOWARD A. *
     MUSIC FOR STUDY..A SOURCE BOOK OF EXCERPTS
MUSICIANS ADVISORY SERVICE
     MUSICIANS ADVISORY SERVICE FIRST MUSIC READER FOR PIANO..TEACHERS
MUSIC EDUCATION LEAGUE
     COMPREHENSIVE GUIDE FOR PIANO TEACHERS AND PIANO AUDITION SYLLABUS
MUSIC EDUCATORS NATIONAL CONFERENCE
     KEYBOARD EXPERIENCE AND CLASS PIANO INSTRUCTION
MUSIC EDUCATORS NATIONAL CONFERENCE
     TEACHING PIANO IN CLASSROOM AND STUDIO
MUSIC PROJECT--NEW YORK CITY
     TEACHER'S GUIDE..A CREATIVE APPROACH TO PIANO CLASS TEACHING, BY
NEAL, HARRY LEE
     WAVE AS YOU PASS
NEUHAUS, HEINRICH
     ART OF PIANO PLAYING, THE
NEWMAN, ELIZABETH
     HOW TO TEACH MUSIC TO BEGINNERS
NEWMAN, WILLIAM S.
     PERFORMANCE PRACTICES IN BEETHOVEN'S PIANO SONATAS..AN
NEWMAN, WILLIAM S.
     PIANIST'S PROBLEMS, THE ..A MODERN APPROACH TO EFFICIENT PRACTICE
NEW ENGLAND CONSERVATORY
     NEW ENGLAND CONSERVATORY METHOD FOR THE PIANO-FORTE, THE
NICCHIA, LILLIAN
     PIANOFORTE STUDY..HINTS ON PIANO PLAYING
NICHOLS, JULIA F.
     COMMON SENSE CATECHISM..OR, PIANO AND ORGAN PUPIL'S COMPANION
NILES BRYANT SCHOOL OF PIANO TUNING
     CORRESPONDENCE COURSE IN 12 LESSONS, A
NIMITZ, DANIEL
     KEYBOARD MASTERS..STUDY GUIDE
NIXON, W.
     GUIDE TO INSTRUCTION ON THE PIANOFORTE, A --IN A SERIES OF SHORT
O'REAR, MRS. ASBURY S.
     SELF READING NOTES
O'TOOLE, WILLIAM
     KEYBOARD HARMONY---DUPLICATED FROM MANUSCRIPT
OLIVER, EDWARD B.
     PRACTICAL TEXT-BOOK OF MUSIC, AS CONNECTED WITH THE ART OF PLAYING
OREM, PRESTON WARE
     MANUAL OF MODULATION
ORLIK, JULES
     CREATIVE APPROACH TO PIANO CLASS TEACHING, A ---REPRODUCED FROM
ORREY, LESLIE
     MUSIC AT THE KEYBOARD
PACE, ROBERT
     MUSIC ESSENTIALS FOR CLASSROOM TEACHERS--2ND. ED.---1961
PACE, ROBERT
     PIANO FOR CLASSROOM MUSIC--2ND. ED.---1956
PAIN, EVA
     BEGINNING TO PLAY THE PIANO..A MANUAL FOR TEACHERS
PALME, RUDOLPH
     FIRST MONTHS IN PIANOFORTE INSTRUCTION, THE ---1870, IN GERMAN
PALMER, ANNIE L.
     MUSIC TEACHERS' GUIDE TO THE GOLDBECK PIANO METHOD
PALMER, HORATIO R.
     PALMER'S PIANO PRIMER
PALMER, KING
     TEACH YOURSELF MUSIC
PALMER, KING
     TEACH YOURSELF TO PLAY THE PIANO

PARSONS, ALBERT R.
     SCIENCE OF PIANO PRACTICE, THE
PARSONS, ALBERT R.
     SYNTHETIC METHOD FOR THE PIANOFORTE, THE
PARSONS, MARY H.
     RHYTHMIC WAY, THE
PASQUALI, NICOLO
     ART OF FINGERING THE HARPSICHORD, THE
PATTON, VICTOR S.
     LEARN TO PLAY POPULAR PIANO BY NOTE IN 20 EASY LESSONS...HOME
PEARCE, CHARLES WILLIAM
     ART OF THE PIANO TEACHER, THE
PEDERSON, GALE
     KEY TO THE KEYS..A SELF-TAUGHT PIANO METHOD FOR ADULTS AND TEEN
PEDERSON, OLAF
     MEMORY TESTS FOR PIANOFORTE PLAYING ---7 PIECES WITH INSTRUCTIONS
PERRY, ADELAIDE TROWBRIDGE *
     GUIDE TO PIANO STUDY FOR CLASS OR INDIVIDUAL INSTRUCTION, A
PETERS, WILLIAM C.
     ECLECTIC PIANOFORTE SCHOOL, THE ..ARRANGED FROM THE WORKS OF THE
PETERSILEA, CARLYLE
     PIANO PLAYING..GENERAL MUSICAL INSTRUCTION FROM BEGINNING TO END
PETERSON, FRANKLIN
     THEORETIC COMPANION TO PRACTICE--PART I OF THE PIANIST'S HANDBOOK
PETRI, LILLIAN JEFFREY
     MIND OVER MUSCLE..A TECHNICAL ECONOMY FOR PIANISTS
PFEFFERKORN, OTTO W.
     PIANISTIC HINTS
PHILIPP, LILLIE H.
     PIANO STUDY..APPLICATION AND TECHNIQUE
PHILLIPSON, WENTWORTH
     GUIDE TO YOUNG PIANOFORTE TEACHERS AND STUDENTS
PLAIDY, LOUIS
     PIANOFORTE TEACHER'S GUIDE, THE
PLAIDY, LOUIS
     PIANO TEACHER, THE
PLATT, CAROLYN
     CAROLYN PLATT METHOD FOR PIANO, THE --GROUP INSTRUCTION--TEACHER'S
PLAYFORD, JOHN
     MUSICKS HAND-MAID..NEW LESSONS AND INSTRUCTIONS FOR THE VIRGINALS
POINTER SYSTEM, INC.
     GUIDE TO THE MODERN PIANIST, A
POTAMKIN, FRANK
     MODERN PIANO PEDAGOGY
POWERS-WADSWORTH, L.
     PIANIST'S GUIDE TO TECHNICAL FREEDOM, THE ..2 VOLS. IN 1
PRATT, SILAS G.
     PIANIST'S MENTAL VELOCITY, THE ..A SYSTEMATIC PREPARATION OF THE
PRELLEUR, PETER
     HARPSICHORD ILLUSTRATED AND IMPROV'D, WHEREIN IS SHEWN THE ITALIAN
PRENTICE, THOMAS RIDLEY
     MUSICIAN, THE ..A GUIDE FOR PIANOFORTE STUDENTS--6 VOLS.
PRENTNER, MARIE
     MODERN PIANIST..BEING MY EXPERIENCES IN THE TECHNIQUE AND
PRIESING, DOROTHY *
     LANGUAGE OF THE PIANO..A WORKBOOK IN THEORY AND KEYBOARD HARMONY
PROCTOR, CHARLES
     HARMONIZATION AT THE KEYBOARD
PSTROKONSKY, JULES DE
     NEW METHOD OF TEACHING THE PIANOFORTE
PUPIN, ANNIE
     HOW TO PRACTICE..OR HINTS TO PIANO-FORTE STUDENTS ON THE METHOD OF
PUPIN, ANNIE
     SCALES, THE ..THEIR FORMATION, FINGERING, AND HOW TO PRACTICE
QUINN, MARCUS LUCIUS
     HOW TO STUDY MUSIC AND LEARN TO PLAY PIANO OR ORGAN
RABSON, GRACE RUBIN
     INFLUENCE OF ANALYTICAL PRESTUDY IN MEMORIZING PIANO MUSIC, THE
RAMUL, PETER
     PSYCHO-PHYSICAL FOUNDATIONS OF MODERN PIANO TECHNIQUE, THE
RAST, LAURENCE R.
     LET'S FIND OUT ABOUT MUSIC..WURLITZER ELEMENTARY PIANO WORKBOOKS,
REDDIE, CHARLES FREDERICK
     PIANOFORTE PLAYING ON ITS TECHNICAL AND AESTHETIC SIDES
REEVES, BETTY
     APPROACH TO PIANO TEACHING---ALSO CATALOGUED UNDER
REEVES, BETTY
     AURAL TRAINING--MONOGRAPH ON THE ART OF PIANO TEACHING, NO. 2
REEVES, WILLIAM
     REEVES' POPULAR PIANOFORTE TUTOR..RUDIMENTS OF MUSIC, EXERCISES
REINAGLE, CAROLINE
     FEW WORDS ON PIANOFORTE PLAYING, A
RENAUD, EMILIANO
     RENAUD-PHONE PIANO METHOD..A PIANO COURSE THROUGH THE MEDIUM OF
REZITS, JOSEPH
     SOURCE MATERIALS FOR PIANO TECHNIQUES
REZITS, JOSEPH
     TEACHER'S GUIDE TO THE NEW SCRIBNER MUSIC LIBRARY
RHODES, ALFRED
     CURIOSITIES OF THE KEY-BOARD AND THE STAFF...SHOWN TO BE UPON A
RICHARDSON, NATHAN
     INKLINGS FOR THE LOVERS OF MUSIC, PART 1...CULTIVATION OF THE ART
RICHARDSON, NATHAN
     NEW METHOD FOR THE PIANOFORTE..ADDED, RUDIMENTS OF HARMONY AND
RICHTER, ADA
     TEACHING HINTS
RICKER, EARL
     MUSIC LESSONS FOR YOUR CHILD
RIEMANN, HUGO
     CATECHISM OF PIANOFORTE PLAYING---1888, IN GERMAN
ROBBINS, EDGAR A.
     AMERICAN METHOD FOR THE PIANOFORTE
ROBERT, WALTER
     PIANO STUDY IN SOVIET-RUSSIAN SCHOOLS OF MUSIC--REPRINT..'JOURNAL
ROBILLIARD, EILEEN D.
     PERSISTENT PIANIST, THE ..A BOOK FOR THE LATE BEGINNER AND THE
ROBINSON, HELENE
     BASIC PIANO FOR ADULTS
ROBYN, LOUISE
     HOW TO TEACH PIANO TO THE CHILD BEGINNER..A TEXT BOOK FOR TEACHERS
ROBYN, LOUISE
     ROBYN-HANKS HARMONY, THE ..A JUNIOR COURSE--BKS. 1-3, 1936-1938
ROEDER, ELWOOD S.
     TIME-SPACE CONCEPTION OF THE GEOMETRY AND SPEED OF MOTION AT THE
ROOT, CATHERINE ADAMS *
     LISTEN, SING AND PLAY..CLASS LESSONS FOR PIANO AND VOICE
ROSENTHAL, MORIZ
     OLD AND THE NEW SCHOOL OF PIANO PLAYING, THE --TYPEWRITTEN COPY
ROTHSCHILD, FRITZ
     LOST TRADITION IN MUSIC, THE --PT. 1..RHYTHM AND TEMPO IN J. S.
ROTHSCHILD, FRITZ
     LOST TRADITION IN MUSIC, THE --PT. 2..MUSICAL PERFORMANCE IN THE
ROWLEY, ALEC
     DO'S AND DONT'S FOR MUSICIANS..A HANDBOOK FOR TEACHERS AND
ROWLEY, ALEC *
     GRADED TESTS IN PRACTICAL MUSICIANSHIP AND MUSICAL INITIATIVE--IN

ROWLEY, ALEC *
    MELODY MAKING AT THE PIANO--IN THREE STAGES
ROWLEY, ALEC
    PRACTICAL MUSICIANSHIP, A HANDBOOK FOR TEACHERS AND STUDENTS
RUBINSTEIN, BERYL
    OUTLINE OF PIANO PEDAGOGY--REV. ED.----1929
RUBINSTEIN, BERYL
    PIANIST'S APPROACH TO SIGHT READING AND MEMORIZING, THE
SAFONOFF, WASSILI
    NEW FORMULA FOR THE PIANO TEACHER AND PIANO STUDENT
SAULS, RANDY
    THINKING MUSICIANS' APPLICATION OF MODERN HARMONY, THE ..HOW TO
SAVLER, ROBERTA--EDITOR
    SELECTIONS FROM THE PIANO TEACHER, 1958-1963
SCHAAF, EDWARD O.
    ART OF PIANO PLAYER TRANSCRIPTION, THE ..MAKING OF PERFORATED
SCHAAF, EDWARD O.
    FUNDAMENTAL PRINCIPLES INVOLVED IN THE COMPOSING AND ARRANGING OF
SCHAAF, EDWARD O.
    MUSICAL INDIVIDUALITY OF THE PLAYER PIANO, THE ---EXCERPTS..'THE
SCHAUFFLER, ROBERT HAVEN
    MUSICAL AMATEUR, THE
SCHAUFFLER, ROBERT HAVEN
    SCIENCE OF PRACTICE, THE
SCHELLING, ERNEST *
    OXFORD PIANO COURSE, TEACHER'S FIRST MANUAL
SCHELLING, ERNEST *
    OXFORD PIANO COURSE, TEACHER'S SECOND MANUAL
SCHERER, HERBERT
    PIANO PRACTICING
SCHLIEDER, FREDERICK W.
    LYRIC COMPOSITION THROUGH IMPROVISATION--2 VOLS., 1927-1946
SCHMITZ, ELIE ROBERT
    CAPTURE OF INSPIRATION, THE
SCHNEIDER, HANS
    WORKING OF THE MIND IN PIANO TEACHING AND PLAYING, THE
SCHOTT, HOWARD
    PLAYING THE HARPSICHORD
SCHUMANN, ROBERT
    ADVICE TO YOUNG MUSICIANS--FROM 'MUSIC AND MUSICIANS'---1876
SCHUMANN, ROBERT
    RULES AND MAXIMS FOR YOUNG MUSICIANS--FROM 'MUSIC AND MUSICIANS'
SCIONTI, SILVIO
    L'ARTE PIANISTICA..SYSTEM OF PIANO ARTISTRY---IN ITALIAN AND
SCONCIA, JOHN A.
    ANALYTICAL INSTRUCTOR FOR THE PIANO FORTE, CONTAINING THE
SCONCIA, JOHN A.
    SCONCIA'S NEW SYSTEM OF INSTRUCTION IN MUSIC AS A SCIENCE..OR, A
SCOTT, MARY M.
    WHAT CAN I PLAY..A BOOK ABOUT MUSICAL INSTRUMENTS
SEGUEL, MANIA
    CHOPIN'S TEMPO RUBATO
SEROFF, VICTOR
    COMMON SENSE IN PIANO STUDY
SEYMOUR, HARRIET AYER
    HOME MUSIC LESSONS..HOW TO FIND YOUR MUSICAL SELF
SEYMOUR, HARRIET AYER
    HOW TO THINK MUSIC
SEYMOUR, HARRIET AYER
    PHILOSOPHY OF MUSIC, THE ..WHAT MUSIC CAN DO FOR YOU
SHEEHY, EMMA DICKSON
    THERE'S MUSIC IN CHILDREN--REV. ED.----1946
SHEFTEL, PAUL
    EXPLORING KEYBOARD FUNDAMENTALS
SHELDON, JAY
    ALL ABOUT MUSIC..A COMPLETE BOOK OF MUSICAL THEORY FOR PIANISTS
SHELDON, ROBERT--COMPILER
    EGON PETRI-ALEXANDER LIBERMANN NOTES ON THE ART AND TECHNIQUE OF
SHEPARD, FRANK H.
    PIANO TOUCH AND SCALES..AN ANALYSIS OF THE FUNDAMENTAL PRINCIPLES
SHEPARD, ROBERT
    COMPLETE SCALE AND ARPEGGIO MANUAL
SHERWOOD MUSIC SCHOOL
    PIANO LESSONS AND TESTS--4TH. REV. ED.----1945+
SHINN, FREDERICK G.
    MUSICAL MEMORY AND ITS CULTIVATION
SHUMWAY, STANLEY
    HARMONY AND EAR TRAINING AT THE KEYBOARD
SHUTER, ROSAMUND
    PSYCHOLOGY OF MUSICAL ABILITY, THE
SKUTLEY, MILDRED A.
    MUSIC FOR YOU..A SUPPLEMENTAL WORK BOOK FOR INDIVIDUAL OR CLASS
SLENCZYNSKA, RUTH *
    MUSIC AT YOUR FINGERTIPS
SMELTZER, JEANNIE R.--COMPILER
    OUTLINES AND GRADES FOR THE USE OF PIANO TEACHERS
SMITH, A. G. WARREN
    BEGINNER'S GUIDE, THE ..FOR ALL COMMENCING THE STUDY OF THE
SMITH, EDWIN S.
    PIANO BY EAR
SMITH, THOMAS
    LITTLE DIFFICULTIES WHICH OCCUR IN PIANOFORTE PLAYING
SMITH, USELMA CLARK
    KEYBOARD HARMONY..LEARNING BY HEARING
SOREL, CLAUDETTE
    COMPENDIUM OF PIANO TECHNIQUE--39 ETUDES SELECTED FROM OVER 4000,
SPENCER, ALLEN
    FOUNDATION OF PIANO TECHNIC, THE
SPENCER, BERNARD
    POPULAR PIANO...A CORRESPONDENCE COURSE OF THE EASTERN SCHOOLS OF
SPENCER, CHARLES C.
    RUDIMENTS OF THE ART OF PLAYING THE PIANOFORTE, THE ...WITH
SQUIRE, RUSSEL N. *
    CLASS PIANO FOR ADULT BEGINNERS--2ND. ED.----1964
STANLEY, JANE
    BASIC ROUTINES IN ELEMENTARY PIANO TEACHING THROUGH THE FIRST
STARKEY, EVELYN
    PIANO CLASS WORKBOOK FOR FIRST YEAR STUDENTS
STEIN, ERWIN
    FORM AND PERFORMANCE
STEPHENSON, LILIAN E.
    BEGONE, DULL PRACTICE..SUGGESTIONS FOR STUDENTS AND
STERNBERG, CONSTANTIN I. VON
    ETHICS AND ESTHETICS OF PIANO PLAYING
STERNBERG, CONSTANTIN I. VON
    TEMPO RUBATO AND OTHER ESSAYS
STEVENS, WILLIAM S.
    TREATISE ON PIANO-FORTE, CONTAINING THE PRINCIPLES OF FINE PLAYING
STEWART, REID
    HOW TO PASS MUSIC EXAMINATIONS--PIANO--A GUIDE FOR TEACHERS AND
STORMEN, WIN
    FIFTY YEARS OF POPULAR PIANO TECHNIQUES IN THE U.S.A.
STORMEN, WIN
    POPULAR PIANO SELF-TAUGHT---1956
SUMMY-BIRCHARD COMPANY
    HANDBOOK FOR PIANO TEACHERS..COLLECTED ARTICLES ON SUBJECTS

SUZUKI, SHIN'ICHI
    SUZUKI PIANO SCHOOL--4 VOLS.
SWENSON, LUCILE B.
    DISCOVERING THE PIANO..THE MULTIPLE KEY APPROACH..STUDY GUIDE AND
TANKARD, GEOFFREY
    FOUNDATIONS OF PIANOFORTE TECHNIQUE
TANKARD, GEOFFREY
    PIANOFORTE DIPLOMAS
TANKARD, GEOFFREY
    SPECIMEN ANSWERS TO THE QUESTIONS IN PIANOFORTE DIPLOMAS
TAPPER, THOMAS
    ABC OF KEYBOARD HARMONY, THE
TAPPER, THOMAS
    EDUCATION OF THE MUSIC TEACHER, THE
TAYLER, E. DOUGLAS
    MIND-POWER IN MUSIC FOR STUDENTS, TEACHERS AND PERFORMERS
TAYLER, E. DOUGLAS
    SECRET OF SUCCESSFUL PRACTICE, THE
TAYLOR, FRANKLIN
    PRIMER OF PIANOFORTE PLAYING
TAYLOR, FRANKLIN
    TECHNIQUE AND EXPRESSION IN PIANOFORTE PLAYING
TAYLOR, GEORGE C.
    FIRST STEPS TO THE PIANOFORTE
TERWILLIGER, GORDON B.
    PIANO TEACHERS PROFESSIONAL HANDBOOK
THACKRAY, RUPERT M.
    PLAYING FOR DANCE..THE PLACE OF THE PIANIST IN THE TEACHING OF
THOMPSON, JOHN
    TEACHING PIANO IN CLASSES
TOBIN, JOSEPH RAYMOND
    ADVENTURES IN MUSICIANSHIP
TOBIN, JOSEPH RAYMOND
    COMMON SENSE IN SIGHT READING..A GUIDE FOR PIANO TEACHERS
TOBIN, JOSEPH RAYMOND
    HOW TO IMPROVISE PIANO ACCOMPANIMENTS
TOBIN, JOSEPH RAYMOND
    MEMORY PLAYING AT THE PIANO
TOBIN, JOSEPH RAYMOND
    PREPARING FOR KEYBOARD TESTS IN MUSICIANSHIP EXAMINATIONS, JUNIOR
TOBIN, JOSEPH RAYMOND
    READ AND REMEMBER..TWELVE STUDY PIECES TO FACILITATE PLAYING FROM
TOWNSEND, WILLIAM
    BALANCE OF ARM IN PIANO TECHNIQUE--4TH. REV. ED.----1903
TURECK, ROSALYN
    INTRODUCTION TO THE PERFORMANCE OF BACH, AN--3 VOLS.
UNDERWOOD, REX
    GHOST NOTE PATTERN BUILDERS FOR VISUALIZING THE STRUCTURE OF
UNSCHULD, MARIE VON
    PIANIST'S HAND, THE ..A SYSTEMATIC METHOD...ACCORDING TO THE
VANTYN, SIDNEY
    MODERN PIANOFORTE TECHNIQUE
VAN APPLEDORN, MARY J.
    KEYBOARD, SINGING AND DICTATION MANUAL
VAN DER VELPEN, JEAN
    HARMONY AND THOROUGH BASS--2 VOLS., 1909-1910
VENABLE, MARY
    INTERPRETATION OF PIANO MUSIC, THE
VENINO, ALBERT F.
    PEDAL METHOD FOR THE PIANO, A
VINING, HARRISON S.
    SIMPLE AND COMPLETE PRIMER FOR THE PIANOFORTE, THE
VINING, HARRISON S.
    WHYS AND WHEREFORES..QUESTIONS AND ANSWERS FOR PIANO STUDENTS
VIRGIL, ALMON K.
    EDUCATION IN MUSIC..LESSONS TO TEACHERS IN THE INSTRUCTION OF
VIRGIL, ALMON K.
    FOUNDATION EXERCISES IN PIANO PLAYING FROM FIRST RUDIMENTS TO
VIRGIL, ALMON K.
    PUPIL'S RECORD BOOK, THE ..SHOWING HOW TO SUCCEED AND HOW TO FAIL
VIRGIL, ALMON K.
    STEP BY STEP...TEXTBOOK IN PIANO PLAYING..HANDBOOK FOR TEACHERS
VIRGIL, ANTHA MINERVA
    ELEMENTARY EXERCISES IN SIGHT READING...FROM THE VIRGIL METHOD
VIRGIL, ANTHA MINERVA
    INSTRUCTIVE TALKS TO PIANO STUDENTS
VIRGIL, ANTHA MINERVA
    VIRGIL METHOD OF PIANOFORTE TECHNIC, THE --2 VOLS.
WEBBE, SAMUEL
    HARMONY EPITOMIZED, BEING A SHORT EXPLANATION OF FIGURED BASSES,
WEBBE, WILLIAM H.
    PIANISTS' 'ABC' PRIMER AND GUIDE--WITH AN APPENDIX
WEISER, ADOLPH
    TWO RIGHT HANDS..A GUIDE FOR THE DEVELOPMENT OF PIANO TECHNIQUE
WELLS, HOWARD
    EARS, BRAIN AND FINGERS..A TEXT BOOK FOR PIANO TEACHERS AND PUPILS
WELLS, HOWARD
    PIANIST'S THUMB, THE
WELSH, J. ROBERT
    MAKING MUSIC AT THE KEYBOARD..BEGINNING PIANO...CLASS...AND EAR
WEST, GEORGE FREDERICK
    HINTS TO YOUNG TEACHERS OF THE PIANOFORTE
WESTBROOK, BENJAMIN V.
    SYSTEM OF STUDY OF SCALES AND CHORDS, A ..BEING CHAPTERS ON THE
WESTRUP, SIR JACK ALLAN
    MUSICAL INTERPRETATION---THIS BOOK ACCOMPANIED A SERIES OF B.B.C.
WEYLAND, RUDOLPH H.
    LEARNING TO READ MUSIC
WHEELER, BERTHA H.
    MIND AND MECHANISM..THOUGHTS ON TEACHING AND THE PIANISTIC ART
WHITE, WILLIAM BRAID
    PLAYER-PIANIST, THE ..A GUIDE TO THE APPRECIATION AND
WHITEMORE, CUTHBERT
    COMMONSENSE IN PIANOFORTE PLAYING
WHITESIDE, ABBY
    INDISPENSABLES OF PIANO PLAYING--2ND. ED.---1955
WIECK, FRIEDRICH
    PIANO AND SONG..HOW TO TEACH, HOW TO LEARN, AND HOW TO FORM A
WIER, ALBERT
    PIANO, THE ..ITS HISTORY, MAKERS, PLAYERS AND MUSIC
WILKINS-GUTMANN, EMMA
    TALKS WITH PIANO TEACHERS
WILLIAMS, JEAN E. *
    MIND IN MUSIC, THE
WILLIAMS, JEAN E.
    MODERN METHOD OF PIANO INSTRUCTION, A ..TEACHERS MANUAL
WILLIAMS, JOHN M.
    WHAT TO TEACH AT THE VERY FIRST LESSON
WILLIS, AUBREY
    AUBREY WILLIS HOME STUDY COURSE IN PIANO TUNING AND REPAIRING
WILLS, VERA G. *
    PARENT'S GUIDE TO MUSIC LESSONS, A
WILSON, MORRIS E.
    HOW TO HELP YOUR CHILD WITH MUSIC--2ND. ED.----1951
WILSON, MORRIS E.
    HOW TO PLAY BY EAR

WILSON, WILLIAM
    NEW FINGERING NOTATION FOR KEYBOARD MUSIC---REPRODUCED FROM
WINNER, SEPTIMUS
    WINNER'S NEW SCHOOL FOR THE PIANO, IN WHICH THE INSTRUCTIONS ARE
WOLFF, ERNST VICTOR
    WITH REASON AND RHYME
WOLLENHAUPT, HEINRICH
    METHOD FOR THE PIANOFORTE AND METHODICAL GUIDE FOR THE PIANO FORTE
WOLLNER, GERTRUDE PRICE
    IMPROVISATION IN MUSIC..WAYS TOWARDS CAPTURING MUSICAL IDEAS AND
WOODHOUSE, GEORGE
    ARTIST AT THE PIANO, THE ..THE ART OF MUSICAL INTERPRETATION
WOODHOUSE, GEORGE
    FROM KEYBOARD TO MUSIC
WOODHOUSE, GEORGE
    NEW PATH FOR PIANISTS, A ..THE MUTANO--MUTE PIANO--SYSTEM, ETC.
WOODHOUSE, GEORGE
    REALISTIC APPROACH TO PIANO PLAYING, A
WRIGHT, WILLIAM C.
    GOLDEN MONITOR, FOR THE PIANOFORTE AND CABINET ORGAN, DESIGNED AS
WRIGHT, WILLIAM C.
    PIANOFORTE MANUAL, THE ..DESIGNED AS A COMPLETE PIANOFORTE PRIMER
WYMAN, ADDISON P.
    WYMAN'S PIANO TEXTBOOK..CONTAINING A COMPLETE SYSTEM OF MUSICAL
YATES, PETER
    AMATEUR AT THE KEYBOARD, AN
ZEITLIN, POLDI *
    THEORY PAPERS, THE --C.M.P. PIANO LIBRARY--2 VOLS., 1961-1963
ZEPER, M. E. P.
    READING OF MUSIC, THE ..A RATIONAL METHOD--NO. 1 OF A SERIES ON
ZUCH, ANNETT V. *
    PIANO TEACHER, THE ..A BOOK OF SELF-INSTRUCTION

The Art of Teaching

ABBOTT, A. T.
    METHOD FOR GAINING A PERFECT KNOWLEDGE OF THE NOTES, ETC., FOR
ADAMS, JAMES B.
    FAMILIAR INTRODUCTION TO THE FIRST PRINCIPLES OF MUSIC, A ...FOR
ADAMS, JULIETTE
    RECENT DEVELOPMENTS IN TEACHING CHILDREN TO PLAY THE PIANO
AEOLIAN COMPANY, THE
    DUO-ART BOOK OF MUSIC, THE
AGUILAR, EMANUEL
    HOW TO LEARN THE PIANOFORTE
AGUILAR, EMANUEL
    LITTLE BOOK ABOUT LEARNING THE PIANOFORTE, A
AHEARN, ELLA MASON *
    ADULT EXPLORER AT THE PIANO, THE
AHRENS, CORA B. *
    FOR ALL PIANO TEACHERS
ALBIG, GEORGE L.
    HOW TO PLAY THE PLAYER
ALLEN, MARGARET *
    CREATIVE MOTION
ALLISON, IRL
    LET'S LEARN ALL THE NOTES AND READ BETTER..FOR ALL PIANO PUPILS,
AMERICAN SCHOOL OF PIANO TUNING
    TRAINING AS A PIANO TECHNICIAN--8 VOLS. IN 1
ANDERSON, WILLIAM P.
    MUSIC AS A CAREER
ANON
    ADVICE TO A NOBLEMAN...ON THE MANNER IN WHICH HIS CHILDREN SHOULD
ANON
    CHILD'S INTRODUCTION TO THOROUGH BASS, THE ..IN CONVERSATIONS OF A
ANON
    COMPLEAT TUTOR FOR THE HARPSICHORD OR SPINNET, WHEREIN IS SHEWN
ANON
    DIGITORIUM, THE --MINIATURE DUMB PIANO
ANON
    FASHIONABLE PRECEPTOR, FOR THE PIANO-FORTE AND HARPSICHORD,
ANON
    FIRST STEPS TO THOROUGH BASE, IN 12 FAMILIAR LESSONS BETWEEN A
ANON
    GENERAL OBSERVATIONS ON MUSIC AND REMARKS ON MR. LOGIER'S SYSTEM
ANON
    HOW TO LEARN TO PLAY THE PIANO WELL, BY ONE WHO HAS TAUGHT HIMSELF
ANON
    NEW AND COMPLETE INSTRUCTIONS FOR THE HARPSICHORD, PIANO FORTE OR
ANON
    NEW INSTRUCTIONS FOR PLAYING THE HARPSICHORD, PIANOFORTE OR
ANON
    PIANO IN TWELVE LESSONS
ANON
    PRECEPTOR, FOR THE PIANOFORTE, THE ORGAN OR HARPSICHORD, THE
ANON
    RULES..OR A SHORT AND COMPLEAT METHOD FOR ATTAINING TO PLAY A
ANON
    THOROUGH BASS AT ONE VIEW, WITH DIRECTIONS FOR ACCOMPANIMENT AND
ANTCLIFFE, HERBERT
    SUCCESSFUL MUSIC TEACHER, THE ..WORDS OF ADVICE
ANTRIM, DORAN K.
    TEACHING MUSIC AND MAKING IT PAY
APPEL, PEARL *
    HARMONY AT THE PIANO LESSON, A COMPANION TO PIANO STUDY
ARIZONA STATE MUSIC TEACHERS ASSOCIATION
    GUIDE TO TEACHING PIANO--REV. ED.---1958
ARNOLD, FRANCK THOMAS
    ART OF ACCOMPANIMENT FROM A THOROUGH-BASS, AS PRACTICED IN THE
ASHBURNHAM, GEORGE
    STORY OF UNIQUE PIANO TUITION, THE
AXTENS, FLORENCE
    FIRST SIX MONTHS IN THE PIANO CLASS, THE ..A MANUAL FOR TEACHERS
AXTENS, FLORENCE
    PIANO CLASS INSTRUCTION FOR CHILDREN AND ADULT CLASSES..A MANUAL
AXTENS, FLORENCE
    PIANO CLASS METHOD..THE FIRST TWELVE MONTHS IN THE PIANO CLASS
BABBITT, WILLIAM
    PHYSIOLOGICAL METHOD FOR PLAYING THE PIANO-FORTE, DESIGNED AS A
BACON, ERNST
    NOTES ON THE PIANO
BAILLIE, ALEXANDER--SUPPOSED AUTHOR
    INTRODUCTION TO THE KNOWLEDGE AND PRACTICE OF THE THORO' BASS, AN
BAKER, HENRIETTE
    PRACTICAL METHOD FOR THE PIANOFORTE FOR PRIVATE CLASS LESSONS--2
BARNWELL, V. T.
    BARNWELL'S NORMAL KEYBOARD AND STAFF STUDIES--THE MENTAL
BARTHELEMON, FRANCOIS H.
    NEW TUTOR FOR THE HARPSICHORD OR PIANO FORTE, WHEREIN THE FIRST
BARTOK, BELA *
    BARTOK-RESCHOVSKY PIANO METHOD---1913
BASTIEN, JAMES W. *
    BEGINNING PIANO FOR ADULTS

BASTIEN, JAMES W.
    HOW TO TEACH PIANO SUCCESSFULLY
BAUER, HAROLD *
    PIANO METHOD FOR CLASS AND INDIVIDUAL INSTRUCTION--2 VOLS.
BAUGHAN, EDWARD ALGERNON
    IGNACE JAN PADEREWSKI
BAVIN, JOHN T.
    PIANO CLASS INSTRUCTOR
BAXTER, JAMES
    INDUCTIVE GRAMMAR OF MUSIC, FOR CLASS, PRIVATE LESSON, OR SELF
BAXTER, JAMES
    NEW SCHOOL OF MUSIC, THE ..PRACTICAL THOROUGH BASE CULTURE, FOR
BECKERMAN, H. J.
    AMERICAN SCHOOL OF RAGTIME PIANO PLAYING, THE
BEMETZRIEDER, ANTON
    ABSTRACT OF A NEW METHOD OF TEACHING THE PRINCIPLES OF MUSIC,
BEMETZRIEDER, ANTON
    COMPENDIUM OF A NEW METHOD OF MUSIC...WITH THE AUTHOR'S PRINCIPLES
BEMETZRIEDER, ANTON
    GAMUT AND COMMON CHORD IN ALL KEYS, FINGERED FOR THE HARPSICHORD,
BEMETZRIEDER, ANTON
    MUSIC MADE EASY TO EVERY CAPACITY, IN A SERIES OF DIALOGUES..BEING
BENDEP, GEORGE CHARLES
    BUSINESS MANUAL FOR PIANO TEACHERS
BENEDICT, LADY *
    HOW TO PLAY THE PIANOFORTE
BENEDICT, MILO ELLSWORTH
    THIRTY-THREE SUGGESTIONS IN ONE LESSON..FOR THE GUIDANCE AND
BENNER, LORA
    BENNER BLUE BOOK, THE ..PRACTICAL MANUAL OF PIANO TEACHING--4TH.
BENNER, LORA
    BENNER GOLD BOOK, THE ..PIANO MATERIAL AND TEACHING METHODS--3RD.
BENNER, LORA
    THEORY FOR PIANO STUDENTS--1ST. YEAR, PRIVATE OR CLASS--5 VOLS.,
BENNETT, BEULAH VARNER
    PIANO CLASSES FOR EVERYONE..A PRACTICAL GUIDE FOR PIANO TEACHERS
BERGER, FRANCESCO
    FIRST STEPS AT THE PIANOFORTE
BERLIN, BORIS *
    BORIS BERLIN MUSICAL KINDERGARTEN PIANO METHOD, THE.. GUIDE FOR
BERNING, ALICE B. *
    KEYBOARD EXPERIENCES FOR CLASSROOM TEACHERS
BEVITT, ZAY RECTOR
    CLASS PROCEDURE FOR 40 LESSONS IN PIANO PLAYING BY HARMONY
BEVITT, ZAY RECTOR
    PIANO PLAYING BY HARMONY DIAGRAMS..STUDENT'S BOOK
BEVITT, ZAY RECTOR
    PIANO PLAYING BY HARMONY DIAGRAMS..TEACHER'S MANUAL
BIART, VICTOR
    PIANIST'S GUIDE, THE ..A SERIES OF PAMPHLETS ON THE TEACHING AND
BLAKE, DOROTHY
    FIRST STEPS IN CHORD PLAYING
BLAKE, DOROTHY
    FIRST STEPS IN THE USE OF THE PEDAL FOR PIANO
BOAL, DEAN *
    CONCEPTS AND SKILLS FOR THE PIANO..TEACHER'S MANUAL 1---CLASS
BOLTON, HETTY
    ON TEACHING THE PIANO
BOOTH, VICTOR
    WE PIANO TEACHERS--REVISED BY ADELE FRANKLIN---1946
BORST, ALBERT W.
    ADVICE TO YOUNG STUDENTS OF THE PIANOFORTE
BOSWORTH, HARRIETTE DEXTER
    IDEAS FOR YOUNG PIANO TEACHERS
BOTTOMLEY, JOSEPH
    NEW SYSTEM OF PRACTICING AND TEACHING THE PIANOFORTE, A
BOWEN, CAROLYN
    OUTLINES FOR TRAINING PIANO TEACHERS
BRECKENRIDGE, WILLIAM KILGORE
    HINTS FOR PIANO NORMAL STUDIES
BREMNER, ROBERT
    HARPSICHORD OR SPINNET MISCELLANY, THE --KEYBOARD
BRIED, FREDERICK
    STIMULATION IN PIANO STUDY..HOW PARENTS CAN STIMULATE AND MAINTAIN
BROTHERHOOD, JAMES
    IMPROVED METHOD IN PIANO TEACHING, AND RECENT IDEAS OF LEADING
BROTHERHOOD, JAMES
    SCIENCE AND ART AS TWIN SISTERS..BEING A SECOND TREATISE UPON THE
BROTHERHOOD, JAMES
    TECHNICON, THE..A TREATISE UPON THE DEVELOPMENT OF PIANOFORTE
BROUGHTON, JULIA *
    SIXTEEN LESSON PLANS..A MANUAL FOR PROGRESSIVE SERIES
BROUGHTON, JULIA
    SUCCESS IN PIANO TEACHING
BROWER, HARRIETTE
    ART OF THE PIANIST, THE
BROWER, HARRIETTE
    HOME HELP IN MUSIC STUDY
BROWER, HARRIETTE
    MODERN MASTERS OF THE KEYBOARD
BROWER, HARRIETTE
    PIANO MASTERY..TALKS WITH MASTER PIANISTS AND TEACHERS...
BROWER, HARRIETTE
    PIANO MASTERY, SECOND SERIES
BROWER, HARRIETTE
    SELF-HELP IN PIANO STUDY
BUCK, PERCY
    PSYCHOLOGY FOR MUSICIANS
BUONAMICI, GIUSEPPE
    ART OF SCALE STUDY FOR THE PIANOFORTE, THE ...AS TAUGHT TO HIS
BURROWES, JOHN FRECKLETON
    PIANOFORTE PRIMER, THE ..CONTAINING THE RUDIMENTS OF MUSIC
BURROWES, JOHN FRECKLETON
    THOROUGH-BASS PRIMER, THE ..CONTAINING EXPLANATIONS AND EXAMPLES
BURROWS, RAYMOND
    ADVANCED PIANO CLASS, THE --REPRINT..PROCEEDINGS OF THE M.E.N.C.,
BURROWS, RAYMOND
    ELEMENTARY PIANO INSTRUCTION IN COLLEGE
BURROWS, RAYMOND
    HANDBOOK FOR TEACHING PIANO CLASSES
BURROWS, RAYMOND
    PIANO IN SCHOOL, A MEMORANDUM FOR SCHOOL ADMINISTRATORS
CALLAGHAN, JAMES
    ZIP CHORDMASTER..BEGINNERS HOME COURSE FOR PIANO AND ORGAN
CALLENDER, ROMAINE
    TEACHER'S MANUAL, A WORK DESIGNED TO SUPPLEMENT...'THE FIRST TEN
CAPEN, C. L.
    MUSIC TEACHER'S VADE-MECUM, THE ..A GUIDE IN THE CHOICE OF MUSIC
CARPE, ADOLPH
    PIANIST AND THE ART OF MUSIC, THE ..A TREATISE ON PIANO PLAYING
CARRE, JOHN
    PSYCHOLOGY OF PIANO TEACHING, THE ..A TEXTBOOK FOR TEACHERS,
CARTER, BUENTA
    BEGINNER'S PIANO BOOK FOR OLDER STUDENTS...DESIGNED FOR THE OLDER
CARY, MRS. C. S. P.
    PIANO-FORTE CLASS BOOK, CONTAINING PRACTICAL RUDIMENTAL LESSONS

CAVALLARO, CARMEN
    KEYBOARD HARMONY..A NEW MODERN PIANO METHOD---POPULAR IDIOM
CHAPPLE, STANLEY
    CLASS WAY TO THE KEYBOARD, THE
CHAROL, SIMON
    NEW APPROACH TO THE STUDY OF THE PIANOFORTE, A ---IN ITALIAN AND
CHASTEK, WINIFRED
    KEYBOARD SKILLS..SIGHT READING, TRANSPOSITION, HARMONIZATION,
CHEYETTE, IRVING
    BASIC PIANO FOR THE MUSIC EDUCATOR AND CLASSROOM TEACHER
CHILDERS, LEMUEL
    CHORD DICTIONARY..DESIGNED FOR TEACHERS, STUDENTS AND SELF-TAUGHT
CHING, JAMES
    BETTER BEGINNINGS..A FIRST BOOK FOR EVERYONE WHO WANTS TO BECOME A
CHING, JAMES
    CANDIDATE'S COMPANION TO THE EXERCISES, SCALES, BROKEN CHORDS,
CHING, JAMES
    ENTIRELY NEW SOLUTION TO THE PROBLEMS OF PIANO STUDY AT HOME, AN
CHING, JAMES
    LET'S PLAY THE PIANO..THE FIRST MUSIC BOOK FOR CHILDREN OF ALL
CHING, JAMES
    ON TEACHING PIANO TECHNIQUE TO CHILDREN
CHING, JAMES
    PERFORMER AND AUDIENCE..AN INVESTIGATION INTO THE PSYCHOLOGICAL
CHING, JAMES
    PIANIST'S HOME STUDY COURSES, THE
CHING, JAMES
    PIANO PLAYING, A PRACTICAL METHOD--A NEW EDITION OF 'PIANO
CHING, JAMES
    PLAYING AND TEACHING OF BACH, THE ..A GUIDE FOR TEACHERS, STUDENTS
CHING, JAMES
    TEACHING OF TECHNIQUE TO CHILDREN, THE --4 PTS.
CHING, JOAN ELIZABETH
    OURSELVES AND OUR PUPILS---ALSO CATALOGUED UNDER AUTHORSHIP..BETTY
CHITTENDEN, KATE S.
    SYNTHETIC CATECHISM, THE ..538 QUESTIONS AND ANSWERS FOR USE IN
CHURCHILL, VIRGINIA PEAKES
    MODERN TEACHER'S GUIDE TO PIANO AND PIANO CLASS TEACHING
CHURCHILL, VIRGINIA PEAKES
    NINETEEN FIFTY-SIX SUPPLEMENT TO THE MODERN TEACHER'S GUIDE TO
CLARKE, HUGH ARCHIBALD
    ART OF PIANOFORTE PLAYING, THE --TEXT BOOK FOR BEGINNERS
CLIFFORD, S. M.
    ADVENTURES IN PIANOLAND..TWELVE LESSONS FOR TEACHERS OF PIANO
COCHRAN, MARY
    ULTIMATE PRINCIPLES OF PIANOFORTE TEACHING AND PLAYING
COGGINS, JOSEPH
    GOVERNESS'S MUSICAL ASSISTANT, CONTAINING ALL THAT IS TRULY USEFUL
COLEMAN, H. P.
    PIANO CLASS, THE
COOK, J. LAWRENCE
    PIANO HANDBOOK ON BOOGIE WOOGIE, BLUES, AND BARRELHOUSE..3 EASY TO
COOKE, JAMES FRANCIS
    GREAT MEN AND FAMOUS MUSICIANS ON THE ART OF MUSIC
COOKE, MAX
    HOW TO PREPARE FOR PIANOFORTE...SUGGESTIONS FOR A.M.E.B.
COPP, EVELYN A.
    WHAT IS THE FLETCHER MUSIC METHOD
CRAMER, JOHN BAPTIST
    INSTRUCTIONS FOR THE PIANOFORTE---CONTAINS ALSO A SET OF 28
CROTCH, WILLIAM
    PRELUDES FOR THE PIANO FORTE, COMPOSED IN VARIOUS STYLES..TO WHICH
CURWEN, ANNIE JESSY
    CHILD PIANIST, THE
CURWEN, ANNIE JESSY
    PSYCHOLOGY APPLIED TO MUSIC TEACHING
CURWEN, ANNIE JESSY
    TEACHER'S GUIDE...TO MRS. CURWEN'S PIANOFORTE METHOD, 'THE CHILD
CZERNY, CARL
    LETTERS ON THOROUGH-BASS...FORMING THE SECOND PART OF THE LETTERS
DAHL, ANTON
    SOUL OF GENIUS, THE ..ITS MUSICAL DEVELOPMENT AND HOW THE WORLD AT
DANIELS, BESS
    PIANO COURSE..TEACHER'S BOOK, FOR CLASS OR INDIVIDUAL INSTRUCTION
DANIELS, BESS *
    PIANO COURSE EITHER FOR CLASS OR FOR INDIVIDUAL INSTRUCTION
DANIELS, BESS *
    WORLD OF MUSIC, THE ..PIANO COURSE..TEACHERS' BOOK, FOR CLASS OR
DARDENELLE, LOUISE
    HARMONY-FIRST METHOD FOR THE PIANO...FOR CHILD AND ADULT
DAVIS, HARRY
    INSTANT PIANO..A UNIQUE METHOD OF READING AND CHORDING FROM THE
DAVIS, LUCILE
    READ AND PLAY..RAPID CHORD CONSTRUCTION--REV. ED.---1943
DAVIS, MARILYN K.
    GROUP ACTIVITIES AT THE KEYBOARD
DAVISON, JUNE *
    PIANO PROGRESS..AN APPROACH TO MUSIC FOR THE PARTIALLY SIGHTED--2
DECKER, TOM W.
    CONSOLE SYSTEM, THE ..A TEXT FOR MODERN PIANO AND ORGAN TO BE USED
DENT, EDWARD J.
    FERRUCCIO BUSONI, A BIOGRAPHY
DENVER--PUBLIC SCHOOLS
    CLASS-PIANO TEACHERS HANDBOOK
DEUTSCH, LEONHARD
    PIANO..GUIDED SIGHT-READING
DE WITT, EDYTHE
    EDYTHE DE WITT'S METHOD FOR CLASS PIANO...WRITTEN TO GIVE CORRECT
DIEHL, ALICE M.
    MUSICAL MEMORIES--SOME LESSONS WITH HENSELT
DILLER, ANGELA
    FIRST PEDAL-STUDIES FOR THE PIANO, 24 PROGRESSIVE EXERCISES AND
DILLER, ANGELA
    KEYBOARD MUSIC STUDY..A CREATIVE METHOD BASED ON EAR-TRAINING--IN
DILLER, ANGELA
    SPLENDOR OF MUSIC, THE
DITSON COMPANY
    TEACHING PIECES AND HOW TO TEACH THEM
DOBBIE, E. A.
    AUSTRALIAN PIANOFORTE TUTOR
DUCKWORTH, GUY
    KEYBOARD MUSICIANSHIP
DUFFEE, GERTRUDE BANKS
    PIANO STUDY..A GUIDE TO TEACHER AND STUDENT
DUMM, ROBERT W.
    IN BLACK AND WHITE
DUTTON, CHUCK *
    MUSIC FOR FUN..PROFESSIONAL COURSE USING THE CHUCK DUTTON
EDWARDS, RUTH
    COMPLEAT MUSIC TEACHER FOR TEACHERS, PARENTS AND STUDENTS
EGBERT, MARION S.
    SEEING WHAT WE SING, AN AID THROUGH KEYBOARD EXPERIENCE TO THE
EISENBERG, JACOB
    ARTISTIC PIANIST, THE ..NATURAL TECHNICS IN PIANO MASTERY..FROM
EISENBERG, JACOB
    WEIGHT AND RELAXATION METHOD FOR THE PIANOFORTE

ELKAN, IDA
    TECHNICAL WORK IN EAR-TRAINING FOR THE PIANO..A METHOD FOR PRIVATE
ENGLBRECHT, J. G.
    MATERIA MUSICA, OR MATERIALS FOR THE PIANIST..A CLASS BOOK
ERWIN, GARNET PARKER
    KEYBOARD STORIES FOR CLASS AND INDIVIDUAL INSTRUCTION---1939
EVERHART, POWELL
    PIANIST'S ART, THE ..A COMPREHENSIVE MANUAL ON PIANO PLAYING FOR
FAELTEN, CARL
    TEACHER'S MANUAL FOR PIANOFORTE COURSE, THE
FAELTEN, CARL *
    TRANSPOSITION READER--FUNDAMENTAL TRAINING COURSE FOR PIANOFORTE
FAELTEN, REINHOLD
    CATECHISM OF THE FAELTEN SYSTEM, A
FALKENER, ROBERT
    INSTRUCTIONS FOR PLAYING THE HARPSICHORD..WHEREIN IS FULLY
FAY, AMY
    MUSIC STUDY IN GERMANY---1880
FIELDEN, THOMAS
    SCIENCE OF PIANOFORTE TECHNIC, THE --2ND. REV. ED.---1927
FILLINGHAM, ARTHUR H.
    GUIDE TO THE A.º.C.M. AND OTHER EXAMINATIONS IN THE ART OF
FINCK, EDWARD J.
    AMERICAN PRIZE METHOD FOR PIANOFORTE
FISHER, HENRY
    PIANIST'S MENTOR..A TEXT BOOK FOR STUDENTS OF ALL GRADES--2ND. ED.
FISHER, HENRY
    PSYCHOLOGY FOR MUSIC TEACHERS..THE LAWS OF THOUGHT APPLIED TO
FRAY, JACQUES *
    HOW TO PLAY BY THE JACQUES FRAY SPEED METHOD
FREDRICH, FRANK
    PLAYING BY SEEING..A STUDY IN TRAINING AND PERCEPTION FOR BETTER
FRYER, HERBERT
    HINTS FOR PIANOFORTE PRACTICE--A SUGGESTED PLAN FOR DAILY
FULLER, JANET E.
    COMPLETE KNOWLEDGE OF THE ESSENTIALS OF PIANOFORTE PLAYING, A
GALLICO, PAOLO
    NEW METHOD FOR SYNCHRONIZED SCALE FINGERINGS, A
GARROWAY, WILL
    PIANISM
GEARY, ELEANOR MARGARET
    MUSICAL EDUCATION, WITH PRACTICAL OBSERVATIONS ON THE ART OF
GEMINIANI, FRANCESCO
    RULES FOR PLAYING IN A TRUE TASTE ON THE VIOLIN, GERMAN FLUTE,
GERMER, HEINRICH
    HOW OUGHT ONE TO STUDY PIANO-TECHNIC---1881, IN GERMAN
GERMER, HEINRICH
    TECHNICS OF PIANOFORTE PLAYING REARRANGED AS A METHODICAL PLAN OF
GEST, ELIZABETH
    KEYBOARD HARMONY FOR JUNIORS
GIBBS, GEORGE A., JR.
    SELF INSTRUCTION IN THE PIANO
GIBBS, POLLY
    LISTS AND SUGGESTIONS FOR PIANO TEACHING
GIDDINGS, THADDEUS P.
    GIDDING'S PUBLIC SCHOOL CLASS METHOD FOR THE PIANO
GIFFORD, ALEXANDER M.
    PIANOFORTE AND HOW TO STUDY IT, THE
GLASFORD, IRENE A.
    RHYTHM, REASON AND RESPONSE FOR THE MUSICIAN, PIANIST AND TEACHER
GOODRICH, ALFRED JOHN
    GUIDE TO PRACTICAL MUSICIANSHIP--INTENDED TO SUPERCEDE ROTE
GRAHAM, GEORGE FARQUHAR
    GENERAL OBSERVATIONS UPON MUSIC AND REMARKS ON MR. LOGIER'S SYSTEM
GRAHAM, JAMES L.
    MUSIC MADE EASY, PIANOFORTE TUTOR ON A NEW PLAN
GRAHAM, MARY JANE
    LETTER TO A YOUNG PIANOFORTE PLAYER, A
GRAY, WILLIAM L.
    SELECTED AND GRADED LIST OF STUDIES AND PIECES FOR TEACHERS OF
GREW, SIDNEY
    ART OF THE PLAYER-PIANO, THE ..A TEXTBOOK FOR STUDENT AND TEACHER
GRIFFIN, RUSSELL B.
    PIANOFORTE TELEGRAPHY, THE --THE MORSE TELEGRAPH CODE--INSTRUCTOR
GRIFFIN, SISTER MARY ANNAROSE
    PIANO MATERIALS..GRADED AND COMPILED AS AN AID TO INSTRUCTORS
GRIMALDI, MARIA LOUISA
    ART OF PIANOFORTE PLAYING AND TEACHING, THE
GRINDEA, CAROLA
    FIRST TEN LESSONS, THE ..A NEW APPROACH TO PIANO TEACHING
HALLE, SIR CHARLES
    CHARLES HALLE'S PRACTICAL PIANOFORTE SCHOOL--9 VOLS.
HAMBOURG, MARK
    HOW TO PREPARE FOR PLAYING IN CONCERT
HAMILTON, CLARENCE G.
    FUTURE OF PIANO STUDY, THE ---FROM 'M.T.N.A. PROCEEDINGS', SERIES
HAMILTON, CLARENCE G.
    PIANO TEACHING..ITS PRINCIPLES AND PROBLEMS
HANSMANN, RICHARD
    THEORETICAL AND PRACTICAL PIANO-FORTE SCHOOL FOR THE JANKO
HARGISS, GENEVIEVE
    MUSIC FOR ELEMENTARY TEACHERS..A PROGRAMMED COURSE IN BASIC THEORY
HARKNESS, ROBERT
    BEGINNERS PIANO COURSE IN HYMN PLAYING BY CORRESPONDENCE
HARKNESS, ROBERT
    GOSPEL SONG ACCOMPANIMENT..THE ROBERT HARKNESS METHOD FOR PIANO
HARKNESS, ROBERT
    GOSPEL SONG PIANO ACCOMPANIMENT..THE ROBERT HARKNESS
HARKNESS, ROBERT
    HOME STUDY CORRESPONDENCE COURSE IN EVANGELISTIC HYMN PLAYING, FOR
HARRISON, SIDNEY
    BEGINNING TO PLAY THE PIANO--A TEACHER'S HANDBOOK, INCLUDING THE
HARTLINE, ELIZABETH DILL *
    KEYBOARD MUSICIANSHIP, GROUP PIANO FOR ADULTS
HARVEY, ROBERT
    MAGIC KEY TO KEYBOARD SUCCESS, THE
HECK, JOHANN CASPAR
    ART OF FINGERING, THE ..OR, THE EASIEST AND SUREST METHOD HOW TO
HECK, JOHANN CASPAR
    ART OF PLAYING THE HARPSICHORD, ILLUSTRATED BY A VARIETY OF
HEIDELBERGER, PAULINE
    MASTER METHOD..PIANO NORMAL AND TEACHER'S MANUAL
HENDERSON, ARCHIBALD
    MUSICAL MEMORIES---CONCERNS SEVERAL PIANISTS
HERZOG, SIGMUND *
    PIANO TEACHER'S MANUAL, THE
HILES, JOHN
    CATECHISM FOR THE PIANOFORTE STUDENT, A ..CONTAINING A FULL
HILES, JOHN
    KEY TO THE EXERCISES IN THE CATECHISM OF HARMONY, THOROUGH-BASS
HODGES, SISTER MABELLE L.
    CATALOGUE OF REPRESENTATIVE TEACHING MATERIALS FOR PIANO SINCE
HOFHEIMER, GRACE
    TEACHING TECHNIQUES FOR THE PIANO
HOPKINS, GEORGE P.
    PIANO PLAYING FOR FUN--4 VOLS.

HORROCKS, CYRIL P. H.
   STUDENT'S GUIDE TO THE ART OF TEACHING THE PIANOFORTE, THE --2ND.
HOWE, JAMES H.
   PIANO-FORTE INSTRUCTOR, A ..OR, PREPARATORY SYSTEM OF PIANOFORTE
HUENTEN, FRANZ
   ABRIDGED EDITION OF F. HUENTEN'S CELEBRATED INSTRUCTIONS FOR THE
HUENTEN, FRANZ
   FRANZ HUENTEN'S CELEBRATED INSTRUCTIONS FOR THE PIANOFORTE--2ND.
HULL, ARTHUR EAGLEFIELD
   THREE HUNDRED QUESTIONS ON PIANOFORTE TEACHING IN 30 GRADUATED
HUNEKER, JAMES GIBBONS
   FRANZ LISZT
HUNTEN, WILLIAM
   HUNTEN'S CELEBRATED PIANOFORTE SCHOOL
HUTT, DOREEN
   PIANO CLASS METHOD--BKS. 1 AND 2
ISAACS, EDWARD
   BLIND PIANO TEACHER, THE
IVES, WILLIAM
   SURE TEACHER..OR, CHILD'S FIRST COURSE FOR THE PIANOFORTE, THE
JEWETT, ALBERT DEWEY
   IDIOMATIC COURSE OF PIANO INSTRUCTION FOR CLASS WORK
JOHNSON, ARTEMAS N.
   INSTRUCTIONS IN THE ART OF PLAYING CHURCH MUSIC UPON THE MELODEON,
JOHNSON, ARTEMAS N.
   INSTRUCTIONS IN THOROUGH BASE..BEING A NEW AND EASY METHOD FOR
JOHNSON, SARAH S.
   HELPS TO TEACHER AND STUDENT ON THE FAELTEN SYSTEM
JOHNSTONE, J. ALFRED
   ART OF TEACHING PIANOFORTE PLAYING, THE --2ND. REV. ED.---1910
JOHNSTONE, J. ALFRED
   ESSENTIALS IN PIANOFORTE PLAYING, AND OTHER MUSICAL STUDIES...
JOUSSE, JOHN
   JOUSSE'S CATECHISM OF MUSIC, AND BURROWES' PIANOFORTE PRIMER AND
KARLIN, AARON
   KARLIN'S HARMONIC COURSE FOR PIANO IMPROVISING--4
KENYON, CHARLES FREDERICK
   HOW TO MEMORIZE MUSIC
KING, AUDREY
   PIANO CLASSES IN ELEMENTARY SCHOOLS
KIRBY, MAY B. KELLY
   KELLY KIRBY KINDERGARTEN PIANO METHOD, TEACHERS' COURSE, THE
KLAVARSKRIBO, SLEKKERVIER, HOLLAND
   PRACTICAL CORRESPONDENCE COURSE FOR PIANOFORTE
KNORR, JULIUS
   KNORR'S METHODICAL GUIDE FOR TEACHERS OF MUSIC ON THE PIANOFORTE
KOTZSCHMAR, MARY ANN
   HALF-HOUR LESSONS IN MUSIC..CLASS WORK FOR BEGINNERS AT THE PIANO
KRUSZYNSKI, MICHAL
   APPROACH TO THE PSYCHOLOGY OF PIANO TEACHING, AN
KULLAK, ADOLPH
   AESTHETICS OF PIANOFORTE PLAYING, THE ---1861 IN GERMAN--1ST.
KULLAK, ADOLPH
   ART OF THE TOUCH, THE ..A WORK FOR THE USE OF ADVANCED PLAYERS AND
LAMAR, RICHARD
   COLLEGE PIANO PEDAGOGY
LAMPE, JOHN F.
   PLAIN AND COMPENDIOUS METHOD OF TEACHING THOROUGH BASS, A ..WITH
LANDOWSKA, WANDA
   LANDOWSKA ON MUSIC--EDITED BY DENISE RESTOUT
LASSIMONNE, DENISE
   OPENING THE SHUTTERS..A SHORT EXPOSITION ON THE TEACHINGS AND
LATOUR, T.
   LATOUR'S NEW AND IMPROVED METHOD OF INSTRUCTION FOR THE PIANO
LEACH, JOHN R.
   FUNCTIONAL PIANO FOR THE TEACHER
LEAVEY, LILIAN
   JUNIOR SCHOOL PIANIST, THE --ADDRESSED TO THE NEW MUSIC TEACHER
LEVINE, JACK
   WHAT MUSICAL INSTRUMENT FOR ME
LEVINSKAYA, MARIA
   LEVINSKAYA SYSTEM OF PIANOFORTE TECHNIC AND TONE COLOR, THE
LE COUPPEY, FELIX
   PIANO TEACHING..ADVICE TO PUPILS AND YOUNG TEACHERS---1868 IN
LE ROY, PERRY J.
   HOW TO PLAY THE PIANO BY EAR..THE QUICK, EASY, SIMPLE WAY
LINDO, ALGERNON H.
   AURAL TESTS FOR EXAMINATIONS--SPECIALLY WRITTEN FOR TEACHERS AND
LINDO, ALGERNON H.
   PIANOFORTE STUDY..HINTS FOR TEACHERS AND STUDENTS
LINLEY, FRANCIS
   NEW ASSISTANT TO THE PIANO-FORTE OR HARPSICHORD, A ...RULES FOR
LITTLE, FRED W.
   LITTLE SYSTEM OF PLAYING THE PIANO BY EAR, THE
LOGIER, JOHANN BERNHARD
   AUTHENTIC ACCOUNT OF THE EXAMINATION OF PUPILS, INSTRUCTED IN THE
LOGIER, JOHANN BERNHARD
   EXPLANATION AND DESCRIPTION OF THE ROYAL PATENT CHIROPLAST, OR
LOGIER, JOHANN BERNHARD
   FIRST COMPANION TO THE ROYAL PATENT CHIROPLAST OR HAND-DIRECTOR,
LOGIER, JOHANN BERNHARD
   LOGIER'S SYSTEM OF THE SCIENCE OF MUSIC, HARMONY, AND PRACTICAL
LOGIER, JOHANN BERNHARD
   LOGIER'S THEORETICAL AND PRACTICAL STUDY FOR THE PIANO FORTE,
LOGIER, JOHANN BERNHARD
   REFUTATION OF THE FALLACIES AND MISREPRESENTATIONS CONTAINED IN A
LOGIER, JOHANN BERNHARD
   SEQUEL TO THE FIRST COMPANION TO THE CHIROPLAST
LOGIER, JOHANN BERNHARD
   SHORT ACCOUNT OF THE PROGRESS OF J. B. LOGIER'S SYSTEM OF MUSICAL
LOGIER, JOHANN BERNHARD
   SYLLABUS OF THE SECOND EXAMINATION OF MR. LOGIER'S PUPILS, ON HIS
LOMAS, LULU GRAHAM
   FIRST TEN PIANO LESSONS, LAID OUT FOR YOUNG TEACHERS, WITH
LONDON--A COMMITTEE OF PROFESSORS
   EXPOSITION OF THE MUSICAL SYSTEM OF MR. LOGIER..WITH STRICTURES ON
LOVELOCK, WILLIAM
   COMMON SENSE IN MUSIC TEACHING
LOVELOCK, WILLIAM
   ORNAMENTS AND ABBREVIATIONS FOR EXAMINATION CANDIDATES
LOVELOCK, WILLIAM
   TESTS IN SIGHT READING, FOR PIANO..FROM FIRST GRADE TO DIPLOMA--3
LOWE, CLAUDE EDGERTON
   CANDIDATES GUIDE TO QUESTIONS AND ANSWERS AT PRACTICAL LOCAL
LOWE, CLAUDE EDGERTON
   PIANOFORTE TEACHER'S VADE MECUM, THE ..A CYCLOPEDIA FOR THE
LOWERY, HAPPY
   GUIDE TO MUSICAL ACOUSTICS, A ---1956
LOYNES, W. H.
   HOW TO PLAY THE PIANO IN ONE HOUR WITHOUT A TEACHER
LUBIT, JULIA
   PIANOFORTE THEORY COURSE FOR BEGINNERS' PIANO CLASS
MACEWAN, DESIREE
   FIRST TWO YEARS OF PIANOFORTE STUDY, THE
MACKLIN, CHARLES B.
   ELEMENTARY PIANO PEDAGOGY, A GUIDE BOOK FOR YOUNG PIANO TEACHERS

MACLEAN, CHARLES D.
   PRINCIPLES OF PIANOFORTE PRACTICE, THE
MAHONY, CORNELIUS
   SELF-INSTRUCTOR FOR THE PIANOFORTE, CONTAINING C. MAHONY'S NEW
MAIER, GUY
   PIANO TEACHER'S COMPANION, THE
MAIER, GUY *
   PLAYING THE PIANO..A COURSE OF ROTE TRAINING FOR BEGINNERS--CLASS
MAIER, GUY *
   PLAYING THE PIANO--TEACHER'S MANUAL
MANHIRE, WILSON
   CANDIDATE'S SCALE AND ARPEGGIO TESTS FOR THE PIANOFORTE, ETC., THE
MANHIRE, WILSON
   GUIDE TO THE A.R.C.M. AND OTHER EXAMINATIONS IN
MANHIRE, WILSON
   MODEL ANSWERS TO QUESTIONS ON 'TOUCH' FOR CANDIDATES PREPARING FOR
MARIAL, R.
   METHODS APPLICABLE TO GROUP TEACHING OR PRIVATE PIANO INSTRUCTION
MARX, ADOLF BERNHARD
   INTRODUCTION TO THE INTERPRETATION OF BEETHOVEN'S PIANO
MASON, ELLA H. *
   ANSWERS TO CRITICISMS OF PIANO CLASS INSTRUCTION
MASON, WILLIAM G. *
   METHOD FOR THE PIANO-FORTE, A
MASON, WILLIAM G. *
   PRIMER OF MUSIC, A ..BEING THE FIRST STEPS IN MUSICIANSHIP..FOR
MATHEWS, WILLIAM S. B.
   TEACHER'S MANUAL OF MASON'S PIANOFORTE TECHNICS
MATTHAY, TOBIAS A.
   ACT OF TOUCH IN ALL ITS DIVERSITY, THE ..AN ANALYSIS AND SYNTHESIS
MATTHAY, TOBIAS A.
   CHILD'S FIRST STEPS IN PIANOFORTE PLAYING, THE
MATTHAY, TOBIAS A.
   FOREARM ROTATION PRINCIPLE IN PIANOFORTE PLAYING, THE ..ITS
MATTHAY, TOBIAS A.
   INTRODUCTION TO PSYCHOLOGY FOR MUSIC TEACHERS, AN --THREE LECTURES
MATTHAY, TOBIAS A.
   MUSICAL INTERPRETATION..ITS LAWS AND PRINCIPLES---1913
MATTHAY, TOBIAS A.
   ON METHOD IN TEACHING
MATTHAY, TOBIAS A. *
   PIANIST'S FIRST MUSIC MAKING, THE --3 VOLS.
MATTHAY, TOBIAS A.
   PIANOFORTE TONE-PRODUCTION---SAME AS 'THE ACT OF TOUCH IN ALL ITS
MCCLINTOCK, LORENE
   TEACH YOURSELF TO PLAY THE PIANO..BASED ON THE INTERVAL METHOD
MCFERRIN, CHARLES BETTEYS
   MOTHER'S PART IN HER CHILD'S MUSICAL EDUCATION, A ..OR, THE THINGS
MCHOSE, ALLEN IRVINE *
   KEYBOARD AND DICTATION MANUAL
MCHOSE, ALLEN IRVINE
   TEACHERS DICTATION MANUAL
MCLAIN, MARGARET STARR
   CLASS PIANO
MEHR, NORMAN
   GROUP PIANO TEACHING
MEKOTA, BETH ANNA
   TEACHING APPLIED MUSIC BY CLASS METHOD
MERRILL, MYRTLE
   SIGHT-READING AT THE PIANO
MIESSNER, WILLIAM OTTO
   MELODY WAY COURSE FOR CLASS OR PRIVATE PIANO INSTRUCTION, THE
MILLER, ALLAN
   BEGINNING PIANO FOR ADULTS
MILLER, EDWARD
   INSTITUTES OF MUSIC, OR, EASY INSTRUCTIONS FOR THE HARPSICHORD
MINNESOTA MUSIC TEACHERS ASSOCIATION
   PIANO-THEORY EXAMINATION SYLLABUS
MOKREJS, JOHN
   STORY OF NANYNKA, THE ..FIRST PIANO LESSONS FOR CHILDREN, PRIVATE
MOLLER, JOHN CHRISTOPHER
   SETT OF PROGRESSIVE LESSONS FOR THE HARPSICHORD OR PIANO FORTE, A
MONTI, H. DE
   STRICTURES ON MR. LOGIER'S SYSTEM OF MUSICAL EDUCATION
MOORE, HENRY K.
   CHILD'S PIANOFORTE BOOK, THE ..BEING A FIRST YEAR'S COURSE AT THE
MUSICIANS ADVISORY SERVICE
   MUSICIANS ADVISORY SERVICE FIRST MUSIC READER FOR PIANO..TEACHERS
MUSIC EDUCATION LEAGUE
   COMPREHENSIVE GUIDE FOR PIANO TEACHERS AND PIANO AUDITION SYLLABUS
MUSIC EDUCATORS NATIONAL CONFERENCE
   HANDBOOK FOR TEACHING PIANO CLASSES
MUSIC EDUCATORS NATIONAL CONFERENCE
   KEYBOARD EXPERIENCE AND CLASS PIANO INSTRUCTION
MUSIC EDUCATORS NATIONAL CONFERENCE
   MUSIC BEGINS WITH THE PIANO
MUSIC EDUCATORS NATIONAL CONFERENCE
   TEACHING PIANO IN CLASSROOM AND STUDIO
MUSIC EDUCATORS NATIONAL CONFERENCE
   TRAVELING THE CIRCUIT WITH PIANO CLASSES
MUSIC PROJECT--NEW YORK CITY
   TEACHER'S GUIDE..A CREATIVE APPROACH TO PIANO CLASS TEACHING, BY
NATIONAL BUREAU FOR THE ADVANCEMENT OF MUSIC
   GUIDE FOR CONDUCTING PIANO CLASSES IN THE SCHOOLS, A
NATIONAL BUREAU FOR THE ADVANCEMENT OF MUSIC
   NATIONAL SURVEY OF PIANO CLASSES IN OPERATION
NATIONAL BUREAU FOR THE ADVANCEMENT OF MUSIC
   PIANO CLASSES AND THE PRIVATE TEACHER
NATIONAL BUREAU FOR THE ADVANCEMENT OF MUSIC
   PIANO CLASSES IN THE SCHOOLS..EDUCATIONAL VALUE OF IMPORTANT NEW
NATIONAL BUREAU FOR THE ADVANCEMENT OF MUSIC
   PIANO CLASS INSTRUCTION
NATIONAL PIANO FOUNDATION
   GREATER REWARDS THROUGH CREATIVE PIANO TEACHING
NATIONAL PIANO FOUNDATION
   KEYS TO SUCCESSFUL PIANO STUDIO ORGANIZATION
NEUHAUS, HEINRICH
   ART OF PIANO PLAYING, THE
NEWCOMB, ETHEL
   LESCHETIZKY AS I KNEW HIM---1923
NEWMAN, ELIZABETH
   HOW TO TEACH MUSIC TO BEGINNERS
NEWMAN, ELIZABETH
   TEACHING MATERIAL GRADED ACCORDING TO HARMONIC STRUCTURE,
NEW ENGLAND CONSERVATORY
   NEW ENGLAND CONSERVATORY METHOD FOR THE PIANO-FORTE, THE
NEW SCHOOL FOR MUSIC STUDY
   STUDY GUIDE FOR PIANO TEACHERS
NILES BRYANT SCHOOL OF PIANO TUNING
   CORRESPONDENCE COURSE IN 12 LESSONS, A
NIMITZ, DANIEL
   KEYBOARD MASTERS..STUDY GUIDE
NIXON, W.
   GUIDE TO INSTRUCTION ON THE PIANOFORTE, A --IN A SERIES OF SHORT
O'TOOLE, WILLIAM
   CREATIVE PIANO TECHNIC

OREGON MUSIC TEACHERS ASSOCIATION
    PIANO MATERIALS
ORLIK, JULES
    CREATIVE APPROACH TO PIANO CLASS TEACHING, A --REPRODUCED FROM
PACE, ROBERT
    MUSIC ESSENTIALS FOR CLASSROOM TEACHERS--2ND. ED.---1961
PACE, ROBERT
    PIANO FOR CLASSROOM MUSIC--2ND. ED.---1956
PAIN, EVA
    BEGINNING TO PLAY THE PIANO..A MANUAL FOR TEACHERS
PALMER, ANNIE L.
    MUSIC TEACHERS' GUIDE TO THE GOLDBECK PIANO METHOD
PALMER, HORATIO R.
    PALMER'S PIANO PRIMER
PALMER, KING
    TEACH YOURSELF MUSIC
PASQUALI, NICOLO
    ART OF FINGERING THE HARPSICHORD, THE
PATTON, VICTOR S.
    LEARN TO PLAY POPULAR PIANO BY NOTE IN 20 EASY LESSONS...HOME
PEARCE, CHARLES WILLIAM
    ART OF THE PIANO TEACHER, THE
PEDERSON, GALE
    KEY TO THE KEYS..A SELF-TAUGHT PIANO METHOD FOR ADULTS AND TEEN
PERRY, ADELAIDE TROWBRIDGE *
    GUIDE TO PIANO STUDY FOR CLASS OR INDIVIDUAL INSTRUCTION, A
PETERSILIA, FRANZ
    STUDY WITH AMUSEMENT, A SERIES OF PROGRESSIVE LESSONS FOR THE
PETERSON, HOUSTON--EDITOR
    GREAT TEACHERS, PORTRAYED BY THOSE WHO STUDIED UNDER
PETRI, LILLIAN JEFFREY
    MIND OVER MUSCLE..A TECHNICAL ECONOMY FOR PIANISTS
PHILIPP, LILLIE H.
    PIANO STUDY..APPLICATION AND TECHNIQUE
PHILLIPSON, WENTWORTH
    GUIDE TO YOUNG PIANOFORTE TEACHERS AND STUDENTS
PICHIER, PAUL
    PIANIST'S TOUCH, THE ..METHOD AND THEORY OF PAUL PICHIER
PLAIDY, LOUIS
    PIANOFORTE TEACHER'S GUIDE, THE
PLAIDY, LOUIS
    PIANO TEACHER, THE
PLATT, CAROLYN
    CAROLYN PLATT METHOD FOR PIANO, THE --GROUP INSTRUCTION--TEACHER'S
PLAYFORD, JOHN
    MUSICKS HAND-MAID..NEW LESSONS AND INSTRUCTIONS FOR THE VIRGINALS
POINTER SYSTEM, INC.
    GUIDE TO THE MODERN PIANIST, A
PORTER, FRANK A. *
    TEACHERS' MANUAL FOR THE PORTER PIANOFORTE COURSE
POTAMKIN, FRANK
    MODERN PIANO PEDAGOGY
POWERS-WADSWORTH, L.
    PIANIST'S GUIDE TO TECHNICAL FREEDOM, THE ..2 VOLS. IN 1
PRATT, SILAS G.
    PIANIST'S MENTAL VELOCITY, THE ..A SYSTEMATIC PREPARATION OF THE
PRENTNER, MARIE
    MODERN PIANIST..BEING MY EXPERIENCES IN THE TECHNIQUE AND
PSTROKONSKY, JULES DE
    NEW METHOD OF TEACHING THE PIANOFORTE
PUGNO, RAOUL
    LESSONS OF RAOUL PUGNO, THE ..WITH A BIOGRAPHY OF CHOPIN BY M.
QUINN, MARCUS LUCIUS
    HOW TO STUDY MUSIC AND LEARN TO PLAY PIANO OR ORGAN
RAINBOW, BERNARR J. G.--EDITOR
    HANDBOOK FOR MUSIC TEACHERS--2 VOLS.
REEVES, BETTY
    OURSELVES AND OUR PUPILS--MONOGRAPH ON THE ART OF PIANO TEACHING,
REEVES, WILLIAM
    REEVES' POPULAR PIANOFORTE TUTOR..RUDIMENTS OF MUSIC, EXERCISES
REINECKE, KARL H.
    WHAT SHALL WE PLAY--NOT UNLIKE CZERNY'S 'LETTERS TO A YOUNG
RENAUD, EMILIANO
    RENAUD-PHONE PIANO METHOD..A PIANO COURSE THROUGH THE MEDIUM OF
REZITS, JOSEPH
    SOURCE MATERIALS FOR PIANO TECHNIQUES
RICHARDSON, NATHAN
    INKLINGS FOR THE LOVERS OF MUSIC, PART 1..CULTIVATION OF THE ART
RICHARDSON, NATHAN
    NEW METHOD FOR THE PIANOFORTE..ADDED, RUDIMENTS OF HARMONY AND
RICHTER, ADA
    TEACHING HINTS
RICKER, EARL
    MUSIC LESSONS FOR YOUR CHILD
RIEMANN, HUGO
    COMPARATIVE PIANOFORTE SCHOOL--4 BKS.---BK. 3 TRANSLATED BY J. C.
ROBBINS, EDGAR A.
    AMERICAN METHOD FOR THE PIANOFORTE
ROBERT, WALTER
    PIANO STUDY IN SOVIET-RUSSIAN SCHOOLS OF MUSIC--REPRINT..'JOURNAL
ROBILLIARD, EILEEN D.
    PERSISTENT PIANIST, THE ..A BOOK FOR THE LATE BEGINNER AND THE
ROBINSON, HELENE
    BASIC PIANO FOR ADULTS
ROBYN, LOUISE
    HOW TO TEACH PIANO TO THE CHILD BEGINNER..A TEXT BOOK FOR TEACHERS
RODMAN, MOLLY C.
    LET'S TRY SOMETHING NEW..A BOOK OF RECITAL AND TEACHING IDEAS FOR
ROOT, CATHERINE ADAMS *
    LISTEN, SING AND PLAY..CLASS LESSONS FOR PIANO AND VOICE
ROWLEY, ALEC
    DO'S AND DONT'S FOR MUSICIANS..A HANDBOOK FOR TEACHERS AND
ROWLEY, ALEC
    PRACTICAL MUSICIANSHIP, A HANDBOOK FOR TEACHERS AND STUDENTS
ROWLEY, DAISY WOODRUFF
    NINE HUNDRED MODEL LESSONS FOR PIANO TEACHERS
RUBINSTEIN, BERYL
    OUTLINE OF PIANO PEDAGOGY--REV. ED.---1929
SAVLER, ROBERTA--EDITOR
    SELECTIONS FROM THE PIANO TEACHER, 1958-1963
SCHELLING, ERNEST *
    OXFORD PIANO COURSE, TEACHER'S FIRST MANUAL
SCHELLING, ERNEST *
    OXFORD PIANO COURSE, TEACHER'S SECOND MANUAL
SCHIRMER, G.
    NEW PIANO-TEACHER'S GUIDE..A GRADED AND CLASSIFIED LIST OF PIANO
SCHLIEDER, FREDERICK W.
    LYRIC COMPOSITION THROUGH IMPROVISATION--2 VOLS., 1927-1946
SCHNEIDER, HANS
    WORKING OF THE MIND IN PIANO TEACHING AND PLAYING, THE
SCHULTZ, ARNOLD
    RIDDLE OF THE PIANIST'S FINGER, THE
SCHUMANN, ROBERT
    ADVICE TO YOUNG MUSICIANS--FROM 'MUSIC AND MUSICIANS'---1876
SCHUMANN, ROBERT
    RULES AND MAXIMS FOR YOUNG MUSICIANS--FROM 'MUSIC AND MUSICIANS'

SCONCIA, JOHN A.
    ANALYTICAL INSTRUCTOR FOR THE PIANO FORTE, CONTAINING THE
SEROFF, VICTOR
    COMMON SENSE IN PIANO STUDY
SEYMOUR, HARRIET AYER
    HOME MUSIC LESSONS..HOW TO FIND YOUR MUSICAL SELF
SEYMOUR, HARRIET AYER
    HOW TO THINK MUSIC
SEYMOUR, HARRIET AYER
    PHILOSOPHY OF MUSIC, THE ..WHAT MUSIC CAN DO FOR YOU
SHERWOOD MUSIC SCHOOL
    PIANO LESSONS AND TESTS--4TH. REV. ED.---1945+
SHUTER, ROSAMUND
    PSYCHOLOGY OF MUSICAL ABILITY, THE
SKUTLEY, MILDRED A.
    MUSIC FOR YOU..A SUPPLEMENTAL WORK BOOK FOR INDIVIDUAL OR CLASS
SLENCZYNSKA, RUTH *
    MUSIC AT YOUR FINGERTIPS
SMELTZER, JEANNIE R.--COMPILER
    OUTLINES AND GRADES FOR THE USE OF PIANO TEACHERS
SMITH, A. G. WARREN
    BEGINNER'S GUIDE, THE ..FOR ALL COMMENCING THE STUDY OF THE
SMITH, EDWIN S.
    PIANO BY EAR
SMITH, HOWARD G.
    ANYONE CAN PLAY THE PIANO BY EAR IN FIVE EASY LESSONS..A-B-C PIANO
SMITH, THOMAS
    HOW TO LEARN TO PLAY THE PIANO WELL
SMITH, VERA K.
    YOUNG PIANO TEACHER, WITH 75 HELPFUL TEACHING QUESTIONS, THE
SMITHERS, WELSFORD
    PIANO TEACHER'S GUIDE, THE ..A HUNDRED QUESTIONS FOR YOUNG
SORABJI, KAIKHOSRU
    AROUND MUSIC---PACHMAN, CHOPIN AND LISZT
SOREL, CLAUDETTE *
    INDEPENDENT LEARNING APPROACH TO PIANO SIGHT READING, AN
SQUIRE, RUSSEL N. *
    CLASS PIANO FOR ADULT BEGINNERS--2ND. ED.---1964
STANLEY, JANE
    BASIC ROUTINES IN ELEMENTARY PIANO TEACHING THROUGH THE FIRST
STARKEY, EVELYN
    PIANO CLASS WORKBOOK FOR FIRST YEAR STUDENTS
STARR, WILLIAM J. *
    BASIC PIANO TECHNIQUE FOR THE CLASSROOM TEACHER
STEINER, ERIC
    MASTER TUNES AND MUSIC TESTS FOR THE PIANO STUDENT
STEVENS, A. M.
    HOW TO PLAY THE PIANO AND ORGAN..OR, KEY TO THE SCIENCE AND THEORY
STEWART, REID
    HOW TO PASS MUSIC EXAMINATIONS--PIANO--A GUIDE FOR TEACHERS AND
STORMEN, WIN
    POPULAR PIANO SELF-TAUGHT---1956
STUCKENSCHMIDT, HANS H.
    FERRUCCIO BUSONI..CHRONICLE OF A EUROPEAN---1967, IN GERMAN
SUDDS, WILLIAM F.
    NATIONAL SCHOOL FOR PIANOFORTE, THE
SUMMY-BIRCHARD COMPANY
    HANDBOOK FOR PIANO TEACHERS..COLLECTED ARTICLES ON SUBJECTS
SUR, WILLIAM R.--EDITOR
    KEYBOARD EXPERIENCE AND PIANO CLASS INSTRUCTION
SUR, WILLIAM R.--EDITOR
    PIANO INSTRUCTION IN THE SCHOOLS
SUTHERLAND, ADELAIDE K.--COMPILER
    WHAT SHALL I PLAY..PREFERENCES FOR PIANO AND ORGAN..GUIDE TO
SWENSON, LUCILE B.
    DISCOVERING THE PIANO..THE MULTIPLE KEY APPROACH..STUDY GUIDE AND
SWISHER, WALTER SAMUEL
    PSYCHOLOGY FOR THE MUSIC TEACHER
TANKARD, GEOFFREY
    SPECIMEN ANSWERS TO THE QUESTIONS IN PIANOFORTE DIPLOMAS
TAPPER, THOMAS
    EDUCATION OF THE MUSIC TEACHER, THE
TAYLER, E. DOUGLAS
    MIND-POWER IN MUSIC FOR STUDENTS, TEACHERS AND PERFORMERS
TAYLOR, GEORGE C.
    FIRST STEPS TO THE PIANOFORTE
TERWILLIGER, GORDON B.
    PIANO TEACHERS PROFESSIONAL HANDBOOK
THIMAN, ERIC H.
    PIANOFORTE TESTS IN INITIATIVE AND INTELLIGENCE AS SET IN DIPLOMA
THOMPSON, JOHN
    TEACHING PIANO IN CLASSES
TOBIN, JOSEPH RAYMOND
    FUN WITH FINGERING, A FIRST-OF-ALL BOOK ON EASY FINGERING AND
TOBIN, JOSEPH RAYMOND
    PREPARING FOR KEYBOARD TESTS IN MUSICIANSHIP EXAMINATIONS, JUNIOR
TOWNSEND, WILLIAM
    MODERN PIANO TEACHING
VAN DER WEYDE, PETER H.
    INSTRUCTIONS IN PLAYING THE PIANO-FORTE WITH AEOLIAN ATTACHMENT
VILLOING, ALEXANDER
    RUBINSTEIN'S FINGER EXERCISES..TECHNICAL STUDIES FROM THE
VINING, HARRISON S.
    SIMPLE AND COMPLETE PRIMER FOR THE PIANOFORTE, THE
VIRGIL, ALMON K.
    EDUCATION IN MUSIC..LESSONS TO TEACHERS IN THE INSTRUCTION OF
VIRGIL, ALMON K.
    FOUNDATION EXERCISES IN PIANO PLAYING FROM FIRST RUDIMENTS TO
VIRGIL, ALMON K.
    PUPIL'S RECORD BOOK, THE ..SHOWING HOW TO SUCCEED AND HOW TO FAIL
VIRGIL, ALMON K.
    SPECIAL TECHNIC COURSE IN THE VIRGIL CLAVIER METHOD--6 PTS.
VIRGIL, ALMON K.
    STEP BY STEP..TEXTBOOK IN PIANO PLAYING..HANDBOOK FOR TEACHERS
VIRGIL, ALMON K.
    VIRGIL CLAVIER METHOD, THE --2 VOLS.
VISUOLA CORPORATION
    BLAZING A NEW TRAIL IN PIANO PLAYING
WAIT, WILLIAM B.
    NORMAL COURSE OF PIANO TECHNIC, THE
WALKER, ALAN--EDITOR
    FRANZ LISZT, THE MAN AND HIS MUSIC---ESSAYS BY SACHEVERALL SITWELL
WARRINER, JOHN
    HANDBOOK ON THE ART OF TEACHING AS APPLIED TO MUSIC..FOR THE USE
WASHINGTON STATE MUSIC TEACHERS ASSOCIATION
    PIANO TEACHING GUIDE--GRADES 1-8
WEBBE, WILLIAM H.
    PIANISTS' 'ABC' PRIMER AND GUIDE--WITH AN APPENDIX
WELBOURNE, EVE V.
    WELBOURNE WAY TO HOBBY PIANO PLAYING FOR ADULTS, THE --9 LESSONS
WELLS, HOWARD
    EARS, BRAIN AND FINGERS..A TEXT BOOK FOR PIANO TEACHERS AND PUPILS
WELSH, J. ROBERT
    MAKING MUSIC AT THE KEYBOARD..BEGINNING PIANO...CLASS...AND EAR
WEST, GEORGE FREDERICK
    HINTS TO YOUNG TEACHERS OF THE PIANOFORTE

WESTERBY, HERBERT
LISZT, COMPOSER, AND HIS PIANO WORKS..DESCRIPTIVE GUIDE AND
WHEELER, BERTHA H.
MIND AND MECHANISM..THOUGHTS ON TEACHING AND THE PIANISTIC ART
WHITESIDE, ABBY
INDISPENSABLES OF PIANO PLAYING--2ND. ED.---1955
WHITESIDE, ABBY
MASTERING THE CHOPIN ETUDES AND OTHER ESSAYS
WHITESIDE, ABBY
PIANIST'S MECHANISM, THE
WHITFORD, ROBERT
PIANO AND ITS MUSIC, THE --FROM 'MODERN PIANO COURSE'
WHITING, ARTHUR B.
LESSON OF THE CLAVICHORD, THE --REPRINT..'NEW MUSIC REVIEW'
WIECK, FRIEDRICH
PIANO AND SONG..HOW TO TEACH, HOW TO LEARN, AND HOW TO FORM A
WIER, ALBERT
PIANO, THE ..ITS HISTORY, MAKERS, PLAYERS AND MUSIC
WILKINS-GUTMANN, EMMA
TALKS WITH PIANO TEACHERS
WILLIAMS, GUY BEVIER
PIANISM..A COURSE IN NORMAL TRAINING
WILLIAMS, JEAN E.
MODERN METHOD OF PIANO INSTRUCTION, A ..TEACHERS MANUAL
WILLIAMS, JOHN M.
WHAT TO TEACH AT THE VERY FIRST LESSON
WILLIS, AUBREY
AUBREY WILLIS HOME STUDY COURSE IN PIANO TUNING AND REPAIRING
WILLS, VERA G. *
PARENT'S GUIDE TO MUSIC LESSONS, A
WILSON, MORRIS E.
HOW TO HELP YOUR CHILD WITH MUSIC--2ND. ED.---1951
WILSON, MORRIS E.
HOW TO PLAY BY EAR
WOLFF, ERNST VICTOR
WITH REASON AND RHYME
WOLLENHAUPT, HEINRICH
METHOD FOR THE PIANOFORTE AND METHODICAL GUIDE FOR THE PIANO FORTE
WOLLNER, GERTRUDE PRICE
IMPROVISATION IN MUSIC..WAYS TOWARDS CAPTURING MUSICAL IDEAS AND
WOODHOUSE, GEORGE
NEW PATH FOR PIANISTS, A ..THE MUTANO--MUTE PIANO--SYSTEM, ETC.
WRIGHT, WILLIAM C.
GOLDEN MONITOR, FOR THE PIANOFORTE AND CABINET ORGAN, DESIGNED AS
ZIMMERMAN, ALEX H. *
BASIC PIANO FOR THE COLLEGE STUDENT
ZUCH, ANNETT V. *
PIANO TEACHER, THE ..A BOOK OF SELF-INSTRUCTION

Piano Technique

AGUILAR, EMANUEL
LITTLE BOOK ABOUT LEARNING THE PIANOFORTE, A
AHRENS, CORA B. *
FOR ALL PIANO TEACHERS
ALLEN, MARGARET *
CREATIVE MOTION
AMEY, ELLEN
CONSCIOUS CONTROL IN PIANO STUDY
ANDERSON, J. CLARK
GOOD MUSIC EXPLAINED..WHAT ALL GOOD PIANISTS SHOULD KNOW
ANON
COMPLEAT TUTOR FOR THE HARPSICHORD OR SPINNET, WHEREIN IS SHEWN
ANON
ESSAY ON THE CHIROGYMNAST..OR, FINGER EXERCISES APPLIED TO...ALL
ANON
FASHIONABLE PRECEPTOR, FOR THE PIANO-FORTE AND HARPSICHORD,
ANON
GENERAL OBSERVATIONS ON MUSIC AND REMARKS ON MR. LOGIER'S SYSTEM
ANON
GUIDE TO THE MUSICAL TUITION OF VERY YOUNG CHILDREN, BY AN OLD
ANON
NEW AND COMPLETE INSTRUCTIONS FOR THE HARPSICHORD, PIANO FORTE OR
ANON
NEW INSTRUCTIONS FOR PLAYING THE HARPSICHORD, PIANOFORTE OR
ANON
PLAYING THE HARPSICHORD, SPINET OR PIANO FORTE MADE EASY BY NEW
ANON
PRECEPTOR, FOR THE PIANOFORTE, THE ORGAN OR HARPSICHORD, THE
ARNIM, ANNA L.
COMPLETE COURSE OF WRIST AND FINGER GYMNASTICS, A --3RD.
AULD, WILDA J.
HANDBOOK FOR THE CHURCH PIANIST, A
AXTENS, FLORENCE
PIANO CLASS METHOD..THE FIRST TWELVE MONTHS IN THE PIANO CLASS
BABBITT, WILLIAM
PHYSIOLOGICAL METHOD FOR PLAYING THE PIANO-FORTE, DESIGNED AS A
BABITZ, SOL
ON USING EARLY KEYBOARD FINGERING--REPRINT OF 3 ARTICLES FROM THE
BACH, CARL PHILIPP EMANUEL
ESSAY ON THE TRUE ART OF PLAYING KEYBOARD INSTRUMENTS---TWO PTS.,
BACON, ERNST
NOTES ON THE PIANO
BAKER, DAVID
JAZZ IMPROVISATION..A COMPREHENSIVE METHOD OF STUDY FOR ALL
BANTLY, BENEDICT
SIMPLE TREATISE ON SCALES AND ARPEGGIOS FOR PIANO, A --3 VOLS.
BARNETT, DAVID
PERFORMANCE OF MUSIC, THE ..A STUDY IN TERMS OF THE PIANOFORTE
BARNWELL, V. T.
BARNWELL'S NORMAL KEYBOARD AND STAFF STUDIES--THE MENTAL
BARTH, HANS
TECHNIC..FOR DEVELOPING AN EARLY FOUNDATION IN PIANO PLAYING
BARTH, HANS
TECHNIC..THE ENTIRE 25 BRANCHES FOR DEVELOPING TECHNIC NECESSARY
BARTHELEMON, FRANCOIS H.
NEW TUTOR FOR THE HARPSICHORD OR PIANO FORTE, WHEREIN THE FIRST
BASTIEN, JAMES W. *
BEGINNING PIANO FOR ADULTS
BAUER, HAROLD
PIANIST'S WARMING-UP EXERCISES FOR THE MAINTENANCE AND IMPROVEMENT
BECKERMAN, H. J.
AMERICAN SCHOOL OF RAGTIME PIANO PLAYING, THE
BEMETZRIEDER, ANTON
ACCOUNT OF A NEW WAY OF CONSIDERING MUSICK, AND TEACHING
BEMETZRIEDER, ANTON
GAMUT AND COMMON CHORD IN ALL KEYS, FINGERED FOR THE HARPSICHORD,
BEMETZRIEDER, ANTON
NEW GUIDE TO MUSIC, IN FRENCH AND ENGLISH, A
BENNER, LORA
BENNER GOLD BOOK, THE ..PIANO MATERIAL AND TEACHING METHODS--3RD.
BERGER, FRANCESCO
FIRST STEPS AT THE PIANOFORTE

BERTINI, HENRI
BERTINI'S SELF-TEACHING CATECHISM OF MUSIC FOR THE PIANOFORTE
BLOCKLEY, JOHN
PIANIST'S CATECHISM, THE ---1880
BOLTON, HETTY
HOW TO PRACTICE
BOLTON, HETTY
ON TEACHING THE PIANO
BONPENSIERE, LUIGI
NEW PATHWAYS TO PIANO TECHNIQUE..A STUDY OF THE RELATIONS BETWEEN
BOOTH, VICTOR
WE PIANO TEACHERS--REVISED BY ADELE FRANKLIN---1946
BOWEN, CAROLYN
OUTLINES FOR TRAINING PIANO TEACHERS
BOWEN, YORK
PEDALLING THE MODERN PIANOFORTE---1936
BOWEN, YORK
SIMPLICITY OF PIANO TECHNIQUE, THE
BRANDT, LEONIE
SCIENCE IN MODERN PIANOFORTE PLAYING
BRECKENRIDGE, WILLIAM KILGORE
HINTS FOR PIANO NORMAL STUDIES
BREE, MADAME MALWINE
GROUNDWORK OF THE LESCHETIZKY METHOD, THE ---1902
BREITHAUPT, RUDOLPH MARIA
NATURAL PIANO-TECHNIC..SCHOOL OF WEIGHT TOUCH--2 VOLS.
BRIGGS, GILBERT A.
PIANOS, PIANISTS AND SONICS
BRIGHAM, ELEANOR
SCALES..THEIR HISTORY, THEORY, FINGERING AND TECHNICAL USE ON THE
BROTHERHOOD, JAMES
BROTHERHOOD 'TECHNICON' AND HOW TO USE IT, THE
BROTHERHOOD, JAMES
DEVELOPMENT OF THE HAND FOR PIANO-FORTE PLAYING BY MEANS OF A
BROTHERHOOD, JAMES
KNOWLEDGE OF THE RELATION OF PHYSIOLOGY AND ANATOMY TO PIANO
BROTHERHOOD, JAMES
MUSCLES USED IN PIANO-PLAYING..WITH EXPLANATORY NOTES AND DIAGRAMS
BROTHERHOOD, JAMES
SCIENCE AND ART AS TWIN SISTERS..BEING A SECOND TREATISE UPON THE
BROTHERHOOD, JAMES
SENSITIVE PIANO TOUCH AND WAYS AND MEANS TO ITS ACQUIREMENT---A
BROTHERHOOD, JAMES
TECHNICON, THE..A TREATISE UPON THE DEVELOPMENT OF PIANOFORTE
BROWER, HARRIETTE
ART OF THE PIANIST, THE
BROWER, HARRIETTE
HOW A DEPENDABLE PIANO TECHNIQUE WAS WON
BROWER, HARRIETTE
PIANO MASTERY..TALKS WITH MASTER PIANISTS AND TEACHERS...
BROWER, HARRIETTE
PIANO MASTERY, SECOND SERIES
BROWER, HARRIETTE
SELF-HELP IN PIANO STUDY
BROWN, JEAN PARKMAN
INTERVALS, CHORDS AND EAR TRAINING FOR YOUNG PIANOFORTE STUDENTS
BRUXNER, MERVYN
MASTERING THE PIANO
BUCHAROFF, SIMON
MODERN PIANIST'S TEXT BOOK, THE
BUCK, PERCY
PSYCHOLOGY FOR MUSICIANS
BUCKLEY, OLIVIA DUSSEK
MUSICAL TRUTHS..OR, AN ANALYSIS OF MUSIC AND AN ESSAY ON THE PAST
BUELOW, HANS GUIDO VON
APPLIED PIANO TECHNIC..300 EXTRACTS FOR DAILY PRACTICE FROM
BUONAMICI, GIUSEPPE
ART OF SCALE STUDY FOR THE PIANOFORTE, THE ...AS TAUGHT TO HIS
BURROWES, JOHN FRECKLETON
GUIDE TO PRACTICE ON THE PIANOFORTE
CALAND, ELIZABETH
ARTISTIC PIANO PLAYING, AS TAUGHT BY LUDWIG DEPPE
CALLENDER, ROMAINE
TEACHER'S MANUAL, A WORK DESIGNED TO SUPPLEMENT...'THE FIRST TEN
CAMPBELL, LE ROY B.
TRUE FUNCTION OF RELAXATION IN PIANO PLAYING, THE
CAMPBELL, LE ROY B.
VELOCITY PLUS
CARMIENCKE, ALBERT G.
MECHANICS OF PIANO PLAYING, THE
CARPE, ADOLPH
PIANIST AND THE ART OF MUSIC, THE ..A TREATISE ON PIANO PLAYING
CARR, BENJAMIN
ANALYTICAL INSTRUCTOR FOR THE PIANO FORTE, OP. 15, THE --IN 3 PTS.
CARRE, JOHN
PSYCHOLOGY OF PIANO TEACHING, THE ..A TEXTBOOK FOR TEACHERS,
CARRENO, TERESA
POSSIBILITIES OF TONE COLOR BY ARTISTIC USE OF PEDALS
CARTER, BUENTA
BEGINNER'S PIANO BOOK FOR OLDER STUDENTS...DESIGNED FOR THE OLDER
CARUTHERS, JULIA LOIS
PIANO TECHNIC FOR CHILDREN
CARY, MRS. C. S. P.
PIANO-FORTE CLASS BOOK, CONTAINING PRACTICAL RUDIMENTAL LESSONS
CASTELLINI, JOHN EDWARD
RUDIMENTS OF MUSIC..A NEW APPROACH WITH APPLICATION TO THE
CHAPOL, SIMON
NEW APPROACH TO THE STUDY OF THE PIANOFORTE, A ---IN ITALIAN AND
CHASE, MARY WOOD
NATURAL LAWS IN PIANO TECHNIC
CHEYETTE, IRVING
BASIC PIANO FOR THE MUSIC EDUCATOR AND CLASSROOM TEACHER
CHING, JAMES
AMATEUR PIANIST'S COMPANION, THE
CHING, JAMES
CANDIDATE'S COMPANION TO THE EXERCISES, SCALES, BROKEN CHORDS,
CHING, JAMES
FOREARM ROTATION---A SEQUEL TO 'THE ROTARY ROAD'--15 PHOTOS AND
CHING, JAMES
MUSCULAR RELAXATION, A SIMPLE EXPLANATION
CHING, JAMES
ON TEACHING PIANO TECHNIQUE TO CHILDREN
CHING, JAMES
PIANO PLAYING, A PRACTICAL METHOD--A NEW EDITION OF 'PIANO
CHING, JAMES
PIANO TECHNIQUE..FOUNDATION PRINCIPLES
CHING, JAMES
POINTS ON PEDALLING
CHING, JAMES
ROTARY ROAD, AN EASY PILGRIMAGE BY EIGHT SHORT STEPS, THE
CHING, JAMES
SIDELIGHTS ON TOUCH..TOGETHER WITH 101 QUESTIONS, SUITABLE FOR
CHING, JAMES
STUDIES FOR BASIC PIANO TECHNIQUE..WRITTEN AND SELECTED WITH
CHING, JAMES
TEACHING OF TECHNIQUE TO CHILDREN, THE --4 PTS.

CHING, JOAN ELIZABETH
    APPROACH TO PIANO TEACHING---ALSO CATALOGUED UNDER
CHITY, R.
    NEW SCHOOL OF SCALE PLAYING--COLOR PATTERNS
CHRISTIANI, ADOLPH FRIEDRICH
    PRINCIPLES OF EXPRESSION IN PIANOFORTE PLAYING, THE
CHURCHILL, VIRGINIA PEAKES
    MODERN TEACHER'S GUIDE TO PIANO AND PIANO CLASS TEACHING
CHURCHILL, VIRGINIA PEAKES
    NINETEEN FIFTY-SIX SUPPLEMENT TO THE MODERN TEACHER'S GUIDE TO
CLEMENTI, MUZIO
    INTRODUCTION TO THE ART OF PLAYING ON THE PIANOFORTE---1801+
COHEN, HARRIET
    MUSIC'S HANDMAID
COOKE, CHARLES
    PLAYING THE PIANO FOR PLEASURE--REV. ED.---1941
COOKE, JAMES FRANCIS
    GREAT MEN AND FAMOUS MUSICIANS ON THE ART OF MUSIC
COOKE, JAMES FRANCIS
    GREAT PIANISTS ON PIANO PLAYING..STUDY TALKS WITH FOREMOST
COPP, EVELYN A.
    WHAT IS THE FLETCHER MUSIC METHOD
CORTOT, ALFRED
    RATIONAL PRINCIPLES OF PIANOFORTE TECHNIQUE
COUPERIN, FRANCOIS
    ART DE TOUCHER LE CLAVECIN, L' ---IN FRENCH, GERMAN AND ENGLISH
COVIELLO, AMBROSE
    FOUNDATIONS OF PIANOFORTE TECHNIC
COVIELLO, AMBROSE
    WHAT MATTHAY MEANT
CRAMER, JOHN BAPTIST
    INSTRUCTIONS FOR THE PIANOFORTE---CONTAINS ALSO A SET OF 28
CROUCH, M. S.
    SYSTEMATIC FINGERING OF THE ARPEGGIOS OF COMMON CHORDS, ETC., THE
CURCIO, LOUISE
    MUSICIAN'S HANDBOOK FOR THE DEVELOPMENT OF MANUAL SUPPLENESS AND
CURCIO, LOUISE
    SINGLE NOTE, THE
CURWEN, ANNIE JESSY
    PSYCHOLOGY APPLIED TO MUSIC TEACHING
CURWEN, ANNIE JESSY
    TEACHER'S GUIDE...TO MRS. CURWEN'S PIANOFORTE METHOD, 'THE CHILD
CZERNY, CARL
    COMPLETE THEORETICAL AND PRACTICAL PIANO FORTE SCHOOL, FROM THE
CZERNY, CARL
    LETTERS TO A YOUNG LADY ON THE ART OF PLAYING THE PIANOFORTE
D'ABREU, GERALD
    PLAYING THE PIANO WITH CONFIDENCE---1964
DAHL, ANTON
    SOUL OF GENIUS, THE ..ITS MUSICAL DEVELOPMENT AND HOW THE WORLD AT
DALE, KATHLEEN
    NINETEENTH CENTURY PIANO MUSIC, A HANDBOOK FOR PIANISTS
DANIELS, BESS *
    WORLD OF MUSIC, THE ..PIANO COURSE..TEACHERS' BOOK, FOR CLASS OR
DENHAM, GEORGE
    MASTERY OF THE KEYBOARD
DEUTSCH, LEONHARD
    PIANO..GUIDED SIGHT-READING
DE SOLIS, SOLITO
    THREE POSITIONS OF HARMONIZED SCALES, THE --SHOWN IN ALL KEYS
DE WITT, EDYTHE
    EDYTHE DE WITT'S METHOD FOR CLASS PIANO...WRITTEN TO GIVE CORRECT
DICKERSON, RUTH A.
    NEW APPROACH TO PIANO TECHNIQUE, A
DILLER, ANGELA
    SPLENDOR OF MUSIC, THE
DOBBIE, E. A.
    AUSTRALIAN PIANOFORTE TUTOR
DOLMETSCH, ARNOLD
    INTERPRETATION OF MUSIC OF THE SEVENTEENTH AND EIGHTEENTH
DRAKE, KENNETH
    SONATAS OF BEETHOVEN AS HE PLAYED AND TAUGHT THEM, THE
DUCKWORTH, GUY
    KEYBOARD MUSICIANSHIP
DUFFEE, GERTRUDE BANKS
    PIANO STUDY..A GUIDE TO TEACHER AND STUDENT
DUMESNIL, MAURICE
    HOW TO PLAY AND TEACH DEBUSSY
DUMM, ROBERT W.
    IN BLACK AND WHITE
DUNN, JOHN PETRIE
    BASIS OF PIANOFORTE PLAYING, THE
DUSSEK, JOHANN L.
    DUSSEK'S INSTRUCTIONS ON THE ART OF PLAYING THE PIANOFORTE OR
EBERHARDT, GOBY
    MY SYSTEM FOR PRACTICING THE VIOLIN AND PIANO, BASED UPON
EHRENFECTER, C. A.
    TECHNICAL STUDY IN THE ART OF PIANOFORTE PLAYING--DEPPE'S
EHRLICH, ALFRED HEINRICH
    HOW TO PRACTICE ON THE PIANO..REFLECTIONS AND SUGGESTIONS
EISENBERG, JACOB
    ARTISTIC PIANIST, THE ..NATURAL TECHNICS IN PIANO MASTERY..FROM
EISENBERG, JACOB
    WEIGHT AND RELAXATION METHOD FOR THE PIANOFORTE
ENGEL, CARL
    PIANIST'S HANDBOOK, THE ..A GUIDE FOR THE RIGHT COMPREHENSION AND
ENGELBRECHT, J. G.
    MATERIA MUSICA, OR MATERIALS FOR THE PIANIST..A CLASS BOOK
EVERHART, POWELL
    PIANIST'S ART, THE ..A COMPREHENSIVE MANUAL ON PIANO PLAYING FOR
FALKENER, ROBERT
    INSTRUCTIONS FOR PLAYING THE HARPSICHORD..WHEREIN IS FULLY
FAY, AMY
    DEPPE FINGER EXERCISES FOR RAPIDLY DEVELOPING AN ARTISTIC TOUCH IN
FERGUSON, DONALD NIVISON
    PIANO MUSIC OF SIX GREAT COMPOSERS---1947
FIELDEN, THOMAS
    MARKS AND REMARKS..MUSICAL EXAMINATIONS AND THEIR PROBLEMS
FIELDEN, THOMAS
    NEW APPROACH TO SCALES AND ARPEGGIOS, A
FIELDEN, THOMAS
    SCIENCE OF PIANOFORTE TECHNIC, THE --2ND. REV. ED.---1927
FILLMORE, JOHN C.
    PIANOFORTE MUSIC..ITS HISTORY, WITH BIOGRAPHICAL SKETCHES AND
FOLDES, ANDOR
    KEYS TO THE KEYBOARD, A BOOK FOR PIANISTS
FOOTE, ARTHUR W.
    SOME PRACTICAL THINGS IN PIANO PLAYING
FORD, DONALD
    SINGING CLASS PIANIST AND ON PIANOFORTE ACCOMPANYING IN GENERAL,
FRISKIN, JAMES
    PRINCIPLES OF PIANOFORTE PRACTICE, THE
FROST, EDWARD
    THALBEGARIAN (SIC) EXERCISES..OR, THE PIANIST'S DESIDERATA
FULLER, JANET E.
    COMPLETE KNOWLEDGE OF PIANO TECHNIQUE, A

GALLICO, PAOLO
    NEW METHOD FOR SYNCHRONIZED SCALE FINGERINGS, A
GARRATT, PERCIVAL
    ART OF PIANOFORTE PLAYING, THE
GARROWAY, WILL
    PIANISM
GAT, JOZSEF
    TECHNIQUE OF PIANO PLAYING, THE, --2ND. ED.---1958
GEARY, ELEANOR MARGARET
    MUSICAL EDUCATION, WITH PRACTICAL OBSERVATIONS ON THE ART OF
GEBHARD, HEINRICH
    ART OF PEDALLING, THE
GEIB, WILLIAM
    GEIB'S PIANO-FORTE PRECEPTOR, AND MUSICAL GRAMMAR...A TREATISE ON
GERMER, HEINRICH
    HOW OUGHT ONE TO STUDY PIANO-TECHNIC---1881, IN GERMAN
GERMER, HEINRICH
    MANUAL OF TONE-PRODUCTION IN PIANOFORTE PLAYING, FROM 'TECHNICS OF
GERMER, HEINRICH
    TECHNICS OF PIANOFORTE PLAYING, THE ..MUSICAL ORNAMENTATION,
GERMER, HEINRICH
    TECHNICS OF PIANOFORTE PLAYING REARRANGED AS A METHODICAL PLAN OF
GERMER, HEINRICH
    THEORETICO-PRACTICAL ELEMENTARY PIANO-FORTE SCHOOL FOR STUDENTS OF
GIDDINGS, THADDEUS P.
    GIDDING'S PUBLIC SCHOOL CLASS METHOD FOR THE PIANO
GIESEKING, WALTER *
    PIANO TECHNIQUE---COMBINED REPUBLICATION OF..'THE SHORTEST WAY TO
GILBERT, RUSSELL S.
    EMBRYO MUSICIAN, THE ..A METHOD OF INTRODUCING MUSIC TO LITTLE
GILLESPIE, JOHN
    FIVE CENTURIES OF KEYBOARD MUSIC..AN HISTORIC SURVEY FOR
GLASFORD, IRENE A.
    RHYTHM, REASON AND RESPONSE FOR THE MUSICIAN, PIANIST AND TEACHER
GORDON, STEPHEN T.
    GORDON'S NEW SCHOOL FOR THE PIANO-FORTE
GRABILL, ETHELBERT WARREN
    MECHANICS OF PIANO TECHNIC, THE
GRAHAM, JAMES L.
    MUSIC MADE EASY, PIANOFORTE TUTOR ON A NEW PLAN
GRAUPNER, GOTTLIEB
    RUDIMENTS OF THE ART OF PLAYING ON THE PIANOFORTE...A PLAIN
GRIFFIN, SISTER MARY ANNAROSE
    PIANO MATERIALS..GRADED AND COMPILED AS AN AID TO INSTRUCTORS
GRUNDY, ENID
    HAPPY PIANIST, THE
HAMBOURG, MARK
    HOW TO PLAY THE PIANO--NEW AND ENLARGED EDITION OF 'HOW TO BECOME
HAMBOURG, MARK
    HOW TO PREPARE FOR PLAYING IN CONCERT
HAMILTON, CLARENCE G.
    PIANO TEACHING..ITS PRINCIPLES AND PROBLEMS
HAMILTON, CLARENCE G.
    TOUCH AND EXPRESSION IN PIANO PLAYING
HAMILTON, CLARENCE G.
    WHAT EVERY PIANO PUPIL SHOULD KNOW
HANSMANN, RICHARD
    THEORETICAL AND PRACTICAL PIANO-FORTE SCHOOL FOR THE JANKO
HARICH-SCHNEIDER, ETA
    HARPSICHORD, THE ..AN INTRODUCTION TO TECHNIQUE, STYLE AND THE
HARKNESS, ROBERT
    BEGINNERS PIANO COURSE IN HYMN PLAYING BY CORRESPONDENCE
HARKNESS, ROBERT
    HARKNESS PIANO METHOD OF EVANGELISTIC HYMN PLAYING, THE ..A
HARRISON, SIDNEY
    BEGINNING TO PLAY THE PIANO--A TEACHER'S HANDBOOK, INCLUDING THE
HARRISON, SIDNEY
    PIANO TECHNIQUE
HARRISON, SIDNEY
    YOUNG PERSON'S GUIDE TO PLAYING THE PIANO, THE
HARVEY, ROBERT
    MAGIC KEY TO KEYBOARD SUCCESS, THE
HECK, JOHANN CASPAR
    ART OF FINGERING, THE ..OR, THE EASIEST AND SUREST METHOD HOW TO
HEERINGEN, ERNEST VON
    CELEBRATED INSTRUCTION BOOK FOR THE PIANOFORTE, CONTAINING THE
HEIDELBERGER, PAULINE
    MASTER METHOD..PIANO NORMAL AND TEACHER'S MANUAL
HELD, ERNST
    RULES AND REASONS FOR CORRECT SCALE-FINGERING
HELMANN, JACOB N.
    CONSCIOUSLY CONTROLLED PIANO TONE, THE --REV. ED.---1950
HENDERSON, WILLIAM JAMES
    PRELUDES AND STUDIES..MUSICAL THEMES OF THE DAY--SECTION 3..THE
HERZ, HENRI
    MEISSNER'S MODERN, PRACTICAL SYSTEM OF TUNING THE PIANOFORTE..WITH
HERZ, HENRI
    NEW AND COMPLETE PIANOFORTE SCHOOL
HIPKINS, ALFRED JAMES
    HOW CHOPIN PLAYED...FROM CONTEMPORARY IMPRESSIONS COLLECTED FROM
HOFFMAN, CARL
    HABIT IN PIANOFORTE PLAYING--ANALYTICAL STUDY OF CONTROL OF
HOFHEIMER, GRACE
    TEACHING TECHNIQUES FOR THE PIANO
HOFMANN, JOSEF
    PIANO PLAYING..A LITTLE BOOK OF SIMPLE SUGGESTIONS--REPRINTED FROM
HOFMANN, JOSEF
    PIANO PLAYING, WITH PIANO QUESTIONS ANSWERED---PUBLISHED EARLIER
HOOK, JAMES
    GUIDA DI MUSICA..SECOND PART, CONSISTING OF SEVERAL HUNDRED
HOPE, ERIC
    AIDS TO TECHNIQUE
HOPE, ERIC
    HANDBOOK OF PIANO PLAYING, A
HORROCKS, CYRIL R. H.
    STUDENT'S GUIDE TO THE ART OF TEACHING THE PIANOFORTE, THE --2ND.
HOWARD, GEORGE HENRY
    OUTLINE OF TECHNIQUE..A GUIDE IN THE THEORY AND PRACTICE OF
HOWE, JAMES H.
    PIANO-FORTE INSTRUCTOR, A ..OR, PREPARATORY SYSTEM OF PIANOFORTE
HUENTEN, FRANZ
    ABRIDGED EDITION OF F. HUENTEN'S CELEBRATED INSTRUCTIONS FOR THE
HULL, ARTHUR EAGLEFIELD
    THREE HUNDRED QUESTIONS ON PIANOFORTE TEACHING IN 30 GRADUATED
HUMMEL, JOHANN NEPOMUK
    COMPLETE THEORETICAL AND PRACTICAL COURSE OF INSTRUCTIONS ON THE
HUTCHESON, ERNEST
    ELEMENTS OF PIANO TECHNIQUE, THE
HUTCHESON, ERNEST *
    LITERATURE OF THE PIANO, THE ..A GUIDE FOR AMATEUR AND
ISAACS, EDWARD
    BLIND PIANO TEACHER, THE
JACKSON, EDWIN WARD
    GYMNASTICS FOR THE FINGERS AND WRIST
JEANS, SIR JAMES HOPWOOD
    SCIENCE AND MUSIC

JEWETT, ALBERT DEWEY
IDIOMATIC COURSE OF PIANO INSTRUCTION FOR CLASS WORK
JOHNS, CLAYTON
ESSENTIALS OF PIANOFORTE PLAYING, THE
JOHNSON, REGINALD
COMMONSENSE IN SCALE AND ARPEGGIO PLAYING
JOHNSON, VERA A.
SCIENTIFIC SIDE OF MUSIC IN SIMPLE, PRACTICAL FORM FOR TEACHERS
JOHNSTONE, J. ALFRED
ART OF TEACHING PIANOFORTE PLAYING, THE --2ND. REV. ED.---1910
JOHNSTONE, J. ALFRED
ESSENTIALS IN PIANOFORTE PLAYING, AND OTHER MUSICAL STUDIES...
JOHNSTONE, J. ALFRED
TOUCH, PHRASING AND INTERPRETATION
JONAS, ALBERTO
MASTER SCHOOL OF MODERN PIANO PLAYING AND VIRTUOSITY--3 PARTS IN 7
JONAS, ALBERTO
PIANOSCRIPT BOOK..AN INVALUABLE AID TO TEACHER AND STUDENT IN
JONES, GRIFFITH
COMPLEAT INSTRUCTOR FOR THE HARPSICHORD OR PIANOFORTE, THE
KENYON, CHARLES FREDERICK
HOW TO MEMORIZE MUSIC
KIRBY, MAY B. KELLY
KELLY KIRBY KINDERGARTEN PIANO METHOD, TEACHERS' COURSE, THE
KLECZYNSKI, JAN
HOW TO PLAY CHOPIN--THREE LECTURES
KNOTT, THOMAS B.
PIANOFORTE FINGERING, ITS PRINCIPLES AND APPLICATIONS
KOCHEVITSKY, GEORGE
ART OF PIANO PLAYING, THE ..A SCIENTIFIC APPROACH
KRUSZYNSKI, MICHAL
APPROACH TO THE PSYCHOLOGY OF PIANO TEACHING, AN
KUERSTEINER, JEAN PAUL
EXPERT AID TO ARTISTIC PIANO PLAYING
KULLAK, ADOLPH
AESTHETICS OF PIANOFORTE PLAYING, THE ---1861 IN GERMAN--1ST.
KULLAK, ADOLPH
ART OF THE TOUCH, THE ..A WORK FOR THE USE OF ADVANCED PLAYERS AND
LAMAR, RICHARD
COLLEGE PIANO PEDAGOGY
LANDOWSKA, WANDA
LANDOWSKA ON MUSIC--EDITED BY DENISE RESTOUT
LANG, EDITH *
MUSICAL ACCOMPANIMENT OF MOVING PICTURES..A PRACTICAL MANUAL FOR
LAST, JOAN
INTERPRETATION FOR THE PIANO STUDENT
LAST, JOAN
YOUNG PIANIST, THE ..A NEW APPROACH FOR TEACHERS AND
LAWRENCE, FREDERIC LOCKE
RATIONALE OF PIANO TECHNIQUE, THE
LEFRANK, E.
HUMAN HAND, THE ..ITS CONSTRUCTION, MUSCLES, NERVES AND TENDONS IN
LEIMER, KARL *
RHYTHMICS, DYNAMICS, PEDAL, AND OTHER PROBLEMS OF PIANO
LEIMER, KARL *
SHORTEST WAY TO PIANISTIC PERFECTION, THE
LEVINE, HENRY
KNOW YOUR SCALES..FOR PIANO STUDENTS OF ALL GRADES
LEVINSKAYA, MARIA
LEVINSKAYA SYSTEM OF PIANOFORTE TECHNIC AND TONE COLOR, THE
LEWIS, THOMAS C.
PROTEST AGAINST THE MODERN DEVELOPMENT OF UNMUSICAL TONE, A
LE COUPPEY, FELIX
PIANO TEACHING..ADVICE TO PUPILS AND YOUNG TEACHERS---1868 IN
LHEVINNE, JOSEF
BASIC PRINCIPLES IN PIANOFORTE PLAYING---1924
LINDO, ALGERNON H. *
INDIVIDUALITY IN PIANO TOUCH
LOGIER, JOHANN BERNHARD
AUTHENTIC ACCOUNT OF THE EXAMINATION OF PUPILS, INSTRUCTED IN THE
LOGIER, JOHANN BERNHARD
COMPANION TO THE ROYAL PATENT CHIROPLAST, OR HAND-DIRECTOR, A ..A
LOGIER, JOHANN BERNHARD
EXPLANATION AND DESCRIPTION OF THE ROYAL PATENT CHIROPLAST, OR
LOGIER, JOHANN BERNHARD
FIRST COMPANION TO THE ROYAL PATENT CHIROPLAST OR HAND-DIRECTOR,
LOGIER, JOHANN BERNHARD
REFUTATION OF THE FALLACIES AND MISREPRESENTATIONS CONTAINED IN A
LOGIER, JOHANN BERNHARD
SEQUEL TO THE FIRST COMPANION TO THE CHIROPLAST
LOGIER, JOHANN BERNHARD
SHORT ACCOUNT OF THE PROGRESS OF J. B. LOGIER'S SYSTEM OF MUSICAL
LOGIER, JOHANN BERNHARD
SYLLABUS OF THE SECOND EXAMINATION OF MR. LOGIER'S PUPILS, ON HIS
LOMAS, LULU GRAHAM
FIRST TEN PIANO LESSONS, LAID OUT FOR YOUNG TEACHERS, WITH
LONDON--A COMMITTEE OF PROFESSORS
EXPOSITION OF THE MUSICAL SYSTEM OF MR. LOGIER..WITH STRICTURES ON
LONGSTREET, H. P.
PRACTICAL FINGER CONTROL--10TH. ED.
MACKINNON, LILIAS
MUSICAL SECRETS ON THE TECHNIQUE OF PIANO PLAYING
MACLEAN, CHARLES D.
PRINCIPLES OF PIANOFORTE PRACTICE, THE
MAIER, GUY
PIANO TEACHER'S COMPANION, THE
MAIER, GUY *
PLAYING THE PIANO--TEACHER'S MANUAL
MANHIRE, WILSON
CANDIDATE'S SCALE AND ARPEGGIO TESTS FOR THE PIANOFORTE, ETC., THE
MANHIRE, WILSON
EXAMINATION CANDIDATE'S GUIDE TO SCALE AND ARPEGGIO PLAYING, ETC.,
MANHIRE, WILSON
MODEL ANSWERS TO QUESTIONS ON 'TOUCH' FOR CANDIDATES PREPARING FOR
MANSFELDT, HUGO L.
TECHNIC..A SYSTEM OF THE MOST NECESSARY DAILY EXERCISES TO PRODUCE
MARIAL, R.
METHODS APPLICABLE TO GROUP TEACHING OR PRIVATE PIANO INSTRUCTION
MARKS, ADOLF B.
INTRODUCTION TO THE INTERPRETATION OF BEETHOVEN'S PIANO-FORTE
MARX, ADOLF BERNHARD
INTRODUCTION TO THE INTERPRETATION OF BEETHOVEN'S PIANO
MASON, DANIEL GREGORY
NEGLECTED SENSE IN PIANO PLAYING, A
MASON, MARY B.
BOY MUSIC, A FIRST PIANO METHOD FOR BOYS BETWEEN 8 AND 16
MASON, WILLIAM G.
ACCENTUAL TREATMENT OF EXERCISES AS APPLIED TO PIANOFORTE
MASON, WILLIAM G. *
PRIMER OF MUSIC, A ..BEING THE FIRST STEPS IN MUSICIANSHIP..FOR
MASON, WILLIAM G. *
SYSTEM FOR BEGINNERS IN THE ART OF PLAYING UPON THE PIANOFORTE, A
MASON, WILLIAM G.
SYSTEM OF TECHNICAL EXERCISES FOR THE PIANO-FORTE, A
MASON, WILLIAM G.
TOUCH, AS APPLIED TO PIANOFORTE PRACTICE--ESSAY FOR THE 10TH.

MASON, WILLIAM G.
TOUCH AND TECHNIC..FOR ARTISTIC PIANO PLAYING, OP. 44--4 VOLS. IN
MATHEWS, WILLIAM S. B.
MASON'S PRINCIPLES OF VELOCITY AND ARM TOUCHES
MATHEWS, WILLIAM S. B.
TEACHER'S MANUAL OF MASON'S PIANOFORTE TECHNICS
MATTHAY, TOBIAS A.
ACT OF TOUCH IN ALL ITS DIVERSITY, THE ..AN ANALYSIS AND SYNTHESIS
MATTHAY, TOBIAS A.
CHILD'S FIRST STEPS IN PIANOFORTE PLAYING, THE
MATTHAY, TOBIAS A.
EPITOME OF THE LAWS OF PIANOFORTE TECHNIQUE, AN
MATTHAY, TOBIAS A.
FIRST LIGHTS ON PIANO-PLAYING
MATTHAY, TOBIAS A.
FIRST PRINCIPLES OF PIANOFORTE PLAYING--EXTRACT FROM 'THE ACT OF
MATTHAY, TOBIAS A.
FOREARM ROTATION PRINCIPLE IN PIANOFORTE PLAYING, THE ..ITS
MATTHAY, TOBIAS A.
MUSICAL INTERPRETATION..ITS LAWS AND PRINCIPLES---1913
MATTHAY, TOBIAS A.
NINE STEPS TOWARDS 'FINGER INDIVIDUALIZATION' THROUGH FOREARM
MATTHAY, TOBIAS A.
ON COLORING AS DISTINCT FROM TONE-INFLECTION--A LECTURE
MATTHAY, TOBIAS A.
ON METHOD IN TEACHING
MATTHAY, TOBIAS A. *
PIANIST'S FIRST MUSIC MAKING, THE --3 VOLS.
MATTHAY, TOBIAS A.
PIANOFORTE TONE-PRODUCTION---SAME AS 'THE ACT OF TOUCH IN ALL ITS
MATTHAY, TOBIAS A.
PIANO FALLACIES OF TODAY
MATTHAY, TOBIAS A.
PRACTICE TRIANGLE, THE ..EXERCISES FOR FOREARM ROTATION
MATTHAY, TOBIAS A.
PRINCIPLES OF FINGERING AND LAWS OF PEDALLING
MATTHAY, TOBIAS A.
PROBLEMS OF AGILITY, THE
MATTHAY, TOBIAS A.
RELAXATION STUDIES IN THE MUSCULAR DISCRIMINATION REQUIRED FOR
MATTHAY, TOBIAS A.
SOME COMMENTARIES ON THE TEACHING OF PIANOFORTE TECHNIC..A
MATTHAY, TOBIAS A.
TEACHING OF PIANOFORTE TECHNIQUE, THE ..A SUPPLEMENT TO THE ACT OF
MATTHAY, TOBIAS A.
VISIBLE AND INVISIBLE IN PIANOFORTE TECHNIC, THE ..BEING A DIGEST
MCALL, REGINALD L.
PRACTICAL CHURCH SCHOOL MUSIC..METHODS AND TRAINING FOR SUCCESSFUL
MCARTHUR, ALEXANDER
PIANOFORTE STUDY..HINTS ON PIANO PLAYING
MCFERRIN, CHARLES BETTEYS
MOTHER'S PART IN HER CHILD'S MUSICAL EDUCATION, A ..OR, THE THINGS
MCMILLAN, FIONA
FINGERING OF SCALES AND ARPEGGIOS, THE
MEHEGAN, JOHN F.
TOUCH AND RHYTHM TECHNIQUES FOR THE JAZZ PIANIST
MEIER, NELLIE SIMMONS
LIONS' PAWS..THE STORY OF FAMOUS HANDS--INCLUDES MUSICIANS..JOSE
MERGES, P.
PRACTICAL RULES FOR PIANOFORTE PLAYING..TEXT BOOK FOR TEACHERS AND
MERRICK, FRANK
PRACTICING THE PIANO
MERRILL, MYRTLE
SIGHT-READING AT THE PIANO
MIDKIFF, HELEN T.
CHURCH PIANIST, THE
MILLER, ALLAN
BEGINNING PIANO FOR ADULTS
MILLER, EDWARD
INSTITUTES OF MUSIC, OR, EASY INSTRUCTIONS FOR THE HARPSICHORD
MININBERG, IAN
VISUAL APPROACH TO PIANO TECHNIQUE, A
MINNESOTA MUSIC TEACHERS ASSOCIATION
PIANO-THEORY EXAMINATION SYLLABUS
MOKREJS, JOHN
SCIENCE OF FINGERING, THE ---FOR PIANO
MONTI, H. DE
STRICTURES ON MR. LOGIER'S SYSTEM OF MUSICAL EDUCATION
MOOR, WINIFRED
TECHNICAL EXERCISES FOR THE EMANUEL MOOR DOUBLE KEYBOARD
MOORE, MARY BURNHAM
LURE OF THE PIANO THROUGH COORDINATION AND CONCENTRATION, THE
MORRILL, HENRY H.
MANUAL OF PIANO FOR PUPILS AND TEACHERS
MOTT, ISAAC H. R.
ADVICE AND INSTRUCTIONS FOR PLAYING THE PIANOFORTE WITH EXPRESSION
MUSAFIA, JULIEN
ART OF FINGERING IN PIANO PLAYING, THE
MUSIC EDUCATORS NATIONAL CONFERENCE
TEACHING PIANO IN CLASSROOM AND STUDIO
MUSIC PROJECT--NEW YORK CITY
TEACHER'S GUIDE..A CREATIVE APPROACH TO PIANO CLASS TEACHING, BY
NALDER, LAWRENCE MARCUS
MODERN PIANO, THE
NETZORG, BENDETSON
KEY-BOTTOM TONE
NEUHAUS, HEINRICH
ART OF PIANO PLAYING, THE
NEWMAN, ELIZABETH
HOW TO TEACH MUSIC TO BEGINNERS
NEWMAN, WILLIAM S.
PERFORMANCE PRACTICES IN BEETHOVEN'S PIANO SONATAS..AN
NEWMAN, WILLIAM S.
PIANIST'S PROBLEMS, THE ..A MODERN APPROACH TO EFFICIENT PRACTICE
NICCHIA, LILLIAN
PIANOFORTE STUDY..HINTS ON PIANO PLAYING
NIXON, W.
GUIDE TO INSTRUCTION ON THE PIANOFORTE, A --IN A SERIES OF SHORT
O'REAR, MRS. ASBURY S.
SELF READING NOTES
O'TOOLE, WILLIAM
CREATIVE PIANO TECHNIC
OLIVER, EDWARD B.
PRACTICAL TEXT-BOOK OF MUSIC, AS CONNECTED WITH THE ART OF PLAYING
ORLIK, JULES
CREATIVE APPROACH TO PIANO CLASS TEACHING, A ---REPRODUCED FROM
ORTMANN, OTTO
PHYSICAL BASIS OF PIANO TOUCH AND TONE, THE
ORTMANN, OTTO
PHYSIOLOGICAL MECHANICS OF PIANO TECHNIQUE, THE ---1929
OSTROVSKY, HENRY
LESSON COURSE...THE COMPLETE OSTROVSKY FINGER EXERCISE, FOR
OSTROVSKY, HENRY
TECHNIQUE AND HAND DEVELOPMENT---USE OF A MACHINE
PALME, RUDOLPH
FIRST MONTHS IN PIANOFORTE INSTRUCTION, THE ---1870, IN GERMAN

PALMER, ANNIE L.
  MUSIC TEACHERS' GUIDE TO THE GOLDBECK PIANO METHOD
PALMER, HORATIO R.
  PALMER'S PIANO PRIMER
PALMER, KING
  TEACH YOURSELF TO PLAY THE PIANO
PARSONS, ALBERT R.
  SCIENCE OF PIANO PRACTICE, THE
PARSONS, ALBERT R.
  SYNTHETIC METHOD FOR THE PIANOFORTE, THE
PARSONS, MARY H.
  RHYTHMIC WAY, THE
PASQUALI, NICOLO
  ART OF FINGERING THE HARPSICHORD, THE
PEARCE, CHARLES WILLIAM
  ART OF THE PIANO TEACHER, THE
PERRY, ADELAIDE TROWBRIDGE *
  GUIDE TO PIANO STUDY FOR CLASS OR INDIVIDUAL INSTRUCTION, A
PETERS, WILLIAM C.
  ECLECTIC PIANOFORTE SCHOOL, THE ..ARRANGED FROM THE WORKS OF THE
PETERSON, FRANKLIN
  THEORETIC COMPANION TO PRACTICE--PART I OF THE PIANIST'S HANDBOOK
PETRI, LILLIAN JEFFREY
  MIND OVER MUSCLE..A TECHNICAL ECONOMY FOR PIANISTS
PFEFFERKORN, OTTO W.
  PIANISTIC HINTS
PHILIPP, ISIDOR
  TRILL IN THE WORKS OF BEETHOVEN, THE
PHILIPP, LILLIE H.
  PIANO STUDY..APPLICATION AND TECHNIQUE
PHILLIPSON, WENTWORTH
  GUIDE TO YOUNG PIANOFORTE TEACHERS AND STUDENTS
PICHIER, PAUL
  PIANIST'S TOUCH, THE ..METHOD AND THEORY OF PAUL PICHIER
PLAIDY, LOUIS
  PIANOFORTE TEACHER'S GUIDE, THE
PLAIDY, LOUIS
  PIANO TEACHER, THE
PLATT, CAROLYN
  CAROLYN PLATT METHOD FOR PIANO, THE --GROUP INSTRUCTION--TEACHER'S
POINTER SYSTEM, INC.
  GUIDE TO THE MODERN PIANIST, A
POTAMKIN, FRANK
  MODERN PIANO PEDAGOGY
POWERS-WADSWORTH, L.
  PIANIST'S GUIDE TO TECHNICAL FREEDOM, THE ..2 VOLS. IN 1
PRATT, SILAS G.
  PIANIST'S MENTAL VELOCITY, THE ..A SYSTEMATIC PREPARATION OF THE
PRELLEUR, PETER
  HARPSICHORD ILLUSTRATED AND IMPROV'D, WHEREIN IS SHEWN THE ITALIAN
PRENTICE THOMAS RIDLEY
  HAND GYMNASTICS, FOR THE SCIENTIFIC DEVELOPMENT OF THE MUSCLES
PRENTNER, MARIE
  MODERN PIANIST..BEING MY EXPERIENCES IN THE TECHNIQUE AND
PRIESING, DOROTHY *
  LANGUAGE OF THE PIANO..A WORKBOOK IN THEORY AND KEYBOARD HARMONY
PSTROKONSKY, JULES DE
  NEW METHOD OF TEACHING THE PIANOFORTE
PUPIN, ANNIE
  HOW TO PRACTICE..OR HINTS TO PIANO-FORTE STUDENTS ON THE METHOD OF
PUPIN, ANNIE
  SCALES, THE ..THEIR FORMATION, FINGERING, AND HOW TO PRACTICE
RAMUL, PETER
  PSYCHO-PHYSICAL FOUNDATIONS OF MODERN PIANO TECHNIQUE, THE
REDDIE, CHARLES FREDERICK
  PIANOFORTE PLAYING ON ITS TECHNICAL AND AESTHETIC SIDES
REEDER, BETAH
  SINGING TOUCH, THE
REEVES, BETTY
  APPROACH TO PIANO TEACHING---ALSO CATALOGUED UNDER
REEVES, WILLIAM
  REEVES' POPULAR PIANOFORTE TUTOR..RUDIMENTS OF MUSIC, EXERCISES
REINAGLE, CAROLINE
  FEW WORDS ON PIANOFORTE PLAYING, A
RENNIE, BLANCHE H.
  HAND CULTURE FOR PIANISTS, VIOLINISTS AND 'CELLISTS--FINGER, HAND
REZITS, JOSEPH
  SOURCE MATERIALS FOR PIANO TECHNIQUES
REZITS, JOSEPH
  TEACHER'S GUIDE TO THE NEW SCRIBNER MUSIC LIBRARY
RHODES, ALFRED
  CURIOSITIES OF THE KEY-BOARD AND THE STAFF...SHOWN TO BE UPON A
RICHARDSON, NATHAN
  NEW METHOD FOR THE PIANOFORTE..ADDED, RUDIMENTS OF HARMONY AND
RICHTER, ADA
  TEACHING HINTS
RICKER, EARL
  MUSIC LESSONS FOR YOUR CHILD
RIEMANN, HUGO
  CATECHISM OF PIANOFORTE PLAYING---1888, IN GERMAN
ROBBINS, EDGAR A.
  AMERICAN METHOD FOR THE PIANOFORTE
ROBILLIARD, EILEEN D.
  PERSISTENT PIANIST, THE ..A BOOK FOR THE LATE BEGINNER AND THE
ROBYN, LOUISE
  HAND BUILDING AND HAND STRETCHING EXERCISES
ROBYN, LOUISE
  HOW TO TEACH PIANO TO THE CHILD BEGINNER..A TEXT BOOK FOR TEACHERS
ROBYN, LOUISE
  TECHNIC TALES FOR THE CHILD AT THE PIANO--BKS. 1-3..TEACHER'S
ROEDER, CARL M.
  LIBERATION AND DELIBERATION IN PIANO TECHNIC
ROEDER, ELWOOD S.
  TIME-SPACE CONCEPTION OF THE GEOMETRY AND SPEED OF MOTION AT THE
ROOT, CATHERINE ADAMS *
  LISTEN, SING AND PLAY..CLASS LESSONS FOR PIANO AND VOICE
ROSENTHAL, MORIZ
  OLD AND THE NEW SCHOOL OF PIANO PLAYING, THE --TYPEWRITTEN COPY
ROSTAND, CLAUDE
  LISZT
ROTHSCHILD, FRITZ
  LOST TRADITION IN MUSIC, THE --PT. 1..RHYTHM AND TEMPO IN J. S.
ROTHSCHILD, FRITZ
  LOST TRADITION IN MUSIC, THE --PT. 2..MUSICAL PERFORMANCE IN THE
ROWLEY, ALEC
  DO'S AND DONT'S FOR MUSICIANS..A HANDBOOK FOR TEACHERS AND
ROWLEY, ALEC
  PRACTICAL MUSICIANSHIP, A HANDBOOK FOR TEACHERS AND STUDENTS
RUBINSTEIN, BERYL
  OUTLINE OF PIANO PEDAGOGY--REV. ED.---1929
RUSSELL, LOUIS ARTHUR
  DEVELOPMENT OF ARTISTIC PIANOFORTE TOUCH
SAFONOFF, WASSILI
  NEW FORMULA FOR THE PIANO TEACHER AND PIANO STUDENT
SAVLER, ROBERTA--EDITOR
  SELECTIONS FROM THE PIANO TEACHER, 1958-1963

SCHAAF, EDWARD O.
  ART OF PIANO PLAYER TRANSCRIPTION, THE ..MAKING OF PERFORATED
SCHAAF, EDWARD O.
  FUNDAMENTAL PRINCIPLES INVOLVED IN THE COMPOSING AND ARRANGING OF
SCHAAF, EDWARD O.
  MUSICAL INDIVIDUALITY OF THE PLAYER PIANO, THE ---EXCERPTS..'THE
SCHAUFFLER, LAWRENCE
  PIANO TECHNIC..MYTH OR SCIENCE
SCHELLING, ERNEST *
  OXFORD PIANO COURSE, TEACHER'S FIRST MANUAL
SCHELLING, ERNEST *
  OXFORD PIANO COURSE, TEACHER'S SECOND MANUAL
SCHERER, HERBERT
  PIANO PRACTICING
SCHMITZ, ELIE ROBERT
  CAPTURE OF INSPIRATION, THE
SCHNEIDER, HANS
  WORKING OF THE MIND IN PIANO TEACHING AND PLAYING, THE
SCHOTT, HOWARD
  PLAYING THE HARPSICHORD
SCHULTZ, ARNOLD
  RIDDLE OF THE PIANIST'S FINGER, THE
SCIONTI, SILVIO
  L'ARTE PIANISTICA..SYSTEM OF PIANO ARTISTRY---IN ITALIAN AND
SCONCIA, JOHN A.
  SCONCIA'S NEW SYSTEM OF INSTRUCTION IN MUSIC AS A SCIENCE..OR, A
SEROFF, VICTOR
  COMMON SENSE IN PIANO STUDY
SHEFTEL, PAUL
  EXPLORING KEYBOARD FUNDAMENTALS
SHELDON, ROBERT--COMPILER
  EGON PETRI-ALEXANDER LIBERMANN NOTES ON THE ART AND TECHNIQUE OF
SHEPARD, FRANK H.
  PIANO TOUCH AND SCALES..AN ANALYSIS OF THE FUNDAMENTAL PRINCIPLES
SHEPARD, ROBERT
  COMPLETE SCALE AND ARPEGGIO MANUAL
SHERWOOD MUSIC SCHOOL
  PIANO LESSONS AND TESTS--4TH. REV. ED.---1945+
SIMPSON, ELIZABETH
  BASIC PIANOFORTE TECHNIQUE...BASED ON THE SCIENCE OF PIANOFORTE
SIMPSON, KENNETH
  KEYBOARD HARMONY AND IMPROVISATION
SLENCZYNSKA, RUTH *
  MUSIC AT YOUR FINGERTIPS
SMELTZER, JEANNIE R.--COMPILER
  OUTLINES AND GRADES FOR THE USE OF PIANO TEACHERS
SMITH, A. G. WARREN
  BEGINNER'S GUIDE, THE ..FOR ALL COMMENCING THE STUDY OF THE
SMITH, MACDONALD
  FROM BRAIN TO KEYBOARD..A SYSTEM OF HAND AND FINGER CONTROL FOR
SORABJI, KAIKHOSRU
  AROUND MUSIC---PACHMAN, CHOPIN AND LISZT
SOREL, CLAUDETTE
  COMPENDIUM OF PIANO TECHNIQUE--39 ETUDES SELECTED FROM OVER 4000,
SPENCER, ALLEN
  FOUNDATION OF PIANO TECHNIC, THE
SPENCER, BERNARD
  POPULAR PIANO...A CORRESPONDENCE COURSE OF THE EASTERN SCHOOLS OF
SQUIRE, RUSSEL N. *
  CLASS PIANO FOR ADULT BEGINNERS--2ND. ED.---1964
STANLEY, JANE
  BASIC ROUTINES IN ELEMENTARY PIANO TEACHING THROUGH THE FIRST
STARKEY, EVELYN
  PIANO CLASS WORKBOOK FOR FIRST YEAR STUDENTS
STEVENS, EVERETT
  CHORDS, CADENCES, AND ARPEGGIOS
STEVENS, WILLIAM S.
  TREATISE ON PIANO-FORTE, CONTAINING THE PRINCIPLES OF FINE PLAYING
STEWART; REID
  HOW TO PASS MUSIC EXAMINATIONS--PIANO--A GUIDE FOR TEACHERS AND
STORMEN, WIN
  FIFTY YEARS OF POPULAR PIANO TECHNIQUES IN THE U.S.A.
SUMMY-BIRCHARD COMPANY
  HANDBOOK FOR PIANO TEACHERS..COLLECTED ARTICLES ON SUBJECTS
SWENSON, LUCILE B.
  DISCOVERING THE PIANO..THE MULTIPLE KEY APPROACH..STUDY GUIDE AND
TANKARD, GEOFFREY
  FOUNDATIONS OF PIANOFORTE TECHNIQUE
TANKARD, GEOFFREY
  PIANOFORTE DIPLOMAS
TANKARD, GEOFFREY
  SPECIMEN ANSWERS TO THE QUESTIONS IN PIANOFORTE DIPLOMAS
TAYLER, E. DOUGLAS
  SECRET OF SUCCESSFUL PRACTICE, THE
TAYLOR, FRANKLIN
  PRIMER OF PIANOFORTE PLAYING
TAYLOR, FRANKLIN
  TECHNIQUE AND EXPRESSION IN PIANOFORTE PLAYING
THAYER, E. D.
  SHORT CUTS TO PIANO TECHNIQUE
TOBIN, JOSEPH RAYMOND
  COMMON SENSE IN SIGHT READING..A GUIDE FOR PIANO TEACHERS
TOBIN, JOSEPH RAYMOND
  FUN WITH FINGERING, A FIRST-OF-ALL BOOK ON EASY FINGERING AND
TOMLINSON, ANNA M.
  ANNA M. TOMLINSON'S FORTY LESSONS ON HOW TO DEVELOP A PIANO HAND
TOWNSEND, WILLIAM
  BALANCE OF ARM IN PIANO TECHNIQUE--4TH. REV. ED.---1903
TUFTS, JOHN W.
  TECHNIC AND NOTATION AS APPLIED TO THE PIANOFORTE
TURECK, ROSALYN
  INTRODUCTION TO THE PERFORMANCE OF BACH, AN--3 VOLS.
UNDERWOOD, REX
  GHOST NOTE PATTERN BUILDERS FOR VISUALIZING THE STRUCTURE OF
UNSCHULD, MARIE VON
  PIANIST'S HAND, THE ..A SYSTEMATIC METHOD...ACCORDING TO THE
VANTYN, SIDNEY
  MODERN PIANOFORTE TECHNIQUE
VENABLE, MARY
  INTERPRETATION OF PIANO MUSIC, THE
VERNAZZA, MARCELLE
  BASIC MATERIALS FOR THE PIANO STUDENT
VIARD-LOUIS, JENNY
  MUSIC AND THE PIANO
VILLOING, ALEXANDER
  RUBINSTEIN'S FINGER EXERCISES..TECHNICAL STUDIES FROM THE
VINING, HARRISON S.
  SIMPLE AND COMPLETE PRIMER FOR THE PIANOFORTE, THE
VIRGIL, ALMON K.
  EDUCATION IN MUSIC..LESSONS TO TEACHERS IN THE INSTRUCTION OF
VIRGIL, ALMON K.
  FOUNDATION EXERCISES IN PIANO PLAYING FROM FIRST RUDIMENTS TO
VIRGIL, ALMON K.
  SPECIAL TECHNIC COURSE IN THE VIRGIL CLAVIER METHOD--6 PTS.
VIRGIL, ALMON K.
  STEP BY STEP..TEXTBOOK IN PIANO PLAYING..HANDBOOK FOR TEACHERS

VIRGIL, ALMON K.
TECHNIPHONE MANUAL..INSTRUCTIONS AND EXERCISES IN THE USE OF THE
VIRGIL, ANTHA MINERVA
ELEMENTARY EXERCISES IN SIGHT READING...FROM THE VIRGIL METHOD
VIRGIL, ANTHA MINERVA
INSTRUCTIVE TALKS TO PIANO STUDENTS
VIRGIL, ANTHA MINERVA
VIRGIL METHOD OF PIANOFORTE TECHNIC, THE --2 VOLS.
WAIT, WILLIAM B.
NORMAL COURSE OF PIANO TECHNIC, THE
WEISER, ADOLPH
TWO RIGHT HANDS..A GUIDE FOR THE DEVELOPMENT OF PIANO TECHNIQUE
WELLS, HOWARD
EARS, BRAIN AND FINGERS..A TEXT BOOK FOR PIANO TEACHERS AND PUPILS
WELLS, HOWARD
PIANIST'S THUMB, THE
WESTBROOK, BENJAMIN V.
SYSTEM OF STUDY OF SCALES AND CHORDS, A ..BEING CHAPTERS ON THE
WESTERBY, HERBERT
APPROACH TO LISZT, THE ..A COURSE OF MODERN TONAL TECHNIQUE FOR
WESTERBY, HERBERT
LISZT, COMPOSER, AND HIS PIANO WORKS..DESCRIPTIVE GUIDE AND
WHEELER, BERTHA H.
MIND AND MECHANISM..THOUGHTS ON TEACHING AND THE PIANISTIC ART
WHITE, WILLIAM BRAID
PIANO TUNING AND ALLIED ARTS--5TH. ED.---1917
WHITE, WILLIAM BRAID
PLAYER-PIANIST, THE ..A GUIDE TO THE APPRECIATION AND
WHITEMORE, CUTHBERT
COMMONSENSE IN PIANOFORTE PLAYING
WHITESIDE, ABBY
INDISPENSABLES OF PIANO PLAYING--2ND. ED.---1955
WHITESIDE, ABBY
MASTERING THE CHOPIN ETUDES AND OTHER ESSAYS
WHITESIDE, ABBY
PIANIST'S MECHANISM, THE
WIER, ALBERT
PIANO, THE ..ITS HISTORY, MAKERS, PLAYERS AND MUSIC
WILKINS-GUTMANN, EMMA
TALKS WITH PIANO TEACHERS
WILLIAMS, JEAN E. *
MIND IN MUSIC, THE
WILLIAMS, JEAN E.
MODERN METHOD OF PIANO INSTRUCTION, A ..TEACHERS MANUAL
WILLIAMS, JOHN M.
WHAT TO TEACH AT THE VERY FIRST LESSON
WILSON, CHARLES J.
SCALES TAUGHT IN ONE EASY LESSON, THE
WILSON, DAVID M.
PLAYER-PIANO, THE ..ITS CONSTRUCTION..HOW TO PLAY, WHAT TO PLAY
WILSON, MORRIS E.
HOW TO PLAY BY EAR
WILSON, WILLIAM
NEW FINGERING NOTATION FOR KEYBOARD MUSIC---REPRODUCED FROM
WINNER, SEPTIMUS
WINNER'S NEW SCHOOL FOR THE PIANO, IN WHICH THE INSTRUCTIONS ARE
WOLFF, ERNST VICTOR
WITH REASON AND RHYME
WOLFF, KONRAD
TEACHING OF ARTUR SCHNABEL, THE ..A GUIDE TO INTERPRETATION
WOLLNER, GERTRUDE PRICE
IMPROVISATION IN MUSIC..WAYS TOWARDS CAPTURING MUSICAL IDEAS AND
WOOD, CHARLES W.
FINGER AND WRIST GYMNASTICS--WITHOUT USE OF PIANO--FOR PIANO
WOODHOUSE, GEORGE
ARTIST AT THE PIANO, THE ..THE ART OF MUSICAL INTERPRETATION
WOODHOUSE, GEORGE
CREATIVE TECHNIQUE, FOR ARTISTS IN GENERAL AND PIANISTS IN
WOODHOUSE, GEORGE
FINGER EXERCISES FOR THE POCKET MUTANO
WOODHOUSE, GEORGE
FROM KEYBOARD TO MUSIC
WOODHOUSE, GEORGE
NEW PATH FOR PIANISTS, A ..THE MUTANO--MUTE PIANO--SYSTEM, ETC.
WOODHOUSE, GEORGE
NEW WAY TO PIANO TECHNIQUE, THE --8 VOLS.
WOODHOUSE, GEORGE
REALISTIC APPROACH TO PIANO PLAYING, A
WRIGHT, WILLIAM C.
GOLDEN MONITOR, FOR THE PIANOFORTE AND CABINET ORGAN, DESIGNED AS
WRIGHT, WILLIAM C.
PIANOFORTE MANUAL, THE ..DESIGNED AS A COMPLETE PIANOFORTE PRIMER
WYMAN, ADDISON P.
WYMAN'S PIANO TEXTBOOK..CONTAINING A COMPLETE SYSTEM OF MUSICAL
YOUNG, PERCY M.
KEYBOARD MUSICIANS OF THE WORLD
ZIMMERMAN, ALEX H. *
BASIC PIANO FOR THE COLLEGE STUDENT

Keyboard Skills

ADAMS, JOHN S.
FIVE THOUSAND MUSICAL TERMS..A COMPLETE DICTIONARY WITH A TREATISE
ADLER, KURT
ART OF ACCOMPANYING AND COACHING, THE ---1965
AEBERSOLD, JAMEY
NEW APPROACH TO JAZZ IMPROVISATION, A --VOL. 1
AHRENS, CORA B. *
FOR ALL PIANO TEACHERS
ALBRECHTSBERGER, JOHANN GEORG
ALBRECHTSBERGER'S COLLECTED WRITINGS ON THOROUGH-BASS, HARMONY AND
ALBRECHTSBERGER, JOHANN GEORG
ALBRECHTSBERGER'S ELEMENTARY WORK ON THE SCIENCE OF
ALBRECHTSBERGER, JOHANN GEORG
METHODS OF HARMONY, FIGURED BASE, AND COMPOSITION...ADAPTED FOR
ALBRECHTSBERGER, JOHANN GEORG
PRINCIPLES OF ACCOMPANIMENT OR THOROUGH BASS
ALCHIN, CARRIE A.
APPLIED HARMONY--REVISED AND WITH ADDITIONAL CHAPTERS BY VINCENT
ALCHIN, CARRIE A.
KEYBOARD HARMONY--3 VOLS. IN 1, 1923-1926
ALLISON, IRL
LET'S LEARN ALL THE NOTES AND READ BETTER..FOR ALL PIANO PUPILS,
AMEY, ELLEN
CONSCIOUS CONTROL IN PIANO STUDY
ANDERSON, J. CLARK
GOOD MUSIC EXPLAINED..WHAT ALL GOOD PIANISTS SHOULD KNOW
ANON
CHILD'S INTRODUCTION TO THOROUGH BASS, THE ..IN CONVERSATIONS OF A
ANON
COMPLEAT TUTOR FOR THE HARPSICHORD OR SPINNET, WHEREIN IS SHEWN
ANON
FIRST STEPS TO THOROUGH BASE, IN 12 FAMILIAR LESSONS BETWEEN A

ANON
NEW AND COMPLETE INSTRUCTIONS FOR THE HARPSICHORD, PIANO FORTE OR
ANON
NEW INSTRUCTIONS FOR PLAYING THE HARPSICHORD, PIANOFORTE OR
ANON
PIANOFORTE POCKET COMPANION, THE ..OR, A POPULAR VIEW OF THE
ANON
PLAYING THE HARPSICHORD, SPINET OR PIANO FORTE MADE EASY BY NEW
ANON
PRECEPTOR, FOR THE PIANOFORTE, THE ORGAN OR HARPSICHORD, THE
ANON
RULES..OR A SHORT AND COMPLEAT METHOD FOR ATTAINING TO PLAY A
ANON
THOROUGH BASS AT ONE VIEW, WITH DIRECTIONS FOR ACCOMPANIMENT AND
APPEL, PEARL *
HARMONY AT THE PIANO LESSON, A COMPANION TO PIANO STUDY
ARNOLD, FRANCK THOMAS
ART OF ACCOMPANIMENT FROM A THOROUGH-BASS, AS PRACTICED IN THE
AULD, WILDA J.
HANDBOOK FOR THE CHURCH PIANIST, A
BACH, CARL PHILIPP EMANUEL
ESSAY ON THE TRUE ART OF PLAYING KEYBOARD INSTRUMENTS---TWO PTS.,
BAILLIE, ALEXANDER--SUPPOSED AUTHOR
INTRODUCTION TO THE KNOWLEDGE AND PRACTICE OF THE THORO' BASS, AN
BAKER, DAVID
JAZZ IMPROVISATION..A COMPREHENSIVE METHOD OF STUDY FOR ALL
BAKER, PERCY
STUDIES IN MODULATION FOR PRACTICAL AND THEORETICAL PURPOSES
BANISTER, HENRY C.
ART OF MODULATING, THE --A SERIES OF PAPERS ON MODULATION AT THE
BANISTER, HENRY C.
HARMONIZING OF MELODIES, THE ..A TEXT-BOOK FOR STUDENTS AND
BARNWELL, V. T.
BARNWELL'S NORMAL KEYBOARD AND STAFF STUDIES--THE MENTAL
BASTIEN, JAMES W. *
BEGINNING PIANO FOR ADULTS
BAUER, HAROLD
PRIMER FOR PRACTICAL KEYBOARD MODULATION, A
BAXTER, JAMES
INDUCTIVE GRAMMAR OF MUSIC, FOR CLASS, PRIVATE LESSON, OR SELF
BAXTER, JAMES
NEW SCHOOL OF MUSIC, THE ..PRACTICAL THOROUGH BASE CULTURE, FOR
BECKER, JULIUS
CONCISE TREATISE ON HARMONY, ACCOMPANIMENT, AND COMPOSITION, FOR
BECKERMAN, H. J.
AMERICAN SCHOOL OF RAGTIME PIANO PLAYING, THE
BEMETZRIEDER, ANTON
ABSTRACT OF A NEW METHOD OF TEACHING THE PRINCIPLES OF MUSIC,
BEMETZRIEDER, ANTON
ACCOUNT OF A NEW WAY OF CONSIDERING MUSICK, AND TEACHING
BEMETZRIEDER, ANTON
ART OF MODULATING, ILLUSTRATED, THE
BEMETZRIEDER, ANTON
COMPENDIUM OF A NEW METHOD OF MUSIC...WITH THE AUTHOR'S PRINCIPLES
BEMETZRIEDER, ANTON
MUSIC MADE EASY TO EVERY CAPACITY, IN A SERIES OF DIALOGUES..BEING
BEMETZRIEDER, ANTON
NEW GUIDE TO MUSIC, IN FRENCH AND ENGLISH, A
BEMETZRIEDER, ANTON
NEW LESSONS FOR THE HARPSICHORD
BENNER, LORA
THEORY FOR PIANO STUDENTS--1ST. YEAR, PRIVATE OR CLASS--5 VOLS.,
BERNING, ALICE B. *
KEYBOARD EXPERIENCES FOR CLASSROOM TEACHERS
BERNSTEIN, MARTIN--COMPILER
SCORE READING..A SERIES OF GRADED EXCERPTS
BEVITT, ZAY RECTOR
CLASS PROCEDURE FOR 40 LESSONS IN PIANO PLAYING BY HARMONY
BISHOP, DOROTHY
CHORDS IN ACTION
BLAKE, DOROTHY
FIRST STEPS IN CHORD PLAYING
BOLTON, HETTY
ON TEACHING THE PIANO
BONPENSIERE, LUIGI
NEW PATHWAYS TO PIANO TECHNIQUE..A STUDY OF THE RELATIONS BETWEEN
BOOTH, VICTOR
WE PIANO TEACHERS--REVISED BY ADELE FRANKLIN---1946
BOWEN, CAROLYN
OUTLINES FOR TRAINING PIANO TEACHERS
BOYD, MALCOLM
BACH'S INSTRUMENTAL COUNTERPOINT
BOYD, MALCOLM
HARMONIZING 'BACH' CHORALES
BRECKENRIDGE, WILLIAM KILGORE
HINTS FOR PIANO NORMAL STUDIES
BRIDGER, JOHN HENRY
HOW TO HARMONIZE MELODIES, WITH HINTS ON WRITING FOR STRINGS AND
BROUGHTON, JULIA
SUCCESS IN PIANO TEACHING
BROWN, JEAN PARKMAN
INTERVALS, CHORDS AND EAR TRAINING FOR YOUNG PIANOFORTE STUDENTS
BUCHAROFF, SIMON
MODERN PIANIST'S TEXT BOOK, THE
BUCK, PERCY
UNFIGURED HARMONY--2ND. ED.---1911
BUELOW, GEORGE J.
THOROUGH-BASS ACCOMPANIMENT ACCORDING TO JOHANN DAVID HEINICHEN
BURROWES, JOHN FRECKLETON
GUIDE TO PRACTICE ON THE PIANOFORTE
BURROWES, JOHN FRECKLETON
THOROUGH-BASS PRIMER, THE ..CONTAINING EXPLANATIONS AND EXAMPLES
BURROWS, RAYMOND
ELEMENTARY PIANO INSTRUCTION IN COLLEGE
BUSSLER, LUDWIG
HARMONIC EXERCISES AT THE PIANOFORTE FOR BEGINNERS AND ADVANCED
CALLAGHAN, JAMES
ZIP CHORDMASTER..BEGINNERS HOME COURSE FOR PIANO AND ORGAN
CAPPS, STANLEY M.
CAPPS SYSTEM OF IMPROVISING FOR PIANO, THE --A MODERN COURSE OF
CARL, SYLVESTER
CARL'S DICTIONARY OF CHORDS...REFERENCE BOOK FOR CUED-IN HARMONY
CARTER, BUENTA
ADVANCED KEYBOARD HARMONY WITH ILLUSTRATIVE PIANO PIECES
CARTER, BUENTA
KEYBOARD HARMONY WITH ILLUSTRATIVE PIANO PIECES
CARTER, BUENTA
TRANSPOSITION PATTERNS, FOR THE PIANO...APPROACHED THROUGH
CARY, MRS. C. S. P.
PIANO-FORTE CLASS BOOK, CONTAINING PRACTICAL RUDIMENTAL LESSONS
CASTELLINI, JOHN EDWARD
RUDIMENTS OF MUSIC..A NEW APPROACH WITH APPLICATION TO THE
CAVALLARO, CARMEN
KEYBOARD HARMONY..A NEW MODERN PIANO METHOD---POPULAR IDIOM
CHAPPLE, STANLEY
CLASS WAY TO THE KEYBOARD, THE

CHASTEK, WINIFRED
KEYBOARD SKILLS..SIGHT READING, TRANSPOSITION, HARMONIZATION,
CHEYETTE, IRVING
BASIC PIANO FOR THE MUSIC EDUCATOR AND CLASSROOM TEACHER
CHILDERS, LEMUEL
CHORD DICTIONARY..DESIGNED FOR TEACHERS, STUDENTS AND SELF-TAUGHT
CHILDERS, LEMUEL
PLAYING THE PIANO BY EAR
CHING, JAMES
CANDIDATE'S COMPANION TO THE EXERCISES, SCALES, BROKEN CHORDS,
CHING, JAMES
NEW GRADED SIGHT READING FOR PIANO, THE --BKS. 1 AND
CHING, JOAN ELIZABETH
APPROACH TO PIANO TEACHING---ALSO CATALOGUED UNDER
CHRISTIANSEN, FREDERICK M.
PRACTICAL MODULATION FOR ADVANCED STUDENTS---43 LESSONS
CHURCHILL, VIRGINIA PEAKES
MODERN TEACHER'S GUIDE TO PIANO AND PIANO CLASS TEACHING
CHURCHILL, VIRGINIA PEAKES
NINETEEN FIFTY-SIX SUPPLEMENT TO THE MODERN TEACHER'S GUIDE TO
CLARE, EDWARD
ANALYSIS OF PRACTICAL THOROUGH BASS
CLARE, EDWARD
NEW TREATISE OF PRACTICAL THOROUGH BASS, A
CLARKE, HUGH ARCHIBALD
THEORY EXPLAINED TO PIANO STUDENTS..OR PRACTICAL LESSONS IN
CLEMENTI, MUZIO
CLEMENTI'S SELECTION OF PRACTICAL HARMONY FOR THE ORGAN OR
COKER, JERRY
IMPROVISING JAZZ
COLOMBATTI, HAROLD
PRACTICAL COURSE IN TRANSPOSITION, A
COLOMBATTI, HAROLD
PROGRESSIVE SIGHT READING EXERCISES---FOR PIANO
CONKLIN-HAPP, SUZANNE
APPLIED KEYBOARD HARMONY
COOK, J. LAWRENCE
PIANO HANDBOOK ON BOOGIE WOOGIE, BLUES, AND BARRELHOUSE..3 EASY TO
COOKE, CHARLES
PLAYING THE PIANO FOR PLEASURE--REV. ED.---1941
COOKE, JAMES FRANCIS
GREAT MEN AND FAMOUS MUSICIANS ON THE ART OF MUSIC
COPP, EVELYN A.
WHAT IS THE FLETCHER MUSIC METHOD
COPPAGE, HOWARD W.
PIANO, CHORDS AND HARMONY---REPRODUCED FROM MANUSCRIPT
CORFE, JOSEPH
THOROUGH BASS SIMPLIFIED
CRAMER, JOHN BAPTIST
INSTRUCTIONS FOR THE PIANOFORTE---CONTAINS ALSO A SET OF 28
CRANMER, PHILIP
TECHNIQUE OF ACCOMPANIMENT, THE --THE STUDENT'S MUSIC LIBRARY
CRAWFORD, THOMAS J.
CRAWFORD SYSTEM OF KEYBOARD HARMONY AND TRANSPOSITION, THE
CROTCH, WILLIAM
ELEMENTS OF MUSICAL COMPOSITION..COMPREHENDING THE RULES OF
CROTCH, WILLIAM
PRACTICAL THOROUGH BASS, OR, THE ART OF PLAYING FROM A FIGURED
CURWEN, ANNIE JESSY
TEACHER'S GUIDE...TO MRS. CURWEN'S PIANOFORTE METHOD, 'THE CHILD
CZERNY, CARL
COMPLETE THEORETICAL AND PRACTICAL PIANO FORTE SCHOOL, FROM THE
CZERNY, CARL
LETTERS ON THOROUGH-BASS...FORMING THE SECOND PART OF THE LETTERS
CZERNY, CARL
LETTERS TO A YOUNG LADY ON THE ART OF PLAYING THE PIANOFORTE
CZERNY, CARL
NEW EXERCISES ON HARMONY AND THOROUGH BASS...FORMING A PRACTICAL
DALE, BENJAMIN J.
HARMONY, COUNTERPOINT AND IMPROVISATION
DANIELS, BESS
PLAYING PIANO AT SIGHT--MECHANICS FOR THE ADULT BEGINNER
DANIELS, BESS *
WORLD OF MUSIC, THE ..PIANO COURSE..TEACHERS' BOOK, FOR CLASS OR
DARDENELLE, LOUISE
HARMONY-FIRST METHOD FOR THE PIANO...FOR CHILD AND ADULT
DAVIS, HARRY
INSTANT PIANO..A UNIQUE METHOD OF READING AND CHORDING FROM THE
DAVIS, LUCILE
READ AND PLAY..RAPID CHORD CONSTRUCTION--REV. ED.---1943
DAWSON, FREDERICK
PIANOFORTE, THE
DEUTSCH, LEONHARD
PIANO..GUIDED SIGHT-READING
DE SOLIS, SOLITO
THREE POSITIONS OF HARMONIZED SCALES, THE --SHOWN IN ALL KEYS
DE WITT, EDYTHE
EDYTHE DE WITT'S METHOD FOR CLASS PIANO...WRITTEN TO GIVE CORRECT
DILLER, ANGELA
KEYBOARD HARMONY COURSE..A CREATIVE METHOD BASED ON
DILLER, ANGELA
SPLENDOR OF MUSIC, THE
DOBBIE, E. A.
AUSTRALIAN PIANOFORTE TUTOR
DOLMETSCH, ARNOLD
INTERPRETATION OF MUSIC OF THE SEVENTEENTH AND EIGHTEENTH
DONINGTON, ROBERT
INTERPRETATION OF EARLY MUSIC, THE
DONINGTON, ROBERT
PERFORMER'S GUIDE TO BAROQUE MUSIC, A
DUCKWORTH, GUY
KEYBOARD MUSICIANSHIP
DUNHAM, ROWLAND W.
PRACTICAL TRANSPOSITION, FOR PIANISTS AND ORGANISTS
DUNWELL, WILFRID
PIANOFORTE ACCOMPANIMENT WRITING
DUTTON, CHUCK *
MUSIC FOR FUN..PROFESSIONAL COURSE USING THE CHUCK DUTTON
EGBERT, MARION S.
KEYBOARD EXPERIENCE IN THE CLASSROOM MUSIC PROGRAM..HANDBOOK FOR
EGBERT, MARION S.
SEEING WHAT WE SING, AN AID THROUGH KEYBOARD EXPERIENCE TO THE
ELKAN, IDA
PIANO SIGHTREADING CAN BE TAUGHT
ELKAN, IDA
PRACTICAL PIANO PLAYING MANUAL AND THEORY WRITING BOOK
ELKAN, IDA
TECHNICAL WORK IN EAR-TRAINING FOR THE PIANO..A METHOD FOR PRIVATE
ENGEL, CARL
PIANIST'S HANDBOOK, THE ..A GUIDE FOR THE RIGHT COMPREHENSION AND
ETHIER, JOSEPH A.
ETHIER'S GREAT NON-SUCH SELF-INSTRUCTOR IN THE ART OF ACCOMPANYING
EVANS, EDWIN
HOW TO ACCOMPANY AT THE PIANO
EVANS, EVERETT J.
SELF-TEACHING CHORD BOOK FOR THE PIANO OR ORGAN..SHOWS HOW TO PLAY

EVERHART, POWELL
PIANIST'S ART, THE ..A COMPREHENSIVE MANUAL ON PIANO PLAYING FOR
FAELTEN, CARL *
TRANSPOSITION READER--FUNDAMENTAL TRAINING COURSE FOR PIANOFORTE
FALKENER, ROBERT
INSTRUCTIONS FOR PLAYING THE HARPSICHORD..WHEREIN IS FULLY
FERAND, ERNEST T.
IMPROVISATION IN NINE CENTURIES OF WESTERN MUSIC
FETIS, FRANCOIS JOSEPH
HOW TO PLAY FROM SCORE...ON THE ORGAN OR PIANOFORTE
FIELDEN, THOMAS
MARKS AND REMARKS..MUSICAL EXAMINATIONS AND THEIR PROBLEMS
FISKE, ROGER
SCORE READING--BK. 3..CONCERTOS
FISKE, ROGER
SCORE READING--BK. 4..ORATORIOS
FOOTE, ARTHUR W.
MODULATION AND RELATED HARMONIC QUESTIONS
FORD, DONALD
SINGING CLASS PIANIST AND ON PIANOFORTE ACCOMPANYING IN GENERAL,
FORTE, ALLEN
COMPOSITIONAL MATRIX, THE ..MONOGRAPHS IN THEORY AND COMPOSITION
FOWLES, ERNEST
HARMONY IN PIANOFORTE-STUDY..FOR THE INDIVIDUAL STUDENT--2 VOLS.,
FRACKENPOHL, ARTHUR
HARMONIZATION AT THE PIANO--2ND. ED.---1962
FREDRICH, FRANK
PLAYING BY SEEING..A STUDY IN TRAINING AND PERCEPTION FOR BETTER
FRICK, PHILIPP J.
ART OF MUSICAL MODULATION RENDERED EASY AND FAMILIAR, THE
FRICK, PHILIPP J.
TREATISE ON THOROUGH BASS, A
FRISKIN, JAMES
PRINCIPLES OF PIANOFORTE PRACTICE, THE
FULLER, ESTHER MARY
KEYBOARD MODULATIONS FOR ALL KEYBOARD INSTRUMENTS..552 TWO-MEASURE
GARRATT, PERCIVAL
ART OF PIANOFORTE PLAYING, THE
GARROWAY, WILL
PIANISM
GASPARINI, FRANCESCO
PRACTICAL HARMONIST AT THE HARPSICHORD, THE ---1708
GAT, JOZSEF
TECHNIQUE OF PIANO PLAYING, THE, --2ND. ED.---1958
GEIB, WILLIAM
GEIB'S PIANO-FORTE PRECEPTOR, AND MUSICAL GRAMMAR...A TREATISE ON
GEIB, WILLIAM
TREATISE ON PRACTICAL HARMONIC INTONATION, A ..ALSO, A SYNOPSIS OF
GEMINIANI, FRANCESCO
ART OF ACCOMPANIMENT, OR A NEW AND WELL DIGESTED METHOD TO LEARN
GEMINIANI, FRANCESCO
GUIDA ARMONICA, A DIZIONARIO ARMONICO..BEING A SURE GUIDE TO
GEMINIANI, FRANCESCO
RULES FOR PLAYING IN A TRUE TASTE ON THE VIOLIN, GERMAN FLUTE,
GEST, ELIZABETH
KEYBOARD HARMONY FOR JUNIORS
GIBBS, GEORGE A., JR.
FIRST STEPS IN HARMONIZING MELODIES
GIBBS, GEORGE A., JR.
HARMONIZING MELODIES AT SIGHT
GIBBS, GEORGE A., JR.
MODERN CHORD CONSTRUCTION AND ANALYSIS, FOR ALL INSTRUMENTS...AN
GIDDINGS, THADDEUS P.
GIDDING'S PUBLIC SCHOOL CLASS METHOD FOR THE PIANO
GILBERT, RUSSELL S.
EMBRYO MUSICIAN, THE ..A METHOD OF INTRODUCING MUSIC TO LITTLE
GILBERT, RUSSELL S.
SUGGESTED PIANO STUDY FOR THE VOCAL STUDENT
GILBERTSON, ARNOLD B.
TEACHERS MANUAL FOR POPULAR PIANO PLAYING, DESIGNED FOR ALL
GLEN, ANNIE
HOW TO ACCOMPANY..A GUIDE TO THE ARTISTIC ACCOMPANIMENT OF ANY
GORDON, STEPHEN T.
GORDON'S NEW SCHOOL FOR THE PIANO-FORTE
GOSS, JOHN
INTRODUCTION TO HARMONY AND THOROUGH-BASS WITH NUMEROUS EXAMPLES
GRAF, HENRY C.
SIMPLIFIED KEYBOARD HARMONY
GRANTHAM, BILLY
HELLO TO THE BLUES..FUN WITH CHORDS..FUN AND INFORMATION ON
GREW, SIDNEY
FIRST BOOK OF THE PLAYER-PIANIST, THE
GRIMM, CARL W.
HARMONY STUDY AT THE PIANO
GRINDEA, CAROLA
FIRST TEN LESSONS, THE ..A NEW APPROACH TO PIANO TEACHING
GRUNDY, ENID
HAPPY PIANIST, THE
GUTMANN, EMMA WILKINS
TALKS WITH PIANO TEACHERS
HAMBOURG, MARK
HOW TO PREPARE FOR PLAYING IN CONCERT
HAMILTON, ANNA H.
KEYBOARD HARMONY AND TRANSPOSITION..A PRACTICAL COURSE OF KEYBOARD
HAMILTON, CLARENCE G.
MUSIC THEORY FOR PIANO STUDENTS
HAMILTON, CLARENCE G.
PIANO TEACHING..ITS PRINCIPLES AND PROBLEMS
HAMILTON, JAMES ALEXANDER
CATECHISM OF THE RUDIMENTS OF HARMONY AND THOROUGHBASS, A ---1833
HARGISS, GENEVIEVE
MUSIC FOR ELEMENTARY TEACHERS..A PROGRAMMED COURSE IN BASIC THEORY
HARICH-SCHNEIDER, ETA
HARPSICHORD, THE ..AN INTRODUCTION TO TECHNIQUE, STYLE AND THE
HARKNESS, ROBERT
BEGINNERS PIANO COURSE IN HYMN PLAYING BY CORRESPONDENCE
HARKNESS, ROBERT
HARKNESS PIANO METHOD OF EVANGELISTIC HYMN PLAYING, THE ..A
HARTLINE, ELIZABETH DILL *
KEYBOARD MUSICIANSHIP, GROUP PIANO FOR ADULTS
HARVEY, ROBERT
MAGIC KEY TO KEYBOARD SUCCESS, THE
HAVILL, LORINA
YOU CAN SIGHT READ..THE PLEASURES OF PIANO SIGHT READING THROUGH
HAWKINS, JOHN SIDNEY
INQUIRY INTO THE NATURE AND PRINCIPLES OF THROUGH BASS, ON A NEW
HEACOX, ARTHUR EDWARD
HARMONY FOR EAR, EYE, AND KEYBOARD--1ST. YEAR
HEACOX, ARTHUR EDWARD
KEYBOARD TRAINING IN HARMONY--PTS. 1 AND 2--725 GRADED
HECK, JOHANN CASPAR
ART OF PLAYING THOROUGH BASS WITH CORRECTNESS ACCORDING TO THE
HECK, JOHANN CASPAR
COMPLETE SYSTEM OF HARMONY..OR A REGULAR AND EASY METHOD TO ATTAIN
HECK, JOHANN CASPAR
SHORT AND FUNDAMENTAL INSTRUCTIONS FOR LEARNING THOROUGH BASS

HEIDELBERGER, PAULINE
    MASTER METHOD..PIANO NORMAL AND TEACHER'S MANUAL
HERZ, HENRI
    NEW AND COMPLETE PIANOFORTE SCHOOL
HIGGS, JAMES
    MODULATION--'NOVELLO'S MUSIC PRIMERS', NO. 31
HILES, JOHN
    CATECHISM OF HARMONY, THOROUGH-BASS, AND MODULATION, A ..WITH
HILES, JOHN
    KEY TO THE EXERCISES IN THE CATECHISM OF HARMONY, THOROUGH-BASS
HILL, FRANK W.
    HARMONY AT THE KEYBOARD
HILL, JIM
    ART OF IMPROVISING, THE ..HOW TO PLAY POPULAR SONGS IN A MODERN
HILL, JIM
    ART OF TRANSPOSING FOR THE PIANO AT SIGHT, THE
HILL, JIM
    CREATIVE IMPROVISING FOR THE RIGHT HAND..CREATIVE STUDIES IN
HILL, JIM
    CREATIVE WORLD OF SCALES AND CHORDS, THE ..CREATIVE STUDIES IN
HILL, PAUL
    PIANO-MASTER CHORD CHART--CONSTRUCTION, ACCOMPANIMENT, AND SWING
HOLDER, WILLIAM
    TREATISE ON THE NATURAL GROUNDS AND PRINCIPLES OF HARMONY, A ..TO
HOLLIDAY, MARGARET M.
    KEYBOARD MUSICIANSHIP--BKS. 1 AND 2
HOLT, HILDA
    HARMONY AT YOUR KEYBOARD
HOLTZ, GUY
    PIANO PROJECTS...A NEW APPROACH TO THE STUDY OF MODERN POPULAR
HOME, ETHEL
    FIRST STEPS IN HARMONIZING MELODIES
HOME, ETHEL
    IMPROVISING..A SIMPLE METHOD OF TEACHING THE SUBJECT TO CHILDREN
HORROCKS, CYRIL R. H.
    STUDENT'S GUIDE TO THE ART OF TEACHING THE PIANOFORTE, THE --2ND.
HOUGHTON, WINIFRED E.
    TEXTBOOK OF PRACTICAL HARMONY AT THE KEYBOARD
HOWELL, DOROTHY
    KEYBOARD WORK FOR HARMONY STUDENTS
HULL, ARTHUR EAGLEFIELD
    THREE HUNDRED QUESTIONS ON PIANOFORTE TEACHING IN 30 GRADUATED
HUMMEL, JOHANN NEPOMUK
    COMPLETE THEORETICAL AND PRACTICAL COURSE OF INSTRUCTIONS ON THE
HUNT, REGINALD H.
    EXTEMPORIZATION FOR MUSIC STUDENTS
HUNT, REGINALD H.
    HARMONY AT THE KEYBOARD
HUNT, REGINALD H.
    TRANSPOSITION FOR MUSIC STUDENTS
INTERNATIONAL MUSIC INSTITUTE FOR FREE IMPROVISATION
    METHODICAL WAY TO FREE IMPROVISATION, THE --AVANT-GARDE
IRWIN, WILLIAM
    RHYTHM ACCOMPANIMENT MAGIC, FOR THE POPULAR PIANIST
JACOB, GORDON P.
    HOW TO READ A SCORE
JOHNSON, ARTEMAS N.
    INSTRUCTIONS IN THE ART OF PLAYING CHURCH MUSIC UPON THE MELODEON,
JOHNSON, ARTEMAS N.
    INSTRUCTIONS IN THOROUGH BASE..BEING A NEW AND EASY METHOD FOR
JOHNSON, ARTEMAS N.
    JOHNSON'S NEW METHOD FOR THOROUGH BASE..AN INSTRUCTION BOOK IN THE
JOHNSON, ARTEMAS N.
    THOROUGH BASE, MELODEON, ORGAN AND HARMONY INSTRUCTION BOOK, WITH
JOHNSON, JOHN BARHAM
    KEYBOARD HARMONY FOR BEGINNERS
JOHNSON, VERA A.
    SCIENTIFIC SIDE OF MUSIC IN SIMPLE, PRACTICAL FORM FOR TEACHERS
JONES, JOHN H.
    PRACTICAL GUIDE TO THOROUGH BASS, A ..OR, HARMONY ILLUSTRATED AND
JOUSSE, JOHN
    GUIDA ARMONICA, IN WHICH...CHORDS, ARE CLEARLY EXPLAINED AND
KANZELL, MAXWELL
    HOW TO READ MUSIC..A COMPLETELY NEW AND SIMPLIFIED APPROACH TO
KARLIN, AARON
    KARLIN'S HARMONIC COURSE FOR PIANO IMPROVISING--4
KEDDINGTON, J. BLAINE
    CHORD-O-GRAPH METHOD OF KEYBOARD HARMONY---PRINTED FROM TYPED COPY
KEILMAN, WILHELM
    INTRODUCTION TO SIGHT READING
KELLER, GOTTFRIED
    COMPLEAT METHOD, FOR ATTAINING TO PLAY A THOROUGH BASS UPON EITHER
KELLER, HERMANN
    THOROUGHBASS METHOD--NUMEROUS EXAMPLES FROM THE LITERATURE OF THE
KENYON, CHARLES FREDERICK
    HOW TO MEMORIZE MUSIC
KERN, ALICE M.
    HARMONIZATION-TRANSPOSITION AT THE KEYBOARD
KIRBY, MAY B. KELLY
    KELLY KIRBY KINDERGARTEN PIANO METHOD, TEACHERS' COURSE, THE
KLING, HENRI
    TRANSPOSITION...A PRACTICAL AND AUTHORITATIVE GUIDE FOR ALL
KLOSE, F. J.
    PRACTICAL HINTS FOR ACQUIRING THOROUGH BASS
KOLANDER, MAX
    KOLANDER'S ACCOMPANIMENT INSTRUCTOR FOR THE PIANO OR ORGAN
KOLLMANN, AUGUST F.
    INTRODUCTION TO THE ART OF PRELUDING AND EXTEMPORISING IN SIX
KOLLMANN, AUGUST F.
    PRACTICAL GUIDE TO THOROUGH-BASS, A
KOLLMANN, AUGUST F.
    SECOND PRACTICAL GUIDE TO THOROUGH BASS, A
KRAEHENBUEHL, DAVID
    KEYBOARD THEORY--6 VOLS.
KREBS, T. L.
    MANUAL OF MODULATION...FOR THE USE OF PIANISTS AND ORGANISTS
KRUSZYNSKI, MICHAL
    APPROACH TO THE PSYCHOLOGY OF PIANO TEACHING, AN
LAMAR, RICHARD
    COLLEGE PIANO PEDAGOGY
LAMPE, JOHN F.
    PLAIN AND COMPENDIOUS METHOD OF TEACHING THOROUGH BASS, A ..WITH
LANG, CRAIG SELLAR
    HARMONY AT THE KEYBOARD
LANG, EDITH *
    MUSICAL ACCOMPANIMENT OF MOVING PICTURES..A PRACTICAL MANUAL FOR
LAST, JOAN
    YOUNG PIANIST, THE ..A NEW APPROACH FOR TEACHERS AND
LAVIGNAC, ALBERT
    MUSIC AND MUSICIANS---1895, IN FRENCH
LAWRENCE, LUCILE
    ART OF MODULATING, THE ..FOR HARPISTS, PIANISTS, ORGANISTS
LAWRENCE, SIDNEY
    GUIDE TO REMEDIAL SIGHT READING FOR THE PIANO STUDENT, A
LEACH, JOHN R.
    FUNCTIONAL PIANO FOR THE TEACHER

LEHMER, ISABEL
    KEYBOARD HARMONY..A COMPREHENSIVE APPROACH TO MUSICIANSHIP
LEIGHTON, GEORGE A.
    HARMONY, ANALYTICAL AND APPLIED
LE ROY, PERRY J.
    HOW TO PLAY THE PIANO BY EAR..THE QUICK, EASY, SIMPLE WAY
LIEBERMAN, MAURICE
    ELEMENTARY KEYBOARD HARMONY
LIEBERMAN, MAURICE
    KEYBOARD HARMONY AND IMPROVISATION--2 VOLS.
LINDO, ALGERNON H.
    ART OF ACCOMPANYING, THE
LINDO, ALGERNON H.
    AURAL TESTS FOR EXAMINATIONS--SPECIALLY WRITTEN FOR TEACHERS AND
LINDO, ALGERNON H.
    TREATISE ON MODULATION WITH TYPICAL EXAMPLES FROM WELL-KNOWN
LINLEY, FRANCIS
    NEW ASSISTANT TO THE PIANO-FORTE OR HARPSICHORD, A ...RULES FOR
LITTLE, FRED W.
    LITTLE SYSTEM OF PLAYING THE PIANO BY EAR, THE
LOCKE, MATTHEW
    MELOTHESIA..OR, CERTAIN GENERAL RULES FOR PLAYING UPON A
LOGIER, JOHANN BERNHARD
    LOGIER'S SYSTEM OF THE SCIENCE OF MUSIC, HARMONY, AND PRACTICAL
LOGIER, JOHANN BERNHARD
    SEQUEL TO THE FIRST COMPANION TO THE CHIROPLAST
LOGIER, JOHANN BERNHARD
    SYSTEM OF THE SCIENCE OF MUSIC AND PRACTICAL
LOMAS, LULU GRAHAM
    FIRST TEN PIANO LESSONS, LAID OUT FOR YOUNG TEACHERS, WITH
LONDON--A COMMITTEE OF PROFESSORS
    EXPOSITION OF THE MUSICAL SYSTEM OF MR. LOGIER..WITH STRICTURES ON
LONG, NOEL
    HARMONY AND STYLE--3 VOLS.
LOVELOCK, WILLIAM
    ELEMENTARY ACCOMPANIMENT WRITING--CHIEFLY MUSIC, FOR EXAM
LOVELOCK, WILLIAM
    TESTS IN SIGHT READING, FOR PIANO..FROM FIRST GRADE TO DIPLOMA--3
LOVELOCK, WILLIAM
    TRANSPOSITION AT THE KEYBOARD..PIANO..26 PAGES OF GRADED EXERCISES
LOWRY, MARGARET
    KEYBOARD APPROACH TO HARMONY
LUBIN, ERNEST
    PIANISTS CHORD MANUAL, THE
LUBIT, JULIA
    PIANOFORTE THEORY COURSE FOR BEGINNERS' PIANO CLASS
LUCKE, KATHARINE E.
    PRACTICAL DRILL IN KEYBOARD HARMONY--2 VOLS., 1932-1940
LUDDEN, WILLIAM
    THOROUGH BASS SCHOOL, THE ..AN EASY AND PROGRESSIVE COURSE FOR
MACEWAN, DESIREE
    FIRST TWO YEARS OF PIANOFORTE STUDY, THE
MACK, GLEN
    ADVENTURES IN IMPROVISATION AT THE KEYBOARD
MACLEAN, CHARLES D.
    PRINCIPLES OF PIANOFORTE PRACTICE, THE
MAIER, GUY
    PIANO TEACHER'S COMPANION, THE
MAIER, GUY *
    PLAYING THE PIANO..A COURSE OF ROTE TRAINING FOR BEGINNERS--CLASS
MAIER, GUY *
    PLAYING THE PIANO--TEACHER'S MANUAL
MARIAL, R.
    METHODS APPLICABLE TO GROUP TEACHING OR PRIVATE PIANO INSTRUCTION
MARSDEN AND COMPANY
    HOW TO EXTEMPORIZE PIANO ACCOMPANIMENTS...RAPID AND SIMPLE METHOD
MARSH, JOHN
    RUDIMENTS OF THOROUGH BASS, THE
MASON, WILLIAM G. *
    PRIMER OF MUSIC, A ..BEING THE FIRST STEPS IN MUSICIANSHIP..FOR
MATTHESON, JOHANN
    COMPLETE TREATISE OF THOROUGH BASS, A
MCALL, REGINALD L.
    PRACTICAL CHURCH SCHOOL MUSIC..METHODS AND TRAINING FOR SUCCESSFUL
MCCARTHY, ALBERT J.--EDITOR
    PIANO JAZZ..ESSAYS--2 VOLS., 1945-1946
MCCLINTOCK, LORENE
    TEACH YOURSELF TO PLAY THE PIANO..BASED ON THE INTERVAL METHOD
MCHOSE, ALLEN IRVINE *
    KEYBOARD AND DICTATION MANUAL
MCHOSE, ALLEN IRVINE
    TEACHERS DICTATION MANUAL
MCLAIN, MARGARET STARR
    CLASS PIANO
MEHEGAN, JOHN F.
    JAZZ IMPROVISATION..TONAL AND RHYTHMIC PRINCIPLES--4 VOLS.
MEHEGAN, JOHN F.
    JAZZ PIANIST, THE ..STUDIES IN THE ART AND PRACTICE OF JAZZ
MEHEGAN, JOHN F.
    STUDIES IN JAZZ HARMONY
MEHEGAN, JOHN F.
    STYLES FOR THE JAZZ PIANIST--BK. 1..THE RHYTHMIC SCHOOL
MEHEGAN, JOHN F.
    TOUCH AND RHYTHM TECHNIQUES FOR THE JAZZ PIANIST
MEHER, DONOVAN
    HOW TO VAMP AT SIGHT..THE EASIEST AND CLEAREST METHOD OF
MEHR, NORMAN
    GROUP PIANO TEACHING
MELCHER, ROBERT A. *
    MUSIC FOR ADVANCED STUDY..A SOURCE BOOK OF EXCERPTS
MELCHER, ROBERT A. *
    MUSIC FOR KEYBOARD HARMONY
MELCHER, ROBERT A. *
    MUSIC FOR SCORE READING
MELLERS, WILFRED
    FRANCOIS COUPERIN AND THE FRENCH CLASSICAL TRADITION
MELLING, E. H.
    EXTEMPORIZING AT THE PIANO MADE EASY
MERRICK, FRANK
    PRACTICING THE PIANO
MERRILL, MYRTLE
    SIGHT-READING AT THE PIANO
MILLER, EDWARD
    ELEMENTS OF THOROUGH BASS AND COMPOSITION
MILLER, EDWARD
    INSTITUTES OF MUSIC, OR, EASY INSTRUCTIONS FOR THE HARPSICHORD
MINNESOTA MUSIC TEACHERS ASSOCIATION
    PIANO-THEORY EXAMINATION SYLLABUS
MOKREJS, JOHN
    GREAT HARMONIC LAW OF CHORD PROGRESSION AND IMPROVISING, THE
MOKREJS, JOHN
    LESSONS IN SIGHT READING AT THE PIANO
MOORE, GERALD
    UNASHAMED ACCOMPANIST, THE
MOORE, MARY BURNHAM
    LURE OF THE PIANO THROUGH COORDINATION AND CONCENTRATION, THE

MORDEN, HARRY
    PLAYING THE PIANO BY EAR--3 PTS.
MORRIS, REGINALD OWEN
    FIGURED HARMONY AT THE KEYBOARD---PRINCIPALLY EXERCISES
MUFFAT, GEORG
    ESSAY ON THOROUGHBASS, AN --MUSICOLOGICAL STUDIES AND DOCUMENTS,
MURPHY, HOWARD A. *
    MUSIC FOR STUDY..A SOURCE BOOK OF EXCERPTS
MUSIC EDUCATORS NATIONAL CONFERENCE
    TEACHING PIANO IN CLASSROOM AND STUDIO
MUSIC PROJECT--NEW YORK CITY
    TEACHER'S GUIDE..A CREATIVE APPROACH TO PIANO CLASS TEACHING, BY
NEILL, JACK
    NEILL IMPROVISING SYSTEM
NEVINS, WILLARD I. *
    HARMONY AT THE KEYBOARD
NEWMAN, ELIZABETH
    HOW TO TEACH MUSIC TO BEGINNERS
NEWMAN, WILLIAM S.
    PIANIST'S PROBLEMS, THE ..A MODERN APPROACH TO EFFICIENT PRACTICE
NEWTON, ERNEST
    ELEMENTARY STUDIES IN TRANSPOSITION--BKS. 1 AND 2
NICCHIA, LILLIAN
    PIANOFORTE STUDY..HINTS ON PIANO PLAYING
NICHOL, HENRY E.
    TRANSPOSITION AT SIGHT..FOR STUDENTS OF THE ORGAN AND
NICHOLLS, FREDERICK *
    ADVENTURES IN IMPROVISATION
NICHOLSON, JAMES
    CONCISE TREATISE ON THOROUGHBASS, A
O'REAR, MRS. ASBURY S.
    SELF READING NOTES
O'TOOLE, WILLIAM
    KEYBOARD HARMONY---DUPLICATED FROM MANUSCRIPT
OREM, PRESTON WARE
    MANUAL OF MODULATION
ORREY, LESLIE
    MUSIC AT THE KEYBOARD
OTTERSTROEN, THORVALD
    THEORY OF MODULATION, A ---DUAL TEXT..ENGLISH AND GERMAN
PACE, ROBERT
    MUSIC ESSENTIALS FOR CLASSROOM TEACHERS--2ND. ED.---1961
PACE, ROBERT
    PIANO FOR CLASSROOM MUSIC--2ND. ED.---1956
PASFIELD, WILLIAM R.
    MELODY MAKING, KEYBOARD HARMONY AND EXTEMPORISATION
PASQUALI, NICOLO
    THOROUGH-BASS MADE EASY..OR, PRACTICAL RULES FOR FINDING AND
PATTON, VICTOR S.
    LEARN TO PLAY POPULAR PIANO BY NOTE IN 20 EASY LESSONS...HOME
PAULSON, JOSEPH
    MODERN KEYBOARD HARMONY AND IMPROVISATION
PEARCE, CHARLES WILLIAM
    ART OF THE PIANO TEACHER, THE
PEERY, ROB ROY
    PRACTICAL KEYBOARD MODULATION
PELZ, WILLIAM
    BASIC KEYBOARD SKILLS--2ND. ED.---1963
PERRY, ADELAIDE TROWBRIDGE *
    GUIDE TO PIANO STUDY FOR CLASS OR INDIVIDUAL INSTRUCTION, A
PETERS, WILLIAM C.
    ECLECTIC PIANOFORTE SCHOOL, THE ..ARRANGED FROM THE WORKS OF THE
PETERS, WILLIAM C.
    ELEMENTS OF THOROUGH BASE, ADAPTED TO THE WANTS OF YOUNG PUPILS
PETERSILIA, FRANZ
    STUDY WITH AMUSEMENT, A SERIES OF PROGRESSIVE LESSONS FOR THE
PETERSON, FRANKLIN
    THEORETIC COMPANION TO PRACTICE--PART I OF THE PIANIST'S HANDBOOK
PFEFFERKORN, OTTO W.
    PIANISTIC HINTS
PHILIPP, LILLIE H.
    PIANO STUDY..APPLICATION AND TECHNIQUE
PIERCE, DORA *
    INTRODUCTION TO SIGHT READING, AN
PIERCE, DORA *
    READ AND ENJOY--2 VOLS.
PIERCE, DORA *
    SIGHT READING TESTS FOR BEGINNERS--2 VOLS., 1930-1933
PILLING, DOROTHY
    HARMONIZATION OF MELODIES AT THE KEYBOARD--BKS. 1 AND 2
PILLING, DOROTHY
    KEY TO THE HARMONIZATION OF MELODIES AT THE KEYBOARD--BK. 1
PLATT, CAROLYN
    CAROLYN PLATT METHOD FOR PIANO, THE --GROUP INSTRUCTION--TEACHER'S
POINTER SYSTEM, INC.
    GUIDE TO THE MODERN PIANIST, A
POTAMKIN, FRANK
    MODERN PIANO PEDAGOGY
PRATT, SILAS G.
    PIANIST'S MENTAL VELOCITY, THE ..A SYSTEMATIC PREPARATION OF THE
PRELLEUR, PETER
    HARPSICHORD ILLUSTRATED AND IMPROV'D, WHEREIN IS SHEWN THE ITALIAN
PRIESING, DOROTHY *
    LANGUAGE OF THE PIANO..A WORKBOOK IN THEORY AND KEYBOARD HARMONY
PROCTOR, CHARLES
    HARMONIZATION AT THE KEYBOARD
QUINTE, MICHAEL S.
    MODULATIONARY HARMONY BOOK
QUIST, BOBBIE LEE *
    LISTEN TO LEARN--KEYBOARD HARMONY
RABINOF, SYLVIA
    MUSICIANSHIP THROUGH IMPROVISATION AT THE KEYBOARD--BK.
RAST, LAURENCE R.
    LET'S FIND OUT ABOUT MUSIC..WURLITZER ELEMENTARY PIANO WORKBOOKS,
REDDIE, CHARLES FREDERICK
    PIANOFORTE PLAYING ON ITS TECHNICAL AND AESTHETIC SIDES
REED, CLARE OSBORNE
    CONSTRUCTIVE HARMONY AND IMPROVISATION
REES-DAVIES, IVAN
    TRANSPOSITION AT THE KEYBOARD
REEVES, BETTY
    APPROACH TO PIANO TEACHING---ALSO CATALOGUED UNDER
REGER, MAX
    ON THE THEORY OF MODULATION
REGER, MAX
    SUPPLEMENT TO THE THEORY OF MODULATION
REINAGLE, CAROLINE
    FEW WORDS ON PIANOFORTE PLAYING, A
RELFE, JOHN
    REMARKS ON THE PRESENT STATE OF MUSICAL INSTRUCTION...THOROUGH
REZITS, JOSEPH
    SOURCE MATERIALS FOR PIANO TECHNIQUES
RHODES, ALFRED
    CURIOSITIES OF THE KEY-BOARD AND THE STAFF...SHOWN TO BE UPON A
RICHARDSON, ALFRED M.
    EXTEMPORE PLAYING..FORTY LESSONS IN THE ART OF KEYBOARD

RICHTER, ADA
    TEACHING HINTS
RICKER, EARL
    MUSIC LESSONS FOR YOUR CHILD
RIEMANN, HUGO
    INTRODUCTION TO PLAYING FROM SCORE
ROBBINS, EDGAR A.
    AMERICAN METHOD FOR THE PIANOFORTE
ROBINSON, HELENE
    BASIC PIANO FOR ADULTS
ROBYN, LOUISE
    FIRST YEAR ESSENTIALS IN KEYBOARD HARMONY
ROBYN, LOUISE
    HOW TO TEACH PIANO TO THE CHILD BEGINNER..A TEXT BOOK FOR TEACHERS
ROBYN, LOUISE
    ROBYN-HANKS HARMONY, THE ..A JUNIOR COURSE--BKS. 1-3, 1936-1938
ROEDER, CARL M.
    PRACTICAL KEYBOARD HARMONY, A
ROOT, CATHERINE ADAMS *
    LISTEN, SING AND PLAY..CLASS LESSONS FOR PIANO AND VOICE
ROWBOTHAM, JOHN F.
    HOW TO VAMP..A PRACTICAL GUIDE TO THE ACCOMPANIMENT OF SONGS BY
ROWLEY, ALEC
    DO'S AND DONT'S FOR MUSICIANS..A HANDBOOK FOR TEACHERS AND
ROWLEY, ALEC *
    GRADED TESTS IN PRACTICAL MUSICIANSHIP AND MUSICAL INITIATIVE--IN
ROWLEY, ALEC *
    HARMONIZATION AT THE PIANO--IN THREE STAGES
ROWLEY, ALEC *
    MELODY MAKING AT THE PIANO--IN THREE STAGES
ROWLEY, ALEC
    PRACTICAL MUSICIANSHIP, A HANDBOOK FOR TEACHERS AND STUDENTS
ROWLEY, ALEC *
    SIGHT READING AT THE PIANO--IN THREE STAGES
RUBINSTEIN, BERYL
    PIANIST'S APPROACH TO SIGHT READING AND MEMORIZING, THE
SAULS, RANDY
    HOW TO READ KEYBOARD MUSIC
SAULS, RANDY
    THINKING MUSICIANS' APPLICATION OF MODERN HARMONY, THE ..HOW TO
SAWYER, FRANK J.
    EXTEMPORIZATION
SCHAAF, EDWARD C.
    FUNDAMENTAL PRINCIPLES INVOLVED IN THE COMPOSING AND ARRANGING OF
SCHELLING, ERNEST *
    OXFORD PIANO COURSE, TEACHER'S FIRST MANUAL
SCHELLING, ERNEST *
    OXFORD PIANO COURSE, TEACHER'S SECOND MANUAL
SCHLIEDER, FREDERICK W.
    LYRIC COMPOSITION THROUGH IMPROVISATION--2 VOLS., 1927-1946
SCHNEIDER, FRIEDRICH
    SCHNEIDER'S TREATISE ON THOROUGH BASS AND HARMONY
SCHULER, GEORGE S.
    ACCOMPANIST'S MANUAL, THE
SCHULER, GEORGE S.
    EVANGELISTIC PIANO PLAYING
SCONCIA, JOHN A.
    SCONCIA'S NEW SYSTEM OF INSTRUCTION IN MUSIC AS A SCIENCE..OR, A
SCOTT, WAYNE
    HANDBOOK OF CHORD PROGRESSIONS
SCOVILL, MODENA
    KEYBOARD HARMONY--REV. ED.---1939
SEYMOUR, HARRIET AYER
    HOME MUSIC LESSONS..HOW TO FIND YOUR MUSICAL SELF
SEYMOUR, HARRIET AYER
    HOW TO THINK MUSIC
SHEFTE, ARTHUR G.
    KEYBOARD HARMONY SIMPLIFIED
SHEFTE, ARTHUR G.
    PIANO IMPROVISING--2 VOLS., 1936-1938
SHEFTEL, PAUL
    EXPLORING KEYBOARD FUNDAMENTALS
SHELDON, JAY
    ALL ABOUT MUSIC..A COMPLETE BOOK OF MUSICAL THEORY FOR PIANISTS
SHEPARD, FRANK H.
    HOW TO MODULATE..MODULATING FROM ANY KEY TO ANY OTHER
SHEPARD, ROBERT
    HARMONIZING..HOW TO PLAY SIMPLE ACCOMPANIMENTS TO A MELODY AT THE
SHUMWAY, STANLEY
    HARMONY AND EAR TRAINING AT THE KEYBOARD
SIMPSON, ELIZABETH
    BASIC PIANOFORTE TECHNIQUE...BASED ON THE SCIENCE OF PIANOFORTE
SIMPSON, KENNETH
    KEYBOARD HARMONY AND IMPROVISATION
SMELTZER, JEANNIE R.--COMPILER
    OUTLINES AND GRADES FOR THE USE OF PIANO TEACHERS
SMITH, EDWIN S.
    PIANO BY EAR
SMITH, HOWARD G.
    ANYONE CAN PLAY THE PIANO BY EAR IN FIVE EASY LESSONS..A-B-C PIANO
SMITH, THOMAS
    ART OF PLAYING AT SIGHT, THE
SMITH, THOMAS
    CONCISE AND PRACTICAL EXPLANATION OF THE RULES OF SIMPLE HARMONY
SMITH, USELMA CLARK
    KEYBOARD HARMONY..LEARNING BY HEARING
SOREL, CLAUDETTE *
    INDEPENDENT LEARNING APPROACH TO PIANO SIGHT READING, AN
SPENCER, BERNARD
    POPULAR PIANO...A CORRESPONDENCE COURSE OF THE EASTERN SCHOOLS OF
SQUIRE, RUSSEL N. *
    CLASS PIANO FOR ADULT BEGINNERS--2ND. ED.---1964
STANLEY, JANE
    BASIC ROUTINES IN ELEMENTARY PIANO TEACHING THROUGH THE FIRST
STARKEY, EVELYN
    PIANO CLASS WORKBOOK FOR FIRST YEAR STUDENTS
STEVENS, A. M.
    HOW TO PLAY THE PIANO AND ORGAN..OR, KEY TO THE SCIENCE AND THEORY
STEVENS, EVERETT
    CHORDS, CADENCES, AND ARPEGGIOS
STEWART, REID
    HOW TO PASS MUSIC EXAMINATIONS--PIANO--A GUIDE FOR TEACHERS AND
STORMEN, WIN
    FIFTY YEARS OF POPULAR PIANO TECHNIQUES IN THE U.S.A.
STORMEN, WIN
    JAZZ PIANO..DIXIELAND TO MODERN JAZZ, BLUES, BOOGIE, RAGTIME,
STORMEN, WIN
    JAZZ PIANO..EARLY BLUES TO CONTEMPORARY MODERN JAZZ, HOW TO PLAY
STORMEN, WIN
    LINK TO MODERN MUSIC INSTRUCTION, THE
STORMEN, WIN
    MODERN PIANO IMPROVISATION..BASIC PRINCIPLES ADAPTED FROM THE
STORMEN, WIN
    POPULAR ACCOMPANYING
STORMEN, WIN
    POPULAR KEYBOARD HARMONY

STORMEN, WIN
    POPULAR PIANO SELF-TAUGHT---1956
STORMEN, WIN
    YOUR GUIDE TO PLAYING AND WRITING POPULAR MUSIC--REV. ED.
SUMNER, WILLIAM L.
    PIANOFORTE, THE --3RD. ED.---1966
SWENSON, LUCILE B.
    DISCOVERING THE PIANO..THE MULTIPLE KEY APPROACH..STUDY GUIDE AND
TANKARD, GEOFFREY
    PIANOFORTE DIPLOMAS
TAPPER, THOMAS
    ABC OF KEYBOARD HARMONY, THE
TAYLER, E. DOUGLAS
    MODULATION MADE EASY
TAYLOR, ERIC R.
    INTRODUCTION TO SCORE PLAYING, AN
TAYLOR, ERIC R.
    PLAYING FROM AN ORCHESTRAL SCORE
TAYLOR, FRANCIS
    REEVES' VAMPING TUTOR FOR PLAYING BY EAR
TAYLOR, FRANKLIN
    PRIMER OF PIANOFORTE PLAYING
THACKRAY, RUPERT M.
    PLAYING FOR DANCE..THE PLACE OF THE PIANIST IN THE TEACHING OF
TISCHLER, HANS
    PRACTICAL HARMONY, AN INTEGRATED COURSE IN THE PRINCIPLES OF
TOBIN, JOSEPH RAYMOND
    ADVENTURES IN MUSICIANSHIP
TOBIN, JOSEPH RAYMOND
    COMMON SENSE IN SIGHT READING..A GUIDE FOR PIANO TEACHERS
TOBIN, JOSEPH RAYMOND
    HOW TO IMPROVISE PIANO ACCOMPANIMENTS
TOBIN, JOSEPH RAYMOND
    MODULATION AT THE PIANO--IN THREE STAGES
TOBIN, JOSEPH RAYMOND
    READ AND REMEMBER..TWELVE STUDY PIECES TO FACILITATE PLAYING FROM
TOBIN, JOSEPH RAYMOND
    TRANSPOSING AT THE PIANO--IN THREE STAGES
TRACY, GEORGE L.
    PRACTICAL GUIDE TO THE STUDY OF TRANSPOSITION, A
TRUE, LYLE C.
    HOW AND WHAT TO PLAY FOR MOVING PICTURES..A MANUAL AND GUIDE FOR
UNITED STATES TRAINING SERVICE
    COURSES OF INSTRUCTION IN PIANO MAKING, TOGETHER WITH A SECTION ON
VAN DER VELPEN, JEAN
    HARMONY AND THOROUGH BASS--2 VOLS., 1909-1910
VENDEN, LEONARD
    MUSICIAN'S LIGHTNING MODULATION GUIDE..INFORMATION, EXAMPLES,
VERNAZZA, MARCELLE
    BASIC MATERIALS FOR THE PIANO STUDENT
VINING, HARRISON S.
    SIMPLE AND COMPLETE PRIMER FOR THE PIANOFORTE, THE
VIRGIL, ALMON K.
    FOUNDATION EXERCISES IN PIANO PLAYING FROM FIRST RUDIMENTS TO
VIRGIL, ANTHA MINERVA
    ELEMENTARY EXERCISES IN SIGHT READING...FROM THE VIRGIL METHOD
VIRGIL, ANTHA MINERVA
    PRACTICAL EXERCISES IN THEORY AND HARMONY PLAYING...LEADING TO
VIRGIL, ANTHA MINERVA
    VIRGIL METHOD OF PIANOFORTE TECHNIC, THE --2 VOLS.
WAGNER, JOHN J.
    NUMERICAL METHOD OF PIANO ACCOMPANIMENTS, A --WITH CHARTS
WARRINER, JOHN
    TRANSPOSITION, KEYBOARD AND ORCHESTRAL--2 PTS., 1893-1908
WEBBE, SAMUEL
    HARMONY EPITOMIZED, BEING A SHORT EXPLANATION OF FIGURED BASSES,
WEDGE, GEORGE ANSON
    KEYBOARD HARMONY
WEISSBUCH, ANTONIA
    KEYBOARD HARMONY MADE SIMPLE..THE NATURAL ROAD TO MUSICIANSHIP
WELLS, HOWARD
    EARS, BRAIN AND FINGERS..A TEXT BOOK FOR PIANO TEACHERS AND PUPILS
WESTRUP, SIR JACK ALLAN
    MUSICAL INTERPRETATION---THIS BOOK ACCOMPANIED A SERIES OF B.B.C.
WHITMER, THOMAS C.
    ART OF IMPROVISATION, THE ..A HANDBOOK OF PRINCIPLES AND METHODS
WIER, ALBERT
    PIANO, THE ..ITS HISTORY, MAKERS, PLAYERS AND MUSIC
WILLIAMS, JEAN E. *
    MIND IN MUSIC, THE
WILLIAMS, JEAN E.
    MODERN METHOD OF PIANO INSTRUCTION, A ..TEACHERS MANUAL
WILLIAMS, JOHN M.
    WHAT TO TEACH AT THE VERY FIRST LESSON
WILLIAMS, PETER F.
    FIGURED BASS ACCOMPANIMENT--2 VOLS.
WILSON, MORRIS E.
    HOW TO HELP YOUR CHILD WITH MUSIC--2ND. ED.---1951
WILSON, MORRIS E.
    HOW TO PLAY BY EAR
WOLFF, KONRAD
    TEACHING OF ARTUR SCHNABEL, THE ..A GUIDE TO INTERPRETATION
WOLFRAM, THEODOR
    PRACTICAL MODULATOR, OR, HOW TO LEARN TO MODULATE FROM ANY ONE KEY
WOLLNER, GERTRUDE PRICE
    IMPROVISATION IN MUSIC..WAYS TOWARDS CAPTURING MUSICAL IDEAS AND
WRIGHT, WILLIAM C.
    GOLDEN MONITOR, FOR THE PIANOFORTE AND CABINET ORGAN, DESIGNED AS
WRIGHT, WILLIAM C.
    PIANOFORTE MANUAL, THE ..DESIGNED AS A COMPLETE PIANOFORTE PRIMER
ZEITLIN, POLDI *
    THEORY PAPERS, THE --C.M.P. PIANO LIBRARY--2 VOLS., 1961-1963
ZEPP, ARTHUR
    LET'S IMPROVISE--2 VOLS.
ZUR HEIDE, KARL GERT
    DEEP SOUTH PIANO..THE STORY OF LITTLE BROTHER MONTGOMERY

Piano Music

ABRAHAM, GERALD
    CHOPIN'S MUSICAL STYLE---1939
ADAMS, JULIETTE
    WHAT THE PIANO WRITING OF EDWARD MACDOWELL MEANS TO THE PIANO
AEOLIAN COMPANY, THE
    CATALOG OF AEOLIAN MUSIC ARRANGED FOR 46-NOTE INSTRUMENTS
AEOLIAN COMPANY, THE
    CATALOG OF METROSTYLE AND THEMODIST MUSIC FOR THE PIANOLA AND
AEOLIAN COMPANY, THE
    CATALOG OF MUSIC-ROLLS FOR THE DUO-ART REPRODUCING PIANO
AEOLIAN COMPANY, THE
    CATALOG OF MUSIC AND MUSICAL LITERATURE---PIANOLA RECORDS
AEOLIAN COMPANY, THE
    CATALOG OF MUSIC FOR THE PIANOLA, PIANOLA PIANO AND

AEOLIAN COMPANY, THE
    COMPLETE CATALOG OF MUSIC ROLLS FOR THE DUO-ART REPRODUCING PIANO
AEOLIAN COMPANY, THE
    DUO-ART PIANO MUSIC...RECORDED BY MORE THAN 250 PIANISTS
AEOLIAN COMPANY, THE
    DUO-ART PIANO MUSIC
AEOLIAN COMPANY, THE
    LIBRARY OF DUO-ART MUSIC ROLLS
AEOLIAN COMPANY, THE
    METROSTYLE-THEMODIST AND METRO-ART MUSIC ROLLS FOR THE PIANOLA AND
AEOLIAN COMPANY, THE
    METROSTYLE, THE
AEOLIAN COMPANY, THE
    METROSTYLE AND THEMODIST MUSIC CATALOG FOR THE PIANOLA AND PIANOLA
AEOLIAN COMPANY, THE
    MUSIC FOR THE AEOLIAN GRAND--SUPPLEMENT
AEOLIAN COMPANY, THE
    MUSIC FOR THE AEOLIAN GRAND
AEOLIAN COMPANY, THE
    MUSIC FOR THE ORCHESTRELLE AND AEOLIAN GRAND
AEOLIAN COMPANY, THE
    MUSIC FOR THE PIANOLA AND THE AERIAL PIANO--4 VOLS.
AEOLIAN COMPANY, THE
    NEW MUSIC FOR THE AEOLIAN GRAND, THE PIANOLA, AND THE AERIOL PIANO
AEOLIAN COMPANY, THE
    PIANOLA AND PIANOLA PIANO MUSIC CATALOG, THE ..SIXTY-FIVE NOTE
AEOLIAN COMPANY, THE
    SUPPLEMENTARY CATALOG OF MUSIC FOR THE AEOLIAN GRAND AND
ALBRECHTSBERGER, JOHANN GEORG
    ALBRECHTSBERGER'S COLLECTED WRITINGS ON THOROUGH-BASS, HARMONY AND
ALBRECHTSBERGER, JOHANN GEORG
    METHODS OF HARMONY, FIGURED BASE, AND COMPOSITION...ADAPTED FOR
ALLEN, MARGARET *
    CREATIVE MOTION
ALTMAN, FRANCES
    GEORGE GERSHWIN, MASTER COMPOSER
AMERICAN PIANO CORPORATION
    CATALOGUE OF MUSIC FOR THE AMPICO, A ..A LIST OF THE RECORDINGS OF
AMERICAN PIANO CORPORATION
    CATALOGUE OF MUSIC FOR THE AMPICO, A --A LIST OF THE RECORDINGS OF
AMPICO CORPORATION
    AMPICO REPRODUCING PIANO..A SUPPLEMENT TO *PIANO MUSIC, ITS
AMPICO CORPORATION
    SUPREMACY OF AMPICO MUSIC..UNIT TWO OF A COURSE IN AMPICO
ANDERSON, WILLIAM R.
    RACHMANINOV AND HIS PIANO CONCERTOS
ANON
    GUIDE TO THE PROPER USE OF THE PIANOFORTE PEDALS, WITH EXAMPLES
ANON
    LIFE AND WORKS OF GUSTAVE SATTER, THE ..A BIOGRAPHICAL SKETCH IN
ANON
    LIFE AND WORKS OF STEPHEN HELLER, THE PIANOFORTE COMPOSER, THE ..A
ANSON, GEORGE
    CONTEMPORARY PIANO MUSIC OF THE AMERICAS, COMPILED BY GEORGE ANSON
APEL, WILLI
    HISTORY OF KEYBOARD MUSIC TO 1700, THE --TRANSLATED AND REVISED BY
APEL, WILLI
    MASTERS OF THE KEYBOARD
ARONSON, MAURICE
    KEY TO THE MINIATURES OF LEOPOLD GODOWSKY, A ..ANALYTICAL ESSAYS
ARPIN, PAUL
    LIFE OF LOUIS MOREAU GOTTSCHALK
ASSOCIATION FOR RECORDED SOUND COLLECTIONS
    PRELIMINARY DIRECTORY OF SOUND RECORDING COLLECTIONS IN THE UNITED
AULD, WILDA J.
    HANDBOOK FOR THE CHURCH PIANIST, A
AZULAY, GERTRUDE
    CHOPIN..THE STORY OF THE BOY WHO MADE BEAUTIFUL MELODIES
BACHE, CONSTANCE
    BROTHER MUSICIANS..REMINISCENCES OF EDWARD AND WALTER BACHE
BACON, ERNST
    NOTES ON THE PIANO
BADURA-SKODA, EVA *
    INTERPRETING MOZART ON THE KEYBOARD---1957, IN GERMAN
BAGGER, EUGENE S.
    EMINENT EUROPEANS..STUDIES IN CONTINENTAL REALITY---PADEREWSKI
BARBEDETTE, HIPPOLYTE
    STEPHEN HELLER..HIS LIFE AND WORKS
BARFORD, PHILIP
    KEYBOARD MUSIC OF C. P. E. BACH, THE ..CONSIDERED IN RELATION TO
BARTELS, LEO F. *
    PERFORATING OF MUSIC ROLLS WITH THE LEABARJAN PERFORATOR, THE
BASTIEN, JAMES W.
    HOW TO TEACH PIANO SUCCESSFULLY
BAUGHAN, EDWARD ALGERNON
    IGNACE JAN PADEREWSKI
BEAUFORT, RAPHAEL
    FRANZ LISZT, THE STORY OF HIS LIFE--TO WHICH IS ADDED..'LISZT AS A
BECKETT, WALTER
    LISZT
BEDBROOK, GERALD STARES
    KEYBOARD MUSIC FROM THE MIDDLE AGES TO THE BEGINNINGS OF THE
BEHREND, WILLIAM
    LUDWIG VAN BEETHOVEN'S PIANOFORTE SONATAS
BENNER, LORA
    BENNER BLUE BOOK, THE ..PRACTICAL MANUAL OF PIANO TEACHING--4TH.
BENNER, LORA
    BENNER GOLD BOOK, THE ..PIANO MATERIAL AND TEACHING METHODS--3RD.
BENNETT, JOSEPH
    FREDERIC CHOPIN--NOVELLO'S BIOGRAPHY PRIMERS
BIART, VICTOR
    PIANIST'S GUIDE, THE ..A SERIES OF PAMPHLETS ON THE TEACHING AND
BIDOU, HENRI
    CHOPIN
BIE, OSKAR
    HISTORY OF THE PIANOFORTE AND PIANOFORTE PLAYERS, A ---1899
BLOM, ERIC
    BEETHOVEN'S PIANOFORTE SONATAS DISCUSSED---1938
BLOM, ERIC
    ROMANCE OF THE PIANO, THE ---1928
BODKY, ERWIN
    INTERPRETATION OF BACH'S KEYBOARD WORKS, THE
BOGIANCKINO, MASSIMO
    HARPSICHORD MUSIC OF DOMENICO SCARLATTI, THE
BORREN, CHARLES VAN DEN
    SOURCES OF KEYBOARD MUSIC IN ENGLAND, THE ---1913
BOWEN, CATHERINE DRINKER
    FREE ARTIST..THE STORY OF ANTON AND NICHOLAS RUBINSTEIN
BOWEN, YORK
    PEDALLING THE MODERN PIANOFORTE---1936
BOWMAN, EDWARD M.
    MASTER LESSONS IN PIANOFORTE PLAYING, 'LETTERS FROM A MUSICIAN TO
BOYD, MALCOLM
    BACH'S INSTRUMENTAL COUNTERPOINT
BOYD, MALCOLM
    HARMONIZING 'BACH' CHORALES

BRANSON, DAVID
    JOHN FIELD AND CHOPIN
BREMNER, ROBERT
    HARPSICHORD OR SPINNET MISCELLANY, THE --KEYBOARD
BRESLIN, HOWARD
    CONCERT GRAND---GOTTSCHALK
BRIDGER, JOHN HENRY
    HOW TO HARMONIZE MELODIES, WITH HINTS ON WRITING FOR STRINGS AND
BRINKMAN, JOSEPH *
    PIANO MUSIC..AVAILABLE EDITIONS RECOMMENDED---ADDENDA, 1959
BRISKIER, ARTHUR
    NEW APPROACH TO PIANO TRANSCRIPTIONS AND INTERPRETATION OF JOHANN
BRITISH BROADCASTING CORPORATION--CENTRAL MUSIC LIBRARY
    CHAMBER MUSIC CATALOGUE
BRITISH BROADCASTING CORPORATION--CENTRAL MUSIC LIBRARY
    PIANO AND ORGAN CATALOGUE--2 VOLS.
BRITISH COLUMBIA--DEPT. OF EDUCATION
    PIANOFORTE AND VIOLIN FOR HIGH SCHOOL STUDENTS
BROADWOOD, JOHN AND SONS
    BROADWOOD CONCERTS--HISTORICAL NOTES BY ROBIN H.
BROCKWAY, WALLACE *
    MEN OF MUSIC..THEIR LIVES, TIMES, AND ACHIEVEMENTS--REV.
BROWER, HARRIETTE
    MODERN MASTERS OF THE KEYBOARD
BROWER, HARRIETTE
    STORY-LIVES OF MASTER MUSICIANS
BROWER, HARRIETTE
    WHAT TO PLAY--WHAT TO TEACH
BROWN, MAURICE J. E.
    CHOPIN..AN INDEX OF HIS WORKS IN CHRONOLOGICAL ORDER--2ND. REV.
BROWN, MAURICE J. E.
    SCHUBERT'S VARIATIONS
BRUXNER, MERVYN
    MASTERING THE PIANO
BUECKELMANN, BERNARDUS
    EIGHT FUGUES FROM J. S. BACH'S 'W.T.C.', WITH ANALYTICAL NOTES IN
BULL, STORM
    INDEX TO BIOGRAPHIES OF CONTEMPORARY COMPOSERS
BURROWS, RAYMOND
    ELEMENTARY PIANO INSTRUCTION IN COLLEGE
BUTLER, STANLEY
    GUIDE TO THE BEST IN CONTEMPORARY PIANO MUSIC..AN ANNOTATED LIST
BYRON, MAY CLARISSA
    DAY WITH FREDERIC CHOPIN, A
CALDWELL, JOHN
    ENGLISH KEYBOARD MUSIC BEFORE THE NINETEENTH CENTURY---EXTENSIVE
CALLENDER, ROMAINE
    TEACHER'S MANUAL, A WORK DESIGNED TO SUPPLEMENT...'THE FIRST TEN
CANAVE, PAZ CORAZON G.
    RE-EVALUATION OF THE ROLE PLAYED BY C. P. E. BACH IN THE
CAPEN, C. L.
    MUSIC TEACHER'S VADE-MECUM, THE ..A GUIDE IN THE CHOICE OF MUSIC
CARLSON, EFFIE B.
    BIO-BIBLIOGRAPHICAL DICTIONARY OF TWELVE-TONE AND SERIAL
CARPE, ADOLPH
    PIANIST AND THE ART OF MUSIC, THE ..A TREATISE ON PIANO PLAYING
CAUCHI, PAUL
    CHOPIN..CENTENNIAL MEMORY 1849-1949..A LECTURE
CHASINS, ABRAM
    SPEAKING OF PIANISTS
CHISSELL, JOAN
    CHOPIN--'GREAT COMPOSERS' SERIES
CHISSELL, JOAN
    SCHUMANN PIANO MUSIC--B.B.C. MUSIC GUIDE, NO. 25
CHURCHILL, VIRGINIA PEAKES
    MODERN TEACHER'S GUIDE TO PIANO AND PIANO CLASS TEACHING
CHURCHILL, VIRGINIA PEAKES
    NINETEEN FIFTY-SIX SUPPLEMENT TO THE MODERN TEACHER'S GUIDE TO
CLARE, EDWARD
    ANALYSIS OF PRACTICAL THOROUGH BASS
COCKSHOOT, JOHN V.
    FUGUE IN BEETHOVEN'S PIANO MUSIC, THE
COHEN, HARRIET
    MUSIC'S HANDMAID
COOKE, JAMES FRANCIS
    LOUIS MOREAU GOTTSCHALK..A SHORT BIOGRAPHY
CORDER, FREDERICK
    FERENCZ LISZT--HALF-TITLE..MASTERS OF MUSIC
CORTOT, ALFRED
    ALFRED CORTOT'S STUDIES IN MUSICAL INTERPRETATION, SET DOWN BY
CORTOT, ALFRED
    FRENCH PIANO MUSIC
CORTOT, ALFRED
    IN SEARCH OF CHOPIN
CORTOT, ALFRED
    PIANO MUSIC OF CLAUDE DEBUSSY, THE
COUPERIN, FRANCOIS
    ART DE TOUCHER LE CLAVECIN, L' ---IN FRENCH, GERMAN AND ENGLISH
COVIELLO, AMBROSE
    CHOICE OF A BEETHOVEN SONATA FOR DIPLOMA EXAMINATIONS, THE --NOTES
COVIELLO, AMBROSE
    DIFFICULTIES OF BEETHOVEN PIANOFORTE SONATAS, AN ANALYSIS OF
CRONK, CUTHBERT H.
    WORKS OF ANTON RUBINSTEIN, NOV. 1829-NOV. 1894, THE ..A STUDY
CULSHAW, JOHN
    CONCERTO, THE
CULSHAW, JOHN
    SERGEI RACHMANINOFF..THE MAN AND HIS MUSIC
CURTIS, ALAN
    SWEELINCK'S KEYBOARD MUSIC..A STUDY OF ENGLISH ELEMENTS IN
CZERNY, CARL
    COMPLETE THEORETICAL AND PRACTICAL PIANO FORTE SCHOOL, FROM THE
CZERNY, CARL
    LETTERS TO A YOUNG LADY ON THE ART OF PLAYING THE PIANOFORTE
CZERNY, CARL
    ON THE PROPER PERFORMANCE OF ALL BEETHOVEN'S WORKS FOR THE PIANO
DALE, KATHLEEN
    NINETEENTH CENTURY PIANO MUSIC, A HANDBOOK FOR PIANISTS
DARRELL, ROBERT D.--COMPILER
    SCHIRMER'S GUIDE TO BOOKS ON MUSIC AND MUSICIANS--A PRACTICAL
DART, THURSTON
    INTERPRETATION OF MUSIC, THE --4TH. ED.---1954
DAVISON, JAMES W.
    FREDERICK CHOPIN..A MEMOIR
DAVISON, JAMES W.
    FREDERIC FRANCOIS CHOPIN..CRITICAL AND APPRECIATIVE ESSAY---1843
DAWES, FRANCIS E.
    DEBUSSY PIANO MUSIC--B.B.C. MUSIC GUIDE---COMPOSITIONAL ASPECT
DELUXE REPRODUCING ROLL CORPORATION
    LIBRARY OF DELUXE--REPRODUCING--MUSIC RECORDS
DELUXE ROLL CORPORATION
    LIBRARY OF DELUXE WELTE-MIGNON MUSIC RECORDS FOR REPRODUCING
DEMUTH, NORMAN
    FRENCH PIANO MUSIC..A SURVEY WITH NOTES ON ITS PERFORMANCE
DENT, EDWARD J.
    FERRUCCIO BUSONI, A BIOGRAPHY

DENVER--PUBLIC SCHOOLS
    CLASS-PIANO TEACHERS HANDBOOK
DICKINSON, ALLAN E.
    BACH'S FUGAL WORKS
DIDIMUS, HENRY
    BIOGRAPHY OF LOUIS MOREAU GOTTSCHALK, THE AMERICAN PIANIST AND
DITSON COMPANY
    TEACHING PIECES AND HOW TO TEACH THEM
DONINGTON, ROBERT
    PERFORMER'S GUIDE TO BAROQUE MUSIC, A
DORIAN, FREDERICK
    HISTORY OF MUSIC IN PERFORMANCE, THE ---1942
DRAKE, KENNETH
    SONATAS OF BEETHOVEN AS HE PLAYED AND TAUGHT THEM, THE
DRY, WAKELING
    CHOPIN--'MUSIC OF THE MASTERS' SERIES
DUMESNIL, MAURICE
    HOW TO PLAY AND TEACH DEBUSSY
DUNLOP, AGNES MARY
    DUET---STORY OF CLARA AND ROBERT SCHUMANN
DUNN, JOHN PETRIE
    ORNAMENTATION IN THE WORKS OF FREDERIC CHOPIN---1921
EDWARDS, RUTH
    COMPLEAT MUSIC TEACHER FOR TEACHERS, PARENTS AND STUDENTS
EHRLICH, ALFRED HEINRICH
    ORNAMENTATION IN BEETHOVEN'S PIANOFORTE-WORKS, THE
EICHBERG, OSCAR
    ANALYTICAL AND HISTORICAL REMARKS ON ANTON RUBINSTEIN'S CYCLE OF
EMERICH, PAUL
    ROAD TO MODERN MUSIC, THE
EMERY, WALTER
    BACH'S ORNAMENTS
EMERY, WALTER
    EDITIONS AND MUSICIANS
ENGEL, CARL
    PIANIST'S HANDBOOK, THE ..A GUIDE FOR THE RIGHT COMPREHENSION AND
EVANS, EDWIN
    HANDBOOK TO THE PIANOFORTE WORKS OF JOHANNES BRAHMS---1936
EVANS MUSIC COMPANY
    EVANS' GRADED STUDY GUIDE FOR THE PIANOFORTE AND DICTIONARY OF
EWEN, DAVID
    COMPOSERS SINCE 1900..A BIOGRAPHICAL AND CRITICAL GUIDE
EWEN, DAVID
    GREAT COMPOSERS, 1300-1900..A BIOGRAPHICAL AND CRITICAL GUIDE
EWEN, DAVID
    WORLD OF GREAT COMPOSERS, THE
EXECUTIVE COMMITTEE OF CHOPIN YEAR 1949
    CHOPIN YEAR 1949 IN POLAND, THE
FAELTEN, CARL
    TEACHER'S MANUAL FOR PIANOFORTE COURSE, THE
FERGUSON, DONALD NIVISON
    PIANO INTERPRETATION
FERGUSON, DONALD NIVISON
    PIANO MUSIC OF SIX GREAT COMPOSERS---1947
FERRIS, GEORGE TITUS
    GREAT MUSICAL COMPOSERS..GERMAN, FRENCH, AND ITALIAN
FILLMORE, JOHN C.
    PIANOFORTE MUSIC..ITS HISTORY, WITH BIOGRAPHICAL SKETCHES AND
FILLMORE, THOMAS H.
    FILLMORE'S LIST OF CAREFULLY SELECTED AND GRADED WORKS FOR THE
FINCK, HENRY T.
    CHOPIN AND OTHER MUSICAL ESSAYS---1889
FINCK, HENRY T.
    PADEREWSKI AND HIS ART
FINCK, HENRY T.
    TWENTY MUSICAL EVENINGS---PIANOLA PROGRAMS WITH NOTES AND COMMENTS
FISCHER, EDWIN
    BEETHOVEN'S PIANOFORTE SONATAS, A GUIDE FOR STUDENTS AND
FISCHER, EDWIN
    REFLECTIONS ON MUSIC
FISKE, ROGER
    BEETHOVEN CONCERTOS AND OVERTURES
FLOOD, WILLIAM HENRY GRATTAN
    JOHN FIELD OF DUBLIN, THE INVENTOR OF THE NOCTURNE---1920
FOLDES, ANDOR
    KEYS TO THE KEYBOARD, A BOOK FOR PIANISTS
FORMAN, DENIS
    MOZART'S CONCERTO FORM..THE FIRST MOVEMENTS OF THE PIANO CONCERTOS
FORTE, ALLEN
    COMPOSITIONAL MATRIX, THE ..MONOGRAPHS IN THEORY AND COMPOSITION
FRISKIN, JAMES *
    MUSIC FOR THE PIANO..A HANDBOOK OF CONCERT AND TEACHING MATERIAL
FULLER-MAITLAND, J. A.
    FORTY-EIGHT, THE ..BACH'S WOHLTEMPERIRTES CLAVIER, FROM 'THE
FULLER-MAITLAND, J. A.
    KEYBOARD SUITES OF J. S. BACH, THE
FULLER-MAITLAND, J. A.
    ROBERT SCHUMANN--'THE GREAT MUSICIANS' SERIES
FULLER-MAITLAND, J. A.
    SCHUMANN'S PIANOFORTE WORKS
GABRIEL, GILBERT W.
    GREAT PIANISTS AND COMPOSERS
GANZ, RUDOLPH
    RUDOLPH GANZ EVALUATES MODERN PIANO MUSIC
GARVIN, FLORENCE HOLLISTER
    BEGINNINGS OF THE ROMANTIC PIANO CONCERTO, THE
GEARY, ELEANOR MARGARET
    MUSICAL EDUCATION, WITH PRACTICAL OBSERVATIONS ON THE ART OF
GERMER, HEINRICH
    THEORETICO-PRACTICAL ELEMENTARY PIANO-FORTE SCHOOL FOR STUDENTS OF
GIBBS, POLLY
    LISTS AND SUGGESTIONS FOR PIANO TEACHING
GIDE, ANDRE
    NOTES ON CHOPIN
GILLESPIE, JOHN
    FIVE CENTURIES OF KEYBOARD MUSIC..AN HISTORIC SURVEY FOR
GIRDLESTONE, CUTHBERT
    MOZART AND HIS PIANO CONCERTOS---FIRST PUBLISHED IN 1948 AS
GLENNON, JAMES
    MAKING FRIENDS WITH PIANO MUSIC..THE HISTORY AND ANALYTICAL NOTES
GLENNON, JAMES
    MAKING FRIENDS WITH PIANO MUSIC--SUPPLEMENT
GLENNON, JAMES
    MAKING FRIENDS WITH THE CONCERTO..HISTORICAL AND ANALYTICAL NOTES
GLINSKI, MATEUSZ
    CHOPIN THE UNKNOWN
GLOYNE, HOWARD F.--M.D.
    CARL A. PREYER, THE LIFE OF A KANSAS MUSICIAN
GLYN, MARGARET H.
    ABOUT ELIZABETHAN VIRGINAL MUSIC AND ITS COMPOSERS..NEW ISSUE,
GLYN, MARGARET H.
    NATIONAL SCHOOL OF VIRGINAL MUSIC IN ELIZABETHAN TIMES, THE
GOODRICH, ALFRED JOHN
    GUIDE TO MEMORIZING MUSIC, A
GOODRICH, ALFRED JOHN
    THEORY OF INTERPRETATION, APPLIED TO ARTISTIC MUSICAL PERFORMANCE

GORDON, PHILIP
  SYLLABUS FOR PIANO AUDITIONS
GORDON, STEPHEN T.
  GORDON'S NEW SCHOOL FOR THE PIANO-FORTE
GOTTSCHALD, ERNEST
  BEETHOVEN'S PIANOFORTE SONATAS EXPLAINED FOR THE LOVERS OF THE
GRAY, CECIL
  BACH AND DAS WOHLTEMPERIRTE KLAVIER..ANALYTICAL NOTES, WITH AN
GRAY, CECIL
  CONTINGENCIES AND OTHER ESSAYS---LISZT
GRAY, CECIL
  FORTY-EIGHT PRELUDES AND FUGUES OF J. S. BACH, THE
GRAY, WILLIAM L.
  SELECTED AND GRADED LIST OF STUDIES AND PIECES FOR TEACHERS OF
GREW, SIDNEY
  ART OF THE PLAYER-PIANO, THE ..A TEXTBOOK FOR STUDENT AND TEACHER
GREW, SIDNEY
  FIRST BOOK OF THE PLAYER-PIANIST, THE
GRIFFIN, SISTER MARY ANNAROSE
  PIANO MATERIALS..GRADED AND COMPILED AS AN AID TO INSTRUCTORS
GUTMANN, EMMA WILKINS
  TALKS WITH PIANO TEACHERS
HADDEN, JAMES CUTHBERT
  CHOPIN--'MASTER MUSICIANS' SERIES
HADOW, SIR WILLIAM HENRY
  SONATA FORM---1896
HADOW, SIR WILLIAM HENRY
  STUDIES IN MODERN MUSIC--2ND. SERIES--9TH. ED.---CHOPIN
HALL, CONSTANCE HUNTINGTON
  HELEN HOPEKIRK, 1856-1945
HALLE, SIR CHARLES
  AUTOBIOGRAPHY OF CHARLES HALLE, WITH CORRESPONDENCE AND DIARIES,
HALLE, SIR CHARLES
  ST. JAMES HALL...C. HALLE'S PIANOFORTE RECITALS..MAY 5-JUNE 29,
HALLE, SIR CHARLES
  ST. JAMES HALL...MR. HALLE'S BEETHOVEN RECITALS, MAY 23-JULY 11,
HAMBOURG, MARK
  EIGHTH OCTAVE, THE ---CONTINUES THE RECORD, BEGUN IN 'FROM PIANO
HAMILTON, CLARENCE G.
  PIANO MUSIC, ITS COMPOSERS AND CHARACTERISTICS
HAMILTON, CLARENCE G.
  PIANO TEACHING..ITS PRINCIPLES AND PROBLEMS
HAMILTON, CLARENCE G.
  SUPPLEMENT TO PIANO MUSIC, ITS COMPOSERS AND CHARACTERISTICS, A
HANSON, JOHN R.
  FORM IN SELECTED TWENTIETH-CENTURY PIANO CONCERTOS
HARDING, BERTITA
  CONCERTO, THE STORY OF CLARA SCHUMANN
HARDING, HENRY ALFRED
  ANALYSIS OF FORM AS DISPLAYED IN BEETHOVEN'S 32 PIANOFORTE
HARDING, HENRY ALFRED
  THREE HUNDRED AND FIFTY QUESTIONS ON THE FORM AND TONALITY OF
HARRISON, SIDNEY
  BEGINNING TO PLAY THE PIANO--A TEACHER'S HANDBOOK, INCLUDING THE
HARRISON, SIDNEY
  TEACHER NEVER TOLD ME--TIPS FOR STUDENTS
HARRISON, W. WELLS
  SCHUBERT'S COMPOSITIONS FOR PIANO AND STRINGS--STRAD HANDBOOK NO.
HARSANYI, ZSOLT
  IMMORTAL FRANZ..THE LIFE AND LOVES OF A GENIUS---FRANZ LISZT
HARTSHORN, WILLIAM C.
  CONCERTO, THE --ANALYTICAL GUIDES---FIVE FOLDOUTS--EIGHT PAGES
HEDLEY, ARTHUR
  CHOPIN--'MASTER MUSICIAN' SERIES--INCLUDES CATALOGUE OF
HENDERSON, WILLIAM JAMES
  PRELUDES AND STUDIES..MUSICAL THEMES OF THE DAY--SECTION 3..THE
HERVEY, ARTHUR
  FRANZ LISZT AND HIS MUSIC
HERVEY, ARTHUR
  FRENCH MUSIC IN THE NINETEENTH CENTURY---CHOPIN
HERVEY, ARTHUR
  RUBINSTEIN--'MAYFAIR BIOGRAPHIES', NO. 11
HERVEY, ARTHUR
  SAINT-SAENS---1921
HEUSCHNEIDER, KARIN
  PIANO SONATA OF THE EIGHTEENTH CENTURY IN GERMANY, THE
HEUSCHNEIDER, KARIN
  PIANO SONATA OF THE EIGHTEENTH CENTURY IN ITALY, THE
HILL, GEORGE R.
  PRELIMINARY CHECKLIST OF RESEARCH ON THE CLASSIC SYMPHONY AND
HILL, RALPH--EDITOR
  CONCERTO, THE
HILL, RALPH
  LISZT
HINSON, MAURICE
  GUIDE TO THE PIANIST'S REPERTOIRE
HINSON, MAURICE
  PIANO TEACHER'S SOURCE BOOK--BIBLIOGRAPHY OF BOOKS ABOUT PIANOS
HODGES, SISTER MABELLE L.
  CATALOGUE OF REPRESENTATIVE TEACHING MATERIALS FOR PIANO SINCE
HOLCMAN, JAN
  LEGACY OF CHOPIN, THE
HOLMES, EDWARD
  ANALYTICAL AND THEMATIC INDEX OF MOZART'S PIANO WORKS
HOLMES, GEORGE AUGUSTUS *
  ANALYSIS OF PIANOFORTE COMPOSITIONS FROM THE CLASSICAL AND
HOOK, JAMES
  GUIDA DI MUSICA..BEING A COMPLETE BOOK OF INSTRUCTIONS FOR
HOPKINS, ANTHONY
  TALKING ABOUT CONCERTOS..AN ANALYTICAL STUDY OF A NUMBER OF
HOPKINS, ANTHONY
  TALKING ABOUT SONATAS..A BOOK OF ANALYTICAL STUDIES, BASED ON A
HOPKINSON, CECIL
  BIBLIOGRAPHICAL THEMATIC CATALOGUE OF THE WORKS OF JOHN FIELD,
HORROCKS, CYRIL R. H.
  STUDENT'S GUIDE TO THE ART OF TEACHING THE PIANOFORTE, THE --2ND.
HUBBARD, ELBERT
  LITTLE JOURNEYS TO THE HOMES OF GREAT MUSICIANS--VOL. 8, NO.
HUBBARD, ELBERT
  LITTLE JOURNEYS TO THE HOMES OF GREAT MUSICIANS--VOL. 9, NO.
HUEFFER, FRANCIS
  HALF A CENTURY OF MUSIC IN ENGLAND, 1837-1887..LISZT IN ENGLAND
HUEFFER, FRANCIS
  MUSICAL STUDIES..A SERIES OF CONTRIBUTIONS BY FRANCIS HUEFFER,
HULL, ARTHUR EAGLEFIELD
  THREE HUNDRED QUESTIONS ON PIANOFORTE TEACHING IN 30 GRADUATED
HUMISTON, WILLIAM H.
  ANTON RUBINSTEIN--'LITTLE BIOGRAPHIES'
HUMISTON, WILLIAM H.
  CHOPIN--'LITTLE BIOGRAPHIES'
HUMISTON, WILLIAM H.
  LISZT--'LITTLE BIOGRAPHIES'
HUMISTON, WILLIAM H.
  PADEREWSKI--'LITTLE BIOGRAPHIES'
HUMISTON, WILLIAM H.
  RACHMANINOFF--'LITTLE BIOGRAPHIES'

HUNEKER, JAMES GIBBONS
  CHOPIN..THE MAN AND HIS MUSIC---1901
HUNEKER, JAMES GIBBONS
  DEVELOPMENT OF PIANO MUSIC FROM THE DAYS OF THE CLAVICHORD AND
HUNEKER, JAMES GIBBONS
  FRANZ LISZT
HUNEKER, JAMES GIBBONS
  MELOMANIACS...ESSAYS---CHOPIN AND LISZT
HUNEKER, JAMES GIBBONS
  MEZZOTINTS IN MODERN MUSIC--6TH. ED.---CHOPIN AND LISZT--1901
HUNEKER, JAMES GIBBONS
  OLD FOGY, HIS MUSICAL OPINIONS AND GROTESQUES---D'ALBERT,
HUNEKER, JAMES GIBBONS
  UNICORNS---CHOPIN
HUNEKER, JAMES GIBBONS
  VARIATIONS---CHOPIN, LISZT, AND PACHMANN
HUTCHESON, ERNEST
  GREAT MASTERS OF PIANO MUSIC, THE ..BACH, BEETHOVEN, SCHUMANN,
HUTCHESON, ERNEST *
  LITERATURE OF THE PIANO, THE ..A GUIDE FOR AMATEUR AND
HUTCHESON, ERNEST
  LITERATURE OF THE PIANO, THE --FROM THE 16TH. CENTURY TO THE
HUTCHINGS, ARTHUR
  BAROQUE CONCERTO, THE
HUTCHINGS, ARTHUR
  COMPANION TO MOZART'S PIANO CONCERTOS, A
ILIFFE, FREDERICK
  FORTY-EIGHT PRELUDES AND FUGUES OF JOHANN SEBASTIAN BACH ANALYZED
INTERNATIONAL MUSICOLOGICAL CONGRESS..FIRST--1960--WORKS OF FREDERICK
  BOOK OF THE FIRST INTERNATIONAL MUSICOLOGICAL CONGRESS DEVOTED TO
ISAACSON, CHARLES D.
  FACE TO FACE WITH GREAT MUSICIANS---CHOPIN AND LISZT
IWASZKIEWICZ, JAROSLAW
  SUMMER AT NOHANT..A PLAY IN THREE ACTS---CHOPIN
JAMES, BURNETT
  BRAHMS..A CRITICAL STUDY
JOHNS, CLAYTON
  ESSENTIALS OF PIANOFORTE PLAYING, THE
JOHNSTONE, J. ALFRED
  ART OF TEACHING PIANOFORTE PLAYING, THE --2ND. REV. ED.---1910
JOHNSTONE, J. ALFRED
  NOTES ON THE INTERPRETATION OF 24 FAMOUS PIANO SONATAS OF
JOHNSTONE, J. ALFRED
  TOUCH, PHRASING AND INTERPRETATION
JONSON, GEORGE CHARLES
  HANDBOOK TO CHOPIN'S WORKS, A
KACZMAREK, REGINA A.
  CATALOG OF SELECTED PIANO ROLLS FROM THE LIBRARY OF CONGRESS
KARASOWSKI, MORITZ
  FREDERIC CHOPIN..HIS LIFE, LETTERS AND WORKS--3RD. REV. ED.---1879
KASTNER, RUDOLPH
  BEETHOVEN'S PIANO SONATAS AND ARTUR SCHNABEL
KASTNER, SANTIAGO
  PARALLELS AND DISCREPANCIES BETWEEN ENGLISH AND SPANISH KEYBOARD
KATOWICE, POLAND--BIBLIOTECA PANSTWOWEJ
  CHOPINIANA IN THE HIGH MUSIC SCHOOL LIBRARY IN
KEEFER, LUBOV
  INFLUENCE OF ADAM MICKIEWICZ ON THE BALLADES OF CHOPIN, THE
KELBERINE, ALEXANDER
  FOUR FAMOUS PIANOFORTE SONATAS OF BEETHOVEN, THE --OP. 13, OP. 27,
KELLEY, EDGAR STILLMAN
  CHOPIN THE COMPOSER---1913
KENYON, MAX
  HARPSICHORD MUSIC..THE INSTRUMENTS, THE COMPOSERS, THE PLAYERS
KERN, ALICE M. *
  TEACHER'S GUIDEBOOK TO PIANO LITERATURE, THE --REV. ED.---1954+
KIRBY, FRANK EUGENE
  SHORT HISTORY OF KEYBOARD MUSIC, A
KIRKPATRICK, JOHN
  OBSERVATIONS ON FOUR VOLUMES AND SUPPLEMENT OF THE WORKS OF L. M.
KIRKPATRICK, RALPH
  DOMENICO SCARLATTI---1953
KLECZYNSKI, JAN
  CHOPIN'S GREATER WORKS...HOW THEY SHOULD BE UNDERSTOOD...INCLUDING
KLECZYNSKI, JAN
  HOW TO PLAY CHOPIN--THREE LECTURES
KLECZYNSKI, JAN
  WORKS OF FREDERIC CHOPIN, THE ..THEIR PROPER INTERPRETATION--6TH.
KNOLLER, JACOB
  FREE WILL OR DESTINY..ONE ACT PLAY AROUND CHOPIN---EARLY SUMMER,
KOBBE, GUSTAV
  PIANOLIST, THE ..A GUIDE FOR PIANOLA PLAYERS
KOBYLANSKA, KRYSTYNA--EDITOR
  CHOPIN IN HIS OWN LAND..DOCUMENTS AND SOUVENIRS
KOCH, CASPAR
  PIANO STUDENT'S GRADUS AD PARNASSUM, THE ..PRESENTING THE
KORSTEN, BJARNE
  RECENT NORWEGIAN PIANO MUSIC
KOTZSCHMAR, MARY ANN
  HALF-HOUR LESSONS IN MUSIC..CLASS WORK FOR BEGINNERS AT THE PIANO
KULLAK, FRANZ
  BEETHOVEN'S PIANO PLAYING, WITH AN ESSAY ON THE EXECUTION OF THE
LAMAR, RICHARD
  COLLEGE PIANO PEDAGOGY
LAMOND, FREDERICK ARCHIBALD
  BEETHOVEN..NOTES ON THE SONATAS...
LANDOWSKA, WANDA
  LANDOWSKA ON MUSIC--EDITED BY DENISE RESTOUT
LANDOWSKA, WANDA
  MUSIC OF THE PAST
LANDOWSKI, ALICE-WANDA
  DOMENICO SCARLATTI--NOTES TO ACCOMPANY GRAMOPHONE RECORDINGS
LANNING, RUSSELL
  BACH ORNAMENTATION
LEICHTENTRITT, HUGO
  COMPLETE PIANOFORTE SONATAS OF BEETHOVEN, THE ---ANALYTICAL NOTES
LEIMER, KARL *
  SHORTEST WAY TO PIANISTIC PERFECTION, THE
LEONHARDT, GUSTAV M.
  ART OF FUGUE, BACH'S LAST HARPSICHORD WORK, THE ..AN ARGUMENT
LESSMANN, W. J. OTTO
  FRANZ LISZT..EINE HULDIGUNG--FRANZ LISZT..A TRIBUTE
LINGG, ANN M.
  MEPHISTO WALTZ, THE STORY OF FRANZ LISZT
LISZT, FRANZ
  FREDERIC CHOPIN--A BIOGRAPHICAL AND CRITICAL NOTICE---1852
LISZT, FRANZ
  LIFE OF CHOPIN--TRANSLATED ONLY IN PART BY MARTHA WALKER COOK
LITZMANN, BERTHOLD
  CLARA SCHUMANN..AN ARTIST'S LIFE BASED ON MATERIAL FOUND IN
LIVERPOOL--PUBLIC LIBRARIES, MUSEUMS AND ART GALLERY
  PIANO, ITS MUSIC AND LITERATURE, THE ..CATALOGUE OF THE MUSIC
LOCKWOOD, ALBERT
  NOTES ON THE LITERATURE OF THE PIANO--RE-EDITED BY BROTHER, SAMUEL
LONG, MARGUERITE
  AT THE PIANO WITH DEBUSSY---1960, IN FRENCH

LOVELOCK, WILLIAM
  FORMAL ANALYSIS OF THE SENIOR AND ADVANCED SENIOR PIANOFORTE
LOWE, CLAUDE EDGERTON
  BEETHOVEN'S PIANOFORTE SONATAS..HINTS ON THEIR RENDERING, FORM...
LOWE, CLAUDE EDGERTON
  FORM IN PIANOFORTE MUSIC--FOR THEORETICAL AND PRACTICAL EXAMS
LOWE, CLAUDE EDGERTON
  WORD-PHRASES TO BACH'S 48 FUGUES, WITH HINTS ON THE RENDERINGS OF
LUBIN, ERNEST
  PIANO DUET, THE ...A GUIDE FOR PIANISTS
LYKE, JAMES
  SELECTED LIST OF PIANO TEACHING MATERIALS PUBLISHED SINCE 1960, A
LYLE, WATSON
  CAMILLE SAINT-SAENS, HIS LIFE AND ART---DISCUSSES CONCERTI AND
MACKENZIE, SIR ALEXANDER
  LISZT--'THE MAYFAIR BIOGRAPHIES', NO. 3
MACKENZIE, SIR ALEXANDER
  LISZT--MASTERPIECES OF MUSIC
MACPHERSON, STEWART
  COMMENTARY ON BKS. 1 AND 2 OF THE FORTY-EIGHT PRELUDES AND FUGUES
MAIER, GUY
  PIANO TEACHER'S COMPANION, THE
MAINE, BASIL
  CHOPIN--'GREAT LIVES' SERIES
MARKS, ADOLF B.
  INTRODUCTION TO THE INTERPRETATION OF BEETHOVEN'S PIANO-FORTE
MARKS, F. HELENA
  QUESTIONS ON MOZART'S PIANO SONATAS, DESIGNED AS A COMPANION
MARKS, F. HELENA
  SONATA, ITS FORM AND MEANING AS EXEMPLIFIED IN THE PIANO SONATAS
MARTENS, FREDERICK HERMAN
  PADEREWSKI--'LITTLE BIOGRAPHIES', VOL. 2
MARX, ADOLF BERNHARD
  INTRODUCTION TO THE INTERPRETATION OF BEETHOVEN'S PIANO
MASON, DANIEL GREGORY
  ROMANTIC COMPOSERS, THE ---CHOPIN AND LISZT
MATHEWS, WILLIAM S. B.
  GREAT IN MUSIC, THE ..A SYSTEMATIC COURSE OF STUDY IN THE MUSIC OF
MATTHEWS, DENIS--EDITOR
  KEYBOARD MUSIC--ESSAYS ON KEYBOARD LITERATURE, EXCLUDING ORGAN
MATTHEWS, DENIS
  BEETHOVEN PIANO SONATAS--B.B.C. MUSIC GUIDE, NO. 1
MAUROIS, ANDRE
  FREDERIC CHOPIN---FOR YOUNGER READERS
MAY, FLORENCE
  GIRLHOOD OF CLARA SCHUMANN, THE ..CLARA WIECK AND HER TIME
MCARTHUR, ALEXANDER
  ANTON RUBINSTEIN, A BIOGRAPHICAL SKETCH
MCARTHUR, ALEXANDER
  PIANOFORTE STUDY..HINTS ON PIANO PLAYING
MCCLANAHAN, RICHARD
  CADENCE, KEY TO MUSICAL CLARITY, THE ..A SIMPLE AND PRACTICAL
MCEWEN, JOHN B.
  INTRODUCTION TO AN UNPUBLISHED EDITION OF THE PIANOFORTE SONATAS
MCLAIN, MARGARET STARR
  CLASS PIANO
MCMILLAN, MARY LEE *
  MY HELENKA---IGNACE PADEREWSKI
MCNABB, GEORGE
  SELECTED LIST OF GRADED TEACHING MATERIAL FOR THE PIANO, A --3RD.
MEL-O-DEE MUSIC COMPANY
  MELODEE MUSIC ROLLS..SEPTEMBER, 1920
MELLERS, WILFRED
  FRANCOIS COUPERIN AND THE FRENCH CLASSICAL TRADITION
MELLERS, WILFRED
  SONATA PRINCIPLE, THE --CIRCA 1750
MICHIGAN MUSIC TEACHERS ASSOCIATION
  PIANO TEACHER'S GUIDE
MILLER, JEWELL
  POLONAISE MILITAIRE..THE LIFE AND WORK OF FREDERIC CHOPIN..A
MILNE, ALFRED FORBES
  BEETHOVEN..THE PIANOFORTE SONATAS--2 VOLS.
MINNESOTA MUSIC TEACHERS ASSOCIATION
  PIANO-THEORY EXAMINATION SYLLABUS
MIZWA, STEPHEN P.--EDITOR
  FREDERIC CHOPIN, 1810-1849
MOLDENHAUER, HANS
  DUO-PIANISM---PUBLISHED DISSERTATION
MONTAGU-NATHAN, M.
  CONTEMPORARY RUSSIAN COMPOSERS---RACHMANINOFF
MONTAGU-NATHAN, M.
  HANDBOOK TO THE PIANO WORKS OF SCRIABIN
MORGAN, ORLANDO
  J. S. BACH..48 PRELUDES AND FUGUES..ANALYSIS OF THE FUGUES
MORRILL, HENRY H.
  MANUAL OF PIANO FOR PUPILS AND TEACHERS
MOSCHELES, CHARLOTTE
  RECENT MUSIC AND MUSICIANS, AS DESCRIBED IN THE DIARIES AND
MURDOCH, WILLIAM
  BRAHMS..WITH AN ANALYTICAL STUDY OF THE COMPLETE PIANOFORTE WORKS
MURDOCH, WILLIAM
  CHOPIN..HIS LIFE---1935
MURGIA, ADELAIDE
  LIFE AND TIMES OF CHOPIN, THE
MUSIC EDUCATION LEAGUE, INC.
  PIANO AUDITIONS SYLLABUS AND COMPREHENSIVE GUIDE FOR PIANO
MUSIC EDUCATION LEAGUE
  COMPREHENSIVE GUIDE FOR PIANO TEACHERS AND PIANO AUDITION SYLLABUS
MUSIC EDUCATORS NATIONAL CONFERENCE
  TEACHING PIANO IN CLASSROOM AND STUDIO
MUSIC PROJECT--NEW YORK CITY
  TEACHER'S GUIDE..A CREATIVE APPROACH TO PIANO CLASS TEACHING, BY
NATIONAL BUREAU FOR THE ADVANCEMENT OF MUSIC
  GIVING OF HIGH SCHOOL CREDITS FOR PRIVATE MUSIC STUDY, THE ..A
NAYLOR, EDWARD W.
  ELIZABETHAN VIRGINAL BOOK, AN ..A CRITICAL ESSAY ON THE CONTENTS
NELSON, WENDELL
  CONCERTO, THE --BROWN 'MUSIC HORIZON' SERIES
NEWMAN, ELIZABETH
  TEACHING MATERIAL GRADED ACCORDING TO HARMONIC STRUCTURE,
NEWMAN, ERNEST
  MAN LISZT, THE ..A STUDY OF THE TRAGI-COMEDY OF A SOUL DIVIDED
NEWMAN, WILLIAM S.
  PERFORMANCE PRACTICES IN BEETHOVEN'S PIANO SONATAS..AN
NEWMAN, WILLIAM S.
  SELECTED LIST OF MUSIC RECOMMENDED FOR PIANO STUDENTS, A --4TH.
NEWMAN, WILLIAM S.
  SONATA IN THE BAROQUE ERA, THE --A HISTORY OF THE SONATA IDEA,
NEWMAN, WILLIAM S.
  SONATA IN THE CLASSIC ERA, THE --A HISTORY OF THE SONATA IDEA,
NEWMAN, WILLIAM S.
  SONATA SINCE BEETHOVEN, THE --A HISTORY OF THE SONATA IDEA, VOL. 3
NEWMAN, WILLIAM S.
  THIRTEEN KEYBOARD SONATAS OF THE EIGHTEENTH AND NINETEENTH
NEW ENGLAND CONSERVATORY
  TEACHERS' GRADED LIST FOR THE PIANOFORTE

NEW YORK--PUBLIC LIBRARY
  LIST OF PIANO MUSIC IN THE CIRCULATION DEPARTMENT OF THE NEW YORK
NEW YORK STATE MUSIC TEACHERS' ASSOCIATION
  SYLLABUS FOR PIANO, 1970
NICCHIA, LILLIAN
  PIANOFORTE STUDY..HINTS ON PIANO PLAYING
NIECKS, FREDERICK
  FREDERICK CHOPIN AS A MAN AND MUSICIAN--2 VOLS.---1888
NIMITZ, DANIEL
  KEYBOARD MASTERS..STUDY GUIDE
O'TOOLE, WILLIAM
  FIVE YEAR GUIDE TO PIANO TEACHING, A
OFFERGELD, ROBERT
  CENTENNIAL CATALOGUE OF THE PUBLISHED AND UNPUBLISHED COMPOSITIONS
OREGON MUSIC TEACHERS ASSOCIATION
  PIANO MATERIALS
ORLIK, JULES
  CREATIVE APPROACH TO PIANO CLASS TEACHING, A ---REPRODUCED FROM
PALMER, ANNIE L.
  MUSIC TEACHERS' GUIDE TO THE GOLDBECK PIANO METHOD
PALMER, HORATIO R.
  PALMER'S PIANO PRIMER
PALMER, WILLARD A.--EDITOR
  CHOPIN..AN INTRODUCTION TO HIS PIANO WORKS
PARKER, DOUGLAS C.
  PERCY ALDRIDGE GRAINGER, A STUDY
PARRISH, CARL
  EARLY PIANO AND ITS INFLUENCE ON KEYBOARD TECHNIQUE AND
PARSONS, ALBERT R.
  SCIENCE OF PIANO PRACTICE, THE
PAUER, ERNST
  DICTIONARY OF PIANISTS AND COMPOSERS FOR THE PIANOFORTE..WITH AN
PAUER, ERNST
  ERNST PAUER'S SIX HISTORICAL PERFORMANCES OF PIANOFORTE MUSIC
PEABODY INSTITUTE, BALTIMORE
  GRADED LIST OF SOME USEFUL WORKS FOR PIANO STUDY---REVISED BY
PEARCE, CHARLES WILLIAM
  ART OF THE PIANO TEACHER, THE
PEDERSON, GALE
  KEY TO THE KEYS..A SELF-TAUGHT PIANO METHOD FOR ADULTS AND TEEN
PELZ, WILLIAM
  BASIC KEYBOARD SKILLS--2ND. ED.---1963
PERRY, ADELAIDE TROWBRIDGE
  COMPENDIUM OF PIANO MATERIAL--2ND. ED.---1929
PERRY, EDWARD B.
  DESCRIPTIVE ANALYSES OF PIANO WORKS, FOR THE USE OF TEACHERS,
PERRY, EDWARD B.
  STORIES OF STANDARD TEACHING PIECES FOR THE PIANOFORTE
PETERSON, FRANKLIN
  HANDBOOK OF MUSICAL FORM--PART 2 OF THE PIANIST'S HANDBOOK
PETERSON, FRANKLIN
  THEORETIC COMPANION TO PRACTICE--PART I OF THE PIANIST'S HANDBOOK
PHILLIPS, CHARLES
  PADEREWSKI..THE STORY OF A MODERN IMMORTAL
PIGGOTT, PATRICK
  LIFE AND MUSIC OF JOHN FIELD, 1782-1837, THE
PIRANI, EUGENIO DI
  SECRETS OF THE SUCCESS OF GREAT MUSICIANS
PLAIDY, LOUIS
  PIANO TEACHER, THE
PLANTIGA, LEON B.
  SCHUMANN AS CRITIC
POLISH RESEARCH AND INFORMATION SERVICE
  FREDERIC CHOPIN--CENTENNIAL 1849-1949, BACKGROUND
POLISH RESEARCH AND INFORMATION SERVICE
  FREDERIC CHOPIN CENTENNIAL--1949---EIGHT ARTICLES
PORTE, JOHN F.
  CHOPIN, THE COMPOSER AND HIS MUSIC
PORTE, JOHN F.
  EDWARD MACDOWELL, A GREAT AMERICAN TONE POET..HIS LIFE AND MUSIC
POTAMKIN, FRANK
  MODERN PIANO PEDAGOGY
POURTALES, GUY DE
  FRANZ LISZT, THE MAN OF LOVE
POURTALES, GUY DE
  POLONAISE, THE LIFE OF CHOPIN---ENGLISH EDITION, 'FREDERICK
PRENTICE, THOMAS RIDLEY
  MUSICIAN, THE ..A GUIDE FOR PIANOFORTE STUDENTS--6 VOLS.
PROSNAK, JAN
  FREDERIC CHOPIN INTERNATIONAL PIANO COMPETITIONS, THE
PUGNO, RAOUL
  LESSONS OF RAOUL PUGNO, THE ..WITH A BIOGRAPHY OF CHOPIN BY M.
RACHMANINOFF, SERGEI
  RACHMANINOFF'S RECOLLECTIONS, TOLD TO OSKAR VON RIESEMANN---1934
RADCLIFFE, PHILIP
  SCHUBERT PIANO SONATAS--B.B.C. MUSIC GUIDE, NO. 17
RAPEE, ERNO--ARRANGER
  ERNO RAPEE'S ENCYCLOPEDIA OF MUSIC FOR PICTURES---LISTED BOTH BY
RAPEE, ERNO--ARRANGER
  MOTION PICTURE MOODS FOR PIANISTS AND ORGANISTS
RAYSON, ETHEL
  POLISH MUSIC AND CHOPIN ITS LAUREATE, ETC.
REINECKE, KARL H.
  BEETHOVEN PIANOFORTE SONATAS, THE ..LETTERS TO A LADY
REINECKE, KARL H.
  WHAT SHALL WE PLAY--NOT UNLIKE CZERNY'S 'LETTERS TO A YOUNG
RENAUD, EMILIANO
  RENAUD-PHONE PIANO METHOD..A PIANO COURSE THROUGH THE MEDIUM OF
RETI, RUDOLPH
  THEMATIC PATTERNS IN SONATAS OF BEETHOVEN
REZITS, JOSEPH
  TEACHER'S GUIDE TO THE NEW SCRIBNER MUSIC LIBRARY
RICHARDSON, NATHAN
  NEW METHOD FOR THE PIANOFORTE..ADDED, RUDIMENTS OF HARMONY AND
RICHNER, THOMAS
  ORIENTATION FOR INTERPRETING MOZART'S PIANO SONATAS
RIEMANN, HUGO
  ANALYSIS OF J. S. BACH'S WOHLTEMPIERTES KLAVIER--2 PTS.
RIEMANN, HUGO
  PRACTICAL GUIDE TO THE ART OF PHRASING...ANALYSIS OF CLASSIC AND
ROBERT, WALTER
  PIANO STUDY IN SOVIET-RUSSIAN SCHOOLS OF MUSIC--REPRINT..'JOURNAL
ROEHL, HARVEY
  PLAYER PIANO TREASURY..THE SCRAPBOOK HISTORY OF THE MECHANICAL
ROLLAND, ROMAIN
  BEETHOVEN..WITH A BRIEF ANALYSIS OF THE SONATAS...BY A. EAGLEFIELD
ROSTAND, CLAUDE
  LISZT
ROTHSCHILD, FRITZ
  HANDBOOK TO THE PERFORMANCE OF THE 48 PRELUDES AND FUGUES OF J. S.
ROTHSCHILD, FRITZ
  LOST TRADITION IN MUSIC, THE --PT. 1..RHYTHM AND TEMPO IN J. S.
ROTHSCHILD, FRITZ
  LOST TRADITION IN MUSIC, THE --PT. 2..MUSICAL PERFORMANCE IN THE
ROWBOTHAM, JOHN F.
  PRIVATE LIFE OF THE GREAT COMPOSERS, THE ---CHOPIN AND LISZT

ROWLEY, ALEC
  FOUR HANDS--ONE PIANO..A LIST OF WORKS FOR DUET PLAYERS--A GUIDE
ROWLEY, ALEC *
  MUSICAL FORM AT THE PIANO
RUBINSTEIN, ANTON
  CONVERSATION ON MUSIC, A
RUBINSTEIN, BERYL
  OUTLINE OF PIANO PEDAGOGY--REV. ED.---1929
RUBINSTEIN, BERYL
  PIANIST'S APPROACH TO SIGHT READING AND MEMORIZING, THE
RUTTKAY, GEORGE
  CHOPIN, HIS LIFE TOLD IN ANECDOTAL FORM---FOR YOUNGER READERS
RYAN, THOMAS
  RECOLLECTIONS OF AN OLD MUSICIAN---GOTTSCHALK, JONAS CHICKERING,
SACHS, CURT
  EVOLUTION OF PIANO MUSIC, 1350-1700, THE
SALSBURY, JANET
  CONCISE ANALYSIS OF BEETHOVEN'S 32 PIANOFORTE SONATAS, A
SALSBURY, JANET
  SHORT AND CONCISE ANALYSIS OF MOZART'S 22 PIANOFORTE SONATAS, A
SAMPSON, BROOK
  DIGEST OF THE ANALYSES OF THE 48 FUGUES IN THE WELL-TEMPERED
SAMPSON, BROOK
  OUTLINE ANALYSIS OF EACH OF BACH'S FORTY-EIGHT FUGUES--IN THE 'DAS
SAVLER, ROBERTA--EDITOR
  SELECTIONS FROM THE PIANO TEACHER, 1958-1963
SCHAAF, EDWARD O.
  ART OF PIANO PLAYER TRANSCRIPTION, THE ..MAKING OF PERFORATED
SCHAAF, EDWARD O.
  FUNDAMENTAL PRINCIPLES INVOLVED IN THE COMPOSING AND ARRANGING OF
SCHALLENBERG, EVERT W.
  FREDERIC CHOPIN--SYMPHONIA BOOKS..'HISTORY OF MUSIC' SERIES
SCHAUFFLER, ROBERT HAVEN
  FLORESTAN..THE LIFE AND WORK OF ROBERT SCHUMANN---1945
SCHELLING, ERNEST *
  OXFORD PIANO COURSE, TEACHER'S SECOND MANUAL
SCHENKER, HEINRICH
  FIVE GRAPHIC MUSIC ANALYSES---INCLUDES TWO CHOPIN ETUDES..OP. 10,
SCHIRMER, G.
  NEW PIANO-TEACHER'S GUIDE..A GRADED AND CLASSIFIED LIST OF PIANO
SCHMITZ, ELIE ROBERT
  PIANO WORKS OF CLAUDE DEBUSSY, THE
SCHNITTKIND, HENRY T.
  LIVING BIOGRAPHIES OF GREAT COMPOSERS---CHOPIN AND LISZT
SCHOLES, PERCY
  APPRECIATION OF MUSIC BY MEANS OF THE PIANOLA AND DUO-ART, THE
SCHONBERG, HAROLD
  COLLECTOR'S CHOPIN AND SCHUMANN, THE --KEYSTONE BOOKS
SCHONBERG, HAROLD
  LIVES OF THE GREAT COMPOSERS, THE ---CHOPIN AND LISZT
SCHOTT, HOWARD
  PLAYING THE HARPSICHORD
SCHUMANN, ROBERT
  ON MUSIC AND MUSICIANS---1854, IN GERMAN--FIRST ENGLISH EDITION IN
SCHWIMMER, FRANCISKA
  GREAT MUSICIANS AS CHILDREN
SEARLE, HUMPHREY
  MUSIC OF LISZT, THE --2ND. REV. ED.---1954
SEYMOUR, HARRIET AYER
  HOW TO THINK MUSIC
SHATTUCK, ARTHUR
  MEMOIRS OF ARTHUR SHATTUCK, THE ..WITH AN ACCOUNT OF HIS CAREER BY
SHEDLOCK, JOHN S.
  BEETHOVEN'S PIANOFORTE SONATAS..THE ORIGIN AND RESPECTIVE VALUES
SHEDLOCK, JOHN S.
  PIANOFORTE SONATA, THE ..ITS ORIGIN AND DEVELOPMENT---1895
SHERWOOD MUSIC SCHOOL
  PIANO LESSONS AND TESTS--4TH. REV. ED.---1945+
SITWELL, SACHEVERELL
  BACKGROUND FOR DOMENICO SCARLATTI..1685-1757, WRITTEN FOR HIS
SITWELL, SACHEVERELL
  LISZT---1934
SMITH, BILLYE MULLINS
  PIANO REPERTOIRE GUIDE
SMITH, JULIA
  MASTER PIANIST..THE CAREER AND TEACHING OF CARL FRIEDBERG
SMITHERS, WELSFORD
  PIANO TEACHER'S GUIDE, THE ..A HUNDRED QUESTIONS FOR YOUNG
SORABJI, KAIKHOSRU
  AROUND MUSIC---PACHMAN, CHOPIN AND LISZT
SOREL, CLAUDETTE
  COMPENDIUM OF PIANO TECHNIQUE--39 ETUDES SELECTED FROM OVER 4000,
SOREL, CLAUDETTE *
  INDEPENDENT LEARNING APPROACH TO PIANO SIGHT READING, AN
SPAETH, SIGMUND *
  AMPICO IN MUSIC STUDY, THE
STAINKAMPH, EILEEN
  FORM AND ANALYSES OF MOZART'S PIANOFORTE SONATAS, THE
STAINKAMPH, EILEEN
  FORM AND ANALYSIS OF THE COMPLETE BEETHOVEN'S PIANOFORTE SONATAS
STATHAM, HENRY H.
  MY THOUGHTS ON MUSIC AND MUSICIANS---CHOPIN AND LISZT
STEIN, ERWIN
  FORM AND PERFORMANCE
STERNBERG, CONSTANTIN I. VON
  ETHICS AND ESTHETICS OF PIANO PLAYING
STOOKES, SACHA
  ART OF ROBERT CASADESUS, THE
STRACHEY, MARJORIE C.
  NIGHTINGALE, THE ..A LIFE OF CHOPIN--IN THE FORM OF FICTION
STUCKENSCHMIDT, HANS H.
  FERRUCCIO BUSONI..CHRONICLE OF A EUROPEAN---1967, IN GERMAN
STUCKENSCHMIDT, HANS H.
  MAURICE RAVEL..VARIATIONS ON HIS LIFE AND WORK
SUCHOFF, B.
  GUIDE TO THE MIKROKOSMOS OF BELA BARTOK, A --PUBLISHED
SUMMY-BIRCHARD COMPANY
  HANDBOOK FOR PIANO TEACHERS..COLLECTED ARTICLES ON SUBJECTS
SUMNER, WILLIAM L.
  PIANOFORTE, THE --3RD. ED.---1966
SUTHERLAND, ADELAIDE K.--COMPILER
  WHAT SHALL I PLAY..PREFERENCES FOR PIANO AND ORGAN..GUIDE TO
SZIGETI, JOSEPH
  TEN BEETHOVEN SONATAS FOR PIANO AND VIOLIN, THE
TANKARD, GEOFFREY
  PIANOFORTE DIPLOMAS
TARCZYNSKI-ALF, TADEUSZ
  HOMAGE TO CHOPIN---TEXT IN POLISH AND ENGLISH
TAWASTSTJERNA, ERIK
  PIANOFORTE COMPOSITIONS OF SIBELIUS, THE
TAYLOR, ERIC R.
  INTRODUCTION TO SCORE PLAYING, AN
TAYLOR, ROBERT L.
  RUNNING PIANIST, THE ---PERCY GRAINGER
TEMPLIER, PIERRE D.
  ERIK SATIE---1932, IN FRENCH

THOMPSON, KENNETH
  DICTIONARY OF TWENTIETY-CENTURY COMPOSERS, A --1911-1971
THOMPSON, OSCAR
  DEBUSSY, MAN AND ARTIST---1937
TISCHLER, HANS
  STRUCTURAL ANALYSIS OF MOZART'S PIANO CONCERTOS, A --MUSICOLOGICAL
TOBIN, JOSEPH RAYMOND
  MOZART AND THE SONATA FORM..A COMPANION BOOK TO ANY EDITION OF
TOVEY, DONALD FRANCIS
  COMPANION TO BEETHOVEN'S PIANO SONATAS, A ..COMPLETE
TURECK, ROSALYN
  INTRODUCTION TO THE PERFORMANCE OF BACH, AN--3 VOLS.
TYSON, ALAN
  AUTHENTIC ENGLISH EDITIONS OF BEETHOVEN, THE --'ALL SOULS
TYSON, ALAN
  THEMATIC CATALOG OF THE WORKS OF MUZIO CLEMENTI
VALLAS, LEON
  THEORIES OF CLAUDE DEBUSSY, MUSICIEN FRANCAIS, THE ---1929
VEINUS, ABRAHAM
  CONCERTO, THE ---1944
VEINUS, ABRAHAM
  VICTOR BOOK OF CONCERTOS
VENABLE, MARY
  INTERPRETATION OF PIANO MUSIC, THE
VERNAZZA, MARCELLE
  BASIC MATERIALS FOR THE PIANO STUDENT
VIARD-LOUIS, JENNY
  MUSIC AND THE PIANO
VUILLERMOZ, EMILE
  GABRIEL FAURE
WALKER, ALAN--EDITOR
  CHOPIN COMPANION, THE ..PROFILES OF THE MAN AND THE
WALKER, ALAN--EDITOR
  FRANZ LISZT, THE MAN AND HIS MUSIC---ESSAYS BY SACHEVERALL SITWELL
WALKER, ALAN--EDITOR
  ROBERT SCHUMANN..THE MAN AND HIS MUSIC---SYMPOSIUM--13 AUTHORS
WALKER, ALAN
  LISZT
WALLACE, WILLIAM
  LISZT, WAGNER, AND THE PRINCESS
WARRACK, JOHN H.
  SIX GREAT COMPOSERS---CHOPIN
WARRACK JOHN H.
  CHAIKOVSKY SYMPHONIES AND CONCERTOS--B.B.C. MUSIC GUIDES, NO. 16
WARREN, CLARENCE H.--EDITOR
  MEN BEHIND THE MUSIC, THE ---CHOPIN AND LISZT
WASHINGTON STATE MUSIC TEACHERS ASSOCIATION
  PIANO TEACHING GUIDE--GRADES 1-8
WEINSTOCK, HERBERT
  CHOPIN, THE MAN AND HIS MUSIC
WEISER, BERNHARD D.
  KEYBOARD MUSIC--16TH.-20TH. CENTURIES
WEITZMANN, CARL F.
  HISTORY OF PIANOFORTE-PLAYING AND PIANOFORTE-LITERATURE, A
WELTE-MIGNON CORPORATION
  LIBRARY OF DELUXE WELTE-MIGNON MUSIC RECORDS FOR REPRODUCING
WELTE-MIGNON CORPORATION
  LIBRARY OF WELTE-MIGNON MUSIC RECORDS
WELTE ARTISTIC PLAYER-PIANO COMPANY
  LIST OF MUSIC FOR THE WELTE-MIGNON PIANO--WITH SUPPLEMENT
WESTERBY, HERBERT
  APPROACH TO LISZT, THE ..A COURSE OF MODERN TONAL TECHNIQUE FOR
WESTERBY, HERBERT
  BEETHOVEN AND HIS PIANO WORKS
WESTERBY, HERBERT
  HISTORY OF PIANOFORTE MUSIC, THE ---1924
WESTERBY, HERBERT
  HOW TO STUDY THE PIANOFORTE WORKS OF THE GREAT COMPOSERS
WESTERBY, HERBERT
  INTRODUCTION TO RUSSIAN PIANO MUSIC--REPRINT..'MUSICAL OPINION'
WESTERBY, HERBERT
  LISZT, COMPOSER, AND HIS PIANO WORKS..DESCRIPTIVE GUIDE AND
WESTRUP, SIR JACK ALLAN
  LISZT--NOVELLO'S BIOGRAPHIES OF GREAT MUSICIANS
WHEELER, OPAL
  FREDERIC CHOPIN, SON OF POLAND, EARLY YEARS--2 VOLS.---YOUNGER
WHITE, WILLIAM BRAID
  PLAYER-PIANIST, THE ..A GUIDE TO THE APPRECIATION AND
WHITESIDE, ABBY
  MASTERING THE CHOPIN ETUDES AND OTHER ESSAYS
WIER, ALBERT
  PIANO, THE ..ITS HISTORY, MAKERS, PLAYERS AND MUSIC
WIERZYNSKI, CASIMIR
  LIFE AND DEATH OF CHOPIN, THE
WILKINSON, CHARLES W.
  HOW TO INTERPRET MENDELSSOHN'S SONGS WITHOUT WORDS
WILKINSON, CHARLES W.
  HOW TO PLAY BACH'S 48 PRELUDES AND FUGUES
WILKINSON, CHARLES W.
  HOW TO PLAY 110 FAVOURITE PIANO SOLOS
WILKINSON, CHARLES W.
  WELL-KNOWN PIANO SOLOS..HOW TO PLAY THEM WITH UNDERSTANDING,
WILLEBY, CHARLES
  FREDERIC FRANCOIS CHOPIN
WILLS, VERA G. *
  PARENT'S GUIDE TO MUSIC LESSONS, A
WILSON, DAVID M.
  INSTRUCTION BOOK ON THE PIANO-PLAYER AND PLAYER-PIANO, AN
WOLFF, ERNST VICTOR
  WITH REASON AND RHYME
WOLFF, KONRAD
  TEACHING OF ARTUR SCHNABEL, THE ..A GUIDE TO INTERPRETATION
WOLFRAM, VICTOR
  SOSTENUTO PEDAL, THE
WOLLENHAUPT, HEINRICH
  METHOD FOR THE PIANOFORTE AND METHODICAL GUIDE FOR THE PIANO FORTE
WOODHOUSE, GEORGE
  NEW PATH FOR PIANISTS, A ..THE MUTANO--MUTE PIANO--SYSTEM, ETC.
YATES, PETER
  AMATEUR AT THE KEYBOARD, AN
YOUNG, PERCY M.
  CONCERTO--'PHOENIX MUSIC GUIDES', NO. 1
YOUNG, PERCY M.
  KEYBOARD MUSICIANS OF THE WORLD

The Art of Performing

ADLER, KURT
  ART OF ACCOMPANYING AND COACHING, THE ---1965
AEOLIAN COMPANY, THE
  WEIGHT OF EVIDENCE ON THE TRUE MUSICAL WORTH OF THE PIANOLA AND

AHRENS, CORA B. *
    FOR ALL PIANO TEACHERS
ALBIG, GEORGE L.
    HOW TO PLAY THE PLAYER
ALDRICH, PUTNAM
    PRINCIPAL AGREMENTS OF THE SEVENTEENTH AND EIGHTEENTH CENTURIES, *
ALLEN, MARGARET *
    CREATIVE MOTION
AMEY, ELLEN
    CONSCIOUS CONTROL IN PIANO STUDY
ANDERSON, J. CLARK
    GOOD MUSIC EXPLAINED..WHAT ALL GOOD PIANISTS SHOULD KNOW
ANDERSON, WILLIAM P.
    MUSIC AS A CAREER
ANON
    COMPLEAT TUTOR FOR THE HARPSICHORD OR SPINNET, WHEREIN IS SHEWN
ANON
    FASHIONABLE PRECEPTOR, FOR THE PIANO-FORTE AND HARPSICHORD,
ANON
    GUIDE TO THE PROPER USE OF THE PIANOFORTE PEDALS, WITH EXAMPLES
ANON
    NEW AND COMPLETE INSTRUCTIONS FOR THE HARPSICHORD, PIANO FORTE OR
ANON
    NEW INSTRUCTIONS FOR PLAYING THE HARPSICHORD, PIANOFORTE OR
ANON
    PLAYING THE HARPSICHORD, SPINET OR PIANO FORTE MADE EASY BY NEW
ANON
    PRECEPTOR, FOR THE PIANOFORTE, THE ORGAN OR HARPSICHORD, THE
APEL, WILLI
    MASTERS OF THE KEYBOARD
AULD, WILDA J.
    HANDBOOK FOR THE CHURCH PIANIST, A
BABBITT, WILLIAM
    PHYSIOLOGICAL METHOD FOR PLAYING THE PIANO-FORTE, DESIGNED AS A
BACH, CARL PHILIPP EMANUEL
    ESSAY ON THE TRUE ART OF PLAYING KEYBOARD INSTRUMENTS---TWO PTS.,
BACON, ERNST
    NOTES ON THE PIANO
BADURA-SKODA, EVA *
    INTERPRETING MOZART ON THE KEYBOARD---1957, IN GERMAN
BALLANTINE, BILL
    PIANO, THE ..AN INTRODUCTION TO THE INSTRUMENT
BARFORD, PHILIP
    KEYBOARD MUSIC OF C. P. E. BACH, THE ..CONSIDERED IN RELATION TO
BARNETT, DAVID
    PERFORMANCE OF MUSIC, THE ..A STUDY IN TERMS OF THE PIANOFORTE
BASTIEN, JAMES W.
    HOW TO TEACH PIANO SUCCESSFULLY
BEMETZRIEDER, ANTON
    COMPENDIUM OF A NEW METHOD OF MUSIC...WITH THE AUTHOR'S PRINCIPLES
BEMETZRIEDER, ANTON
    GAMUT AND COMMON CHORD IN ALL KEYS, FINGERED FOR THE HARPSICHORD,
BEMETZRIEDER, ANTON
    NEW GUIDE TO MUSIC, IN FRENCH AND ENGLISH, A
BLAKE, DOROTHY
    FIRST STEPS IN THE USE OF THE PEDAL FOR PIANO
BLOM, ERIC
    BEETHOVEN'S PIANOFORTE SONATAS DISCUSSED---1938
BODKY, ERWIN
    INTERPRETATION OF BACH'S KEYBOARD WORKS, THE
BOLTON, HETTY
    HOW TO PRACTICE
BOLTON, HETTY
    ON TEACHING THE PIANO
BOOTH, VICTOR
    WE PIANO TEACHERS--REVISED BY ADELE FRANKLIN---1946
BORREN, CHARLES VAN DEN
    SOURCES OF KEYBOARD MUSIC IN ENGLAND, THE ---1913
BOS, COENRAAD V.
    WELL-TEMPERED ACCOMPANIST, THE
BOWEN, YORK
    PEDALLING THE MODERN PIANOFORTE---1936
BRANSON, DAVID
    JOHN FIELD AND CHOPIN
BRECKENRIDGE, WILLIAM KILGORE
    HINTS FOR PIANO NORMAL STUDIES
BREE, MADAME MALWINE
    GROUNDWORK OF THE LESCHETIZKY METHOD, THE ---1902
BRIGGS, GILBERT A.
    PIANOS, PIANISTS AND SONICS
BRISKIER, ARTHUR
    NEW APPROACH TO PIANO TRANSCRIPTIONS AND INTERPRETATION OF JOHANN
BROWER, HARRIETTE
    ART OF THE PIANIST, THE
BROWER, HARRIETTE
    MODERN MASTERS OF THE KEYBOARD
BROWER, HARRIETTE
    PIANO MASTERY..TALKS WITH MASTER PIANISTS AND TEACHERS...
BROWER, HARRIETTE
    PIANO MASTERY, SECOND SERIES
BROWN, MAURICE J. E.
    SCHUBERT'S VARIATIONS
BUCHAROFF, SIMON
    MODERN PIANIST'S TEXT BOOK, THE
BUCKLEY, OLIVIA DUSSEK
    MUSICAL TRUTHS..OR, AN ANALYSIS OF MUSIC AND AN ESSAY ON THE PAST
BUONAMICI, CARLO
    PRACTICAL POINTS ON PIANO PLAYING
CALAND, ELIZABETH
    ARTISTIC PIANO PLAYING, AS TAUGHT BY LUDWIG DEPPE
CANAVE, PAZ CORAZON G.
    RE-EVALUATION OF THE ROLE PLAYED BY C. P. E. BACH IN THE
CARPE, ADOLPH
    GROUPING, ARTICULATING AND PHRASING IN MUSICAL INTERPRETATION..A
CARPE, ADOLPH
    PIANIST AND THE ART OF MUSIC, THE ..A TREATISE ON PIANO PLAYING
CARR, BENJAMIN
    ANALYTICAL INSTRUCTOR FOR THE PIANO FORTE, OP. 15, THE --IN 3 PTS.
CARRE, JOHN
    PSYCHOLOGY OF PIANO TEACHING, THE ..A TEXTBOOK FOR TEACHERS,
CARRENO, TERESA
    POSSIBILITIES OF TONE COLOR BY ARTISTIC USE OF PEDALS
CARTER, BUENTA
    BEGINNER'S PIANO BOOK FOR OLDER STUDENTS...DESIGNED FOR THE OLDER
CASTELLINI, JOHN EDWARD
    RUDIMENTS OF MUSIC..A NEW APPROACH WITH APPLICATION TO THE
CHAPPLE, STANLEY
    CLASS WAY TO THE KEYBOARD, THE
CHASE, MARY WOOD
    NATURAL LAWS IN PIANO TECHNIC
CHASINS, ABRAM
    SPEAKING OF PIANISTS
CHILDERS, LEMUEL
    PLAYING THE PIANO BY EAR
CHING, JAMES
    NEW GRADED PEDALLING FOR PIANO, THE --BKS. 1 AND 2

CHING, JAMES
    PERFORMER AND AUDIENCE..AN INVESTIGATION INTO THE PSYCHOLOGICAL
CHING, JAMES
    PIANO PLAYING, A PRACTICAL METHOD--A NEW EDITION OF 'PIANO
CHING, JAMES
    POINTS ON PEDALLING
CHING, JAMES
    STUDIES FOR BASIC PIANO TECHNIQUE..WRITTEN AND SELECTED WITH
CHING, JOAN ELIZABETH
    APPROACH TO PIANO TEACHING---ALSO CATALOGUED UNDER
CHRISTIANI, ADOLPH FRIEDRICH
    PRINCIPLES OF EXPRESSION IN PIANOFORTE PLAYING, THE
CLARKE, HUGH ARCHIBALD
    ART OF PIANOFORTE PLAYING, THE --TEXT BOOK FOR BEGINNERS
CLEMENTI, MUZIO
    INTRODUCTION TO THE ART OF PLAYING ON THE PIANOFORTE---1801+
COCHRAN, MARY
    ULTIMATE PRINCIPLES OF PIANOFORTE TEACHING AND PLAYING
COHEN, HARRIET
    MUSIC'S HANDMAID
COOK, J. LAWRENCE
    PIANO HANDBOOK ON BOOGIE WOOGIE, BLUES, AND BARRELHOUSE..3 EASY TO
COOKE, JAMES FRANCIS
    GREAT PIANISTS ON PIANO PLAYING..STUDY TALKS WITH FOREMOST
COPP, LAURA R.
    SOME SECRETS OF SUCCESS IN PLAYING IN PUBLIC
COUPERIN, FRANCOIS
    ART DE TOUCHER LE CLAVECIN, L' ---IN FRENCH, GERMAN AND ENGLISH
COVIELLO, AMBROSE
    DIFFICULTIES OF BEETHOVEN PIANOFORTE SONATAS, AN ANALYSIS OF
COVIELLO, AMBROSE
    FOUNDATIONS OF PIANOFORTE TECHNIC
COVIELLO, AMBROSE
    WHAT MATTHAY MEANT
CRAMER, JOHN BAPTIST
    INSTRUCTIONS FOR THE PIANOFORTE---CONTAINS ALSO A SET OF 28
CULSHAW, JOHN
    CONCERTO, THE
CZERNY, CARL
    COMPLETE THEORETICAL AND PRACTICAL PIANO FORTE SCHOOL, FROM THE
CZERNY, CARL
    LETTERS TO A YOUNG LADY ON THE ART OF PLAYING THE PIANOFORTE
CZERNY, CARL
    ON THE PROPER PERFORMANCE OF ALL BEETHOVEN'S WORKS FOR THE PIANO
D'ABREU, GERALD
    PLAYING THE PIANO WITH CONFIDENCE---1964
DAHL, ANTON
    SOUL OF GENIUS, THE ..ITS MUSICAL DEVELOPMENT AND HOW THE WORLD AT
DALE, BENJAMIN J.
    HARMONY, COUNTERPOINT AND IMPROVISATION
DANIELS, BESS *
    WORLD OF MUSIC, THE ..PIANO COURSE..TEACHERS' BOOK, FOR CLASS OR
DANNREUTHER, EDWARD
    MUSICAL ORNAMENTATION--IN TWO PARTS
DART, THURSTON
    INTERPRETATION OF MUSIC, THE --4TH. ED.---1954
DILLER, ANGELA
    FIRST PEDAL-STUDIES FOR THE PIANO, 24 PROGRESSIVE EXERCISES AND
DILLER, ANGELA
    SPLENDOR OF MUSIC, THE
DOLMETSCH, ARNOLD
    INTERPRETATION OF MUSIC OF THE SEVENTEENTH AND EIGHTEENTH
DONINGTON, ROBERT
    INTERPRETATION OF EARLY MUSIC, THE
DONINGTON, ROBERT
    PERFORMER'S GUIDE TO BAROQUE MUSIC, A
DORIAN, FREDERICK
    HISTORY OF MUSIC IN PERFORMANCE, THE ---1942
DRAKE, KENNETH
    SONATAS OF BEETHOVEN AS HE PLAYED AND TAUGHT THEM, THE
DUMESNIL, MAURICE
    HOW TO PLAY AND TEACH DEBUSSY
DUMM, ROBERT W.
    IN BLACK AND WHITE
DUNN, JOHN PETRIE
    ORNAMENTATION IN THE WORKS OF FREDERIC CHOPIN---1921
EDWARDS, RUTH
    COMPLEAT MUSIC TEACHER FOR TEACHERS, PARENTS AND STUDENTS
EHRENFECTER, C. A.
    DELIVERY IN THE ART OF PIANOFORTE PLAYING
EHRENFECTER, C. A.
    TECHNICAL STUDY IN THE ART OF PIANOFORTE PLAYING--DEPPE'S
EHRLICH, ALFRED HEINRICH
    ORNAMENTATION IN BEETHOVEN'S PIANOFORTE-WORKS, THE
EHRLICH, ALFRED HEINRICH
    ORNAMENTATION IN JOH. SEB. BACH'S PIANOFORTE-WORKS, THE
EISENBERG, JACOB
    ARTISTIC PIANIST, THE ..NATURAL TECHNICS IN PIANO MASTERY..FROM
EISENBERG, JACOB
    WEIGHT AND RELAXATION METHOD FOR THE PIANOFORTE
ELLINGHAM, HARRY
    HOW TO USE A PLAYER-PIANO
EMERICH, PAUL
    ROAD TO MODERN MUSIC, THE
EMERY, WALTER
    BACH'S ORNAMENTS
ENGEL, CARL
    PIANIST'S HANDBOOK, THE ..A GUIDE FOR THE RIGHT COMPREHENSION AND
ENGELBRECHT, J. G.
    MATERIA MUSICA, OR MATERIALS FOR THE PIANIST..A CLASS BOOK
EVANS, EDWIN
    HANDBOOK TO THE PIANOFORTE WORKS OF JOHANNES BRAHMS---1936
EVERHART, POWELL
    PIANIST'S ART, THE ..A COMPREHENSIVE MANUAL ON PIANO PLAYING FOR
FAELTEN, CARL
    PEDAL EXERCISES FOR PIANOFORTE
FARJEON, HARRY
    ART OF PIANO PEDALLING, THE ..TWO VOLUMES IN ONE
FARJEON, HARRY
    ART OF PIANO PHRASING, THE
FERGUSON, DONALD NIVISON
    PIANO INTERPRETATION
FIELDEN, THOMAS
    MARKS AND REMARKS..MUSICAL EXAMINATIONS AND THEIR PROBLEMS
FINCK, HENRY T.
    PADEREWSKI AND HIS ART
FISCHER, EDWIN
    BEETHOVEN'S PIANOFORTE SONATAS, A GUIDE FOR STUDENTS AND
FISCHER, EDWIN
    REFLECTIONS ON MUSIC
FOLDES, ANDOR
    KEYS TO THE KEYBOARD, A BOOK FOR PIANISTS
FOOTE, ARTHUR W.
    SOME PRACTICAL THINGS IN PIANO PLAYING
FORD, DONALD
    SINGING CLASS PIANIST AND ON PIANOFORTE ACCOMPANYING IN GENERAL,

FOWLES, ERNEST
    HARMONY IN PIANOFORTE-STUDY..FOR THE INDIVIDUAL STUDENT--2 VOLS.,
FULLER-MAITLAND, J. A.
    MUSICIAN'S PILGRIMAGE, THE ..A STUDY IN ARTISTIC DEVELOPMENT
GABRIEL, GILBERT W.
    GREAT PIANISTS AND COMPOSERS
GARRATT, PERCIVAL
    ART OF PIANOFORTE PLAYING, THE
GARROWAY, WILL
    PIANISM
GASPARINI, FRANCESCO
    PRACTICAL HARMONIST AT THE HARPSICHORD, THE ---1708
GAT, JOZSEF
    TECHNIQUE OF PIANO PLAYING, THE, --2ND. ED.---1958
GEARY, ELEANOR MARGARET
    MUSICAL EDUCATION, WITH PRACTICAL OBSERVATIONS ON THE ART OF
GEBHARD, HEINRICH
    ART OF PEDALLING, THE
GERMER, HEINRICH
    MUSICAL ORNAMENTATION..DIDACTICO-CRITICAL TREATISE ON ALL OF THE
GERMER, HEINRICH
    TECHNICS OF PIANOFORTE PLAYING, THE ..MUSICAL ORNAMENTATION,
GERMER, HEINRICH
    THEORETICO-PRACTICAL ELEMENTARY PIANO-FORTE SCHOOL FOR STUDENTS OF
GIESEKING, WALTER *
    PIANO TECHNIQUE---COMBINED REPUBLICATION OF..'THE SHORTEST WAY TO
GILBERTSON, ARNOLD B.
    TEACHERS MANUAL FOR POPULAR PIANO PLAYING, DESIGNED FOR ALL
GIRDLESTONE, CUTHBERT
    MOZART AND HIS PIANO CONCERTOS---FIRST PUBLISHED IN 1948 AS
GIVENS, LARRY
    RE-ENACTING THE ARTIST..A STORY OF THE AMPICO REPRODUCING PIANO
GOLDTHWAITE, SCOTT
    ORNAMENTATION IN MUSIC FOR THE KEYBOARD
GOODRICH, ALFRED JOHN
    THEORY OF INTERPRETATION, APPLIED TO ARTISTIC MUSICAL PERFORMANCE
GORDON, STEPHEN T.
    GORDON'S NEW SCHOOL FOR THE PIANO-FORTE
GOSS, JOHN
    INTRODUCTION TO HARMONY AND THOROUGH-BASS WITH NUMEROUS EXAMPLES
GRANTHAM, BILLY
    HELLO TO THE BLUES..FUN WITH CHORDS..FUN AND INFORMATION ON
GRAUPNER, GOTTLIEB
    RUDIMENTS OF THE ART OF PLAYING ON THE PIANOFORTE...A PLAIN
GRAY, CECIL
    BACH AND DAS WOHLTEMPERIRTE KLAVIER..ANALYTICAL NOTES, WITH AN
GRAY, CECIL
    CONTINGENCIES AND OTHER ESSAYS---LISZT
GRAY, CECIL
    FORTY-EIGHT PRELUDES AND FUGUES OF J. S. BACH, THE
GREW, SIDNEY
    ART OF THE PLAYER-PIANO, THE ..A TEXTBOOK FOR STUDENT AND TEACHER
GREW, SIDNEY
    FIRST BOOK OF THE PLAYER-PIANIST, THE
GRUNDY, ENID
    HAPPY PIANIST, THE
GUTMANN, EMMA WILKINS
    TALKS WITH PIANO TEACHERS
HAMBOURG, MARK
    HOW TO PLAY THE PIANO--NEW AND ENLARGED EDITION OF 'HOW TO BECOME
HAMBOURG, MARK
    HOW TO PREPARE FOR PLAYING IN CONCERT
HAMILTON, CLARENCE G.
    ORNAMENTS IN CLASSICAL AND MODERN MUSIC
HAMILTON, CLARENCE G.
    PIANO TEACHING..ITS PRINCIPLES AND PROBLEMS
HAMILTON, CLARENCE G.
    TOUCH AND EXPRESSION IN PIANO PLAYING
HAMILTON, CLARENCE G.
    WHAT EVERY PIANO PUPIL SHOULD KNOW
HANSMANN, RICHARD
    THEORETICAL AND PRACTICAL PIANO-FORTE SCHOOL FOR THE JANKO
HARDING, HENRY ALFRED
    MUSICAL ORNAMENTS SIMPLY EXPLAINED...NUMEROUS EXAMPLES...WITH 100
HARICH-SCHNEIDER, ETA
    HARPSICHORD, THE ..AN INTRODUCTION TO TECHNIQUE, STYLE AND THE
HARKNESS, ROBERT
    HARKNESS PIANO METHOD OF EVANGELISTIC HYMN PLAYING, THE ..A
HARRISON, SIDNEY
    PIANO TECHNIQUE
HARRISON, SIDNEY
    TEACHER NEVER TOLD ME--TIPS FOR STUDENTS
HARRISON, SIDNEY
    YOUNG PERSON'S GUIDE TO PLAYING THE PIANO, THE
HECK, JOHANN CASPAR
    ART OF PLAYING THE HARPSICHORD, ILLUSTRATED BY A VARIETY OF
HEPLER, EFFIE A.
    EXERCISES IN TIME AND RHYTHM..A CONTRIBUTION TO MODERN PIANO
HERZ, HENRI
    NEW AND COMPLETE PIANOFORTE SCHOOL
HEUSCHNEIDER, KARIN
    PIANO SONATA OF THE EIGHTEENTH CENTURY IN ITALY, THE
HIPKINS, ALFRED JAMES
    HOW CHOPIN PLAYED...FROM CONTEMPORARY IMPRESSIONS COLLECTED FROM
HOFHEIMER, GRACE
    TEACHING TECHNIQUES FOR THE PIANO
HOFMANN, JOSEF
    PIANO PLAYING..A LITTLE BOOK OF SIMPLE SUGGESTIONS--REPRINTED FROM
HOFMANN, JOSEF
    PIANO PLAYING, WITH PIANO QUESTIONS ANSWERED---PUBLISHED EARLIER
HOLCMAN, JAN
    LEGACY OF CHOPIN, THE
HOOK, JAMES
    GUIDA DI MUSICA..BEING A COMPLETE BOOK OF INSTRUCTIONS FOR
HOPE, ERIC
    HANDBOOK OF PIANO PLAYING, A
HOPKINS, ANTHONY
    TALKING ABOUT SONATAS..A BOOK OF ANALYTICAL STUDIES, BASED ON A
HORROCKS, CYRIL R. H.
    STUDENT'S GUIDE TO THE ART OF TEACHING THE PIANOFORTE, THE --2ND.
HOWELL, DOROTHY
    KEYBOARD WORK FOR HARMONY STUDENTS
HUENTEN, FRANZ
    ABRIDGED EDITION OF F. HUENTEN'S CELEBRATED INSTRUCTIONS FOR THE
HUENTEN, FRANZ
    FRANZ HUENTEN'S CELEBRATED INSTRUCTIONS FOR THE PIANOFORTE--2ND.
HULL, ARTHUR EAGLEFIELD
    THREE HUNDRED QUESTIONS ON PIANOFORTE TEACHING IN 30. GRADUATED
HUMMEL, JOHANN NEPOMUK
    COMPLETE THEORETICAL AND PRACTICAL COURSE OF INSTRUCTIONS ON THE
HUNEKER, JAMES GIBBONS
    DEVELOPMENT OF PIANO MUSIC FROM THE DAYS OF THE CLAVICHORD AND
HUTCHESON, ERNEST *
    LITERATURE OF THE PIANO, THE ..A GUIDE FOR AMATEUR AND
HUTCHINGS, ARTHUR
    COMPANION TO MOZART'S PIANO CONCERTOS, A

ILIFFE, FREDERICK
    FORTY-EIGHT PRELUDES AND FUGUES OF JOHANN SEBASTIAN BACH ANALYZED
INTERNATIONAL MUSICOLOGICAL CONGRESS..FIRST--1960--WORKS OF FREDERICK
    BOOK OF THE FIRST INTERNATIONAL MUSICOLOGICAL CONGRESS DEVOTED TO
ISAACS, EDWARD
    BLIND PIANO TEACHER, THE
JEWETT, ALBERT DEWEY
    IDIOMATIC COURSE OF PIANO INSTRUCTION FOR CLASS WORK
JOHNS, CLAYTON
    ESSENTIALS OF PIANOFORTE PLAYING, THE
JOHNSON, THOMAS A.
    PRINCIPLES OF PIANOFORTE PEDALLING, THE
JOHNSTONE, J. ALFRED
    ART OF EXPRESSION IN PIANOFORTE PLAYING, THE
JOHNSTONE, J. ALFRED
    ART OF TEACHING PIANOFORTE PLAYING, THE --2ND. REV. ED.---1910
JOHNSTONE, J. ALFRED
    HOW TO USE THE PEDAL IN PIANO PLAYING
JOHNSTONE, J. ALFRED
    PHRASING IN PIANO PLAYING..AN ELEMENTARY GUIDE WITH EXAMPLES
JOHNSTONE, J. ALFRED
    RUBATO, OR THE SECRET OF EXPRESSION IN PIANOFORTE PLAYING
JOHNSTONE, J. ALFRED
    TOUCH, PHRASING AND INTERPRETATION
JONAS, ALBERTO
    PIANOSCRIPT BOOK..AN INVALUABLE AID TO TEACHER AND STUDENT IN
JONES, GRIFFITH
    COMPLEAT INSTRUCTOR FOR THE HARPSICHORD OR PIANOFORTE, THE
KASTNER, SANTIAGO
    PARALLELS AND DISCREPANCIES BETWEEN ENGLISH AND SPANISH KEYBOARD
KELLER, HERMANN
    PHRASING AND ARTICULATION---152 MUSICAL EXAMPLES
KELLEY, EDGAR STILLMAN
    CHOPIN THE COMPOSER---1913
KIRKPATRICK, RALPH
    DOMENICO SCARLATTI---1953
KLAUWELL, OTTO
    ON MUSICAL EXECUTION...PRIMARILY WITH REFERENCE TO PIANO-PLAYING
KLECZYNSKI, JAN
    HOW TO PLAY CHOPIN--THREE LECTURES
KLECZYNSKI, JAN
    WORKS OF FREDERIC CHOPIN, THE ..THEIR PROPER INTERPRETATION--6TH.
KOBBE, GUSTAV
    STRAIGHT TO THE HEART OF MUSIC---PLAYER-PIANO
KOCH, CASPAR
    PIANO STUDENT'S GRADUS AD PARNASSUM, THE ..PRESENTING THE
KOCHEVITSKY, GEORGE
    ART OF PIANO PLAYING, THE ..A SCIENTIFIC APPROACH
KRUSZYNSKI, MICHAL
    APPROACH TO THE PSYCHOLOGY OF PIANO TEACHING, AN
KULLAK, ADOLPH
    AESTHETICS OF PIANOFORTE PLAYING, THE ---1861 IN GERMAN--1ST.
KULLAK, FRANZ
    BEETHOVEN'S PIANO PLAYING, WITH AN ESSAY ON THE EXECUTION OF THE
LAMAR, RICHARD
    COLLEGE PIANO PEDAGOGY
LANDOWSKA, WANDA
    LANDOWSKA ON MUSIC--EDITED BY DENISE RESTOUT
LANG, EDITH *
    MUSICAL ACCOMPANIMENT OF MOVING PICTURES..A PRACTICAL MANUAL FOR
LANNING, RUSSELL
    BACH ORNAMENTATION
LAST, JOAN
    INTERPRETATION FOR THE PIANO STUDENT
LAST, JOAN
    INTRODUCTION TO PEDALLING
LAST, JOAN
    YOUNG PIANIST, THE ..A NEW APPROACH FOR TEACHERS AND
LAWRENCE, FREDERIC LOCKE
    RATIONALE OF PIANO TECHNIQUE, THE
LEIMER, KARL *
    RHYTHMICS, DYNAMICS, PEDAL, AND OTHER PROBLEMS OF PIANO
LEIMER, KARL *
    SHORTEST WAY TO PIANISTIC PERFECTION, THE
LEONHARDT, GUSTAV M.
    ART OF FUGUE, BACH'S LAST HARPSICHORD WORK, THE ..AN ARGUMENT
LEVINSKAYA, MARIA
    LEVINSKAYA SYSTEM OF PIANOFORTE TECHNIC AND TONE COLOR, THE
LHEVINNE, JOSEF
    BASIC PRINCIPLES IN PIANOFORTE PLAYING---1924
LIEBERMAN, MAURICE
    KEYBOARD HARMONY AND IMPROVISATION--2 VOLS.
LINDO, ALGERNON H. *
    INDIVIDUALITY IN PIANO TOUCH
LINDO, ALGERNON H.
    PEDALLING IN PIANOFORTE MUSIC
LOGIER, JOHANN BERNHARD
    SYLLABUS OF THE SECOND EXAMINATION OF MR. LOGIER'S PUPILS, ON HIS
LOVELOCK, WILLIAM
    ORNAMENTS AND ABBREVIATIONS FOR EXAMINATION CANDIDATES
LOWE, CLAUDE EDGERTON
    SUGGESTIONS FOR THE APPRECIATION AND INTERPRETATION OF PIANOFORTE
LOWE, CLAUDE EDGERTON
    VIVA VOCE..250 QUESTIONS AND ANSWERS FOR PIANOFORTE DIPLOMA
LUDDEN, WILLIAM
    THOROUGH BASS SCHOOL, THE ..AN EASY AND PROGRESSIVE COURSE FOR
MACPHERSON, STEWART
    STUDIES IN PHRASING AND FORM
MAIER, GUY
    PIANO TEACHER'S COMPANION, THE
MARKS, ADOLF B.
    INTRODUCTION TO THE INTERPRETATION OF BEETHOVEN'S PIANO-FORTE
MASON, WILLIAM G. *
    PRIMER OF MUSIC, A ..BEING THE FIRST STEPS IN MUSICIANSHIP..FOR
MASON, WILLIAM G.
    SYSTEM OF TECHNICAL EXERCISES FOR THE PIANO-FORTE, A
MASON, WILLIAM G.
    TOUCH AND TECHNIC..FOR ARTISTIC PIANO PLAYING, OP. 44--4 VOLS. IN
MATHEWS, WILLIAM S. B.
    SCHOOL OF THE PIANO PEDAL
MATHEWS, WILLIAM S. B.
    STUDIES IN PHRASING, MEMORIZING AND INTERPRETATION
MATHEWS, WILLIAM S. B.
    STUDIES IN PHRASING SELECTED FROM THE WORKS OF THE BEST CLASSIC
MATHEWS, WILLIAM S. B.
    TEACHER'S MANUAL OF MASON'S PIANOFORTE TECHNICS
MATTHAY, TOBIAS A.
    ACT OF TOUCH IN ALL ITS DIVERSITY, THE ..AN ANALYSIS AND SYNTHESIS
MATTHAY, TOBIAS A.
    FIRST PRINCIPLES OF PIANOFORTE PLAYING--EXTRACT FROM 'THE ACT OF
MATTHAY, TOBIAS A.
    MUSICAL INTERPRETATION..ITS LAWS AND PRINCIPLES---1913
MATTHAY, TOBIAS A.
    ON COLORING AS DISTINCT FROM TONE-INFLECTION--A LECTURE
MATTHAY, TOBIAS A.
    PIANOFORTE TONE-PRODUCTION---SAME AS 'THE ACT OF TOUCH IN ALL ITS

MATTHAY, TOBIAS A.
    PRINCIPLES OF FINGERING AND LAWS OF PEDALLING
MATTHAY, TOBIAS A.
    SLUR OR COUPLET OF NOTES IN ALL ITS VARIETY, THE ..ITS
MATTHEWS, DENIS--EDITOR
    KEYBOARD MUSIC--ESSAYS ON KEYBOARD LITERATURE, EXCLUDING ORGAN
MCARTHUR, ALEXANDER
    PIANOFORTE STUDY..HINTS ON PIANO PLAYING
MCCLANAHAN, RICHARD
    CADENCE, KEY TO MUSICAL CLARITY, THE ..A SIMPLE AND PRACTICAL
MCEWEN, JOHN B.
    INTRODUCTION TO AN UNPUBLISHED EDITION OF THE PIANOFORTE SONATAS
MCEWEN, JOHN B.
    PRINCIPLES OF PHRASING AND ARTICULATION IN MUSIC, THE
MEHEGAN, JOHN F.
    STYLES FOR THE JAZZ PIANIST--BK. 1..THE RHYTHMIC SCHOOL
MELLERS, WILFRED
    FRANCOIS COUPERIN AND THE FRENCH CLASSICAL TRADITION
MERGES, P.
    PRACTICAL RULES FOR PIANOFORTE PLAYING..TEXT BOOK FOR TEACHERS AND
MERRICK, FRANK
    PRACTICING THE PIANO
MILLER, ALLAN
    BEGINNING PIANO FOR ADULTS
MILLER, EDWARD
    INSTITUTES OF MUSIC, OR, EASY INSTRUCTIONS FOR THE HARPSICHORD
MILNE, ALFRED FORBES
    BEETHOVEN..THE PIANOFORTE SONATAS--2 VOLS.
MOLLER, JOHN CHRISTOPHER
    SETT OF PROGRESSIVE LESSONS FOR THE HARPSICHORD OR PIANO FORTE, A
MOORE, MARY BURNHAM
    LURE OF THE PIANO THROUGH COORDINATION AND CONCENTRATION, THE
MORRILL, HENRY H.
    MANUAL OF PIANO FOR PUPILS AND TEACHERS
MOTT, ISAAC H. R.
    ADVICE AND INSTRUCTIONS FOR PLAYING THE PIANOFORTE WITH EXPRESSION
MUSIC EDUCATORS NATIONAL CONFERENCE
    TEACHING PIANO IN CLASSROOM AND STUDIO
MUSIC PROJECT--NEW YORK CITY
    TEACHER'S GUIDE..A CREATIVE APPROACH TO PIANO CLASS TEACHING, BY
NALDER, LAWRENCE MARCUS
    MODERN PIANO, THE
NAYLOR, EDWARD W.
    ELIZABETHAN VIRGINAL BOOK, AN ..A CRITICAL ESSAY ON THE CONTENTS
NEUHAUS, HEINRICH
    ART OF PIANO PLAYING, THE
NEWMAN, ELIZABETH
    HOW TO TEACH MUSIC TO BEGINNERS
NEWMAN, ERNEST
    PIANO-PLAYER AND ITS MUSIC, THE
NEWMAN, WILLIAM S.
    PERFORMANCE PRACTICES IN BEETHOVEN'S PIANO SONATAS..AN
NEWMAN, WILLIAM S.
    PIANIST'S PROBLEMS, THE ..A MODERN APPROACH TO EFFICIENT PRACTICE
NEWMAN, WILLIAM S.
    SONATA IN THE BAROQUE ERA, THE --A HISTORY OF THE SONATA IDEA,
NEWMAN, WILLIAM S.
    SONATA IN THE CLASSIC ERA, THE --A HISTORY OF THE SONATA IDEA,
NEWTON, IVOR
    AT THE PIANO--IVOR NEWTON..THE WORLD OF AN ACCOMPANIST
NICCHIA, LILLIAN
    PIANOFORTE STUDY..HINTS ON PIANO PLAYING
O'REAR, MRS. ASBURY S.
    SELF READING NOTES
OLIVER, EDWARD B.
    PRACTICAL TEXT-BOOK OF MUSIC, AS CONNECTED WITH THE ART OF PLAYING
PALMER, ANNIE L.
    MUSIC TEACHERS' GUIDE TO THE GOLDBECK PIANO METHOD
PALMER, HORATIO R.
    PALMER'S PIANO PRIMER
PALMER, KING
    TEACH YOURSELF TO PLAY THE PIANO
PALMER, WILLARD A.--EDITOR
    CHOPIN..AN INTRODUCTION TO HIS PIANO WORKS
PARSONS, ALBERT R.
    SYNTHETIC METHOD FOR THE PIANOFORTE, THE
PASQUALI, NICOLO
    ART OF FINGERING THE HARPSICHORD, THE
PAUER, ERNST
    ART OF PIANOFORTE PLAYING, THE
PEARCE, CHARLES WILLIAM
    ART OF THE PIANO TEACHER, THE
PERRY, EDWARD B.
    DESCRIPTIVE ANALYSES OF PIANO WORKS, FOR THE USE OF TEACHERS,
PERRY, EDWARD B.
    STORIES OF STANDARD TEACHING PIECES FOR THE PIANOFORTE
PETERSILEA, CARLYLE
    PIANO PLAYING..GENERAL MUSICAL INSTRUCTION FROM BEGINNING TO END
PETERSON, FRANKLIN
    THEORETIC COMPANION TO PRACTICE--PART I OF THE PIANIST'S HANDBOOK
PFEFFERKORN, OTTO W.
    PIANISTIC HINTS
PHILIPP, ISIDOR
    SOME REFLECTIONS ON PIANO PLAYING
PHILIPP, LILLIE H.
    PIANO STUDY..APPLICATION AND TECHNIQUE
PHILLIPSON, WENTWORTH
    GUIDE TO YOUNG PIANOFORTE TEACHERS AND STUDENTS
PINCHERLE, MARC
    WORLD OF THE VIRTUOSO, THE
PLATT, CAROLYN
    CAROLYN PLATT METHOD FOR PIANO, THE --GROUP INSTRUCTION--TEACHER'S
POINTER SYSTEM, INC.
    GUIDE TO THE MODERN PIANIST, A
PORTE, JOHN F.
    CHOPIN, THE COMPOSER AND HIS MUSIC
POTAMKIN, FRANK
    MODERN PIANO PEDAGOGY
PRELLEUR, PETER
    HARPSICHORD ILLUSTRATED AND IMPROV'D, WHEREIN IS SHEWN THE ITALIAN
PRENTICE, THOMAS RIDLEY
    MUSICIAN, THE ..A GUIDE FOR PIANOFORTE STUDENTS--6 VOLS.
PRENTNER, MARIE
    MODERN PIANIST..BEING MY EXPERIENCES IN THE TECHNIQUE AND
PROSNAK, JAN
    FREDERIC CHOPIN INTERNATIONAL PIANO COMPETITIONS, THE
QUINTE, MICHAEL S.
    MODULATIONARY HARMONY BOOK
RAMUL, PETER
    PSYCHO-PHYSICAL FOUNDATIONS OF MODERN PIANO TECHNIQUE, THE
REDDIE, CHARLES FREDERICK
    PIANOFORTE PLAYING ON ITS TECHNICAL AND AESTHETIC SIDES
REEDER, BETAH
    SINGING TOUCH, THE
REEVES, BETTY
    APPROACH TO PIANO TEACHING---ALSO CATALOGUED UNDER

REINAGLE, CAROLINE
    FEW WORDS ON PIANOFORTE PLAYING, A
REZITS, JOSEPH
    TEACHER'S GUIDE TO THE NEW SCRIBNER MUSIC LIBRARY
RICHNER, THOMAS
    ORIENTATION FOR INTERPRETING MOZART'S PIANO SONATAS
RICHTER, ADA
    TEACHING HINTS
RIEFLING, REIMAR
    PIANO PEDALLING---1957, IN NORWEGIAN
RIEMANN, HUGO
    CATECHISM OF PIANOFORTE PLAYING---1888, IN GERMAN
RIEMANN, HUGO
    PRACTICAL GUIDE TO THE ART OF PHRASING...ANALYSIS OF CLASSIC AND
ROBBINS, EDGAR A.
    AMERICAN METHOD FOR THE PIANOFORTE
ROBYN, LOUISE
    HOW TO TEACH PIANO TO THE CHILD BEGINNER..A TEXT BOOK FOR TEACHERS
ROEDER, CARL M.
    LIBERATION AND DELIBERATION IN PIANO TECHNIC
ROSENTHAL, MORIZ
    OLD AND THE NEW SCHOOL OF PIANO PLAYING, THE --TYPEWRITTEN COPY
ROSS, CHARLES
    RIGHT FOOT FORWARD..A FIRST BOOK ON PEDALLING FOR ADULT STUDENTS
ROSTAND, CLAUDE
    LISZT
ROTHSCHILD, FRITZ
    LOST TRADITION IN MUSIC, THE --PT. 1..RHYTHM AND TEMPO IN J. S.
ROTHSCHILD, FRITZ
    LOST TRADITION IN MUSIC, THE --PT. 2..MUSICAL PERFORMANCE IN THE
ROWLEY, ALEC
    DO'S AND DONT'S FOR MUSICIANS..A HANDBOOK FOR TEACHERS AND
ROWLEY, ALEC *
    GRADED TESTS IN PRACTICAL MUSICIANSHIP AND MUSICAL INITIATIVE--IN
ROWLEY, ALEC
    PRACTICAL MUSICIANSHIP, A HANDBOOK FOR TEACHERS AND STUDENTS
RUBINSTEIN, BERYL
    OUTLINE OF PIANO PEDAGOGY--REV. ED.----1929
RUSSELL, LOUIS ARTHUR
    EMBELLISHMENTS OF MUSIC, THE ..A STUDY OF THE ENTIRE RANGE OF
SAVLER, ROBERTA--EDITOR
    SELECTIONS FROM THE PIANO TEACHER, 1958-1963
SCHAAF, EDWARD O.
    ART OF PIANO PLAYER TRANSCRIPTION, THE ..MAKING OF PERFORATED
SCHAAF, EDWARD O.
    FUNDAMENTAL PRINCIPLES INVOLVED IN THE COMPOSING AND ARRANGING OF
SCHAAF, EDWARD O.
    MUSICAL INDIVIDUALITY OF THE PLAYER PIANO, THE ---EXCERPTS..'THE
SCHELLING, ERNEST *
    OXFORD PIANO COURSE, TEACHER'S FIRST MANUAL
SCHELLING, ERNEST *
    OXFORD PIANO COURSE, TEACHER'S SECOND MANUAL
SCHERER, HERBERT
    PIANO PRACTICING
SCHLIEDER, FREDERICK W.
    LYRIC COMPOSITION THROUGH IMPROVISATION--2 VOLS., 1927-1946
SCHMITT, HANS
    NATURAL LAWS OF MUSICAL EXPRESSION, THE
SCHMITT, HANS
    PEDALS OF THE PIANOFORTE, THE --FOUR LECTURES
SCHMITZ, ELIE ROBERT
    CAPTURE OF INSPIRATION, THE
SCHMITZ, ELIE ROBERT
    PIANO WORKS OF CLAUDE DEBUSSY, THE
SCHNABEL, KARL ULRICH
    MODERN TECHNIQUE OF THE PEDAL
SCHNEIDER, HANS
    WORKING OF THE MIND IN PIANO TEACHING AND PLAYING, THE
SCHOTT, HOWARD
    PLAYING THE HARPSICHORD
SCHUMANN, ROBERT
    ON MUSIC AND MUSICIANS---1854, IN GERMAN--FIRST ENGLISH EDITION IN
SEGUEL, MANIA
    CHOPIN'S TEMPO RUBATO
SHEDLOCK, JOHN S.
    BEETHOVEN'S PIANOFORTE SONATAS..THE ORIGIN AND RESPECTIVE VALUES
SHELDON, ROBERT--COMPILER
    EGON PETRI-ALEXANDER LIBERMANN NOTES ON THE ART AND TECHNIQUE OF
SHERWOOD MUSIC SCHOOL
    PIANO LESSONS AND TESTS--4TH. REV. ED.---1945+
SLENCZYNSKA, RUTH *
    MUSIC AT YOUR FINGERTIPS
SMELTZER, JEANNIE R.--COMPILER
    OUTLINES AND GRADES FOR THE USE OF PIANO TEACHERS
SMITH, THOMAS
    LITTLE DIFFICULTIES WHICH OCCUR IN PIANOFORTE PLAYING
SOREL, CLAUDETTE
    MIND YOUR MUSICAL MANNERS, OFF AND ON STAGE..A HANDBOOK OF STAGE
SQUIRE, RUSSEL N. *
    CLASS PIANO FOR ADULT BEGINNERS--2ND. ED.---1964
STARKEY, EVELYN
    PIANO CLASS WORKBOOK FOR FIRST YEAR STUDENTS
STEIN, ERWIN
    FORM AND PERFORMANCE
STEINERT, MORRIS
    MORRIS STEINERT COLLECTION OF KEYED AND STRINGED INSTRUMENTS, THE
STEPHENSON, LILIAN E.
    BEGONE, DULL PRACTICE..SUGGESTIONS FOR STUDENTS AND
STERNBERG, CONSTANTIN I. VON
    ETHICS AND ESTHETICS OF PIANO PLAYING
STERNBERG, CONSTANTIN I. VON
    TEMPO RUBATO AND OTHER ESSAYS
STEWART, REID
    HOW TO PASS MUSIC EXAMINATIONS--PIANO--A GUIDE FOR TEACHERS AND
STORMEN, WIN
    JAZZ PIANO..DIXIELAND TO MODERN JAZZ, BLUES, BOOGIE, RAGTIME,
STORMEN, WIN
    JAZZ PIANO..EARLY BLUES TO CONTEMPORARY MODERN JAZZ, HOW TO PLAY
SUMMY-BIRCHARD COMPANY
    HANDBOOK FOR PIANO TEACHERS..COLLECTED ARTICLES ON SUBJECTS
TANKARD, GEOFFREY
    FOUNDATIONS OF PIANOFORTE TECHNIQUE
TANKARD, GEOFFREY
    PIANOFORTE DIPLOMAS
TANKARD, GEOFFREY
    SPECIMEN ANSWERS TO THE QUESTIONS IN PIANOFORTE DIPLOMAS
TAPPER, THOMAS
    ABC OF KEYBOARD HARMONY, THE
TAYLER, E. DOUGLAS
    MIND-POWER IN MUSIC FOR STUDENTS, TEACHERS AND PERFORMERS
TAYLER, E. DOUGLAS
    SECRET OF MUSICAL EXPRESSION, WITH SPECIAL REFERENCE TO PIANOFORTE
TAYLER, E. DOUGLAS
    SECRET OF SUCCESSFUL PRACTICE, THE
TAYLOR, FRANKLIN
    PRIMER OF PIANOFORTE PLAYING

TAYLOR, FRANKLIN
TECHNIQUE AND EXPRESSION IN PIANOFORTE PLAYING
TAYLOR, H.
ORNAMENTS IN MUSIC
TOBIN, JOSEPH RAYMOND
COMMON SENSE IN SIGHT READING..A GUIDE FOR PIANO TEACHERS
TRUE, LYLE C.
HOW AND WHAT TO PLAY FOR MOVING PICTURES..A MANUAL AND GUIDE FOR
TURECK, ROSALYN
INTRODUCTION TO THE PERFORMANCE OF BACH, AN--3 VOLS.
UNSCHULD, MARIE VON
PIANIST'S HAND, THE ..A SYSTEMATIC METHOD...ACCORDING TO THE
VANTYN, SIDNEY
MODERN PIANOFORTE TECHNIQUE
VAN DER WEYDE, PETER H.
INSTRUCTIONS IN PLAYING THE PIANO-FORTE WITH AEOLIAN ATTACHMENT
VEINUS, ABRAHAM
CONCERTO, THE ---1944
VENABLE, MARY
INTERPRETATION OF PIANO MUSIC, THE
VENINO, ALBERT F.
PEDAL METHOD FOR THE PIANO, A
VERNAZZA, MARCELLE
BASIC MATERIALS FOR THE PIANO STUDENT
VIARD-LOUIS, JENNY
MUSIC AND THE PIANO
VINING, HARRISON S.
SIMPLE AND COMPLETE PRIMER FOR THE PIANOFORTE, THE
VINQUIST, MARY *
PERFORMANCE PRACTICE..A BIBLIOGRAPHY
VIRGIL, ALMON K.
STEP BY STEP..TEXTBOOK IN PIANO PLAYING..HANDBOOK FOR TEACHERS
VIRGIL, ANTHA MINERVA
PIANO PEDALS, THE
WARRINER, JOHN
TRANSPOSITION, KEYBOARD AND ORCHESTRAL--2 PTS., 1893-1908
WELLS, HOWARD
EARS, BRAIN AND FINGERS..A TEXT BOOK FOR PIANO TEACHERS AND PUPILS
WESTERBY, HERBERT
HOW TO STUDY THE PIANOFORTE WORKS OF THE GREAT COMPOSERS
WESTERBY, HERBERT
LISZT, COMPOSER, AND HIS PIANO WORKS..DESCRIPTIVE GUIDE AND
WESTRUP, SIR JACK ALLAN
MUSICAL INTERPRETATION---THIS BOOK ACCOMPANIED A SERIES OF B.B.C.
WHITE, WILLIAM BRAID
PLAYER-PIANIST, THE ..A GUIDE TO THE APPRECIATION AND
WHITEMORE, CUTHBERT
COMMONSENSE IN PIANOFORTE PLAYING
WHITESIDE, ABBY
INDISPENSABLES OF PIANO PLAYING--2ND. ED.---1955
WHITESIDE, ABBY
MASTERING THE CHOPIN ETUDES AND OTHER ESSAYS
WHITFORD, ROBERT
PIANO AND ITS MUSIC, THE --FROM 'MODERN PIANO COURSE'
WIECK, FRIEDRICH
PIANO AND SONG..HOW TO TEACH, HOW TO LEARN, AND HOW TO FORM A
WIER, ALBERT
PIANO, THE ..ITS HISTORY, MAKERS, PLAYERS AND MUSIC
WILKINS-GUTMANN, EMMA
TALKS WITH PIANO TEACHERS
WILKINSON, CHARLES W.
HOW TO PLAY 110 FAVOURITE PIANO SOLOS
WILKINSON, CHARLES W.
WELL-KNOWN PIANO SOLOS..HOW TO PLAY THEM WITH UNDERSTANDING,
WILLIAMS, JEAN E.
MODERN METHOD OF PIANO INSTRUCTION, A ..TEACHERS MANUAL
WILLIAMS, JOHN M.
WHAT TO TEACH AT THE VERY FIRST LESSON
WILSON, DAVID M.
INSTRUCTION BOOK ON THE PIANO-PLAYER AND PLAYER-PIANO, AN
WILSON, MORRIS E.
HOW TO PLAY BY EAR
WINN, CYRIL
DO YOU ACCOMPANY
WINNER, SEPTIMUS
WINNER'S NEW SCHOOL FOR THE PIANO, IN WHICH THE INSTRUCTIONS ARE
WOLFF, ERNST VICTOR
WITH REASON AND RHYME
WOLFF, KONRAD
TEACHING OF ARTUR SCHNABEL, THE ..A GUIDE TO INTERPRETATION
WOLFRAM, VICTOR
SOSTENUTO PEDAL, THE
WOODHOUSE, GEORGE
ARTIST AT THE PIANO, THE ..THE ART OF MUSICAL INTERPRETATION
WOODHOUSE, GEORGE
CREATIVE TECHNIQUE, FOR ARTISTS IN GENERAL AND PIANISTS IN
WOODHOUSE, GEORGE
FROM KEYBOARD TO MUSIC
WOODHOUSE, GEORGE
REALISTIC APPROACH TO PIANO PLAYING, A
WRIGHT, WILLIAM C.
GOLDEN MONITOR, FOR THE PIANOFORTE AND CABINET ORGAN, DESIGNED AS
YOUNG, PERCY M.
CONCERTO--'PHOENIX MUSIC GUIDES', NO. 1
YOUNG, PERCY M.
KEYBOARD MUSICIANS OF THE WORLD

Ensemble Playing

ADLER, KURT
ART OF ACCOMPANYING AND COACHING, THE ---1965
AEOLIAN COMPANY, THE
DUO-ART BOOK OF MUSIC, THE
ALBRECHTSBERGER, JOHANN GEORG
PRINCIPLES OF ACCOMPANIMENT OR THOROUGH BASS
ARNOLD, FRANCK THOMAS
ART OF ACCOMPANIMENT FROM A THOROUGH-BASS, AS PRACTICED IN THE
BACH, CARL PHILIPP EMANUEL
ESSAY ON THE TRUE ART OF PLAYING KEYBOARD INSTRUMENTS---TWO PTS.,
BACON, ERNST
NOTES ON THE PIANO
BASTIEN, JAMES W. *
BEGINNING PIANO FOR ADULTS
BECKER, JULIUS
CONCISE TREATISE ON HARMONY, ACCOMPANIMENT, AND COMPOSITION, FOR
BEMETZRIEDER, ANTON
ABSTRACT OF A NEW METHOD OF TEACHING THE PRINCIPLES OF MUSIC,
BEMETZRIEDER, ANTON
ACCOUNT OF A NEW WAY OF CONSIDERING MUSICK, AND TEACHING
BEMETZRIEDER, ANTON
COMPENDIUM OF A NEW METHOD OF MUSIC...WITH THE AUTHOR'S PRINCIPLES
BENNER, LORA
BENNER GOLD BOOK, THE ..PIANO MATERIAL AND TEACHING METHODS--3RD.

BOS, COENRAAD V.
WELL-TEMPERED ACCOMPANIST, THE
BRIDGER, JOHN HENRY
HOW TO HARMONIZE MELODIES, WITH HINTS ON WRITING FOR STRINGS AND
BRITISH BROADCASTING CORPORATION--CENTRAL MUSIC LIBRARY
CHAMBER MUSIC CATALOGUE
BROUGHTON, JULIA
SUCCESS IN PIANO TEACHING
BRUXNER, MERVYN
MASTERING THE PIANO
BUELOW, GEORGE J.
THOROUGH-BASS ACCOMPANIMENT ACCORDING TO JOHANN DAVID HEINICHEN
BURROWS, RAYMOND
ELEMENTARY PIANO INSTRUCTION IN COLLEGE
CASTELLINI, JOHN EDWARD
RUDIMENTS OF MUSIC..A NEW APPROACH WITH APPLICATION TO THE
CAVALLARO, CARMEN
KEYBOARD HARMONY..A NEW MODERN PIANO METHOD---POPULAR IDIOM
CHAPPLE, STANLEY
CLASS WAY TO THE KEYBOARD, THE
CHEYETTE, IRVING
BASIC PIANO FOR THE MUSIC EDUCATOR AND CLASSROOM TEACHER
CRANMER, PHILIP
TECHNIQUE OF ACCOMPANIMENT, THE --THE STUDENT'S MUSIC LIBRARY
CULSHAW, JOHN
SERGEI RACHMANINOFF..THE MAN AND HIS MUSIC
CURWEN, ANNIE JESSY
CHILD PIANIST, THE
DALE, KATHLEEN
NINETEENTH CENTURY PIANO MUSIC, A HANDBOOK FOR PIANISTS
DAVID, ELIZABETH HARBISON
I PLAYED THEIR ACCOMPANIMENTS
DENVER--PUBLIC SCHOOLS
CLASS-PIANO TEACHERS HANDBOOK
DONINGTON, ROBERT
INSTRUMENTS OF MUSIC, THE --3RD. REV. ED.---1949
DONINGTON, ROBERT
INTERPRETATION OF EARLY MUSIC, THE
DONINGTON, ROBERT
PERFORMER'S GUIDE TO BAROQUE MUSIC, A
EGBERT, MARION S.
KEYBOARD EXPERIENCE IN THE CLASSROOM MUSIC PROGRAM..HANDBOOK FOR
ELLINGHAM, HARRY
HOW TO USE A PLAYER-PIANO
ETHIER, JOSEPH A.
ETHIER'S GREAT NON-SUCH SELF-INSTRUCTOR IN THE ART OF ACCOMPANYING
EVANS, EDWIN
HOW TO ACCOMPANY AT THE PIANO
EVANS, EVERETT J.
SELF-TEACHING CHORD BOOK FOR THE PIANO OR ORGAN..SHOWS HOW TO PLAY
FALKENER, ROBERT
INSTRUCTIONS FOR PLAYING THE HARPSICHORD..WHEREIN IS FULLY
FETIS, FRANCOIS JOSEPH
HOW TO PLAY FROM SCORE...ON THE ORGAN OR PIANOFORTE
FILLMORE, THOMAS H.
FILLMORE'S LIST OF CAREFULLY SELECTED AND GRADED WORKS FOR THE
FORD, DONALD
SINGING CLASS PIANIST AND ON PIANOFORTE ACCOMPANYING IN GENERAL,
GARRATT, PERCIVAL
ART OF PIANOFORTE PLAYING, THE
GARROWAY, WILL
PIANISM
GEBHARD, HEINRICH
ART OF PEDALLING, THE
GEMINIANI, FRANCESCO
ART OF ACCOMPANIMENT, OR A NEW AND WELL DIGESTED METHOD TO LEARN
GLEN, ANNIE
HOW TO ACCOMPANY..A GUIDE TO THE ARTISTIC ACCOMPANIMENT OF ANY
GOODRICH, ALFRED JOHN
THEORY OF INTERPRETATION, APPLIED TO ARTISTIC MUSICAL PERFORMANCE
GRAY, CECIL
CONTINGENCIES AND OTHER ESSAYS---LISZT
HARKNESS, ROBERT
GOSPEL SONG ACCOMPANIMENT..THE ROBERT HARKNESS METHOD FOR PIANO
HARKNESS, ROBERT
GOSPEL SONG PIANO ACCOMPANIMENT..THE ROBERT HARKNESS
HARKNESS, ROBERT
HARKNESS PIANO METHOD OF EVANGELISTIC HYMN PLAYING, THE ..A
HARKNESS, ROBERT
HOME STUDY CORRESPONDENCE COURSE IN EVANGELISTIC HYMN PLAYING, FOR
HARRISON, SIDNEY
YOUNG PERSON'S GUIDE TO PLAYING THE PIANO, THE
HAVILL, LORINA
YOU CAN SIGHT READ..THE PLEASURES OF PIANO SIGHT READING THROUGH
HECK, JOHANN CASPAR
COMPLETE SYSTEM OF HARMONY..OR A REGULAR AND EASY METHOD TO ATTAIN
HEIDELBERGER, PAULINE
MASTER METHOD..PIANO NORMAL AND TEACHER'S MANUAL
HERBERT, JOHN BUNYAN
HOW TO WRITE AN ACCOMPANIMENT..HELPS AND HINTS FOR STUDENTS AND
HICKIN, WELTON
PIANOFORTE ACCOMPANIMENT--'NOVELLO'S MUSIC PRIMERS', NO. 99
HOME, ETHEL
IMPROVISING..A SIMPLE METHOD OF TEACHING THE SUBJECT TO CHILDREN
HULL, ARTHUR EAGLEFIELD
THREE HUNDRED QUESTIONS ON PIANOFORTE TEACHING IN 30 GRADUATED
IRWIN, WILLIAM
RHYTHM ACCOMPANIMENT MAGIC, FOR THE POPULAR PIANIST
JOUSSE, JOHN
GUIDA ARMONICA, IN WHICH...CHORDS, ARE CLEARLY EXPLAINED AND
KOLANDER, MAX
KOLANDER'S ACCOMPANIMENT INSTRUCTOR FOR THE PIANO OR ORGAN
LAMAR, RICHARD
COLLEGE PIANO PEDAGOGY
LANG, EDITH *
MUSICAL ACCOMPANIMENT OF MOVING PICTURES..A PRACTICAL MANUAL FOR
LEAVEY, LILIAN
JUNIOR SCHOOL PIANIST, THE --ADDRESSED TO THE NEW MUSIC TEACHER
LE MASSENA, CLARENCE E.
SONGS OF SCHUBERT, A GUIDE FOR SINGERS, TEACHERS AND ACCOMPANISTS,
LINDO, ALGERNON H.
ART OF ACCOMPANYING, THE
LUBIN, ERNEST
PIANO DUET, THE ...A GUIDE FOR PIANISTS
MACLEAN, CHARLES D.
PRINCIPLES OF PIANOFORTE PRACTICE, THE
MAIER, GUY
PIANO TEACHER'S COMPANION, THE
MARSDEN AND COMPANY
HOW TO EXTEMPORIZE PIANO ACCOMPANIMENTS..RAPID AND SIMPLE METHOD
MATHIS, WILLIAM STEPHAN
PIANIST AND CHURCH MUSIC, THE
MEHER, DONOVAN
HOW TO VAMP AT SIGHT..THE EASIEST AND CLEAREST METHOD OF
MERGES, P.
PRACTICAL RULES FOR PIANOFORTE PLAYING..TEXT BOOK FOR TEACHERS AND

MIDKIFF, HELEN T.
CHURCH PIANIST, THE
MOLDENHAUER, HANS
DUO-PIANISM---PUBLISHED DISSERTATION
MOORE, GERALD
AM I TOO LOUD..MEMOIRS OF AN ACCOMPANIST
MOORE, GERALD
SINGER AND ACCOMPANIST..THE PERFORMANCE OF FIFTY SONGS
MOORE, GERALD
UNASHAMED ACCOMPANIST, THE
MURDOCH, WILLIAM
BRAHMS..WITH AN ANALYTICAL STUDY OF THE COMPLETE PIANOFORTE WORKS
MUSIC EDUCATION LEAGUE
COMPREHENSIVE GUIDE FOR PIANO TEACHERS AND PIANO AUDITION SYLLABUS
MUSIC PROJECT--NEW YORK CITY
TEACHER'S GUIDE..A CREATIVE APPROACH TO PIANO CLASS TEACHING, BY
NEAL, HARRY LEE
WAVE AS YOU PASS
NEWMAN, WILLIAM S.
SONATA IN THE BAROQUE ERA, THE --A HISTORY OF THE SONATA IDEA,
NEWMAN, WILLIAM S.
SONATA IN THE CLASSIC ERA, THE --A HISTORY OF THE SONATA IDEA,
NEWTON, ERNEST
ELEMENTARY STUDIES IN TRANSPOSITION--BKS. 1 AND 2
NEWTON, IVOR
AT THE PIANO--IVOR NEWTON..THE WORLD OF AN ACCOMPANIST
NEW ENGLAND CONSERVATORY
TEACHERS' GRADED LIST FOR THE PIANOFORTE
ORLIK, JULES
CREATIVE APPROACH TO PIANO CLASS TEACHING, A ---REPRODUCED FROM
PALMER, KING
TEACH YOURSELF TO PLAY THE PIANO
PATTERSON, ANNIE WILSON
PROFESSION OF MUSIC AND HOW TO PREPARE FOR IT, THE
PEABODY INSTITUTE, BALTIMORE
GRADED LIST OF SOME USEFUL WORKS FOR PIANO STUDY---REVISED BY
PEARCE, CHARLES WILLIAM
ART OF THE PIANO TEACHER, THE
PETERSON, FRANKLIN
THEORETIC COMPANION TO PRACTICE--PART I OF THE PIANIST'S HANDBOOK
RAPEE, ERNO--ARRANGER
ERNO RAPEE'S ENCYCLOPEDIA OF MUSIC FOR PICTURES---LISTED BOTH BY
RAPEE, ERNO--ARRANGER
MOTION PICTURE MOODS FOR PIANISTS AND ORGANISTS
REES-DAVIES, IVAN
TRANSPOSITION AT THE KEYBOARD
REZITS, JOSEPH
SOURCE MATERIALS FOR PIANO TECHNIQUES
REZITS, JOSEPH
TEACHER'S GUIDE TO THE NEW SCRIBNER MUSIC LIBRARY
ROOT, CATHERINE ADAMS *
LISTEN, SING AND PLAY..CLASS LESSONS FOR PIANO AND VOICE
ROWBOTHAM, JOHN F.
HOW TO VAMP..A PRACTICAL GUIDE TO THE ACCOMPANIMENT OF SONGS BY
ROWLEY, ALEC
FOUR HANDS--ONE PIANO..A LIST OF WORKS FOR DUET PLAYERS--A GUIDE
SCHAUFFLER, ROBERT HAVEN
FLORESTAN..THE LIFE AND WORK OF ROBERT SCHUMANN---1945
SCHOTT, HOWARD
PLAYING THE HARPSICHORD
SCHULER, GEORGE S.
ACCOMPANIST'S MANUAL, THE
SCHULER, GEORGE S.
EVANGELISTIC PIANO PLAYING
SEARLE, HUMPHREY
MUSIC OF LISZT, THE --2ND. REV. ED.---1954
SHEPARD, ROBERT
HARMONIZING..HOW TO PLAY SIMPLE ACCOMPANIMENTS TO A MELODY AT THE
SPENCER, BERNARD
POPULAR PIANO...A CORRESPONDENCE COURSE OF THE EASTERN SCHOOLS OF
SQUIRE, RUSSEL N. *
CLASS PIANO FOR ADULT BEGINNERS--2ND. ED.---1964
STEWART, REID
HOW TO PASS MUSIC EXAMINATIONS--PIANO--A GUIDE FOR TEACHERS AND
STORMEN, WIN
POPULAR ACCOMPANYING
STORMEN, WIN
YOUR GUIDE TO PLAYING AND WRITING POPULAR MUSIC--REV. ED.
TERWILLIGER, GORDON B.
PIANO TEACHERS PROFESSIONAL HANDBOOK
THACKRAY, RUPERT M.
PLAYING FOR DANCE..THE PLACE OF THE PIANIST IN THE TEACHING OF
TOBIN, JOSEPH RAYMOND
HOW TO IMPROVISE PIANO ACCOMPANIMENTS
WAGNER, JOHN J.
NUMERICAL METHOD OF PIANO ACCOMPANIMENTS, A --WITH CHARTS
WALKER, ALAN--EDITOR
ROBERT SCHUMANN..THE MAN AND HIS MUSIC---SYMPOSIUM--13 AUTHORS
WARRINER, JOHN
TRANSPOSITION, KEYBOARD AND ORCHESTRAL--2 PTS., 1893-1908
WEBBE, SAMUEL
HARMONY EPITOMIZED, BEING A SHORT EXPLANATION OF FIGURED BASSES,
WELTE-MIGNON CORPORATION
LIBRARY OF DELUXE WELTE-MIGNON MUSIC RECORDS FOR REPRODUCING
WELTE-MIGNON CORPORATION
LIBRARY OF WELTE-MIGNON MUSIC RECORDS
WESTERBY, HERBERT
LISZT, COMPOSER, AND HIS PIANO WORKS..DESCRIPTIVE GUIDE AND
WIER, ALBERT
PIANO, THE ..ITS HISTORY, MAKERS, PLAYERS AND MUSIC
WILLIAMS, JOHN M.
WHAT TO TEACH AT THE VERY FIRST LESSON
WILSON, MORRIS E.
HOW TO PLAY BY EAR
WINN, CYRIL
DO YOU ACCOMPANY
WOLFF, ERNST VICTOR
WITH REASON AND RHYME
WOLLENHAUPT, HEINRICH
METHOD FOR THE PIANOFORTE AND METHODICAL GUIDE FOR THE PIANO FORTE
WOLLNER, GERTRUDE PRICE
IMPROVISATION IN MUSIC..WAYS TOWARDS CAPTURING MUSICAL IDEAS AND
WOODHOUSE, GEORGE
NEW PATH FOR PIANISTS, A ..THE MUTANO--MUTE PIANO--SYSTEM, ETC.
YATES, PETER
AMATEUR AT THE KEYBOARD, AN

General Interest

ADAMS, JOHN S.
FIVE THOUSAND MUSICAL TERMS..A COMPLETE DICTIONARY WITH A TREATISE
AEOLIAN COMPANY, THE
CATALOG OF THE AEOLIAN

AEOLIAN COMPANY, THE
CONFIDENTIAL MANUAL FOR SALESMEN OF THE DUO-ART REPRODUCING
AEOLIAN COMPANY, THE
DUO-ART PIANO MUSIC
AEOLIAN COMPANY, THE
LIBRARY OF DUO-ART MUSIC ROLLS
AEOLIAN COMPANY, THE
MUSIC FOR THE AEOLIAN GRAND
AEOLIAN COMPANY, THE
PIANISTS WHO HAVE MADE RECORDS FOR THE DUO-ART PIANO
AEOLIAN COMPANY, THE
SPECIAL SURVEY CONDUCTED--IN 1889--FOR LYON AND HEALY, INC.,
AEOLIAN COMPANY, THE
WEIGHT OF EVIDENCE ON THE TRUE MUSICAL WORTH OF THE PIANOLA AND
AHRENS, CORA B. *
FOR ALL PIANO TEACHERS
AMERICAN PIANO CORPORATION
CATALOGUE OF MUSIC FOR THE AMPICO, A ..A LIST OF THE RECORDINGS OF
AMERICAN PIANO CORPORATION
CATALOGUE OF MUSIC FOR THE AMPICO, A --A LIST OF THE RECORDINGS OF
AMERICAN SCHOOL OF PIANO TUNING
TRAINING AS A PIANO TECHNICIAN--8 VOLS. IN 1
AMERICAN STEEL AND WIRE COMPANY
NERVES OF STEEL..THE STORY OF AMERICAN PIANO WIRE AND ITS
AMPICO CORPORATION
AMPICO REPRODUCING PIANO..A SUPPLEMENT TO 'PIANO MUSIC, ITS
AMPICO CORPORATION
SUPREMACY OF AMPICO MUSIC..UNIT TWO OF A COURSE IN AMPICO
ANDERSON-MULDER COMPANY
DEALER'S HANDBOOK OF PIANOS AND THEIR MAKERS
ANDERSON, WILLIAM P.
MUSIC AS A CAREER
ANTCLIFFE, HERBERT
SUCCESSFUL MUSIC TEACHER, THE ..WORDS OF ADVICE
ANTRIM, DORAN K.
TEACHING MUSIC AND MAKING IT PAY
ARPIN, PAUL
LIFE OF LOUIS MOREAU GOTTSCHALK
ASSOCIATION FOR RECORDED SOUND COLLECTIONS
PRELIMINARY DIRECTORY OF SOUND RECORDING COLLECTIONS IN THE UNITED
AUTO PNEUMATIC ACTION COMPANY
WELTE-MIGNON BOOK...OF FAMOUS ARTISTS, THE
AZULAY, GERTRUDE
CHOPIN..THE STORY OF THE BOY WHO MADE BEAUTIFUL MELODIES
BACON, ERNST
NOTES ON THE PIANO
BAGGER, EUGENE S.
EMINENT EUROPEANS..STUDIES IN CONTINENTAL REALITY---PADEREWSKI
BALLANTINE, BILL
PIANO, THE ..AN INTRODUCTION TO THE INSTRUMENT
BALTIMORE--MUSEUM OF ART
MUSICAL INSTRUMENTS AND THEIR PORTRAYAL IN
BAMBERGER, LOUIS
MEMORIES OF SIXTY YEARS IN THE TIMBER AND PIANOFORTE TRADES
BARRY, KEITH LEWIS
CHOPIN AND HIS FOURTEEN DOCTORS
BARTELS, LEO F. *
PERFORATING OF MUSIC ROLLS WITH THE LEABARJAN PERFORATOR, THE
BASTIEN, JAMES W.
HOW TO TEACH PIANO SUCCESSFULLY
BAUGHAN, EDWARD ALGERNON
IGNACE JAN PADEREWSKI
BECKER, JULIUS
CONCISE TREATISE ON HARMONY, ACCOMPANIMENT, AND COMPOSITION, FOR
BENDER, GEORGE CHARLES
BUSINESS MANUAL FOR PIANO TEACHERS
BENNER, LORA
BENNER BLUE BOOK, THE ..PRACTICAL MANUAL OF PIANO TEACHING--4TH.
BOWERS, Q. DAVID
ENCYCLOPEDIA OF AUTOMATIC MUSICAL INSTRUMENTS---INCLUDES A
BRECKENRIDGE, WILLIAM KILGORE
HINTS FOR PIANO NORMAL STUDIES
BRIED, FREDERICK
STIMULATION IN PIANO STUDY..HOW PARENTS CAN STIMULATE AND MAINTAIN
BRIGGS, GILBERT A.
MUSICAL INSTRUMENTS AND AUDIO
BRIGGS, GILBERT A.
PIANOS, PIANISTS AND SONICS
BROUGHTON, JULIA
SUCCESS IN PIANO TEACHING
BRUXNER, MERVYN
MASTERING THE PIANO
BUCK, PERCY
PSYCHOLOGY FOR MUSICIANS
BURCH, GLADYS
FAMOUS PIANISTS FOR BOYS AND GIRLS
BURCH, GLADYS
MODERN COMPOSERS FOR YOUNG PEOPLE---FIRST PUBLISHED AS 'A CHILD'S
BURROWS, RAYMOND
ELEMENTARY PIANO INSTRUCTION IN COLLEGE
BURROWS, RAYMOND
PIANO IN SCHOOL, A MEMORANDUM FOR SCHOOL ADMINISTRATORS
BYERLY, DOROTHEA J.
ADVENTURES OF PETER THE PIANO, THE ..AN ILLUSTRATED STORY FOR
BYRON, MAY CLARISSA
DAY WITH FREDERIC CHOPIN, A
CARMI, AVNER *
IMMORTAL PIANO, THE
CARRE, JOHN
PSYCHOLOGY OF PIANO TEACHING, THE ..A TEXTBOOK FOR TEACHERS,
CHASINS, ABRAM
SPEAKING OF PIANISTS
CHICKERING AND SONS
COMMEMORATION OF THE FOUNDING OF THE HOUSE OF CHICKERING AND SONS,
CHICKERING AND SONS
HISTORICAL MUSICAL EXHIBITION..CATALOGUE OF THE EXHIBITION,
CHILTON, CARROLL B.
DE-ASSIFICATION OF MUSIC, THE ..A PROPAGANDIST MAGAZINE, OF ONE
CHING, JAMES
AMATEUR PIANIST'S COMPANION, THE
CHING, JAMES
PERFORMER AND AUDIENCE..AN INVESTIGATION INTO THE PSYCHOLOGICAL
CHING, JAMES
PLAYING AND TEACHING OF BACH, THE ..A GUIDE FOR TEACHERS, STUDENTS
CHRISTENSEN, INGA
INGA - PLAY--MEMOIRS
CHURCHILL, WILLIAM--SUPPOSED AUTHOR
MARVELLOUS YEAR, THE ...CRITICAL SKETCHES OF CELEBRATED MEN, THE
CLARK, MADAM STEINEGER
RELIGION AND ROMANCE OF A PIANIST'S LIFE---AUTOBIOGRAPHY
COIT, LOTTIE ELLSWORTH
CHILD CHOPIN, THE ...WITH DIRECTIONS FOR PRESENTATION WITH A
COOKE, CHARLES
PLAYING THE PIANO FOR PLEASURE--REV. ED.---1941
COOKE, JAMES FRANCIS
GREAT PIANISTS ON PIANO PLAYING..STUDY TALKS WITH FOREMOST

D'ABREU, GERALD
  PLAYING THE PIANO WITH CONFIDENCE---1964
DAHL, ANTON
  SOUL OF GENIUS, THE ..ITS MUSICAL DEVELOPMENT AND HOW THE WORLD AT
DARLOW, DENYS
  MUSICAL INSTRUMENTS--JUNIOR REFERENCE BOOKS, NO. 12--2ND. ED.
DAVIS, LIONEL
  KEYBOARD INSTRUMENTS..THE STORY OF THE PIANO---YOUNGER READERS
DENVER--PUBLIC SCHOOLS
  CLASS-PIANO TEACHERS HANDBOOK
DE BOER, JOSEPHINE
  MALLORCAN MOODS IN CONTEMPORARY ART AND LITERATURE--CONTAINS
DUNLOP, AGNES MARY
  DUET---STORY OF CLARA AND ROBERT SCHUMANN
EDWARDS, RUTH
  COMPLEAT MUSIC TEACHER FOR TEACHERS, PARENTS AND STUDENTS
EISENBERG, JACOB
  ARTISTIC PIANIST, THE ..NATURAL TECHNICS IN PIANO MASTERY..FROM
EISENBERG, JACOB
  LET ME HELP YOU, MY ANCESTORS AND I..A COMPREHENSIVE JUVENILE
EISENBERG, JACOB
  WEIGHT AND RELAXATION METHOD FOR THE PIANOFORTE
ELLINGHAM, HARRY
  HOW TO USE A PLAYER-PIANO
EXECUTIVE COMMITTEE OF CHOPIN YEAR 1949
  CHOPIN YEAR 1949 IN POLAND, THE
FAIRLIE, GERARD
  PIANIST SHOOTS FIRST, THE ---PSYCHOLOGICAL STORY
FERRA I PERELLO, BARTOLOME
  CHOPIN AND GEORGE SAND IN THE CARTUJA DE VALLDEMOSA...
FIELDEN, THOMAS
  MARKS AND REMARKS..MUSICAL EXAMINATIONS AND THEIR PROBLEMS
FILLINGHAM, ARTHUR H.
  GUIDE TO THE A.R.C.M. AND OTHER EXAMINATIONS IN THE ART OF
FILLINGHAM, ARTHUR H.
  PIANOFORTE TEACHERS' EXAMINATION FOR THE A.R.C.M. DIPLOMA..A GUIDE
FINCK, HENRY T.
  PADEREWSKI AND HIS ART
FINNEGAN, BILL
  PIANO FACTS
FOLDES, LILI
  TWO ON A CONTINENT
FOX, LILLA M.
  INSTRUMENTS OF POPULAR MUSIC..A HISTORY OF MUSICAL
FREDERIC CHOPIN INTERNATIONAL COMPETITION--FIFTH
  FREDERIC CHOPIN INTERNATIONAL COMPETITIONS IN POLAND
FREDRICH, FRANK
  KEY TO PIANO PLEASURE
FULLER-MAITLAND, J. A.
  MUSICIAN'S PILGRIMAGE, THE ..A STUDY IN ARTISTIC DEVELOPMENT
GEPPERT, WILLIAM
  OFFICIAL GUIDE TO PIANO QUALITY, THE ---4TH. ED.
GEST, ELIZABETH
  KEYBOARD HARMONY FOR JUNIORS
GIDDINGS, THADDEUS P.
  GIDDING'S PUBLIC SCHOOL CLASS METHOD FOR THE PIANO
GIFFORD, ALEXANDER M.
  PIANOFORTE AND HOW TO STUDY IT, THE
GLENNON, JAMES
  AUSTRALIAN MUSIC AND MUSICIANS
GORDON, PHILIP
  SYLLABUS FOR PIANO AUDITIONS
GRAHAM, L. SIBLEY
  TALES OF THE OLD VIRTUOSO..THE SPANISH COURT PIANIST--MARQUIS DON
GRIFFIN, RUSSELL B.
  PIANOFORTE TELEGRAPHY, THE --THE MORSE TELEGRAPH CODE--INSTRUCTOR
GRONOWICZ, ANTONI
  CHOPIN---YOUNGER READERS
GRONOWICZ, ANTONI
  PADEREWSKI, PIANIST AND PATRIOT
GRONOWICZ, ANTONI
  SERGEI RACHMANINOFF
GRUNDY, ENID
  HAPPY PIANIST, THE
HALLE, SIR CHARLES
  ST. JAMES HALL...C. HALLE'S PIANOFORTE RECITALS..MAY 5-JUNE 29,
HALLE, SIR CHARLES
  ST. JAMES HALL...MR. HALLE'S BEETHOVEN RECITALS, MAY 23-JULY 11,
HAMBOURG, MARK
  EIGHTH OCTAVE, THE ---CONTINUES THE RECORD, BEGUN IN 'FROM PIANO
HANSMANN, RICHARD
  THEORETICAL AND PRACTICAL PIANO-FORTE SCHOOL FOR THE JANKO
HARDING, BERTITA
  CONCERTO, THE STORY OF CLARA SCHUMANN
HARRISON, SIDNEY
  TEACHER NEVER TOLD ME--TIPS FOR STUDENTS
HAWEIS, HUGH R.
  MUSIC AND MORALS---CHOPIN
HEINE, HEINRICH
  HEINE IN ART AND LETTERS---CHOPIN AND LISZT--1837
HENDERSON, ARCHIBALD
  CONTEMPORARY IMMORTALS---PADEREWSKI
HILL, GEORGE R.
  PRELIMINARY CHECKLIST OF RESEARCH ON THE CLASSIC SYMPHONY AND
HINSON, MAURICE
  KEYBOARD BIBLIOGRAPHY--'NEW RESOURCES' SERIES
HIPKINS, ALFRED JAMES
  HOW CHOPIN PLAYED...FROM CONTEMPORARY IMPRESSIONS COLLECTED FROM
HUBBARD, ELBERT
  LITTLE JOURNEYS TO THE HOMES OF GREAT MUSICIANS--VOL. 8, NO.
HUBBARD, ELBERT
  LITTLE JOURNEYS TO THE HOMES OF GREAT MUSICIANS--VOL. 9, NO.
HULL, ANNE
  MAESTRO SPINETTI'S MUSIC SHOP--HARPSICHORD, CLAVICHORD,
HULLAH, M. E.
  FEW WORDS ABOUT MUSIC, CONTAINING HINTS TO AMATEUR PIANISTS, A
HUME, RUTH *
  LION OF POLAND, THE ..THE STORY OF PADEREWSKI--JUNIOR BIOGRAPHIES
INTERNATIONAL MUSICOLOGICAL CONGRESS..FIRST--1960--WORKS OF FREDERICK
  BOOK OF THE FIRST INTERNATIONAL MUSICOLOGICAL CONGRESS DEVOTED TO
IWASZKIEWICZ, JAROSLAW
  SUMMER AT NOHANT..A PLAY IN THREE ACTS---CHOPIN
JOHNSON, HARRIETT
  YOUR CAREER IN MUSIC
KAISER, JOACHIM
  GREAT PIANISTS OF OUR TIME
KAUFMANN, HELEN LOEB
  ARTISTS IN MUSIC OF TODAY
KEEFER, LUBOV
  INFLUENCE OF ADAM MICKIEWICZ ON THE BALLADES OF CHOPIN, THE
KEELER, WALTER B.
  THEORY OF THE NEW KEYBOARD, ARRANGED BY W. B. KEELER AND E. K.
KELLEY, EDGAR STILLMAN
  MUSICAL INSTRUMENTS--3RD. YEAR OF A STUDY COURSE IN MUSIC
KNOLLER, JACOB
  FREE WILL OR DESTINY..ONE ACT PLAY AROUND CHOPIN---EARLY SUMMER,

KOBBE, GUSTAV
  PIANOLIST, THE ..A GUIDE FOR PIANOLA PLAYERS
KRAUS, ALESSANDRO B.
  ONE-KEYBOARDED CLAVICYTHERIUM OF THE KRAUS COLLECTION IN FLORENCE,
LANDOWSKI, ALICE-WANDA
  DOMENICO SCARLATTI--NOTES TO ACCOMPANY GRAMOPHONE RECORDINGS
LANG, EDITH *
  MUSICAL ACCOMPANIMENT OF MOVING PICTURES..A PRACTICAL MANUAL FOR
LESSMANN, W. J. OTTO
  FRANZ LISZT..EINE HULDIGUNG--FRANZ LISZT..A TRIBUTE
LEVINE, JACK *
  UNDERSTANDING MUSICAL INSTRUMENTS..HOW TO SELECT YOUR
LE MASSENA, CLARENCE E.
  PADEREWSKI, 'THE MASTER OF MASTERS' ---REPRODUCED FROM TYPEWRITTEN
LOESSER, ARTHUR
  MEN, WOMEN AND PIANOS..A SOCIAL HISTORY
LONG, ESMOND R.--PATHOLOGIST
  HISTORY OF THE THERAPY OF TUBERCULOSIS, AND THE CASE OF FREDERIC
LOWE, CLAUDE EDGERTON
  PIANOFORTE TEACHER'S VADE MECUM, THE ..A CYCLOPEDIA FOR THE
LOWE, CLAUDE EDGERTON
  SUGGESTIONS FOR THE APPRECIATION AND INTERPRETATION OF PIANOFORTE
LOWE, CLAUDE EDGERTON
  VIVA VOCE..250 QUESTIONS AND ANSWERS FOR PIANOFORTE DIPLOMA
MACQUOID, PERCY *
  DICTIONARY OF ENGLISH FURNITURE, THE --VOL. 3---16 ILLUSTRATIONS
MANHIRE, WILSON
  EXAMINATION CANDIDATE'S GUIDE TO SCALE AND ARPEGGIO PLAYING, ETC.,
MANHIRE, WILSON
  GUIDE TO THE A.R.C.M. AND OTHER EXAMINATIONS IN
MANHIRE, WILSON
  HINTS TO CANDIDATES FOR THE L.R.A.M. ASSOCIATED BOARD AND OTHER
MANHIRE, WILSON
  MODEL ANSWERS TO QUESTIONS ON 'TOUCH' FOR CANDIDATES PREPARING FOR
MANITOBA--DEPARTMENT OF EDUCATION
  PLAN FOR CREDITING OUTSIDE STUDY IN MUSIC UNDER PRIVATE
MARTENS, FREDERICK HERMAN
  PADEREWSKI--'LITTLE BIOGRAPHIES', VOL. 2
MATHEWS, WILLIAM S. B.
  GREAT IN MUSIC, THE ..A SYSTEMATIC COURSE OF STUDY IN THE MUSIC OF
MATHIS, WILLIAM STEPHAN
  PIANIST AND CHURCH MUSIC, THE
MATTHEWS, DENIS
  IN PURSUIT OF MUSIC
MAUROIS, ANDRE
  FREDERIC CHOPIN---FOR YOUNGER READERS
MAYO, WALDO
  CHOPIN---FOR YOUNGER READERS
MCARTHUR, ALEXANDER
  PIANOFORTE STUDY..HINTS ON PIANO PLAYING
MCCARTHY, ALBERT J.--EDITOR
  PIANO JAZZ..ESSAYS--2 VOLS., 1945-1946
MCCLINTOCK, LORENE
  TEACH YOURSELF TO PLAY THE PIANO..BASED ON THE INTERVAL METHOD
MEIER, NELLIE SIMMONS
  LIONS' PAWS..THE STORY OF FAMOUS HANDS--INCLUDES MUSICIANS..JOSE
MILLER, JEWELL
  POLONAISE MILITAIRE..THE LIFE AND WORK OF FREDERIC CHOPIN..A
MINNESOTA MUSIC TEACHERS ASSOCIATION
  PIANO-THEORY EXAMINATION SYLLABUS
MOOR, WINIFRED
  TECHNICAL EXERCISES FOR THE EMANUEL MOOR DOUBLE KEYBOARD
MOORE, GERALD
  AM I TOO LOUD..MEMOIRS OF AN ACCOMPANIST
MUSIC EDUCATION LEAGUE, INC.
  PIANO AUDITIONS SYLLABUS AND COMPREHENSIVE GUIDE FOR PIANO
MUSIC EDUCATION LEAGUE
  COMPREHENSIVE GUIDE FOR PIANO TEACHERS AND PIANO AUDITION SYLLABUS
MUSIC EDUCATORS NATIONAL CONFERENCE
  HANDBOOK FOR TEACHING PIANO CLASSES
MUSIC EDUCATORS NATIONAL CONFERENCE
  MUSIC BEGINS WITH THE PIANO
MUSIC INDUSTRY COUNCIL
  MUSIC EDUCATOR'S BUSINESS HANDBOOK, THE ---PUBLISHED OCCASIONALLY
NATIONAL BUREAU FOR THE ADVANCEMENT OF MUSIC
  GIVING OF HIGH SCHOOL CREDITS FOR PRIVATE MUSIC STUDY, THE ..A
NATIONAL BUREAU FOR THE ADVANCEMENT OF MUSIC
  GUIDE FOR CONDUCTING PIANO CLASSES IN THE SCHOOLS, A
NATIONAL BUREAU FOR THE ADVANCEMENT OF MUSIC
  NATIONAL SURVEY OF PIANO CLASSES IN OPERATION
NATIONAL BUREAU FOR THE ADVANCEMENT OF MUSIC
  PIANO CLASSES AND THE PRIVATE TEACHER
NATIONAL BUREAU FOR THE ADVANCEMENT OF MUSIC
  PIANO CLASSES IN THE SCHOOLS..EDUCATIONAL VALUE OF IMPORTANT NEW
NATIONAL GUILD OF PIANO TEACHERS
  GUILD SYLLABUS, THE ..STREAMLINED EDITION
NATIONAL GUILD OF PIANO TEACHERS
  NATIONAL AUDITIONS FOR AMERICAN PIANO PUPILS
NATIONAL GUILD OF PIANO TEACHERS
  STUDENT'S HANDBOOK FOR ENTRANTS IN THE NATIONAL PIANO PLAYING
NATIONAL PIANO FOUNDATION
  GREATER REWARDS THROUGH CREATIVE PIANO TEACHING
NATIONAL PIANO FOUNDATION
  KEYS TO SUCCESSFUL PIANO STUDIO ORGANIZATION
NATIONAL PIANO MANUFACTURERS ASSOCIATION OF AMERICA
  STENCILLING OF PIANOS, THE
NATIONAL PIANO MANUFACTURERS ASSOCIATION
  CONSUMER INVESTIGATION FOR NATIONAL PIANO MANUFACTURERS
NATIONAL PIANO TRAVELERS ASSOCIATION
  PIANO TRAVELERS ASSOCIATION BOOK, THE ..A REFERENCE BOOK
NEUHAUS, HEINRICH
  ART OF PIANO PLAYING, THE
NEWMAN, ELIZABETH
  HOW TO TEACH MUSIC TO BEGINNERS
NEW YORK STATE MUSIC TEACHERS' ASSOCIATION
  SYLLABUS FOR PIANO, 1970
NIMITZ, DANIEL
  KEYBOARD MASTERS..STUDY GUIDE
NOSSIG, ALFRED
  METHODS OF THE MASTERS OF PIANO TEACHING IN EUROPE, THE ..THE
PALMER, KING
  TEACH YOURSELF TO PLAY THE PIANO
PATTERSON, ANNIE WILSON
  PROFESSION OF MUSIC AND HOW TO PREPARE FOR IT, THE
PEARCE, CHARLES WILLIAM
  ART OF THE PIANO TEACHER, THE
PENGELLY, J. BRADFORD
  PENGELLY BLUE BOOK OF STYLE, THE ...A STUDY OF THE ART OF STYLING
PIANO, ORGAN AND MUSICAL INSTRUMENT WORKERS INTERNATIONAL UNION OF
  CONSTITUTION OF THE PIANO, ORGAN AND MUSICAL INSTRUMENT WORKERS'
PIGGOTT, PATRICK
  LIFE AND MUSIC OF JOHN FIELD, 1782-1837, THE
PLANTIGA, LEON B.
  SCHUMANN AS CRITIC
POWERS, J. HAROLD
  MUSIC'S GLAMOROUS HALL OF FAME..SHORT ARTICLES ABOUT FAMOUS NAMES,

PROSNAK, JAN
    FREDERIC CHOPIN INTERNATIONAL PIANO COMPETITIONS, THE
PUGNO, RAOUL
    LESSONS OF RAOUL PUGNO, THE ..WITH A BIOGRAPHY OF CHOPIN BY M.
RAPEE, ERNO--ARRANGER
    ERNO RAPEE'S ENCYCLOPEDIA OF MUSIC FOR PICTURES---LISTED BOTH BY
RAPEE, ERNO--ARRANGER
    MOTION PICTURE MOODS FOR PIANISTS AND ORGANISTS
REED, MARY G.
    KEYBOARD ROAD IN MUSIC LAND, AND OTHER STORIES---FOR CHILDREN
REMBUSCH, JOSEPH ADAM
    PIANOS AND MUSICAL INSTRUMENTS DISCUSSED FROM AN UNSANITARY
PEZITS, JOSEPH
    TEACHER'S GUIDE TO THE NEW SCRIBNER MUSIC LIBRARY
RIGBY, CHARLES
    SIR CHARLES HALLE..A PORTRAIT FOR TODAY
ROBILLIARD, EILEEN D.
    PERSISTENT PIANIST, THE ..A BOOK FOR THE LATE BEGINNER AND THE
ROEHL, HARVEY
    PLAYER PIANO TREASURY..THE SCRAPBOOK HISTORY OF THE MECHANICAL
ROWLEY, ALEC
    DO'S AND DONT'S FOR MUSICIANS..A HANDBOOK FOR TEACHERS AND
ROWLEY, ALEC
    PRACTICAL MUSICIANSHIP, A HANDBOOK FOR TEACHERS AND STUDENTS
RUBINSTEIN, ARTUR
    MY YOUNG YEARS
RUTTKAY, GEORGE
    CHOPIN, HIS LIFE TOLD IN ANECDOTAL FORM---FOR YOUNGER READERS
SACKETT, SHELTON
    NOCTURNE..A CHOPIN-PLAY IN ONE ACT
SCHAAF, EDWARD O.
    ART OF PIANO PLAYER TRANSCRIPTION, THE ..MAKING OF PERFORATED
SCHAUFFLER, ROBERT HAVEN
    MUSICAL AMATEUR, THE
SCHELLING, ERNEST *
    OXFORD PIANO COURSE, TEACHER'S FIRST MANUAL
SCHELLING, ERNEST *
    OXFORD PIANO COURSE, TEACHER'S SECOND MANUAL
SCHNABEL, ARTUR
    MUSIC AND THE LINE OF MOST RESISTANCE---1942
SCHNABEL, ARTUR
    MY LIFE AND MUSIC
SCHWIMMER, FRANCISKA
    GREAT MUSICIANS AS CHILDREN
SEYMOUR, HARRIET AYER
    HOME MUSIC LESSONS..HOW TO FIND YOUR MUSICAL SELF
SEYMOUR, HARRIET AYER
    PHILOSOPHY OF MUSIC, THE ..WHAT MUSIC CAN DO FOR YOU
SHATTUCK, ARTHUR
    MEMOIRS OF ARTHUR SHATTUCK, THE ..WITH AN ACCOUNT OF HIS CAREER BY
SHINN, DUANE
    HOW PEOPLE MAKE MONEY IN MUSIC
SMITH, CYRIL
    DUET FOR THREE HANDS...AS TOLD TO JOYCE EGGINTON
SORABJI, KAIKHOSRU
    AROUND MUSIC---PACHMAN, CHOPIN AND LISZT
SOREL, CLAUDETTE
    MIND YOUR MUSICAL MANNERS, OFF AND ON STAGE..A HANDBOOK OF STAGE
SPAETH, SIGMUND *
    AMPICO IN MUSIC STUDY, THE
SPAETH, SIGMUND
    MAXIMS TO MUSIC..TRADITIONAL PROVERBS, MOTTOES AND MAXIMS OF THE
SPILLANE, DANIEL
    HISTORY OF THE AMERICAN PIANOFORTE..ITS TECHNICAL DEVELOPMENT, AND
STANLEY, JANE
    BASIC ROUTINES IN ELEMENTARY PIANO TEACHING THROUGH THE FIRST
STECK AND COMPANY
    ILLUSTRATED CATALOG...GRAND AND UPRIGHT PIANOS
STEINWAY, THEODORE E.
    PEOPLE AND PIANOS..A CENTURY OF SERVICE TO MUSIC---1853-1953
STEINWAY AND SONS
    ILLUSTRATED CATALOGUE OF--STEINWAY AND SONS...PIANOFORTES
STEINWAY AND SONS
    ILLUSTRATED CATALOGUE OF STEINWAY AND SONS' PIANOS
STEINWAY AND SONS
    ILLUSTRATED CIRCULAR AND CATALOGUE OF PIANOFORTES--MANUFACTURERS
STEINWAY AND SONS
    INIMITABLE TONE...'PRICE LIST OF PIANOS MADE BY STEINWAY AND SONS,
STEINWAY AND SONS
    PIANOFORTES
STEINWAY AND SONS
    PORTRAITS OF MUSICAL CELEBRITIES
STEINWAY AND SONS
    PORTRAITS OF MUSICAL CELEBRITIES
STEINWAY AND SONS
    PORTRAITS OF MUSICAL CELEBRITIES
STEINWAY AND SONS
    PORTRAITS OF MUSICAL CELEBRITIES
STEINWAY AND SONS
    PORTRAITS OF MUSICAL CELEBRITIES
STEINWAY AND SONS
    PORTRAITS OF MUSICAL CELEBRITIES
STEINWAY AND SONS
    STEINWAY..YESTERDAY, TODAY, TOMORROW
STEINWAY AND SONS
    STEINWAY AND SONS' PIANO-FORTE MANUFACTORY AT 'STEINWAY', LONG
STEINWAY AND SONS
    STEINWAY PROGRESS..AN APPRECIATION BY I. J. PADEREWSKI
STERNBERG, CONSTANTIN I. VON
    ETHICS AND ESTHETICS OF PIANO PLAYING
STEVENS, FLOYD A.
    COMPLETE COURSE IN PROFESSIONAL PIANO TUNING, REPAIR, AND
STEVENS, WILLIAM S.
    TREATISE ON PIANO-FORTE, CONTAINING THE PRINCIPLES OF FINE PLAYING
STRAUCH BROTHERS
    MANUFACTURE OF PIANOFORTE ACTION, THE ..ITS RISE AND DEVELOPMENT
STUCKENSCHMIDT, HANS H.
    FERRUCCIO BUSONI..CHRONICLE OF A EUROPEAN---1967, IN GERMAN
SUR, WILLIAM R.--EDITOR
    KEYBOARD EXPERIENCE AND PIANO CLASS INSTRUCTION
SUR, WILLIAM R.--EDITOR
    PIANO INSTRUCTION IN THE SCHOOLS
TANKARD, GEOFFREY
    PIANOFORTE DIPLOMAS
TAPPER, THOMAS
    EDUCATION OF THE MUSIC TEACHER, THE
TAYLER, E. DOUGLAS
    MIND-POWER IN MUSIC FOR STUDENTS, TEACHERS AND PERFORMERS
TAYLOR, ROBERT L.
    RUNNING PIANIST, THE ---PERCY GRAINGER
TERWILLIGER, GORDON B.
    PIANO TEACHERS PROFESSIONAL HANDBOOK
THACKRAY, RUPERT M.
    PLAYING FOR DANCE..THE PLACE OF THE PIANIST IN THE TEACHING OF
TRAVIS, JOHN W.
    GUIDE TO RESTRINGING, A
UMINSKA, ZOFIA *
    CHOPIN, THE CHILD AND THE LAD
UNITED STATES--NATIONAL RECOVERY ADMINISTRATION
    CODE OF FAIR COMPETITION FOR THE PIANO MANUFACTURING INDUSTRY AS
UNITED STATES PATENT OFFICE
    COLLECTION OF LETTERS PATENT RELATING TO THE CONSTRUCTION OF
VERNE, MATHILDE
    CHORDS OF REMEMBRANCE---BY A PUPIL OF CLARA SCHUMANN
VIRGIL, ALMON K.
    EDUCATION IN MUSIC..LESSONS TO TEACHERS IN THE INSTRUCTION OF
WAGNER, CHARLES A.
    HOW TO SELECT A GOOD PIANO
WALKER, ALAN
    LISZT
WALKER, BETTINA
    MY MUSICAL EXPERIENCES
WEBER PIANO COMPANY
    WEBER GRAND, SQUARE AND UPRIGHT PIANO-FORTES, THE
WELBOURNE, EVE V.
    WELBOURNE WAY TO HOBBY PIANO PLAYING FOR ADULTS, THE --9 LESSONS
WHEELER, OPAL
    FREDERIC CHOPIN, SON OF POLAND, EARLY YEARS--2 VOLS.---YOUNGER
WHITE, WILLIAM BRAID
    PLAYER-PIANIST, THE ..A GUIDE TO THE APPRECIATION AND
WIENER, HILDA
    PENCIL PORTRAITS OF CONCERT CELEBRITIES---INCLUDES 24 PIANISTS
WILLS, VERA G. *
    PARENT'S GUIDE TO MUSIC LESSONS, A
WILSON, MORRIS E.
    HOW TO HELP YOUR CHILD WITH MUSIC--2ND. ED.---1951
WILSON, ROBINA BECKLES
    MUSICAL INSTRUMENTS--THE 'BYWAYS LIBRARY'
WOLFF, ERNST VICTOR
    WITH REASON AND RHYME
WOLFRAM, VICTOR
    SOSTENUTO PEDAL, THE
YATES, PETER
    AMATEUR AT THE KEYBOARD, AN
YOUFF, ULV
    ULVEN, WRITTEN DURING RETIREMENT IN SWITZERLAND--AUTOBIOGRAPHY OF

Notable Pianists and Piano Teachers

General

APEL, WILLI
HISTORY OF KEYBOARD MUSIC TO 1700, THE --TRANSLATED AND REVISED BY
FAY, AMY
MUSIC STUDY IN GERMANY---1880
FINCK, HENRY T.
MASTERS OF THE PIANO
LOESSER, ARTHUR
MEN, WOMEN AND PIANOS..A SOCIAL HISTORY
SCHONBERG, HAROLD
GREAT PIANISTS, THE
WIER, ALBERT
PIANO, THE ..ITS HISTORY, MAKERS, PLAYERS AND MUSIC

Miscellaneous

COIT, LOTTIE ELLSWORTH
CHILD CHOPIN, THE ...WITH DIRECTIONS FOR PRESENTATION WITH A
FAY, AMY
MUSIC STUDY IN GERMANY---1880
FINCK, HENRY T.
MASTERS OF THE PIANO
KOCHEVITSKY, GEORGE
ART OF PIANO PLAYING, THE ..A SCIENTIFIC APPROACH
KULLAK, ADOLPH
AESTHETICS OF PIANOFORTE PLAYING, THE ---1861 IN GERMAN--1ST.
LOESSER, ARTHUR
MEN, WOMEN AND PIANOS..A SOCIAL HISTORY
MATTHAY, TOBIAS A.
PIANO FALLACIES OF TODAY
MCARTHUR, ALEXANDER
PIANOFORTE STUDY..HINTS ON PIANO PLAYING
REVESZ, GEZA
PSYCHOLOGY OF A MUSICAL PRODIGY, THE ---1925
SCHONBERG, HAROLD
GREAT PIANISTS, THE
STEINWAY, THEODORE E.
PEOPLE AND PIANOS..A CENTURY OF SERVICE TO MUSIC---1853-1953
STEINWAY AND SONS
PORTRAITS OF MUSICAL CELEBRITIES
WIER, ALBERT
PIANO, THE ..ITS HISTORY, MAKERS, PLAYERS AND MUSIC

Professional Scope

BACHE, CONSTANCE
BROTHER MUSICIANS..REMINISCENCES OF EDWARD AND WALTER BACHE
BARFORD, PHILIP
KEYBOARD MUSIC OF C. P. E. BACH, THE ..CONSIDERED IN RELATION TO
BEAUFORT, RAPHAEL
FRANZ LISZT, THE STORY OF HIS LIFE--TO WHICH IS ADDED..'LISZT AS A
BECKETT, WALTER
LISZT
BERTENSSON, SERGEI *
SERGEI RACHMANINOFF, A LIFETIME IN MUSIC
BIE, OSKAR
HISTORY OF THE PIANOFORTE AND PIANOFORTE PLAYERS, A ---1899
BOGIANCKINO, MASSIMO
HARPSICHORD MUSIC OF DOMENICO SCARLATTI, THE
BONE, AUDREY E.
JANE WILHELMINA STIRLING, 1804-1859..THE FIRST STUDY OF THE LIFE
BOWEN, CATHERINE DRINKER
FREE ARTIST..THE STORY OF ANTON AND NICHOLAS RUBINSTEIN
BRANSON, DAVID
JOHN FIELD AND CHOPIN
BROOK, DONALD
MASTERS OF THE KEYBOARD
BURCH, GLADYS
FAMOUS PIANISTS FOR BOYS AND GIRLS
CANAVE, PAZ CORAZON G.
RE-EVALUATION OF THE ROLE PLAYED BY C. P. E. BACH IN THE
CHAPIN, VICTOR
GIANTS OF THE KEYBOARD
CHASINS, ABRAM
SPEAKING OF PIANISTS
CHASINS, ABRAM *
VAN CLIBURN LEGEND, THE
CORDER, FREDERICK
FERENCZ LISZT--HALF-TITLE..MASTERS OF MUSIC
CORTOT, ALFRED
IN SEARCH OF CHOPIN
CULSHAW, JOHN
SERGEI RACHMANINOFF..THE MAN AND HIS MUSIC
DENT, EDWARD J.
FERRUCCIO BUSONI, A BIOGRAPHY
DRY, WAKELING
CHOPIN--'MUSIC OF THE MASTERS' SERIES
EHRLICH, ALFRED HEINRICH
CELEBRATED PIANISTS OF THE PAST AND PRESENT--139 BIOGRAPHIES, WITH
EICHMANN, A. H. *
WILHELM BACKHAUS
EXECUTIVE COMMITTEE OF CHOPIN YEAR 1949
CHOPIN YEAR 1949 IN POLAND, THE
FINCK, HENRY T.
SUCCESS IN MUSIC, AND HOW IT IS WON
FRIEDHEIM, ARTHUR
LIFE AND LISZT..THE RECOLLECTIONS OF A CONCERT PIANIST
GAVOTY, BERNARD *
ALFRED CORTOT
GAVOTY, BERNARD *
ARTHUR RUBINSTEIN
GAVOTY, BERNARD *
WALTER GIESEKING
GAVOTY, BERNARD *
WANDA LANDOWSKA
GLINSKI, MATEUSZ
CHOPIN THE UNKNOWN
GLOYNE, HOWARD F.--M.D.
CARL A. PREYER, THE LIFE OF A KANSAS MUSICIAN
HADOW, SIR WILLIAM HENRY
STUDIES IN MODERN MUSIC--2ND. SERIES--9TH. ED.---CHOPIN
HARDING, BERTITA
CONCERTO, THE STORY OF CLARA SCHUMANN
HERVEY, ARTHUR
FRANZ LISZT AND HIS MUSIC
HERVEY, ARTHUR
SAINT-SAENS---1921
HILL, RALPH
LISZT
HOFMANN, JOSEF
PIANO PLAYING, WITH PIANO QUESTIONS ANSWERED---PUBLISHED EARLIER

HOLCMAN, JAN
LEGACY OF CHOPIN, THE
HULLAH, ANNA
THEODORE LESCHETIZKY
HUMMEL, JOHANN NEPOMUK
COMPLETE THEORETICAL AND PRACTICAL COURSE OF INSTRUCTIONS ON THE
HUNEKER, JAMES GIBBONS
CHOPIN..THE MAN AND HIS MUSIC---1901
HUNEKER, JAMES GIBBONS
FRANZ LISZT
JAMES, BURNETT
BRAHMS..A CRITICAL STUDY
JONSON, GEORGE CHARLES
HANDBOOK TO CHOPIN'S WORKS, A
KASTNER, RUDOLPH
BEETHOVEN'S PIANO SONATAS AND ARTUR SCHNABEL
KELLEY, EDGAR STILLMAN
CHOPIN THE COMPOSER---1913
KIRKPATRICK, RALPH
DOMENICO SCARLATTI---1953
KOBYLANSKA, KRYSTYNA--EDITOR
CHOPIN IN HIS OWN LAND..DOCUMENTS AND SOUVENIRS
KULLAK, ADOLPH
AESTHETICS OF PIANOFORTE PLAYING, THE ---1861 IN GERMAN--1ST.
KULLAK, FRANZ
BEETHOVEN'S PIANO PLAYING, WITH AN ESSAY ON THE EXECUTION OF THE
LAHEE, HENRY C.
FAMOUS PIANISTS OF TODAY AND YESTERDAY
LANDOWSKA, WANDA
LANDOWSKA ON MUSIC--EDITED BY DENISE RESTOUT
LASSIMONNE, DENISE *
MYRA HESS, BY HER FRIENDS
LENZ, WILHELM VON
GREAT PIANO VIRTUOSOS OF OUR TIME, FROM PERSONAL ACQUAINTANCE, THE
LEVINSKAYA, MARIA
LEVINSKAYA SYSTEM OF PIANOFORTE TECHNIC AND TONE COLOR, THE
LISZT, FRANZ
FREDERIC CHOPIN--A BIOGRAPHICAL AND CRITICAL NOTICE---1852
LISZT, FRANZ
LIFE OF CHOPIN--TRANSLATED BY JOHN BROADHOUSE
LISZT, FRANZ
LIFE OF CHOPIN--TRANSLATED ONLY IN PART BY MARTHA WALKER COOK
LITZMANN, BERTHOLD
CLARA SCHUMANN..AN ARTIST'S LIFE BASED ON MATERIAL FOUND IN
LYLE, WATSON
CAMILLE SAINT-SAENS, HIS LIFE AND ART---DISCUSSES CONCERTI AND
LYLE, WATSON
RACHMANINOFF, A BIOGRAPHY
MASON, WILLIAM G.
MEMORIES OF A MUSICAL LIFE
MATTHAY, JESSIE H.
LIFE AND WORKS OF TOBIAS MATTHAY, THE
MAY, FLORENCE
GIRLHOOD OF CLARA SCHUMANN, THE ..CLARA WIECK AND HER TIME
MCARTHUR, ALEXANDER
ANTON RUBINSTEIN, A BIOGRAPHICAL SKETCH
MCARTHUR, ALEXANDER
PIANOFORTE STUDY..HINTS ON PIANO PLAYING
MILINOWSKI, MARTA
TERESA CARRENO, 'BY THE GRACE OF GOD'
MIZWA, STEPHEN P.--EDITOR
FREDERIC CHOPIN, 1810-1849
MOSCHELES, CHARLOTTE
RECENT MUSIC AND MUSICIANS, AS DESCRIBED IN THE DIARIES AND
MURDOCH, WILLIAM
BRAHMS..WITH AN ANALYTICAL STUDY OF THE COMPLETE PIANOFORTE WORKS
MURDOCH, WILLIAM
CHOPIN..HIS LIFE---1935
MURGIA, ADELAIDE
LIFE AND TIMES OF CHOPIN, THE
NEAL, HARRY LEE
WAVE AS YOU PASS
NEWCOMB, ETHEL
LESCHETIZKY AS I KNEW HIM---1923
NEWMAN, ERNEST
MAN LISZT, THE ..A STUDY OF THE TRAGI-COMEDY OF A SOUL DIVIDED
NEWMAN, WILLIAM S.
PERFORMANCE PRACTICES IN BEETHOVEN'S PIANO SONATAS..AN
NIECKS, FREDERICK
FREDERICK CHOPIN AS A MAN AND MUSICIAN--2 VOLS.---1888
NOSSIG, ALFRED
METHODS OF THE MASTERS OF PIANO TEACHING IN EUROPE, THE ..THE
PAUER, ERNST
DICTIONARY OF PIANISTS AND COMPOSERS FOR THE PIANOFORTE..WITH AN
PAYNE, ALBERT
CELEBRATED PIANISTS OF THE PAST AND PRESENT--139 BIOGRAPHIES, WITH
PHILLIPS, CHARLES
PADEREWSKI..THE STORY OF A MODERN IMMORTAL
PIGGOTT, PATRICK
LIFE AND MUSIC OF JOHN FIELD, 1782-1837, THE
PORTE, JOHN F.
CHOPIN, THE COMPOSER AND HIS MUSIC
POTOCKA, COMTESSE ANGELE
THEODOR LESCHETIZKY
POURTALES, GUY DE
POLONAISE, THE LIFE OF CHOPIN---ENGLISH EDITION, 'FREDERICK
REVESZ, GEZA
PSYCHOLOGY OF A MUSICAL PRODIGY, THE ---1925
RIGBY, CHARLES
SIR CHARLES HALLE..A PORTRAIT FOR TODAY
ROLLAND, ROMAIN
BEETHOVEN..WITH A BRIEF ANALYSIS OF THE SONATAS...BY A. EAGLEFIELD
ROSTAND, CLAUDE
LISZT
SAERCHINGER, CESAR
ARTUR SCHNABEL, A BIOGRAPHY
SALESKI, GDAL
FAMOUS MUSICIANS OF JEWISH ORIGIN
SCHAUFFLER, ROBERT HAVEN
FLORESTAN..THE LIFE AND WORK OF ROBERT SCHUMANN---1945
SCHMITZ, ELIE ROBERT
PIANO WORKS OF CLAUDE DEBUSSY, THE
SCHUMANN, ROBERT
ON MUSIC AND MUSICIANS---1854, IN GERMAN--FIRST ENGLISH EDITION IN
SEARLE, HUMPHREY
MUSIC OF LISZT, THE --2ND. REV. ED.---1954
SEROFF, VICTOR
RACHMANINOFF
SITWELL, SACHEVERELL
BACKGROUND FOR DOMENICO SCARLATTI..1685-1757, WRITTEN FOR HIS
SITWELL, SACHEVERELL
LISZT---1934
SMITH, JULIA
MASTER PIANIST..THE CAREER AND TEACHING OF CARL FRIEDBERG
STUCKENSCHMIDT, HANS H.
FERRUCCIO BUSONI..CHRONICLE OF A EUROPEAN---1967, IN GERMAN

STUCKENSCHMIDT, HANS H.
    MAURICE RAVEL..VARIATIONS ON HIS LIFE AND WORK
SZABOLCSI, BENCE
    TWILIGHT OF F. LISZT, THE
TAYLOR, ROBERT L.
    RUNNING PIANIST, THE ---PERCY GRAINGER
THOMPSON, OSCAR
    DEBUSSY, MAN AND ARTIST---1937
THRELFALL, ROBERT
    SERGEI RACHMANINOFF
WALKER, ALAN--EDITOR
    CHOPIN COMPANION, THE ..PROFILES OF THE MAN AND THE
WALKER, ALAN--EDITOR
    FRANZ LISZT, THE MAN AND HIS MUSIC---ESSAYS BY SACHEVERALL SITWELL
WALKER, ALAN--EDITOR
    ROBERT SCHUMANN..THE MAN AND HIS MUSIC---SYMPOSIUM--13 AUTHORS
WALKER, ALAN
    LISZT
WALKER, BETTINA
    MY MUSICAL EXPERIENCES
WEINSTOCK, HERBERT
    CHOPIN, THE MAN AND HIS MUSIC
WEITZMANN, CARL F.
    HISTORY OF PIANOFORTE-PLAYING AND PIANOFORTE-LITERATURE, A
WESTERBY, HERBERT
    LISZT, COMPOSER, AND HIS PIANO WORKS..DESCRIPTIVE GUIDE AND
WIERZYNSKI, CASIMIR
    LIFE AND DEATH OF CHOPIN, THE
WILLEBY, CHARLES
    FREDERIC FRANCOIS CHOPIN
WOLFF, KONRAD
    TEACHING OF ARTUR SCHNABEL, THE ..A GUIDE TO INTERPRETATION
WOODHOUSE, GEORGE
    FROM KEYBOARD TO MUSIC
YOUNG, PERCY M.
    KEYBOARD MUSICIANS OF THE WORLD

Biography - Narrative

ALBRECHTSBERGER, JOHANN GEORG
    METHODS OF HARMONY, FIGURED BASE, AND COMPOSITION...ADAPTED FOR
ALTMAN, FRANCES
    GEORGE GERSHWIN, MASTER COMPOSER
ANDERSON, WILLIAM R.
    RACHMANINOV AND HIS PIANO CONCERTOS
ANON
    LIFE AND WORKS OF GUSTAVE SATTER, THE ..A BIOGRAPHICAL SKETCH IN
ANON
    LIFE AND WORKS OF STEPHEN HELLER, THE PIANOFORTE COMPOSER, THE ..A
ARPIN, PAUL
    LIFE OF LOUIS MOREAU GOTTSCHALK
AZULAY, GERTRUDE
    CHOPIN..THE STORY OF THE BOY WHO MADE BEAUTIFUL MELODIES
BAGBY, ALBERT MORRIS
    LISZT'S WEIMAR
BAGGER, EUGENE S.
    EMINENT EUROPEANS..STUDIES IN CONTINENTAL REALITY---PADEREWSKI
BARBEDETTE, HIPPOLYTE
    STEPHEN HELLER..HIS LIFE AND WORKS
BARRY, KEITH LEWIS
    CHOPIN AND HIS FOURTEEN DOCTORS
BAUGHAN, EDWARD ALGERNON
    IGNACE JAN PADEREWSKI
BENNETT, JOSEPH
    FREDERIC CHOPIN--NOVELLO'S BIOGRAPHY PRIMERS
BIDOU, HENRI
    CHOPIN
BIE, OSKAR
    HISTORY OF THE PIANOFORTE AND PIANOFORTE PLAYERS, A ---1899
BREMONT, ANNA
    WORLD OF MUSIC, THE --THE GREAT COMPOSERS
BRESLIN, HOWARD
    CONCERT GRAND---GOTTSCHALK
BROCKWAY, WALLACE *
    MEN OF MUSIC..THEIR LIVES, TIMES, AND ACHIEVEMENTS--REV.
BROOK, DONALD
    MASTERS OF THE KEYBOARD
BROOKSHAW, SUSANNA
    CONCERNING CHOPIN IN MANCHESTER--ON A CONCERT, AT WHICH CHOPIN
BROWER, HARRIETTE
    MODERN MASTERS OF THE KEYBOARD
BUELOW, HANS GUIDO VON
    HANS VON BUELOW..A BIOGRAPHICAL SKETCH..HIS VISIT TO AMERICA
BURCH, GLADYS
    FAMOUS PIANISTS FOR BOYS AND GIRLS
BURK, JOHN N.
    CLARA SCHUMANN..A ROMANTIC BIOGRAPHY
BYRON, MAY CLARISSA
    DAY WITH FREDERIC CHOPIN, A
CAUCHI, PAUL
    CHOPIN..CENTENNIAL MEMORY 1849-1949..A LECTURE
CHAPIN, VICTOR
    GIANTS OF THE KEYBOARD
CHASINS, ABRAM
    SPEAKING OF PIANISTS
CHASINS, ABRAM *
    VAN CLIBURN LEGEND, THE
CHISSELL, JOAN
    CHOPIN--'GREAT COMPOSERS' SERIES
CLEMENS, CLARA
    MY HUSBAND GABRILOWITSCH
COATES, HENRY
    CHOPIN--NOVELLO'S BIOGRAPHIES OF GREAT MUSICIANS
COOKE, JAMES FRANCIS
    IGNACE JAN PADEREWSKI
COOKE, JAMES FRANCIS
    LOUIS MOREAU GOTTSCHALK..A SHORT BIOGRAPHY
CORTOT, ALFRED
    IN SEARCH OF CHOPIN
DAVISON, JAMES W.
    FREDERICK CHOPIN..A MEMOIR
DAVISON, JAMES W.
    FREDERIC FRANCOIS CHOPIN..CRITICAL AND APPRECIATIVE ESSAY---1843
DE BOER, JOSEPHINE
    MALLORCAN MOODS IN CONTEMPORARY ART AND LITERATURE--CONTAINS
DIDIMUS, HENRY
    BIOGRAPHY OF LEOPOLD DE MEYER...ROYAL COURT PIANIST...TO THEIR
DIDIMUS, HENRY
    BIOGRAPHY OF LOUIS MOREAU GOTTSCHALK, THE AMERICAN PIANIST AND
DIEHL, ALICE M.
    MUSICAL MEMORIES--SOME LESSONS WITH HENSELT
DUNLOP, AGNES MARY
    DUET---STORY OF CLARA AND ROBERT SCHUMANN
EHRLICH, ALFRED HEINRICH
    CELEBRATED PIANISTS OF THE PAST AND PRESENT--139 BIOGRAPHIES, WITH

EICHMANN, A. H. *
    WILHELM BACKHAUS
FAY, AMY
    MUSIC STUDY IN GERMANY---1880
FERRA I PERELLO, BARTOLOME
    CHOPIN AND GEORGE SAND IN THE CARTUJA DE VALLDEMOSA...
FERRIS, GEORGE TITUS
    GREAT VIOLINISTS AND PIANISTS, THE ---1881
FINCK, HENRY T.
    PADEREWSKI AND HIS ART
FINCK, HENRY T.
    SUCCESS IN MUSIC, AND HOW IT IS WON
FISCHER, EDWIN
    REFLECTIONS ON MUSIC
FLOOD, WILLIAM HENRY GRATTAN
    JOHN FIELD OF DUBLIN, THE INVENTOR OF THE NOCTURNE---1920
FORSEE, AYLESA
    ARTUR RUBINSTEIN, KING OF THE KEYBOARD
FRIEDHEIM, ARTHUR
    LIFE AND LISZT..THE RECOLLECTIONS OF A CONCERT PIANIST
GAVOTY, BERNARD *
    ALFRED CORTOT
GAVOTY, BERNARD *
    ARTHUR RUBINSTEIN
GAVOTY, BERNARD *
    CLAUDIO ARRAU
GAVOTY, BERNARD *
    SAMSON FRANCOIS
GAVOTY, BERNARD *
    WALTER GIESEKING
GAVOTY, BERNARD *
    WANDA LANDOWSKA
GAVOTY, BERNARD *
    WITOLD MALCUZYNSKI
GRAHAM, L. SIBLEY
    TALES OF THE OLD VIRTUOSO..THE SPANISH COURT PIANIST--MARQUIS DON
GRAYDON, NELL *
    AMAZING MARRIAGE OF MARIE EUSTIS AND JOSEF HOFMANN, THE
GRONOWICZ, ANTONI
    CHOPIN---YOUNGER READERS
GRONOWICZ, ANTONI
    PADEREWSKI, PIANIST AND PATRIOT
GRONOWICZ, ANTONI
    SERGEI RACHMANINOFF
HADDEN, JAMES CUTHBERT
    CHOPIN--'MASTER MUSICIANS' SERIES
HALDANE, CHARLOTTE
    GALLEY SLAVES OF LOVE, THE ..THE STORY OF MARIE D'AGOULT AND FRANZ
HALLE, SIR CHARLES
    SIR C. HALLE..A SKETCH OF HIS CAREER AS A
HARSANYI, ZSOLT
    IMMORTAL FRANZ..THE LIFE AND LOVES OF A GENIUS---FRANZ LISZT
HAWEIS, HUGH R.
    MUSIC AND MORALS---CHOPIN
HEDLEY, ARTHUR
    CHOPIN--'MASTER MUSICIAN' SERIES--INCLUDES CATALOGUE OF
HENDERSON, ARCHIBALD
    CONTEMPORARY IMMORTALS---PADEREWSKI
HERVEY, ARTHUR
    FRENCH MUSIC IN THE NINETEENTH CENTURY---CHOPIN
HERVEY, ARTHUR
    RUBINSTEIN--'MAYFAIR BIOGRAPHIES', NO. 11
HIPKINS, ALFRED JAMES
    HOW CHOPIN PLAYED...FROM CONTEMPORARY IMPRESSIONS COLLECTED FROM
HOPKINSON, CECIL
    BIBLIOGRAPHICAL THEMATIC CATALOGUE OF THE WORKS OF JOHN FIELD,
HUBBARD, ELBERT
    LITTLE JOURNEYS TO THE HOMES OF GREAT MUSICIANS--VOL. 8, NO.
HUBBARD, ELBERT
    LITTLE JOURNEYS TO THE HOMES OF GREAT MUSICIANS--VOL. 9, NO.
HUEFFER, FRANCIS
    MUSICAL STUDIES..A SERIES OF CONTRIBUTIONS BY FRANCIS HUEFFER,
HUME, RUTH *
    LION OF POLAND, THE ..THE STORY OF PADEREWSKI--JUNIOR BIOGRAPHIES
HUMISTON, WILLIAM H.
    ANTON RUBINSTEIN--'LITTLE BIOGRAPHIES'
HUMISTON, WILLIAM H.
    CHOPIN--'LITTLE BIOGRAPHIES'
HUMISTON, WILLIAM H.
    FRIEDMAN--'LITTLE BIOGRAPHIES'
HUMISTON, WILLIAM H.
    LISZT--'LITTLE BIOGRAPHIES'
HUMISTON, WILLIAM H.
    PADEREWSKI--'LITTLE BIOGRAPHIES'
HUMISTON, WILLIAM H.
    RACHMANINOFF--'LITTLE BIOGRAPHIES'
ISAACSON, CHARLES D.
    FACE TO FACE WITH GREAT MUSICIANS---CHOPIN AND LISZT
JOHNS, CLAYTON
    REMINISCENCES OF A MUSICIAN---LISZT AND PADEREWSKI
KAISER, JOACHIM
    GREAT PIANISTS OF OUR TIME
KELLOGG, CHARLOTTE
    PADEREWSKI
KIRKWOOD, KENNETH P.
    GARDEN IN POLAND, A ...ON CHOPIN'S BIRTHPLACE AND BURIAL
KLECZYNSKI, JAN
    HOW TO PLAY CHOPIN--THREE LECTURES
KOSCIUSZKO FOUNDATION
    TO IGNACE JAN PADEREWSKI, ARTIST, PATRIOT, HUMANITARIAN, 1918-1928
LAHEE, HENRY C.
    FAMOUS PIANISTS OF TODAY AND YESTERDAY
LANDAU, ROM
    IGNACE PADEREWSKI, MUSICIAN AND STATESMAN
LANDOWSKA, WANDA
    LANDOWSKA ON MUSIC--EDITED BY DENISE RESTOUT
LASSIMONNE, DENISE
    OPENING THE SHUTTERS..A SHORT EXPOSITION ON THE TEACHINGS AND
LASZLO, SZIGMOND *
    FRANZ LISZT..A BIOGRAPHY IN PICTURES---240 PICTORIAL ENTRIES
LAWRENCE, FREDERIC LOCKE
    MUSICIANS OF SORROW AND ROMANCE---CHOPIN
LEE, JENNETTE B.
    UNFINISHED PORTRAITS..STORIES OF MUSICIANS AND ARTISTS---CHOPIN
LENZ, WILHELM VON
    GREAT PIANO VIRTUOSOS OF OUR TIME, FROM PERSONAL ACQUAINTANCE, THE
LESLIE, DORIS
    POLONAISE---NOVELIZED BIOGRAPHY OF CHOPIN
LESSMANN, W. J. OTTO
    FRANZ LISZT..EINE HULDIGUNG--FRANZ LISZT..A TRIBUTE
LEVANT, OSCAR
    SMATTERING OF IGNORANCE, A
LE MASSENA, CLARENCE E.
    PADEREWSKI, 'THE MASTER OF MASTERS' ---REPRODUCED FROM TYPEWRITTEN
LINGG, ANN M.
    MEPHISTO WALTZ, THE STORY OF FRANZ LISZT

LISZT, FRANZ
    FREDERIC CHOPIN--A BIOGRAPHICAL AND CRITICAL NOTICE---1852
LOCKE, ROBINSON
    BLOOMFIELD-ZEISLER--ROBINSON LOCKE SCRAP BOOKS
LOCKE, ROBINSON
    BUSONI--ROBINSON LOCKE SCRAP BOOKS
LOCKE, ROBINSON
    GABRILOWITSCH--ROBINSON LOCKE SCRAP BOOKS--2 VOLS.
LOCKE, ROBINSON
    HOFMANN--ROBINSON LOCKE SCRAP BOOKS
LOCKE, ROBINSON
    PADEREWSKI--ROBINSON LOCKE SCRAP BOOKS--2 VOLS.
LOGGINS, VERNON
    WHERE THE WORD ENDS..THE LIFE OF LOUIS MOREAU GOTTSCHALK
LONG, ESMOND R.--PATHOLOGIST
    HISTORY OF THE THERAPY OF TUBERCULOSIS, AND THE CASE OF FREDERIC
MACKENZIE, SIR ALEXANDER
    LISZT--'THE MAYFAIR BIOGRAPHIES', NO. 3
MACKENZIE, SIR ALEXANDER
    LISZT--MASTERPIECES OF MUSIC
MACKENZIE, SIR ALEXANDER
    MUSICIAN'S NARRATIVE, A ---CLARA SCHUMANN, VON BUELOW AND LISZT
MAINE, BASIL
    CHOPIN--'GREAT LIVES' SERIES
MANUEL, ROLAND
    FREDERIC CHOPIN--'GREAT ANNIVERSARIES' SERIES
MARTENS, FREDERICK HERMAN
    PADEREWSKI--'LITTLE BIOGRAPHIES', VOL. 2
MARTENS, FREDERICK HERMAN
    RACHMANINOFF--'LITTLE BIOGRAPHIES', VOL. 2
MARTIN, THOMAS CARLAW
    FRANZ LISZT..A SKETCH OF HIS LIFE AND PERSONALITY
MASON, DANIEL GREGORY
    ROMANTIC COMPOSERS, THE ---CHOPIN AND LISZT
MASON, WILLIAM G.
    MEMORIES OF A MUSICAL LIFE
MASON, WILLIAM G.
    PADEREWSKI..A CRITICAL STUDY--'CENTURY LIBRARY OF MUSIC', VOL. 18
MATHEWS, WILLIAM S. B.
    GREAT IN MUSIC, THE ..A SYSTEMATIC COURSE OF STUDY IN THE MUSIC OF
MATTHAY, JESSIE H.
    LIFE AND WORKS OF TOBIAS MATTHAY, THE
MAUROIS, ANDRE
    FREDERIC CHOPIN---FOR YOUNGER READERS
MAYO, WALDO
    CHOPIN---FOR YOUNGER READERS
MCMILLAN, MARY LEE *
    MY HELENKA---IGNACE PADEREWSKI
MILLER, JEWELL
    POLONAISE MILITAIRE..THE LIFE AND WORK OF FREDERIC CHOPIN..A
MOISEIVITCH, MAURICE
    MOISEIVITCH--BENNO--, BIOGRAPHY OF A CONCERT PIANIST
MONTAGU-NATHAN, M.
    CONTEMPORARY RUSSIAN COMPOSERS---RACHMANINOFF
MOORE, GERALD
    AM I TOO LOUD..MEMOIRS OF AN ACCOMPANIST
NEAL, HARRY LEE
    WAVE AS YOU PASS
NEWCOMB, ETHEL
    LESCHETIZKY AS I KNEW HIM---1923
NOHL, LUDWIG
    LIFE OF LISZT--'BIOGRAPHIES OF MUSICIANS', VOL. 5
OFFERGELD, ROBERT
    CENTENNIAL CATALOGUE OF THE PUBLISHED AND UNPUBLISHED COMPOSITIONS
PADEREWSKI FOUNDATION
    IGNACY JAN PADEREWSKI, 1860-1941..MEMORIAL ALBUM---IN ENGLISH AND
PARKER, DOUGLAS C.
    PERCY ALDRIDGE GRAINGER, A STUDY
PAYNE, ALBERT
    CELEBRATED PIANISTS OF THE PAST AND PRESENT--139 BIOGRAPHIES, WITH
POLISH RESEARCH AND INFORMATION SERVICE
    FREDERIC CHOPIN--CENTENNIAL 1849-1949, BACKGROUND
POLISH RESEARCH AND INFORMATION SERVICE
    FREDERIC CHOPIN CENTENNIAL--1949---EIGHT ARTICLES
PORTE, JOHN F.
    EDWARD MACDOWELL, A GREAT AMERICAN TONE POET..HIS LIFE AND MUSIC
POTOCKA, COMTESSE ANGELE
    THEODOR LESCHETIZKY
POURTALES, GUY DE
    FRANZ LISZT, THE MAN OF LOVE
RAMANN, LINA
    FRANZ LISZT, ARTIST AND MAN--2 VOLS.---ONLY VOL. 1, 1811-1840,
RAYSON, ETHEL
    POLISH MUSIC AND CHOPIN ITS LAUREATE, ETC.
REVESZ, GEZA
    PSYCHOLOGY OF A MUSICAL PRODIGY, THE ---1925
RICHARDSON, NATHAN
    INKLINGS FOR THE LOVERS OF MUSIC, PART 1..CULTIVATION OF THE ART
ROSENTHAL, MORIZ
    OLD AND THE NEW SCHOOL OF PIANO PLAYING, THE --TYPEWRITTEN COPY
ROUSSELOT, JEAN
    FRANZ LISZT
ROWBOTHAM, JOHN F.
    PRIVATE LIFE OF THE GREAT COMPOSERS, THE ---CHOPIN AND LISZT
RUTTKAY, GEORGE
    CHOPIN, HIS LIFE TOLD IN ANECDOTAL FORM---FOR YOUNGER READERS
SACKETT, SHELTON
    NOCTURNE..A CHOPIN-PLAY IN ONE ACT
SAERCHINGER, CESAR
    ARTUR SCHNABEL, A BIOGRAPHY
SALESKI, GDAL
    FAMOUS MUSICIANS OF JEWISH ORIGIN
SCHALLENBERG, EVERT W.
    FREDERIC CHOPIN--SYMPHONIA BOOKS..'HISTORY OF MUSIC' SERIES
SCHONBERG, HAROLD
    COLLECTOR'S CHOPIN AND SCHUMANN, THE --KEYSTONE BOOKS
SCHONBERG, HAROLD
    GREAT PIANISTS, THE
SCHUMANN, ROBERT
    ON MUSIC AND MUSICIANS---1854, IN GERMAN--FIRST ENGLISH EDITION IN
SEGUEL, MANIA
    CHOPIN'S TEMPO RUBATO
SEROFF, VICTOR
    DEBUSSY, MUSICIAN OF FRANCE
SEROFF, VICTOR
    FRANZ LISZT
SEROFF, VICTOR
    FREDERIC CHOPIN
SEROFF, VICTOR
    MAURICE RAVEL
SEROFF, VICTOR
    RACHMANINOFF
SEROFF, VICTOR
    WOLFGANG AMADEUS MOZART
SEYMOUR, MARY ALICE IVES
    LIFE AND LETTERS OF LOUIS MOREAU GOTTSCHALK

SILOTI, ALEXANDER
    MY MEMORIES OF LISZT
SMITH, JULIA
    MASTER PIANIST..THE CAREER AND TEACHING OF CARL FRIEDBERG
SPAETH, SIGMUND
    DEDICATION, THE LOVE STORY OF CLARA AND ROBERT SCHUMANN
STOCKES, SACHA
    ART OF ROBERT CASADESUS, THE
STRACHEY, MARJORIE C.
    NIGHTINGALE, THE ..A LIFE OF CHOPIN--IN THE FORM OF FICTION
STRAKACZ, ANIELA
    PADEREWSKI AS I KNEW HIM
SZABOLCSI, BENCE
    TWILIGHT OF F. LISZT, THE
TARCZYNSKI-ALF, TADEUSZ
    HOMAGE TO CHOPIN---TEXT IN POLISH AND ENGLISH
TARNOWSKI, STANISLAS
    CHOPIN..AS REVEALED BY EXTRACTS FROM HIS DIARY--2ND. ED.---1905
THOMPSON, OSCAR
    DEBUSSY, MAN AND ARTIST---1937
UMINSKA, ZOFIA *
    CHOPIN, THE CHILD AND THE LAD
WARREN, CLARENCE H.--EDITOR
    MEN BEHIND THE MUSIC, THE ---CHOPIN AND LISZT
WEITZMANN, CARL F.
    HISTORY OF PIANOFORTE-PLAYING AND PIANOFORTE-LITERATURE, A
WELTE-MIGNON CORPORATION
    LIBRARY OF DELUXE WELTE-MIGNON MUSIC RECORDS FOR REPRODUCING
WELTE-MIGNON CORPORATION
    LIBRARY OF WELTE-MIGNON MUSIC RECORDS
WESTRUP, SIR JACK ALLAN
    LISZT--NOVELLO'S BIOGRAPHIES OF GREAT MUSICIANS
WHEELER, OPAL
    FREDERIC CHOPIN, SON OF POLAND, EARLY YEARS--2 VOLS.---YOUNGER
YOUNG, PERCY M.
    KEYBOARD MUSICIANS OF THE WORLD
ZUR HEIDE, KARL GERT
    DEEP SOUTH PIANO..THE STORY OF LITTLE BROTHER MONTGOMERY

Biography - Historical Survey

AEOLIAN COMPANY, THE
    DUO-ART PIANO MUSIC...RECORDED BY MORE THAN 250 PIANISTS
AEOLIAN COMPANY, THE
    PIANISTS WHO HAVE MADE RECORDS FOR THE DUO-ART PIANO
AMERICAN PIANO CORPORATION
    CATALOGUE OF MUSIC FOR THE AMPICO, A --A LIST OF THE RECORDINGS OF
ANDERSON, ARVID C.
    MASTERS OF MUSIC---CHOPIN AND LISZT
AUTO PNEUMATIC ACTION COMPANY
    WELTE-MIGNON BOOK...OF FAMOUS ARTISTS, THE
BALLANTINE, BILL
    PIANO, THE ..AN INTRODUCTION TO THE INSTRUMENT
BREMONT, ANNA
    WORLD OF MUSIC, THE --THE GREAT VIRTUOSI
BROOK, DONALD
    MASTERS OF THE KEYBOARD
BROWER, HARRIETTE
    MODERN MASTERS OF THE KEYBOARD
BUCKLEY, OLIVIA DUSSEK
    MUSICAL TRUTHS..OR, AN ANALYSIS OF MUSIC AND AN ESSAY ON THE PAST
BURCH, GLADYS
    FAMOUS PIANISTS FOR BOYS AND GIRLS
BURCH, GLADYS
    MODERN COMPOSERS FOR YOUNG PEOPLE---FIRST PUBLISHED AS 'A CHILD'S
CARLSON, EFFIE B.
    BIO-BIBLIOGRAPHICAL DICTIONARY OF TWELVE-TONE AND SERIAL
CHAPIN, VICTOR
    GIANTS OF THE KEYBOARD
CHASINS, ABRAM
    SPEAKING OF PIANISTS
CHURCHILL, WILLIAM--SUPPOSED AUTHOR
    MARVELLOUS YEAR, THE ...CRITICAL SKETCHES OF CELEBRATED MEN, THE
COOKE, JAMES FRANCIS
    MUSIC MASTERS OLD AND NEW..A SERIES OF EDUCATIONAL BIOGRAPHIES...
DOLE, NATHAN H.
    FAMOUS COMPOSERS--2 VOLS.---CHOPIN AND LISZT--1891+
DOLE, NATHAN H.
    LIVES OF THE MUSICIANS, THE ...WITH PORTRAITS
EHRLICH, ALFRED HEINRICH
    CELEBRATED PIANISTS OF THE PAST AND PRESENT--139 BIOGRAPHIES, WITH
EWEN, DAVID
    COMPOSERS OF YESTERDAY..A BIOGRAPHICAL AND CRITICAL GUIDE TO THE
EWEN, DAVID
    COMPOSERS SINCE 1900..A BIOGRAPHICAL AND CRITICAL GUIDE
EWEN, DAVID
    GREAT COMPOSERS, 1300-1900..A BIOGRAPHICAL AND CRITICAL GUIDE
EWEN, DAVID
    MEN AND WOMEN WHO MAKE MUSIC
EWEN, DAVID
    MEN AND WOMEN WHO MAKE MUSIC
EWEN, DAVID
    MEN AND WOMEN WHO MAKE MUSIC
EWEN, DAVID
    WORLD OF GREAT COMPOSERS, THE
FARNSWORTH, EDWARD C.
    THREE GREAT EPOCH-MAKERS IN MUSIC---CHOPIN
FAY, AMY
    MUSIC STUDY IN GERMANY---1880
FERRIS, GEORGE TITUS
    GREAT MUSICAL COMPOSERS..GERMAN, FRENCH, AND ITALIAN
FERRIS, GEORGE TITUS
    GREAT VIOLINISTS AND PIANISTS, THE ---1881
FERRIS, GEORGE TITUS
    SKETCHES OF GREAT PIANISTS AND GREAT VIOLINISTS, BIOGRAPHICAL AND
FINCK, HENRY T.
    SUCCESS IN MUSIC, AND HOW IT IS WON
FRIEDHEIM, ARTHUR
    LIFE AND LISZT..THE RECOLLECTIONS OF A CONCERT PIANIST
FULLER-MAITLAND, J. A.
    MASTERS OF GERMAN MUSIC---CLARA SCHUMANN
GABRIEL, GILBERT W.
    GREAT PIANISTS AND COMPOSERS
GELATT, ROLAND
    MUSIC MAKERS..SOME OUTSTANDING MUSICAL PERFORMERS OF OUR DAY
GLENNON, JAMES
    AUSTRALIAN MUSIC AND MUSICIANS
GLYN, MARGARET H.
    ABOUT ELIZABETHAN VIRGINAL MUSIC AND ITS COMPOSERS..NEW ISSUE,
GREW, SIDNEY
    MAKERS OF MUSIC..THE STORY OF SINGERS AND INSTRUMENTALISTS
HADDEN, JAMES CUTHBERT
    MASTER MUSICIANS..A BOOK FOR PLAYERS, SINGERS AND LISTENERS
HADDEN, JAMES CUTHBERT
    MODERN MUSICIANS..A BOOK FOR PLAYERS, SINGERS AND LISTENERS

HENDERSON, WILLIAM JAMES
PRELUDES AND STUDIES..MUSICAL THEMES OF THE DAY--SECTION 3..THE
HUNEKER, JAMES GIBBONS
FRANZ LISZT
HUNEKER, JAMES GIBBONS
MEZZOTINTS IN MODERN MUSIC--6TH. ED.---CHOPIN AND LISZT--1901
KAUFMANN, HELEN LOEB
ARTISTS IN MUSIC OF TODAY
KENYON, CHARLES FREDERICK
IMAGINARY INTERVIEWS WITH GREAT COMPOSERS..A SERIES OF VIVID PEN
KREHBIEL, HENRY
PIANOFORTE AND ITS MUSIC, THE ---1911
KULLAK, ADOLPH
AESTHETICS OF PIANOFORTE PLAYING, THE ---1861 IN GERMAN--1ST.
LAHEE, HENRY C.
FAMOUS PIANISTS OF TODAY AND YESTERDAY
LAVIGNAC, ALBERT
MUSIC AND MUSICIANS---1895, IN FRENCH
LENZ, WILHELM VON
GREAT PIANO VIRTUOSOS OF OUR TIME, FROM PERSONAL ACQUAINTANCE, THE
LOESSER, ARTHUR
MEN, WOMEN AND PIANOS..A SOCIAL HISTORY
MASON, WILLIAM G.
MEMORIES OF A MUSICAL LIFE
NICCHIA, LILLIAN
PIANOFORTE STUDY..HINTS ON PIANO PLAYING
PAYNE, ALBERT
CELEBRATED PIANISTS OF THE PAST AND PRESENT--139 BIOGRAPHIES, WITH
PIRANI, EUGENIO DI
SECRETS OF THE SUCCESS OF GREAT MUSICIANS
POWERS, J. HAROLD
MUSIC'S GLAMOROUS HALL OF FAME..SHORT ARTICLES ABOUT FAMOUS NAMES,
REESER, EDUARD
SONS OF BACH, THE
SACHS, CURT
EVOLUTION OF PIANO MUSIC, 1350-1700, THE
SALAMAN, CHARLES
PIANISTS OF THE PAST..PERSONAL RECOLLECTIONS BY THE LATE CHARLES
SALESKI, GDAL
FAMOUS MUSICIANS OF A WANDERING RACE
SALESKI, GDAL
FAMOUS MUSICIANS OF JEWISH ORIGIN
SCHNITTKIND, HENRY T. *
FORTY FAMOUS COMPOSERS---CHOPIN AND LISZT
SCHONBERG, HAROLD
GREAT PIANISTS, THE
SCHONBERG, HAROLD
LIVES OF THE GREAT COMPOSERS, THE ---CHOPIN AND LISZT
SCHWIMMER, FRANCISKA
GREAT MUSICIANS AS CHILDREN
SORABJI, KAIKHOSRU
AROUND MUSIC---PACHMAN, CHOPIN AND LISZT
STATHAM, HENRY H.
MY THOUGHTS ON MUSIC AND MUSICIANS---CHOPIN AND LISZT
THOMPSON, KENNETH
DICTIONARY OF TWENTIETY-CENTURY COMPOSERS, A --1911-1971
VIARD-LOUIS, JENNY
MUSIC AND THE PIANO
WALLACE, WILLIAM
LISZT, WAGNER, AND THE PRINCESS
WARRACK, JOHN H.
SIX GREAT COMPOSERS---CHOPIN
WEITZMANN, CARL F.
HISTORY OF PIANOFORTE-PLAYING AND PIANOFORTE-LITERATURE, A
WELTE-MIGNON CORPORATION
LIBRARY OF DELUXE WELTE-MIGNON MUSIC RECORDS FOR REPRODUCING
WELTE-MIGNON CORPORATION
LIBRARY OF WELTE-MIGNON MUSIC RECORDS
WIENER, HILDA
PENCIL PORTRAITS OF CONCERT CELEBRITIES---INCLUDES 24 PIANISTS
WIER, ALBERT
PIANO, THE ..ITS HISTORY, MAKERS, PLAYERS AND MUSIC
YOUNG, PERCY M.
KEYBOARD MUSICIANS OF THE WORLD
YOUNG, PERCY M.
MASTERS OF MUSIC
ZOFF, OTTO--EDITOR
GREAT COMPOSERS THROUGH THE EYES OF THEIR CONTEMPORARIES---CHOPIN

Autobiography, Essays, Letters, Lectures and Diaries

ADAMS, JULIETTE
CHAPTERS FROM A MUSICAL LIFE
AEOLIAN COMPANY, THE
AUDIOGRAPHIC MUSIC
AEOLIAN COMPANY, THE
WEIGHT OF EVIDENCE ON THE TRUE MUSICAL WORTH OF THE PIANOLA AND
AGUILAR, EMANUEL
LITTLE BOOK ABOUT LEARNING THE PIANOFORTE, A
ALLEY, MARGUERITE *
PASSIONATE FRIENDSHIP, A ..CLARA SCHUMANN AND BRAHMS---LETTERS TO
ANDERSON, WILLIAM P.
MUSIC AS A CAREER
ANON
ESSAY ON THE CHIROGYMNAST..OR, FINGER EXERCISES APPLIED TO...ALL
ANON
GENERAL OBSERVATIONS ON MUSIC AND REMARKS ON MR. LOGIER'S SYSTEM
ANON
HUMANISTIC STUDIES IN HONOR OF JOHN CALVIN METCALF---INCLUDES
ANON
LIFE AND WORKS OF STEPHEN HELLER, THE PIANOFORTE COMPOSER, THE ..A
ARONSON, MAURICE
KEY TO THE MINIATURES OF LEOPOLD GODOWSKY, A ..ANALYTICAL ESSAYS
BACH, CARL PHILIPP EMANUEL
CARL PHILIPP EMANUEL BACH'S AUTOBIOGRAPHY..FACSIMILE OF ORIGINAL
BACHE, CONSTANCE
BROTHER MUSICIANS..REMINISCENCES OF EDWARD AND WALTER BACHE
BAMBERGER, LOUIS
MEMORIES OF SIXTY YEARS IN THE TIMBER AND PIANOFORTE TRADES
BARNETT, JOHN FRANCIS
MUSICAL REMINISCENCES AND IMPRESSIONS---TEACHER, PIANIST,
BAUER, HAROLD
HAROLD BAUER, HIS BOOK---1948
BEREGSZASZY, LAJOS
OBSERVATIONS CONCERNING IMPROVEMENTS IN THE CONSTRUCTION OF THE
BERINGER, OSCAR
FIFTY YEARS EXPERIENCE OF PIANOFORTE TEACHING AND PLAYING
BOS, COENRAAD V.
WELL-TEMPERED ACCOMPANIST, THE
BOWMAN, EDWARD M.
MASTER LESSONS IN PIANOFORTE PLAYING, 'LETTERS FROM A MUSICIAN TO
BROTHERHOOD, JAMES
DEVELOPMENT OF THE HAND FOR PIANO-FORTE PLAYING BY MEANS OF A
BROTHERHOOD, JAMES
IMPROVED METHOD IN PIANO TEACHING, AND RECENT IDEAS OF LEADING

BROTHERHOOD, JAMES
SENSITIVE PIANO TOUCH AND WAYS AND MEANS TO ITS ACQUIREMENT---A
BUELOW, HANS GUIDO VON
CORRESPONDENCE OF HANS VON BUELOW AND RICHARD STRAUSS
BUELOW, HANS GUIDO VON
EARLY CORRESPONDENCE OF HANS VON BUELOW, THE ---EDITED BY HIS
BUELOW, HANS GUIDO VON
LETTERS OF HANS VON BUELOW---INCLUDES CORRESPONDENCE TO KARL
BUSONI, FERRUCCIO
FERRUCCIO BUSONI--LETTERS TO HIS WIFE--1895
CAUCHI, PAUL
CHOPIN..CENTENNIAL MEMORY 1849-1949..A LECTURE
CHICKERING AND SONS
JONAS CHICKERING CENTENNIAL CELEBRATION, THE ..A TRIBUTE TO THE
CHOPIN, FREDERIC
CHOPIN'S LETTERS--COLLECTED BY HENRY OPIENSKI..TRANSLATED BY E. L.
CHOPIN, FREDERIC
SELECTED CORRESPONDENCE OF FREDERYK F. CHOPIN--COLLECTED BY
CHRISTENSEN, INGA
INGA - PLAY--MEMOIRS
CLARK, MADAM STEINEGER
RELIGION AND ROMANCE OF A PIANIST'S LIFE---AUTOBIOGRAPHY
COHEN, HARRIET
BUNDLE OF TIME, A ..THE MEMOIRS OF HARRIET COHEN
COOKE, JAMES FRANCIS
HOW TO MEMORIZE MUSIC
CZERNY, CARL
LETTERS ON THOROUGH-BASS...FORMING THE SECOND PART OF THE LETTERS
DAVID, ELIZABETH HARBISON
I PLAYED THEIR ACCOMPANIMENTS
DAVISON, JAMES W.
FREDERIC FRANCOIS CHOPIN..CRITICAL AND APPRECIATIVE ESSAY---1843
DE LARA, ADELINA
FINALE---MEMOIRS OF LAST SURVIVING PUPIL OF CLARA SCHUMANN
DIEHL, ALICE M.
TRUE STORY OF MY LIFE, THE
DUCAT, EVA
ANOTHER WAY OF MUSIC---AUTOBIOGRAPHY
EHLERT, LOUIS
FROM THE TONE WORLD--ESSAYS---TAUSIG, CHOPIN AND LISZT--2ND.
EHLERT, LOUIS
LETTERS ON MUSIC, TO A LADY
ELLIS, HAVELOCK
AFFIRMATIONS--LITERARY ESSAYS---CHOPIN
ELLIS, HAVELOCK
NEW SPIRIT, THE --ESSAYS---CHOPIN--1891
FINCK, HENRY T.
CHOPIN AND OTHER MUSICAL ESSAYS---1889
FISCHER, EDWIN
REFLECTIONS ON MUSIC
FOLDES, LILI
TWO ON A CONTINENT
FOSS, HUBERT J.--EDITOR
HERITAGE OF MUSIC, THE --SECOND SERIES OF ESSAYS---CHOPIN AND
GLINSKI, MATEUSZ
CHOPIN'S LETTERS TO DELFINA
GOTTSCHALK, LOUIS MOREAU
NOTES OF A PIANIST--EDITED BY JEANNE BEHREND---1881
GRAHAM, GEORGE FARQUHAR
GENERAL OBSERVATIONS UPON MUSIC AND REMARKS ON MR. LOGIER'S SYSTEM
GRAY, CECIL
CONTINGENCIES AND OTHER ESSAYS---LISZT
GRAY, CECIL
MUSICAL CHAIRS..OR, BETWEEN TWO STOOLS, BEING THE LIFE AND MEMOIRS
HABETS, ALFRED
BORODIN AND LISZT--VOL. 2--LISZT, AS SKETCHED IN THE LETTERS OF
HALL, CONSTANCE HUNTINGTON
HELEN HOPEKIRK, 1856-1945
HALLE, SIR CHARLES
AUTOBIOGRAPHY OF CHARLES HALLE, WITH CORRESPONDENCE AND DIARIES,
HAMBOURG, MARK
EIGHTH OCTAVE, THE ---CONTINUES THE RECORD, BEGUN IN 'FROM PIANO
HAMBOURG, MARK
FROM PIANO TO FORTE..A THOUSAND AND ONE NOTES---AUTOBIOGRAPHY
HEINE, HEINRICH
HEINE IN ART AND LETTERS---CHOPIN AND LISZT--1837
HENDERSON, ARCHIBALD
MUSICAL MEMORIES---CONCERNS SEVERAL PIANISTS
HERZ, HENRI
MY TRAVELS IN AMERICA---1840+
HOFFMAN, RICHARD
SOME MUSICAL RECOLLECTIONS OF FIFTY YEARS---INCLUDES LEOPOLD DE
HOFMANN, JOSEF
PIANO QUESTIONS ANSWERED..A LITTLE BOOK OF DIRECT ANSWERS TO TWO
HUEFFER, FRANCIS
HALF A CENTURY OF MUSIC IN ENGLAND, 1837-1887..LISZT IN ENGLAND
HUNEKER, JAMES GIBBONS
INTIMATE LETTERS OF JAMES GIBBONS HUNEKER, COLLECTED AND EDITED BY
HUNEKER, JAMES GIBBONS
MELOMANIACS..ESSAYS---CHOPIN AND LISZT
HUNEKER, JAMES GIBBONS
OLD FOGY, HIS MUSICAL OPINIONS AND GROTESQUES---D'ALBERT,
HUNEKER, JAMES GIBBONS
UNICORNS---CHOPIN
HUNEKER, JAMES GIBBONS
VARIATIONS---CHOPIN, LISZT, AND PACHMANN
JOHNS, CLAYTON
REMINISCENCES OF A MUSICIAN---LISZT AND PADEREWSKI
JOHNSTONE, J. ALFRED
MODERN TENDENCIES AND OLD STANDARDS IN MUSICAL ART
KARASOWSKI, MORITZ
FREDERIC CHOPIN..HIS LIFE, LETTERS AND WORKS--3RD. REV. ED.----1879
KUHE, WILHELM
MY MUSICAL RECOLLECTIONS---CHOPIN
LAMOND, FREDERICK ARCHIBALD
MEMOIRS OF FREDERICK LAMOND, THE
LANDOWSKA, WANDA
LANDOWSKA ON MUSIC--EDITED BY DENISE RESTOUT
LEVANT, OSCAR
MEMOIRS OF AN AMNESIAC
LEVANT, OSCAR
SMATTERING OF IGNORANCE, A
LEVANT, OSCAR
UNIMPORTANCE OF BEING OSCAR, THE
LISZT, FRANZ
LETTERS OF FRANZ LISZT--COLLECTED AND EDITED BY LA
LISZT, FRANZ
LETTERS OF FRANZ LISZT TO MARIE ZU SAYN-WITTGENSTEIN, THE
LITZMANN, BERTHOLD
CLARA SCHUMANN..AN ARTIST'S LIFE BASED ON MATERIAL FOUND IN
LOCKE, ROBINSON
BLOOMFIELD-ZEISLER--ROBINSON LOCKE SCRAP BOOKS
LOCKE, ROBINSON
BUSONI--ROBINSON LOCKE SCRAP BOOKS
LOCKE, ROBINSON
GABRILOWITSCH--ROBINSON LOCKE SCRAP BOOKS--2 VOLS.

LOCKE, ROBINSON
    HOFMANN--ROBINSON LOCKE SCRAP BOOKS
LOCKE, ROBINSON
    PADEREWSKI--ROBINSON LOCKE SCRAP BOOKS--2 VOLS.
LOEHR, JOHANN JOSEPH
    ESSAY ON THE THEORY AND PRACTICE OF TUNING, AN ...PIANOFORTES AND
LOGIER, JOHANN BERNHARD
    AUTHENTIC ACCOUNT OF THE EXAMINATION OF PUPILS, INSTRUCTED IN THE
LOGIER, JOHANN BERNHARD
    REFUTATION OF THE FALLACIES AND MISREPRESENTATIONS CONTAINED IN A
LONDON--A COMMITTEE OF PROFESSORS
    EXPOSITION OF THE MUSICAL SYSTEM OF MR. LOGIER..WITH STRICTURES ON
MACDOWELL, MARIAN GRISWOLD
    RANDOM NOTES ON EDWARD MACDOWELL AND HIS MUSIC
MACKENZIE, SIR ALEXANDER
    MUSICIAN'S NARRATIVE, A ---CLARA SCHUMANN, VON BUELOW AND LISZT
MASON, WILLIAM G.
    MEMORIES OF A MUSICAL LIFE
MATHEWS, WILLIAM S. B.
    GREAT IN MUSIC, THE ..A SYSTEMATIC COURSE OF STUDY IN THE MUSIC OF
MATTHEWS, DENIS--EDITOR
    KEYBOARD MUSIC--ESSAYS ON KEYBOARD LITERATURE, EXCLUDING ORGAN
MATTHEWS, DENIS
    IN PURSUIT OF MUSIC
MCCARTHY, ALBERT J.--EDITOR
    PIANO JAZZ..ESSAYS--2 VOLS., 1945-1946
MCDOWELL, LOUISE
    PAST AND PRESENT--A CANADIAN MUSICIAN'S REMINISCENSES
MOORE, GERALD
    AM I TOO LOUD..MEMOIRS OF AN ACCOMPANIST
MOSCHELES, CHARLOTTE
    RECENT MUSIC AND MUSICIANS, AS DESCRIBED IN THE DIARIES AND
NALDER, LAWRENCE MARCUS
    ESSAYS IN PIANOFORTE TECHNOLOGY
NEAL, HARRY LEE
    WAVE AS YOU PASS
NEWTON, IVOR
    AT THE PIANO--IVOR NEWTON..THE WORLD OF AN ACCOMPANIST
OSBORNE, GEORGE A.
    REMINISCENSES OF FREDERIC CHOPIN
PADEREWSKI, IGNACE JAN
    CHOPIN..A DISCOURSE
PADEREWSKI, IGNACE JAN *
    PADEREWSKI MEMOIRS, THE ---1938
PARKER, HENRY T.
    EIGHTH NOTES, VOICES AND FIGURES OF MUSIC AND THE DANCE---CHAPTER
PARKER, RICHARD G.
    TRIBUTE TO THE LIFE AND CHARACTER OF JONAS CHICKERING, 1798-1853,
PETERSON, HOUSTON--EDITOR
    GREAT TEACHERS, PORTRAYED BY THOSE WHO STUDIED UNDER
PHILIPP, ISIDOR
    SOME REFLECTIONS ON PIANO PLAYING
POLISH RESEARCH AND INFORMATION SERVICE
    FREDERIC CHOPIN--CENTENNIAL 1849-1949, BACKGROUND
POLISH RESEARCH AND INFORMATION SERVICE
    FREDERIC CHOPIN CENTENNIAL--1949----EIGHT ARTICLES
PORTE, JOHN F.
    EDWARD MACDOWELL, A GREAT AMERICAN TONE POET..HIS LIFE AND MUSIC
PUGNO, RAOUL
    LESSONS OF RAOUL PUGNO, THE ..WITH A BIOGRAPHY OF CHOPIN BY M.
RACHMANINOFF, SERGEI
    RACHMANINOFF'S RECOLLECTIONS, TOLD TO OSKAR VON RIESEMANN---1934
ROSE, ALGERNON SIDNEY
    A439, BEING THE AUTOBIOGRAPHY OF A PIANO BY 25 MUSICAL
RUBINSTEIN, ANTON
    AUTOBIOGRAPHY OF ANTON RUBINSTEIN, 1829-1889, THE ---1890
RUBINSTEIN, ANTON
    CONVERSATION ON MUSIC, A
RUBINSTEIN, ARTUR
    MY YOUNG YEARS
RYAN, THOMAS
    RECOLLECTIONS OF AN OLD MUSICIAN---GOTTSCHALK, JONAS CHICKERING,
SAINT-SAENS, CAMILLE
    MUSICAL MEMORIES---LISZT
SAMAROFF, OLGA
    AMERICAN MUSICIAN'S STORY, AN
SCHAAF, EDWARD O.
    ESSAYS AND ARTICLES ON MUSICAL SUBJECTS, PARTICULARLY
SCHNABEL, ARTUR
    MUSIC AND THE LINE OF MOST RESISTANCE---1942
SCHNABEL, ARTUR
    MY LIFE AND MUSIC
SCHNABEL, ARTUR
    REFLECTIONS ON MUSIC..A LECTURE---IN ENGLISH AND GERMAN
SCHUMANN, CLARA
    LETTERS OF CLARA SCHUMANN AND JOHANNES BRAHMS, 1853-1896--2
SCHUMANN, EUGENIE
    MEMOIRS OF EUGENIE SCHUMANN---1927
SCHUMANN, FERDINAND
    REMINISCENCES OF CLARA SCHUMANN AS FOUND IN THE DIARY OF HER
SCHUMANN, ROBERT
    ADVICE TO YOUNG MUSICIANS--FROM 'MUSIC AND MUSICIANS'---1876
SCHUMANN, ROBERT
    EARLY LETTERS OF ROBERT SCHUMANN, ORIGINALLY PUBLISHED BY HIS
SCHUMANN, ROBERT
    LETTERS OF ROBERT SCHUMANN, THE --SELECTED AND EDITED BY KARL
SCHUMANN, ROBERT
    LIFE OF ROBERT SCHUMANN TOLD IN HIS LETTERS, THE --2 VOLS.
SCHUYLER, PHILLIPA DUKE
    ADVENTURES IN BLACK AND WHITE--AUTOBIOGRAPHY
SEYMOUR, MARY ALICE IVES
    LIFE AND LETTERS OF LOUIS MOREAU GOTTSCHALK
SHATTUCK, ARTHUR
    MEMOIRS OF ARTHUR SHATTUCK, THE ..WITH AN ACCOUNT OF HIS CAREER BY
SLENCZYNSKA, RUTH *
    FORBIDDEN CHILDHOOD
SMITH, CYRIL
    DUET FOR THREE HANDS...AS TOLD TO JOYCE EGGINTON
STEINERT, MORRIS
    REMINISCENCES OF MORRIS STEINERT, COMPILED AND ARRANGED BY JANE
STEINWAY AND SONS
    PORTRAITS OF MUSICAL CELEBRITIES
STEINWAY AND SONS
    PORTRAITS OF MUSICAL CELEBRITIES
STEINWAY AND SONS
    STEINWAY PROGRESS..AN APPRECIATION BY I. J. PADEREWSKI
STERNBERG, CONSTANTIN I. VON
    TEMPO RUBATO AND OTHER ESSAYS
TARNOWSKI, STANISLAS
    CHOPIN..AS REVEALED BY EXTRACTS FROM HIS DIARY--2ND. ED.---1905
TONK, WILLIAM
    MEMOIRS OF A--PIANO--MANUFACTURER
UPTON, GEORGE P.
    MUSICAL MEMORIES..MY RECOLLECTIONS OF CELEBRITIES OF THE HALF
VERNE, MATHILDE
    CHORDS OF REMEMBRANCE---BY A PUPIL OF CLARA SCHUMANN

WALKER, ALAN--EDITOR
    CHOPIN COMPANION, THE ..PROFILES OF THE MAN AND THE
WALKER, ALAN--EDITOR
    FRANZ LISZT, THE MAN AND HIS MUSIC---ESSAYS BY SACHEVERALL SITWELL
WALKER, BETTINA
    MY MUSICAL EXPERIENCES
WEATHERLY, FREDERICK EDWARD
    PIANO AND GOWN--REMINISCENCES
WEBBE, WILLIAM H.
    PIANOFORTE PLAYING..JOTTINGS BY W. H. WEBBE--2ND. ED.
WESTERBY, HERBERT
    LISZT, COMPOSER, AND HIS PIANO WORKS..DESCRIPTIVE GUIDE AND
WOHL, JANKA
    FRANCOIS LISZT..RECOLLECTIONS OF A COMPATRIOT
WOLFF, ERNST VICTOR
    WITH REASON AND RHYME
WOOD, CHARLES W.
    LETTERS FROM MAJORCA---CHOPIN--NUMEROUS ILLUSTRATIONS
WULSIN, LUCIEN
    DWIGHT HAMILTON BALDWIN AND THE BALDWIN PIANO
YOUFF, ULV
    ULVEN, WRITTEN DURING RETIREMENT IN SWITZERLAND--AUTOBIOGRAPHY OF

Critical Review

ANDERSON, WILLIAM P.
    MUSIC AS A CAREER
ANON
    GENERAL OBSERVATIONS ON MUSIC AND REMARKS ON MR. LOGIER'S SYSTEM
BROWER, HARRIETTE
    WHAT TO PLAY--WHAT TO TEACH
COHEN, HARRIET
    MUSIC'S HANDMAID
CORTOT, ALFRED
    IN SEARCH OF CHOPIN
DIDIMUS, HENRY
    BIOGRAPHY OF LEOPOLD DE MEYER...ROYAL COURT PIANIST...TO THEIR
EHRENFECTER, C. A.
    TECHNICAL STUDY IN THE ART OF PIANOFORTE PLAYING--DEPPE'S
EICHBERG, OSCAR
    ANALYTICAL AND HISTORICAL REMARKS ON ANTON RUBINSTEIN'S CYCLE OF
GRAHAM, GEORGE FARQUHAR
    GENERAL OBSERVATIONS UPON MUSIC AND REMARKS ON MR. LOGIER'S SYSTEM
HALLE, SIR CHARLES
    ST. JAMES HALL...C. HALLE'S PIANOFORTE RECITALS..MAY 5-JUNE 29,
HALLE, SIR CHARLES
    ST. JAMES HALL...MR. HALLE'S BEETHOVEN RECITALS, MAY 23-JULY 11,
HARRISON, SIDNEY
    TEACHER NEVER TOLD ME--TIPS FOR STUDENTS
KLECZYNSKI, JAN
    HOW TO PLAY CHOPIN--THREE LECTURES
LEVINSKAYA, MARIA
    LEVINSKAYA SYSTEM OF PIANOFORTE TECHNIC AND TONE COLOR, THE
LONDON--A COMMITTEE OF PROFESSORS
    EXPOSITION OF THE MUSICAL SYSTEM OF MR. LOGIER..WITH STRICTURES ON
MONTI, H. DE
    STRICTURES ON MR. LOGIER'S SYSTEM OF MUSICAL EDUCATION
PLANTIGA, LEON B.
    SCHUMANN AS CRITIC
SCHULTZ, ARNOLD
    RIDDLE OF THE PIANIST'S FINGER, THE
SCHUMANN, ROBERT
    ON MUSIC AND MUSICIANS---1854, IN GERMAN--FIRST ENGLISH EDITION IN
SMITH, JULIA
    MASTER PIANIST..THE CAREER AND TEACHING OF CARL FRIEDBERG
STOOKES, SACHA
    ART OF ROBERT CASADESUS, THE
SZABOLCSI, BENCE
    TWILIGHT OF F. LISZT, THE

Interviews

BASTIEN, JAMES W.
    HOW TO TEACH PIANO SUCCESSFULLY
BRIGGS, GILBERT A.
    PIANOS, PIANISTS AND SONICS
BROWER, HARRIETTE
    MODERN MASTERS OF THE KEYBOARD
BROWER, HARRIETTE
    PIANO MASTERY..TALKS WITH MASTER PIANISTS AND TEACHERS...
BROWER, HARRIETTE
    PIANO MASTERY, SECOND SERIES
CHASINS, ABRAM
    SPEAKING OF PIANISTS
COOKE, JAMES FRANCIS
    GREAT MEN AND FAMOUS MUSICIANS ON THE ART OF MUSIC
COOKE, JAMES FRANCIS
    GREAT PIANISTS ON PIANO PLAYING..STUDY TALKS WITH FOREMOST
GAVOTY, BERNARD *
    ALFRED CORTOT
GAVOTY, BERNARD *
    ARTHUR RUBINSTEIN
KENYON, CHARLES FREDERICK
    IMAGINARY INTERVIEWS WITH GREAT COMPOSERS..A SERIES OF VIVID PEN
ROSTAND, CLAUDE
    LISZT
SALESKI, GDAL
    FAMOUS MUSICIANS OF JEWISH ORIGIN
STRELEZKI, ANTON
    PERSONAL RECOLLECTIONS OF CHATS WITH LISZT, IN 1869---1893

Keyboard Instruments

General

AEOLIAN COMPANY, THE
    SPECIAL SURVEY CONDUCTED--IN 1889--FOR LYON AND HEALY, INC.,
AHRENS, CORA B. *
    FOR ALL PIANO TEACHERS
AMERICAN NEWS COMPANY
    ROMANCE OF A PIANO, THE
APEL, WILLI
    HISTORY OF KEYBOARD MUSIC TO 1700, THE --TRANSLATED AND REVISED BY
APEL, WILLI
    MASTERS OF THE KEYBOARD
BAMBERGER, LOUIS
    MEMORIES OF SIXTY YEARS IN THE TIMBER AND PIANOFORTE TRADES
BRAGARD, ROGER
    MUSICAL INSTRUMENTS IN ART AND HISTORY
BRINSMEAD, E.
    HISTORY OF THE PIANOFORTE, THE ..WITH AN AN ACCOUNT OF THE THEORY
BROADWOOD, JOHN AND SONS
    PIANOFORTES..WITH USEFUL AND INTERESTING INFORMATION CONCERNING

BUNGER, RICHARD
    WELL-PREPARED PIANO, THE
BYERLY, DOROTHEA J.
    ADVENTURES OF PETER THE PIANO, THE ..AN ILLUSTRATED STORY FOR
DONALDSON, GEORGE
    CATALOGUE OF THE MUSICAL INSTRUMENTS AND OBJECTS FORMING THE
FOX, LILLA M.
    INSTRUMENTS OF POPULAR MUSIC..A HISTORY OF MUSICAL
GALPIN, FRANCIS W.
    OLD ENGLISH INSTRUMENTS OF MUSIC--4TH. ED.---1910
GALPIN, FRANCIS W.
    TEXTBOOK OF EUROPEAN MUSICAL INSTRUMENTS, A ---1937
HARICH-SCHNEIDER, ETA
    HARPSICHORD, THE ..AN INTRODUCTION TO TECHNIQUE, STYLE AND THE
HIPKINS, ALFRED JAMES
    DESCRIPTION AND HISTORY OF THE PIANOFORTE AND OLDER KEYBOARD
HIRT, FRANZ JOSEF
    STRINGED KEYBOARD INSTRUMENTS 1440-1880---1955, IN GERMAN
HUBBARD, FRANK
    HARPSICHORD REGULATING AND REPAIRING
HUBBARD, FRANK
    THREE CENTURIES OF HARPSICHORD MAKING
LOESSER, ARTHUR
    MEN, WOMEN AND PIANOS..A SOCIAL HISTORY
MOOR, WINIFRED
    TECHNICAL EXERCISES FOR THE EMANUEL MOOR DOUBLE KEYBOARD
PRESTO PUBLISHING COMPANY
    PRESTO BUYERS' GUIDE TO PLAYER-PIANOS AND PIANOS
REED, MARY G.
    KEYBOARD ROAD IN MUSIC LAND, AND OTHER STORIES---FOR CHILDREN
REMBUSCH, JOSEPH ADAM
    PIANOS AND MUSICAL INSTRUMENTS DISCUSSED FROM AN UNSANITARY
RIEMANN, HUGO
    CATECHISM OF PIANOFORTE PLAYING---1888, IN GERMAN
SQUIRE, RUSSEL N. *
    CLASS PIANO FOR ADULT BEGINNERS--2ND. ED.---1964
STANLEY, ALBERT A.
    CATALOGUE OF THE STEARNS COLLECTION OF MUSICAL INSTRUMENTS
TRAVIS, JOHN W.
    LET'S TUNE UP
WEISER, BERNHARD D.
    KEYBOARD MUSIC--16TH.-20TH. CENTURIES
WILSON, ROBINA BECKLES
    MUSICAL INSTRUMENTS--THE 'BYWAYS LIBRARY'
WRIGHT, WILLIAM C.
    PIANOFORTE MANUAL, THE ..DESIGNED AS A COMPLETE PIANOFORTE PRIMER

Miscellaneous

AMERICAN NEWS COMPANY
    ROMANCE OF A PIANO, THE
ANON
    DIGITORIUM, THE --MINIATURE DUMB PIANO
ANON
    OLD PIANO, THE ..A FANTASIA, WITH VARIATIONS HIGH FANTASTICAL,
ANON
    PIANO LOVER, THE ..BY VARIOUS AUTHORS
APEL, WILLI
    MASTERS OF THE KEYBOARD
BRAGARD, ROGER
    MUSICAL INSTRUMENTS IN ART AND HISTORY
BRINSMEAD, E.
    HISTORY OF THE PIANOFORTE, THE ..WITH AN AN ACCOUNT OF THE THEORY
BROADWOOD, JAMES SHUDI
    SOME NOTES--ON THE HARPSICHORD AND PIANOFORTE--MADE BY J. S.
BROADWOOD, JOHN AND SONS
    CATALOGUE OF JOHN BROADWOOD AND SONS, LTD. LATEST MODELS,
BROADWOOD, JOHN AND SONS
    PIANOFORTES..WITH USEFUL AND INTERESTING INFORMATION CONCERNING
DARBYSHIRE, JOHN H.
    CONSTANT K--18600, THE ..ITS USE IN THEORY AND PRACTICE
DOLGE, ALFRED
    PIANOS AND THEIR MAKERS..A COMPREHENSIVE HISTORY OF THE
GLYN, MARGARET H.
    NATIONAL SCHOOL OF VIRGINAL MUSIC IN ELIZABETHAN TIMES, THE
HARICH-SCHNEIDER, ETA
    HARPSICHORD, THE ..AN INTRODUCTION TO TECHNIQUE, STYLE AND THE
HIPKINS, ALFRED JAMES
    DESCRIPTION AND HISTORY OF THE PIANOFORTE AND OLDER KEYBOARD
HIRT, FRANZ JOSEF
    STRINGED KEYBOARD INSTRUMENTS 1440-1880---1955, IN GERMAN
LOESSER, ARTHUR
    MEN, WOMEN AND PIANOS..A SOCIAL HISTORY
NALDER, LAWRENCE MARCUS
    FIRST STEPS IN PIANO TUNING AND OTHER ESSAYS IN PIANOFORTE
ORD-HUME, ARTHUR W. J. G.
    PLAYER PIANO, THE HISTORY OF THE MECHANICAL PIANO AND HOW TO
VAN NOORDEN, C.
    FREAK PIANOS---SCRAPBOOK
WING AND SONS
    BOOK OF COMPLETE INFORMATION ABOUT PIANOS, THE ...1868-1918, A

History

ADLER, KURT
    ART OF ACCOMPANYING AND COACHING, THE ---1965
AEOLIAN COMPANY, THE
    PIANOLA PIANO, THE
ALBARDA, JAN H.
    WOOD, WIRE AND QUILL..AN INTRODUCTION TO THE HARPSICHORD
AMERICAN PHOTO PLAYER COMPANY
    INSTALLATION, CARE AND OPERATION OF THE PHOTOPLAYER---1920+
AMERICAN PIANO CORPORATION
    AMPICO REPRODUCING PIANO, INSPECTOR'S REFERENCE BOOK, THE ---1923
AMERICAN PIANO CORPORATION
    AMPICO REPRODUCING PIANO, THE ..INSPECTOR'S INSTRUCTION BOOK,
AMERICAN STEEL AND WIRE COMPANY
    NERVES OF STEEL..THE STORY OF AMERICAN PIANO WIRE AND ITS
ANON
    HOW TO TUNE YOUR OWN PIANOFORTE..OR, THE WAY TO KEEP YOUR
APEL, WILLI
    HISTORY OF KEYBOARD MUSIC TO 1700, THE --TRANSLATED AND REVISED BY
BADURA-SKODA, EVA *
    INTERPRETING MOZART ON THE KEYBOARD---1957, IN GERMAN
BAINES, ANTHONY
    EUROPEAN AND AMERICAN MUSICAL INSTRUMENTS
BAINES, ANTHONY
    MUSICAL INSTRUMENTS THROUGH THE AGES--REV. ED.---1961
BALLANTINE, BILL
    PIANO, THE ..AN INTRODUCTION TO THE INSTRUMENT
BARTHOLOMEW, RALPH T.
    MAKING OF A STEINWAY, THE
BESSARABOFF, NICHOLAS
    ANCIENT EUROPEAN MUSICAL INSTRUMENTS...IN THE LESLIE LINDSAY MASON

BIE, OSKAR
    HISTORY OF THE PIANOFORTE AND PIANOFORTE PLAYERS, A ---1899
BLOM, ERIC
    ROMANCE OF THE PIANO, THE ---1928
BOALCH, DONALD HOWARD
    MAKERS OF THE HARPSICHORD AND CLAVICHORD, 1440 TO 1840
BODDINGTON, HENRY
    CATALOGUE OF MUSICAL INSTRUMENTS, PRINCIPALLY ILLUSTRATIVE OF THE
BODKY, ERWIN
    INTERPRETATION OF BACH'S KEYBOARD WORKS, THE
BORREN, CHARLES VAN DEN
    SOURCES OF KEYBOARD MUSIC IN ENGLAND, THE ---1913
BRAGARD, ROGER
    MUSICAL INSTRUMENTS IN ART AND HISTORY
BRIGGS, GILBERT A.
    MUSICAL INSTRUMENTS AND AUDIO
BRIGGS, GILBERT A.
    PIANOS, PIANISTS AND SONICS
BRINSMEAD, E.
    HISTORY OF THE PIANOFORTE, THE ..WITH AN AN ACCOUNT OF THE THEORY
BROADWOOD, JAMES SHUDI
    SOME NOTES--ON THE HARPSICHORD AND PIANOFORTE--MADE BY J. S.
BROADWOOD, JOHN AND SONS
    CATALOGUE OF JOHN BROADWOOD AND SONS, LTD. LATEST MODELS,
BROADWOOD, JOHN AND SONS
    PIANOFORTES..WITH USEFUL AND INTERESTING INFORMATION CONCERNING
BUCHNER, ALEXANDER
    MUSICAL INSTRUMENTS THROUGH THE AGES
CASTELLINI, JOHN EDWARD
    RUDIMENTS OF MUSIC..A NEW APPROACH WITH APPLICATION TO THE
CHAPIN, VICTOR
    GIANTS OF THE KEYBOARD
CHICKERING AND SONS
    ACHIEVEMENT..AN ASCENDING SCALE, BEING A SHORT HISTORY OF THE
CHICKERING AND SONS
    CHICKERING CENTENNIAL CELEBRATION, APRIL 1823-1923
CHICKERING AND SONS
    JONAS CHICKERING CENTENNIAL CELEBRATION, 1823-1923..IN
CLEMENCIC, RENE
    OLD MUSICAL INSTRUMENTS
CLOSSON, ERNEST
    HISTORY OF THE PIANO
CURCIO, LOUISE
    SINGLE NOTE, THE
DALE, KATHLEEN
    NINETEENTH CENTURY PIANO MUSIC, A HANDBOOK FOR PIANISTS
DARLOW, DENYS
    MUSICAL INSTRUMENTS--JUNIOR REFERENCE BOOKS, NO. 12--2ND. ED.
DART, THURSTON
    INTERPRETATION OF MUSIC, THE --4TH. ED.---1954
DAVIS, LIONEL
    KEYBOARD INSTRUMENTS..THE STORY OF THE PIANO---YOUNGER READERS
DENSMORE, FRANCES
    HANDBOOK OF THE COLLECTION OF MUSICAL INSTRUMENTS IN THE UNITED
DOLGE, ALFRED
    PIANOS AND THEIR MAKERS..A COMPREHENSIVE HISTORY OF THE
DOLMETSCH, ARNOLD
    INTERPRETATION OF MUSIC OF THE SEVENTEENTH AND EIGHTEENTH
DONINGTON, ROBERT
    INSTRUMENTS OF MUSIC, THE --3RD. REV. ED.---1949
DUFFEE, GERTRUDE BANKS
    PIANO STUDY..A GUIDE TO TEACHER AND STUDENT
EDINBURGH UNIVERSITY--DEPT. OF EARLY KEYBOARD INSTRUMENTS
    RUSSELL COLLECTION AND OTHER EARLY KEYBOARD INSTRUMENTS IN ST.
EISENBERG, JACOB
    LET ME HELP YOU, MY ANCESTORS AND I..A COMPREHENSIVE JUVENILE
EISENBERG, JACOB
    ROMANCE OF KEYS AND TONES..THE PIANO, ITS ORIGIN AND DEVELOPMENT,
ELLINGHAM, HARRY
    HOW TO USE A PLAYER-PIANO
ENGEL, CARL
    MUSICAL INSTRUMENTS--REV. ED.---1876
ENGEL, CARL
    PIANIST'S HANDBOOK, THE ..A GUIDE FOR THE RIGHT COMPREHENSION AND
FISCHER, JERRY CREE
    PIANO TUNING, REGULATING AND REPAIRING...SELF INSTRUCTION...FOR
FOX, LILLA M.
    INSTRUMENTS OF POPULAR MUSIC..A HISTORY OF MUSICAL
GABRY, GYORGY
    OLD MUSICAL INSTRUMENTS
GALPIN, FRANCIS W.
    OLD ENGLISH INSTRUMENTS OF MUSIC--4TH. ED.---1910
GALPIN, FRANCIS W.
    TEXTBOOK OF EUROPEAN MUSICAL INSTRUMENTS, A ---1937
GARRATT, PERCIVAL
    ART OF PIANOFORTE PLAYING, THE
GATES, WILLEY F.
    PIPE AND STRINGS..THREE HISTORIC AND DESCRIPTIVE SKETCHES...THE
GEIRINGER, KARL
    MUSICAL INSTRUMENTS, THEIR HISTORY IN WESTERN CULTURE FROM THE
GILLESPIE, JOHN
    FIVE CENTURIES OF KEYBOARD MUSIC..AN HISTORIC SURVEY FOR
GLOVER, ELLYE HOWELL
    HOW THE PIANO CAME TO BE
GUENTHER, FELIX
    PIANO AND ITS ANCESTORS, THE
HAMILTON, CLARENCE G.
    PIANO MUSIC, ITS COMPOSERS AND CHARACTERISTICS
HARDING, ROSAMUND
    PIANOFORTE, THE ..ITS HISTORY TRACED TO THE GREAT EXHIBITION OF
HENDERSON, WILLIAM JAMES
    EVOLUTION OF THE PIANO, THE
HENDERSON, WILLIAM JAMES
    PRELUDES AND STUDIES..MUSICAL THEMES OF THE DAY--SECTION 3..THE
HINDLEY, GEOFFREY
    MUSICAL INSTRUMENTS
HIPKINS, ALFRED JAMES
    DESCRIPTION AND HISTORY OF THE PIANOFORTE AND OLDER KEYBOARD
HIPKINS, ALFRED JAMES
    HISTORY OF THE PIANOFORTE, THE --REPRINT
HIPKINS, ALFRED JAMES
    MUSICAL INSTRUMENTS, HISTORIC, RARE AND UNIQUE---1888
HIRT, FRANZ JOSEF
    STRINGED KEYBOARD INSTRUMENTS 1440-1880---1955, IN GERMAN
HOOVER, CYNTHIA A.
    HARPSICHORDS AND CLAVICHORDS
HORNIMAN MUSEUM AND LIBRARY, LONDON
    HANDBOOK TO THE MUSEUM'S COLLECTION, BY JEAN L. JENKINS--2ND.
HORNIMAN MUSEUM AND LIBRARY, LONDON
    MUSICAL INSTRUMENTS
HUBBARD, ELBERT
    STORY OF THE STEINWAYS, THE --REPRINT FROM 'FRA' MAGAZINE
HUBBARD, FRANK
    HARPSICHORD REGULATING AND REPAIRING
HUBBARD, FRANK
    THREE CENTURIES OF HARPSICHORD MAKING

HUNEKER, JAMES GIBBONS
 DEVELOPMENT OF PIANO MUSIC FROM THE DAYS OF THE CLAVICHORD AND
JAMES, PHILIP BRUTTON
 EARLY KEYBOARD INSTRUMENTS, FROM THEIR BEGINNINGS TO THE YEAR
KELLEY, EDGAR STILLMAN
 MUSICAL INSTRUMENTS--3RD. YEAR OF A STUDY COURSE IN MUSIC
KENDALL, ALAN
 WORLD OF MUSICAL INSTRUMENTS, THE ---CHIEFLY ILLUSTRATIONS
KENYON, MAX
 HARPSICHORD MUSIC..THE INSTRUMENTS, THE COMPOSERS, THE PLAYERS
KINSKY, GEORG--EDITOR
 HISTORY OF MUSIC IN PICTURES, A
KIRBY, FRANK EUGENE
 SHORT HISTORY OF KEYBOARD MUSIC, A
KOCHEVITSKY, GEORGE
 ART OF PIANO PLAYING, THE ..A SCIENTIFIC APPROACH
KREHBIEL, HENRY
 PIANOFORTE AND ITS MUSIC, THE ---1911
LANDOWSKA, WANDA
 LANDOWSKA ON MUSIC--EDITED BY DENISE RESTOUT
LAVIGNAC, ALBERT
 MUSIC AND MUSICIANS---1895, IN FRENCH
LOESCHMANN, DAVID
 DESCRIPTION AND USE OF THE PATENT ENHARMONIC PIANOFORTE
LOESSER, ARTHUR
 MEN, WOMEN AND PIANOS..A SOCIAL HISTORY
LYONS, SISTER MARIE STEPHEN
 REAWAKENING OF INTEREST IN THE HARPSICHORD IN THE 20TH. CENTURY,
MACQUOID, PERCY *
 DICTIONARY OF ENGLISH FURNITURE, THE --VOL. 3---16 ILLUSTRATIONS
MARKS, ADOLF B.
 INTRODUCTION TO THE INTERPRETATION OF BEETHOVEN'S PIANO-FORTE
MARX, ADOLF BERNHARD
 INTRODUCTION TO THE INTERPRETATION OF BEETHOVEN'S PIANO
MASON, HENRY LOWELL
 HOW HAS THE PIANOFORTE AS AN INSTRUMENT DEVELOPED SINCE
MCTAMMANY, JOHN
 EVOLUTION OF THE PLAYER-PIANO MECHANISM---EXCERPT FROM 'PRESTO',
MCTAMMANY, JOHN
 HISTORY OF THE PLAYER-PIANO, THE
MCTAMMANY, JOHN
 TECHNICAL HISTORY OF THE PLAYER
METROPOLITAN MUSEUM OF ART, NEW YORK
 CATALOGUE OF THE CROSBY BROWN COLLECTION OF MUSICAL INSTRUMENTS OF
METROPOLITAN MUSEUM OF ART, NEW YORK
 KEYBOARD INSTRUMENTS IN THE METROPOLITAN MUSEUM OF ART..A PICTURE
MICHEL, NORMAN ELWOOD
 HISTORICAL PIANOS, HARPSICHORDS AND CLAVICHORDS---1963
MICHEL, NORMAN ELWOOD
 MICHEL'S PIANO ATLAS---REPUBLISHED IN 1965 UNDER AUTHORSHIP..B.
MICHEL, NORMAN ELWOOD
 OLD PIANOS
NEUPERT, HANNS
 CLAVICHORD, THE ---1956, IN GERMAN
NEUPERT, HANNS
 HARPSICHORD MANUAL..A HISTORY AND TECHNICAL DEVELOPMENT--2ND.
NEWMAN, WILLIAM S.
 SONATA IN THE BAROQUE ERA, THE --A HISTORY OF THE SONATA IDEA,
NEWMAN, WILLIAM S.
 SONATA IN THE CLASSIC ERA, THE --A HISTORY OF THE SONATA IDEA,
O'NEILL, J. A.
 DESCRIPTION AND HISTORY OF THE PIANOFORTE, A
ORD-HUME, ARTHUR W. J. G.
 CLOCKWORK MUSIC..AN ILLUSTRATED HISTORY OF MECHANICAL MUSICAL
ORD-HUME, ARTHUR W.
 PLAYER PIANO, THE HISTORY OF THE MECHANICAL PIANO AND HOW TO
PAGE, C. E.
 MUSICAL INSTRUMENTS--MECHANICAL AGE LIBRARY
PARRISH, CARL
 EARLY PIANO AND ITS INFLUENCE ON KEYBOARD TECHNIQUE AND
PELZ, EDWARD
 ON PIANOFORTE MANUFACTURE, ESPECIALLY IN AMERICA
PENGELLY, J. BRADFORD
 PENGELLY BLUE BOOK OF STYLE, THE ...A STUDY OF THE ART OF STYLING
PETERSON, FRANKLIN
 THEORETIC COMPANION TO PRACTICE--PART I OF THE PIANIST'S HANDBOOK
PINCHERLE, MARC
 WORLD OF THE VIRTUOSO, THE
PULVER, JEFFREY
 DICTIONARY OF OLD ENGLISH MUSIC AND MUSICAL INSTRUMENTS, A
REEDER, BETAH
 SINGING TOUCH, THE
RHODES, ALFRED
 CURIOSITIES OF THE KEY-BOARD AND THE STAFF...SHOWN TO BE UPON A
RICHNER, THOMAS
 ORIENTATION FOR INTERPRETING MOZART'S PIANO SONATAS
RIEFLING, REIMAR
 PIANO PEDALLING---1957, IN NORWEGIAN
RIMBAULT, EDWARD FRANCIS
 PIANOFORTE, THE ..ITS ORIGIN, PROCESS AND CONSTRUCTION
RIPIN, EDWIN M.--EDITOR
 KEYBOARD INSTRUMENTS..STUDIES IN KEYBOARD ORGANOLOGY---10 ESSAYS
ROEHL, HARVEY
 KEYS TO A MUSICAL PAST...ILLUSTRATED TREATISE ON THE VARIOUS TYPES
ROEHL, HARVEY
 PLAYER PIANO, AN HISTORICAL SCRAPBOOK, THE
ROEHL, HARVEY
 PLAYER PIANO TREASURY..THE SCRAPBOOK HISTORY OF THE MECHANICAL
RUBINSTEIN, ANTON
 CONVERSATION ON MUSIC, A
RUSSELL, RAYMOND
 EARLY KEYBOARD INSTRUMENTS--VICTORIA AND ALBERT MUSEUM..'SMALL
RUSSELL, RAYMOND
 HARPSICHORD AND THE CLAVICHORD, THE --2ND. ED., REVISED BY HOWARD
SACHS, CURT
 EVOLUTION OF PIANO MUSIC, 1350-1700, THE
SACHS, CURT
 HISTORY OF MUSICAL INSTRUMENTS, THE
SCHOTT, HOWARD
 PLAYING THE HARPSICHORD
SCHULZE, RICHARD ALLEN
 HOW TO BUILD A BAROQUE CONCERT HARPSICHORD
SKINNER, BELLE
 BELLE SKINNER COLLECTION OF OLD MUSICAL INSTRUMENTS, HOLYOKE,
SMITH, FANNY MORRIS
 NOBLE ART, A ..THREE LECTURES ON THE EVOLUTION AND CONSTRUCTION OF
SOUTH KENSINGTON MUSEUM, LONDON
 DESCRIPTIVE CATALOGUE OF THE MUSICAL INSTRUMENTS IN THE SOUTH
SOUTH KENSINGTON MUSEUM, LONDON
 DESCRIPTIVE CATALOGUE OF THE MUSICAL INSTRUMENTS IN THE SOUTH
SPILLANE, DANIEL
 HISTORY OF THE AMERICAN PIANOFORTE..ITS TECHNICAL DEVELOPMENT, AND
STANLEY, ALBERT A.
 CATALOGUE OF THE STEARNS COLLECTION OF MUSICAL INSTRUMENTS
STEGLICH, RUDOLF
 MOZARTS FLUEGEL KLINGT WIEDER--MOZART'S PIANO SOUNDS AGAIN---WITH

STEINERT, MORRIS
 MORRIS STEINERT COLLECTION OF KEYED AND STRINGED INSTRUMENTS, THE
STEINWAY, THEODORE E.
 PEOPLE AND PIANOS..A CENTURY OF SERVICE TO MUSIC---1853-1953
STEINWAY AND SONS
 ILLUSTRATED CIRCULAR AND CATALOGUE OF PIANOFORTES--MANUFACTURERS
STEINWAY AND SONS
 PIANOFORTES
STEINWAY AND SONS
 STEINWAY..YESTERDAY, TODAY, TOMORROW
STEINWAY AND SONS
 STEINWAY OF TODAY, THE ..A FAMILY OF PIANO MANUFACTURERS THROUGH
STEVENS, FLOYD A.
 COMPLETE COURSE IN PROFESSIONAL PIANO TUNING, REPAIR, AND
STEVENS, PARAN
 REPORT UPON MUSICAL INSTRUMENTS..PARIS UNIVERSAL EXPOSITION, 1867
STODDARD, HOPE
 FROM THESE COMES MUSIC
STRAUCH BROTHERS
 MANUFACTURE OF PIANOFORTE ACTION, THE ..ITS RISE AND DEVELOPMENT
SUMNER, WILLIAM L.
 PIANOFORTE, THE --3RD. ED.---1966
TANKARD, GEOFFREY
 PIANOFORTE DIPLOMAS
TRAVIS, JOHN W.
 LET'S TUNE UP
VAN NOORDEN, C.
 FREAK PIANOS---SCRAPBOOK
VICTORIA AND ALBERT MUSEUM, SOUTH KENSINGTON
 EXAMPLES OF ART WORKMANSHIP OF VARIOUS AGES AND COUNTRIES..MUSICAL
VICTORIA AND ALBERT MUSEUM, SOUTH KENSINGTON
 MUSICAL INSTRUMENTS AS WORKS OF ART..VOL. 1, KEYBOARD
WALKER, ADAM
 PHILOSOPHY OF THE HARPSICHORD, EXPLAINING HOW THAT INSTRUMENT IS
WEITZMANN, CARL F.
 HISTORY OF PIANOFORTE-PLAYING AND PIANOFORTE-LITERATURE, A
WESTERBY, HERBERT
 HISTORY OF THE PIANOFORTE
WHITE, WILLIAM BRAID
 PIANO PLAYING MECHANISMS
WHITE, WILLIAM BRAID
 PLAYER-PIANO UP TO DATE, THE
WHITE, WILLIAM BRAID
 THEORY AND PRACTICE OF PIANOFORTE BUILDING
WIER, ALBERT
 PIANO, THE ..ITS HISTORY, MAKERS, PLAYERS AND MUSIC
WILSON, DAVID M.
 INSTRUCTION BOOK ON THE PIANO-PLAYER AND PLAYER-PIANO, AN
WILSON, DAVID M.
 PLAYER-PIANO, THE ..ITS CONSTRUCTION..HOW TO PLAY, WHAT TO PLAY
WING AND SONS
 BOOK OF COMPLETE INFORMATION ABOUT PIANOS, THE ...1868-1918, A
WINTERNITZ, EMANUEL
 MUSICAL INSTRUMENTS AND THEIR SYMBOLISM IN WESTERN ART
WINTERNITZ, EMANUEL
 MUSICAL INSTRUMENTS OF THE WESTERN WORLD
WOLFRAM, VICTOR
 SOSTENUTO PEDAL, THE
WORCH, HUGO
 PIANO MAKERS OF THE EVOLUTIONARY PERIOD..RARE ENGLISH AND AMERICAN
WORCH, HUGO
 WORCH PIANOS, AND A BRIEF SKETCH OF THE PIANOFORTE
YATES, PETER
 AMATEUR AT THE KEYBOARD, AN
YOUNG, PERCY M.
 KEYBOARD MUSICIANS OF THE WORLD
ZUCKERMANN, WOLFGANG JOACHIM
 MODERN HARPSICHORD, THE ..TWENTIETH CENTURY INSTRUMENTS AND THEIR

Selection

AEOLIAN COMPANY, THE
 CATALOG OF THE AEOLIAN
AEOLIAN COMPANY, THE
 PIANOLA PIANO, THE
ANON
 HUMANISTIC STUDIES IN HONOR OF JOHN CALVIN METCALF---INCLUDES
BABBINGTON, CHARLES
 TUNING AND REPAIRING PIANOFORTES..THE AMATEURS GUIDE--2ND. ED.
BRIED, FREDERICK
 STIMULATION IN PIANO STUDY..HOW PARENTS CAN STIMULATE AND MAINTAIN
BRIGGS, GILBERT A.
 PIANOS, PIANISTS AND SONICS
BROADWOOD, JOHN AND SONS
 INFORMATION CONCERNING PIANOFORTES OF USE AND OF INTEREST..A VADE
CARY, MRS. C. S. P.
 PIANO-FORTE CLASS BOOK, CONTAINING PRACTICAL RUDIMENTAL LESSONS
CHICKERING AND SONS
 HISTORICAL MUSICAL EXHIBITION..CATALOGUE OF THE EXHIBITION,
CHICKERING AND SONS
 ILLUSTRATED CATALOGUE OF PIANO FORTES
DOLGE, ALFRED
 PIANOS AND THEIR MAKERS..A COMPREHENSIVE HISTORY OF THE
ELLINGHAM, HARRY
 HOW TO USE A PLAYER-PIANO
EPWORTH PIANOS
 BOOK ABOUT PIANOS IN GENERAL AND THE EPWORTH IN PARTICULAR, A
FINNEGAN, BILL
 PIANO FACTS
FUNKE, OTTO
 PIANO AND HOW TO CARE FOR IT, THE ..PIANO TUNING IN THEORY AND
GEPPERT, WILLIAM
 OFFICIAL GUIDE TO PIANO QUALITY, THE ---4TH. ED.
GOULD, BRIAN M.
 BUYING A SQUARE PIANO
HARDING, ROSAMUND
 PIANOFORTE, THE ..ITS HISTORY TRACED TO THE GREAT EXHIBITION OF
HARRIS, REGINALD
 HOW TO CHOOSE AN INSTRUMENT..PIANO AND STRINGS
HARRISON, SIDNEY
 YOUNG PERSON'S GUIDE TO PLAYING THE PIANO, THE
HASLUCK, PAUL N.
 PIANOS..THEIR CONSTRUCTION, TUNING AND REPAIR
HOBBS, HENRY
 PIANO IN INDIA, THE ..HOW TO KEEP IT IN ORDER, PRACTICAL
HOWE, ALFRED H.
 SCIENTIFIC PIANO TUNING AND SERVICING--REV. ED.---1941
KRUSZYNSKI, MICHAL
 APPROACH TO THE PSYCHOLOGY OF PIANO TEACHING, AN
LEVINE, JACK *
 UNDERSTANDING MUSICAL INSTRUMENTS..HOW TO SELECT YOUR
LEVINE, JACK
 WHAT MUSICAL INSTRUMENT FOR ME
MATTHAY, TOBIAS A.
 ACT OF TOUCH IN ALL ITS DIVERSITY, THE ..AN ANALYSIS AND SYNTHESIS

MATTHAY, TOBIAS A.
    PIANOFORTE TONE-PRODUCTION---SAME AS 'THE ACT OF TOUCH IN ALL ITS
MCFERRIN, CHARLES BETTEYS
    MOTHER'S PART IN HER CHILD'S MUSICAL EDUCATION, A ..OR, THE THINGS
NALDER, LAWRENCE MARCUS
    ESSAYS IN PIANOFORTE TECHNOLOGY
PAETKAU, DAVID H.
    GROWTH OF INSTRUMENTS AND INSTRUMENTAL MUSIC, THE
PALMER, KING
    TEACH YOURSELF TO PLAY THE PIANO
PHILLIPSON, WENTWORTH
    GUIDE TO YOUNG PIANOFORTE TEACHERS AND STUDENTS
PLAYER-PIANO, THE
    FOUR HUNDRED OF THE BEST ADS OF 1911 DEVOTED TO PIANOS AND
PRESTO--EDITORIAL STAFF
    MUSICAL INSTRUMENTS AT THE WORLD'S COLUMBIAN EXPOSITION, CHICAGO,
PRESTO PUBLISHING COMPANY
    PRESTO BUYERS' GUIDE TO PLAYER-PIANOS AND PIANOS
RICKER, EARL
    MUSIC LESSONS FOR YOUR CHILD
ROEHL, HARVEY
    KEYS TO A MUSICAL PAST...ILLUSTRATED TREATISE ON THE VARIOUS TYPES
ROEHL, HARVEY
    PLAYER PIANO, AN HISTORICAL SCRAPBOOK, THE
ROSE, ALGERNON SIDNEY
    ON CHOOSING A PIANO
SCHMECKEL, CARL D.
    PIANO OWNER'S GUIDE, THE
SCHOTT, HOWARD
    PLAYING THE HARPSICHORD
SCOTT, MARY M.
    WHAT CAN I PLAY..A BOOK ABOUT MUSICAL INSTRUMENTS
SEROFF, VICTOR
    COMMON SENSE IN PIANO STUDY
SMITH, FANNY MORRIS
    NOBLE ART, A ..THREE LECTURES ON THE EVOLUTION AND CONSTRUCTION OF
STECK AND COMPANY
    ILLUSTRATED CATALOG...GRAND AND UPRIGHT PIANOS
STEINWAY AND SONS
    BOOK OF ART PIANO CASES
STEINWAY AND SONS
    ILLUSTRATED CATALOGUE OF--STEINWAY AND SONS...PIANOFORTES
STEINWAY AND SONS
    ILLUSTRATED CATALOGUE OF PIANOS
STEINWAY AND SONS
    ILLUSTRATED CATALOGUE OF STEINWAY AND SONS' PIANOS
STEINWAY AND SONS
    ILLUSTRATED CIRCULAR AND CATALOGUE OF PIANOFORTES--MANUFACTURERS
STEINWAY AND SONS
    INIMITABLE TONE..'PRICE LIST OF PIANOS MADE BY STEINWAY AND SONS,
STEINWAY AND SONS
    PIANOFORTES
STEINWAY AND SONS
    PORTRAITS OF MUSICAL CELEBRITIES
STEINWAY AND SONS
    PORTRAITS OF MUSICAL CELEBRITIES
STEINWAY AND SONS
    PORTRAITS OF MUSICAL CELEBRITIES
STEINWAY AND SONS
    PORTRAITS OF MUSICAL CELEBRITIES
STEVENS, FLOYD A.
    COMPLETE COURSE IN PROFESSIONAL PIANO TUNING, REPAIR, AND
VANTYN, SIDNEY
    MODERN PIANOFORTE TECHNIQUE
WAGNER, CHARLES A.
    HOW TO SELECT A GOOD PIANO
WEBER PIANO COMPANY
    WEBER GRAND, SQUARE AND UPRIGHT PIANO-FORTES, THE
WILSON, DAVID M.
    PLAYER-PIANO, THE ..ITS CONSTRUCTION..HOW TO PLAY, WHAT TO PLAY
WILSON, MORRIS E.
    HOW TO HELP YOUR CHILD WITH MUSIC--2ND. ED.---1951
WING AND SONS
    BOOK OF COMPLETE INFORMATION ABOUT PIANOS, THE ...1868-1918, A
WOODMAN, HENRY STAUNTON
    HOW TO TUNE A PIANO..HOW TO BUY A USED PIANO..HOW TO KEEP YOUR
WORCH, HUGO
    WORCH PIANOS, AND A BRIEF SKETCH OF THE PIANOFORTE
WYMAN, ADDISON P.
    WYMAN'S PIANO TEXTBOOK...CONTAINING A COMPLETE SYSTEM OF MUSICAL
YOUNG, THOMAS C.
    MAKING OF MUSICAL INSTRUMENTS, THE ---1939

Construction

ADLER, KURT
    ART OF ACCOMPANYING AND COACHING, THE ---1965
AEOLIAN COMPANY, THE
    CATALOG OF THE AEOLIAN
AEOLIAN COMPANY, THE
    PIANOLA PIANO, THE
AEOLIAN COMPANY, THE
    WEIGHT OF EVIDENCE ON THE TRUE MUSICAL WORTH OF THE PIANOLA AND
ALBARDA, JAN H.
    WOOD, WIRE AND QUILL..AN INTRODUCTION TO THE HARPSICHORD
AMERICAN PHOTO PLAYER COMPANY
    INSTALLATION, CARE AND OPERATION OF THE PHOTOPLAYER---1920+
AMERICAN PIANO CORPORATION
    AMPICO, THE ..A DESCRIPTION OF ITS PERFORMANCE...
AMERICAN PIANO CORPORATION
    AMPICO, THE ..SERVICE MANUAL 1929
AMERICAN PIANO CORPORATION
    AMPICO REPRODUCING PIANO, INSPECTOR'S REFERENCE BOOK, THE ---1923
AMERICAN PIANO CORPORATION
    AMPICO REPRODUCING PIANO, THE ..INSPECTOR'S INSTRUCTION BOOK,
ANON
    NEW PIANOFORTE KEYBOARD, THE ..CARD AND GAME, THE A.B.C. OF MUSIC
ANON
    PIANOFORTE POCKET COMPANION, THE ..OR, A POPULAR VIEW OF THE
ANON
    QUESTIONS AND ANSWERS ON THE SCIENCE AND ART OF PIANOFORTE
APEL, WILLI
    HISTORY OF KEYBOARD MUSIC TO 1700, THE --TRANSLATED AND REVISED BY
APEL, WILLI
    MASTERS OF THE KEYBOARD
AUTOPIANO COMPANY
    PLAYER PIANO POINTERS
AUTO PNEUMATIC ACTION COMPANY
    HOW TO TEST AND REGULATE THE WELTE-MIGNON REPRODUCING PIANO
BAINES, ANTHONY
    EUROPEAN AND AMERICAN MUSICAL INSTRUMENTS
BAINES, ANTHONY
    MUSICAL INSTRUMENTS THROUGH THE AGES--REV. ED.---1961
BAINTON, HERBERT G.
    PIANO, ITS CONSTRUCTION AND CARE, THE
BALLANTINE, BILL
    PIANO, THE ..AN INTRODUCTION TO THE INSTRUMENT

BAMBERGER, LOUIS
    MEMORIES OF SIXTY YEARS IN THE TIMBER AND PIANOFORTE TRADES
BARTHOLOMEW, RALPH I.
    MAKING OF A STEINWAY, THE
BEREGSZASZY, LAJOS
    OBSERVATIONS CONCERNING IMPROVEMENTS IN THE CONSTRUCTION OF THE
BESSARABOFF, NICHOLAS
    ANCIENT EUROPEAN MUSICAL INSTRUMENTS...IN THE LESLIE LINDSAY MASON
BLOM, ERIC
    ROMANCE OF THE PIANO, THE ---1928
BOALCH, DONALD HOWARD
    MAKERS OF THE HARPSICHORD AND CLAVICHORD, 1440 TO 1840
BOWEN, YORK
    PEDALLING THE MODERN PIANOFORTE---1936
BRAGARD, ROGER
    MUSICAL INSTRUMENTS IN ART AND HISTORY
BRIGGS, GILBERT A.
    MUSICAL INSTRUMENTS AND AUDIO
BRIGGS, GILBERT A.
    PIANOS, PIANISTS AND SONICS
BRINSMEAD, F.
    HISTORY OF THE PIANOFORTE, THE ..WITH AN AN ACCOUNT OF THE THEORY
BROADWOOD, JOHN AND SONS
    INFORMATION CONCERNING PIANOFORTES OF USE AND OF INTEREST..A VADE
CARRENO, TERESA
    POSSIBILITIES OF TONE COLOR BY ARTISTIC USE OF PEDALS
CHICKERING AND SONS
    NEW ILLUSTRATED CATALOGUE OF PIANOFORTES, A
CHICKERING BROTHERS, CHICAGO
    PIANO-FORTES AND THEIR MANUFACTURE, WITH ILLUSTRATED CATALOGUE
CLEMENCIC, RENE
    OLD MUSICAL INSTRUMENTS
CLOSSON, ERNEST
    HISTORY OF THE PIANO
DARLOW, DENYS
    MUSICAL INSTRUMENTS--JUNIOR REFERENCE BOOKS, NO. 12--2ND. ED.
DAVIS, LIONEL
    KEYBOARD INSTRUMENTS..THE STORY OF THE PIANO---YOUNGER READERS
DIETZ, FRANZ RUDOLF
    REGULIEREN VON FLUEGELN BEI STEINWAY, DAS --REGULATION OF THE
DOLGE, ALFRED
    PIANOS AND THEIR MAKERS..A COMPREHENSIVE HISTORY OF THE
DONINGTON, ROBERT
    INSTRUMENTS OF MUSIC, THE --3RD. REV. ED.---1949
DRAKE, HARRY
    PLAYER-PIANO EXPLAINED, THE --PAMPHLET
DUNN, JOHN PETRIE
    BASIS OF PIANOFORTE PLAYING, THE
EARL, S. G.
    REPAIRING THE PLAYER PIANO..INFORMATION USEFUL TO PIANOFORTE
EDINBURGH UNIVERSITY--DEPT. OF EARLY KEYBOARD INSTRUMENTS
    RUSSELL COLLECTION AND OTHER EARLY KEYBOARD INSTRUMENTS IN ST.
EISENBERG, JACOB
    LET ME HELP YOU, MY ANCESTORS AND I..A COMPREHENSIVE JUVENILE
ELLINGHAM, HARRY
    HOW TO USE A PLAYER-PIANO
ENGEL, CARL
    MUSICAL INSTRUMENTS--REV. ED.---1876
ENGEL, CARL
    PIANIST'S HANDBOOK, THE ..A GUIDE FOR THE RIGHT COMPREHENSION AND
EPWORTH PIANOS
    BOOK ABOUT PIANOS IN GENERAL AND THE EPWORTH IN PARTICULAR, A
FERGUSON, DONALD NIVISON
    PIANO MUSIC OF SIX GREAT COMPOSERS---1947
FISCHER, JERRY CREE
    PIANO TUNING, REGULATING AND REPAIRING...SELF INSTRUCTION...FOR
FOX, LILLA M.
    INSTRUMENTS OF POPULAR MUSIC..A HISTORY OF MUSICAL
FUNKE, OTTO
    PIANO AND HOW TO CARE FOR IT, THE ..PIANO TUNING IN THEORY AND
FUREY, J.
    BUILDING OF THE PIANO, THE
GABRY, GYORGY
    OLD MUSICAL INSTRUMENTS
GALPIN, FRANCIS W.
    OLD ENGLISH INSTRUMENTS OF MUSIC--4TH. ED.---1910
GALPIN, FRANCIS W.
    TEXTBOOK OF EUROPEAN MUSICAL INSTRUMENTS, A ---1937
GATES, WILLEY F.
    PIPE AND STRINGS..THREE HISTORIC AND DESCRIPTIVE SKETCHES...THE
GEIRINGER, KARL
    MUSICAL INSTRUMENTS, THEIR HISTORY IN WESTERN CULTURE FROM THE
GILLESPIE, JOHN
    FIVE CENTURIES OF KEYBOARD MUSIC..AN HISTORIC SURVEY FOR
GLOVER, ELLYE HOWELL
    HOW THE PIANO CAME TO BE
HAMILTON, CLARENCE G.
    PIANO MUSIC, ITS COMPOSERS AND CHARACTERISTICS
HANSING, SIEGFRIED
    PIANOFORTE AND ITS ACOUSTIC PROPERTIES, THE --2ND. REV.
HARDING, ROSAMUND
    PIANOFORTE, THE ..ITS HISTORY TRACED TO THE GREAT EXHIBITION OF
HARICH-SCHNEIDER, ETA
    HARPSICHORD, THE ..AN INTRODUCTION TO TECHNIQUE, STYLE AND THE
HARRIS, REGINALD
    HOW TO CHOOSE AN INSTRUMENT..PIANO AND STRINGS
HASLUCK, PAUL N.
    PIANOS..THEIR CONSTRUCTION, TUNING AND REPAIR
HENDERSON, WILLIAM JAMES
    PRELUDES AND STUDIES..MUSICAL THEMES OF THE DAY--SECTION 3..THE
HINDLEY, GEOFFREY
    MUSICAL INSTRUMENTS
HIPKINS, ALFRED JAMES
    DESCRIPTION AND HISTORY OF THE PIANOFORTE AND OLDER KEYBOARD
HIPKINS, ALFRED JAMES
    MUSICAL INSTRUMENTS, HISTORIC, RARE AND UNIQUE---1888
HIRT, FRANZ JOSEF
    STRINGED KEYBOARD INSTRUMENTS 1440-1880---1955, IN GERMAN
HOBBS, HENRY
    PIANO IN INDIA, THE ..HOW TO KEEP IT IN ORDER, PRACTICAL
HOFMANN, JOSEF
    PIANO PLAYING..A LITTLE BOOK OF SIMPLE SUGGESTIONS--REPRINTED FROM
HOOVER, CYNTHIA A.
    HARPSICHORDS AND CLAVICHORDS
HORNIMAN MUSEUM AND LIBRARY, LONDON
    HANDBOOK TO THE MUSEUM'S COLLECTION, BY JEAN L. JENKINS--2ND.
HORNIMAN MUSEUM AND LIBRARY, LONDON
    MUSICAL INSTRUMENTS
HOWE, ALFRED H.
    SCIENTIFIC PIANO TUNING AND SERVICING--REV. ED.---1941
HUBBARD, FRANK
    HARPSICHORD REGULATING AND REPAIRING
HUBBARD, FRANK
    THREE CENTURIES OF HARPSICHORD MAKING
HULL, ANNE
    MAESTRO SPINETTI'S MUSIC SHOP--HARPSICHORD, CLAVICHORD,
HUMMEL, JOHANN NEPOMUK
    COMPLETE THEORETICAL AND PRACTICAL COURSE OF INSTRUCTIONS ON THE

JAMES, PHILIP BRUTTON
  EARLY KEYBOARD INSTRUMENTS, FROM THEIR BEGINNINGS TO THE YEAR
KEELER, WALTER B.
  THEORY OF THE NEW KEYBOARD, ARRANGED BY W. B. KEELER AND E. K.
KELLEY, EDGAR STILLMAN
  MUSICAL INSTRUMENTS--3RD. YEAR OF A STUDY COURSE IN MUSIC
KENDALL, ALAN
  WORLD OF MUSICAL INSTRUMENTS, THE ---CHIEFLY ILLUSTRATIONS
KENYON, MAX
  HARPSICHORD MUSIC..THE INSTRUMENTS, THE COMPOSERS, THE PLAYERS
KIRBY, FRANK EUGENE
  SHORT HISTORY OF KEYBOARD MUSIC, A
KRAUS, ALESSANDRO B.
  ONE-KEYBOARDED CLAVICYTHERIUM OF THE KRAUS COLLECTION IN FLORENCE,
LANDOWSKA, WANDA
  LANDOWSKA ON MUSIC--EDITED BY DENISE RESTOUT
LEWIS, THOMAS C.
  PROTEST AGAINST THE MODERN DEVELOPMENT OF UNMUSICAL TONE, A
LOESCHMANN, DAVID
  DESCRIPTION AND USE OF THE PATENT ENHARMONIC PIANOFORTE
LOESSER, ARTHUR
  MEN, WOMEN AND PIANOS..A SOCIAL HISTORY
MASON, HENRY LOWELL
  MODERN ARTISTIC PIANOFORTE, THE ..ITS CONSTRUCTION
MATTHAY, TOBIAS A.
  ACT OF TOUCH IN ALL ITS DIVERSITY, THE ..AN ANALYSIS AND SYNTHESIS
MATTHAY, TOBIAS A.
  PIANOFORTE TONE-PRODUCTION---SAME AS 'THE ACT OF TOUCH IN ALL ITS
METROPOLITAN MUSEUM OF ART, NEW YORK
  CATALOGUE OF THE CROSBY BROWN COLLECTION OF MUSICAL INSTRUMENTS OF
METROPOLITAN MUSEUM OF ART, NEW YORK
  KEYBOARD INSTRUMENTS IN THE METROPOLITAN MUSEUM OF ART..A PICTURE
MICHEL, NORMAN ELWOOD
  OLD PIANOS
NALDER, LAWRENCE MARCUS
  FIRST STEPS IN PIANO TUNING AND OTHER ESSAYS IN PIANOFORTE
NALDER, LAWRENCE MARCUS
  MODERN PIANO, THE
NALDER, LAWRENCE MARCUS
  PIANOFORTE CONSTRUCTION
NALDER, LAWRENCE MARCUS
  REPAIRING THE PIANOFORTE
NATIONAL PIANO MANUFACTURERS ASSOCIATION OF AMERICA
  STENCILLING OF PIANOS, THE
NEUPERT, HANNS
  CLAVICHORD, THE ---1956, IN GERMAN
NEUPERT, HANNS
  HARPSICHORD MANUAL..A HISTORY AND TECHNICAL DEVELOPMENT--2ND.
NEWMAN, WILLIAM S.
  PERFORMANCE PRACTICES IN BEETHOVEN'S PIANO SONATAS..AN
NORTON, EDWARD Q.
  CONSTRUCTION, TUNING AND CARE OF THE PIANOFORTE--EDITED AND
O'NEILL, J. A.
  DESCRIPTION AND HISTORY OF THE PIANOFORTE, A
ORD-HUME, ARTHUR W. J. G.
  CLOCKWORK MUSIC..AN ILLUSTRATED HISTORY OF MECHANICAL MUSICAL
ORD-HUME, ARTHUR W. J. G.
  PLAYER PIANO, THE HISTORY OF THE MECHANICAL PIANO AND HOW TO
ORTMANN, OTTO
  PHYSICAL BASIS OF PIANO TOUCH AND TONE, THE
PAETKAU, DAVID H.
  GROWTH OF INSTRUMENTS AND INSTRUMENTAL MUSIC, THE
PAGE, C. E.
  MUSICAL INSTRUMENTS--MECHANICAL AGE LIBRARY
PARRISH, CARL
  EARLY PIANO AND ITS INFLUENCE ON KEYBOARD TECHNIQUE AND
PENGELLY, J. BRADFORD
  PENGELLY BLUE BOOK OF STYLE, THE ...A STUDY OF THE ART OF STYLING
PETERSON, FRANKLIN
  THEORETIC COMPANION TO PRACTICE--PART I OF THE PIANIST'S HANDBOOK
PFEIFFER, WALTER
  PIANO KEY AND WHIPPEN, THE ..AN ANALYSIS OF THEIR RELATIONSHIPS IN
PINCHERLE, MARC
  WORLD OF THE VIRTUOSO, THE
PRESTO--EDITORIAL STAFF
  MUSICAL INSTRUMENTS AT THE WORLD'S COLUMBIAN EXPOSITION, CHICAGO,
PRESTO PUBLISHING COMPANY
  PRESTO BUYERS' GUIDE TO PLAYER-PIANOS AND PIANOS
PULVER, JEFFREY
  DICTIONARY OF OLD ENGLISH MUSIC AND MUSICAL INSTRUMENTS, A
RIMBAULT, EDWARD FRANCIS
  PIANOFORTE, THE ..ITS ORIGIN, PROCESS AND CONSTRUCTION
RIPIN, EDWIN M.--EDITOR
  KEYBOARD INSTRUMENTS..STUDIES IN KEYBOARD ORGANOLOGY---10 ESSAYS
ROEHL, HARVEY
  KEYS TO A MUSICAL PAST...ILLUSTRATED TREATISE ON THE VARIOUS TYPES
ROEHL, HARVEY
  PLAYER PIANO, AN HISTORICAL SCRAPBOOK, THE
ROEHL, HARVEY
  PLAYER PIANO TREASURY..THE SCRAPBOOK HISTORY OF THE MECHANICAL
ROSENCRANTZ, ISIDOR B.
  PIANO, ITS CONSTRUCTION AND RELATION TO TONE, PITCH AND
RUSSELL, RAYMOND
  CATALOGUE OF THE BENTON FLETCHER COLLECTION OF EARLY KEYBOARD
RUSSELL, RAYMOND
  HARPSICHORD AND THE CLAVICHORD, THE --2ND. ED., REVISED BY HOWARD
SACHS, CURT
  HISTORY OF MUSICAL INSTRUMENTS, THE
SCHMECKEL, CARL D.
  PIANO OWNER'S GUIDE, THE
SCHULZE, RICHARD ALLEN
  HOW TO BUILD A BAROQUE CONCERT HARPSICHORD
SHORTRIDGE, JOHN D.
  ITALIAN HARPSICHORD BUILDING IN THE 16TH. AND 17TH.
SKINNER, BELLE
  BELLE SKINNER COLLECTION OF OLD MUSICAL INSTRUMENTS, HOLYOKE,
SMITH, FANNY MORRIS
  NOBLE ART, A ..THREE LECTURES ON THE EVOLUTION AND CONSTRUCTION OF
SMITH, HERMANN
  ART OF TUNING THE PIANOFORTE, THE ...ON THE THEORY OF EQUAL
SOUTH KENSINGTON MUSEUM, LONDON
  CATALOGUE OF THE SPECIAL EXHIBITION OF ANCIENT MUSICAL INSTRUMENTS
SOUTH KENSINGTON MUSEUM, LONDON
  DESCRIPTIVE CATALOGUE OF THE MUSICAL INSTRUMENTS IN THE SOUTH
SOUTH KENSINGTON MUSEUM, LONDON
  DESCRIPTIVE CATALOGUE OF THE MUSICAL INSTRUMENTS IN THE SOUTH
SPILLANE, DANIEL
  HISTORY OF THE AMERICAN PIANOFORTE..ITS TECHNICAL DEVELOPMENT, AND
STANDARD PLAYER ACTION COMPANY
  PRINCIPLES OF PLAYER ACTION OPERATION--3RD. ED.
STANDARD PNEUMATIC ACTION COMPANY
  DESCRIPTION OF STANDARD PNEUMATIC PLAYER ACTION, WITH SUGGESTIONS
STEINERT, MORRIS
  MORRIS STEINERT COLLECTION OF KEYED AND STRINGED INSTRUMENTS, THE
STEINWAY, THEODORE E.
  PEOPLE AND PIANOS..A CENTURY OF SERVICE TO MUSIC---1853-1953

STEINWAY AND SONS
  BOOK OF ART PIANO CASES
STEINWAY AND SONS
  ILLUSTRATED CATALOGUE OF--STEINWAY AND SONS...PIANOFORTES
STEINWAY AND SONS
  ILLUSTRATED CATALOGUE OF PIANOS
STEINWAY AND SONS
  ILLUSTRATED CATALOGUE OF STEINWAY AND SONS' PIANOS
STEINWAY AND SONS
  ILLUSTRATED CIRCULAR AND CATALOGUE OF PIANOFORTES--MANUFACTURERS
STEINWAY AND SONS
  STEINWAY..YESTERDAY, TODAY, TOMORROW
STEINWAY AND SONS
  STEINWAY AND SONS' PIANO-FORTE MANUFACTORY AT 'STEINWAY', LONG
STEVENS, FLOYD A.
  COMPLETE COURSE IN PROFESSIONAL PIANO TUNING, REPAIR, AND
STEVENS, PARAN
  REPORT UPON MUSICAL INSTRUMENTS..PARIS UNIVERSAL EXPOSITION, 1867
STODDARD, HOPE
  FROM THESE COMES MUSIC
STRAUCH BROTHERS
  MANUFACTURE OF PIANOFORTE ACTION, THE ..ITS RISE AND DEVELOPMENT
STROHBER PIANO COMPANY
  PNEUMATIC PLAYER MECHANISM AND DESCRIPTIVE CATALOG OF STROHBER AND
SUMNER, WILLIAM L.
  PIANOFORTE, THE --3RD. ED.---1966
TRAVIS, JOHN W.
  LET'S TUNE UP
UNITED STATES PATENT OFFICE
  COLLECTION OF LETTERS PATENT RELATING TO THE CONSTRUCTION OF
VAN ATTA, HARRISON LOUIS--EDITOR
  TREATISE ON THE PIANO AND PLAYER PIANO, A
VAN NOORDEN, C.
  FREAK PIANOS---SCRAPBOOK
VICTORIA AND ALBERT MUSEUM, SOUTH KENSINGTON
  CATALOGUE OF MUSICAL INSTRUMENTS..VOL. 1, KEYBOARD
VICTORIA AND ALBERT MUSEUM, SOUTH KENSINGTON
  EXAMPLES OF ART WORKMANSHIP OF VARIOUS AGES AND COUNTRIES..MUSICAL
WAGNER, CHARLES A.
  HOW TO SELECT A GOOD PIANO
WEBER PIANO COMPANY
  WEBER GRAND, SQUARE AND UPRIGHT PIANO-FORTES, THE
WEITZMANN, CARL F.
  HISTORY OF PIANOFORTE-PLAYING AND PIANOFORTE-LITERATURE, A
WHITE, WILLIAM BRAID
  PIANO PLAYING MECHANISMS
WHITE, WILLIAM BRAID
  PIANO TUNING AND ALLIED ARTS--5TH. ED.---1917
WHITE, WILLIAM BRAID
  PLAYER-PIANO UP TO DATE, THE
WHITE, WILLIAM BRAID
  REGULATION AND REPAIR OF PIANO AND PLAYER PIANO MECHANISM
WHITE, WILLIAM BRAID
  TECHNICAL TREATISE ON PLAYER PIANO MECHANISM, A
WHITE, WILLIAM BRAID
  THEORY AND PRACTICE OF PIANOFORTE BUILDING
WIER, ALBERT
  PIANO, THE ..ITS HISTORY, MAKERS, PLAYERS AND MUSIC
WILLIS, AUBREY
  AUBREY WILLIS HOME STUDY COURSE IN PIANO TUNING AND REPAIRING
WILSON, DAVID M.
  INSTRUCTION BOOK ON THE PIANO-PLAYER AND PLAYER-PIANO, AN
WILSON, DAVID M.
  PLAYER-PIANO, THE ..ITS CONSTRUCTION..HOW TO PLAY, WHAT TO PLAY
WING AND SONS
  BOOK OF COMPLETE INFORMATION ABOUT PIANOS, THE ...1868-1918, A
WINTERNITZ, EMANUEL
  MUSICAL INSTRUMENTS OF THE WESTERN WORLD
WOLFENDEN, S.
  TREATISE ON THE ART OF PIANOFORTE CONSTRUCTION, A --SUPPLEMENT
WOLFENDEN, S.
  TREATISE ON THE ART OF PIANOFORTE CONSTRUCTION, A
WOLFRAM, VICTOR
  SOSTENUTO PEDAL, THE
WOODMAN, HENRY STAUNTON
  HOW TO TUNE A PIANO..HOW TO BUY A USED PIANO..HOW TO KEEP YOUR
WORCH, HUGO
  PIANO MAKERS OF THE EVOLUTIONARY PERIOD..RARE ENGLISH AND AMERICAN
WORCH, HUGO
  WORCH PIANOS, AND A BRIEF SKETCH OF THE PIANOFORTE
YALE UNIVERSITY--ART GALLERY
  MUSICAL INSTRUMENTS AT YALE..A SELECTION OF WESTERN INSTRUMENTS
YATES, PETER
  AMATEUR AT THE KEYBOARD, AN
YOUNG, THOMAS C.
  MAKING OF MUSICAL INSTRUMENTS, THE ---1939
ZUCKERMANN, WOLFGANG JOACHIM
  MODERN HARPSICHORD, THE ..TWENTIETH CENTURY INSTRUMENTS AND THEIR

Mechanism

ADLER, KURT
  ART OF ACCOMPANYING AND COACHING, THE ---1965
AEOLIAN COMPANY, THE
  AEOLIAN PIANOS, THE ---WEBER, STECK, STROUD
AEOLIAN COMPANY, THE
  CATALOG OF THE AEOLIAN
AEOLIAN COMPANY, THE
  PIANOLA PIANO, THE
ALBARDA, JAN H.
  WOOD, WIRE AND QUILL..AN INTRODUCTION TO THE HARPSICHORD
AMERICAN PHOTO PLAYER COMPANY
  INSTALLATION, CARE AND OPERATION OF THE PHOTOPLAYER---1920+
AMERICAN PIANO CORPORATION
  AMPICO, THE ..A DESCRIPTION OF ITS PERFORMANCE...
AMERICAN PIANO CORPORATION
  AMPICO, THE ..SERVICE MANUAL 1929
AMERICAN PIANO CORPORATION
  AMPICO REPRODUCING PIANO, INSPECTOR'S REFERENCE BOOK, THE ---1923
AMERICAN PIANO CORPORATION
  AMPICO REPRODUCING PIANO, THE ..INSPECTOR'S INSTRUCTION BOOK,
AMERICAN STEEL AND WIRE COMPANY
  NERVES OF STEEL..THE STORY OF AMERICAN PIANO WIRE AND ITS
ANON
  REPAIRING THE PIANOFORTE, WITH CHAPTERS ON REGULATING, TONING,
APEL, WILLI
  HISTORY OF KEYBOARD MUSIC TO 1700, THE --TRANSLATED AND REVISED BY
APEL, WILLI
  MASTERS OF THE KEYBOARD
AUTOPIANO COMPANY
  PLAYER PIANO POINTERS
AUTO PNEUMATIC ACTION COMPANY
  HOW TO TEST AND REGULATE THE WELTE-MIGNON REPRODUCING PIANO
BAINES, ANTHONY
  EUROPEAN AND AMERICAN MUSICAL INSTRUMENTS

BAINES, ANTHONY
    MUSICAL INSTRUMENTS THROUGH THE AGES--REV. ED.---1961
BAINTON, HERBERT G.
    PIANO, ITS CONSTRUCTION AND CARE, THE
BALLANTINE, BILL
    PIANO, THE ..AN INTRODUCTION TO THE INSTRUMENT
BARTHOLOMEW, RALPH I.
    MAKING OF A STEINWAY, THE
BESSARABOFF, NICHOLAS
    ANCIENT EUROPEAN MUSICAL INSTRUMENTS...IN THE LESLIE LINDSAY MASON
BLOM, ERIC
    ROMANCE OF THE PIANO, THE ---1928
BORREN, CHARLES VAN DEN
    SOURCES OF KEYBOARD MUSIC IN ENGLAND, THE ---1913
BOWEN, YORK
    PEDALLING THE MODERN PIANOFORTE---1936
BOWEN, YORK
    SIMPLICITY OF PIANO TECHNIQUE, THE
BRAGARD, ROGER
    MUSICAL INSTRUMENTS IN ART AND HISTORY
BRIGGS, GILBERT A.
    MUSICAL INSTRUMENTS AND AUDIO
BRIGGS, GILBERT A.
    PIANOS, PIANISTS AND SONICS
BRINSMEAD, E.
    HISTORY OF THE PIANOFORTE, THE ..WITH AN AN ACCOUNT OF THE THEORY
BROADWOOD, JOHN AND SONS
    INFORMATION CONCERNING PIANOFORTES OF USE AND OF INTEREST..A VADE
BUNGER, RICHARD
    WELL-PREPARED PIANO, THE
CLEMENCIC, RENE
    OLD MUSICAL INSTRUMENTS
CLOSSON, ERNEST
    HISTORY OF THE PIANO
COVIELLO, AMBROSE
    WHAT MATTHAY MEANT
DAHL, ANTON
    SOUL OF GENIUS, THE ..ITS MUSICAL DEVELOPMENT AND HOW THE WORLD AT
DALE, KATHLEEN
    NINETEENTH CENTURY PIANO MUSIC, A HANDBOOK FOR PIANISTS
DARLOW, DENYS
    MUSICAL INSTRUMENTS--JUNIOR REFERENCE BOOKS, NO. 12--2ND. ED.
DIETZ, FRANZ RUDOLF
    REGULIEREN VON FLUEGELN BEI STEINWAY, DAS --REGULATION OF THE
DOLGE, ALFRED
    PIANOS AND THEIR MAKERS..A COMPREHENSIVE HISTORY OF THE
DONINGTON, ROBERT
    INSTRUMENTS OF MUSIC, THE --3RD. REV. ED.---1949
DRAKE, HARRY
    PLAYER-PIANO EXPLAINED, THE --PAMPHLET
DUNN, JOHN PETRIE
    BASIS OF PIANOFORTE PLAYING, THE
EARL, S. G.
    REPAIRING THE PLAYER PIANO..INFORMATION USEFUL TO PIANOFORTE
EDINBURGH UNIVERSITY--DEPT. OF EARLY KEYBOARD INSTRUMENTS
    RUSSELL COLLECTION AND OTHER EARLY KEYBOARD INSTRUMENTS IN ST.
EISENBERG, JACOB
    ARTISTIC PIANIST, THE ..NATURAL TECHNICS IN PIANO MASTERY..FROM
EISENBERG, JACOB
    LET ME HELP YOU, MY ANCESTORS AND I..A COMPREHENSIVE JUVENILE
ELLINGHAM, HARRY
    HOW TO USE A PLAYER-PIANO
ENGEL, CARL
    MUSICAL INSTRUMENTS---78 WOODCUT ILLUSTRATIONS
ENGEL, CARL
    MUSICAL INSTRUMENTS--REV. ED.---1876
EPWORTH PIANOS
    BOOK ABOUT PIANOS IN GENERAL AND THE EPWORTH IN PARTICULAR, A
FERGUSON, DONALD NIVISON
    PIANO MUSIC OF SIX GREAT COMPOSERS---1947
FISCHER, JERRY CREE
    PIANO TUNING, REGULATING AND REPAIRING...SELF INSTRUCTION...FOR
FOOTE, ARTHUR W.
    SOME PRACTICAL THINGS IN PIANO PLAYING
FUNKE, OTTO
    PIANO AND HOW TO CARE FOR IT, THE ..PIANO TUNING IN THEORY AND
FUREY, J.
    BUILDING OF THE PIANO, THE
GABRY, GYORGY
    OLD MUSICAL INSTRUMENTS
GALPIN, FRANCIS W.
    TEXTBOOK OF EUROPEAN MUSICAL INSTRUMENTS, A ---1937
GATES, WILLEY F.
    PIPE AND STRINGS..THREE HISTORIC AND DESCRIPTIVE SKETCHES...THE
GILLESPIE, JOHN
    FIVE CENTURIES OF KEYBOARD MUSIC..AN HISTORIC SURVEY FOR
HAMILTON, CLARENCE G.
    PIANO MUSIC, ITS COMPOSERS AND CHARACTERISTICS
HANSING, SIEGFRIED
    PIANOFORTE AND ITS ACOUSTIC PROPERTIES, THE --2ND. REV.
HARDING, ROSAMUND
    PIANOFORTE, THE ..ITS HISTORY TRACED TO THE GREAT EXHIBITION OF
HARRISON, SIDNEY
    YOUNG PERSON'S GUIDE TO PLAYING THE PIANO, THE
HASLUCK, PAUL N.
    PIANOS..THEIR CONSTRUCTION, TUNING AND REPAIR
HENDERSON, WILLIAM JAMES
    PRELUDES AND STUDIES..MUSICAL THEMES OF THE DAY--SECTION 3..THE
HINDLEY, GEOFFREY
    MUSICAL INSTRUMENTS
HIPKINS, ALFRED JAMES
    DESCRIPTION AND HISTORY OF THE PIANOFORTE AND OLDER KEYBOARD
HIPKINS, ALFRED JAMES
    MUSICAL INSTRUMENTS, HISTORIC, RARE AND UNIQUE---1888
HIRT, FRANZ JOSEF
    STRINGED KEYBOARD INSTRUMENTS 1440-1880---1955, IN GERMAN
HOBBS, HENRY
    PIANO IN INDIA, THE ..HOW TO KEEP IT IN ORDER, PRACTICAL
HORNIMAN MUSEUM AND LIBRARY, LONDON
    HANDBOOK TO THE MUSEUM'S COLLECTION, BY JEAN L. JENKINS--2ND.
HORNIMAN MUSEUM AND LIBRARY, LONDON
    MUSICAL INSTRUMENTS
HOWE, ALFRED H.
    SCIENTIFIC PIANO TUNING AND SERVICING--REV. ED.---1941
HUBBARD, FRANK
    HARPSICHORD REGULATING AND REPAIRING
HUBBARD, FRANK
    THREE CENTURIES OF HARPSICHORD MAKING
HULL, ANNE
    MAESTRO SPINETTI'S MUSIC SHOP--HARPSICHORD, CLAVICHORD,
HUMMEL, JOHANN NEPOMUK
    COMPLETE THEORETICAL AND PRACTICAL COURSE OF INSTRUCTIONS ON THE
HUTCHESON, ERNEST *
    LITERATURE OF THE PIANO, THE ..A GUIDE FOR AMATEUR AND
JAMES, PHILIP BRUTTON
    EARLY KEYBOARD INSTRUMENTS, FROM THEIR BEGINNINGS TO THE YEAR

JEANS, SIR JAMES HOPWOOD
    SCIENCE AND MUSIC
KEELER, WALTER B.
    THEORY OF THE NEW KEYBOARD, ARRANGED BY W. B. KEELER AND E. K.
KENDALL, ALAN
    WORLD OF MUSICAL INSTRUMENTS, THE ---CHIEFLY ILLUSTRATIONS
KENYON, MAX
    HARPSICHORD MUSIC..THE INSTRUMENTS, THE COMPOSERS, THE PLAYERS
KIRBY, FRANK EUGENE
    SHORT HISTORY OF KEYBOARD MUSIC, A
KRAUS, ALESSANDRO B.
    ONE-KEYBOARDED CLAVICYTHERIUM OF THE KRAUS COLLECTION IN FLORENCE,
LANDOWSKA, WANDA
    LANDOWSKA ON MUSIC--EDITED BY DENISE RESTOUT
LAVIGNAC, ALBERT
    MUSIC AND MUSICIANS---1895, IN FRENCH
LEWIS, THOMAS C.
    PROTEST AGAINST THE MODERN DEVELOPMENT OF UNMUSICAL TONE, A
LINDO, ALGERNON H.
    PEDALLING IN PIANOFORTE MUSIC
LOESSER, ARTHUR
    MEN, WOMEN AND PIANOS..A SOCIAL HISTORY
MATTHAY, TOBIAS A.
    ACT OF TOUCH IN ALL ITS DIVERSITY, THE ..AN ANALYSIS AND SYNTHESIS
MATTHAY, TOBIAS A.
    FIRST PRINCIPLES OF PIANOFORTE PLAYING--EXTRACT FROM 'THE ACT OF
MATTHAY, TOBIAS A.
    PIANOFORTE TONE-PRODUCTION---SAME AS 'THE ACT OF TOUCH IN ALL ITS
MCTAMMANY, JOHN
    EVOLUTION OF THE PLAYER-PIANO MECHANISM---EXCERPT FROM 'PRESTO',
METROPOLITAN MUSEUM OF ART, NEW YORK
    CATALOGUE OF THE CROSBY BROWN COLLECTION OF MUSICAL INSTRUMENTS OF
METROPOLITAN MUSEUM OF ART, NEW YORK
    KEYBOARD INSTRUMENTS IN THE METROPOLITAN MUSEUM OF ART..A PICTURE
MICHEL, NORMAN ELWOOD
    OLD PIANOS
MININBERG, IAN
    VISUAL APPROACH TO PIANO TECHNIQUE, A
NALDER, LAWRENCE MARCUS
    FIRST STEPS IN PIANO TUNING AND OTHER ESSAYS IN PIANOFORTE
NALDER, LAWRENCE MARCUS
    MODERN PIANO, THE
NALDER, LAWRENCE MARCUS
    PIANOFORTE CONSTRUCTION
NALDER, LAWRENCE MARCUS
    REPAIRING THE PIANOFORTE
NEUPERT, HANNS
    CLAVICHORD, THE ---1956, IN GERMAN
NEUPERT, HANNS
    HARPSICHORD MANUAL..A HISTORY AND TECHNICAL DEVELOPMENT--2ND.
NEWMAN, WILLIAM S.
    PERFORMANCE PRACTICES IN BEETHOVEN'S PIANO SONATAS..AN
O'NEILL, J. A.
    DESCRIPTION AND HISTORY OF THE PIANOFORTE, A
ORD-HUME, ARTHUR W. J. G.
    CLOCKWORK MUSIC..AN ILLUSTRATED HISTORY OF MECHANICAL MUSICAL
ORD-HUME, ARTHUR W. J. G.
    PLAYER PIANO, THE HISTORY OF THE MECHANICAL PIANO AND HOW TO
ORTMANN, OTTO
    PHYSICAL BASIS OF PIANO TOUCH AND TONE, THE
PAETKAU, DAVID H.
    GROWTH OF INSTRUMENTS AND INSTRUMENTAL MUSIC, THE
PAGE, C. E.
    MUSICAL INSTRUMENTS--MECHANICAL AGE LIBRARY
PALME, RUDOLPH
    FIRST MONTHS IN PIANOFORTE INSTRUCTION, THE ---1870, IN GERMAN
PARRISH, CARL
    EARLY PIANO AND ITS INFLUENCE ON KEYBOARD TECHNIQUE AND
PETERSON, FRANKLIN
    THEORETIC COMPANION TO PRACTICE--PART I OF THE PIANIST'S HANDBOOK
PFEIFFER, WALTER
    PIANO KEY AND WHIPPEN, THE ..AN ANALYSIS OF THEIR RELATIONSHIPS IN
PULVER, JEFFREY
    DICTIONARY OF OLD ENGLISH MUSIC AND MUSICAL INSTRUMENTS, A
REEDER, BETAH
    SINGING TOUCH, THE
RIMBAULT, EDWARD FRANCIS
    CHAPPELL AND CO.'S PRACTICAL DIRECTIONS UPON THE ART OF TUNING THE
RIMBAULT, EDWARD FRANCIS
    PIANOFORTE, THE ..ITS ORIGIN, PROCESS AND CONSTRUCTION
RIPIN, EDWIN M.--EDITOR
    KEYBOARD INSTRUMENTS..STUDIES IN KEYBOARD ORGANOLOGY---10 ESSAYS
ROEHL, HARVEY
    KEYS TO A MUSICAL PAST...ILLUSTRATED TREATISE ON THE VARIOUS TYPES
ROEHL, HARVEY
    PLAYER PIANO, AN HISTORICAL SCRAPBOOK, THE
ROEHL, HARVEY
    PLAYER PIANO TREASURY..THE SCRAPBOOK HISTORY OF THE MECHANICAL
ROSENCRANTZ, ISIDOR B.
    PIANO, ITS CONSTRUCTION AND RELATION TO TONE, PITCH AND
RUSSELL, RAYMOND
    CATALOGUE OF THE BENTON FLETCHER COLLECTION OF EARLY KEYBOARD
RUSSELL, RAYMOND
    HARPSICHORD AND THE CLAVICHORD, THE --2ND. ED., REVISED BY HOWARD
SACHS, CURT
    HISTORY OF MUSICAL INSTRUMENTS, THE
SCHMECKEL, CARL D.
    PIANO OWNER'S GUIDE, THE
SCHULZE, RICHARD ALLEN
    HOW TO BUILD A BAROQUE CONCERT HARPSICHORD
SEROFF, VICTOR
    COMMON SENSE IN PIANO STUDY
SKINNER, BELLE
    BELLE SKINNER COLLECTION OF OLD MUSICAL INSTRUMENTS, HOLYOKE,
SMITH, FANNY MORRIS
    NOBLE ART, A ..THREE LECTURES ON THE EVOLUTION AND CONSTRUCTION OF
SMITH, HERMANN
    ART OF TUNING THE PIANOFORTE, THE ...ON THE THEORY OF EQUAL
SOUTH KENSINGTON MUSEUM, LONDON
    CATALOGUE OF THE SPECIAL EXHIBITION OF ANCIENT MUSICAL INSTRUMENTS
SOUTH KENSINGTON MUSEUM, LONDON
    DESCRIPTIVE CATALOGUE OF THE MUSICAL INSTRUMENTS IN THE SOUTH
SOUTH KENSINGTON MUSEUM, LONDON
    DESCRIPTIVE CATALOGUE OF THE MUSICAL INSTRUMENTS IN THE SOUTH
SPILLANE, DANIEL
    HISTORY OF THE AMERICAN PIANOFORTE..ITS TECHNICAL DEVELOPMENT, AND
STANDARD PLAYER ACTION COMPANY
    PRINCIPLES OF PLAYER ACTION OPERATION--3RD. ED.
STANDARD PNEUMATIC ACTION COMPANY
    DESCRIPTION OF STANDARD PNEUMATIC PLAYER ACTION, WITH SUGGESTIONS
STEGLICH, RUDOLF
    MOZARTS FLUEGEL KLINGT WIEDER--MOZART'S PIANO SOUNDS AGAIN---WITH
STEINERT, MORRIS
    MORRIS STEINERT COLLECTION OF KEYED AND STRINGED INSTRUMENTS, THE
STEINWAY, THEODORE E.
    PEOPLE AND PIANOS..A CENTURY OF SERVICE TO MUSIC---1853-1953

STEINWAY AND SONS
  ILLUSTRATED CATALOGUE OF--STEINWAY AND SONS...PIANOFORTES
STEINWAY AND SONS
  ILLUSTRATED CATALOGUE OF STEINWAY AND SONS' PIANOS
STEINWAY AND SONS
  ILLUSTRATED CIRCULAR AND CATALOGUE OF PIANOFORTES--MANUFACTURERS
STEVENS, FLOYD A.
  COMPLETE COURSE IN PROFESSIONAL PIANO TUNING, REPAIR, AND
STODDARD, HOPE
  FROM THESE COMES MUSIC
STRAUCH BROTHERS
  MANUFACTURE OF PIANOFORTE ACTION, THE ..ITS RISE AND DEVELOPMENT
STROHBER PIANO COMPANY
  PNEUMATIC PLAYER MECHANISM AND DESCRIPTIVE CATALOG OF STROHBER AND
SUMMER, WILLIAM L.
  PIANOFORTE, THE --3RD. ED.---1966
TANKARD, GEOFFREY
  PIANOFORTE DIPLOMAS
TRAVIS, JOHN W.
  LET'S TUNE UP
VANT, ALBERT B.
  PIANO SCALE MAKING
VAN ATTA, HARRISON LOUIS--EDITOR
  TREATISE ON THE PIANO AND PLAYER PIANO, A
VENABLE, MARY
  INTERPRETATION OF PIANO MUSIC, THE
VICTORIA AND ALBERT MUSEUM, SOUTH KENSINGTON
  CATALOGUE OF MUSICAL INSTRUMENTS..VOL. 1, KEYBOARD
WAGNER, CHARLES A.
  HOW TO SELECT A GOOD PIANO
WEITZMANN, CARL F.
  HISTORY OF PIANOFORTE-PLAYING AND PIANOFORTE-LITERATURE, A
WHITE, WILLIAM BRAID
  PIANO PLAYING MECHANISMS
WHITE, WILLIAM BRAID
  PIANO TUNING AND ALLIED ARTS--5TH. ED.---1917
WHITE, WILLIAM BRAID
  PLAYER-PIANO UP TO DATE, THE
WHITE, WILLIAM BRAID
  REGULATION AND REPAIR OF PIANO AND PLAYER PIANO MECHANISM
WHITE, WILLIAM BRAID
  TECHNICAL TREATISE ON PLAYER PIANO MECHANISM, A
WHITE, WILLIAM BRAID
  THEORY AND PRACTICE OF PIANOFORTE BUILDING
WIER, ALBERT
  PIANO, THE ..ITS HISTORY, MAKERS, PLAYERS AND MUSIC
WILLIS, AUBREY
  AUBREY WILLIS HOME STUDY COURSE IN PIANO TUNING AND REPAIRING
WILSON, DAVID M.
  INSTRUCTION BOOK ON THE PIANO-PLAYER AND PLAYER-PIANO, AN
WILSON, DAVID M.
  PLAYER-PIANO, THE ..ITS CONSTRUCTION..HOW TO PLAY, WHAT TO PLAY
WING AND SONS
  BOOK OF COMPLETE INFORMATION ABOUT PIANOS, THE ...1868-1918, A
WINTERNITZ, EMANUEL
  MUSICAL INSTRUMENTS OF THE WESTERN WORLD
WOLFRAM, VICTOR
  SOSTENUTO PEDAL, THE
WOODHOUSE, GEORGE
  REALISTIC APPROACH TO PIANO PLAYING, A
WOODMAN, HENRY STAUNTON
  HOW TO TUNE A PIANO..HOW TO BUY A USED PIANO..HOW TO KEEP YOUR
WORCH, HUGO
  PIANO MAKERS OF THE EVOLUTIONARY PERIOD..RARE ENGLISH AND AMERICAN
WORCH, HUGO
  WORCH PIANOS, AND A BRIEF SKETCH OF THE PIANOFORTE
YALE UNIVERSITY--ART GALLERY
  MUSICAL INSTRUMENTS AT YALE..A SELECTION OF WESTERN INSTRUMENTS
YATES, PETER
  AMATEUR AT THE KEYBOARD, AN
YOUNG, THOMAS C.
  MAKING OF MUSICAL INSTRUMENTS, THE ---1939
ZUCKERMANN, WOLFGANG JOACHIM
  MODERN HARPSICHORD, THE ..TWENTIETH CENTURY INSTRUMENTS AND THEIR

Acoustics

AEOLIAN COMPANY, THE
  AEOLIAN PIANOS, THE ---WEBER, STECK, STROUD
APEL, WILLI
  MASTERS OF THE KEYBOARD
BRIGGS, GILBERT A.
  MUSICAL INSTRUMENTS AND AUDIO
BRIGGS, GILBERT A.
  PIANOS, PIANISTS AND SONICS
BRINSMEAD, E.
  HISTORY OF THE PIANOFORTE, THE ..WITH AN AN ACCOUNT OF THE THEORY
BUNGER, RICHARD
  WELL-PREPARED PIANO, THE
CLEMENCIC, RENE
  OLD MUSICAL INSTRUMENTS
DARLOW, DENYS
  MUSICAL INSTRUMENTS--JUNIOR REFERENCE BOOKS, NO. 12--2ND. ED.
DOLGE, ALFRED
  PIANOS AND THEIR MAKERS..A COMPREHENSIVE HISTORY OF THE
DONINGTON, ROBERT
  INSTRUMENTS OF MUSIC, THE --3RD. REV. ED.---1949
DUNN, JOHN PETRIE
  BASIS OF PIANOFORTE PLAYING, THE
EISENBERG, JACOB
  LET ME HELP YOU, MY ANCESTORS AND I..A COMPREHENSIVE JUVENILE
ENGEL, CARL
  MUSICAL INSTRUMENTS---78 WOODCUT ILLUSTRATIONS
ENGEL, CARL
  MUSICAL INSTRUMENTS--REV. ED.---1876
HANSING, SIEGFRIED
  PIANOFORTE AND ITS ACOUSTIC PROPERTIES, THE --2ND. REV.
HARDING, ROSAMUND
  PIANOFORTE, THE ..ITS HISTORY TRACED TO THE GREAT EXHIBITION OF
HOWE, ALFRED H.
  SCIENTIFIC PIANO TUNING AND SERVICING--REV. ED.---1941
JEANS, SIR JAMES HOPWOOD
  SCIENCE AND MUSIC
KENDALL, ALAN
  WORLD OF MUSICAL INSTRUMENTS, THE ---CHIEFLY ILLUSTRATIONS
LOWERY, HARRY
  GUIDE TO MUSICAL ACOUSTICS, A ---1956
MATTHAY, TOBIAS A.
  ACT OF TOUCH IN ALL ITS DIVERSITY, THE ..AN ANALYSIS AND SYNTHESIS
MATTHAY, TOBIAS A.
  PIANOFORTE TONE-PRODUCTION---SAME AS 'THE ACT OF TOUCH IN ALL ITS
NALDER, LAWRENCE MARCUS
  MODERN PIANO, THE
ORTMANN, OTTO
  PHYSICAL BASIS OF PIANO TOUCH AND TONE, THE

PAETKAU, DAVID H.
  GROWTH OF INSTRUMENTS AND INSTRUMENTAL MUSIC, THE
PRESTO--EDITORIAL STAFF
  MUSICAL INSTRUMENTS AT THE WORLD'S COLUMBIAN EXPOSITION, CHICAGO,
REEDER, BETAH
  SINGING TOUCH, THE
RIPIN, EDWIN M.--EDITOR
  KEYBOARD INSTRUMENTS..STUDIES IN KEYBOARD ORGANOLOGY---10 ESSAYS
ROEHL, HARVEY
  KEYS TO A MUSICAL PAST...ILLUSTRATED TREATISE ON THE VARIOUS TYPES
SEROFF, VICTOR
  COMMON SENSE IN PIANO STUDY
SKINNER, BELLE
  BELLE SKINNER COLLECTION OF OLD MUSICAL INSTRUMENTS, HOLYOKE,
SMITH, FANNY MORRIS
  NOBLE ART, A ..THREE LECTURES ON THE EVOLUTION AND CONSTRUCTION OF
SOUTH KENSINGTON MUSEUM, LONDON
  DESCRIPTIVE CATALOGUE OF THE MUSICAL INSTRUMENTS IN THE SOUTH
STEGLICH, RUDOLF
  MOZARTS FLUEGEL KLINGT WIEDER--MOZART'S PIANO SOUNDS AGAIN---WITH
STEINERT, MORRIS
  MORRIS STEINERT COLLECTION OF KEYED AND STRINGED INSTRUMENTS, THE
STEINWAY AND SONS
  ILLUSTRATED CIRCULAR AND CATALOGUE OF PIANOFORTES--MANUFACTURERS
STEINWAY AND SONS
  PORTRAITS OF MUSICAL CELEBRITIES
STEVENS, FLOYD A.
  COMPLETE COURSE IN PROFESSIONAL PIANO TUNING, REPAIR, AND
STODDARD, HOPE
  FROM THESE COMES MUSIC
TANKARD, GEOFFREY
  PIANOFORTE DIPLOMAS
TRAVIS, JOHN W.
  LET'S TUNE UP
VANT, ALBERT B.
  PIANO SCALE MAKING
VICTORIA AND ALBERT MUSEUM, SOUTH KENSINGTON
  CATALOGUE OF MUSICAL INSTRUMENTS..VOL. 1, KEYBOARD
WEITZMANN, CARL F.
  HISTORY OF PIANOFORTE-PLAYING AND PIANOFORTE-LITERATURE, A
WHITE, WILLIAM BRAID
  PIANO TUNING AND ALLIED ARTS--5TH. ED.---1917
WHITE, WILLIAM BRAID
  THEORY AND PRACTICE OF PIANOFORTE BUILDING
WILSON, DAVID M.
  PLAYER-PIANO, THE ..ITS CONSTRUCTION..HOW TO PLAY, WHAT TO PLAY
WOOD, ALEXANDER
  PHYSICS OF MUSIC, THE --4TH. ED.---1944
WOODMAN, HENRY STAUNTON
  HOW TO TUNE A PIANO..HOW TO BUY A USED PIANO..HOW TO KEEP YOUR
YATES, PETER
  AMATEUR AT THE KEYBOARD, AN
YOUNG, THOMAS C.
  MAKING OF MUSICAL INSTRUMENTS, THE ---1939

Maintenance, Tuning and Repair

AEOLIAN COMPANY, THE
  DUO-ART REPRODUCING PIANO, THE ..THE DUO-ART REPRODUCING PIANO
AMERICAN PHOTO PLAYER COMPANY
  INSTALLATION, CARE AND OPERATION OF THE PHOTOPLAYER---1920+
AMERICAN PIANO CORPORATION
  AMPICO, THE ..A DESCRIPTION OF ITS PERFORMANCE...
AMERICAN PIANO CORPORATION
  AMPICO, THE ..SERVICE MANUAL 1929
AMERICAN PIANO CORPORATION
  AMPICO REPRODUCING PIANO, INSPECTOR'S REFERENCE BOOK, THE ---1923
AMERICAN PIANO CORPORATION
  AMPICO REPRODUCING PIANO, THE ..INSPECTOR'S INSTRUCTION BOOK,
AMERICAN SCHOOL OF PIANO TUNING
  TRAINING AS A PIANO TECHNICIAN--8 VOLS. IN 1
ANON
  COMPLEAT TUTOR FOR THE HARPSICHORD OR SPINNET, WHEREIN IS SHEWN
ANON
  HOW TO TUNE YOUR OWN PIANOFORTE..OR, THE WAY TO KEEP YOUR
ANON
  NEW INSTRUCTIONS FOR PLAYING THE HARPSICHORD, PIANOFORTE OR
ANON
  PIANOFORTE POCKET COMPANION, THE ..OR, A POPULAR VIEW OF THE
ANON
  PLAYING THE HARPSICHORD, SPINET OR PIANO FORTE MADE EASY BY NEW
ANON
  PRECEPTOR, FOR THE PIANOFORTE, THE ORGAN OR HARPSICHORD, THE
ANON
  REPAIRING THE PIANOFORTE, WITH CHAPTERS ON REGULATING, TONING,
ANON
  SHORT INSTRUCTIONS FOR TUNING A PIANO-FORTE..WRITTEN BY 'MUSICUS
AUTOPIANO COMPANY
  PLAYER PIANO POINTERS
AUTO PNEUMATIC ACTION COMPANY
  HOW TO TEST AND REGULATE THE WELTE-MIGNON REPRODUCING PIANO
BABBINGTON, CHARLES
  TUNING AND REPAIRING PIANOFORTES..THE AMATEURS GUIDE--2ND. ED.
BAINTON, HERBERT G.
  PIANO, ITS CONSTRUCTION AND CARE, THE
BALDWIN PIANO COMPANY
  MANUALO, THE PLAYER PIANO THAT IS ALL BUT HUMAN, THE ..CARE,
BALLANTINE, BILL
  PIANO, THE ..AN INTRODUCTION TO THE INSTRUMENT
BARBOUR, JAMES MURRAY
  TUNING AND TEMPERAMENT---1951
BEMETZRIEDER, ANTON
  ART OF TUNING OUR INSTRUMENTS MADE INTERESTING AND EASY TO ALL
BERNER, ALFRED *
  PRESERVATION AND RESTORATION OF MUSICAL INSTRUMENTS..PROVISIONAL
BILL, EDWARD LYMAN
  PIANO SAVING AND HOW TO ACCOMPLISH IT
BLYTHER, JAMES H.
  HOW TO TUNE YOUR OWN PIANO
BRIGGS, GILBERT A.
  MUSICAL INSTRUMENTS AND AUDIO
BRIGGS, GILBERT A.
  PIANOS, PIANISTS AND SONICS
COOKE, JAMES FRANCIS
  EVERY MAN HIS OWN TUNER..AN EASY AND CERTAIN GUIDE TO TUNING THE
DANIELL, CHARLES A.
  TRUE PIANO-TUNER, THE ..CONTAINING SIMPLE DIRECTIONS FOR TUNING,
DICKEY, ALBERT W.
  PRACTICAL PIANO TUNING..A METHOD WITH A DO-IT-YOURSELF OUTLOOK
DIETZ, FRANZ RUDOLF
  INTONIEREN VON FLUEGELN, DAS --GRAND VOICING---IN GERMAN, ENGLISH,
DIETZ, FRANZ RUDOLF
  REGULIEREN VON FLUEGELN BEI STEINWAY, DAS --REGULATION OF THE
DOLGE, ALFRED
  PIANOS AND THEIR MAKERS..A COMPREHENSIVE HISTORY OF THE

DRAKE, HARRY
    FROM PIANO TUNER TO PLAYER EXPERT
DRAKE, HARRY
    PNEUMATIC PLAYER, THE ..THE REGULATION AND REPAIR OF SOME MODERN
DRAKE, HARRY
    REPAIRING THE PLAYER PIANO
EARL, S. G.
    REPAIRING THE PLAYER PIANO..INFORMATION USEFUL TO PIANOFORTE
ELLINGHAM, HARRY
    HOW TO USE A PLAYER-PIANO
FALKENER, ROBERT
    INSTRUCTIONS FOR PLAYING THE HARPSICHORD..WHEREIN IS FULLY
FAUST, OLIVER C.
    PIANOFORTE TUNER'S POCKET COMPANION, THE ..COMPILED FROM THE NOTES
FISCHER, JERRY CREE
    PIANO TUNING, REGULATING AND REPAIRING...SELF INSTRUCTION...FOR
FUNKE, OTTO
    PIANO AND HOW TO CARE FOR IT, THE ..PIANO TUNING IN THEORY AND
GEIB, WILLIAM
    GEIB'S PIANO-FORTE PRECEPTOR, AND MUSICAL GRAMMAR...A TREATISE ON
GEIB, WILLIAM
    TREATISE ON PRACTICAL HARMONIC INTONATION, A ..ALSO, A SYNOPSIS OF
GEIB, WILLIAM
    TUNING THE PIANOFORTE..A NEW AND EASY METHOD OF HARMONIZING THE
GIESKE, GEORGE
    CARE OF THE PIANO AND PLAYER PIANO IN THE HOME, THE
GIVENS, LARRY
    REBUILDING THE PLAYER PIANO
GOULD, BRIAN M.
    BUYING A SQUARE PIANO
GRIMM, CARL W.
    HARMONY STUDY AT THE PIANO
GULBRANSEN-DICKINSON COMPANY
    GULBRANSEN SERVICE MANUAL---PLAYER PIANO
HAFER, HOWARD W.
    STUDY IN EQUAL TEMPERAMENT, A
HAMBOURG, MARK
    HOW TO PLAY THE PIANO--NEW AND ENLARGED EDITION OF "HOW TO BECOME
HAMILTON, JAMES ALEXANDER
    HAMILTON'S PRACTICAL INTRODUCTION TO THE ART OF TUNING THE
HARDING, ROSAMUND
    PIANOFORTE, THE ..ITS HISTORY TRACED TO THE GREAT EXHIBITION OF
HARRIS, BEATRIX O.
    YOUR PIANO AND HOW TO CARE FOR IT
HARRIS, REGINALD
    HOW TO CHOOSE AN INSTRUMENT..PIANO AND STRINGS
HASLUCK, PAUL N.
    PIANOS..THEIR CONSTRUCTION, TUNING AND REPAIR
HERZ, HENRI
    MEISSNER'S MODERN, PRACTICAL SYSTEM OF TUNING THE PIANOFORTE..WITH
HILL, SUMNER *
    TUNER'S MANUAL, THE
HOBBS, HENRY
    PIANO IN INDIA, THE ..HOW TO KEEP IT IN ORDER, PRACTICAL
HOLDER, WILLIAM
    TREATISE ON THE NATURAL GROUNDS AND PRINCIPLES OF HARMONY, A ..TO
HOWE, ALFRED H.
    SCIENTIFIC PIANO TUNING AND SERVICING--REV. ED.---1941
HUBBARD, FRANK
    HARPSICHORD REGULATING AND REPAIRING
HUBBARD, FRANK
    THREE CENTURIES OF HARPSICHORD MAKING
HUMMEL, JOHANN NEPOMUK
    COMPLETE THEORETICAL AND PRACTICAL COURSE OF INSTRUCTIONS ON THE
LOEHR, JOHANN JOSEPH
    ESSAY ON THE THEORY AND PRACTICE OF TUNING, AN ...PIANOFORTES AND
MACKENZIE, SIR ALEXANDER
    MUSICIAN'S NARRATIVE, A ---CLARA SCHUMANN, VON BUELOW AND LISZT
MAITLAND, GEORGE L.
    HOW TO CHANGE PITCH OF PIANOS, IN FOUR LESSONS
MARTIN, H. T.
    EVERY WOMAN HER OWN PIANO TUNER..OR, HINTS AND AIDS TO PIANO
MAYBERRY, JOHN HENRY
    PRACTICAL COURSE IN PIANO TUNING
MOORE, HENRY K.
    MANUAL OF PIANOFORTE TUNING, A
MOSCOW, CHARLES E.
    PRACTICAL PIANO TUNER, THE ..A COMPREHENSIVE SIMPLE SET OF RULES
MURATA, KOH
    SECTIONAL TUNING OF THE PIANO
MUSICAL OPINION AND MUSIC TRADE REVIEW
    REPAIRING THE REED ORGAN AND HARMONIUM..INFORMATION USEFUL TO
MUSIC EDUCATORS NATIONAL CONFERENCE
    HANDBOOK FOR TEACHING PIANO CLASSES
NALDER, LAWRENCE MARCUS
    ESSAYS IN PIANOFORTE TECHNOLOGY
NALDER, LAWRENCE MARCUS
    FIRST STEPS IN PIANO TUNING AND OTHER ESSAYS IN PIANOFORTE
NALDER, LAWRENCE MARCUS
    MODERN PIANO, THE
NALDER, LAWRENCE MARCUS
    REPAIRING THE PIANOFORTE
NEUPERT, HANNS
    CLAVICHORD, THE ---1956, IN GERMAN
NEUPERT, HANNS
    HARPSICHORD MANUAL..A HISTORY AND TECHNICAL DEVELOPMENT--2ND.
NILES BRYANT SCHOOL OF PIANO TUNING
    CORRESPONDENCE COURSE IN 12 LESSONS, A
NORTON, EDWARD Q.
    CONSTRUCTION, TUNING AND CARE OF THE PIANOFORTE--EDITED AND
ORD-HUME, ARTHUR W. J. G.
    PLAYER PIANO, THE HISTORY OF THE MECHANICAL PIANO AND HOW TO
PALMER, KING
    TEACH YOURSELF TO PLAY THE PIANO
PARKINSON, HANS B.
    PIANO, THE ..ITS CARE
PELTIER, LOUIS O.
    PIANO TUNER'S GUIDE, THE
PFEIFFER, WALTER
    PIANO KEY AND WHIPPEN, THE ..AN ANALYSIS OF THEIR RELATIONSHIPS IN
PRELLEUR, PETER
    HARPSICHORD ILLUSTRATED AND IMPROV'D, WHEREIN IS SHEWN THE ITALIAN
PYLE, HOWARD WILLETT
    PRACTICAL TREATISE ON TUNING AND REPAIRING THE PIANOFORTE, A
RIMBAULT, EDWARD FRANCIS
    CHAPPELL AND CO.'S PRACTICAL DIRECTIONS UPON THE ART OF TUNING THE
RIMBAULT, EDWARD FRANCIS
    PIANOFORTE, THE ..ITS ORIGIN, PROCESS AND CONSTRUCTION
ROSENCRANTZ, ISIDOR B.
    PIANO, ITS CONSTRUCTION AND RELATION TO TONE, PITCH AND
RUSSELL, RAYMOND
    HARPSICHORD AND THE CLAVICHORD, THE --2ND. ED., REVISED BY HOWARD
SCHMECKEL, CARL D.
    PIANO OWNER'S GUIDE, THE
SCHOTT, HOWARD
    PLAYING THE HARPSICHORD

SMITH, HERMANN
    ART OF TUNING THE PIANOFORTE, THE ...ON THE THEORY OF EQUAL
SMITH, THOMAS
    HOW TO TUNE YOUR OWN PIANO
SPILLANE, DANIEL
    HISTORY OF THE AMERICAN PIANOFORTE..ITS TECHNICAL DEVELOPMENT, AND
SPILLANE, DANIEL
    PIANO, THE ..SCIENTIFIC, TECHNICAL, AND PRACTICAL INSTRUCTIONS
STANDARD PLAYER ACTION COMPANY
    PRINCIPLES OF PLAYER ACTION OPERATION--3RD. ED.
STANDARD PNEUMATIC ACTION COMPANY
    DESCRIPTION OF STANDARD PNEUMATIC PLAYER ACTION, WITH SUGGESTIONS
STEINWAY AND SONS
    ILLUSTRATED CATALOGUE OF--STEINWAY AND SONS...PIANOFORTES
STEINWAY AND SONS
    ILLUSTRATED CATALOGUE OF PIANOS
STEVENS, FLOYD A.
    COMPLETE COURSE IN PROFESSIONAL PIANO TUNING, REPAIR, AND
STROHBER PIANO COMPANY
    PNEUMATIC PLAYER MECHANISM AND DESCRIPTIVE CATALOG OF STROHBER AND
SUMNER, WILLIAM L.
    PIANOFORTE, THE --3RD. ED.---1966
TERWILLIGER, GORDON B.
    PIANO TEACHERS PROFESSIONAL HANDBOOK
TRAVIS, JOHN W.
    GUIDE TO RESTRINGING, A
TRAVIS, JOHN W.
    LET'S TUNE UP
VAN ATTA, HARRISON LOUIS--EDITOR
    TREATISE ON THE PIANO AND PLAYER PIANO, A
WALKER, ADAM
    PHILOSOPHY OF THE HARPSICHORD, EXPLAINING HOW THAT INSTRUMENT IS
WEBER PIANO COMPANY
    WEBER GRAND, SQUARE AND UPRIGHT PIANO-FORTES, THE
WELTE-MIGNON CORPORATION
    HOW TO TEST AND REGULATE THE AUTO DE LUXE WELTE-MIGNON REPRODUCING
WHITE, WILLIAM BRAID
    PIANO PLAYING MECHANISMS
WHITE, WILLIAM BRAID
    PIANO TUNING AND ALLIED ARTS--5TH. ED.---1917
WHITE, WILLIAM BRAID
    PLAYER-PIANO UP TO DATE, THE
WHITE, WILLIAM BRAID
    REGULATION AND REPAIR OF PIANO AND PLAYER PIANO MECHANISM
WHITE, WILLIAM BRAID
    TECHNICAL TREATISE ON PLAYER PIANO MECHANISM, A
WHITE, WILLIAM BRAID
    THEORY AND PRACTICE OF PIANOFORTE BUILDING
WIER, ALBERT
    PIANO, THE ..ITS HISTORY, MAKERS, PLAYERS AND MUSIC
WILLIS, AUBREY
    AUBREY WILLIS HOME STUDY COURSE IN PIANO TUNING AND REPAIRING
WILSON, DAVID M.
    INSTRUCTION BOOK ON THE PIANO-PLAYER AND PLAYER-PIANO, AN
WILSON, DAVID M.
    PLAYER-PIANO, THE ..ITS CONSTRUCTION..HOW TO PLAY, WHAT TO PLAY
WILSON, MORRIS E.
    HOW TO HELP YOUR CHILD WITH MUSIC--2ND. ED.---1951
WOLFENDEN, S.
    TREATISE ON THE ART OF PIANOFORTE CONSTRUCTION, A
WOODMAN, HENRY STAUNTON
    HOW TO TUNE A PIANO..HOW TO BUY A USED PIANO..HOW TO KEEP YOUR
WRIGHT, WILLIAM C.
    GOLDEN MONITOR, FOR THE PIANOFORTE AND CABINET ORGAN, DESIGNED AS
ZUCKERMANN, WOLFGANG JOACHIM
    MODERN HARPSICHORD, THE ..TWENTIETH CENTURY INSTRUMENTS AND THEIR

Aesthetic Qualities

AEOLIAN COMPANY, THE
    AEOLIAN PIANOS, THE ---WEBER, STECK, STROUD
AEOLIAN COMPANY, THE
    AUDIOGRAPHIC MUSIC
AEOLIAN COMPANY, THE
    CATALOG OF THE AEOLIAN
AEOLIAN COMPANY, THE
    PIANOLA PIANO, THE
ALBARDA, JAN H.
    WOOD, WIRE AND QUILL..AN INTRODUCTION TO THE HARPSICHORD
ANON
    PIANO LOVER, THE ..BY VARIOUS AUTHORS
APEL, WILLI
    HISTORY OF KEYBOARD MUSIC TO 1700, THE --TRANSLATED AND REVISED BY
APEL, WILLI
    MASTERS OF THE KEYBOARD
BADURA-SKODA, EVA *
    INTERPRETING MOZART ON THE KEYBOARD---1957, IN GERMAN
BAINES, ANTHONY
    EUROPEAN AND AMERICAN MUSICAL INSTRUMENTS
BALLANTINE, BILL
    PIANO, THE ..AN INTRODUCTION TO THE INSTRUMENT
BALTIMORE--MUSEUM OF ART
    MUSICAL INSTRUMENTS AND THEIR PORTRAYAL IN
BLOM, ERIC
    ROMANCE OF THE PIANO, THE ---1928
BORREN, CHARLES VAN DEN
    SOURCES OF KEYBOARD MUSIC IN ENGLAND, THE ---1913
BRAGARD, ROGER
    MUSICAL INSTRUMENTS IN ART AND HISTORY
BRIGGS, GILBERT A.
    PIANOS, PIANISTS AND SONICS
BRISKIER, ARTHUR
    NEW APPROACH TO PIANO TRANSCRIPTIONS AND INTERPRETATION OF JOHANN
CHICKERING AND SONS
    HISTORICAL MUSICAL EXHIBITION..CATALOGUE OF THE EXHIBITION,
CHICKERING AND SONS
    ILLUSTRATED CATALOGUE OF PIANO FORTES
CLEMENCIC, RENE
    OLD MUSICAL INSTRUMENTS
CLOSSON, ERNEST
    HISTORY OF THE PIANO
DARLOW, DENYS
    MUSICAL INSTRUMENTS--JUNIOR REFERENCE BOOKS, NO. 12--2ND. ED.
DART, THURSTON
    INTERPRETATION OF MUSIC, THE --4TH. ED.---1954
DOLGE, ALFRED
    PIANOS AND THEIR MAKERS..A COMPREHENSIVE HISTORY OF THE
DOLMETSCH, ARNOLD
    INTERPRETATION OF MUSIC OF THE SEVENTEENTH AND EIGHTEENTH
DONALDSON, GEORGE
    CATALOGUE OF THE MUSICAL INSTRUMENTS AND OBJECTS FORMING THE
DONINGTON, ROBERT
    INSTRUMENTS OF MUSIC, THE --3RD. REV. ED.---1949
EDINBURGH UNIVERSITY--DEPT. OF EARLY KEYBOARD INSTRUMENTS
    RUSSELL COLLECTION AND OTHER EARLY KEYBOARD INSTRUMENTS IN ST.

EISENBERG, JACOB
    LET ME HELP YOU, MY ANCESTORS AND I..A COMPREHENSIVE JUVENILE
ENGEL, CARL
    MUSICAL INSTRUMENTS--REV. ED.---1876
EPWORTH PIANOS
    BOOK ABOUT PIANOS IN GENERAL AND THE EPWORTH IN PARTICULAR, A
FERGUSON, DONALD NIVISON
    PIANO MUSIC OF SIX GREAT COMPOSERS---1947
FINCK, HENRY T.
    AEOLIAN, THE ..ITS ARTISTIC MERITS, DISTINCTION FROM MECHANICAL
GABRY, GYORGY
    OLD MUSICAL INSTRUMENTS
GALPIN, FRANCIS W.
    OLD ENGLISH INSTRUMENTS OF MUSIC--4TH. ED.---1910
GALPIN, FRANCIS W.
    TEXTBOOK OF EUROPEAN MUSICAL INSTRUMENTS, A ---1937
GEIRINGER, KARL
    MUSICAL INSTRUMENTS, THEIR HISTORY IN WESTERN CULTURE FROM THE
GEPPERT, WILLIAM
    OFFICIAL GUIDE TO PIANO QUALITY, THE ---4TH. ED.
GLOVER, ELLYE HOWELL
    HOW THE PIANO CAME TO BE
HARDING, ROSAMUND
    PIANOFORTE, THE ..ITS HISTORY TRACED TO THE GREAT EXHIBITION OF
HARICH-SCHNEIDER, ETA
    HARPSICHORD, THE ..AN INTRODUCTION TO TECHNIQUE, STYLE AND THE
HARRIS, REGINALD
    HOW TO CHOOSE AN INSTRUMENT..PIANO AND STRINGS
HENDERSON, WILLIAM JAMES
    PRELUDES AND STUDIES..MUSICAL THEMES OF THE DAY--SECTION 3..THE
HINDLEY, GEOFFREY
    MUSICAL INSTRUMENTS
HIPKINS, ALFRED JAMES
    MUSICAL INSTRUMENTS, HISTORIC, RARE AND UNIQUE---1888
HORNIMAN MUSEUM AND LIBRARY, LONDON
    HANDBOOK TO THE MUSEUM'S COLLECTION, BY JEAN L. JENKINS--2ND.
HORNIMAN MUSEUM AND LIBRARY, LONDON
    MUSICAL INSTRUMENTS
HUBBARD, FRANK
    THREE CENTURIES OF HARPSICHORD MAKING
HULL, ANNE
    MAESTRO SPINETTI'S MUSIC SHOP--HARPSICHORD, CLAVICHORD,
HUTCHESON, ERNEST *
    LITERATURE OF THE PIANO, THE ..A GUIDE FOR AMATEUR AND
JAMES, PHILIP BRUTTON
    EARLY KEYBOARD INSTRUMENTS, FROM THEIR BEGINNINGS TO THE YEAR
JEANS, SIR JAMES HOPWOOD
    SCIENCE AND MUSIC
KELLEY, EDGAR STILLMAN
    MUSICAL INSTRUMENTS--3RD. YEAR OF A STUDY COURSE IN MUSIC
KENDALL, ALAN
    WORLD OF MUSICAL INSTRUMENTS, THE ---CHIEFLY ILLUSTRATIONS
KENYON, MAX
    HARPSICHORD MUSIC..THE INSTRUMENTS, THE COMPOSERS, THE PLAYERS
KIRKPATRICK, RALPH
    DOMENICO SCARLATTI---1953
LANDOWSKA, WANDA
    LANDOWSKA ON MUSIC--EDITED BY DENISE RESTOUT
LAVIGNAC, ALBERT
    MUSIC AND MUSICIANS---1895, IN FRENCH
LOESSER, ARTHUR
    MEN, WOMEN AND PIANOS..A SOCIAL HISTORY
LYONS, SISTER MARIE STEPHEN
    REAWAKENING OF INTEREST IN THE HARPSICHORD IN THE 20TH. CENTURY,
MATTHAY, TOBIAS A.
    ACT OF TOUCH IN ALL ITS DIVERSITY, THE ..AN ANALYSIS AND SYNTHESIS
MATTHAY, TOBIAS A.
    PIANOFORTE TONE-PRODUCTION---SAME AS 'THE ACT OF TOUCH IN ALL ITS
METROPOLITAN MUSEUM OF ART, NEW YORK
    KEYBOARD INSTRUMENTS IN THE METROPOLITAN MUSEUM OF ART..A PICTURE
NALDER, LAWRENCE MARCUS
    MODERN PIANO, THE
NEUPERT, HANNS
    CLAVICHORD, THE ---1956, IN GERMAN
NEWMAN, WILLIAM S.
    SONATA IN THE BAROQUE ERA, THE --A HISTORY OF THE SONATA IDEA,
NEWMAN, WILLIAM S.
    SONATA IN THE CLASSIC ERA, THE --A HISTORY OF THE SONATA IDEA,
ORD-HUME, ARTHUR W. J. G.
    CLOCKWORK MUSIC..AN ILLUSTRATED HISTORY OF MECHANICAL MUSICAL
ORTMANN, OTTO
    PHYSICAL BASIS OF PIANO TOUCH AND TONE, THE
PAETKAU, DAVID H.
    GROWTH OF INSTRUMENTS AND INSTRUMENTAL MUSIC, THE
PENGELLY, J. BRADFORD
    PENGELLY BLUE BOOK OF STYLE, THE ...A STUDY OF THE ART OF STYLING
PLAYER-PIANO, THE
    FOUR HUNDRED OF THE BEST ADS OF 1911 DEVOTED TO PIANOS AND
PRESTO--EDITORIAL STAFF
    MUSICAL INSTRUMENTS AT THE WORLD'S COLUMBIAN EXPOSITION, CHICAGO,
REEDER, BETAH
    SINGING TOUCH, THE
RIPIN, EDWIN M.--EDITOR
    KEYBOARD INSTRUMENTS..STUDIES IN KEYBOARD ORGANOLOGY---10 ESSAYS
ROEHL, HARVEY
    KEYS TO A MUSICAL PAST...ILLUSTRATED TREATISE ON THE VARIOUS TYPES
ROEHL, HARVEY
    PLAYER PIANO, AN HISTORICAL SCRAPBOOK, THE
ROEHL, HARVEY
    PLAYER PIANO TREASURY..THE SCRAPBOOK HISTORY OF THE MECHANICAL
RUSSELL, RAYMOND
    CATALOGUE OF THE BENTON FLETCHER COLLECTION OF EARLY KEYBOARD
RUSSELL, RAYMOND
    HARPSICHORD AND THE CLAVICHORD, THE --2ND. ED., REVISED BY HOWARD
SACHS, CURT
    HISTORY OF MUSICAL INSTRUMENTS, THE
SCHULZE, RICHARD ALLEN
    HOW TO BUILD A BAROQUE CONCERT HARPSICHORD
SKINNER, BELLE
    BELLE SKINNER COLLECTION OF OLD MUSICAL INSTRUMENTS, HOLYOKE,
SMITH, FANNY MORRIS
    NOBLE ART, A ..THREE LECTURES ON THE EVOLUTION AND CONSTRUCTION OF
SOUTH KENSINGTON MUSEUM, LONDON
    CATALOGUE OF THE SPECIAL EXHIBITION OF ANCIENT MUSICAL INSTRUMENTS
SOUTH KENSINGTON MUSEUM, LONDON
    DESCRIPTIVE CATALOGUE OF THE MUSICAL INSTRUMENTS IN THE SOUTH
SOUTH KENSINGTON MUSEUM, LONDON
    DESCRIPTIVE CATALOGUE OF THE MUSICAL INSTRUMENTS IN THE SOUTH
SPILLANE, DANIEL
    HISTORY OF THE AMERICAN PIANOFORTE..ITS TECHNICAL DEVELOPMENT, AND
STECK AND COMPANY
    ILLUSTRATED CATALOG...GRAND AND UPRIGHT PIANOS
STEGLICH, RUDOLF
    MOZARTS FLUEGEL KLINGT WIEDER--MOZART'S PIANO SOUNDS AGAIN---WITH
STEINERT, MORRIS
    MORRIS STEINERT COLLECTION OF KEYED AND STRINGED INSTRUMENTS, THE

STEINWAY, THEODORE E.
    PEOPLE AND PIANOS..A CENTURY OF SERVICE TO MUSIC---1853-1953
STEINWAY AND SONS
    BOOK OF ART PIANO CASES
STEINWAY AND SONS
    ILLUSTRATED CATALOGUE OF PIANOS
STEINWAY AND SONS
    ILLUSTRATED CATALOGUE OF STEINWAY AND SONS' PIANOS
STEINWAY AND SONS
    ILLUSTRATED CIRCULAR AND CATALOGUE OF PIANOFORTES--MANUFACTURERS
STEINWAY AND SONS
    INIMITABLE TONE..'PRICE LIST OF PIANOS MADE BY STEINWAY AND SONS,
STEINWAY AND SONS
    PIANOFORTES
STEINWAY AND SONS
    PORTRAITS OF MUSICAL CELEBRITIES
STEINWAY AND SONS
    PORTRAITS OF MUSICAL CELEBRITIES
STEINWAY AND SONS
    PORTRAITS OF MUSICAL CELEBRITIES
STEINWAY AND SONS
    PORTRAITS OF MUSICAL CELEBRITIES
STEINWAY AND SONS
    PORTRAITS OF MUSICAL CELEBRITIES
STEINWAY AND SONS
    STEINWAY..YESTERDAY, TODAY, TOMORROW
STEINWAY AND SONS
    STEINWAY PROGRESS..AN APPRECIATION BY I. J. PADEREWSKI
SUMNER, WILLIAM L.
    PIANOFORTE, THE --3RD. ED.---1966
VAN NOORDEN, C.
    FREAK PIANOS---SCRAPBOOK
VICTORIA AND ALBERT MUSEUM, SOUTH KENSINGTON
    CATALOGUE OF MUSICAL INSTRUMENTS..VOL. 1, KEYBOARD
VICTORIA AND ALBERT MUSEUM, SOUTH KENSINGTON
    EXAMPLES OF ART WORKMANSHIP OF VARIOUS AGES AND COUNTRIES..MUSICAL
VICTORIA AND ALBERT MUSEUM, SOUTH KENSINGTON
    MUSICAL INSTRUMENTS AS WORKS OF ART..VOL. 1, KEYBOARD
WEBER PIANO COMPANY
    WEBER GRAND, SQUARE AND UPRIGHT PIANO-FORTES, THE
WHITE, WILLIAM BRAID
    THEORY AND PRACTICE OF PIANOFORTE BUILDING
WINTERNITZ, EMANUEL
    MUSICAL INSTRUMENTS AND THEIR SYMBOLISM IN WESTERN ART
WINTERNITZ, EMANUEL
    MUSICAL INSTRUMENTS OF THE WESTERN WORLD
WOLFRAM, VICTOR
    SOSTENUTO PEDAL, THE
WORCH, HUGO
    PIANO MAKERS OF THE EVOLUTIONARY PERIOD..RARE ENGLISH AND AMERICAN
YALE UNIVERSITY--ART GALLERY
    MUSICAL INSTRUMENTS AT YALE..A SELECTION OF WESTERN INSTRUMENTS
ZUCKERMANN, WOLFGANG JOACHIM
    MODERN HARPSICHORD, THE ..TWENTIETH CENTURY INSTRUMENTS AND THEIR

Mechanical Pianos

AEOLIAN COMPANY, THE
    AUDIOGRAPHIC MUSIC
AEOLIAN COMPANY, THE
    CATALOG OF AEOLIAN MUSIC ARRANGED FOR 46-NOTE INSTRUMENTS
AEOLIAN COMPANY, THE
    CATALOG OF METROSTYLE AND THEMODIST MUSIC FOR THE PIANOLA AND
AEOLIAN COMPANY, THE
    CATALOG OF MUSIC-ROLLS FOR THE DUO-ART REPRODUCING PIANO
AEOLIAN COMPANY, THE
    CATALOG OF MUSIC AND MUSICAL LITERATURE---PIANOLA RECORDS
AEOLIAN COMPANY, THE
    CATALOG OF MUSIC FOR THE PIANOLA, PIANOLA PIANO AND
AEOLIAN COMPANY, THE
    CATALOG OF THE AEOLIAN
AEOLIAN COMPANY, THE
    COMPLETE CATALOG OF MUSIC ROLLS FOR THE DUO-ART REPRODUCING PIANO
AEOLIAN COMPANY, THE
    DUO-ART BOOK OF MUSIC, THE
AEOLIAN COMPANY, THE
    DUO-ART PIANO MUSIC...RECORDED BY MORE THAN 250 PIANISTS
AEOLIAN COMPANY, THE
    DUO-ART PIANO MUSIC
AEOLIAN COMPANY, THE
    DUO-ART REPRODUCING PIANO, THE ..THE DUO-ART REPRODUCING PIANO
AEOLIAN COMPANY, THE
    LIBRARY OF DUO-ART MUSIC ROLLS
AEOLIAN COMPANY, THE
    METROSTYLE-THEMODIST AND METRO-ART MUSIC ROLLS FOR THE PIANOLA AND
AEOLIAN COMPANY, THE
    METROSTYLE, THE
AEOLIAN COMPANY, THE
    METROSTYLE AND THEMODIST MUSIC CATALOG FOR THE PIANOLA AND PIANOLA
AEOLIAN COMPANY, THE
    MUSIC FOR THE AEOLIAN GRAND--SUPPLEMENT
AEOLIAN COMPANY, THE
    MUSIC FOR THE AEOLIAN GRAND
AEOLIAN COMPANY, THE
    MUSIC FOR THE ORCHESTRELLE AND AEOLIAN GRAND
AEOLIAN COMPANY, THE
    MUSIC FOR THE PIANOLA AND THE AERIAL PIANO--4 VOLS.
AEOLIAN COMPANY, THE
    NEW MUSIC FOR THE AEOLIAN GRAND, THE PIANOLA, AND THE AERIOL PIANO
AEOLIAN COMPANY, THE
    PIANISTS WHO HAVE MADE RECORDS FOR THE DUO-ART PIANO
AEOLIAN COMPANY, THE
    PIANOLA AND PIANOLA PIANO MUSIC CATALOG, THE ..SIXTY-FIVE NOTE
AEOLIAN COMPANY, THE
    PIANOLA PIANO, THE
AEOLIAN COMPANY, THE
    SUPPLEMENTARY CATALOG OF MUSIC FOR THE AEOLIAN GRAND AND
AEOLIAN COMPANY, THE
    WEIGHT OF EVIDENCE ON THE TRUE MUSICAL WORTH OF THE PIANOLA AND
ALBIG, GEORGE L.
    HOW TO PLAY THE PLAYER
AMERICAN PHOTO PLAYER COMPANY
    INSTALLATION, CARE AND OPERATION OF THE PHOTOPLAYER---1920+
AMERICAN PIANO CORPORATION
    AMPICO, THE ..A DESCRIPTION OF ITS PERFORMANCE...
AMERICAN PIANO CORPORATION
    AMPICO, THE ..SERVICE MANUAL 1929
AMERICAN PIANO CORPORATION
    AMPICO REPRODUCING PIANO, INSPECTOR'S REFERENCE BOOK, THE ---1923
AMERICAN PIANO CORPORATION
    AMPICO REPRODUCING PIANO, THE ..INSPECTOR'S INSTRUCTION BOOK,
AMERICAN PIANO CORPORATION
    CATALOGUE OF MUSIC FOR THE AMPICO, A ..A LIST OF THE RECORDINGS OF
AMERICAN PIANO CORPORATION
    CATALOGUE OF MUSIC FOR THE AMPICO, A --A LIST OF THE RECORDINGS OF

AMPICO CORPORATION
    AMPICO REPRODUCING PIANO..A SUPPLEMENT TO 'PIANO MUSIC, ITS
AMPICO CORPORATION
    SUPREMACY OF AMPICO MUSIC..UNIT TWO OF A COURSE IN AMPICO
ANON
    DIGITORIUM, THE --MINIATURE DUMB PIANO
ASSOCIATION FOR RECORDED SOUND COLLECTIONS
    PRELIMINARY DIRECTORY OF SOUND RECORDING COLLECTIONS IN THE UNITED
AUTOPIANO COMPANY
    PLAYER PIANO POINTERS
AUTO PNEUMATIC ACTION COMPANY
    HOW TO TEST AND REGULATE THE WELTE-MIGNON REPRODUCING PIANO
AUTO PNEUMATIC ACTION COMPANY
    WELTE-MIGNON BOOK...OF FAMOUS ARTISTS, THE
BALDWIN PIANO COMPANY
    MANUALO, THE PLAYER PIANO THAT IS ALL BUT HUMAN, THE ..CARE,
BAMBERGER, LOUIS
    MEMORIES OF SIXTY YEARS IN THE TIMBER AND PIANOFORTE TRADES
BARTELS, LEO F. *
    PERFORATING OF MUSIC ROLLS WITH THE LEABARJAN PERFORATOR, THE
BOWERS, Q. DAVID
    ENCYCLOPEDIA OF AUTOMATIC MUSICAL INSTRUMENTS---INCLUDES A
BOWERS, Q. DAVID
    GUIDEBOOK OF AUTOMATIC MUSICAL INSTRUMENTS, A. --2 VOLS.
BOWERS, Q. DAVID
    PUT ANOTHER NICKEL IN..A HISTORY OF COIN-OPERATED PIANOS
BRIGGS, GILBERT A.
    MUSICAL INSTRUMENTS AND AUDIO
BROADWOOD, JOHN AND SONS
    CATALOGUE OF JOHN BROADWOOD AND SONS, LTD. LATEST MODELS,
BUCHNER, ALEXANDER
    MECHANICAL MUSICAL INSTRUMENTS---174 NUMBERED PLATES
CHILTON, CARROLL B.
    DE-ASSIFICATION OF MUSIC, THE ..A PROPAGANDIST MAGAZINE, OF ONE
DELUXE ROLL CORPORATION
    LIBRARY OF DELUXE WELTE-MIGNON MUSIC RECORDS FOR REPRODUCING
DOLGE, ALFRED
    PIANOS AND THEIR MAKERS..A COMPREHENSIVE HISTORY OF THE
DRAKE, HARRY
    FROM PIANO TUNER TO PLAYER EXPERT
DRAKE, HARRY
    PLAYER-PIANO EXPLAINED, THE --PAMPHLET
DRAKE, HARRY
    PNEUMATIC PLAYER, THE ..THE REGULATION AND REPAIR OF SOME MODERN
DRAKE, HARRY
    REPAIRING THE PLAYER PIANO
EISENBERG, JACOB
    LET ME HELP YOU, MY ANCESTORS AND I..A COMPREHENSIVE JUVENILE
FINCK, HENRY T.
    AEOLIAN, THE ..ITS ARTISTIC MERITS, DISTINCTION FROM MECHANICAL
FINCK, HENRY T.
    TWENTY MUSICAL EVENINGS---PIANOLA PROGRAMS WITH NOTES AND COMMENTS
GEPPERT, WILLIAM
    OFFICIAL GUIDE TO PIANO QUALITY, THE ---4TH. ED.
GIESKE, GEORGE
    CARE OF THE PIANO AND PLAYER PIANO IN THE HOME, THE
GIVENS, LARRY
    RE-ENACTING THE ARTIST..A STORY OF THE AMPICO REPRODUCING PIANO
GIVENS, LARRY
    REBUILDING THE PLAYER PIANO
GOW, GEORGE C.
    PROS AND CONS OF THE MECHANICAL PLAYER, THE --REPRINT..M.T.N.A.
GREW, SIDNEY
    ART OF THE PLAYER-PIANO, THE ..A TEXTBOOK FOR STUDENT AND TEACHER
GREW, SIDNEY
    FIRST BOOK OF THE PLAYER-PIANIST, THE
GULBRANSEN-DICKINSON COMPANY
    GULBRANSEN SERVICE MANUAL---PLAYER PIANO
HAMILTON, CLARENCE G.
    SUPPLEMENT TO PIANO MUSIC, ITS COMPOSERS AND CHARACTERISTICS, A
HANSMANN, RICHARD
    THEORETICAL AND PRACTICAL PIANO-FORTE SCHOOL FOR THE JANKO
HOBBS, HENRY
    PIANO IN INDIA, THE ..HOW TO KEEP IT IN ORDER, PRACTICAL
HOOVER, CYNTHIA A.
    MUSIC MACHINES--AMERICAN STYLE..A CATALOG OF THE EXHIBITION
KACZMAREK, REGINA A.
    CATALOG OF SELECTED PIANO ROLLS FROM THE LIBRARY OF CONGRESS
KOBBE, GUSTAV
    PIANOLIST, THE ..A GUIDE FOR PIANOLA PLAYERS
KOBBE, GUSTAV
    STRAIGHT TO THE HEART OF MUSIC---PLAYER-PIANO
LOESSER, ARTHUR
    MEN, WOMEN AND PIANOS..A SOCIAL HISTORY
MCTAMMANY, JOHN
    EVOLUTION OF THE PLAYER-PIANO MECHANISM---EXCERPT FROM 'PRESTO',
MCTAMMANY, JOHN
    HISTORY OF THE PLAYER-PIANO, THE
MCTAMMANY, JOHN
    TECHNICAL HISTORY OF THE PLAYER
MEL-O-DEE MUSIC COMPANY
    MELODEE MUSIC ROLLS..SEPTEMBER, 1920
NEWMAN, ERNEST
    PIANO-PLAYER AND ITS MUSIC, THE
NICCHIA, LILLIAN
    PIANOFORTE STUDY..HINTS ON PIANO PLAYING
ORD-HUME, ARTHUR W. J. G.
    CLOCKWORK MUSIC..AN ILLUSTRATED HISTORY OF MECHANICAL MUSICAL
ORD-HUME, ARTHUR W. J. G.
    PLAYER PIANO, THE HISTORY OF THE MECHANICAL PIANO AND HOW TO
RIMBAULT, EDWARD FRANCIS
    PIANOFORTE, THE ..ITS ORIGIN, PROCESS AND CONSTRUCTION
ROEHL, HARVEY
    KEYS TO A MUSICAL PAST...ILLUSTRATED TREATISE ON THE VARIOUS TYPES
ROEHL, HARVEY
    PLAYER PIANO, AN HISTORICAL SCRAPBOOK, THE
ROEHL, HARVEY
    PLAYER PIANO TREASURY..THE SCRAPBOOK HISTORY OF THE MECHANICAL
SCHAAF, EDWARD O.
    ART OF PIANO PLAYER TRANSCRIPTION, THE ..MAKING OF PERFORATED
SCHAAF, EDWARD O.
    ESSAYS AND ARTICLES ON MUSICAL SUBJECTS, PARTICULARLY
SCHAAF, EDWARD O.
    FUNDAMENTAL PRINCIPLES INVOLVED IN THE COMPOSING AND ARRANGING OF
SCHAAF, EDWARD O.
    MUSICAL INDIVIDUALITY OF THE PLAYER PIANO, THE ---EXCERPTS..'THE
SCHOLES, PERCY
    APPRECIATION OF MUSIC BY MEANS OF THE PIANOLA AND DUO-ART, THE
SPAETH, SIGMUND *
    AMPICO IN MUSIC STUDY, THE
STANDARD PLAYER ACTION COMPANY
    PRINCIPLES OF PLAYER ACTION OPERATION--3RD. ED.
STANDARD PNEUMATIC ACTION COMPANY
    DESCRIPTION OF STANDARD PNEUMATIC PLAYER ACTION, WITH SUGGESTIONS
STROHBER PIANO COMPANY
    PNEUMATIC PLAYER MECHANISM AND DESCRIPTIVE CATALOG OF STROHBER AND

TAPPER, THOMAS
    EDUCATION OF THE MUSIC TEACHER, THE
TONK, WILLIAM
    MEMOIRS OF A--PIANO--MANUFACTURER
UNITED STATES--LIBRARY OF CONGRESS..DIVISION OF BIBLIOGRAPHY
    BRIEF LIST OF REFERENCES ON THE PIANO AND THE PIANO PLAYER
VAN ATTA, HARRISON LOUIS--EDITOR
    TREATISE ON THE PIANO AND PLAYER PIANO, A
VAN DER WEYDE, PETER H.
    INSTRUCTIONS IN PLAYING THE PIANO-FORTE WITH AEOLIAN ATTACHMENT
VIRGIL, ALMON K.
    TECHNIPHONE MANUAL..INSTRUCTIONS AND EXERCISES IN THE USE OF THE
WELTE-MIGNON CORPORATION
    HOW TO TEST AND REGULATE THE AUTO DE LUXE WELTE-MIGNON REPRODUCING
WELTE-MIGNON CORPORATION
    LIBRARY OF DELUXE WELTE-MIGNON MUSIC RECORDS FOR REPRODUCING
WELTE-MIGNON CORPORATION
    LIBRARY OF WELTE-MIGNON MUSIC RECORDS
WELTE ARTISTIC PLAYER-PIANO COMPANY
    LIST OF MUSIC FOR THE WELTE-MIGNON PIANO--WITH SUPPLEMENT
WHITE, WILLIAM BRAID
    PIANO PLAYING MECHANISMS
WHITE, WILLIAM BRAID
    PLAYER-PIANIST, THE ..A GUIDE TO THE APPRECIATION AND
WHITE, WILLIAM BRAID
    PLAYER-PIANO UP TO DATE, THE
WHITE, WILLIAM BRAID
    REGULATION AND REPAIR OF PIANO AND PLAYER PIANO MECHANISM
WHITE, WILLIAM BRAID
    TECHNICAL TREATISE ON PLAYER PIANO MECHANISM, A
WHITE, WILLIAM BRAID
    THEORY AND PRACTICE OF PIANOFORTE BUILDING
WIER, ALBERT
    PIANO, THE ..ITS HISTORY, MAKERS, PLAYERS AND MUSIC
WILSON, DAVID M.
    INSTRUCTION BOOK ON THE PIANO-PLAYER AND PLAYER-PIANO, AN
WILSON, DAVID M.
    PLAYER-PIANO, THE ..ITS CONSTRUCTION..HOW TO PLAY, WHAT TO PLAY
WOLFRAM, VICTOR
    SOSTENUTO PEDAL, THE

Electronic Instruments

AMERICAN PIANO CORPORATION
    AMPICO, THE ..A DESCRIPTION OF ITS PERFORMANCE...
AMERICAN PIANO CORPORATION
    AMPICO, THE ..SERVICE MANUAL 1929
BRIGGS, GILBERT A.
    MUSICAL INSTRUMENTS AND AUDIO
DECKER, TOM W.
    CONSOLE SYSTEM, THE ..A TEXT FOR MODERN PIANO AND ORGAN TO BE USED
LUND, VICTOR E.
    EVALUATION OF ELECTRONIC SELF-INSTRUCTION ON PIANO KEYBOARD, THE
STEVENS, FLOYD A.
    COMPLETE COURSE IN PROFESSIONAL PIANO TUNING, REPAIR, AND
WILLS, VERA G. *
    PARENT'S GUIDE TO MUSIC LESSONS, A

Makers

AEOLIAN COMPANY, THE
    AEOLIAN PIANOS, THE ---WEBER, STECK, STROUD
AEOLIAN COMPANY, THE
    AUDIOGRAPHIC MUSIC
AEOLIAN COMPANY, THE
    CATALOG OF THE AEOLIAN
AEOLIAN COMPANY, THE
    PIANOLA PIANO, THE
AEOLIAN COMPANY, THE
    SPECIAL SURVEY CONDUCTED--IN 1889--FOR LYON AND HEALY, INC.,
AEOLIAN COMPANY, THE
    WEIGHT OF EVIDENCE ON THE TRUE MUSICAL WORTH OF THE PIANOLA AND
ALBARDA, JAN H.
    WOOD, WIRE AND QUILL..AN INTRODUCTION TO THE HARPSICHORD
AMERICAN PHOTO PLAYER COMPANY
    INSTALLATION, CARE AND OPERATION OF THE PHOTOPLAYER---1920+
AMERICAN STEEL AND WIRE COMPANY
    NERVES OF STEEL..THE STORY OF AMERICAN PIANO WIRE AND ITS
ANDERSON-MULDER COMPANY
    DEALER'S HANDBOOK OF PIANOS AND THEIR MAKERS
AUTOPIANO COMPANY
    PLAYER PIANO POINTERS
BABBINGTON, CHARLES
    TUNING AND REPAIRING PIANOFORTES..THE AMATEURS GUIDE--2ND. ED.
BAINES, ANTHONY
    EUROPEAN AND AMERICAN MUSICAL INSTRUMENTS
BAINES, ANTHONY
    MUSICAL INSTRUMENTS THROUGH THE AGES--REV. ED.---1961
BALDWIN PIANO COMPANY
    MANUALO, THE PLAYER PIANO THAT IS ALL BUT HUMAN, THE ..CARE,
BALLANTINE, BILL
    PIANO, THE ..AN INTRODUCTION TO THE INSTRUMENT
BALTIMORE--MUSEUM OF ART
    MUSICAL INSTRUMENTS AND THEIR PORTRAYAL IN
BAMBERGER, LOUIS
    MEMORIES OF SIXTY YEARS IN THE TIMBER AND PIANOFORTE TRADES
BARTHOLOMEW, RALPH I.
    MAKING OF A STEINWAY, THE
BESSARABOFF, NICHOLAS
    ANCIENT EUROPEAN MUSICAL INSTRUMENTS...IN THE LESLIE LINDSAY MASON
BLOM, ERIC
    ROMANCE OF THE PIANO, THE ---1928
BOWERS, Q. DAVID
    ENCYCLOPEDIA OF AUTOMATIC MUSICAL INSTRUMENTS--- INCLUDES A
BROADWOOD, JAMES SHUDI
    SOME NOTES--ON THE HARPSICHORD AND PIANOFORTE--MADE BY J. S.
BROADWOOD, JOHN AND SONS
    CATALOGUE OF BOOKS IN THE LIBRARY OF JOHN BROADWOOD AND SONS'
BROADWOOD, JOHN AND SONS
    CATALOGUE OF JOHN BROADWOOD AND SONS, LTD. LATEST MODELS,
BROADWOOD, JOHN AND SONS
    INFORMATION CONCERNING PIANOFORTES OF USE AND OF INTEREST..A VADE
BROADWOOD, JOHN AND SONS
    INTERNATIONAL EXHIBITION, 1862..LIST OF PIANOFORTES AND
CARMI, AVNER *
    IMMORTAL PIANO, THE
CHICKERING AND SONS
    ACHIEVEMENT..AN ASCENDING SCALE, BEING A SHORT HISTORY OF THE
CHICKERING AND SONS
    CHICKERING AND SONS, MANUFACTURER OF GRAND, SQUARE AND UPRIGHT
CHICKERING AND SONS
    CHICKERING AND SONS PIANOFORTES AT THE CENTENNIAL EXHIBITION,
CHICKERING AND SONS
    CHICKERING CENTENNIAL CELEBRATION, APRIL 1823-1923
CHICKERING AND SONS
    COMMEMORATION OF THE FOUNDING OF THE HOUSE OF CHICKERING AND SONS,

CHICKERING AND SONS
    HISTORICAL MUSICAL EXHIBITION..CATALOGUE OF THE EXHIBITION,
CHICKERING AND SONS
    ILLUSTRATED CATALOGUE OF PIANO FORTES
CHICKERING AND SONS
    JONAS CHICKERING CENTENNIAL CELEBRATION, THE ..A TRIBUTE TO THE
CHICKERING AND SONS
    JONAS CHICKERING CENTENNIAL CELEBRATION, 1823-1923..IN
CHICKERING AND SONS
    NEW ILLUSTRATED CATALOGUE OF PIANOFORTES, A
CHICKERING AND SONS
    PIANO-FORTES AT THE EXHIBITION OF 1856
CHICKERING BROTHERS, CHICAGO
    PIANO-FORTES AND THEIR MANUFACTURE, WITH ILLUSTRATED CATALOGUE
CLEMENCIC, RENE
    OLD MUSICAL INSTRUMENTS
DALE, WILLIAM
    TSCHUDI THE HARPSICHORD MAKER
DARLOW, DENYS
    MUSICAL INSTRUMENTS--JUNIOR REFERENCE BOOKS, NO. 12--2ND. ED.
DIETZ, FRANZ RUDOLF
    REGULIEREN VON FLUEGELN BEI STEINWAY, DAS --REGULATION OF THE
EDINBURGH UNIVERSITY--DEPT. OF EARLY KEYBOARD INSTRUMENTS
    RUSSELL COLLECTION AND OTHER EARLY KEYBOARD INSTRUMENTS IN ST.
EISENBERG, JACOB
    LET ME HELP YOU, MY ANCESTORS AND I..A COMPREHENSIVE JUVENILE
EISENBERG, JACOB
    ROMANCE OF KEYS AND TONES..THE PIANO, ITS ORIGIN AND DEVELOPMENT,
EPWORTH PIANOS
    BOOK ABOUT PIANOS IN GENERAL AND THE EPWORTH IN PARTICULAR, A
FINCK, HENRY T.
    AEOLIAN, THE ..ITS ARTISTIC MERITS, DISTINCTION FROM MECHANICAL
GABRY, GYORGY
    OLD MUSICAL INSTRUMENTS
GATES, WILLEY F.
    PIPE AND STRINGS..THREE HISTORIC AND DESCRIPTIVE SKETCHES...THE
GEIRINGER, KARL
    MUSICAL INSTRUMENTS, THEIR HISTORY IN WESTERN CULTURE FROM THE
GEPPERT, WILLIAM
    OFFICIAL GUIDE TO PIANO QUALITY, THE ---4TH. ED.
GLOVER, ELLYE HOWELL
    HOW THE PIANO CAME TO BE
HARDING, ROSAMUND
    PIANOFORTE, THE ..ITS HISTORY TRACED TO THE GREAT EXHIBITION OF
HINDLEY, GEOFFREY
    MUSICAL INSTRUMENTS
HOBBS, HENRY
    PIANO IN INDIA, THE ..HOW TO KEEP IT IN ORDER, PRACTICAL
HUBBARD, ELBERT
    STORY OF THE STEINWAYS, THE --REPRINT FROM 'FRA' MAGAZINE
KIRBY, FRANK EUGENE
    SHORT HISTORY OF KEYBOARD MUSIC, A
LOESSER, ARTHUR
    MEN, WOMEN AND PIANOS..A SOCIAL HISTORY
MACQUOID, PERCY *
    DICTIONARY OF ENGLISH FURNITURE, THE --VOL. 3---16 ILLUSTRATIONS
MASON AND HAMLIN ORGAN AND PIANO COMPANY
    CATALOGUE OF PIANOFORTES EMBODYING LATEST IMPROVEMENTS
MICHEL, NORMAN ELWOOD
    MICHEL'S PIANO ATLAS---REPUBLISHED IN 1965 UNDER AUTHORSHIP..B.
NATIONAL PIANO MANUFACTURERS ASSOCIATION OF AMERICA
    STENCILLING OF PIANOS, THE
NATIONAL PIANO MANUFACTURERS ASSOCIATION
    CONSUMER INVESTIGATION FOR NATIONAL PIANO MANUFACTURERS
NATIONAL PIANO TRAVELERS ASSOCIATION
    PIANO TRAVELERS ASSOCIATION BOOK, THE ..A REFERENCE BOOK
PARKER, RICHARD G.
    TRIBUTE TO THE LIFE AND CHARACTER OF JONAS CHICKERING, 1798-1853,
PARRISH, CARL
    EARLY PIANO AND ITS INFLUENCE ON KEYBOARD TECHNIQUE AND
PAUER, ERNST
    DICTIONARY OF PIANISTS AND COMPOSERS FOR THE PIANOFORTE..WITH AN
PENGELLY, J. BRADFORD
    PENGELLY BLUE BOOK OF STYLE, THE ...A STUDY OF THE ART OF STYLING
PIANO, ORGAN AND MUSICAL INSTRUMENT WORKERS INTERNATIONAL UNION OF
    CONSTITUTION OF THE PIANO, ORGAN AND MUSICAL INSTRUMENT WORKERS'
PIERCE, B.
    PIERCE PIANO ATLAS--6TH. ED.---ORIGINALLY PUBLISHED AS 'MICHEL'S
PLAYER-PIANO, THE
    FOUR HUNDRED OF THE BEST ADS OF 1911 DEVOTED TO PIANOS AND
PRESTO--EDITORIAL STAFF
    MUSICAL INSTRUMENTS AT THE WORLD'S COLUMBIAN EXPOSITION, CHICAGO,
PRESTO PUBLISHING COMPANY
    PRESTO BUYERS' GUIDE TO PLAYER-PIANOS AND PIANOS
RIMBAULT, EDWARD FRANCIS
    PIANOFORTE, THE ..ITS ORIGIN, PROCESS AND CONSTRUCTION
RIPIN, EDWIN M.--EDITOR
    KEYBOARD INSTRUMENTS..STUDIES IN KEYBOARD ORGANOLOGY---10 ESSAYS
ROEHL, HARVEY
    KEYS TO A MUSICAL PAST...ILLUSTRATED TREATISE ON THE VARIOUS TYPES
ROEHL, HARVEY
    PLAYER PIANO, AN HISTORICAL SCRAPBOOK, THE
ROEHL, HARVEY
    PLAYER PIANO TREASURY..THE SCRAPBOOK HISTORY OF THE MECHANICAL
RUSSELL, RAYMOND
    CATALOGUE OF THE BENTON FLETCHER COLLECTION OF EARLY KEYBOARD
RUSSELL, RAYMOND
    HARPSICHORD AND THE CLAVICHORD, THE --2ND. ED., REVISED BY HOWARD
SOUTH KENSINGTON MUSEUM, LONDON
    CATALOGUE OF THE SPECIAL EXHIBITION OF ANCIENT MUSICAL INSTRUMENTS
SOUTH KENSINGTON MUSEUM, LONDON
    DESCRIPTIVE CATALOGUE OF THE MUSICAL INSTRUMENTS IN THE SOUTH
SPILLANE, DANIEL
    HISTORY OF THE AMERICAN PIANOFORTE..ITS TECHNICAL DEVELOPMENT, AND
STANDARD PNEUMATIC ACTION COMPANY
    DESCRIPTION OF STANDARD PNEUMATIC PLAYER ACTION, WITH SUGGESTIONS
STECK AND COMPANY
    ILLUSTRATED CATALOG...GRAND AND UPRIGHT PIANOS
STEGLICH, RUDOLF
    MOZARTS FLUEGEL KLINGT WIEDER--MOZART'S PIANO SOUNDS AGAIN---WITH
STEINERT, MORRIS
    MORRIS STEINERT COLLECTION OF KEYED AND STRINGED INSTRUMENTS, THE
STEINWAY, THEODORE E.
    PEOPLE AND PIANOS..A CENTURY OF SERVICE TO MUSIC---1853-1953
STEINWAY AND SONS
    BOOK OF ART PIANO CASES
STEINWAY AND SONS
    ILLUSTRATED CATALOGUE OF STEINWAY AND SONS' PIANOS
STEINWAY AND SONS
    ILLUSTRATED CIRCULAR AND CATALOGUE OF PIANOFORTES--MANUFACTURERS
STEINWAY AND SONS
    INIMITABLE TONE..'PRICE LIST OF PIANOS MADE BY STEINWAY AND SONS,
STEINWAY AND SONS
    PIANOFORTES
STEINWAY AND SONS
    PORTRAITS OF MUSICAL CELEBRITIES

STEINWAY AND SONS
    PORTRAITS OF MUSICAL CELEBRITIES
STEINWAY AND SONS
    PORTRAITS OF MUSICAL CELEBRITIES
STEINWAY AND SONS
    PORTRAITS OF MUSICAL CELEBRITIES
STEINWAY AND SONS
    PORTRAITS OF MUSICAL CELEBRITIES
STEINWAY AND SONS
    PORTRAITS OF MUSICAL CELEBRITIES
STEINWAY AND SONS
    STEINWAY..YESTERDAY, TODAY, TOMORROW
STEINWAY AND SONS
    STEINWAY AND SONS' PIANO-FORTE MANUFACTORY AT 'STEINWAY', LONG
STEINWAY AND SONS
    STEINWAY OF TODAY, THE ..A FAMILY OF PIANO MANUFACTURERS THROUGH
STEINWAY AND SONS
    STEINWAY PROGRESS..AN APPRECIATION BY I. J. PADEREWSKI
STEVENS, PARAN
    REPORT UPON MUSICAL INSTRUMENTS..PARIS UNIVERSAL EXPOSITION, 1867
STRAUCH BROTHERS
    MANUFACTURE OF PIANOFORTE ACTION, THE ..ITS RISE AND DEVELOPMENT
STROHBER PIANO COMPANY
    PNEUMATIC PLAYER MECHANISM AND DESCRIPTIVE CATALOG OF STROHBER AND
SUMNER, WILLIAM L.
    PIANOFORTE, THE --3RD. ED.---1966
TONK, WILLIAM
    MEMOIRS OF A--PIANO--MANUFACTURER
UNITED STATES--LIBRARY OF CONGRESS..DIVISION OF BIBLIOGRAPHY
    BRIEF LIST OF REFERENCES ON THE PIANO AND THE PIANO PLAYER
UNITED STATES--NATIONAL RECOVERY ADMINISTRATION
    CODE OF FAIR COMPETITION FOR THE PIANO MANUFACTURING INDUSTRY AS
UNITED STATES PATENT OFFICE
    COLLECTION OF LETTERS PATENT RELATING TO THE CONSTRUCTION OF
VICTORIA AND ALBERT MUSEUM, SOUTH KENSINGTON
    CATALOGUE OF MUSICAL INSTRUMENTS..VOL. 1, KEYBOARD
WEBER PIANO COMPANY
    WEBER GRAND, SQUARE AND UPRIGHT PIANO-FORTES, THE
WEITZMANN, CARL F.
    HISTORY OF PIANOFORTE-PLAYING AND PIANOFORTE-LITERATURE, A
WIER, ALBERT
    PIANO, THE ..ITS HISTORY, MAKERS, PLAYERS AND MUSIC
WILSON, DAVID M.
    PLAYER-PIANO, THE ..ITS CONSTRUCTION..HOW TO PLAY, WHAT TO PLAY
WINTERNITZ, EMANUEL
    MUSICAL INSTRUMENTS OF THE WESTERN WORLD
WOLFRAM, VICTOR
    SOSTENUTO PEDAL, THE
WORCH, HUGO
    PIANO MAKERS OF THE EVOLUTIONARY PERIOD..RARE ENGLISH AND AMERICAN
WORCH, HUGO
    WORCH PIANOS, AND A BRIEF SKETCH OF THE PIANOFORTE
YALE UNIVERSITY--ART GALLERY
    MUSICAL INSTRUMENTS AT YALE..A SELECTION OF WESTERN INSTRUMENTS
YALE UNIVERSITY--ART GALLERY
    YALE COLLECTION OF MUSICAL INSTRUMENTS..CHECKLIST
YOUNG, THOMAS C.
    MAKING OF MUSICAL INSTRUMENTS, THE ---1939

Pictorial

AEOLIAN COMPANY, THE
    AUDIOGRAPHIC MUSIC
AEOLIAN COMPANY, THE
    CATALOG OF THE AEOLIAN
AEOLIAN COMPANY, THE
    PIANOLA PIANO, THE
ALBARDA, JAN H.
    WOOD, WIRE AND QUILL..AN INTRODUCTION TO THE HARPSICHORD
APEL, WILLI
    MASTERS OF THE KEYBOARD
BAINES, ANTHONY
    EUROPEAN AND AMERICAN MUSICAL INSTRUMENTS
BAINES, ANTHONY
    MUSICAL INSTRUMENTS THROUGH THE AGES--REV. ED.---1961
BALLANTINE, BILL
    PIANO, THE ..AN INTRODUCTION TO THE INSTRUMENT
BALTIMORE--MUSEUM OF ART
    MUSICAL INSTRUMENTS AND THEIR PORTRAYAL IN
BLOM, ERIC
    ROMANCE OF THE PIANO, THE ---1928
BODDINGTON, HENRY
    CATALOGUE OF MUSICAL INSTRUMENTS, PRINCIPALLY ILLUSTRATIVE OF THE
BOWERS, Q. DAVID
    ENCYCLOPEDIA OF AUTOMATIC MUSICAL INSTRUMENTS---INCLUDES A
BOWERS, Q. DAVID
    GUIDEBOOK OF AUTOMATIC MUSICAL INSTRUMENTS, A. --2 VOLS.
BOWERS, Q. DAVID
    PUT ANOTHER NICKEL IN...A HISTORY OF COIN-OPERATED PIANOS
BRAGARD, ROGER
    MUSICAL INSTRUMENTS IN ART AND HISTORY
BRIGGS, GILBERT A.
    PIANOS, PIANISTS AND SONICS
BROADWOOD, JOHN AND SONS
    BROADWOOD COLLECTION OF ANTIQUE INSTRUMENTS, THE ..FORERUNNERS OF
BROADWOOD, JOHN AND SONS
    CATALOGUE OF JOHN BROADWOOD AND SONS, LTD. LATEST MODELS,
BUCHNER, ALEXANDER
    MECHANICAL MUSICAL INSTRUMENTS---174 NUMBERED PLATES
BUCHNER, ALEXANDER
    MUSICAL INSTRUMENTS THROUGH THE AGES
CARMI, AVNER *
    IMMORTAL PIANO, THE
CHICKERING AND SONS
    ILLUSTRATED CATALOGUE OF PIANO FORTES
CHICKERING AND SONS
    NEW ILLUSTRATED CATALOGUE OF PIANOFORTES, A
CLEMENCIC, RENE
    OLD MUSICAL INSTRUMENTS
DARLOW, DENYS
    MUSICAL INSTRUMENTS--JUNIOR REFERENCE BOOKS, NO. 12--2ND. ED.
DONINGTON, ROBERT
    INSTRUMENTS OF MUSIC, THE --3RD. REV. ED.---1949
EDINBURGH UNIVERSITY--DEPT. OF EARLY KEYBOARD INSTRUMENTS
    RUSSELL COLLECTION AND OTHER EARLY KEYBOARD INSTRUMENTS IN ST.
EISENBERG, JACOB
    LET ME HELP YOU, MY ANCESTORS AND I..A COMPREHENSIVE JUVENILE
ENGEL, CARL
    MUSICAL INSTRUMENTS---78 WOODCUT ILLUSTRATIONS
ENGEL, CARL
    MUSICAL INSTRUMENTS--REV. ED.---1876
EPWORTH PIANOS
    BOOK ABOUT PIANOS IN GENERAL AND THE EPWORTH IN PARTICULAR, A
FINCK, HENRY T.
    AEOLIAN, THE ..ITS ARTISTIC MERITS, DISTINCTION FROM MECHANICAL

FOX, LILLA M.
    INSTRUMENTS OF POPULAR MUSIC..A HISTORY OF MUSICAL
GABRY, GYORGY
    OLD MUSICAL INSTRUMENTS
GALPIN, FRANCIS W.
    OLD ENGLISH INSTRUMENTS OF MUSIC--4TH. ED.---1910
GALPIN, FRANCIS W.
    TEXTBOOK OF EUROPEAN MUSICAL INSTRUMENTS, A ---1937
GEIRINGER, KARL
    MUSICAL INSTRUMENTS, THEIR HISTORY IN WESTERN CULTURE FROM THE
GILLESPIE, JOHN
    FIVE CENTURIES OF KEYBOARD MUSIC..AN HISTORIC SURVEY FOR
GLOVER, ELLYE HOWELL
    HOW THE PIANO CAME TO BE
HARDING, ROSAMUND
    PIANOFORTE, THE ..ITS HISTORY TRACED TO THE GREAT EXHIBITION OF
HINDLEY, GEOFFREY
    MUSICAL INSTRUMENTS
HIPKINS, ALFRED JAMES
    MUSICAL INSTRUMENTS, HISTORIC, RARE AND UNIQUE---1888
HIRT, FRANZ JOSEF
    STRINGED KEYBOARD INSTRUMENTS 1440-1880---1955, IN GERMAN
HOOVER, CYNTHIA A.
    MUSIC MACHINES--AMERICAN STYLE..A CATALOG OF THE EXHIBITION
HORNIMAN MUSEUM AND LIBRARY, LONDON
    HANDBOOK TO THE MUSEUM'S COLLECTION, BY JEAN L. JENKINS--2ND.
HORNIMAN MUSEUM AND LIBRARY, LONDON
    MUSICAL INSTRUMENTS
JAMES, PHILIP BRUTTON
    EARLY KEYBOARD INSTRUMENTS, FROM THEIR BEGINNINGS TO THE YEAR
KELLEY, EDGAR STILLMAN
    MUSICAL INSTRUMENTS--3RD. YEAR OF A STUDY COURSE IN MUSIC
KENDALL, ALAN
    WORLD OF MUSICAL INSTRUMENTS, THE ---CHIEFLY ILLUSTRATIONS
KINSKY, GEORG--EDITOR
    HISTORY OF MUSIC IN PICTURES, A
LAVIGNAC, ALBERT
    MUSIC AND MUSICIANS---1895, IN FRENCH
MACQUOID, PERCY *
    DICTIONARY OF ENGLISH FURNITURE, THE --VOL. 3----16 ILLUSTRATIONS
MARCUSE, SIBYL
    MUSICAL INSTRUMENTS..A COMPREHENSIVE DICTIONARY
METROPOLITAN MUSEUM OF ART, NEW YORK
    KEYBOARD INSTRUMENTS IN THE METROPOLITAN MUSEUM OF ART..A PICTURE
MICHEL, NORMAN ELWOOD
    HISTORICAL PIANOS, HARPSICHORDS AND CLAVICHORDS---1963
ORD-HUME, ARTHUR W. J. G.
    CLOCKWORK MUSIC..AN ILLUSTRATED HISTORY OF MECHANICAL MUSICAL
PENGELLY, J. BRADFORD
    PENGELLY BLUE BOOK OF STYLE, THE ...A STUDY OF THE ART OF STYLING
PIERCE, B.
    PIERCE PIANO ATLAS--6TH. ED.---ORIGINALLY PUBLISHED AS 'MICHEL'S
PLAYER-PIANO, THE
    FOUR HUNDRED OF THE BEST ADS OF 1911 DEVOTED TO PIANOS AND
PRESTO--EDITORIAL STAFF
    MUSICAL INSTRUMENTS AT THE WORLD'S COLUMBIAN EXPOSITION, CHICAGO,
RIMBAULT, EDWARD FRANCIS
    CHAPPELL AND CO.'S PRACTICAL DIRECTIONS UPON THE ART OF TUNING THE
RIMBAULT, EDWARD FRANCIS
    PIANOFORTE, THE ..ITS ORIGIN, PROCESS AND CONSTRUCTION
RIPIN, EDWIN M.--EDITOR
    KEYBOARD INSTRUMENTS..STUDIES IN KEYBOARD ORGANOLOGY---10 ESSAYS
ROEHL, HARVEY
    KEYS TO A MUSICAL PAST...ILLUSTRATED TREATISE ON THE VARIOUS TYPES
ROEHL, HARVEY
    PLAYER PIANO, AN HISTORICAL SCRAPBOOK, THE
ROEHL, HARVEY
    PLAYER PIANO TREASURY..THE SCRAPBOOK HISTORY OF THE MECHANICAL
RUSSELL, RAYMOND
    HARPSICHORD AND THE CLAVICHORD, THE --2ND. ED., REVISED BY HOWARD
SMITH, FANNY MORRIS
    NOBLE ART, A ..THREE LECTURES ON THE EVOLUTION AND CONSTRUCTION OF
SOUTH KENSINGTON MUSEUM, LONDON
    CATALOGUE OF THE SPECIAL EXHIBITION OF ANCIENT MUSICAL INSTRUMENTS
SOUTH KENSINGTON MUSEUM, LONDON
    DESCRIPTIVE CATALOGUE OF THE MUSICAL INSTRUMENTS IN THE SOUTH
SPILLANE, DANIEL
    HISTORY OF THE AMERICAN PIANOFORTE..ITS TECHNICAL DEVELOPMENT, AND
STANDARD PNEUMATIC ACTION COMPANY
    DESCRIPTION OF STANDARD PNEUMATIC PLAYER ACTION, WITH SUGGESTIONS
STECK AND COMPANY
    ILLUSTRATED CATALOG...GRAND AND UPRIGHT PIANOS
STEINERT, MORRIS
    MORRIS STEINERT COLLECTION OF KEYED AND STRINGED INSTRUMENTS, THE
STEINWAY, THEODORE E.
    PEOPLE AND PIANOS..A CENTURY OF SERVICE TO MUSIC---1853-1953
STEINWAY AND SONS
    BOOK OF ART PIANO CASES
STEINWAY AND SONS
    ILLUSTRATED CATALOGUE OF PIANOS
STEINWAY AND SONS
    ILLUSTRATED CIRCULAR AND CATALOGUE OF PIANOFORTES--MANUFACTURERS
STEINWAY AND SONS
    INIMITABLE TONE..'PRICE LIST OF PIANOS MADE BY STEINWAY AND SONS,
STEINWAY AND SONS
    PIANOFORTES
STEINWAY AND SONS
    STEINWAY AND SONS' PIANO-FORTE MANUFACTORY AT 'STEINWAY', LONG
STRAUCH BROTHERS
    MANUFACTURE OF PIANOFORTE ACTION, THE ..ITS RISE AND DEVELOPMENT
STROHBER PIANO COMPANY
    PNEUMATIC PLAYER MECHANISM AND DESCRIPTIVE CATALOG OF STROHBER AND
VAN ATTA, HARRISON LOUIS--EDITOR
    TREATISE ON THE PIANO AND PLAYER PIANO, A
VICTORIA AND ALBERT MUSEUM, SOUTH KENSINGTON
    CATALOGUE OF MUSICAL INSTRUMENTS...VOL. 1, KEYBOARD
VICTORIA AND ALBERT MUSEUM, SOUTH KENSINGTON
    EXAMPLES OF ART WORKMANSHIP OF VARIOUS AGES AND COUNTRIES..MUSICAL
VICTORIA AND ALBERT MUSEUM, SOUTH KENSINGTON
    LIST OF PHOTOGRAPHS OF OBJECTS IN THE VICTORIA AND ALBERT
VICTORIA AND ALBERT MUSEUM, SOUTH KENSINGTON
    MUSICAL INSTRUMENTS AS WORKS OF ART..VOL. 1, KEYBOARD
VICTORIA AND ALBERT MUSEUM, SOUTH KENSINGTON
    PICTURE BOOK OF KEYBOARD MUSICAL INSTRUMENTS, A
WEBER PIANO COMPANY
    WEBER GRAND, SQUARE AND UPRIGHT PIANO-FORTES, THE
WINTERNITZ, EMANUEL
    MUSICAL INSTRUMENTS AND THEIR SYMBOLISM IN WESTERN ART
WINTERNITZ, EMANUEL
    MUSICAL INSTRUMENTS OF THE WESTERN WORLD
WORCH, HUGO
    PIANO MAKERS OF THE EVOLUTIONARY PERIOD..RARE ENGLISH AND AMERICAN
WORCH, HUGO
    WORCH PIANOS, AND A BRIEF SKETCH OF THE PIANOFORTE
YALE UNIVERSITY--ART GALLERY
    MUSICAL INSTRUMENTS AT YALE..A SELECTION OF WESTERN INSTRUMENTS

Early Instruments
ALBARDA, JAN H.
    WOOD, WIRE AND QUILL..AN INTRODUCTION TO THE HARPSICHORD
ANON
    DIGITORIUM, THE --MINIATURE DUMB PIANO
ANON
    HUMANISTIC STUDIES IN HONOR OF JOHN CALVIN METCALF---INCLUDES
ANON
    NEW INSTRUCTIONS FOR PLAYING THE HARPSICHORD, PIANOFORTE OR
ANON
    PRECEPTOR, FOR THE PIANOFORTE, THE ORGAN OR HARPSICHORD, THE
APEL, WILLI
    HISTORY OF KEYBOARD MUSIC TO 1700, THE --TRANSLATED AND REVISED BY
APEL, WILLI
    MASTERS OF THE KEYBOARD
BABITZ, SOL
    ON USING EARLY KEYBOARD FINGERING--REPRINT OF 3 ARTICLES FROM THE
BAINES, ANTHONY
    MUSICAL INSTRUMENTS THROUGH THE AGES--REV. ED.---1961
BALTIMORE--MUSEUM OF ART
    MUSICAL INSTRUMENTS AND THEIR PORTRAYAL IN
BEDBROOK, GERALD STARES
    KEYBOARD MUSIC FROM THE MIDDLE AGES TO THE BEGINNINGS OF THE
BEMETZRIEDER, ANTON
    ACCOUNT OF A NEW WAY OF CONSIDERING MUSICK, AND TEACHING
BEMETZRIEDER, ANTON
    NEW LESSONS FOR THE HARPSICHORD
BERKOWITZ, FREDA
    ON LUTES, RECORDERS AND HARPSICHORDS..MEN AND MUSIC OF THE BAROQUE
BESSARABOFF, NICHOLAS
    ANCIENT EUROPEAN MUSICAL INSTRUMENTS...IN THE LESLIE LINDSAY MASON
BLOM, ERIC
    ROMANCE OF THE PIANO, THE ---1928
BOALCH, DONALD HOWARD
    MAKERS OF THE HARPSICHORD AND CLAVICHORD, 1440 TO 1840
BODKY, ERWIN
    INTERPRETATION OF BACH'S KEYBOARD WORKS, THE
BOGIANCKINO, MASSIMO
    HARPSICHORD MUSIC OF DOMENICO SCARLATTI, THE
BORREN, CHARLES VAN DEN
    SOURCES OF KEYBOARD MUSIC IN ENGLAND, THE ---1913
BRAGARD, ROGER
    MUSICAL INSTRUMENTS IN ART AND HISTORY
BRIGGS, GILBERT A.
    PIANOS, PIANISTS AND SONICS
BRINSMEAD, E.
    HISTORY OF THE PIANOFORTE, THE ..WITH AN AN ACCOUNT OF THE THEORY
BROADWOOD, JAMES SHUDI
    SOME NOTES--ON THE HARPSICHORD AND PIANOFORTE--MADE BY J. S.
BROADWOOD, JOHN AND SONS
    BROADWOOD COLLECTION OF ANTIQUE INSTRUMENTS, THE ..FORERUNNERS OF
BUCHNER, ALEXANDER
    MECHANICAL MUSICAL INSTRUMENTS---174 NUMBERED PLATES
BUCHNER, ALEXANDER
    MUSICAL INSTRUMENTS THROUGH THE AGES
CLEMENCIC, RENE
    OLD MUSICAL INSTRUMENTS
DALE, WILLIAM
    TSCHUDI THE HARPSICHORD MAKER
DARLOW, DENYS
    MUSICAL INSTRUMENTS--JUNIOR REFERENCE BOOKS, NO. 12--2ND. ED.
DENSMORE, FRANCES
    HANDBOOK OF THE COLLECTION OF MUSICAL INSTRUMENTS IN THE UNITED
DOLMETSCH, ARNOLD
    INTERPRETATION OF MUSIC OF THE SEVENTEENTH AND EIGHTEENTH
DONINGTON, ROBERT
    INSTRUMENTS OF MUSIC, THE --3RD. REV. ED.---1949
DONINGTON, ROBERT
    INTERPRETATION OF EARLY MUSIC, THE
DONINGTON, ROBERT
    PERFORMER'S GUIDE TO BAROQUE MUSIC, A
EDINBURGH UNIVERSITY--DEPT. OF EARLY KEYBOARD INSTRUMENTS
    RUSSELL COLLECTION AND OTHER EARLY KEYBOARD INSTRUMENTS IN ST.
EISENBERG, JACOB
    LET ME HELP YOU, MY ANCESTORS AND I..A COMPREHENSIVE JUVENILE
ENGEL, CARL
    MUSICAL INSTRUMENTS---78 WOODCUT ILLUSTRATIONS
ENGEL, CARL
    MUSICAL INSTRUMENTS--REV. ED.---1876
GABRIEL, GILBERT W.
    GREAT PIANISTS AND COMPOSERS
GABRY, GYORGY
    OLD MUSICAL INSTRUMENTS
GALPIN, FRANCIS W.
    OLD ENGLISH INSTRUMENTS OF MUSIC--4TH. ED.---1910
GALPIN, FRANCIS W.
    TEXTBOOK OF EUROPEAN MUSICAL INSTRUMENTS, A ---1937
GATES, WILLEY F.
    PIPE AND STRINGS..THREE HISTORIC AND DESCRIPTIVE SKETCHES...THE
GEIPINGER, KARL
    MUSICAL INSTRUMENTS, THEIR HISTORY IN WESTERN CULTURE FROM THE
GILLESPIE, JOHN
    FIVE CENTURIES OF KEYBOARD MUSIC..AN HISTORIC SURVEY FOR
GLOVER, ELLYE HOWELL
    HOW THE PIANO CAME TO BE
GUENTHER, FELIX
    PIANO AND ITS ANCESTORS, THE
HAMILTON, CLARENCE G.
    PIANO MUSIC, ITS COMPOSERS AND CHARACTERISTICS
HARDING, ROSAMUND
    PIANOFORTE, THE ..ITS HISTORY TRACED TO THE GREAT EXHIBITION OF
HARICH-SCHNEIDER, ETA
    HARPSICHORD, THE ..AN INTRODUCTION TO TECHNIQUE, STYLE AND THE
HECK, JOHANN CASPAR
    ART OF PLAYING THE HARPSICHORD, ILLUSTRATED BY A VARIETY OF
HENDERSON, WILLIAM JAMES
    EVOLUTION OF THE PIANO, THE
HINDLEY, GEOFFREY
    MUSICAL INSTRUMENTS
HIPKINS, ALFRED JAMES
    DESCRIPTION AND HISTORY OF THE PIANOFORTE AND OLDER KEYBOARD
HIPKINS, ALFRED JAMES
    MUSICAL INSTRUMENTS, HISTORIC, RARE AND UNIQUE---1888
HIRT, FRANZ JOSEF
    STRINGED KEYBOARD INSTRUMENTS 1440-1880---1955, IN GERMAN
HOOVER, CYNTHIA A.
    HARPSICHORDS AND CLAVICHORDS
HORNIMAN MUSEUM AND LIBRARY, LONDON
    HANDBOOK TO THE MUSEUM'S COLLECTION, BY JEAN L. JENKINS--2ND.
HORNIMAN MUSEUM AND LIBRARY, LONDON
    MUSICAL INSTRUMENTS
HUBBARD, FRANK
    HARPSICHORD REGULATING AND REPAIRING

LITERATURE ON THE PIANISTIC ART

HUBBARD, FRANK
    THREE CENTURIES OF HARPSICHORD MAKING
HULL, ANNE
    MAESTRO SPINETTI'S MUSIC SHOP--HARPSICHORD, CLAVICHORD,
HUNEKER, JAMES GIBBONS
    DEVELOPMENT OF PIANO MUSIC FROM THE DAYS OF THE CLAVICHORD AND
HUTCHESON, ERNEST *
    LITERATURE OF THE PIANO, THE ..A GUIDE FOR AMATEUR AND
JAMES, PHILIP BRUTTON
    EARLY KEYBOARD INSTRUMENTS, FROM THEIR BEGINNINGS TO THE YEAR
KELLEY, EDGAR STILLMAN
    MUSICAL INSTRUMENTS--3RD. YEAR OF A STUDY COURSE IN MUSIC
KENDALL, ALAN
    WORLD OF MUSICAL INSTRUMENTS, THE ---CHIEFLY ILLUSTRATIONS
KINSKY, GEORG--EDITOR
    HISTORY OF MUSIC IN PICTURES, A
KIRBY, FRANK EUGENE
    SHORT HISTORY OF KEYBOARD MUSIC, A
KIRKPATRICK, RALPH
    DOMENICO SCARLATTI---1953
LANDOWSKA, WANDA
    LANDOWSKA ON MUSIC--EDITED BY DENISE RESTOUT
LYONS, SISTER MARIE STEPHEN
    REAWAKENING OF INTEREST IN THE HARPSICHORD IN THE 20TH. CENTURY,
MACQUOID, PERCY *
    DICTIONARY OF ENGLISH FURNITURE, THE --VOL. 3----16 ILLUSTRATIONS
METROPOLITAN MUSEUM OF ART, NEW YORK
    KEYBOARD INSTRUMENTS IN THE METROPOLITAN MUSEUM OF ART..A PICTURE
MICHEL, NORMAN ELWOOD
    HISTORICAL PIANOS, HARPSICHORDS AND CLAVICHORDS---1963
NEUPERT, HANNS
    CLAVICHORD, THE ---1956, IN GERMAN
NEUPERT, HANNS
    HARPSICHORD MANUAL..A HISTORY AND TECHNICAL DEVELOPMENT--2ND.
NEWMAN, WILLIAM S.
    SONATA IN THE BAROQUE ERA, THE --A HISTORY OF THE SONATA IDEA,
NEWMAN, WILLIAM S.
    SONATA IN THE CLASSIC ERA, THE --A HISTORY OF THE SONATA IDEA,
PAETKAU, DAVID H.
    GROWTH OF INSTRUMENTS AND INSTRUMENTAL MUSIC, THE
PARRISH, CARL
    EARLY PIANO AND ITS INFLUENCE ON KEYBOARD TECHNIQUE AND
PINCHERLE, MARC
    WORLD OF THE VIRTUOSO, THE
PLAYFORD, JOHN
    MUSICKS HAND-MAID..NEW LESSONS AND INSTRUCTIONS FOR THE VIRGINALS
PULVER, JEFFREY
    DICTIONARY OF OLD ENGLISH MUSIC AND MUSICAL INSTRUMENTS, A
RIMBAULT, EDWARD FRANCIS
    PIANOFORTE, THE ..ITS ORIGIN, PROCESS AND CONSTRUCTION
RIPIN, EDWIN M.--EDITOR
    KEYBOARD INSTRUMENTS..STUDIES IN KEYBOARD ORGANOLOGY---10 ESSAYS
RIPIN, EDWIN M.
    COUPLET HARPSICHORD IN THE CROSBY BROWN COLLECTION, THE --FROM
RUSSELL, RAYMOND
    CATALOGUE OF THE BENTON FLETCHER COLLECTION OF EARLY KEYBOARD
RUSSELL, RAYMOND
    EARLY KEYBOARD INSTRUMENTS--VICTORIA AND ALBERT MUSEUM..'SMALL
RUSSELL, RAYMOND
    HARPSICHORD AND THE CLAVICHORD, THE --2ND. ED., REVISED BY HOWARD
SACHS, CURT
    EVOLUTION OF PIANO MUSIC, 1350-1700, THE
SACHS, CURT
    HISTORY OF MUSICAL INSTRUMENTS, THE
SCHOLES, PERCY
    APPRECIATION OF MUSIC BY MEANS OF THE PIANOLA AND DUO-ART, THE
SCHULZE, RICHARD ALLEN
    HOW TO BUILD A BAROQUE CONCERT HARPSICHORD
SHORTRIDGE, JOHN D.
    ITALIAN HARPSICHORD BUILDING IN THE 16TH. AND 17TH.
SKINNER, BELLE
    BELLE SKINNER COLLECTION OF OLD MUSICAL INSTRUMENTS, HOLYOKE,
SOUTH KENSINGTON MUSEUM, LONDON
    CATALOGUE OF THE SPECIAL EXHIBITION OF ANCIENT MUSICAL INSTRUMENTS
SOUTH KENSINGTON MUSEUM, LONDON
    DESCRIPTIVE CATALOGUE OF THE MUSICAL INSTRUMENTS IN THE SOUTH
SOUTH KENSINGTON MUSEUM, LONDON
    DESCRIPTIVE CATALOGUE OF THE MUSICAL INSTRUMENTS IN THE SOUTH
SPILLANE, DANIEL
    HISTORY OF THE AMERICAN PIANOFORTE..ITS TECHNICAL DEVELOPMENT, AND
STANLEY, ALBERT A.
    CATALOGUE OF THE STEARNS COLLECTION OF MUSICAL INSTRUMENTS
STEGLICH, RUDOLF
    MOZARTS FLUEGEL KLINGT WIEDER--MOZART'S PIANO SOUNDS AGAIN---WITH
STEINERT, MORRIS
    CATALOGUE OF THE M. STEINERT COLLECTION OF KEYED AND STRING
STEINERT, MORRIS
    MORRIS STEINERT COLLECTION OF KEYED AND STRINGED INSTRUMENTS, THE
STODDARD, HOPE
    FROM THESE COMES MUSIC
STRAUCH BROTHERS
    MANUFACTURE OF PIANOFORTE ACTION, THE ..ITS RISE AND DEVELOPMENT
UNITED STATES MUSEUM OF HISTORY AND TECHNOLOGY
    CHECKLIST OF KEYBOARD INSTRUMENTS AT THE SMITHSONIAN INSTITUTION,
VICTORIA AND ALBERT MUSEUM, SOUTH KENSINGTON
    CATALOGUE OF MUSICAL INSTRUMENTS..VOL. 1, KEYBOARD
VICTORIA AND ALBERT MUSEUM, SOUTH KENSINGTON
    EXAMPLES OF ART WORKMANSHIP OF VARIOUS AGES AND COUNTRIES..MUSICAL
VICTORIA AND ALBERT MUSEUM, SOUTH KENSINGTON
    MUSICAL INSTRUMENTS AS WORKS OF ART..VOL. 1, KEYBOARD
VICTORIA AND ALBERT MUSEUM, SOUTH KENSINGTON
    PICTURE BOOK OF KEYBOARD MUSICAL INSTRUMENTS, A
WALKER, ADAM
    PHILOSOPHY OF THE HARPSICHORD, EXPLAINING HOW THAT INSTRUMENT IS
WEITZMANN, CARL F.
    HISTORY OF PIANOFORTE-PLAYING AND PIANOFORTE-LITERATURE, A
WHITING, ARTHUR B.
    LESSON OF THE CLAVICHORD, THE --REPRINT..'NEW MUSIC REVIEW'
WIER, ALBERT
    PIANO, THE ..ITS HISTORY, MAKERS, PLAYERS AND MUSIC
WINTERNITZ, EMANUEL
    MUSICAL INSTRUMENTS AND THEIR SYMBOLISM IN WESTERN ART
WINTERNITZ, EMANUEL
    MUSICAL INSTRUMENTS OF THE WESTERN WORLD
YALE UNIVERSITY--ART GALLERY
    YALE COLLECTION OF MUSICAL INSTRUMENTS..CHECKLIST
YATES, PETER
    AMATEUR AT THE KEYBOARD, AN
YOUNG, PERCY M.
    KEYBOARD MUSICIANS OF THE WORLD

Catalogs, Collections, Dictionaries and Bibliographies

AEOLIAN COMPANY, THE
    AUDIOGRAPHIC MUSIC
AEOLIAN COMPANY, THE
    CATALOG OF MUSIC AND MUSICAL LITERATURE---PIANOLA RECORDS

SUB-CLASSIFICATION INDEX

AEOLIAN COMPANY, THE
    CATALOG OF THE AEOLIAN
AEOLIAN COMPANY, THE
    PIANOLA PIANO, THE
ASSOCIATION FOR RECORDED SOUND COLLECTIONS
    PRELIMINARY DIRECTORY OF SOUND RECORDING COLLECTIONS IN THE UNITED
BALTIMORE--MUSEUM OF ART
    MUSICAL INSTRUMENTS AND THEIR PORTRAYAL IN
BODDINGTON, HENRY
    CATALOGUE OF MUSICAL INSTRUMENTS, PRINCIPALLY ILLUSTRATIVE OF THE
BOWERS, Q. DAVID
    ENCYCLOPEDIA OF AUTOMATIC MUSICAL INSTRUMENTS---INCLUDES A
BROADWOOD, JOHN AND SONS
    BROADWOOD COLLECTION OF ANTIQUE INSTRUMENTS, THE ..FORERUNNERS OF
BROADWOOD, JOHN AND SONS
    CATALOGUE OF BOOKS IN THE LIBRARY OF JOHN BROADWOOD AND SONS'
BROADWOOD, JOHN AND SONS
    CATALOGUE OF JOHN BROADWOOD AND SONS, LTD. LATEST MODELS,
BROADWOOD, JOHN AND SONS
    INTERNATIONAL EXHIBITION, 1862..LIST OF PIANOFORTES AND
CHICKERING AND SONS
    CHICKERING AND SONS, MANUFACTURER OF GRAND, SQUARE AND UPRIGHT
CHICKERING AND SONS
    CHICKERING AND SONS PIANOFORTES AT THE CENTENNIAL EXHIBITION,
CHICKERING AND SONS
    HISTORICAL MUSICAL EXHIBITION..CATALOGUE OF THE EXHIBITION,
CHICKERING AND SONS
    ILLUSTRATED CATALOGUE OF PIANO FORTES
CHICKERING AND SONS
    NEW ILLUSTRATED CATALOGUE OF PIANOFORTES, A
CHICKERING AND SONS
    PIANO-FORTES AT THE EXHIBITION OF 1856
CHICKERING BROTHERS, CHICAGO
    PIANO-FORTES AND THEIR MANUFACTURE, WITH ILLUSTRATED CATALOGUE
CHURCHILL, VIRGINIA PEAKES
    NINETEEN FIFTY-SIX SUPPLEMENT TO THE MODERN TEACHER'S GUIDE TO
CLEMENCIC, RENE
    OLD MUSICAL INSTRUMENTS
DENSMORE, FRANCES
    HANDBOOK OF THE COLLECTION OF MUSICAL INSTRUMENTS IN THE UNITED
DONALDSON, GEORGE
    CATALOGUE OF THE MUSICAL INSTRUMENTS AND OBJECTS FORMING THE
EDINBURGH UNIVERSITY--DEPT. OF EARLY KEYBOARD INSTRUMENTS
    RUSSELL COLLECTION AND OTHER EARLY KEYBOARD INSTRUMENTS IN ST.
EVANS MUSIC COMPANY
    EVANS' GRADED STUDY GUIDE FOR THE PIANOFORTE AND DICTIONARY OF
GABRY, GYORGY
    OLD MUSICAL INSTRUMENTS
HINSON, MAURICE
    PIANO TEACHER'S SOURCE BOOK--BIBLIOGRAPHY OF BOOKS ABOUT PIANOS
HIPKINS, ALFRED JAMES
    GUIDE TO THE LOAN COLLECTION--OF THE INTERNATIONAL INVENTIONS
HIPKINS, ALFRED JAMES
    MUSICAL INSTRUMENTS, HISTORIC, RARE AND UNIQUE---1888
HORNIMAN MUSEUM AND LIBRARY, LONDON
    HANDBOOK TO THE MUSEUM'S COLLECTION, BY JEAN L. JENKINS--2ND.
HORNIMAN MUSEUM AND LIBRARY, LONDON
    MUSICAL INSTRUMENTS
JAMES, PHILIP BRUTTON
    EARLY KEYBOARD INSTRUMENTS, FROM THEIR BEGINNINGS TO THE YEAR
MACQUOID, PERCY *
    DICTIONARY OF ENGLISH FURNITURE, THE --VOL. 3---16 ILLUSTRATIONS
MARCUSE, SIBYL
    MUSICAL INSTRUMENTS..A COMPREHENSIVE DICTIONARY
MASON AND HAMLIN ORGAN AND PIANO COMPANY
    CATALOGUE OF PIANOFORTES EMBODYING LATEST IMPROVEMENTS
METROPOLITAN MUSEUM OF ART, NEW YORK
    CATALOGUE OF THE CROSBY BROWN COLLECTION OF MUSICAL INSTRUMENTS OF
METROPOLITAN MUSEUM OF ART, NEW YORK
    KEYBOARD INSTRUMENTS IN THE METROPOLITAN MUSEUM OF ART..A PICTURE
NEBLING, ALBERT N. *
    MUSIC INSTRUMENT CHECKLIST
PAUER, ERNST
    DICTIONARY OF PIANISTS AND COMPOSERS FOR THE PIANOFORTE..WITH AN
PIERCE, B.
    PIERCE PIANO ATLAS--6TH. ED.---ORIGINALLY PUBLISHED AS 'MICHEL'S
PRESTO--EDITORIAL STAFF
    MUSICAL INSTRUMENTS AT THE WORLD'S COLUMBIAN EXPOSITION, CHICAGO,
PULVER, JEFFREY
    DICTIONARY OF OLD ENGLISH MUSIC AND MUSICAL INSTRUMENTS, A
RIPIN, EDWIN M.--EDITOR
    KEYBOARD INSTRUMENTS..STUDIES IN KEYBOARD ORGANOLOGY---10 ESSAYS
ROEHL, HARVEY
    PLAYER PIANO, AN HISTORICAL SCRAPBOOK, THE
ROEHL, HARVEY
    PLAYER PIANO TREASURY..THE SCRAPBOOK HISTORY OF THE MECHANICAL
RUSSELL, RAYMOND
    CATALOGUE OF THE BENTON FLETCHER COLLECTION OF EARLY KEYBOARD
RUSSELL, RAYMOND
    EARLY KEYBOARD INSTRUMENTS--VICTORIA AND ALBERT MUSEUM..'SMALL
RUSSELL, RAYMOND
    HARPSICHORD AND THE CLAVICHORD, THE --2ND. ED., REVISED BY HOWARD
SMITH, FANNY MORRIS
    NOBLE ART, A ..THREE LECTURES ON THE EVOLUTION AND CONSTRUCTION OF
SOUTH KENSINGTON MUSEUM, LONDON
    CATALOGUE OF THE SPECIAL EXHIBITION OF ANCIENT MUSICAL INSTRUMENTS
SOUTH KENSINGTON MUSEUM, LONDON
    DESCRIPTIVE CATALOGUE OF THE MUSICAL INSTRUMENTS IN THE SOUTH
STANLEY, ALBERT A.
    CATALOGUE OF THE STEARNS COLLECTION OF MUSICAL INSTRUMENTS
STECK AND COMPANY
    ILLUSTRATED CATALOG...GRAND AND UPRIGHT PIANOS
STEINERT, MORRIS
    CATALOGUE OF THE M. STEINERT COLLECTION OF KEYED AND STRING
STEINWAY AND SONS
    BOOK OF ART PIANO CASES
STEINWAY AND SONS
    ILLUSTRATED CATALOGUE OF PIANOS
STEINWAY AND SONS
    ILLUSTRATED CATALOGUE OF STEINWAY AND SONS' PIANOS
STEINWAY AND SONS
    ILLUSTRATED CIRCULAR AND CATALOGUE OF PIANOFORTES--MANUFACTURERS
STEINWAY AND SONS
    INIMITABLE TONE.. 'PRICE LIST OF PIANOS MADE BY STEINWAY AND SONS,
STROHBER PIANO COMPANY
    PNEUMATIC PLAYER MECHANISM AND DESCRIPTIVE CATALOG OF STROHBER AND
UNITED STATES MUSEUM OF HISTORY AND TECHNOLOGY
    CHECKLIST OF KEYBOARD INSTRUMENTS AT THE SMITHSONIAN INSTITUTION,
VICTORIA AND ALBERT MUSEUM, SOUTH KENSINGTON
    CATALOGUE OF MUSICAL INSTRUMENTS..VOL. 1, KEYBOARD
VICTORIA AND ALBERT MUSEUM, SOUTH KENSINGTON
    LIST OF PHOTOGRAPHS OF OBJECTS IN THE VICTORIA AND ALBERT
VICTORIA AND ALBERT MUSEUM, SOUTH KENSINGTON
    PICTURE BOOK OF KEYBOARD MUSICAL INSTRUMENTS, A
WINTERNITZ, EMANUEL
    MUSICAL INSTRUMENTS AND THEIR SYMBOLISM IN WESTERN ART
WINTERNITZ, EMANUEL
    MUSICAL INSTRUMENTS OF THE WESTERN WORLD

YALE UNIVERSITY--ART GALLERY
    YALE COLLECTION OF MUSICAL INSTRUMENTS..CHECKLIST
YALE UNIVERSITY SCHOOL OF MUSIC
    CHECK-LIST OF WESTERN INSTRUMENTS IN THE COLLECTION OF MUSICAL

Process of Learning

General

AGUILAR, EMANUEL
    LITTLE BOOK ABOUT LEARNING THE PIANOFORTE, A
BONPENSIERE, LUIGI
    NEW PATHWAYS TO PIANO TECHNIQUE..A STUDY OF THE RELATIONS BETWEEN
BOOTH, VICTOR
    WE PIANO TEACHERS--REVISED BY ADELE FRANKLIN---1946
BUONAMICI, CARLO
    PRACTICAL POINTS ON PIANO PLAYING
CHING, JAMES
    PLAYING AND TEACHING OF BACH, THE ..A GUIDE FOR TEACHERS, STUDENTS
CHRISTIANI, ADOLPH FRIEDRICH
    PRINCIPLES OF EXPRESSION IN PIANOFORTE PLAYING, THE
COCHRAN, MARY
    ULTIMATE PRINCIPLES OF PIANOFORTE TEACHING AND PLAYING
COOKE, JAMES FRANCIS
    GREAT PIANISTS ON PIANO PLAYING..STUDY TALKS WITH FOREMOST
DODD, FLORENCE
    BERLIN TEST CLASS, THE ..OR, FORTY-EIGHT PROGRESSIVE LESSONS IN
DUFFEE, GERTRUDE BANKS
    PIANO STUDY..A GUIDE TO TEACHER AND STUDENT
EARLES, ADELAIDE L. S. T.
    PIANO PLAYING OF THE FUTURE, FOR EVERY GOOD PIANIST, THE
EARLES, ADELAIDE L. S. T.
    SHORT ESSAY ON THE GENERAL NEED FOR SCIENTIFIC PIANOFORTE PLAYING,
EVERHART, POWELL
    PIANIST'S ART, THE ..A COMPREHENSIVE MANUAL ON PIANO PLAYING FOR
FISK, BEATRICE H.
    KEYBOARD FUNDAMENTALS
GIFFORD, ALEXANDER M.
    PIANOFORTE AND HOW TO STUDY IT, THE
GRIMALDI, MARIA LOUISA
    ART OF PIANOFORTE PLAYING AND TEACHING, THE
GRUNDY, ENID
    HAPPY PIANIST, THE
HOFMANN, JOSEF
    PIANO PLAYING, WITH PIANO QUESTIONS ANSWERED---PUBLISHED EARLIER
HULLAH, M. E.
    FEW WORDS ABOUT MUSIC, CONTAINING HINTS TO AMATEUR PIANISTS, A
LENHART, A.
    ELEMENTS OF MUSIC..A CLEAR AND SYSTEMATIC ARRANGEMENT OF RULES FOR
LINDO, ALGERNON H.
    PIANOFORTE STUDY..HINTS FOR TEACHERS AND STUDENTS
LOWE, CLAUDE EDGERTON
    SUGGESTIONS FOR THE APPRECIATION AND INTERPRETATION OF PIANOFORTE
LOWE, CLAUDE EDGERTON
    VIVA VOCE..250 QUESTIONS AND ANSWERS FOR PIANOFORTE DIPLOMA
NICHOLS, JULIA E.
    COMMON SENSE CATECHISM..OR, PIANO AND ORGAN PUPIL'S COMPANION
PETERSILEA, CARLYLE
    PIANO PLAYING..GENERAL MUSICAL INSTRUCTION FROM BEGINNING TO END
POWERS-WADSWORTH, L.
    PIANIST'S GUIDE TO TECHNICAL FREEDOM, THE ..2 VOLS. IN 1
RIEMANN, HUGO
    CATECHISM OF PIANOFORTE PLAYING---1888, IN GERMAN
SCOTT, MARY M.
    WHAT CAN I PLAY..A BOOK ABOUT MUSICAL INSTRUMENTS
SHELDON, ROBERT--COMPILER
    EGON PETRI-ALEXANDER LIBERMANN NOTES ON THE ART AND TECHNIQUE OF
SHUTER, ROSAMUND
    PSYCHOLOGY OF MUSICAL ABILITY, THE
WIECK, FRIEDRICH
    PIANO AND SONG..HOW TO TEACH, HOW TO LEARN, AND HOW TO FORM A

Miscellaneous

ANON
    ADVICE TO A NOBLEMAN...ON THE MANNER IN WHICH HIS CHILDREN SHOULD
ANON
    NEW PIANOFORTE KEYBOARD, THE ..CARD AND GAME, THE A.B.C. OF MUSIC
BEMETZRIEDER, ANTON
    NEW LESSONS FOR THE HARPSICHORD
BENEDICT, LADY *
    HOW TO PLAY THE PIANOFORTE
BENEDICT, MILO ELLSWORTH
    THIRTY-THREE SUGGESTIONS IN ONE LESSON..FOR THE GUIDANCE AND
BEVITT, ZAY RECTOR
    PIANO PLAYING BY HARMONY DIAGRAMS..STUDENT'S BOOK
BEVITT, ZAY RECTOR
    PIANO PLAYING BY HARMONY DIAGRAMS..TEACHER'S MANUAL
BONPENSIERE, LUIGI
    NEW PATHWAYS TO PIANO TECHNIQUE..A STUDY OF THE RELATIONS BETWEEN
BOOTH, VICTOR
    WE PIANO TEACHERS--REVISED BY ADELE FRANKLIN---1946
BOTTOMLEY, JOSEPH
    NEW SYSTEM OF PRACTICING AND TEACHING THE PIANOFORTE, A
CHING, JAMES
    ENTIRELY NEW SOLUTION TO THE PROBLEMS OF PIANO STUDY AT HOME, AN
CHING, JAMES
    PIANIST'S HOME STUDY COURSES, THE
CHRISTIANI, ADOLPH FRIEDRICH
    PRINCIPLES OF EXPRESSION IN PIANOFORTE PLAYING, THE
COOKE, JAMES FRANCIS
    GREAT PIANISTS ON PIANO PLAYING..STUDY TALKS WITH FOREMOST
DODD, FLORENCE
    BERLIN TEST CLASS, THE ..OR, FORTY-EIGHT PROGRESSIVE LESSONS IN
EARLES, ADELAIDE L. S. T.
    PIANO PLAYING OF THE FUTURE, FOR EVERY GOOD PIANIST, THE
EARLES, ADELAIDE L. S. T.
    SHORT ESSAY ON THE GENERAL NEED FOR SCIENTIFIC PIANOFORTE PLAYING,
EISENBERG, JACOB
    ARTISTIC PIANIST, THE ..NATURAL TECHNICS IN PIANO MASTERY..FROM
FRISKIN, JAMES
    PRINCIPLES OF PIANOFORTE PRACTICE, THE
GIFFORD, ALEXANDER M.
    PIANOFORTE AND HOW TO STUDY IT, THE
GRAHAM, MARY JANE
    LETTER TO A YOUNG PIANOFORTE PLAYER, A
GRUNDY, ENID
    HAPPY PIANIST, THE
HAMILTON, CLARENCE G.
    WHAT EVERY PIANO PUPIL SHOULD KNOW
KLAVARSKRIBO, SLEKKERVIER, HOLLAND
    PRACTICAL CORRESPONDENCE COURSE FOR PIANOFORTE

LAMOTTE, J.
    PIANO AND MUSICAL MATTERS
LENHART, A.
    ELEMENTS OF MUSIC..A CLEAR AND SYSTEMATIC ARRANGEMENT OF RULES FOR
MASON, DANIEL GREGORY
    NEGLECTED SENSE IN PIANO PLAYING, A
MCARTHUR, ALEXANDER
    PIANOFORTE STUDY..HINTS ON PIANO PLAYING
NICHOLS, JULIA E.
    COMMON SENSE CATECHISM..OR, PIANO AND ORGAN PUPIL'S COMPANION
PETERSILEA, CARLYLE
    PIANO PLAYING..GENERAL MUSICAL INSTRUCTION FROM BEGINNING TO END
POWERS-WADSWORTH, L.
    PIANIST'S GUIDE TO TECHNICAL FREEDOM, THE ..2 VOLS. IN 1
REZITS, JOSEPH
    SOURCE MATERIALS FOR PIANO TECHNIQUES
SAVLER, ROBERTA--EDITOR
    SELECTIONS FROM THE PIANO TEACHER, 1958-1963
SHELDON, ROBERT--COMPILER
    EGON PETRI-ALEXANDER LIBERMANN NOTES ON THE ART AND TECHNIQUE OF
SPENCER, CHARLES C.
    RUDIMENTS OF THE ART OF PLAYING THE PIANOFORTE, THE ...WITH
TAYLOR, GEORGE C.
    FIRST STEPS TO THE PIANOFORTE
TOBIN, JOSEPH RAYMOND
    ADVENTURES IN MUSICIANSHIP
VIRGIL, ALMON K.
    PUPIL'S RECORD BOOK, THE ..SHOWING HOW TO SUCCEED AND HOW TO FAIL

Psychological Applications

ALLEN, MARGARET *
    CREATIVE MOTION
AMEY, ELLEN
    CONSCIOUS CONTROL IN PIANO STUDY
BOLTON, HETTY
    ON TEACHING THE PIANO
BONPENSIERE, LUIGI
    NEW PATHWAYS TO PIANO TECHNIQUE..A STUDY OF THE RELATIONS BETWEEN
BOWEN, CAROLYN
    OUTLINES FOR TRAINING PIANO TEACHERS
BRIED, FREDERICK
    STIMULATION IN PIANO STUDY..HOW PARENTS CAN STIMULATE AND MAINTAIN
BUCK, PERCY
    PSYCHOLOGY FOR MUSICIANS
CHING, JAMES
    PERFORMER AND AUDIENCE..AN INVESTIGATION INTO THE PSYCHOLOGICAL
CHING, JAMES
    PIANO PLAYING, A PRACTICAL METHOD--A NEW EDITION OF 'PIANO
COGGINS, JOSEPH
    COMPANION TO THE MUSICAL ASSISTANT, A ..CONTAINING ALL THAT IS
CURWEN, ANNIE JESSY
    PSYCHOLOGY APPLIED TO MUSIC TEACHING
DAHL, ANTON
    SOUL OF GENIUS, THE ..ITS MUSICAL DEVELOPMENT AND HOW THE WORLD AT
DUCKWORTH, GUY
    KEYBOARD MUSICIANSHIP
DUSSEK, JOHANN L.
    DUSSEK'S INSTRUCTIONS ON THE ART OF PLAYING THE PIANOFORTE OR
EBERHARDT, GOBY
    MY SYSTEM FOR PRACTICING THE VIOLIN AND PIANO, BASED UPON
EVERHART, POWELL
    PIANIST'S ART, THE ..A COMPREHENSIVE MANUAL ON PIANO PLAYING FOR
FREDRICH, FRANK
    PLAYING BY SEEING..A STUDY IN TRAINING AND PERCEPTION FOR BETTER
GIFFORD, ALEXANDER M.
    PIANOFORTE AND HOW TO STUDY IT, THE
GLASFORD, IRENE A.
    RHYTHM, REASON AND RESPONSE FOR THE MUSICIAN, PIANIST AND TEACHER
HOFFMAN, CARL
    HABIT IN PIANOFORTE PLAYING--ANALYTICAL STUDY OF CONTROL OF
HOFMANN, JOSEF
    PIANO PLAYING, WITH PIANO QUESTIONS ANSWERED---PUBLISHED EARLIER
KIRBY, MAY B. KELLY
    KELLY KIRBY KINDERGARTEN PIANO METHOD, TEACHERS' COURSE, THE
KRUSZYNSKI, MICHAL
    APPROACH TO THE PSYCHOLOGY OF PIANO TEACHING, AN
LE COUPPEY, FELIX
    PIANO TEACHING..ADVICE TO PUPILS AND YOUNG TEACHERS---1868 IN
MASON, WILLIAM G.
    SYSTEM OF TECHNICAL EXERCISES FOR THE PIANO-FORTE, A
MATTHAY, TOBIAS A.
    ACT OF MUSICAL CONCENTRATION, THE
MATTHAY, TOBIAS A.
    CHILD'S FIRST STEPS IN PIANOFORTE PLAYING, THE
MATTHAY, TOBIAS A.
    EPITOME OF THE LAWS OF PIANOFORTE TECHNIQUE, AN
MATTHAY, TOBIAS A.
    INTRODUCTION TO PSYCHOLOGY FOR MUSIC TEACHERS, AN --THREE LECTURES
MEHR, NORMAN
    GROUP PIANO TEACHING
MUSIC EDUCATORS NATIONAL CONFERENCE
    KEYBOARD EXPERIENCE AND CLASS PIANO INSTRUCTION
SCHMITZ, ELIE ROBERT
    CAPTURE OF INSPIRATION, THE
SCHNEIDER, HANS
    WORKING OF THE MIND IN PIANO TEACHING AND PLAYING, THE
SPENCER, ALLEN
    FOUNDATION OF PIANO TECHNIC, THE
STERNBERG, CONSTANTIN I. VON
    ETHICS AND ESTHETICS OF PIANO PLAYING
TAPPER, THOMAS
    EDUCATION OF THE MUSIC TEACHER, THE
TAYLER, E. DOUGLAS
    MIND-POWER IN MUSIC FOR STUDENTS, TEACHERS AND PERFORMERS
TOWNSEND, WILLIAM
    BALANCE OF ARM IN PIANO TECHNIQUE--4TH. REV. ED.---1903
WOODHOUSE, GEORGE
    ARTIST AT THE PIANO, THE ..THE ART OF MUSICAL INTERPRETATION

Rudiments, Notation

ABBOTT, A. T.
    METHOD FOR GAINING A PERFECT KNOWLEDGE OF THE NOTES, ETC., FOR
ADAMS, JAMES B.
    FAMILIAR INTRODUCTION TO THE FIRST PRINCIPLES OF MUSIC, A ...FOR
AGUILAR, EMANUEL
    HOW TO LEARN THE PIANOFORTE
AHEARN, ELLA MASON *
    ADULT EXPLORER AT THE PIANO, THE
ALCHIN, CARRIE A.
    APPLIED HARMONY--REVISED AND WITH ADDITIONAL CHAPTERS BY VINCENT
ALCHIN, CARRIE A.
    KEYBOARD HARMONY--3 VOLS. IN 1, 1923-1926

ALLEN, MARGARET *
   CREATIVE MOTION
ALLISON, IRL
   LET'S LEARN ALL THE NOTES AND READ BETTER..FOR ALL PIANO PUPILS,
AMEY, ELLEN
   CONSCIOUS CONTROL IN PIANO STUDY
ANDERSON, J. CLARK
   GOOD MUSIC EXPLAINED..WHAT ALL GOOD PIANISTS SHOULD KNOW
ANON
   ADVICE TO A NOBLEMAN...ON THE MANNER IN WHICH HIS CHILDREN SHOULD
ANON
   COMPLEAT TUTOR FOR THE HARPSICHORD OR SPINNET, WHEREIN IS SHEWN
ANON
   FASHIONABLE PRECEPTOR, FOR THE PIANO-FORTE AND HARPSICHORD,
ANON
   NEW AND COMPLETE INSTRUCTIONS FOR THE HARPSICHORD, PIANO FORTE OR
ANON
   NEW INSTRUCTIONS FOR PLAYING THE HARPSICHORD, PIANOFORTE OR
ANON
   NEW PIANOFORTE KEYBOARD, THE ..CARD AND GAME, THE A.B.C. OF MUSIC
ANON
   PIANOFORTE POCKET COMPANION, THE ..OR, A POPULAR VIEW OF THE
ANON
   PIANO IN TWELVE LESSONS
ANON
   PLAYING THE HARPSICHORD, SPINET OR PIANO FORTE MADE EASY BY NEW
ANON
   PRECEPTOR, FOR THE PIANOFORTE, THE ORGAN OR HARPSICHORD, THE
ARNOLD, FRANCK THOMAS
   ART OF ACCOMPANIMENT FROM A THOROUGH-BASS, AS PRACTICED IN THE
AULD, WILDA J.
   HANDBOOK FOR THE CHURCH PIANIST, A
AXTENS, FLORENCE
   FIRST SIX MONTHS IN THE PIANO CLASS, THE ..A MANUAL FOR TEACHERS
AXTENS, FLORENCE
   PIANO CLASS METHOD..THE FIRST TWELVE MONTHS IN THE PIANO CLASS
BAILLIE, ALEXANDER--SUPPOSED AUTHOR
   INTRODUCTION TO THE KNOWLEDGE AND PRACTICE OF THE THORO' BASS, AN
BARNETT, DAVID
   PERFORMANCE OF MUSIC, THE ..A STUDY IN TERMS OF THE PIANOFORTE
BARNWELL, V. T.
   BARNWELL'S NORMAL KEYBOARD AND STAFF STUDIES--THE MENTAL
BARTHELEMON, FRANCOIS H.
   NEW TUTOR FOR THE HARPSICHORD OR PIANO FORTE, WHEREIN THE FIRST
BASTIEN, JAMES W. *
   BEGINNING PIANO FOR ADULTS
BASTIEN, JAMES W.
   HOW TO TEACH PIANO SUCCESSFULLY
BAVIN, JOHN T.
   PIANO CLASS INSTRUCTOR
BAXTER, JAMES
   INDUCTIVE GRAMMAR OF MUSIC, FOR CLASS, PRIVATE LESSON, OR SELF
BAXTER, JAMES
   NEW SCHOOL OF MUSIC, THE ..PRACTICAL THOROUGH BASE CULTURE, FOR
BECKER, JULIUS
   CONCISE TREATISE ON HARMONY, ACCOMPANIMENT, AND COMPOSITION, FOR
BECKERMAN, H. J.
   AMERICAN SCHOOL OF RAGTIME PIANO PLAYING, THE
BEMETZRIEDER, ANTON
   ABSTRACT OF A NEW METHOD OF TEACHING THE PRINCIPLES OF MUSIC,
BEMETZRIEDER, ANTON
   COMPENDIUM OF A NEW METHOD OF MUSIC...WITH THE AUTHOR'S PRINCIPLES
BEMETZRIEDER, ANTON
   GAMUT AND COMMON CHORD IN ALL KEYS, FINGERED FOR THE HARPSICHORD,
BEMETZRIEDER, ANTON
   MUSIC MADE EASY TO EVERY CAPACITY, IN A SERIES OF DIALOGUES..BEING
BEMETZRIEDER, ANTON
   NEW GUIDE TO MUSIC, IN FRENCH AND ENGLISH, A
BEMETZRIEDER, ANTON
   NEW LESSONS FOR THE HARPSICHORD
BENNER, LORA
   BENNER BLUE BOOK, THE ..PRACTICAL MANUAL OF PIANO TEACHING--4TH.
BENNER, LORA
   BENNER GOLD BOOK, THE ..PIANO MATERIAL AND TEACHING METHODS--3RD.
BENNER, LORA
   THEORY FOR PIANO STUDENTS--1ST. YEAR, PRIVATE OR CLASS--5 VOLS.,
BERGER, FRANCESCO
   FIRST STEPS AT THE PIANOFORTE
BERNING, ALICE B. *
   KEYBOARD EXPERIENCES FOR CLASSROOM TEACHERS
BERTINI, HENRI
   BERTINI'S SELF-TEACHING CATECHISM OF MUSIC FOR THE PIANOFORTE
BLAKE, DOROTHY
   FIRST STEPS IN CHORD PLAYING
BLOCKLEY, JOHN
   PIANIST'S CATECHISM, THE ---1880
BOLTON, HETTY
   ON TEACHING THE PIANO
BOOTH, VICTOR
   WE PIANO TEACHERS--REVISED BY ADELE FRANKLIN---1946
BOWEN, CAROLYN
   OUTLINES FOR TRAINING PIANO TEACHERS
BREMNER, ROBERT
   HARPSICHORD OR SPINNET MISCELLANY, THE --KEYBOARD
BROWER, HARRIETTE
   HOME HELP IN MUSIC STUDY
BROWER, HARRIETTE
   HOW A DEPENDABLE PIANO TECHNIQUE WAS WON
BROWER, HARRIETTE
   SELF-HELP IN PIANO STUDY
BROWN, JEAN PARKMAN
   INTERVALS, CHORDS AND EAR TRAINING FOR YOUNG PIANOFORTE STUDENTS
BURROWES, JOHN FRECKLETON
   PIANOFORTE PRIMER, THE ..CONTAINING THE RUDIMENTS OF MUSIC
BURROWS, RAYMOND
   ELEMENTARY PIANO INSTRUCTION IN COLLEGE
CALLENDER, ROMAINE
   TEACHER'S MANUAL, A WORK DESIGNED TO SUPPLEMENT...'THE FIRST TEN
CARPE, ADOLPH
   PIANIST AND THE ART OF MUSIC, THE ..A TREATISE ON PIANO PLAYING
CARP, BENJAMIN
   ANALYTICAL INSTRUCTOR FOR THE PIANO FORTE, OP. 15, THE --IN 3 PTS.
CARRE, JOHN
   PSYCHOLOGY OF PIANO TEACHING, THE ..A TEXTBOOK FOR TEACHERS,
CARTER, BUENTA
   BEGINNER'S PIANO BOOK FOR OLDER STUDENTS...DESIGNED FOR THE OLDER
CARY, MRS. C. S. P.
   PIANO-FORTE CLASS BOOK, CONTAINING PRACTICAL RUDIMENTAL LESSONS
CASTELLINI, JOHN EDWARD
   RUDIMENTS OF MUSIC..A NEW APPROACH WITH APPLICATION TO THE
CHAPPLE, STANLEY
   CLASS WAY TO THE KEYBOARD, THE
CHASTEK, WINIFRED
   KEYBOARD SKILLS..SIGHT READING, TRANSPOSITION, HARMONIZATION,
CHEYETTE, IRVING
   BASIC PIANO FOR THE MUSIC EDUCATOR AND CLASSROOM TEACHER

CHING, JAMES
   BETTER BEGINNINGS..A FIRST BOOK FOR EVERYONE WHO WANTS TO BECOME A
CHING, JAMES
   LET'S PLAY THE PIANO..THE FIRST MUSIC BOOK FOR CHILDREN OF ALL
CHING, JAMES
   STUDIES FOR BASIC PIANO TECHNIQUE..WRITTEN AND SELECTED WITH
CHING, JOAN ELIZABETH
   APPROACH TO PIANO TEACHING---ALSO CATALOGUED UNDER
CHITTENDEN, KATE S.
   SYNTHETIC CATECHISM, THE ..538 QUESTIONS AND ANSWERS FOR USE IN
CHRISTIANI, ADOLPH FRIEDRICH
   PRINCIPLES OF EXPRESSION IN PIANOFORTE PLAYING, THE
CHURCHILL, VIRGINIA PEAKES
   MODERN TEACHER'S GUIDE TO PIANO AND PIANO CLASS TEACHING
CLARKE, HUGH ARCHIBALD
   ART OF PIANOFORTE PLAYING, THE --TEXT BOOK FOR BEGINNERS
CLEMENTI, MUZIO
   INTRODUCTION TO THE ART OF PLAYING ON THE PIANOFORTE---1801+
COGGINS, JOSEPH
   GOVERNESS'S MUSICAL ASSISTANT, CONTAINING ALL THAT IS TRULY USEFUL
COKER, JERRY
   IMPROVISING JAZZ
CONKLIN-HAPP, SUZANNE
   APPLIED KEYBOARD HARMONY
COOKE, CHARLES
   PLAYING THE PIANO FOR PLEASURE--REV. ED.---1941
COUPERIN, FRANCOIS
   ART DE TOUCHER LE CLAVECIN, L' ---IN FRENCH, GERMAN AND ENGLISH
CRAMER, JOHN BAPTIST
   INSTRUCTIONS FOR THE PIANOFORTE---CONTAINS ALSO A SET OF 28
CROTCH, WILLIAM
   PRELUDES FOR THE PIANO FORTE, COMPOSED IN VARIOUS STYLES..TO WHICH
CURWEN, ANNIE JESSY
   CHILD PIANIST, THE
CURWEN, ANNIE JESSY
   TEACHER'S GUIDE...TO MRS. CURWEN'S PIANOFORTE METHOD, 'THE CHILD
CZERNY, CARL
   COMPLETE THEORETICAL AND PRACTICAL PIANO FORTE SCHOOL, FROM THE
CZERNY, CARL
   LETTERS TO A YOUNG LADY ON THE ART OF PLAYING THE PIANOFORTE
DANIELS, BESS *
   WORLD OF MUSIC, THE ..PIANO COURSE..TEACHERS' BOOK, FOR CLASS OR
DAVIS, LIONEL
   KEYBOARD INSTRUMENTS..THE STORY OF THE PIANO---YOUNGER READERS
DENVER--PUBLIC SCHOOLS
   CLASS-PIANO TEACHERS HANDBOOK
DE WITT, EDYTHE
   EDYTHE DE WITT'S METHOD FOR CLASS PIANO...WRITTEN TO GIVE CORRECT
DILLER, ANGELA
   SPLENDOR OF MUSIC, THE
DOBBIE, E. A.
   AUSTRALIAN PIANOFORTE TUTOR
DUCKWORTH, GUY
   KEYBOARD MUSICIANSHIP
DUSSEK, JOHANN L.
   DUSSEK'S INSTRUCTIONS ON THE ART OF PLAYING THE PIANOFORTE OR
EGBERT, MARION S.
   KEYBOARD EXPERIENCE IN THE CLASSROOM MUSIC PROGRAM..HANDBOOK FOR
EGBERT, MARION S.
   SEEING WHAT WE SING, AN AID THROUGH KEYBOARD EXPERIENCE TO THE
ELKAN, IDA
   PRACTICAL PIANO PLAYING MANUAL AND THEORY WRITING BOOK
ENGELBRECHT, J. G.
   MATERIA MUSICA, OR MATERIALS FOR THE PIANIST..A CLASS BOOK
EVERHART, POWELL
   PIANIST'S ART, THE ..A COMPREHENSIVE MANUAL ON PIANO PLAYING FOR
FAELTEN, CARL *
   TRANSPOSITION READER--FUNDAMENTAL TRAINING COURSE FOR PIANOFORTE
FALKENER, ROBERT
   INSTRUCTIONS FOR PLAYING THE HARPSICHORD..WHEREIN IS FULLY
FIELDEN, THOMAS
   NEW APPROACH TO SCALES AND ARPEGGIOS, A
FISK, BEATRICE H.
   KEYBOARD FUNDAMENTALS
FRACKENPOHL, ARTHUR
   HARMONIZATION AT THE PIANO--2ND. ED.---1962
FRAY, JACQUES *
   HOW TO PLAY BY THE JACQUES FRAY SPEED METHOD
FREDRICH, FRANK
   PLAYING BY SEEING..A STUDY IN TRAINING AND PERCEPTION FOR BETTER
FULLER, JANET E.
   COMPLETE KNOWLEDGE OF THE ESSENTIALS OF PIANOFORTE PLAYING, A
GASPARINI, FRANCESCO
   PRACTICAL HARMONIST AT THE HARPSICHORD, THE ---1708
GAT, JOZSEF
   TECHNIQUE OF PIANO PLAYING, THE, --2ND. ED.---1958
GEARY, ELEANOR MARGARET
   MUSICAL EDUCATION, WITH PRACTICAL OBSERVATIONS ON THE ART OF
GEIB, WILLIAM
   GEIB'S PIANO-FORTE PRECEPTOR, AND MUSICAL GRAMMAR...A TREATISE ON
GERMER, HEINRICH
   THEORETICO-PRACTICAL ELEMENTARY PIANO-FORTE SCHOOL FOR STUDENTS OF
GEST, ELIZABETH
   KEYBOARD HARMONY FOR JUNIORS
GIFFORD, ALEXANDER M.
   PIANOFORTE AND HOW TO STUDY IT, THE
GILBERT, RUSSELL S.
   EMBRYO MUSICIAN, THE ..A METHOD OF INTRODUCING MUSIC TO LITTLE
GILBERT, RUSSELL S.
   SUGGESTED PIANO STUDY FOR THE VOCAL STUDENT
GILBERTSON, ARNOLD R.
   TEACHERS MANUAL FOR POPULAR PIANO PLAYING, DESIGNED FOR ALL
GORDON, STEPHEN T.
   GORDON'S NEW SCHOOL FOR THE PIANO-FORTE
GRAHAM, GEOGRE FARQUHAR
   GENERAL OBSERVATIONS UPON MUSIC AND REMARKS ON MR. LOGIER'S SYSTEM
GRAHAM, JAMES L.
   MUSIC MADE EASY, PIANOFORTE TUTOR ON A NEW PLAN
GRAUPNER, GOTTLIEB
   RUDIMENTS OF THE ART OF PLAYING ON THE PIANOFORTE...A PLAIN
GRIMM, CARL W.
   HARMONY STUDY AT THE PIANO
GRINDEA, CAROLA
   FIRST TEN LESSONS, THE ..A NEW APPROACH TO PIANO TEACHING
GRUNDY, ENID
   HAPPY PIANIST, THE
HAAKE, CHARLES JOHN *
   TEACHING MUSIC READING IN THE OXFORD PIANO COURSE
HAMILTON, CLARENCE G.
   WHAT EVERY PIANO PUPIL SHOULD KNOW
HARGISS, GENEVIEVE
   MUSIC FOR ELEMENTARY TEACHERS..A PROGRAMMED COURSE IN BASIC THEORY
HARRISON, SIDNEY
   BEGINNING TO PLAY THE PIANO--A TEACHER'S HANDBOOK, INCLUDING THE
HARTLINE, ELIZABETH DILL *
   KEYBOARD MUSICIANSHIP, GROUP PIANO FOR ADULTS

HARVEY, ROBERT
   MAGIC KEY TO KEYBOARD SUCCESS, THE
HEERINGEN, ERNEST VON
   CELEBRATED INSTRUCTION BOOK FOR THE PIANOFORTE, CONTAINING THE
HEIDELBERGER, PAULINE
   MASTER METHOD..PIANO NORMAL AND TEACHER'S MANUAL
HERZ, HENRI
   NEW AND COMPLETE PIANOFORTE SCHOOL
HILES, JOHN
   CATECHISM FOR THE PIANOFORTE STUDENT, A ..CONTAINING A FULL
HOOK, JAMES
   GUIDA DI MUSICA..BEING A COMPLETE BOOK OF INSTRUCTIONS FOR
HORROCKS, CYRIL R. H.
   STUDENT'S GUIDE TO THE ART OF TEACHING THE PIANOFORTE, THE --2ND.
HUENTEN, FRANZ
   ABRIDGED EDITION OF F. HUENTEN'S CELEBRATED INSTRUCTIONS FOR THE
HUENTEN, FRANZ
   FRANZ HUENTEN'S CELEBRATED INSTRUCTIONS FOR THE PIANOFORTE--2ND.
HUMMEL, JOHANN NEPOMUK
   COMPLETE THEORETICAL AND PRACTICAL COURSE OF INSTRUCTIONS ON THE
ISAACS, EDWARD
   BLIND PIANO TEACHER, THE
JEWETT, ALBERT DEWEY
   IDIOMATIC COURSE OF PIANO INSTRUCTION FOR CLASS WORK
JOHNS, CLAYTON
   ESSENTIALS OF PIANOFORTE PLAYING, THE
JOHNSON, JOHN BARHAM
   KEYBOARD HARMONY FOR BEGINNERS
JOHNSON, REGINALD
   COMMONSENSE IN SCALE AND ARPEGGIO PLAYING
JONES, GRIFFITH
   COMPLEAT INSTRUCTOR FOR THE HARPSICHORD OR PIANOFORTE, THE
JOUSSE, JOHN
   GUIDA ARMONICA, IN WHICH...CHORDS, ARE CLEARLY EXPLAINED AND
KANZELL, MAXWELL
   HOW TO READ MUSIC..A COMPLETELY NEW AND SIMPLIFIED APPROACH TO
KEILMAN, WILHELM
   INTRODUCTION TO SIGHT READING
KERN, ALICE M.
   HARMONIZATION-TRANSPOSITION AT THE KEYBOARD
KING, AUDREY
   PIANO CLASSES IN ELEMENTARY SCHOOLS
KIRBY, MAY B. KELLY
   KELLY KIRBY KINDERGARTEN PIANO METHOD, TEACHERS' COURSE, THE
KLAVARSKRIBO, SLEKKERVIER, HOLLAND
   PRACTICAL CORRESPONDENCE COURSE FOR PIANOFORTE
KOLLMANN, AUGUST F.
   INTRODUCTION TO THE ART OF PRELUDING AND EXTEMPORISING IN SIX
KOTZSCHMAR, MARY ANN
   HALF-HOUR LESSONS IN MUSIC..CLASS WORK FOR BEGINNERS AT THE PIANO
KRUSZYNSKI, MICHAL
   APPROACH TO THE PSYCHOLOGY OF PIANO TEACHING, AN
LAST, JOAN
   INTERPRETATION FOR THE PIANO STUDENT
LAST, JOAN
   YOUNG PIANIST, THE ..A NEW APPROACH FOR TEACHERS AND
LEACH, JOHN R.
   FUNCTIONAL PIANO FOR THE TEACHER
LENHART, A.
   ELEMENTS OF MUSIC..A CLEAR AND SYSTEMATIC ARRANGEMENT OF RULES FOR
LHEVINNE, JOSEF
   BASIC PRINCIPLES IN PIANOFORTE PLAYING---1924
LINDO, ALGERNON H.
   AURAL TESTS FOR EXAMINATIONS--SPECIALLY WRITTEN FOR TEACHERS AND
LOCKE, MATTHEW
   MELOTHESIA..OR, CERTAIN GENERAL RULES FOR PLAYING UPON A
LOGIER, JOHANN BERNHARD
   AUTHENTIC ACCOUNT OF THE EXAMINATION OF PUPILS, INSTRUCTED IN THE
LOGIER, JOHANN BERNHARD
   COMPANION TO THE ROYAL PATENT CHIROPLAST, OR HAND-DIRECTOR, A ..A
LOGIER, JOHANN BERNHARD
   EXPLANATION AND DESCRIPTION OF THE ROYAL PATENT CHIROPLAST, OR
LOGIER, JOHANN BERNHARD
   FIRST COMPANION TO THE ROYAL PATENT CHIROPLAST OR HAND-DIRECTOR,
LOGIER, JOHANN BERNHARD
   REFUTATION OF THE FALLACIES AND MISREPRESENTATIONS CONTAINED IN A
LOGIER, JOHANN BERNHARD
   SYLLABUS OF THE SECOND EXAMINATION OF MR. LOGIER'S PUPILS, ON HIS
LONDON--A COMMITTEE OF PROFESSORS
   EXPOSITION OF THE MUSICAL SYSTEM OF MR. LOGIER..WITH STRICTURES ON
LUDDEN, WILLIAM
   THOROUGH BASS SCHOOL, THE ..AN EASY AND PROGRESSIVE COURSE FOR
MACEWAN, DESIREE
   FIRST TWO YEARS OF PIANOFORTE STUDY, THE
MACEWEN, JOHN B.
   INTRODUCTION TO AN UNPUBLISHED EDITION OF THE PIANOFORTE SONATAS
MACPHERSON, D.
   CATECHISM OF MUSIC, CHIEFLY ADAPTED FOR LEARNERS ON THE
MAIER, GUY *
   PLAYING THE PIANO..A COURSE OF ROTE TRAINING FOR BEGINNERS--CLASS
MAIER, GUY *
   PLAYING THE PIANO--TEACHER'S MANUAL
MASON, MARY B.
   BOY MUSIC, A FIRST PIANO METHOD FOR BOYS BETWEEN 8 AND 16
MASON, WILLIAM G. *
   METHOD FOR THE PIANO-FORTE, A
MASON, WILLIAM G. *
   PRIMER OF MUSIC, A ..BEING THE FIRST STEPS IN MUSICIANSHIP..FOR
MASON, WILLIAM G. *
   SYSTEM FOR BEGINNERS IN THE ART OF PLAYING UPON THE PIANOFORTE, A
MASON, WILLIAM G.
   TOUCH AND TECHNIC..FOR ARTISTIC PIANO PLAYING, OP. 44--4 VOLS. IN
MATTHAY, TOBIAS A.
   CHILD'S FIRST STEPS IN PIANOFORTE PLAYING, THE
MATTHAY, TOBIAS A.
   FIRST LIGHTS ON PIANO-PLAYING
MATTHAY, TOBIAS A.
   MUSICAL INTERPRETATION..ITS LAWS AND PRINCIPLES---1913
MCCLINTOCK, LORENE
   TEACH YOURSELF TO PLAY THE PIANO..BASED ON THE INTERVAL METHOD
MCEWEN, JOHN B.
   INTRODUCTION TO AN UNPUBLISHED EDITION OF THE PIANOFORTE SONATAS
MCLAIN, MARGARET STARR
   CLASS PIANO
MEHR, NORMAN
   GROUP PIANO TEACHING
MERRILL, MYRTLE
   SIGHT-READING AT THE PIANO
MIDDLEMISS, CHARLES S.
   NEW GRAPHIC NOTATION FOR KEYBOARD MUSIC, A
MILLER, ALLAN
   BEGINNING PIANO FOR ADULTS
MILLER, EDWARD
   INSTITUTES OF MUSIC, OR, EASY INSTRUCTIONS FOR THE HARPSICHORD
MINNESOTA MUSIC TEACHERS ASSOCIATION
   PIANO-THEORY EXAMINATION SYLLABUS

MOKREJS, JOHN
   STORY OF NANYNKA, THE ..FIRST PIANO LESSONS FOR CHILDREN, PRIVATE
MONTI, H. DE
   STRICTURES ON MR. LOGIER'S SYSTEM OF MUSICAL EDUCATION
MOORE, MARY BURNHAM
   LURE OF THE PIANO THROUGH COORDINATION AND CONCENTRATION, THE
MOTT, ISAAC H. R.
   ADVICE AND INSTRUCTIONS FOR PLAYING THE PIANOFORTE WITH EXPRESSION
MUSIC EDUCATORS NATIONAL CONFERENCE
   TEACHING PIANO IN CLASSROOM AND STUDIO
NEWMAN, ELIZABETH
   HOW TO TEACH MUSIC TO BEGINNERS
NEW ENGLAND CONSERVATORY
   NEW ENGLAND CONSERVATORY METHOD FOR THE PIANO-FORTE, THE
NILES BRYANT SCHOOL OF PIANO TUNING
   CORRESPONDENCE COURSE IN 12 LESSONS, A
OLIVER, EDWARD B.
   PRACTICAL TEXT-BOOK OF MUSIC, AS CONNECTED WITH THE ART OF PLAYING
OREM, PRESTON WARE
   MANUAL OF MODULATION
ORLIK, JULES
   CREATIVE APPROACH TO PIANO CLASS TEACHING, A ---REPRODUCED FROM
ORREY, LESLIE
   MUSIC AT THE KEYBOARD
PACE, ROBERT
   MUSIC ESSENTIALS FOR CLASSROOM TEACHERS--2ND. ED.---1961
PACE, ROBERT
   PIANO FOR CLASSROOM MUSIC--2ND. ED.---1956
PAIN, EVA
   BEGINNING TO PLAY THE PIANO..A MANUAL FOR TEACHERS
PALMER, HORATIO R.
   PALMER'S PIANO PRIMER
PALMER, KING
   TEACH YOURSELF TO PLAY THE PIANO
PARSONS, ALBERT R.
   SYNTHETIC METHOD FOR THE PIANOFORTE, THE
PASQUALI, NICOLO
   ART OF FINGERING THE HARPSICHORD, THE
PETERS, WILLIAM C.
   ECLECTIC PIANOFORTE SCHOOL, THE ..ARRANGED FROM THE WORKS OF THE
PETERSON, FRANKLIN
   THEORETIC COMPANION TO PRACTICE--PART I OF THE PIANIST'S HANDBOOK
PLAIDY, LOUIS
   PIANOFORTE TEACHER'S GUIDE, THE
PLAYFORD, JOHN
   MUSICKS HAND-MAID..NEW LESSONS AND INSTRUCTIONS FOR THE VIRGINALS
POTAMKIN, FRANK
   MODERN PIANO PEDAGOGY
PRATT, SILAS G.
   PIANIST'S MENTAL VELOCITY, THE ..A SYSTEMATIC PREPARATION OF THE
PRELLEUR, PETER
   HARPSICHORD ILLUSTRATED AND IMPROV'D, WHEREIN IS SHEWN THE ITALIAN
PRIESING, DOROTHY *
   LANGUAGE OF THE PIANO..A WORKBOOK IN THEORY AND KEYBOARD HARMONY
PROCTOR, CHARLES
   HARMONIZATION AT THE KEYBOARD
RAST, LAURENCE R.
   LET'S FIND OUT ABOUT MUSIC..WURLITZER ELEMENTARY PIANO WORKBOOKS,
REEVES, BETTY
   APPROACH TO PIANO TEACHING---ALSO CATALOGUED UNDER
REEVES, WILLIAM
   REEVES' POPULAR PIANOFORTE TUTOR..RUDIMENTS OF MUSIC, EXERCISES
RHODES, ALFRED
   CURIOSITIES OF THE KEY-BOARD AND THE STAFF...SHOWN TO BE UPON A
RICHARDSON, NATHAN
   INKLINGS FOR THE LOVERS OF MUSIC, PART 1..CULTIVATION OF THE ART
RICHARDSON, NATHAN
   NEW METHOD FOR THE PIANOFORTE..ADDED, RUDIMENTS OF HARMONY AND
RICHTER, ADA
   TEACHING HINTS
ROBBINS, EDGAR A.
   AMERICAN METHOD FOR THE PIANOFORTE
ROBILLIARD, EILEEN D.
   PERSISTENT PIANIST, THE ..A BOOK FOR THE LATE BEGINNER AND THE
ROBINSON, HELENE
   BASIC PIANO FOR ADULTS
ROBYN, LOUISE
   HOW TO TEACH PIANO TO THE CHILD BEGINNER..A TEXT BOOK FOR TEACHERS
ROOT, CATHERINE ADAMS *
   LISTEN, SING AND PLAY..CLASS LESSONS FOR PIANO AND VOICE
ROWLEY, ALEC
   DO'S AND DONT'S FOR MUSICIANS..A HANDBOOK FOR TEACHERS AND
ROWLEY, ALEC *
   GRADED TESTS IN PRACTICAL MUSICIANSHIP AND MUSICAL INITIATIVE--IN
ROWLEY, ALEC
   PRACTICAL MUSICIANSHIP, A HANDBOOK FOR TEACHERS AND STUDENTS
SCHELLING, ERNEST *
   OXFORD PIANO COURSE, TEACHER'S FIRST MANUAL
SCHLIEDER, FREDERICK W.
   LYRIC COMPOSITION THROUGH IMPROVISATION--2 VOLS., 1927-1946
SCONCIA, JOHN A.
   ANALYTICAL INSTRUCTOR FOR THE PIANO FORTE, CONTAINING THE
SCONCIA, JOHN A.
   SCONCIA'S NEW SYSTEM OF INSTRUCTION IN MUSIC AS A SCIENCE..OR, A
SEYMOUR, HARRIET AYER
   HOW TO THINK MUSIC
SEYMOUR, HARRIET AYER
   PHILOSOPHY OF MUSIC, THE ..WHAT MUSIC CAN DO FOR YOU
SHEFTEL, PAUL
   EXPLORING KEYBOARD FUNDAMENTALS
SHELDON, JAY
   ALL ABOUT MUSIC..A COMPLETE BOOK OF MUSICAL THEORY FOR PIANISTS
SHERWOOD MUSIC SCHOOL
   PIANO LESSONS AND TESTS--4TH. REV. ED.---1945+
SKUTLEY, MILDRED A.
   MUSIC FOR YOU..A SUPPLEMENTAL WORK BOOK FOR INDIVIDUAL OR CLASS
SMELTZER, JEANNIE R.--COMPILER
   OUTLINES AND GRADES FOR THE USE OF PIANO TEACHERS
SMITH, A. G. WARREN
   BEGINNER'S GUIDE, THE ..FOR ALL COMMENCING THE STUDY OF THE
SMITH, EDWIN S.
   PIANO BY EAR
SMITH, THOMAS
   LITTLE DIFFICULTIES WHICH OCCUR IN PIANOFORTE PLAYING
SMITH, USELMA CLARK
   KEYBOARD HARMONY..LEARNING BY HEARING
SPENCER, BERNARD
   POPULAR PIANO...A CORRESPONDENCE COURSE OF THE EASTERN SCHOOLS OF
SPENCER, CHARLES C.
   RUDIMENTS OF THE ART OF PLAYING THE PIANOFORTE, THE ...WITH
SQUIRE, RUSSEL N. *
   CLASS PIANO FOR ADULT BEGINNERS--2ND. ED.---1964
STANLEY, JANE
   BASIC ROUTINES IN ELEMENTARY PIANO TEACHING THROUGH THE FIRST
STARKEY, EVELYN
   PIANO CLASS WORKBOOK FOR FIRST YEAR STUDENTS

TAPPER, THOMAS
    ABC OF KEYBOARD HARMONY, THE
TAYLOR, GEORGE C.
    FIRST STEPS TO THE PIANOFORTE
THOMPSON, JOHN
    TEACHING PIANO IN CLASSES
TOBIN, JOSEPH RAYMOND
    ADVENTURES IN MUSICIANSHIP
TOBIN, JOSEPH RAYMOND
    HOW TO IMPROVISE PIANO ACCOMPANIMENTS
UNDERWOOD, REX
    GHOST NOTE PATTERN BUILDERS FOR VISUALIZING THE STRUCTURE OF
VAN APPLEDORN, MARY J.
    KEYBOARD, SINGING AND DICTATION MANUAL
VAN DER VELPEN, JEAN
    HARMONY AND THOROUGH BASS--2 VOLS., 1909-1910
VENABLE, MARY
    INTERPRETATION OF PIANO MUSIC, THE
VINING, HARRISON S.
    SIMPLE AND COMPLETE PRIMER FOR THE PIANOFORTE, THE
VINING, HARRISON S.
    WHYS AND WHEREFORES..QUESTIONS AND ANSWERS FOR PIANO STUDENTS
VIRGIL, ALMON K.
    EDUCATION IN MUSIC..LESSONS TO TEACHERS IN THE INSTRUCTION OF
VIRGIL, ANTHA MINERVA
    ELEMENTARY EXERCISES IN SIGHT READING...FROM THE VIRGIL METHOD
WEBBE, SAMUEL
    HARMONY EPITOMIZED, BEING A SHORT EXPLANATION OF FIGURED BASSES,
WEBBE, WILLIAM H.
    PIANISTS' 'ABC' PRIMER AND GUIDE--WITH AN APPENDIX
WELLS, HOWARD
    EARS, BRAIN AND FINGERS..A TEXT BOOK FOR PIANO TEACHERS AND PUPILS
WELSH, J. ROBERT
    MAKING MUSIC AT THE KEYBOARD..BEGINNING PIANO...CLASS...AND EAR
WEST, GEORGE FREDERICK
    HINTS TO YOUNG TEACHERS OF THE PIANOFORTE
WESTRUP, SIR JACK ALLAN
    MUSICAL INTERPRETATION---THIS BOOK ACCOMPANIED A SERIES OF B.B.C.
WEYLAND, RUDOLPH H.
    LEARNING TO READ MUSIC
WHEELER, BERTHA H.
    MIND AND MECHANISM..THOUGHTS ON TEACHING AND THE PIANISTIC ART
WILLIAMS, JEAN E. *
    MIND IN MUSIC, THE
WILLIAMS, JEAN E.
    MODERN METHOD OF PIANO INSTRUCTION, A ..TEACHERS MANUAL
WILLIAMS, JOHN M.
    WHAT TO TEACH AT THE VERY FIRST LESSON
WILSON, MORRIS E.
    HOW TO HELP YOUR CHILD WITH MUSIC--2ND. ED.---1951
WILSON, MORRIS E.
    HOW TO PLAY BY EAR
WILSON, WILLIAM
    NEW FINGERING NOTATION FOR KEYBOARD MUSIC---REPRODUCED FROM
WINNER, SEPTIMUS
    WINNER'S NEW SCHOOL FOR THE PIANO, IN WHICH THE INSTRUCTIONS ARE
WOLLENHAUPT, HEINRICH
    METHOD FOR THE PIANOFORTE AND METHODICAL GUIDE FOR THE PIANO FORTE
WRIGHT, WILLIAM C.
    GOLDEN MONITOR, FOR THE PIANOFORTE AND CABINET ORGAN, DESIGNED AS
WRIGHT, WILLIAM C.
    PIANOFORTE MANUAL, THE ..DESIGNED AS A COMPLETE PIANOFORTE PRIMER
WYMAN, ADDISON P.
    WYMAN'S PIANO TEXTBOOK..CONTAINING A COMPLETE SYSTEM OF MUSICAL
YATES, PETER
    AMATEUR AT THE KEYBOARD, AN
ZEITLIN, POLDI *
    THEORY PAPERS, THE --C.M.P. PIANO LIBRARY--2 VOLS., 1961-1963
ZEPER, M. E. P.
    READING OF MUSIC, THE ..A RATIONAL METHOD--NO. 1 OF A SERIES ON

Analytical Procedures

AMEY, ELLEN
    CONSCIOUS CONTROL IN PIANO STUDY
BARNETT, DAVID
    PERFORMANCE OF MUSIC, THE ..A STUDY IN TERMS OF THE PIANOFORTE
BASTIEN, JAMES W. *
    BEGINNING PIANO FOR ADULTS
BOLTON, HETTY
    HOW TO PRACTICE
BONPENSIERE, LUIGI
    NEW PATHWAYS TO PIANO TECHNIQUE..A STUDY OF THE RELATIONS BETWEEN
BOOTH, VICTOR
    WE PIANO TEACHERS--REVISED BY ADELE FRANKLIN---1946
BROWER, HARRIETTE
    SELF-HELP IN PIANO STUDY
CARR, BENJAMIN
    ANALYTICAL INSTRUCTOR FOR THE PIANO FORTE, OP. 15, THE --IN 3 PTS.
CHRISTIANI, ADOLPH FRIEDRICH
    PRINCIPLES OF EXPRESSION IN PIANOFORTE PLAYING, THE
CZERNY, CARL
    COMPLETE THEORETICAL AND PRACTICAL PIANO FORTE SCHOOL, FROM THE
DAVIS, HARRY
    INSTANT PIANO..A UNIQUE METHOD OF READING AND CHORDING FROM THE
DUCKWORTH, GUY
    KEYBOARD MUSICIANSHIP
DUFFEE, GERTRUDE BANKS
    PIANO STUDY..A GUIDE TO TEACHER AND STUDENT
FORMAN, DENIS
    MOZART'S CONCERTO FORM..THE FIRST MOVEMENTS OF THE PIANO CONCERTOS
FREDRICH, FRANK
    PLAYING BY SEEING..A STUDY IN TRAINING AND PERCEPTION FOR BETTER
GIBBS, GEORGE A., JR.
    MODERN CHORD CONSTRUCTION AND ANALYSIS, FOR ALL INSTRUMENTS...AN
GILBERTSON, ARNOLD B.
    TEACHERS MANUAL FOR POPULAR PIANO PLAYING, DESIGNED FOR ALL
GLASFORD, IRENE A.
    RHYTHM, REASON AND RESPONSE FOR THE MUSICIAN, PIANIST AND TEACHER
GRIMM, CARL W.
    HARMONY STUDY AT THE PIANO
HARKNESS, ROBERT
    HARKNESS PIANO METHOD OF EVANGELISTIC HYMN PLAYING, THE ..A
HOFMANN, JOSEF
    PIANO PLAYING, WITH PIANO QUESTIONS ANSWERED---PUBLISHED EARLIER
HULL, ARTHUR EAGLEFIELD
    THREE HUNDRED QUESTIONS ON PIANOFORTE TEACHING IN 30 GRADUATED
HUMMEL, JOHANN NEPOMUK
    COMPLETE THEORETICAL AND PRACTICAL COURSE OF INSTRUCTIONS ON THE
JOHNS, CLAYTON
    ESSENTIALS OF PIANOFORTE PLAYING, THE
JOHNSON, VERA A.
    SCIENTIFIC SIDE OF MUSIC IN SIMPLE, PRACTICAL FORM FOR TEACHERS
KENYON, CHARLES FREDERICK
    HOW TO MEMORIZE MUSIC
LANDOWSKI, ALICE-WANDA
    DOMENICO SCARLATTI--NOTES TO ACCOMPANY GRAMOPHONE RECORDINGS

LAST, JOAN
    INTERPRETATION FOR THE PIANO STUDENT
MACLEAN, CHARLES D.
    PRINCIPLES OF PIANOFORTE PRACTICE, THE
MACPHERSON, STEWART
    STUDIES IN PHRASING AND FORM
MARIAL, R.
    METHODS APPLICABLE TO GROUP TEACHING OR PRIVATE PIANO INSTRUCTION
MATTHAY, TOBIAS A.
    ACT OF MUSICAL CONCENTRATION, THE
MATTHAY, TOBIAS A.
    INTRODUCTION TO PSYCHOLOGY FOR MUSIC TEACHERS, AN --THREE LECTURES
MATTHAY, TOBIAS A.
    MUSICAL INTERPRETATION..ITS LAWS AND PRINCIPLES---1913
MATTHAY, TOBIAS A.
    ON MEMORIZING AND PLAYING FROM MEMORY
MCCLANAHAN, RICHARD
    CADENCE, KEY TO MUSICAL CLARITY, THE ..A SIMPLE AND PRACTICAL
MIDKIFF, HELEN T.
    CHURCH PIANIST, THE
MURPHY, HOWARD A. *
    MUSIC FOR STUDY..A SOURCE BOOK OF EXCERPTS
NEWMAN, WILLIAM S.
    PIANIST'S PROBLEMS, THE ..A MODERN APPROACH TO EFFICIENT PRACTICE
PARSONS, MARY H.
    RHYTHMIC WAY, THE
PERRY, ADELAIDE TROWBRIDGE *
    GUIDE TO PIANO STUDY FOR CLASS OR INDIVIDUAL INSTRUCTION, A
PRATT, SILAS G.
    PIANIST'S MENTAL VELOCITY, THE ..A SYSTEMATIC PREPARATION OF THE
PUPIN, ANNIE
    HOW TO PRACTICE..OR HINTS TO PIANO-FORTE STUDENTS ON THE METHOD OF
REZITS, JOSEPH
    SOURCE MATERIALS FOR PIANO TECHNIQUES
REZITS, JOSEPH
    TEACHER'S GUIDE TO THE NEW SCRIBNER MUSIC LIBRARY
SCHELLING, ERNEST *
    OXFORD PIANO COURSE, TEACHER'S SECOND MANUAL
SCHMITZ, ELIE ROBERT
    CAPTURE OF INSPIRATION, THE
SCHOTT, HOWARD
    PLAYING THE HARPSICHORD
SHEPARD, FRANK H.
    PIANO TOUCH AND SCALES..AN ANALYSIS OF THE FUNDAMENTAL PRINCIPLES
SWENSON, LUCILE B.
    DISCOVERING THE PIANO..THE MULTIPLE KEY APPROACH..STUDY GUIDE AND
TAYLOR, FRANKLIN
    TECHNIQUE AND EXPRESSION IN PIANOFORTE PLAYING
TURECK, ROSALYN
    INTRODUCTION TO THE PERFORMANCE OF BACH, AN--3 VOLS.

Listening

BOLTON, HETTY
    HOW TO PRACTICE
BOLTON, HETTY
    ON TEACHING THE PIANO
BROWER, HARRIETTE
    ART OF THE PIANIST, THE
BROWER, HARRIETTE
    HOME HELP IN MUSIC STUDY
BROWER, HARRIETTE
    HOW A DEPENDABLE PIANO TECHNIQUE WAS WON
CHAPPLE, STANLEY
    CLASS WAY TO THE KEYBOARD, THE
DUCKWORTH, GUY
    KEYBOARD MUSICIANSHIP
DUMM, ROBERT W.
    IN BLACK AND WHITE
FOLDES, ANDOR
    KEYS TO THE KEYBOARD, A BOOK FOR PIANISTS
GRINDEA, CAROLA
    FIRST TEN LESSONS, THE ..A NEW APPROACH TO PIANO TEACHING
JEWETT, ALBERT DEWEY
    IDIOMATIC COURSE OF PIANO INSTRUCTION FOR CLASS WORK
KENYON, CHARLES FREDERICK
    HOW TO MEMORIZE MUSIC
LAST, JOAN
    INTERPRETATION FOR THE PIANO STUDENT
MATHEWS, WILLIAM S. B.
    SCHOOL OF THE PIANO PEDAL
MATTHAY, TOBIAS A.
    ACT OF MUSICAL CONCENTRATION, THE
MATTHAY, TOBIAS A.
    ACT OF TOUCH IN ALL ITS DIVERSITY, THE ..AN ANALYSIS AND SYNTHESIS
MATTHAY, TOBIAS A.
    EPITOME OF THE LAWS OF PIANOFORTE TECHNIQUE, AN
MATTHAY, TOBIAS A.
    FIRST PRINCIPLES OF PIANOFORTE PLAYING--EXTRACT FROM 'THE ACT OF
MATTHAY, TOBIAS A.
    MUSICAL INTERPRETATION..ITS LAWS AND PRINCIPLES---1913
MATTHAY, TOBIAS A.
    PIANOFORTE TONE-PRODUCTION---SAME AS 'THE ACT OF TOUCH IN ALL ITS
MCCLANAHAN, RICHARD
    CADENCE, KEY TO MUSICAL CLARITY, THE ..A SIMPLE AND PRACTICAL
MCLAIN, MARGARET STARR
    CLASS PIANO
MEHR, NORMAN
    GROUP PIANO TEACHING
NIMITZ, DANIEL
    KEYBOARD MASTERS..STUDY GUIDE
PACE, ROBERT
    MUSIC ESSENTIALS FOR CLASSROOM TEACHERS--2ND. ED.---1961
PHILIPP, LILLIE A.
    PIANO STUDY..APPLICATION AND TECHNIQUE
PLAIDY, LOUIS
    PIANO TEACHER, THE
REZITS, JOSEPH
    TEACHER'S GUIDE TO THE NEW SCRIBNER MUSIC LIBRARY
ROWLEY, ALEC
    DO'S AND DONT'S FOR MUSICIANS..A HANDBOOK FOR TEACHERS AND
ROWLEY, ALEC
    PRACTICAL MUSICIANSHIP, A HANDBOOK FOR TEACHERS AND STUDENTS
SCHAUFFLER, ROBERT HAVEN
    MUSICAL AMATEUR, THE
SCHNEIDER, HANS
    WORKING OF THE MIND IN PIANO TEACHING AND PLAYING, THE
SEYMOUR, HARRIET AYER
    HOME MUSIC LESSONS..HOW TO FIND YOUR MUSICAL SELF
SEYMOUR, HARRIET AYER
    HOW TO THINK MUSIC
SHEEHY, EMMA DICKSON
    THERE'S MUSIC IN CHILDREN--REV. ED.---1946
SHERWOOD MUSIC SCHOOL
    PIANO LESSONS AND TESTS--4TH. REV. ED.---1945+
SLENCZYNSKA, RUTH *
    MUSIC AT YOUR FINGERTIPS

SQUIRE, RUSSEL N. *
CLASS PIANO FOR ADULT BEGINNERS--2ND. ED.---1964
STEPHENSON, LILIAN E.
BEGONE, DULL PRACTICE..SUGGESTIONS FOR STUDENTS AND
STERNBERG, CONSTANTIN I. VON
ETHICS AND ESTHETICS OF PIANO PLAYING
SUZUKI, SHIN'ICHI
SUZUKI PIANO SCHOOL--4 VOLS.
TANKARD, GEOFFREY
PIANOFORTE DIPLOMAS
TOBIN, JOSEPH RAYMOND
ADVENTURES IN MUSICIANSHIP
WHITEMORE, CUTHBERT
COMMONSENSE IN PIANOFORTE PLAYING
WOLLNER, GERTRUDE PRICE
IMPROVISATION IN MUSIC..WAYS TOWARDS CAPTURING MUSICAL IDEAS AND
WOODHOUSE, GEORGE
ARTIST AT THE PIANO, THE ..THE ART OF MUSICAL INTERPRETATION
WOODHOUSE, GEORGE
NEW PATH FOR PIANISTS, A ..THE MUTANO--MUTE PIANO--SYSTEM, ETC.
YATES, PETER
AMATEUR AT THE KEYBOARD, AN

Practice Procedures

AGUILAR, EMANUEL
LITTLE BOOK ABOUT LEARNING THE PIANOFORTE, A
AHRENS, CORA B. *
FOR ALL PIANO TEACHERS
AMEY, ELLEN
CONSCIOUS CONTROL IN PIANO STUDY
ANON
GUIDE TO THE MUSICAL TUITION OF VERY YOUNG CHILDREN, BY AN OLD
ANON
MASTER RULES FOR SUCCESSFUL PIANO PRACTICE..A COLLECTION OF
BACON, ERNST
NOTES ON THE PIANO
BARNETT, DAVID
PERFORMANCE OF MUSIC, THE ..A STUDY IN TERMS OF THE PIANOFORTE
BASTIEN, JAMES W. *
BEGINNING PIANO FOR ADULTS
BEMETZRIEDER, ANTON
MUSIC MADE EASY TO EVERY CAPACITY, IN A SERIES OF DIALOGUES..BEING
BENNER, LORA
BENNER BLUE BOOK, THE ..PRACTICAL MANUAL OF PIANO TEACHING--4TH.
BLOCKLEY, JOHN
PIANIST'S CATECHISM, THE ---1880
BOLTON, HETTY
HOW TO PRACTICE
BOLTON, HETTY
ON TEACHING THE PIANO
BONPENSIERE, LUIGI
NEW PATHWAYS TO PIANO TECHNIQUE..A STUDY OF THE RELATIONS BETWEEN
BOOTH, VICTOR
WE PIANO TEACHERS--REVISED BY ADELE FRANKLIN---1946
BOTTOMLEY, JOSEPH
NEW SYSTEM OF PRACTICING AND TEACHING THE PIANOFORTE, A
BRANDT, LEONIE
SCIENCE IN MODERN PIANOFORTE PLAYING
BRECKENRIDGE, WILLIAM KILGORE
HINTS FOR PIANO NORMAL STUDIES
BREE, MADAME MALWINE
GROUNDWORK OF THE LESCHETIZKY METHOD, THE ---1902
BREITHAUPT, RUDOLPH MARIA
NATURAL PIANO-TECHNIC..SCHOOL OF WEIGHT TOUCH--2 VOLS.
BRIGGS, GILBERT A.
PIANOS, PIANISTS AND SONICS
BROTHERHOOD, JAMES
BROTHERHOOD 'TECHNICON' AND HOW TO USE IT, THE
BROWER, HARRIETTE
ART OF THE PIANIST, THE
BROWER, HARRIETTE
HOME HELP IN MUSIC STUDY
BROWER, HARRIETTE
HOW A DEPENDABLE PIANO TECHNIQUE WAS WON
BROWER, HARRIETTE
MODERN MASTERS OF THE KEYBOARD
BROWER, HARRIETTE
PIANO MASTERY..TALKS WITH MASTER PIANISTS AND TEACHERS...
BROWER, HARRIETTE
PIANO MASTERY, SECOND SERIES
BROWER, HARRIETTE
SELF-HELP IN PIANO STUDY
BRUXNER, MERVYN
MASTERING THE PIANO
BURROWES, JOHN FRECKLETON
GUIDE TO PRACTICE ON THE PIANOFORTE
CALAND, ELIZABETH
ARTISTIC PIANO PLAYING, AS TAUGHT BY LUDWIG DEPPE
CAMPBELL, LE ROY B.
VELOCITY PLUS
CARPE, ADOLPH
PIANIST AND THE ART OF MUSIC, THE ..A TREATISE ON PIANO PLAYING
CARUTHERS, JULIA LOIS
PIANO TECHNIC FOR CHILDREN
CARY, MRS. C. S. P.
PIANO-FORTE CLASS BOOK, CONTAINING PRACTICAL RUDIMENTAL LESSONS
CASTELLINI, JOHN EDWARD
RUDIMENTS OF MUSIC..A NEW APPROACH WITH APPLICATION TO THE
CHASE, MARY WOOD
NATURAL LAWS IN PIANO TECHNIC
CHING, JAMES
AMATEUR PIANIST'S COMPANION, THE
CHING, JAMES
FOREARM ROTATION---A SEQUEL TO 'THE ROTARY ROAD'--15 PHOTOS AND
CHING, JAMES
PERFORMER AND AUDIENCE..AN INVESTIGATION INTO THE PSYCHOLOGICAL
CHING, JAMES
PIANO PLAYING, A PRACTICAL METHOD--A NEW EDITION OF 'PIANO
CHURCHILL, VIRGINIA PEAKES
MODERN TEACHER'S GUIDE TO PIANO AND PIANO CLASS TEACHING
COGGINS, JOSEPH
COMPANION TO THE MUSICAL ASSISTANT, A ..CONTAINING ALL THAT IS
COGGINS, JOSEPH
GOVERNESS'S MUSICAL ASSISTANT, CONTAINING ALL THAT IS TRULY USEFUL
COOKE, CHARLES
PLAYING THE PIANO FOR PLEASURE--REV. ED.---1941
COOKE, JAMES FRANCIS
GREAT PIANISTS ON PIANO PLAYING..STUDY TALKS WITH FOREMOST
COUPERIN, FRANCOIS
ART DE TOUCHER LE CLAVECIN, L' ---IN FRENCH, GERMAN AND ENGLISH
COVIELLO, AMBROSE
WHAT MATTHAY MEANT
CURWEN, ANNIE JESSY
PSYCHOLOGY APPLIED TO MUSIC TEACHING
D'ABREU, GERALD
PLAYING THE PIANO WITH CONFIDENCE---1964

DAHL, ANTON
SOUL OF GENIUS, THE ..ITS MUSICAL DEVELOPMENT AND HOW THE WORLD AT
DANIELS, BESS *
WORLD OF MUSIC, THE ..PIANO COURSE..TEACHERS' BOOK, FOR CLASS OR
DILLER, ANGELA
SPLENDOR OF MUSIC, THE
DUCKWORTH, GUY
KEYBOARD MUSICIANSHIP
DUSSEK, JOHANN L.
DUSSEK'S INSTRUCTIONS ON THE ART OF PLAYING THE PIANOFORTE OR
EDWARDS, RUTH
COMPLEAT MUSIC TEACHER FOR TEACHERS, PARENTS AND STUDENTS
EHRLICH, ALFRED HEINRICH
HOW TO PRACTICE ON THE PIANO..REFLECTIONS AND SUGGESTIONS
EHRLICH, ALFRED HEINRICH
HOW TO PRACTICE THE PIANOFORTE..SPECULATIONS AND ADVICE
EISENBERG, JACOB
WEIGHT AND RELAXATION METHOD FOR THE PIANOFORTE
ENGEL, CARL
PIANIST'S HANDBOOK, THE ..A GUIDE FOR THE RIGHT COMPREHENSION AND
FOLDES, ANDOR
KEYS TO THE KEYBOARD, A BOOK FOR PIANISTS
FRANZ, FREDERICK
METRONOME TECHNIQUES
FRAY, JACQUES *
HOW TO PLAY BY THE JACQUES FRAY SPEED METHOD
FRISKIN, JAMES
PRINCIPLES OF PIANOFORTE PRACTICE, THE
FROST, EDWARD
THALBEGARIAN (SIC) EXERCISES..OR, THE PIANIST'S DESIDERATA
FRYER, HERBERT
HINTS FOR PIANOFORTE PRACTICE--A SUGGESTED PLAN FOR DAILY
GARRATT, PERCIVAL
ART OF PIANOFORTE PLAYING, THE
GARROWAY, WILL
PIANISM
GAT, JOZSEF
TECHNIQUE OF PIANO PLAYING, THE, --2ND. ED.---1958
GEARY, ELEANOR MARGARET
MUSICAL EDUCATION, WITH PRACTICAL OBSERVATIONS ON THE ART OF
GIFFORD, ALEXANDER M.
PIANOFORTE AND HOW TO STUDY IT, THE
GLASFORD, IRENE A.
RHYTHM, REASON AND RESPONSE FOR THE MUSICIAN, PIANIST AND TEACHER
GORDON, STEPHEN T.
GORDON'S NEW SCHOOL FOR THE PIANO-FORTE
GRABILL, ETHELBERT WARREN
MECHANICS OF PIANO TECHNIC, THE
GRINDEA, CAROLA
FIRST TEN LESSONS, THE ..A NEW APPROACH TO PIANO TEACHING
GRUNDY, ENID
HAPPY PIANIST, THE
HAMBOURG, MARK
HOW TO PLAY THE PIANO--NEW AND ENLARGED EDITION OF 'HOW TO BECOME
HAMILTON, CLARENCE G.
WHAT EVERY PIANO PUPIL SHOULD KNOW
HARRISON, SIDNEY
PIANO TECHNIQUE
HARRISON, SIDNEY
TEACHER NEVER TOLD ME--TIPS FOR STUDENTS
HARRISON, SIDNEY
YOUNG PERSON'S GUIDE TO PLAYING THE PIANO, THE
HARVEY, ROBERT
MAGIC KEY TO KEYBOARD SUCCESS, THE
HEIDELBERGER, PAULINE
MASTER METHOD..PIANO NORMAL AND TEACHER'S MANUAL
HOFHEIMER, GRACE
TEACHING TECHNIQUES FOR THE PIANO
HOFMANN, JOSEF
PIANO PLAYING, WITH PIANO QUESTIONS ANSWERED---PUBLISHED EARLIER
HOPE, ERIC
AIDS TO TECHNIQUE
HORROCKS, CYRIL R. H.
STUDENT'S GUIDE TO THE ART OF TEACHING THE PIANOFORTE, THE --2ND.
HUENTEN, FRANZ
ABRIDGED EDITION OF F. HUENTEN'S CELEBRATED INSTRUCTIONS FOR THE
JOHNS, CLAYTON
ESSENTIALS OF PIANOFORTE PLAYING, THE
JOHNSTONE, J. ALFRED
ART OF TEACHING PIANOFORTE PLAYING, THE --2ND. REV. ED.---1910
JONAS, ALBERTO
PIANOSCRIPT BOOK..AN INVALUABLE AID TO TEACHER AND STUDENT IN
KOCHEVITSKY, GEORGE
ART OF PIANO PLAYING, THE ..A SCIENTIFIC APPROACH
KRUSZYNSKI, MICHAL
APPROACH TO THE PSYCHOLOGY OF PIANO TEACHING, AN
LAMAR, RICHARD
COLLEGE PIANO PEDAGOGY
LAMPE, JOHN F.
PLAIN AND COMPENDIOUS METHOD OF TEACHING THOROUGH BASS, A ..WITH
LANDOWSKA, WANDA
LANDOWSKA ON MUSIC--EDITED BY DENISE RESTOUT
LAST, JOAN
INTERPRETATION FOR THE PIANO STUDENT
LAST, JOAN
YOUNG PIANIST, THE ..A NEW APPROACH FOR TEACHERS AND
LEIMER, KARL *
RHYTHMICS, DYNAMICS, PEDAL, AND OTHER PROBLEMS OF PIANO
LEIMER, KARL *
SHORTEST WAY TO PIANISTIC PERFECTION, THE
LEVINE, HENRY
KNOW YOUR SCALES..FOR PIANO STUDENTS OF ALL GRADES
LE COUPPEY, FELIX
PIANO TEACHING..ADVICE TO PUPILS AND YOUNG TEACHERS---1868 IN
LHEVINNE, JOSEF
BASIC PRINCIPLES IN PIANOFORTE PLAYING---1924
LOGIER, JOHANN BERNHARD
SYLLABUS OF THE SECOND EXAMINATION OF MR. LOGIER'S PUPILS, ON HIS
LOWE, CLAUDE EDGERTON
ART OF PIANOFORTE PRACTICING, THE
MACLEAN, CHARLES D.
PRINCIPLES OF PIANOFORTE PRACTICE, THE
MAIER, GUY
PIANO TEACHER'S COMPANION, THE
MAIER, GUY *
PLAYING THE PIANO..A COURSE OF ROTE TRAINING FOR BEGINNERS--CLASS
MAIER, GUY *
PLAYING THE PIANO--TEACHER'S MANUAL
MASON, WILLIAM G.
ACCENTUAL TREATMENT OF EXERCISES AS APPLIED TO PIANOFORTE
MASON, WILLIAM G. *
PRIMER OF MUSIC, A ..BEING THE FIRST STEPS IN MUSICIANSHIP..FOR
MASON, WILLIAM G.
SYSTEM OF TECHNICAL EXERCISES FOR THE PIANO-FORTE, A
MASON, WILLIAM G.
TOUCH, AS APPLIED TO PIANOFORTE PRACTICE--ESSAY FOR THE 10TH.
MASON, WILLIAM G.
TOUCH AND TECHNIC..FOR ARTISTIC PIANO PLAYING, OP. 44--4 VOLS. IN

MATHEWS, WILLIAM S. B.
TEACHER'S MANUAL OF MASON'S PIANOFORTE TECHNICS
MATTHAY, TOBIAS A.
ACT OF TOUCH IN ALL ITS DIVERSITY, THE ..AN ANALYSIS AND SYNTHESIS
MATTHAY, TOBIAS A.
CHILD'S FIRST STEPS IN PIANOFORTE PLAYING, THE
MATTHAY, TOBIAS A.
EPITOME OF THE LAWS OF PIANOFORTE TECHNIQUE, AN
MATTHAY, TOBIAS A.
MUSICAL INTERPRETATION..ITS LAWS AND PRINCIPLES---1913
MATTHAY, TOBIAS A.
PIANOFORTE TONE-PRODUCTION---SAME AS 'THE ACT OF TOUCH IN ALL ITS
MCARTHUR, ALEXANDER
PIANOFORTE STUDY..HINTS ON PIANO PLAYING
MCFERRIN, CHARLES BETTEYS
MOTHER'S PART IN HER CHILD'S MUSICAL EDUCATION, A ..OR, THE THINGS
MCLAIN, MARGARET STARR
CLASS PIANO
MERGES, P.
PRACTICAL RULES FOR PIANOFORTE PLAYING..TEXT BOOK FOR TEACHERS AND
MERRICK, FRANK
PRACTICING THE PIANO
MOLDENHAUER, HANS
DUO-PIANISM---PUBLISHED DISSERTATION
MOORE, GERALD
AM I TOO LOUD..MEMOIRS OF AN ACCOMPANIST
MOTT, ISAAC H. R.
ADVICE AND INSTRUCTIONS FOR PLAYING THE PIANOFORTE WITH EXPRESSION
NEWMAN, WILLIAM S.
PIANIST'S PROBLEMS, THE ..A MODERN APPROACH TO EFFICIENT PRACTICE
NICCHIA, LILLIAN
PIANOFORTE STUDY..HINTS ON PIANO PLAYING
NIXON, W.
GUIDE TO INSTRUCTION ON THE PIANOFORTE, A --IN A SERIES OF SHORT
O'REAR, MRS. ASBURY S.
SELF READING NOTES
PACE, ROBERT
MUSIC ESSENTIALS FOR CLASSROOM TEACHERS--2ND. ED.---1961
PALMER, KING
TEACH YOURSELF TO PLAY THE PIANO
PARSONS, ALBERT R.
SCIENCE OF PIANO PRACTICE, THE
PATTON, VICTOR S.
LEARN TO PLAY POPULAR PIANO BY NOTE IN 20 EASY LESSONS...HOME
PEARCE, CHARLES WILLIAM
ART OF THE PIANO TEACHER, THE
PETERSON, FRANKLIN
THEORETIC COMPANION TO PRACTICE--PART I OF THE PIANIST'S HANDBOOK
PETRI, LILLIAN JEFFREY
MIND OVER MUSCLE..A TECHNICAL ECONOMY FOR PIANISTS
PHILIPP, LILLIE H.
PIANO STUDY..APPLICATION AND TECHNIQUE
PHILLIPSON, WENTWORTH
GUIDE TO YOUNG PIANOFORTE TEACHERS AND STUDENTS
PLATT, CAROLYN
CAROLYN PLATT METHOD FOR PIANO, THE --GROUP INSTRUCTION--TEACHER'S
POTAMKIN, FRANK
MODERN PIANO PEDAGOGY
PRENTNER, MARIE
MODERN PIANIST..BEING MY EXPERIENCES IN THE TECHNIQUE AND
PSTROKONSKY, JULES DE
NEW METHOD OF TEACHING THE PIANOFORTE
PUPIN, ANNIE
HOW TO PRACTICE..OR HINTS TO PIANO-FORTE STUDENTS ON THE METHOD OF
PUPIN, ANNIE
SCALES, THE ..THEIR FORMATION, FINGERING, AND HOW TO PRACTICE
RAMUL, PETER
PSYCHO-PHYSICAL FOUNDATIONS OF MODERN PIANO TECHNIQUE, THE
REZITS, JOSEPH
SOURCE MATERIALS FOR PIANO TECHNIQUES
REZITS, JOSEPH
TEACHER'S GUIDE TO THE NEW SCRIBNER MUSIC LIBRARY
RICHTER, ADA
TEACHING HINTS
RICKER, EARL
MUSIC LESSONS FOR YOUR CHILD
ROBILLIARD, EILEEN O.
PERSISTENT PIANIST, THE ..A BOOK FOR THE LATE BEGINNER AND THE
ROBINSON, HELENE
BASIC PIANO FOR ADULTS
ROOT, CATHERINE ADAMS *
LISTEN, SING AND PLAY..CLASS LESSONS FOR PIANO AND VOICE
ROWLEY, ALEC
PRACTICAL MUSICIANSHIP, A HANDBOOK FOR TEACHERS AND STUDENTS
RUBINSTEIN, BERYL
OUTLINE OF PIANO PEDAGOGY--REV. ED.---1929
SCHAUFFLER, ROBERT HAVEN
SCIENCE OF PRACTICE, THE
SCHELLING, ERNEST *
OXFORD PIANO COURSE, TEACHER'S FIRST MANUAL
SCHERER, HERBERT
PIANO PRACTICING
SCHMITZ, ELIE ROBERT
CAPTURE OF INSPIRATION, THE
SCHNEIDER, HANS
WORKING OF THE MIND IN PIANO TEACHING AND PLAYING, THE
SEROFF, VICTOR
COMMON SENSE IN PIANO STUDY
SHEFTEL, PAUL
EXPLORING KEYBOARD FUNDAMENTALS
SHEPARD, ROBERT
COMPLETE SCALE AND ARPEGGIO MANUAL
SHERWOOD MUSIC SCHOOL
PIANO LESSONS AND TESTS--4TH. REV. ED.---1945+
SLENCZYNSKA, RUTH *
MUSIC AT YOUR FINGERTIPS
SMELTZER, JEANNIE R.--COMPILER
OUTLINES AND GRADES FOR THE USE OF PIANO TEACHERS
SMITH, A. G. WARREN
BEGINNER'S GUIDE, THE ..FOR ALL COMMENCING THE STUDY OF THE
SOREL, CLAUDETTE
COMPENDIUM OF PIANO TECHNIQUE--39 ETUDES SELECTED FROM OVER 4000,
SQUIRE, RUSSEL N. *
CLASS PIANO FOR ADULT BEGINNERS--2ND. ED.---1964
STANLEY, JANE
BASIC ROUTINES IN ELEMENTARY PIANO TEACHING THROUGH THE FIRST
STEPHENSON, LILIAN E.
BEGONE, DULL PRACTICE..SUGGESTIONS FOR STUDENTS AND
STEWART, REID
HOW TO PASS MUSIC EXAMINATIONS--PIANO--A GUIDE FOR TEACHERS AND
SUZUKI, SHIN'ICHI
SUZUKI PIANO SCHOOL--4 VOLS.
TANKARD, GEOFFREY
PIANOFORTE DIPLOMAS
TAYLER, E. DOUGLAS
SECRET OF SUCCESSFUL PRACTICE, THE

TAYLOR, FRANKLIN
TECHNIQUE AND EXPRESSION IN PIANOFORTE PLAYING
TERWILLIGER, GORDON B.
PIANO TEACHERS PROFESSIONAL HANDBOOK
TOWNSEND, WILLIAM
BALANCE OF ARM IN PIANO TECHNIQUE--4TH. REV. ED.---1903
UNSCHULD, MARIE VON
PIANIST'S HAND, THE ..A SYSTEMATIC METHOD...ACCORDING TO THE
VANTYN, SIDNEY
MODERN PIANOFORTE TECHNIQUE
VIRGIL, ALMON K.
EDUCATION IN MUSIC..LESSONS TO TEACHERS IN THE INSTRUCTION OF
VIRGIL, ALMON K.
FOUNDATION EXERCISES IN PIANO PLAYING FROM FIRST RUDIMENTS TO
VIRGIL, ALMON K.
STEP BY STEP..TEXTBOOK IN PIANO PLAYING..HANDBOOK FOR TEACHERS
VIRGIL, ANTHA MINERVA
INSTRUCTIVE TALKS TO PIANO STUDENTS
WEISER, ADOLPH
TWO RIGHT HANDS..A GUIDE FOR THE DEVELOPMENT OF PIANO TECHNIQUE
WELLS, HOWARD
PIANIST'S THUMB, THE
WESTBROOK, BENJAMIN V.
SYSTEM OF STUDY OF SCALES AND CHORDS, A ..BEING CHAPTERS ON THE
WHITEMORE, CUTHBERT
COMMONSENSE IN PIANOFORTE PLAYING
WILLIAMS, JEAN E. *
MIND IN MUSIC, THE
WILLIAMS, JOHN M.
WHAT TO TEACH AT THE VERY FIRST LESSON
WILLS, VERA G. *
PARENT'S GUIDE TO MUSIC LESSONS, A
WILSON, MORRIS E.
HOW TO HELP YOUR CHILD WITH MUSIC--2ND. ED.---1951
WOLLENHAUPT, HEINRICH
METHOD FOR THE PIANOFORTE AND METHODICAL GUIDE FOR THE PIANO FORTE
WOODHOUSE, GEORGE
NEW PATH FOR PIANISTS, A ..THE MUTANO--MUTE PIANO--SYSTEM, ETC.

Memorizing

AEOLIAN COMPANY, THE
DUO-ART BOOK OF MUSIC, THE
AHRENS, CORA B. *
FOR ALL PIANO TEACHERS
AMEY, ELLEN
CONSCIOUS CONTROL IN PIANO STUDY
ANDERSON, J. CLARK
GOOD MUSIC EXPLAINED..WHAT ALL GOOD PIANISTS SHOULD KNOW
BASTIEN, JAMES W.
HOW TO TEACH PIANO SUCCESSFULLY
BOLTON, HETTY
HOW TO PRACTICE
BOLTON, HETTY
ON TEACHING THE PIANO
BRECKENRIDGE, WILLIAM KILGORE
HINTS FOR PIANO NORMAL STUDIES
BRIGGS, GILBERT A.
PIANOS, PIANISTS AND SONICS
BROUGHTON, JULIA
SUCCESS IN PIANO TEACHING
BROWER, HARRIETTE
ART OF THE PIANIST, THE
BROWER, HARRIETTE
MODERN MASTERS OF THE KEYBOARD
BROWER, HARRIETTE
SELF-HELP IN PIANO STUDY
BUCK, PERCY
PSYCHOLOGY FOR MUSICIANS
BURROWS, RAYMOND
ELEMENTARY PIANO INSTRUCTION IN COLLEGE
CALAND, ELIZABETH
ARTISTIC PIANO PLAYING, AS TAUGHT BY LUDWIG DEPPE
CARRE, JOHN
PSYCHOLOGY OF PIANO TEACHING, THE ..A TEXTBOOK FOR TEACHERS,
CHASE, MARY WOOD
NATURAL LAWS IN PIANO TECHNIC
COHEN, HARRIET
MUSIC'S HANDMAID
COOKE, CHARLES
PLAYING THE PIANO FOR PLEASURE--REV. ED.---1941
COOKE, JAMES FRANCIS
HOW TO MEMORIZE MUSIC
COVIELLO, AMBROSE
WHAT MATTHAY MEANT
CURWEN, ANNIE JESSY
PSYCHOLOGY APPLIED TO MUSIC TEACHING
CZERNY, CARL
COMPLETE THEORETICAL AND PRACTICAL PIANO FORTE SCHOOL, FROM THE
D'ABREU, GERALD
PLAYING THE PIANO WITH CONFIDENCE---1964
DEUTSCH, LEONHARD
PIANO..GUIDED SIGHT-READING
DILLER, ANGELA
SPLENDOR OF MUSIC, THE
DUMM, ROBERT W.
IN BLACK AND WHITE
EVERHART, POWELL
PIANIST'S ART, THE ..A COMPREHENSIVE MANUAL ON PIANO PLAYING FOR
FOLDES, ANDOR
KEYS TO THE KEYBOARD, A BOOK FOR PIANISTS
FRANZ, FREDERICK
METRONOME TECHNIQUES
GARRATT, PERCIVAL
ART OF PIANOFORTE PLAYING, THE
GARROWAY, WILL
PIANISM
GOODRICH, ALFRED JOHN
GUIDE TO MEMORIZING MUSIC, A
GUTMANN, EMMA WILKINS
TALKS WITH PIANO TEACHERS
HAMBOURG, MARK
HOW TO PLAY THE PIANO--NEW AND ENLARGED EDITION OF 'HOW TO BECOME
HAMILTON, CLARENCE G.
WHAT EVERY PIANO PUPIL SHOULD KNOW
HARKNESS, ROBERT
HARKNESS PIANO METHOD OF EVANGELISTIC HYMN PLAYING, THE ..A
HARRISON, SIDNEY
TEACHER NEVER TOLD ME--TIPS FOR STUDENTS
HARRISON, SIDNEY
YOUNG PERSON'S GUIDE TO PLAYING THE PIANO, THE
HEIDELBERGER, PAULINE
MASTER METHOD..PIANO NORMAL AND TEACHER'S MANUAL
HOFFZIMMER, ERNST
MUSICAL MEMORY, THE --INDIANA UNIVERSITY STUDIES, NO. 92

HOFHEIMER, GRACE
   TEACHING TECHNIQUES FOR THE PIANO
HOLCMAN, JAN
   LEGACY OF CHOPIN, THE
HOLDER, WILLIAM
   TREATISE ON THE NATURAL GROUNDS AND PRINCIPLES OF HARMONY, A ..TO
HORROCKS, CYRIL R. H.
   STUDENT'S GUIDE TO THE ART OF TEACHING THE PIANOFORTE, THE --2ND.
KENYON, CHARLES FREDERICK
   HOW TO MEMORIZE MUSIC
KENYON, CHARLES FREDERICK
   MEMORIZING MUSIC
LAMAR, RICHARD
   COLLEGE PIANO PEDAGOGY
LE COUPPEY, FELIX
   PIANO TEACHING..ADVICE TO PUPILS AND YOUNG TEACHERS---1868 IN
LHEVINNE, JOSEF
   BASIC PRINCIPLES IN PIANOFORTE PLAYING---1924
MACKINNON, LILIAS
   MUSIC BY HEART
MACLEAN, CHARLES D.
   PRINCIPLES OF PIANOFORTE PRACTICE, THE
MATHEWS, WILLIAM S. B.
   STUDIES IN PHRASING, MEMORIZING AND INTERPRETATION
MATHEWS, WILLIAM S. B.
   STUDIES IN PHRASING SELECTED FROM THE WORKS OF THE BEST CLASSIC
MATTHAY, TOBIAS A.
   INTRODUCTION TO PSYCHOLOGY FOR MUSIC TEACHERS, AN --THREE LECTURES
MATTHAY, TOBIAS A.
   MUSICAL INTERPRETATION..ITS LAWS AND PRINCIPLES---1913
MATTHAY, TOBIAS A.
   ON MEMORIZING AND PLAYING FROM MEMORY
MCLAIN, MARGARET STARR
   CLASS PIANO
MERRICK, FRANK
   PRACTICING THE PIANO
MUSIC EDUCATORS NATIONAL CONFERENCE
   TEACHING PIANO IN CLASSROOM AND STUDIO
NEAL, HARRY LEE
   WAVE AS YOU PASS
NEWMAN, ELIZABETH
   HOW TO TEACH MUSIC TO BEGINNERS
NEWMAN, WILLIAM S.
   PIANIST'S PROBLEMS, THE ..A MODERN APPROACH TO EFFICIENT PRACTICE
PALMER, ANNIE L.
   MUSIC TEACHERS' GUIDE TO THE GOLDBECK PIANO METHOD
PEARCE, CHARLES WILLIAM
   ART OF THE PIANO TEACHER, THE
PEDERSON, OLAF
   MEMORY TESTS FOR PIANOFORTE PLAYING ---7 PIECES WITH INSTRUCTIONS
PETERSON, FRANKLIN
   THEORETIC COMPANION TO PRACTICE--PART I OF THE PIANIST'S HANDBOOK
PHILIPP, LILLIE H.
   PIANO STUDY..APPLICATION AND TECHNIQUE
PLATT, CAROLYN
   CAROLYN PLATT METHOD FOR PIANO, THE --GROUP INSTRUCTION--TEACHER'S
POTAMKIN, FRANK
   MODERN PIANO PEDAGOGY
PUPIN, ANNIE
   HOW TO PRACTICE..OR HINTS TO PIANO-FORTE STUDENTS ON THE METHOD OF
RABSON, GRACE RUBIN
   INFLUENCE OF ANALYTICAL PRESTUDY IN MEMORIZING PIANO MUSIC, THE
RAMUL, PETER
   PSYCHO-PHYSICAL FOUNDATIONS OF MODERN PIANO TECHNIQUE, THE
RICHTER, ADA
   TEACHING HINTS
RICKER, EARL
   MUSIC LESSONS FOR YOUR CHILD
ROBINSON, HELENE
   BASIC PIANO FOR ADULTS
ROBYN, LOUISE
   HOW TO TEACH PIANO TO THE CHILD BEGINNER..A TEXT BOOK FOR TEACHERS
RUBINSTEIN, BERYL
   PIANIST'S APPROACH TO SIGHT READING AND MEMORIZING, THE
SCHNEIDER, HANS
   WORKING OF THE MIND IN PIANO TEACHING AND PLAYING, THE
SHERWOOD MUSIC SCHOOL
   PIANO LESSONS AND TESTS--4TH. REV. ED.---1945+
SHINN, FREDERICK G.
   MUSICAL MEMORY AND ITS CULTIVATION
SMELTZER, JEANNIE R.--COMPILER
   OUTLINES AND GRADES FOR THE USE OF PIANO TEACHERS
STANLEY, JANE
   BASIC ROUTINES IN ELEMENTARY PIANO TEACHING THROUGH THE FIRST
STEWART, REID
   HOW TO PASS MUSIC EXAMINATIONS--PIANO--A GUIDE FOR TEACHERS AND
SUZUKI, SHIN'ICHI
   SUZUKI PIANO SCHOOL--4 VOLS.
SWENSON, LUCILE B.
   DISCOVERING THE PIANO..THE MULTIPLE KEY APPROACH..STUDY GUIDE AND
TANKARD, GEOFFREY
   PIANOFORTE DIPLOMAS
TOBIN, JOSEPH RAYMOND
   COMMON SENSE IN SIGHT READING..A GUIDE FOR PIANO TEACHERS
TOBIN, JOSEPH RAYMOND
   HOW TO IMPROVISE PIANO ACCOMPANIMENTS
TOBIN, JOSEPH RAYMOND
   MEMORY PLAYING AT THE PIANO
TOBIN, JOSEPH RAYMOND
   READ AND REMEMBER..TWELVE STUDY PIECES TO FACILITATE PLAYING FROM
UNSCHULD, MARIE VON
   PIANIST'S HAND, THE ..A SYSTEMATIC METHOD...ACCORDING TO THE
VIRGIL, ALMON K.
   STEP BY STEP..TEXTBOOK IN PIANO PLAYING..HANDBOOK FOR TEACHERS
WELLS, HOWARD
   EARS, BRAIN AND FINGERS..A TEXT BOOK FOR PIANO TEACHERS AND PUPILS
WHITESIDE, ABBY
   INDISPENSABLES OF PIANO PLAYING--2ND. ED.---1955
WIER, ALBERT
   PIANO, THE ..ITS HISTORY, MAKERS, PLAYERS AND MUSIC
WILKINS-GUTMANN, EMMA
   TALKS WITH PIANO TEACHERS
WILLIAMS, JEAN E.
   MODERN METHOD OF PIANO INSTRUCTION, A ..TEACHERS MANUAL
WILSON, MORRIS E.
   HOW TO HELP YOUR CHILD WITH MUSIC--2ND. ED.---1951
WILSON, MORRIS E.
   HOW TO PLAY BY EAR
WOODHOUSE, GEORGE
   FROM KEYBOARD TO MUSIC

Repertoire Building

ADLER, KURT
   ART OF ACCOMPANYING AND COACHING, THE ---1965
BOOTH, VICTOR
   WE PIANO TEACHERS--REVISED BY ADELE FRANKLIN---1946

CARPE, ADOLPH
   PIANIST AND THE ART OF MUSIC, THE ..A TREATISE ON PIANO PLAYING
COOKE, CHARLES
   PLAYING THE PIANO FOR PLEASURE--REV. ED.---1941
DEUTSCH, LEONHARD
   PIANO..GUIDED SIGHT-READING
DUCKWORTH, GUY
   KEYBOARD MUSICIANSHIP
DUFFEE, GERTRUDE BANKS
   PIANO STUDY..A GUIDE TO TEACHER AND STUDENT
GARRATT, PERCIVAL
   ART OF PIANOFORTE PLAYING, THE
HAMILTON, CLARENCE G.
   WHAT EVERY PIANO PUPIL SHOULD KNOW
HARVEY, ROBERT
   MAGIC KEY TO KEYBOARD SUCCESS, THE
HERZ, HENRI
   NEW AND COMPLETE PIANOFORTE SCHOOL
HOLCMAN, JAN
   LEGACY OF CHOPIN, THE
HUTCHESON, ERNEST
   LITERATURE OF THE PIANO, THE --FROM THE 16TH. CENTURY TO THE
ISAACS, EDWARD
   BLIND PIANO TEACHER, THE
JONAS, ALBERTO
   PIANOSCRIPT BOOK..AN INVALUABLE AID TO TEACHER AND STUDENT IN
KENYON, CHARLES FREDERICK
   HOW TO MEMORIZE MUSIC
MOLDENHAUER, HANS
   DUO-PIANISM---PUBLISHED DISSERTATION
MUSIC EDUCATION LEAGUE
   COMPREHENSIVE GUIDE FOR PIANO TEACHERS AND PIANO AUDITION SYLLABUS
NEWMAN, WILLIAM S.
   PIANIST'S PROBLEMS, THE ..A MODERN APPROACH TO EFFICIENT PRACTICE
PALMER, KING
   TEACH YOURSELF TO PLAY THE PIANO
PERRY, ADELAIDE TROWBRIDGE *
   GUIDE TO PIANO STUDY FOR CLASS OR INDIVIDUAL INSTRUCTION, A
PFEFFERKORN, OTTO W.
   PIANISTIC HINTS
PHILLIPSON, WENTWORTH
   GUIDE TO YOUNG PIANOFORTE TEACHERS AND STUDENTS
PRENTICE, THOMAS RIDLEY
   MUSICIAN, THE ..A GUIDE FOR PIANOFORTE STUDENTS--6 VOLS.
ROBERT, WALTER
   PIANO STUDY IN SOVIET-RUSSIAN SCHOOLS OF MUSIC--REPRINT..'JOURNAL
SCHELLING, ERNEST *
   OXFORD PIANO COURSE, TEACHER'S FIRST MANUAL
SHERWOOD MUSIC SCHOOL
   PIANO LESSONS AND TESTS--4TH. REV. ED.---1945+
SLENCZYNSKA, RUTH *
   MUSIC AT YOUR FINGERTIPS
SQUIRE, RUSSEL N. *
   CLASS PIANO FOR ADULT BEGINNERS--2ND. ED.---1964
STANLEY, JANE
   BASIC ROUTINES IN ELEMENTARY PIANO TEACHING THROUGH THE FIRST
TANKARD, GEOFFREY
   PIANOFORTE DIPLOMAS
TANKARD, GEOFFREY
   SPECIMEN ANSWERS TO THE QUESTIONS IN PIANOFORTE DIPLOMAS
WOLFF, ERNST VICTOR
   WITH REASON AND RHYME
YATES, PETER
   AMATEUR AT THE KEYBOARD, AN

Ear Training

AHEARN, ELLA MASON *
   ADULT EXPLORER AT THE PIANO, THE
AHRENS, CORA B. *
   FOR ALL PIANO TEACHERS
BAKER, DAVID
   JAZZ IMPROVISATION..A COMPREHENSIVE METHOD OF STUDY FOR ALL
BASTIEN, JAMES W. *
   BEGINNING PIANO FOR ADULTS
BENNER, LORA
   BENNER BLUE BOOK, THE ..PRACTICAL MANUAL OF PIANO TEACHING--4TH.
BOLTON, HETTY
   ON TEACHING THE PIANO
BOWEN, CAROLYN
   OUTLINES FOR TRAINING PIANO TEACHERS
BROWER, HARRIETTE
   HOME HELP IN MUSIC STUDY
BROWN, JEAN PARKMAN
   INTERVALS, CHORDS AND EAR TRAINING FOR YOUNG PIANOFORTE STUDENTS
BURROWS, RAYMOND
   ELEMENTARY PIANO INSTRUCTION IN COLLEGE
CHAPPLE, STANLEY
   CLASS WAY TO THE KEYBOARD, THE
CHEYETTE, IRVING
   BASIC PIANO FOR THE MUSIC EDUCATOR AND CLASSROOM TEACHER
CHING, JAMES
   CANDIDATE'S COMPANION TO THE EXERCISES, SCALES, BROKEN CHORDS,
CHING, JOAN ELIZABETH
   APPROACH TO PIANO TEACHING---ALSO CATALOGUED UNDER
CHURCHILL, VIRGINIA PEAKES
   MODERN TEACHER'S GUIDE TO PIANO AND PIANO CLASS TEACHING
CHURCHILL, VIRGINIA PEAKES
   NINETEEN FIFTY-SIX SUPPLEMENT TO THE MODERN TEACHER'S GUIDE TO
COVIELLO, AMBROSE
   WHAT MATTHAY MEANT
CURCIO, LOUISE
   SINGLE NOTE, THE
CURWEN, ANNIE JESSY
   TEACHER'S GUIDE...TO MRS. CURWEN'S PIANOFORTE METHOD, 'THE CHILD
DEUTSCH, LEONHARD
   PIANO..GUIDED SIGHT-READING
DILLER, ANGELA
   KEYBOARD HARMONY COURSE..A CREATIVE METHOD BASED ON
DILLER, ANGELA
   KEYBOARD MUSIC STUDY..A CREATIVE METHOD BASED ON EAR-TRAINING--IN
DILLER, ANGELA
   SPLENDOR OF MUSIC, THE
DUCKWORTH, GUY
   KEYBOARD MUSICIANSHIP
ELKAN, IDA
   PRACTICAL PIANO PLAYING MANUAL AND THEORY WRITING BOOK
ELKAN, IDA
   TECHNICAL WORK IN EAR-TRAINING FOR THE PIANO..A METHOD FOR PRIVATE
FIELDEN, THOMAS
   MARKS AND REMARKS..MUSICAL EXAMINATIONS AND THEIR PROBLEMS
FREDRICH, FRANK
   PLAYING BY SEEING..A STUDY IN TRAINING AND PERCEPTION FOR BETTER
FRISKIN, JAMES
   PRINCIPLES OF PIANOFORTE PRACTICE, THE
GARROWAY, WILL
   PIANISM

GUTMANN, EMMA WILKINS
TALKS WITH PIANO TEACHERS
HARRIS, CUTHBERT
FIRST STEPS IN EAR-TRAINING--FOR THE PIANO STUDENT
HARRISON, SIDNEY
YOUNG PERSON'S GUIDE TO PLAYING THE PIANO, THE
HEIDELBERGER, PAULINE
MASTER METHOD..PIANO NORMAL AND TEACHER'S MANUAL
HORROCKS, CYRIL R. H.
STUDENT'S GUIDE TO THE ART OF TEACHING THE PIANOFORTE, THE --2ND.
JEWETT, ALBERT DEWEY
IDIOMATIC COURSE OF PIANO INSTRUCTION FOR CLASS WORK
LAST, JOAN
YOUNG PIANIST, THE ..A NEW APPROACH FOR TEACHERS AND
LEIMER, KARL *
SHORTEST WAY TO PIANISTIC PERFECTION, THE
LHEVINNE, JOSEF
BASIC PRINCIPLES IN PIANOFORTE PLAYING---1924
LINDO, ALGERNON H.
AURAL TESTS FOR EXAMINATIONS--SPECIALLY WRITTEN FOR TEACHERS AND
MACEWAN, DESIREE
FIRST TWO YEARS OF PIANOFORTE STUDY, THE
MATTHAY, TOBIAS A.
MUSICAL INTERPRETATION..ITS LAWS AND PRINCIPLES---1913
MATTHAY, TOBIAS A.
SOME COMMENTARIES ON THE TEACHING OF PIANOFORTE TECHNIC..A
MCHOSE, ALLEN IRVINE *
KEYBOARD AND DICTATION MANUAL
MCHOSE, ALLEN IRVINE
TEACHERS DICTATION MANUAL
MCLAIN, MARGARET STARR
CLASS PIANO
MELCHER, ROBERT A. *
MUSIC FOR ADVANCED STUDY..A SOURCE BOOK OF EXCERPTS
MOORE, MARY BURNHAM
LURE OF THE PIANO THROUGH COORDINATION AND CONCENTRATION, THE
MURPHY, HOWARD A. *
MUSIC FOR STUDY..A SOURCE BOOK OF EXCERPTS
MUSIC PROJECT--NEW YORK CITY
TEACHER'S GUIDE..A CREATIVE APPROACH TO PIANO CLASS TEACHING, BY
NEWMAN, ELIZABETH
HOW TO TEACH MUSIC TO BEGINNERS
NEWMAN, WILLIAM S.
PIANIST'S PROBLEMS, THE ..A MODERN APPROACH TO EFFICIENT PRACTICE
O'TOOLE, WILLIAM
KEYBOARD HARMONY---DUPLICATED FROM MANUSCRIPT
ORLIK, JULES
CREATIVE APPROACH TO PIANO CLASS TEACHING, A ---REPRODUCED FROM
PACE, ROBERT
MUSIC ESSENTIALS FOR CLASSROOM TEACHERS--2ND. ED.---1961
PALME, RUDOLPH
FIRST MONTHS IN PIANOFORTE INSTRUCTION, THE ---1870, IN GERMAN
PLATT, CAROLYN
CAROLYN PLATT METHOD FOR PIANO, THE --GROUP INSTRUCTION--TEACHER'S
POTAMKIN, FRANK
MODERN PIANO PEDAGOGY
REEVES, BETTY
APPROACH TO PIANO TEACHING---ALSO CATALOGUED UNDER
REEVES, BETTY
AURAL TRAINING--MONOGRAPH ON THE ART OF PIANO TEACHING, NO. 2
REZITS, JOSEPH
SOURCE MATERIALS FOR PIANO TECHNIQUES
ROBINSON, HELENE
BASIC PIANO FOR ADULTS
ROBYN, LOUISE
HOW TO TEACH PIANO TO THE CHILD BEGINNER..A TEXT BOOK FOR TEACHERS
ROBYN, LOUISE
ROBYN-HANKS HARMONY, THE ..A JUNIOR COURSE--BKS. 1-3, 1936-1938
ROWLEY, ALEC
DO'S AND DONT'S FOR MUSICIANS..A HANDBOOK FOR TEACHERS AND
SAULS, RANDY
THINKING MUSICIANS' APPLICATION OF MODERN HARMONY, THE ..HOW TO
SCHELLING, ERNEST *
OXFORD PIANO COURSE, TEACHER'S FIRST MANUAL
SHUMWAY, STANLEY
HARMONY AND EAR TRAINING AT THE KEYBOARD
SQUIRE, RUSSEL N. *
CLASS PIANO FOR ADULT BEGINNERS--2ND. ED.---1964
STARKEY, EVELYN
PIANO CLASS WORKBOOK FOR FIRST YEAR STUDENTS
STEWART, REID
HOW TO PASS MUSIC EXAMINATIONS--PIANO--A GUIDE FOR TEACHERS AND
TOBIN, JOSEPH RAYMOND
ADVENTURES IN MUSICIANSHIP
VAN APPLEDORN, MARY J.
KEYBOARD, SINGING AND DICTATION MANUAL
VIRGIL, ALMON K.
FOUNDATION EXERCISES IN PIANO PLAYING FROM FIRST RUDIMENTS TO
VIRGIL, ANTHA MINERVA
VIRGIL METHOD OF PIANOFORTE TECHNIC, THE --2 VOLS.
WELLS, HOWARD
EARS, BRAIN AND FINGERS..A TEXT BOOK FOR PIANO TEACHERS AND PUPILS
WELSH, J. ROBERT
MAKING MUSIC AT THE KEYBOARD..BEGINNING PIANO...CLASS...AND EAR
WILKINS-GUTMANN, EMMA
TALKS WITH PIANO TEACHERS
WILLIAMS, JEAN E.
MODERN METHOD OF PIANO INSTRUCTION, A ..TEACHERS MANUAL

Self-Instruction

ALBRECHTSBERGER, JOHANN GEORG
ALBRECHTSBERGER'S COLLECTED WRITINGS ON THOROUGH-BASS, HARMONY AND
ANON
HOW TO LEARN TO PLAY THE PIANO WELL, BY ONE WHO HAS TAUGHT HIMSELF
BASTIEN, JAMES W. *
BEGINNING PIANO FOR ADULTS
BAXTER, JAMES
INDUCTIVE GRAMMAR OF MUSIC, FOR CLASS, PRIVATE LESSON, OR SELF
BAXTER, JAMES
NEW SCHOOL OF MUSIC, THE ..PRACTICAL THOROUGH BASE CULTURE, FOR
BENEDICT, LADY *
HOW TO PLAY THE PIANOFORTE
BERTINI, HENRI
BERTINI'S SELF-TEACHING CATECHISM OF MUSIC FOR THE PIANOFORTE
BONPENSIERE, LUIGI
NEW PATHWAYS TO PIANO TECHNIQUE..A STUDY OF THE RELATIONS BETWEEN
BROWER, HARRIETTE
SELF-HELP IN PIANO STUDY
CALLAGHAN, JAMES
ZIP CHORDMASTER..BEGINNERS HOME COURSE FOR PIANO AND ORGAN
CHILDERS, LEMUEL
CHORD DICTIONARY..DESIGNED FOR TEACHERS, STUDENTS AND SELF-TAUGHT
CHING, JAMES
ENTIRELY NEW SOLUTION TO THE PROBLEMS OF PIANO STUDY AT HOME, AN
CHING, JAMES
PIANIST'S HOME STUDY COURSES, THE

DAVIS, HARRY
INSTANT PIANO..A UNIQUE METHOD OF READING AND CHORDING FROM THE
DEUTSCH, LEONHARD
PIANO..GUIDED SIGHT-READING
DUSSEK, JOHANN L.
DUSSEK'S INSTRUCTIONS ON THE ART OF PLAYING THE PIANOFORTE OR
ETHIER, JOSEPH A.
ETHIER'S GREAT NON-SUCH SELF-INSTRUCTOR IN THE ART OF ACCOMPANYING
EVANS, EVERETT J.
SELF-TEACHING CHORD BOOK FOR THE PIANO OR ORGAN..SHOWS HOW TO PLAY
FISCHER, JERRY CREE
PIANO TUNING, REGULATING AND REPAIRING...SELF INSTRUCTION...FOR
FRAY, JACQUES *
HOW TO PLAY BY THE JACQUES FRAY SPEED METHOD
GIBBS, GEORGE A., JR.
SELF INSTRUCTION IN THE PIANO
GRUNDY, ENID
HAPPY PIANIST, THE
HARGISS, GENEVIEVE
MUSIC FOR ELEMENTARY TEACHERS..A PROGRAMMED COURSE IN BASIC THEORY
HARKNESS, ROBERT
BEGINNERS PIANO COURSE IN HYMN PLAYING BY CORRESPONDENCE
HARKNESS, ROBERT
GOSPEL SONG ACCOMPANIMENT..THE ROBERT HARKNESS METHOD FOR PIANO
HARKNESS, ROBERT
GOSPEL SONG PIANO ACCOMPANIMENT..THE ROBERT HARKNESS
HARKNESS, ROBERT
HOME STUDY CORRESPONDENCE COURSE IN EVANGELISTIC HYMN PLAYING, FOR
JONAS, ALBERTO
PIANOSCRIPT BOOK..AN INVALUABLE AID TO TEACHER AND STUDENT IN
JONES, JOHN H.
PRACTICAL GUIDE TO THOROUGH BASS, A ..OR, HARMONY ILLUSTRATED AND
KLAVARSKRIBO, SLEKKERVIER, HOLLAND
PRACTICAL CORRESPONDENCE COURSE FOR PIANOFORTE
KOBBE, GUSTAV
PIANOLIST, THE ..A GUIDE FOR PIANOLA PLAYERS
KRAUSE, E. W.
STUDIES IN MEASURE AND RHYTHM...FOR TEACHERS AND PUPILS, ALSO FOR
KRAUSE, E. W.
STUDIES IN MEASURE AND RHYTHM, FOR THE PIANOFORTE, TO DEVELOP AN
LEACH, JOHN R.
FUNCTIONAL PIANO FOR THE TEACHER
LOYNES, W. H.
HOW TO PLAY THE PIANO IN ONE HOUR WITHOUT A TEACHER
LUND, VICTOR E.
EVALUATION OF ELECTRONIC SELF-INSTRUCTION ON PIANO KEYBOARD, THE
MAHONY, CORNELIUS
SELF-INSTRUCTOR FOR THE PIANOFORTE, CONTAINING C. MAHONY'S NEW
MATTHAY, TOBIAS A.
CHILD'S FIRST STEPS IN PIANOFORTE PLAYING, THE
MCCLINTOCK, LORENE
TEACH YOURSELF TO PLAY THE PIANO..BASED ON THE INTERVAL METHOD
MCLAIN, MARGARET STARR
CLASS PIANO
MILLER, ALLAN
BEGINNING PIANO FOR ADULTS
MOSCOW, CHARLES E.
PRACTICAL PIANO TUNER, THE ..A COMPREHENSIVE SIMPLE SET OF RULES
MOTT, ISAAC H. R.
ADVICE AND INSTRUCTIONS FOR PLAYING THE PIANOFORTE WITH EXPRESSION
NICHOLS, JULIA E.
COMMON SENSE CATECHISM..OR, PIANO AND ORGAN PUPIL'S COMPANION
NILES BRYANT SCHOOL OF PIANO TUNING
CORRESPONDENCE COURSE IN 12 LESSONS, A
PALMER, KING
TEACH YOURSELF MUSIC
PATTON, VICTOR S.
LEARN TO PLAY POPULAR PIANO BY NOTE IN 20 EASY LESSONS...HOME
PEDERSON, GALE
KEY TO THE KEYS..A SELF-TAUGHT PIANO METHOD FOR ADULTS AND TEEN
PRENTICE, THOMAS RIDLEY
MUSICIAN, THE ..A GUIDE FOR PIANOFORTE STUDENTS--6 VOLS.
QUINN, MARCUS LUCIUS
HOW TO STUDY MUSIC AND LEARN TO PLAY PIANO OR ORGAN
RENAUD, EMILIANO
RENAUD-PHONE PIANO METHOD..A PIANO COURSE THROUGH THE MEDIUM OF
REZITS, JOSEPH
SOURCE MATERIALS FOR PIANO TECHNIQUES
REZITS, JOSEPH
TEACHER'S GUIDE TO THE NEW SCRIBNER MUSIC LIBRARY
ROBINSON, HELENE
BASIC PIANO FOR ADULTS
SCONCIA, JOHN A.
ANALYTICAL INSTRUCTOR FOR THE PIANO FORTE, CONTAINING THE
SCONCIA, JOHN A.
SCONCIA'S NEW SYSTEM OF INSTRUCTION IN MUSIC AS A SCIENCE..OR, A
SEYMOUR, HARRIET AYER
HOME MUSIC LESSONS..HOW TO FIND YOUR MUSICAL SELF
SHERWOOD MUSIC SCHOOL
PIANO LESSONS AND TESTS--4TH. REV. ED.---1945+
SPENCER, BERNARD
POPULAR PIANO...A CORRESPONDENCE COURSE OF THE EASTERN SCHOOLS OF
STARKEY, EVELYN
PIANO CLASS WORKBOOK FOR FIRST YEAR STUDENTS
STORMEN, WIN
POPULAR PIANO SELF-TAUGHT---1956
TOBIN, JOSEPH RAYMOND
ADVENTURES IN MUSICIANSHIP
WILLIS, AUBREY
AUBREY WILLIS HOME STUDY COURSE IN PIANO TUNING AND REPAIRING
WINNER, SEPTIMUS
WINNER'S NEW SCHOOL FOR THE PIANO, IN WHICH THE INSTRUCTIONS ARE
WOODHOUSE, GEORGE
NEW PATH FOR PIANISTS, A ..THE MUTANO--MUTE PIANO--SYSTEM, ETC.
ZUCH, ANNETT V. *
PIANO TEACHER, THE ..A BOOK OF SELF-INSTRUCTION

Rhythm, Metrics, Tempo

ADAMS, JAMES B.
FAMILIAR INTRODUCTION TO THE FIRST PRINCIPLES OF MUSIC, A ...FOR
ADAMS, JOHN S.
FIVE THOUSAND MUSICAL TERMS..A COMPLETE DICTIONARY WITH A TREATISE
ADLER, KURT
ART OF ACCOMPANYING AND COACHING, THE ---1965
AHRENS, CORA B. *
FOR ALL PIANO TEACHERS
ALBRECHTSBERGER, JOHANN GEORG
ALBRECHTSBERGER'S ELEMENTARY WORK ON THE SCIENCE OF
ALLEN, MARGARET *
CREATIVE MOTION
ANDERSON, J. CLARK
GOOD MUSIC EXPLAINED..WHAT ALL GOOD PIANISTS SHOULD KNOW
ANON
COMPLEAT TUTOR FOR THE HARPSICHORD OR SPINNET, WHEREIN IS SHEWN
ANON
FASHIONABLE PRECEPTOR, FOR THE PIANO-FORTE AND HARPSICHORD,

ANON
    GUIDE TO THE MUSICAL TUITION OF VERY YOUNG CHILDREN, BY AN OLD
ANON
    NEW AND COMPLETE INSTRUCTIONS FOR THE HARPSICHORD, PIANO FORTE OR
ANON
    NEW INSTRUCTIONS FOR PLAYING THE HARPSICHORD, PIANOFORTE OR
ANON
    PRECEPTOR, FOR THE PIANOFORTE, THE ORGAN OR HARPSICHORD, THE
AULD, WILDA J.
    HANDBOOK FOR THE CHURCH PIANIST, A
AXTENS, FLORENCE
    PIANO CLASS METHOD..THE FIRST TWELVE MONTHS IN THE PIANO CLASS
BADURA-SKODA, EVA *
    INTERPRETING MOZART ON THE KEYBOARD---1957, IN GERMAN
BANISTER, HENRY C.
    HARMONIZING OF MELODIES, THE ..A TEXT-BOOK FOR STUDENTS AND
BARNETT, DAVID
    PERFORMANCE OF MUSIC, THE ..A STUDY IN TERMS OF THE PIANOFORTE
BARTH, HANS
    TECHNIC..THE ENTIRE 25 BRANCHES FOR DEVELOPING TECHNIC NECESSARY
BARTHELEMON, FRANCOIS H.
    NEW TUTOR FOR THE HARPSICHORD OR PIANO FORTE, WHEREIN THE FIRST
BASTIEN, JAMES W. *
    BEGINNING PIANO FOR ADULTS
BEMETZRIEDER, ANTON
    MUSIC MADE EASY TO EVERY CAPACITY, IN A SERIES OF DIALOGUES..BEING
BEMETZRIEDER, ANTON
    NEW GUIDE TO MUSIC, IN FRENCH AND ENGLISH, A
BERGER, FRANCESCO
    FIRST STEPS AT THE PIANOFORTE
BODKY, ERWIN
    INTERPRETATION OF BACH'S KEYBOARD WORKS, THE
BOLTON, HETTY
    HOW TO PRACTICE
BOOTH, VICTOR
    WE PIANO TEACHERS--REVISED BY ADELE FRANKLIN---1946
BOSWORTH, HARRIETTE DEXTER
    IDEAS FOR YOUNG PIANO TEACHERS
BOWEN, CAROLYN
    OUTLINES FOR TRAINING PIANO TEACHERS
BRANDT, LEONIE
    SCIENCE IN MODERN PIANOFORTE PLAYING
BRECKENRIDGE, WILLIAM KILGORE
    HINTS FOR PIANO NORMAL STUDIES
BROUGHTON, JULIA
    SUCCESS IN PIANO TEACHING
BROWER, HARRIETTE
    HOME HELP IN MUSIC STUDY
BROWER, HARRIETTE
    SELF-HELP IN PIANO STUDY
BUCHAROFF, SIMON
    MODERN PIANIST'S TEXT BOOK, THE
BUCKLEY, OLIVIA DUSSEK
    MUSICAL TRUTHS..OR, AN ANALYSIS OF MUSIC AND AN ESSAY ON THE PAST
CALLENDER, ROMAINE
    TEACHER'S MANUAL, A WORK DESIGNED TO SUPPLEMENT...'THE FIRST TEN
CARMIENCKE, ALBERT G.
    MECHANICS OF PIANO PLAYING, THE
CARPE, ADOLPH
    GROUPING, ARTICULATING AND PHRASING IN MUSICAL INTERPRETATION..A
CARR, BENJAMIN
    ANALYTICAL INSTRUCTOR FOR THE PIANO FORTE, OP. 15, THE --IN 3 PTS.
CARUTHERS, JULIA LOIS
    PIANO TECHNIC FOR CHILDREN
CARY, MRS. C. S. P.
    PIANO-FORTE CLASS BOOK, CONTAINING PRACTICAL RUDIMENTAL LESSONS
CASTELLINI, JOHN EDWARD
    RUDIMENTS OF MUSIC..A NEW APPROACH WITH APPLICATION TO THE
CHAPPLE, STANLEY
    CLASS WAY TO THE KEYBOARD, THE
CHASE, MARY WOOD
    NATURAL LAWS IN PIANO TECHNIC
CHILDERS, LEMUEL
    PLAYING THE PIANO BY EAR
CHING, JAMES
    AMATEUR PIANIST'S COMPANION, THE
CHING, JAMES
    NEW GRADED TIME EXERCISES, FOR PIANO, THE
CHING, JAMES
    STUDIES FOR BASIC PIANO TECHNIQUE..WRITTEN AND SELECTED WITH
CHURCHILL, VIRGINIA PEAKES
    NINETEEN FIFTY-SIX SUPPLEMENT TO THE MODERN TEACHER'S GUIDE TO
CLEMENTI, MUZIO
    INTRODUCTION TO THE ART OF PLAYING ON THE PIANOFORTE---1801+
COHEN, HARRIET
    MUSIC'S HANDMAID
CONKLIN-HAPP, SUZANNE
    APPLIED KEYBOARD HARMONY
COOKE, CHARLES
    PLAYING THE PIANO FOR PLEASURE--REV. ED.---1941
COUPERIN, FRANCOIS
    ART DE TOUCHER LE CLAVECIN, L' ---IN FRENCH, GERMAN AND ENGLISH
COVIELLO, AMBROSE
    WHAT MATTHAY MEANT
CRAMER, JOHN BAPTIST
    INSTRUCTIONS FOR THE PIANOFORTE---CONTAINS ALSO A SET OF 28
CURWEN, ANNIE JESSY
    TEACHER'S GUIDE...TO MRS. CURWEN'S PIANOFORTE METHOD, 'THE CHILD
CZERNY, CARL
    COMPLETE THEORETICAL AND PRACTICAL PIANO FORTE SCHOOL, FROM THE
CZERNY, CARL
    LETTERS TO A YOUNG LADY ON THE ART OF PLAYING THE PIANOFORTE
D'ABREU, GERALD
    PLAYING THE PIANO WITH CONFIDENCE---1964
DANIELS, BESS *
    WORLD OF MUSIC, THE ..PIANO COURSE..TEACHERS' BOOK, FOR CLASS OR
DEUTSCH, LEONHARD
    PIANO..GUIDED SIGHT-READING
DE WITT, EDYTHE
    EDYTHE DE WITT'S METHOD FOR CLASS PIANO...WRITTEN TO GIVE CORRECT
DILLER, ANGELA
    SPLENDOR OF MUSIC, THE
DOBBIE, E. A.
    AUSTRALIAN PIANOFORTE TUTOR
DOLMETSCH, ARNOLD
    INTERPRETATION OF MUSIC OF THE SEVENTEENTH AND EIGHTEENTH
DONINGTON, ROBERT
    INTERPRETATION OF EARLY MUSIC, THE
DONINGTON, ROBERT
    PERFORMER'S GUIDE TO BAROQUE MUSIC, A
DRAKE, KENNETH
    SONATAS OF BEETHOVEN AS HE PLAYED AND TAUGHT THEM, THE
DUCKWORTH, GUY
    KEYBOARD MUSICIANSHIP
DUFFEE, GERTRUDE BANKS
    PIANO STUDY..A GUIDE TO TEACHER AND STUDENT

DUMM, ROBERT W.
    IN BLACK AND WHITE
DUSSEK, JOHANN L.
    DUSSEK'S INSTRUCTIONS ON THE ART OF PLAYING THE PIANOFORTE OR
EHRENFECTER, C. A.
    DELIVERY IN THE ART OF PIANOFORTE PLAYING
EISENBERG, JACOB
    WEIGHT AND RELAXATION METHOD FOR THE PIANOFORTE
ELKAN, IDA
    PRACTICAL PIANO PLAYING MANUAL AND THEORY WRITING BOOK
ENGELBRECHT, J. G.
    MATERIA MUSICA, OR MATERIALS FOR THE PIANIST..A CLASS BOOK
EVERHART, POWELL
    PIANIST'S ART, THE ..A COMPREHENSIVE MANUAL ON PIANO PLAYING FOR
FALKENER, ROBERT
    INSTRUCTIONS FOR PLAYING THE HARPSICHORD..WHEREIN IS FULLY
FIELDEN, THOMAS
    MARKS AND REMARKS..MUSICAL EXAMINATIONS AND THEIR PROBLEMS
FOOTE, ARTHUR W.
    SOME PRACTICAL THINGS IN PIANO PLAYING
FRANZ, FREDERICK
    METRONOME TECHNIQUES
GARRATT, PERCIVAL
    ART OF PIANOFORTE PLAYING, THE
GEARY, ELEANOR MARGARET
    MUSICAL EDUCATION, WITH PRACTICAL OBSERVATIONS ON THE ART OF
GEBHARD, HEINRICH
    ART OF PEDALLING, THE
GERMER, HEINRICH
    RHYTHMICAL PROBLEMS..SPECIAL STUDIES FOR MASTERING RHYTHMS
GIESEKING, WALTER *
    PIANO TECHNIQUE---COMBINED REPUBLICATION OF..'THE SHORTEST WAY TO
GILBERT, RUSSELL S.
    EMBRYO MUSICIAN, THE ..A METHOD OF INTRODUCING MUSIC TO LITTLE
GILBERT, RUSSELL S.
    SUGGESTED PIANO STUDY FOR THE VOCAL STUDENT
GILBERTSON, ARNOLD B.
    TEACHERS MANUAL FOR POPULAR PIANO PLAYING, DESIGNED FOR ALL
GLASFORD, IRENE A.
    RHYTHM, REASON AND RESPONSE FOR THE MUSICIAN, PIANIST AND TEACHER
GOODRICH, ALFRED JOHN
    THEORY OF INTERPRETATION, APPLIED TO ARTISTIC MUSICAL PERFORMANCE
GORDON, STEPHEN T.
    GORDON'S NEW SCHOOL FOR THE PIANO-FORTE
GOSS, JOHN
    INTRODUCTION TO HARMONY AND THOROUGH-BASS WITH NUMEROUS EXAMPLES
GRAHAM, JAMES L.
    MUSIC MADE EASY, PIANOFORTE TUTOR ON A NEW PLAN
GRAUPNER, GOTTLIEB
    RUDIMENTS OF THE ART OF PLAYING ON THE PIANOFORTE...A PLAIN
GREW, SIDNEY
    ART OF THE PLAYER-PIANO, THE ..A TEXTBOOK FOR STUDENT AND TEACHER
GREW, SIDNEY
    FIRST BOOK OF THE PLAYER-PIANIST, THE
GRINDEA, CAROLA
    FIRST TEN LESSONS, THE ..A NEW APPROACH TO PIANO TEACHING
GUTMANN, EMMA WILKINS
    TALKS WITH PIANO TEACHERS
HAMILTON, CLARENCE G.
    PIANO TEACHING..ITS PRINCIPLES AND PROBLEMS
HAMILTON, CLARENCE G.
    TOUCH AND EXPRESSION IN PIANO PLAYING
HARPIS, CUTHBERT
    FIRST STEPS IN EAR-TRAINING--FOR THE PIANO STUDENT
HEERINGEN, ERNEST VON
    CELEBRATED INSTRUCTION BOOK FOR THE PIANOFORTE, CONTAINING THE
HEIDELBERGER, PAULINE
    MASTER METHOD..PIANO NORMAL AND TEACHER'S MANUAL
HEPLER, EFFIE A.
    EXERCISES IN TIME AND RHYTHM..A CONTRIBUTION TO MODERN PIANO
HOFHEIMER, GRACE
    TEACHING TECHNIQUES FOR THE PIANO
HOLCMAN, JAN
    LEGACY OF CHOPIN, THE
HOOK, JAMES
    GUIDA DI MUSICA..BEING A COMPLETE BOOK OF INSTRUCTIONS FOR
HORROCKS, CYRIL R. H.
    STUDENT'S GUIDE TO THE ART OF TEACHING THE PIANOFORTE, THE --2ND.
HUENTEN, FRANZ
    ABRIDGED EDITION OF F. HUENTEN'S CELEBRATED INSTRUCTIONS FOR THE
HUENTEN, FRANZ
    FRANZ HUENTEN'S CELEBRATED INSTRUCTIONS FOR THE PIANOFORTE--2ND.
HUMMEL, JOHANN NEPOMUK
    COMPLETE THEORETICAL AND PRACTICAL COURSE OF INSTRUCTIONS ON THE
IRWIN, WILLIAM
    RHYTHM ACCOMPANIMENT MAGIC, FOR THE POPULAR PIANIST
JEWETT, ALBERT DEWEY
    IDIOMATIC COURSE OF PIANO INSTRUCTION FOR CLASS WORK
JOHNSTONE, J. ALFRED
    ART OF TEACHING PIANOFORTE PLAYING, THE --2ND. REV. ED.---1910
JOHNSTONE, J. ALFRED
    METRONOMIC INDICATIONS FOR BACH'S PRELUDES AND FUGUES AND THE
JONES, GRIFFITH
    COMPLEAT INSTRUCTOR FOR THE HARPSICHORD OR PIANOFORTE, THE
KIRBY, MAY B. KELLY
    KELLY KIRBY KINDERGARTEN PIANO METHOD, TEACHERS' COURSE, THE
KOCH, CASPAR
    PIANO STUDENT'S GRADUS AD PARNASSUM, THE ..PRESENTING THE
KRAUSE, E. W.
    STUDIES IN MEASURE AND RHYTHM...FOR TEACHERS AND PUPILS, ALSO FOR
KRAUSE, E. W.
    STUDIES IN MEASURE AND RHYTHM, FOR THE PIANOFORTE, TO DEVELOP AN
KRAUSE, E. W.
    STUDY OF TIME AND MEASURE, THE --FOR PIANO STUDENTS
KULLAK, FRANZ
    BEETHOVEN'S PIANO PLAYING, WITH AN ESSAY ON THE EXECUTION OF THE
LAMAR, RICHARD
    COLLEGE PIANO PEDAGOGY
LANDOWSKA, WANDA
    LANDOWSKA ON MUSIC---EDITED BY DENISE RESTOUT
LANNING, RUSSELL
    BACH ORNAMENTATION
LAST, JOAN
    INTERPRETATION FOR THE PIANO STUDENT
LAST, JOAN
    YOUNG PIANIST, THE ..A NEW APPROACH FOR TEACHERS AND
LEACH, JOHN R.
    FUNCTIONAL PIANO FOR THE TEACHER
LEIMER, KARL *
    RHYTHMICS, DYNAMICS, PEDAL, AND OTHER PROBLEMS OF PIANO
LHEVINNE, JOSEF
    BASIC PRINCIPLES IN PIANOFORTE PLAYING---1924
LINDO, ALGERNON H.
    AURAL TESTS FOR EXAMINATIONS--SPECIALLY WRITTEN FOR TEACHERS AND
LOGIER, JOHANN BERNHARD
    FIRST COMPANION TO THE ROYAL PATENT CHIROPLAST OR HAND-DIRECTOR,

MACEWAN, DESIREE
    FIRST TWO YEARS OF PIANOFORTE STUDY, THE
MACEWEN, JOHN B.
    INTRODUCTION TO AN UNPUBLISHED EDITION OF THE PIANOFORTE SONATAS
MACPHERSON, D.
    CATECHISM OF MUSIC, CHIEFLY ADAPTED FOR LEARNERS ON THE
MAIER, GUY
    PIANO TEACHER'S COMPANION, THE
MAIER, GUY *
    PLAYING THE PIANO..A COURSE OF ROTE TRAINING FOR BEGINNERS--CLASS
MAIER, GUY *
    PLAYING THE PIANO--TEACHER'S MANUAL
MANSFELDT, HUGO L.
    TECHNIC..A SYSTEM OF THE MOST NECESSARY DAILY EXERCISES TO PRODUCE
MARKS, ADOLF B.
    INTRODUCTION TO THE INTERPRETATION OF BEETHOVEN'S PIANO-FORTE
MARX, ADOLF BERNHARD
    INTRODUCTION TO THE INTERPRETATION OF BEETHOVEN'S PIANO
MASON, WILLIAM G. *
    PRIMER OF MUSIC, A ..BEING THE FIRST STEPS IN MUSICIANSHIP..FOR
MASON, WILLIAM G. *
    SYSTEM FOR BEGINNERS IN THE ART OF PLAYING UPON THE PIANOFORTE, A
MASON, WILLIAM G.
    SYSTEM OF TECHNICAL EXERCISES FOR THE PIANO-FORTE, A
MASON, WILLIAM G.
    TOUCH AND TECHNIC..FOR ARTISTIC PIANO PLAYING, OP. 44--4 VOLS. IN
MATHEWS, WILLIAM S. B.
    MASON'S PRINCIPLES OF VELOCITY AND ARM TOUCHES
MATTHAY, TOBIAS A.
    FIRST LIGHTS ON PIANO-PLAYING
MATTHAY, TOBIAS A.
    FIRST PRINCIPLES OF PIANOFORTE PLAYING--EXTRACT FROM 'THE ACT OF
MATTHAY, TOBIAS A.
    MUSICAL INTERPRETATION..ITS LAWS AND PRINCIPLES---1913
MCALL, REGINALD L.
    PRACTICAL CHURCH SCHOOL MUSIC..METHODS AND TRAINING FOR SUCCESSFUL
MCCLINTOCK, LORENE
    TEACH YOURSELF TO PLAY THE PIANO..BASED ON THE INTERVAL METHOD
MCEWEN, JOHN B.
    INTRODUCTION TO AN UNPUBLISHED EDITION OF THE PIANOFORTE SONATAS
MCEWEN, JOHN B.
    TEMPO RUBATO, OR TIME VARIATION IN MUSICAL PERFORMANCE
MCHOSE, ALLEN IRVINE *
    KEYBOARD AND DICTATION MANUAL
MCHOSE, ALLEN IRVINE
    TEACHERS DICTATION MANUAL
MCLAIN, MARGARET STARR
    CLASS PIANO
MEHR, NORMAN
    GROUP PIANO TEACHING
MELLERS, WILFRED
    FRANCOIS COUPERIN AND THE FRENCH CLASSICAL TRADITION
MERRICK, FRANK
    PRACTICING THE PIANO
MILLER, EDWARD
    INSTITUTES OF MUSIC, OR, EASY INSTRUCTIONS FOR THE HARPSICHORD
MINNESOTA MUSIC TEACHERS ASSOCIATION
    PIANO-THEORY EXAMINATION SYLLABUS
MORRILL, HENRY H.
    MANUAL OF PIANO FOR PUPILS AND TEACHERS
MOTT, ISAAC H. R.
    ADVICE AND INSTRUCTIONS FOR PLAYING THE PIANOFORTE WITH EXPRESSION
MUSICIANS ADVISORY SERVICE
    MUSICIANS ADVISORY SERVICE FIRST MUSIC READER FOR PIANO..TEACHERS
NEUHAUS, HEINRICH
    ART OF PIANO PLAYING, THE
NEWMAN, ELIZABETH
    HOW TO TEACH MUSIC TO BEGINNERS
NEWMAN, WILLIAM S.
    PERFORMANCE PRACTICES IN BEETHOVEN'S PIANO SONATAS..AN
NEWMAN, WILLIAM S.
    PIANIST'S PROBLEMS, THE ..A MODERN APPROACH TO EFFICIENT PRACTICE
NIXON, W.
    GUIDE TO INSTRUCTION ON THE PIANOFORTE, A --IN A SERIES OF SHORT
OLIVER, EDWARD B.
    PRACTICAL TEXT-BOOK OF MUSIC, AS CONNECTED WITH THE ART OF PLAYING
ORREY, LESLIE
    MUSIC AT THE KEYBOARD
PACE, ROBERT
    MUSIC ESSENTIALS FOR CLASSROOM TEACHERS--2ND. ED.---1961
PALME, RUDOLPH
    FIRST MONTHS IN PIANOFORTE INSTRUCTION, THE ---1870, IN GERMAN
PARSONS, ALBERT R.
    SYNTHETIC METHOD FOR THE PIANOFORTE, THE
PARSONS, MARY H.
    RHYTHMIC WAY, THE
PEARCE, CHARLES WILLIAM
    ART OF THE PIANO TEACHER, THE
PETERSON, FRANKLIN
    THEORETIC COMPANION TO PRACTICE--PART I OF THE PIANIST'S HANDBOOK
PFEFFERKORN, OTTO W.
    PIANISTIC HINTS
PHILLIPSON, WENTWORTH
    GUIDE TO YOUNG PIANOFORTE TEACHERS AND STUDENTS
POTAMKIN, FRANK
    MODERN PIANO PEDAGOGY
PRENTNER, MARIE
    MODERN PIANIST..BEING MY EXPERIENCES IN THE TECHNIQUE AND
RAMUL, PETER
    PSYCHO-PHYSICAL FOUNDATIONS OF MODERN PIANO TECHNIQUE, THE
REDDIE, CHARLES FREDERICK
    PIANOFORTE PLAYING ON ITS TECHNICAL AND AESTHETIC SIDES
REINAGLE, CAROLINE
    FEW WORDS ON PIANOFORTE PLAYING, A
REZITS, JOSEPH
    TEACHER'S GUIDE TO THE NEW SCRIBNER MUSIC LIBRARY
RICHARDSON, NATHAN
    NEW METHOD FOR THE PIANOFORTE..ADDED, RUDIMENTS OF HARMONY AND
RICKER, EARL
    MUSIC LESSONS FOR YOUR CHILD
ROBINSON, HELENE
    BASIC PIANO FOR ADULTS
ROBYN, LOUISE
    HOW TO TEACH PIANO TO THE CHILD BEGINNER..A TEXT BOOK FOR TEACHERS
ROEDER, ELWOOD S.
    TIME-SPACE CONCEPTION OF THE GEOMETRY AND SPEED OF MOTION AT THE
ROTHSCHILD, FRITZ
    LOST TRADITION IN MUSIC, THE --PT. 1..RHYTHM AND TEMPO IN J. S.
ROTHSCHILD, FRITZ
    LOST TRADITION IN MUSIC, THE --PT. 2..MUSICAL PERFORMANCE IN THE
ROWLEY, ALEC *
    GRADED TESTS IN PRACTICAL MUSICIANSHIP AND MUSICAL INITIATIVE--IN
RUBINSTEIN, BERYL
    OUTLINE OF PIANO PEDAGOGY--REV. ED.---1929
SAFONOFF, WASSILI
    NEW FORMULA FOR THE PIANO TEACHER AND PIANO STUDENT

SCHAAF, EDWARD O.
    ART OF PIANO PLAYER TRANSCRIPTION, THE ..MAKING OF PERFORATED
SCHAAF, EDWARD O.
    MUSICAL INDIVIDUALITY OF THE PLAYER PIANO, THE ---EXCERPTS..'THE
SCHELLING, ERNEST *
    OXFORD PIANO COURSE, TEACHER'S FIRST MANUAL
SCHELLING, ERNEST *
    OXFORD PIANO COURSE, TEACHER'S SECOND MANUAL
SCHERER, HERBERT
    PIANO PRACTICING
SCHNEIDER, HANS
    WORKING OF THE MIND IN PIANO TEACHING AND PLAYING, THE
SCHOTT, HOWARD
    PLAYING THE HARPSICHORD
SCIONTI, SILVIO
    L'ARTE PIANISTICA..SYSTEM OF PIANO ARTISTRY---IN ITALIAN AND
SEGUEL, MANIA
    CHOPIN'S TEMPO RUBATO
SEYMOUR, HARRIET AYER
    HOW TO THINK MUSIC
SHEPARD, FRANK H.
    PIANO TOUCH AND SCALES..AN ANALYSIS OF THE FUNDAMENTAL PRINCIPLES
SHERWOOD MUSIC SCHOOL
    PIANO LESSONS AND TESTS--4TH. REV. ED.---1945+
SLENCZYNSKA, RUTH *
    MUSIC AT YOUR FINGERTIPS
SMELTZER, JEANNIE R.---COMPILER
    OUTLINES AND GRADES FOR THE USE OF PIANO TEACHERS
SMITH, A. G. WARREN
    BEGINNER'S GUIDE, THE ..FOR ALL COMMENCING THE STUDY OF THE
SMITH, EDWIN S.
    PIANO BY EAR
SMITH, THOMAS
    LITTLE DIFFICULTIES WHICH OCCUR IN PIANOFORTE PLAYING
SPENCER, BERNARD
    POPULAR PIANO...A CORRESPONDENCE COURSE OF THE EASTERN SCHOOLS OF
SQUIRE, RUSSEL N. *
    CLASS PIANO FOR ADULT BEGINNERS--2ND. ED.---1964
STANLEY, JANE
    BASIC ROUTINES IN ELEMENTARY PIANO TEACHING THROUGH THE FIRST
STARKEY, EVELYN
    PIANO CLASS WORKBOOK FOR FIRST YEAR STUDENTS
STEIN, ERWIN
    FORM AND PERFORMANCE
STERNBERG, CONSTANTIN I. VON
    ETHICS AND ESTHETICS OF PIANO PLAYING
STERNBERG, CONSTANTIN I. VON
    TEMPO RUBATO AND OTHER ESSAYS
STEWART, REID
    HOW TO PASS MUSIC EXAMINATIONS--PIANO--A GUIDE FOR TEACHERS AND
STORMEN, WIN
    FIFTY YEARS OF POPULAR PIANO TECHNIQUES IN THE U.S.A.
SUMMY-BIRCHARD COMPANY
    HANDBOOK FOR PIANO TEACHERS..COLLECTED ARTICLES ON SUBJECTS
TANKARD, GEOFFREY
    FOUNDATIONS OF PIANOFORTE TECHNIQUE
TANKARD, GEOFFREY
    SPECIMEN ANSWERS TO THE QUESTIONS IN PIANOFORTE DIPLOMAS
TAYLOR, FRANKLIN
    PRIMER OF PIANOFORTE PLAYING
TAYLOR, FRANKLIN
    TECHNIQUE AND EXPRESSION IN PIANOFORTE PLAYING
TOBIN, JOSEPH RAYMOND
    COMMON SENSE IN SIGHT READING..A GUIDE FOR PIANO TEACHERS
VANTYN, SIDNEY
    MODERN PIANOFORTE TECHNIQUE
VAN APPLEDORN, MARY J.
    KEYBOARD, SINGING AND DICTATION MANUAL
VENINO, ALBERT F.
    PEDAL METHOD FOR THE PIANO, A
VINING, HARRISON S.
    SIMPLE AND COMPLETE PRIMER FOR THE PIANOFORTE, THE
VIRGIL, ALMON K.
    FOUNDATION EXERCISES IN PIANO PLAYING FROM FIRST RUDIMENTS TO
VIRGIL, ALMON K.
    STEP BY STEP..TEXTBOOK IN PIANO PLAYING..HANDBOOK FOR TEACHERS
VIRGIL, ANTHA MINERVA
    INSTRUCTIVE TALKS TO PIANO STUDENTS
VIRGIL, ANTHA MINERVA
    VIRGIL METHOD OF PIANOFORTE TECHNIC, THE --2 VOLS.
WELLS, HOWARD
    EARS, BRAIN AND FINGERS..A TEXT BOOK FOR PIANO TEACHERS AND PUPILS
WESTBROOK, BENJAMIN V.
    SYSTEM OF STUDY OF SCALES AND CHORDS, A ..BEING CHAPTERS ON THE
WESTRUP, SIR JACK ALLAN
    MUSICAL INTERPRETATION---THIS BOOK ACCOMPANIED A SERIES OF B.B.C.
WHITE, WILLIAM BRAID
    PLAYER-PIANIST, THE ..A GUIDE TO THE APPRECIATION AND
WHITEMORE, CUTHBERT
    COMMONSENSE IN PIANOFORTE PLAYING
WHITESIDE, ABBY
    INDISPENSABLES OF PIANO PLAYING--2ND. ED.---1955
WILKINS-GUFMANN, EMMA
    TALKS WITH PIANO TEACHERS
WILLIAMS, JEAN E. *
    MIND IN MUSIC, THE
WILLIAMS, JEAN E.
    MODERN METHOD OF PIANO INSTRUCTION, A ..TEACHERS MANUAL
WILSON, MORRIS E.
    HOW TO PLAY BY EAR
WOLLNER, GERTRUDE PRICE
    IMPROVISATION IN MUSIC...WAYS TOWARDS CAPTURING MUSICAL IDEAS AND
WOODHOUSE, GEORGE
    ARTIST AT THE PIANO, THE ..THE ART OF MUSICAL INTERPRETATION
WRIGHT, WILLIAM C.
    GOLDEN MONITOR, FOR THE PIANOFORTE AND CABINET ORGAN, DESIGNED AS
WRIGHT, WILLIAM C.
    PIANOFORTE MANUAL, THE ..DESIGNED AS A COMPLETE PIANOFORTE PRIMER
WYMAN, ADDISON P.
    WYMAN'S PIANO TEXTBOOK..CONTAINING A COMPLETE SYSTEM OF MUSICAL
YATES, PETER
    AMATEUR AT THE KEYBOARD, AN
ZEITLIN, POLDI *
    THEORY PAPERS, THE --C.M.P. PIANO LIBRARY--2 VOLS., 1961-1963

Creativity

ALCHIN, CARRIE A.
    APPLIED HARMONY--REVISED AND WITH ADDITIONAL CHAPTERS BY VINCENT
ALLEN, MARGARET *
    CREATIVE MOTION
AMEY, ELLEN
    CONSCIOUS CONTROL IN PIANO STUDY
BASTIEN, JAMES W. *
    BEGINNING PIANO FOR ADULTS

BROWER, HARRIETTE
    HOME HELP IN MUSIC STUDY
CHAPPLE, STANLEY
    CLASS WAY TO THE KEYBOARD, THE
DANIELS, BESS *
    WORLD OF MUSIC, THE ..PIANO COURSE..TEACHERS' BOOK, FOR CLASS OR
DUCKWORTH, GUY
    KEYBOARD MUSICIANSHIP
EDWARDS, RUTH
    COMPLEAT MUSIC TEACHER FOR TEACHERS, PARENTS AND STUDENTS
GILBERT, RUSSELL S.
    EMBRYO MUSICIAN, THE ..A METHOD OF INTRODUCING MUSIC TO LITTLE
GRINDEA, CAROLA
    FIRST TEN LESSONS, THE ..A NEW APPROACH TO PIANO TEACHING
HERZ, HENRI
    NEW AND COMPLETE PIANOFORTE SCHOOL
HILL, JIM
    CREATIVE WORLD OF SCALES AND CHORDS, THE ..CREATIVE STUDIES IN
HOME, ETHEL
    IMPROVISING..A SIMPLE METHOD OF TEACHING THE SUBJECT TO CHILDREN
MCLAIN, MARGARET STARR
    CLASS PIANO
MEHR, NORMAN
    GROUP PIANO TEACHING
MUSIC EDUCATORS NATIONAL CONFERENCE
    TEACHING PIANO IN CLASSROOM AND STUDIO
NEWMAN, ELIZABETH
    HOW TO TEACH MUSIC TO BEGINNERS
PACE, ROBERT
    MUSIC ESSENTIALS FOR CLASSROOM TEACHERS--2ND. ED.---1961
PACE, ROBERT
    PIANO FOR CLASSROOM MUSIC--2ND. ED.---1956
PAIN, EVA
    BEGINNING TO PLAY THE PIANO..A MANUAL FOR TEACHERS
PERRY, ADELAIDE TROWBRIDGE *
    GUIDE TO PIANO STUDY FOR CLASS OR INDIVIDUAL INSTRUCTION, A
RAST, LAURENCE R.
    LET'S FIND OUT ABOUT MUSIC..WURLITZER ELEMENTARY PIANO WORKBOOKS,
REZITS, JOSEPH
    SOURCE MATERIALS FOR PIANO TECHNIQUES
ROBINSON, HELENE
    BASIC PIANO FOR ADULTS
ROWLEY, ALEC *
    MELODY MAKING AT THE PIANO--IN THREE STAGES
SCHELLING, ERNEST *
    OXFORD PIANO COURSE, TEACHER'S FIRST MANUAL
SCHELLING, ERNEST *
    OXFORD PIANO COURSE, TEACHER'S SECOND MANUAL
SEYMOUR, HARRIET AYER
    HOME MUSIC LESSONS..HOW TO FIND YOUR MUSICAL SELF
SHEEHY, EMMA DICKSON
    THERE'S MUSIC IN CHILDREN--REV. ED.---1946
STARKEY, EVELYN
    PIANO CLASS WORKBOOK FOR FIRST YEAR STUDENTS
THACKRAY, RUPERT M.
    PLAYING FOR DANCE..THE PLACE OF THE PIANIST IN THE TEACHING OF
WOODHOUSE, GEORGE
    REALISTIC APPROACH TO PIANO PLAYING, A

Musicianship, Expression

AMEY, ELLEN
    CONSCIOUS CONTROL IN PIANO STUDY
BASTIEN, JAMES W. *
    BEGINNING PIANO FOR ADULTS
BOLTON, HETTY
    HOW TO PRACTICE
BOLTON, HETTY
    ON TEACHING THE PIANO
CHING, JOAN ELIZABETH
    APPROACH TO PIANO TEACHING---ALSO CATALOGUED UNDER
CHURCHILL, VIRGINIA PEAKES
    NINETEEN FIFTY-SIX SUPPLEMENT TO THE MODERN TEACHER'S GUIDE TO
CONKLIN-HAPP, SUZANNE
    APPLIED KEYBOARD HARMONY
COVIELLO, AMBROSE
    WHAT MATTHAY MEANT
DONINGTON, ROBERT
    PERFORMER'S GUIDE TO BAROQUE MUSIC, A
FIELDEN, THOMAS
    MARKS AND REMARKS..MUSICAL EXAMINATIONS AND THEIR PROBLEMS
GOODRICH, ALFRED JOHN
    GUIDE TO PRACTICAL MUSICIANSHIP--INTENDED TO SUPERCEDE ROTE
HAMBOURG, MARK
    HOW TO PLAY THE PIANO--NEW AND ENLARGED EDITION OF 'HOW TO BECOME
HARKNESS, ROBERT
    HARKNESS PIANO METHOD OF EVANGELISTIC HYMN PLAYING, THE ..A
HEIDELBERGER, PAULINE
    MASTER METHOD..PIANO NORMAL AND TEACHER'S MANUAL
HERZ, HENRI
    NEW AND COMPLETE PIANOFORTE SCHOOL
HUMMEL, JOHANN NEPOMUK
    COMPLETE THEORETICAL AND PRACTICAL COURSE OF INSTRUCTIONS ON THE
JOHNSON, VERA A.
    SCIENTIFIC SIDE OF MUSIC IN SIMPLE, PRACTICAL FORM FOR TEACHERS
JOHNSTONE, J. ALFRED
    ESSENTIALS IN PIANOFORTE PLAYING, AND OTHER MUSICAL STUDIES...
LAST, JOAN
    INTERPRETATION FOR THE PIANO STUDENT
LEVINE, JACK
    WHAT MUSICAL INSTRUMENT FOR ME
LE COUPPEY, FELIX
    PIANO TEACHING..ADVICE TO PUPILS AND YOUNG TEACHERS---1868 IN
LHEVINNE, JOSEF
    BASIC PRINCIPLES IN PIANOFORTE PLAYING---1924
MATTHAY, TOBIAS A.
    EPITOME OF THE LAWS OF PIANOFORTE TECHNIQUE, AN
MATTHAY, TOBIAS A.
    FIRST PRINCIPLES OF PIANOFORTE PLAYING--EXTRACT FROM 'THE ACT OF
MCLAIN, MARGARET STARR
    CLASS PIANO
MEHR, NORMAN
    GROUP PIANO TEACHING
MOTT, ISAAC H. R.
    ADVICE AND INSTRUCTIONS FOR PLAYING THE PIANOFORTE WITH EXPRESSION
NICCHIA, LILLIAN
    PIANOFORTE STUDY..HINTS ON PIANO PLAYING
PACE, ROBERT
    MUSIC ESSENTIALS FOR CLASSROOM TEACHERS--2ND. ED.---1961
PACE, ROBERT
    PIANO FOR CLASSROOM MUSIC--2ND. ED.---1956
PLATT, CAROLYN
    CAROLYN PLATT METHOD FOR PIANO, THE --GROUP INSTRUCTION--TEACHER'S
PROCTOR, CHARLES
    HARMONIZATION AT THE KEYBOARD
REEVES, BETTY
    APPROACH TO PIANO TEACHING---ALSO CATALOGUED UNDER

REZITS, JOSEPH
    SOURCE MATERIALS FOR PIANO TECHNIQUES
RICKER, EARL
    MUSIC LESSONS FOR YOUR CHILD
ROBINSON, HELENE
    BASIC PIANO FOR ADULTS
ROWLEY, ALEC *
    GRADED TESTS IN PRACTICAL MUSICIANSHIP AND MUSICAL INITIATIVE--IN
ROWLEY, ALEC
    PRACTICAL MUSICIANSHIP, A HANDBOOK FOR TEACHERS AND STUDENTS
SCHELLING, ERNEST *
    OXFORD PIANO COURSE, TEACHER'S FIRST MANUAL
SCHUMANN, ROBERT
    ADVICE TO YOUNG MUSICIANS--FROM 'MUSIC AND MUSICIANS'---1876
SCHUMANN, ROBERT
    RULES AND MAXIMS FOR YOUNG MUSICIANS--FROM 'MUSIC AND MUSICIANS'
SHERWOOD MUSIC SCHOOL
    PIANO LESSONS AND TESTS--4TH. REV. ED.---1945+
STARKEY, EVELYN
    PIANO CLASS WORKBOOK FOR FIRST YEAR STUDENTS
STERNBERG, CONSTANTIN I. VON
    TEMPO RUBATO AND OTHER ESSAYS
STEVENS, WILLIAM S.
    TREATISE ON PIANO-FORTE, CONTAINING THE PRINCIPLES OF FINE PLAYING
SUZUKI, SHIN'ICHI
    SUZUKI PIANO SCHOOL--4 VOLS.
TANKARD, GEOFFREY
    SPECIMEN ANSWERS TO THE QUESTIONS IN PIANOFORTE DIPLOMAS
TOBIN, JOSEPH RAYMOND
    PREPARING FOR KEYBOARD TESTS IN MUSICIANSHIP EXAMINATIONS, JUNIOR
UNSCHULD, MARIE VON
    PIANIST'S HAND, THE ..A SYSTEMATIC METHOD...ACCORDING TO THE
VINING, HARRISON S.
    WHYS AND WHEREFORES..QUESTIONS AND ANSWERS FOR PIANO STUDENTS
WESTRUP, SIR JACK ALLAN
    MUSICAL INTERPRETATION---THIS BOOK ACCOMPANIED A SERIES OF B.B.C.
WILLS, VERA G. *
    PARENT'S GUIDE TO MUSIC LESSONS, A

Dynamics

ANDERSON, J. CLARK
    GOOD MUSIC EXPLAINED..WHAT ALL GOOD PIANISTS SHOULD KNOW
BARNETT, DAVID
    PERFORMANCE OF MUSIC, THE ..A STUDY IN TERMS OF THE PIANOFORTE
BARTH, HANS
    TECHNIC..THE ENTIRE 25 BRANCHES FOR DEVELOPING TECHNIC NECESSARY
BASTIEN, JAMES W. *
    BEGINNING PIANO FOR ADULTS
BERGER, FRANCESCO
    FIRST STEPS AT THE PIANOFORTE
BUCKLEY, OLIVIA DUSSEK
    MUSICAL TRUTHS..OR, AN ANALYSIS OF MUSIC AND AN ESSAY ON THE PAST
CARR, BENJAMIN
    ANALYTICAL INSTRUCTOR FOR THE PIANO FORTE, OP. 15, THE --IN 3 PTS.
CHING, JAMES
    STUDIES FOR BASIC PIANO TECHNIQUE..WRITTEN AND SELECTED WITH
COVIELLO, AMBROSE
    WHAT MATTHAY MEANT
CRAMER, JOHN BAPTIST
    INSTRUCTIONS FOR THE PIANOFORTE---CONTAINS ALSO A SET OF 28
CZERNY, CARL
    COMPLETE THEORETICAL AND PRACTICAL PIANO FORTE SCHOOL, FROM THE
DONINGTON, ROBERT
    INTERPRETATION OF EARLY MUSIC, THE
DONINGTON, ROBERT
    PERFORMER'S GUIDE TO BAROQUE MUSIC, A
DRAKE, KENNETH
    SONATAS OF BEETHOVEN AS HE PLAYED AND TAUGHT THEM, THE
GARROWAY, WILL
    PIANISM
GERMER, HEINRICH
    THEORETICO-PRACTICAL ELEMENTARY PIANO-FORTE SCHOOL FOR STUDENTS OF
GIESEKING, WALTER *
    PIANO TECHNIQUE---COMBINED REPUBLICATION OF..'THE SHORTEST WAY TO
GRINDEA, CAROLA
    FIRST TEN LESSONS, THE ..A NEW APPROACH TO PIANO TEACHING
HERZ, HENRI
    NEW AND COMPLETE PIANOFORTE SCHOOL
HOLCMAN, JAN
    LEGACY OF CHOPIN, THE
HUENTEN, FRANZ
    FRANZ HUENTEN'S CELEBRATED INSTRUCTIONS FOR THE PIANOFORTE--2ND.
MASON, WILLIAM G. *
    SYSTEM FOR BEGINNERS IN THE ART OF PLAYING UPON THE PIANOFORTE, A
MCLAIN, MARGARET STARR
    CLASS PIANO
MOKREJS, JOHN
    SCIENCE OF FINGERING, THE ---FOR PIANO
O'REAR, MRS. ASBURY S.
    SELF READING NOTES
PALMER, ANNIE L.
    MUSIC TEACHERS' GUIDE TO THE GOLDBECK PIANO METHOD
PARSONS, ALBERT R.
    SYNTHETIC METHOD FOR THE PIANOFORTE, THE
PEARCE, CHARLES WILLIAM
    ART OF THE PIANO TEACHER, THE
PFEFFERKORN, OTTO W.
    PIANISTIC HINTS
PHILIPP, LILLIE H.
    PIANO STUDY..APPLICATION AND TECHNIQUE
PHILLIPSON, WENTWORTH
    GUIDE TO YOUNG PIANOFORTE TEACHERS AND STUDENTS
POINTER SYSTEM, INC.
    GUIDE TO THE MODERN PIANIST, A
ROBINSON, HELENE
    BASIC PIANO FOR ADULTS
ROSENTHAL, MORIZ
    OLD AND THE NEW SCHOOL OF PIANO PLAYING, THE --TYPEWRITTEN COPY
SCHAAF, EDWARD O.
    ART OF PIANO PLAYER TRANSCRIPTION, THE ..MAKING OF PERFORATED
SCHAAF, EDWARD O.
    FUNDAMENTAL PRINCIPLES INVOLVED IN THE COMPOSING AND ARRANGING OF
SCHAAF, EDWARD O.
    MUSICAL INDIVIDUALITY OF THE PLAYER PIANO, THE ---EXCERPTS..'THE
SMITH, A. G. WARREN
    BEGINNER'S GUIDE, THE ..FOR ALL COMMENCING THE STUDY OF THE
SMITH, THOMAS
    LITTLE DIFFICULTIES WHICH OCCUR IN PIANOFORTE PLAYING
STARKEY, EVELYN
    PIANO CLASS WORKBOOK FOR FIRST YEAR STUDENTS
STERNBERG, CONSTANTIN I. VON
    ETHICS AND ESTHETICS OF PIANO PLAYING
WRIGHT, WILLIAM C.
    PIANOFORTE MANUAL, THE ..DESIGNED AS A COMPLETE PIANOFORTE PRIMER
WYMAN, ADDISON P.
    WYMAN'S PIANO TEXTBOOK..CONTAINING A COMPLETE SYSTEM OF MUSICAL

The Art of Teaching

General

ANDERSON, WILLIAM P.
    MUSIC AS A CAREER
ANTCLIFFE, HERBERT
    SUCCESSFUL MUSIC TEACHER, THE ..WORDS OF ADVICE
ANTRIM, DORAN K.
    TEACHING MUSIC AND MAKING IT PAY
ARIZONA STATE MUSIC TEACHERS ASSOCIATION
    GUIDE TO TEACHING PIANO--REV. ED.---1958
ASHBURNHAM, GEORGE
    STORY OF UNIQUE PIANO TUITION, THE
BACON, ERNST
    NOTES ON THE PIANO
BASTIEN, JAMES W.
    HOW TO TEACH PIANO SUCCESSFULLY
BENNETT, BEULAH VARNER
    PIANO CLASSES FOR EVERYONE..A PRACTICAL GUIDE FOR PIANO TEACHERS
BOOTH, VICTOR
    WE PIANO TEACHERS--REVISED BY ADELE FRANKLIN---1946
BORST, ALBERT W.
    ADVICE TO YOUNG STUDENTS OF THE PIANOFORTE
BROWER, HARRIETTE
    MODERN MASTERS OF THE KEYBOARD
BROWER, HARRIETTE
    PIANO MASTERY..TALKS WITH MASTER PIANISTS AND TEACHERS...
BROWER, HARRIETTE
    PIANO MASTERY, SECOND SERIES
CARPE, ADOLPH
    PIANIST AND THE ART OF MUSIC, THE ..A TREATISE ON PIANO PLAYING
CHING, JAMES
    PLAYING AND TEACHING OF BACH, THE ..A GUIDE FOR TEACHERS, STUDENTS
COCHRAN, MARY
    ULTIMATE PRINCIPLES OF PIANOFORTE TEACHING AND PLAYING
COOKE, JAMES FRANCIS
    GREAT MEN AND FAMOUS MUSICIANS ON THE ART OF MUSIC
DILLER, ANGELA
    SPLENDOR OF MUSIC, THE
DITSON COMPANY
    TEACHING PIECES AND HOW TO TEACH THEM
DUMM, ROBERT W.
    IN BLACK AND WHITE
EDWARDS, RUTH
    COMPLEAT MUSIC TEACHER FOR TEACHERS, PARENTS AND STUDENTS
FAY, AMY
    MUSIC STUDY IN GERMANY---1880
FILLINGHAM, ARTHUR H.
    GUIDE TO THE A.R.C.M. AND OTHER EXAMINATIONS IN THE ART OF
GIBBS, POLLY
    LISTS AND SUGGESTIONS FOR PIANO TEACHING
GRIMALDI, MARIA LOUISA
    ART OF PIANOFORTE PLAYING AND TEACHING, THE
HARRISON, SIDNEY
    BEGINNING TO PLAY THE PIANO--A TEACHER'S HANDBOOK, INCLUDING THE
HERZOG, SIGMUND *
    PIANO TEACHER'S MANUAL, THE
HOFHEIMER, GRACE
    TEACHING TECHNIQUES FOR THE PIANO
JOHNSTONE, J. ALFRED
    ART OF TEACHING PIANOFORTE PLAYING, THE --2ND. REV. ED.---1910
KNORR, JULIUS
    KNORR'S METHODICAL GUIDE FOR TEACHERS OF MUSIC ON THE PIANOFORTE
KULLAK, ADOLPH
    ART OF THE TOUCH, THE ..A WORK FOR THE USE OF ADVANCED PLAYERS AND
LAMAR, RICHARD
    COLLEGE PIANO PEDAGOGY
LANDOWSKA, WANDA
    LANDOWSKA ON MUSIC--EDITED BY DENISE RESTOUT
LINDO, ALGERNON H.
    PIANOFORTE STUDY..HINTS FOR TEACHERS AND STUDENTS
LOVELOCK, WILLIAM
    COMMON SENSE IN MUSIC TEACHING
LOWE, CLAUDE EDGERTON
    PIANOFORTE TEACHER'S VADE MECUM, THE ..A CYCLOPEDIA FOR THE
MACKLIN, CHARLES B.
    ELEMENTARY PIANO PEDAGOGY, A GUIDE BOOK FOR YOUNG PIANO TEACHERS
MUSIC EDUCATION LEAGUE
    COMPREHENSIVE GUIDE FOR PIANO TEACHERS AND PIANO AUDITION SYLLABUS
MUSIC EDUCATORS NATIONAL CONFERENCE
    TEACHING PIANO IN CLASSROOM AND STUDIO
NEWMAN, ELIZABETH
    HOW TO TEACH MUSIC TO BEGINNERS
NEW SCHOOL FOR MUSIC STUDY
    STUDY GUIDE FOR PIANO TEACHERS
O'TOOLE, WILLIAM
    CREATIVE PIANO TECHNIC
PLAIDY, LOUIS
    PIANOFORTE TEACHER'S GUIDE, THE
POWERS-WADSWORTH, L.
    PIANIST'S GUIDE TO TECHNICAL FREEDOM, THE ..2 VOLS. IN 1
RAINBOW, BERNARR J. G.--EDITOR
    HANDBOOK FOR MUSIC TEACHERS--2 VOLS.
SCHELLING, ERNEST *
    OXFORD PIANO COURSE, TEACHER'S FIRST MANUAL
SCHELLING, ERNEST *
    OXFORD PIANO COURSE, TEACHER'S SECOND MANUAL
STEWART, REID
    HOW TO PASS MUSIC EXAMINATIONS--PIANO--A GUIDE FOR TEACHERS AND
SUMMY-BIRCHARD COMPANY
    HANDBOOK FOR PIANO TEACHERS..COLLECTED ARTICLES ON SUBJECTS
TAPPER, THOMAS
    EDUCATION OF THE MUSIC TEACHER, THE
TERWILLIGER, GORDON B.
    PIANO TEACHERS PROFESSIONAL HANDBOOK
TOWNSEND, WILLIAM
    MODERN PIANO TEACHING
WASHINGTON STATE MUSIC TEACHERS ASSOCIATION
    PIANO TEACHING GUIDE--GRADES 1-8
WELLS, HOWARD
    EARS, BRAIN AND FINGERS..A TEXT BOOK FOR PIANO TEACHERS AND PUPILS
WEST, GEORGE FREDERICK
    HINTS TO YOUNG TEACHERS OF THE PIANOFORTE
WHEELER, BERTHA H.
    MIND AND MECHANISM..THOUGHTS ON TEACHING AND THE PIANISTIC ART
WHITESIDE, ABBY
    INDISPENSABLES OF PIANO PLAYING--2ND. ED.---1955
WHITESIDE, ABBY
    MASTERING THE CHOPIN ETUDES AND OTHER ESSAYS
WIECK, FRIEDRICH
    PIANO AND SONG..HOW TO TEACH, HOW TO LEARN, AND HOW TO FORM A

WIER, ALBERT
    PIANO, THE ..ITS HISTORY, MAKERS, PLAYERS AND MUSIC
WILKINS-GUTMANN, EMMA
    TALKS WITH PIANO TEACHERS
WILLIAMS, GUY BEVIER
    PIANISM..A COURSE IN NORMAL TRAINING

Miscellaneous

ANON
    HOW TO LEARN TO PLAY THE PIANO WELL, BY ONE WHO HAS TAUGHT HIMSELF
ASHBURNHAM, GEORGE
    STORY OF UNIQUE PIANO TUITION, THE
BASTIEN, JAMES W.
    HOW TO TEACH PIANO SUCCESSFULLY
BENEDICT, MILO ELLSWORTH
    THIRTY-THREE SUGGESTIONS IN ONE LESSON..FOR THE GUIDANCE AND
BOOTH, VICTOR
    WE PIANO TEACHERS--REVISED BY ADELE FRANKLIN---1946
BOTTOMLEY, JOSEPH
    NEW SYSTEM OF PRACTICING AND TEACHING THE PIANOFORTE, A
BROUGHTON, JULIA
    SUCCESS IN PIANO TEACHING
CARRE, JOHN
    PSYCHOLOGY OF PIANO TEACHING, THE ..A TEXTBOOK FOR TEACHERS,
DUMM, ROBERT W.
    IN BLACK AND WHITE
GRAHAM, MARY JANE
    LETTER TO A YOUNG PIANOFORTE PLAYER, A
HARRISON, SIDNEY
    BEGINNING TO PLAY THE PIANO--A TEACHER'S HANDBOOK, INCLUDING THE
HERZOG, SIGMUND *
    PIANO TEACHER'S MANUAL, THE
JOHNSTONE, J. ALFRED
    ART OF TEACHING PIANOFORTE PLAYING, THE --2ND. REV. ED.---1910
KNORR, JULIUS
    KNORR'S METHODICAL GUIDE FOR TEACHERS OF MUSIC ON THE PIANOFORTE
KULLAK, ADOLPH
    ART OF THE TOUCH, THE ..A WORK FOR THE USE OF ADVANCED PLAYERS AND
LOWE, CLAUDE EDGERTON
    PIANOFORTE TEACHER'S VADE MECUM, THE ..A CYCLOPEDIA FOR THE
MACKLIN, CHARLES B.
    ELEMENTARY PIANO PEDAGOGY, A GUIDE BOOK FOR YOUNG PIANO TEACHERS
MAIER, GUY
    PIANO TEACHER'S COMPANION, THE
NEWMAN, ELIZABETH
    HOW TO TEACH MUSIC TO BEGINNERS
NEW SCHOOL FOR MUSIC STUDY
    STUDY GUIDE FOR PIANO TEACHERS
OREGON MUSIC TEACHERS ASSOCIATION
    PIANO MATERIALS
POWERS-WADSWORTH, L.
    PIANIST'S GUIDE TO TECHNICAL FREEDOM, THE ..2 VOLS. IN 1
SAVLER, ROBERTA--EDITOR
    SELECTIONS FROM THE PIANO TEACHER, 1958-1963
SCHELLING, ERNEST *
    OXFORD PIANO COURSE, TEACHER'S FIRST MANUAL
SUR, WILLIAM R.--EDITOR
    PIANO INSTRUCTION IN THE SCHOOLS
TAPPER, THOMAS
    EDUCATION OF THE MUSIC TEACHER, THE
TERWILLIGER, GORDON B.
    PIANO TEACHERS PROFESSIONAL HANDBOOK
TOWNSEND, WILLIAM
    MODERN PIANO TEACHING
WASHINGTON STATE MUSIC TEACHERS ASSOCIATION
    PIANO TEACHING GUIDE--GRADES 1-8
WELLS, HOWARD
    EARS, BRAIN AND FINGERS..A TEXT BOOK FOR PIANO TEACHERS AND PUPILS
WHEELER, BERTHA H.
    MIND AND MECHANISM..THOUGHTS ON TEACHING AND THE PIANISTIC ART
WHITESIDE, ABBY
    MASTERING THE CHOPIN ETUDES AND OTHER ESSAYS
WIER, ALBERT
    PIANO, THE ..ITS HISTORY, MAKERS, PLAYERS AND MUSIC
WILLIAMS, GUY BEVIER
    PIANISM..A COURSE IN NORMAL TRAINING

Philosophy and Psychology of Teaching

AHRENS, CORA B. *
    FOR ALL PIANO TEACHERS
ALLEN, MARGARET *
    CREATIVE MOTION
ANTCLIFFE, HERBERT
    SUCCESSFUL MUSIC TEACHER, THE ..WORDS OF ADVICE
ANTRIM, DORAN K.
    TEACHING MUSIC AND MAKING IT PAY
BASTIEN, JAMES W.
    HOW TO TEACH PIANO SUCCESSFULLY
BAUGHAN, EDWARD ALGERNON
    IGNACE JAN PADEREWSKI
BEMETZRIEDER, ANTON
    COMPENDIUM OF A NEW METHOD OF MUSIC...WITH THE AUTHOR'S PRINCIPLES
BENNER, LORA
    BENNER GOLD BOOK, THE ..PIANO MATERIAL AND TEACHING METHODS--3RD.
BOAL, DEAN *
    CONCEPTS AND SKILLS FOR THE PIANO..TEACHER'S MANUAL 1---CLASS
BOLTON, HETTY
    ON TEACHING THE PIANO
BOOTH, VICTOR
    WE PIANO TEACHERS--REVISED BY ADELE FRANKLIN---1946
BOSWORTH, HARRIETTE DEXTER
    IDEAS FOR YOUNG PIANO TEACHERS
BRECKENRIDGE, WILLIAM KILGORE
    HINTS FOR PIANO NORMAL STUDIES
BROTHERHOOD, JAMES
    IMPROVED METHOD IN PIANO TEACHING, AND RECENT IDEAS OF LEADING
BROUGHTON, JULIA
    SUCCESS IN PIANO TEACHING
BROWER, HARRIETTE
    ART OF THE PIANIST, THE
BROWER, HARRIETTE
    SELF-HELP IN PIANO STUDY
BUCK, PERCY
    PSYCHOLOGY FOR MUSICIANS
CALLENDER, ROMAINE
    TEACHER'S MANUAL, A WORK DESIGNED TO SUPPLEMENT...'THE FIRST TEN
CARRE, JOHN
    PSYCHOLOGY OF PIANO TEACHING, THE ..A TEXTBOOK FOR TEACHERS,
CHING, JAMES
    PERFORMER AND AUDIENCE..AN INVESTIGATION INTO THE PSYCHOLOGICAL
CHING, JAMES
    PIANO PLAYING, A PRACTICAL METHOD--A NEW EDITION OF 'PIANO
CHING, JOAN ELIZABETH
    OURSELVES AND OUR PUPILS---ALSO CATALOGUED UNDER AUTHORSHIP..BETTY

COPP, EVELYN A.
    WHAT IS THE FLETCHER MUSIC METHOD
CURWEN, ANNIE JESSY
    PSYCHOLOGY APPLIED TO MUSIC TEACHING
CURWEN, ANNIE JESSY
    TEACHER'S GUIDE...TO MRS. CURWEN'S PIANOFORTE METHOD, 'THE CHILD
DAVISON, JUNE *
    PIANO PROGRESS..AN APPROACH TO MUSIC FOR THE PARTIALLY SIGHTED--2
DEUTSCH, LEONHARD
    PIANO..GUIDED SIGHT-READING
DUFFEE, GERTRUDE BANKS
    PIANO STUDY..A GUIDE TO TEACHER AND STUDENT
DUMM, ROBERT W.
    IN BLACK AND WHITE
EDWARDS, RUTH
    COMPLEAT MUSIC TEACHER FOR TEACHERS, PARENTS AND STUDENTS
EISENBERG, JACOB
    ARTISTIC PIANIST, THE ..NATURAL TECHNICS IN PIANO MASTERY..FROM
FISHER, HENRY
    PSYCHOLOGY FOR MUSIC TEACHERS..THE LAWS OF THOUGHT APPLIED TO
FREDRICH, FRANK
    PLAYING BY SEEING..A STUDY IN TRAINING AND PERCEPTION FOR BETTER
HAMILTON, CLARENCE G.
    FUTURE OF PIANO STUDY, THE ---FROM 'M.T.N.A. PROCEEDINGS', SERIES
HAMILTON, CLARENCE G.
    PIANO TEACHING..ITS PRINCIPLES AND PROBLEMS
HEIDELBERGER, PAULINE
    MASTER METHOD..PIANO NORMAL AND TEACHER'S MANUAL
HORROCKS, CYRIL R. H.
    STUDENT'S GUIDE TO THE ART OF TEACHING THE PIANOFORTE, THE --2ND.
ISAACS, EDWARD
    BLIND PIANO TEACHER, THE
JOHNSTONE, J. ALFRED
    ESSENTIALS IN PIANOFORTE PLAYING. AND OTHER MUSICAL STUDIES...
KIRBY, MAY B. KELLY
    KELLY KIRBY KINDERGARTEN PIANO METHOD, TEACHERS' COURSE, THE
KOTZSCHMAR, MARY ANN
    HALF-HOUR LESSONS IN MUSIC..CLASS WORK FOR BEGINNERS AT THE PIANO
KRUSZYNSKI, MICHAL
    APPROACH TO THE PSYCHOLOGY OF PIANO TEACHING, AN
LASSIMONNE, DENISE
    OPENING THE SHUTTERS..A SHORT EXPOSITION ON THE TEACHINGS AND
LE COUPPEY, FELIX
    PIANO TEACHING..ADVICE TO PUPILS AND YOUNG TEACHERS---1868 IN
LOMAS, LULU GRAHAM
    FIRST TEN PIANO LESSONS, LAID OUT FOR YOUNG TEACHERS, WITH
LOVELOCK, WILLIAM
    COMMON SENSE IN MUSIC TEACHING
MAIER, GUY
    PIANO TEACHER'S COMPANION, THE
MAIER, GUY *
    PLAYING THE PIANO--TEACHER'S MANUAL
MASON, WILLIAM G. *
    PRIMER OF MUSIC, A ..BEING THE FIRST STEPS IN MUSICIANSHIP..FOR
MATTHAY, TOBIAS A.
    MUSICAL INTERPRETATION..ITS LAWS AND PRINCIPLES---1913
MATTHAY, TOBIAS A.
    ON METHOD IN TEACHING
MEHR, NORMAN
    GROUP PIANO TEACHING
MUSIC EDUCATORS NATIONAL CONFERENCE
    TEACHING PIANO IN CLASSROOM AND STUDIO
NATIONAL BUREAU FOR THE ADVANCEMENT OF MUSIC
    PIANO CLASSES AND THE PRIVATE TEACHER
PETERSON, HOUSTON--EDITOR
    GREAT TEACHERS, PORTRAYED BY THOSE WHO STUDIED UNDER
PLAIDY, LOUIS
    PIANO TEACHER, THE
PLATT, CAROLYN
    CAROLYN PLATT METHOD FOR PIANO, THE --GROUP INSTRUCTION--TEACHER'S
PORTER, FRANK A. *
    TEACHERS' MANUAL FOR THE PORTER PIANOFORTE COURSE
POTAMKIN, FRANK
    MODERN PIANO PEDAGOGY
QUINN, MARCUS LUCIUS
    HOW TO STUDY MUSIC AND LEARN TO PLAY PIANO OR ORGAN
REEVES, BETTY
    OURSELVES AND OUR PUPILS--MONOGRAPH ON THE ART OF PIANO TEACHING,
REINECKE, KARL H.
    WHAT SHALL WE PLAY--NOT UNLIKE CZERNY'S 'LETTERS TO A YOUNG
ROBERT, WALTER
    PIANO STUDY IN SOVIET-RUSSIAN SCHOOLS OF MUSIC--REPRINT..'JOURNAL
ROBILLIARD, EILEEN D.
    PERSISTENT PIANIST, THE ..A BOOK FOR THE LATE BEGINNER AND THE
ROWLEY, ALEC
    DO'S AND DONT'S FOR MUSICIANS..A HANDBOOK FOR TEACHERS AND
ROWLEY, ALEC
    PRACTICAL MUSICIANSHIP, A HANDBOOK FOR TEACHERS AND STUDENTS
RUBINSTEIN, BERYL
    OUTLINE OF PIANO PEDAGOGY--REV. ED.---1929
SCHELLING, ERNEST *
    OXFORD PIANO COURSE, TEACHER'S FIRST MANUAL
SCHELLING, ERNEST *
    OXFORD PIANO COURSE, TEACHER'S SECOND MANUAL
SCHNEIDER, HANS
    WORKING OF THE MIND IN PIANO TEACHING AND PLAYING, THE
SCHUMANN, ROBERT
    ADVICE TO YOUNG MUSICIANS--FROM 'MUSIC AND MUSICIANS'---1876
SCHUMANN, ROBERT
    RULES AND MAXIMS FOR YOUNG MUSICIANS--FROM 'MUSIC AND MUSICIANS'
SEYMOUR, HARRIET AYER
    HOW TO THINK MUSIC
SEYMOUR, HARRIET AYER
    PHILOSOPHY OF MUSIC, THE ..WHAT MUSIC CAN DO FOR YOU
SHUTER, ROSAMUND
    PSYCHOLOGY OF MUSICAL ABILITY, THE
SMITH, VERA K.
    YOUNG PIANO TEACHER, WITH 75 HELPFUL TEACHING QUESTIONS, THE
SUMMY-BIRCHARD COMPANY
    HANDBOOK FOR PIANO TEACHERS..COLLECTED ARTICLES ON SUBJECTS
SWISHER, WALTER SAMUEL
    PSYCHOLOGY FOR THE MUSIC TEACHER
TAPPER, THOMAS
    EDUCATION OF THE MUSIC TEACHER, THE
TAYLER, E. DOUGLAS
    MIND-POWER IN MUSIC FOR STUDENTS, TEACHERS AND PERFORMERS
TERWILLIGER, GORDON B.
    PIANO TEACHERS PROFESSIONAL HANDBOOK
THOMPSON, JOHN
    TEACHING PIANO IN CLASSES
VIRGIL, ALMON K.
    EDUCATION IN MUSIC..LESSONS TO TEACHERS IN THE INSTRUCTION OF
WARRINER, JOHN
    HANDBOOK ON THE ART OF TEACHING AS APPLIED TO MUSIC..FOR THE USE
WHEELER, BERTHA H.
    MIND AND MECHANISM..THOUGHTS ON TEACHING AND THE PIANISTIC ART

Methods or Systems of Instruction

ABBOTT, A. T.
    METHOD FOR GAINING A PERFECT KNOWLEDGE OF THE NOTES, ETC., FOR
ADAMS, JAMES B.
    FAMILIAR INTRODUCTION TO THE FIRST PRINCIPLES OF MUSIC, A ...FOR
AGUILAR, EMANUEL
    HOW TO LEARN THE PIANOFORTE
AHEARN, ELLA MASON *
    ADULT EXPLORER AT THE PIANO, THE
ALBIG, GEORGE L.
    HOW TO PLAY THE PLAYER
ALLISON, IRL
    LET'S LEARN ALL THE NOTES AND READ BETTER..FOR ALL PIANO PUPILS,
AMERICAN SCHOOL OF PIANO TUNING
    TRAINING AS A PIANO TECHNICIAN--8 VOLS. IN 1
ANON
    ADVICE TO A NOBLEMAN...ON THE MANNER IN WHICH HIS CHILDREN SHOULD
ANON
    COMPLEAT TUTOR FOR THE HARPSICHORD OR SPINNET, WHEREIN IS SHEWN
ANON
    DIGITORIUM, THE --MINIATURE DUMB PIANO
ANON
    FASHIONABLE PRECEPTOR, FOR THE PIANO-FORTE AND HARPSICHORD,
ANON
    FIRST STEPS TO THOROUGH BASE, IN 12 FAMILIAR LESSONS BETWEEN A
ANON
    GENERAL OBSERVATIONS ON MUSIC AND REMARKS ON MR. LOGIER'S SYSTEM
ANON
    HOW TO LEARN TO PLAY THE PIANO WELL, BY ONE WHO HAS TAUGHT HIMSELF
ANON
    NEW AND COMPLETE INSTRUCTIONS FOR THE HARPSICHORD, PIANO FORTE OR
ANON
    NEW INSTRUCTIONS FOR PLAYING THE HARPSICHORD, PIANOFORTE OR
ANON
    PIANO IN TWELVE LESSONS
ANON
    PRECEPTOR, FOR THE PIANOFORTE, THE ORGAN OR HARPSICHORD, THE
ANON
    RULES..OR A SHORT AND COMPLEAT METHOD FOR ATTAINING TO PLAY A
ANON
    THOROUGH BASS AT ONE VIEW, WITH DIRECTIONS FOR ACCOMPANIMENT AND
APPEL, PEARL *
    HARMONY AT THE PIANO LESSON, A COMPANION TO PIANO STUDY
ARNOLD, FRANCK THOMAS
    ART OF ACCOMPANIMENT FROM A THOROUGH-BASS, AS PRACTICED IN THE
ASHBURNHAM, GEORGE
    STORY OF UNIQUE PIANO TUITION, THE
AXTENS, FLORENCE
    FIRST SIX MONTHS IN THE PIANO CLASS, THE ..A MANUAL FOR TEACHERS
AXTENS, FLORENCE
    PIANO CLASS METHOD..THE FIRST TWELVE MONTHS IN THE PIANO CLASS
BABBITT, WILLIAM
    PHYSIOLOGICAL METHOD FOR PLAYING THE PIANO-FORTE, DESIGNED AS A
BAILLIE, ALEXANDER--SUPPOSED AUTHOR
    INTRODUCTION TO THE KNOWLEDGE AND PRACTICE OF THE THORO' BASS, AN
BAKER, HENRIETTE
    PRACTICAL METHOD FOR THE PIANOFORTE FOR PRIVATE CLASS LESSONS--2
BARNWELL, V. T.
    BARNWELL'S NORMAL KEYBOARD AND STAFF STUDIES--THE MENTAL
BARTHELEMON, FRANCOIS H.
    NEW TUTOR FOR THE HARPSICHORD OR PIANO FORTE, WHEREIN THE FIRST
BARTOK, BELA *
    BARTOK-RESCHOVSKY PIANO METHOD---1913
BASTIEN, JAMES W. *
    BEGINNING PIANO FOR ADULTS
BAUER, HAROLD *
    PIANO METHOD FOR CLASS AND INDIVIDUAL INSTRUCTION--2 VOLS.
BAVIN, JOHN T.
    PIANO CLASS INSTRUCTOR
BAXTER, JAMES
    INDUCTIVE GRAMMAR OF MUSIC, FOR CLASS, PRIVATE LESSON, OR SELF
BAXTER, JAMES
    NEW SCHOOL OF MUSIC, THE ..PRACTICAL THOROUGH BASE CULTURE, FOR
BECKERMAN, H. J.
    AMERICAN SCHOOL OF RAGTIME PIANO PLAYING, THE
BEMETZRIEDER, ANTON
    ABSTRACT OF A NEW METHOD OF TEACHING THE PRINCIPLES OF MUSIC,
BEMETZRIEDER, ANTON
    COMPENDIUM OF A NEW METHOD OF MUSIC...WITH THE AUTHOR'S PRINCIPLES
BEMETZRIEDER, ANTON
    GAMUT AND COMMON CHORD IN ALL KEYS, FINGERED FOR THE HARPSICHORD,
BEMETZRIEDER, ANTON
    MUSIC MADE EASY TO EVERY CAPACITY, IN A SERIES OF DIALOGUES..BEING
BENEDICT, LADY *
    HOW TO PLAY THE PIANOFORTE
BENNER, LORA
    BENNER BLUE BOOK, THE ..PRACTICAL MANUAL OF PIANO TEACHING--4TH.
BENNER, LORA
    THEORY FOR PIANO STUDENTS--1ST. YEAR, PRIVATE OR CLASS--5 VOLS.,
BERGER, FRANCESCO
    FIRST STEPS AT THE PIANOFORTE
BERLIN, BORIS *
    BORIS BERLIN MUSICAL KINDERGARTEN PIANO METHOD, THE.. GUIDE FOR
BERNING, ALICE B. *
    KEYBOARD EXPERIENCES FOR CLASSROOM TEACHERS
BEVITT, ZAY RECTOR
    CLASS PROCEDURE FOR 40 LESSONS IN PIANO PLAYING BY HARMONY
BEVITT, ZAY RECTOR
    PIANO PLAYING BY HARMONY DIAGRAMS..STUDENT'S BOOK
BEVITT, ZAY RECTOR
    PIANO PLAYING BY HARMONY DIAGRAMS..TEACHER'S MANUAL
BIART, VICTOR
    PIANIST'S GUIDE, THE ..A SERIES OF PAMPHLETS ON THE TEACHING AND
BLAKE, DOROTHY
    FIRST STEPS IN CHORD PLAYING
BLAKE, DOROTHY
    FIRST STEPS IN THE USE OF THE PEDAL FOR PIANO
BOAL, DEAN *
    CONCEPTS AND SKILLS FOR THE PIANO..TEACHER'S MANUAL 1---CLASS
BOLTON, HETTY
    ON TEACHING THE PIANO
BOTTOMLEY, JOSEPH
    NEW SYSTEM OF PRACTICING AND TEACHING THE PIANOFORTE, A
BREMNER, ROBERT
    HARPSICHORD OR SPINNET MISCELLANY, THE --KEYBOARD
BROTHERHOOD, JAMES
    IMPROVED METHOD IN PIANO TEACHING, AND RECENT IDEAS OF LEADING
BROTHERHOOD, JAMES
    SCIENCE AND ART AS TWIN SISTERS..BEING A SECOND TREATISE UPON THE
BROTHERHOOD, JAMES
    TECHNICON, THE..A TREATISE UPON THE DEVELOPMENT OF PIANOFORTE
BROUGHTON, JULIA *
    SIXTEEN LESSON PLANS..A MANUAL FOR PROGRESSIVE SERIES

LOGIER, JOHANN BERNHARD
    EXPLANATION AND DESCRIPTION OF THE ROYAL PATENT CHIROPLAST, OR
LOGIER, JOHANN BERNHARD
    FIRST COMPANION TO THE ROYAL PATENT CHIROPLAST OR HAND-DIRECTOR,
LOGIER, JOHANN BERNHARD
    LOGIER'S SYSTEM OF THE SCIENCE OF MUSIC, HARMONY, AND PRACTICAL
LOGIER, JOHANN BERNHARD
    LOGIER'S THEORETICAL AND PRACTICAL STUDY FOR THE PIANO FORTE,
LOGIER, JOHANN BERNHARD
    REFUTATION OF THE FALLACIES AND MISREPRESENTATIONS CONTAINED IN A
LOGIER, JOHANN BERNHARD
    SEQUEL TO THE FIRST COMPANION TO THE CHIROPLAST
LOGIER, JOHANN BERNHARD
    SHORT ACCOUNT OF THE PROGRESS OF J. B. LOGIER'S SYSTEM OF MUSICAL
LOGIER, JOHANN BERNHARD
    SYLLABUS OF THE SECOND EXAMINATION OF MR. LOGIER'S PUPILS, ON HIS
LOMAS, LULU GRAHAM
    FIRST TEN PIANO LESSONS, LAID OUT FOR YOUNG TEACHERS, WITH
LONDON--A COMMITTEE OF PROFESSORS
    EXPOSITION OF THE MUSICAL SYSTEM OF MR. LOGIER..WITH STRICTURES ON
LOYNES, W. H.
    HOW TO PLAY THE PIANO IN ONE HOUR WITHOUT A TEACHER
MACEWAN, DESIREE
    FIRST TWO YEARS OF PIANOFORTE STUDY, THE
MACLEAN, CHARLES D.
    PRINCIPLES OF PIANOFORTE PRACTICE, THE
MAHONY, CORNELIUS
    SELF-INSTRUCTOR FOR THE PIANOFORTE, CONTAINING C. MAHONY'S NEW
MANHIRE, WILSON
    MODEL ANSWERS TO QUESTIONS ON 'TOUCH' FOR CANDIDATES PREPARING FOR
MARTAL, R.
    METHODS APPLICABLE TO GROUP TEACHING OR PRIVATE PIANO INSTRUCTION
MARX, ADOLF BERNHARD
    INTRODUCTION TO THE INTERPRETATION OF BEETHOVEN'S PIANO
MASON, MARY B.
    BOY MUSIC, A FIRST PIANO METHOD FOR BOYS BETWEEN 8 AND 16
MASON, WILLIAM G. *
    METHOD FOR THE PIANO-FORTE, A
MASON, WILLIAM G. *
    PRIMER OF MUSIC, A ..BEING THE FIRST STEPS IN MUSICIANSHIP..FOR
MATHEWS, WILLIAM S. B.
    TEACHER'S MANUAL OF MASON'S PIANOFORTE TECHNICS
MATTHAY, TOBIAS A.
    ACT OF TOUCH IN ALL ITS DIVERSITY, THE ..AN ANALYSIS AND SYNTHESIS
MATTHAY, TOBIAS A.
    FOREARM ROTATION PRINCIPLE IN PIANOFORTE PLAYING, THE ..ITS
MATTHAY, TOBIAS A.
    INTRODUCTION TO PSYCHOLOGY FOR MUSIC TEACHERS, AN --THREE LECTURES
MATTHAY, TOBIAS A.
    ON METHOD IN TEACHING
MATTHAY, TOBIAS A. *
    PIANIST'S FIRST MUSIC MAKING, THE --3 VOLS.
MATTHAY, TOBIAS A.
    PIANOFORTE TONE-PRODUCTION---SAME AS 'THE ACT OF TOUCH IN ALL ITS
MCCLINTOCK, LORENE
    TEACH YOURSELF TO PLAY THE PIANO..BASED ON THE INTERVAL METHOD
MCHOSE, ALLEN IRVINE
    TEACHERS DICTATION MANUAL
MCLAIN, MARGARET STARR
    CLASS PIANO
MEHR, NORMAN
    GROUP PIANO TEACHING
MILLER, EDWARD
    INSTITUTES OF MUSIC, OR, EASY INSTRUCTIONS FOR THE HARPSICHORD
MOKREJS, JOHN
    STORY OF NANYNKA, THE ..FIRST PIANO LESSONS FOR CHILDREN, PRIVATE
MOLLER, JOHN CHRISTOPHER
    SETT OF PROGRESSIVE LESSONS FOR THE HARPSICHORD OR PIANO FORTE, A
MONTI, H. DE
    STRICTURES ON MR. LOGIER'S SYSTEM OF MUSICAL EDUCATION
MOORE, HENRY K.
    CHILD'S PIANOFORTE BOOK, THE ..BEING A FIRST YEAR'S COURSE AT THE
MUSICIANS ADVISORY SERVICE
    MUSICIANS ADVISORY SERVICE FIRST MUSIC READER FOR PIANO..TEACHERS
MUSIC EDUCATORS NATIONAL CONFERENCE
    HANDBOOK FOR TEACHING PIANO CLASSES
MUSIC EDUCATORS NATIONAL CONFERENCE
    TEACHING PIANO IN CLASSROOM AND STUDIO
MUSIC EDUCATORS NATIONAL CONFERENCE
    TRAVELING THE CIRCUIT WITH PIANO CLASSES
MUSIC PROJECT--NEW YORK CITY
    TEACHER'S GUIDE..A CREATIVE APPROACH TO PIANO CLASS TEACHING, BY
NATIONAL BUREAU FOR THE ADVANCEMENT OF MUSIC
    PIANO CLASSES AND THE PRIVATE TEACHER
NATIONAL PIANO FOUNDATION
    GREATER REWARDS THROUGH CREATIVE PIANO TEACHING
NEWCOMB, ETHEL
    LESCHETIZKY AS I KNEW HIM---1923
NEW ENGLAND CONSERVATORY
    NEW ENGLAND CONSERVATORY METHOD FOR THE PIANO-FORTE, THE
NILES BRYANT SCHOOL OF PIANO TUNING
    CORRESPONDENCE COURSE IN 12 LESSONS, A
NIMITZ, DANIEL
    KEYBOARD MASTERS..STUDY GUIDE
NIXON, W.
    GUIDE TO INSTRUCTION ON THE PIANOFORTE, A --IN A SERIES OF SHORT
O'TOOLE, WILLIAM
    CREATIVE PIANO TECHNIC
PACE, ROBERT
    MUSIC ESSENTIALS FOR CLASSROOM TEACHERS--2ND. ED.---1961
PAIN, EVA
    BEGINNING TO PLAY THE PIANO..A MANUAL FOR TEACHERS
PALMER, ANNIE L.
    MUSIC TEACHERS' GUIDE TO THE GOLDBECK PIANO METHOD.
PALMER, KING
    TEACH YOURSELF MUSIC
PATTON, VICTOR S.
    LEARN TO PLAY POPULAR PIANO BY NOTE IN 20 EASY LESSONS...HOME
PEARCE, CHARLES WILLIAM
    ART OF THE PIANO TEACHER, THE
PEDERSON, GALE
    KEY TO THE KEYS..A SELF-TAUGHT PIANO METHOD FOR ADULTS AND TEEN
PETERSILIA, FRANZ
    STUDY WITH AMUSEMENT, A SERIES OF PROGRESSIVE LESSONS FOR THE
PETRI, LILLIAN JEFFREY
    MIND OVER MUSCLE..A TECHNICAL ECONOMY FOR PIANISTS
PHILIPP, LILLIE H.
    PIANO STUDY..APPLICATION AND TECHNIQUE
PHILLIPSON, WENTWORTH
    GUIDE TO YOUNG PIANOFORTE TEACHERS AND STUDENTS
PICHIER, PAUL
    PIANIST'S TOUCH, THE ..METHOD AND THEORY OF PAUL PICHIER
PLAYFORD, JOHN
    MUSICKS HAND-MAID..NEW LESSONS AND INSTRUCTIONS FOR THE VIRGINALS
PORTER, FRANK A. *
    TEACHERS' MANUAL FOR THE PORTER PIANOFORTE COURSE

PRATT, SILAS G.
    PIANIST'S MENTAL VELOCITY, THE ..A SYSTEMATIC PREPARATION OF THE
PRENTNER, MARIE
    MODERN PIANIST..BEING MY EXPERIENCES IN THE TECHNIQUE AND
PSTROKONSKY, JULES DE
    NEW METHOD OF TEACHING THE PIANOFORTE
QUINN, MARCUS LUCIUS
    HOW TO STUDY MUSIC AND LEARN TO PLAY PIANO OR ORGAN
REEVES, WILLIAM
    REEVES' POPULAR PIANOFORTE TUTOR..RUDIMENTS OF MUSIC, EXERCISES
RENAUD, EMILIANO
    RENAUD-PHONE PIANO METHOD..A PIANO COURSE THROUGH THE MEDIUM OF
RICHARDSON, NATHAN
    INKLINGS FOR THE LOVERS OF MUSIC, PART 1..CULTIVATION OF THE ART
RICHARDSON, NATHAN
    NEW METHOD FOR THE PIANOFORTE..ADDED, RUDIMENTS OF HARMONY AND
RICHTER, ADA
    TEACHING HINTS
RIEMANN, HUGO
    COMPARATIVE PIANOFORTE SCHOOL--4 BKS.---BK. 3 TRANSLATED BY J. C.
ROBBINS, EDGAR A.
    AMERICAN METHOD FOR THE PIANOFORTE
ROBINSON, HELENE
    BASIC PIANO FOR ADULTS
ROWLEY, DAISY WOODRUFF
    NINE HUNDRED MODEL LESSONS FOR PIANO TEACHERS
RUBINSTEIN, BERYL
    OUTLINE OF PIANO PEDAGOGY--REV. ED.---1929
SCHELLING, ERNEST *
    OXFORD PIANO COURSE, TEACHER'S FIRST MANUAL
SCHELLING, ERNEST *
    OXFORD PIANO COURSE, TEACHER'S SECOND MANUAL
SCHULTZ, ARNOLD
    RIDDLE OF THE PIANIST'S FINGER, THE
SCONCIA, JOHN A.
    ANALYTICAL INSTRUCTOR FOR THE PIANO FORTE, CONTAINING THE
SEYMOUR, HARRIET AYER
    HOW TO THINK MUSIC
SHERWOOD MUSIC SCHOOL
    PIANO LESSONS AND TESTS--4TH. REV. ED.---1945+
SKUTLEY, MILDRED A.
    MUSIC FOR YOU..A SUPPLEMENTAL WORK BOOK FOR INDIVIUAL OR CLASS
SMITH, EDWIN S.
    PIANO BY EAR
SMITH, HOWARD G.
    ANYONE CAN PLAY THE PIANO BY EAR IN FIVE EASY LESSONS..A-B-C PIANO
SMITH, THOMAS
    HOW TO LEARN TO PLAY THE PIANO WELL
SORABJI, KAIKHOSRU
    AROUND MUSIC---PACHMAN, CHOPIN AND LISZT
STARKEY, EVELYN
    PIANO CLASS WORKBOOK FOR FIRST YEAR STUDENTS
STARR, WILLIAM J. *
    BASIC PIANO TECHNIQUE FOR THE CLASSROOM TEACHER
STEVENS, A. M.
    HOW TO PLAY THE PIANO AND ORGAN..OR, KEY TO THE SCIENCE AND THEORY
STORMEN, WIN
    POPULAR PIANO SELF-TAUGHT---1956
SUDDS, WILLIAM F.
    NATIONAL SCHOOL FOR PIANOFORTE, THE
SUR, WILLIAM R.--EDITOR
    KEYBOARD EXPERIENCE AND PIANO CLASS INSTRUCTION
SWENSON, LUCILE B.
    DISCOVERING THE PIANO..THE MULTIPLE KEY APPROACH..STUDY GUIDE AND
TAYLOR, GEORGE C.
    FIRST STEPS TO THE PIANOFORTE
THOMPSON, JOHN
    TEACHING PIANO IN CLASSES
TOBIN, JOSEPH RAYMOND
    FUN WITH FINGERING, A FIRST-OF-ALL BOOK ON EASY FINGERING AND
TOBIN, JOSEPH RAYMOND
    PREPARING FOR KEYBOARD TESTS IN MUSICIANSHIP EXAMINATIONS, JUNIOR
VAN DER WEYDE, PETER H.
    INSTRUCTIONS IN PLAYING THE PIANO-FORTE WITH AEOLIAN ATTACHMENT
VILLOING, ALEXANDER
    RUBINSTEIN'S FINGER EXERCISES..TECHNICAL STUDIES FROM THE
VINING, HARRISON S.
    SIMPLE AND COMPLETE PRIMER FOR THE PIANOFORTE, THE
VIRGIL, ALMON K.
    EDUCATION IN MUSIC..LESSONS TO TEACHERS IN THE INSTRUCTION OF
VIRGIL, ALMON K.
    FOUNDATION EXERCISES IN PIANO PLAYING FROM FIRST RUDIMENTS TO
VIRGIL, ALMON K.
    PUPIL'S RECORD BOOK, THE ..SHOWING HOW TO SUCCEED AND HOW TO FAIL
VIRGIL, ALMON K.
    SPECIAL TECHNIC COURSE IN THE VIRGIL CLAVIER METHOD--6 PTS.
VIRGIL, ALMON K.
    VIRGIL CLAVIER METHOD, THE --2 VOLS.
VISUOLA CORPORATION
    BLAZING A NEW TRAIL IN PIANO PLAYING
WAIT, WILLIAM B.
    NORMAL COURSE OF PIANO TECHNIC, THE
WEBBE, WILLIAM H.
    PIANISTS' 'ABC' PRIMER AND GUIDE--WITH AN APPENDIX
WELBOURNE, EVE V.
    WELBOURNE WAY TO HOBBY PIANO PLAYING FOR ADULTS, THE --9 LESSONS
WELLS, HOWARD
    EARS, BRAIN AND FINGERS..A TEXT BOOK FOR PIANO TEACHERS AND PUPILS
WELSH, J. ROBERT
    MAKING MUSIC AT THE KEYBOARD..BEGINNING PIANO...CLASS...AND EAR
WHITESIDE, ABBY
    PIANIST'S MECHANISM, THE
WHITFORD, ROBERT
    PIANO AND ITS MUSIC, THE --FROM 'MODERN PIANO COURSE'
WHITING, ARTHUR B.
    LESSON OF THE CLAVICHORD, THE --REPRINT..'NEW MUSIC REVIEW'
WILLIS, AUBREY
    AUBREY WILLIS HOME STUDY COURSE IN PIANO TUNING AND REPAIRING
WOLLENHAUPT, HEINRICH
    METHOD FOR THE PIANOFORTE AND METHODICAL GUIDE FOR THE PIANO FORTE
WRIGHT, WILLIAM C.
    GOLDEN MONITOR, FOR THE PIANOFORTE AND CABINET ORGAN, DESIGNED AS
ZIMMERMAN, ALEX H. *
    BASIC PIANO FOR THE COLLEGE STUDENT
ZUCH, ANNETT V. *
    PIANO TEACHER, THE ..A BOOK OF SELF-INSTRUCTION

Child Approach

ADAMS, JULIETTE
    RECENT DEVELOPMENTS IN TEACHING CHILDREN TO PLAY THE PIANO
AHRENS, CORA B. *
    FOR ALL PIANO TEACHERS
ANON
    ADVICE TO A NOBLEMAN...ON THE MANNER IN WHICH HIS CHILDREN SHOULD

ANON
    CHILD'S INTRODUCTION TO THOROUGH BASS, THE ..IN CONVERSATIONS OF A
AXTENS, FLORENCE
    PIANO CLASS METHOD..THE FIRST TWELVE MONTHS IN THE PIANO CLASS
BASTIEN, JAMES W.
    HOW TO TEACH PIANO SUCCESSFULLY
BAUER, HAROLD *
    PIANO METHOD FOR CLASS AND INDIVIDUAL INSTRUCTION--2 VOLS.
BEMETZRIEDER, ANTON
    COMPENDIUM OF A NEW METHOD OF MUSIC...WITH THE AUTHOR'S PRINCIPLES
BENNER, LORA
    BENNER BLUE BOOK, THE ..PRACTICAL MANUAL OF PIANO TEACHING--4TH.
BENNER, LORA
    BENNER GOLD BOOK, THE ..PIANO MATERIAL AND TEACHING METHODS--3RD.
BERLIN, BORIS
    BORIS BERLIN MUSICAL KINDERGARTEN PIANO METHOD, THE.. GUIDE FOR
BOSWORTH, HARRIETTE DEXTER
    IDEAS FOR YOUNG PIANO TEACHERS
BRIED, FREDERICK
    STIMULATION IN PIANO STUDY..HOW PARENTS CAN STIMULATE AND MAINTAIN
BROWER, HARRIETTE
    ART OF THE PIANIST, THE
BROWER, HARRIETTE
    PIANO MASTERY..TALKS WITH MASTER PIANISTS AND TEACHERS...
BROWER, HARRIETTE
    PIANO MASTERY, SECOND SERIES
BURROWS, RAYMOND
    ELEMENTARY PIANO INSTRUCTION IN COLLEGE
CALLENDER, ROMAINE
    TEACHER'S MANUAL, A WORK DESIGNED TO SUPPLEMENT...'THE FIRST TEN
CHAPPLE, STANLEY
    CLASS WAY TO THE KEYBOARD, THE
CHING, JAMES
    LET'S PLAY THE PIANO..THE FIRST MUSIC BOOK FOR CHILDREN OF ALL
CHING, JAMES
    ON TEACHING PIANO TECHNIQUE TO CHILDREN
CHING, JAMES
    TEACHING OF TECHNIQUE TO CHILDREN, THE --4 PTS.
CHING, JOAN ELIZABETH
    OURSELVES AND OUR PUPILS---ALSO CATALOGUED UNDER AUTHORSHIP..BETTY
CHURCHILL, VIRGINIA PEAKES
    NINETEEN FIFTY-SIX SUPPLEMENT TO THE MODERN TEACHER'S GUIDE TO
CURWEN, ANNIE JESSY
    TEACHER'S GUIDE...TO MRS. CURWEN'S PIANOFORTE METHOD, 'THE CHILD
DARDENELLE, LOUISE
    HARMONY-FIRST METHOD FOR THE PIANO...FOR CHILD AND ADULT
DAVIS, MARILYN K.
    GROUP ACTIVITIES AT THE KEYBOARD
DENVER--PUBLIC SCHOOLS
    CLASS-PIANO TEACHERS HANDBOOK
DILLER, ANGELA
    SPLENDOR OF MUSIC, THE
DUMM, ROBERT W.
    IN BLACK AND WHITE
EDWARDS, RUTH
    COMPLEAT MUSIC TEACHER FOR TEACHERS, PARENTS AND STUDENTS
GEST, ELIZABETH
    KEYBOARD HARMONY FOR JUNIORS
GRINDEA, CAROLA
    FIRST TEN LESSONS, THE ..A NEW APPROACH TO PIANO TEACHING
HARRISON, SIDNEY
    BEGINNING TO PLAY THE PIANO--A TEACHER'S HANDBOOK, INCLUDING THE
HORROCKS, CYRIL R. H.
    STUDENT'S GUIDE TO THE ART OF TEACHING THE PIANOFORTE, THE --2ND.
IVES, WILLIAM
    SURE TEACHER..OR, CHILD'S FIRST COURSE FOR THE PIANOFORTE, THE
KING, AUDREY
    PIANO CLASSES IN ELEMENTARY SCHOOLS
KOTZSCHMAR, MARY ANN
    HALF-HOUR LESSONS IN MUSIC..CLASS WORK FOR BEGINNERS AT THE PIANO
KRUSZYNSKI, MICHAL
    APPROACH TO THE PSYCHOLOGY OF PIANO TEACHING, AN
LE COUPPEY, FELIX
    PIANO TEACHING..ADVICE TO PUPILS AND YOUNG TEACHERS---1868 IN
LOGIER, JOHANN BERNHARD
    COMPANION TO THE ROYAL PATENT CHIROPLAST, OR HAND-DIRECTOR, A ..A
LOGIER, JOHANN BERNHARD
    EXPLANATION AND DESCRIPTION OF THE ROYAL PATENT CHIROPLAST, OR
LOMAS, LULU GRAHAM
    FIRST TEN PIANO LESSONS, LAID OUT FOR YOUNG TEACHERS, WITH
MACLEAN, CHARLES D.
    PRINCIPLES OF PIANOFORTE PRACTICE, THE
MAIER, GUY
    PIANO TEACHER'S COMPANION, THE
MAIER, GUY *
    PLAYING THE PIANO..A COURSE OF ROTE TRAINING FOR BEGINNERS--CLASS
MASON, MARY B.
    BOY MUSIC, A FIRST PIANO METHOD FOR BOYS BETWEEN 8 AND 16
MATTHAY, TOBIAS A.
    CHILD'S FIRST STEPS IN PIANOFORTE PLAYING, THE
MATTHAY, TOBIAS A. *
    PIANIST'S FIRST MUSIC MAKING, THE --3 VOLS.
MEHR, NORMAN
    GROUP PIANO TEACHING
MOKREJS, JOHN
    STORY OF NANYNKA, THE ..FIRST PIANO LESSONS FOR CHILDREN, PRIVATE
MOORE, HENRY K.
    CHILD'S PIANOFORTE BOOK, THE ..BEING A FIRST YEAR'S COURSE AT THE
MUSIC EDUCATORS NATIONAL CONFERENCE
    HANDBOOK FOR TEACHING PIANO CLASSES
MUSIC EDUCATORS NATIONAL CONFERENCE
    KEYBOARD EXPERIENCE AND CLASS PIANO INSTRUCTION
MUSIC EDUCATORS NATIONAL CONFERENCE
    TEACHING PIANO IN CLASSROOM AND STUDIO
MUSIC EDUCATORS NATIONAL CONFERENCE
    TRAVELING THE CIRCUIT WITH PIANO CLASSES
NATIONAL PIANO FOUNDATION
    GREATER REWARDS THROUGH CREATIVE PIANO TEACHING
NEWMAN, ELIZABETH
    HOW TO TEACH MUSIC TO BEGINNERS
ORLIK, JULES
    CREATIVE APPROACH TO PIANO CLASS TEACHING, A ---REPRODUCED FROM
PAIN, EVA
    BEGINNING TO PLAY THE PIANO..A MANUAL FOR TEACHERS
PASQUALI, NICOLO
    ART OF FINGERING THE HARPSICHORD, THE
POWERS-WADSWORTH, L.
    PIANIST'S GUIDE TO TECHNICAL FREEDOM, THE ..2 VOLS. IN 1
REEVES, BETTY
    OURSELVES AND OUR PUPILS---MONOGRAPH ON THE ART OF PIANO TEACHING,
RICHTER, ADA
    TEACHING HINTS
RICKER, EARL
    MUSIC LESSONS FOR YOUR CHILD
ROBYN, LOUISE
    HOW TO TEACH PIANO TO THE CHILD BEGINNER..A TEXT BOOK FOR TEACHERS

ROWLEY, ALEC
    DO'S AND DONT'S FOR MUSICIANS..A HANDBOOK FOR TEACHERS AND
SCHELLING, ERNEST *
    OXFORD PIANO COURSE, TEACHER'S FIRST MANUAL
SCHELLING, ERNEST *
    OXFORD PIANO COURSE, TEACHER'S SECOND MANUAL
SEYMOUR, HARRIET AYER
    HOW TO THINK MUSIC
SEYMOUR, HARRIET AYER
    PHILOSOPHY OF MUSIC, THE ..WHAT MUSIC CAN DO FOR YOU
SHERWOOD MUSIC SCHOOL
    PIANO LESSONS AND TESTS--4TH. REV. ED.---1945+
SKUTLEY, MILDRED A.
    MUSIC FOR YOU..A SUPPLEMENTAL WORK BOOK FOR INDIVIDUAL OR CLASS
SLENCZYNSKA, RUTH *
    MUSIC AT YOUR FINGERTIPS
STARR, WILLIAM J. *
    BASIC PIANO TECHNIQUE FOR THE CLASSROOM TEACHER
SUMMY-BIRCHARD COMPANY
    HANDBOOK FOR PIANO TEACHERS..COLLECTED ARTICLES ON SUBJECTS
SUR, WILLIAM R.--EDITOR
    PIANO INSTRUCTION IN THE SCHOOLS
TERWILLIGER, GORDON B.
    PIANO TEACHERS PROFESSIONAL HANDBOOK
VIRGIL, ALMON K.
    EDUCATION IN MUSIC..LESSONS TO TEACHERS IN THE INSTRUCTION OF
WELLS, HOWARD
    EARS, BRAIN AND FINGERS..A TEXT BOOK FOR PIANO TEACHERS AND PUPILS
WILSON, MORRIS E.
    HOW TO HELP YOUR CHILD WITH MUSIC--2ND. ED.---1951

Adult Approach

AHEARN, ELLA MASON *
    ADULT EXPLORER AT THE PIANO, THE
AHRENS, CORA B. *
    FOR ALL PIANO TEACHERS
BASTIEN, JAMES W. *
    BEGINNING PIANO FOR ADULTS
BASTIEN, JAMES W.
    HOW TO TEACH PIANO SUCCESSFULLY
BEMETZRIEDER, ANTON
    COMPENDIUM OF A NEW METHOD OF MUSIC...WITH THE AUTHOR'S PRINCIPLES
BROUGHTON, JULIA
    SUCCESS IN PIANO TEACHING
BURROWS, RAYMOND
    ELEMENTARY PIANO INSTRUCTION IN COLLEGE
CHASTEK, WINIFRED
    KEYBOARD SKILLS..SIGHT READING, TRANSPOSITION, HARMONIZATION,
COOKE, JAMES FRANCIS
    GREAT MEN AND FAMOUS MUSICIANS ON THE ART OF MUSIC
CURWEN, ANNIE JESSY
    TEACHER'S GUIDE...TO MRS. CURWEN'S PIANOFORTE METHOD, 'THE CHILD
DARDENELLE, LOUISE
    HARMONY-FIRST METHOD FOR THE PIANO...FOR CHILD AND ADULT
DILLER, ANGELA
    SPLENDOR OF MUSIC, THE
DUCKWORTH, GUY
    KEYBOARD MUSICIANSHIP
EDWARDS, RUTH
    COMPLEAT MUSIC TEACHER FOR TEACHERS, PARENTS AND STUDENTS
GIFFORD, ALEXANDER M.
    PIANOFORTE AND HOW TO STUDY IT, THE
HARTLINE, ELIZABETH DILL *
    KEYBOARD MUSICIANSHIP, GROUP PIANO FOR ADULTS
LEACH, JOHN R.
    FUNCTIONAL PIANO FOR THE TEACHER
MCLAIN, MARGARET STARR
    CLASS PIANO
MILLER, ALLAN
    BEGINNING PIANO FOR ADULTS
MUSIC EDUCATORS NATIONAL CONFERENCE
    HANDBOOK FOR TEACHING PIANO CLASSES
MUSIC EDUCATORS NATIONAL CONFERENCE
    TEACHING PIANO IN CLASSROOM AND STUDIO
MUSIC EDUCATORS NATIONAL CONFERENCE
    TRAVELING THE CIRCUIT WITH PIANO CLASSES
ORLIK, JULES
    CREATIVE APPROACH TO PIANO CLASS TEACHING, A ---REPRODUCED FROM
PACE, ROBERT
    MUSIC ESSENTIALS FOR CLASSROOM TEACHERS--2ND. ED.---1961
PACE, ROBERT
    PIANO FOR CLASSROOM MUSIC--2ND. ED.---1956
PASQUALI, NICOLO
    ART OF FINGERING THE HARPSICHORD, THE
PHILIPP, LILLIE H.
    PIANO STUDY..APPLICATION AND TECHNIQUE
POWERS-WADSWORTH, L.
    PIANIST'S GUIDE TO TECHNICAL FREEDOM, THE ..2 VOLS. IN 1
REZITS, JOSEPH
    SOURCE MATERIALS FOR PIANO TECHNIQUES
ROBINSON, HELENE
    BASIC PIANO FOR ADULTS
SHERWOOD MUSIC SCHOOL
    PIANO LESSONS AND TESTS--4TH. REV. ED.---1945+
SQUIRE, RUSSEL N. *
    CLASS PIANO FOR ADULT BEGINNERS--2ND. ED.---1964
STARKEY, EVELYN
    PIANO CLASS WORKBOOK FOR FIRST YEAR STUDENTS
TERWILLIGER, GORDON B.
    PIANO TEACHERS PROFESSIONAL HANDBOOK

Group Teaching

AGUILAR, EMANUEL
    LITTLE BOOK ABOUT LEARNING THE PIANOFORTE, A
AHEARN, ELLA MASON *
    ADULT EXPLORER AT THE PIANO, THE
AXTENS, FLORENCE
    FIRST SIX MONTHS IN THE PIANO CLASS, THE ..A MANUAL FOR TEACHERS
AXTENS, FLORENCE
    PIANO CLASS INSTRUCTION FOR CHILDREN AND ADULT CLASSES..A MANUAL
AXTENS, FLORENCE
    PIANO CLASS METHOD..THE FIRST TWELVE MONTHS IN THE PIANO CLASS
BAKER, HENRIETTE
    PRACTICAL METHOD FOR THE PIANOFORTE FOR PRIVATE CLASS LESSONS--2
BARNWELL, V. T.
    BARNWELL'S NORMAL KEYBOARD AND STAFF STUDIES--THE MENTAL
BASTIEN, JAMES W. *
    BEGINNING PIANO FOR ADULTS
BASTIEN, JAMES W.
    HOW TO TEACH PIANO SUCCESSFULLY
BAUER, HAROLD *
    PIANO METHOD FOR CLASS AND INDIVIDUAL INSTRUCTION--2 VOLS.

BAVIN, JOHN T.
    PIANO CLASS INSTRUCTOR
BAXTER, JAMES
    INDUCTIVE GRAMMAR OF MUSIC, FOR CLASS, PRIVATE LESSON, OR SELF
BAXTER, JAMES
    NEW SCHOOL OF MUSIC, THE ..PRACTICAL THOROUGH BASE CULTURE, FOR
BENNETT, BEULAH VARNER
    PIANO CLASSES FOR EVERYONE..A PRACTICAL GUIDE FOR PIANO TEACHERS
BERNING, ALICE B. *
    KEYBOARD EXPERIENCES FOR CLASSROOM TEACHERS
BEVITT, ZAY RECTOR
    CLASS PROCEDURE FOR 40 LESSONS IN PIANO PLAYING BY HARMONY
BOAL, DEAN *
    CONCEPTS AND SKILLS FOR THE PIANO..TEACHER'S MANUAL 1---CLASS
BOWEN, CAROLYN
    OUTLINES FOR TRAINING PIANO TEACHERS
BROUGHTON, JULIA
    SUCCESS IN PIANO TEACHING
BROWER, HARRIETTE
    HOME HELP IN MUSIC STUDY
BURROWES, JOHN FRECKLETON
    PIANOFORTE PRIMER, THE ..CONTAINING THE RUDIMENTS OF MUSIC
BURROWS, RAYMOND
    ADVANCED PIANO CLASS, THE --REPRINT..PROCEEDINGS OF THE M.E.N.C.,
BURROWS, RAYMOND
    ELEMENTARY PIANO INSTRUCTION IN COLLEGE
BURROWS, RAYMOND
    HANDBOOK FOR TEACHING PIANO CLASSES
BURROWS, RAYMOND
    PIANO IN SCHOOL, A MEMORANDUM FOR SCHOOL ADMINISTRATORS
CARRE, JOHN
    PSYCHOLOGY OF PIANO TEACHING, THE ..A TEXTBOOK FOR TEACHERS,
CARTER, BUENTA
    BEGINNER'S PIANO BOOK FOR OLDER STUDENTS...DESIGNED FOR THE OLDER
CHAPPLE, STANLEY
    CLASS WAY TO THE KEYBOARD, THE
CHASTEK, WINIFRED
    KEYBOARD SKILLS..SIGHT READING, TRANSPOSITION, HARMONIZATION,
CHEYETTE, IRVING
    BASIC PIANO FOR THE MUSIC EDUCATOR AND CLASSROOM TEACHER
CHING, JAMES
    ON TEACHING PIANO TECHNIQUE TO CHILDREN
CHURCHILL, VIRGINIA PEAKES
    MODERN TEACHER'S GUIDE TO PIANO AND PIANO CLASS TEACHING
CHURCHILL, VIRGINIA PEAKES
    NINETEEN FIFTY-SIX SUPPLEMENT TO THE MODERN TEACHER'S GUIDE TO
CLIFFORD, S. M.
    ADVENTURES IN PIANOLAND..TWELVE LESSONS FOR TEACHERS OF PIANO
COLEMAN, H. P.
    PIANO CLASS, THE
DANIELS, BESS
    PIANO COURSE..TEACHER'S BOOK, FOR CLASS OR INDIVIDUAL INSTRUCTION
DANIELS, BESS *
    PIANO COURSE EITHER FOR CLASS OR FOR INDIVIDUAL INSTRUCTION
DANIELS, BESS *
    WORLD OF MUSIC, THE ..PIANO COURSE..TEACHERS' BOOK, FOR CLASS OR
DARDENELLE, LOUISE
    HARMONY-FIRST METHOD FOR THE PIANO...FOR CHILD AND ADULT
DAVIS, MARILYN K.
    GROUP ACTIVITIES AT THE KEYBOARD
DECKER, TOM W.
    CONSOLE SYSTEM, THE ..A TEXT FOR MODERN PIANO AND ORGAN TO BE USED
DENVER--PUBLIC SCHOOLS
    CLASS-PIANO TEACHERS HANDBOOK
DE WITT, EDYTHE
    EDYTHE DE WITT'S METHOD FOR CLASS PIANO...WRITTEN TO GIVE CORRECT
DILLER, ANGELA
    SPLENDOR OF MUSIC, THE
DUCKWORTH, GUY
    KEYBOARD MUSICIANSHIP
EDWARDS, RUTH
    COMPLEAT MUSIC TEACHER FOR TEACHERS, PARENTS AND STUDENTS
EGBERT, MARION S.
    SEEING WHAT WE SING, AN AID THROUGH KEYBOARD EXPERIENCE TO THE
ELKAN, IDA
    TECHNICAL WORK IN EAR-TRAINING FOR THE PIANO..A METHOD FOR PRIVATE
ENGELBRECHT, J. G.
    MATERIA MUSICA, OR MATERIALS FOR THE PIANIST..A CLASS BOOK
ERWIN, GARNET PARKER
    KEYBOARD STORIES FOR CLASS AND INDIVIDUAL INSTRUCTION---1939
FAELTEN, CARL
    TEACHER'S MANUAL FOR PIANOFORTE COURSE, THE
FREDRICH, FRANK
    PLAYING BY SEEING..A STUDY IN TRAINING AND PERCEPTION FOR BETTER
GIDDINGS, THADDEUS P.
    GIDDING'S PUBLIC SCHOOL CLASS METHOD FOR THE PIANO
HARGISS, GENEVIEVE
    MUSIC FOR ELEMENTARY TEACHERS..A PROGRAMMED COURSE IN BASIC THEORY
HARTLINE, ELIZABETH DILL *
    KEYBOARD MUSICIANSHIP, GROUP PIANO FOR ADULTS
HEIDELBERGER, PAULINE
    MASTER METHOD..PIANO NORMAL AND TEACHER'S MANUAL
HUTT, DOREEN
    PIANO CLASS METHOD--BKS. 1 AND 2
JEWETT, ALBERT DEWEY
    IDIOMATIC COURSE OF PIANO INSTRUCTION FOR CLASS WORK
KING, AUDREY
    PIANO CLASSES IN ELEMENTARY SCHOOLS
KOTZSCHMAR, MARY ANN
    HALF-HOUR LESSONS IN MUSIC..CLASS WORK FOR BEGINNERS AT THE PIANO
LEACH, JOHN R.
    FUNCTIONAL PIANO FOR THE TEACHER
LONDON--A COMMITTEE OF PROFESSORS
    EXPOSITION OF THE MUSICAL SYSTEM OF MR. LOGIER..WITH STRICTURES ON
LUBIT, JULIA
    PIANOFORTE THEORY COURSE FOR BEGINNERS' PIANO CLASS
MAIER, GUY *
    PLAYING THE PIANO..A COURSE OF ROTE TRAINING FOR BEGINNERS---CLASS
MAIER, GUY *
    PLAYING THE PIANO--TEACHER'S MANUAL
MARIAL, R.
    METHODS APPLICABLE TO GROUP TEACHING OR PRIVATE PIANO INSTRUCTION
MASON, ELLA H. *
    ANSWERS TO CRITICISMS OF PIANO CLASS INSTRUCTION
MCHOSE, ALLEN IRVINE *
    KEYBOARD AND DICTATION MANUAL
MCHOSE, ALLEN IRVINE
    TEACHERS DICTATION MANUAL
MCLAIN, MARGARET STARR
    CLASS PIANO
MEHR, NORMAN
    GROUP PIANO TEACHING
MEKOTA, BETH ANNA
    TEACHING APPLIED MUSIC BY CLASS METHOD
MERRILL, MYRTLE
    SIGHT-READING AT THE PIANO

MIESSNER, WILLIAM OTTO
    MELODY WAY COURSE FOR CLASS OR PRIVATE PIANO INSTRUCTION, THE
MILLER, ALLAN
    BEGINNING PIANO FOR ADULTS
MOKREJS, JOHN
    STORY OF NANYNKA, THE ..FIRST PIANO LESSONS FOR CHILDREN, PRIVATE
MUSIC EDUCATORS NATIONAL CONFERENCE
    HANDBOOK FOR TEACHING PIANO CLASSES
MUSIC EDUCATORS NATIONAL CONFERENCE
    KEYBOARD EXPERIENCE AND CLASS PIANO INSTRUCTION
MUSIC EDUCATORS NATIONAL CONFERENCE
    MUSIC BEGINS WITH THE PIANO
MUSIC EDUCATORS NATIONAL CONFERENCE
    TRAVELING THE CIRCUIT WITH PIANO CLASSES
MUSIC PROJECT--NEW YORK CITY
    TEACHER'S GUIDE..A CREATIVE APPROACH TO PIANO CLASS TEACHING, BY
NATIONAL BUREAU FOR THE ADVANCEMENT OF MUSIC
    GUIDE FOR CONDUCTING PIANO CLASSES IN THE SCHOOLS, A
NATIONAL BUREAU FOR THE ADVANCEMENT OF MUSIC
    NATIONAL SURVEY OF PIANO CLASSES IN OPERATION
NATIONAL BUREAU FOR THE ADVANCEMENT OF MUSIC
    PIANO CLASSES AND THE PRIVATE TEACHER
NATIONAL BUREAU FOR THE ADVANCEMENT OF MUSIC
    PIANO CLASSES IN THE SCHOOLS..EDUCATIONAL VALUE OF IMPORTANT NEW
NATIONAL BUREAU FOR THE ADVANCEMENT OF MUSIC
    PIANO CLASS INSTRUCTION
NATIONAL PIANO FOUNDATION
    GREATER REWARDS THROUGH CREATIVE PIANO TEACHING
NATIONAL PIANO FOUNDATION
    KEYS TO SUCCESSFUL PIANO STUDIO ORGANIZATION
ORLIK, JULES
    CREATIVE APPROACH TO PIANO CLASS TEACHING, A ---REPRODUCED FROM
PACE, ROBERT
    MUSIC ESSENTIALS FOR CLASSROOM TEACHERS--2ND. ED.---1961
PACE, ROBERT
    PIANO FOR CLASSROOM MUSIC--2ND. ED.---1956
PALMER, HORATIO R.
    PALMER'S PIANO PRIMER
PERRY, ADELAIDE TROWBRIDGE *
    GUIDE TO PIANO STUDY FOR CLASS OR INDIVIDUAL INSTRUCTION, A
PLATT, CAROLYN
    CAROLYN PLATT METHOD FOR PIANO, THE --GROUP INSTRUCTION--TEACHER'S
REZITS, JOSEPH
    SOURCE MATERIALS FOR PIANO TECHNIQUES
ROBINSON, HELENE
    BASIC PIANO FOR ADULTS
ROOT, CATHERINE ADAMS *
    LISTEN, SING AND PLAY..CLASS LESSONS FOR PIANO AND VOICE
SCHELLING, ERNEST *
    OXFORD PIANO COURSE, TEACHER'S FIRST MANUAL
SCHELLING, ERNEST *
    OXFORD PIANO COURSE, TEACHER'S SECOND MANUAL
SCONCIA, JOHN A.
    ANALYTICAL INSTRUCTOR FOR THE PIANO FORTE, CONTAINING THE
SKUTLEY, MILDRED A.
    MUSIC FOR YOU..A SUPPLEMENTAL WORK BOOK FOR INDIVIDUAL OR CLASS
SMELTZER, JEANNIE R.--COMPILER
    OUTLINES AND GRADES FOR THE USE OF PIANO TEACHERS
SQUIRE, RUSSEL N. *
    CLASS PIANO FOR ADULT BEGINNERS--2ND. ED.---1964
STARKEY, EVELYN
    PIANO CLASS WORKBOOK FOR FIRST YEAR STUDENTS
STARR, WILLIAM J. *
    BASIC PIANO TECHNIQUE FOR THE CLASSROOM TEACHER
SUR, WILLIAM R.--EDITOR
    KEYBOARD EXPERIENCE AND PIANO CLASS INSTRUCTION
SUR, WILLIAM R.--EDITOR
    PIANO INSTRUCTION IN THE SCHOOLS
THOMPSON, JOHN
    TEACHING PIANO IN CLASSES
WELSH, J. ROBERT
    MAKING MUSIC AT THE KEYBOARD..BEGINNING PIANO...CLASS...AND EAR
WIER, ALBERT
    PIANO, THE ..ITS HISTORY, MAKERS, PLAYERS AND MUSIC
WILSON, MORRIS E.
    HOW TO HELP YOUR CHILD WITH MUSIC--2ND. ED.---1951
WOLLNER, GERTRUDE PRICE
    IMPROVISATION IN MUSIC..WAYS TOWARDS CAPTURING MUSICAL IDEAS AND
WOODHOUSE, GEORGE
    NEW PATH FOR PIANISTS, A ..THE MUTANO--MUTE PIANO--SYSTEM, ETC.
ZIMMERMAN, ALEX H. *
    BASIC PIANO FOR THE COLLEGE STUDENT

Studio Organization and Equipment

ANTRIM, DORAN K.
    TEACHING MUSIC AND MAKING IT PAY
BASTIEN, JAMES W.
    HOW TO TEACH PIANO SUCCESSFULLY
BENNER, LORA
    BENNER BLUE BOOK, THE ..PRACTICAL MANUAL OF PIANO TEACHING--4TH.
DANIELS, BESS *
    WORLD OF MUSIC, THE ..PIANO COURSE..TEACHERS' BOOK, FOR CLASS OR
DECKER, TOM W.
    CONSOLE SYSTEM, THE ..A TEXT FOR MODERN PIANO AND ORGAN TO BE USED
DENVER--PUBLIC SCHOOLS
    CLASS-PIANO TEACHERS HANDBOOK
DILLER, ANGELA
    SPLENDOR OF MUSIC, THE
FREDRICH, FRANK
    PLAYING BY SEEING..A STUDY IN TRAINING AND PERCEPTION FOR BETTER
GEARY, ELEANOR MARGARET
    MUSICAL EDUCATION, WITH PRACTICAL OBSERVATIONS ON THE ART OF
HEIDELBERGER, PAULINE
    MASTER METHOD..PIANO NORMAL AND TEACHER'S MANUAL
KIRBY, MAY B. KELLY
    KELLY KIRBY KINDERGARTEN PIANO METHOD, TEACHERS' COURSE, THE
MUSIC EDUCATORS NATIONAL CONFERENCE
    HANDBOOK FOR TEACHING PIANO CLASSES
MUSIC EDUCATORS NATIONAL CONFERENCE
    TEACHING PIANO IN CLASSROOM AND STUDIO
MUSIC EDUCATORS NATIONAL CONFERENCE
    TRAVELING THE CIRCUIT WITH PIANO CLASSES
NATIONAL BUREAU FOR THE ADVANCEMENT OF MUSIC
    NATIONAL SURVEY OF PIANO CLASSES IN OPERATION
NATIONAL BUREAU FOR THE ADVANCEMENT OF MUSIC
    PIANO CLASSES AND THE PRIVATE TEACHER
NATIONAL BUREAU FOR THE ADVANCEMENT OF MUSIC
    PIANO CLASSES IN THE SCHOOLS..EDUCATIONAL VALUE OF IMPORTANT NEW
NATIONAL PIANO FOUNDATION
    GREATER REWARDS THROUGH CREATIVE PIANO TEACHING
NATIONAL PIANO FOUNDATION
    KEYS TO SUCCESSFUL PIANO STUDIO ORGANIZATION
PACE, ROBERT
    PIANO FOR CLASSROOM MUSIC--2ND. ED.---1956

PEARCE, CHARLES WILLIAM
    ART OF THE PIANO TEACHER, THE
PERRY, ADELAIDE TROWBRIDGE *
    GUIDE TO PIANO STUDY FOR CLASS OR INDIVIDUAL INSTRUCTION, A
SCHELLING, ERNEST *
    OXFORD PIANO COURSE, TEACHER'S FIRST MANUAL
SCHELLING, ERNEST *
    OXFORD PIANO COURSE, TEACHER'S SECOND MANUAL
SUR, WILLIAM R.--EDITOR
    PIANO INSTRUCTION IN THE SCHOOLS
TERWILLIGER, GORDON B.
    PIANO TEACHERS PROFESSIONAL HANDBOOK
THOMPSON, JOHN
    TEACHING PIANO IN CLASSES
VIRGIL, ALMON K.
    STEP BY STEP..TEXTBOOK IN PIANO PLAYING..HANDBOOK FOR TEACHERS
WIER, ALBERT
    PIANO, THE ..ITS HISTORY, MAKERS, PLAYERS AND MUSIC

Student Recitals

ANTRIM, DORAN K.
    TEACHING MUSIC AND MAKING IT PAY
BASTIEN, JAMES W.
    HOW TO TEACH PIANO SUCCESSFULLY
BENDER, GEORGE CHARLES
    BUSINESS MANUAL FOR PIANO TEACHERS
BENNER, LORA
    BENNER BLUE BOOK, THE ..PRACTICAL MANUAL OF PIANO TEACHING--4TH.
BOWEN, CAROLYN
    OUTLINES FOR TRAINING PIANO TEACHERS
CARRE, JOHN
    PSYCHOLOGY OF PIANO TEACHING, THE ..A TEXTBOOK FOR TEACHERS,
CHING, JOAN ELIZABETH
    OURSELVES AND OUR PUPILS---ALSO CATALOGUED UNDER AUTHORSHIP..BETTY
DENVER--PUBLIC SCHOOLS
    CLASS-PIANO TEACHERS HANDBOOK
DILLER, ANGELA
    SPLENDOR OF MUSIC, THE
EDWARDS, RUTH
    COMPLEAT MUSIC TEACHER FOR TEACHERS, PARENTS AND STUDENTS
GIDDINGS, THADDEUS P.
    GIDDING'S PUBLIC SCHOOL CLASS METHOD FOR THE PIANO
HAMBOURG, MARK
    HOW TO PREPARE FOR PLAYING IN CONCERT
HEIDELBERGER, PAULINE
    MASTER METHOD..PIANO NORMAL AND TEACHER'S MANUAL
LE COUPPEY, FELIX
    PIANO TEACHING..ADVICE TO PUPILS AND YOUNG TEACHERS---1868 IN
LOGIER, JOHANN BERNHARD
    SYLLABUS OF THE SECOND EXAMINATION OF MR. LOGIER'S PUPILS, ON HIS
MAIER, GUY
    PIANO TEACHER'S COMPANION, THE
NEUHAUS, HEINRICH
    ART OF PIANO PLAYING, THE
PLATT, CAROLYN
    CAROLYN PLATT METHOD FOR PIANO, THE --GROUP INSTRUCTION--TEACHER'S
POTAMKIN, FRANK
    MODERN PIANO PEDAGOGY
REEVES, BETTY
    OURSELVES AND OUR PUPILS--MONOGRAPH ON THE ART OF PIANO TEACHING,
RICKER, EARL
    MUSIC LESSONS FOR YOUR CHILD
RODMAN, MOLLY C.
    LET'S TRY SOMETHING NEW..A BOOK OF RECITAL AND TEACHING IDEAS FOR
SEROFF, VICTOR
    COMMON SENSE IN PIANO STUDY
TERWILLIGER, GORDON B.
    PIANO TEACHERS PROFESSIONAL HANDBOOK
WILLIAMS, JEAN E.
    MODERN METHOD OF PIANO INSTRUCTION, A ..TEACHERS MANUAL
WILLIAMS, JOHN M.
    WHAT TO TEACH AT THE VERY FIRST LESSON
WILSON, MORRIS E.
    HOW TO HELP YOUR CHILD WITH MUSIC--2ND. ED.---1951
WOLFF, ERNST VICTOR
    WITH REASON AND RHYME

Testing and Evaluation

AEOLIAN COMPANY, THE
    DUO-ART BOOK OF MUSIC, THE
ANDERSON, WILLIAM P.
    MUSIC AS A CAREER
BIART, VICTOR
    PIANIST'S GUIDE, THE ..A SERIES OF PAMPHLETS ON THE TEACHING AND
BROWER, HARRIETTE
    SELF-HELP IN PIANO STUDY
CHING, JAMES
    CANDIDATE'S COMPANION TO THE EXERCISES, SCALES, BROKEN CHORDS,
CHING, JOAN ELIZABETH
    OURSELVES AND OUR PUPILS---ALSO CATALOGUED UNDER AUTHORSHIP..BETTY
CHITTENDEN, KATE S.
    SYNTHETIC CATECHISM, THE ..538 QUESTIONS AND ANSWERS FOR USE IN
COOKE, MAX
    HOW TO PREPARE FOR PIANOFORTE...SUGGESTIONS FOR A.M.E.B.
DE WITT, EDYTHE
    EDYTHE DE WITT'S METHOD FOR CLASS PIANO...WRITTEN TO GIVE CORRECT
GARROWAY, WILL
    PIANISM
LE COUPPEY, FELIX
    PIANO TEACHING..ADVICE TO PUPILS AND YOUNG TEACHERS---1868 IN
LINDO, ALGERNON H.
    AURAL TESTS FOR EXAMINATIONS--SPECIALLY WRITTEN FOR TEACHERS AND
LOGIER, JOHANN BERNHARD
    AUTHENTIC ACCOUNT OF THE EXAMINATION OF PUPILS, INSTRUCTED IN THE
LOVELOCK, WILLIAM
    ORNAMENTS AND ABBREVIATIONS FOR EXAMINATION CANDIDATES
LOVELOCK, WILLIAM
    TESTS IN SIGHT READING, FOR PIANO..FROM FIRST GRADE TO DIPLOMA--3
LOWE, CLAUDE EDGERTON
    CANDIDATES GUIDE TO QUESTIONS AND ANSWERS AT PRACTICAL LOCAL
LOWERY, HARRY
    GUIDE TO MUSICAL ACOUSTICS, A ---1956
MANHIRE, WILSON
    CANDIDATE'S SCALE AND ARPEGGIO TESTS FOR THE PIANOFORTE, ETC., THE
MINNESOTA MUSIC TEACHERS ASSOCIATION
    PIANO-THEORY EXAMINATION SYLLABUS
POINTER SYSTEM, INC.
    GUIDE TO THE MODERN PIANIST, A
REEVES, BETTY
    OURSELVES AND OUR PUPILS--MONOGRAPH ON THE ART OF PIANO TEACHING,
ROWLEY, ALEC
    PRACTICAL MUSICIANSHIP, A HANDBOOK FOR TEACHERS AND STUDENTS
SCHLIEDER, FREDERICK W.
    LYRIC COMPOSITION THROUGH IMPROVISATION--2 VOLS., 1927-1946

SHERWOOD MUSIC SCHOOL
    PIANO LESSONS AND TESTS--4TH. REV. ED.---1945+
SHUTER, ROSAMUND
    PSYCHOLOGY OF MUSICAL ABILITY, THE
SKUTLEY, MILDRED A.
    MUSIC FOR YOU..A SUPPLEMENTAL WORK BOOK FOR INDIVIDUAL OR CLASS
SMITH, A. G. WARREN
    BEGINNER'S GUIDE, THE ..FOR ALL COMMENCING THE STUDY OF THE
SMITHERS, WELSFORD
    PIANO TEACHER'S GUIDE, THE ..A HUNDRED QUESTIONS FOR YOUNG
SOREL, CLAUDETTE *
    INDEPENDENT LEARNING APPROACH TO PIANO SIGHT READING, AN
STEINER, ERIC
    MASTER TUNES AND MUSIC TESTS FOR THE PIANO STUDENT
STEWART, REID
    HOW TO PASS MUSIC EXAMINATIONS--PIANO--A GUIDE FOR TEACHERS AND
SWENSON, LUCILE B.
    DISCOVERING THE PIANO..THE MULTIPLE KEY APPROACH..STUDY GUIDE AND
TANKARD, GEOFFREY
    SPECIMEN ANSWERS TO THE QUESTIONS IN PIANOFORTE DIPLOMAS
TAPPER, THOMAS
    EDUCATION OF THE MUSIC TEACHER, THE
THIMAN, ERIC H.
    PIANOFORTE TESTS IN INITIATIVE AND INTELLIGENCE AS SET IN DIPLOMA
VIRGIL, ALMON K.
    EDUCATION IN MUSIC..LESSONS TO TEACHERS IN THE INSTRUCTION OF

Teacher Qualifications

ANTCLIFFE, HERBERT
    SUCCESSFUL MUSIC TEACHER, THE ..WORDS OF ADVICE
ANTRIM, DORAN K.
    TEACHING MUSIC AND MAKING IT PAY
BOLTON, HETTY
    ON TEACHING THE PIANO
BROWER, HARRIETTE
    SELF-HELP IN PIANO STUDY
CARY, MRS. C. S. P.
    PIANO-FORTE CLASS BOOK, CONTAINING PRACTICAL RUDIMENTAL LESSONS
CURWEN, ANNIE JESSY
    TEACHER'S GUIDE...TO MRS. CURWEN'S PIANOFORTE METHOD, 'THE CHILD
EDWARDS, RUTH
    COMPLEAT MUSIC TEACHER FOR TEACHERS, PARENTS AND STUDENTS
EISENBERG, JACOB
    WEIGHT AND RELAXATION METHOD FOR THE PIANOFORTE
GREW, SIDNEY
    ART OF THE PLAYER-PIANO, THE ..A TEXTBOOK FOR STUDENT AND TEACHER
HARVEY, ROBERT
    MAGIC KEY TO KEYBOARD SUCCESS, THE
HULL, ARTHUR EAGLEFIELD
    THREE HUNDRED QUESTIONS ON PIANOFORTE TEACHING IN 30 GRADUATED
ISAACS, EDWARD
    BLIND PIANO TEACHER, THE
JOHNSON, SARAH S.
    HELPS TO TEACHER AND STUDENT ON THE FAELTEN SYSTEM
KRUSZYNSKI, MICHAL
    APPROACH TO THE PSYCHOLOGY OF PIANO TEACHING, AN
LEAVEY, LILIAN
    JUNIOR SCHOOL PIANIST, THE --ADDRESSED TO THE NEW MUSIC TEACHER
LEVINE, JACK
    WHAT MUSICAL INSTRUMENT FOR ME
LE COUPPEY, FELIX
    PIANO TEACHING..ADVICE TO PUPILS AND YOUNG TEACHERS---1868 IN
LOMAS, LULU GRAHAM
    FIRST TEN PIANO LESSONS, LAID OUT FOR YOUNG TEACHERS, WITH
MANHIRE, WILSON
    GUIDE TO THE A.R.C.M. AND OTHER EXAMINATIONS IN
MATTHAY, TOBIAS A.
    MUSICAL INTERPRETATION..ITS LAWS AND PRINCIPLES---1913
MCFERRIN, CHARLES BETTEYS
    MOTHER'S PART IN HER CHILD'S MUSICAL EDUCATION, A ..OR, THE THINGS
MUSIC EDUCATORS NATIONAL CONFERENCE
    HANDBOOK FOR TEACHING PIANO CLASSES
MUSIC EDUCATORS NATIONAL CONFERENCE
    TEACHING PIANO IN CLASSROOM AND STUDIO
PEARCE, CHARLES WILLIAM
    ART OF THE PIANO TEACHER, THE
PHILLIPSON, WENTWORTH
    GUIDE TO YOUNG PIANOFORTE TEACHERS AND STUDENTS
QUINN, MARCUS LUCIUS
    HOW TO STUDY MUSIC AND LEARN TO PLAY PIANO OR ORGAN
RICKER, EARL
    MUSIC LESSONS FOR YOUR CHILD
ROWLEY, DAISY WOODRUFF
    NINE HUNDRED MODEL LESSONS FOR PIANO TEACHERS
RUBINSTEIN, BERYL
    OUTLINE OF PIANO PEDAGOGY--REV. ED.---1929
SCHELLING, ERNEST *
    OXFORD PIANO COURSE, TEACHER'S FIRST MANUAL
SMITH, VERA K.
    YOUNG PIANO TEACHER, WITH 75 HELPFUL TEACHING QUESTIONS, THE
SMITHERS, WELSFORD
    PIANO TEACHER'S GUIDE, THE ..A HUNDRED QUESTIONS FOR YOUNG
STANLEY, JANE
    BASIC ROUTINES IN ELEMENTARY PIANO TEACHING THROUGH THE FIRST
SUR, WILLIAM R.--EDITOR
    PIANO INSTRUCTION IN THE SCHOOLS
THOMPSON, JOHN
    TEACHING PIANO IN CLASSES
VIRGIL, ALMON K.
    EDUCATION IN MUSIC..LESSONS TO TEACHERS IN THE INSTRUCTION OF
WHITFORD, ROBERT
    PIANO AND ITS MUSIC, THE --FROM 'MODERN PIANO COURSE'
WIER, ALBERT
    PIANO, THE ..ITS HISTORY, MAKERS, PLAYERS AND MUSIC
WILSON, MORRIS E.
    HOW TO HELP YOUR CHILD WITH MUSIC--2ND. ED.---1951
WILSON, MORRIS E.
    HOW TO PLAY BY EAR

Master Classes

DENT, EDWARD J.
    FERRUCCIO BUSONI, A BIOGRAPHY
DIEHL, ALICE M.
    MUSICAL MEMORIES--SOME LESSONS WITH HENSELT
HENDERSON, ARCHIBALD
    MUSICAL MEMORIES---CONCERNS SEVERAL PIANISTS
HUNEKER, JAMES GIBBONS
    FRANZ LISZT
PETERSON, HOUSTON--EDITOR
    GREAT TEACHERS, PORTRAYED BY THOSE WHO STUDIED UNDER
PUGNO, RAOUL
    LESSONS OF RAOUL PUGNO, THE ..WITH A BIOGRAPHY OF CHOPIN BY M.
STUCKENSCHMIDT, HANS H.
    FERRUCCIO BUSONI..CHRONICLE OF A EUROPEAN---1967, IN GERMAN
TERWILLIGER, GORDON B.
    PIANO TEACHERS PROFESSIONAL HANDBOOK

WALKER, ALAN--EDITOR
   FRANZ LISZT, THE MAN AND HIS MUSIC---ESSAYS BY SACHEVERALL SITWELL
WESTERBY, HERBERT
   LISZT, COMPOSER, AND HIS PIANO WORKS..DESCRIPTIVE GUIDE AND

Teacher-Student-Parent Interrelationships

ANON
   ADVICE TO A NOBLEMAN...ON THE MANNER IN WHICH HIS CHILDREN SHOULD
ANTCLIFFE, HERBERT
   SUCCESSFUL MUSIC TEACHER, THE ..WORDS OF ADVICE
ANTRIM, DORAN K.
   TEACHING MUSIC AND MAKING IT PAY
BASTIEN, JAMES W.
   HOW TO TEACH PIANO SUCCESSFULLY
BRIED, FREDERICK
   STIMULATION IN PIANO STUDY..HOW PARENTS CAN STIMULATE AND MAINTAIN
BROWER, HARRIETTE
   SELF-HELP IN PIANO STUDY
CARY, MRS. C. S. P.
   PIANO-FORTE CLASS BOOK, CONTAINING PRACTICAL RUDIMENTAL LESSONS
CHING, JOAN ELIZABETH
   OURSELVES AND OUR PUPILS---ALSO CATALOGUED UNDER AUTHORSHIP..BETTY
DIEHL, ALICE M.
   MUSICAL MEMORIES--SOME LESSONS WITH HENSELT
HEIDELBERGER, PAULINE
   MASTER METHOD..PIANO NORMAL AND TEACHER'S MANUAL
HUNEKER, JAMES GIBBONS
   FRANZ LISZT
MAIER, GUY *
   PLAYING THE PIANO--TEACHER'S MANUAL
MCFERRIN, CHARLES BETTEYS
   MOTHER'S PART IN HER CHILD'S MUSICAL EDUCATION, A ..OR, THE THINGS
NATIONAL PIANO FOUNDATION
   GREATER REWARDS THROUGH CREATIVE PIANO TEACHING
NEUHAUS, HEINRICH
   ART OF PIANO PLAYING, THE
REEVES, BETTY
   OURSELVES AND OUR PUPILS--MONOGRAPH ON THE ART OF PIANO TEACHING,
RICKER, EARL
   MUSIC LESSONS FOR YOUR CHILD
ROBYN, LOUISE
   HOW TO TEACH PIANO TO THE CHILD BEGINNER..A TEXT BOOK FOR TEACHERS
SEYMOUR, HARRIET AYER
   HOME MUSIC LESSONS..HOW TO FIND YOUR MUSICAL SELF
VIRGIL, ALMON K.
   EDUCATION IN MUSIC..LESSONS TO TEACHERS IN THE INSTRUCTION OF
WHITFORD, ROBERT
   PIANO AND ITS MUSIC, THE --FROM 'MODERN PIANO COURSE'
WILLS, VERA G. *
   PARENT'S GUIDE TO MUSIC LESSONS, A
WOLFF, ERNST VICTOR
   WITH REASON AND RHYME

Selecting Instructional Materials

ANTRIM, DORAN K.
   TEACHING MUSIC AND MAKING IT PAY
BASTIEN, JAMES W.
   HOW TO TEACH PIANO SUCCESSFULLY
BIART, VICTOR
   PIANIST'S GUIDE, THE ..A SERIES OF PAMPHLETS ON THE TEACHING AND
BROUGHTON, JULIA *
   SIXTEEN LESSON PLANS..A MANUAL FOR PROGRESSIVE SERIES
CAPEN, C. L.
   MUSIC TEACHER'S VADE-MECUM, THE ..A GUIDE IN THE CHOICE OF MUSIC
GRAY, WILLIAM L.
   SELECTED AND GRADED LIST OF STUDIES AND PIECES FOR TEACHERS OF
GRIFFIN, SISTER MARY ANNAROSE
   PIANO MATERIALS..GRADED AND COMPILED AS AN AID TO INSTRUCTORS
HODGES, SISTER MABELLE L.
   CATALOGUE OF REPRESENTATIVE TEACHING MATERIALS FOR PIANO SINCE
MUSIC EDUCATORS NATIONAL CONFERENCE
   HANDBOOK FOR TEACHING PIANO CLASSES
MUSIC EDUCATORS NATIONAL CONFERENCE
   TEACHING PIANO IN CLASSROOM AND STUDIO
NEWMAN, ELIZABETH
   TEACHING MATERIAL GRADED ACCORDING TO HARMONIC STRUCTURE,
RAINBOW, BERNARR J. G.--EDITOR
   HANDBOOK FOR MUSIC TEACHERS--2 VOLS.
REINECKE, KARL H.
   WHAT SHALL WE PLAY--NOT UNLIKE CZERNY'S 'LETTERS TO A YOUNG
SCHIRMER, G.
   NEW PIANO-TEACHER'S GUIDE..A GRADED AND CLASSIFIED LIST OF PIANO
SUTHERLAND, ADELAIDE K.--COMPILER
   WHAT SHALL I PLAY..PREFERENCES FOR PIANO AND ORGAN..GUIDE TO

Piano Technique

General

AHRENS, CORA B. *
   FOR ALL PIANO TEACHERS
ANDERSON, J. CLARK
   GOOD MUSIC EXPLAINED..WHAT ALL GOOD PIANISTS SHOULD KNOW
AULD, WILDA J.
   HANDBOOK FOR THE CHURCH PIANIST, A
BABBITT, WILLIAM
   PHYSIOLOGICAL METHOD FOR PLAYING THE PIANO-FORTE, DESIGNED AS A
BARTH, HANS
   TECHNIC..THE ENTIRE 25 BRANCHES FOR DEVELOPING TECHNIC NECESSARY
BEMETZRIEDER, ANTON
   ACCOUNT OF A NEW WAY OF CONSIDERING MUSICK, AND TEACHING
BENNER, LORA
   BENNER GOLD BOOK, THE ..PIANO MATERIAL AND TEACHING METHODS--3RD.
BOLTON, HETTY
   HOW TO PRACTICE
BOLTON, HETTY
   ON TEACHING THE PIANO
BOWEN, YORK
   SIMPLICITY OF PIANO TECHNIQUE, THE
BRANDT, LEONIE
   SCIENCE IN MODERN PIANOFORTE PLAYING
BROWER, HARRIETTE
   ART OF THE PIANIST, THE
BROWER, HARRIETTE
   MODERN MASTERS OF THE KEYBOARD
BROWER, HARRIETTE
   PIANO MASTERY..TALKS WITH MASTER PIANISTS AND TEACHERS...
BROWER, HARRIETTE
   PIANO MASTERY, SECOND SERIES
CAMPBELL, LE ROY B.
   TRUE FUNCTION OF RELAXATION IN PIANO PLAYING, THE

CAMPBELL, LE ROY B.
   VELOCITY PLUS
CARPE, ADOLPH
   PIANIST AND THE ART OF MUSIC, THE ..A TREATISE ON PIANO PLAYING
CHING, JAMES
   AMATEUR PIANIST'S COMPANION, THE
CHING, JAMES
   PIANO PLAYING, A PRACTICAL METHOD--A NEW EDITION OF 'PIANO
CHING, JAMES
   PIANO TECHNIQUE..FOUNDATION PRINCIPLES
CHING, JAMES
   STUDIES FOR BASIC PIANO TECHNIQUE..WRITTEN AND SELECTED WITH
CHING, JAMES
   TEACHING OF TECHNIQUE TO CHILDREN, THE --4 PTS.
CHING, JOAN ELIZABETH
   APPROACH TO PIANO TEACHING---ALSO CATALOGUED UNDER
CHRISTIANI, ADOLPH FRIEDRICH
   PRINCIPLES OF EXPRESSION IN PIANOFORTE PLAYING, THE
CHURCHILL, VIRGINIA PEAKES
   MODERN TEACHER'S GUIDE TO PIANO AND PIANO CLASS TEACHING
CHURCHILL, VIRGINIA PEAKES
   NINETEEN FIFTY-SIX SUPPLEMENT TO THE MODERN TEACHER'S GUIDE TO
COOKE, CHARLES
   PLAYING THE PIANO FOR PLEASURE--REV. ED.---1941
COPP, EVELYN A.
   WHAT IS THE FLETCHER MUSIC METHOD
CORTOT, ALFRED
   RATIONAL PRINCIPLES OF PIANOFORTE TECHNIQUE
D'ABREU, GERALD
   PLAYING THE PIANO WITH CONFIDENCE---1964
DICKERSON, RUTH A.
   NEW APPROACH TO PIANO TECHNIQUE, A
DILLER, ANGELA
   SPLENDOR OF MUSIC, THE
EVERHART, POWELL
   PIANIST'S ART, THE ..A COMPREHENSIVE MANUAL ON PIANO PLAYING FOR
FERGUSON, DONALD NIVISON
   PIANO MUSIC OF SIX GREAT COMPOSERS---1947
FIELDEN, THOMAS
   SCIENCE OF PIANOFORTE TECHNIC, THE --2ND. REV. ED.---1927
FILLMORE, JOHN C.
   PIANOFORTE MUSIC..ITS HISTORY, WITH BIOGRAPHICAL SKETCHES AND
FULLER, JANET E.
   COMPLETE KNOWLEDGE OF PIANO TECHNIQUE, A
GARROWAY, WILL
   PIANISM
GAT, JOZSEF
   TECHNIQUE OF PIANO PLAYING, THE, --2ND. ED.---1958
GERMER, HEINRICH
   HOW OUGHT ONE TO STUDY PIANO-TECHNIC---1881, IN GERMAN
GERMER, HEINRICH
   MANUAL OF TONE-PRODUCTION IN PIANOFORTE PLAYING, FROM 'TECHNICS OF
GERMER, HEINRICH
   TECHNICS OF PIANOFORTE PLAYING REARRANGED AS A METHODICAL PLAN OF
GIESEKING, WALTER *
   PIANO TECHNIQUE---COMBINED REPUBLICATION OF..'THE SHORTEST WAY TO
HAMBOURG, MARK
   HOW TO PLAY THE PIANO--NEW AND ENLARGED EDITION OF 'HOW TO BECOME
HAMILTON, CLARENCE G.
   PIANO TEACHING..ITS PRINCIPLES AND PROBLEMS
HARKNESS, ROBERT
   HARKNESS PIANO METHOD OF EVANGELISTIC HYMN PLAYING, THE ..A
HARRISON, SIDNEY
   PIANO TECHNIQUE
HARVEY, ROBERT
   MAGIC KEY TO KEYBOARD SUCCESS, THE
HELMANN, JACOB N.
   CONSCIOUSLY CONTROLLED PIANO TONE, THE --REV. ED.---1950
HOFMANN, JOSEF
   PIANO PLAYING, WITH PIANO QUESTIONS ANSWERED---PUBLISHED EARLIER
HOPE, ERIC
   HANDBOOK OF PIANO PLAYING, A
HORROCKS, CYRIL R. H.
   STUDENT'S GUIDE TO THE ART OF TEACHING THE PIANOFORTE, THE --2ND.
HOWARD, GEORGE HENRY
   OUTLINE OF TECHNIQUE..A GUIDE IN THE THEORY AND PRACTICE OF
HOWE, JAMES H.
   PIANO-FORTE INSTRUCTOR, A ..OR, PREPARATORY SYSTEM OF PIANOFORTE
HUTCHESON, ERNEST
   ELEMENTS OF PIANO TECHNIQUE, THE
HUTCHESON, ERNEST *
   LITERATURE OF THE PIANO, THE ..A GUIDE FOR AMATEUR AND
ISAACS, EDWARD
   BLIND PIANO TEACHER, THE
JEWETT, ALBERT DEWEY
   IDIOMATIC COURSE OF PIANO INSTRUCTION FOR CLASS WORK
JOHNSTONE, J. ALFRED
   ART OF TEACHING PIANOFORTE PLAYING, THE --2ND. REV. ED.---1910
KIRBY, MAY B. KELLY
   KELLY KIRBY KINDERGARTEN PIANO METHOD, TEACHERS' COURSE, THE
LE COUPPEY, FELIX
   PIANO TEACHING..ADVICE TO PUPILS AND YOUNG TEACHERS---1868 IN
LHEVINNE, JOSEF
   BASIC PRINCIPLES IN PIANOFORTE PLAYING---1924
MACKINNON, LILIAS
   MUSICAL SECRETS ON THE TECHNIQUE OF PIANO PLAYING
MARKS, ADOLF B.
   INTRODUCTION TO THE INTERPRETATION OF BEETHOVEN'S PIANO-FORTE
MASON, WILLIAM G. *
   PRIMER OF MUSIC, A ..BEING THE FIRST STEPS IN MUSICIANSHIP..FOR
MATTHAY, TOBIAS A.
   FIRST LIGHTS ON PIANO-PLAYING
MATTHAY, TOBIAS A.
   TEACHING OF PIANOFORTE TECHNIQUE, THE ..A SUPPLEMENT TO THE ACT OF
MATTHAY, TOBIAS A.
   VISIBLE AND INVISIBLE IN PIANOFORTE TECHNIC, THE ..BEING A DIGEST
MIDKIFF, HELEN T.
   CHURCH PIANIST, THE
MILLER, ALLAN
   BEGINNING PIANO FOR ADULTS
MINNESOTA MUSIC TEACHERS ASSOCIATION
   PIANO-THEORY EXAMINATION SYLLABUS
MORRILL, HENRY H.
   MANUAL OF PIANO FOR PUPILS AND TEACHERS
MUSIC EDUCATORS NATIONAL CONFERENCE
   TEACHING PIANO IN CLASSROOM AND STUDIO
NEUHAUS, HEINRICH
   ART OF PIANO PLAYING, THE
NEWMAN, ELIZABETH
   HOW TO TEACH MUSIC TO BEGINNERS
NEWMAN, WILLIAM S.
   PERFORMANCE PRACTICES IN BEETHOVEN'S PIANO SONATAS..AN
O'TOOLE, WILLIAM
   CREATIVE PIANO TECHNIC
ORTMANN, OTTO
   PHYSIOLOGICAL MECHANICS OF PIANO TECHNIQUE, THE ---1929
OSTROVSKY, HENRY
   TECHNIQUE AND HAND DEVELOPMENT---USE OF A MACHINE

PALMER, KING
    TEACH YOURSELF TO PLAY THE PIANO
PERRY, ADELAIDE TROWBRIDGE *
    GUIDE TO PIANO STUDY FOR CLASS OR INDIVIDUAL INSTRUCTION, A
PLAIDY, LOUIS
    PIANO TEACHER, THE
PLATT, CAROLYN
    CAROLYN PLATT METHOD FOR PIANO, THE --GROUP INSTRUCTION--TEACHER'S
POWERS-WADSWORTH, L.
    PIANIST'S GUIDE TO TECHNICAL FREEDOM, THE ..2 VOLS. IN 1
REEVES, BETTY
    APPROACH TO PIANO TEACHING---ALSO CATALOGUED UNDER
RICHTER, ADA
    TEACHING HINTS
RIEMANN, HUGO
    CATECHISM OF PIANOFORTE PLAYING---1888, IN GERMAN
ROBYN, LOUISE
    TECHNIC TALES FOR THE CHILD AT THE PIANO--BKS. 1-3..TEACHER'S
ROEDER, CARL M.
    LIBERATION AND DELIBERATION IN PIANO TECHNIC
ROSTAND, CLAUDE
    LISZT
RUBINSTEIN, BERYL
    OUTLINE OF PIANO PEDAGOGY--REV. ED.---1929
SAFONOFF, WASSILI
    NEW FORMULA FOR THE PIANO TEACHER AND PIANO STUDENT
SCHAUFFLER, LAWRENCE
    PIANO TECHNIC..MYTH OR SCIENCE
SCHELLING, ERNEST *
    OXFORD PIANO COURSE, TEACHER'S FIRST MANUAL
SCHELLING, ERNEST *
    OXFORD PIANO COURSE, TEACHER'S SECOND MANUAL
SCIONTI, SILVIO
    L'ARTE PIANISTICA..SYSTEM OF PIANO ARTISTRY---IN ITALIAN AND
SEROFF, VICTOR
    COMMON SENSE IN PIANO STUDY
SHELDON, ROBERT--COMPILER
    EGON PETRI-ALEXANDER LIBERMANN NOTES ON THE ART AND TECHNIQUE OF
SHERWOOD MUSIC SCHOOL
    PIANO LESSONS AND TESTS--4TH. REV. ED.---1945+
SIMPSON, KENNETH
    KEYBOARD HARMONY AND IMPROVISATION
SMELTZER, JEANNIE R.--COMPILER
    OUTLINES AND GRADES FOR THE USE OF PIANO TEACHERS
SMITH, MACDONALD
    FROM BRAIN TO KEYBOARD..A SYSTEM OF HAND AND FINGER CONTROL FOR
STANLEY, JANE
    BASIC ROUTINES IN ELEMENTARY PIANO TEACHING THROUGH THE FIRST
THAYER, E. D.
    SHORT CUTS TO PIANO TECHNIQUE
VIRGIL, ANTHA MINERVA
    INSTRUCTIVE TALKS TO PIANO STUDENTS
WESTERBY, HERBERT
    LISZT, COMPOSER, AND HIS PIANO WORKS..DESCRIPTIVE GUIDE AND
WHITE, WILLIAM BRAID
    PLAYER-PIANIST, THE ..A GUIDE TO THE APPRECIATION AND
WHITESIDE, ABBY
    MASTERING THE CHOPIN ETUDES AND OTHER ESSAYS
WIER, ALBERT
    PIANO, THE ..ITS HISTORY, MAKERS, PLAYERS AND MUSIC
WILLIAMS, JEAN E. *
    MIND IN MUSIC, THE
WILLIAMS, JOHN M.
    WHAT TO TEACH AT THE VERY FIRST LESSON
WILSON, DAVID M.
    PLAYER-PIANO, THE ..ITS CONSTRUCTION..HOW TO PLAY, WHAT TO PLAY
WOLFF, KONRAD
    TEACHING OF ARTUR SCHNABEL, THE ..A GUIDE TO INTERPRETATION
WOODHOUSE, GEORGE
    FROM KEYBOARD TO MUSIC
ZIMMERMAN, ALEX H. *
    BASIC PIANO FOR THE COLLEGE STUDENT

Miscellaneous

BOLTON, HETTY
    HOW TO PRACTICE
BRANDT, LEONIE
    SCIENCE IN MODERN PIANOFORTE PLAYING
BROTHERHOOD, JAMES
    TECHNICON, THE..A TREATISE UPON THE DEVELOPMENT OF PIANOFORTE
BROWER, HARRIETTE
    ART OF THE PIANIST, THE
BUCK, PERCY
    PSYCHOLOGY FOR MUSICIANS
CALAND, ELIZABETH
    ARTISTIC PIANO PLAYING, AS TAUGHT BY LUDWIG DEPPE
CAMPBELL, LE ROY B.
    TRUE FUNCTION OF RELAXATION IN PIANO PLAYING, THE
CAMPBELL, LE ROY B.
    VELOCITY PLUS
CHING, JAMES
    AMATEUR PIANIST'S COMPANION, THE
CHING, JAMES
    PIANO PLAYING, A PRACTICAL METHOD--A NEW EDITION OF 'PIANO
CORTOT, ALFRED
    RATIONAL PRINCIPLES OF PIANOFORTE TECHNIQUE
CURCIO, LOUISE
    MUSICIAN'S HANDBOOK FOR THE DEVELOPMENT OF MANUAL SUPPLENESS AND
DEUTSCH, LEONHARD
    PIANO..GUIDED SIGHT-READING
EVERHART, POWELL
    PIANIST'S ART, THE ..A COMPREHENSIVE MANUAL ON PIANO PLAYING FOR
FIELDEN, THOMAS
    SCIENCE OF PIANOFORTE TECHNIC, THE --2ND. REV. ED.---1927
FILLMORE, JOHN C.
    PIANOFORTE MUSIC..ITS HISTORY, WITH BIOGRAPHICAL SKETCHES AND
FORD, DONALD
    SINGING CLASS PIANIST AND ON PIANOFORTE ACCOMPANYING IN GENERAL,
FULLER, JANET E.
    COMPLETE KNOWLEDGE OF PIANO TECHNIQUE, A
GAT, JOZSEF
    TECHNIQUE OF PIANO PLAYING, THE, --2ND. ED.---1958
GIDDINGS, THADDEUS P.
    GIDDING'S PUBLIC SCHOOL CLASS METHOD FOR THE PIANO
HAMILTON, CLARENCE G.
    WHAT EVERY PIANO PUPIL SHOULD KNOW
JOHNSTONE, J. ALFRED
    ART OF TEACHING PIANOFORTE PLAYING, THE --2ND. REV. ED.---1910
LEIMER, KARL *
    RHYTHMICS, DYNAMICS, PEDAL, AND OTHER PROBLEMS OF PIANO
LEVINSKAYA, MARIA
    LEVINSKAYA SYSTEM OF PIANOFORTE TECHNIC AND TONE COLOR, THE
LHEVINNE, JOSEF
    BASIC PRINCIPLES IN PIANOFORTE PLAYING---1924
MACKINNON, LILIAS
    MUSICAL SECRETS ON THE TECHNIQUE OF PIANO PLAYING

MASON, DANIEL GREGORY
    NEGLECTED SENSE IN PIANO PLAYING, A
MATTHAY, TOBIAS A.
    FOREARM ROTATION PRINCIPLE IN PIANOFORTE PLAYING, THE ..ITS
MATTHAY, TOBIAS A.
    MUSICAL INTERPRETATION..ITS LAWS AND PRINCIPLES---1913
MATTHAY, TOBIAS A.
    RELAXATION STUDIES IN THE MUSCULAR DISCRIMINATION REQUIRED FOR
MATTHAY, TOBIAS A.
    TEACHING OF PIANOFORTE TECHNIQUE, THE ..A SUPPLEMENT TO THE ACT OF
MATTHAY, TOBIAS A.
    VISIBLE AND INVISIBLE IN PIANOFORTE TECHNIC, THE ..BEING A DIGEST
O'TOOLE, WILLIAM
    CREATIVE PIANO TECHNIC
ORTMANN, OTTO
    PHYSIOLOGICAL MECHANICS OF PIANO TECHNIQUE, THE ---1929
PHILIPP, ISIDOR
    TRILL IN THE WORKS OF BEETHOVEN, THE
POWERS-WADSWORTH, L.
    PIANIST'S GUIDE TO TECHNICAL FREEDOM, THE ..2 VOLS. IN 1
PRENTICE THOMAS RIDLEY
    HAND GYMNASTICS, FOR THE SCIENTIFIC DEVELOPMENT OF THE MUSCLES
REZITS, JOSEPH
    TEACHER'S GUIDE TO THE NEW SCRIBNER MUSIC LIBRARY
ROBYN, LOUISE
    TECHNIC TALES FOR THE CHILD AT THE PIANO--BKS. 1-3..TEACHER'S
SAVLER, ROBERTA--EDITOR
    SELECTIONS FROM THE PIANO TEACHER, 1958-1963
SCHAUFFLER, LAWRENCE
    PIANO TECHNIC..MYTH OR SCIENCE
SCHELLING, ERNEST *
    OXFORD PIANO COURSE, TEACHER'S FIRST MANUAL
SHELDON, ROBERT--COMPILER
    EGON PETRI-ALEXANDER LIBERMANN NOTES ON THE ART AND TECHNIQUE OF
THAYER, E. D.
    SHORT CUTS TO PIANO TECHNIQUE
VIRGIL, ALMON K.
    SPECIAL TECHNIC COURSE IN THE VIRGIL CLAVIER METHOD--6 PTS.
WEISER, ADOLPH
    TWO RIGHT HANDS..A GUIDE FOR THE DEVELOPMENT OF PIANO TECHNIQUE
WELLS, HOWARD
    PIANIST'S THUMB, THE
WESTERBY, HERBERT
    APPROACH TO LISZT, THE ..A COURSE OF MODERN TONAL TECHNIQUE FOR
WHITESIDE, ABBY
    MASTERING THE CHOPIN ETUDES AND OTHER ESSAYS
WOODHOUSE, GEORGE
    CREATIVE TECHNIQUE, FOR ARTISTS IN GENERAL AND PIANISTS IN
WOODHOUSE, GEORGE
    FROM KEYBOARD TO MUSIC

Physiology and Anatomy

ALLEN, MARGARET *
    CREATIVE MOTION
BABBITT, WILLIAM
    PHYSIOLOGICAL METHOD FOR PLAYING THE PIANO-FORTE, DESIGNED AS A
BACON, ERNST
    NOTES ON THE PIANO
BARNETT, DAVID
    PERFORMANCE OF MUSIC, THE ..A STUDY IN TERMS OF THE PIANOFORTE
BONPENSIERE, LUIGI
    NEW PATHWAYS TO PIANO TECHNIQUE..A STUDY OF THE RELATIONS BETWEEN
BOWEN, YORK
    SIMPLICITY OF PIANO TECHNIQUE, THE
BRANDT, LEONIE
    SCIENCE IN MODERN PIANOFORTE PLAYING
BREE, MADAME MALWINE
    GROUNDWORK OF THE LESCHETIZKY METHOD, THE ---1902
BREITHAUPT, RUDOLPH MARIA
    NATURAL PIANO-TECHNIC..SCHOOL OF WEIGHT TOUCH--2 VOLS.
BROTHERHOOD, JAMES
    DEVELOPMENT OF THE HAND FOR PIANO-FORTE PLAYING BY MEANS OF A
BROTHERHOOD, JAMES
    KNOWLEDGE OF THE RELATION OF PHYSIOLOGY AND ANATOMY TO PIANO
BROTHERHOOD, JAMES
    MUSCLES USED IN PIANO-PLAYING..WITH EXPLANATORY NOTES AND DIAGRAMS
BROTHERHOOD, JAMES
    SENSITIVE PIANO TOUCH AND WAYS AND MEANS TO ITS ACQUIREMENT---A
BROTHERHOOD, JAMES
    TECHNICON, THE..A TREATISE UPON THE DEVELOPMENT OF PIANOFORTE
BROWER, HARRIETTE
    PIANO MASTERY..TALKS WITH MASTER PIANISTS AND TEACHERS...
BROWER, HARRIETTE
    PIANO MASTERY, SECOND SERIES
CALAND, ELIZABETH
    ARTISTIC PIANO PLAYING, AS TAUGHT BY LUDWIG DEPPE
CAMPBELL, LE ROY B.
    TRUE FUNCTION OF RELAXATION IN PIANO PLAYING, THE
CHAROL, SIMON
    NEW APPROACH TO THE STUDY OF THE PIANOFORTE, A ---IN ITALIAN AND
CHASE, MARY WOOD
    NATURAL LAWS IN PIANO TECHNIC
CHING, JAMES
    AMATEUR PIANIST'S COMPANION, THE
CHING, JAMES
    FOREARM ROTATION---A SEQUEL TO 'THE ROTARY ROAD'--15 PHOTOS AND
CHING, JAMES
    MUSCULAR RELAXATION, A SIMPLE EXPLANATION
CHING, JAMES
    ON TEACHING PIANO TECHNIQUE TO CHILDREN
CHING, JAMES
    PIANO PLAYING, A PRACTICAL METHOD--A NEW EDITION OF 'PIANO
COOKE, JAMES FRANCIS
    GREAT MEN AND FAMOUS MUSICIANS ON THE ART OF MUSIC
COVIELLO, AMBROSE
    FOUNDATIONS OF PIANOFORTE TECHNIC
COVIELLO, AMBROSE
    WHAT MATTHAY MEANT
CURCIO, LOUISE
    MUSICIAN'S HANDBOOK FOR THE DEVELOPMENT OF MANUAL SUPPLENESS AND
CURCIO, LOUISE
    SINGLE NOTE, THE
DICKERSON, RUTH A.
    NEW APPROACH TO PIANO TECHNIQUE, A
DILLER, ANGELA
    SPLENDOR OF MUSIC, THE
DUNN, JOHN PETRIE
    BASIS OF PIANOFORTE PLAYING, THE
EBERHARDT, GOBY
    MY SYSTEM FOR PRACTICING THE VIOLIN AND PIANO, BASED UPON
EISENBERG, JACOB
    ARTISTIC PIANIST, THE ..NATURAL TECHNICS IN PIANO MASTERY..FROM
EISENBERG, JACOB
    WEIGHT AND RELAXATION METHOD FOR THE PIANOFORTE
EVERHART, POWELL
    PIANIST'S ART, THE ..A COMPREHENSIVE MANUAL ON PIANO PLAYING FOR

FIELDEN, THOMAS
    SCIENCE OF PIANOFORTE TECHNIC, THE --2ND. REV. ED.---1927
GAT, JOZSEF
    TECHNIQUE OF PIANO PLAYING, THE, --2ND. ED.---1958
GIESEKING, WALTER *
    PIANO TECHNIQUE---COMBINED REPUBLICATION OF..'THE SHORTEST WAY TO
GLASFORD, IRENE A.
    RHYTHM, REASON AND RESPONSE FOR THE MUSICIAN, PIANIST AND TEACHER
GRABILL, ETHELBERT WARREN
    MECHANICS OF PIANO TECHNIC, THE
HARRISON, SIDNEY
    YOUNG PERSON'S GUIDE TO PLAYING THE PIANO, THE
HOFFMAN, CARL
    HABIT IN PIANOFORTE PLAYING--ANALYTICAL STUDY OF CONTROL OF
JACKSON, EDWIN WARD
    GYMNASTICS FOR THE FINGERS AND WRIST
JOHNSTONE, J. ALFRED
    ESSENTIALS IN PIANOFORTE PLAYING, AND OTHER MUSICAL STUDIES...
KOCHEVITSKY, GEORGE
    ART OF PIANO PLAYING, THE ..A SCIENTIFIC APPROACH
LAWRENCE, FREDERIC LOCKE
    RATIONALE OF PIANO TECHNIQUE, THE
LEFRANK, E.
    HUMAN HAND, THE ..ITS CONSTRUCTION, MUSCLES, NERVES AND TENDONS IN
LEVINSKAYA, MARIA
    LEVINSKAYA SYSTEM OF PIANOFORTE TECHNIC AND TONE COLOR, THE
MAIER, GUY
    PIANO TEACHER'S COMPANION, THE
MASON, WILLIAM G.
    SYSTEM OF TECHNICAL EXERCISES FOR THE PIANO-FORTE, A
MATTHAY, TOBIAS A.
    ACT OF TOUCH IN ALL ITS DIVERSITY, THE ..AN ANALYSIS AND SYNTHESIS
MATTHAY, TOBIAS A.
    EPITOME OF THE LAWS OF PIANOFORTE TECHNIQUE, AN
MATTHAY, TOBIAS A.
    FIRST PRINCIPLES OF PIANOFORTE PLAYING--EXTRACT FROM 'THE ACT OF
MATTHAY, TOBIAS A.
    PIANOFORTE TONE-PRODUCTION---SAME AS 'THE ACT OF TOUCH IN ALL ITS
MATTHAY, TOBIAS A.
    PIANO FALLACIES OF TODAY
MATTHAY, TOBIAS A.
    VISIBLE AND INVISIBLE IN PIANOFORTE TECHNIC, THE ..BEING A DIGEST
MEIER, NELLIE SIMMONS
    LIONS' PAWS..THE STORY OF FAMOUS HANDS--INCLUDES MUSICIANS...JOSE
MININBERG, IAN
    VISUAL APPROACH TO PIANO TECHNIQUE, A
NEWMAN, WILLIAM S.
    PIANIST'S PROBLEMS, THE ..A MODERN APPROACH TO EFFICIENT PRACTICE
ORTMANN, OTTO
    PHYSIOLOGICAL MECHANICS OF PIANO TECHNIQUE, THE ---1929
OSTROVSKY, HENRY
    TECHNIQUE AND HAND DEVELOPMENT---USE OF A MACHINE
PEARCE, CHARLES WILLIAM
    ART OF THE PIANO TEACHER, THE
PRENTICE THOMAS RIDLEY
    HAND GYMNASTICS, FOR THE SCIENTIFIC DEVELOPMENT OF THE MUSCLES
RAMUL, PETER
    PSYCHO-PHYSICAL FOUNDATIONS OF MODERN PIANO TECHNIQUE, THE
REEDER, BETAH
    SINGING TOUCH, THE
ROBILLIARD, EILEEN D.
    PERSISTENT PIANIST, THE ..A BOOK FOR THE LATE BEGINNER AND THE
RUBINSTEIN, BERYL
    OUTLINE OF PIANO PEDAGOGY--REV. ED.----1929
SCHAUFFLER, LAWRENCE
    PIANO TECHNIC..MYTH OR SCIENCE
SCHMITZ, ELIE ROBERT
    CAPTURE OF INSPIRATION, THE
SCHNEIDER, HANS
    WORKING OF THE MIND IN PIANO TEACHING AND PLAYING, THE
SCHULTZ, ARNOLD
    RIDDLE OF THE PIANIST'S FINGER, THE
SMITH, MACDONALD
    FROM BRAIN TO KEYBOARD..A SYSTEM OF HAND AND FINGER CONTROL FOR
SUMMY-BIRCHARD COMPANY
    HANDBOOK FOR PIANO TEACHERS..COLLECTED ARTICLES ON SUBJECTS
TAYLER, E. DOUGLAS
    SECRET OF SUCCESSFUL PRACTICE, THE
VANTYN, SIDNEY
    MODERN PIANOFORTE TECHNIQUE
VENABLE, MARY
    INTERPRETATION OF PIANO MUSIC, THE
WEISER, ADOLPH
    TWO RIGHT HANDS..A GUIDE FOR THE DEVELOPMENT OF PIANO TECHNIQUE
WELLS, HOWARD
    PIANIST'S THUMB, THE
WHITEMORE, CUTHBERT
    COMMONSENSE IN PIANOFORTE PLAYING
WHITESIDE, ABBY
    INDISPENSABLES OF PIANO PLAYING--2ND. ED.----1955
WHITESIDE, ABBY
    MASTERING THE CHOPIN ETUDES AND OTHER ESSAYS
WHITESIDE, ABBY
    PIANIST'S MECHANISM, THE
WIER, ALBERT
    PIANO, THE ..ITS HISTORY, MAKERS, PLAYERS AND MUSIC
WOODHOUSE, GEORGE
    CREATIVE TECHNIQUE, FOR ARTISTS IN GENERAL AND PIANISTS IN

Physical Attitude

ALLEN, MARGARET *
    CREATIVE MOTION
ANON
    GUIDE TO THE MUSICAL TUITION OF VERY YOUNG CHILDREN, BY AN OLD
BARTH, HANS
    TECHNIC..FOR DEVELOPING AN EARLY FOUNDATION IN PIANO PLAYING
BERGER, FRANCESCO
    FIRST STEPS AT THE PIANOFORTE
BERTINI, HENRI
    BERTINI'S SELF-TEACHING CATECHISM OF MUSIC FOR THE PIANOFORTE
BLOCKLEY, JOHN
    PIANIST'S CATECHISM, THE ---1880
BOLTON, HETTY
    ON TEACHING THE PIANO
BONPENSIERE, LUIGI
    NEW PATHWAYS TO PIANO TECHNIQUE..A STUDY OF THE RELATIONS BETWEEN
BOOTH, VICTOR
    WE PIANO TEACHERS--REVISED BY ADELE FRANKLIN---1946
BOWEN, CAROLYN
    OUTLINES FOR TRAINING PIANO TEACHERS
BOWEN, YORK
    SIMPLICITY OF PIANO TECHNIQUE, THE
BRANDT, LEONIE
    SCIENCE IN MODERN PIANOFORTE PLAYING
BREE, MADAME MALWINE
    GROUNDWORK OF THE LESCHETIZKY METHOD, THE ---1902

BREITHAUPT, RUDOLPH MARIA
    NATURAL PIANO-TECHNIC..SCHOOL OF WEIGHT TOUCH--2 VOLS.
BROWER, HARRIETTE
    ART OF THE PIANIST, THE
BROWER, HARRIETTE
    HOW A DEPENDABLE PIANO TECHNIQUE WAS WON
BROWER, HARRIETTE
    SELF-HELP IN PIANO STUDY
BRUXNER, MERVYN
    MASTERING THE PIANO
CALAND, ELIZABETH
    ARTISTIC PIANO PLAYING, AS TAUGHT BY LUDWIG DEPPE
CALLENDER, ROMAINE
    TEACHER'S MANUAL, A WORK DESIGNED TO SUPPLEMENT...'THE FIRST TEN
CAMPBELL, LE ROY B.
    TRUE FUNCTION OF RELAXATION IN PIANO PLAYING, THE
CAMPBELL, LE ROY B.
    VELOCITY PLUS
CARPE, ADOLPH
    PIANIST AND THE ART OF MUSIC, THE ..A TREATISE ON PIANO PLAYING
CARRE, JOHN
    PSYCHOLOGY OF PIANO TEACHING, THE ..A TEXTBOOK FOR TEACHERS,
CARRENO, TERESA
    POSSIBILITIES OF TONE COLOR BY ARTISTIC USE OF PEDALS
CARUTHERS, JULIA LOIS
    PIANO TECHNIC FOR CHILDREN
CARY, MRS. C. S. P.
    PIANO-FORTE CLASS BOOK, CONTAINING PRACTICAL RUDIMENTAL LESSONS
CHAPOL, SIMON
    NEW APPROACH TO THE STUDY OF THE PIANOFORTE, A ---IN ITALIAN AND
CHASE, MARY WOOD
    NATURAL LAWS IN PIANO TECHNIC
CHING, JAMES
    AMATEUR PIANIST'S COMPANION, THE
CHING, JAMES
    FOREARM ROTATION---A SEQUEL TO 'THE ROTARY ROAD'--15 PHOTOS AND
CHING, JAMES
    ON TEACHING PIANO TECHNIQUE TO CHILDREN
CHING, JAMES
    PIANO PLAYING, A PRACTICAL METHOD--A NEW EDITION OF 'PIANO
CHING, JAMES
    SIDELIGHTS ON TOUCH..TOGETHER WITH 101 QUESTIONS, SUITABLE FOR
COVIELLO, AMBROSE
    FOUNDATIONS OF PIANOFORTE TECHNIC
COVIELLO, AMBROSE
    WHAT MATTHAY MEANT
CZERNY, CARL
    COMPLETE THEORETICAL AND PRACTICAL PIANO FORTE SCHOOL, FROM THE
DANIELS, BESS *
    WORLD OF MUSIC, THE ..PIANO COURSE..TEACHERS' BOOK, FOR CLASS OR
DENHAM, GEORGE
    MASTERY OF THE KEYBOARD
DICKERSON, RUTH A.
    NEW APPROACH TO PIANO TECHNIQUE, A
DUFFEE, GERTRUDE BANKS
    PIANO STUDY..A GUIDE TO TEACHER AND STUDENT
DUMM, ROBERT W.
    IN BLACK AND WHITE
DUNN, JOHN PETRIE
    BASIS OF PIANOFORTE PLAYING, THE
DUSSEK, JOHANN L.
    DUSSEK'S INSTRUCTIONS ON THE ART OF PLAYING THE PIANOFORTE OR
EBERHARDT, GOBY
    MY SYSTEM FOR PRACTICING THE VIOLIN AND PIANO, BASED UPON
EHRENFECTER, C. A.
    TECHNICAL STUDY IN THE ART OF PIANOFORTE PLAYING--DEPPE'S
EHRLICH, ALFRED HEINRICH
    HOW TO PRACTICE ON THE PIANO..REFLECTIONS AND SUGGESTIONS
EISENBERG, JACOB
    ARTISTIC PIANIST, THE ..NATURAL TECHNICS IN PIANO MASTERY..FROM
EISENBERG, JACOB
    WEIGHT AND RELAXATION METHOD FOR THE PIANOFORTE
EVERHART, POWELL
    PIANIST'S ART, THE ..A COMPREHENSIVE MANUAL ON PIANO PLAYING FOR
FERGUSON, DONALD NIVISON
    PIANO MUSIC OF SIX GREAT COMPOSERS---1947
FROST, EDWARD
    THALBEGARIAN (SIC) EXERCISES..OR, THE PIANIST'S DESIDERATA
GARROWAY, WILL
    PIANISM
GAT, JOZSEF
    TECHNIQUE OF PIANO PLAYING, THE, --2ND. ED.---1958
GEARY, ELEANOR MARGARET
    MUSICAL EDUCATION, WITH PRACTICAL OBSERVATIONS ON THE ART OF
GEIB, WILLIAM
    GEIB'S PIANO-FORTE PRECEPTOR, AND MUSICAL GRAMMAR...A TREATISE ON
GERMER, HEINRICH
    THEORETICO-PRACTICAL ELEMENTARY PIANO-FORTE SCHOOL FOR STUDENTS OF
GIESEKING, WALTER *
    PIANO TECHNIQUE---COMBINED REPUBLICATION OF..'THE SHORTEST WAY TO
GLASFORD, IRENE A.
    RHYTHM, REASON AND RESPONSE FOR THE MUSICIAN, PIANIST AND TEACHER
HAMILTON, CLARENCE G.
    TOUCH AND EXPRESSION IN PIANO PLAYING
HANSMANN, RICHARD
    THEORETICAL AND PRACTICAL PIANO-FORTE SCHOOL FOR THE JANKO
HARKNESS, ROBERT
    BEGINNERS PIANO COURSE IN HYMN PLAYING BY CORRESPONDENCE
HARRISON, SIDNEY
    PIANO TECHNIQUE
HEERINGEN, ERNEST VON
    CELEBRATED INSTRUCTION BOOK FOR THE PIANOFORTE, CONTAINING THE
HEIDELBERGER, PAULINE
    MASTER METHOD..PIANO NORMAL AND TEACHER'S MANUAL
HELMANN, JACOB N.
    CONSCIOUSLY CONTROLLED PIANO TONE, THE --REV. ED.---1950
HOFFMAN, CARL
    HABIT IN PIANOFORTE PLAYING--ANALYTICAL STUDY OF CONTROL OF
HOFHEIMER, GRACE
    TEACHING TECHNIQUES FOR THE PIANO
HOFMANN, JOSEF
    PIANO PLAYING..A LITTLE BOOK OF SIMPLE SUGGESTIONS--REPRINTED FROM
HOPE, ERIC
    HANDBOOK OF PIANO PLAYING, A
HORROCKS, CYRIL R. H.
    STUDENT'S GUIDE TO THE ART OF TEACHING THE PIANOFORTE, THE --2ND.
HUENTEN, FRANZ
    ABRIDGED EDITION OF F. HUENTEN'S CELEBRATED INSTRUCTIONS FOR THE
HUMMEL, JOHANN NEPOMUK
    COMPLETE THEORETICAL AND PRACTICAL COURSE OF INSTRUCTIONS ON THE
JOHNS, CLAYTON
    ESSENTIALS OF PIANOFORTE PLAYING, THE
JOHNSTONE, J. ALFRED
    ART OF TEACHING PIANOFORTE PLAYING, THE --2ND. REV. ED.---1910
JONAS, ALBERTO
    PIANOSCRIPT BOOK..AN INVALUABLE AID TO TEACHER AND STUDENT IN
KLECZYNSKI, JAN
    HOW TO PLAY CHOPIN--THREE LECTURES

KOCHEVITSKY, GEORGE
  ART OF PIANO PLAYING, THE ..A SCIENTIFIC APPROACH
KRUSZYNSKI, MICHAL
  APPROACH TO THE PSYCHOLOGY OF PIANO TEACHING, AN
LANG, EDITH *
  MUSICAL ACCOMPANIMENT OF MOVING PICTURES..A PRACTICAL MANUAL FOR
LAST, JOAN
  YOUNG PIANIST, THE ..A NEW APPROACH FOR TEACHERS AND
LAWRENCE, FREDERIC LOCKE
  RATIONALE OF PIANO TECHNIQUE, THE
LEFRANK, E.
  HUMAN HAND, THE ..ITS CONSTRUCTION, MUSCLES, NERVES AND TENDONS IN
LEIMER, KARL *
  RHYTHMICS, DYNAMICS, PEDAL, AND OTHER PROBLEMS OF PIANO
LEIMER, KARL *
  SHORTEST WAY TO PIANISTIC PERFECTION, THE
LEVINSKAYA, MARIA
  LEVINSKAYA SYSTEM OF PIANOFORTE TECHNIC AND TONE COLOR, THE
LHEVINNE, JOSEF
  BASIC PRINCIPLES IN PIANOFORTE PLAYING---1924
LOMAS, LULU GRAHAM
  FIRST TEN PIANO LESSONS, LAID OUT FOR YOUNG TEACHERS, WITH
MAIER, GUY
  PIANO TEACHER'S COMPANION, THE
MASON, WILLIAM G. *
  SYSTEM FOR BEGINNERS IN THE ART OF PLAYING UPON THE PIANOFORTE, A
MATHEWS, WILLIAM S. B.
  TEACHER'S MANUAL OF MASON'S PIANOFORTE TECHNICS
MATTHAY, TOBIAS A.
  ACT OF TOUCH IN ALL ITS DIVERSITY, THE ..AN ANALYSIS AND SYNTHESIS
MATTHAY, TOBIAS A.
  CHILD'S FIRST STEPS IN PIANOFORTE PLAYING, THE
MATTHAY, TOBIAS A.
  EPITOME OF THE LAWS OF PIANOFORTE TECHNIQUE, AN
MATTHAY, TOBIAS A.
  FIRST LIGHTS ON PIANO-PLAYING
MATTHAY, TOBIAS A.
  FOREARM ROTATION PRINCIPLE IN PIANOFORTE PLAYING, THE ..ITS
MATTHAY, TOBIAS A.
  ON METHOD IN TEACHING
MATTHAY, TOBIAS A.
  PIANOFORTE TONE-PRODUCTION---SAME AS 'THE ACT OF TOUCH IN ALL ITS
MATTHAY, TOBIAS A.
  PIANO FALLACIES OF TODAY
MATTHAY, TOBIAS A.
  PROBLEMS OF AGILITY, THE
MATTHAY, TOBIAS A.
  RELAXATION STUDIES IN THE MUSCULAR DISCRIMINATION REQUIRED FOR
MATTHAY, TOBIAS A.
  SOME COMMENTARIES ON THE TEACHING OF PIANOFORTE TECHNIC..A
MATTHAY, TOBIAS A.
  VISIBLE AND INVISIBLE IN PIANOFORTE TECHNIC, THE ..BEING A DIGEST
MCARTHUR, ALEXANDER
  PIANOFORTE STUDY..HINTS ON PIANO PLAYING
MCFERRIN, CHARLES BETTEYS
  MOTHER'S PART IN HER CHILD'S MUSICAL EDUCATION, A ..OR, THE THINGS
MERGES, P.
  PRACTICAL RULES FOR PIANOFORTE PLAYING..TEXT BOOK FOR TEACHERS AND
MERRICK, FRANK
  PRACTICING THE PIANO
MININBERG, IAN
  VISUAL APPROACH TO PIANO TECHNIQUE, A
MOTT, ISAAC H. R.
  ADVICE AND INSTRUCTIONS FOR PLAYING THE PIANOFORTE WITH EXPRESSION
NICCHIA, LILLIAN
  PIANOFORTE STUDY..HINTS ON PIANO PLAYING
NIXON, W.
  GUIDE TO INSTRUCTION ON THE PIANOFORTE, A --IN A SERIES OF SHORT
OLIVER, EDWARD B.
  PRACTICAL TEXT-BOOK OF MUSIC, AS CONNECTED WITH THE ART OF PLAYING
ORTMANN, OTTO
  PHYSIOLOGICAL MECHANICS OF PIANO TECHNIQUE, THE ---1929
PALME, RUDOLPH
  FIRST MONTHS IN PIANOFORTE INSTRUCTION, THE ---1870, IN GERMAN
PHILIPP, LILLIE H.
  PIANO STUDY..APPLICATION AND TECHNIQUE
PLAIDY, LOUIS
  PIANOFORTE TEACHER'S GUIDE, THE
POTAMKIN, FRANK
  MODERN PIANO PEDAGOGY
PRENTNER, MARIE
  MODERN PIANIST..BEING MY EXPERIENCES IN THE TECHNIQUE AND
REEDER, BETAH
  SINGING TOUCH, THE
RHODES, ALFRED
  CURIOSITIES OF THE KEY-BOARD AND THE STAFF...SHOWN TO BE UPON A
RICHARDSON, NATHAN
  NEW METHOD FOR THE PIANOFORTE..ADDED, RUDIMENTS OF HARMONY AND
RICKER, EARL
  MUSIC LESSONS FOR YOUR CHILD
ROBYN, LOUISE
  TECHNIC TALES FOR THE CHILD AT THE PIANO--BKS. 1-3..TEACHER'S
ROEDER, ELWOOD S.
  TIME-SPACE CONCEPTION OF THE GEOMETRY AND SPEED OF MOTION AT THE
ROOT, CATHERINE ADAMS *
  LISTEN, SING AND PLAY..CLASS LESSONS FOR PIANO AND VOICE
RUBINSTEIN, BERYL
  OUTLINE OF PIANO PEDAGOGY--REV. ED.---1929
SCHAUFFLER, LAWRENCE
  PIANO TECHNIC..MYTH OR SCIENCE
SCHELLING, ERNEST *
  OXFORD PIANO COURSE, TEACHER'S FIRST MANUAL
SCHULTZ, ARNOLD
  RIDDLE OF THE PIANIST'S FINGER, THE
SIMPSON, ELIZABETH
  BASIC PIANOFORTE TECHNIQUE...BASED ON THE SCIENCE OF PIANOFORTE
SPENCER, ALLEN
  FOUNDATION OF PIANO TECHNIC, THE
SUMMY-BIRCHARD COMPANY
  HANDBOOK FOR PIANO TEACHERS..COLLECTED ARTICLES ON SUBJECTS
TOBIN, JOSEPH RAYMOND
  FUN WITH FINGERING, A FIRST-OF-ALL BOOK ON EASY FINGERING AND
TOMLINSON, ANNA M.
  ANNA M. TOMLINSON'S FORTY LESSONS ON HOW TO DEVELOP A PIANO HAND
TUFTS, JOHN W.
  TECHNIC AND NOTATION AS APPLIED TO THE PIANOFORTE
UNSCHULD, MARIE VON
  PIANIST'S HAND, THE ..A SYSTEMATIC METHOD...ACCORDING TO THE
VANTYN, SIDNEY
  MODERN PIANOFORTE TECHNIQUE
VENABLE, MARY
  INTERPRETATION OF PIANO MUSIC, THE
VIRGIL, ALMON K.
  EDUCATION IN MUSIC..LESSONS TO TEACHERS IN THE INSTRUCTION OF
VIRGIL, ALMON K.
  FOUNDATION EXERCISES IN PIANO PLAYING FROM FIRST RUDIMENTS TO

VIRGIL, ALMON K.
  STEP BY STEP..TEXTBOOK IN PIANO PLAYING..HANDBOOK FOR TEACHERS
WEISER, ADOLPH
  TWO RIGHT HANDS..A GUIDE FOR THE DEVELOPMENT OF PIANO TECHNIQUE
WELLS, HOWARD
  EARS, BRAIN AND FINGERS..A TEXT BOOK FOR PIANO TEACHERS AND PUPILS
WELLS, HOWARD
  PIANIST'S THUMB, THE
WESTBROOK, BENJAMIN V.
  SYSTEM OF STUDY OF SCALES AND CHORDS, A ..BEING CHAPTERS ON THE
WHITEMORE, CUTHBERT
  COMMONSENSE IN PIANOFORTE PLAYING
WHITESIDE, ABBY
  INDISPENSABLES OF PIANO PLAYING--2ND. ED.---1955
WHITESIDE, ABBY
  MASTERING THE CHOPIN ETUDES AND OTHER ESSAYS
WHITESIDE, ABBY
  PIANIST'S MECHANISM, THE
WILKINS-GUTMANN, EMMA
  TALKS WITH PIANO TEACHERS
WILLIAMS, JEAN E.
  MODERN METHOD OF PIANO INSTRUCTION, A ..TEACHERS MANUAL
WINNER, SEPTIMUS
  WINNER'S NEW SCHOOL FOR THE PIANO, IN WHICH THE INSTRUCTIONS ARE
WOODHOUSE, GEORGE
  FROM KEYBOARD TO MUSIC
WOODHOUSE, GEORGE
  REALISTIC APPROACH TO PIANO PLAYING, A
WRIGHT, WILLIAM C.
  PIANOFORTE MANUAL, THE ..DESIGNED AS A COMPLETE PIANOFORTE PRIMER

Gymnastics

ANON
  ESSAY ON THE CHIROGYMNAST..OR, FINGER EXERCISES APPLIED TO...ALL
ARNIM, ANNA E.
  COMPLETE COURSE OF WRIST AND FINGER GYMNASTICS, A --3RD.
BAUER, HAROLD
  PIANIST'S WARMING-UP EXERCISES FOR THE MAINTENANCE AND IMPROVEMENT
BRECKENRIDGE, WILLIAM KILGORE
  HINTS FOR PIANO NORMAL STUDIES
BROTHERHOOD, JAMES
  BROTHERHOOD 'TECHNICON' AND HOW TO USE IT, THE
BROTHERHOOD, JAMES
  DEVELOPMENT OF THE HAND FOR PIANO-FORTE PLAYING BY MEANS OF A
BROTHERHOOD, JAMES
  SCIENCE AND ART AS TWIN SISTERS..BEING A SECOND TREATISE UPON THE
BROWER, HARRIETTE
  HOW A DEPENDABLE PIANO TECHNIQUE WAS WON
BROWER, HARRIETTE
  SELF-HELP IN PIANO STUDY
CALAND, ELIZABETH
  ARTISTIC PIANO PLAYING, AS TAUGHT BY LUDWIG DEPPE
CALLENDER, ROMAINE
  TEACHER'S MANUAL, A WORK DESIGNED TO SUPPLEMENT...'THE FIRST TEN
CAMPBELL, LE ROY B.
  TRUE FUNCTION OF RELAXATION IN PIANO PLAYING, THE
CARMIENCKE, ALBERT G.
  MECHANICS OF PIANO PLAYING, THE
CHING, JAMES
  FOREARM ROTATION---A SEQUEL TO 'THE ROTARY ROAD'--15 PHOTOS AND
CURCIO, LOUISE
  MUSICIAN'S HANDBOOK FOR THE DEVELOPMENT OF MANUAL SUPPLENESS AND
FIELDEN, THOMAS
  SCIENCE OF PIANOFORTE TECHNIC, THE --2ND. REV. ED.---1927
GARRATT, PERCIVAL
  ART OF PIANOFORTE PLAYING, THE
GAT, JOZSEF
  TECHNIQUE OF PIANO PLAYING, THE, --2ND. ED.---1958
GLASFORD, IRENE A.
  RHYTHM, REASON AND RESPONSE FOR THE MUSICIAN, PIANIST AND TEACHER
HEIDELBERGER, PAULINE
  MASTER METHOD..PIANO NORMAL AND TEACHER'S MANUAL
HOPE, ERIC
  AIDS TO TECHNIQUE
JACKSON, EDWIN WARD
  GYMNASTICS FOR THE FINGERS AND WRIST
KRUSZYNSKI, MICHAL
  APPROACH TO THE PSYCHOLOGY OF PIANO TEACHING, AN
MACLEAN, CHARLES D.
  PRINCIPLES OF PIANOFORTE PRACTICE, THE
MATTHAY, TOBIAS A.
  NINE STEPS TOWARDS 'FINGER INDIVIDUALIZATION' THROUGH FOREARM
O'REAR, MRS. ASBURY S.
  SELF READING NOTES
PARSONS, ALBERT R.
  SCIENCE OF PIANO PRACTICE, THE
PARSONS, ALBERT R.
  SYNTHETIC METHOD FOR THE PIANOFORTE, THE
PHILIPP, LILLIE H.
  PIANO STUDY..APPLICATION AND TECHNIQUE
POWERS-WADSWORTH, L.
  PIANIST'S GUIDE TO TECHNICAL FREEDOM, THE ..2 VOLS. IN 1
PRENTICE THOMAS RIDLEY
  HAND GYMNASTICS, FOR THE SCIENTIFIC DEVELOPMENT OF THE MUSCLES
RENNIE, BLANCHE H.
  HAND CULTURE FOR PIANISTS, VIOLINISTS AND 'CELLISTS--FINGER, HAND
ROBYN, LOUISE
  HAND BUILDING AND HAND STRETCHING EXERCISES
ROBYN, LOUISE
  HOW TO TEACH PIANO TO THE CHILD BEGINNER..A TEXT BOOK FOR TEACHERS
ROEDER, CARL M.
  LIBERATION AND DELIBERATION IN PIANO TECHNIC
SCHULTZ, ARNOLD
  RIDDLE OF THE PIANIST'S FINGER, THE
SMITH, MACDONALD
  FROM BRAIN TO KEYBOARD..A SYSTEM OF HAND AND FINGER CONTROL FOR
TAYLER, E. DOUGLAS
  SECRET OF SUCCESSFUL PRACTICE, THE
TOWNSEND, WILLIAM
  BALANCE OF ARM IN PIANO TECHNIQUE--4TH. REV. ED.---1903
VIRGIL, ALMON K.
  EDUCATION IN MUSIC..LESSONS TO TEACHERS IN THE INSTRUCTION OF
VIRGIL, ALMON K.
  FOUNDATION EXERCISES IN PIANO PLAYING FROM FIRST RUDIMENTS TO
VIRGIL, ALMON K.
  STEP BY STEP..TEXTBOOK IN PIANO PLAYING..HANDBOOK FOR TEACHERS
VIRGIL, ALMON K.
  TECHNIPHONE MANUAL..INSTRUCTIONS AND EXERCISES IN THE USE OF THE
VIRGIL, ANTHA MINERVA
  INSTRUCTIVE TALKS TO PIANO STUDENTS
VIRGIL, ANTHA MINERVA
  VIRGIL METHOD OF PIANOFORTE TECHNIC, THE --2 VOLS.
WOOD, CHARLES W.
  FINGER AND WRIST GYMNASTICS--WITHOUT USE OF PIANO--FOR PIANO

Fingering

AHRENS, CORA B. *
  FOR ALL PIANO TEACHERS
AMEY, ELLEN
  CONSCIOUS CONTROL IN PIANO STUDY
ANON
  COMPLEAT TUTOR FOR THE HARPSICHORD OR SPINNET, WHEREIN IS SHEWN
ANON
  FASHIONABLE PRECEPTOR, FOR THE PIANO-FORTE AND HARPSICHORD,
ANON
  NEW AND COMPLETE INSTRUCTIONS FOR THE HARPSICHORD, PIANO FORTE OR
ANON
  NEW INSTRUCTIONS FOR PLAYING THE HARPSICHORD, PIANOFORTE OR
ANON
  PLAYING THE HARPSICHORD, SPINET OR PIANO FORTE MADE EASY BY NEW
ANON
  PRECEPTOR, FOR THE PIANOFORTE, THE ORGAN OR HARPSICHORD, THE
BABBITT, WILLIAM
  PHYSIOLOGICAL METHOD FOR PLAYING THE PIANO-FORTE, DESIGNED AS A
BABITZ, SOL
  ON USING EARLY KEYBOARD FINGERING--REPRINT OF 3 ARTICLES FROM THE
BACH, CARL PHILIPP EMANUEL
  ESSAY ON THE TRUE ART OF PLAYING KEYBOARD INSTRUMENTS---TWO PTS.,
BARTHELEMON, FRANCOIS H.
  NEW TUTOR FOR THE HARPSICHORD OR PIANO FORTE, WHEREIN THE FIRST
BEMETZRIEDER, ANTON
  GAMUT AND COMMON CHORD IN ALL KEYS, FINGERED FOR THE HARPSICHORD,
BEMETZRIEDER, ANTON
  NEW GUIDE TO MUSIC, IN FRENCH AND ENGLISH, A
BOLTON, HETTY
  HOW TO PRACTICE
BONPENSIERE, LUIGI
  NEW PATHWAYS TO PIANO TECHNIQUE..A STUDY OF THE RELATIONS BETWEEN
BOOTH, VICTOR
  WE PIANO TEACHERS--REVISED BY ADELE FRANKLIN---1946
BRANDT, LEONIE
  SCIENCE IN MODERN PIANOFORTE PLAYING
BREE, MADAME MALWINE
  GROUNDWORK OF THE LESCHETIZKY METHOD, THE ---1902
BRIGHAM, ELEANOR
  SCALES..THEIR HISTORY, THEORY, FINGERING AND TECHNICAL USE ON THE
BROWER, HARRIETTE
  HOW A DEPENDABLE PIANO TECHNIQUE WAS WON
BROWER, HARRIETTE
  SELF-HELP IN PIANO STUDY
BUCHAROFF, SIMON
  MODERN PIANIST'S TEXT BOOK, THE
BUCKLEY, OLIVIA DUSSEK
  MUSICAL TRUTHS..OR, AN ANALYSIS OF MUSIC AND AN ESSAY ON THE PAST
CARPE, ADOLPH
  PIANIST AND THE ART OF MUSIC, THE ..A TREATISE ON PIANO PLAYING
CARR, BENJAMIN
  ANALYTICAL INSTRUCTOR FOR THE PIANO FORTE, OP. 15, THE --IN 3 PTS.
CARRE, JOHN
  PSYCHOLOGY OF PIANO TEACHING, THE ..A TEXTBOOK FOR TEACHERS,
CARUTHERS, JULIA LOIS
  PIANO TECHNIC FOR CHILDREN
CHAROL, SIMON
  NEW APPROACH TO THE STUDY OF THE PIANOFORTE, A ---IN ITALIAN AND
CHING, JAMES
  CANDIDATE'S COMPANION TO THE EXERCISES, SCALES, BROKEN CHORDS,
CLEMENTI, MUZIO
  INTRODUCTION TO THE ART OF PLAYING ON THE PIANOFORTE---1801+
COPP, EVELYN A.
  WHAT IS THE FLETCHER MUSIC METHOD
COUPERIN, FRANCOIS
  ART DE TOUCHER LE CLAVECIN, L' ---IN FRENCH, GERMAN AND ENGLISH
COVIELLO, AMBROSE
  FOUNDATIONS OF PIANOFORTE TECHNIC
COVIELLO, AMBROSE
  WHAT MATTHAY MEANT
CRAMER, JOHN BAPTIST
  INSTRUCTIONS FOR THE PIANOFORTE---CONTAINS ALSO A SET OF 28
CROUCH, M. S.
  SYSTEMATIC FINGERING OF THE ARPEGGIOS OF COMMON CHORDS, ETC., THE
CURCIO, LOUISE
  SINGLE NOTE, THE
CURWEN, ANNIE JESSY
  PSYCHOLOGY APPLIED TO MUSIC TEACHING
CZERNY, CARL
  LETTERS TO A YOUNG LADY ON THE ART OF PLAYING THE PIANOFORTE
DEUTSCH, LEONHARD
  PIANO..GUIDED SIGHT-READING
DE WITT, EDYTHE
  EDYTHE DE WITT'S METHOD FOR CLASS PIANO...WRITTEN TO GIVE CORRECT
DILLER, ANGELA
  SPLENDOR OF MUSIC, THE
DOBBIE, E. A.
  AUSTRALIAN PIANOFORTE TUTOR
DOLMETSCH, ARNOLD
  INTERPRETATION OF MUSIC OF THE SEVENTEENTH AND EIGHTEENTH
DUCKWORTH, GUY
  KEYBOARD MUSICIANSHIP
DUFFEE, GERTRUDE BANKS
  PIANO STUDY..A GUIDE TO TEACHER AND STUDENT
DUMESNIL, MAURICE
  HOW TO PLAY AND TEACH DEBUSSY
DUSSEK, JOHANN L.
  DUSSEK'S INSTRUCTIONS ON THE ART OF PLAYING THE PIANOFORTE OR
EBERHARDT, GOBY
  MY SYSTEM FOR PRACTICING THE VIOLIN AND PIANO, BASED UPON
EHRENFECTER, C. A.
  TECHNICAL STUDY IN THE ART OF PIANOFORTE PLAYING--DEPPE'S
EISENBERG, JACOB
  ARTISTIC PIANIST, THE ..NATURAL TECHNICS IN PIANO MASTERY..FROM
EISENBERG, JACOB
  WEIGHT AND RELAXATION METHOD FOR THE PIANOFORTE
FALKENER, ROBERT
  INSTRUCTIONS FOR PLAYING THE HARPSICHORD..WHEREIN IS FULLY
FERGUSON, DONALD NIVISON
  PIANO MUSIC OF SIX GREAT COMPOSERS---1947
FIELDEN, THOMAS
  MARKS AND REMARKS..MUSICAL EXAMINATIONS AND THEIR PROBLEMS
FIELDEN, THOMAS
  SCIENCE OF PIANOFORTE TECHNIC, THE --2ND. REV. ED.---1927
FOOTE, ARTHUR W.
  SOME PRACTICAL THINGS IN PIANO PLAYING
GARRATT, PERCIVAL
  ART OF PIANOFORTE PLAYING, THE
GARROWAY, WILL
  PIANISM
GAT, JOZSEF
  TECHNIQUE OF PIANO PLAYING, THE, --2ND. ED.---1958
GEARY, ELEANOR MARGARET
  MUSICAL EDUCATION, WITH PRACTICAL OBSERVATIONS ON THE ART OF
GEIB, WILLIAM
  GEIB'S PIANO-FORTE PRECEPTOR, AND MUSICAL GRAMMAR...A TREATISE ON

GIESEKING, WALTER *
  PIANO TECHNIQUE---COMBINED REPUBLICATION OF.. 'THE SHORTEST WAY TO
GRABILL, ETHELBERT WARREN
  MECHANICS OF PIANO TECHNIC, THE
GRUNDY, ENID
  HAPPY PIANIST, THE
HAMBOURG, MARK
  HOW TO PLAY THE PIANO--NEW AND ENLARGED EDITION OF 'HOW TO BECOME
HAMBOURG, MARK
  HOW TO PREPARE FOR PLAYING IN CONCERT
HANSMANN, RICHARD
  THEORETICAL AND PRACTICAL PIANO-FORTE SCHOOL FOR THE JANKO
HARICH-SCHNEIDER, ETA
  HARPSICHORD, THE ..AN INTRODUCTION TO TECHNIQUE, STYLE AND THE
HECK, JOHANN CASPAR
  ART OF FINGERING, THE ..OR, THE EASIEST AND SUREST METHOD HOW TO
HEIDELBERGER, PAULINE
  MASTER METHOD..PIANO NORMAL AND TEACHER'S MANUAL
HELD, ERNST
  RULES AND REASONS FOR CORRECT SCALE-FINGERING
HENDERSON, WILLIAM JAMES
  PRELUDES AND STUDIES..MUSICAL THEMES OF THE DAY--SECTION 3..THE
HERZ, HENRI
  NEW AND COMPLETE PIANOFORTE SCHOOL
HUENTEN, FRANZ
  ABRIDGED EDITION OF F. HUENTEN'S CELEBRATED INSTRUCTIONS FOR THE
HULL, ARTHUR EAGLEFIELD
  THREE HUNDRED QUESTIONS ON PIANOFORTE TEACHING IN 30 GRADUATED
HUTCHESON, ERNEST *
  LITERATURE OF THE PIANO, THE ..A GUIDE FOR AMATEUR AND
ISAACS, EDWARD
  BLIND PIANO TEACHER, THE
JOHNSTONE, J. ALFRED
  ART OF TEACHING PIANOFORTE PLAYING, THE --2ND. REV. ED.---1910
JONAS, ALBERTO
  MASTER SCHOOL OF MODERN PIANO PLAYING AND VIRTUOSITY--3 PARTS IN 7
JONES, GRIFFITH
  COMPLEAT INSTRUCTOR FOR THE HARPSICHORD OR PIANOFORTE, THE
KLECZYNSKI, JAN
  HOW TO PLAY CHOPIN--THREE LECTURES
KNOTT, THOMAS B.
  PIANOFORTE FINGERING, ITS PRINCIPLES AND APPLICATIONS
KOCHEVITSKY, GEORGE
  ART OF PIANO PLAYING, THE ..A SCIENTIFIC APPROACH
KUERSTEINER, JEAN PAUL
  EXPERT AID TO ARTISTIC PIANO PLAYING
LAMAR, RICHARD
  COLLEGE PIANO PEDAGOGY
LANDOWSKA, WANDA
  LANDOWSKA ON MUSIC--EDITED BY DENISE RESTOUT
LAST, JOAN
  YOUNG PIANIST, THE ..A NEW APPROACH FOR TEACHERS AND
LEVINE, HENRY
  KNOW YOUR SCALES..FOR PIANO STUDENTS OF ALL GRADES
LOGIER, JOHANN BERNHARD
  FIRST COMPANION TO THE ROYAL PATENT CHIROPLAST OR HAND-DIRECTOR,
LONGSTREET, H. P.
  PRACTICAL FINGER CONTROL--10TH. ED.
MACLEAN, CHARLES D.
  PRINCIPLES OF PIANOFORTE PRACTICE, THE
MAIER, GUY
  PIANO TEACHER'S COMPANION, THE
MARKS, ADOLF B.
  INTRODUCTION TO THE INTERPRETATION OF BEETHOVEN'S PIANO-FORTE
MARX, ADOLF BERNHARD
  INTRODUCTION TO THE INTERPRETATION OF BEETHOVEN'S PIANO
MASON, WILLIAM G. *
  PRIMER OF MUSIC, A ..BEING THE FIRST STEPS IN MUSICIANSHIP..FOR
MASON, WILLIAM G. *
  SYSTEM FOR BEGINNERS IN THE ART OF PLAYING UPON THE PIANOFORTE, A
MATTHAY, TOBIAS A.
  EPITOME OF THE LAWS OF PIANOFORTE TECHNIQUE, AN
MATTHAY, TOBIAS A.
  FIRST PRINCIPLES OF PIANOFORTE PLAYING--EXTRACT FROM 'THE ACT OF
MATTHAY, TOBIAS A.
  MUSICAL INTERPRETATION..ITS LAWS AND PRINCIPLES---1913
MATTHAY, TOBIAS A.
  PRINCIPLES OF FINGERING AND LAWS OF PEDALLING
MATTHAY, TOBIAS A.
  VISIBLE AND INVISIBLE IN PIANOFORTE TECHNIC, THE ..BEING A DIGEST
MERGES, P.
  PRACTICAL RULES FOR PIANOFORTE PLAYING..TEXT BOOK FOR TEACHERS AND
MERRICK, FRANK
  PRACTICING THE PIANO
MILLER, EDWARD
  INSTITUTES OF MUSIC, OR, EASY INSTRUCTIONS FOR THE HARPSICHORD
MOKREJS, JOHN
  SCIENCE OF FINGERING, THE ---FOR PIANO
MUSAFIA, JULIEN
  ART OF FINGERING IN PIANO PLAYING, THE
NETZORG, BENDETSON
  KEY-BOTTOM TONE
NEUHAUS, HEINRICH
  ART OF PIANO PLAYING, THE
NEWMAN, WILLIAM S.
  PIANIST'S PROBLEMS, THE ..A MODERN APPROACH TO EFFICIENT PRACTICE
NIXON, W.
  GUIDE TO INSTRUCTION ON THE PIANOFORTE, A --IN A SERIES OF SHORT
OLIVER, EDWARD B.
  PRACTICAL TEXT-BOOK OF MUSIC, AS CONNECTED WITH THE ART OF PLAYING
ORTMANN, OTTO
  PHYSIOLOGICAL MECHANICS OF PIANO TECHNIQUE, THE ---1929
PALME, RUDOLPH
  FIRST MONTHS IN PIANOFORTE INSTRUCTION, THE ---1870, IN GERMAN
PALMER, HORATIO R.
  PALMER'S PIANO PRIMER
PALMER, KING
  TEACH YOURSELF TO PLAY THE PIANO
PASQUALI, NICOLO
  ART OF FINGERING THE HARPSICHORD, THE
PEARCE, CHARLES WILLIAM
  ART OF THE PIANO TEACHER, THE
PETERSON, FRANKLIN
  THEORETIC COMPANION TO PRACTICE--PART I OF THE PIANIST'S HANDBOOK
PHILIPP, LILLIE H.
  PIANO STUDY..APPLICATION AND TECHNIQUE
PHILLIPSON, WENTWORTH
  GUIDE TO YOUNG PIANOFORTE TEACHERS AND STUDENTS
PRELLEUR, PETER
  HARPSICHORD ILLUSTRATED AND IMPROV'D, WHEREIN IS SHEWN THE ITALIAN
PUPIN, ANNIE
  SCALES, THE ..THEIR FORMATION, FINGERING, AND HOW TO PRACTICE
REINAGLE, CAROLINE
  FEW WORDS ON PIANOFORTE PLAYING, A
RENNIE, BLANCHE H.
  HAND CULTURE FOR PIANISTS, VIOLINISTS AND 'CELLISTS--FINGER, HAND
REZITS, JOSEPH
  SOURCE MATERIALS FOR PIANO TECHNIQUES

REZITS, JOSEPH
    TEACHER'S GUIDE TO THE NEW SCRIBNER MUSIC LIBRARY
RICKER, EARL
    MUSIC LESSONS FOR YOUR CHILD
ROBYN, LOUISE
    TECHNIC TALES FOR THE CHILD AT THE PIANO--BKS. 1-3..TEACHER'S
SCHAUFFLER, LAWRENCE
    PIANO TECHNIC..MYTH OR SCIENCE
SCHERER, HERBERT
    PIANO PRACTICING
SCHMITZ, ELIE ROBERT
    CAPTURE OF INSPIRATION, THE
SCHOTT, HOWARD
    PLAYING THE HARPSICHORD
SCHULTZ, ARNOLD
    RIDDLE OF THE PIANIST'S FINGER, THE
SCONCIA, JOHN A.
    SCONCIA'S NEW SYSTEM OF INSTRUCTION IN MUSIC AS A SCIENCE..OR, A
SEROFF, VICTOR
    COMMON SENSE IN PIANO STUDY
SHEFTEL, PAUL
    EXPLORING KEYBOARD FUNDAMENTALS
SHEPARD, ROBERT
    COMPLETE SCALE AND ARPEGGIO MANUAL
SIMPSON, ELIZABETH
    BASIC PIANOFORTE TECHNIQUE...BASED ON THE SCIENCE OF PIANOFORTE
SLENCZYNSKA, RUTH *
    MUSIC AT YOUR FINGERTIPS
SOREL, CLAUDETTE
    COMPENDIUM OF PIANO TECHNIQUE--39 ETUDES SELECTED FROM OVER 4000,
SPENCER, ALLEN
    FOUNDATION OF PIANO TECHNIC, THE
SQUIRE, RUSSEL N. *
    CLASS PIANO FOR ADULT BEGINNERS--2ND. ED.---1964
SWENSON, LUCILE B.
    DISCOVERING THE PIANO..THE MULTIPLE KEY APPROACH..STUDY GUIDE AND
TAYLER, E. DOUGLAS
    SECRET OF SUCCESSFUL PRACTICE, THE
TAYLOR, FRANKLIN
    PRIMER OF PIANOFORTE PLAYING
TAYLOR, FRANKLIN
    TECHNIQUE AND EXPRESSION IN PIANOFORTE PLAYING
TOBIN, JOSEPH RAYMOND
    COMMON SENSE IN SIGHT READING..A GUIDE FOR PIANO TEACHERS
TOBIN, JOSEPH RAYMOND
    FUN WITH FINGERING, A FIRST-OF-ALL BOOK ON EASY FINGERING AND
TOWNSEND, WILLIAM
    BALANCE OF ARM IN PIANO TECHNIQUE--4TH. REV. ED.---1903
TUFTS, JOHN W.
    TECHNIC AND NOTATION AS APPLIED TO THE PIANOFORTE
TURECK, ROSALYN
    INTRODUCTION TO THE PERFORMANCE OF BACH, AN--3 VOLS.
VANTYN, SIDNEY
    MODERN PIANOFORTE TECHNIQUE
VENABLE, MARY
    INTERPRETATION OF PIANO MUSIC, THE
VINING, HARRISON S.
    SIMPLE AND COMPLETE PRIMER FOR THE PIANOFORTE, THE
VIRGIL, ALMON K.
    EDUCATION IN MUSIC..LESSONS TO TEACHERS IN THE INSTRUCTION OF
VIRGIL, ALMON K.
    FOUNDATION EXERCISES IN PIANO PLAYING FROM FIRST RUDIMENTS TO
VIRGIL, ALMON K.
    STEP BY STEP..TEXTBOOK IN PIANO PLAYING..HANDBOOK FOR TEACHERS
WEISEP, ADOLPH
    TWO RIGHT HANDS..A GUIDE FOR THE DEVELOPMENT OF PIANO TECHNIQUE
WESTBROOK, BENJAMIN V.
    SYSTEM OF STUDY OF SCALES AND CHORDS, A ..BEING CHAPTERS ON THE
WILSON, WILLIAM
    NEW FINGERING NOTATION FOR KEYBOARD MUSIC---REPRODUCED FROM
WINNER, SEPTIMUS
    WINNER'S NEW SCHOOL FOR THE PIANO, IN WHICH THE INSTRUCTIONS ARE
WOODHOUSE, GEORGE
    FROM KEYBOARD TO MUSIC
WRIGHT, WILLIAM C.
    GOLDEN MONITOR, FOR THE PIANOFORTE AND CABINET ORGAN, DESIGNED AS
ZIMMERMAN, ALEX H. *
    BASIC PIANO FOR THE COLLEGE STUDENT

Relaxation

BOLTON, HETTY
    ON TEACHING THE PIANO
BOOTH, VICTOR
    WE PIANO TEACHERS--REVISED BY ADELE FRANKLIN---1946
BREITHAUPT, RUDOLPH MARIA
    NATURAL PIANO-TECHNIC..SCHOOL OF WEIGHT TOUCH--2 VOLS.
BROWER, HARRIETTE
    HOW A DEPENDABLE PIANO TECHNIQUE WAS WON
BROWER, HARRIETTE
    MODERN MASTERS OF THE KEYBOARD
BROWER, HARRIETTE
    PIANO MASTERY..TALKS WITH MASTER PIANISTS AND TEACHERS...
BROWER, HARRIETTE
    PIANO MASTERY, SECOND SERIES
BROWER, HARRIETTE
    SELF-HELP IN PIANO STUDY
CAMPBELL, LE ROY B.
    TRUE FUNCTION OF RELAXATION IN PIANO PLAYING, THE
CAMPBELL, LE ROY B.
    VELOCITY PLUS
CHING, JAMES
    MUSCULAR RELAXATION, A SIMPLE EXPLANATION
CHING, JAMES
    PIANO PLAYING, A PRACTICAL METHOD--A NEW EDITION OF 'PIANO
CHING, JAMES
    SIDELIGHTS ON TOUCH..TOGETHER WITH 101 QUESTIONS, SUITABLE FOR
COVIELLO, AMBROSE
    FOUNDATIONS OF PIANOFORTE TECHNIC
COVIELLO, AMBROSE
    WHAT MATTHAY MEANT
D'ABREU, GERALD
    PLAYING THE PIANO WITH CONFIDENCE---1964
DEUTSCH, LEONHARD
    PIANO..GUIDED SIGHT-READING
EBERHARDT, GOBY
    MY SYSTEM FOR PRACTICING THE VIOLIN AND PIANO, BASED UPON
EISENBERG, JACOB
    ARTISTIC PIANIST, THE ..NATURAL TECHNICS IN PIANO MASTERY..FROM
EISENBERG, JACOB
    WEIGHT AND RELAXATION METHOD FOR THE PIANOFORTE
FIELDEN, THOMAS
    SCIENCE OF PIANOFORTE TECHNIC, THE --2ND. REV. ED.---1927
FOOTE, ARTHUR W.
    SOME PRACTICAL THINGS IN PIANO PLAYING
GAT, JOZSEF
    TECHNIQUE OF PIANO PLAYING, THE, --2ND. ED.---1958

GIESEKING, WALTER *
    PIANO TECHNIQUE--COMBINED REPUBLICATION OF..'THE SHORTEST WAY TO
HAMILTON, CLARENCE G.
    TOUCH AND EXPRESSION IN PIANO PLAYING
HARRISON, SIDNEY
    PIANO TECHNIQUE
HARRISON, SIDNEY
    YOUNG PERSON'S GUIDE TO PLAYING THE PIANO, THE
HELMANN, JACOB N.
    CONSCIOUSLY CONTROLLED PIANO TONE, THE --REV. ED.---1950
JOHNSTONE, J. ALFRED
    ESSENTIALS IN PIANOFORTE PLAYING, AND OTHER MUSICAL STUDIES...
KOCHEVITSKY, GEORGE
    ART OF PIANO PLAYING, THE ..A SCIENTIFIC APPROACH
LAMAR, RICHARD
    COLLEGE PIANO PEDAGOGY
LEIMER, KARL *
    SHORTEST WAY TO PIANISTIC PERFECTION, THE
LEVINSKAYA, MARIA
    LEVINSKAYA SYSTEM OF PIANOFORTE TECHNIC AND TONE COLOR, THE
MAIER, GUY
    PIANO TEACHER'S COMPANION, THE
MATHEWS, WILLIAM S. B.
    TEACHER'S MANUAL OF MASON'S PIANOFORTE TECHNICS
MATTHAY, TOBIAS A.
    ACT OF TOUCH IN ALL ITS DIVERSITY, THE ..AN ANALYSIS AND SYNTHESIS
MATTHAY, TOBIAS A.
    EPITOME OF THE LAWS OF PIANOFORTE TECHNIQUE, AN
MATTHAY, TOBIAS A. *
    PIANIST'S FIRST MUSIC MAKING, THE --3 VOLS.
MATTHAY, TOBIAS A.
    PIANOFORTE TONE-PRODUCTION---SAME AS 'THE ACT OF TOUCH IN ALL ITS
MATTHAY, TOBIAS A.
    PIANO FALLACIES OF TODAY
MATTHAY, TOBIAS A.
    PROBLEMS OF AGILITY, THE
MATTHAY, TOBIAS A.
    RELAXATION STUDIES IN THE MUSCULAR DISCRIMINATION REQUIRED FOR
MATTHAY, TOBIAS A.
    SOME COMMENTARIES ON THE TEACHING OF PIANOFORTE TECHNIC..A
MATTHAY, TOBIAS A.
    VISIBLE AND INVISIBLE IN PIANOFORTE TECHNIC, THE ..BEING A DIGEST
NETZORG, BENDETSON
    KEY-BOTTOM TONE
NEUHAUS, HEINRICH
    ART OF PIANO PLAYING, THE
ORTMANN, OTTO
    PHYSIOLOGICAL MECHANICS OF PIANO TECHNIQUE, THE ---1929
PETRI, LILLIAN JEFFREY
    MIND OVER MUSCLE..A TECHNICAL ECONOMY FOR PIANISTS
PFEFFERKORN, OTTO W.
    PIANISTIC HINTS
RAMUL, PETER
    PSYCHO-PHYSICAL FOUNDATIONS OF MODERN PIANO TECHNIQUE, THE
REEDER, BETAH
    SINGING TOUCH, THE
ROBYN, LOUISE
    TECHNIC TALES FOR THE CHILD AT THE PIANO--BKS. 1-3..TEACHER'S
RUBINSTEIN, BERYL
    OUTLINE OF PIANO PEDAGOGY--REV. ED.---1929
SCHAUFFLER, LAWRENCE
    PIANO TECHNIC..MYTH OR SCIENCE
SCHERER, HERBERT
    PIANO PRACTICING
SCHULTZ, ARNOLD
    RIDDLE OF THE PIANIST'S FINGER, THE
SHEPARD, FRANK H.
    PIANO TOUCH AND SCALES..AN ANALYSIS OF THE FUNDAMENTAL PRINCIPLES
SIMPSON, ELIZABETH
    BASIC PIANOFORTE TECHNIQUE...BASED ON THE SCIENCE OF PIANOFORTE
VIARD-LOUIS, JENNY
    MUSIC AND THE PIANO
WILLIAMS, JEAN E.
    MODERN METHOD OF PIANO INSTRUCTION, A ..TEACHERS MANUAL

Touch-tone

AHRENS, CORA B. *
    FOR ALL PIANO TEACHERS
AMEY, ELLEN
    CONSCIOUS CONTROL IN PIANO STUDY
BABBITT, WILLIAM
    PHYSIOLOGICAL METHOD FOR PLAYING THE PIANO-FORTE, DESIGNED AS A
BACON, ERNST
    NOTES ON THE PIANO
BERGER, FRANCESCO
    FIRST STEPS AT THE PIANOFORTE
BLOCKLEY, JOHN
    PIANIST'S CATECHISM, THE ---1880
BOLTON, HETTY
    HOW TO PRACTICE
BOOTH, VICTOR
    WE PIANO TEACHERS--REVISED BY ADELE FRANKLIN---1946
BOWEN, YORK
    PEDALLING THE MODERN PIANOFORTE---1936
BOWEN, YORK
    SIMPLICITY OF PIANO TECHNIQUE, THE
BRANDT, LEONIE
    SCIENCE IN MODERN PIANOFORTE PLAYING
BRECKENRIDGE, WILLIAM KILGORE
    HINTS FOR PIANO NORMAL STUDIES
BREE, MADAME MALWINE
    GROUNDWORK OF THE LESCHETIZKY METHOD, THE ---1902
BREITHAUPT, RUDOLPH MARIA
    NATURAL PIANO-TECHNIC..SCHOOL OF WEIGHT TOUCH--2 VOLS.
BRIGGS, GILBERT A.
    PIANOS, PIANISTS AND SONICS
BROTHERHOOD, JAMES
    SENSITIVE PIANO TOUCH AND WAYS AND MEANS TO ITS ACQUIREMENT---A
BROWER, HARRIETTE
    ART OF THE PIANIST, THE
BROWER, HARRIETTE
    HOW A DEPENDABLE PIANO TECHNIQUE WAS WON
BROWER, HARRIETTE
    PIANO MASTERY..TALKS WITH MASTER PIANISTS AND TEACHERS...
BROWER, HARRIETTE
    PIANO MASTERY, SECOND SERIES
BROWER, HARRIETTE
    SELF-HELP IN PIANO STUDY
BURROWES, JOHN FRECKLETON
    GUIDE TO PRACTICE ON THE PIANOFORTE
CALAND, ELIZABETH
    ARTISTIC PIANO PLAYING, AS TAUGHT BY LUDWIG DEPPE
CAMPBELL, LE ROY B.
    TRUE FUNCTION OF RELAXATION IN PIANO PLAYING, THE
CAMPBELL, LE ROY B.
    VELOCITY PLUS

CARPE, ADOLPH
    PIANIST AND THE ART OF MUSIC, THE ..A TREATISE ON PIANO PLAYING
CARTER, BUENTA
    BEGINNER'S PIANO BOOK FOR OLDER STUDENTS...DESIGNED FOR THE OLDER
CARY, MRS. C. S. P.
    PIANO-FORTE CLASS BOOK, CONTAINING PRACTICAL RUDIMENTAL LESSONS
CHASE, MARY WOOD
    NATURAL LAWS IN PIANO TECHNIC
CHING, JAMES
    CANDIDATE'S COMPANION TO THE EXERCISES, SCALES, BROKEN CHORDS,
CHING, JAMES
    ON TEACHING PIANO TECHNIQUE TO CHILDREN
CHING, JAMES
    PIANO PLAYING, A PRACTICAL METHOD--A NEW EDITION OF 'PIANO
CHING, JAMES
    POINTS ON PEDALLING
CHING, JAMES
    SIDELIGHTS ON TOUCH..TOGETHER WITH 101 QUESTIONS, SUITABLE FOR
CHING, JAMES
    STUDIES FOR BASIC PIANO TECHNIQUE..WRITTEN AND SELECTED WITH
CHING, JOAN ELIZABETH
    APPROACH TO PIANO TEACHING---ALSO CATALOGUED UNDER
COHEN, HARRIET
    MUSIC'S HANDMAID
COOKE, JAMES FRANCIS
    GREAT MEN AND FAMOUS MUSICIANS ON THE ART OF MUSIC
COOKE, JAMES FRANCIS
    GREAT PIANISTS ON PIANO PLAYING..STUDY TALKS WITH FOREMOST
COVIELLO, AMBROSE
    FOUNDATIONS OF PIANOFORTE TECHNIC
COVIELLO, AMBROSE
    WHAT MATTHAY MEANT
CURCIO, LOUISE
    SINGLE NOTE, THE
CZERNY, CARL
    COMPLETE THEORETICAL AND PRACTICAL PIANO FORTE SCHOOL, FROM THE
CZERNY, CARL
    LETTERS TO A YOUNG LADY ON THE ART OF PLAYING THE PIANOFORTE
DAHL, ANTON
    SOUL OF GENIUS, THE ..ITS MUSICAL DEVELOPMENT AND HOW THE WORLD AT
DANIELS, BESS *
    WORLD OF MUSIC, THE ..PIANO COURSE..TEACHERS' BOOK, FOR CLASS OR
DENHAM, GEORGE
    MASTERY OF THE KEYBOARD
DEUTSCH, LEONHARD
    PIANO..GUIDED SIGHT-READING
DICKERSON, RUTH A.
    NEW APPROACH TO PIANO TECHNIQUE, A
DILLER, ANGELA
    SPLENDOR OF MUSIC, THE
DOBBIE, E. A.
    AUSTRALIAN PIANOFORTE TUTOR
DRAKE, KENNETH
    SONATAS OF BEETHOVEN AS HE PLAYED AND TAUGHT THEM, THE
DUMESNIL, MAURICE
    HOW TO PLAY AND TEACH DEBUSSY
DUNN, JOHN PETRIE
    BASIS OF PIANOFORTE PLAYING, THE
EHRENFECTER, C. A.
    TECHNICAL STUDY IN THE ART OF PIANOFORTE PLAYING--DEPPE'S
EISENBERG, JACOB
    ARTISTIC PIANIST, THE ..NATURAL TECHNICS IN PIANO MASTERY..FROM
EISENBERG, JACOB
    WEIGHT AND RELAXATION METHOD FOR THE PIANOFORTE
ENGEL, CARL
    PIANIST'S HANDBOOK, THE ..A GUIDE FOR THE RIGHT COMPREHENSION AND
ENGELBRECHT, J. G.
    MATERIA MUSICA, OR MATERIALS FOR THE PIANIST..A CLASS BOOK
FAY, AMY
    DEPPE FINGER EXERCISES FOR RAPIDLY DEVELOPING AN ARTISTIC TOUCH IN
FERGUSON, DONALD NIVISON
    PIANO MUSIC OF SIX GREAT COMPOSERS---1947
FIELDEN, THOMAS
    MARKS AND REMARKS..MUSICAL EXAMINATIONS AND THEIR PROBLEMS
FIELDEN, THOMAS
    SCIENCE OF PIANOFORTE TECHNIC, THE --2ND. REV. ED.---1927
FOOTE, ARTHUR W.
    SOME PRACTICAL THINGS IN PIANO PLAYING
FRISKIN, JAMES
    PRINCIPLES OF PIANOFORTE PRACTICE, THE
GARRATT, PERCIVAL
    ART OF PIANOFORTE PLAYING, THE
GARROWAY, WILL
    PIANISM
GAT, JOZSEF
    TECHNIQUE OF PIANO PLAYING, THE, --2ND. ED.---1958
GEARY, ELEANOR MARGARET
    MUSICAL EDUCATION, WITH PRACTICAL OBSERVATIONS ON THE ART OF
GEBHARD, HEINRICH
    ART OF PEDALLING, THE
GERMER, HEINRICH
    MANUAL OF TONE-PRODUCTION IN PIANOFORTE PLAYING, FROM 'TECHNICS OF
GERMER, HEINRICH
    TECHNICS OF PIANOFORTE PLAYING, THE ..MUSICAL ORNAMENTATION,
GERMER, HEINRICH
    THEORETICO-PRACTICAL ELEMENTARY PIANO-FORTE SCHOOL FOR STUDENTS OF
GIESEKING, WALTER *
    PIANO TECHNIQUE---COMBINED REPUBLICATION OF..'THE SHORTEST WAY TO
GILBERT, RUSSELL S.
    EMBRYO MUSICIAN, THE ..A METHOD OF INTRODUCING MUSIC TO LITTLE
GORDON, STEPHEN T.
    GORDON'S NEW SCHOOL FOR THE PIANO-FORTE
GRABILL, ETHELBERT WARREN
    MECHANICS OF PIANO TECHNIC, THE
HAMILTON, CLARENCE G.
    TOUCH AND EXPRESSION IN PIANO PLAYING
HARICH-SCHNEIDER, ETA
    HARPSICHORD, THE ..AN INTRODUCTION TO TECHNIQUE, STYLE AND THE
HARRISON, SIDNEY
    PIANO TECHNIQUE
HARRISON, SIDNEY
    YOUNG PERSON'S GUIDE TO PLAYING THE PIANO, THE
HELMANN, JACOB N.
    CONSCIOUSLY CONTROLLED PIANO TONE, THE --REV. ED.---1950
HIPKINS, ALFRED JAMES
    HOW CHOPIN PLAYED...FROM CONTEMPORARY IMPRESSIONS COLLECTED FROM
HOFHEIMER, GRACE
    TEACHING TECHNIQUES FOR THE PIANO
HOFMANN, JOSEF
    PIANO PLAYING..A LITTLE BOOK OF SIMPLE SUGGESTIONS--REPRINTED FROM
HOFMANN, JOSEF
    PIANO PLAYING, WITH PIANO QUESTIONS ANSWERED---PUBLISHED EARLIER
HOPE, ERIC
    HANDBOOK OF PIANO PLAYING, A
HORROCKS, CYRIL R. H.
    STUDENT'S GUIDE TO THE ART OF TEACHING THE PIANOFORTE, THE --2ND.

HULL, ARTHUR EAGLEFIELD
    THREE HUNDRED QUESTIONS ON PIANOFORTE TEACHING IN 30 GRADUATED
HUMMEL, JOHANN NEPOMUK
    COMPLETE THEORETICAL AND PRACTICAL COURSE OF INSTRUCTIONS ON THE
JEANS, SIR JAMES HOPWOOD
    SCIENCE AND MUSIC
JEWETT, ALBERT DEWEY
    IDIOMATIC COURSE OF PIANO INSTRUCTION FOR CLASS WORK
JOHNSTONE, J. ALFRED
    TOUCH, PHRASING AND INTERPRETATION
JONAS, ALBERTO
    MASTER SCHOOL OF MODERN PIANO PLAYING AND VIRTUOSITY--3 PARTS IN 7
JONAS, ALBERTO
    PIANOSCRIPT BOOK..AN INVALUABLE AID TO TEACHER AND STUDENT IN
KENYON, CHARLES FREDERICK
    HOW TO MEMORIZE MUSIC
KOCHEVITSKY, GEORGE
    ART OF PIANO PLAYING, THE ..A SCIENTIFIC APPROACH
KUERSTEINER, JEAN PAUL
    EXPERT AID TO ARTISTIC PIANO PLAYING
KULLAK, ADOLPH
    ART OF THE TOUCH, THE ..A WORK FOR THE USE OF ADVANCED PLAYERS AND
LAMAR, RICHARD
    COLLEGE PIANO PEDAGOGY
LANDOWSKA, WANDA
    LANDOWSKA ON MUSIC--EDITED BY DENISE RESTOUT
LANG, EDITH *
    MUSICAL ACCOMPANIMENT OF MOVING PICTURES..A PRACTICAL MANUAL FOR
LAST, JOAN
    INTERPRETATION FOR THE PIANO STUDENT
LAST, JOAN
    YOUNG PIANIST, THE ..A NEW APPROACH FOR TEACHERS AND
LEIMER, KARL *
    RHYTHMICS, DYNAMICS, PEDAL, AND OTHER PROBLEMS OF PIANO
LEIMER, KARL *
    SHORTEST WAY TO PIANISTIC PERFECTION, THE
LEVINSKAYA, MARIA
    LEVINSKAYA SYSTEM OF PIANOFORTE TECHNIC AND TONE COLOR, THE
LEWIS, THOMAS C.
    PROTEST AGAINST THE MODERN DEVELOPMENT OF UNMUSICAL TONE, A
LHEVINNE, JOSEF
    BASIC PRINCIPLES IN PIANOFORTE PLAYING---1924
LINDO, ALGERNON H. *
    INDIVIDUALITY IN PIANO TOUCH
MAIER, GUY
    PIANO TEACHER'S COMPANION, THE
MAIER, GUY *
    PLAYING THE PIANO--TEACHER'S MANUAL
MANHIRE, WILSON
    MODEL ANSWERS TO QUESTIONS ON 'TOUCH' FOR CANDIDATES PREPARING FOR
MASON, WILLIAM G. *
    PRIMER OF MUSIC, A ..BEING THE FIRST STEPS IN MUSICIANSHIP..FOR
MASON, WILLIAM G. *
    SYSTEM FOR BEGINNERS IN THE ART OF PLAYING UPON THE PIANOFORTE, A
MASON, WILLIAM G.
    SYSTEM OF TECHNICAL EXERCISES FOR THE PIANO-FORTE, A
MASON, WILLIAM G.
    TOUCH, AS APPLIED TO PIANOFORTE PRACTICE--ESSAY FOR THE 10TH.
MASON, WILLIAM G.
    TOUCH AND TECHNIC..FOR ARTISTIC PIANO PLAYING, OP. 44--4 VOLS. IN
MATHEWS, WILLIAM S. B.
    MASON'S PRINCIPLES OF VELOCITY AND ARM TOUCHES
MATHEWS, WILLIAM S. B.
    TEACHER'S MANUAL OF MASON'S PIANOFORTE TECHNICS
MATTHAY, TOBIAS A.
    ACT OF TOUCH IN ALL ITS DIVERSITY, THE ..AN ANALYSIS AND SYNTHESIS
MATTHAY, TOBIAS A.
    EPITOME OF THE LAWS OF PIANOFORTE TECHNIQUE, AN
MATTHAY, TOBIAS A.
    FIRST PRINCIPLES OF PIANOFORTE PLAYING--EXTRACT FROM 'THE ACT OF
MATTHAY, TOBIAS A.
    MUSICAL INTERPRETATION..ITS LAWS AND PRINCIPLES---1913
MATTHAY, TOBIAS A.
    ON COLORING AS DISTINCT FROM TONE-INFLECTION--A LECTURE
MATTHAY, TOBIAS A. *
    PIANIST'S FIRST MUSIC MAKING, THE --3 VOLS.
MATTHAY, TOBIAS A.
    PIANOFORTE TONE-PRODUCTION---SAME AS 'THE ACT OF TOUCH IN ALL ITS
MATTHAY, TOBIAS A.
    PIANO FALLACIES OF TODAY
MATTHAY, TOBIAS A.
    PRINCIPLES OF FINGERING AND LAWS OF PEDALLING
MATTHAY, TOBIAS A.
    PROBLEMS OF AGILITY, THE
MATTHAY, TOBIAS A.
    RELAXATION STUDIES IN THE MUSCULAR DISCRIMINATION REQUIRED FOR
MATTHAY, TOBIAS A.
    SOME COMMENTARIES ON THE TEACHING OF PIANOFORTE TECHNIC..A
MATTHAY, TOBIAS A.
    VISIBLE AND INVISIBLE IN PIANOFORTE TECHNIC, THE ..BEING A DIGEST
MCALL, REGINALD L.
    PRACTICAL CHURCH SCHOOL MUSIC..METHODS AND TRAINING FOR SUCCESSFUL
MCARTHUR, ALEXANDER
    PIANOFORTE STUDY..HINTS ON PIANO PLAYING
MEHEGAN, JOHN F.
    TOUCH AND RHYTHM TECHNIQUES FOR THE JAZZ PIANIST
MERRICK, FRANK
    PRACTICING THE PIANO
MERRILL, MYRTLE
    SIGHT-READING AT THE PIANO
MININBERG, IAN
    VISUAL APPROACH TO PIANO TECHNIQUE, A
MOKREJS, JOHN
    SCIENCE OF FINGERING, THE ---FOR PIANO
MORRILL, HENRY H.
    MANUAL OF PIANO FOR PUPILS AND TEACHERS
NALDER, LAWRENCE MARCUS
    MODERN PIANO, THE
NETZORG, BENDETSON
    KEY-BOTTOM TONE
NEWMAN, WILLIAM S.
    PIANIST'S PROBLEMS, THE ..A MODERN APPROACH TO EFFICIENT PRACTICE
NICCHIA, LILLIAN
    PIANOFORTE STUDY..HINTS ON PIANO PLAYING
OLIVER, EDWARD B.
    PRACTICAL TEXT-BOOK OF MUSIC, AS CONNECTED WITH THE ART OF PLAYING
ORTMANN, OTTO
    PHYSICAL BASIS OF PIANO TOUCH AND TONE, THE
ORTMANN, OTTO
    PHYSIOLOGICAL MECHANICS OF PIANO TECHNIQUE, THE ---1929
PALME, RUDOLPH
    FIRST MONTHS IN PIANOFORTE INSTRUCTION, THE ---1870, IN GERMAN
PALMER, HORATIO R.
    PALMER'S PIANO PRIMER
PEARCE, CHARLES WILLIAM
    ART OF THE PIANO TEACHER, THE

PETRI, LILLIAN JEFFREY
  MIND OVER MUSCLE..A TECHNICAL ECONOMY FOR PIANISTS
PHILIPP, LILLIE H.
  PIANO STUDY..APPLICATION AND TECHNIQUE
PHILLIPSON, WENTWORTH
  GUIDE TO YOUNG PIANOFORTE TEACHERS AND STUDENTS
PICHIER, PAUL
  PIANIST'S TOUCH, THE ..METHOD AND THEORY OF PAUL PICHIER
PLAIDY, LOUIS
  PIANO TEACHER, THE
POINTER SYSTEM, INC.
  GUIDE TO THE MODERN PIANIST, A
POTAMKIN, FRANK
  MODERN PIANO PEDAGOGY
PRENTNER, MARIE
  MODERN PIANIST..BEING MY EXPERIENCES IN THE TECHNIQUE AND
RAMUL, PETER
  PSYCHO-PHYSICAL FOUNDATIONS OF MODERN PIANO TECHNIQUE, THE
REDDIE, CHARLES FREDERICK
  PIANOFORTE PLAYING ON ITS TECHNICAL AND AESTHETIC SIDES
REEDER, BETAH
  SINGING TOUCH, THE
REEVES, BETTY
  APPROACH TO PIANO TEACHING---ALSO CATALOGUED UNDER
REINAGLE, CAROLINE
  FEW WORDS ON PIANOFORTE PLAYING, A
RICHARDSON, NATHAN
  NEW METHOD FOR THE PIANOFORTE..ADDED, RUDIMENTS OF HARMONY AND
RICHTER, ADA
  TEACHING HINTS
RICKER, EARL
  MUSIC LESSONS FOR YOUR CHILD
ROSENTHAL, MORIZ
  OLD AND THE NEW SCHOOL OF PIANO PLAYING, THE --TYPEWRITTEN COPY
ROTHSCHILD, FRITZ
  LOST TRADITION IN MUSIC, THE --PT. 1..RHYTHM AND TEMPO IN J. S.
ROTHSCHILD, FRITZ
  LOST TRADITION IN MUSIC, THE --PT. 2..MUSICAL PERFORMANCE IN THE
ROWLEY, ALEC
  DO'S AND DONT'S FOR MUSICIANS..A HANDBOOK FOR TEACHERS AND
RUBINSTEIN, BERYL
  OUTLINE OF PIANO PEDAGOGY--REV. ED.---1929
RUSSELL, LOUIS ARTHUR
  DEVELOPMENT OF ARTISTIC PIANOFORTE TOUCH
SAFONOFF, WASSILI
  NEW FORMULA FOR THE PIANO TEACHER AND PIANO STUDENT
SCHAAF, EDWARD O.
  ART OF PIANO PLAYER TRANSCRIPTION, THE ..MAKING OF PERFORATED
SCHAAF, EDWARD O.
  FUNDAMENTAL PRINCIPLES INVOLVED IN THE COMPOSING AND ARRANGING OF
SCHAAF, EDWARD O.
  MUSICAL INDIVIDUALITY OF THE PLAYER PIANO, THE ---EXCERPTS..'THE
SCHAUFFLER, LAWRENCE
  PIANO TECHNIC..MYTH OR SCIENCE
SCHELLING, ERNEST *
  OXFORD PIANO COURSE, TEACHER'S FIRST MANUAL
SCHELLING, ERNEST *
  OXFORD PIANO COURSE, TEACHER'S SECOND MANUAL
SCHERER, HERBERT
  PIANO PRACTICING
SCHNEIDER, HANS
  WORKING OF THE MIND IN PIANO TEACHING AND PLAYING, THE
SCHOTT, HOWARD
  PLAYING THE HARPSICHORD
SCHULTZ, ARNOLD
  RIDDLE OF THE PIANIST'S FINGER, THE
SCIONTI, SILVIO
  L'ARTE PIANISTICA..SYSTEM OF PIANO ARTISTRY---IN ITALIAN AND
SHEPARD, FRANK H.
  PIANO TOUCH AND SCALES..AN ANALYSIS OF THE FUNDAMENTAL PRINCIPLES
SIMPSON, ELIZABETH
  BASIC PIANOFORTE TECHNIQUE...BASED ON THE SCIENCE OF PIANOFORTE
SMELTZER, JEANNIE R.--COMPILER
  OUTLINES AND GRADES FOR THE USE OF PIANO TEACHERS
SORABJI, KAIKHOSRU
  AROUND MUSIC---PACHMAN, CHOPIN AND LISZT
STANLEY, JANE
  BASIC ROUTINES IN ELEMENTARY PIANO TEACHING THROUGH THE FIRST
STEVENS, WILLIAM S.
  TREATISE ON PIANO-FORTE, CONTAINING THE PRINCIPLES OF FINE PLAYING
STEWART, REID
  HOW TO PASS MUSIC EXAMINATIONS--PIANO--A GUIDE FOR TEACHERS AND
SUMMY-BIRCHARD COMPANY
  HANDBOOK FOR PIANO TEACHERS..COLLECTED ARTICLES ON SUBJECTS
TANKARD, GEOFFREY
  FOUNDATIONS OF PIANOFORTE TECHNIQUE
TANKARD, GEOFFREY
  PIANOFORTE DIPLOMAS
TANKARD, GEOFFREY
  SPECIMEN ANSWERS TO THE QUESTIONS IN PIANOFORTE DIPLOMAS
TAYLOR, FRANKLIN
  PRIMER OF PIANOFORTE PLAYING
TAYLOR, FRANKLIN
  TECHNIQUE AND EXPRESSION IN PIANOFORTE PLAYING
TOBIN, JOSEPH RAYMOND
  COMMON SENSE IN SIGHT READING..A GUIDE FOR PIANO TEACHERS
TOWNSEND, WILLIAM
  BALANCE OF ARM IN PIANO TECHNIQUE--4TH. REV. ED.---1903
TUFTS, JOHN W.
  TECHNIC AND NOTATION AS APPLIED TO THE PIANOFORTE
UNSCHULD, MARIE VON
  PIANIST'S HAND, THE ..A SYSTEMATIC METHOD...ACCORDING TO THE
VANTYN, SIDNEY
  MODERN PIANOFORTE TECHNIQUE
VENABLE, MARY
  INTERPRETATION OF PIANO MUSIC, THE
VIRGIL, ALMON K.
  FOUNDATION EXERCISES IN PIANO PLAYING FROM FIRST RUDIMENTS TO
VIRGIL, ALMON K.
  STEP BY STEP..TEXTBOOK IN PIANO PLAYING..HANDBOOK FOR TEACHERS
VIRGIL, ALMON K.
  TECHNIPHONE MANUAL..INSTRUCTIONS AND EXERCISES IN THE USE OF THE
VIRGIL, ANTHA MINERVA
  ELEMENTARY EXERCISES IN SIGHT READING...FROM THE VIRGIL METHOD
WEISER, ADOLPH
  TWO RIGHT HANDS..A GUIDE FOR THE DEVELOPMENT OF PIANO TECHNIQUE
WESTERBY, HERBERT
  APPROACH TO LISZT, THE ..A COURSE OF MODERN TONAL TECHNIQUE FOR
WHITE, WILLIAM BRAID
  PIANO TUNING AND ALLIED ARTS--5TH. ED.---1917
WHITEMORE, CUTHBERT
  COMMONSENSE IN PIANOFORTE PLAYING
WIER, ALBERT
  PIANO, THE ..ITS HISTORY, MAKERS, PLAYERS AND MUSIC
WILLIAMS, JEAN E.
  MODERN METHOD OF PIANO INSTRUCTION, A ..TEACHERS MANUAL

WILLIAMS, JOHN M.
  WHAT TO TEACH AT THE VERY FIRST LESSON
WOODHOUSE, GEORGE
  ARTIST AT THE PIANO, THE ..THE ART OF MUSICAL INTERPRETATION
WOODHOUSE, GEORGE
  CREATIVE TECHNIQUE, FOR ARTISTS IN GENERAL AND PIANISTS IN
WOODHOUSE, GEORGE
  FROM KEYBOARD TO MUSIC
WOODHOUSE, GEORGE
  NEW PATH FOR PIANISTS, A ..THE MUTANO--MUTE PIANO--SYSTEM, ETC.
WOODHOUSE, GEORGE
  REALISTIC APPROACH TO PIANO PLAYING, A
WRIGHT, WILLIAM C.
  GOLDEN MONITOR, FOR THE PIANOFORTE AND CABINET ORGAN, DESIGNED AS
WRIGHT, WILLIAM C.
  PIANOFORTE MANUAL, THE ..DESIGNED AS A COMPLETE PIANOFORTE PRIMER

Scales, Arpeggios and Chord Formations

AHRENS, CORA B. *
  FOR ALL PIANO TEACHERS
AMEY, ELLEN
  CONSCIOUS CONTROL IN PIANO STUDY
ANON
  FASHIONABLE PRECEPTOR, FOR THE PIANO-FORTE AND HARPSICHORD,
ANON
  GUIDE TO THE MUSICAL TUITION OF VERY YOUNG CHILDREN, BY AN OLD
ANON
  NEW INSTRUCTIONS FOR PLAYING THE HARPSICHORD, PIANOFORTE OR
ANON
  PRECEPTOR, FOR THE PIANOFORTE, THE ORGAN OR HARPSICHORD, THE
AXTENS, FLORENCE
  PIANO CLASS METHOD..THE FIRST TWELVE MONTHS IN THE PIANO CLASS
BACON, ERNST
  NOTES ON THE PIANO
BAKER, DAVID
  JAZZ IMPROVISATION..A COMPREHENSIVE METHOD OF STUDY FOR ALL
BANTLY, BENEDICT
  SIMPLE TREATISE ON SCALES AND ARPEGGIOS FOR PIANO, A --3 VOLS.
BARNWELL, V. T.
  BARNWELL'S NORMAL KEYBOARD AND STAFF STUDIES--THE MENTAL
BARTH, HANS
  TECHNIC..FOR DEVELOPING AN EARLY FOUNDATION IN PIANO PLAYING
BASTIEN, JAMES W. *
  BEGINNING PIANO FOR ADULTS
BENNER, LORA
  BENNER GOLD BOOK, THE ..PIANO MATERIAL AND TEACHING METHODS--3RD.
BERGER, FRANCESCO
  FIRST STEPS AT THE PIANOFORTE
BERTINI, HENRI
  BERTINI'S SELF-TEACHING CATECHISM OF MUSIC FOR THE PIANOFORTE
BOLTON, HETTY
  ON TEACHING THE PIANO
BOWEN, YORK
  SIMPLICITY OF PIANO TECHNIQUE, THE
BRANDT, LEONIE
  SCIENCE IN MODERN PIANOFORTE PLAYING
BRECKENRIDGE, WILLIAM KILGORE
  HINTS FOR PIANO NORMAL STUDIES
BREE, MADAME MALWINE
  GROUNDWORK OF THE LESCHETIZKY METHOD, THE ---1902
BREITHAUPT, RUDOLPH MARIA
  NATURAL PIANO-TECHNIC..SCHOOL OF WEIGHT TOUCH--2 VOLS.
BRIGHAM, ELEANOR
  SCALES..THEIR HISTORY, THEORY, FINGERING AND TECHNICAL USE ON THE
BROWER, HARRIETTE
  ART OF THE PIANIST, THE
BROWER, HARRIETTE
  HOW A DEPENDABLE PIANO TECHNIQUE WAS WON
BROWER, HARRIETTE
  SELF-HELP IN PIANO STUDY
BROWN, JEAN PARKMAN
  INTERVALS, CHORDS AND EAR TRAINING FOR YOUNG PIANOFORTE STUDENTS
BRUXNER, MERVYN
  MASTERING THE PIANO
BUCHAROFF, SIMON
  MODERN PIANIST'S TEXT BOOK, THE
BUONAMICI, GIUSEPPE
  ART OF SCALE STUDY FOR THE PIANOFORTE, THE ...AS TAUGHT TO HIS
BURROWES, JOHN FRECKLETON
  GUIDE TO PRACTICE ON THE PIANOFORTE
CALAND, ELIZABETH
  ARTISTIC PIANO PLAYING, AS TAUGHT BY LUDWIG DEPPE
CALLENDER, ROMAINE
  TEACHER'S MANUAL, A WORK DESIGNED TO SUPPLEMENT...'THE FIRST TEN
CAMPBELL, LE ROY B.
  VELOCITY PLUS
CARMIENCKE, ALBERT G.
  MECHANICS OF PIANO PLAYING, THE
CARPE, ADOLPH
  PIANIST AND THE ART OF MUSIC, THE ..A TREATISE ON PIANO PLAYING
CARRENO, TERESA
  POSSIBILITIES OF TONE COLOR BY ARTISTIC USE OF PEDALS
CARTER, BUENTA
  BEGINNER'S PIANO BOOK FOR OLDER STUDENTS...DESIGNED FOR THE OLDER
CARUTHERS, JULIA LOIS
  PIANO TECHNIC FOR CHILDREN
CASTELLINI, JOHN EDWARD
  RUDIMENTS OF MUSIC..A NEW APPROACH WITH APPLICATION TO THE
CHAPOL, SIMON
  NEW APPROACH TO THE STUDY OF THE PIANOFORTE, A ---IN ITALIAN AND
CHASE, MARY WOOD
  NATURAL LAWS IN PIANO TECHNIC
CHING, JAMES
  CANDIDATE'S COMPANION TO THE EXERCISES, SCALES, BROKEN CHORDS,
CHING, JOAN ELIZABETH
  APPROACH TO PIANO TEACHING---ALSO CATALOGUED UNDER
CHITY, R.
  NEW SCHOOL OF SCALE PLAYING--COLOR PATTERNS
CLEMENTI, MUZIO
  INTRODUCTION TO THE ART OF PLAYING ON THE PIANOFORTE---1801+
COPP, EVELYN A.
  WHAT IS THE FLETCHER MUSIC METHOD
COVIELLO, AMBROSE
  FOUNDATIONS OF PIANOFORTE TECHNIC
CRAMER, JOHN BAPTIST
  INSTRUCTIONS FOR THE PIANOFORTE---CONTAINS ALSO A SET OF 28
CROUCH, M. S.
  SYSTEMATIC FINGERING OF THE ARPEGGIOS OF COMMON CHORDS, ETC., THE
CURWEN, ANNIE JESSY
  PSYCHOLOGY APPLIED TO MUSIC TEACHING
CURWEN, ANNIE JESSY
  TEACHER'S GUIDE...TO MRS. CURWEN'S PIANOFORTE METHOD, 'THE CHILD
CZERNY, CARL
  COMPLETE THEORETICAL AND PRACTICAL PIANO FORTE SCHOOL, FROM THE

DENHAM, GEORGE
    MASTERY OF THE KEYBOARD
DE SOLIS, SOLITO
    THREE POSITIONS OF HARMONIZED SCALES, THE --SHOWN IN ALL KEYS
DICKERSON, RUTH A.
    NEW APPROACH TO PIANO TECHNIQUE, A
DOBBIE, E. A.
    AUSTRALIAN PIANOFORTE TUTOR
DUCKWORTH, GUY
    KEYBOARD MUSICIANSHIP
DUFFEE, GERTRUDE BANKS
    PIANO STUDY..A GUIDE TO TEACHER AND STUDENT
DUNN, JOHN PETRIE
    BASIS OF PIANOFORTE PLAYING, THE
DUSSEK, JOHANN L.
    DUSSEK'S INSTRUCTIONS ON THE ART OF PLAYING THE PIANOFORTE OR
EBERHARDT, GOBY
    MY SYSTEM FOR PRACTICING THE VIOLIN AND PIANO, BASED UPON
EHRENFECTER, C. A.
    TECHNICAL STUDY IN THE ART OF PIANOFORTE PLAYING--DEPPE'S
EHRLICH, ALFRED HEINRICH
    HOW TO PRACTICE ON THE PIANO..REFLECTIONS AND SUGGESTIONS
EISENBERG, JACOB
    ARTISTIC PIANIST, THE ..NATURAL TECHNICS IN PIANO MASTERY..FROM
EISENBERG, JACOB
    WEIGHT AND RELAXATION METHOD FOR THE PIANOFORTE
ENGELBRECHT, J. G.
    MATERIA MUSICA, OR MATERIALS FOR THE PIANIST..A CLASS BOOK
EVERHART, POWELL
    PIANIST'S ART, THE ..A COMPREHENSIVE MANUAL ON PIANO PLAYING FOR
FERGUSON, DONALD NIVISON
    PIANO MUSIC OF SIX GREAT COMPOSERS---1947
FIELDEN, THOMAS
    MARKS AND REMARKS..MUSICAL EXAMINATIONS AND THEIR PROBLEMS
FIELDEN, THOMAS
    NEW APPROACH TO SCALES AND ARPEGGIOS, A
FIELDEN, THOMAS
    SCIENCE OF PIANOFORTE TECHNIC, THE --2ND. REV. ED.---1927
FOLDES, ANDOR
    KEYS TO THE KEYBOARD, A BOOK FOR PIANISTS
FOOTE, ARTHUR W.
    SOME PRACTICAL THINGS IN PIANO PLAYING
FROST, EDWARD
    THALBEGARIAN (SIC) EXERCISES..OR, THE PIANIST'S DESIDERATA
GALLICO, PAOLO
    NEW METHOD FOR SYNCHRONIZED SCALE FINGERINGS, A
GARROWAY, WILL
    PIANISM
GAT, JOZSEF
    TECHNIQUE OF PIANO PLAYING, THE, --2ND. ED.---1958
GERMER, HEINRICH
    TECHNICS OF PIANOFORTE PLAYING, THE ..MUSICAL ORNAMENTATION,
GIESEKING, WALTER *
    PIANO TECHNIQUE---COMBINED REPUBLICATION OF..'THE SHORTEST WAY TO
GORDON, STEPHEN T.
    GORDON'S NEW SCHOOL FOR THE PIANO-FORTE
GRABILL, ETHELBERT WARREN
    MECHANICS OF PIANO TECHNIC, THE
GRAHAM, JAMES L.
    MUSIC MADE EASY, PIANOFORTE TUTOR ON A NEW PLAN
GRAUPNER, GOTTLIEB
    RUDIMENTS OF THE ART OF PLAYING ON THE PIANOFORTE...A PLAIN
GRUNDY, ENID
    HAPPY PIANIST, THE
HAMBOURG, MARK
    HOW TO PLAY THE PIANO--NEW AND ENLARGED EDITION OF 'HOW TO BECOME
HANSMANN, RICHARD
    THEORETICAL AND PRACTICAL PIANO-FORTE SCHOOL FOR THE JANKO
HARRISON, SIDNEY
    BEGINNING TO PLAY THE PIANO--A TEACHER'S HANDBOOK, INCLUDING THE
HEIDELBERGER, PAULINE
    MASTER METHOD..PIANO NORMAL AND TEACHER'S MANUAL
HELD, ERNST
    RULES AND REASONS FOR CORRECT SCALE-FINGERING
HENDERSON, WILLIAM JAMES
    PRELUDES AND STUDIES..MUSICAL THEMES OF THE DAY--SECTION 3..THE
HERZ, HENRI
    NEW AND COMPLETE PIANOFORTE SCHOOL
HOFHEIMER, GRACE
    TEACHING TECHNIQUES FOR THE PIANO
HORROCKS, CYRIL R. H.
    STUDENT'S GUIDE TO THE ART OF TEACHING THE PIANOFORTE, THE --2ND.
HULL, ARTHUR EAGLEFIELD
    THREE HUNDRED QUESTIONS ON PIANOFORTE TEACHING IN 30 GRADUATED
HUTCHESON, ERNEST
    ELEMENTS OF PIANO TECHNIQUE, THE
JEWETT, ALBERT DEWEY
    IDIOMATIC COURSE OF PIANO INSTRUCTION FOR CLASS WORK
JOHNS, CLAYTON
    ESSENTIALS OF PIANOFORTE PLAYING, THE
JOHNSON, REGINALD
    COMMONSENSE IN SCALE AND ARPEGGIO PLAYING
JOHNSON, VERA A.
    SCIENTIFIC SIDE OF MUSIC IN SIMPLE, PRACTICAL FORM FOR TEACHERS
JOHNSTONE, J. ALFRED
    ART OF TEACHING PIANOFORTE PLAYING, THE --2ND. REV. ED.---1910
JONAS, ALBERTO
    MASTER SCHOOL OF MODERN PIANO PLAYING AND VIRTUOSITY--3 PARTS IN 7
JONAS, ALBERTO
    PIANOSCRIPT BOOK..AN INVALUABLE AID TO TEACHER AND STUDENT IN
KLECZYNSKI, JAN
    HOW TO PLAY CHOPIN--THREE LECTURES
KRUSZYNSKI, MICHAL
    APPROACH TO THE PSYCHOLOGY OF PIANO TEACHING, AN
LAMAR, RICHARD
    COLLEGE PIANO PEDAGOGY
LAST, JOAN
    YOUNG PIANIST, THE ..A NEW APPROACH FOR TEACHERS AND
LAWRENCE, FREDERIC LOCKE
    RATIONALE OF PIANO TECHNIQUE, THE
LEIMER, KARL *
    RHYTHMICS, DYNAMICS, PEDAL, AND OTHER PROBLEMS OF PIANO
LEIMER, KARL *
    SHORTEST WAY TO PIANISTIC PERFECTION, THE
LOGIER, JOHANN BERNHARD
    SEQUEL TO THE FIRST COMPANION TO THE CHIROPLAST
LOMAS, LULU GRAHAM
    FIRST TEN PIANO LESSONS, LAID OUT FOR YOUNG TEACHERS, WITH
MACLEAN, CHARLES D.
    PRINCIPLES OF PIANOFORTE PRACTICE, THE
MAIER, GUY
    PIANO TEACHER'S COMPANION, THE
MANHIRE, WILSON
    CANDIDATE'S SCALE AND ARPEGGIO TESTS FOR THE PIANOFORTE, ETC., THE
MANHIRE, WILSON
    EXAMINATION CANDIDATE'S GUIDE TO SCALE AND ARPEGGIO PLAYING, ETC.,

MANSFELDT, HUGO L.
    TECHNIC..A SYSTEM OF THE MOST NECESSARY DAILY EXERCISES TO PRODUCE
MARIAL, R.
    METHODS APPLICABLE TO GROUP TEACHING OR PRIVATE PIANO INSTRUCTION
MASON, WILLIAM G. *
    PRIMER OF MUSIC, A ..BEING THE FIRST STEPS IN MUSICIANSHIP..FOR
MASON, WILLIAM G. *
    SYSTEM FOR BEGINNERS IN THE ART OF PLAYING UPON THE PIANOFORTE, A
MASON, WILLIAM G.
    SYSTEM OF TECHNICAL EXERCISES FOR THE PIANO-FORTE, A
MATHEWS, WILLIAM S. B.
    TEACHER'S MANUAL OF MASON'S PIANOFORTE TECHNICS
MATTHAY, TOBIAS A. *
    PIANIST'S FIRST MUSIC MAKING, THE --3 VOLS.
MATTHAY, TOBIAS A.
    PIANO FALLACIES OF TODAY
MATTHAY, TOBIAS A.
    RELAXATION STUDIES IN THE MUSCULAR DISCRIMINATION REQUIRED FOR
MCMILLAN, FIONA
    FINGERING OF SCALES AND ARPEGGIOS, THE
MERGES, P.
    PRACTICAL RULES FOR PIANOFORTE PLAYING..TEXT BOOK FOR TEACHERS AND
MERRICK, FRANK
    PRACTICING THE PIANO
MINNESOTA MUSIC TEACHERS ASSOCIATION
    PIANO-THEORY EXAMINATION SYLLABUS
MOKREJS, JOHN
    SCIENCE OF FINGERING, THE ---FOR PIANO
MOTT, ISAAC H. R.
    ADVICE AND INSTRUCTIONS FOR PLAYING THE PIANOFORTE WITH EXPRESSION
MUSIC PROJECT--NEW YORK CITY
    TEACHER'S GUIDE..A CREATIVE APPROACH TO PIANO CLASS TEACHING, BY
NEWMAN, ELIZABETH
    HOW TO TEACH MUSIC TO BEGINNERS
NEWMAN, WILLIAM S.
    PIANIST'S PROBLEMS, THE ..A MODERN APPROACH TO EFFICIENT PRACTICE
O'REAR, MRS. ASBURY S.
    SELF READING NOTES
ORLIK, JULES
    CREATIVE APPROACH TO PIANO CLASS TEACHING, A ---REPRODUCED FROM
ORTMANN, OTTO
    PHYSIOLOGICAL MECHANICS OF PIANO TECHNIQUE, THE ---1929
PALMER, HORATIO R.
    PALMER'S PIANO PRIMER
PARSONS, ALBERT R.
    SYNTHETIC METHOD FOR THE PIANOFORTE, THE
PARSONS, MARY H.
    RHYTHMIC WAY, THE
PASQUALI, NICOLO
    ART OF FINGERING THE HARPSICHORD, THE
PEARCE, CHARLES WILLIAM
    ART OF THE PIANO TEACHER, THE
PETERS, WILLIAM C.
    ECLECTIC PIANOFORTE SCHOOL, THE ..ARRANGED FROM THE WORKS OF THE
PETRI, LILLIAN JEFFREY
    MIND OVER MUSCLE..A TECHNICAL ECONOMY FOR PIANISTS
PHILIPP, LILLIE H.
    PIANO STUDY..APPLICATION AND TECHNIQUE
PLAIDY, LOUIS
    PIANOFORTE TEACHER'S GUIDE, THE
PLAIDY, LOUIS
    PIANO TEACHER, THE
PLATT, CAROLYN
    CAROLYN PLATT METHOD FOR PIANO, THE --GROUP INSTRUCTION--TEACHER'S
POTAMKIN, FRANK
    MODERN PIANO PEDAGOGY
PRATT, SILAS G.
    PIANIST'S MENTAL VELOCITY, THE ..A SYSTEMATIC PREPARATION OF THE
PRENTNER, MARIE
    MODERN PIANIST..BEING MY EXPERIENCES IN THE TECHNIQUE AND
PRIESING, DOROTHY *
    LANGUAGE OF THE PIANO..A WORKBOOK IN THEORY AND KEYBOARD HARMONY
PUPIN, ANNIE
    HOW TO PRACTICE..OR HINTS TO PIANO-FORTE STUDENTS ON THE METHOD OF
PUPIN, ANNIE
    SCALES, THE ..THEIR FORMATION, FINGERING, AND HOW TO PRACTICE
REEVES, BETTY
    APPROACH TO PIANO TEACHING---ALSO CATALOGUED UNDER
REEVES, WILLIAM
    REEVES' POPULAR PIANOFORTE TUTOR..RUDIMENTS OF MUSIC, EXERCISES
REZITS, JOSEPH
    SOURCE MATERIALS FOR PIANO TECHNIQUES
RICHARDSON, NATHAN
    NEW METHOD FOR THE PIANOFORTE..ADDED, RUDIMENTS OF HARMONY AND
ROBYN, LOUISE
    HOW TO TEACH PIANO TO THE CHILD BEGINNER..A TEXT BOOK FOR TEACHERS
ROWLEY, ALEC
    PRACTICAL MUSICIANSHIP, A HANDBOOK FOR TEACHERS AND STUDENTS
RUBINSTEIN, BERYL
    OUTLINE OF PIANO PEDAGOGY--REV. ED.---1929
SAFONOFF, WASSILI
    NEW FORMULA FOR THE PIANO TEACHER AND PIANO STUDENT
SCHAAF, EDWARD O.
    MUSICAL INDIVIDUALITY OF THE PLAYER PIANO, THE ---EXCERPTS..'THE
SCHAUFFLER, LAWRENCE
    PIANO TECHNIC..MYTH OR SCIENCE
SCHERER, HERBERT
    PIANO PRACTICING
SCHMITZ, ELIE ROBERT
    CAPTURE OF INSPIRATION, THE
SCIONTI, SILVIO
    L'ARTE PIANISTICA..SYSTEM OF PIANO ARTISTRY---IN ITALIAN AND
SHEPARD, FRANK H.
    PIANO TOUCH AND SCALES..AN ANALYSIS OF THE FUNDAMENTAL PRINCIPLES
SHEPARD, ROBERT
    COMPLETE SCALE AND ARPEGGIO MANUAL
SIMPSON, ELIZABETH
    BASIC PIANOFORTE TECHNIQUE...BASED ON THE SCIENCE OF PIANOFORTE
SLENCZYNSKA, RUTH A.
    MUSIC AT YOUR FINGERTIPS
SMELTZER, JEANNIE R.--COMPILER
    OUTLINES AND GRADES FOR THE USE OF PIANO TEACHERS
SMITH, A. G. WARREN
    BEGINNER'S GUIDE, THE ..FOR ALL COMMENCING THE STUDY OF THE
SMITH, MACDONALD
    FROM BRAIN TO KEYBOARD..A SYSTEM OF HAND AND FINGER CONTROL FOR
SOREL, CLAUDETTE
    COMPENDIUM OF PIANO TECHNIQUE--39 ETUDES SELECTED FROM OVER 4000,
SPENCER, ALLEN
    FOUNDATION OF PIANO TECHNIC, THE
SPENCER, BERNARD
    POPULAR PIANO...A CORRESPONDENCE COURSE OF THE EASTERN SCHOOLS OF
SQUIRE, RUSSEL N. *
    CLASS PIANO FOR ADULT BEGINNERS--2ND. ED.---1964
STANLEY, JANE
    BASIC ROUTINES IN ELEMENTARY PIANO TEACHING THROUGH THE FIRST

STARKEY, EVELYN
    PIANO CLASS WORKBOOK FOR FIRST YEAR STUDENTS
STEVENS, EVERETT
    CHORDS, CADENCES, AND ARPEGGIOS
STEWART, REID
    HOW TO PASS MUSIC EXAMINATIONS--PIANO--A GUIDE FOR TEACHERS AND
SWENSON, LUCILE B.
    DISCOVERING THE PIANO..THE MULTIPLE KEY APPROACH..STUDY GUIDE AND
TANKARD, GEOFFREY
    PIANOFORTE DIPLOMAS
TANKARD, GEOFFREY
    SPECIMEN ANSWERS TO THE QUESTIONS IN PIANOFORTE DIPLOMAS
TAYLOR, FRANKLIN
    TECHNIQUE AND EXPRESSION IN PIANOFORTE PLAYING
TUFTS, JOHN W.
    TECHNIC AND NOTATION AS APPLIED TO THE PIANOFORTE
UNDERWOOD, REX
    GHOST NOTE PATTERN BUILDERS FOR VISUALIZING THE STRUCTURE OF
UNSCHULD, MARIE VON
    PIANIST'S HAND, THE ..A SYSTEMATIC METHOD...ACCORDING TO THE
VANTYN, SIDNEY
    MODERN PIANOFORTE TECHNIQUE
VERNAZZA, MARCELLE
    BASIC MATERIALS FOR THE PIANO STUDENT
VINING, HARRISON S.
    SIMPLE AND COMPLETE PRIMER FOR THE PIANOFORTE, THE
VIRGIL, ALMON K.
    FOUNDATION EXERCISES IN PIANO PLAYING FROM FIRST RUDIMENTS TO
VIRGIL, ANTHA MINERVA
    VIRGIL METHOD OF PIANOFORTE TECHNIC, THE --2 VOLS.
WEISER, ADOLPH
    TWO RIGHT HANDS..A GUIDE FOR THE DEVELOPMENT OF PIANO TECHNIQUE
WELLS, HOWARD
    EARS, BRAIN AND FINGERS..A TEXT BOOK FOR PIANO TEACHERS AND PUPILS
WELLS, HOWARD
    PIANIST'S THUMB, THE
WESTBROOK, BENJAMIN V.
    SYSTEM OF STUDY OF SCALES AND CHORDS, A ..BEING CHAPTERS ON THE
WHEELER, BERTHA H.
    MIND AND MECHANISM..THOUGHTS ON TEACHING AND THE PIANISTIC ART
WHITESIDE, ABBY
    INDISPENSABLES OF PIANO PLAYING--2ND. ED.---1955
WIER, ALBERT
    PIANO, THE ..ITS HISTORY, MAKERS, PLAYERS AND MUSIC
WILLIAMS, JEAN E. *
    MIND IN MUSIC, THE
WILLIAMS, JEAN E.
    MODERN METHOD OF PIANO INSTRUCTION, A ..TEACHERS MANUAL
WILLIAMS, JOHN M.
    WHAT TO TEACH AT THE VERY FIRST LESSON
WILSON, CHARLES J.
    SCALES TAUGHT IN ONE EASY LESSON, THE
WILSON, MORRIS E.
    HOW TO PLAY BY EAR
WOLFF, ERNST VICTOR
    WITH REASON AND RHYME
WOLLNER, GERTRUDE PRICE
    IMPROVISATION IN MUSIC..WAYS TOWARDS CAPTURING MUSICAL IDEAS AND
WOODHOUSE, GEORGE
    NEW WAY TO PIANO TECHNIQUE, THE --8 VOLS.
WOODHOUSE, GEORGE
    REALISTIC APPROACH TO PIANO PLAYING, A
WRIGHT, WILLIAM C.
    GOLDEN MONITOR, FOR THE PIANOFORTE AND CABINET ORGAN, DESIGNED AS
WYMAN, ADDISON P.
    WYMAN'S PIANO TEXTBOOK..CONTAINING A COMPLETE SYSTEM OF MUSICAL
ZIMMERMAN, ALEX H. *
    BASIC PIANO FOR THE COLLEGE STUDENT

Exercises for Keyboard Facility

AGUILAR, EMANUEL
    LITTLE BOOK ABOUT LEARNING THE PIANOFORTE, A
AHRENS, CORA B. *
    FOR ALL PIANO TEACHERS
AMEY, ELLEN
    CONSCIOUS CONTROL IN PIANO STUDY
ANON
    GENERAL OBSERVATIONS ON MUSIC AND REMARKS ON MR. LOGIER'S SYSTEM
ANON
    GUIDE TO THE MUSICAL TUITION OF VERY YOUNG CHILDREN, BY AN OLD
BARTH, HANS
    TECHNIC..FOR DEVELOPING AN EARLY FOUNDATION IN PIANO PLAYING
BASTIEN, JAMES W. *
    BEGINNING PIANO FOR ADULTS
BAUER, HAROLD
    PIANIST'S WARMING-UP EXERCISES FOR THE MAINTENANCE AND IMPROVEMENT
BECKERMAN, H. J.
    AMERICAN SCHOOL OF RAGTIME PIANO PLAYING, THE
BENNER, LORA
    BENNER GOLD BOOK, THE ..PIANO MATERIAL AND TEACHING METHODS--3RD.
BERGER, FRANCESCO
    FIRST STEPS AT THE PIANOFORTE
BOOTH, VICTOR
    WE PIANO TEACHERS--REVISED BY ADELE FRANKLIN---1946
BRANDT, LEONIE
    SCIENCE IN MODERN PIANOFORTE PLAYING
BRECKENRIDGE, WILLIAM KILGORE
    HINTS FOR PIANO NORMAL STUDIES
BREE, MADAME MALWINE
    GROUNDWORK OF THE LESCHETIZKY METHOD, THE ---1902
BREITHAUPT, RUDOLPH MARIA
    NATURAL PIANO-TECHNIC..SCHOOL OF WEIGHT TOUCH--2 VOLS.
BROWER, HARRIETTE
    ART OF THE PIANIST, THE
BROWER, HARRIETTE
    HOW A DEPENDABLE PIANO TECHNIQUE WAS WON
BROWER, HARRIETTE
    SELF-HELP IN PIANO STUDY
BUCHAROFF, SIMON
    MODERN PIANIST'S TEXT BOOK, THE
BUELOW, HANS GUIDO VON
    APPLIED PIANO TECHNIC..300 EXTRACTS FOR DAILY PRACTICE FROM
BURROWES, JOHN FRECKLETON
    GUIDE TO PRACTICE ON THE PIANOFORTE
CALAND, ELIZABETH
    ARTISTIC PIANO PLAYING, AS TAUGHT BY LUDWIG DEPPE
CAMPBELL, LE ROY B.
    TRUE FUNCTION OF RELAXATION IN PIANO PLAYING, THE
CAMPBELL, LE ROY B.
    VELOCITY PLUS
CARMIENCKE, ALBERT G.
    MECHANICS OF PIANO PLAYING, THE
CARPE, ADOLPH
    PIANIST AND THE ART OF MUSIC, THE ..A TREATISE ON PIANO PLAYING
CARPE, JOHN
    PSYCHOLOGY OF PIANO TEACHING, THE ..A TEXTBOOK FOR TEACHERS,

CARTER, BUENTA
    BEGINNER'S PIANO BOOK FOR OLDER STUDENTS...DESIGNED FOR THE OLDER
CARUTHERS, JULIA LOIS
    PIANO TECHNIC FOR CHILDREN
CHAROL, SIMON
    NEW APPROACH TO THE STUDY OF THE PIANOFORTE, A ---IN ITALIAN AND
CHASE, MARY WOOD
    NATURAL LAWS IN PIANO TECHNIC
CHEYETTE, IRVING
    BASIC PIANO FOR THE MUSIC EDUCATOR AND CLASSROOM TEACHER
CHING, JAMES
    CANDIDATE'S COMPANION TO THE EXERCISES, SCALES, BROKEN CHORDS,
CHING, JAMES
    FOREARM ROTATION---A SEQUEL TO 'THE ROTARY ROAD'--15 PHOTOS AND
CHING, JAMES
    ON TEACHING PIANO TECHNIQUE TO CHILDREN
CHING, JAMES
    PIANO PLAYING, A PRACTICAL METHOD--A NEW EDITION OF 'PIANO
CHING, JAMES
    ROTARY ROAD, AN EASY PILGRIMAGE BY EIGHT SHORT STEPS, THE
CHING, JAMES
    SIDELIGHTS ON TOUCH..TOGETHER WITH 101 QUESTIONS, SUITABLE FOR
CHING, JOAN ELIZABETH
    APPROACH TO PIANO TEACHING---ALSO CATALOGUED UNDER
COVIELLO, AMBROSE
    FOUNDATIONS OF PIANOFORTE TECHNIC
CURCIO, LOUISE
    MUSICIAN'S HANDBOOK FOR THE DEVELOPMENT OF MANUAL SUPPLENESS AND
CURWEN, ANNIE JESSY
    TEACHER'S GUIDE...TO MRS. CURWEN'S PIANOFORTE METHOD, 'THE CHILD
CZERNY, CARL
    COMPLETE THEORETICAL AND PRACTICAL PIANO FORTE SCHOOL, FROM THE
D'ABREU, GERALD
    PLAYING THE PIANO WITH CONFIDENCE---1964
DUFFEE, GERTRUDE BANKS
    PIANO STUDY..A GUIDE TO TEACHER AND STUDENT
DUNN, JOHN PETRIE
    BASIS OF PIANOFORTE PLAYING, THE
EBERHARDT, GOBY
    MY SYSTEM FOR PRACTICING THE VIOLIN AND PIANO, BASED UPON
EHRENFECTER, C. A.
    TECHNICAL STUDY IN THE ART OF PIANOFORTE PLAYING--DEPPE'S
EHRLICH, ALFRED HEINRICH
    HOW TO PRACTICE ON THE PIANO..REFLECTIONS AND SUGGESTIONS
EISENBERG, JACOB
    ARTISTIC PIANIST, THE ..NATURAL TECHNICS IN PIANO MASTERY..FROM
EISENBERG, JACOB
    WEIGHT AND RELAXATION METHOD FOR THE PIANOFORTE
FAY, AMY
    DEPPE FINGER EXERCISES FOR RAPIDLY DEVELOPING AN ARTISTIC TOUCH IN
FERGUSON, DONALD NIVISON
    PIANO MUSIC OF SIX GREAT COMPOSERS---1947
FIELDEN, THOMAS
    NEW APPROACH TO SCALES AND ARPEGGIOS, A
FOLDES, ANDOR
    KEYS TO THE KEYBOARD, A BOOK FOR PIANISTS
FRISKIN, JAMES
    PRINCIPLES OF PIANOFORTE PRACTICE, THE
GAT, JOZSEF
    TECHNIQUE OF PIANO PLAYING, THE, --2ND. ED.---1958
GERMER, HEINRICH
    TECHNICS OF PIANOFORTE PLAYING, THE ..MUSICAL ORNAMENTATION,
GERMER, HEINRICH
    THEORETICO-PRACTICAL ELEMENTARY PIANO-FORTE SCHOOL FOR STUDENTS OF
GORDON, STEPHEN T.
    GORDON'S NEW SCHOOL FOR THE PIANO-FORTE
GRABILL, ETHELBERT WARREN
    MECHANICS OF PIANO TECHNIC, THE
HAMBOURG, MARK
    HOW TO PLAY THE PIANO--NEW AND ENLARGED EDITION OF 'HOW TO BECOME
HEIDELBERGER, PAULINE
    MASTER METHOD..PIANO NORMAL AND TEACHER'S MANUAL
HERZ, HENRI
    NEW AND COMPLETE PIANOFORTE SCHOOL
HOOK, JAMES
    GUIDA DI MUSICA..SECOND PART, CONSISTING OF SEVERAL HUNDRED
HOPE, ERIC
    AIDS TO TECHNIQUE
HORROCKS, CYRIL R. H.
    STUDENT'S GUIDE TO THE ART OF TEACHING THE PIANOFORTE, THE --2ND.
HULL, ARTHUR EAGLEFIELD
    THREE HUNDRED QUESTIONS ON PIANOFORTE TEACHING IN 30 GRADUATED
HUTCHESON, ERNEST
    ELEMENTS OF PIANO TECHNIQUE, THE
JOHNSTONE, J. ALFRED
    ART OF TEACHING PIANOFORTE PLAYING, THE --2ND. REV. ED.---1910
JONAS, ALBERTO
    PIANOSCRIPT BOOK..AN INVALUABLE AID TO TEACHER AND STUDENT IN
KLECZYNSKI, JAN
    HOW TO PLAY CHOPIN--THREE LECTURES
KRUSZYNSKI, MICHAL
    APPROACH TO THE PSYCHOLOGY OF PIANO TEACHING, AN
KUERSTEINER, JEAN PAUL
    EXPERT AID TO ARTISTIC PIANO PLAYING
LAMAR, RICHARD
    COLLEGE PIANO PEDAGOGY
LAWRENCE, FREDERIC LOCKE
    RATIONALE OF PIANO TECHNIQUE, THE
LEIMER, KARL *
    RHYTHMICS, DYNAMICS, PEDAL, AND OTHER PROBLEMS OF PIANO
LEIMER, KARL *
    SHORTEST WAY TO PIANISTIC PERFECTION, THE
LOGIER, JOHANN BERNHARD
    SEQUEL TO THE FIRST COMPANION TO THE CHIROPLAST
LONGSTREET, H. P.
    PRACTICAL FINGER CONTROL--10TH. ED.
MACLEAN, CHARLES D.
    PRINCIPLES OF PIANOFORTE PRACTICE, THE
MAIER, GUY
    PIANO TEACHER'S COMPANION, THE
MANSFELDT, HUGO L.
    TECHNIC..A SYSTEM OF THE MOST NECESSARY DAILY EXERCISES TO PRODUCE
MASON, WILLIAM G.
    ACCENTUAL TREATMENT OF EXERCISES AS APPLIED TO PIANOFORTE
MASON, WILLIAM G. *
    SYSTEM FOR BEGINNERS IN THE ART OF PLAYING UPON THE PIANOFORTE, A
MASON, WILLIAM G.
    SYSTEM OF TECHNICAL EXERCISES FOR THE PIANO-FORTE, A
MATHEWS, WILLIAM S. B.
    TEACHER'S MANUAL OF MASON'S PIANOFORTE TECHNICS
MATTHAY, TOBIAS A.
    FIRST LIGHTS ON PIANO-PLAYING
MATTHAY, TOBIAS A.
    NINE STEPS TOWARDS 'FINGER INDIVIDUALIZATION' THROUGH FOREARM
MATTHAY, TOBIAS A.
    PRACTICE TRIANGLE, THE ..EXERCISES FOR FOREARM ROTATION
MATTHAY, TOBIAS A.
    RELAXATION STUDIES IN THE MUSCULAR DISCRIMINATION REQUIRED FOR

MEHEGAN, JOHN F.
    TOUCH AND RHYTHM TECHNIQUES FOR THE JAZZ PIANIST
MERGES, P.
    PRACTICAL RULES FOR PIANOFORTE PLAYING..TEXT BOOK FOR TEACHERS AND
MOORE, MARY BURNHAM
    LURE OF THE PIANO THROUGH COORDINATION AND CONCENTRATION, THE
NETZORG, BENDETSON
    KEY-BOTTOM TONE
NEWMAN, WILLIAM S.
    PIANIST'S PROBLEMS, THE ..A MODERN APPROACH TO EFFICIENT PRACTICE
OSTROVSKY, HENRY
    LESSON COURSE...THE COMPLETE OSTROVSKY FINGER EXERCISE, FOR
PALME, RUDOLPH
    FIRST MONTHS IN PIANOFORTE INSTRUCTION, THE ---1870, IN GERMAN
PEARCE, CHARLES WILLIAM
    ART OF THE PIANO TEACHER, THE
PETERSON, FRANKLIN
    THEORETIC COMPANION TO PRACTICE--PART I OF THE PIANIST'S HANDBOOK
PETRI, LILLIAN JEFFREY
    MIND OVER MUSCLE..A TECHNICAL ECONOMY FOR PIANISTS
PHILIPP, LILLIE H.
    PIANO STUDY..APPLICATION AND TECHNIQUE
PHILLIPSON, WENTWORTH
    GUIDE TO YOUNG PIANOFORTE TEACHERS AND STUDENTS
PLAIDY, LOUIS
    PIANOFORTE TEACHER'S GUIDE, THE
POINTER SYSTEM, INC.
    GUIDE TO THE MODERN PIANIST, A
PRENTNER, MARIE
    MODERN PIANIST..BEING MY EXPERIENCES IN THE TECHNIQUE AND
PSTROKONSKY, JULES DE
    NEW METHOD OF TEACHING THE PIANOFORTE
PUPIN, ANNIE
    HOW TO PRACTICE..OR HINTS TO PIANO-FORTE STUDENTS ON THE METHOD OF
REEVES, BETTY
    APPROACH TO PIANO TEACHING---ALSO CATALOGUED UNDER
RENNIE, BLANCHE H.
    HAND CULTURE FOR PIANISTS, VIOLINISTS AND 'CELLISTS--FINGER, HAND
RICHARDSON, NATHAN
    NEW METHOD FOR THE PIANOFORTE..ADDED, RUDIMENTS OF HARMONY AND
ROBBINS, EDGAR A.
    AMERICAN METHOD FOR THE PIANOFORTE
ROBYN, LOUISE
    HAND BUILDING AND HAND STRETCHING EXERCISES
ROBYN, LOUISE
    TECHNIC TALES FOR THE CHILD AT THE PIANO--BKS. 1-3..TEACHER'S
RUBINSTEIN, BERYL
    OUTLINE OF PIANO PEDAGOGY--REV. ED.---1929
SAFONOFF, WASSILI
    NEW FORMULA FOR THE PIANO TEACHER AND PIANO STUDENT
SCHAUFFLER, LAWRENCE
    PIANO TECHNIC..MYTH OR SCIENCE
SCHELLING, ERNEST *
    OXFORD PIANO COURSE, TEACHER'S SECOND MANUAL
SCHERER, HERBERT
    PIANO PRACTICING
SCHMITZ, ELIE ROBERT
    CAPTURE OF INSPIRATION, THE
SCIONTI, SILVIO
    L'ARTE PIANISTICA..SYSTEM OF PIANO ARTISTRY---IN ITALIAN AND
SCONCIA, JOHN A.
    SCONCIA'S NEW SYSTEM OF INSTRUCTION IN MUSIC AS A SCIENCE..OR, A
SHEFTEL, PAUL
    EXPLORING KEYBOARD FUNDAMENTALS
SHEPARD, FRANK H.
    PIANO TOUCH AND SCALES..AN ANALYSIS OF THE FUNDAMENTAL PRINCIPLES
SIMPSON, KENNETH
    KEYBOARD HARMONY AND IMPROVISATION
SMITH, MACDONALD
    FROM BRAIN TO KEYBOARD..A SYSTEM OF HAND AND FINGER CONTROL FOR
SQUIRE, RUSSEL N. *
    CLASS PIANO FOR ADULT BEGINNERS--2ND. ED.---1964
TANKARD, GEOFFREY
    FOUNDATIONS OF PIANOFORTE TECHNIQUE
TANKARD, GEOFFREY
    PIANOFORTE DIPLOMAS
TAYLOR, FRANKLIN
    PRIMER OF PIANOFORTE PLAYING
TOMLINSON, ANNA M.
    ANNA M. TOMLINSON'S FORTY LESSONS ON HOW TO DEVELOP A PIANO HAND
UNSCHULD, MARIE VON
    PIANIST'S HAND, THE ..A SYSTEMATIC METHOD...ACCORDING TO THE
VANTYN, SIDNEY
    MODERN PIANOFORTE TECHNIQUE
VENABLE, MARY
    INTERPRETATION OF PIANO MUSIC, THE
VERNAZZA, MARCELLE
    BASIC MATERIALS FOR THE PIANO STUDENT
VILLOING, ALEXANDER
    RUBINSTEIN'S FINGER EXERCISES..TECHNICAL STUDIES FROM THE
VIRGIL, ALMON K.
    EDUCATION IN MUSIC..LESSONS TO TEACHERS IN THE INSTRUCTION OF
VIRGIL, ALMON K.
    FOUNDATION EXERCISES IN PIANO PLAYING FROM FIRST RUDIMENTS TO
VIRGIL, ALMON K.
    STEP BY STEP..TEXTBOOK IN PIANO PLAYING..HANDBOOK FOR TEACHERS
VIRGIL, ALMON K.
    TECHNIPHONE MANUAL..INSTRUCTIONS AND EXERCISES IN THE USE OF THE
VIRGIL, ANTHA MINERVA
    VIRGIL METHOD OF PIANOFORTE TECHNIC, THE --2 VOLS.
WAIT, WILLIAM B.
    NORMAL COURSE OF PIANO TECHNIC, THE
WEISER, ADOLPH
    TWO RIGHT HANDS..A GUIDE FOR THE DEVELOPMENT OF PIANO TECHNIQUE
WELLS, HOWARD
    PIANIST'S THUMB, THE
WHITESIDE, ABBY
    INDISPENSABLES OF PIANO PLAYING--2ND. ED.---1955
WIER, ALBERT
    PIANO, THE ..ITS HISTORY, MAKERS, PLAYERS AND MUSIC
WILLIAMS, JEAN E.
    MODERN METHOD OF PIANO INSTRUCTION, A ..TEACHERS MANUAL
WILLIAMS, JOHN M.
    WHAT TO TEACH AT THE VERY FIRST LESSON
WOODHOUSE, GEORGE
    FINGER EXERCISES FOR THE POCKET MUTANO
WOODHOUSE, GEORGE
    FROM KEYBOARD TO MUSIC
WOODHOUSE, GEORGE
    NEW WAY TO PIANO TECHNIQUE, THE --8 VOLS.
WOODHOUSE, GEORGE
    REALISTIC APPROACH TO PIANO PLAYING, A
WRIGHT, WILLIAM C.
    GOLDEN MONITOR, FOR THE PIANOFORTE AND CABINET ORGAN, DESIGNED AS

Studies

BARTH, HANS
    TECHNIC..THE ENTIRE 25 BRANCHES FOR DEVELOPING TECHNIC NECESSARY
BENNER, LORA
    BENNER GOLD BOOK, THE ..PIANO MATERIAL AND TEACHING METHODS--3RD.
BOLTON, HETTY
    ON TEACHING THE PIANO
CHASE, MARY WOOD
    NATURAL LAWS IN PIANO TECHNIC
CHING, JAMES
    STUDIES FOR BASIC PIANO TECHNIQUE..WRITTEN AND SELECTED WITH
CZERNY, CARL
    COMPLETE THEORETICAL AND PRACTICAL PIANO FORTE SCHOOL, FROM THE
DALE, KATHLEEN
    NINETEENTH CENTURY PIANO MUSIC, A HANDBOOK FOR PIANISTS
EHRLICH, ALFRED HEINRICH
    HOW TO PRACTICE ON THE PIANO..REFLECTIONS AND SUGGESTIONS
GAT, JOZSEF
    TECHNIQUE OF PIANO PLAYING, THE, --2ND. ED.---1958
GEARY, ELEANOR MARGARET
    MUSICAL EDUCATION, WITH PRACTICAL OBSERVATIONS ON THE ART OF
GILLESPIE, JOHN
    FIVE CENTURIES OF KEYBOARD MUSIC..AN HISTORIC SURVEY FOR
GRUNDY, ENID
    HAPPY PIANIST, THE
HOOK, JAMES
    GUIDA DI MUSICA..SECOND PART, CONSISTING OF SEVERAL HUNDRED
HORROCKS, CYRIL R. H.
    STUDENT'S GUIDE TO THE ART OF TEACHING THE PIANOFORTE, THE --2ND.
HULL, ARTHUR EAGLEFIELD
    THREE HUNDRED QUESTIONS ON PIANOFORTE TEACHING IN 30 GRADUATED
JOHNSTONE, J. ALFRED
    ART OF TEACHING PIANOFORTE PLAYING, THE --2ND. REV. ED.---1910
JONAS, ALBERTO
    MASTER SCHOOL OF MODERN PIANO PLAYING AND VIRTUOSITY--3 PARTS IN 7
JONAS, ALBERTO
    PIANOSCRIPT BOOK..AN INVALUABLE AID TO TEACHER AND STUDENT IN
LAMAR, RICHARD
    COLLEGE PIANO PEDAGOGY
LEIMER, KARL *
    RHYTHMICS, DYNAMICS, PEDAL, AND OTHER PROBLEMS OF PIANO
LEIMER, KARL *
    SHORTEST WAY TO PIANISTIC PERFECTION, THE
LE COUPPEY, FELIX
    PIANO TEACHING..ADVICE TO PUPILS AND YOUNG TEACHERS---1868 IN
MOOR, WINIFRED
    TECHNICAL EXERCISES FOR THE EMANUEL MOOR DOUBLE KEYBOARD
PALMER, ANNIE L.
    MUSIC TEACHERS' GUIDE TO THE GOLDBECK PIANO METHOD
PALMER, HORATIO R.
    PALMER'S PIANO PRIMER
PARSONS, ALBERT R.
    SCIENCE OF PIANO PRACTICE, THE
PASQUALI, NICOLO
    ART OF FINGERING THE HARPSICHORD, THE
PHILIPP, LILLIE H.
    PIANO STUDY..APPLICATION AND TECHNIQUE
PSTROKONSKY, JULES DE
    NEW METHOD OF TEACHING THE PIANOFORTE
ROSTAND, CLAUDE
    LISZT
SAFONOFF, WASSILI
    NEW FORMULA FOR THE PIANO TEACHER AND PIANO STUDENT
SCHELLING, ERNEST *
    OXFORD PIANO COURSE, TEACHER'S SECOND MANUAL
SQUIRE, RUSSEL N. *
    CLASS PIANO FOR ADULT BEGINNERS--2ND. ED.---1964
VIRGIL, ALMON K.
    FOUNDATION EXERCISES IN PIANO PLAYING FROM FIRST RUDIMENTS TO

History of Technique

HENDERSON, WILLIAM JAMES
    PRELUDES AND STUDIES..MUSICAL THEMES OF THE DAY--SECTION 3..THE
KOCHEVITSKY, GEORGE
    ART OF PIANO PLAYING, THE ..A SCIENTIFIC APPROACH
KULLAK, ADOLPH
    AESTHETICS OF PIANOFORTE PLAYING, THE ---1861 IN GERMAN--1ST.
REEDER, BETAH
    SINGING TOUCH, THE
SOREL, CLAUDETTE
    COMPENDIUM OF PIANO TECHNIQUE--39 ETUDES SELECTED FROM OVER 4000,
STORMEN, WIN
    FIFTY YEARS OF POPULAR PIANO TECHNIQUES IN THE U.S.A.
WIER, ALBERT
    PIANO, THE ..ITS HISTORY, MAKERS, PLAYERS AND MUSIC
WOODHOUSE, GEORGE
    CREATIVE TECHNIQUE, FOR ARTISTS IN GENERAL AND PIANISTS IN
YOUNG, PERCY M.
    KEYBOARD MUSICIANS OF THE WORLD

Compilations of Technical Material

BUELOW, HANS GUIDO VON
    APPLIED PIANO TECHNIC..300 EXTRACTS FOR DAILY PRACTICE FROM
GRIFFIN, SISTER MARY ANNAROSE
    PIANO MATERIALS..GRADED AND COMPILED AS AN AID TO INSTRUCTORS
JONAS, ALBERTO
    MASTER SCHOOL OF MODERN PIANO PLAYING AND VIRTUOSITY--3 PARTS IN 7
SOREL, CLAUDETTE
    COMPENDIUM OF PIANO TECHNIQUE--39 ETUDES SELECTED FROM OVER 4000,
WEISER, ADOLPH
    TWO RIGHT HANDS..A GUIDE FOR THE DEVELOPMENT OF PIANO TECHNIQUE
WELLS, HOWARD
    PIANIST'S THUMB, THE

Mechanical Devices

ANON
    ESSAY ON THE CHIROGYMNAST..OR, FINGER EXERCISES APPLIED TO...ALL
ANON
    GENERAL OBSERVATIONS ON MUSIC AND REMARKS ON MR. LOGIER'S SYSTEM
BROTHERHOOD, JAMES
    BROTHERHOOD 'TECHNICON' AND HOW TO USE IT, THE
BROTHERHOOD, JAMES
    DEVELOPMENT OF THE HAND FOR PIANO-FORTE PLAYING BY MEANS OF A
BROTHERHOOD, JAMES
    SCIENCE AND ART AS TWIN SISTERS..BEING A SECOND TREATISE UPON THE
BROTHERHOOD, JAMES
    TECHNICON, THE..A TREATISE UPON THE DEVELOPMENT OF PIANOFORTE
GEARY, ELEANOR MARGARET
    MUSICAL EDUCATION, WITH PRACTICAL OBSERVATIONS ON THE ART OF
HERZ, HENRI
    MEISSNER'S MODERN, PRACTICAL SYSTEM OF TUNING THE PIANOFORTE..WITH

KOCHEVITSKY, GEORGE
    ART OF PIANO PLAYING, THE ..A SCIENTIFIC APPROACH
LOGIER, JOHANN BERNHARD
    AUTHENTIC ACCOUNT OF THE EXAMINATION OF PUPILS, INSTRUCTED IN THE
LOGIER, JOHANN BERNHARD
    COMPANION TO THE ROYAL PATENT CHIROPLAST, OR HAND-DIRECTOR, A ..A
LOGIER, JOHANN BERNHARD
    EXPLANATION AND DESCRIPTION OF THE ROYAL PATENT CHIROPLAST, OR
LOGIER, JOHANN BERNHARD
    REFUTATION OF THE FALLACIES AND MISREPRESENTATIONS CONTAINED IN A
LOGIER, JOHANN BERNHARD
    SHORT ACCOUNT OF THE PROGRESS OF J. B. LOGIER'S SYSTEM OF MUSICAL
LOGIER, JOHANN BERNHARD
    SYLLABUS OF THE SECOND EXAMINATION OF MR. LOGIER'S PUPILS, ON HIS
LONDON—A COMMITTEE OF PROFESSORS
    EXPOSITION OF THE MUSICAL SYSTEM OF MR. LOGIER..WITH STRICTURES ON
MONTI, H. DE
    STRICTURES ON MR. LOGIER'S SYSTEM OF MUSICAL EDUCATION
OSTROVSKY, HENRY
    TECHNIQUE AND HAND DEVELOPMENT---USE OF A MACHINE
PARSONS, ALBERT R.
    SCIENCE OF PIANO PRACTICE, THE
PRENTICE THOMAS RIDLEY
    HAND GYMNASTICS, FOR THE SCIENTIFIC DEVELOPMENT OF THE MUSCLES
VIRGIL, ANTHA MINERVA
    VIRGIL METHOD OF PIANOFORTE TECHNIC, THE --2 VOLS.
WIER, ALBERT
    PIANO, THE ..ITS HISTORY, MAKERS, PLAYERS AND MUSIC
WOODHOUSE, GEORGE
    FINGER EXERCISES FOR THE POCKET MUTANO

Keyboard Skills

General

AMEY, ELLEN
    CONSCIOUS CONTROL IN PIANO STUDY
BISHOP, DOROTHY
    CHORDS IN ACTION
DAWSON, FREDERICK
    PIANOFORTE, THE
HAMILTON, CLARENCE G.
    PIANO TEACHING..ITS PRINCIPLES AND PROBLEMS
LAMAR, RICHARD
    COLLEGE PIANO PEDAGOGY
SCHELLING, ERNEST *
    OXFORD PIANO COURSE, TEACHER'S FIRST MANUAL

Miscellaneous

BISHOP, DOROTHY
    CHORDS IN ACTION
DAWSON, FREDERICK
    PIANOFORTE, THE
HARICH-SCHNEIDER, ETA
    HARPSICHORD, THE ..AN INTRODUCTION TO TECHNIQUE, STYLE AND THE
REZITS, JOSEPH
    SOURCE MATERIALS FOR PIANO TECHNIQUES
ROWLEY, ALEC *
    MELODY MAKING AT THE PIANO--IN THREE STAGES
TRUE, LYLE C.
    HOW AND WHAT TO PLAY FOR MOVING PICTURES..A MANUAL AND GUIDE FOR

Sight Reading

AHRENS, CORA B. *
    FOR ALL PIANO TEACHERS
ALLISON, IRL
    LET'S LEARN ALL THE NOTES AND READ BETTER..FOR ALL PIANO PUPILS,
BARNWELL, V. T.
    BARNWELL'S NORMAL KEYBOARD AND STAFF STUDIES--THE MENTAL
BASTIEN, JAMES W. *
    BEGINNING PIANO FOR ADULTS
BEMETZRIEDER, ANTON
    ACCOUNT OF A NEW WAY OF CONSIDERING MUSICK, AND TEACHING
BEMETZRIEDER, ANTON
    COMPENDIUM OF A NEW METHOD OF MUSIC...WITH THE AUTHOR'S PRINCIPLES
BOLTON, HETTY
    ON TEACHING THE PIANO
BONPENSIERE, LUIGI
    NEW PATHWAYS TO PIANO TECHNIQUE..A STUDY OF THE RELATIONS BETWEEN
BOOTH, VICTOR
    WE PIANO TEACHERS--REVISED BY ADELE FRANKLIN---1946
BOWEN, CAROLYN
    OUTLINES FOR TRAINING PIANO TEACHERS
BRECKENRIDGE, WILLIAM KILGORE
    HINTS FOR PIANO NORMAL STUDIES
BROUGHTON, JULIA
    SUCCESS IN PIANO TEACHING
BURROWS, RAYMOND
    ELEMENTARY PIANO INSTRUCTION IN COLLEGE
CHAPPLE, STANLEY
    CLASS WAY TO THE KEYBOARD, THE
CHASTEK, WINIFRED
    KEYBOARD SKILLS..SIGHT READING, TRANSPOSITION, HARMONIZATION,
CHING, JAMES
    CANDIDATE'S COMPANION TO THE EXERCISES, SCALES, BROKEN CHORDS,
CHING, JAMES
    NEW GRADED SIGHT READING FOR PIANO, THE --BKS. 1 AND
CHING, JOAN ELIZABETH
    APPROACH TO PIANO TEACHING---ALSO CATALOGUED UNDER
CHURCHILL, VIRGINIA PEAKES
    MODERN TEACHER'S GUIDE TO PIANO AND PIANO CLASS TEACHING
CHURCHILL, VIRGINIA PEAKES
    NINETEEN FIFTY-SIX SUPPLEMENT TO THE MODERN TEACHER'S GUIDE TO
COLOMBATTI, HAROLD
    PROGRESSIVE SIGHT READING EXERCISES---FOR PIANO
COOKE, CHARLES
    PLAYING THE PIANO FOR PLEASURE--REV. ED.---1941
CZERNY, CARL
    COMPLETE THEORETICAL AND PRACTICAL PIANO FORTE SCHOOL, FROM THE
DANIELS, BESS
    PLAYING PIANO AT SIGHT--MECHANICS FOR THE ADULT BEGINNER
DAVIS, LUCILE
    READ AND PLAY..RAPID CHORD CONSTRUCTION--REV. ED.---1943
DEUTSCH, LEONHARD
    PIANO..GUIDED SIGHT-READING
DE WITT, EDYTHE
    EDYTHE DE WITT'S METHOD FOR CLASS PIANO...WRITTEN TO GIVE CORRECT
DUCKWORTH, GUY
    KEYBOARD MUSICIANSHIP
ELKAN, IDA
    PIANO SIGHTREADING CAN BE TAUGHT
ELKAN, IDA
    PRACTICAL PIANO PLAYING MANUAL AND THEORY WRITING BOOK
ELKAN, IDA
    TECHNICAL WORK IN EAR-TRAINING FOR THE PIANO..A METHOD FOR PRIVATE
ENGEL, CARL
    PIANIST'S HANDBOOK, THE ..A GUIDE FOR THE RIGHT COMPREHENSION AND
EVERHART, POWELL
    PIANIST'S ART, THE ..A COMPREHENSIVE MANUAL ON PIANO PLAYING FOR
FIELDEN, THOMAS
    MARKS AND REMARKS..MUSICAL EXAMINATIONS AND THEIR PROBLEMS
FORD, DONALD
    SINGING CLASS PIANIST AND ON PIANOFORTE ACCOMPANYING IN GENERAL,
FREDRICH, FRANK
    PLAYING BY SEEING..A STUDY IN TRAINING AND PERCEPTION FOR BETTER
FRISKIN, JAMES
    PRINCIPLES OF PIANOFORTE PRACTICE, THE
GARRATT, PERCIVAL
    ART OF PIANOFORTE PLAYING, THE
GARROWAY, WILL
    PIANISM
GIDDINGS, THADDEUS P.
    GIDDING'S PUBLIC SCHOOL CLASS METHOD FOR THE PIANO
GLEN, ANNIE
    HOW TO ACCOMPANY..A GUIDE TO THE ARTISTIC ACCOMPANIMENT OF ANY
GRUNDY, ENID
    HAPPY PIANIST, THE
GUTMANN, EMMA WILKINS
    TALKS WITH PIANO TEACHERS
HARKNESS, ROBERT
    HARKNESS PIANO METHOD OF EVANGELISTIC HYMN PLAYING, THE ..A
HARTLINE, ELIZABETH DILL *
    KEYBOARD MUSICIANSHIP, GROUP PIANO FOR ADULTS
HARVEY, ROBERT
    MAGIC KEY TO KEYBOARD SUCCESS, THE
HAVILL, LORINA
    YOU CAN SIGHT READ..THE PLEASURES OF PIANO SIGHT READING THROUGH
HEIDELBERGER, PAULINE
    MASTER METHOD..PIANO NORMAL AND TEACHER'S MANUAL
HORROCKS, CYRIL R. H.
    STUDENT'S GUIDE TO THE ART OF TEACHING THE PIANOFORTE, THE --2ND.
HULL, ARTHUR EAGLEFIELD
    THREE HUNDRED QUESTIONS ON PIANOFORTE TEACHING IN 30 GRADUATED
KANZELL, MAXWELL
    HOW TO READ MUSIC..A COMPLETELY NEW AND SIMPLIFIED APPROACH TO
KARLIN, AARON
    KARLIN'S HARMONIC COURSE FOR PIANO IMPROVISING--4
KEILMAN, WILHELM
    INTRODUCTION TO SIGHT READING
KENYON, CHARLES FREDERICK
    HOW TO MEMORIZE MUSIC
KIRBY, MAY B. KELLY
    KELLY KIRBY KINDERGARTEN PIANO METHOD, TEACHERS' COURSE, THE
KRUSZYNSKI, MICHAL
    APPROACH TO THE PSYCHOLOGY OF PIANO TEACHING, AN
LAMAR, RICHARD
    COLLEGE PIANO PEDAGOGY
LAST, JOAN
    YOUNG PIANIST, THE ..A NEW APPROACH FOR TEACHERS AND
LAWRENCE, SIDNEY
    GUIDE TO REMEDIAL SIGHT READING FOR THE PIANO STUDENT, A
LINDO, ALGERNON H.
    ART OF ACCOMPANYING, THE
LOMAS, LULU GRAHAM
    FIRST TEN PIANO LESSONS, LAID OUT FOR YOUNG TEACHERS, WITH
LOVELOCK, WILLIAM
    TESTS IN SIGHT READING, FOR PIANO..FROM FIRST GRADE TO DIPLOMA--3
MACEWAN, DESIREE
    FIRST TWO YEARS OF PIANOFORTE STUDY, THE
MACLEAN, CHARLES D.
    PRINCIPLES OF PIANOFORTE PRACTICE, THE
MAIER, GUY
    PIANO TEACHER'S COMPANION, THE
MARIAL, R.
    METHODS APPLICABLE TO GROUP TEACHING OR PRIVATE PIANO INSTRUCTION
MCCLINTOCK, LORENE
    TEACH YOURSELF TO PLAY THE PIANO..BASED ON THE INTERVAL METHOD
MCLAIN, MARGARET STARR
    CLASS PIANO
MELCHER, ROBERT A. *
    MUSIC FOR ADVANCED STUDY..A SOURCE BOOK OF EXCERPTS
MERRICK, FRANK
    PRACTICING THE PIANO
MERRILL, MYRTLE
    SIGHT-READING AT THE PIANO
MINNESOTA MUSIC TEACHERS ASSOCIATION
    PIANO-THEORY EXAMINATION SYLLABUS
MOKREJS, JOHN
    LESSONS IN SIGHT READING AT THE PIANO
MOORE, GERALD
    UNASHAMED ACCOMPANIST, THE
MURPHY, HOWARD A. *
    MUSIC FOR STUDY..A SOURCE BOOK OF EXCERPTS
MUSIC EDUCATORS NATIONAL CONFERENCE
    TEACHING PIANO IN CLASSROOM AND STUDIO
NEWMAN, WILLIAM S.
    PIANIST'S PROBLEMS, THE ..A MODERN APPROACH TO EFFICIENT PRACTICE
O'REAR, MRS. ASBURY S.
    SELF READING NOTES
ORREY, LESLIE
    MUSIC AT THE KEYBOARD
PATTON, VICTOR S.
    LEARN TO PLAY POPULAR PIANO BY NOTE IN 20 EASY LESSONS...HOME
PELZ, WILLIAM
    BASIC KEYBOARD SKILLS--2ND. ED.---1963
PERRY, ADELAIDE TROWBRIDGE *
    GUIDE TO PIANO STUDY FOR CLASS OR INDIVIDUAL INSTRUCTION, A
PETERSON, FRANKLIN
    THEORETIC COMPANION TO PRACTICE--PART I OF THE PIANIST'S HANDBOOK
PHILIPP, LILLIE H.
    PIANO STUDY..APPLICATION AND TECHNIQUE
PIERCE, DORA *
    INTRODUCTION TO SIGHT READING, AN
PIERCE, DORA *
    READ AND ENJOY--2 VOLS.
PIERCE, DORA *
    SIGHT READING TESTS FOR BEGINNERS--2 VOLS., 1930-1933
POINTER SYSTEM, INC.
    GUIDE TO THE MODERN PIANIST, A
POTAMKIN, FRANK
    MODERN PIANO PEDAGOGY
PEDDIE, CHARLES FREDERICK
    PIANOFORTE PLAYING ON ITS TECHNICAL AND AESTHETIC SIDES
REES-DAVIES, IVAN
    TRANSPOSITION AT THE KEYBOARD
REEVES, BETTY
    APPROACH TO PIANO TEACHING---ALSO CATALOGUED UNDER
REINAGLE, CAROLINE
    FEW WORDS ON PIANOFORTE PLAYING, A

REZITS, JOSEPH
SOURCE MATERIALS FOR PIANO TECHNIQUES
RHODES, ALFRED
CURIOSITIES OF THE KEY-BOARD AND THE STAFF...SHOWN TO BE UPON A
RICHTER, ADA
TEACHING HINTS
RICKER, EARL
MUSIC LESSONS FOR YOUR CHILD
ROBINSON, HELENE
BASIC PIANO FOR ADULTS
ROOT, CATHERINE ADAMS *
LISTEN, SING AND PLAY..CLASS LESSONS FOR PIANO AND VOICE
ROWLEY, ALEC
DO'S AND DONT'S FOR MUSICIANS..A HANDBOOK FOR TEACHERS AND
ROWLEY, ALEC
PRACTICAL MUSICIANSHIP, A HANDBOOK FOR TEACHERS AND STUDENTS
ROWLEY, ALEC *
SIGHT READING AT THE PIANO--IN THREE STAGES
RUBINSTEIN, BERYL
PIANIST'S APPROACH TO SIGHT READING AND MEMORIZING, THE
SAULS, RANDY
HOW TO READ KEYBOARD MUSIC
SCHELLING, ERNEST *
OXFORD PIANO COURSE, TEACHER'S FIRST MANUAL
SCHELLING, ERNEST *
OXFORD PIANO COURSE, TEACHER'S SECOND MANUAL
SHEFTEL, PAUL
EXPLORING KEYBOARD FUNDAMENTALS
SHEPARD, FRANK H.
HOW TO MODULATE..MODULATING FROM ANY KEY TO ANY OTHER
SIMPSON, ELIZABETH
BASIC PIANOFORTE TECHNIQUE...BASED ON THE SCIENCE OF PIANOFORTE
SMELTZER, JEANNIE R.--COMPILER
OUTLINES AND GRADES FOR THE USE OF PIANO TEACHERS
SMITH, THOMAS
ART OF PLAYING AT SIGHT, THE
SOREL, CLAUDETTE *
INDEPENDENT LEARNING APPROACH TO PIANO SIGHT READING, AN
STARKEY, EVELYN
PIANO CLASS WORKBOOK FOR FIRST YEAR STUDENTS
STEWART, REID
HOW TO PASS MUSIC EXAMINATIONS--PIANO--A GUIDE FOR TEACHERS AND
SWENSON, LUCILE B.
DISCOVERING THE PIANO..THE MULTIPLE KEY APPROACH..STUDY GUIDE AND
TANKARD, GEOFFREY
PIANOFORTE DIPLOMAS
TOBIN, JOSEPH RAYMOND
COMMON SENSE IN SIGHT READING..A GUIDE FOR PIANO TEACHERS
TOBIN, JOSEPH RAYMOND
READ AND REMEMBER..TWELVE STUDY PIECES TO FACILITATE PLAYING FROM
VIRGIL, ALMON K.
FOUNDATION EXERCISES IN PIANO PLAYING FROM FIRST RUDIMENTS TO
VIRGIL, ANTHA MINERVA
ELEMENTARY EXERCISES IN SIGHT READING...FROM THE VIRGIL METHOD
VIRGIL, ANTHA MINERVA
VIRGIL METHOD OF PIANOFORTE TECHNIC, THE --2 VOLS.
WARRINER, JOHN
TRANSPOSITION, KEYBOARD AND ORCHESTRAL--2 PTS., 1893-1908
WIER, ALBERT
PIANO, THE ..ITS HISTORY, MAKERS, PLAYERS AND MUSIC
WILLIAMS, JEAN E.
MODERN METHOD OF PIANO INSTRUCTION, A ..TEACHERS MANUAL
WILSON, MORRIS E.
HOW TO PLAY BY EAR

Keyboard Harmony and Theory

ALBRECHTSBERGER, JOHANN GEORG
ALBRECHTSBERGER'S COLLECTED WRITINGS ON THOROUGH-BASS, HARMONY AND
ALBRECHTSBERGER, JOHANN GEORG
ALBRECHTSBERGER'S ELEMENTARY WORK ON THE SCIENCE OF
ALCHIN, CARRIE A.
APPLIED HARMONY--REVISED AND WITH ADDITIONAL CHAPTERS BY VINCENT
ALCHIN, CARRIE A.
KEYBOARD HARMONY--3 VOLS. IN 1, 1923-1926
ANDERSON, J. CLARK
GOOD MUSIC EXPLAINED..WHAT ALL GOOD PIANISTS SHOULD KNOW
ANON
NEW INSTRUCTIONS FOR PLAYING THE HARPSICHORD, PIANOFORTE OR
ANON
PIANOFORTE POCKET COMPANION, THE ..OR, A POPULAR VIEW OF THE
ANON
PRECEPTOR, FOR THE PIANOFORTE, THE ORGAN OR HARPSICHORD, THE
APPEL, PEARL *
HARMONY AT THE PIANO LESSON, A COMPANION TO PIANO STUDY
ARNOLD, FRANCK THOMAS
ART OF ACCOMPANIMENT FROM A THOROUGH-BASS, AS PRACTICED IN THE
AULD, WILDA J.
HANDBOOK FOR THE CHURCH PIANIST, A
BAKER, DAVID
JAZZ IMPROVISATION..A COMPREHENSIVE METHOD OF STUDY FOR ALL
BANISTER, HENRY C.
HARMONIZING OF MELODIES, THE ..A TEXT-BOOK FOR STUDENTS AND
BARNWELL, V. T.
BARNWELL'S NORMAL KEYBOARD AND STAFF STUDIES--THE MENTAL
BASTIEN, JAMES W. *
BEGINNING PIANO FOR ADULTS
BECKER, JULIUS
CONCISE TREATISE ON HARMONY, ACCOMPANIMENT, AND COMPOSITION, FOR
BEMETZRIEDER, ANTON
ACCOUNT OF A NEW WAY OF CONSIDERING MUSICK, AND TEACHING
BEMETZRIEDER, ANTON
COMPENDIUM OF A NEW METHOD OF MUSIC...WITH THE AUTHOR'S PRINCIPLES
BEMETZRIEDER, ANTON
MUSIC MADE EASY TO EVERY CAPACITY, IN A SERIES OF DIALOGUES..BEING
BEMETZRIEDER, ANTON
NEW GUIDE TO MUSIC, IN FRENCH AND ENGLISH, A
BEMETZRIEDER, ANTON
NEW LESSONS FOR THE HARPSICHORD
BENNER, LORA
THEORY FOR PIANO STUDENTS--1ST. YEAR, PRIVATE OR CLASS--5 VOLS.,
BEVITT, ZAY RECTOR
CLASS PROCEDURE FOR 40 LESSONS IN PIANO PLAYING BY HARMONY
BISHOP, DOROTHY
CHORDS IN ACTION
BLAKE, DOROTHY
FIRST STEPS IN CHORD PLAYING
BOWEN, CAROLYN
OUTLINES FOR TRAINING PIANO TEACHERS
BOYD, MALCOLM
BACH'S INSTRUMENTAL COUNTERPOINT
BOYD, MALCOLM
HARMONIZING 'BACH' CHORALES
BRIDGER, JOHN HENRY
HOW TO HARMONIZE MELODIES, WITH HINTS ON WRITING FOR STRINGS AND
BUCK, PERCY
UNFIGURED HARMONY--2ND. ED.---1911

BURROWES, JOHN FRECKLETON
THOROUGH-BASS PRIMER, THE ..CONTAINING EXPLANATIONS AND EXAMPLES
BUSSLER, LUDWIG
HARMONIC EXERCISES AT THE PIANOFORTE FOR BEGINNERS AND ADVANCED
CALLAGHAN, JAMES
ZIP CHORDMASTER..BEGINNERS HOME COURSE FOR PIANO AND ORGAN
CAPPS, STANLEY M.
CAPPS SYSTEM OF IMPROVISING FOR PIANO, THE --A MODERN COURSE OF
CARL, SYLVESTER
CARL'S DICTIONARY OF CHORDS...REFERENCE BOOK FOR CUED-IN HARMONY
CARTER, BUENTA
ADVANCED KEYBOARD HARMONY WITH ILLUSTRATIVE PIANO PIECES
CARTER, BUENTA
KEYBOARD HARMONY WITH ILLUSTRATIVE PIANO PIECES
CASTELLINI, JOHN EDWARD
RUDIMENTS OF MUSIC..A NEW APPROACH WITH APPLICATION TO THE
CAVALLARO, CARMEN
KEYBOARD HARMONY..A NEW MODERN PIANO METHOD---POPULAR IDIOM
CHAPPLE, STANLEY
CLASS WAY TO THE KEYBOARD, THE
CHASTEK, WINIFRED
KEYBOARD SKILLS..SIGHT READING, TRANSPOSITION, HARMONIZATION,
CHEYETTE, IRVING
BASIC PIANO FOR THE MUSIC EDUCATOR AND CLASSROOM TEACHER
CHILDERS, LEMUEL
CHORD DICTIONARY..DESIGNED FOR TEACHERS, STUDENTS AND SELF-TAUGHT
CHILDERS, LEMUEL
PLAYING THE PIANO BY EAR
CLAPKE, HUGH ARCHIBALD
THEORY EXPLAINED TO PIANO STUDENTS..OR PRACTICAL LESSONS IN
CLEMENTI, MUZIO
CLEMENTI'S SELECTION OF PRACTICAL HARMONY FOR THE ORGAN OR
CONKLIN-HAPP, SUZANNE
APPLIED KEYBOARD HARMONY
COPP, EVELYN A.
WHAT IS THE FLETCHER MUSIC METHOD
COPPAGE, HOWARD W.
PIANO, CHORDS AND HARMONY---REPRODUCED FROM MANUSCRIPT
CRAWFORD, THOMAS J.
CRAWFORD SYSTEM OF KEYBOARD HARMONY AND TRANSPOSITION, THE
CZERNY, CARL
LETTERS TO A YOUNG LADY ON THE ART OF PLAYING THE PIANOFORTE
CZERNY, CARL
NEW EXERCISES ON HARMONY AND THOROUGH BASS...FORMING A PRACTICAL
DALE, BENJAMIN J.
HARMONY, COUNTERPOINT AND IMPROVISATION
DANIELS, BESS *
WORLD OF MUSIC, THE ..PIANO COURSE..TEACHERS' BOOK, FOR CLASS OR
DARDENELLE, LOUISE
HARMONY-FIRST METHOD FOR THE PIANO...FOR CHILD AND ADULT
DAVIS, HARRY
INSTANT PIANO..A UNIQUE METHOD OF READING AND CHORDING FROM THE
DAVIS, LUCILE
READ AND PLAY..RAPID CHORD CONSTRUCTION--REV. ED.----1943
DE SOLIS, SOLITO
THREE POSITIONS OF HARMONIZED SCALES, THE --SHOWN IN ALL KEYS
DILLER, ANGELA
KEYBOARD HARMONY COURSE..A CREATIVE METHOD BASED ON
DILLER, ANGELA
SPLENDOR OF MUSIC, THE
DOBBIE, E. A.
AUSTRALIAN PIANOFORTE TUTOR
DONINGTON, ROBERT
INTERPRETATION OF EARLY MUSIC, THE
DUCKWORTH, GUY
KEYBOARD MUSICIANSHIP
DUNWELL, WILFRID
PIANOFORTE ACCOMPANIMENT WRITING
DUTTON, CHUCK *
MUSIC FOR FUN..PROFESSIONAL COURSE USING THE CHUCK DUTTON
EGBERT, MARION S.
SEEING WHAT WE SING, AN AID THROUGH KEYBOARD EXPERIENCE TO THE
ELKAN, IDA
PRACTICAL PIANO PLAYING MANUAL AND THEORY WRITING BOOK
EVANS, EDWIN
HOW TO ACCOMPANY AT THE PIANO
EVANS, EVERETT J.
SELF-TEACHING CHORD BOOK FOR THE PIANO OR ORGAN..SHOWS HOW TO PLAY
FOOTE, ARTHUR W.
MODULATION AND RELATED HARMONIC QUESTIONS
FOWLES, ERNEST
HARMONY IN PIANOFORTE-STUDY..FOR THE INDIVIDUAL STUDENT--2 VOLS.,
FRACKENPOHL, ARTHUR
HARMONIZATION AT THE PIANO--2ND. ED.---1962
FREDRICH, FRANK
PLAYING BY SEEING..A STUDY IN TRAINING AND PERCEPTION FOR BETTER
GARROWAY, WILL
PIANISM
GASPARINI, FRANCESCO
PRACTICAL HARMONIST AT THE HARPSICHORD, THE ---1708
GEIB, WILLIAM
GEIB'S PIANO-FORTE PRECEPTOR, AND MUSICAL GRAMMAR...A TREATISE ON
GEIB, WILLIAM
TREATISE ON PRACTICAL HARMONIC INTONATION, A ..ALSO, A SYNOPSIS OF
GEMINIANI, FRANCESCO
ART OF ACCOMPANIMENT, OR A NEW AND WELL DIGESTED METHOD TO LEARN
GEMINIANI, FRANCESCO
GUIDA ARMONICA, A DIZIONARIO ARMONICO..BEING A SURE GUIDE TO
GEST, ELIZABETH
KEYBOARD HARMONY FOR JUNIORS
GIBBS, GEORGE A., JR.
FIRST STEPS IN HARMONIZING MELODIES
GIBBS, GEORGE A., JR.
HARMONIZING MELODIES AT SIGHT
GIBBS, GEORGE A., JR.
MODERN CHORD CONSTRUCTION AND ANALYSIS, FOR ALL INSTRUMENTS...AN
GILBERT, RUSSELL S.
SUGGESTED PIANO STUDY FOR THE VOCAL STUDENT
GILBERTSON, ARNOLD B.
TEACHERS MANUAL FOR POPULAR PIANO PLAYING, DESIGNED FOR ALL
GORDON, STEPHEN T.
GORDON'S NEW SCHOOL FOR THE PIANO-FORTE
GOSS, JOHN
INTRODUCTION TO HARMONY AND THOROUGH-BASS WITH NUMEROUS EXAMPLES
GRAF, HENRY C.
SIMPLIFIED KEYBOARD HARMONY
GREW, SIDNEY
FIRST BOOK OF THE PLAYER-PIANIST, THE
GRIMM, CARL W.
HARMONY STUDY AT THE PIANO
GRINDEA, CAROLA
FIRST TEN LESSONS, THE ..A NEW APPROACH TO PIANO TEACHING
HAMBOURG, MARK
HOW TO PREPARE FOR PLAYING IN CONCERT
HAMILTON, ANNA H.
KEYBOARD HARMONY AND TRANSPOSITION..A PRACTICAL COURSE OF KEYBOARD
HAMILTON, CLARENCE G.
MUSIC THEORY FOR PIANO STUDENTS

HAMILTON, JAMES ALEXANDER
    CATECHISM OF THE RUDIMENTS OF HARMONY AND THOROUGHBASS, A ---1833
HARGISS, GENEVIEVE
    MUSIC FOR ELEMENTARY TEACHERS..A PROGRAMMED COURSE IN BASIC THEORY
HARKNESS, ROBERT
    BEGINNERS PIANO COURSE IN HYMN PLAYING BY CORRESPONDENCE
HARTLINE, ELIZABETH DILL *
    KEYBOARD MUSICIANSHIP, GROUP PIANO FOR ADULTS
HAVILL, LORINA
    YOU CAN SIGHT READ..THE PLEASURES OF PIANO SIGHT READING THROUGH
HEACOX, ARTHUR EDWARD
    HARMONY FOR EAR, EYE, AND KEYBOARD--1ST. YEAR
HEACOX, ARTHUR EDWARD
    KEYBOARD TRAINING IN HARMONY--PTS. 1 AND 2--725 GRADED
HECK, JOHANN CASPAR
    COMPLETE SYSTEM OF HARMONY..OR A REGULAR AND EASY METHOD TO ATTAIN
HEIDELBERGER, PAULINE
    MASTER METHOD..PIANO NORMAL AND TEACHER'S MANUAL
HILES, JOHN
    KEY TO THE EXERCISES IN THE CATECHISM OF HARMONY, THOROUGH-BASS
HILL, FRANK W.
    HARMONY AT THE KEYBOARD
HILL, JIM
    CREATIVE WORLD OF SCALES AND CHORDS, THE ..CREATIVE STUDIES IN
HILL, PAUL
    PIANO-MASTER CHORD CHART--CONSTRUCTION, ACCOMPANIMENT, AND SWING
HOLDER, WILLIAM
    TREATISE ON THE NATURAL GROUNDS AND PRINCIPLES OF HARMONY, A ..TO
HOLLIDAY, MARGARET M.
    KEYBOARD MUSICIANSHIP--BKS. 1 AND 2
HOLT, HILDA
    HARMONY AT YOUR KEYBOARD
HOME, ETHEL
    FIRST STEPS IN HARMONIZING MELODIES
HOUGHTON, WINIFRED E.
    TEXTBOOK OF PRACTICAL HARMONY AT THE KEYBOARD
HOWELL, DOROTHY
    KEYBOARD WORK FOR HARMONY STUDENTS
HUNT, REGINALD H.
    HARMONY AT THE KEYBOARD
JOHNSON, JOHN BARHAM
    KEYBOARD HARMONY FOR BEGINNERS
JOHNSON, VERA A.
    SCIENTIFIC SIDE OF MUSIC IN SIMPLE, PRACTICAL FORM FOR TEACHERS
JOUSSE, JOHN
    GUIDA ARMONICA, IN WHICH...CHORDS, ARE CLEARLY EXPLAINED AND
KEDDINGTON, J. BLAINE
    CHORD-O-GRAPH METHOD OF KEYBOARD HARMONY---PRINTED FROM TYPED COPY
KELLER, HERMANN
    THOROUGHBASS METHOD--NUMEROUS EXAMPLES FROM THE LITERATURE OF THE
KERN, ALICE M.
    HARMONIZATION-TRANSPOSITION AT THE KEYBOARD
KOLLMANN, AUGUST F.
    INTRODUCTION TO THE ART OF PRELUDING AND EXTEMPORISING IN SIX
KRAEHENBUEHL, DAVID
    KEYBOARD THEORY--6 VOLS.
LANG, CRAIG SELLAR
    HARMONY AT THE KEYBOARD
LAVIGNAC, ALBERT
    MUSIC AND MUSICIANS---1895, IN FRENCH
LEACH, JOHN R.
    FUNCTIONAL PIANO FOR THE TEACHER
LEHMER, ISABEL
    KEYBOARD HARMONY..A COMPREHENSIVE APPROACH TO MUSICIANSHIP
LEIGHTON, GEORGE A.
    HARMONY, ANALYTICAL AND APPLIED
LIEBERMAN, MAURICE
    ELEMENTARY KEYBOARD HARMONY
LIEBERMAN, MAURICE
    KEYBOARD HARMONY AND IMPROVISATION--2 VOLS.
LINDO, ALGERNON H.
    AURAL TESTS FOR EXAMINATIONS--SPECIALLY WRITTEN FOR TEACHERS AND
LOGIER, JOHANN BERNHARD
    LOGIER'S SYSTEM OF THE SCIENCE OF MUSIC, HARMONY, AND PRACTICAL
LOGIER, JOHANN BERNHARD
    SEQUEL TO THE FIRST COMPANION TO THE CHIROPLAST
LONDON--A COMMITTEE OF PROFESSORS
    EXPOSITION OF THE MUSICAL SYSTEM OF MR. LOGIER..WITH STRICTURES ON
LOWRY, MARGARET
    KEYBOARD APPROACH TO HARMONY
LUBIN, ERNEST
    PIANISTS CHORD MANUAL, THE
LUBIT, JULIA
    PIANOFORTE THEORY COURSE FOR BEGINNERS' PIANO CLASS
LUCKE, KATHARINE E.
    PRACTICAL DRILL IN KEYBOARD HARMONY--2 VOLS., 1932-1940
MAIER, GUY *
    PLAYING THE PIANO..A COURSE OF ROTE TRAINING FOR BEGINNERS--CLASS
MAIER, GUY *
    PLAYING THE PIANO--TEACHER'S MANUAL
MARIAL, R.
    METHODS APPLICABLE TO GROUP TEACHING OR PRIVATE PIANO INSTRUCTION
MASON, WILLIAM G. *
    PRIMER OF MUSIC, A ..BEING THE FIRST STEPS IN MUSICIANSHIP..FOR
MCALL, REGINALD L.
    PRACTICAL CHURCH SCHOOL MUSIC..METHODS AND TRAINING FOR SUCCESSFUL
MCCLINTOCK, LORENE
    TEACH YOURSELF TO PLAY THE PIANO..BASED ON THE INTERVAL METHOD
MCHOSE, ALLEN IRVINE *
    KEYBOARD AND DICTATION MANUAL
MCHOSE, ALLEN IRVINE
    TEACHERS DICTATION MANUAL
MCLAIN, MARGARET STARR
    CLASS PIANO
MEHR, NORMAN
    GROUP PIANO TEACHING
MELCHER, ROBERT A. *
    MUSIC FOR ADVANCED STUDY..A SOURCE BOOK OF EXCERPTS
MELCHER, ROBERT A. *
    MUSIC FOR KEYBOARD HARMONY
MELLERS, WILFRED
    FRANCOIS COUPERIN AND THE FRENCH CLASSICAL TRADITION
MINNESOTA MUSIC TEACHERS ASSOCIATION
    PIANO-THEORY EXAMINATION SYLLABUS
MOKREJS, JOHN
    GREAT HARMONIC LAW OF CHORD PROGRESSION AND IMPROVISING, THE
MOORE, MARY BURNHAM
    LURE OF THE PIANO THROUGH COORDINATION AND CONCENTRATION, THE
MORRIS, REGINALD OWEN
    FIGURED HARMONY AT THE KEYBOARD---PRINCIPALLY EXERCISES
MURPHY, HOWARD A. *
    MUSIC FOR STUDY..A SOURCE BOOK OF EXCERPTS
MUSIC PROJECT--NEW YORK CITY
    TEACHER'S GUIDE..A CREATIVE APPROACH TO PIANO CLASS TEACHING, BY
NEVINS, WILLARD I. *
    HARMONY AT THE KEYBOARD
NEWMAN, ELIZABETH
    HOW TO TEACH MUSIC TO BEGINNERS

NEWMAN, WILLIAM S.
    PIANIST'S PROBLEMS, THE ..A MODERN APPROACH TO EFFICIENT PRACTICE
NICCHIA, LILLIAN
    PIANOFORTE STUDY..HINTS ON PIANO PLAYING
O'TOOLE, WILLIAM
    KEYBOARD HARMONY---DUPLICATED FROM MANUSCRIPT
ORREY, LESLIE
    MUSIC AT THE KEYBOARD
PACE, ROBERT
    MUSIC ESSENTIALS FOR CLASSROOM TEACHERS--2ND. ED.---1961
PACE, ROBERT
    PIANO FOR CLASSROOM MUSIC--2ND. ED.---1956
PATTON, VICTOR S.
    LEARN TO PLAY POPULAR PIANO BY NOTE IN 20 EASY LESSONS...HOME
PAULSON, JOSEPH
    MODERN KEYBOARD HARMONY AND IMPROVISATION
PEARCE, CHARLES WILLIAM
    ART OF THE PIANO TEACHER, THE
PETERSILIA, FRANZ
    STUDY WITH AMUSEMENT, A SERIES OF PROGRESSIVE LESSONS FOR THE
PFEFFERKORN, OTTO W.
    PIANISTIC HINTS
PILLING, DOROTHY
    HARMONIZATION OF MELODIES AT THE KEYBOARD--BKS. 1 AND 2
PILLING, DOROTHY
    KEY TO THE HARMONIZATION OF MELODIES AT THE KEYBOARD--BK. 1
POINTER SYSTEM, INC.
    GUIDE TO THE MODERN PIANIST, A
PRATT, SILAS G.
    PIANIST'S MENTAL VELOCITY, THE ..A SYSTEMATIC PREPARATION OF THE
PRIESING, DOROTHY *
    LANGUAGE OF THE PIANO..A WORKBOOK IN THEORY AND KEYBOARD HARMONY
PROCTOR, CHARLES
    HARMONIZATION AT THE KEYBOARD
QUINTE, MICHAEL S.
    MODULATIONARY HARMONY BOOK
QUIST, BOBBIE LEE *
    LISTEN TO LEARN--KEYBOARD HARMONY
RAST, LAURENCE R.
    LET'S FIND OUT ABOUT MUSIC..WURLITZER ELEMENTARY PIANO WORKBOOKS,
REED, CLARE OSBORNE
    CONSTRUCTIVE HARMONY AND IMPROVISATION
REINAGLE, CAROLINE
    FEW WORDS ON PIANOFORTE PLAYING, A
REZITS, JOSEPH
    SOURCE MATERIALS FOR PIANO TECHNIQUES
RICKER, EARL
    MUSIC LESSONS FOR YOUR CHILD
ROBBINS, EDGAR A.
    AMERICAN METHOD FOR THE PIANOFORTE
ROBINSON, HELENE
    BASIC PIANO FOR ADULTS
ROBYN, LOUISE
    FIRST YEAR ESSENTIALS IN KEYBOARD HARMONY
ROBYN, LOUISE
    ROBYN-HANKS HARMONY, THE ..A JUNIOR COURSE--BKS. 1-3, 1936-1938
ROEDER, CARL M.
    PRACTICAL KEYBOARD HARMONY, A
ROWLEY, ALEC *
    HARMONIZATION AT THE PIANO--IN THREE STAGES
ROWLEY, ALEC
    PRACTICAL MUSICIANSHIP, A HANDBOOK FOR TEACHERS AND STUDENTS
SAULS, RANDY
    THINKING MUSICIANS' APPLICATION OF MODERN HARMONY, THE ..HOW TO
SCHELLING, ERNEST *
    OXFORD PIANO COURSE, TEACHER'S SECOND MANUAL
SCHLIEDER, FREDERICK W.
    LYRIC COMPOSITION THROUGH IMPROVISATION--2 VOLS., 1927-1946
SCHULER, GEORGE S.
    EVANGELISTIC PIANO PLAYING
SCONCIA, JOHN A.
    SCONCIA'S NEW SYSTEM OF INSTRUCTION IN MUSIC AS A SCIENCE..OR, A
SCOTT, WAYNE
    HANDBOOK OF CHORD PROGRESSIONS
SCOVILL, MODENA
    KEYBOARD HARMONY--REV. ED.---1939
SEYMOUR, HARRIET AYER
    HOME MUSIC LESSONS...HOW TO FIND YOUR MUSICAL SELF
SEYMOUR, HARRIET AYER
    HOW TO THINK MUSIC
SHEFTE, ARTHUR G.
    KEYBOARD HARMONY SIMPLIFIED
SHEFTE, ARTHUR G.
    PIANO IMPROVISING--2 VOLS., 1936-1938
SHEFTEL, PAUL
    EXPLORING KEYBOARD FUNDAMENTALS
SHELDON, JAY
    ALL ABOUT MUSIC..A COMPLETE BOOK OF MUSICAL THEORY FOR PIANISTS
SHEPARD, ROBERT
    HARMONIZING..HOW TO PLAY SIMPLE ACCOMPANIMENTS TO A MELODY AT THE
SHUMWAY, STANLEY
    HARMONY AND EAR TRAINING AT THE KEYBOARD
SIMPSON, KENNETH
    KEYBOARD HARMONY AND IMPROVISATION
SMITH, THOMAS
    CONCISE AND PRACTICAL EXPLANATION OF THE RULES OF SIMPLE HARMONY
SMITH, USELMA CLARK
    KEYBOARD HARMONY..LEARNING BY HEARING
SPENCER, BERNARD
    POPULAR PIANO...A CORRESPONDENCE COURSE OF THE EASTERN SCHOOLS OF
SQUIRE, RUSSEL N. *
    CLASS PIANO FOR ADULT BEGINNERS--2ND. ED.---1964
STANLEY, JANE
    BASIC ROUTINES IN ELEMENTARY PIANO TEACHING THROUGH THE FIRST
STARKEY, EVELYN
    PIANO CLASS WORKBOOK FOR FIRST YEAR STUDENTS
STEVENS, A. M.
    HOW TO PLAY THE PIANO AND ORGAN..OR, KEY TO THE SCIENCE AND THEORY
STEVENS, EVERETT
    CHORDS, CADENCES, AND ARPEGGIOS
STORMEN, WIN
    FIFTY YEARS OF POPULAR PIANO TECHNIQUES IN THE U.S.A.
STORMEN, WIN
    LINK TO MODERN MUSIC INSTRUCTION, THE
STORMEN, WIN
    MODERN PIANO IMPROVISATION..BASIC PRINCIPLES ADAPTED FROM THE
STORMEN, WIN
    POPULAR KEYBOARD HARMONY
STORMEN, WIN
    YOUR GUIDE TO PLAYING AND WRITING POPULAR MUSIC--REV. ED.
SWENSON, LUCILE B.
    DISCOVERING THE PIANO..THE MULTIPLE KEY APPROACH..STUDY GUIDE AND
TAPPER, THOMAS
    ABC OF KEYBOARD HARMONY, THE
TAYLOR, FRANKLIN
    PRIMER OF PIANOFORTE PLAYING
THACKRAY, RUPERT M.
    PLAYING FOR DANCE..THE PLACE OF THE PIANIST IN THE TEACHING OF

TISCHLER, HANS
    PRACTICAL HARMONY, AN INTEGRATED COURSE IN THE PRINCIPLES OF
VAN DER VELPEN, JEAN
    HARMONY AND THOROUGH BASS--2 VOLS., 1909-1910
VERNAZZA, MARCELLE
    BASIC MATERIALS FOR THE PIANO STUDENT
VINING, HARRISON S.
    SIMPLE AND COMPLETE PRIMER FOR THE PIANOFORTE, THE
VIRGIL, ANTHA MINERVA
    PRACTICAL EXERCISES IN THEORY AND HARMONY PLAYING...LEADING TO
WEDGE, GEORGE ANSON
    KEYBOARD HARMONY
WEISSBUCH, ANTONIA
    KEYBOARD HARMONY MADE SIMPLE..THE NATURAL ROAD TO MUSICIANSHIP
WELLS, HOWARD
    EARS, BRAIN AND FINGERS..A TEXT BOOK FOR PIANO TEACHERS AND PUPILS
WILLIAMS, JEAN E.
    MODERN METHOD OF PIANO INSTRUCTION, A ..TEACHERS MANUAL
WILSON, MORRIS E.
    HOW TO PLAY BY EAR
WRIGHT, WILLIAM C.
    GOLDEN MONITOR, FOR THE PIANOFORTE AND CABINET ORGAN, DESIGNED AS
WRIGHT, WILLIAM C.
    PIANOFORTE MANUAL, THE ..DESIGNED AS A COMPLETE PIANOFORTE PRIMER
ZEITLIN, POLDI *
    THEORY PAPERS, THE --C.M.P. PIANO LIBRARY--2 VOLS., 1961-1963

Improvisation - Traditional

BACH, CARL PHILIPP EMANUEL
    ESSAY ON THE TRUE ART OF PLAYING KEYBOARD INSTRUMENTS---TWO PTS.,
BASTIEN, JAMES W. *
    BEGINNING PIANO FOR ADULTS
BERNING, ALICE B. *
    KEYBOARD EXPERIENCES FOR CLASSROOM TEACHERS
BISHOP, DOROTHY
    CHORDS IN ACTION
BONPENSIERE, LUIGI
    NEW PATHWAYS TO PIANO TECHNIQUE..A STUDY OF THE RELATIONS BETWEEN
BURROWS, RAYMOND
    ELEMENTARY PIANO INSTRUCTION IN COLLEGE
CAPPS, STANLEY M.
    CAPPS SYSTEM OF IMPROVISING FOR PIANO, THE --A MODERN COURSE OF
CASTELLINI, JOHN EDWARD
    RUDIMENTS OF MUSIC..A NEW APPROACH WITH APPLICATION TO THE
CHAPPLE, STANLEY
    CLASS WAY TO THE KEYBOARD, THE
CHASTEK, WINIFRED
    KEYBOARD SKILLS..SIGHT READING, TRANSPOSITION, HARMONIZATION,
CZERNY, CARL
    COMPLETE THEORETICAL AND PRACTICAL PIANO FORTE SCHOOL, FROM THE
CZERNY, CARL
    LETTERS TO A YOUNG LADY ON THE ART OF PLAYING THE PIANOFORTE
DONINGTON, ROBERT
    INTERPRETATION OF EARLY MUSIC, THE
DONINGTON, ROBERT
    PERFORMER'S GUIDE TO BAROQUE MUSIC, A
DUCKWORTH, GUY
    KEYBOARD MUSICIANSHIP
EVANS, EDWIN
    HOW TO ACCOMPANY AT THE PIANO
FERAND, ERNEST T.
    IMPROVISATION IN NINE CENTURIES OF WESTERN MUSIC
GAT, JOZSEF
    TECHNIQUE OF PIANO PLAYING, THE, --2ND. ED.---1958
GIBBS, GEORGE A., JR.
    HARMONIZING MELODIES AT SIGHT
GRINDEA, CAROLA
    FIRST TEN LESSONS, THE ..A NEW APPROACH TO PIANO TEACHING
HARKNESS, ROBERT
    HARKNESS PIANO METHOD OF EVANGELISTIC HYMN PLAYING, THE ..A
HARTLINE, ELIZABETH DILL *
    KEYBOARD MUSICIANSHIP, GROUP PIANO FOR ADULTS
HERZ, HENRI
    NEW AND COMPLETE PIANOFORTE SCHOOL
HILL, JIM
    CREATIVE IMPROVISING FOR THE RIGHT HAND..CREATIVE STUDIES IN
HOME, ETHEL
    IMPROVISING..A SIMPLE METHOD OF TEACHING THE SUBJECT TO CHILDREN
HUMMEL, JOHANN NEPOMUK
    COMPLETE THEORETICAL AND PRACTICAL COURSE OF INSTRUCTIONS ON THE
HUNT, REGINALD H.
    EXTEMPORIZATION FOR MUSIC STUDENTS
INTERNATIONAL MUSIC INSTITUTE FOR FREE IMPROVISATION
    METHODICAL WAY TO FREE IMPROVISATION, THE --AVANT-GARDE
KARLIN, AARON
    KARLIN'S HARMONIC COURSE FOR PIANO IMPROVISING--4
KOLANDER, MAX
    KOLANDER'S ACCOMPANIMENT INSTRUCTOR FOR THE PIANO OR ORGAN
KOLLMANN, AUGUST F.
    INTRODUCTION TO THE ART OF PRELUDING AND EXTEMPORISING IN SIX
LANG, EDITH *
    MUSICAL ACCOMPANIMENT OF MOVING PICTURES..A PRACTICAL MANUAL FOR
LAVIGNAC, ALBERT
    MUSIC AND MUSICIANS---1895, IN FRENCH
LIEBERMAN, MAURICE
    KEYBOARD HARMONY AND IMPROVISATION--2 VOLS.
MACK, GLEN
    ADVENTURES IN IMPROVISATION AT THE KEYBOARD
MARSDEN AND COMPANY
    HOW TO EXTEMPORIZE PIANO ACCOMPANIMENTS...RAPID AND SIMPLE METHOD
MCHOSE, ALLEN IRVINE *
    KEYBOARD AND DICTATION MANUAL
MCLAIN, MARGARET STARR
    CLASS PIANO
MELLING, E. H.
    EXTEMPORIZING AT THE PIANO MADE EASY
MOKREJS, JOHN
    GREAT HARMONIC LAW OF CHORD PROGRESSION AND IMPROVISING, THE
NEILL, JACK
    NEILL IMPROVISING SYSTEM
NICHOLLS, FREDERICK *
    ADVENTURES IN IMPROVISATION
ORREY, LESLIE
    MUSIC AT THE KEYBOARD
PACE, ROBERT
    MUSIC ESSENTIALS FOR CLASSROOM TEACHERS--2ND. ED.---1961
PACE, ROBERT
    PIANO FOR CLASSROOM MUSIC--2ND. ED.---1956
PASFIELD, WILLIAM R.
    MELODY MAKING, KEYBOARD HARMONY AND EXTEMPORISATION
PATTON, VICTOR S.
    LEARN TO PLAY POPULAR PIANO BY NOTE IN 20 EASY LESSONS...HOME
PAULSON, JOSEPH
    MODERN KEYBOARD HARMONY AND IMPROVISATION
PELZ, WILLIAM
    BASIC KEYBOARD SKILLS--2ND. ED.---1963

PRIESING, DOROTHY *
    LANGUAGE OF THE PIANO..A WORKBOOK IN THEORY AND KEYBOARD HARMONY
PROCTOR, CHARLES
    HARMONIZATION AT THE KEYBOARD
RABINOF, SYLVIA
    MUSICIANSHIP THROUGH IMPROVISATION AT THE KEYBOARD--BK.
REZITS, JOSEPH
    SOURCE MATERIALS FOR PIANO TECHNIQUES
RICHARDSON, ALFRED M.
    EXTEMPORE PLAYING..FORTY LESSONS IN THE ART OF KEYBOARD
ROBINSON, HELENE
    BASIC PIANO FOR ADULTS
SAWYER, FRANK J.
    EXTEMPORIZATION
SCHULER, GEORGE S.
    EVANGELISTIC PIANO PLAYING
SHEFTE, ARTHUR G.
    PIANO IMPROVISING--2 VOLS., 1936-1938
SHEFTEL, PAUL
    EXPLORING KEYBOARD FUNDAMENTALS
SHEPARD, ROBERT
    HARMONIZING..HOW TO PLAY SIMPLE ACCOMPANIMENTS TO A MELODY AT THE
SIMPSON, KENNETH
    KEYBOARD HARMONY AND IMPROVISATION
SMELTZER, JEANNIE R.--COMPILER
    OUTLINES AND GRADES FOR THE USE OF PIANO TEACHERS
STARKEY, EVELYN
    PIANO CLASS WORKBOOK FOR FIRST YEAR STUDENTS
STORMEN, WIN
    LINK TO MODERN MUSIC INSTRUCTION, THE
THACKRAY, RUPERT M.
    PLAYING FOR DANCE..THE PLACE OF THE PIANIST IN THE TEACHING OF
TISCHLER, HANS
    PRACTICAL HARMONY, AN INTEGRATED COURSE IN THE PRINCIPLES OF
TOBIN, JOSEPH RAYMOND
    HOW TO IMPROVISE PIANO ACCOMPANIMENTS
UNITED STATES TRAINING SERVICE
    COURSES OF INSTRUCTION IN PIANO MAKING, TOGETHER WITH A SECTION ON
VERNAZZA, MARCELLE
    BASIC MATERIALS FOR THE PIANO STUDENT
VIRGIL, ANTHA MINERVA
    PRACTICAL EXERCISES IN THEORY AND HARMONY PLAYING...LEADING TO
WESTRUP, SIR JACK ALLAN
    MUSICAL INTERPRETATION---THIS BOOK ACCOMPANIED A SERIES OF B.B.C.
WHITMER, THOMAS C.
    ART OF IMPROVISATION, THE ..A HANDBOOK OF PRINCIPLES AND METHODS
WOLLNER, GERTRUDE PRICE
    IMPROVISATION IN MUSIC..WAYS TOWARDS CAPTURING MUSICAL IDEAS AND
WRIGHT, WILLIAM C.
    GOLDEN MONITOR, FOR THE PIANOFORTE AND CABINET ORGAN, DESIGNED AS
ZEPP, ARTHUR
    LET'S IMPROVISE--2 VOLS.

Improvisation - Jazz

AEBERSOLD, JAMEY
    NEW APPROACH TO JAZZ IMPROVISATION, A --VOL. 1
BAKER, DAVID
    JAZZ IMPROVISATION..A COMPREHENSIVE METHOD OF STUDY FOR ALL
BECKERMAN, H. J.
    AMERICAN SCHOOL OF RAGTIME PIANO PLAYING, THE
CAVALLARO, CARMEN
    KEYBOARD HARMONY..A NEW MODERN PIANO METHOD---POPULAR IDIOM
CHILDERS, LEMUEL
    CHORD DICTIONARY..DESIGNED FOR TEACHERS, STUDENTS AND SELF-TAUGHT
COKER, JERRY
    IMPROVISING JAZZ
COOK, J. LAWRENCE
    PIANO HANDBOOK ON BOOGIE WOOGIE, BLUES, AND BARRELHOUSE..3 EASY TO
COOKE, JAMES FRANCIS
    GREAT MEN AND FAMOUS MUSICIANS ON THE ART OF MUSIC
DUTTON, CHUCK
    MUSIC FOR FUN..PROFESSIONAL COURSE USING THE CHUCK DUTTON
GIBBS, GEORGE A., JR.
    MODERN CHORD CONSTRUCTION AND ANALYSIS, FOR ALL INSTRUMENTS...AN
GILBERTSON, ARNOLD B.
    TEACHERS MANUAL FOR POPULAR PIANO PLAYING, DESIGNED FOR ALL
GRANTHAM, BILLY
    HELLO TO THE BLUES..FUN WITH CHORDS..FUN AND INFORMATION ON
HILL, JIM
    ART OF IMPROVISING, THE ..HOW TO PLAY POPULAR SONGS IN A MODERN
HILL, JIM
    CREATIVE IMPROVISING FOR THE RIGHT HAND..CREATIVE STUDIES IN
HILL, JIM
    CREATIVE WORLD OF SCALES AND CHORDS, THE ..CREATIVE STUDIES IN
HILL, PAUL
    PIANO-MASTER CHORD CHART--CONSTRUCTION, ACCOMPANIMENT, AND SWING
HOLTZ, GUY
    PIANO PROJECTS...A NEW APPROACH TO THE STUDY OF MODERN POPULAR
IRWIN, WILLIAM
    RHYTHM ACCOMPANIMENT MAGIC, FOR THE POPULAR PIANIST
MCCARTHY, ALBERT J.--EDITOR
    PIANO JAZZ..ESSAYS--2 VOLS., 1945-1946
MEHEGAN, JOHN F.
    JAZZ IMPROVISATION..TONAL AND RHYTHMIC PRINCIPLES--4 VOLS.
MEHEGAN, JOHN F.
    JAZZ PIANIST, THE ..STUDIES IN THE ART AND PRACTICE OF JAZZ
MEHEGAN, JOHN F.
    STUDIES IN JAZZ HARMONY
MEHEGAN, JOHN F.
    STYLES FOR THE JAZZ PIANIST--BK. 1..THE RHYTHMIC SCHOOL
MEHEGAN, JOHN F.
    TOUCH AND RHYTHM TECHNIQUES FOR THE JAZZ PIANIST
MEHER, DONOVAN
    HOW TO VAMP AT SIGHT..THE EASIEST AND CLEAREST METHOD OF
PATTON, VICTOR S.
    LEARN TO PLAY POPULAR PIANO BY NOTE IN 20 EASY LESSONS...HOME
REED, CLARE OSBORNE
    CONSTRUCTIVE HARMONY AND IMPROVISATION
ROWBOTHAM, JOHN F.
    HOW TO VAMP..A PRACTICAL GUIDE TO THE ACCOMPANIMENT OF SONGS BY
SMITH, HOWARD G.
    ANYONE CAN PLAY THE PIANO BY EAR IN FIVE EASY LESSONS..A-B-C PIANO
SPENCER, BERNARD
    POPULAR PIANO...A CORRESPONDENCE COURSE OF THE EASTERN SCHOOLS OF
STORMEN, WIN
    FIFTY YEARS OF POPULAR PIANO TECHNIQUES IN THE U.S.A.
STORMEN, WIN
    JAZZ PIANO..DIXIELAND TO MODERN JAZZ, BLUES, BOOGIE, RAGTIME,
STORMEN, WIN
    JAZZ PIANO..EARLY BLUES TO CONTEMPORARY MODERN JAZZ, HOW TO PLAY
STORMEN, WIN
    MODERN PIANO IMPROVISATION..BASIC PRINCIPLES ADAPTED FROM THE
STORMEN, WIN
    POPULAR ACCOMPANYING
STORMEN, WIN
    POPULAR KEYBOARD HARMONY

STORMEN, WIN
    POPULAR PIANO SELF-TAUGHT---1956
STORMEN, WIN
    YOUR GUIDE TO PLAYING AND WRITING POPULAR MUSIC--REV. ED.
UNITED STATES TRAINING SERVICE
    COURSES OF INSTRUCTION IN PIANO MAKING, TOGETHER WITH A SECTION ON
ZUR HEIDE, KARL GERT
    DEEP SOUTH PIANO..THE STORY OF LITTLE BROTHER MONTGOMERY

Transposition

ADLER, KURT
    ART OF ACCOMPANYING AND COACHING, THE ---1965
AULD, WILDA J.
    HANDBOOK FOR THE CHURCH PIANIST, A
BARNWELL, V. T.
    BARNWELL'S NORMAL KEYBOARD AND STAFF STUDIES--THE MENTAL
BASTIEN, JAMES W. *
    BEGINNING PIANO FOR ADULTS
BEMETZRIEDER, ANTON
    NEW GUIDE TO MUSIC, IN FRENCH AND ENGLISH, A
BISHOP, DOROTHY
    CHORDS IN ACTION
BOWEN, CAROLYN
    OUTLINES FOR TRAINING PIANO TEACHERS
BURROWES, JOHN FRECKLETON
    GUIDE TO PRACTICE ON THE PIANOFORTE
BURROWS, RAYMOND
    ELEMENTARY PIANO INSTRUCTION IN COLLEGE
CARL, SYLVESTER
    CARL'S DICTIONARY OF CHORDS...REFERENCE BOOK FOR CUED-IN HARMONY
CARTER, BUENTA
    TRANSPOSITION PATTERNS, FOR THE PIANO...APPROACHED THROUGH
CARY, MRS. C. S. P.
    PIANO-FORTE CLASS BOOK, CONTAINING PRACTICAL RUDIMENTAL LESSONS
CASTELLINI, JOHN EDWARD
    RUDIMENTS OF MUSIC..A NEW APPROACH WITH APPLICATION TO THE
CHAPPLE, STANLEY
    CLASS WAY TO THE KEYBOARD, THE
CHASTEK, WINIFRED
    KEYBOARD SKILLS..SIGHT READING, TRANSPOSITION, HARMONIZATION,
COLOMBATTI, HAROLD
    PRACTICAL COURSE IN TRANSPOSITION, A
CRAMER, JOHN BAPTIST
    INSTRUCTIONS FOR THE PIANOFORTE---CONTAINS ALSO A SET OF 28
CRAWFORD, THOMAS J.
    CRAWFORD SYSTEM OF KEYBOARD HARMONY AND TRANSPOSITION, THE
CURWEN, ANNIE JESSY
    TEACHER'S GUIDE...TO MRS. CURWEN'S PIANOFORTE METHOD, 'THE CHILD
CZERNY, CARL
    COMPLETE THEORETICAL AND PRACTICAL PIANO FORTE SCHOOL, FROM THE
DALE, BENJAMIN J.
    HARMONY, COUNTERPOINT AND IMPROVISATION
DARDENELLE, LOUISE
    HARMONY-FIRST METHOD FOR THE PIANO...FOR CHILD AND ADULT
DUNHAM, ROWLAND W.
    PRACTICAL TRANSPOSITION, FOR PIANISTS AND ORGANISTS
EGBERT, MARION S.
    KEYBOARD EXPERIENCE IN THE CLASSROOM MUSIC PROGRAM..HANDBOOK FOR
ELKAN, IDA
    PRACTICAL PIANO PLAYING MANUAL AND THEORY WRITING BOOK
FAELTEN, CARL *
    TRANSPOSITION READER--FUNDAMENTAL TRAINING COURSE FOR PIANOFORTE
FALKENER, ROBERT
    INSTRUCTIONS FOR PLAYING THE HARPSICHORD..WHEREIN IS FULLY
FIELDEN, THOMAS
    MARKS AND REMARKS..MUSICAL EXAMINATIONS AND THEIR PROBLEMS
FORD, DONALD
    SINGING CLASS PIANIST AND ON PIANOFORTE ACCOMPANYING IN GENERAL,
GARPATT, PERCIVAL
    ART OF PIANOFORTE PLAYING, THE
GASPARINI, FRANCESCO
    PRACTICAL HARMONIST AT THE HARPSICHORD, THE ---1708
GILBERT, RUSSELL S.
    EMBRYO MUSICIAN, THE ..A METHOD OF INTRODUCING MUSIC TO LITTLE
GILBERT, RUSSELL S.
    SUGGESTED PIANO STUDY FOR THE VOCAL STUDENT
GILBERTSON, ARNOLD B.
    TEACHERS MANUAL FOR POPULAR PIANO PLAYING, DESIGNED FOR ALL
GRIMM, CARL W.
    HARMONY STUDY AT THE PIANO
HAMILTON, ANNA H.
    KEYBOARD HARMONY AND TRANSPOSITION..A PRACTICAL COURSE OF KEYBOARD
HARGISS, GENEVIEVE
    MUSIC FOR ELEMENTARY TEACHERS..A PROGRAMMED COURSE IN BASIC THEORY
HARKNESS, ROBERT
    HARKNESS PIANO METHOD OF EVANGELISTIC HYMN PLAYING, THE ..A
HAVILL, LORINA
    YOU CAN SIGHT READ..THE PLEASURES OF PIANO SIGHT READING THROUGH
HEIDELBERGER, PAULINE
    MASTER METHOD..PIANO NORMAL AND TEACHER'S MANUAL
HILL, JIM
    ART OF TRANSPOSING FOR THE PIANO AT SIGHT, THE
HOLDER, WILLIAM
    TREATISE ON THE NATURAL GROUNDS AND PRINCIPLES OF HARMONY, A ..TO
HOLLIDAY, MARGARET M.
    KEYBOARD MUSICIANSHIP--BKS. 1 AND 2
HOLTZ, GUY
    PIANO PROJECTS...A NEW APPROACH TO THE STUDY OF MODERN POPULAR
HULL, ARTHUR EAGLEFIELD
    THREE HUNDRED QUESTIONS ON PIANOFORTE TEACHING IN 30 GRADUATED
HUNT, REGINALD H.
    TRANSPOSITION FOR MUSIC STUDENTS
KLING, HENRI
    TRANSPOSITION...A PRACTICAL AND AUTHORITATIVE GUIDE FOR ALL
LANG, EDITH *
    MUSICAL ACCOMPANIMENT OF MOVING PICTURES..A PRACTICAL MANUAL FOR
LIEBERMAN, MAURICE
    KEYBOARD HARMONY AND IMPROVISATION--2 VOLS.
LINDO, ALGERNON H.
    ART OF ACCOMPANYING, THE
LOVELOCK, WILLIAM
    TRANSPOSITION AT THE KEYBOARD..PIANO..26 PAGES OF GRADED EXERCISES
MASON, WILLIAM G. *
    PRIMER OF MUSIC, A ..BEING THE FIRST STEPS IN MUSICIANSHIP..FOR
MCLAIN, MARGARET STARR
    CLASS PIANO
MERRICK, FRANK
    PRACTICING THE PIANO
MILLER, EDWARD
    INSTITUTES OF MUSIC, OR, EASY INSTRUCTIONS FOR THE HARPSICHORD
MOORE, GERALD
    UNASHAMED ACCOMPANIST, THE
MUSIC PROJECT--NEW YORK CITY
    TEACHER'S GUIDE..A CREATIVE APPROACH TO PIANO CLASS TEACHING, BY
NEWMAN, ELIZABETH
    HOW TO TEACH MUSIC TO BEGINNERS

NEWTON, ERNEST
    ELEMENTARY STUDIES IN TRANSPOSITION--BKS. 1 AND 2
NICHOL, HENRY E.
    TRANSPOSITION AT SIGHT..FOR STUDENTS OF THE ORGAN AND
ORREY, LESLIE
    MUSIC AT THE KEYBOARD
PACE, ROBERT
    MUSIC ESSENTIALS FOR CLASSROOM TEACHERS--2ND. ED.---1961
PACE, ROBERT
    PIANO FOR CLASSROOM MUSIC--2ND. ED.---1956
PELZ, WILLIAM
    BASIC KEYBOARD SKILLS--2ND. ED.---1963
PLATT, CAROLYN
    CAROLYN PLATT METHOD FOR PIANO, THE --GROUP INSTRUCTION--TEACHER'S
PRELLEUR, PETER
    HARPSICHORD ILLUSTRATED AND IMPROV'D, WHEREIN IS SHEWN THE ITALIAN
QUINTE, MICHAEL J.
    MODULATIONARY HARMONY BOOK
REES-DAVIES, IVAN
    TRANSPOSITION AT THE KEYBOARD
REZITS, JOSEPH
    SOURCE MATERIALS FOR PIANO TECHNIQUES
ROBINSON, HELENE
    BASIC PIANO FOR ADULTS
ROBYN, LOUISE
    HOW TO TEACH PIANO TO THE CHILD BEGINNER..A TEXT BOOK FOR TEACHERS
ROWLEY, ALEC *
    GRADED TESTS IN PRACTICAL MUSICIANSHIP AND MUSICAL INITIATIVE--IN
SAULS, RANDY
    THINKING MUSICIANS' APPLICATION OF MODERN HARMONY, THE ..HOW TO
SCHELLING, ERNEST *
    OXFORD PIANO COURSE, TEACHER'S SECOND MANUAL
SCHULER, GEORGE S.
    EVANGELISTIC PIANO PLAYING
SMELTZER, JEANNIE R.--COMPILER
    OUTLINES AND GRADES FOR THE USE OF PIANO TEACHERS
STARKEY, EVELYN
    PIANO CLASS WORKBOOK FOR FIRST YEAR STUDENTS
STORMEN, WIN
    LINK TO MODERN MUSIC INSTRUCTION, THE
STORMEN, WIN
    YOUR GUIDE TO PLAYING AND WRITING POPULAR MUSIC--REV. ED.
SUMNER, WILLIAM L.
    PIANOFORTE, THE --3RD. ED.---1966
SWENSON, LUCILE B.
    DISCOVERING THE PIANO..THE MULTIPLE KEY APPROACH..STUDY GUIDE AND
TOBIN, JOSEPH RAYMOND
    ADVENTURES IN MUSICIANSHIP
TOBIN, JOSEPH RAYMOND
    TRANSPOSING AT THE PIANO--IN THREE STAGES
TRACY, GEORGE L.
    PRACTICAL GUIDE TO THE STUDY OF TRANSPOSITION, A
VINING, HARRISON S.
    SIMPLE AND COMPLETE PRIMER FOR THE PIANOFORTE, THE
WARRINER, JOHN
    TRANSPOSITION, KEYBOARD AND ORCHESTRAL--2 PTS., 1893-1908
WHITMER, THOMAS C.
    ART OF IMPROVISATION, THE ..A HANDBOOK OF PRINCIPLES AND METHODS
WILLIAMS, JEAN E.
    MODERN METHOD OF PIANO INSTRUCTION, A ..TEACHERS MANUAL
WILLIAMS, JOHN M.
    WHAT TO TEACH AT THE VERY FIRST LESSON
WRIGHT, WILLIAM C.
    GOLDEN MONITOR, FOR THE PIANOFORTE AND CABINET ORGAN, DESIGNED AS
WRIGHT, WILLIAM C.
    PIANOFORTE MANUAL, THE ..DESIGNED AS A COMPLETE PIANOFORTE PRIMER

Modulation

ALCHIN, CARRIE A.
    APPLIED HARMONY--REVISED AND WITH ADDITIONAL CHAPTERS BY VINCENT
ANON
    PIANOFORTE POCKET COMPANION, THE ..OR, A POPULAR VIEW OF THE
AULD, WILDA J.
    HANDBOOK FOR THE CHURCH PIANIST, A
BAILLIE, ALEXANDER--SUPPOSED AUTHOR
    INTRODUCTION TO THE KNOWLEDGE AND PRACTICE OF THE THORO' BASS, AN
BAKER, PERCY
    STUDIES IN MODULATION FOR PRACTICAL AND THEORETICAL PURPOSES
BANISTER, HENRY C.
    ART OF MODULATING, THE --A SERIES OF PAPERS ON MODULATION AT THE
BANISTER, HENRY C.
    HARMONIZING OF MELODIES, THE ..A TEXT-BOOK FOR STUDENTS AND
BAUER, HAROLD
    PRIMER FOR PRACTICAL KEYBOARD MODULATION, A
BECKER, JULIUS
    CONCISE TREATISE ON HARMONY, ACCOMPANIMENT, AND COMPOSITION, FOR
BEMETZRIEDER, ANTON
    ABSTRACT OF A NEW METHOD OF TEACHING THE PRINCIPLES OF MUSIC,
BEMETZRIEDEP, ANTON
    ART OF MODULATING, ILLUSTRATED, THE
BRIDGER, JOHN HENRY
    HOW TO HARMONIZE MELODIES, WITH HINTS ON WRITING FOR STRINGS AND
BROWN, JEAN PARKMAN
    INTERVALS, CHORDS AND EAR TRAINING FOR YOUNG PIANOFORTE STUDENTS
BUCHAROFF, SIMON
    MODERN PIANIST'S TEXT BOOK, THE
BUCK, PERCY
    UNFIGURED HARMONY--2ND. ED.---1911
BUSSLER, LUDWIG
    HARMONIC EXERCISES AT THE PIANOFORTE FOR BEGINNERS AND ADVANCED
CARL, SYLVESTER
    CARL'S DICTIONARY OF CHORDS...REFERENCE BOOK FOR CUED-IN HARMONY
CHAPPLE, STANLEY
    CLASS WAY TO THE KEYBOARD, THE
CHILDERS, LEMUEL
    PLAYING THE PIANO BY EAR
CHRISTIANSEN, FREDERICK M.
    PRACTICAL MODULATION FOR ADVANCED STUDENTS---43 LESSONS
CRAWFORD, THOMAS J.
    CRAWFORD SYSTEM OF KEYBOARD HARMONY AND TRANSPOSITION, THE
CZERNY, CARL
    LETTERS ON THOROUGH-BASS...FORMING THE SECOND PART OF THE LETTERS
DOBBIE, E. A.
    AUSTRALIAN PIANOFORTE TUTOR
FOOTE, ARTHUR W.
    MODULATION AND RELATED HARMONIC QUESTIONS
FOWLES, ERNEST
    HARMONY IN PIANOFORTE-STUDY..FOR THE INDIVIDUAL STUDENT--2 VOLS.,
FRICK, PHILIPP J.
    ART OF MUSICAL MODULATION RENDERED EASY AND FAMILIAR, THE
FULLER, ESTHER MARY
    KEYBOARD MODULATIONS FOR ALL KEYBOARD INSTRUMENTS..552 TWO-MEASURE
GASPARINI, FRANCESCO
    PRACTICAL HARMONIST AT THE HARPSICHORD, THE ---1708
GEMINIANI, FRANCESCO
    GUIDA ARMONICA, A DIZIONARIO ARMONICO..BEING A SURE GUIDE TO

GILBERT, RUSSELL S.
    SUGGESTED PIANO STUDY FOR THE VOCAL STUDENT
GILBERTSON, ARNOLD B.
    TEACHERS MANUAL FOR POPULAR PIANO PLAYING, DESIGNED FOR ALL
GORDON, STEPHEN T.
    GORDON'S NEW SCHOOL FOR THE PIANO-FORTE
GOSS, JOHN
    INTRODUCTION TO HARMONY AND THOROUGH-BASS WITH NUMEROUS EXAMPLES
GRIMM, CARL W.
    HARMONY STUDY AT THE PIANO
HARKNESS, ROBERT
    HARKNESS PIANO METHOD OF EVANGELISTIC HYMN PLAYING, THE ..A
HIGGS, JAMES
    MODULATION--'NOVELLO'S MUSIC PRIMERS', NO. 31
HILES, JOHN
    CATECHISM OF HARMONY, THOROUGH-BASS, AND MODULATION, A ..WITH
HILES, JOHN
    KEY TO THE EXERCISES IN THE CATECHISM OF HARMONY, THOROUGH-BASS
HOLLIDAY, MARGARET M.
    KEYBOARD MUSICIANSHIP--BKS. 1 AND 2
HOWELL, DOROTHY
    KEYBOARD WORK FOR HARMONY STUDENTS
HUNT, REGINALD H.
    EXTEMPORIZATION FOR MUSIC STUDENTS
JOUSSE, JOHN
    GUIDA ARMONICA, IN WHICH...CHORDS, ARE CLEARLY EXPLAINED AND
KANZELL, MAXWELL
    HOW TO READ MUSIC..A COMPLETELY NEW AND SIMPLIFIED APPROACH TO
KERN, ALICE M.
    HARMONIZATION-TRANSPOSITION AT THE KEYBOARD
KREBS, T. L.
    MANUAL OF MODULATION...FOR THE USE OF PIANISTS AND ORGANISTS
LANG, EDITH *
    MUSICAL ACCOMPANIMENT OF MOVING PICTURES..A PRACTICAL MANUAL FOR
LAWRENCE, LUCILE
    ART OF MODULATING, THE ..FOR HARPISTS, PIANISTS, ORGANISTS
LEHMER, ISABEL
    KEYBOARD HARMONY..A COMPREHENSIVE APPROACH TO MUSICIANSHIP
LEIGHTON, GEORGE A.
    HARMONY, ANALYTICAL AND APPLIED
LIEBERMAN, MAURICE
    ELEMENTARY KEYBOARD HARMONY
LIEBERMAN, MAURICE
    KEYBOARD HARMONY AND IMPROVISATION--2 VOLS.
LINDO, ALGERNON H.
    TREATISE ON MODULATION WITH TYPICAL EXAMPLES FROM WELL-KNOWN
LONG, NOEL
    HARMONY AND STYLE--3 VOLS.
MCHOSE, ALLEN IRVINE *
    KEYBOARD AND DICTATION MANUAL
MCHOSE, ALLEN IRVINE
    TEACHERS DICTATION MANUAL
MCLAIN, MARGARET STARR
    CLASS PIANO
NEVINS, WILLARD I. *
    HARMONY AT THE KEYBOARD
OREM, PRESTON WARE
    MANUAL OF MODULATION
OTTERSTROEN, THORVALD
    THEORY OF MODULATION, A ---DUAL TEXT..ENGLISH AND GERMAN
PEARCE, CHARLES WILLIAM
    ART OF THE PIANO TEACHER, THE
PEERY, ROB ROY
    PRACTICAL KEYBOARD MODULATION
PETERS, WILLIAM C.
    ELEMENTS OF THOROUGH BASE, ADAPTED TO THE WANTS OF YOUNG PUPILS
PILLING, DOROTHY
    HARMONIZATION OF MELODIES AT THE KEYBOARD--BKS. 1 AND 2
PROCTOR, CHARLES
    HARMONIZATION AT THE KEYBOARD
QUINTE, MICHAEL S.
    MODULATIONARY HARMONY BOOK
REED, CLARE OSBORNE
    CONSTRUCTIVE HARMONY AND IMPROVISATION
REGER, MAX
    ON THE THEORY OF MODULATION
REGER, MAX
    SUPPLEMENT TO THE THEORY OF MODULATION
REZITS, JOSEPH
    SOURCE MATERIALS FOR PIANO TECHNIQUES
RHODES, ALFRED
    CURIOSITIES OF THE KEY-BOARD AND THE STAFF...SHOWN TO BE UPON A
RICHARDSON, ALFRED M.
    EXTEMPORE PLAYING..FORTY LESSONS IN THE ART OF KEYBOARD
ROBBINS, EDGAR A.
    AMERICAN METHOD FOR THE PIANOFORTE
ROBINSON, HELENE
    BASIC PIANO FOR ADULTS
ROWLEY, ALEC *
    GRADED TESTS IN PRACTICAL MUSICIANSHIP AND MUSICAL INITIATIVE--IN
ROWLEY, ALEC
    PRACTICAL MUSICIANSHIP, A HANDBOOK FOR TEACHERS AND STUDENTS
SCHAAF, EDWARD O.
    FUNDAMENTAL PRINCIPLES INVOLVED IN THE COMPOSING AND ARRANGING OF
SCHELLING, ERNEST *
    OXFORD PIANO COURSE, TEACHER'S SECOND MANUAL
SCHLIEDER, FREDERICK W.
    LYRIC COMPOSITION THROUGH IMPROVISATION--2 VOLS., 1927-1946
SHEPARD, FRANK H.
    HOW TO MODULATE..MODULATING FROM ANY KEY TO ANY OTHER
SHUMWAY, STANLEY
    HARMONY AND EAR TRAINING AT THE KEYBOARD
SMITH, USELMA CLARK
    KEYBOARD HARMONY..LEARNING BY HEARING
STORMEN, WIN
    LINK TO MODERN MUSIC INSTRUCTION, THE
SWENSON, LUCILE B.
    DISCOVERING THE PIANO..THE MULTIPLE KEY APPROACH..STUDY GUIDE AND
TAYLER, E. DOUGLAS
    MODULATION MADE EASY
TISCHLER, HANS
    PRACTICAL HARMONY, AN INTEGRATED COURSE IN THE PRINCIPLES OF
TOBIN, JOSEPH RAYMOND
    ADVENTURES IN MUSICIANSHIP
TOBIN, JOSEPH RAYMOND
    HOW TO IMPROVISE PIANO ACCOMPANIMENTS
TOBIN, JOSEPH RAYMOND
    MODULATION AT THE PIANO--IN THREE STAGES
VENDEN, LEONARD
    MUSICIAN'S LIGHTNING MODULATION GUIDE..INFORMATION, EXAMPLES,
VERNAZZA, MARCELLE
    BASIC MATERIALS FOR THE PIANO STUDENT
VINING, HARRISON S.
    SIMPLE AND COMPLETE PRIMER FOR THE PIANOFORTE, THE
VIRGIL, ANTHA MINERVA
    PRACTICAL EXERCISES IN THEORY AND HARMONY PLAYING...LEADING TO

WARRINER, JOHN
    TRANSPOSITION, KEYBOARD AND ORCHESTRAL--2 PTS., 1893-1908
WEBBE, SAMUEL
    HARMONY EPITOMIZED, BEING A SHORT EXPLANATION OF FIGURED BASSES,
WHITMER, THOMAS C.
    ART OF IMPROVISATION, THE ..A HANDBOOK OF PRINCIPLES AND METHODS
WILLIAMS, JEAN E. *
    MIND IN MUSIC, THE
WOLFRAM, THEODOR
    PRACTICAL MODULATOR, OR, HOW TO LEARN TO MODULATE FROM ANY ONE KEY

Score Reading

BERNSTEIN, MARTIN--COMPILER
    SCORE READING..A SERIES OF GRADED EXCERPTS
CZERNY, CARL
    COMPLETE THEORETICAL AND PRACTICAL PIANO FORTE SCHOOL, FROM THE
FETIS, FRANCOIS JOSEPH
    HOW TO PLAY FROM SCORE...ON THE ORGAN OR PIANOFORTE
FISKE, ROGER
    SCORE READING--BK. 3..CONCERTOS
FISKE, ROGER
    SCORE READING--BK. 4..ORATORIOS
FORD, DONALD
    SINGING CLASS PIANIST AND ON PIANOFORTE ACCOMPANYING IN GENERAL,
GARROWAY, WILL
    PIANISM
JACOB, GORDON P.
    HOW TO READ A SCORE
MELCHER, ROBERT A. *
    MUSIC FOR SCORE READING
MURPHY, HOWARD A. *
    MUSIC FOR STUDY..A SOURCE BOOK OF EXCERPTS
RIEMANN, HUGO
    INTRODUCTION TO PLAYING FROM SCORE
TAYLOR, ERIC R.
    INTRODUCTION TO SCORE PLAYING, AN
TAYLOR, ERIC R.
    PLAYING FROM AN ORCHESTRAL SCORE
WOLFF, KONRAD
    TEACHING OF ARTUR SCHNABEL, THE ..A GUIDE TO INTERPRETATION

Figured Bass Playing

ADAMS, JOHN S.
    FIVE THOUSAND MUSICAL TERMS..A COMPLETE DICTIONARY WITH A TREATISE
ALBRECHTSBERGER, JOHANN GEORG
    ALBRECHTSBERGER'S COLLECTED WRITINGS ON THOROUGH-BASS, HARMONY AND
ALBRECHTSBERGER, JOHANN GEORG
    ALBRECHTSBERGER'S ELEMENTARY WORK ON THE SCIENCE OF
ALBRECHTSBERGER, JOHANN GEORG
    METHODS OF HARMONY, FIGURED BASE, AND COMPOSITION...ADAPTED FOR
ALBRECHTSBERGER, JOHANN GEORG
    PRINCIPLES OF ACCOMPANIMENT OR THOROUGH BASS
ANON
    CHILD'S INTRODUCTION TO THOROUGH BASS, THE ..IN CONVERSATIONS OF A
ANON
    COMPLEAT TUTOR FOR THE HARPSICHORD OR SPINNET, WHEREIN IS SHEWN
ANON
    FIRST STEPS TO THOROUGH BASE, IN 12 FAMILIAR LESSONS BETWEEN A
ANON
    NEW AND COMPLETE INSTRUCTIONS FOR THE HARPSICHORD, PIANO FORTE OR
ANON
    NEW INSTRUCTIONS FOR PLAYING THE HARPSICHORD, PIANOFORTE OR
ANON
    PLAYING THE HARPSICHORD, SPINET OR PIANO FORTE MADE EASY BY NEW
ANON
    PRECEPTOR, FOR THE PIANOFORTE, THE ORGAN OR HARPSICHORD, THE
ANON
    RULES..OR A SHORT AND COMPLEAT METHOD FOR ATTAINING TO PLAY A
ANON
    THOROUGH BASS AT ONE VIEW, WITH DIRECTIONS FOR ACCOMPANIMENT AND
ARNOLD, FRANCK THOMAS
    ART OF ACCOMPANIMENT FROM A THOROUGH-BASS, AS PRACTICED IN THE
BACH, CARL PHILIPP EMANUEL
    ESSAY ON THE TRUE ART OF PLAYING KEYBOARD INSTRUMENTS---TWO PTS.,
BAILLIE, ALEXANDER--SUPPOSED AUTHOR
    INTRODUCTION TO THE KNOWLEDGE AND PRACTICE OF THE THORO' BASS, AN
BAXTER, JAMES
    INDUCTIVE GRAMMAR OF MUSIC, FOR CLASS, PRIVATE LESSON, OR SELF
BAXTER, JAMES
    NEW SCHOOL OF MUSIC, THE ..PRACTICAL THOROUGH BASE CULTURE, FOR
BEMETZRIEDER, ANTON
    COMPENDIUM OF A NEW METHOD OF MUSIC...WITH THE AUTHOR'S PRINCIPLES
BUCK, PERCY
    UNFIGURED HARMONY--2ND. ED.---1911
BUELOW, GEORGE J.
    THOROUGH-BASS ACCOMPANIMENT ACCORDING TO JOHANN DAVID HEINICHEN
BURROWES, JOHN FRECKLETON
    THOROUGH-BASS PRIMER, THE ..CONTAINING EXPLANATIONS AND EXAMPLES
CLARE, EDWARD
    ANALYSIS OF PRACTICAL THOROUGH BASS
CLARE, EDWARD
    NEW TREATISE OF PRACTICAL THOROUGH BASS, A
CORFE, JOSEPH
    THOROUGH BASS SIMPLIFIED
CROTCH, WILLIAM
    ELEMENTS OF MUSICAL COMPOSITION..COMPREHENDING THE RULES OF
CROTCH, WILLIAM
    PRACTICAL THOROUGH BASS, OR, THE ART OF PLAYING FROM A FIGURED
CZERNY, CARL
    LETTERS ON THOROUGH-BASS...FORMING THE SECOND PART OF THE LETTERS
CZERNY, CARL
    LETTERS TO A YOUNG LADY ON THE ART OF PLAYING THE PIANOFORTE
CZERNY, CARL
    NEW EXERCISES ON HARMONY AND THOROUGH BASS...FORMING A PRACTICAL
DOLMETSCH, ARNOLD
    INTERPRETATION OF MUSIC OF THE SEVENTEENTH AND EIGHTEENTH
DONINGTON, ROBERT
    INTERPRETATION OF EARLY MUSIC, THE
DONINGTON, ROBERT
    PERFORMER'S GUIDE TO BAROQUE MUSIC, A
FALKENER, ROBERT
    INSTRUCTIONS FOR PLAYING THE HARPSICHORD..WHEREIN IS FULLY
FISKE, ROGER
    SCORE READING--BK. 3..CONCERTOS
FORTE, ALLEN
    COMPOSITIONAL MATRIX, THE ..MONOGRAPHS IN THEORY AND COMPOSITION
FRICK, PHILIPP J.
    TREATISE ON THOROUGH BASS, A
GASPARINI, FRANCESCO
    PRACTICAL HARMONIST AT THE HARPSICHORD, THE ---1708
GEMINIANI, FRANCESCO
    ART OF ACCOMPANIMENT, OR A NEW AND WELL DIGESTED METHOD TO LEARN
GEMINIANI, FRANCESCO
    GUIDA ARMONICA, A DIZIONARIO ARMONICO..BEING A SURE GUIDE TO

GEMINIANI, FRANCESCO
RULES FOR PLAYING IN A TRUE TASTE ON THE VIOLIN, GERMAN FLUTE,
GORDON, STEPHEN T.
GORDON'S NEW SCHOOL FOR THE PIANO-FORTE
GOSS, JOHN
INTRODUCTION TO HARMONY AND THOROUGH-BASS WITH NUMEROUS EXAMPLES
HAMILTON, JAMES ALEXANDER
CATECHISM OF THE RUDIMENTS OF HARMONY AND THOROUGHBASS, A ---1833
HAWKINS, JOHN SIDNEY
INQUIRY INTO THE NATURE AND PRINCIPLES OF THROUGH BASS, ON A NEW
HECK, JOHANN CASPAR
ART OF PLAYING THOROUGH BASS WITH CORRECTNESS ACCORDING TO THE
HECK, JOHANN CASPAR
COMPLETE SYSTEM OF HARMONY..OR A REGULAR AND EASY METHOD TO ATTAIN
HECK, JOHANN CASPAR
SHORT AND FUNDAMENTAL INSTRUCTIONS FOR LEARNING THOROUGH BASS
HILES, JOHN
CATECHISM OF HARMONY, THOROUGH-BASS, AND MODULATION, A ..WITH
HILES, JOHN
KEY TO THE EXERCISES IN THE CATECHISM OF HARMONY, THOROUGH-BASS
HOLDER, WILLIAM
TREATISE ON THE NATURAL GROUNDS AND PRINCIPLES OF HARMONY, A ..TO
JOHNSON, ARTEMAS N.
INSTRUCTIONS IN THE ART OF PLAYING CHURCH MUSIC UPON THE MELODEON,
JOHNSON, ARTEMAS N.
INSTRUCTIONS IN THOROUGH BASE..BEING A NEW AND EASY METHOD FOR
JOHNSON, ARTEMAS N.
JOHNSON'S NEW METHOD FOR THOROUGH BASE..AN INSTRUCTION BOOK IN THE
JOHNSON, ARTEMAS N.
THOROUGH BASE, MELODEON, ORGAN AND HARMONY INSTRUCTION BOOK, WITH
JONES, JOHN H.
PRACTICAL GUIDE TO THOROUGH BASS, A ..OR, HARMONY ILLUSTRATED AND
JOUSSE, JOHN
GUIDA ARMONICA, IN WHICH...CHORDS, ARE CLEARLY EXPLAINED AND
KELLER, GOTTFRIED
COMPLEAT METHOD, FOR ATTAINING TO PLAY A THOROUGH BASS UPON EITHER
KELLER, HERMANN
THOROUGHBASS METHOD--NUMEROUS EXAMPLES FROM THE LITERATURE OF THE
KLOSE, F. J.
PRACTICAL HINTS FOR ACQUIRING THOROUGH BASS
KOLLMANN, AUGUST F.
PRACTICAL GUIDE TO THOROUGH-BASS, A
KOLLMANN, AUGUST F.
SECOND PRACTICAL GUIDE TO THOROUGH BASS, A
LAMPE, JOHN F.
PLAIN AND COMPENDIOUS METHOD OF TEACHING THOROUGH BASS, A ..WITH
LINDO, ALGERNON H.
ART OF ACCOMPANYING, THE
LINLEY, FRANCIS
NEW ASSISTANT TO THE PIANO-FORTE OR HARPSICHORD, A ...RULES FOR
LOCKE, MATTHEW
MELOTHESIA..OR, CERTAIN GENERAL RULES FOR PLAYING UPON A
LOGIER, JOHANN BERNHARD
LOGIER'S SYSTEM OF THE SCIENCE OF MUSIC, HARMONY, AND PRACTICAL
LOGIER, JOHANN BERNHARD
SYSTEM OF THE SCIENCE OF MUSIC AND PRACTICAL
LUDDEN, WILLIAM
THOROUGH BASS SCHOOL, THE ..AN EASY AND PROGRESSIVE COURSE FOR
MARSH, JOHN
RUDIMENTS OF THOROUGH BASS, THE
MATTHESON, JOHANN
COMPLETE TREATISE OF THOROUGH BASS, A
MCHOSE, ALLEN IRVINE *
KEYBOARD AND DICTATION MANUAL
MCHOSE, ALLEN IRVINE
TEACHERS DICTATION MANUAL
MILLER, EDWARD
ELEMENTS OF THOROUGH BASS AND COMPOSITION
MORRIS, REGINALD OWEN
FIGURED HARMONY AT THE KEYBOARD---PRINCIPALLY EXERCISES
MUFFAT, GEORG
ESSAY ON THOROUGHBASS, AN --MUSICOLOGICAL STUDIES AND DOCUMENTS,
NICHOLSON, JAMES
CONCISE TREATISE ON THOROUGHBASS, A
ORREY, LESLIE
MUSIC AT THE KEYBOARD
PASQUALI, NICOLO
THOROUGH-BASS MADE EASY..OR, PRACTICAL RULES FOR FINDING AND
PETERS, WILLIAM C.
ECLECTIC PIANOFORTE SCHOOL, THE ..ARRANGED FROM THE WORKS OF THE
PETERS, WILLIAM C.
ELEMENTS OF THOROUGH BASE, ADAPTED TO THE WANTS OF YOUNG PUPILS
PILLING, DOROTHY
HARMONIZATION OF MELODIES AT THE KEYBOARD--BKS. 1 AND 2
PRELLEUR, PETER
HARPSICHORD ILLUSTRATED AND IMPROV'D, WHEREIN IS SHEWN THE ITALIAN
RELFE, JOHN
REMARKS ON THE PRESENT STATE OF MUSICAL INSTRUCTION...THOROUGH
SCHNEIDER, FRIEDRICH
SCHNEIDER'S TREATISE ON THOROUGH BASS AND HARMONY
SMITH, THOMAS
CONCISE AND PRACTICAL EXPLANATION OF THE RULES OF SIMPLE HARMONY
UNITED STATES TRAINING SERVICE
COURSES OF INSTRUCTION IN PIANO MAKING, TOGETHER WITH A SECTION ON
VAN DER VELPEN, JEAN
HARMONY AND THOROUGH BASS--2 VOLS., 1909-1910
WEBBE, SAMUEL
HARMONY EPITOMIZED, BEING A SHORT EXPLANATION OF FIGURED BASSES,
WESTRUP, SIR JACK ALLAN
MUSICAL INTERPRETATION---THIS BOOK ACCOMPANIED A SERIES OF B.B.C.
WILLIAMS, PETER F.
FIGURED BASS ACCOMPANIMENT--2 VOLS.

Accompaniment Writing

ALBRECHTSBERGER, JOHANN GEORG
PRINCIPLES OF ACCOMPANIMENT OR THOROUGH BASS
ARNOLD, FRANCK THOMAS
ART OF ACCOMPANIMENT FROM A THOROUGH-BASS, AS PRACTICED IN THE
BECKER, JULIUS
CONCISE TREATISE ON HARMONY, ACCOMPANIMENT, AND COMPOSITION, FOR
BEMETZRIEDER, ANTON
ABSTRACT OF A NEW METHOD OF TEACHING THE PRINCIPLES OF MUSIC,
BEMETZRIEDER, ANTON
ACCOUNT OF A NEW WAY OF CONSIDERING MUSICK, AND TEACHING
BRIDGER, JOHN HENRY
HOW TO HARMONIZE MELODIES, WITH HINTS ON WRITING FOR STRINGS AND
BUELOW, GEORGE J.
THOROUGH-BASS ACCOMPANIMENT ACCORDING TO JOHANN DAVID HEINICHEN
CRANMER, PHILIP
TECHNIQUE OF ACCOMPANIMENT, THE --THE STUDENT'S MUSIC LIBRARY
DUNWELL, WILFRID
PIANOFORTE ACCOMPANIMENT WRITING
LINDO, ALGERNON H.
ART OF ACCOMPANYING, THE
LOVELOCK, WILLIAM
ELEMENTARY ACCOMPANIMENT WRITING--CHIEFLY MUSIC, FOR EXAM

PACE, ROBERT
MUSIC ESSENTIALS FOR CLASSROOM TEACHERS--2ND. ED.---1961
ROWLEY, ALEC *
MELODY MAKING AT THE PIANO--IN THREE STAGES
SCHULER, GEORGE S.
ACCOMPANIST'S MANUAL, THE
WAGNER, JOHN J.
NUMERICAL METHOD OF PIANO ACCOMPANIMENTS, A --WITH CHARTS

Playing by Ear

CHILDERS, LEMUEL
PLAYING THE PIANO BY EAR
ETHIER, JOSEPH A.
ETHIER'S GREAT NON-SUCH SELF-INSTRUCTOR IN THE ART OF ACCOMPANYING
LE ROY, PERRY J.
HOW TO PLAY THE PIANO BY EAR..THE QUICK, EASY, SIMPLE WAY
LITTLE, FRED W.
LITTLE SYSTEM OF PLAYING THE PIANO BY EAR, THE
MORDEN, HARRY
PLAYING THE PIANO BY EAR--3 PTS.
ORREY, LESLIE
MUSIC AT THE KEYBOARD
ROWLEY, ALEC
PRACTICAL MUSICIANSHIP, A HANDBOOK FOR TEACHERS AND STUDENTS
SMITH, EDWIN S.
PIANO BY EAR
SMITH, HOWARD G.
ANYONE CAN PLAY THE PIANO BY EAR IN FIVE EASY LESSONS..A-B-C PIANO
TAYLOR, FRANCIS
REEVES' VAMPING TUTOR FOR PLAYING BY EAR
WILSON, MORRIS E.
HOW TO HELP YOUR CHILD WITH MUSIC--2ND. ED.---1951
WILSON, MORRIS E.
HOW TO PLAY BY EAR

Piano Music

General

ADAMS, JULIETTE
WHAT THE PIANO WRITING OF EDWARD MACDOWELL MEANS TO THE PIANO
APEL, WILLI
HISTORY OF KEYBOARD MUSIC TO 1700, THE --TRANSLATED AND REVISED BY
EDWARDS, RUTH
COMPLEAT MUSIC TEACHER FOR TEACHERS, PARENTS AND STUDENTS
FILLMORE, JOHN C.
PIANOFORTE MUSIC..ITS HISTORY, WITH BIOGRAPHICAL SKETCHES AND
RUBINSTEIN, BERYL
OUTLINE OF PIANO PEDAGOGY--REV. ED.---1929
YATES, PETER
AMATEUR AT THE KEYBOARD, AN

Miscellaneous

AMERICAN PIANO CORPORATION
CATALOGUE OF MUSIC FOR THE AMPICO, A ..A LIST OF THE RECORDINGS OF
BRISKIER, ARTHUR
NEW APPROACH TO PIANO TRANSCRIPTIONS AND INTERPRETATION OF JOHANN
LOWE, CLAUDE EDGERTON
WORD-PHRASES TO BACH'S 48 FUGUES, WITH HINTS ON THE RENDERINGS OF
POTAMKIN, FRANK
MODERN PIANO PEDAGOGY
SAVLER, ROBERTA--EDITOR
SELECTIONS FROM THE PIANO TEACHER, 1958-1963
YATES, PETER
AMATEUR AT THE KEYBOARD, AN

Composers and Compositional Techniques

ABRAHAM, GERALD
CHOPIN'S MUSICAL STYLE---1939
ADAMS, JULIETTE
WHAT THE PIANO WRITING OF EDWARD MACDOWELL MEANS TO THE PIANO
ALBRECHTSBERGER, JOHANN GEORG
ALBRECHTSBERGER'S COLLECTED WRITINGS ON THOROUGH-BASS, HARMONY AND
ALBRECHTSBERGER, JOHANN GEORG
METHODS OF HARMONY, FIGURED BASE, AND COMPOSITION...ADAPTED FOR
ALTMAN, FRANCES
GEORGE GERSHWIN, MASTER COMPOSER
AMPICO CORPORATION
AMPICO REPRODUCING PIANO..A SUPPLEMENT TO 'PIANO MUSIC, ITS
ANON
LIFE AND WORKS OF GUSTAVE SATTER, THE ..A BIOGRAPHICAL SKETCH IN
ANON
LIFE AND WORKS OF STEPHEN HELLER, THE PIANOFORTE COMPOSER, THE ..A
APEL, WILLI
HISTORY OF KEYBOARD MUSIC TO 1700, THE --TRANSLATED AND REVISED BY
APEL, WILLI
MASTERS OF THE KEYBOARD
ARONSON, MAURICE
KEY TO THE MINIATURES OF LEOPOLD GODOWSKY, A ..ANALYTICAL ESSAYS
ARPIN, PAUL
LIFE OF LOUIS MOREAU GOTTSCHALK
AZULAY, GERTRUDE
CHOPIN..THE STORY OF THE BOY WHO MADE BEAUTIFUL MELODIES
BAGGER, EUGENE S.
EMINENT EUROPEANS..STUDIES IN CONTINENTAL REALITY---PADEREWSKI
BARBEDETTE, HIPPOLYTE
STEPHEN HELLER..HIS LIFE AND WORKS
BARFORD, PHILIP
KEYBOARD MUSIC OF C. P. E. BACH, THE ..CONSIDERED IN RELATION TO
BAUGHAN, EDWARD ALGERNON
IGNACE JAN PADEREWSKI
BEOBROOK, GERALD STARES
KEYBOARD MUSIC FROM THE MIDDLE AGES TO THE BEGINNINGS OF THE
BEHREND, WILLIAM
LUDWIG VAN BEETHOVEN'S PIANOFORTE SONATAS
BENNER, LORA
BENNER GOLD BOOK, THE ..PIANO MATERIAL AND TEACHING METHODS--3RD.
BENNETT, JOSEPH
FREDERIC CHOPIN--NOVELLO'S BIOGRAPHY PRIMERS
BIART, VICTOR
PIANIST'S GUIDE, THE ..A SERIES OF PAMPHLETS ON THE TEACHING AND
BIDOU, HENRI
CHOPIN
BIE, OSKAR
HISTORY OF THE PIANOFORTE AND PIANOFORTE PLAYERS, A ---1899
BLOM, ERIC
BEETHOVEN'S PIANOFORTE SONATAS DISCUSSED---1938
BODKY, ERWIN
INTERPRETATION OF BACH'S KEYBOARD WORKS, THE

BOGIANCKINO, MASSIMO
    HARPSICHORD MUSIC OF DOMENICO SCARLATTI, THE
BORREN, CHARLES VAN DEN
    SOURCES OF KEYBOARD MUSIC IN ENGLAND, THE ---1913
BOWEN, CATHERINE DRINKER
    FREE ARTIST..THE STORY OF ANTON AND NICHOLAS RUBINSTEIN
BOYD, MALCOLM
    HARMONIZING 'BACH' CHORALES
BRANSON, DAVID
    JOHN FIELD AND CHOPIN
BRESLIN, HOWARD
    CONCERT GRAND---GOTTSCHALK
BRISKIER, ARTHUR
    NEW APPROACH TO PIANO TRANSCRIPTIONS AND INTERPRETATION OF JOHANN
BROCKWAY, WALLACE *
    MEN OF MUSIC..THEIR LIVES, TIMES, AND ACHIEVEMENTS--REV.
BROWER, HARRIETTE
    MODERN MASTERS OF THE KEYBOARD
BROWER, HARRIETTE
    STORY-LIVES OF MASTER MUSICIANS
BROWER, HARRIETTE
    WHAT TO PLAY---WHAT TO TEACH
BROWN, MAURICE J. E.
    SCHUBERT'S VARIATIONS
BULL, STORM
    INDEX TO BIOGRAPHIES OF CONTEMPORARY COMPOSERS
BYRON, MAY CLARISSA
    DAY WITH FREDERIC CHOPIN, A
CALDWELL, JOHN
    ENGLISH KEYBOARD MUSIC BEFORE THE NINETEENTH CENTURY---EXTENSIVE
CANAVE, PAZ CORAZON G.
    RE-EVALUATION OF THE ROLE PLAYED BY C. P. E. BACH IN THE
CARLSON, EFFIE B.
    BIO-BIBLIOGRAPHICAL DICTIONARY OF TWELVE-TONE AND SERIAL
CAUCHI, PAUL
    CHOPIN..CENTENNIAL MEMORY 1849-1949..A LECTURE
CHASINS, ABRAM
    SPEAKING OF PIANISTS
CHISSELL, JOAN
    CHOPIN--'GREAT COMPOSERS' SERIES
CHISSELL, JOAN
    SCHUMANN PIANO MUSIC--B.B.C. MUSIC GUIDE, NO. 25
COCKSHOOT, JOHN V.
    FUGUE IN BEETHOVEN'S PIANO MUSIC, THE
COHEN, HARRIET
    MUSIC'S HANDMAID
COOKE, JAMES FRANCIS
    LOUIS MOREAU GOTTSCHALK..A SHORT BIOGRAPHY
CORDER, FREDERICK
    FERENCZ LISZT--HALF-TITLE..MASTERS OF MUSIC
CORTOT, ALFRED
    ALFRED CORTOT'S STUDIES IN MUSICAL INTERPRETATION, SET DOWN BY
CORTOT, ALFRED
    FRENCH PIANO MUSIC
CORTOT, ALFRED
    PIANO MUSIC OF CLAUDE DEBUSSY, THE
COVIELLO, AMBROSE
    CHOICE OF A BEETHOVEN SONATA FOR DIPLOMA EXAMINATIONS, THE --NOTES
CRONK, CUTHBERT H.
    WORKS OF ANTON RUBINSTEIN, NOV. 1829-NOV. 1894, THE ..A STUDY
CULSHAW, JOHN
    CONCERTO, THE
CULSHAW, JOHN
    SERGEI RACHMANINOFF..THE MAN AND HIS MUSIC
CURTIS, ALAN
    SWEELINCK'S KEYBOARD MUSIC..A STUDY OF ENGLISH ELEMENTS IN
CZERNY, CARL
    ON THE PROPER PERFORMANCE OF ALL BEETHOVEN'S WORKS FOR THE PIANO
DALE, KATHLEEN
    NINETEENTH CENTURY PIANO MUSIC, A HANDBOOK FOR PIANISTS
DART, THURSTON
    INTERPRETATION OF MUSIC, THE --4TH. ED.---1954
DAVISON, JAMES W.
    FREDERICK CHOPIN..A MEMOIR
DAVISON, JAMES W.
    FREDERIC FRANCOIS CHOPIN..CRITICAL AND APPRECIATIVE ESSAY---1843
DAWES, FRANCIS E.
    DEBUSSY PIANO MUSIC--B.B.C. MUSIC GUIDE---COMPOSITIONAL ASPECT
DEMUTH, NORMAN
    FRENCH PIANO MUSIC..A SURVEY WITH NOTES ON ITS PERFORMANCE
DENT, EDWARD J.
    FERRUCCIO BUSONI, A BIOGRAPHY
DICKINSON, ALLAN E.
    BACH'S FUGAL WORKS
DIDIMUS, HENRY
    BIOGRAPHY OF LOUIS MOREAU GOTTSCHALK, THE AMERICAN PIANIST AND
DONINGTON, ROBERT
    PERFORMER'S GUIDE TO BAROQUE MUSIC, A
DORIAN, FREDERICK
    HISTORY OF MUSIC IN PERFORMANCE, THE ---1942
DRAKE, KENNETH
    SONATAS OF BEETHOVEN AS HE PLAYED AND TAUGHT THEM, THE
DRY, WAKELING
    CHOPIN--'MUSIC OF THE MASTERS' SERIES
DUMESNIL, MAURICE
    HOW TO PLAY AND TEACH DEBUSSY
DUNLOP, AGNES MARY
    DUET---STORY OF CLARA AND ROBERT SCHUMANN
DUNN, JOHN PETRIE
    ORNAMENTATION IN THE WORKS OF FREDERIC CHOPIN---1921
EHRLICH, ALFRED HEINRICH
    ORNAMENTATION IN BEETHOVEN'S PIANOFORTE-WORKS, THE
EMERY, WALTER
    BACH'S ORNAMENTS
EVANS, EDWIN
    HANDBOOK TO THE PIANOFORTE WORKS OF JOHANNES BRAHMS---1936
EWEN, DAVID
    COMPOSERS SINCE 1900..A BIOGRAPHICAL AND CRITICAL GUIDE
EWEN, DAVID
    GREAT COMPOSERS, 1300-1900..A BIOGRAPHICAL AND CRITICAL GUIDE
EWEN, DAVID
    WORLD OF GREAT COMPOSERS, THE
EXECUTIVE COMMITTEE OF CHOPIN YEAR 1949
    CHOPIN YEAR 1949 IN POLAND, THE
FERGUSON, DONALD NIVISON
    PIANO INTERPRETATION
FERGUSON, DONALD NIVISON
    PIANO MUSIC OF SIX GREAT COMPOSERS---1947
FERRIS, GEORGE TITUS
    GREAT MUSICAL COMPOSERS..GERMAN, FRENCH, AND ITALIAN
FILLMORE, JOHN C.
    PIANOFORTE MUSIC..ITS HISTORY, WITH BIOGRAPHICAL SKETCHES AND
FINCK, HENRY T.
    CHOPIN AND OTHER MUSICAL ESSAYS---1889
FINCK, HENRY T.
    PADEREWSKI AND HIS ART
FISCHER, EDWIN
    BEETHOVEN'S PIANOFORTE SONATAS, A GUIDE FOR STUDENTS AND

FISCHER, EDWIN
    REFLECTIONS ON MUSIC
FISKE, ROGER
    BEETHOVEN CONCERTOS AND OVERTURES
FORMAN, DENIS
    MOZART'S CONCERTO FORM..THE FIRST MOVEMENTS OF THE PIANO CONCERTOS
FORTE, ALLEN
    COMPOSITIONAL MATRIX, THE ..MONOGRAPHS IN THEORY AND COMPOSITION
FULLER-MAITLAND, J. A.
    KEYBOARD SUITES OF J. S. BACH, THE
FULLER-MAITLAND, J. A.
    ROBERT SCHUMANN--'THE GREAT MUSICIANS' SERIES
FULLER-MAITLAND, J. A.
    SCHUMANN'S PIANOFORTE WORKS
GABRIEL, GILBERT W.
    GREAT PIANISTS AND COMPOSERS
GARVIN, FLORENCE HOLLISTER
    BEGINNINGS OF THE ROMANTIC PIANO CONCERTO, THE
GIDE, ANDRE
    NOTES ON CHOPIN
GILLESPIE, JOHN
    FIVE CENTURIES OF KEYBOARD MUSIC..AN HISTORIC SURVEY FOR
GIRDLESTONE, CUTHBERT
    MOZART AND HIS PIANO CONCERTOS---FIRST PUBLISHED IN 1948 AS
GLENNON, JAMES
    MAKING FRIENDS WITH PIANO MUSIC..THE HISTORY AND ANALYTICAL NOTES
GLINSKI, MATEUSZ
    CHOPIN THE UNKNOWN
GLOYNE, HOWARD F.--M.D.
    CARL A. PREYER, THE LIFE OF A KANSAS MUSICIAN
GOTTSCHALD, ERNEST
    BEETHOVEN'S PIANOFORTE SONATAS EXPLAINED FOR THE LOVERS OF THE
GRAY, CECIL
    BACH UND DAS WOHLTEMPERIRTE KLAVIER..ANALYTICAL NOTES, WITH AN
GRAY, CECIL
    FORTY-EIGHT PRELUDES AND FUGUES OF J. S. BACH, THE
HADDEN, JAMES CUTHBERT
    CHOPIN--'MASTER MUSICIANS' SERIES
HADOW, SIR WILLIAM HENRY
    SONATA FORM---1896
HADOW, SIR WILLIAM HENRY
    STUDIES IN MODERN MUSIC--2ND. SERIES--9TH. ED.---CHOPIN
HALLE, SIR CHARLES
    ST. JAMES HALL...C. HALLE'S PIANOFORTE RECITALS..MAY 5-JUNE 29,
HALLE, SIR CHARLES
    ST. JAMES HALL...MR. HALLE'S BEETHOVEN RECITALS, MAY 23-JULY 11,
HAMILTON, CLARENCE G.
    PIANO MUSIC, ITS COMPOSERS AND CHARACTERISTICS
HARDING, HENRY ALFRED
    ANALYSIS OF FORM AS DISPLAYED IN BEETHOVEN'S 32 PIANOFORTE
HARRISON, W. WELLS
    SCHUBERT'S COMPOSITIONS FOR PIANO AND STRINGS--STRAD HANDBOOK NO.
HARSANYI, ZSOLT
    IMMORTAL FRANZ..THE LIFE AND LOVES OF A GENIUS---FRANZ LISZT
HEDLEY, ARTHUR
    CHOPIN--'MASTER MUSICIAN' SERIES--INCLUDES CATALOGUE OF
HENDERSON, WILLIAM JAMES
    PRELUDES AND STUDIES..MUSICAL THEMES OF THE DAY--SECTION 3..THE
HERVEY, ARTHUR
    FRANZ LISZT AND HIS MUSIC
HERVEY, ARTHUR
    FRENCH MUSIC IN THE NINETEENTH CENTURY---CHOPIN
HERVEY, ARTHUR
    RUBINSTEIN--'MAYFAIR BIOGRAPHIES', NO. 11
HERVEY, ARTHUR
    SAINT-SAENS---1921
HEUSCHNEIDER, KARIN
    PIANO SONATA OF THE EIGHTEENTH CENTURY IN GERMANY, THE
HEUSCHNEIDER, KARIN
    PIANO SONATA OF THE EIGHTEENTH CENTURY IN ITALY, THE
HILL, RALPH
    LISZT
HOLCMAN, JAN
    LEGACY OF CHOPIN, THE
HOLMES, EDWARD
    ANALYTICAL AND THEMATIC INDEX OF MOZART'S PIANO WORKS
HOPKINS, ANTHONY
    TALKING ABOUT CONCERTOS..AN ANALYTICAL STUDY OF A NUMBER OF
HOPKINSON, CECIL
    BIBLIOGRAPHICAL THEMATIC CATALOGUE OF THE WORKS OF JOHN FIELD,
HUBBARD, ELBERT
    LITTLE JOURNEYS TO THE HOMES OF GREAT MUSICIANS--VOL. 8, NO.
HUBBARD, ELBERT
    LITTLE JOURNEYS TO THE HOMES OF GREAT MUSICIANS--VOL. 9, NO.
HUEFFER, FRANCIS
    HALF A CENTURY OF MUSIC IN ENGLAND, 1837-1887..LISZT IN ENGLAND
HUEFFER, FRANCIS
    MUSICAL STUDIES..A SERIES OF CONTRIBUTIONS BY FRANCIS HUEFFER,
HUMISTON, WILLIAM H.
    ANTON RUBINSTEIN--'LITTLE BIOGRAPHIES'
HUMISTON, WILLIAM H.
    CHOPIN--'LITTLE BIOGRAPHIES'
HUMISTON, WILLIAM H.
    LISZT--'LITTLE BIOGRAPHIES'
HUMISTON, WILLIAM H.
    PADEREWSKI--'LITTLE BIOGRAPHIES'
HUMISTON, WILLIAM H.
    RACHMANINOFF--'LITTLE BIOGRAPHIES'
HUNEKER, JAMES GIBBONS
    CHOPIN..THE MAN AND HIS MUSIC---1901
HUNEKER, JAMES GIBBONS
    FRANZ LISZT
HUNEKER, JAMES GIBBONS
    MELOMANIACS..ESSAYS---CHOPIN AND LISZT
HUNEKER, JAMES GIBBONS
    MEZZOTINTS IN MODERN MUSIC--6TH. ED.---CHOPIN AND LISZT--1901
HUNEKER, JAMES GIBBONS
    UNICORNS---CHOPIN
HUNEKER, JAMES GIBBONS
    VARIATIONS---CHOPIN, LISZT, AND PACHMANN
HUTCHESON, ERNEST
    GREAT MASTERS OF PIANO MUSIC, THE ..BACH, BEETHOVEN, SCHUMANN,
HUTCHESON, ERNEST *
    LITERATURE OF THE PIANO, THE ..A GUIDE FOR AMATEUR AND
HUTCHINGS, ARTHUR
    COMPANION TO MOZART'S PIANO CONCERTOS, A
ILIFFE, FREDERICK
    FORTY-EIGHT PRELUDES AND FUGUES OF JOHANN SEBASTIAN BACH ANALYZED
INTERNATIONAL MUSICOLOGICAL CONGRESS..FIRST--1960--WORKS OF FREDERICK
    BOOK OF THE FIRST INTERNATIONAL MUSICOLOGICAL CONGRESS DEVOTED TO
ISAACSON, CHARLES D.
    FACE TO FACE WITH GREAT MUSICIANS---CHOPIN AND LISZT
IWASZKIEWICZ, JAROSLAW
    SUMMER AT NOHANT..A PLAY IN THREE ACTS---CHOPIN
JAMES, BURNETT
    BRAHMS..A CRITICAL STUDY
JOHNSTONE, J. ALFRED
    NOTES ON THE INTERPRETATION OF 24 FAMOUS PIANO SONATAS OF

JOHNSTONE, J. ALFRED
TOUCH, PHRASING AND INTERPRETATION
JONSON, GEORGE CHARLES
HANDBOOK TO CHOPIN'S WORKS, A
KARASOWSKI, MORITZ
FREDERIC CHOPIN..HIS LIFE, LETTERS AND WORKS--3RD. REV. ED.---1879
KASTNER, RUDOLPH
BEETHOVEN'S PIANO SONATAS AND ARTUR SCHNABEL
KEEFER, LUBOV
INFLUENCE OF ADAM MICKIEWICZ ON THE BALLADES OF CHOPIN, THE
KELBERINE, ALEXANDER
FOUR FAMOUS PIANOFORTE SONATAS OF BEETHOVEN, THE --OP. 13, OP. 27,
KELLEY, EDGAR STILLMAN
CHOPIN THE COMPOSER---1913
KENYON, MAX
HARPSICHORD MUSIC..THE INSTRUMENTS, THE COMPOSERS, THE PLAYERS
KIRBY, FRANK EUGENE
SHORT HISTORY OF KEYBOARD MUSIC, A
KIRKPATRICK, RALPH
DOMENICO SCARLATTI---1953
KLECZYNSKI, JAN
CHOPIN'S GREATER WORKS...HOW THEY SHOULD BE UNDERSTOOD...INCLUDING
KLECZYNSKI, JAN
HOW TO PLAY CHOPIN--THREE LECTURES
KLECZYNSKI, JAN
WORKS OF FREDERIC CHOPIN, THE ..THEIR PROPER INTERPRETATION--6TH.
KNOLLER, JACOB
FREE WILL OR DESTINY..ONE ACT PLAY AROUND CHOPIN---EARLY SUMMER,
KOBYLANSKA, KRYSTYNA--EDITOR
CHOPIN IN HIS OWN LAND..DOCUMENTS AND SOUVENIRS
KOCH, CASPAR
PIANO STUDENT'S GRADUS AD PARNASSUM, THE ..PRESENTING THE
KORSTEN, BJARNE
RECENT NORWEGIAN PIANO MUSIC
LAMAR, RICHARD
COLLEGE PIANO PEDAGOGY
LANDOWSKA, WANDA
LANDOWSKA ON MUSIC--EDITED BY DENISE RESTOUT
LANDOWSKA, WANDA
MUSIC OF THE PAST
LANNING, RUSSELL
BACH ORNAMENTATION
LEIMER, KARL *
SHORTEST WAY TO PIANISTIC PERFECTION, THE
LESSMANN, W. J. OTTO
FRANZ LISZT..EINE HULDIGUNG--FRANZ LISZT..A TRIBUTE
LINGG, ANN M.
MEPHISTO WALTZ, THE STORY OF FRANZ LISZT
LISZT, FRANZ
LIFE OF CHOPIN--TRANSLATED ONLY IN PART BY MARTHA WALKER COOK
LOCKWOOD, ALBERT
NOTES ON THE LITERATURE OF THE PIANO--RE-EDITED BY BROTHER, SAMUEL
LONG, MARGUERITE
AT THE PIANO WITH DEBUSSY---1960, IN FRENCH
LUBIN, ERNEST
PIANO DUET, THE ..A GUIDE FOR PIANISTS
LYLE, WATSON
CAMILLE SAINT-SAENS, HIS LIFE AND ART---DISCUSSES CONCERTI AND
MACKENZIE, SIR ALEXANDER
LISZT--'THE MAYFAIR BIOGRAPHIES', NO. 3
MACKENZIE, SIR ALEXANDER
LISZT--MASTERPIECES OF MUSIC
MAINE, BASIL
CHOPIN--'GREAT LIVES' SERIES
MARKS, F. HELENA
QUESTIONS ON MOZART'S PIANO SONATAS, DESIGNED AS A COMPANION
MARKS, F. HELENA
SONATA, ITS FORM AND MEANING AS EXEMPLIFIED IN THE PIANO SONATAS
MARTENS, FREDERICK HERMAN
PADEREWSKI--'LITTLE BIOGRAPHIES', VOL. 2
MARX, ADOLF BERNHARD
INTRODUCTION TO THE INTERPRETATION OF BEETHOVEN'S PIANO
MASON, DANIEL GREGORY
ROMANTIC COMPOSERS, THE ---CHOPIN AND LISZT
MATHEWS, WILLIAM S. B.
GREAT IN MUSIC, THE ..A SYSTEMATIC COURSE OF STUDY IN THE MUSIC OF
MATTHEWS, DENIS--EDITOR
KEYBOARD MUSIC--ESSAYS ON KEYBOARD LITERATURE, EXCLUDING ORGAN
MATTHEWS, DENIS
BEETHOVEN PIANO SONATAS--B.B.C. MUSIC GUIDE, NO. 1
MAUROIS, ANDRE
FREDERIC CHOPIN---FOR YOUNGER READERS
MCARTHUR, ALEXANDER
ANTON RUBINSTEIN, A BIOGRAPHICAL SKETCH
MCMILLAN, MARY LEE *
MY HELENKA---IGNACE PADEREWSKI
MELLERS, WILFRED
FRANCOIS COUPERIN AND THE FRENCH CLASSICAL TRADITION
MELLERS, WILFRED
SONATA PRINCIPLE, THE --CIRCA 1750
MILLER, JEWELL
POLONAISE MILITAIRE..THE LIFE AND WORK OF FREDERIC CHOPIN..A
MILNE, ALFRED FORBES
BEETHOVEN..THE PIANOFORTE SONATAS--2 VOLS.
MIZWA, STEPHEN P.--EDITOR
FREDERIC CHOPIN, 1810-1849
MOLDENHAUER, HANS
DUO-PIANISM---PUBLISHED DISSERTATION
MONTAGU-NATHAN, M.
CONTEMPORARY RUSSIAN COMPOSERS---RACHMANINOFF
MONTAGU-NATHAN, M.
HANDBOOK TO THE PIANO WORKS OF SCRIABIN
MORGAN, ORLANDO
J. S. BACH..48 PRELUDES AND FUGUES..ANALYSIS OF THE FUGUES
MURDOCH, WILLIAM
BRAHMS..WITH AN ANALYTICAL STUDY OF THE COMPLETE PIANOFORTE WORKS
MURDOCH, WILLIAM
CHOPIN..HIS LIFE---1935
MURGIA, ADELAIDE
LIFE AND TIMES OF CHOPIN, THE
NAYLOR, EDWARD W.
ELIZABETHAN VIRGINAL BOOK, AN ..A CRITICAL ESSAY ON THE CONTENTS
NEWMAN, ERNEST
MAN LISZT, THE ..A STUDY OF THE TRAGI-COMEDY OF A SOUL DIVIDED
NEWMAN, WILLIAM S.
PERFORMANCE PRACTICES IN BEETHOVEN'S PIANO SONATAS..AN
NEWMAN, WILLIAM S.
SONATA IN THE BAROQUE ERA, THE --A HISTORY OF THE SONATA IDEA,
NEWMAN, WILLIAM S.
SONATA IN THE CLASSIC ERA, THE --A HISTORY OF THE SONATA IDEA,
NEWMAN, WILLIAM S.
SONATA SINCE BEETHOVEN, THE --A HISTORY OF THE SONATA IDEA, VOL. 3
NEWMAN, WILLIAM S.
THIRTEEN KEYBOARD SONATAS OF THE EIGHTEENTH AND NINETEENTH
NICCHIA, LILLIAN
PIANOFORTE STUDY..HINTS ON PIANO PLAYING
NIECKS, FREDERICK
FREDERIC CHOPIN AS A MAN AND MUSICIAN--2 VOLS.---1888

OFFERGELD, ROBERT
CENTENNIAL CATALOGUE OF THE PUBLISHED AND UNPUBLISHED COMPOSITIONS
PALMER, WILLARD A.--EDITOR
CHOPIN..AN INTRODUCTION TO HIS PIANO WORKS
PARRISH, CARL
EARLY PIANO AND ITS INFLUENCE ON KEYBOARD TECHNIQUE AND
PAUER, ERNST
DICTIONARY OF PIANISTS AND COMPOSERS FOR THE PIANOFORTE..WITH AN
PAUER, ERNST
ERNST PAUER'S SIX HISTORICAL PERFORMANCES OF PIANOFORTE MUSIC
PERRY, EDWARD B.
DESCRIPTIVE ANALYSES OF PIANO WORKS, FOR THE USE OF TEACHERS,
PERRY, EDWARD B.
STORIES OF STANDARD TEACHING PIECES FOR THE PIANOFORTE
PETERSON, FRANKLIN
HANDBOOK OF MUSICAL FORM--PART 2 OF THE PIANIST'S HANDBOOK
PHILLIPS, CHARLES
PADEREWSKI..THE STORY OF A MODERN IMMORTAL
PIGGOTT, PATRICK
LIFE AND MUSIC OF JOHN FIELD, 1782-1837, THE
PIRANI, EUGENIO DI
SECRETS OF THE SUCCESS OF GREAT MUSICIANS
POLISH RESEARCH AND INFORMATION SERVICE
FREDERIC CHOPIN--CENTENNIAL 1849-1949, BACKGROUND
POLISH RESEARCH AND INFORMATION SERVICE
FREDERIC CHOPIN CENTENNIAL--1949---EIGHT ARTICLES
PORTE, JOHN F.
CHOPIN, THE COMPOSER AND HIS MUSIC
PORTE, JOHN F.
EDWARD MACDOWELL, A GREAT AMERICAN TONE POET..HIS LIFE AND MUSIC
POURTALES, GUY DE
FRANZ LISZT, THE MAN OF LOVE
POURTALES, GUY DE
POLONAISE, THE LIFE OF CHOPIN---ENGLISH EDITION, 'FREDERICK
PRENTICE, THOMAS RIDLEY
MUSICIAN, THE ..A GUIDE FOR PIANOFORTE STUDENTS--6 VOLS.
PROSNAK, JAN
FREDERIC CHOPIN INTERNATIONAL PIANO COMPETITIONS, THE
PUGNO, RAOUL
LESSONS OF RAOUL PUGNO, THE ..WITH A BIOGRAPHY OF CHOPIN BY M.
RAYSON, ETHEL
POLISH MUSIC AND CHOPIN ITS LAUREATE, ETC.
RICHNER, THOMAS
ORIENTATION FOR INTERPRETING MOZART'S PIANO SONATAS
RIEMANN, HUGO
ANALYSIS OF J. S. BACH'S WOHLTEMPIERTES KLAVIER--2 PTS.
ROLLAND, ROMAIN
BEETHOVEN..WITH A BRIEF ANALYSIS OF THE SONATAS...BY A. EAGLEFIELD
ROSTAND, CLAUDE
LISZT
ROTHSCHILD, FRITZ
LOST TRADITION IN MUSIC, THE --PT. 1..RHYTHM AND TEMPO IN J. S.
ROTHSCHILD, FRITZ
LOST TRADITION IN MUSIC, THE --PT. 2..MUSICAL PERFORMANCE IN THE
ROWBOTHAM, JOHN F.
PRIVATE LIFE OF THE GREAT COMPOSERS, THE ---CHOPIN AND LISZT
RUBINSTEIN, ANTON
CONVERSATION ON MUSIC, A
RUBINSTEIN, BERYL
OUTLINE OF PIANO PEDAGOGY--REV. ED.---1929
RUTTKAY, GEORGE
CHOPIN, HIS LIFE TOLD IN ANECDOTAL FORM---FOR YOUNGER READERS
RYAN, THOMAS
RECOLLECTIONS OF AN OLD MUSICIAN---GOTTSCHALK, JONAS CHICKERING,
SCHAAF, EDWARD O.
FUNDAMENTAL PRINCIPLES INVOLVED IN THE COMPOSING AND ARRANGING OF
SCHALLENBERG, EVERT W.
FREDERIC CHOPIN--SYMPHONIA BOOKS..'HISTORY OF MUSIC' SERIES
SCHAUFFLER, ROBERT HAVEN
FLORESTAN..THE LIFE AND WORK OF ROBERT SCHUMANN---1945
SCHMITZ, ELIE ROBERT
PIANO WORKS OF CLAUDE DEBUSSY, THE
SCHNITTKIND, HENRY T.
LIVING BIOGRAPHIES OF GREAT COMPOSERS---CHOPIN AND LISZT
SCHOLES, PERCY
APPRECIATION OF MUSIC BY MEANS OF THE PIANOLA AND DUO-ART, THE
SCHONBERG, HAROLD
COLLECTOR'S CHOPIN AND SCHUMANN, THE --KEYSTONE BOOKS
SCHONBERG, HAROLD
LIVES OF THE GREAT COMPOSERS, THE ---CHOPIN AND LISZT
SCHUMANN, ROBERT
ON MUSIC AND MUSICIANS---1854, IN GERMAN--FIRST ENGLISH EDITION IN
SCHWIMMER, FRANCISKA
GREAT MUSICIANS AS CHILDREN
SEARLE, HUMPHREY
MUSIC OF LISZT, THE --2ND. REV. ED.---1954
SHEDLOCK, JOHN S.
BEETHOVEN'S PIANOFORTE SONATAS..THE ORIGIN AND RESPECTIVE VALUES
SHEDLOCK, JOHN S.
PIANOFORTE SONATA, THE ..ITS ORIGIN AND DEVELOPMENT---1895
SITWELL, SACHEVERELL
BACKGROUND FOR DOMENICO SCARLATTI..1685-1757, WRITTEN FOR HIS
SITWELL, SACHEVERELL
LISZT---1934
SORABJI, KAIKHOSRU
AROUND MUSIC---PACHMAN, CHOPIN AND LISZT
SOREL, CLAUDETTE
COMPENDIUM OF PIANO TECHNIQUE--39 ETUDES SELECTED FROM OVER 4000,
SPAETH, SIGMUND *
AMPICO IN MUSIC STUDY, THE
STATHAM, HENRY H.
MY THOUGHTS ON MUSIC AND MUSICIANS---CHOPIN AND LISZT
STEIN, ERWIN
FORM AND PERFORMANCE
STOOKES, SACHA
ART OF ROBERT CASADESUS, THE
STRACHEY, MARJORIE C.
NIGHTINGALE, THE ..A LIFE OF CHOPIN--IN THE FORM OF FICTION
STUCKENSCHMIDT, HANS H.
FERRUCCIO BUSONI..CHRONICLE OF A EUROPEAN---1967, IN GERMAN
STUCKENSCHMIDT, HANS H.
MAURICE RAVEL..VARIATIONS ON HIS LIFE AND WORK
SUMMY-BIRCHARD COMPANY
HANDBOOK FOR PIANO TEACHERS..COLLECTED ARTICLES ON SUBJECTS
SUMNER, WILLIAM L.
PIANOFORTE, THE --3RD. ED.---1966
SZIGETI, JOSEPH
TEN BEETHOVEN SONATAS FOR PIANO AND VIOLIN, THE
TANKARD, GEOFFREY
PIANOFORTE DIPLOMAS
TARCZYNSKI-ALF, TADEUSZ
HOMAGE TO CHOPIN---TEXT IN POLISH AND ENGLISH
TAWASTSTJERNA, ERIK
PIANOFORTE COMPOSITIONS OF SIBELIUS, THE
TEMPLIER, PIERRE D.
ERIK SATIE---1932, IN FRENCH
THOMPSON, KENNETH
DICTIONARY OF TWENTIETY-CENTURY COMPOSERS, A --1911-1971

TISCHLER, HANS
    STRUCTURAL ANALYSIS OF MOZART'S PIANO CONCERTOS, A --MUSICOLOGICAL
TURECK, ROSALYN
    INTRODUCTION TO THE PERFORMANCE OF BACH, AN--3 VOLS.
TYSON, ALAN
    AUTHENTIC ENGLISH EDITIONS OF BEETHOVEN, THE --'ALL SOULS
VALLAS, LEON
    THEORIES OF CLAUDE DEBUSSY, MUSICIEN FRANCAIS, THE ---1929
VEINUS, ABRAHAM
    CONCERTO, THE ---1944
VENABLE, MARY
    INTERPRETATION OF PIANO MUSIC, THE
VIARD-LOUIS, JENNY
    MUSIC AND THE PIANO
VUILLERMOZ, EMILE
    GABRIEL FAURE
WALKER, ALAN--EDITOR
    CHOPIN COMPANION, THE ..PROFILES OF THE MAN AND THE
WALKER, ALAN--EDITOR
    FRANZ LISZT, THE MAN AND HIS MUSIC---ESSAYS BY SACHEVERALL SITWELL
WALKER, ALAN--EDITOR
    ROBERT SCHUMANN..THE MAN AND HIS MUSIC---SYMPOSIUM--13 AUTHORS
WALKER, ALAN
    LISZT
WALLACE, WILLIAM
    LISZT, WAGNER, AND THE PRINCESS
WARRACK, JOHN H.
    SIX GREAT COMPOSERS---CHOPIN
WARRACK JOHN H.
    CHAIKOVSKY SYMPHONIES AND CONCERTOS--B.B.C. MUSIC GUIDES, NO. 16
WARREN, CLARENCE H.--EDITOR
    MEN BEHIND THE MUSIC, THE ---CHOPIN AND LISZT
WEINSTOCK, HERBERT
    CHOPIN, THE MAN AND HIS MUSIC
WEISER, BERNHARD D.
    KEYBOARD MUSIC--16TH.-20TH. CENTURIES
WEITZMANN, CARL F.
    HISTORY OF PIANOFORTE-PLAYING AND PIANOFORTE-LITERATURE, A
WESTERBY, HERBERT
    APPROACH TO LISZT, THE ..A COURSE OF MODERN TONAL TECHNIQUE FOR
WESTERBY, HERBERT
    BEETHOVEN AND HIS PIANO WORKS
WESTERBY, HERBERT
    HISTORY OF PIANOFORTE MUSIC, THE ---1924
WESTERBY, HERBERT
    HOW TO STUDY THE PIANOFORTE WORKS OF THE GREAT COMPOSERS
WESTERBY, HERBERT
    LISZT, COMPOSER, AND HIS PIANO WORKS..DESCRIPTIVE GUIDE AND
WESTRUP, SIR JACK ALLAN
    LISZT--NOVELLO'S BIOGRAPHIES OF GREAT MUSICIANS
WHEELER, OPAL
    FREDERIC CHOPIN, SON OF POLAND, EARLY YEARS--2 VOLS.---YOUNGER
WIER, ALBERT
    PIANO, THE ..ITS HISTORY, MAKERS, PLAYERS AND MUSIC
WIERZYNSKI, CASIMIR
    LIFE AND DEATH OF CHOPIN, THE
WILKINSON, CHARLES W.
    HOW TO PLAY 110 FAVOURITE PIANO SOLOS
WILKINSON, CHARLES W.
    WELL-KNOWN PIANO SOLOS..HOW TO PLAY THEM WITH UNDERSTANDING,
WILLEBY, CHARLES
    FREDERIC FRANCOIS CHOPIN
WOLFRAM, VICTOR
    SOSTENUTO PEDAL, THE
YATES, PETER
    AMATEUR AT THE KEYBOARD, AN
YOUNG, PERCY M.
    CONCERTO--'PHOENIX MUSIC GUIDES', NO. 1
YOUNG, PERCY M.
    KEYBOARD MUSICIANS OF THE WORLD

Editions

APEL, WILLI
    HISTORY OF KEYBOARD MUSIC TO 1700, THE --TRANSLATED AND REVISED BY
BACON, ERNST
    NOTES ON THE PIANO
BADURA-SKODA, EVA *
    INTERPRETING MOZART ON THE KEYBOARD---1957, IN GERMAN
BARFORD, PHILIP
    KEYBOARD MUSIC OF C. P. E. BACH, THE ..CONSIDERED IN RELATION TO
BASTIEN, JAMES W.
    HOW TO TEACH PIANO SUCCESSFULLY
BENNER, LORA
    BENNER BLUE BOOK, THE ..PRACTICAL MANUAL OF PIANO TEACHING--4TH.
BODKY, ERWIN
    INTERPRETATION OF BACH'S KEYBOARD WORKS, THE
BOWEN, YORK
    PEDALLING THE MODERN PIANOFORTE---1936
BREMNER, ROBERT
    HARPSICHORD OR SPINNET MISCELLANY, THE --KEYBOARD
BROWER, HARRIETTE
    WHAT TO PLAY--WHAT TO TEACH
DRY, WAKELING
    CHOPIN--'MUSIC OF THE MASTERS' SERIES
EMERY, WALTER
    EDITIONS AND MUSICIANS
FRISKIN, JAMES *
    MUSIC FOR THE PIANO..A HANDBOOK OF CONCERT AND TEACHING MATERIAL
HEUSCHNEIDER, KARIN
    PIANO SONATA OF THE EIGHTEENTH CENTURY IN GERMANY, THE
HORROCKS, CYRIL R. H.
    STUDENT'S GUIDE TO THE ART OF TEACHING THE PIANOFORTE, THE --2ND.
JOHNSTONE, J. ALFRED
    TOUCH, PHRASING AND INTERPRETATION
KERN, ALICE M. *
    TEACHER'S GUIDEBOOK TO PIANO LITERATURE, THE --REV. ED.---1954+
MCARTHUR, ALEXANDER
    PIANOFORTE STUDY..HINTS ON PIANO PLAYING
MCEWEN, JOHN B.
    INTRODUCTION TO AN UNPUBLISHED EDITION OF THE PIANOFORTE SONATAS
MCNABB, GEORGE
    SELECTED LIST OF GRADED TEACHING MATERIAL FOR THE PIANO, A --3RD.
MELLERS, WILFRED
    FRANCOIS COUPERIN AND THE FRENCH CLASSICAL TRADITION
MILNE, ALFRED FORBES
    BEETHOVEN..THE PIANOFORTE SONATAS--2 VOLS.
MUSIC EDUCATION LEAGUE, INC.
    PIANO AUDITIONS SYLLABUS AND COMPREHENSIVE GUIDE FOR PIANO
MUSIC EDUCATION LEAGUE
    COMPREHENSIVE GUIDE FOR PIANO TEACHERS AND PIANO AUDITION SYLLABUS
MUSIC EDUCATORS NATIONAL CONFERENCE
    TEACHING PIANO IN CLASSROOM AND STUDIO
NEWMAN, WILLIAM S.
    PERFORMANCE PRACTICES IN BEETHOVEN'S PIANO SONATAS..AN
NEWMAN, WILLIAM S.
    SONATA IN THE BAROQUE ERA, THE --A HISTORY OF THE SONATA IDEA,

NEWMAN, WILLIAM S.
    SONATA IN THE CLASSIC ERA, THE --A HISTORY OF THE SONATA IDEA,
NICCHIA, LILLIAN
    PIANOFORTE STUDY..HINTS ON PIANO PLAYING
ROTHSCHILD, FRITZ
    LOST TRADITION IN MUSIC, THE --PT. 1..RHYTHM AND TEMPO IN J. S.
ROTHSCHILD, FRITZ
    LOST TRADITION IN MUSIC, THE --PT. 2..MUSICAL PERFORMANCE IN THE
RUBINSTEIN, BERYL
    OUTLINE OF PIANO PEDAGOGY--REV. ED.---1929
SCHOTT, HOWARD
    PLAYING THE HARPSICHORD
SEARLE, HUMPHREY
    MUSIC OF LISZT, THE --2ND. REV. ED.---1954
SHEDLOCK, JOHN S.
    BEETHOVEN'S PIANOFORTE SONATAS..THE ORIGIN AND RESPECTIVE VALUES
TAYLOR, ROBERT L.
    RUNNING PIANIST, THE ---PERCY GRAINGER
TURECK, ROSALYN
    INTRODUCTION TO THE PERFORMANCE OF BACH, AN--3 VOLS.
TYSON, ALAN
    AUTHENTIC ENGLISH EDITIONS OF BEETHOVEN, THE --'ALL SOULS
VEINUS, ABRAHAM
    VICTOR BOOK OF CONCERTOS
WESTERBY, HERBERT
    BEETHOVEN AND HIS PIANO WORKS
WESTERBY, HERBERT
    HOW TO STUDY THE PIANOFORTE WORKS OF THE GREAT COMPOSERS

Bibliographies

AEOLIAN COMPANY, THE
    DUO-ART PIANO MUSIC...RECORDED BY MORE THAN 250 PIANISTS
APEL, WILLI
    HISTORY OF KEYBOARD MUSIC TO 1700, THE --TRANSLATED AND REVISED BY
BENNER, LORA
    BENNER GOLD BOOK, THE ..PIANO MATERIAL AND TEACHING METHODS--3RD.
BRIDGER, JOHN HENRY
    HOW TO HARMONIZE MELODIES, WITH HINTS ON WRITING FOR STRINGS AND
BROWER, HARRIETTE
    WHAT TO PLAY--WHAT TO TEACH
BURROWS, RAYMOND
    ELEMENTARY PIANO INSTRUCTION IN COLLEGE
CALDWELL, JOHN
    ENGLISH KEYBOARD MUSIC BEFORE THE NINETEENTH CENTURY---EXTENSIVE
CANAVE, PAZ CORAZON G.
    RE-EVALUATION OF THE ROLE PLAYED BY C. P. E. BACH IN THE
CARPE, ADOLPH
    PIANIST AND THE ART OF MUSIC, THE ..A TREATISE ON PIANO PLAYING
CHURCHILL, VIRGINIA PEAKES
    MODERN TEACHER'S GUIDE TO PIANO AND PIANO CLASS TEACHING
CHURCHILL, VIRGINIA PEAKES
    NINETEEN FIFTY-SIX SUPPLEMENT TO THE MODERN TEACHER'S GUIDE TO
CORTOT, ALFRED
    IN SEARCH OF CHOPIN
DARRELL, ROBERT D.--COMPILER
    SCHIRMER'S GUIDE TO BOOKS ON MUSIC AND MUSICIANS--A PRACTICAL
EVANS, EDWIN
    HANDBOOK TO THE PIANOFORTE WORKS OF JOHANNES BRAHMS---1936
FRISKIN, JAMES *
    MUSIC FOR THE PIANO..A HANDBOOK OF CONCERT AND TEACHING MATERIAL
GLENNON, JAMES
    MAKING FRIENDS WITH PIANO MUSIC..THE HISTORY AND ANALYTICAL NOTES
HAMILTON, CLARENCE G.
    PIANO MUSIC, ITS COMPOSERS AND CHARACTERISTICS
HINSON, MAURICE
    PIANO TEACHER'S SOURCE BOOK--BIBLIOGRAPHY OF BOOKS ABOUT PIANOS
HOPKINSON, CECIL
    BIBLIOGRAPHICAL THEMATIC CATALOGUE OF THE WORKS OF JOHN FIELD,
HORROCKS, CYRIL R. H.
    STUDENT'S GUIDE TO THE ART OF TEACHING THE PIANOFORTE, THE --2ND.
HUTCHESON, ERNEST *
    LITERATURE OF THE PIANO, THE ..A GUIDE FOR AMATEUR AND
KARASOWSKI, MORITZ
    FREDERIC CHOPIN..HIS LIFE, LETTERS AND WORKS--3RD. REV. ED.---1879
KATOWICE, POLAND--BIBLIOTECA PANSTWOWEJ
    CHOPINIANA IN THE HIGH MUSIC SCHOOL LIBRARY IN
KORSTEN, BJARNE
    RECENT NORWEGIAN PIANO MUSIC
MILNE, ALFRED FORBES
    BEETHOVEN..THE PIANOFORTE SONATAS--2 VOLS.
MONTAGU-NATHAN, M.
    HANDBOOK TO THE PIANO WORKS OF SCRIABIN
NEWMAN, ELIZABETH
    TEACHING MATERIAL GRADED ACCORDING TO HARMONIC STRUCTURE,
NEWMAN, WILLIAM S.
    SONATA IN THE BAROQUE ERA, THE --A HISTORY OF THE SONATA IDEA,
NEWMAN, WILLIAM S.
    SONATA IN THE CLASSIC ERA, THE --A HISTORY OF THE SONATA IDEA,
NEWMAN, WILLIAM S.
    SONATA SINCE BEETHOVEN, THE --A HISTORY OF THE SONATA IDEA, VOL. 3
NEW YORK--PUBLIC LIBRARY
    LIST OF PIANO MUSIC IN THE CIRCULATION DEPARTMENT OF THE NEW YORK
NEW YORK STATE MUSIC TEACHERS' ASSOCIATION
    SYLLABUS FOR PIANO, 1970
NIMITZ, DANIEL
    KEYBOARD MASTERS..STUDY GUIDE
RADCLIFFE, PHILIP
    SCHUBERT PIANO SONATAS--B.B.C. MUSIC GUIDE, NO. 17
SCHAUFFLER, ROBERT HAVEN
    FLORESTAN..THE LIFE AND WORK OF ROBERT SCHUMANN---1945
SHEDLOCK, JOHN S.
    BEETHOVEN'S PIANOFORTE SONATAS..THE ORIGIN AND RESPECTIVE VALUES
TANKARD, GEOFFREY
    PIANOFORTE DIPLOMAS
WEISER, BERNHARD D.
    KEYBOARD MUSIC--16TH.-20TH. CENTURIES
WEITZMANN, CARL F.
    HISTORY OF PIANOFORTE-PLAYING AND PIANOFORTE-LITERATURE, A
WESTERBY, HERBERT
    HOW TO STUDY THE PIANOFORTE WORKS OF THE GREAT COMPOSERS
WIER, ALBERT
    PIANO, THE ..ITS HISTORY, MAKERS, PLAYERS AND MUSIC
WILLS, VERA G. *
    PARENT'S GUIDE TO MUSIC LESSONS, A

Lists, Graded and Ungraded

ABRAHAM, GERALD
    CHOPIN'S MUSICAL STYLE---1939
AEOLIAN COMPANY, THE
    CATALOG OF AEOLIAN MUSIC ARRANGED FOR 46-NOTE INSTRUMENTS
AEOLIAN COMPANY, THE
    CATALOG OF METROSTYLE AND THEMODIST MUSIC FOR THE PIANOLA AND
AEOLIAN COMPANY, THE
    CATALOG OF MUSIC-ROLLS FOR THE DUO-ART REPRODUCING PIANO

AEOLIAN COMPANY, THE
    CATALOG OF MUSIC FOR THE PIANOLA, PIANOLA PIANO AND
AEOLIAN COMPANY, THE
    COMPLETE CATALOG OF MUSIC ROLLS FOR THE DUO-ART REPRODUCING PIANO
AEOLIAN COMPANY, THE
    LIBRARY OF DUO-ART MUSIC ROLLS
AEOLIAN COMPANY, THE
    METROSTYLE-THEMODIST AND METRO-ART MUSIC ROLLS FOR THE PIANOLA AND
AEOLIAN COMPANY, THE
    METROSTYLE, THE
AEOLIAN COMPANY, THE
    METROSTYLE AND THEMODIST MUSIC CATALOG FOR THE PIANOLA AND PIANOLA
AEOLIAN COMPANY, THE
    MUSIC FOR THE AEOLIAN GRAND--SUPPLEMENT
AEOLIAN COMPANY, THE
    MUSIC FOR THE AEOLIAN GRAND
AEOLIAN COMPANY, THE
    MUSIC FOR THE ORCHESTRELLE AND AEOLIAN GRAND
AEOLIAN COMPANY, THE
    MUSIC FOR THE PIANOLA AND THE AERIAL PIANO--4 VOLS.
AEOLIAN COMPANY, THE
    NEW MUSIC FOR THE AEOLIAN GRAND, THE PIANOLA, AND THE AERIOL PIANO
AEOLIAN COMPANY, THE
    PIANOLA AND PIANOLA PIANO MUSIC CATALOG, THE ..SIXTY-FIVE NOTE
AEOLIAN COMPANY, THE
    SUPPLEMENTARY CATALOG OF MUSIC FOR THE AEOLIAN GRAND AND
ALBRECHTSBERGER, JOHANN GEORG
    METHODS OF HARMONY, FIGURED BASE, AND COMPOSITION...ADAPTED FOR
AMERICAN PIANO CORPORATION
    CATALOGUE OF MUSIC FOR THE AMPICO, A ..A LIST OF THE RECORDINGS OF
AMERICAN PIANO CORPORATION
    CATALOGUE OF MUSIC FOR THE AMPICO, A --A LIST OF THE RECORDINGS OF
AMPICO CORPORATION
    AMPICO REPRODUCING PIANO..A SUPPLEMENT TO 'PIANO MUSIC, ITS
ANON
    LIFE AND WORKS OF STEPHEN HELLER, THE PIANOFORTE COMPOSER, THE ..A
ANSON, GEORGE
    CONTEMPORARY PIANO MUSIC OF THE AMERICAS, COMPILED BY GEORGE ANSON
BACHE, CONSTANCE
    BROTHER MUSICIANS..REMINISCENCES OF EDWARD AND WALTER BACHE
BARBEDETTE, HIPPOLYTE
    STEPHEN HELLER..HIS LIFE AND WORKS
BENNER, LORA
    BENNER BLUE BOOK, THE ..PRACTICAL MANUAL OF PIANO TEACHING--4TH.
BENNER, LORA
    BENNER GOLD BOOK, THE ..PIANO MATERIAL AND TEACHING METHODS--3RD.
BOWEN, CATHERINE DRINKER
    FREE ARTIST..THE STORY OF ANTON AND NICHOLAS RUBINSTEIN
BRINKMAN, JOSEPH *
    PIANO MUSIC..AVAILABLE EDITIONS RECOMMENDED---ADDENDA, 1959
BRITISH BROADCASTING CORPORATION--CENTRAL MUSIC LIBRARY
    CHAMBER MUSIC CATALOGUE
BRITISH BROADCASTING CORPORATION--CENTRAL MUSIC LIBRARY
    PIANO AND ORGAN CATALOGUE--2 VOLS.
BRITISH COLUMBIA--DEPT. OF EDUCATION
    PIANOFORTE AND VIOLIN FOR HIGH SCHOOL STUDENTS
BROWER, HARRIETTE
    WHAT TO PLAY--WHAT TO TEACH
BROWN, MAURICE J. E.
    CHOPIN..AN INDEX OF HIS WORKS IN CHRONOLOGICAL ORDER--2ND. REV.
BURROWS, RAYMOND
    ELEMENTARY PIANO INSTRUCTION IN COLLEGE
BUTLER, STANLEY
    GUIDE TO THE BEST IN CONTEMPORARY PIANO MUSIC..AN ANNOTATED LIST
CALDWELL, JOHN
    ENGLISH KEYBOARD MUSIC BEFORE THE NINETEENTH CENTURY---EXTENSIVE
CALLENDER, ROMAINE
    TEACHER'S MANUAL, A WORK DESIGNED TO SUPPLEMENT...'THE FIRST TEN
CAPEN, C. L.
    MUSIC TEACHER'S VADE-MECUM, THE ..A GUIDE IN THE CHOICE OF MUSIC
CHISSELL, JOAN
    SCHUMANN PIANO MUSIC--B.B.C. MUSIC GUIDE, NO. 25
CHURCHILL, VIRGINIA PEAKES
    MODERN TEACHER'S GUIDE TO PIANO AND PIANO CLASS TEACHING
CHURCHILL, VIRGINIA PEAKES
    NINETEEN FIFTY-SIX SUPPLEMENT TO THE MODERN TEACHER'S GUIDE TO
CORDER, FREDERICK
    FERENCZ LISZT--HALF-TITLE..MASTERS OF MUSIC
CULSHAW, JOHN
    SERGEI RACHMANINOFF..THE MAN AND HIS MUSIC
DAVISON, JAMES W.
    FREDERIC FRANCOIS CHOPIN..CRITICAL AND APPRECIATIVE ESSAY---1843
DENT, EDWARD J.
    FERRUCCIO BUSONI, A BIOGRAPHY
DENVER--PUBLIC SCHOOLS
    CLASS-PIANO TEACHERS HANDBOOK
DITSON COMPANY
    TEACHING PIECES AND HOW TO TEACH THEM
EMERICH, PAUL
    ROAD TO MODERN MUSIC, THE
EVANS MUSIC COMPANY
    EVANS' GRADED STUDY GUIDE FOR THE PIANOFORTE AND DICTIONARY OF
EWEN, DAVID
    WORLD OF GREAT COMPOSERS, THE
FAELTEN, CARL
    TEACHER'S MANUAL FOR PIANOFORTE COURSE, THE
FERGUSON, DONALD NIVISON
    PIANO MUSIC OF SIX GREAT COMPOSERS---1947
FILLMORE, THOMAS H.
    FILLMORE'S LIST OF CAREFULLY SELECTED AND GRADED WORKS FOR THE
FOLDES, ANDOR
    KEYS TO THE KEYBOARD, A BOOK FOR PIANISTS
FULLER-MAITLAND, J. A.
    ROBERT SCHUMANN--'THE GREAT MUSICIANS' SERIES
GABRIEL, GILBERT W.
    GREAT PIANISTS AND COMPOSERS
GANZ, RUDOLPH
    RUDOLPH GANZ EVALUATES MODERN PIANO MUSIC
GEARY, ELEANOR MARGARET
    MUSICAL EDUCATION, WITH PRACTICAL OBSERVATIONS ON THE ART OF
GIBBS, POLLY
    LISTS AND SUGGESTIONS FOR PIANO TEACHING
GOODRICH, ALFRED JOHN
    GUIDE TO MEMORIZING MUSIC, A
GORDON, PHILIP
    SYLLABUS FOR PIANO AUDITIONS
GRAY, WILLIAM L.
    SELECTED AND GRADED LIST OF STUDIES AND PIECES FOR TEACHERS OF
GREW, SIDNEY
    FIRST BOOK OF THE PLAYER-PIANIST, THE
GRIFFIN, SISTER MARY ANNAROSE
    PIANO MATERIALS..GRADED AND COMPILED AS AN AID TO INSTRUCTORS
GUTMANN, EMMA WILKINS
    TALKS WITH PIANO TEACHERS
HALL, CONSTANCE HUNTINGTON
    HELEN HOPEKIRK, 1856-1945
HALLE, SIR CHARLES
    AUTOBIOGRAPHY OF CHARLES HALLE, WITH CORRESPONDENCE AND DIARIES,

HAMILTON, CLARENCE G.
    PIANO TEACHING..ITS PRINCIPLES AND PROBLEMS
HARDING, BERTITA
    CONCERTO, THE STORY OF CLARA SCHUMANN
HEDLEY, ARTHUR
    CHOPIN--'MASTER MUSICIAN' SERIES--INCLUDES CATALOGUE OF
HERVEY, ARTHUR
    SAINT-SAENS---1921
HODGES, SISTER MABELLE L.
    CATALOGUE OF REPRESENTATIVE TEACHING MATERIALS FOR PIANO SINCE
HOLMES, EDWARD
    ANALYTICAL AND THEMATIC INDEX OF MOZART'S PIANO WORKS
HOOK, JAMES
    GUIDA DI MUSICA..BEING A COMPLETE BOOK OF INSTRUCTIONS FOR
HOPKINSON, CECIL
    BIBLIOGRAPHICAL THEMATIC CATALOGUE OF THE WORKS OF JOHN FIELD,
HORPOCKS, CYRIL R. H.
    STUDENT'S GUIDE TO THE ART OF TEACHING THE PIANOFORTE, THE --2ND.
HUTCHESON, ERNEST
    LITERATURE OF THE PIANO, THE --FROM THE 16TH. CENTURY TO THE
HUTCHINGS, ARTHUR
    COMPANION TO MOZART'S PIANO CONCERTOS, A
JOHNSTONE, J. ALFRED
    ART OF TEACHING PIANOFORTE PLAYING, THE --2ND. REV. ED.---1910
JONSON, GEORGE CHARLES
    HANDBOOK TO CHOPIN'S WORKS, A
KERN, ALICE M. *
    TEACHER'S GUIDEBOOK TO PIANO LITERATURE, THE --REV. ED.---1954+
KIRKPATRICK, RALPH
    DOMENICO SCARLATTI---1953
KOTZSCHMAR, MARY ANN
    HALF-HOUR LESSONS IN MUSIC..CLASS WORK FOR BEGINNERS AT THE PIANO
LITZMANN, BERTHOLD
    CLARA SCHUMANN..AN ARTIST'S LIFE BASED ON MATERIAL FOUND IN
LIVERPOOL--PUBLIC LIBRARIES, MUSEUMS AND ART GALLERY
    PIANO, ITS MUSIC AND LITERATURE, THE ..CATALOGUE OF THE MUSIC
LOCKWOOD, ALBERT
    NOTES ON THE LITERATURE OF THE PIANO--RE-EDITED BY BROTHER, SAMUEL
LUBIN, ERNEST
    PIANO DUET, THE ...A GUIDE FOR PIANISTS
LYKE, JAMES
    SELECTED LIST OF PIANO TEACHING MATERIALS PUBLISHED SINCE 1960, A
LYLE, WATSON
    CAMILLE SAINT-SAENS, HIS LIFE AND ART---DISCUSSES CONCERTI AND
MAY, FLORENCE
    GIRLHOOD OF CLARA SCHUMANN, THE ..CLARA WIECK AND HER TIME
MCARTHUR, ALEXANDER
    ANTON RUBINSTEIN, A BIOGRAPHICAL SKETCH
MCLAIN, MARGARET STARR
    CLASS PIANO
MCNABB, GEORGE
    SELECTED LIST OF GRADED TEACHING MATERIAL FOR THE PIANO, A --3RD.
MELLERS, WILFRED
    FRANCOIS COUPERIN AND THE FRENCH CLASSICAL TRADITION
MICHIGAN MUSIC TEACHERS ASSOCIATION
    PIANO TEACHER'S GUIDE
MINNESOTA MUSIC TEACHERS ASSOCIATION
    PIANO-THEORY EXAMINATION SYLLABUS
MOLDENHAUER, HANS
    DUO-PIANISM---PUBLISHED DISSERTATION
MORRILL, HENRY H.
    MANUAL OF PIANO FOR PUPILS AND TEACHERS
MOSCHELES, CHARLOTTE
    RECENT MUSIC AND MUSICIANS, AS DESCRIBED IN THE DIARIES AND
MURDOCH, WILLIAM
    BRAHMS..WITH AN ANALYTICAL STUDY OF THE COMPLETE PIANOFORTE WORKS
MURDOCH, WILLIAM
    CHOPIN..HIS LIFE---1935
MUSIC EDUCATION LEAGUE, INC.
    PIANO AUDITIONS SYLLABUS AND COMPREHENSIVE GUIDE FOR PIANO
MUSIC EDUCATION LEAGUE
    COMPREHENSIVE GUIDE FOR PIANO TEACHERS AND PIANO AUDITION SYLLABUS
MUSIC EDUCATORS NATIONAL CONFERENCE
    TEACHING PIANO IN CLASSROOM AND STUDIO
MUSIC PROJECT--NEW YORK CITY
    TEACHER'S GUIDE..A CREATIVE APPROACH TO PIANO CLASS TEACHING, BY
NATIONAL BUREAU FOR THE ADVANCEMENT OF MUSIC
    GIVING OF HIGH SCHOOL CREDITS FOR PRIVATE MUSIC STUDY, THE ..A
NEWMAN, ELIZABETH
    TEACHING MATERIAL GRADED ACCORDING TO HARMONIC STRUCTURE,
NEWMAN, WILLIAM S.
    PERFORMANCE PRACTICES IN BEETHOVEN'S PIANO SONATAS..AN
NEWMAN, WILLIAM S.
    SELECTED LIST OF MUSIC RECOMMENDED FOR PIANO STUDENTS, A --4TH.
NEW ENGLAND CONSERVATORY
    TEACHERS' GRADED LIST FOR THE PIANOFORTE
NEW YORK--PUBLIC LIBRARY
    LIST OF PIANO MUSIC IN THE CIRCULATION DEPARTMENT OF THE NEW YORK
NEW YORK STATE MUSIC TEACHERS' ASSOCIATION
    SYLLABUS FOR PIANO, 1970
NIECKS, FREDERICK
    FREDERICK CHOPIN AS A MAN AND MUSICIAN--2 VOLS.---1888
O'TOOLE, WILLIAM
    FIVE YEAR GUIDE TO PIANO TEACHING, A
OFFERGELD, ROBERT
    CENTENNIAL CATALOGUE OF THE PUBLISHED AND UNPUBLISHED COMPOSITIONS
OREGON MUSIC TEACHERS ASSOCIATION
    PIANO MATERIALS
ORLIK, JULES
    CREATIVE APPROACH TO PIANO CLASS TEACHING, A ---REPRODUCED FROM
PALMER, ANNIE L.
    MUSIC TEACHERS' GUIDE TO THE GOLDBECK PIANO METHOD
PARKER, DOUGLAS C.
    PERCY ALDRIDGE GRAINGER, A STUDY
PARRISH, CARL
    EARLY PIANO AND ITS INFLUENCE ON KEYBOARD TECHNIQUE AND
PEABODY INSTITUTE, BALTIMORE
    GRADED LIST OF SOME USEFUL WORKS FOR PIANO STUDY---REVISED BY
PELZ, WILLIAM
    BASIC KEYBOARD SKILLS--2ND. ED.---1963
PERRY, ADELAIDE TROWBRIDGE
    COMPENDIUM OF PIANO MATERIAL--2ND. ED.---1929
PERRY, EDWARD B.
    STORIES OF STANDARD TEACHING PIECES FOR THE PIANOFORTE
PHILLIPS, CHARLES
    PADEREWSKI..THE STORY OF A MODERN IMMORTAL
PORTE, JOHN F.
    EDWARD MACDOWELL, A GREAT AMERICAN TONE POET..HIS LIFE AND MUSIC
PRENTICE, THOMAS RIDLEY
    MUSICIAN, THE ..A GUIDE FOR PIANOFORTE STUDENTS--6 VOLS.
RACHMANINOFF, SERGEI
    RACHMANINOFF'S RECOLLECTIONS, TOLD TO OSKAR VON RIESEMANN---1934
REINECKE, KARL H.
    WHAT SHALL WE PLAY--NOT UNLIKE CZERNY'S 'LETTERS TO A YOUNG
REZITS, JOSEPH
    TEACHER'S GUIDE TO THE NEW SCRIBNER MUSIC LIBRARY
ROBERT, WALTER
    PIANO STUDY IN SOVIET-RUSSIAN SCHOOLS OF MUSIC--REPRINT..'JOURNAL

ROLLAND, ROMAIN
    BEETHOVEN..WITH A BRIEF ANALYSIS OF THE SONATAS...BY A. EAGLEFIELD
ROWLEY, ALEC
    FOUR HANDS--ONE PIANO..A LIST OF WORKS FOR DUET PLAYERS--A GUIDE
RUBINSTEIN, BERYL
    PIANIST'S APPROACH TO SIGHT READING AND MEMORIZING, THE
SCHAUFFLER, ROBERT HAVEN
    FLORESTAN..THE LIFE AND WORK OF ROBERT SCHUMANN---1945
SCHELLING, ERNEST *
    OXFORD PIANO COURSE, TEACHER'S SECOND MANUAL
SCHIRMER, G.
    NEW PIANO-TEACHER'S GUIDE..A GRADED AND CLASSIFIED LIST OF PIANO
SCHMITZ, ELIE ROBERT
    PIANO WORKS OF CLAUDE DEBUSSY, THE
SCHONBERG, HAROLD
    COLLECTOR'S CHOPIN AND SCHUMANN, THE --KEYSTONE BOOKS
SEARLE, HUMPHREY
    MUSIC OF LISZT, THE --2ND. REV. ED.---1954
SEYMOUR, HARRIET AYER
    HOW TO THINK MUSIC
SITWELL, SACHEVERELL
    LISZT---1934
SMITH, BILLYE MULLINS
    PIANO REPERTOIRE GUIDE
SMITHERS, WELSFORD
    PIANO TEACHER'S GUIDE, THE ..A HUNDRED QUESTIONS FOR YOUNG
SOREL, CLAUDETTE *
    INDEPENDENT LEARNING APPROACH TO PIANO SIGHT READING, AN
SPAETH, SIGMUND *
    AMPICO IN MUSIC STUDY, THE
SUTHERLAND, ADELAIDE K.--COMPILER
    WHAT SHALL I PLAY..PREFERENCES FOR PIANO AND ORGAN..GUIDE TO
TANKARD, GEOFFREY
    PIANOFORTE DIPLOMAS
TAYLOR, ERIC R.
    INTRODUCTION TO SCORE PLAYING, AN
THOMPSON, KENNETH
    DICTIONARY OF TWENTIETY-CENTURY COMPOSERS, A --1911-1971
TYSON, ALAN
    THEMATIC CATALOG OF THE WORKS OF MUZIO CLEMENTI
VERNAZZA, MARCELLE
    BASIC MATERIALS FOR THE PIANO STUDENT
VUILLERMOZ, EMILE
    GABRIEL FAURE
WALKER, ALAN--EDITOR
    CHOPIN COMPANION, THE ..PROFILES OF THE MAN AND THE
WALKER, ALAN--EDITOR
    FRANZ LISZT, THE MAN AND HIS MUSIC---ESSAYS BY SACHEVERALL SITWELL
WALKER, ALAN--EDITOR
    ROBERT SCHUMANN..THE MAN AND HIS MUSIC---SYMPOSIUM--13 AUTHORS
WASHINGTON STATE MUSIC TEACHERS ASSOCIATION
    PIANO TEACHING GUIDE--GRADES 1-8
WELTE ARTISTIC PLAYER-PIANO COMPANY
    LIST OF MUSIC FOR THE WELTE-MIGNON PIANO--WITH SUPPLEMENT
WESTERBY, HERBERT
    LISZT, COMPOSER, AND HIS PIANO WORKS..DESCRIPTIVE GUIDE AND
WILLEBY, CHARLES
    FREDEPIC FRANCOIS CHOPIN
WOLLENHAUPT, HEINRICH
    METHOD FOR THE PIANOFORTE AND METHODICAL GUIDE FOR THE PIANO FORTE

History

ANON
    GUIDE TO THE PROPER USE OF THE PIANOFORTE PEDALS, WITH EXAMPLES
APEL, WILLI
    HISTORY OF KEYBOARD MUSIC TO 1700, THE --TRANSLATED AND REVISED BY
APEL, WILLI
    MASTERS OF THE KEYBOARD
BEDBROOK, GERALD STARES
    KEYBOARD MUSIC FROM THE MIDDLE AGES TO THE BEGINNINGS OF THE
BIE, OSKAR
    HISTORY OF THE PIANOFORTE AND PIANOFORTE PLAYERS, A ---1899
BLOM, ERIC
    BEETHOVEN'S PIANOFORTE SONATAS DISCUSSED---1938
BLOM, ERIC
    ROMANCE OF THE PIANO, THE ---1928
BODKY, ERWIN
    INTERPRETATION OF BACH'S KEYBOARD WORKS, THE
BORREN, CHARLES VAN DEN
    SOURCES OF KEYBOARD MUSIC IN ENGLAND, THE ---1913
BROADWOOD, JOHN AND SONS
    BROADWOOD CONCERTS--HISTORICAL NOTES BY ROBIN H.
CALDWELL, JOHN
    ENGLISH KEYBOARD MUSIC BEFORE THE NINETEENTH CENTURY---EXTENSIVE
CANAVE, PAZ CORAZON G.
    RE-EVALUATION OF THE ROLE PLAYED BY C. P. E. BACH IN THE
COUPERIN, FRANCOIS
    ART DE TOUCHER LE CLAVECIN, L' ---IN FRENCH, GERMAN AND ENGLISH
CULSHAW, JOHN
    CONCERTO, THE
CURTIS, ALAN
    SWEELINCK'S KEYBOARD MUSIC..A STUDY OF ENGLISH ELEMENTS IN
DEMUTH, NORMAN
    FRENCH PIANO MUSIC..A SURVEY WITH NOTES ON ITS PERFORMANCE
DONINGTON, ROBERT
    PERFORMER'S GUIDE TO BAROQUE MUSIC, A
DORIAN, FREDERICK
    HISTORY OF MUSIC IN PERFORMANCE, THE ---1942
DRAKE, KENNETH
    SONATAS OF BEETHOVEN AS HE PLAYED AND TAUGHT THEM, THE
EICHBERG, OSCAR
    ANALYTICAL AND HISTORICAL REMARKS ON ANTON RUBINSTEIN'S CYCLE OF
EMERICH, PAUL
    ROAD TO MODERN MUSIC, THE
EVANS, EDWIN
    HANDBOOK TO THE PIANOFORTE WORKS OF JOHANNES BRAHMS---1936
FERGUSON, DONALD NIVISON
    PIANO MUSIC OF SIX GREAT COMPOSERS---1947
FILLMORE, JOHN C.
    PIANOFORTE MUSIC..ITS HISTORY, WITH BIOGRAPHICAL SKETCHES AND
GARVIN, FLORENCE HOLLISTER
    BEGINNINGS OF THE ROMANTIC PIANO CONCERTO, THE
GILLESPIE, JOHN
    FIVE CENTURIES OF KEYBOARD MUSIC..AN HISTORIC SURVEY FOR
GLENNON, JAMES
    MAKING FRIENDS WITH PIANO MUSIC--SUPPLEMENT
GLOYNE, HOWARD F.--M.D.
    CARL A. PREYER, THE LIFE OF A KANSAS MUSICIAN
GLYN, MARGARET H.
    ABOUT ELIZABETHAN VIRGINAL MUSIC AND ITS COMPOSERS..NEW ISSUE,
GLYN, MARGARET H.
    NATIONAL SCHOOL OF VIRGINAL MUSIC IN ELIZABETHAN TIMES, THE
GOODRICH, ALFRED JOHN
    THEORY OF INTERPRETATION, APPLIED TO ARTISTIC MUSICAL PERFORMANCE
GOTTSCHALD, ERNEST
    BEETHOVEN'S PIANOFORTE SONATAS EXPLAINED FOR THE LOVERS OF THE

HAMILTON, CLARENCE G.
    PIANO MUSIC, ITS COMPOSERS AND CHARACTERISTICS
HARRISON, SIDNEY
    TEACHER NEVER TOLD ME--TIPS FOR STUDENTS
HENDERSON, WILLIAM JAMES
    PRELUDES AND STUDIES..MUSICAL THEMES OF THE DAY--SECTION 3..THE
HEUSCHNEIDER, KARIN
    PIANO SONATA OF THE EIGHTEENTH CENTURY IN GERMANY, THE
HEUSCHNEIDER, KARIN
    PIANO SONATA OF THE EIGHTEENTH CENTURY IN ITALY, THE
HILL, GEORGE R.
    PRELIMINARY CHECKLIST OF RESEARCH ON THE CLASSIC SYMPHONY AND
HUNEKER, JAMES GIBBONS
    DEVELOPMENT OF PIANO MUSIC FROM THE DAYS OF THE CLAVICHORD AND
HUTCHESON, ERNEST *
    LITERATURE OF THE PIANO, THE ..A GUIDE FOR AMATEUR AND
HUTCHESON, ERNEST
    LITERATURE OF THE PIANO, THE --FROM THE 16TH. CENTURY TO THE
HUTCHINGS, ARTHUR
    BAROQUE CONCERTO, THE
HUTCHINGS, ARTHUR
    COMPANION TO MOZART'S PIANO CONCERTOS, A
KASTNER, RUDOLPH
    BEETHOVEN'S PIANO SONATAS AND ARTUR SCHNABEL
KASTNER, SANTIAGO
    PARALLELS AND DISCREPANCIES BETWEEN ENGLISH AND SPANISH KEYBOARD
KENYON, MAX
    HARPSICHORD MUSIC..THE INSTRUMENTS, THE COMPOSERS, THE PLAYERS
KERN, ALICE M. *
    TEACHER'S GUIDEBOOK TO PIANO LITERATURE, THE --REV. ED.---1954+
KIRBY, FRANK EUGENE
    SHORT HISTORY OF KEYBOARD MUSIC, A
KOCH, CASPAR
    PIANO STUDENT'S GRADUS AD PARNASSUM, THE ..PRESENTING THE
LANDOWSKA, WANDA
    LANDOWSKA ON MUSIC--EDITED BY DENISE RESTOUT
LANDOWSKA, WANDA
    MUSIC OF THE PAST
MATTHEWS, DENIS--EDITOR
    KEYBOARD MUSIC--ESSAYS ON KEYBOARD LITERATURE, EXCLUDING ORGAN
MATTHEWS, DENIS
    BEETHOVEN PIANO SONATAS--B.B.C. MUSIC GUIDE, NO. 1
MILNE, ALFRED FORBES
    BEETHOVEN..THE PIANOFORTE SONATAS--2 VOLS.
MOLDENHAUER, HANS
    DUO-PIANISM---PUBLISHED DISSERTATION
NAYLOR, EDWARD W.
    ELIZABETHAN VIRGINAL BOOK, AN ..A CRITICAL ESSAY ON THE CONTENTS
NEWMAN, WILLIAM S.
    SONATA IN THE BAROQUE ERA, THE --A HISTORY OF THE SONATA IDEA,
NEWMAN, WILLIAM S.
    SONATA IN THE CLASSIC ERA, THE --A HISTORY OF THE SONATA IDEA,
NEWMAN, WILLIAM S.
    SONATA SINCE BEETHOVEN, THE --A HISTORY OF THE SONATA IDEA, VOL. 3
NEWMAN, WILLIAM S.
    THIRTEEN KEYBOARD SONATAS OF THE EIGHTEENTH AND NINETEENTH
NIMITZ, DANIEL
    KEYBOARD MASTERS..STUDY GUIDE
PARRISH, CARL
    EARLY PIANO AND ITS INFLUENCE ON KEYBOARD TECHNIQUE AND
PAUER, ERNST
    ERNST PAUER'S SIX HISTORICAL PERFORMANCES OF PIANOFORTE MUSIC
PETERSON, FRANKLIN
    HANDBOOK OF MUSICAL FORM--PART 2 OF THE PIANIST'S HANDBOOK
RADCLIFFE, PHILIP
    SCHUBERT PIANO SONATAS--B.B.C. MUSIC GUIDE, NO. 17
RICHNER, THOMAS
    ORIENTATION FOR INTERPRETING MOZART'S PIANO SONATAS
ROWLEY, ALEC
    FOUR HANDS--ONE PIANO..A LIST OF WORKS FOR DUET PLAYERS--A GUIDE
RUBINSTEIN, ANTON
    CONVERSATION ON MUSIC, A
SACHS, CURT
    EVOLUTION OF PIANO MUSIC, 1350-1700, THE
SCHMITZ, ELIE ROBERT
    PIANO WORKS OF CLAUDE DEBUSSY, THE
SHEDLOCK, JOHN S.
    PIANOFORTE SONATA, THE ..ITS ORIGIN AND DEVELOPMENT---1895
STERNBERG, CONSTANTIN I. VON
    ETHICS AND ESTHETICS OF PIANO PLAYING
VEINUS, ABRAHAM
    CONCERTO, THE ---1944
VIARD-LOUIS, JENNY
    MUSIC AND THE PIANO
WEISER, BERNHARD D.
    KEYBOARD MUSIC--16TH.-20TH. CENTURIES
WEITZMANN, CARL F.
    HISTORY OF PIANOFORTE-PLAYING AND PIANOFORTE-LITERATURE, A
WESTERBY, HERBERT
    HISTORY OF PIANOFORTE MUSIC, THE ---1924
WESTERBY, HERBERT
    HOW TO STUDY THE PIANOFORTE WORKS OF THE GREAT COMPOSERS
WHITE, WILLIAM BRAID
    PLAYER-PIANIST, THE ..A GUIDE TO THE APPRECIATION AND
WIER, ALBERT
    PIANO, THE ..ITS HISTORY, MAKERS, PLAYERS AND MUSIC
YATES, PETER
    AMATEUR AT THE KEYBOARD, AN
YOUNG, PERCY M.
    CONCERTO--'PHOENIX MUSIC GUIDES', NO. 1
YOUNG, PERCY M.
    KEYBOARD MUSICIANS OF THE WORLD

Analysis - Theoretical

ABRAHAM, GERALD
    CHOPIN'S MUSICAL STYLE---1939
ANDERSON, WILLIAM R.
    RACHMANINOV AND HIS PIANO CONCERTOS
APEL, WILLI
    HISTORY OF KEYBOARD MUSIC TO 1700, THE --TRANSLATED AND REVISED BY
APEL, WILLI
    MASTERS OF THE KEYBOARD
ARONSON, MAURICE
    KEY TO THE MINIATURES OF LEOPOLD GODOWSKY, A ..ANALYTICAL ESSAYS
BADURA-SKODA, EVA *
    INTERPRETING MOZART ON THE KEYBOARD---1957, IN GERMAN
BARFORD, PHILIP
    KEYBOARD MUSIC OF C. P. E. BACH, THE ..CONSIDERED IN RELATION TO
BECKETT, WALTER
    LISZT
BIART, VICTOR
    PIANIST'S GUIDE, THE ..A SERIES OF PAMPHLETS ON THE TEACHING AND
BLOM, ERIC
    BEETHOVEN'S PIANOFORTE SONATAS DISCUSSED---1938
BODKY, ERWIN
    INTERPRETATION OF BACH'S KEYBOARD WORKS, THE

BOYD, MALCOLM
BACH'S INSTRUMENTAL COUNTERPOINT
BRANSON, DAVID
JOHN FIELD AND CHOPIN
BROWN, MAURICE J. E.
SCHUBERT'S VARIATIONS
BRUXNER, MERVYN
MASTERING THE PIANO
BUECKELMANN, BERNARDUS
EIGHT FUGUES FROM J. S. BACH'S 'W.T.C.', WITH ANALYTICAL NOTES IN
CALDWELL, JOHN
ENGLISH KEYBOARD MUSIC BEFORE THE NINETEENTH CENTURY---EXTENSIVE
CANAVE, PAZ CORAZON G.
RE-EVALUATION OF THE ROLE PLAYED BY C. P. E. BACH IN THE
CLARE, EDWARD
ANALYSIS OF PRACTICAL THOROUGH BASS
COCKSHOOT, JOHN V.
FUGUE IN BEETHOVEN'S PIANO MUSIC, THE
CORTOT, ALFRED
FRENCH PIANO MUSIC
COVIELLO, AMBROSE
CHOICE OF A BEETHOVEN SONATA FOR DIPLOMA EXAMINATIONS, THE --NOTES
COVIELLO, AMBROSE
DIFFICULTIES OF BEETHOVEN PIANOFORTE SONATAS, AN ANALYSIS OF
CULSHAW, JOHN
CONCERTO, THE
CULSHAW, JOHN
SERGEI RACHMANINOFF..THE MAN AND HIS MUSIC
CURTIS, ALAN
SWEELINCK'S KEYBOARD MUSIC..A STUDY OF ENGLISH ELEMENTS IN
DAVISON, JAMES W.
FREDERIC FRANCOIS CHOPIN..CRITICAL AND APPRECIATIVE ESSAY---1843
DAWES, FRANCIS E.
DEBUSSY PIANO MUSIC--B.B.C. MUSIC GUIDE---COMPOSITIONAL ASPECT
DEMUTH, NORMAN
FRENCH PIANO MUSIC..A SURVEY WITH NOTES ON ITS PERFORMANCE
DICKINSON, ALLAN E.
BACH'S FUGAL WORKS
DONINGTON, ROBERT
PERFORMER'S GUIDE TO BAROQUE MUSIC, A
DRAKE, KENNETH
SONATAS OF BEETHOVEN AS HE PLAYED AND TAUGHT THEM, THE
EMERICH, PAUL
ROAD TO MODERN MUSIC, THE
ENGEL, CARL
PIANIST'S HANDBOOK, THE ..A GUIDE FOR THE RIGHT COMPREHENSION AND
EVANS, EDWIN
HANDBOOK TO THE PIANOFORTE WORKS OF JOHANNES BRAHMS---1936
FERGUSON, DONALD NIVISON
PIANO MUSIC OF SIX GREAT COMPOSERS---1947
FISCHER, EDWIN
BEETHOVEN'S PIANOFORTE SONATAS, A GUIDE FOR STUDENTS AND
FISKE, ROGER
BEETHOVEN CONCERTOS AND OVERTURES
FORMAN, DENIS
MOZART'S CONCERTO FORM..THE FIRST MOVEMENTS OF THE PIANO CONCERTOS
FORTE, ALLEN
COMPOSITIONAL MATRIX, THE ..MONOGRAPHS IN THEORY AND COMPOSITION
FULLER-MAITLAND, J. A.
FORTY-EIGHT, THE ..BACH'S WOHLTEMPERIRTES CLAVIER, FROM 'THE
FULLER-MAITLAND, J. A.
KEYBOARD SUITES OF J. S. BACH, THE
FULLER-MAITLAND, J. A.
SCHUMANN'S PIANOFORTE WORKS
GARVIN, FLORENCE HOLLISTER
BEGINNINGS OF THE ROMANTIC PIANO CONCERTO, THE
GILLESPIE, JOHN
FIVE CENTURIES OF KEYBOARD MUSIC..AN HISTORIC SURVEY FOR
GIRDLESTONE, CUTHBERT
MOZART AND HIS PIANO CONCERTOS---FIRST PUBLISHED IN 1948 AS
GLENNON, JAMES
MAKING FRIENDS WITH THE CONCERTO..HISTORICAL AND ANALYTICAL NOTES
GRAY, CECIL
BACH AND DAS WOHLTEMPERIRTE KLAVIER..ANALYTICAL NOTES, WITH AN
GRAY, CECIL
FORTY-EIGHT PRELUDES AND FUGUES OF J. S. BACH, THE
HADOW, SIR WILLIAM HENRY
SONATA FORM---1896
HALLE, SIR CHARLES
ST. JAMES HALL...C. HALLE'S PIANOFORTE RECITALS..MAY 5-JUNE 29,
HALLE, SIR CHARLES
ST. JAMES HALL...MR. HALLE'S BEETHOVEN RECITALS, MAY 23-JULY 11,
HAMILTON, CLARENCE G.
PIANO MUSIC, ITS COMPOSERS AND CHARACTERISTICS
HANSON, JOHN R.
FORM IN SELECTED TWENTIETH-CENTURY PIANO CONCERTOS
HARDING, HENRY ALFRED
ANALYSIS OF FORM AS DISPLAYED IN BEETHOVEN'S 32 PIANOFORTE
HARDING, HENRY ALFRED
THREE HUNDRED AND FIFTY QUESTIONS ON THE FORM AND TONALITY OF
HARRISON, W. WELLS
SCHUBERT'S COMPOSITIONS FOR PIANO AND STRINGS--STRAD HANDBOOK NO.
HARTSHORN, WILLIAM C.
CONCERTO, THE --ANALYTICAL GUIDES---FIVE FOLDOUTS--EIGHT PAGES
HEUSCHNEIDER, KARIN
PIANO SONATA OF THE EIGHTEENTH CENTURY IN GERMANY, THE
HEUSCHNEIDER, KARIN
PIANO SONATA OF THE EIGHTEENTH CENTURY IN ITALY, THE
HILL, RALPH--EDITOR
CONCERTO, THE
HOLMES, EDWARD
ANALYTICAL AND THEMATIC INDEX OF MOZART'S PIANO WORKS
HOLMES, GEORGE AUGUSTUS *
ANALYSIS OF PIANOFORTE COMPOSITIONS FROM THE CLASSICAL AND
HOPKINS, ANTHONY
TALKING ABOUT CONCERTOS..AN ANALYTICAL STUDY OF A NUMBER OF
HULL, ARTHUR EAGLEFIELD
THREE HUNDRED QUESTIONS ON PIANOFORTE TEACHING IN 30 GRADUATED
HUTCHESON, ERNEST *
LITERATURE OF THE PIANO, THE ..A GUIDE FOR AMATEUR AND
HUTCHESON, ERNEST
LITERATURE OF THE PIANO, THE --FROM THE 16TH. CENTURY TO THE
HUTCHINGS, ARTHUR
BAROQUE CONCERTO, THE
HUTCHINGS, ARTHUR
COMPANION TO MOZART'S PIANO CONCERTOS, A
ILIFFE, FREDERICK
FORTY-EIGHT PRELUDES AND FUGUES OF JOHANN SEBASTIAN BACH ANALYZED
INTERNATIONAL MUSICOLOGICAL CONGRESS..FIRST--1960--WORKS OF FREDERICK
BOOK OF THE FIRST INTERNATIONAL MUSICOLOGICAL CONGRESS DEVOTED TO
JOHNS, CLAYTON
ESSENTIALS OF PIANOFORTE PLAYING, THE
JOHNSTONE, J. ALFRED
NOTES ON THE INTERPRETATION OF 24 FAMOUS PIANO SONATAS OF
KASTNER, RUDOLF
BEETHOVEN'S PIANO SONATAS AND ARTUR SCHNABEL
KELBERINE, ALEXANDER
FOUR FAMOUS PIANOFORTE SONATAS OF BEETHOVEN, THE --OP. 13, OP. 27,

KIRBY, FRANK EUGENE
SHORT HISTORY OF KEYBOARD MUSIC, A
KORSTEN, BJARNE
RECENT NORWEGIAN PIANO MUSIC
LANDOWSKA, WANDA
LANDOWSKA ON MUSIC--EDITED BY DENISE RESTOUT
LEICHTENTRITT, HUGO
COMPLETE PIANOFORTE SONATAS OF BEETHOVEN, THE ---ANALYTICAL NOTES
LEIMER, KARL *
SHORTEST WAY TO PIANISTIC PERFECTION, THE
LOVELOCK, WILLIAM
FORMAL ANALYSIS OF THE SENIOR AND ADVANCED SENIOR PIANOFORTE
LOWE, CLAUDE EDGERTON
BEETHOVEN'S PIANOFORTE SONATAS..HINTS ON THEIR RENDERING, FORM...
LUBIN, ERNEST
PIANO DUET, THE ...A GUIDE FOR PIANISTS
MACPHERSON, STEWART
COMMENTARY ON BKS. 1 AND 2 OF THE FORTY-EIGHT PRELUDES AND FUGUES
MARKS, F. HELENA
QUESTIONS ON MOZART'S PIANO SONATAS, DESIGNED AS A COMPANION
MARKS, F. HELENA
SONATA, ITS FORM AND MEANING AS EXEMPLIFIED IN THE PIANO SONATAS
MARX, ADOLF BERNHARD
INTRODUCTION TO THE INTERPRETATION OF BEETHOVEN'S PIANO
MATTHEWS, DENIS--EDITOR
KEYBOARD MUSIC--ESSAYS ON KEYBOARD LITERATURE, EXCLUDING ORGAN
MATTHEWS, DENIS
BEETHOVEN PIANO SONATAS--B.B.C. MUSIC GUIDE, NO. 1
MCCLANAHAN, RICHARD
CADENCE, KEY TO MUSICAL CLARITY, THE ..A SIMPLE AND PRACTICAL
MILNE, ALFRED FORBES
BEETHOVEN..THE PIANOFORTE SONATAS--2 VOLS.
MORGAN, ORLANDO
J. S. BACH..48 PRELUDES AND FUGUES..ANALYSIS OF THE FUGUES
MURDOCH, WILLIAM
BRAHMS..WITH AN ANALYTICAL STUDY OF THE COMPLETE PIANOFORTE WORKS
NAYLOR, EDWARD W.
ELIZABETHAN VIRGINAL BOOK, AN ..A CRITICAL ESSAY ON THE CONTENTS
NELSON, WENDELL
CONCERTO, THE --BROWN 'MUSIC HORIZON' SERIES
NEWMAN, WILLIAM S.
SONATA IN THE BAROQUE ERA, THE --A HISTORY OF THE SONATA IDEA,
NEWMAN, WILLIAM S.
SONATA IN THE CLASSIC ERA, THE --A HISTORY OF THE SONATA IDEA,
NEWMAN, WILLIAM S.
SONATA SINCE BEETHOVEN, THE --A HISTORY OF THE SONATA IDEA, VOL. 3
NEWMAN, WILLIAM S.
THIRTEEN KEYBOARD SONATAS OF THE EIGHTEENTH AND NINETEENTH
NICCHIA, LILLIAN
PIANOFORTE STUDY..HINTS ON PIANO PLAYING
PALMER, WILLARD A.--EDITOR
CHOPIN..AN INTRODUCTION TO HIS PIANO WORKS
PRENTICE, THOMAS RIDLEY
MUSICIAN, THE ..A GUIDE FOR PIANOFORTE STUDENTS--6 VOLS.
RADCLIFFE, PHILIP
SCHUBERT PIANO SONATAS--B.B.C. MUSIC GUIDE, NO. 17
REINECKE, KARL H.
BEETHOVEN PIANOFORTE SONATAS, THE ..LETTERS TO A LADY
RETI, RUDOLPH
THEMATIC PATTERNS IN SONATAS OF BEETHOVEN
RICHNER, THOMAS
ORIENTATION FOR INTERPRETING MOZART'S PIANO SONATAS
RIEMANN, HUGO
ANALYSIS OF J. S. BACH'S WOHLTEMPIERTES KLAVIER--2 PTS.
RIEMANN, HUGO
PRACTICAL GUIDE TO THE ART OF PHRASING...ANALYSIS OF CLASSIC AND
ROLLAND, ROMAIN
BEETHOVEN..WITH A BRIEF ANALYSIS OF THE SONATAS...BY A. EAGLEFIELD
ROTHSCHILD, FRITZ
HANDBOOK TO THE PERFORMANCE OF THE 48 PRELUDES AND FUGUES OF J. S.
ROTHSCHILD, FRITZ
LOST TRADITION IN MUSIC, THE --PT. 1..RHYTHM AND TEMPO IN J. S.
ROTHSCHILD, FRITZ
LOST TRADITION IN MUSIC, THE --PT. 2..MUSICAL PERFORMANCE IN THE
SALSBURY, JANET
CONCISE ANALYSIS OF BEETHOVEN'S 32 PIANOFORTE SONATAS, A
SALSBURY, JANET
SHORT AND CONCISE ANALYSIS OF MOZART'S 22 PIANOFORTE SONATAS, A
SAMPSON, BROOK
DIGEST OF THE ANALYSES OF THE 48 FUGUES IN THE WELL-TEMPERED
SAMPSON, BROOK
OUTLINE ANALYSIS OF EACH OF BACH'S FORTY-EIGHT FUGUES--IN THE 'DAS
SCHAUFFLER, ROBERT HAVEN
FLORESTAN..THE LIFE AND WORK OF ROBERT SCHUMANN---1945
SCHELLING, ERNEST *
OXFORD PIANO COURSE, TEACHER'S SECOND MANUAL
SCHENKER, HEINRICH
FIVE GRAPHIC MUSIC ANALYSES--- INCLUDES TWO CHOPIN ETUDES..OP. 10,
SCHMITZ, ELIE ROBERT
PIANO WORKS OF CLAUDE DEBUSSY, THE
SCHOLES, PERCY
APPRECIATION OF MUSIC BY MEANS OF THE PIANOLA AND DUO-ART, THE
SCHONBERG, HAROLD
COLLECTOR'S CHOPIN AND SCHUMANN, THE --KEYSTONE BOOKS
SCHONBERG, HAROLD
LIVES OF THE GREAT COMPOSERS, THE ---CHOPIN AND LISZT
SEARLE, HUMPHREY
MUSIC OF LISZT, THE --2ND. REV. ED.---1954
SHEDLOCK, JOHN S.
BEETHOVEN'S PIANOFORTE SONATAS..THE ORIGIN AND RESPECTIVE VALUES
SHEDLOCK, JOHN S.
PIANOFORTE SONATA, THE ..ITS ORIGIN AND DEVELOPMENT---1895
SHERWOOD MUSIC SCHOOL
PIANO LESSONS AND TESTS--4TH. REV. ED.---1945+
STAINKAMPH, EILEEN
FORM AND ANALYSES OF MOZART'S PIANOFORTE SONATAS, THE
STAINKAMPH, EILEEN
FORM AND ANALYSIS OF THE COMPLETE BEETHOVEN'S PIANOFORTE SONATAS
STEIN, ERWIN
FORM AND PERFORMANCE
STUCKENSCHMIDT, HANS H.
MAURICE RAVEL..VARIATIONS ON HIS LIFE AND WORK
SUCHOFF, B.
GUIDE TO THE MIKROKOSMOS OF BELA BARTOK, A --PUBLISHED
SZIGETI, JOSEPH
TEN BEETHOVEN SONATAS FOR PIANO AND VIOLIN, THE
TISCHLER, HANS
STRUCTURAL ANALYSIS OF MOZART'S PIANO CONCERTOS, A --MUSICOLOGICAL
TOBIN, JOSEPH RAYMOND
MOZART AND THE SONATA FORM..A COMPANION BOOK TO ANY EDITION OF
TOVEY, DONALD FRANCIS
COMPANION TO BEETHOVEN'S PIANO SONATAS, A ..COMPLETE
TURECK, ROSALYN
INTRODUCTION TO THE PERFORMANCE OF BACH, AN--3 VOLS.
VEINUS, ABRAHAM
CONCERTO, THE ---1944
VEINUS, ABRAHAM
VICTOR BOOK OF CONCERTOS

VENABLE, MARY
    INTERPRETATION OF PIANO MUSIC, THE
VUILLERMOZ, EMILE
    GABRIEL FAURE
WALKER, ALAN--EDITOR
    CHOPIN COMPANION, THE ..PROFILES OF THE MAN AND THE
WALKER, ALAN--EDITOR
    ROBERT SCHUMANN..THE MAN AND HIS MUSIC---SYMPOSIUM--13 AUTHORS
WARRACK JOHN H.
    CHAIKOVSKY SYMPHONIES AND CONCERTOS--B.B.C. MUSIC GUIDES, NO. 16
WESTERBY, HERBERT
    BEETHOVEN AND HIS PIANO WORKS
WESTERBY, HERBERT
    HOW TO STUDY THE PIANOFORTE WORKS OF THE GREAT COMPOSERS
WESTERBY, HERBERT
    LISZT, COMPOSER, AND HIS PIANO WORKS..DESCRIPTIVE GUIDE AND
WILKINSON, CHARLES W.
    HOW TO INTERPRET MENDELSSOHN'S SONGS WITHOUT WORDS
WILKINSON, CHARLES W.
    HOW TO PLAY BACH'S 48 PRELUDES AND FUGUES
WILKINSON, CHARLES W.
    HOW TO PLAY 110 FAVOURITE PIANO SOLOS

Analysis - Interpretative

ABRAHAM, GERALD
    CHOPIN'S MUSICAL STYLE---1939
ALLEN, MARGARET *
    CREATIVE MOTION
ANDERSON, WILLIAM R.
    RACHMANINOV AND HIS PIANO CONCERTOS
APEL, WILLI
    HISTORY OF KEYBOARD MUSIC TO 1700, THE --TRANSLATED AND REVISED BY
ARONSON, MAURICE
    KEY TO THE MINIATURES OF LEOPOLD GODOWSKY, A ..ANALYTICAL ESSAYS
BADURA-SKODA, EVA *
    INTERPRETING MOZART ON THE KEYBOARD---1957, IN GERMAN
BARFORD, PHILIP
    KEYBOARD MUSIC OF C. P. E. BACH, THE ..CONSIDERED IN RELATION TO
BEAUFORT, RAPHAEL
    FRANZ LISZT, THE STORY OF HIS LIFE--TO WHICH IS ADDED..'LISZT AS A
BECKETT, WALTER
    LISZT
BEHREND, WILLIAM
    LUDWIG VAN BEETHOVEN'S PIANOFORTE SONATAS
BLOM, ERIC
    BEETHOVEN'S PIANOFORTE SONATAS DISCUSSED---1938
BODKY, ERWIN
    INTERPRETATION OF BACH'S KEYBOARD WORKS, THE
BRANSON, DAVID
    JOHN FIELD AND CHOPIN
BROWER, HARRIETTE
    WHAT TO PLAY--WHAT TO TEACH
BROWN, MAURICE J. E.
    SCHUBERT'S VARIATIONS
CANAVE, PAZ CORAZON G.
    RE-EVALUATION OF THE ROLE PLAYED BY C. P. E. BACH IN THE
CORTOT, ALFRED
    ALFRED CORTOT'S STUDIES IN MUSICAL INTERPRETATION, SET DOWN BY
CORTOT, ALFRED
    FRENCH PIANO MUSIC
CORTOT, ALFRED
    PIANO MUSIC OF CLAUDE DEBUSSY, THE
CULSHAW, JOHN
    CONCERTO, THE
CULSHAW, JOHN
    SERGEI RACHMANINOFF..THE MAN AND HIS MUSIC
CURTIS, ALAN
    SWEELINCK'S KEYBOARD MUSIC..A STUDY OF ENGLISH ELEMENTS IN
DALE, KATHLEEN
    NINETEENTH CENTURY PIANO MUSIC, A HANDBOOK FOR PIANISTS
DAVISON, JAMES W.
    FREDERIC FRANCOIS CHOPIN..CRITICAL AND APPRECIATIVE ESSAY---1843
DAWES, FRANCIS E.
    DEBUSSY PIANO MUSIC--B.B.C. MUSIC GUIDE---COMPOSITIONAL ASPECT
DEMUTH, NORMAN
    FRENCH PIANO MUSIC..A SURVEY WITH NOTES ON ITS PERFORMANCE
DITSON COMPANY
    TEACHING PIECES AND HOW TO TEACH THEM
DONINGTON, ROBERT
    PERFORMER'S GUIDE TO BAROQUE MUSIC, A
DRAKE, KENNETH
    SONATAS OF BEETHOVEN AS HE PLAYED AND TAUGHT THEM, THE
DRY, WAKELING
    CHOPIN--'MUSIC OF THE MASTERS' SERIES
DUMESNIL, MAURICE
    HOW TO PLAY AND TEACH DEBUSSY
DUNN, JOHN PETRIE
    ORNAMENTATION IN THE WORKS OF FREDERIC CHOPIN---1921
EVANS, EDWIN
    HANDBOOK TO THE PIANOFORTE WORKS OF JOHANNES BRAHMS---1936
FERGUSON, DONALD NIVISON
    PIANO INTERPRETATION
FERGUSON, DONALD NIVISON
    PIANO MUSIC OF SIX GREAT COMPOSERS---1947
FISCHER, EDWIN
    REFLECTIONS ON MUSIC
FORMAN, DENIS
    MOZART'S CONCERTO FORM..THE FIRST MOVEMENTS OF THE PIANO CONCERTOS
FRISKIN, JAMES *
    MUSIC FOR THE PIANO..A HANDBOOK OF CONCERT AND TEACHING MATERIAL
FULLER-MAITLAND, J. A.
    ROBERT SCHUMANN--'THE GREAT MUSICIANS' SERIES
FULLER-MAITLAND, J. A.
    SCHUMANN'S PIANOFORTE WORKS
GARVIN, FLORENCE HOLLISTER
    BEGINNINGS OF THE ROMANTIC PIANO CONCERTO, THE
GIRDLESTONE, CUTHBERT
    MOZART AND HIS PIANO CONCERTOS---FIRST PUBLISHED IN 1948 AS
GLENNON, JAMES
    MAKING FRIENDS WITH PIANO MUSIC..THE HISTORY AND ANALYTICAL NOTES
GLENNON, JAMES
    MAKING FRIENDS WITH PIANO MUSIC--SUPPLEMENT
GLENNON, JAMES
    MAKING FRIENDS WITH THE CONCERTO..HISTORICAL AND ANALYTICAL NOTES
GOTTSCHALD, ERNEST
    BEETHOVEN'S PIANOFORTE SONATAS EXPLAINED FOR THE LOVERS OF THE
GRAY, CECIL
    BACH AND DAS WOHLTEMPERIRTE KLAVIER..ANALYTICAL NOTES, WITH AN
GRAY, CECIL
    CONTINGENCIES AND OTHER ESSAYS---LISZT
GRAY, CECIL
    FORTY-EIGHT PRELUDES AND FUGUES OF J. S. BACH, THE
HADOW, SIR WILLIAM HENRY
    STUDIES IN MODERN MUSIC--2ND. SERIES--9TH. ED.---CHOPIN
HAMILTON, CLARENCE G.
    PIANO MUSIC, ITS COMPOSERS AND CHARACTERISTICS

HENDERSON, WILLIAM JAMES
    PRELUDES AND STUDIES..MUSICAL THEMES OF THE DAY--SECTION 3..THE
HERVEY, ARTHUR
    SAINT-SAENS---1921
HILL, RALPH--EDITOR
    CONCERTO, THE
HOLMES, EDWARD
    ANALYTICAL AND THEMATIC INDEX OF MOZART'S PIANO WORKS
HOLMES, GEORGE AUGUSTUS *
    ANALYSIS OF PIANOFORTE COMPOSITIONS FROM THE CLASSICAL AND
HOPKINS, ANTHONY
    TALKING ABOUT SONATAS..A BOOK OF ANALYTICAL STUDIES, BASED ON A
HUNEKER, JAMES GIBBONS
    FRANZ LISZT
HUTCHESON, ERNEST *
    LITERATURE OF THE PIANO, THE ..A GUIDE FOR AMATEUR AND
HUTCHINGS, ARTHUR
    BAROQUE CONCERTO, THE
HUTCHINGS, ARTHUR
    COMPANION TO MOZART'S PIANO CONCERTOS, A
INTERNATIONAL MUSICOLOGICAL CONGRESS..FIRST--1960--WORKS OF FREDERICK
    BOOK OF THE FIRST INTERNATIONAL MUSICOLOGICAL CONGRESS DEVOTED TO
JOHNS, CLAYTON
    ESSENTIALS OF PIANOFORTE PLAYING, THE
JOHNSTONE, J. ALFRED
    TOUCH, PHRASING AND INTERPRETATION
JONSON, GEORGE CHARLES
    HANDBOOK TO CHOPIN'S WORKS, A
KASTNER, RUDOLPH
    BEETHOVEN'S PIANO SONATAS AND ARTUR SCHNABEL
KASTNER, SANTIAGO
    PARALLELS AND DISCREPANCIES BETWEEN ENGLISH AND SPANISH KEYBOARD
KIRBY, FRANK EUGENE
    SHORT HISTORY OF KEYBOARD MUSIC, A
KIRKPATRICK, JOHN
    OBSERVATIONS ON FOUR VOLUMES AND SUPPLEMENT OF THE WORKS OF L. M.
KLECZYNSKI, JAN
    CHOPIN'S GREATER WORKS...HOW THEY SHOULD BE UNDERSTOOD...INCLUDING
KLECZYNSKI, JAN
    HOW TO PLAY CHOPIN--THREE LECTURES
KLECZYNSKI, JAN
    WORKS OF FREDERIC CHOPIN, THE ..THEIR PROPER INTERPRETATION--6TH.
LAMAR, RICHARD
    COLLEGE PIANO PEDAGOGY
LANDOWSKA, WANDA
    LANDOWSKA ON MUSIC--EDITED BY DENISE RESTOUT
LANDOWSKI, ALICE-WANDA
    DOMENICO SCARLATTI--NOTES TO ACCOMPANY GRAMOPHONE RECORDINGS
LEIMER, KARL *
    SHORTEST WAY TO PIANISTIC PERFECTION, THE
LEONHARDT, GUSTAV M.
    ART OF FUGUE, BACH'S LAST HARPSICHORD WORK, THE ..AN ARGUMENT
LINGG, ANN M.
    MEPHISTO WALTZ, THE STORY OF FRANZ LISZT
LONG, MARGUERITE
    AT THE PIANO WITH DEBUSSY---1960, IN FRENCH
LOWE, CLAUDE EDGERTON
    BEETHOVEN'S PIANOFORTE SONATAS..HINTS ON THEIR RENDERING, FORM...
LOWE, CLAUDE EDGERTON
    WORD-PHRASES TO BACH'S 48 FUGUES, WITH HINTS ON THE RENDERINGS OF
LUBIN, ERNEST
    PIANO DUET, THE ...A GUIDE FOR PIANISTS
LYLE, WATSON
    CAMILLE SAINT-SAENS, HIS LIFE AND ART---DISCUSSES CONCERTI AND
MACPHERSON, STEWART
    COMMENTARY ON BKS. 1 AND 2 OF THE FORTY-EIGHT PRELUDES AND FUGUES
MARKS, ADOLF B.
    INTRODUCTION TO THE INTERPRETATION OF BEETHOVEN'S PIANO-FORTE
MARKS, F. HELENA
    QUESTIONS ON MOZART'S PIANO SONATAS, DESIGNED AS A COMPANION
MARKS, F. HELENA
    SONATA, ITS FORM AND MEANING AS EXEMPLIFIED IN THE PIANO SONATAS
MARX, ADOLF BERNHARD
    INTRODUCTION TO THE INTERPRETATION OF BEETHOVEN'S PIANO
MATTHEWS, DENIS--EDITOR
    KEYBOARD MUSIC--ESSAYS ON KEYBOARD LITERATURE, EXCLUDING ORGAN
MATTHEWS, DENIS
    BEETHOVEN PIANO SONATAS--B.B.C. MUSIC GUIDE, NO. 1
MCCLANAHAN, RICHARD
    CADENCE, KEY TO MUSICAL CLARITY, THE ..A SIMPLE AND PRACTICAL
MILNE, ALFRED FORBES
    BEETHOVEN..THE PIANOFORTE SONATAS--2 VOLS.
MONTAGU-NATHAN, M.
    CONTEMPORARY RUSSIAN COMPOSERS---RACHMANINOFF
MONTAGU-NATHAN, M.
    HANDBOOK TO THE PIANO WORKS OF SCRIABIN
MURDOCH, WILLIAM
    BRAHMS..WITH AN ANALYTICAL STUDY OF THE COMPLETE PIANOFORTE WORKS
NAYLOR, EDWARD W.
    ELIZABETHAN VIRGINAL BOOK, AN ..A CRITICAL ESSAY ON THE CONTENTS
NEWMAN, WILLIAM S.
    SONATA IN THE BAROQUE ERA, THE --A HISTORY OF THE SONATA IDEA,
NEWMAN, WILLIAM S.
    SONATA IN THE CLASSIC ERA, THE --A HISTORY OF THE SONATA IDEA,
NEWMAN, WILLIAM S.
    SONATA SINCE BEETHOVEN, THE --A HISTORY OF THE SONATA IDEA, VOL. 3
NEWMAN, WILLIAM S.
    THIRTEEN KEYBOARD SONATAS OF THE EIGHTEENTH AND NINETEENTH
NIMITZ, DANIEL
    KEYBOARD MASTERS..STUDY GUIDE
PAUER, ERNST
    ERNST PAUER'S SIX HISTORICAL PERFORMANCES OF PIANOFORTE MUSIC
PERRY, EDWARD B.
    STORIES OF STANDARD TEACHING PIECES FOR THE PIANOFORTE
PETERSON, FRANKLIN
    THEORETIC COMPANION TO PRACTICE--PART I OF THE PIANIST'S HANDBOOK
PORTE, JOHN F.
    EDWARD MACDOWELL, A GREAT AMERICAN TONE POET..HIS LIFE AND MUSIC
PRENTICE, THOMAS RIDLEY
    MUSICIAN, THE ..A GUIDE FOR PIANOFORTE STUDENTS--6 VOLS.
RADCLIFFE, PHILIP
    SCHUBERT PIANO SONATAS--B.B.C. MUSIC GUIDE, NO. 17
REINECKE, KARL H.
    BEETHOVEN PIANOFORTE SONATAS, THE ..LETTERS TO A LADY
REZITS, JOSEPH
    TEACHER'S GUIDE TO THE NEW SCRIBNER MUSIC LIBRARY
RICHNER, THOMAS
    ORIENTATION FOR INTERPRETING MOZART'S PIANO SONATAS
RIEMANN, HUGO
    ANALYSIS OF J. S. BACH'S WOHLTEMPIERTES KLAVIER--2 PTS.
ROLLAND, ROMAIN
    BEETHOVEN..WITH A BRIEF ANALYSIS OF THE SONATAS...BY A. EAGLEFIELD
ROSTAND, CLAUDE
    LISZT
ROTHSCHILD, FRITZ
    HANDBOOK TO THE PERFORMANCE OF THE 48 PRELUDES AND FUGUES OF J. S.
ROTHSCHILD, FRITZ
    LOST TRADITION IN MUSIC, THE --PT. 1..RHYTHM AND TEMPO IN J. S.

ROTHSCHILD, FRITZ
LOST TRADITION IN MUSIC, THE --PT. 2..MUSICAL PERFORMANCE IN THE
RUBINSTEIN, ANTON
CONVERSATION ON MUSIC, A
SCHAUFFLER, ROBERT HAVEN
FLORESTAN..THE LIFE AND WORK OF ROBERT SCHUMANN---1945
SCHELLING, ERNEST *
OXFORD PIANO COURSE, TEACHER'S SECOND MANUAL
SCHMITZ, ELIE ROBERT
PIANO WORKS OF CLAUDE DEBUSSY, THE
SCHOLES, PERCY
APPRECIATION OF MUSIC BY MEANS OF THE PIANOLA AND DUO-ART, THE
SCHONBERG, HAROLD
COLLECTOR'S CHOPIN AND SCHUMANN, THE --KEYSTONE BOOKS
SCHONBERG, HAROLD
LIVES OF THE GREAT COMPOSERS, THE ---CHOPIN AND LISZT
SCHUMANN, ROBERT
ON MUSIC AND MUSICIANS---1854, IN GERMAN--FIRST ENGLISH EDITION IN
SEARLE, HUMPHREY
MUSIC OF LISZT, THE --2ND. REV. ED.---1954
SHEDLOCK, JOHN S.
BEETHOVEN'S PIANOFORTE SONATAS..THE ORIGIN AND RESPECTIVE VALUES
SHERWOOD MUSIC SCHOOL
PIANO LESSONS AND TESTS--4TH. REV. ED.---1945+
STEIN, ERWIN
FORM AND PERFORMANCE
STOOKES, SACHA
ART OF ROBERT CASADESUS, THE
STUCKENSCHMIDT, HANS H.
MAURICE RAVEL..VARIATIONS ON HIS LIFE AND WORK
SUCHOFF, B.
GUIDE TO THE MIKROKOSMOS OF BELA BARTOK, A --PUBLISHED
SZIGETI, JOSEPH
TEN BEETHOVEN SONATAS FOR PIANO AND VIOLIN, THE
TAWASTSTJERNA, ERIK
PIANOFORTE COMPOSITIONS OF SIBELIUS, THE
TEMPLIER, PIERRE D.
ERIK SATIE---1932, IN FRENCH
TURECK, ROSALYN
INTRODUCTION TO THE PERFORMANCE OF BACH, AN--3 VOLS.
VEINUS, ABRAHAM
CONCERTO, THE ---1944
VEINUS, ABRAHAM
VICTOR BOOK OF CONCERTOS
VENABLE, MARY
INTERPRETATION OF PIANO MUSIC, THE
VUILLERMOZ, EMILE
GABRIEL FAURE
WALKER, ALAN--EDITOR
CHOPIN COMPANION, THE ..PROFILES OF THE MAN AND THE
WALKER, ALAN--EDITOR
FRANZ LISZT, THE MAN AND HIS MUSIC---ESSAYS BY SACHEVERALL SITWELL
WALKER, ALAN--EDITOR
ROBERT SCHUMANN..THE MAN AND HIS MUSIC---SYMPOSIUM--13 AUTHORS
WARRACK JOHN H.
CHAIKOVSKY SYMPHONIES AND CONCERTOS--B.B.C. MUSIC GUIDES, NO. 16
WESTERBY, HERBERT
BEETHOVEN AND HIS PIANO WORKS
WESTERBY, HERBERT
LISZT, COMPOSER, AND HIS PIANO WORKS..DESCRIPTIVE GUIDE AND
WILKINSON, CHARLES W.
HOW TO INTERPRET MENDELSSOHN'S SONGS WITHOUT WORDS
WILKINSON, CHARLES W.
HOW TO PLAY 110 FAVOURITE PIANO SOLOS
WILKINSON, CHARLES W.
WELL-KNOWN PIANO SOLOS..HOW TO PLAY THEM WITH UNDERSTANDING,
WILLEBY, CHARLES
FREDERIC FRANCOIS CHOPIN
WOLFF, ERNST VICTOR
WITH REASON AND RHYME
WOLFF, KONRAD
TEACHING OF ARTUR SCHNABEL, THE ..A GUIDE TO INTERPRETATION
YOUNG, PERCY M.
CONCERTO--'PHOENIX MUSIC GUIDES', NO. 1

Criticism

BLOM, ERIC
BEETHOVEN'S PIANOFORTE SONATAS DISCUSSED---1938
CZERNY, CARL
LETTERS TO A YOUNG LADY ON THE ART OF PLAYING THE PIANOFORTE
ENGEL, CARL
PIANIST'S HANDBOOK, THE ..A GUIDE FOR THE RIGHT COMPREHENSION AND
EVANS, EDWIN
HANDBOOK TO THE PIANOFORTE WORKS OF JOHANNES BRAHMS---1936
GILLESPIE, JOHN
FIVE CENTURIES OF KEYBOARD MUSIC..AN HISTORIC SURVEY FOR
GORDON, STEPHEN T.
GORDON'S NEW SCHOOL FOR THE PIANO-FORTE
HAMILTON, CLARENCE G.
PIANO TEACHING..ITS PRINCIPLES AND PROBLEMS
HOLCMAN, JAN
LEGACY OF CHOPIN, THE
HULL, ARTHUR EAGLEFIELD
THREE HUNDRED QUESTIONS ON PIANOFORTE TEACHING IN 30 GRADUATED
HUNEKER, JAMES GIBBONS
OLD FOGY, HIS MUSICAL OPINIONS AND GROTESQUES---D'ALBERT,
LOCKWOOD, ALBERT
NOTES ON THE LITERATURE OF THE PIANO--RE-EDITED BY BROTHER, SAMUEL
MCNABB, GEORGE
SELECTED LIST OF GRADED TEACHING MATERIAL FOR THE PIANO, A --3RD.
PALMER, HORATIO R.
PALMER'S PIANO PRIMER
PARSONS, ALBERT R.
SCIENCE OF PIANO PRACTICE, THE
PLAIDY, LOUIS
PIANO TEACHER, THE
PLANTIGA, LEON B.
SCHUMANN AS CRITIC
RICHARDSON, NATHAN
NEW METHOD FOR THE PIANOFORTE..ADDED, RUDIMENTS OF HARMONY AND
SORABJI, KAIKHOSRU
AROUND MUSIC---PACHMAN, CHOPIN AND LISZT
SUTHERLAND, ADELAIDE K.--COMPILER
WHAT SHALL I PLAY..PREFERENCES FOR PIANO AND ORGAN..GUIDE TO
WHITE, WILLIAM BRAID
PLAYER-PIANIST, THE ..A GUIDE TO THE APPRECIATION AND
WILSON, DAVID M.
INSTRUCTION BOOK ON THE PIANO-PLAYER AND PLAYER-PIANO, AN

Master Lessons

BADUPA-SKODA, EVA *
INTERPRETING MOZART ON THE KEYBOARD---1957, IN GERMAN
BLOM, ERIC
BEETHOVEN'S PIANOFORTE SONATAS DISCUSSED---1938

BOWMAN, EDWARD M.
MASTER LESSONS IN PIANOFORTE PLAYING, *LETTERS FROM A MUSICIAN TO
BROWEP, HARRIETTE
WHAT TO PLAY--WHAT TO TEACH
COHEN, HARRIET
MUSIC'S HANDMAID
CORTOT, ALFRED
FRENCH PIANO MUSIC
COUPERIN, FRANCOIS
ART DE TOUCHER LE CLAVECIN, L' ---IN FRENCH, GERMAN AND ENGLISH
HARRISON, SIDNEY
BEGINNING TO PLAY THE PIANO--A TEACHER'S HANDBOOK, INCLUDING THE
HUTCHESON, ERNEST *
LITERATURE OF THE PIANO, THE ..A GUIDE FOR AMATEUR AND
KELBERINE, ALEXANDER
FOUR FAMOUS PIANOFORTE SONATAS OF BEETHOVEN, THE --OP. 13, OP. 27,
LANDOWSKA, WANDA
LANDOWSKA ON MUSIC--EDITED BY DENISE RESTOUT
LEIMER, KARL *
SHORTEST WAY TO PIANISTIC PERFECTION, THE
MAIER, GUY
PIANO TEACHER'S COMPANION, THE
MATTHEWS, DENIS
BEETHOVEN PIANO SONATAS--B.B.C. MUSIC GUIDE, NO. 1
NAYLOR, EDWARD W.
ELIZABETHAN VIRGINAL BOOK, AN ..A CRITICAL ESSAY ON THE CONTENTS
PUGNO, RAOUL
LESSONS OF RAOUL PUGNO, THE ..WITH A BIOGRAPHY OF CHOPIN BY M.
REINECKE, KAPL H.
BEETHOVEN PIANOFORTE SONATAS, THE ..LETTERS TO A LADY
RICHNER, THOMAS
ORIENTATION FOR INTERPRETING MOZART'S PIANO SONATAS
SMITH, JULIA
MASTER PIANIST..THE CAREER AND TEACHING OF CARL FRIEDBERG
SUCHOFF, B.
GUIDE TO THE MIKROKOSMOS OF BELA BARTOK, A --PUBLISHED
SUMMY-BIRCHARD COMPANY
HANDBOOK FOR PIANO TEACHERS..COLLECTED ARTICLES ON SUBJECTS
VENABLE, MARY
INTERPRETATION OF PIANO MUSIC, THE
WHITESIDE, ABBY
MASTERING THE CHOPIN ETUDES AND OTHER ESSAYS
WILKINSON, CHARLES W.
HOW TO PLAY 110 FAVOURITE PIANO SOLOS
WILKINSON, CHARLES W.
WELL-KNOWN PIANO SOLOS..HOW TO PLAY THEM WITH UNDERSTANDING,

Recordings

AEOLIAN COMPANY, THE
CATALOG OF AEOLIAN MUSIC ARRANGED FOR 46-NOTE INSTRUMENTS
AEOLIAN COMPANY, THE
CATALOG OF METROSTYLE AND THEMODIST MUSIC FOR THE PIANOLA AND
AEOLIAN COMPANY, THE
CATALOG OF MUSIC-ROLLS FOR THE DUO-ART REPRODUCING PIANO
AEOLIAN COMPANY, THE
CATALOG OF MUSIC AND MUSICAL LITERATURE---PIANOLA RECORDS
AEOLIAN COMPANY, THE
CATALOG OF MUSIC FOR THE PIANOLA, PIANOLA PIANO AND
AEOLIAN COMPANY, THE
DUO-ART PIANO MUSIC...RECORDED BY MORE THAN 250 PIANISTS
AEOLIAN COMPANY, THE
DUO-ART PIANO MUSIC
AEOLIAN COMPANY, THE
LIBRARY OF DUO-ART MUSIC ROLLS
AEOLIAN COMPANY, THE
METROSTYLE-THEMODIST AND METRO-ART MUSIC ROLLS FOR THE PIANOLA AND
AEOLIAN COMPANY, THE
METROSTYLE, THE
AEOLIAN COMPANY, THE
METROSTYLE AND THEMODIST MUSIC CATALOG FOR THE PIANOLA AND PIANOLA
AEOLIAN COMPANY, THE
MUSIC FOR THE AEOLIAN GRAND--SUPPLEMENT
AEOLIAN COMPANY, THE
MUSIC FOR THE AEOLIAN GRAND
AEOLIAN COMPANY, THE
MUSIC FOR THE ORCHESTRELLE AND AEOLIAN GRAND
AEOLIAN COMPANY, THE
MUSIC FOR THE PIANOLA AND THE AERIAL PIANO--4 VOLS.
AEOLIAN COMPANY, THE
NEW MUSIC FOR THE AEOLIAN GRAND, THE PIANOLA, AND THE AERIOL PIANO
AEOLIAN COMPANY, THE
PIANOLA AND PIANOLA PIANO MUSIC CATALOG, THE ..SIXTY-FIVE NOTE
AEOLIAN COMPANY, THE
SUPPLEMENTARY CATALOG OF MUSIC FOR THE AEOLIAN GRAND AND
AMERICAN PIANO CORPORATION
CATALOGUE OF MUSIC FOR THE AMPICO, A ..A LIST OF THE RECORDINGS OF
AMERICAN PIANO CORPORATION
CATALOGUE OF MUSIC FOR THE AMPICO, A --A LIST OF THE RECORDINGS OF
AMPICO CORPORATION
AMPICO REPRODUCING PIANO..A SUPPLEMENT TO 'PIANO MUSIC, ITS
AMPICO CORPORATION
SUPREMACY OF AMPICO MUSIC..UNIT TWO OF A COURSE IN AMPICO
ANDERSON, WILLIAM R.
RACHMANINOV AND HIS PIANO CONCERTOS
ASSOCIATION FOR RECORDED SOUND COLLECTIONS
PRELIMINARY DIRECTORY OF SOUND RECORDING COLLECTIONS IN THE UNITED
BARTELS, LEO F. *
PERFORATING OF MUSIC ROLLS WITH THE LEABARJAN PERFORATOR, THE
CORTOT, ALFRED
IN SEARCH OF CHOPIN
DELUXE REPRODUCING ROLL CORPORATION
LIBRARY OF DELUXE--REPRODUCING--MUSIC RECORDS
DELUXE ROLL CORPORATION
LIBRARY OF DELUXE WELTE-MIGNON MUSIC RECORDS FOR REPRODUCING
HAMILTON, CLARENCE G.
SUPPLEMENT TO PIANO MUSIC, ITS COMPOSERS AND CHARACTERISTICS, A
KACZMAREK, REGINA A.
CATALOG OF SELECTED PIANO ROLLS FROM THE LIBRARY OF CONGRESS
KORSTEN, BJARNE
RECENT NORWEGIAN PIANO MUSIC
LANDOWSKA, WANDA
LANDOWSKA ON MUSIC--EDITED BY DENISE RESTOUT
LANDOWSKA, WANDA
MUSIC OF THE PAST
MEL-O-DEE MUSIC COMPANY
MELODEE MUSIC ROLLS..SEPTEMBER, 1920
MOLDENHAUER, HANS
DUO-PIANISM---PUBLISHED DISSERTATION
NIMITZ, DANIEL
KEYBOARD MASTERS..STUDY GUIDE
PEDERSON, GALE
KEY TO THE KEYS..A SELF-TAUGHT PIANO METHOD FOR ADULTS AND TEEN
RENAUD, EMILIANO
RENAUD-PHONE PIANO METHOD..A PIANO COURSE THROUGH THE MEDIUM OF
ROEHL, HARVEY
PLAYER PIANO TREASURY..THE SCRAPBOOK HISTORY OF THE MECHANICAL

SCHAUFFLER, ROBERT HAVEN
    FLORESTAN..THE LIFE AND WORK OF ROBERT SCHUMANN---1945
SCHONBERG, HAROLD
    COLLECTOR'S CHOPIN AND SCHUMANN, THE --KEYSTONE BOOKS
VERNAZZA, MARCELLE
    BASIC MATERIALS FOR THE PIANO STUDENT
VUILLERMOZ, EMILE
    GABRIEL FAURE
WEISER, BERNHARD D.
    KEYBOARD MUSIC--16TH.-20TH. CENTURIES
WELTE-MIGNON CORPORATION
    LIBRARY OF DELUXE WELTE-MIGNON MUSIC RECORDS FOR REPRODUCING
WELTE-MIGNON CORPORATION
    LIBRARY OF WELTE-MIGNON MUSIC RECORDS
WILSON, DAVID M.
    INSTRUCTION BOOK ON THE PIANO-PLAYER AND PLAYER-PIANO, AN
WOODHOUSE, GEORGE
    NEW PATH FOR PIANISTS, A ..THE MUTANO--MUTE PIANO--SYSTEM, ETC.

Descriptive Analysis, Program Notes

APEL, WILLI
    MASTERS OF THE KEYBOARD
BECKETT, WALTER
    LISZT
BORREN, CHARLES VAN DEN
    SOURCES OF KEYBOARD MUSIC IN ENGLAND, THE ---1913
BROADWOOD, JOHN AND SONS
    BROADWOOD CONCERTS--HISTORICAL NOTES BY ROBIN H.
BROWER, HARRIETTE
    WHAT TO PLAY--WHAT TO TEACH
EICHBERG, OSCAR
    ANALYTICAL AND HISTORICAL REMARKS ON ANTON RUBINSTEIN'S CYCLE OF
FINCK, HENRY T.
    TWENTY MUSICAL EVENINGS---PIANOLA PROGRAMS WITH NOTES AND COMMENTS
FISCHER, EDWIN
    BEETHOVEN'S PIANOFORTE SONATAS, A GUIDE FOR STUDENTS AND
FRISKIN, JAMES *
    MUSIC FOR THE PIANO..A HANDBOOK OF CONCERT AND TEACHING MATERIAL
FULLER-MAITLAND, J. A.
    SCHUMANN'S PIANOFORTE WORKS
GILLESPIE, JOHN
    FIVE CENTURIES OF KEYBOARD MUSIC..AN HISTORIC SURVEY FOR
GIRDLESTONE, CUTHBERT
    MOZART AND HIS PIANO CONCERTOS---FIRST PUBLISHED IN 1948 AS
HAMBOURG, MARK
    EIGHTH OCTAVE, THE ---CONTINUES THE RECORD, BEGUN IN 'FROM PIANO
HUTCHESON, ERNEST
    GREAT MASTERS OF PIANO MUSIC, THE ..BACH, BEETHOVEN, SCHUMANN,
HUTCHESON, ERNEST *
    LITERATURE OF THE PIANO, THE ..A GUIDE FOR AMATEUR AND
HUTCHESON, ERNEST
    LITERATURE OF THE PIANO, THE --FROM THE 16TH. CENTURY TO THE
KELBERINE, ALEXANDER
    FOUR FAMOUS PIANOFORTE SONATAS OF BEETHOVEN, THE --OP. 13, OP. 27,
KLECZYNSKI, JAN
    CHOPIN'S GREATER WORKS...HOW THEY SHOULD BE UNDERSTOOD...INCLUDING
KOBBE, GUSTAV
    PIANOLIST, THE ..A GUIDE FOR PIANOLA PLAYERS
LAMOND, FREDERICK ARCHIBALD
    BEETHOVEN..NOTES ON THE SONATAS...
LANDOWSKA, WANDA
    MUSIC OF THE PAST
LANDOWSKI, ALICE-WANDA
    DOMENICO SCARLATTI--NOTES TO ACCOMPANY GRAMOPHONE RECORDINGS
MARKS, F. HELENA
    QUESTIONS ON MOZART'S PIANO SONATAS, DESIGNED AS A COMPANION
MARKS, F. HELENA
    SONATA, ITS FORM AND MEANING AS EXEMPLIFIED IN THE PIANO SONATAS
NEWMAN, WILLIAM S.
    PERFORMANCE PRACTICES IN BEETHOVEN'S PIANO SONATAS..AN
PERRY, EDWARD B.
    DESCRIPTIVE ANALYSES OF PIANO WORKS, FOR THE USE OF TEACHERS,
PRENTICE, THOMAS RIDLEY
    MUSICIAN, THE ..A GUIDE FOR PIANOFORTE STUDENTS--6 VOLS.
RAPEE, ERNO--ARRANGER
    ERNO RAPEE'S ENCYCLOPEDIA OF MUSIC FOR PICTURES---LISTED BOTH BY
RAPEE, ERNO--ARRANGER
    MOTION PICTURE MOODS FOR PIANISTS AND ORGANISTS
REZITS, JOSEPH
    TEACHER'S GUIDE TO THE NEW SCRIBNER MUSIC LIBRARY
ROSTAND, CLAUDE
    LISZT
ROTHSCHILD, FRITZ
    LOST TRADITION IN MUSIC, THE --PT. 1..RHYTHM AND TEMPO IN J. S.
ROTHSCHILD, FRITZ
    LOST TRADITION IN MUSIC, THE --PT. 2..MUSICAL PERFORMANCE IN THE
SACHS, CURT
    EVOLUTION OF PIANO MUSIC, 1350-1700, THE
SHATTUCK, ARTHUR
    MEMOIRS OF ARTHUR SHATTUCK, THE ..WITH AN ACCOUNT OF HIS CAREER BY
THOMPSON, OSCAR
    DEBUSSY, MAN AND ARTIST---1937
WELTE-MIGNON CORPORATION
    LIBRARY OF DELUXE WELTE-MIGNON MUSIC RECORDS FOR REPRODUCING
WELTE-MIGNON CORPORATION
    LIBRARY OF WELTE-MIGNON MUSIC RECORDS
WESTERBY, HERBERT
    HOW TO STUDY THE PIANOFORTE WORKS OF THE GREAT COMPOSERS
WESTERBY, HERBERT
    INTRODUCTION TO RUSSIAN PIANO MUSIC--REPRINT..'MUSICAL OPINION'

Compositional Forms

ABRAHAM, GERALD
    CHOPIN'S MUSICAL STYLE---1939
APEL, WILLI
    HISTORY OF KEYBOARD MUSIC TO 1700, THE --TRANSLATED AND REVISED BY
APEL, WILLI
    MASTERS OF THE KEYBOARD
AULD, WILDA J.
    HANDBOOK FOR THE CHURCH PIANIST, A
BARFORD, PHILIP
    KEYBOARD MUSIC OF C. P. E. BACH, THE ..CONSIDERED IN RELATION TO
BEDBROOK, GERALD STARES
    KEYBOARD MUSIC FROM THE MIDDLE AGES TO THE BEGINNINGS OF THE
BEHREND, WILLIAM
    LUDWIG VAN BEETHOVEN'S PIANOFORTE SONATAS
BIART, VICTOR
    PIANIST'S GUIDE, THE ..A SERIES OF PAMPHLETS ON THE TEACHING AND
BODKY, ERWIN
    INTERPRETATION OF BACH'S KEYBOARD WORKS, THE
BORREN, CHARLES VAN DEN
    SOURCES OF KEYBOARD MUSIC IN ENGLAND, THE ---1913
BOYD, MALCOLM
    BACH'S INSTRUMENTAL COUNTERPOINT

BOYD, MALCOLM
    HARMONIZING 'BACH' CHORALES
BRANSON, DAVID
    JOHN FIELD AND CHOPIN
BROWN, MAURICE J. E.
    SCHUBERT'S VARIATIONS
BUECKELMANN, BERNARDUS
    EIGHT FUGUES FROM J. S. BACH'S 'W.T.C.', WITH ANALYTICAL NOTES IN
CALDWELL, JOHN
    ENGLISH KEYBOARD MUSIC BEFORE THE NINETEENTH CENTURY---EXTENSIVE
CANAVE, PAZ CORAZON G.
    RE-EVALUATION OF THE ROLE PLAYED BY C. P. E. BACH IN THE
CARLSON, EFFIE B.
    BIO-BIBLIOGRAPHICAL DICTIONARY OF TWELVE-TONE AND SERIAL
COCKSHOOT, JOHN V.
    FUGUE IN BEETHOVEN'S PIANO MUSIC, THE
CORTOT, ALFRED
    ALFRED CORTOT'S STUDIES IN MUSICAL INTERPRETATION, SET DOWN BY
COVIELLO, AMBROSE
    CHOICE OF A BEETHOVEN SONATA FOR DIPLOMA EXAMINATIONS, THE --NOTES
COVIELLO, AMBROSE
    DIFFICULTIES OF BEETHOVEN PIANOFORTE SONATAS, AN ANALYSIS OF
CULSHAW, JOHN
    CONCERTO, THE
CULSHAW, JOHN
    SERGEI RACHMANINOFF..THE MAN AND HIS MUSIC
CURTIS, ALAN
    SWEELINCK'S KEYBOARD MUSIC..A STUDY OF ENGLISH ELEMENTS IN
CZERNY, CARL
    COMPLETE THEORETICAL AND PRACTICAL PIANO FORTE SCHOOL, FROM THE
DALE, KATHLEEN
    NINETEENTH CENTURY PIANO MUSIC, A HANDBOOK FOR PIANISTS
DAVISON, JAMES W.
    FREDERIC FRANCOIS CHOPIN..CRITICAL AND APPRECIATIVE ESSAY---1843
DAWES, FRANCIS E.
    DEBUSSY PIANO MUSIC--B.B.C. MUSIC GUIDE---COMPOSITIONAL ASPECT
DICKINSON, ALLAN E.
    BACH'S FUGAL WORKS
DONINGTON, ROBERT
    PERFORMER'S GUIDE TO BAROQUE MUSIC, A
DRAKE, KENNETH
    SONATAS OF BEETHOVEN AS HE PLAYED AND TAUGHT THEM, THE
DRY, WAKELING
    CHOPIN--'MUSIC OF THE MASTERS' SERIES
EHRLICH, ALFRED HEINRICH
    ORNAMENTATION IN BEETHOVEN'S PIANOFORTE-WORKS, THE
FERGUSON, DONALD NIVISON
    PIANO INTERPRETATION
FISCHER, EDWIN
    BEETHOVEN'S PIANOFORTE SONATAS, A GUIDE FOR STUDENTS AND
FISKE, ROGER
    BEETHOVEN CONCERTOS AND OVERTURES
FLOOD, WILLIAM HENRY GRATTAN
    JOHN FIELD OF DUBLIN, THE INVENTOR OF THE NOCTURNE---1920
FORMAN, DENIS
    MOZART'S CONCERTO FORM..THE FIRST MOVEMENTS OF THE PIANO CONCERTOS
FRISKIN, JAMES *
    MUSIC FOR THE PIANO..A HANDBOOK OF CONCERT AND TEACHING MATERIAL
FULLER-MAITLAND, J. A.
    FORTY-EIGHT, THE ..BACH'S WOHLTEMPERIRTES CLAVIER, FROM 'THE
FULLER-MAITLAND, J. A.
    KEYBOARD SUITES OF J. S. BACH, THE
FULLER-MAITLAND, J. A.
    SCHUMANN'S PIANOFORTE WORKS
GABRIEL, GILBERT W.
    GREAT PIANISTS AND COMPOSERS
GERMER, HEINRICH
    THEORETICO-PRACTICAL ELEMENTARY PIANO-FORTE SCHOOL FOR STUDENTS OF
GILLESPIE, JOHN
    FIVE CENTURIES OF KEYBOARD MUSIC..AN HISTORIC SURVEY FOR
GIRDLESTONE, CUTHBERT
    MOZART AND HIS PIANO CONCERTOS---FIRST PUBLISHED IN 1948 AS
GLENNON, JAMES
    MAKING FRIENDS WITH THE CONCERTO..HISTORICAL AND ANALYTICAL NOTES
GOODRICH, ALFRED JOHN
    THEORY OF INTERPRETATION, APPLIED TO ARTISTIC MUSICAL PERFORMANCE
GOTTSCHALD, ERNEST
    BEETHOVEN'S PIANOFORTE SONATAS EXPLAINED FOR THE LOVERS OF THE
GREW, SIDNEY
    ART OF THE PLAYER-PIANO, THE ..A TEXTBOOK FOR STUDENT AND TEACHER
HADOW, SIR WILLIAM HENRY
    SONATA FORM---1896
HALLE, SIR CHARLES
    ST. JAMES HALL...C. HALLE'S PIANOFORTE RECITALS..MAY 5-JUNE 29,
HALLE, SIR CHARLES
    ST. JAMES HALL...MR. HALLE'S BEETHOVEN RECITALS, MAY 23-JULY 11,
HAMILTON, CLARENCE G.
    PIANO MUSIC, ITS COMPOSERS AND CHARACTERISTICS
HANSON, JOHN R.
    FORM IN SELECTED TWENTIETH-CENTURY PIANO CONCERTOS
HARRISON, W. WELLS
    SCHUBERT'S COMPOSITIONS FOR PIANO AND STRINGS--STRAD HANDBOOK NO.
HARTSHORN, WILLIAM C.
    CONCERTO, THE --ANALYTICAL GUIDES---FIVE FOLDOUTS--EIGHT PAGES
HENDERSON, WILLIAM JAMES
    PRELUDES AND STUDIES..MUSICAL THEMES OF THE DAY--SECTION 3..THE
HERVEY, ARTHUR
    SAINT-SAENS---1921
HEUSCHNEIDER, KARIN
    PIANO SONATA OF THE EIGHTEENTH CENTURY IN GERMANY, THE
HILL, GEORGE R.
    PRELIMINARY CHECKLIST OF RESEARCH ON THE CLASSIC SYMPHONY AND
HOLMES, EDWARD
    ANALYTICAL AND THEMATIC INDEX OF MOZART'S PIANO WORKS
HOPKINS, ANTHONY
    TALKING ABOUT CONCERTOS..AN ANALYTICAL STUDY OF A NUMBER OF
HULL, ARTHUR EAGLEFIELD
    THREE HUNDRED QUESTIONS ON PIANOFORTE TEACHING IN 30 GRADUATED
HUNEKER, JAMES GIBBONS
    CHOPIN..THE MAN AND HIS MUSIC---1901
INTERNATIONAL MUSICOLOGICAL CONGRESS..FIRST--1960--WORKS OF FREDERICK
    BOOK OF THE FIRST INTERNATIONAL MUSICOLOGICAL CONGRESS DEVOTED TO
JOHNSTONE, J. ALFRED
    NOTES ON THE INTERPRETATION OF 24 FAMOUS PIANO SONATAS OF
KARASOWSKI, MORITZ
    FREDERIC CHOPIN..HIS LIFE, LETTERS AND WORKS--3RD. REV. ED.---1879
KASTNER, RUDOLPH
    BEETHOVEN'S PIANO SONATAS AND ARTUR SCHNABEL
KELLEY, EDGAR STILLMAN
    CHOPIN THE COMPOSER---1913
KIRBY, FRANK EUGENE
    SHORT HISTORY OF KEYBOARD MUSIC, A
KIRKPATRICK, RALPH
    DOMENICO SCARLATTI---1953
KLECZYNSKI, JAN
    CHOPIN'S GREATER WORKS...HOW THEY SHOULD BE UNDERSTOOD...INCLUDING
KLECZYNSKI, JAN
    HOW TO PLAY CHOPIN--THREE LECTURES

KLECZYNSKI, JAN
    WORKS OF FREDERIC CHOPIN, THE ..THEIR PROPER INTERPRETATION--6TH.
KULLAK, FRANZ
    BEETHOVEN'S PIANO PLAYING, WITH AN ESSAY ON THE EXECUTION OF THE
LAMOND, FREDERICK ARCHIBALD
    BEETHOVEN..NOTES ON THE SONATAS...
LANDOWSKA, WANDA
    LANDOWSKA ON MUSIC--EDITED BY DENISE RESTOUT
LANDOWSKA, WANDA
    MUSIC OF THE PAST
LEICHTENTRITT, HUGO
    COMPLETE PIANOFORTE SONATAS OF BEETHOVEN, THE ---ANALYTICAL NOTES
LISZT, FRANZ
    FREDERIC CHOPIN--A BIOGRAPHICAL AND CRITICAL NOTICE---1852
LISZT, FRANZ
    LIFE OF CHOPIN--TRANSLATED ONLY IN PART BY MARTHA WALKER COOK
LOWE, CLAUDE EDGERTON
    BEETHOVEN'S PIANOFORTE SONATAS..HINTS ON THEIR RENDERING, FORM...
LOWE, CLAUDE EDGERTON
    FORM IN PIANOFORTE MUSIC--FOR THEORETICAL AND PRACTICAL EXAMS
LOWE, CLAUDE EDGERTON
    WORD-PHRASES TO BACH'S 48 FUGUES, WITH HINTS ON THE RENDERINGS OF
LUBIN, ERNEST
    PIANO DUET, THE ...A GUIDE FOR PIANISTS
LYLE, WATSON
    CAMILLE SAINT-SAENS, HIS LIFE AND ART---DISCUSSES CONCERTI AND
MARX, ADOLF BERNHARD
    INTRODUCTION TO THE INTERPRETATION OF BEETHOVEN'S PIANO
MATTHEWS, DENIS--EDITOR
    KEYBOARD MUSIC--ESSAYS ON KEYBOARD LITERATURE, EXCLUDING ORGAN
MELLERS, WILFRED
    FRANCOIS COUPERIN AND THE FRENCH CLASSICAL TRADITION
MELLERS, WILFRED
    SONATA PRINCIPLE, THE --CIRCA 1750
NELSON, WENDELL
    CONCERTO, THE --BROWN 'MUSIC HORIZON' SERIES
NEWMAN, WILLIAM S.
    SONATA IN THE BAROQUE ERA, THE --A HISTORY OF THE SONATA IDEA,
NEWMAN, WILLIAM S.
    SONATA IN THE CLASSIC ERA, THE --A HISTORY OF THE SONATA IDEA,
NEWMAN, WILLIAM S.
    SONATA SINCE BEETHOVEN, THE --A HISTORY OF THE SONATA IDEA, VOL. 3
NEWMAN, WILLIAM S.
    THIRTEEN KEYBOARD SONATAS OF THE EIGHTEENTH AND NINETEENTH
PALMER, WILLARD A.--EDITOR
    CHOPIN..AN INTRODUCTION TO HIS PIANO WORKS
PARRISH, CARL
    EARLY PIANO AND ITS INFLUENCE ON KEYBOARD TECHNIQUE AND
PEABODY INSTITUTE, BALTIMORE
    GRADED LIST OF SOME USEFUL WORKS FOR PIANO STUDY---REVISED BY
PEARCE, CHARLES WILLIAM
    ART OF THE PIANO TEACHER, THE
PERRY, EDWARD B.
    DESCRIPTIVE ANALYSES OF PIANO WORKS, FOR THE USE OF TEACHERS,
PETERSON, FRANKLIN
    HANDBOOK OF MUSICAL FORM--PART 2 OF THE PIANIST'S HANDBOOK
PIGGOTT, PATRICK
    LIFE AND MUSIC OF JOHN FIELD, 1782-1837, THE
PORTE, JOHN F.
    CHOPIN, THE COMPOSER AND HIS MUSIC
PRENTICE, THOMAS RIDLEY
    MUSICIAN, THE ..A GUIDE FOR PIANOFORTE STUDENTS--6 VOLS.
ROLLAND, ROMAIN
    BEETHOVEN..WITH A BRIEF ANALYSIS OF THE SONATAS...BY A. EAGLEFIELD
ROSTAND, CLAUDE
    LISZT
ROTHSCHILD, FRITZ
    LOST TRADITION IN MUSIC, THE --PT. 1..RHYTHM AND TEMPO IN J. S.
ROTHSCHILD, FRITZ
    LOST TRADITION IN MUSIC, THE --PT. 2..MUSICAL PERFORMANCE IN THE
ROWLEY, ALEC *
    MUSICAL FORM AT THE PIANO
SALSBURY, JANET
    CONCISE ANALYSIS OF BEETHOVEN'S 32 PIANOFORTE SONATAS, A
SALSBURY, JANET
    SHORT AND CONCISE ANALYSIS OF MOZART'S 22 PIANOFORTE SONATAS, A
SCHAAF, EDWARD O.
    ART OF PIANO PLAYER TRANSCRIPTION, THE ..MAKING OF PERFORATED
SCHAUFFLER, ROBERT HAVEN
    FLORESTAN..THE LIFE AND WORK OF ROBERT SCHUMANN---1945
SCHMITZ, ELIE ROBERT
    PIANO WORKS OF CLAUDE DEBUSSY, THE
SCHOLES, PERCY
    APPRECIATION OF MUSIC BY MEANS OF THE PIANOLA AND DUO-ART, THE
SCHONBERG, HAROLD
    COLLECTOR'S CHOPIN AND SCHUMANN, THE --KEYSTONE BOOKS
SCHONBERG, HAROLD
    LIVES OF THE GREAT COMPOSERS, THE ---CHOPIN AND LISZT
SHEDLOCK, JOHN S.
    PIANOFORTE SONATA, THE ..ITS ORIGIN AND DEVELOPMENT---1895
SORABJI, KAIKHOSRU
    AROUND MUSIC---PACHMAN, CHOPIN AND LISZT
STAINKAMPH, EILEEN
    FORM AND ANALYSES OF MOZART'S PIANOFORTE SONATAS, THE
STAINKAMPH, EILEEN
    FORM AND ANALYSIS OF THE COMPLETE BEETHOVEN'S PIANOFORTE SONATAS
STEIN, ERWIN
    FORM AND PERFORMANCE
STUCKENSCHMIDT, HANS H.
    MAURICE RAVEL..VARIATIONS ON HIS LIFE AND WORK
SZIGETI, JOSEPH
    TEN BEETHOVEN SONATAS FOR PIANO AND VIOLIN, THE
TISCHLER, HANS
    STRUCTURAL ANALYSIS OF MOZART'S PIANO CONCERTOS, A --MUSICOLOGICAL
TOVEY, DONALD FRANCIS
    COMPANION TO BEETHOVEN'S PIANO SONATAS, A ..COMPLETE
VEINUS, ABRAHAM
    CONCERTO, THE ---1944
VEINUS, ABRAHAM
    VICTOR BOOK OF CONCERTOS
VUILLERMOZ, EMILE
    GABRIEL FAURE
WALKER, ALAN--EDITOR
    CHOPIN COMPANION, THE ..PROFILES OF THE MAN AND THE
WALKER, ALAN--EDITOR
    ROBERT SCHUMANN..THE MAN AND HIS MUSIC---SYMPOSIUM--13 AUTHORS
WARRACK JOHN H.
    CHAIKOVSKY SYMPHONIES AND CONCERTOS--B.B.C. MUSIC GUIDES, NO. 16
WEITZMANN, CARL F.
    HISTORY OF PIANOFORTE-PLAYING AND PIANOFORTE-LITERATURE, A
WESTERBY, HERBERT
    HOW TO STUDY THE PIANOFORTE WORKS OF THE GREAT COMPOSERS
WESTERBY, HERBERT
    LISZT, COMPOSER, AND HIS PIANO WORKS..DESCRIPTIVE GUIDE AND
WILKINSON, CHARLES W.
    HOW TO INTERPRET MENDELSSOHN'S SONGS WITHOUT WORDS
WILKINSON, CHARLES W.
    HOW TO PLAY BACH'S 48 PRELUDES AND FUGUES

YOUNG, PERCY M.
    CONCERTO--'PHOENIX MUSIC GUIDES', NO. 1

Guides to Keyboard Literature

APEL, WILLI
    MASTERS OF THE KEYBOARD
AULD, WILDA J.
    HANDBOOK FOR THE CHURCH PIANIST, A
BADURA-SKODA, EVA *
    INTERPRETING MOZART ON THE KEYBOARD---1957, IN GERMAN
BEDBROOK, GERALD STARES
    KEYBOARD MUSIC FROM THE MIDDLE AGES TO THE BEGINNINGS OF THE
BLOM, ERIC
    BEETHOVEN'S PIANOFORTE SONATAS DISCUSSED---1938
BORREN, CHARLES VAN DEN
    SOURCES OF KEYBOARD MUSIC IN ENGLAND, THE ---1913
BRINKMAN, JOSEPH *
    PIANO MUSIC..AVAILABLE EDITIONS RECOMMENDED---ADDENDA, 1959
BROWER, HARRIETTE
    WHAT TO PLAY--WHAT TO TEACH
BROWN, MAURICE J. E.
    CHOPIN..AN INDEX OF HIS WORKS IN CHRONOLOGICAL ORDER--2ND. REV.
BROWN, MAURICE J. E.
    SCHUBERT'S VARIATIONS
CORTOT, ALFRED
    FRENCH PIANO MUSIC
CORTOT, ALFRED
    PIANO MUSIC OF CLAUDE DEBUSSY, THE
COVIELLO, AMBROSE
    DIFFICULTIES OF BEETHOVEN PIANOFORTE SONATAS, AN ANALYSIS OF
CULSHAW, JOHN
    CONCERTO, THE
DALE, KATHLEEN
    NINETEENTH CENTURY PIANO MUSIC, A HANDBOOK FOR PIANISTS
DARRELL, ROBERT D.--COMPILER
    SCHIRMER'S GUIDE TO BOOKS ON MUSIC AND MUSICIANS--A PRACTICAL
DEMUTH, NORMAN
    FRENCH PIANO MUSIC..A SURVEY WITH NOTES ON ITS PERFORMANCE
DICKINSON, ALLAN E.
    BACH'S FUGAL WORKS
DITSON COMPANY
    TEACHING PIECES AND HOW TO TEACH THEM
EVANS, EDWIN
    HANDBOOK TO THE PIANOFORTE WORKS OF JOHANNES BRAHMS---1936
FERGUSON, DONALD NIVISON
    PIANO MUSIC OF SIX GREAT COMPOSERS---1947
FISCHER, EDWIN
    BEETHOVEN'S PIANOFORTE SONATAS, A GUIDE FOR STUDENTS AND
FRISKIN, JAMES *
    MUSIC FOR THE PIANO..A HANDBOOK OF CONCERT AND TEACHING MATERIAL
FULLER-MAITLAND, J. A.
    FORTY-EIGHT, THE ..BACH'S WOHLTEMPERIRTES CLAVIER, FROM 'THE
FULLER-MAITLAND, J. A.
    SCHUMANN'S PIANOFORTE WORKS
GANZ, RUDOLPH
    RUDOLPH GANZ EVALUATES MODERN PIANO MUSIC
GARVIN, FLORENCE HOLLISTER
    BEGINNINGS OF THE ROMANTIC PIANO CONCERTO, THE
GILLESPIE, JOHN
    FIVE CENTURIES OF KEYBOARD MUSIC..AN HISTORIC SURVEY FOR
GIRDLESTONE, CUTHBERT
    MOZART AND HIS PIANO CONCERTOS---FIRST PUBLISHED IN 1948 AS
GRAY, CECIL
    BACH AND DAS WOHLTEMPERIRTE KLAVIER..ANALYTICAL NOTES, WITH AN
GRAY, CECIL
    FORTY-EIGHT PRELUDES AND FUGUES OF J. S. BACH, THE
HAMILTON, CLARENCE G.
    PIANO MUSIC, ITS COMPOSERS AND CHARACTERISTICS
HARDING, HENRY ALFRED
    ANALYSIS OF FORM AS DISPLAYED IN BEETHOVEN'S 32 PIANOFORTE
HARDING, HENRY ALFRED
    THREE HUNDRED AND FIFTY QUESTIONS ON THE FORM AND TONALITY OF
HEUSCHNEIDER, KARIN
    PIANO SONATA OF THE EIGHTEENTH CENTURY IN ITALY, THE
HILL, GEORGE R.
    PRELIMINARY CHECKLIST OF RESEARCH ON THE CLASSIC SYMPHONY AND
HINSON, MAURICE
    GUIDE TO THE PIANIST'S REPERTOIRE
HOLMES, GEORGE AUGUSTUS *
    ANALYSIS OF PIANOFORTE COMPOSITIONS FROM THE CLASSICAL AND
HOPKINS, ANTHONY
    TALKING ABOUT CONCERTOS..AN ANALYTICAL STUDY OF A NUMBER OF
HORROCKS, CYPIL R. H.
    STUDENT'S GUIDE TO THE ART OF TEACHING THE PIANOFORTE, THE --2ND.
HUNEKER, JAMES GIBBONS
    CHOPIN..THE MAN AND HIS MUSIC---1901
HUTCHESON, ERNEST *
    LITERATURE OF THE PIANO, THE ..A GUIDE FOR AMATEUR AND
HUTCHINGS, ARTHUR
    COMPANION TO MOZART'S PIANO CONCERTOS, A
ILIFFE, FREDERICK
    FORTY-EIGHT PRELUDES AND FUGUES OF JOHANN SEBASTIAN BACH ANALYZED
JONSON, GEORGE CHARLES
    HANDBOOK TO CHOPIN'S WORKS, A
KELBERINE, ALEXANDER
    FOUR FAMOUS PIANOFORTE SONATAS OF BEETHOVEN, THE --OP. 13, OP. 27,
KERN, ALICE M. *
    TEACHER'S GUIDEBOOK TO PIANO LITERATURE, THE --REV. ED.---1954+
KIRBY, FRANK EUGENE
    SHORT HISTORY OF KEYBOARD MUSIC, A
KIRKPATRICK, RALPH
    DOMENICO SCARLATTI---1953
KLECZYNSKI, JAN
    CHOPIN'S GREATER WORKS...HOW THEY SHOULD BE UNDERSTOOD...INCLUDING
KLECZYNSKI, JAN
    HOW TO PLAY CHOPIN--THREE LECTURES
KORSTEN, BJARNE
    RECENT NORWEGIAN PIANO MUSIC
LANDOWSKA, WANDA
    LANDOWSKA ON MUSIC--EDITED BY DENISE RESTOUT
LANDOWSKA, WANDA
    MUSIC OF THE PAST
LOCKWOOD, ALBERT
    NOTES ON THE LITERATURE OF THE PIANO--RE-EDITED BY BROTHER, SAMUEL
MACPHERSON, STEWART
    COMMENTARY ON BKS. 1 AND 2 OF THE FORTY-EIGHT PRELUDES AND FUGUES
MCNABB, GEORGE
    SELECTED LIST OF GRADED TEACHING MATERIAL FOR THE PIANO, A --3RD.
MELLERS, WILFRED
    SONATA PRINCIPLE, THE --CIRCA 1750
MICHIGAN MUSIC TEACHERS ASSOCIATION
    PIANO TEACHER'S GUIDE
MILNE, ALFRED FORBES
    BEETHOVEN..THE PIANOFORTE SONATAS--2 VOLS.
MOLDENHAUER, HANS
    DUO-PIANISM---PUBLISHED DISSERTATION

MONTAGU-NATHAN, M.
   HANDBOOK TO THE PIANO WORKS OF SCRIABIN
MURDOCH, WILLIAM
   BRAHMS..WITH AN ANALYTICAL STUDY OF THE COMPLETE PIANOFORTE WORKS
NEWMAN, WILLIAM S.
   SELECTED LIST OF MUSIC RECOMMENDED FOR PIANO STUDENTS, A --4TH.
NEWMAN, WILLIAM S.
   SONATA IN THE BAROQUE ERA, THE --A HISTORY OF THE SONATA IDEA,
NEWMAN, WILLIAM S.
   SONATA IN THE CLASSIC ERA, THE --A HISTORY OF THE SONATA IDEA,
NEWMAN, WILLIAM S.
   THIRTEEN KEYBOARD SONATAS OF THE EIGHTEENTH AND NINETEENTH
O'TOOLE, WILLIAM
   FIVE YEAR GUIDE TO PIANO TEACHING, A
PERRY, ADELAIDE TROWBRIDGE
   COMPENDIUM OF PIANO MATERIAL--2ND. ED.---1929
PERRY, EDWARD B.
   DESCRIPTIVE ANALYSES OF PIANO WORKS, FOR THE USE OF TEACHERS,
PERRY, EDWARD B.
   STORIES OF STANDARD TEACHING PIECES FOR THE PIANOFORTE
PRENTICE, THOMAS RIDLEY
   MUSICIAN, THE ..A GUIDE FOR PIANOFORTE STUDENTS--6 VOLS.
REINECKE, KARL H.
   BEETHOVEN PIANOFORTE SONATAS, THE ..LETTERS TO A LADY
REZITS, JOSEPH
   TEACHER'S GUIDE TO THE NEW SCRIBNER MUSIC LIBRARY
RICHNER, THOMAS
   ORIENTATION FOR INTERPRETING MOZART'S PIANO SONATAS
RIEMANN, HUGO
   ANALYSIS OF J. S. BACH'S WOHLTEMPIERTES KLAVIER--2 PTS.
ROTHSCHILD, FRITZ
   HANDBOOK TO THE PERFORMANCE OF THE 48 PRELUDES AND FUGUES OF J. S.
ROWLEY, ALEC
   FOUR HANDS--ONE PIANO..A LIST OF WORKS FOR DUET PLAYERS--A GUIDE
SACHS, CURT
   EVOLUTION OF PIANO MUSIC, 1350-1700, THE
SAMPSON, BROOK
   DIGEST OF THE ANALYSES OF THE 48 FUGUES IN THE WELL-TEMPERED
SCHAUFFLER, ROBERT HAVEN
   FLORESTAN..THE LIFE AND WORK OF ROBERT SCHUMANN---1945
SCHMITZ, ELIE ROBERT
   PIANO WORKS OF CLAUDE DEBUSSY, THE
SEARLE, HUMPHREY
   MUSIC OF LISZT, THE --2ND. REV. ED.---1954
SHEDLOCK, JOHN S.
   BEETHOVEN'S PIANOFORTE SONATAS..THE ORIGIN AND RESPECTIVE VALUES
SHEDLOCK, JOHN S.
   PIANOFORTE SONATA, THE ..ITS ORIGIN AND DEVELOPMENT---1895
SMITH, BILLYE MULLINS
   PIANO REPERTOIRE GUIDE
SUCHOFF, B.
   GUIDE TO THE MIKROKOSMOS OF BELA BARTOK, A --PUBLISHED
THOMPSON, OSCAR
   DEBUSSY, MAN AND ARTIST---1937
TOBIN, JOSEPH RAYMOND
   MOZART AND THE SONATA FORM..A COMPANION BOOK TO ANY EDITION OF
TOVEY, DONALD FRANCIS
   COMPANION TO BEETHOVEN'S PIANO SONATAS, A ..COMPLETE
VENABLE, MARY
   INTERPRETATION OF PIANO MUSIC, THE
WEITZMANN, CARL F.
   HISTORY OF PIANOFORTE-PLAYING AND PIANOFORTE-LITERATURE, A
WESTERBY, HERBERT
   BEETHOVEN AND HIS PIANO WORKS
WESTERBY, HERBERT
   HISTORY OF PIANOFORTE MUSIC, THE ---1924
WESTERBY, HERBERT
   HOW TO STUDY THE PIANOFORTE WORKS OF THE GREAT COMPOSERS
WESTERBY, HERBERT
   INTRODUCTION TO RUSSIAN PIANO MUSIC--REPRINT..'MUSICAL OPINION'
WESTERBY, HERBERT
   LISZT, COMPOSER, AND HIS PIANO WORKS..DESCRIPTIVE GUIDE AND
WIER, ALBERT
   PIANO, THE ..ITS HISTORY, MAKERS, PLAYERS AND MUSIC
WILKINSON, CHARLES W.
   HOW TO INTERPRET MENDELSSOHN'S SONGS WITHOUT WORDS
WILKINSON, CHARLES W.
   HOW TO PLAY BACH'S 48 PRELUDES AND FUGUES
WILKINSON, CHARLES W.
   HOW TO PLAY 110 FAVOURITE PIANO SOLOS
WILKINSON, CHARLES W.
   WELL-KNOWN PIANO SOLOS..HOW TO PLAY THEM WITH UNDERSTANDING,

The Art of Performing

General

AHRENS, CORA B. *
   FOR ALL PIANO TEACHERS
ANDERSON, WILLIAM P.
   MUSIC AS A CAREER
ANON
   GUIDE TO THE PROPER USE OF THE PIANOFORTE PEDALS, WITH EXAMPLES
BUONAMICI, CARLO
   PRACTICAL POINTS ON PIANO PLAYING
CLARKE, HUGH ARCHIBALD
   ART OF PIANOFORTE PLAYING, THE --TEXT BOOK FOR BEGINNERS
COCHRAN, MARY
   ULTIMATE PRINCIPLES OF PIANOFORTE TEACHING AND PLAYING
COPP, LAURA R.
   SOME SECRETS OF SUCCESS IN PLAYING IN PUBLIC
D'ABREU, GERALD
   PLAYING THE PIANO WITH CONFIDENCE---1964
FOLDES, ANDOR
   KEYS TO THE KEYBOARD, A BOOK FOR PIANISTS
FULLER-MAITLAND, J. A.
   MUSICIAN'S PILGRIMAGE, THE ..A STUDY IN ARTISTIC DEVELOPMENT
GABRIEL, GILBERT W.
   GREAT PIANISTS AND COMPOSERS
HOFMANN, JOSEF
   PIANO PLAYING, WITH PIANO QUESTIONS ANSWERED---PUBLISHED EARLIER
ISAACS, EDWARD
   BLIND PIANO TEACHER, THE
KLAUWELL, OTTO
   ON MUSICAL EXECUTION...PRIMARILY WITH REFERENCE TO PIANO-PLAYING
KOBBE, GUSTAV
   STRAIGHT TO THE HEART OF MUSIC---PLAYER-PIANO
LOWE, CLAUDE EDGERTON
   VIVA VOCE..250 QUESTIONS AND ANSWERS FOR PIANOFORTE DIPLOMA
NEUHAUS, HEINRICH
   ART OF PIANO PLAYING, THE
PAUER, ERNST
   ART OF PIANOFORTE PLAYING, THE
PETERSILEA, CARLYLE
   PIANO PLAYING..GENERAL MUSICAL INSTRUCTION FROM BEGINNING TO END

PHILIPP, ISIDOR
   SOME REFLECTIONS ON PIANO PLAYING
RIEMANN, HUGO
   CATECHISM OF PIANOFORTE PLAYING---1888, IN GERMAN
SHELDON, ROBERT--COMPILER
   EGON PETRI-ALEXANDER LIBERMANN NOTES ON THE ART AND TECHNIQUE OF
WHITESIDE, ABBY
   MASTERING THE CHOPIN ETUDES AND OTHER ESSAYS
WIECK, FRIEDRICH
   PIANO AND SONG..HOW TO TEACH, HOW TO LEARN, AND HOW TO FORM A

Miscellaneous

CLARKE, HUGH ARCHIBALD
   ART OF PIANOFORTE PLAYING, THE --TEXT BOOK FOR BEGINNERS
COPP, LAURA R.
   SOME SECRETS OF SUCCESS IN PLAYING IN PUBLIC
HAMILTON, CLARENCE G.
   WHAT EVERY PIANO PUPIL SHOULD KNOW
LAST, JOAN
   YOUNG PIANIST, THE ..A NEW APPROACH FOR TEACHERS AND
NEWMAN, WILLIAM S.
   PIANIST'S PROBLEMS, THE ..A MODERN APPROACH TO EFFICIENT PRACTICE
PAUER, ERNST
   ART OF PIANOFORTE PLAYING, THE
PETERSILEA, CARLYLE
   PIANO PLAYING..GENERAL MUSICAL INSTRUCTION FROM BEGINNING TO END
RICHTER, ADA
   TEACHING HINTS
SAVLER, ROBERTA--EDITOR
   SELECTIONS FROM THE PIANO TEACHER, 1958-1963
SHELDON, ROBERT--COMPILER
   EGON PETRI-ALEXANDER LIBERMANN NOTES ON THE ART AND TECHNIQUE OF
TRUE, LYLE C.
   HOW AND WHAT TO PLAY FOR MOVING PICTURES..A MANUAL AND GUIDE FOR
WHITESIDE, ABBY
   MASTERING THE CHOPIN ETUDES AND OTHER ESSAYS
WOODHOUSE, GEORGE
   FROM KEYBOARD TO MUSIC

Performance Practices

ALBIG, GEORGE L.
   HOW TO PLAY THE PLAYER
APEL, WILLI
   MASTERS OF THE KEYBOARD
BALLANTINE, BILL
   PIANO, THE ..AN INTRODUCTION TO THE INSTRUMENT
BARFORD, PHILIP
   KEYBOARD MUSIC OF C. P. E. BACH, THE ..CONSIDERED IN RELATION TO
BARNETT, DAVID
   PERFORMANCE OF MUSIC, THE ..A STUDY IN TERMS OF THE PIANOFORTE
BLOM, ERIC
   BEETHOVEN'S PIANOFORTE SONATAS DISCUSSED---1938
BODKY, ERWIN
   INTERPRETATION OF BACH'S KEYBOARD WORKS, THE
BORREN, CHARLES VAN DEN
   SOURCES OF KEYBOARD MUSIC IN ENGLAND, THE ---1913
BOS, COENRAAD V.
   WELL-TEMPERED ACCOMPANIST, THE
BRISKIER, ARTHUR
   NEW APPROACH TO PIANO TRANSCRIPTIONS AND INTERPRETATION OF JOHANN
CHING, JAMES
   PERFORMER AND AUDIENCE..AN INVESTIGATION INTO THE PSYCHOLOGICAL
CHRISTIANI, ADOLPH FRIEDRICH
   PRINCIPLES OF EXPRESSION IN PIANOFORTE PLAYING, THE
CLARKE, HUGH ARCHIBALD
   ART OF PIANOFORTE PLAYING, THE --TEXT BOOK FOR BEGINNERS
COPP, LAURA R.
   SOME SECRETS OF SUCCESS IN PLAYING IN PUBLIC
COUPERIN, FRANCOIS
   ART DE TOUCHER LE CLAVECIN, L' ---IN FRENCH, GERMAN AND ENGLISH
CULSHAW, JOHN
   CONCERTO, THE
CZERNY, CARL
   ON THE PROPER PERFORMANCE OF ALL BEETHOVEN'S WORKS FOR THE PIANO
DART, THURSTON
   INTERPRETATION OF MUSIC, THE --4TH. ED.---1954
DONINGTON, ROBERT
   INTERPRETATION OF EARLY MUSIC, THE
DONINGTON, ROBERT
   PERFORMER'S GUIDE TO BAROQUE MUSIC, A
DORIAN, FREDERICK
   HISTORY OF MUSIC IN PERFORMANCE, THE ---1942
DRAKE, KENNETH
   SONATAS OF BEETHOVEN AS HE PLAYED AND TAUGHT THEM, THE
DUMESNIL, MAURICE
   HOW TO PLAY AND TEACH DEBUSSY
ELLINGHAM, HARRY
   HOW TO USE A PLAYER-PIANO
EVANS, EDWIN
   HANDBOOK TO THE PIANOFORTE WORKS OF JOHANNES BRAHMS---1936
FISCHER, EDWIN
   BEETHOVEN'S PIANOFORTE SONATAS, A GUIDE FOR STUDENTS AND
FISCHER, EDWIN
   REFLECTIONS ON MUSIC
GIRDLESTONE, CUTHBERT
   MOZART AND HIS PIANO CONCERTOS---FIRST PUBLISHED IN 1948 AS
GIVENS, LARRY
   RE-ENACTING THE ARTIST..A STORY OF THE AMPICO REPRODUCING PIANO
GOODRICH, ALFRED JOHN
   THEORY OF INTERPRETATION, APPLIED TO ARTISTIC MUSICAL PERFORMANCE
GRAY, CECIL
   FORTY-EIGHT PRELUDES AND FUGUES OF J. S. BACH, THE
HECK, JOHANN CASPAR
   ART OF PLAYING THE HARPSICHORD, ILLUSTRATED BY A VARIETY OF
HEUSCHNEIDER, KARIN
   PIANO SONATA OF THE EIGHTEENTH CENTURY IN ITALY, THE
HIPKINS, ALFRED JAMES
   HOW CHOPIN PLAYED...FROM CONTEMPORARY IMPRESSIONS COLLECTED FROM
HUMMEL, JOHANN NEPOMUK
   COMPLETE THEORETICAL AND PRACTICAL COURSE OF INSTRUCTIONS ON THE
HUNEKER, JAMES GIBBONS
   DEVELOPMENT OF PIANO MUSIC FROM THE DAYS OF THE CLAVICHORD AND
HUTCHESON, ERNEST *
   LITERATURE OF THE PIANO, THE ..A GUIDE FOR AMATEUR AND
HUTCHINGS, ARTHUR
   COMPANION TO MOZART'S PIANO CONCERTOS, A
ILIFFE, FREDERICK
   FORTY-EIGHT PRELUDES AND FUGUES OF JOHANN SEBASTIAN BACH ANALYZED
INTERNATIONAL MUSICOLOGICAL CONGRESS..FIRST--1960--WORKS OF FREDERICK
   BOOK OF THE FIRST INTERNATIONAL MUSICOLOGICAL CONGRESS DEVOTED TO
JOHNSTONE, J. ALFRED
   TOUCH, PHRASING AND INTERPRETATION
KASTNER, SANTIAGO
   PARALLELS AND DISCREPANCIES BETWEEN ENGLISH AND SPANISH KEYBOARD

KELLEY, EDGAR STILLMAN
    CHOPIN THE COMPOSER---1913
KIRKPATRICK, RALPH
    DOMENICO SCARLATTI---1953
KLECZYNSKI, JAN
    HOW TO PLAY CHOPIN--THREE LECTURES
KLECZYNSKI, JAN
    WORKS OF FREDERIC CHOPIN, THE ..THEIR PROPER INTERPRETATION--6TH.
KOCH, CASPAR
    PIANO STUDENT'S GRADUS AD PARNASSUM, THE ..PRESENTING THE
KULLAK, FRANZ
    BEETHOVEN'S PIANO PLAYING, WITH AN ESSAY ON THE EXECUTION OF THE
LANDOWSKA, WANDA
    LANDOWSKA ON MUSIC--EDITED BY DENISE RESTOUT
LEONHARDT, GUSTAV M.
    ART OF FUGUE, BACH'S LAST HARPSICHORD WORK, THE ..AN ARGUMENT
MATTHEWS, DENIS--EDITOR
    KEYBOARD MUSIC--ESSAYS ON KEYBOARD LITERATURE, EXCLUDING ORGAN
MCCLANAHAN, RICHARD
    CADENCE, KEY TO MUSICAL CLARITY, THE ..A SIMPLE AND PRACTICAL
MELLERS, WILFRED
    FRANCOIS COUPERIN AND THE FRENCH CLASSICAL TRADITION
MILNE, ALFRED FORBES
    BEETHOVEN..THE PIANOFORTE SONATAS--2 VOLS.
NAYLOR, EDWARD W.
    ELIZABETHAN VIRGINAL BOOK, AN ..A CRITICAL ESSAY ON THE CONTENTS
NEWMAN, ERNEST
    PIANO-PLAYER AND ITS MUSIC, THE
NEWMAN, WILLIAM S.
    PERFORMANCE PRACTICES IN BEETHOVEN'S PIANO SONATAS..AN
NEWMAN, WILLIAM S.
    SONATA IN THE BAROQUE ERA, THE --A HISTORY OF THE SONATA IDEA,
NEWMAN, WILLIAM S.
    SONATA IN THE CLASSIC ERA, THE --A HISTORY OF THE SONATA IDEA,
PALMER, HORATIO R.
    PALMER'S PIANO PRIMER
PINCHERLE, MARC
    WORLD OF THE VIRTUOSO, THE
PORTE, JOHN F.
    CHOPIN, THE COMPOSER AND HIS MUSIC
ROSTAND, CLAUDE
    LISZT
ROTHSCHILD, FRITZ
    LOST TRADITION IN MUSIC, THE --PT. 1..RHYTHM AND TEMPO IN J. S.
ROTHSCHILD, FRITZ
    LOST TRADITION IN MUSIC, THE --PT. 2..MUSICAL PERFORMANCE IN THE
SCHMITZ, ELIE ROBERT
    PIANO WORKS OF CLAUDE DEBUSSY, THE
SCHNEIDER, HANS
    WORKING OF THE MIND IN PIANO TEACHING AND PLAYING, THE
SEGUEL, MANIA
    CHOPIN'S TEMPO RUBATO
SHEDLOCK, JOHN S.
    BEETHOVEN'S PIANOFORTE SONATAS..THE ORIGIN AND RESPECTIVE VALUES
SHERWOOD MUSIC SCHOOL
    PIANO LESSONS AND TESTS--4TH. REV. ED.---1945+
STEIN, ERWIN
    FORM AND PERFORMANCE
STEINERT, MORRIS
    MORRIS STEINERT COLLECTION OF KEYED AND STRINGED INSTRUMENTS, THE
STERNBERG, CONSTANTIN I. VON
    TEMPO RUBATO AND OTHER ESSAYS
SUMMY-BIRCHARD COMPANY
    HANDBOOK FOR PIANO TEACHERS..COLLECTED ARTICLES ON SUBJECTS
TURECK, ROSALYN
    INTRODUCTION TO THE PERFORMANCE OF BACH, AN--3 VOLS.
VAN DER WEYDE, PETER H.
    INSTRUCTIONS IN PLAYING THE PIANO-FORTE WITH AEOLIAN ATTACHMENT
VEINUS, ABRAHAM
    CONCERTO, THE ---1944
VENABLE, MARY
    INTERPRETATION OF PIANO MUSIC, THE
VINQUIST, MARY *
    PERFORMANCE PRACTICE..A BIBLIOGRAPHY
WESTRUP, SIR JACK ALLAN
    MUSICAL INTERPRETATION---THIS BOOK ACCOMPANIED A SERIES OF B.B.C.
WILSON, DAVID M.
    INSTRUCTION BOOK ON THE PIANO-PLAYER AND PLAYER-PIANO, AN
WOLFF, KONRAD
    TEACHING OF ARTUR SCHNABEL, THE ..A GUIDE TO INTERPRETATION
WOLFRAM, VICTOR
    SOSTENUTO PEDAL, THE
YOUNG, PERCY M.
    CONCERTO--'PHOENIX MUSIC GUIDES', NO. 1

Interpretation and Style

ADLER, KURT
    ART OF ACCOMPANYING AND COACHING, THE ---1965
ALLEN, MARGARET *
    CREATIVE MOTION
ANDERSON, J. CLARK
    GOOD MUSIC EXPLAINED..WHAT ALL GOOD PIANISTS SHOULD KNOW
APEL, WILLI
    MASTERS OF THE KEYBOARD
BARFORD, PHILIP
    KEYBOARD MUSIC OF C. P. E. BACH, THE ..CONSIDERED IN RELATION TO
BARNETT, DAVID
    PERFORMANCE OF MUSIC, THE ..A STUDY IN TERMS OF THE PIANOFORTE
BLOM, ERIC
    BEETHOVEN'S PIANOFORTE SONATAS DISCUSSED---1938
BODKY, ERWIN
    INTERPRETATION OF BACH'S KEYBOARD WORKS, THE
BOLTON, HETTY
    HOW TO PRACTICE
BOLTON, HETTY
    ON TEACHING THE PIANO
BOOTH, VICTOR
    WE PIANO TEACHERS--REVISED BY ADELE FRANKLIN---1946
BORREN, CHARLES VAN DEN
    SOURCES OF KEYBOARD MUSIC IN ENGLAND, THE ---1913
BOS, COENRAAD V.
    WELL-TEMPERED ACCOMPANIST, THE
BRANSON, DAVID
    JOHN FIELD AND CHOPIN
BRECKENRIDGE, WILLIAM KILGORE
    HINTS FOR PIANO NORMAL STUDIES
BREE, MADAME MALWINE
    GROUNDWORK OF THE LESCHETIZKY METHOD, THE ---1902
BRISKIER, ARTHUR
    NEW APPROACH TO PIANO TRANSCRIPTIONS AND INTERPRETATION OF JOHANN
BROWER, HARRIETTE
    ART OF THE PIANIST, THE
BROWER, HARRIETTE
    MODERN MASTERS OF THE KEYBOARD
BROWER, HARRIETTE
    PIANO MASTERY..TALKS WITH MASTER PIANISTS AND TEACHERS...

BROWER, HARRIETTE
    PIANO MASTERY, SECOND SERIES
BROWN, MAURICE J. E.
    SCHUBERT'S VARIATIONS
CALAND, ELIZABETH
    ARTISTIC PIANO PLAYING, AS TAUGHT BY LUDWIG DEPPE
CARPE, ADOLPH
    PIANIST AND THE ART OF MUSIC, THE ..A TREATISE ON PIANO PLAYING
CHASE, MARY WOOD
    NATURAL LAWS IN PIANO TECHNIC
CHASINS, ABRAM
    SPEAKING OF PIANISTS
CHING, JAMES
    PIANO PLAYING, A PRACTICAL METHOD--A NEW EDITION OF 'PIANO
CHING, JOAN ELIZABETH
    APPROACH TO PIANO TEACHING---ALSO CATALOGUED UNDER
CHRISTIANI, ADOLPH FRIEDRICH
    PRINCIPLES OF EXPRESSION IN PIANOFORTE PLAYING, THE
CLARKE, HUGH ARCHIBALD
    ART OF PIANOFORTE PLAYING, THE --TEXT BOOK FOR BEGINNERS
COHEN, HARRIET
    MUSIC'S HANDMAID
COOK, J. LAWRENCE
    PIANO HANDBOOK ON BOOGIE WOOGIE, BLUES, AND BARRELHOUSE..3 EASY TO
COPP, LAURA R.
    SOME SECRETS OF SUCCESS IN PLAYING IN PUBLIC
COUPERIN, FRANCOIS
    ART DE TOUCHER LE CLAVECIN, L' ---IN FRENCH, GERMAN AND ENGLISH
COVIELLO, AMBROSE
    DIFFICULTIES OF BEETHOVEN PIANOFORTE SONATAS, AN ANALYSIS OF
CULSHAW, JOHN
    CONCERTO, THE
CZERNY, CARL
    COMPLETE THEORETICAL AND PRACTICAL PIANO FORTE SCHOOL, FROM THE
CZERNY, CARL
    ON THE PROPER PERFORMANCE OF ALL BEETHOVEN'S WORKS FOR THE PIANO
D'ABREU, GERALD
    PLAYING THE PIANO WITH CONFIDENCE---1964
DART, THURSTON
    INTERPRETATION OF MUSIC, THE --4TH. ED.---1954
DONINGTON, ROBERT
    INTERPRETATION OF EARLY MUSIC, THE
DONINGTON, ROBERT
    PERFORMER'S GUIDE TO BAROQUE MUSIC, A
DORIAN, FREDERICK
    HISTORY OF MUSIC IN PERFORMANCE, THE ---1942
DRAKE, KENNETH
    SONATAS OF BEETHOVEN AS HE PLAYED AND TAUGHT THEM, THE
DUMESNIL, MAURICE
    HOW TO PLAY AND TEACH DEBUSSY
DUMM, ROBERT W.
    IN BLACK AND WHITE
EDWARDS, RUTH
    COMPLEAT MUSIC TEACHER FOR TEACHERS, PARENTS AND STUDENTS
EHRENFECTER, C. A.
    DELIVERY IN THE ART OF PIANOFORTE PLAYING
EISENBERG, JACOB
    ARTISTIC PIANIST, THE ..NATURAL TECHNICS IN PIANO MASTERY..FROM
EISENBERG, JACOB
    WEIGHT AND RELAXATION METHOD FOR THE PIANOFORTE
EMERICH, PAUL
    ROAD TO MODERN MUSIC, THE
EVANS, EDWIN
    HANDBOOK TO THE PIANOFORTE WORKS OF JOHANNES BRAHMS---1936
FERGUSON, DONALD NIVISON
    PIANO INTERPRETATION
FINCK, HENRY T.
    PADEREWSKI AND HIS ART
FISCHER, EDWIN
    BEETHOVEN'S PIANOFORTE SONATAS, A GUIDE FOR STUDENTS AND
GARRATT, PERCIVAL
    ART OF PIANOFORTE PLAYING, THE
GIESEKING, WALTER *
    PIANO TECHNIQUE---COMBINED REPUBLICATION OF..'THE SHORTEST WAY TO
GIRDLESTONE, CUTHBERT
    MOZART AND HIS PIANO CONCERTOS---FIRST PUBLISHED IN 1948 AS
GOODRICH, ALFRED JOHN
    THEORY OF INTERPRETATION, APPLIED TO ARTISTIC MUSICAL PERFORMANCE
GRANTHAM, BILLY
    HELLO TO THE BLUES..FUN WITH CHORDS..FUN AND INFORMATION ON
GRAY, CECIL
    BACH AND DAS WOHLTEMPERIRTE KLAVIER..ANALYTICAL NOTES, WITH AN
GRAY, CECIL
    FORTY-EIGHT PRELUDES AND FUGUES OF J. S. BACH, THE
HAMILTON, CLARENCE G.
    PIANO TEACHING..ITS PRINCIPLES AND PROBLEMS
HAMILTON, CLARENCE G.
    TOUCH AND EXPRESSION IN PIANO PLAYING
HARKNESS, ROBERT
    HARKNESS PIANO METHOD OF EVANGELISTIC HYMN PLAYING, THE ..A
HARRISON, SIDNEY
    TEACHER NEVER TOLD ME--TIPS FOR STUDENTS
HEUSCHNEIDER, KARIN
    PIANO SONATA OF THE EIGHTEENTH CENTURY IN ITALY, THE
HOFHEIMER, GRACE
    TEACHING TECHNIQUES FOR THE PIANO
HOFMANN, JOSEF
    PIANO PLAYING..A LITTLE BOOK OF SIMPLE SUGGESTIONS--REPRINTED FROM
HOFMANN, JOSEF
    PIANO PLAYING, WITH PIANO QUESTIONS ANSWERED---PUBLISHED EARLIER
HOLCMAN, JAN
    LEGACY OF CHOPIN, THE
HOPE, ERIC
    HANDBOOK OF PIANO PLAYING, A
HOPKINS, ANTHONY
    TALKING ABOUT SONATAS..A BOOK OF ANALYTICAL STUDIES, BASED ON A
HORROCKS, CYRIL R. H.
    STUDENT'S GUIDE TO THE ART OF TEACHING THE PIANOFORTE, THE --2ND.
HUNEKER, JAMES GIBBONS
    DEVELOPMENT OF PIANO MUSIC FROM THE DAYS OF THE CLAVICHORD AND
HUTCHESON, ERNEST *
    LITERATURE OF THE PIANO, THE ..A GUIDE FOR AMATEUR AND
HUTCHINGS, ARTHUR
    COMPANION TO MOZART'S PIANO CONCERTOS, A
ILIFFE, FREDERICK
    FORTY-EIGHT PRELUDES AND FUGUES OF JOHANN SEBASTIAN BACH ANALYZED
INTERNATIONAL MUSICOLOGICAL CONGRESS..FIRST--1960--WORKS OF FREDERICK
    BOOK OF THE FIRST INTERNATIONAL MUSICOLOGICAL CONGRESS DEVOTED TO
JOHNSTONE, J. ALFRED
    ART OF EXPRESSION IN PIANOFORTE PLAYING, THE
JOHNSTONE, J. ALFRED
    ART OF TEACHING PIANOFORTE PLAYING, THE --2ND. REV. ED.---1910
JOHNSTONE, J. ALFRED
    RUBATO, OR THE SECRET OF EXPRESSION IN PIANOFORTE PLAYING
JOHNSTONE, J. ALFRED
    TOUCH, PHRASING AND INTERPRETATION
KIRKPATRICK, RALPH
    DOMENICO SCARLATTI---1953

KLECZYNSKI, JAN
    HOW TO PLAY CHOPIN--THREE LECTURES
KLECZYNSKI, JAN
    WORKS OF FREDERIC CHOPIN, THE ..THEIR PROPER INTERPRETATION--6TH.
KOCH, CASPAR
    PIANO STUDENT'S GRADUS AD PARNASSUM, THE ..PRESENTING THE
KRUSZYNSKI, MICHAL
    APPROACH TO THE PSYCHOLOGY OF PIANO TEACHING, AN
KULLAK, ADOLPH
    AESTHETICS OF PIANOFORTE PLAYING, THE ---1861 IN GERMAN--1ST.
KULLAK, FRANZ
    BEETHOVEN'S PIANO PLAYING, WITH AN ESSAY ON THE EXECUTION OF THE
LAMAR, RICHARD
    COLLEGE PIANO PEDAGOGY
LANDOWSKA, WANDA
    LANDOWSKA ON MUSIC--EDITED BY DENISE RESTOUT
LAST, JOAN
    INTERPRETATION FOR THE PIANO STUDENT
LAST, JOAN
    YOUNG PIANIST, THE ..A NEW APPROACH FOR TEACHERS AND
LEIMER, KARL *
    RHYTHMICS, DYNAMICS, PEDAL, AND OTHER PROBLEMS OF PIANO
LEIMER, KARL *
    SHORTEST WAY TO PIANISTIC PERFECTION, THE
LEONHARDT, GUSTAV M.
    ART OF FUGUE, BACH'S LAST HARPSICHORD WORK, THE ..AN ARGUMENT
LOWE, CLAUDE EDGERTON
    SUGGESTIONS FOR THE APPRECIATION AND INTERPRETATION OF PIANOFORTE
MAIER, GUY
    PIANO TEACHER'S COMPANION, THE
MARKS, ADOLF B.
    INTRODUCTION TO THE INTERPRETATION OF BEETHOVEN'S PIANO-FORTE
MATHEWS, WILLIAM S. B.
    STUDIES IN PHRASING, MEMORIZING AND INTERPRETATION
MATHEWS, WILLIAM S. B.
    STUDIES IN PHRASING SELECTED FROM THE WORKS OF THE BEST CLASSIC
MATTHAY, TOBIAS A.
    MUSICAL INTERPRETATION..ITS LAWS AND PRINCIPLES---1913
MATTHAY, TOBIAS A.
    ON COLORING AS DISTINCT FROM TONE-INFLECTION--A LECTURE
MATTHEWS, DENIS--EDITOR
    KEYBOARD MUSIC--ESSAYS ON KEYBOARD LITERATURE, EXCLUDING ORGAN
MCARTHUR, ALEXANDER
    PIANOFORTE STUDY..HINTS ON PIANO PLAYING
MCCLANAHAN, RICHARD
    CADENCE, KEY TO MUSICAL CLARITY, THE ..A SIMPLE AND PRACTICAL
MCEWEN, JOHN B.
    INTRODUCTION TO AN UNPUBLISHED EDITION OF THE PIANOFORTE SONATAS
MEHEGAN, JOHN F.
    STYLES FOR THE JAZZ PIANIST--BK. 1..THE RHYTHMIC SCHOOL
MILNE, ALFRED FORBES
    BEETHOVEN..THE PIANOFORTE SONATAS--2 VOLS.
MOTT, ISAAC H. R.
    ADVICE AND INSTRUCTIONS FOR PLAYING THE PIANOFORTE WITH EXPRESSION
MUSIC EDUCATORS NATIONAL CONFERENCE
    TEACHING PIANO IN CLASSROOM AND STUDIO
MUSIC PROJECT--NEW YORK CITY
    TEACHER'S GUIDE..A CREATIVE APPROACH TO PIANO CLASS TEACHING, BY
NAYLOR, EDWARD W.
    ELIZABETHAN VIRGINAL BOOK, AN ..A CRITICAL ESSAY ON THE CONTENTS
NEWMAN, WILLIAM S.
    PERFORMANCE PRACTICES IN BEETHOVEN'S PIANO SONATAS..AN
NEWMAN, WILLIAM S.
    PIANIST'S PROBLEMS, THE ..A MODERN APPROACH TO EFFICIENT PRACTICE
NEWMAN, WILLIAM S.
    SONATA IN THE BAROQUE ERA, THE --A HISTORY OF THE SONATA IDEA,
NEWMAN, WILLIAM S.
    SONATA IN THE CLASSIC ERA, THE --A HISTORY OF THE SONATA IDEA,
NEWTON, IVOR
    AT THE PIANO--IVOR NEWTON..THE WORLD OF AN ACCOMPANIST
NICCHIA, LILLIAN
    PIANOFORTE STUDY..HINTS ON PIANO PLAYING
OLIVER, EDWARD B.
    PRACTICAL TEXT-BOOK OF MUSIC, AS CONNECTED WITH THE ART OF PLAYING
PALMER, ANNIE L.
    MUSIC TEACHERS' GUIDE TO THE GOLDBECK PIANO METHOD
PALMER, KING
    TEACH YOURSELF TO PLAY THE PIANO
PALMER, WILLARD A.--EDITOR
    CHOPIN..AN INTRODUCTION TO HIS PIANO WORKS
PERRY, EDWARD B.
    DESCRIPTIVE ANALYSES OF PIANO WORKS, FOR THE USE OF TEACHERS,
PETERSON, FRANKLIN
    THEORETIC COMPANION TO PRACTICE--PART I OF THE PIANIST'S HANDBOOK
PINCHERLE, MARC
    WORLD OF THE VIRTUOSO, THE
POINTER SYSTEM, INC.
    GUIDE TO THE MODERN PIANIST, A
PRENTICE, THOMAS RIDLEY
    MUSICIAN, THE ..A GUIDE FOR PIANOFORTE STUDENTS--6 VOLS.
PROSNAK, JAN
    FREDERIC CHOPIN INTERNATIONAL PIANO COMPETITIONS, THE
REDDIE, CHARLES FREDERICK
    PIANOFORTE PLAYING ON ITS TECHNICAL AND AESTHETIC SIDES
REEVES, BETTY
    APPROACH TO PIANO TEACHING---ALSO CATALOGUED UNDER
REZITS, JOSEPH
    TEACHER'S GUIDE TO THE NEW SCRIBNER MUSIC LIBRARY
RIEFLING, REIMAR
    PIANO PEDALLING---1957, IN NORWEGIAN
RIEMANN, HUGO
    CATECHISM OF PIANOFORTE PLAYING---1888, IN GERMAN
ROSTAND, CLAUDE
    LISZT
ROTHSCHILD, FRITZ
    LOST TRADITION IN MUSIC, THE --PT. 1..RHYTHM AND TEMPO IN J. S.
ROTHSCHILD, FRITZ
    LOST TRADITION IN MUSIC, THE --PT. 2..MUSICAL PERFORMANCE IN THE
ROWLEY, ALEC
    DO'S AND DONT'S FOR MUSICIANS..A HANDBOOK FOR TEACHERS AND
RUBINSTEIN, BERYL
    OUTLINE OF PIANO PEDAGOGY--REV. ED.---1929
SCHAAF, EDWARD O.
    FUNDAMENTAL PRINCIPLES INVOLVED IN THE COMPOSING AND ARRANGING OF
SCHAAF, EDWARD O.
    MUSICAL INDIVIDUALITY OF THE PLAYER PIANO, THE ---EXCERPTS..'THE
SCHELLING, ERNEST *
    OXFORD PIANO COURSE, TEACHER'S FIRST MANUAL
SCHELLING, ERNEST *
    OXFORD PIANO COURSE, TEACHER'S SECOND MANUAL
SCHERER, HERBERT
    PIANO PRACTICING
SCHMITT, HANS
    NATURAL LAWS OF MUSICAL EXPRESSION, THE
SCHMITZ, ELIE ROBERT
    CAPTURE OF INSPIRATION, THE
SCHMITZ, ELIE ROBERT
    PIANO WORKS OF CLAUDE DEBUSSY, THE

SCHNABEL, KARL ULRICH
    MODERN TECHNIQUE OF THE PEDAL
SCHUMANN, ROBERT
    ON MUSIC AND MUSICIANS---1854, IN GERMAN--FIRST ENGLISH EDITION IN
SEGUEL, MANIA
    CHOPIN'S TEMPO RUBATO
SHEDLOCK, JOHN S.
    BEETHOVEN'S PIANOFORTE SONATAS..THE ORIGIN AND RESPECTIVE VALUES
SHERWOOD MUSIC SCHOOL
    PIANO LESSONS AND TESTS--4TH. REV. ED.---1945+
SMELTZER, JEANNIE R.--COMPILER
    OUTLINES AND GRADES FOR THE USE OF PIANO TEACHERS
STEIN, ERWIN
    FORM AND PERFORMANCE
STERNBERG, CONSTANTIN I. VON
    ETHICS AND ESTHETICS OF PIANO PLAYING
STORMEN, WIN
    JAZZ PIANO..DIXIELAND TO MODERN JAZZ, BLUES, BOOGIE, RAGTIME,
STORMEN, WIN
    JAZZ PIANO..EARLY BLUES TO CONTEMPORARY MODERN JAZZ, HOW TO PLAY
SUMMY-BIRCHARD COMPANY
    HANDBOOK FOR PIANO TEACHERS..COLLECTED ARTICLES ON SUBJECTS
TANKARD, GEOFFREY
    PIANOFORTE DIPLOMAS
TAYLER, E. DOUGLAS
    SECRET OF MUSICAL EXPRESSION, WITH SPECIAL REFERENCE TO PIANOFORTE
TAYLOR, FRANKLIN
    TECHNIQUE AND EXPRESSION IN PIANOFORTE PLAYING
TURECK, ROSALYN
    INTRODUCTION TO THE PERFORMANCE OF BACH, AN--3 VOLS.
VEINUS, ABRAHAM
    CONCERTO, THE ---1944
VENABLE, MARY
    INTERPRETATION OF PIANO MUSIC, THE
VIARD-LOUIS, JENNY
    MUSIC AND THE PIANO
WESTERBY, HERBERT
    HOW TO STUDY THE PIANOFORTE WORKS OF THE GREAT COMPOSERS
WESTRUP, SIR JACK ALLAN
    MUSICAL INTERPRETATION---THIS BOOK ACCOMPANIED A SERIES OF B.B.C.
WHITE, WILLIAM BRAID
    PLAYER-PIANIST, THE ..A GUIDE TO THE APPRECIATION AND
WHITEMORE, CUTHBERT
    COMMONSENSE IN PIANOFORTE PLAYING
WHITFORD, ROBERT
    PIANO AND ITS MUSIC, THE --FROM 'MODERN PIANO COURSE'
WIECK, FRIEDRICH
    PIANO AND SONG..HOW TO TEACH, HOW TO LEARN, AND HOW TO FORM A
WIER, ALBERT
    PIANO, THE ..ITS HISTORY, MAKERS, PLAYERS AND MUSIC
WILKINSON, CHARLES W.
    HOW TO PLAY 110 FAVOURITE PIANO SOLOS
WILKINSON, CHARLES W.
    WELL-KNOWN PIANO SOLOS..HOW TO PLAY THEM WITH UNDERSTANDING,
WILLIAMS, JEAN F.
    MODERN METHOD OF PIANO INSTRUCTION, A ..TEACHERS MANUAL
WILSON, MORRIS E.
    HOW TO PLAY BY EAR
WOLFF, ERNST VICTOR
    WITH REASON AND RHYME
WOLFF, KONRAD
    TEACHING OF ARTUR SCHNABEL, THE ..A GUIDE TO INTERPRETATION
WOODHOUSE, GEORGE
    ARTIST AT THE PIANO, THE ..THE ART OF MUSICAL INTERPRETATION
WOODHOUSE, GEORGE
    CREATIVE TECHNIQUE, FOR ARTISTS IN GENERAL AND PIANISTS IN
WOODHOUSE, GEORGE
    REALISTIC APPROACH TO PIANO PLAYING, A
WRIGHT, WILLIAM C.
    GOLDEN MONITOR, FOR THE PIANOFORTE AND CABINET ORGAN, DESIGNED AS
YOUNG, PERCY M.
    CONCERTO--'PHOENIX MUSIC GUIDES', NO. 1
YOUNG, PERCY M.
    KEYBOARD MUSICIANS OF THE WORLD

Aesthetics

APEL, WILLI
    MASTERS OF THE KEYBOARD
BOS, COENRAAD V.
    WELL-TEMPERED ACCOMPANIST, THE
BRISKIER, ARTHUR
    NEW APPROACH TO PIANO TRANSCRIPTIONS AND INTERPRETATION OF JOHANN
CHRISTIANI, ADOLPH FRIEDRICH
    PRINCIPLES OF EXPRESSION IN PIANOFORTE PLAYING, THE
CLARKE, HUGH ARCHIBALD
    ART OF PIANOFORTE PLAYING, THE --TEXT BOOK FOR BEGINNERS
DORIAN, FREDERICK
    HISTORY OF MUSIC IN PERFORMANCE, THE ---1942
DUMM, ROBERT W.
    IN BLACK AND WHITE
GARROWAY, WILL
    PIANISM
GIRDLESTONE, CUTHBERT
    MOZART AND HIS PIANO CONCERTOS---FIRST PUBLISHED IN 1948 AS
JOHNSTONE, J. ALFRED
    ART OF EXPRESSION IN PIANOFORTE PLAYING, THE
JOHNSTONE, J. ALFRED
    RUBATO, OR THE SECRET OF EXPRESSION IN PIANOFORTE PLAYING
KLECZYNSKI, JAN
    HOW TO PLAY CHOPIN--THREE LECTURES
KOCHEVITSKY, GEORGE
    ART OF PIANO PLAYING, THE ..A SCIENTIFIC APPROACH
KULLAK, ADOLPH
    AESTHETICS OF PIANOFORTE PLAYING, THE ---1861 IN GERMAN--1ST.
LANDOWSKA, WANDA
    LANDOWSKA ON MUSIC--EDITED BY DENISE RESTOUT
LEVINSKAYA, MARIA
    LEVINSKAYA SYSTEM OF PIANOFORTE TECHNIC AND TONE COLOR, THE
NEWMAN, WILLIAM S.
    SONATA IN THE BAROQUE ERA, THE --A HISTORY OF THE SONATA IDEA,
NEWMAN, WILLIAM S.
    SONATA IN THE CLASSIC ERA, THE --A HISTORY OF THE SONATA IDEA,
NEWTON, IVOR
    AT THE PIANO--IVOR NEWTON..THE WORLD OF AN ACCOMPANIST
PERRY, EDWARD B.
    DESCRIPTIVE ANALYSES OF PIANO WORKS, FOR THE USE OF TEACHERS,
PERRY, EDWARD B.
    STORIES OF STANDARD TEACHING PIECES FOR THE PIANOFORTE
ROTHSCHILD, FRITZ
    LOST TRADITION IN MUSIC, THE --PT. 1..RHYTHM AND TEMPO IN J. S.
ROTHSCHILD, FRITZ
    LOST TRADITION IN MUSIC, THE --PT. 2..MUSICAL PERFORMANCE IN THE
RUBINSTEIN, BERYL
    OUTLINE OF PIANO PEDAGOGY--REV. ED.---1929
SCHELLING, ERNEST *
    OXFORD PIANO COURSE, TEACHER'S SECOND MANUAL

SCHMITT, HANS
    NATURAL LAWS OF MUSICAL EXPRESSION, THE
SCHMITZ, ELIE ROBERT
    PIANO WORKS OF CLAUDE DEBUSSY, THE
SCHUMANN, ROBERT
    ON MUSIC AND MUSICIANS---1854, IN GERMAN--FIRST ENGLISH EDITION IN
STEIN, ERWIN
    FORM AND PERFORMANCE
TAYLER, E. DOUGLAS
    SECRET OF MUSICAL EXPRESSION, WITH SPECIAL REFERENCE TO PIANOFORTE
VANTYN, SIDNEY
    MODERN PIANOFORTE TECHNIQUE
WHITESIDE, ABBY
    INDISPENSABLES OF PIANO PLAYING--2ND. ED.---1955
WOODHOUSE, GEORGE
    ARTIST AT THE PIANO, THE ..THE ART OF MUSICAL INTERPRETATION
WOODHOUSE, GEORGE
    REALISTIC APPROACH TO PIANO PLAYING, A

Phrasing, Articulation

ADLER, KURT
    ART OF ACCOMPANYING AND COACHING, THE ---1965
AHRENS, CORA B. *
    FOR ALL PIANO TEACHERS
ANDERSON, J. CLARK
    GOOD MUSIC EXPLAINED..WHAT ALL GOOD PIANISTS SHOULD KNOW
BODKY, ERWIN
    INTERPRETATION OF BACH'S KEYBOARD WORKS, THE
BOLTON, HETTY
    ON TEACHING THE PIANO
BUCKLEY, OLIVIA DUSSEK
    MUSICAL TRUTHS..OR, AN ANALYSIS OF MUSIC AND AN ESSAY ON THE PAST
CARPE, ADOLPH
    GROUPING, ARTICULATING AND PHRASING IN MUSICAL INTERPRETATION..A
CARPE, ADOLPH
    PIANIST AND THE ART OF MUSIC, THE ..A TREATISE ON PIANO PLAYING
CARRENO, TERESA
    POSSIBILITIES OF TONE COLOR BY ARTISTIC USE OF PEDALS
CHAPPLE, STANLEY
    CLASS WAY TO THE KEYBOARD, THE
CHING, JAMES
    POINTS ON PEDALLING
CHING, JAMES
    STUDIES FOR BASIC PIANO TECHNIQUE..WRITTEN AND SELECTED WITH
CHRISTIANI, ADOLPH FRIEDRICH
    PRINCIPLES OF EXPRESSION IN PIANOFORTE PLAYING, THE
CLARKE, HUGH ARCHIBALD
    ART OF PIANOFORTE PLAYING, THE --TEXT BOOK FOR BEGINNERS
COPP, LAURA R.
    SOME SECRETS OF SUCCESS IN PLAYING IN PUBLIC
DALE, BENJAMIN J.
    HARMONY, COUNTERPOINT AND IMPROVISATION
DANIELS, BESS *
    WORLD OF MUSIC, THE ..PIANO COURSE..TEACHERS' BOOK, FOR CLASS OR
DILLER, ANGELA
    SPLENDOR OF MUSIC, THE
DONINGTON, ROBERT
    PERFORMER'S GUIDE TO BAROQUE MUSIC, A
DRAKE, KENNETH
    SONATAS OF BEETHOVEN AS HE PLAYED AND TAUGHT THEM, THE
DUMM, ROBERT W.
    IN BLACK AND WHITE
EHRENFECTER, C. A.
    DELIVERY IN THE ART OF PIANOFORTE PLAYING
EVERHART, POWELL
    PIANIST'S ART, THE ..A COMPREHENSIVE MANUAL ON PIANO PLAYING FOR
FARJEON, HARRY
    ART OF PIANO PHRASING, THE
FOOTE, ARTHUR W.
    SOME PRACTICAL THINGS IN PIANO PLAYING
GEBHARD, HEINRICH
    ART OF PEDALLING, THE
GERMER, HEINRICH
    THEORETICO-PRACTICAL ELEMENTARY PIANO-FORTE SCHOOL FOR STUDENTS OF
GIESEKING, WALTER *
    PIANO TECHNIQUE---COMBINED REPUBLICATION OF..'THE SHORTEST WAY TO
GOODRICH, ALFRED JOHN
    THEORY OF INTERPRETATION, APPLIED TO ARTISTIC MUSICAL PERFORMANCE
GORDON, STEPHEN T.
    GORDON'S NEW SCHOOL FOR THE PIANO-FORTE
GREW, SIDNEY
    ART OF THE PLAYER-PIANO, THE ..A TEXTBOOK FOR STUDENT AND TEACHER
GREW, SIDNEY
    FIRST BOOK OF THE PLAYER-PIANIST, THE
GUTMANN, EMMA WILKINS
    TALKS WITH PIANO TEACHERS
HAMILTON, CLARENCE G.
    TOUCH AND EXPRESSION IN PIANO PLAYING
HARICH-SCHNEIDER, ETA
    HARPSICHORD, THE ..AN INTRODUCTION TO TECHNIQUE, STYLE AND THE
HARKNESS, ROBERT
    HARKNESS PIANO METHOD OF EVANGELISTIC HYMN PLAYING, THE ..A
HARRISON, SIDNEY
    PIANO TECHNIQUE
HARRISON, SIDNEY
    YOUNG PERSON'S GUIDE TO PLAYING THE PIANO, THE
HEPLER, EFFIE A.
    EXERCISES IN TIME AND RHYTHM..A CONTRIBUTION TO MODERN PIANO
HOFMANN, JOSEF
.   PIANO PLAYING, WITH PIANO QUESTIONS ANSWERED---PUBLISHED EARLIER
HOLCMAN, JAN
    LEGACY OF CHOPIN, THE
HORROCKS, CYPIL R. H.
    STUDENT'S GUIDE TO THE ART OF TEACHING THE PIANOFORTE, THE --2ND.
HOWELL, DOROTHY
    KEYBOARD WORK FOR HARMONY STUDENTS
HUENTEN, FRANZ
    ABRIDGED EDITION OF F. HUENTEN'S CELEBRATED INSTRUCTIONS FOR THE
HULL, ARTHUR EAGLEFIELD
    THREE HUNDRED QUESTIONS ON PIANOFORTE TEACHING IN 30 GRADUATED
JEWETT, ALBERT DEWEY
    IDIOMATIC COURSE OF PIANO INSTRUCTION FOR CLASS WORK
JOHNS, CLAYTON
    ESSENTIALS OF PIANOFORTE PLAYING, THE
JOHNSTONE, J. ALFRED
    ART OF EXPRESSION IN PIANOFORTE PLAYING, THE
JOHNSTONE, J. ALFRED
    PHRASING IN PIANO PLAYING..AN ELEMENTARY GUIDE WITH EXAMPLES
JOHNSTONE, J. ALFRED
    RUBATO, OR THE SECRET OF EXPRESSION IN PIANOFORTE PLAYING
JOHNSTONE, J. ALFRED
    TOUCH, PHRASING AND INTERPRETATION
KELLER, HERMANN
    PHRASING AND ARTICULATION---152 MUSICAL EXAMPLES
KIRKPATRICK, RALPH
    DOMENICO SCARLATTI----1953

KULLAK, FRANZ
    BEETHOVEN'S PIANO PLAYING, WITH AN ESSAY ON THE EXECUTION OF THE
LAMAR, RICHARD
    COLLEGE PIANO PEDAGOGY
LANDOWSKA, WANDA
    LANDOWSKA ON MUSIC--EDITED BY DENISE RESTOUT
LAST, JOAN
    INTERPRETATION FOR THE PIANO STUDENT
LEIMER, KARL *
    RHYTHMICS, DYNAMICS, PEDAL, AND OTHER PROBLEMS OF PIANO
MACPHERSON, STEWART
    STUDIES IN PHRASING AND FORM
MASON, WILLIAM G.
    TOUCH AND TECHNIC..FOR ARTISTIC PIANO PLAYING, OP. 44--4 VOLS. IN
MATHEWS, WILLIAM S. B.
    STUDIES IN PHRASING, MEMORIZING AND INTERPRETATION
MATHEWS, WILLIAM S. B.
    STUDIES IN PHRASING SELECTED FROM THE WORKS OF THE BEST CLASSIC
MATTHAY, TOBIAS A.
    SLUR OR COUPLET OF NOTES IN ALL ITS VARIETY, THE ..ITS
MCEWEN, JOHN B.
    PRINCIPLES OF PHRASING AND ARTICULATION IN MUSIC, THE
MELLERS, WILFRED
    FRANCOIS COUPERIN AND THE FRENCH CLASSICAL TRADITION
NEWMAN, ELIZABETH
    HOW TO TEACH MUSIC TO BEGINNERS
NEWMAN, WILLIAM S.
    PERFORMANCE PRACTICES IN BEETHOVEN'S PIANO SONATAS..AN
NEWMAN, WILLIAM S.
    PIANIST'S PROBLEMS, THE ..A MODERN APPROACH TO EFFICIENT PRACTICE
PALMER, ANNIE L.
    MUSIC TEACHERS' GUIDE TO THE GOLDBECK PIANO METHOD
PARSONS, ALBERT R.
    SYNTHETIC METHOD FOR THE PIANOFORTE, THE
PHILIPP, LILLIE H.
    PIANO STUDY..APPLICATION AND TECHNIQUE
PLATT, CAROLYN
    CAROLYN PLATT METHOD FOR PIANO, THE --GROUP INSTRUCTION--TEACHER'S
POINTER SYSTEM, INC.
    GUIDE TO THE MODERN PIANIST, A
POTAMKIN, FRANK
    MODERN PIANO PEDAGOGY
REDDIE, CHARLES FREDERICK
    PIANOFORTE PLAYING ON ITS TECHNICAL AND AESTHETIC SIDES
REEDER, BETAH
    SINGING TOUCH, THE
REINAGLE, CAROLINE
    FEW WORDS ON PIANOFORTE PLAYING, A
RIEMANN, HUGO
    CATECHISM OF PIANOFORTE PLAYING---1888, IN GERMAN
RIEMANN, HUGO
    PRACTICAL GUIDE TO THE ART OF PHRASING...ANALYSIS OF CLASSIC AND
ROBBINS, EDGAR A.
    AMERICAN METHOD FOR THE PIANOFORTE
ROTHSCHILD, FRITZ
    LOST TRADITION IN MUSIC, THE --PT. 1..RHYTHM AND TEMPO IN J. S.
ROTHSCHILD, FRITZ
    LOST TRADITION IN MUSIC, THE --PT. 2..MUSICAL PERFORMANCE IN THE
ROWLEY, ALEC *
    GRADED TESTS IN PRACTICAL MUSICIANSHIP AND MUSICAL INITIATIVE--IN
ROWLEY, ALEC
    PRACTICAL MUSICIANSHIP, A HANDBOOK FOR TEACHERS AND STUDENTS
RUBINSTEIN, BERYL
    OUTLINE OF PIANO PEDAGOGY--REV. ED.---1929
SCHAAF, EDWARD O.
    ART OF PIANO PLAYER TRANSCRIPTION, THE ..MAKING OF PERFORATED
SCHAAF, EDWARD O.
    FUNDAMENTAL PRINCIPLES INVOLVED IN THE COMPOSING AND ARRANGING OF
SCHELLING, ERNEST *
    OXFORD PIANO COURSE, TEACHER'S SECOND MANUAL
SCHLIEDER, FREDERICK W.
    LYRIC COMPOSITION THROUGH IMPROVISATION--2 VOLS., 1927-1946
SCHMITZ, ELIE ROBERT
    PIANO WORKS OF CLAUDE DEBUSSY, THE
SCHOTT, HOWARD
    PLAYING THE HARPSICHORD
SHERWOOD MUSIC SCHOOL
    PIANO LESSONS AND TESTS--4TH. REV. ED.---1945+
SMELTZER, JEANNIE R.--COMPILER
    OUTLINES AND GRADES FOR THE USE OF PIANO TEACHERS
SMITH, THOMAS
    LITTLE DIFFICULTIES WHICH OCCUR IN PIANOFORTE PLAYING
STEIN, ERWIN
    FORM AND PERFORMANCE
STEPHENSON, LILIAN E.
    BEGONE, DULL PRACTICE..SUGGESTIONS FOR STUDENTS AND
STERNBERG, CONSTANTIN I. VON
    ETHICS AND ESTHETICS OF PIANO PLAYING
TANKARD, GEOFFREY
    FOUNDATIONS OF PIANOFORTE TECHNIQUE
TAPPER, THOMAS
    ABC OF KEYBOARD HARMONY, THE
TAYLOR, FRANKLIN
    PRIMER OF PIANOFORTE PLAYING
TAYLOR, FRANKLIN
    TECHNIQUE AND EXPRESSION IN PIANOFORTE PLAYING
TOBIN, JOSEPH RAYMOND
    COMMON SENSE IN SIGHT READING..A GUIDE FOR PIANO TEACHERS
VANTYN, SIDNEY
    MODERN PIANOFORTE TECHNIQUE
VENABLE, MARY
    INTERPRETATION OF PIANO MUSIC, THE
VIRGIL, ALMON K.
    STEP BY STEP..TEXTBOOK IN PIANO PLAYING..HANDBOOK FOR TEACHERS
WELLS, HOWARD
    EARS, BRAIN AND FINGERS..A TEXT BOOK FOR PIANO TEACHERS AND PUPILS
WHITE, WILLIAM BRAID
    PLAYER-PIANIST, THE ..A GUIDE TO THE APPRECIATION AND
WIER, ALBERT
    PIANO, THE ..ITS HISTORY, MAKERS, PLAYERS AND MUSIC
WILKINS-GUTMANN, EMMA
    TALKS WITH PIANO TEACHERS
WILLIAMS, JOHN M.
    WHAT TO TEACH AT THE VERY FIRST LESSON

Ornamentation

ADLER, KURT
    ART OF ACCOMPANYING AND COACHING, THE ---1965
ALDRICH, PUTNAM
    PRINCIPAL AGREMENTS OF THE SEVENTEENTH AND EIGHTEENTH CENTURIES,
AMEY, ELLEN
    CONSCIOUS CONTROL IN PIANO STUDY
ANON
    COMPLEAT TUTOR FOR THE HARPSICHORD OR SPINNET, WHEREIN IS SHEWN
ANON
    FASHIONABLE PRECEPTOR, FOR THE PIANO-FORTE AND HARPSICHORD,

ANON
  NEW AND COMPLETE INSTRUCTIONS FOR THE HARPSICHORD, PIANO FORTE OR
ANON
  NEW INSTRUCTIONS FOR PLAYING THE HARPSICHORD, PIANOFORTE OR
ANON
  PLAYING THE HARPSICHORD, SPINET OR PIANO FORTE MADE EASY BY NEW
ANON
  PRECEPTOR, FOR THE PIANOFORTE, THE ORGAN OR HARPSICHORD, THE
BABBITT, WILLIAM
  PHYSIOLOGICAL METHOD FOR PLAYING THE PIANO-FORTE, DESIGNED AS A
BACH, CARL PHILIPP EMANUEL
  ESSAY ON THE TRUE ART OF PLAYING KEYBOARD INSTRUMENTS---TWO PTS.,
BACON, ERNST
  NOTES ON THE PIANO
BADURA-SKODA, EVA *
  INTERPRETING MOZART ON THE KEYBOARD---1957, IN GERMAN
BASTIEN, JAMES W.
  HOW TO TEACH PIANO SUCCESSFULLY
BEMETZRIEDER, ANTON
  COMPENDIUM OF A NEW METHOD OF MUSIC...WITH THE AUTHOR'S PRINCIPLES
BEMETZRIEDER, ANTON
  GAMUT AND COMMON CHORD IN ALL KEYS, FINGERED FOR THE HARPSICHORD,
BEMETZRIEDER, ANTON
  NEW GUIDE TO MUSIC, IN FRENCH AND ENGLISH, A
BODKY, ERWIN
  INTERPRETATION OF BACH'S KEYBOARD WORKS, THE
BUCHAROFF, SIMON
  MODERN PIANIST'S TEXT BOOK, THE
CANAVE, PAZ CORAZON G.
  RE-EVALUATION OF THE ROLE PLAYED BY C. P. E. BACH IN THE
CARR, BENJAMIN
  ANALYTICAL INSTRUCTOR FOR THE PIANO FORTE, OP. 15, THE --IN 3 PTS.
CARRE, JOHN
  PSYCHOLOGY OF PIANO TEACHING, THE ..A TEXTBOOK FOR TEACHERS,
CHAPPLE, STANLEY
  CLASS WAY TO THE KEYBOARD, THE
CLEMENTI, MUZIO
  INTRODUCTION TO THE ART OF PLAYING ON THE PIANOFORTE---1801+
COUPERIN, FRANCOIS
  ART DE TOUCHER LE CLAVECIN, L' ---IN FRENCH, GERMAN AND ENGLISH
CZERNY, CARL
  COMPLETE THEORETICAL AND PRACTICAL PIANO FORTE SCHOOL, FROM THE
CZERNY, CARL
  LETTERS TO A YOUNG LADY ON THE ART OF PLAYING THE PIANOFORTE
DALE, BENJAMIN J.
  HARMONY, COUNTERPOINT AND IMPROVISATION
DANNREUTHER, EDWARD
  MUSICAL ORNAMENTATION--IN TWO PARTS
DART, THURSTON
  INTERPRETATION OF MUSIC, THE --4TH. ED.---1954
DOLMETSCH, ARNOLD
  INTERPRETATION OF MUSIC OF THE SEVENTEENTH AND EIGHTEENTH
DONINGTON, ROBERT
  INTERPRETATION OF EARLY MUSIC, THE
DONINGTON, ROBERT
  PERFORMER'S GUIDE TO BAROQUE MUSIC, A
DRAKE, KENNETH
  SONATAS OF BEETHOVEN AS HE PLAYED AND TAUGHT THEM, THE
DUNN, JOHN PETRIE
  ORNAMENTATION IN THE WORKS OF FREDERIC CHOPIN---1921
EHRLICH, ALFRED HEINRICH
  ORNAMENTATION IN BEETHOVEN'S PIANOFORTE-WORKS, THE
EHRLICH, ALFRED HEINRICH
  ORNAMENTATION IN JOH. SEB. BACH'S PIANOFORTE-WORKS, THE
EMERY, WALTER
  BACH'S ORNAMENTS
ENGELBRECHT, J. G.
  MATERIA MUSICA, OR MATERIALS FOR THE PIANIST..A CLASS BOOK
EVERHART, POWELL
  PIANIST'S ART, THE ..A COMPREHENSIVE MANUAL ON PIANO PLAYING FOR
GARROWAY, WILL
  PIANISM
GASPARINI, FRANCESCO
  PRACTICAL HARMONIST AT THE HARPSICHORD, THE ---1708
GERMER, HEINRICH
  MUSICAL ORNAMENTATION..DIDACTICO-CRITICAL TREATISE ON ALL OF THE
GERMER, HEINRICH
  TECHNICS OF PIANOFORTE PLAYING, THE ..MUSICAL ORNAMENTATION,
GILBERTSON, ARNOLD B.
  TEACHERS MANUAL FOR POPULAR PIANO PLAYING, DESIGNED FOR ALL
GOLDTHWAITE, SCOTT
  ORNAMENTATION IN MUSIC FOR THE KEYBOARD
GOODRICH, ALFRED JOHN
  THEORY OF INTERPRETATION, APPLIED TO ARTISTIC MUSICAL PERFORMANCE
GORDON, STEPHEN T.
  GORDON'S NEW SCHOOL FOR THE PIANO-FORTE
GOSS, JOHN
  INTRODUCTION TO HARMONY AND THOROUGH-BASS WITH NUMEROUS EXAMPLES
GRAUPNER, GOTTLIEB
  RUDIMENTS OF THE ART OF PLAYING ON THE PIANOFORTE...A PLAIN
GRAY, CECIL
  BACH AND DAS WOHLTEMPERIRTE KLAVIER..ANALYTICAL NOTES, WITH AN
GRAY, CECIL
  FORTY-EIGHT PRELUDES AND FUGUES OF J. S. BACH, THE
HAMILTON, CLARENCE G.
  ORNAMENTS IN CLASSICAL AND MODERN MUSIC
HARDING, HENRY ALFRED
  MUSICAL ORNAMENTS SIMPLY EXPLAINED...NUMEROUS EXAMPLES...WITH 100
HARICH-SCHNEIDER, ETA
  HARPSICHORD, THE ..AN INTRODUCTION TO TECHNIQUE, STYLE AND THE
HOOK, JAMES
  GUIDA DI MUSICA..BEING A COMPLETE BOOK OF INSTRUCTIONS FOR
HUENTEN, FRANZ
  ABRIDGED EDITION OF F. HUENTEN'S CELEBRATED INSTRUCTIONS FOR THE
HUENTEN, FRANZ
  FRANZ HUENTEN'S CELEBRATED INSTRUCTIONS FOR THE PIANOFORTE--2ND.
HUMMEL, JOHANN NEPOMUK
  COMPLETE THEORETICAL AND PRACTICAL COURSE OF INSTRUCTIONS ON THE
JOHNSTONE, J. ALFRED
  TOUCH, PHRASING AND INTERPRETATION
JONES, GRIFFITH
  COMPLEAT INSTRUCTOR FOR THE HARPSICHORD OR PIANOFORTE, THE
KASTNER, SANTIAGO
  PARALLELS AND DISCREPANCIES BETWEEN ENGLISH AND SPANISH KEYBOARD
KELLEY, EDGAR STILLMAN
  CHOPIN THE COMPOSER---1913
KIRKPATRICK, RALPH
  DOMENICO SCARLATTI---1953
KOCH, CASPAR
  PIANO STUDENT'S GRADUS AD PARNASSUM, THE ..PRESENTING THE
KULLAK, FRANZ
  BEETHOVEN'S PIANO PLAYING, WITH AN ESSAY ON THE EXECUTION OF THE
LAMAR, RICHARD
  COLLEGE PIANO PEDAGOGY
LANDOWSKA, WANDA
  LANDOWSKA ON MUSIC--EDITED BY DENISE RESTOUT
LANNING, RUSSELL
  BACH ORNAMENTATION

LAST, JOAN
  INTERPRETATION FOR THE PIANO STUDENT
LIEBERMAN, MAURICE
  KEYBOARD HARMONY AND IMPROVISATION--2 VOLS.
LOVELOCK, WILLIAM
  ORNAMENTS AND ABBREVIATIONS FOR EXAMINATION CANDIDATES
LUDDEN, WILLIAM
  THOROUGH BASS SCHOOL, THE ..AN EASY AND PROGRESSIVE COURSE FOR
MASON, WILLIAM G.
  TOUCH AND TECHNIC..FOR ARTISTIC PIANO PLAYING, OP. 44--4 VOLS. IN
MELLERS, WILFRED
  FRANCOIS COUPERIN AND THE FRENCH CLASSICAL TRADITION
MILLER, EDWARD
  INSTITUTES OF MUSIC, OR, EASY INSTRUCTIONS FOR THE HARPSICHORD
MOLLER, JOHN CHRISTOPHER
  SETT OF PROGRESSIVE LESSONS FOR THE HARPSICHORD OR PIANO FORTE, A
MOTT, ISAAC H. R.
  ADVICE AND INSTRUCTIONS FOR PLAYING THE PIANOFORTE WITH EXPRESSION
NEWMAN, WILLIAM S.
  PERFORMANCE PRACTICES IN BEETHOVEN'S PIANO SONATAS..AN
NEWMAN, WILLIAM S.
  PIANIST'S PROBLEMS, THE ..A MODERN APPROACH TO EFFICIENT PRACTICE
NEWMAN, WILLIAM S.
  SONATA IN THE BAROQUE ERA, THE --A HISTORY OF THE SONATA IDEA,
NEWMAN, WILLIAM S.
  SONATA IN THE CLASSIC ERA, THE --A HISTORY OF THE SONATA IDEA,
O'REAR, MRS. ASBURY S.
  SELF READING NOTES
PALMER, HORATIO R.
  PALMER'S PIANO PRIMER
PALMER, WILLARD A.--EDITOR
  CHOPIN..AN INTRODUCTION TO HIS PIANO WORKS
PASQUALI, NICOLO
  ART OF FINGERING THE HARPSICHORD, THE
PEARCE, CHARLES WILLIAM
  ART OF THE PIANO TEACHER, THE
PETERSON, FRANKLIN
  THEORETIC COMPANION TO PRACTICE--PART I OF THE PIANIST'S HANDBOOK
PFEFFERKORN, OTTO W.
  PIANISTIC HINTS
PHILIPP, LILLIE H.
  PIANO STUDY..APPLICATION AND TECHNIQUE
PHILLIPSON, WENTWORTH
  GUIDE TO YOUNG PIANOFORTE TEACHERS AND STUDENTS
PRELLEUR, PETER
  HARPSICHORD ILLUSTRATED AND IMPROV'D, WHEREIN IS SHEWN THE ITALIAN
REINAGLE, CAROLINE
  FEW WORDS ON PIANOFORTE PLAYING, A
RICHNER, THOMAS
  ORIENTATION FOR INTERPRETING MOZART'S PIANO SONATAS
RIEFLING, REIMAR
  PIANO PEDALLING---1957, IN NORWEGIAN
RUSSELL, LOUIS ARTHUR
  EMBELLISHMENTS OF MUSIC, THE ..A STUDY OF THE ENTIRE RANGE OF
SCHAAF, EDWARD O.
  ART OF PIANO PLAYER TRANSCRIPTION, THE ..MAKING OF PERFORATED
SCHAAF, EDWARD O.
  FUNDAMENTAL PRINCIPLES INVOLVED IN THE COMPOSING AND ARRANGING OF
SCHAAF, EDWARD O.
  MUSICAL INDIVIDUALITY OF THE PLAYER PIANO, THE ---EXCERPTS..'THE
SCHOTT, HOWARD
  PLAYING THE HARPSICHORD
SHERWOOD MUSIC SCHOOL
  PIANO LESSONS AND TESTS--4TH. REV. ED.---1945+
SLENCZYNSKA, RUTH *
  MUSIC AT YOUR FINGERTIPS
SMITH, THOMAS
  LITTLE DIFFICULTIES WHICH OCCUR IN PIANOFORTE PLAYING
SQUIRE, RUSSEL N. *
  CLASS PIANO FOR ADULT BEGINNERS--2ND. ED.---1964
SUMMY-BIRCHARD COMPANY
  HANDBOOK FOR PIANO TEACHERS..COLLECTED ARTICLES ON SUBJECTS
TAYLOR, FRANKLIN
  PRIMER OF PIANOFORTE PLAYING
TAYLOR, FRANKLIN
  TECHNIQUE AND EXPRESSION IN PIANOFORTE PLAYING
TAYLOR, H.
  ORNAMENTS IN MUSIC
TURECK, ROSALYN
  INTRODUCTION TO THE PERFORMANCE OF BACH, AN--3 VOLS.
VENABLE, MARY
  INTERPRETATION OF PIANO MUSIC, THE
VINING, HARRISON S.
  SIMPLE AND COMPLETE PRIMER FOR THE PIANOFORTE, THE
WARRINER, JOHN
  TRANSPOSITION, KEYBOARD AND ORCHESTRAL--2 PTS., 1893-1908
WESTRUP, SIR JACK ALLAN
  MUSICAL INTERPRETATION---THIS BOOK ACCOMPANIED A SERIES OF B.B.C.
WINNER, SEPTIMUS
  WINNER'S NEW SCHOOL FOR THE PIANO, IN WHICH THE INSTRUCTIONS ARE
WRIGHT, WILLIAM C.
  GOLDEN MONITOR, FOR THE PIANOFORTE AND CABINET ORGAN, DESIGNED AS

Pedalling

AEOLIAN COMPANY, THE
  WEIGHT OF EVIDENCE ON THE TRUE MUSICAL WORTH OF THE PIANOLA AND
AHRENS, CORA B. *
  FOR ALL PIANO TEACHERS
ANDERSON, J. CLARK
  GOOD MUSIC EXPLAINED..WHAT ALL GOOD PIANISTS SHOULD KNOW
ANON
  GUIDE TO THE PROPER USE OF THE PIANOFORTE PEDALS, WITH EXAMPLES
AULD, WILDA J.
  HANDBOOK FOR THE CHURCH PIANIST, A
BACON, ERNST
  NOTES ON THE PIANO
BADURA-SKODA, EVA *
  INTERPRETING MOZART ON THE KEYBOARD---1957, IN GERMAN
BLAKE, DOROTHY
  FIRST STEPS IN THE USE OF THE PEDAL FOR PIANO
BODKY, ERWIN
  INTERPRETATION OF BACH'S KEYBOARD WORKS, THE
BOOTH, VICTOR
  WE PIANO TEACHERS--REVISED BY ADELE FRANKLIN---1946
BOWEN, YORK
  PEDALLING THE MODERN PIANOFORTE---1936
BRECKENRIDGE, WILLIAM KILGORE
  HINTS FOR PIANO NORMAL STUDIES
BREE, MADAME MALWINE
  GROUNDWORK OF THE LESCHETIZKY METHOD, THE ---1902
BRIGGS, GILBERT A.
  PIANOS, PIANISTS AND SONICS
BROWER, HARRIETTE
  ART OF THE PIANIST, THE
CALAND, ELIZABETH
  ARTISTIC PIANO PLAYING, AS TAUGHT BY LUDWIG DEPPE

CAPRE, JOHN
    PSYCHOLOGY OF PIANO TEACHING, THE ..A TEXTBOOK FOR TEACHERS,
CARRENO, TERESA
    POSSIBILITIES OF TONE COLOR BY ARTISTIC USE OF PEDALS
CARTER, BUENTA
    BEGINNER'S PIANO BOOK FOR OLDER STUDENTS...DESIGNED FOR THE OLDER
CASTELLINI, JOHN EDWARD
    RUDIMENTS OF MUSIC..A NEW APPROACH WITH APPLICATION TO THE
CHASE, MARY WOOD
    NATURAL LAWS IN PIANO TECHNIC
CHILDERS, LEMUEL
    PLAYING THE PIANO BY EAR
CHING, JAMES
    NEW GRADED PEDALLING FOR PIANO, THE --BKS. 1 AND 2
CHING, JAMES
    POINTS ON PEDALLING
CHING, JOAN ELIZABETH
    APPROACH TO PIANO TEACHING---ALSO CATALOGUED UNDER
COVIELLO, AMBROSE
    FOUNDATIONS OF PIANOFORTE TECHNIC
COVIELLO, AMBROSE
    WHAT MATTHAY MEANT
CRAMER, JOHN BAPTIST
    INSTRUCTIONS FOR THE PIANOFORTE---CONTAINS ALSO A SET OF 28
CZERNY, CARL
    COMPLETE THEORETICAL AND PRACTICAL PIANO FORTE SCHOOL, FROM THE
DAHL, ANTON
    SOUL OF GENIUS, THE ..ITS MUSICAL DEVELOPMENT AND HOW THE WORLD AT
DANIELS, BESS *
    WORLD OF MUSIC, THE ..PIANO COURSE..TEACHERS' BOOK, FOR CLASS OR
DILLER, ANGELA
    FIRST PEDAL-STUDIES FOR THE PIANO, 24 PROGRESSIVE EXERCISES AND
DRAKE, KENNETH
    SONATAS OF BEETHOVEN AS HE PLAYED AND TAUGHT THEM, THE
DUMESNIL, MAURICE
    HOW TO PLAY AND TEACH DEBUSSY
DUMM, ROBERT W.
    IN BLACK AND WHITE
EHRENFECTER, C. A.
    TECHNICAL STUDY IN THE ART OF PIANOFORTE PLAYING--DEPPE'S
EISENBERG, JACOB
    ARTISTIC PIANIST, THE ..NATURAL TECHNICS IN PIANO MASTERY..FROM
ENGEL, CARL
    PIANIST'S HANDBOOK, THE ..A GUIDE FOR THE RIGHT COMPREHENSION AND
ENGELBRECHT, J. G.
    MATERIA MUSICA, OR MATERIALS FOR THE PIANIST..A CLASS BOOK
EVERHART, POWELL
    PIANIST'S ART, THE ..A COMPREHENSIVE MANUAL ON PIANO PLAYING FOR
FAELTEN, CARL
    PEDAL EXERCISES FOR PIANOFORTE
FARJEON, HARRY
    ART OF PIANO PEDALLING, THE ..TWO VOLUMES IN ONE
FOOTE, ARTHUR W.
    SOME PRACTICAL THINGS IN PIANO PLAYING
FORD, DONALD
    SINGING CLASS PIANIST AND ON PIANOFORTE ACCOMPANYING IN GENERAL,
FOWLES, ERNEST
    HARMONY IN PIANOFORTE-STUDY..FOR THE INDIVIDUAL STUDENT--2 VOLS.,
GAT, JOZSEF
    TECHNIQUE OF PIANO PLAYING, THE, --2ND. ED.---1958
GEARY, ELEANOR MARGARET
    MUSICAL EDUCATION, WITH PRACTICAL OBSERVATIONS ON THE ART OF
GEBHARD, HEINRICH
    ART OF PEDALLING, THE
GIESEKING, WALTER *
    PIANO TECHNIQUE---COMBINED REPUBLICATION OF..'THE SHORTEST WAY TO
GILBERTSON, ARNOLD B.
    TEACHERS MANUAL FOR POPULAR PIANO PLAYING, DESIGNED FOR ALL
GRAUPNER, GOTTLIEB
    RUDIMENTS OF THE ART OF PLAYING ON THE PIANOFORTE...A PLAIN
GREW, SIDNEY
    ART OF THE PLAYER-PIANO, THE ..A TEXTBOOK FOR STUDENT AND TEACHER
GREW, SIDNEY
    FIRST BOOK OF THE PLAYER-PIANIST, THE
GRUNDY, ENID
    HAPPY PIANIST, THE
GUTMANN, EMMA WILKINS
    TALKS WITH PIANO TEACHERS
HAMILTON, CLARENCE G.
    TOUCH AND EXPRESSION IN PIANO PLAYING
HANSMANN, RICHARD
    THEORETICAL AND PRACTICAL PIANO-FORTE SCHOOL FOR THE JANKO
HARKNESS, ROBERT
    HARKNESS PIANO METHOD OF EVANGELISTIC HYMN PLAYING, THE ..A
HARRISON, SIDNEY
    PIANO TECHNIQUE
HARRISON, SIDNEY
    YOUNG PERSON'S GUIDE TO PLAYING THE PIANO, THE
HERZ, HENRI
    NEW AND COMPLETE PIANOFORTE SCHOOL
HOFHEIMER, GRACE
    TEACHING TECHNIQUES FOR THE PIANO
HOFMANN, JOSEF
    PIANO PLAYING..A LITTLE BOOK OF SIMPLE SUGGESTIONS--REPRINTED FROM
HOLCMAN, JAN
    LEGACY OF CHOPIN, THE
HOPE, ERIC
    HANDBOOK OF PIANO PLAYING, A
HORROCKS, CYRIL R. H.
    STUDENT'S GUIDE TO THE ART OF TEACHING THE PIANOFORTE, THE --2ND.
HUMMEL, JOHANN NEPOMUK
    COMPLETE THEORETICAL AND PRACTICAL COURSE OF INSTRUCTIONS ON THE
JOHNS, CLAYTON
    ESSENTIALS OF PIANOFORTE PLAYING, THE
JOHNSON, THOMAS A.
    PRINCIPLES OF PIANOFORTE PEDALLING, THE
JOHNSTONE, J. ALFRED
    ART OF TEACHING PIANOFORTE PLAYING, THE --2ND. REV. ED.---1910
JOHNSTONE, J. ALFRED
    HOW TO USE THE PEDAL IN PIANO PLAYING
JONAS, ALBERTO
    PIANOSCRIPT BOOK..AN INVALUABLE AID TO TEACHER AND STUDENT IN
KLECZYNSKI, JAN
    HOW TO PLAY CHOPIN--THREE LECTURES
KRUSZYNSKI, MICHAL
    APPROACH TO THE PSYCHOLOGY OF PIANO TEACHING, AN
LAMAR, RICHARD
    COLLEGE PIANO PEDAGOGY
LANG, EDITH *
    MUSICAL ACCOMPANIMENT OF MOVING PICTURES..A PRACTICAL MANUAL FOR
LAST, JOAN
    INTERPRETATION FOR THE PIANO STUDENT
LAST, JOAN
    INTRODUCTION TO PEDALLING
LAST, JOAN
    YOUNG PIANIST, THE ..A NEW APPROACH FOR TEACHERS AND

LAWRENCE, FREDERIC LOCKE
    RATIONALE OF PIANO TECHNIQUE, THE
LEIMER, KARL *
    RHYTHMICS, DYNAMICS, PEDAL, AND OTHER PROBLEMS OF PIANO
LHEVINNE, JOSEF
    BASIC PRINCIPLES IN PIANOFORTE PLAYING---1924
LINDO, ALGERNON H. *
    INDIVIDUALITY IN PIANO TOUCH
LINDO, ALGERNON H.
    PEDALLING IN PIANOFORTE MUSIC
MAIER, GUY
    PIANO TEACHER'S COMPANION, THE
MASON, WILLIAM G. *
    PRIMER OF MUSIC, A ..BEING THE FIRST STEPS IN MUSICIANSHIP..FOR
MASON, WILLIAM G.
    SYSTEM OF TECHNICAL EXERCISES FOR THE PIANO-FORTE, A
MATHEWS, WILLIAM S. B.
    SCHOOL OF THE PIANO PEDAL
MATHEWS, WILLIAM S. B.
    TEACHER'S MANUAL OF MASON'S PIANOFORTE TECHNICS
MATTHAY, TOBIAS A.
    ACT OF TOUCH IN ALL ITS DIVERSITY, THE ..AN ANALYSIS AND SYNTHESIS
MATTHAY, TOBIAS A.
    FIRST PRINCIPLES OF PIANOFORTE PLAYING--EXTRACT FROM 'THE ACT OF
MATTHAY, TOBIAS A.
    MUSICAL INTERPRETATION..ITS LAWS AND PRINCIPLES---1913
MATTHAY, TOBIAS A.
    PIANOFORTE TONE-PRODUCTION---SAME AS 'THE ACT OF TOUCH IN ALL ITS
MATTHAY, TOBIAS A.
    PRINCIPLES OF FINGERING AND LAWS OF PEDALLING
MCARTHUR, ALEXANDER
    PIANOFORTE STUDY..HINTS ON PIANO PLAYING
MERGES, P.
    PRACTICAL RULES FOR PIANOFORTE PLAYING..TEXT BOOK FOR TEACHERS AND
MERRICK, FRANK
    PRACTICING THE PIANO
MOORE, MARY BURNHAM
    LURE OF THE PIANO THROUGH COORDINATION AND CONCENTRATION, THE
MORRILL, HENRY H.
    MANUAL OF PIANO FOR PUPILS AND TEACHERS
NALDER, LAWRENCE MARCUS
    MODERN PIANO, THE
NEUHAUS, HEINRICH
    ART OF PIANO PLAYING, THE
NEWMAN, WILLIAM S.
    PIANIST'S PROBLEMS, THE ..A MODERN APPROACH TO EFFICIENT PRACTICE
PALMER, WILLARD A.--EDITOR
    CHOPIN..AN INTRODUCTION TO HIS PIANO WORKS
PEARCE, CHARLES WILLIAM
    ART OF THE PIANO TEACHER, THE
PHILIPP, LILLIE H.
    PIANO STUDY..APPLICATION AND TECHNIQUE
PHILLIPSON, WENTWORTH
    GUIDE TO YOUNG PIANOFORTE TEACHERS AND STUDENTS
PLATT, CAROLYN
    CAROLYN PLATT METHOD FOR PIANO, THE --GROUP INSTRUCTION--TEACHER'S
POINTER SYSTEM, INC.
    GUIDE TO THE MODERN PIANIST, A
POTAMKIN, FRANK
    MODERN PIANO PEDAGOGY
PRENTNER, MARIE
    MODERN PIANIST..BEING MY EXPERIENCES IN THE TECHNIQUE AND
QUINTE, MICHAEL S.
    MODULATIONARY HARMONY BOOK
RAMUL, PETER
    PSYCHO-PHYSICAL FOUNDATIONS OF MODERN PIANO TECHNIQUE, THE
REDDIE, CHARLES FREDERICK
    PIANOFORTE PLAYING ON ITS TECHNICAL AND AESTHETIC SIDES
REEDER, BETAH
    SINGING TOUCH, THE
REEVES, BETTY
    APPROACH TO PIANO TEACHING---ALSO CATALOGUED UNDER
RICHTER, ADA
    TEACHING HINTS
RIEFLING, REIMAR
    PIANO PEDALLING---1957, IN NORWEGIAN
ROBYN, LOUISE
    HOW TO TEACH PIANO TO THE CHILD BEGINNER..A TEXT BOOK FOR TEACHERS
ROEDER, CARL M.
    LIBERATION AND DELIBERATION IN PIANO TECHNIC
ROSENTHAL, MORIZ
    OLD AND THE NEW SCHOOL OF PIANO PLAYING, THE --TYPEWRITTEN COPY
ROSS, CHARLES
    RIGHT FOOT FORWARD..A FIRST BOOK ON PEDALLING FOR ADULT STUDENTS
ROWLEY, ALEC
    DO'S AND DONT'S FOR MUSICIANS..A HANDBOOK FOR TEACHERS AND
RUBINSTEIN, BERYL
    OUTLINE OF PIANO PEDAGOGY--REV. ED.---1929
SCHAAF, EDWARD O.
    MUSICAL INDIVIDUALITY OF THE PLAYER PIANO, THE ---EXCERPTS..'THE
SCHELLING, ERNEST *
    OXFORD PIANO COURSE, TEACHER'S SECOND MANUAL
SCHERER, HERBERT
    PIANO PRACTICING
SCHMITT, HANS
    PEDALS OF THE PIANOFORTE, THE --FOUR LECTURES
SCHMITZ, ELIE ROBERT
    CAPTURE OF INSPIRATION, THE
SCHMITZ, ELIE ROBERT
    PIANO WORKS OF CLAUDE DEBUSSY, THE
SCHNABEL, KARL ULRICH
    MODERN TECHNIQUE OF THE PEDAL
SMELTZER, JEANNIE R.--COMPILER
    OUTLINES AND GRADES FOR THE USE OF PIANO TEACHERS
SMITH, THOMAS
    LITTLE DIFFICULTIES WHICH OCCUR IN PIANOFORTE PLAYING
SQUIRE, RUSSEL N. *
    CLASS PIANO FOR ADULT BEGINNERS--2ND. ED.---1964
STARKEY, EVELYN
    PIANO CLASS WORKBOOK FOR FIRST YEAR STUDENTS
STEWART, REID
    HOW TO PASS MUSIC EXAMINATIONS--PIANO--A GUIDE FOR TEACHERS AND
SUMMY-BIRCHARD COMPANY
    HANDBOOK FOR PIANO TEACHERS..COLLECTED ARTICLES ON SUBJECTS
TANKARD, GEOFFREY
    FOUNDATIONS OF PIANOFORTE TECHNIQUE
TANKARD, GEOFFREY
    SPECIMEN ANSWERS TO THE QUESTIONS IN PIANOFORTE DIPLOMAS
TAYLOR, FRANKLIN
    PRIMER OF PIANOFORTE PLAYING
TAYLOR, FRANKLIN
    TECHNIQUE AND EXPRESSION IN PIANOFORTE PLAYING
TURECK, ROSALYN
    INTRODUCTION TO THE PERFORMANCE OF BACH, AN--3 VOLS.
UNSCHULD, MARIE VON
    PIANIST'S HAND, THE ..A SYSTEMATIC METHOD...ACCORDING TO THE

VANTYN, SIDNEY
    MODERN PIANOFORTE TECHNIQUE
VENABLE, MARY
    INTERPRETATION OF PIANO MUSIC, THE
VENINO, ALBERT F.
    PEDAL METHOD FOR THE PIANO, A
VERNAZZA, MARCELLE
    BASIC MATERIALS FOR THE PIANO STUDENT
VIRGIL, ANTHA MINERVA
    PIANO PEDALS, THE
WELLS, HOWARD
    EARS, BRAIN AND FINGERS..A TEXT BOOK FOR PIANO TEACHERS AND PUPILS
WHITEMORE, CUTHBERT
    COMMONSENSE IN PIANOFORTE PLAYING
WHITESIDE, ABBY
    INDISPENSABLES OF PIANO PLAYING--2ND. ED.---1955
WIER, ALBERT
    PIANO, THE ..ITS HISTORY, MAKERS, PLAYERS AND MUSIC
WILSON, MORRIS E.
    HOW TO PLAY BY EAR
WINN, CYRIL
    DO YOU ACCOMPANY
WOLFRAM, VICTOR
    SOSTENUTO PEDAL, THE
WOODHOUSE, GEORGE
    REALISTIC APPROACH TO PIANO PLAYING, A
WRIGHT, WILLIAM C.
    GOLDEN MONITOR, FOR THE PIANOFORTE AND CABINET ORGAN, DESIGNED AS

Demeanor and Poise

ANDERSON, WILLIAM P.
    MUSIC AS A CAREER
BRECKENRIDGE, WILLIAM KILGORE
    HINTS FOR PIANO NORMAL STUDIES
BUCKLEY, OLIVIA DUSSEK
    MUSICAL TRUTHS..OR, AN ANALYSIS OF MUSIC AND AN ESSAY ON THE PAST
CHASE, MARY WOOD
    NATURAL LAWS IN PIANO TECHNIC
CHING, JAMES
    PERFORMER AND AUDIENCE..AN INVESTIGATION INTO THE PSYCHOLOGICAL
CHING, JAMES
    STUDIES FOR BASIC PIANO TECHNIQUE..WRITTEN AND SELECTED WITH
COOKE, JAMES FRANCIS
    GREAT PIANISTS ON PIANO PLAYING..STUDY TALKS WITH FOREMOST
COPP, LAURA R.
    SOME SECRETS OF SUCCESS IN PLAYING IN PUBLIC
COUPERIN, FRANCOIS
    ART DE TOUCHER LE CLAVECIN, L' ---IN FRENCH, GERMAN AND ENGLISH
D'ABREU, GERALD
    PLAYING THE PIANO WITH CONFIDENCE---1964
DILLER, ANGELA
    SPLENDOR OF MUSIC, THE
DUMM, ROBERT W.
    IN BLACK AND WHITE
EISENBERG, JACOB
    ARTISTIC PIANIST, THE ..NATURAL TECHNICS IN PIANO MASTERY..FROM
FIELDEN, THOMAS
    MARKS AND REMARKS..MUSICAL EXAMINATIONS AND THEIR PROBLEMS
FOLDES, ANDOR
    KEYS TO THE KEYBOARD, A BOOK FOR PIANISTS
GARROWAY, WILL
    PIANISM
GEARY, ELEANOR MARGARET
    MUSICAL EDUCATION, WITH PRACTICAL OBSERVATIONS ON THE ART OF
GORDON, STEPHEN T.
    GORDON'S NEW SCHOOL FOR THE PIANO-FORTE
GRAY, CECIL
    CONTINGENCIES AND OTHER ESSAYS---LISZT
HAMBOURG, MARK
    HOW TO PLAY THE PIANO--NEW AND ENLARGED EDITION OF 'HOW TO BECOME
HAMBOURG, MARK
    HOW TO PREPARE FOR PLAYING IN CONCERT
HAMILTON, CLARENCE G.
    PIANO TEACHING..ITS PRINCIPLES AND PROBLEMS
HAMILTON, CLARENCE G.
    WHAT EVERY PIANO PUPIL SHOULD KNOW
HARRISON, SIDNEY
    PIANO TECHNIQUE
HARRISON, SIDNEY
    TEACHER NEVER TOLD ME--TIPS FOR STUDENTS
KOCHEVITSKY, GEORGE
    ART OF PIANO PLAYING, THE ..A SCIENTIFIC APPROACH
LAST, JOAN
    INTERPRETATION FOR THE PIANO STUDENT
LOGIER, JOHANN BERNHARD
    SYLLABUS OF THE SECOND EXAMINATION OF MR. LOGIER'S PUPILS, ON HIS
MAIER, GUY
    PIANO TEACHER'S COMPANION, THE
MATTHAY, TOBIAS A.
    FIRST PRINCIPLES OF PIANOFORTE PLAYING--EXTRACT FROM 'THE ACT OF
MILLER, ALLAN
    BEGINNING PIANO FOR ADULTS
NEWMAN, WILLIAM S.
    PIANIST'S PROBLEMS, THE ..A MODERN APPROACH TO EFFICIENT PRACTICE
NEWTON, IVOR
    AT THE PIANO--IVOR NEWTON..THE WORLD OF AN ACCOMPANIST
ROWLEY, ALEC
    DO'S AND DONT'S FOR MUSICIANS..A HANDBOOK FOR TEACHERS AND
SCHMITZ, ELIE ROBERT
    CAPTURE OF INSPIRATION, THE
SLENCZYNSKA, RUTH *
    MUSIC AT YOUR FINGERTIPS
SOREL, CLAUDETTE
    MIND YOUR MUSICAL MANNERS, OFF AND ON STAGE..A HANDBOOK OF STAGE
SUMMY-BIRCHARD COMPANY
    HANDBOOK FOR PIANO TEACHERS..COLLECTED ARTICLES ON SUBJECTS
TANKARD, GEOFFREY
    PIANOFORTE DIPLOMAS
TAYLER, E. DOUGLAS
    MIND-POWER IN MUSIC FOR STUDENTS, TEACHERS AND PERFORMERS
TAYLER, E. DOUGLAS
    SECRET OF SUCCESSFUL PRACTICE, THE
WESTERBY, HERBERT
    LISZT, COMPOSER, AND HIS PIANO WORKS..DESCRIPTIVE GUIDE AND
WESTRUP, SIR JACK ALLAN
    MUSICAL INTERPRETATION---THIS BOOK ACCOMPANIED A SERIES OF B.B.C.
WHITESIDE, ABBY
    MASTERING THE CHOPIN ETUDES AND OTHER ESSAYS
WOODHOUSE, GEORGE
    FROM KEYBOARD TO MUSIC
WOODHOUSE, GEORGE
    REALISTIC APPROACH TO PIANO PLAYING, A

Ensemble Playing

General

BACON, ERNST
    NOTES ON THE PIANO
BRITISH BROADCASTING CORPORATION--CENTRAL MUSIC LIBRARY
    CHAMBER MUSIC CATALOGUE
BROUGHTON, JULIA
    SUCCESS IN PIANO TEACHING
BRUXNER, MERVYN
    MASTERING THE PIANO
DENVER--PUBLIC SCHOOLS
    CLASS-PIANO TEACHERS HANDBOOK
FILLMORE, THOMAS H.
    FILLMORE'S LIST OF CAREFULLY SELECTED AND GRADED WORKS FOR THE
HEIDELBERGER, PAULINE
    MASTER METHOD..PIANO NORMAL AND TEACHER'S MANUAL
LEAVEY, LILIAN
    JUNIOR SCHOOL PIANIST, THE --ADDRESSED TO THE NEW MUSIC TEACHER
MACLEAN, CHARLES D.
    PRINCIPLES OF PIANOFORTE PRACTICE, THE
MUSIC EDUCATION LEAGUE
    COMPREHENSIVE GUIDE FOR PIANO TEACHERS AND PIANO AUDITION SYLLABUS
MUSIC PROJECT--NEW YORK CITY
    TEACHER'S GUIDE..A CREATIVE APPROACH TO PIANO CLASS TEACHING, BY
NEW ENGLAND CONSERVATORY
    TEACHERS' GRADED LIST FOR THE PIANOFORTE
PALMER, KING
    TEACH YOURSELF TO PLAY THE PIANO
PEABODY INSTITUTE, BALTIMORE
    GRADED LIST OF SOME USEFUL WORKS FOR PIANO STUDY---REVISED BY
SCHOTT, HOWARD
    PLAYING THE HARPSICHORD
SQUIRE, RUSSEL N. *
    CLASS PIANO FOR ADULT BEGINNERS--2ND. ED.---1964
WALKER, ALAN--EDITOR
    ROBERT SCHUMANN..THE MAN AND HIS MUSIC---SYMPOSIUM--13 AUTHORS

Miscellaneous

ADLER, KURT
    ART OF ACCOMPANYING AND COACHING, THE ---1965
MATHIS, WILLIAM STEPHAN
    PIANIST AND CHURCH MUSIC, THE
MUSIC EDUCATION LEAGUE
    COMPREHENSIVE GUIDE FOR PIANO TEACHERS AND PIANO AUDITION SYLLABUS
ORLIK, JULES
    CREATIVE APPROACH TO PIANO CLASS TEACHING, A ---REPRODUCED FROM

Chamber Music Playing

AEOLIAN COMPANY, THE
    DUO-ART BOOK OF MUSIC, THE
DONINGTON, ROBERT
    INSTRUMENTS OF MUSIC, THE --3RD. REV. ED.---1949
GEBHARD, HEINRICH
    ART OF PEDALLING, THE
LINDO, ALGERNON H.
    ART OF ACCOMPANYING, THE
MURDOCH, WILLIAM
    BRAHMS..WITH AN ANALYTICAL STUDY OF THE COMPLETE PIANOFORTE WORKS
NEWMAN, WILLIAM S.
    SONATA IN THE BAROQUE ERA, THE --A HISTORY OF THE SONATA IDEA,
NEWMAN, WILLIAM S.
    SONATA IN THE CLASSIC ERA, THE --A HISTORY OF THE SONATA IDEA,
SCHAUFFLER, ROBERT HAVEN
    FLORESTAN..THE LIFE AND WORK OF ROBERT SCHUMANN---1945
WIER, ALBERT
    PIANO, THE ..ITS HISTORY, MAKERS, PLAYERS AND MUSIC
YATES, PETER
    AMATEUR AT THE KEYBOARD, AN

Duet Playing

BASTIEN, JAMES W. *
    BEGINNING PIANO FOR ADULTS
BENNER, LORA
    BENNER GOLD BOOK, THE ..PIANO MATERIAL AND TEACHING METHODS--3RD.
CURWEN, ANNIE JESSY
    CHILD PIANIST, THE
DALE, KATHLEEN
    NINETEENTH CENTURY PIANO MUSIC, A HANDBOOK FOR PIANISTS
FILLMORE, THOMAS H.
    FILLMORE'S LIST OF CAREFULLY SELECTED AND GRADED WORKS FOR THE
LAMAR, RICHARD
    COLLEGE PIANO PEDAGOGY
MUSIC EDUCATION LEAGUE
    COMPREHENSIVE GUIDE FOR PIANO TEACHERS AND PIANO AUDITION SYLLABUS
NEWMAN, WILLIAM S.
    SONATA IN THE BAROQUE ERA, THE --A HISTORY OF THE SONATA IDEA,
NEWMAN, WILLIAM S.
    SONATA IN THE CLASSIC ERA, THE --A HISTORY OF THE SONATA IDEA,
REZITS, JOSEPH
    TEACHER'S GUIDE TO THE NEW SCRIBNER MUSIC LIBRARY
ROWLEY, ALEC
    FOUR HANDS--ONE PIANO..A LIST OF WORKS FOR DUET PLAYERS--A GUIDE
SCHAUFFLER, ROBERT HAVEN
    FLORESTAN..THE LIFE AND WORK OF ROBERT SCHUMANN---1945
SQUIRE, RUSSEL N. *
    CLASS PIANO FOR ADULT BEGINNERS--2ND. ED.---1964
TERWILLIGER, GORDON B.
    PIANO TEACHERS PROFESSIONAL HANDBOOK
WOLLENHAUPT, HEINRICH
    METHOD FOR THE PIANOFORTE AND METHODICAL GUIDE FOR THE PIANO FORTE
YATES, PETER
    AMATEUR AT THE KEYBOARD, AN

Two Piano Playing

BENNER, LORA
    BENNER GOLD BOOK, THE ..PIANO MATERIAL AND TEACHING METHODS--3RD.
LAMAR, RICHARD
    COLLEGE PIANO PEDAGOGY
LUBIN, ERNEST
    PIANO DUET, THE ...A GUIDE FOR PIANISTS
MAIER, GUY
    PIANO TEACHER'S COMPANION, THE
MOLDENHAUER, HANS
    DUO-PIANISM---PUBLISHED DISSERTATION
MUSIC EDUCATION LEAGUE
    COMPREHENSIVE GUIDE FOR PIANO TEACHERS AND PIANO AUDITION SYLLABUS
NEAL, HARRY LEE
    WAVE AS YOU PASS

NEWMAN, WILLIAM S.
    SONATA IN THE CLASSIC ERA, THE --A HISTORY OF THE SONATA IDEA,
SCHAUFFLER, ROBERT HAVEN
    FLORESTAN..THE LIFE AND WORK OF ROBERT SCHUMANN---1945
TERWILLIGER, GORDON B.
    PIANO TEACHERS PROFESSIONAL HANDBOOK
WIER, ALBERT
    PIANO, THE ..ITS HISTORY, MAKERS, PLAYERS AND MUSIC
WOLLENHAUPT, HEINRICH
    METHOD FOR THE PIANOFORTE AND METHODICAL GUIDE FOR THE PIANO FORTE

Accompanying and Coaching

ADLER, KURT
    ART OF ACCOMPANYING AND COACHING, THE ---1965
AEOLIAN COMPANY, THE
    DUO-ART BOOK OF MUSIC, THE
ALBRECHTSBERGER, JOHANN GEORG
    PRINCIPLES OF ACCOMPANIMENT OR THOROUGH BASS
ARNOLD, FRANCK THOMAS
    ART OF ACCOMPANIMENT FROM A THOROUGH-BASS, AS PRACTICED IN THE
BACH, CARL PHILIPP EMANUEL
    ESSAY ON THE TRUE ART OF PLAYING KEYBOARD INSTRUMENTS---TWO PTS.,
BECKER, JULIUS
    CONCISE TREATISE ON HARMONY, ACCOMPANIMENT, AND COMPOSITION, FOR
BEMETZRIEDER, ANTON
    ABSTRACT OF A NEW METHOD OF TEACHING THE PRINCIPLES OF MUSIC,
BEMETZRIEDER, ANTON
    ACCOUNT OF A NEW WAY OF CONSIDERING MUSICK, AND TEACHING
BEMETZRIEDER, ANTON
    COMPENDIUM OF A NEW METHOD OF MUSIC...WITH THE AUTHOR'S PRINCIPLES
BOS, COENRAAD V.
    WELL-TEMPERED ACCOMPANIST, THE
BRIDGER, JOHN HENRY
    HOW TO HARMONIZE MELODIES, WITH HINTS ON WRITING FOR STRINGS AND
BUELOW, GEORGE J.
    THOROUGH-BASS ACCOMPANIMENT ACCORDING TO JOHANN DAVID HEINICHEN
BURROWS, RAYMOND
    ELEMENTARY PIANO INSTRUCTION IN COLLEGE
CASTELLINI, JOHN EDWARD
    RUDIMENTS OF MUSIC..A NEW APPROACH WITH APPLICATION TO THE
CAVALLARO, CARMEN
    KEYBOARD HARMONY..A NEW MODERN PIANO METHOD---POPULAR IDIOM
CHAPPLE, STANLEY
    CLASS WAY TO THE KEYBOARD, THE
CHEYETTE, IRVING
    BASIC PIANO FOR THE MUSIC EDUCATOR AND CLASSROOM TEACHER
CRANMER, PHILIP
    TECHNIQUE OF ACCOMPANIMENT, THE --THE STUDENT'S MUSIC LIBRARY
DAVID, ELIZABETH HARBISON
    I PLAYED THEIR ACCOMPANIMENTS
DONINGTON, ROBERT
    INTERPRETATION OF EARLY MUSIC, THE
DONINGTON, ROBERT
    PERFORMER'S GUIDE TO BAROQUE MUSIC, A
EGBERT, MARION S.
    KEYBOARD EXPERIENCE IN THE CLASSROOM MUSIC PROGRAM..HANDBOOK FOR
ELLINGHAM, HARRY
    HOW TO USE A PLAYER-PIANO
ETHIER, JOSEPH A.
    ETHIER'S GREAT NON-SUCH SELF-INSTRUCTOR IN THE ART OF ACCOMPANYING
EVANS, EDWIN
    HOW TO ACCOMPANY AT THE PIANO
EVANS, EVERETT J.
    SELF-TEACHING CHORD BOOK FOR THE PIANO OR ORGAN..SHOWS HOW TO PLAY
FALKENER, ROBERT
    INSTRUCTIONS FOR PLAYING THE HARPSICHORD..WHEREIN IS FULLY
FETIS, FRANCOIS JOSEPH
    HOW TO PLAY FROM SCORE...ON THE ORGAN OR PIANOFORTE
FORD, DONALD
    SINGING CLASS PIANIST AND ON PIANOFORTE ACCOMPANYING IN GENERAL,
GARRATT, PERCIVAL
    ART OF PIANOFORTE PLAYING, THE
GARROWAY, WILL
    PIANISM
GEMINIANI, FRANCESCO
    ART OF ACCOMPANIMENT, OR A NEW AND WELL DIGESTED METHOD TO LEARN
GLEN, ANNIE
    HOW TO ACCOMPANY..A GUIDE TO THE ARTISTIC ACCOMPANIMENT OF ANY
GOODRICH, ALFRED JOHN
    THEORY OF INTERPRETATION, APPLIED TO ARTISTIC MUSICAL PERFORMANCE
HARKNESS, ROBERT
    GOSPEL SONG ACCOMPANIMENT..THE ROBERT HARKNESS METHOD FOR PIANO
HARKNESS, ROBERT
    GOSPEL SONG PIANO ACCOMPANIMENT..THE ROBERT HARKNESS
HARKNESS, ROBERT
    HARKNESS PIANO METHOD OF EVANGELISTIC HYMN PLAYING, THE ..A
HARKNESS, ROBERT
    HOME STUDY CORRESPONDENCE COURSE IN EVANGELISTIC HYMN PLAYING, FOR
HARRISON, SIDNEY
    YOUNG PERSON'S GUIDE TO PLAYING THE PIANO, THE
HAVILL, LORINA
    YOU CAN SIGHT READ..THE PLEASURES OF PIANO SIGHT READING THROUGH
HECK, JOHANN CASPAR
    COMPLETE SYSTEM OF HARMONY..OR A REGULAR AND EASY METHOD TO ATTAIN
HERBERT, JOHN BUNYAN
    HOW TO WRITE AN ACCOMPANIMENT..HELPS AND HINTS FOR STUDENTS AND
HICKIN, WELTON
    PIANOFORTE ACCOMPANIMENT--'NOVELLO'S MUSIC PRIMERS', NO. 99
HOME, ETHEL
    IMPROVISING..A SIMPLE METHOD OF TEACHING THE SUBJECT TO CHILDREN
HULL, ARTHUR EAGLEFIELD
    THREE HUNDRED QUESTIONS ON PIANOFORTE TEACHING IN 30 GRADUATED
IRWIN, WILLIAM
    RHYTHM ACCOMPANIMENT MAGIC, FOR THE POPULAR PIANIST
JOUSSE, JOHN
    GUIDA ARMONICA, IN WHICH...CHORDS, ARE CLEARLY EXPLAINED AND
KOLANDER, MAX
    KOLANDER'S ACCOMPANIMENT INSTRUCTOR FOR THE PIANO OR ORGAN
LANG, EDITH *
    MUSICAL ACCOMPANIMENT OF MOVING PICTURES..A PRACTICAL MANUAL FOR
LEAVEY, LILIAN
    JUNIOR SCHOOL PIANIST, THE --ADDRESSED TO THE NEW MUSIC TEACHER
LE MASSENA, CLARENCE E.
    SONGS OF SCHUBERT, A GUIDE FOR SINGERS, TEACHERS AND ACCOMPANISTS,
LINDO, ALGERNON H.
    ART OF ACCOMPANYING, THE
MARSDEN AND COMPANY
    HOW TO EXTEMPORIZE PIANO ACCOMPANIMENTS...RAPID AND SIMPLE METHOD
MATHIS, WILLIAM STEPHAN
    PIANIST AND CHURCH MUSIC, THE
MEHER, DONOVAN
    HOW TO VAMP AT SIGHT..THE EASIEST AND CLEAREST METHOD OF
MERGES, P.
    PRACTICAL RULES FOR PIANOFORTE PLAYING..TEXT BOOK FOR TEACHERS AND
MIDKIFF, HELEN T.
    CHURCH PIANIST, THE

MOORE, GERALD
    AM I TOO LOUD..MEMOIRS OF AN ACCOMPANIST
MOORE, GERALD
    SINGER AND ACCOMPANIST..THE PERFORMANCE OF FIFTY SONGS
MOORE, GERALD
    UNASHAMED ACCOMPANIST, THE
NEWMAN, WILLIAM S.
    SONATA IN THE BAROQUE ERA, THE --A HISTORY OF THE SONATA IDEA,
NEWMAN, WILLIAM S.
    SONATA IN THE CLASSIC ERA, THE --A HISTORY OF THE SONATA IDEA,
NEWTON, ERNEST
    ELEMENTARY STUDIES IN TRANSPOSITION--BKS. 1 AND 2
NEWTON, IVOR
    AT THE PIANO--IVOR NEWTON..THE WORLD OF AN ACCOMPANIST
PATTERSON, ANNIE WILSON
    PROFESSION OF MUSIC AND HOW TO PREPARE FOR IT, THE
PEARCE, CHARLES WILLIAM
    ART OF THE PIANO TEACHER, THE
PETERSON, FRANKLIN
    THEORETIC COMPANION TO PRACTICE--PART I OF THE PIANIST'S HANDBOOK
RAPEE, ERNO--ARRANGER
    ERNO RAPEE'S ENCYCLOPEDIA OF MUSIC FOR PICTURES---LISTED BOTH BY
RAPEE, ERNO--ARRANGER
    MOTION PICTURE MOODS FOR PIANISTS AND ORGANISTS
REES-DAVIES, IVAN
    TRANSPOSITION AT THE KEYBOARD
REZITS, JOSEPH
    SOURCE MATERIALS FOR PIANO TECHNIQUES
REZITS, JOSEPH
    TEACHER'S GUIDE TO THE NEW SCRIBNER MUSIC LIBRARY
ROOT, CATHERINE ADAMS *
    LISTEN, SING AND PLAY..CLASS LESSONS FOR PIANO AND VOICE
ROWBOTHAM, JOHN F.
    HOW TO VAMP..A PRACTICAL GUIDE TO THE ACCOMPANIMENT OF SONGS BY
SCHULER, GEORGE S.
    ACCOMPANIST'S MANUAL, THE
SCHULER, GEORGE S.
    EVANGELISTIC PIANO PLAYING
SHEPARD, ROBERT
    HARMONIZING..HOW TO PLAY SIMPLE ACCOMPANIMENTS TO A MELODY AT THE
SPENCER, BERNARD
    POPULAR PIANO...A CORRESPONDENCE COURSE OF THE EASTERN SCHOOLS OF
SQUIRE, RUSSEL N. *
    CLASS PIANO FOR ADULT BEGINNERS--2ND. ED.---1964
STEWART, REID
    HOW TO PASS MUSIC EXAMINATIONS--PIANO--A GUIDE FOR TEACHERS AND
STORMEN, WIN
    POPULAR ACCOMPANYING
STORMEN, WIN
    YOUR GUIDE TO PLAYING AND WRITING POPULAR MUSIC--REV. ED.
TERWILLIGER, GORDON B.
    PIANO TEACHERS PROFESSIONAL HANDBOOK
THACKRAY, RUPERT M.
    PLAYING FOR DANCE..THE PLACE OF THE PIANIST IN THE TEACHING OF
TOBIN, JOSEPH RAYMOND
    HOW TO IMPROVISE PIANO ACCOMPANIMENTS
WAGNER, JOHN J.
    NUMERICAL METHOD OF PIANO ACCOMPANIMENTS, A --WITH CHARTS
WARRINER, JOHN
    TRANSPOSITION, KEYBOARD AND ORCHESTRAL--2 PTS., 1893-1908
WEBBE, SAMUEL
    HARMONY EPITOMIZED, BEING A SHORT EXPLANATION OF FIGURED BASSES,
WELTE-MIGNON CORPORATION
    LIBRARY OF DELUXE WELTE-MIGNON MUSIC RECORDS FOR REPRODUCING
WELTE-MIGNON CORPORATION
    LIBRARY OF WELTE-MIGNON MUSIC RECORDS
WIER, ALBERT
    PIANO, THE ..ITS HISTORY, MAKERS, PLAYERS AND MUSIC
WILLIAMS, JOHN M.
    WHAT TO TEACH AT THE VERY FIRST LESSON
WILSON, MORRIS E.
    HOW TO PLAY BY EAR
WINN, CYRIL
    DO YOU ACCOMPANY
WOLFF, ERNST VICTOR
    WITH REASON AND RHYME
WOLLNER, GERTRUDE PRICE
    IMPROVISATION IN MUSIC..WAYS TOWARDS CAPTURING MUSICAL IDEAS AND
WOODHOUSE, GEORGE
    NEW PATH FOR PIANISTS, A ..THE MUTANO--MUTE PIANO--SYSTEM, ETC.
YATES, PETER
    AMATEUR AT THE KEYBOARD, AN

Concerto Performing

CULSHAW, JOHN
    SERGEI RACHMANINOFF..THE MAN AND HIS MUSIC
GRAY, CECIL
    CONTINGENCIES AND OTHER ESSAYS---LISZT
MURDOCH, WILLIAM
    BRAHMS..WITH AN ANALYTICAL STUDY OF THE COMPLETE PIANOFORTE WORKS
SEARLE, HUMPHREY
    MUSIC OF LISZT, THE --2ND. REV. ED.---1954
WALKER, ALAN--EDITOR
    ROBERT SCHUMANN..THE MAN AND HIS MUSIC---SYMPOSIUM--13 AUTHORS
WESTERBY, HERBERT
    LISZT, COMPOSER, AND HIS PIANO WORKS..DESCRIPTIVE GUIDE AND
WOODHOUSE, GEORGE
    NEW PATH FOR PIANISTS, A ..THE MUTANO--MUTE PIANO--SYSTEM, ETC.

General Interest

Miscellaneous

AEOLIAN COMPANY, THE
    SPECIAL SURVEY CONDUCTED--IN 1889--FOR LYON AND HEALY, INC.,
BRECKENRIDGE, WILLIAM KILGORE
    HINTS FOR PIANO NORMAL STUDIES
HINSON, MAURICE
    KEYBOARD BIBLIOGRAPHY--'NEW RESOURCES' SERIES
LOESSER, ARTHUR
    MEN, WOMEN AND PIANOS..A SOCIAL HISTORY
MATHIS, WILLIAM STEPHAN
    PIANIST AND CHURCH MUSIC, THE
NATIONAL BUREAU FOR THE ADVANCEMENT OF MUSIC
    GIVING OF HIGH SCHOOL CREDITS FOR PRIVATE MUSIC STUDY, THE ..A
SCHNABEL, ARTUR
    MUSIC AND THE LINE OF MOST RESISTANCE---1942
SCHNABEL, ARTUR
    MY LIFE AND MUSIC
VIRGIL, ALMON K.
    EDUCATION IN MUSIC..LESSONS TO TEACHERS IN THE INSTRUCTION OF

Appreciation

AEOLIAN COMPANY, THE
SPECIAL SURVEY CONDUCTED--IN 1889--FOR LYON AND HEALY, INC.,
AHRENS, CORA B. *
FOR ALL PIANO TEACHERS
AMPICO CORPORATION
AMPICO REPRODUCING PIANO..A SUPPLEMENT TO 'PIANO MUSIC, ITS
BACON, ERNST
NOTES ON THE PIANO
BUCK, PERCY
PSYCHOLOGY FOR MUSICIANS
BURROWS, RAYMOND
ELEMENTARY PIANO INSTRUCTION IN COLLEGE
EISENBERG, JACOB
ARTISTIC PIANIST, THE ..NATURAL TECHNICS IN PIANO MASTERY..FROM
EISENBERG, JACOB
WEIGHT AND RELAXATION METHOD FOR THE PIANOFORTE
FREDRICH, FRANK
KEY TO PIANO PLEASURE
HARRISON, SIDNEY
TEACHER NEVER TOLD ME--TIPS FOR STUDENTS
LANDOWSKI, ALICE-WANDA
DOMENICO SCARLATTI--NOTES TO ACCOMPANY GRAMOPHONE RECORDINGS
LOESSER, ARTHUR
MEN, WOMEN AND PIANOS..A SOCIAL HISTORY.
LOWE, CLAUDE EDGERTON
SUGGESTIONS FOR THE APPRECIATION AND INTERPRETATION OF PIANOFORTE
LOWE, CLAUDE EDGERTON
VIVA VOCE..250 QUESTIONS AND ANSWERS FOR PIANOFORTE DIPLOMA
MANHIRE, WILSON
MODEL ANSWERS TO QUESTIONS ON 'TOUCH' FOR CANDIDATES PREPARING FOR
MCARTHUR, ALEXANDER
PIANOFORTE STUDY..HINTS ON PIANO PLAYING
MUSIC EDUCATORS NATIONAL CONFERENCE
MUSIC BEGINS WITH THE PIANO
NATIONAL BUREAU FOR THE ADVANCEMENT OF MUSIC
GIVING OF HIGH SCHOOL CREDITS FOR PRIVATE MUSIC STUDY, THE ..A
NEWMAN, ELIZABETH
HOW TO TEACH MUSIC TO BEGINNERS
NIMITZ, DANIEL
KEYBOARD MASTERS..STUDY GUIDE
REZITS, JOSEPH
TEACHER'S GUIDE TO THE NEW SCRIBNER MUSIC LIBRARY
ROWLEY, ALEC
DO'S AND DONT'S FOR MUSICIANS..A HANDBOOK FOR TEACHERS AND
ROWLEY, ALEC
PRACTICAL MUSICIANSHIP, A HANDBOOK FOR TEACHERS AND STUDENTS
SCHELLING, ERNEST *
OXFORD PIANO COURSE, TEACHER'S FIRST MANUAL
SCHELLING, ERNEST *
OXFORD PIANO COURSE, TEACHER'S SECOND MANUAL
SEYMOUR, HARRIET AYER
PHILOSOPHY OF MUSIC, THE ..WHAT MUSIC CAN DO FOR YOU
STEVENS, WILLIAM S.
TREATISE ON PIANO-FORTE, CONTAINING THE PRINCIPLES OF FINE PLAYING
TAPPER, THOMAS
EDUCATION OF THE MUSIC TEACHER, THE
WHITE, WILLIAM BRAID
PLAYER-PIANIST, THE ..A GUIDE TO THE APPRECIATION AND
WILSON, MORRIS E.
HOW TO HELP YOUR CHILD WITH MUSIC--2ND. ED.---1951

Audiences

AEOLIAN COMPANY, THE
SPECIAL SURVEY CONDUCTED--IN 1889--FOR LYON AND HEALY, INC.,
CHING, JAMES
PERFORMER AND AUDIENCE..AN INVESTIGATION INTO THE PSYCHOLOGICAL
COOKE, JAMES FRANCIS
GREAT PIANISTS ON PIANO PLAYING..STUDY TALKS WITH FOREMOST
D'ABREU, GERALD
PLAYING THE PIANO WITH CONFIDENCE----1964
DAHL, ANTON
SOUL OF GENIUS, THE ..ITS MUSICAL DEVELOPMENT AND HOW THE WORLD AT
HARRISON, SIDNEY
TEACHER NEVER TOLD ME--TIPS FOR STUDENTS
LOESSER, ARTHUR
MEN, WOMEN AND PIANOS..A SOCIAL HISTORY
MOORE, GERALD
AM I TOO LOUD..MEMOIRS OF AN ACCOMPANIST
SORABJI, KAIKHOSRU
AROUND MUSIC---PACHMAN, CHOPIN AND LISZT
STERNBERG, CONSTANTIN I. VON
ETHICS AND ESTHETICS OF PIANO PLAYING
TAYLER, E. DOUGLAS
MIND-POWER IN MUSIC FOR STUDENTS, TEACHERS AND PERFORMERS
WOLFF, ERNST VICTOR
WITH REASON AND RHYME

Recording Procedures

AEOLIAN COMPANY, THE
LIBRARY OF DUO-ART MUSIC ROLLS
AEOLIAN COMPANY, THE
MUSIC FOR THE AEOLIAN GRAND
ASSOCIATION FOR RECORDED SOUND COLLECTIONS
PRELIMINARY DIRECTORY OF SOUND RECORDING COLLECTIONS IN THE UNITED
BARTELS, LEO F. *
PERFORATING OF MUSIC ROLLS WITH THE LEABARJAN PERFORATOR, THE
BRIGGS, GILBERT A.
MUSICAL INSTRUMENTS AND AUDIO
BRIGGS, GILBERT A.
PIANOS, PIANISTS AND SONICS
CHASINS, ABRAM
SPEAKING OF PIANISTS
KAISER, JOACHIM
GREAT PIANISTS OF OUR TIME
MATTHEWS, DENIS
IN PURSUIT OF MUSIC
MOORE, GERALD
AM I TOO LOUD..MEMOIRS OF AN ACCOMPANIST
SPAETH, SIGMUND *
AMPICO IN MUSIC STUDY, THE

Business Aspects

AEOLIAN COMPANY, THE
CATALOG OF THE AEOLIAN
AEOLIAN COMPANY, THE
CONFIDENTIAL MANUAL FOR SALESMEN OF THE DUO-ART REPRODUCING
AEOLIAN COMPANY, THE
SPECIAL SURVEY CONDUCTED--IN 1889--FOR LYON AND HEALY, INC.,
AMERICAN SCHOOL OF PIANO TUNING
TRAINING AS A PIANO TECHNICIAN--8 VOLS. IN 1

AMERICAN STEEL AND WIRE COMPANY
NERVES OF STEEL..THE STORY OF AMERICAN PIANO WIRE AND ITS
AMPICO CORPORATION
SUPREMACY OF AMPICO MUSIC..UNIT TWO OF A COURSE IN AMPICO
ANDERSON-MULDER COMPANY
DEALER'S HANDBOOK OF PIANOS AND THEIR MAKERS
ANDERSON, WILLIAM P.
MUSIC AS A CAREER
ANTCLIFFE, HERBERT
SUCCESSFUL MUSIC TEACHER, THE ..WORDS OF ADVICE
ANTRIM, DORON K.
TEACHING MUSIC AND MAKING IT PAY
BAMBERGER, LOUIS
MEMORIES OF SIXTY YEARS IN THE TIMBER AND PIANOFORTE TRADES
BASTIEN, JAMES W.
HOW TO TEACH PIANO SUCCESSFULLY
BENDER, GEORGE CHARLES
BUSINESS MANUAL FOR PIANO TEACHERS
BENNER, LORA
BENNER BLUE BOOK, THE ..PRACTICAL MANUAL OF PIANO TEACHING--4TH.
BOWERS, Q. DAVID
ENCYCLOPEDIA OF AUTOMATIC MUSICAL INSTRUMENTS---INCLUDES A
BROUGHTON, JULIA
SUCCESS IN PIANO TEACHING
CARRE, JOHN
PSYCHOLOGY OF PIANO TEACHING, THE ..A TEXTBOOK FOR TEACHERS,
CHASINS, ABRAM
SPEAKING OF PIANISTS
CHICKERING AND SONS
COMMEMORATION OF THE FOUNDING OF THE HOUSE OF CHICKERING AND SONS,
CHICKERING AND SONS
HISTORICAL MUSICAL EXHIBITION..CATALOGUE OF THE EXHIBITION,
FINNEGAN, BILL
PIANO FACTS
GEPPERT, WILLIAM
OFFICIAL GUIDE TO PIANO QUALITY, THE ---4TH. ED.
GIDDINGS, THADDEUS P.
GIDDING'S PUBLIC SCHOOL CLASS METHOD FOR THE PIANO
HARRISON, SIDNEY
TEACHER NEVER TOLD ME--TIPS FOR STUDENTS
LOESSER, ARTHUR
MEN, WOMEN AND PIANOS..A SOCIAL HISTORY
MUSIC INDUSTRY COUNCIL
MUSIC EDUCATOR'S BUSINESS HANDBOOK, THE ---PUBLISHED OCCASIONALLY
NATIONAL BUREAU FOR THE ADVANCEMENT OF MUSIC
NATIONAL SURVEY OF PIANO CLASSES IN OPERATION
NATIONAL BUREAU FOR THE ADVANCEMENT OF MUSIC
PIANO CLASSES IN THE SCHOOLS..EDUCATIONAL VALUE OF IMPORTANT NEW
NATIONAL GUILD OF PIANO TEACHERS
GUILD SYLLABUS, THE ..STREAMLINED EDITION
NATIONAL PIANO FOUNDATION
GREATER REWARDS THROUGH CREATIVE PIANO TEACHING
NATIONAL PIANO FOUNDATION
KEYS TO SUCCESSFUL PIANO STUDIO ORGANIZATION
NATIONAL PIANO MANUFACTURERS ASSOCIATION OF AMERICA
STENCILLING OF PIANOS, THE
NATIONAL PIANO MANUFACTURERS ASSOCIATION
CONSUMER INVESTIGATION FOR NATIONAL PIANO MANUFACTURERS
NATIONAL PIANO TRAVELERS ASSOCIATION
PIANO TRAVELERS ASSOCIATION BOOK, THE ..A REFERENCE BOOK
PATTERSON, ANNIE WILSON
PROFESSION OF MUSIC AND HOW TO PREPARE FOR IT, THE
PEARCE, CHARLES WILLIAM
ART OF THE PIANO TEACHER, THE
PENGELLY, J. BRADFORD
PENGELLY BLUE BOOK OF STYLE, THE ...A STUDY OF THE ART OF STYLING
SCHELLING, ERNEST *
OXFORD PIANO COURSE, TEACHER'S FIRST MANUAL
SHINN, DUANE
HOW PEOPLE MAKE MONEY IN MUSIC
SOREL, CLAUDETTE
MIND YOUR MUSICAL MANNERS, OFF AND ON STAGE..A HANDBOOK OF STAGE
STANLEY, JANE
BASIC ROUTINES IN ELEMENTARY PIANO TEACHING THROUGH THE FIRST
STEINWAY, THEODORE E.
PEOPLE AND PIANOS..A CENTURY OF SERVICE TO MUSIC---1853-1953
STEINWAY AND SONS
BOOK OF ART PIANO CASES
STEINWAY AND SONS
ILLUSTRATED CATALOGUE OF--STEINWAY AND SONS...PIANOFORTES
STEINWAY AND SONS
ILLUSTRATED CATALOGUE OF PIANOS
STEINWAY AND SONS
ILLUSTRATED CATALOGUE OF STEINWAY AND SONS' PIANOS
STEINWAY AND SONS
ILLUSTRATED CIRCULAR AND CATALOGUE OF PIANOFORTES--MANUFACTURERS
STEINWAY AND SONS
INIMITABLE TONE..'PRICE LIST OF PIANOS MADE BY STEINWAY AND SONS,
STEINWAY AND SONS
PIANOFORTES
STEINWAY AND SONS
STEINWAY..YESTERDAY, TODAY, TOMORROW
STEINWAY AND SONS
STEINWAY AND SONS' PIANO-FORTE MANUFACTORY AT 'STEINWAY', LONG
STEVENS, FLOYD A.
COMPLETE COURSE IN PROFESSIONAL PIANO TUNING, REPAIR, AND
STRAUCH BROTHERS
MANUFACTURE OF PIANOFORTE ACTION, THE ..ITS RISE AND DEVELOPMENT
SUR, WILLIAM R.--EDITOR
PIANO INSTRUCTION IN THE SCHOOLS
TANKARD, GEOFFREY
PIANOFORTE DIPLOMAS
TERWILLIGER, GORDON B.
PIANO TEACHERS PROFESSIONAL HANDBOOK
TRAVIS, JOHN W.
GUIDE TO RESTRINGING, A
UNITED STATES--NATIONAL RECOVERY ADMINISTRATION
CODE OF FAIR COMPETITION FOR THE PIANO MANUFACTURING INDUSTRY AS
UNITED STATES PATENT OFFICE
COLLECTION OF LETTERS PATENT RELATING TO THE CONSTRUCTION OF
WAGNER, CHARLES A.
HOW TO SELECT A GOOD PIANO
WEBER PIANO COMPANY
WEBER GRAND, SQUARE AND UPRIGHT PIANO-FORTES, THE
WOLFRAM, VICTOR
SOSTENUTO PEDAL, THE

Clubs and Organizations

AEOLIAN COMPANY, THE
SPECIAL SURVEY CONDUCTED--IN 1889--FOR LYON AND HEALY, INC.,
ANDERSON, WILLIAM P.
MUSIC AS A CAREER
BENNER, LORA
BENNER BLUE BOOK, THE ..PRACTICAL MANUAL OF PIANO TEACHING--4TH.
DENVER--PUBLIC SCHOOLS
CLASS-PIANO TEACHERS HANDBOOK

EXECUTIVE COMMITTEE OF CHOPIN YEAR 1949
    CHOPIN YEAR 1949 IN POLAND, THE
FOX, LILLA M.
    INSTRUMENTS OF POPULAR MUSIC..A HISTORY OF MUSICAL
INTERNATIONAL MUSICOLOGICAL CONGRESS..FIRST--1960--WORKS OF FREDERICK
    BOOK OF THE FIRST INTERNATIONAL MUSICOLOGICAL CONGRESS DEVOTED TO
KELLEY, EDGAR STILLMAN
    MUSICAL INSTRUMENTS--3RD. YEAR OF A STUDY COURSE IN MUSIC
MATHEWS, WILLIAM S. B.
    GREAT IN MUSIC, THE ..A SYSTEMATIC COURSE OF STUDY IN THE MUSIC OF
NATIONAL GUILD OF PIANO TEACHERS
    GUILD SYLLABUS, THE ..STREAMLINED EDITION
NATIONAL GUILD OF PIANO TEACHERS
    NATIONAL AUDITIONS FOR AMERICAN PIANO PUPILS
NATIONAL GUILD OF PIANO TEACHERS
    STUDENT'S HANDBOOK FOR ENTRANTS IN THE NATIONAL PIANO PLAYING
NATIONAL PIANO TRAVELERS ASSOCIATION
    PIANO TRAVELERS ASSOCIATION BOOK, THE ..A REFERENCE BOOK
NEW YORK STATE MUSIC TEACHERS' ASSOCIATION
    SYLLABUS FOR PIANO, 1970
SOREL, CLAUDETTE
    MIND YOUR MUSICAL MANNERS, OFF AND ON STAGE..A HANDBOOK OF STAGE
TAPPER, THOMAS
    EDUCATION OF THE MUSIC TEACHER, THE
TERWILLIGER, GORDON B.
    PIANO TEACHERS PROFESSIONAL HANDBOOK
WILLS, VEPA G. *
    PARENT'S GUIDE TO MUSIC LESSONS, A

Music Therapy

EDWARDS, RUTH
    COMPLEAT MUSIC TEACHER FOR TEACHERS, PARENTS AND STUDENTS

Institutional Applications

BASTIEN, JAMES W.
    HOW TO TEACH PIANO SUCCESSFULLY
BURROWS, RAYMOND
    ELEMENTARY PIANO INSTRUCTION IN COLLEGE
BURROWS, RAYMOND
    PIANO IN SCHOOL, A MEMORANDUM FOR SCHOOL ADMINISTRATORS
GIDDINGS, THADDEUS P.
    GIDDING'S PUBLIC SCHOOL CLASS METHOD FOR THE PIANO
MANITOBA--DEPARTMENT OF EDUCATION
    PLAN FOR CREDITING OUTSIDE STUDY IN MUSIC UNDER PRIVATE
MUSIC EDUCATORS NATIONAL CONFERENCE
    HANDBOOK FOR TEACHING PIANO CLASSES
MUSIC EDUCATORS NATIONAL CONFERENCE
    MUSIC BEGINS WITH THE PIANO
NATIONAL BUREAU FOR THE ADVANCEMENT OF MUSIC
    GUIDE FOR CONDUCTING PIANO CLASSES IN THE SCHOOLS, A
NATIONAL BUREAU FOR THE ADVANCEMENT OF MUSIC
    NATIONAL SURVEY OF PIANO CLASSES IN OPERATION
NATIONAL BUREAU FOR THE ADVANCEMENT OF MUSIC
    PIANO CLASSES AND THE PRIVATE TEACHER
NATIONAL BUREAU FOR THE ADVANCEMENT OF MUSIC
    PIANO CLASSES IN THE SCHOOLS..EDUCATIONAL VALUE OF IMPORTANT NEW
NIMITZ, DANIEL
    KEYBOARD MASTERS..STUDY GUIDE
SCHELLING, ERNEST *
    OXFORD PIANO COURSE, TEACHER'S FIRST MANUAL
SUR, WILLIAM R.--EDITOR
    KEYBOARD EXPERIENCE AND PIANO CLASS INSTRUCTION
SUR, WILLIAM R.--EDITOR
    PIANO INSTRUCTION IN THE SCHOOLS
TAPPER, THOMAS
    EDUCATION OF THE MUSIC TEACHER, THE
TERWILLIGER, GORDON B.
    PIANO TEACHERS PROFESSIONAL HANDBOOK

Competitions, Auditions, Examinations and Festivals

AHRENS, CORA B. *
    FOR ALL PIANO TEACHERS
ANDERSON, WILLIAM P.
    MUSIC AS A CAREER
BASTIEN, JAMES W.
    HOW TO TEACH PIANO SUCCESSFULLY
CARRE, JOHN
    PSYCHOLOGY OF PIANO TEACHING, THE ..A TEXTBOOK FOR TEACHERS,
CHING, JAMES
    PLAYING AND TEACHING OF BACH, THE ..A GUIDE FOR TEACHERS, STUDENTS
DENVER--PUBLIC SCHOOLS
    CLASS-PIANO TEACHERS HANDBOOK
FIELDEN, THOMAS
    MARKS AND REMARKS..MUSICAL EXAMINATIONS AND THEIR PROBLEMS
FILLINGHAM, ARTHUR H.
    GUIDE TO THE A.R.C.M. AND OTHER EXAMINATIONS IN THE ART OF
FILLINGHAM, ARTHUR H.
    PIANOFORTE TEACHERS' EXAMINATION FOR THE A.R.C.M. DIPLOMA..A GUIDE
FREDERIC CHOPIN INTERNATIONAL COMPETITION--FIFTH
    FREDERIC CHOPIN INTERNATIONAL COMPETITIONS IN POLAND
GORDON, PHILIP
    SYLLABUS FOR PIANO AUDITIONS
HARRISON, SIDNEY
    TEACHER NEVER TOLD ME--TIPS FOR STUDENTS
LOWE, CLAUDE EDGERTON
    PIANOFORTE TEACHER'S VADE MECUM, THE ..A CYCLOPEDIA FOR THE
MANHIRE, WILSON
    EXAMINATION CANDIDATE'S GUIDE TO SCALE AND ARPEGGIO PLAYING, ETC.,
MANHIRE, WILSON
    GUIDE TO THE A.R.C.M. AND OTHER EXAMINATIONS IN
MANHIRE, WILSON
    HINTS TO CANDIDATES FOR THE L.R.A.M. ASSOCIATED BOARD AND OTHER
MINNESOTA MUSIC TEACHERS ASSOCIATION
    PIANO-THEORY EXAMINATION SYLLABUS
MUSIC EDUCATION LEAGUE, INC.
    PIANO AUDITIONS SYLLABUS AND COMPREHENSIVE GUIDE FOR PIANO
MUSIC EDUCATION LEAGUE
    COMPREHENSIVE GUIDE FOR PIANO TEACHERS AND PIANO AUDITION SYLLABUS
NATIONAL GUILD OF PIANO TEACHERS
    NATIONAL AUDITIONS FOR AMERICAN PIANO PUPILS
NATIONAL GUILD OF PIANO TEACHERS
    STUDENT'S HANDBOOK FOR ENTRANTS IN THE NATIONAL PIANO PLAYING
PROSNAK, JAN
    FREDERIC CHOPIN INTERNATIONAL PIANO COMPETITIONS, THE
ROWLEY, ALEC
    DO'S AND DONT'S FOR MUSICIANS..A HANDBOOK FOR TEACHERS AND
SCHELLING, ERNEST *
    OXFORD PIANO COURSE, TEACHER'S FIRST MANUAL
SOREL, CLAUDETTE
    MIND YOUR MUSICAL MANNERS, OFF AND ON STAGE..A HANDBOOK OF STAGE
TANKARD, GEOFFREY
    PIANOFORTE DIPLOMAS

TAPPER, THOMAS
    EDUCATION OF THE MUSIC TEACHER, THE
TERWILLIGER, GORDON B.
    PIANO TEACHERS PROFESSIONAL HANDBOOK
WILSON, MORRIS E.
    HOW TO HELP YOUR CHILD WITH MUSIC--2ND. ED.---1951

Books for Younger Readers

AZULAY, GERTRUDE
    CHOPIN..THE STORY OF THE BOY WHO MADE BEAUTIFUL MELODIES
BALLANTINE, BILL
    PIANO, THE ..AN INTRODUCTION TO THE INSTRUMENT
BURCH, GLADYS
    FAMOUS PIANISTS FOR BOYS AND GIRLS
BURCH, GLADYS
    MODERN COMPOSERS FOR YOUNG PEOPLE---FIRST PUBLISHED AS 'A CHILD'S
BYERLY, DOROTHEA J.
    ADVENTURES OF PETER THE PIANO, THE ..AN ILLUSTRATED STORY FOR
BYRON, MAY CLARISSA
    DAY WITH FREDERIC CHOPIN, A
COIT, LOTTIE ELLSWORTH
    CHILD CHOPIN, THE ...WITH DIRECTIONS FOR PRESENTATION WITH A
DARLOW, DENYS
    MUSICAL INSTRUMENTS--JUNIOR REFERENCE BOOKS, NO. 12--2ND. ED.
DAVIS, LIONEL
    KEYBOARD INSTRUMENTS..THE STORY OF THE PIANO---YOUNGER READERS
DUNLOP, AGNES MARY
    DUET---STORY OF CLARA AND ROBERT SCHUMANN
EISENBERG, JACOB
    LET ME HELP YOU, MY ANCESTORS AND I..A COMPREHENSIVE JUVENILE
GEST, ELIZABETH
    KEYBOARD HARMONY FOR JUNIORS
GRONOWICZ, ANTONI
    CHOPIN---YOUNGER READERS
GRONOWICZ, ANTONI
    PADEREWSKI, PIANIST AND PATRIOT
GRONOWICZ, ANTONI
    SERGEI RACHMANINOFF
HUBBARD, ELBERT
    LITTLE JOURNEYS TO THE HOMES OF GREAT MUSICIANS--VOL. 8, NO.
HUBBARD, ELBERT
    LITTLE JOURNEYS TO THE HOMES OF GREAT MUSICIANS--VOL. 9, NO.
HULL, ANNE
    MAESTRO SPINETTI'S MUSIC SHOP--HARPSICHORD, CLAVICHORD,
HUME, RUTH *
    LION OF POLAND, THE ..THE STORY OF PADEREWSKI--JUNIOR BIOGRAPHIES
LEVINE, JACK *
    UNDERSTANDING MUSICAL INSTRUMENTS..HOW TO SELECT YOUR
MAUROIS, ANDRE
    FREDERIC CHOPIN---FOR YOUNGER READERS
MAYO, WALDO
    CHOPIN---FOR YOUNGER READERS
REED, MARY G.
    KEYBOARD ROAD IN MUSIC LAND, AND OTHER STORIES---FOR CHILDREN
RUTTKAY, GEORGE
    CHOPIN, HIS LIFE TOLD IN ANECDOTAL FORM---FOR YOUNGER READERS
SCHWIMMER, FRANCISKA
    GREAT MUSICIANS AS CHILDREN
SPAETH, SIGMUND
    MAXIMS TO MUSIC..TRADITIONAL PROVERBS, MOTTOES AND MAXIMS OF THE
UMINSKA, ZOFIA *
    CHOPIN, THE CHILD AND THE LAD
WALKER, ALAN
    LISZT
WHEELER, OPAL
    FREDERIC CHOPIN, SON OF POLAND, EARLY YEARS--2 VOLS.---YOUNGER
WILSON, ROBINA BECKLES
    MUSICAL INSTRUMENTS--THE 'BYWAYS LIBRARY'

The Amateur Pianist

BECKER, JULIUS
    CONCISE TREATISE ON HARMONY, ACCOMPANIMENT, AND COMPOSITION, FOR
BRIED, FREDERICK
    STIMULATION IN PIANO STUDY..HOW PARENTS CAN STIMULATE AND MAINTAIN
BRUXNER, MERVYN
    MASTERING THE PIANO
CHING, JAMES
    AMATEUR PIANIST'S COMPANION, THE
COOKE, CHARLES
    PLAYING THE PIANO FOR PLEASURE--REV. ED.---1941
GIFFORD, ALEXANDER M.
    PIANOFORTE AND HOW TO STUDY IT, THE
GRUNDY, ENID
    HAPPY PIANIST, THE
HULLAH, M. E.
    FEW WORDS ABOUT MUSIC, CONTAINING HINTS TO AMATEUR PIANISTS, A
KOBBE, GUSTAV
    PIANOLIST, THE ..A GUIDE FOR PIANOLA PLAYERS
MCARTHUR, ALEXANDER
    PIANOFORTE STUDY..HINTS ON PIANO PLAYING
MCCLINTOCK, LORENE
    TEACH YOURSELF TO PLAY THE PIANO..BASED ON THE INTERVAL METHOD
PALMER, KING
    TEACH YOURSELF TO PLAY THE PIANO
ROBILLIARD, EILEEN D.
    PERSISTENT PIANIST, THE ..A BOOK FOR THE LATE BEGINNER AND THE
SCHAUFFLER, ROBERT HAVEN
    MUSICAL AMATEUR, THE
SEYMOUR, HARRIET AYER
    HOME MUSIC LESSONS..HOW TO FIND YOUR MUSICAL SELF
WELBOURNE, EVE V.
    WELBOURNE WAY TO HOBBY PIANO PLAYING FOR ADULTS, THE --9 LESSONS
WILSON, MORRIS E.
    HOW TO HELP YOUR CHILD WITH MUSIC--2ND. ED.---1951
YATES, PETER
    AMATEUR AT THE KEYBOARD, AN

Esoterica

ADAMS, JOHN S.
    FIVE THOUSAND MUSICAL TERMS..A COMPLETE DICTIONARY WITH A TREATISE
ASSOCIATION FOR RECORDED SOUND COLLECTIONS
    PRELIMINARY DIRECTORY OF SOUND RECORDING COLLECTIONS IN THE UNITED
BARRY, KEITH LEWIS
    CHOPIN AND HIS FOURTEEN DOCTORS
CHILTON, CARROLL B.
    DE-ASSIFICATION OF MUSIC, THE ..A PROPAGANDIST MAGAZINE, OF ONE
CHURCHILL, WILLIAM--SUPPOSED AUTHOR
    MARVELLOUS YEAR, THE ...CRITICAL SKETCHES OF CELEBRATED MEN, THE
COIT, LOTTIE ELLSWORTH
    CHILD CHOPIN, THE ...WITH DIRECTIONS FOR PRESENTATION WITH A
FAIRLIE, GERARD
    PIANIST SHOOTS FIRST, THE ---PSYCHOLOGICAL STORY

GRIFFIN, RUSSELL B.
    PIANOFORTE TELEGRAPHY, THE --THE MORSE TELEGRAPH CODE--INSTRUCTOR
HANSMANN, RICHARD
    THEORETICAL AND PRACTICAL PIANO-FORTE SCHOOL FOR THE JANKO
IWASZKIEWICZ, JAROSLAW
    SUMMER AT NOHANT..A PLAY IN THREE ACTS---CHOPIN
KEEFER, LUBOV
    INFLUENCE OF ADAM MICKIEWICZ ON THE BALLADES OF CHOPIN, THE
KEELER, WALTER B.
    THEORY OF THE NEW KEYBOARD, ARRANGED BY W. B. KEELER AND E. K.
KNOLLER, JACOB
    FREE WILL OR DESTINY..ONE ACT PLAY AROUND CHOPIN---EARLY SUMMER,
KRAUS, ALESSANDRO B.
    ONE-KEYBOARDED CLAVICYTHERIUM OF THE KRAUS COLLECTION IN FLORENCE,
LANG, EDITH *
    MUSICAL ACCOMPANIMENT OF MOVING PICTURES..A PRACTICAL MANUAL FOR
LOESSER, ARTHUR
    MEN, WOMEN AND PIANOS..A SOCIAL HISTORY
LONG, ESMOND R.--PATHOLOGIST
    HISTORY OF THE THERAPY OF TUBERCULOSIS, AND THE CASE OF FREDERIC
MEIER, NELLIE SIMMONS
    LIONS' PAWS..THE STORY OF FAMOUS HANDS--INCLUDES MUSICIANS...JOSE
MOOR, WINIFRED
    TECHNICAL EXERCISES FOR THE EMANUEL MOOR DOUBLE KEYBOARD
RAPEE, ERNO--ARRANGER
    ERNO RAPEE'S ENCYCLOPEDIA OF MUSIC FOR PICTURES---LISTED BOTH BY
RAPEE, ERNO--ARRANGER
    MOTION PICTURE MOODS FOR PIANISTS AND ORGANISTS
SACKETT, SHELTON
    NOCTURNE..A CHOPIN-PLAY IN ONE ACT
SPAETH, SIGMUND
    MAXIMS TO MUSIC..TRADITIONAL PROVERBS, MOTTOES AND MAXIMS OF THE
STECK AND COMPANY
    ILLUSTRATED CATALOG...GRAND AND UPRIGHT PIANOS

Pianistic Careers

AEOLIAN COMPANY, THE
    DUO-ART PIANO MUSIC
AEOLIAN COMPANY, THE
    LIBRARY OF DUO-ART MUSIC ROLLS
AEOLIAN COMPANY, THE
    PIANISTS WHO HAVE MADE RECORDS FOR THE DUO-ART PIANO
AEOLIAN COMPANY, THE
    WEIGHT OF EVIDENCE ON THE TRUE MUSICAL WORTH OF THE PIANOLA AND
AMERICAN PIANO CORPORATION
    CATALOGUE OF MUSIC FOR THE AMPICO, A ..A LIST OF THE RECORDINGS OF
AMERICAN PIANO CORPORATION
    CATALOGUE OF MUSIC FOR THE AMPICO, A --A LIST OF THE RECORDINGS OF
ARPIN, PAUL
    LIFE OF LOUIS MOREAU GOTTSCHALK
AUTO PNEUMATIC ACTION COMPANY
    WELTE-MIGNON BOOK...OF FAMOUS ARTISTS, THE
BAGGER, EUGENE S.
    EMINENT EUROPEANS..STUDIES IN CONTINENTAL REALITY---PADEREWSKI
BASTIEN, JAMES W.
    HOW TO TEACH PIANO SUCCESSFULLY
BAUGHAN, EDWARD ALGERNON
    IGNACE JAN PADEREWSKI
CARRE, AVNER *
    IMMORTAL PIANO, THE
CHING, JAMES
    PERFORMER AND AUDIENCE..AN INVESTIGATION INTO THE PSYCHOLOGICAL
CHRISTENSEN, INGA
    INGA - PLAY--MEMOIRS
CLARK, MADAM STEINEGER
    RELIGION AND ROMANCE OF A PIANIST'S LIFE---AUTOBIOGRAPHY
DAHL, ANTON
    SOUL OF GENIUS, THE ..ITS MUSICAL DEVELOPMENT AND HOW THE WORLD AT
EISENBERG, JACOB
    ARTISTIC PIANIST, THE ..NATURAL TECHNICS IN PIANO MASTERY..FROM
FINCK, HENRY T.
    PADEREWSKI AND HIS ART
FOLDES, LILI
    TWO ON A CONTINENT
FULLER-MAITLAND, J. A.
    MUSICIAN'S PILGRIMAGE, THE ..A STUDY IN ARTISTIC DEVELOPMENT
GLENNON, JAMES
    AUSTRALIAN MUSIC AND MUSICIANS
GRAHAM, L. SIBLEY
    TALES OF THE OLD VIRTUOSO..THE SPANISH COURT PIANIST--MARQUIS DON
GRONOWICZ, ANTONI
    PADEREWSKI, PIANIST AND PATRIOT
HALLE, SIR CHARLES
    ST. JAMES HALL...C. HALLE'S PIANOFORTE RECITALS..MAY 5-JUNE 29,
HALLE, SIR CHARLES
    ST. JAMES HALL...MR. HALLE'S BEETHOVEN RECITALS, MAY 23-JULY 11,
HAMBOURG, MARK
    EIGHTH OCTAVE, THE ---CONTINUES THE RECORD, BEGUN IN 'FROM PIANO
HARDING, BERTITA
    CONCERTO, THE STORY OF CLARA SCHUMANN
HIPKINS, ALFRED JAMES
    HOW CHOPIN PLAYED...FROM CONTEMPORARY IMPRESSIONS COLLECTED FROM
JOHNSON, HARRIETT
    YOUR CAREER IN MUSIC
KAISER, JOACHIM
    GREAT PIANISTS OF OUR TIME
KAUFMANN, HELEN LOEB
    ARTISTS IN MUSIC OF TODAY
LESSMANN, W. J. OTTO
    FRANZ LISZT..EINE HULDIGUNG--FRANZ LISZT..A TRIBUTE
LE MASSENA, CLARENCE E.
    PADEREWSKI, 'THE MASTER OF MASTERS' ---REPRODUCED FROM TYPEWRITTEN
MARTENS, FREDERICK HERMAN
    PADEREWSKI--'LITTLE BIOGRAPHIES', VOL. 2
MATHIS, WILLIAM STEPHAN
    PIANIST AND CHURCH MUSIC, THE
MCARTHUR, ALEXANDER
    PIANOFORTE STUDY..HINTS ON PIANO PLAYING
MCCARTHY, ALBERT J.--EDITOR
    PIANO JAZZ..ESSAYS--2 VOLS., 1945-1946
NOSSIG, ALFRED
    METHODS OF THE MASTERS OF PIANO TEACHING IN EUROPE, THE ..THE

PATTERSON, ANNIE WILSON
    PROFESSION OF MUSIC AND HOW TO PREPARE FOR IT, THE
PIGGOTT, PATRICK
    LIFE AND MUSIC OF JOHN FIELD, 1782-1837, THE
POWERS, J. HAROLD
    MUSIC'S GLAMOROUS HALL OF FAME..SHORT ARTICLES ABOUT FAMOUS NAMES,
PUGNO, RAOUL
    LESSONS OF RAOUL PUGNO, THE ..WITH A BIOGRAPHY OF CHOPIN BY M.
RIGBY, CHARLES
    SIR CHARLES HALLE..A PORTRAIT FOR TODAY
RUBINSTEIN, ARTUR
    MY YOUNG YEARS
SHATTUCK, ARTHUR
    MEMOIRS OF ARTHUR SHATTUCK, THE ..WITH AN ACCOUNT OF HIS CAREER BY
SMITH, CYRIL
    DUET FOR THREE HANDS...AS TOLD TO JOYCE EGGINTON
SOREL, CLAUDETTE
    MIND YOUR MUSICAL MANNERS, OFF AND ON STAGE..A HANDBOOK OF STAGE
STEINWAY AND SONS
    PORTRAITS OF MUSICAL CELEBRITIES
STEINWAY AND SONS
    PORTRAITS OF MUSICAL CELEBRITIES
STEINWAY AND SONS
    PORTRAITS OF MUSICAL CELEBRITIES
STEINWAY AND SONS
    PORTRAITS OF MUSICAL CELEBRITIES
STEINWAY AND SONS
    PORTRAITS OF MUSICAL CELEBRITIES
STEINWAY AND SONS
    PORTRAITS OF MUSICAL CELEBRITIES
STEINWAY AND SONS
    STEINWAY PROGRESS..AN APPRECIATION BY I. J. PADEREWSKI
STUCKENSCHMIDT, HANS H.
    FERRUCCIO BUSONI..CHRONICLE OF A EUROPEAN---1967, IN GERMAN
TAPPER, THOMAS
    EDUCATION OF THE MUSIC TEACHER, THE
TAYLER, E. DOUGLAS
    MIND-POWER IN MUSIC FOR STUDENTS, TEACHERS AND PERFORMERS
TAYLOR, ROBERT L.
    RUNNING PIANIST, THE ---PERCY GRAINGER
TERWILLIGER, GORDON B.
    PIANO TEACHERS PROFESSIONAL HANDBOOK
VERNE, MATHILDE
    CHORDS OF REMEMBRANCE---BY A PUPIL OF CLARA SCHUMANN
WALKER, BETTINA
    MY MUSICAL EXPERIENCES
WIENER, HILDA
    PENCIL PORTRAITS OF CONCERT CELEBRITIES---INCLUDES 24 PIANISTS
WOLFF, ERNST VICTOR
    WITH REASON AND RHYME
YOUFF, ULV
    ULVEN, WRITTEN DURING RETIREMENT IN SWITZERLAND--AUTOBIOGRAPHY OF

Research

ELLINGHAM, HARRY
    HOW TO USE A PLAYER-PIANO
HILL, GEORGE R.
    PRELIMINARY CHECKLIST OF RESEARCH ON THE CLASSIC SYMPHONY AND
SCHAAF, EDWARD O.
    ART OF PIANO PLAYER TRANSCRIPTION, THE ..MAKING OF PERFORATED

Related Arts

BALTIMORE--MUSEUM OF ART
    MUSICAL INSTRUMENTS AND THEIR PORTRAYAL IN
BARRY, KEITH LEWIS
    CHOPIN AND HIS FOURTEEN DOCTORS
CHURCHILL, WILLIAM--SUPPOSED AUTHOR
    MARVELLOUS YEAR, THE ...CRITICAL SKETCHES OF CELEBRATED MEN, THE
DE BOER, JOSEPHINE
    MALLORCAN MOODS IN CONTEMPORARY ART AND LITERATURE--CONTAINS
FAIRLIE, GERARD
    PIANIST SHOOTS FIRST, THE ---PSYCHOLOGICAL STORY
FERRA I PERELLO, BARTOLOME
    CHOPIN AND GEORGE SAND IN THE CARTUJA DE VALLDEMOSA...
GRIFFIN, RUSSELL B.
    PIANOFORTE TELEGRAPHY, THE --THE MORSE TELEGRAPH CODE--INSTRUCTOR
HAWEIS, HUGH R.
    MUSIC AND MORALS---CHOPIN
HEINE, HEINRICH
    HEINE IN ART AND LETTERS---CHOPIN AND LISZT--1837
HENDERSON, ARCHIBALD
    CONTEMPORARY IMMORTALS---PADEREWSKI
IWASZKIEWICZ, JAROSLAW
    SUMMER AT NOHANT..A PLAY IN THREE ACTS---CHOPIN
KEEFER, LUBOV
    INFLUENCE OF ADAM MICKIEWICZ ON THE BALLADES OF CHOPIN, THE
KNOLLER, JACOB
    FREE WILL OR DESTINY..ONE ACT PLAY AROUND CHOPIN---EARLY SUMMER,
LANG, EDITH *
    MUSICAL ACCOMPANIMENT OF MOVING PICTURES..A PRACTICAL MANUAL FOR
LONG, ESMOND R.--PATHOLOGIST
    HISTORY OF THE THERAPY OF TUBERCULOSIS, AND THE CASE OF FREDERIC
MACQUOID, PERCY *
    DICTIONARY OF ENGLISH FURNITURE, THE --VOL. 3----16 ILLUSTRATIONS
MILLER, JEWELL
    POLONAISE MILITAIRE..THE LIFE AND WORK OF FREDERIC CHOPIN..A
PENGELLY, J. BRADFORD
    PENGELLY BLUE BOOK OF STYLE, THE ...A STUDY OF THE ART OF STYLING
PIANO, ORGAN AND MUSICAL INSTRUMENT WORKERS INTERNATIONAL UNION OF
    CONSTITUTION OF THE PIANO, ORGAN AND MUSICAL INSTRUMENT WORKERS'
PLANTIGA, LEON B.
    SCHUMANN AS CRITIC
REMBUSCH, JOSEPH ADAM
    PIANOS AND MUSICAL INSTRUMENTS DISCUSSED FROM AN UNSANITARY
SACKETT, SHELTON
    NOCTURNE..A CHOPIN-PLAY IN ONE ACT
SPAETH, SIGMUND
    MAXIMS TO MUSIC..TRADITIONAL PROVERBS, MOTTOES AND MAXIMS OF THE
THACKRAY, RUPERT M.
    PLAYING FOR DANCE..THE PLACE OF THE PIANIST IN THE TEACHING OF

Aeolian Company.
DUO-ART PIANO MUSIC.
New York: The Aeolian Company, 1927.

When player-piano popularity was at its height, piano-roll catalogs were veritable encyclopedias. They were annotated and cross-indexed and contained photographs, biographical sketches, testimonials to the manufacturer and program notes.

Competition between the Aeolian Company, publisher of the Duo-Art piano-roll catalog, and the Welte-Mignon Corporation, publisher of the Welte-Mignon catalog, was intense.[1] The Duo-Art catalog was almost half again as large as the Welte-Mignon and contained, in addition, such bonuses as a special children's section and a suggested basic (five foot!) library. The rosters of both catalogs were equally stellar. There was relatively little duplication of names, although such "greats" as Busoni, Carreno, Gabrilowitsch, Ganz, Landowska, de Pachmann, Paderewski and Saint-Saens appeared on the lists of both companies. Some of the Duo-Art "exclusives" were Backhaus, Bauer, Cadman, Chaminade, Cortot, Friedman, Gershwin, Godowsky, Grainger, Griffes, Jonas, Leginska, Palmgren, Prokofieff, Anton Rubinstein, Schmitz and Stravinsky.

Piano-roll manufacturers can certainly be complimented on their foresightedness (all commercialism aside) to include the art of composers-as-pianists for posterity.

[1]See review of *Library of Welte-Mignon Music Records*, Welte-Mignon Corporation, on page 955.

Ahrens, Cora B. and G. D. Atkinson.
FOR ALL PIANO TEACHERS.
Oakville, Ontario: Frederick Harris Music Co., 1955.

For All Piano Teachers is truly a pedagogical text. Its directness and conciseness is never diminished by narrative filling. Much of the information is presented in outline form, facilitating its use as a ready reference. All elements of superficiality are avoided as the authors probe deeply into their chosen subject matter.

Probably one of the most difficult tasks facing an author who writes on the multiple facets of piano pedagogy is the delineation of topic headings with a minimum of overlapping. Authors Ahrens and Atkinson have certainly succeeded as well as any writers, past or present, in this respect. I like especially the separate and broad-based chapter on psychology; it is far more effective in this single unit than if the subject were allowed to run as a nebulous thread through a host of other topics.

There is no need to give a resume of chapter headings, since all the traditional pedagogical areas are covered. A bibliography and set of questions are included at the end of each chapter. The bibliographical references are chosen not merely to illustrate or support the author's opinions; instead, diametrically opposed points of view are often represented in these lists. The questions are not merely routine inquiries based upon the text, but rather are questions involving dynamic issues that could well precipitate active class discussions.

Anderson, W. R.
RACHMANINOV AND HIS PIANOFORTE CONCERTOS.
London: Hinrichsen Edition Limited.

This little volume covers even more than its title would suggest: lists of recordings (which I assume are now collector's items), musical examples, a sketch of Rachmaninov's life and highly descriptive analyses of his piano concertos (with special consideration given to the *Second in C minor*), the *Rhapsody on a Theme of Paganini*, selections for piano solo and some notable works for other media.

Although a number of far more complete volumes are available on Rachmaninov as a pianist-composer, this book represents a useful compromise between extended biographical works and relatively brief periodical articles (which are not found in abundance). The selected biographical material is concise and relevant; the analyses are sensitive and colorful and contain pertinent musicological and historical data.

Auld, Wilda J.
A HANDBOOK FOR THE CHURCH PIANIST.
Kansas City: Lillenas Publishing Company, 1964.

Wilda Auld's *Handbook* is designed to aid the church pianist who, generally speaking, will serve in this capacity when the more traditional organist cannot be obtained.

As, in many instances, the pianist in this situation will be a person with relatively little musical training, a substantial amount of the book is devoted to musical rudiments and other assorted essentials. However, its most valuable contributions are in the specific areas of ecclesiastical use that would not be covered in a more general do-it-yourself piano playing guide.

Such topics as the following are included: transcribing and arranging hymns, especially by means of embellishment and amplification; creating hymn introductions; choosing basic materials for use in various parts of the service; demeanor and responsibilities before, during and after the service; placement and care of the instrument; specific suggestions for developing and maintaining the performance techniques vital to successful service-playing.

Bacon, Ernst.
NOTES ON THE PIANO.
Syracuse: Syracuse University Press, 1963.

Notes on the Piano is unique in one major respect: the pianistic arts are discussed from the independent but overlapping viewpoints of the performer, learner, writer, composer, teacher, observer and critic, each infused with the validity of Mr. Bacon's involvement in that particular area.

This book is powerful, convincing and authoritative, yet sensitive, compassionate and understanding. I must admit, however, that I experienced a feeling of edginess while reading the concluding chapter, "The Observer." In this section, the subdivision "Of the Environment" presents perhaps a harsh, though hardly unrealistic, picture of the current musical scene. The final part, "Commonplaces," consists of many brief "pearls-of-wisdom" type sayings, veritably out of place in a book of such high caliber and taste.

Notwithstanding these possible minor flaws, *Notes on the Piano* can easily take its place as one of the outstanding piano books of our day. Bacon's absorbing style of writing, his knowledge and command of vocabulary, his pin-point accuracy in the use of terminology all lead to a type of reference that will initiate the uninitiated and re-educate the experienced.

A particularly revealing section consists of an evaluation of our schools. The effect of this section will be quite pronounced on anyone who has worked in any level of our educational system. I found myself alternately howling with laughter and tearfully admitting, *"touche!"*

More evidence of Mr. Bacon's skillful writing may be found in the perfect length of individual topics and the variable degrees of intensity with which he presents them. He writes with the scholarly precision of a William Newman, the fervency of a Harry Pleasants, the varied colors of an Abram Chasins and the devotion of an Angela Diller. This volume is a "must" for your book shelf.

Badura-Skoda, Eva, and Paul Badura-Skoda.
INTERPRETING MOZART ON THE KEYBOARD.
London: Barrie and Rockliff, 1962.

Often the pianist feels, with some justification, that musicological orientation can be carried to the extreme. Superficially, it would seem that this volume, which is fairly substantial in size, would support this premise. Happily, the complete opposite is true. There is hardly a redundancy in the entire work, and many may feel as I did when I completed reading it, "How did I ever get along without it?".

Dialectic areas are discussed in fine detail and with great flexibility; e.g., how to achieve the delicate balance between

the composer's intentions and the interpreter's wishes; how to determine the validity of the "old" or the "new" sound; how to decide upon the use of the pedal in its quantitative aspect. The authors are fully sensitive to the illusory nature of piano sound and, in a tonal sense, successfully link tradition with present-day performance practices.

Mozart was much more specific in his directions to the performer than most of his contemporaries, but certain inconsistencies (or what may percolate down to the performer as misunderstandings) in notation could present great difficulties to the uninitiated. The Badura-Skodas have worked out in minute detail, replete with examples, a superb clarification of these aspects. Included in this category are slur markings (which were never used by Mozart as an indication of phrasing), articulation and ornamentation. Examples of Mozart's non-piano works are brought in as needed to expand on the more purely pianistic points.

Notwithstanding the intricacy and detail of the subject matter, this book is not difficult reading. Indeed, the unfolding of musical reasoning is so smooth and logical in its progression, one feels that much of it is "common-artistic-sense" created by rules of sound musicianship. This is a reassuring thought to the dedicated musician!

Bastien, James W.
HOW TO TEACH PIANO SUCCESSFULLY.
Park Ridge, Illinois: Neil A. Kjos Music Company, 1973.

Any author who chooses a "How to . . ." title accepts a very special challenge. These two introductory words should imply that the writer is an authority in the field and that he is capable of disseminating information on his subject in a lucid and thorough manner. Mr. Bastien has met this challenge admirably. In what might well be considered a magnum opus in the field of piano pedagogy, Mr. Bastien encompasses a wide range of material and goes into fine detail when such meticulous consideration is desirable.

James Bastien has a wealth of personal experience to support his writing. His teaching endeavors to include every step of pianistic achievement—individually and in groups, and at the college as well as private studio level. Therefore, his advice is not merely academic or theoretical representation.

As stated in the preface, "The book is designed to be used as a basic text for piano pedagogy classes and as a general reference book for the piano teacher." To this end, Mr. Bastien has included exhaustive references to the pianistic art; e.g., (to list but a few topics) the teacher's background and training, the teacher's personality, learning how to teach, and the teacher's studio. Sections on procedures and techniques include such topics as how to obtain students, how to advertise, how to interview prospective students, lesson fees, procedures of payment and so forth.

Detailed lesson plans, extensive bibliographies and evaluative reports and surveys make this book a major source of essential pedagogical material. Special subjects such as "Contests and Festivals for the Young Pianist," "The College Preparatory Department," and "Editions of Keyboard Music" are presented by contributing authors. Another highlight of the book is the section devoted to interviews with notable musicians: Rosina Lhevinne, Irl Allison, Adele Marcus and James Dick.

As an all-purpose text for piano pedagogy, no book can surpass *How to Teach Piano Successfully* in completeness, authenticity and readability.

Bauer, Harold.
HAROLD BAUER, HIS BOOK.
New York: W. W. Norton & Company, Inc., 1948.

My first experience with the writing of Mr. Bauer was in reading his article, "Artistic Aspects of Piano Study," from *Great Pianists on Piano Playing.*[2] Greatly impressed with Bauer's musical views, I summarily thought of him as a marvelous combination of iconoclast, eclectic and innovator. My acquaintance with his autobiography has done nothing to modify my original opinion, but I would like to add a fourth title—raconteur *extraordinaire*.

The reader may be disappointed in finding the book far more anecdotal than instructive. In view of the very limited amount of other material written either by or about Mr. Bauer, it is unfortunate that this volume does not contain more references to the purely artistic side of pianism. Notwithstanding, it presents valuable information about the other musical "greats" of his time, much of which is not obtainable from other sources.

Bauer is truly a "self-made" pianist. His period of formal study was relatively short. He eschewed the popular doctrines and his approach was basically empirical. Uncanny accuracy in finding technical short-cuts, often dictated by necessity, point to his being what is called, in the profession, a "natural."

Acoustics, physics and aesthetics were delicately and accurately balanced in his musical philosophy. I was awed by his analysis of tonal variety—a theory that was developed, strangely enough, as a result of his experience with the pianola (player piano). A number of years later, his beliefs were proven accurate by intricate scientific investigation.

[2]See review of *Great Pianists On Piano Playing* by James Francis Cooke, on page 940.

Bie, Oscar.
A HISTORY OF THE PIANOFORTE
AND PIANOFORTE PLAYERS.
London: J. M. Dent and Company, 1899. (Da Capo reprint. New York: Da Capo Press, 1966.)

Although books about pianists and pianist-composers seem to have appeared through the years almost at regular intervals (with a stretto in the last decade or so), no single issue can be dismissed as a repetition of another. Although much of the purely factual material is not dissimilar, the position of the author (in his particular portion of the artistic cycle) and his proximity to the era of the subject combine to form a unique perspective. That which may be described as a culmination at the turn of the century may be considered a transition seventy years later, or vice versa.

The reader will be attracted by many examples of this perspective in action. As a particularly noteworthy point, it must be said (again, as I have said it elsewhere) that the past generations, as compared with the present generations, seemed more accurate, more in agreement with each other and often more prophetic in evaluating works of their contemporary composers. Could this be explained in part by the possible fact that in the nineteenth century there may have been a greater incidence of insipidity than of camouflage?

Mr. Bie makes no effort to cushion his negative comments; such terms as "lowest type," "vapid" and "hollow" are used as he feels the necessity! Commentaries of individual works also attain an interesting perspective. According to the author, the *Moonlight* and *Pathetique* sonatas of Beethoven had already appeared on high levels of appreciation and popularity while Mendelssohn's *Rondo Cappricioso* had already been "worn out" before the dawn of the twentieth century.

There is another phenomenon in Bie's evaluation of contemporary pianists. Understandably, Liszt emerged as the pianistic giant of the century, and his pupils, however blessed with the touch of greatness, were swept off the front page, as it were, by the big news of the day. Consequently, Paderewski (already at the height of his career when this book was written), Sauer, Siloti, Friedheim, Rosenthal, Gabrilowitsch, Rachmaninoff and Hofmann received but passing recognition.

As if Bie's masterful writing is not enough to recommend this book as a "must," the illustrations are superb and in many instances unique. However, perhaps a touch of morbidity is reflected in the choice of some of the photographs: Bach's skull, Bulow on his deathbed, Liszt lying in state, etc.

Blockley, John.
THE PIANIST'S CATECHISM.
London: Ascherberg, Hopwood and Crew, 1955.

I am very much in favor of a catechistic approach to learning the rudiments of music. In such an area, where the infor-

mation includes a numerous quantity of related facts, the "question and answer" method serves to underline the vital points as well as to form a basis for quick review of the material studied. Indeed, modern programmed texts would seem to be an outgrowth of the catechism rather than of the conventional textbook.

Mr. Blockley does not confine his book to music fundamentals; he also incorporates certain applied and aesthetic topics usually covered only by prose; e.g., hand position, touch, expression, etc.

Bolton, Hetty.
HOW TO PRACTICE.
London: Elkin and Company, Ltd., 1937.

The art of practicing is a difficult subject on which to expound. Although books on how to play form a major part of the pianistic bibliography, books on how to practice constitute a negligible percentage of the total. In some contemporary pedagogical circles, even the word "practice" is avoided; "play" is often substituted. Perhaps the former word symbolizes work and consequently might make the student feel uncomfortable!

Miss Bolton's fine book came about as a result of the compiling of a myriad of notes, written over a period of many years and originally recording ideas for her own use. I like to think of this treatise as a guide to awareness—awareness of listening procedures, of technical control, of musical functions in general. In another sense, it is a guide to the act of concentration, which is a basic requisite to successful practicing. Although generally philosophical in character, this book also includes concrete suggestions for specific methods of practicing, sample practice outlines and time tables. Generic classification of practice problem-areas are covered in individual chapters.

Bopensiere, Luigi.
NEW PATHWAYS TO PIANO TECHNIQUE.
New York: Philosophical Library, 1953.

Are these pathways really new? In terminology and manner of expression, yes. In finding a heretofore undiscovered means of musical production, no. What Mr. Bonpensiere has done, essentially and effectively, is to isolate and delineate certain psychological and physical principles that the great "natural" talents have been using unwittingly. Basically, this involves a fusing of the conscious and subconscious, or more accurately, a matter of the conscious-self "getting out of the way" to allow the subconscious-self the freedom to do things as they should be done. Consequently, there should exist a greater awareness of the musical goals themselves rather than of the means of producing or obtaining them.

It would be impractical for me to attempt to describe in more detail, in a small amount of space, the essence of Bonpensiere's theory. Perhaps it will suffice to say that all takes place on a highly philosophical, even a religious or metaphysical plane. With all its complexity, the author's unfolding of this theory is fascinating.

In the application of Mr. Bonpensiere's principles there are problems. I would think that complete mental detachment from conscious physical activity could result in superficiality of interpretation. Secondly, there is no real "guarantee" that such physical principles could be incorporated by a musician who has less than a superb natural talent. Thirdly, it would be virtually impossible to follow all of Bonpensiere's concepts literally, as they seem to be at odds with certain accepted truths relating to muscle tensions, note-thinking and the trial-and-error means of experimentation.

Bonpensiere's utilization of his theory in sight reading, that is, looking at the material used without being conscious of content, might serve its purpose in terms of immediate visual grasp. However, it would seem that the spirit and understanding of the music would be missing. It might remind one of successful touch-typing, when the typist can perform faster and more accurately if he is unaware of content.

Bosworth, Harriette Dexter.
IDEAS FOR YOUNG PIANO TEACHERS.
Boston: Oliver Ditson Company, 1931.

Although the author in her preface (called the "Prelude") specifies that her book is directed to young piano teachers and parents, I would venture to add that this volume could effectively serve to refresh or rejuvenate the older, more experienced teacher as well.

No less than twenty-eight topics are covered in a span of sixty-seven pages; however, because of the excellent subdivision of subject matter, one does not feel that any particular idea is slighted in terms of space.

The book commences with discussions of the more practical aspects of the child's beginning study and leads to the philosophical and psychological considerations of the teacher-pupil relationship. Although this book was written in 1931, one has the feeling that Miss Bosworth has accurately foreshadowed many of our "modern" pedagogical ideas. Richness of imagination and unusual artistic devotion characterize this fine work.

Bowen, York.
PEDALLING THE MODERN PIANOFORTE.
London: Oxford University Press, 1936.

Mr. Bowen's book on piano pedalling is remarkably complete for its modest size. A section is devoted to mechanical features, including criteria for selecting an instrument in terms of pedal construction: precise location of pedals, proper amount of spring tension and free motion, and depth of stroke. Even the choice of shoes is discussed!

Another unique feature of this book is Mr. Bowen's examination of the important subject of pedal-release. As pianos tend to be less than precise in their release mechanism, information in this area is especially valuable.

Bowen's discussion on the use of the soft pedal is particularly enlightening; his extensive knowledge of the instrument, as pianist and composer, is reflected in a most sensitive analysis of the functions of this pedal. Interestingly, his preference for the shifting mechanism, currently used in all grand pianos, is not always that of other writers; most prefer (I do not, myself) the upright-type mechanism which will not alter the tone quality of the piano when used.

Bowen dismisses many questionable pedal markings by composers, especially of the classic and romantic periods, as merely careless or erroneous—a highly dialectic point!

Several minor inconveniences to the reader must be mentioned. Bowen's use of the marking **P** to indicate the depressing of the pedal is somewhat old-fashioned (of course it is better than the older *Ped.* but neither marking is as precise as a thin line). Although the general format of the book is excellent, the interrupted columns and the very small print may present visual problems.

Bowen, York.
THE SIMPLICITY OF PIANO TECHNIQUE.
London: Augener Ltd., 1961.

The Simplicity of Piano Technique is the product of a mature musician with many years of experience in virtually all phases of pianistic activity. It is always comforting to read a text book when one feels confident that the author has transcended the viscossitudes of experimentation and has come up with a definite product, accessible to and workable by all.

Mr. Bowen is especially careful to avoid semantic misunderstanding. His words are very discreetly chosen, a fact which in no way interferes with the free flow and continuity of the text. No musical term or expression, no matter how universally used and interpreted, is inserted without definition and clarification if the need is present. The much-used and mis-used term "rotation," for example, is a case in point.

I am a little surprised, however, to find a certain imbalance between the amount of space devoted to the intricacies of muscular coordination and control, and to the mechanism of the instrument to which all of this is directed. If one considers the possibility that the bulk of the reader's knowledge in these areas could be obtained from this particular volume (and no

writer could realistically assume that such a thing could never happen), there is ever-present danger that pre-occupation with so-called "touch" could impair the vital listening process. After all, it is important to know what the piano can and can't do as well as to know the physiological mechanism that activates the instrument. In other words, one cannot eschew certain quantitative elements and still "tell the whole story."

I can see real value in this book as a buffer between the purely scientific studies and the highly intuitive works of many of the great artists. Mr. Bowen is a "gentleman of the old school" who wishes to adapt his heritage to present-day needs.

Breckenridge, W. K.
HINTS FOR PIANO NORMAL STUDIES.
New York: Vantage Press, Inc., 1955.

The author has provided an accurate title for his book. Mr. Breckenridge touches on a multitude of subject areas, pinpoints the problems and outlines the means of solution without becoming involved in great detail. I can see value in this approach for the beginning teacher; it will serve to clarify the scope and definition of problems and enable the teacher, as necessary, to refer to other more selective and detailed texts.

Interspersed among the pedagogical "tips" are sections on rather basic pianistic information (musical rudiments, clarification of terms, elementary practice procedures, etc.) which, on superficial reading, may seem to be redundant. However, one may soon feel that such material is too often taken for granted. It is not infrequent that the author of a pedagogy manual may leave a gap by overestimating the reader's previous knowledge.

A substantial appendix (sixty-seven pages) lists various categories of piano music—exercises, studies and compositions—plus ensemble works and a bibliography of books on musical subjects.

Briggs, G. A.
PIANOS, PIANISTS AND SONICS.
Bradford, England: Wharfedale Wireless Works, 1951.

Pianos, Pianists and Sonics is written by a piano technologist who is vitally interested in the aesthetic as well as the technical side of the maker's art.

A brief historical introduction leads to the details of construction, the explanation of mechanism and the exposition of acoustic principles. Line drawings and photographs (including photomicrographs) amply illustrate the text. Virtually all areas of technological interest are covered: action, pedals, strings, uprights versus grands, toning, tuning, touch-tone, vibration, analysis of sound by means of oscillograms, the choosing of an instrument, its care, room acoustics, recording and reproduction. Unlike most texts covering this type of subject matter, the manner of presentation is eminently suited to the non-technically-minded pianist. A lucid style, combined with occasional touches of humor to lighten the seriousness of the subject, add up to probably the best book available in this field.

A high point in the content of this book is the chapter entitled, "Pianists and Their Views." Mr. Briggs balances the artistic and scientific sides of piano playing by asking a number of well-known English artists certain questions that were of particular interest to the author; e.g., at what age did you begin to play? How do you memorize? Do you attribute success as a concert pianist mainly to talent or to hard work? Do you believe that you are able to alter the tone of a piano by the method of key depression, as distinct from the speed?

Brinsmead, Edgar.
THE HISTORY OF THE PIANOFORTE.
London: Simpkin, Marshall and Company, 1889.

Edgar Brinsmead was the son of the famous English piano maker, John Brinsmead, and "bring[s] to [his] subject practical experience as a pianoforte manufacturer."

His book is divided into two main sections: "Sound" and "History of the Pianoforte." In "Sound," many of the early experiments and conclusions (based upon the work of Chladni,

Herschel, Hemholtz, Tyndall and others) are vividly described. The second (and by far the largest) section, "History of the Pianoforte," is valable for two principal reasons: it offers a contemporary perspective of progress in the development of the piano; and it is an excellent source of little-known information, both consequential and trivial. For example, no less than five hundred and twenty-one inventions (concerning the piano and other keyboard instruments), patented between the years 1693 and 1886, are listed, many of which warrant more complete description in the text. "In 1774 Joseph Merlin tried to effect a compromise between the harpsichord and the piano which had nearly superseded it. He patented a compound harpsichord and piano, five octaves in compass, the two instruments being played together or separately at will . . . In 1792 John Geib, the inventor of an action well known as the 'grasshopper,' attempted to revive the clavichord in combination with the pianoforte, with separate sets of keys, but he had little success." Somewhat more bizarre is the following: "In a patent dated December 16, 1854, [Daniel Hewitt] proposed affixing a wrest-plank and bent side (the two parts that together carry the strings) to the brick or stone wall of an apartment, so as to avoid the necessity for constructing costly framework . . . "

Brook, Donald.
MASTERS OF THE KEYBOARD.
London: Rockliff, 1946.

Here is an especially valuable contribution to the "Great Pianist" family. The perspective is definitely English, a fact which is apparent in both the choice of keyboard masters and/or their particular activities within the British Empire. Part I of this book contains material on the virtuosi of the past, from Dr. John Bull to Sergei Rachmaninoff; Part II describes nine pianists who were prominent in Great Britain at the time of writing.

In Part I *Masters of the Keyboard* differs from its cousins in several ways. The author has attempted to be as objective as possible in his presentation of biographical facts. The colorful narrative usually associated with this type of book is generally absent. Quotes from writings of Brook's contemporaries are liberally inserted, giving a more balanced perspective in time. Many of the more personal items in the lives of the artists are presented without undue modesty.

In Part II the selections, although brought forth from a lesser amount of source material than Part I, are infused with sensitivity, warmth and genuine respect. One wishes that our fine American pianists of today could be reviewed in this manner, instead of being represented by the hurried, superficial interviews that seem to be so popular within our mass communication media of today.

A superb set of illustrations accompanies the text.

Broughton, Julia.
SUCCESS IN PIANO TEACHING.
New York: Vantage Press, 1956.

This informally-written, unsophisticated teacher's manual will be of special value to the beginning teacher who wishes to avoid the myriad of pitfalls inherent to the profession. More experienced teachers will not fail to find helpful suggestions and observations of procedures that may have been forgotten or neglected over the years. One can easily overlook the occasional *non sequitur*, omitted comma, or time-worn phrase, in favor of the overwhelming sincerity of Miss Broughton's approach.

Although the book is only one hundred and twenty-three pages in length, a multiplicity of pedagogical topics is covered, including the often-avoided "touchy" subjects such as advertising the profession, self-analysis, the piano teacher's relationships with the public school administration and the personal appearance of the teacher.

This book is liberally spiced with quotes from a number of professional musicians. Subject divisions are neat and accurate, allowing the reader easy access to specific content.

Brower, Harriette.
MODERN MASTERS OF THE KEYBOARD.
New York: Frederick A. Stokes Co., 1926.

This book of artist-interviews, published less than a decade after the appearance of the author's *Piano Mastery, Second Series,*[3] contains a roster of pianists who, in many instances, settled only recently into the pages of history: Gieseking, Landowska, Dohnanyi, Moiseivitch and Hess, among others. To my knowledge, only one, Alexander Brailowsky, is currently active in concert work.

It is interesting to note that virtually without exception, the artists included in *Modern Masters* were the giants of the era, and their names, even to this day, are instantly familiar. This is in contrast to Miss Brower's selections for the *Piano Mastery* series; notwithstanding her inclusion of the noted masters of the time, a number of these chosen pianists were destined to pass soon into oblivion.

[3]See review of *Piano Mastery, Second Series* by Harriette Bower, below.

Brower, Harriette.
PIANO MASTERY.
New York: Frederick A. Stokes Co., 1915.

PIANO MASTERY, SECOND SERIES.
New York: Frederick A. Stokes Co., 1917.

Harriette Brower was a prolific writer who specialized in interviewing the famous keyboard artists of her time. These two books, although somewhat similar to James Francis Cooke's *Great Pianists on Piano Playing,*[4] do not carry the degree of sophistication represented in Cooke's work. As implied elsewhere, Miss Brower's sentimentality of approach may cause some initial discomfort to the "modern" reader. Despite this minor point, these interviews, written in the days when the Saint-Saens *G minor* and the Rubinstein *D minor* were considered to be modern piano concertos and the works of Debussy, Rachmaninoff, Reger and Liadow to be products of the "ultramodern" school, are valuable mementos of that grand era of pianism. Also, unlike *Great Pianists,* in which only the "giants" are listed, *Piano Mastery* includes younger and/or relatively unknown pianists, some of whom subsequently became renowned.

The "relaxationist school" of pianism was in full flower at that time; the "weight and relaxation" techniques and their links to beautiful tone quality were discussed and extolled at great length by virtually all except the more scientifically oriented Harold Bauer.

Some of the notable pianists who are considered in these volumes are Paderewski, Stojowski, Ganz, Leginska, Busoni, Carreno, Backhaus, Gabrilowitsch, Von Bulow, Grainger, Hofmann, Novaes, Godowski, Levitzky and Joseffy.

[4]See review of *Great Pianists On Piano Playing* by James Francis Cooke, on Page 940.

Brower, Harriette.
WHAT TO PLAY—WHAT TO TEACH.
Philadelphia: Theodore Presser Company, 1925.

This book is essentially an extended treatise on program building. Part I consists of a series of nine sample programs selected by the author and graded according to difficulty; e.g., program no. 1 contains such selections as easy Bach *Minuets* and excerpts from Schumann's *Album for the Young;* program no. 9 is represented by Schumann's *Kreisleriana* and Liszt's *Hungarian Rhapsody No. 4.* Each program is discussed in fine detail, incorporating specific suggestions for practicing, descriptive and stylistic analyses of the chosen works, biographical material on the composers, evaluation of editions, and comments on the performance of these works by contemporary artists.

In Part II eight single compositions are discussed individually in even greater detail than above. Part III consists of "blow-by-blow" reviews of programs performed by the celebrated pianists of the era: Rachmaninoff, Hofmann, Cortot, Backhaus, Gabrilowitsch, Friedman, Bauer, Hess, Novaes and Paderewski. Subsequent sections include opinions of various pianists and teachers on program building, representative "unusual" programs and teaching-studio glimpses of Cortot and Schmitz.

Miss Brower writes with picturesqueness and vivid imagination, although with a degree of sentimentality that could make today's reader somewhat uncomfortable.

Caland, Elizabeth.
ARTISTIC PIANO PLAYING, AS TAUGHT BY LUDWIG DEPPE.
Nashville, Tennessee: Olympian Publishing Company, 1903.

Deppe's principles seem to have the element of "tone quality" as a foundation. He believed that piano tones must be produced according to certain laws for the ultimate in beauty; and, in this respect, he was not unlike Matthay, who insisted that a specific muscular combination is needed to produce a certain quality of sound.[5]

Deppe, however, inserted a visual element; he maintained that if the physical action looks correct, it is correct. He also claimed that only "necessary" movements should be used. To state these physiological and aesthetic conclusions another way, beauty of movement was equated with beauty of tone. Of course, in a sense, this is correct, but how can it be standardized? As Rudolf Serkin almost cracks his head on the piano's fall-board, he produces some of the most exquisite music on this side of Heaven; Walter Gieseking often needed no more physical manifestation than the slight lifting of an eyebrow; another noted pianist (who shall remain unnamed) weaves about as if he is balancing himself on a tight-rope.

I think it is safe to say that in Deppe's system, as in other celebrated systems, the real value lies in the by-products of method: results that are often obtained for reasons other than those claimed by the originator. Deppe made his pupils listen to what they were doing; he made them concentrate on what they were doing; he made them develop acute aesthetic values; he made them develop a consciousness of physical grace and of the conservation of energy. He thus arranged a wedding of musical concepts and "technique" and, in short, gave his students a philosophy of music-making based upon purity and objectivity.

To say that Deppe had confidence in his system would be a gross understatement. According to Amy Fay in *Music Study in Germany,*[6] Deppe claimed that "Gifted people play by the grace of God, but everybody could master the technique in my system."

[5]See review of Tobias Matthay's works and biography on page 948.
[6]See review of *Music Study In Germany* by Amy Fay on page 942.

Campbell, Le Roy B.
THE TRUE FUNCTION OF RELAXATION IN PIANO PLAYING.
St. Louis: Art Publication Society, 1922.

Basically, this is an excellent work. It is a product of its era, and much of the information that could have been accepted as valid at the time of publication has since been proved wrong. However, the author deals with many physiological truths and his clarified the term "relaxation" as applied to the pianistic art. Such definition stands out in bold relief among the hazy principles of the so-called "relaxationist school" of piano playing.

The author's thesis, and it is a perfectly valid one, is that the sensation of relaxation must be known and experienced in all possible ways so that it can be incorporated and utilized as needed. To this end, he has devised a number of exercises (not unlike Thomas Fielden in *The Science of Pianoforte Technique*[7]) to aid the player. These exercises are quite detailed—obviously the result of careful thinking; and they involve (hopefully) each important muscle of the piano-playing organism.

I sometimes speak of "literary traps"; and here I must say that Mr. Campbell has fallen into the "new-way-is-better-than-the-old-way-because-it-is-new" genre. Moreover, one finds an overabundandance of *non sequiturs,* erroneous analogies and oversimplifications. Notwithstanding, the book is a valuable one. The interested and astute reader will be able to glean much useable information.

[7]See review of *The Science of Pianoforte Technique* by Thomas Fielden, on page 942.

Carré, John F.
THE PSYCHOLOGY OF PIANO TEACHING.
Racine, Wisconsin: Conservatory Publishing Company, 1933. (Reprinted by Belwin-Mills Publishing Corp.)

The title *The Psychology of Piano Teaching* is somewhat of a misnomer, since the strictly psychological factors are covered in a rather small section of the book—only five and a half pages—or, if the reader wishes to stretch the topic a bit, no more than eleven pages. Otherwise, this book could be considered a general teaching manual, and a rather good one at that.

As is the case with a multitude of sister volumes, a large number of individual topics are touched upon, perhaps so that both author and reader can feel that little of importance has been left out. It is not without justification that this genre of guide-book exists. Windows, or at least peep-holes, are opened to the subject areas in which prospective teachers are going to have to think analytically. Such a volume can logically spur them to seek more detailed references or to experiment in more clearly-defined channels.

Often, however, the author of such a work may have a favorite area which he covers in special depth. In Mr. Carré's case, this area is the business aspect of the teaching profession. Although this book was first published in the deepest depths of the Great Depression, Mr. Carré's astute observations, procedures and suggestions are entirely pertinent to the needs and problems of the present day. Obviously, the fee structures have changed enormously; otherwise, his discussions of the ethics of competition and advertising, professional announcements, interviewing, bookkeeping, scheduling and so forth will be of value to the reader of the current decade.

Carreño, Teresa.
POSSIBILITIES OF TONE COLOR BY ARTISTIC USE OF PEDALS.
Cincinnati: The John Church Company, 1919.

It is refreshing to read a book on a technical subject based almost entirely on the intuitive reasoning of a great artist. Although the end result would hardly be the last word in scientific accuracy, there exists an ingredient of artistic involvement which, in a number of ways, can often clarify an issue in a most definitive manner.

Of course this highly subjective approach can pose problems as well. It is all too easy, under the spell of an artistic situation, to imagine effects that simply aren't there. For example, Miss Carreño states that the key must remain depressed through the entire note value (insofar as possible), even though the pedal is used for sustaining purposes, in order to avoid any interruption of the sound. Miss Carreño goes so far as to insist that substitute fingering be employed to ensure maximum legato in pedalled passages involving consecutive chords. This misconception is in no way connected to any lack of mechanistic knowledge at the time; Theodor Leschetizky stated many years before, "After all, you do not need your foot and your hands both. If the hands hold the note you don't need the foot to hold it, and if the foot holds it, then why the hand, too?"[8] Moreover, it cannot be considered as an illusion in the genre of the touch-tone quality relationship. In the latter, a difference in volume is noted primarily, and sometimes exclusively, as a change of quality. However, even the most perceptive listener cannot possibly detect a change in sound if the keys are released while the pedal remains depressed.

[8]Quotation from *Leschetizky as I Knew Him* by Ethel Newcomb. Reprinted by permission of Meredith Press.

Chasins, Abram.
SPEAKING OF PIANISTS.
New York: Alfred A. Knopf, 1958.

Books about pianists seem to have unusual appeal. They have been written, from time to time, almost since the invention of the instrument; and no doubt they will continue to be written as long as there are pianists to write about. Especially popular is the "Great-Pianists-of-the-Past-and-Present" genre. Author Chasins, however, has given us far more than a series of interviews and biographical sketches. He treats the past generation with due reverence and the present generation with objectivity. In addition, Mr. Chasins uses his book as a logical and effective sounding board for such timely and vital subjects as concert management, the recording industry and musical subsidy. He includes a wealth of information about interpretation, teaching, the great composers who wrote for the piano and many of their monumental works.

This book is not merely informative; it is provocative. Disturbing questions will come to the mind of the reader. What has happened to the pianistic arts in the eyes and ears of the public? What has happened to the glamor that was part and parcel of the pianist of yesteryear? What is the author's reason for writing twenty pages on Josef Hofmann, yet only listing forty-five present-day pianists on one page?

Nevertheless, Mr. Chasins is indeed a crusader for the American pianist; his exposé of certain aspects of the American musical scene of the '50s could certainly have placed him as a target for the fire of large and influential commercial bodies. Is is comforting to realize that there has been much improvement in the pianist's lot during the last decade.

Chasins, Abram, and Villa Stiles.
THE VAN CLIBURN LEGEND.
New York: Doubleday and Company, 1959.

The Van Cliburn Legend is a double-sided mirror: an engrossing narrative on what is perhaps the most unique American-pianist success story of the century and a pointed commentary on the commercially guided musical tastes of the day. The latter could be considered a follow-up to Chasins' treatment of similar material in his book *Speaking of Pianists.*[9] Searching, often unanswerable questions were implied in this earlier book, and they are continued here; e.g., why does the American public so often need a "gimmick" to enable them to appreciate a native-born artist? Why were ears that were deaf to legitimate music-making suddenly "tuned-in" to the "classics" when an attractive non-musical situation is added? Why does the "winner-take-all" philosophy often dominate the American musical scene? With consumate writing skill, Mr. Chasins and his collaborator, Villa Stiles, place these inequities (and many others) in bold relief without in any way negating the significant accomplishments and well-deserved approbation of Mr. Cliburn.

Now, in the perspective of a later decade, one still cannot lose sight of Mr. Cliburn's immeasurable contribution to the artistic world, of the growing prestige and increased status of the young American musician, and of the international aspects of Mr. Cliburn's achievement.

[9]See review of *Speaking of Pianists* by Abram Chasins, above.

Ching, James.
PIANO PLAYING—A PRACTICAL METHOD.
London: Bosworth and Co., Ltd., 1946.

I do not believe that there is a single author, living or dead, who could synthesize the physical, physiological and psychological aspects of pianism as intelligently and effectively as James Ching has done. *Piano Playing—A Practical Method* is a collection of lectures presented by the author in London during 1944-1945 and covers primarily a variety of technical approaches. The genius of James Ching lies in his capacity for analysis: taking into consideration all factors of a problem and coming up with a valid solution; determining what makes a technical "system" work and facilitating its utilization. Within the pages of his book it would be difficult, perhaps impossible,

to find any legitimate approach to piano technique that has not been described, analyzed, dissected and put into practical application by furnishing step-by-step, "how-to-do-it" information. A case in point is as follows: There is much space devoted to an intricate system involving the use of the wrist (undulating wrist, as he terms it) that can be recognized as a fundamental part of the method of the great Russian pedagogue, Isabelle Vengerova. Although Mr. Ching may have had no direct contact with Mme. Vengerova or her method, he accomplishes here what few writers can do; he reduces this "magic touch" to a rational, easily understood procedure, complete with aesthetic justification and scientific reasoning.

Much has been written, both good and bad, about the psychology of piano teaching. Less has been said about the psychology of piano practicing, and virtually nothing has emerged about the psychology of piano playing. In three chapters entitled, respectively, "The Psychology of the Learning Process," "Freudian Psychology and the Pianistic Art," and "The Relaxation Motif: A Psychological Analysis," Ching explores these areas with his characteristic insight and thoroughness.

Ching, James.
POINTS ON PEDALLING.
London: Forsyth Brothers, Ltd., 1930.

I have great admiration for Mr. Ching's writings; and I looked forward to reading his book on pedalling with much anticipation. His style of writing is invariably captivating. He involves the reader with the subject matter immediately, a "try-this-on-your-piano" approach. In asking the reader to explore with him, Mr. Ching is presently a prototype (1930 style) of what we now call "discovery learning."

Mr. Ching likes to emphasize the "why" of things; and that, I believe, will preclude the possibility of the reader being burdened with a multiplicity of unanswered questions. Some chapter divisions are classified in terms of purpose rather than in terms of effect or by composer, as in some other books on the subject. His explanations are assisted not only by musical examples, but by exercises. Non-musical examples or anecdotes are inserted as necessary to clarify essential principles.

No detail that might be misunderstood is slurred over. For example, in the category "half-pedalling" (which has as many definitions as writers attempting to give one), Mr. Ching makes a logical distinction between "half-pedalling" and "half-damping."

If this book pleases you, do not fail to read Mr. Ching's *Piano Playing—a Practical Method.*[10]

[10]See review of *Piano Playing,—a Practical Method* by James Ching on page 938.

Cohen, Harriet.
MUSIC'S HANDMAID.
London: Faber and Faber, Ltd., 1936.

Miss Cohen refreshingly departs from what might be called the standard pattern for so many volumes on the subject of piano playing.

Her book is divided into three main parts: The Composer, The Performer, and The Technique of the Approach to Music. In Part One Miss Cohen discusses with great insight and perspective the innovator's perpetual struggle for public acceptance of his ideas and justification for his break with tradition. A brief Part Two touches on the subjects of interpretation, technique, rhythm, touch, memorization and the great pianists. Part Three may be described as "master lessons" on a variety of piano compositions.

It is on the highly controversial subject of tone that I would like to make an observation. Throughout the book various adjectives describing piano tone quality are present: " . . . fat, bland kind of tone . . . clear piano or mezzo-piano . . . a thin quality or a thick quality . . . a mezzo-piano which is sharpened up . . . the tone . . . must have a living quality . . .

tone which stabbed one to the heart . . . tone here should be sensitive and nervous . . . a warm glowing quality should be infused into the tone . . . "[11]

I am in no way denying the great value of words that will stimulate the imagination and therefore aid the musical comprehension and projection; however, it will be difficult for the player to avoid frustration if he is not thoroughly familiar with all technical and acoustical considerations involved. May I strongly urge the reader who contemplates using this volume to become familiar with Miss Cohen's brilliant article in *Etude* magazine, December 1940, entitled "The Pianist's Technic and Tone." This is truly a remarkable synthesis of artistic thought and scientific understanding and will serve as the logical complement to *Music's Handmaid.*

[11]Quotation reprinted by permission of Faber and Faber, Ltd.

Cooke, Charles.
PLAYING THE PIANO FOR PLEASURE.
New York: Simon and Schuster, Inc., 1941.

Most books written for the amateur pianist are by professional pianists or teachers, who are often amateur authors. In this case the situation is reversed, as Mr. Cooke is a professional writer but an amateur pianist. Within this reversal of roles a new perspective has emerged—and a product that will be of great value to both the professional and non-professional pianist. Mr. Cooke has had frequent personal contact with notable pianists of the present generation, and he has supplemented this musical nourishment by extensive reading of the wisdom of past generations. Consequently, his writing is frequently spiced by pertinent quotations from masters of the pianistic arts. Above all, Mr. Cooke writes with the unbridled joy that is part and parcel of the true amateur's realm.

Mr. Cooke sets his goals and objectives on a very high plane and presents a most convincing case for the validity of this approach. Accurate physiology, sound pedagogy and irresistible psychology are all interwoven into a unique fabric of inspiration.

Cooke, James Francis.
GREAT MEN AND FAMOUS MUSICIANS.
Philadelphia: Theodore Presser Company, 1925.

This book contains commentaries on the art of music by sixty-three well-known (at least at the time of writing) personages. Although many branches of both the musical and non-musical professions are represented, Mr. Cooke is somewhat partial to pianists, since more than a third of his contributors belong to this genre of artist.

I have implied elsewhere that despite the diversity of opinions expressed by a composite of master musicians of a particular era, certain "common denominators" can be found. Among the pianists of *Great Men and Famous Musicians* it seems that the elements of versatility and adaptability are well in evidence; or, to express this in another way, it is freely admitted that there are many roads to technical and artistic competence. No one expressed this feeling more lucidly than the English pianist, Ethel Leginska.

Strong differences of opinion in other areas add interest for the reader; e.g., Rachmaninoff believed that pianistic standards at the time of his interview were markedly lower than in the days of Anton Rubinstein; on the other hand, Rosenthal and Friedman were in agreement that their contemporary pianistic standards would certainly equal or surpass those of all by-gone eras.

As many of the artist-writers were former students of Leschetizky, here is another source of first-hand information about that king of pedagogues.

A wealth of non-pianistic miscellany may be found in this book—encompassing topics from the acoustic observations of Thomas A. Edison to the incident that inspired Franz Drdla's "Souvenir."

Cooke, James Francis.
GREAT PIANISTS ON PIANO PLAYING.
Philadelphia: Theodore Presser Co., 1913, 1917.

Great Pianists on Piano Playing is a powerful book; it represents the essence of pianistic thinking in the early part of this century. Mr. Cooke describes his book as "A Series of Personal Educational Conferences With Renowned Masters of the Keyboard, Presenting the Most Modern Ideas Upon the Subjects of Technic, Interpretation, Style and Expression."

Over fifty years later, one hardly needs to alter the title; the chosen pianists are legendary, and, in a surprising number of instances, their ideas are as modern (or in some cases as dated) as their counterparts of today. I was especially impressed by the thoughts of Harold Bauer, who physiologically and psychologically was far ahead of his time. Much of his theory has been scientifically validated since the granting of his interview. Interestingly, Bauer's close friend and colleague, Ossip Gabrilowitsch, held views that in many ways were diametrically opposed to those of Bauer. Many readers will appreciate Alfred Reisenauer's early criticism of the "middle C approach" (he was interviewed in 1907) and his reluctance to introduce musical notation at the commencement of piano studies. Not surprisingly, most pianists seemed to feel the need for extreme concentration during practice, the musical and technical need for Bach, the need for careful listening at all times and the need for cultivation of individuality in technical analysis and interpretation. The greatest variances of opinion were prompted by the controversy over organized technic versus "technic from the music itself."

I should like to point out two significant "threads" of thought that would not be in evidence if such a volume were to be compiled today. First, professional pianistic goals reflected a polarity that no longer exists. Generally speaking, one either rose to the "height" of the concert stage or tacked up his shingle on the front door. Many and varied opportunities in the academic world simply did not exist. Secondly, these pianists often expressed a not-too-successfully camouflaged dislike for mechanical means of musical reproduction, i.e., player pianos and phonograph records. I do not think this was meant to be a summary dismissal of these devises *per se*, but rather to show distrust of what many considered a soulless means of producing and hearing music. In their minds the "touch" was missing, and, therefore, the individuality was destroyed!

Coviello, Ambrose.
WHAT MATTHAY MEANT.
London: Bosworth and Company, Ltd., 1948.

All devotees of Tobias Matthay can give a rousing cheer of appreciation to Mr. Coviello for his noteworthy contribution. His was a difficult task: the pitfalls of becoming involved in what might be described as a "second generation method" are manifold. It is impossible to be truly objective in such a project, since the personal opinions and prejudices of the commentator cannot help but come through in some measure. Some readers would be tempted to create another book entitled "What Coviello Meant," and so on, ad infinitum.

Although loyal to Matthay, Mr. Coviello has apparently come under the influence of Otto Ortmann's findings. In attempting to reconcile certain principles of Matthay with opposing principles, Mr. Coviello has brought together the irresistible force with the immovable object!

This book should definitely be read before moving on to any of Tobias Matthay's writings. Coviello fully admits the confusing aspects of Matthay's textual works and proceeds to effect a clarification by means of summarization and simplification. Matthay's technical theories are condensed into twenty-three key statements; his musical theories are also noted in concise fashion. However, Coviello feels that Matthay's most important contribution by far was his teaching approach. It would be difficult to disagree with this conclusion. It is common knowledge that Tobias Matthay taught with a degree of devotion that was virtually unsurpassed; he had an uncanny, instinctive knowledge of what was "right" and "wrong" in both pianistic approach and musical taste.

Flexible partisan that he is, Coviello does not avoid discussing fallacies as well as salient points in Matthay's approach. As an example, Coviello compares Matthay's views on rubato with those of another prominent pedagogue. Coviello admits to agreeing with the latter, and suggests that the reader compare both theories, subsequently hear a variety of competent performers and then make a decision!

Curcio, Louise.
THE MUSICIAN'S HANDBOOK FOR THE DEVELOPMENT OF MANUAL SUPPLENESS AND STRENGTH.
New York: The Joseph Patelson Music House, 1968.

This book is devoted entirely to a set of exercises designed to achieve the goal stated in the title. It is recommended by the author to both musicians and non-musicians; in short, to anyone who wishes to achieve greater efficiency, strength, facility and coordination in manual operation.

The author has made a special attempt to be concise. In a book that measures 3½" x 7" and contains twenty-three pages, one hundred and fifty-four exercises are described. This is made possible by a rather intricate system of cross-reference involving an anatomical sketch in the cover, a page of definitions, eighteen photographs (on one page) and a single page of both instructions and physiological orientation.

I would consider the absence of more detailed instructions and more specific precautionary measures a significant shortcoming of this book.

D'Abreu, Gerald.
PLAYING THE PIANO WITH CONFIDENCE.
London: Faber and Faber, Ltd., 1964.

In this volume, Mr. D'Abreu attempts to cover a great deal of material; indeed, his book carries the sub-title of "An Analysis of Technique, Interpretation, Memory and Performance." In scarcely over one hundred pages of text, however, it is not possible to do justice to all of these formidable subjects. Nevertheless, as a general introduction to a more detailed or sophisticated discussion of pianistic art, this book may be of value. Mr. D'Abreu's section on performance is especially well written for both the performer and the teacher of performance.

Mr. D'Abreu's frequent use of generalizations and oversimplifications could easily confuse the reader by not allowing him to have sufficient information to make a point lucid and convincing. In his preface he states, "Pianoforte practice is no longer a blind struggle towards improving technique, interpretation, memory and the rest."[12] Consequently, the reader could easily assume that pianoforte practice was a blind struggle through the days of C. P. E. Bach, Liszt, Chopin and the other keyboard giants from a bygone era.

Later, Mr. D'Abreu states, "We must have uppermost in our minds the thought that the obstacles we meet have been met and overcome by others, and that therefore there is no reason why we should not be able to do the same thing ourselves." If the reader accepts this statement literally and presupposes that any problem may be solved just by educated effort, he may be flirting with severe disillusionment.

In his section on "Touch," Mr. D'Abreu asserts, "The production of tone is a technique in itself, and it therefore has to be approached scientifically." Later on the same page he states, "It is common knowledge that muscular tension is responsible for harshness of sound." The inclusion of such an oversimplification without clarification and qualification could be entirely confusing to the uninitiated.

Within the section on syncopation, Mr. D'Abreu presents the following: "Syncopation disturbs the rhythmic flow. Used to advantage by both Romantic and contemporary composers . . . it is an excellent device for creating surprise or for adding impetus and excitement to normal movement." If I were reading this book and did not have advance knowledge of the subject, I would naturally believe that the use of syncopation began in the Romantic era. It would be perhaps unnecessary for Mr. D'Abreu to discuss its vital role in fourteenth century

music or even its use in the late works of Beethoven, but certainly almost everyone knows the little Bach *Musette* where syncopation often takes its first hold on the budding pianist.

[12]Quotations reprinted by permission of Faber and Faber, Ltd.

Dickerson, Ruth A.
A NEW APPROACH TO PIANO TECHNIQUE.
New York: Pageant Press, Inc., 1962.

Habitually, one looks askance at the term "new" when applied to piano methods or approches. The "newness" of Miss Dickerson's approach may not be taken as literally by some readers as by others; however, the author presents an interesting description of her version of the role of the finger in piano playing: "The finger does a sort of 'push-up' from the bottom of the key, upward and slightly outward, then immediately returns to the curved position, never losing contact with the key and moving exactly with it both down and up."[13]

One may logically think that this is more of a psychological than a physical aid to piano technic; nevertheless, it is a well-taken observation, and the reader may be interested in pursuing the principle involved. I can recall other similar types of aid, such as thinking of the upstroke of an adjacent finger to provide the motive power for the downstroke of the playing finger (from Dr. D. C. Dounis); or, thinking of "pulling" rather than pushing on the normally contracted finger in playing position, to avoid any "breaking-in" of the nail joint.

Unfortunately, Miss Dickerson is severely handicapped in her overall presentation by linking her "new" technical ideas to antiquated notions about the mechanism of the piano.

[13]Quotation reprinted by permission of Ruth A. Dickerson.

Diller, Angela.
THE SPLENDOR OF MUSIC.
New York: G. Schirmer, Inc., 1957.

The very title of this excellent volume presents a most significant clue, not to its content, but rather to the attitude of the author; Miss Diller's writing attests to her awe and respect for the art of music. Such a superlative degree of appreciation is rare.

This is primarily a book on the pedagogical aspects of pianism. Miss Diller covers such general areas as the transition from studying to teaching, a teacher's qualifications, group and individual piano sessions, choosing music for study, practical details, phrasing, ear training, practicing, memorizing and piano technique. The controversial subject of pupil recitals is discussed with insight and understanding. Piano teachers will be especially interested in a "case history" section which consists of a narrative of significant parts of actual interviews, auditions and lessons.

Although some readers may feel that Miss Diller's approach to piano technique *per se* is a bit "old-fashioned," (leaning more heavily on tradition than on physiological and acoustical truths), it cannot be denied that her vivid illustrations, lucid descriptions, vital explanations and imaginative comparisons combine to make this one of the most readable and worthwhile books in the realm of piano pedagogy.

Ehrlich, Alfred Heinrich.
HOW TO PRACTICE ON THE PIANO.
New York: G. Schirmer, Inc., 1901.

Mr. Ehrlich approaches the art of practicing from a primarily technical standpoint—a contrast to, for example, the all-encompassing attitude of Hetty Bolton.[14] The author initially assures the reader that his work is not a method *per se*, but rather a supplement to existing methods.

Historically speaking, Mr. Ehrlich's book reached the public at an interesting time. First published in Germany in 1879, it came about in the wake of a number of practice devices (various kinds of mechanical contrivances and hand-guides), and the refutation of the necessity of using these devices is a primary thesis. However, it was not possible for Mr. Ehrlich to divorce himself entirely from the philosophy behind them, as a certain rigidity in technical approach is strongly implied. It might be said, in effect, that his technical principles were directly opposed to those of Matthay;[15] Ehrlich supported the high finger motion, brisk attack, etc. However, the idea of reducing unnecessary motion is common to both technical theories.

The final portion of this book is devoted to directions for practicing the Tausig-Ehrlich daily studies.

[14]See review of *How to Practice* by Hetty Bolton on page 935.
[15]See review of Tobias Matthay's works and biography on page 948.

Evans, Edwin.
HOW TO ACCOMPANY AT THE PIANO.
London: William Reeves, 1917.

This is a representative sample of the textbook of yesteryear: carefully written in impeccable and proper English, dryly factual, meticulously detailed in certain areas and highly organized into numbered paragraphs.

I do not think that the modern reader would support the degree of emphasis given to what the author has classified as the various forms and styles of accompaniment. Alternating hand motions, ostinato figures, broken chord accompaniments, uses of the holding-note, sustained harmonies, among many others, are each given recognition in individual chapters. Perhaps a general heading of "ensemble syntax" would cover a variety of these items, enabling the prospective accompanist to utilize the resources of his own ear rather than an intricate network of musical subdivisions. One must keep in mind that this portion of the text deals with playing accompaniments, not creating them.

Enigmatically, the sections on modulation and transposition are relatively brief, presenting only introductory material for these complex skills.

Faelten, Carl.
TEACHER'S MANUAL FOR PIANOFORTE COURSE.
Boston: New England Conservatory of Music, 1889.

Many of the teacher's manuals published by individuals who head their own private music schools take on the character of a house-organ, and this book is no exception. However, such a fact attaches no stigma to this prophetic and historically valuable treatise.

It will be of great interest to today's more progressive piano teachers to know that Mr. Faelten was a real pioneer in both class piano instruction and functional pianistic skills. To my knowledge, he was the first in this country to institute group piano in a private music school, noting that it " . . . will produce better results in cultivating general proficiency than exclusive private instruction." Keyboard harmony, sight reading, transposition, analysis, etc. were incorporated as the basic necessities of versatile pianism.

A substantial part of the book is devoted to lists of selected piano literature, including the turn-of-the-century studies which were characteristically high in opus number and low in quality. However, his carefully subdivided classifications of much now-standard piano solo music can be of value to us, three-fourths of a century later. His inclusion, in the listings, of his own contemporaries—Chaminade, Heller, d'Albert, Kullak, MacDowell, Moskowski, Henselt, *et al.*—gives us valuable information about the pedagogical tastes of that era.

Fay, Amy.
MUSIC STUDY IN GERMANY.
Chicago: A. C. McClurg & Company, 1880. (Reprinted by Dover Publications, Inc., 1965.)

In a most absorbing narrative, Miss Fay presents a vivid picture of musical and non-musical life in Germany during the years from 1869 to 1875. A compilation of letters written to her family in America, *Music Study in Germany* contains significant pianistic history on the immensely enjoyable level of back-fence gossip!

Miss Fay's book had wide influence during its early years of availability (there were twenty-one printings in America alone, followed by translations and re-publications in other countries); and it was instrumental in creating great interest in the United States for European music study. It sparked an international awareness of the principles of Ludwig Deppe,[16] who could be considered one of the pioneers in a physiological approach to piano teaching.

Miss Fay studied with four celebrated teachers: Tausig, Kullak, Liszt and the aforementioned Deppe. Her boundless enthusiasm and lack of affectation in describing her lessons and personal experiences leaves us with far more than an academic chronicle; she has bequeathed to us a living record of this colorful "golden age" of pianism.

[16]See reviews of *Artistic Piano Playing, As Taught by Ludwig Deppe* by Elizabeth Caland on page 937.

Fielden, Thomas.
THE SCIENCE OF PIANOFORTE TECHNIQUE.
London: Macmillan & Co., Ltd., 1927.

The solemn proclamation (in the first sentence of the preface) that this book is a scientific treatise could easily frighten away the prospective reader. However, *The Science of Pianoforte Technique* is entirely readable without being in the least condescending to the non-scientifically oriented musician.

Unfortunately, Mr. Friedlen is placed in the unenviable position of the proverbial scientist who was finally able to present "convincing" proof that the world was flat, just as Columbus discovered the New World. (The "Columbus" in this case is, of course, Otto Ortmann.[17]) This is not to say that the book is not a valuable physiological reference; it simply means that Fielden, being unaware of the true capacities of the piano's mechanism, has on occasion become mired in the confusion of unresolved variables.

Otherwise, the book is extremely well organized and quite revealing. His comparisons of the "methods" of Leschetizky, Breithaupt and Deppe disclose the fact that these "old-timers" knew more about physiology than we would generally give them credit for. Fielden's own well-illustrated section on physiology as related to the piano-playing organism is one of the best to be found anywhere.

I was especially impressed by the chapter on "Gymnastics." As defined by the author, this heading is not to be confused with traditional (arm, wrist or finger) exercises. The gymnastics described are designed not for strengthening the muscles (a usual purpose of gymnastics), but rather for enabling the pianist to experience accurately the sensations of tension and relaxation and allowing these sensations to be recognized as needed. This basic principle is hardly old-fashioned; in a higher degree of refinement, it is the "latest thing" in a specific branch of psychiatric therapy.

[17]See review of *The Physiological Mechanics of Piano Technique* by Otto Ortmann on page 950.

Fillmore, John Comfort.
PIANOFORTE MUSIC.
Philadelphia: F. A. North & Co., 1888.

This book is divided into five parts, the first three of which trace the evolution of keyboard music through the Romantic period of the 1870's. Although expertly and concisely written, these three parts do not differ greatly in content from material which is currently available and readily accessible to us.

It is in the last two sections, "The Development of Piano-forte Technic" and "Minor Composers and Virtuosi of the different Epochs," that the phenomenal insight of the author and inestimable value of the book is revealed. Mr. Fillmore gives a graphic picture of the interaction of the avant-garde performer and the capacities of the keyboard instruments themselves. This is written with the perspective of a man who was living while Liszt was still in the process of transforming the art of pianist. One can see from the inside, as it were, the inevitable forcing of the piano beyond its boundaries and capacities, and how the search for more and more "technique" led many of its seekers into blind alleys and tunnels of erroneous thought.

I am amazed by Mr. Fillmore's evaluation of his own era. His profile of Liszt, in terms of an evaluation of his works, his place in musical history and his influence on future generations, was uncannily prophetic. His classification of "major and minor" composers remains virtually identical to similar classifications written almost a century later, through artificial artistic cycles created by the ebb and flow of the waves of changing tastes.

As for his predictions of the future, here is a musical Jules Verne. In speaking of future keyboard instruments, he states, " . . . perhaps the coming instrument may employ tuning forks instead of strings, and may even give the player command at will of all the varieties of tone-color producible by the orchestra. Who knows?".

Electronic piano makers, take heed.

Foldes, Andor.
KEYS TO THE KEYBOARD.
London: Oxford University Press, 1950.

Mr. Foldes has prepared a brief, direct volume that expresses his very personal views on several vital pianistic subjects. Sincerity, honesty and unpretentiousness are paramount qualities in Mr. Foldes' work; one never receives the impression, "Do this because it is what I have done (and therefore correct)," but rather, "I have experienced this and it has worked for me. Perhaps it will work for you as well."

This book can hardly be described as an all-inclusive text. The subject matter is narrowly selective and consequently, despite the volume's small size, one feels that what is covered is done so with thoroughness. I can picture this book as an ideal supplement to almost any volume that is more universal in content; one need not fear duplication.

Throughout the volume, I constantly detect a feeling of what I might call "artistic reassurance," giving the reader a sense of comfort rather than of apprehension. This is especially noticeable in his sections on preparation for (and involvement in) public performance and memorization.

A high degree of organization is apparent in Mr. Foldes' discussion on the art of practicing; a true balance of values may be perceived. The author outlines what practicing can and cannot do. Practice goals are clearly and specifically delineated; practice problems are anticipated and explained; special exercises are suggested for basic problems; aesthetic and practical considerations are outlined in significant detail. Even intricate plans of practice organization are discussed which may be adapted to the needs of the individual pianist.

Ford, Donald.
THE SINGING-CLASS PIANIST.
London: Joseph Williams Limited.

There are relatively few books available on the art of accompanying, and virtually all of these are directed to the professional rather than to the amateur pianist. However, *The Singing-Class Pianist* is a book written for the inexperienced and perhaps untrained accompanist. Therefore, even though this work is quite brief, it fulfills a definite need.

The term "singing class" as used by the author may be stretched, in view of the book's usefulness, to include the choral organization, church choir and even the individual soloist. General and specific musical suggestions are volunteered; pertinent areas covered include sight reading techniques and related skills with which the accompanist may find himself involved (i.e., conducting from the piano).

Franz, Frederick.
METRONOME TECHNIQUES.
New Haven: Yale University Press, 1947.

To my knowledge, this is the only volume ever available which is devoted exclusively to the use of the metronome. For this reason alone, it would be a worthwhile addition to one's library; it should at least be included in one's professional reading schedule.

Mr. Franz discusses the metronome's use in non-pianistic areas as well as pianistic ones; e.g., in controlling instrumental and vocal vibrato. However, the primary value of this treatise to the pianist lies in its description of various techniques over and above the conventional means of setting tempo and maintaining constant speed in practicing.

As the name Franz immediately brings to mind the well-known electric metronome, it is good to note that this volume is in no sense an advertisement or instruction book for his product. Indeed, only a two-sentence reference at the end of the book is made to the Franz Electric Metronome.

In a final section consisting of various statements and testimonials attesting the value of the metronome, the inadvisability of watching the pendulum of the Maelzel (mechanical) type while listening to the clicks is mentioned. I cannot help but disagree with this statement, and I have often suggested to my students the purchase of the Maelzel-type purely because of the visual-aid factor: at a very slow setting, the observation of the pendulum by the peripheral vision of the player can be an enormous aid to rhythmic accuracy.

Garvin, Florence Hollister.
THE BEGINNINGS OF THE ROMANTIC PIANO CONCERTO.
New York: Vantage Press, Inc., 1952.

Miss Garvin has covered a segment of musical history about which many pianists have been only passively curious. It is all too easy to accept the periods of classic and romantic concerto writing as separate eras without actively considering the brief but noteworthy time of transition.

Miss Garvin approaches her subject with understanding and projects her information with clarity and conciseness. Many examples from the piano concertos of the three outstanding composers representing this era—Hummel, 1778-1837; Weber, 1786-1826; Mendelssohn, 1809-1847—supplement the text.

Gat, Jozsef.
THE TECHNIQUE OF PIANO PLAYING.
Budapest: Corvina Press, 1965.

The Technique of Piano Playing is one of the finest and most comprehensive available texts devoted to this subject. Translated from the original Hungarian, the second edition reflects the able assistance of Dr. Howard Gloyne, M. D., the Kansas pianist-internist who fused his expertise in two areas to correct and improve the original edition.

There are no wasted words in this book. The reader must concentrate heavily and read carefully in order to absorb properly the immense amount of material covered. Gat has created his own terminology in many instances: e.g., "swing-stroke" and "weight-effect," and although his descriptive words accurately reflect their function, it takes time to become familiar with them. One may even have the feeling that the text is too detailed and consequently, one may learn more about physical and physiological interrelationships than is really necessary or desirable.[18]

A unique facet of presentation is the series of motion picture frames illustrating technical approaches and analyzing technical problems. Although the action can be followed effectively by looking at a number of individual "stills," how much more effectual it might be to have these photos on the sides of consecutive pages (or as an independent supplement) so that they may be viewed like old-fashioned "flipbooks."

Detailed explanations in areas often neglected by other writers, e.g., seating height or application of noise-effects, contribute to the high value of this book. Hardly a scientific approach excluding true musical values, *The Technique of Piano Playing* interrelates such vital forces as emotional con-

tent, musical imagination, body positions, breathing and muscle action. Questions on practice procedures are explored: Is endless repetition of any value or can actual damage be done by this approach? Can an emotion be exactly repeated? What are the real effects of mood or fatigue on practicing? How can the pianist listen to himself with real objectivity? What is the difference between slow practicing and playing in a slow tempo?

Little of value is left uncovered in this volume. Jozsef Gat has the rare gift of being able to synthesize theory, fact and practical application.

[18]See review of *The Artist at the Piano* by George Woodhouse on page 956.

Gebhard, Heinrich.
THE ART OF PEDALING.
New York: Franco Colombo, Inc., 1963.

Leonard Bernstein's eulogistic introduction furnishes a perfect setting for the reading of this artistically and inspiringly written book.

As in the volume by Karl Ulrich Schnabel,[19] over-detailed text is eschewed and more extensive use is made of the musical examples. It must be noted that this is the only book in which the piano's capacity for effect is challenged, as it were, by the author's occasional substitution of subjective auditory illusion for scientific fact about the piano's mechanism.

Gebhard's views on the pedalling of Bach's music reflect the "old school" of conservative pedal treatment; his ideas on the pedalling of Romantic music seem to be both authoritative and highly imaginative.

Not often found elsewhere are valuable sections on unusual combining of pedals and on the use of the pedal in chamber-music.

[19]See review of *Modern Technique of the Pedal* by Karl Ulrich Schnabel on page 952.

Giddings, Thaddeus P., and Wilma A. Gilman.
GIDDINGS' PUBLIC SCHOOL
CLASS METHOD FOR THE PIANO.
Boston: Oliver Ditson Company, 1919.

T. P. Giddings was one of the pioneers of class-piano instruction as we know it today. Although this book was written over a half-century ago, many of his basic organizational ideas and educational purposes have survived—and thrived—to the present time. The greatest change over the years—and, of course, this would be expected—was in actual class procedure.

Although the prospective or practicing class-piano teacher may not glean a great deal of material from this book that is directly usable in teaching, I strongly recommend the work for its historical value. Mr. Giddings gives a fascinating account of the initial class program in the Minnesota Public Schools: the early experiments, pedagogically and artistically, and the financial problems (most amusing in the light of present-day inflation).

Mr. Giddings writes in a most informal style. He wastes no words and furnishes many light moments with his subtle sense of humor. It is easy to see how a man of the caliber of Thaddeus P. Giddings gave a mighty fillip to the cause of Music Education.

Grundy, Enid.
THE HAPPY PIANIST.
London: Oxford University Press, 1947.

The Happy Pianist is directed to the individual who contemplates music study on the level of the amateur. Carefully and concisely written, this book is designed to supplement a course of instruction rather than to substitute for it. The author's style is well-suited to the subject matter, involving gentle but forceful repetition of important points, clear delineation of topics and just the right amount of humor to lighten an otherwise over-serious heading.

Miss Grundy rides the crest of the Matthay wave,[20] but in no way tries to reflect the intricacy of his approach to the uninitiated amateur. Both idealistic and practical in nature, *The Happy Pianist* may well serve as the turning point for the undecided dilettante.

[20]See reviews of Tobias Matthay's works and biography on page 948.

Hamilton, Clarence G.
WHAT EVERY PIANO PUPIL SHOULD KNOW.
Philadelphia: Theodore Presser Co., 1928.

Most books on the art of pianism are directed to the teacher or to the advanced student, and of course this involves an element of musical sophistication. Here is a book, however, that is truly meant for the musical neophyte. In his presentation, Mr. Hamilton combines an infectious enthusiasm with an easy-going informality. His book is totally disarming, non-technical in approach and infused with warmth and sincerity.

Although the greater part of the volume deals with material introductory to the skills and basic knowledge of elementary piano playing (including music fundamentals and a history of the instrument), a convincing case is made for the why of piano study, which in other treatises is all too often obliterated by the how. The sensitive and meaningful relationship between teacher and student is discussed in fine detail, enabling the prospective pupil to be emotionally prepared for this experience.

Harris, Reginald, and Edwina Palmer.
HOW TO CHOOSE AN INSTRUMENT: PIANO AND STRINGS.
London: The Fountain Press, 1953.

This book is designed to aid the prospective piano (and stringed instrument) buyer by establishing criteria for intelligent selection. The emphasis is on the evaluation of used pianos rather than new pianos, a point of view brought about by the fact that at the time of writing, new pianos were almost impossible to obtain in Great Britain.

Although the book is small in size, the significant points are amply covered. Both the objective (construction, physical condition) and subjective (tone, appearance) elements are discussed; a comparison is made of the relative merits of grands and uprights; a "what to avoid" roster is incorporated, including, for example, "modernized" ancient pianos and "practice" pianos obtained on the thought that any instrument is good enough for a beginner.

Suggestions are made for choosing and maintaining pianos for institutional use (especially for the school, church and "village hall"); and in this category the check-points of heating, ventilation, placement and the effect of wear and tear are brought forth.

Although primarily written for the British market, this book will be of value also to the American consumer.

Harrison, Sidney.
TEACHER NEVER TOLD ME.
London: Elek Books Limited, 1961.

Although this book may have been designed more for entertainment than for instruction, it most certainly must take its place in the "must-reading" catagory. It is described as "delightfully irreverent" on the dust cover, and this terse evaluation gives a revealing clue to its content. Time-honored (but not always time-tested) theories topple before his witty observations, and revered masters shrink to the size of ordinary mortals.

In speaking of an early teacher's views on tone production, Harrison states, "He told me that relaxation improved tone. I couldn't see why. It seemed to me that the way to improve tone was to buy a better piano."[21]

In discussing Tobias Matthay, Harrison reflects, " . . . [he] was the sort of author who tells you something in ordinary type, rams it home in italics, adds an N. B. in block capitals, and then, via a footnote, refers you to one of his other books." This is balanced with "Matthayites . . . nearly all had one great merit; a piano under their fingers often sounded better than it really was."

Readers who are looking for specific pianistic or pedagogical catagories will find especially valuable Mr. Harrison's discussions on the role of patronage in music history, the dance forms from Bach to Gershwin, what people think about when they play, nervousness as a natural hazard, adjudicating in festivals and competitions, and television as an educational medium (in this instance, establishing a frontier for TV piano lessons). (Note: these are my own composite headings, and they do not necessarily coincide with the author's chapter classifications.)

[21]Quotations reprinted by permission of Elek Books Limited.

Harrison, Sidney.
THE YOUNG PERSON'S GUIDE TO PLAYING THE PIANO.
London: Faber and Faber, 1966.

Here is a delightful book for young people of all ages. It is many-sided in terms of potential use: an introductory work to serve as a prelude to actual music study; a pedagogical text to aid the teacher in finding new and more pleasant ways to offer basic instruction; a student's handbook that can be used not only to answer specific questions but, because of its unusual appeal, for reading and re-reading from time to time in order to allow its many salient points to be fully absorbed.

In less than seventy pages, Mr. Harrison is able t· ·ack in the real pianistic essentials, but never in a crowded t. hion. The book is replete with masterfully constructed examples and word-pictures; often made by using fascinatingly onomatopoetic British terms.

May I suggest this book as a "number one" gift for your teen-age student?

Hipkins, A. J.
A DESCRIPTION AND HISTORY OF THE PIANOFORTE.
London: Novello Ewer and Co., 1896.

This remarkable volume is divided into three parts: a detailed treatise on the construction of what can be called the modern piano; an historical survey of the keyboard stringed instruments which preceded the piano; and the development of the early piano up to the time of introducing iron into its construction.

My own use (above) of the term "modern" may appear paradoxical in view of the fact that this book was published in 1896. Most pianists, however, will agree that any "improvements" to the instrument during the twentieth century are relatively insignificant compared to the large-scale modifications that occurred during the nineteenth century. Consequently, Mr. Hipkins, actually living through the piano's golden era of growth (the author was born in 1826 and died in 1903), has been able to present a stirring account of this phase of the piano's progress.

Many rarely found, but exceedingly important, facts are included; for example, piano keyboards until almost the midpoint of the nineteenth century were made with shorter keys, necessitating (as we know it) an unconventional position of the player's hand since the thumb could not assume what we now consider a "normal" position. Yet, in many historical surveys of piano technique, only the modification of the keyboard action in weight and depth is deemed responsible for muscular changes in technical approach.

Another example of important facts included is the revealing explanation of why the real una-corda pedal (which had a provision for the use of one or two strings) could not be incorporated into the modern piano: the hammers used in Beethoven's day were small and made of leather, but a felt hammer would soon be cut up by the multiple movements demanded.

Hofheimer, Grace.
TEACHING TECHNIQUES FOR THE PIANO.
Rockville Centre, N. Y.: Belwin, Inc., 1954.

This book may be best described as a potpourri of musical thoughts. The organization of material is somewhat loose, which actually works out to advantage, as much peripheral knowledge is incorporated which otherwise might be excluded in a more tightly-knit organizational scheme. Miss Hofheimer has a highly developed musical conscience, and this is no more strongly represented than by her unwillingness to compromise standards for the musical hobbyist. She believes that the difference in accomplishment between the serious student and the dilletante should be purely quantitative, a premise with which I can agree in large measure.

The author states in the preface that science and art are both integral factors in the aesthetic result, and attempts to follow through in both these channels. Unfortunately, on the scientific side, Miss Hofheimer confuses what might be called "musical control" with "muscular formulae," resulting in a multiplicity of quasi-scientific conclusions that produce the very element of confusion that she is expressly trying to avoid. In a number of instances, her conclusions are downright erroneous; e.g., the implication that slow practicing or playing is merely a "slow motion" technical counterpart of the faster motion used in an "a tempo" rendition.

A wide variance in quality of material presented is apparent in this work. However, it could easily be said that its greatest value lies in the author's account of the philosophical and psychological aspects of piano teaching.

Hume, Ruth, and Paul Hume.
THE LION OF POLAND—THE STORY OF PADEREWSKI.
New York: Hawthorn Books, Inc., 1962.

This book is classified by the publisher as a "Junior Biography," and many piano techers will be very grateful for the existence of such a work. There is certainly a dearth of biographical material at this level of readability, and we are fortunate to have a book of this caliber accessible to our students.

The period of time from Paderewski's early childhood to his death is covered in smooth transition. Paderewski's pianistic accomplishments and political endeavors are interwoven in remarkable perspective. Be sure to read this book before you present it to a young student; there is much to be learned from it.

Hutchings, Arthur.
A COMPANION TO MOZART'S PIANO CONCERTOS.
London: Oxford University Press, 1948.

The subject of Mozart seems to be an ever-flowing fountain whence an endless variety of descriptive, biographical and analytical substance can flow. Because of the diversity of attitudes and approaches of the authors, the prospective reader of such works has the tremendous advantage of rarely having to anticipate repetition of material. Consequently, this book emerges not only as a companion to Mozart's piano concertos, but also as a companion to the other significant works on this composer.

This volume moves along at a highly sophisticated level, and although it cannot be classified as difficult reading, it is most certainly slow reading. One simply cannot skim through such a book without missing a great deal of tightly-packed and relevant information. The author's formidable background allows no unlinked elements; a devastating wit and unusual command of vocabulary will fascinate the astute reader.

In addition to a discussion of Mozartian concepts, spheres of influence and performance practices, this volume includes a detailed examination of each Mozart piano concerto.

Johnson, Thomas Arnold.
THE PRINCIPLES OF PIANOFORTE PEDALLING.
London: A. Weeks & Co., Ltd., 1953.

More of a pamphlet than a book (it contains only twelve pages), *The Principles of Pianoforte Pedalling* covers certain vital points on pedal technique and is amply illustrated for its length. Unfortunately, it does not go into sufficient detail to avoid possible misconceptions or misunderstandings. In addition, the author's supplementary hints are much too general to be of value and could possibly be of harm. For example, it is suggested that the player should not use the pedal for scale passages, excepting only those scales that are in the treble and which are used in conjunction with chords. The author further suggests avoiding the use of the pedal in seventeenth and eighteenth century music.

Kelberine, Alexander.
THE FOUR FAMOUS PIANOFORTE SONATAS OF BEETHOVEN.
Glen Rock, N. J.: J. Fischer and Bro., 1939.

The works chosen by the author as the four famous sonatas of Beethoven are the following: *Op. 13 in C minor (Pathetique), Op. 27, No. 2 in C sharp minor (Moonlight), Op. 53 in C minor (Waldstein), and Op. 57 in F minor (Appassionata).*

These analyses are no mere academic representations. The writer becomes deeply involved in each analysis, which may be described as *ad hoc* in nature; i.e., relating to no established traditional format. Structural and interpretative elements dominate; pedagogical aspects are eschewed almost entirely.

Mr. Kelberine writes with uncommon scope; he incorporates historical setting, observations of other brilliant scholars and significant events in the life of the composer as related to the particular sonata involved. Kelberine's affinity for Beethoven is overwhelmingly apparent.

Above all, this book is fascinating reading—unusual for analytical material.

Kullak, Adolph.
THE AESTHETICS OF PIANOFORTE PLAYING.
New York: G. Schirmer, 1895. (Third Edition).

This is a book of both historical significance and timeless musical perspective. Although the first edition was published almost a century ago, several revisions by Hans Bischoff (the third edition was completed in 1889) have materially changed the essence of the work; indeed, Mr. Bischoff's modifications and additions comprise, in my opinion, the most valuable parts of the volume.

In *The Aesthetics of Pianoforte Playing*, one may find a background for some of the general concepts of the present day. The "singing tone" idea was very much in the foreground, not really spoken of in an illusional manner but rather as the "striving" of a relatively imperfect instrument for an elusive vocal quality. Likewise, the decay of piano sound was a disturbing factor; I do not think it had been fully accepted as an irrevocable element, but merely compromised as not being really a part of the Romantic ideal.

Very often, an artistic generation will blame the immediately preceding generation for intolerable lack of taste! In this context, the author (really Bischoff) speaks of virtuosity for its own sake as the crime of a past era: " . . . the pianoforte was for a time an arena for jugglers with effect." This is followed by the classic "Now-a-days, of course, the sole value of virtuosity lies in carrying out the artistic intention."

Actually, only a relatively small portion of this book deals with musical aesthetics *per se*. The bulk of the text covers the more conventional aspects of technique and interpretation which, although understandably somewhat dated, are nevertheless extremely well-written. Along with the previously noted aesthetic considerations, the chapters "History of Clavier Virtuosity" and "Critical and Historical Reviews of Pianoforte Methods, and of Writings on Pianoforte Playing" should be of special interest to the reader.

Kürsteiner, Jean Paul.
EXPERT AID TO ARTISTIC PIANO PLAYING.
New York: Unz and Company, 1910.

Jean Paul Kürsteiner was an American pianist and teacher who occupied a twig on the pianistic family tree; he studied at the Leipzig Conservatory with Robert Teichmüller, who in turn worked with Carl Reinecke at the same institution. This small volume contains several essays, imaginatively and picturesquely written: "The Thumb as King Pin," "Conservation of Energy," "Equal Finger Development," "Punctuation in Music," "A Plea for Harmony as a Help to Music Study" and "Atmosphere—the Aura of an Artist."

Last, Joan.
THE YOUNG PIANIST.
London: Oxford University Press, 1954.

I would venture to say that this is the most authoritative book available on the subject of early piano instruction. One cannot feel that Miss Last is merely experimenting or propounding theoretical knowledge; she simply knows what she is talking about.

The most striking manifestation of Miss Last's pedagogical genius lies in her ability to convert the commonplace into the attractive. The most basic or elementary finger exercise turns to gold by means of a certain musical twist or a captivating set of words. An aptly chosen title immediately clarifies the purpose of an otherwise meaningless finger drill.

Miss Last does not believe in artistic compromise and asserts that the young player can be musically aware during every phase of the learning process. Indeed, it would be hard to imagine an unmusical product of her inspired and devoted teaching.

Detailed advice is given in all pertinent pedagogical areas. Of special importance is Miss Last's description of her approach to the very first lesson and her suggestions for choosing first pieces.

Leimer, Karl, and Walter Gieseking.
RHYTHMICS, DYNAMICS, PEDAL.
Philadelphia: Theodore Presser Company, 1938.

Rhythmics, Dynamics, Pedal is an outgrowth of and supplement to Mr. Leimer's and Mr. Gieseking's first book, *The Shortest Way to Pianistic Perfection.*[22] As can be expected, the areas listed in the title are expanded here, but not without frequent references to the earlier book. Invariably, opinions expressed in no way conflict with or contradict those contained in *The Shortest Way*, notwithstanding the fact that seven or eight years elapsed between the writing of these two named works.

It becomes increasingly evident that Leimer's link to greatness (if this can be assumed from the artistic success of his greatest pupil, Walter Gieseking) is due in large measure to his thoroughness rather than to any revolutionary approach. There is nothing "new" or startling in his teaching, but there is constantly apparent a supreme logic, a continuity of presentation and an endless flow of patience in explaining detail. Furthermore, Leimer did not work in isolation; he frequently refers, by name, to other renowned pedagogues and their ideas.

It seems to me that this book, in some ways, lacks the clarity of presentation of the first volume. This is due, in some measure, to the use of a number of terms that may not be familiar to the reader, either because of obsolescence, rare usage or ambiguity in translation.

The reader may be especially interested in Leimer's discussion of pedalling. In describing what he terms "time-treading," meaning that the pedal is depressed exactly with the note or chord to be played, the author claims that all the Beethoven Sonatas can be pedalled in this manner.

[22]See review of *The Shortest Way to Pianistic Perfection* by Karl Leimer and Walter Gieseking.

Leimer, Karl, and Walter Geiseking.
THE SHORTEST WAY TO PIANISTIC PERFECTION.
Philadelphia: Theodore Presser Company, 1930.

Although Mr. Leimer himself refers to this treatise as presenting his method or system, it seems to me that the procedure is too non-specific and eclectic to be objectively classified in those terms; I would prefer to call it a philosophy of teaching. Certain basic tenets are in evidence: a minimum of physical exertion (eradication of superfluous physical movements) and a maximum of mental exertion (an acute awareness of musical values during the act of playing). Leimer's suggested process of learning a composition involves particular steps and concepts: 1) a highly detailed structural analysis must be made immediately to facilitate rapid (even immediate) memorization; 2) the process of interpretation must commence only after the technical foundation is prepared; 3) the acquiring of a ready technique can be accomplished basically from the music itself.

The author's musical integrity is well established by such beliefs as the necessity of studying fewer compositions with greater intensity when the artistic results would suffer otherwise (this is not as much of a platitude as it might initially seem to be, since being "repertoire-happy" is a very common fault, especially at a high artistic level); and also the belief that the irrevocable artistic duty is to adhere to the will of the composer, i.e., the artist must effect a wedding of accuracy (first) and subjectivity (second).

It must be said that ambiguities occur more often than they should. What is an "absolute" legato or "perfect" relaxation? If the latter were interpreted literally, the player would soon be snoozing on the piano bench. Even the word "perfection" in a place as obvious as the title smacks of the unobtainable rather than the realistic.

Lenz, Wilhelm von.
THE GREAT PIANO VIRTUOSOS OF OUR TIME.
New York: G. Schirmer, Inc., 1899.

This is not the typical "Great Pianist" book in which a sizeable number of artists are effectively described in an objective manner. Mr. von Lenz concentrates upon four virtuosi—Liszt, Chopin, Tausig and Henselt—and bases his material upon personal acquaintance with the artists involved.

Not surprisingly, Liszt emerges as a god rather than as a mortal. Unfettered by the external reality of perspective, von Lenz is uninhibited in his evaluation of the master. "Liszt is a phenomenon of universal musical virtuosity, such as had never before been known: not simply a pianistic wonder. Liszt is a phenomenon spreading over the whole domain of musical production, and creating a universal standard of comparison . . . Nothing could be more foolish than to attempt to imitate Liszt, or even to use him as a measure by which to criticise others. Where Liszt appears, all other pianists disappear; there remains only the piano, and that trembles in its whole body!".

By means of anecdotes, the author is able to present a significant profile of Chopin's personal life as well as of his musical views and opinions. A seemingly definitive answer to the somewhat controversial question on the Chopin rubato might be as follows: "'The left hand,' I often heard him (Chopin) say, 'is the conductor; it must not waver, or lose ground; do with the right hand what you will and can.' He taught: 'Supposing that a piece lasts a given number of minutes; it may take ust so long to perform the whole, but in the details deviations may occur!'"

Levinskaya, Maria.
THE LEVINSKAYA SYSTEM OF PIANOFORTE TECHNIQUE THROUGH MENTAL AND MUSCULAR CONTROL.
London: J. M. Dent and Sons, Ltd., 1930.

This book represents an almost unbelievable enigma in musical thinking. The author, in a convincing, readable and erudite style, has unfolded a highly detailed and complex system (she does not wish to use the term "method" of piano

playing), all based upon a fallacy. This is not to say that the book has no value or that much of her reasoning is not without worth. As an historical reference, it is almost unsurpassed as a source of descriptions of the methods and doctrines of the celebrated teachers of the nineteenth century. In a technical way, she analyzes and compares the "older school" of "stiff fingers" with the "newer school" of "relaxation," concluding, logically, that the correct approaches may involve both schools.

As I was reading through the concluding portions of this book, I could not help thinking, "This woman has a highly analytical and searching mind. If only she had written a decade or two later and had allowed her ideas to be shaped and tempered by such scholars as Ortmann, Schauffler or Schultz!" Subsequently, I came across a statement that she had recently read Ortmann's *The Physiological Basis of Piano Touch and Tone*, and that this scientific treatise supported her theories. Instantly I realized that such a basic misunderstanding of principle could stem from only one cause (and this can apply to many other earlier writers as well), namely, the possession of a very respectable knowledge of physiology and almost complete ignorance of the tone-actuating mechanism of the piano.

It could be said that Miss Levinskaya's system deals with physical or muscular sensations, not in the all-encompassing rhythmic sense of Whiteside, but rather in the tonal sense of Matthay.[23]

I think there is much to be gained, at least indirectly, from this book. Please, however, read *Piano Technic, Myth or Science?* by Lawrence Schauffler, or its equivalent, as an antidote.

[23] See reviews of *The Pianist's Mechanism* by Abby Whiteside on page 955 and Tobias Matthay's works and biography on page 948.

Lindo, Algernon H.
PEDALLING IN PIANOFORTE MUSIC.
London: Kegan Paul, Trench, Trubner & Co., Ltd., 1922.

Lindo's book is the largest treatise (one hundred and eighty-five pages) on the subject of pedalling that is listed in this bibliography. The author makes no particular effort to be concise, and it is somewhat refreshing to find a book on pedalling that is not overly terse.

Unlike the authors of most other pedal-books, Mr. Lindo cites as "ordinary" pedalling the depressing of the pedal at the instant of striking the note or chord. In more modern pedalling techniques, the so-called syncopated pedalling is considered the norm and point of departure for other special uses and effects.

A common theme in most books on pedalling is that of placing unlimited blame upon composer and editor alike for insufficient clarity in pedal notation. While there is undoubtedly a certain amount of censure to be channeled in that direction, I cannot help but think of the automobile-safety controversies in similar context. The manufacturers can be justifiably criticized for building cars that are less-than-safe, but let us not forget the "nut at the wheel" as a very possible source of trouble as well!

One may feel that this volume is somewhat over-classified. There are many rules and exceptions to rules; there are many sub-divisions of categories. It is possible that such a system of piano pedalling, if taken too literally, may not allow sufficient flexibility for individual artistic tastes.

The section on special effects is excellent; and it should be an invaluable source of reference. An example is the creating, with the assistance of the pedal, of a *ff* to *ppp* trill by illusory effect. It is one of the most fascinating sounds that can be made by a modern instrument.

Lockwood, Norman.
NOTES ON THE LITERATURE OF THE PIANO.
Ann Arbor: University of Michigan Press, 1940.

Through the years books devoted exclusively to piano literature appear far less frequently than books on piano ped-

agogy. Therefore, each one that exists carries a certain degree of importance. When this volume was published, only a handful had been written up to that time, and it filled a rather substantial void in this area.

This work is written in an ultra-conservative manner, which is surprising for a book that emanates from the late 1930's or early 1940's. Contemporary American composers are lumped together in a miscellaneous category; Bloch, Copland, Gershwin, Griffes, Harris, Ives, Riegger and Sessions are classified, without comment, along with George T. Strong, Alexander Macfadyen, J. Albert Jefferey and Louis Campbell-Tipton. It is curious and perhaps significant that Mr. Lockwood wished to make no value judgment on these composers or their works; other writers of similar evaluative books could be surprisingly selective, accurate and prophetic.

Bartók is virtually dismissed as a collector of folk tunes, although a condescending note is made of his potential for greatness after he will have completed his folk-tune collecting.

Although many of the composers included are represented by a list of piano works and accompanying descriptive or historical material, other national groups are often represented in a way similar to that which is used for the American composers. Consequently, Hindemith, Kodaly and Schoenberg are equated with Alexander Jemnitz, Geza V. Zagon and Siegfried Karg-Elert under the classification of "Miscellaneous German and Hungarian Composers."

Mr. Lockwood obviously has, however, some strong preferences. Liszt commands twenty-two pages in his book; Beethoven, four and one-half; J. S. Bach receives somewhat less than four. Benjamin Godard is covered in slightly over one page, while Satie and Stravinsky receive several lines each.

I do not wish to criticize Mr. Lockwood for his personal judgments; yet, one cannot simply dismiss what one does not understand in a work which purports to enlighten the reader in such a wide subject area. One must balance subjectivity with scholarliness.

Notwithstanding these limitations, it can be said that Mr. Lockwood writes with erudition and imagination. There is much valuable information, especially of a peripheral nature, that will supplement the more objective surveys that are currently available.

MacEwan, Desirée.
THE FIRST TWO YEARS OF PIANOFORTE STUDY.
London: Oxford University Press, 1930.

The title of this book might lead one to think that it is a succession of detailed lesson-plans, involving the step-by-step process of an instructional method. Actually, it consists of a master-outline divided into six terms, each of which is categorized into fundamental units of study: rhythm, aural training, specific pianistic activities and a composite of notation and sight reading. Each of these categories is discussed in detail, combining guided experiences for the student (in the five to eight year range) with a wealth of pedagogical suggestions for the teacher. This volume may serve as an idea supplement to any "method" or system the teacher wishes to use.

Although one has the feeling that Mr. Tobias Matthay is looking over Ms. MacEwan's shoulder, the influence does not dominate in any way.

Mason, Ella H., and Ramond Burrows.
ANSWERS TO CRITICISMS OF CLASS PIANO INSTRUCTION.
New York: National Bureau for the Advancement of Music, 1930.

Most treatises on the subject of class piano emphasize the positive aspects. This booklet goes one step further in delineating specific criticisms, analyzing the issues involved and presenting definite countermeasures (if the criticism is justifiable) or adequate defense (if the criticism is not justifiable).

I would highly recommend the reading of this work to individuals who wish further orientation on the subject or who want to formulate their own organized perspective on the advantages and disadvantages of this popular teaching medium. Thirty-six questions are presented, involving such areas as sight reading, individual development, playing time during lessons, individual technical drill, the recognition of individual differences among students, financial considerations, "keeping up" with the group, standards of interpretation, problems in teaching techniques, problems of discipline, the furnishing of incentive for practicing at home and the maintenance of student interest.

Matthay, Jessie H.
THE LIFE AND WORKS OF TOBIAS MATTHAY.
London: Boosey and Hawkes, 1945.

Much critical material has been written about the theories or doctrines of Tobias Matthay. Neutrality is not generally shown. One of his students may eulogize or defend him in glowing terms or a scholar with opposing ideas may attack him unmercifully. Mrs. Matthay's loving account of Tobias Matthay's life contains a dimension that no other descriptive writings include: that is, an informal chronology of his theories and discoveries complete with the particular incidents that precipitated them. From this body of information emerged his unique terminology and "laws" of piano playing.

We can see that Tobias Matthay's task was not an easy one. The relative standardization of the instruments of today did not exist in Matthay's early years (e.g., the Erard was not equipped with front weights, making the action unusually heavy); and Matthay's attempt to accommodate piano technique to basic principles was confounded by the multiplicity of variables in the pianos themselves. However, the subsequent "explosion" of much of his theory does not negate his enormous contribution to the pianistic art.

Mrs. Matthay gives a fascinating account of Tobias Matthay's early years: his activities as a performing pianist and composer, his association with other notable musicians of his time and his initial attempts at writing, all leading up to and climaxed by his first major work, *The Act of Touch* (1903). It must be noted here that this book is the basic work of Matthay and that much of his later writing involves explanations, amplifications, simplifications or condensations of this treatise.

Matthay's pedagogical activities at the Royal Academy of Music and at his own Pianoforte School are described at length. Special mention is made of his stellar pupils, many of whom will be familiar to the reader.

Matthay, Tobias.
ON MEMORIZING AND PLAYING FROM MEMORY.
London: Oxford University Press, 1926.

Tobias Matthay was probably the most prolific writer on pianistic subjects who ever lived. His works have precipitated strong controversies and have indeed accounted for much of the twentieth century pianistic (verbal) literature, created in opposition to his theories. His most vulnerable area was the realm of piano mechanics; and, as science tended to prove more of his theories erroneous, the controversies became increasingly "heated." However, his stature as psychologist-teacher was almost never questioned; and, when his writing involves the subject of practical psychology, one can find little with which to disagree and, conversely, a great deal to consider and accept.

Consequently, in a treatise such as this, the reader is best able to appreciate Matthay's forceful style, boundless enthusiasm and a terminology which necessarily transcends the boundaries of the English language. One can easily forgive a certain amount of physiological truth-stretching when it is done in good faith and with the supreme purpose of driving a point home in the most effective way possible.

Matthay, Tobias.
PIANO FALLACIES OF TODAY.
London: Oxford University Press, 1939.

One can hardly obtain a perspective on the history of piano pedagogy without becoming involved in some of the works of Matthay. Because of the large quantity of his writing, however, the element of selectivity can pose a problem for the reader. I would place this volume high on the priority list, since it (despite the small size) not only serves to clarify his own principles in a relatively succinct manner, but it also affords Matthay the opportunity to defend himself against a newer generation of scientifically-oriented musicians, notably Schultz and Ortmann, who seek to topple his pianistic structures.

The result is often a compounding of musical misunderstandings. Mr. Matthay regrets that he is often misunderstood (although this could be the inevitable result of his making the obvious sound complex); and he feels that he must further clarify his stand on certain musical matters. Yet, it is obvious that he himself misunderstands the scholarly attempts of Schultz and Ortmann. The issues are further confounded by what amounts to cross-attacks on the futility of over-terminology!

A very important point is made by Matthay in his discussion of the relative merits of the various sciences in their application to music and to piano playing in particular. He stresses the importance of psychology; and he decries the over-use of facts when this very over-use may not be pedagogically (or psychologically) sound. He infers that if such an imbalance exists in this relationship, it is unscientific, despite the accuracy of the factual material. I agree. An interesting analogy might relate to a performance of old music that is meant to be authentic. Great care is taken to match the conditions that existed when the music was created to the point where, in terms of "modern" ears, communication with the audience is lost and, consequently, the very link to authenticity that was hopefully being approached.

Melling, E. H.
EXTEMPORIZING AT THE PIANO MADE EASY.
London: William Reeves, 1931.

This small volume could best be classified as an introduction to the art of improvisation rather than a detailed manual for acquiring skill in that area. Its range of usefulness is very narrow, since it assumes an adequate knowledge of elementary harmony as a prerequisite and covers a relatively brief amount of territory immediately beyond this stage. However, it does have the notable quality of consciseness (more common in older methodological works than in newer ones); and it presents suggestions that are not covered in similar fashion elsewhere.

Merrick, Frank.
PRACTICING THE PIANO.
London: Barrie and Rockliff, 1958.

Frank Merrick was a pupil of the celebrated Theodor Leschetizky and has been strongly influenced by the master's teaching. This is not to say that his book merely reflects Leschetizky's principles; on the contrary, Mr. Merrick's varied and comprehensive suggestions for piano practice are highly original. In an area of writing where "new" and "original" material can often be found in a variety of sources, such a remark denotes high praise; much of the substance of this volume simply cannot be found elsewhere.

Numerous and pertinent quotations from the wisdom of Leschetizky are included, but these are preceded by annotations to enhance modern understanding: e.g., Leschetizky " . . . loved pithy overstatements" or "Leschetizky always expected us to season his utterances with the salt of common sense."[21]

Practicing the Piano is not always easy reading. Packed into its one hundred and eleven pages are no less than twenty-six individual headings, including such fanciful and imagina-

tive subjects as "Delayed Continuity," "Practicing on the Surface of the Keys," "The Postman's Knock," "Practicing with One Finger," "Body Stillness and Dramatic Significance." These, of course, are in addition to such down-to-earth topics as the ways of practicing chords, finger passages, the preparation of hand positions, the beauty of tone and so forth.

A delightful sense of humor is always in evidence; and Mr. Merrick's devotion to the art of teaching is well reflected in the dedication: "To all my pupils past and present from whom I may well have learnt more than they can have learnt from me".

[24]Quotations reprinted by permission of Mr. Merrick.

Michel, N. E.
MICHEL'S PIANO ATLAS.
Pico Rivera, California, 1961.

This unique volume is basically an index of piano manufacturers. One can express only amazement and praise for the scope of this reference; no less than six thousand, five hundred and eighty names have been incorporated—far beyond the wildest expectation of the unsuspecting reader.

Probably the greatest value of this book is that it enables the reader to determine the age of any given piano by referring to the serial numbers, classified by year of manufacture. In addition, Mr. Michel provides capsule information as available, including pertinent historical facts and other useful "tidbits," photographs of various pianos through the ages, statistical information and antique piano advertisements from the nineteenth century.

Milinowski, Marta.
TERESA CARREÑO.
New Haven: Yale University Press, 1940.

Teresa Carreño deserves special recognition for being (to my knowledge) the only extended work on this celebrated artist; indeed, its comprehensiveness would seem to preclude any further attempt to detail the life of Mme. Correño. Perhaps cognizant of the uniqueness of her work, Professor Milinowski writes with an inclusiveness and timelessness that should make her book gratifying and readable for future generations as well as for the present. Over-documentation and over-romanticizing are avoided; the essence of Carreño's professional and personal life are deftly interwoven; acknowledgment is made of the fact that a negative as well as a positive side of a great person does exist, and should not be disguised or eliminated in a definitive and evaluative work of this genre.

The many anecdotes and humorous stories incorporated into the text seem especially well-chosen. Ample space is devoted to the teaching philosophy of Mme. Carreño; and a generous quantity of well-reproduced photographs represent the artist in many phases of her career.

Moldenhauer, Hans.
DUO-PIANISM.
New York: Coleman-Ross Company, 1950.

One could not begin to imagine a more exhaustive treatment of this subject. Virtually every conceivable topic within the duo-pianistic realm has been unearthed, explored and discussed. The thoroughness with which Mr. Moldenhauer has gathered his information is constantly a source of admiration, yet the fine detail that would naturally result from this approach is never dry or uninteresting. Especially gratifying are the sections devoted to the classification of information obtained by interviewing (by both personal contact and questionnaire) well-known duo-pianists and composers of duo-piano music.

Since this book also covers the purely pedagogical aspects of the physical existence of two pianos in proximity to each other (as a studio teaching aid, for example), it will be a valuable reference volume for anyone engaged in piano teaching, not merely for two-piano-performance enthusiasts. There is only one genre of piano-music lover who may be disap-

pointed, even annoyed with this book: the one-piano, four-hand partisan. Moldenhauer does little to disguise his basic conviction that whatever the piano duet can do the two-piano ensemble can do better. It would perhaps have been more prudent for Mr. Moldenhauer to admit the validity of one-piano, four-hands as another effective musical medium rather than to have used its existence as a basis for elevating the the two-piano domain.

Moore, Gerald.
AM I TOO LOUD?
London: The Macmillan Company, 1962.

Rarely does an artist write as artistically and eloquently as he plays; the exception can certainly be found in Gerald Moore's *Am I Too Loud?*

Perhaps unashamed but hardly insensitive about his calling, Mr. Moore plunges another large nail into the coffin of the "accompanist-is-an-accessory" belief that is all too prevalent, even to the present day. Moore's unflagging sense of humor is both his feather tickler and rapier. Many of his personal-professional experiences are described in a way that will draw involuntary bursts of laughter from the reader. On the other hand, individuals who, by dint of conceit or stupidity, interrupt the smooth flow of activity are skewered unmercifully (and deservedly!). Mr. Moore combines with great sensitivity his natural sense of modesty with a realistic appraisal of his own gifts; consequently, his reminiscences of making music with some of the greatest singers and instrumentalists of our time emerge with a rare objectivity.

The scope of this book involves far more than musical anecdotes. Topics of vital interest to the ensemble player (accompanist, if you will) include ensemble technique, balance, the art of transposition (including the hair-raising story of how a beautiful friendship was destroyed by an adventure in transposing), acoustical considerations, stage lighting, page turning and many more. Of special historical significance are his unparalleled (at least in my reading experience) accounts of pre-electrical recording sessions.

Neal, Harry Lee.
WAVE AS YOU PASS.
Philadelphia and New York: J. B. Lippincott Company, 1958.

This autobiographical work is a delight from beginning to end. Although the total amount of space devoted to pedagogical topics is relatively small, there are valuable references to the teaching of Isabelle Vengerova and to the rehearsal and performance techniques of two-piano playing.

In a chapter entitled "Isabelle Vengerova," Mr. Neal provides a sensitive, searching and at times hilarious account of his experiences with this celebrated pedagogue.

As a veteran of many seasons of duo-piano performing (with his wife Allison Nelson), Mr. Neal is eminently qualified to discuss the aesthetic as well as the organizational aspects of his art.

Newcomb, Ethel.
LESCHETIZKY AS I KNEW HIM.
New York: D. Appelton Company, 1921. Reprinted by Da Capo Press, 1967.

No one with a love for his pianistic heritage can afford to ignore this chronicle of a bygone era. Even allowing for an understandable degree of romanticizing in Miss Newcomb's writing, Leschetizky emerges as a truly outstanding psychologist and philosopher of his day. Much has been said about the Leschetizky "method," and perhaps even more has been said about his absence of method. This book, I believe, will clarify that controversy, which in reality is almost purely semantic in nature. In a conversation with the author, Leschetizky states (in speaking of Malwine Bree's forthcoming book on his "method"), "One has to call it something, if one must write a book at all about the way to study." Subsequently, he offers, "Don't have a method; it is far better to

leave your mind a blank for the pupil to fill in . . . I have no method and will have no method. Write over your music-room door the motto: NO METHOD."[25]

Common sense as well as psychological insight were vital ingredients in Leschetizky's evaluation of pianistic problems. In discussing the use of the damper pedal, Leschetizky by-passes much of the pedagogical subjectivity and psuedo-science yet to come: "Why does one need pedal marks? It is the people who don't listen who need the pedal marked for them! After all, you do not need your foot and your hands both. If the hands hold the note you don't need the foot to hold it, and if the foot holds it, then why the hand, too? . . . You don't need rules for the pedal—you need common sense and your ear to direct you."

In reading this book, one cannot help but reflect on the gradually increasing role of the academic in the education of the musician. Total involvement or saturation in musical experience during the formative years is now almost a thing of the past, and one wonders how much has been lost or gained.

A more prophetic portion of the book reads as follows: " . . . turning to a row of long-haired young men standing at the back of the room, he said, 'Come up here, one of you, and see if your long hair will help you to do it any better.' " Perhaps times have not really changed so much.

[25]Quotations reprinted by permission of Meredith Press.

Newman, William S.
THE PIANIST'S PROBLEMS.
New York: Harper and Row, 1956.

William Newman's book is certainly one of our present-day pedagogical classics, and for many excellent reasons. At the risk of sounding trite, I will have to say that there is truly "something for everyone" in this volume. The skilled professional will undoubtedly find much material that will be of interest to him; the serious amateur will discover new concepts and procedures that will enhance his comprehension and appreciation. Perhaps I am not the only reader who found himself nodding frequently in approval or reminiscence.

The general subjects, Musicianship, Technique, Practice, and Performance, comprise the major part of the content, with subdivisions and supplements combining to form a surprisingly large amount of material for this slender volume.

An experienced author, Dr. Newman can pack a substantial amount of information in pithy statements. Noteworthy examples: "The pianist . . . can control but two things: the volume of the tone at the instant of attack and the duration of the tone while it lasts. That is all. On these two controls he must depend for everything that constitutes style and interpretation in piano music." [Interpretation is] " . . . the sum of understanding, experience and talent." " . . . the learning process does not distinguish between accidents and conscious efforts." "Neither teacher nor student should encircle the mistakes with a pencil. (One soon learns to recognize the age of such mistakes, like the age of trees, by the number of rings.)"[26]

Despite its concentrated and weighty material, it cannot be said that *The Pianist's Problems* is difficult reading. Newman's style reflects a clarity, conciseness and conviction that can only be the product of a high order of intelligence.

Many readers will be fascinated by Dr. Newman's suggestions for use of the metronome, an area usually neglected in modern pedagogical writing.

[26]Quotations reprinted by permission of Harper and Row, Publishers, Inc.

Ortmann, Otto.
THE PHYSIOLOGICAL MECHANICS OF PIANO TECHNIQUE.
New York: E. P. Dutton and Co., Inc., 1962.

Otto Ortmann's *The Physiological Mechanics of Piano Technique* remains the most detailed and comprehensive study ever made to relate the physical and physiological aspects of piano playing. It is hardly a book with which one can curl up by

the fireside and read for relaxation; it is a fundamental text that will be referred to time and time again—studied, digested, applied and re-studied. The principles so clearly outlined by Ortmann percolated down to many treatises written after the publication (1929) of his study; consequently, much of the validity and authenticity of the so-called technical manuals of later generations are the result of Ortmann's dedication. Pedagogical ideas, previously accepted as law despite their hazy beginnings and scanty proof of effectiveness, had to be revised in the reflected light of this study.

The book is divided into three main sections. Part I, "The Physiological Organism," deals with physiological and anatomical orientation. Part II, "General Aspects of Physiological Movement," covers the larger movements and functions. Part III, "The Touch Forms of Piano Technique," explains the specific approaches used in the act of piano playing; e.g., arm legato, tremolo, staccato, etc., leading up to a primary goal in any technical approach—the obtaining of the tone quality desired by the player.

Palmer, King.
TEACH YOURSELF TO PLAY THE PIANO.
London: The English Universities Press, Ltd., 1957.

Most musicians will feel that the learning of music is hardly a "do-it-yourself" project; however, *Teach Yourself to Play the Piano* can be recommended with certain reservations. It must also be noted that since this book was first published, a number of effective programmed units in music fundamentals have appeared, providing a more logical approach to self-study than a purely textual format.

There is much to say in favor of this book: it is written in a manner that will be easy for the musical layman to understand; certain basic pianistic concepts (such as fingering) have been covered in a concise but highly logical manner; and despite its modest size, no significant point for the beginner has been overlooked. Even the English and American names of note-values quaver = eighth note, etc.) have been compared in a chart to avoid any possible misunderstanding.

However, by the very nature of the previously noted textual format, the book tends to be too compartmentalized in chapter areas, making it difficult for the student to achieve a basic continuity on his own. The asset of brevity can occasionally be turned into a disadvantage when oversimplification is allowed to obscure fundamental truths. In some cases, rigidity in musical "rules" might prove to be over-restricting interpretatively; e.g., the admonition that a staccato note is to be held down for half its full value.

I can see this book as an excellent supplement to a more detailed step-by-step piano course or as a ready reference for the professionally-guided amateur.

Potamkin, Frank.
MODERN PIANO PEDAGOGY.
Philadelphia: Elkan-Vogel Company, 1936.

It becomes immediately apparent that Mr. Potamkin's book is not the conventional pedagogical manual. He does not attempt to cover the entire realm of pedagogical subjects and divide them more or less equally within the pages of his book. An extended discussion on musical memory covers no less than seventy-one pages; the subjects of tone-production and pedalling receive similar in-depth treatment. Subsequently, other pertinent topics receive more brief but equally careful attention.

Some readers may feel that Mr. Potamkin's selections on memorizing and tone production may be overdrawn and/or over-theoretical. They are infused with long quotations from "authorities" which, after all, do not really substitute for authors' paraphrases and can interfere in some measure with basic continuity. This is also the case in the section on tone production, where the author quotes copiously from both Matthay and Ortmann who, in many ways, are incompatible in basic physical theory.[27] Conflict is avoided, as Potamkin uses no quotation from Ortmann that would disagree with one

of Matthay! Although Ortmann's main contribution to this pianistic area, the quantitative aspects of quality, is not noted in the main body of the author's chapter on tone production (it is, of course, in opposition to Matthay's theories), it is succinctly, if paradoxically, implied in the chapter's resumé.

I feel that the best sections of this book are those that reflect the personal experiences of the author—e.g., slow practicing, separate-hand practicing, sight reading, fingering, harmony, phrasing, etc.—rather than those that are the result of scholarly research.

[27]See reviews of Tobias Matthay's works and biography on page 948 and *The Physiological Mechanics of Piano Technique* by Otto Ortmann on page 950.

Prentice, Ridley.
HAND GYMNASTICS.
London: Novello and Company, Ltd., 1908.

From time to time, treatises on gymnastics appear, either as independent works or as parts of more comprehensive pianistic "how-to-do-it" manuals. (Gymnastics may be identified as a form of muscular development of the whole or parts of the piano-playing organism without recourse to the instrument itself.) The utilization of this form of exercise has never really been out of fashion; Prentice's book was the third significant one to appear in the latter part of the nineteenth century, and today one can find detailed sections on the gymnastic art in notable books such as Gat's *The Technique of Piano Playing*.[28] (It should be said here that Gat used Prentice's book as a reference for his own section on gymnastics.) However, opinions differ as to whether such exercises should be used in place of, or in conjunction with, exercises at the keyboard. Mr. Prentice maintains that the latter method is most practical.

In justification of the necessity of using hand gymnastics, Prentice states that parts of the body other than the hand have had the chance to develop in the normal course of activity. However, this is not the case with the hand. If the brain conveys messages to a hand that is not capable of responding, inefficiency will result. The author's premise is that the keyboard *per se* is simply not designed for the purpose of developing the hand in a truly organized fashion.

As a training manual, *Hand Gymnastics* seems very well put together. The author prepares his reader with a psychologically oriented introduction; precautionary measures are inserted so that any possible physical harm can be avoided; all points are presented in fine detail and clearly illustrated with drawings. The author further suggests that for maximum efficiency, procedures be carried out in classes.

[28]See review of *The Technique of Piano Playing* by Jozsef Gat on page 943.

Prentice, Ridley.
THE MUSICIAN—A GUIDE FOR PIANOFORTE STUDENTS.
Volumes I - VI. Philadelphia: Theodore Presser Company, 1886.

This remarkable six-volume work is best described by the author himself: "My object . . . has been to supply, in a convenient form, such facts regarding the structure and meaning of music as a teacher would naturally explain during his lesson; and to add to the interest, I have, wherever it was possible, inserted particulars as to the time and place of writing, with anecdotes throwing light on the composer's method." "The whole work will be divided into Six Grades, distinguished by the varying degrees of difficulty in the pieces analyzed."

In an introductory section by F. L. Ritter, it is stated that " . . . every contribution to musical literature which aims at a higher artistic end than mere superficial virtuosity, and which at the same time helps to remove the old slovenly empirical method of teaching, must be welcomed by every intelligent, earnest art teacher. Mr. Ridley Prentice's work . . . is a contribution of such a healthy nature."

We are familiar with this type of statement, the "commercial." that runs through the pages of history, saying in effect, "At last we have found the 'right' way!". It must be admitted, nevertheless, that the pedagogical principle of such an analytical and descriptive work will always remain sound; i.e., any factual information that can be presented in written form will release the teacher to present ideas; in this way, the maximum benefit of study can be obtained.

Reeder, Betah.
THE SINGING TOUCH.
New York: Galaxy Music Corporation, 1943.

The vast majority of books devoted to the ways of varying tone quality by means of specific manners of key-depression were published up through the 1920's and to a much lesser degree in the 1930's. It is uncommon to find a book of this sort emerging in the 1940's, when overwhelming proof of the fallacy of this premise had been evident for some time. I am tempted to classify Miss Reeder as a latter-day Levinskaya; however, unlike Mme. Levinskaya, Miss Reeder's knowledge of basic piano mechanism is considerable—a fact that makes her conclusions all the more curious.

On the positive side, it must be said that her well-organized factual material in areas of musical acoustics and piano action is lucid and well-illustrated. Historical materials are given, describing the physiological adjustments made necessary as keyboard instruments progressed from clavichord to harpsichord to various stages of the pianoforte.

Excellent material is presented on the interaction of artist's desire and manufacturer's fulfillment.

Richner, Thomas.
ORIENTATION FOR INTERPRETING MOZART'S PIANO SONATAS.
New York: Teachers College, Columbia University, 1963.

Thomas Richner, who is one of our country's leading Mozart specialists, has presented us with an invaluable introduction to the study of Mozart's piano works. Obviously the result of an overwhelming love for Mozart's music, a deep understanding of interpretative intricacies and an all-encompassing interest in the peripheral aspects of Mozart's creative process, this volume presents an overview of much that is necessary and desirable for the would-be interpreter of Mozart.

The book is divided into a number of independent sections, both delineating and linking various aspects of orientation. The role of Mozart's contemporaries is discussed, outlining an interesting balance among the great and not-so-great composers who were instrumental in shaping Mozart's genius. A chapter on the pianos of Mozart's time gives valuable clues to the range of tonal variety needed for authentic interpretation.

A sensitive analysis of Mozart's tonalities and harmonies gives much insight into the unity of Mozart's works. Mozart's own ideas on piano performance are incorporated, referring to the use of the body mechanism, tempi, physical attitudes, demeanor and general interpretative means. A clear and concise chapter on ornamentation should serve as the last word in authenticity.

The second half of Mr. Richner's book is devoted to specific structural, stylistic and interpretative analyses of the works themselves.

In view of the general excellence and wide scope of this volume, I hesitate to infer that anything is missing. However, is not a significant facet of Mozart's genius his unparalleled gift for rhythmic texture? If the work of one of Mozart's contemporories can almost be mistaken for a work of Mozart's, it is often the subtle interplay of note values that will separate the great from the near-great work. Of course, involvement in this area could result in an extended study in itself. Perhaps someday Mr. Richner will favor us with such a work.

Riefling, Reimar.
PIANO PEDALLING.
London: Oxford University Press, 1962.

As I commenced reading seven books on the subject of pedalling that were currently available to me, I felt that perhaps the age of overspecialization had come to the art of pianism. Writing a book exclusively on the technic of pedalling, it seemed to me, was analogous to an ear, nose and throat doctor's specializing in the right nostril. I was soon to change my mind. Not only were there absences of redundancies, but in each book there were points covered that were totally missing in the others. Therefore, a truly sizeable composite volume could well be imagined.

Piano Pedalling is a very well-written book, perhaps the best of those available for the musician who requires a straightforward, accurate and lucid account of pedal techniques. In an historical section, a fascinating description is given of a double-shifting soft pedal that would be able to give accurate representations of una corda, due corde and tutte le corde. Such a pedal would be highly desirable for producing the tonal effects prescribed by Beethoven in certain later works.

Every book written on piano pedalling speaks in some measure of how musical notation influences the use of the pedal. Unique, however, is the author's chapter on how the use of the pedal has influenced musical notation. In the latter classification, Mr. Riefling demonstrates the type of musical shorthand that has evolved from the more recent composers in their desire to express effect rather than to be bound by notational accuracy.

In my opinion, the supreme enigma has been left in limbo by all writers. I am referring to the many examples, especially in the works of Beethoven and Chopin, where rests plus pedal, following the emission of sound, were substituted for longer duration of the notes themselves. Was it because the visual concept of the phrase would be clearer? Would it promote a seemingly greater ease of execution by enabling the player to think in terms of a rest to aid an awkward leap? Or, was it because the composer actually believed that the aural effect would be different between notes held by both the hand and the pedal and those held by the pedal alone?

Robilliard, Eileen D.
THE PERSISTENT PIANIST.
London: Oxford University Press, 1967.

Rarely is an author able to combine the ingredients of realism and optimism in a subject as delicate to handle as the role of the amateur pianist. Specially directed to the adult beginner or "re-starter," *The Persistent Pianist* anticipates and answers the disturbing questions that tend to plague the prospective hobbyist.

This is no mere outpouring of the subjective thinking of the writer. Miss Robilliard has combined the results of her own extensive survey with the essence of the latest psychological research to produce a highly organized body of useful and valid information. Authoritative quotations are frequently interspersed throughout the book, never breaking the continuity of approach but rather acting as an adhesive to hold the substance of each chapter within a clearly outlined frame.

I can also suggest this book as a confidence-builder for the experienced professional, since the fallacy of equating diminishing pianistic powers with advancing years is realistically discussed.

Saleski, Gdal.
FAMOUS MUSICIANS OF JEWISH ORIGIN.
New York: Bloch Publishing Company, 1949.

Although this book is not devoted exclusively to pianists (also included are other instrumentalists, composers, conductors and singers), it is significant insofar as the biograph-

ical sketches of eighty-four pianists, many of whom are very well known, are presented. In most instances comprehensive biographical material is eschewed in favor of personal glimpses and anecdotes, making this book especially useful in supplementing the more purely factual and critical information that can be found elsewhere.

Gdal Saleski compiled much of his material by interviewing the artists, their families and friends. As an active professional musician, Mr. Saleski had ample opportunity to make the numerous contacts necessary for accumulating this large body of information.

Schauffler, Lawrence.
PIANO TECHNIQUE—MYTH OR SCIENCE.
Chicago: Gamble Hinged Music Company, 1937.

Although volumes have been written on the touch-tone-quality controversy, no single work remains as convincing as this one in outlining the dialectic points, defining them, bringing in all relevant information and formulating conclusions. Intensely readable, spiced with humor (sometimes with devastating wit), this book makes an ideal reference for piano pedagogy classes. Indeed, I have used it for this purpose for many years. My preliminary step before assigning the reading is to interrogate, by means of a questionnaire, the students regarding their views on touch-tone relationships. In perhaps ninety percent of all cases it is revealed that students are not only unaware of the factors that determine tone quality, but actually resist any acceptance of factual information that would contradict their beliefs. After one careful reading of the first forty pages of this book, the majority of attitudes are substantially changed.

Despite its high degree of accuracy, this book is not exempt from errors. On page sixty-three Mr. Schauffler states, "Playing with a high wrist position and no finger or hand action, the forearm can repeat the same tone at a speed almost, if not fully, equal to that of the hand or a single finger, and with equally fine control whether pp or ff." More recent physiological findings have determined that different and specific velocity maximums can be applied to various parts of the piano-playing organism, the wrist being the fastest (ten to eleven movements per second) and the forearm the slowest (three to four flexions per second). In assuming that the forearm is capable of moving at great speed, Mr. Schauffler is perhaps not taking into consideration that what appears to be a forearm stroke is amply supplemented by a vibrating wrist motion as well as a "shaking" motion of the shoulder.

Schnabel, Karl Ulrich.
MODERN TECHNIQUE OF THE PEDAL.
New York: Mills Music, Inc., 1950, 1954.

Mr. Schnabel's book commences in a manner that is common to virtually all books that deal with the pedal: it is stated that pedalling is a generally neglected subject, too much guesswork is involved, etc, etc. Beyond that, the book is a model of imaginative thinking and practical reasoning. It is good to see musical examples that are not already overworked in other similar volumes. In *Modern Technique of the Pedal* these examples are numerous and the amount of text is minimized—an ideal arrangement.

Certain subtle effects are introduced, such as one-fourth pedal or three-fourths pedal, that are completely by-passed in other treatises.

This is the most scholarly of existing pedal-books, and Mr. Schnabel does not hesitate to tread on ground that is often avoided, e.g., exploring the use of the sostenuto pedal as a more-frequent-than-usual substitute for the damper pedal and justifying the retaining of the composer's original pedal markings, especially in Beethoven, with only slight adaptations.

An experienced concert pianist with a remarkable heritage, Mr. Schnabel is eminently qualified to write this authoritative reference work.

Schnabel, Artur.
MUSIC AND THE LINE OF MOST RESISTANCE.
Princeton: Princeton University Press, 1942.

Mr. Schnabel, in a very brief preface, apologizes for the fact that English is not his mother tongue and subsequently proceeds to write in a most elegant and erudite fashion.

Although this book is not devoted to a particular phase of the art of pianism in the more specific manner of other works described, it is supremely important as the philosophical voice of one of the world's most respected musicians. It is impossible to "classify" the content in terms of subject matter; the chapters have no headings and there is no division of material in the usual sense. One can open up the book to any point and find that which is both timely and timeless.

Schnabel, Artur.
MY LIFE AND MUSIC.
New York: St. Martin's Press, 1963.

This eminently readable book presents a profile of one of the most remarkable musicians of the first half of the twentieth century. Transcribed from a series of talks given at the University of Chicago in 1945, the content is divided into two sections: twelve autobiographical lectures, and questions and answers over a wide range of both musical and non-musical subjects.

It seems obvious to me that, among a multitude of personal and pianistic virtues, Mr. Schnabel's very special quality of honesty comes to the fore at all times. There are no contradictions, no piling on of erudition for its own sake, no involvement with false musical values. At no time in his life did he "play down" to an audience or adjust his standards to the degree of audience appreciation. (I am reminded of the headline of a review that appeared some years ago in the Chicago *Tribune*: "Schnabel plays for Artur and his Friends.")

Especially revealing are his many scattered references to Leschetizky, with whom Schnabel studied as a child. Devotees of Leschetizky's teaching will be pleased that Mr. Schnabel drives another large nail into the coffin of the so-called "Leschetizky method" legend and furnishes the following terse evaluation of his teaching: "He succeeded in releasing all the vitality and elan and sense of beauty a student had in his nature . . . "[29]

Schnabel's attitude toward many of the musical conventionalities is both fresh and pointed. "The 'direct' musician . . . is a gardener; the 'indirect' musician is a botanist." In speaking of press notices, he states, " . . . reviews are addressed to the customer, not the salesman . . . " In replying to a piano manufacturer's representative who posed the question, "Your famous colleagues all want to please and serve the man in the street. Why not you?" Schnabel answered, "I don't want to bother him." The inevitable question on musical memory was given to him: " . . . do you have theories of your own about memorizing?". Schnabel replied, "No, I let the memory do it."

Schnabel was devoted to the chamber-music literature and decried the fact that there were insufficient opportunities for presentation of the great works. He would have been very pleased to know that, by virtue of the increasing decentralization of music (from relatively few large cities to many college campuses), his wish has been realized.

[29]Quotations reprinted by permission of St. Martin's Press, Inc.

Schultz, Arnold.
THE RIDDLE OF THE PIANIST'S FINGER.
New York: Carl Fischer, Inc., 1936.

This work is one of the most significant to appear in the wake of Otto Ortmann's monumental studies.[30] A changeover from empirical to scientific thinking was emphasized in a number of treatises written during the period following the publication of Ortmann's discoveries, and it is most natural that the older "systems" of piano technic would be open to much critical analysis. The "methods" of such noted figures as Matthay, Breithaupt and Leschetizky are dissected with great discernment as Mr. Schultz attempts to balance quasi-

scientific conclusions with the sincere attempts on the part of these celebrated teachers to record and apply the physical sensations as they feel them.

Schultz crusades against any misuse of the term "scientific," best expressed by his own words: "Numerous writers in the fields of both vocal and piano technique have cheapened the term by applying it indiscriminately to whatever conclusions they happen to believe correct; or at best they have given only an illusion of an honest claim upon it by borrowing heavily from the vocabularies of the anatomist or physicist."[31]

Readers, however, may object to a certain overemphasis on semantic misunderstandings, as Mr. Schultz does pick rather unmercifully at the terminology and/or vocabulary of those less erudite than he.

Mr. Schultz's physiological description of the piano-playing organism is among the most analytical, accurate and detailed to be found anywhere. What a pity that Mr. Schultz's own suggestion, " . . . I earnestly recommend that schools of music inaugurate courses in physiological mechanics," has not found fruition in our present academic scheme.

May I suggest to the reader two other volumes to be read in conjunction with Mr. Schultz's work: Schauffler's *Piano Technic—Myth or Science* for a contemporary (to Mr. Schultz) simplification of certain physiological points; and Gat's *The Technique of Piano Playing*, for more recent additions in terminology.[32]

[30]See review of *The Physiological Mechanics of Piano Technique* by Otto Ortmann on page 950. Also refer to Ortmann's book *The Physical Basis of Touch and Tone*.

[31]Quotations reprinted by permission of Carl Fischer, Inc.

[32]See review of Schauffler's book on page 952 and review of Gat's book on page 943.

Schumann, Ferdinand.
REMINISCENCES OF CLARA SCHUMANN
AS FOUND IN THE DIARY OF HER GRANDSON
FERDINAND SCHUMANN OF DRESDEN.
Rochester, N. Y.: Schumann Memorial Foundation, 1949.

Clara Schumann seems to have earned her place in history in a variety of ways: obviously as the wife of Robert, notably as a composer and editor, and, of course, as one of the most respected pianists of her century. Less has been said, however, of the fact that she was the first of the great women pianists, setting a tradition that continues to grow with each generation.

This small book covers the period of the final two years of her life (1894-1896, when she was between seventy-five and seventy-seven years of age). It is valuable not for highly professional reasons but rather for a day by day account of Clara Schumann's personal life, with a record of her observations and commentaries. She expressed, for example, her aversion to the music of Wagner and Liszt, although she respected and admired the latter as a pianist.

Has the reader ever felt curious about the out-of-place "G" in her husband's "Hunting Song" from *Album for the Young?* Read the book and find the explanation!

Slenczynska, Ruth, and Louis Leopold Biancolli.
FORBIDDEN CHILDHOOD.
New York: Doubleday and Company, 1957.

It is not a rare occurrence when a child prodigy has his brilliant but fleeting moment; it is far rarer for a child prodigy to re-ascend to another high artistic peak; it is rarer still for the prodigy to tell the tale in such a way that the reader can hardly put the book down. Such is the case in Ruth Slenczynska's *Forbidden Childhood*. With understandable ambivalence, Miss Slenczynska reveals the character of her despotic father and his enormous, almost total influence on her early life. New dimensions on the teaching of Cortot, Schnabel, Boulanger, Rachmaninoff and Backhaus are presented as Miss Slenczynska unfolds detailed descriptions of her work with them during her early childhood.

It is difficult to say whether or not the era of the child prodigy is over. Certainly, at the present time it seems that the music-appreciating public prefers the seasoned artist to the very small child who will sweep the audience to its feet in an incredible demonstration of virtuosity. In any event, this "Truth-is-stranger-than-fiction" account of an era immediately past is especially valuable to the reader of today by virtue of its insight into that difficult period of transition that, to a certain degree, affects every musician who is involved in artistic growth through childhood, adolescence and adulthood. I am speaking of that elusive, awkward period when the juvenile flare begins to disappear and must be substituted by the objective thinking and hard work of maturity.

Slenczynska, Ruth.
MUSIC AT YOUR FINGERTIPS.
New York: Doubleday and Company, 1961.

Early in her book, Miss Slenczynska states, "We receive sparks of inspiration, store them carefully in our memories, and, when released, they fire our own re-creative power."[33] Coming from Miss Slenczynska, this declaration carries more than passing significance to me, as I can vividly recall my own first real spark of pianistic inspiration in the form of Ruth Slenczynska's first Carnegie Hall recital. (She was ten and I was nine.)

Music at Your Fingertips will be valuable to the professional and amateur alike. Few authors have the gift of condensing essential information in a small amount of space; in only one hundred and seventeen pages, Miss Slenczynska projects her no-nonsense, immensely practical counsel. Despite this brevity, she is able to cut a diagonal swath across the traditional pedagogical headings and speak of "Music as a Language," "Personality Factors," "Absorption and Projection," along with the perenially relevant sections on acquiring repertoire, building concert programs and so fourth. One soon receives the impression that Ruth Slenczynska is a deep and accurate thinker, and that she is more than willing to share her pianistic "secrets" after they have been thoroughly tested within the realm of her own performing and teaching experience.

Her very enthusiasm and picturesqueness of speech, or desire for emphasis, may occasionally lead the reader to a misunderstanding of content. Therefore, one must be prepared to insert, as needed, the proverbial grain of salt. Note the following, for example: "Ritardandi must be as gentle as possible. Only the pianist must know that they are there at all." "The point I'm trying to make is that the pianistic problem doesn't exist that cannot be solved by determined imagination."[34] "The pedal should be used only to enhance harmony and to help bind legato that the fingers can't manage . . . Never use the pedal when you can do without it." "There is no such thing as 'good' music or 'bad' music."

[33]Quotations reprinted by permission of Ruth Slenczynska.
[34]See review of *Playing the Piano With Confidence* by Gerald D'Abreu on page 940.

Stookes, Sacha.
THE ART OF ROBERT CASSADESUS.
London: Fortune Press, 1960.

To the majority of prospective readers of this book, the word "art" as used in the title would seem to imply the performance art, as the name of Robert Cassadesus is a highly respected one in pianistic circles. However, in *The Art of Robert Cassadesus* Mr. Stookes concentrates on Robert Cassadesus as a composer. Contained in this volume are astute decriptive analyses of Mr. Cassadesus' published works, as well as a list of works still in manuscript, a discography and a biographical sketch.

Sumner, William Leslie.
THE PIANOFORTE.
London: Macdonald and Company, Ltd., 1966.

As the author states in his introduction, "This book is an account of the pianoforte as a link in the chain between the composer and the listener."[35]

Eschewing the oft-used pedantic approach to this subject-area, Mr. Sumner (who is an Honorary Fellow of the Institute of Musical Instrument Technology) writes with the perspective of the technician rather than of the professional musicologist, pianist or teacher.

The reader will discover that Mr. Sumner's flowing style may make the book as difficult to put down before completion as the latest "whodunit" novel. Amply covered are sections on early keyboard instruments, the early pianoforte, nineteenth century progress in pianoforte making, pianoforte construction and great pianoforte makers. Of special interest to the pianist are the chapters on the aforementioned "links in the chain of music" and "Musicians and the Pianoforte." In the latter section many of the great composer-pianists (C. P. E. Bach, Mozart, Beethoven, Chopin, Liszt, etc.) are " . . . considered only as far as their work throws some light on the development of the piano and the sounds which it makes."

The Pianoforte has much to offer both the active professional and the interested amateur. Replete with illustrations, diagrams and bibliographies, it promises to be a handy reference for the piano-lover's bookshelf.

[35]Quotations reprinted by permission of Macdonald and Company, Ltd.

Tayler, E. Douglas.
THE SECRET OF SUCCESSFUL PRACTICE.
London: Bosworth and Company, Ltd.

As explained by the author, the purpose of *The Secret of Successful Practice* is to present valid "short cuts" and consequently avoid any needless waste of practice time. Despite the attractiveness of both the title and its implication, I do not think that either "secrets" or "short cuts" are presented, but rather a time-tested and completely logical outline of practice methods. There is a basic difference between this book and many other manuals with similar content: Mr. Tayler does not claim that educated effort will smooth out all problems, but he does venture to imply that one's possibilities for development are unlimited.

Various areas of practice techniques are discussed, such as practice tempi, making corrections, analyzing difficult spots, etc. Vivid word-pictures greatly facilitate the reader's understanding and contribute to a conciseness of manner.

Upon reading this fine series of "pointers," the advanced musician may think, "Oh, but I already know that!". However, the real thought should be, "Am I doing it?". Doesn't one find, at a very advanced stage of formal learning, that the greater part of the teacher's statements are reminders of what one already knows but is not putting into practice?

Tobin, J. Raymond.
MOZART AND THE SONATA FORM.
London: William Reeves, 1916.

This straightforward work commences with a brief description of general plans and characteristics of "the" Mozart sonata—an archtype, so to speak, from which the reader may be duly oriented.

Subsequently, each sonata is analyzed individually in detail. The author's approach remains constant for each work: first, the skeletal form is presented (i.e., delineation of the main sections identified by bar numbers and keys); secondly, a descriptive analysis is made of the entire work. Since the latter is primarily structural rather than interpretative, this book may serve as a companion rather than as a guide to one's chosen edition of the music.

Vantyn, Sidney.
MODERN PIANOFORTE TECHNIQUE.
London: Kegan Paul, Trench, Trubner & Co., Ltd., 1919.

The information contained in this book reflects an unusually wide range of quality. On the positive side, it can be said that Mr. Vantyn displays a gift for clarity of presentation. When his knowledge of a particular subject is sufficient, the resulting text is easily understood, unsparing in pertinent detail and infused with "common sense." This approach is especially apparent in such topics as the choosing of fingerings, the discussing of rubato and the selecting of finger-flexibility exercises.

Unfortunately, the book cannot otherwise be suggested for reading except as a means of achieving a perspective on his era of pianism. Moreover, Mr. Vantyn has fallen into the literary trap of setting the degree of importance for a subject-area by stating that others have consistently neglected it. Overgeneralization in areas where his knowledge is insufficient could pose a great handicap for the believing reader. His views on "how to practice" are dated, even for 1919. Three stages of the practice routine are recommended: 1) consideration of note-correctness only, in pianissimo; 2) working out all technical difficulties, still in pianissimo; and 3) folding in all other "details."

The elusive area of aesthetics has posed the greatest problem to the author, who becomes hopelessly mired in ludicrous analogies and expanded misinformation. One should compare Vantyn's views with those expressed by Kullak and Bischoff, several decades earlier.[36]

[36]See review of Kullak's book *The Aesthetics of Pianoforte Playing*, revised by Bischoff, on page 945.

Weitzmann, C. F.
A HISTORY OF PIANOFORTE PLAYING AND PIANOFORTE LITERATURE.
New York: G. Schirmer, Inc., 1893.

It is evident that every chronicler must make some decision, however informal or nebulous it may be, as to what is ancient (or "earlier") history and what is modern. Where he makes that division is a vital factor in presenting his historical perspective. Since Weitzmann created his work almost a century ago, it is understandable that what the author considers a modern history commences with Haydn and Mozart. And, since most critics of "modern" history are reluctant to make qualitative decisions as to the significance or importance of the creative artists of their own (or "modern") era, this volume contains copious references to those whom we now consider the "lesser lights." Within the text, each name appears in large print, facilitating the browsing operation of the reader.

I do not wish to imply that Mr. Weitzmann excluded his personal opinions from his writing; the element of subjectivity is hardly lacking. His separation of "good" salon music from inconsequential salon music is especially revealing.

This book concludes with a history of keyboard instruments, excluding the organ, made especially readable by the author's frequent "side-trips"—detailed accounts of inventions and/or improvements that never received public recognition or that had a relatively brief vogue, e.g., the double-pianoforte, the Logier Chiroplast, Bohner's automatic handguide and early attempts at what eventually turned out to be the player-piano.

Welte-Mignon Corporation.
LIBRARY OF WELTE-MIGNON MUSIC RECORDS.
New York: De Luxe Reproducing Roll Corporation, 1927.

As stated earlier in the review of *Duo-Art Piano Music*,[37] when player-piano popularity was at its height, piano-roll catalogs were veritable encyclopedias. They were annotated and cross-indexed; they contained photographs, biographical sketches, testimonials to the manufacturer and program notes. In addition, the Welte-Mignon catalog included pictures of the recording studio and an explanation of the recording process.

One could not imagine a more star-studded register of contemporary pianism and composition: d'Albert, Busoni, Carreño, Debussy, Dohnanyi, Essipoff, Fauré, Friedheim, Gabrilowitsch, Granados, Grieg, Humperdinck, Landowska, Leoncavallo, Leschetizky, Lhevinne, dePachmann, Paderewski, Reger, Ravel. Saint-Saens, Samaroff, Scriabin and Strauss—to name but a few.

A number of piano parts to chamber works and vocal accompaniments were also listed, making up a former day "music-minus-one" roster. The unseen and unheard instrumentalist or vocalist who collaborated in the recording was hardly relegated to anonymity; the artist was identified by stating, "violin interpretation of . . . ," "vocal interpretation of . . . ," etc.

[37]See review on page 933.

Whiteside, Abby.
INDISPENSABLES OF PIANO PLAYING.
New York: Coleman-Ross Company, Inc., 1955, 1961.

This book is a searching analysis of the "whys" and "hows" in piano playing. Abstruse, even bordering on the esoteric, *Indispensables of Piano Playing* will challenge the reader's capacity for understanding. As explained in the Foreword, the principles and instructional methods of the author dealt largely with physical sensation; it is understandable that this is a particularly elusive area in terms of verbal descriptions. An admitted iconoclast, Miss Whiteside often considers many of the traditional elements of pianism as the dispensables of piano playing!

The fervent belief that an underlying, fundamental rhythm is necessary and vital to all music is the crux of Miss Whiteside's philosophy. Although the reader may be reluctant to apply many of Miss Whiteside's suggestions literally, he must realize that the real value of this book transcends a so-called practical application. It will be impossible for anyone who reads the book with a reasonable degree of thoroughness not to absorb the essence of the author's thoughts and incorporate them in his own musical being.

Interspersed throughout the book are discussions that stand out in bold relief above all possible controversy; e.g., why a soloist cannot be judged by the same standards in a solo recital and as a soloist with orchestra; why "mannerisms" are often necessary for emotional expression; and why the pianist has greater difficulty than other instrumentalists in matters of musical projection.

Whiteside, Abby.
THE PIANIST'S MECHANISM.
New York: G. Schirmer, Inc., 1929.

This is Abby Whiteside's first book, published twenty-six years before the currently available *Indispensables of Piano Playing*. Miss Whiteside writes with authority on physiological and mechanical topics at a time when most authors were floundering in a mass of misinformation.

Oddly, much of the text is devoted to the premise that women as a group are unable to generate sufficient "power" to play the piano as easily as men. Miss Whiteside has reduced this premise to specific examples; e.g., "wrist octaves" can be played successfully by men, but almost never by women. Perhaps if she were able to re-evaluate this study at the present time, considerations other than purely physiological would be incorporated, bringing forth the possibility of different conclusions.

Although this book may not be easy to digest, the fundamental ideas are entirely clear and direct. Miss Whiteside believes, for example, in basic economy of motion (perhaps too much so, as she would exclude many of the "carry through" movements that many pianists feel are essential to their technic efficiency); she believes in by-passing the gradual technic-building procedures when it is possible to enter the more complex or advanced schemes without organized preparation.

The author describes the function of each part of the playing mechanism and its relationship to the whole. The concept of physical sensation is germinated here to be carried through in much greater detail in her second book.

One might feel that much of Miss Whiteside's writing is overdetailed, making application difficult. At any rate, it is worthwhile reading.

Wilkins-Gutmann, Emma.
TALKS WITH PIANO TEACHERS.
Chicago: The Clayton F. Summy Co., 1897.

Here is another volume devoted to the young piano teacher; no one seems to be looking out for the older ones! Although the author specifies that the ideas presented have been taken from various sources and that no special method is involved, it is nevertheless interesting to note that her own study includes work with the renowned Leschetizky.

Miss Wilkins-Gutmann advocates a "singing approach" to many phases of early piano instruction, an approach that makes its appearances through the history of piano pedagogy, often heralded as "new" when the cycle re-commences.

As is to be expected, certain fallacies and naivetes of that era filter through the text. The author's views on legato are perhaps unique and merit quoting here: "A hard tone, caused by striking the key suddenly, has very little resonance; therefore, even though it is held down until the next key is struck, a listener can hear no connection between them. This mechanical idea of legato only hinders the pupil, making him careless in listening to the quality of the tone produced and the pure legato touch is not developed. It is not the physical control of two keys which produces a legato, but the quality of the tone. Legato can be played with a single finger, by first producing a musical tone with the pressure touch, the singing quality of which will carry it to the next."

I strongly approve of the author's use of the term "reading" in lieu of our currently used and ambiguous term "sight-reading." Would one "sight-read" the evening newspaper?

I am always fascinated to read about pedagogical problems that exist as strongly now as they did in the last century. In the athor's chapter on "Material for Teaching," her first sentence is revealing: "There is plenty of good material for all the grades, with the exception of the first." Subsequently, the author quotes from W. S. B. Mathews: "There is something so ideal in the Kindergarten conception, something which reaches out in so many directions into the later life of the child, for which every step in the Kindergarten is to be in some sense a preparation, that it is hardly to be wondered at that the composers fail when brought face to face with this mighty problem of writing music true to the heart of the child, and at the same time having in it the prophecy and potency of the ultimate musical taste which the grown-up child may be hoped to develop."

Woodhouse, George.
THE ARTIST AT THE PIANO—
THE ART OF MUSICAL INTERPRETATION.
London: William Reeves, 1925.

The Artist at the Piano is essentially a philosophical treatise on the aesthetic aspects of pianism. Mr. Woodhouse's ideas are, for the most part, an interesting blend of conservatism and far-sightedness. This may be attributed to his particular place (at the time of writing this book) in musical history: in the midst of a tug-of-war between the Leschetizky school and the emerging "relaxationist" school. His main premise outlines the necessity of eliminating the theoretical side of pianism (which, roughly paraphrased, may be defined as a mechanical and physiological analysis), since it is both unnecessary and detrimental to the success of practice and performance. Paradoxically, however, Mr. Woodhouse equates theory with method, which in my opinion can only result in erroneous conclusions. Another way of stating his premise is to say that the act of successful piano-playing, as a pouring out, so to speak, of the artist's soul, cannot exist with the necessary freedom if the facts relating to its production are known to the artist. This is akin, perhaps, to saying that religion and science cannot co-exist.

Actually, having a scientific knowledge of the piano as an instrument and of the body as a piano-playing organism is of basic value simply because one then knows what can or cannot be done; and, in turn, this gives the player a sense of freedom that will enhance, not restrict, the artistic result.

Mr. Woodhouse is far ahead of his time in other pianistic matters, notably his analysis of "weight-touch," which closely approximates the recent findings of Jozsef Gat[38] (more accurately defined by the latter as apportioning of resistance). His observations on the subject of pianistic illusion are as searching and valid as any that have ever appeared.

[38]See review of *The Technique of Piano Playing* by Joseph Gat on page 943.

Woodhouse, George.
CREATIVE TECHNIQUE FOR
ARTISTS IN GENERAL AND PIANISTS IN PARTICULAR.
London: Augener, Ltd., 1921.

In *Creative Technique*, written approximately twelve years after *The Artist at the Piano*,[39] we find a somewhat more mellow and flexible Mr. Woodhouse. Although hardly less vitriolic about contemporary pedagogues such as Matthay and Johnstone, Mr. Woodhouse confines his content mainly to a subject that does not directly involve his colleagues—the necessity for individuality in technical approach. This may sound paradoxical when we are discussing method; however, was there ever a teacher worth his title who did not claim or at least attempt (despite any affiliation with a specific method) to mold a pupil along the latter's individual lines?

It is interesting to note that Mr. Woodhouse chooses to place Matthay and Johnstone together in the enemy camp. Modern perspective shows us that, in reality, Woodhouse could be placed (from the standpoint of piano technique) in dead center with the other two at opposite poles.

Especially noticeable in this book are substantial references to the interrelationship and interdependence of the "schools" of piano playing.

[39]See review of *The Artist at the Piano* by George Woodhouse above.

Woodhouse, George.
FROM KEYBOARD TO MUSIC.
London: Augener, Ltd., 1949.

An interim of twenty-eight years elapsed between the writing of Woodhouse's second book *Creative Technique* and *From Keyboard to Music*, and this latest work presents still another phase of his musical approach. Far more encompassing and tolerant than in his other works, the author draws together the entities of art and science—a philosophy which in goal and procedure is foreign to the Woodhouse of 1911. Paradoxes and enigmas are dissected, explained and rationalized. Scientific facts are presented as support for mechanical or physiological conclusions. Nowhere have I read a more lucid and practical explanation of the "follow-through motions" that are so vital to the pianist's technical freedom.

Exercises are presented in detail—not gymnastics, for which the author has no use, but rather experimental exercises in the sense that they will enable the student to find and apply those motions which are especially appropriate for piano playing.

The work concludes with an admirable section on the effects of nerves on memory in performance and an appreciation of Theodor Leschetizky, to whom this book is dedicated.

```
ABRAM, JACQUES
  BIOGRAPHICAL MATERIAL
    SALESKI, G.                              BFMOJO   P441
ABSOLUTE PITCH
  GEN INFO
    FOLDES, A.                               BKTTK    P44
ACCENTED PASSAGES
  DEPPE'S APPROACH
    CALAND, E.                               BAPP     P81-87
ACCENTS
  AGOGIC
    AHRENS, C. * ATKINSON, G.                BFAPT    P85
  DYNAMIC
    AHRENS, C. * ATKINSON, G.                BFAPT    P85
  FINGER MOVEMENT IN
    SCHAUFFLER, L.                           BPTMOS   P92-94
ACCOMPANIMENT
  ALTERNATED HAND MOTION IN
    EVANS, E.                                BHTAAT   P122-29
  FIGURATION ON THE MAJOR TRIAD
    EVANS, E.                                BHTAAT   P73-81
  FIGURATION ON THE MINOR TRIAD
    EVANS, E.                                BHTAAT   P149-63
  FORMED BY TRIAD DISPERSIONS
    EVANS, E.                                BHTAAT   P82-101
  FORMED FROM BROKEN CHORDS
    EVANS, E.                                BHTAAT   P102-11
  GENERAL SURVEY OF FORMATIONS
    EVANS, E.                                BHTAAT   P3-16
  HOLDING NOTE, USES OF THE
    EVANS, E.                                BHTAAT   P44-54
  MELODY AS BASS OR INNER VOICE, WITH
    EVANS, E.                                BHTAAT   P55-64
  OSTINATO FIGURES OF
    EVANS, E.                                BHTAAT   P130-45
  POLYPHONIC
    EVANS, E.                                BHTAAT   P65-70
  RHYTHMICAL FIGURES OF
    EVANS, E.                                BHTAAT   P112-21
  SIMPLE HARMONIZATION, BY
    EVANS, E.                                BHTAAT   P35-43
  SUSTAINED HARMONIES IN
    EVANS, E.                                BHTAAT   P25-34
  TETRAD POSITIONS REQUIRED IN
    EVANS, E.                                BHTAAT   P170-77
  TRIADIC POSITIONS REQUIRED IN
    EVANS, E.                                BHTAAT   P164-69
  UNISON
    EVANS, E.                                BHTAAT   P17-24
ACCOMPANYING
  CONDUCTING FROM THE PIANO
    FORD, D.                                 BSCP     P7
  GEN INFO
    HARRISON, S.                             BYPGTP   P62-63
  GEN INFO
    FORD, D.                                 BSCP     P3
  GEN INFO
    BRIGGS, G. A.                            BPPAS    P179-80
  INTRODUCTIONS AND INTERLUDES
    FORD, D.                                 BSCP     P7
  LEFT-HAND TECHNIQUE
    FORD, D.                                 BSCP     P4
  PAGE-TURNING
    MOORE, G.                                BAITL    P212-15
  PEDAL, USE OF THE
    FORD, D.                                 BSCP     P4-5
  PROBLEMS OF THE ACCOMPANIST--NON-MUSICAL
    MOORE, G.                                BAITL    P179-87
  PSYCHOLOGICAL CONSIDERATIONS
    MOORE, G.                                BAITL    P200-208
  READING BY PHRASES
    FORD, D.                                 BSCP     P3
  READING FROM OPEN SCORE
    FORD, D.                                 BSCP     P7
  READING WORDS OF SONG, IMPORTANCE OF
    FORD, D.                                 BSCP     P3
  REHEARSAL AND PERFORMANCE TECHNIQUES
    MOORE, G.                                BAITL    P188-99
  REHEARSAL TECHNIQUES IN THE SINGING CLASS
    FORD, D.                                 BSCP     P5
  SIGHT READING IN
    FORD, D.                                 BSCP     P5-6
  TONE GRADATIONS IN
    FORD, D.                                 BSCP     P5
  TRANSPOSITION IN
    FORD, D.                                 BSCP     P6-7
  VOCAL AS DISTINCT FROM INSTRUMENTAL
    FORD, D.                                 BSCP     P3
ACOUSTICS
  ENSEMBLE PERFORMANCE, IN
    MOORE, G.                                BAITL    P209-10
ACTION AND REACTION
  APPLIED TO MUSCULAR CONTRACTIONS
    CAMPBELL, L.                             BTFORI   P16-17
ADAPTING MOVEMENTS
  GEN INFO
    GAT, J.                                  BTOPP    P33-36
ADJUDICATION
  GEN INFO
    HARRISON, S.                             BTNTM    P135-50
ADLER, CLARENCE
  BIOGRAPHICAL MATERIAL
    SALESKI, G.                              BFMOJO   P442-43
ADULT BEGINNER
  ANALYZING MUSIC
    DILLER, A.                               BSOM     P165-66
  APPROACH TO STUDY
    DABREU, G.                               BPTPWC   P23-24
  GEN INFO
    BROUGHTON, J.                            BSIPT    P61-62
  LISTENING TO MUSIC
    DILLER, A.                               BSOM     P165-66
  PLAYING BY EAR
    DILLER, A.                               BSOM     P162-63
  READING MUSIC
    DILLER, A.                               BSOM     P165
  ROTE LEARNING
    DILLER, A.                               BSOM     P163-65
  STUDYING KEYBOARD HARMONY
    DILLER, A.                               BSOM     P162-63
ADVERTISING
  METHODS
    BROUGHTON, J.                            BSIPT    P15-18
  TEACHING PROFESSION, IN THE
    CARRE, J.                                BPOPT    P64-65

AESTHETICS
  GEN INFO
    VANTYN, S.                               BMPT     P118-42
AESTHETIC CONSIDERATIONS
  PIANO PLAYING, IN
    KULLAK, A.                               BAOPP    P1-9
AESTHETIC VALUES
  IMPOSSIBILITY OF STANDARDIZING
    LEVINSKAYA, M.                           BLSOPT   P240-44
AGILITY
  FINGER WORK, IN
    MATTHAY, T.                              BPFOT    P14-20
AGOGICS
  GEN INFO
    BRECKENRIDGE, W.                         BHFPNS   P43
ALLISON, IRL
  INTERVIEW
    BASTIEN, J. W.                           BHTTPS   P401-7
AMATEUR PIANIST
  ABILITY TO LEARN THROUGH ADVANCING YEARS
    ROBILLIARD, E.                           BPP      P20-22
  CHOOSING MUSIC, SUGGESTIONS FOR
    PALMER, K.                               BTYTPT   P83-86
  DISCUSSION OF COMPOSITIONS
    COOKE, C.                                BPTPFP   P145-71
  ELEMENTARY INTERPRETATION
    PALMER, K.                               BTYTPT   P57-60
  ELEMENTARY PRINCIPLES OF FINGERING
    PALMER, K.                               BTYTPT   P61-66
  ENSEMBLE MUSIC
    PALMER, K.                               BTYTPT   P87-97
  HARMONY, ELEMENTARY
    PALMER, K.                               BTYTPT   P122-30
  MATERIALS
    COOKE, C.                                BPTPFP   P35-38
  MEMORIZING
    COOKE, C.                                BPTPFP   P71-82
  MEMORY AIDS
    COOKE, C.                                BPTPFP   P82-90
  MUSICAL EAR
    ROBILLIARD, E.                           BPP      P49-52
  MUSICAL TALENT
    ROBILLIARD, E.                           BPP      P53-55
  OBJECTIVES
    COOKE, C.                                BPTPFP   P29-32
  PIANIST'S HAND, THE
    ROBILLIARD, E.                           BPP      P43-48
  PLACE OF MUSIC, THE
    COOKE, C.                                BPTPFP   P21-25
  PLAYING FOR OTHERS
    COOKE, C.                                BPTPFP   P107-11
  POSITIVE APPROACH TO STUDY
    ROBILLIARD, E.                           BPP      P1-5
  PRACTICE, HOW TO
    PALMER, K.                               BTYTPT   P71-82
  PRACTICE TECHNIQUES
    ROBILLIARD, E.                           BPP      P28-42
  PRACTICING DIFFICULT SPOTS
    COOKE, C.                                BPTPFP   P49-70
  PRACTICING
    COOKE, C.                                BPTPFP   P39-42
  REASONS FOR CHOOSING THE PIANO
    ROBILLIARD, E.                           BPP      P17-19
  REASONS FOR PLAYING THE PIANO
    ROBILLIARD, E.                           BPP      P10-13
  RETENTION OF MEMORIZED PIECES
    COOKE, C.                                BPTPFP   P102-107
  SETTING GOALS
    ROBILLIARD, E.                           BPP      P6-9,23-27
  SIGHT READING
    COOKE, C.                                BPTPFP   P141-44
  STARTING OUT
    PALMER, K.                               BTYTPT   P9-11
  SUGGESTIONS FOR REPERTOIRE
    COOKE, C.                                BPTPFP   P46-49
  TECHNIQUE, ELEMENTARY
    PALMER, K.                               BTYTPT   P52-56
  TECHNIQUE
    COOKE, C.                                BPTPFP   P113-40
  THEORY, ELEMENTARY
    PALMER, K.                               BTYTPT   P19-37,98-1
AMATEUR
  MUSICAL ROLE OF
    BROUGHTON, J.                            BSIPT    P96-97
ANALYSIS IN PRACTICING--GOODSON
  GEN INFO
    COOKE, J. F.                             BGPOPP   P143-55
ANALYSIS
  MOVEMENT IN PRACTICING, OF
    TAYLER, E. O.                            BSOSP    P15-16
ANTAL, ISTVAN
  PHOTOGRAPHIC ANALYSIS OF PERFORMANCE
    GAT, J.                                  BTOPP    P64
ANXIETY
  CAUSE OF MUSCULAR RESTRICTION, AS
    DABREU, G.                               BPTPWC   P30-31
APPOGGIATURA
  MOZART, IN--ACCENTED
    BADURA-SKODA, E. * BADURA-SKODA, P.      BIMOTK   P71-76
  MOZART, IN--COMPOUND
    BADURA-SKODA, E. * BADURA-SKODA, P.      BIMOTK   P95-99
  MOZART, IN--GEN INFO
    RICHNER, T.                              BOFIMP   P30-31
  MOZART, IN--SINGLE
    BADURA-SKODA, E. * BADURA-SKODA, P.      BIMOTK   P70-71
  MOZART, IN--UNACCENTED
    BADURA-SKODA, E. * BADURA-SKODA, P.      BIMOTK   P76-88
  MOZART, IN--VOCAL
    BADURA-SKODA, E. * BADURA-SKODA, P.      BIMOTK   P88-95
  MUSICAL MEANING
    BACON, E.                                BNOTP    P17
APPRECIATION
  MUSIC, OF
    AHRENS, C. * ATKINSON, G.                BFAPT    P103-7
APPRECIATORS
  NEED FOR
    BACON, E.                                BNOTP    P103-4
ARM-LEGATO
  GEN INFO
    ORTMANN, O.                              BPMOPT   P177-82
  WEIGHT DISTRIBUTION
    ORTMANN, O.                              BPMOPT   P180-82
  WRIST MOVEMENT IN
    ORTMANN, O.                              BPMOPT   P178-80
ARM TOUCHES
  ANALYSIS OF EXAMPLES
    CHING, J.                                BPPAPM   P195-206
```

APPLICATION OF PRINCIPLE TO PRACTICE
   CHING, J.   BPPAPM P167-82
CHOICE OF CORRECT MOVEMENT
   CHING, J.   BPPAPM P167-82
EXERCISES FOR HIGH SPEEDS
   CHING, J.   BPPAPM P195-206
GENERAL PRINCIPLES
   CHING, J.   BPPAPM P195-206
NECESSITY FOR DETAILED MENTAL ANALYSIS
   CHING, J.   BPPAPM P167-82
OBLIQUE WHOLE-ARM TOUCH
   CHING, J.   BPPAPM P167-82
ARM WEIGHT, CESSATION OF
MATTHAY'S APPROACH
   COVIELLO, A.   BWMM P17
ARM WEIGHT
MATTHAY'S APPROACH
   COVIELLO, A.   BWMM P15
ARM
ARM-DROP
   SCHULTZ, A.   BROTPF P174-76
ARM-LEGATO
   SCHULTZ, A.   BROTPF P177-78
FOREARM ROTATION
   SCHULTZ, A.   BROTPF P177
INDIVIDUAL DIFFERENCES
   ORTMANN, O.   BPMOPT P297-300
LATERAL MOVEMENTS
   SCHAUFFLER, L.   BPTMOS P95-96
PRINCIPAL ACCOMMODATING MOVEMENTS
   BACON, E.   BNOTP P39-43
RESOURCES OF
   DILLER, A.   BSOM P106-7
ROTARY MOVEMENTS
   SCHULTZ, A.   BROTPF P180-93
ARPEGGIOS
FINGERING PROBLEMS
   NEWMAN, W.   BPP P38-42
FINGERING
   AHRENS, C. * ATKINSON, G.   BFAPT P44-45
FINGER MOVEMENT IN
   SCHAUFFLER, L.   BPTMOS P91-92
FINGER MOVEMENT
   ORTMANN, O.   BPMOPT P270-71
GEN INFO
   WHITESIDE, A.   BIOPP P103-22
GEN INFO
   ORTMANN, O.   BPMOPT P262-76
INTENSITY
   ORTMANN, O.   BPMOPT P273-76
PRACTICE SUGGESTIONS FOR AMATEURS
   GRUNDY, E.   BHP P34-37
PRACTICING, WAYS OF
   VANTYN, S.   BMPT P52-58
PRACTICING OF
   GAT, J.   BTOPP P167-69
TEMPO
   ORTMANN, O.   BPMOPT P271-73
WEIGHT
   ORTMANN, O.   BPMOPT P262-70
ARPEGGIO PLAYING
DEPPE'S APPROACH
   CALAND, E.   BAPP P91-96
ARRAU, CLAUDIO
BIOGRAPHICAL MATERIAL
   CHASINS, A.   BSOP P154
ARRIOLA, PEPITO
BIO-CONF--STORY OF A WONDER CHILD, THE
   COOKE, J. F.   BGPOPP P40-50
ARTIST-TEACHER, THE
GEN INFO
   CHASINS, A.   BSOP P80-84
ARTISTIC DESIRES
MECHANICAL INNOVATIONS, RELATIONSHIP TO
   REEDER, B.   BST P63-64
ASSOCIATIVE LEARNING
GEN INFO
   POTAMKIN, F. J.   BMPP P39-40
AUDITORY-MOTOR IMAGERY
GEN INFO
   POTAMKIN, F. J.   BMPP P40-41
AURAL TRAINING
CHILD, OF THE
   LAST, J.   BYP P52-62
GEN INFO
   AHRENS, C. * ATKINSON, G.   BFAPT P73-75
AUS DER OHE, ADELE
CONF--ARTIST AT HOME, AN
   BROWER, H.   BPM P142-46
AWARDS
PIANO STUDENTS, TO
   CARRE, J.   BPOPT P76-77
BACH, C. P. E.
KEYBOARD WORKS
   BIE, O.   BHOTPA P138-48
ROLE IN THE DEVELOPMENT OF THE PF AND PF PLAYING
   SUMNER, W.   BP P135-42
BACH, J. S.
ALLEMANDE FROM FRENCH SUITE IN E...MASTER LESSON
   LEIMER, K. * GIESEKING, W.   BRDP P7-13
GEN INFO
   BROOK, D.   BMOTK P19-27
INFLUENCE ON W. A. MOZART
   RICHNER, T.   BOFIMP P9-11
INFLUENCE ON W. A. MOZART
   RICHNER, T.   BOFIMP P14-17
KEYBOARD WORKS
   BIE, O.   BHOTPA P91-125
TECHNICAL APPROACH TO CLAVIER PLAYING
   KULLAK, A.   BAOPP P11-14
THREE-PART INVENTION IN C.. MASTER LESSON
   LEIMER, K. * GIESEKING, W.   BSWTPP P28-32
TWO-PART INVENTION IN C..MASTER LESSON
   LEIMER, K. * GIESEKING, W.   BSWTPP P23-28
WORKS FOR PIANO DUO
   MOLDENHAUER, H.   BDP P20-45
BACHAUER, GINA
BIOGRAPHICAL MATERIAL
   CHASINS, A.   BSOP P151
BACKHAUS, WILHELM
BIO-CONF--PIANIST OF TOMORROW, THE
   COOKE, J. F.   BGPOPP P51-62
BIO-CONF--THE HARDEST THINGS TO MASTER IN MUSIC
   COOKE, J. F.   BGMAFM P418-22
BIOGRAPHICAL MATERIAL
   CHASINS, A.   BSOP P98-102

CONF--TECHNICAL PROBLEMS DISCUSSED
   BROWER, H.   BPM P168-74
REVIEW OF RECITAL
   BROWER, H.   BWTPWT P178-83
BACON, KATHERINE
BIOGRAPHICAL MATERIAL
   BROWER, H.   BMMOTK P292-96
BAD HABITS
PIANO PLAYING, IN
   VANTYN, S.   BMPT P154-56
BALANCE
ARM-WEIGHT
   REEDER, B.   BST P45
CULTIVATED TOUCH
   REEDER, B.   BST P48
DRIVING FORCE
   REEDER, B.   BST P46
FOLLOW-THROUGH
   REEDER, B.   BST P46
MECHANICS OF TOUCH
   REEDER, B.   BST P47
PERSONAL EQUATION
   REEDER, B.   BST P47-48
SMOOTH APPROACH
   REEDER, B.   BST P46
TRAINING
   REEDER, B.   BST P46
BALSAM, ARTUR
BIOGRAPHICAL MATERIAL
   SALESKI, G.   BFMOJO P443
BARERE, SIMON
BIOGRAPHICAL MATERIAL
   SALESKI, G.   BFMOJO P444-45
BIOGRAPHICAL MATERIAL
   CHASINS, A.   BSOP P157
BARTOK, BELA
PIANO WORKS
   CHASINS, A.   BSOP P270-71
BAUER, HAROLD
AUTOBIOGRAPHY--HAROLD BAUER, HIS BOOK
   BAUER, H.   BHBHB P7-302
BIO-CONF--ARTISTIC ASPECTS OF PIANO STUDY
   COOKE, J. F.   BGPOPP P63-78
BIO-CONF--PIANIST'S PALETTE, THE
   COOKE, J. F.   BGMAFM P293-99
BIOGRAPHICAL MATERIAL
   SALESKI, G.   BFMOJO P446-47
CONF--THE QUESTION OF PIANO TONE
   BROWER, H.   BPM P95-106
REVIEW OF RECITAL
   BROWER, H.   BWTPWT P194-200
BAY, EMANUEL
BIOGRAPHICAL MATERIAL
   SALESKI, G.   BFMOJO P448
BEAUTY OF TONE
PROBLEMS AND SOLUTIONS
   HARRISON, S.   BYPGTP P40-48
BEETHOVEN, LUDWIG VAN
BEETHOVEN'S SLOW MOVEMENTS
   KELBERINE, A.   BFFPSO P53-59
BIOGRAPHICAL MATERIAL
   BIE, O.   BHOTPA P157-82
PIANO WORKS
   CHASINS, A.   BSOP P214-19
ROLE IN THE DEVELOPMENT OF THE PF AND PF PLAYING
   SUMNER, W.   BP P146-54
SONATA, OP. 13--STRUCTURAL AND INTERPRETATIVE ANALYSIS
   KELBERINE, A.   BFFPSO P9-16
SONATA, OP. 27 NO. 2-- STRUCTURAL AND INTERPRETATIVE ANALYSIS
   KELBERINE, A.   BFFPSO P17-27
SONATA, OP. 53--STRUCTURAL AND INTERPRETATIVE ANALYSIS
   KELBERINE, A.   BFFPSO P28-40
SONATA, OP. 57--STRUCTURAL AND INTERPRETATIVE ANALYSIS
   KELBERINE, A.   BFFPSO P41-52
SONATA IN F MINOR, OP. 2 NO. 1...MASTER LESSON
   LEIMER, K. * GIESEKING, W.   BSWTPP P32-42
TECHNICAL APPROACH TO CLAVIER PLAYING
   KULLAK, A.   BAOPP P17-20
BEGINNING PIANO STUDENT
AVERAGE AGE BEGINNERS
   BASTIEN, J. W.   BHTTPS P131-74
SURVEY OF METHODS
   BASTIEN, J. W.   BHTTPS P63-105
VERY YOUNG BEGINNERS
   BASTIEN, J. W.   BHTTPS P109-30
BENT FINGER
MATTHAY'S APPROACH
   COVIELLO, A.   BWMM P16-17
BERINGER, OSCAR
BIOGRAPHICAL MATERIAL
   FAY, A.   BMSIG P63, 100-1
BERUMEN, ERNESTO
CONF--MIND THE MOTIVE POWER IN PIANO PLAYING
   BROWER, H.   BMMOTK P260-72
BLOOMFIELD-ZEISLER, FANNY
BIO-CONF--APPEARING IN PUBLIC
   COOKE, J. F.   BGPOPP P79-95
BODY POSTURE
GEN INFO
   GAT, J.   BTOPP P49-58
BOOKKEEPING
TEACHING PROFESSION, IN THE
   CARRE, J.   BPOPT P70-73
BOOKS
TEACHERS, AS
   GRUNDY, E.   BHP P61-66
BOROWSKI, ALEXANDER
BIOGRAPHICAL MATERIAL
   SALESKI, G.   BFMOJO P449-51
CONF--NATURAL TECHNIC, A
   BROWER, H.   BMMOTK P215-22
BRAHMS, JOHANNES
PIANO WORKS
   CHASINS, A.   BSOP P240-45
ROLE IN THE DEVELOPMENT OF THE PF AND PF PLAYING
   SUMNER, W.   BP P174-75
WORKS FOR PIANO DUO
   MOLDENHAUER, H.   BDP P93-109
BRAILOWSKY, ALEXANDER
BIO-CONF--SECRETS OF A GREAT TEACHER--LESCHETIZKY
   COOKE, J. F.   BGMAFM P282-87
BIOGRAPHICAL MATERIAL
   SALESKI, G.   BFMOJO P451-53
BIOGRAPHICAL MATERIAL
   CHASINS, A.   BSOP P150-51
CONF--THOUGHT AND FEELING IN PIANO PLAYING
   BROWER, H.   BMMOTK P55-63

BREE, MALWINE
  REVIEW OF--THE GROUNDWORK OF THE LESCHETIZKY METHOD
    SCHULTZ, A.   BROTPF   P218-36
BREITHAUPT, RUDOLF MARIA
  CRITICAL ANALYSIS OF TECHNICAL THEORIES
    SCHULTZ, A.   BROTPF   P266-91
  TECHNICAL APPROACH
    FIELDEN, T.   BSOPT   P5-7
  TECHNICAL APPROACH
    LEVINSKAYA, MARIA   BLSOPT   P54-57
BRILLIANCE
  PIANO PLAYING, IN
    BACON, E.   BNOTP   P16-17
BROCHURES
  PIANO TEACHER, FOR THE
    CARRE, J.   BPOPT   P65-66
BROKEN CHORDS
  SPECIAL PROBLEMS IN PRACTICING
    LEIMER, K. * GIESEKING, W.   BSWTPP   P55-56
BULL, JOHN
  BIOGRAPHICAL MATERIAL
    BROOK, D.   BMOTK   P13-18
BULOW, HANS VON
  BIOGRAPHICAL MATERIAL
    FAY, A.   BMSIG   P176-77,
  TEACHER AND INTERPRETER, AS
    BROWER, H.   BPM   P232-47
BUSINESS ASPECTS
  PIANO TEACHING, OF
    CARRE, J.   BPOPT   P58-61
BUSINESS OF PIANO TEACHING
  LESSON FEES
    BASTIEN, J. W.   BHTTPS   P52-61
  PAYMENT PROCEDURES
    BASTIEN, J. W.   BHTTPS   P51-52
BUSONI, FERRUCCIO
  BIO-CONF--IMPORTANT DETAILS IN PIANO STUDY
    COOKE, J. F.   BGPOPP   P96-107
  BIOGRAPHICAL MATERIAL
    SALESKI, G.   BFMOJO   P454-57
  BIOGRAPHICAL MATERIAL
    BROOK, D.   BMOTK   P111-24
  CONF--ARTIST AT HOME
    BROWER, H.   BPM   P137-41
  DESCRIPTION OF PERFORMANCE
    COHEN, H.   BMH   P56
CANTILENA
  DESCRIPTION OF
    VANTYN, S.   BMPT   P113-17
CARRENO, TERESA
  BIO-CONF--DISTINCTIVE PIANO PLAYING
    COOKE, J. F.   BGPOPP   P108-20
  CONF--EARLY TECHNICAL TRAINING
    BROWER, H.   BPM   P160-67
  TECHNICAL APPROACH
    LEVINSKAYA, MARIA   BLSOPT   P37-38
CASADESUS, ROBERT
  BIOGRAPHICAL MATERIAL
    STOOKES, S.   BAORC   P9-13
  BIOGRAPHICAL MATERIAL
    CHASINS, A.   BSOP   P125-29
  DESCRIPTIVE ANALYSES OF WORKS
    STOOKES, S.   BAORC   P15-68
  DISCOGRAPHY OF WORKS
    STOOKES, S.   BAORC   P72
  LIST OF PUBLISHED AND UNPUBLISHED WORKS
    STOOKES, S.   BAORC   P69-70
CHASINS, ABRAM
  BIOGRAPHICAL MATERIAL
    SALESKI, G.   BFMOJO   P457-58
CHERKASSKY, SHURA
  BIOGRAPHICAL MATERIAL
    SALESKI, G.   BFMOJO   P459-60
CHILDREN
  CHOOSING MUSIC FOR CHILDREN TO STUDY
    DILLER, A.   BSOM   P19-23
  EARLY TRAINING--PUGNO
    BROWER, H.   BPM   P107-17
  EASY CLASSICS FOR STUDY
    DILLER, A.   BSOM   P20
  FOLK MUSIC FOR STUDY
    DILLER, A.   BSOM   P19
  HOLDING THE CHILD'S ATTENTION AT THE LESSON
    BOSWORTH, H.   BIFYPT   P3-4
  INDIVIDUAL PIANO LESSON, THE
    DILLER, A.   BSOM   P12-16
  LESSON PLAN FOR PRIVATE STUDY, A
    DILLER, A.   BSOM   P14-16
  PRACTICE RECORD
    DILLER, A.   BSOM   P35-36
  PUPIL'S RECITALS
    DILLER, A.   BSOM   P131-46
  ROUTINE OF PIANO LESSON
    DILLER, A.   BSOM   P12-13
CHITTENDEN, KATE S.
  CONF--SIMPLIFIED PIANO TECHNIC
    BROWER, H.   BPMSS   P255-63
CHOICE OF MATERIAL
  PRACTICING, FOR
    BRECKENRIDGE, W.   BHFPNS   P2-4
CHOOSING OFFETORY MATERIALS
  CHURCH PIANIST, FOR THE
    AULD, W.   BHFTCP   P85-89
CHOPIN, FREDERIC
  BIOGRAPHICAL MATERIAL
    BROOK, D.   BMOTK   P54-72
  CHOICE OF FIVE-NOTE SERIES FOR EXERCISES
    VANTYN, S.   BMPT   P21
  PIANO WORKS
    BIE, O.   BHOTPA   P255-70
  PIANO WORKS
    CHASINS, A.   BSOP   P220-26
  RECOLLECTIONS OF W. VON LENZ
    LENZ, W. VON   BGPVOO   P27-74
  ROLE IN THE DEVELOPMENT OF THE PF AND PF PLAYING
    SUMNER, W.   BP   P160-69
CHORDS
  BROKEN CHORDS
    GAT, J.   BTOPP   P165-67
  DEPPE'S APPROACH
    CALAND, E.   BAPP   P81-87
  DYNAMIC SHAPING OF
    GAT, J.   BTOPP   P147-48
  FORMATION IN PRACTICING
    AHRENS, C. * ATKINSON, G.   BFAPT   P41-43
  PRACTICING, WAYS OF
    BRECKENRIDGE, W.   BHFPNS   P9-10

PRACTICING, WAYS OF
  DICKERSON, R.   BNATPT   P28-29
PRACTICING, WAYS OF
  FOLDES, A.   BKTTK   P49-50
PRACTICING, WAYS OF
  MERRICK, F.   BPTP   P14-16
PRACTICING OF
  GAT, J.   BTOPP   P157-60
SKIPPING
  GAT, J.   BTOPP   P177-83
SPECIAL PROBLEMS IN PRACTICING
  LEIMER, K. * GIESEKING, W.   BSWTPP   P56-57
CHORD PROGRESSIONS
  ADVANCED PROGRESSIONS FOR TECHNICAL PRACTICE
    MERRICK, F.   BPTP   P10-16
CHROMATIC SCALE PASSAGES
  TECHNICAL CONSIDERATIONS
    BOWEN, Y.   BSOPT   P13
CHROMATIC SCALE
  THIRDS, IN
    VANTYN, S.   BMPT   P50-51
CHURCH PIANIST
  CHOOSING OFFETORY MATERIALS
    AULD, W.   BHFTCP   P85-89
  HYMN INTRODUCTIONS
    AULD, W.   BHFTCP   P75-81
  INTERPRETATION
    AULD, W.   BHFTCP   P90-96
  MODULATION
    AULD, W.   BHFTCP   P48-50
  MUSICAL TASTE
    AULD, W.   BHFTCP   P82-84
  PREPAREDNESS
    AULD, W.   BHFTCP   P70-73
  TIME
    AULD, W.   BHFTCP   P51-57
  TRANSCRIPTIONS AND ARRANGEMENTS
    AULD, W.   BHFTCP   P58-59
  TRANSPOSITION
    AULD, W.   BHFTCP   P46-47
CHURCH PIANO
  PROBLEMS OF HEATING AND VENTILATION
    HARRIS, R. J.   BHTCAA   P126-27
  PROTECTION AND MAINTENENCE OF
    HARRIS, R. J.   BHTCAA   P125-26
  PURCHASE OF
    HARRIS, R. J.   BHTCAA   P124-25
  TECHNICAL ADVICE
    HARRIS, R. J.   BHTCAA   P125
CIRCLE OF FIFTHS
  TEACHING OF KEY RELATIONSHIPS, IN
    NEWMAN, W.   BPP   P9
CLASS INSTRUCTION
  COMPARED TO PRIVATE INSTRUCTION
    GIDDINGS, T. P.   BGPSCM   P1-6
CLAVICHORD
  GEN INFO
    BIE, O.   BHOTPA   P20-22
  GEN INFO
    HIPKINS, A.   BDAHOT   P57-65
  GEN INFO
    REEDER, B.   BST   P56
  HISTORY AND CONSTRUCTION
    SUMNER, W.   BP   P22-24
  ORIGIN AND DEVELOPMENT
    WEITZMANN, C.   BHOPPA   P219-22
CLAVICIMBALU
  GEN INFO
    SUMNER, W.   BP   P35-36
CLAVICITERIU
  GEN INFO
    SUMNER, W.   BP   P37
CLAVICORDIU
  GEN INFO
    SUMNER, W.   BP   P35
CLAVICYMBAL
  GEN INFO
    BIE, O.   BHOTPA   P23-24
CLAVICYTERIUM
  GEN INFO
    SUMNER, W.   BP   P35
CLAVICYTHERIUM
  GEN INFO
    HIPKINS, A.   BDAHOT   P74-76
CLAVIER-PLAYING
  C.P.E. BACH AND HIS PREDECESSORS
    WEITZMANN, C.   BHOPPA   P48-64
  CONTRAPUNTAL ORGAN STYLE
    WEITZMANN, C.   BHOPPA   P3-23
  EARLIER DANCE FORMS
    WEITZMANN, C.   BHOPPA   P65-74
  EARLIER ENGLISH SCHOOL
    WEITZMANN, C.   BHOPPA   P24-26
  EARLIER FRENCH SCHOOL
    WEITZMANN, C.   BHOPPA   P26-30
  EARLIER GERMAN SCHOOL
    WEITZMANN, C.   BHOPPA   P31-47
  EARLIER ITALIAN SCHOOL
    WEITZMANN, C.   BHOPPA   P3-23
  FREER CLAVIER STYLE
    WEITZMANN, C.   BHOPPA   P3-23
CLAVIERS AND THE PIANO
  GEN INFO
    HAMILTON, C.   BWEPPS   P59-72
CLAVIER VIRTUOSITY
  HISTORY OF
    KULLAK, A.   BAOPP   P9-34
CLAVIER
  RELATIONSHIP TO EARLIER INSTRUMENTS
    WEITZMANN, C.   BHOPPA   P216-18
CLAVIORGANUM
  GEN INFO
    HIPKINS, A.   BDAHOT   P94-95
CLEMENTI, MUZIO
  ITINERANT VIRTUOSO, AS
    BIE, O.   BHOTPA   P193
  ROLE IN THE DEVELOPMENT OF THE PF AND PF PLAYING
    SUMNER, W.   BP   P178-79
  TECHNICAL APPROACH TO CLAVIER PLAYING
    KULLAK, A.   BAOPP   P15-17
COHEN, HARRIET
  BIOGRAPHICAL MATERIAL
    SALESKI, G.   BFMOJO   P463-64
  BIOGRAPHICAL MATERIAL
    BROOK, D.   BMOTK   P151-52
COLLEGE PIANO MAJOR
  GEN INFO
    BASTIEN, J. W.   BHTTPS   P347-61

COLLEGE PREPARATORY DEPARTMENT
  GEN INFO
    BASTIEN, J. W.   BHTTPS   P339-45
COMPANIONSHIP
  MUSIC, IN
    BOSWORTH, H.   BIFYPT   P65-67
COMPETITIONS AND EXAMINATIONS
  GEN INFO
    AHRENS, C. * ATKINSON, G.   BFAPT   P98-102
COMPETITIONS
  GEN INFO
    HARRISON, S.   BTNTM   P135-50
COMPETITION
  TEACHING PROFESSION, IN THE
    CARRE, J.   BPOPT   P61-64
COMPOSERS
  DISTINGUISHING CHARACTERISTICS
    BRECKENRIDGE, W.   BHFPNS   P80-83
COMPOSER
  OBSERVATIONS OF THE COMPOSER'S ROLE
    BACON, E.   BNOTP   P114-32
  STRUGGLE FOR PUBLIC ACCEPTANCE OF NEW IDEAS
    COHEN, H.   BMH   P17-39
CONCENTRATION IN MUSIC STUDY--SAMAROFF
  GEN INFO
    COOKE, J. F.   BGPOPP   P334-47
CONCENTRATION
  PIANO PLAYING, IN
    BOLTON, H.   BHTP   P6-9
  PRACTICING, IN
    AHRENS, C. * ATKINSON, G.   BFAPT   P48
  PRACTICING AND PLAYING, IN
    HOFHEIMER, G.   BTTFTP   P67-72
CONCERTO--PIANO
  DEVELOPMENT
    GARVIN, F. H.   BBOTRP   P12-19
CONCERTOS
  KEYBOARD CONCERTOS BEFORE MOZART
    HUTCHINGS, A.   BCTMPC   P26-35
CONCERT MANAGEMENT
  MANNER OF OPERATION
    CHASINS, A.   BSOP   P177-86
CONCERT NERVES
  INHIBITION
    CHING, J.   BPPAPM   P323-41
CONSCIOUSNESS AND INSPIRATION
  GEN INFO
    GAT, J.   BTOPP   P75-76
CONSTRUCTION
  FACTORS IN
    HIPKINS, A.   BDAHOT   P3-10
CONTESTS AND FESTIVALS
  YOUNG PIANIST, FOR THE
    BASTIEN, J. W.   BHTTPS   P311-37
CONTINUITY
  CHOPIN'S FINGERING
    WOODHOUSE, G.   BFKTM   P41-44
  GEN INFO
    WOODHOUSE, G.   BFKTM   P33
  LEGATO TONE CONNECTIONS
    WOODHOUSE, G.   BFKTM   P33-40
CONTRA-FIXATION MOVEMENT
  GEN INFO
    SCHULTZ, A.   BROTPF   P62-82
  PEDAGOGY OF
    SCHULTZ, A.   BROTPF   P135-47
CONTRACTION AND FIXATION
  GEN INFO
    FIELDEN T.   BSOPT   P83-88
COOPERATION
  BETWEEN CHILD, TEACHER AND PARENT
    BOSWORTH, H.   BIFYPT   P20-21
COORDINATION AND INCOORDINATION
  GEN INFO
    ORTMANN, O.   BPMOPT   P282-94
CORRECTIONS
  PRACTICE, IN
    TAYLER, E. D.   BSOSP   P10-11
CORTOT, ALFRED
  CONF--PRACTICAL ASPECTS OF MODERN PIANO STUDY
    BROWER, H.   BMMOTK   P22-31
  REVIEW OF RECITAL
    BROWER, H.   BWTPWT   P170-77
COUNTING ALOUD
  GEN INFO
    BROUGHTON, J.   BSIPT   P36-40
COUNTING
  AID TO CORRECT RHYTHM, AS AN
    NEWMAN, W.   BPP   P81-87
  GEN INFO
    DILLER, A.   BSOM   P60-73
COURAGE
  EARLY MUSICAL SUCCESS, IN
    BOSWORTH, H.   BIFYPT   P56-57
CRAMER, JOHN BAPTIST
  ROLE IN THE DEVELOPMENT OF THE PF AND PF PLAYING
    SUMNER, W.   BP   P179-80
CURZON, CLIFFORD
  BIOGRAPHICAL MATERIAL
    BROOK, D.   BMOTK   P153-57
  BIOGRAPHICAL MATERIAL
    CHASINS, A.   BSOP   P153
  INTERVIEW BY G. A. BRIGGS
    BRIGGS, G. A.   BPPAS   P149-51
CZERNY, CARL
  FATHER OF MECHANICAL GYMNASTICS, AS
    BIE, O.   BHOTPA   P188-89+
  ROLE IN THE DEVELOPMENT OF THE PF AND PF PLAYING
    SUMNER, W.   BP   P179
  TECHNICAL APPROACH
    LEVINSKAYA, M.   BLSOPT   P28-29
DANCE FORMS
  PIANO MUSIC, IN
    HARRISON, S.   BTNTM   P68-73
DANCE MOVEMENTS
  ANCIENT AND MODERN
    BRECKENRIDGE, W.   BHFPNS   P50-53
DEBUSSY, CLAUDE
  ROLE IN THE DEVELOPMENT OF THE PF AND PF PLAYING
    SUMNER, W.   BP   P175-77
DEMONSTRATION
  VALUE IN TEACHING
    CARRE, J.   BPOPT   P9
DEPACHMANN, VLADIMIR
  BIOGRAPHICAL MATERIAL
    SALESKI, G.   BFMOJO   P534-37

DEPPE, LUDWIG--TEACHING APPROACH
  GEN INFO
    CALAND, E.   BAPP   P17-109
DEPPE, LUDWIG
  TECHNICAL APPROACH
    FIELDEN, T.   BSOPT   P3-5
  TECHNICAL APPROACH
    LEVINSKAYA, M.   BLSOPT   P49-53
DETERMINATION
  LEARNING, IN
    DABREU, G.   BPTPWC   P27-29
DICK, JAMES
  INTERVIEW
    BASTIEN, J. W.   BHTTPS   P415-24
DIFFICULTIES PECULIAR TO THE PIANO
  GEN INFO
    WHITESIDE, A.   BIOPP   P18-22
DISCIPLINE
  PIANO LESSONS, AT
    BROUGHTON, J.   BSIPT   P24-27
DODGING
  RE-ARRANGING FINGERING, IN
    TAYLER, E. D.   BSOSP   P26
DOHNANYI, ERNST VON
  BIO-CONF--FREEDOM IN MUSIC TEACHING METHODS
    COOKE, J. F.   BGMAFM   P89-94
  CONF--TECHNICAL MATERIAL DISCUSSED
    BROWER, H.   BMMOTK   P104-12
DORFMANN, ANIA
  BIOGRAPHICAL MATERIAL
    SALESKI, G.   BFMOJO   P464
DOUBLE-JOINTEDNESS
  GEN INFO
    ORTMANN, O.   BPMOPT   P324-26
DOUBLE MOVEMENT
  ATTACK, IN
    VANTYN, S.   BMPT   P59-61
DOUBLE NOTES
  FINGER MOVEMENT IN
    SCHAUFFLER, L.   BPTMOS   P96
  THIRDS, FOURTHS AND SIXTHS
    WHITESIDE, A.   BIOPP   P96-97
DOUBLE SIXTHS
  FINGERING
    NEWMAN, W.   BPP   P43
DOUBLE THIRDS
  FINGERING
    MERRICK, F.   BPTP   P35-42
  FINGERING
    NEWMAN, W.   BPP   P42-43
  PRACTICING, WAYS OF
    MERRICK, F.   BPTP   P35-42
DRAMATIC SIGNIFICANCE
  MUSICAL WORKS, IN
    MERRICK, F.   BPTP   P102-4
DULCE MELOS
  GEN INFO
    HIPKINS, A.   BDAHOT   P53-57
DULCIMER
  GEN INFO
    SUMNER, W.   BP   P32-34
DUMMY KEYBOARDS
  GEN INFO
    FOLDES, A.   BKTTK   P54-55
DUO-PIANISM
  ART OF PERFORMANCE, THE
    MOLDENHAUER, H.   BDP   P241-57
  COMPOSERS OF TWO-PIANO WORKS
    MOLDENHAUER, H.   BDP   P137-54
  CREATIVE MEDIUM, AS A
    MOLDENHAUER, H.   BDP   P258-85
  EDUCATIONAL AND PEDAGOGICAL APPLICATIONS
    MOLDENHAUER, H.   BDP   P286-310
  HISTORY
    MOLDENHAUER, H.   BDP   P7-170
  ORIGINAL TWO-PIANO MUSIC
    MOLDENHAUER, H.   BDP   P340-62
  PRACTICE AND REHEARSAL TECHNIQUES
    MOLDENHAUER, H.   BDP   P195-224
  PROGRAM BUILDING
    MOLDENHAUER, H.   BDP   P225-40
  RECORDED TWO-PIANO MUSIC--1950
    MOLDENHAUER, H.   BDP   P363-73
  STANDARD TWO-PIANO REPERTOIRE--1950
    MOLDENHAUER, H.   BDP   P312-39
  TWO-PIANO TEAMS ACTIVE IN THE 1950S
    MOLDENHAUER, H.   BDP   P129-36
  TWO-PIANO TEAMS OF A PAST ERA
    MOLDENHAUER, H.   BDP   P126-28
DUPLICATION
  PRACTICING, IN
    MERRICK, F.   BPTP   P94
DURATION, TERMS FOR
  LEGATISSIMO
    REEDER, B.   BST   P40
  LEGATO
    REEDER, B.   BST   P39-40
  NON-LEGATO
    REEDER, B.   BST   P39
  PORTAMENTO
    REEDER, B.   BST   P39
  STACCATISSIMO
    REEDER, B.   BST   P39
  STACCATO
    REEDER, B.   BST   P39
DURATIONS
  MATTHAY'S APPROACH
    COVIELLO, A.   BWMM   P21
DUSSEK, JAN LADISLAV
  ROLE IN THE DEVELOPMENT OF THE PF AND PF PLAYING
    SUMNER, W.   BP   P181
DYNAMICS
  GEN INFO
    LEIMER, K. * GIESEKING, W.   BRDP   P27-28
  SENSATION OF LOUDNESS
    SUMNER, W.   BP   P98-99
DYNAMIC CONTOUR
  WEIGHT-EFFECT AND CONTROL IN SHAPING
    GAT, J.   BTOPP   P29
DYNAMIC EXPRESSION
  REVIVAL OF
    REEDER, B.   BST   P60-61
EARLY KEYBOARD INSTRUMENTS
  GEN INFO
    SUMNER, W.   BP   P19-38
EARLY TECHNIQUE
  CHILD, FOR THE
    LAST, J.   BYP   P21-32

EAR TRAINING AND HARMONY
  GEN INFO
    POTAMKIN, F. J.   BMPP   P162-67
EAR TRAINING
  GEN INFO
    WILKINS-GUTMANN, E.   BTWPT   P11-23
  GEN INFO
    DILLER, A.   BSOM   P74-86
  GEN INFO
    LEIMER, K. * GIESEKING, W.   BSWTPP   P9-12
  IDENTIFYING RHYTHMIC DESIGN
    DILLER, A.   BSOM   P76-77
  PLAYING BY EAR
    DILLER, A.   BSOM   P77-78
  PLAYING BY EAR
    NEWMAN, W.   BPP   P6-17
  TEACHING SONGS TO ADULTS
    DILLER, A.   BSOM   P81-85
ECHIQUIER
  GEN INFO
    HIPKINS, A.   BDAHOT   P53-57
ECKARDT, JOHANN
  INFLUENCE ON W. A. MOZART
    RICHNER, T.   BOFIMP   P7-8
EDITIONS
  CHOICE OF
    BACON, E.   BNOTP   P63
  KEYBOARD MUSIC, OF
    BASTIEN, J. W.   BHTTPS   P387-94
  PROBLEMS IN MOZART WORKS
    BADURA-SKODA, E. * BADURA-SKODA, P. BIMOTK   P127-45
EIGHTEENTH CENTURY KEYBOARD MUSIC
  ORNAMENTS AND EMBELLISHMENTS
    BASTIEN, J. W.   BHTTPS   P371-85
ELBOW
  FUNCTION IN THE PLAYING MECHANISM
    WHITESIDE, A.   BPM   P22-23
ELECTRONIC PIANOS
  EARLY ATTEMPTS IN MANUFACTURING
    BRIGGS, G. A.   BPPAS   P15-16
EMOTIONAL ACTIVITIES
  PIANO PLAYING, IN
    CHING, J.   BPPAPM   P1-15
EMOTIONAL CONTENT, THE
  GEN INFO
    GAT, J.   BTOPP   P76-78
EMOTION
  CHANNELLING OF
    WHITESIDE, A.   BIOPP   P65-66
EMPIRICAL APPROACH
  PIANO PLAYING, TO
    NEWMAN, W.   BPP   P65-66
ENCOURAGEMENT
  STIMULANT TO MUSICAL GROWTH, AS A
    BOSWORTH, H.   BIFYPT   P40-41
ENDURANCE
  GEN INFO
    SCHULTZ, A.   BROTPF   P209-15
ENERGY
  CONSERVATION OF IN PIANO PRACTICE--GANZ
    BROWER, H.   BPM   P32-37
ENGLISH CLAVIER SCHOOL, EARLY
  GEN INFO
    BIE, O.   BHOTPA   P1-39
ENJOYMENT
  PIANO PLAYING, IN
    GRUNDY, E.   BHP   P1-2
ENSEMBLE PLAYING
  GEN INFO
    BACON, E.   BNOTP   P109-13
  GEN INFO
    BROUGHTON, J.   BSIPT   P58-60
  MEANS OF AWAKENING TO MUSICAL VALUES, AS A
    NEWMAN, W.   BPP   P25-26
ERARD, SEBASTIAN
  BIOGRAPHICAL MATERIAL
    SUMNER, W.   BP   P54-56
ESCAPEMENT
  DEVELOPMENT IN EARLY PIANOS
    SUMNER, W.   BP   P44-47
ESCHAQUEIL D'ANGLETERRE
  GEN INFO
    HIPKINS, A.   BDAHOT   P53-57
ETUDES
  PLAYING OF
    GAT, J.   BTOPP   P233-35
  SPECIAL PROBLEMS IN PRACTICING
    LEIMER, K. * GIESEKING, W.   BSWTPP   P50-51
ETUDE
  GROWTH OF THE FORM
    BIE, O.   BHOTPA   P202-8
EURHYTHMICS
  VALUE IN DEVELOPING RHYTHMIC SENSE
    BOLTON, H.   BHTP   P13
EVANGELISTIC PIANIST
  GEN INFO
    AULD, W.   BHFTCP   P9
EXAMINATIONS AND COMPETITIONS
  GEN INFO
    AHRENS, C. * ATKINSON, G.   BFAPT   P98-102
EXAMINATIONS
  YOUNG STUDENT, FOR THE
    LAST, J.   BYP   P147-51
EXERCISES
  CREATED FROM MUSICAL CONTEXT
    NEWMAN, W.   BPP   P45-47
  DEVELOPMENT OF MANUAL SUPPLENESS AND STRENGTH, FOR THE
    CURCIO, L.   BMHFTD   P1-24
  FINGER, FOR EACH
    VANTYN, S.   BMPT   P18-24
EXPRESSION
  PIANO PLAYING, IN
    BRECKENRIDGE, W.   BHFPNS   P68-73
  PIANO PLAYING, IN
    AHRENS, C. * ATKINSON, G.   BFAPT   P84
FATIGUE
  PROBLEMS OF
    CHING, J.   BPPAPM   P285-306
FEES
  PIANO TEACHING, FOR
    CARRE, J.   BPOPT   P61-64
FESTIVALS
  GEN INFO
    AHRENS, C. * ATKINSON, G.   BFAPT   P112-13
  YOUNG STUDENT, FOR THE
    LAST, J.   BYP   P151-55

FINGER-STROKE
  ANGLE OF MUSCULAR PULL
    ORTMANN, O.   BPMOPT   P217-18
  CURVED FINGER-STROKE
    ORTMANN, O.   BPMOPT   P220-22
  EFFECT OF INTENSITY ON FINGER STROKE
    ORTMANN, O.   BPMOPT   P234-35
  EFFECT OF PLAYING UNIT UPON FINGER-STROKE
    ORTMANN, O.   BPMOPT   P239-41
  ELLIPTICAL STROKE
    ORTMANN, O.   BPMOPT   P228-29
  FINGER-KEY PERCUSSION
    ORTMANN, O.   BPMOPT   P229-31
  FINGER-LIFT
    ORTMANN, O.   BPMOPT   P235-36
  FINGER POSITION AND KEY RESISTANCE
    ORTMANN, O.   BPMOPT   P227-28
  FLAT-FINGER STROKE
    ORTMANN, O.   BPMOPT   P218-20
  GEN INFO
    ORTMANN, O.   BPMOPT   P217-50
  ISOLATION
    ORTMANN, O.   BPMOPT   P237-39
  MECHANICS OF THE ARCHED HAND
    ORTMANN, O.   BPMOPT   P249-50
  NAIL-JOINT, THE
    ORTMANN, O.   BPMOPT   P225-27
  PERCUSSIVE AND NON-PERCUSSIVE TOUCH
    ORTMANN, O.   BPMOPT   P231-34
  PHYSIOLOGICAL CONTRAST
    ORTMANN, O.   BPMOPT   P222-25
  RELAXATION AND RIGIDITY
    ORTMANN, O.   BPMOPT   P241-43
  REPEATED TONES
    ORTMANN, O.   BPMOPT   P246-47
  SPREAD OF TENSION
    ORTMANN, O.   BPMOPT   P236-37
  TEMPO AND FINGER-STROKE
    ORTMANN, O.   BPMOPT   P248-49
  TONE QUALITIES
    ORTMANN, O.   BPMOPT   P243-46
  WRIST POSITION
    ORTMANN, O.   BPMOPT   P247-48
FINGERING
  ACCENTS
    SCHAUFFLER, L.   BPTMOS   P100
  ADAPTING MOVEMENTS
    GAT, J.   BTOPP   P242
  ARPEGGIOS
    SCHAUFFLER, L.   BPTMOS   P103
  AVOIDANCE OF STRETCHING
    SCHAUFFLER, L.   BPTMOS   P98-99
  CHOICE OF
    DILLER, A.   BSOM   P119-20
  COMPARISON OF ENGLISH AND CONTINENTAL SYSTEMS
    VANTYN, S.   BMPT   P23
  CROSSING
    GAT, J.   BTOPP   P239-40
  DEPENDENCE ON ARRANGEMENT OF KEYS
    SCHAUFFLER, L.   BPTMOS   P98
  DEPENDENCE ON PHRASING
    SCHAUFFLER, L.   BPTMOS   P99
  DEPENDENCE ON PITCH OF NOTES
    SCHAUFFLER, L.   BPTMOS   P97
  DOUBLE THIRDS, SIXTHS AND OCTAVES
    SCHAUFFLER, L.   BPTMOS   104-5
  DOUBLE THIRDS
    MERRICK, F.   BPTP   P35-42
  EARLY STUDY, IN
    LAST, J.   BYP   P86-94
  FINE-TONE GROUP
    SCHAUFFLER, L.   BPTMOS   P103-4
  GENERAL RULES
    AHRENS, C. * ATKINSON, G.   BFAPT   P38-39
  GEN INFO
    FIELDEN, T.   BSOPT   P168-79
  GEN INFO
    ORTMANN, O.   BPMOPT   P278-80
  HINTS FOR THE AMATEUR
    GRUNDY, E.   BHP   P21-23
  IMPORTANCE OF PROPER CHOICE
    NEWMAN, W.   BPP   P74-81
  LITTLE FINGER, ROLE OF
    GAT, J.   BTOPP   P236-37
  MATTHAY'S APPROACH
    COVIELLO, A.   BWMM   P23
  PASSING OVER AND UNDER
    GAT, J.   BTOPP   P237
  PLAN FOR EVALUATING AND CHOOSING
    VANTYN, S.   BMPT   P89-103
  PRESERVING LEGATO
    SLENCZYNSKA, R.   BMAYF   P45-46
  RELATIONSHIP TO PEDALLING
    SCHAUFFLER, L.   BPTMOS   P100-1
  REPEATED NOTES
    SCHAUFFLER, L.   BPTMOS   P104
  SCALES
    SCHAUFFLER, L.   BPTMOS   P101-3
  SEQUENCES IN
    GAT, J.   BTOPP   P243
  SEQUENCES
    SCHAUFFLER, L.   BPTMOS   P99-100
  SHIFTING THE CENTER OF GRAVITY
    GAT, J.   BTOPP   P241
  SYNTHESIZING MOVEMENTS
    GAT, J.   BTOPP   P238-39
  THUMB, ROLE OF THE
    GAT, J.   BTOPP   P236-37
FINGERS
  ACCENTS
    SCHAUFFLER, L.   BPTMOS   P92-94
  ARPEGGIOS, PLAYING OF
    SCHAUFFLER, L.   BPTMOS   P91-92
  DOUBLE NOTES, PLAYING OF
    SCHAUFFLER, L.   BPTMOS   P94
  PIANO PLAYING, SPECIFIC USE IN
    FIELDEN, T.   BSOPT   P96-107
  PIANO PLAYING, SPECIFIC USE IN
    NEWMAN, W.   BPP   P54-60
  PLAYING MOVEMENTS
    SCHAUFFLER, L.   BPTMOS   P83-87
  PLAYING POSITIONS
    SCHAUFFLER, L.   BPTMOS   P80-83
  REACTIONS
    SCHAUFFLER, L.   BPTMOS   P87-88
  SCALES, PLAYING OF
    SCHAUFFLER, L.   BPTMOS   P88-91

TRILLS, PLAYING OF
    SCHAUFFLER, L.   BPTMOS   P92-93
FINGER ACTION
  GEN INFO
    HARRISON, S.   BYPGTP   P33-36
  GEN INFO
    CARRE, J.   BPOPT   P52-57
FINGER INDEPENDENCE
  GEN INFO
    WOODHOUSE, G.   BFKTM   P14-16
FINGER STRENGTHENING
  MECHANICAL MEANS
    VANTYN, S.   BMPT   P152-53
FINGER STROKE
  CURVED
    SCHAUFFLER, L.   BPTMOS   P84-85
  FLAT
    SCHAUFFLER, L.   BPTMOS   P83-84
  HIGH
    SCHAUFFLER, L.   BPTMOS   P84
  RELEASE
    SCHAUFFLER, L.   BPTMOS   P85-86
  REPETITION
    SCHAUFFLER, L.   BPTMOS   P85
  THUMB STROKE
    SCHAUFFLER, L.   BPTMOS   P86-87
FINGER TOUCHES
  ARM MOVEMENTS IN FINGER PASSAGES
    CHING, J.   BPPAPM   P234-50
  CONTROL OF FINGER MOVEMENTS
    CHING, J.   BPPAPM   P207-19
  CONVENTIONAL AND NON-CONVENTIONAL FINGERING
    CHING, J.   BPPAPM   P251-68
  CURVILINEAR MOVEMENTS
    CHING, J.   BPPAPM   P269-84
  DIFFICULTIES OF FINGER INDIVIDUALIZATION
    CHING, J.   BPPAPM   P207-19
  FINGERING IN RELATION TO TECHNICAL GROUPING
    CHING, J.   BPPAPM   P251-68
  FOREARM ROTATION
    CHING, J.   BPPAPM   P207-19
  METHOD OF TECHNICAL GROUPING
    CHING, J.   BPPAPM   P234-50
  PIANIST'S CRAMP, A CURE FOR
    CHING, J.   BPPAPM   P269-84
  PLAYING OF SCALES AND ARPEGGIOS
    CHING, J.   BPPAPM   P234-50
  POSTURE, IMPORTANCE OF
    CHING, J.   BPPAPM   P220-33
  PRACTICAL RULES
    CHING, J.   BPPAPM   P269-84
  PREVENTION OF ROTARY MOVEMENTS
    CHING, J.   BPPAPM   P207-19
  RELATIONSHIP BETWEEN RHYTHM AND TONE GRADATION
    CHING, J.   BPPAPM   P220-33
  REVERSAL OF DIRECTION
    CHING, J.   BPPAPM   P269-84
  TONAL GRADATIONS IN FINGER PASSAGES
    CHING, J.   BPPAPM   P220-33
  TONE QUALITY IN FINGER PASSAGES
    CHING, J.   BPPAPM   P251-68
FINGER TOUCH
  GEN INFO
    HOFHEIMER, G.   BTTFTP   P6-12
FINGER TRAINING
  GEN INFO
    WILKINS-GUTMANN, E.   BTWPT   P32-37
FINGER
  BENT VS. FLAT FINGERS
    SCHULTZ, A.   BROTPF   P130-33
  COORDINATION OF MUSCULAR UNITS
    SCHULYZ, A.   BROTPF   P106-28
  GEN INFO
    SCHULTZ, A.   BROTPF   P101-34
  GYMNASTIC EXERCISES
    FIELDEN, T.   BSOPT   P40-44
  MUSCULATURE
    SCHULTZ, A.   BROTPF   P103-6
  PEDAGOGY OF FINGER COORDINATION
    SCHULTZ, A.   BROTPF   P148-64
  POSITION
    SCHULTZ, A.   BROTPF   P128-30
  PRELIMINARY LIFTING
    BOWEN, Y.   BSOPT   P11-12
  SIMPLE FINGER TOUCH
    BOWEN, Y.   BSOPT   P7-8
FIRST LESSON
  PIANO, AT THE
    LAST, J.   BYP   P6-17
FIRST PIECES
  CHILD, FOR THE
    LAST, J.   BYP   P32-40
FISCHER, ANNIE
  PHOTOGRAPHIC ANALYSIS OF PERFORMANCE
    GAT, J.   BTOPP   P60-61
FLEISCHER, LEON
  BIOGRAPHICAL MATERIAL
    SALESKI, G.   BFMOJO   P465
FOREARM ROTATION
  GEN INFO
    MATTHAY, T.   BPFOT   P20-27
  MATTHAY'S APPROACH
    COVIELLO, A.   BWMM   P24-26
  PASSAGE WORK, USE IN
    CHING, J.   BPPAPM   P285-305
FOREARM
  ARM DROP
    SCHAUFFLER, L.   BPTMOS   P67-69
  ARM LEGATO
    SCHAUFFLER, L.   BPTMOS   P69-71
  ARM STACCATO
    SCHAUFFLER, L.   BPTMOS   P62-67
  BALANCE
    SCHAUFFLER, L.   BPTMOS   P73-74
  CONCENTRATION OF ENERGY IN
    SCHAUFFLER, L.   BPTMOS   P61-62
  EXERCISES
    FIELDEN, T.   BSOPT   P39-40
  PIANO PLAYING, SPECIFIC USE IN
    NEWMAN, W.   BPP   P64-65
  PIANO PLAYING, SPECIFIC USE IN
    WHITESIDE, A.   BIOPP   P39-45
  REBOUNDS
    SCHAUFFLER, L.   BPTMOS   P71-73
  RELEASE
    SCHAUFFLER, L.   BPTMOS   P71
  ROTATION
    SCHAUFFLER, L.   BPTMOS   P74-78

VARIOUS TOUCHES
    BOWEN, Y.   BSOPT   P20-23
FOREIGN STUDY
  AMERICAN MUSIC STUDENTS, FOR
    BRECKENRIDGE, W.   BHFPNS   P91-93
FORM, TECHNIC AND EXPRESSION
  GEN INFO--HAMBOURG
    BROWER, H.   BPM   P78-83
FORM AND STYLE
  GEN INFO
    BACON, E.   BNOTP   P27-33
FORTISSIMO PRACTICING
  GEN INFO
    VANTYN, S.   BMPT   P6
FORTISSIMO
  RELATIVE TERM, AS A
    VANTYN, S.   BMPT   P104-8
FORWARD AND BACKWARD MOVEMENT
  PASSING FROM BLACK TO WHITE KEYS, IN
    VANTYN, S.   BMPT   P62-63
FREEDOM
  PERFORMANCE, IN
    BACON, E.   BNOTP   P108
FRENCH KEYBOARD MUSIC, EARLY
  GEN INFO
    BIE, O.   BHOTPA   P40-67
FRENCH MUSIC--MODERN
  INTERPRETATION BY SCHMITZ
    BROWER, H.   BMMMOTK   P128-37
FREUDIAN PSYCHOLOGY AND THE PIANISTIC ART
  CONCERT AND EXAMINATION NERVES
    CHING, J.   BPPAPM   P323-41
  INHIBITION
    CHING, J.   BPPAPM   P323-41
  MEMORY FAILURE
    CHING, J.   BPPAPM   P323-41
  MUSIC AND CIVILIZATION
    CHING, J.   BPPAPM   P323-41
  RELATION OF UNCONSCIOUS TO ARTISTIC EXPRESSION
    CHING, J.   BPPAPM   P323-41
  TEACHER-PUPIL RELATIONSHIP
    CHING, J.   BPPAPM   P323-41
FRIEDBERG, CARL
  BIOGRAPHICAL MATERIAL
    SALESKI, G.   BFMOJO   P465-66
  CONF--DISCUSSION ON PIANO PLAYING
    BROWER, H.   BPMSS   P80-87
FRIEDHEIM, ARTHUR
  BIO-CONF--INTIMATE THOUGHTS ON PIANO STUDY
    COOKE, J. F.   BGMAFM   P404-7
  BIOGRAPHICAL MATERIAL
    SALESKI, G.   BFMOJO   P466-67
FRIEDMAN, IGNAZ
  BIOGRAPHICAL MATERIAL
    SALESKI, G.   BFMOJO   P467-69
  REVIEW OF RECITAL
    BROWER, H.   BWTPWT   P189-93
FRIEDMANN, IGNAZ
  BIO-CONF--MOST DIFFICULT THING IN PIANO PLAYING, THE
    COOKE, J. F.   BGMAFM   P73-78
  CONF--SELF-DEVELOPMENT A NECESSITY FOR THE PIANIST
    BROWER, H.   BMMOTK   P43-54
FUGUES
  PRACTICE SUGGESTIONS
    HARRISON, S.   BYPGTP   P49-51
  PRACTICING, WAYS OF
    MERRICK, F.   BPTP   P63-67
FUGUE
  GEN INFO
    BACON, E.   BNOTP   P31-33
FUTURISM
  MUSIC, IN--PROKOFIEFF
    BROWER, H.   BMMOTK   P223-34
GABRILOWITSCH, OSSIP
  BIO-CONF--ESSENTIALS OF TOUCH
    COOKE, J. F.   BGPOPP   P121-31
  BIOGRAPHICAL MATERIAL
    SALESKI, G.   BFMOJO   P469-71
  BIOGRAPHICAL MATERIAL
    CHASINS, A.   BSOP   P145-46
  CONF--CHARACTERISTIC TOUCH ON THE PIANO
    BROWER, H.   BPM   P225-31
  REVIEW OF RECITAL
    BROWER, H.   BWTPWT   P184-88
GALANT SCHOOL
  GEN INFO
    BIE, O.   BHOTPA   P128-56
GANZ, RUDOLPH
  BIO-CONF--OPPORTUNITIES...IN PIANOFORTE PLAYING
    COOKE, J. F.   BGPOPP   P310-20
  CONF--CONSERVING ENERGY IN PIANO PRACTICE
    BROWER, H.   BPM   P32-37
GENEALOGY
  MODERN PIANO, OF THE
    SUMNER, W.   BP   P17
GERSHWIN, GEORGE
  PIANO WORKS
    CHASINS, A.   BSOP   P259-66
GESTURE
  TECHNICAL AID, AS A
    DILLER, A.   BSOM   P120-29
  TONE PRODUCTION, IN
    BACON, E.   BNOTP   P20
GIESEKING, WALTER
  BIOGRAPHICAL MATERIAL
    CHASINS, A.   BSOP   P112-17
  CONF--RELAXATION A PRIME ESSENTIAL
    BROWER, H.   BMMOTK   P64-71
GLISSANDO
  GEN INFO
    GAT, J.   BTOPP   P188-89
  MATTHAY'S APPROACH
    COVIELLO, A.   BWMM   P26
GODOWSKY, LEOPOLD
  BIO-CONF--REAL SIGNIFICANCE OF TECHNIC, THE
    COOKE, J. F.   BGPOPP   P132-42
  BIOGRAPHICAL MATERIAL
    SALESKI, G.   BFMOJO   P472-76
  BIOGRAPHICAL MATERIAL
    CHASINS, A.   BSOP   P27-39,
  LAWS GOVERNING TECHNIC AND INTERPRETATION, THE
    BROWER, H.   BPMSS   P61-79
GOLDSAND, ROBERT
  BIOGRAPHICAL MATERIAL
    SALESKI, G.   BFMOJO   P476-77
GOODSON, KATHERINE
  BIO-CONF--ANALYZING MASTERPIECES
    COOKE, J. F.   BGPOPP   P143-55

CONF--ARTIST AT HOME, AN
   BROWER, H.   BPM   P72-77
GOOD TASTE
  DEVELOPMENT OF
   AHRENS, C. * ATKINSON, G.   BFAPT   P84
GORODNITZKI, SASCHA
  BIOGRAPHICAL MATERIAL
   SALESKI, G.   BFMOJO   P479
GOULD, GLENN
  BIOGRAPHICAL MATERIAL
   CHASINS, A.   BSOP   P167-68
GRAINGER, PERCY
  BIO-CONF--JAZZ AND THE MUSIC OF THE FUTURE
   COOKE, J. F.   BGMAFM   P308-13
  BIO-CONF--MODERNISM IN PIANOFORTE STUDY
   COOKE, J. F.   BGPOPP   P363-81
  CONF--FREEDOM OF THOUGHT IN PIANO STUDY
   BROWER, H.   BPMSS   P1-17
GROUP PIANO INSTRUCTION
  ADEQUACY OF INSTRUCTION
   MASON, E. * BURROWS, R.   BATCOC   P5
  CARDBOARD KEYBOARDS, USE OF
   MASON, E. * BURROWS, R.   BATCOC   P18
  CHALLENGE TO TEACHER
   MASON, E. * BURROWS, R.   BATCOC   P19-20
  CLASS PIANO CURRICULUM IN COLLEGE
   BASTIEN, J. W.   BHTTPS   P295-300
  COLLEGE PIANO MINORS, FOR
   BASTIEN, J. W.   BHTTPS   P285-309
  COMBINING GROUP AND PRIVATE LESSONS
   BASTIEN, J. W.   BHTTPS   P44-47
  COMPARED TO PRIVATE TEACHING
   CARRE, J.   BPOPT   P24-25
  DROPOUTS
   MASON, E. * BURROWS, R.   BATCOC   P12-13
  EQUIPMENT AND FACILITIES
   BASTIEN, J. W.   BHTTPS   P287-91
  FALLING BEHIND THE GROUP
   MASON, E. * BURROWS, R.   BATCOC   P11-12
  FEE STRUCTURE
   MASON, E. * BURROWS, R.   BATCOC   P23-24
  GEN INFO
   BASTIEN, J. W.   BHTTPS   P285-309
  GEN INFO
   DILLER, A.   BSOM   P24-25
  HOMOGENEOUS GROUPS, ASSENBLING OF
   MASON, E. * BURROWS, R.   BATCOC   P8-9
  INCENTIVE FOR HOME PRACTICE
   MASON, E. * BURROWS, R.   BATCOC   P21
  INDIVIDUAL DIFFERENCES, RECOGNITION OF
   MASON, E. * BURROWS, R.   BATCOC   P7
  INDIVIDUAL DRILL
   MASON, E. * BURROWS, R.   BATCOC   P6-7
  INSPIRATION, MAINTAINING OF
   MASON, E. * BURROWS, R.   BATCOC   P16
  LENGTH OF SESSION
   MASON, E. * BURROWS, R.   BATCOC   P24
  MATERIAL FOR HOME PRACTICE
   MASON, E. * BURROWS, R.   BATCOC   P7-8
  MONOTONY, POSSIBILITY OF
   MASON, E. * BURROWS, R.   BATCOC   P6
  ORGANIZATION OF CLASSES
   BASTIEN, J. W.   BHTTPS   P293-95
  PARENT-TEACHER COOPERATION
   MASON, E. * BURROWS, R.   BATCOC   P24
  PLACEMENT OF INSTRUMENTS
   BASTIEN, J. W.   BHTTPS   P291-92
  PLAYING TIME IN A LARGE CLASS
   MASON, E. * BURROWS, R.   BATCOC   P5-6
  PROFICIENCY EXAMINATION REQUIREMENTS
   BASTIEN, J. W.   BHTTPS   P300-1
  PROGRESS, RATE OF
   MASON, E. * BURROWS, R.   BATCOC   P22
  QUALITIES NECESSARY FOR SUCCESSFUL TEACHER
   MASON, E. * BURROWS, R.   BATCOC   P20-21
  REARRANGING CLASSES
   MASON, E. * BURROWS, R.   BATCOC   P12
  SELECTING MUSIC FOR NEEDS OF STUDENTS
   MASON, E. * BURROWS, R.   BATCOC   P14
  SIGHT READING
   MASON, E. * BURROWS, R.   BATCOC   P16-17
  SPECIAL TRAINING FOR TEACHER
   MASON, E. * BURROWS, R.   BATCOC   P20
  STANDARDS FOR INTERPRETATION AND FINESSE
   MASON, E. * BURROWS, R.   BATCOC   P14-15
  STEREOTYPING, AVOIDANCE OF
   MASON, E. * BURROWS, R.   BATCOC   P13-14
  TALENTED PUPIL, PROGRESS OF
   MASON, E. * BURROWS, R.   BATCOC   P9-10
  TALENTED PUPIL, SPECIAL ATTENTION TO
   MASON, E. * BURROWS, R.   BATCOC   PP9
  TEACHING PROCEDURES
   BROUGHTON, J.   BSIPT   P19-23
  TECHNICAL DEVELOPMENT
   MASON, E. * BURROWS, R.   BATCOC   P17-18
  TECHNICAL FOUNDATION
   MASON, E. * BURROWS, R.   BATCOC   P19
  TONAL CONSIDERATIONS
   MASON, E. * BURROWS, R.   BATCOC   P22
  WEAKER PUPIL, SPECIAL ATTENTION TO
   MASON, E. * BURROWS, R.   BATCOC   P11
GYMNASTICS
  PRACTICE, IN
   TAYLER, E. D.   BSOSP   P11
  TECHNICAL TRAINING, USED IN
   FIELDEN, T.   BSOPT   P34-44
GYMNASTIC EXERCISES
  GEN INFO
   GAT, J.   BTOPP   P249-65
HALF-PEDALLING
  MATTHAY'S APPROACH
   COVIELLO, A.   BWMM   P27
HALF DAMPING
  MATTHAY'S APPROACH
   COVIELLO, A.   BWMM   P27
HAMBOURG, MARK
  BIO-CONF--INSURING PROGRESS IN MUSIC STUDY
   COOKE, J. F.   BGPOPP   P348-62
  BIOGRAPHICAL MATERIAL
   SALESKI, G.   BFMOJO   P480-81
  BIOGRAPHICAL MATERIAL
   BROOK, D.   BMOTK   P158-63
  CONF--FORM, TECHNIC AND EXPRESSION
   BROWER, H.   BPM   P78-83
HANDS
  SYNCHRONIZATION OF
   LAST, J.   BYP   P114-15

  UNIT, USE OF AS A
   GAT, J.   BTOPP   P145-47
HAND ADJUSTING PRINCIPLE
  GEN INFO
   WOODHOUSE, G.   BFKTM   P22-27
HAND AND ARM, POSITION OF
  DEPPE'S APPROACH
   CALAND, E.   BAPP   P26-32
HAND POSITION
  AWKWARDNESS OF
   LAST, J.   BYP   P125-26
HAND
  DEVELOPMENT BY DISJUNCTION OF THE FINGERS
   VANTYN, S.   BMPT   P64-67
  DOUBLE-JOINTEDNESS
   ORTMANN, O.   BPMOPT   P324-26
  FINGER-TIP
   ORTMANN, O.   BPMOPT   P335-36
  FORM OF
   GAT, J.   BTOPP   P139-41
  FUNCTION IN THE PLAYING MECHANISM
   WHITESIDE, A.   BPM   P24-28
  HAND TYPES
   ORTMANN, O.   BPMOPT   P326-35
  INDIVIDUAL DIFFERENCES
   ORTMANN, O.   BPMOPT   P311-36
  PIANIST, OF THE--SCHELLING
   BROWER, H.   BPM   P12-16
  POSITION IN PIANO PLAYING
   DILLER, A.   BSCM   P108-9
  POSITION IN PIANO PLAYING
   VANTYN, S.   BMPT   P15-17
  PRINCIPAL ACCOMMODATING MOVEMENTS
   BACON, E.   BNOTP   P39-43
  RELEASE AT END OF PASSAGE
   BOWEN, Y.   BSOPT   P33
  SPECIFIC USE IN PIANO PLAYING
   DICKERSON, R.   BNATPT   P10-12
  SPECIFIC USE IN PIANO PLAYING
   NEWMAN, W.   BPP   P60-63
  STIFFNESS IN
   ORTMANN, O.   BPMOPT   P321-24
  STRUCTURE OF
   GAT, J.   BTOPP   P131-38
HANON EXERCISES
  PRACTICING, WAYS OF
   AHRENS, C. * ATKINSON, G.   BFAPT   P45-46
HARMONY
  INTRODUCTION TO THE AMATEUR
   GRUNDY, E.   BHP   P54-60
HARPSICHORD
  GEN INFO
   HIPKINS, A.   BDAHOT   76-94
  GEN INFO
   REEDER, B.   BST   P56-57
  HISTORY AND CONSTRUCTION
   SUMNER, W.   BP   P25-31
  ORIGIN AND DEVELOPMENT
   WEITZMANN, C.   BHOPPA   P223-25
  TRANSITION FROM HARPSICHORD TO PIANO
   SUMNER, W.   BP   P50-53
HAYDN, FRANZ JOSEPH
  INFLUENCE ON W. A. MOZART
   RICHNER, T.   BOFIMP   P12-14
HAYDN, JOSEPH
  KEYBOARD WORKS
   BIE, O.   BHOTPA   P149-51
HAYDN, MICHAEL
  INFLUENCE ON W. A. MOZART
   RICHNER, T.   BOFIMP   P11-12
HELLER, STEPHEN
  ROLE IN THE DEVELOPMENT OF THE PF AND PF PLAYING
   SUMNER, W.   BP   P181-82
HENSELT, ADOLF VON
  BIOGRAPHICAL MATERIAL
   FAY, A.   BMSIG   P229
  RECOLLECTIONS OF W. VON LENZ
   LENZ, W. VON   BGPVOO   P119-58
  ROLE IN THE DEVELOPMENT OF THE PF AND PF PLAYING
   SUMNER, W.   BP   P181
  TECHNICAL APPROACH
   LEVINSKAYA, M.   BLSOPT   P34-35
HERZ, HENRI
  BIOGRAPHICAL MATERIAL
   SALESKI, G.   BFMOJO   P481-82
HESS, MYRA
  BIOGRAPHICAL MATERIAL
   SALESKI, G.   BFMOJO   P482-85
  BIOGRAPHICAL MATERIAL
   BROOK, D.   BMOTK   P164-66
  BIOGRAPHICAL MATERIAL
   CHASINS, A.   BSOP   P152-53
  CONF--GLIMPSES OF PRESENT-DAY PIANO STUDY
   BROWER, H.   BMMOTK   P193-202
  REVIEW OF RECITAL
   BROWER, H.   BWTPWT   P201-207
HOFMANN, JOSEF
  BIO-CONF--PROGRESS IN PIANO STUDY
   COOKE, J. F.   BGPOPP   P156-68
  BIOGRAPHICAL MATERIAL
   CHASINS, A.   BSOP   P7-26,
  CONF--INSPIRATION IN PIANO PLAYING
   BROWER, H.   BPMSS   P18-29
  REVIEW OF RECITAL
   BROWER, H.   BWTPWT   P163-69
HOROWITZ, VLADIMIR
  BIOGRAPHICAL MATERIAL
   SALESKI, G.   BFMOJO   P486-91
  BIOGRAPHICAL MATERIAL
   CHASINS, A.   BSOP   P136-44
HUGHES, EDWIN
  CONF--SOME ESSENTIALS OF PIANO PLAYING
   BROWER, H.   BPM   P127-36
HUMMEL, JOHANN NEPOMUK
  PIANISTIC THEORETICIAN, AS
   BIE, O.   BHOTPA   P186-88+
  ROLE IN DEV OF ROMANTIC PIANO CONCERTO
   GARVIN, F. H.   BBOTRP   P20-23
  ROLE IN THE DEVELOPMENT OF THE PF AND PF PLAYING
   SUMNER, W.   BP   P178
HURDY-GURDY
  GEN INFO
   HIPKINS, A.   BDAHOT   P95-98
  GEN INFO
   SUMNER, W.   BP   P21
HUTCHESON, ERNEST
  BIO-CONF--ADULTS AND PIANO STUDY
   COOKE, J. F.   BGMAFM   P345-49

BIO-CONF--UNIVERSALITY IN PIANO TEACHING METHODS
    COOKE, J. F.   BGPOPP   P321-32
CONF--TECHNIC AND INTERPRETATION
    BROWER, H.   BPMSS   P100-13
HYMN INTRODUCTIONS
  CHURCH PIANIST, FOR THE
    AULD, W.   BHFTCP   P75-81
IDEALS
  INDIVIDUAL STUDENT, FOR THE
    BOSWORTH, H.   BIFYPT   P53-55
IDEAS
  STIMULATE THE CHILD'S IMAGINATION, TO
    BOSWORTH, H.   BIFYPT   P7-8, 15-16
IMAGERY
  GEN INFO
    WHITESIDE, A.   BIOPP   P59-61
IMAGINATION
  PIANO PLAYING, IN
    BRECKENRIDGE, W.   BHFPNS   P76-79
IMITATION
  TEACHER BY THE CHILD, OF
    BOSWORTH, H.   BIFYPT   P31-32
IMPROVISATION
  GEN INFO
    MELLING, E.   BEATPM   P1-15
INDIVIDUALISM
  INDIVIDUALISM IN PIANO STUDY
    COOKE, J. F.   BGMAFM   P149-57
INSPIRATION
  PIANO PLAYING, IN--HOFMANN
    BROWER, H.   BPMSS   P18-29
INSTRUCTION
  ADULT BEGINNER, FOR THE
    AHRENS, C. * ATKINSON, G. BFAPT   P94-96
  FIRST IMPRESSIONS
    AHRENS, C. * ATKINSON, G. BFAPT   P92
  PRE-SCHOOL CHILD, FOR THE
    AHRENS, C. * ATKINSON, G. BFAPT   P90-94
INTERPRETATION, NATURAL
  GEN INFO
    LEIMER, K. * GIESEKING, W. BSWTPP   P43-45
INTERPRETATION
  ART OF, THE
    COHEN, H.   BMH   P45
  CHURCH PIANIST, FOR THE
    AULD, W.   BHFTCP   P90-96
  COMPOSERS' VIEWS
    CHASINS, A.   BSOP   P71-79
  DEPPE'S APPROACH
    CALAND, E.   BAPP   P65-72
  GEN INFO
    BACON, E.   BNOTP   P7-19
  GEN INFO
    BRECKENRIDGE, W.   BHFPNS   P74-75
  GEN INFO
    NEWMAN, W.   BPP   P91-104
  GEN INFO
    BOLTON, H.   BHTP   P26-29
  IMAGINATION, ROLE OF
    BOLTON, H.   BHTP   P26-27
  INSPIRATION, ROLE OF
    BOLTON, H.   BHTP   P28-29
  MID-NINETEENTH CENTURY VIEWPOINT, A
    KULLAK, A.   BAOPP   P214-26
  NEED FOR UNDERSTANDING IN
    NEWMAN, W.   BPP   P92-93
  PATHWAYS TO
    LAST, J.   BYP   P129-42
  REPEATED NOTES, OF
    DABREU, G.   BPTPWC   P71-72
  REPETITION OF PHRASES
    DABREU, G.   BPTPWC   P70-71
  REST THAT REPLACES THE DOT, THE
    DABREU, G.   BPTPWC   P83-84
  SEQUENCES, OF
    DABREU, G.   BPTPWC   P68-70
  SILENCES AND PAUSES
    DABREU, G.   BPTPWC   P81-83
INTERVIEWS
  PROSPECTIVE STUDENTS, WITH
    CARRE, J.   BPOPT   P67-68
ITURBI, JOSE
  BIOGRAPHICAL MATERIAL
    CHASINS, A.   BSOP   P149-50
IVES, CHARLES
  PIANO WORKS
    CHASINS, A.   BSOP   P276
JANIS, BYRON
  BIOGRAPHICAL MATERIAL
    SALESKI, G.   BFMOJO   P491-92
JAZZ
  JAZZ AND THE MUSIC OF THE FUTURE--GRAINGER
    COOKE, J. F.   BGMAFM   P308-13
JOINTS, ROLES OF VARIOUS
  ELBOW AND RADIO-ULNAR JOINT
    GAT, J.   BTOPP   P122-24
  FINGER-JOINTS
    GAT, J.   BTOPP   P127-29
  HIPS
    GAT, J.   BTOPP   P118
  SHOULDER JOINT
    GAT, J.   BTOPP   P118-19
  UPPER ARM
    GAT, J.   BTOPP   P119-21
  WRIST
    GAT, J.   BTOPP   P125-26
JONAS, ALBERTO
  BIO-CONF--NERVOUSNESS IN PIANO PLAYING
    COOKE, J. F.   BGPOPP   P397-418
  BIOGRAPHICAL MATERIAL
    SALESKI, G.   BFMOJO   P492-93
JOSEFFY, RAFAEL
  BIOGRAPHICAL MATERIAL
    SALESKI, G.   BFMOJO   P496
  COMMENTARIES BY SOME OF HIS PUPILS
    BROWER, H.   BPMSS   P242-54
JOYCE, EILEEN
  BIOGRAPHICAL MATERIAL
    BROOK, D.   BMOTK   P167-71
KALKBRENNER, FRIEDRICH WILHELM
  ROLE IN THE DEVELOPMENT OF THE PF AND PF PLAYING
    SUMNER, W.   BP   P181
KAPELL, WILLIAM
  BIOGRAPHICAL MATERIAL
    SALESKI, G.   BFMOJO   P497-99
  BIOGRAPHICAL MATERIAL
    CHASINS, A.   BSOP   P164-65

KENTNER, LOUIS
  BIOGRAPHICAL MATERIAL
    BROOK, D.   BMOTK   P172-74
  BIOGRAPHICAL MATERIAL
    CHASINS, A.   BSOP   P153-54
KEY-BEDDING
  GEN INFO
    LEVINSKAYA, M.   BLSOPT   P177-98
KEY-DESCENT
  CONTROLLED
    SCHULTZ, A.   BROTPF   P1-2
KEY-HITTING
  GEN INFO
    MATTHAY, T.   BPFOT   P29-31
KEY-RESISTANCE
  MATTHAY'S APPROACH
    COVIELLO, A.   BWMM   P28-29
KEY-SENSE
  GEN INFO
    MATTHAY, T.   BPFOT   P27-29
KEYBOARD HARMONY
  DOMINANT EMBELLISHMENTS, USE OF
    NEWMAN, W.   BPP   P14-17
  EFFECTIVE AND EXCLUSIVE USE OF I, IV, AND V
    NEWMAN, W.   BPP   P13-14
KEYBOARD INSTRUMENTS, UNDETERMINED
  DULCE MELOS
    HIPKINS, A.   BDAHOT   P53-57
  ECHIQUIER
    HIPKINS, A.   BDAHOT   P53-57
  ESCHAQUEIL D'ANGLETERRE
    HIPKINS, A.   BDAHOT   P53-57
  SYMPHONIA
    HIPKINS, A.   BDAHOT   P53-57
KEYBOARD INSTRUMENTS
  PRECEDING THE PIANO
    BRINSMEAD, E.   BHOTP   P83-106
KEYBOARD MUSIC
  EDITIONS
    BASTIEN, J. W.   BHTTPS   P387-94
KEYBOARD
  EARLY HISTORY
    HIPKINS, A.   BDAHOT   P47-53
KEY AND HAMMER
  MATTHAY'S PRINCIPLES
    COVIELLO, A.   BWMM   P29
KEY DEPRESSION
  SUDDEN VS. GRADUAL
    BOWEN, Y.   BSOPT   P24
KEY MOVEMENT
  MATTHAY'S APPROACH
    COVIELLO, A.   BWMM   P29
KEY RELEASE
  GEN INFO
    DICKERSON, R.   BNATPT   P19
KEY RESISTANCE
  MATTHAY'S PRINCIPLES
    COVIELLO, A.   BWMM   P30-32
KINESTHETIC SENSATIONS
  IMPORTANCE OF
    CHING, J.   BPPAPM   P15-19
KNOWLEDGE VS. ROUTINE PRACTICE
  GEN INFO
    CHING, J.   BPPAPM   P1-15
KULLAK, ADOLPH
  PIANO TECHNIQUE, APPROACH TO
    LEVINSKAYA, M.   BLSOPT   P32-33,
KULLAK, THEODOR
  BIOGRAPHICAL MATERIAL
    FAY, A.   BMSIG   P102-3,
LAMBERT, ALEXANDER
  BIO-CONF--PROFITABLE PRACTICE VS. WASTED PRACTICE
    COOKE, J. F.   BGPOPP   P382-96
  CONF--AMERICAN AND EUROPEAN TEACHERS
    BROWER, H.   BPM   P175-79
LAMOND, FREDERICK
  CONF--REQUISITES FOR A DEPENDABLE PIANO TECHNIC
    BROWER, H.   BMMOTK   P94-103
LANDOWSKA, WANDA
  BIOGRAPHICAL MATERIAL
    SALESKI, G.   BFMOJO   P505-6
  BIOGRAPHICAL MATERIAL
    CHASINS, A.   BSOP   P92-97
  CONF--CHARMS OF OLD MUSIC, THE
    BROWER, H.   BMMOTK   P83-93
LAWS OF TECHNIQUE
  MATTHAY'S APPROACH
    COVIELLO, A.   BWMM   P32
LEARNING PROCESS
  GENERAL EFFICIENCY IN LEARNING
    CHING, J.   BPPAPM   P306-22
  PSYCHOLOGY OF
    CHING, J.   BPPAPM   P306-22
LEARNING
  CHOOSING A COMPOSITION
    NEWMAN, W.   BPP   P131-33
  FINAL STEPS IN THE LEARNING OF A COMPOSITION
    NEWMAN, W.   BPP   P152-56
  FIRST READINGS AND ANALYSIS OF A COMPOSITION
    NEWMAN, W.   BPP   P133-37
  LEARNING THE NOTES OF A NEW COMPOSITION
    NEWMAN, W.   BPP   P150-52
  MENTAL ATTITUDE
    DABREU, G.   BPTPWC   P103-4
  PLANNING PRIOR TO ORGANIZED PRACTICING
    NEWMAN, W.   BPP   P137-50
  PLAN FOR LEARNING A NEW WORK--SCHELLING
    COOKE, J. F.   BGPOPP   P267-77
  PLAN FOR LEARNING A NEW WORK
    DABREU, G.   BPTPWC   P105-6
  RHYTHM, WITH A
    WHITESIDE, A.   BIOPP   P125-47
  SIGHT READING APPROACH FOR BEGINNERS
    NEWMAN, W.   BPP   P157-62
  TEMPO OF
    BACON, E.   BNOTP   P63
LEGATO AND STACCATO
  DIFFERENT STYLES, IN
    GAT, J.   BTOPP   P73
  TECHNIQUE OF
    GAT, J.   BTOPP   P72-73
LEGATO CHORDS
  GEN INFO
    LAST, J.   BYP   P126-29
LEGATO PLAYING
  DEPPE'S APPROACH
    CALAND, E.   BAPP   P88-90

DEPPE'S APPROACH
    CALAND, E.   BAPP   P33-46
LEGATO
  CANTILENA
    GAT, J.   BTOPP   P70
  INACCURACY OF DYNAMIC CONTOUR IN
    GAT, J.   BTOPP   P68-69
  LAWS OF
    GAT, J.   BTOPP   P69
  MAINTAINING CONTINUITY
    LAST, J.   BYP   P115-19
  MAINTAINING LINE BETWEEN HANDS
    LAST, J.   BYP   P115-16
  MEANS OF PRODUCING
    BOWEN, Y.   BSOPT   P25-26
  NOISES
    GAT, J.   BTOPP   P68
  PAUSE BETWEEN THE NOTES
    GAT, J.   BTOPP   P68
  SUDDEN DYNAMIC CHANGES IN
    GAT, J.   BTOPP   P68
LEGINSKA, ETHEL
  BIO-CONF--INDIVIDUALISM IN PIANOFORTE STUDY
    COOKE, J. F.   BGMAFM   P149-57
  CONF--RELAXATION THE KEYNOTE OF MODERN PIANO PLAYING
    BROWER, H.   BPM   P47-53
LESCHETIZKY, THEODOR
  BIBLIOGRAPHY
    NEWCOMB, E.   BLAIKH   P301-8
  BIOGRAPHICAL MATERIAL
    BROOK, D.   BMOTK   P102-10
  BIOGRAPHY--LESCHETIZKY AS I KNEW HIM
    NEWCOMB, E.   BLAIKH   P1-300
  CHRONOLOGY--1830 - 1915
    NEWCOMB, E.   BLAIKH   P309-10
  CRITICAL ANALYSIS OF THEORIES OF TECHNIQUE
    SCHULTZ, A.   BROTPF   P218-36
  INTERVIEW WITH MME. M. R. LESCHETIZKY
    COOKE, J. F.   BGMAFM   P199-209
  PEDAGOGICAL PRINCIPLES
    WOODHOUSE, G.   BFKTM   P50-54
  PIANO TEACHING, APPROACH TO
    NEAL, H.   BWAYP   P74-77
  PIANO TECHNIQUE, APPROACH TO
    FIELDEN, T.   BSOPT   P4-5
  PIANO TECHNIQUE, APPROACH TO
    LEVINSKAYA, M.   BLSOPT   P38-40
  PIANO WORKS
    NEWCOMB, E.   BLAIKH   P311-13
LEVANT, OSCAR
  BIOGRAPHICAL MATERIAL
    SALESKI, G.   BFMOJO   P510-12
LEVERS
  PIANO PLAYING MECHANISM, IN THE
    CAMPBELL, L.   BTFORI   P13-15
LEVINSKAYA, MARIA
  SYSTEM OF MENTAL AND MUSCULAR CONTROL
    LEVINSKAYA, M.   BLSOPT   P98-155
  THEORY OF TONE-COLOR TECHNIQUE
    LEVINSKAYA, M.   BLSOPT   P212-26
LEVITZKY, MISCHA
  BIO-CONF--GETTING A START AS A VIRTUOSO
    COOKE, J. F.   BGMAFM   P175-80
  BIOGRAPHICAL MATERIAL
    SALESKI, G.   BFMOJO   P512-14
  BIOGRAPHICAL MATERIAL
    CHASINS, A.   BSOP   P156-57
  CONF--THE DEVELOPMENT OF A NATURAL TECHNIC
    BROWER, H.   BPMSS   P224-32
LHEVINNE, JOSEF
  BIO-CONF--PIANO STUDY IN RUSSIA
    COOKE, J. F.   BGPOPP   P169-80
  BIO-CONF--PRACTICAL IDEAS IN PIANOFORTE STUDY
    COOKE, J. F.   BGMAFM   P128-32
  BIOGRAPHICAL MATERIAL
    SALESKI, G.   BFMOJO   P515-17
  BIOGRAPHICAL MATERIAL
    CHASINS, A.   BSOP   P155-56
  CONF--ART OF MODERN PIANISM, THE
    BROWER, H.   BMMOTK   P72-82
LHEVINNE, ROSINA
  INTERVIEW
    BASTIEN, J. W.   BHTTPS   P397-400
LIGHTING
  PERFORMANCE, FOR A
    MOORE, G.   BAITL   P210
LIPATTI, DINU
  BIOGRAPHICAL MATERIAL
    CHASINS, A.   BSOP   P164-65
LISTENING
  ART, AS AN
    SLENCZYNSKA, R.   BMAYF   P96-102
  GEN INFO
    BOLTON, H.   BHTP   P19-22
  INDEPENDENT LISTENING AS AN AID TO PRACTICING
    FOLDES, A.   BKTTK   P7-12
  MATTHAY'S APPROACH
    COVIELLO, A.   BWMM   P33
  PITCH
    BOLTON, H.   BHTP   P19
  TONE QUALITY
    BOLTON, H.   BHTP   P20
  TONE VARIETY
    BOLTON, H.   BHTP   P19-21
LISZT, FRANZ
  BIOGRAPHICAL MATERIAL
    BROOK, D.   BMOTK   P73-80
  BIOGRAPHICAL MATERIAL
    FAY, A.   BMSIG   P205-71
  INFLUENCE UPON HIS TIME
    BIE, O.   BHOTPA   P271-95
  PIANO TECHNIQUE, APPROACH TO
    FIELDEN, T.   BSOPT   P2-3
  PIANO TECHNIQUE, APPROACH TO
    LEVINSKAYA, M.   BLSOPT   P35-37
  PIANO WORKS
    CHASINS, A.   BSOP   P234-39
  RECOLLECTIONS OF W. VON LENZ
    LENZ, W. VON   BGPVOO   P1-23
  ___E IN THE DEVELOPMENT OF THE PF AND PF PLAYING
    SUMNER, W.   BP   P169-74
___ARTHUR
___PHICAL MATERIAL
    ___ESKI, G.   BFMOJO   P521-22
  ___ BY G. A. BRIGGS
    ___, G. A.   BPPAS   P152-54

LYMPANY, MOURA
  INTERVIEW BY G. A. BRIGGS
    BRIGGS, G. A.   BPPAS   P155-57
MACDOWELL, EDWARD
  COMMENTARY BY MRS. EDWARD MACDOWELL
    BROWER, H.   BPMSS   P125-33
MANNERISMS
  GEN INFO
    BACON, E.   BNOTP   P98-99
  GEN INFO
    BRECKENRIDGE, W.   BHFPNS   P58
MARCUS, ADELE
  INTERVIEW
    BASTIEN, J. W.   BHTTPS   P409-14
MARLOWE, SYLVIA
  BIOGRAPHICAL MATERIAL
    SALESKI, G.   BFMOJO   P522-23
MARX, ADOLPH
  PIANO TECHNIQUE, APPROACH TO
    LEVINSKAYA, M.   BLSOPT   P44-47
MASON, WILLIAM
  HINTS ON INTERPRETATION
    BROWER, H.   BPM   P258-63
MASTER LESSONS
  BACH..CHORAL PRELUDE--BELOVED JESU, WE ARE HERE
    COHEN, H.   BMH   P77-80
  BACH..PRELUDES AND FUGUES, VOL I..C MAJ, C SHARP MIN
    COHEN, H.   BMH   P83-92
  BARTOK..SIX DANCES IN BULGARIAN RHYTHM
    COHEN, H.   BMH   P153-62
  BAX..NEREID
    COHEN, H.   BMH   P163-68
  BRAHMS..INTERMEZZO OP. 117 NO. 3
    COHEN, H.   BMH   P126-33
  CHOPIN..ETUDE OP. 25 NO. 5
    COHEN, H.   BMH   P112-17
  CHOPIN..NOCTURNE IN F MAJOR
    COHEN, H.   BMH   P117-25
  DEBUSSY..CLAIR DE LUNE
    COHEN, H.   BMH   P142-47
  DE FALLA..DANSE DU MEUNIER
    COHEN, H.   BMH   P134-41
  ELIZABETHAN KEYBOARD MUSIC
    COHEN, H.   BMH   P65-75
  MOZART..SONATA IN C MAJOR, K330
    COHEN, H.   BMH   P93-110
  VAUGHAN WILLIAMS..HYMN-TUNE PRELUDE
    COHEN, H.   BMH   P148-52
MATTHAY, TOBIAS
  CONF--WATCHING THE ARTIST TEACHER AT WORK
    BROWER, H.   BPM   P84-94
  CRITICAL ANALYSIS OF THEORIES OF PIANO TECHNIQUE
    SCHULTZ, A.   BROTPF   P237-65
  CRITICAL APPRECIATION AND OUTLINE OF 'MATTHAY METHOD'
    COVIELLO, A.   BWMM   P1-13
  DEFENSE AGAINST CRITICS
    MATTHAY, T.   BPFOT   P34-40
  EVALUATION OF DOCTRINE
    HARRISON, S.   BTNTM   P21-23
  MUSICAL THEORIES
    COVIELLO, A.   BWMM   P7-13
  PIANO TECHNIQUE, APPROACH TO
    FIELDEN, T.   BSOPT   P5-10
  PIANO TECHNIQUE, APPROACH TO
    LEVINSKAYA, M.   BLSOPT   P61-63
  TEACHING METHODS
    COVIELLO, A.   BWMM   P10-13
  TECHNICAL THEORIES
    COVIELO * 1 * 5002836 *   BWMM   P4-7
  TONE INFLECTION, THEORY OF
    COVIELLO, A.   BWMM   P9
MATTHEWS, DENIS
  INTERVIEW BY G. A. BRIGGS
    BRIGGS, G. A.   BPPAS   P158-60
MECHANICAL ACTIVITIES
  PIANO PLAYING, IN
    CHING, J.   BPPAPM   P1-15
MEDTNER, NICHOLAS
  CONF--CLASSIC VERSUS ULTRA-MODERN MUSIC
    BROWER, H.   BMMOTK   P138-45
MELODY
  GEN INFO
    BACON, E.   BNOTP   P20-26
MEMORIZING
  ACTION OF MEMORY IN PERFORMANCE
    MATTHAY, T.   BOMAPF   P5-7
  ADVANTAGE AND CONVENIENCE TO ARTISTIC PLAYING, AS AN
    NEWMAN, W.   BPP   P112-16
  AGE TO BEGIN
    POTAMKIN, F. J.   BMPP   P44-46
  ANALYSIS, BY
    MATTHAY, T.   BOMAPF   P8, 10-11
  ANALYSIS IN
    AHRENS, C. * ATKINSON, G.   BFAPT   P81
  ASSOCIATION, PROCESS OF
    DILLER, A.   BSOM   P96-97
  AUDITORY MEMORIZING
    NEWMAN, W.   BPP   P112-13
  AUDITORY MEMORIZING
    AHRENS, C. * ATKINSON, G.   BFAPT   P80
  AWAY FROM THE PIANO
    DILLER, A.   BSOM   P100-3
  BUILDING CONFIDENCE
    DABREU, G.   BPTPWC   P99-102
  COMMITTING TO MEMORY
    MATTHAY, T.   BOMAPF   P1-5
  COMPOSITIONS, OF
    POTAMKIN, F. J.   BMPP   P46-56
  CONDITIONS NECESSITATING USE OF SCORE
    MATTHAY, T.   BOMAPF   P19-20
  CONTINUITY IN
    DILLER, A.   BSOM   P97
  CORRECT IMPRESSIONS, IMPORTANCE OF
    MATTHAY, T.   BOMAPF   P18-19
  DEPPE'S APPROACH
    CALAND, E.   BAPP   P56-60
  DIFFERENCES IN METHOD
    HARRISON, S.   BTNTM   P36-37,
  DURING LEARNING
    DILLER, A.   BSOM   P97-98
  EMERGENCY MEASURES
    DILLER, A.   BSOM   P99-100
  FINGER MEMORY
    DILLER, A.   BSOM   P98-99
  GEN INFO
    HARRISON, S.   BYPGTP   P59-61

GEN INFO
    AHRENS, C. * ATKINSON, G.   BFAPT   P80-83
GEN INFO
    BRECKENRIDGE, W.   BHFPNS   P40-41
GEN INFO
    BROUGHTON, J.   BSIPT   P41-44
GEN INFO
    CARRE, J.   BPOPT   P33-35
GEN INFO
    COHEN, H.   BMH   P53-54
GEN INFO
    FOLDES, A.   BKTTK   P30-34
GEN INFO
    MERRICK, F.   BPTP   P105-8
GEN INFO
    WHITESIDE, A.   BIOPP   P61-63
GEN INFO
    WILKINS-GUTMANN, E.   BTWPT   P47-53
GEN INFO
    BOLTON, H.   BHTP   P21-22
HAZARDS
    NEAL, H.   BWAYP   P169-71
IMPLICATION OF ASSOCIATION
    MATTHAY, T.   BOMAPF   P4-5
INTELLECTUAL MEMORY
    NEWMAN, W.   BPP   P113-14
KINDS OF MEMORY
    NEWMAN, W.   BPP   P112-14
KINESTHETIC MEMORY
    AHRENS, C. * ATKINSON, G.   BFAPT   P81
MATTHAY'S APPROACH
    COVIELLO, A.   BWMM   P33
MEMORIZING TWENTIETH CENTURY MUSIC
    DABREU, G.   BPTPWC   P94-96
METHODS OF
    FOLDES, A.   BKTTK   P32
PRACTICE PROCEDURES
    POTAMKIN, F. J.   BMPP   P50-51
PROCEDURES AT THE PIANO--ROTE AND NOTE
    POTAMKIN, F. J.   BMPP   P57-63
PROCEDURES AWAY FROM THE PIANO
    POTAMKIN, F. J.   BMPP   P63-64
PROCEDURES
    DICKERSON, R.   BNATPT   P37-41
PROCEDURES
    HAMILTON, C.   BWEPPS   P96-98
PROCEDURES
    NEWMAN, W.   BPP   P114-16
RECALL
    POTAMKIN, F. J.   BMPP   P52-53
REPETITION, VALUE OF
    POTAMKIN, F. J.   BMPP   P48-50
REPETITION IN
    FOLDES, A.   BKTTK   P33
ROUTINE FOR
    MATTHAY, T.   BOMAPF   P3-4
SELF-CONFIDENCE IN
    FOLDES, A.   BKTTK   P33
THROUGH THE MIND'S EYE--NIKISCH
    BROWER, H.   BMMOTK   P183-92
VITAL PROCESS, AS A
    MATTHAY, T.   BOMAPF   P1
WAYS OF
    DABREU, G.   BPTPWC   P91-99
WHOLE VS PART
    POTAMKIN, F. J.   BMPP   P47-48
MEMORY FAILURES
  INHIBITION
    CHING, J.   BPPAPM   P323-41
MEMORY
  AUDITORY-MOTOR
    POTAMKIN, F. J.   BMPP   P38-39
  AUDITORY
    POTAMKIN, F. J.   BMPP   P26-27
  CLASSIFICATIONS
    POTAMKIN, F. J.   BMPP   P20-23
  DEFINITIONS
    POTAMKIN, F. J.   BMPP   P19-20
  EAR
    HOFHEIMER, G.   BTTFTP   P70
  FUNCTION
    POTAMKIN, F. J.   BMPP   P41-43
  MOTOR
    POTAMKIN, F. J.   BMPP   P35
  MUSCULAR
    MATTHAY, T.   BOMAPF   P9-10
  MUSCULAR
    HOFHEIMER, G.   BTTFTP   P70
  MUSICAL--HARMONIC, MELODIC, RHYTHMIC
    MATTHAY, T.   BOMAPF   P9
  MUSICAL
    POTAMKIN, F. J.   BMPP   P24-26
  PHOTOGRAPHIC
    HOFHEIMER, G.   BTTFTP   P70
  PITCH
    POTAMKIN, F. J.   BMPP   P28-32
  TACTUAL
    AHRENS, C. * ATKINSON, G.   BFAPT   P80-81
  TOUCH
    NEWMAN, W.   BPP   P113
  TYPES OF
    DABREU, G.   BPTPWC   P89-90
  TYPES OF
    FOLDES, A.   BKTTK   P31
  VISUAL
    POTAMKIN, F. J.   BMPP   P33-34
  VISUAL
    MATTHAY, T.   BOMAPF   P9
  VISUAL
    NEWMAN, W.   BPP   P113
  VISUAL
    AHRENS, C. * ATKINSON, G.   BFAPT   P80
MENDELSSOHN, FELIX
  PIANO WORKS
    BIE, O.   BHOTPA   P249-53
  ROLE IN DEV OF ROMANTIC PIANO CONCERTO
    GARVIN, F. H.   BBOTRP   P27-29
  ROLE IN THE DEVELOPMENT OF THE PF AND PF PLAYING
    SUMNER, W.   BP   P157
MENTAL PROBLEMS
  PIANO STUDY, IN--NEWCOMB
    BROWER, H.   BPMSS   P233-41
MERO, YOLANDA
  BIO-CONF--THOROUGHNESS IN HUNGARIAN MUSIC STUDY
    COOKE, J. F.   BGPOPP   P301-9
  BIOGRAPHICAL MATERIAL
    SALESKI, G.   BFMOJO   P523

CONF--THE BEAUTIFUL IN MUSIC
    BROWER, H.   BPMSS   P88-89
METHODOLOGY
  STEPS TO BE TAKEN IN LEARNING A NEW WORK
    NEWMAN, W.   BPP   P129-56
METRONOME
  ADVANTAGE OF ITS USE IN PRACTICING
    NEWMAN, W.   BPP   P82-83, 93,
  AID IN MEMORIZING, AS AN
    FRANZ, F.   BMT   P35-36
  CHECKING ACCURACY OF METRONOME
    FRANZ, F.   BMT   P16-17
  CHECKING UNIFORMITY OF METRONOME BEAT
    FRANZ, F.   BMT   P18
  CONTROLLING GRADUAL TEMPO CHANGES
    FRANZ, F.   BMT   P13-15
  DEVELOPING TEMPO MEMORY
    FRANZ, F.   BMT   P13
  DIVISION OF BEATS
    FRANZ, F.   BMT   P19-21
  DRILL IN PRACTICING
    SLENCZYNSKA, R.   BMAYF   P31-34
  EXPLANATION OF SYMBOLS
    FRANZ, F.   BMT   P9
  HISTORY OF
    FRANZ, F.   BMT   P46-48
  LEARNING COMPLEX RHYTHMS, USE IN
    FRANZ, F.   BMT   P22-28
  MEASURING TEMPI SET BY OTHER PERFORMERS
    FRANZ, F.   BMT   P10-11
  OBTAINING SETTING FROM APPROX. TEMPO DESIGNATION
    FRANZ, F.   BMT   P11-12
  PRACTICING, USE IN
    DILLER, A.   BSOM   P93-94
  PRACTICING, USE IN
    FOLDES, A.   BKTTK   P52
MEZZO-LEGATO PLAYING
  DEPPE'S APPROACH
    CALAND, E.   BAPP   P88-90
MIND
  MOTIVE POWER IN PIANO PLAYING, AS--BERUMEN
    BROWER, H.   BMMOTK   P260-72
  PIANO PRACTICE, IN
    TAYLER, E. D.   BSOSP   P5-8
  PIANO STUDY, IN--STOJOWSKI
    BROWER, H.   BPM   P25-31
MIROVITCH, ALFRED
  BIOGRAPHICAL MATERIAL
    SALESKI, G.   BFMOJO   P524-25
MISSED LESSONS
  PROBLEMS AND SOLUTIONS
    BROUGHTON, J.   BSIPT   P89-90
MODERN MUSIC
  PEDAGOGICAL USE
    POTAMKIN, F. J.   BMPP   P187-220
MODULATION
  CHURCH PIANIST, FOR THE
    AULD, W.   BHFTCP   P48-50
MOISEIVITCH, BENNO
  BIO-CONF--NEW TENDENCIES IN PIANISTIC ART
    COOKE, J. F.   BGMAFM   P165-69
  BIOGRAPHICAL MATERIAL
    BROOK, D.   BMOTK   P175-76
  BIOGRAPHICAL MATERIAL
    SALESKI, G.   BFMOJO   P525-28
  CONF--STUDY AND ART OF PIANO PLAYING, THE
    BROWER, H.   BMMOTK   P169-82
MONOCHORD
  DEVELOPMENT OF
    BIE, O.   BHOTPA   P19-20
  GEN INFO
    SUMNER, W.   BP   P20-22
MOSCHELES, IGNAZ
  BIOGRAPHICAL MATERIAL
    BROOK, D.   BMOTK   P43-53
  BIOGRAPHICAL MATERIAL
    SALESKI, G.   BFMOJO   P529-30
  ROLE IN THE DEVELOPMENT OF THE PF AND PF PLAYING
    SUMNER, W.   BP   P177
MOVEMENTS IN PIANO PLAYING
  FIXATION
    SCHAUFFLER, L.   BPTMOS   P52-53
  FREE, RAPID MOVEMENT
    SCHAUFFLER, L.   BPTMOS   P50-52
  PREPARATORY AND ADJUSTING MOVEMENTS
    SCHAUFFLER, L.   BPTMOS   P53
  REACTION
    SCHAUFFLER, L.   BPTMOS   P53-55
MOVEMENTS
  EXERCISES AT AND AWAY FROM KEYBOARD
    CHING, J.   BPPAPM   P30-43
MOZART, LEOPOLD
  INFLUENCE ON W. A. MOZART
    RICHNER, T.   BOFIMP   P5-7
MOZART, W. A.
  AGOGICS AND RUBATO IN THE MUSIC OF
    BADURA-SKODA, E. * BADURA-SKODA, P.   BIMOTK   P40-46
  ANALYSIS OF CONCERTOS FROM K449 TO K595
    HUTCHINGS, A.   BCTMPC   P81-197
  ANALYSIS OF THE PIANO SONATAS
    RICHNER, T.   BOFIMP   P45-93
  APPROACH TO CLAVIER PLAYING
    KULLAK, A.   BAOPP   P14-16
  ARTICULATION IN THE MUSIC OF
    BADURA-SKODA, E. * BADURA-SKODA, P.   BIMOTK   P53-68
  BIOGRAPHICAL MATERIAL
    BROOK, D.   BMOTK   P32-42
  CADENZAS IN MOZART'S PIANO CONCERTOS
    BADURA-SKODA, E. * BADURA-SKODA, P.   BIMOTK   P214-34
  CHOICE OF TONALITIES IN THE WORKS OF
    RICHNER, T.   BOFIMP   P23-28
  CONCEPTS IN COMPOSITION
    HUTCHINGS, A.   BCTMPC   P4-25
  CONCERTO IN A MAJOR, K488--REMARKS
    BADURA-SKODA, E. * BADURA-SKODA, P.   BIMOTK   P256-66
  CONCERTO IN C MINOR, K491--REMARKS
    BADURA-SKODA, E. * BADURA-SKODA, P.   BIMOTK   P266-90
  CONCERTO IN D MINOR, K466--REMARKS
    BADURA-SKODA, E. * BADURA-SKODA, P.   BIMOTK   P243-
  CONTINUO PLAYING IN THE MUSIC OF
    BADURA-SKODA, E. * BADURA-SKODA, P.   BIMOTK   P
  EARLY VIENNA CONCERTOS
    HUTCHINGS, A.   BCTMPC
  IDEAS ON PIANO PERFORMANCE
    RICHNER, T.   BOFIMP
  IMPROVISED EMBELLISHMENTS IN THE MUSIC OF
    BADURA-SKODA, E. * BADURA-SKODA, P.   BIMO

INFLUENCE OF CONTEMPORARY COMPOSERS
  RICHNER, T.   BOFIMP   P5-17
KEYBOARD WORKS
  BIE, O.   BHOTPA   P151-56
LEAD-INS IN THE MUSIC OF
  BADURA-SKODA, E. * BADURA-SKODA, P.   BIMOTK   P234-41
MODERN PERFORMANCE PRACTICES
  HUTCHINGS, A.   BCTMPC   P198-207
MOZART SOUND, THE
  BADURA-SKODA, E. * BADURA-SKODA, P.   BIMOTK   P6-26
ORNAMENTATION IN THE MUSIC OF
  BADURA-SKODA, E. * BADURA-SKODA, P.   BIMOTK   P69-126
PEDAL, USE IN MOZART'S PIANO MUSIC
  BADURA-SKODA, E. * BADURA-SKODA, P.   BIMOTK   P10-11
PIANO WORKS
  CHASINS, A.   BSOP   P205-13
PLAYING IN TIME
  BADURA-SKODA, E. * BADURA-SKODA, P.   BIMOTK   P38-40
PROBLEMS IN RHYTHMIC NOTATION IN THE MUSIC OF
  BADURA-SKODA, E. * BADURA-SKODA, P.   BIMOTK   P47-52
PROBLEMS OF ACCOMPANIMENT IN THE MUSIC OF
  BADURA-SKODA, E. * BADURA-SKODA, P.   BIMOTK   P209-13
PROBLEMS OF TEMPI IN THE MUSIC OF
  BADURA-SKODA, E. * BADURA-SKODA, P.   BIMOTK   P27-38
ROLE IN THE DEVELOPMENT OF THE PF AND PF PLAYING
  SUMNER, W.   BP   P142-46
SALZBURG CONCERTOS
  HUTCHINGS, A.   BCTMPC   P48-66
TASTE AND FEELING IN PERFORMANCE OF THE MUSIC OF
  BADURA-SKODA, E. * BADURA-SKODA, P.   BIMOTK   P158-76
TECHNICAL QUESTIONS IN PIANO WORKS
  BADURA-SKODA, E. * BADURA-SKODA, P.   BIMOTK   P146-57
WORKS FOR PIANO DUO
  MOLDENHAUER, H.   BDP   P46-68
MOZART'S PIANO CONCERTOS
MOVEMENTS IN VARIATION FORM
  HUTCHINGS, A.   BCTMPC   P36-47
THEMATIC GUIDE
  HUTCHINGS, A.   BCTMPC   P22-14
MOZART SONATAS, THE
ANALYSES OF THE SONATAS
  TOBIN, J.   BMATSF   P23-148
CHARACTER AND PLAN
  TOBIN, J.   BMATSF   P11-19
NUMBERING IN VARIOUS EDITIONS
  TOBIN, J.   BMATSF   P8
MUSCLES
COMPLEX SUSTAINED CONTRACTION
  ORTMANN, O.   BPMOPT   P51-52
CONTRACTILITY
  ORTMANN, O.   BPMOPT   P50-51
DEGREES OF CONTRACTION
  ORTMANN, O.   BPMOPT   P52-53
DOCTRINE OF RELAXATION
  SCHULTZ, A.   BROTPF   P23-28
FATIGUE, EFFECT OF
  ORTMANN, O.   BPMOPT   P56-57
FATIGUE IN
  SCHULTZ, A.   BROTPF   P17-18
FOREARM MUSCLES
  ORTMANN, O.   BPMOPT   P42-43
GENERAL ASPECTS OF MUSCLE BEHAVIOR
  SCHULTZ, A.   BROTPF   P14-16
GRADED RESPONSE
  ORTMANN, O.   BPMOPT   P53-55
HAND MUSCLES
  ORTMANN, O.   BPMOPT   P43-46
INDIVIDUAL DIFFERENCES
  ORTMANN, O.   BPMOPT   P300-2
MUSCLE-TONE
  SCHULTZ, A.   BROTPF   P16-17
MUSCLE TONE
  ORTMANN, O.   BPMOPT   P59
MUSCULAR FREEDOM
  BOWEN, Y.   BSOPT   P4-5
MUSCULAR STRENGTH
  SCHULTZ, A.   BROTPF   P21-23
MUSCULAR VIBRATO
  SCHULTZ, A.   BROTPF   P28-30,
MUSCULAR WORK
  ORTMANN, O.   BPMOPT   P55-56
PIANO-PLAYING ORGANISM, OF
  SCHAUFFLER, L.   BPTMOS   P43-46
RELAXATION
  ORTMANN, O.   BPMOPT   P59-63
RIGIDITY
  ORTMANN, O.   BPMOPT   P57-59
SHAPE OF
  ORTMANN, O.   BPMOPT   P40
SHOULDER MUSCLES
  ORTMANN, O.   BPMOPT   P40-41
SIMPLE CONTRACTION
  ORTMANN, O.   BPMOPT   P51
SYMPATHETIC CONTRACTION
  CAMPBELL, L.   BTFORI   P18-20
TEMPERATURE, EFFECT OF
  ORTMANN, O.   BPMOPT   P56
THUMB MUSCLES
  ORTMANN, O.   BPMOPT   P46-47
TONAL INTENSITY AND THE DEGREE OF CONTRACTION
  SCHULTZ, A.   BROTPF   P20-21
TONAL INTENSITY AND THE SIZE OF THE PLAYING UNIT
  SCHULTZ, A.   BROTPF   P21
UPPER-ARM MUSCLES
  ORTMANN, O.   BPMOPT   P41-42
USED IN PIANOFORTE PLAYING
  FIELDEN, T.   BSOPT   P18-33
VELOCITY AND THE DEGREE OF CONTRACTION
  SCHULTZ, A.   BROTPF   P18-19
VELOCITY AND THE SIZE OF THE ARM-UNIT
  SCHULTZ, A.   BROTPF   P19-20
MUSCLE ACTION
NATURAL LAWS
  CHING, J.   BPPAPM   P30-43
RELATIONSHIP TO MUSICAL IMAGINATION
  GAT, J.   BTOPP   P79-81
RELATIONSHIP TO VOLUNTARY MOVEMENTS
  CHING, J.   BPPAPM   P30-43
MUSCULAR DISCRIMINATIONS
MATTHAY'S APPROACH
  COVIELLO, A.   BWMM   P34-35
MUSCULAR SENSITIVITY
KINESTHETIC SENSE
  REEDER, B.   BST   P45
MOTOR NERVES
  REEDER, B.   BST   P44-45

NERVOUS VITALITY
  REEDER, B.   BST   P44
SENSORY NERVES
  REEDER, B.   BST   P44
TOUCH SENSE
  REEDER, B.   BST   P44
MUSCULAR TESTS
MATTHAY'S APPROACH
  COVIELLO, A.   BWMM   P50-51
MUSCULAR TRAINING
MATTHAY'S APPROACH
  COVIELLO, A.   BWMM   P36
MUSICAL CONCEPT, THE
GEN INFO
  GAT, J.   BTOPP   P78-79
MUSICAL CRITICISM
GEN INFO
  MOORE, G.   BAITL   P222-27
MUSICAL EAR
TRAINING OF THE
  LEIMER, K. * GIESEKING, W.   BSWTPP   P9-12
MUSICAL ENVIRONMENT
GEN INFO
  BACON, E.   BNOTP   P135-49
MUSICAL IMAGINATION
RELATIONSHIP TO MUSCLE ACTION
  GAT, J.   BTOPP   P79-81
MUSICAL MIND
ESSENTIAL QUALITIES
  BOSWORTH, H.   BIFYPT   P60-62
MUSICAL TASTE
CHURCH PIANIST, FOR THE
  AULD, W.   BHFTCP   P82-84
MUSICIANSHIP
DEVELOPMENT AT COMMENCEMENT OF PIANO STUDY
  DILLER, A.   BSOM   P26-31
TESTS FOR
  AHRENS, C. * ATKINSON, G.   BFAPT   P92
MUSICOLOGY
ROLE IN INTERPRETATION OF PIANO MUSIC
  NEWMAN, W.   BPP   P99
MUSIC APPRECIATION
GEN INFO
  AHRENS, C. * ATKINSON, G.   BFAPT   P103-7
MUSIC FESTIVALS
GEN INFO
  AHRENS, C. * ATKINSON, G.   BFAPT   P112-13
MUSIC LIBRARY
FORMATION OF PERSONAL COLLECTION
  HAMILTON, C.   BWEPPS   P152-56
MUSIC PROFESSION
QUALIFICATIONS FOR ENTERING
  GRUNDY, E.   BHP   P70-73
MUSIC READING
GEN INFO
  HARRISON, S.   BYPGTP   P19-23
INITIAL ATTEMPTS IN A NEW WORK
  FOLDES, A.   BKTTK   P7-12
MUSIC STUDY
WHY, THE
  GIDDINGS, T. P.   BGPSCM   P1-7
MUSIC
LANGUAGE, AS A
  SLENCZYNSKA, R.   BMAYF   P18-26
NAIL-JOINTS
STRENGTHENING WEAK NAIL-JOINTS
  AHRENS, C. * ATKINSON, G.   BFAPT   P46
NATURAL INTERPRETATION
GEN INFO
  LEIMER, K. * GIESEKING, W.   BSWTPP   P43-45
NATURAL MOVEMENTS IN PLAYING
BREATHING
  GAT, J.   BTOPP   P89-90
EFFECT OF EMOTIONAL CONTENT ON BODY POSITION
  GAT, J.   BTOPP   P92
EYES, DIRECTION OF THE
  GAT, J.   BTOPP   P91-92
GEN INFO
  GAT, J.   BTOPP   P89-98
PARTICIPATION OF THE WHOLE BODY
  GAT, J.   BTOPP   P90-91
NATURAL TALENT
PREREQUISITE IN MUSIC STUDY, AS A
  CARRE, J.   BPOPT   P13-15
NATURE STUDY
MUSICAL ILLUSTRATION, IN
  BOSWORTH, H.   BIFYPT   P17-19
NERVES, MEMORY AND PERFORMANCE
GEN INFO
  WOODHOUSE, G.   BFKTM   P45-49
NERVOUSNESS
CAUSES AND REMEDIES
  GRUNDY, E.   BHP   P67-69
PERFORMANCE, IN
  HOFHEIMER, G.   BTTFTP   P70-71
PIANO PLAYING, IN--JONAS
  COOKE, J. F.   BGPOPP   P398-418
PIANO PLAYING, IN
  TAYLER, E. D.   BSOSP   P29-30
REASONS FOR
  HARRISON, S.   BTNTM   P112-14
NEURAL AND CIRCULATORY SYSTEMS
BLOOD VESSELS
  ORTMANN, O.   BPMOPT   P67
CIRCULATION, THE
  ORTMANN, O.   BPMOPT   P67-68
CIRCULATORY SYSTEM
  ORTMANN, O.   BPMOPT   P66-67
CIRCULATORY VARIATIONS
  ORTMANN, O.   BPMOPT   P68-71
NEURAL SYSTEM
  ORTMANN, O.   BPMOPT   P64-66
NEWCOMB, ETHEL
CONF--MENTAL PROBLEMS IN PIANO STUDY
  BROWER, H.   BPMSS   P233-41
NEY, ELLY
CONF--BRING OUT THE MEANING OF THE MUSIC
  BROWER, H.   BMMOTK   P203-14
NIKISCH, MITJA
CONF--MEMORIZING THROUGH THE MIND'S EYE
  BROWER, H.   BMMOTK   P183-92
NOTE-READING
GEN INFO
  POTAMKIN, F. J.   BMPP   P154-57
NOTEBOOKS
PUPIL'S
  DILLER, A.   BSOM   P34

        TEACHER'S
            DILLER, A.   BSOM   P33
NOTE DURATION
        COMPARISON OF AMERICAN AND ENGLISH TERMS
            BRECKENRIDGE, W.   BHFPNS   P84
NOVAES, GUIOMAR
        BIO-CONF--POETRY AND PRACTICE
            COOKE, J. F.   BGMAFM   P117-22
        BIOGRAPHICAL MATERIAL
            CHASINS, A.   BSOP   P118-24
        CONF--GIFT OF MUSIC, THE
            BROWER, H.   BPMSS   P30-38
        REVIEW OF RECITAL
            BROWER, H.   BWTPWT   P208-15
OBSERVATIONAL LEARNING
        GEN INFO
            POTAMKIN, F. J.   BMPP   P34-35
OCTAVES
        BROKEN OCTAVES
            GAT, J.   BTOPP   P175-76
        FINGERING OF
            GAT, J.   BTOPP   P156
        FOREARM, ROLE OF
            GAT, J.   BTOPP   P148-49
        GEN INFO
            WHITESIDE, A.   BIOPP   P97-103
        LEGATO
            MERRICK, F.   BPTP   P53-54
        MEASURING BY
            TAYLER, E. D.   BSOSP   P25-26
        PRACTICE SUGGESTIONS FOR AMATEURS
            GRUNDY, E.   BHP   P38-40
        PRACTICING, WAYS OF
            BRECKENRIDGE, W.   BHFPNS   P7-8
        PRACTICING, WAYS OF
            DICKERSON, R.   BNATPT   P30-32
        PRACTICING, WAYS OF
            FOLDES, A.   BKTTK   P46-47
        PRACTICING, WAYS OF
            MERRICK, F.   BPTP   P51-54
        PRACTICING OF
            GAT, J.   BTOPP   P160-65
        SKIPS
            GAT, J.   BTOPP   P184-85
        STACCATO
            MERRICK, F.   BPTP   P52-53
        VIBRATO IN
            GAT, J.   BTOPP   P154-56
        WRIST MOTION
            GAT, J.   BTOPP   P150-53
ORCHESTRAL SCORES
        READING AT THE PIANO
            BACON, E.   BNOTP   P68
ORGANISED SPINET--CLAVIORGANUM
        GEN INFO
            HIPKINS, A.   BDAHOT   P94-95
ORGANISTRUM
        GEN INFO
            SUMNER, W.   BP   P21
ORIGINALITY
        AVOIDING MONOTONY IN STUDY, AS A MEANS OF
            BOSWORTH, H.   BIFYPT   P12-14
ORNAMENTATION
        BASIC PRINCIPLES
            NEWMAN, W.   BPP   P100-1
        EIGHTEENTH CENTURY KEYBOARD MUSIC, IN
            BASTIEN, J. W.   BHTTPS   P371-85
        GEN INFO
            CAPRE, J.   BPOPT   P45-48
        MOZART, IN THE MUSIC OF
            RICHNER, T.   BOFIMP   P29-34
ORNSTEIN, LEO
        BIOGRAPHICAL MATERIAL
            SALESKI, G.   BFMOJO   P530-33
        CONF--SANITY IN MUSIC STUDY
            BROWER, H.   BPMSS   P188-200
ORTMANN, OTTO
        EVALUATION OF HIS CONTRIBUTION TO PIANO PLAYING
            SCHULTZ, A.   BROTPF   P292-310
OVERCONFIDENT PUPIL
        GEN INFO
            BRECKENRIDGE, W.   BHFPNS   P47
PACHMANN, VLADIMIR DE
        BIO-CONF--SEEKING ORIGINALITY
            COOKE, J. F.   BGPOPP   P181-95
        BIO-CONF--VELVETY PIANOFORTE TOUCH, A
            COOKE, J. F.   BGMAFM   P103-10
        BIOGRAPHICAL MATERIAL
            CHASINS, A.   BSOP   P147-48
        CONF--DISTINCTIVE METHOD OF PIANO PLAYING, A
            BROWER, H.   BMMOTK   P32-42
PADEREWSKI, IGNACE JAN
        ANALYSIS OF PERFORMANCE
            COHEN, H.   BMH   P54-56
        BIO-CONF--BREADTH IN MUSICAL ART
            COOKE, J. F.   BGPOPP   P289-300
        BIOGRAPHICAL MATERIAL
            BROOK, D.   BMOTK   P125-39
        BIOGRAPHICAL MATERIAL
            CHASINS, A.   BSOP   P87-91
        CHOPIN RECITAL, AND THE
            BROWER, H.   BWTPWT   P233-39
        LION OF POLAND, THE - THE STORY OF PADEREWSKI
            HUME, R. * HUME, P.   BLOPTS   P1-188
        TEACHER, AS A
            BROWER, H.   BPM   P1-11
PAGE-TURNING
        GEN INFO
            MOORE, G.   BAITL   P212-215
PARENT
        CONTRIBUTION TO ENSEMBLE PLAYING AND SINGING
            DILLER, A.   BSOM   P149-51
        ROLE IN MUSIC STUDY
            BROUGHTON, J.   BSIPT   P83-88
        ROLE IN THE CHILD'S PIANO STUDY
            DILLER, A.   BSOM   P147-60
PASSAGES
        PRACTICING OF
            GAT, J.   BTOPP   P219-24
PASSAGE WORK
        DAILY EXERCISES IN
            CHING, J.   BPPAPM   P104-16
        PREPARATION FOR
            CHING, J.   BPPAPM   P104-16
PATRONAGE IN MUSIC
        GEN INFO
            HARRISON, S.   BTNTM   P44-58

PAUER, MAX
        BIO-CONF--MODERN PIANISTIC PROBLEMS
            COOKE, J. F.   BGPOPP   P196-206
PEDAGOGICAL CONSIDERATIONS
        GEN INFO
            BASTIEN, J. W.   BHTTPS   P3-15
PEDAGOGICAL TECHNIQUES
        AVERAGE AGE BEGINNERS
            BASTIEN, J. W.   BHTTPS   P131-74
        GEN INFO
            BASTIEN, J. W.   BHTTPS   P109-281
        INTERMEDIATE STUDENTS
            BASTIEN, J. W.   BHTTPS   P239-81
        SECOND YEAR STUDENTS
            BASTIEN, J. W.   BHTTPS   P175-200
        THIRD YEAR STUDENTS
            BASTIEN, J. W.   BHTTPS   P201-37
        VERY YOUNG BEGINNERS
            BASTIEN, J. W.   BHTTPS   P109-30
PEDAL-BOARD
        MOZART'S PIANO, IN
            BADURA-SKODA, E. * BADURA-SKODA, P.   BIMOTK   P13-15
PEDALLING
        ACCENTUATE RHYTHM, TO
            GEBHARD, H.   BAOP   P16
        AGAINST THE PHRASE
            GEBHARD, H.   BAOP   P14-15
        AID TO INDIVIDUALITY OF INTERPRETATION, AS
            CHING, J.   BPOP   P36-38
        AID TO PHRASING, AS
            CHING, J.   BPOP   P26
        BACH, IN
            CHING, J.   BPOP   P31-33
        BACH, IN
            LINDO, A.   BPIPM   P160-68
        BACH, IN
            RIEFLING, R.   BPP   P33-37
        BAROQUE MUSIC, IN
            GEBHARD, H.   BAOP   P32-33
        BEETHOVEN, IN
            LINDO, A.   BPIPM   P169-74
        BEETHOVEN, IN
            RIEFLING, R.   BPP   P42-44
        BLENDING UPPER AND LOWER REGISTERS
            GEBHARD, H.   BAOP   P8-11
        BRAHMS, IN
            RIEFLING, R.   BPP   P52-53
        BRINGING OUT MIDDLE VOICES
            GEBHARD, H.   BAOP   P29
        CHAMBER-MUSIC, IN
            GEBHARD, H.   BAOP   P49-50
        CHOPIN, IN
            RIEFLING, R.   BPP   P47-50
        CHORDS WHICH ARE HARMONICALLY DIFFERENT, FOR
            LEIMER, K. * GIESEKING, W.   BRDP   P59
        CHORD PROGRESSIONS, IN
            LEIMER, K. * GIESEKING, W.   BRDP   P51-56
        CHROMATIC SCALE PROGRESSIONS, IN
            LEIMER, K. * GIESEKING, W.   BRDP   P57-58
        CLASSICAL WORKS, IN
            GEBHARD, H.   BAOP   P33-34
        COLOR, FOR
            CHING, J.   BPOP   P22-24
        COLOR, FOR
            GEBHARD, H.   BAOP   P20-24
        COMMENCEMENT OF COMPOSITION, AT
            BOWEN, Y.   BPTMP   P20
        COMMON CHORD, THE
            LINDO, A.   BPIPM   P23-39
        COMPOSERS' INDICATIONS
            RIEFLING, R.   BPP   P4-9
        CONDITIONS AFFECTING
            BOWEN, Y.   BPTMP   P13
        CONSECUTIVE THIRDS, IN
            CARRENO, T.   BPOTCB   P28-29
        CONTRADICTIONS OF COMPOSER
            SCHNABEL, K. U.   BMTOTP   P35-38
        CONTRAPUNTAL MUSIC, IN
            BOWEN, Y.   BPTMP   P15-16
        CONTRASTS
            GEBHARD, H.   BAOP   P31-32
        CREATING ILLUSION OF CRESCENDO
            CARRENO, T.   BPOTCB   P30
        CURRENT NOTATION
            RIEFLING, R.   BPP   P11-16
        DAMPER-PEDAL, USE OF
            DABREU, G.   BPTPWC   P85-88
        DANCE-LIKE PASSAGES
            GEBHARD, H.   BAOP   P17-20
        DEBUSSY, IN
            RIEFLING, R.   BPP   P57-59
        DEGREE OF DEPRESSION
            CARRENO, T.   BPOTCB   P29-33
        DEPRESSION WHILE OR BEFORE NOTES ARE PLAYED
            SCHNABEL, K. U.   BMTOTP   P8-14
        DIATONIC SCALE PROGRESSIONS, IN
            LEIMER, K. * GIESEKING, W.   BRDP   P56-57
        DIRECT
            JOHNSON, T.   BPOPP   P9-10
        EARLY STUDY, IN
            LAST, J.   BYP   P94-103
        EMPHASIS, FOR
            CHING, J.   BPOP   P26
        ERRORS IN SCORE
            BOWEN, Y.   BPTMP   P21-22
        EXTREME FINGER EXPANSIONS, FOR
            LEIMER, K. * GIESEKING, W.   BRDP   P60-61
        FOOT TECHNIC
            GEBHARD, H.   BAOP   P1
        GENERAL PRINCIPLES
            LINDO, A.   BPIPM   P2-21
        GEN INFO
            POTAMKIN, F. J.   BMPP   P119-37
        GEN INFO
            HARRISON, S.   BYPGTP   P25-27
        GEN INFO
            BRECKENRIDGE, W.   BHFPNS   P18-20
        GEN INFO
            CARRE, J.   BPOPT   P42-45
        GEN INFO
            HOFHEIMER, G.   BTTFTP   P53-58
        GEN INFO
            MERRICK, F.   BPTP   P21-26
        GEN INFO
            NEWMAN, W.   BPP   P69-71
        GEN INFO
            VANTYN, S.   BMPT   P75-84

GEN INFO			
WHITESIDE, A.		BIOPP	P63-64
GEN INFO			
WILKINS-GUTMANN, E.		BTWPT	P54-61
GEN INFO			
LEIMER, K. * GIESEKING, W.		BRDP	P48-51
GEN INFO			
AULD, W.		BHFTCP	P26-27
GLISSANDO SCALES			
LINDO, A.		BPIPM	P75-77
GRIEG, IN			
RIEFLING, R.		BPP	P53-57
HALF-DAMPING			
AHRENS, C. * ATKINSON, G.		BFAPT	P29
HALF-DAMPING			
CHING, J.		BPOP	P29
HALF-PEDALLING			
AHRENS, C. * ATKINSON, G.		BFAPT	P28
HALF-PEDALLING			
BOWEN, Y.		BPTMP	P11-12
HALF-PEDALLING			
CHING, J.		BPOP	P28-29
HALF-PEDALLING			
GEBHARD, H.		BAOP	P35-36
HALF-PEDALLING			
JOHNSON, T.		BPOPP	P10-11
HALF-PEDALLING			
LINDO, A.		BPIPM	P114-17
HALF-PEDALLING			
SCHNABEL, K. U.		BMTOTP	P18-24
HISTORICAL SIGNIFICANCE			
POTAMKIN, F. J.		BMPP	P120
INDISPENSABLE PEDALLINGS			
BOWEN, Y.		BPTMP	P19-20
INFLUENCE OF TONE QUANTITY AND REGISTER			
CHING, J.		BPOP	P20-21
ISOLATED CHORDS, FOR			
LINDO, A.		BPIPM	P40-44
LEFT FOOT, WITH THE			
BOWEN, Y.		BPTMP	P26
LEGATISSIMO			
REEDER, B.		BST	P50
LEGATO CHORDS, IN			
POTAMKIN, F. J.		BMPP	P124-26
LEGATO CHORDS, IN			
CARRENO, T.		BPOTCB	P8-15
LEGATO PURPOSES, FOR			
CHING, J.		BPOP	P14-21
LEGATO			
REEDER, B.		BST	P50
LISZT, IN			
RIEFLING, R.		BPP	P50-52
MANNER OF DEPRESSING PEDAL			
REEDER, B.		BST	P50-51
MATTHAY'S APPROACH			
COVIELLO, A.		BWMM	P37-38
MELODIES WITH PASSING NOTES			
GEBHARD, H.		BAOP	P5-8
MODERN MUSIC, IN			
CHING, J.		BPOP	P34-35
MODERN MUSIC, IN			
GEBHARD, H.		BAOP	P34-35
MOZART, IN			
RIEFLING, R.		BPP	P37-41
MUSICIANS' VIEWS			
RIEFLING, R.		BPP	P17-18
NOMENCLATURE--ENGLISH, FRENCH, GERMAN AND ITALIAN			
RIEFLING, R.		BPP	P10
NON-LEGATO, IN			
BOWEN, Y.		BPTMP	P7-8
NON-LEGATO WITH PEDAL			
GEBHARD, H.		BAOP	P11-13
ONE-FOURTH PEDALLING			
SCHNABEL, K. U.		BMTOTP	P15-18
ORNAMENTS			
RIEFLING, R.		BPP	P26
OVERTONES			
POTAMKIN, F. J.		BMPP	P127-29
PASSING NOTES			
CHING, J.		BPOP	P17-20
PASSING NOTES			
LINDO, A.		BPIPM	P51-82
PEDAL-RELEASE			
BOWEN, Y.		BPTMP	P14
PEDAL LEGATO WHERE FINGER LEGATO IS DIFFICULT			
GEBHARD, H.		BAOP	P25
PEDAL NOTATION			
SCHNABEL, K. U.		BMTOTP	P3
PEDAL POINT, IN			
LINDO, A.		BPIPM	P102-13
PHRASE, THROUGH THE			
GEBHARD, H.		BAOP	P15
PHRASE, WITH THE			
GEBHARD, H.		BAOP	P14
POLYPHONIC PLAYING, IN			
LEIMER, K. * GIESEKING, W.		BRDP	P59-60
POSITION OF THE FEET			
CARRENO, T.		BPOTCB	P9-10
POST-TREADING, SYNCOPATED			
LEIMER, K. * GIESEKING, W.		BRDP	P48-51
PREPARATORY EXERCISES			
MERRICK, F.		BPTP	P17-21
PUMPING EFFECT			
WILKINS-GUTMANN, E.		BTWPT	P57
QUICK CHANGE			
BOWEN, Y.		BPTMP	P23-24
RAPID PASSAGES, IN			
BOWEN, Y.		BPTMP	P16-18
REASONS FOR CHANGING PEDAL			
BOWEN, Y.		BPTMP	P9-11
RELATIONSHIP TO FINGERING AND ARTICULATION			
RIEFLING, R.		BPP	P25-26
RELATIONSHIP TO HARMONIC STRUCTURE			
CHING, J.		BPOP	P8-10
RESTS, IN			
CHING, J.		BPOP	P25
RESTS IN			
LINDO, A.		BPIPM	P83-93
RHYTHMIC PEDALLING			
MERRICK, F.		BPTP	P25
ROMANTIC MUSIC, IN			
LINDO, A.		BPIPM	P175-80
SCALES IN CONTRARY MOTION			
LINDO, A.		BPIPM	P74-75
SCALE AND ARPEGGIO FORMATIONS, IN			
BOWEN, Y.		BPTMP	P16-18

SCALE PASSAGES, OF			
CHING, J.		BPOP	P27
SCHUMANN, IN			
RIEFLING, R.		BPP	P44-47
SINGLE UNCONNECTED NOTES, OF			
GEBHARD, H.		BAOP	P1-2
SLURS, IN			
CHING, J.		BPOP	P26
SLURS, IN			
JOHNSON, T.		BPOPP	P11
SOFT DAMPING			
BOWEN, Y.		BPTMP	P11-12
SOFT PEDAL, USE OF			
AHRENS, C. * ATKINSON, G.		BFAPT	P31-32
SOFT PEDAL, USE OF			
BOWEN, Y.		BPTMP	P27-28
SOFT PEDAL, USE OF			
CHING, J.		BPOP	P29-30
SOFT PEDAL, USE OF			
GEBHARD, H.		BAOP	P45-48
SOFT PEDAL, USE OF			
JOHNSON, T.		BPOPP	P6
SOFT PEDAL, USE OF			
LINDO, A.		BPIPM	P141-49
SOFT PEDAL, USE OF			
RIEFLING, R.		BPP	P28-30
SOFT PEDAL, USE OF			
LEIMER, K. * GIESEKING, W.		BRDP	P64
SOSTENUTO PEDAL, USE OF			
AHRENS, C. * ATKINSON, G.		BFAPT	P32-33
SOSTENUTO PEDAL, USE OF			
GEBHARD, H.		BAOP	P37-41
SOSTENUTO PEDAL, USE OF			
RIEFLING, R.		BPP	P30-31
SOSTENUTO PEDAL, USE OF			
SCHNABEL, K. U.		BMTOTP	P27-29
SOSTENUTO PEDAL WITH DAMPER PEDAL, USE OF			
GEBHARD, H.		BAOP	P42-44
SPECIAL EFFECTS			
BOWEN, Y.		BPTMP	P25-26
SPECIAL EFFECTS			
GEBHARD, H.		BAOP	P30-31
SPECIAL EFFECTS			
LINDO, A.		BPIPM	P120-36
SPECIAL EFFECTS			
RIEFLING, R.		BPP	P26-27
SPECIAL EFFECTS			
SCHNABEL, K. U.		BMTOTP	P29-38
STACCATO, IN			
CHING, J.		BPOP	P24-25
STACCATO, IN			
GEBHARD, H.		BAOP	P26-29
STACCATO, IN			
LINDO, A.		BPIPM	P93-101
SUGGESTIONS FOR THE AMATEUR			
GRUNDY, E.		BHP	P44-46
SUPER-LEGATO			
BOWEN, Y.		BPTMP	P13
SUSTAINING PURPOSES, FOR			
CHING, J.		BPOP	P11-13
SYMPATHETIC VIBRATION OF OVERTONES			
AHRENS, C. * ATKINSON, G.		BFAPT	P27-28
SYMPATHETIC VIBRATION			
POTAMKIN, F. J.		BMPP	P126
SYNCOPATED			
AHRENS, C. * ATKINSON, G.		BFAPT	P28-30
SYNCOPATED			
GEBHARD, H.		BAOP	P3-5
SYNCOPATED			
JOHNSON, T.		BPOPP	P7-9
SYNCOPATED			
LINDO, A.		BPIPM	P45-50
SYNCOPATION, IN			
LEIMER, K. * GIESEKING, W.		BRDP	P63
TEACHING THE PEDAL			
CHING, J.		BPOP	P36
TECHNIQUES			
RIEFLING, R.		BPP	P19-25
THREE-FOURTHS PEDALLING			
SCHNABEL, K. U.		BMTOTP	P24-27
TIME-TREADING			
LEIMER, K. * GIESEKING, W.		BRDP	P48-51
TONE-PAINTING, FOR			
LEIMER, K. * GIESEKING, W.		BRDP	P62-63
TONE AND TIMBRE, EFFECT ON			
RIEFLING, R.		BPP	P3
TONE QUANTITY, EFFECT ON			
BOWEN, Y.		BPTMP	P23
TOUCH AND CONTROL			
BOWEN, Y.		BPTMP	P5
TREMOLO			
LINDO, A.		BPIPM	P117-19
TRILLS, FOR			
LEIMER, K. * GIESEKING, W.		BRDP	P64
UNIFORM CHORDS IN VARIOUS POSITIONS, FOR			
LEIMER, K. * GIESEKING, W.		BRDP	P58-59
VIBRATING PEDAL			
BOWEN, Y.		BPTMP	P11-12
VIBRATING PEDAL			
SCHNABEL, K. U.		BMTOTP	P7-8
WALTZ PEDALLING			
MERRICK, F.		BPTP	P25
WHEN TO INTRODUCE			
POTAMKIN, F. J.		BMPP	P121-22
PEDAL			
ACTION IN EXTENDED CHORDS			
CARRENO, T.		BPOTCB	P20-28
ACTION			
RIEFLING, R.		BPP	P3
APPLICATION IN EXPRESSING SOUND DIFFERENCES			
LEIMER, K. * GIESEKING, W.		BRDP	P61-64
APPLICATION IN OBTAINING LEGATO EFFECTS			
LEIMER, K. * GIESEKING, W.		BRDP	P58-61
DESCRIPTION OF PEDALS			
JOHNSON, T.		BPOPP	P4-5
EFFECT ON RESTS OR PAUSES			
CARRENO, T.		BPOTCB	P18-20
FUNCTION OF			
BOWEN, Y.		BPTMP	P6-7
HISTORICAL NOTES			
RIEFLING, R.		BPP	P2
IMPORTANCE OF			
CHING, J.		BPOP	P5-6
INFLUENCE ON HARMONIC CONTENT OF SOUND			
BRIGGS, G. A.		BPPAS	P35-36
INFLUENCE ON MUSICAL NOTATION			
RIEFLING, R.		BPP	P60-64

MECHANISM AND ACTION
    CARRENO, T.   BPOTCB   P7-8
MECHANISM
    CHING, J.   BPOP   P5
MECHANISM
    LINDO, A.   BPIPM   P137-40
MODERN USAGE
    REEDER, B.   BST   P51
PHRASING, USE IN
    CARRENO, T.   BPOTCB   P15-18
PRINCIPLES AND FUNCTIONS
    BACON, E.   BNOTP   P51-55
UTILIZATION IN ATTAINMENT OF TONE VOLUME
    LEIMER, K. * GIESEKING, W.   BRDP   P51-58
VARIOUS USES
    AHRENS, C. * ATKINSON, G.   BFAPT   P30-31
PERFORMANCE
    ADAPTABILITY TO SITUATIONS
        DABREU, G.   BPTPWC   P117
    APPROACH TO AN AUDIENCE
        DABREU, G.   BPTWC   P121
    CONTROL OVER NERVOUSNESS
        DABREU, G.   BPTPWC   P121-22
    DESIRE TO PERFORM
        DABREU, G.   BPTPWC   P120-21
    FEAR OF FAILURE
        DABREU, G.   BPTPWC   P119-20
    FIRST APPEARANCE, THE
        FOLDES, A.   BKTTK   P35-36
    INFORMAL OCCASIONS
        HAMILTON, C.   BWEPPS   P101-2
    MEANING OF
        WOODHOUSE, G.   BFKTM   P7-10
    MEMORIZATION TECHNIQUES LEADING TOWARD
        BASTIEN, J. W.   BHTTPS   P363-69
    MOZART'S IDEAS
        RICHNER, T.   BOFIMP   P35-42
    OBJECTIVITY AND SUBJECTIVITY
        AHRENS, C. * ATKINSON, G.   BFAPT   P84-85
    PERFORMING VS. RE-CREATING
        FOLDES, A.   BKTTK   P39-43
    PRE-CONCERT NERVOUSNESS
        FOLDES, A.   BKTTK   P35
    PREPARATION FOR
        BACON, E.   BNOTP   P97-102
    READING TECHNIQUES LEADING TOWARD
        BASTIEN, J. W.   BHTTPS   P363-69
    REASONS FOR UNSATISFACTORY PERFORMANCE
        NEWMAN, W.   BPP   P121
    SAFE MEMORY-PLAYING IN
        DABREU, G.   BPTPWC   P119
    SEPARATE SKILL, AS A
        DABREU, G.   BPTPWC   P116-17
    SPECIFIC PREPARATION FOR
        DABREU, G.   BPTPWC   P118
    STAGE APPROACH
        DABREU, G.   BPTPWC   P123
    STAGE CONDUCT
        HAMILTON, C.   BWEPPS   P103-4
    TECHNICAL ANXIETY IN
        DABREU, G.   BPTPWC   P117-18
    THOUGHTS WHILE PLAYING
        HAMILTON, C.   BWEPPS   P104-6
    TRYING OUT A COMPOSITION
        HAMILTON, C.   BWEPPS   P101
    WARMING-UP EXERCISES
        FOLDES, A.   BKTTK   P36-38
    YOUNG STUDENT, FOR THE
        LAST, J.   BYP   P142-47
PERSONALITY FACTOR
    GEN INFO
        SLENCZYNSKA, R.   BMAYF   P15-17
PHRASING, DYNAMIC
    ART OF
        REEDER, B.   BST   P33
PHRASING MARKS
    CURVED LINE
        REEDER, B.   BST   P39
    DOT
        REEDER, B.   BST   P39
    SLUR
        REEDER, B.   BST   P38
    TIE
        REEDER, B.   BST   P38
PHRASING
    ART, AS AN
        VANTYN, S.   BMPT   P157-61
    ART OF INTERPRETATION, IN THE
        LEIMER, K. * GIESEKING, W.   BRDP   P44-47
    GEN INFO
        POTAMKIN, F. J.   BMPP   P171-73
    GEN INFO
        HARRISON, S.   BYPGTP   P24-25
    GEN INFO
        AHRENS, C. * ATKINSON, G.   BFAPT   P86-87
    GEN INFO
        WILKINS-GUTMANN, E.   BTWPT   P38-46
    GEN INFO
        DILLER, A.   BSOM   P40-59
    GUIDES TO INTELLIGENT PHRASING
        NEWMAN, W.   BPP   P94-99
    MARKS IN NOTATION
        LEIMER, K. * GIESEKING, W.   BRDP   P44
PHYSICAL CONDITION OF STUDENT
    RELATIONSHIP TO MENTAL CONDITION
        AHRENS, C. * ATKINSON, G.   BFAPT   P20
PHYSIOLOGICAL ACTIVITIES
    PIANO PLAYING, IN
        CHING, J.   BPPAPM   P1-15
PHYSIOLOGICAL DIFFERENCES, INDIVIDUAL
    ARM
        ORTMANN, O.   BPMOPT   P297-300
    CIRCULATORY
        ORTMANN, O.   BPMOPT   P307-8
    HAND
        ORTMANN, O.   BPMOPT   P311-36
    METABOLIC
        ORTMANN, O.   BPMOPT   P309-10
    MUSCLES
        ORTMANN, O.   BPMOPT   P300-2
    NEURAL
        ORTMANN, O.   BPMOPT   P308-9
    PATHOLOGICAL AND NON-PATHOLOGICAL
        ORTMANN, O.   BPMOPT   P304-7
    STRENGTH
        ORTMANN, O.   BPMOPT   P302-4

PHYSIOLOGICAL MOVEMENT, GENERAL ASPECTS OF
    ACTION AND REACTION
        ORTMANN, O.   BPMOPT   P82-89
    ACTIVITY AND PASSIVITY
        ORTMANN, O.   BPMOPT   P90-98
    COORDINATION AND INCOORDINATION
        ORTMANN, O.   BPMOPT   P99-123
    GEOMETRICS
        ORTMANN, O.   BPMOPT   P75-81
    LATERAL ARM MOVEMENT
        ORTMANN, O.   BPMOPT   P160-74
    RELAXATION
        ORTMANN, O.   BPMOPT   P124-33
    VERTICAL ARM MOVEMENT
        ORTMANN, O.   BPMOPT   P149-59
    WEIGHT-TRANSFER
        ORTMANN, O.   BPMOPT   P134-48
PHYSIOLOGICAL ORGANISM, THE
    MECHANICAL PRINCIPLES
        ORTMANN, O.   BPMOPT   P3-12
    MUSCLES, THE
        ORTMANN, O.   BPMOPT   P40-49
    NEURAL AND CIRCULATORY SYSTEMS
        ORTMANN, O.   BPMOPT   P64-71
    SKELETON, THE
        ORTMANN, O.   BPMOPT   P13-39
    STATES AND PROPERTIES OF MUSCLES
        ORTMANN, O.   BPMOPT   P50-63
PHYSIOLOGICAL PROCESSES
    COORDINATION AND DIFFERENTIATION OF
        CHING, J.   BPPAPM   P91-103
    EXERCISES FOR GRADATION OF TONE QUANTITY
        CHING, J.   BPPAPM   P69-78
    TRIAL AND ERROR METHODS AT THE KEYBOARD
        CHING, J.   BPPAPM   P69-78
    VOLUNTARY CONTROL OF
        CHING, J.   BPPAPM   P69-78
PHYSIOLOGY
    PLAYING MECHANISM, OF THE
        AHRENS, C. * ATKINSON, G.   BFAPT   P20-21
PIANISTIC HINDRANCES
    GEN INFO
        WHITESIDE, A.   BPM   P9-17
PIANISTS
    LIGHT, HEAVY AND JAZZ
        HARRISON, S.   BYPGTP   P67-69
    MINOR PIANISTS THROUGH THE ROMANTIC ERA
        FILLMORE, J.   BPM   P211-34
    VIRTUOSO OF THE EARLY 1900S, THE
        COOKE, J. F.   BGPOPP   P5-39
PIANIST
    TEACHER, AS--B. RUBINSTEIN
        BROWER, H.   BMMOTK   P252-59
PIANO--UPRIGHT
    INVENTION AND PROGRESS
        BRINSMEAD, E.   BHOTP   P134-45
PIANO-MAKERS
    BECHSTEIN
        SUMNER, W.   BP   P118-19
    BLUTHNER
        SUMNER, W.   BP   P120-21
    BOSENDORFER
        SUMNER, W.   BP   P125-28
    BROADWOOD
        SUMNER, W.   BP   P103-31
    CHICKERING AND SONS
        SUMNER, W.   BP   P121-22
    GAVEAU
        SUMNER, W.   BP   P129
    GEN INFO
        SUMNER, W.   BP   P118-34
    GROTIAN-STEINWEG
        SUMNER, W.   BP   P124-25
    IBACH
        SUMNER, W.   BP   P119-20
    MASON AND HAMLIN
        SUMNER, W.   BP   P123-24
    PLEYEL
        SUMNER, W.   BP   P129
    SCHIEDMAYER
        SUMNER, W.   BP   P119
    STEINWAY AND SONS
        SUMNER, W.   BP   P122-23
PIANOFORTE--MAKING
    ENGMAND, IN
        WEITZMANN, C.   BHOPPA   P271
    FRANCE, IN
        WEITZMANN, C.   BHOPPA   P272-74
    GERMANY, IN
        WEITZMANN, C.   BHOPPA   P275-76
PIANOFORTE PLAYING, WRITINGS ON
    CRITICAL AND HISTORICAL REVIEW
        KULLAK, A.   BAOPP   P34-94
PIANOFORTE STYLE--BRILLIANT
    FRANCE, IN
        WEITZMANN, C.   BHOPPA   P147-55
    GERMANY AND ITALY
        WEITZMANN, C.   BHOPPA   P126-31
    HENSELT
        WEITZMANN, C.   BHOPPA   P146
    MENDELSSOHN
        WEITZMANN, C.   BHOPPA   P142-45
    MOSCHELES
        WEITZMANN, C.   BHOPPA   P136-38
    TOMASCHEK
        WEITZMANN, C.   BHOPPA   P132-34
    WEBER, VON
        WEITZMANN, C.   BHOPPA   P139-41
PIANOFORTE STYLE--DRAMATIC
    BEETHOVEN
        WEITZMANN, C.   BHOPPA   P115-23
    SCHUBERT
        WEITZMANN, C.   BHOPPA   P124-25
PIANOFORTE STYLE--LYRICAL
    CLEMENTI'S PUPILS
        WEITZMANN, C.   BHOPPA   P104-9
    CLEMENTI
        WEITZMANN, C.   BHOPPA   P93-95
    CONTEMPORARIES OF HAYDN AND MOZART
        WEITZMANN, C.   BHOPPA   P96-103
    HAYDN AND MOZART
        WEITZMANN, C.   BHOPPA   P75-92
    HUMMEL
        WEITZMANN, C.   BHOPPA   P110
PIANOFORTE STYLE--ROMANTIC
    BRAHMS AND RUBINSTEIN
        WEITZMANN, C.   BHOPPA   P198-202

CHOPIN
    WEITZMANN, C.   BHOPPA   P156-59
  CONTEMPORARIES OF MENDELSSOHN
    WEITZMANN, C.   BHOPPA   P168-69
  GRIEG, SAINT-SAENS AND TCHAIKOWSKY
    WEITZMANN, C.   BHOPPA   P203-14
  LISZT'S PUPILS AND CONTEMPORARIES
    WEITZMANN, C.   BHOPPA   P192-97
  LISZT
    WEITZMANN, C.   BHOPPA   P180-91
  SCHUMANN'S SUCCESSORS
    WEITZMANN, C.   BHOPPA   P165-67
  SCHUMANN
    WEITZMANN, C.   BHOPPA   P160-64
PIANOFORTE TEACHING
  MATTHAY'S APPROACH
    COVIELLO, A.   BWMM   P40-41
PIANOFORTE
  GEN INFO
    REEDER, B.   BST   P58-59
PIANOS, EARLY
  GEN INFO
    REEDER, B.   BST   P59-60
PIANOS, ELECTRONIC
  EARLY ATTEMPTS IN MANUFACTURING
    BRIGGS, G. A.   BPPAS   P15-16
PIANOS
  UPRIGHTS AND GRANDS, A COMPARISON
    BRIGGS, G. A.   BPPAS   P42-45
PIANO ACTION
  BALANCIER
    REEDER, B.   BST   P14
  BOSENDORFER
    HIPKINS, A.   BDAHOT   P33-34
  BROADWOOD
    HIPKINS, A.   BDAHOT   P32-33
  DAMPERS
    BRIGGS, G. A.   BPPAS   P34-35
  DAMPER
    REEDER, B.   BST   P19
  DOUBLE ACTION
    SUMNER, W.   BP   P45-46
  DOUBLE ESCAPEMENT
    REEDER, B.   BST   P60
  EARLY DESIGN
    BRIGGS, G. A.   BPPAS   P29-30
  EARLY DEVELOPMENT
    SUMNER, W.   BP   P43-50
  ERARD
    HIPKINS, A.   BDAHOT   P34-35
  ESCAPEMENT
    REEDER, B.   BST   P22
  HERZ-ERARD
    HIPKINS, A.   BDAHOT   P35-36
  JACK REGULATING SCREW
    REEDER, B.   BST   P21
  JACK
    REEDER, B.   BST   P17
  KEY
    REEDER, B.   BST   P15-16
  KNUCKLE
    REEDER, B.   BST   P19
  LET-OFF SCREW
    REEDER, B.   BST   P21
  MODERN DESIGN
    BRIGGS, G. A.   BPPAS   P31
  POINT OF LET-OFF
    REEDER, B.   BST   P21
  REPETITION ACTION
    REEDER, B.   BST   P21-22
  REQUIREMENTS
    BRIGGS, G. A.   BPPAS   P29
  STICKER
    HARRIS, R. J.   BHTCAA   P108-9
  SUPPORT
    REEDER, B.   BST   P17
  TAPE-CHECK
    HARRIS, R. J.   BHTCAA   P109
  TOUCH REGULATING BUTTON
    REEDER, B.   BST   P21
  UNDER-DAMPER
    HARRIS. R. J.   BHTCAA   P109-10
  UPRIGHT..WORNUM
    HIPKINS, A.   BDAHOT   P36-38
  VIENNESE OR GERMAN
    SUMNER, W.   BP   P46-50
  WEIGHT OF TOUCH
    BRIGGS, G. A.   BPPAS   P32-34
PIANO CLASSES - 1919
  APPROACH TO PIANO TECHNIQUE
    GIDDINGS, T. P.   BGPSCM   P65-68
  INFORMAL RECITALS
    GIDDINGS, T. P.   BGPSCM   P69-71
  MATERIAL USED
    GIDDINGS, T. P.   BGPSCM   P19-23
  ORGANIZATION
    GIDDINGS, T. P.   BGPSCM   P14-18
  PROCEDURES
    GIDDINGS, T. P.   BGPSCM   P24-64
  STEPS LEADING TO ORGANIZATION
    GIDDINGS, T. P.   BGPSCM   P8-13
PIANO CONSTRUCTION
  ACTION
    SUMNER, W.   BP   P78-81
  CASE
    SUMNER, W.   BP   P90-91
  HAMMERS
    SUMNER, W.   BP   P85-88
  KEYBOARDS AND KEYS
    SUMNER, W.   BP   P81-85
  METAL FRAME
    SUMNER, W.   BP   P71-74
  PEDAL, DAMPER
    SUMNER, W.   BP   P88-89
  PEDAL, SOFT
    SUMNER, W.   BP   P89-90
  PEDAL, SOSTENUTO
    SUMNER, W.   BP   P90
  PIN-BLOCK
    SUMNER, W.   BP   P77-78
  SOUNDBOARD
    SUMNER, W.   BP   P68-71
  STRINGS AND STRINGING
    SUMNER, W.   BP   P74-77
PIANO DUETS
  ENSEMBLE ADVANTAGES
    NEWMAN, W.   BPP   P23-24

PIANO FACTORIES
  EARLY ESTABLISHMENTS
    BIE, O.   BHOTPA   P132-36
PIANO INDUSTRY
  ENGLAND, IN
    BRIGGS, G. A.   BPPAS   P15
PIANO IN THE CHURCH
  ADVENT OF
    AULD, W.   BHFTCP   P9-10
PIANO KEYBOARDS
  LIMITATIONS
    ORTMANN, O.   BPMOPT   P280-82
PIANO KEY
  WHERE TO PLAY ON
    DILLER, A.   BSOM   P115-19
PIANO LESSONS
  INTERRUPTIONS AND DIVERSIONS
    BOSWORTH, H.   BIFYPT   P5-6
PIANO METHODS
  CRITICAL AND HISTORICAL REVIEW
    KULLAK, A.   BAOPP   P34-94
PIANO MUSIC
  ACQUIRING A BASIC LIBRARY
    NEWMAN, W.   BPP   P26-30
PIANO PLAYING ORGANISM
  GEN INFO
    HARRISON, S.   BYPGTP   P28-32
PIANO STRINGS
  BASS STRINGS
    BRIGGS, G. A.   BPPAS   P39
  FALSE NOTES
    BRIGGS, G. A.   BPPAS   P39
  HARMONICS
    BRIGGS, G. A.   BPPAS   P36
  NODES
    BRIGGS, G. A.   BPPAS   P37-39
  RUST
    BRIGGS, G. A.   BPPAS   P39-41
  STRIKE POSITION
    BRIGGS, G. A.   BPPAS   P37
  STRIKING-PLACE
    HIPKINS, A.   BDAHOT   P39-41
  WIRE SIZE
    BRIGGS, G. A.   BPPAS   P36
PIANO STUDENT
  INTERMEDIATE LEVEL, DURING THE
    BASTIEN, J. W.   BHTTPS   P239-81
  SECOND YEAR, DURING THE
    BASTIEN, J. W.   BHTTPS   P175-200
  THIRD YEAR, DURING THE
    BASTIEN, J. W.   BHTTPS   P201-37
PIANO STUDY
  COMMENCEMENT OF
    FOLDES, A.   BKTTK   P1-6
  PLEASURES OF
    HAMILTON, C.   BWEPPS   P7-8
  WHY OF, THE
    HAMILTON, C.   BWEPPS   P7-12
PIANO TEACHER
  BACKGROUND AND TRAINING
    BASTIEN, J. W.   BHTTPS   P4-8
  CHANGING TEACHERS
    HAMILTON, C.   BWEPPS   P20-21
  CHOOSING A TEACHER
    HAMILTON, C.   BWEPPS   P13-14
  COLLEGE TRAINING
    BASTIEN, J. W.   BHTTPS   P8-9
  CONCEPT OF TEACHING
    BASTIEN, J. W.   BHTTPS   P3-4
  CRITIC, AS A
    HAMILTON, C.   BEWPPS   P19-20
  FIRST MEETING WITH THE PUPIL
    BOSWORTH, H.   BIFYPT   P1-2
  GENERAL ADVICE TO
    AHRENS, C. * ATKINSON, G.   BFAPT   P119-23
  GUIDE, AS A
    HAMILTON, C.   BWEPPS   P14-15
  LEARNING HOW TO TEACH
    DILLER, A.   BSOM   P10-11
  OBLIGATIONS OF THE STUDENT
    HAMILTON, C.   BWEPPS   P16-17
  PEDAGOGICAL TRAINING, NEED FOR
    GIDDINGS, T. P.   BGPSCM   P10-13
  PERSONALITY OF
    BASTIEN, J. W.   BHTTPS   P9-15
  PITFALLS IN THE PATH OF THE YOUNG TEACHER
    DILLER, A.   BSOM   P17-18
  PROBLEMS--ROEDER
    BROWER, H.   BPM   P61-71
  PROPER ATTIRE
    BROUGHTON, J.   BSIPT   P94-95
  QUALIFICATIONS AND BACKGROUND
    CARRE, J.   BPOPT   P27-29
  QUALIFICATIONS
    BROUGHTON, J.   BSIPT   P11-14
  QUALIFICATIONS
    DILLER, A.   BSOM   P9
  ROLE IN SELECTION OF MUSIC
    HAMILTON, C.   BWEPPS   P18-19
  SUGGESTIONS FOR CHOOSING A
    GRUNDY, E.   BHP   P47-50
  SUGGESTIONS FOR THE PROSPECTIVE TEACHER
    DILLER, A.   BSOM   P10-11
  WRITING LESSON ASSIGNMENTS FOR THE STUDENT
    SLENCZYNSKA, R.   BMAYF   P104-5
PIANO TEACHING
  BUSINESS OF
    BASTIEN, J. W.   BHTTPS   P51-61
  FINGERING, TEACHING OF
    CARRE, J.   BPOPT   P42
  KEY SIGNATURES, TEACHING OF
    CARRE, J.   BPOPT   P40-41
  NOTES AND RESTS, TEACHING OF
    CARRE, J.   BPOPT   P38-39
  NOTE RECOGNITION, TEACHING OF
    CARRE, J.   BPOPT   P37-38
  PSYCHOLOGICAL CONSIDERATIONS
    CARRE, J.   BPOPT   P30-33
  TIME SIGNATURES, TEACHING OF
    CARRE, J.   BPOPT   P39-40
PIANO TECHNIQUE
  FUNDAMENTAL PLAYING FORMS
    GAT, J.   BTOPP   142-43
PIANO TUNING
  ACCURACY IN
    BRIGGS, G. A.   BPPAS   P79
  BEATS
    BRIGGS, G. A.   BPPAS   P73-75

EQUAL TEMPERAMENT
    BRIGGS, G. A.   BPPAS   P72
FREQUENCY CALCULATION
    BRIGGS, G. A.   BPPAS   P72
HUMIDITY TESTS
    BRIGGS, G. A.   BPPAS   P81-83
JUST INTONATION
    BRIGGS, G. A.   BPPAS   P72
MUSICAL INTERVALS
    BRIGGS, G. A.   BPPAS   P76
PITCH
    BRIGGS, G. A.   BPPAS   P75
PROCEDURES
    SUMNER, W.   BP   P105-14
SHARP OVERTONES
    BRIGGS, G. A.   BPPAS   P76-78
TEMPERING THE SCALE
    BRIGGS, G. A.   BPPAS   P72-73
VARIATIONS
    BRIGGS, G. A.   BPPAS   P79-81
PIANO
ACTION, THE
    HIPKINS, A.   BDAHOT   P28-39
AMERICAN PIANOS IN THE NINETEENTH CENTURY
    SUMNER, W.   BP   P64-66
APPEARANCE AND TONE
    HARRIS, R. J.   BHTCAA   P114-15
BEGINNING OF THE NINETEENTH CENTURY, AT THE
    GARVIN, F. H.   BBOTRP   P5-8
BRIDGES, THE
    HIPKINS, A.   BDAHOT   · P27-28
CARE OF INSTRUMENT
    BRIGGS, G. A.   BPPAS   P119
CASE AND FRAMING, THE
    HIPKINS, A.   BDAHOT   P14-24
CHOICE OF INSTRUMENT
    BRIGGS, G. A.   BPPAS   P117-18
CHOOSING AN INSTRUMENT
    PALMER, K.   BTYPPT   P14-16
CHOOSING AN INSTRUMENT
    VANTYN, S.   BMPT   P149-51
CHOOSING AN INSTRUMENT
    HARRIS, R. J.   BHTCAA   P105-6
CONSTRUCTION, ILLUSTRATED
    BRIGGS, G. A.   BPPAS   P25-28
CRITERIA FOR JUDGEMENT IN PURCHASE
    HARRISON, S.   BYPGTP   P15-16
DESCRIPTION OF MECHANISM
    HARRISON, S.   BYPGTP   P9-14
DEVICES FOR ALTERING TONE IN 18TH CEN. PIANOS
    BADURA-SKODA, E. * BADURA-SKODA, P.   BIMOTK   P16-17
DIFFERENCES BETWEEN GRAND AND UPRIGHT
    AHRENS, C. * ATKINSON, G.   BFAPT   P25
EARLY INSTRUMENTS..1709 - 1820
    HIPKINS, A.   BDAHOT   P99-112
EARLY INSTRUMENTS
    SUMNER, W.   BP   P39-53
EFFECT OF PIANISTS ON IMPROVING THE INSTRUMENT
    BRINSMEAD, E.   BHOTP   P146-70
ENGLISH PIANOS IN THE NINETEENTH CENTURY
    SUMNER, W.   BP   P62-64
FRIENDSHIP WITH THE INSTRUMENT
    HARRISON, S.   BYPGTP   P17-18
HAMMERS, THE
    HIPKINS, A.   BDAHOT   P30-31
HISTORICAL DEVELOPMENT
    CARRE, J.   BPOPT   P16-23
HISTORY, A BRIEF
    AHRENS, C. * ATKINSON, G.   BFAPT   P23-24
HISTORY, ILLUSTRATED
    BRIGGS, G. A.   BPPAS   P17-24
HOME, IN THE
    HARRIS, R. J.   BHTCAA   P111-20
IMPROVEMENTS TOWARD END OF NINETEENTH CENTURY
    BRINSMEAD, E.   BHOTP   P171-82
INVENTION OF, AND EARLY PROGRESS
    BRINSMEAD, E.   BHOTP   P107-17
IRON FRAME
    HARRIS, R. J.   BHTCAA   P107-8
MAINTENANCE
    PALMER, K.   BTYTPT   P16-17
MAKERS OF EARLY INSTRUMENTS...CRISTOFORI
    SUMNER, W.   BP   P39-46
MAKERS OF EARLY INSTRUMENTS...SILBERMANN
    SUMNER, W.   BP   P42-43
MAKERS OF EARLY INSTRUMENTS...STEIN
    SUMNER, W.   BP   P44-47
MAKERS OF EARLY INSTRUMENTS...ZUMPE
    SUMNER, W.   BP   P45
MECHANISM BRIEFLY EXPLAINED
    BOWEN, Y.   BSOPT   P3
MINIATURE
    HARRIS, R. J.   BHTCAA   P115-16
MODERNIZED
    HARRIS, R. J.   BHTCAA   P115
MOZART'S TIME, IN
    BADURA-SKODA, E. * BADURA-SKODA, P.   BIMOTK   P6-26
MOZART'S TIME, IN
    RICHNER, T.   BOFIMP   P18-22
NINETEENTH CENTURY EFFECTS
    SUMNER, W.   BP   P56-62
NINETEENTH CENTURY PROGRESS IN PIANO-MAKING
    SUMNER, W.   BP   P54-67
ORCHESTRA, REGARDED AS AN
    HOFHEIMER, G.   BTTFTP   P47-48
OUTLOOK IN GREAT BRITIAN--1966
    SUMNER, W.   BP   P197-202
PEDALS OF THE
    HIPKINS, A.   BDAHOT   P41-43
PERCUSSION INSTRUMENT, AS A
    WOODHOUSE, G.   BFKTM   P33
PIN-BLOCK, THE
    HIPKINS, A.   BDAHOT   P13-14
PROGRESS FROM ITS INTRODUCTION INTO ENGLAND
    BRINSMEAD, E.   BHOTP   P118-33
QUALITY OF TONE, FACTORS AFFECTING
    HIPKINS, A.   BDAHOT   P7-10
REASONS FOR ITS PRE-EMINENCE
    BRIGGS, G. A.   BPPAS   P13
RECORDING AND REPRODUCTION
    BRIGGS, G. A.   BPPAS   P138-43
SCHOOL, IN THE
    HARRIS, R. J.   BHTCAA   P121-23
SOUND-BOARD, THE
    HIPKINS, A.   BDAHOT   P24-27
STRINGS, THE
    HIPKINS, A.   BDAHOT   P10-13

SUITABLE FOR LEARNER
    HARRIS, R. J.   BHTCAA   P113-14
SUITING TO ROOM AND REQUIREMENTS
    HARRIS, R. J.   BHTCAA   P112-13
UNUSUAL KEYBOARDS
    SUMNER, W.   BP   P192-94
UPRIGHT PIANO AS 19TH CENTURY DEVELOPMENT
    SUMNER, W.   BP   P66-67
UPRIGHT VERSUS GRAND
    HARRIS, R. J.   BHTCAA   P111-12
VILLAGE OR CHURCH HALL, IN THE
    HARRIS, R. J.   BHTCAA   PP124-27
PLAYER PIANO
GEN INFO
    SUMNER, W.   BP   P194-95
PLAYING BY EAR
GEN INFO
    HARRISON, S.   BYPGTP   P57-58
PLAYING MECHANISM
ANALYSIS, AN
    WHITESIDE, A.   BPM   P18-28
DISTANCE, USE OF
    WHITESIDE, A.   BIOPP   P67-75
POWER PLUS DISTANCE, USE OF
    WHITESIDE, A.   BIOPP   P76-124
POLYPHYTHMS
SOLVING PROBLEMS IN
    COOKE, C.   BPTPFP   P172-82
PORTAMENTO
GEN INFO
    VANTYN, S.   BMPT   P109-12
POSITION
MATTHAY'S APPROACH
    COVIELLO, A.   BWMM   P42-43
PIANO, AT THE
    POTAMKIN, F. J.   BMPP   P98-104
POSTURE
PIANO, AT THE
    BOWEN, Y.   BSOPT   P34-35
PIANO, AT THE
    CARRE, J.   BPOPT   P51-52
PIANO, AT THE
    DICKERSON, R.   BNATPT   P8-9
PIANO, AT THE
    DILLER, A.   BSOM   P105-6
PIANO, AT THE
    HOFHEIMER, G.   BTTFTP   P5
PIANO, AT THE
    VANTYN, S.   BMPT   P12-14
POWELL, JOHN
CONF--ART THE EXPRESSION OF LIFE
    BROWER, H.   BPMSS   P39-52
PRACTICE RECORDS
STUDENTS, FOR
    CARRE, J.   BPOPT   P77
PRACTICE
THREE TYPES OF
    CHING, J.   BPPAPM   P306-22
PRACTICING
AMATEUR, BY THE
    GRUNDY, E.   BHP   P3-5
ANALYZING PASSAGES
    DABREU, G.   BPTPWC   P34-35
ART OF, THE
    FOLDES, A.   BKTTK   P18-29
ATHLETIC FORM IN
    MERRICK, F.   BPTP   P98-100
ATTENTION SPAN IN
    GAT, J.   BTOPP   P103-4
BACK END FIRST
    DILLER, A.   BSOM   P89-91
BASIC PROCEDURES
    LEIMER, K. * GIESEKING, W.   BSWTPP   P13-23,46-4
BODILY STILLNESS IN
    MERRICK, F.   BPTP   P96-97
CHILDREN..HOW MUCH, WHEN, WHERE
    DILLER, A.   BSOM   P156-58
CHORDS, OF
    DICKERSON, R.   BNATPT   P28-29
CHORDS AS SOLIDIFIED HARMONIES
    MERRICK, F.   BPTP   P47-50
CONDUCTING WHILE PRACTICING
    MERRICK, F.   BPTP   P7-9
CONVERTING CHORDS TO MELODIC SKELETONS
    DABREU, G.   BPTPWC   P56-57
CONVERTING PASSAGES TO CHORD-BLOCKS
    DABREU, G.   BPTPWC   P53-56
DELAYED CONTINUITY
    MERRICK, F.   BPTP   P1-6
DEPPE'S APPROACH
    CALAND, E.   BAPP   P47-55
DETERMINING QUANTITY
    POTAMKIN, F. J.   BMPP   P180-82
DIFFERENCES IN ATTITUDE AND METHOD
    HARRISON, S.   BTNTM   P31-34
DIVISION OF TIME IN
    HAMILTON, C.   BWEPPS   P91-93
DOES NOT ALWAYS MAKE PERFECT
    DILLER, A.   BSOM   P94-95
DOTTED-RHYTHM SEQUENCES, OF
    DABREU, G.   BPTPWC   P35-41
EFFICIENCY IN METHODS OF
    NEWMAN, W.   BPP   P104-10
ENDURANCE IN
    MERRICK, F.   BPTP   P98-100
FINGER INDEPENDENCE, FOR
    SCHAUFFLER, L.   BPTMOS   P111-12
FINGER LEGATO
    SCHAUFFLER, L.   BPTMOS   P113-15
FINGER STRENGTH, FOR
    SCHAUFFLER, L.   BPTMOS   P112-13
FINGER STRETCHES
    SCHAUFFLER, L.   BPTMOS   P117
FOUR-NOTE RHYTHMS, OF
    DABREU, G.   BPTPWC   P45-46
FUNDAMENTAL RULES IN
    AHRENS, C. * ATKINSON, G.   BFAPT   P49
FUTILITY OF FAST PRACTICE
    DABREU, G.   BPTPWC   P32
GENERAL SUGGESTIONS AND PROCEDURES
    BRECKENRIDGE, W.   BHFPNS   P59-67
GENERAL SUGGESTIONS
    HARRISON, S.   BYPGTP   P52-56
GEN INFO
    EHRLICH, H.   BHTPOT   P1-28
GEN INFO
    BOLTON, H.   BHTP   P5-36

GOALS IN
      FOLDES, A.   BKTTK   P19
GYMNASTICS
      SCHAUFFLER, L.   BPTMOS   P118
HANDS SEPARATELY
      FOLDES, A.   BKTTK   P59-60
HOW, WHAT AND WHY OF
      HOFHEIMER, G.   BTTFTP   P59-66
HOW NOT TO PRACTICE
      DILLER, A.   BSOM   P92-95
HOW TO PRACTICE
      DILLER, A.   BSOM   P87-92
HOW TO PRACTICE
      VANTYN, S.   BMPT   P85-88
JUMPING OF HANDS
      SLENCZYNSKA, R.   BMAYF   P40-41
LATERLA ARM MOVEMENTS
      SCHAUFFLER, L.   BPTMOS   P119-20
LEAPS, OF
      DABREU, G.   BPTPWC   P49-53
LENGTH OF PRACTICE PERIODS
      BACON, E.   BNOTP   P66-67
LENGTH OF PRACTICE PERIOD
      AHRENS, C. * ATKINSON, G.   BFAPT   P49
MARKING BEATS WITH NON-PLAYING HAND
      MERRICK, F.   BPTP   P29-30
METHOD IN
      HAMILTON, C.   BWEPPS   P90-91
METHOD IN
      BOLTON, H.   BHTP   P30-32
MISTAKES IN
      HAMILTON, C.   BWEPPS   P91
NOTE-ADDING, METHOD OF
      DABREU, G.   BPTPWC   P47-49
OCTAVES, OF
      DICKERSON, R.   BNATPT   P30-32
OCTAVES
      SCHAUFFLER, L.   BPTMOS   P117-18
OCTAVE MOLD IN
      SLENCZYNSKA, R.   BMAYF   P39-40
ONE FINGER, WITH...AS AID TO NOTE-LEARNING
      MERRICK, F.   BPTP   P60-62
ORNAMENTATION, OF
      SLENCZYNSKA, R.   BMAYF   P42-43
OUTLINES FOR PRACTICE PROCEDURE
      BOLTON, H.   BHTP   P33-36
PHRASES, IN
      DILLER, A.   BSOM   P89
POSTURE IN
      BACON, E.   BNOTP   P67-68
PRACTICE CONDITIONS
      HAMILTON, C.   BWEPPS   P89-90
PRACTICE PLANS AND METHODS
      AHRENS, C. * ATKINSON, G.   BFAPT   P50-52
PRACTICE SCHEMES
      HAMILTON, C.   BWEPPS   P93-96
PREPARING OF HAND POSITION
      MERRICK, F.   BPTP   P76-79
REFLECTIONS AND SUGGESTIONS
      EHRLICH, H.   BHTPOT   P1-28
REGULARITY AND AMOUNT
      HAMILTON, C.   BWEPPS   P87-89
REPEATED NOTES, OF
      SLENCZYNSKA, R.   BMAYF   P41
REPETITION IN
      GAT, J.   BTOPP   P99-102
RHYTHMS AND ACCENTS, WITH
      SLENCZYNSKA, R.   BMAYF   P38
SAMPLE CHART OF PRACTICE ROUTINE
      FOLDES, A.   BKTTK   P29
SCALES AND ARPEGGIOS
      SCHAUFFLER, L.   BPTMOS   P115-16
SCIENCE OF, THE
      FOLDES, A.   BKTTK   P18-29
SECTIONAL
      TAYLER, E. D.   BSOSP   P10
SEPARATE HANDS, WITH
      POTAMKIN, F. J.   BMPP   P143-45
SHORT GROUPS, IN
      MERRICK, F.   BPTP   P28-29
SIMPLIFIED VERSIONS OF DIFFICULT PASSAGES
      MERRICK, F.   BPTP   P55-59
SINGING WHILE PRACTICING
      MERRICK, F.   BPTP   P7-9
SIX-NOTE RHYTHMS, OF
      DABREU, G.   BPTPWC   P46-47
SLOW-MOTION, IN
      DICKERSON, R.   BNATPT   P17-18
SLOW PRACTICING
      SCHAUFFLER, L.   BPTMOS   P118-19
SLOW TEMPO, IN
      POTAMKIN, F. J.   BMPP   P141-43
SLOW TEMPO, IN
      GAT, J.   BTOPP   P105
SUGGESTIONS FOR THE CHILD
      LAST, J.   BYP   P103-10
SUPERVISION OF
      DILLER, A.   BSOM   P158
SUPERVISION OF
      AHRENS, C. * ATKINSON, G.   BFAPT   P48
SURFACE OF THE KEYS, ON THE
      MERRICK, F.   BPTP   P43-44
SYNCOPATION, OF
      SLENCZYNSKA, R.   BMAYF   P43-44
TAUSIG-EHRLICH DAILY STUDIES
      EHRLICH, H.   BHTPOT   P29-60
TECHNICAL PRACTICE IN LEARNING A NEW WORK
      DABREU, G.   BPTPWC   P107-13
THREE-NOTE RHYTHMS, OF
      DABREU, G.   BPTPWC   P41-15
TRILLS, OF
      MERRICK, F.   BPTP   P83-87
WAYS AND MEANS OF
      BACON, E.   BNOTP   P59-74
WAYS AND MEANS OF
      FOLDES, A.   BKTTK   P20-29
WITHOUT THE MUSIC
      FOLDES, A.   BKTTK   P55
WRONG HAND, WITH THE
      MERRICK, F.   BPTP   P94-95
PRALLTRILLER
   MOZART, IN
      BADURA-SKODA, E. * BADURA-SKODA, P.   BIMOTK   P123-26
PREPAREDNESS
   CHURCH PIANIST, FOR THE
      AULD, W.   BHFTCP   P70-73

PRESSLER, MENAHEM
   BIOGRAPHICAL MATERIAL
      SALESKI, G.   BFMOJO   P538-39
PRIVATE INSTRUCTION
   COMPARED WITH GROUP INSTRUCTION
      GIDDINGS, T. P.   BGPSCM   P1-6
   COMPARED WITH GROUP INSTRUCTION
      CARRE, J.   BPOPT   P24-25
PRIVATE TEACHING
   ADVERTISING
      BASTIEN, J. W.   BHTTPS   P30-34
   ASPECTS OF
      BASTIEN, J. W.   BHTTPS   P17-49
   INTERVIEWING PROSPECTIVE STUDENTS
      BASTIEN, J. W.   BHTTPS   P34-36
   LESSON SCHEDULING
      BASTIEN, J. W.   BHTTPS   P38-45
   TRANSFER STUDENTS
      BASTIEN, J. W.   BHTTPS   P37-38
PROGRAM-MUSIC
   INTERPRETATION OF
      HARRISON, S.   BTNTM   P117-18
   PORTRAYING TITLES IN
      DABREU, G.   BPTPWC   P63-66
PROGRAM BUILDING
   GEN INFO
      SLENCZYNSKA, R.   BMAYF   P72-86
   ORDER OF COMPOSITIONS
      SLENCZYNSKA, R.   BMAYF   P75-78
   PREPARING A PROGRAM
      SLENCZYNSKA, R.   BMAYF   P87-95
   REPRESENTATIVE CONCERT PROGRAMS
      SLENCZYNSKA, R.   BMAYF   P78-86
PROGRESSION
   MATTHAY'S APPROACH
      COVIELLO, A.   BWMM   P41-42
PROJECTION
   PART OF THE LEARNING PROCESS, AS
      SLENCZYNSKA, R.   BMAYF   P58-60
PROKOFIEFF, SERGEI
   CONF--FUTURISM IN MUSIC
      BROWER, H.   BMMOTK   P223-34
   PIANO WORKS
      CHASINS, A.   BSOP   P267-70
PROPORTION
   RELATED SOUNDS, IN
      BACON, E.   BNOTP   P20-21
PSALTERY
   GEN INFO
      SUMNER, W.   BP   P33-34
PSEUDO-SCIENCE
   DEFINITION OF
      MATTHAY, T.   BPFOT   P31-32
PSYCHOLOGICAL ACTIVITIES
   PIANO PLAYING, IN
      CHING, J.   BPPAPM   P1-15
PSYCHOLOGY OF PIANO TEACHING
   EMOTIONAL RESPONSES
      AHRENS, C. * ATKINSON, G.   BFAPT   P6-8
   ENVIRONMENTAL FACTORS
      AHRENS, C. * ATKINSON, G.   BFAPT   P14-15
   HABIT
      AHRENS, C. * ATKINSON, G.   BFAPT   P15-16
   IDEAS AS PROCESSES
      AHRENS, C. * ATKINSON, G.   BFAPT   P8-9
   IMAGINATION
      AHRENS, C. * ATKINSON, G.   BFAPT   P11-13
   INTEREST AND ATTENTION
      AHRENS, C. * ATKINSON, G.   BFAPT   P13-14
   LEARNING PROCESS, THE
      AHRENS, C. * ATKINSON, G.   BFAPT   P9-11
   MENTAL HEALTH
      AHRENS, C. * ATKINSON, G.   BFAPT   P16-17
   MENTAL REACTIONS
      AHRENS, C. * ATKINSON, G.   BFAPT   P17
   MUSICAL STIMULI, EFFECT OF
      AHRENS, C. * ATKINSON, G.   BFAPT   P3-6
   PRIMARY FACTORS
      AHRENS, C. * ATKINSON, G.   BFAPT   P1-2
PUBLIC PERFORMANCE
   COMMERCIAL ASPECTS
      HARRISON, S.   BTNTM   P99-103
PUBLIC SCHOOL
   RELATIONSHIP OF PIANO TEACHER TO
      BROUGHTON, J.   BSIPT   P91-93
PUGNO, RAOUL
   CONF--TRAINING THE CHILD
      BROWER, H.   BPM   P107-17
PUPILS' RECITALS
   GEN INFO
      BROUGHTON, J.   BSIPT   P66-69
   GEN INFO
      DILLER, A.   BSOM   P131-46
PUPIL
   FIRST MEETING WITH THE TEACHER
      BOSWORTH, H.   BIFYPT   P1-2
   UNDERSTOOD BY THE TEACHER, AS
      BOSWORTH, H.   BIFYPT   P24-25
PURISTS
   ARTS, IN THE
      BACON, E.   BNOTP   P104-5
RACHMANINOFF, SERGEI
   ANALYSES OF PIANO WORKS
      ANDERSON, W.   BRAHPC   P8-20
   BIO-CONF--ESSENTIALS OF ARTISTIC PLAYING
      COOKE, J. F.   BGPOPP   P207-20
   BIOGRAPHICAL MATERIAL
      BROOK, D.   BMOTK   P140-47
   BIOGRAPHICAL MATERIAL
      CHASINS, A.   BSOP   P40-47,
   BIOGRAPHICAL MATERIAL
      ANDERSON, W.   BRAHPC   P5-8
   CONF--SERIOUS PIANO PRACTICE A NECESSITY IN AMERICA
      BROWER, H.   BMMOTK   P1-11
   PIANO WORKS
      CHASINS, A.   BSOP   P254-58
   REVIEW OF PERFORMANCE--CHOPIN'S B FLAT MINOR SONATA
      COHEN, H.   BMH   P54-56
   REVIEW OF RECITAL
      BROWER, H.   BWTPWT   P154-62
REALIZATION
   MUSIC, OF THE
      HOFHEIMER, G.   BTTFTP   P78
RECORDING INDUSTRY
   GEN INFO
      CHASINS, A.   BSOP   P187-92

RECORDING
  PRE-ELECTRICAL PROCEDURES
    MOORE, G.   BAITL   P48-55
  PRESENT-DAY PROCEDURES
    MOORE, G.   BAITL   P228-33
REISENAUER, ALFRED
  BIO-CONF--SYSTEMATIC MUSICAL TRAINING
    COOKE, J. F.   BGPOPP   P221-34
RELAXATION AND ROTATION
  GEN INFO
    LEVINSKAYA, M.   BLSOPT   P82-89
RELAXATION METHOD
  INFLUENCED BY MODERN INSTRUMENTS, AS
    CAMPBELL, L.   BTFORI   P24-27
RELAXATION MOTIF
  PSYCHOLOGICAL ANALYSIS
    CHING, J.   BPPAPM   P342-57
RELAXATION STUDY
  BY-PRODUCTS--MENTAL
    CAMPBELL, L.   BTFORI   P71-73
  BY-PRODUCTS--PHYSICAL
    CAMPBELL, L.   BTFORI   P74-80
RELAXATION
  ARM POSITION
    ORTMANN, O.   BPMOPT   P124-26
  CONSCIOUS CONTROL, ATTAINMENT OF
    CAMPBELL, L.   BTFORI   P38-42
  DOCTRINE OF RELAXATION
    SCHULTZ, A.   BROTPF   P23-28
  EXERCISES FOR CONTROL OF
    CHING, J.   BPPAPM   P56-68
  FALLACIES
    FIELDEN, T.   BSOPT   P75-82
  FINGER EXERCISES FOR
    CAMPBELL, L.   BTFORI   P52-70
  FIXATION
    ORTMANN, O.   BPMOPT   P136-27
  GEN INFO
    HARRISON, S.   BYPGTP   P37-39
  KEYNOTE OF MODERN PIANO PLAYING, AS THE--LEGINSKA
    BROWER, H.   BPM   P47-53
  MATTHAY'S APPROACH
    COVIELLO, A.   BWMM   P43
  MENTAL CONSCIOUSNESS
    CAMPBELL, L.   BTFORI   P28-37
  MISUNDERSTANDINGS AND MISINTERPRETATIONS
    MATTHAY, T.   BPFOT   P1-4
  PIANO PLAYING, IN
    SCHAUFFLER, L.   BPTMOS   P57-58
  PLAYING THE PIANO, IN
    DABREU, G.   BPTPWC   P31-32
  PRIME ESSENTIAL, A--GIESEKING
    BROWER, H.   BMMOTK   P64-71
  SHOULDER, WRIST AND ELBOW EXERCISES FOR
    CAMPBELL, L.   BTFORI   P47-51
  STIFFNESS AND JOINT POSITION
    ORTMANN, O.   BPMOPT   P131-33
  TIMING OF
    CHING, J.   BPPAPM   P56-68
  WEIGHT DISTRIBUTION
    ORTMANN, O.   BPMOPT   P127-31
REPERTOIRE CLASS
  GEN INFO
    POTAMKIN, F. J.   BMPP   P64-65
REPERTOIRE
  ACQUISITION OF
    SLENCZYNSKA, R.   BMAYF   P64-71
REPETITION OF SINGLE TONES
  DEPPE'S APPROACH
    CALAND, E.   BAPP   P101-3
REPETITION
  TECHNIQUE OF
    GAT, J.   BTOPP   P229-32
RESILIENCE
  PSYCHOLOGY OF
    FIELDEN, T.   BSOPT   P75-82
RETENTION
  PIANO PROFICIENCY, OF
    BOSWORTH, H.   BIFYPT   P42-44
RETURN OF EFFORT
  VITAL FORCE IN PUPIL'S PROGRESS, AS
    BOSWORTH, H.   BIFYPT   P38-39
REWARDS AND INCENTIVES
  GEN INFO
    BROUGHTON, J.   BSIPT   P63-65
RHYTHMICS
  GEN INFO
    LEIMER, K. * GIESEKING, W.   BRDP   P17-19
  PEDAGOGICAL HINTS
    LEIMER, K. * GIESEKING, W.   BRDP   P19-21
  SYNCOPATION
    LEIMER, K. * GIESEKING, W.   BRDP   P21-24
  TEMPO
    LEIMER, K. * GIESEKING, W.   BRDP   P24-26
RHYTHM AND DYNAMICS
  GEN INFO
    HOFHEIMER, G.   BTTFTP   P33-44
RHYTHM AND TIME
  GEN INFO
    POTAMKIN, F. J.   BMPP   P168-71
RHYTHM
  ANALYZING COMPLEX GROUPINGS
    DABREU, G.   BPTPWC   P72-77
  BASIS OF ALL PIANO PLAYING, AS THE
    WHITESIDE, A.   BIOPP   P3-17
  BEGINNING STUDY FOR CHILDREN
    BOSWORTH, H.   BIFYPT   P28-30
  CONCEPTS OF
    SLENCZYNSKA, R.   BMAYF   P28-29
  ELEMENTS OF
    NEWMAN, W.   BPP   P81-91
  EURHYTHMICS, VALUE OF
    BOLTON, H.   BHTP   P13
  GEN INFO
    BOLTON, H.   BHTP   P13-18
  KEEPING TIME
    BRECKENRIDGE, W.   BHFPNS   P25
  METRONOME, USE OF
    BOLTON, H.   BHTP   P13-14
  MUSICAL ELEMENT, AS A
    BRECKENRIDGE, W.   BHFPNS   P11-12
  PRACTICE SUGGESTIONS
    BOLTON, H.   BHTP   P13-18
  PRACTICING WITH ACCENTS
    BOLTON, H.   BHTP   P16-17
  SYNCOPATION
    DABREU, G.   BPTPWC   P77-79
  TEACHING COMPLICATED RHYTHMIC PASSAGES
    AHRENS, C. * ATKINSON, G.   BFAPT   P70-71
  TEACHING OF POLYRHYTHMS
    AHRENS, C. * ATKINSON, G.   BFAPT   P65-68
  TEACHING RHYTHM TO CHILDREN
    AHRENS, C. * ATKINSON, G.   BFAPT   P63-64
  TEACHING SYNCOPATION
    AHRENS, C. * ATKINSON, G.   BFAPT   P65
  TECHNICAL COMMAND
    COHEN, H.   BMH   P46
RICHTER, SVIATOSLAV
  PHOTOGRAPHIC ANALYSIS OF PERFORMANCE
    GAT, J.   BTOPP   P62
  SLOW MOTION STUDIES OF
    GAT, J.   BTOPP   P38-47
RITARDANDO
  EXTENDED DEFINITION
    BRECKENRIDGE, W.   BHFPNS   P16-17
ROEDER, CARL M.
  CONF--PROBLEMS OF PIANO TEACHERS
    BROWER, H.   BPM   P61-71
ROLLED CHORDS
  GEN INFO
    DILLER, A.   BSOM   P121-22
ROOM ACOUSTICS
  ABSORBTION OF SOUND
    BRIGGS, G. A.   BPPAS   P124-26
  BUILD-UP OF SOUND
    BRIGGS, G. A.   BPPAS   P122-24
  CONVEX SURFACES
    BRIGGS, G. A.   BPPAS   P128
  DOORS
    BRIGGS, G. A.   BPPAS   P134
  GEN INFO
    BRIGGS, G. A.   BPPAS   P120-21
  HIGH FREQUENCIES
    BRIGGS, G. A.   BPPAS   P136-37
  POSITION OF INSTRUMENT
    BRIGGS, G. A.   BPPAS   P131-32
  REFLECTION OF SOUND
    BRIGGS, G. A.   BPPAS   P126-28
  REVERBERATION
    BRIGGS, G. A.   BPPAS   P121-22
  ROOM RESONANCE
    BRIGGS, G. A.   BPPAS   P129-31
  SOUND INSULATION
    BRIGGS, G. A.   BPPAS   P132-33
  STRUCTURE-BORNE SOUND
    BRIGGS, G. A.   BPPAS   P135-36
  WALLS
    BRIGGS, G. A.   BPPAS   P133
  WINDOWS
    BRIGGS, G. A.   BPPAS   P135
ROSENTHAL, MORIZ
  BIO-CONF--IF FRANZ LISZT SHOULD COME BACK AGAIN
    COOKE, J. F.   BGMAFM   P60-66
  BIOGRAPHICAL MATERIAL
    SALESKI, G.   BFMOJO   P542-44
  CONF--BUILDING A CONCERT TECHNIC
    BROWER, H.   BMMOTK   P12-21
ROTATION
  THEORY OF
    FIELDEN, T.   BSOPT   P89-95
RUBATO
  EXAGGERATION OF
    FOLDES, A.   BKTTK   P56
  GEN INFO
    HARRISON, S.   BYPGTP   P45-46
  GEN INFO
    BACON, E.   BNOTP   P9-10, 13
  GEN INFO
    BRECKENRIDGE, W.   BHFPNS   P21
  GEN INFO
    MERRICK, F.   BPTP   P72-75
  GEN INFO
    VANTYN, S.   BMPT   P143-48
  MATTHAY'S APPROACH
    COVIELLO, A.   BWMM   P45-46
RUBINSTEIN, ANTON
  BIOGRAPHICAL MATERIAL
    BROOK, D.   BMOTK   P96-101
  BIOGRAPHICAL MATERIAL
    FAY, A.   BMSIG   P37, 47+
RUBINSTEIN, ARTUR
  BIOGRAPHICAL MATERIAL
    SALESKI, G.   BFMOJO   P545-50
  BIOGRAPHICAL MATERIAL
    CHASINS, A.   BSOP   P103-11
RUBINSTEIN, BERYL
  BIOGRAPHICAL MATERIAL
    SALESKI, G.   BFMOJO   P550
  CONF--PIANIST AS TEACHER, THE
    BROWER, H.   BMMOTK   P252-59
RUBINSTEIN, NICOLAI
  BIOGRAPHICAL MATERIAL
    SALESKI, G.   BFMOJO   P551-52
RUDIMENTS
  CHURCH PIANIST, FOR THE
    AULD, W.   BHFTCP   P28-45
SAFONOFF, VASSILY
  PIANO TECHNIQUE, APPROACH TO
    LEVINSKAYA, M.   BLSOPT   P40-43
SAMAROFF, OLGA
  BIO-CONF--CONCENTRATION IN MUSIC STUDY
    COOKE, J. F.   BGPOPP   P333-47
  CONF--PIANISTIC PROBLEMS
    BROWER, H.   BMMOTK   P146-59
SAMUEL, HAROLD
  BIOGRAPHICAL MATERIAL
    SALESKI, G.   BFMOJO   P553-54
  BIOGRAPHICAL MATERIAL
    BROWER, H.   BMMOTK   P288-92
SANDOR, GYORGY
  BIOGRAPHICAL MATERIAL
    SALESKI, G.   BFMOJO   P554-55
SANITY
  MUSIC STUDY, IN
    BROWER, H.   BPMSS   P188-200
SAUER, EMIL VON
  BIO-CONF--TRAINING OF THE VIRTUOSO, THE
    COOKE, J. F.   BGPOPP   P235-50
  BIOGRAPHICAL MATERIAL
    SALESKI, G.   BFMOJO   P556
SCALES AND ARPEGGIOS
  PRACTICING, WAYS OF
    SLENCZYNSKA, R.   BMAYF   P110-15

SCALES
   AGOGIC EFFECTS
      ORTMANN, O.   BPMOPT   P256-59,261
   ASYMMETRY
      ORTMANN, O.   BPMOPT   P253-54
   BUILDING MAJOR SCALES
      NEWMAN, W.   BPP   P8-9
   DYNAMIC EFFECTS
      ORTMANN, O.   BPMOPT   P260
   EXERCISES, AS
      POTAMKIN, F. J.   BMPP   P146-53
   FINGER MOVEMENT IN
      SCHAUFFLER, L.   BPTMOS   P88-91
   FINGER STACCATO, IN
      VANTYN, S.   BMPT   P43-44
   GEN INFO
      WHITESIDE, A.   BIOPP   P123-24
   OCTAVE DIATONIC SCALES
      ORTMANN, O.   BPMOPT   P258
   PRACTICE SCHEME
      FIELDEN, T.   BSOPT   P156-60
   PRACTICE SUGGESTIONS FOR AMATEURS
      GRUNDY, E.   BHP   P24-33
   PREPARATION
      ORTMANN, O.   BPMOPT   P254-56
   PRINCIPLES OF FINGERING
      BACON, E.   BNOTP   P45-47
   ROUTINE FOR PRACTICING
      NEWMAN, W.   BPP   P37-38
   SPECIAL PROBLEMS IN PRACTICING
      LEIMER, K. * GIESEKING, W.   BSWTPP   P51-55
   SPEED IN PRACTICING
      FOLDES, A.   BKTTK   P44-45
   SUGGESTIONS FOR PRACTICING
      VANTYN, S.   BMPT   P29-42
   SUGGESTIONS FOR TEACHING
      AHRENS, C. * ATKINSON, G.   BFAPT   P40
   THIRDS, IN
      VANTYN, S.   BMPT   P45-49
   THIRDS, IN
      GAT, J.   BTOPP   P215-18
   VARIETY IN PRACTICING
      AHRENS, C. * ATKINSON, G.   BFAPT   P41
SCALE AND KEY
   GEN INFO
      LAST, J.   BYP   P40-52
SCALE PLAYING
   ARM MOVEMENT IN
      GAT, J.   BTOPP   P206-7
   DEPPE'S APPROACH
      CALAND, E.   BAPP   P33-46
   HAND POSITION CHANGES IN
      GAT, J.   BTOPP   P207-9
   THUMB STROKE IN
      GAT, J.   BTOPP   P209-10
SCALE PRACTICING
   GEN INFO
      MATTHAY, T.   BPFOT   P40-45
SCARLATTI, DOMENICO
   BIOGRAPHICAL MATERIAL
      BROOK, D.   BMOTK   P28-31
   KEYBOARD WORKS
      BIE, O.   BHOTPA   P68-90
SCHARWENKA, XAVER
   BIO-CONF--ECONOMY IN MUSIC STUDY
      COOKE, J. F.   BGPOPP   P251-65
SCHELLING, ERNEST
   BIO-CONF--LEARNING A NEW PIECE
      COOKE, J. F.   BGPOPP   P266-77
   BIO-CONF--THE HUMAN ELEMENT IN PIANO PLAYING
      COOKE, J. F.   BGMAFM   P329-35
   CONF--HAND OF A PIANIST, THE
      BROWER, H.   BPM   P12-16
SCHMITZ, E. ROBERT
   BIO-CONF--MODERN PF TECHNIC FROM A FRENCH STANDPOINT
      COOKE, J. F.   BGMAFM   P423-30
   CONF--INTERPRETATION OF MODERN FRENCH MUSIC, THE
      BROWER, H.   BMMOTK   P128-37
SCHNABEL, ARTUR
   AUTOBIOGRAPHICAL TALKS GIVEN IN 1945
      SCHNABEL, A.   BMLAM   P3-117
   BIO-CONF--HAND AND THE KEYBOARD, THE
      COOKE, J. F.   BGMAFM   P186-90
   BIOGRAPHICAL MATERIAL
      SALESKI, G.   BFMOJO   P557-58
   BIOGRAPHICAL MATERIAL
      CHASINS, A.   BSOP   P48-55,
   CONF--WORK OF THE TEACHER, THE
      BROWER, H.   BMMOTK   P160-68
   QUESTION AND ANSWER SESSIONS, U. OF CHICAGO
      SCHNABEL, A.   BMLAM   P121-223
   RECORDINGS AVAILABLE IN U. S. 1964
      SCHNABEL, A.   BMLAM   P224
SCHOBERT, JOHANN
   INFLUENCE ON W. A. MOZART
      RICHNER, T.   BOFIMP   P8-9
SCHOENBERG, ARNOLD
   PIANO WORKS
      CHASINS, A.   BSOP   P273
SCHOOLS OF MUSIC
   GEN INFO
      BACON, E.   BNOTP   P82-93
SCHOOL PIANO
   FIRST IMPRESSIONS
      HARRIS, R. J.   BHTCAA   P121-22
   MAINTENENCE
      HARRIS, R. J.   BHTCAA   P122
   PLACING OF
      HARRIS, R. J.   BHTCAA   P122
   SPECIAL REQUIREMENTS
      HARRIS, R. J.   BHTCAA   P121
   WEAR AND TEAR
      HARRIS, R. J.   BHTCAA   P122-23
SCHUBERT, FRANZ
   PIANO WORKS
      BIE, O.   BHOTPA   P225-30
   ROLE IN THE DEVELOPMENT OF THE PF AND PF PLAYING
      SUMNER, W.   BP   P155-57
SCHUMANN, CLARA
   BIOGRAPHICAL MATERIAL
      BROOK, D.   BMOTK   P81-95
   BIOGRAPHICAL MATERIAL
      FAY, A.   BMSIG   P25-27,
   REMINISCENSES
      SCHUMANN, F.   BROCSF   P10-41
   ROLE IN THE DEVELOPMENT OF THE PF AND PF PLAYING
      SUMNER, W.   BP   P157-60

SCHUMANN, ROBERT
   PIANO WORKS
      BIE, O.   BHOTPA   P230-49,253
   PIANO WORKS
      CHASINS, A.   BSOP   P227-33
   ROLE IN THE DEVELOPMENT OF THE PF AND PF PLAYING
      SUMNER, W.   BP   P157-60
SCIENTIFIC TECHNIQUE
   ARTISTIC INTERPRETATION, RELATIONSHIP TO
      CHING, J.   BPPAPM   P15-29
   EMPLOYMENT OF
      CHING, J.   BPPAPM   P15-19
   EXERCISES AND EXPERIMENTS AWAY FROM KEYBOARD
      CHING, J.   BPPAPM   P15-29
SELF-ANALYSIS
   PIANO TEACHERS, FOR
      BROUGHTON, J.   BSIPT   P79-80
SELF-CRITICISM
   GEN INFO
      DABREU, G.   BPTPWC   P26
SELF-DEVELOPMENT
   NECESSITY FOR THE PIANIST, A--FRIEDMANN
      BROWER, H.   BMMOTK   P43-54
SELLICK, PHYLLIS
   INTERVIEW BY G. A. BRIGGS
      BRIGGS, G. A.   BPPAS   P161-63
SEQUENCES
   INTERPRETATION OF
      DABREU, G.   BPTPWC   P68-70
SERKIN, RUDOLF
   BIOGRAPHICAL MATERIAL
      SALESKI, G.   BFMOJO   P559-61
   BIOGRAPHICAL MATERIAL
      CHASINS, A.   BSOP   P130-35
SETTING-UP EXERCISES
   GEN INFO
      BRECKENRIDGE, W.   BHFPNS   P22-24
SHAKING MOVEMENTS
   DEPPE'S APPROACH
      CALAND, E.   BAPP   P97-100
SHATTUCK, ARTHUR
   CONF--PIANIST SHOULD CULTIVATE MANY SIDES OF ART, THE
      BROWER, H.   BPMSS   P53-60
SHERWOOD, WILLIAM H.
   HINTS ON INTERPRETATION
      BROWER, H.   BPM   P248-58
SHOULDER
   EXERCISES FOR
      FIELDEN, T.   BSOPT   P36-38
   FUNCTION IN THE PLAYING MECHANISM
      WHITESIDE, A.   BPM   P19-22
   LOOSENESS IN
      MERRICK, F.   BPTP   P68-70
SHY PUPIL
   GEN INFO
      BRECKENRIDGE, W.   BHFPNS   P46
SIGHT READING
   AMATEUR, FOR THE
      GRUNDY, E.   BHP   P6-10
   APPROACH IN INTRODUCING THE PIANO
      NEWMAN, W.   BPP   P157-62
   BASIC LITERATURE, VALUE IN COVERING
      NEWMAN, W.   BPP   P18-21
   CHILD, FOR THE
      LAST, J.   BYP   P78-86
   COUNTING, IMPORTANCE OF
      HAMILTON, C.   BWEPPS   P141
   DANGERS IN
      HAMILTON, C.   BWEPPS   P140-41
   FLUENCY, VALUE OF
      NEWMAN, W.   BPP   P17-18
   GEN INFO
      POTAMKIN, F. J.   BMPP   P157-59
   GEN INFO
      AHRENS, C. * ATKINSON, G.   BFAPT   P76-79
   GEN INFO
      BRECKENRIDGE, W.   BHFPNS   P37-38
   GEN INFO
      BROUGHTON, J.   BSIPT   P45-50
   MENTAL PROCESS
      MERRICK, F.   BPTP   P88-90
   PROBLEMS IN
      NEWMAN, W.   BPP   P20-22
   SPECIAL VALUE FOR THE PIANIST
      GIDDINGS, T. P.   BGPSCM   P5-6
SILOTI, ALEXANDER
   BIO-CONF--MANY ROADS TO ARTISTIC PIANO PLAYING
      COOKE, J. F.   BGMAFM   P314-18
   CONF--GLIMPSES OF RUBINSTEIN AND LISZT
      BROWER, H.   BMMOTK   P113-27
SIMON, ABBEY
   BIOGRAPHICAL MATERIAL
      SALESKI, G.   BFMOJO   P561-62
SIMPLE MOVEMENTS
   ANALYSIS OF
      CHING, J.   BPPAPM   P30-43
SINGING TOUCH
   REVIVAL OF
      REEDER, B.   BST   P62-63
SITTING POSTURE
   GEN INFO
      GAT, J.   BTOPP   P49-58
   GEN INFO
      LEIMER, K. * GIESEKING, W.   BSWTPP   P13
SKELETON, THE
   ELBOW JOINT, THE
      ORTMANN, O.   BPMOPT   P15
   FINGER JOINTS
      ORTMANN, O.   BPMOPT   P18-19
   HAND JOINTS, THE
      ORTMANN, O.   BPMOPT   P17-18
   HORIZONTAL MOVEMENTS
      ORTMANN, O.   BPMOPT   P25-29
   KEYBOARD APPLICATIONS
      ORTMANN, O.   BPMOPT   P30-39
   MULTI-PLANAR MOVEMENTS
      ORTMANN, O.   BPMOPT   P29-30
   PHYSIOLOGICAL ORGANISM INVOLVED IN PIANO PLAYING
      SCHULTZ, A.   BROTPF   P3-12
   RADIO-ULNAR JOINT
      ORTMANN, O.   BPMOPT   P15-17
   SHOULDER-GIRDLE
      ORTMANN, O.   BPMOPT   P19
   SHOULDER JOINT
      ORTMANN, O.   BPMOPT   P20-21
   SKELETAL STRUCTURE
      ORTMANN, O.   BPMOPT   P13-14

VERTICAL MOVEMENTS
  ORTMANN, O.   BPMOPT   P19-25
WRIST JOINT, THE
  ORTMANN, O.   BPMOPT   P17
SKOLOVSKY, ZADEL
  BIOGRAPHICAL MATERIAL
    SALESKI, G.   BFMOJO   P562-63
SLOW-MOTION
  GEN INFO
    DICKERSON, R.   BNATPT   P17-18
SLOW PRACTICING
  ADAPTING MOVEMENTS
    GAT, J.   BTOPP   P114-15
  APPLICATION OF
    GAT, J.   BTOPP   P110-11
  DEVELOPMENT OF VELOCITY, IN
    GAT, J.   BTOPP   P107
  FAST PLAYING, OF
    GAT, J.   BTOPP   P105-15
  RHYTHMIC VARIANTS
    GAT, J.   BTOPP   P111-13
  SYNTHESIZING MOVEMENTS IN
    GAT, J.   BTOPP   P114
SLUR
  DIFFICULTIES IN TEACHING
    LAST, J.   BYP   P123-25
SMITH, CYRIL
  INTERVIEW BY G. A. BRIGGS
    BRIGGS, G. A.   BPPAS   P164-66
SOLOMON
  BIOGRAPHICAL MATERIAL
    SALESKI, G.   BFMOJO   P564-67
  BIOGRAPHICAL MATERIAL
    MOORE, G.   BAITL   P39-47
  BIOGRAPHICAL MATERIAL
    BROWER, H.   BMMOTK   P296-300
  BIOGRAPHICAL MATERIAL
    BROOK, D.   BMOTK   P180-83
  BIOGRAPHICAL MATERIAL
    CHASINS, A.   BSOP   P153
SOSTENENTE KEYBOARD INSTRUMENTS
  GEN INFO
    HIPKINS, A.   BDAHOT   P95-98
SOUND, CESSATION OF
  MATTHAY'S APPROACH
    COVIELLO, A.   BWMM   P17
SOUND, THEORY OF
  GEN INFO, CA. 1899
    BRINSMEAD, E.   BHOTP   P1-54
SPACING
  KEYBOARD, AT THE
    HOFHEIMER, G.   BTTFTP   P21-26
SPECIALIZATION
  ADVANTAGES AND DISADVANTAGES
    CARRE, J.   BPOPT   P10-12
SPEED
  PIANO PLAYING, IN
    DICKERSON, R.   BNATPT   P23-27
  PRACTICE, IN
    TAYLER, E. D.   BSOSP   P8-9
SPINET
  GEN INFO
    HIPKINS, A.   BDAHOT   P65-74
  GEN INFO
    SUMNER, W.   BP   P34
STACCATO PLAYING
  DEPPE'S APPROACH
    CALAND, E.   BAPP   P88-90
STACCATO
  ACCURACY IN OBSERVATION
    LAST, J.   BYP   P120-23
  AGOGIC VARIATIONS
    OPTMANN, O.   BPMOPT   P207-9
  ARM STACCATO
    ORTMANN, O.   BPMOPT   P203-4
  CHANGE OF POSITION
    ORTMANN, O.   BPMOPT   P204-5
  DOUBLE RAP
    MERRICK, F.   BPTP   P45-46
  DYNAMIC VARIATIONS
    ORTMANN, O.   BPMOPT   P205
  FINGER STACCATO
    ORTMANN, O.   BPMOPT   P215-16
  GEN INFO
    ORTMANN, O.   BPMOPT   P196-216
  HAND AND WRIST EXTENSION
    ORTMANN, O.   BPMOPT   P212-13
  HAND STACCATO
    MERRICK, F.   BPTP   P27-28
  HAND STACCATO
    ORTMANN, O.   BPMOPT   P198-203
  LAWS OF
    GAT, J.   BTOPP   P71-72
  MATTHAY'S APPROACH
    COVIELLO, A.   BWMM   P44-45
  NEURAL PHASE
    ORTMANN, O.   BPMOPT   P213-14
  NOTATION
    BACON, E.   BNOTP   P13-14
  PRACTICING
    FOLDES, A.   BKTTK   P45-46
  PRODUCTION, MEANS OF
    BOWEN, Y.   BSOPT   P25-26
  TECHNIQUE OF
    GAT, J.   BTOPP   P72-73
  VIBRATO
    ORTMANN, O.   BPMOPT   P209-12
  WRIST TOUCH
    BOWEN, Y.   BSOPT   P16-18
STAGE DEPORTMENT
  GEN INFO
    BRECKENRIDGE, W.   BHFPNS   P94-95
STAGE FRIGHT
  FACTS, ATTITUDES AND PROCEDURES
    NEWMAN, W.   BPP   P124-28
STEINHAUSEN, F. A.
  PIANO TECHNIQUE, APPROACH TO
    LEVINSKAYA, M.   BLSOPT   P53-54
STIFFNESS VS. RELAXATION
  GEN INFO
    LEVINSKAYA, M.   BLSOPT   P90-97
STIFFNESS
  IMPROPER USE OF ANTAGONISTIC MUSCLES, CAUSED BY
    MATTHAY, T.   BPFOT   P4-9
  MATTHAY'S APPROACH
    COVIELLO, A.   BWMM   P48

STOJOWSKI, SIGISMOND
  BIO-CONF—WHAT INTERPRETATION REALLY IS
    COOKE, J. F.   BGPOPP   P278-88
  CONF—MIND IN PIANO STUDY
    BROWER, H.   BPM   P25-31
STRAVINSKY, IGOR
  PIANO WORKS
    CHASINS, A.   BSOP   P272
STRENGTH
  INDIVIDUAL DIFFERENCES IN
    ORTMANN, O.   BPMOPT   P302-4
STUDENT RECITALS
  GEN INFO
    POTAMKIN, F. J.   BMPP   P66-69
  GEN INFO
    CARRE, J.   BPOPT   P78-85
STUDIES
  AMATEUR, USES FOR THE
    GRUNDY, E.   BHP   P41-43
  CHOOSING IN PROPER ORDER
    VANTYN, S.   BMPT   P162-66
STUDIO
  ARRANGEMENT
    DILLER, A.   BSOM   P33
  EQUIPMENT
    BASTIEN, J. W.   BHTTPS   P24-27
  EQUIPMENT
    DILLER, A.   BSOM   P32-33
  HOME, IN THE
    BASTIEN, J. W.   BHTTPS   P22
  HOME, OUTSIDE THE
    BASTIEN, J. W.   BHTTPS   P22-23
STUDYING ALONE
  GEN INFO
    GRUNDY, E.   BHP   P51-53
STUDY
  HABITS AND SUGGESTIONS
    BACON, E.   BNOTP   P59-74
STYLE
  KNOWLEDGE OF ESSENTIAL TO GOOD TASTE IN DYNAMICS
    NEWMAN, W.   BPP   P202-4
SUBSIDY OF THE ARTS
  FEDERAL AID, NEED FOR
    CHASINS, A.   BSOP   P193-202
SWING-STROKE
  CONTROL IN
    GAT, J.   BTOPP   P26
  DIRECT
    GAT, J.   BTOPP   P25
  FACTORS OF
    GAT, J.   BTOPP   P24
  INDIRECT
    GAT, J.   BTOPP   P25-26
SYMMETRICAL INVERSION
  GEN INFO
    BACON, E.   BNOTP   P47-49
SYMPHONIA
  GEN INFO
    HIPKINS, A.   BDAHOT   P53-57
SYNCOPATION
  TEACHING OF
    AHRENS, C. * ATKINSON, G.   BFAPT   P65
SYNTHESIZING PROCESS
  GEN INFO
    GAT, J.   BTOPP   P31-32
TASTE
  PIANO PLAYING, IN
    BRECKENRIDGE, W.   BHFPNS   P56
TAUSIG-EHRLICH DAILY STUDIES
  DIRECTIONS FOR PRACTICING
    EHRLICH, H.   BHTPOT   P29-60
TAUSIG, CARL
  BIOGRAPHICAL MATERIAL
    SALESKI, G.   BFMOJO   P567-68
  BIOGRAPHICAL MATERIAL
    FAY, A.   BMSIG   P26, 35-36+
  RECOLLECTIONS OF W. VON LENZ
    LENZ, W. VON   BGPVOO   P77-116
TAYLOR, KENDALL
  INTERVIEW BY G. A. BRIGGS
    BRIGGS, G. A.   BPPAS   P167-70
TCHAIKOWSKY, PETER ILYITCH
  PIANO WORKS
    CHASINS, A.   BSOP   P246-53
TEACHER
  SETTING GOALS FOR THE PUPIL, ROLE IN
    DABREU, G.   BPTPWC   P24-25
TEACHING HINTS
  GEN INFO
    BROUGHTON, J.   BSIPT   P70-78
TEACHING TECHNIQUES
  GEN INFO
    WHITESIDE, A.   BPM   P38-51
TEACHING
  ARTIST-TEACHER, THE
    CHASINS, A.   BSOP   P80-84
  COMMON ERRORS IN
    CARRE, J.   BPOPT   P25-27
  GENERAL OBSERVATIONS
    BACON, E.   BNOTP   P75-81
  LIMITING OF EXPLANATIONS
    BACON, E.   BNOTP   P76
TECHNICAL ANALYSIS, METHOD OF
  ARM TOUCHES
    CHING, J.   BPPAPM   P167-206
  FINGER TOUCHES
    CHING, J.   BPPAPM   P207-84
TECHNICAL DEVELOPMENT
  GEN INFO
    CARRE, J.   BPOPT   P49-50
  MENTAL FACTOR IN
    FIELDEN, T.   BSOPT   P11-13
  MUSCULAR FACTOR IN
    FIELDEN, T.   BSOPT   P15-17
  NERVOUS FACTOR IN
    FIELDEN, T.   BSOPT   P13-15
TECHNIQUE, BASIC PRINCIPLES OF
  CONTINUITY
    WOODHOUSE, G.   BFKTM   P14-16
  HAND ADJUSTMENT
    WOODHOUSE, G.   BFKTM   P14-16
  INDEPENDENT FINGER
    WOODHOUSE, G.   BFKTM   P14-16
  TIMED FOLLOW-THROUGH
    WOODHOUSE, G.   BFKTM   P14-16
TECHNIQUE, FINGER
  ANATOMICAL CONSIDERATIONS
    GAT, J.   BTOPP   P192-93

APPLICATION OF NOISE EFFECTS IN
  GAT, J. — BTOPP — P197
EXERCISES FOR DEVELOPMENT OF
  GAT, J. — BTOPP — P198-205
GEN INFO
  GAT, J. — BTOPP — P190-205
POSITIVE CONCENTRATION IN
  GAT, J. — BTOPP — P191-92
PREREQUISITE OF GOOD TONE IN
  GAT, J. — BTOPP — P196
TECHNIQUE AND INTERPRETATION
GEN INFO--HUTCHESON
  BROWER, H. — BPMSS — P100-13
GEN INFO
  HAMILTON, C. — BWEPPS — P73-86
LAWS GOVERNING--GODOWSKY
  BROWER, H. — BPMSS — P61-79
TECHNIQUE
ARM, RESOURCES OF
  DILLER, A. — BSOM — P106-7
ARM WEIGHT
  BOWEN, Y. — BSOPT — P28-31
BIOLOGICAL INSTINCTS, RELATIONSHIP TO
  CHING, J. — BPPAPM — P1-15
CHURCH PIANIST, FOR THE
  AULD, W. — BHFTCP — P10-25
COMBINING OF FINGER AND HAND ACTIVITY
  BOWEN, Y. — BSOPT — P14-15
COMPARISON OF OLD AND NEW SCHOOLS
  LEVINSKAYA, M. — BLSOPT — P25-72
CREATIVE IMAGINATION IN
  WOODHOUSE, G. — BCT — P31-34
DAILY PRACTICE
  FIELDEN, T. — BSOPT — P144-55
DEFINITION OF TERM
  NEWMAN, W. — BPP — P31-32
EVOLUTION OF
  WOODHOUSE, G. — BCT — P5-16
FINGER INDEPENDENCE
  SCHAUFFLER, L. — BPTMOS — P111-12
FINGER LEGATO
  SCHAUFFLER, L. — BPTMOS — P113-15
FINGER STRENGTH
  SCHAUFFLER, L. — BPTMOS — P112-13
FINGER STRETCHES
  SCHAUFFLER, L. — BPTMOS — P117
FORMAL STUDIES--CZERNY, HANON ET AL
  NEWMAN, W. — BPP — P33-36
GEN INFO
  DILLER, A. — BSOM — P104-30
GEN INFO
  FOLDES, A. — BKTTK — P13-17
GEN INFO
  BOLTON, H. — BHTP — P10-12
GESTURE AS A TECHNICAL AID
  DILLER, A. — BSOM — P120-29
GLISSANDO
  GAT, J. — BTOPP — P188-89
GYMNASTICS
  SCHAUFFLER, L. — BPTMOS — P118
HAND POSITION
  DILLER, A. — BSOM — P108-9
HINTS FOR THE AMATEUR
  GRUNDY, E. — BHP — P11-20
HISTORICAL BACKGROUND
  AHRENS, C. * ATKINSON, G. — BFAPT — P35-36
HISTORICAL DEVELOPMENT--BAROQUE ERA
  FILLMORE, J. — BPM — P181-87
HISTORICAL DEVELOPMENT--CLASSIC TO ROMANTIC PERIOD
  FILLMORE, J. — BPM — P193-95
HISTORICAL DEVELOPMENT--ROMANTIC PERIOD
  FILLMORE, J. — BPM — P196-208
HISTORY OF METHODS
  FIELDEN, T. — BSOPT — P1-10
ILLUSIONS
  WOODHOUSE, G. — BCT — P34-40
INTERPRETATION, RELATIONSHIP TO
  WOODHOUSE, G. — BCT — P49-54
INTERPRETATION, RELATIONSHIP TO
  CHING, J. — BPPAPM — P1-15
LATERAL ARM MOVEMENTS
  SCHAUFFLER, L. — BPTMOS — P119-20
LATERAL MOVEMENTS
  BOWEN, Y. — BSOPT — P27
MATERIAL USED IN TRAINING
  SCHAUFFLER, L. — BPTMOS — P106-110
MEANING OF
  CHING, J. — BPPAPM — P1-15
MENTAL WORK, THROUGH
  LEIMER, K. * GIESEKING, W. — BRDP — P14-16
MID-NINETEENTH CENTURY VIEWPOINT
  KULLAK, A. — BAOPP — P95-214
NATURAL--BOROWSKI
  BROWER, H. — BMMOTK — P215-22
NATURAL DEVELOPMENT--LESCHETIZKY
  BROWER, H. — BPMSS — P224-32
OCTAVES AND CHORDS, OF
  GAT, J. — BTOPP — P145-69
OCTAVES
  SCHAUFFLER, L. — BPTMOS — P117-18
PHILOSOPHY OF
  FIELDEN, T. — BSOPT — P161-64
PHYSIOLOGY OF
  SCHAUFFLER, L. — BPTMOS — P40-42
PIANO CLASSES, APPROACH IN
  GIDDINGS, T. P. — BGPSCM — P65-68
PLAYING MECHANISMS--FINGERS, HAND, ARM
  NEWMAN, W. — BPP — P51-65
POSITION AT THE PIANO
  AHRENS, C. * ATKINSON, G. — BFAPT — P37
POSITION AT THE PIANO
  NEWMAN, W. — BPP — P48-51
PRACTICE PROCEDURES
  BOLTON, H. — BHTP — P10-12
PROBLEMS, ANALYSIS OF
  CHING, J. — BPPAPM — P1-15
PROBLEMS OF BEGINNERS
  GAT, J. — BTOPP — P266-76
ROTARY ACTION
  COHEN, H. — BMH — P49-50
SCALES AND ARPEGGIOS
  SCHAUFFLER, L. — BPTMOS — P115-16
SCIENTIFIC APPROACH
  AHRENS, C. * ATKINSON, G. — BFAPT — P36
SCIENTIFIC TECHNIQUE, IMPORTANCE OF
  CHING, J. — BPPAPM — P1-15

SLOW PRACTICING
  SCHAUFFLER, L. — BPTMOS — P118-19
SUGGESTIONS FOR TEACHING
  FIELDEN, T. — BSOPT — P132-43
TEMPERAMENT, RELATIONSHIP TO
  WOODHOUSE, G. — BCT — P41-44
THEORY OF
  WOODHOUSE, G. — BCT — P17-23
UNWANTED AND UNNECESSARY MOVEMENTS
  CHING, J. — BPPAPM — P30-43
VIBRATO
  FIELDEN, T. — BSOPT — P108-22
WEIGHT-DISTRIBUTION
  DILLER, A. — BSOM — P112-13
WEIGHT-TOUCH
  DILLER, A. — BSOM — P109-10
WRIST POSITION
  DILLER, A. — BSOM — P113-15
TELEVISION TEACHING
GEN INFO
  HARRISON, S. — BTNTM — P173-200
TELEVISION
PERFORMING ON
  MOORE, G. — BAITL — P278-84
TEMPERAMENT AND TUNING
GEN INFO
  SUMNER, W. — BP — P100-1
TEMPERAMENT
EQUAL
  SUMNER, W. — BP — P102-4
MEAN-TONE
  SUMNER, W. — BP — P102
TEMPO
RUBATO
  AHRENS, C. * ATKINSON, G. — BFAPT — P86
TABLE OF BASIC TEMPI
  NEWMAN, W. — BPP — P88-89
TENSION, SPEED AND TONE
FUNDAMENTAL PRINCIPLES
  CHING, J. — BPPAPM — P129-40
PRACTICAL EXERCISES
  CHING, J. — BPPAPM — P129-40
RELATIONSHIPS
  CHING, J. — BPPAPM — P129-40
RELAXATION, REAL FUNCTION OF
  CHING, J. — BPPAPM — P129-40
TENSIONS
GOOD AND BAD
  HOFHEIMER, G. — BTTFTP — P13-20
TENSION AND SPEED
BIOLOGICALLY DETERMINED RELATIONSHIP
  CHING, J. — BPPAPM — P117-28
EXPERIMENTS AND EXERCISES
  CHING, J. — BPPAPM — P117-28
PROBLEMS OF HIGH SPEEDS
  CHING, J. — BPPAPM — P117-28
TENSION
CORRECT AND INCORRECT METHODS OF
  CHING, J. — BPPAPM — P91-103
EXERCISES FOR ACQUIRING NECESSARY COORDINATION
  CHING, J. — BPPAPM — P91-103
EXERCISES FOR CONTROL OF
  CHING, J. — BPPAPM — P56-68
GEN INFO
  MATTHAY, T. — BPFOT — P32-33
HOW MUCH IS NECESSARY
  CHING, J. — BPPAPM — P56-68
MECHANICS OF LIMB STABILIZATION
  CHING, J. — BPPAPM — P56-68
TIMING OF
  CHING, J. — BPPAPM — P56-68
TONE CONTROL, NECESSARY CONDITIONS FOR
  CHING, J. — BPPAPM — P56-68
WHERE IT IS NECESSARY
  CHING, J. — BPPAPM — P56-68
TESTS
MUSICIANSHIP, FOR
  AHRENS, C. * ATKINSON, G. — BFAPT — P92
THALBERG, SIGISMOND
PIANO TECHNIQUE, APPROACH TO
  LEVINSKAYA, M. — BLSOPT — P31-32
ROLE IN THE DEVELOPMENT OF THE PF AND PF PLAYING
  SUMNER, W. — BP — P180
THINKING CLEARLY
PIANO PLAYING, IN
  BOLTON, H. — BHTP — P6-9
THIRDS, SIXTHS AND OCTAVES
DEPPE'S APPROACH
  CALAND, E. — BAPP — P101-3
THOUGHT AND FEELING
PIANO PLAYING, IN--BRAILOWSKY
  BROWER, H. — BMMOTK — P55-63
THUMB
CONTROL OF
  BOWEN, Y. — BSOPT — P9-10
EXERCISES FOR DOUBLE-JOINTED THUMB
  AHRENS, C. * ATKINSON, G. — BFAPT — P46
FUNCTION IN THE PIANO PLAYING MECHANISM
  WHITESIDE, A. — BPM — P29-37
GEN INFO
  BRECKENRIDGE, W. — BHFPNS — P5-6
TECHNICAL DIFFICULTIES TRACEABLE TO
  TAYLER, E. D. — BSOSP — P17-19
TIMED FOLLOW-THROUGH
THEORETICAL AND PRACTICAL APPLICATIONS
  WOODHOUSE, G. — BFKTM — P17-21
TIME AND RHYTHM
GEN INFO
  LAST, J. — BYP — P62-78
GEN INFO
  WILKINS-GUTMANN, E. — BTWPT — P24-31
TIME FAULTS
MATTHAY'S APPROACH
  COVIELLO, A. — BWMM — P50
TIME
CHURCH PIANIST, FOR THE
  AULD, W. — BHFTCP — P51-57
GRADATIONS
  AHRENS, C. * ATKINSON, G. — BFAPT — P85
GRADATIONS
  MERRICK, F. — BPTP — P72-75
INFLECTION
  AHRENS, C. * ATKINSON, G. — BFAPT — P85
SIMPLE AND COMPOUND
  AHRENS, C. * ATKINSON, G. — BFAPT — P69
TEACHING BY ARITHMETICAL APPROACH
  AHRENS, C. * ATKINSON, G. — BFAPT — P70

TIMING
    PIANO PLAYING, IN
        SCHAUFFLER, L.   BPTMOS   P58-60
TONE-COLOR
    GEN INFO
        SUMNER, W.   BP   P94-98
TONE, FAILURE TO CONTROL
    COMMON CAUSES
        CHING, J.   BPPAPM   P30-43
TONE, PIANO
    BRIGHTNESS
        REEDER, B.   BST   P10
    CHARACTERISTICS
        REEDER, B.   BST   P7-11
    DEFINITION OF
        BRIGGS, G. A.   BPPAS   P46-49
    DEPTH OF
        BRIGGS, G. A.   BPPAS   P52
    FACTORS THAT INFLUENCE QUALITY...ACOUSTICAL ENVIRONMENT
        SUMNER, W.   BP   P114-17
    FACTORS THAT INFLUENCE QUALITY...ACTION, INC. HAMMERS
        SUMNER, W.   BP   P95-96
    FACTORS THAT INFLUENCE QUALITY...AGOGICS
        GAT, J.   BTOPP   P15-16
    FACTORS THAT INFLUENCE QUALITY...CONSTRUCTION OF INSTRUMENT
        SUMNER, W.   BP   P95
    FACTORS THAT INFLUENCE QUALITY...DURATION
        SCHULTZ, A.   BROTPF   P200-2
    FACTORS THAT INFLUENCE QUALITY...DYNAMICS
        GAT, J.   BTOPP   P15-16
    FACTORS THAT INFLUENCE QUALITY...EFFECT OF THE IMAGINATION
        SCHULTZ, A.   BROTPF   P202-3
    FACTORS THAT INFLUENCE QUALITY...HARMONIES
        MERRICK, F.   BPTP   P80-81
    FACTORS THAT INFLUENCE QUALITY...INTENSITY
        SCHULTZ, A.   BROTPF   P200-2
    FACTORS THAT INFLUENCE QUALITY...MECHANICAL CONSIDERATIONS
        GAT, J.   BTOPP   P12-13
    FACTORS THAT INFLUENCE QUALITY...NATURE OF SOUND-BOARD
        SUMNER, W.   BP   P95
    FACTORS THAT INFLUENCE QUALITY...NOISE ELEMENTS
        GAT, J.   BTOPP   P14-15
    FACTORS THAT INFLUENCE QUALITY...NON-LEGATO TOUCH
        SCHULTZ, A.   BROTPF   P196-99
    FACTORS THAT INFLUENCE QUALITY...OVERTONE STRUCTURE
        GAT, J.   BTOPP   P11
    FACTORS THAT INFLUENCE QUALITY...PEDAL
        MERRICK, F.   BPTP   P80-81
    FACTORS THAT INFLUENCE QUALITY...PERCUSSIVE NOISES
        SCHULTZ, A.   BROTPF   P199-200
    FACTORS THAT INFLUENCE QUALITY...PITCH
        SCHULTZ, A.   BROTPF   P200-2
    FACTORS THAT INFLUENCE QUALITY...PSYCHOLOGICAL CONSIDERATIONS
        GAT, J.   BTOPP   P20-21
    FACTORS THAT INFLUENCE QUALITY...TEMPERAMENT
        SUMNER, W.   BP   P97
    FACTORS THAT INFLUENCE QUALITY...TUNING
        SUMNER, W.   BP   P97
    FACTORS THAT INFLUENCE QUALITY...UNCONTROLLED INTENSITY
        SCHULTZ, A.   BROTPF   P200
    FACTORS THAT INFLUENCE QUALITY...VERTICAL BALANCE
        GAT, J.   BTOPP   P18-19
    FACTORS THAT INFLUENC E QUALITY...NATURE OF THE STRING
        SUMNER, W.   BP   P95
    HAMMERS
        BRIGGS, G. A.   BPPAS   P51
    HARMONICS IN
        BRIGGS, G. A.   BPPAS   P49-50
    HARMONIC ANALYSIS
        BRIGGS, G. A.   BPPAS   P99-116
    HARSHNESS
        REEDER, B.   BST   P11
    LAWS GOVERNING PRODUCTION
        CAMPBELL, L.   BTFORI   P21-23
    LUSTRE
        BRIGGS, G. A.   BPPAS   P52
    OVERSTRINGING, EFFECTS OF
        BRIGGS, G. A.   BPPAS   P54
    PARTIAL TONE SCALE
        REEDER, B.   BST   P8-9
    PEDALS, EFFECT OF
        BRIGGS, G. A.   BPPAS   P53
    QUALITATIVE AND QUANTITATIVE FACTORS
        SCHAUFFLER, L.   BPTMOS   P1-39
    QUALITATIVE DIFFERENCES IN
        SCHULTZ, A.   BROTPF   P194-96
    QUALITIES
        REEDER, B.   BST   P9-11
    RELATIONSHIP TOUCH
        DICKERSON, R.   BNATPT   P20-21
    RELATIONSHIP TO TECHNIQUE
        SCHULTZ, A.   BROTPF   P203-5
    RELATIONSHIP TO TOUCH
        NEWMAN, W.   BPP   P65-69
    ROOM EFFECTS
        BRIGGS, G. A.   BPPAS   P53
    SINGING TONE
        BRIGGS, G. A.   BPPAS   P52-53
    SUSTAINING POWER
        BRIGGS, G. A.   BPPAS   P55
    TEST FOR OVERTONES
        BRIGGS, G. A.   BPPAS   P50-51
    VOLUME
        REEDER, B.   BST   P10
TONE, SUSTAINING OF
    DURATION, TERMS FOR
        REEDER, B.   BST   P39-43
    PHRASING MARKS
        REEDER, B.   BST   P38-39
TONE CONTROL
    DEPTH OF TOUCH
        CHING, J.   BPPAPM   P44-55
    FORCE ESTIMATION
        CHING, J.   BPPAPM   P44-55
    PHYSIOLOGICAL MECHANICS
        CHING, J.   BPPAPM   P44-55
    PRACTICAL EXERCISES IN
        CHING, J.   BPPAPM   P44-55
    PRACTICAL EXERCISES
        CHING, J.   BPPAPM   P44-55
    USELESSNESS OF 'FEELING THE KEYS'
        CHING, J.   BPPAPM   P44-55
TONE INFLECTION
    MATTHAY'S APPROACH
        COVIELLO, A.   BWMM   P51-52

TONE PRODUCTION
    DEPPE'S APPROACH
        CALAND, E.   BAPP   P26-32
    DYNAMICS IN
        AHRENS, C. * ATKINSON, G.   BFAPT   P58
    EXERCISES AT AND AWAY FROM THE KEYBOARD
        CHING, J.   BPPAPM   P30-43
    MATTHAY'S APPROACH
        COVIELLO, A.   BWMM   P52-53
    PHYSICAL BASIS
        POTAMKIN, F. J.   BMPP   P75-85
    PHYSIOLOGICAL ASPECTS
        CHING, J.   BPPAPM   P30-43
    PSYCHOLOGICAL ASPECTS
        CHING, J.   BPPAPM   P30-43
    PSYCHOLOGICAL BASIS
        POTAMKIN, F. J.   BMPP   P86-97
    RELATIONSHIP TO TOUCH
        AHRENS, C. * ATKINSON, G.   BFAPT   P55-58
    TECHNICAL CONSIDERATIONS
        AHRENS, C. * ATKINSON, G.   BFAPT   P59-60
    THEORY OF
        DICKERSON, R.   BNATPT   P6-7
TONE QUALITY
    APPLICATION OF SCIENTIFIC THEORIES TO KEYBOARD WORK
        CHING, J.   BPPAPM   P154-66
    BELL-LIKE
        ORTMANN, O.   BPMOPT   P342
    BRITTLE
        ORTMANN, O.   BPMOPT   P344-45
    CRISP
        ORTMANN, O.   BPMOPT   P341
    DRY
        ORTMANN, O.   BPMOPT   P342-44
    ELEMENTS OF
        ORTMANN, O.   BPMOPT   P354-55
    FACTS AND FALLACIES
        CHING, J.   BPPAPM   P141-53
    GEN INFO
        ORTMANN, O.   BPMOPT   P337-61
    IMAGERY, ROLE OF
        ORTMANN, O.   BPMOPT   P356-58
    KEY RELEASE, EFFECT OF
        ORTMANN, O.   BPMOPT   P352-54
    LAWS OF QUALITATIVE VARIATION
        CHING, J.   BPPAPM   P141-53
    MATTHAY'S APPROACH
        COVIELLO, A.   BWMM   P53-54
    OLDER THEORIES, REVIEW OF
        CHING, J.   BPPAPM   P141-53
    PEARLY
        ORTMANN, O.   BPMOPT   P350-52
    PRACTICAL CONSIDERATIONS
        CHING, J.   BPPAPM   P154-66
    PRACTICAL DEMONSTRATION OF CURRENT SCIENTIFIC THEORIES
        CHING, J.   BPPAPM   P141-53
    SCIENTIFIC OUTLOOK
        CHING, J.   BPPAPM   P141-53
    SINGING
        ORTMANN, O.   BPMOPT   P345-46
    SPARKLING
        ORTMANN, O.   BPMOPT   P339-40
    SURFACE TONE
        ORTMANN, O.   BPMOPT   P348-50
    VELVETY
        ORTMANN, O.   BPMOPT   P340
TONE VOLUME
    REGULATION OF
        GAT, J.   BTOPP   P27-28
TONE
    BEAUTY OF
        MERRICK, F.   BPTP   P80-82
    QUESTION OF, THE--BAUER
        BROWER, H.   BPM   P95-106
TONING, PIANO
    AMERICAN VIEW
        BRIGGS, G. A.   BPPAS   P64-65
    PROCEDURES
        BRIGGS, G. A.   BPPAS   P57-70
TORSO
    SPECIFIC USE IN PIANO PLAYING
        WHITESIDE, A.   BIOPP   P31-33
TOUCH-SENSING EXERCISES
    GEN INFO
        CAMPBELL, L.   BTFORI   P64-70
TOUCH-TONE CONTROVERSY
    GEN INFO
        REEDER, B.   BST   P64
TOUCH, MANNER OF
    IMPULSIVE
        REEDER, B.   BST   P28
    NON-PERCUSSIVE
        REEDER, B.   BST   P28
    PERCUSSIVE
        REEDER, B.   BST   P27
TOUCH, MODES OF
    FREE FALL
        LEIMER, K. * GIESEKING, W.   BRDP   P31
    GEN INFO
        LEIMER, K. * GIESEKING, W.   BRDP   P30, 34-36
    LEGATO
        LEIMER, K. * GIESEKING, W.   BRDP   P37
    NON-LEGATO, PORTAMENTO, STACCATO
        LEIMER, K. * GIESEKING, W.   BRDP   P37-38
    OCTAVES, SIXTHS, THIRDS
        LEIMER, K. * GIESEKING, W.   BRDP   P39-42
    POLYPHONIC PLAYING, IN
        LEIMER, K. * GIESEKING, W.   BRDP   P42-43
    PRESSURE
        LEIMER, K. * GIESEKING, W.   BRDP   P33-34
    ROLL
        LEIMER, K. * GIESEKING, W.   BRDP   P32-33
    SWING
        LEIMER, K. * GIESEKING, W.   BRDP   P32
    TECHNICAL STUDIES, IN
        LEIMER, K. * GIESEKING, W.   BRDP   P38-39
    THROW AND STROKE
        LEIMER, K. * GIESEKING, W.   BRDP   P31-32
TOUCH, PHASES OF
    AFTER-TOUCH
        REEDER, B.   BST   P25
    DRIVING FORCE
        REEDER, B.   BST   P25
    KEY RESISTANCE
        REEDER, B.   BST   P25

TOUCH, SINGING
   ADDED IMPETUS
      REEDER, B.   BST   P28
   EARLY TIMING
      REEDER, B.   BST   P29
   LATE TIMIMG
      REEDER, B.   BST   P29
   SMOOTH APPROACH
      REEDER, B.   BST   P28
TOUCHES, CLASSIFICATION OF
   MATTHAY'S APPROACH
      COVIELLO, A.   BWMM   P18-20
TOUCHES
   PERCUSSIVE AND NON-PERCUSSIVE
      POTAMKIN, F. J.   BMPP   P106-108
   STACCATO AND LEGATO
      POTAMKIN, F. J.   BMPP   P109-12
   VARIETY OF
      BRECKENRIDGE, W.   BHFPNS   P13-14
TOUCH AND TONE-COLOR
   GEN INFO
      LEVINSKAYA, M.   BLSOPT   P199-201
TOUCH AND TONE
   GEN INFO
      BRIGGS, G. A.   BPPAS   P85-90
TOUCH DIFFERENCES
   CLAVICHORD, HARPSICHORD, PIANO
      REEDER, B.   BST   P56-57
TOUCH TYPES
   CANTABILE
      REEDER, B.   BST   P35
   LEGGIERO
      REEDER, B.   BST   P35
   SFORZATO
      REEDER, B.   BST   P35-36
   TENUTO
      REEDER, B.   BST   P35
TOUCH
   ANALYSIS OF MOVEMENTS
      CHING, J.   BPPAPM   P79-90
   ARM-LEGATO
      ORTMANN, O.   BPMOPT   P177-82
   ARPEGGIOS
      ORTMANN, O.   BPMOPT   P262-76
   BASIC APPROACH
      LEIMER, K. * GIESEKING, W.   BSWTPP   P19-22
   CHARACTERISTIC TOUCH ON THE PIANO--GABRILOWITSCH
      BROWER, H.   BPM   P225-31
   CONSCIOUS CONTROL
      REEDER, B.   BST   P25-27
   ENIGMA OF
      WOODHOUSE, G.   BFKTM   P11-13
   ESSENTIALS--GABRILOWITSCH
      COOKE, J. F.   BGPOPP   P122-30
   EVOLUTION OF
      REEDER, B.   BST   P56-64
   EXERCISES IN BODILY DIFFERENTIATION OF MOVEMENTS
      CHING, J.   BPPAPM   P79-90
   FINGER-STROKE
      ORTMANN, O.   BPMOPT   P217-250
   FINGER ATTITUDES--MATTHAY'S APPROACH
      COVIELLO, A.   BWMM   P57
   FOREARM ROTATIONAL ADJUSTMENTS--MATTHAY'S APPROACH
      COVIELLO, A.   BWMM   P56-57
   GEN INFO--MATTHAY'S APPROACH
      COVIELLO, A.   BWMM   P54-55
   GEN INFO
      FIELDEN, T.   BSOPT   P45-68
   HAMMER, CONTROL OF
      REEDER, B.   BST   P27
   INDIVIDUAL DIFFERENCES...GENERAL
      ORTMANN, O.   BPMOPT   P297-310
   INDIVIDUAL DIFFERENCES...THE HAND
      ORTMANN, O.   BPMOPT   P311-36
   MANNER OF
      REEDER, B.   BST   P27-28
   MATTHAY'S APPROACH
      COVIELLO, A.   BWMM   P54-58
   MISCELLANEOUS MOVEMENTS
      ORTMANN, O.   BPMOPT   P277-96
   PHASES OF
      REEDER, B.   BST   P25
   PHYSIOLOGICAL BASIS FOR CLASSIFICATION OF TOUCH FORMS
      CHING, J.   BPPAPM   P79-90
   PHYSIOLOGICAL FACTORS
      SCHAUFFLER, L.   BPTMOS   P47-60
   PRACTICING EXERCISES
      CHING, J.   BPPAPM   P79-90
   RELATIONSHIP BETWEEN EASE AND EFFICIENCY
      CHING, J.   BPPAPM   P79-90
   RELATIONSHIP TO TONE
      DICKERSON, R.   BNATPT   P20-21
   RELATIONSHIP TO TONE
      NEWMAN, W.   BP   P65-69
   SCALES
      ORTMANN, O.   BPMOPT   P251-61
   SINGING TOUCH
      REEDER, B.   BST   P28-29
   SPECIES--MATTHAY'S PRINCIPLES
      COVIELLO, A.   BWMM   P55-56
   STACCATO
      ORTMANN, O.   BPMOPT   P196-210
   STYLE
      ORTMANN, O.   BPMOPT   P362-75
   TECHNICAL CONSIDERATIONS
      COHEN, H.   BMH   P50-52
   TONE QUALITIES
      ORTMANN, O.   BPMOPT   P337-61
   TOUCH-ACTION, CONTROL OF
      REEDER, B.   BST   P25-27
   TREMOLO
      ORTMANN, O.   BPMOPT   P183-95
   VELVETY PIANOFORTE TOUCH, A--DEPACHMANN
      COOKE, J. F.   BGMAFM   P103-10
TOVEY, DONALD FRANCIS
   BIOGRAPHICAL MATERIAL
      CHASINS, A.   BSOP   P65-70
TRADITIONAL TEACHING METHODS
   QUESTIONS AND ANSWERS
      WHITESIDE, A.   BIOPP   P46-58
TRANQUILITY
   MOVEMENT, IN
      LEIMER, K. * GIESEKING, W.   BSWTPP   P58-59
TRANS-FIXATION MOVEMENTS
   GEN INFO
      SCHULTZ, A.   BROTPF   P83-100

TRANS-MOVEMENTS
   PEDAGOGY OF
      SCHULTZ, A.   BROTPF   P165-72
TRANS-PRESSURE MOVEMENTS
   GEN INFO
      SCHULTZ, A.   BROTPF   P83-100
TRANS-WEIGHT MOVEMENTS
   GEN INFO
      SCHULTZ, A.   BROTPF   P83-100
TRANSCRIPTIONS AND ARRANGEMENTS
   CHURCH PIANIST, FOR THE
      AULD, W.   BHFTCP   P58-69
TRANSPOSITION
   AID TO PRACTICING DIFFICULT PASSAGES, AS AN
      MERRICK, F.   BPTP   P93-94
   CHURCH PIANIST, FOR THE
      AULD, W.   BHFTCP   P46-47
   MECHANICAL KEYBOARD DEVICES FOR
      SUMNER, W.   BP   P195-96
TREMOLO
   ASYMMETRY
      ORTMANN, O.   BPMOPT   P193-94
   DYNAMICS
      ORTMANN, O.   BPMOPT   P192
   FINGER-TREMOLO
      ORTMANN, O.   BPMOPT   P188-89
   FINGERING IN
      ORTMANN, O.   BPMOPT   P189-91
   GEN INFO
      ORTMANN, O.   BPMOPT   P183-95
   INTENSITY IN
      ORTMANN, O.   BPMOPT   P192
   MOVEMENT-PHASE
      ORTMANN, O.   BPMOPT   P195
   PRACTICING OF
      GAT, J.   BTOPP   P170-74
   RELATIVE INTENSITY
      ORTMANN, O.   BPMOPT   P194-95
   SPEED IN
      ORTMANN, O.   BPMOPT   P191-92
   TREMOLO TRILLS
      ORTMANN, O.   BPMOPT   P185-88
   WEIGHT TRANSFER
      ORTMANN, O.   BPMOPT   P184-85
TRILLS IN MOZART
   GEN INFO
      RICHNER, T.   BOFIMP   P31-32
   TRILL-BEGINNINGS
      BADURA-SKODA, E. * BADURA-SKODA, P.   BIMOTK   P108-21
   TRILL-ENDINGS
      BADURA-SKODA, E. * BADURA-SKODA, P.   BIMOTK   P121-23
TRILLS
   ALTERNATING FINGERS, WITH
      GAT, J.   BTOPP   P227
   DEPPE'S APPROACH
      CALAND, E.   BAPP   P104-9
   DOUBLE THIRDS, IN
      WHITESIDE, A.   BIOPP   P95
   FINGER MOVEMENT IN
      SCHAUFFLER, L.   BPTMOS   P92-93
   FOREARM ROTATION, USE OF
      MERRICK, F.   BPTP   P83-87
   FUNDAMENTAL PIANO EXERCISE, AS A
      NEWMAN, W.   BPP   P36-37
   GEN INFO
      GAT, J.   BTOPP   P225-28
   OCTAVE TRILL
      WHITESIDE, A.   BIOPP   P81-88
   PRACTICING, WAYS OF
      MERRICK, F.   BPTP   P83-87
   PRACTICING, WAYS OF
      VANTYN, S.   BMPT   P25-28
   PRACTICING OF
      GAT, J.   BTOPP   P228
   SINGLE TRILL
      WHITESIDE, A.   BIOPP   P88-94
   SPECIAL PROBLEMS IN PRACTICING
      LEIMER, K. * GIESEKING, W.   BSWTPP   P57-58
   TREMOLO TRILLS
      GAT, J.   BTOPP   P227
TUNING
   HISTORICAL CONSIDERATIONS
      HIPKINS, A.   BDAHOT   P43-46
TURECK, ROSALYN
   BIOGRAPHICAL MATERIAL
      SALESKI, G.   BFMOJO   P568-70
TURK, DANIEL G.
   PIANO TECHNIQUE, APPROACH TO
      LEVINSKAYA, M.   BLSOPT   P30-31
TURNS
   MOZART, IN
      BADURA-SKODA, E. * BADURA-SKODA, P.   BIMOTK   P99-108
   MOZART, IN
      RICHNER, T.   BOFIMP   P32-34
TWO-PIANO PLAYING
   PROBLEMS IN
      NEAL, H.   BWAYP   P118-21
UNCONSCIOUS PHYSIOLOGICAL MOTIVATION
   CONCEPT OF
      CHING, J.   BPPAPM   P30-43
UNGAR, IMRE
   PHOTOGRAPHIC ANALYSIS OF PERFORMANCE
      GAT, J.   BTOPP   P63
UNINSKY, ALEXANDER
   BIOGRAPHICAL MATERIAL
      SALESKI, G.   BFMOJO   P570-71
UNTALENTED CHILD
   PROPER ENCOURAGEMENT FOR
      BOSWORTH, H.   BIFYPT   P33-35
UPPER ARM
   EXERCISES FOR
      FIELDEN, T.   BSOPT   P38-39
   SPECIFIC USE IN PIANO PLAYING
      NEWMAN, W.   BPP   P64-65
   SPECIFIC USE IN PIANO PLAYING
      WHITESIDE, A.   BIOPP   P33
UPRIGHT SPINET
   GEN INFO
      HIPKINS, A.   BDAHOT   P74-76
VARIATION FORM
   GEN INFO
      BACON, E.   BNOTP   P30-31
VASARY, TAMAS
   PHOTOGRAPHIC ANALYSIS OF PERFORMANCE
      GAT, J.   BTOPP   P65

VELOCITY PLAYING
   ANALYSIS OF
      GAT, J.   BTOPP   P107-9
VELOCITY
   SCHOOL OF
      REEDER, B.   BST   P61
VENGEROVA, ISABELLE
   BIOGRAPHICAL MATERIAL
      SALESKI, G.   BFMOJO   P573
   BIOGRAPHICAL MATERIAL
      NEAL, H.   BWAYP   P73-111
VIBRATION
   EFFECT ON PIANO TONE QUALITY
      BRIGGS, G. A.   BPPAS   P91-98
VIBRATO
   PIANO TECHNIQUE, AS A FORM OF
      FIELDEN, T.   BSOPT   P108-22
VIENNESE PIANO
   GEN INFO
      REEDER, B.   BST   P59
VIRGIL, MR AND MRS A. K.
   CONF--THE NECESSITY OF A THOROUGH FOUNDATION
      BROWER, H.   BPMSS   P114-24
VIRGINAL
   GEN INFO
      BIE, O.   BHOTPA   P18-19
   GEN INFO
      HIPKINS, A.   BDAHOT   P65-74
   GEN INFO
      SUMNER, W.   BP   P34-35
VISUALIZATION
   MUSICAL LEARNING, IN
      LEIMER, K. * GIESEKING, W.   BSWTPP   P11-12+
VISUAL PERCEPTION
   GEN INFO
      BOLTON, H.   BHTP   P23-25
WEBER, CARL MARIA VON
   ROLE IN DEV OF ROMANTIC PIANO CONCERTO
      GARVIN, F. H.   BBOTRP   P24-26
WEIGHT-TOUCH
   GEN INFO
      DILLER, A.   BSOM   P109-10
   MISCONCEPTIONS
      MATTHAY, T.   BPFOT   P9-14
WEIGHT-TRANSFER
   ARM WEIGHT
      ORTMANN, O.   BPMOPT   P147-48
   EFFECT OF INTENSITY
      ORTMANN, O.   BPMOPT   P136-37
   EFFECT OF PERCUSSIVENESS
      ORTMANN, O.   BPMOPT   P144-46
   EFFECT OF SPEED
      ORTMANN, O.   BPMOPT   P137-41
   FINGER REPETITION
      ORTMANN, O.   BPMOPT   P141-43
   INERTIA
      ORTMANN, O.   BPMOPT   P146
   MECHANICAL DETERMINANTS
      ORTMANN, O.   BPMOPT   P234-36
   SCALES
      ORTMANN, O.   BPMOPT   P143-44

WEIGHT AND RELAXATION
   GEN INFO
      BACON, E.   BNOTP   P38-39
WEIGHT EFFECT
   GEN INFO
      GAT, J.   BTOPP   P26-27
WEIGHT
   CONTRA-WEIGHT MOVEMENT
      SCHULTZ, A.   BROTPF   P45-51
   DISTINCTION BETWEEN MASS AND WEIGHT
      SCHULTZ, A.   BROTPF   P36-38
   DISTRIBUTION OF
      DILLER, A.   BSOM   P112-13
   MISCONCEPTIONS
      CHING, J.   BPPAPM   P30-43
   PEDAGOGY OF
      SCHULTZ, A.   BROTPF   P173-79
   WEIGHT-MOVEMENT
      SCHULTZ, A.   BROTPF   P38-45
   WEIGHT-TRANSFERENCE
      SCHULTZ, A.   BROTPF   P51-61
WIECK, FREDERICK
   BIOGRAPHICAL MATERIAL
      FAY, A.   BMSIG   P163, 168
WINGED STROKE
   FOREARM-WRIST-FINGER STROKE
      WOODHOUSE, G.   BFKTM   P32
   HAND AND FOREARM TECHNIQUE
      WOODHOUSE, G.   BFKTM   P31-32
   LEGATISSIMO
      WOODHOUSE, G.   BFKTM   P30
   LEGATO
      WOODHOUSE, G.   BFKTM   P30-31
   LEGGIERO
      WOODHOUSE, G.   BFKTM   P31
   NON-LEGATO
      WOODHOUSE, G.   BFKTM   P29-30
   VARIOUS FORMS
      WOODHOUSE, G.   BFKTM   P28-32
WOMEN PIANISTS
   SPECIFIC MUSCULAR PROBLEMS
      WHITESIDE, A.   BPM   P4-8
WRIST
   EXERCISES FOR WRIST FREEDOM
      DICKERSON, R.   BNATPT   P13-14
   EXERCISES FOR
      VANTYN, S.   BMPT   P68-74
   FUNCTION IN THE PLAYING MECHANISM
      WHITESIDE, A.   BPM   P23-24
   POSITION OF
      DILLER, A.   BSOM   P113-15
   UNDULATORY MOVEMENT OF
      FIELDEN, T.   BSOPT   P69-74
ZEISLER, FANNY BLOOMFIELD
   BIOGRAPHICAL MATERIAL
      SALESKI, G.   BFMOJO   P448-49
   CONF--SCOPE OF PIANO TECHNIC, THE
      BROWER, H.   BPM   P180-97

The *Publishers Index* is a listing of all publishers included in *Piano Music in Print, Literature on the Pianistic Art* and the *Piano Reader's Guide*. The reader should be aware that many publishing houses are no longer in existence; in such cases, the addresses given are the last known place of publication. All publishers addresses are as complete as were obtainable at the publication deadline of this volume. Agents, distributors or representatives of publishers are shown in parentheses.

ABELARD-SCHUMAN, LTD.
257 PARK AVENUE SOUTH
NEW YORK, N. Y. 10010

ABINGDON MUSIC PRESS
201 8TH AVENUE SOUTH
NASHVILLE, TENN. 37203

ADAMS AND DENT
40 GAY ST.
BATH, SOMERSET
ENGLAND

C. ADAMS
CHICAGO, ILL.

JAMES B. ADAMS
LONDON
ENGLAND

ADVANCED MUSIC CORP.
(WARNER BROS. PUBLISHERS)

JAMEY AEBERSOLD
NEW ALBANY, IND.

THE AEOLIAN COMPANY
NEW YORK, N. Y.

THE AEOLIAN CORPORATION
E. ROCHESTER, N. Y. 14445

AFFILIATED MUSIC PUBLISHERS, LTD.
134/140 CHARING CROSS RD.
LONDON WC2H OLD
ENGLAND

GEORGE L. ALBIG
RIDGEFIELD, N. J.

C. A. ALCHIN
LOS ANGELES, CALIF.

ALDINE PUBLISHING CO.
529 S. WABASH AVE.
CHICAGO, ILL. 60605

ALERT PUBLISHING COMPANY
CHICAGO, ILL.

ALFRED PUBLISHING COMPANY, INC.
75 CHANNEL DRIVE
PORT WASHINGTON, N. Y. 11050

ALLAN'S MUSIC, PTY. LTD.
276 COLLINS ST.
MELBOURNE, VIC.
AUSTRALIA

ALLEGRO MUSICAL ART LEAGUE OF AMERICA
NEW YORK, N. Y.

ALLEN AND COMPANY, LTD.
43 ESSEX ST.
LONDON WC2R 35G
ENGLAND

ALLEN AND UNWIN, LTD.
RUSKIN HOUSE
24 MUSEUM ST.
LONDON WC 1
ENGLAND

I. ALLISON, PUBLISHER
BOX 1807
AUSTIN, TEX. 78767

ALLYN AND BACON, INC.
470 ATLANTIC AVENUE
BOSTON, MASS. 02110

AMERICAN INSTITUTE OF MUSICOLOGY
ROME
ITALY

AMERICAN MUSIC EDITION
263 EAST 7TH ST.
NEW YORK, N. Y. 10009

AMERICAN MUSICAL COLLEGE
CHICAGO, ILL.

AMERICAN NEWS COMPANY
NEW YORK, N. Y.

AMERICAN PIANO CORPORATION
NEW YORK, N. Y.

AMERICAN PIANO SUPPLY COMPANY
CLIFTON, N. J.

AMERICAN SCHOOL OF PIANO TUNING
NEW YORK, N. Y.

AMERICAN STEEL AND WIRE COMPANY
NEW YORK, N. Y.

AMERICAN STRING TEACHERS ASSN.
2596 PRINCETON PIKE
TRENTON, N. J. 08638

AMPICO CORPORATION
NEW YORK, N. Y.

AMSCO MUSIC
(MUSIC SALES CORP.)

ANDERSON-MULDER COMPANY
CHICAGO, ILL.

JOHN M. ANDREWS, TREASURER
HOUGHTON, N. Y.

THE ANGLO-FRENCH MUSIC COMPANY
LONDON
ENGLAND

ANGUS AND ROBERTSON, LTD., PUBLISHERS
102 GLOVER ST.
CREMORNE N.S.W. 2090
AUSTRALIA

APEX PIANO PUBLISHERS
SHEBOYGAN, WIS.

APPEL-ALEXANDER
CHICAGO, ILL.

APPLETON-CENTURY-CROFTS, INC.
440 PARK AVENUE SOUTH
NEW YORK, N. Y. 10016

ARCHIVES OF PSYCHOLOGY
NEW YORK, N. Y.

ARCO PUBLISHING COMPANY, INC.
219 PARK AVE. S.
NEW YORK, N. Y. 10003

ARIZONA STATE MUSIC TEACHERS
PHOENIX, ARIZ.

E. ARNOLD AND COMPANY, LTD.
(ST. MARTIN'S PRESS)

ARTCRAFT LITHOGRAPH PRINTING COMPANY
NEW YORK, N. Y.

ART PUBLICATION SOCIETY
P. O. BOX 11970
ST. LOUIS, MO. 63112

ARTIA
(BOOSEY AND HAWKES)

ASCHERBERG, HOPWOOD AND CREW
(BRODT MUSIC CO., CHAPPELL AND COMPANY,
G. SCHIRMER, INC.)

ASHBURNHAM SCHOOL OF MUSIC
WOKING, SURREY
ENGLAND

EDWIN ASHDOWN, LTD.
(ASSOCIATED MUSIC PUBLISHERS,
BOOSEY AND HAWKES, BRODT MUSIC CO.)

ASHDOWN AND PARRY
LONDON
ENGLAND

ASHLEY PUBLICATIONS, INC.
263 VETERANS BLVD.
CARLSTADT, N. J. 07072

H. B. ASHMEAD
PHILADELPHIA, PENN.

ASSOCIATED MUSIC PUBLISHERS, INC.
866 THIRD AVE.
NEW YORK, N. Y. 10022

ASSUMPTION UNIVERSITY OF WINDSOR PRESS
WINDSOR
CANADA

ASTOR PUBLISHING, INC.
103 UNION ST.
LODI, N. J. 07644

G. ASTOR
LONDON
ENGLAND

ATHENEUM PUBLISHERS
122 E. 42ND ST.
NEW YORK, N. Y. 10017

AUGENER, LTD.
(GALAXY MUSIC CORP.)

AUGSBURG PUBLISHING HOUSE
426 S. FIFTH ST.
MINNEAPOLIS, MINN. 55415

AUTO PNEUMATIC ACTION COMPANY
NEW YORK, N. Y.

BACH SOCIETY PUBLICATIONS
LONDON
ENGLAND

BARENREITER VERLAG
(JOSEPH BOONIN, MAGNAMUSIC-BATON,
G. SCHIRMER, INC.)

ALEXANDER BAILLIE
EDINBURGH
SCOTLAND

BAKER PRINTING COMPANY
NEWARK, N. J.

PRESS OF E. L. BALCH
BOSTON, MASS.

BALDWIN, CRADOCK AND JOY
LONDON
ENGLAND

THE BALDWIN PIANO COMPANY
1801 GILBERT AVE.
CINCINNATI, OHIO 45202

A. A. BALKEMA (PTY) LTD, PUBLISHER
POSBUS 3117
CAPE TOWN
SOUTH AFRICA

BALTIMORE MUSEUM OF ART
BALTIMORE, MD.

C. F. BANFIELD
VICTORIA
BRITISH COLUMBIA

BANKS AND SON LTD.
(BRODT MUSIC CO.)

A. S. BARNES AND COMPANY, INC.
BOX 421
CRANBURY, N. J. 08512

BARNES AND NOBLE
(HARPER AND ROW PUBLISHERS)

C. L. BARNHOUSE COMPANY
1008 AVENUE EAST
OSKALOOSA, IOWA 52577

V. T. BARNWELL
ATLANTA, GA.

M. BARON CO.
P. O. BOX 149
OYSTER BAY, N. Y. 11771

BARRIE AND JENKINS, LTD.
24 HIGHWAY CRESCENT
LONDON N5 1RX
ENGLAND

BARRIE AND ROCKLIFF
(BARRIE AND JENKINS, LTD.)

BARTA PRINTERS
BOSTON, MASS.

FRANCOIS H. BARTHELEMON
LONDON
ENGLAND

BATCHWORTH PRESS
LONDON
ENGLAND

RICHARD BATES
MANCHESTER
ENGLAND

W. C. BATES
LONDON
ENGLAND

B. T. BATSFORD
LONDON
ENGLAND

BATTLE CREEK REVIEW AND HERALD
BATTLE CREEK, MICH.

J. BAXTER AND COMPANY
FRIENDSHIP, N. Y.

MEL BAY PUBLICATIONS, INC.
107 WEST JEFFERSON AVE.
KIRKWOOD, MO. 63122

THE BAYARD PRESS
WILLIAMSPORT, PENN.

BBC PUBLICATIONS
35 MARYLEBONE HIGH ST.
LONDON W1A 4AA
ENGLAND

I. BECKET AND J. PORTER
LONDON
ENGLAND

BECK ENGRAVING COMPANY
PHILADELPHIA, PENN.

G. BELL
LONDON
ENGLAND

PUBLISHERS INDEX

G. BELL AND SONS, LTD.
YORK HOUSE
6 PORTUGAL STREET
LONDON W. C. 2
ENGLAND

BELWIN, INC.
(BELWIN-MILLS)

BELWIN-MILLS PUBLISHING CORPORATION
25 DESCHON DRIVE
MELVILLE, N.Y. 11746

ANTON BEMETZRIEDER
LONDON
ENGLAND

ERNEST BENN, LTD.
BOUVERIE HOUSE
154-160 FLEET ST.
LONDON, E.C.4
ENGLAND

BENNER PUBLISHERS
1739 RANDOLPH RD.
SCHENECTADY, N. Y. 12308

R. BENTLEY AND SON
LONDON
ENGLAND

ROBERT BENTLEY, INC.
872 MASSACHUSETTS AVE.
CAMBRIDGE, MASS. 02139

BERKLEE PRESS PUBLICATIONS
(FRANK DISTRIBUTING CORP.)

BERNING MUSIC SCHOOL
5320 W. LAWRENCE
CHICAGO, ILL.

BIBLE INSTITUTE COLPORTAGE
CHICAGO, ILL.

BIBLIOTECA PANSTWOWEJ
KATOWICE
POLAND

BIG BELLS
33 HOVEY AVE.
TRENTON, N. J. 08610

THE BIG THREE MUSIC CORPORATION
1775 BROADWAY
NEW YORK, N.Y. 10019

E. L. BILL
NEW YORK, N. Y.

GERARD BILLAUDOT EDITIONS MUSICALES
(THEODORE PRESSER COMPANY)

C. C. BIRCHARD AND COMPANY
BOSTON, MASS.

A. AND C. BLACK, LTD.
4-6 SOHO SQUARE
LONDON W1V 6AD
ENGLAND

BLAND AND WELLER'S MUSIC WAREHOUSE
LONDON
ENGLAND

BLOCH PUBLISHING COMPANY
915 BROADWAY
NEW YORK, N. Y. 10010

BENJAMIN BLOM, INC.
2521 BROADWAY
NEW YORK, N. Y. 10025

BLYTHER'S PIANO COMPANY
CAMDEN, N. J.

AUDREY BONE
GERRARDS CROSS
BUCKS
ENGLAND

BONI AND LIVERIGHT
(LIVERIGHT)

BOOKS FOR LIBRARIES PRESS, INC.
50 LIBERTY AVENUE
FREEPORT, L. I.
NEW YORK 11520

JOSEPH BOONIN, INC.
P.O. BOX 2124
HACKENSACK, N.J. 07606

BOOSEY AND COMPANY, LTD.
(BOOSEY AND HAWKES)

BOOSEY AND HAWKES, INC.
P. O. BOX 130
OCEANSIDE, N. Y. 11572

BOSTON BOOK AND ART, PUBLISHERS
655 BOYLSTON ST.
BOSTON, MASS. 02116

BOSTON MUSIC COMPANY
(FRANK DISTRIBUTING CORP.)

BOSWORTH AND COMPANY, LTD.
14/18 HEDDON ST.
LONDON W1R 8DP
ENGLAND

BOURNE COMPANY
(CHAPPELL AND CO.)

WILLIAM BRADFORD PRESS
NEW YORK, N. Y.

C. BRADLEE
BOSTON, MASS.

THE S. BRAINARDS AND SONS COMPANY
NEW YORK, N. Y.

BREITKOPF AND HARTEL
(ASSOCIATED MUSIC PUBLISHERS, INC.,
ALEXANDER BROUDE, INC.)

R. BREMNER
EDINBURGH
SCOTLAND

THE BRENAN PUBLISHING COMPANY
GAINESVILLE, GA.

BRENTANO
NEW YORK, N. Y.

S. BREWER AND COMPANY
(MOONCREST LTD.)

BRITISH BROADCASTING CORP.
(BBC PUBLICATIONS)

A. V. BROADHURST
LONDON
ENGLAND

BROADMAN PRESS
127 NINTH AVE., N.
NASHVILLE, TENN. 37234

BROADWOOD AND SONS
LONDON
ENGLAND

BRODT MUSIC COMPANY
BOX 1207
CHARLOTTE, N. C. 28201

ALEXANDER BROUDE, INC.
225 WEST 57TH STREET
NEW YORK, N.Y. 10019

BROUDE BROTHERS, LTD.
56 WEST 45TH STREET
NEW YORK, N. Y. 10036

O. B. BROWN
BOSTON, MASS.

SIR THOMAS BROWN INSTITUTE
LONDON
ENGLAND

WM. C. BROWN COMPANY, PUBLISHERS
2460 KERPER BLVD.
DUBUQUE, IOWA 52001

BROWNE AND HOWELL COMPANY
CHICAGO, ILL.

BUCKLEY, OLIVIA DUSSEK
LONDON
ENGLAND

BUDD AND CALKIN
LONDON
ENGLAND

BULMAN BROTHERS, LTD.
WINNIPEG
CANADA

BURKE PUBLISHING COMPANY, LTD.
LONDON
ENGLAND

BUSINESS TRAINING CORPORATION
NEW YORK, N. Y.

BUTLER AND TANNER, LTD.
LONDON
ENGLAND

C. M. CADY
NEW YORK, N. Y.

CALLAGHAN AND COMPANY
6141 N. CICERO AVE.
CHICAGO, ILL. 60646

JAMES CALLAGHAN
UNIVERSITY CITY, CALIF.

CAMPUS PUBLISHERS
711 NORTH UNIVERSITY
ANN ARBOR, MICH.

CANADIAN MUSIC SALES CORPORATION
TORONTO
CANADA

CANYON PRESS, INC.
BOX 1235
CINCINNATI, OHIO 45201

JONATHAN CAPE, LTD.
30 BEDFORD SQUARE
LONDON, W.C.1
ENGLAND

CAPELLA MUSIC
(BOURNE COMPANY)

CAPITOL SONGS
NEW YORK, N. Y.

CARDINAL STRITCH COLLEGE
6801 N. YATES RD.
MILWAUKEE, WIS. 53217

SYLVESTER CARL, PUBLISHERS
BROOKLYN, N. Y.

CARLTON PRESS, INC.
84 FIFTH AVE.
NEW YORK, N. Y. 10011

E. P. CARPENTER COMPANY
BRATTLEBORO, VT.

BENJAMIN CARR
PHILADELPHIA, PENN.

J. CARR
LONDON
ENGLAND

J. CARRICK
DUBLIN
IRELAND

CASSELL AND COMPANY, LTD.
35 RED LION SQUARE
LONDON WC1R 4SG
ENGLAND

CATHOLIC UNIVERSITY OF AMERICA PRESS
620 MICHIGAN AVE. N.E.
WASHINGTON, D.C. 20017

CAVALLARO PUBLICATIONS
NEW YORK, N. Y.

THE CAXTON INSTITUTE, INC.
NEW YORK, N. Y.

CAXTON PRINTERS, LTD.
312 MAIN ST.
CALDWELL, IDAHO 83605

CENTRAL PRINTING COMPANY
BLOOMINGTON, IND.

THE CENTURY COMPANY
NEW YORK, N. Y.

CENTURY HOUSE, INC.
IVY MUSIC
WATSON GLEN, N. Y. 14891

THE CENTURY LIBRARY OF MUSIC
NEW YORK, N. Y.

CENTURY MUSIC PUBLISHING COMPANY, INC.
(ASHLEY PUBLICATIONS, INC.)

CHAPMAN AND DODD, LTD.
LONDON
ENGLAND

CHAPMAN AND HALL, LTD.
(BARNES AND NOBLE)

CHAPPELL AND COMPANY, INC.
609 FIFTH AVENUE
NEW YORK, N. Y. 10017

CHARLTON
LONDON
ENGLAND

SIMON CHAROL
ROME
ITALY

J. AND W. CHESTER, LTD.
(MAGNAMUSIC-BATON, G. SCHIRMER, INC.)

CHICKERING AND SONS
(AEOLIAN CORP.)

CHICKERING BROTHERS
CHICAGO, ILL.

LEMUEL CHILDERS
TULSA, OKLA.

CHILTON BOOK COMPANY
CHILTON WAY
RADNOR, PENN. 19089

C. B. CHILTON
NEW YORK, N. Y.

JAMES CHING
SEDLESCOMBE
SUSSEX
ENGLAND

CHISWICK PRESS
LONDON
ENGLAND

C. G. CHRISTMAN
NEW YORK, N. Y.

CHRISTOPHER PUBLISHING HOUSE
53 BILLINGS RD. N.
QUINCY, MASS. 02171

THE JOHN CHURCH COMPANY
(THEODORE PRESSER COMPANY)

CIMINO PUBLICATIONS, INC.
1646 NEW HIGHWAY
FARMINGDALE, L. I., N. Y. 11735

CLARENDON PRESS
(OXFORD UNIVERSITY PRESS)

CLARK MIMEOGRAPH-BOOK PUBLISHING
LOS ANGELES, CALIF.

CLAUS AND BARCLAY, PRINTERS
ST. LOUIS, MO.

CLEF MUSIC PUBLISHING CORPORATION
351 WEST 52ND ST.
NEW YORK, N. Y. 10019

CLEMENTI AND COMPANY
LONDON
ENGLAND

WILLIAM CLOWES
LONDON
ENGLAND

COACH HOUSE PRESS
TORONTO
CANADA

L. COCKS
LONDON
ENGLAND

R. COCKS AND COMPANY
LONDON
ENGLAND

JOSEPH COGGINS
LONDON
ENGLAND

M. M. COLE PUBLISHING COMPANY
251 EAST GRAND AVE.
CHICAGO, ILL. 60611

COLEMAN-ROSS COMPANY
NEW YORK, N. Y.

CHARLES COLIN MUSIC PUBLISHERS
315 WEST 53RD STREET
NEW YORK, N. Y. 10019

FRANCO COLOMBO PUBLICATIONS
(BELWIN-MILLS)

THE COLONIAL WILLIAMSBURG FOUNDATION
BOX C
WILLIAMSBURG, VA. 23185

THE COLORADO COLLEGE MUSIC PRESS
COLORADO SPRINGS, COLO. 80903

COMPOSERS AUTOGRAPH PUBLICATIONS
1527 1/2 N. VINE STREET
HOLLYWOOD, CALIF. 90028

COMPOSERS PRESS, INC.
177 E. 87TH ST.
NEW YORK, N. Y. 10028

CONCORDIA PUBLISHING HOUSE
3558 S. JEFFERSON AVE.
ST. LOUIS, MO. 63118

CONCORDIA TEACHERS COLLEGE
SEWARD, NEB.

CONSERVATORY PUBLISHING COMPANY
RACINE, WIS.

CONSOLIDATED MUSIC PUBLISHERS, INC.
(MUSIC SALES CORP.)

CONSTABLE AND COMPANY, LTD.
10-12 ORANGE ST.
LONDON W.C.2
ENGLAND

CONTINENTAL BOOK COMPANY
STOCKHOLM
SWEDEN

CONVENTION PRESS
NASHVILLE, TENN.

COOPER SQUARE PUBLISHERS
NEW YORK, N. Y.

EVELYN A. COPP
BROOKLINE, MASS.

COPPAGE ENTERPRISES
PHOENIX, ARIZ.

CORRELATION MUSIC INDUSTRIES
P.O. BOX 751
LA CANADA, CALIF. 91011

CORRI, DUSSEK AND COMPANY
LONDON
ENGLAND

CORVINA PRESS
BUDAPEST V.
VOEROSMARTY TER 1
HUNGARY

CORWOOD PUBLISHERS
HUNTINGTON, N. Y.

COUNTRY LIFE LIMITED FOR
THE NATIONAL TRUST
LONDON
ENGLAND

CRAMER
(BRODT MUSIC CO.)

J. C. CRANDALL
FRIENDSHIP, N. Y.

CREATIVE MUSIC PUBLISHERS
1701 DEL OGIER
GLENVIEW, ILL. 60025

CRESCENDO MUSIC SALES
P. O. BOX 395   8 BUNTING LANE
NAPERVILLE, ILL. 60540

CRESCENDO PUBLISHERS
NEW YORK, N. Y.

F. S. CROFTS AND COMPANY
NEW YORK, N. Y.

CROKE PRINTING COMPANY
BOSTON, MASS.

CROSBY LOCKWOOD STAPLES, LTD.
3 UPPER JAMES ST.
GOLDEN SQUARE
LONDON W1R 4BP
ENGLAND

THOMAS Y. CROWELL CO.
666 FIFTH AVE.
NEW YORK, N. Y. 10019

CROWN PUBLISHERS
419 PARK AVE. S.
NEW YORK, N. Y. 10016

JOHN CULLEN
LONDON
ENGLAND

J. CURWEN AND SONS, LTD.
(G. SCHIRMER, INC.)

DA CAPO PRESS
227 W. 17TH ST.
NEW YORK, N. Y. 10011

D'ALMAINE AND COMPANY
LONDON
ENGLAND

J. E. DALLAS AND SONS, LTD.
LONDON
ENGLAND

DARWIN PUBLICATIONS
STERLING, ILL.

PETER DAVIES, LTD.
15-16 QUEENS ST.
LONDON W.C.1
ENGLAND

H. DAVIS INSTANT MUSIC
WESTBURY, LONG ISLAND, N. Y.

LUCILE DAVIS
SPOKANE, WASH.

DEACON AND PETERSON, PRINTERS
PHILADELPHIA, PENN.

DECKER CONSOLE SYSTEM
MOBILE, ALA.

DELLAMO PRODUCTIONS
HOLLYWOOD, CALIF.

DELPHI MUSIC PUBLISHERS
NEW YORK, N. Y.

DELRIEU ET CIE.
(GALAXY MUSIC CORP.)

DELUXE REPRODUCING ROLL CORPORATION
NEW YORK, N. Y.

DELUXE ROLL CORPORATION
CHICAGO, ILL.

T. S. DENISON AND COMPANY, INC.
5100 W. 82ND ST.
MINNEAPOLIS, MINN. 55437

DENISON AND SMITH, PRINTER
NEW YORK. N. Y.

DENISON MUSIC COMPANY
(HANDY FOLIO MUSIC CO.)

J. M. DENT AND SONS, LTD. PUBLISHERS
ALDINE HOUSE
10-13 BEDFORD ST.
LONDON W.C.2
ENGLAND

DENVER PUBLIC SCHOOLS--DIV. OF
DENVER, COLO.

DEPARTMENT OF HEALTH, EDUCATION,
AND WELFARE
WASHINGTON, D. C.

DESANTIS
(BELWIN-MILLS)

DE PAUL UNIVERSITY PRESS
25 E. JACKSON BLVD.
CHICAGO, ILL. 60604

THE DE VINNE PRESS
NEW YORK. N. Y.

W. DICEY
LONDON
ENGLAND

DIGBY, LONG AND COMPANY
LONDON
ENGLAND

DISPATCH PRINTING COMPANY
BIRMINGHAM, ALA.

OLIVER DITSON COMPANY
(THEODORE PRESSER COMPANY)

DOBSON BOOKS, LTD.
80 KENSINGTON CHURCH ST.
LONDON W.8
ENGLAND

DODD, MEAD AND COMPANY, INC.
79 MADISON AVE.
NEW YORK, N. Y. 10016

THE DOLPHIN PRESS
MANCHESTER
ENGLAND

R. R. DONNELLEY AND SONS COMPANY
2223 SOUTH PARK WAY
CHICAGO, ILL. 60616

DOUBLEDAY AND COMPANY, INC.
501 FRANKLIN AVE.
GARDEN CITY, N. Y. 11531

DORAN DOUBLEDAY
GARDEN CITY, N. Y.

DOUBLEDAY, PAGE AND COMPANY
NEW YORK, N. Y.

DOVER PUBLICATIONS, INC.
180 VARICK STREET
NEW YORK, N. Y. 10014

J. DRAKE
CINCINNATI, OHIO

DROKE HOUSE/HALLUX
1372 PEACHTREE ST. N.E.
ATLANTA, GA. 30303

DROKE HOUSE PUBLISHERS
ANDERSON, S. C.

DUELL, SLOAN AND PEARCE, INC.
NEW YORK, N. Y.

CHUCK DUTTON
BERKLEY, CALIF.

E. P. DUTTON AND COMPANY, INC.
201 PARK AVE. S.
NEW YORK, N. Y. 10003

EARLY MUSIC LABORATORY
LOS ANGELES, CALIF.

EASTMAN SCHOOL OF MUSIC
(CARL FISCHER, INC.)

EDINBURGH UNIVERSITY PRESS
(ALDINE PUBLISHING, INC.)

EDITIO MUSICA
BUDAPEST
HUNGARY

EDICIONES MEXICANAS DE MUSICA, A. C.
(PEER SOUTHERN ORGANIZATION)

EDITIONS M. SENART
PARIS
FRANCE

LES EDITIONS OUVRIERES
(GALAXY MUSIC CORP.)

EDITIONS SALABERT, INC.
575 MADISON AVENUE
NEW YORK, N. Y. 10022

EDITORIAL ARGENTINA DE MUSICA
(PEER SOUTHERN ORGANIZATION)

EDITORIAL COOPERATIVA INTER-AMERICANA
DE COMPOSITORES
(PEER SOUTHERN ORGANIZATION)

EDITORIAL SARACENO, BUENOS AIRES
(PEER SOUTHERN ORGANIZATION)

EDIZIONI BERBEN
(THEODORE PRESSER COMPANY)

EDIZIONI CURCI
(THE BIG THREE MUSIC CORPORATION)

J. W. EDWARDS
ANN ARBOR, MICH.

JACOB EISENBERG PUBLISHING COMPANY
NEW YORK, N. Y.

PAUL ELEK, LTD.
54 CALADONIAN RD.
LONDON N1 9RN
ENGLAND

HENRI ELKAN MUSIC PUBLISHER
1316 WALNUT STREET
PHILADELPHIA, PENN. 19107

ELKAN-VOGEL, INC.
(THEODORE PRESSER COMPANY)

ELKIN AND COMPANY, LTD.
(GALAXY MUSIC CORP.)

EMB MUSIC SERVICE
(SUMMY-BIRCHARD COMPANY)

EMPIRE SERVICE CORPORATION
PORTLAND, ORE.

THE ENGLISH UNIVERSITIES PRESS, LTD.
ST. PAUL'S HOUSE
WARWICK LANE
LONDON
ENGLAND

EPOCH DELIVERY COMPANY
HADLEIGH
SUFFOLK
ENGLAND

J. A. ETHIER
BUFFALO, N. Y.

PUBLISHERS INDEX

EVANS BROTHERS, LTD.
MONTAGUE HOUSE
RUSSELL SQUARE
LONDON W.C.1
ENGLAND

EVERETT J. EVANS
EAST ORANGE, N. J.

EVANS MUSIC COMPANY
(CARL FISCHER, INC.)

EVANS PRINTING COMPANY
PROVIDENCE, R. I.

EVELYN, ADAMS AND MACKAY
(ADAMS AND DENT)

POWELL EVERHART
ATLANTA, GA.

EWER AND COMPANY
LONDON
ENGLAND

EXECUTIVE COMMITTEE OF CHOPIN YEAR 1949
WARSAW
POLAND

THE EXPOSITION PRESS
50 JERICHO TURNPIKE
JERICHO, N. Y. 11753

EYE GATE HOUSE, INC.
JAMAICA, N. Y.

FABER MUSIC, LTD.
(G. SCHIRMER, INC.)

ROBERT FALKENER
LONDON
ENGLAND

G. FALKNER AND SONS
MANCHESTER
ENGLAND

FARRAR, STRAUS AND GIROUX, INC.
19 UNION SQUARE W.
NEW YORK, N. Y. 10003

FARRAR, STRAUSS AND CUDAHY
NEW YORK, N. Y.

LEO FEIST, INC.
(THE BIG THREE MUSIC CORPORATION)

FEMA MUSIC PUBLICATIONS
(CRESCENDO MUSIC SALES)

ARTHUR H. FILLINGHAM
LEEDS
ENGLAND

T. H. FILLMORE
PASADENA, CALIF.

FILLMORE MUSIC HOUSE
(CARL FISCHER, INC.)

FINE ART, PHILATELIST
MUSKOGEE, OKLA.

FIRTH AND HALL
NEW YORK, N. Y.

CARL FISCHER, INC.
62 COOPER SQUARE
NEW YORK, N. Y. 10003

G. FISCHER
NEW YORK, N. Y.

J. FISCHER AND BRO.
(BELWIN-MILLS)

H. T. FITZSIMONS COMPANY
615 NORTH LASALLE STREET
CHICAGO, ILL. 60610

HAROLD FLAMMER, INC.
(SHAWNEE PRESS, INC.)

CHARLES FOLEY, INC.
(CARL FISCHER, INC.)

J. H. FOOTE
NEW YORK, N. Y.

FORSTER MUSIC PUBLISHERS, INC.
216 SOUTH WABASH AVE.
CHICAGO, ILL. 60604

FORSYTH BROTHERS, LTD.
(BELWIN-MILLS, BRODT MUSIC CO.)

FORTUNE PRESS
LONDON
ENGLAND

MARK FOSTER MUSIC CO.
P. O. BOX 4012
CHAMPAIGN, ILL. 61820

G. T. FOULIS AND COMPANY
LONDON
ENGLAND

T. N. FOULIS
LONDON
ENGLAND

W. FOULSHAM AND CO.
200 FIFTH AVE.
NEW YORK, N. Y. 10010

THE FOUNTAIN PRESS
(MORGAN AND MORGAN)

SAM FOX PUBLISHING COMPANY, INC.
(CARL FISCHER, INC.)

FRANK DISTRIBUTING CORPORATION
116 BOYLSTON STREET
BOSTON, MASS. 02116

FRANK MUSIC CORPORATION
(FRANK DISTRIBUTING CORP.)

BURT FRANKLIN
(SUBS. OF LENOX HILL PUBL.
AND DISTR. CORP.)
235 E. 44TH ST.
NEW YORK, N. Y. 10017

FREDERIC CHOPIN SOCIETY
WARSAW
POLAND

FREE PRESS
(MACMILLAN CO.)

W. H. FREEMAN AND CO. PUBLISHERS
600 MARKET ST.
SAN FRANCISCO, CALIF. 94104

SAMUEL FRENCH, INC.
25 WEST 45TH ST.
NEW YORK, N. Y. 10036

PHILLIP J. FRICK
LONDON
ENGLAND

IRA J. FRIEDMAN, INC.
90 S. BAYLES AVE.
PORT WASHINGTON, N. Y. 11050

FUNK AND WAGNALLS, INC.
53 E. 77TH ST.
NEW YORK, N. Y. 10021

GAKUSHOBO
TOKYO
JAPAN

GALAXY MUSIC CORPORATION
2121 BROADWAY
NEW YORK, N. Y. 10023

GALE RESEARCH COMPANY
BOOK TOWER
DETROIT, MICH. 48226

GAMBLE HINGED MUSIC CO.
(CARL FISCHER, CHICAGO)

GARDEN CITY PUBLISHING COMPANY, INC.
NEW YORK, N. Y.

W. GARDNER, DARTON AND COMPANY, LTD.
LONDON
ENGLAND

WILLIAM GEIB
PHILADELPHIA, PENN.

FRANCESCO GEMINIANI
LONDON
ENGLAND

GENERAL MUSIC PUBLISHING COMPANY, INC.
BOX 267
HASTINGS-ON-HUDSON, N. Y. 10706

GENERAL WORDS AND MUSIC COMPANY
(NEIL A. KJOS MUSIC CO.)

EVAN GEORGEOFF MUSIC PUBLISHING CO.
(BOURNE COMPANY)

WILLIAM GEPPERT, INC.
NEW YORK, N. Y.

GERON-X, INC.
BOX 1108
LOS ALTOS, CALIF. 94022

W. W. GIBBINGS
LONDON
ENGLAND

RUSSELL S. GILBERT
ORANGE, N. J.

ARNOLD B. GILBERTSON
MINNEAPOLIS, MINN.

GILES COMPANY
NEW YORK, N. Y.

L. UPCOTT GILL
LONDON
ENGLAND

GINN AND COMPANY
191 SPRING ST.
LEXINGTON, MASS. 02173

THE GLADSTONE PUBLISHING COMPANY
CHICAGO, ILL.

W. J. GOLBOURN
LONDON
ENGLAND

VICTOR GOLLANCZ, LTD.
14 HENRIETTA ST.
COVENT GARDEN, LONDON, W.C.2
ENGLAND

S. T. GORDON AND SON
NEW YORK, N. Y.

THE GORHAM PRESS
NORWALK, CONN.

S. GOSNELL
LONDON
ENGLAND

GOULDING, PHIPPS AND D'ALMAINE
LONDON
ENGLAND

GOVERNMENT PRINTING OFFICE
WASHINGTON, D. C.

GRAND CONSERVATORY PUBLISHING COMPANY
NEW YORK, N. Y.

BILLY GRANTHAM
GREENSBORO, N. C.

GRANT EDUCATIONAL COMPANY, LTD.
LONDON
ENGLAND

G. GRAUPNER
BOSTON, MASS.

H. W. GRAY COMPANY, INC.
(BELWIN-MILLS)

I. GREEN
LONDON
ENGLAND

J. GREEN
LONDON
ENGLAND

S. W. GREEN
NEW YORK, N. Y.

GREENWOOD PRESS, INC.
51 RIVERSIDE AVE.
WESTPORT, CONN. 06880

H. GREVEL AND COMPANY
LONDON
ENGLAND

GRIFFITH AND FARRAN
LONDON
ENGLAND

GRIFFITH MUSIC FOUNDATION
NEWARK, N. J.

GROOMBRIDGE AND SONS
LONDON
ENGLAND

GROSSET AND DUNLAP, INC.
51 MADISON AVE.
NEW YORK, N. Y. 10010

GROSSMAN PUBLISHERS
625 MADISON AVE.
NEW YORK, N. Y. 10022

GULBRANSEN-DICKINSON COMPANY
CHICAGO, ILL.

GWYN PUBLISHING COMPANY
P.O. BOX 5900
SHERMAN OAKS, CALIF. 91413

THEODORE HAGEN
NEW YORK, N. Y.

HALCYON HOUSE
GARDEN CITY, N. Y.

CONSTANCE HUNTINGTON HALL
CAMBRIDGE, MASS.

HALL, LTD.
OXFORD
ENGLAND

W. HALL AND SON
NEW YORK, N. Y.

C. B. HAMILTON AND COMPANY
TOPEKA, KAN.

HAMISH HAMILTON, LTD.
90 GREAT RUSSELL ST.
LONDON, W.C.1
ENGLAND

THE HAMLYN PUBLISHING GROUP
(PAUL HAMLYN, INC.)

PAUL HAMLYN, INC.
205 E. 42ND ST.
NEW YORK, N. Y. 10017

HAMMOND, INC.
515 VALLEY ST.
MAPLEWOOD, N. J. 07040

HANDY FOLIO MUSIC COMPANY
5100 WEST 82ND STREET
MINNEAPOLIS, MINN. 55431

CHARLES H. HANSEN MUSIC
1842 WEST AVENUE
MIAMI BEACH, FLA. 33139

HANSEN PUBLICATIONS, INC.
(CHARLES H. HANSEN MUSIC)

SIEGFRIED HANSING
SCHWERIN
GERMANY

HARCOURT BRACE JOVANOVICH, INC.
757 THIRD AVE.
NEW YORK, N. Y. 10017

HARGAIL MUSIC, INC.
28 WEST 38TH ST.
NEW YORK, N. Y. 10018

ROBERT HARKNESS
SOUTH PASADENA, CALIF.

HARMS, INC.
(WARNER BROS. PUBLISHERS)

HARPER AND BROS.
(HARPER AND ROW)

HARPER AND ROW PUBLISHERS
10 E. 53RD ST.
NEW YORK, N. Y. 10022

GEORGE HARRAP AND CO., LTD, PUBLISHERS
182 HIGH HOLBORN
LONDON, W.C.1
ENGLAND

BEATRIX O. HARRIS
NUTLEY, N. J.

FREDERICK HARRIS MUSIC CO.
(BRODT MUSIC CO.)

RUPERT HART-DAVIS, LTD.
1-3 UPPER JAMES ST.
LONDON W.1
ENGLAND

HARVARD UNIVERSITY
CAMBRIDGE, MASS. 02138

HARVARD UNIVERSITY PRESS
79 GARDEN ST.
CAMBRIDGE, MASS. 02138

THE HARVILL PRESS, LTD.
30A PAVILLON RD.
LONDON, S.W . 1
ENGLAND

HASKELL HOUSE PUBLISHERS
280 LAFAYETTE ST.
NEW YORK, N. Y. 10012

J. HATCHARD, ET AL
LONDON
ENGLAND

HATCH MUSIC COMPANY
PHILADELPHIA, PENN.

HAWKES AND SON
(BOOSEY AND HAWKES)

HAWTHORN BOOKS, INC.
260 MADISON AVE.
NEW YORK, N. Y. 10016

JOHANN CASPAR HECK
LONDON
ENGLAND

THE HEIDELBERG PRESS
PHILADELPHIA, PENN.

HEINEMANN EDUCATIONAL BOOKS, LTD.
48 CHARLES ST.
LONDON, W1X 8AH
ENGLAND

WILLIAM HEINEMANN, LTD.
15-16 QUEENS ST.
MAYFAIR, W1X 8BE
LONDON
ENGLAND

W. S. HEINMAN
1966 BROADWAY
NEW YORK, N. Y. 10023

HEINTZMAN AND COMPANY, LTD.
25 SCARSDALE RD.
DON MILLS
ONTARIO
CANADA

F. W. HELMICK
CINCINNATI, OHIO

HENDERSON AND SPALDING
LONDON
ENGLAND

G. HENLE MUSIKVERLAG
(BRODT MUSIC CO., MAGNAMUSIC-BATON)

HERITAGE MUSIC PUBLISHING COMPANY, INC.
(ASHLEY PUBLICATIONS, INC.)

J. HERZ
BUDAPEST
HUNGARY

HER MAJESTY'S STATIONERY OFFICE
LONDON
ENGLAND

HEUGEL ET CIE.
(THEODORE PRESSER COMPANY)

A. H. HEUSSER
PATERSON, N. J.

J. HEYWOOD
MANCHESTER
ENGLAND

HEYWOOD AND SON
MANCHESTER
ENGLAND

HIGHLAND MUSIC CO.
1011 NORTH HIGHLAND AVE.
HOLLYWOOD, CALIF. 90028

HIMA EDITION
LAUSANNE
SWITZERLAND

HINRICHSEN EDITION, LTD.
(C. F. PETERS CORP.)

HODDER AND STOUGHTON, LTD.
ST. PAUL'S HOUSE
8-12 WARWICK LANE
LONDON, E.C. 4
ENGLAND

P. HODGSON
LONDON
ENGLAND

W. HODSOLL AND E. RILEY
LONDON
ENGLAND

FRIEDRICH HOFMEISTER MUSIKVERLAG
(ASSOCIATED MUSIC PUBLISHERS, INC.)

THE HOLLAND PRESS
LONDON
ENGLAND

HOLT, HENRY, AND COMPANY
NEW YORK, N. Y.

HOLT, RINEHART AND WINSTON, INC.
383 MADISON AVE.
NEW YORK, N. Y. 10017

HOME AND VAN THAL
LONDON
ENGLAND

C. W. HOMEYER AND CO., INC.
(CARL FISCHER, INC.)

HOPE AND COMPANY
LONDON
ENGLAND

HOPE PUBLISHING COMPANY
380 S. MAIN PLACE
CAROL STREAM, ILL. 60187

CECIL HOPKINSON
LONDON
ENGLAND

HOUGHTON MIFFLIN COMPANY
2 PARK ST.
BOSTON, MASS. 02107

G. E. HOWARD
WASHINGTON, D. C.

A. J. HOWE
NEW YORK, N. Y.

B. W. HUEBSCH
NEW YORK, N. Y.

HUG, GEBRUDER, AND COMPANY
(C. F. PETERS CORP.)

BRUCE HUMPHRIES
68 BEACON ST.
SOMMERVILLE, MASS. 02143

R. HUNTER
LONDON
ENGLAND

F. J. HUNTINGTON
NEW YORK, N. Y.

HUNTINGTON AND SAVAGE
NEW YORK, N. Y.

HUTCHINGS AND CROWSLEY
LONDON
ENGLAND

HUTCHINSON AND COMPANY, LTD.
LONDON
ENGLAND

HYPERION PRESS
WESTPORT, CONN.

IMPERO-VERLAG
(THEODORE PRESSER COMPANY)

INDIANA UNIVERSITY PRESS
TENTH AND MORTON STREETS
BLOOMINGTON, IND. 47401

INDIANA UNIVERSITY SCHOOL OF MUSIC
BLOOMINGTON, IND. 47401

INDIANA UNIVERSITY BOOKSTORE
INDIANA MEMORIAL UNION
BLOOMINGTON, IND. 47401

INNER LONDON EDUCATIONAL AUTHORITY
LONDON
ENGLAND

INSTITUTE OF MEDIAEVAL MUSIC, LTD.
BROOKLYN, N. Y.

INSTITUTE OF MUSICAL INSTRUMENT
TECHNOLOGY
LONDON
ENGLAND

INSTITUTION FOR THE BLIND
PHILADELPHIA, PENN.

INSTITUTO ESPAÑOL DE MUSICOLOGIA
DEL C. S. I. C.
BARCELONA
SPAIN

INSTRUCTOR'S PUBLICATIONS
VAN NUYS, CALIF.

THE INSTRUMENTALIST
1418 LAKE ST.
EVANSTON, ILL. 60204

INTERNATIONAL EXHIBITION OF 1862
LONDON
ENGLAND

INTERNATIONAL LIBRARY OF PIANO MUSIC
(UNIVERSITY SOCIETY, INC.)

INTERNATIONAL MUSIC COMPANY
511 FIFTH AVENUE
NEW YORK, N. Y. 10017

IONE PRESS, INC.
(E. C. SCHIRMER MUSIC CO.)

ISBISTER AND COMPANY, LTD.
LONDON
ENGLAND

ISRAEL MUSIC INSTITUTE
(BOOSEY AND HAWKES)

JANKO CONSERVATORY OF MUSIC
NEW YORK, N. Y.

JANSEN, MCCLURG AND COMPANY
CHICAGO, ILL.

JAY-ROGER MUSIC COMPANY
NORTH BERGEN, N. J.

JAZZ MUSIC BOOKS
LONDON
ENGLAND

JENKINS, LTD.
LONDON
ENGLAND

THE GEORGE B. JENNINGS COMPANY
CINCINNATI, OHIO

JERRY JOHNSON, INC.
R.D. 1
LEBANON, N. J. 08833

W. S. JOHNSON AND COMPANY
LONDON
ENGLAND

MARSHALL JONES CO.
FRANCESTOWN, N. H. 03043

JOURNAL OF THE SOCIETY OF ARTS
LONDON
ENGLAND

C. F. KAHNT, NACHFOLGER
LEIPZIG
E. GERMANY

EDWIN F. KALMUS
P. O. BOX 1007
OPA-LOCKA, FLA. 33054

AARON KARLIN
BROOKLYN, N. Y.

J. B. KEDDINGTON
SALT LAKE CITY, UTAH

LUBOV KEEFER
BALTIMORE, MD.

C. H. KELLEY
LONDON
ENGLAND

KENYON PUBLICATIONS
17 WEST 60TH STREET
NEW YORK, N. Y. 10023

KEYBOARD PUBLICATIONS, INC.
1346 CHAPEL STREET
NEW HAVEN, CONN. 06511

KIMBALL PRESS
FAIR LAWN, N. J.

KING AND JARRETT, LTD.
LONDON
ENGLAND

KING MUSIC PUBLISHING CORP.
351 WEST 52ND ST.
NEW YORK, N. Y. 10019

KENNETH P. KIRKWOOD
KARACHI
PAKISTAN

RENE KISTER
GENEVA
SWITZERLAND

NEIL A. KJOS MUSIC COMPANY
525 BUSSE HIGHWAY
PARK RIDGE, ILL. 60068

KLAVARSKRIBO
BENEDENRIJWEG 355
SLIKKERVEER
HOLLAND

J. KNOLLER
NEW YORK, N. Y.

PUBLISHERS INDEX

ALFRED A. KNOPF, INC.
201 EAST 50TH ST.
NEW YORK, N. Y. 10022

W. KNOWLES
NEW YORK, N. Y.

FRITS A. M. KNUF
HILVERSUM
THE NETHERLANDS

WILLIAM KOHLING AND COMPANY
MILWAUKEE, WIS.

MAX KOLANDER MUSIC HOUSE
SAN FRANCISCO, CALIF.

AUGUST F. KOLLMANN
LONDON
ENGLAND

KOSCIUSZKO FOUNDATION
NEW YORK, N. Y.

KRANZ MUSIC COMPANY
BALTIMORE, MD.

J. M. KRONHEIM AND COMPANY
LONDON
ENGLAND

KULTURA
(BOOSEY AND HAWKES)

KUSTANNUSOSAKEY-HITO OTAVA
HELSINKI
FINLAND

S. LANDI
FLORENCE
ITALY

JOHN LANE, LTD.
LONDON
ENGLAND

J. H. LARWAY
LONDON
ENGLAND

LATONA SCHOOL OF POPULAR MUSIC
CHICAGO, ILL.

LAWSON-GOULD MUSIC PUBLISHERS, INC.
(G. SCHIRMER, INC.)

THE LEABARJAN MANUFACTURING COMPANY
HAMILTON, OHIO

ALPHONSE LEDUC
(M. BARON CO., BRODT MUSIC CO., THEODORE
PRESSER COMPANY, SOUTHERN MUSIC CO.)

LEE AND WALKER
PHILADELPHIA, PENN.

A. LENGNICK AND COMPANY, LTD.
(FREDERICK HARRIS MUSIC CO.)

HAL LEONARD PUBLISHING CO.
64 EAST 2ND STREET
WINONA, MINN. 55987

S. M. LERNER PUBLICATIONS
7560 HOLLYWOOD BLVD.
WEST HOLLYWOOD, CALIF. 90046

LESTER BOOK AND STATIONERY COMPANY
ATLANTA, GA.

CLARENCE E. LE MASSENA
NEW YORK, N. Y.

LIBBY AND SHERWOOD PRINTING COMPANY
CHICAGO, ILL.

LIBRARY OF CONGRESS
WASHINGTON, D.C. 20540

LILLENAS PUBLISHING COMPANY
P. O. BOX 527
KANSAS CITY, MO.

LINDEN PRESS
MONTREAT, N. C.

J. B. LIPPINCOTT COMPANY
EAST WASHINGTON SQUARE
PHILADELPHIA, PA. 19105

LITTLE, BROWN AND CO., INC
34 BEACON ST.
BOSTON, MASS. 02106

LIVERIGHT PUBLISHING CORP.
386 PARK AVE. S.
NEW YORK, N. Y. 10016

LIVERPOOL PUBLIC LIBRARIES
LIVERPOOL
ENGLAND

ROBINSON LOCKE
TOLEDO, OHIO

LO-KNO-PLA
P. O. BOX 6767
CORPUS CHRISTI, TEXAS 78411

LULU G. LOMAS
OAK PARK, ILL.

LONDON BOARD OF EDUCATION
LONDON
ENGLAND

LONDON COUNTY COUNCIL
LONDON
ENGLAND

LONGMAN AND BRODERIP
LONDON
ENGLAND

LONGMAN, HURST, REES, ORME AND BROWN
LONDON
ENGLAND

LONGMAN, LUKEY AND COMPANY
LONDON
ENGLAND

LONGMANS, GREEN AND COMPANY, LTD.
LONDON
ENGLAND

LOOKER-ON PUBLISHING COMPANY
NEW YORK, N. Y.

LORENZ PUBLISHING COMPANY
501 EAST 3RD STREET
DAYTON, OHIO 45401

J. LORING
BOSTON, MASS.

LOUISIANA STATE UNIVERSITY PRESS
HILL MEMORIAL BLDG.
LOUISIANA STATE UNIVERSITY
BATON ROUGE, LA. 70803

LOUISIANA STATE UNIVERSITY PRESS
BATON ROUGE, LA.

S. LOW, MARSTON AND COMPANY, LTD.
LONDON
ENGLAND

LUCKHARDT AND BELDER
NEW YORK, N. Y.

LUDWIG INDUSTRIES
1728 N. DAMEN AVE.
CHICAGO, ILL. 60647

LYNNE PUBLICATIONS
MEDINA, OHIO

LYON AND HEALY MUSIC COMPANY
243 S. WABASH AVE.
CHICAGO, ILL. 60604

T. MACCOUN
CHICAGO, ILL.

MACDONALD AND CO., LTD.
2 PORTMAN ST.
LONDON, E.C. 1
ENGLAND

ROBERT MACLEHOSE AND COMPANY
GLASGOW
SCOTLAND

WILLIAM MACLELLAN
GLASGOW
SCOTLAND

THE MACMILLAN COMPANY
866 THIRD AVE.
NEW YORK, N. Y. 10022

MAGNAMUSIC-BATON
10370 PAGE INDUSTRIAL BLVD.
ST. LOUIS, MO. 63132

MAGNAMUSIC DISTRIBUTORS, INC.
SHARON, CONN. 06069

J. MAHER
CHICAGO, ILL.

THE MAIN STREET PUBLISHING COMPANY
WAYNE, MICH.

G. L. MAITLAND
PHILADELPHIA, PENN.

MANITOBA DEPARTMENT OF EDUCATION
WINNIPEG
CANADA

MAR DE MAR MUSIC COMPANY
WINONA, MINN.

EDWARD B. MARKS MUSIC CORP.
(BELWIN-MILLS)

MARSDEN AND COMPANY
NEW YORK, N. Y.

H. T. MARTIN
BEAVER FALLS, PENN.

M. MARTIN
LONDON
ENGLAND

N. V. MARTINUS NYHOFF'S BOEKHANDEL
EN UITGEVERSMAATSCHAPPIG
LANGE VOORHOUT 9-11
BOX 269
THE HAGUE
NETHERLANDS

HENRY LOWELL MASON
CAMBRIDGEPORT, MASS.

MASON AND HAMLIN ORGAN AND PIANO
COMPANY
(AEOLIAN CORP.)

MASON BROTHERS
NEW YORK, N. Y.

MASSACHUSETTS INSTITUTE OF TECHNOLOGY
PRESS
28 CARLTON ST.
CAMBRIDGE, MASS 02142

MCA MUSIC
(BELWIN-MILLS)

ROBERT M. MCBRIDE AND COMPANY
NEW YORK, N. Y.

RICHARD MCCLANAHAN
CLEVELAND, OHIO

MCCLURE PRINTING CO. INC.
BOX 936
VERONA, VA. 24482

A. C. MCCLURG
CHICAGO, ILL.

MCCLURG AND COMPANY
CHICAGO, ILL.

MCGRAW-HILL BOOK CO.
1221 AVE. OF THE AMERICAS
NEW YORK, N. Y. 10020

JOHN MCTAMMANY
NEW YORK, N. Y.

MEL-O-DEE MUSIC COMPANY
NEW YORK, N. Y.

MENTOR ASSOCIATES
NEW YORK, N. Y.

MERLIN PRESS, INC.
NEW YORK, N. Y.

MERLIN PRESS, LTD.
11 FITZROY SQUARE
LONDON, W.1
ENGLAND

METHUEN AND CO. LTD.
(HARPER AND ROW PUBLISHERS, INC.)

METHUEN-SIMPSON, LTD.
EDINBURGH
SCOTLAND

METROPOLITAN MUSEUM OF ART
5TH AVE. AND 82ND ST.
NEW YORK, N. Y. 10028

M-F COMPANY
BOX 351
EVANSTON, ILL. 60204

N. E. MICHEL
PICO RIVERA, CALIF.

MICHIGAN STATE UNIVERSITY PRESS
MANLY MILES BLDG.
1405 S. HARRISON RD.
EAST LANSING, MICH. 48823

MIDDLEBURG PRESS
MIDDLEBURG, VA.

CHARLES S. MIDDLEMISS
CROWBRIDGE
SUSSEX
ENGLAND

H. MILES
LONDON
ENGLAND

MILLS MUSIC, INC.
(BELWIN-MILLS)

MINERVA PUBLISHING COMPANY
LONDON
ENGLAND

MINNESOTA MUSIC TEACHERS ASSOCIATION
MINNEAPOLIS, MINN.

THE MITRE PRESS
(FUDGE AND CO. LTD.)
52 LINCOLNS INN FIELDS
LONDON, W.C. 2
ENGLAND

THE MODERN LIBRARY
NEW YORK, N. Y.

MOFFAT, YARD AND COMPANY
NEW YORK, N. Y.

MOONCREST, LTD.
37 SOHO SQ.
LONDON W1
ENGLAND

A. K. MOORE
TROY, N. Y.

M. B. MOORE
LOS ANGELES, CALIF.

MOORE PUBLISHING CO.
BOX 3143
W. DURHAM STATION
DURHAM, N. C . 27705

MORDEN SCHOOL OF MUSIC
LONDON
ENGLAND

MORGAN AND MORGAN, INC.
400 WARBURTON AVE.
HASTINGS-ON-HUDSON, N. Y. 10706

THE MORSE ART COMPANY
QUINCY, ILL.

ISAAC H. R. MOTT
LONDON
ENGLAND

MOYER AND SCHLICH
LOUISVILLE, KY.

FREDERICK MULLER, LTD.
LUDGATE HOUSE
110 FLEET ST.
LONDON, EC4 2AP
ENGLAND

H. P. MUNROE
CAMBRIDGE, MASS.

WILLIAM MURDOCH COMPANY
LONDON
ENGLAND

MUSEUM PRESS, LTD.
39 PARKER ST.
LONDON, W.C. 2
ENGLAND

MUSIC CENTER FOR THE HAND
INCAPACITATED
DENVER, COLO.

MUSIC CORPORATION OF AMERICA, INC.
NEW YORK, N. Y.

MUSIC EDUCATION LEAGUE, INC.
NEW YORK, N. Y.

MUSIC EDUCATORS NATIONAL CONFERENCE
8150 LEESBURG PIKE
VIENNA, VA. 22180

MUSIC MAGAZINE PUBLISHING COMPANY
CHICAGO, ILL.

MUSIC PUBLISHERS HOLDING CORP.
1250 AVE. OF THE AMERICAS
NEW YORK, N. Y.

MUSIC SALES CORPORATION
33 WEST 60TH STREET
NEW YORK, N. Y. 10023

MUSIC SIGHTREADING PUBLICATIONS
NEW YORK, N. Y.

MUSIC SUPPLY COMPANY
SAN FRANCISCO, CALIF.

MUSIC TEACHERS NATIONAL ASSN.
1831 CAREW TOWER
CINCINNATI, OHIO 45202

MUSIC TIMES COMPANY
CHICAGO, ILL.

MUSIC TRADE REVIEW
NEW YORK, N. Y.

MUSIC TREASURE PUBLICATIONS
P. O. BOX 127
HIGHBRIDGE STATION
BRONX, N. Y. 10452

MUSICA OBSCURA
410 S. MICHIGAN AVENUE
SUITE 730
CHICAGO, ILL. 60605

MUSICAL BOUQUET OFFICE
LONDON
ENGLAND

MUSICAL INSTRUMENT WORKERS
CHICAGO, ILL.

MUSICAL MAGAZINE PUBLISHING COMPANY
CHICAGO, ILL.

MUSICAL OPINION AND MUSIC TRADE REVIEW
LONDON
ENGLAND

MUSICAL SCOPE PUBLISHERS
BOX 125
AUDUBON STATION
NEW YORK, N. Y. 10032

MUSICIANS ADVISORY SERVICE, INC.
NEW YORK, N. Y.

MUSICORD PUBLICATIONS, INC.
P. O. 87
STATEN ISLAND, N. Y. 10314

MUSIQUEST PUBLISHING COMPANY
EUGENE, ORE.

BARROWS MUSSEY
NEW YORK, N. Y.

MYKLAS PRESS
BOX 929
BOULDER, COLO. 80302

W. NAPIER
LONDON
ENGLAND

NAPLES PRESS
BIRMINGHAM
ENGLAND

NATIONAL BUREAU FOR THE ADVANCEMENT
OF MUSIC
NEW YORK, N. Y.

NATIONAL BUREAU OF ENGRAVING
PHILADELPHIA, PENN.

NATIONAL GUILD OF PIANO TEACHERS
P.O. BOX 1807
AUSTIN, TEXAS 78767

NATIONAL KEYBOARD ARTS ASSOCIATES
UNIVERSITY PARK
PRINCETON, N. J. 05840

NATIONAL LIBRARY PRESS
NEW YORK, N. Y.

NATIONAL MUSEUM OF HISTORY AND
TECHNOLOGY
WASHINGTON, D. C.

NATIONAL PIANO FOUNDATION
CHICAGO, ILL.

NATIONAL PIANO MANUFACTURERS ASSN.
OF AMERICA
435 NORTH MICHIGAN AVE.
CHICAGO, ILL. 60611

THE NEILL COMPANY
CHICAGO, ILL.

THOMAS NELSON, INC.
407 SEVENTH AVE., S.
NASHVILLE, TENN. 37203

NELSON-HALL COMPANY
325 W. JACKSON BLVD.
CHICAGO, ILL. 60606

G. F. NESBITT AND COMPANY
NEW YORK, N. Y.

B. NETZORG
DETROIT, MICH.

NEWCOMER SOCIETY IN NORTH AMERICA
NEW YORK, N. Y.

NEW ENGLAND CONSERVATORY
(FRANK DISTRIBUTING CORP.)

ELIZABETH NEWMAN
NEW YORK, N. Y.

NEWMAN AND IVISON
NEW YORK, N. Y.

NEW ERA PRINTING COMPANY
DEEP RIVER, CONN.

NEW MUSIC REVIEW
BOSTON, MASS.

NEW SCHOOL FOR MUSIC STUDY
PRINCETON, N. J.

NEW WORLD MUSIC CORPORATION
(WARNER BROS. PUBLISHERS)

NEW YORK PUBLIC LIBRARY
MUSIC PUBLICATIONS
(C. F. PETERS CORP.)

NEW YORK UNIVERSITY PRESS
WASHINGTON SQUARE
NEW YORK, N. Y. 10003

MARTINUS NIJHOFF
THE HAGUE
NETHERLANDS

NILES BRYANT SCHOOL OF PIANO TUNING
WASHINGTON, D. C.

NORSK MUSIKFORLAG A/S
KARL JOHANS GATE 39
P. O. BOX 1499 VIKA
OSLO
NORWAY

NORTHEASTERN MUSIC COMPANY
(BOURNE COMPANY)

W. W. NORTON AND CO., INC.
55 FIFTH AVE.
NEW YORK, N. Y. 10003

NOVELLO, EWER AND COMPANY
LONDON
ENGLAND

NOVELLO AND COMPANY, LTD.
(BIG BELLS)

J. A. NOVELLO
LONDON
ENGLAND

J. F. NUNNS
NEW YORK, N. Y.

OAK PUBLICATIONS
(MUSIC SALES CORP.)

B. O'CONNOR
MANCHESTER
ENGLAND

OCTOBER HOUSE, INC.
160 AVENUE OF THE AMERICAS
NEW YORK, N. Y. 10013

ODOWAN PUBLISHING COMPANY
CEDAR RAPIDS, IOWA

OHIO PRINTING COMPANY
DAYTON, OHIO

OKLAHOMA STATE UNIVERSITY
STILLWATER, OKLA. 74074

OLD PARSONAGE PRESS
ALTHAM
LANCASHIRE
ENGLAND

C. AND J. OLLIER
LONDON
ENGLAND

OLYMPIAN PUBLISHING COMPANY
NASHVILLE, TENN.

OMEGA MUSIC EDITION
NEW YORK, N. Y.

ONGAKU NO TOMO SHA
(THEODORE PRESSER COMPANY)

ORANGE CHRONICLE PRESS
ORANGE, N. J.

OREGON MUSIC TEACHERS ASSOCIATION
PORTLAND, ORE.

OREGON STATE SYSTEM OF HIGHER EDUCATION
MONMOUTH, ORE.

ORTMAN, HART AND COMPANY
LONDON
ENGLAND

JAMES G. OSBOURNE
PHILADELPHIA, PENN.

OSGOOD, MCILVAINE AND COMPANY
LONDON
ENGLAND

HENRY OSTROVSKY
LONDON
ENGLAND

OSTROVSKY MUSICIANS' HAND DEVELOPMENT
COMPANY
LONDON
ENGLAND

WILLIAM O'TOOLE
NEW YORK, N. Y.

OXFORD UNIVERSITY PRESS
200 MADISON AVENUE
NEW YORK, N. Y. 10016

PACIFIC SCHOOL OF MUSIC
FRESNO, CALIF.

PADEREWSKI FOUNDATION
NEW YORK. N. Y.

C. L. PAGE AND COMPANY
BOSTON, MASS.

PAGEANT PRESS, INC.
NEW YORK, N. Y.

W. H. PALING AND COMPANY, LTD.
SYDNEY
AUSTRALIA

C. PALMER
LONDON
ENGLAND

H. R. PALMER
NEW YORK, N. Y.

PALMER AND CLAYTON
LONDON
ENGLAND

PALMER AND HAYWARD
LONDON
ENGLAND

PAN AMERICAN UNION
(PEER SOUTHERN ORGANIZATION)

PANTHEON BOOKS, INC.
(RANDOM HOUSE, INC.)

HANS B. PARKINSON
LOS ANGELES, CALIF.

MAX PARRISH AND COMPANY, LTD.
LONDON
ENGLAND

JOSEPH PATELSON MUSIC HOUSE
160 WEST 56TH ST.
NEW YORK, N. Y. 10019

PATERSON SONS AND COMPANY
GLASGOW
SCOTLAND

PAUL, KEGAN, TRENCH, TRUBNER AND
COMPANY
LONDON
ENGLAND

PAULL-PIONEER MUSIC CORPORATION
NEW YORK, N. Y.

E. T. PAULL MUSIC COMPANY
NEW YORK, N. Y.

PEABODY CONSERVATORY
1 E. MT VERNON PLACE
BALTIMORE, MD. 21202

C. A. PEARSON
LONDON
ENGLAND

PEER INTERNATIONAL CORPORATION
(PEER SOUTHERN ORGANIZATION)

PUBLISHERS INDEX

PEER SOUTHERN ORGANIZATION
1740 BROADWAY
NEW YORK, N. Y. 10019

L. O. PELTIER
SOMERVILLE, MASS.

PENGUIN BOOKS, INC.
7110 AMBASSADOR RD.
BALTIMORE, MD. 21207

PEPAMAR MUSIC CORPORATION
(WARNER BROS. PUBLISHERS)

J. W. PEPPER AND SON, INC.
VALLEY FORGE CORPORATE CENTER
VALLEY FORGE, PENN. 19482

PERELIN PUBLISHERS
MARSHALL, CALIF.

C. F. PETERS CORP.
373 PARK AVENUE SOUTH
NEW YORK, N. Y. 10016

W. C. PETERS AND SONS
CINCINNATI, OHIO

W. M. PETERS
NEW YORK, N. Y.

C. U. PHILLIPS
LONDON
ENGLAND

PHILLIPS AND PAGE
LONDON
ENGLAND

WENTWORTH PHILLIPSON
LONDON
ENGLAND

PHILOSOPHICAL LIBRARY, INC.
15 EAST 40TH ST.
NEW YORK, N. Y. 10016

PHOENIX HOUSE, LTD.
LONDON
ENGLAND

PIANOHAUS WILHELM RUECH
NUERNBERG
GERMANY

PIANOPHONE TUITION, LTD.
LONDON
ENGLAND

PIANO PLAYHOUSE
WILMINGTON, DEL.

B. PIERCE
LONG BEACH, CALIF.

PINE HILL PRESS
FREEMAN, S. D.

PITMAN, HART AND COMPANY, LTD.
LONDON
ENGLAND

I. PITMAN AND SONS, LTD.
LONDON
ENGLAND

PITMAN PUBLISHING CORP.
6 EAST 43RD ST.
NEW YORK, N. Y. 10017

THE PLAYER-PIANO
NEW YORK, N. Y.

J. PLAYFORD
LONDON
ENGLAND

POINTER PUBLICATIONS
(HAL LEONARD PUBLISHING CO.)

POLISH LIBRARY
GLASGOW
SCOTLAND

POLISH RESEARCH AND INFORMATION
SERVICE
NEW YORK, N. Y.

POLISH SCIENTIFIC PUBLISHERS
WARSAW
POLAND

W. A. POND AND COMPANY
NEW YORK, N. Y.

C. P. POTTER
NORWICH, CONN.

J. POWER
LONDON
ENGLAND

FREDERICK A. PRAEGER
NEW YORK, N. Y.

PRAEGER PUBLISHERS, INC.
111 FOURTH AVE.
NEW YORK, N. Y. 10003

PRENTICE-HALL, INC.
ENGLEWOOD CLIFFS, N. J. 07632

THEODORE PRESSER COMPANY
PRESSER PLACE
BRYN MAWR, PENN. 19010

PRESTON-STEVENS MUSIC CO., LTD.
LANSDOWNE HOUSE
LANSDOWNE RD.
LONDON W11
ENGLAND

PRESTO PUBLISHING COMPANY
CHICAGO, ILL.

PRINCETON UNIVERSITY PRESS
PRINCETON, N. J. 08540

PRO-ART PUBLICATIONS, INC.
469 UNION AVENUE
WESTBURY, N. Y. 11590

PROGRESS MUSIC PUBLICATIONS
2109 BROADWAY
NEW YORK, N. Y. 10023

KEITH PROWSE MUSIC PUBLISHING CO.
(AFFILIATED MUSIC PUBLISHERS, LTD.)

PRUETT PUBLISHING COMPANY
P.O. BOX 1560
BOULDER, COLO. 80302

PUBLISHING SERVS. PARTNERSHIP
QUEEN ANN'S RD.
GREAT YARMOUTH
NORFOLK
ENGLAND

PUGET MUSIC PUBLICATIONS, INC.
P.O. BOX 471
KENMORE, WASH. 98020

Z. T. PURDAY
LONDON
ENGLAND

R. PURDIE
EDINBURGH
SCOTLAND

PURE MUSIC SOCIETY
LONDON
ENGLAND

G. P. PUTNAM'S SONS
200 MADISON AVE.
NEW YORK, N. Y. 10016

QUALITY PRESS, LTD.
LONDON
ENGLAND

MARCUS LUCIUS QUINN CONSERVATORY
OF MUSIC
CHICAGO, ILL.

QUINTE RECORDING COMPANY
WEST HOLLYWOOD, CALIF.

W. RANDALL AND I. ABELL
LONDON
ENGLAND

RAND MCNALLY AND CO.
BOX 7600
CHICAGO, ILL. 60680

RANDOM HOUSE, INC.
201 EAST 50TH ST.
NEW YORK, N. Y. 10022

THE READERS PRESS
NEW YORK, N. Y.

REBAY AND ROBITSCHEK
VIENNA
AUSTRIA

G. P. REED
BOSTON, MASS.

WILLIAM REEVES, LTD.
(BRODT MUSIC CO.)

H. REGNERY COMPANY
114 W. ILLINOIS
CHICAGO, ILL. 60610

REL. TR. SOC.
LONDON
ENGLAND

REMICK
(WARNER BROS. PUBLISHERS)

RENAUD-PHONE PIANO METHOD, INC.
NEW YORK, N. Y.

RESEARCH MICROFILM PUBLISHERS
SUPERIOR, WIS.

REVIEW AND HERALD PUBLISHING ASSOC.
TAKOMA PARK
WASHINGTON, D. C. 20012

G. RICHARDS, LTD.
LONDON
ENGLAND

NATHAN RICHARDSON
BOSTON, MASS.

THE RICHARDS PRESS, LTD.
LONDON
ENGLAND

RICH AND COWAN
LONDON
ENGLAND

RIGBY, LTD.
(TRI-OCEANA BOOKS)

F. RILEY
NEW YORK, N. Y.

W. RITCHIE-LESCARD
LONDON
ENGLAND

E. A. ROBBINS
BOSTON, MASS.

ROBBINS MUSIC CORP.
(THE BIG THREE MUSIC CORPORATION)

LEE ROBERTS MUSIC PUBLICATIONS, INC.
P. O. BOX 225
KATONAH, N. Y. 10536

ROBERTS PRESS
GZIRA
EAST MALTA

ROBYN TEACHING SERVICE
CHICAGO, ILL.

ROCHESTER MUSIC PUBLISHERS, INC.
358 ALDRICH ROAD
FAIRPORT, N. Y. 14450

ROCKLIFF PUBLISHING CORPORATION
LONDON
ENGLAND

E. S. ROEDER
ALLENTOWN, PENN.

W. ROLFING
MILWAUKEE, WIS.

GEORGE RONALD PUBLISHER
46 HIGH ST.
KIDLINGTON
OXFORD OX5 2DN
ENGLAND

MORIZ ROSENTHAL
ST. LOUIS, MO.

ROSE EDUCATION PUBLISHERS
NEWARK, N. J.

H. A. ROST
NEW YORK, N. Y.

G. ROUTLEDGE AND SONS, LTD.
LONDON
ENGLAND

ROUTLEDGE AND KEGAN PAUL, LTD.
9 PARK ST.
BOSTON, MASS. 02108

ROY PUBLISHERS, INC.
30 EAST 74TH ST.
NEW YORK, N. Y. 10021

ROYAL HARMONIC INSTITUTION
LONDON
ENGLAND

THE ROYCROFTERS
EAST AURORA, N. Y.

RUBANK, INC.
16215 N. W. 15TH AVENUE
MIAMI, FLA. 33169

RUSSELL AND TOLMAN
BOSTON, MASS.

RUTGERS UNIVERSITY PRESS
30 COLLEGE AVE.
NEW BRUNSWICK, N. J. 08901

ST. MARTIN'S PRESS, INC.
175 FIFTH AVE.
NEW YORK, N. Y. 10010

SAMPSON, LOW, MARSTON, SEARLE,
AND RIVINGTON
LONDON
ENGLAND

SANDS AND COMPANY
LONDON
ENGLAND

SANTA MARIA TIMES
SANTA MARIA, CALIF.

SAXTON AND CHALONER
SHEFFIELD
ENGLAND

SCARECROW PRESS, INC.
52 LIBERTY ST.
BOX 656
METUCHEN, N. J. 08840

H. B. SCHAAD
NEW YORK, N. Y.

E. O. SCHAAF
NEW YORK, N. Y.

SCHAUM PUBLICATIONS, INC.
2018 E. NORTH AVE.
MILWAUKEE, WIS. 53202

E. C. SCHIRMER MUSIC CO.
112 SOUTH STREET
BOSTON, MASS. 02111

G. SCHIRMER, INC.
866 THIRD AVE.
NEW YORK, N.Y. 10022

A. P. SCHMIDT COMPANY
(SUMMY-BIRCHARD)

SCHMITT, HALL AND MCCREARY COMPANY
110 NORTH 5TH STREET
MINNEAPOLIS, MINN. 55403

HANS SCHNEIDER
TUTZING
GERMANY

SCHOLARLY PRESS
ST. CLAIR SHORES, MICH.

SCHOTT AND CO., LTD.
(BELWIN-MILLS)

D. L. SCHROEDER PUBLICATIONS, INC.
(ASHLEY PUBLICATIONS, INC.)

SCHROEDER AND GUNTHER, INC.
(ASSOCIATED MUSIC PUBLISHERS, INC.)

EDWARD SCHUBERTH AND COMPANY
(ASHLEY PUBLICATIONS, INC.)

J. SCHUBERTH AND COMPANY
LEIPZIG
E. GERMANY

HENRY SCHUMANN
NEW YORK, N. Y.

SCHUMANN MEMORIAL FOUNDATION
ROCHESTER, N. Y.

JOHN A. SCONCIA
BALTIMORE, MD.

WALTER SCOTT, LTD.
LONDON
ENGLAND

SCREEN GEMS — COLUMBIA PUBLICATIONS
6744 N.E. 4TH AVE.
MIAMI, FLA. 33138

CHARLES SCRIBNER'S SONS
597 FIFTH AVENUE
NEW YORK, N. Y. 10017

SECRETARIAT--5TH F. CHOPIN
INTERNATIONAL COMPETITION
WARSAW
POLAND

SEELEY SERVICE AND CO., LTD.
196 SHAFTESBURY AVE.
LONDON WC2H 8JL
ENGLAND

SEESAW MUSIC CORPORATION
177 E. 87TH ST.
NEW YORK, N. Y. 10028

SEIFERT AND SMITH, PRINTERS
MACON, GA.

SENTINEL BOOK PUBLISHERS, INC.
17 EAST 22ND ST.
NEW YORK, N. Y. 10010

SENTINEL PRINTING COMPANY
FITCHBURG, MASS.

SHAPIRO, BERNSTEIN AND CO., INC.
17 WEST 60TH STREET
NEW YORK, N. Y. 10023

ARTHUR SHATTUCK
NEENAH, WIS.

J. P. SHAW
ROCHESTER, N. Y.

SHAWNEE PRESS, INC.
DELAWARE WATER GAP, PENN. 18327

FRANK H. SHEPARD
BETHEL, CONN.

SHERMAN CLAY AND COMPANY
SAN FRANCISCO, CALIF.

SHERWOOD MUSIC SCHOOL
1014 S. MICHIGAN AVE.
CHICAGO, ILL.

SHINN MUSIC AIDS
P.O. BOX 192
MEDFORD, ORE. 97501

SIGHT AND SOUND SYSTEMS, INC.
6055 W. FOND DU LAC AVE.
MILWAUKEE, WIS. 53218

SILVER BURDETT COMPANY
250 JAMES ST.
MORRISTOWN, N. J. 07960

SIMON AND SCHUSTER, INC.
630 FIFTH AVENUE
NEW YORK, N. Y. 10020

SIMPKIN, MARSHALL AND COMPANY
LONDON
ENGLAND

SISTERS OF MERCY CONVENT
NEW HAVEN, CONN.

SKEFFINGTON AND SONS, LTD.
LONDON
ENGLAND

T. SKILLERN
LONDON
ENGLAND

M. A. SKUTLEY
PHOENIX, ARIZ.

SMALL, MAYNARD AND COMPANY
BOSTON, MASS.

SMITH, ELDER AND COMPANY
LONDON
ENGLAND

P. SMITH
MAGNOLIA, MISS.

SMITH AND SALE, PRINTERS
PORTLAND, ORE.

SMITHSONIAN INSTITUTION PRESS
WASHINGTON, D.C. 20560

W. S. SONNENSCHEIN AND COMPANY
LONDON
ENGLAND

SOUTHERN MUSIC COMPANY
1100 BROADWAY
SAN ANTONIO, TEXAS 78215

SOUTHERN MUSIC PUBLISHING COMPANY, INC.
(PEER SOUTHERN ORGANIZATION)

ROBERT SPELLER AND SONS, PUBLISHERS, INC.
10 EAST 3RD ST.
NEW YORK, N. Y. 10010

BERNARD SPENCER
NEW YORK, N. Y.

SPRATT MUSIC PUBLISHERS
17 WEST 60TH STREET
NEW YORK, N. Y. 10023

SPRING BOOKS
(HAMLYN)

STANDARD PLAYER ACTION COMPANY
3465 BAYLISS AVE.
MEMPHIS, TENN. 38122

STANDARD PNEUMATIC ACTION COMPANY
NEW YORK, N. Y.

STANDARD PRINTING COMPANY
LOS ANGELES, CALIF.

JANE STANLEY
LONG BEACH, CALIF.

STAPLES PRESS
(CROSBY LOCKWOOD STAPLES)

STATE HISTORICAL SOCIETY OF WISCONSIN
THE SOCIETY PRESS
816 STATE ST.
MADISON, WIS. 53706

STATE UNIVERSITY COLLEGE
FREDONIA, N. Y.

STATE UNIVERSITY OF NEW YORK PRESS
99 WASHINGTON AVE.
ALBANY, N. Y. 12210

STATIONER'S HALL
LONDON
ENGLAND

GEORGE STECK AND COMPANY
(AEOLIAN CORP.)

STEIN AND DAY, PUBLISHERS
7 EAST 48TH ST.
NEW YORK, N. Y. 10017

STEINWAY AND SONS
STEINWAY PLACE
LONG ISLAND CITY, N.Y. 11105

STEREO REVIEW
P.O. BOX 1099
FLUSHING, N.Y. 11352

STERLING PUBLISHING COMPANY
419 PARK AVE. S.
NEW YORK, N. Y. 10016

A. M. STEVENS
FARGO, N. D.

DUNCAN STEVENSON AND COMPANY
EDINBURGH
SCOTLAND

STIPES PUBLISHING COMPANY
10-12 CHESTER STREET
CHAMPAIGN, ILL. 61820

FREDERICK A. STOKES COMPANY
NEW YORK, N. Y.

STRAHAN AND COMPANY, PUBLISHERS
LONDON
ENGLAND

J. STRANGEWAYS
LONDON
ENGLAND

S. W. STRAUB AND COMPANY
CHICAGO, ILL.

STROHBER PIANO COMPANY
CHICAGO, ILL.

STUDIO TREND PUBLISHERS
BROOKLYN, N. Y.

STUDIO VISTA PUBLISHERS
(ST. MARTIN'S PRESS)

SUMMY-BIRCHARD COMPANY
1834 RIDGE AVENUE
EVANSTON, ILL. 60204

THE SUNDIAL PRESS
NEW YORK, N. Y.

SUPERINTENDENT OF DOCUMENTS
U.S. GOVT. PRINTING OFFICE
WASHINGTON, D.C. 20402

J. SUTHERLAND
EDINBURGH
SCOTLAND

LUCILE B. SWENSON
SALT LAKE CITY, UTAH

SYRACUSE UNIVERSITY PRESS
BOX 8, UNIVERSITY STATION
SYRACUSE, N.Y. 13210

TAPLINGER PUBLISHING CO., INC.
200 PARK AVE. S.
NEW YORK, N. Y. 10003

TEACHERS COLLEGE PRESS
COLUMBIA UNIVERSITY
1234 AMSTERDAM AVE.
NEW YORK, N. Y. 10027

THE TECHNIPHONE COMPANY
NEW YORK, N. Y.

W. P. TEWKSBURY
BOSTON, MASS.

THACKER, SPINK AND COMPANY
CALCUTTA
INDIA

C. AND S. THOMPSON
LONDON
ENGLAND

C. W. THOMPSON AND COMPANY
BOSTON, MASS.

THOMPSON'S WAREHOUSE
LONDON
ENGLAND

ANNA M. TOMLINSON
BERWYN, ILL.

JOHN W. TRAVIS
TACOMA PARK, MD.

CHARLES F. TRETBAR
NEW YORK, N. Y.

TRIBUNE PRINTING COMPANY
BAY CITY, TEX.

TRINITY COLLEGE
LONDON
ENGLAND

TRI-OCEANA, INC.
62 TOWNSEND ST.
SAN FRANCISCO, CALIF. 94107

TRO SONGWAYS SERVICE, INC.
17 WEST 60TH STREET
NEW YORK, N. Y. 10023

N. TRUEBNER AND COMPANY
LONDON
ENGLAND

THE TUNELLA COMPANY
CHICAGO, ILL.

TUNERS SUPPLY COMPANY, INC.
NEW YORK, N. Y.

W. TURNBULL
GLASGOW
SCOTLAND

TUTTLE, MOREHOUSE AND TAYLOR
NEW HAVEN, CONN.

U.N.E.S.C.O.--DISTR. BY COLUMBIA
UNIVERSITY PRESS
PARIS
FRANCE

REX UNDERWOOD
EUGENE, ORE.

UNICORN PRESS
STUDIO 126
EL PASEO
SANTA BARBARA, CALIF. 93105

UNITED STATES PATENT OFFICE
WASHINGTON, D. C.

UNITED STATES SCHOOL OF MUSIC
NEW YORK, N. Y.

UNIVERSAL EDITION
(THEODORE PRESSER COMPANY)

UNIVERSE BOOKS, INC.
381 PARK AVE. S.
NEW YORK, N.Y. 10016

THE UNIVERSITY PRESS
BOSTON, MASS.

UNIVERSITY OF CALIFORNIA PRESS
2223 FULTON ST.
BERKELEY, CALIF. 94720

PUBLISHERS INDEX

UNIVERSITY OF CHICAGO PRESS
5801 ELLIS AVE.
CHICAGO, ILL. 60637

UNIVERSITY OF ILLINOIS PRESS
URBANA, ILL. 61801

UNIVERSITY OF MICHIGAN PRESS
ANN ARBOR, MICH. 48106

UNIVERSITY OF MINNESOTA PRESS
2037 UNIVERSITY AVE. S.E.
MINNEAPOLIS, MINN. 55455

UNIVERSITY OF MISSOURI
COLUMBIA, MO.

UNIVERSITY OF MISSOURI PRESS
107 SWALLOW HALL
COLUMBIA, MO. 65201

UNIVERSITY OF NORTH CAROLINA PRESS
BOX 2288
CHAPEL HILL, N.C. 27514

UNIVERSITY OF SOUTH CAROLINA PRESS
COLUMBIA, S.C. 29208

UNIVERSITY OF SOUTHERN CALIFORNIA PRESS
LOS ANGELES, CALIF. 90007

UNIVERSITY OF WASHINGTON PRESS
(GALAXY MUSIC CORP.)

UNIVERSITY PRESS OF KANSAS
366 WATSON LIBRARY
LAWRENCE, KAN. 66044

UNIVERSITY PRESS OF VIRGINIA
BOX 3608, UNIVERSITY STA.
CHARLOTTESVILLE, VA . 22903

THE UNIVERSITY SOCIETY, INC.
25 COTTAGE STREET
MIDLAND PARK, N. J. 07432

UNWIN BROS., LTD.
LONDON
ENGLAND

UNZ AND COMPANY
NEW YORK, N. Y.

VANGUARD PRESS
424 MADISON AVE.
NEW YORK, N.Y. 10017

ALBERT B. VANT
NEW YORK, N. Y.

PETER H. VAN DER WEYDE
NEW YORK, N. Y.

C. VAN NOORDEN
LONDON
ENGLAND

VANTAGE PRESS, INC.
516 WEST 34TH ST .
NEW YORK, N.Y. 10001

LEONARD VENDEN
COLLEGE PLACE, WASH.

VERLAG DAS MUSIKINSTRUMENT
FRANKFURT AM MAIN
GERMANY

VESTAL PRESS
NEW YORK, N. Y.

VICTORIA AND ALBERT MUSEUM
LONDON
ENGLAND

VIENNA HOUSE, INC.
342 MADISON AVE.
NEW YORK, N. Y. 10017

THE VIKING PRESS, INC.
625 MADISON AVE.
NEW YORK, N.Y. 10022

THE VINCENT MUSIC COMPANY, LTD.
LONDON
ENGLAND

A. K. VIRGIL
NEW YORK, N. Y.

MRS. A. M. VIRGIL
NEW YORK, N. Y.

VIRGIL PIANO CONSERVATORY,
PUBLICATION DEPARTMENT
NEW YORK, N. Y.

VIRGIL PIANO SCHOOL COMPANY
NEW YORK, N. Y.

VIRGIL PRACTICE CLAVIER COMPANY
LONDON
ENGLAND

VISUOLA CORPORATION
NEW YORK, N. Y.

A. VOLK, VERLAG
COLOGNE
GERMANY

VOLKWEIN BROS.
117 SANDUSKY STREET
PITTSBURGH, PENN. 15212

WADSWORTH PUBLISHING CO., INC.
BELMONT, CALIF. 94002

CHARLES A. WAGNER
BELDING, MICH.

HENRY Z. WALCK, INC., PUBLISHERS
19 UNION SQUARE W.
NEW YORK, N.Y. 10003

WALSH, HOLMES AND COMPANY
LONDON
ENGLAND

I. WALSH
LONDON
ENGLAND

JOHN WANAMAKER
NEW YORK, N. Y.

WARD AND COMPANY
LONDON
ENGLAND

WARD AND DOWNEY
LONDON
ENGLAND

FREDERICK WARNE AND CO., INC.
101 FIFTH AVE.
NEW YORK, N.Y. 10003

WARNER BROTHERS PUBLISHERS
75 ROCKEFELLER PLAZA
NEW YORK, N.Y. 10019

WARNER-TAMERLANE PUBLISHING COMPANY
(WARNER BROS. PUBLISHERS)

WARREN AND PHILLIPS
LONDON
ENGLAND

WASHBURN AND THOMAS
CAMBRIDGE, MASS.

WASHINGTON STATE MUSIC TEACHERS
SEATTLE, WASH.

WATERLOO MUSIC COMPANY
(BRODT MUSIC CO.)

WATSON-GUPTILL PUBLICATIONS
1 ASTOR PLAZA
NEW YORK, N.Y. 10036

FRANKLIN WATTS, INC.
845 THIRD AVE.
NEW YORK, N.Y. 10022

WB MUSIC CORPORATION
(WARNER BROS. PUBLISHERS)

WEALE
LONDON
ENGLAND

F. H. WEBB
NEW YORK, N. Y.

WEBER PIANO COMPANY
(AEOLIAN CORP.)

A. WEEKES AND COMPANY, LTD.
(PUBLISHING SERVS. PARTNERSHIP)

WEILL-BRECHT-HARMS COMPANY, INC.
(WARNER BROS. PUBLISHERS)

JOSEF WEINBERGER
(BOOSEY AND HAWKES)

WEINTRAUB MUSIC COMPANY
(MUSIC SALES CORP.)

WELCKER
LONDON
ENGLAND

WELSH AND HAWES
LONDON
ENGLAND

WELTE ARTISTIC PLAYER-PIANO COMPANY
NEW YORK, N. Y.

WESTERN INTERNATIONAL MUSIC, INC.
2859 HOLT AVENUE
LOS ANGELES, CALIF. 90034

WHARFEDALE WIRELESS WORKS
BRADFORD
SOMERSET
ENGLAND

WHEATON COLLEGE
WHEATON, ILL.

B. B. WHITE
HUDDERSFIELD
YORKS
ENGLAND

WHITE, SMITH AND PERRY
BOSTON, MASS.

ROBERT WHITFORD PUBLICATIONS
DEPT. C
8277 N. E. SECOND AVE.
MIAMI, FLA. 33138

WIENER URTEXT EDITION
(THEODORE PRESSER COMPANY,
MAGNAMUSIC-BATON)

J. WILCOX
LONDON
ENGLAND

A. WILLIAMS
LONDON
ENGLAND

JEAN E. WILLIAMS
ST. LOUIS, MO.

JOSEPH WILLIAMS, LTD.
(GALAXY MUSIC CORP.)

WILLIAMS AND NORGATE
LONDON
ENGLAND

WILLIAMS ORGAN AND PIANO COMPANY
CHICAGO, ILL.

WILLIS MUSIC COMPANY
7380 INDUSTRIAL HIGHWAY
(P. O. BOX 433)
FLORENCE, KY. 41042

H. W. WILSON COMPANY
950 UNIVERSITY AVE.
BRONX, N.Y. 10452

WILLIAM WILSON
EDINBURGH
SCOTLAND

AUBREY WILLIS SCHOOL OF PIANO TUNING
ORLANDO, FLA.

WINDSOR PRESS
P. O. BOX 11957
ATLANTA, GA. 30305

WING AND SONS, INC.
NEW YORK, N. Y.

S. WINTER
NEW HAVEN, CONN.

WITHERBY AND COMPANY
LONDON
ENGLAND

WITMARK AND SONS
(WARNER BROS. PUBLISHERS)

B. F. WOOD
(BELWIN-MILLS)

WOODBURY MUSIC CORPORATION
P. O. BOX 447
WOODBURY, CONN. 06798

H. WORCH
WASHINGTON, D. C.

WORKSHOP MUSIC TEACHING PUBLICATIONS
HEWLITT, N. Y.

WORKS PROGRESS ADMINISTRATION--MUSIC
NEW YORK, N. Y.

WORK PROJECTS ADMINISTRATION--MUS.
NEW YORK, N. Y.

R. WORNUM
LONDON
ENGLAND

W. C. WRIGHT
AUGUSTA, GA.

WURLITZER COMPANY
1700 PLEASANT ST.
DEKALB, ILL. 60115

A. A. WYN, INC.
NEW YORK, N. Y.

YALE UNIVERSITY PRESS
149 YORK ST.
NEW HAVEN, CONN. 06520

YORKTOWN MUSIC PRESS
(MUSIC SALES CORP.)

THOMAS YOSELOFF, INC., PUBLISHERS
BOX 421
CRANBURY, N.J. 08512

MASTER CODE LIST

CODE IDENTIFICATION

AP   The Art of Performing
      AP1—General
      AP2—Miscellaneous
      AP3—Performance Practices
      AP4—Interpretation and Style
      AP5—Aesthetics
      AP6—Phrasing, Articulation
      AP7—Ornamentation
      AP8—Pedalling
      AP9—Demeanor and Poise
APP   Appendices
AS   Arizona State University Library
AT   The Art of Teaching
      AT1—General
      AT2—Miscellaneous
      AT3—Philosophy and Psychology
          of Teaching
      AT4—Methods or Systems of
          Instruction
      AT5—Child Approach
      AT6—Adult Approach
      AT7—Group Teaching
      AT8—Studio Organization and
          Equipment
      AT9—Student Recitals
      AT10—Testing and Evaluation
      AT11—Teacher Qualifications
      AT12—Master Classes
      AT13—Teacher-Student-Parent
          Interrelationships
      AT14—Selecting Instructional
          Materials
B   Book
BIB   Bibliographies
BP   Boston Public Library
BR   British Museum
CHR   Charts, Graphs or Diagrams
CNG   Chronologies
CP   Chicago Public Library
CU   University of Colorado Library
DIS   Discographies
EP   Ensemble Playing
      EP1—General
      EP2—Miscellaneous
      EP3—Chamber Music Playing
      EP4—Duet Playing
      EP5—Two Piano Playing
      EP6—Accompanying and Coaching
      EP7—Concerto Performing
ES   Eastman School of Music Library
GI   General Interest
      GI1—Miscellaneous
      GI2—Appreciation
      GI3—Audiences
      GI4—Recording Procedures
      GI5—Business Aspects
      GI6—Clubs and Organizations
      GI7—Music Therapy
      GI8—Institutional Applications
      GI9—Competitions, Auditions,
          Examinations and Festivals
      GI10—Books for Younger Readers
      GI11—The Amateur Pianist
      GI12—Esoterica
      GI13—Pianistic Careers

CODE IDENTIFICATION

(GI General Interest, cont.)

      GI14—Research
      GI15—Related Arts
GLO   Glossaries
ILL   Illustrations
IND   Indices
IU   Indiana University Library
KI   Keyboard Instruments
      KI1—General
      KI2—Miscellaneous
      KI3—History
      K14—Selection
      KI5—Construction
      KI6—Mechanism
      KI7—Acoustics
      KI8—Maintenance, Tuning and
          Repair
      KI9—Aesthetic Qualities
      KI10—Mechanical Pianos
      KI11—Electronic Instruments
      KI12—Makers
      KI13—Pictorial
      KI14—Early Instruments
      KI15—Catalogs, Collections,
          Dictionaries and
          Bibliographies
KS   Keyboard Skills
      KS1—General
      KS2—Miscellaneous
      KS3—Sight Reading
      KS4—Keyboard Harmony and
          Theory
      KS5—Improvisation—Traditional
      KS6—Improvisation—Jazz
      KS7—Transposition
      KS8—Modulation
      KS9—Score Reading
      KS10—Figured Bass Playing
      KS11—Accompaniment Writing
      KS12—Playing by Ear
LC   Library of Congress
LDR   Line Drawings
MEX   Musical Examples
MI   University of Minnesota Library
MSF   Manuscript Facsimilies
NP   New York Public Library
NP   Notable Pianists and Piano Teachers
      NP1—General
      NP2—Miscellaneous
      NP3—Professional Scope
      NP4—Biography—Narrative
      NP5—Biography—Historical Survey
      NP6—Autobiography, Essays,
          Letters, Lectures and
          Diaries
      NP7—Critical Review
      NP8—Interviews
OC   Oberlin College Library
PHO   Photographs
PL   Processes of Learning
      PL1—General
      PL2—Miscellaneous
      PL3—Psychological Applications
      PL4—Rudiments, Notation

CODE IDENTIFICATION

(PL Processes of Learning, cont.)

      PL5—Analytical Procedures
      PL6—Listening
      PL7—Practice Procedures
      PL8—Memorizing
      PL9—Repertoire Building
      PL10—Ear Training
      PL11—Self-Instruction
      PL12—Rhythm, Metrics, Tempo
      PL13—Creativity
      PL14—Musicianship, Expression
      PL15—Dynamics
PM   Piano Music
      PM1—General
      PM2—Miscellaneous
      PM3—Composers and
          Compositional Techniques
      PM4—Editions
      PM5—Bibliographies
      PM6—Lists, Graded and Ungraded
      PM7—History
      PM8—Analysis—Theoretical
      PM9—Analysis—Interpretative
      PM10—Criticism
      PM11—Master Lessons
      PM12—Recordings
      PM13—Descriptive Analysis,
          Program Notes
      PM14—Compositional Forms
      PM15—Guides to Keyboard
          Literature
PT   Piano Technique
      PT1—General
      PT2—Miscellaneous
      PT3—Physiology and Anatomy
      PT4—Physical Attitude
      PT5—Gymnastics
      PT6—Fingering
      PT7—Relaxation
      PT8—Touch-tone
      PT9—Scales, Arpeggios and
          Chord Formations
      PT10—Exercises for Keyboard
          Facility
      PT11—Studies
      PT12—History of Technique
      PT13—Compilations of Technical
          Material
      PT14—Mechanical Devices
TAB   Tables
TO   University of Toronto Library
UA   University of Arizona Library
UC   University of California at Berkeley
          Library
UI   University of Illinois Library
UK   University of Kansas Library
UM   University of Michigan Library
UO   University of Oregon Library
US   University of Southern California
          Library
UT   University of Texas Library
UU   University of Utah Library
UW   University of Washington Library
YU   Yale University Library

CODE IDENTIFICATION

AP   The Art of Performing
    AP1—General
    AP2—Miscellaneous
    AP3—Performance Practices
    AP4—Interpretation and Style
    AP5—Aesthetics
    AP6—Phrasing, Articulation
    AP7—Ornamentation
    AP8—Pedalling
    AP9—Demeanor and Poise
APP Appendices
AS   Arizona State University Library
AT   The Art of Teaching
    AT1—General
    AT2—Miscellaneous
    AT3—Philosophy and Psychology
       of Teaching
    AT4—Methods or Systems of
       Instruction
    AT5—Child Approach
    AT6—Adult Approach
    AT7—Group Teaching
    AT8—Studio Organization and
       Equipment
    AT9—Student Recitals
    AT10—Testing and Evaluation
    AT11—Teacher Qualifications
    AT12—Master Classes
    AT13—Teacher-Student-Parent
       Interrelationships
    AT14—Selecting Instructional
       Materials

B   Book
BIB Bibliographies
BP   Boston Public Library
BR   British Museum
CHR Charts, Graphs or Diagrams
CNG Chronologies
CP   Chicago Public Library
CU   University of Colorado Library
DIS Discographies
EP   Ensemble Playing
    EP1—General
    EP2—Miscellaneous
    EP3—Chamber Music Playing
    EP4—Duet Playing
    EP5—Two Piano Playing
    EP6—Accompanying and Coaching
    EP7—Concerto Performing
ES   Eastman School of Music Library
GI   General Interest
    GI1—Miscellaneous
    GI2—Appreciation
    GI3—Audiences
    GI4—Recording Procedures
    GI5—Business Aspects
    GI6—Clubs and Organizations
    GI7—Music Therapy
    GI8—Institutional Applications
    GI9—Competitions, Auditions,
       Examinations and Festivals
    GI10—Books for Younger Readers
    GI11—The Amateur Pianist
    GI12—Esoterica
    GI13—Pianistic Careers

CODE IDENTIFICATION

(GI General Interest, cont.)

    GI14—Research
    GI15—Related Arts
GLO Glossaries
ILL Illustrations
IND Indices
IU   Indiana University Library
KI   Keyboard Instruments
    KI1—General
    KI2—Miscellaneous
    KI3—History
    K14—Selection
    KI5—Construction
    KI6—Mechanism
    KI7—Acoustics
    KI8—Maintenance, Tuning and
       Repair
    KI9—Aesthetic Qualities
    KI10—Mechanical Pianos
    KI11—Electronic Instruments
    KI12—Makers
    KI13—Pictorial
    KI14—Early Instruments
    KI15—Catalogs, Collections,
       Dictionaries and
       Bibliographies
KS   Keyboard Skills
    KS1—General
    KS2—Miscellaneous
    KS3—Sight Reading
    KS4—Keyboard Harmony and
       Theory
    KS5—Improvisation—Traditional
    KS6—Improvisation—Jazz
    KS7—Transposition
    KS8—Modulation
    KS9—Score Reading
    KS10—Figured Bass Playing
    KS11—Accompaniment Writing
    KS12—Playing by Ear
LC   Library of Congress
LDR Line Drawings
MEX Musical Examples
MI   University of Minnesota Library
MSF Manuscript Facsimilies
NP   New York Public Library
NP   Notable Pianists and Piano Teachers
    NP1—General
    NP2—Miscellaneous
    NP3—Professional Scope
    NP4—Biography—Narrative
    NP5—Biography—Historical Survey
    NP6—Autobiography, Essays,
       Letters, Lectures and
       Diaries
    NP7—Critical Review
    NP8—Interviews
OC   Oberlin College Library
PHO Photographs
PL   Processes of Learning
    PL1—General
    PL2—Miscellaneous
    PL3—Psychological Applications
    PL4—Rudiments, Notation

CODE IDENTIFICATION

(PL Processes of Learning, cont.)

    PL5—Analytical Procedures
    PL6—Listening
    PL7—Practice Procedures
    PL8—Memorizing
    PL9—Repertoire Building
    PL10—Ear Training
    PL11—Self-Instruction
    PL12—Rhythm, Metrics, Tempo
    PL13—Creativity
    PL14—Musicianship, Expression
    PL15—Dynamics
PM   Piano Music
    PM1—General
    PM2—Miscellaneous
    PM3—Composers and
       Compositional Techniques
    PM4—Editions
    PM5—Bibliographies
    PM6—Lists, Graded and Ungraded
    PM7—History
    PM8—Analysis—Theoretical
    PM9—Analysis—Interpretative
    PM10—Criticism
    PM11—Master Lessons
    PM12—Recordings
    PM13—Descriptive Analysis,
       Program Notes
    PM14—Compositional Forms
    PM15—Guides to Keyboard
       Literature
PT   Piano Technique
    PT1—General
    PT2—Miscellaneous
    PT3—Physiology and Anatomy
    PT4—Physical Attitude
    PT5—Gymnastics
    PT6—Fingering
    PT7—Relaxation
    PT8—Touch-tone
    PT9—Scales, Arpeggios and
       Chord Formations
    PT10—Exercises for Keyboard
       Facility
    PT11—Studies
    PT12—History of Technique
    PT13—Compilations of Technical
       Material
    PT14—Mechanical Devices
TAB Tables
TO   University of Toronto Library
UA   University of Arizona Library
UC   University of California at Berkeley
    Library
UI   University of Illinois Library
UK   University of Kansas Library
UM   University of Michigan Library
UO   University of Oregon Library
US   University of Southern California
    Library
UT   University of Texas Library
UU   University of Utah Library
UW University of Washington Library
YU   Yale University Library

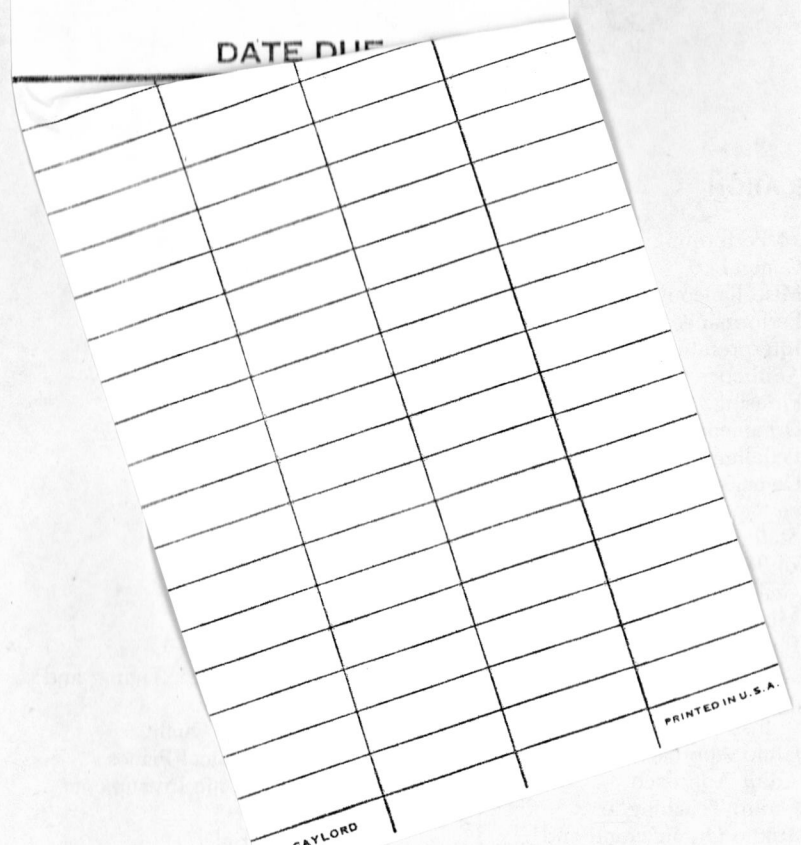

DATE DUE

GAYLORD

PRINTED IN U.S.A.